Merriam-Webster's Intermediate Dictionary

Merriam-Webster's Intermediate Dictionary

Merriam-Webster, Incorporated
Springfield, Massachusetts, U.S.A.

Copyright © 2016 by Merriam-Webster, Incorporated

Library of Congress Cataloging-in-Publication Data

Merriam-Webster's intermediate dictionary.
       p. cm.
    Summary: Provides definitions, pronunciation, etymology, part of speech designation, and other appropriate information. Intended for use by students in grades six to eight.
    ISBN 978-0-87779-697-8
    1. English language—Dictionaries, Juvenile [1. English language—Dictionaries.] I. Title: Intermediate dictionary. II. Merriam-Webster, Inc.

PE1628.5.M44 2004
423—dc22

2004045792

Merriam-Webster's Intermediate Dictionary principal copyright 1986

Made in the United States of America

4th printing   Quad Graphics   Versailles KY   8/2018

Contents

Preface   6a

Using Your Dictionary   7a

Abbreviations Used in This Dictionary   15a

Pronunciation Symbols   16a

A Dictionary of the English Language   **1**

Abbreviations and Symbols for Chemical Elements   943

Biographical, Biblical, and Mythological Names   949

Geographical Names   965

Signs and Symbols   999

A Handbook of Style   1002

Preface

Merriam-Webster's Intermediate Dictionary is part of a series of dictionaries prepared especially for elementary and secondary students. It is preceded by *Merriam-Webster's Elementary Dictionary* and followed by *Merriam-Webster's School Dictionary. Merriam-Webster's Intermediate Dictionary* is intended for use primarily by students in middle school and junior high school. The range of vocabulary covered is suited to the needs of older students, but the definitions have been written in everyday language that will be clear to younger students.

The dictionary has been written and edited by Merriam-Webster's permanent staff of trained and experienced lexicographers. They have included words chiefly on the basis of their occurrence in textbooks and other materials in all subjects. The editors have also had access to the many millions of examples of English words used in context that form the extensive Merriam-Webster citation files and that underlie the entire family of Merriam-Webster dictionaries, including *Webster's Third New International Dictionary* and *Merriam-Webster's Collegiate Dictionary.*

By basing their work on this broad body of evidence, the editors have ensured that the current general vocabulary of English has received its proper share of attention, while also giving the language of special subjects—such as mathematics, science, social studies, and computers—the full coverage that today's students need.

Merriam-Webster's Intermediate Dictionary will give students all of the information they need about how words are spelled, how they are pronounced, and what they mean. In addition, it also has some features found in more advanced dictionaries. For example, word history paragraphs at many entries, each followed by a traditional dictionary etymology, introduce the fascinating study of where words come from and build dictionary skills in understanding etymologies. Synonym paragraphs introduce students to the small but important differences in meaning that make one word more appropriate than another in a particular context.

Over a thousand illustrations of animals, plants, vehicles, musical instruments, articles of clothing, and many other kinds of things supplement and enrich the information given in definitions. Special tables throughout the book answer questions about such matters as the name of a chemical element, the relation of a U.S. measure to its metric equivalent, or the diameter of a planet in our solar system.

In the back of the dictionary there are separate sections giving information about common abbreviations; names of figures from history, mythology, and the Bible; names of places; and signs and symbols.

Merriam-Webster's Intermediate Dictionary can become a very valuable book for students facing the special challenges of developing language skills and basic knowledge across a broad range of topics. The more a student uses the dictionary, the more useful it becomes. However, using a dictionary is not always an easy and obvious matter. To assist students in building necessary dictionary skills, this dictionary includes an introductory section called "Using Your Dictionary." Students should read this section carefully and become thoroughly familiar with what it tells them about the variety of type styles, symbols, special words, and abbreviations used in this dictionary. By doing this, students will be sure to get the most from their dictionary.

Using Your Dictionary

Dictionary Entries

The entries in the dictionary are all the words printed in **boldface** type. The **main entries** are the entries that are listed in alphabetical order at the far left in a column. Most main entries are provided with a pronunciation, a part-of-speech label, and a definition.

Most main entries are single words, but some are not. A main entry can also be a prefix like **¹a-**, a suffix like **-ability**, a combining form like **bio-**, a combination of words like **abominable snowman** and **about–face**, a combination of letters like **IOU**, or a combination of a numeral and a letter like **3-D**.

Run-on Entries

At the end of many entries are additional boldface words and sometimes boldface phrases introduced with a dash. These are known as **run-on entries**. These words and compounds are derived from the main-entry word in different ways. They may come about through a shift in function (as the noun *implant* comes from the verb *implant*) or they may be formed by the addition of suffixes (as the adverb *closely* and the noun *closeness* come from the adjective *close*). The derived words are run on without definitions when their meanings are easy to figure out. But if the meaning of the run-on word is not easy to figure out from the meaning of the base word and the meaning of any added suffix, we always enter it as a main entry with a definition.

The boldface phrases run on at the end of many entries are common idioms whose meanings are more than the sum of the meanings of the individual words. These phrases are generally entered under the first major element (for example, a noun or verb or sometimes an adjective or adverb, rather than a preposition or article).

For example, the phrases *on board, in any case*, and *to date* will appear at the entries **board, case,** and **date,** respectively. *Break camp, cast lots,* and *now and then* will appear respectively under **break, cast,** and **now.**

Order of Entries

Throughout the dictionary, main entries are alphabetized by first letter, then second letter, and so on, regardless of any spaces or hyphens that may appear in them. When a main entry contains a numeral, consider the numeral as though it were a spelled-out word and you will find it at its alphabetical place. For example, **4–H** appears between **four–footed** and **four–in–hand.** Likewise, when a word is usually spelled with an abbreviation, such as **St. Bernard**, consider the spelled-out form (in this case **Saint**) and you will find it at its alphabetical place between **Saint Andrew's cross** and **sainted.**

When main entries are spelled exactly alike but have different functions in a sentence (such as noun and verb) or have different origins, they are called **homographs.** Each homograph is indicated by a small raised numeral at the very beginning of the word. For example, **¹account** and **²account** are entered as separate homographs because they have different functions (the first is a noun, the second is a verb). The entries **¹calf** and **²calf** are separate homographs because they have different origins (the first from an Old English word, the second from a Norse word). In general, homographs are listed and numbered in the order in which they came into the language. The word *calf* meaning a young cow came into the language before the word *calf* meaning a part of the leg.

When main entries are spelled alike except that one of them is capitalized, the one not capitalized is listed first. For example, **frank** is listed before **Frank.**

When main entries are compounds, such as **layoff, lay off, long–distance,** and **long distance,** the solid form is entered first, then the hyphenated form, and then the open form with a space between the parts. Thus, **layoff** comes before **lay off,** and **long–distance** comes before **long distance.**

Guide Words

At the top of each page are two large boldface words separated by a dot. These are called **guide words.** They show the alphabetical range of the entries on that page, and you can use them to help you find a word quickly. For example, if you are looking up the word *aplomb*, flip through the pages looking at the guide words. Stop when you come to the guide words between which the word *aplomb* alphabetically falls. The page having the guide words **apace • apparatus** (page 35) is the page you want. If you stop at the preceding page

(page 34), the guide words **antimatter • ap-** tell you that you are not yet where you want to be. If you stop at the following page (page 36), the guide words **apparel • appointment** tell you that you have gone too far.

The guide words are usually the first and last main entries on the page, but there are exceptions. Actually, the guide words are the first and last entries alphabetically on the page, and this includes all the boldface entries, not just the main entries. A guide word is most often a main entry, but it may also be a variant spelling, an inflected form, or a run-on entry.

Look, for example, at the guide words on page 45. The first guide word, **assemblywoman**, is also the first main entry. But the second guide word is **assuredness**, while the last main entry is **assured**. **Assuredness** is an undefined run-on entry at the main entry **assured**, but it is alphabetically the last entry on the page and so is the proper guide word.

Like main entries, guide words are always in alphabetical order from page to page throughout the book. Once in a while, this presents a problem where the alphabetically last entry on a page—the one that would normally be chosen as the second guide word—is actually later in alphabetical order than the first guide word on the next page. When this happens, a different second guide word must be chosen, one that does not disturb the alphabetical order of the guide words from page to page.

Look, for example, at pages 508 and 509. Notice that the first guide word on page 509 is **moneybags**, because it is the alphabetically first entry on the page. Now look at page 508: you notice that the alphabetically last entry on the page is **monies**, a plural of **money**, yet it is not the second guide word. The second guide word is **money**, which is in alphabetical order with **moneybags** on the next page. If **monies** were used as the second guide word, alphabetical order would be broken, so it is ignored.

Variant Spellings

A number of main entries have a second and sometimes a third spelling also shown in boldface. These alternate spellings are called **variants**.

Variants that are separated by the word *or* are equal variants. This means that either spelling is equally acceptable with the other in current English. Equal variants are usually listed in alphabetical order.

bobby socks *or* **bobby sox**

However, if one of the equal variants is used slightly more frequently, that one is entered first even though it may not fall alphabetically first.

pol·ly·wog *or* **pol·li·wog**

Variants that are separated by the word *also* are not equal variants, and the one listed before the word *also* is quite a bit more common than the one that follows the word *also*. So, at the entry

glam·or·ous *also* **glam·our·ous**

the first spelling is used more often than the second, but both spellings are considered acceptable.

Occasionally both *or* and *also* are used to separate a number of variants at a single entry. The example below indicates that neither **bogy** nor **bogie** is as commonly used as **bogey**, but all three are considered acceptable.

bo·gey *also* **bo·gy** *or* **bo·gie**

Some variants are entered separately at their own alphabetical places. These are followed by the italicized words *variant of* and a cross-reference in small capital letters to the more common spelling or form.

lichee *variant of* LYCHEE

despatch *chiefly British variant of* DISPATCH

Variants that are standard in American English are given at the main entry and are entered again at their own alphabetical places only if they fall one column or more away from the main entry. Variants that are restricted in some way (as by being chiefly British or dialect) are found only at their own alphabetical places.

When one variant is more common for a particular meaning than for other meanings, it is given before the definition with an indication of how common it is.

¹**disk** *or* **disc** . . . **2** : a thin circular object: as **a** *usually disc* : a phonograph record

¹**nick·el** . . . **2 a** *also* **nick·le** : the U.S. five-cent piece made of nickel and copper

If the variant is shown in boldface at the beginning of the entry, as **disc** is, it appears in italic before the definition. If it is not shown at the beginning of the entry, as **nickle** is not, it appears in boldface before the definition.

Centered Dots and Hyphenation

This dictionary shows you how to divide words for two distinct purposes: for end-of-line division by the use of **centered dots** in the entry word, and second, for syllabification by the use of **hyphens** in the pronunciations.

The boldface centered dots in entries indicate the acceptable places to put a hyphen when the word is divided at the end of a line. For example, the dots in the entry **in·ter·con·ti·nen·tal** indicate that the word may be broken at the end of a line as follows:

in-
tercontinental

or

inter-
continental

or

intercon-
tinental

or

interconti-
nental

or

intercontinen-
tal

It is customary to avoid dividing a word so that a single letter is left at the end of one line or the beginning of the next line. For this reason this dictionary does not show any division in such words as **eject, away,** and **lily.**

It is very important to understand that the dots that show end-of-line division do *not* always separate the syllables of a word. Syllables are shown only in the pronunciation, explained in the next section.

In the case of homographs, the divisions are usually indicated only in the first homograph. The divisions shown in the first homograph apply to all the following homographs.

> ¹**mas·ter** . . . *n*
>
> ²**master** *adj*
>
> ³**master** *vb*

A word in a compound made up of two or more separate words is divided only when no individual entry exists for that word.

> **Dew·ey decimal classification** . . . *n*
>
> **diabetes mel·li·tus** . . . *n*
>
> **ha·be·as cor·pus** . . . *n*

There are no separate entries for *Dewey, mellitus, habeas,* or *corpus.*

This dictionary also uses a special double hyphen ⸗ at the end of a line when the word being broken is usually spelled with a hyphen at that point. For example, at the entry **duckbill** on page 242 the word in italics is broken at the end of the first line with a double hyphen so as to show that the word is spelled *duck-billed platypus* and not *duckbilled platypus.*

Pronunciation

It is often difficult to tell how a word is pronounced from its spelling. For example, in *bat, late, any,* and *above* the letter *a* stands for a different sound in each word. In addition, there are many words that are pronounced in more than one way, even though there may be only one accepted spelling.

In order to represent the sounds of spoken English in a written form, a special set of pronunciation symbols is used. Each symbol stands for only one sound and each sound is represented by only one symbol.

The pronunciation of most entry words is shown immediately following the boldface entry. To make it clear that pronunciation symbols are being used and not regular letters, the symbols are always shown between slant lines \ \.

A complete list of pronunciation symbols used in this dictionary appears on page 16a. A shorter list of symbols you may need to be reminded of is printed at the bottom of the right column on odd-numbered pages throughout the dictionary. After most of the symbols in the chart are words containing the sound of that symbol. The boldface letters in these words are the letters which have the same sound as the symbol.

For example, following the symbol **j** are the words **j**ob, **g**em, e**dge**. The boldface **j** in **j**ob, the **g** in **g**em, and the **dge** in e**dge** are all pronounced \j\.

At the beginning of the list of pronunciation symbols is the symbol ə, called a **schwa** \'shwä\. This symbol often represents the sound of an unstressed vowel (as the first and last vowels in *America*), but it may also represent the sound of a stressed vowel (as the first vowel of *brother*).

Hyphens are used in the pronunciation to indicate the syllables of a word.

> **noisy** \'nȯi-zē\ (2 syllables)
>
> **no·tice·able** \'nōt-ə-sə-bəl\ (4 syllables)

Of course, the syllables of words are not separated when we speak. One sound follows right after another without pause. It is obvious in the example *noticeable* above that the number and position of hyphens are not the same as the number and position of dots in the entry word. Only the hyphens show syllables; the dots mark acceptable places to divide the word at the end of a line.

Some syllables are spoken with greater force or stress than others. In this dictionary the primary (strongest) stress is shown by a high-set vertical mark \'\ placed immediately *before* the stressed syllable. Secondary (slightly weaker) stress is shown by a low-set vertical mark \ˌ\ also placed immediately *before* the stressed syllable. In the word *notify*, for example, the first syllable receives primary stress and the last syllable receives secondary stress. The middle syllable receives weak stress and is not marked in the dictionary. All of this is shown in the pronunciation \'nōt-ə-ˌfī\.

Many words can be pronounced in more than one way. Variant pronunciations are separated by commas, and sometimes groups of variants are separated by semicolons. When the word *also* separates variant pronunciations, the one following the *also* is not as common as the one preceding it. All the variant pronunciations shown in this dictionary are quite acceptable and are used by educated speakers of English.

Sometimes when a variant pronunciation is shown, only part of the pronunciation of the word changes. When that happens, only the part that changes may be shown. To get the full pronunciation, add the part that changes to the part that stays the same.

>**ec·o·nom·ic** \ˌek-ə-'näm-ik, ˌē-kə-\
>
>**¹ei·ther** \'ē-_thər_ *also* 'ī-\
>
>**ex·pi·ra·to·ry** \ik-'spī-rə-ˌtōr-ē, ek-, -ˌtor-; 'ek-sp(ə-)rə-\

If a variant is used mostly in a particular region of the U.S. or a part of the English-speaking world outside the U.S., that location is identified.

>**¹sure** \'shu̇(ə)r, *especially Southern* 'shō(ə)r\
>
>**¹sched·ule** \'skej-ü(ə)l, -əl, *Canadian also* 'shej-, *British usually* 'shed-yü(ə)l\

When a pronunciation symbol is enclosed in parentheses, that sound may or may not be pronounced.

>**¹ear** \'i(ə)r\

The parentheses at **¹ear** indicate that *ear* may be pronounced \'ir\ or \'iər\.

If an incomplete pronunciation is given for an entry word, the missing portion may be found at a preceding entry.

>**cat·bird** \'kat-ˌbərd\
>
>**cat·boat** \-ˌbōt\

Thus, the full pronunciation of *catboat* is \'kat-ˌbōt\. In the case of homographs, if the pronunciation is the same for each homograph, the pronunciation is given only for the first.

>**¹cheer** \'chi(ə)r\ *n*
>
>**²cheer** *vb*
>
>**¹her·ald** \'her-əld\ *n*
>
>**²herald** *vb*

Many entries for compounds made up of two or more separate words will also have missing pronunciations. Look at the entries for the separate words to determine the pronunciation. If one of the words has no entry of its own, however, the pronunciation of that word will be shown at the entry for the compound.

>**monarch butterfly** *n*
>
>**hog·nose snake** \ˌhȯg-ˌnōz-, ˌhäg-\ *n*

Some undefined run-on entries show no pronunciation. In these cases, the pronunciation of the run-on is the pronunciation of the main entry plus the pronunciation of the suffix, which may be found at its own alphabetical place.

>**bossy** \'bȯ-sē\ *adj* . . . — **boss·i·ness** *n*

Thus, the pronunciation of **bossiness** is \'bȯ-sē-nəs\; it is not shown because it is simply \'bȯ-sē\ plus \nəs\.

The Functions of Words

Words are used in many different ways in a sentence. A word may serve as the name of something, or be used to indicate an action or to describe a thing or the way something happens. The several different grammatical functions of words are known as parts of speech. This dictionary identifies the function of most entry words with one of the eight traditional part-of-speech labels, abbreviated, italicized, and placed after the boldface entry itself or after the pronunciation, when one is given.

>**bur·glar** . . . *n* (noun)
>
>**cease** . . . *vb* (verb)
>
>**de·li·cious** . . . *adj* (adjective)
>
>**fair·ly** . . . *adv* (adverb)
>
>**you** . . . *pron* (pronoun)
>
>**in·to** . . . *prep* (preposition)
>
>**or** . . . *conj* (conjunction)
>
>**ouch** . . . *interj* (interjection)

When a noun is always used in the plural, the label *n pl* is used. A noun so labeled always takes a plural verb.

>**munch·ies** . . . *n pl*

Sometimes an entry word that is spelled as a

plural may take either a singular or a plural verb, depending on its use. For example, although the word *acrobatics* is plural in form, it may be singular in such uses as "Acrobatics is a strenuous activity" or plural in "You make these acrobatics look easy." To indicate such uses, the word *acrobatics* is given the label *n sing or pl*.

In addition to the traditional part-of-speech labels, there are a number of other functional labels used in this dictionary.

> **may** . . . *helping verb*
>
> **me·thinks** . . . *impersonal verb*
>
> **avast** . . . *imperative verb*
>
> **an** . . . *indefinite article*
>
> **the** . . . *definite article*
>
> **Fris·bee** . . . *trademark*
>
> **Re·al·tor** . . . *collective mark*
>
> **NC–17** . . . *certification mark*
>
> **-gram** . . . *n combining form*
>
> **-ous** . . . *adj suffix*
>
> **non-** . . . *prefix*
>
> **-nd** . . . *symbol*

Inflected Forms

The plural forms of nouns, the past tense, past participle, and present participle forms of verbs, and the comparative and superlative forms of adjectives and adverbs are known as **inflected forms**. In most instances, these forms are regular (that is, they are formed by the addition of *-s* or *-es* to nouns, *-ed* and *-ing* to verbs, and *-er* and *-est* to adjectives and adverbs). These regular inflected forms are not shown in this dictionary. Irregular inflected forms, such as those that involve a change in the spelling of the root word or a doubling of a final letter, are shown in boldface.

Just as with variants of main entries, variants of inflected forms are equal when they are separated by *or*. If they are out of alphabetical order, the one shown first is slightly more common. Variants separated by *also* are not equal, however, and the one shown first is considerably more common than the other. Even so, both variants are acceptable.

An effort is usually made to save space in showing inflected forms by showing only the last part for words of more than two syllables. The form is usually cut back to the point that corresponds to the last indicated end-of-line division in the main entry.

> **can·di·da·cy** . . . *n, pl* **-cies**
>
> **or·ga·nize** . . . *vb* **-nized; -niz·ing**

Inflected forms whose own alphabetical places are more than one column away from the main entry are given separate entry there with a cross-reference in small capital letters to the main entry.

> **geese** *plural of* GOOSE
>
> **brought** *past and past participle of* BRING

PLURALS OF NOUNS

Nouns that form their plurals simply by the addition of *-s* or *-es* are not shown unless there is a chance that they may be mistaken or misspelled.

> **mon·key** . . . *n, pl* **monkeys** (not *monkies*)
>
> **mon·goose** . . . *n, pl* **mon·goos·es** (not *mongeese*)

Nouns that form their plurals in any other way than by the addition of *-s* or *-es* to an unchanged base have such plurals shown.

> **cad·dy** . . . *n, pl* **caddies** (*-y* changes to *-i-*)
>
> **child** . . . *n, pl* **chil·dren** (irregular ending)
>
> **knife** . . . *n, pl* **knives** (*-f-* changes to *-v-*)
>
> **oa·sis** . . . *n, pl* **oa·ses** (Greek plural)
>
> **se·ta** . . . *n, pl* **se·tae** (Latin plural)
>
> **ser·aph** . . . *n, pl* **ser·a·phim** . . . (Hebrew plural)
>
> **deer** . . . *n, pl* **deer** (no change at all)

Most compound nouns form their plural by pluralizing the final element. Such plurals are not shown when the final element is a recognizable word entered at its own place (such as *blueberry* and *eyetooth*). Plurals for compounds that pluralize any but the last element are shown.

> **moth·er–in–law** . . . *n, pl* **moth·ers–in–law**
>
> **postmaster general** *n, pl* **postmasters general**

Plurals are also given for all entries that have variant plural forms.

> ¹**in·dex** . . . *n, pl* **in·dex·es** . . . *or* **in·di·ces**
>
> **mon·si·gnor** . . . *n, pl* **monsignors** *or* **mon·si·gno·ri**
>
> **ban·jo** . . . *n, pl* **banjos** *also* **banjoes**

Irregular plural forms are also entered at their own alphabetical place in this dictionary when they fall more than one column away from the singular entry. You will find the plural form **feet**, for example, entered at its own alphabetical place between **feeling** and **feetfirst** because it falls more than a column away from the singular **foot**. However, the irregular plural **oxen** is not shown at its own place because it does not fall more than a column away from **ox**. Irregular plurals that are shown at their own alphabetical place have a cross-reference in small capital letters to the singular form.

>**lice** *plural of* LOUSE

>**media** *plural of* MEDIUM

FORMS OF VERBS

Some inflected forms of a verb are especially important because they are used to form all of the verb tenses. These forms are the present tense, past tense, past participle, and present participle. Most verbs in English form the past tense and past participle by the addition of *-ed* to the base form, which is also the present tense form. They form the present participle by the addition of *-ing* to the base form. These verbs are considered to be regular, and their inflected forms are not shown in this dictionary.

Inflected forms are shown if they are created in any other way, even if it is no more than a matter of dropping a final *-e* before the ending is added. Variants of inflected forms are always shown. When the past participle has the same form as the past tense, only one form is shown.

>**¹blow** . . . *vb* **blew** . . . ; **blown** . . . ; **blow·ing**

>**¹fade** . . . *vb* **fad·ed; fad·ing**

>**¹chop** . . . *vb* **chopped; chop·ping**

>**²bias** *vb* **bi·ased** *or* **bi·assed; bi·as·ing** *or* **bi·as·sing**

>**²picnic** *vb* **pic·nicked; pic·nick·ing**

>**¹fry** . . . *vb* **fried; fry·ing**

FORMS OF ADJECTIVES AND ADVERBS

Most adjectives and adverbs form their comparative and superlative forms with the words *more* or *most* or with the addition of *-er* and *-est* to the simple form. These adjectives and adverbs are considered regular, and such forms are not shown in this dictionary. Any other spelling changes (such as the changing of *-y* to *-i-*, the doubling of the final consonant, or the dropping of *-e*) are shown. All variant forms are shown. To save space, superlative forms are often cut back to the ending **-est**.

>**¹good** . . . *adj* **bet·ter** . . . ; **best**

>**mad** . . . *adj* **mad·der; mad·dest**

>**²dandy** *adj* **dan·di·er; -est**

>**³fine** *adj* **fin·er; fin·est**

>**¹ear·ly** . . . *adv* **ear·li·er; -est**

>**²much** *adv* **more; most**

>**spry** . . . *adj* **spri·er** *or* **spry·er** . . . ; **spri·est** *or* **spry·est**

Definitions

A definition is the statement of the meaning of an entry word. In this dictionary each definition is introduced by a boldface colon.

>**³fan** *n* : an enthusiastic follower or admirer

>**op·ti·mis·tic** . . . *adj* : showing optimism : expecting everything to come out all right : HOPEFUL

Often, instead of a statement or in addition to it, one or more cross-references to synonyms are given in small capital letters.

>**law·mak·er** . . . *n* : LEGISLATOR

>**mer·i·to·ri·ous** . . . *adj* : deserving reward or honor : PRAISEWORTHY

This tells you that the meaning of *lawmaker* and the meaning of *legislator* are the same, and the meaning of *meritorious* and the meaning of *praiseworthy* are the same.

When an entry word has more than one sense, the appropriate number precedes each sense.

>**hoax** . . . *n* **1** : an act intended to trick or deceive **2** : something false passed off or accepted as genuine

Sometimes a particular relationship between two meanings is shown by the use of an italic label. Two labels are used: *esp* (for *especially*) and *also*. The divider *esp* is used to introduce the most common meaning that is included in the general definition just before it. The divider *also* is used to introduce a meaning that is closely related to the meaning given just before it but is not as common.

>**opus** . . . *n* . . . : ¹WORK 7; *esp* : a musical composition or set of compositions

>**demi·tasse** . . . *n* : a small cup of black coffee; *also* : the cup used to serve it

A numbered sense can be further divided into subsenses preceded by small boldface letters. Sometimes an unnumbered sense is divided into lettered subsenses.

>**erode** . . . *vb* . . . **1 a** : to destroy gradually by chemical means : CORRODE **b** : to wear away by or as if by the action of water, wind, or glacial ice **2** : to undergo erosion

>**²scope** *n* : any of various instruments for viewing: as **a** : MICROSCOPE **b** : ¹TELESCOPE **c** : OSCILLOSCOPE

In this dictionary, the definitions of senses of a word are generally listed in historical order, just as homographs are. This means that sense 1 was used in English before sense 2, sense 2 before sense 3, and so forth. It does not mean, however, that sense 3 necessarily developed from sense 2. It may have done so, or sense 2 and sense 3 may have developed independently from sense 1. Sometimes it is possible to see that one sense developed out of another just by the way their definitions are worded.

> **¹branch** . . . *n* **1** : a natural division of a plant stem (as a bough growing from a trunk or twig from a bough) **2** : something extending from a main line or source ⟨river *branch*⟩ ⟨a railroad *branch*⟩ **3** : a separate or subordinate division or part of a central system ⟨executive *branch* of the government⟩ ⟨a *branch* of a bank⟩

In the above entry, phrases are provided within angle brackets ⟨ ⟩ to illustrate common ways of using the entry word in the indicated sense. These phrases are called **verbal illustrations**.

Sometimes, in addition to or in place of a definition, you will find a cross-reference to a table in which other similar terms are listed or a cross-reference that sends you to another entry for related information.

> **Leo** . . . *n* . . . **2 a** : the fifth sign of the zodiac — see ZODIAC table
>
> **Dan·iel** . . . *n* — see BIBLE table
>
> **digital computer** *n* : a computer that operates with numbers expressed as digits (as in the binary system) — compare ANALOG COMPUTER

Capitalization

When an entry word is usually capitalized in ordinary writing, it is entered in this dictionary with a capital letter. Other entries begin with a lowercase letter. A few such entries also have an italic label *often cap*. This label indicates that the word is capitalized about as often as not.

> **Oc·to·ber** . . . *n*
>
> **back·ground** . . . *n*
>
> **an·gli·cize** . . . *vb* . . . *often cap*

Some words have special meanings when capitalized that they do not have when they are written without a capital letter. This dictionary shows the use of the capital with such entries by putting the label *cap* or *often cap* at the appropriate sense.

> **re·nais·sance** . . . *n* **1** *cap* : the period of European history between the 14th and 17th centuries marked by a flourishing of art and literature inspired by ancient times and by the beginnings of modern science **2** *often cap* : a movement or period of great activity (as in literature, science, and the arts)

Occasionally, some words that are almost always capitalized in their usual meanings have special meanings in which they are not capitalized. In this dictionary the labels *not cap* or *often not cap* are given at the proper sense.

> **DJ** . . . *n, often not cap* : DISC JOCKEY
>
> **²Roman** *adj* **1** : of or relating to Rome or the Romans or the empire of which Rome was the original capital **2 a** . . . **b** . . . **3** *not cap* : of or relating to a type style with upright characters (as in "these definitions")

Special Usage Labels and Guide Phrases

For many entries italic labels identify the kind of context in which the word or a sense of the word is usually found. Some of the most commonly used labels in this dictionary are the following:

archaic (once standard but now used only in special contexts)

slang (very informal usage not usually found in formal writing)

substandard (not normally used by educated speakers and writers)

nonstandard (sometimes used by well-educated people but not always considered appropriate for good usage)

British (common only in Great Britain or the British Commonwealth countries)

Scottish (common only in Scotland)

dialect (common only in one or more regions of the U.S.)

Regional labels like the last three in the list above are often preceded by the word *chiefly*. This modifier indicates that the word or meaning is most common in the named region but has some use outside of it.

The following examples illustrate the use of such special usage labels:

> **¹fain** . . . *adj* **1** *archaic* : GLAD, HAPPY
>
> **lid** . . . *n* . . . **3** *slang* : HAT
>
> **learn** . . . *vb* . . . **4** *substandard* : to cause to learn : TEACH
>
> **¹lay** . . . *vb* . . . **4** *nonstandard* : ¹LIE
>
> **³chap** *n, chiefly British* : ¹FELLOW 4a
>
> **auld** . . . *adj, chiefly Scottish* : OLD
>
> **craw·dad** . . . *n, dialect* : CRAYFISH 1

At a few entries an italicized **guide phrase** may be provided before a definition to identify the reference of a special meaning.

> **¹bounce** . . . *vb* . . . **5** *of a check* : to be returned by a bank . . .

Usage Notes

For some entries, a note beginning with a phrase such as "used as," "used in," or "used to" may be added to a definition. This **usage note** is set off by a dash.

> **le·ga·to** . . . *adv or adj* : in a manner that is smooth and connected — used as a direction in music
>
> **²cave** *vb* . . . : to fall or cause to fall in or down : COL- LAPSE — usually used with *in*
>
> **¹chamber** . . . *n* . . . **3** . . . **b** : a room where a judge con- ducts business out of court — usually used in plural

When a word has a special use that cannot eas- ily or clearly be explained in a definition, a usage note may take the place of a definition.

> **ouch** . . . *interj* — used to express sudden pain
>
> **²let** *vb* . . . **3** . . . **b** — used to introduce a request

Synonym Paragraphs

At selected entries, the boldface italic word *synonyms* introduces a paragraph of explanation at the end of the definition. This *synonym para- graph* explains and illustrates with examples the relation of words that are similar in meaning to the main entry. Following is one such paragraph:

> **¹de·cline** . . . *vb* . . . **5** . . .
> **synonyms** DECLINE, REFUSE, REJECT mean to ex- press unwillingness to go along with a demand or re- quest. DECLINE suggests a polite negative response ⟨*decline* an invitation to a party⟩. REFUSE suggests a forceful or absolute denial ⟨*refused* to see him at all⟩. REJECT may suggest an unwillingness even to consider a demand or request ⟨*rejected* her plan before she could explain it⟩.

Notice that the words being discussed are listed at the beginning of the paragraph in small capital letters, followed by a statement of the meaning which they have in common. Next something is said about the special element of meaning each word has that makes it different from the other words in the list. A verbal illustration follows showing the special meaning of the word in ac- tion.

At the main entries for these words (except the first word) you will find a cross-reference to this synonym paragraph. This cross-reference is also introduced by the boldface italic word *synonyms* following the definition.

> **¹re·fuse** . . . *vb* . . . **3** . . . *synonyms* see DECLINE
>
> **¹re·ject** . . . *vb* . . . **4** . . . *synonyms* see DECLINE

Etymologies

At many entries, the origin of the entry word is shown by tracing it or its parts back to the earli- est known forms and meanings. Such informa- tion is called an **etymology**. In this dictionary the etymologies are shown within square brackets [ ] generally just after the definition.

Names of languages in etymologies are given in full rather than abbreviated. No attempt has been made to distinguish the major historical periods of languages other than English. The appearance of the phrase "derived from" before a new lan- guage name and form indicates that one or more minor stages of development have been omitted for clarity and simplicity. Language forms within etymologies are given in italics, and their mean- ings are placed inside quotation marks. If no lan- guage name appears before a form, the language is the last one named. Thus, in the etymology of **abbreviate**, *abbreviare* and *brevis* are Latin words and *ad-* is a Latin prefix.

> **li·co·rice** . . . *n* . . . [Middle English *licorice* "licorice," from early French *licoris* (same meaning), from Latin *liquiritia* (same meaning), derived from Greek *glykyr- rhiza,* literally "sweet root"]
>
> **ab·bre·vi·ate** . . . *vb* . . . [Middle English *abbreviaten* "abbreviate," from Latin *abbreviatus* "made short," from *abbreviare* "to shorten," from earlier *ad-* "to" and *brevis* "short" — related to ABRIDGE, BRIEF]

Sometimes an etymology explains how the word came to be applied to something.

> **red—let·ter** . . . *adj* : worth remembering especially in a happy or joyful way ⟨a *red-letter* day⟩ [from the prac- tice of marking holy days in red letters in church calen- dars]

When a word comes from the name of a per- son, the name of a place, or some other proper name, this fact is often given in the etymology.

> **sax·o·phone** . . . *n* [named for Antoine "Adolph" *Sax* 1814–1894 a Belgian maker of musical instruments]
>
> **pan·de·mo·ni·um** . . . *n* . . . [from *Pandemonium,* name of the place of demons in *Paradise Lost* by John Mil- ton, from Greek *pan-* "all, every, completely" and Greek *daimon* "evil spirit, demon"]
>
> **Wal·dorf salad** . . . *n* . . . [named for the *Waldorf*-Astoria Hotel in New York City]

To some extent words exist in families, just as people do. Particularly with borrowings into En- glish from Latin and Greek, many words may be derived from a single ancestor. Sometimes the connection is evident when you see the words to- gether, as in the case of *final, define, finish,* and *infinity.* Sometimes, however, the connection may have been blurred somewhat by changes in spelling, pronunciation, and meaning over the centuries, as in the case of *nautical, nausea,* and *noise.* Such connections between words are inter- esting in themselves, and they can also be helpful to you in learning new words. Your attention is drawn to such connections in etymologies by a note that begins "—related to" and continues with one or more cross-references in small capital letters to the related entries. Each of the entries named will have its own etymology and a similar note.

¹cross . . . *n* . . . [Old English *cros*, probably from an early Norse or an early Irish word derived from Latin *crux* "cross" — related to CRUCIAL, CRUISE, CRUSADE, CRUX, EXCRUCIATING]

cru·cial . . . *adj* . . . [from French *crucial* "having the form of a cross, being or involving a crisis," from Latin *cruc-, crux* "cross, trouble, torture" — related to CROSS, CRUCIFY, CRUX]

cruise . . . *vb* . . . [from Dutch *kruisen* "to cruise, move crosswise," from early Dutch *crūce* "cross," from Latin *crux* "cross" — related to CROSS, CRUCIAL]

¹cru·sade . . . *n* . . . [derived from early French *croisade* and Spanish *cruzada*, both meaning literally "an expedition of persons marked with or bearing the sign of the cross" and both derived from Latin *cruc-, crux* "cross" — related to CROSS]

crux . . . *n* . . . [from Latin *crux* "cross, torture, trouble" — related to CROSS, CRUCIAL, CRUCIFY]

ex·cru·ci·at·ing . . . *adj* . . . [derived from Latin *excruciatus*, past participle of *excruciare* "to torture," from *ex-* "out of, from" and *cruciare* "to torment, crucify," from *cruc-, crux* "cross" — related to CROSS, CRUCIAL, CRUCIFY]

Word Histories

Some of the many English words that have interesting histories are provided with a *Word History* paragraph. Such a paragraph follows the definition and is followed by the etymology.

can·di·date . . . *n* . . .
Word History In ancient Rome it was the custom for a person who wanted to be elected to public office to wear a toga that had been rubbed with chalk to make it white. The Latin word for "dressed in white" was *candidatus*. In time this word came to be used for the person himself, or the candidate. The Latin word *candidatus* came from *candidus*, meaning "bright, shining white." This in turn came from *candēre*, a verb meaning "to shine, be bright." Latin *candēre* has given us two other English words: *candid*, which at first meant "white, free from prejudice" but now usually means "honest, natural," and *candle*, the mass of wax with a wick that is burned to give off a bright light. [from Latin *candidatus* "candidate," from *candidatus* (adjective) "dressed in white," from *candidus* "shining white," from *candēre* "to be bright, shine" —related to CANDID, CANDLE]

Lists of Undefined Words

Lists of words appear without definitions at the following prefix entries in this dictionary:

non-	re-
over-	un-

The meanings of the listed compounds formed with these prefixes are easily understandable from the meaning of the prefix and the meaning of the base word. Compounds that are not easily understandable in this way are entered at their own place with definitions. For example, **nonobjective** is entered and defined at its own place because its meaning is not easily understandable as the sum of the meanings of **non-** and **objective**.

Abbreviations Used in This Dictionary

A.D.	anno Domini		**n pl**	noun plural
adj	adjective		**NW**	northwest, northwestern
adv	adverb		**pl**	plural
a.m.	ante meridiem		**p.m.**	post meridiem
B.C.	before Christ		**prep**	preposition
C	Celsius, centigrade		**pron**	pronoun
cap	capitalized		**S**	south, southern
conj	conjunction		**SE**	southeast, southeastern
constr	construction		**sing**	singular
E	east, eastern		**SSE**	south-southeast
ENE	east-northeast		**SSW**	south-southwest
ESE	east-southeast		**SW**	southwest, southwestern
esp	especially		**U.S.**	United States
F	Fahrenheit		**U.S.S.R.**	Union of Soviet Socialist Republics
interj	interjection		**usu**	usually
n	noun		**vb**	verb
N	north, northern		**W**	west, western
NE	northeast, northeastern		**WNW**	west-northwest
NNE	north-northeast		**WSW**	west-southwest
NNW	north-northwest			

Pronunciation Symbols

ə	....	(called *schwa* \'shwä\) banana, collide, abut; in stressed syllables as in humdrum, mother, abut
ə	....	used before \l\, \n\, and \m\, as in battle, mitten, and one pronunciation of open \'ōp-əm\
ər	....	further, merger
a	....	ax, map
ā	....	age, vacation, day
ä	....	father, cot, cart
à	....	used for a sound between \a\ and \ä\, as in an eastern New England pronunciation of aunt, half
au̇	....	out, now
b	....	baby, rib
ch	....	chin, match, nature \'nā-chər\
d	....	did, ladder
e	....	less
ē	....	seaweed, any, serial, cereal
f	....	fifty, cuff, phone
g	....	gift, pig, bigger
h	....	hat, ahead
hw	....	whale as pronounced by those who do not pronounce *whale* and *wail* the same
i	....	trip
ī	....	life, buy, my
j	....	job, gem, edge
k	....	kin, cook, chasm
k̲	....	used for a rasping sound between \k\ and \h\, as in German ich, Buch, one pronunciation of loch, chutzpah
l	....	lily, pool, mortal
m	....	murmur
n	....	nine, cotton
ŋ	....	sing, singer, finger, ink
ō	....	low, bone, cooperate
ȯ	....	moth, law, sort, all
œ	....	French boeuf, German Hölle
œ̄	....	French feu, German Höhle
ȯi	....	coin, destroy
p	....	pepper, lip
r	....	rarity
s	....	spice, less
sh	....	shy, dish, machine, mission, special
t	....	tight, latter
th	....	thin, ether
th̲	....	this, either
ü	....	boot, rule
u̇	....	foot, pull
ᵫ	....	German füllen, hübsch
ᵫ̄	....	French rue, German fühlen
v	....	give, vivid
w	....	we, away
y	....	you, yet
yü	....	few, union, mule, youth
yu̇	....	furious
z	....	zone, raise
zh	....	vision, beige
\ \	....	slant lines used in pairs to mark the beginning and end of a pronunciation: \'pen\
'	....	mark at the beginning of a syllable that has primary (strongest) stress: \'pen-ə-ˌtrāt\
ˌ	....	mark at the beginning of a syllable that has secondary (next-strongest) stress: \'pen-ə-ˌtrāt\
-	....	mark of syllable division in pronunciations [the mark of end-of-line division in boldface entry words is a centered dot · and the position of the two kinds of division often does not agree, as in build·ing \'bil-diŋ\, spe·cial \'spesh-əl\, ca·ter \'kāt-ər\]
( )	....	parentheses indicate that what is between is present in some utterances but not in others: at fac·to·ry, \'fak-t(ə-)rē\ = \'fak-tə-rē, 'fak-trē\ or \'fak-trē, 'fak-tə-rē\

A

¹a \'ā\ *n, pl* **a's** *or* **as** *often cap* **1** : the first letter of the English alphabet **2** : a musical note referred to by the letter A : the sixth tone of a C-major scale **3** : a grade rating a student's work as superior

²a \ə, (')ā\ *indefinite article* **1** : someone or something unspecified ⟨*a* man in the street⟩ ⟨*a* dozen⟩ **2** : the same : ONE ⟨two of *a* kind⟩ ⟨birds of *a* feather⟩ **3** : of whatever kind : ANY ⟨*a* person who is sick can't work well⟩ — used in all senses before words beginning with a consonant sound; compare AN [Old English *ān* "one"]

³a \ə, (')ā\ *prep* : in each : to each : for each ⟨twice *a* week⟩ ⟨one *a* piece⟩ [Old English *a-, an, on* "on"]

¹a- \ə\ *prefix* **1** : on : in : at ⟨abed⟩ **2** : in a specified state or condition ⟨afire⟩ **3** : in a specified manner ⟨aloud⟩ **4** : in the act or process of ⟨gone *a*-hunting⟩ [Old English *a-* "on, in, at"]

²a- \(')ā\ *or* **an-** \(')an\ *prefix* : not : without ⟨asexual⟩ — *a-* before consonants other than *h* and sometimes before *h*, *an-* before vowels and usually before *h* ⟨anhydrate⟩ [Greek *a-, an-* "not"]

aard·vark \'ärd-ˌvärk\ *n* : a large burrowing African mammal that feeds on insects and especially termites with its long sticky tongue [from early Afrikaans (now *erdvark*), "earth pig"]

ab- *prefix* : from : away : departing from ⟨abnormal⟩ [Latin *ab-* "from, away"]

ab·a·ca \ˌab-ə-'kä, 'ab-ə-ˌkä\ *n* : a strong fiber that comes from a banana plant native to the Philippines — called also *Manila hemp*

aback \ə-'bak\ *adv* **1** *archaic* : ²BACK 1, BACKWARD **2** : by surprise : UNAWARES ⟨taken *aback* by the turn of events⟩

aba·cus \'ab-ə-kəs, ə-'bak-əs\ *n, pl* **aba·ci** \'ab-ə-ˌsī, -ˌkē; ə-'bak-ˌī\ *or* **aba·cus·es** : an instrument for making calculations by sliding counters along rods or in grooves

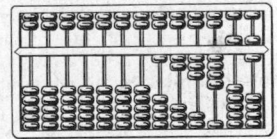
aardvark

abacus

¹abaft \ə-'baft\ *adv* : toward the stern : at the stern

²abaft *prep* : to the rear of; *esp* : toward the stern from

ab·a·lo·ne \ˌab-ə-'lō-nē, 'ab-ə-ˌ\ *n* : a mollusk with a flattened slightly spiral shell that has holes along the edge and is lined with mother-of-pearl

¹aban·don \ə-'ban-dən\ *vb* **1** : to give up completely **2** : to withdraw from often in the face of danger ⟨*abandon* ship⟩ **3** : to withdraw protection, support, or help from ⟨*abandoned* the dog⟩ **4** : to give oneself up to an emotion — **abandoner** *n* — **aban·don·ment** \-mənt\ *n*

synonyms ABANDON, DESERT, FORSAKE mean to leave without intending to return. ABANDON suggests that the person or thing left behind is helpless or needs protection ⟨the baby was *abandoned* on the steps of the church⟩. DESERT suggests the breaking of a promise, duty, or relationship ⟨*deserted* the cause when there was trouble⟩ ⟨mining towns that were *deserted* after the gold rush⟩. FORSAKE stresses leaving behind something known or loved well ⟨could not *forsake* her friends⟩.

²abandon *n* : a complete yielding to natural impulses; *esp* : ENTHUSIASM 1, EXUBERANCE

aban·doned \ə-'ban-dənd\ *adj* **1** : that has been deserted : left empty or unused ⟨an *abandoned* house⟩ **2** : completely free from restraint ⟨*abandoned* laughter⟩

abase \ə-'bās\ *vb* **abased; abas·ing** : to lower in rank or position : HUMBLE, DEGRADE — **abase·ment** \-mənt\ *n*

abash \ə-'bash\ *vb* : to destroy the self-control or self-confidence of **synonyms** see EMBARRASS — **abash·ment** \-mənt\ *n*

abate \ə-'bāt\ *vb* **abat·ed; abat·ing** : to make or become less ⟨the wind *abated*⟩ ⟨*abated* their prices⟩ — **abat·er** *n*

abate·ment \ə-'bāt-mənt\ *n* **1** : the act or process of abating : the state of being abated **2** : an amount abated (as from a tax)

ab·at·toir \'ab-ə-ˌtwär\ *n* : SLAUGHTERHOUSE

ab·bess \'ab-əs\ *n* : the head of a convent of nuns

ab·bey \'ab-ē\ *n, pl* **abbeys** **1 a** : MONASTERY **b** : CONVENT **2** : a church that once belonged to an abbey ⟨Westminster *Abbey*⟩

ab·bot \'ab-ət\ *n* : the head of a monastery for men

ab·bre·vi·ate \ə-'brē-vē-ˌāt\ *vb* **-at·ed; -at·ing** : to make briefer : SHORTEN; *esp* : to reduce (as a word) to a shorter form intended to stand for the whole [Middle English *abbreviaten* "abbreviate," from Latin *abbreviatus* "made short," from *abbreviare* "to shorten," from earlier *ad-* "to" and *brevis* "short" — related to ABRIDGE, BRIEF]

ab·bre·vi·a·tion \ə-ˌbrē-vē-'ā-shən\ *n* **1** : the act or result of abbreviating : ABRIDGMENT **2** : a shortened form of a written word or phrase used in place of the whole

Ab·di·as \ab-'dī-əs\ *n* : OBADIAH

ab·di·cate \'ab-di-ˌkāt\ *vb* **-cat·ed; -cat·ing** : to formally give up sovereign power, office, or responsibility — **ab·di·ca·tion** \ˌab-di-'kā-shən\ *n*

ab·do·men \'ab-də-mən, ab-'dō-mən\ *n* **1 a** : the part of the body between the chest and the hips **b** : the body cavity containing the chief digestive organs — called also *abdominal cavity* **2** : the hind portion of the body behind the thorax in an arthropod — see INSECT illustration — **ab·dom·i·nal** \ab-'däm-ən-ᵊl, -nᵊl\ *adj* — **ab·dom·i·nal·ly** \-ē\ *adv*

ab·duct \ab-'dəkt\ *vb* **1** : to carry (a person) off by force **2** : to draw (a part of the body) away from a middle plane or line that divides the body or a bodily part into right and left halves — **ab·duc·tion** \-'dək-shən\ *n*

ab·duc·tor \ab-'dək-tər\ *n* : one that abducts; *esp* : a muscle that draws a body part (as an arm or finger) away from a plane or a line that divides the body or a hand or foot into right and left halves

abeam \ə-'bēm\ *adv or adj* : at right angles to a ship or plane's length

abed \ə-'bed\ *adv or adj* : in bed

Ab·er·deen An·gus \ˌab-ər-ˌdē-'naŋ-gəs\ *n* : ANGUS

ab·er·rant \ə-'ber-ənt, 'ab-ə-rənt\ *adj* : being different from the usual or natural type

ab·er·ra·tion \ˌab-ə-'rā-shən\ *n* **1** : the act of differing especially from a moral standard or normal state **2** : unsoundness or disorder of the mind **3** : a small regularly occurring change of apparent position in heavenly bodies due to the combined effect of the motion of light and the motion of the observer

\ə\ abut	\au̇\ out	\i\ tip	\ȯ\ saw	\u̇\ foot
\ər\ further	\ch\ chin	\ī\ life	\ȯi\ coin	\y\ yet
\a\ mat	\e\ pet	\j\ job	\th\ thin	\yü\ few
\ā\ take	\ē\ easy	\ŋ\ sing	\t̲h̲\ this	\yu̇\ cure
\ä\ cot, cart	\g\ go	\ō\ bone	\ü\ food	\zh\ vision

abet \ə-'bet\ *vb* **abet·ted; abet·ting** : to actively encourage or aid — **abet·ment** \-mənt\ *n* — **abet·tor** *also* **abet·ter** \-'bet-ər\ *n*

abey·ance \ə-'bā-ən(t)s\ *n* : a temporary interruption of activity ⟨plans held in *abeyance*⟩ — **abey·ant** \-ənt\ *adj*

ab·hor \əb-'hȯ(ə)r, ab-\ *vb* **ab·horred; ab·hor·ring** : to shrink from in disgust *synonyms* see HATE — **ab·hor·rence** \-'hȯr-ən(t)s, -'här-\ *n* — **ab·hor·rer** \-'hȯr-ər\ *n*

ab·hor·rent \əb-'hȯr-ənt, -'här-, ab-\ *adj* **1** : causing or deserving strong dislike **2** : not agreeable : CONTRARY ⟨a notion *abhorrent* to their beliefs⟩ — **ab·hor·rent·ly** *adv*

abide \ə-'bīd\ *vb* **abode** \-'bōd\ *or* **abid·ed; abid·ing** **1** : to wait for **2** : to bear patiently : TOLERATE **3** : ¹LAST 1, ENDURE ⟨an *abiding* friendship⟩ **4** : to live or continue in a place : DWELL — **abid·ance** \ə-'bīd-ən(t)s\ *n* — **abid·er** *n* — **abide by** : to accept the terms of : be obedient to ⟨*abide by* the rules⟩

abil·i·ty \ə-'bil-ət-ē\ *n, pl* **-ties** **1 a** : the quality or state of being able : power to do something **b** : competence in doing : SKILL **2** : natural or learned skill
   synonyms ABILITY, APTITUDE, TALENT mean the capacity for doing or achieving something. ABILITY suggests having from birth the power to do a thing especially well ⟨always has had the *ability* to run fast⟩. APTITUDE suggests a quickness to learn and a natural liking usually for a field or activity ⟨people with a natural *aptitude* for computers⟩. TALENT suggests a great ability to create things and one that needs to be developed ⟨you should work on your *talent* for writing short stories⟩.

-abil·i·ty *also* **-ibil·i·ty** \ə-'bil-ət-ē\ *n suffix, pl* **-ties** : ability, fitness, or likeliness to act or be acted on in (such) a way ⟨read*ability*⟩ [derived from Latin *-abilitas, -ibilitas* "-ability"]

abi·ot·ic \,ā-bī-'ät-ik\ *adj* : not living or composed of living things ⟨water and soil are *abiotic* parts of an environment⟩

ab·ject \'ab-,jekt\ *adj* : very low in spirit or hope : WRETCHED ⟨*abject* misery⟩ ⟨an *abject* coward⟩ — **ab·ject·ly** \'ab-,jek-(t)lē, ab-'jek-\ *adv* — **ab·ject·ness** \-,jek(t)-nəs, -'jek(t)-\ *n*

ab·jure \ab-'jů(ə)r\ *vb* **ab·jured; ab·jur·ing** : to give up, abandon, or reject solemnly ⟨*abjure* allegiance⟩

ab·late \a-'blāt\ *vb* **ab·lat·ed; ab·lat·ing** : to remove or become removed by cutting, wearing away, evaporating, or vaporizing

ab·la·tion \a-'blā-shən\ *n* : the process of ablating: as **a** : surgical cutting and removal **b** : removal of a part (as the outside of a nose cone) by melting or vaporization

ablaze \ə-'blāz\ *adj* **1** : being on fire **2** : radiant with light or bright color

able \'ā-bəl\ *adj* **abler** \-b(ə-)lər\; **ablest** \-b(ə-)ləst\ **1 a** : having enough power, skill, or resources to do something ⟨*able* to swim⟩ **b** : not prevented ⟨*able* to vote⟩ **2** : SKILLFUL, COMPETENT ⟨an *able* editor⟩ [Middle English *able* "able," from early French *able* (same meaning), from Latin *habilis* "easily managed, skillful," from *habēre* "to have"]

-able *also* **-ible** \ə-bəl\ *adj suffix* **1** : capable of, fit for, or worthy of being ⟨collect*ible*⟩ **2** : tending, given, or likely to ⟨perish*able*⟩ ⟨agree*able*⟩ [derived from Latin *-abilis, -ibilis* "-able"]

able–bod·ied \,ā-bəl-'bäd-ēd\ *adj* : having a healthy strong body : physically fit

abloom \ə-'blüm\ *adj* : being in bloom

ab·lu·tion \ə-'blü-shən, a-'blü-\ *n* : washing oneself especially as a religious rite

ably \'ā-blē\ *adv* : in an able manner

ABM \,ā-(,)bē-'em\ *n* : ANTIBALLISTIC MISSILE

ab·ne·gate \'ab-ni-,gāt\ *vb* **-gat·ed; -gat·ing** **1** : to give up a right or privilege ⟨*abnegate* her power⟩ **2** : to deny to oneself : RENOUNCE ⟨*abnegating* outdated beliefs⟩ — **ab·ne·ga·tion** \,ab-ni-'gā-shən\ *n*

ab·nor·mal \(')ab-'nȯr-məl\ *adj* : differing from the normal or average : UNUSUAL — **ab·nor·mal·ly** \-mə-lē\ *adv*

ab·nor·mal·i·ty \,ab-nər-'mal-ət-ē, -(,)nȯr-\ *n, pl* **-ties** **1** : the state of being abnormal **2** : something abnormal

¹**aboard** \ə-'bōrd, -'bȯrd\ *adv* : on, onto, or within a vehicle (as a car, ship, or airplane)

²**aboard** *prep* : on or into especially as a passenger ⟨go *aboard* ship⟩

abode \ə-'bōd\ *n* : the place where one stays or lives

abol·ish \ə-'bäl-ish\ *vb* : to do away with completely : put an end to — **abol·ish·able** \-ə-bəl\ *adj* — **abol·ish·er** *n* — **abol·ish·ment** \-mənt\ *n*

ab·o·li·tion \,ab-ə-'lish-ən\ *n* **1** : the act of abolishing : the state of being abolished **2** : the abolishing of slavery — **ab·o·li·tion·ary** \-'lish-ə-,ner-ē\ *adj*

ab·o·li·tion·ist \ab-ə-'lish-(ə-)nəst\ *n* : a person who is in favor of abolishing especially slavery — **ab·o·li·tion·ism** \-'lish-ə-,niz-əm\ *n*

A–bomb \'ā-,bäm\ *n* : ATOMIC BOMB

abom·i·na·ble \ə-'bäm-(ə-)nə-bəl\ *adj* **1** : deserving or causing disgust : HATEFUL, DETESTABLE ⟨*abominable* behavior⟩ **2** : quite disagreeable ⟨*abominable* weather⟩ — **abom·i·na·bly** \-blē\ *adv*

abominable snow·man \-'snō-mən, -,man\ *n, often cap A&S* : a creature somewhat resembling a human being or ape that is reported to exist in the Himalayas

abom·i·nate \ə-'bäm-ə-,nāt\ *vb* **-nat·ed; -nat·ing** : HATE, LOATHE — **abom·i·na·tor** \-,nāt-ər\ *n*

abom·i·na·tion \ə-,bäm-ə-'nā-shən\ *n* **1** : something detestable **2** : extreme disgust and hatred : LOATHING

ab·orig·i·nal \,ab-ə-'rij-nəl, -ən-ᵊl\ *adj* **1** : being the first of its kind in a region : INDIGENOUS **2** : of, relating to, or being aborigines — **ab·orig·i·nal·ly** \-ē\ *adv*

ab·orig·i·ne \,ab-ə-'rij-ə-(,)nē\ *n* **1** : a member of the original people to live in an area : NATIVE **2** *often cap* : a member of any of the native people of Australia [from Latin *aborigines* "original inhabitants," from *ab origine* "from the beginning," from *origin-, origo* "beginning, source," from *oriri* "to rise" — related to ORIGIN]

abort \ə-'bȯrt\ *vb* **1** : to bring forth premature or stillborn offspring **2** : to become checked in development **3** : to put an end to before completion ⟨*abort* a project⟩

abor·tion \ə-'bȯr-shən\ *n* **1** : a premature birth whether natural or caused artificially that occurs before the fetus can survive **2** : failure of a project or action to reach full development; *also* : a result of such failure

abor·tion·ist \ə-'bȯr-sh(ə-)nəst\ *n* : one who produces abortions

abor·tive \ə-'bȯrt-iv\ *adj* **1** : unsuccessful in achieving the desired conclusion or result ⟨an *abortive* escape attempt⟩ **2** : imperfectly formed or developed : RUDIMENTARY — **abor·tive·ly** *adv* — **abor·tive·ness** *n*

abound \ə-'baůnd\ *vb* **1** : to be present in large numbers or in great quantity ⟨wildlife *abounds*⟩ **2** : to be filled or abundantly supplied ⟨a stream *abounding* in fish⟩

¹**about** \ə-'baůt\ *adv* **1** : on all sides : AROUND ⟨wander *about*⟩ ⟨people standing *about*⟩ **2 a** : reasonably close to : APPROXIMATELY, NEARLY ⟨*about* three years⟩ ⟨*about* ready to go⟩ **b** : on the verge of ⟨is *about* to go home⟩ **3** : in the opposite direction ⟨face *about*⟩

²**about** *prep* **1** : on every side of : AROUND ⟨houses *about* the lake⟩ **2 a** : ²NEAR **b** : in the possession of ⟨had no pencil *about* her⟩ **c** : in the control of ⟨keeps her wits *about* her⟩ **3** : in the act or process of doing ⟨do it well while you're *about* it⟩ **4** : having to do with : CONCERNING ⟨tell me *about* it⟩ ⟨a book *about* birds⟩ **5** : over or in different parts of ⟨traveled *about* the country⟩

about–face \ə-'baůt-'fās\ *n* **1** : a reversal of direction **2** : a reversal of attitude or point of view — **about–face** *vb*

¹**above** \ə-'bəv\ *adv* **1** : in or to a higher place : OVERHEAD **2** : higher on the same or a preceding page **3** : in or to a higher rank or number

²above *prep* **1** : in or to a higher place than : OVER **2** : superior to ⟨a captain is *above* a lieutenant⟩ ⟨*above* criticism⟩ **3** : too proud or honorable to stoop to ⟨*above* such mean tricks⟩ **4** : exceeding in number, quantity, or size : more than ⟨*above* the average⟩ **5** : as distinct from and in addition to ⟨heard the bell *above* the roar of the crowd⟩

³above *adj* : written above

above·board \ə-'bəv-ˌbōrd, -ˌbȯrd\ *adv or adj* : without concealment or deceit

above·ground \ə-'bəv-ˌgraůnd\ *adj* : located or happening on or above the surface of the ground ⟨an *above-ground* swimming pool⟩

ab·ra·ca·dab·ra \ˌab-rə-kə-'dab-rə\ *n* **1** : a magical charm or word **2** : unintelligible language : JARGON

abrade \ə-'brād\ *vb* **abrad·ed; abrad·ing** **1** : to rub or wear away especially by friction **2** : to irritate or roughen by rubbing — **abrad·er** *n*

abra·sion \ə-'brā-zhən\ *n* **1** : a rubbing, grinding, or wearing away by friction **2** : a place where the surface has been rubbed or scraped off ⟨an *abrasion* on her knee⟩

¹abra·sive \ə-'brā-siv, -ziv\ *adj* : having the effect of abrading — **abra·sive·ly** *adv* — **abra·sive·ness** *n*

²abrasive *n* : a substance (as sand) used for grinding, smoothing, or polishing

abreast \ə-'brest\ *adv or adj* **1** : side by side with bodies in line ⟨lined up three *abreast*⟩ **2** : up to a standard or level especially of knowledge ⟨keep *abreast* of the times⟩

abridge \ə-'brij\ *vb* **abridged; abridg·ing** **1** : to make less : DIMINISH ⟨forbidden to *abridge* the rights of citizens⟩ **2** : to shorten in duration or extent **3** : to shorten by omission of words : CONDENSE [Middle English *abregen* "deprive, reduce," from early French *abreger* (same meaning), from Latin *abbreviare* "to shorten" — related to ABBREVIATE] — **abridg·er** *n*

abridg·ment *or* **abridge·ment** \ə-'brij-mənt\ *n* **1 a** : the action of abridging **b** : the state of being abridged **2** : a shortened form of a written work

abroad \ə-'brȯd\ *adv or adj* **1** : over a wide area **2** : away from one's home ⟨doesn't go *abroad* at night⟩ **3** : in or to foreign countries ⟨travel *abroad*⟩ **4** : in wide circulation ⟨rumors were *abroad*⟩

ab·ro·gate \'ab-rə-ˌgāt\ *vb* **-gat·ed; -gat·ing** : to do away with or cancel by authority ⟨*abrogate* a law⟩ — **ab·ro·ga·tion** \ˌab-rə-'gā-shən\ *n*

abrupt \ə-'brəpt\ *adj* **1 a** : SUDDEN 1a ⟨an *abrupt* change in the weather⟩ **b** : rudely brief : CURT ⟨an *abrupt* manner⟩ **2** : ¹STEEP 1 ⟨the high *abrupt* bank of a stream⟩ — **abrupt·ly** \ə-'brup-(t)lē\ *adv* — **abrupt·ness** \ə-'brəp(t)-nəs\ *n*

　　Word History If a person is rudely brief in speech or manner or stops you before you finish talking, you could say that that person is abrupt. If a road ends suddenly, you could say that the road comes to an abrupt end. In both of these cases you might think of something that is abrupt as "breaking off." *Abrupt* comes from the Latin word *abruptus,* meaning "broken off, ending suddenly." That word is formed (with the addition of the prefix *ab-,* meaning "from") from the Latin word *rumpere,* meaning "to break." Latin *rumpere* has given us several other English words that carry the idea of breaking: *interrupt, rupture,* and *corrupt.* [from Latin *abruptus* "abrupt," derived from *abrumpere* "to break off," from *ab-* "from" and *rumpere* "to break" — related to CORRUPT, INTERRUPT, RUPTURE]

ab·scess \'ab-ˌses\ *n* : a collection of pus surrounded by inflamed tissue at some point in the body — **ab·scessed** \-ˌsest\ *adj*

ab·scis·sa \ab-'sis-ə\ *n* : the number in an ordered pair of numbers (as *x* in (*x, y*)) that gives the location of a point along the x-axis — called also *x-coordinate;* compare ORDINATE

ab·scis·sion \ab-'sizh-ən\ *n* **1** : the act or process of cutting off **2** : the natural separation of flowers, fruit, or leaves from plants

ab·scond \ab-'skänd, əb-\ *vb* : to leave secretly and hide oneself — **ab·scond·er** *n*

ab·sence \'ab-sən(t)s\ *n* **1** : the state of being absent **2** : the time that one is absent **3** : ²WANT 1a, LACK ⟨*absence* of detail⟩

¹ab·sent \'ab-sənt\ *adj* **1** : not present or attending : MISSING **2** : not existing ⟨enthusiasm was *absent*⟩ **3** : lost in thought : PREOCCUPIED — **ab·sent·ly** *adv*

²ab·sent \ab-'sent\ *vb* : to keep (oneself) away

ab·sen·tee \ˌab-sən-'tē\ *n* : a person who is absent — **absentee** *adj*

ab·sent·mind·ed \ˌab-sənt-'mīn-dəd\ *adj* : lost in thought and unaware of one's surroundings or actions — **ab·sent·mind·ed·ly** *adv* — **ab·sent·mind·ed·ness** *n*

ab·so·lute \'ab-sə-ˌlüt, ˌab-sə-'lüt\ *adj* **1 a** : free from imperfection : PERFECT **b** : free or nearly free from mixture : PURE ⟨*absolute* alcohol⟩ **2** : free from restraint or limitation ⟨*absolute* power⟩ ⟨an *absolute* monarch⟩ **3** : having no exceptions ⟨an *absolute* requirement⟩ ⟨*absolute* freedom⟩ **4** : free from doubt : CERTAIN ⟨*absolute* proof⟩ **5 a** : independent of standards of measurement that reflect individual choice : ACTUAL ⟨*absolute* brightness of a star⟩ ⟨*absolute* motion⟩ **b** : relating to or coming from the basic units of length, mass, and time ⟨*absolute* electric units⟩ **c** : relating to the absolute-temperature scale ⟨10° *absolute*⟩ — **ab·so·lute·ness** \-ˌlüt-nəs, -'lüt-\ *n*

ab·so·lute·ly \'ab-sə-ˌlüt-lē, ˌab-sə-'lüt-\ *adv* : in an absolute way : completely or definitely ⟨you are *absolutely* right⟩

absolute temperature *n* : temperature measured on a scale that has absolute zero as the zero point

absolute value *n* : a nonnegative number that is equal to a given number with any negative sign removed ⟨the *absolute value* of -3 is 3⟩

absolute zero *n* : a hypothetical temperature that has never been reached, represents no heat at all, and is equal to approximately −273.15°C or −459.67°F

ab·so·lu·tion \ˌab-sə-'lü-shən\ *n* : the act of absolving; *esp* : a forgiving of sins

ab·solve \əb-'zälv, -'sälv, -'zȯlv, -'sȯlv\ *vb* **ab·solved; ab·solv·ing** : to set free from an obligation or punishment — **ab·solv·er** *n*

ab·sorb \əb-'sȯrb, -'zȯrb\ *vb* **1** : to take in or suck or swallow up ⟨a sponge *absorbs* water⟩ ⟨plant roots *absorb* water⟩ **2** : to hold the interest of : ENGROSS ⟨*absorbed* in thought⟩ **3 a** : to receive without giving back ⟨a sound-*absorbing* surface⟩ **b** : to transform (radiant energy) into a different form usually with a resulting rise in temperature ⟨the earth *absorbs* the sun's rays⟩ — **ab·sorb·abil·i·ty** \əb-ˌsȯr-bə-'bil-ət-ē, -ˌzȯr-\ *n* — **ab·sorb·able** \əb-'sȯr-bə-bəl, -'zȯr-\ *adj* — **ab·sorb·er** *n*

ab·sor·bent \əb-'sȯr-bənt, -'zȯr-\ *adj* : able to absorb ⟨as *absorbent* as a sponge⟩ — **ab·sor·ben·cy** \əb-'sȯr-bən-sē, -'zȯr-\ *n* — **absorbent** *n*

ab·sorp·tion \əb-'sȯrp-shən, -'zȯrp-\ *n* **1** : the process of absorbing or being absorbed: as **a** : the passing of di-

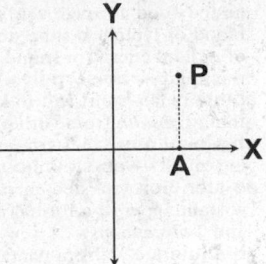

abscissa: *A* is the abscissa of point *P*

\ə\ abut	\aů\ out	\i\ tip	\ȯ\ saw	\ů\ foot
\ər\ further	\ch\ chin	\ī\ life	\ȯi\ coin	\y\ yet
\a\ mat	\e\ pet	\j\ job	\th\ thin	\yü\ few
\ā\ take	\ē\ easy	\ŋ\ sing	\th\ this	\yů\ cure
\ä\ cot, cart	\g\ go	\ō\ bone	\ü\ food	\zh\ vision

gested food through the wall of the intestines into the blood or lymph **b** : the stopping and taking in especially of radiant energy or sound waves **2** : entire occupation of the mind — **ab·sorp·tive** \-'sȯrp-tiv, -'zȯrp-\ *adj*

ab·stain \əb-'stān\ *vb* : to keep oneself from doing something ⟨*abstain* from voting⟩ — **ab·stain·er** *n*

ab·ste·mi·ous \ab-'stē-mē-əs\ *adj* : not eating and drinking much — **ab·ste·mi·ous·ly** *adv*

ab·sten·tion \əb-'sten-chən, ab-\ *n* : the act or practice of abstaining; *esp* : a formal refusal to vote ⟨3 ayes, 5 nays, and 2 *abstentions*⟩

ab·sti·nence \'ab-stə-nən(t)s\ *n* **1** : an abstaining from giving in to an appetite or from eating some foods **2 a** : habitual abstaining from drinking alcoholic beverages **b** : abstention from sexual intercourse — **ab·sti·nent** \-nənt\ *adj* — **ab·sti·nent·ly** *adv*

¹**ab·stract** \ab-'strakt, 'ab-ˌstrakt\ *adj* **1** : expressing a quality or idea without reference to an actual person or thing ⟨"honesty" is an *abstract* word⟩ **2** : difficult to understand : HARD ⟨*abstract* problems⟩ **3** : using elements of form (as color, line, or texture) with little or no attempt at creating a realistic picture ⟨*abstract* art⟩ [from Latin *abstractus* "abstract," from earlier *abstrahere* "to draw away," from *abs-, ab-* "from, away" and *trahere* "to draw" — related to ATTRACT, ¹TRACE, ³TRACE] — **ab·stract·ly** \ab-'strak-(t)lē, 'ab-ˌstrak-\ *adv* — **ab·stract·ness** \ab-'strak(t)-nəs, 'ab-ˌstrak(t)-\ *n*

²**ab·stract** \'ab-ˌstrakt\ *n* : a brief statement of the main points or facts : SUMMARY

³**ab·stract** \ab-'strakt, 'ab-ˌstrakt, *in sense 3 usually* 'ab-ˌstrakt\ *vb* **1** : to take out : REMOVE ⟨*abstract* a diamond from a pile of sand⟩ **2** : to consider apart from a particular instance ⟨*abstract* the idea of roundness from a ball⟩ **3** : to make an abstract of : SUMMARIZE **4** : to draw away the attention of — **ab·strac·tor** *or* **ab·stract·er** \-'strak-tər, -ˌstrak-\ *n*

ab·stract·ed \ab-'strak-təd, 'ab-ˌstrak-\ *adj* : PREOCCUPIED 1, ABSENTMINDED — **ab·stract·ed·ly** *adv* — **ab·stract·ed·ness** *n*

ab·strac·tion \ab-'strak-shən\ *n* **1 a** : the act or process of abstracting : the state of being abstracted **b** : an abstract idea or term **2** : an artistic composition or creation having designs that do not represent actual objects — **ab·strac·tive** \-'strak-tiv\ *adj*

ab·struse \əb-'strüs, ab-\ *adj* : hard to understand — **ab·struse·ly** *adv* — **ab·struse·ness** *n*

ab·surd \əb-'sərd, -'zərd\ *adj* : completely unreasonable or untrue : RIDICULOUS — **ab·sur·di·ty** \-'sərd-ət-ē, -'zərd-\ *n* — **ab·surd·ly** *adv* — **ab·surd·ness** *n*

abun·dance \ə-'bən-dən(t)s\ *n* **1** : a large quantity : PLENTY **2** : WEALTH 1

abun·dant \ə-'bən-dənt\ *adj* : existing in or possessing abundance : ABOUNDING *synonyms* see PLENTIFUL — **abun·dant·ly** *adv*

¹**abuse** \ə-'byüz\ *vb* **abused; abus·ing 1 a** : to use wrongly : MISUSE ⟨*abuse* a privilege⟩ **b** : to use excessively ⟨*abuse* alcohol⟩ **2** : to treat cruelly : MISTREAT ⟨*abuse* a dog⟩ **3** : to attack in words : scold rudely — **abus·er** *n*

²**abuse** \ə-'byüs\ *n* **1** : a corrupt practice or custom ⟨election *abuses*⟩ **2 a** : improper or excessive use or treatment : MISUSE ⟨*abuse* of privileges⟩ ⟨drug *abuse*⟩ **b** : physical mistreatment **3** : harsh insulting language

abu·sive \ə-'byü-siv, -ziv\ *adj* : using or characterized by abuse — **abu·sive·ly** *adv* — **abu·sive·ness** *n*

abut \ə-'bət\ *vb* **abut·ted; abut·ting** : to touch along a border or with a part that sticks out — **abut·ter** *n*

abut·ment \ə-'bət-mənt\ *n* **1** : the place of abutting **2** : something against

abutment 2

which another thing rests its weight or pushes with force ⟨*abutments* that support a bridge⟩

abys·mal \ə-'biz-məl\ *adj* **1** : resembling an abyss in huge extent ⟨*abysmal* ignorance⟩ **2** : ABYSSAL — **abys·mal·ly** \-mə-lē\ *adv*

abyss \ə-'bis\ *n* : a gulf so deep or a space so great that it cannot be measured

abys·sal \ə-'bis-əl\ *adj* : of or relating to the bottom waters of the ocean depths

ac- — see AD-

aca·cia \ə-'kā-shə\ *n* **1** : GUM ARABIC **2** : any of numerous shrubs and trees of the legume family that grow in warm areas and have white or yellow flower clusters

acacia 2

ac·a·dem·ic \ˌak-ə-'dem-ik\ *adj* **1** : of or relating to school or college **2** : literary or general rather than technical ⟨took the *academic* course⟩ **3** : having no practical importance : THEORETICAL ⟨an *academic* question⟩ — **ac·a·dem·i·cal·ly** \-'dem-i-k(ə-)lē\ *adv*

acad·e·my \ə-'kad-ə-mē\ *n, pl* **-mies** **1 a** : ¹SCHOOL 1a; *esp* : a private high school **b** : an institution for training in special subjects or skills ⟨military *academy*⟩ **2** : an organization of people specializing in knowledge in a particular subject

Word History Our word *academy* comes from the Greek word *Akadēmeia,* the name of the park or grove outside of ancient Athens where the philosopher Plato taught his students. Just as schools and parks today are often named after famous persons, the *Akadēmeia* had been named in honor of a Greek hero, *Akadēmos.* [Greek *Akadēmeia,* the grove outside Athens where Plato had his school]

a cap·pel·la *also* **a ca·pel·la** \ˌäk-ə-'pel-ə\ *adv or adj* : without accompanying instrumental music ⟨sing *a cappella*⟩ [from Italian *a cappella* "in chapel style"]

ac·cede \ak-'sēd, ik-\ *vb* **ac·ced·ed; ac·ced·ing 1** : to give consent : AGREE ⟨*accede* to a proposed plan⟩ **2** : to enter upon an office or position ⟨*acceded* to the throne in 1838⟩

ac·ce·le·ran·do \(ˌ)ä-ˌchel-ə-'rän-dō\ *adv or adj* : gradually faster — used as a direction in music

ac·cel·er·ate \ik-'sel-ə-ˌrāt, ak-\ *vb* **-at·ed; -at·ing 1** : to bring about earlier ⟨*accelerated* our departure⟩ **2** : to move or cause to move faster — **ac·cel·er·a·tive** \-ˌrāt-iv\ *adj*

ac·cel·er·a·tion \ik-ˌsel-ə-'rā-shən, ak-\ *n* **1** : the act or process of accelerating : the state of being accelerated **2** : the rate of change of velocity with respect to time; *also* : change in velocity

acceleration of gravity : the acceleration of a freely falling body under the influence of gravity that is expressed as the rate of increase of velocity per unit of time and that amounts to a value of about 9.81 meters (32.2 feet) per second per second

ac·cel·er·a·tor \ik-'sel-ə-ˌrāt-ər, ak-\ *n* **1** : one that accelerates **2** : a device (as a pedal) in a motor vehicle used to control the speed of the motor **3** : a device that is used to give high velocities to charged particles (as electrons and protons)

ac·cel·er·om·e·ter \ik-ˌsel-ə-'räm-ət-ər, ak-\ *n* : an instrument for measuring acceleration or for detecting and measuring vibrations

¹**ac·cent** \'ak-ˌsent\ *n* **1** : a way of talking shared by a group (as the people of a country) **2** : greater stress or force given to a syllable of a word in speaking ⟨*before* has the *accent* on the last syllable⟩ **3** : a mark (as ´, `, or ˆ accents) identifying a syllable that is stressed in speaking **4**

: greater stress given to a beat in music **5** : an emphasized detail used for contrast

²ac·cent \ak-'sent, 'ak-¸sent\ *vb* **1** : to make noticeable : EMPHASIZE **2 a** : to say with an accent : STRESS **b** : to mark with a written or printed accent

accent mark *n* **1** : ¹ACCENT 3 **2** : one of several symbols used to indicate musical stress

ac·cen·tu·ate \ik-'sen-chə-¸wāt, ak-\ *vb* **-at·ed; -at·ing** **1** : to pronounce or mark with an accent **2** : EMPHA-SIZE ⟨the blue shirt *accentuates* your eyes⟩ — **ac·cen·tu·a·tion** \ik-¸sen-chə-'wā-shən, (¸)ak-\ *n*

accent mark 2

ac·cept \ik-'sept, ak-\ *vb* **1 a** : to receive or take willingly ⟨*accept* a gift⟩ ⟨*accepted* her as a member⟩ **b** : to be able or designed to take or hold (something applied or added) ⟨a surface that will not *accept* ink⟩ ⟨a computer program ready to *accept* commands⟩ **2 a** : to agree to ⟨*accept* an offer⟩ **b** : to agree to undertake (a responsibility) ⟨*accept* a job⟩ **c** : to take on an obligation to pay; *also* : to take in payment ⟨don't *accept* checks⟩ **3** : to think of as proper or normal ⟨the idea is widely *accepted*⟩ [Middle English *accepten* "receive, accept," from early French *accepter* (same meaning), derived from Latin *accipere* "receive," from *ac-, ad-* "to" and *capere* "to take" — related to CAPTURE, EXCEPT, RECEIVE] — **ac·cept·er** *or* **ac·cep·tor** \-'sep-tər\ *n*

ac·cept·able \ik-'sep-tə-bəl, ak-\ *adj* **1** : capable or worthy of being accepted : SATISFACTORY ⟨an *acceptable* excuse⟩ **2** : barely good enough ⟨plays an *acceptable* game⟩ — **ac·cept·abil·i·ty** \ik-¸sep-tə-'bil-ət-ē, ak-\ *n* — **ac·cept·ably** \ik-'sep-tə-blē, ak-\ *adv*

ac·cep·tance \ik-'sep-tən(t)s, ak-\ *n* **1** : the act of accepting **2** : the quality or state of being accepted or acceptable

ac·cep·ta·tion \¸ak-¸sep-'tā-shən\ *n* : the generally understood meaning of a word or expression

¹ac·cess \'ak-¸ses\ *n* **1** : permission or power to enter, approach, or make use of ⟨*access* to secret information⟩ ⟨Internet *access*⟩ **2** : a way or means of approach ⟨a nation's *access* to the sea⟩

²access *vb* : to get at : gain access to

ac·ces·si·ble \ik-'ses-ə-bəl, ak-\ *adj* **1** : capable of being reached ⟨a resort *accessible* by train or bus⟩ **2** : capable of being used, seen, or known : OBTAINABLE ⟨*accessible* information⟩ — **ac·ces·si·bil·i·ty** \ik-¸ses-ə-'bil-ət-ē, ak-\ *n* — **ac·ces·si·bly** \-blē\ *adv*

ac·ces·sion \ik-'sesh-ən, ak-\ *n* **1** : something added : ACQUISITION **2** : increase by something added **3** : the act of agreeing ⟨*accession* to a proposal⟩ **4** : the act of coming to office or power ⟨the *accession* of a king⟩

ac·ces·so·rize \ik-'ses-ə-¸rīz, ak-\ *vb* **-rized; -riz·ing** : to wear or decorate with accessories

¹ac·ces·so·ry \ik-'ses-(ə-)rē, ak-\ *n, pl* **-ries** **1** : something (as an object or device) that is not necessary in itself but adds to the beauty, convenience, or effectiveness of something else **2** : a person who aids another in doing wrong or in an attempt to escape justice

²accessory *adj* : aiding or helping in a secondary way : SUPPLEMENTARY

accessory fruit *n* : a fruit (as the strawberry, apple, or fig) of which a conspicuous part consists of tissue other than that of the ripened ovary

access time *n* : the time lag between the time stored information (as in a computer) is requested and the time it is delivered

ac·ci·dent \'ak-səd-ənt, -sə-¸dent\ *n* **1 a** : an event occurring by chance or from unknown causes **b** : ¹CHANCE 1

⟨we met by *accident*⟩ **2** : an unintended and usually sudden and unexpected event resulting in loss or injury ⟨an automobile *accident*⟩

¹ac·ci·den·tal \¸ak-sə-'dent-ᵊl\ *adj* **1** : happening unexpectedly or by chance ⟨an *accidental* discovery of oil⟩ **2** : not happening or done on purpose ⟨an *accidental* fall⟩ — **ac·ci·den·tal·ly** \-'dent-lē, -'dent-ᵊl-ē\ *adv*

²accidental *n* : a musical note whose pitch is changed (as by a sharp or a flat) from the pitch shown in the key signature

ac·cip·i·ter \ak-'sip-ət-ər\ *n* : any of various low-flying hawks that have short wings and long tails

¹ac·claim \ə-'klām\ *vb* **1** : to welcome with applause or great praise ⟨a novel *acclaimed* by the critics⟩ **2** : to proclaim by or as if by acclamation [from Latin *acclamare*, literally "to shout at," from *ac-, ad-* "to, toward" and *clamare* "to shout" — related to CLAIM, CLAMOR] — **ac·claim·er** *n*

²acclaim *n* **1** : the act of acclaiming **2** : APPLAUSE, PRAISE

ac·cla·ma·tion \¸ak-lə-'mā-shən\ *n* **1** : a loud eager expression of approval, praise, or agreement **2** : an overwhelming positive vote by voice ⟨elected by *acclamation*⟩

ac·cli·mate \'ak-lə-¸māt, ə-'klī-mət, -¸māt\ *vb* **-mat·ed; -mat·ing** : to adapt to a new climate, environment, or situation — **ac·cli·ma·tion** \¸ak-lə-'mā-shən, ¸ak-¸lī-\ *n*

ac·cli·ma·tize \ə-'klī-mə-¸tīz\ *vb* **-tized; -tiz·ing** : ACCLI-MATE — **ac·cli·ma·ti·za·tion** \ə-¸klī-mət-ə-'zā-shən\ *n*

ac·co·lade \'ak-ə-¸lād\ *n* **1** : a formal salute (as a tap on the shoulder with the blade of a sword) that marks the conferring of knighthood **2** : a mark of recognition of merit : PRAISE

ac·com·mo·date \ə-'käm-ə-¸dāt\ *vb* **-dat·ed; -dat·ing** **1** : ADAPT **2** : to bring into agreement ⟨*accommodate* the differences⟩ **3** : to do a favor for : OBLIGE 2b ⟨*accommodated* me with a ride⟩ **4** : to provide with something desired: as **a** : to provide with lodgings **b** : to make or have room for ⟨the table *accommodates* 12 comfortably⟩ **5** : to undergo visual accommodation ⟨the lens of the eye *accommodates*⟩ *synonyms* see CONTAIN — **ac·com·mo·da·tive** \-¸dāt-iv\ *adj* — **ac·com·mo·da·tive·ness** *n*

accommodating *adj* : ready and willing to help : OBLIG-ING — **ac·com·mo·dat·ing·ly** *adv*

ac·com·mo·da·tion \ə-¸käm-ə-'dā-shən\ *n* **1 a** : something supplied that is useful and handy **b** *pl* : lodging and meals or traveling space and related services ⟨overnight *accommodations*⟩ **2** : the act of accommodating : the state of being accommodated **3** : the automatic adjustment of the eye for seeing at different distances **4** : an adjustment of differences : SETTLEMENT

ac·com·pa·ni·ment \ə-'kəmp-(ə-)nē-mənt\ *n* **1** : music played along with a solo part to enrich it **2** : an accompanying object, situation, or event

ac·com·pa·nist \ə-'kəmp-(ə-)nəst\ *n* : a musician who plays an accompaniment

ac·com·pa·ny \ə-'kəmp-(ə-)nē\ *vb* **-nied; -ny·ing** **1** : to go with or attend as a companion **2** : to perform an accompaniment to or for **3** : to occur at the same time as or along with ⟨a thunderstorm *accompanied* by high winds⟩ [Middle English *accompanien* "to accompany," from early French *acompaigner* (same meaning), from *a-* "to" and *cumpaing* "companion," from Latin *companio* "companion" — related to COMPANION, COMPANY]

synonyms ACCOMPANY, ATTEND, ESCORT mean to go along with. ACCOMPANY stresses the closeness of the re-

\ə\ abut	\au̇\ out	\i\ tip	\ȯ\ saw	\u̇\ foot
\ər\ further	\ch\ chin	\ī\ life	\ȯi\ coin	\y\ yet
\a\ mat	\e\ pet	\j\ job	\th\ thin	\yü\ few
\ā\ take	\ē\ easy	\ŋ\ sing	\t͟h\ this	\yu̇\ cure
\ä\ cot, cart	\g\ go	\ō\ bone	\ü\ food	\zh\ vision

lationship and stresses that the people are equals ⟨my friends *accompanied* me to the movies⟩. ATTEND suggests waiting upon and serving someone of higher rank ⟨assistants and bodyguards *attended* the President⟩. ESCORT suggests that one is going along as a matter of protection, ceremony, or courtesy ⟨a marching band *escorted* the heroes⟩.

ac·com·plice \ə-'käm-pləs, -'kəm-\ *n* : someone associated with another in wrongdoing

ac·com·plish \ə-'käm-plish, -'kəm-\ *vb* : to bring to a successful finish : PERFORM — **ac·com·plish·able** \-ə-bəl\ *adj*

ac·com·plished \-pisht\ *adj* **1 a** : skilled or polished through practice or training : EXPERT ⟨an *accomplished* pianist⟩ **b** : having done or achieved many good or important things **2** : shown or known to be true ⟨an *accomplished* fact⟩

ac·com·plish·ment \ə-'käm-plish-mənt, -'kəm-\ *n* **1** : the act of accomplishing : COMPLETION **2** : something accomplished : ACHIEVEMENT **3** : an ability, social quality, or skill gained through training or practice

¹ac·cord \ə-'kórd\ *vb* **1** : to grant as suitable or proper ⟨rights *accorded* to citizens⟩ **2** : to be in harmony : AGREE ⟨a theory that *accords* with known fact⟩

²accord *n* **1 a** : AGREEMENT 1b, HARMONY **b** : an agreement between parties ⟨reach an *accord*⟩ **2** : willingness to act or do something ⟨went of their own *accord*⟩

ac·cor·dance \ə-'kórd-²n(t)s\ *n* : AGREEMENT 1b, CONFORMITY ⟨in *accordance* with a rule⟩

ac·cord·ing as \ə-'kórd-iŋ-\ *conj* **1** : in accord with the way in which **2** : depending on how or whether

ac·cord·ing·ly \ə-'kórd-iŋ-lē\ *adv* **1** : in accordance : CORRESPONDINGLY **2** : CONSEQUENTLY, SO

according to *prep* **1** : in agreement with ⟨did everything *according to* the rules⟩ **2** : as stated by ⟨*according to* the experts⟩ **3** : depending on ⟨dress *according to* the weather⟩

¹ac·cor·di·on \ə-'kórd-ē-ən\ *n* : a musical instrument that has a keyboard and a bellows and that produces tones when air is forced past metal reeds — **ac·cor·di·on·ist** \-ē-ə-nəst\ *n*

²accordion *adj* : creased to fold like an accordion ⟨*accordion* doors⟩

¹accordion

ac·cost \ə-'kóst, -'käst\ *vb* : to approach and speak to often in a challenging or aggressive way

¹ac·count \ə-'kaúnt\ *n* **1** : a record of money paid out and money received **2** : a statement listing purchases and credits : BILL **3 a** : ¹VALUE 3 ⟨a man of little *account*⟩ **b** : ¹REGARD 2a ⟨held in high *account*⟩ **4** : ¹PROFIT 1, ADVANTAGE ⟨labored to no *account*⟩ **5 a** : a statement of reasons, causes, or motives ⟨gave an *account* of her actions⟩ **b** : a statement of facts ⟨*accounts* of the game⟩ **c** : a reason for an action ⟨on that *account* I must refuse⟩ **6 a** : a sum of money deposited in a bank **b** : an arrangement in which a person uses the Internet or e-mail services of a particular company [Middle English *acount, accompt* "the act or result of counting," from early French *acunte* (same meaning), from *acunter* (verb) "to add, count," from *a-* "to" and *cunter* "to count," from Latin *computare* "to count, compute" — related to COMPUTE, ¹COUNT] *synonyms* see NARRATIVE — **on account of** : for the sake of : by reason of : BECAUSE OF — **on no account** : in no circumstances

²account *vb* **1** : to think of as ⟨*accounts* herself lucky⟩ **2** : to give an explanation ⟨have to *account* for the money I spent⟩ **3** : to be the cause ⟨illness *accounts* for so many absences⟩

ac·count·able \ə-'kaúnt-ə-bəl\ *adj* **1** : responsible for giving an account (as of one's acts) ⟨will be held *accountable*⟩ **2** : capable of being accounted for : EXPLAINABLE — **ac·count·abil·i·ty** \-,kaúnt-ə-'bil-ət-ē\ *n* — **ac·count·ably** \-'kaúnt-ə-blē\ *adv*

ac·coun·tant \ə-'kaúnt-²nt\ *n* : a person professionally trained in accounting

ac·count·ing \ə-'kaúnt-iŋ\ *n* **1** : the system or practice of recording the amounts of money made and spent by a person or business **2** : a statement explaining one's conduct : ACCOUNT 5a

ac·cou·tre *or* **ac·cou·ter** \ə-'küt-ər\ *vb* **-cou·tred** *or* **-cou·tered; -cou·tring** *or* **-cou·ter·ing** \-'küt-ə-riŋ, -'kü-triŋ\ : to provide with equipment : OUTFIT

ac·cou·tre·ment *or* **ac·cou·ter·ment** \ə-'kü-trə-mənt, -'küt-ər-mənt\ *n* : an accessory item of clothing or equipment — usually used in plural

ac·cred·it \ə-'kred-ət\ *vb* **1** : to send with credentials and authority to act as representative ⟨*accredit* an ambassador to France⟩ **2** : to certify as in agreement with a standard ⟨an *accredited* school⟩ **3** : to give credit to — **ac·cred·i·ta·tion** \ə-,kred-ə-'tā-shən, -'dā-\ *n*

ac·cre·tion \ə-'krē-shən\ *n* **1** : the process of growth or enlargement; *esp* : increase or growth by addition on the outside **2** : a product or result of accretion

ac·crue \ə-'krü\ *vb* **ac·crued; ac·cru·ing** **1** : to come about as a natural growth or addition ⟨benefits *accrue* to society from education⟩ **2** : to accumulate over a period of time ⟨*accrued* interest⟩ — **ac·cru·al** \-'krü-əl\ *n*

ac·cu·mu·late \ə-'kyü-myə-,lāt\ *vb* **-lat·ed; -lat·ing** **1** : to gather or pile up especially little by little : AMASS ⟨*accumulate* a fortune⟩ **2** : to increase in quantity, number, or amount ⟨rubbish *accumulates* quickly⟩

ac·cu·mu·la·tion \ə-,kyü-myə-'lā-shən\ *n* **1** : a collecting together : AMASSING **2** : increase or growth by addition **3** : something accumulated : COLLECTION

ac·cu·mu·la·tor \ə-'kyü-m(y)ə-,lāt-ər\ *n* : one that accumulates; *esp* : a part (as in a computer) where numbers are totaled or stored

ac·cu·ra·cy \'ak-yə-rə-sē\ *n, pl* **-cies** **1** : freedom from error : CORRECTNESS **2** : conformity to a standard : EXACTNESS

ac·cu·rate \'ak-yə-rət\ *adj* **1** : free from mistakes especially as the result of care ⟨an *accurate* count⟩ **2** : agreeing exactly with truth or a standard ⟨an *accurate* copy⟩ **3** : able to give an accurate result ⟨an *accurate* gauge⟩ [from Latin *accuratus* "accurate," from *accurare* "to take care of," from *ac-, ad-* "to" and *cura* "care" — related to CURE, CURIOUS; see *Word History* at CURE] *synonyms* see CORRECT — **ac·cu·rate·ly** \-yə-rət-lē, -yərt-\ *adv* — **ac·cu·rate·ness** \-nəs\ *n*

ac·cursed \ə-'kər-səd, -'kər-səd\ *or* **ac·curst** \ə-'kərst\ *adj* **1** : being under a curse **2** : DAMNABLE 2, DETESTABLE — **ac·curs·ed·ly** \-'kər-səd-lē\ *adv* — **ac·curs·ed·ness** \-'kər-səd-nəs\ *n*

ac·cu·sa·tion \,ak-yə-'zā-shən, -yü-\ *n* **1** : the act of accusing : the fact of being accused **2** : a charge of wrongdoing

ac·cu·sa·tive \ə-'kyü-zət-iv\ *adj* : of, relating to, or being the grammatical case that marks the direct object of a verb or the object of a preposition — **accusative** *n*

ac·cu·sa·to·ry \ə-'kyü-zə-,tōr-ē, -,tór-\ *adj* : containing or expressing accusation ⟨an *accusatory* look⟩

ac·cuse \ə-'kyüz\ *vb* **ac·cused; ac·cus·ing** : to blame for wrongdoing : to charge with a fault and especially with a crime — **ac·cus·er** *n* — **ac·cus·ing·ly** \-'kyü-ziŋ-lē\ *adv*

ac·cused \ə-'kyüzd\ *n, pl* **accused** : one charged with wrongdoing; *esp* : the defendant in a criminal case

ac·cus·tom \ə-'kəs-təm\ *vb* : to make familiar

ac·cus·tomed \ə-'kəs-təmd\ *adj* **1** : CUSTOMARY ⟨my *ac-customed* lunch hour⟩ **2** : familiar with **3** : being in the habit or custom ⟨*accustomed* to making decisions⟩

¹**ace** \'ās\ *n* **1** : a playing card with one large figure in its center **2** : a very small amount or degree ⟨within an *ace* of winning⟩ **3** : a point scored on a serve (as in tennis) that an opponent fails to touch **4** : a golf hole made in one stroke **5 a** : a combat pilot who has shot down at least five enemy airplanes **b** : a person who is expert at something

²**ace** *vb* **aced**; **ac·ing** **1** : to score an ace against ⟨the tennis player *aced* her opponent⟩ **2** : to earn the grade of A on (an examination)

³**ace** *adj* : of first or high rank or quality

acel·lu·lar \(')ā-'sel-yə-lər\ *adj* : not made up of cells

-a·ceous \'ā-shəs\ *adj suffix* : consisting of ⟨carbon*aceous*⟩ : having the nature or form of ⟨herb*aceous*⟩ [from Latin *-aceus* "consisting of"]

acet·amin·o·phen \ə-ˌsēt-ə-'min-ə-fən\ *n* : a crystalline compound used in medicine to relieve pain and fever

ac·e·tate \'as-ə-ˌtāt\ *n* **1** : a chemical compound formed by the reaction of acetic acid with another substance **2** : made from acetate or from cellulose and acetate combined

ace·tic \ə-'sēt-ik\ *adj* : of, relating to, or producing acetic acid or vinegar

acetic acid *n* : a colorless strong-smelling liquid acid that gives the sour taste to vinegar and that is used especially in making chemical compounds (as plastics)

ac·e·tone \'as-ə-ˌtōn\ *n* : an easily evaporated fragrant flammable liquid compound used chiefly to dissolve or to make chemical compounds

ace·tyl·cho·line \ə-ˌset-ᵊl-'kō-ˌlēn, -ˌsēt-; 'as-ə-ˌtēl-\ *n* : a compound released at autonomic nerve endings that functions in carrying nerve impulses

acet·y·lene \ə-'set-ᵊl-ən, -ᵊl-ˌēn\ *n* : a compound of carbon and hydrogen that is a colorless gas used chiefly in welding and soldering and in making chemical compounds

ace·tyl·sal·i·cyl·ic acid \ə-ˌsēt-ᵊl-ˌsal-ə-ˌsil-ik-\ *n* : ASPIRIN 1

¹**ache** \'āk\ *vb* **ached**; **ach·ing** **1** : to suffer a dull persistent pain **2** : to long painfully : YEARN

²**ache** *n* : a dull persistent pain — **achy** \'ā-kē\ *adj*

achene \ā-'kēn\ *n* : a small dry one-seeded fruit (as of the sunflower) that ripens without bursting open — **ache·ni·al** \ə-'kē-nē-əl\ *adj*

achieve \ə-'chēv\ *vb* **achieved**; **achiev·ing** **1** : ACCOMPLISH ⟨*achieved* our purpose⟩ **2** : to get by effort ⟨*achieve* greatness⟩ [Middle English *acheven* "achieve," from early French *achever* "to finish," from *a-* "to" and *cheef* "end, head," from Latin *caput* "head" — related to CAPITAL, CHIEF] — **achiev·able** \-'chē-və-bəl\ *adj* — **achiev·er** *n*

achieve·ment \ə-'chēv-mənt\ *n* **1** : the act of achieving **2** : something achieved

Achil·les' heel \ə-ˌkil-ēz-\ *n* : a special or personal weakness

> **Word History** In Greek legend, Achilles' mother protected him from harm by dipping him in the River Styx. However, she held him by the heel while doing it. As a result this heel did not get wet and thus was not protected. Later, during the Trojan War, Achilles was killed by Paris, a Trojan prince, who shot him in the unprotected heel with an arrow. The term *Achilles' heel* has since come to refer to any weak spot or point. [named for *Achilles*, warrior in Greek legend]

Achilles tendon *n* : the strong tendon joining the muscles in the calf of the leg to the bone of the heel

ach·ro·mat·ic \ˌak-rə-'mat-ik\ *adj* **1** : giving an image practically free from colors not in the object ⟨an *achromatic* lens⟩ **2** : being black, gray, or white

¹**ac·id** \'as-əd\ *adj* **1** : sour, bitter, or stinging to the taste : resembling vinegar in taste **2** : sharp or sour in temper : CROSS ⟨*acid* remarks⟩ **3** : of, relating to, or having the characteristics of an acid ⟨*acid* soil⟩ ⟨*acid* indigestion⟩ — **ac·id·ly** *adv* — **ac·id·ness** *n*

²**acid** *n* **1** : a sour substance **2** : a compound that usually dissolves in water, has a sour taste, reacts with a base to form a salt, and turns litmus paper red **3** : LSD

ac·id–fast \'as-əd-ˌfast\ *adj* : not easily made to lose color by acids

acid·ic \ə-'sid-ik, a-\ *adj* **1** : acid-forming **2** : ACID

acid·i·fy \ə-'sid-ə-ˌfī\ *vb* **-fied**; **-fy·ing** **1** : to make acid **2** : to change into an acid — **acid·i·fi·ca·tion** \ə-ˌsid-ə-fə-'kā-shən\ *n*

acid·i·ty \ə-'sid-ət-ē, a-\ *n, pl* **-ties** **1** : the quality, state, or degree of being acid **2** : the state of being extremely acid

acid precipitation *n* : precipitation (as rain or snow) with increased acidity that is caused by environmental factors

acid rain *n* : rain with increased acidity that is caused by environmental factors (as atmospheric pollutants)

ac·knowl·edge \ik-'näl-ij, ak-\ *vb* **-edged**; **-edg·ing** **1** : to recognize the rights or authority of **2** : to admit the truth or existence of **3** : to make known that something has been received or noticed ⟨*acknowledge* a letter⟩

> **synonyms** ACKNOWLEDGE, ADMIT, OWN, CONFESS mean to make public something one would rather keep private. ACKNOWLEDGE suggests revealing something that has been or might be concealed ⟨the company *acknowledged* that it had been polluting the lake⟩. ADMIT stresses a demand to reveal and an unwillingness to do so ⟨why don't you *admit* that you made a mistake?⟩. OWN suggests acknowledging something of a personal nature ⟨I *own* that I can be rude sometimes⟩. CONFESS suggests an admission of weakness, failure, or guilt ⟨*confessed* involvement in the scam⟩.

ac·knowl·edged \ik-'näl-ijd, ak-\ *adj* : generally recognized or accepted ⟨the *acknowledged* leader⟩

ac·knowl·edg·ment *also* **ac·knowl·edge·ment** \ik-'näl-ij-mənt, ak-\ *n* **1 a** : the act of acknowledging **b** : an act of acknowledging some deed or achievement **2** : something done or given in return for something received

ac·me \'ak-mē\ *n* : the highest point : PEAK ⟨the *acme* of perfection⟩

ac·ne \'ak-nē\ *n* : a disorder of the skin caused by inflammation of skin glands and hair follicles and marked by pimples especially on the face

ac·o·lyte \'ak-ə-ˌlīt\ *n* : a person who assists a member of the clergy in a service

ac·o·nite \'ak-ə-ˌnīt\ *n* **1** : MONKSHOOD **2** : a drug obtained from the poisonous root of the common Old World monkshood

acorn \'ā-ˌkȯrn, -kərn\ *n* : the roundish one-seeded thin-shelled nut of an oak tree usually having a woody cap

acorn squash *n* : an acorn-shaped winter squash with ridges on its dark green outer surface and somewhat sweet yellow to orange flesh

acous·tic \ə-'kü-stik\ *or* **acous·ti·cal** \-sti-kəl\ *adj* **1** : of or relating to the sense or organs of hearing, to sound, or to the science of sounds: as **a** : deadening or absorbing sound **b** : operated by or using sound

acorn squash

\ə\ abut	\au̇\ out	\i\ tip	\ȯ\ saw	\u̇\ foot
\ər\ further	\ch\ chin	\ī\ life	\ȯi\ coin	\y\ yet
\a\ mat	\e\ pet	\j\ job	\th\ thin	\yü\ few
\ā\ take	\ē\ easy	\ŋ\ sing	\th\ this	\yu̇\ cure
\ä\ cot, cart	\g\ go	\ō\ bone	\ü\ food	\zh\ vision

waves **2** : of, relating to, or being a musical instrument whose sound is not electronically modified ⟨*acoustic* guitar⟩ — **acous·ti·cal·ly** \-sti-k(ə-)lē\ *adv*

acous·tics \ə-'kü-stiks\ *n sing or pl* **1** : a science dealing with sound **2** *also* **acous·tic** \-stik\ : the qualities in an enclosed space (as an auditorium) that make it easy or hard for a person in it to hear distinctly

ac·quaint \ə-'kwānt\ *vb* **1** : to cause to know socially ⟨became *acquainted* at school⟩ **2** : to cause to know firsthand : INFORM ⟨*acquaint* her with her duties⟩

ac·quain·tance \ə-'kwānt-ᵊn(t)s\ *n* **1** : knowledge gained by personal experience ⟨had some *acquaintance* with the subject⟩ **2** : a person one knows slightly — **ac·quain·tance·ship** \-ˌship\ *n*

ac·qui·esce \ˌak-wē-'es\ *vb* **-esced; -esc·ing** : to accept, agree, or give consent by keeping silent or by not raising objections — **ac·qui·es·cence** \-'es-ᵊn(t)s\ *n*

ac·qui·es·cent \ˌak-wē-'es-ᵊnt\ *adj* : acquiescing or tending to acquiesce — **ac·qui·es·cent·ly** *adv*

ac·quire \ə-'kwī(ə)r\ *vb* **ac·quired; ac·quir·ing** : to come to have often by one's own efforts : GAIN — **ac·quir·able** \-'kwī-rə-bəl\ *adj*

acquired *adj* **1** : gained by or as a result of effort or experience **2** : caused by environmental forces and not passed from parent to offspring in the genes ⟨*acquired* characteristics⟩

acquired immune deficiency syndrome *n* : AIDS

acquired immunity *n* : immunity that develops following exposure (as through infection or vaccination) to something that causes disease

ac·quire·ment \ə-'kwī(ə)r-mənt\ *n* **1** : the act of acquiring **2** : ACCOMPLISHMENT 3

ac·qui·si·tion \ˌak-wə-'zish-ən\ *n* **1** : the act of acquiring **2** : something acquired

ac·quis·i·tive \ə-'kwiz-ət-iv\ *adj* : having a strong wish to acquire things — **ac·quis·i·tive·ness** *n*

ac·quit \ə-'kwit\ *vb* **ac·quit·ted; ac·quit·ting** **1** : to declare innocent of a crime or wrongdoing **2** : to conduct (oneself) usually satisfactorily

ac·quit·tal \ə-'kwit-ᵊl\ *n* : the freeing (as by verdict) of a person from the charge of a crime

acre \'ā-kər\ *n* **1** *pl* : property consisting of land : ESTATE **2** : a unit of area equal to 43,560 square feet (about 4047 square meters) — see MEASURE table [Old English *æcer* "field, cultivated land"]

acre·age \'ā-k(ə-)rij\ *n* : area in acres

acre–foot *n* : the volume (as of irrigation water) that would cover one acre to a depth of one foot

ac·rid \'ak-rəd\ *adj* **1** : biting or bitter in taste or odor **2** : bitterly irritating to the feelings ⟨an *acrid* remark⟩ — **ac·rid·ly** *adv* — **ac·rid·ness** *n*

ac·ri·mo·ny \'ak-rə-ˌmō-nē\ *n, pl* **-nies** : harsh or biting sharpness especially of words, manner, or disposition — **ac·ri·mo·ni·ous** \ˌak-rə-'mō-nē-əs\ *adj* — **ac·ri·mo·ni·ous·ly** *adv* — **ac·ri·mo·ni·ous·ness** *n*

ac·ro·bat \'ak-rə-ˌbat\ *n* : a person (as a circus performer) who is very good at stunts like jumping, balancing, tumbling, and swinging from things — **ac·ro·bat·ic** \ˌak-rə-'bat-ik\ *adj* — **ac·ro·bat·i·cal·ly** \-i-k(ə-)lē\ *adv*

ac·ro·bat·ics \ˌak-rə-'bat-iks\ *n sing or pl* **1** : the art or performance of an acrobat **2** : stunts of or resembling those of an acrobat ⟨airplane *acrobatics*⟩

ac·ro·nym \'ak-rə-ˌnim\ *n* : a word (as *radar*) formed from the beginning letter or letters of each or most of the parts of a compound term

ac·ro·pho·bia \ˌak-rə-'fō-bē-ə\ *n* : fear of heights

acrop·o·lis \ə-'kräp-ə-ləs\ *n* : the upper fortified part of an ancient Greek city

¹**across** \ə-'krós\ *adv* **1** : from one side to the other ⟨boards sawed directly *across*⟩ **2** : to or on the opposite side ⟨got *across* in a boat⟩ **3** : so as to be understandable or successful ⟨get the message *across*⟩

²**across** *prep* **1** : to or on the opposite side of ⟨*across* the street⟩ **2** : so as to cross or pass at an angle ⟨lay one stick *across* another⟩

acros·tic \ə-'krós-tik, -'kräs-\ *n* : a poem in which a set of letters (as the first letter of the lines) taken in order form a word or phrase

acryl·ic \ə-'kril-ik\ *n* **1** : ACRYLIC FIBER **2** : a paint containing an acrylic resin

acrylic fiber *n* : a quick-drying synthetic fiber used for woven and knitted cloth

acrylic resin *n* : a glassy synthetic plastic used for cast and molded parts or as coatings and adhesives

¹**act** \'akt\ *n* **1** : something that is done ⟨an *act* of kindness⟩ **2** : the doing of something ⟨caught in the *act*⟩ **3** : a law made by a governing body ⟨an *act* of Congress⟩ **4 a** : one of the main divisions of a play or opera **b** : one of the parts of a variety show or circus **5** : a display of behavior that is not sincere ⟨just putting on an *act*⟩ [Middle English *act* "act, deed," from Latin *actus* "action of doing" and from Latin *actum* "something done," both from *agere* "to drive, do" — related to AGENT]

²**act** *vb* **1** : to perform by action especially on the stage **2** : to play the part of ⟨*act* the man of the world⟩ **3 a** : to behave in a manner suitable to ⟨*act* your age⟩ **b** : to conduct oneself ⟨*act* like a fool⟩ **4** : to take action : MOVE ⟨think before you *act*⟩ **5 a** : to perform a function : SERVE ⟨*act* as mayor⟩ **b** : to produce an effect : WORK ⟨wait for a medicine to *act*⟩

ac·tin \'ak-tən\ *n* : a protein of muscle that with myosin is active in muscular contraction

act·ing \'ak-tiŋ\ *adj* : serving temporarily or in place of another ⟨*acting* president⟩

ac·tin·i·um \ak-'tin-ē-əm\ *n* : a radioactive metallic element found especially in pitchblende — see ELEMENT table

ac·tion \'ak-shən\ *n* **1** : a legal proceeding in a court by which one demands one's right or the correction of a wrong **2** : the working of one thing on another so as to produce a change ⟨the *action* of acids on metals⟩ **3** : the process or manner of acting or functioning; *also* : such an action expressed by a verb **4 a** : a thing done : DEED **b** *pl* : BEHAVIOR, CONDUCT **5** : combat in war : BATTLE **6** : the plot of a drama or work of fiction

action figure *n* : a small-scale figure (as of a superhero) used especially as a toy

action verb *n* : a verb that expresses action ⟨"lingered" in "they lingered over dinner" and "bring" in "bring me the broom" are *action verbs*⟩ — compare LINKING VERB

ac·ti·vate \'ak-tə-ˌvāt\ *vb* **-vat·ed; -vat·ing** **1** : to make active **2** : to make (as molecules) more chemically active **3** : to make (a substance) give off radioactive particles, give off light at low temperatures, be easily affected by light, or carry an electric charge under the influence of light or other electromagnetic radiation **4** : to treat (as carbon or alumina) so as to improve the amount of adsorption **5** : to place on active military duty ⟨*activate* the reserves⟩ — **ac·ti·va·tion** \ˌak-tə-'vā-shən\ *n* — **ac·ti·va·tor** \'ak-tə-ˌvāt-ər\ *n*

activation energy *n* : the least amount of energy required to change a stable molecule into a reactive molecule

ac·tive \'ak-tiv\ *adj* **1** : producing or involving action or movement **2** : representing the subject as performing the action expressed by the verb ⟨"hits" in "she hits the ball" is an *active* verb⟩ **3** : having or requiring quick or energetic movements ⟨an *active* child⟩ ⟨*active* sports⟩ **4 a** : ready for action ⟨takes an *active* interest⟩ **b** : engaged or participating in an action or activity ⟨an *active* member⟩ **c** : erupting or likely to erupt ⟨an *active* volcano⟩ **5** : engaged in or requiring full-time service especially in the armed forces ⟨*active* duty⟩ **6** : marked by present action or use ⟨an *active* account⟩ ⟨a student's *active* vocabulary⟩ **7 a** : capable of acting or reacting ⟨*active* ingredients⟩ **b** : tending to progress or increase ⟨*active tuberculosis*⟩ — **ac·tive·ly** *adv* — **ac·tive·ness** *n*

active immunity *n* : immunity produced by the individual when exposed to an antigen — compare PASSIVE IMMUNITY

active transport *n* : the movement (as across a cell membrane) of substances from regions of lower concentration to regions of higher concentration by the use of energy

ac·tive-wear \'ak-tiv-ˌwa(ə)r, -ˌwe(ə)r\ *n* : SPORTSWEAR

ac·tiv·ist \'ak-ti-vəst\ *n* : a person who believes in forceful action (as a mass demonstration) for political purposes — **ac·tiv·ism** \-ˌviz-əm\ *n*

ac·tiv·i·ty \ak-'tiv-ət-ē\ *n, pl* **-ties** **1** : the quality or state of being active **2** : forceful or energetic action **3** : a natural, normal, or assigned function: as **a** : a process that an organism carries on or participates in by virtue of being alive **b** : a similar process that involves or is capable of involving mental function **4** : an educational exercise designed to teach by firsthand experience **5** : an active ⟨solar *activity*⟩ **6 a** : something done especially for relaxation or fun **b** : a form of organized recreation

ac·tor \'ak-tər\ *n* : one that acts; *esp* : a person who acts especially in a play or movie or on television

act out *vb* **1** : to represent in action ⟨children *act out* what they read⟩ **2** : to behave badly especially as a way of letting out painful emotions

ac·tress \'ak-trəs\ *n* : a woman or girl who acts especially in a play or movie or on television

Acts \'ak(t)s\ *or* **Acts of the Apostles** — see BIBLE table

ac·tu·al \'ak-ch(ə-w)əl, 'ak-sh(ə-w)əl\ *adj* : existing in fact and not merely as a possibility **synonyms** see REAL — **ac·tu·al·i·ty** \ˌak-chə-'wal-ət-ē, -shə-\ *n* — **ac·tu·al·i·za·tion** \'ak-ch(ə-w)ə-lə-'zā-shən, -sh(ə-w)ə-\ *n* — **ac·tu·al·ize** \-ˌīz\ *vb*

ac·tu·al·ly \'ak-ch(ə-w)ə-lē, 'ak-sh(ə-w)ə-lē\ *adv* : in fact or in truth : REALLY ⟨she *actually* spoke Spanish⟩ ⟨*actually*, I didn't want to go⟩

ac·tu·ary \'ak-chə-ˌwer-ē, -shə-\ *n, pl* **-ar·ies** : a person who calculates insurance premiums and dividends — **ac·tu·ar·i·al** \ˌak-chə-'wer-ē-əl\ *adj*

ac·tu·ate \'ak-chə-ˌwāt, -shə-\ *vb* **-at·ed; -at·ing** **1** : to put into action ⟨the windmill *actuates* the pump⟩ **2** : to arouse to action ⟨*actuated* by the hope of winning⟩

act up *vb* : to act in an unruly, abnormal, or annoying way

acu·ity \ə-'kyü-ət-ē\ *n* : sharpness of perception

acu·men \ə-'kyü-mən, 'ak-yə-mən\ *n* : keenness of mind : SHREWDNESS

acu·punc·ture \'ak-yə-ˌpəŋ(k)-chər\ *n* : an originally Chinese practice of inserting fine needles through the skin at specified points especially to cure disease or relieve pain [Latin *acus* "needle" and English *puncture*]

acute \ə-'kyüt\ *adj* **acut·er; acut·est** **1 a** : SEVERE 3, SHARP ⟨*acute* pain⟩ **b** : having a sudden onset and short duration ⟨*acute* disease⟩ **2** : being or forming an angle measuring less than 90 degrees ⟨an *acute* angle⟩ **3 a** : marked by keen awareness : SHREWD ⟨*acute* observation⟩ **b** : having sharp perceptions : OBSERVANT **4** : needing speedy attention : URGENT ⟨an *acute* shortage of blood plasma⟩ **5** : felt or experienced intensely ⟨*acute* distress⟩ **synonyms** see SHARP — **acute·ly** *adv* — **acute·ness** *n*

ad \'ad\ *n* : ADVERTISEMENT 2

ad- *or* **ac-** *or* **af-** *or* **ag-** *or* **al-** *or* **ap-** *or* **as-** *or* **at-** *prefix* : to : toward — usually *ac-* before *c, k,* or *q* and *af-* before *f* and *ag-* before *g* and *al-* before *l* and *ap-* before *p* and *as-* before *s* and *at-* before *t* and *ad-* before other sounds but sometimes *ad-* even before one of the listed consonants [Latin *ad-* "to, toward"]

ad·age \'ad-ij\ *n* : an old familiar saying : PROVERB

¹**ada·gio** \ə-'däj-ō, -'däj-ē-ˌō, -'däzh-\ *adv or adj* : in an easy graceful manner : SLOWLY — used as a direction in music

²**adagio** *n* **1** : a musical composition or movement in adagio tempo **2** : a ballet duet or trio displaying difficult feats of balance, lifting, or spinning

¹**ad·a·mant** \'ad-ə-mənt, -ˌmant\ *n* **1** : an imaginary stone of great hardness **2** : an unbreakable or extremely hard substance [Middle English *adamant* "an imaginary stone of great hardness, diamond," from early French *adamant* (same meaning), from Latin *adamant-, adamas* "hardest metal, diamond," from Greek *adamant-, adamas* (same meaning) — related to DIAMOND; see *Word History* at DIAMOND]

²**adamant** *adj* : firmly fixed or decided especially against something : UNYIELDING — **ad·a·mant·ly** *adv*

ad·a·man·tine \ˌad-ə-'man-ˌtēn, -ˌtīn\ *adj* **1** : made of or having the quality of adamant **2** : ²ADAMANT

Ad·am's apple \'ad-əmz-\ *n* : the lump in the front of the neck formed by the largest cartilage of the larynx

adapt \ə-'dapt\ *vb* : to make or become suitable; *esp* : to change so as to fit a new or specific use or situation ⟨*adapt* to life in a new school⟩ ⟨*adapt* the novel for children⟩ [from French *adapter* and Latin *adaptare*, both meaning "to adapt," from Latin *ad-* "to" and *aptus* "apt, fit" — related to APT] — **adapt·abil·i·ty** \-ˌdap-tə-'bil-ət-ē\ *n* — **adapt·able** \-'dap-tə-bəl\ *adj*

ad·ap·ta·tion \ˌad-ˌap-'tā-shən, -əp-\ *n* **1 a** : the act or process of adapting **b** : the state of being adapted **2** : adjustment to environmental conditions: as **a** : adjustment of a sense organ to the degree or quality of stimulation **b** : change in an organism or its parts that fits it better for the conditions of its environment; *also* : a structure resulting from this change **3** : something that is adapted; *esp* : a composition rewritten into a new form — **ad·ap·ta·tion·al** \-shnəl, -shən-ᵊl\ *adj* — **ad·ap·ta·tion·al·ly** \-ē\ *adv*

adapt·ed \ə-'dap-təd\ *adj* : suited by nature or design to a particular use, purpose, or situation

adapt·er *also* **adap·tor** \ə-'dap-tər\ *n* **1** : someone or something that adapts **2 a** : a device for connecting two parts (as of different diameters) of a usually larger device **b** : an attachment for adapting a device for uses not originally intended

add \'ad\ *vb* **1 a** : to join or unite to a thing so as to increase or improve it ⟨*add* a wing to the house⟩ ⟨color *adds* a creative touch⟩ **b** : to unite or combine in a single whole **c** : to include as a member of a group ⟨*add* me in⟩ **2** : to say something more ⟨*add* to her remarks⟩ **3** : to combine (numbers) into a single number that has the same total value — **add·able** *or* **add·ible** \'ad-ə-bəl\ *adj*

ad·dend \'ad-ˌend\ *n* : a number that is to be added to another

ad·den·dum \ə-'den-dəm\ *n, pl* **-den·da** \-'den-də\ : something added (as to a book)

¹**ad·der** \'ad-ər\ *n* **1** : a poisonous European viper; *also* : any of several related snakes **2** : any of several harmless North American snakes (as the hognose snakes)

²**add·er** \'ad-ər\ *n* : one that adds

ad·der's-tongue \'ad-ərz-ˌtəŋ\ *n* **1** : a fern whose spore-bearing stalk resembles a serpent's tongue **2** : DOGTOOTH VIOLET

¹**ad·dict** \ə-'dikt\ *vb* **1** : to devote or surrender oneself to something habitually ⟨*addicted* to detective stories⟩ **2** : to cause to make a habit of using a drug ⟨nicotine is *addicting*⟩

²**ad·dict** \'ad-(ˌ)ikt\ *n* **1** : one who is addicted (as to a drug) **2** : a person devoted to something ⟨a TV *addict*⟩

adder's-tongue 1

\ə\ **abut**	\au̇\ **out**	\i\ **tip**	\ȯ\ **saw**	\u̇\ **foot**	
\ər\ **further**	\ch\ **chin**	\ī\ **life**	\ȯi\ **coin**	\y\ **yet**	
\a\ **mat**	\e\ **pet**	\j\ **job**	\th\ **thin**	\yü\ **few**	
\ā\ **take**	\ē\ **easy**	\ŋ\ **sing**	\th\ **this**	\yu̇\ **cure**	
\ä\ **cot, cart**	\g\ **go**	\ō\ **bone**	\ü\ **food**	\zh\ **vision**	

ad·dic·tion \ə-'dik-shən, a-\ *n* : the quality or state of being addicted; *esp* : uncontrollable use of habit-forming drugs

ad·dic·tive \ə-'dik-tiv, a-\ *adj* : causing or characterized by addiction ⟨an *addictive* drug⟩ ⟨an *addictive* game⟩

ad·di·tion \ə-'dish-ən, a-\ *n* **1** : the result of adding : IN-CREASE **2** : the act, process, or operation of adding **3** : a part added (as to a building) — **in addition** : as something more : BESIDES — **in addition to** : ²BESIDES

ad·di·tion·al \ə-'dish-nəl, -ən-ᵊl\ *adj* : being an addition : EXTRA — **ad·di·tion·al·ly** \-ē\ *adv*

¹**ad·di·tive** \'ad-ət-iv\ *adj* : relating to or produced by addition — **ad·di·tive·ly** *adv*

²**additive** *n* : a substance added to another in small amounts to give or improve desirable qualities or decrease unwanted qualities ⟨a gasoline *additive*⟩ ⟨*additives* which color, flavor, or preserve food⟩

additive identity *n* : an element (as zero in the set of real numbers) of a mathematical set that leaves every element of the set unchanged when added to it

additive inverse *n* : a number that when added to a given number sums to zero ⟨the *additive inverse* of 4 is −4⟩ — compare ²OPPOSITE 3

ad·dle \'ad-ᵊl\ *vb* **ad·dled; ad·dling** \'ad-liŋ, -ᵊl-iŋ\ **1** : to make or become confused **2** : to become rotten : SPOIL ⟨*addled* eggs⟩

¹**ad·dress** \ə-'dres, a-\ *vb* **1 a** : to direct the attention of oneself ⟨*addressed* themselves to the problem⟩ **b** : to deal with ⟨prepares to *address* the problem⟩ **2 a** : to communicate directly ⟨*address* a petition to the governor⟩ **b** : to deliver a formal speech to ⟨*address* the convention⟩ **3** : to mark directions for delivery on ⟨*address* a letter⟩ **4** : to greet by a prescribed form **5** : to identify (as a computer peripheral or a piece of information) by an address or name for information transfer — **ad·dress·er** *n*

²**ad·dress** \ə-'dres, 'ad-₁res\ *n* **1** : manner of speaking : DE-LIVERY **2** : a rehearsed speech **3 a** : a place where a person or organization can usually be reached **b** : the directions for delivery on mail **4 a** : a location (as in the memory of a computer) where particular information is stored **b** : a series of symbols (as numerals or letters) that identifies the location of information in a computer's memory or on the Internet or that specifies the source or destination of an e-mail message

ad·dress·able \ə-'dres-ə-bəl\ *adj* : able to be reached through an address ⟨*addressable* registers in a computer⟩

ad·dress·ee \₁ad-₁res-'ē, ə-₁dres-'ē\ *n* : one to whom mail is addressed

ad·duce \ə-'d(y)üs\ *vb* **ad·duced; ad·duc·ing** : to offer as example, reason, or proof

ad·duct \ə-'dəkt\ *vb* : to draw (a part of the body) toward or past a middle plane or line that divides the body or a bodily part into right and left halves

ad·duc·tor \ə-'dək-tər\ *n* : a muscle that draws a body part (as an arm or finger) toward or past a plane or a line that divides the body or a hand or foot into right and left halves

add up *vb* **1 a** : to come to a total and especially the expected total **b** : to make sense ⟨her story just doesn't *add up*⟩ **2** : to amount to a lot ⟨just a little each time, but it all *adds up*⟩

ad·e·nine \'ad-ᵊn-ēn\ *n* : one of the bases which make up the genetic code of DNA and RNA — compare CYTO-SINE, GUANINE, THYMINE, URACIL

¹**ad·e·noid** \'ad-ᵊn-₁oid, 'ad-₁noid\ *n* : either of two masses of tissue at the back of the pharynx that usually interfere with breathing when abnormally enlarged — usually used in plural

²**adenoid** *adj* **1** : of or relating to the adenoids **2** : relating to or affected with abnormally enlarged adenoids

ad·e·noi·dal \₁ad-ᵊn-'oid-ᵊl\ *adj* : exhibiting the signs (as a nasal voice) of one affected with abnormally enlarged ad-

enoids : ADENOID ⟨an *adenoidal* singer⟩ — not usually used technically

aden·o·sine di·phos·phate \ə-'den-ə-₁sēn-dī-'fäs-₁fāt\ *n* : ADP

adenosine tri·phos·phate \-trī-'fäs-₁fāt\ *n* : ATP

¹**ad·ept** \'ad-₁ept\ *n* : a highly skilled or well-trained individual : EXPERT

²**adept** \ə-'dept\ *adj* : very good at something **synonyms** see SKILLFUL — **adept·ly** *adv* — **adept·ness** \-'dep(t)-nəs\ *n*

ad·e·qua·cy \'ad-i-kwə-sē\ *n, pl* **-cies** : the quality or state of being adequate

ad·e·quate \'ad-i-kwət\ *adj* **1** : suitable or enough for a requirement ⟨food and water *adequate* for six people⟩ **2** : good enough ⟨your grades are barely *adequate*⟩ — **ad·e·quate·ly** *adv* — **ad·e·quate·ness** *n*

ad·here \ad-'hi(ə)r, əd-\ *vb* **ad·hered; ad·her·ing** **1** : to stay loyal (as to a cause or promise) **2** : to stick by or as if by gluing, suction, grasping, or melting **3** : to agree to observe ⟨*adhere* to the rules⟩

ad·her·ence \ad-'hir-ən(t)s, əd-\ *n* **1** : the action or quality of adhering **2** : steady or faithful attachment ⟨*adherence* to the truth⟩

¹**ad·her·ent** \ad-'hir-ənt, əd-\ *adj* : able or tending to adhere

²**adherent** *n* : a person who adheres to a leader, belief, or group

ad·he·sion \ad-'hē-zhən, əd-\ *n* **1** : steady or firm attachment; *esp* : a sticking together **2** : abnormal union of tissues following inflammation (as after surgery) **3** : the molecular attraction between surfaces of bodies in contact

¹**ad·he·sive** \ad-'hē-siv, əd-, -ziv\ *adj* : tending to adhere : prepared for adhering — **ad·he·sive·ness** *n*

²**adhesive** *n* : an adhesive substance (as glue or cement)

adhesive tape *n* : tape that is coated on one side with an adhesive and is used especially for medical purposes

adi·a·bat·ic \₁ad-ē-ə-'bat-ik, ₁ā-dī-ə-\ *adj* : occurring without loss or gain of heat ⟨*adiabatic* expansion of a gas⟩ — **ad·i·a·bat·i·cal·ly** \-'bat-i-k(ə-)lē\ *adv*

adieu \ə-'d(y)ü, a-\ *n, pl* **adieus** *or* **adieux** \-'d(y)üz\ : ²FAREWELL 1 — often used interjectionally [Middle English *adieu* "farewell," from early French *adieu* (same meaning), from *a Dieu,* literally "(I commit you) to God," from Latin *Deus* "God" — related to ADIOS, DEITY]

adi·os \₁ad-ē-'ōs, ₁äd-\ *interj* — used to express farewell [from Spanish *adiós* "farewell," from *a Dios,* literally "(I commit you) to God," from Latin *Deus* "God" — related to ADIEU, DEITY]

ad·i·pose \'ad-ə-₁pōs\ *adj* : of or relating to animal fat : FATTY — **ad·i·pos·i·ty** \₁ad-ə-'päs-ət-ē\ *n*

adipose tissue *n* : tissue in which fat is stored and which has the cells swollen by droplets of fat

ad·ja·cent \ə-'jās-ᵊnt\ *adj* **1** : lying next or near : having a border or point in common ⟨a field *adjacent* to the road⟩ **2** : having a vertex or a vertex and side in common ⟨*adjacent* angles⟩ ⟨*adjacent* sides of a rectangle⟩ — **ad·ja·cent·ly** *adv*

ad·jec·tive \'aj-ik-tiv\ *n* : a word that modifies a noun by describing a quality of the thing named, indicating its quantity or extent, or specifying a thing as distinct from something else — **adjective** *adj* — **ad·jec·ti·val** \₁aj-ik-'tī-vəl\ *adj or n* — **ad·jec·ti·val·ly** \-və-lē\ *adv*

ad·join \ə-'jöin, a-\ *vb* **1** : to add or attach by joining **2** : to lie next to or in contact with

ad·journ \ə-'jərn\ *vb* **1** : to bring or come to a close for a period of time ⟨Congress *adjourned*⟩ ⟨*adjourn* a meeting⟩ **2** : to move to another place ⟨let us *adjourn* to the sitting room⟩ — **ad·journ·ment** \-mənt\ *n*

ad·judge \ə-'jəj\ *vb* **ad·judged; ad·judg·ing** **1** : to decide or rule upon as a judge : ADJUDICATE **2** : to consider or say to be : DEEM ⟨they *adjudged* the play a success⟩

ad·ju·di·cate \ə-'jüd-i-ˌkāt\ *vb* **-cat·ed; -cat·ing** : to decide, award, or sentence judicially ⟨*adjudicate* a claim⟩
— **ad·ju·di·ca·tion** \-ˌjüd-i-'kā-shən\ *n*

ad·junct \'aj-ˌən(k)t\ *n* : ¹ACCESSORY 1

ad·jure \ə-'jủ(ə)r\ *vb* **ad·jured; ad·jur·ing** : to command
solemnly under or as if under oath — **ad·ju·ra·tion** \ˌaj-
ə-'rā-shən\ *n*

ad·just \ə-'jəst\ *vb* **1** : to bring to a better state : set right
⟨*adjust* conflicts⟩ ⟨*adjust* the error⟩ **2** : to move the parts
of an instrument or a piece of machinery until they fit
together in the best working order ⟨*adjust* a watch⟩ ⟨*adjust* the brakes on a car⟩ **3** : to determine the amount of
an insurance claim **4** : to adapt oneself to conditions
⟨had trouble *adjusting* to the new job⟩ — **ad·just·able**
\-'jəs-tə-bəl\ *adj* — **ad·just·er** *also* **ad·jus·tor** \-'jəs-tər\ *n*

ad·just·ment \ə-'jəs(t)-mənt\ *n* **1** : the act or process of
adjusting **2** : a settlement of a claim or debt **3** : the state
of being adjusted **4** : a means of adjusting one part (as in
a machine) in relation to another ⟨an *adjustment* for focusing a microscope⟩

ad·ju·tant \'aj-ət-ənt\ *n* **1** : an officer (as in the army) who
assists the commanding officer in clerical work **2** : AS-
SISTANT

¹**ad–lib** \(ˈ)ad-'lib\ *vb* **ad–libbed; ad–lib·bing** : to impro-
vise especially lines or a speech

²**ad–lib** *adj* : spoken, composed, or performed without
preparation ⟨an *ad-lib* speech⟩

ad lib *adv* : without restraint or limit ⟨known for talking
ad lib⟩

ad li·bi·tum \(ˈ)ad-'lib-ət-əm\ *adj* : freely as one wishes —
used as a direction in music [modern Latin, "according to
one's desire"]

ad·min·is·ter \əd-'min-ə-stər\ *vb* **ad·min·is·tered; ad-
min·is·ter·ing** \-st(ə-)riŋ\ **1** : to direct the affairs of
: MANAGE ⟨*administer* a government⟩ **2** : to give out as
deserved ⟨*administer* justice⟩ **3** : to give formally or cer-
emonially ⟨*administer* the sacraments⟩ **4** : to give as
treatment ⟨*administer* a drug⟩

ad·min·is·tra·tion \əd-ˌmin-ə-'strā-shən, ad-\ *n* **1** : the act
or process of administering **2** : performance of supervising duties : MANAGEMENT **3** : the work involved in managing public affairs as distinguished from policy-making
4 a : a group of persons who administer **b** *cap* : the executive branch of a government

ad·min·is·tra·tive \əd-'min-ə-ˌstrāt-iv, -strət-\ *adj* : of or
relating to administration ⟨an *administrative* position⟩

ad·min·is·tra·tor \əd-'min-ə-ˌstrāt-ər\ *n* : a person who administers especially business, school, or government affairs

ad·min·is·tra·trix \əd-ˌmin-ə-'strā-triks\ *n, pl* **-tra·tri·ces**
\-'strā-trə-ˌsēz\ : a woman who is an administrator

ad·mi·ra·ble \ˌad-mə-rə-bəl, -mrə-bəl\ *adj* : deserving to
be admired : EXCELLENT — **ad·mi·ra·ble·ness** *n* — **ad-
mi·ra·bly** \-blē\ *adv*

ad·mi·ral \'ad-mə-rəl, -mrəl\ *n* **1** : a naval commissioned
officer with a rank above that of captain; *esp* : an officer
with a rank just above that of vice admiral **2** : any of
several brightly colored butterflies

Word History It is a curiosity of history that *admiral*, a
word meaning "naval commander," ultimately has its
source in Arabic, the language of a desert people who
acquired their seafaring skills largely from the Mediterranean peoples they dominated after the great expansion
of Islam in the 7th century A.D. As the name for a Muslim chieftain, the Arabic word *amīr* appears as a loanword in the 9th century in Medieval Latin documents, in
spellings such as *amiratus, admirandus,* and *admirallus.*
These words display a variety of suffixes and an extra *d,*
through confusion with the Latin verb *admirari,* "to
admire." The ending *-allus* is probably from the Arabic
definite article *al,* which actually belongs to the following word in phrases such as *amīr al-'alī,* "supreme

commander." The specific application of *admirallus* to a
commander of a fleet originated in 12th century Sicily.
The usage was acquired by the Genoese and then spread
to the rest of western Europe, including France and
England. [Middle English *admiral* "naval commander,"
from early French *amiral* "commander" and Latin *admirallus* "naval commander," from Arabic *amīr-al-*
"commander of the" (as in *amīr al-'alī* "supreme
commander")]

¹**ad·mi·ral·ty** *n* **1** : a group of officials formerly in charge of
the British navy **2** : the court having authority over questions of maritime law; *also* : the system of law administered by admiralty courts

²**ad·mi·ral·ty** \'ad-mə-rəl-tē, -mrəl-\ *adj* : of or relating to
conduct on the sea

ad·mi·ra·tion \ˌad-mə-'rā-shən\ *n* **1** : an object of admiring regard **2** : a feeling of great and delighted approval

ad·mire \əd-'mī(ə)r\ *vb* **ad·mired; ad·mir·ing** **1** : to look
at with admiration ⟨*admire* the scenery⟩ **2** : to have high
regard for ⟨*admired* her courage⟩ [from early French *admirer* "to marvel at," from Latin *admirari* (same meaning), from *ad-* "at" and *mirari* "to wonder" — related to
MIRACLE] — **ad·mir·er** \-'mīr-ər\ *n*

ad·mis·si·ble \əd-'mis-ə-bəl\ *adj* : that can be or is worthy
to be admitted or allowed ⟨*admissible* evidence⟩ — **ad-
mis·si·bil·i·ty** \-ˌmis-ə-'bil-ət-ē\ *n*

ad·mis·sion \əd-'mish-ən, ad-\ *n* **1** : the act of admitting;
esp : an admitting of something that has not been proved
⟨an *admission* of guilt⟩ **2** : the right or permission to
enter ⟨standards of *admission* to a school⟩ **3** : the price
of entrance

ad·mit \əd-'mit, ad-\ *vb* **ad·mit·ted; ad·mit·ting** **1 a** : to
allow room for : PERMIT ⟨a question that *admits* two an-
swers⟩ **b** : to make known usually with some unwillingness ⟨*admitted* that he really didn't know⟩ ⟨*admit* a mis-
take⟩ **2** : to allow entry : let in ⟨*admit* a state to the
Union⟩ **synonyms** see ACKNOWLEDGE

ad·mit·tance \əd-'mit-ən(t)s, ad-\ *n* : permission to enter
: ENTRANCE

ad·mit·ted·ly \-'mit-əd-lē\ *adv* : acknowledged as true

ad·mix·ture \ad-'miks-chər\ *n* **1 a** : the act of mixing **b**
: the fact of being mixed **2 a** : something added by mixing
b : a product of mixing

ad·mon·ish \əd-'män-ish\ *vb* **1** : to criticize or warn gently
but seriously : warn of a fault **2** : to give friendly advice or
encouragement to ⟨*admonished* them to keep trying⟩ **synonyms** see REBUKE — **ad·mon·ish·ment** \-mənt\ *n*

ad·mo·ni·tion \ˌad-mə-'nish-ən\ *n* : a gentle or friendly
criticism or warning

ad·mon·i·to·ry \əd-'män-ə-ˌtōr-ē, -ˌtòr-\ *adj* : expressing
admonition : WARNING

ado \ə-'dü\ *n* : ¹FUSS 1, TROUBLE ⟨much *ado* about noth-
ing⟩

ado·be \ə-'dō-bē\ *n* **1** : a brick or building material made
of a sun-dried mixture of
earth and straw **2** : a building made of adobe bricks
[Spanish]

ad·o·les·cence \ˌad-ᵊl-'es-
ᵊn(t)s\ *n* : the state or process of growing up; *also* : the
period of life from puberty
to maturity [Middle English
adolescence "adolescence,"
from early French *adolescence* (same meaning), from

adobe 2

Latin *adolescentia* (same meaning), from *adolescere* "to grow up" — related to ADULT] — **ad·o·les·cent** \-ᵊnt\ *adj or n*

adopt \ə-'däpt\ *vb* **1** : to take legally as one's own child ⟨*adopted* a baby girl⟩ **2** : to take as one's own ⟨*adopt* a point of view⟩ **3** : to accept formally ⟨the assembly *adopted* a constitution⟩ — **adopt·able** \ə-'däp-tə-bəl\ *adj* — **adopt·er** *n*

adop·tion \ə-'däp-shən\ *n* : the act of adopting : the state of being adopted

adop·tive \ə-'däp-tiv\ *adj* : made by or associated with adoption ⟨the *adoptive* parents⟩

ador·able \ə-'dōr-ə-bəl, -'dȯr-\ *adj* **1** : deserving to be adored **2** : CHARMING, LOVELY ⟨an *adorable* child⟩ — **ador·able·ness** *n* — **ador·ably** \-blē\ *adv*

adore \ə-'dō(ə)r, -'dȯ(ə)r\ *vb* **adored; ador·ing 1** : ²WORSHIP 1 ⟨*adore* God⟩ **2** : to be very fond of [from early French *adourer* "to adore," from Latin *adorare* (same meaning), from *ad-* "to" and *orare* "to speak, pray" — related to ORACLE, ORATION] — **ad·o·ra·tion** \,ad-ə-'rā-shən\ *n* — **ador·er** \ə-'dōr-ər, -'dȯr-\ *n*

adorn \ə-'dȯrn\ *vb* : to enhance the appearance of with ornaments

synonyms ADORN, DECORATE, EMBELLISH, BEAUTIFY mean to improve the appearance by adding something that is not essential. ADORN suggests that the thing added is beautiful in itself ⟨a gold star *adorned* the tree⟩. DECORATE suggests adding color or design to something that is plain or dull ⟨*decorated* her room with posters⟩. EMBELLISH stresses the adding of something not needed ⟨dishes *embellished* with a leaf design⟩. BEAUTIFY stresses the improvement of something plain or ugly ⟨flower boxes *beautify* the street⟩.

adorn·ment \ə-'dȯrn-mənt\ *n* **1** : the action of adorning : the state of being adorned **2** : something that adorns

ADP \,ā-,dē-'pē, ā-,dē-,pē\ *n* : a compound formed in living cells that reacts to form ATP

¹**ad·re·nal** \ə-'drē-nᵊl\ *adj* : of, relating to, or derived from the adrenal glands or their secretions

²**adrenal** *n* : ADRENAL GLAND

adrenal gland *n* : either of a pair of endocrine glands that are located near the kidney and produce the hormone epinephrine

adren·a·line \ə-'dren-ᵊl-ən\ *n* : EPINEPHRINE

adrift \ə-'drift\ *adv or adj* **1** : without power or anchor ⟨a ship *adrift* in the storm⟩ **2** : without guidance or purpose ⟨alone and *adrift* in the city⟩

adroit \ə-'drȯit\ *adj* : having or showing great skill or cleverness ⟨an *adroit* leader⟩ ⟨the candidate's *adroit* use of television⟩ — **adroit·ly** *adv* — **adroit·ness** *n*

ad·sorb \ad-'sȯrb, -'zȯrb\ *vb* : to take up and hold or to become taken up by adsorption

ad·sorp·tion \-'sȯrp-shən, -'zȯrp-\ *n* : the sticking of molecules (as of a gas or liquid) in a very thin layer to the surfaces of solid objects or liquids which the molecules come in contact with

ad·u·late \'aj-ə-,lāt\ *vb* **-lat·ed; -lat·ing** : to flatter or admire slavishly — **ad·u·la·tion** \,aj-ə-'lā-shən\ *n* — **ad·u·la·tor** \'aj-ə-,lāt-ər\ *n* — **ad·u·la·to·ry** \'aj-ə-lə-,tōr-ē, -,tȯr-\ *adj*

¹**adult** \ə-'dəlt, 'ad-,əlt\ *adj* **1** : fully developed and mature **2** : of, relating to, or characteristic of adults [from Latin *adultus* "having grown up," from *adolescere* "to grow up" — related to ADOLESCENCE] — **adult·hood** \ə-'dəlt-,hùd\ *n* — **adult·ness** \ə-'dəlt-nəs, 'ad-,əlt-\ *n*

²**adult** *n* : a fully grown person, animal, or plant — **adult·like** \ə-'dəlt-,līk\ *adj*

adul·ter·ant \ə-'dəl-tə-rənt\ *n* : something used to adulterate another thing

adul·ter·ate \ə-'dəl-tə-,rāt\ *vb* **-at·ed; -at·ing** : to make impure or weaker by adding an unnecessary or lower-grade substance; *esp* : to prepare for sale by using in

whole or in part a substance that reduces value or strength [from Latin *adulterare* "to make impure," from *ad-* "to" and *alter* "other" — related to ALTER] — **adul·ter·a·tion** \ə-,dəl-tə-'rā-shən\ *n* — **adul·ter·a·tor** \ə-'dəl-tə-,rāt-ər\ *n*

adul·tery \ə-'dəl-t(ə-)rē\ *n, pl* **-ter·ies** : voluntary sexual intercourse between a married person and someone other than his or her spouse — **adul·ter·er** \-tər-ər\ *n* — **adul·ter·ess** \-t(ə-)rəs\ *n* — **adul·ter·ous** \-t(ə-)rəs\ *adj*

¹**ad·vance** \əd-'van(t)s\ *vb* **ad·vanced; ad·vanc·ing 1** : to move forward ⟨*advance* a few yards⟩ **2** : to help the progress of ⟨sacrifices that *advance* the cause of freedom⟩ **3** : to raise to a higher rank or position : PROMOTE ⟨was *advanced* from clerk to assistant manager⟩ **4** : to give and expect to be paid back ⟨*advance* a loan⟩ **5** : SUGGEST 1, PROPOSE ⟨*advance* a new plan⟩ — **ad·vanc·er** *n*

²**advance** *n* **1** : a forward movement **2** : progress in development : IMPROVEMENT ⟨recent *advances* in medicine⟩ **3** : a rise in price, value, or amount **4** : a first step or approach ⟨an unfriendly look discourages *advances*⟩ **5 a** : the giving of something in payment (as money) before goods or services are received ⟨I need an *advance* on my salary⟩ **b** : the money or goods given — **in advance** : ¹BEFORE, BEFOREHAND ⟨knew of the change two weeks *in advance*⟩ — **in advance of** : AHEAD OF

³**advance** *adj* **1** : made, sent, or furnished ahead of time ⟨an *advance* payment⟩ **2** : going or situated before ⟨an *advance* guard⟩ ⟨an *advance* scout⟩

ad·vanced \əd-'van(t)st\ *adj* **1** : far on in time or course ⟨a man *advanced* in years⟩ **2** : being beyond the elementary or introductory level ⟨*advanced* mathematics⟩ **3** : being far along in progress or development ⟨an *advanced* civilization⟩ ⟨a disease in an *advanced* stage⟩ **4** : having changed from a more primitive state found in an ancestor ⟨*advanced* insects like the wasps and bees⟩

ad·vance·ment \əd-'van(t)-smənt\ *n* **1** : the action of advancing : the state of being advanced **2 a** : a raising or being raised to a higher rank or position **b** : progression to a higher stage of development **3** : an improved feature

ad·van·tage \əd-'vant-ij\ *n* **1** : the fact of being in a better position or condition ⟨gain the *advantage*⟩ **2** : ¹BENEFIT 1, GAIN **3** : something that helps the one it belongs to ⟨speed is an *advantage* in sports⟩ — **to advantage** : so as to give a favorable impression

ad·van·ta·geous \,ad-,van-'tā-jəs, -vən-\ *adj* : giving an advantage : HELPFUL, FAVORABLE — **ad·van·ta·geous·ly** *adv* — **ad·van·ta·geous·ness** *n*

ad·vent \'ad-,vent\ *n* **1** *cap* : the season beginning four Sundays before Christmas **2** : the first appearance : ARRIVAL ⟨the *advent* of spring⟩ [Middle English *advent* "Christmas season," from Latin *adventus* (same meaning), from earlier *advent* "arrival"]

ad·ven·ti·tious \,ad-(,)ven-'tish-əs, -vən-\ *adj* **1** : coming from an outside source and not an essential part : ACCIDENTAL **2** : appearing in other than the usual or normal place ⟨*adventitious* roots⟩ — **ad·ven·ti·tious·ly** *adv*

¹**ad·ven·ture** \əd-'ven-chər\ *n* **1** : an action involving unknown risks or dangers **2** : the encountering of risks ⟨the spirit of *adventure*⟩ **3** : an unusual or exciting experience ⟨the field trip was an *adventure*⟩

²**adventure** *vb* **-ven·tured; -ven·tur·ing** \-'vench-(ə-)riŋ\ **1** : ²RISK 1, VENTURE **2** : to venture upon ⟨explorers *adventuring* the wilderness⟩

ad·ven·tur·er \əd-'vench-(ə-)rər\ *n* **1** : a person who looks for adventures **2** : a person who tries to become wealthy or powerful by trickery

ad·ven·ture·some \əd-'ven-chər-səm\ *adj* : ADVENTUROUS 1

ad·ven·tur·ous \əd-'vench-(ə-)rəs\ *adj* **1** : ready to take risks or to deal with the new and unknown ⟨*adventurous* explorers⟩ **2** : having unknown dangers and risks ⟨an

adventurous voyage⟩ — **ad·ven·tur·ous·ly** adv — **ad·ven·tur·ous·ness** n

synonyms ADVENTUROUS, VENTURESOME, DARING mean exposing oneself to more danger than one has to. ADVENTUROUS suggests a willingness to accept risks but does not rule out showing good sense ⟨adventurous campers backpacking in the mountains⟩. VENTURESOME suggests a lively eagerness for dangerous undertakings ⟨venturesome deep-sea explorers⟩. DARING stresses lack of fear and even boldness in looking for danger ⟨racing-car drivers are often very daring⟩.

ad·verb \'ad-ˌvərb\ n : a word used to modify a verb, an adjective, another adverb, a preposition, a phrase, a clause, or a sentence and often used to show degree, manner, place, or time — **adverb** adj — **ad·ver·bi·al** \ad-'vər-bē-əl\ adj or n — **ad·ver·bi·al·ly** \-bē-ə-lē\ adv

¹**ad·ver·sary** \'ad-və(r)-ˌser-ē\ n, pl **-sar·ies** : someone or something that struggles with, opposes, or resists : ENEMY, OPPONENT

²**adversary** adj : involving two persons or two sides who oppose each other ⟨our adversary system of justice⟩

ad·verse \ad-'vərs, 'ad-ˌvərs\ adj **1** : acting in an opposite direction ⟨adverse winds⟩ **2** : opposed to one's interests ⟨adverse testimony⟩; esp : not friendly or favorable ⟨adverse criticism⟩ **3** : causing harm : HARMFUL ⟨adverse effects of a drug⟩ — **ad·verse·ly** adv — **ad·verse·ness** n

ad·ver·si·ty \ad-'vər-sət-ē\ n, pl **-ties** : an instance or condition of serious or continued misfortune

ad·vert \ad-'vərt\ vb : to make a reference : REFER ⟨advert to a previous remark⟩

ad·ver·tise \'ad-vər-ˌtīz\ vb **-tised; -tis·ing 1** : to announce publicly especially by a printed notice or a broadcast ⟨advertise a sale⟩ **2** : to call public attention to especially by pointing out desirable qualities so as to create a desire to buy or to do business with ⟨advertise a cereal⟩ ⟨advertise a store⟩ **3** : to give a public notice or advertisement ⟨advertise for a lost dog⟩ — **ad·ver·tis·er** n

ad·ver·tise·ment \ˌad-vər-'tīz-mənt, əd-'vərt-əz-\ n **1** : the act or process of advertising **2** : a public notice; esp : one published or broadcast

ad·ver·tis·ing \'ad-vər-ˌtī-ziŋ\ n **1** : the action of calling something to the attention of the public especially by paid announcements **2** : published or broadcast advertisements **3** : the business of preparing advertisements

ad·vice \əd-'vīs\ n : an opinion or suggestion offered about a decision or course of conduct : COUNSEL

ad·vis·able \əd-'vī-zə-bəl\ adj : reasonable or proper under the circumstances : WISE, PRUDENT — **ad·vis·abil·i·ty** \-ˌvī-zə-'bil-ət-ē\ n — **ad·vis·ably** \-'vī-zə-blē\ adv

ad·vise \əd-'vīz\ vb **ad·vised; ad·vis·ing 1 a** : to give advice to : COUNSEL ⟨advised them to wait⟩ **b** : RECOMMEND **3** ⟨advised caution⟩ **2** : to give information or notice to : INFORM **1** ⟨were advised of the news⟩ **3** : to talk over a problem or decision : CONSULT ⟨advised with her parents⟩ — **ad·vis·er** or **ad·vi·sor** \-'vī-zər\ n

ad·vised \əd-'vīzd\ adj : thought about : CONSIDERED ⟨an ill-advised plan⟩ — **ad·vis·ed·ly** \-'vī-zəd-lē\ adv

ad·vise·ment \əd-'vīz-mənt\ n : careful consideration ⟨take a matter under advisement⟩

ad·vi·so·ry \əd-'vīz-(ə-)rē\ adj **1** : having the power or right to advise ⟨an advisory committee⟩ **2** : giving or containing advice ⟨an advisory opinion⟩

ad·vo·ca·cy \'ad-və-kə-sē\ n : the act or process of advocating : SUPPORT

¹**ad·vo·cate** \'ad-və-kət, -ˌkāt\ n **1** : a person who argues for the cause of another especially in a court of law **2** : a person who argues for, recommends, or supports a cause or policy ⟨an advocate of civil rights⟩ [Middle English advocat "one that pleads a case for another (in court)," from early French advocat (same meaning), from Latin advocatus (same meaning), derived from advocare "to call to

one's aid, summon," from ad- "to, toward, near" and vocare "to call" — related to PROVOKE, REVOKE, VOCATION]

²**ad·vo·cate** \'ad-və-ˌkāt\ vb **-cat·ed; -cat·ing** : to speak in favor of : argue for

adze also **adz** \'adz\ n : a cutting tool that has a thin arched blade set at right angles to the handle and is used chiefly for shaping wood

aë·des \ā-'ēd-ēz\ n, pl **aëdes** : any of a genus of mosquitoes including carriers of disease (as yellow fever)

ae·gis \'ē-jəs\ n **1** : PROTECTION **1a**, DEFENSE ⟨under the aegis of the law⟩ **2** : PATRONAGE **1**, SPONSORSHIP ⟨under the aegis of the museum⟩

adze

aeolian variant of EOLIAN

ae·on or **eon** \'ē-ən, 'ē-ˌän\ n **1** : a very long period of time : AGE **2 a** usu eon : a very large division of geologic time usually longer than an era **b** : a unit of geologic time equal to one billion years

aer- or **aero-** combining form **1** : air : atmosphere ⟨aerate⟩ ⟨aerobic⟩ **2** : gas ⟨aerosol⟩ **3** : aviation ⟨aeronautics⟩ [from Greek aer-, aero- "air"]

aer·ate \'a(-ə)r-ˌāt, 'e(-ə)r-\ vb **aer·at·ed; aer·at·ing 1** : to expose to or supply or fill to the limit with air ⟨aerate the soil⟩ **2** : to supply (blood) with oxygen by respiration **3** : to combine or fill with gas — **aer·a·tion** \ˌa(-ə)r-'ā-shən, ˌe(-ə)r-\ n — **aer·a·tor** \'a(-ə)r-ˌāt-ər, 'e(-ə)r-\ n

¹**ae·ri·al** \'ar-ē-əl, 'er-\ adj **1 a** : of, relating to, or occurring in the air or atmosphere ⟨an aerial display on a trapeze⟩ **b** : living or growing in the air rather than on the ground or in water **c** : running on cables or rails that are raised above the ground ⟨an aerial railway⟩ **2 a** : of or relating to aircraft ⟨aerial navigation⟩ **b** : designed for use in, taken from, or operating from aircraft ⟨aerial photograph⟩ — **aer·i·al·ly** \-ē-ə-lē\ adv

²**aerial** n **1** : ANTENNA **2 2** : FORWARD PASS

aerial root n : a root (as for clinging to a wall) that does not enter the soil

aer·ie \'a(-ə)r-ē, 'e(-ə)r-, 'i(-ə)r-\ n **1** : the nest of a bird on a cliff or a mountaintop **2** : a dwelling placed high up

aer·o·bat·ics \ˌar-ə-'bat-iks, ˌer-\ n sing or pl : spectacular flying feats and maneuvers — **aer·o·bat·ic** \-ik\ adj

aer·o·bic \ˌa(-ə)r-'ō-bik, ˌe(-ə)r-\ adj **1** : living, active, or occurring only in the presence of oxygen **2** : of, relating to, or caused by aerobic organisms (as bacteria) **3** : involving or increasing oxygen use ⟨aerobic exercise⟩ — **aer·o·bi·cal·ly** \-bi-k(ə-)lē\ adv

aer·o·bics \ˌa(-ə)r-'ō-biks, ˌe(-ə)r-\ n sing or pl : a system of exercises intended to improve the body's ability to take in and use oxygen

A aerial root

aero·drome \'ar-ə-ˌdrōm, 'er-\ n, British : AIRPORT, AIRFIELD

aero·dy·nam·ics \ˌar-ō-dī-'nam-iks, ˌer-\ n : a science that deals with the motion of fluids (as air) that are gases and with the forces acting on bodies exposed to them — **aero·dy·nam·ic** \-ik\ adj

\ə\	**abut**	\aù\	**out**	\i\	**tip**	\ò\	**saw**	\ù\	**foot**
\ər\	**further**	\ch\	**chin**	\ī\	**life**	\òi\	**coin**	\y\	**yet**
\a\	**mat**	\e\	**pet**	\j\	**job**	\th\	**thin**	\yü\	**few**
\ā\	**take**	\ē\	**easy**	\ŋ\	**sing**	\th\	**this**	\yù\	**cure**
\ä\	**cot, cart**	\g\	**go**	\ō\	**bone**	\ü\	**food**	\zh\	**vision**

aero·naut \'ar-ə-ˌnȯt, 'er-, -nät\ *n* : a person who operates or travels in an airship or a balloon

aero·nau·tics \ˌar-ə-'nȯt-iks, ˌer-\ *n* **1** : a science dealing with the operation of aircraft **2** : the art or science of flight — **aero·nau·ti·cal** \-'nȯt-i-kəl\ *adj*

aero·plane \'ar-ə-ˌplān, 'er-\ *chiefly British variant of* AIR-PLANE

aero·sol \'ar-ə-ˌsäl, 'er-, -ˌsȯl\ *n* : a mixture of fine solid or liquid particles and gas ⟨smoke and fog are *aerosols*⟩

¹aero·space \'ar-ō-ˌspās, 'er-\ *n* **1** : the earth's atmosphere and the space beyond **2** : a science dealing with aerospace

²aerospace *adj* : of or relating to aerospace, to the vehicles used in aerospace or their manufacture, or to travel in aerospace ⟨*aerospace* medicine⟩

aes·thet·ic *or* **es·thet·ic** \es-'thet-ik, is-\ *adj* : of or relating to beauty or what is beautiful — **aes·thet·i·cal·ly** \-i-k(ə)-lē\ *adv*

aes·thet·ics *also* **es·thet·ics** \es-'thet-iks, is-\ *n* : a branch of philosophy that studies and explains the principles and forms of beauty especially in art and literature

aestivate, aestivation *variant of* ESTIVATE, ESTIVATION

af- — see AD-

¹afar \ə-'fär\ *adv* : from, to, or at a great distance

²afar *n* : a great distance ⟨a voice from *afar*⟩

af·fa·ble \'af-ə-bəl\ *adj* : being at ease and pleasant especially in conversation ⟨an *affable* host⟩ **synonyms** see GRACIOUS — **af·fa·bil·i·ty** \ˌaf-ə-'bil-ət-ē\ *n* — **af·fa·bly** \'af-ə-blē\ *adv*

af·fair \ə-'fa(ə)r, -'fe(ə)r\ *n* **1 a** *pl* : commercial, professional, public, or personal business ⟨government *affairs*⟩ ⟨arranged my *affairs* before leaving⟩ **b** : ²CONCERN 1, MATTER ⟨not your *affair* at all⟩ **2 a** : EVENT 1b, ACTIVITY ⟨a social *affair*⟩ **b** : PRODUCT 2, THING ⟨the house was a two-story *affair*⟩ **3** : a brief romantic relationship

¹af·fect \ə-'fekt, a-\ *vb* **1** : to show a liking for : FANCY ⟨*affect* flashy clothes⟩ **2** : FEIGN 1, PRETEND ⟨*affect* indifference⟩

²affect *vb* : to produce an effect upon: as **a** : to produce a significant influence upon or change in ⟨paralysis *affected* his limbs⟩ **b** : to act upon (as a person or a person's feelings) so as to cause a response ⟨the criticism *affected* her deeply⟩

af·fec·ta·tion \ˌaf-ˌek-'tā-shən\ *n* : an unnatural form of behavior usually intended to impress others ⟨the accent was an *affectation*⟩

af·fect·ed \ə-'fek-təd, a-\ *adj* : not natural or genuine — **af·fect·ed·ly** *adv* — **af·fect·ed·ness** *n*

af·fect·ing \ə-'fek-tiŋ, a-\ *adj* : causing a feeling of pity, sympathy, or sorrow — **af·fect·ing·ly** \-tiŋ-lē\ *adv*

af·fec·tion \ə-'fek-shən\ *n* **1** : a quality or feeling of liking and caring for another **2** : DISEASE, DISORDER ⟨an *affection* of the brain⟩

af·fec·tion·ate \ə-'fek-sh(ə-)nət\ *adj* : feeling or showing a great liking for a person or thing : LOVING — **af·fec·tion·ate·ly** *adv*

af·fer·ent \'af-ə-rənt, 'af-ˌer-ənt\ *adj* : bearing or conducting inward; *esp* : conveying impulses toward the central nervous system — **af·fer·ent·ly** *adv*

af·fi·ance \ə-'fī-ən(t)s\ *vb* **-anced; -anc·ing** : to promise in marriage

af·fi·da·vit \ˌaf-ə-'dā-vət\ *n* : a sworn statement in writing

¹af·fil·i·ate \ə-'fil-ē-ˌāt\ *vb* **-at·ed; -at·ing** : to connect closely often as a member, branch, or associate — **af·fil·i·a·tion** \-ˌfil-ē-'ā-shən\ *n*

²af·fil·i·ate \ə-'fil-ē-ət\ *n* : an affiliated person or organization

af·fin·i·ty \ə-'fin-ət-ē\ *n, pl* **-ties** **1** : relationship by marriage **2 a** : a feeling of closeness or sympathy because of shared interests **b** : ATTRACTION; *esp* : an attractive force between substances or particles that causes them to enter into and remain in chemical combination

af·firm \ə-'fərm\ *vb* : to state positively or with confidence **synonyms** see ASSERT — **af·fir·ma·tion** \ˌaf-ər-'mā-shən\ *n*

¹af·fir·ma·tive \ə-'fər-mət-iv\ *adj* **1** : declaring that the fact is so ⟨gave an *affirmative* answer⟩ **2** : being positive or helpful ⟨take an *affirmative* approach⟩ — **af·fir·ma·tive·ly** *adv*

²affirmative *n* **1** : an expression (as the word *yes*) of agreement **2** : the affirmative side in a debate or vote

affirmative action *n* : an active effort to improve the educational and employment opportunities of members of minority groups and women

¹af·fix \ə-'fiks, a-\ *vb* **1** : to attach physically : FASTEN ⟨*affix* a stamp to a letter⟩ **2** : to attach in any way : ADD ⟨*affix* a signature to a document⟩

²af·fix \'af-ˌiks\ *n* : a letter or a group of letters attached to the beginning or end of a word that serves to produce a derivative word or an inflectional form

af·flict \ə-'flikt\ *vb* : to cause suffering or unhappiness to

af·flic·tion \ə-'flik-shən\ *n* **1** : the state of being afflicted **2** : something that causes pain or unhappiness

af·flu·ence \'af-ˌlü-ən(t)s *also* a-'flü-, ə-'flü-\ *n* : the state of having much wealth or property

af·flu·ent \'af-ˌlü-ənt *also* a-'flü-, ə-'flü-\ *adj* : having plenty of money and the things money can buy [Middle English *affluent* "abundant," derived from Latin *ad-* "to" and *fluere* "to flow" — related to FLUID] — **af·flu·ent·ly** *adv*

af·ford \ə-'fȯrd, -'fȯrd\ *vb* **1** : to be able to do or to bear without serious harm ⟨you can't *afford* to waste your strength⟩ **2** : to be able to pay for ⟨unable to *afford* a new car⟩ **3** : to supply one with : PROVIDE, FURNISH ⟨tennis *affords* good exercise⟩ — **af·ford·able** \-'fȯrd-ə-bəl, -'fȯrd-\ *adj*

af·fray \ə-'frā\ *n* : a noisy quarrel or fight

af·fright \ə-'frīt\ *vb, archaic* : FRIGHTEN 1, ALARM

¹af·front \ə-'frənt\ *vb* : to insult openly : OFFEND

²affront *n* : a deliberately insulting or disrespectful act or utterance

Af·ghan \'af-ˌgan\ *n* **1** : a person born or living in Afghanistan **2** *not cap* : a blanket or shawl made of knitted or crocheted colored wool — **Afghan** *or* **Af·ghani** \af-'gan-ē, -'gän-\ *adj*

Afghan hound *n* : any of a breed of tall swift hunting dogs originating in Afghanistan with a coat of long silky hair and a long silky bunch of hair on the head

afi·cio·na·do \ə-ˌfish-(ē-)ə-'näd-ō, -ˌfis-ē-\ *n, pl* **-dos** : a person who really likes and appreciates something ⟨an *aficionado* of Mexican food⟩ ⟨science fiction *aficionados*⟩ [Spanish, derived from Latin *affectio* "affection"]

Afghan hound

afield \ə-'fēld\ *adv* **1** : to, in, or on the field **2** : away from home **3** : out of a regular, planned, or proper course : ASTRAY

afire \ə-'fī(ə)r\ *adj or adv* : being on fire

aflame \ə-'flām\ *adj or adv* : AFIRE

afloat \ə-'flōt\ *adj or adv* **1 a** : carried on or as if on the water **b** : being at sea **2** : circulating about : RUMORED ⟨there was a story *afloat*⟩

aflut·ter \ə-'flət-ər\ *adj* **1** : flapping quickly **2** : nervously excited

afoot \ə-'fut\ *adv or adj* **1** : on foot ⟨travels *afoot*⟩ **2** : in the process of development : UNDER WAY ⟨a plan was *afoot* to seize power⟩

afore \ə-'fō(ə)r, -'fȯ(ə)r\ *adv or conj or prep, chiefly dialect* : BEFORE

afore·men·tioned \-ˌmen-chənd\ *adj* : mentioned before

afore·said \-ˌsed\ *adj* : said or named before

afore·thought \-ˌthȯt\ *adj* : thought of or planned beforehand : PREMEDITATED ⟨with malice *aforethought*⟩

afoul of \ə-ˈfau̇-ləv\ *prep* **1** : in or into collision or entanglement with ⟨one ship ran *afoul of* the other⟩ **2** : in or into conflict with ⟨they fell *afoul of* the law⟩

afraid \ə-ˈfrād, *Southern also* -ˈfre(ə)d\ *adj* **1** : filled with fear or dread ⟨*afraid* of snakes⟩ **2** : filled with concern or regret ⟨*afraid* she might be late⟩ **3** : having a dislike for something ⟨not *afraid* to work hard⟩ [Middle English *affraied* "filled with fear," from *affraien* "to frighten," from early French *affraier, effreer* "to frighten" — related to ¹FRAY]

afresh \ə-ˈfresh\ *adv* : from a new start : AGAIN

Af·ri·can \ˈaf-ri-kən\ *n* **1** : a person born or living in Africa **2** : a person of African ancestry — **African** *adj*

African–American *n* : an American having African and especially black African ancestors — **African–American** *adj*

African elephant *n* : ELEPHANT a

African sleeping sickness *n* : SLEEPING SICKNESS 1

African violet *n* : a tropical African plant widely grown as a houseplant for its velvety fleshy leaves and showy purple, pink, or white flowers

Af·ri·kaans \ˌaf-ri-ˈkän(t)s, -ˈkänz\ *n* : a language developed from 17th century Dutch and used in the Republic of South Africa

Af·ri·ka·ner \ˌaf-ri-ˈkän-ər\ *n* : a person born in South Africa whose native language is Afrikaans and whose ancestors were from Europe

Afro \ˈaf-rō\ *n* : a hairdo of tight curls in a full evenly rounded shape — **Af·roed** \-rōd\ *adj*

Af·ro–Amer·i·can \ˌaf-rō-ə-ˈmer-ə-kən\ *n* : AFRICAN-AMERICAN — **Afro–American** *adj*

Afro

aft \ˈaft\ *adv* : near, toward, or in the stern of a ship or the tail of an aircraft

¹af·ter \ˈaf-tər\ *adv* : following in time or place : LATER, BEHIND [Old English *æfter* "behind, later"]

²after *prep* **1 a** : behind in time or place ⟨following *after* us⟩ ⟨*after* dinner⟩ **b** : below in rank or order ⟨the highest mountain *after* Mount Everest⟩ **2** : for the reason of catching, seizing, or getting ⟨ran *after* the ball⟩ ⟨go *after* gold⟩ **3 a** : with the name of or a name derived from that of ⟨named *after* his father⟩ **b** : in imitation of ⟨patterned *after* a Gothic cathedral⟩

³after *conj* : later than the time when ⟨opened the door *after* she knocked⟩

⁴after *adj* **1** : later in time ⟨in *after* years⟩ **2** : located toward the stern of a ship or tail of an aircraft

after all *adv* : in spite of what was indicated or expected ⟨decided to go *after all*⟩ ⟨it rained *after all*⟩

af·ter·birth \ˈaf-tər-ˌbərth\ *n* : the placenta and membranes of the fetus that are expelled after childbirth

af·ter·burn·er \-ˌbər-nər\ *n* : a burner attached to the tail pipe of a turbojet engine for forcing fuel into the hot exhaust gases and burning it to provide extra forward push

af·ter·deck \-ˌdek\ *n* : the rear half of the deck of a ship

af·ter·ef·fect \-ə-ˌfekt\ *n* : an effect that arises after the first or immediate effect has decreased or disappeared ⟨a medicine with no noticeable *aftereffects*⟩

af·ter·glow \-ˌglō\ *n* **1** : a glow remaining (as in the sky after sunsets) where a light has disappeared **2** : a pleasant feeling that lingers after something is done, experienced, or achieved ⟨the *afterglow* of success⟩

af·ter·guard \-ˌgärd\ *n* : the sailors stationed on the poop or after part of a ship

af·ter·im·age \-ˌim-ij\ *n* : a usually visual sensation continuing after the stimulus causing it has ended

af·ter·life \-ˌlīf\ *n* **1** : an existence after death **2** : a later period in one's life

af·ter·math \ˈaf-tər-ˌmath\ *n* **1** : ²RESULT 1, CONSEQUENCE ⟨felt tired as an *aftermath* of the race⟩ **2** : the period immediately following a usually destructive event ⟨the *aftermath* of war⟩

Word History The second part of *aftermath* comes from the Old English word *mæth,* meaning "the result of a mowing or harvesting," that is, a crop. This word was derived from the Old English verb *māwan,* which survives today as our modern English *mow.* During a good growing season in England, a second and sometimes a third crop of hay could be grown after the first mowing. When this crop was cut, it was the aftermath. Since the 17th century, the meaning of *aftermath* has broadened to include all kinds of results, not just those of a second mowing. [Old English *mæth* "mowing," from *māwan* "to mow"]

af·ter·noon \ˌaf-tər-ˈnün\ *n* : the part of day between noon and sunset — **afternoon** *adj*

af·ter·shave \ˈaf-tər-ˌshāv\ *n* : a lotion for use on the face after shaving

af·ter·taste \-ˌtāst\ *n* : a sensation (as of flavor) continuing after the stimulus causing it has ended

af·ter·thought \-ˌthȯt\ *n* **1** : a later thought about something one has done or said **2** : something not thought of originally

af·ter·ward \ˈaf-tə(r)-wərd\ *or* **af·ter·wards** \-wərdz\ *adv* : at a later time

ag- — see AD-

again \ə-ˈgen, -ˈgin, -ˈgān\ *adv* **1** : in return ⟨send the message and bring us word *again*⟩ **2** : another time : ANEW ⟨come see us *again*⟩ **3** : in addition ⟨half as much *again*⟩ **4** : on the other hand ⟨I may, and *again* I may not⟩ **5** : MOREOVER, FURTHER ⟨*again,* there is another matter to consider⟩ [Old English *ongēan* "opposite, back"]

against \ə-ˈgen(t)st, -ˈgin(t)st, -ˈgān(t)st\ *prep* **1 a** : opposed to ⟨a campaign *against* disease⟩ ⟨play *against* each other⟩ **b** : contrary to ⟨*against* the law⟩ **2** : ⁴OPPOSITE ⟨over *against* the park⟩ **3 a** : in preparation for ⟨storing food *against* the winter⟩ **b** : as a protection from ⟨a shield *against* aggression⟩ **4** : in or into contact with ⟨ran *against* a tree⟩ ⟨leaning *against* the wall⟩ **5** : in a direction opposite to ⟨*against* the wind⟩ **6** : before the background of ⟨green trees *against* the blue sky⟩

agape \ə-ˈgāp *also* ə-ˈgap\ *adj* : having the mouth open in wonder or surprise ⟨the crowd stood *agape* at the sight⟩

agar \ˈäg-ər\ *also* **agar–agar** \ˈäg-ə-ˈräg-ər\ *n* **1** : a jellylike substance obtained from a red alga and used especially in culture media or to give firmness to foods **2** : a culture medium containing agar

ag·ate \ˈag-ət\ *n* **1** : a smooth-looking quartz having its colors arranged in stripes or forms that look like clouds or moss **2** : a playing marble of agate or glass

aga·ve \ə-ˈgäv-ē\ *n* : any of a genus of plants (as the century plant) that have spiny-edged leaves and flowers in tall branched clusters and include some cultivated for fiber or for ornament

¹age \ˈāj\ *n* **1 a** : the time of life when a person attains some right or capacity ⟨the voting *age* is 18⟩; *esp* : MAJORITY 1 ⟨come of *age*⟩ **b** : the time from birth to a specified date ⟨a child six years of *age*⟩ **c** : normal lifetime **d** : the later part of life ⟨youth and *age*⟩ **2** : a period of time associated with a particular person or thing ⟨machine *age*⟩

\ə\ **abut**	\au̇\ **out**	\i\ **tip**	\ȯ\ **saw**	\u̇\ **foot**
\ər\ **further**	\ch\ **chin**	\ī\ **life**	\ȯi\ **coin**	\y\ **yet**
\a\ **mat**	\e\ **pet**	\j\ **job**	\th\ **thin**	\yü\ **few**
\ā\ **take**	\ē\ **easy**	\ŋ\ **sing**	\th\ **this**	\yu̇\ **cure**
\ä\ **cot, cart**	\g\ **go**	\ō\ **bone**	\ü\ **food**	\zh\ **vision**

⟨*Age* of Discovery⟩ **3** : a long period of time ⟨did it *ages* ago⟩ **synonyms** see PERIOD

²**age** *vb* **aged; ag·ing** *or* **age·ing** **1** : to become or cause to become old or old in appearance ⟨his troubles *aged* him⟩ **2** : to become or cause to become mellow or mature : RIPEN ⟨letting cheese *age*⟩

-age \ij\ *n suffix* **1** : total amount : collection ⟨mile*age*⟩ **2 a** : action : process ⟨cover*age*⟩ **b** : result of ⟨break*age*⟩ **c** : rate of ⟨dos*age*⟩ **3** : house or place of ⟨orphan*age*⟩ **4** : state : status ⟨bond*age*⟩ **5** : fee : charge ⟨post*age*⟩ [Middle English *-age* "collection," from early French *-age* (same meaning), from Latin *-aticum,* suffix of mass and abstract nouns]

aged *adj* **1** \'ā-jəd\ : very old ⟨an *aged* oak⟩ **2** \'ājd\ : having reached a specified age ⟨a child *aged* ten⟩ — **ag·ed·ness** \'ā-jəd-nəs\ *n*

age·ism \'ā-(,)jiz-əm\ *n* : prejudice or discrimination against people of a particular age and especially against the elderly — **age·ist** \-jist\ *adj*

age·less \'āj-ləs\ *adj* **1** : not growing old or showing the effects of age ⟨an *ageless* face⟩ **2** : ETERNAL 1, TIMELESS ⟨an *ageless* story⟩ — **age·less·ly** *adv* — **age·less·ness** *n*

agen·cy \'ā-jən-sē\ *n, pl* **-cies** **1** : the office or function of an agent **2** : a person or thing through which power is used or something is achieved : MEANS **3** : an establishment doing business for another ⟨an insurance *agency*⟩ **4** : a part of a government that manages projects in a certain area ⟨a health *agency*⟩

agen·da \ə-'jen-də\ *n* : a list of items of business to be considered (as at a meeting)

agent \'ā-jənt\ *n* **1 a** : something that produces an effect ⟨a cleansing *agent*⟩ **b** : a chemically, physically, or biologically active substance **2** : a person who acts or does business for another ⟨government *agents*⟩ ⟨a real estate *agent*⟩ [Middle English *agent* "one that produces an effect," derived from Latin *agere* "to drive, act, do" — related to ACT, AGILE]

Age of Fishes : the Devonian period

Age of Mammals : the Cenozoic era

Age of Reptiles : the Mesozoic era

age–old \'a-,jōld\ *adj* : having existed for ages : ANCIENT ⟨an *age-old* story⟩

ag·er·a·tum \,aj-ə-'rāt-əm\ *n* : any of a large genus of tropical American herbs related to the daisies and often cultivated for their small showy heads of blue or white flowers

Ag·ge·us \a-'gē-əs\ *n* : HAGGAI

¹**ag·glom·er·ate** \ə-'gläm-ə-,rāt\ *vb* **-at·ed; -at·ing** : to gather into a ball, mass, or cluster

²**ag·glom·er·ate** \ə-'gläm-ə-rət\ *n* **1** : a jumbled mass or collection **2** : a rock composed of volcanic pieces of various sizes

ag·glom·er·a·tion \ə-,gläm-ə-'rā-shən\ *n* **1** : the action or process of collecting in a mass **2** : a heap or cluster of dissimilar elements — **ag·glom·er·a·tive** \ə-'gläm-ə-,rāt-iv\ *adj*

ag·glu·ti·nate \ə-'glüt-ᵊn-āt\ *vb* **-nat·ed; -nat·ing** **1** : to cause to stick : FASTEN **2** : to cause to clump or experience agglutination **3** : to unite into a group or gather into a mass

ag·glu·ti·na·tion \ə-,glüt-ᵊn-'ā-shən\ *n* **1** : the action or process of agglutinating **2** : a mass or group formed by the union of separate elements **3** : a reaction in which particles (as red blood cells or bacteria) suspended in a liquid collect into clumps usually as a response to a specific antibody — **ag·glu·ti·na·tive** \-'glüt-ᵊn-,āt-iv, -ət-\ *adj*

ag·glu·ti·nin \ə-'glüt-ᵊn-ən\ *n* : an antibody causing agglutination

ag·gran·dize \ə-'gran-,dīz *also* 'ag-rən-\ *vb* **-dized; -diz·ing** : to make great or greater (as in power, wealth, or reputation) — **ag·gran·dize·ment** \ə-'gran-dəz-mənt, -,dīz- *also* ,ag-rən-'dīz-mənt\ *n* — **ag·gran·diz·er** *n*

ag·gra·vate \'ag-rə-,vāt\ *vb* **-vat·ed; -vat·ing** **1** : to make more serious or severe ⟨*aggravate* an injury⟩ **2** : to make angry by bothering again and again [from Latin *aggravare* "to make heavier," from *ad-* "to" and *gravare* "to burden," from *gravis* "heavy" — related to ³GRAVE, GRAVITY, GRIEVE]

ag·gra·va·tion \,ag-rə-'vā-shən\ *n* **1** : the act or result of aggravating **2** : something that aggravates

¹**ag·gre·gate** \'ag-ri-gət\ *adj* **1** : formed by the collection of units or particles into one mass or sum ⟨*aggregate* expenses⟩ **2** : clustered in a dense mass or head ⟨an *aggregate* flower⟩ [Middle English *aggregat* "made up of a collection," derived from Latin *aggregare* "to cause to join together," from *ag-, ad-* "to, toward" and *greg-, grex* "flock, herd" — related to CONGREGATE, SEGREGATE]

²**ag·gre·gate** \'ag-ri-,gāt\ *vb* **-gat·ed; -gat·ing** **1** : to collect or gather into a mass or whole **2** : to amount to as a whole : TOTAL

³**ag·gre·gate** \'ag-ri-gət\ *n* **1** : a collection or sum of units or parts **2 a** : a hard material (as sand or gravel) used especially in making concrete **b** : a clustered mass of individual soil particles considered the basic structural unit of soil

aggregate fruit *n* : a compound fruit (as a raspberry) made up of the several separate ripened ovaries of a single flower

ag·gre·ga·tion \,ag-ri-'gā-shən\ *n* **1** : the collecting of units or parts into a mass or whole **2** : a group, body, or mass composed of many distinct parts

ag·gres·sion \ə-'gresh-ən\ *n* **1** : an attack made without reasonable cause **2** : the practice of making attacks **3** : hostile or destructive behavior or outlook [derived from Latin *aggredi* "to attack," from *ad-* "to" and *gradi* "to step, go"]

ag·gres·sive \ə-'gres-iv\ *adj* **1 a** : showing readiness to attack ⟨an *aggressive* dog⟩ **b** : practicing aggression ⟨an *aggressive* nation⟩ **2** : being forceful in getting things done ⟨an *aggressive* sales campaign⟩ **3** : growing, developing, or spreading rapidly ⟨*aggressive* weeds⟩ — **ag·gres·sive·ly** *adv* — **ag·gres·sive·ness** *n*

ag·gres·sor \ə-'gres-ər\ *n* : a person or country that attacks without reasonable cause

ag·grieved \ə-'grēvd\ *adj* **1** : troubled or distressed in spirit **2** : having a cause for complaint; *esp* : suffering from injury or loss

aghast \ə-'gast\ *adj* : struck with terror, amazement, or horror

ag·ile \'aj-əl, -,īl\ *adj* **1** : able to move quickly and easily : NIMBLE ⟨an *agile* gymnast⟩ **2** : mentally quick ⟨an *agile* thinker⟩ [Latin *agilis* "nimble, agile," from *agere* "to drive, act, do" — related to ACT, AGENT] — **ag·ile·ly** \-ə(l)-lē, -,ī(l)-lē\ *adv* — **agil·i·ty** \ə-'jil-ət-ē\ *n*

aging *present participle of* AGE

ag·i·tate \'aj-ə-,tāt\ *vb* **-tat·ed; -tat·ing** **1** : to move with an irregular, rapid, or violent action ⟨water *agitated* by wind⟩ **2** : to stir up : EXCITE, DISTURB ⟨*agitated* by bad news⟩ **3** : to try to stir up public feeling ⟨*agitate* for equal rights⟩ — **ag·i·tat·ed·ly** \-,tāt-əd-lē\ *adv* — **ag·i·ta·tion** \,aj-ə-'tā-shən\ *n*

ag·i·ta·tor \'aj-ə-,tāt-ər\ *n* **1** : a person who stirs up public feeling **2** : a device for stirring or shaking

aglit·ter \ə-'glit-ər\ *adj* : glittering by reflecting light

aglow \ə-'glō\ *adj* : glowing with warmth or excitement

ag·nos·tic \ag-'näs-tik, əg-\ *n* : a person who believes that whether God exists is not known and probably cannot be known [from Greek *agnōstos* "unknown," from *a-* "not" and *gnōstos* "known"] — **agnostic** *adj* — **ag·nos·ti·cism** \-'näs-tə-,siz-əm\ *n*

ago \ə-'gō\ *adj or adv* : earlier than the present time ⟨many years *ago*⟩

agog \ə-'gäg\ *adj* : full of interest or excitement ⟨kids all *agog* over new toys⟩

ag·o·nize \'ag-ə-,nīz\ *vb* **-nized; -niz·ing** : to suffer or cause to suffer extreme pain or anguish of body or mind — **ag·o·niz·ing·ly** \-,nī-zin-lē\ *adv*

ag·o·ny \'ag-ə-nē\ *n, pl* **-nies** **1** : intense pain of mind or body **2** : a strong sudden display of emotion : OUTBURST ⟨an *agony* of delight⟩

> *Word History* In ancient Greece a public gathering was called *agōn*. Since the Greeks placed a high value on sports and athletic competition, there were almost always athletic events at gatherings on festival days. The struggle to win the prize in such contests came to be called *agōnia*. This term came also to be used for any difficult physical struggle and then for the pain that went with it, physical or mental. Our English word *agony*, meaning "intense pain of mind or body," thus comes from a word that originally meant a happy celebration. [Middle English *agonie* "agony," from Latin *agonia* (same meaning), from Greek *agōnia* "struggle," from *agōn* "gathering, contest for a prize"]

ag·o·ra \'ag-ə-rə\ *n, pl* **agoras** \-rəz\ *or* **ag·o·rae** \-,rē, -,rī\ : the marketplace or gathering place in an ancient Greek city

ag·o·ra·pho·bia \,a-gə-rə-'fō-bē-ə\ *n* : abnormal fear of being helpless in a situation which is embarrassing or inescapable and that leads to the avoidance of open or public places — **ag·o·ra·pho·bic** \-'fō-bik\ *adj*

agou·ti \ə-'güt-ē\ *n* **1** : a tropical American rodent about the size of a rabbit **2** : a gray-streaked color of fur resulting from the barring of each hair in several alternate dark and light bands

agouti 1

agrar·i·an \ə-'grer-ē-ən, -'grar-\ *adj* **1** : of or relating to fields or lands or their ownership ⟨*agrarian* reforms⟩ **2** : of, relating to, or concerned with farmers or farming interests ⟨an *agrarian* political party⟩ **3** : AGRICULTURAL 2 ⟨an *agrarian* country⟩

agree \ə-'grē\ *vb* **agreed; agree·ing** **1** : to give one's approval : CONSENT ⟨*agree* to a plan⟩ **2** : ADMIT 1b, CONCEDE ⟨all *agreed* they had been wrong⟩ **3** : to be alike : CORRESPOND ⟨both copies *agree*⟩ **4** : to get along well **5** : to come to an understanding ⟨*agree* on a price⟩ **6** : to be fitting, pleasing, or healthful : SUIT ⟨the climate *agrees* with you⟩ **7** : to be alike or correspond grammatically in gender, number, case, or person ⟨a verb should *agree* with its subject⟩ [Middle English *agreen* "admit, accept," from early French *agreer* (same meaning), from *a-* "to, toward" and *gre* "will, pleasure," derived from Latin *gratus* "pleasing, thankful, agreeable" — related to GRACE]

agree·able \ə-'grē-ə-bəl\ *adj* **1** : pleasing to the mind or senses : PLEASANT ⟨an *agreeable* taste⟩ **2** : ready or willing to agree ⟨I'm *agreeable* to the idea⟩ **3** : being in harmony : CONSONANT — **agree·able·ness** *n* — **agree·ably** \-blē\ *adv*

agree·ment \ə-'grē-mənt\ *n* **1 a** : the act of agreeing **b** : harmony of opinion, action, or character : CONCORD ⟨all are in *agreement*⟩ **2 a** : an arrangement or understanding (as a contract or treaty) about action to be taken **b** : a written record of such an agreement **3** : the fact of agreeing grammatically

> *synonyms* AGREEMENT, CONTRACT, BARGAIN mean an arrangement between persons on a matter of common interest. AGREEMENT suggests a shared understanding that is arrived at after some discussion ⟨an *agreement* to work as a team⟩. CONTRACT suggests a formal often written agreement ⟨a *contract* with a recording studio⟩. BARGAIN applies to a firm agreement especially about purchase and sale ⟨we made a *bargain* to sell the land⟩.

ag·ri·cul·tur·al \,ag-ri-'kəlch-(ə-)rəl\ *adj* **1** : of, relating to, or used in agriculture ⟨*agricultural* machinery⟩ **2** : engaged in or concerned with agriculture ⟨an *agricultural* society⟩ — **ag·ri·cul·tur·al·ly** \-ē\ *adv*

ag·ri·cul·ture \'ag-ri-,kəl-chər\ *n* : the science or occupation of cultivating the soil, producing crops, and raising livestock : FARMING — **ag·ri·cul·tur·ist** \,ag-ri-'kəlch-(ə-)rəst\ *or* **ag·ri·cul·tur·al·ist** \-(ə-)rə-ləst\ *n*

agron·o·my \ə-'grän-ə-mē\ *n* : a branch of agriculture that deals with the raising of crops and the care of the soil — **agron·o·mist** \-məst\ *n*

aground \ə-'graund\ *adv or adj* : on or onto the shore or the bottom of a body of water ⟨the ship ran *aground*⟩

ague \'ā-gyü\ *n* **1** : a fever (as malaria) marked by outbreaks of chills, fever, and sweating that recur at regular intervals **2** : a fit of shivering : CHILL

ah \'ä\ *interj* — used to express delight, relief, regret, or scorn

aha \ä-'hä\ *interj* — used to express surprise, triumph, or scorn

ahead \ə-'hed\ *adv or adj* **1** : in or toward the front ⟨the road *ahead*⟩ ⟨go *ahead*⟩ **2** : in, into, or for the future ⟨think *ahead*⟩ **3** : in or toward a better position ⟨came out $20 *ahead* on the deal⟩ **4** : at or to an earlier time : in advance ⟨make payments *ahead*⟩

ahead of *prep* : in or at a place or time before ⟨got *ahead of* me⟩ ⟨we're *ahead of* schedule⟩

A ho·ri·zon \'ä-hə-,rī-zən\ *n* : the outer dark-colored soil with a light texture consisting usually of soil rich in debris obtained from living things in various stages of disintegration

ahoy \ə-'hoi\ *interj* — used in calling out to a passing ship or boat

¹aid \'ād\ *vb* : to provide with what is useful or necessary : HELP, ASSIST — **aid·er** *n*

²aid *n* **1 a** : the act of helping **b** : help given : ASSISTANCE **2** : ASSISTANT **3** : someone or something that is of help or assistance ⟨a visual *aid*⟩

aide \'ād\ *n* : a person who acts as an assistant

aide–de–camp \,ād-di-'kamp, -'kän\ *n, pl* **aides–de–camp** \,ād(z)-di-\ : an aide to a high military or naval officer

AIDS \'ādz\ *n* : a serious disease of the human immune system marked by destruction of a large proportion of the helper T cells in the body due to infection by the HIV virus commonly transmitted especially in blood and semen

AIDS virus *n* : HIV

ai·ki·do \,ī-ki-'dō, ī-'kē-,dō\ *n* : a Japanese art of self-defense characterized by the use of techniques that force an opponent's own weight to work against him or her

ail \'āl\ *vb* **1** : to be the matter with : TROUBLE ⟨what *ails* you?⟩ **2** : to have something the matter; *esp* : to suffer ill health ⟨has been *ailing* for years⟩

ai·lan·thus \ā-'lan(t)-thəs\ *n* : TREE OF HEAVEN

ai·le·ron \'ā-lə-,rän\ *n* : a movable part (as a flap) of an airplane wing or a movable body apart from the wing for giving a rolling motion and as a result providing control sideways

ail·ment \'āl-mənt\ *n* : a bodily disorder : SICKNESS

¹aim \'ām\ *vb* **1** : to point a weapon **2** : ASPIRE, INTEND ⟨*aims* to please⟩ **3** : to direct to or toward an object or goal ⟨*aim* a camera⟩

²aim *n* **1** : the directing of a weapon or a missile at a mark **2** : GOAL 2, PURPOSE

\ə\ abut	\au̇\ out	\i\ tip	\ȯ\ saw	\u̇\ foot
\ər\ further	\ch\ chin	\ī\ life	\ȯi\ coin	\y\ yet
\a\ mat	\e\ pet	\j\ job	\th\ thin	\yü\ few
\ā\ take	\ē\ easy	\ŋ\ sing	\th\ this	\yu̇\ cure
\ä\ cot, cart	\g\ go	\ō\ bone	\ü\ food	\zh\ vision

aim·less \\'ām-ləs\\ *adj* : lacking a goal or purpose ⟨*aimless* wandering⟩ — **aim·less·ly** *adv* — **aim·less·ness** *n*

ain't \\(')ānt\\ **1 a** : are not **b** : is not **c** : am not **2 a** : have not **b** : has not — used by many educated speakers and writers in certain set phrases (as "two out of three ain't bad" or "and that ain't hay") and to catch attention but more common in less educated speech

¹**air** \\'a(ə)r, 'e(ə)r\\ *n* **1 a** : the invisible mixture of odorless tasteless gases (as nitrogen and oxygen) that surrounds the earth **b** : a light breeze **2** : the state of being empty or nothing — usually used in the phrase *into thin air* ⟨vanished into thin *air*⟩ **3** : ¹TUNE 1, MELODY **4 a** : outward appearance : apparent nature ⟨an *air* of mystery⟩ **b** *pl* : an artificial way of acting ⟨put on *airs*⟩ **5** : COMPRESSED AIR ⟨put *air* in a soft bicycle tire⟩ **6 a** : AIRCRAFT ⟨travel by *air*⟩ ⟨*air* attack⟩ **b** : AVIATION ⟨*air* safety⟩ **7 a** : the substance through which radio waves travel **b** : a radio or television broadcast ⟨went on the *air*⟩ **8** : an air-conditioning system ⟨turn on the *air*⟩ **9** : the height achieved in performing a maneuver in the air ⟨a skateboarder catching big *air*⟩

²**air** *vb* **1** : to place in the air for cooling, freshening, or cleaning ⟨*air* blankets⟩ **2** : to make known in public ⟨*air* one's complaints⟩ **3** : to broadcast on radio or television ⟨*air* a talk show⟩

air bag *n* : an automobile safety device consisting of a bag designed to inflate automatically especially in front of a rider in case of a collision

air base *n* : a base of operations for military aircraft

air bladder *n* **1** : SWIM BLADDER **2** : a cavity found in various algae that contains gases and serves to keep the algae afloat

air·borne \\'a(ə)r-ˌbōrn, -ˌbȯrn, 'e(ə)r-\\ *adj* : supported or transported by air ⟨*airborne* troops⟩

air brake *n* **1** : a brake operated by a piston driven by compressed air **2** : a surface that may be quickly positioned into the air for lowering the speed of an airplane

air·brush \\'a(ə)r-ˌbrəsh, 'e(ə)r-\\ *n* : a device that uses compressed air to apply a liquid (as paint or a protective coating) as a fine spray — **airbrush** *vb*

air–con·di·tion \\ˌa(ə)r-kən-'dish-ən, ˌe(ə)r-\\ *vb* : to equip with a device for cleaning air and controlling its humidity and temperature — **air con·di·tion·er** \\-'dish-(ə-)nər\\ *n* — **air–con·di·tion·ing** \\-'dish-(ə-)niŋ\\ *n*

air–cool \\'a(ə)r-'kül, 'e(ə)r-\\ *vb* : to cool (as an internal combustion engine) by air

air·craft \\'a(ə)r-ˌkraft, 'e(ə)r-\\ *n, pl* **aircraft** : a machine (as an airplane, glider, or helicopter) that can travel through the air and that is supported either by its own buoyancy or by the action of the air against its surfaces

aircraft carrier *n* : a warship with a deck from which aircraft can take off and on which they can land

air–cushion vehicle *n* : HOVERCRAFT

air·drome \\'a(ə)r-ˌdrōm, 'e(ə)r-\\ *n* : AIRPORT

air·drop \\-ˌdräp\\ *n* : delivery of cargo, supplies, or people by parachute from an airplane — **air–drop** \\-ˌdräp\\ *vb*

Aire·dale \\'a(ə)r-ˌdāl, 'e(ə)r-\\ *n* : any of a breed of large terriers with a black and tan coat

air·field \\'a(ə)r-ˌfēld, 'e(ə)r-\\ *n* **1** : the landing field of an airport **2** : AIRPORT

air·flow \\-ˌflō\\ *n* : a flow of air; *esp* : the motion of air (as around parts of an airplane in flight) compared to the surface of a body surrounded by the air

air·foil \\-ˌfȯil\\ *n* : an airplane surface (as a wing or

Airedale

rudder) designed to produce reaction from the air through which it moves

air force *n* : the military organization of a nation for air warfare

air·frame \\'a(ə)r-ˌfrām, 'e(ə)r-\\ *n* : the structure of an aircraft, rocket vehicle, or missile without the engine and related parts

air gun *n* **1** : a gun that fires with a compressed gas (as air or carbon dioxide) **2** : any of various hand tools that work by compressed air; *esp* : AIRBRUSH

air lane *n* : a route followed by airplanes

air letter *n* **1** : an airmail letter **2** : a sheet of airmail writing paper that can be folded and sealed with the message inside and the address outside

air·lift \\'a(ə)r-ˌlift, 'e(ə)r-\\ *n* : a system of transporting cargo or passengers by aircraft to or from an area otherwise impossible to reach — **airlift** *vb*

air·line \\-ˌlīn\\ *n* : a system of transportation by airplanes including its routes, equipment, and workers

air·lin·er \\-ˌlī-nər\\ *n* : a large passenger airplane operated by an airline

air lock *n* : an air space with two airtight doors that permits movement between two spaces with different pressures or different temperatures

air·mail \\'a(ə)r-ˌmāl, 'e(ə)r-, -ˌmȧl\\ *n* **1** : the system of transporting mail by aircraft **2** : mail transported by air — **airmail** *vb*

air·man \\-mən\\ *n* **1** : ¹PILOT 3, AVIATOR **2 a** : an enlisted person in the air force **b** : an enlisted person in the air force with a rank below that of sergeant; *esp* : one with the rank just below that of airman first class

airman basic *n* : an enlisted person of the lowest rank in the air force

airman first class *n* : an enlisted person in the air force with a rank just below that of sergeant

air mass *n* : a body of air extending hundreds or thousands of miles sideways and sometimes as high as the stratosphere and having nearly the same conditions of temperature and humidity at any single level

air·plane \\'a(ə)r-ˌplān, 'e(ə)r-\\ *n* : a fixed-wing heavier-than-air aircraft that is driven by a propeller or by a forceful stream of gases backward and is supported by the reaction of the air against its wings

airplane: *1* cockpit, *2* wing, *3* vertical stabilizer, *4* horizontal stabilizer, *5* flaps, *6* jet engine

air plant *n* **1** : EPIPHYTE **2** : any of several kalanchoes

air pocket *n* : a condition of the atmosphere that causes an airplane to drop suddenly

air·port \\'a(ə)r-ˌpōrt, 'e(ə)r-, -ˌpȯrt\\ *n* : an area of land or water where airplanes may land to take on and let off passengers or cargo and that usually has equipment for the shelter, supply, and repair of planes

air pump *n* : a pump for removing air from a closed space or for compressing air or forcing it through other equipment

air raid *n* : an attack by airplanes (as bombers) on a surface target

air sac *n* **1** : one of the air-filled spaces connected with the lungs of a bird **2** : one of the thin-walled microscopic pouches in which gases are exchanged in the lungs

air·ship \\'a(ə)r-ˌship, 'e(ə)r-\\ *n* : a lighter-than-air aircraft with its own power and steering

air·sick \-ˌsik\ *adj* : sick to one's stomach while riding in an airplane because of its motion — **air·sick·ness** *n*

air·speed \-ˌspēd\ *n* : the speed of an airplane according to measurements of the surrounding air rather than of the ground below

air·strip \-ˌstrip\ *n* : a runway without normal air base or airport equipment

air·tight \-ˈtīt\ *adj* **1** : so tightly sealed that no air can get in or out ⟨an *airtight* container⟩ **2** : too strong or effective to fail or be defeated ⟨an *airtight* argument⟩

air·wave \-ˌwāv\ *n* : ¹AIR 7a — usually used in plural

air·way \-ˌwā\ *n* **1** : a passage for a current of air; *esp* : one through which air passes to and from the lungs **2** : a regular route for aircraft; *esp* : one equipped with aids for guiding aircraft **3** : AIRLINE

air·wor·thy \-ˌwər-thē\ *adj* : fit or safe for operation in the air ⟨a very *airworthy* plane⟩ — **air·wor·thi·ness** *n*

airy \ˈa(ə)r-ē, ˈe(ə)r-\ *adj* **air·i·er; -est 1 a** : of or relating to air : ATMOSPHERIC **b** : high in the air : LOFTY ⟨*airy* perches⟩ **c** : performed in air ⟨*airy* leaps⟩ **2** : lacking a sound or solid basis ⟨*airy* romance⟩ **3 a** : light and graceful in movement and manner ⟨an *airy* dancer⟩ **b** : extremely light, delicate, or refined ⟨an *airy* perfume⟩ **4** : open to the air : BREEZY ⟨an *airy* room⟩ — **air·i·ly** \ˈar-ə-lē, ˈer-\ *adv* — **air·i·ness** \ˈar-ē-nəs, ˈer-\ *n*

aisle \ˈī(ə)l\ *n* **1** : a passage between sections of seats (as in a church or theater) **2** : a passage between shelves (as in a store)

ajar \ə-ˈjär\ *adv or adj* : slightly open ⟨left the door *ajar*⟩

akim·bo \ə-ˈkim-bō\ *adj or adv* **1** : having the hand on the hip and the elbow turned outward **2** : set in a bent position ⟨legs *akimbo*⟩ [Middle English *in kenebowe* "akimbo"]

akin \ə-ˈkin\ *adj* **1** : related by blood **2** : essentially similar or related

Ak·ka·di·an \ə-ˈkäd-ē-ən\ *n* **1** : an extinct Semitic language of ancient Mesopotamia **2** : a member of a Semitic people living in Mesopotamia before 2000 B.C. — **Akkadian** *adj*

al- — see AD-

¹-al \əl, ᵊl\ *adj suffix* : of, relating to, or characterized by ⟨direction*al*⟩ ⟨fiction*al*⟩ [Middle English *-al* "relating to," from early French *-al* (same meaning), from Latin *-alis* "relating to"]

²-al *n suffix* : action : process ⟨rehears*al*⟩ [Middle English *-aille* "action, process," from early French *-aille* (same meaning), derived from Latin *-alis* "relating to"]

al·a·bas·ter \ˈal-ə-ˌbas-tər\ *n* **1** : a smooth usually white and nearly transparent gypsum used for carving (as vases) **2** : a hard calcite that is nearly transparent and sometimes has stripes

à la carte *also* **a la carte** \ˌal-ə-ˈkärt, ˌäl-\ *adv or adj* : with a separate price for each item on the menu or list ⟨an *à la carte* dinner⟩ [from French *à la carte,* literally "by the bill of fare"]

alac·ri·ty \ə-ˈlak-rət-ē\ *n* : a cheerful readiness to do something ⟨accepted with *alacrity*⟩ — **alac·ri·tous** \-rət-əs\ *adj*

à la mode *also* **a la mode** \ˌal-ə-ˈmōd, ˌäl-\ *adj* **1** : STYLISH, FASHIONABLE **2** : topped with ice cream ⟨pie *à la mode*⟩ [from French *à la mode,* literally "according to the fashion"]

al·a·nine \ˈal-ə-ˌnēn\ *n* : an amino acid formed especially by the breakdown of proteins

¹alarm \ə-ˈlärm\ *n* **1** : a warning of danger **2** : a device that warns or signals (as by a bell, buzzer, or whistle) ⟨sound the *alarm*⟩ ⟨set the *alarm* for six o'clock⟩ **3** : the fear caused by a sudden sense of danger **synonyms** see FEAR

Word History Today we usually think of an alarm as a loud noise that awakens us or warns us of fire or some other danger. Its first use, however, was as a call to arms to soldiers in Italy. The Italian phrase *all'arme!* means literally "to arms" or "to your weapons." It was still used

this way when borrowed into other languages, but gradually this call came to be shortened to *alarme* in early French and Middle English. The final *-e* was later dropped in English. The word also came to be used as the name for the cry, as for example to "give the alarm." Then it came to be used for any warning. A bell or gun used to sound a warning was called an *alarm bell* or an *alarm gun.* It wasn't long before people started thinking of *alarm* as the signal device itself. Then they dropped the second part of the phrase. Since an alarm can cause fright or worry, such feelings also came to be known as *alarm.* By the 17th century, the word was used as a verb, meaning "to warn of danger" and then "to frighten." [Middle English *alarme* "a call to arms," from early French *alarme* (same meaning), derived from early Italian *all'arme,* literally "to arms," from *all'* "to the" and *arme* "weapon," from Latin *arma* "weapon" — related to ³ARM]

²alarm *vb* **1** : to warn of danger **2** : to cause to feel a sense of danger : FRIGHTEN ⟨*alarmed* by the noise⟩ — **alarm·ing·ly** \ə-ˈlär-miŋ-lē\ *adv*

alarm clock *n* : a clock that can be set to sound an alarm at any desired time

alarm·ist \ə-ˈlär-məst\ *n* : a person who alarms others especially needlessly — **alarm·ism** \-ˌmiz-əm\ *n*

alas \ə-ˈlas\ *interj* — used to express unhappiness, pity, or concern

Alas·kan malamute \ə-ˌlas-kən-\ *n* : any of a breed of strong heavy-coated working dogs developed in Alaska for pulling sleds

Alas·ka time \ə-ˈlas-kə-\ *n* : the time of the ninth time zone west of Greenwich that includes most of Alaska

alb \ˈalb\ *n* : a full-length white linen vestment worn by priests at the Eucharist

al·ba·core \ˈal-bə-ˌkō(ə)r, -ˌkò(ə)r\ *n, pl* **-core** *or* **-cores** : a large tuna with long pectoral fins that is the source of most canned tuna

Al·ba·nian \al-ˈbā-nē-ən, -nyən\ *n* **1** : a person born or living in Albania **2** : the Indo-European language of the Albanian people — **Albanian** *adj*

al·ba·tross \ˈal-bə-ˌtrós, -ˌträs\ *n, pl* **-tross** *or* **-tross·es** : any of various large web-footed seabirds that are related to the petrels and include the largest birds of the sea

albatross

al·be·it \ȯl-ˈbē-ət, al-\ *conj* : even though : ALTHOUGH

al·bi·no \al-ˈbī-nō\ *n, pl* **-nos** : an organism deficient in coloring matter; *esp* : a human being or animal that is born with a lack of pigment and usually a milky skin, white or colorless hair, and eyes with pink or blue iris and deep red pupil — **al·bi·nism** \ˈal-bə-ˌniz-əm, al-ˈbī-\ *n* — **albino** *adj*

al·bite \ˈal-ˌbīt\ *n* : a usually white feldspar containing sodium

al·bum \ˈal-bəm\ *n* **1 a** : a book with blank pages in which to put a collection (as of autographs, stamps, or photographs) **b** : a container for a phonograph record **c** : one or more recordings (as on tape or disc) produced as a single collection **2** : a collection usually in book form of literary selections, musical compositions, or pictures : ANTHOLOGY

\ə\ **abut**	\au̇\ **out**	\i\ **tip**	\ȯ\ **saw**	\u̇\ **foot**
\ər\ **further**	\ch\ **chin**	\ī\ **life**	\ȯi\ **coin**	\y\ **yet**
\a\ **mat**	\e\ **pet**	\j\ **job**	\th\ **thin**	\yü\ **few**
\ā\ **take**	\ē\ **easy**	\ŋ\ **sing**	\th\ **this**	\yu̇\ **cure**
\ä\ **cot, cart**	\g\ **go**	\ō\ **bone**	\ü\ **food**	\zh\ **vision**

al·bu·men \al-ˈbyü-mən\ *n* **1** : the white of an egg **2** : AL-
BUMIN

al·bu·min \al-ˈbyü-mən\ *n* : any of numerous proteins that
dissolve in water and are found especially in blood, the
whites of eggs, and various animal and plant tissues

al·che·my \ˈal-kə-mē\ *n* : a medieval chemical science
with the goals of changing less valuable metals into gold,
discovering a single cure for all diseases, and discovering
how to live forever [Middle English *alkamie, alquemie,*
from early French *alquemie* or Latin *alchymia* (both
same meaning), from Arabic *al-kīmiyā'* (same meaning),
from *al* "the" and *kīmiyā'* "alchemy," from Greek *chēmeia* "alchemy" — related to CHEMO-, CHEMISTRY]

al·co·hol \ˈal-kə-ˌhȯl\ *n* **1 a** : ethanol especially when used
as the substance in fermented or distilled liquors (as beer
or whiskey) that can make one drunk **b** : drink (as beer,
wine, or whiskey) containing ethanol **2** : any of various
carbon compounds that are similar to ethanol in having
one or more hydroxyl groups

¹al·co·hol·ic \ˌal-kə-ˈhȯl-ik, -ˈhäl-\ *adj* **1** : of, relating to, or
containing alcohol **2** : affected with alcoholism — **al·co-
hol·i·cal·ly** \-i-k(ə-)lē\ *adv*

²alcoholic *n* : a person affected with alcoholism

al·co·hol·ism \ˈal-kə-ˌhȯ-ˌliz-əm\ *n* : continued, uncontrolled, and greater than normal use of alcoholic drinks;
also : an abnormal bodily state associated with such use

al·cove \ˈal-ˌkōv\ *n* **1** : a small section of a room set back
from the rest of it **2** : an arched opening (as in a wall)
: NICHE

Al·deb·a·ran \al-ˈdeb-ə-rən\ *n* : a very bright red star in
Taurus

al·der \ˈȯl-dər\ *n* : any of a genus of toothed-leaved trees
or shrubs related to the birches

al·der·man \ˈȯl-dər-mən\ *n* : a member of a city legislative
body — **al·der·man·ic** \ˌȯl-dər-ˈman-ik\ *adj*

al·der·wom·an \-ˌwu̇m-ən\ *n* : a female member of a city
legislative body

al·drin \ˈȯl-drən, al-\ *n* : a very poisonous long-acting insecticide that is no longer used

ale \ˈā(ə)l\ *n* : an alcoholic drink made from malt and flavored with hops that is usually more bitter than beer

alee \ə-ˈlē\ *adv or adj* : on or toward the lee

¹alert \ə-ˈlərt\ *adj* **1 a** : being watchful and ready to meet
danger **b** : quick to understand and act **2** : ACTIVE 3,
BRISK **synonyms** see INTELLIGENT — **alert·ly** *adv* —
alert·ness *n*

²alert *n* **1** : a signal of danger **2** : the period during which
an alert is in effect — **on the alert** : on the lookout especially for danger or opportunity

³alert *vb* : to call to a state of readiness : WARN

A level *n* : the later of two British examinations in a secondary school subject

ale·wife \ˈā(ə)l-ˌwīf\ *n*
: a food fish that is re-
lated to the herrings
and is common along
the Atlantic coast of
the U.S.

al·fal·fa \al-ˈfal-fə\ *n* : a
deep-rooted southwest
Asian plant of the le-
gume family with pur-

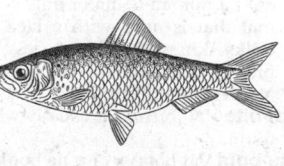

alewife

ple flowers and leaves like clover that is widely grown for
hay and forage

al·ga \ˈal-gə\ *n, pl* **al·gae** \ˈal-(ˌ)jē\ : any plant or plantlike
organism (as a seaweed) that includes forms mostly grow-
ing in water, lacking a system of vessels for carrying fluids, and often having chlorophyll masked by brown or red
coloring matter — **al·gal** \ˈal-gəl\ *adj*

al·ge·bra \ˈal-jə-brə\ *n* : a branch of mathematics that uses
letters to represent numbers and that studies numbers
and the operations (as multiplication and addition) that

are used on them — **al·ge·bra·ic** \ˌal-jə-ˈbrā-ik\ *adj* — **al-
ge·bra·i·cal·ly** \-ˈbrā-ə-k(ə-)lē\ *adv*

al·gin \ˈal-jən\ *n* : a substance obtained from marine
brown algae that is used especially in food and paints to
give thickness or firmness or to make a stable liquid mixture in which drops of one liquid are scattered evenly
throughout the other

AL·GOL *or* **Al·gol** \ˈal-ˌgäl, -ˌgȯl\ *n* : a computer programming language that is used especially in mathematics and
science [from *algorithm* and *language*]

Al·gon·qui·an \al-ˈgän-kwē-ən, -ˈgän-\ *n* **1** : a family of
American Indian languages spoken from Labrador to the
Carolinas and westward to the Great Plains **2** : a member
of any of the peoples speaking Algonquian languages

al·go·rithm \ˈal-gə-ˌrith-əm\ *n* : a step-by-step method for
solving a problem (as finding the greatest common divisor) or accomplishing a goal

¹alias \ˈā-lē-əs, ˈāl-yəs\ *adv* : otherwise called : otherwise
known as ⟨John Doe *alias* Richard Roe⟩

²alias *n* : an assumed or additional name

¹al·i·bi \ˈal-ə-ˌbī\ *n, pl* **-bis** \-ˌbīz\ **1** : the plea made by a
person accused of a crime of having been at another place
when the crime occurred **2** : an excuse intended to avoid
blame [from Latin *alibi* "elsewhere"]

²alibi *vb* **-bied; -bi·ing** **1** : to make an excuse for **2** : to
offer an excuse ⟨tried to *alibi* for showing up late⟩

¹alien \ˈā-lē-ən, ˈāl-yən\ *adj* **1** : relating or belonging to
another country : FOREIGN ⟨*alien* residents⟩ **2** : EXOTIC
1 **3** : wholly different in nature or character ⟨opinions
alien to his outlook⟩

²alien *n* **1** : a resident who was born elsewhere and is not a
citizen of the country in which he or she now lives **2** : a
being that comes from or lives in another world : EXTRA-
TERRESTRIAL **3** : EXOTIC

alien·ate \ˈā-lē-ə-ˌnāt, ˈāl-yə-ˌnāt\ *vb* **-at·ed; -at·ing** **1** : to
transfer (as a title, property, or right) to another **2** : to
cause (one who used to be friendly or loyal) to become
unfriendly or disloyal

alien·ation \ˌā-lē-ə-ˈnā-shən, ˌāl-yə-ˈnā-\ *n* **1** : a withdrawing or separation of a person or a person's affection from
an object of past attachment **2** : a transfer of property to
another

¹alight \ə-ˈlīt\ *vb* **alight·ed** \-ˈlīt-əd\ *also* **alit** \ə-ˈlit\; **alight·
ing** **1** : to get down : DISMOUNT **2** : to descend from the
air and settle : LAND ⟨the bird *alighted* on a twig⟩

²alight *adj* : full of light : lighted up ⟨the sky was *alight* with
stars⟩

align *also* **aline** \ə-ˈlīn\ *vb* **1** : to bring into or be in line or
alignment **2** : to cause to be for or against something (as
a belief or political party) ⟨*aligned* himself with the op-
position⟩ — **align·er** *n*

align·ment *also* **aline·ment** \ə-ˈlīn-mənt\ *n* **1 a** : the act
of aligning : the state of being aligned **b** : the proper adjustment of parts in relation to each other **2** : an arrangement of groups or forces ⟨a new political *alignment*⟩

¹alike \ə-ˈlīk\ *adj* : SIMILAR 1 — **alike·ness** *n*

²alike *adv* : in the same manner, form, or degree ⟨we think
alike⟩

al·i·ment \ˈal-ə-mənt\ *n* : FOOD 1, NUTRIMENT; *also* : food
for the mind or spirit

al·i·men·ta·ry \ˌal-ə-ˈment-ə-rē, -ˈmen-trē\ *adj* : of or relating to nourishment or nutrition [from Latin *alimentarius*
"relating to or involving the nourishing process," derived
from *alere* "to nourish" — related to ALUMNUS, ALMA
MATER]

alimentary canal *n* : a long tube made up of the esophagus, stomach, small intestine, and large intestine into
which food is taken and digested and from which wastes
are passed out

al·i·mo·ny \ˈal-ə-ˌmō-nē\ *n* : money paid to one spouse by
the other for support during or after divorce or separation

A–line \'ā-ˌlīn\ *adj* : having a flared bottom and a close= fitting top ⟨an *A-line* skirt⟩

alive \ə-'līv\ *adj* **1** : having life : not dead **2** : still in existence, force, or operation : ACTIVE ⟨kept hope *alive*⟩ **3** : extremely aware or conscious : SENSITIVE ⟨*alive* to the beauty of life⟩ **4** : marked by much life or activity ⟨blossoms *alive* with bees⟩ — **alive·ness** *n*

aliz·a·rin \ə-'liz-ə-rən\ *n* : a compound of orange or red crystals that is used as a red dye and in making red pigments

al·ka·li \'al-kə-ˌlī\ *n, pl* **-lies** *or* **-lis** **1** : a substance (as a hydroxide) that has a bitter taste and neutralizes acids **2** : ALKALI METAL **3** : a salt or mixture of salts easily dissolved in water and present in some soils of very dry regions [Middle English *alkali* "alkali," from Latin *alkali* (same meaning), from Arabic *al-qili* "ashes of a particular plant"]

alkali metal *n* : any of the metals in the group that consists of lithium, sodium, potassium, rubidium, cesium, and francium

al·ka·line \'al-kə-lən, -ˌlīn\ *adj* : of, relating to, or having the characteristics of an alkali : BASIC — **al·ka·lin·i·ty** \ˌal-kə-'lin-ət-ē\ *n*

alkaline battery *n* : a long-lasting battery containing alkaline chemicals

alkaline–earth metal *n* : any of the strongly basic metals consisting of beryllium, magnesium, calcium, strontium, barium, and radium — called also *alkaline earth*

al·kane \'al-ˌkān\ *n* : any of a series of compounds of carbon and hydrogen atoms in which each carbon atom is attached to four other atoms

al·kyd \'al-kəd\ *n* : any of numerous synthetic resins used especially for protective coatings ⟨as paint⟩

¹**all** \'ȯl\ *adj* **1 a** : the whole of ⟨sat up *all* night⟩ **b** : as much as possible ⟨in *all* seriousness⟩ **2** : every one of ⟨*all* students can go⟩ **3** : any whatever ⟨beyond *all* doubt⟩

²**all** *adv* **1** : WHOLLY, ALTOGETHER ⟨sat *all* alone⟩ ⟨*all* across the country⟩ **2** : so much ⟨*all* the better for it⟩ **3** : for each side : APIECE ⟨the score is two *all*⟩

³**all** *pron* **1 a** : the whole number, quantity, or amount ⟨*all* that I have⟩ ⟨*all* of us⟩ **b** — used in such phrases as *for all I know*, *for all I care*, and *for all the good it does* to show a lack of knowledge, interest, or effectiveness **2** : EVERYONE, EVERYTHING ⟨known to *all*⟩ ⟨sacrificed *all* for love⟩ — **all in all** : on the whole ⟨*all in all*, it could be worse⟩ — **and all** : and everything else especially of a kind mentioned before

Al·lah \'al-ə, 'äl-ə, 'äl-ˌä, ä-'lä\ *n* : GOD 1 — used in Islam [Arabic *allāh*]

all along *adv* : all the time ⟨knew the truth *all along*⟩

all–Amer·i·can \ˌȯ-lə-'mer-ə-kən\ *adj* **1** : representing or typical of the U.S. or its ideals ⟨an *all-American* boy⟩ **2** : selected as the best in the U.S. ⟨the *all-American* football team⟩ — **all–American** *n*

al·lar·gan·do \ˌäl-ˌär-'gän-dō\ *adv or adj* : gradually slower with crescendo — used as a direction in music

all–around \ˌȯ-lə-'raůnd\ *also* **all–round** *adj* **1** : considered as a whole or including all parts ⟨the best *all-around* performance so far⟩ **2** : good in many fields ⟨an *all= around* athlete⟩ **3** : having general usefulness ⟨*all-around* tools⟩ — **all around** *adv*

al·lay \ə-'lā, ə-'\ *vb* **-layed; -lay·ing** **1** : to make less severe : RELIEVE ⟨*allay* pain⟩ **2** : to make quiet : CALM ⟨*allay* fears⟩

all but *adv* : very nearly : ALMOST ⟨would be *all but* impossible⟩

al·le·ga·tion \ˌal-i-'gā-shən\ *n* **1** : the act of alleging **2** : something alleged; *esp* : a statement not supported by proof or evidence ⟨*allegations* of criminal involvement⟩

al·lege \ə-'lej\ *vb* **al·leged; al·leg·ing** **1** : to state as a fact but without proof ⟨*allege* a person's guilt⟩ **2** : to offer as a reason or excuse ⟨*allege* illness to avoid work⟩ — **al-**

leged \ə-'lejd, -'lej-əd\ *adj* — **al·leg·ed·ly** \ə-'lej-əd-lē\ *adv*

al·le·giance \ə-'lē-jən(t)s\ *n* **1** : loyalty and obedience owed to one's country or government **2** : devotion or loyalty to a person, group, or cause

al·le·go·ry \'al-ə-ˌgōr-ē, -ˌgȯr-\ *n, pl* **-ries** : a story in which the characters and events are symbols that stand for truths about human life — **al·le·gor·i·cal** \ˌal-ə-'gȯr-i-kəl, -'gär-\ *adj* — **al·le·gor·i·cal·ly** \-i-k(ə-)lē\ *adv*

al·le·gret·to \ˌal-ə-'gret-ō, ˌäl-\ *adv or adj* : faster than andante but not so fast as allegro — used as a direction in music

¹**al·le·gro** \ə-'leg-rō, -'lā-grō\ *n, pl* **-gros** : a piece or movement in allegro tempo

²**allegro** *adv or adj* : in a brisk lively manner — used as a direction in music

al·lele \ə-'lē(ə)l\ *n* : one of several forms of a gene that determine alternate forms of one or more genetic traits and occupy identical places on two chromosomes having the same genes arranged in the same order — **al·le·lic** \-'lē-lik, -'lel-ik\ *adj*

al·le·lu·ia \ˌal-ə-'lü-yə\ *interj* : ¹HALLELUJAH

Al·len wrench \'al-ən-\ *n* : an L-shaped hexagonal metal bar used to turn a screw or bolt

al·ler·gen \'al-ər-jən\ *n* : a substance (as pollen) that causes allergy — **al·ler·gen·ic** \ˌal-ər-'jen-ik\ *adj*

al·ler·gic \ə-'lər-jik\ *adj* **1** : of, relating to, affected with, or caused by allergy ⟨an *allergic* reaction⟩ **2** : having a dislike for something ⟨*allergic* to hard work⟩

al·ler·gist \'al-ər-jəst\ *n* : a specialist in treating allergies

al·ler·gy \'al-ər-jē\ *n, pl* **-gies** **1** : exaggerated or abnormal reaction (as by sneezing, itching, or rashes) to substances, situations, or physical states that do not have such a strong effect on most people **2** : a feeling of dislike

allergy shot *n* : an injection containing very small amounts of an allergen (as mold or grass pollen) to which a person is sensitive that is given at regular intervals usually over a period of several years to desensitize the immune system and reduce allergic symptoms

al·le·vi·ate \ə-'lē-vē-ˌāt\ *vb* **-at·ed; -at·ing** : to make easier to put up with : RELIEVE — **al·le·vi·a·tion** \ə-ˌlē-vē-'ā-shən\ *n*

al·ley \'al-ē\ *n, pl* **alleys** **1** : a garden or park walk bordered by trees or bushes **2** : a narrow wooden floor on which balls are rolled in bowling; *also* : a room or building housing a number of such alleys **3** : a narrow street or passageway between buildings

alley cat *n* : a stray cat

al·ley·way \'al-ē-ˌwā\ *n* : ALLEY 3

All Fools' Day *n* : APRIL FOOLS' DAY

all fours *n pl* : all four legs of a four-legged animal or the two legs and two arms of a person ⟨got down on *all fours*⟩

All·hal·lows \ȯl-'hal-ōz, -əz\ *n* : ALL SAINTS' DAY

all hours *n pl* : a very late time ⟨stayed up until *all hours*⟩

al·li·ance \ə-'lī-ən(t)s\ *n* **1** : the state of being allied **2 a** : a union between persons, families, or parties **b** : a union between nations for assistance and protection **3** : a treaty of alliance

al·lied \ə-'līd, 'al-ˌīd\ *adj* **1** : being related or connected in some way ⟨*chemistry* and *allied* subjects⟩ **2 a** : joined in alliance ⟨*allied* nations⟩ **b** *cap* : of or relating to the nations united against Germany and its allies in World War I or World War II

allies *plural of* ALLY

\ə\ **abut**	\aů\ **out**	\i\ **tip**	\ȯ\ **saw**	\ů\ **foot**
\ər\ **further**	\ch\ **chin**	\ī\ **life**	\ȯi\ **coin**	\y\ **yet**
\a\ **mat**	\e\ **pet**	\j\ **job**	\th\ **thin**	\yü\ **few**
\ā\ **take**	\ē\ **easy**	\ŋ\ **sing**	\th\ **this**	\yů\ **cure**
\ä\ **cot, cart**	\g\ **go**	\ō\ **bone**	\ü\ **food**	\zh\ **vision**

al·li·ga·tor \'al-ə-ˌgāt-ər\ *n* **1** : either of two large short-legged reptiles resembling crocodiles but having a shorter and broader snout **2** : leather made from alligator's hide [from Spanish *el lagarto* "the lizard"]

alligator 1

alligator clip *n* : a clip that has jaws resembling an alligator's and is used to make temporary electrical connections

alligator gar *n* : a large freshwater gar of the central U.S.

alligator pear *n* : AVOCADO

all–im·por·tant \ˌȯ-lim-ˈpȯrt-ᵊnt, -ənt\ *adj* : of very great importance ⟨an *all-important* question⟩

al·lit·er·a·tion \ə-ˌlit-ə-ˈrā-shən\ *n* : the repetition of a sound at the beginning of two or more neighboring words (as in *wild and woolly* or *a babbling brook*) — **al·lit·er·a·tive** \ə-ˈlit-ə-ˌrāt-iv, -rət-\ *adj* — **al·lit·er·a·tive·ly** *adv*

al·lo·cate \'al-ə-ˌkāt\ *vb* **-cat·ed; -cat·ing** **1** : to divide and distribute for a special reason or to particular persons or things ⟨*allocate* funds among charities⟩ **2** : to set apart for a particular purpose ⟨*allocate* materials for a project⟩ — **al·lo·ca·tion** \ˌal-ə-ˈkā-shən\ *n*

al·lo·sau·rus \ˌal-ə-ˈsȯr-əs\ *n* : any of several very large meat-eating dinosaurs of the Jurassic period that were related to the tyrannosaur

al·lot \ə-ˈlät\ *vb* **al·lot·ted; al·lot·ting** : to assign as a share or portion ⟨*allot* 10 minutes for the speech⟩

al·lot·ment \ə-ˈlät-mənt\ *n* **1** : the act of allotting **2** : something allotted

al·lot·ro·py \ə-ˈlä-trə-pē\ *n* : the existence of a substance and especially a chemical element in two or more different forms ⟨diamond and graphite show the *allotropy* of carbon⟩ — **al·lo·trope** \'al-ə-ˌtrōp\ *n* — **al·lo·trop·ic** \ˌal-ə-ˈträp-ik\ *adj*

all–out \'ȯ-ˈlaut\ *adj* : made with maximum effort : EXTREME ⟨an *all-out* attempt to finish on time⟩

all out *adv* : with maximum effort ⟨went *all out* to win⟩

all–over \'ȯ-ˌlō-vər\ *adj* : covering the whole surface of something ⟨a sweater with an *allover* pattern⟩

¹all over *adv* : EVERYWHERE

²all over *prep* **1** : in very affectionate, attentive, or aggressive pursuit of ⟨the band's fans were *all over* them⟩ **2** : in or into a state marked by all-out criticism of ⟨reporters were *all over* the coach after the loss⟩

al·low \ə-ˈlau\ *vb* **1 a** : to assign as a share or suitable amount (as of time or money) **b** : to take into consideration as a deduction or an addition ⟨*allow* a gallon for leakage⟩ **2** : ADMIT 1b, CONCEDE ⟨*allowed* that the situation was serious⟩ **3** : ¹PERMIT ⟨gaps *allow* passage⟩ ⟨will not *allow* smoking⟩ **4** : to give thought to what will probably happen later ⟨*allow* for growth⟩ — **al·low·able** \-ə-bəl\ *adj* — **al·low·ably** \-blē\ *adv*

al·low·ance \ə-ˈlau-ən(t)s\ *n* **1 a** : a share or portion given out **b** : a sum given ⟨gets a weekly *allowance*⟩ ⟨an *allowance* for expenses⟩ **c** : a reduction from a stated price ⟨a trade-in *allowance* on a car⟩ **2** : an allowed difference between parts that fit together in a machine **3** : the act of allowing : PERMISSION **4** : an allowing for things that may partly excuse an offense or mistake or for things that may happen ⟨make *allowance* for age⟩

¹al·loy \'al-ˌȯi, ə-ˈlȯi\ *n* : a substance consisting of two or more metals or of a metal and a nonmetal united usually by being melted together

²al·loy \ə-ˈlȯi, 'al-ˌȯi\ *vb* **1** : to reduce the purity of by mixing with a less valuable metal **2** : to mix so as to form an alloy **3** : to make worse by mixing with something else

all–pow·er·ful \'ȯl-ˈpau(-ə)r-fəl\ *adj* : having complete power ⟨an *all-powerful* leader⟩

all–pur·pose \-ˈpər-pəs\ *adj* : suitable for many uses ⟨an *all-purpose* tool⟩

¹all right *adj* **1** : SATISFACTORY, CORRECT ⟨it is *all right* with me⟩ **2** : ¹SAFE 1, WELL ⟨he was sick but he's *all right* now⟩

²all right *adv* **1** : very well : YES ⟨*all right*, I'll come⟩ — used as an interjection especially to show agreement or acceptance or to show the continuation of a discussion **2** : beyond doubt : CERTAINLY ⟨that's the one *all right*⟩ **3** : reasonably well ⟨does *all right* in school⟩

all–round *variant of* ALL-AROUND

All Saints' Day *n* : November 1 observed as a church festival in honor of the Christian saints

All Souls' Day *n* : November 2 observed in some Christian churches as a day of prayer for the dead

all·spice \'ȯl-ˌspīs\ *n* **1** : the berry of a West Indian tree related to the myrtle **2** : a spice made from dried allspice berries

all–star \ˌȯl-ˌstär\ *adj* : made up chiefly or entirely of stars ⟨an *all-star* team⟩ — **all–star** \'ȯl-ˌstär\ *n*

all–terrain vehicle *n* : a small motor vehicle with three or four wheels for use on various types of ground

al·lude \ə-ˈlüd\ *vb* **allud·ed; allud·ing** : to speak of or hint at without mentioning directly

¹al·lure \ə-ˈlu̇(ə)r\ *vb* **al·lured; al·lur·ing** : to try to attract or influence by offering what seems to be a benefit or pleasure — **al·lure·ment** \-mənt\ *n*

²allure *n* : power of attraction : CHARM

al·lu·sion \ə-ˈlü-zhən\ *n* : a reference made to something that is not directly mentioned ⟨the book contains many *allusions* to earlier books⟩ — **al·lu·sive** \-ˈlü-siv, -ziv\ *adj* — **al·lu·sive·ly** *adv* — **al·lu·sive·ness** *n*

al·lu·vi·al \ə-ˈlü-vē-əl\ *adj* : relating to, composed of, or found in alluvium

al·lu·vi·um \ə-ˈlü-vē-əm\ *n, pl* **-vi·ums** *or* **-via** \-vē-ə\ : soil material (as clay, silt, sand, or gravel) deposited by running water

all–wheel drive *n* : a system that applies engine power directly to all four wheels of a vehicle together or separately

¹al·ly \ə-ˈlī, 'al-ˌī\ *vb* **al·lied; al·ly·ing** : to form a connection or relation between : UNITE; *esp* : to join in an alliance [Middle English *allien* "unite," from early French *alier* (same meaning), derived from Latin *al-, ad-* "to" and *ligare* "to bind" — related to LIGAMENT]

²al·ly \'al-ˌī, ə-ˈlī\ *n, pl* **al·lies** **1** : a plant or animal linked to another by genetic or evolutionary relationship ⟨ferns and their *allies*⟩ **2 a** : one associated or united with another for some common purpose **b** *pl, cap* : the Allied nations in World War I or World War II

-al·ly \(ə-)lē\ *adv suffix* : ²-ly [from ¹-*al* + -*ly*]

al·ma ma·ter \ˌal-mə-ˈmät-ər\ *n* : a school, college, or university that one has attended [Latin, literally "fostering mother," from *almus* "nourishing" (from *alire* "to nourish") and *mater* "mother" — related to ALIMENTARY, MATERNAL]

al·ma·nac \'ȯl-mə-ˌnak, 'al-\ *n* : a book containing a calendar of days, weeks, and months and usually facts about the rising and setting of the sun and moon, changes in the tides, and information of general interest

al·man·dine \'al-mən-ˌdēn, -ˌdīn\ *n* : ALMANDITE

al·man·dite \'al-mən-ˌdīt\ *n* : a deep red garnet containing iron and aluminum

al·mighty \ȯl-ˈmīt-ē\ *adj, often cap* : having unlimited power ⟨*Almighty* God⟩

Almighty *n* : GOD 1 — used with *the*

al·mond \'äm-ənd, 'am-; 'äl-mənd, 'al-\ *n* : a small tree related to the roses and having flowers like those of a peach tree; *also* : the edible kernel of its fruit used as a nut

al·mo·ner \'al-mə-nər, 'äm-ə-\ *n* : a person who gives out alms

al·most \'ȯl-ˌmōst, ȯl-'mōst\ *adv* : only a little less than : NEARLY ⟨we're *almost* finished⟩

alms \'ämz, 'älmz\ *n, pl* **alms** : something and especially money given to help the poor : CHARITY — **alms·giv·er** \-ˌgiv-ər\ *n* — **alms·giv·ing** \-ˌgiv-iŋ\ *n*

alms·house \-ˌhaus\ *n* : POORHOUSE

al·ni·co \'al-ni-ˌkō\ *n* : a powerful permanent-magnet alloy containing iron, nickel, aluminum, and one or more of the elements cobalt, copper, and titanium

al·oe \'al-ō\ *n* 1 : any of a large genus of chiefly southern African plants related to lilies and having spikes of often showy flowers 2 : the dried bitter juice of the leaves of an aloe used especially formerly as a strong laxative and tonic — usually used in plural 3 : ALOE VERA

aloe vera \-'ver-ə, -'vir-\ *n* : an aloe plant whose leaves contain a jelly-like substance that is soothing to the skin; *also* : such a substance or a preparation consisting mostly of such a substance

aloft \ə-'lȯft\ *adv or adj* 1 : in the air; *esp* : in flight 2 : at, on, or to the higher rigging of a sailing ship

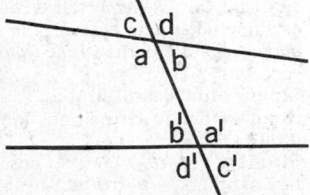

aloe 1

alo·ha \ə-'lō-ə, -ˌhä; ä-'lō-ˌhä\ *interj* — used to express greeting or farewell [from Hawaiian *aloha* "love"]

¹**alone** \ə-'lōn\ *adj* 1 : separated from others ⟨*alone* in her room⟩ 2 : not including anyone or anything else ⟨money *alone* is not enough⟩

²**alone** *adv* 1 : SOLELY 1 ⟨the proof rests on that statement *alone*⟩ 2 : without company, aid, or support ⟨did it *alone*⟩

¹**along** \ə-'lȯŋ\ *prep* 1 : in a line matching the length or direction of ⟨walk *along* the beach⟩ ⟨lined up *along* the wall⟩ 2 : at a point or points on ⟨stopped *along* the way⟩ 3 : in accordance with ⟨a new agreement *along* the lines of the first⟩

²**along** *adv* 1 : ¹ONWARD, FORWARD ⟨move *along*⟩ 2 : as a companion or associate ⟨brought my best friend *along*⟩ 3 : in addition : ALSO ⟨the bill came *along* with the package⟩ 4 : at or on hand ⟨had a camera *along*⟩

along·shore \-ˌshō(ə)r, -ˌshȯ(ə)r\ *adv or adj* : along the shore or coast

¹**along·side** \-ˌsīd\ *adv* : along or close at the side : in parallel position ⟨a guard with a prisoner *alongside*⟩

²**alongside** *prep* : side by side with; *esp* : parallel to ⟨boats *alongside* the dock⟩

¹**aloof** \ə-'lüf\ *adv* : at a distance : out of involvement

²**aloof** *adj* : removed or distant in interest or feeling : RESERVED — **aloof·ly** *adv* — **aloof·ness** *n*

aloud \ə-'laud\ *adv* : so as to be clearly heard ⟨read *aloud*⟩

alp \'alp\ *n* : a high rugged mountain

al·paca \al-'pak-ə\ *n* 1 : a mammal with fine long woolly hair domesticated in Peru and related to the llama 2 : wool of the alpaca or a cloth made of it; *also* : a rayon or cotton imitation of this cloth [Spanish]

al·pha \'al-fə\ *n* 1 : the first letter of the Greek alphabet — A or α 2 : something that is first : BEGINNING

al·pha·bet \'al-fə-ˌbet, -bət\ *n* 1 : the letters of a language arranged in their usual order 2 : a system of signs or signals that serve as equivalents for letters [Middle English *alphabete* "alphabet," derived from Greek *alphabētos* "alphabet," from *alpha* and *bēta*, the first and second letters of the Greek alphabet]

al·pha·bet·i·cal \ˌal-fə-'bet-i-kəl\ *also* **al·pha·bet·ic** \ˌal-fə-'bet-ik\ *adj* : arranged in the order of the letters of the alphabet — **al·pha·bet·i·cal·ly** \-i-k(ə-)lē\ *adv*

al·pha·bet·ize \'al-fə-bə-ˌtīz\ *vb* **-ized; -iz·ing** : to arrange in alphabetical order — **al·pha·bet·i·za·tion** \ˌal-fə-bet-ə-'zā-shən\ *n* — **al·pha·bet·iz·er** *n*

alpha particle *n* : a positively charged particle that is identical with the nucleus of a helium atom, consists of 2 protons and 2 neutrons, and is thrown at high speed from a radioactive atomic nucleus

alpha ray *n* 1 : an alpha particle moving at high speed 2 : a stream of alpha particles — called also *alpha radiation*

al·pine \'al-ˌpīn\ *adj, often cap* 1 a : of, relating to, or resembling mountains and especially the Alps b : of, relating to, or growing on upland slopes above the highest elevation where trees grow 2 *cap* : of or relating to competitive ski events consisting of slalom and downhill racing

al·ready \ȯl-'red-ē, 'ȯl-ˌred-ē\ *adv* : before a certain time : by the time ⟨I had *already* left when you called⟩

al·right \ȯl-'rīt, 'ȯl-ˌrīt\ *adv or adj* : ALL RIGHT

Al·sa·tian \al-'sā-shən\ *n* : GERMAN SHEPHERD

al·sike clover \ˌal-ˌsak-, -ˌsīk-\ *n* : a European perennial clover widely grown as food for browsing or grazing animals

al·so \'ȯl-sō\ *adv* 1 : LIKEWISE 1 2 : in addition : TOO

al·so-ran \-ˌran\ *n* 1 : a horse or dog that does not finish in the first three places in a race 2 : a contestant that does not win

al·tar \'ȯl-tər\ *n* 1 : a raised place on which sacrifices are offered 2 : a platform or table used as a center of worship

altar boy *n* : a boy who assists the priest in a church service

altar server *n* : a boy or girl who assists the priest in a church service

al·ter \'ȯl-tər\ *vb* 1 : to change partly but usually not completely ⟨*alter* a dress⟩ 2 : CASTRATE, SPAY [Middle English *alteren* "to make different," from Latin *alterare* (same meaning), from Latin *alter* "other (of two)" — related to ADULTERATE] — **al·ter·abil·i·ty** \ˌȯl-t(ə-)rə-'bil-ə-tē\ *n* — **al·ter·able** \'ȯl-t(ə-)rə-bəl\ *adj* — **al·ter·er** *n*

al·ter·ation \ˌȯl-tə-'rā-shən\ *n* 1 a : the act or process of altering b : the state of being altered 2 : the result of altering : MODIFICATION

al·ter·ca·tion \ˌȯl-tər-'kā-shən\ *n* : a noisy or angry dispute

al·ter ego \ˌȯl-tər-'ē-gō\ *n* 1 : a trusted friend or personal representative 2 : the opposite side of a personality

¹**al·ter·nate** \'ȯl-tər-nət *also* 'al-\ *adj* 1 : occurring or following by turns ⟨a day of *alternate* sunshine and rain⟩ 2 a : occurring first on one side and then on the other at different levels along an axis ⟨*alternate* leaves on a plant stem⟩ b : arranged one above, beside, or next to another ⟨*alternate* layers of meat and cheese⟩ 3 : every other : every second ⟨works on *alternate* days⟩ 4 : being one of the things between which a choice is to be made ⟨we took an *alternate* route⟩ — **al·ter·nate·ly** *adv*

²**al·ter·nate** \'ȯl-tər-ˌnāt *also* 'al-\ *vb* **-nat·ed; -nat·ing** 1 : to do, occur, or act by turns 2 : to cause to alternate

³**al·ter·nate** \-nət\ *n* : a person named to take the place of another when necessary

alternate angle *n* 1 : one of a pair of angles on opposite sides of a line intersecting two other lines and between the two inner lines

alternate angle 1 and 2: alternate interior angles *a, a', b, b'*, alternate exterior angles *c, c', d, d'*

tersected lines — called also *alternate interior angle* **2** : one of a pair of angles on opposite sides of a line intersecting two other lines and outside the two intersected lines — called also *alternate exterior angle*

alternating current *n* : an electric current that reverses its direction at regular intervals — abbreviation *AC*

al·ter·na·tion \ˌȯl-tər-ˈnā-shən *also* ˌal-\ *n* **1** : the act or process of alternating **2** : alternate position or occurrence : SUCCESSION **3** : regular reversal in direction of flow ⟨an *alternation* of an electric current⟩

alternation of generations : the alternate occurrence of two or more forms and especially of a sexual and an asexual generation in the life cycle of a plant or animal

¹**al·ter·na·tive** \ȯl-ˈtər-nət-iv *also* al-\ *adj* **1** : offering or expressing a choice ⟨*alternative* plans⟩ **2** : being one of the things between which a choice is to be made : ALTERNATE ⟨an *alternative* route⟩ — **al·ter·na·tive·ly** *adv* — **al·ter·na·tive·ness** *n*

²**alternative** *n* **1** : a chance to choose between two or more things only one of which may be chosen ⟨the *alternative* of going by bus or car⟩ **2** : one of the things between which a choice is to be made

alternative medicine *n* : any of various systems of healing or treating disease (as herbal medicine) involving approaches not customarily taught or practiced in the U.S.

al·ter·na·tor \ˈȯl-tər-ˌnāt-ər *also* ˈal-\ *n* : an electric generator for producing alternating current

alt·horn \ˈalt-ˌhȯ(ə)rn\ *n* : an alto horn often used in bands in place of the French horn

al·though *also* **al·tho** \ȯl-ˈthō\ *conj* : in spite of the fact that : THOUGH

al·tim·e·ter \al-ˈtim-ət-ər, ˈal-tə-ˌmēt-ər\ *n* : an instrument for measuring altitude; *esp* : a barometer that registers changes in atmospheric pressure accompanying changes in altitude

al·ti·tude \ˈal-tə-ˌt(y)üd\ *n* **1 a** : the angular height of a celestial object above the horizon **b** : the vertical distance of an object above a given level (as sea level) **c** : a perpendicular line from a vertex of a geometric figure (as a triangle) to the opposite side or from one side or face to a parallel side or face; *also* : the length of such a line **2** : an elevated region — usually used in plural **synonyms** see HEIGHT

al·to \ˈal-tō\ *n, pl* **altos** **1 a** : CONTRALTO **b** : the second highest of the four voice parts of a mixed chorus — compare ²BASS 1a, ²SOPRANO 1, TENOR 2a **2** : the second highest member of a family of musical instruments; *esp* : ALTHORN

al·to·cu·mu·lus \ˌal-tō-ˈkyü-myə-ləs\ *n* : a fleecy cloud formation consisting of large whitish globular masses with shaded portions

al·to·geth·er \ˌȯl-tə-ˈgeth-ər\ *adv* **1** : WHOLLY, THOROUGHLY ⟨an *altogether* different problem⟩ **2** : with everything taken into account : in all ⟨the bill came to $25 *altogether*⟩ **3** : on the whole ⟨*altogether* their efforts were successful⟩

al·to·stra·tus \ˌal-tō-ˈstrāt-əs, -ˈstrat-\ *n* : a layer of gray cloud similar to cirrostratus but darker and at a lower level

al·tru·ism \ˈal-trü-ˌiz-əm\ *n* : unselfish interest in the welfare of others — **al·tru·ist** \-trü-əst\ *n* — **al·tru·is·tic** \ˌal-trü-ˈis-tik\ *adj* — **al·tru·is·ti·cal·ly** \-ˈis-ti-k(ə-)lē\ *adv*

al·um \ˈal-əm\ *n* **1** : either of two colorless crystalline compounds containing aluminum that are used in medicine (as to check local sweating or to stop bleeding) **2** : ALUMINUM SULFATE

alu·mi·na \ə-ˈlü-mə-nə\ *n* : the oxide of aluminum that occurs in nature as corundum and in bauxite and is used as a source of aluminum, as an abrasive, and as an absorbent

al·u·min·i·um \ˌal-yə-ˈmin-ē-əm\ *n, chiefly British* : ALUMINUM

alu·mi·nize \ə-ˈlü-mə-ˌnīz\ *vb* **-nized; -niz·ing** : to treat or coat with aluminum

alu·mi·num \ə-ˈlü-mə-nəm\ *n* : a silver-white malleable light element that conducts electricity and heat well, is highly resistant to oxidation, and is the most abundant metal in the earth's crust — see ELEMENT table

aluminum oxide *n* : ALUMINA

aluminum sulfate *n* : a white salt made from bauxite and used in making paper, purifying water, and tanning

alum·na \ə-ˈləm-nə\ *n, pl* **-nae** \-(ˌ)nē\ : a girl or woman who has attended or graduated from a particular school, college, or university

alum·nus \ə-ˈləm-nəs\ *n, pl* **-ni** \-ˌnī\ : a person who has attended or has graduated from a particular school, college, or university [Latin, literally "foster son," from *alere* "to nourish" — related to ALIMENTARY, ALMA MATER]

al·ve·o·lar \al-ˈvē-ə-lər\ *adj* : of, relating to, resembling, or having alveoli

al·ve·o·lus \al-ˈvē-ə-ləs\ *n, pl* **-li** \-ˌlī, -ˌlē\ : a small cavity or pit; *esp* : an air cell of the lungs

al·ways \ˈȯl-wēz, -wəz, -ˌwāz\ *adv* **1** : at all times : INVARIABLY ⟨*always* ready for a party⟩ **2** : throughout all time : FOREVER ⟨I'll remember you *always*⟩

Alz·hei·mer's disease \ˈälts-ˌhī-mərz, ˈalts-\ *n* : a brain disease of later life that is characterized by changes in brain tissue with gradual loss of memory and mental abilities — called also *Alzheimer's*

am *present 1st singular of* BE

AM \ˈā-ˌem\ *n* : a system of broadcasting using amplitude modulation; *also* : a receiver of radio waves broadcast by such a system — **AM** *adj*

amain \ə-ˈmān\ *adv* **1** : with all one's might **2 a** : at full speed **b** : in great haste

amal·gam \ə-ˈmal-gəm\ *n* **1** : an alloy of mercury with some other metal or metals that is used especially for tooth filling **2** : a combination or mixture of different elements ⟨an *amalgam* of fact and fiction⟩

amal·gam·ate \ə-ˈmal-gə-ˌmāt\ *vb* **-at·ed; -at·ing** **1** : to unite into an amalgam **2** : to combine into a single body : MERGE

amal·gam·ation \ə-ˌmal-gə-ˈmā-shən\ *n* **1 a** : the act or process of amalgamating ⟨made by the *amalgamation* of mercury with silver⟩ **b** : the state of being amalgamated **2** : a combination of different elements into a single body

am·a·ni·ta \ˌam-ə-ˈnīt-ə, -ˈnēt-\ *n* : any of various mostly poisonous fungi with white spores and a globe-shaped swelling about the base of the stem

aman·u·en·sis \ə-ˌman-yə-ˈwen(t)-səs\ *n, pl* **-en·ses** \-ˈwen(t)-ˌsēz\ : a person employed to write from dictation or to copy manuscript : SECRETARY

am·a·ranth \ˈam-ə-ˌran(t)th\ *n* : any of various herbs including some considered weeds and others grown for their colorful leaves or spikes of flowers

am·a·ryl·lis \ˌam-ə-ˈril-əs\ *n* : any of various plants of a group related to the lilies; *esp* : an African herb having a bulb and grown for its cluster of large showy flowers

amass \ə-ˈmas\ *vb* : to collect into a mass : ACCUMULATE — **amass·er** *n*

am·a·teur \ˈam-ə-ˌtər, -ət-ər, -ə-ˌt(y)ù(ə)r, -ə-ˌchù(ə)r, -ə-chər\ *n* **1** : a person who takes part in an activity (as a study or sport) for pleasure and not for pay **2** : a person who engages in something without experience or skill ⟨mistakes made only by an *amateur*⟩ [from French *amateur* "one who admires or is devoted to something," derived from Latin *amare* "to love" — re-

amaryllis

lated to AMOROUS] — **amateur** *adj* — **am·a·teur·ish** \ˌam-ə-'tər-ish, -'t(y)u̇(ə)r-ish\ *adj* — **am·a·teur·ish·ly** *adv* — **am·a·teur·ish·ness** *n*

am·a·to·ry \'am-ə-ˌtōr-ē, -ˌtȯr-\ *adj* : of, relating to, or expressing sexual love

amaze \ə-'māz\ *vb* **amazed; amaz·ing** : to surprise or astonish greatly : fill with wonder — **amaz·ing·ly** *adv*

amaze·ment \ə-'māz-mənt\ *n* : great surprise or astonishment

amazing *adj* : causing amazement, great wonder, or surprise

am·a·zon \'am-ə-ˌzän, -ə-zən\ *n* **1** *cap* : a member of a race of female warriors of ancient Greek mythology **2** *often cap* : a tall strong woman

Am·a·zo·nian \ˌam-ə-'zō-nē-ən, -'zō-nyən\ *adj* **1** : of or resembling an Amazon **2** : of or relating to the Amazon River or its valley

am·bas·sa·dor \am-'bas-əd-ər, əm-, -'bas-ə-dȯ(ə)r\ *n* **1** : a person sent as the chief representative of his or her own government in another country **2** : an official representative or messenger — **am·bas·sa·do·ri·al** \(ˌ)am-ˌbas-ə-'dōr-ē-əl, -ˌdȯr-, əm-\ *adj* — **am·bas·sa·dor·ship** \am-'bas-əd-ər-ˌship, əm-\ *n*

am·ber \'am-bər\ *n* **1** : a hard yellowish partly transparent resin from trees long dead that can be highly polished and is used for ornamental objects (as beads) **2** : a dark orange yellow — **amber** *adj*

Amber alert *n* : a widely publicized bulletin that alerts the public to a recently abducted or missing child

am·ber·gris \'am-bər-ˌgris, -ˌgrēs\ *n* : a waxy substance from the sperm whale that is used to make perfumes

am·bi·dex·trous \ˌam-bi-'dek-strəs\ *adj* : using both hands with equal ease — **am·bi·dex·trous·ly** *adv*

am·bi·ence *or* **am·bi·ance** \'am-bē-ən(t)s, 'äm-bē-än(t)s\ *n* : a feeling or mood that is related to a particular place, person, or thing

am·bi·ent \'am-bē-ənt\ *adj* : surrounding on all sides

am·bi·gu·ity \ˌam-bə-'gyü-ət-ē\ *n, pl* **-ities** **1** : the fact or state of being ambiguous **2** : something ambiguous

am·big·u·ous \am-'big-yə-wəs\ *adj* : able to be understood in more than one way [from Latin *ambiguus* "ambiguous," from *ambigere* "to be undecided," from *ambi* "around, both," and *agere* "to drive, do" — related to ACT, AGENT] — **am·big·u·ous·ly** *adv* — **am·big·u·ous·ness** *n*

am·bi·tion \am-'bish-ən\ *n* **1 a** : an eager desire for social standing, fame, or power **b** : desire to achieve a particular goal : ASPIRATION **2** : the particular goal of ambition

Word History When political candidates in ancient Rome wanted to be elected, they had to do what modern candidates must do. They had to spend their time going around the city urging the citizens to vote for them. The Latin word for this effort was *ambitio*, which came from *ambire*, a verb meaning "to go around." Since this "ambition" was caused by a desire for honor or power, the word eventually came to mean "the desire for honor or power." This word came into French and English as *ambition* in the late Middle Ages. Later its meaning broadened to include "an admirable desire for advancement or improvement" and still later "the object of this desire." [Middle English *ambition* "desire for power," from early French *ambition* (same meaning), derived from Latin *ambire* "to go around," from *ambi-* "around" and *ire* "to go"]

am·bi·tious \am-'bish-əs\ *adj* **1** : controlled by or having ambition ⟨*ambitious* to be captain of the team⟩ **2** : showing ambition ⟨an *ambitious* plan⟩ — **am·bi·tious·ly** *adv*

¹am·ble \'am-bəl\ *vb* **am·bled; am·bling** \-b(ə-)liŋ\ : to go at an amble [Middle English *amblen* "to walk in a leisurely manner," from early French *ambler* (same meaning), from Latin *ambulare* "to walk" — related to AMBU-

LANCE; see *Word History* at AMBULANCE] — **am·bler** \-b(ə-)lər\ *n*

²amble *n* **1** : an easy gait of a horse in which the legs on the same side of the body move together **2** : a leisurely way of walking

am·bly·opia \ˌam-blē-'ō-pē-ə\ *n* : reduced vision in one eye that results from poor development of the part of the brain which serves the affected eye — called also *lazy eye*

am·bro·sia \am-'brō-zh(ē-)ə\ *n* **1** : the food of the Greek and Roman gods **2** : something extremely pleasing to taste or smell **3** : a dessert made of oranges and shredded coconut — **am·bro·sial** \-zh(ē-)əl\ *adj*

am·bu·lance \'am-byə-lən(t)s\ *n* : a vehicle that is equipped for transporting the injured or the sick

Word History When the term *ambulance* first came into use, it did not refer to a vehicle. To meet the urgent needs of the wounded during war, the French about 200 years ago set up temporary movable hospitals close to the battlefields. They called such a hospital *hôpital ambulant*, meaning literally "walking hospital." The French adjective *ambulant* can be traced back to the Latin verb *ambulare*, meaning "to walk." In time the French dropped the word *hôpital* from the phrase and changed the adjective to the noun *ambulance*. This word was also later applied to the wagon used for transporting the wounded to the field hospital. Before long, the word *ambulance* came to be used for civilian temporary hospitals set up during emergencies and also for the vehicles used to take the sick and injured to the hospital. English borrowed the word from French to refer to such vehicles. [from French *ambulance* "field hospital," from *(hôpital) ambulant*, literally "traveling hospital," derived from Latin *ambulare* "to walk" — related to AMBLE]

am·bu·la·to·ry \'am-byə-lə-ˌtōr-ē, -ˌtȯr-\ *adj* **1** : of or relating to walking **2** : able to walk about

am·bus·cade \'am-bə-ˌskād, ˌam-bə-'skād\ *n* : ²AMBUSH — **ambuscade** *vb* — **am·bus·cad·er** *n*

¹am·bush \'am-ˌbu̇sh\ *vb* : to attack from an ambush

²ambush *n* : a trap in which hidden persons wait to attack by surprise

ame·ba, ame·boid *variant of* AMOEBA, AMOEBOID

am·e·bi·a·sis \ˌam-i-'bī-ə-səs\ *n, pl* **-a·ses** \-'bī-ə-ˌsēz\ : infection with or disease caused by amoebas

amebic dysentery *n* : severe amebiasis affecting the intestines of human beings and marked by dysentery, pain, and injury to the intestine

ame·lio·rate \ə-'mēl-yə-ˌrāt\ *vb* **-rat·ed; -rat·ing** : to make or grow better or more tolerable — **ame·lio·ra·tion** \-ˌmēl-yə-'rā-shən, -ˌmē-lē-ə-\ *n* — **ame·lio·ra·tive** \-'mēl-yə-ˌrāt-iv, -'mē-lē-ə-\ *adj*

amen \(')ä-'men, (')ā-; 'ä- *when sung*\ *interj* — used to express agreement or approval

ame·na·ble \ə-'mē-nə-bəl, -'men-ə-\ *adj* : readily giving in or agreeing ⟨*amenable* to our wishes⟩ — **ame·na·bil·i·ty** \ə-ˌmē-nə-'bil-ət-ē, -ˌmen-ə-\ *n* — **ame·na·bly** \ə-'mē-nə-blē, -'men-ə-\ *adv*

amend \ə-'mend\ *vb* **1** : to change for the better : IMPROVE **2** : to change the wording or meaning of : ALTER ⟨*amend* a legislative bill⟩ **synonyms** see CORRECT — **amend·able** \-'men-də-bəl\ *adj* — **amend·er** *n*

amend·ment \ə-'men(d)-mənt\ *n* **1** : the act or process of amending especially for the better **2** : a change in wording or meaning especially in a law, bill, or motion

amends \ə-'men(d)z\ *n sing or pl* : something done or given by a person to make up for a loss or injury he or she has caused ⟨make *amends*⟩

\ə\ **abut**	\au̇\ **out**	\i\ **tip**	\ȯ\ **saw**	\u̇\ **foot**
\ər\ **further**	\ch\ **chin**	\ī\ **life**	\ȯi\ **coin**	\y\ **yet**
\a\ **mat**	\e\ **pet**	\j\ **job**	\th\ **thin**	\yü\ **few**
\ā\ **take**	\ē\ **easy**	\ŋ\ **sing**	\th\ **this**	\yu̇\ **cure**
\ä\ **cot, cart**	\g\ **go**	\ō\ **bone**	\ü\ **food**	\zh\ **vision**

ame·ni·ty \ə-'men-ət-ē, -'mē-nət-\ *n, pl* **-ties** **1** : the quality of being pleasant or agreeable **2** : something (as good manners or household appliances) that makes life easier or more pleasant — usually used in plural

ament \'am-ənt, 'ā-mənt\ *n* : CATKIN

¹Amer·i·can \ə-'mer-ə-kən\ *n* **1** : a person born or living in North America or South America; *esp* : a citizen of the U.S. **2** : the English language used in the U.S.

²American *adj* **1** : of or relating to North or South America or their residents ⟨*American* coastline⟩ **2** : of or relating to the U.S. or its citizens

American chameleon *n* : GREEN ANOLE

American elm *n* : a large ornamental tree common in the eastern U.S.

American Indian *n* : a member of any of the native peoples of the western hemisphere except often the Eskimos; *esp* : an American Indian of North America and especially the U.S. — **American Indian** *adj*

Amer·i·can·ism \ə-'mer-ə-kə-,niz-əm\ *n* **1** : a word or meaning of a word that is common only in American English **2** : loyalty to the traditions, interests, or standards of the U.S. **3** : a custom or attitude common only to Americans

Amer·i·can·ize \ə-'mer-ə-kə-,nīz\ *vb* **-ized; -iz·ing** : to make or become American (as in customs, habits, dress, or speech) — **Amer·i·can·i·za·tion** \ə-,mer-ə-kə-nə-'zā-shən\ *n*

American pit bull terrier *n* : any of a breed of medium-sized dogs with a stocky build, powerful jaws, and great strength

American Sign Language *n* : a sign language for the deaf

American Spanish *n* : any of the varieties of Spanish used in North, Central, and South America and in the West Indies

American Standard Version *n* : an American revision of the Authorized Version of the Bible published in 1901 — called also *American Revised Version*

am·er·i·ci·um \,am-ə-'ris-ē-əm, -'rish-\ *n* : a radioactive metallic element produced by bombardment of plutonium with high-energy neutrons — see ELEMENT table

Am·er·in·di·an \,am-ə-'rin-dē-ən\ *also* **Am·er·ind** \'a-mə-,rind\ *n* : AMERICAN INDIAN — **Amerindian** *also* **Amerind** *adj*

am·e·thyst \'am-ə-thəst, -(,)thist\ *n* **1** : a clear purple or bluish violet variety of crystallized quartz used as a gem **2** : a medium purple

> ***Word History*** Gems were once believed to have magical qualities. An amethyst, for example, was supposed to have the power to prevent or cure drunkenness in its wearer. For this reason the Greeks gave it the name *amethystos*, which comes from the prefix *a-*, meaning "not," and *methyein* "to be drunk." [Middle English *amatiste* "amethyst," from early French *amatiste* and Latin *amethystus* (both with the same meaning), from Greek *amethystos*, literally "remedy against drunkenness," from *a-* "not" and *methyein* "to be drunk," from *methy* "wine"]

ami·a·ble \'ā-mē-ə-bəl\ *adj* : generally agreeable : having a friendly and pleasant manner ⟨an *amiable* comedy⟩ — **ami·a·bil·i·ty** \,ā-mē-ə-'bil-ət-ē\ *n* — **ami·a·ble·ness** \'ā-mē-ə-bəl-nəs\ *n* — **ami·a·bly** \-blē\ *adv*

am·i·ca·ble \'am-i-kə-bəl\ *adj* : showing kindness or goodwill : PEACEABLE ⟨neighbors maintaining *amicable* relations⟩ — **am·i·ca·bil·i·ty** \,am-i-kə-'bil-ət-ē\ *n* — **am·i·ca·bly** \'am-i-kə-blē\ *adv*

am·ice \'am-əs\ *n* : a white linen cloth worn around the neck and shoulders under other vestments by a priest at Mass

amid \ə-'mid\ *or* **amidst** \-'midst\ *prep* : in or into the middle of ⟨*amid* the crowd⟩

amid·ships \ə-'mid-,ships\ *adv* : in or near the middle of a ship

amine \ə-'mēn, 'am-,ēn\ *n* : any of various carbon compounds derived from ammonia

ami·no acid \ə-'mē-nō-\ *n* : any of numerous acids that include some which are the building blocks of proteins and are made by living cells from simpler compounds or are obtained in the diet

Amish \'äm-ish, 'am-, 'ām-\ *adj* : of or relating to the Mennonites who were followers of Amman and settled in America [probably from German *amisch*, from Jacob *Amman* or *Amen*, flourished 1693–97, Swiss Mennonite bishop] — **Amish** *n*

¹amiss \ə-'mis\ *adv* **1** : in the wrong way ⟨don't take this remark *amiss*⟩ **2** : ASTRAY 2 ⟨something had gone *amiss*⟩

²amiss *adj* **1 a** : not in accordance with the right order **b** : FAULTY, IMPROPER ⟨something is *amiss* here⟩ **2** : out of place in given circumstances

am·i·ty \'am-ət-ē\ *n, pl* **-ties** : FRIENDSHIP; *esp* : friendly relations between nations

am·me·ter \'am-,ēt-ər\ *n* : an instrument for measuring electric current in amperes

am·mo \'am-ō\ *n* : AMMUNITION

am·mo·nia \ə-'mō-nyə\ *n* **1** : a colorless gas that is a compound of nitrogen and hydrogen, has a sharp smell and taste, is easily dissolved in water, can easily be made a liquid by cold and pressure, is used to make ice, fertilizers, and explosives, and is the chief nitrogen-containing waste product of many organisms that live in water **2** : a solution of ammonia in water [from Latin *sal ammoniacus* "ammonium chloride," literally "salt of Ammon," named for the Egyptian god Ammon near whose temple the salt was extracted] — **am·mo·ni·a·cal** \,am-ə-'nī-ə-kəl\ *adj*

am·mo·nite \'am-ə-,nīt\ *n* : any of numerous flat spiral fossil shells of mollusks related to the nautilus that are especially abundant in the Mesozoic era of geological history — **am·mo·nit·ic** \,am-ə-'nit-ik\ *adj*

am·mo·ni·um \ə-'mō-nē-əm\ *n* : an ion that comes from the combination of ammonia with a hydrogen ion

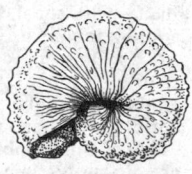
ammonite

ammonium chloride *n* : a white crystalline volatile salt used in dry cells and to cause the discharge of mucus from the respiratory tract

ammonium hydroxide *n* : a compound that is formed when ammonia dissolves in water and that exists only in solution

ammonium nitrate *n* : a colorless crystalline salt used in explosives and fertilizers

ammonium sulfate *n* : a colorless crystalline salt used chiefly as a fertilizer

am·mu·ni·tion \,am-yə-'nish-ən\ *n* **1 a** : objects (as bullets) fired from guns **b** : explosive objects (as bombs) used in war **2** : material that may be used in attacking or defending a position ⟨results of the study provided more *ammunition*⟩

am·ne·sia \am-'nē-zhə\ *n* : severe loss of memory — **am·ne·si·ac** \-z(h)ē-,ak\ *adj or n*

am·nes·ty \'am-nə-stē\ *n, pl* **-ties** : the granting of pardon (as by a government) to a large number of persons

am·nio·cen·te·sis \,am-nē-ō-(,)sen-'tē-səs\ *n, pl* **-te·ses** \-'tē-,sēz\ : the procedure of inserting a hollow needle through the wall of the abdomen and into the uterus of a pregnant female to withdraw a sample of the fluid surrounding the fetus that is used to find out its sex and especially to check for abnormal chromosomes which may predict a birth defect

am·ni·on \'am-nē-,än\ *n* : a thin membrane forming a closed sac about the embryo or fetus of a reptile, bird, or mammal and containing a watery fluid in which the embryo or fetus is immersed

am·ni·ot·ic \ˌam-nē-'ät-ik\ *adj* : of or relating to the am-nion ⟨*amniotic* fluid⟩

amoe·ba *also* **ame·ba** \ə-'mē-bə\ *n, pl* **-bas** *or* **-bae** \-(ˌ)bē\ : any of a large genus of protozoans that have no permanent cell or-gans or structures, that change shape to form temporary lobes for moving and taking in food, and that are widespread in fresh and salt water and in moist soils — **amoe·bic** \-bik\ *adj*

amoe·boid *also* **ame·boid** \ə-'mē-ˌbȯid\ *adj* : resembling an amoeba especially in moving or changing shape by means of the flow of cytoplasm

amoeba: 1 pseudopo-dium, 2 nucleus, 3 contractile vacuole, 4 food vacuole

amok \ə-'mək, -'mäk\ *or* **amuck** \ə-'mək\ *adv* **1** : in a violently excited state ⟨run *amok*⟩ **2** : in an undisciplined, uncontrolled, or faulty manner ⟨paper shredded by a copier run *amok*⟩

among \ə-'məŋ\ *also* **amongst** \-'məŋ(k)st\ *prep* **1** : in or through the midst of ⟨*among* the crowd⟩ **2** : in company with ⟨you're *among* friends⟩ **3** : through all or most of ⟨discontent *among* the poor⟩ **4** : in the class of ⟨*among* my good qualities is modesty⟩ **5** : in shares to each of ⟨divided *among* the heirs⟩

amon·til·la·do \ə-ˌmän-tə-'läd-(ˌ)ō\ *n, pl* **-dos** : a medium dry sherry

amor·al \ā-'mȯr-əl, -'mär-\ *adj* : not being moral nor im-moral — **amor·al·ly** \-ə-lē\ *adv*

am·o·rous \'am-(ə-)rəs\ *adj* **1** : tending to love : easily falling in love ⟨an *amorous* nature⟩ **2** : of, relating to, or caused by love ⟨an *amorous* glance⟩ [Middle English *amorous* "moved by love," from early French *amorous* (same meaning), derived from Latin *amare* "to love" — related to AMATEUR] — **am·o·rous·ly** *adv* — **am·o·rous·ness** *n*

amor·phous \ə-'mȯr-fəs\ *adj* : having no fixed form ⟨an *amorphous* cloud⟩ — **amor·phous·ly** *adv* — **amor-phous·ness** *n*

Amos \'ā-məs\ *n* — see BIBLE table

¹amount \ə-'maȯnt\ *vb* **1** : to add up ⟨the bill *amounted* to ten dollars⟩ **2** : to be the same in meaning or effect ⟨acts that *amount* to treason⟩

²amount *n* : the total number or quantity : AGGREGATE ⟨the *amount* to be paid⟩ **2** : a given or particular quan-tity or number ⟨add the same *amount* to both columns⟩

amour \ə-'mu̇(ə)r, ä-, a-\ *n* : a love affair; *esp* : a secret love affair

amp \'amp\ *n* **1** : AMPERE **2** : AMPLIFIER

am·per·age \'am-p(ə-)rij, -ˌpi(ə)r-ij\ *n* : the rate of flow of a current of electricity expressed in amperes

am·pere \'am-ˌpi(ə)r\ *n* : a unit for measuring the rate of flow of an electric current

am·per·sand \'am-pər-ˌsand\ *n* : a character & standing for the word *and* [from older *and per se and,* spoken form of the phrase *& per se and,* which followed *Z* in early lists of letters of the alphabet and meant "(the character) & by itself (stands for) *and*"]

am·phet·amine \am-'fet-ə-ˌmēn, -mən\ *n* : a compound or one made from it used medically to increase the activity of the central nervous system but often abused for its stimulant effects

am·phib·ia \am-'fib-ē-ə\ *n pl* : AMPHIBIANS

am·phib·i·an \am-'fib-ē-ən\ *n* **1** : any organism that is able to live both on land and in water; *esp* : any of a class of cold-blooded vertebrate animals (as frogs and salaman-ders) that in many respects are between fishes and reptiles **2** : an airplane designed to take off from and land on ei-ther land or water — **amphibian** *adj*

am·phib·i·ous \am-'fib-ē-əs\ *adj* **1** : able to live both on land and in water ⟨*amphibious* plants⟩ **2 a** : designed for use on both land and water ⟨*amphibious* vehicles⟩ **b** : carried out by land, sea, and air forces acting together ⟨an *amphibious* assault⟩ [from Greek *amphibios* "living a double life," from *amphi-* "around, on both sides" and *bios* "mode of life"] — **am·phib·i·ous·ly** *adv* — **am-phib·i·ous·ness** *n*

am·phi·bole \'am(p)-fə-ˌbōl\ *n* : any of a group of rock-forming minerals of similar crystal structure that contain silicon, oxygen, calcium, magnesium, iron, aluminum, and sodium

am·phi·ox·us \ˌam(p)-fē-'äk-səs\ *n, pl* **-oxi** \-'äk-ˌsī\ *or* **-ox·us·es** : LANCELET

am·phi·pod \'am(p)-fə-fi-ˌpäd\ *n* : any of a large group of small crustaceans including the sand fleas and related forms — **amphipod** *adj*

am·phi·the·a·ter \'am(p)-fə-ˌthē-ət-ər\ *n* **1** : a building with seats rising in curved rows around an open space on which games and plays take place **2** : something (as a piece of level ground surrounded by hills) that resembles an amphitheater

am·pho·ra \'am(p)-fə-rə\ *n, pl* **-pho·rae** \-fə-ˌrē, -ˌrī\ *or* **-pho·ras** \-rəz\ : an an-cient Greek jar or vase with two handles; *also* : such a jar or vase used elsewhere in the ancient world

amphora

am·ple \'am-pəl\ *adj* **am·pler** \-p(ə-)lər\; **am·plest** \-p(ə-)ləst\ **1** : generous in size, scope, or capacity : COPIOUS ⟨*ample* room for a garden⟩ **2** : enough to satisfy a need ⟨*ample* money for the trip⟩ **syn-onyms** see PLENTIFUL — **am·ple·ness** *n* — **am·ply** \-plē\ *adv*

am·pli·fi·ca·tion \ˌam-plə-fə-'kā-shən\ *n* : an act, example, or product of amplify-ing

am·pli·fi·er \'am-plə-ˌfī(-ə)r\ *n* : one that amplifies; *esp* : a device usually using electron tubes or transistors to obtain an increase of voltage, current, or power

am·pli·fy \'am-plə-ˌfī\ *vb* **-fied; -fy·ing 1** : ENLARGE **2**; *esp* : to add details or illustrations to ⟨*amplify* a statement⟩ **2** : to increase (voltage, current, or power) in magnitude or strength

am·pli·tude \'am-plə-ˌt(y)üd\ *n* **1** : the quality or state of being ample : FULLNESS, ABUNDANCE **2** : EXTENT 1, RANGE **3 a** : the extent of a back-and-forth movement (as of a pendulum) measured from the midpoint to an ex-treme **b** : one half of the up-and-down extent of the vi-bration of a wave (as of alternating current)

amplitude modulation *n* **1** : changes in the amplitude of a radio carrier wave according to the strength of the sig-nal **2** : a broadcasting system using amplitude modula-tion

am·pu·tate \'am-pyə-ˌtāt\ *vb* **-tat·ed; -tat·ing** : to cut off; *esp* : to cut off an arm or leg from the body — **am·pu·ta-tion** \ˌam-pyə-'tā-shən\ *n*

am·pu·tee \ˌam-pyə-'tē\ *n* : one that has had an arm or leg amputated

amuck *variant of* AMOK

am·u·let \'am-yə-lət\ *n* : a small object worn as a charm against evil

amuse \ə-'myüz\ *vb* **amused; amus·ing 1** : to occupy with something pleasant ⟨*amuse* a child with a toy⟩ **2** : to please the sense of humor of ⟨the story *amused* everyone⟩ — **amus·ed·ly** \-'myü-zəd-lē\ *adv* — **amus·ing·ly** \-'myü-ziŋ-lē\ *adv*

\ə\ abut	\au̇\ out	\i\ tip	\ȯ\ saw	\u̇\ foot
\ər\ further	\ch\ chin	\ī\ life	\ȯi\ coin	\y\ yet
\a\ mat	\e\ pet	\j\ job	\th\ thin	\yü\ few
\ā\ take	\ē\ easy	\ŋ\ sing	\t̲h̲\ this	\yu̇\ cure
\ä\ cot, cart	\g\ go	\ō\ bone	\ü\ food	\zh\ vision

synonyms AMUSE, DIVERT, ENTERTAIN mean to pass or cause to pass the time pleasantly. AMUSE suggests that one's attention is lightly held ⟨*amused* herself by playing solitaire⟩. DIVERT suggests turning the attention from worry or routine to something funny ⟨the patients found the play *diverting*⟩. ENTERTAIN suggests amusing with specially prepared activity or performance ⟨put on a show to *entertain* the troops⟩.

amuse·ment \ə-'myüz-mənt\ *n* **1** : something that amuses **2** : the condition of being amused

amusement park *n* : a park with many rides (as a roller coaster or merry-go-round) and games for entertainment

am·yl acetate \'am-əl-\ *n* : BANANA OIL

am·y·lase \'am-ə-ˌlās, -ˌlāz\ *n* : an enzyme that speeds up the digestion of starch or glycogen — called also *diastase*

an \ən, (')an\ *indefinite article* : ²A — used before words beginning with a vowel sound ⟨*an* oak⟩ ⟨*an* hour⟩

an- — see ²A-

¹-an *or* **-ian** *also* **-ean** *n suffix* **1** : one that belongs to ⟨American⟩ ⟨Bostonian⟩ **2** : one skilled in or specializing in ⟨magician⟩ [derived from Latin *-anus, -ianus* (adjective and noun suffixes)]

²-an *or* **-ian** *also* **-ean** *adj suffix* **1** : of or belonging to ⟨American⟩ **2** : characteristic of : resembling ⟨Herculean⟩

ana- *or* **an-** *prefix* : up : upward ⟨*ana*bolism⟩ [derived from Greek *ana* "up, back"]

anabolic steroid *n* : any of several man-made hormones that are used in medicine to help tissue grow, that are sometimes abused by athletes to increase muscle size and strength, and that may have harmful effects (as stunted growth in teenagers)

anab·o·lism \ə-'nab-ə-ˌliz-əm\ *n* : the part of metabolism concerned with the building up of the substance of plants and animals — **an·a·bol·ic** \ˌan-ə-'bäl-ik\ *adj*

anach·ro·nism \ə-'nak-rə-ˌniz-əm\ *n* **1** : the placing of persons, events, objects, or customs in times to which they do not belong **2** : a person or a thing out of place in time and especially the present time **3** : the state or condition of being out of place in time [probably from Greek *anachronismos* "anachronism," derived from earlier *anachronizein* "to be late," from *ana-* "up" and *chronos* "time" — related to CHRONIC, CHRONICLE, SYNCHRONOUS] — **anach·ro·nis·tic** \ə-ˌnak-rə-'nis-tik\ *adj* — **anach·ro·nis·ti·cal·ly** \-ti-k(ə-)lē\ *adv*

an·a·con·da \ˌan-ə-'kän-də\ *n* : a large South American snake that crushes its prey in its coils; *also* : any large snake that crushes its prey like an anaconda

anad·ro·mous \ə-'nad-rə-məs\ *adj* : traveling up rivers from the sea to breed ⟨*anadromous* shad and salmon⟩

anae·mia *chiefly British variant of* ANEMIA

an·aer·obe \'an-ə-ˌrōb; (')an-'a(-ə)r-ˌōb, -'e(-ə)r-\ *n* : an anaerobic organism

an·aer·o·bic \ˌan-ə-'rō-bik; ˌan-ˌa-(ə-)'rō-, -ˌe-(ə-)'rō-\ *adj* : living, active, or occurring in the absence of free oxygen ⟨*anaerobic* bacteria⟩ — **an·aer·o·bi·cal·ly** \ˌan-ə-'rō-bi-k(ə-)lē; ˌan-ˌa-(ə-)'rō-, -ˌe-(ə-)'ro-\ *adv*

an·aes·the·sia, an·aes·thet·ic *chiefly British variant of* ANESTHESIA, ANESTHETIC

ana·gram \'an-ə-ˌgram\ *n* : a word or phrase made out of another by changing the order of the letters ⟨"rebate" is an *anagram* of "beater"⟩

anal \'ān-ᵊl\ *adj* : of, relating to, situated near, or involving the anus — **anal·ly** \-ᵊl-ē\ *adv*

anal fin *n* : a single fin located on the lower back part of the body of a fish behind the excretory opening

an·al·ge·sia \ˌan-ᵊl-'jē-zhə, -z(h)ē-ə\ *n* : loss of the ability to feel pain while awake — **an·al·ge·sic** \-'jē-zik, -sik\ *adj or n*

analog computer *n* : a computer that works with numbers represented by directly measurable quantities (as voltages or resistances) — compare DIGITAL COMPUTER

anal·o·gous \ə-'nal-ə-gəs\ *adj* **1** : showing analogy : SIMILAR ⟨the two stories are *analogous*⟩ **2** : related by analogy — **anal·o·gous·ly** *adv* — **anal·o·gous·ness** *n*

an·a·logue *or* **an·a·log** \'an-ᵊl-ˌȯg, -ˌäg\ *n* **1** : something that is analogous to something else **2** : an organ or part similar in function to an organ or part of another animal or plant but different in structure and origin **3** : of or relating to an analog computer **4** : being a clock or watch that has hour and minute hands

anal·o·gy \ə-'nal-ə-jē\ *n, pl* **-gies** **1 a** : resemblance in some details between things otherwise unlike : SIMILARITY **b** : comparison based on such resemblance **2** : similarity in function between bodily parts of different structure and origin — **an·a·log·i·cal** \ˌan-ᵊl-'läj-i-kəl\ *adj* — **an·a·log·i·cal·ly** \-k(ə)lē\ *adv*

anal·y·sis \ə-'nal-ə-səs\ *n, pl* **-y·ses** \-ə-ˌsēz\ **1 a** : an examination of a whole to discover its elements and their relations **b** : a statement of such an analysis **2** : an explanation of the nature and meaning of something ⟨*analysis* of the news⟩ **3** : the identification or separation of the parts of a substance **4** : PSYCHOANALYSIS [derived from Greek, from *analyein* "to break up," from *ana-* "up" and *lyein* "to loosen"]

an·a·lyst \'an-ᵊl-əst\ *n* **1** : a person who analyzes or who is skilled in analysis ⟨news *analyst*⟩ **2** : PSYCHOANALYST

an·a·lyt·ic \ˌan-ə-'lit-ik\ *or* **an·a·lyt·i·cal** \-i-kəl\ *adj* **1 a** : of or relating to analysis **b** : separating something into its parts or elements **2** : skilled in or using analysis ⟨a keenly *analytic* person⟩ — **an·a·lyt·i·cal·ly** \-i-k(ə-)lē\ *adv*

an·a·lyze \'an-ᵊl-ˌīz\ *vb* **-lyzed; -lyz·ing** : to study or find out the nature and relationship of the parts by analysis — **an·a·lyz·able** \-ˌī-zə-bəl\ *adj* — **an·a·lyz·er** *n*

an·a·pest \'an-ə-ˌpest\ *n* : a metrical foot consisting of two unaccented syllables followed by one accented syllable (as in *the accused*) — **an·a·pes·tic** \ˌan-ə-'pes-tik\ *adj*

ana·phase \'an-ə-ˌfāz\ *n* : a stage of mitosis or meiosis in which the chromosomes move from the center toward the opposite ends of a dividing cell

an·ar·chic \a-'när-kik, ə-\ *adj* : of or relating to anarchy — **an·ar·chi·cal·ly** \-ki-k(ə-)lē\ *adv*

an·ar·chism \'an-ər-ˌkiz-əm, -ˌär-\ *n* : a political theory that government is not necessary

an·ar·chist \'an-ər-kəst, -ˌär-\ *n* : a person who believes in anarchism or anarchy or practices anarchy — **anarchist** *or* **an·ar·chis·tic** \ˌan-ər-'kis-tik, -(ˌ)är-\ *adj*

an·ar·chy \'an-ər-kē, -ˌär-\ *n* **1** : the condition of a country where there is no government **2** : a state of lawlessness, confusion, or disorder

anath·e·ma \ə-'nath-ə-mə\ *n* **1 a** : a ban or curse declared by church authority and accompanied by excommunication **b** : ¹CURSE 1 **2** : a person or thing that is cursed or strongly disliked ⟨taxation without representation was *anathema* to the colonists⟩

anat·o·mist \ə-'nat-ə-məst\ *n* : a specialist in anatomy

anat·o·mize \ə-'nat-ə-ˌmīz\ *vb* **-mized; -miz·ing** : to cut up carefully so as to show or to examine the structure and use of the parts

anat·o·my \ə-'nat-ə-mē\ *n, pl* **-mies** **1** : a branch of knowledge that deals with the structure of organisms; *also* : a book on bodily structure **2** : structural makeup especially of an organism or any of its parts — **an·a·tom·ic** \ˌan-ə-'täm-ik\ *or* **an·a·tom·i·cal** \-'täm-i-kəl\ *adj* — **an·a·tom·i·cal·ly** \-i-k(ə-)lē\ *adv*

-ance \ən(t)s, ᵊn(t)s\ *n suffix* **1** : action or process ⟨avoid*ance*⟩ ⟨perform*ance*⟩ **2** : quality or state : instance of a quality or state ⟨protuber*ance*⟩ **3** : amount or degree ⟨conduct*ance*⟩ [derived from Latin *-antia* "-ancy"]

an·ces·tor \'an-ˌses-tər\ *n* **1** : one from whom an individual, group, or species is descended **2** : something from which something else has developed : FORERUNNER [Middle English *ancestre* "ancestor," from early French *ancestre* (same meaning), from Latin *antecessor* "one that goes before," derived from earlier *antecedere* "to go before," from *ante-* "before" and *cedere* "to go, yield" — related to CONCEDE, PREDECESSOR]

an·ces·tral \an-'ses-trəl\ *adj* : of, relating to, or developed from an ancestor ⟨*ancestral* home⟩ — **an·ces·tral·ly** \-trə-lē\ *adv*

an·ces·tress \'an-ˌses-trəs\ *n* : a female ancestor

an·ces·try \'an-ˌses-trē\ *n* **1** : line of descent **2** : one's ancestors

¹an·chor \'aŋ-kər\ *n* **1** : a device usually of metal that is attached to a boat or ship by a cable and that when thrown overboard digs into the earth and holds the boat or ship in place **2** : something that serves to hold an object firmly or that gives a feeling of stability ⟨the *anchor* of a bridge⟩ **3** : ANCHORPERSON

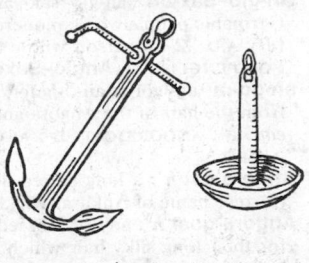

¹anchor 1

²anchor *vb* **an·chored; an·chor·ing** \-k(ə-)riŋ\ **1** : to hold in place by means of an anchor ⟨*anchor* a ship⟩ **2** : to fasten to a firm foundation ⟨*anchor* the cables of a bridge⟩ **3** : to drop anchor : become anchored ⟨the boat *anchored* in the harbor⟩

an·chor·age \'aŋ-k(ə-)rij\ *n* **1** : a place where boats may be anchored **2** : a firm hold to resist a strong pull **3** : a means of security

an·cho·rite \'aŋ-kə-ˌrīt\ *n* : HERMIT 1

an·chor·man \'aŋ-kər-ˌman\ *n* **1** : one who competes or is placed last **2** : an anchorperson who is a man

an·chor·per·son \-ˌpər-s°n\ *n* : a broadcaster who reads the news and introduces the reports of other broadcasters

an·chor·wom·an \-ˌwùm-ən\ *n* **1** : a woman who competes or is placed last **2** : an anchorperson who is a woman

an·cho·vy \'an-ˌchō-vē, an-'chō-vē\ *n, pl* **-vies** *or* **-vy** : any of numerous small fishes resembling herrings that include several that are important food fishes used especially for sauces and relishes

¹an·cient \'ān-shənt, -chənt; 'āŋ(k)-shənt\ *adj* **1** : having existed for many years ⟨*ancient* customs⟩ **2** : of or relating to a period of time long past **3 a** : AGED, VENERABLE **b** : OLD-FASHIONED 1, ANTIQUE **synonyms** see OLD — **an·cient·ness** *n*

²ancient *n* **1** : an aged person **2** *pl* : the civilized peoples of ancient times and especially of Greece and Rome

an·cient·ly \'ān-shənt-lē, -chənt-; 'āŋ(k)-shənt-lē\ *adv* : in ancient times

-an·cy \ən-sē, °n-sē\ *n suffix, pl* **-ancies** : quality or state ⟨vacancy⟩ [derived from Latin *-antia* "quality or state"]

and \ən(d), (')an(d)\ *conj* **1** : added to ⟨2 *and* 2 make 4⟩ **2** : AS WELL AS — used to join words or word groups ⟨ice cream *and* cake⟩ ⟨strong *and* healthy⟩ ⟨swerved *and* avoided an accident⟩ — **and so on 1** : and others or more of the same or similar kind **2** : further in the same or similar manner **3** : and the rest **4** : and other things

¹an·dan·te \än-'dän-ˌtā, an-'dant-ē\ *adv or adj* : slow but not too slow — used as a direction in music

²andante *n* : a musical piece or movement in andante tempo

an·des·ite \'an-di-ˌzīt\ *n* : a usually dark grayish rock of feldspar that is formed from lava — **an·des·it·ic** \ˌan-di-'zit-ik\ *adj*

and·iron \'an-ˌdī(-ə)rn\ *n* : one of a pair of metal supports for firewood in a fireplace

an·dra·dite \an-'dräd-ˌīt, 'an-drə-ˌdīt\ *n* : a garnet ranging from yellow and green to brown and black and containing calcium and iron

an·dro·gen \'an-drə-jən\ *n* : a male sex hormone (as testosterone)

an·drog·y·nous \an-'drä-jə-nəs\ *adj* : having both male and female characteristics — **an·drog·y·nous·ly** *adv* — **an·drog·y·ny** \-nē\ *n*

An·drom·e·da \an-'dräm-əd-ə\ *n* : a northern group of stars in a straight line south of Cassiopeia between Pegasus and Perseus [from Greek *Andromedē,* a mythological princess]

-ane \ˌān\ *n suffix* : a carbon compound in which each carbon atom is attached to four atoms [altered form of *-ene*]

an·ec·dote \'an-ik-ˌdōt\ *n* : a brief story about something interesting or funny in a person's life — **an·ec·dot·al** \ˌan-ik-'dōt-°l\ *adj* — **an·ec·dot·al·ly** \-°l-ē\ *adv*

ane·mia \ə-'nē-mē-ə\ *n* : a condition in which the blood has less than the normal amount of red blood cells, hemoglobin, or total volume and which is usually marked by weakness, exhaustion, pale skin, shortness of breath, and abnormal heartbeat — **ane·mic** \-mik\ *adj*

an·e·mom·e·ter \ˌan-ə-'mäm-ət-ər\ *n* : an instrument for measuring the force or speed of the wind

anem·o·ne \ə-'nem-ə-nē\ *n* **1** : any of a large genus of herbs related to the buttercups that have showy flowers **2** : SEA ANEMONE

anemone 1

aneroid barometer *n* : an instrument in which atmospheric pressure bends a metallic surface which in turn moves a pointer

an·es·the·sia \ˌan-əs-'thē-zhə\ *n* : loss of bodily sensation with or without loss of consciousness

an·es·the·si·ol·o·gist \ˌan-əs-ˌthē-zē-'äl-ə-jist\ *n* : ANESTHETIST; *esp* : a doctor specializing in giving anesthetics to patients

¹an·es·thet·ic \ˌan-əs-'thet-ik\ *adj* : of, relating to, or capable of producing anesthesia — **an·es·thet·i·cal·ly** \-'thet-i-k(ə-)lē\ *adv*

²anesthetic *n* : a substance that produces anesthesia in part or all of the body

anes·the·tist \ə-'nes-thət-əst\ *n* : one who gives anesthetics to patients

anes·the·tize \ə-'nes-thə-ˌtīz\ *vb* **-tized; -tiz·ing** : to make insensible to pain especially by the use of an anesthetic

anew \ə-'n(y)ü\ *adv* **1** : over again : for another time ⟨begin *anew*⟩ **2** : in a new or different form ⟨a story told *anew* as a movie⟩

an·gel \'ān-jəl\ *n* **1** : a spiritual being serving God especially as a messenger or as a guardian of human beings **2** : MESSENGER, HARBINGER ⟨*angel* of death⟩ **3** : a person as pure, lovely, or good as an angel [Middle English *angel* "spiritual being," from Old English *engel* and early French *angele* (both, same meaning), derived from Greek *angelos* "messenger"] — **an·gel·ic** \an-'jel-ik\ *or* **an·gel·i·cal** \-i-kəl\ *adj* — **an·gel·i·cal·ly** \-i-k(ə-)lē\ *adv*

an·gel·fish \'ān-jəl-ˌfish\ *n* **1** : any of several brightly colored bony fishes that are very thin from side to side and live in warm seas **2** : a similarly thin black and silver South American fish popular in aquariums

\ə\ abut	\aú\ out	\i\ tip	\ò\ saw	\ù\ foot
\ər\ further	\ch\ chin	\ī\ life	\òi\ coin	\y\ yet
\a\ mat	\e\ pet	\j\ job	\th\ thin	\yü\ few
\ā\ take	\ē\ easy	\ŋ\ sing	\th\ this	\yú\ cure
\ä\ cot, cart	\g\ go	\ō\ bone	\ü\ food	\zh\ vision

angel food cake *n* : a usually white sponge cake made of flour, sugar, and whites of eggs

¹an·ger \'aŋ-gər\ *n* : a strong feeling of displeasure and usually of opposition toward someone or something

> **synonyms** ANGER, RAGE, FURY, WRATH mean an intense emotional state caused by displeasure. ANGER is a broad term that applies to various levels of emotion that may or may not be shown ⟨kept her *anger* inside herself⟩. RAGE suggests loss of self-control from great anger ⟨screaming with *rage*⟩. FURY suggests loss of self-control from violence of emotion ⟨could not contain his *fury*⟩. WRATH suggests a desire to gain revenge or to punish ⟨they feared her *wrath* if caught⟩.

²anger *vb* **an·gered; an·ger·ing** \-g(ə-)riŋ\ : to make angry

an·gi·na \an-'jī-nə, 'an-jə-nə\ *n* : a disorder marked by sudden bursts of intense pain; *esp* : ANGINA PECTORIS — **an·gi·nal** \an-'jīn-ᵊl, 'an-jən-\ *adj*

angina pec·to·ris \-'pek-t(ə-)rəs\ *n* : a heart disorder in which the heart muscle receives too little oxygen and which is marked by brief attacks of intense chest pain that occur again and again

an·gio·sperm \'an-jē-ə-,spərm\ *n* : FLOWERING PLANT — **an·gio·sper·mous** \,an-jē-ə-'spər-məs\ *adj*

¹an·gle \'aŋ-gəl\ *n* **1** : a sharp projecting corner **2** : the figure formed by two lines extending from the same point **3** : a measure of the amount that one line of an angle would have to be turned to be in exactly the same place as the other line ⟨a 90-degree *angle*⟩ **4** : POINT OF VIEW, ASPECT ⟨consider a problem from a new *angle*⟩ **5** : an often improper way of getting an advantage ⟨a cheater looking for an *angle*⟩ **6** : a sharply curving course or direction ⟨the road went off at an *angle*⟩ [Middle English *angle* "corner," from early French *angle* (same meaning), from Latin *angulus* "angle"] — **an·gled** \-gəld\ *adj*

²angle *vb* **an·gled; an·gling** \-g(ə-)liŋ\ **1** : to turn, move, or direct at an angle **2** : to present (as a news story) from a particular point of view : SLANT

³angle *vb* **an·gled; an·gling** \-g(ə-)liŋ\ **1** : to fish with hook and line **2** : to try to get what one wants in a sly way ⟨*angling* for a promotion⟩ [derived from Old English *angel* "fishhook," from *anga* "hook"]

angle bracket *n* : BRACKET 3b

angle of incidence : the angle that a ray meeting a surface makes with a perpendicular to the surface at the point of contact

angle of reflection : the angle between a reflected ray and the perpendicular to a reflecting surface drawn at the point of contact

an·gler \'aŋ-glər\ *n* **1** : a person who fishes with hook and line especially for pleasure **2** : ANGLERFISH

an·gler·fish \-,fish\ *n* : a bottom-dwelling marine fish that has a large flat head with parts that stick out and lure other fish within reach of its broad mouth

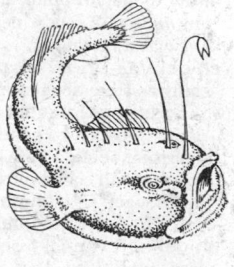

anglerfish

An·gles \'aŋ-gəlz\ *n pl* : a Germanic people conquering England with the Saxons and Jutes in the 5th century A.D. and joining with them to form the Anglo-Saxon people [from Latin *Angli* "the Angles," of Germanic origin]

an·gle·worm \'aŋ-gəl-,wərm\ *n* : EARTHWORM

An·gli·can \'aŋ-gli-kən\ *adj* : of or relating to the established Church of England — **Anglican** *n* — **An·gli·can·ism** \-kə-,niz-əm\ *n*

an·gli·cize \'aŋ-glə-sīz\ *vb* **-cized; -ciz·ing** *often cap* : to make English (as in habits, speech, or outlook)

an·gling \'aŋ-gliŋ\ *n* : fishing with hook and line for pleasure

An·glo *combining form* **1** \'aŋ-,glō, -glə\ : English ⟨*Anglo*-Norman⟩ **2** \-,glō\ : English and ⟨*Anglo*-Japanese⟩ [derived from Latin *Angli* "the Angles"]

An·glo–Amer·i·can \,aŋ-glō-ə-'mer-ə-kən\ *n* **1** : a person living in the U.S. who was born in or whose ancestors were born in England **2** : a North American whose native language is English and especially whose culture is of European origin — **Anglo–American** *adj*

An·glo–Sax·on \,aŋ-glō-'sak-sən\ *n* **1** : a member of the Germanic people who conquered England in the 5th century A.D. **2** : a person whose ancestors were English **3** : OLD ENGLISH — **Anglo–Saxon** *adj*

an·go·ra \aŋ-'gōr-ə, an-, -'gòr-\ *n* **1** : yarn or cloth made from the hair of the Angora goat or the Angora rabbit **2** *cap* **a** : ANGORA CAT **b** : ANGORA GOAT **c** : ANGORA RABBIT

Angora cat *n* : a long-haired domestic cat [from *Angora* (former name of Ankara, Turkey)]

Angora goat *n* : any of a breed of domestic goats raised for their long silky hair which is used to make true mohair fabrics

Angora rabbit *n* : a usually white rabbit raised for its long fine soft hair

an·gry \'aŋ-grē\ *adj* **an·gri·er; -est 1 a** : feeling or showing anger **b** : threatening as if in anger ⟨an *angry* sky⟩ **2** : painfully inflamed ⟨an *angry* rash⟩ — **an·gri·ly** \-grə-lē\ *adv* — **an·gri·ness** \-grē-nəs\ *n*

angst \'äŋ(k)st, 'aŋ(k)st\ *n* : a feeling of anxiety : DREAD

ang·strom \'aŋ-strəm\ *n* : a unit of length used especially of wavelengths (as of light) and equal to one ten-billionth of a meter — abbreviation *Å*

an·guish \'aŋ-gwish\ *n* : extreme pain or distress of body or mind — **an·guished** \-gwisht\ *adj*

an·gu·lar \'aŋ-gyə-lər\ *adj* **1** : having one or more angles : sharp-cornered : POINTED ⟨an *angular* mountain peak⟩ **2** : measured by an angle ⟨the *angular* distance between two stars as observed from earth⟩ **3** : being lean and bony ⟨an *angular* face⟩ — **an·gu·lar·i·ty** \,aŋ-gyə-'lar-ət-ē\ *n* — **an·gu·lar·ly** \'aŋ-gyə-lər-lē\ *adv*

An·gus \'aŋ-gəs\ *n* : any of a breed of usually black hornless beef cattle originating in Scotland

an·hin·ga \an-'hiŋ-gə\ *n* : a fish-eating bird having a long neck and sharply pointed bill and occurring from the southern U.S. to Argentina

an·hy·dride \(')an-'hī-,drīd\ *n* : a compound that comes from another (as an acid) by removal of water

an·hy·drite \(')an-'hī-,drīt\ *n* : a mineral consisting of calcium sulfate free from water

an·hy·drous \(')an-'hī-drəs\ *adj* : free from water

an·i·line \'an-ᵊl-ən\ *n* : an oily poisonous liquid that is used in making dyes

¹an·i·mal \'an-ə-məl\ *n* **1** : any of a kingdom of living things composed of many cells typically differing from plants in capacity for active movement, in rapid response to stimulation, in being unable to carry on photosynthesis, and in lack of cellulose cell walls **2 a** : one of the lower animals as distinguished from human beings **b** : MAMMAL

> **Word History** Latin *anima* means "breath" or "soul," and *animalis,* the adjective that comes from it, means "having breath or soul." An animal such as a cat or dog can be seen to breathe. Plants breathe too, by taking in certain gases from the atmosphere and releasing others. However, this process cannot be observed by the naked eye. So the noun *animal,* which comes from *animalis,* was borrowed from Latin for that group of living beings that breathe visibly. [from Latin *animal* "living being that can move," derived from *animalis* "animate," from *anima* "soul, breath" — related to ANIMATE; see *Word History* at ANIMATE]

²**animal** *adj* **1** : of, relating to, or derived from animals **2** : of or relating to the body rather than the mind

an·i·mal·cule \ˌan-ə-'mal-kyül\ *n* : a very small organism that is invisible or nearly invisible to the naked eye — **an·i·mal·cu·lar** \-'mal-kyə-lər\ *adj*

animal heat *n* : heat produced in the body of a living animal by its chemical and physical activity

animal husbandry *n* : a branch of agriculture concerned with raising domestic animals

animal kingdom *n* : a basic group of natural objects that includes all living and extinct animals — compare MINERAL KINGDOM, PLANT KINGDOM

¹**an·i·mate** \'an-ə-mət\ *adj* **1** : having life : ALIVE **2** : ANIMATED 1, LIVELY — **an·i·mate·ly** *adv*

> **Word History** The same Latin word *anima* meaning "breath, soul" that gave us *animal* has given us other words. The English adjective *animate* meaning "alive" comes from the Latin verb *animare* meaning "to give life to," which in turn came from *anima*. A characteristic of animals is their ability to move about. When a cartoon is drawn and filmed in such a way that lifelike movement is produced, we say it is *animated*. An *animated* film seems to have a life of its own. [Middle English *animate* "alive," from Latin *animatus* (same meaning), derived from *anima* "soul, breath" — related to ANIMAL; see *Word History* at ANIMAL]

²**an·i·mate** \'an-ə-ˌmāt\ *vb* **-mat·ed; -mat·ing 1** : to give life to : make alive **2** : to give spirit and vigor to : ENLIVEN **3** : to make as an animated cartoon ⟨*animate* a story⟩

an·i·mat·ed \'an-ə-ˌmāt-əd\ *adj* **1** : full of life and energy : LIVELY **2** : appearing to be alive or moving **3** : made in the form of an animated cartoon ⟨an *animated* movie⟩ **synonyms** see LIVELY — **an·i·mat·ed·ly** *adv*

animated cartoon *n* : a movie that is made from a series of drawings, computer graphics, or photographs of inanimate objects (as puppets) and that gives the appearance of motion by small changes in each frame

an·i·ma·tion \ˌan-ə-'mā-shən\ *n* **1** : the state of being animate or animated **2 a** : a film made by photographing a series of positions of objects (as puppets) **b** : ANIMATED CARTOON **3** : the making of animations

an·i·ma·tor \'an-ə-ˌmāt-ər\ *n* : someone who makes an animated cartoon

an·i·me \'an-ə-ˌmā, 'ä-nē-\ *n* : a style of animation originating in Japan that has stark colorful graphics, action-filled plots, and often fantastic or futuristic themes [from Japanese, literally, "animation," short for *animēshiyon* (from English)]

an·i·mos·i·ty \ˌan-ə-'mäs-ət-ē\ *n, pl* **-ties** : a feeling of dislike or hatred

an·ion \'an-ˌī-ən\ *n* : a negatively charged ion

an·ise \'an-əs\ *n* : an herb that is related to the carrot and produces seeds with an aroma; *also* : ANISEED

ani·seed \'an-ə(s)-ˌsēd\ *n* : the seed of anise often used as a flavoring

an·iso·trop·ic \ˌan-ˌī-sə-'träp-ik\ *adj* : having properties that differ when measured in different directions ⟨an *anisotropic* crystal⟩

an·kle \'aŋ-kəl\ *n* : the joint between the foot and the leg; *also* : the region of this joint

an·kle·bone \-'bōn, -ˌbōn\ *n* : the bone that in human beings bears the weight of the body and with the tibia and fibula forms the ankle joint

an·klet \'aŋ-klət\ *n* **1** : something (as an ornament) worn around the ankle **2** : a short sock reaching slightly above the ankle

an·ky·lo·saur \'aŋ-kə-lō-ˌsȯr\ *n* : any of several plant-eating dinosaurs of the Cretaceous period having a thickset body with bony plates covering the back

an·nal·ist \'an-ᵊl-əst\ *n* : a writer of annals : HISTORIAN — **an·nal·is·tic** \ˌan-ᵊl-'is-tik\ *adj*

an·nals \'an-ᵊlz\ *n pl* **1** : a record of events arranged in yearly order **2** : historical records

an·nat·to \ə-'nät-ō\ *n, pl* **-tos** : a yellowish red substance used for dyeing that is made from the pulp around the seeds of a tropical tree

an·neal \ə-'nē(ə)l\ *vb* : to heat and then cool so as to toughen and make less brittle

an·ne·lid \'an-ᵊl-əd, 'an-ə-lid\ *n* : any of a phylum of long invertebrate animals that have segments and a body cavity and include the earthworms, leeches, and related forms — **annelid** *adj*

¹**an·nex** \ə-'neks, 'an-ˌeks\ *vb* **1** : to attach as an addition : APPEND **2** : to add (a territory) to one's own territory to form a larger country ⟨the United States *annexed* Texas in 1845⟩ — **an·nex·a·tion** \ˌan-ek-'sā-shən\ *n*

²**an·nex** \'an-ˌeks, 'an-iks\ *n* : something annexed; *esp* : an added part of a building

an·ni·hi·late \ə-'nī-ə-ˌlāt\ *vb* **-lat·ed; -lat·ing** : to destroy completely — **an·ni·hi·la·tion** \ə-ˌnī-ə-'lā-shən\ *n* — **an·ni·hi·la·tor** \ə-'nī-ə-ˌlāt-ər\ *n*

an·ni·ver·sa·ry \ˌan-ə-'vərs-(ə-)rē\ *n, pl* **-ries 1 a** : the annual return of the date of a special event **b** : a date that follows such an event by a specified period of time ⟨the 6-month *anniversary* of the accident⟩ **2** : the celebration of an anniversary [Middle English *anniversarie* "anniversary," from Latin *anniversarium* (same meaning), literally "turning of the year," from *annus* "year" and *versus* "turned," from *vertere* "to turn" — related to CONVERSE, UNIVERSE, VERSATILE]

an·no Do·mi·ni \ˌan-ō-'däm-ə-nē, -'dō-mə-, -ˌnī\ *adv, often cap A* — used to indicate that a time division falls within the period dating from the birth of Christ [Latin, literally "in the year of the Lord"]

an·no·tate \'an-ə-ˌtāt\ *vb* **-tat·ed; -tat·ing** : to make or add explanatory notes — **an·no·ta·tor** \-ˌtāt-ər\ *n*

an·no·ta·tion \ˌan-ə-'tā-shən\ *n* **1** : the act of annotating **2** : a note added as a comment or explanation

an·nounce \ə-'naun(t)s\ *vb* **an·nounced; an·nounc·ing 1** : to make known publicly : PROCLAIM **2** : to give notice of the coming, arrival, or presence of

an·nounce·ment \ə-'naun(t)s-mənt\ *n* **1** : the act of announcing **2** : a public notice announcing something

an·nounc·er \ə-'naun(t)-sər\ *n* : one who announces: as **a** : a person who introduces television or radio programs, makes commercial announcements, or gives station identification **b** : a person who describes and comments on the action in a broadcast sports event

an·noy \ə-'nȯi\ *vb* : to disturb or irritate especially by repeated acts : VEX — **an·noy·er** *n*

an·noy·ance \ə-'nȯi-ən(t)s\ *n* **1 a** : the act of annoying **b** : the feeling of being annoyed **2** : a source of annoyance : NUISANCE

an·noy·ing \ə-'nȯi-iŋ\ *adj* : causing annoyance ⟨an *annoying* habit⟩ — **an·noy·ing·ly** *adv*

¹**an·nu·al** \'an-y(ə-w)əl\ *adj* **1** : covering the period of a year ⟨*annual* rainfall⟩ **2** : occurring or performed once a year : YEARLY ⟨an *annual* meeting⟩ **3** : completing the life cycle in one growing season or single year ⟨*annual* plants⟩ [Middle English *annual* "for a year," from early French *annuel* and Latin *annualis* (both, same meaning), derived from Latin *annus* "year"] — **an·nu·al·ly** \-ē\ *adv*

²**annual** *n* **1** : a publication appearing yearly **2** : an annual plant

annual ring *n* : the layer of wood produced by a single year's growth of a woody plant — called also *tree ring*

\ə\ **abut**	\au̇\ **out**	\i\ **tip**	\ȯ\ **saw**	\u̇\ **foot**
\ər\ **further**	\ch\ **chin**	\ī\ **life**	\ȯi\ **coin**	\y\ **yet**
\a\ **mat**	\e\ **pet**	\j\ **job**	\th\ **thin**	\yü\ **few**
\ā\ **take**	\ē\ **easy**	\ŋ\ **sing**	\th̲\ **this**	\yu̇\ **cure**
\ä\ **cot, cart**	\g\ **go**	\ō\ **bone**	\ü\ **food**	\zh\ **vision**

an·nu·ity \ə-'n(y)ü-ət-ē\ *n, pl* **-ities 1** : a sum of money paid at regular intervals **2** : an insurance contract providing for the payment of an annuity

an·nul \ə-'nəl\ *vb* **an·nulled; an·nul·ling 1** : to make ineffective : NEUTRALIZE **2** : to bring to an end legally ⟨*annul* a marriage⟩ — **an·nul·ment** \ə-'nəl-mənt\ *n*

an·nu·lar \'an-yə-lər\ *adj* : of, relating to, or forming a ring

annular eclipse *n* : an eclipse in which a thin outer ring of the sun's disk is not covered by the moon's dark disk

An·nun·ci·a·tion \ə-,nən(t)-sē-'ā-shən\ *n* : the announcement to the Virgin Mary that she was to be the mother of the Messiah; *also* : March 25 observed as a church festival in honor of the Annunciation

an·ode \'an-,ōd\ *n* **1** : the positive electrode of an electrolytic cell to which the negative ions are attracted — compare CATHODE **2** : the negative terminal of a battery that is delivering electric current **3** : the electron-collecting electrode of an electron tube — **an·od·ic** \a-'näd-ik\ *adj*

an·od·ize \'an-ə-,dīz\ *vb* **-ized; -iz·ing** : to cause (a metal) to undergo electrolytic action as the anode of a cell in order to coat with a protective or decorative film

anoint \ə-'nȯint\ *vb* **1** : to rub over with oil or an oily substance **2** : to put oil on as part of a religious ceremony — **anoint·er** *n* — **anoint·ment** \-mənt\ *n*

ano·le \ə-'nō-lē\ *n* : any of various chiefly tropical lizards that are able to change color and in the males have a usually brightly colored flap of skin on the throat

anom·a·lous \ə-'näm-ə-ləs\ *adj* : not following a general rule or method : IRREGULAR, UNUSUAL — **anom·a·lous·ly** *adv* — **anom·a·lous·ness** *n*

anom·a·ly \ə-'näm-ə-lē\ *n, pl* **-lies 1** : an act or instance of not following the general rule or method **2** : something anomalous : something different, abnormal, strange, or not easily described

anon \ə-'nän\ *adv* : SOON 1; *also* : at a later time ⟨more of that *anon*⟩

an·o·nym·i·ty \,an-ə-'nim-ət-ē\ *n, pl* **-ties** : the quality or state of being anonymous

anon·y·mous \ə-'nän-ə-məs\ *adj* **1** : not named or identified ⟨the donor remained *anonymous*⟩ **2** : made or done by someone unknown ⟨*anonymous* gifts⟩ ⟨an *anonymous* poem⟩ [from Latin *anonymus* "anonymous," from Greek *anonymos* (same meaning), from *an-, a-* "not, without" and *onyma, onoma* "name" — related to SYNONYMOUS] — **anon·y·mous·ly** *adv* — **anon·y·mous·ness** *n*

anoph·e·les \ə-'näf-ə-,lēz\ *n* : any of a genus of mosquitoes that includes all mosquitoes which transmit malaria to human beings — **anoph·e·line** \-,līn\ *adj or n*

an·orex·ia \,an-ə-'rek-sē-ə\ *n* : ANOREXIA NERVOSA

anorexia ner·vo·sa \-(,)nər-'vō-sə, -zə\ *n* : a serious eating disorder especially of young women in their teens in which an abnormal fear of weight gain leads to faulty eating habits and extreme weight loss

an·orex·ic \,an-ə-'rek-sik\ *adj* : affected with anorexia nervosa

an·or·thite \ə-'nȯr-,thīt\ *n* : a white, grayish, or reddish calcium-containing feldspar

¹an·oth·er \ə-'nəth-ər\ *adj* **1** : different or distinct from the first one considered ⟨viewed from *another* angle⟩ **2** : some other ⟨at *another* time⟩ ⟨choose *another* book⟩ **3** : one more in addition ⟨have *another* piece of toast⟩

²another *pron* **1** : one more of the same kind ⟨I've had one piece, but I think I'll have *another*⟩ **2** : one that is different : someone or something else ⟨living in *another's* house⟩ **3** : one of a group that is not specified ⟨at one time or *another*⟩

an·ox·ia \a-'näk-sē-ə\ *n* : a condition in which too little oxygen (as at high altitudes) reaches the tissues

¹an·swer \'an(t)-sər\ *n* **1 a** : something spoken or written in reply especially to a question **b** : a correct response ⟨knew the *answer*⟩ **c** : a solution of a problem **2** : something said or done in response

²answer *vb* **an·swered; an·swer·ing** \'an(t)s-(ə-)riŋ\ **1** : to speak or write in reply **2 a** : to take responsibility for something ⟨*answered* for the children's safety⟩ **b** : to make amends ⟨must *answer* for their crime⟩ **3** : CONFORM 2, CORRESPOND ⟨*answered* to the description⟩ **4** : to be what is needed for : SERVE ⟨*answered* the purpose⟩ **5** : to find a solution for ⟨*answer* a riddle⟩ — **an·swer·er** \'an(t)-sər-ər\ *n*

an·swer·able \'an(t)s-(ə-)rə-bəl\ *adj* **1** : getting the credit or blame for one's acts or decisions : RESPONSIBLE **2** : capable of being answered or proved wrong — **an·swer·abil·i·ty** \,an(t)s-(ə-)rə-'bil-ət-ē\ *n*

answering machine *n* : a machine that receives telephone calls by recording messages from callers

answering service *n* : a commercial service that answers telephone calls for its clients

ant \'ant\ *n* : any of a family of small insects that are related to the bees and wasps and live in colonies in which different types of individuals perform special duties — **ants in one's pants** : impatience for action or activity : RESTLESSNESS

ant- — see ANTI-

¹-ant \ənt, ⁿnt\ *n suffix* **1** : one that performs a specified action ⟨cool*ant*⟩ ⟨deodor*ant*⟩ **2** : thing that is acted upon in a specified manner ⟨inhal*ant*⟩ [derived from Latin *-ant* (verb or adjective suffix)]

²-ant *adj suffix* **1** : performing a specified action or being in a specified condition ⟨propell*ant*⟩ **2** : causing a specified action or process

ant·ac·id \(')ant-'as-əd\ *adj* : tending to prevent or neutralize acidity ⟨*antacid* tablets⟩ — **antacid** *n*

an·tag·o·nism \an-'tag-ə-,niz-əm\ *n* : a state of being opposed to something or unfriendly toward someone

an·tag·o·nist \an-'tag-ə-nəst\ *n* : one that opposes another

an·tag·o·nis·tic \(,)an-,tag-ə-'nis-tik\ *adj* : showing antagonism — **an·tag·o·nis·ti·cal·ly** \-ti-k(ə-)lē\ *adv*

an·tag·o·nize \an-'tag-ə-,nīz\ *vb* **-nized; -niz·ing** : to stir up dislike or anger in

ant·arc·tic \(')ant-'ärk-tik, -'ärt-ik\ *adj, often cap* : of or relating to the South Pole or to the region near it

antarctic circle *n, often cap A&C* : the parallel of latitude that is approximately 66½ degrees south of the equator

ant bear *n* : AARDVARK

ant cow *n* : an aphid which secretes a sugary substance used by ants

ante- *prefix* **1 a** : prior : earlier ⟨*ante*date⟩ **b** : before or toward the front : forward ⟨*ante*room⟩ **2** : prior to : earlier than ⟨*ante*diluvian⟩ [derived from Latin *ante* "before, in front"]

ant·eat·er \'ant-,ēt-ər\ *n* : any of several mammals (as an echidna or aardvark) that feed on ants

an·te·bel·lum \,ant-i-'bel-əm\ *adj* : existing before a war; *esp* : existing before the American Civil War

¹an·te·ced·ent \,ant-ə-'sēd-ənt\ *n* **1** : a noun, pronoun, phrase, or clause referred to by a pronoun ⟨in "the house that we live in," "house" is the *antecedent* of "that"⟩ **2** : an event or cause coming before something **3** *pl* : one's ancestors or parents

²antecedent *adj* : coming earlier in time or order — **an·te·ced·ent·ly** *adv*

an·te·cham·ber \'ant-i-,chām-bər\ *n* : ANTEROOM

an·te·date \'ant-i-,dāt\ *vb* **1** : to date with a date earlier than that of actual writing ⟨*antedate* a check⟩ **2** : to come before in time ⟨automobiles *antedate* airplanes⟩

an·te·di·lu·vi·an \,ant-i-də-'lü-vē-ən, -dī-\ *adj* **1** : of or relating to the period before the Flood described in the Bible **2** : very old or old-fashioned — **antediluvian** *n*

an·te·lope \'ant-ᵊl-,ōp\ *n, pl* **-lope** *or* **-lopes 1** : any of various cud-chewing mammals chiefly of Africa and southwest Asia that are related to the goats and oxen and that have a slender lean build and usually horns directed

upward and backward **2**
: PRONGHORN

an·te me·ri·di·em \ˌant-i-
mə-'rid-ē-əm, -ē-ˌem\ *adj*
: being before noon —
abbreviation *a.m.* [Latin]

an·ten·na \an-'ten-ə\ *n, pl*
-ten·nae \-'ten-(ˌ)ē\ *or*
-tennas 1 *pl usually* an-
tennae : one of a pair of
slender movable organs
of sensation on the head
of an arthropod (as an insect or a crab) that are
made up of segments **2** *pl*
usually antennas : a de-

antelope

vice (as a rod or wire) for sending or receiving radio
waves

an·ten·nule \an-'ten-(ˌ)yü(ə)l\ *n* : a small antenna (as of a
crayfish)

an·te·ri·or \an-'tir-ē-ər\ *adj* **1** : placed or being before or
toward the front **2** : coming before in time — **an·te·ri·or·**
ly *adv*

an·te·room \ant-i-ˌrüm, -ˌrùm\ *n* : a room used as an entrance to another

an·them \'an(t)-thəm\ *n* **1** : a sacred composition with
words usually from the Scriptures **2** : a song of praise or
gladness

an·ther \'an(t)-thər\ *n* : the part of the stamen of a flower
that produces and contains pollen and is usually borne on
a stalk

ant·hill \'ant-ˌhil\ *n* : a mound made by ants in digging
their nest

an·tho·cy·a·nin \ˌan(t)-thə-'sī-ə-nən\ *n* : any of various
soluble pigments producing blue to red coloring in flowers and plants

an·thol·o·gy \an-'thäl-ə-jē\ *n, pl* **-gies** : a collection of literary pieces — **an·thol·o·gist** \-jəst\ *n*

an·thra·cite \'an(t)-thrə-ˌsīt\ *n* : a hard glossy coal that
burns without much smoke or flame

an·thrax \'an-ˌthraks\ *n* : an infectious and usually fatal
disease of warm-blooded animals (as cattle and sheep)
caused by a bacterium and transmissible to humans; *also*
: a bacterium causing anthrax

¹**an·thro·poid** \'an(t)-thrə-ˌpòid\ *adj* : of, relating to, or being an anthropoid ⟨*anthropoid* apes⟩

²**anthropoid** *n* **1** : APE 1b **2** : a person resembling an ape
(as in behavior)

an·thro·pol·o·gy \ˌan(t)-thrə-'päl-ə-jē\ *n* : the science of
human beings and especially of their physical characteristics, their origin, their environment and social relations,
and their culture — **an·thro·po·log·i·cal** \-pə-'läj-i-kəl\
adj — **an·thro·pol·o·gist** \-'päl-ə-jəst\ *n*

anti- \ant-i, ˌant-ē, ˌan-ˌtī\ *or* **ant-** *or* **anth-** *prefix* **1** : opposite in kind, position, or action ⟨*anti*histamine⟩ **2** : opposed to ⟨*anti*social⟩ **3** : working against ⟨*anti*bacterial⟩
⟨*anti*pollution⟩ [derived from Greek *anti-* "against"]

an·ti·air·craft \ˌant-ē-'a(ə)r-ˌkraft, -'e(ə)r-\ *adj* : designed
or used for defense against aircraft ⟨an *antiaircraft* gun⟩

an·ti·bac·te·ri·al \ˌant-ē-ˌbak-'tir-ē-əl, ˌan-ˌtī-ˌbak-\ *adj*
: directed or effective against bacteria ⟨*antibacterial*
soap⟩

an·ti·bal·lis·tic missile \ˌant-i-bə-'lis-tik-, ˌan-ˌtī-\ *n* : a
missile for stopping and destroying ballistic missiles

an·ti·bi·ot·ic \ˌant-i-bī-'ät-ik, ˌan-ˌtī-, ˌant-i-bē-\ *n* : a substance produced by an organism (as a fungus or bacteri-
um) that in dilute solution inhibits or kills a harmful microscopic plant or animal and especially one that causes
disease — **antibiotic** *adj*

an·ti·body \'ant-i-ˌbäd-ē\ *n* : a substance produced by special cells of the body that combines with an antigen and

counteracts its effects or those of the microscopic plant
or animal on which the antigen may occur

¹**an·tic** \'ant-ik\ *n* : a wildly playful or funny act or action

²**antic** *adj* : wildly playful : FROLICSOME

an·tic·i·pate \an-'tis-ə-ˌpāt\ *vb* **-pat·ed; -pat·ing 1** : to
foresee and deal with or provide for beforehand ⟨*antici-*
pated their objections⟩ ⟨*anticipated* my every need⟩ **2**
: to expect especially with pleasure ⟨*anticipate* your visit
next week⟩ [from Latin *anticipatus* "having dealt with
ahead of time," from *anticipare* "anticipate," literally "to
occupy beforehand," from *anti-*, altered form of *ante-*
"before" and *-cipare,* derived from *capere* "to take" —
related to ACCEPT, CAPTURE] — **an·tic·i·pa·tor** \-ˌpāt-ər\
n

an·tic·i·pa·tion \(ˌ)an-ˌtis-ə-'pā-shən\ *n* **1** : an earlier ac-
tion that takes into account and deals with or prevents a
later action **2** : pleasurable expectation **3** : the act of
providing for an expected event or state — **an·tic·i·pa·to·**
ry \an-'tis-ə-pə-ˌtòr-ē, -ˌtór-\ *adj*

an·ti·cli·max \ˌant-i-'klī-ˌmaks\ *n* **1** : a shift in writing or
speaking from an important idea to an unimportant or
silly one **2** : an event, result, or ending that is strikingly
less important than expected — **an·ti·cli·mac·tic** \-klī-
'mak-tik, -klə-\ *adj*

an·ti·cline \'ant-i-ˌklīn\
n : an arch of rock ar-
ranged in layers that
bend downward in op-
posite directions from
the top — compare
SYNCLINE

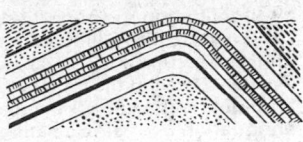

anticline

an·ti·cy·clone \ˌant-i-
'sī-ˌklōn\ *n* : a system
of winds that rotates about a center of high atmospheric
pressure clockwise in the northern hemisphere, that usually advances at 20 to 30 miles (about 30 to 50 kilometers)
per hour, and that usually has a diameter of 1500 to 2500
miles (about 2400 to 4000 kilometers) — **an·ti·cy·clon·ic**
\-sī-'klän-ik\ *adj*

an·ti·dote \'ant-i-ˌdōt\ *n* : a remedy to counteract the effects of poison — **an·ti·dot·al** \ˌant-i-'dōt-ᵊl\ *adj* — **an·ti·**
dot·al·ly \-ᵊl-ē\ *adv*

an·ti·drug \'an-ˌtī-ˌdrəg\ *adj* : acting against or opposing
illegal drugs ⟨*antidrug* programs⟩

an·ti–fed·er·al·ist \ˌant-i-'fed-(ə)re-ləst\ *n, often cap A&F*
: a member of the group that opposed the adoption of the
U.S. Constitution

an·ti·freeze \'ant-i-ˌfrēz\ *n* : a substance added to a liquid
(as the water in an automobile radiator) to prevent freezing

an·ti·gen \'ant-i-jən, -ˌjen\ *n* : a substance (as a protein)
that causes the body to form antibodies against it when it
is introduced into the body either alone or as part of a
microscopic plant or animal — **an·ti·gen·ic** \ˌant-i-'jen-
ik\ *adj*

an·ti·his·ta·mine \ˌant-i-'his-tə-ˌmēn, -mən, ˌan-ˌtī-\ *n*
: any of various drugs used for treating allergic reactions
and cold symptoms

an·ti·knock \ˌant-i-'näk, ˌan-ˌtī-\ *n* : a substance that is
added to the fuel of an internal combustion engine to
help prevent knocking

an·ti·lock \'an-ˌtī-ˌläk, 'an-ti-\ *adj* : being a braking system
for a motor vehicle designed to keep the wheels from
locking and skidding

an·ti·ma·lar·i·al \ˌant-i-mə-'ler-ē-əl, ˌan-ˌtī-\ *adj* : serving
to prevent, control, or cure malaria — **antimalarial** *n*

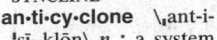

\ə\ abut	\aù\ out	\i\ tip	\ò\ saw	\ù\ foot
\ər\ further	\ch\ chin	\ī\ life	\òi\ coin	\y\ yet
\a\ mat	\e\ pet	\j\ job	\th\ thin	\yü\ few
\ā\ take	\ē\ easy	\ŋ\ sing	\t̲h̲\ this	\yù\ cure
\ä\ cot, cart	\g\ go	\ō\ bone	\ü\ food	\zh\ vision

an·ti·mat·ter \'ant-i-ˌmat-ər\ *n* : matter whose parts match parts of ordinary matter except in having some opposite properties (as a positive instead of a negative charge)

an·ti·mo·ny \'ant-ə-ˌmō-nē\ *n* : a metallic silvery white element that is used especially in alloys and medicine — see ELEMENT table

an·ti·neu·tron \ˌant-i-'n(y)ü-ˌträn, ˌan-ˌtī-\ *n* : the uncharged part of antimatter that is related to the neutron

an·ti·ox·i·dant \ˌant-ē-'äk-səd-ənt, ˌan-ˌtī-\ *n* : a substance that opposes oxidation or prevents or makes difficult reactions made easier by oxygen

an·ti·par·ti·cle \'ant-i-ˌpärt-i-kəl, 'an-ˌtī-\ *n* : an elementary particle identical to another elementary particle in mass but opposite to it in electric or magnetic properties

an·tip·a·thy \an-'tip-ə-thē\ *n, pl* **-thies** 1 : a strong dislike 2 : a person or thing that arouses strong dislike — **an·ti·pa·thet·ic** \ˌant-i-pə-'thet-ik\ *adj*

an·ti·per·spi·rant \ˌant-i-'pər-sp(ə-)rənt, ˌan-ˌtī-\ *n* : a preparation used to stop or reduce perspiration

an·ti·pode \'ant-ə-ˌpōd\ *n, pl* **an·tip·o·des** \an-'tip-ə-ˌdēz\ 1 : the parts of the earth opposite each other at a distance of the earth's diameter — usually used in plural 2 : the exact opposite — **an·tip·o·dal** \an-'tip-əd-ᵊl\ *adj* — **an·tip·o·de·an** \ˌ(ˌ)an-tip-ə-'dē-ən\ *adj*

an·ti·pol·lu·tion \ˌant-i-pə-'lü-shən, ˌan-ˌtī-\ *adj* : designed to stop or reduce pollution ⟨*antipollution* laws⟩

an·ti·pro·ton \ˌant-i-'prō-ˌtän, ˌan-ˌtī-\ *n* : the part of antimatter related to the proton

¹an·ti·quar·i·an \ˌant-ə-'kwer-ē-ən\ *n* : ANTIQUARY

²antiquarian *adj* : of or relating to antiquaries or antiquities

an·ti·quary \'ant-ə-ˌkwer-ē\ *n, pl* **-quar·ies** : a person who collects or studies antiquities

an·ti·quate \'ant-ə-ˌkwāt\ *vb* **-quat·ed; -quat·ing** : to make old or obsolete — **an·ti·qua·tion** \ˌant-ə-'kwā-shən\ *n*

an·ti·quat·ed \'ant-ə-ˌkwāt-əd\ *adj* 1 : OBSOLETE 1 2 : OLD-FASHIONED 1, OUTMODED ⟨*antiquated* methods of farming⟩ 3 : advanced in age

¹an·tique \an-'tēk\ *n* : an object of an earlier period; *esp* : a work of art, piece of furniture, or decorative object made at an earlier period

²antique *adj* 1 : belonging to antiquity 2 : belonging to earlier periods ⟨*antique* furniture⟩ 3 : belonging to or resembling a former style or fashion ⟨silver of an *antique* design⟩ *synonyms* see OLD

an·tiq·ui·ty \an-'tik-wət-ē\ *n, pl* **-ties** 1 : ancient times; *esp* : those before the Middle Ages 2 : very great age 3 *pl* : objects or monuments from ancient times

¹an·ti·sep·tic \ˌant-ə-'sep-tik\ *adj* 1 : killing or preventing the growth of germs that cause disease or decay 2 : relating to or characterized by the use of antiseptic substances — **an·ti·sep·ti·cal·ly** \-ti-k(ə-)lē\ *adv*

²antiseptic *n* : a substance that helps stop the growth or action of microorganisms especially in or on living tissue

an·ti·se·rum \'ant-i-ˌsir-əm, 'an-ˌtī-\ *n* : a serum that contains specific antibodies and is used to prevent or cure disease

an·ti·slav·ery \ˌant-i-'slāv-(ə-)rē, ˌan-ˌtī-\ *adj* : opposing slavery

an·ti·so·cial \ˌant-i-'sō-shəl, ˌan-ˌtī-\ *adj* 1 : UNFRIENDLY 1 2 : being against or bad for society; *esp* : being or exhibiting behavior that is very different from accepted behavior

an·ti·stat·ic \ˌant-i-'stat-ik, ˌan-ˌtī-\ *adj* : reducing, removing, or preventing the collection of static electricity

an·ti·tank \ˌant-i-'taŋk\ *adj* : designed to destroy or stop tanks

an·tith·e·sis \an-'tith-ə-səs\ *n, pl* **-tith·e·ses** \-'tith-ə-ˌsēz\ : the exact opposite : CONTRARY — **an·ti·thet·i·cal** \ˌant-ə-'thet-i-kəl\ *adj*

an·ti·tox·in \ˌant-i-'täk-sən\ *n* : an antibody that is formed in response to a foreign and usually poisonous substance introduced into the body and that can often be produced in animals for use in treating human diseases (as tetanus) — **an·ti·tox·ic** \-sik\ *adj*

an·ti·ven·in \ˌant-i-'ven-ən, ˌan-ˌtī-\ *n* : a serum containing an antitoxin to a poison of an animal (as a snake)

an·ti·ven·om \ˌant-i-'ven-əm, ˌan-ˌtī-\ *n* : ANTIVENIN

ant·ler \'ant-lər\ *n* : the solid often branched horn of a deer or one of its close relatives that is cast off and grown anew each year; *also* : a branch of such horn — **ant·lered** \-lərd\ *adj* — **ant·ler·less** \-ləs\ *adj*

ant lion *n* : a four-winged insect that when a larva digs a cone-shaped pit in which it lies in wait to catch insects (as ants) on which it feeds

ant·onym \'ant-ə-ˌnim\ *n* : a word of opposite meaning ⟨"hot" and "cold" are *antonyms*⟩ — **an·ton·y·mous** \an-'tän-ə-məs\ *adj*

ant·sy \'ant-sē\ *adj* : RESTLESS 3, IMPATIENT

anus \'ā-nəs\ *n* : the lower or posterior opening of the alimentary canal

an·vil \'an-vəl\ *n* 1 : a heavy iron block on which metal is shaped (as by hammering) 2 : the middle bone of the chain of three small bones in the ear of a mammal — called also *incus*

anx·i·ety \aŋ-'zī-ət-ē\ *n, pl* **-eties** 1 : fear or nervousness about what might happen 2 : fearful concern or interest ⟨*anxiety* to succeed⟩

anx·ious \'aŋ(k)-shəs\ *adj* 1 : afraid or nervous about what may happen : WORRIED ⟨*anxious* about their son's health⟩ 2 : desiring earnestly ⟨*anxious* to make good⟩ *synonyms* see EAGER — **anx·ious·ly** *adv* — **anx·ious·ness** *n*

anvil 1

¹any \'en-ē\ *adj* 1 : one taken at random ⟨*any* person you meet⟩ 2 : EVERY 1 ⟨*any* child knows that⟩ 3 : of whatever number or amount ⟨haven't *any* money⟩

²any *pron sing or pl* 1 : any individuals ⟨are *any* of you ready⟩ 2 : any number or amount ⟨there isn't *any* left⟩

³any *adv* : to the least amount or degree ⟨can't get it *any* clearer⟩ ⟨was never *any* good⟩

any·body \'en-ē-ˌbäd-ē, -bəd-ē\ *pron* : ANYONE

any·how \'en-ē-ˌhaů\ *adv* 1 : in any way, manner, or order 2 : without regard to or in spite of other considerations : in any case

any·more \ˌen-ē-'mō(ə)r, -'mó(ə)r\ *adv* : at the present time : NOWADAYS ⟨never see them *anymore*⟩

any·one \'en-ē-(ˌ)wən\ *pron* : any person at all

any·place \'en-ē-ˌplās\ *adv* : ANYWHERE

any·thing \'en-ē-ˌthiŋ\ *pron* : a thing of any kind

any·way \'en-ē-ˌwā\ *adv* : ANYHOW

any·where \'en-ē-ˌ(h)we(ə)r, -ˌ(h)wa(ə)r\ *adv* : in, at, or to any place

any·wise \'en-ē-ˌwīz\ *adv* : in any way whatever

A–OK \ˌā-(ˌ)ō-'kā\ *adv or adj* : very well or fine

A1 \'ā-'wən\ *adj* : of the very best kind

aor·ta \ā-'ȯrt-ə\ *n, pl* **aortas** *or* **aor·tae** \-'ȯrt-ē\ : the main artery that carries blood from the heart to branch arteries by which it is carried throughout the body — **aor·tic** \-'ȯrt-ik\ *adj*

aou·dad \'aů-ˌdad, 'ä-ủ-\ *n* : a wild sheep of North Africa

¹ap- — see AD-

²ap- — see APO-

aoudad

apace \ə-'pās\ *adv* : at a quick pace : FAST

Apache \ə-'pach-ē\ *n, pl* **Apache** *or* **Apaches** : a member of a group of American Indian peoples of the American Southwest

¹apart \ə-'pärt\ *adv* **1** : away from each other ⟨towns five miles *apart*⟩ **2** : as a separate unit : SEPARATELY ⟨considered *apart* from other points⟩ **3** : in or into two or more parts : to pieces ⟨took the clock *apart*⟩ **4** : one from another ⟨can't tell the twins *apart*⟩

²apart *adj* : separate from others ⟨in a place *apart*⟩ — **apart·ness** *n*

apart·heid \ə-'pär-,tāt, -,tīt\ *n* : racial segregation; *esp* : a policy of racial segregation formerly practiced in the Republic of South Africa

apart·ment \ə-'pärt-mənt\ *n* **1** : a room or set of rooms used as a dwelling **2** : APARTMENT BUILDING

apartment building *n* : a building containing several individual apartments

ap·a·thet·ic \,ap-ə-'thet-ik\ *adj* : having or showing little or no feeling or interest — **ap·a·thet·i·cal·ly** \-'thet-i-k(ə-)lē\ *adv*

ap·a·thy \'ap-ə-thē\ *n* : lack of feeling or of interest

ap·a·tite \'ap-ə-,tīt\ *n* : any of a group of variously colored minerals that are phosphates of calcium and that are used as a source of phosphorus and its compounds

apato·sau·rus \ə-,pat-ə-'sȯr-əs\ *n* : BRONTOSAURUS

¹ape \'āp\ *n* **1 a** : ¹MONKEY 1; *esp* : one of the larger tailless or short-tailed forms   **b** : any of two families of large primates including the chimpanzee, gorilla, orangutan, and gibbon **2** : ³MIMIC 1 **3** : a large uncouth person

²ape *vb* **aped; ap·ing** : to copy closely but often clumsily *synonyms* see IMITATE — **ap·er** *n*

ape—man \'āp-,man, -,man\ *n* : a primate (as an australopithecine) between human beings and the higher apes in character

ap·er·ture \'ap-ə(r)-,chú(ə)r, -chər\ *n* **1** : an opening or open space : HOLE **2 a** : the opening in a camera lens that allows light through   **b** : the diameter of the opening in a camera lens

apex \'ā-,peks\ *n, pl* **apex·es** *or* **api·ces** \'ā-pə-,sēz, 'ap-ə-\ **1** : the uppermost point : TOP ⟨*apex* of a mountain⟩ **2** : ⁴TIP 1 ⟨*apex* of the tongue⟩ **3** : the highest point ⟨at the *apex* of her career⟩

aph·elion \a-'fēl-yən\ *n, pl* **aph·elia** \-yə\ : the point in the orbit of a heavenly body (as a planet) that is farthest from the sun

aphid \'ā-fəd *also* 'af-əd\ *n* : any of numerous small soft-bodied insects that suck the juices of plants

aphid lion *n* : any of several insect larvae (as a lacewing or ladybug larva) that feed on aphids

aphis \'ā-fəs, 'af-əs\ *n, pl* **aphi·des** \'ā-fə-,dēz, 'af-ə-\ : APHID

aph·o·rism \'af-ə-,riz-əm\ *n* : a short statement of a general truth or idea — **aph·o·rist** \-rəst\ *n* — **aph·o·ris·tic** \,af-ə-'ris-tik\ *adj* — **aph·o·ris·ti·cal·ly** \-ti-k(ə-)lē\ *adv*

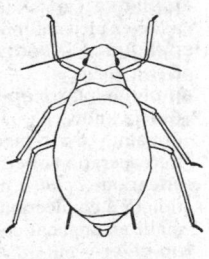

aphid

api·ary \'ā-pē-,er-ē\ *n, pl* **-ar·ies** : a place where bees are kept; *esp* : a collection of hives of bees kept for their honey — **api·a·rist** \'ā-pē-ə-rəst\ *n*

apiece \ə-'pēs\ *adv* : for each one

ap·ish \'ā-pish\ *adj* **1** : very silly ⟨*apish* antics⟩ **2** : imitating closely — **ap·ish·ly** *adv* — **ap·ish·ness** *n*

aplomb \ə-'pläm, -'pləm\ *n* : complete freedom from nervousness or uncertainty

apo- *or* **ap-** *prefix* : away from : off ⟨*aphelion*⟩ [from Greek *apo* "away, off"]

Apoc·a·lypse \ə-'päk-ə-,lips\ *n* — see BIBLE table

Apoc·ry·pha \ə-'päk-rə-fə\ *n sing or pl* — see BIBLE table

apo·gee \'ap-ə-(,)jē\ *n* : the point farthest from the center of a heavenly body (as the earth or the moon) reached by an object (as a satellite) orbiting it — compare PERIGEE

apol·o·get·ic \ə-,päl-ə-'jet-ik\ *adj* **1** : offered by way of apology ⟨an *apologetic* smile⟩ **2** : sorry for having done something wrong ⟨they were *apologetic* about the mistake⟩ — **apol·o·get·i·cal·ly** \-'jet-i-k(ə-)lē\ *adv*

apol·o·gist \ə-'päl-ə-jəst\ *n* : one who speaks or writes in defense of a faith, cause, or institution

apol·o·gize \ə-'päl-ə-,jīz\ *vb* **-gized; -giz·ing** : to make an apology — **apol·o·giz·er** *n*

apol·o·gy \ə-'päl-ə-jē\ *n, pl* **-gies** **1** : an expression of regret (as for a mistake or a discourtesy) **2** : a poor substitute

ap·o·plec·tic \,ap-ə-'plek-tik\ *adj* **1** : of, relating to, or caused by stroke ⟨*apoplectic* symptoms⟩ **2** : affected with or inclined to stroke ⟨*apoplectic* patients⟩ **3** : seeming likely to cause stroke ⟨an *apoplectic* rage⟩; *also* : very excited or angry ⟨was *apoplectic* over the news⟩

ap·o·plexy \'ap-ə-,plek-sē\ *n, pl* **-plex·ies** : ²STROKE 5

apos·ta·sy \ə-'päs-tə-sē\ *n, pl* **-sies** : a giving up of a religious faith or a previous loyalty

apos·tate \ə-'päs-,tāt, -tət\ *n* : one who commits apostasy — **apostate** *adj*

apos·tle \ə-'päs-əl\ *n* **1 a** : one of a group made up of Christ's twelve original disciples and Paul **b** : the first Christian missionary to a region **2 a** : the person who first puts forward an important belief or starts a great reform **b** : a loyal supporter : ADHERENT [Middle English *apostle* "teacher sent out by Christ," from Old English *apostol* and early French *apostle* (both, same meaning), derived from Greek *apostolos* "one sent on a mission"] — **apos·tle·ship** \-,ship\ *n*

ap·os·tol·ic \,ap-ə-'stäl-ik\ *adj* **1** : of or relating to an apostle or the apostles **2** : PAPAL

¹apos·tro·phe \ə-'päs-trə-(,)fē\ *n* : the addressing of an absent person as if present or of an object or abstract idea as if capable of understanding (as in "O grave, where is thy victory?")

²apostrophe *n* : a mark ' used to show that letters or figures are missing (as in *can't* for *cannot* or *'76* for *1776*) or to show the possessive case (as in *Steven's*) or the plural of letters or figures (as in "cross your *t's*")

apoth·e·car·ies' measure \ə-'päth-ə-,ker-ēz-\ *n* : a measure of capacity used chiefly by pharmacists

apothecaries' weight *n* : a system of weights used chiefly by pharmacists — see MEASURE table

apoth·e·cary \ə-'päth-ə-,ker-ē\ *n, pl* **-car·ies** : DRUGGIST

app \'ap\ *n* : APPLICATION 6

ap·pall \ə-'pȯl\ *vb* : to overcome or shock with horror ⟨we were *appalled* by his rude behavior⟩

ap·pall·ing \ə-'pȯl-iŋ\ *adj* : inspiring horror or dismay : SHOCKING — **ap·pall·ing·ly** *adv*

Ap·pa·loo·sa \,ap-ə-'lü-sə\ *n* : any of a breed of saddle horses developed in western North America that have small dark spots on a white or solid-colored coat

ap·pa·nage \'ap-ə-nij\ *n* **1** : a grant (as of land) made by a ruler to a member of the royal family **2** : a customary right or privilege

ap·pa·ra·tus \,ap-ə-'rat-əs, -'rät-əs\ *n, pl* **-tus·es** *or*

Appaloosa

\ə\ **abut**	\aú\ **out**	\i\ **tip**	\ȯ\ **saw**	\ú\ **foot**
\ər\ **further**	\ch\ **chin**	\ī\ **life**	\ȯi\ **coin**	\y\ **yet**
\a\ **mat**	\e\ **pet**	\j\ **job**	\th\ **thin**	\yú\ **few**
\ā\ **take**	\ē\ **easy**	\ŋ\ **sing**	\th\ **this**	\yü\ **cure**
\ä\ **cot, cart**	\g\ **go**	\ō\ **bone**	\ü\ **food**	\zh\ **vision**

-tus 1 : the equipment or material for a particular use or job ⟨laboratory *apparatus*⟩ **2** : a complicated instrument or device

ap·par·el \ə-'par-əl\ *n* : things that are worn : CLOTHING

ap·par·ent \ə-'par-ənt, -'per-\ *adj* **1** : open to view : VISIBLE **2** : clear to the understanding : EVIDENT ⟨*apparent* that the road was little used⟩ **3** : appearing to be true or real ⟨the *apparent* meaning of the speech⟩

ap·par·ent·ly \ə-'par-ənt-lē, -'per-\ *adv* : it seems apparent : EVIDENTLY ⟨the door had *apparently* been forced open⟩ ⟨*apparently*, we're supposed to wait here⟩

ap·pa·ri·tion \ˌap-ə-'rish-ən\ *n* **1** : an unusual or unexpected sight **2** : GHOST

¹ap·peal \ə-'pē(ə)l\ *n* **1** : a legal proceeding by which a case is brought to a higher court for review **2** : an asking for something badly needed or wanted : PLEA ⟨an *appeal* for help⟩ **3** : the power to cause enjoyment : ATTRACTION ⟨movies had a great *appeal* for him⟩

²appeal *vb* **1** : to make a legal appeal **2** : to call upon another for a decision ⟨*appealed* to the umpire⟩ **3** : to ask for something badly needed or wanted **4** : to be pleasing or attractive ⟨the idea *appeals* to her⟩

ap·pear \ə-'pi(ə)r\ *vb* **1** : to come into sight : become plain : SHOW ⟨stars *appeared* in the sky⟩ **2** : to present oneself formally (as to answer a charge) ⟨*appear* in court⟩ **3** : SEEM 1, LOOK ⟨things are not always as they *appear*⟩ ⟨*appears* to be tired⟩ **4** : to come before the public ⟨*appears* on television⟩

ap·pear·ance \ə-'pir-ən(t)s\ *n* **1** : the way someone or something looks ⟨the room has a cool *appearance*⟩ ⟨gave every *appearance* of being healthy⟩ ⟨keep up *appearances*⟩ **2** : the act, process, or an instance of appearing **3** : something that appears

ap·pease \ə-'pēz\ *vb* **ap·peased; ap·peas·ing 1** : to make calm or quiet **2** : to make less severe : RELIEVE ⟨*appeased* my hunger⟩ **3** : to give in to even when it is wrong to do so [Middle English *appesen* "to appease," from early French *apaiser* (same meaning), from *a-* "to" and *pais* "peace," from Latin *pac-, pax* "peace" — related to PACIFY, PEACE] *synonyms* see PACIFY — **ap·pease·ment** \-mənt\ *n* — **ap·peas·er** *n*

ap·pel·lant \ə-'pel-ənt\ *n* : one that appeals; *esp* : one that appeals a judicial decision

ap·pel·late \ə-'pel-ət\ *adj* : having the power to review the decisions of a lower court ⟨an *appellate* court⟩

ap·pel·la·tion \ˌap-ə-'lā-shən\ *n* : an identifying or descriptive name or title

ap·pel·lee \ˌap-ə-'lē\ *n* : one against whom an appeal is taken

ap·pend \ə-'pend\ *vb* : to add as something extra ⟨*append* a postscript to a letter⟩

ap·pend·age \ə-'pen-dij\ *n* **1** : something attached to a larger or more important thing **2** : a projecting part (as an antenna) of an animal or plant body; *esp* : an arm, leg, or similar part

ap·pen·dec·to·my \ˌap-ən-'dek-tə-mē, ˌap-ˌen-\ *n, pl* **-mies** : surgical removal of the human appendix

ap·pen·di·ci·tis \ə-ˌpen-də-'sīt-əs\ *n* : inflammation of the appendix

ap·pen·dix \ə-'pen-diks\ *n, pl* **-dix·es** *or* **-di·ces** \-də-ˌsēz\ **1** : additional material attached at the end of a piece of writing **2** : a small tube that is closed at one end and projects from the pouch marking the beginning of the large intestine in the lower right side of the abdomen

ap·per·tain \ˌap-ər-'tān\ *vb* : PERTAIN 1

ap·pe·tite \'ap-ə-ˌtīt\ *n* **1** : a natural desire especially for food **2** : ²TASTE 4 ⟨an *appetite* for adventure⟩

ap·pe·tiz·er \'ap-ə-ˌtī-zər\ *n* **1** : a food or drink usually served before a meal to make one hungrier **2** : something that creates a desire for more

ap·pe·tiz·ing \'ap-ə-ˌtī-ziŋ\ *adj* : appealing to the appetite — **ap·pe·tiz·ing·ly** *adv*

ap·plaud \ə-'plȯd\ *vb* **1** : PRAISE 1, APPROVE ⟨*applaud* their efforts⟩ **2** : to show approval especially by clapping the hands [from early French *aplaudir* "to applaud," from Latin *applaudere* (same meaning), from *ap-, ad-* "to, toward" and *plaudere* "to clap" — related to EXPLODE, PLAUDIT, PLAUSIBLE; see *Word History* at EXPLODE, PLAUSIBLE] — **ap·plaud·able** \-ə-bəl\ *adj* — **ap·plaud·er** *n*

ap·plause \ə-'plȯz\ *n* : approval shown especially by clapping the hands

ap·ple \'ap-əl\ *n* : a rounded fruit with a red, yellow, or green skin, firm white flesh and a seedy core; *also* : the tree of the rose family that bears this fruit

ap·ple–pie \ˌap-əl-ˌpī\ *adj* : just right : PERFECT ⟨in *apple-pie* order⟩

ap·ple·sauce \-ˌsȯs\ *n* : a sauce or dessert made of sweetened stewed apples

ap·plet \'ap-lət\ *n* : a small computer application

ap·pli·ance \ə-'plī-ən(t)s\ *n* **1** : a piece of equipment for making a tool or machine suitable for a special purpose : ATTACHMENT **2** : a device designed for a particular use ⟨a fire-fighting *appliance*⟩ ⟨an *appliance* serving as an artificial arm⟩ **3** : a household device (as a stove, fan, or refrigerator) or piece of office equipment that runs on gas or electricity

ap·pli·ca·ble \'ap-li-kə-bəl *also* ə-'plik-ə-\ *adj* : capable of being put to use or put into practice : APPROPRIATE — **ap·pli·ca·bil·i·ty** \ˌap-li-kə-'bil-ət-ē *also* ə-ˌplik-ə-\ *n*

ap·pli·cant \'ap-li-kənt\ *n* : one who applies for something ⟨an *applicant* for work⟩

ap·pli·ca·tion \ˌap-lə-'kā-shən\ *n* **1 a** : an act of applying ⟨*application* of paint to a house⟩ **b** : an act of putting to use ⟨*application* of a new method⟩ **c** : the use to which something is put **2** : ability to fix one's attention on a task **3 a** : a request made personally or in writing ⟨an *application* for a job⟩ **b** : a form used for making a request ⟨fill out a job *application*⟩ **4** : something put or spread on a surface ⟨hot *applications* on a sprained ankle⟩ **5** : ability to be put to practical use **6** : a computer program that performs one of the major tasks for which a computer is used

ap·pli·ca·tor \'ap-lə-ˌkāt-ər\ *n* : a device for applying a substance (as medicine or polish)

ap·plied \ə-'plīd\ *adj* : put to use in practice or action; *esp* : applying general principles to solve problems that have clear limits ⟨*applied* sciences⟩

¹ap·pli·qué \ˌap-lə-'kā\ *n* : a cutout decoration fastened to a larger piece of material

²appliqué *vb* **-quéd; -qué·ing** : to apply an appliqué to a larger surface

ap·ply \ə-'plī\ *vb* **ap·plied; ap·ply·ing 1 a** : to put to use ⟨*apply* knowledge⟩ **b** : to lay or spread on ⟨*apply* a coat of paint⟩ **c** : to place in contact ⟨*apply* heat⟩ **d** : to put into operation or effect ⟨*apply* a law⟩ **2** : to give one's full attention ⟨*applied* myself to the work⟩ **3** : to have relation or a connection ⟨this law *applies* to everyone⟩ **4** : to make an application : make a request ⟨*apply* for a job⟩ — **ap·pli·er** \-'plī-(ə)r\ *n*

ap·point \ə-'pȯint\ *vb* **1** : to decide on usually from a position of authority ⟨the teacher *appointed* a time for our meeting⟩ **2** : to choose for some job or offices ⟨I was *appointed* to wash the dishes⟩ ⟨the school board *appointed* three new teachers⟩ ⟨the president *appoints* a cabinet⟩

ap·point·ed \ə-'pȯin-təd\ *adj* : provided with furnishings and equipment ⟨a well-*appointed* house⟩

ap·poin·tee \ə-ˌpȯin-'tē, ˌa-ˌpȯin-\ *n* : a person appointed to a position or an office

ap·point·ive \ə-'pȯint-iv\ *adj* : of, relating to, or filled by appointment ⟨an *appointive* office⟩

ap·point·ment \ə-'pȯint-mənt\ *n* **1** : the act or an instance of appointing ⟨holds office by *appointment*⟩ **2** : a position or office to which a person is named ⟨holds an *ap-*

pointment from the president⟩ **3** : an agreement to meet at a fixed time ⟨an *appointment* with the dentist⟩ **4** : FURNISHINGS — usually used in plural

ap·por·tion \ə-'pōr-shən, -'por-\ *vb* **-tioned; -tion·ing** \-sh(ə-)niŋ\ : to divide and distribute in proportion — **ap·por·tion·ment** \-shən-mənt\ *n*

ap·po·site \'ap-ə-zət\ *adj* : highly appropriate : PERTINENT, APT ⟨*apposite* remarks⟩ — **ap·po·site·ly** *adv* — **ap·po·site·ness** *n*

ap·po·si·tion \,ap-ə-'zish-ən\ *n* : a grammatical construction in which a noun or noun equivalent is followed by another that explains it ⟨in "my friend the doctor," the word "doctor" is in *apposition* with "friend"⟩

¹**ap·pos·i·tive** \ə-'päz-ət-iv, a-\ *adj* : of, relating to, or standing in apposition — **ap·pos·i·tive·ly** *adv*

²**appositive** *n* : the second of a pair of nouns or noun equivalents in apposition

ap·prais·al \ə-'prā-zəl\ *n* : an act or instance of appraising

ap·praise \ə-'prāz\ *vb* **ap·praised; ap·prais·ing** **1** : to set a value on **2** : to judge how good someone or something is — **ap·praise·ment** \-mənt\ *n* — **ap·prais·er** *n*

ap·pre·cia·ble \ə-'prē-shə-bəl, ə-'prish(-ē)-ə-bəl\ *adj* : large enough to be noticed or measured ⟨no *appreciable* difference⟩ — **ap·pre·cia·bly** \-blē\ *adv*

ap·pre·ci·ate \ə-'prē-shē-,āt, ə-'prish-ē-,āt\ *vb* **-at·ed; -at·ing** **1** : to see the worth, quality, or significance of ⟨*appreciate* the difference between right and wrong⟩ **2** : to admire highly ⟨*appreciates* the artist's work⟩ **3** : to be fully aware of ⟨must experience it to *appreciate* it⟩ **4** : to be grateful for ⟨we *appreciate* your help⟩ **5** : to increase in number or value ⟨savings *appreciate* over time⟩ [from Latin *appretiatus* "having put a value on," derived from *ap-, ad-* "to" and *pretium* "price" — related to PRICE] — **ap·pre·ci·a·tion** \ə-,prē-shē-'ā-shən, -,prish-ē-\ — **ap·pre·cia·tive** \ə-'prē-shət-iv, -,prish-ət-\ *adj* — **ap·pre·cia·tive·ly** *adv* — **ap·pre·cia·tive·ness** *n*

ap·pre·hend \,ap-ri-'hend\ *vb* **1** : ¹ARREST 2 ⟨*apprehend* a burglar⟩ **2** : to look forward to with fear and uncertainty **3** : UNDERSTAND 1a

ap·pre·hen·sion \,ap-ri-'hen-chən\ *n* **1** : ²ARREST 2 **2** : an understanding of something **3** : fear of or uncertainty about what may be coming

ap·pre·hen·sive \,ap-ri-'hen(t)-siv\ *adj* : fearful of what may be coming — **ap·pre·hen·sive·ly** *adv* — **ap·pre·hen·sive·ness** *n*

¹**ap·pren·tice** \ə-'prent-əs\ *n* : a person who is learning a trade or art by experience under a skilled worker

²**apprentice** *vb* **-ticed; -tic·ing** : to set at work as an apprentice

ap·pren·tice·ship \ə-'prent-əs-,ship\ *n* **1** : service as an apprentice **2** : the period during which a person serves as an apprentice

ap·prise \ə-'prīz\ *vb* **ap·prised; ap·pris·ing** : to give notice to : INFORM ⟨*apprised* him of his rights⟩

¹**ap·proach** \ə-'prōch\ *vb* **1** : to come near or nearer **2** : to begin to deal with ⟨*approach* a problem⟩

²**approach** *n* **1** : an act or instance of approaching **2** : a beginning step toward an end **3** : way of dealing with something ⟨try a new *approach*⟩ **4** : a way (as a path or road) to get to some place

ap·proach·able \ə-'prō-chə-bəl\ *adj* : easy to meet or deal with ⟨a friendly and *approachable* teacher⟩ — **ap·pro·ach·abil·i·ty** \-,prō-chə-'bil-ət-ē\ *n*

ap·pro·ba·tion \,ap-rə-'bā-shən\ *n* : APPROVAL

¹**ap·pro·pri·ate** \ə-'prō-prē-,āt\ *vb* **-at·ed; -at·ing** **1** : to take for one's own often without right **2** : to set apart for a particular purpose or use ⟨*appropriate* funds for research⟩

²**ap·pro·pri·ate** \ə-'prō-prē-ət\ *adj* : especially suitable or fitting **synonyms** see FIT — **ap·pro·pri·ate·ly** *adv* — **ap·pro·pri·ate·ness** *n*

ap·pro·pri·a·tion \ə-,prō-prē-'ā-shən\ *n* **1** : an act or instance of appropriating **2** : a sum of money appropriated for a specific use

ap·prov·al \ə-'prü-vəl\ *n* : an act or instance of approving — **on approval** : for a customer to buy or send back ⟨goods sent *on approval*⟩

ap·prove \ə-'prüv\ *vb* **ap·proved; ap·prov·ing** **1** : to think well of **2** : to accept as satisfactory — **ap·prov·ing·ly** \-'prü-viŋ-lē\ *adv*

¹**ap·prox·i·mate** \ə-'präk-sə-mət\ *adj* : nearly correct or exact ⟨the *approximate* cost⟩ ⟨*approximate* rhyme⟩

²**ap·prox·i·mate** \ə-'präk-sə-,māt\ *vb* **-mat·ed; -mat·ing** **1** : to bring near or close **2** : to come near in position, value, or characteristics : APPROACH ⟨tried to *approximate* the singer's style⟩

ap·prox·i·mate·ly \-mət-lē\ *adv* : reasonably close to ⟨*approximately* 5 miles⟩ ⟨at *approximately* six o'clock⟩

ap·prox·i·ma·tion \ə-,präk-sə-'mā-shən\ *n* **1** : a coming near or close (as in value) **2** : something approximate; *esp* : an estimate or figure that is almost exact

apri·cot \'ap-rə-,kät, 'ā-prə-\ *n* : an oval orange-colored fruit resembling the related peach and plum in flavor; *also* : a tree that bears apricots

April \'ā-prəl\ *n* : the 4th month of the year

Word History The English word *April* comes from the Latin *Aprilis,* the name given to the month by the ancient Romans. No one knows for certain why the Romans named it as they did. Some Roman authors thought that *Aprilis* was related to the Latin verb *aperire* meaning "to open," because April "opened" the buds of leaves and flowers. A more likely theory is that the name was based on *Apru,* an Etruscan form of the name of the Greek goddess Aphrodite. [Middle English *April* "April," from early French *avrill* and Latin *Aprilis* (both meaning "April")]

April fool *n* : one who is tricked on April Fools' Day

April Fools' Day *also* **April Fool's Day** : April 1 on which many people like to play practical jokes

apron \'ā-prən, -pərn\ *n* **1** : a garment worn on the front of the body to keep the clothing from getting dirty **2** : something that suggests or resembles an apron in shape, position, or use: **a** : the part of the stage in front of the curtain **b** : the paved part of an airport next to the terminal area or hangars [from Middle English *napron* "protective garment" (*a napron* was mistaken for *an apron*), derived from early French *nape* "cloth," from Latin *mappa* "napkin" — related to MAP, NAPKIN]

¹**ap·ro·pos** \,ap-rə-'pō, 'ap-rə-,pō\ *adv* : at the right time

²**apropos** *adj* : being to the point : PERTINENT

apropos of *prep* : CONCERNING

apse \'aps\ *n* : a part of a building (as a church) that sticks out from one end of the building, is usually semicircular, has an arched roof, and is often richly decorated especially in Gothic churches

apt \'apt\ *adj* **1** : just right; *esp* : being to the point : RELEVANT ⟨an *apt* remark⟩ **2** : having a tendency : INCLINED, LIKELY ⟨*apt* to become angry⟩ **3** : quick to learn ⟨an *apt* pupil⟩ [Middle English *apt* "suitable," from Latin *aptus* "apt, fit" — related to ADAPT] **synonyms** see QUICK — **apt·ly** *adv* — **apt·ness** \'ap(t)-nəs\ *n*

ap·ti·tude \'ap-tə-,t(y)üd\ *n* **1** : ability to learn : APTNESS **2** : a natural ability ⟨an *aptitude* for mathematics⟩ **synonyms** see ABILITY

aqua \'ak-wə, 'äk-\ *n* : a light greenish blue

aqua·cade \'ak-wə-,kād, 'äk-\ *n* : a water spectacle that consists usually of exhibitions of swimming and diving accompanied by music

\ə\ **abut**	\aú\ **out**	\i\ **tip**	\ò\ **saw**	\ú\ **foot**
\ər\ **further**	\ch\ **chin**	\ī\ **life**	\òi\ **coin**	\y\ **yet**
\a\ **mat**	\e\ **pet**	\j\ **job**	\th\ **thin**	\yü\ **few**
\ā\ **take**	\ē\ **easy**	\ŋ\ **sing**	\th\ **this**	\yú\ **cure**
\ä\ **cot, cart**	\g\ **go**	\ō\ **bone**	\ü\ **food**	\zh\ **vision**

aqua·cul·ture \'ak-wə-ˌkəl-ˌchər, äk-\ *n* : the cultivation of living things (as fish or shellfish) naturally occurring in water — **aqua·cul·tur·ist** \-ˈkəlch-(ə-)rəst\ *n*

aqua·ma·rine \ˌak-wə-mə-ˈrēn, ˌäk-\ *n* **1** : a transparent beryl that is blue, blue-green, or green **2** : a pale blue to light greenish blue

aqua·naut \'ak-wə-ˌnȯt, 'äk-\ *n* : a person who lives for a long while in an underwater shelter used as a base for research

aqua·plane \'ak-wə-ˌplān, 'äk-\ *n* : a board towed behind a motorboat and ridden by a person standing on it — **aquaplane** *vb* — **aqua·plan·er** *n*

aqua re·gia \ˌak-wə-ˈrē-j(ē-)ə, ˌäk-\ *n* : a mixture of nitric and hydrochloric acids that dissolves gold or platinum

aquar·ist \ə-ˈkwar-əst, -ˈkwer-\ *n* : one who keeps an aquarium

aquar·i·um \ə-ˈkwar-ē-əm, -ˈkwer-\ *n, pl* **-i·ums** *or* **-ia** \-ē-ə\ : a container (as a glass tank) in which living water animals or plants are kept; *also* : an establishment where collections of such animals or plants are kept and shown

Aquar·i·us \ə-ˈkwar-ē-əs, -ˈkwer-\ *n* **1 a** : the 11th sign of the zodiac — see ZODIAC table **b** : a person whose sign of the zodiac is Aquarius **2** : a group of stars between Capricorn and Pisces usually pictured as a man pouring water

¹aquat·ic \ə-ˈkwät-ik, -ˈkwat-\ *adj* **1** : growing or living in or often found in water ⟨*aquatic* animals⟩ **2** : performed in or on water ⟨*aquatic* sports⟩

²aquatic *n* : an aquatic animal or plant

aq·ue·duct \'ak-wə-ˌdəkt\ *n* **1** : an artificial channel for water; *esp* : one for carrying a large quantity of flowing water

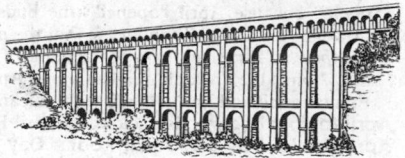

aqueduct 2

2 : a structure that carries the water of a canal across a river or hollow [from Latin *aquaeductus* "aqueduct," from *aquae,* form of *aqua* "water," and *ductus* "act of conducting or leading" — related to DUCT]

aque·ous \'ā-kwē-əs, 'ak-wē-\ *adj* **1 a** : of, relating to, or resembling water **b** : made from, by, or with water ⟨an *aqueous* solution⟩ **2** : of or relating to the aqueous humor

aqueous humor *n* : a clear fluid between the lens and the cornea of the eye

aqui·fer \'ak-wə-fər, 'äk-\ *n* : a water-bearing layer of rock, sand, or gravel capable of absorbing water — **aquif·er·ous** \a-ˈkwif-ə-rəs, ä-\ *adj*

aq·ui·line \'ak-wə-ˌlīn, -lən\ *adj* **1** : of or resembling an eagle **2** : curving like an eagle's beak ⟨an *aquiline* nose⟩ — **aq·ui·lin·i·ty** \ˌak-wə-ˈlin-ət-ē\ *n*

-ar \ər *also* ˌär\ *adj suffix* : of or relating to ⟨molecul*ar*⟩ : being ⟨spectacul*ar*⟩ : resembling ⟨oracul*ar*⟩ [derived from Latin *-aris* (adjective suffix)]

Ar·ab \'ar-əb\ *n* **1 a** : a member of the Semitic people of the Arabian Peninsula **b** : a member of an Arabic-speaking people **2** : ARABIAN HORSE — **Arab** *adj*

ar·a·besque \ˌar-ə-ˈbesk\ *n* : an ornament or style of decoration that uses outlines of flowers, leaves, branches, or fruit and sometimes animal and human figures to produce a pattern of lines that cross over one another — **arabesque** *adj*

Ara·bi·an \ə-ˈrā-bē-ən\ *adj* : of, relating to, or characteristic of Arabia or its people — **Arabian** *n*

Arabian camel *n* : DROMEDARY

Arabian horse *n* : a horse of a breed originally used in Arabia and nearby areas and noted for its graceful build, intelligence, and spirit

¹Ar·a·bic \'ar-ə-bik\ *adj* **1** : ARABIAN, ARAB **2** : expressed in or making use of Arabic numerals

²Arabic *n* : a Semitic language that is the chief language of a wide region of southwestern Asia and northern Africa

Arabic numeral *n* : any of the number symbols 1, 2, 3, 4, 5, 6, 7, 8, 9, and 0

ar·a·ble \'ar-ə-bəl\ *adj* : fit for or cultivated by plowing : suitable for producing crops ⟨*arable* soil⟩ — **ar·a·bil·i·ty** \ˌar-ə-ˈbil-ət-ē\ *n*

arach·nid \ə-ˈrak-nəd, -ˌnid\ *n* : any of a class of arthropods including the spiders, scorpions, mites, and ticks and having a segmented body divided into two regions of which the front part bears four pairs of legs but no antennae — **arachnid** *adj*

ara·go·nite \ə-ˈrag-ə-ˌnīt, 'ar-ə-gə-\ *n* : a mineral that is chemically the same as calcite but heavier per unit volume and with different crystalline form

Ar·a·mae·an \ˌar-ə-ˈmē-ən\ *n* **1** : a member of a Semitic people of the 2nd millennium B.C. in Syria and northern Mesopotamia **2** : ARAMAIC — **Aramaean** *adj*

Ar·a·ma·ic \ˌar-ə-ˈmā-ik\ *n* : a Semitic language of the Aramaeans

ar·a·mid \'ar-ə-məd, -ˌmid\ *n* : any of a group of light but very strong heat-resistant synthetic materials used especially in woven fabrics and plastics

Arap·a·ho *or* **Arap·a·hoe** \ə-ˈrap-ə-ˌhō\ *n, pl* **-ho** *or* **-hos** *or* **-hoe** *or* **-hoes** : a member of an American Indian people of the plains region extending from Saskatchewan and Manitoba to New Mexico and Texas

Ar·a·wak \'ar-ə-ˌwäk\ *n, pl* **-wak** *or* **-waks** : a member of an Indian people chiefly of Guyana

ar·bi·ter \'är-bət-ər\ *n* **1** : ARBITRATOR **2** : a person whose judgment or opinion decides what is right or proper ⟨an *arbiter* of⟩

ar·bi·trary \'är-bə-ˌtrer-ē\ *adj* **1** : coming from or given to free exercise of the will without thought of fairness or right ⟨an *arbitrary* punishment⟩ ⟨an *arbitrary* ruler⟩ **2 a** : based on or determined by a person's preference or opinion ⟨an *arbitrary* choice⟩ **b** : seeming to have been chosen by chance ⟨an *arbitrary* sampling⟩ — **ar·bi·trari·ly** \ˌär-bə-ˈtrer-ə-lē\ *adv* — **ar·bi·trari·ness** \'är-bə-ˌtrer-ē-nəs\ *n*

ar·bi·trate \'är-bə-ˌtrāt\ *vb* **-trat·ed; -trat·ing** **1** : to settle a disagreement after hearing the arguments of both sides ⟨*arbitrate* between management and labor⟩ **2** : to refer a dispute to others for settlement : submit to arbitration

ar·bi·tra·tion \ˌär-bə-ˈtrā-shən\ *n* : the act of arbitrating; *esp* : the settling of a dispute in which both sides present their arguments to a third person or group for settlement

ar·bi·tra·tor \'är-bə-ˌtrāt-ər\ *n* : a person chosen to settle differences in a disagreement

ar·bor \'är-bər\ *n* : a shelter of vines or branches or a structure of crossed wood or metal strips covered with climbing shrubs or vines

Arbor Day *n* : a day in April set aside as a day to plant trees

ar·bo·re·al \är-ˈbōr-ē-əl, -ˈbȯr-\ *adj* **1** : of, relating to, or resembling a tree **2** : living in or often found in trees

ar·bo·re·tum \ˌär-bə-ˈrēt-əm\ *n, pl* **-retums** *or* **-re·ta** \-ˈrēt-ə\ : a place where trees and plants are grown for scientific and educational purposes

ar·bor·ist \'är-bə-rəst\ *n* : a specialist in the care of trees

ar·bor·vi·tae \ˌär-bər-ˈvīt-ē\ *n* : any of various evergreen trees and shrubs with closely overlapping scalelike leaves that are often grown for ornament and hedges [modern Latin *arbor vitae,* literally "tree of life"]

ar·bu·tus \är-ˈbyüt-əs\ *n* : TRAILING ARBUTUS

¹arc \'ärk\ *n* **1 a** : something curved **b** : a curved path **2** : a glowing flow of electricity across a gap in a circuit or between electrodes **3** : a continuous portion of a curved line (as part of the circumference of a circle)

²arc *vb* **1** : to form an electric arc **2** : to follow an arc-shaped course

ar·cade \är-'kād\ *n* **1** : a row of arches with the columns that support them **2** : an arched or covered passageway (as between shops) **3** : a place with many games to be played by putting coins in them

arcade 1

arcade game *n* : VIDEO GAME

¹arch \'ärch\ *n* **1** : a usually curved part of a structure that is over an opening and serves as a support **2** : something resembling an arch in form or function; *esp* : either of two portions of the bony structure of the foot that give it flexibility **3** : ARCHWAY [Middle English *arche* "arch," from early French *arche* (same meaning), derived from Latin *arcus* "bow (weapon)"]

²arch *vb* **1** : to cover or provide with an arch **2** : to form into an arch **3** : to take an arch-shaped path

³arch *adj* **1** : PRINCIPAL, CHIEF ⟨an *arch* opponent⟩ **2** : being clever and mischievous ⟨an *arch* look⟩ [from *arch-* (prefix)] — **arch·ly** *adv* — **arch·ness** *n*

arch- *prefix* : chief : principal ⟨*arch*enemy⟩ [derived from Greek *archein* "to begin, rule"]

ar·chaea \är-'kē-ə\ *n pl* : single-celled organisms that are prokaryotes often of harsh environments (as hot springs) and include forms that produce methane

ar·chae·ol·o·gy *or* **ar·che·ol·o·gy** \ˌär-kē-'äl-ə-jē\ *n* : the science that deals with past human life as shown by fossil relics and the monuments and tools left by ancient peoples — **ar·chae·o·log·i·cal** \-kē-ə-'läj-i-kəl\ *adj* — **ar·chae·ol·o·gist** \-kē-'äl-ə-jəst\ *n*

ar·chae·op·ter·yx \ˌär-kē-'äp-tə-riks\ *n* : a primitive extinct bird of the Jurassic period of geological history in Europe having characteristics (as teeth) of a reptile as well as wings and feathers

ar·cha·ic \är-'kā-ik\ *adj* : of, relating to, characteristic of, or surviving from an earlier time; *esp* : no longer in general use ⟨the *archaic* words "methinks" and "saith"⟩ **synonyms** see OLD

ar·cha·ism \'är-kē-ˌiz-əm, -kā-\ *n* **1** : the use of archaic words **2** : an archaic word or expression

arch·an·gel \'ärk-ˌān-jəl\ *n* : an angel of high rank — **arch·an·gel·ic** \ˌärk-ˌan-'jel-ik\ *adj*

arch·bish·op \(')ärch-'bish-əp\ *n* : the bishop of highest rank in a group of dioceses

arch·bish·op·ric \(')ärch-'bish-ə-(ˌ)prik\ *n* : the office or area of authority of an archbishop

arch·dea·con \(')ärch-'dē-kən\ *n* : a church official who assists a bishop

arch·di·o·cese \(')ärch-'dī-ə-səs, -ˌsēz, -ˌsēs\ *n* : the diocese of an archbishop

Ar·che·an *or* **Ar·chae·an** \är-'kē-ən\ *adj* : of, relating to, or being the earliest eon of geological history or the corresponding system of rocks — see GEOLOGIC TIME table — **Archean** *n*

arch·en·e·my \(')ärch-'en-ə-mē\ *n* : a principal enemy

Ar·cheo·zo·ic \ˌär-kē-ə-'zō-ik\ *adj* : ARCHEAN — **Archeozoic** *n*

ar·cher \'är-chər\ *n* : a person who shoots with a bow and arrow

ar·chery \'ärch-(ə-)rē\ *n* : the art, practice, or skill of shooting with bow and arrow

ar·che·type \'är-ki-ˌtīp\ *n* : the original pattern or model from which something is copied — **ar·che·typ·al** \ˌär-ki-'tī-pəl\ *adj*

arch·foe \(ˌ)ärch-'fō\ *n* : a principal foe : ARCHENEMY

ar·chi·epis·co·pal \ˌär-kē-ə-'pis-kə-pəl\ *adj* : of or relating to an archbishop

Ar·chi·me·des' principle \ˌär-kə-'mēd-ēz-\ *n* : a law of fluid mechanics: a body in a fluid is lifted up with a force equal to the weight of the fluid whose place was taken by the body

ar·chi·pel·a·go \ˌär-kə-'pel-ə-ˌgō, ˌär-chə-\ *n, pl* **-goes** *or* **-gos** : a wide stretch of water with many scattered islands; *also* : a group of islands

ar·chi·tect \'är-kə-ˌtekt\ *n* : a person who designs buildings and advises in their construction

ar·chi·tec·ture \'är-kə-ˌtek-chər\ *n* **1** : the art or science of designing and building structures and especially ones that can be lived in **2** : architectural product or work **3** : a method or style of building — **ar·chi·tec·tur·al** \ˌär-kə-'tek-chə-rəl, -'tek-shrəl\ *adj* — **ar·chi·tec·tur·al·ly** \-ē\ *adv*

¹ar·chive \'är-ˌkīv\ *n* **1** : a place in which public records or historical documents are preserved; *also* : the material preserved — usually used in plural **2** : a collection of information

²archive *vb* **ar·chived; ar·chiv·ing** : to file or collect in or as if in an archive ⟨was *archiving* documents⟩

ar·chi·vist \'är-kə-vəst, -ˌkī-\ *n* : a person in charge of archives

arch·ri·val \(ˌ)ärch-'rī-vəl\ *n* : a principal rival

arch·way \'ärch-ˌwā\ *n* : a passage under an arch; *also* : an arch over a passage

-archy \ˌär-kē, *in some words also* ər-kē\ *n combining form, pl* **-archies** : rule : government ⟨matri*archy*⟩ [derived from Greek *archein* "to rule"]

arc lamp *n* : a lamp that produces light when an electric current passes between two hot electrodes surrounded by gas — called also *arc light*

¹arc·tic \'ärk-tik, 'ärt-tik\ *adj* **1** *often cap* : of, relating to, or suitable for use at the north pole or the region around it ⟨*arctic* waters⟩ ⟨*arctic* animals⟩ ⟨*arctic* clothing⟩ **2** : very cold : FRIGID [Middle English *artik* "arctic," derived from Greek *arktikos* "arctic," from *Arktos* "the Bear," name of the most easily recognizable constellation near the north pole of the sky]

²arc·tic \'ärt-tik, 'ärk-tik\ *n* : a rubber overshoe : GALOSH

arctic circle *n, often cap A&C* : the parallel of latitude that is approximately 66½ degrees north of the equator

arctic fox *n* : a small fox of arctic regions having fur that is blue-gray or brownish in summer and white in winter

arctic hare *n* : a large hare of arctic America that is almost completely white in winter

Arc·tu·rus \ärk-'t(y)ur-əs\ *n* : a very large bright star in Boötes that does not appear to move

arctic fox

ar·dent \'ärd-ᵊnt\ *adj* **1** : showing or having warmth of feeling : PASSIONATE ⟨an *ardent* admirer⟩ **2** : ZEALOUS, DEVOTED ⟨an *ardent* supporter⟩ — **ar·dent·ly** *adv*

ar·dor \'ärd-ər\ *n* **1** : a warmth of feeling **2** : great eagerness : ZEAL

ar·du·ous \'ärj-(ə-)wəs\ *adj* : extremely difficult : LABORIOUS ⟨an *arduous* climb⟩ — **ar·du·ous·ly** *adv* — **ar·du·ous·ness** *n*

¹are *present 2nd singular or present plural of* BE [Old English *earun* "are"]

\ə\ **abut**		\aů\ **out**	\i\ **tip**		\ó\ **saw**		\ů\ **foot**
\ər\ **further**		\ch\ **chin**	\ī\ **life**		\ói\ **coin**		\y\ **yet**
\a\ **mat**		\e\ **pet**	\j\ **job**		\th\ **thin**		\yů\ **few**
\ā\ **take**		\ē\ **easy**	\ŋ\ **sing**		\th\ **this**		\yů\ **cure**
\ä\ **cot, cart**		\g\ **go**	\ō\ **bone**		\ü\ **food**		\zh\ **vision**

²are \'a(ə)r, 'e(ə)r, 'är\ *n* — see METRIC SYSTEM table [from French *are* (unit of measure), from Latin *area* "open space, area"]

ar·ea \'ar-ē-ə, 'er-\ *n* **1** : a particular piece of ground or extent of space often set aside for special use ⟨a picnic *area*⟩ ⟨a waiting *area*⟩ **2** : the surface inside a figure or shape; *esp* : the number of unit squares equal to the amount of space the surface covers ⟨a circle with an *area* of 500 square meters⟩ **3** : REGION 2a ⟨a farming *area*⟩ **4** : a field of activity or study **5** : a part of the brain having a particular function (as vision or hearing) [from Latin "open space, threshing floor" — related to AERIE]

area code *n* : a usually three-digit number that represents each telephone service area in a country (as the U.S. or Canada)

area·way \'ar-ē-ə-,wā, 'er-\ *n* : a sunken space providing entrance to and air and light for a basement

are·na \ə-'rē-nə\ *n* **1** : an enclosed area used for public entertainment **2** : a building containing an arena **3** : a field of activity ⟨the political *arena*⟩

aren't \(')ärnt, 'är-ənt\ : are not

are·o·la \ə-'rē-ə-lə\ *n, pl* **-lae** \-,lē\ *or* **-las** : a colored ring (as about the nipple) — **are·o·lar** \-lər\ *adj*

ar·gent \'är-jənt\ *adj* : resembling silver : SILVERY, WHITE

ar·gen·tite \'är-jən-,tīt\ *n* : a dark gray mineral with a metallic luster that is a sulfide of silver and an ore of silver

ar·gil·la·ceous \,är-jə-'lā-shəs\ *adj* : of, relating to, or containing clay or the minerals of clay

ar·gi·nine \'är-jə-,nēn\ *n* : an amino acid that is found in various proteins

Ar·give \'är-,jīv, -,gīv\ *adj* : of or relating to the Greeks or Greece and especially to the city of Argos — **Argive** *n*

ar·gon \'är-,gän\ *n* : a colorless odorless element that is a gas found in the air and in volcanic gases and used especially in electric bulbs — see ELEMENT table

ar·go·naut \'är-gə-,nȯt, -,nät\ *n* **1** *cap* : one of a band of heroes sailing with Jason in search of the Golden Fleece **2** : PAPER NAUTILUS

ar·go·sy \'är-gə-sē\ *n, pl* **-sies** : a large merchant ship

ar·got \'är-gət, -gō\ *n* : a more or less private vocabulary used by a particular class or group

ar·gu·able \'är-gyü-ə-bəl\ *adj* : open to argument, dispute, or question — **ar·gu·ably** \-(ə-)blē\ *adv*

ar·gue \'är-gyü\ *vb* **ar·gued; ar·gu·ing** **1** : to give reasons for or against ⟨*argue* in favor of lowering taxes⟩ **2** : to talk about some matter usually with different points of view ⟨*argue* about politics⟩ **3** : to persuade by giving reasons ⟨tried to *argue* their parents into getting a new car⟩ *synonyms* see DISCUSS — **ar·gu·er** *n*

ar·gu·ment \'är-gyə-mənt\ *n* **1 a** : a reason for or against something **b** : a discussion in which arguments are presented : DEBATE **2** : an angry disagreement : QUARREL

ar·gu·men·ta·tive \,är-gyə-'ment-ət-iv\ *adj* : marked by or given to argument : QUARRELSOME — **ar·gu·men·ta·tive·ly** *adv*

aria \'är-ē-ə\ *n* : a song in an opera sung by a single voice

ar·id \'ar-əd\ *adj* : very dry; *esp* : not having enough rainfall to support agriculture — **arid·i·ty** \ə-'rid-ət-ē, a-\ *n*

Ar·i·es \'er-(ē-),ēz, 'ar-\ *n* **1 a** : the first sign of the zodiac — see ZODIAC table **b** : a person whose sign of the zodiac is Aries **2** : a group of stars between Pisces and Taurus usually pictured as a ram

aright \ə-'rīt\ *adv* : so as to be correct : RIGHTLY ⟨if I remember *aright*⟩

arise \ə-'rīz\ *vb* **arose** \-'rōz\; **aris·en** \-'riz-ən\; **aris·ing** \-'rī-ziŋ\ **1** : to get up from sleep or after lying down ⟨*arising* at dawn⟩ **2 a** : to begin at a source ⟨arteries that *arise* from the aorta⟩ **b** : to come into being or to attention ⟨a question *arose*⟩ **3** : to move upward ⟨mist *arose* from the valley⟩

ar·is·toc·ra·cy \,ar-ə-'stäk-rə-sē\ *n, pl* **-cies** **1** : a government run by a small class of people **2 a** : an upper class

that is usually based on birth and is richer and more powerful than the rest of society **b** : persons thought to be better than the rest of the community

aris·to·crat \ə-'ris-tə-,krat, a-; 'ar-ə-stə-\ *n* **1** : a member of an aristocracy **2** : a person who has habits and ideas like those of the aristocracy — **aris·to·crat·ic** \ə-,ris-tə-'krat-ik, a-,ris-tə-, ,ar-ə-stə-\ *adj* — **aris·to·crat·i·cal·ly** \-i-k(ə-)lē\ *adv*

arith·me·tic \ə-'rith-mə-,tik\ *n* **1** : a branch of mathematics that deals with real numbers and their addition, subtraction, multiplication, and division **2** : an act or method of computing — **ar·ith·met·ic** \,ar-ith-'met-ik\ *or* **ar·ith·met·i·cal** \-'met-i-kəl\ *adj* — **ar·ith·met·i·cal·ly** \-i-k(ə-)lē\ *adv* — **arith·me·ti·cian** \ə-,rith-mə-'tish-ən\ *n*

arithmetic mean \,ar-ith-,met-ik-\ *n* : a number equal to the sum of a set of numbers divided by how many numbers are in the set ⟨the *arithmetic mean* of 3, 4, 6, and 7 is 5⟩

ark \'ärk\ *n* **1** : the ship in which Noah and his family were saved from the Flood **2 a** : a sacred chest in which the ancient Hebrews kept the two tablets of the Law **b** : a place in a synagogue for the scrolls of the Torah

¹arm \'ärm\ *n* **1 a** : a human upper limb; *esp* : the part between the shoulder and wrist **b** : a corresponding limb of a lower vertebrate animal **2** : something resembling an arm in shape or position ⟨an *arm* of the sea⟩ ⟨the *arm* of a chair⟩ **3** : POWER 1a ⟨the long *arm* of the law⟩ **4** : SLEEVE 1 [Old English *earm* "arm"] — **armed** \'ärmd\ *adj* — **arm·less** \'ärm-ləs\ *adj* — **arm·like** \-,līk\ *adj* — **arm in arm** : with arms linked together ⟨walked down the street *arm in arm*⟩

²arm *vb* **1** : to provide with weapons ⟨*arm* a regiment⟩ **2** : to provide with a way of fighting, competing, or succeeding ⟨*armed* herself with facts⟩ **3** : to make ready for action or use ⟨*arm* a bomb⟩

³arm *n* **1 a** : WEAPON; *esp* : FIREARM **b** : a branch of an army **c** : a branch of the military forces **2** *pl* : the designs on a shield or flag of a family or a government **3** *pl* : actual fighting : WARFARE ⟨a call to *arms*⟩ **b** : military service [Middle English *armes* "weapons," from early French *armes* (same meaning), from Latin *arma* "weapons" — related to ALARM; see *Word History* at ALARM]

ar·ma·da \är-'mäd-ə, -'mād-\ *n* **1** : a large fleet of warships **2** : a large force or group of usually moving things ⟨an *armada* of fishing boats⟩ [from Spanish *armada* "fleet," derived from Latin *arma* "weapons"]

ar·ma·dil·lo \,är-mə-'dil-ō\ *n, pl* **-los** : any of several small burrowing mammals of warm parts of the Americas whose head and body are protected by hard bony armor

ar·ma·ment \'är-mə-mənt\ *n* **1** : the military strength and equipment of a nation **2** : a supply of war materials **3** : the process of preparing for war

armadillo

ar·ma·ture \'är-mə-chər, -,chu̇(ə)r\ *n* **1** : a covering or structure (as the spines of a cactus) used for protection or defense **2** : the part of an electric generator that consists of coils of wire around an iron core and that induces an electric current when it is rotated in a magnetic field **3** : the part of an electric motor that consists of coils of wire around an iron core and that is caused to rotate in a magnetic field when an electric current is passed through the coils **4** : the movable part of an electromagnetic device (as a loudspeaker)

arm·chair \'ärm-,che(ə)r, -,cha(ə)r; 'arm-'che(ə)r, -'cha(ə)r\ *n* : a chair with supports for a person's arms

armed *adj* **1** : furnished with weapons ⟨an *armed* guard⟩ **2** : furnished with something that provides security or strength ⟨*armed* with knowledge⟩

armed forces *n pl* : the military, naval, and air forces of a nation

Ar·me·nian \är-'mē-nē-ən, -nyən\ *n* **1** : a member of a people native to Armenia **2** : the Indo-European language of the Armenians — **Armenian** *adj*

arm·ful \'ärm-ˌfůl\ *n, pl* **arm·fuls** \-ˌfůlz\ *or* **arms·ful** \'ärmz-ˌfůl\ : as much as a person's arm can hold ⟨an *armful* of books⟩

arm·hole \'ärm-ˌhōl\ *n* : an opening for the arm in a garment

ar·mi·stice \'är-mə-stəs\ *n* : a pause in fighting brought about by agreement between the two sides

Armistice Day *n* : VETERANS DAY

arm·let \'ärm-lət\ *n* : a band (as of cloth or metal) worn around the upper arm

ar·mor \'är-mər\ *n* **1** : a covering (as of metal) to protect the body in battle **2** : a protective covering (as the steel sides of a battleship or the covering of an animal or plant) **3** : armored forces and vehicles (as tanks)

ar·mored \'är-mərd\ *adj* **1** : protected by armor ⟨an *armored* car⟩ ⟨*armored* reptiles⟩ **2** : supplied with armored equipment ⟨an *armored* force⟩

ar·mor·er \'är-mər-ər\ *n* **1** : one that makes armor or arms **2** : a person who repairs, puts together, and tests firearms

ar·mo·ri·al \är-'mōr-ē-əl, -'mȯr-\ *adj* : of, relating to, or carrying designs on a shield or flag of a family or a government

ar·mory \'ärm-(ə-)rē\ *n, pl* **ar·mor·ies** **1** : a supply of weapons **2** : a place where arms are kept and where soldiers are often trained **3** : a place where arms are made

arm·pit \'ärm-ˌpit\ *n* : the hollow beneath the spot where the arm and shoulder join

ar·my \'är-mē\ *n, pl* **ar·mies** **1 a** : a large body of men and women organized for land warfare **b** *often cap* : the complete military organization of a nation for land warfare **2** : a great number of persons or things **3** : a body of persons organized to promote an idea [Middle English *armee* "army," from early French *armee* (same meaning), derived from Latin *arma* "weapons"]

army ant *n* : any of various ants that live in groups, move from place to place in search of food, are found from Mexico to South America, and feed especially on insects and spiders

ar·my·worm \-ˌwərm\ *n* : any of numerous moths that in the larval stage travel in large numbers from field to field destroying crops (as grass or grain)

aro·ma \ə-'rō-mə\ *n* : a noticeable and usually pleasant smell ⟨the *aroma* of coffee⟩

ar·o·mat·ic \ˌar-ə-'mat-ik\ *adj* : of, relating to, or having aroma — **aromatic** *n*

arose *past of* ARISE

¹around \ə-'raůnd\ *adv* **1** : in circumference ⟨a tree five feet *around*⟩ **2** : in or along a curving path **3** : on all sides ⟨papers lying *around*⟩ **4** : NEARBY ⟨stick *around* a while⟩ **5** : here and there in various places ⟨travel *around*⟩ **6** : to each in turn ⟨pass the fruit *around*⟩ **7** : from beginning to end ⟨mild the year *around*⟩ **8** : in or to an opposite direction or position ⟨turn *around*⟩ **9** : close to : APPROXIMATELY ⟨costs *around* $20⟩

²around *prep* **1 a** : on all sides of ⟨were fields *around* the village⟩ **b** : so as to encircle or enclose ⟨people seated *around* the table⟩ **c** : on or to another side of ⟨voyage *around* Cape Horn⟩ **d** : near to ⟨lives *around* Chicago⟩ **2** : here and there in or throughout ⟨travel *around* the country⟩

arouse \ə-'raůz\ *vb* **aroused; arous·ing** **1** : to awaken from sleep **2** : to rouse to action : EXCITE

ar·peg·gio \är-'pej-ō, -'pej-ē-ˌō\ *n, pl* **-gios** **1** : the playing of the tones of a chord in succession and not at the same time **2** : a chord played in arpeggio

arquebus *variant of* HARQUEBUS

ar·raign \ə-'rān\ *vb* : to call before a court to answer to a charge — **ar·raign·ment** \-mənt\ *n*

ar·range \ə-'rānj\ *vb* **ar·ranged; ar·rang·ing** **1** : to put in order; *esp* : to put in a particular order ⟨*arrange* books on shelves⟩ **2** : to make plans for ⟨*arrange* a program⟩ **3** : to come to an agreement about : SETTLE ⟨*arrange* a time for the meeting⟩ **4** : to make a musical arrangement of — **ar·rang·er** *n*

ar·range·ment \ə-'rānj-mənt\ *n* **1** : a putting in order : the order in which things are put ⟨the *arrangement* of furniture in a room⟩ **2** : preparation or planning done in advance ⟨make *arrangements* for a trip⟩ **3** : something made by arranging ⟨a flower *arrangement*⟩ **4** : a changing of a piece of music to suit voices or instruments other than those for which it was first written

ar·rant \'ar-ənt\ *adj* : OUT-AND-OUT, COMPLETE ⟨an *arrant* fool⟩ — **ar·rant·ly** *adv*

¹ar·ray \ə-'rā\ *vb* **1** : to set in order : DRAW UP ⟨soldiers *arrayed* for review⟩ **2** : to dress especially in fine clothing : ADORN — **ar·ray·er** *n*

²array *n* **1** : regular order or arrangement; *also* : persons (as troops) in array **2** : rich or beautiful clothing **3** : an impressive group : large number ⟨a whole *array* of problems⟩; *also* : VARIETY 2, ASSORTMENT **4** : a group of mathematical elements (as numbers or letters) arranged in rows and columns

ar·rears \ə-'ri(ə)rz\ *n pl* **1** : the state of being behind in the paying of debts ⟨two months in *arrears*⟩ **2** : unpaid and overdue debts

¹ar·rest \ə-'rest\ *vb* **1 a** : to stop the progress or movement of **b** : ²CHECK 3, SLOW ⟨*arrest* a disease⟩ **2** : to take or keep in one's control by authority of law ⟨*arrest* someone on suspicion of robbery⟩ **3** : to attract and hold the attention of ⟨colors that *arrest* the eye⟩

²arrest *n* **1 a** : the act of stopping **b** : the state of being stopped **2** : the act of taking or holding in one's control by authority of law

ar·rest·ing \ə-'res-tiŋ\ *adj* : catching the attention ⟨an *arresting* painting⟩

ar·riv·al \ə-'rī-vəl\ *n* **1** : the act of arriving ⟨await the *arrival* of guests⟩ **2** : a person or thing that has arrived ⟨late *arrivals* at a concert⟩

ar·rive \ə-'rīv\ *vb* **ar·rived; ar·riv·ing** **1** : to reach the place one started out for ⟨*arrive* home at six o'clock⟩ **2** : COME 4 ⟨the time *arrived* to begin⟩ **3** : to be successful — **arrive at** : to reach by effort or thought ⟨*arrive at* a decision⟩

ar·ro·gance \'ar-ə-gən(t)s\ *n* : a sense of one's own importance that shows itself in a proud and insulting way

ar·ro·gant \'ar-ə-gənt\ *adj* **1** : overly proud of oneself or one's own opinions **2** : marked by arrogance ⟨*arrogant* remarks⟩ — **ar·ro·gant·ly** *adv*

ar·ro·gate \'ar-ə-ˌgāt\ *vb* **-gat·ed; -gat·ing** **1** : to take or claim for one's own without right **2** : to attribute to another especially without good reason — **ar·ro·ga·tion** \ˌar-ə-'gā-shən\ *n*

ar·row \'ar-ō\ *n* **1** : a weapon that is made to be shot from a bow and is usually a stick with a point at one end and feathers at the other **2** : a mark (as on a map) to show direction

ar·row·head \-ˌhed\ *n* **1** : the wedge-shaped striking end of an arrow **2** : something (as a mark) resembling an arrowhead

ar·row·root \-ˌrüt, -ˌrůt\ *n* **1** : any of several plants of warm regions of Central and South America with starchy

\ə\ **abut**	\aů\ **out**	\i\ **tip**	\ȯ\ **saw**	\ů\ **foot**
\ər\ **further**	\ch\ **chin**	\ī\ **life**	\ȯi\ **coin**	\y\ **yet**
\a\ **mat**	\e\ **pet**	\j\ **job**	\th\ **thin**	\yü\ **few**
\ā\ **take**	\ē\ **easy**	\ŋ\ **sing**	\th\ **this**	\yů\ **cure**
\ä\ **cot, cart**	\g\ **go**	\ō\ **bone**	\ü\ **food**	\zh\ **vision**

roots **2** : an edible starch from the roots of an arrowroot plant

arrow worm *n* : any of various small ocean animals that look like worms

ar·roy·o \ə-'rȯi-ə, -'rȯi-(ˌ)ō\ *n, pl* **-royos 1** : a waterway (as a creek) in a dry region **2** : an often dry gully or channel carved by water

ar·se·nal \'ärs-nəl, -ᵊn-əl\ *n* **1** : a place for the manufacture or storage of arms **2** : a collection of weapons

ar·se·nic \'ärs-nik, -ᵊn-ik\ *n* **1** : a solid poisonous element that is commonly metallic steel-gray and brittle — see ELEMENT table **2** : a white or transparent extremely poisonous oxide of arsenic used especially in insecticides

ar·se·no·py·rite \ˌärs-ᵊn-ō-'pī-ˌrīt\ *n* : a hard bluish or grayish white mineral consisting of iron, arsenic, and sulfur

ar·sine \är-'sēn, 'är-ˌsēn\ *n* : a colorless flammable extremely poisonous gas with an odor like garlic

ar·son \'är-sᵊn\ *n* : the illegal burning of a building or other property — **ar·son·ist** \-əst\ *n*

¹art \(')ärt, ərt\ *archaic present 2nd singular of* BE [Old English *eart* "art"]

²art \'ärt\ *n* **1** : skill that comes through experience or study ⟨the *art* of making friends⟩ **2** : a branch of learning; *esp* : one of the nonscientific branches of learning (as literature) — usually used in plural ⟨a degree in the *arts*⟩ **3** : an occupation that requires knowledge or skill ⟨cooking is an *art*⟩ **4** : the use of skill and creativity especially in the making of things that are beautiful to look at, listen to, or read **5** : the works (as pictures, poems, or songs) produced by artists [Middle English *art* "art, skill," from early French *art* (same meaning), from Latin *art-, ars* "skill"]

ar·te·ri·al \är-'tir-ē-əl\ *adj* **1 a** : of or relating to an artery **b** : being the bright red oxygen-rich blood present in most arteries **2** : of, relating to, or being routes for through traffic ⟨*arterial* highways⟩ — **ar·te·ri·al·ly** \-ē-ə-lē\ *adv*

ar·te·ri·ole \är-'tir-ē-ˌōl\ *n* : a very small artery connecting a larger artery to capillaries — **ar·te·ri·o·lar** \är-ˌtir-ē-'ō-ˌlär, -lər\ *adj*

ar·te·rio·scle·ro·sis \är-ˌtir-ē-ō-sklə-'rō-səs\ *n* : a disease characterized by abnormal thickening and hardening of the walls of the arteries — **ar·te·rio·scle·rot·ic** \-'rät-ik\ *adj or n*

ar·tery \'ärt-ə-rē\ *n, pl* **-ter·ies 1** : one of the tube-shaped branching muscular-walled and elastic-walled vessels that carry blood from the heart to all parts of the body **2** : a channel (as a river or highway) of transportation or communication; *esp* : the main channel in a branching system

ar·te·sian well \är-ˌtē-zhən-\ *n* **1** : a drilled well from which water flows up like a fountain **2** : a deep well

art·ful \'ärt-fəl\ *adj* **1** : done with or showing art or skill **2** : clever at taking advantage — **art·ful·ly** \-fə-lē\ *adv* — **art·ful·ness** *n*

ar·thri·tis \är-'thrīt-əs\ *n* : inflammation of the joints — **ar·thrit·ic** \-'thrit-ik\ *adj or n*

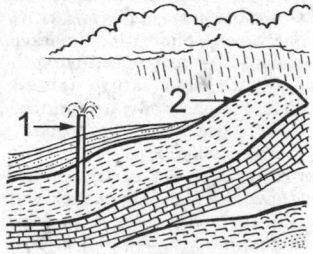

artesian well 1: *1* well, *2* catchment area

ar·thro·pod \'är-thrə-ˌpäd\ *n* : any of a phylum of invertebrate animals (as insects, arachnids, and crustaceans) having a segmented body, jointed limbs, and a shell of chitin that is shed periodically — **arthropod** *adj*

ar·ti·choke \'ärt-ə-ˌchōk\ *n* : a tall plant related to the daisies and having a flower head which is cooked and eaten as a vegetable

ar·ti·cle \'ärt-i-kəl\ *n* **1** : a separate part of a document dealing with a single subject ⟨the third *article* of the U.S. Constitution⟩ **2** : a piece of writing other than fiction or poetry that forms an independent part of a publication (as a magazine) **3** : a word (as *a, an,* or *the*) used with a noun to limit it or make it clearer **4** : a member of a class of things ⟨*articles* of clothing⟩

ar·tic·u·lar \är-'tik-yə-lər\ *adj* : of or relating to a joint

¹ar·tic·u·late \är-'tik-yə-lət\ *adj* **1 a** : clearly understandable ⟨an *articulate* argument⟩ **b** : able to express oneself clearly and well ⟨an *articulate* speaker⟩ **2** : consisting of segments united by joints : JOINTED ⟨*articulate* animals⟩ — **ar·tic·u·late·ly** *adv* — **ar·tic·u·late·ness** *n*

²ar·tic·u·late \är-'tik-yə-ˌlāt\ *vb* **-lat·ed; -lat·ing 1 a** : to speak in clear syllables or words **b** : to express clearly **2** : to unite or become united or connected by or as if by a joint — **ar·tic·u·la·tor** \-ˌlāt-ər\ *n*

ar·tic·u·la·tion \(ˌ)är-ˌtik-yə-'lā-shən\ *n* **1** : the making of articulate sounds (as in pronunciation) **2** : a joint between rigid parts of an animal; *esp* : one between bones or cartilages

ar·ti·fact \'ärt-i-ˌfakt\ *n* : a usually simple object (as a tool or ornament) showing human work and representing a culture or a stage in the development of a culture

ar·ti·fice \'ärt-ə-fəs\ *n* **1 a** : a clever device : TRICK **b** : false or dishonest behavior ⟨social *artifice*⟩ **2** : clever skill ⟨a vase made with much *artifice*⟩

ar·ti·fi·cer \är-'tif-ə-sər, 'ärt-ə-fə-sər\ *n* : a skilled or artistic worker

ar·ti·fi·cial \ˌärt-ə-'fish-əl\ *adj* **1** : made, produced, or performed by human beings often following a natural model or process ⟨*artificial* flowers⟩ ⟨*artificial* pollination⟩ **2** : not genuine or sincere : FORCED ⟨an *artificial* smile⟩ [Middle English *artificial* "made or done by humans rather than occurring in nature," from early French *artificiel* (same meaning) or Latin *artificialis* "contrived by art," from Latin *artificium* "skill, artistry, craft," derived from *arti-* (from *art-, ars* "skill") and *facere* "to make, do" — related to FASHION, MANUFACTURE, PERFECT] — **ar·ti·fi·ci·al·i·ty** \ˌärt-ə-ˌfish-ē-'al-ət-ē\ *n* — **ar·ti·fi·cial·ly** \ˌärt-ə-'fish-(ə-)lē\ *adv*

artificial heart *n* : a device designed to maintain the flow of blood to the tissues of the body

artificial intelligence *n* : the power of a machine to imitate intelligent human behavior

artificial respiration *n* : the rhythmic forcing of air into and out of the lungs of a person whose breathing has stopped

artificial selection *n* : the process of modifying living things (as plants and animals) by selective breeding controlled by human beings

ar·til·lery \är-'til-(ə-)rē\ *n, pl* **-ler·ies 1** : large firearms (as cannon or rockets) **2** : a branch of an army armed with artillery — **ar·til·lery·man** \-mən\ *n*

ar·ti·san \'ärt-ə-zən, -sən\ *n* : a skilled worker; *esp* : one (as a carpenter) whose occupation requires skill with the hands

art·ist \'ärt-əst\ *n* **1** : a person skilled in one of the arts (as painting, sculpture, music, or writing) **2** : a person showing unusual ability in an occupation requiring skill

ar·tis·tic \är-'tis-tik\ *adj* **1** : relating to or characteristic of art or artists **2** : showing skill and imagination — **ar·tis·ti·cal·ly** \-'tis-ti-k(ə-)lē\ *adv*

art·ist·ry \'ärt-ə-strē\ *n* **1** : artistic quality of effect or skill ⟨the *artistry* of her novel⟩ **2** : artistic ability

art·less \'ärt-ləs\ *adj* **1** : lacking art, knowledge, or skill : UNCULTURED **2 a** : made without skill ⟨an *artless* attempt to win⟩ **b** : being simple and sincere : NATURAL ⟨*artless* grace⟩ **3** : not trying to deceive others — **art·less·ly** *adv* — **art·less·ness** *n*

ar·um \'ar-əm, 'er-\ *n* : any of a family of plants (as the jack-in-the-pulpit or the skunk cabbage) having heart=

shaped or sword-shaped leaves and flowers in a fleshy spike enclosed in a leafy covering

¹**ary** \usually ˌer-ē after an unstressed syllable, ə-rē or rē after a stressed syllable\ n suffix, pl **-aries** : thing or person belonging to or connected with ⟨boundary⟩ [derived from Latin -arius, -aria, -arium (noun suffix), from -arius (adjective suffix)]

²**ary** adj suffix : of, relating to, or connected with ⟨legendary⟩ [derived from Latin -arius (adjective suffix)]

Ary·an \'ar-ē-ən, 'er-, 'är-yən\ n 1 : INDO-EUROPEAN 2 2 : a member of the subgroup of Indo-European speakers ancestral to speakers of Indo-Aryan and Iranian languages — **Aryan** adj

¹**as** \əz, (ˌ)az\ adv 1 : to the same degree or amount ⟨as cold as ice⟩ ⟨a number twice as large⟩ 2 : for example ⟨various trees, as oak or pine⟩

²**as** conj 1 : in or to the same degree that ⟨mad as a hornet⟩ 2 : in the way or manner that ⟨do as I say⟩ 3 : at the same time that : WHILE, WHEN ⟨sang as they marched along⟩ 4 : ²THOUGH ⟨improbable as it seems, it's true⟩ 5 : BECAUSE, SINCE ⟨stayed home, as I had no car⟩ 6 : that the result is ⟨so clearly guilty as to leave no doubt⟩ — **as is** : in the present condition without any changes ⟨bought the clock at an auction as is⟩

³**as** pron 1 : ¹THAT, WHO, WHICH — used after same or such ⟨had the same name as my cousin⟩ 2 : a fact that ⟨they are smart, as you know⟩ ⟨as I said before, it's time to go⟩

⁴**as** prep 1 : ⁴LIKE 2 ⟨came dressed as a clown⟩ 2 : in the position or role of ⟨working as an editor⟩

as- — see AD-

asa·fet·i·da or **asa·foe·ti·da** \ˌas-ə-'fet-əd-ə\ n : a hard gum that has an unpleasant smell, comes from several Asian plants related to the carrot, is used in Indian cooking, and was once thought to prevent disease

as·bes·tos \as-'bes-təs, az-\ n : a grayish mineral that easily separates into long flexible fibers, that is used to make materials that are fireproof, do not conduct electricity, and are chemically resistant, and that can cause serious lung disease if inhaled as a dust

as·cend \ə-'send\ vb : to go up : CLIMB, RISE ⟨ascend a hill⟩ ⟨smoke ascends⟩ — **as·cend·able** or **as·cend·ible** \-'sen-də-bəl\ adj

as·cen·dance \ə-'sen-dən(t)s\ n : ASCENDANCY

as·cen·dan·cy \ə-'sen-dən-sē\ n : controlling influence

¹**as·cen·dant** \ə-'sen-dənt\ n : a state or position of commanding power

²**ascendant** adj 1 : moving up : RISING 2 a : in a superior position b : inclined to control

as·cen·sion \ə-'sen-chən\ n : the act or process of ascending

Ascension Day n : the Thursday 40 days after Easter observed by Christians in honor of Christ's ascension into heaven after the Resurrection

as·cent \ə-'sent, a-\ n 1 : the act of rising or climbing up ⟨began their ascent of the mountain⟩ 2 : an upward slope

as·cer·tain \ˌas-ər-'tān\ vb : to learn with certainty : FIND OUT ⟨could not ascertain the correct date⟩ — **as·cer·tain·able** \-'tā-nə-bəl\ adj — **as·cer·tain·ment** \-'tān-mənt\ n

as·cet·ic \ə-'set-ik, a-\ adj 1 : following a practice of not giving in to one's desires especially as a means of religious discipline ⟨an ascetic way of life⟩ 2 : harshly simple : AUSTERE ⟨ascetic surroundings⟩ — **ascetic** n — **as·cet·i·cism** \ə-'set-ə-ˌsiz-əm\ n

ASCII \'as-(ˌ)kē\ n : a computer code for expressing numerals, letters of the alphabet, and other symbols [American Standard Code for Information Interchange]

as·co·my·cete \ˌas-kō-'mī-ˌsēt, -mī-'sēt\ n : any of a class of higher fungi (as yeasts and molds) that have the hyphae divided by partitions and the spores produced in sacs — called also sac fungus

ascor·bic acid \ə-ˌskòr-bik-\ n : VITAMIN C

as·cot \'as-kət, -ˌkät\ n : a broad neck scarf that is looped under the chin

as·cribe \ə-'skrīb\ vb **as·cribed; as·crib·ing** : to think of as coming from a specified cause, source, or author ⟨a statement ascribed to Plato⟩ — **as·crib·able** \-'skrī-bə-bəl\ adj

as·crip·tion \ə-'skrip-shən\ n : the act of ascribing : ATTRIBUTION

-ase \ˌās, ˌāz\ n suffix : enzyme ⟨maltase⟩ [French -ase (suffix), from the enzyme diastase]

asep·sis \(')ā-'sep-səs, ə-\ n : the condition of being aseptic; also : the methods of making or keeping aseptic

asep·tic \(')ā-'sep-tik, ə-\ adj : preventing infection; also : free or freed from disease-causing germs — **asep·ti·cal·ly** \-ti-k(ə-)lē\ adv

asex·u·al \(')ā-'seksh-(ə-)wəl, -'sek-shəl\ adj 1 : lacking sex ⟨asexual organisms⟩ 2 : occurring or formed without the production and union of two kinds of gametes ⟨asexual reproduction⟩ ⟨asexual spores⟩ — **asex·u·al·ly** \-ē\ adv

as for prep : CONCERNING ⟨as for me⟩

As·gard \'as-ˌgärd, 'az-\ n : the home of the Norse gods

¹**ash** \'ash\ n 1 : any of a genus of trees related to the olive and having bark with grooves and ridges and winged seeds 2 : the hard strong wood of an ash [Old English æsc "ash tree"]

²**ash** n 1 a : the solid that remains after material is thoroughly burned or is oxidized by chemical means b : fine particles of mineral matter from a volcanic vent 2 pl : the remains of something destroyed : RUINS 3 pl : the remains of the dead human body especially after cremation [Old English asce "the remains of something burned"]

ashamed \ə-'shāmd\ adj 1 : feeling shame, guilt, or disgrace ⟨ashamed of my behavior⟩ 2 : kept from doing something by an expectation of shame ⟨ashamed to beg⟩ — **asham·ed·ly** \-'shā-məd-lē\ adv

Ashan·ti \ə-'shant-ē, -'shänt-\ n, pl **Ashanti** or **Ashantis** : a member of a people of southern Ghana

ash·en \'ash-ən\ adj 1 : of the color of ashes 2 : deadly pale ⟨ashen with fear⟩

ashore \ə-'shō(ə)r, -'shó(ə)r\ adv : on or to the shore

ash·tray \'ash-ˌtrā\ n : a container for tobacco ashes and for cigar and cigarette butts

Ash Wednesday n : the first day of Lent

ashy \'ash-ē\ adj **ash·i·er; -est** 1 : of, relating to, or resembling ashes 2 : ASHEN 2

Asian \'ā-zhən, 'ā-shən\ adj : of, relating to, or characteristic of Asia or its people — **Asian** n

Asian–American \-ə-'mer-ə-kən\ n : an American who has Asian ancestors — **Asian–American** adj

Asian elephant n : ELEPHANT b

Asi·at·ic \ˌā-zhē-'at-ik, -zē-\ adj, sometimes offensive : ASIAN — **Asiatic** n, sometimes offensive

¹**aside** \ə-'sīd\ adv 1 : to or toward the side ⟨stepped aside⟩ 2 : out of the way especially for future use : AWAY ⟨put money aside for school⟩ 3 : away from one's thought or consideration ⟨all kidding aside⟩

²**aside** n : words meant not to be heard by someone; esp : an actor's words supposedly not heard by others on the stage

aside from prep : with the exception of : EXCEPT FOR ⟨aside from a few pieces of bread, the food is gone⟩

as if conj 1 : the way it would be if ⟨it was as if we had never left⟩ 2 : the way one would do if ⟨they acted as if they'd never heard of us⟩ 3 : ²THAT 1a ⟨it seemed as if the day would never end⟩

\ə\ abut	\aú\ out	\i\ tip	\ò\ saw	\ú\ foot
\ər\ further	\ch\ chin	\ī\ life	\òi\ coin	\y\ yet
\a\ mat	\e\ pet	\j\ job	\th\ thin	\yü\ few
\ā\ take	\ē\ easy	\ŋ\ sing	\th\ this	\yú\ cure
\ä\ cot, cart	\g\ go	\ō\ bone	\ü\ food	\zh\ vision

as·i·nine \\'as-ᵊn-ˌīn\ *adj* : extremely foolish ⟨an *asinine* excuse⟩ — **as·i·nine·ly** *adv* — **as·i·nin·i·ty** \ˌas-ᵊn-'in-ət-ē\ *n*

ask \'ask, 'ȧsk\ *vb* **1** : to seek information : INQUIRE ⟨*asked* about our trip⟩ **2 a** : to make a request ⟨*ask* for help⟩ **b** : to make a request to ⟨*ask* your teacher to help you⟩ **3** : to set as a price : DEMAND ⟨*asked* $20 for the bicycle⟩ **4** : ¹INVITE 2a ⟨*asked* friends to a party⟩ **5** : to behave as if looking ⟨*asking* for trouble⟩ — **ask·er** *n*

askance \ə-'skan(t)s\ *adv* **1** : with a side glance **2** : with distrust or disapproval ⟨eyed the stranger *askance*⟩

askew \ə-'skyü\ *adv or adj* : out of line : AWRY 1

aslant \ə-'slant\ *adv or adj* : in a slanting direction

¹asleep \ə-'slēp\ *adj* **1** : being in a state of sleep **2** : lacking sensation : NUMB ⟨my foot was *asleep*⟩

²asleep *adv* : into a state of sleep

as of *prep* : ¹ON 3, AT ⟨we begin work *as of* Tuesday⟩ ⟨*as of* the moment, things are fine⟩

asp \'asp\ *n* : a small poisonous snake of Egypt

as·par·a·gus \ə-'spar-ə-gəs\ *n* : a tall branching long-lived herb related to the lilies and widely grown for its thick edible young shoots

as·par·tic acid \ə-ˌspärt-ik-\ *n* : an amino acid found especially in plants

as·pect \'as-ˌpekt\ *n* **1** : a position facing a certain direction : EXPOSURE **2** : a certain way in which something appears or may be regarded ⟨studied every *aspect* of the question⟩ **3** : the appearance of something : LOOK

aspect ratio *n* : a comparison of one dimension (as width) to another (as height)

as·pen \'as-pən\ *n* : any of several poplars with leaves that flutter in the lightest breeze

asparagus

as·per·i·ty \a-'sper-ət-ē, ə-'sper-\ *n, pl* **-ties** **1** : something making for hardship : RIGOR, SEVERITY **2** : harshness of temper, manner, or tone

as·perse \ə-'spərs, a-\ *vb* **as·persed; as·pers·ing** : to attack with evil reports or false charges : SLANDER

as·per·sion \ə-'spər-zhən\ *n* : an evil report or false charge ⟨cast *aspersions* on a person⟩

¹as·phalt \'as-ˌfȯlt\ *n* **1** : a brown to black substance that is found in natural beds or obtained as something left in petroleum or coal-tar refining and that consists chiefly of compounds of carbon and hydrogen **2** : any of various compositions of asphalt having different uses (as for pavement or for waterproof cement or paint) — **as·phal·tic** \as-'fȯl-tik\ *adj*

²asphalt *vb* : to cover with asphalt

as·pho·del \'as-fə-ˌdel\ *n* : any of several herbs related to the lilies and bearing white or yellow flowers in long upright spikes

as·phyx·ia \as-'fik-sē-ə\ *n* : a lack of oxygen or excess of carbon dioxide in the body usually caused by interruption of breathing or insufficient oxygen supply and resulting in unconsciousness and often death

as·phyx·i·ate \as-'fik-sē-ˌāt\ *vb* **-at·ed; -at·ing** : to cause asphyxia in — **as·phyx·i·a·tion** \(ˌ)as-ˌfik-sē-'ā-shən\ *n*

as·pic \'as-pik\ *n* : a jelly of fish or meat stock used especially to make a mold of meat, fish, or vegetables

as·pi·dis·tra \ˌas-pə-'dis-trə\ *n* : an Asian plant related to the lilies, having large leaves at the base of the stem, and often grown as a houseplant

as·pi·rant \'as-p(ə-)rənt, ə-'spī-rənt\ *n* : a person who aspires

¹as·pi·rate \'as-pə-ˌrāt\ *vb* **-rat·ed; -rat·ing** **1** : to pronounce with an initial \h\ **2** : to remove (as blood) by suction

²as·pi·rate \'as-p(ə-)rət\ *n* : the sound \h\ or a letter or symbol representing it

as·pi·ra·tion \ˌas-pə-'rā-shən\ *n* **1** : pronunciation with or as an aspirate **2** : a drawing of something in, out, up, or through by suction **3 a** : a strong desire to achieve something high or great **b** : an object of such desire

as·pi·ra·tor \'as-pə-ˌrāt-ər\ *n* : an apparatus for producing suction or moving or collecting materials by suction

as·pire \ə-'spī(ə)r\ *vb* **as·pired; as·pir·ing** : to work to get something high or great — **as·pir·er** *n*

as·pi·rin \'as-p(ə-)rən\ *n* **1** : a white drug used as a remedy for pain and fever **2** : a tablet of aspirin

ass \'as\ *n* **1** : any of several mammals resembling but smaller than the related horses and having a shorter mane, shorter hair on the tail, and longer ears; *esp* : DONKEY **2** *sometimes vulgar* : a stupid or stubborn person

as·sail \ə-'sā(ə)l\ *vb* : to attack violently with blows or words — **as·sail·able** \-'sā-lə-bəl\ *adj* — **as·sail·ant** \-'sā-lənt\ *n*

as·sas·sin \ə-'sas-ən\ *n* : a person who kills another person; *esp* : one who murders a politically important person either for pay or from loyalty to a cause

as·sas·si·nate \ə-'sas-ᵊn-ˌāt\ *vb* **-nat·ed; -nat·ing** : to murder a usually important person by a surprise or secret attack **synonyms** see KILL — **as·sas·si·na·tion** \ə-ˌsas-ᵊn-'ā-shən\ *n*

as·sault \ə-'sȯlt\ *n* **1** : a violent or sudden attack **2** : an unlawful attempt or threat to do harm to another [Middle English *assaut* "assault," from early French *assaut* (same meaning), derived from Latin *assilire, adsilire* "to leap upon," from *as-, ad-* "to, toward" and *salire* "to leap, spring" — related to INSULT, RESILIENT] — **assault** *vb*

assault rifle *n* : any of various especially automatic rifles designed for military use — called also *assault weapon*

¹as·say \'as-ˌā, a-'sā\ *n* : examination (as of an ore, metal, or drug) for the purpose of determining the presence, absence, or amount of one or more substances

²as·say \a-'sā, 'as-ˌā\ *vb* **1** : ¹TRY 4, ATTEMPT **2** : to analyze (as an ore) for one or more valuable substances — **as·say·er** *n*

as·sem·blage \ə-'sem-blij, *for 3 also* ˌas-ˌäm-'bläzh\ *n* **1** : a collection or gathering of persons or things **2** : the act of assembling **3** : an artistic composition made by putting together scraps or junk

as·sem·ble \ə-'sem-bəl\ *vb* **-bled; -bling** \-b(ə-)liŋ\ **1** : to collect into one place or group ⟨*assembled* the crew⟩ **2** : to fit together the parts of ⟨*assemble* a toy⟩ **3** : to meet together ⟨the right to *assemble* peacefully⟩ [Middle English *assemblen* "to bring together, assemble," from early French *assembler* (same meaning), derived from Latin *ad-* "to" and *simul* "together" — related to ENSEMBLE, SIMULTANEOUS] **synonyms** see GATHER

as·sem·bler \ə-'sem-b(ə-)lər\ *n* **1** : one that assembles **2** : a computer program that turns instructions written in assembly language into machine language

as·sem·bly \ə-'sem-blē\ *n, pl* **-blies** **1** : a body of persons gathered together (as to make laws or for discussion, worship, or entertainment) **2** *cap* : a governing body; *esp* : the lower house of a legislature **3** : the act of gathering together or state of being assembled **4** : a signal for troops to assemble **5** : a collection of parts that go to make up a complete machine, structure, or unit of a machine **6** : the translation of assembly language to machine language by an assembler **7** : a meeting of a student body and usually teachers for educational or recreational purposes

assembly language *n* : a code for programming a computer that is a close approximation of machine language but is more easily understood by humans

assembly line *n* : an arrangement of machines, equipment, and workers in which work passes from operation to operation in direct line until the product is assembled

as·sem·bly·man \ə-'sem-blē-mən\ *n* : a member of a legislative assembly

as·sem·bly·wom·an \-,wùm-ən\ *n* : a woman who is a member of a legislative assembly

as·sent \ə-'sent, a-\ *vb* : to give one's approval : agree to something — **assent** *n*

as·sert \ə-'sərt, a-\ *vb* **1** : to state clearly and strongly **2** : to make others aware of ⟨*assert* your rights⟩ — **assert oneself** : to act or speak up so others are aware of one's interests and opinions

> **synonyms** ASSERT, DECLARE, AFFIRM, AVOW mean to state positively usually in the face of denial or objection. ASSERT suggests declaring with confidence often without need for proof or evidence ⟨I *assert* that our team can win the game⟩. DECLARE stresses an open or public statement ⟨*declared* that she would run for the senate⟩. AFFIRM suggests a firm belief based on evidence, experience, or faith ⟨*affirmed* that there is good in everyone⟩. AVOW suggests an open and forceful statement that declares responsibility ⟨the newspaper *avowed* responsibility for its mistake⟩.

as·ser·tion \ə-'sər-shən, a-\ *n* : the act of asserting; *also* : something asserted : DECLARATION

as·ser·tive \ə-'sərt-iv, a-\ *adj* : having a bold or confident manner — **as·ser·tive·ly** *adv* — **as·ser·tive·ness** *n*

as·sess \ə-'ses, a-\ *vb* **1** : to set the rate or amount of ⟨the jury *assessed* damages of $5000⟩ **2** : to set a value on (as property) for tax purposes ⟨a house *assessed* at $163,000⟩ **3** : to put a tax or charge on ⟨the city *assessed* all car owners $25⟩ **4** : to find out or decide the importance, size, or value of ⟨*assess* the problem⟩ — **as·sess·able** \-'ses-ə-bəl\ *adj*

as·sess·ment \ə-'ses-mənt, a-\ *n* **1** : the act of assessing **2** : the amount or value assessed

as·ses·sor \ə-'ses-ər\ *n* : an official who assesses property for taxes

as·set \'as-,et\ *n* **1** *pl* : all the property of a person, corporation, or estate that may be used in payment of debts **2** : a quality or thing that can be used to advantage ⟨a real *asset* to the team⟩

as·sid·u·ous \ə-'sij-(ə-)wəs\ *adj* : constantly attentive : DILIGENT — **as·si·du·ity** \,as-ə-'d(y)ü-ət-ē\ *n* — **as·sid·u·ous·ly** *adv* — **as·sid·u·ous·ness** *n*

as·sign \ə-'sīn\ *vb* **1** : to give (as a title or right) to someone legally **2** : to pick for a specific use or job ⟨*assigned* them to work in the kitchen⟩ **3** : to give out as a portion or task ⟨parts in the play were *assigned* to each person⟩ ⟨*assign* homework⟩ **4** : to give a certain quality, role, or importance to ⟨events *assigned* to certain periods of history⟩ ⟨*assign* number values to different letters⟩ — **as·sign·able** \ə-'sī-nə-bəl\ *adj* — **as·sign·er** \ə-'sī-nər\ *or* **as·sign·or** \ə-'sī-nər; ,as-ə-'nó(ə)r, ,as-,ī-, ə-,sī-\ *n* — **as·sign·ment** \ə-'sīn-mənt\ *n*

as·sign·ee \,as-ə-'nē, ,as-,ī-, ə-,sī-\ *n* : a person to whom something is assigned

as·sim·i·late \ə-'sim-ə-,lāt\ *vb* **-lat·ed; -lat·ing** : to take something in and make it part of the thing it has joined

as·sim·i·la·tion \ə-,sim-ə-'lā-shən\ *n* : the act or process of assimilating ⟨the *assimilation* of immigrants⟩; *esp* : the bodily process of changing nutrients (as of digested food) into cells and tissues

¹**as·sist** \ə-'sist\ *vb* : to give support or aid : HELP

²**assist** *n* **1** : an act of assisting **2** : the action of a player who by passing a ball or puck makes it possible for a teammate to make a putout or score a goal

as·sis·tance \ə-'sis-tən(t)s\ *n* : the act of assisting; *also* : the help given

as·sis·tant \ə-'sis-tənt\ *n* : a person who assists another : HELPER — **assistant** *adj*

as·size \ə-'sīz\ *n* : a session of an English court formerly held by judges traveling through various counties — usually used in plural

¹**as·so·ci·ate** \ə-'sō-shē-,āt, -sē-,āt\ *vb* **-at·ed; -at·ing** **1** : to join or come together as partners, friends, or companions **2** : to connect in thought ⟨*associate* hot chocolate with winter⟩ **3** : to combine or join with other parts : UNITE [Middle English *associat* "connected, related," derived from Latin *associare* "to unite," from *ad-* "to" and *sociare* "to join," from *socius* "companion" — related to SOCIABLE]

²**as·so·ci·ate** \ə-'sō-shē-ət, -sē-ət, -shət, -shē-,āt, -sē-,āt\ *n* **1** : a fellow worker : COLLEAGUE **2** : ¹COMPANION 1, FRIEND **3** *often cap* : a degree given especially by a junior college ⟨*associate* in arts⟩ — **associate** *adj*

as·so·ci·a·tion \ə-,sō-sē-'ā-shən, -,sō-shē-\ *n* **1** : the act of associating : the state of being associated **2** : an organization of persons having a common interest ⟨an athletic *association*⟩ **3** : a feeling, memory, or thought connected with a person, place, or thing ⟨pleasant *associations* with the beach⟩ **4** : the formation of loosely bound groups of ions or molecules

association neuron *n* : INTERNEURON

as·so·cia·tive \ə-'sō-shē-,āt-iv, -sē-, -shət-iv\ *adj* **1** : of or relating to association **2** : of, having, or being the property of producing the same mathematical value no matter how an expression's elements are grouped so long as the order of those elements is the same ⟨addition is *associative* since $(a + b) + c = a + (b + c)$⟩ — **as·so·cia·tive·ly** *adv* — **as·so·cia·tiv·i·ty** \ə-,sō-shē-ə-'tiv-ət-ē, -,sō-sē-, -,sō-shə-'tiv-\ *n*

as·so·nance \'as-ə-nən(t)s\ *n* : the repetition of vowel sounds but not consonants in words (as "red hen") for poetic effect — **as·so·nant** \-nənt\ *adj*

as soon as *conj* : immediately at or just after the time that ⟨left *as soon as* the meeting was over⟩

as·sort \ə-'sò(ə)rt\ *vb* : to sort into groups

as·sort·ed \ə-'sòrt-əd\ *adj* **1** : consisting of various kinds ⟨*assorted* cheeses⟩ **2** : matching or fitting together ⟨an ill-*assorted* pair⟩

as·sort·ment \ə-'sò(ə)rt-mənt\ *n* **1 a** : arrangement in classes **b** : the quality or state of being made up of various kinds **2** : a collection of different things or persons

as·suage \ə-'swāj\ *vb* **as·suaged; as·suag·ing** **1** : to lessen or make easier to bear : SOOTHE, EASE **2** : SATISFY 2b, QUENCH — **as·suage·ment** \-mənt\ *n*

as·sume \ə-'süm\ *vb* **as·sumed; as·sum·ing** **1** : to take upon oneself ⟨*assume* control⟩ ⟨*assumed* the presidency⟩ **2** : TAKE ON 3, RECEIVE ⟨it *assumes* greater importance now⟩ **3** : to pretend to have or be : PUT ON ⟨immediately *assumed* a look of innocence⟩ **4** : to take as true : SUPPOSE ⟨I *assumed* he knew⟩

as·sump·tion \ə-'səm(p)-shən\ *n* **1** *cap* : August 15 observed as a church festival to mark the taking up of the Virgin Mary into heaven **2 a** : the act of taking upon oneself or taking possession of something **3 a** : the belief that something is true **b** : a fact or statement taken for granted

as·sur·ance \ə-'shùr-ən(t)s\ *n* **1** : the act of assuring **2** : the state of being sure or certain **3** *chiefly British* : INSURANCE 1 **4** : SELF-CONFIDENCE

as·sure \ə-'shù(ə)r\ *vb* **as·sured; as·sur·ing** **1** : to provide a guarantee of ⟨*assure* security⟩ **2** : to give words of comfort or confidence to : REASSURE ⟨tried to *assure* the worried children⟩ **3** : to cause to be sure or certain ⟨*assure* himself that the door was locked⟩ **4** : to inform positively ⟨can *assure* you of her dependability⟩

as·sured \ə-'shù(ə)rd\ *adj* **1** : made sure or certain **2** : very confident ⟨rest *assured* we will be there⟩ — **as·sur·ed·ly** \-'shùr-əd-lē\ *adv* — **as·sur·ed·ness** \-əd-nəs\ *n*

\ə\ abut	\aú\ out	\i\ tip	\ò\ saw	\ù\ foot
\ər\ **further**	\ch\ **chin**	\ī\ **life**	\òi\ **coin**	\y\ **yet**
\a\ **mat**	\e\ **pet**	\j\ **job**	\th\ **thin**	\yü\ **few**
\ā\ **take**	\ē\ **easy**	\ŋ\ **sing**	\th\ **this**	\yù\ **cure**
\ä\ **cot, cart**	\g\ **go**	\ō\ **bone**	\ü\ **food**	\zh\ **vision**

as·ta·tine \\'as-tə-ˌtēn\ *n* : a radioactive element discovered by bombarding bismuth with helium nuclei — see ELEMENT table

as·ter \\'as-tər\ *n* : any of various mostly fall-blooming leafy-stemmed herbs related to the daisies usually with showy white, pink, purple, or yellow flower heads

as·ter·isk \\'as-tə-ˌrisk\ *n* : a symbol * used especially to refer a reader to a note [Middle English *astarisc* "asterisk," derived from Greek *asteriskos,* literally "little star," from *aster-, astēr* "star"]

astern \ə-'stərn\ *adv* 1 : in, at, or toward the stern 2 : in a reverse direction : BACKWARD ⟨full speed *astern*⟩

as·ter·oid \\'as-tə-ˌrȯid\ *n* : one of thousands of small rocky bodies between Mars and Jupiter with diameters from a fraction of a kilometer to nearly 800 kilometers

asteroid belt *n* : the region of interplanetary space between the orbits of Mars and Jupiter in which most asteroids are found

asth·ma \\'az-mə\ *n* : a condition that is marked by difficulty in breathing with wheezing, a feeling of tightness in the chest, and coughing — **asth·mat·ic** \az-'mat-ik\ *adj or n* — **asth·mat·i·cal·ly** \-'mat-i-k(ə-)lē\ *adv*

as though *conj* : AS IF

astig·ma·tism \ə-'stig-mə-ˌtiz-əm\ *n* : a defect of an optical system (as of the eye) that prevents light from focusing accurately and results in a blurred image or unclear vision — **as·tig·mat·ic** \ˌas-tig-'mat-ik\ *adj*

astir \ə-'stər\ *adj* 1 : being in a state of activity : STIRRING 2 : being out of bed : UP

as to *prep* 1 : with respect to : ABOUT ⟨confused *as to* what happened⟩ 2 : ACCORDING TO 1 ⟨graded *as to* size⟩

as·ton·ish \ə-'stän-ish\ *vb* : to strike with sudden wonder or surprise — **as·ton·ish·ing·ly** \-iŋ-lē\ *adv* — **as·ton·ish·ment** \-mənt\ *n*

as·tound \ə-'staûnd\ *vb* : to fill with puzzled wonder

astrad·dle \ə-'strad-ᵊl\ *adv or prep* : ASTRIDE

as·tra·khan \\'as-trə-kən, -ˌkan\ *n, often cap* 1 : sheepskin of the karakul lamb from Russia 2 : a cloth made to look like karakul sheepskin

as·tral \\'as-trəl\ *adj* : of or relating to the stars

astray \ə-'strā\ *adv or adj* 1 : off the right path or route 2 : in or into error

¹**astride** \ə-'strīd\ *adv* : with one leg on each side

²**astride** *prep* : on or above and with one leg on each side of ⟨*astride* a horse⟩

as·trin·gen·cy \ə-'strin-jən-sē\ *n* : the quality or state of being astringent

¹**as·trin·gent** \ə-'strin-jənt\ *adj* : able or tending to shrink body tissues ⟨*astringent* lotions⟩ — **as·trin·gent·ly** *adv*

²**astringent** *n* : an astringent substance

astro- *combining form* : star : heavens : outer space : astronomical ⟨*astro*physics⟩ [Latin *astro-* "star," derived from Greek *astēr, astron* "star"]

as·tro·labe \\'as-trə-ˌlāb\ *n* : an instrument for observing the positions of heavenly bodies that was used before the sextant was invented

astrolabe

as·trol·o·gy \ə-'sträl-ə-jē\ *n* : the study of the supposed influences of the stars on human affairs by their positions in relation to each other — **as·trol·o·ger** \-jər\ *n* — **as·tro·log·i·cal** \ˌas-trə-'läj-i-kəl\ *adj* — **as·tro·log·i·cal·ly** \-k(ə-)lē\ *adv*

as·tro·naut \\'as-trə-ˌnȯt, -ˌnät\ *n* : a traveler in a spacecraft [from *astro-* "star, heavens" (derived from Greek *astron* "star") and *-naut* (derived from Greek *nautēs* "sailor," from *naus* "ship") — related to NAUSEA, NAUTICAL; see

Word History at NAUSEA] — **as·tro·nau·tic** \ˌas-trə-'nȯt-ik\ *or* **as·tro·nau·ti·cal** \-i-kəl, -nät-\ *adj*

as·tro·nau·tics \ˌas-trə-'nȯt-iks, -nät-\ *n* : the science of the construction and operation of spacecraft

as·tro·nom·i·cal \ˌas-trə-'näm-i-kəl\ *also* **as·tro·nom·ic** \-'näm-ik\ *adj* 1 : of or relating to astronomy 2 : extremely or unbelievably large ⟨the cost was *astronomical*⟩ — **as·tro·nom·i·cal·ly** \-'näm-i-k(ə-)lē\ *adv*

astronomical unit *n* : a unit of length used in astronomy equal to the average distance of the earth from the sun or about 93 million miles (150 million kilometers)

as·tron·o·my \ə-'strän-ə-mē\ *n, pl* **-mies** : the science of the heavenly bodies and of their sizes, motions, and composition — **as·tron·o·mer** \-mər\ *n*

as·tro·phys·ics \ˌas-trə-'fiz-iks\ *n* : a branch of astronomy dealing with the physical and chemical measurements of the heavenly bodies — **as·tro·phys·i·cal** \-'fiz-i-kəl\ *adj* — **as·tro·phys·i·cist** \-'fiz-ə-səst\ *n*

as·tute \ə-'st(y)üt, a-\ *adj* : having or showing understanding and the skill to make good choices or decisions : WISE, SHREWD ⟨an *astute* investor⟩ — **as·tute·ly** *adv* — **as·tute·ness** *n*

asun·der \ə-'sən-dər\ *adv or adj* 1 : into parts ⟨torn *asunder*⟩ 2 : far apart

¹**as well as** *conj* : and in addition ⟨catch fish for food *as well as* for sport⟩

²**as well as** *prep* : in addition to : BESIDES ⟨is a real scholar *as well as* being a poet⟩

asy·lum \ə-'sī-ləm\ *n* 1 : a place of safety : SHELTER 2 : protection given especially to political refugees 3 : an institution for the care of those unable to care for themselves and especially for the insane

asym·met·ri·cal \ˌā-sə-'me-tri-kəl\ *or* **asym·met·ric** \-trik\ *adj* : not symmetrical — **asym·met·ri·cal·ly** \-tri-k(ə-)lē\ *adv* — **asym·me·try** \(')ā-'sim-ə-trē\ *n*

asymp·tom·at·ic \ˌā-ˌsim(p)-tə-'mat-ik\ *adj* : presenting no signs of disease

at \ət, (')at\ *prep* 1 — used to indicate location in space or time ⟨staying *at* a hotel⟩ ⟨be here *at* six⟩ ⟨sick *at* heart⟩ 2 — used to indicate a goal that an action is aimed towards ⟨aim *at* the target⟩ ⟨laugh *at* him⟩ 3 — used to indicate a condition one is in ⟨*at* work⟩ ⟨*at* liberty⟩ ⟨*at* rest⟩ 4 — used to indicate how or why ⟨sold *at* auction⟩ ⟨angry *at* his answer⟩ 5 — used to indicate the rate, degree, age, or position in a scale or series ⟨the temperature *at* 90⟩ ⟨retire *at* 65⟩

at- — see AD-

at all \ət-'ȯl, ə-'tȯl, at-'ȯl\ *adv* : in any way : under any circumstances ⟨will go anywhere *at all*⟩ ⟨doesn't mind *at all*⟩ ⟨not *at all* likely⟩

at·a·vis·tic \ˌat-ə-'vis-tik\ *adj* : coming from or associated with one's most primitive ancestors ⟨*atavistic* behavior⟩

atax·ia \ə-'tak-sē-ə, (')ā-\ *n* : inability to coordinate voluntary muscular movements — **atax·ic** \-sik\ *adj*

ate *past of* EAT

¹**-ate** \ət, ˌāt\ *n suffix* : office : function : rank : group of persons holding a specified office or rank [derived from Latin *-atus* (noun suffix)]

²**-ate** *adj suffix* : marked by having ⟨chord*ate*⟩ [derived from Latin *-atus* (adjective suffix)]

³**-ate** \ˌāt\ *vb suffix* 1 : cause to be modified or affected by ⟨hydrogen*ate*⟩ 2 : cause to become ⟨activ*ate*⟩ 3 : furnish with ⟨aer*ate*⟩ [derived from ²-ate]

a tem·po \ä-'tem-pō\ *adv or adj* : in time — used as a direction in music to return to the original speed

athe·ism \\'ā-thē-ˌiz-əm\ *n* : the belief that there is no God — **athe·ist** \-thē-əst\ *n* — **athe·is·tic** \ˌā-thē-'is-tik\ *adj*

ath·ero·scle·ro·sis \ˌath-ə-rō-sklə-'rō-səs\ *n* : hardening and thickening of the walls of arteries due to deposit of fatty substances in the inner layer

athirst \ə-'thərst\ *adj* : EAGER ⟨*athirst* for knowledge⟩

ath·lete \'ath-,lēt\ *n* : a person who is trained in or good at games and exercises that require physical skill, endurance, and strength

athlete's foot *n* : ringworm of the feet

ath·let·ic \ath-'let-ik\ *adj* **1** : of, relating to, or characteristic of athletes or athletics **2** : VIGOROUS 1, ACTIVE **3** : STRONG 1, MUSCULAR — **ath·let·i·cal·ly** \-'let-i-k(ə)lē\ *adv*

ath·let·ics \ath-'let-iks\ *n sing or pl* : games, sports, and exercises requiring strength and skill

athletic supporter *n* : an elastic pouch to support the male genitals worn especially while playing sports

¹athwart \ə-'thwȯ(ə)rt, *nautical often* -thȯ(ə)rt\ *prep* **1** : ²ACROSS 1 **2** : in opposition to

²athwart *adv* : ¹ACROSS 1

-a·tion \'ā-shən\ *n suffix* **1** : action or process ⟨flirt*ation*⟩ **2** : something connected with an action or process ⟨discolor*ation*⟩ [derived from Latin *-ation-*, *-atio* (noun suffix)]

-a·tive \,āt-iv, ət-iv\ *adj suffix* **1** : of, relating to, or connected with ⟨authorit*ative*⟩ **2** : tending to ⟨talk*ative*⟩ [derived from Latin *-ativus* (adjective suffix)]

At·lan·tic salmon \ət-'lant-ik-, at-\ *n* : SALMON 1a

Atlantic time *n* : the time of the fourth time zone west of Greenwich that includes the Canadian Maritime Provinces, Puerto Rico, and the Virgin Islands

at·las \'at-ləs\ *n* : a book of maps

> *Word History* Atlas was one of the giants of Greek mythology who ruled the world in an early age. Their rule was overthrown after a mighty battle with other gods. After their defeat, the story goes, Atlas was forced to hold up the sky on his shoulders. In the 16th century the Flemish mapmaker Gerardus Mercator published a collection of maps. On the title page he showed a picture of Atlas supporting his burden. Mercator gave the book the title *Atlas.* Later collections of maps included similar pictures of Atlas, and such books came to be called *atlases.* [named for Atlas, a giant in Greek mythology]

ATM \,ā-,tē-'em\ *n* : a computerized machine that performs basic banking functions (as issuing cash withdrawals) [*a*utomatic *t*eller *m*achine]

at·mo·sphere \'at-mə-,sfi(ə)r\ *n* **1 a** : the whole mass of air surrounding the earth **b** : a mass of gases surrounding a heavenly body (as a planet) **2** : the air in a particular place ⟨the stuffy *atmosphere* of this room⟩ **3 a** : a surrounding influence or set of conditions ⟨a friendly *atmosphere*⟩ **b** : the main mood or feeling in a creative work **c** : a unique or appealing effect or mood ⟨a restaurant with *atmosphere*⟩ **4** : a unit of pressure equal to the pressure of the air at sea level or about 10 newtons per square centimeter (about 14.7 pounds per square inch) [derived from Greek *atmos* "vapor" and Latin *sphaera* "sphere"]

at·mo·spher·ic \,at-mə-'sfi(ə)r-ik, -'sfer-\ *adj* : of or relating to the atmosphere ⟨*atmospheric* pressure⟩ — **at·mo·spher·i·cal·ly** \-i-k(ə-)lē\ *adv*

atoll \'a-,tȯl, -,täl, -,tōl, 'ā-\ *n* : a coral island consisting of a coral reef surrounding a lagoon

atoll

at·om \'at-əm\ *n* **1** : a tiny particle : BIT **2** : the smallest particle of an element that has the properties of the element and can exist either alone or in combination **3** : the atom considered as a source of vast potential energy [Middle English *atom* "particle," from Latin *atomus* (same meaning), derived from Greek *atomos* "unable to be divided," from *a-* "not" and *temnein* "to cut"]

atom·ic \ə-'täm-ik\ *adj* **1** : of, relating to, or concerned with atoms, atomic bombs, or nuclear energy ⟨*atomic* physics⟩ ⟨the *atomic* age⟩ ⟨*atomic* energy⟩ **2** : extremely small **3** : found in the state of separate atoms ⟨*atomic* hydrogen⟩

atomic bomb *n* **1** : a bomb whose violent explosive power is due to the sudden release of energy resulting from the splitting of nuclei of a heavy chemical element (as plutonium or uranium) by neutrons — called also *atom bomb* **2** : HYDROGEN BOMB

atomic clock *n* : an extremely exact clock that depends for its operation on the natural vibrations of atoms (as of cesium)

atomic mass *n* : the mass of any kind of atom usually expressed in atomic mass units

atomic mass unit *n* : a unit of mass for expressing masses of atoms, molecules, or nuclear particles that is equal to $\frac{1}{12}$ of the atomic mass of the most abundant kind of carbon

atomic number *n* : a number that is characteristic of a chemical element and represents the number of protons in the nucleus

atomic pile *n* : REACTOR 2

atomic reactor *n* : REACTOR 2

atomic theory *n* **1** : a theory of the nature of matter: all material substances consist of very tiny particles or atoms of not really many kinds and all the atoms of the same kind are uniform in size, weight, and other properties **2** : any of several theories of the structure of the atom; *esp* : one saying that the atom consists essentially of a small positively charged heavy nucleus in relation to a large arrangement of electrons that surround the nucleus

atomic weight *n* : the average atomic mass of an element compared to $\frac{1}{12}$ the mass of the most abundant kind of carbon

at·om·ize \'at-ə-,mīz\ *vb* **-ized; -iz·ing** : to reduce to very tiny particles or to a fine spray

at·om·iz·er \'at-ə-,mī-zər\ *n* : a device for giving a very fine spray of a liquid (as a perfume)

atomizer

atom smasher *n* : ACCELERATOR 3

aton·al \(')ā-'tōn-əl, (')a-\ *adj* : being music written without traditional organization based on a scale — **ato·nal·i·ty** \,ā-tō-'nal-ət-ē\ *n* — **aton·al·ly** \(')ā-'tōn-ə-lē, (')a-\ *adv*

atone \ə-'tōn\ *vb* **atoned; aton·ing** : to do something to make up for a wrong that has been done

atone·ment \ə-'tōn-mənt\ *n* **1** : the return to a state of love and harmony between God and human beings through the death of Jesus Christ **2** : something that makes up for an offense or injury

atop \ə-'täp\ *prep* : on top of

ATP \,ā-,tē-'pē, ,ā-'tē-,pē\ *n* : a compound that occurs widely in living tissue and serves as a major source of energy for many cellular processes

atri·um \'ā-trē-əm\ *n, pl* **atria** \-trē-ə\ *also* **atri·ums** : a chamber of the heart receiving blood from the veins and forcing it into a ventricle that in lung-breathing vertebrates (as frogs and human beings) is one of two chambers of which the right receives blood full of carbon dioxide from the body and the left receives oxygen-rich blood from the lungs but in gill-breathing vertebrates (as fishes) is only a single chamber

atro·cious \ə-'trō-shəs\ *adj* **1** : savagely wicked, brutal, or cruel **2** : very bad ⟨*atrocious* weather⟩ — **atro·cious·ly** *adv* — **atro·cious·ness** *n*

\ə\ abut	\aú\ out	\i\ tip	\ȯ\ saw	\ú\ foot
\ər\ further	\ch\ chin	\ī\ life	\ȯi\ coin	\y\ yet
\a\ mat	\e\ pet	\j\ job	\th\ thin	\yü\ few
\ā\ take	\ē\ easy	\ŋ\ sing	\th\ this	\yú\ cure
\ä\ cot, cart	\g\ go	\ō\ bone	\ü\ food	\zh\ vision

atroc·i·ty \ə-'träs-ət-ē\ *n, pl* **-ties** **1** : the quality or state of being atrocious **2** : something that is atrocious

¹at·ro·phy \'a-trə-fē\ *n, pl* **-phies** : decrease in size or wasting away of a body part or tissue

²atrophy *vb* **-phied; -phy·ing** : to undergo atrophy

at·ro·pine \'a-trə-ˌpēn\ *n* : a poisonous white compound from belladonna and related plants used especially to relieve spasms and to dilate the pupil of the eye

at sign *n* : the symbol @ especially when used as part of an e-mail address

at·tach \ə-'tach\ *vb* **1** : to take money or property by legal authority especially to gain or force payment of a debt ⟨*attach* a person's salary⟩ **2** : to fasten or join one thing to another ⟨*attach* a light to a bicycle⟩ ⟨*attach* a file to an e-mail⟩ **3** : to tie or bind by feelings of affection ⟨the children were *attached* to their dog⟩ **4** : to assign (an individual or unit in the military) temporarily ⟨*attach* an officer to a headquarters⟩ **5** : to think of as belonging to something ⟨*attach* no importance to a remark⟩ — **at·tach·able** \-ə-bəl\ *adj*

at·ta·ché \ˌat-ə-'shā, ˌa-ˌta-, ə-ˌta-\ *n* : a technical expert on a diplomatic staff ⟨military *attaché*⟩

at·taché case \ˌa-ˌta-'shā-, ˌat-ə-; ə-'tash-(ˌ)ā-\ *n* : a small suitcase especially for carrying papers and documents

at·tach·ment \ə-'tach-mənt\ *n* **1** : a legal taking of property **2** : strong affection : FONDNESS **3** : a device with a special use that is attached to a machine or tool ⟨*attachments* for a vacuum cleaner⟩ **4** : the connection by which one thing is attached to another **5** : the process of physically attaching **6** : a document or file that is sent with e-mail

¹at·tack \ə-'tak\ *vb* **1** : to take strong action against ⟨the dog *attacked* a skunk⟩ **2** : to use unfriendly or bitter words against **3** : to begin to cause something harmful or destructive to happen to ⟨*attacked* by fever⟩ **4** : to start work on ⟨*attack* a problem⟩ — **at·tack·er** *n*

²attack *n* **1** : the act or action of attacking : ASSAULT **2** : a beginning of work on something (as a problem or project) **3** : a spell of sickness; *esp* : one of a disease that is long-lasting or that tends to occur over and over again

attack dog *n* : a dog trained to attack upon receiving a command or upon seeing a certain object (as a person)

at·tain \ə-'tān\ *vb* **1** : to reach as a goal : ACCOMPLISH, ACHIEVE **2** : to come to possess : OBTAIN **3** : to arrive at : REACH ⟨*attain* the top of the mountain⟩ — often used with *to* — **at·tain·abil·i·ty** \ə-ˌtā-nə-'bil-ət-ē\ *n* — **at·tain·able** \-'tā-nə-bəl\ *adj*

at·tain·der \ə-'tān-dər\ *n* : the taking away of a person's civil rights when that person has been declared an outlaw or sentenced to death

at·tain·ment \ə-'tān-mənt\ *n* **1** : the act of attaining : the state of being attained **2** : something attained : ACCOMPLISHMENT

at·tar \'at-ər, 'a-ˌtär\ *n* : a fragrant oil that comes from a plant (as the rose) and is used in perfumes or flavorings; *also* : FRAGRANCE

¹at·tempt \ə-'tem(p)t\ *vb* **1** : to try to do or perform ⟨*attempt* an escape⟩ **2** : to make an effort : TRY ⟨*attempt* to solve the problem⟩

²attempt *n* **1** : the act or an instance of attempting; *esp* : an unsuccessful effort **2** : ²ATTACK 1 ⟨an *attempt* on the president's life⟩

at·tend \ə-'tend\ *vb* **1 a** : to pay attention to ⟨*attend* my words⟩ **b** : to give one's attention ⟨*attend* to business⟩ **2** : to go or stay with especially as a companion or servant ⟨*attend* the sick⟩ **3** : to be present with ⟨a cold *attended* by fever⟩ **4** : to go or to be present at especially to take part in or observe ⟨*attend* a party⟩ ⟨*attend* school⟩ **5** : to take charge of : look after ⟨a doorman *attending* the entrance⟩ **synonyms** see ACCOMPANY

at·ten·dance \ə-'ten-dən(t)s\ *n* **1** : the act of attending **2 a** : the number of persons attending **b** : the number of times a person attends ⟨perfect *attendance*⟩

¹at·ten·dant \ə-'ten-dənt\ *adj* : accompanying or following as a result

²attendant *n* **1** : one who goes with or serves another ⟨a bride and her *attendants*⟩ **2** : an employee who waits on customers ⟨a gas station *attendant*⟩

at·ten·tion \ə-'ten-chən\ *n* **1** : the act or power of fixing one's mind upon something : careful listening or watching ⟨pay *attention*⟩ **2 a** : a state of being aware : AWARENESS, NOTICE ⟨attract *attention*⟩ **b** : consideration with the idea of taking action ⟨a problem that needs prompt *attention*⟩ **3** : an act of kindness, care, or courtesy **4** : a posture taken by a soldier with the body stiff and straight, heels together, and arms at the sides

attention deficit disorder *n* : a condition that is characterized by an inability to maintain attention or by excessively active and impulsive behavior or by a combination of both and that interferes with one's ability to function in school, home, work, or with others

attention span *n* : the length of time during which one is able to concentrate or remain interested

at·ten·tive \ə-'tent-iv\ *adj* **1** : paying attention **2** : thoughtful for the welfare or comfort of others : COURTEOUS — **at·ten·tive·ly** *adv* — **at·ten·tive·ness** *n*

at·ten·u·ate \ə-'ten-yə-ˌwāt\ *vb* **-at·ed; -at·ing** **1** : to make thin or slender **2** : to make less in amount, force, or value : WEAKEN **3** : to become thin, fine, or less — **at·ten·u·a·tion** \ə-ˌten-yə-'wā-shən\ *n*

at·test \ə-'test\ *vb* : to give proof of : testify to ⟨the result *attests* the truth of that statement⟩ ⟨I can *attest* to your innocence⟩ — **at·tes·ta·tion** \ˌa-ˌtes-'tā-shən\ *n* — **at·test·er** \ə-'tes-tər\ *n*

at·tic \'at-ik\ *n* : a room or a space just below the roof of a building

Word History In ancient Greece the region around Athens was known as Attica, and many of the buildings in Attica had a special feature of a second wall that extended above the top of the main wall or row of columns supporting the roof. When builders in Europe later copied this feature of Attica's buildings, their buildings were said to be in the style of Attica, or the Attic style. Eventually, the word *attic* came to be used as a noun to refer to this upper wall and later to a room behind the wall under the roof. Today we refer to any room just underneath the roof as the attic, even when the building is not in the style of those in ancient Attica. [from French *attique* "attic," from *attique* (an adjective) "of Attica," from Latin *Atticus* "of Attica"]

At·tic \'at-ik\ *adj* : of or relating to Athens

¹at·tire \ə-'tī(ə)r\ *vb* **at·tired; at·tir·ing** : to put clothes and especially special or fine clothes on

²attire *n* : CLOTHING 1; *esp* : fine clothes

at·ti·tude \'at-ə-ˌt(y)üd\ *n* **1** : a position of the body or a figure : POSTURE **2** : a particular feeling or way of thinking about something else **3** : the position of something in relation to something else

at·tor·ney \ə-'tər-nē\ *n, pl* **-neys** : a person who is appointed to conduct business for another; *esp* : LAWYER

attorney general *n, pl* **attorneys general** *or* **attorney generals** : the chief law officer of a nation or state who represents the government in legal matters

at·tract \ə-'trakt\ *vb* **1** : to pull to or toward oneself or itself ⟨a magnet *attracts* iron⟩ **2** : to draw by appealing to interest or feeling ⟨*attract* attention⟩ [Middle English *attracten* "attract, cause to adhere," derived from Latin *attrahere*, literally "to draw near," from *at-*, *ad-* "to, toward" and *trahere* "to draw" — related to ABSTRACT, ¹TRACE, ³TRACE]

at·trac·tant \ə-'trak-tənt\ *n* : something that attracts; *esp* : a substance that attracts animals (as insects)

at·trac·tion \ə-'trak-shən\ *n* **1** : the act, process, or power of attracting **2** : something that attracts or pleases **3** : a force acting between particles of matter, tending to draw them together, and resisting their separation

at·trac·tive \ə-'trak-tiv\ *adj* : having the power or quality of attracting; *esp* : CHARMING, PLEASING — **at·trac·tive·ly** *adv* — **at·trac·tive·ness** *n*

¹at·tri·bute \'a-trə-ˌbyüt\ *n* **1** : a quality belonging to a particular person or thing **2** : a word that indicates a quality; *esp* : ADJECTIVE

²at·trib·ute \ə-'trib-yət, -ˌyüt\ *vb* **-ut·ed; -ut·ing** **1** : to explain as the cause of ⟨*attribute* our success to hard work⟩ **2** : to think of as likely to be a quality of a person or thing ⟨*attribute* stubbornness to mules⟩ — **at·trib·ut·able** \-yət-ə-bəl\ *adj* — **at·tri·bu·tion** \ˌa-trə-'byü-shən\ *n*

at·trib·u·tive \ə-'trib-yət-iv\ *adj* : joined directly to a modified noun without a verb ⟨"city" in "city streets" is *attributive*⟩ — compare PREDICATE

at·tri·tion \ə-'trish-ən, a-\ *n* **1** : the act of wearing down by or as if by friction **2** : a reduction in numbers usually as a result of resignation, retirement, or death

at·tune \ə-'t(y)ün\ *vb* : to bring into harmony : TUNE — **at·tune·ment** \-mənt\ *n*

ATV \ˌā-(ˌ)tē-'vē\ *n* : ALL-TERRAIN VEHICLE

atyp·i·cal \(ˈ)ā-'tip-i-kəl\ *adj* : not typical : IRREGULAR — **atyp·i·cal·ly** \-i-k(ə-)lē\ *adv*

au·burn \'ò-bərn\ *adj* : of a reddish brown color ⟨*auburn* hair⟩

¹auc·tion \'òk-shən\ *n* : a sale at which things are sold to those who offer to pay the most [from Latin *auction-, auctio,* from *augēre* "to increase" — related to AUGMENT]

²auction *vb* **auc·tioned; auc·tion·ing** \-sh(ə-)niŋ\ : to sell at auction

auc·tion·eer \ˌòk-shə-'ni(ə)r\ *n* : a person in charge of an auction — **auctioneer** *vb*

au·da·cious \ò-'dā-shəs\ *adj* **1** : very bold and daring : FEARLESS **2** : showing a lack of proper respect — **au·da·cious·ly** *adv* — **au·da·cious·ness** *n*

au·dac·i·ty \ò-'das-ət-ē\ *n, pl* **-ties** : the quality or fact of being audacious

au·di·ble \'òd-ə-bəl\ *adj* : heard or capable of being heard ⟨the sound was barely *audible*⟩ — **au·di·bil·i·ty** \ˌòd-ə-'bil-ət-ē\ *n* — **au·di·bly** \'òd-ə-blē\ *adv*

au·di·ence \'òd-ē-ən(t)s\ *n* **1** : a group that listens or watches (as at a play or concert) **2** : an interview with a person of high rank **3** : those of the general public who give attention to something said, done, or written ⟨books with an *audience* of millions⟩

¹au·dio \'òd-ē-ˌō\ *adj* **1** : of or relating to electrical or other frequencies occurring in the range of sound waves that can be heard **2 a** : of or relating to sound or its reproduction and especially accurate reproduction ⟨bought new *audio* equipment⟩ **b** : relating to or used in sending or receiving sound — compare ²VIDEO 1

²audio *n* **1** : the sending, receiving, or reproducing of sound **2** : the part of television or motion-picture equipment that deals with sound

audio- *combining form* **1** : hearing ⟨*audio*meter⟩ **2** : sound ⟨*audio*phile⟩ **3** : auditory and ⟨*audio*visual⟩ [derived from Latin *audire* "to hear"]

au·dio·book \'òd-ē-ō-ˌbùk\ *n* : a recording of a book being read

au·dio–lin·gual \ˌòd-ē-ō-'liŋ-g(yə-)wəl\ *adj* : involving the use of listening and speaking drills in language learning

au·di·ol·o·gist \ˌòd-ē-'äl-ə-jəst\ *n* : a person who specializes in audiology

au·di·ol·o·gy \ˌòd-ē-'äl-ə-jē\ *n* : a branch of science concerned with hearing and especially with the treatment of individuals having trouble with their hearing

au·di·om·e·ter \ˌòd-ē-'äm-ət-ər\ *n* : an instrument used to measure the keenness of hearing — **au·dio·met·ric** \ˌòd-ē-ō-'me-trik\ *adj* — **au·di·om·e·try** \ˌòd-ē-'äm-ə-trē\ *n*

au·dio·tape \'òd-ē-ō-ˌtāp\ *n* : a tape recording of sound

au·dio·vi·su·al \ˌòd-ē-ō-'vizh(-ə)-wəl, -'vizh-əl\ *adj* : of, relating to, or using both sound and sight ⟨*audiovisual* teaching aids⟩

au·dio·vi·su·als \ˌòd-ē-ō-'vizh(-ə)-wəlz, -'vizh-əlz\ *n pl* : audiovisual teaching materials

¹au·dit \'òd-ət\ *n* **1** : a thorough check of accounts especially of a business **2** : a careful check or review ⟨an energy *audit* of our house⟩

²audit *vb* : to make an audit of

¹au·di·tion \ò-'dish-ən\ *n* **1** : the power or sense of hearing **2** : a short performance to test the talents of a musician, singer, dancer, or actor

²audition *vb* **-di·tioned; -di·tion·ing** \-'dish-(ə-)niŋ\ : to test or try out in an audition

au·di·tor \'òd-ət-ər\ *n* **1** : a person who listens to or hears something or someone; *esp* : a member of an audience **2** : a person who audits accounts

au·di·to·ri·um \ˌòd-ə-'tòr-ē-əm, -'tòr-\ *n* **1** : the part of a public building where an audience sits **2** : a room, hall, or building used for public gatherings

au·di·to·ry \'òd-ə-ˌtòr-ē, -ˌtòr-\ *adj* : of or relating to hearing or to the sense or organs of hearing

auditory canal *n* : the passage leading from the opening of the external ear to the eardrum

auditory nerve *n* : a nerve connecting the inner ear with the brain and carrying nerve impulses concerned with hearing and balance

au·ger \'ò-gər\ *n* : any of various tools made like a spiral or screw and used for boring holes or moving loose material

Word History The tool called an *auger* has nothing to do with people's navels, but the words *auger* and *navel* are related. This tool was first used to bore a hole for the axle in the nave or hub of a wheel. Such a nave was called *nafu* in Old English. *Nafu* is related to the word *nafela,* which has become our word *navel.* The Old English ancestor of *auger* was *nafogār,* which was made up of *nafu* and *gār,* meaning "spear." By Middle English *nafogār* had lost a syllable and shrunk to *nauger,* and it no longer made sense as a compound. Since *a nauger* sounds just like *an auger,* many people began to write *an auger.* That is how our modern spelling of the word was born. [Middle English *auger* "auger," an altered form of *nauger,* from Old English *nafogār* "tool for boring holes in the hub of a wheel"]

¹aught \' òt, 'ät\ *pron* : ³ALL 1 ⟨for *aught* we know⟩ [Old English *āwiht* "anything," from *ā* "ever, always" and *wiht* "creature, thing"]

²aught *n* **1** : ¹ZERO 1 **2** : the first decade of a century [from *naught* "zero," from mistaking *a naught* for *an aught*]

au·gite \'ò-ˌjīt\ *n* : a black to dark green variety of pyroxene

aug·ment \òg-'ment\ *vb* **1** : to increase especially in size, amount, or degree **2** : to add to : SUPPLEMENT [Middle English *augmenten* "to increase," from early French *augmenter* (same meaning), derived from Latin *augēre* "to increase" — related to AUCTION] — **aug·men·ta·tion** \ˌòg-mən-'tā-shən, -ˌmen-\ *n*

augmented reality *n* : an enhanced version of reality created by the use of technology to overlay digital information on an image of something being viewed through a device (as a smartphone camera); *also* : the technology used to create augmented reality

au gratin \ō-'grat-ᵊn, ò-, -'grät-\ *adj* : covered with bread crumbs or grated cheese and browned

\ə\ **abut**	\aù\ **out**	\i\ **tip**	\ò\ **saw**	\ù\ **foot**
\ər\ **further**	\ch\ **chin**	\ī\ **life**	\òi\ **coin**	\y\ **yet**
\a\ **mat**	\e\ **pet**	\j\ **job**	\th\ **thin**	\yü\ **few**
\ā\ **take**	\ē\ **easy**	\ŋ\ **sing**	\th\ **this**	\yù\ **cure**
\ä\ **cot, cart**	\g\ **go**	\ō\ **bone**	\ü\ **food**	\zh\ **vision**

¹**au·gur** \'ȯ-gər\ *n* : a person (as in ancient Rome) who fore-tells the future by omens

²**augur** *vb* **1** : to predict from signs or omens **2** : to give promise of ⟨this *augurs* well for the future⟩

au·gu·ry \'ȯ-gyə-rē, -gə-\ *n, pl* **-ries** **1** : predicting the future especially from omens **2** : a sign of the future : OMEN

au·gust \ȯ-'gəst\ *adj* : being grand and noble : MAJESTIC — **au·gust·ly** *adv* — **au·gust·ness** *n*

Au·gust \'ȯ-gəst\ *n* : the eighth month of the year

Word History The first calendar used by the ancient Romans began the year with March. The month that we now call August was then the sixth month of the year and was known by the name *Sextilis,* a Latin word meaning "sixth." When the emperor Augustus Caesar was in power, however, he wished to have a month named after himself. The Roman senate satisfied him by changing *Sextilis* to *Augustus.* The English word *August* comes from the Latin *Augustus.* [Old English *August* "the eighth month," from Latin *Augustus* "August," from *Augustus (Caesar)*]

auk \'ȯk\ *n* : any of several black-and-white short-necked diving seabirds that breed in colder parts of the northern hemisphere

auld \'ȯl(d), 'äl(d)\ *adj, chiefly Scottish* : OLD

auld lang syne \ˌōl-ˌ(d)aŋ-'zīn, ˌōl-ˌ(d)laŋ-, ˌȯl-\ *n* : the good old times [from Scots, literally "old long ago"]

aunt \'ant, 'änt\ *n* **1** : the sister of one's father or mother **2** : the wife of one's uncle

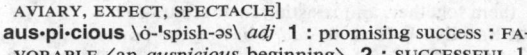

auk

au·ra \'ȯr-ə\ *n* : a special quality or impression associated with something ⟨an *aura* of holiness⟩

au·ral \'ȯr-əl\ *adj* : of or relating to the ear or sense of hearing — **au·ral·ly** \-ə-lē\ *adv*

au·re·ole \'ȯr-ē-ˌōl\ *or* **au·re·o·la** \ȯ-'rē-ə-lə\ *n* **1** : a radiant light around the head or body in a picture of a sacred person **2** : a bright area surrounding a bright light (as of the sun's disk) when seen through thin cloud or mist

au re·voir \ˌōr-əv-'wär, ˌȯr-\ *n* : GOOD-BYE [French, literally "till seeing again"]

au·ri·cle \'ȯr-i-kəl\ *n* **1** : PINNA 2 **2** : a small pouch in each atrium of the human heart

au·ric·u·lar \ȯ-'rik-yə-lər\ *adj* **1** : of or relating to the ear or the sense of hearing **2** : told privately ⟨*auricular* confession⟩ **3** : learned or recognized through the sense of hearing **4** : of or relating to an auricle

Au·ri·ga \ȯ-'rī-gə\ *n* : a group of stars between Perseus and Gemini

au·rochs \'au̇(ə)r-ˌäks, ˌȯ(ə)r-\ *n* : an extinct large long-horned wild ox of Europe that is the wild ancestor of domestic cattle

au·ro·ra \ə-'rōr-ə, ȯ-'rȯr-, -'rȯr-\ *n, pl* **-ras** *or* **-rae** \-ē\ **1** : ²DAWN 1 **2** : AURORA BOREALIS **3** : AURORA AUSTRALIS — **au·ro·ral** \-əl\ *adj*

aurora aus·tra·lis \-ȯ-'strā-ləs, -ä-'strä-\ *n* : a display of light that is the same as the aurora borealis but occurs in the southern hemisphere — called also *southern lights*

aurora bo·re·al·is \-ˌbȯr-ē-'al-əs, -ˌbȯr-\ *n* : broad bands of light that have a magnetic and electrical source and that appear in the sky at night especially in the arctic region — called also *northern lights*

aus·pice \'ȯ-spəs\ *n, pl* **aus·pic·es** \-spə-səz, -ˌsēz\ **1** : predicting the future especially according to the flight of birds **2** : OMEN; *esp* : a favorable sign **3** *pl* : support and guidance of a sponsor ⟨a concert given under the *auspices* of the school⟩ [from Latin *auspicium* "auspice," derived

from *avis* "bird" and *specere* "to look at" — related to AVIARY, EXPECT, SPECTACLE]

aus·pi·cious \ȯ-'spish-əs\ *adj* **1** : promising success : FAVORABLE ⟨an *auspicious* beginning⟩ **2** : SUCCESSFUL 1, PROSPEROUS ⟨has been an *auspicious* year⟩ — **aus·pi·cious·ly** *adv* — **aus·pi·cious·ness** *n*

Word History In ancient Rome the flight of birds was thought to be a sign from the gods. If a bird swooped down or soared up, it might mean good or bad luck for a person. But only special people were thought to be able to read these signs. Such a person was called in Latin an *auspex,* meaning literally "bird observer." The word was formed from Latin *avis,* meaning "bird," and the Latin verb *specere,* meaning "to see." The art of predicting the future in this way came to be called *auspicium.* A reading of bird actions was taken each time a person or the state was about to take an important step, such as marriage, a new business, or war. The word was taken into English by borrowing the Latin stem *auspici-* of *auspicium* and adding the adjective suffix *-ous.* Although *auspicium* could mean either good news or bad news, when *auspicious* came to be used in English, it was always used of something favorable. [from Latin *auspicium* "reading the future from the flight of birds" and English *-ous* (adjective suffix)]

aus·tere \ȯ-'sti(ə)r\ *adj* **1** : stern and unfriendly in appearance and manner **2** : living a harsh life with few pleasures : ASCETIC **3** : SIMPLE 4a, UNADORNED ⟨an *austere* room⟩ — **aus·tere·ly** *adv*

aus·ter·i·ty \ȯ-'ster-ət-ē\ *n, pl* **-ties** **1** : the quality or state of being austere **2** : an austere act, manner, or attitude **3** : a way of living with few or no luxuries

Aus·tra·lian \ȯ-'strāl-yən, ä-\ *adj* : of, relating to, or characteristic of Australia or its people

Aus·tra·loid \'ȯs-trə-ˌlȯid, 'äs-\ *adj* : of or relating to a human population group including the Australian aborigines and related peoples — **Australoid** *n*

aus·tra·lo·pith·e·cine \ȯ-ˌstrā-lō-'pith-ə-ˌsīn, ä-ˌstrā-; ˌȯs-trə-, ˌäs-trə-\ *adj* : of or relating to a group of extinct southern African apes that stood upright, walked on two legs, and had teeth somewhat like those of human beings but had a smaller brain — **australopithecine** *n*

aut- *or* **auto-** *combining form* : self : same one ⟨*auto*biography⟩ [derived from Greek *aut-* "self," from *autos* "self, same"]

au·then·tic \ə-'thent-ik, ȯ-\ *adj* **1** : being really what it seems to be : GENUINE ⟨*authentic* examples of Hopi jewelry⟩ **2** : made to be or look just like an original ⟨*authentic* colonial costumes⟩ ⟨*authentic* French-style mustard⟩ — **au·then·ti·cal·ly** \-'thent-i-k(ə)lē\ *adv* — **au·then·tic·i·ty** \ˌȯ-ˌthen-'tis-ət-ē, -thən-\ *n*

au·then·ti·cate \ə-'thent-i-ˌkāt, ȯ-\ *vb* **-cat·ed; -cat·ing** : to prove or serve to prove that something is authentic — **au·then·ti·ca·tion** \-ˌthent-i-'kā-shən\ *n*

au·thor \'ȯ-thər\ *n* **1** : a person who creates a written work : WRITER **2** : one that starts or creates ⟨*author* of a plan for education⟩ — **author** *vb*

au·thor·i·tar·i·an \ȯ-ˌthär-ə-'ter-ē-ən, ə-, -ˌthȯr-\ *adj* **1** : expecting strict obedience to one's authority ⟨had *authoritarian* parents⟩ **2** : based on the principle that the leaders and not the people have the final authority ⟨an *authoritarian* state⟩ — **authoritarian** *n* — **au·thor·i·tar·i·an·ism** \-ē-ə-ˌniz-əm\ *n*

au·thor·i·ta·tive \ə-'thär-ə-ˌtāt-iv, ȯ-, -'thȯr-\ *adj* : having or coming from authority — **au·thor·i·ta·tive·ly** *adv* — **au·thor·i·ta·tive·ness** *n*

au·thor·i·ty \ə-'thär-ət-ē, ȯ-, -'thȯr-\ *n, pl* **-ties** **1 a** : a fact or statement that is used to support a position or decision **b** : a person looked to as an expert **2** : the right to give commands : the power to influence the behavior of others ⟨the *authority* to hire workers⟩ **3** : persons having powers of government ⟨local *authorities*⟩ **4** : the quality of being convincing ⟨spoke with *authority*⟩

au·tho·rize \'o-thə-ˌrīz\ *vb* **-rized; -riz·ing 1** : to give authority to **2** : to give legal or official approval to — **au·tho·ri·za·tion** \ˌo-th(ə-)rə-'zā-shən\ *n* — **au·tho·riz·er** \'o-thə-ˌrī-zər\

Authorized Version *n* : a revision of the English Bible made under James I, published in 1611, and widely used by Protestants

au·thor·ship \'o-thər-ˌship\ *n* **1** : writing as an occupation **2** : the origin especially of a written work

au·tism \'o-ˌtiz-əm\ *n* : a disorder that is characterized especially by problems in interacting and communicating with other people and by doing some activities over and over again

au·to \'ot-ō-, 'ät-\ *n, pl* **au·tos** : AUTOMOBILE

auto- — see AUT-

au·to·bi·og·ra·phy \ˌot-ə-bī-'äg-rə-fē, -bē-\ *n* : a biography written by the person it is about — **au·to·bi·og·ra·pher** \-rə-fər\ *n* — **au·to·bio·graph·i·cal** \-ˌbī-ə-'graf-i-kəl\ *also* **au·to·bio·graph·ic** \-'graf-ik\ *adj* — **au·to·bio·graph·i·cal·ly** \-i-k(ə-)lē\ *adv*

au·to·clave \'ot-ō-ˌklāv\ *n* : a device (as for sterilizing) that uses steam under pressure

au·toc·ra·cy \o-'täk-rə-sē\ *n, pl* **-cies** : government in which one person has unlimited power

au·to·crat \'ot-ə-ˌkrat\ *n* : a person who rules with unlimited authority

au·to·crat·ic \ˌot-ə-'krat-ik\ *adj* : of, relating to, or resembling autocracy or an autocrat — **au·to·crat·i·cal·ly** \-'krat-i-k(ə-)lē\ *adv*

¹**au·to·graph** \'ot-ə-ˌgraf\ *n* : a person's signature written by hand

²**autograph** *vb* : to write one's signature in or on

au·to·im·mune \ˌot-ō-im-'yün\ *adj* : relating to or caused by an abnormal condition in which an organism's immune system attacks and destroys parts of its own cells or tissues ⟨multiple sclerosis is an *autoimmune* disease⟩

au·to·mate \'ot-ə-ˌmāt\ *vb* **-mat·ed; -mat·ing 1** : to operate by automation **2** : to convert to mainly automatic operation

¹**au·to·mat·ic** \ˌot-ə-'mat-ik\ *adj* **1 a** : largely or wholly involuntary; *esp* : REFLEX **2 b** : acting or done without conscious thought or intention ⟨an *automatic* reply⟩ ⟨an *automatic* smile⟩ **2** : having devices or mechanisms (as timers) that permit operation without help from a person ⟨*automatic* washer⟩ **3** : firing repeatedly until the trigger is released ⟨an *automatic* rifle⟩ — **au·to·mat·i·cal·ly** \-'mat-i-k(ə-)lē\ *adv*

²**automatic** *n* : an automatic machine or device; *esp* : an automatic firearm

au·to·ma·tion \ˌot-ə-'mā-shən\ *n* **1** : the method of making a device, a process, or a system operate by itself **2** : automatic operation of a device, process, or system by mechanical or electronic devices that replace human operators

au·tom·a·tize \o-'täm-ə-ˌtīz\ *vb* **-tized; -tiz·ing** : to make automatic — **au·tom·a·ti·za·tion** \o-ˌtäm-ət-ə-'zā-shən\ *n*

au·tom·a·ton \o-'täm-ət-ən, -'täm-ə-ˌtän\ *n, pl* **-atons** *or* **-a·ta** \-ət-ə\ : a machine that can move by itself; *esp* : ROBOT 1a

¹**au·to·mo·bile** \'ot-ə-mō-ˌbēl, ˌot-ə-mō-'bē(ə)l, ˌot-ə-'mō-ˌbēl\ *adj* : of or relating to automobiles

²**automobile** *n* : a usually four-wheeled vehicle with its own power system (as an internal combustion engine) designed for passenger transportation on streets and roadways — **automobile** *vb* — **au·to·mo·bil·ist** \-mō-'bē-ləst\ *n*

au·to·mo·tive \ˌot-ə-'mot-iv\ *adj* **1** : SELF-PROPELLED **2** : of, relating to, or concerned with automobiles, trucks, or buses

au·to·nom·ic \ˌot-ə-'näm-ik\ *adj* : of, relating to, controlled by, or being part of the autonomic nervous system

autonomic nervous system *n* : the part of the vertebrate nervous system that controls actions that are mostly automatic (as breathing and heart rate) and that is made up of the sympathetic nervous system and parasympathetic nervous system

au·ton·o·mous \o-'tän-ə-məs\ *adj* **1** : having autonomy : SELF-GOVERNING **2** : existing independent of anything else — **au·ton·o·mous·ly** *adv*

au·ton·o·my \o-'tän-ə-mē\ *n, pl* **-mies** : the power or right of self-government

au·top·sy \'o-ˌtäp-sē, 'ot-əp-\ *n, pl* **-sies** : an examination of a dead body especially to find out the cause of death [from Greek *autopsia* "the act of seeing with one's own eyes," from *aut-* "self" and *opsis* "sight," from *opsesthai* "to be going to see" — related to OPTIC] — **autopsy** *vb*

au·to·ra·dio·graph \ˌot-ō-'rād-ē-ə-ˌgraf\ *n* : an image made on a photographic film or plate by the radiation from a radioactive substance in a nearby object

autos *plural of* AUTO

au·to·troph \'ot-ə-ˌtrōf, -ˌträf\ *n* : an organism (as a plant) that can make its own food from substances that do not come from other living things — **au·to·troph·ic** \ˌot-ə-'trō-fik\ *adj*

au·tumn \'ot-əm\ *n* **1** : the season between summer and winter including in the northern hemisphere usually the months of September, October, and November — called also *fall* **2** : a time late in an existence ⟨in the *autumn* of life⟩ — **au·tum·nal** \o-'təm-nəl\ *adj*

¹**aux·il·ia·ry** \og-'zil-yə-rē, -'zil-(ə-)rē\ *adj* : available to provide something extra when needed ⟨*auxiliary* police⟩

²**auxiliary** *n, pl* **-ries** : an auxiliary person, group, or device

auxiliary verb *n* : HELPING VERB

aux·in \'ok-sən\ *n* : a plant hormone that causes the shoot to grow in length and usually controls other growth processes (as root formation)

¹**avail** \ə-'vā(ə)l\ *vb* : to be of use or help ⟨our best efforts did not *avail*⟩ — **avail oneself of** : to make use of : take advantage of ⟨they *availed themselves of* his services⟩

²**avail** *n* : help toward reaching a goal : USE ⟨effort was of little *avail*⟩

avail·able \ə-'vā-lə-bəl\ *adj* **1** : present in a form that a plant or animal can use ⟨a food that contains *available* iron⟩ **2** : easy or possible to get, get to, or use ⟨kept emergency supplies *available*⟩ ⟨called every *available* hardware store⟩ — **avail·abil·i·ty** \ə-ˌvā-lə-'bil-ət-ē\ *n* — **avail·able·ness** *n* — **avail·ably** \ə-'vā-lə-blē\ *adv*

av·a·lanche \'av-ə-ˌlanch\ *n* **1** : a large mass of snow and ice or of earth and rock sliding down a mountainside **2** : a sudden large amount ⟨an *avalanche* of words⟩

av·a·rice \'av-(ə-)rəs\ *n* : strong desire for riches : GREED

av·a·ri·cious \ˌav-ə-'rish-əs\ *adj* : greedy for riches — **av·a·ri·cious·ly** *adv* — **av·a·ri·cious·ness** *n*

avast \ə-'vast\ *imperative verb* — a command to stop or cease used by sailors

avaunt \ə-'vont, -'vänt\ *adv* : AWAY 2

avenge \ə-'venj\ *vb* **avenged; aveng·ing** : to take vengeance for (an action) or on behalf of (a person) — **aveng·er** *n*

av·e·nue \'av-ə-ˌn(y)ü\ *n* **1** : a way or route to a place or goal : PATH **2** : a usually wide street

aver \ə-'vər\ *vb* **averred; aver·ring** : to declare positively : ASSERT

¹**av·er·age** \'av-(ə-)rij\ *n* **1** : ARITHMETIC MEAN **2** : a level typical of a group, class, or series ⟨their work is above the

\ə\ abut	\au̇\ out	\i\ tip	\o̊\ saw	\u̇\ foot
\ər\ further	\ch\ chin	\ī\ life	\o̊i\ coin	\y\ yet
\a\ mat	\e\ pet	\j\ job	\th\ thin	\yü\ few
\ā\ take	\ē\ easy	\ŋ\ sing	\t̲h̲\ this	\yu̇\ cure
\ä\ cot, cart	\g\ go	\ō\ bone	\ü\ food	\zh\ vision

average⟩ **3** : a ratio of successful tries to total tries ⟨batting *average*⟩

²**average** *adj* **1** : equaling or close to an arithmetic mean **2** : being ordinary or usual ⟨the *average* person⟩ ⟨an *average* day⟩ — **av·er·age·ly** *adv* — **av·er·age·ness** *n*

³**average** *vb* **-aged; -ag·ing 1** : to amount to on the average ⟨they *average* four feet in height⟩ **2** : to do or get usually ⟨she *averaged* 40 miles a day⟩ **3** : to find the average of ⟨*average* the grades⟩

averse \ə-'vərs\ *adj* : having an active and strong dislike ⟨*averse* to exercise⟩ — **averse·ly** *adv* — **averse·ness** *n*

aver·sion \ə-'vər-zhən\ *n* **1** : a strong dislike **2** : something strongly disliked

avert \ə-'vərt\ *vb* **1** : to turn away ⟨*avert* one's eyes⟩ **2** : to keep from happening ⟨*averted* an accident⟩

avi·an \'ā-vē-ən\ *adj* : of, relating to, or derived from birds

avi·ary \'ā-vē-ˌer-ē\ *n, pl* **-ar·ies** : a place (as a large cage or a building) where many live birds are kept usually for exhibition [from Latin *aviarium* "place to keep birds," from *avis* "bird"]

avi·a·tion \ˌā-vē-ˈā-shən, ˌav-ē-\ *n* : the operation of aircraft (as airplanes or helicopters) that are heavier than air

avi·a·tor \'ā-vē-ˌāt-ər, 'av-ē-\ *n* : ¹PILOT 3

av·id \'av-əd\ *adj* **1** : having so much desire for something as to be greedy ⟨*avid* for attention⟩ **2** : very eager : ENTHUSIASTIC ⟨an *avid* football fan⟩ — **avid·ity** \ə-'vid-ət-ē, a-\ *n* — **av·id·ly** \'av-əd-lē\ *adv* — **av·id·ness** *n*

av·o·ca·do \ˌav-ə-'käd-ō, ˌäv-\ *n, pl* **-dos** *also* **-does** : the usually green pear-shaped edible fruit of a tropical American tree that has a rich oily flesh; *also* : the tree that bears this fruit

av·o·ca·tion \ˌav-ə-'kā-shən\ *n* **1** : customary employment : VOCATION **2** : an activity one engages in regularly for enjoyment rather than as a job : HOBBY — **av·o·ca·tion·al** \-shnəl, -shən-ᵊl\ *adj*

av·o·cet \'av-ə-ˌset\ *n* : any of several rather large long-legged shorebirds with webbed feet and a slender bill that curves upward

avoid \ə-'void\ *vb* **1** : to keep away from ⟨they have been *avoiding* me⟩ **2** : to keep from happening ⟨*avoid* an accident⟩ **3** : to keep from doing or being ⟨*avoid* getting too tired⟩ — **avoid·able** \-ə-bəl\ *adj* — **avoid·ably** \-blē\ *adv* — **avoid·er** *n*

avoid·ance \ə-'void-ᵊn(t)s\ *n* : the act or an instance of avoiding something

av·oir·du·pois \ˌav-ərd-ə-'poiz, 'av-ərd-ə-ˌpoiz\ *n* **1** : AVOIRDUPOIS WEIGHT **2** : the fact or quality of being heavy : WEIGHT [Middle English *avoir de pois* "goods sold by weight," from early French, literally "goods of weight"]

avoirdupois weight *n* : the series of units of weight based on the pound of 16 ounces and the ounce of 16 drams — see MEASURE table

avouch \ə-'vauch\ *vb* **1** : to declare positively as a fact : AFFIRM **2** : to give a guarantee of : vouch for ⟨*avouched* her reputation⟩ — **avouch·ment** \-mənt\ *n*

avow \ə-'vau\ *vb* : to declare or acknowledge openly and frankly **synonyms** see ASSERT

avow·al \ə-'vau(-ə)l\ *n* : an open declaration or admission

avowed \ə-'vaud\ *adj* : openly declared or admitted — **avowed·ly** \ə-'vau-əd-lē\ *adv*

aw \'o\ *interj* — used to express mild sympathy, pleading, disbelief, or disappointment

await \ə-'wāt\ *vb* **1** : to wait for : EXPECT ⟨*await* a train⟩ **2** : to be ready or waiting for ⟨a reward *awaits* you⟩

¹**awake** \ə-'wāk\ *vb* **awoke** \-'wōk\ *also* **awaked** \-'wākt\; **awo·ken** \-'wō-kən\ *or* **awaked** *also* **awoke; awak·ing 1** : to arouse from sleep : wake up **2** : to become aware of something ⟨*awoke* to their danger⟩ **3** : to make or become active : STIR ⟨*awoke* old memories⟩

²**awake** *adj* **1** : not sleeping **2** : ¹ALERT 1a

awak·en \ə-'wā-kən\ *vb* **awak·ened; awak·en·ing** \-'wāk-(ə-)niŋ\ : ¹AWAKE — **awak·en·er** \-(ə-)nər\ *n*

¹**award** \ə-'wo(ə)rd\ *vb* **1** : to give by court decision (as after a lawsuit) ⟨*award* damages⟩ **2** : to give or grant as a reward ⟨*award* a prize to the best speaker⟩

²**award** *n* : something (as a prize) that is awarded

aware \ə-'wa(ə)r, -'we(ə)r\ *adj* : having or showing understanding or knowledge : CONSCIOUS — **aware·ness** *n*

awash \ə-'wosh, -'wäsh\ *adj* **1** : washed by waves or tide **2** : floating about **3 a** : flooded or covered with water **b** : filled or covered as if by a flood ⟨an event *awash* in emotion⟩

¹**away** \ə-'wā\ *adv* **1** : on the way ⟨get *away* early⟩ **2** : from this or that place ⟨go *away*⟩ **3** : in or to another place or direction ⟨turn *away*⟩ **4** : to an end : out of existence ⟨echoes dying *away*⟩ **5** : from one's possession ⟨gave *away* a fortune⟩ **6** : without stopping or slowing down ⟨talk *away*⟩ **7** : at or to a great distance in space or time : FAR ⟨*away* back in 1910⟩

²**away** *adj* **1** : absent from a place : GONE ⟨he is *away* from home⟩ **2** : distant in space or time ⟨a lake not far *away*⟩ ⟨the season is two months *away*⟩

¹**awe** \'o\ *n* : a feeling of mixed fear, respect, and wonder

²**awe** *vb* **awed; aw·ing** : to fill with awe

awe·some \'o-səm\ *adj* **1** : showing awe **2** : causing a feeling of awe **3** : TERRIFIC 2, EXTRAORDINARY ⟨had an *awesome* time⟩ — **awe·some·ly** *adv* — **awe·some·ness** *n*

awe·struck \'o-ˌstrək\ *adj* : filled with awe

¹**aw·ful** \'o-fəl\ *adj* **1** : AWESOME 2 **2** : extremely disagreeable or unpleasant **3** : very great ⟨took an *awful* chance⟩ — **aw·ful·ness** *n*

²**awful** *adv* : ²VERY 1 ⟨*awful* tired⟩

aw·ful·ly \usually 'o-fə-lē *in sense 1*, 'o-flē *in sense 2*\ *adv* **1** : in a disagreeable or unpleasant manner **2** : ²VERY 1 ⟨*awfully* nice of you⟩

awhile \ə-'hwī(ə)l, ə-'wī(ə)l\ *adv* : for a while : for a short time ⟨sit and rest *awhile*⟩

awhirl \ə-'hwərl, ə-'wərl\ *adj* : being in a whirl

awk·ward \'o-kwərd\ *adj* **1** : lacking skill and flexibility (as in the use of the hands) **2** : not graceful : CLUMSY **3** : causing embarrassment ⟨an *awkward* situation⟩ **4** : difficult to use or handle ⟨an *awkward* tool⟩ — **awk·ward·ly** *adv* — **awk·ward·ness** *n*

awl \'ol\ *n* : a pointed tool for marking surfaces or for making small holes (as in leather or wood)

aw·ning \'o-niŋ, 'än-\ *n* : a cover (as of canvas) that shades or shelters like a roof

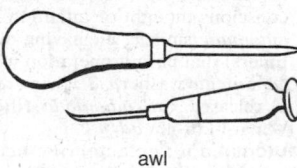

awl

awoke *past and past participle of* AWAKE

awoken *past participle of* AWAKE

AWOL \'ā-ˌwol, ˌā-ˌdəb-əl-yü-ˌō-'el\ *n* : a person who is absent without permission [*a*bsent *w*ith*o*ut *l*eave] — **AWOL** *adv or adj*

awry \ə-'rī\ *adv or adj* **1** : turned or twisted to one side **2** : off the right course : WRONG ⟨their plans went *awry*⟩

ax *or* **axe** \'aks\ *n* : a cutting tool that consists of a heavy edged head attached to a handle and that is used for chopping and splitting wood

ax·i·al \'ak-sē-əl\ *adj* **1** : of, relating to, or having the characteristics of an axis **2** : situated around, in the direction of, on, or along an axis ⟨*axial* flowers⟩ — **ax·i·al·ly** \-sē-ə-lē\ *adv*

ax·il·la \ag-'zil-ə, ak-'sil-\ *n* : ARMPIT

ax·i·om \'ak-sē-əm\ *n* : a rule or principle widely accepted as obviously true and not needing to be proved

ax·i·om·at·ic \ˌak-sē-ə-'mat-ik\ *adj* **1** : of or relating to an axiom **2** : resembling an axiom — **ax·i·om·at·i·cal·ly** \-'mat-i-k(ə-)lē\ *adv*

ax·is \'ak-səs\ *n, pl* **ax·es** \'ak-ˌsēz\ **1 a** : a straight line about which a body or a geometric figure rotates or may be supposed to rotate ⟨the earth's *axis*⟩ **b** : a straight line with respect to which a body or figure is symmetrical — called also *axis of symmetry* **c** : one of the reference lines of a coordinate system **2 a** : a bodily structure around which parts are arranged in a symmetrical way **b** : the main stem of a plant from which leaves and branches arise

ax·le \'ak-səl\ *n* : a pin, pole, or bar on or with which a wheel revolves

ax·o·lotl \'ak-sə-ˌlät-əl\ *n* : any of several salamanders of mountain lakes of Mexico and the western U.S. that ordinarily live and breed while keeping the larval form

axolotl

ax·on \'ak-ˌsän\ *also* **ax·one** \-ˌsōn\ *n* : a usually long and single process of a neuron that usually carries impulses away from the cell body — compare DENDRITE 2 — **ax·o·nal** \'ak-sən-°l; ak-'sän-, -'sōn-\ *adj*

¹aye *also* **ay** \'ā\ *adv* : FOREVER 1, ALWAYS [Middle English *aye* "always"; of Scandinavian origin]

²aye *also* **ay** \'ī\ *adv* : ¹YES 1 ⟨*aye, aye,* sir⟩ [perhaps from Middle English *ye* "yes, yea"]

³aye *also* **ay** \'ī\ *n, pl* **ayes** : a vote yes or a person who votes yes

aye–aye \'ī-ˌī\ *n* : a lemur of Madagascar that has large eyes and ears and is active at night

Ayr·shire \'a(ə)r-ˌshi(ə)r, 'e(ə)r-, -shər\ *n* : any of a breed of hardy dairy cattle varying in color from white to red or brown

aye-aye

aza·lea \ə-'zāl-yə\ *n* : any of numerous rhododendrons that have funnel-shaped flowers, usually shed their leaves in the fall, and include many grown as ornamental plants

az·i·muth \'az-(ə)məth\ *n* : horizontal direction of an object from a fixed point expressed as an angle

azo \'az-ō\ *adj* : relating to or containing two nitrogen atoms united to each other and at both ends to carbon ⟨an *azo* dye⟩

AZT \ˌā-(ˌ)zē-'tē\ *n* : a drug used to treat AIDS

Az·tec \'az-ˌtek\ *n* : a member of an American Indian people that founded the Mexican empire conquered by Cortes in 1519

azure \'azh-ər\ *n* : the blue color of the clear sky

azur·ite \'azh-ə-ˌrīt\ *n* : a blue mineral that is a carbonate of copper and an ore of copper

B

b \'bē\ *n, often cap* **1** : the second letter of the English alphabet **2** : a musical note referred to by the letter B : the seventh tone of a C-major scale **3** : a grade rating a student's work as good

baa \'ba, 'bä\ *n* : the bleat of a sheep — **baa** *vb*

¹bab·ble \'bab-əl\ *vb* **bab·bled; bab·bling** \'bab-(ə)liŋ\ **1 a** : to make meaningless sounds **b** : to talk foolishly or too much **2** : to make the sound of a brook — **bab·bler** \'bab-(ə)lər\ *n*

²babble *n* **1** : talk that is not clear **2** : the sound of a brook

babe \'bāb\ *n* : ¹BABY 1a ⟨a *babe* in arms⟩

ba·bel \'bā-bəl, 'bab-əl\ *n, often cap* **1** : a confusion of sounds or voices **2** : a scene of noise or confusion [from the Tower of *Babel* in Genesis 11:4–9, the building of which was interrupted by a confusion of languages]

ba·boon \ba-'bün\ *n* : any of several large African and Asian monkeys having long squarish muzzles and usually short tails

ba·bush·ka \bə-'büsh-kə, -'büsh-\ *n* : a kerchief usually folded into a triangle and worn on the head [from Russian *babushka,* "grandmother"]

baboon

¹ba·by \'bā-bē\ *n, pl* **ba·bies** **1 a** : a very young child; *esp* : INFANT **b** : a very young animal **2** : the youngest of a group **3** : a childish person — **ba·by·hood** \-bē-ˌhud\ *n* — **ba·by·ish** \-ish\ *adj*

²baby *adj* **1** : being or relating to a baby ⟨a *baby* deer⟩ ⟨my *baby* sister⟩ ⟨*baby* clothes⟩ **2** : much smaller than usual ⟨a *baby* grand piano⟩ ⟨*baby* carrots⟩ ⟨a *baby* spaceship⟩

³baby *vb* **ba·bied; ba·by·ing** **1** : to use or treat as a baby : PET **2** : to operate or treat with care ⟨*babied* the car⟩

baby boom *n* : a marked rise in a birthrate (as in the U.S. after World War II) — **baby boom·er** \'bü-mər\ *n*

baby oil *n* : a usually pleasant-smelling oil used especially to add moisture to and clean the skin

baby powder *n* : a fine powder composed mainly of talc or cornstarch that is sprinkled or rubbed on the skin especially to absorb moisture and relieve chafing

baby's breath *n* : a tall branching herb that is related to the carnation, has clusters of small fragrant white or pink flowers, and is often used in flower arrangements

ba·by·sit \'bā-bē-ˌsit\ *vb* **-sat** \-ˌsat\; **-sit·ting** : to care for children usually while the parents are away for a short time — **ba·by·sit·ter** *n*

baby talk *n* **1** : the speech used by very young children learning to talk **2** : speech like baby talk sometimes used by adults to speak to very young children

baby tooth *n* : MILK TOOTH

bach·e·lor \'bach-(ə-)lər\ *n* **1** : a person who has received the lowest degree given by a college, university, or professional school ⟨*bachelor* of arts⟩; *also* : the degree itself **2 a** : an unmarried man **b** : an unmated male animal — **bach·e·lor·hood** \-ˌhud\ *n*

bach·e·lor·ette \ˌbach-lə-'ret, ˌbach-ə-\ *n* : an unmarried woman

\ə\ abut	\au̇\ out	\i\ tip	\ȯ\ saw	\u̇\ foot
\ər\ further	\ch\ chin	\ī\ life	\ȯi\ coin	\y\ yet
\a\ mat	\e\ pet	\j\ job	\th\ thin	\yü\ few
\ā\ take	\ē\ easy	\ŋ\ sing	\t͟h\ this	\yu̇\ cure
\ä\ cot, cart	\g\ go	\ō\ bone	\ü\ food	\zh\ vision

bachelor's button *n* : a European plant related to the daisies and often grown for its showy blue, pink, or white flower heads — called also *cornflower*

ba·cil·lus \bə-'sil-əs\ *n, pl* **-cil·li** \-'sil-ī *also* -'sil-ē\ : any of numerous straight rod-shaped bacteria that require oxygen for growth; *also* : a disease-producing bacterium

bachelor's button

¹**back** \'bak\ *n* **1 a** : the rear part of the human body especially from the neck to the end of the spine **b** : the corresponding part of a four-footed or lower animal **2** : the part of something that is opposite or away from the front part **3** : something at or on the back for support ⟨*back* of a chair⟩ **4 a** : a position in some games (as football or soccer) behind the front line of players **b** : a player in this position — **backed** \'bakt\ *adj* — **back·less** \'bak-ləs\ *adj* — **behind one's back** : without one's knowledge : in secret

²**back** *adv* **1 a** : to, toward, or at the rear **b** : in or into the past : AGO **c** : in or into a reclining position **d** : under control : in check ⟨held *back*⟩ **2** : to, toward, or in a place from which a person or thing came **3** : in return or reply ⟨write *back*⟩ ⟨talk *back*⟩ — **back and forth** : backward and forward : from one place to another

⁴**back** *vb* **1** : to give aid or support to **2** : to move or cause to move back or backward **3** : to shift in a counterclockwise direction ⟨the wind *backed* around⟩ **4** : to provide with a back — **back·er** *n*

back·ache \'bak-ˌāk\ *n* : pain usually in the lower back

back·beat \-ˌbēt\ *n* : a steady pronounced rhythm stressing the second and fourth beats of a four-beat measure

back·bite \-ˌbīt\ *vb* **-bit; -bit·ten; -bit·ing** : to say mean things about a person who is not present — **back·bit·er** *n*

back·board \'bak-ˌbōrd, -ˌbȯrd\ *n* : a board placed at the back or serving as a back; *esp* : a rounded or rectangular board behind the basket on a basketball court

back·bone \-'bōn, -ˌbōn\ *n* **1** : the skeleton of the trunk and tail of a vertebrate that consists of a jointed series of vertebrae enclosing and protecting the spinal cord — called also *spinal column* **2** : the foundation or sturdiest part of something **3** : firmness of character ⟨a coward with no *backbone*⟩ — **back·boned** \-'bōnd, -ˌbōnd\ *adj*

back·court \-'kō(ə)rt, -'kȯ(ə)rt\ *n* **1** : a basketball team's defensive half of the court **2** : the positions of the guards on a basketball team; *also* : the guards themselves ⟨a team with a strong *backcourt*⟩

back down *vb* : to retreat from a stand one has taken or from a challenge one has accepted

back·drop \'bak-ˌdräp\ *n* **1** : a painted cloth hung across the rear of a stage **2** : BACKGROUND 1, 3a

back·field \-ˌfēld\ *n* : the football players who line up behind the line of scrimmage

¹**back·fire** \-ˌfī(ə)r\ *n* **1** : a fire that is set to check the spread of a forest fire or a grass fire by burning off a strip of land ahead of it **2** : a loud noise caused by the improperly timed explosion of fuel in the cylinder of an internal combustion engine

²**backfire** *vb* **1** : to make a backfire **2** : to have a result opposite to what was planned ⟨their plans *backfired*⟩

back·flip \-ˌflip\ *n* : a backward somersault especially in the air

back·gam·mon \'bak-ˌgam-ən, ˌbak-'gam-\ *n* : a board game for two played with dice in which the object is to be the first to move all one's pieces around and off the board

back·ground \'bak-ˌgraủnd\ *n* **1** : the scenery or ground that is behind a main figure or object (as in a painting) **2** : a position that attracts little attention ⟨always tries to keep in the *background*⟩ **3 a** : the setting within which something takes place **b** : the events leading up to a situation **c** : information needed to understand a problem or situation **d** : the total of a person's experience, knowledge, and education **4 a** : a somewhat steady level of radiation in the natural environment (as from cosmic rays or radio activity) **b** : undesired sound that is heard in a system (as in radio or a tape recording) that produces sound from other sources

background music *n* : music played to go along with and add to the story or mood of a movie or radio or television show

¹**back·hand** \-ˌhand\ *n* **1 a** : a stroke (as in tennis) made with the back of the hand turned in the direction of movement **b** : a catch made with the arm across the body and the palm turned away from the body **2** : handwriting in which the letters slant to the left

²**backhand** *adj* : using or made with a backhand

³**backhand** *vb* : to do, hit, or catch with a backhand

⁴**backhand** *or* **back·hand·ed** \'bak-'han-dəd\ *adv* : with a backhand

back·hand·ed \'bak-'han-dəd\ *adj* **1** : ²BACKHAND **2** : not sincere ⟨a *backhanded* compliment⟩

back·hoe \-ˌhō\ *n* : a large machine that digs into the earth with a metal scoop drawn toward the machine

back·ing \'bak-iŋ\ *n* **1** : something forming a back **2 a** : ²SUPPORT, AID **b** : ENDORSEMENT 3, APPROVAL

back·lash \'bak-ˌlash\ *n* : a reaction against some political or social development

back·log \-ˌlòg, -ˌläg\ *n* **1** : a large log at the back of a fire in a fireplace **2** : an accumulation of tasks that have not been finished

back of *prep* : ²BEHIND 1 ⟨out *back of* the barn⟩

back off *vb* : BACK DOWN

back order *n* : a business order that is to be fulfilled later because the item is unavailable

¹**back·pack** \'bak-ˌpak\ *n* : a camping pack carried on the back; *also* : KNAPSACK

²**backpack** *vb* : to hike with a backpack — **back·pack·er** *n*

back·rest \'bak-ˌrest\ *n* : a rest for the back

back·side \'bak-'sīd\ *n* : BUTTOCK 2a

back·slash \-ˌslash\ *n* : a mark \ used especially in computer programming

back·slide \'bak-ˌslīd\ *vb* **-slid** \-ˌslid\; **-slid** *or* **-slid·den** \-ˌslid-ᵊn\; **-slid·ing** \-ˌslīd-iŋ\ **1** : to go back to a less religious or less moral condition **2** : to go back to a worse condition — **backslide** *n* — **back·slid·er** \-ˌslīd-ər\ *n*

back·space \-ˌspās\ *vb* : to move back one space in a text with the press of a key — **backspace** *n*

back·spin \-ˌspin\ *n* : a backward spinning motion of a ball

back·stage \'bak-'stāj\ *adv or adj* : in or to an area behind the stage of a theater

back·stop \'bak-ˌstäp\ *n* **1** : a screen or fence to keep a ball from leaving the field of play **2** : a baseball catcher

back·stretch \-ˌstrech, -'strech\ *n* : the side of a racetrack that is opposite the part between the last turn and the finish line

back·stroke \-ˌstrōk\ *n* : a swimming stroke made by a swimmer who lies in the water facing upward

back·swim·mer \-ˌswim-ər\ *n* : any of a family of bugs that live in the water and swim on their backs

back talk *n* : a rude or quarrelsome reply

back·track \'bak-ˌtrak\ *vb* **1** : to go back over a course or path **2** : to reverse a position or stand

back·up \'bak-ˌəp\ *n* **1** : a person or thing that takes the place of or supports another ⟨has a *backup* in case he gets sick⟩ **2** : a gathering or piling up because the flow has been stopped ⟨a traffic *backup*⟩ **3** : a copy of a computer file to protect against loss of data; *also* : the act or an instance of making a backup

back up *vb* **1** : to gather or pile up because the flow has been stopped ⟨traffic *backed up* for miles⟩ **2** : to make a copy of (as a computer file) to protect against loss of data

¹**back·ward** \'bak-wərd\ *or* **back·wards** \-wərdz\ *adv* **1** : toward the back ⟨look *backward*⟩ **2** : with the back first ⟨ride *backward*⟩ **3** : opposite to the usual way : in reverse ⟨count *backward*⟩ **4** : toward a worse state

²**backward** *adj* **1 a** : directed or turned toward the back ⟨a *backward* glance⟩ **b** : done backward **2** : ¹SHY 1, BASHFUL **3** : slow in learning or development ⟨*backward* nations⟩ — **back·ward·ly** *adv* — **back·ward·ness** *n*

back·wash \'bak-ˌwȯsh, -ˌwäsh\ *n* : backward movement (as of water or air) produced by a propelling force (as the motion of oars)

back·wa·ter \'bak-ˌwȯt-ər, -ˌwät-\ *n* **1** : water held or turned back from its course **2** : a backward place or condition

back·woods \'bak-'wu̇dz, -ˌwu̇dz\ *n pl* **1** : wooded or partly cleared areas far from cities **2** : a place that is slow to adopt the ways of the city

back·yard \-'yärd\ *n* **1** : an area in back of a house **2** : an area in which one has a special interest

ba·con \'bā-kən\ *n* **1** : salted and smoked meat from the sides and the back of a pig **2** : money gained through employment or legislation ⟨bring home the *bacon*⟩

bacteria *plural of* BACTERIUM

bac·te·ri·al \bak-'tir-ē-əl\ *adj* : of, relating to, or caused by bacteria

bac·te·ri·ol·o·gist \(ˌ)bak-ˌtir-ē-'äl-ə-jəst\ *n* : a person who specializes in bacteriology

bac·te·ri·ol·o·gy \(ˌ)bak-ˌtir-ē-'äl-ə-jē\ *n* **1** : a science that deals with bacteria and their relations to medicine, industry, and agriculture **2** : bacterial life, facts, and events of scientific interest — **bac·te·ri·o·log·ic** \-ē-ə-'läj-ik\ *or* **bac·te·ri·o·log·i·cal** \-'läj-i-kəl\ *adj*

bac·te·rio·phage \bak-'tir-ē-ə-ˌfāj, -ˌfäzh\ *n* : any of various viruses that specifically attack bacteria

bac·te·ri·um \bak-'tir-ē-əm\ *n, pl* **-ria** \-ē-ə\ : any of a group of single-celled microorganisms that live in soil, water, the bodies of plants and animals, or matter obtained from living things and are important because of their chemical effects and disease-causing abilities

Bac·tri·an camel \ˌbak-trē-ən-\ *n* : CAMEL b

¹**bad** \'bad\ *adj* **worse** \'wərs\; **worst** \'wərst\ **1 a** : below standard : POOR **b** : not favorable ⟨a *bad* impression⟩ **c** : ROTTEN 1 ⟨*bad* meat⟩ **2** : not good or right : morally evil or wrong ⟨a *bad* person⟩ ⟨*bad* behavior⟩ **3** : not enough ⟨*bad* lighting⟩ **4** : DISAGREEABLE 1, UNPLEASANT ⟨*bad* news⟩ **5 a** : HARMFUL ⟨*bad* for the health⟩ **b** : SEVERE 3 ⟨a *bad* cold⟩ **6** : INCORRECT, FAULTY ⟨*bad* spelling⟩ **7** : ¹ILL 2c, SICK ⟨feel *bad*⟩ **8** : SORROWFUL 1, SORRY ⟨don't feel *bad* about losing⟩ — **bad·ness** *n*

²**bad** *n* **1** : a bad thing or part ⟨take the *bad* with the good⟩ **2** : a bad or unhappy state ⟨go to the *bad*⟩

³**bad** *adv* : BADLY ⟨not doing so *bad*⟩

bade *past of* BID

badge \'baj\ *n* : a mark or sign worn to show that a person belongs to a certain group, class, or rank

¹**bad·ger** \'baj-ər\ *n* : any of several sturdy burrowing flesh-eating mammals widely distributed in the northern hemisphere; *also* : the pelt or fur of a badger

²**badger** *vb* **bad·gered; bad·ger·ing** \'baj-(ə-)riŋ\ : to annoy again and again

bad·land \'bad-ˌland\ *n* : a region where natural forces have worn away the soft rocks

¹badger

into sharp and complicated shapes and where plant life is scarce — usually used in plural

bad·ly \'bad-lē\ *adv* **worse** \'wərs\; **worst** \'wərst\ **1** : in a bad manner ⟨played *badly*⟩ **2** : very much ⟨wanted the jeans *badly*⟩

bad·min·ton \'bad-ˌmit-ⁿn\ *n* : a game in which a shuttlecock is hit back and forth over a net by players using light rackets

bad–mouth \-ˌmau̇th, -'mau̇th\ *vb* : to say bad things about

¹**baf·fle** \'baf-əl\ *vb* **baf·fled; baf·fling** \'baf-(ə-)liŋ\ **1** : to defeat or check by confusing : PERPLEX **2** : to check or break the force or flow of by or as if by a baffle — **baf·fle·ment** \-əl-mənt\ *n* — **baf·fler** \-(ə)lər\ *n*

²**baffle** *n* : a device (as a wall or screen) to turn aside, check, or regulate flow (as of a fluid, light, or sound)

¹**bag** \'bag\ *n* **1 a** : a container made of flexible material (as paper or plastic) **b** : ¹PURSE 1, HANDBAG **c** : SUITCASE **2 a** : a pouched or hanging bodily part or organ (as an udder); *also* : a puffy sagging area of loose skin ⟨*bags* under the eyes⟩ **b** : a puffed-out sag or bulge in cloth **c** : a square white stuffed canvas container that marks a base in baseball **3** : the amount contained in a bag **4** : a quantity of game taken or permitted to be taken — **in the bag** : ¹SURE 4, CERTAIN ⟨a win is *in the bag*⟩

²**bag** *vb* **bagged; bag·ging** **1** : to swell out ⟨pants *bag* at the knees⟩ **2** : to put into a bag ⟨*bagging* groceries⟩ **3** : to kill or capture in hunting ⟨the hunter *bagged* a deer⟩

ba·gel \'bā-gəl\ *n* : a firm doughnut-shaped roll

bag·gage \'bag-ij\ *n* : the traveling bags and personal belongings of a traveler : LUGGAGE

Bag·gies \'bag-ēz\ *trademark* — used for clear plastic bags

bag·gy \'bag-ē\ *adj* **bag·gi·er; -est** : loose, puffed out, or hanging like a bag ⟨*baggy* pants⟩ — **bag·gi·ly** \'bag-ə-lē\ *adv* — **bag·gi·ness** \'bag-ē-nəs\ *n*

bag of waters : the double-walled fluid-filled pouch that encloses and protects the fetus in the uterus and that breaks releasing its fluid during the birth process

bag·pipe \'bag-ˌpīp\ *n* : a musical instrument played especially in Scotland that consists of a bag for air, a mouth tube for blowing up the air bag, and pipes which give a sound when air passes through them — often used in plural — **bag·pip·er** \-ˌpī-pər\ *n*

ba·guette \ba-'get\ *n* **1** : a gem (as a diamond) cut in a long narrow rectangle; *also* : the shape itself **2** : a long thin loaf of French bread

bag·worm \'bag-ˌwərm\ *n* : a moth that as a larva lives in a silk case covered with plant debris and is often destructive to the leaves of plants

bagpipe

¹**bail** \'bā(ə)l\ *n* : a container used to remove water from a boat [Middle English *baille* "bucket, bail," from early French *baille* "bucket," from Latin *bajula* "water container," derived from *bajulus* "porter, carrier"]

²**bail** *vb* : to remove (water) from a boat by dipping and throwing over the side — usually used with *out*

³**bail** *n* **1** : the temporary release of a prisoner in exchange for a deposit of money ensuring the later appearance of

the prisoner in court **2** : the deposit of money needed to temporarily free a prisoner **3** : a person who provides bail [Middle English *bail* "custody, bail," derived from early French *baillier* "to give, entrust," derived from Latin *bajulare* "to carry a load," from *bajulus* "porter, carrier"]

⁴bail *vb* : to get the release of (a prisoner) by giving bail

⁵bail *n* **1** : a semicircular support **2** : the handle of a kettle or pail [Middle English *beil, baile* "half hoop, bail"]

bai·liff \'bā-ləf\ *n* **1** : any of various officials; *esp* : a minor officer of some U.S. courts usually serving as a messenger or doorkeeper **2** *chiefly British* : one who manages an estate or farm

bail out *vb* **1** : to jump out of an airplane with a parachute **2** : to help from a difficult situation

bairn \'ba(ə)rn, 'be(ə)rn\ *n, chiefly Scottish* : CHILD 1, 2a

¹bait \'bāt\ *vb* **1** : to torment by repeated attacks **2** : to torment (an animal) with dogs **3** : to put bait on or in ⟨*bait* a hook⟩ [Middle English *baiten* "to tease, torment," from an early Norse word originally meaning "to cause to bite"] — **bait·er** *n*

²bait *n* **1** : something (as food) used to attract animals to a hook or into a trap **2** : a poisonous material put where it will be eaten by and kill harmful or undesirable animals **3** : LURE 1, TEMPTATION [Middle English *bait* "a lure," from two early Norse words, one meaning "pasture" and the other meaning "food"]

baize \'bāz\ *n* : a fabric made to resemble felt

¹bake \'bāk\ *vb* **baked; bak·ing** **1** : to cook or become cooked by dry heat especially in an oven **2** : to dry or harden by heat ⟨*bake* bricks⟩ **3** : to be or become very hot ⟨a sidewalk *baking* in the sun⟩ — **bak·er** *n*

²bake *n* **1** : the act or process of baking **2** : a social gathering at which a baked food is served; *esp* : CLAMBAKE

baker's dozen *n* : THIRTEEN

bakers' yeast *n* : a yeast used or suitable for use in making dough rise

bak·ery \'bā-k(ə-)rē\ *n, pl* **-er·ies** : a place where bread, cakes, and pastry are made or sold

bake sale *n* : a fund-raising event at which usually homemade foods (as cakes and cookies) are sold

bake·shop \'bāk-,shäp\ *n* : BAKERY

bake·ware \'bāk-,wa(ə)r, -,we(ə)r\ *n* : dishes used for baking and serving food

baking powder *n* : a powder that usually consists of sodium bicarbonate, an acidic substance (as cream of tartar), and starch or flour and that makes the dough rise in baked goods (as cakes)

baking soda *n* : SODIUM BICARBONATE

¹bal·ance \'bal-ən(t)s\ *n* **1** : an instrument used for measuring mass or weight **2** : a counterbalancing weight, force, or influence **3** : a vibrating wheel operating with a hairspring to regulate the mechanical motions of a timepiece **4** : a condition in which opposing forces are equal to each other **5** : equality between the totals of the two sides of an account **6** : an orderly and artistic arrangement of elements that is pleasing : HARMONY **7 a** : something left over : REMAINDER **b** : the amount by which one side of an account is greater than the other ⟨a *balance* of $10 on the credit side⟩ **8** : mental and emotional steadiness **9** : the maintenance (as in a natural habitat) of a population in about the same condition and numbers

²balance *vb* **bal·anced; bal·anc·ing** **1** : to figure out the difference between the debits and credits of an account ⟨*balanced* her checkbook⟩ **2 a** : to arrange so that one set of elements exactly equals another ⟨*balance* an equation⟩ **b** : to complete (a chemical equation) so that the same number of atoms and electric charges of each kind appears on each side **3 a** : ²COUNTERBALANCE, OFFSET **b** : to equal or make equal in weight, number, or proportion ⟨*balanced* the powers of the three branches of government⟩ **4** : to weigh against one another : COMPARE **5**

: to bring or come to a state or position of balance — **bal·anc·er** *n*

balance beam *n* : a narrow wooden beam supported in a horizontal position above the floor and used for balancing feats in gymnastics

balance of nature : the fine state of balance in a natural ecosystem due to the effects of the living and nonliving parts of the environment on each other

balance wheel *n* : a wheel that adjusts the motion of a mechanism (as a timepiece or a sewing machine)

bal·co·ny \'bal-kə-nē\ *n, pl* **-nies** **1** : a platform enclosed by a low wall or railing and built out from the side of a building **2** : a platform inside a building extending out over part of the main floor (as of a theater)

¹bald \'bȯld\ *adj* **1** : lacking a natural or usual covering (as of hair) **2** : ²PLAIN 1, UNADORNED ⟨the *bald* facts⟩ — **bald·ly** *adv* — **bald·ness** \'bȯl(d)-nəs\ *n*

²bald *vb* : to become bald ⟨his head is *balding*⟩

bald cypress *n* : either of two large swamp trees related to the pine and found in the southern U.S.

bald eagle *n* : a North American eagle which is mostly brown when young but has white head, neck, and tail feathers when mature

bal·dric \'bȯl-drik\ *n* : a belt worn over one shoulder to provide a device from which to hang a sword or bugle at the opposite hip

¹bale \'bā(ə)l\ *n* : a large bundle of goods tightly tied for storing or shipping ⟨a *bale* of cotton⟩

²bale *vb* **baled; bal·ing** : to make up into a bale — **bal·er** *n*

bald eagle

ba·leen \bə-'lēn, 'bā-,lēn\ *n* : a horny substance found in two rows of long plates which hang down from the upper jaw of baleen whales — called also *whalebone*

baleen whale *n* : any of various usually large whales lacking teeth but having baleen for filtering small ocean animals (as krill) out of seawater — compare TOOTHED WHALE

bale·ful \'bāl-fəl\ *adj* **1** : deadly or harmful in influence **2** : threatening harm or evil ⟨a *baleful* look⟩ — **bale·ful·ly** \-fə-lē\ *adv* — **bale·ful·ness** *n*

¹balk \'bȯk\ *n* **1** : something that prevents movement or action **2** : an illegal motion of a baseball pitcher while in position to pitch with a runner on base

²balk *vb* **1** : to check or stop by or as if by something in the way : BLOCK **2** : to stop and refuse to go ⟨the horse *balked*⟩ **3** : to make a balk in baseball — **balk·er** *n*

balky \'bȯ-kē\ *adj* **balk·i·er; -est** : likely to refuse to act or function as directed or expected ⟨a *balky* mule⟩ ⟨a *balky* engine⟩

¹ball \'bȯl\ *n* **1 a** : something round or roundish ⟨a *ball* of twine⟩ **b** : a usually round object used in a game or sport **c** : a usually round shot for a firearm **d** : the rounded bulge at the base of the thumb; *also* : the rounded wide part of the bottom of the human foot between the toes and arch **2** : a game or sport (as baseball) played with a ball ⟨play *ball*⟩ **3** : a pitched baseball that fails to pass through the strike zone and is not struck at by the batter [Middle English *bal* "ball"]

²ball *vb* : to make or come together into a ball

³ball *n* : a large formal party for dancing [from French *bal* "a dance," derived from Latin *ballare* "to dance" — related to BALLET]

bal·lad \'bal-əd\ *n* **1** : a poem that tells a story of adventure, of romance, or of a hero, that is suitable for singing, and that usually has stanzas of four lines with a rhyme on the second and fourth lines **2** : a simple song **3** : a usually slow or sentimental popular song

ball–and–socket joint *n* : a joint (as in the hip) in which a rounded part moves within a socket so as to allow movements in many directions

¹**bal·last** \'bal-əst\ *n* **1** : heavy material used especially to make a ship steady or to control the rising of a balloon **2** : gravel or broken stone laid in a foundation for a railroad or used in making concrete

²**ballast** *vb* : to provide with ballast

ball bearing *n* **1** : a bearing in which the revolving part turns on steel balls that roll easily in a groove **2** : one of the balls in a ball bearing

ball·car·ri·er \'bòl-,kar-ē-ər\ *n* : a football player who carries the ball on offense

bal·le·ri·na \,bal-ə-'rē-nə\ *n* : a female ballet dancer

bal·let \'bal-ā, ba-'lā\ *n* **1 a** : an art form that uses dancing to tell a story or express a theme **b** : dancing in which poses and steps are combined with leaps and turns **2** : a group that performs ballets [from French *ballet* "ballet," derived from Italian *ballare* "to dance," from Latin *ballare* "to dance" — related to ³BALL]

bal·lis·tic \bə-'lis-tik\ *adj* : of or relating to ballistics

ballistic missile *n* : a missile that moves under its own power, is guided as it rises in a steeply curving path, and falls freely on the way back to earth

bal·lis·tics \bə-'lis-tiks\ *n sing or pl* **1** : the science that deals with the motion of objects (as bullets or rockets) that are thrown or driven forward **2** : the flight characteristics of an object (as a bullet or rocket) that is thrown or driven forward

ball joint *n* : BALL-AND-SOCKET JOINT

¹**bal·loon** \bə-'lün\ *n* **1** : a bag of tough light material filled with heated gas or a gas lighter than air so as to rise and float in the atmosphere and that usually carries a suspended load (as a gondola with passengers) **2** : a toy or decoration consisting of an inflatable bag (as of rubber) **3** : an outline containing words spoken or thought by a character (as in a cartoon)

²**balloon** *vb* **1** : to go up or travel in a balloon **2** : to swell or puff out **3** : to increase rapidly ⟨*ballooning* prices⟩

¹**bal·lot** \'bal-ət\ *n* **1** : a small ball or sheet of paper used to cast a secret vote **2 a** : the action or system of voting **b** : the right to vote **3** : the number of votes cast

Word History Small objects have long been used as a means of tallying votes. In ancient Greece, a word for "pebble," *psēphos,* came to designate any voting token, and then to mean simply "vote," from the practice of dropping a pebble into one of two urns as decisions were made in public assemblies. In medieval Venice, small balls were used in public lotteries and elections; in one such lottery, members of the city's Great Council would draw gold and silver balls from vases to determine nominating committees for officeholders. The word for "small ball" in the Venetian form of Italian was *ballotta,* which was extended to other tokens used in drawing lots and voting, such as scraps of linen or paper. Familiarity with Venetian customs led to the adoption of the word as ballot in English. [from Italian *ballotta* "little ball (used in voting)," from *balla* "ball"]

²**ballot** *vb* : to vote or decide by ballot

ball·park \'bòl-,pärk\ *n* : a park in which ball games are played

ball·point \-,pòint\ *n* : a pen whose writing point is a small metal ball that inks itself from an inner supply

ball·room \'bòl-,rüm, -,rùm\ *n* : a large room for dances

bal·ly·hoo \'bal-ē-,hü\ *n* : extravagant statements and claims made for publicity — **ballyhoo** *vb*

balm \'bäm, 'bälm\ *n* **1** : resin from small tropical evergreen trees **2** : a fragrant healing or soothing preparation (as an ointment) **3** : something that comforts or refreshes

balm of Gil·e·ad \-'gil-ē-əd\ **1** : a small African and Asian tree with fragrant evergreen leaves; *also* : its fragrant oily resin **2** : any of several poplars (as balsam poplar) having buds that are full of resin

balmy \'bäm-ē, 'bäl-mē\ *adj* **balm·i·er; -est 1 a** : gently soothing **b** : TEMPERATE 5 ⟨*balmy* weather⟩ **2** : FOOLISH, INSANE — **balm·i·ly** \'bäm-ə-lē, 'bäl-mə-\ *adv* — **balm·i·ness** \'bäm-ē-nəs, 'bäl-mē-\ *n*

bal·sa \'bòl-sə\ *n* **1** : ¹RAFT; *esp* : one made of two cylinders of metal or wood joined by a frame **2** : a tropical American tree with extremely light strong wood used especially for floats; *also* : its wood

bal·sam \'bòl-səm\ *n* **1 a** : a fragrant and usually oily substance that slowly flows from various plants **b** : a preparation containing or smelling like balsam **2 a** : a balsam-yielding tree (as balsam fir) **b** : IMPATIENS; *esp* : one grown as an ornamental **3** : BALM 2 — **bal·sam·ic** \bòl-'sam-ik\ *adj*

balsam fir *n* : a North American fir tree widely used for pulpwood and as a Christmas tree

balsam poplar *n* : a North American poplar that is often cultivated as a shade tree and has buds coated with a resin

Bal·tic \'bòl-tik\ *adj* **1** : of or relating to the Baltic Sea or to the states of Lithuania, Latvia, and Estonia **2** : of or relating to a branch of the Indo-European languages containing Latvian, Lithuanian, and Old Prussian

balsam fir

Bal·ti·more oriole \,bòl-tə-,mō(ə)r-, -,mò(ə)r-, -mər-\ *n* : an oriole of eastern and central parts of the U.S. that is orange below and in the male mostly black above and in the female mostly greenish-brown above

bal·us·ter \'bal-ə-stər\ *n* : a short post that supports a rail (as of a staircase)

bal·us·trade \'bal-ə-,sträd\ *n* : a row of balusters topped by a rail; *also* : a low wall or barrier

bam·boo \bam-'bü\ *n, pl* **bamboos** : any of various chiefly tropical tall woody grasses including some with strong hollow stems used for building, furniture, or utensils; *also* : the strong woody stem of bamboo — **bamboo** *adj*

¹**ban** \'ban\ *vb* **banned; ban·ning 1** : to forbid especially by law or social pressure **2** : ²BAR 4

²**ban** *n* **1** : ¹CURSE 1 **2** : an official order forbidding something

ba·nal \bə-'nal, ba-, -'näl; bā-'nal; 'bān-ºl\ *adj* : not original, fresh, or exciting : STALE, COMMONPLACE — **ba·nal·i·ty** \bə-'nal-ət-ē *also* bā-ə- or ba-\ *n* — **ba·nal·ly** \bə-'nal-lē, ba-, -'näl-; bā-,nal-; 'bān-ºl-(l)ē\ *adv*

ba·nana \bə-'nan-ə\ *n* : a treelike tropical plant with large leaves and flower clusters that develop into a bunch of finger-shaped fruit which are usually yellow when ripe; *also* : its fruit

banana oil *n* : a colorless liquid acetate that has a fruity odor and is used to dissolve things and to make artificial fruit scents

banana

\ə\ **abut**	\aú\ **out**	\i\ **tip**	\ò\ **saw**	\ú\ **foot**
\ər\ **further**	\ch\ **chin**	\ī\ **life**	\òi\ **coin**	\y\ **yet**
\a\ **mat**	\e\ **pet**	\j\ **job**	\th\ **thin**	\yü\ **few**
\ā\ **take**	\ē\ **easy**	\ŋ\ **sing**	\th\ **this**	\yù\ **cure**
\ä\ **cot, cart**	\g\ **go**	\ō\ **bone**	\ü\ **food**	\zh\ **vision**

ba·nan·as \bə-'nan-əz\ *adj* : CRAZY ⟨you're driving me *bananas*⟩ ⟨the crowd went *bananas*⟩

banana split *n* : ice cream served on a banana split in half lengthwise and usually covered with syrups, fruits, nuts, and whipped cream

¹band \'band\ *n* **1** : something that confines or constricts while allowing some movement **2** : something that binds or restrains legally, morally, or spiritually **3** : a strip serving to join or hold things together **4** : a strip that is different (as in color, texture, or composition) from nearby matter ⟨a black beak with a white *band*⟩ **5** : a range of wavelengths, frequencies, or energies between two specified limits [partly from a word of Norse origin meaning "something that binds" and partly from early French *bande* "stripe"; of Germanic origin] — **band·ed** \'ban-dəd\ *adj*

²band *vb* **1** : to put a band on **2** : to tie up with a band **3** : to join in a group ⟨*banded* together for protection⟩

³band *n* **1** : a group of persons, animals, or things **2** : a group of musicians playing together [from early French *bande* "troop," derived from an earlier word of Germanic origin]

¹ban·dage \'ban-dij\ *n* : a strip of fabric used especially to cover and bind up wounds and as a means of applying healing medicines or ointments

²bandage *vb* **ban·daged; ban·dag·ing** : to bind or cover with a bandage

Band–Aid \'ban-'dād\ *trademark* — used for a small adhesive strip with a gauze pad for covering minor wounds

ban·dan·na *or* **ban·dana** \ban-'dan-ə\ *n* : a large handkerchief usually with a colorful design printed on it

band·box \'ban(d)-,bäks\ *n* : a usually round box of paperboard or thin wood often used for storing a hat

ban·di·coot \'ban-di-,küt\ *n* : any of various small insect-eating and plant-eating marsupial mammals especially of Australia

ban·dit \'ban-dət\ *n, pl* **bandits** *also* **ban·dit·ti** \ban-'dit-ē\ : a person who lives by stealing and often as a member of a band : ROBBER, OUTLAW [from Italian *bandito*, literally, "one who is banished"] — **ban·dit·ry** \'ban-də-trē\ *n*

band·mas·ter \'ban(d)-,mas-tər\ *n* : a conductor of a musical band

band·mate \'ban(d)-,māt\ *n* : a fellow member of a band

ban·do·lier *or* **ban·do·leer** \,ban-də-'li(ə)r\ *n* : a belt worn over the shoulder and across the body along the length of which items (as cartridges) may be carried in loops or pouches

band saw *n* : a saw in the form of a continuous steel band running over pulleys

band·stand \'ban(d)-,stand\ *n* : an outdoor platform on which a band performs

band·wag·on \'ban-,dwag-ən\ *n* **1** : a wagon carrying musicians in a parade **2** : a popular movement or activity that attracts growing support ⟨jump on the *bandwagon*⟩

band·width \'band-,width\ *n* **1** : a range of frequencies **2** : the capacity for or rate of data transfer ⟨a high *bandwidth* Internet connection⟩

¹ban·dy \'ban-dē\ *vb* **ban·died; ban·dy·ing** **1** : to exchange (words) in argument **2** : to discuss or mention in gossip or small talk ⟨several names were *bandied* about⟩

²bandy *adj* : curved especially outward ⟨*bandy* legs⟩

ban·dy–legged \,ban-dē-'leg-(ə)d\ *adj* : having bandy legs

bane \'bān\ *n* **1** : ¹POISON 1 **2** : a source of harm, ruin, or unhappiness ⟨greed is the *bane* of humanity⟩

bane·ful \'bān-fəl\ *adj* : causing destruction or serious harm ⟨a *baneful* influence⟩ — **bane·ful·ly** \-fə-lē\ *adv*

¹bang \'baŋ\ *vb* : to beat, strike, or shut with a loud noise [probably of Scandinavian origin]

²bang *n* **1** : a violent blow **2** : a sudden loud noise **3 a** : a quick burst of energy ⟨start off with a *bang*⟩ **b** : a feeling of being thrilled or pleased ⟨you'll get a *bang* out of this⟩

³bang *n* : hair cut short across the forehead — usually used in plural [probably from earlier *bangtail* "a short tail (on a horse)"]

⁴bang *vb* : to cut (front hair) short and squarely across

ban·gle \'baŋ-gəl\ *n* **1** : a stiff bracelet or anklet **2** : a small ornament hanging from a bracelet or necklace

bang–up \'baŋ-,əp\ *adj* : FIRST-RATE, EXCELLENT ⟨had a *bang-up* time⟩ ⟨a *bang-up* job⟩

ban·ish \'ban-ish\ *vb* **1** : to force to leave a country **2** : to drive away ⟨*banish* fears⟩ — **ban·ish·ment** \-mənt\ *n*

ban·is·ter *also* **ban·nis·ter** \'ban-ə-stər\ *n* **1** : one of the slender posts used to support the handrail of a staircase **2** : a handrail with its supporting posts **3** : the handrail of a staircase

ban·jo \'ban-jō\ *n, pl* **banjos** *also* **banjoes** : a musical instrument with a round body like a drum, a long fretted neck, and four or five strings — **ban·jo·ist** \-,jō-ist\ *n*

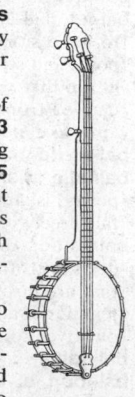

banjo

¹bank \'baŋk\ *n* **1** : a mound, pile, or ridge of earth **2** : a piled-up mass of cloud or fog **3** : a rise in the sea bottom **4** : the rising ground at the edge of a lake, river, or sea **5** : a steep slope (as of a hill) **6** : the inward tilt of a surface along a curve or of a vehicle (as an airplane) when turning [Middle English *bank* "piled up mass"; probably of Scandinavian origin]

²bank *vb* **1** : to raise a bank around **2** : to cover (as a fire) with fresh fuel to reduce the speed of burning **3** : to build with the foundation of a road or railroad sloping upward from the inside edge ⟨*bank* a curve⟩ **4** : to heap or pile in a bank **5** : to rise in or form a bank **6** : to tilt an airplane sideways when turning

³bank *n* **1** : a place of business that lends, exchanges, takes care of, or issues money **2** : a small closed container in which money may be saved **3** : a storage place (as for a reserve supply) ⟨a blood *bank*⟩ [Middle English *bank* "table or counter of a money changer," from early French *banque* (same meaning) or early Italian *banca*, literally, "bench"; of Germanic origin]

⁴bank *vb* **1** : to have an account in a bank **2** : to deposit or store in a bank ⟨*banks* $10 every week⟩ — **bank on** : to depend on ⟨we're *banking on* fair weather for the trip⟩

⁵bank *n* : a group or series of objects arranged close together in a row ⟨a *bank* of seats⟩ [Middle English *bank* "bench for rowers," from early French *banc* "bench"; of Germanic origin]

bank·book \'baŋk-,bu̇k\ *n* : the depositor's book in which a bank enters deposits and withdrawals

bank card *n* : a card (as a credit card or an ATM card) issued by a bank

bank·er \'baŋ-kər\ *n* : a person who is engaged in the business of a bank

bank·ing \'baŋ-kiŋ\ *n* : the business of a bank or banker

bank note *n* : a note issued by a bank that must be paid without interest to anyone presenting it at any time and that may be used as money

bank·roll \'baŋk-,rōl\ *n* : supply of money : FUNDS

¹bank·rupt \'baŋ-(,)krəpt\ *n* : an individual or group who becomes bankrupt; *esp* : one whose property by court order is turned over to be managed for the benefit of the creditors

²bankrupt *adj* **1** : unable to pay one's debts **2** : legally declared bankrupt ⟨the company went *bankrupt*⟩

³bankrupt *vb* : to make bankrupt

bank·rupt·cy \'baŋ-(,)krəp-(t)sē\ *n, pl* **-cies** : the condition of being bankrupt

¹ban·ner \'ban-ər\ *n* **1** : ²FLAG 1 **2** : a strip of cloth with a design, picture, or writing on it

²**banner** *adj* : unusually good : OUTSTANDING ⟨a *banner* year for apples⟩

bannister *variant of* BANISTER

banns \'banz\ *n pl* : public announcement especially in church of a proposed marriage

¹**ban·quet** \'baṅ-kwət, 'ban- *also* -ˌkwet\ *n* : a formal dinner for many people often in honor of someone

²**banquet** *vb* : to treat or be treated with a banquet : FEAST — **ban·quet·er** *n*

ban·shee \'ban-(ˌ)shē, ban-'shē\ *n* : a female spirit in Gaelic folklore whose wailing warns that a death will occur soon [from Irish *bean sídhe* & Scottish Gaelic *bean sìth*, literally, "woman of fairyland"]

ban·tam \'bant-əm\ *n* : any of numerous small domestic fowls that are often miniatures of members of the standard breeds — **bantam** *adj*

ban·tam·weight \-ˌwāt\ *n* : a boxer in a weight division having an upper limit of about 118 pounds

¹**ban·ter** \'bant-ər\ *vb* : to speak in a friendly but teasing or witty way — **ban·ter·er** \-ər-ər\ *n* — **ban·ter·ing·ly** \'bant-ə-riṅ-lē\ *adv*

²**banter** *n* : good-natured teasing or joking

Ban·tu \'ban-(ˌ)tü, 'ban-\ *n, pl* **Bantu** *or* **Bantus** **1** : a group of African languages spoken in central and southern Africa **2** : a member of any of a group of African peoples who speak Bantu languages

ban·yan \'ban-yən\ *n* : a large East Indian tree with branches that send out roots which grow downward into the ground and form new supporting trunks

banyan

bao·bab \'baů-ˌbab, 'bā-ə-\ *n* : a tree native to Africa with a very wide trunk

bap·tism \'bap-ˌtiz-əm\ *n* **1** : the act or ceremony of baptizing **2** : an act or experience that baptizes ⟨a soldier's *baptism* of fire⟩ — **bap·tis·mal** \bap-'tiz-məl\ *adj* — **bap·tis·mal·ly** \-mə-lē\ *adv*

Bap·tist \'bap-təst\ *adj* : of or relating to any of several Protestant denominations practicing baptism by immersion — **Baptist** *n*

bap·tize \bap-'tīz, 'bap-ˌtīz\ *vb* **bap·tized; bap·tiz·ing** **1** : to dip in water or sprinkle water on as a part of the ceremony of receiving into the Christian church **2 a** : to make pure in spirit (as by a painful experience) **b** : ¹INITIATE 3 **3** : to give a name to (as in the ceremony of baptism) : CHRISTEN — **bap·tiz·er** *n*

¹**bar** \'bär\ *n* **1 a** : a straight piece (as of metal or wood) that is longer than it is wide **b** : a usually rectangular piece or block of material ⟨a *bar* of soap⟩ **2** : something that hinders or blocks : OBSTACLE **3** : a bank (as of sand) partly or entirely under water along a shore or in a river **4 a** : the railing in a courtroom around the place where the business of the court is carried on **b** : a court of law **c** : the profession of law **5** : ³STRIPE 1 **6 a** : a counter on which alcoholic drinks or food is served **b** : BARROOM **7 a** : a vertical line across the musical staff before the beginning of a measure **b** : ¹MEASURE 4c **8** : ¹STANDARD 2a ⟨raise the *bar* for improving new medicines⟩ [Middle English *barre* "bar," from early French *barre* (same meaning)] — **behind bars** : in jail

²**bar** *vb* **barred; bar·ring** **1** : to fasten with a bar ⟨*bar* the door⟩ **2** : to mark with bars : STRIPE ⟨gray feathers *barred* with brown⟩ **3** : to block off : CLOSE ⟨*bar* the road with a chain⟩ **4 a** : to keep out : EXCLUDE ⟨*bar* reporters from a meeting⟩ **b** : PREVENT 1, FORBID ⟨the judge *barred* them from talking to reporters⟩

³**bar** *prep* : with the exception of ⟨*bar* none⟩

⁴**bar** *n* : a unit of pressure equal to 100,000 pascals [from German *Bar* "unit of pressure," from Greek *baros* "weight, pressure"]

barb \'bärb\ *n* **1 a** : a sharp point that sticks out and backward (as from the point of an arrow or fishhook) **b** : any of various sharp parts (as the side branch of a feather) that stick out from a plant or animal **2** : an often witty remark intended to hurt a person's feelings [Middle English *barbe* "barb, beard," from early French *barbe* (same meaning), from Latin *barba* "beard" — related to BARBER] — **barb·less** \-ləs\ *adj*

bar·bar·i·an \bär-'ber-ē-ən, bär-'bar-\ *n* : an uncivilized person

bar·bar·ic \bär-'bar-ik\ *adj* **1** : of, relating to, or characteristic of barbarians **2** : CRUEL 2, SAVAGE

bar·ba·rism \'bär-bə-ˌriz-əm\ *n* : the state, ideas, or behavior of a barbarian

bar·bar·i·ty \bär-'bar-ət-ē\ *n, pl* **-ties** **1** : BARBARISM **2 a** : CRUELTY 1 **b** : a cruel act

bar·ba·rous \'bär-b(ə-)rəs\ *adj* **1** : UNCIVILIZED 1 **2** : CRUEL 2, SAVAGE — **bar·ba·rous·ly** *adv* — **bar·ba·rous·ness** *n*

¹**bar·be·cue** \'bär-bi-ˌkyü\ *vb* **-cued; -cu·ing** **1** : to cook over or before an open source of heat (as hot coals) **2** : to cook in a highly seasoned sauce — **bar·be·cu·er** *n*

²**barbecue** *also* **bar·be·que** *n* **1 a** : a large animal (as a hog or steer) roasted or broiled over an open fire **b** : barbecued food **2** : an outdoor social gathering at which barbecued food is eaten [from American Spanish *barbacoa* "a rack for hanging meat over a fire," of Caribbean Indian origin]

barbed wire \'bä(r)b-'(d)wī(ə)r\ *n* : wire (as for a fence) with sharp points spaced evenly along it — called also *barbwire*

bar·bel \'bär-bəl\ *n* : a slender process on the lip of some fishes (as a catfish) that is used for feeling

bar·bell \'bär-ˌbel\ *n* : a bar with adjustable weighted disks attached to each end that is used for exercise and in weight lifting

bar·ber \'bär-bər\ *n* : a person whose business is cutting and dressing hair and shaving beards [Middle English *barber* "barber," from early French *barbour* (same meaning), derived from Latin *barba* "beard" — related to BARB] — **barber** *vb*

bar·ber·ry \'bär-ˌber-ē\ *n* : any of a genus of spiny yellow-flowered shrubs with bright red or blackish berries

bar·ber·shop \'bär-bər-ˌshäp\ *n* : a barber's place of business

bar·bit·u·rate \bär-'bich-ə-rət, -ˌrāt, ˌbär-bə-'t(y)ùr-ət, -'t(y)ù(ə)r-ˌāt\ *n* : any of various drugs related to barbituric acid that are used especially to calm or to produce sleep and are often habit-forming

bar·bi·tu·ric acid \ˌbär-bə-ˌt(y)ùr-ik-\ *n* : an organic acid used in making plastics and drugs

barb·wire \('ˌ)bä(r)b-'wī(ə)r\ *n* : BARBED WIRE

bar·ca·role *or* **bar·ca·rolle** \'bär-kə-ˌrōl\ *n* **1** : a Venetian boat song **2** : a piece of music imitating a barcarole

bar chart *n* : BAR GRAPH

bar code *n* : a code made up of a group of printed and variously spaced bars and sometimes numerals that is designed to be scanned and read into computer memory and that contains information (as identification) about the object it labels

bard \'bärd\ *n* **1** : a person in ancient societies skilled at composing and singing or reciting verses about heroes and their deeds **2** : POET — **bard·ic** \'bärd-ik\ *adj*

\ə\ **abut**		\aů\ **out**	\i\ **tip**		\ò\ **saw**	\ů\ **foot**	
\ər\ **further**		\ch\ **chin**	\ī\ **life**		\òi\ **coin**	\y\ **yet**	
\a\ **mat**		\e\ **pet**	\j\ **job**		\th\ **thin**	\yü\ **few**	
\ā\ **take**		\ē\ **easy**	\ṅ\ **sing**		\th\ **this**	\yů\ **cure**	
\ä\ **cot, cart**		\g\ **go**	\ō\ **bone**		\ü\ **food**	\zh\ **vision**	

¹**bare** \'ba(ə)r, 'be(ə)r\ *adj* **bar·er; bar·est 1 a :** lacking a covering **: NAKED** ⟨trees *bare* of leaves⟩ **b :** lacking any tool or weapon ⟨opened the box with his *bare* hands⟩ **2 :** open to view ⟨the scandal was laid *bare*⟩ **3 :** ¹EMPTY 1 ⟨the cupboard was *bare*⟩ **4 a :** just enough with nothing to spare ⟨a *bare* majority⟩ ⟨the *bare* necessities of life⟩ **b :** not decorated or added to **: PLAIN** ⟨the *bare* facts⟩ ⟨a *bare* outline of the story⟩ — **bare·ly** *adv* — **bare·ness** *n*

²**bare** *vb* **bared; bar·ing :** to make or lay bare **: UNCOVER, REVEAL**

bare·back \'ba(ə)r-ˌbak, 'be(ə)r-\ *or* **bare·backed** \-ˌbakt\ *adv or adj* **:** on the bare back of a horse **:** without a saddle ⟨rode *bareback*⟩ ⟨*bareback* riding⟩

bare·faced \-ˈfāst\ *adj* **:** not pretending to be anything else **:** not appearing to be something different ⟨a *barefaced* lie⟩ ⟨a *barefaced* liar⟩ — **bare·faced·ly** \-ˈfā-səd-lē, -fāst-lē\ *adv* — **bare·faced·ness** \-ˈfā-səd-nəs, -ˈfās(t)-nəs\ *n*

bare·foot \-ˌfu̇t\ *or* **bare·foot·ed** \-ˈfu̇t-əd\ *adv or adj* **:** with the feet bare **:** without shoes

bare·hand·ed \-ˈhan-dəd\ *adv or adj* **1 :** with the hands bare **:** without gloves or mittens **2 :** without tools or weapons ⟨fight an animal *barehanded*⟩

bare·head·ed \-ˈhed-əd\ *adv or adj* **:** with the head bare **:** without a hat

barf \'bärf\ *vb* **:** ²VOMIT

¹**bar·gain** \'bär-gən\ *n* **1 :** an agreement between parties settling what each is to give or receive in a business deal **2 :** something bought or offered for sale at a desirable price **synonyms** see AGREEMENT

²**bargain** *vb* **:** to talk over the terms of a purchase or agreement — **bar·gain·er** *n* — **bargain for :** EXPECT 1 ⟨more trouble than we *bargained for*⟩

¹**barge** \'bärj\ *n* **:** a broad flat-bottomed boat that is usually towed and used chiefly to transport goods in harbors and on rivers and canals

²**barge** *vb* **barged; barg·ing 1 :** to carry by barge **2 :** to move or push oneself clumsily or rudely ⟨*barged* right in⟩

bar graph *n* **:** a graph that shows rectangles with lengths proportional to numbers as a visual way of comparing the numbers — called also *bar chart*

bar·ite \'ba(ə)r-ˌīt, 'be(ə)r-\ *n* **:** a white, yellow, or colorless mineral consisting of barium sulfate and occurring in crystals or as a mass

bar·i·tone \'bar-ə-ˌtōn\ *n* **1 a :** a male singing voice between bass and tenor **b :** a singer having such a voice **2 :** a horn with a range between that of the trumpet and the tuba

bar·i·um \'bar-ē-əm, 'ber-\ *n* **:** a silver-white poisonous metallic element — see ELEMENT table

barium sulfate *n* **:** a colorless crystalline compound that is a sulfate of barium used especially in taking X-ray photographs of the digestive tract

¹**bark** \'bärk\ *vb* **1 :** to make the short loud cry of a dog or a similar noise **2 :** to shout or speak sharply ⟨*bark* out an order⟩ [Old English *beorcan* "to bark"]

²**bark** *n* **:** the sound made by a barking dog

³**bark** *n* **:** the tough covering of a woody root or stem [Middle English *bark* "tree covering," of Scandinavian origin]

⁴**bark** *vb* **1 :** to strip the bark from **2 :** to rub or scrape the skin of ⟨*barked* her knee⟩

⁵**bark** *or* **barque** *n* **1 :** a small sailing ship **2 :** a three-masted ship with the first two masts square-rigged and the last fore-and-aft rigged [Middle English *bark* "a small ship," from early French *barque* (same meaning)]

bark beetle *n* **:** any of a group of beetles that bore under the bark of trees both as larvae and adults

bark·er \'bär-kər\ *n* **:** a person who stands at the entrance to a show and tries to attract customers by loud fast talk

bar·ley \'bär-lē\ *n* **:** a cereal grass with flowers in dense spikes; *also* **:** its seed used especially in malt beverages, in foods (as soups and cereals), or as feed for livestock

bar·ley·corn \-ˌkȯ(ə)rn\ *n* **:** a grain of barley

bar·low \'bär-ˌlō\ *n* **:** a sturdy inexpensive jackknife [named for *Barlow,* a family of 18th century English knife makers]

¹**bar mitz·vah** \bär-ˈmits-və\ *n, often cap B&M* **1 :** a Jewish boy who on his 13th birthday reaches the age of religious duty and responsibility **2 :** the ceremony recognizing a boy as a bar mitzvah [from Hebrew *bar miṣwāh,* literally, "son of the (divine) law"]

²**bar mitzvah** *vb* **bar mitz·vahed; bar mitz·vah·ing :** to administer the ceremony of bar mitzvah to

barn \'bärn\ *n* **:** a building used chiefly for storing grain and hay and for housing farm animals or farm equipment

bar·na·cle \'bär-ni-kəl\ *n* **:** any of numerous small saltwater crustaceans with feathery outgrowths for gathering food that are free-swimming as larvae but as adults are permanently fastened (as to rocks or the bottoms of ships) — **bar·na·cled** \-kəld\ *adj*

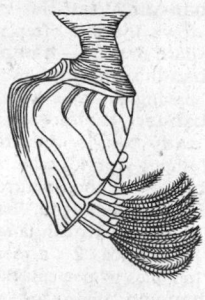

barnacle

barn owl *n* **:** a widely distributed owl with brown, gray, and white feathers that is found near barns and other buildings and preys especially on rodents

barn·storm \'bärn-ˌstȯrm\ *vb* **:** to travel through the country making brief stops to entertain (as with shows or flying stunts) or to campaign for political office — **barn·storm·er** *n*

barn swallow *n* **:** a common swallow that often nests in barns

barn·yard \'bärn-ˌyärd\ *n* **:** a usually fenced area around a barn

baro·graph \'bar-ə-ˌgraf\ *n* **:** a barometer that records pressure changes on a graph

ba·rom·e·ter \bə-ˈräm-ət-ər\ *n* **:** an instrument that measures the pressure of the atmosphere to determine probable weather changes — **baro·met·ric** \ˌbar-ə-ˈme-trik\ *adj*

barometric pressure *n* **:** the pressure of the atmosphere usually expressed as the height of a column of mercury

bar·on \'bar-ən\ *n* **1 :** a member of the lowest rank of the British nobility **2 :** a person of great power or influence ⟨a cattle *baron*⟩

bar·on·ess \'bar-ə-nəs\ *n* **1 :** the wife or widow of a baron **2 :** a woman holding the rank of baron

bar·on·et \'bar-ə-nət *also* ˌbar-ə-ˈnet\ *n* **:** a man holding a rank of honor below a baron but above a knight

ba·ro·ni·al \bə-ˈrō-nē-əl\ *adj* **:** of, relating to, or suitable for a baron ⟨*baronial* splendor⟩

ba·roque \bə-ˈrōk, ba-, -ˈräk\ *adj* **:** of or relating to a style of art and music common in the 17th century that is marked especially by the use of much fancy decoration — **baroque** *n*

barque *variant of* ⁵BARK

bar·racks \'bar-əks, -iks\ *n sing or pl* **:** a building or group of buildings in which soldiers live

bar·ra·cu·da \ˌbar-ə-ˈküd-ə\ *n, pl* **-da** *or* **-das :** any of several large fierce marine fishes of warm seas that have strong jaws and sharp teeth and that include some used for food

bar·rage \bə-ˈräzh, -ˈräj\ *n* **1 :** a barrier formed by continuous artillery or machine-gun fire directed upon a narrow strip of ground **2 :** a rapid or furiously active flow (as of speech or writing)

barred \'bärd\ *adj* **:** having alternate bands of different color

¹**bar·rel** \'bar-əl\ *n* **1 :** a round bulging container that is longer than it is wide and has flat ends **2 a :** the amount held by a barrel **b :** a great quantity ⟨a *barrel* of laughs⟩

3 : a part shaped like a cylinder or tube ⟨gun *barrel*⟩ ⟨the *barrel* of a carburetor⟩ — **bar·reled** \-əld\ *adj*

²**barrel** *vb* **-reled** *or* **-relled; -rel·ing** *or* **-rel·ling** : to travel at a high speed ⟨*barreling* down the highway⟩

barrel cactus *n* : any of various spiny cacti that resemble a barrel in shape, have many ridges on the outside, and are found in Mexico and in nearby parts of the U.S.

barrel organ *n* : an instrument producing music by a series of pegs arranged around a revolving cylinder so that they open valves to admit air from a bellows to a set of pipes

barrel cactus

¹**bar·ren** \'bar-ən\ *adj* **1 a** : not able to produce offspring — used especially of females **b** : usually failing to fruit ⟨*barren* apple trees⟩ **2 a** : producing inferior or little to no vegetation ⟨*barren* soils⟩ **b** : not producing results or gain ⟨a *barren* plan⟩ — **bar·ren·ly** *adv* — **bar·ren·ness** \-ən-nəs\ *n*

²**barren** *n* : a tract of barren land

bar·rette \bä-'ret, bə-\ *n* : a clip or bar for holding a girl's or woman's hair in place

¹**bar·ri·cade** \'bar-ə-ˌkād, ˌbar-ə-'kād\ *vb* **-cad·ed; -cad·ing** : to block off with a barricade

²**barricade** *n* : a barrier usually made in a hurry for protection against attack or for blocking the way

bar·ri·er \'bar-ē-ər\ *n* **1** : something (as a fence, railing, or natural obstacle) that blocks the way **2** : something not material that keeps apart or makes progress difficult ⟨language *barriers*⟩

barrier island *n* : a long broad sandy island parallel to a shore that is built up by the action of waves, currents, and winds

barrier reef *n* : a coral reef roughly parallel to a shore and separated from it by a lagoon

bar·ring \'bär-iŋ\ *prep* **1** : with the exception of ⟨*barring* none⟩ **2** : apart from the possibility of ⟨will be there on time, *barring* accidents⟩

bar·rio \'bär-ē-ˌō, 'bar-\ *n, pl* **-ri·os** : a neighborhood where most of the people speak Spanish

bar·room \'bar-ˌrüm, -ˌrùm\ *n* : a place of business for the sale of alcoholic drinks

¹**bar·row** \'bar-ō\ *n* : a large burial mound of earth or stones [Old English *beorg* "mound"]

²**barrow** *n* **1** : a structure that has handles and sometimes a wheel and is used for carrying things **2** : a cart with a shallow box body, two wheels, and shafts for pushing it : PUSHCART [Old English *bearwe* "barrow"]

bar·tend·er \'bar-ˌten-dər\ *n* : a person who serves alcoholic drinks at a bar — **bar·tend** \'bar-ˌtend\ *vb*

¹**bar·ter** \'bart-ər\ *vb* : to trade one thing for another without the use of money — **bar·ter·er** \'bart-ər-ər\ *n*

²**barter** *n* : the exchange of goods without the use of money

Ba·ruch \bə-'rük, 'bär-ˌük\ *n* — see BIBLE table

bas·al \'bā-səl, -zəl\ *adj* : relating to, located at, or forming a base — **bas·al·ly** \-sə-lē, -zə-lē\ *adv*

basal metabolic rate *n* : the rate at which heat is given off by an organism at complete rest

ba·salt \bə-'sòlt, 'bā-ˌsòlt\ *n* : a dark gray to black usually fine-grained igneous rock — **ba·sal·tic** \bə-'sòl-tik\ *adj*

¹**base** \'bās\ *n, pl* **bas·es** \'bā-səz\ **1 a** : a thing or part on which something rests : BOTTOM, FOUNDATION ⟨the *base* of a lamp⟩ **b** : the part of a plant or animal structure by which it is attached to another more central structure ⟨the *base* of the thumb⟩ **c** : one of the lines or flat surfaces of a geometric figure from which an altitude is or can be constructed ⟨*bases* of a trapezoid⟩; *esp* : one on which the figure stands ⟨*base* of a triangle⟩ **2** : a main

ingredient ⟨paint having a water *base*⟩ **3** : a fundamental part : BASIS **4 a** : the place from which a start is made **b** : a line in a survey that is used to calculate distances or positions **c** : a place where a military force keeps its supplies or from which it starts its operations ⟨naval *base*⟩ ⟨air *base*⟩ **d** : a number equal to the number of units that would be equivalent to one in the next higher place in a given number system ⟨in *base* 10 it takes 10 ones in the units place to equal a one in the tens place⟩; *also* : a system of writing numbers using a given base ⟨convert *base* 10 to *base* 2⟩ **e** : ¹ROOT 5 **5 a** : the starting place or goal in various games **b** : any of the four stations a runner in baseball must touch in order to score **6** : any of various compounds that react with an acid to form a salt, have a bitter taste, and turn red litmus paper blue **7** : a number that is multiplied by a rate or of which a percentage or fraction is calculated ⟨to find the interest on $90 at 10% multiply the *base* 90 by .10⟩ — **based** *adj* — **base·less** \'bās-ləs\ *adj*

²**base** *vb* **based; bas·ing** **1** : to make, form, or serve as a base for **2** : to use as a base or basis for : ESTABLISH

³**base** *adj* **1 a** : being of low value and having less desirable properties when compared with something else ⟨a *base* metal such as iron⟩ **b** : containing more than the usual amount of base metals **2** : not honorable or moral : MEAN ⟨*base* conduct⟩ — **base·ly** *adv* — **base·ness** *n*

base·ball \'bās-ˌbòl\ *n* : a game played with a bat and ball by two teams of nine players each on a field with four bases that mark the course a runner must take to score; *also* : the ball used in this game

baseball cap *n* : a cap of the kind worn by baseball players that has a rounded crown and a long visor

base·board \-ˌbōrd, -ˌbòrd\ *n* : a board placed at or forming the base of something; *esp* : a molding covering the crack between a wall and floor

base-born \-'bòrn\ *adj* **1** : born into a poor family : LOWLY **2** : of illegitimate birth : BASTARD

base exchange *n* : a store at a naval or air force base that sells to military personnel and authorized civilians

base hit *n* : a hit in baseball that allows the batter to reach base safely with no error made and no base runner forced out

base·line \'bās-ˌlīn\ *n* **1** : a line used as a base **2 a** : either of two straight lines on a baseball field leading from home plate to first base and third base and extending into the outfield **b** : BASE PATH

base·ment \'bās-mənt\ *n* : the part of a building that is entirely or partly below ground level

ba·sen·ji \bə-'sen-jē, -'zen-\ *n* : a small curly-tailed hunting dog native to Africa that does not bark

base on balls *n* : an advance to first base given to a baseball batter who takes four pitches that are balls

base path *n* : the area between the bases of a baseball field used by a base runner

base runner *n* : a baseball player of the team at bat who is on base or is trying to reach a base

bash \'bash\ *vb* **1** : to strike violently : BEAT **2** : to smash by a blow **3** : ¹CRASH 1a

bash·ful \'bash-fəl\ *adj* : awkward or afraid around other people *synonyms* see SHY — **bash·ful·ly** \-fə-lē\ *adv* — **bash·ful·ness** *n*

¹**ba·sic** \'bā-sik, -zik\ *adj* **1** : of, relating to, or forming the base or basis : FUNDAMENTAL ⟨*basic* research⟩ **2** : of, relating to, containing, or having the character of a chemical base — **ba·si·cal·ly** \-si-k(ə-)lē, -zi-\ *adv*

²**basic** *n* : something basic : FUNDAMENTAL

\ə\ **abut**	\au̇\ **out**	\i\ **tip**	\ȯ\ **saw**	\u̇\ **foot**
\ər\ **further**	\ch\ **chin**	\ī\ **life**	\ȯi\ **coin**	\y\ **yet**
\a\ **mat**	\e\ **pet**	\j\ **job**	\th\ **thin**	\yü\ **few**
\ā\ **take**	\ē\ **easy**	\ŋ\ **sing**	\th\ **this**	\yu̇\ **cure**
\ä\ **cot, cart**	\g\ **go**	\ō\ **bone**	\ü\ **food**	\zh\ **vision**

BA·SIC \'bā-sik, -zik\ *n* : a simplified language for programming and interacting with a computer [*Beginners All-purpose Symbolic Instruction Code*]

ba·sic·i·ty \bā-'sis-ət-ē\ *n, pl* **-ties** : the quality, state, or extent of being a base

basic training *n* : the first part of training for a military recruit

bas·il \'baz-əl, 'bāz-, 'bas-, 'bās-\ *n* : any of several plants of the mint family; *esp* : SWEET BASIL

ba·sin \'bās-ᵊn\ *n* **1 a** : a wide usually round container with sloping or curving sides for holding liquids **b** : the amount that a basin holds **2** : a hollow area or enclosure containing water; *esp* : a partly enclosed water area for anchoring ships **3 a** : the land drained by a river and its branches **b** : a large or small hollow area in the surface of the land or in the ocean floor **c** : a great hollow area in the surface of the lithosphere filled by an ocean **4** : a broad area of the earth beneath which layers of sedimentary rock dip usually from the sides toward the center

ba·sis \'bā-səs\ *n, pl* **ba·ses** \'bā-sēz\ : something on which some other thing is based or established

bask \'bask\ *vb* : to lie or relax in a pleasant warmth or atmosphere ⟨*bask* in the sun⟩ ⟨*basked* in their success⟩

bas·ket \'bas-kət\ *n* **1 a** : a container made by weaving together materials (as reeds, straw, or strips of wood) **b** : the contents of a basket **2** : something that resembles a basket **3 a** : a net open at the bottom and hung from a metal ring that is the goal in basketball **b** : a score made in basketball by tossing the ball through the basket — **bas·ket·like** \-ˌlīk\ *adj*

bas·ket·ball \-ˌbȯl\ *n* : a court game in which each of two teams tries to toss an inflated ball through a raised goal; *also* : the ball used in this game

bas·ket·ry \'bas-kə-trē\ *n* **1** : the art or craft of making objects (as baskets) by weaving or braiding long slender pieces **2** : objects produced by basketry

basking shark *n* : a large shark that feeds on plankton and may reach 45 feet (13.7 meters) in length

bas mitzvah *variant of* BAT MITZVAH

bas–re·lief \ˌbä-ri-'lēf, ˌbä-riˌlēf\ *n* : a sculpture in which the design is raised very slightly from the background

bas-relief

¹bass \'bas\ *n, pl* **bass** *or* **bass·es** : any of various spiny-finned freshwater or saltwater sport and food fishes [Old English *bærs* "bass"]

²bass \'bās\ *n* **1 a** : the lowest musical part in harmony for four parts — compare ALTO 1b, ²SOPRANO 1, TENOR 2a **b** : the lower half of a musical tone range — compare TREBLE **2 a** : the lowest male singing voice or a person who has this voice **b** : a person or instrument performing the bass part [Middle English *bas* (adjective) "being or having a low solemn tone"] — **bass** *adj*

bass clef *n* **1** : a clef that places the F below middle C on the fourth line of the staff **2** : BASS STAFF

bass drum *n* : a large drum that has two heads and that produces a booming sound

bas·set hound \'bas-ət-\ *n* : any of an old French breed of short-legged long-eared hunting dogs — called also *basset*

bass horn *n* : TUBA

bas·si·net \ˌbas-ə-'net\ *n* : an infant's bed often with a hood over one end

basset hound

bas·so \'bas-(ˌ)ō, 'bäs-\ *n, pl* **bas·sos** *or* **bas·si** \'bäs-ˌē\ **1** : a bass singer; *esp* : an operatic bass **2** : a low deep voice

bas·soon \bə-'sün, ba-\ *n* : the woodwind instrument of the oboe family that plays the lowest part — **bas·soon·ist** \-'sü-nəst\ *n*

bass staff *n* : the musical staff carrying the bass clef

bass viol *n* : DOUBLE BASS

bass·wood \'bas-ˌwu̇d\ *n* : any of several linden trees

bast \'bast\ *n* : a strong woody fiber obtained chiefly from the phloem of plants and used especially in fabrics and ropes or cords

bas·tard \'bas-tərd\ *n* : an illegitimate child — **bastard** *adj*

¹baste \'bāst\ *vb* **bast·ed; bast·ing** : to sew with long loose stitches so as to hold the work temporarily in place — **bast·er** *n*

²baste *vb* **bast·ed; bast·ing** : to moisten with liquid (as melted fat or juices) while roasting — **bast·er** *n*

Bas·tille Day \ba-'stē(ə)l-\ *n* : July 14 observed in France as a national holiday in memory of the capture of the Parisian prison the Bastille by revolutionary forces in 1789

bas·tion \'bas-chən\ *n* : some place or something that gives protection against attack ⟨a *bastion* of democracy⟩

¹bat \'bat\ *n* **1** : a stout solid stick : CLUB **2** : a sharp blow **3** : a usually wooden implement used for hitting the ball in various games (as baseball) **4** : a turn at batting ⟨next at *bat*⟩ [Old English *batt* "club"]

²bat *vb* **bat·ted; bat·ting** **1** : to strike or hit with or as if with a bat **2** : to take one's turn at bat in baseball **3** : to have a batting average of ⟨is *batting* .300⟩

³bat *n* : any of an order of night-flying mammals with the forelimbs modified to form wings [from Middle English *bakke* "flying bat"; probably of Scandinavian origin]

⁴bat *vb* **bat·ted; bat·ting** : to wink especially in surprise or emotion ⟨never *batted* an eye⟩ [probably an altered form of earlier *bate* "to beat the wings in an impatient manner"]

batch \'bach\ *n* **1 a** : a quantity used or made at one time ⟨a *batch* of cookies⟩ **b** : a group of jobs to be run on a computer at one time with the same program ⟨*batch* processing⟩ **2** : a group of persons or things : LOT

bate \'bāt\ *vb* **bat·ed; bat·ing** : to reduce the force or intensity of : RESTRAIN ⟨listen with *bated* breath⟩

bath \'bath, 'bȧth\ *n, pl* **baths** \'ba**t͟h**z, 'baths, 'bȧ**t͟h**z, 'bȧths\ **1** : a washing of the body ⟨take a *bath*⟩ **2 a** : water for bathing ⟨draw a *bath*⟩ **b** : a liquid in which objects are placed so that it can act upon them **3 a** : BATHROOM **b** : a building containing rooms for bathing

bathe \'bā**t͟h**\ *vb* **bathed; bath·ing** **1** : to take a bath **2** : to go swimming **3** : to give a bath to ⟨*bathe* the baby⟩ **4** : to apply a liquid to ⟨*bathe* the eyes⟩ **5** : to cover with or as if with a liquid ⟨a scene *bathed* in moonlight⟩ — **bath·er** \'bā-**t͟h**ər\ *n*

bath·house \'bath-ˌhau̇s, 'bȧth-\ *n* **1** : BATH 3b **2** : a building containing dressing rooms for swimmers

bathing suit *n* : SWIMSUIT

batho·lith \'bath-ə-ˌlith\ *n* : a great mass of igneous rock that forced its way into or between other rocks and that stopped in its rise quite a distance below the surface

bath·robe \'bath-ˌrōb, 'bȧth-\ *n* : a loose robe worn before or after bathing or as a dressing gown

bath·room \-ˌrüm, -ˌru̇m\ *n* **1** : a room containing a bathtub or shower and usually a sink and toilet **2** : LAVATORY 2

bath·tub \-ˌtəb\ *n* : a tub in which to take a bath

bathy·scaphe \'bath-i-ˌskaf, -ˌskāf\ *or* **bathy·scaph** \-ˌskaf\ *n* : a ship that can be guided underwater for deep-sea exploration and has a round watertight cabin attached to its underside

bathy·sphere \'bath-i-ˌsfi(ə)r\ *n* : a strongly built steel ball in which a person can dive to great depth for deep-sea observation

ba·tik \bə-ˈtēk, ˈbat-ik\ *n* **1** : an Indonesian method of hand-printing textiles by coating with wax the parts not to be to be dyed **2** : a design or fabric printed by batik

ba·tiste \bə-ˈtēst, ba-\ *n* : a fine soft sheer fabric of plain weave

¹bat mitz·vah \bät-ˈmits-və\ *also* **bas mitz·vah** \bä-ˈsmits-və\ *n, often cap B&M* **1** : a Jewish girl who at about 12 years of age takes on religious responsibilities **2** : the ceremony recognizing a girl as a bat mitzvah [from Hebrew *bath miṣwāh*, literally, "daughter of the (divine) law"]

²bat mitzvah *also* **bas mitzvah** *vb* **bat mitz·vahed** *also* **bas mitz·vahed; bat mitz·vah·ing** *also* **bas mitz·vah·ing** : to administer the ceremony of bat mitzvah to

ba·ton \bə-ˈtän, ba-\ *n* **1** : a staff borne as a symbol of office **2** : a stick with which a leader directs a band or orchestra **3** : a hollow rod passed from one member of a relay team to another **4** : a staff with a ball at one or both ends carried by a drum major or baton twirler

bat·tal·ion \bə-ˈtal-yən\ *n* **1** : a large body of troops : ARMY **2** : a military unit composed of two or more smaller units (as companies or batteries) **3** : a large body of persons organized to act together

¹bat·ten \ˈbat-ᵊn\ *n* **1** : a thin narrow strip of lumber used especially to seal or strengthen a joint **2** : a strip, bar, or support like or used like a batten (as in a sail)

²batten *vb* **bat·tened; bat·ten·ing** \ˈbat-niŋ, -ᵊn-iŋ\ : to get ready especially for stormy weather by or as if by fastening everything down — usually used with *down* — **batten down the hatches** : to prepare for a difficult or dangerous situation

¹bat·ter \ˈbat-ər\ *vb* **1** : to beat with repeated violent blows ⟨*batter* down the door⟩ **2** : to wear down or injure by hard use ⟨wore a *battered* old hat⟩ [Middle English *bateren* "to beat"] — **bat·ter·er** *n*

²batter *n* : a thin mixture chiefly of flour and liquid beaten together ⟨cake *batter*⟩ [Middle English *bater* "thin mixture," probably derived from *batteren* "to beat"]

³batter *n* : one that bats; *esp* : the baseball player at bat [*bat* and *-er* (noun suffix)]

battering ram *n* **1** : an ancient military machine consisting of a large iron-tipped wooden beam used to beat down walls **2** : a heavy metal bar with handles used (as by firefighters) to batter down doors and walls

bat·tery \ˈbat-ə-rē, ˈba-trē\ *n, pl* **-ter·ies 1 a** : the act of beating **b** : the unlawful beating or use of force upon a person **2** : two or more big military guns that are controlled as a unit **3** : an electric cell or connected electric cells for providing electric current ⟨a flashlight *battery*⟩ **4** : a number of similar articles, items, or

battering ram 1

devices arranged, connected, or used together ⟨a *battery* of tests⟩ **5** : the pitcher and catcher of a baseball team

battery jar *n* : a glass container with straight sides used especially in biology and chemistry laboratories

bat·ting \ˈbat-iŋ\ *n* : layers or sheets of cotton or wool or of synthetic material used mostly for stuffing quilts or packaging goods

batting average *n* : the average of a baseball batter found by dividing the number of official times at bat into the number of base hits

¹bat·tle \ˈbat-ᵊl\ *n* **1** : a fight between two persons ⟨trial by *battle*⟩ **2** : a fight between armies, warships, or airplanes **3** : a long or hard struggle or contest ⟨a *battle* of wits⟩

²battle *vb* **bat·tled; bat·tling** \ˈbat-liŋ, -ᵊl-iŋ\ **1** : to engage in battle **2** : CONTEND 2, STRUGGLE ⟨*battle* for a cause⟩ **3** : to fight against ⟨*battling* a forest fire⟩ — **bat·tler** \-lər, -ᵊl-ər\ *n*

bat·tle–ax *or* **bat·tle–axe** \ˈbat-ᵊl-ˌaks\ *n* : an ax with a broad blade formerly used as a weapon

bat·tle·field \-ˌfēld\ *n* : a place where a battle is fought or was once fought

bat·tle·ground \-ˌgraůnd\ *n* : BATTLEFIELD

bat·tle·ment \ˈbat-ᵊl-mənt\ *n* : a low wall (as at the top of a castle or a tower) with open spaces to shoot through

bat·tle·ship \ˈbat-ᵊl-ˌship\ *n* : a large warship with heavy armor and large guns

bat·ty \ˈbat-ē\ *adj* **bat·ti·er; -est** : mentally unstable : CRAZY

bau·ble \ˈbȯ-bəl, ˈbäb-əl\ *n* : an object of little value

baud \ˈbȯd, ˈbōd\ *n* : a unit of speed (as one bit per second) at which data is sent in communications

baux·ite \ˈbȯk-ˌsīt, ˈbäk-\ *n* : a clayey substance that is the principal ore of aluminum

bawdy \ˈbȯd-ē\ *adj* **bawd·i·er; -est** : morally objectionable : OBSCENE — **bawd·i·ly** \ˈbȯd-ᵊl-ē\ *adv* — **bawd·i·ness** \ˈbȯd-ē-nəs\ *n*

¹bawl \ˈbȯl\ *vb* **1** : to shout or cry out loudly : YELL **2** : to weep noisily — **bawl·er** *n*

²bawl *n* : a loud cry

bawl out *vb* : to scold severely

¹bay \ˈbā\ *adj* : reddish brown ⟨a *bay* mare⟩ [Middle English *bay* "reddish brown," from early French *bai* (same meaning), from Latin *badius* "reddish brown"]

²bay *n* **1** : a horse with a bay-colored body and black mane, tail, and lower legs **2** : a reddish brown

³bay *n* **1** : a section or compartment of a building or vehicle ⟨a bomb *bay*⟩ ⟨a cargo *bay*⟩ **2** : BAY WINDOW [Middle English *bay* "main part of a building," from early French *baee* "opening," derived from earlier *baer* "to be wide open, gape"]

⁴bay *vb* **1** : to bark or bark at with long deep tones ⟨wolves *baying* at the moon⟩ **2** : to cry out : SHOUT **3** : to bring (as an animal) to bay [Middle English *baien, abaien* "to bay," from early French *abaier* (same meaning), originally a word to imitate the sound]

⁵bay *n* **1** : the baying of a dog : a deep bark **2** : the position of an animal or person forced to face pursuers when it is impossible to escape ⟨brought the fox to *bay*⟩ **3** : the position of one restrained or held off ⟨used strong medicines to keep the infection at *bay*⟩

⁶bay *n* : an inlet of a body of water (as the sea) that is usually smaller than a gulf [Middle English *baye* "inlet," from early French *bai*, perhaps from *baer* "to be wide open"]

⁷bay *n* **1 a** : LAUREL 1 **b** : any of several shrubs or trees resembling the laurel **2** : a laurel wreath given as a prize [Middle English *bay* "berry, laurel berry," from early French *baie* (same meaning), from Latin *baca* "berry"]

bay·ber·ry \ˈbā-ˌber-ē\ *n* **1** : any of several wax myrtles; *esp* : a hardy shrub of coastal eastern North America that produces clusters of small berries covered with grayish white wax **2** : the fruit of a bayberry

¹bay·o·net \ˈbā-ə-nət, -ˌnet, ˌbā-ə-ˈnet\ *n* : a weapon like a dagger made to fit on the muzzle end of a rifle

²bayonet *vb* **-net·ed** *also* **-net·ted; -net·ing** *also* **-net·ting** : to stab with a bayonet

bay·ou \ˈbī-ō, ˈbī-ü\ *n* : a marshy or slowly flowing body of water (as a stream or inlet)

bayberry 2

\ə\ **abut**	\au̇\ **out**	\i\ **tip**	\ȯ\ **saw**	\ů\ **foot**
\ər\ **further**	\ch\ **chin**	\ī\ **life**	\ȯi\ **coin**	\y\ **yet**
\a\ **mat**	\e\ **pet**	\j\ **job**	\th\ **thin**	\yů\ **few**
\ā\ **take**	\ē\ **easy**	\ŋ\ **sing**	\th\ **this**	\yü\ **cure**
\ä\ **cot, cart**	\g\ **go**	\ō\ **bone**	\ü\ **food**	\zh\ **vision**

bay rum *n* : a fragrant liquid used as a cologne or after-shave lotion

bay window *n* : a window or set of windows that sticks out from the wall of a building

ba·zaar \bə-'zär\ *n* **1** : a marketplace (as in the Middle East) containing rows of small shops **2** : a place where many kinds of goods are sold **3** : a fair for the sale of articles especially to raise money for charity

ba·zoo·ka \bə-'zü-kə\ *n* : a light portable shoulder weapon that consists of an open tube and shoots an explosive rocket able to pierce the armor of tanks [from *bazooka,* name of a homemade musical instrument consisting of pipes and a funnel]

BB \'bē-,bē\ *n* : a small round piece of shot

bcc \,bē-,sē-'sē\ *vb* **bcc'd; bcc·ing** **1** : to send a blind carbon copy to **2** : to send as a blind carbon copy

B cell \'bē-,sel\ *n* : any of the lymphocytes that produce antigen-binding antibodies and that arise and mature in the bone marrow — compare T CELL

B complex *n* : VITAMIN B COMPLEX

be \(')bē\ *vb, past 1st & 3rd sing* **was** \(')wəz, 'wäz\; *2nd sing* **were** \(')wər\; *pl* **were**; *past subjunctive* **were**; *past participle* **been** \(')bin, *chiefly British* (')bēn\; *present participle* **be·ing** \'bē-iŋ\; *present 1st sing* **am** \əm, (')am\; *2nd sing* **are** \ər, (')är\; *3rd sing* **is** \(')iz, əz\; *pl* **are**; *present subjunctive* **be** **1 a** : to have the same meaning as : serve as a sign for ⟨*January is* the first month⟩ ⟨let *x be* 10⟩ **b** : to have identity with ⟨the first person I met *was* my brother⟩ ⟨she *is* my mother⟩ **c** : to have the quality or character of ⟨the leaves *are* green⟩ **d** : to belong to the class of ⟨the fish *is* a trout⟩ ⟨apes *are* mammals⟩ **2 a** : EXIST 1, LIVE ⟨I think, therefore I *am*⟩ ⟨there once *was* a knight⟩ **b** : to occupy a place, situation, or position ⟨the book *is* on the table⟩ ⟨I *was* sick⟩ **c** : to remain undisturbed or uninterrupted — used only in infinitive form ⟨let *x be*⟩ **d** : to take place : OCCUR ⟨the concert *was* last night⟩ **3** — used with the past participle of transitive verbs to form the passive auxiliary ⟨the money *was* found⟩ ⟨the house is *being* built⟩ **4** — used with the present participle to express continuous action ⟨they *are* studying⟩ ⟨I have *been* sleeping⟩ **5** — used with the infinitive with *to* to express the future or something one must do ⟨she *was* to become famous⟩ ⟨I *am* to leave today⟩

be- *prefix* **1** : on : around : over ⟨*besmear*⟩ **2** : provide with or cover with : dress up with ⟨*bejewel*⟩ ⟨*bewhiskered*⟩ **3** : about : to : upon ⟨*bemoan*⟩ **4** : make : cause to be ⟨*belittle*⟩ ⟨*befriend*⟩ [Old English *be-, bi-* "on, over"]

¹beach \'bēch\ *n* : a sandy or gravelly part of the shore of a body of water

²beach *vb* : to run or drive ashore ⟨*beach* a boat⟩

beach buggy *n* : DUNE BUGGY

beach·comb·er \'bēch-,kō-mər\ *n* **1** : a drifter or loafer especially on a South Pacific island **2** : a person who searches along a beach (as for seashells or items to sell)

beach flea *n* : SAND FLEA 2

beach grass *n* : any of several tough grasses with strong roots that grow on exposed sandy shores and include some planted to bind the soil on dunes or sandy slopes

beach·head \'bēch-,hed\ *n* : an area on an enemy shore held by an advance force of an invading army to protect the later landing of troops or supplies

beach plum *n* : a shrubby plum with showy flowers that grows along the Atlantic coast of the northern U.S. and Canada; *also* : its dark purple fruit often used in preserves

beach towel *n* : a very large usually brightly colored towel made for use at the beach

bea·con \'bē-kən\ *n* **1** : a signal fire commonly on a hill, tower, or pole **2 a** : a guiding or warning signal (as a lighthouse) **b** : a radio station sending out signals to guide airplanes **3** : something that inspires ⟨a *beacon* of hope⟩

¹bead \'bēd\ *n* **1** : a small piece of solid material with a hole by which it can be strung on a thread **2** : a small round mass ⟨*beads* of perspiration⟩ **3** : a small knob on a gun used in taking aim **4** : a rim or molding (as on a board or tire) that sticks out

Word History The beads you might wear around your neck once represented prayers. The Middle English word *bede* at first meant "a prayer." People then, as now, often kept track of the number and order of a series of prayers with the help of a string of little balls. Because each of these balls stands for a prayer, the word *bede* came to be used for the balls themselves. Today this same word, now spelled *bead,* is used to refer to any small piece of material with a hole in it for threading on a string or wire. It has also been used to refer to any small, round object such as a drop of sweat. [Middle English *bede* "prayer, rosary bead," from Old English *bed* "prayer"]

²bead *vb* **1** : to cover with beads or beading **2** : to string together like beads **3** : to form into a bead — **bead·er** *n*

bead·ing \'bēd-iŋ\ *n* : BEADWORK

bead·work \'bēd-,wərk\ *n* : ornamental work made of beads

beady \'bēd-ē\ *adj* **bead·i·er; -est** : resembling beads; *esp* : small, round, and shiny ⟨*beady* eyes⟩

bea·gle \'bē-gəl\ *n* : any of a breed of small hounds with short legs and smooth coats

beak \'bēk\ *n* **1 a** : the bill of a bird; *esp* : the bill of a bird of prey adapted for striking and tearing **b** : any of various rigid mouth structures (as of a turtle) that stick out; *also* : the long sucking mouth of some insects **c** : the human nose **2** : a part shaped like a beak — **beaked** \'bēkt\ *adj*

bea·ker \'bē-kər\ *n* : a deep cup or glass with a wide mouth and usually a lip for pouring

¹beam \'bēm\ *n* **1** : a long heavy piece of timber or metal used especially as a main horizontal support of a building or ship **2** : the bar of a balance from which scales hang **3** : the width of a ship at its widest part **4 a** : a ray of light **b** : a collection of nearly parallel rays (as X-rays) or a stream of particles (as electrons) **5** : a constant radio signal sent out to guide pilots along a course

²beam *vb* **1** : to send out in beams or as a beam **2** : to send out beams of light : SHINE **3** : to smile with joy

bean \'bēn\ *n* **1 a** : BROAD BEAN **b** : the seed or pod of various erect or climbing plants of the legume family **c** : a plant bearing beans **2** : a seed or fruit like a bean ⟨coffee *beans*⟩

bean·bag \'bēn-,bag\ *n* **1** : a cloth bag usually filled with dried beans and used in many games **2** : a bag filled with pellets that is used as a chair

bean curd *n* : TOFU

¹bear \'ba(ə)r, 'be(ə)r\ *n, pl* **bears** **1** *or pl* **bear** : any of a family of large heavy mammals that have long shaggy hair and small tails and feed largely on fruit, plants, and insects as well as on flesh **2** : a rude, burly, or clumsy person ⟨a real *bear* in the morning⟩ ⟨a great *bear* of a man⟩ **3** : a person who sells stocks or bonds in the expectation that the price will go down [Old English *bera* "a bear"] — **bear·ish** \'ba(ə)r-ish, 'be(ə)r-\ *adj*

²bear *vb* **bore** \'bō(ə)r, 'bó(ə)r\; **borne** \'bō(ə)rn, 'bó(ə)rn\ *also* **born** \'bó(ə)rn\; **bear·ing** **1 a** : to move while holding up and supporting ⟨the right to *bear* arms⟩ ⟨arrived *bearing* gifts⟩ **b** : to hold in the mind ⟨*bear* a grudge⟩ **c** : BEHAVE 1 ⟨*bore* himself like a gentleman⟩ **d** : to give as testimony ⟨*bear* false witness⟩ **e** : to have as a feature or characteristic ⟨*bears* marks of suffering⟩ ⟨*bore* a resemblance to her aunt⟩ **2 a** : to give birth to ⟨*bear* children⟩ ⟨the baby was *born* last week⟩ **b** : to bring forth : PRODUCE ⟨*bear* fruit⟩ **3 a** : to hold up : SUPPORT **b** : to put up with : STAND ⟨I can't *bear* the suspense⟩ **c** : ASSUME 1 ⟨*bore* the costs⟩ ⟨*bear* the blame⟩ **4** : to push down on : PRESS ⟨*bears* down on her pencil⟩ **5**

: to move or lie in an indicated direction ⟨*bear* right at the fork in the road⟩ **6 a** : to have a relation to the matter at hand ⟨facts *bearing* on the question⟩ **b** : to exercise force or influence ⟨bring pressure to *bear*⟩ [Old English *beran* "to carry, support"] — **bear in mind** : to think of especially as a warning : REMEMBER — **bear with** : to be indulgent or patient with

bear·able \'bar-ə-bəl, 'ber-\ *adj* : possible to bear

bear·ber·ry \'ba(ə)r-ˌber-ē, 'be(ə)r-\ *n* : a trailing evergreen plant with glossy red berries that is related to the heath

¹**beard** \'bi(ə)rd\ *n* **1** : the hair that grows on a man's face often not including the mustache **2** : a hairy or bristly growth or bunch (as on the chin of a goat) — **beard·ed** \-əd\ *adj* — **beard·less** \-ləs\ *adj*

²**beard** *vb* : to face or challenge boldly ⟨*bearded* his enemy⟩

bear down *vb* : to use all of one's strength and concentration ⟨the pitcher *bore down* and struck out the last batter⟩

bear·er \'bar-ər, 'ber-\ *n* **1** : someone or something that bears, supports, or carries **2** : a person holding a check or order for payment

bear hug *n* : a rough tight hug — **bear–hug** *vb*

bear·ing \'ba(ə)r-iŋ, 'be(ə)r-\ *n* **1** : the manner in which one carries or conducts oneself **2** : a machine part in which another turns or slides **3 a** : the position or direction of one point with respect to another or to the compass **b** : a calculating of position ⟨take a *bearing*⟩ **c** *pl* : understanding of one's location or situation ⟨lost their *bearings*⟩ **4** : CONNECTION 2 ⟨personal feelings had no *bearing* on our decision⟩

bear out *vb* : CONFIRM 4 ⟨the facts *bore out* her story⟩

bear·skin \'ba(ə)r-ˌskin, 'be(ə)r-\ *n* : an article made of the skin of a bear

bear up *vb* : to have the strength or courage ⟨*bear up* under the strain⟩

beast \'bēst\ *n* **1 a** : a four-footed mammal as distinguished from human beings and from lower animals both with and without backbones **b** : a farm animal especially when kept for heavy work **2** : a mean or brutal person

¹**beast·ly** \'bēst-lē\ *adj* **beast·li·er; -est 1** : of, relating to, or resembling a beast : BESTIAL **2** : DISAGREEABLE 1, UNPLEASANT ⟨*beastly* weather⟩ — **beast·li·ness** *n*

²**beastly** *adv* : ²VERY 1 ⟨a *beastly* cold day⟩

beast of burden *n* : an animal (as an ox or horse) used for carrying or pulling heavy loads

¹**beat** \'bēt\ *vb* **beat; beat·en** \'bēt-ᵊn\ *or* **beat; beat·ing 1 a** : to hit again and again ⟨*beat* a drum⟩ ⟨rain *beating* on the roof⟩ — often used with *up* ⟨two bullies *beat* him up⟩ **b** : to flap against ⟨wings *beating* the air⟩ **c** : to mix by stirring : WHIP ⟨*beat* two eggs⟩ **2 a** : to drive or force by blows ⟨*beat* off the intruder⟩ **b** : to make by walking or riding over ⟨*beat* a path⟩ **c** : to shape by blows ⟨*beat* gold into thin strips⟩ **3** : to cause to strike or flap repeatedly ⟨birds *beating* their wings⟩ **4 a** : to win against : DEFEAT **b** : ¹BAFFLE 1 ⟨it *beats* me where they are⟩ **c** : SURPASS 1 ⟨can you *beat* that?⟩ **5 a** : to act ahead of ⟨*beat* me to the punch⟩ **b** : to arrive before ⟨*beat* us home⟩ **6** : to measure or mark off by strokes ⟨*beat* time to the music⟩ **7** : to glare or strike harshly ⟨the sun *beats* down⟩ **8** : PULSATE, THROB ⟨the heart *beating*⟩ — **beat·er** *n* — **beat about the bush** *or* **beat around the bush** : to fail to get to the point — **beat a retreat** : to leave in haste — **beat it** : to hurry away : SCRAM — **beat up on** : to attack physically or verbally ⟨*beat up on* the candidate in campaign ads⟩

²**beat** *n* **1 a** : a stroke or blow especially in a series **b** : PULSATION **c** : a sound produced by or as if by beating ⟨the *beat* of waves against the rock⟩ **2 a** : a rhythmic stress in poetry or music **b** : the tempo given to a musical performer **c** : RHYTHM 2 ⟨likes music with a Latin *beat*⟩ **3**

: a place or area regularly visited in the course of work or duty ⟨a police officer's *beat*⟩ ⟨a reporter's *beat*⟩

³**beat** *adj* **1** : being tired out **2** : having lost one's morale

beat-box \'bēt-ˌbäks\ *n* : an electronic device that adds a backbeat, manipulates sounds, and mimics musical instruments

beat·en \'bēt-ᵊn\ *adj* : worn smooth by passing feet ⟨the *beaten* path⟩

be·atif·ic \ˌbē-ə-'tif-ik\ *adj* : having a blissful appearance ⟨a *beatific* smile⟩

be·at·i·fy \bē-'at-ə-ˌfī\ *vb* **-fied; -fy·ing** : to declare to have reached the blessedness of heaven — **be·at·i·fi·ca·tion** \bē-ˌat-ə-fə-'kā-shən\ *n*

be·at·i·tude \bē-'at-ə-ˌt(y)üd\ *n* : any of the declarations made in the Sermon on the Mount (Matthew 5:3–12) beginning "Blessed are" [derived from Latin *beatus* "happy, blessed"]

beat-up \'bēt-ˌəp, -'əp\ *adj* : worn or damaged by use or neglect ⟨a *beat-up* old car⟩

beau \'bō\ *n, pl* **beaux** \'bōz\ *or* **beaus** \'bōz\ : BOYFRIEND 2 [from French *beau* "boyfriend," from *beau* (adjective) "fine, beautiful," derived from Latin *bellus* "pretty" — related to BEAUTY, BELLE]

Beau·fort scale \ˌbō-fərt-\ *n* : a scale in which the force of the wind is indicated by numbers from 0 to 12

beau ide·al \ˌbō-ī-'dē(-ə)l\ *n, pl* **beau ideals** : a perfect model ⟨the *beau ideal* of a basketball player⟩

beau·te·ous \'byüt-ē-əs\ *adj* : BEAUTIFUL 1 — **beau·te·ous·ly** *adv* — **beau·te·ous·ness** *n*

beau·ti·cian \byü-'tish-ən\ *n* : COSMETOLOGIST

beau·ti·ful \'byüt-i-fəl\ *adj* **1** : having the qualities of beauty **2** : very good : EXCELLENT — **beau·ti·ful·ly** \-f(ə-)lē\ *adv* — **beau·ti·ful·ness** \-fəl-nəs\ *n*

synonyms BEAUTIFUL, PRETTY, LOVELY, HANDSOME mean giving pleasure to the mind or senses. BEAUTIFUL applies to things that give the greatest pleasure and stir the emotions ⟨*beautiful* mountain scenery⟩. PRETTY applies to things that give immediate but often shallow pleasure especially to the senses ⟨a *pretty* dress⟩. LOVELY applies to things that excite the emotions by being very graceful, delicate, or exquisite ⟨a *lovely* melody⟩. HANDSOME applies to things that please the mind because of their good proportions or elegance ⟨the gardens of the mansion are quite *handsome*⟩.

beau·ti·fy \'byüt-ə-ˌfī\ *vb* **-fied; -fy·ing** : to make beautiful or more beautiful **synonyms** see ADORN — **beau·ti·fi·ca·tion** \ˌbyüt-ə-fə-'kā-shən\ *n*

beau·ty \'byüt-ē\ *n, pl* **beauties 1** : the qualities of a person or a thing that give pleasure to the senses **2** : a lovely person or thing; *esp* : a lovely woman **3** : an outstanding example ⟨that's a *beauty* of a black eye⟩ [Middle English *beaute* "beauty," derived from early French *bel* "beautiful," from Latin *bellus* "pretty" — related to BEAU, BELLE]

beauty mark *n* : a small dark mark (as a mole) on the skin especially of the face

beauty shop *n* : a place of business for the care of customers' hair, skin, and nails — called also *beauty parlor, beauty salon*

¹**bea·ver** \'bē-vər\ *n, pl* **beaver** *or* **beavers 1** : a large plant-eating rodent that has webbed hind feet and a broad flat tail and that builds dams and

¹beaver 1

houses of mud and branches which are partly underwater **2** : the fur of a beaver

²beaver *n* : a piece of armor protecting the lower part of the face

be·calm \bi-'käm, -'kälm\ *vb* : to bring to a stop by lack of wind ⟨a ship *becalmed*⟩

be·cause \bi-'kȯz, -(')kəz\ *conj* : for the reason that

because of *prep* : by reason of

beck \'bek\ *n* : a beckoning gesture — **at one's beck and call** : ready to obey any command

beck·on \'bek-ən\ *vb* **beck·oned**; **beck·on·ing** \'bek-(ə)niŋ\ **1** : to call or signal to a person usually by a wave or nod ⟨they *beckoned* us to come over⟩ **2** : to appear inviting ⟨new adventures were *beckoning*⟩

be·cloud \bi-'klau̇d\ *vb* : to hide as if with a cloud

be·come \bi-'kəm\ *vb* **be·came** \-'kām\; **-come; -com·ing** **1** : to come or grow to be ⟨a tadpole *becomes* a frog⟩ ⟨the days *become* shorter as summer ends⟩ **2** : to look well on : SUIT ⟨her suit *becomes* her⟩ — **become of** : to happen to ⟨whatever *became of* our old friend⟩

be·com·ing \bi-'kəm-iŋ\ *adj* : SUITABLE 2; *also* : looking good on a person ⟨a *becoming* hairdo⟩ — **be·com·ing·ly** \-iŋ-lē\ *adv*

¹bed \'bed\ *n* **1 a** : a piece of furniture on which to lie or sleep **b** : ¹SLEEP 1; *also* : a time for sleeping ⟨watched TV before *bed*⟩ **2 a** : a plot of ground prepared for plants **b** : the bottom of a body of water ⟨the *bed* of a river⟩ **3** : a supporting surface or structure : FOUNDATION **4** : ¹LAYER 2 ⟨a *bed* of sandstone⟩

²bed *vb* **bed·ded**; **bed·ding** **1** : to put or go to bed ⟨*bed* down for the night⟩ **2** : to fix in or on a foundation ⟨an argument *bedded* on good sense⟩ **3** : to plant or arrange in beds

bed–and–breakfast *n* : a place for tourists to stay that offers lodging and breakfast

be·daub \bi-'dȯb, -'däb\ *vb* : to smear or soil with something thick, dirty, or sticky

be·daz·zle \bi-'daz-əl\ *vb* : DAZZLE 1 — **be·daz·zle·ment** \-mənt\ *n*

bed·bug \'bed-,bəg\ *n* : a wingless bloodsucking bug sometimes infesting houses and especially beds

bed·cham·ber \-'chām-bər\ *n* : BEDROOM

bed·clothes \-,klō(th)z\ *n pl* : coverings (as sheets and blankets) for a bed

bed·ding \'bed-iŋ\ *n* **1** : BEDCLOTHES **2** : material for a bed

be·deck \bi-'dek\ *vb* : to dress up with showy things ⟨*bedecked* in furs and jewels⟩

be·dev·il \bi-'dev-əl\ *vb* : to trouble or annoy again and again : PESTER, HARASS ⟨*bedeviled* by problems⟩ — **be·dev·il·ment** \-mənt\ *n*

be·dew \bi-'d(y)ü\ *vb* : to wet with or as if with dew

bed·fast \'bed-,fast\ *adj* : BEDRIDDEN

bed·fel·low \'bed-,fel-ō\ *n* : one who shares a bed with another

be·dight \bi-'dīt\ *adj, archaic* : being dressed or decorated

be·dim \bi-'dim\ *vb* **1** : to make less bright : DIM **2** : to make indistinct or obscure

be·di·zen \bi-'dīz-ᵊn, -'diz-ᵊn\ *vb* : to dress or decorate especially with showy finery

bed·lam \'bed-ləm\ *n* : a place or scene of uproar and confusion

Word History Around 1402 the home of a religious community in London was turned into a hospital for the insane. This new hospital kept the name of the community and was known as the Hospital of Saint Mary of Bethlehem. People soon shortened this name to Bethlehem. In

bedbug

Middle English, though, the town of Bethlehem in Palestine was called *Bedlem* or *Bethlem,* so this was the pronunciation used for the hospital's name. In time the name *Bedlem* or *Bedlam* came to refer to any home for the insane. Today we use *bedlam* for any scene of noise and confusion like that found in the early hospitals for the insane. [from Middle English *Bedlem* "Bethlehem"]

Bed·ling·ton terrier \,bed-liŋ-tən-\ : any of a breed of terriers with a narrow head, arched back, and usually curly coat

bed·ou·in \'bed(-ə)-wən\ *n, pl* **-in** *or* **-ins** *often cap* : a nomadic Arab of the Arabian, Syrian, or north African deserts

bed·pan \'bed-,pan\ *n* : a shallow pan for use as a toilet by a person forced to stay in bed

be·drag·gled \bi-'drag-əld\ *adj* : limp, soggy, or dirty from or as if from rain or mud

bed·rid·den \'bed-,rid-ᵊn\ *adj* : forced to stay in bed especially by illness or weakness

bed·rock \'bed-,räk\ *n* **1** : the solid rock lying under surface materials (as soil) that are not in layers **2** : a solid foundation

bed·roll \'bed-,rōl\ *n* : bedding rolled up for carrying

bed·room \-,rüm, -,ru̇m\ *n* : a room used for sleeping

bed·sheet \-,shēt\ *n* : ¹SHEET 1

bed·side \-,sīd\ *n* : the place beside a bed especially of a sick or dying person

bed·sore \-,sō(ə)r, -,sȯ(ə)r\ *n* : a sore caused by constant pressure against a bed (as in a long illness)

bed·spread \-,spred\ *n* : a decorative cover for a bed

bed·stead \-,sted\ *n* : the framework of a bed

bed·straw \-,strȯ\ *n* : any of several herbs related to madder and having squarish stems and small flowers

bed·time \'bed-,tīm\ *n* : time to go to bed

bed–wet·ting \-,wet-iŋ\ *n* : the accidental release of urine especially when occurring in bed during sleep — **bed·wet·ter** \-ər\ *n*

¹bee \'bē\ *n* : any of numerous insects (as the honeybees and bumblebees) that feed on pollen and nectar and sometimes produce honey and that differ from the wasps especially in the heavier hairier body and in having sucking as well as chewing mouthparts [Old English *bēo* "bee"]

²bee *n* : a gathering of people for a specific purpose ⟨a quilting *bee*⟩ [perhaps from a dialect word *been* "help given by neighbors," derived from Old English *bēn* "prayer"]

bee·bread \'bē-,bred\ *n* : a bitter yellowish brown pollen mixture stored in honeycomb cells and used with honey by bees as food

beech \'bēch\ *n, pl* **beech·es** *or* **beech** : any of a genus of trees with smooth gray bark and small edible nuts; *also* : its wood — **beech·en** \'bē-chən\ *adj*

¹beef \'bēf\ *n, pl* **beefs** \'bēfs\ *or* **beeves** \'bēvz\ **1** : the flesh of a steer, cow, or bull **2** : a steer, cow, or bull especially when fattened for food **3** *pl* **beefs** : COMPLAINT 1 — **beef·like** \-,līk\ *adj*

²beef *vb* **1** : to add weight, strength, or power to — usually used with *up* ⟨*beef up* the staff⟩ **2** : COMPLAIN 1

beef cattle *n pl* : cattle developed primarily for effective production of meat

beef·steak \'bēf-,stāk\ *n* : a slice of beef suitable for broiling or frying

beefy \'bē-fē\ *adj* **beef·i·er; -est** **1** : heavily and powerfully built ⟨a *beefy* wrestler⟩ **2** : of or suggesting beef ⟨a *beefy* flavor⟩

¹bee·hive \'bē-,hīv\ *n* **1** : ¹HIVE 1 **2** : ¹HIVE 2 ⟨a *beehive* of activity⟩

²beehive *adj* : resembling a dome-shaped beehive

bee·keep·er \'bē-,kē-pər\ *n* : a person who raises bees — **bee·keep·ing** *n*

bee·line \'bē-,līn\ *n* : a straight direct course

been *past participle of* BE

beep \'bēp\ *n* : a sound that signals or warns — **beep** *vb*

beep·er \'bē-pər\ *n* : PAGER; *esp* : one that beeps

beer \'bi(ə)r\ *n* **1** : an alcoholic drink made from malt and flavored with hops **2** : a nonalcoholic drink made from roots or other parts of plants ⟨birch *beer*⟩

beer belly *n* : POTBELLY 1 — **beer–bel·lied** \'bi(ə)r-ˌbel-ēd\ *adj*

bees·wax \'bēz-ˌwaks\ *n* : ¹WAX 1

beet \'bēt\ *n* : a garden plant with thick long-stalked edible leaves and usually an enlarged purplish red root used as a vegetable, as a source of sugar, or as food for livestock; *also* : this root

¹**bee·tle** \'bēt-ᵊl\ *n* **1** : any of an order of insects having four wings of which the first pair are stiff cases that fold over and protect the second pair when at rest **2** : any of various insects resembling a beetle [Old English *bitula* "beetle," from the root of *bītan* "to bite" — related to BITE]

¹beetle 1

²**beetle** *adj* : sticking out and hanging over ⟨*beetle* brows⟩ [Middle English *bitel-browed* "having overhanging brows," probably from *bitel*, *betylle* "beetle," from Old English *bitula* "beetle"]

³**beetle** *vb* **bee·tled; bee·tling** \'bēt-(ə-)liŋ\ : to stick out or hang over ⟨*beetling* cliffs⟩

be·fall \bi-'fȯl\ *vb* **-fell** \-'fel\; **-fall·en** \-'fȯ-lən\; **-fall·ing** **1** : to take place : HAPPEN **2** : to happen to

be·fit \bi-'fit\ *vb* **be·fit·ted; be·fit·ting** : to be suitable to or proper for ⟨clothes *befitting* the occasion⟩

be·fog \bi-'fȯg, -'fäg\ *vb* **1** : CONFUSE 2 **2** : to make foggy : OBSCURE

¹**be·fore** \bi-'fō(ə)r, -'fȯ(ə)r\ *adv* **1** : in advance : AHEAD ⟨go on *before*⟩ **2** : at an earlier time ⟨was here *before*⟩

²**before** *prep* **1 a** : forward of : in front of ⟨stood *before* a mirror⟩ **b** : in the presence of ⟨spoke *before* the legislature⟩ **2** : under the consideration of ⟨the case *before* the court⟩ **3** : earlier than ⟨got there *before* me⟩ ⟨come *before* six⟩

³**before** *conj* **1** : earlier than the time when ⟨think *before* you speak⟩ **2** : more willingly than ⟨I'd starve *before* I'd steal⟩

be·fore·hand \-ˌhand\ *adv* : ahead of time : in advance

before long *adv* : in the near future : SOON

be·foul \bi-'fau̇l\ *vb* : to make dirty : SOIL

be·friend \bi-'frend\ *vb* : to become or act as a friend to

be·fud·dle \bi-'fəd-ᵊl\ *vb* **-fud·dled; -fud·dling** \-'fəd-liŋ, -ᵊl-iŋ\ **1** : to dull the senses of with or as if with too much drink : STUPEFY **2** : CONFUSE 1a, PERPLEX — **be·fud·dle·ment** \-mənt\ *n*

beg \'beg\ *vb* **begged; beg·ging** **1** : to ask for money, food, or help as charity ⟨*beg* in the streets⟩ **2** : to ask earnestly or politely ⟨*beg* a favor⟩ ⟨*beg* pardon⟩

be·get \bi-'get\ *vb* **-got** \-'gät\ *also* **-gat** \-'gat\; **-got·ten** \-'gät-ᵊn\ *or* **-got; -get·ting** **1** : to become the father of **2** : ²CAUSE — **be·get·ter** *n*

¹**beg·gar** \'beg-ər\ *n* **1** : a person who lives by begging **2** : a very poor person : PAUPER

²**beggar** *vb* **beg·gared; beg·gar·ing** \'beg-(ə-)riŋ\ **1** : to reduce to beggary **2** : to go beyond the ability of ⟨the costumes almost *beggar* description⟩

beg·gar·ly \'beg-ər-lē\ *adj* : MEASLY — **beg·gar·li·ness** *n*

beg·gar–ticks \'beg-ər-ˌtiks\ *also* **beg·gar's–ticks** \-ərz-\ *n sing or pl* : BUR MARIGOLD; *also* : its prickly fruits

beg·gary \'beg-(ə-)rē\ *n* : extreme poverty

be·gin \bi-'gin\ *vb* **be·gan** \-'gan\; **be·gun** \-'gən\; **be·gin·ning** **1** : to do or be the first part of an action or course : START ⟨*begin* your homework⟩ ⟨it *began* to rain⟩ **2** : to come or bring into existence : ORIGINATE ⟨the war *began* in 1939⟩ **3** : to do or succeed in the least degree ⟨does not *begin* to fill our needs⟩

be·gin·ner \bi-'gin-ər\ *n* : a person who is beginning something or doing something for the first time : an inexperienced person

be·gin·ning \bi-'gin-iŋ\ *n* **1** : the point at which something begins ⟨the *beginning* of the year⟩ **2** : the first part ⟨go back to the *beginning* of the song⟩ **3** : an early stage or period ⟨the *beginnings* of American history⟩

be·gone \bi-'gȯn *also* -'gän\ *vb* : to go away — used especially in the imperative mood ⟨*begone* from my sight!⟩

be·go·nia \bi-'gō-nyə\ *n* : any of a large genus of tropical herbs often grown for their colorful leaves and bright waxy flowers

begonia

be·grime \bi-'grīm\ *vb* **be·grimed; be·grim·ing** : to make dirty with grime

be·grudge \bi-'grəj\ *vb* : to give or do reluctantly ⟨*begrudge* a person a favor⟩ — **be·grudg·ing·ly** \-'grəj-iŋ-lē\ *adv*

be·guile \bi-'gī(ə)l\ *vb* **be·guiled; be·guil·ing** **1** : to deceive by cunning means ⟨was *beguiled* into thinking everything was all right⟩ **2** : to draw notice or interest by charm ⟨a *beguiling* manner⟩ ⟨it is the scenery that *beguiles* the tourists⟩ **3** : to cause time to pass pleasantly ⟨*beguile* the time by telling stories⟩ — **be·guile·ment** \-'gī(ə)l-mənt\ *n* — **be·guil·er** \-'gī-lər\ *n*

be·half \bi-'haf, -'háf\ *n* : useful aid : SUPPORT ⟨spoke in my *behalf*⟩ — **in behalf of** *or* **on behalf of** **1** : in the interest of ⟨spoke *in behalf of* the other candidate⟩ **2** : as a representative of ⟨accepted *on behalf of* the whole class⟩

be·have \bi-'hāv\ *vb* **be·haved; be·hav·ing** **1** : to conduct oneself ⟨*behaved* badly at the meeting⟩ **2** : to conduct oneself properly ⟨please *behave*⟩ **3** : to act, function, or react in a particular way ⟨how metals *behave* under heat and pressure⟩

be·hav·ior \bi-'hā-vyər\ *n* **1** : the way in which one conducts oneself **2** : the way in which something (as a machine) behaves **3** : anything that a living being does that involves action and response to stimulation — **be·hav·ior·al** \-vyə-rəl\ *adj*

be·head \bi-'hed\ *vb* : to cut off the head of

be·he·moth \bi-'hē-məth, 'bē-ə-ˌməth, -ˌmäth, -ˌmȯth\ *n* **1** *often cap* : an animal described in the Bible that is probably the hippopotamus **2** : something of monstrous size or power

be·hest \bi-'hest\ *n* : ²ORDER 5b, COMMAND ⟨built monuments at their ruler's *behest*⟩

¹**be·hind** \bi-'hīnd\ *adv or adj* **1 a** : in a place or time that is being or has been departed from ⟨stay *behind*⟩ ⟨left years of poverty *behind*⟩ **b** : at, to, or toward the back ⟨look *behind*⟩ ⟨fall *behind*⟩ **2 a** : not up to the general level ⟨*behind* in school⟩ **b** : not keeping up to a schedule ⟨*behind* in the car payments⟩

²**behind** *prep* **1** : at, to, or toward the back of ⟨look *behind* you⟩ ⟨a garden *behind* the house⟩ **2** : not up to the level of ⟨sales are *behind* those of last year⟩ ⟨*behind* the rest of

\ə\ **abut**	\au̇\ **out**	\i\ **tip**	\ȯ\ **saw**	\u̇\ **foot**
\ər\ **further**	\ch\ **chin**	\ī\ **life**	\ȯi\ **coin**	\y\ **yet**
\a\ **mat**	\e\ **pet**	\j\ **job**	\th\ **thin**	\yü\ **few**
\ā\ **take**	\ē\ **easy**	\ŋ\ **sing**	\th\ **this**	\yu̇\ **cure**
\ä\ **cot, cart**	\g\ **go**	\ō\ **bone**	\ü\ **food**	\zh\ **vision**

the class⟩ **3 a** : in the background of ⟨the reasons *behind* our success⟩ **b** : in support of ⟨we're *behind* you all the way⟩

be·hind·hand \bi-ˈhīnd-ˌhand\ *adv or adj* : not keeping up : BEHIND ⟨*behindhand* with the rent⟩

be·hold \bi-ˈhōld\ *vb* **be·held** \-ˈheld\; **-hold·ing** : to look upon : SEE — **be·hold·er** *n*

be·hold·en \bi-ˈhōl-dən\ *adj* : being indebted for a favor or gift

be·hoof \bi-ˈhüf\ *n* : ¹ADVANTAGE 1, BENEFIT ⟨acted only for his own *behoof*⟩

be·hoove \bi-ˈhüv\ *vb* **be·hooved; be·hoov·ing** : to be necessary, fitting, or proper for ⟨such behavior ill *behooves* you⟩ ⟨it *behooves* a good citizen to obey the law⟩

be·hove \-ˈhōv\ *chiefly British variant of* BEHOOVE

beige \ˈbāzh\ *n* : a light grayish yellowish brown — **beige** *adj*

be·ing \ˈbē-iŋ\ *n* **1** : the state of having life or existence **2** : one that exists in fact or thought **3** : a living thing; *esp* : HUMAN BEING

be·la·bor \bi-ˈlā-bər\ *vb* **1** : to keep explaining or insisting on to excess ⟨I don't want to *belabor* the point⟩ **2** : ASSAIL, ATTACK

be·lat·ed \bi-ˈlāt-əd\ *adj* : delayed beyond the usual time — **be·lat·ed·ly** *adv* — **be·lat·ed·ness** *n*

be·lay \bi-ˈlā\ *vb* **1** : to make (as a rope) fast by turns around a cleat or pin **2** : CEASE, STOP

¹belch \ˈbelch\ *vb* **1** : to force out gas from the stomach through the mouth **2** : to throw out or be thrown out violently ⟨smoke *belching* from the chimney⟩

²belch *n* : a belching of gas

bel·dam *or* **bel·dame** \ˈbel-dəm\ *n* : an old woman

be·lea·guer \bi-ˈlē-gər\ *vb* **-guered; -guer·ing** \-g(ə-)riŋ\ **1** : to surround with an army so as to prevent escape : BESIEGE 1 **2** : to subject to troublesome forces : HARASS ⟨the pests that *beleaguer* farmers⟩

bel·fry \ˈbel-frē\ *n, pl* **belfries** : a tower or a room in a tower for a bell or set of bells

Word History In our day *belfry* means "bell tower"; the first syllable is a perfect match with *bell*, whatever *-fry* might mean. But in fact *belfry* does not derive from *bell*, and the original meaning of its medieval French source, *berfroi*, was not "bell tower," but rather "siege tower." A siege tower was a wheeled wooden structure that was pushed up to the walls of a besieged fortress to provide shelter and a base of attack for the besiegers. A variant of French *berfroi* that was also borrowed into English was *belfroi*. The resemblance of this word to Middle English *belle*, "bell," most likely set in motion a shift in meaning that gave *belfry* its current meaning. [Middle English *belfrey, berfrey* "bell tower, war tower," from early French *berfroi* "war tower," of Germanic origin]

belfry

Bel·gian \ˈbel-jən\ *n* **1** : a person born or living in Belgium **2** : any of a Belgian breed of heavy usually roan or chestnut draft horses — **Belgian** *adj*

Belgian sheepdog *n* : any of a breed of active black dogs developed in Belgium for herding sheep

be·lie \bi-ˈlī\ *vb* **-lied; -ly·ing** **1** : to give a false idea of ⟨her looks *belied* her age⟩ **2** : to show to be false ⟨their actions *belie* their claim to be innocent⟩ — **be·li·er** *n*

be·lief \bə-ˈlēf\ *n* **1** : a feeling sure that someone or something exists or is true or trustworthy ⟨a *belief* in Santa Claus⟩ ⟨a *belief* in democracy⟩ **2** : something that one thinks is true ⟨political *beliefs*⟩

synonyms BELIEF, CREDENCE, FAITH mean an accepting of something or someone as true or reliable without asking for proof. BELIEF may suggest going along without careful thought ⟨the widespread *belief* in flying saucers⟩. CREDENCE suggests ready acceptance of rumors, reports, or opinions as a basis for belief ⟨during the panic people gave *credence* to wild stories⟩. FAITH suggests full trust and confidence in the source ⟨the members of the team had great *faith* in their coach's strategy⟩. **synonyms** see in addition OPINION

be·lieve \bə-ˈlēv\ *vb* **be·lieved; be·liev·ing** **1** : to have a firm religious faith **2** : to have faith or confidence in the existence or worth of ⟨*believe* in ghosts⟩ ⟨*believe* in regular exercise⟩ **3** : to accept as true ⟨*believe* the reports⟩ **4** : to accept the word or evidence of ⟨they *believed* us⟩ ⟨I could hardly *believe* my ears⟩ **5** : to hold as an opinion : THINK ⟨*believe* it will rain⟩ — **be·liev·able** \-ˈlē-və-bəl\ *adj* — **be·liev·ably** \-blē\ *adv* — **be·liev·er** *n*

be·like \bi-ˈlīk\ *adv, archaic* : most likely

be·lit·tle \bi-ˈlit-ᵊl\ *vb* **-lit·tled; -lit·tling** \-ˈlit-ᵊl-iŋ, -ˈlit-liŋ\ : to make (a person or a thing) seem little or unimportant ⟨*belittle* the success of a rival⟩ — **be·lit·tle·ment** \-ᵊl-mənt\ *n* — **be·lit·tler** \-ˈlit-ᵊl-ər, -ˈlit-lər\ *n*

¹bell \ˈbel\ *n* **1** : a hollow usually cup-shaped metallic device that makes a ringing sound when struck **2** : the stroke or sound of a bell that tells the hour **3** : a half hour period of a watch on shipboard indicated by the strokes of a bell **4** : something (as a flower or the mouth of a trumpet) shaped like a bell

SHIP'S BELLS

NUMBER OF BELLS	—— HOUR (A.M. OR P.M.) ——		
1	12:30	4:30	8:30
2	1:00	5:00	9:00
3	1:30	5:30	9:30
4	2:00	6:00	10:00
5	2:30	6:30	10:30
6	3:00	7:00	11:00
7	3:30	7:30	11:30
8	4:00	8:00	12:00

²bell *vb* **1** : to provide with a bell ⟨*bell* a cat⟩ **2** : to take the form of a bell : FLARE

bel·la·don·na \ˌbel-ə-ˈdän-ə\ *n* **1** : a European poisonous herb of the nightshade family with purple or green bell-shaped flowers, glossy black berries, and a root and leaves that are a source of atropine — called also *deadly nightshade* **2** : a drug or extract from the belladonna [from Italian *bella donna*, literally, "beautiful lady"; so called because the extract was formerly used in cosmetics]

bell–bot·toms \ˈbel-ˈbät-əmz\ *n pl* : pants with legs that widen out at the bottom — **bell–bottom** *adj*

bell·boy \ˈbel-ˌbȯi\ *n* : BELLHOP

bell captain *n* : a person in charge of hotel bellhops

belle \ˈbel\ *n* : a popular attractive girl or woman [French *belle* "a beautiful girl," from *belle* (adjective), feminine form of *beau* "beautiful," from Latin *bellus* "pretty" — related to BEAU, BEAUTY]

bell–flow·er \ˈbel-ˌflaů(-ə)r\ *n* : any of various herbs that are often grown for their showy flowers shaped like bells

bell·hop \-ˌhäp\ *n* : a hotel or club employee who takes guests to rooms, carries luggage, and runs errands

bel·li·cose \ˈbel-ə-ˌkōs\ *adj* : likely to quarrel or fight — **bel·li·cos·i·ty** \ˌbel-ə-ˈkäs-ət-ē\ *n*

bel·lig·er·ence \bə-ˈlij-(ə-)rən(t)s\ *n* : a belligerent attitude or disposition

bel·lig·er·en·cy \bə-ˈlij-(ə-)rən-sē\ *n* **1** : the state of being at war **2** : BELLIGERENCE

bel·lig·er·ent \bə-ˈlij-(ə-)rənt\ *adj* **1** : waging war ⟨*belligerent* nations⟩ **2** : eager to or showing eagerness to fight

⟨*belligerent* remarks⟩ — **belligerent** *n* — **bel·lig·er·ent·ly** *adv*

synonyms BELLIGERENT, PUGNACIOUS, QUARRELSOME, CONTENTIOUS mean having an aggressive or fighting attitude. BELLIGERENT suggests either being actually at war ⟨the *belligerent* nations refused to have peace talks⟩ or having angry aggressive feelings ⟨the new girl at school is *belligerent* and is not making many friends⟩. PUGNACIOUS suggests a nature that takes pleasure in conflict ⟨a *pugnacious* fellow always getting into fights⟩. QUARRELSOME stresses a bad-tempered readiness to fight for no good reason ⟨our neighbors are *quarrelsome*⟩. CONTENTIOUS suggests an odd and annoying fondness for arguing ⟨irritated by *contentious* people⟩.

bell jar *n* : a bell-shaped usually glass container, designed to cover objects, hold gases, or keep a vacuum

bel·low \'bel-ō\ *vb* : to make a deep loud roar like that of a bull — **bellow** *n*

bel·lows \'bel-ōz, -əz\ *n sing or pl* **1** : a device that produces a strong current of air when it is spread apart and then pressed together **2** : a part of some cameras that is pleated and can expand

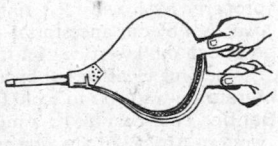

bellows 1

bell·pull \'bel-ˌpul\ *n* : a cord or wire or a handle or knob attached to it that one pulls to ring a bell

bells and whistles *n pl* : items or features that are useful or decorative but not necessary ⟨a new car with lots of *bells and whistles*⟩

bell·weth·er \'bel-ˌweth-ər, -ˌweth-\ *n* : someone or something that leads the way or points out a trend ⟨a *bellwether* of fashion⟩ ⟨a county that is a *bellwether* in national elections⟩ [from earlier *bellwether* "leading sheep (or *wether*) of a flock," from the fact that this sheep wore a bell which told the shepherd where the flock was]

¹bel·ly \'bel-ē\ *n, pl* **bellies** **1 a** : ABDOMEN 1 **b** : the undersurface of an animal's body; *also* : hide from this part **c** : ¹STOMACH 1a **2** : an internal cavity : INTERIOR **3** : a curved or rounded surface or object ⟨the *belly* of an airplane⟩

²belly *vb* **bel·lied; bel·ly·ing** : to swell or bulge out

¹bel·ly·ache \'bel-ē-ˌāk\ *n* : pain in the abdomen and especially in the stomach : STOMACHACHE

²bellyache *vb* : to complain in a whining or irritable way ⟨kept *bellyaching* about the wait⟩ — **bel·ly·ach·er** *n*

belly button *n* : the human navel

belly flop *n* : a dive (as into the water) in which the front of the body lands flat — **belly flop** *vb*

bel·ly·land \'bel-ē-ˌland\ *vb* : to land an airplane without use of landing gear — **belly landing** *n*

be·long \bi-'lȯn\ *vb* **1** : to be in a proper place ⟨this book *belongs* on the top shelf⟩ **2 a** : to be the property of a person or group of persons ⟨the watch *belongs* to me⟩ **b** : to be a member ⟨*belongs* to our club⟩ **3** : to be a part of : be connected with : go with ⟨the parts *belonging* to the clock⟩ **4** : to be classified ⟨whales *belong* among the mammals⟩

be·long·ings \bi-'lȯn-iŋz\ *n pl* : the things that belong to a person : POSSESSIONS

be·loved \bi-'ləv-(ə)d\ *adj* : dearly loved — **be·loved** *n*

¹be·low \bi-'lō\ *adv* **1** : in or to a lower place **2** : on a lower floor or deck **3** : below zero ⟨the temperature was 20 *below*⟩

²below *prep* : lower than ⟨the diver descends *below* 25 meters⟩ ⟨*below* average⟩ ⟨selling *below* cost⟩

¹belt \'belt\ *n* **1** : a strip of flexible material (as leather) worn around a person's body for holding in or supporting something (as clothing, tools, or weapons) or for ornament **2** : a flexible continuous band running around

wheels or pulleys and used for moving or carrying something ⟨a fan *belt* on a car⟩ **3** : a region suited to or producing something or having some special feature ⟨the corn *belt*⟩ ⟨a storm *belt*⟩ — **belt·ed** \'bel-təd\ *adj* — **below the belt** : in an unfair way : UNFAIR — **under one's belt** : as part of one's experience

²belt *vb* **1** : to put a belt on or around **2** : to hit hard ⟨*belt* a home run⟩ **3** : to mark with a band **4** : to sing in a forceful way ⟨*belt* out a song⟩

³belt *n* : a jarring blow

belt·ing \'bel-tiŋ\ *n* : material for making belts

belt–tight·en·ing \'belt-ˌtīt-niŋ, -ᵊn-iŋ\ *n* : a reduction in spending

be·lu·ga \bə-'lü-gə\ *n* : a toothed whale that becomes 10 to 15 feet (3.0 to 5.0 meters) long and white when adult — called also *beluga whale* [from earlier *beluga* "a white sturgeon," from Russian *beluga* (same meaning), from *belyĭ* "white"]

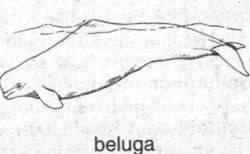

beluga

be·moan \bi-'mōn\ *vb* : to express grief over

be·muse \bi-'myüz\ *vb* **1** : CONFUSE 1a **2** : to cause to have feelings of tolerant amusement ⟨*bemused* by the many rumors⟩

¹bench \'bench\ *n* **1 a** : a long seat for two or more persons **b** : a seat where the members of a team wait for a chance to play **2 a** : the seat where a judge sits in a court of law **b** : the position or rank of a judge ⟨appointed to the *bench*⟩ **c** : a person or persons engaged in judging **3 a** : a long table for holding tools and work **b** : SHELF 2

²bench *vb* **1** : to furnish with benches **2** : to seat on a bench **3** : to remove from or keep out of a game

benchmark *n* **1** *usually* **bench mark** : a mark on a permanent object indicating elevation and serving as a reference in geological surveys **2** : something (as a test) that can be used as a standard to check other things (as computer programs) against

bench·warm·er \'bench-ˌwȯr-mər\ *n* : a reserve player on a sports team

¹bend \'bend\ *vb* **bent** \'bent\; **bend·ing** **1** : to pull tight ⟨*bend* a bow⟩ **2** : to curve or cause a change of shape ⟨*bend* a wire into a circle⟩ **3** : to turn in a certain direction ⟨*bent* their steps toward town⟩ **4** : to apply or apply oneself closely ⟨she *bent* herself to the task⟩ **5** : to curve out of line ⟨the road *bends* to the left⟩ **6** : to curve downward : STOOP ⟨*bend* over and pick it up⟩ — **bend over backward** *or* **bend over backwards** : to make extreme efforts ⟨would *bend over backwards* to help⟩

²bend *n* **1** : the act or process of bending : the state of being bent **2** : something (as a curved part of a stream) that is bent **3** *pl* : a severe disorder marked by pain (as in joints), by difficulty in breathing, and often by collapsing and caused by release of gas bubbles (as of nitrogen) in the tissues upon too rapid a change from an environment of high air pressure to one of lower air pressure — called also *caisson disease, decompression sickness*

¹be·neath \bi-'nēth\ *adv* : in or to a lower position : BELOW

²beneath *prep* **1 a** : lower than : BELOW **b** : directly under **2** : not worthy of ⟨work *beneath* your dignity⟩

bene·dic·tion \ˌben-ə-'dik-shən\ *n* **1** : an expression of good wishes **2** : the short blessing at the end of a religious service [Middle English *benediccioun* "an expression of blessing or good wishes," from Latin *benediction-, benedictio* (same meaning), from *benedicere* "to bless," from

\ə\ **abut**	\au̇\ **out**	\i\ **tip**	\ȯ\ **saw**	\u̇\ **foot**	
\ər\ **further**	\ch\ **chin**	\ī\ **life**	\ȯi\ **coin**	\y\ **yet**	
\a\ **mat**	\e\ **pet**	\j\ **job**	\th\ **thin**	\yü\ **few**	
\ā\ **take**	\ē\ **easy**	\ŋ\ **sing**	\th\ **this**	\yu̇\ **cure**	
\ä\ **cot, cart**	\g\ **go**	\ō\ **bone**	\ü\ **food**	\zh\ **vision**	

earlier *bene dicere* "to praise, speak well," from *bene* "well" and *dicere* "to say" — related to DICTATE]

Ben·e·dict's solution \'ben-ə-,dik(t)s-\ *n* : a blue liquid that is used to detect some sugars (as glucose) with which it reacts when warmed to produce a red, yellow, or orange solid that separates from the liquid

bene·fac·tion \'ben-ə-,fak-shən, ,ben-ə-'fak-\ *n* **1** : the action of benefiting **2** : a benefit given; *esp* : a donation to charity

bene·fac·tor \'ben-ə-,fak-tər\ *n* : one who helps another especially by giving money

bene·fac·tress \'ben-ə-,fak-trəs\ *n* : a woman who is a benefactor

ben·e·fice \'ben-ə-fəs\ *n* : a post held by a member of the clergy that gives the right to use certain property and to receive income from stated sources

be·nef·i·cence \bə-'nef-ə-sən(t)s\ *n* **1** : the quality or state of being beneficent **2** : BENEFACTION

be·nef·i·cent \bə-'nef-ə-sənt\ *adj* : doing or producing good; *esp* : performing acts of kindness or charity — **be·nef·i·cent·ly** *adv*

ben·e·fi·cial \,ben-ə-'fish-əl\ *adj* : producing results that are good for health and happiness — **ben·e·fi·cial·ly** \-'fish-ə-lē\ *adv* — **ben·e·fi·cial·ness** *n*

ben·e·fi·ci·ary \,ben-ə-'fish-ē-,er-ē, -'fish-(ə-)rē\ *n, pl* **-aries** : a person who benefits or is expected to benefit from something ⟨the *beneficiary* of life insurance⟩

¹ben·e·fit \'ben-ə-,fit\ *n* **1 a** : something that does good to a person or thing ⟨the *benefits* of fresh air and sunshine⟩ **b** : useful aid : HELP ⟨had to perform without the *benefit* of a rehearsal⟩ **2 a** : money paid at death or when sick, retired, or unemployed (as by an insurance company or public agency) **b** : something (as health insurance or vacation time) provided to a worker by an employer in addition to pay **3** : an entertainment or social event to raise funds for a person or cause [Middle English *benefet, benefit* "good deed," derived from Latin *bene factum* (same meaning), from *bene factus,* past participle of *bene facere* "to do good," from *bene* "well" (akin to *bonus* "good") and *facere* "to do, make" — related to BONUS, FASHION]

²benefit *vb* **benefit·ed** \-,fit-əd\ *also* **-fit·ted; -fit·ing** *also* **-fit·ting 1** : to be useful or profitable to ⟨medicines that *benefit* all⟩ **2** : to receive benefit ⟨I *benefited* from the experience⟩

be·nev·o·lence \bə-'nev-(ə-)lən(t)s\ *n* : KINDNESS, GENEROSITY

be·nev·o·lent \bə-'nev-(ə-)lənt\ *adj* : having a desire to do good : KINDLY, CHARITABLE ⟨a *benevolent* organization⟩ — **be·nev·o·lent·ly** *adv*

Ben·gali \ben-'gȯ-lē, beŋ-\ *n* **1** : a person born or living in Bengal **2** : the language of Bengal — **Bengali** *adj*

be·night·ed \bi-'nīt-əd\ *adj* : IGNORANT 1, 2

be·nign \bi-'nīn\ *adj* **1** : of a gentle disposition : GRACIOUS **2** : FAVORABLE ⟨a *benign* climate⟩ **3** : of a mild type or character; *esp* : not becoming cancerous ⟨a *benign* tumor⟩ — **be·nig·ni·ty** \-'nig-nət-ē\ *n* — **be·nign·ly** \-'nīn-lē\ *adv*

be·nig·nant \bi-'nig-nənt\ *adj* **1** : showing kindly feelings or intentions **2** : BENEFICIAL — **be·nig·nant·ly** *adv*

ben·i·son \'ben-ə-sən, -zən\ *n* : BLESSING 1

¹bent \'bent\ *n* : BENT GRASS [Middle English *bent* "grassy place, bent grass"]

²bent *adj* **1** : changed by bending : CROOKED ⟨a *bent* pin⟩ **2** : strongly favorable to : quite determined ⟨doctors *bent* on finding a cure⟩ [Middle English *bent* "crooked," from *benden* "to bend"] — **bent out of shape** : extremely upset or angry ⟨got all *bent out of shape* over the news⟩

³bent *n* **1** : a strong natural liking **2** : a special inclination or capacity : TALENT [from *bend* "to turn in a certain direction"]

bent grass *n* : any of a genus of stiff or velvety grasses that are used especially for pastures and lawns

ben·thos \'ben-,thäs\ *n* : the plant and animal life that lives on or in the bottom of a body of water (as an ocean)

ben·ton·ite \'bent-ᵊn-,īt\ *n* : an absorbent clay

be·numb \bi-'nəm\ *vb* : to make numb especially by cold

ben·zene \'ben-,zēn, ben-'zēn\ *n* : a colorless flammable liquid that evaporates easily and is used to make or dissolve other chemicals or as a motor fuel

ben·zine \'ben-,zēn, ben-'zēn\ *n* : any of various flammable chemicals from petroleum that evaporate easily and are used especially to dissolve fatty substances or as motor fuels

ben·zo·ic acid \ben-,zō-ik-\ *n* : a white crystalline organic acid that is used especially to increase the life of foods, to make other chemicals, and in medicine

ben·zo·yl peroxide \'ben-zə-,wil-, -,zȯil-\ *n* : a white crystalline compound used in bleaching and in medicine especially in the treatment of acne

be·queath \bi-'kwēth, -'kwēth\ *vb* **1** : to give or leave property by a will **2** : HAND DOWN 1 ⟨traditions *bequeathed* by our ancestors⟩ — **be·queath·al** \-əl\ *n*

be·quest \bi-'kwest\ *n* **1** : the action of bequeathing **2** : something given or left by a will

be·rate \bi-'rāt\ *vb* : to scold forcefully

Ber·ber \'bər-bər\ *n* **1** : a member of a people of northwestern Africa **2** : any of a group of languages spoken in northwestern Africa

¹be·reaved \bi-'rēvd\ *adj* : suffering the death of a loved one ⟨*bereaved* family members⟩

²bereaved *n, pl* **bereaved** : a person who is bereaved

be·reave·ment \bi-'rēv-mənt\ *n* : the state or fact of being bereaved

be·reft \bi-'reft\ *adj* **1** : not having something needed, wanted, or expected ⟨*bereft* of money⟩ **2** : ¹BEREAVED

be·ret \bə-'rā\ *n* : a soft flat wool cap without a visor

berg \'bərg\ *n* : ICEBERG

ber·i·beri \,ber-ē-'ber-ē\ *n* : a disease marked by weakness, wasting, and damage to nerves and caused by a lack of thiamine in the diet or by an inability to absorb and use it

berke·li·um \'bər-klē-əm\ *n* : an artificially prepared radioactive chemical element — see ELEMENT table

berm \'bərm\ *n* : a shelf or path at the top or bottom of a slope; *also* : a mound or wall of earth

beret

Ber·mu·da grass \bər-'myüd-ə-\ *n* : a trailing grass that is native to Europe and is used for lawns and pasture especially in the southern U.S.

¹ber·ry \'ber-ē\ *n, pl* **berries 1** : a small pulpy and usually edible fruit (as a strawberry or raspberry) **2** : a fruit (as a grape, blueberry, tomato, or cucumber) that develops from a single ovary and has the wall of the ripened ovary pulpy **3** : the dry seed of some plants (as coffee) — **berry·like** \-ē-,līk\ *adj*

²berry *vb* **ber·ried; ber·ry·ing 1** : to bear or produce berries **2** : to gather or look for berries ⟨go *berrying*⟩

¹ber·serk \bə(r)-'sərk, ,bər-, -'zərk; 'bər-,sərk, -,zərk\ *adj* : gone out of control : CRAZY, AMOK — **berserk** *adv*

Word History Many hundreds of years ago in what is now Scandinavia, certain warriors were known for their wild and savage behavior in battle. These fighters wore masks or garments of animal skin and the early Norse word for such a person was *berserkr,* meaning literally, "bear shirt." The word was borrowed into English in the early 19th century when many people became interested in Norse history and legend. From *berserker,* with the sense of "a Scandinavian warrior," the word became *berserk,* a general term for a person whose behavior is reckless and wild. [from early Norse *berserkr,* from *ber-* (derived from the word for "bear") and *serkr* "shirt"]

²**ber·serk** *or* **ber·serk·er** \bə(r)-'sərk-ər, ˌbər-, -'zərk-; 'bər-ˌsərk-ər, -ˌzərk-\ *n* : a Scandinavian warrior of ancient times who fought with great fury in battle and was believed impossible to kill or wound

¹**berth** \'bərth\ *n* **1 a** : enough room to maneuver a ship **b** : a safe distance ⟨give it wide *berth*⟩ **2** : a place where a ship lies at anchor or at a wharf **3** : a place to sleep on a ship or train **4** : JOB 3, POSITION

²**berth** *vb* : to bring or come into a berth

ber·yl \'ber-əl\ *n* : a mineral consisting of a silicate of beryllium and aluminum that has great hardness and occurs in crystals of a variety of colors

be·ryl·li·um \bə-'ril-ē-əm\ *n* : a steel-gray light strong brittle toxic metallic element used chiefly to help harden alloys — see ELEMENT table

be·seech \bi-'sēch\ *vb* **be·sought** \-'sȯt\ *or* **be·seeched**; **be·seech·ing** : to ask earnestly for

be·seem \bi-'sēm\ *vb, archaic* : to be proper for

be·set \bi-'set\ *vb* **-set**; **-set·ting 1** : to trouble with problems **2** : to set upon : ASSAIL

be·set·ting \bi-'set-iŋ\ *adj* : constantly present or attacking ⟨a *besetting* danger⟩

be·side \bi-'sīd\ *prep* **1 a** : by the side of ⟨walk *beside* me⟩ **b** : in comparison with ⟨the kitten looks tiny *beside* that big dog⟩ **2** : ¹BESIDES ⟨was the only one, *beside* me, who objected⟩ **3** : not relating to ⟨*beside* the point⟩ — **beside oneself** : very upset or excited

¹**be·sides** \bi-'sīdz\ *prep* **1** : EXCEPT FOR ⟨no one *besides* me knows about it⟩ **2** : in addition to ⟨*besides* being useful, it looks good⟩

²**besides** *adv* : in addition : ALSO ⟨had a big dinner and dessert *besides*⟩

be·siege \bi-'sēj\ *vb* **be·sieged**; **be·sieg·ing 1** : to surround with armed forces for the purpose of capturing **2** : to trouble with requests **3** : to cause worry or distress to ⟨doubts *besieged* him⟩ — **be·sieg·er** *n*

be·smear \bi-'smi(ə)r\ *vb* : ²SMEAR

be·smirch \bi-'smərch\ *vb* : to make soiled or less pure

be·som \'bē-zəm\ *n* : a broom made of twigs

be·spat·ter \bi-'spat-ər\ *vb* : ¹SPATTER

be·speak \bi-'spēk\ *vb* **be·spoke** \-'spōk\; **be·spo·ken** \-'spō-kən\; **-speak·ing 1** : to ask or arrange for in advance **2** : to make plain : SHOW ⟨her performance *bespeaks* much practice⟩

be·spec·ta·cled \bi-'spek-ti-kəld\ *adj* : wearing glasses

Bessemer process *n* : a process of making steel from pig iron by burning out impurities (as carbon) by means of a blast of air forced through the hot liquid metal

¹**best** \'best\ *adj, superlative of* GOOD **1** : better than all others ⟨my *best* friend⟩ **2** : good or useful in the highest degree : most excellent ⟨my *best* clothes⟩ ⟨the *best* movie I ever saw⟩ ~ **3** : ³MOST, LARGEST ⟨it rained for the *best* part of a week⟩

²**best** *adv, superlative of* WELL **1** : in the best way : to the greatest advantage ⟨some things are *best* left unsaid⟩ **2** : to the highest degree : MOST ⟨*best* able to do the work⟩

³**best** *n, pl* **best 1** : the best state or part ⟨the *best* is yet to come⟩ **2** : one that is best ⟨even the *best* lose once in a while⟩ **3 a** : one's greatest effort ⟨do your *best*⟩ **b** : best performance or achievement ⟨ran a new personal *best*⟩ **4** : best clothes ⟨put on your Sunday *best*⟩ — **at best** : under the best conditions

⁴**best** *vb* : to get the better of : OUTDO ⟨*bested* us in every event⟩

bes·tial \'bes-chəl, 'bēs-\ *adj* **1** : resembling a beast **2** : having or showing qualities like those of a beast : BRUTAL, INHUMAN — **bes·ti·al·i·ty** \ˌbes-chē-'al-ət-ē, ˌbēs-\ *n* — **bes·tial·ly** \-chə-lē\ *adv*

be·stir \bi-'stər\ *vb* : to stir up : rouse to action

be·stow \bi-'stō\ *vb* : to present as a gift — **be·stow·al** \-'stō-əl\ *n* — **be·stow·er** *n*

be·strew \bi-'strü\ *vb* **-strewed; -strewed** *or* **-strewn** \-'strün\; **-strew·ing 1** : STREW 2 **2** : to lie scattered over

be·stride \bi-'strīd\ *vb* **-strode** \-'strōd\; **-strid·den** \-'strid-ən\; **-strid·ing** \-'strīd-iŋ\ : to ride, sit, or stand with one leg on each side of

best–sell·er \'bes(t)-'sel-ər\ *n* : an article (as a book) whose sales are among the highest of its kind — **best–sell·ing** \-'sel-iŋ\ *adj*

¹**bet** \'bet\ *n* **1** : an agreement requiring the person whose guess about the result of a contest or the outcome of an event proves wrong to give something to a person whose guess proves right **2** : the money or thing risked **3** : a choice made by considering what might happen ⟨our best *bet* is to take the back road⟩

²**bet** *vb* **bet** *also* **bet·ted; bet·ting 1** : to risk in a bet ⟨I'll *bet* a nickel⟩ **2** : to make a bet with ⟨I *bet* you he won't⟩ **3** : to be certain enough to bet ⟨I *bet* it will rain⟩

be·ta \'bāt-ə\ *n* : the 2nd letter of the Greek alphabet — B or β

be·ta–car·o·tene \-'kar-ə-ˌtēn\ *n* : a form of carotene found in dark green and dark yellow vegetables and fruits

be·take \bi-'tāk\ *vb* **-took** \-'tuk\; **-tak·en** \-'tā-kən\; **-tak·ing** : to cause (oneself) to go

beta particle *n* : an electron or positron that is thrown out from the nucleus of an atom during radioactive decay; *also* : a high-speed electron or positron

beta ray *n* **1** : BETA PARTICLE **2** : a stream of beta particles

be·ta·tron \'bāt-ə-ˌträn\ *n* : a device that speeds up electrons by the action of a rapidly changing magnetic field

be·tel \'bēt-ᵊl\ *n* : a climbing pepper of southeastern Asia whose dried leaves are chewed together with betel nut and lime to increase the activity of the nervous system

Be·tel·geuse \'bēt-ᵊl-ˌjüs, 'bet-, -ˌjüz, -ˌjə(r)z\ *n* : a red giant star in Orion that changes in brightness

betel nut *n* : the seed of an Asian palm

bête noire \ˌbet-nə-'wär, ˌbāt-\ *n, pl* **bêtes noires** \ˌbet-nə-'wär(z), ˌbāt-\ : a person or thing strongly disliked or feared

beth·el \'beth-əl\ *n* : a place of worship especially for sailors [from Hebrew *bēth'ēl* "house of God"]

be·think \bi-'thiŋk\ *vb* **-thought** \-'thȯt\; **-think·ing 1 a** : REMEMBER 1, RECALL **b** : to cause (oneself) to be reminded **2** : to cause (oneself) to consider

be·tide \bi-'tīd\ *vb* **be·tid·ed; be·tid·ing** : to happen or happen to ⟨woe *betide* you if they ever find out what you've done⟩

be·times \bi-'tīmz\ *adv* : in time : EARLY ⟨was up *betimes* this morning⟩

be·to·ken \bi-'tō-kən\ *vb* **be·to·kened; be·to·ken·ing** \-'tōk-(ə-)niŋ\ : to be a sign of : INDICATE

be·tray \bi-'trā\ *vb* **1** : to give over to an enemy by treachery **2** : to be unfaithful to ⟨*betrayed* our trust⟩ **3** : to reveal without meaning to ⟨*betrayed* their ignorance⟩ **4** : to tell in violation of a trust ⟨*betray* a secret⟩ **synonyms** see REVEAL — **be·tray·al** \-'trā-(ə)l\ *n* — **be·tray·er** \-'trā-ər\ *n*

be·troth \bi-'träth, -'troth, -'trōth, *or with* th\ *vb* : to promise to marry or give in marriage

be·troth·al \-'trōth-əl, -'troth-, -'trōth-\ *n* : an engagement to be married

be·trothed \-'trätht, -'trotht, -'trōthd\ *n* : the person to whom one is betrothed

bet·ta \'bet-ə\ *n* : any of a genus of small brilliantly colored long-finned freshwater fishes of southeastern Asia

\ə\ **abut**	\au̇\ **out**	\i\ **tip**	\ȯ\ **saw**	\u̇\ **foot**
\ər\ **further**	\ch\ **chin**	\ī\ **life**	\ȯi\ **coin**	\y\ **yet**
\a\ **mat**	\e\ **pet**	\j\ **job**	\th\ **thin**	\yü\ **few**
\ā\ **take**	\ē\ **easy**	\ŋ\ **sing**	\th\ **this**	\yu̇\ **cure**
\ä\ **cot, cart**	\g\ **go**	\ō\ **bone**	\ü\ **food**	\zh\ **vision**

¹bet·ter \'bet-ər\ *adj, comparative of* ¹GOOD **1** : improved in health **2** : of higher quality — **better part** : more than half ⟨the *better* part of an hour⟩

²better *adv, comparative of* WELL **1** : in a more excellent manner **2 a** : to a higher or greater degree ⟨knows the story *better* than I do⟩ **b** : ²MORE ⟨*better* than an hour's drive to the lake⟩

³better *n* **1 a** : a better thing or state ⟨a change for the *better*⟩ **b** : a superior especially in merit or rank ⟨be respectful of your *betters*⟩ **2** : ADVANTAGE 1 ⟨get the *better* of someone⟩

⁴better *vb* **1** : to make better **2** : to be or do better than

better half *n* : SPOUSE

bet·ter·ment \'bet-ər-mənt\ *n* : IMPROVEMENT 1

bet·tor *or* **bet·ter** \'bet-ər\ *n* : one that bets

¹be·tween \bi-'twēn\ *prep* **1** : by the common action of ⟨ate six pizzas *between* them⟩ **2** : in the time or space that separates ⟨*between* nine and ten o'clock⟩ ⟨*between* the desk and the wall⟩ **3 a** : from one to the other of ⟨flying *between* Miami and Chicago⟩ **b** : joining or linking in some relationship ⟨the bond *between* friends⟩ ⟨the difference *between* soccer and football⟩ **4** : in comparison of ⟨there's not much to choose *between* the two coats⟩ **5** : staying known by only certain people ⟨a secret *between* you and me⟩ **6** : taking together the combined effect of ⟨*between* school and sports, they have little time for TV⟩

²between *adv* : in an intermediate space or interval ⟨two cars with a truck *between*⟩

be·twixt \bi-'twikst\ *adv or prep* : BETWEEN

¹bev·el \'bev-əl\ *n* **1** : the angle that one surface or line makes with another when they are not at right angles **2** : the slant of a bevel

²bevel *vb* **bev·eled** *or* **bev·elled; bev·el·ing** *or* **bev·el·ling** \'bev-(ə-)liŋ\ : to cut or shape (as an edge) so as to form a bevel

B ¹bevel 2

bev·er·age \'bev-(ə-)rij\ *n* : a liquid for drinking

bevy \'bev-ē\ *n, pl* **bev·ies** : a large group ⟨a *bevy* of girls⟩

be·wail \bi-'wāl\ *vb* : to express great sorrow over ⟨*bewailing* their fate⟩

be·ware \bi-'wa(ə)r, -'we(ə)r\ *vb* **1** : to be on one's guard ⟨*beware* of the dog⟩ **2** : to be suspicious of ⟨*beware* the quick excuse⟩

be·whis·kered \bi-'hwis-kərd, -'wis-\ *adj* : having whiskers

be·wil·der \bi-'wil-dər\ *vb* **-dered; -der·ing** \-d(ə-)riŋ\ : to confuse especially with a great many things to worry about — **be·wil·der·ing·ly** \-d(ə-)riŋ-lē\ *adv* — **be·wil·der·ment** \-dər-mənt\ *n*

be·witch \bi-'wich\ *vb* **1** : to put under a spell **2** : to attract or delight as if by magic — **be·witch·ment** \-mənt\ *n*

be·wray \bi-'rā\ *vb, archaic* : BETRAY, REVEAL

¹be·yond \bē-'änd\ *adv* : on or to the farther side

²beyond *prep* **1** : on or to the farther side of ⟨*beyond* that tree⟩ ⟨*beyond* the sea⟩ **2** : out of the reach or sphere of ⟨*beyond* help⟩ ⟨beautiful *beyond* belief⟩

bi- *combining form* **1** : two ⟨*bi*partisan⟩ **2** : coming or occurring every two ⟨*bi*monthly⟩ **3** : into two parts ⟨*bi*sect⟩ [derived from Latin *bi-* (prefix) "two"]

bi·an·nu·al \(')bī-'an-yə(-wə)l\ *adj* : occurring twice a year — **bi·an·nu·al·ly** \-ē\ *adv*

¹bi·as \'bī-əs\ *n* **1** : a line diagonal to the grain of a fabric **2** : an attitude that always favors one way of feeling or acting over any other : PREJUDICE **3** : a voltage applied to a device (as a transistor control electrode) to establish a reference level for operation

BOOKS OF THE BIBLE

HEBREW BIBLE

Law	Isaiah	Zephaniah	Ruth
Genesis	Jeremiah	Haggai	Lamenta-
Exodus	Ezekiel	Zechariah	tions
Leviticus	Hosea	Malachi	Ecclesiastes
Numbers	Joel	*Writings*	Esther
Deuteronomy	Amos	Psalms	Daniel
Prophets	Obadiah	Proverbs	Ezra
Joshua	Jonah	Job	Nehemiah
Judges	Micah	Song of	1 & 2
1 & 2 Samuel	Nahum	Songs	Chronicles
1 & 2 Kings	Habakkuk		

CHRISTIAN CANON—OLD TESTAMENT

ROMAN CATHOLIC	PROTESTANT	ROMAN CATHOLIC	PROTESTANT
Genesis	Genesis	Wisdom	
Exodus	Exodus	Sirach	
Leviticus	Leviticus	Isaiah	Isaiah
Numbers	Numbers	Jeremiah	Jeremiah
Deuteronomy	Deuteronomy	Lamentations	Lamenta-
Joshua	Joshua		tions
Judges	Judges	Baruch	
Ruth	Ruth	Ezekiel	Ezekiel
1 & 2 Samuel	1 & 2 Samuel	Daniel	Daniel
1 & 2 Kings	1 & 2 Kings	Hosea	Hosea
1 & 2 Chronicles	1 & 2 Chronicles	Joel	Joel
Ezra	Ezra	Amos	Amos
Nehemiah	Nehemiah	Obadiah	Obadiah
Tobit		Jonah	Jonah
Judith		Micah	Micah
Esther	Esther	Nahum	Nahum
Job	Job	Habakkuk	Habakkuk
Psalms	Psalms	Zephaniah	Zephaniah
Proverbs	Proverbs	Haggai	Haggai
Ecclesiastes	Ecclesiastes	Zechariah	Zechariah
Song of Songs	Song of Solomon	Malachi	Malachi
		1 & 2 Maccabees	

PROTESTANT APOCRYPHA

1 & 2 Esdras	Ecclesiasticus	Prayer of	Bel and the
Tobit	or the	Azariah and	Dragon
Judith	Wisdom of	the Song of	The Prayer of
Additions to	Jesus Son	the Three	Manasses
Esther	of Sirach	Holy Children	1 & 2
Wisdom of	Baruch	Susanna	Maccabees
Solomon			

CHRISTIAN CANON—NEW TESTAMENT

Matthew	Romans	1 & 2 Thessa-	James
Mark	1 & 2 Corin-	lonians	1 & 2 Peter
Luke	thians	1 & 2 Timothy	1, 2, 3 John
John	Galatians	Titus	Jude
Acts of the	Ephesians	Philemon	Revelation
Apostles	Philippians	Hebrews	*or* Apoca-
	Colossians		lypse

²bias *vb* **bi·ased** *or* **bi·assed; bi·as·ing** *or* **bi·as·sing** : to give a prejudiced outlook to

bias tape *n* : a narrow strip of cloth cut on the bias, folded, and used for finishing or decorating clothing

bib \'bib\ *n* **1** : a cloth or plastic shield tied under a child's chin to protect the clothes **2** : the upper part of an apron or of overalls

Bi·ble \'bī-bəl\ *n* **1 a** : a book made up of the writings accepted by Christians as coming from God **b** : a book containing the sacred writings of some other religion **2** *not cap* : a publication widely read and considered very important ⟨the *bible* of show business⟩ [Middle English *Bible* "the Bible," from early French *Bible* (same meaning), from Latin *biblia* (same meaning), from Greek *biblia* (plural) "books," derived from *Byblos,* ancient city in Phoenicia from which the Greeks imported papyrus]

bib·li·cal \'bib-li-kəl\ *adj* : relating to, taken from, or found in the Bible — **bib·li·cal·ly** \-k(ə-)lē\ *adv*

bib·li·og·ra·phy \ˌbib-lē-'äg-rə-fē\ *n, pl* **-phies** : a list of writings about a subject or author or by an author — **bib·lio·graph·ic** \ˌbib-lē-ə-'graf-ik\ *or* **bib·lio·graph·i·cal** \-'graf-i-kəl\ *adj*

bib·u·lous \'bib-yə-ləs\ *adj* 1 : highly absorbent 2 : fond of alcoholic drinks — **bib·u·lous·ly** *adv* — **bib·u·lous·ness** *n*

bi·cam·er·al \(')bī-'kam-(ə-)rəl\ *adj* : consisting of two legislative chambers ⟨a *bicameral* legislature⟩

bi·car·bon·ate \(')bī-'kär-bə-ˌnāt, -nət\ *n* : an acid carbonate

bicarbonate of soda : SODIUM BICARBONATE

bi·cen·te·na·ry \ˌbī-(ˌ)sen-'ten-ə-rē, (')bī-'sent-ᵊn-'er-ē, ˌbī-(ˌ)sen-'tē-nə-rē\ *adj* : BICENTENNIAL — **bicentenary** *n*

bi·cen·ten·ni·al \ˌbī-(ˌ)sen-'ten-ē-əl\ *adj* : relating to a 200th anniversary — **bicentennial** *n*

bi·ceps \'bī-ˌseps\ *n, pl* **biceps** : a muscle having the end at which it begins divided into two parts; *esp* : a large muscle of the front of the upper arm

bick·er \'bik-ər\ *vb* **bick·ered; bick·er·ing** \'bik-(ə-)riŋ\ : to quarrel in an irritating way especially over unimportant things — **bick·er·er** *n*

bi·col·ored \'bī-ˌkəl-ərd\ *adj* : two-colored — **bi·col·or** \-ər\ *n*

bi·cul·tur·al \(ˌ)bī-'kəl-chər-əl\ *adj* : of, relating to, or including two distinct cultures ⟨*bicultural* education⟩ — **bi·cul·tur·al·ism** \-ə-ˌliz-əm\ *n*

¹**bi·cus·pid** \(')bī-'kəs-pəd\ *adj* : having or ending in two points

²**bicuspid** *n* : a human tooth located in front of the molar teeth

¹**bi·cy·cle** \'bī-ˌsik-əl, -ˌsīk-\ *n* : a light vehicle with two wheels behind one another, handlebars, a saddle seat, and pedals by which it is made to move

²**bicycle** *vb* **bi·cy·cled; bi·cy·cling** \-ˌsik(-ə-)liŋ\ : to ride a bicycle — **bi·cy·cler** \-lər\ *n* — **bi·cy·clist** \-ləst\ *n*

¹**bid** \'bid\ *vb* **bade** \'bad, 'bād\ *or* **bid; bid·den** \'bid-ᵊn\ *or* **bid; bid·ding** 1 a : ¹ORDER 2a, COMMAND ⟨did as we were *bidden*⟩ b : ¹INVITE 2a 2 : to express to ⟨*bade* me farewell⟩ 3 *past and past participle* **bid** : to make an offer for something (as at an auction) ⟨*bid* $10 for a chair⟩ — **bid·der** *n* — **bid fair** : to seem likely

²**bid** *n* 1 : an offer to pay a certain sum for something or to perform certain work at a stated fee 2 : a turn or opportunity to bid 3 : INVITATION 2 ⟨received a *bid* to the state tournament⟩ 4 a : an announcement of what a card player will try to win b : the amount of such a bid 5 : an attempt to win, achieve, or attract ⟨made a strong *bid* for the job⟩

bid·dy \'bid-ē\ *n, pl* **biddies** : HEN 1; *also* : a young chicken

bide \'bīd\ *vb* **bode** \'bōd\ *or* **bid·ed; bided; bid·ing** : to wait or wait for ⟨*bided* his time before acting⟩

bi·di·rec·tion·al \ˌbī-də-'rek-sh(ə-)nəl, -dī-\ *adj* : involving, moving, or taking place in usually two opposite directions

bi·en·ni·al \(')bī-'en-ē-əl\ *adj* 1 : occurring every two years 2 : growing stalks and leaves one year and flowers and fruit the next before dying — **biennial** *n* — **bi·en·ni·al·ly** \-ē-ə-lē\ *adv*

bier \'bi(ə)r\ *n* : a stand on which a coffin is placed

¹**bi·fo·cal** \(')bī-'fō-kəl\ *adj* : having two focal lengths

²**bifocal** *n* 1 : a bifocal glass or lens 2 *pl* : eyeglasses with bifocal lenses that correct for both near vision and distant vision

¹**big** \'big\ *adj* **big·ger; big·gest** 1 : of great force ⟨a *big* storm⟩ 2 a : large in size, bulk, or extent ⟨a *big* house⟩ ⟨*big* government⟩ ⟨a *big* city⟩ b : large in number or amount ⟨a *big* fleet⟩ ⟨*big* money⟩ c : ¹CAPITAL 2 ⟨*big* letters⟩ 3 : of great importance ⟨my *big* chance⟩ ⟨a *big*

star in movies⟩ 4 : being older ⟨my *big* sister⟩ — **big·ness** *n* — **big on** : very much in favor of : enthusiastic about ⟨is *big on* stamp collecting⟩

²**big** *adv* 1 : in a big way ⟨win *big*⟩ 2 : so as to boast ⟨talk *big*⟩

big·a·my \'big-ə-mē\ *n* : the act of marrying one person while still legally married to another [Middle English *bigamie* "bigamy," derived from Latin *bi-* "two" and Greek *gamia* "marriage"] *n* — **big·a·mous** \-məs\ *adj* — **big·a·mous·ly** *adv*

big bang *n* : the explosion that caused the beginning of the universe according to the big bang theory

big bang theory *n* : a theory that the universe was created billions of years ago as a result of a giant explosion

big cat *n* : a large wild cat (as a leopard or tiger)

Big Dipper *n* : DIPPER 3a

big·foot \'big-ˌfût\ *n, often cap* : a large hairy humanlike creature reported to exist in the Pacific Northwest — called also *Sasquatch*

big game *n* : large animals hunted for sport

big·horn sheep \'big-ˌhorn-\ *n* : a usually grayish brown wild sheep of mountainous western North America — called also *bighorn, Rocky Mountain sheep*

bighorn sheep

bight \'bīt\ *n* 1 : a bend in a coast or the bay it forms 2 : a slack part or loop in a rope

big league *n* : the highest level especially in baseball — **big–league** *adj* — **big leaguer** *n*

big·ot \'big-ət\ *n* : a person who won't listen to anyone whose ideas or beliefs are different from his or her own; *esp* : one who regards or treats the members of a group (as a racial group) with hatred and intolerance — **big·ot·ed** \-ət-əd\ *adj*

big·ot·ry \'big-ə-trē\ *n, pl* **-ries** 1 : the state of mind of a bigot 2 : behavior or beliefs characteristic of a bigot

big shot *n* : an important person

big toe *n* : the innermost and largest toe of the foot

big top *n* 1 : the main tent of a circus 2 : CIRCUS 2

big tree \-ˌtrē\ *n* : GIANT SEQUOIA

big·wig \'big-ˌwig\ *n* : BIG SHOT

bike \'bīk\ *n* 1 : ¹BICYCLE 2 : MOTORCYCLE — **bike** *vb* — **bik·er** *n*

bi·ki·ni \bə-'kē-nē\ *n* : a scanty two-piece bathing suit for a girl or woman [from French *bikini* "two-piece bathing suit," from *Bikini*, atoll in the Marshall Islands]

bi·lat·er·al \(')bī-'lat-ə-rəl, -'la-trəl\ *adj* 1 : having or involving two sides or parties ⟨a *bilateral* treaty⟩ 2 : characterized by bilateral symmetry — **bi·lat·er·al·ly** \-ē\ *adv*

bilateral symmetry *n* : plant and animal symmetry in which similar parts are arranged so that one and only one plane can divide the individual into identical or nearly identical halves — compare RADIAL SYMMETRY

bile \'bī(ə)l\ *n* 1 : a thick bitter yellow or greenish fluid that is secreted by

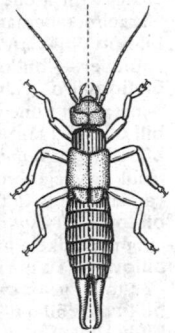

bilateral symmetry

\ə\ **abut**	\au̇\ **out**	\i\ **tip**	\o̅\ **saw**	\u̇\ **foot**	
\ər\ **further**	\ch\ **chin**	\ī\ **life**	\o̅i\ **coin**	\y\ **yet**	
\a\ **mat**	\e\ **pet**	\j\ **job**	\th\ **thin**	\yü\ **few**	
\ā\ **take**	\ē\ **easy**	\ŋ\ **sing**	\th\ **this**	\yu̇\ **cure**	
\ä\ **cot, cart**	\g\ **go**	\ō\ **bone**	\ü\ **food**	\zh\ **vision**	

the liver and aids in the digestion and absorption of fats in the duodenum **2** : ILL WILL, ANGER

¹bilge \'bilj\ *n* **1** : the bulging part of a cask or barrel **2** : the part of a ship's hull between the bottom and the point where the sides begin to rise nearly straight up

²bilge *vb* **bilged; bilg·ing** : to become damaged in the bilge

bilge water *n* : water that collects in a ship's bilge

bil·i·ary \'bil-ē-,er-ē\ *adj* : of, relating to, or conveying bile

bi·lin·gual \(,)bī-'liŋ-g(yə-)wəl\ *adj* **1** : of, expressed in, or using two languages ⟨a *bilingual* dictionary⟩ ⟨*bilingual* signs⟩ **2** : able to use two languages especially with fluency

bil·ious \'bil-yəs\ *adj* **1 a** : of or relating to bile **b** : marked by or suffering from a disorder of liver function **2** : of an irritable disposition : PEEVISH — **bil·ious·ly** *adv* — **bil·ious·ness** *n*

¹bill \'bil\ *n* **1** : the jaws of a bird together with their horny covering **2** : a mouthpart (as the beak of a turtle) resembling a bird's bill **3** : the visor of a cap [Old English *bile* "bill (of a bird)"] — **billed** \'bild\ *adj*

²bill *vb* **1** : to touch bills **2** : to caress affectionately

³bill *n* **1** : a draft of a law presented to a legislature for consideration ⟨introduce a *bill* in Congress⟩ **2** : a record of goods sold, services performed, or work done together with the costs involved ⟨a telephone *bill*⟩ **3** : a sign or poster advertising something **4** : a piece of paper money ⟨a dollar *bill*⟩ [Middle English *bill* "document," perhaps derived from Latin *bulla* "papal seal, bull," from earlier *bulla* "bubble, amulet" — related to ²BOIL, BULLET]

⁴bill *vb* : to send a bill to

bill·board \'bil-,bō(ə)rd, -,bȯ(ə)rd\ *n* : a flat surface on which outdoor advertisements are displayed

¹bil·let \'bil-ət\ *n* **1** : an official order that a soldier be put up in a private home **2** : quarters assigned by or as if by a billet **3** : JOB 3, POSITION [Middle English *bylet* "brief note," from early French *billette*, literally, "little document," derived from Latin *billa* "document"]

²billet *vb* : to assign lodging to : QUARTER

³billet *n* **1** : a chunky piece of wood (as for firewood) **2** : a bar of metal; *esp* : one of iron or steel [Middle English *bylet* "chunk of wood," from early French *billete*, literally, "little log"; of Celtic origin]

bil·let–doux \,bil-ē-'dü, ,bil-(,)ā-\ *n, pl* **bil·lets–doux** \-'dü(z)\ : a love letter [French, literally, "sweet letter"]

bill·fold \'bil-,fōld\ *n* : a folding pocketbook for paper money : WALLET

bil·liards \'bil-yərdz\ *n* : a game played by driving solid balls with a cue into one another or into pockets on a large rectangular table

bil·lion \'bil-yən\ *n* **1** — see NUMBER table **2** : a very large number — **billion** *adj* — **bil·lionth** \-yən(t)th\ *adj or n*

bil·lion·aire \,bil-yə-'na(ə)r, -'ne(ə)r; 'bil-yə-,na(ə)r, -,ne(ə)r\ *n* : one whose wealth is a billion dollars or more

bill of fare : MENU 1

bill of rights *often cap B&R* : a statement of basic rights and privileges guaranteed to a people; *esp* : the first 10 amendments to the U.S. Constitution

¹bil·low \'bil-ō\ *n* **1** : ²WAVE 1; *esp* : a large wave **2** : a rolling mass like a high wave ⟨*billows* of smoke⟩

²billow *vb* **1** : to rise or roll in waves ⟨the *billowing* ocean⟩ **2** : to bulge or swell out ⟨sails *billowing* in the breeze⟩

bil·lowy \'bil-ə-wē\ *adj* **bil·low·i·er; -est** : full of billows

bil·ly \'bil-ē\ *n, pl* **billies** **1** : BILLY CLUB **2** : BILLY GOAT

billy club *n* : a heavy wooden club; *esp* : a police officer's club

billy goat \'bil-ē-\ *n* : a male goat

bi·met·al \'bī-,met-ᵊl\ *adj* : BIMETALLIC

bi·me·tal·lic \,bī-mə-'tal-ik\ *adj* : composed of two different metals — often used of devices having a part in which two metals that expand differently are bonded together

¹bi·month·ly \(')bī-'mən(t)th-lē\ *adj* **1** : occurring every two months **2** : occurring twice a month : SEMIMONTHLY

²bimonthly *adv* **1** : once every two months **2** : twice a month

³bimonthly *n* : a bimonthly publication

bin \'bin\ *n* : a box, frame, or enclosed place for storage

bi·na·ry \'bī-nə-rē\ *adj* **1** : compounded or consisting of or marked by two things or parts **2** : relating to, being, or belonging to a system of numbers having two as its base ⟨the binary digits 0 and 1⟩ **3** : relating exactly two mathematical or logical elements at a time ⟨multiplication is a *binary* operation⟩

binary fission *n* : reproduction of a cell by division into two approximately equal parts

binary star *n* : a system of two stars that revolve around each other under the gravitation of both

binary system *n* : a system of two objects that revolve around each other; *esp* : BINARY STAR

bin·au·ral \(')bī-'nȯr-əl\ *adj* **1** : of, relating to, or used with two or both ears ⟨a *binaural* stethoscope⟩ **2** : of, relating to, or making up sound reproduction involving the use of two separated microphones and two channels over which the sound is sent to get a stereophonic effect — **bin·au·ral·ly** \-ə-lē\ *adv*

¹bind \'bīnd\ *vb* **bound** \'baund\; **bind·ing** **1 a** : to fasten by tying **b** : to hold or restrict by force or obligation ⟨*bound* by an oath⟩ ⟨*bound* by friendship⟩ **2** : ²BANDAGE ⟨*bind* a wound⟩ **3 a** : to stick together **b** : to form a mass that sticks together **c** : to take up and hold (as by chemical forces) : combine with **4** : to make firm or sure ⟨a deposit *binds* the sale⟩ **5 a** : to finish or decorate with a binding **b** : to fasten together and enclose in a cover ⟨*bind* a book⟩

²bind *n* : something that binds — **in a bind** : in trouble

bind·er \'bīn-dər\ *n* **1** : a person or machine that binds something (as books) **2** : a cover for holding together loose sheets of paper **3** : something that holds other substances together ⟨use egg as a *binder* in meat loaf⟩

bind·ery \'bīn-d(ə-)rē\ *n, pl* **-er·ies** : a place where books are bound

bind·ing \'bīn-diŋ\ *n* **1** : the cover and fastenings of a book **2** : a narrow strip of fabric used along the edge of an article of clothing

binding energy *n* : the energy required to break up a molecule, atom, or atomic nucleus completely into the particles that make it up

bind·weed \'bīn-,dwēd\ *n* : any of various twining plants related especially to the morning glorys

binge \'binj\ *n* **1** : SPREE **2** : an act of consuming something (as food) to excess — **binge** *vb*

bin·go \'biŋ-,gō\ *n* : a game that is played by covering a numbered space on a card when the number is matched by one chosen at random and that is won by the first player to cover five spaces in a row

bin·na·cle \'bin-i-kəl\ *n* : a box or stand containing a ship's compass and a lamp

¹bin·oc·u·lar \bī-'näk-yə-lər, bə-\ *adj* : of, relating to, using, or adapted to the use of both eyes ⟨*binocular* vision⟩

²bin·oc·u·lar \bə-'näk-yə-lər, bī-\ *n* **1** : a binocular optical instrument **2** : a handheld instrument for seeing at a distance that consists of two telescopes, a focusing device, and usually prisms — usually used in plural ⟨a pair of *binoculars*⟩

bi·no·mi·al \bī-'nō-mē-əl\ *n* **1** : a mathematical expression consisting of two terms connected by a plus sign or minus sign **2** : a biological species name consisting of two terms according to the system of binomial nomenclature — **binomial** *adj* — **bi·no·mi·al·ly** \-mē-ə-lē\ *adv*

²binocular 2

binomial nomenclature *n* : a system of naming plants and animals in which each species is given a name consisting of two terms of which the first names the genus and the second the species itself

bio- *combining form* **1** : life ⟨*bio*sphere⟩ **2** : living organisms or tissue ⟨*bio*chemistry⟩ [from Greek *bi-, bio-* "life"]

bio·chem·is·try \ˌbī-ō-ˈkem-ə-strē\ *n* : chemistry that deals with the chemical compounds and processes occurring in living things — **bio·chem·i·cal** \-ˈkem-i-kəl\ *adj* — **bio·chem·i·cal·ly** \-i-k(ə-)lē\ *adv* — **bio·chem·ist** \-ˈkem-əst\ *n*

bio·de·grad·able \-di-ˈgrād-ə-bəl\ *adj* : capable of being broken down especially into harmless products by the action of living things (as bacteria) ⟨*biodegradable* trash bags⟩ — **bio·de·grad·abil·i·ty** \-ˌgrād-ə-ˈbil-ət-ē\ *n* — **bio·de·grade** \-di-ˈgrād\ *vb*

bio·die·sel \-ˈdē-zəl, -səl\ *n* : a fuel that is similar to diesel fuel and is usually derived from plants (as soybeans)

bio·di·ver·si·ty \-də-ˈvər-sət-ē, -dī-\ *n* : biological variety in an environment as indicated by numbers of different species of plants and animals

bi·og·ra·phy \bī-ˈäg-rə-fē, bē-\ *n, pl* **-phies** : a history of a person's life — **bi·og·ra·pher** \-fər\ *n* — **bio·graph·i·cal** \ˌbī-ə-ˈgraf-i-kəl\ *adj* — **bio·graph·i·cal·ly** \-i-k(ə-)lē\ *adv*

bio·log·i·cal \ˌbī-ə-ˈläj-i-kəl\ *also* **bio·log·ic** \-ˈläj-ik\ *adj* **1** : of or relating to biology or to life and living things ⟨*biological* activity⟩ **2** : connected by a relationship involving heredity rather than by one involving adoption or marriage ⟨his *biological* father⟩ — **bio·log·i·cal·ly** \-ˈläj-i-k(ə-)lē\ *adv*

biological clock *n* : a mechanism that exists in living things and controls the timing of behaviors and bodily functions which occur in cycles

biological control *n* : attack upon pests by interference with their ecology (as by introduction of parasites or diseases)

biological warfare *n* : warfare involving the use of biological weapons

biological weapon *n* : a harmful living thing (as a disease-causing bacterium) or something (as a poisonous substance) produced by a living thing that is used as a weapon to cause death or disease

bi·ol·o·gy \bī-ˈäl-ə-jē\ *n* **1** : a branch of knowledge that deals with living organisms and life processes **2 a** : the plant and animal life of a region or environment **b** : the life processes of an organism or group [from German *Biologie* "biology," derived from Greek *bi-, bio-* "life" and *-logia* "study, science"] — **bi·ol·o·gist** \-jəst\ *n*

bi·ome \ˈbī-ˌōm\ *n* : a major type of ecological community ⟨the grassland *biome*⟩

bi·on·ic \bī-ˈän-ik\ *adj* **1** : of or relating to bionics **2** : having the normal biological ability to perform a physical task increased by special devices

bi·on·ics \bī-ˈän-iks\ *n* : a branch of science concerned with applying facts about the working of biological systems to the solution of engineering problems

bio·phys·ics \ˈbī-ō-ˌfiz-iks\ *n* : a branch of science concerned with applying the principles and methods of physics to biological problems — **bio·phys·i·cal** \ˌbī-ō-ˈfiz-i-kəl\ *adj* — **bio·phys·i·cist** \-ˈfiz-ə-səst\ *n*

bi·op·sy \ˈbī-ˌäp-sē\ *n, pl* **-sies** : the removal and examination of tissue, cells, or fluids from the living body

bio·sphere \ˈbī-ə-ˌsfi(ə)r\ *n* : the part of the world in which life can exist

bio·syn·the·sis \ˌbī-ō-ˈsin(t)-thə-səs\ *n* : the production of a chemical compound by a living thing

bi·o·ta \bī-ˈōt-ə\ *n* : the plants and animals of a region

bio·tech·nol·o·gy \ˌbī-ō-tek-ˈnäl-ə-jē\ *n* : the manipulation (as by changing genetic material) of living things to produce useful products (as crops resistant to disease)

bio·ter·ror·ism \-ˈter-ər-ˌiz-əm\ *n* : terrorism involving the use of biological weapons — **bio·ter·ror·ist** \-ər-əst\ *n*

bi·ot·ic \bī-ˈät-ik\ *adj* : of, relating to, or caused by living things

bi·o·tin \ˈbī-ə-tən\ *n* : a growth vitamin of the vitamin B complex found especially in yeast, liver, and egg yolk

bi·o·tite \ˈbī-ə-ˌtīt\ *n* : a generally black or dark green mica containing iron, magnesium, potassium, and aluminum

bi·par·ti·san \(ˈ)bī-ˈpärt-ə-zən, -sən\ *adj* : representing, made up of, or organized by members of two political parties ⟨a *bipartisan* foreign policy⟩

bi·par·tite \(ˈ)bī-ˈpär-ˌtīt\ *adj* **1** : being in two parts **2** : shared by two ⟨*bipartite* treaty⟩

bi·ped \ˈbī-ˌped\ *n* : a two-footed animal — **bi·ped·al** \(ˈ)bī-ˈped-ᵊl\ *adj*

bi·plane \ˈbī-ˌplān\ *n* : an airplane with two sets of wings usually placed one above the other

bi·ra·cial \(ˈ)bī-ˈrā-shəl\ *adj* : of, relating to, or involving people from two races ⟨*biracial* communities⟩; *esp* : having biological parents of two different ethnic identities

biplane

¹**birch** \ˈbərch\ *n* **1** : any of a genus of trees or shrubs with typically an outer bark that peels easily in thin layers and leaves that are shed each fall; *also* : its hard pale close-grained wood **2** : a birch rod or bundle of twigs used as a whip — **birch** *or* **birch·en** \ˈbər-chən\ *adj*

²**birch** *vb* : to whip with or as if with a birch

¹**bird** \ˈbərd\ *n* **1** : any of a class of warm-blooded egg-laying vertebrate animals with the body covered with feathers and the forelimbs modified as wings **2** : INDIVIDUAL 2, FELLOW; *esp* : a peculiar person

²**bird** *vb* : to observe or identify wild birds in their natural environment — **bird·er** *n*

bird·bath \ˈbərd-ˌbath, -ˌbäth\ *n* : a basin set up for wild birds to bathe in

bird dog *n* : a dog that has been trained to hunt or bring back game birds

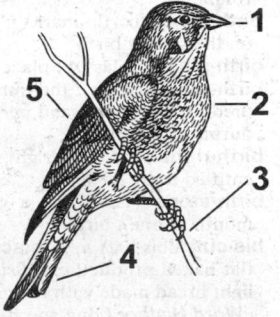
¹bird 1: *1* bill, *2* breast, *3* claw, *4* tail, *5* wing

bird·house \ˈbərd-ˌhaus\ *n* : an artificial nesting place for birds; *also* : AVIARY

bird·like \ˈbərd-ˌlīk\ *adj* : resembling a bird especially in quickness or voice

bird·man \ˈbərd-mən *also* -ˌman\ *n* **1** : one who deals with birds **2** : ¹PILOT 3

bird–of–paradise *n* : a plant from southern Africa that has a colorful flower head resembling the head of a bird with a crest

bird of paradise : any of numerous brilliantly colored birds of the New Guinea area that often have large graceful tail feathers and are related to the crows

bird of passage : a bird that migrates

bird of prey : a meat-eating bird (as a hawk) that feeds partly or completely on the animals it hunts

\ə\ **abut**	\au̇\ **out**	\i\ **tip**	\ȯ\ **saw**	\u̇\ **foot**
\ər\ **further**	\ch\ **chin**	\ī\ **life**	\ȯi\ **coin**	\y\ **yet**
\a\ **mat**	\e\ **pet**	\j\ **job**	\th\ **thin**	\yü\ **few**
\ā\ **take**	\ē\ **easy**	\ŋ\ **sing**	\th\ **this**	\yu̇\ **cure**
\ä\ **cot, cart**	\g\ **go**	\ō\ **bone**	\ü\ **food**	\zh\ **vision**

bird·seed \'bərd-ˌsēd\ n : a mixture of seeds (as of sunflowers and millet) used for feeding birds

bird's-eye \'bərd-ˌzī\ adj **1 a** : seen from above as if by a flying bird ⟨bird's-eye view⟩ **b** : ¹GENERAL 3, CURSORY ⟨a bird's-eye survey of American history⟩ **2** : having spots resembling birds' eyes ⟨bird's-eye maple⟩; also : made of wood containing such spots

bird's-foot trefoil \ˌbərdz-ˌfût-\ n : a European plant with claw-shaped pods that is related to the pea and is widely grown as food for livestock and to control erosion

bird-watch·er \'bərd-ˌwäch-ər\ n : an observer of wild birds — **bird-watch** \-ˌwäch\ vb

bi·ret·ta \bə-'ret-ə\ n : a square cap with three ridges on top worn by Roman Catholic clergymen

birth \'bərth\ n **1 a** : the coming out of a new individual from the body of its parent **b** : the act or process of bringing forth young from the uterus **2** : DESCENT 1, LINEAGE ⟨noble birth⟩ **3** : BEGINNING 1, ORIGIN

birth canal n : the channel through which the fetus of a mammal passes during birth

birth control n **1** : control of the number of births especially by preventing or lessening the occurrence of conception **2** : devices or preparations used to prevent pregnancy

birth control pill n : any of various pills usually taken every day to prevent pregnancy by stopping ovulation

birth·day \'bərth-ˌdā\ n **1** : the day or anniversary of one's birth **2** : the day or anniversary of a beginning

birth defect n : a serious defect (as in physical or mental function) that is present at birth and is inherited or caused by something that happens or exists in the environment

birth·mark \'bərth-ˌmärk\ n : an unusual mark or blemish on the skin at birth

birth·place \-ˌplās\ n : place of birth or origin

birth·rate \-ˌrāt\ n : the number of births for every hundred or every thousand persons in a given area or group during a given time

birth·right \-ˌrīt\ n : a right or possession that a person is entitled to by birth

birth·stone \-ˌstōn\ n : a gemstone associated with the month of one's birth

bis·cuit \'bis-kət\ n, pl **biscuits** also **biscuit** **1** : a crisp flat baked product; esp, British : CRACKER 2 **2** : a small light bread made with baking powder or baking soda

Word History Long ago it was often a great problem to keep food from spoiling, especially on long journeys. One way to preserve the flat loaves of bread made then was to bake them a second time in order to dry them out. In early French, this bread was known as pain bescuit or "bread twice-cooked." Later the term came to be shortened to just bescuit. The idea of being "twicecooked" was lost as the term was used for any crisp, dry, flat bread product or for a type of bread made with baking soda or baking powder instead of yeast. The word was borrowed into Middle English as bisquite but later came to be spelled biscuit on the model of the French spelling. [Middle English bisquite "biscuit," from early French bescuit (same meaning), from earlier pain bescuit "bread twice-cooked"]

bi·sect \'bī-ˌsekt, bī-'sekt\ vb **1** : to divide into two usually equal parts **2** : INTERSECT 1, CROSS

bi·sec·tor \'bī-ˌsek-tər, bī-'sek-tər\ n : one that bisects; esp : a straight line that bisects an angle or a line segment

bi·sex·u·al \(')bī-'seksh-(ə-)wəl, -'sek-shəl\ adj **1** : possessing characters of or having sexual desire for both sexes **2** : of, relating to, or involving two sexes — **bisexual** n — **bi·sex·u·al·i·ty** \ˌbī-ˌsek-shə-'wal-ət-ē\ n

bish·op \'bish-əp\ n **1** : a high-ranking member of various sects of the Christian clergy usually in charge of a diocese **2** : a chess piece that moves diagonally

Word History The Old English word bisceop, from which we get our modern English word bishop, comes to us from the Latin word episcopus. Like many other Latin words connected with religion and the church, this was borrowed from Greek, the language in which the New Testament was written. The Greek word episkopos, meaning literally "overseer," was first used of officials in government and later came to be used for church leaders. In the Bible the word meaning "bishop" and the word meaning "priest" were used for the same thing. It was not until much later that the bishop did indeed become overseer of a large district, or diocese. [Old English bisceop "bishop," from Latin episcopus (same meaning), from Greek episkopos, literally, "overseer," from epi- "on, over" and skopos "watcher, goal, object" — related to EPISCOPAL, HOROSCOPE, SCOPE]

bish·op·ric \'bish-ə-(ˌ)prik\ n **1** : DIOCESE **2** : the position of bishop

bis·muth \'biz-məth\ n : a heavy brittle grayish white metallic element that is chemically like arsenic and antimony and is used in alloys and drugs — see ELEMENT table

bi·son \'bīs-ᵊn, 'bīz-\ n, pl **bison** : any of several large shaggy-maned mammals related to the ox with a large head, short horns, and a large fleshy hump above the shoulders; esp : BUFFALO c

bisque \'bisk\ n : a thick cream soup made with shellfish, meat, or vegetables

bis·tro \'bēs-(ˌ)trō, 'bis-\ n : a small or modest restaurant

bi·sul·fide \(')bī-'səl-ˌfīd\ n : DISULFIDE

¹bit \'bit\ n **1** : the usually metal bar attached to a bridle and put in the mouth of a horse **2** : the biting or cutting edge or part of a tool ⟨the drill bit⟩ [Old English bite "act of biting"]

²bit n **1** : a small piece or amount **2** : a short time ⟨rest a bit⟩ [earlier bit "small piece of food," from Old English bita (same meaning)] — **a bit** : ²SOMEWHAT ⟨was a bit tired⟩

³bit n **1** : a unit of computer information that represents the selection of one of two possible choices (as yes or no, on or off) **2** : something (as an electrical pulse, a magnetized spot, or a punched hole) that physically represents a bit [binary digit]

bitch \'bich\ n : a female dog

¹bite \'bīt\ vb **bit** \'bit\; **bit·ten** \'bit-ᵊn\; **bit·ing** \'bīt-iŋ\ **1** : to seize, grip, or cut into with or as if with teeth ⟨bite an apple⟩ **2** : to wound, pierce, or sting ⟨bitten by a snake⟩ ⟨a mosquito bit me⟩ **3** : to cause to smart : STING ⟨pepper bites the mouth⟩ **4** : to eat into ⟨acid biting into metal⟩ **5** : to take bait ⟨the fish are biting⟩ **6** : to respond to something tempting [Old English bītan "to bite, grip with the teeth" — related to BEETLE] — **bite the dust** : to fall dead especially in battle

²bite n **1 a** : a seizing of something by biting **b** : the grip taken in biting **2 a** : the amount of food taken at a bite **b** : a small amount of food : SNACK **3** : a wound made by biting **4** : a sharp penetrating quality or effect ⟨the bite of the cold wind on our cheeks⟩

bite plate n : a removable usually plastic device used in orthodontics: as **a** : one worn in the upper or lower jaw especially to reposition the jaw or prevent the habit of grinding one's teeth **b** : RETAINER 3

bit·ing \'bīt-iŋ\ adj : causing bodily or mental distress : SHARP, CUTTING ⟨biting wit⟩ ⟨a biting cold⟩

bit·ter \'bit-ər\ adj **1** : having or being a disagreeable sharp taste that is one of the four basic taste sensations ⟨bitter coffee⟩ — compare ³SALT 1b, ¹SOUR 1, ¹SWEET 1b **2** : hard to accept or bear : PAINFUL ⟨bitter disappointment⟩ **3** : sharp and resentful ⟨a bitter reply⟩ **4** : unpleasantly cold ⟨a bitter wind⟩ — **bit·ter·ly** adv — **bit·ter·ness** n

bit·tern \'bit-ərn\ n : any of various small or medium-sized short-necked usually secretive herons

¹bit·ter·sweet \'bit-ər-ˌswēt\ *n* **1** : a poisonous woody vine of the nightshade family with purple flowers and oval reddish orange berries **2** : a North American woody vine with yellow seedcases that open when ripe to show the scarlet seed covers

²bittersweet *adj* : being both bitter and sweet ⟨a *bittersweet* story⟩

bit·ty \'bit-ē\ *adj* : very small : TINY

bi·tu·mi·nous coal \bə-'t(y)ü-mə-nəs-, bī-\ *n* : a coal that when heated yields considerable matter that escapes as gases — called also *soft coal*

bittern

¹bi·valve \'bī-ˌvalv\ *adj* : having or being a shell composed of two movable valves ⟨a *bivalve* mollusk⟩

²bivalve *n* : any of a class of typically marine mollusks (as clams, oysters, and scallops) that have a shell made up of two parts joined by a hinge, are usually filter feeders, and lack a distinct head

¹biv·ouac \'biv-ˌwak, -ə-ˌwak\ *n* : a temporary camp [French, from a German dialect word *biwacht*, literally, "on guard"]

²bivouac *vb* **-ouacked; -ouack·ing** : to camp in a bivouac

¹bi·week·ly \(')bī-'wē-klē\ *adj* **1** : occurring, done, or produced every two weeks **2** : occurring, done, or produced twice a week — **biweekly** *adv*

²biweekly *n* : a biweekly publication

bi·year·ly \(')bī-'yi(ə)r-lē\ *adj* **1** : BIENNIAL 1 **2** : BIANNUAL

bi·zarre \bə-'zär\ *adj* : strikingly unusual or odd : FANTASTIC — **bi·zarre·ly** *adv* — **bi·zarre·ness** *n*

¹blab \'blab\ *n* **1** : TATTLETALE **2** : too much talk : CHATTER — **blab·by** \'blab-ē\ *adj*

²blab *vb* **blabbed; blab·bing** **1** : to make known by careless talk ⟨*blab* a secret⟩ **2** : to talk too much — **blab·ber** *n*

blab·ber·mouth \'blab-ər-ˌmaùth\ *n* : TATTLETALE

¹black \'blak\ *adj* **1 a** : of the color black **b** : very dark **2** *often cap* : of or relating to various peoples having dark skin and especially those of African origin or ancestry ⟨*black* people⟩ **3 a** : ¹EVIL 1, WICKED ⟨a *black* deed⟩ **b** : very sad or gloomy ⟨the outlook was *black*⟩ **c** : SULLEN 1a, HOSTILE — **black·ish** \-ish\ *adj* — **black·ly** *adv* — **black·ness** *n*

²black *n* **1** : a black pigment or dye; *esp* : one consisting largely of carbon **2** : the characteristic color of soot or coal **3** : black clothing ⟨dressed in *black*⟩ **4** : a black animal (as a horse) **5 a** : a person belonging to any of various peoples with dark skin and especially one who has African ancestry **b** : AFRICAN-AMERICAN **6** : absence of light : DARKNESS ⟨the *black* of night⟩ **7** : the condition of making a profit ⟨in the *black*⟩

³black *vb* : BLACKEN 1

black·a·moor \'blak-ə-ˌmú(ə)r\ *n* : a dark-skinned person; *esp* : BLACK 5a

black–and–blue \ˌblak-ən-'blü\ *adj* : darkly discolored as the result of a bruise

¹black·ball \'blak-ˌból\ *n* **1** : a small black ball used to vote against a person **2** : a vote against a person

²blackball *vb* : to vote against; *esp* : to keep (a person) from joining something by voting against

black bass *n* : any of several highly prized freshwater sunfishes native to eastern and central North America

black bean *n* **1** : a black kidney bean commonly used in Latin American cooking **2** : a black soybean commonly used usually fermented in east Asian cooking

black bear *n* : the common usually black-furred bear found in North American forests

black·ber·ry \'blak-ˌber-ē\ *n* **1** : the usually black or dark purple juicy but seedy edible fruit of various prickly bushes **2** : a plant that bears blackberries

black bear

black·bird \'blak-ˌbərd\ *n* : any of various birds of which the males are mostly or entirely black: as **a** : a common European thrush **b** : any of several American birds (as a red-winged blackbird) related to the meadowlarks and orioles

black·board \'blak-ˌbō(ə)rd, -ˌbó(ə)rd\ *n* : CHALKBOARD

black·body \'blak-'bäd-ē\ *n* : a body or surface that absorbs all radiant energy falling upon it with no reflection

black book *n* : a book containing a blacklist

black crappie *n* : a silvery black mottled sunfish of the central and eastern U.S. — called also *calico bass*

black death *n* : plague (as bubonic plague) caused by a bacterium and especially in the epidemic form that spread through Asia and Europe in the 14th century; *also* : the 14th-century epidemic of plague

black diamond *n* : CARBONADO

black·en \'blak-ən\ *vb* **black·ened; black·en·ing** \'blak-(ə-)niŋ\ **1** : to make or become dark or black **2** : to hurt the reputation of : DEFAME — **black·en·er** \-(ə-)nər\ *n*

black eye *n* : a dark discoloration of the skin around the eye as the result of a bruise

black–eyed pea \ˌblak-ˌīd-\ *n* : COWPEA

black–eyed Su·san \-'süz-ᵊn\ *n* : a North American daisy with deep yellow or orange ray flowers and a dark center

black flag *n* : JOLLY ROGER

black·fly \'blak-ˌflī\ *n, pl* **-flies** *or* **-fly** : a two-winged fly that bites and whose larvae live in flowing streams

Black·foot \-ˌfút\ *n, pl* **Black·feet** \-ˌfēt\ *or* **Blackfoot** : a member of an American Indian people of Montana, Alberta, and Saskatchewan

black–foot·ed ferret \'blak-ˌfút-əd-\ *n* : an endangered weasel of western North American prairies having a yellowish coat, black feet and face markings, and a black-tipped tail

black·guard \'blag-ərd, -ˌärd; 'blak-ˌgärd\ *n* : a rude or dishonest person — **black·guard·ly** \-lē\ *adj or adv*

black·head \'blak-ˌhed\ *n* : a small oily bit of material blocking the outlet of a fat-secreting gland in the skin

black hole *n* : an invisible region believed to exist in space having a very strong gravitational field and thought to be caused by the collapse of a star

black ice *n* : a thin film of ice (as on a road) that is difficult to see

black·ing \'blak-iŋ\ *n* : a substance (as a paste or polish) that is applied to an object to make it black

black·jack \'blak-ˌjak\ *n* **1** : a small leather-covered club with a flexible handle **2** : a small oak of the southern U.S. with very dark bark

black light *n* : invisible ultraviolet or infrared light

black·list \'blak-ˌlist\ *n* : a list of persons who are disapproved of and are to be punished (as by refusing them jobs) — **blacklist** *vb*

\ə\ **abut**	\aú\ **out**	\i\ **tip**	\ó\ **saw**	\ú\ **foot**
\ər\ **further**	\ch\ **chin**	\ī\ **life**	\ói\ **coin**	\y\ **yet**
\a\ **mat**	\e\ **pet**	\j\ **job**	\th\ **thin**	\yü\ **few**
\ā\ **take**	\ē\ **easy**	\ŋ\ **sing**	\t̲h̲\ **this**	\yú\ **cure**
\ä\ **cot, cart**	\g\ **go**	\ō\ **bone**	\ü\ **food**	\zh\ **vision**

black lung *n* : a disease of the lungs caused by the repeated breathing in of coal dust over a long time — called also *black lung disease*

black·mail \'blak-ˌmāl\ *n* **1** : the act of forcing a person to do or pay something especially by a threat to reveal a secret **2** : something (as money) obtained through blackmail — **blackmail** *vb* — **black·mail·er** *n*

Word History The word *blackmail* has no connection at all with the postal system. In the 16th and part of the 17th centuries, the area along the border between England and Scotland was not usually protected by the officials on either side. Landholders were beset not only by outlaws but also by their own chieftains, who told them that in return for payment they would not be raided. In Scotland *mail* means "rent" or "payment." This word comes ultimately from an Old Norse word *māl* meaning "agreement" or "speech." The *mail* delivered by a letter carrier originally meant "sack, bag," and referred to the sack in which letters were carried; it is hence completely distinct in origin from the *mail* of *blackmail*. [from *black* (the color) and *mail* "rent, payment," from Old English *māl* "agreement," of Norse origin]

black market *n* : trade that is against government controls (as of prices or rationing); *also* : the place where such trade is carried on — **black mar·ket·er** \-ˈmär-kət-ər\ *or* **black mar·ke·teer** \-ˌmär-kə-ˈti(ə)r\ *n*

black oak *n* : a large timber tree of the central and eastern U.S. with a yellow inner bark used for tanning; *also* : any of several other North American oaks

black·out \'blak-ˌaut\ *n* **1** : a period when lights are kept off to guard against enemy airplane attack in a war **2** : a period when lights are off as a result of an electrical power failure **3** : a temporary dulling or loss of vision or consciousness — **black out** \-ˈaut\ *vb*

black pepper *n* : a spice that is made by grinding the fruit of the East Indian pepper with the black husk still on

black plague *n* : BLACK DEATH

black power *n, often cap B&P* : the use of the political and economic power of American blacks especially to achieve racial fairness

black sheep *n* : a person having a bad reputation in a group with a good reputation

black·smith \'blak-ˌsmith\ *n* : a worker who shapes iron (as into horseshoes) by heating it and then hammering it on an iron block — **black·smith·ing** *n*

black·snake \-ˌsnāk\ *n* **1** : any of several snakes largely black or dark in color; *esp* : either of two large harmless snakes of the U.S. **2** : a long braided leather whip

black·thorn \-ˌthorn\ *n* : a European spiny plum with hard wood and small white flowers

black·top \-ˌtäp\ *n* : a bituminous material (as asphalt) used especially for surfacing roads; *also* : a surface paved with blacktop — **blacktop** *vb*

black walnut *n* : a walnut of eastern North America with hard strong heavy dark brown wood and oily edible nuts; *also* : its wood or nut

black widow *n* : a poisonous New World spider the female of which is black with an hourglass-shaped red mark on the underside of the abdomen

blad·der \'blad-ər\ *n* **1** : a pouch in an animal in which a liquid or gas is stored; *esp* : one into which urine passes from the kidneys and is stored temporarily until discharged by way of the urethra **2** : something resembling

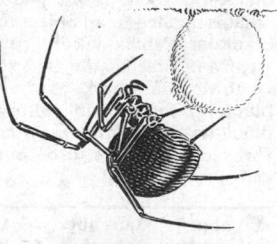
black widow

a bladder; *esp* : a bag or container that can be blown up with air — **blad·der·like** \-ˌlīk\ *adj*

blad·der·wort \-ˌwort, -ˌwȯ(ə)rt\ *n* : any of several plants growing in water or on wet shores and having insect-catching bladders on the stem

blade \'blād\ *n* **1 a** : a leaf of a plant and especially of a grass **b** : the broad flat part of a leaf as distinguished from its stalk **2 a** : the broad flat part of an oar or paddle **b** : an arm of a propeller, electric fan, or steam turbine **3 a** : the cutting part of a tool **b** : SWORD **1 c** : the runner of an ice skate **4** : a bold lively man — **blad·ed** \'blād-əd\ *adj*

blah \'blä\ *adj* : lacking interest or excitement ⟨a *blah* winter day⟩

blahs \'bläz\ *n pl* : a feeling of boredom, lack of energy, or general unhappiness

¹blame \'blām\ *vb* **blamed; blam·ing** **1** : to find fault with : CENSURE **2 a** : to hold responsible ⟨*blame* them for everything⟩ **b** : to place responsibility for ⟨*blames* it on me⟩ [Middle English *blamen* "to find fault with," from early French *blamer, blasmer* (same meaning), from Latin *blasphemare* "to speak ill of," from Greek *blasphemein* "to blaspheme" — related to BLASPHEME] — **blam·able** \'blā-mə-bəl\ *adj* — **blam·ably** \-blē\ *adv* — **blam·er** *n*

²blame *n* **1** : expression of disapproval ⟨receive both *blame* and praise⟩ **2** : responsibility for something that fails : FAULT ⟨take the *blame* for the defeat⟩

blame·less \'blām-ləs\ *adj* : free from blame or fault — **blame·less·ly** *adv* — **blame·less·ness** *n*

blame·wor·thy \'blām-ˌwər-thē\ *adj* : deserving blame — **blame·wor·thi·ness** *n*

blanch \'blanch\ *vb* **1 a** : to take the color out of : BLEACH **b** : to scald in order to remove the skin from or whiten ⟨*blanch* almonds⟩ **2** : to become white or pale — **blanch·er** *n*

bland \'bland\ *adj* **1** : smooth and soothing in manner : GENTLE ⟨a *bland* smile⟩ **2 a** : having soft and soothing qualities : not irritating ⟨*bland* diet⟩ **b** : not interesting : DULL ⟨a *bland* story⟩ — **bland·ly** \'blan-(d)lē\ *adv* — **bland·ness** \'blan(d)-nəs\ *n*

blan·dish \'blan-dish\ *vb* : to coax or persuade with flattery — **blan·dish·ment** \-mənt\ *n*

¹blank \'blaŋk\ *adj* **1** : being without writing, printing, or marks ⟨a *blank* sheet of paper⟩ **2** : having empty spaces to be filled in ⟨a *blank* form⟩ **3** : having no expression ⟨a *blank* look⟩ **4** : lacking variety, change, or accomplishment : EMPTY ⟨a *blank* day⟩ **5** : without exceptions : ABSOLUTE **3** ⟨*blank* refusal⟩ **6** : not shaped into finished form ⟨a *blank* key⟩ — **blank·ly** *adv* — **blank·ness** *n*

²blank *n* **1 a** : an empty space (as on a paper) **b** : a paper with spaces for the entry of information **2** : an empty place ⟨my mind was a *blank*⟩ **3** : a piece of material prepared to be made into something (as a key) **4** : a cartridge loaded with gunpowder but no bullet

³blank *vb* **1** : to keep from scoring ⟨were *blanked* for eight innings⟩ **2** : to become confused ⟨*blanked* out for a moment⟩

¹blan·ket \'blaŋ-kət\ *n* **1** : a large warm usually rectangular covering used for beds **2** : a covering of any kind ⟨a horse *blanket*⟩ ⟨a *blanket* of snow⟩

²blanket *vb* : to cover with or as if with a blanket

³blanket *adj* : covering all instances or members of a group or class ⟨*blanket* approval⟩

blank verse *n* : unrhymed verse; *esp* : unrhymed iambic pentameter verse

¹blare \'bla(ə)r, 'ble(ə)r\ *vb* **blared; blar·ing** **1** : to sound loud and harsh **2** : to sound or say in a harsh noisy manner ⟨loudspeakers *blaring* advertisements⟩

²blare *n* : a loud disagreeable noise ⟨the *blare* of trumpets⟩

blar·ney \'blär-nē\ *n* **1** : skillful flattery : BLANDISHMENT **2** : NONSENSE [from the *Blarney* stone, a stone in the wall of Blarney Castle, Ireland, said to give skill in flattery to those who kiss it] — **blarney** *vb*

blas·pheme \blas-'fēm, 'blas-ˌfēm\ *vb* **blas·phemed; blas·phem·ing 1** : to speak of or talk to with disrespect **2** : to speak blasphemy **3** : REVILE [Middle English *blasfemen* "to blaspheme," from Latin *blasphemare* "to speak ill of, blaspheme," from Greek *blasphēmein* "to blaspheme" — related to BLAME] — **blas·phem·er** *n*

blas·phe·my \'blas-fə-mē\ *n, pl* **-mies** : great disrespect shown to God or to sacred persons or things — **blas·phe·mous** \-məs\ *adj* — **blas·phe·mous·ly** *adv* — **blas·phe·mous·ness** *n*

¹blast \'blast\ *n* **1** : a strong gust of wind **2** : a stream of air or gas forced through an opening **3** : the continuous blowing that ore or metal receives in a blast furnace **4** : the sound made by a wind instrument (as a horn) or by a whistle **5 a** : EXPLOSION 1 **b** : an explosive charge **c** : the sudden air pressure produced around an explosion **6** : a sudden harmful effect from or as if from a hot wind **7** : ¹SPEED 1b, OPERATION ⟨go full *blast*⟩ **8** : a very enjoyable event

²blast *vb* **1** : BLARE ⟨music *blasting* from a radio⟩ **2 a** : to use an explosive **b** : SHOOT **3** : to injure or destroy by or as if by the action of wind ⟨seedlings *blasted* by the hot dry wind⟩ **4** : to shatter by or as if by an explosive **5** : to attack vigorously ⟨*blasted* by the local press⟩ **6** : to cause to blast off ⟨will *blast* themselves from the moon's surface⟩ — **blast·er** *n*

blast furnace *n* : a furnace in which combustion is forced by a stream of air under pressure; *esp* : one for the reduction of iron ore

blast off \'blas-ˌtòf\ *vb* : TAKE OFF 4b — used especially of rocket-driven missiles and vehicles — **blast–off** \-ˌtòf\ *n*

blas·tu·la \'blas-chə-lə\ *n, pl* **-las** \-ləz\ *or* **-lae** \-ˌlē\ : an early embryo typically having the form of a hollow fluid-filled rounded cavity bounded by a single layer of cells — compare GASTRULA

bla·tant \'blāt-ᵊnt\ *adj* **1** : noisy especially in a rude way **2** : completely obvious especially in a disagreeable way ⟨a *blatant* lie⟩ — **bla·tant·ly** *adv*

¹blaze \'blāz\ *n* **1** : a very strongly burning fire **2** : very bright direct light often accompanied by heat ⟨the *blaze* of TV lights⟩ **3** : a sudden outburst ⟨a *blaze* of flame⟩ ⟨a *blaze* of fury⟩ **4** : a dazzling display ⟨a *blaze* of autumn leaves⟩ [Old English *blæse* "torch"]

²blaze *vb* **blazed; blaz·ing 1 a** : to burn brightly **b** : to flare up : FLAME **2** : to be noticeably brilliant ⟨fields *blazing* with flowers⟩ **3** : to shoot rapidly and repeatedly

³blaze *vb* **blazed; blaz·ing** : to make public : PROCLAIM ⟨*blaze* the news⟩ [Middle English *blasen* "to make public," from early Dutch *blāsen* "to blow"]

⁴blaze *n* **1** : a long white mark down the center of the face of an animal **2** : a mark made on a tree usually to leave a trail [perhaps from Dutch or Low German *bles* "a white mark on an animal"]

⁵blaze *vb* **blazed; blaz·ing** : to mark with blazes ⟨*blaze* a trail⟩

blaz·er \'blā-zər\ *n* : a sports jacket in bright stripes or solid color

¹bleach \'blēch\ *vb* **1** : to remove color or stains from **2** : to make whiter or lighter **3** : to grow white : lose color

²bleach *n* **1** : the act or process of bleaching **2** : a chemical used in bleaching

bleach·er \'blē-chər\ *n* : a usually open stand of benches arranged like steps for people to watch from (as at a game) — usually used in plural

bleak \'blēk\ *adj* **1** : open to wind or weather ⟨a *bleak* coast⟩ **2** : ¹COLD 1, RAW ⟨a *bleak* November evening⟩ **3** : DREARY, CHEERLESS ⟨the future looks *bleak*⟩ **4** : very plain — **bleak·ly** *adv* — **bleak·ness** *n*

¹blear \'bli(ə)r\ *vb* **1** : to make (the eyes) sore or watery **2** : ²DIM 1, BLUR ⟨*bleared* sight⟩

²blear *adj* : dim with water or tears — **bleary** \'bli(ə)r-ē\ *adj*

¹bleat \'blēt\ *vb* **1** : to utter a bleat or similar sound **2** : to speak in a bleating way

²bleat *n* : the characteristic cry of a sheep or goat

bleed \'blēd\ *vb* **bled** \'bled\; **bleed·ing 1** : to lose or shed blood **2** : to be wounded ⟨*bleed* for one's country⟩ **3** : to feel pain or deep sympathy ⟨my heart *bleeds* for them⟩ **4** : to ooze or flow from a cut surface **5 a** : to draw liquid from ⟨*bleed* a patient⟩ ⟨*bleed* a carburetor⟩ **b** : to run when wetted ⟨dyes that *bleed*⟩ **6** : to get or force money from

bleed·er \'blēd-ər\ *n* : one that bleeds; *esp* : HEMOPHILIAC

bleeding heart *n* **1** : a garden plant having drooping spikes of deep pink or white heart-shaped flowers **2** : a person who always shows a great amount of sympathy to victims of misfortune or persecution

blem·ish \'blem-ish\ *n* : a mark that makes something imperfect — **blemish** *vb*

synonyms BLEMISH, DEFECT, FLAW mean an imperfection that mars or damages. BLEMISH suggests something that affects only the surface or appearance ⟨peaches with *blemishes* can still be eaten⟩. DEFECT suggests a lack, often hidden, of something that is essential to completeness or perfect functioning ⟨discovered that the car had major *defects*⟩. FLAW suggests a crack, nick, or break in smoothness or a weak spot ⟨the beam of the roof broke because of a *flaw*⟩.

¹blench \'blench\ *vb* : to shrink back out of fear : FLINCH

²blench *vb* : to make or grow pale : BLANCH

¹blend \'blend\ *vb* **1** : to mix thoroughly so that the things mixed cannot be recognized **2** : to shade into each other : MERGE **3** : HARMONIZE 2 ⟨furniture that *blends* with the draperies⟩ **synonyms** see MIX

²blend *n* **1** : a thorough mixture **2** : a product (as coffee) prepared by blending

blend·er \'blen-dər\ *n* : a person or thing that blends; *esp* : an electric appliance with blades for chopping or mixing food

blen·ny \'blen-ē\ *n, pl* **blennies** : any of numerous usually small and relatively long and often scaleless fishes living about rocky seashores

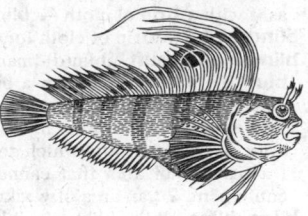

blenny

bless \'bles\ *vb* **blessed** \'blest\ *also* **blest** \'blest\; **bless·ing 1** : to make holy : HALLOW **2** : to make the sign of the cross upon or over **3** : to ask divine care or protection for **4** : to praise or honor as holy **5** : to make successful or happy **6** : ENDOW 2, FAVOR [Old English *blētsian, blēdsian* "to bless, to consecrate (originally with blood)," derived from *blōd* "blood"]

bless·ed \'bles-əd\ *also* **blest** \'blest\ *adj* **1** : HOLY 3 ⟨the *blessed* Trinity⟩ **2** : enjoying happiness — **bless·ed·ly** \'bles-əd-lē\ *adv* — **bless·ed·ness** \'bles-əd-nəs\ *n*

Bless·ed Sacrament \ˌbles-əd-\ *n* : the objects used in Communion; *esp* : ⁴HOST

bless·ing \'bles-iŋ\ *n* **1** : the act or words of one that blesses **2** : APPROVAL ⟨gave my *blessing* to the plan⟩ **3** : something that makes one happy or content **4** : grace said at a meal

\ə\ **abut**	\aù\ **out**	\i\ **tip**	\ò\ **saw**	\ù\ **foot**
\ər\ **further**	\ch\ **chin**	\ī\ **life**	\òi\ **coin**	\y\ **yet**
\a\ **mat**	\e\ **pet**	\j\ **job**	\th\ **thin**	\yü\ **few**
\ā\ **take**	\ē\ **easy**	\ŋ\ **sing**	\th\ **this**	\yù\ **cure**
\ä\ **cot, cart**	\g\ **go**	\ō\ **bone**	\ü\ **food**	\zh\ **vision**

blew *past of* BLOW

¹blight \'blīt\ *n* **1 a** : a disease of plants marked by withering and death of parts (as leaves) **b** : an organism that causes blight **2 a** : something that harms or destroys **b** : a damaged or worsened condition ⟨urban *blight*⟩

²blight *vb* **1** : to affect with blight **2** : to damage or worsen the quality or condition of ⟨slums and *blighted* areas⟩ **3** : to suffer from or become affected with blight

blimp \'blimp\ *n* : an airship filled with gas like a balloon

¹blind \'blīnd\ *adj* **1 a** : SIGHTLESS **b** : having less than ¹/₁₀ normal vision in the best eye even with the aid of glasses **2** : lacking in judgment or understanding **3** : made or done without the aid of sight or knowledge that could provide guidance or cause bias ⟨a *blind* taste test⟩ **4 a** : having only one opening or outlet ⟨a *blind* street⟩ **b** : having no opening ⟨a *blind* wall⟩ — **blind·ly** \'blīn-(d)lē\ *adv* — **blind·ness** \'blīn(d)-nəs\ *n*

blimp

²blind *vb* **1** : to make blind **2** : to make blind for a short time : DAZZLE ⟨*blinded* by the lights⟩ **3** : to take judgment or understanding away from ⟨*blinded* by love⟩

³blind *n* **1** : a device (as a window shade) to prevent sight or keep out light **2** : a hiding place for hunters or wildlife observers

⁴blind *adv* **1** : without seeing outside of an airplane ⟨fly *blind*⟩ **2** : without knowledge of facts that could guide or cause bias

blind carbon copy *n* : a copy of a message (as an e-mail) that is sent without the knowledge of the other recipients

blind·er \'blīn-dər\ *n* : either of two leather flaps on a horse's bridle to keep it from seeing to the side

¹blind·fold \'blīn(d)-,fōld\ *vb* : to cover the eyes of with or as if with a strip of cloth — **blindfold** *adj*

²blindfold *n* : a strip of cloth for covering the eyes

blind·man's buff \,blīn(d)-,manz-'bəf\ *also* **blindman's bluff** *n* : a game in which a blindfolded player tries to catch and identify another

blind spot *n* **1 a** : a point in the retina through which the optic nerve enters and which does not respond to light **b** : a part of an area that cannot be seen with available equipment **2** : an area of weakness (as in judgment)

bling–bling \'blin̪-,blin̪\ *also* **bling** \'blin̪\ *n* : expensive and flashy possessions and especially jewelry

¹blink \'blin̪k\ *vb* **1 a** : to look with half-shut eyes **b** : to close and open the eyes involuntarily **2** : to wink quickly ⟨*blink* back tears⟩ **3** : to shine with a light that goes or seems to go on and off ⟨streetlights *blinking* through rain⟩

²blink *n* **1** : GLIMMER 1a, SPARKLE **2** : a shutting and opening of the eyes — **on the blink** : not working properly ⟨the TV is *on the blink*⟩

blink·er \'blin̪-kər\ *n* **1** : one that blinks; *esp* : a blinking light used as a warning or for signaling **2** : BLINDER

blip \'blip\ *n* : a spot on a screen ⟨a radar *blip*⟩

bliss \'blis\ *n* : complete happiness : JOY — **bliss·ful** \-fəl\ *adj* — **bliss·ful·ly** \-fə-lē\ *adv* — **bliss·ful·ness** *n*

¹blis·ter \'blis-tər\ *n* **1** : a raised area of the outer skin containing liquid — compare WATER BLISTER **2** : a raised spot (as in paint) resembling a blister **3** : something that causes blistering **4** : any of various structures (as a gunner's compartment on an airplane) that bulge out — **blis·tery** \-t(ə-)rē\ *adj*

²blister *vb* **blis·tered; blis·ter·ing** \-t(ə-)rin̪\ **1** : to develop a blister : rise in blisters **2** : to raise a blister on

blister beetle *n* : any of a family of soft-bodied beetles including some whose dried bodies are used in medicine to blister the skin

blis·ter·ing *adj* **1** : very intense ⟨*blistering* heat⟩ **2** : very fast ⟨a *blistering* pace⟩

blithe \'blīth, 'blīth\ *adj* **1** : of a happy carefree nature **2** : HEEDLESS ⟨*blithe* unconcern⟩ — **blithe·ly** *adv*

blithe·some \'blīth-səm, 'blīth-\ *adj* : GAY 1, MERRY

blitz \'blits\ *n* **1 a** : an all-out series of air raids **b** : AIR RAID **2** : a fast thorough campaign ⟨an advertising *blitz* for a new product⟩ — **blitz** *vb*

blitz·krieg \'blits-,krēg\ *n* : a sudden violent enemy attack [German, literally, "lightning war"] — **blitzkrieg** *vb*

bliz·zard \'bliz-ərd\ *n* **1** : a long heavy snowstorm **2** : a very strong cold wind filled with fine snow **3** : an overwhelming rush or deluge ⟨a *blizzard* of mail⟩

bloat \'blōt\ *vb* : to swell by filling with or as if with water or air : puff up

blob \'bläb\ *n* : a small lump of something thick and wet

bloc \'bläk\ *n* : a combination of persons, groups, or nations united by treaty, agreement, or common interest ⟨a *bloc* of voters⟩ [French, literally, "block"]

¹block \'bläk\ *n* **1 a** : a solid piece of material (as stone or wood) usually with one or more flat sides ⟨building *blocks*⟩ **b** : a hollow rectangular piece of material (as of glass or concrete) used for building ⟨cinder *block*⟩ **2 a** : a piece of wood on which condemned persons are beheaded **b** : a mold or support on which something is shaped or displayed **c** : the molded part that contains the cylinders of an internal-combustion engine **3 a** : OBSTACLE **b** : the act of slowing down or stopping an opponent's play in sports **c** : interruption of normal function of bodily processes ⟨a heart *block*⟩; *also* : interruption especially of train of thought ⟨a mental *block*⟩ **4** : a wooden or metal case for one or more pulleys **5** : a number of things forming a group or unit ⟨a *block* of seats⟩ **6** : a large building divided into separate units **7 a** : a usually rectangular space enclosed by streets **b** : the length of the side of such a block ⟨three *blocks* south⟩ **8** : a stand for something to be sold at auction **9** : a hand-carved piece of material from which copies are to be printed

²block *vb* **1 a** : to stop up or close off : OBSTRUCT **b** : to slow down or stop the progress of; *esp* : to interfere with an opponent (as in football) **c** : to shut off from view ⟨*block* the sun⟩ **d** : to prevent normal functioning or action of ⟨*block* a nerve with an anesthetic⟩ **2** : to mark the main lines of ⟨*block* out a sketch⟩ **3** : to shape on, with, or as if with a block **4** : to make (lines of writing or type) even at the left or at both left and right **5** : to secure, support, or provide with a block — **block·er** *n*

block·ade \blä-'kād\ *n* : the cutting off of an area by means of troops or warships to stop the coming in or going out of people or supplies — **blockade** *vb* — **block·ad·er** *n*

block·age \'bläk-ij\ *n* : an act or instance of blocking : the state of being blocked ⟨a *blockage* in an artery⟩

block and tackle *n* : an arrangement of pulley blocks and rope or cable for hoisting or hauling

block·bust·er \'bläk-,bəs-tər\ *n* : one that is very large, successful, or violent ⟨a *blockbuster* of a movie⟩

block·head \-,hed\ *n* : a stupid person

block·house \-,haus\ *n* **1** : a building of heavy timbers or of concrete built with holes in its sides through which persons inside may fire out at an enemy **2** : a building used as an observation point for an operation likely to be accompanied by heat, blast, or radiation hazard

blockhouse 1

block letter *n* : an often hand-printed capital letter having all lines of equal thickness

blog \'blòg, 'bläg\ *n* : a website that contains an online personal journal with reflections, comments, and often hyperlinks provided by the writer; *also* : the contents of such a site [short for *Weblog*, from *Web* + *log* "record of events"] — **blog** *vb* — **blog·ger** *n* — **blog·ging** *n*

bloke \'blōk\ *n, chiefly British* : ¹MAN 1a, FELLOW

¹**blond** *or* **blonde** \'bländ\ *adj* : of a pale yellowish brown color ⟨*blond* hair⟩; *also* : having blond hair ⟨a *blond* actor⟩ — spelled *blond* when used of a boy or man and often *blonde* when used of a girl or woman — **blond·ish** \'blän-dish\ *adj*

²**blond** *or* **blonde** *n* 1 : a blond person — spelled *blond* when used of a boy or man and usually *blonde* when used of a girl or woman 2 : a light yellowish brown to dark grayish yellow

¹**blood** \'bləd\ *n* 1 a : the red fluid that circulates in the heart, arteries, capillaries, and veins of a vertebrate animal and that brings nourishment and oxygen to and carries away waste products from all parts of the body b : a fluid resembling blood 2 a : LINEAGE 2, DESCENT; *esp* : royal lineage b : relationship through a common ancestor : KINSHIP 3 : ²TEMPER 3d [Old English *blōd* "blood"]

²**blood** *vb* : to give experience to [from an earlier sense, meaning "to smear the face of an inexperienced fox hunter with blood of the fox killed on his first hunt"]

blood cell *n* : a cell normally present in blood

blood count *n* : the counting or estimating of the blood cells in a definite volume of blood; *also* : the number of cells counted or estimated in this way

blood·cur·dling \'bləd-ˌkərd-liŋ, -ᵊl-iŋ\ *adj* : causing great horror or fear : TERRIFYING ⟨*bloodcurdling* screams⟩

blood·ed \'bləd-əd\ *adj* 1 : entirely or largely purebred ⟨*blooded* horses⟩ 2 : having blood of a certain type — used in combination ⟨cold-*blooded*⟩

blood group *n* : one of the classes into which people or their blood can be separated on the basis of the presence or absence of specific antigens in their blood — called also *blood type* — **blood grouping** *n*

blood·hound \'bləd-ˌhaùnd\ *n* : any of a breed of large powerful hounds with a wrinkled face and a very good sense of smell

bloodhound

blood·less \'bləd-ləs\ *adj* 1 : having less blood than normal 2 : done without bloodshed ⟨a *bloodless* revolution⟩ 3 : lacking in spirit or feeling — **blood·less·ly** *adv* — **blood·less·ness** *n*

blood·let·ting \'bləd-ˌlet-iŋ\ *n* 1 : the opening of a vein for the purpose of drawing blood 2 : BLOODSHED 2

blood·line \-ˌlīn\ *n* : a sequence of direct ancestors especially in a pedigree; *also* : FAMILY 2, STRAIN 1a

blood·mo·bile \-mō-ˌbēl\ *n* : a motor vehicle staffed and equipped for collecting blood from donors

blood plasma *n* : the fluid portion of whole blood

blood platelet *n* : PLATELET

blood poisoning *n* : a serious condition marked by the passage of disease-causing microorganisms into the blood

blood pressure *n* : pressure of the blood on the walls of blood vessels and especially arteries that varies with physical condition and age

blood·root \'bləd-ˌrüt, -ˌrùt\ *n* : a plant related to the poppies, having a red root and sap, and bearing a single leaf and a white flower in early spring

blood serum *n* : blood plasma from which certain substances (as fibrinogen) involved in the clotting of blood have been removed

blood·shed \-ˌshed\ *n* 1 : the shedding of blood 2 : the taking of life : SLAUGHTER

blood·shot \-ˌshät\ *adj* : red and inflamed ⟨*bloodshot* eyes⟩

blood·stain \-ˌstān\ *n* : a discoloration caused by blood — **blood·stained** \-ˌstānd\ *adj*

blood·stone \-ˌstōn\ *n* : a green quartz with red spots

blood·stream \-ˌstrēm\ *n* : the flowing blood in a living thing with a circulatory system

blood·suck·er \-ˌsək-ər\ *n* : an animal that sucks blood; *esp* : LEECH 1 — **blood·suck·ing** \-ˌsək-iŋ\ *adj*

blood sugar *n* : the glucose in the blood; *esp* : the amount or percentage of such sugar

blood test *n* : a test of the blood (as to detect the presence of disease-causing agents or determine the number of blood cells)

blood·thirsty \'bləd-ˌthər-stē\ *adj* : eager to hurt or kill : CRUEL — **blood·thirst·i·ly** \-stə-lē\ *adv* — **blood·thirst·i·ness** \-stē-nəs\ *n*

blood type *n* : BLOOD GROUP — **blood–type** *vb*

blood vessel *n* : a vessel (as an artery or vein) in which blood circulates in the body of an animal

bloody \'bləd-ē\ *adj* **blood·i·er; -est** 1 a : containing, smeared, or stained with blood ⟨a *bloody* handkerchief⟩ b : dripping blood ⟨a *bloody* nose⟩ 2 : causing or accompanied by bloodshed ⟨a *bloody* battle⟩ 3 : BLOODTHIRSTY, MURDEROUS ⟨a *bloody* deed⟩ — **blood·i·ly** \'bləd-ᵊl-ē\ *adv* — **blood·i·ness** \'bləd-ē-nəs\ *n* — **bloody** *vb*

¹**bloom** \'blüm\ *n* 1 a : ¹BLOSSOM 1 b : the period or state of flowering ⟨the roses are in *bloom*⟩ c : an excessive growth of plankton 2 a : ¹BLOSSOM 3 b : a state or time of beauty, freshness, and strength 3 a : a delicate powdery coating especially on some fruits and leaves b : a rosy appearance of the cheeks

²**bloom** *vb* 1 : to produce flowers : BLOSSOM 2 a : ²BLOSSOM 2 b : to be in a state of youthful beauty or freshness : FLOURISH 3 : to glow with rosy color — **bloom·er** *n*

bloo·mers \'blü-mərz\ *n pl* : full loose pants gathered at the knee and once worn by women for sports; *also* : underpants of similar design worn chiefly by girls [named for Amelia *Bloomer* who introduced the garment]

¹**blos·som** \'bläs-əm\ *n* 1 : the flower of a seed plant ⟨apple *blossoms*⟩; *also* : the mass of such flowers on a single plant ⟨a light *blossom* on the rose bush⟩ 2 : ¹BLOOM 1b 3 : a peak period or stage of development — **blos·somy** \-ə-mē\ *adj*

²**blossom** *vb* 1 : ²BLOOM 1 2 : to grow and do well ⟨students who *blossom* in college⟩

¹**blot** \'blät\ *n* 1 : ¹SPOT 2a, b, STAIN 2 : ¹DISHONOR 1

²**blot** *vb* **blot·ted; blot·ting** 1 : ²SPOT 1, STAIN 2 : ²OBSCURE, DIM 3 : ¹DISGRACE 4 : to dry with something absorbent 5 : to mark or become marked with a blot

blotch \'bläch\ *n* 1 : BLEMISH, FLAW 2 : a large irregular spot (as of color or ink) — **blotch** *vb* — **blotched** \'blächt\ *adj* — **blotchy** \'bläch-ē\ *adj*

blot out *vb* 1 : to make unimportant 2 : to make hard to see or invisible : HIDE 2 : DESTROY 1, KILL

blot·ter \'blät-ər\ *n* 1 : a piece of blotting paper 2 : a book in which entries are made temporarily ⟨a police *blotter*⟩

blotting paper *n* : a spongy paper used to absorb wet ink

blouse \'blaùs *also* 'blaùz\ *n* 1 : a loose outer garment like a shirt or smock varying from hip-length to calf-length 2

\ə\ **abut**	\aú\ **out**	\i\ **tip**	\ò\ **saw**	\ú\ **foot**
\ər\ **further**	\ch\ **chin**	\ī\ **life**	\òi\ **coin**	\y\ **yet**
\a\ **mat**	\e\ **pet**	\j\ **job**	\th\ **thin**	\yü\ **few**
\ā\ **take**	\ē\ **easy**	\ŋ\ **sing**	\th\ **this**	\yù\ **cure**
\ä\ **cot, cart**	\g\ **go**	\ō\ **bone**	\ü\ **food**	\zh\ **vision**

: a usually loose-fitting garment especially for women covering the body from the neck to the waist

¹blow \'blō\ *vb* **blew** \'blü\; **blown** \'blōn\; **blow·ing** 1 : to move or become moved especially rapidly or with power ⟨wind *blowing* from the north⟩ 2 : to send forth a strong stream of air (as from the mouth) ⟨*blow* on your soup⟩ 3 : to drive or become driven by a stream of air ⟨trees *blown* down⟩ 4 a : to make a sound or cause to sound by or as if by blowing ⟨*blow* a horn⟩ ⟨*blow* a whistle⟩ b : to project by blowing ⟨*blow* a kiss⟩ 5 a : to breathe hard or rapidly : PANT b *of a whale* : to force moisture-filled air out of the lungs through the blowhole 6 a : to melt when overloaded ⟨the fuse *blew*⟩ b : to cause (a fuse) to blow 7 : to open or break or tear apart by too much pressure ⟨*blew* a seal⟩ ⟨the tire *blew* out⟩ 8 : to clear by forcing air through ⟨*blew* his nose⟩ 9 : to produce or shape by the action of blown or otherwise forced air ⟨*blow* bubbles⟩ ⟨*blow* glass⟩ 10 : to shatter, burst, or destroy by explosion 11 : to spend recklessly ⟨*blew* all the money in one day⟩ 12 a : ¹BOTCH b : to lose or miss (as an opportunity) especially through clumsiness ⟨*blew* my chance⟩ [Old English *blāwan* "to blow, to move quickly"]

²blow *n* 1 : a blowing of wind especially when strong or violent 2 : a forcing of air from the mouth or nose or through an instrument

³blow *vb* **blew** \'blü\; **blown** \'blōn\; **blow·ing** : ²FLOWER 1, BLOOM [Old English *blōwan* "to bloom"]

⁴blow *n* 1 : a hard hit using a part of the body or an instrument 2 : an unfriendly act : COMBAT ⟨come to *blows*⟩ 3 : a sudden act or effort ⟨solve all our problems with one *blow*⟩ 4 : a sudden disaster ⟨a heavy *blow* to the nation⟩ [Middle English *blaw* "stroke"]

blow–dry \'blō-ˌdrī\ *vb* : to dry and usually style (hair) with a blow-dryer

blow–dry·er \-ˌdrī(-ə)r\ *n* : a handheld hair dryer

blow·er \'blō(-ə)r\ *n* 1 : one that blows 2 : a device for producing a stream of air or gas

blow·fish \'blō-ˌfish\ *n* : PUFFER FISH

blow·fly \'blō-ˌflī\ *n* : any of various two-winged flies (as a bluebottle) that deposit their eggs on meat or in wounds

blow·gun \-ˌgən\ *n* : a long narrow tube from which an arrow or dart may be blown

blow·hole \-ˌhōl\ *n* 1 : a nostril in the top of the head of a whale or related animal 2 : a hole in the ice to which aquatic mammals (as seals) come to breathe

blown \'blōn\ *adj* 1 : being swollen or inflated 2 : being out of breath

blow·out \'blō-ˌaut\ *n* 1 : a big festive party 2 : a bursting of a container (as a tire) by pressure of the contents on a weak spot 3 : an eruption of an oil or gas well that is not under control and is the result of too much natural pressure

blow over *vb* : to come to an end without a lasting effect ⟨hoped the problem would *blow over* soon⟩

blow·pipe \'blō-ˌpīp\ *n* 1 : a small tube for blowing a jet of gas (as air) into a flame so as to increase the heat in a small area 2 : BLOWGUN

blow·torch \-ˌtórch\ *n* : a small burner whose flame is made hotter by a blast of air or oxygen

blow·up \'blō-ˌəp\ *n* 1 : EXPLOSION 1 2 : an outburst of bad temper 3 : a photographic enlargement

blow up \'blō-'əp\ *vb* 1 : to expand or become expanded to extraordinary size 2 : to fill up or become filled with a gas and especially air ⟨*blow up* a balloon⟩ 3 : to make an enlargement of ⟨*blow up* a photograph⟩ 4 a : to destroy or become destroyed by explosion b : to become violently angry

blowy \'blō-ē\ *adj* **blow·i·er; -est** : WINDY 1

BLT \ˌbē-ˌel-'tē\ *n* : a bacon, lettuce, and tomato sandwich

¹blub·ber \'bləb-ər\ *n* 1 : the fat of whales and other large sea mammals 2 : the action of blubbering

²blubber *vb* **blub·bered; blub·ber·ing** \-(ə-)riŋ\ 1 : to weep noisily 2 : to talk and weep at the same time

¹blud·geon \'bləj-ən\ *n* : a short club with one end thicker and heavier than the other

²bludgeon *vb* : to hit very hard : BEAT

¹blue \'blü\ *adj* 1 : of the color blue 2 : low in spirits : MELANCHOLY — **blue·ness** *n*

²blue *n* 1 : the color of the clear daytime sky or of the colors of light between green and violet 2 : blue clothing or cloth 3 a : SKY 1 b : SEA 1a — **out of the blue** : without advance notice : UNEXPECTEDLY ⟨came *out of the blue*⟩

³blue *vb* **blued; blue·ing** *or* **blu·ing** : to make or turn blue

blue baby *n* : an infant with a bluish tint usually from a defect of the heart

blue·bell \'blü-ˌbel\ *n* : any of various plants (as a harebell) with blue bell-shaped flowers

blue·ber·ry \-ˌber-ē, -b(ə-)rē\ *n* : the edible blue or blackish small-seeded berry of any of several plants of the heath family; *also* : a low or tall shrub producing these berries — compare HUCKLEBERRY 1

blue·bird \-ˌbərd\ *n* : any of three small North American songbirds related to the robin but more or less blue above

blue·bon·net \'blü-ˌbän-ət\ *n* : a low-growing annual lupine of Texas with silky leaves and blue flowers

blue·bot·tle \-ˌbät-ᵊl\ *n* : any of several blowflies with a shiny blue abdomen or body

blue cheese *n* : strong-flavored cheese streaked with blue mold

blue chip *n* : a stock issue that has a high value because of public faith in its worth and stability; *also* : a company that issues such stock

blue–collar \'blü-'käl-ər\ *adj* : of or relating to the class of workers whose duties require work clothes

blue·fish \'blü-ˌfish\ *n* : an active saltwater food and sport fish that is bluish above with silvery sides

blue flag *n* : a blue-flowered iris; *esp* : a common wild iris of the eastern U.S.

blue·gill \'blü-ˌgil\ *n* : a common food and sport sunfish of the eastern and central U.S.

blue·grass \-ˌgras\ *n* 1 : any of several grasses with usually bluish green stems; *esp* : KENTUCKY BLUEGRASS 2 : country music played on a small group of instruments (as banjo, fiddle, and mandolin) with melody or harmony often made up by players during a performance

blue–green alga \ˌblü-ˌgrēn-\ *n* : any of a major group of microorganisms that typically live in water and undergo photosynthesis and that are now usually classified as bacteria or sometimes as plants — called also *cyanobacterium*

blue heron *n* : either of two herons with bluish plumage; *esp* : GREAT BLUE HERON

blueing *or* **bluing** *present participle of* BLUE

blue jay \'blü-ˌjā\ *n* : a bright blue North American jay having a small bunch of feathers pointing upward and backward from the top of the head

blue jeans *n pl* : pants usually made of blue denim

blue mold *n* : a fungus and especially a penicillium that produces blue or blue-green growths

blue plate \-ˌplāt\ *adj* : being a main course usually offered at a special price in a restaurant

¹blue·print \'blü-ˌprint\ *n* 1 : a photographic print made with white lines on a blue background and used especially for copying mechanical drawings, maps, and architects' plans 2 : a detailed plan or program of action

²blueprint *vb* : to make a blueprint of or for

blue racer *n* : a blue or greenish blue harmless snake found from southern Ontario to Missouri

blue ribbon *n* : a blue ribbon awarded the first-place winner in a competition

blues \'blüz\ *n pl* 1 : low spirits : MELANCHOLY 2 : a song often expressing sadness and characterized by the continual occurrence of the flatted third, fifth, and seventh tones of a scale in both the melody and harmony

blue shark *n* : an active shark of warm and temperate seas that is blue above and white below and that occasionally attacks people

blue·stem \'blü-ˌstem\ *n* : either of two important grasses of North America with bluish leaf sheaths that are used to feed livestock

blu·et \'blü-ət\ *n* : a low North American herb bearing small bluish or white flowers

blue vitriol *n* : a compound of copper sulfate chemically combined with water

blue whale *n* : a whale that may reach a weight of 150 tons (135 metric tons) and a length of 100 feet (30 meters) and is generally considered the largest living animal

blue whale

¹**bluff** \'bləf\ *adj* **1** : rising steeply with a broad front ⟨a *bluff* coastline⟩ **2** : frank and outspoken in a good-natured manner [from an obsolete Dutch word *blaf* "flat"] — **bluff·ly** *adv* — **bluff·ness** *n*

   synonyms BLUFF, BLUNT, CURT mean speaking in a frank rough manner. BLUFF usually suggests hearty and good-natured roughness ⟨farmers talking in a *bluff* manner⟩. BLUNT may suggest plain speech that disregards the feelings of others ⟨a *blunt* appraisal of the student's work⟩. CURT usually suggests briefness of speech that is upsetting or rude ⟨a *curt* reply to a polite question⟩.

²**bluff** *n* : a high steep bank : CLIFF

³**bluff** *vb* : to deceive or frighten by pretending to have strength or confidence that one does not really have [probably from Dutch *bluffen* "to boast"] — **bluff·er** *n*

⁴**bluff** *n* **1 a** : an act or instance of bluffing **b** : the practice of bluffing **2** : one who bluffs

blu·ing *or* **blue·ing** \'blü-iŋ\ *n* : a mixture used in laundering to prevent yellowing of white fabrics

blu·ish \'blü-ish\ *adj* : somewhat blue

¹**blun·der** \'blən-dər\ *vb* **blun·dered; blun·der·ing** \-d(ə-)riŋ\ **1** : to move unsteadily or blindly **2** : to make a mistake (as through stupidity or carelessness) **3** : to say stupidly or thoughtlessly : BLURT — **blun·der·er** \-dər-ər\ *n*

²**blunder** *n* : a bad or stupid mistake

blun·der·buss \'blən-dər-ˌbəs\ *n* : a muzzle-loader with a short barrel and cone-shaped muzzle to make loading easier [derived from an obsolete Dutch word *donderbus*, literally, "thundergun"]

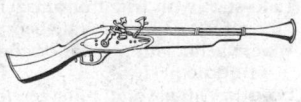

blunderbuss

¹**blunt** \'blənt\ *adj* **1** : slow or lacking in feeling or understanding **2** : having an edge or point that is not sharp **3** : abrupt in speech or manner   *synonyms* see BLUFF — **blunt·ly** *adv* — **blunt·ness** *n*

²**blunt** *vb* : to make or become less sharp

¹**blur** \'blər\ *n* **1** : a smear or stain that dims but does not completely cover **2** : something vague or lacking definite outline — **blur·ry** \-ē\ *adj*

²**blur** *vb* **blurred; blur·ring 1** : to make hard to see or read by smearing **2** : to make or become vague or unclear

blurb \'blərb\ *n* : a short description (as in advertising) praising a product highly

blurt \'blərt\ *vb* : to say suddenly and without thinking — usually used with *out* ⟨*blurt* out a secret⟩

¹**blush** \'bləsh\ *vb* **1** : to become red in the face especially from shame, confusion, or embarrassment **2** : to feel shame or embarrassment **3** : to have a rosy color : BLOOM — **blush·er** *n*

²**blush** *n* **1** : outward appearance : VIEW ⟨at first *blush*⟩ **2** : a reddening of the face especially from shame, confusion, or embarrassment **3** : a red or rosy tint

¹**blus·ter** \'bləs-tər\ *vb* **blus·tered; blus·ter·ing** \-t(ə-)riŋ\ **1** : to blow violently and noisily **2** : to talk or act in a noisy boastful way — **blus·ter·er** \-tər-ər\ *n*

²**bluster** *n* **1** : a violent noise or commotion **2** : loudly boastful or threatening speech — **blus·tery** \-t(ə-)rē\ *adj*

B lymphocyte *n* : B CELL

BMX \ˌbē-(ˌ)em-'eks\ *n* : bicycle racing that is similar to motocross with dirt tracks and jumps and the use of special heavy-duty bicycles

boa \'bō-ə\ *n* **1** : any of various large snakes (as the boa constrictor, anaconda, or python) that crushes its prey **2** : a long fluffy scarf of fur, feathers, or fabric

boa con·stric·tor \-kən-'strik-tər\ *n* : a brown tropical American boa that grows to 10 feet (3 meters) or longer

boar \'bō(ə)r, 'bo(ə)r\ *n* **1** : a male pig; *also* : the male of any of several mammals (as a guinea pig or raccoon) **2** : WILD BOAR

¹**board** \'bō(ə)rd, 'bo(ə)rd\ *n* **1** : the side of a ship **2 a** : a long thin flat piece of lumber **b** : ¹STAGE 2b ⟨trod the *boards* for 40 years⟩ **3 a** : a dining table **b** : daily meals especially when provided for pay ⟨room and *board*⟩ **4** : a group of persons who manage, direct, or investigate ⟨*board* of directors⟩ ⟨*board* of examiners⟩ **5 a** : a flat usually rectangular piece of material designed for a special purpose ⟨cutting *board*⟩ ⟨chess *board*⟩ ⟨diving *board*⟩ **b** : a surface, frame, or device for putting up notices **6** : a sheet of insulating material carrying circuit elements and connectors so that it can be inserted in an electronic device (as a computer) — **on board** : ABOARD

²**board** *vb* **1** : to go or put aboard : get or put on ⟨*board* a plane⟩ **2** : to cover with boards ⟨*board* up a window⟩ **3** : to provide or be provided with regular meals and often lodging usually for pay **4** : to live at a boarding school

board·er \'bōrd-ər, 'bord-\ *n* **1** : one who pays for meals and sometimes lodging at another's house **2** : a person who rides a snowboard

board game *n* : a game of strategy (as chess, checkers, or backgammon) played by moving pieces on a board

board·ing·house \'bōrd-iŋ-ˌhaus, 'bord-\ *n* : a house at which persons are boarded

boarding school *n* : a school at which most of the pupils live during the school term

board·walk \'bō(ə)rd-ˌwok, 'bo(ə)rd-\ *n* : a walk of planks especially along a beach

¹**boast** \'bōst\ *n* **1** : the act of boasting **2** : a cause for pride — **boast·ful** \'bōst-fəl\ *adj* — **boast·ful·ly** \-fə-lē\ *adv* — **boast·ful·ness** *n*

²**boast** *vb* **1** : to praise one's own possessions, qualities, or accomplishments **2** : to have and display proudly ⟨our band *boasted* new uniforms⟩ — **boast·er** *n*

   synonyms BOAST, BRAG, CROW mean to express pride in oneself or what one has done. BOAST often suggests exaggeration ⟨*boasted* that she was the best runner in the school⟩ but sometimes it applies to claims made with justifiable pride ⟨the town *boasts* one of the best hospitals in the area⟩. BRAG suggests crude praising of oneself ⟨always *bragging* about how much money they had⟩. CROW suggests jubilant and noisy bragging ⟨the team *crowed* over their surprise victory⟩.

\ə\ **abut**	\au\ **out**	\i\ **tip**	\o\ **saw**	\u\ **foot**
\ər\ **further**	\ch\ **chin**	\ī\ **life**	\oi\ **coin**	\y\ **yet**
\a\ **mat**	\e\ **pet**	\j\ **job**	\th\ **thin**	\yü\ **few**
\ā\ **take**	\ē\ **easy**	\ŋ\ **sing**	\th\ **this**	\yu\ **cure**
\ä\ **cot, cart**	\g\ **go**	\ō\ **bone**	\ü\ **food**	\zh\ **vision**

¹boat \'bōt\ *n* **1** : a small vessel for travel on water **2** : ¹SHIP 1 **3** : a boat-shaped utensil ⟨gravy *boat*⟩ — **in the same boat** : in the same situation

¹boat 3

²boat *vb* **1** : to put into or carry in a boat **2** : to travel by boat

boat·er \'bōt-ər\ *n* **1** : a person who travels in a boat **2** : a stiff straw hat

boat·house \'bōt-,haús\ *n* : a shelter for boats

boat·load \-,lōd\ *n* **1** : a load that fills a boat **2** : a large amount ⟨a *boatload* of money⟩

boat·man \'bōt-mən\ *n* : a person who manages, works on, or deals in boats

boat·swain *or* **bo·s'n** \'bō-s³n\ *n* : a sailor in the navy or merchant marine responsible for supervising work related to maintenance of the hull

¹bob \'bäb\ *vb* **bobbed; bob·bing 1 a** : to move or cause to move up and down in a short quick movement ⟨*bob* the head⟩ ⟨a cork *bobbing* in the water⟩ **b** : to appear suddenly or unexpectedly ⟨may *bob* up anywhere⟩ **2** : to grasp or make a grab with the teeth ⟨*bob* for apples⟩ [Middle English *boben, bobben* "to hit or beat"]

²bob *n* : a short jerky motion ⟨a *bob* of the head⟩

³bob *n* **1** : a woman's or child's short haircut **2** : a weight hanging from a line **3** : ¹FLOAT 2a [from earlier *bob* "a knot or twist of yarn or hair," from Middle English *bobbe* "bunch, cluster"]

⁴bob *vb* **bobbed; bob·bing 1** : to cut shorter : CROP **2** : to cut (hair) in the style of a bob

bob·ber \'bäb-ər\ *n* : one that bobs; *esp* : ¹FLOAT 2a

bob·bin \'bäb-ən\ *n* : a spool or spindle on which yarn or thread is wound (as in a sewing machine)

bob·ble \'bäb-əl\ *vb* **bob·bled; bob·bling** \'bäb-(ə-)liŋ\ **1** : ¹BOB 1a **2** : to handle in a clumsy or unsure way : FUMBLE — **bobble** *n*

bob·by \'bäb-ē\ *n, pl* **bobbies** *British* : POLICE OFFICER [named for Sir Robert (*Bobby*) Peel 1788–1850 English politician who first organized the London police force]

bob·by pin \'bäb-ē-\ *n* : a flat metal clip with flexible closed tips for holding the hair in place

bobby socks *or* **bobby sox** *n pl* : girls' thick socks reaching above the ankle

bob·by–sox·er \'bäb-ē-,säk-sər\ *n* : an adolescent girl

bob·cat \'bäb-,kat\ *n* : a common usually rusty-colored North American lynx with dark spots

bob·o·link \'bäb-ə-,liŋk\ *n* : an American songbird that has plumage which is streaky brown above and yellowish brown below except for the breeding season when the male is chiefly black and white

bob·sled \'bäb-,sled\ *n* **1** : a short sled usually used as one of a joined pair **2** : a racing sled made with two sets of runners, a hand brake, and often a steering wheel — **bobsled** *vb* — **bob·sled·der** *n*

bob·tail \-,tāl\ *n* **1** : a short or bobbed tail **2** : a horse, dog, or cat with a short or bobbed tail — **bobtail** *or* **bobtailed** \-,tāld\ *adj*

bob·white \(')bäb-'hwīt, -'wīt\ *n* : any of several American quails; *esp* : a gray, white, and reddish game bird of the eastern and central U.S.

¹bode \'bōd\ *vb* **bod·ed; bod·ing** : to indicate (as a future event) by signs : FORESHADOW

²bode *past of* BIDE

bod·ice \'bäd-əs\ *n* : the upper part of a dress

bod·ied \'bäd-ēd\ *adj* : having a body of a certain kind — used in combination ⟨long-*bodied*⟩

bodi·less \'bäd-i-ləs, 'bäd-³l-əs\ *adj* : having no body : INCORPOREAL

¹bodi·ly \'bäd-³l-ē\ *adj* : of or relating to the body : PHYSICAL

²bodily *adv* **1** : in the flesh : by the body ⟨removed them *bodily*⟩ **2** : as a whole : ENTIRELY

bod·kin \'bäd-kən\ *n* **1 a** : DAGGER 1, STILETTO **b** : a sharp slender instrument for making holes in cloth **2** : a blunt needle with a large eye for drawing tape or ribbon through a loop or hem

body \'bäd-ē\ *n, pl* **bod·ies 1 a** : the physical whole of a living or dead organism **b** : the trunk or main part of an organism : PERSON **2** : the main or central part ⟨the *body* of a truck⟩ ⟨the *body* of a letter⟩ **3** : the section of a garment covering the main part of the body **4** : a mass or portion of matter different from other masses ⟨a *body* of water⟩ ⟨a *body* of cold air⟩ **5** : a group of persons or things with a common aim or character ⟨a *body* of troops⟩ ⟨a *body* of laws⟩ **6** : richness or fullness of flavor or texture

body·build·ing \'bäd-ē-,bil-diŋ\ *n* : the developing of the body through exercise and diet — **body·build·er** \-,bil-dər\ *n*

body cavity *n* : a cavity within an animal body; *esp* : COELOM

body·guard \'bäd-ē-,gärd\ *n* : a person or group of persons whose job is to protect someone

body language *n* : movements (as with the hands) or posture used as a means of expression

body louse *n* : a sucking louse that lives in the clothing and feeds on the human body

body mass index *n* : a measure of body fat that is the ratio of the weight of the body in kilograms to the square of its height in meters

body·wash \'bäd-ē-,wósh, -,wäsh\ *n* : a liquid product for washing the body (as in a shower or bath)

Boer \'bō(ə)r, 'bó(ə)r, 'bú(ə)r\ *n* : a South African usually of Dutch descent [Dutch, literally, "farmer"]

¹bog \'bäg, 'bóg\ *n* : wet spongy ground; *esp* : a poorly drained acid area in which dead plant matter accumulates and sphagnum grows in abundance — **bog·gy** \-ē\ *adj*

²bog *vb* **bogged; bog·ging** : to sink or become stuck in or as if in a bog ⟨*bogged* down in too much detail⟩

bo·gey *also* **bo·gy** *or* **bo·gie** *n, pl* **bogeys** *also* **bogies 1** \'búg-ē, 'bō-gē, 'bü-gē\ : GHOST, PHANTOM **2** \'bō-gē *also* 'búg-ē *or* 'bü-gē\ : something one is afraid of especially without reason

bo·gey·man \'búg-ē-,man, 'bō-gē-, 'bü-gē-\ *n* **1** : an imaginary monster used in threatening children **2** : a terrifying or dreaded person or thing

bog·gle \'bä-gəl\ *vb* **bog·gled; bog·gling** \-g(ə-)liŋ\ **1** : to start with fright or amazement ⟨the mind *boggles* at the effort⟩ **2** : to hesitate because of doubt or fear **3** : to overwhelm with wonder or confusion ⟨*boggles* the mind⟩ — **boggle** *n*

bo·gus \'bō-gəs\ *adj* : not genuine : COUNTERFEIT, SHAM

Bo·he·mi·an \bō-'hē-mē-ən\ *n* **1 a** : a person born or living in Bohemia : the Czech dialects used in Bohemia **2** *often not cap* **a** : ²VAGABOND, WANDERER **b** : a person (as an artist or writer) who does not have a typical lifestyle — **bohemian** *adj, often cap* — **bo·he·mi·an·ism** \-mē-ə-,niz-əm\ *n, often cap*

bohr·i·um \'bō(ə)r-ē-əm, 'bó(ə)r-\ *n* : a radioactive element that is produced artificially — see ELEMENT table

¹boil \'bói(ə)l\ *n* : a painful swollen inflamed area of the skin resulting from infection — compare CARBUNCLE 2 [an altered form of Middle English *bile* "a boil," from Old English *bȳl* (same meaning)]

²boil *vb* **1 a** : to produce bubbles of vapor when heated ⟨the water is *boiling*⟩ **b** : to come or bring to the boiling point ⟨the coffee *boiled*⟩ **2** : to churn violently as if boiling ⟨*boiling* floodwaters⟩ **3** : to be excited or stirred up ⟨*boil* with anger⟩ **4** : to go through or cause to go through the action of a boiling liquid ⟨*boil* eggs⟩ [Middle English *boilen* "to boil," from early French *boillir*, derived from Latin *bulla* "a bubble" — related to ³BILL, ²BOWL]

³boil *n* : the act or state of boiling ⟨bring to a *boil*⟩

boil down *vb* : to reduce or become reduced by or as if by boiling ⟨let the sauce *boil down*⟩ ⟨*boil down* a report⟩

boil·er \'bȯi-lər\ *n* **1** : a container in which something is boiled **2** : a strong metal container used in making steam **3** : a tank in which water is heated or hot water is stored

boiling point *n* : the temperature at which a liquid boils

boil over *vb* : to overflow while boiling

bois·ter·ous \'bȯi-st(ə-)rəs\ *adj* **1 a** : noisily rough : ROWDY ⟨a *boisterous* crowd⟩ **b** : marked by high spirits ⟨*boisterous* laughter⟩ **2** : vigorously active : STORMY — **bois·ter·ous·ly** *adv* — **bois·ter·ous·ness** *n*

bo·la \'bō-lə\ *or* **bo·las** \-ləs\ *n, pl* **bo·las** \-ləz\ : a cord with weights attached to the ends for throwing at and entangling an animal [American Spanish *bolas* "bola," from Spanish *bola* "ball"]

bola

bold \'bōld\ *adj* **1 a** : willing to meet danger or take risks : DARING **b** : showing daring spirit ⟨a *bold* plan⟩ **2** : IMPUDENT, SAUCY **3** : ¹STEEP 1 ⟨*bold* cliffs⟩ **4** : standing out in a very noticeable way : CONSPICUOUS ⟨*bold* colors⟩ — **bold·ly** \'bōl-(d)lē\ *adv* — **bold·ness** \'bōl(d)-nəs\ *n*

bold·face \'bōl(d)-ˌfās\ *n* **1** : a type having thick dark lines — compare LIGHTFACE **2** : printing set in boldface

bold–faced \-ˈfāst\ *adj* **1** : bold in manner or conduct **2** *usually* **bold·faced** : being or set in boldface

bole \'bōl\ *n* : the trunk of a tree

bo·le·ro \bə-ˈle(ə)r-ō\ *n, pl* **-ros** **1** : a Spanish dance in ¾ time **2** : a loose waist-length jacket open at the front

bo·li·var \bə-ˈlē-ˌvär, ˈbäl-ə-vər\ *n, pl* **bo·li·vars** *or* **bo·li·va·res** \ˌbäl-ə-ˈvär-ˌās, ˌbō-li-\ **1** : the basic unit of money of Venezuela **2** : a coin representing one bolivar [American Spanish *bolívar* "unit of money," named for Simón *Bolívar*]

boll \'bōl\ *n* : the usually roundish pod of some plants ⟨cotton *bolls*⟩

bol·lard \'bäl-ərd\ *n* : a post of metal or wood on a wharf around which to fasten mooring lines

boll weevil *n* : a gray or brown weevil whose larva lives in and feeds on the buds and bolls of the cotton plant

bo·lo \'bō-lō\ *n, pl* **bolos** : a long heavy single-edged knife used in the Philippines

bo·lo·gna \bə-ˈlō-nē *also* -n(y)ə\ *n* : a large smoked sausage of beef, veal, and pork

Bol·she·vik \'bōl-shə-ˌvik, ˈbȯl-, ˈbäl-, -ˌvēk\ *n, pl* **Bolsheviks** *or* **Bol·she·vi·ki** \ˌbōl-shə-ˈvik-ē, ˌbȯl-, ˌbäl-, -ˈvē-kē\ **1** : a member of the communist party that seized power in Russia by the Revolution of November 1917 **2** : COMMUNIST 2 — **Bolshevik** *adj*

Bol·she·vism \'bōl-shə-ˌviz-əm, ˈbȯl-, ˈbäl-\ *n* : the doctrine or program of the Bolsheviks

¹bol·ster \'bōl-stər\ *n* **1** : a long pillow or cushion **2** : a structural part designed to eliminate friction or provide support

²bolster *vb* **bol·stered; bol·ster·ing** \-st(ə-)riŋ\ : to support with or as if with a bolster; *also* : REINFORCE ⟨came with me to *bolster* my confidence⟩ — **bol·ster·er** \-stər-ər\ *n*

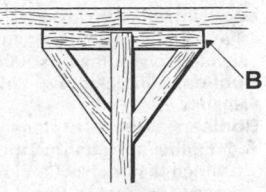
B ¹bolster 2

¹bolt \'bōlt\ *n* **1** : a missile (as an arrow) for a crossbow or catapult **2 a** : a lightning stroke : THUNDERBOLT **b** : a sudden surprise ⟨a *bolt* from the blue⟩ **3** : a sliding bar used to fasten a door **4** : the part of a lock worked by a key **5** : a metal pin or rod usually with a head at one end and a screw thread at the other that is used to hold something in place **6** : a roll of cloth or wallpaper **7** : the device that closes the breech of a firearm

²bolt *vb* **1** : to move suddenly or nervously **2** : to move rapidly : DASH ⟨reporters *bolted* for the door⟩ **3** : RUN AWAY 1 ⟨the horse shied and *bolted*⟩ **4** : to break away from or oppose one's political party **5** : to say thoughtlessly : BLURT **6** : to fasten with a bolt **7** : to swallow hastily or without chewing ⟨*bolted* down my dinner and rushed out⟩ — **bolt·er** *n*

³bolt *n* : an act of bolting

¹bomb \'bäm\ *n* **1 a** : an explosive device that has a fuse and is designed to go off under any of various conditions **b** : ATOMIC BOMB; *also* : nuclear weapons in general — usually used with *the* **2** : a container in which a substance (as an insecticide) is stored under pressure and from which it is released in a fine spray **3** : ²FLOP 2

²bomb *vb* **1** : to attack with bombs **2** : to fail completely

bom·bard \bäm-ˈbärd *also* bəm-\ *vb* **1** : to attack especially with artillery or bombers **2** : to attack forcefully or continuously (as with questions) **3** : to put under the force of rapidly moving particles (as electrons or alpha rays) — **bom·bard·ment** \-mənt\ *n*

bom·bar·dier \ˌbäm-bə(r)-ˈdi(ə)r\ *n* : a bomber-crew member who releases the bombs

bombardier beetle *n* : any of numerous beetles that when disturbed discharge an irritating vapor

bom·bast \'bäm-ˌbast\ *n* : boastful speech or writing — **bom·bas·tic** \bäm-ˈbas-tik\ *adj* — **bom·bas·ti·cal·ly** \-ti-k(ə-)lē\ *adv*

bomb·er \'bäm-ər\ *n* : one that bombs; *esp* : an airplane designed for dropping bombs

bomb·proof \'bäm-ˌprüf\ *adj* : safe against the explosive force of bombs

bomb·shell \-ˌshel\ *n* **1** : ¹BOMB 1a **2** : a great surprise

bo·na fide \'bō-nə-ˌfīd, 'bä-nə-; ˌbō-nə-ˈfīd-ē, -ˈfīd-ə\ *adj* **1** : made or done in good faith ⟨*bona fide* offer⟩ **2** : made with earnest intent : SINCERE **3** : GENUINE 1 ⟨a *bona fide* cowboy⟩ [from Latin *bona fide*, literally, "in good faith"; *bona* from *bonus* "good" and *fide* from *fides* "faith" — related to BONUS, FAITH]

bo·nan·za \bə-ˈnan-zə\ *n* **1** : a large and rich mineral deposit **2** : something that brings a rich return ⟨a box-office *bonanza*⟩

bon·bon \'bän-ˌbän\ *n* : a candy with a soft coating (as chocolate) and a creamy center [French, literally, "good good," from *bon* "good," from Latin *bonus* "good" — related to BONUS, BOUNTY]

¹bond \'bänd\ *n* **1** : something that binds **2 a** : a material or device for binding **b** : a means by which atoms, ions, or groups of atoms are held together in a molecule or crystal **3** : a uniting or binding force or influence : TIE ⟨the *bonds* of friendship⟩ **4 a** : a pledge to do an act or pay a sum on or before a set date or forfeit a sum if the pledge is not fulfilled **b** : a certificate promising payment of a certain sum on or before a stated day and issued by a government or corporation as an evidence of debt **5** : a binding or connection made by overlapping parts of a structure (as in laying brick)

²bond *vb* **1** : to protect or secure by or operate under a bond **2** : to hold together or make solid by or as if by a bond **3** : to form a close relationship especially through

\ə\ **abut**	\au̇\ **out**	\i\ **tip**	\ȯ\ **saw**	\u̇\ **foot**
\ər\ **further**	\ch\ **chin**	\ī\ **life**	\ȯi\ **coin**	\y\ **yet**
\a\ **mat**	\e\ **pet**	\j\ **job**	\th\ **thin**	\yü\ **few**
\ā\ **take**	\ē\ **easy**	\ŋ\ **sing**	\th\ **this**	\yu̇\ **cure**
\ä\ **cot, cart**	\g\ **go**	\ō\ **bone**	\ü\ **food**	\zh\ **vision**

frequent togetherness ⟨the new mother *bonded* with her child⟩ — **bond·able** \'bän-də-bəl\ *adj* — **bond·er** *n*

bond·age \'bän-dij\ *n* : the state of being a slave or serf

bond·hold·er \'bänd-ˌhōl-dər\ *n* : the owner of a government or corporation bond

bond·man \'bän(d)-mən\ *n* : ¹SLAVE 1, SERF

¹**bonds·man** \'bän(d)z-mən\ *n* : BONDMAN

²**bondsman** *n* : one who gives a bond or bail for another

¹**bone** \'bōn\ *n* **1 a** : a hard material which is largely calcium phosphate and of which the skeleton of most vertebrate animals is formed; *also* : one of the hard parts in which this material occurs ⟨break a *bone*⟩ **b** : a hard animal substance (as baleen or ivory) similar to bone **2** : a cause of disagreement — used in the phrases *bone of contention* and *bone to pick* **3** *pl* : something usually or originally made from bone (as dice or clappers) **4 a** : the basic part ⟨cut costs to the *bone*⟩ **b** : the most deeply ingrained part ⟨knew in her *bones* it was wrong⟩ **5** *pl* : BODY ⟨rest my weary *bones*⟩ — **bone·less** \-ləs\ *adj* — **bone·like** \-ˌlīk\ *adj*

²**bone** *vb* **boned; bon·ing** **1** : to remove the bones from ⟨*bone* a fish⟩ **2** : to study hard ⟨*bone* up on math⟩

bone black *n* : the black chiefly carbon matter that is left from bones heated in a closed container and is used especially as a pigment or a material to remove color from other things

bone marrow *n* : a soft tissue rich in blood vessels that fills the cavities of most bones and occurs in two forms: **a** : one that is yellowish and fatty and is found especially in long bones (as the femur) **b** : one that is reddish, is the main place where blood cells are formed, and in adults is limited especially to certain flat or short bones (as the ribs)

bone·meal \'bōn-ˌmē(ə)l\ *n* : crushed or ground bone used especially as fertilizer or animal feed

bon·er \'bō-nər\ *n* : a stupid or ridiculous mistake

bon·fire \'bän-ˌfī(ə)r\ *n* : a large outdoor fire

bon·go \'bäŋ-gō\ *n, pl* **bongos** *also* **bongoes** : either of a pair of small drums of different sizes fitted together and played with the fingers

bo·ni·to \bə-'nēt-ō, -'nēt-ə\ *n, pl* **-tos** *or* **-to** : any of various medium-sized tunas

bon·net \'bän-ət\ *n* **1** : a child's or woman's hat tied under the chin by ribbons or strings **2** : a soft woolen cap worn in Scotland

bon·ny \'bän-ē\ *adj* **bon·ni·er; -est** *chiefly British* : HANDSOME 3, ATTRACTIVE

bon·sai \(')bōn-'sī, 'bōn-ˌsī, 'bän-ˌsī\ *n, pl* **bonsai** : a miniature plant (as a tree) grown in a pot by special methods to restrict its growth; *also* : the art of growing such a plant [Japanese]

bo·nus \'bō-nəs\ *n* : something given to somebody (as a worker) in addition to what is usual or owed [from Latin *bonus* "good" — related to BONA FIDE, BONBON, ²BOON, BOUNTY]

bonsai

bon voy·age \ˌbōn-ˌvwī-'äzh, -ˌvwä-'yäzh, ˌbän-\ *n* : ²FAREWELL 1 — usually used as an interjection [French, literally, "good journey"]

bony \'bō-nē\ *adj* **bon·i·er; -est** **1** : of or relating to bone ⟨the *bony* structure of the body⟩ **2** : full of bones **3** : resembling bone especially in hardness ⟨a *bony* substance⟩ **4** : having large or noticeable bones ⟨a *bony* face⟩ **5** : SKINNY 2, SCRAWNY

bony fish *n* : any of a class of fishes (as eels, mackerels, and trout) with bony rather than cartilaginous skeletons

¹**boo** \'bü\ *interj* — used to express contempt or disapproval or to startle or frighten

²**boo** *n, pl* **boos** **1** : a shout of disapproval or contempt **2** : any sound at all ⟨never said *boo*⟩ — **boo** *vb*

boo–boo \'bü-ˌbü\ *n, pl* **boo-boos** **1** : a usually small bruise or scratch especially on a child **2** : a foolish mistake

boo·by \'bü-bē\ *n, pl* **boobies** **1** : a foolish person : DOPE **2** : any of several tropical seabirds related to the gannets

booby trap *n* : a trap for a careless or unsuspecting person; *esp* : a concealed explosive device set to go off when a harmless-looking object is touched — **boo·by·trap** \'bü-bē-ˌtrap\ *vb*

¹**book** \'buk\ *n* **1** : a set of sheets of paper bound together **2 a** : a long written work **b** : a major division of a written work **3 a** : a volume of business records ⟨the company's *books* show a profit⟩ **b** *pl* : ²RECORD 2b ⟨an outdated law still on the *books*⟩ **4** *cap* : BIBLE 1a **5** : a pack of items bound together ⟨a *book* of matches⟩ — **in one's book** : in one's own opinion — **one for the book** : an act or event worth noting

²**book** *vb* **1** : ¹RESERVE 3 ⟨*book* a hotel room⟩ **2** : to schedule engagements for ⟨*book* a singer⟩ **3** : to enter charges against in a police register ⟨*book* a suspect⟩

³**book** *adj* **1** : gotten from books ⟨*book* learning⟩ **2** : shown by account books ⟨*book* value⟩

book·bind·er \'buk-ˌbīn-dər\ *n* : BINDER 1

book·bind·ing \-ˌbīn-diŋ\ *n* **1** : the binding of a book **2** : the art or trade of binding books

book·case \'buk-ˌkās\ *n* : a set of shelves to hold books

book·end \-ˌend\ *n* : something placed at the end of a row of books to hold them up

book·ish \'buk-ish\ *adj* **1** : fond of reading **2** : tending to rely on knowledge from books rather than practical experience **3** : resembling the language of books : FORMAL — **book·ish·ly** *adv* — **book·ish·ness** *n*

book·keep·er \'buk-ˌkē-pər\ *n* : a person who keeps accounts for a business — **book·keep·ing** \-ˌkē-piŋ\ *n*

book·let \'buk-lət\ *n* : a little book; *esp* : PAMPHLET

book louse *n* : any of several minute wingless insects that feed on and injure books

book lung *n* : a specialized breathing organ of spiders and related animals

book·mak·er \'buk-ˌmā-kər\ *n* : a person who receives and pays off bets

¹**book·mark** \-ˌmärk\ *n* **1** : something placed in a book to mark a page **2** : something on a computer screen that serves as a shortcut (as to a website)

²**bookmark** *vb* : to create a computer bookmark for ⟨*bookmark* a website⟩

book·mo·bile \'buk-mō-ˌbēl\ *n* : a truck that serves as a traveling library

book·plate \'buk-ˌplāt\ *n* : a label pasted inside a book to show who owns it

book·sell·er \-ˌsel-ər\ *n* : a person who owns or works in a bookstore

book·store \-ˌstō(ə)r, -ˌstȯ(ə)r\ *n* : a store that sells mainly books

book·worm \-ˌwərm\ *n* **1** : any of various insect larvae that feed on the binding and paste of books **2** : a person devoted to reading or study

Bool·ean \'bü-lē-ən\ *adj* : of, relating to, or being Boolean algebra

Boolean algebra *n* : any of several logical systems of combining abstract quantities; *esp* : an arithmetic of sets in which the intersection and union of sets are operations [named for George *Boole* 1815–1864 English mathematician]

¹**boom** \'büm\ *n* **1** : a long pole used especially to stretch the bottom of a sail **2 a** : a long beam sticking out from the mast of a derrick to support or guide something that is being lifted **b** : a long arm used to move a microphone

3 : a line of connected floating timbers (as across a river) to obstruct passage or catch floating objects [from Dutch *boom* "tree, wooden beam"]

²**boom** *vb* **1** : to make a deep hollow rumbling sound **2 a** : to increase in importance or popularity **b** : to experience a boom (as in growth) [a word imitating the sound]

³**boom** *n* **1** : a booming sound or cry **2** : a rapid increase in growth, popularity, or prosperity; *esp* : a rapid widespread expansion of business

boom box *n* : a large portable radio and often tape deck or CD player with two attached speakers

¹**boo·mer·ang** \'bü-mə-ˌraŋ\ *n* : a curved club that can be thrown so as to return to the thrower [the native word for this club in Australia]

²**boomerang** *vb* : ²BACKFIRE 2

boom·ing \'bü-miŋ\ *adj* **1** : making a deep sound ⟨his *booming* voice⟩ **2** : forcefully or powerfully done ⟨hit a *booming* serve⟩

boom·town \'büm-ˌtaùn\ *n* : a town experiencing a sudden growth in business and population

¹**boon** \'bün\ *n* **1** : something asked or granted as a favor **2** : something pleasant or helpful that comes at just the right time : BLESSING [Middle English *boon* "favor," from an early Norse word meaning "a request, plea"]

¹boomerang

²**boon** *adj* : MERRY 1 ⟨a *boon* companion⟩ [Middle English *boon, bon* "favorable," from early French *bon* "good," derived from Latin *bonus* "good" — related to BONUS]

boon·docks \'bün-ˌdäks\ *n pl* **1** : rough country filled with dense brush **2** : a rural area

boor \'bù(ə)r\ *n* **1 a** : PEASANT **b** : ²RUSTIC **2** : a crude or impolite person — **boor·ish** \-ish\ *adj* — **boor·ish·ly** *adv* — **boor·ish·ness** *n*

boos *plural of* BOO

¹**boost** \'büst\ *vb* **1** : to push or shove up from below **2** : to increase in force, power, or amount ⟨*boost* production⟩ ⟨*boost* prices⟩ **3** : ²FURTHER, RAISE ⟨*boost* morale⟩ **4** : to support enthusiastically : PLUG

²**boost** *n* **1** : a push upward : an increase in amount ⟨a *boost* in production⟩ **3** : an act that gives help or encouragement

boost·er \'bü-stər\ *n* **1** : one that boosts **2** : an enthusiastic supporter **3** : BOOSTER SHOT **4** : a device for strengthening radio or television signals **5** : the first stage of a multistage rocket providing force for the launching and the first part of the flight

booster shot *n* : an extra dose of an immunizing agent given to maintain or restore the effects of previously established immunity

¹**boot** \'büt\ *n, chiefly dialect* : something given to make a trade equal [Old English *bōt* "remedy"] — **to boot** : ²BESIDES

²**boot** *n* **1** : a covering usually of leather or rubber for the foot and part of the leg **2 a** : ²KICK 1a **b** : a rude dismissal or discharge — used with *the* **3** : a new member of the Navy or Marine Corps while in boot camp [Middle English *boot* "a covering for the foot"]

³**boot** *vb* **1** : to put boots on **2 a** : ¹KICK 1 **b** : to get rid of or dismiss rudely — often used with *out* ⟨was *booted* out of the office⟩ **3 a** : to load (a program) into a computer from a disk **b** : to start or make ready for use especially by booting a program ⟨*boot* a computer⟩

boot·black \'büt-ˌblak\ *n* : a person who shines boots and shoes

boot camp *n* : a camp where recently enlisted members of the Navy or Marine Corps receive their basic training

boot·ee *or* **boot·ie** \'büt-ē\ *n* : an infant's knitted or crocheted sock

Bo·ö·tes \bō-'ōt-ēz\ *n* : a northern group of stars including the bright star Arcturus [Greek *Boōtēs,* literally, "plowman"]

booth \'büth\ *n, pl* **booths** \'büthz, 'büths\ **1** : a covered stand for selling or displaying goods (as at a fair or exhibition) or for providing services ⟨information *booth*⟩ **2** : a small enclosure giving privacy for one person ⟨voting *booth*⟩ ⟨telephone *booth*⟩ **3** : a section of a restaurant consisting of a table between two high-backed benches

boot·jack \'büt-ˌjak\ *n* : a device with a notch used to help pull off one's boots

¹**boot·leg** \-ˌleg\ *vb* **boot·legged; boot·leg·ging** **1** : to make, transport, or sell alcoholic liquor illegally **2 a** : to produce or sell illegally or without permission ⟨*bootlegged* recordings⟩ **b** : SMUGGLE 1 — **boot·leg·ger** *n*

²**bootleg** *n* : something bootlegged; *esp* : MOONSHINE 3 — **bootleg** *adj*

boot·less \'büt-ləs\ *adj* : USELESS, UNPROFITABLE

boo·ty \'büt-ē\ *n* **1** : money or goods taken in war or by robbery : SPOILS **2** : a rich gain or prize

booze \'büz\ *n* : alcoholic liquor

¹**bop** \'bäp\ *vb* **bopped; bop·ping** : ¹HIT 1, SOCK

²**bop** *n* : a blow (as from a fist or club) that strikes a person

bo·rate \'bō(ə)r-ˌāt, 'bȯ(ə)r-\ *n* : a chemical compound formed by the reaction of boric acid with another substance

bo·rax \'bō(ə)r-ˌaks, 'bȯ(ə)r-\ *n* : a borate of sodium that occurs as a mineral and is used in agricultural chemicals, as a cleansing agent, and as a water softener

¹**bor·der** \'bȯrd-ər\ *n* **1** : an outer part or edge **2** : a boundary especially of a country or state **3** : a narrow bed of plants along the edge of a garden or walk **4** : an ornamental design at the edge of a fabric or rug — **bor·dered** \-ərd\ *adj*

    synonyms BORDER, MARGIN, EDGE mean the outermost part of something. BORDER applies to an area on or just within a boundary line ⟨guards were placed along the *border*⟩. MARGIN suggests a border of exact width ⟨do not write in the *margin* of the page⟩. EDGE suggests a sharp line marking a fixed limit ⟨the *edge* of the table⟩.

²**border** *vb* **bor·dered; bor·der·ing** \'bȯrd-(ə-)riŋ\ **1** : to put a border on ⟨*border* the garden with flowers⟩ **2** : to be located close or next to ⟨the U.S. *borders* on Canada⟩ **3** : to come very close to being : VERGE ⟨that remark *borders* on the ridiculous⟩ — **bor·der·er** \-ər-ər\ *n*

bor·der·land \'bȯrd-ər-ˌland\ *n* **1** : territory at or near a border : FRONTIER **2** : an unclear condition or region separating two clearly different ones ⟨the *borderland* between sleeping and waking⟩

bor·der·line \-ˌlīn\ *adj* **1** : situated between two points or states **2** : not quite normal or acceptable

¹**bore** \'bō(ə)r, 'bȯ(ə)r\ *vb* **bored; bor·ing** **1** : to make a hole in especially with a drill **2** : to make (as a hole shaped like a cylinder) by boring or digging away material ⟨*bore* a well⟩ **3** : to move forward steadily especially by overcoming an opposing force ⟨the plane *bored* through the storm⟩ [Old English *borian* "to bore"]

²**bore** *n* **1** : a hole made by or as if by boring **2** : a cavity (as in a gun barrel) shaped like a cylinder **3** : the diameter of a hole or tube; *esp* : the interior diameter of a gun barrel

³**bore** *past of* BEAR

⁴**bore** *n* : a tidal flood with a high abrupt front [probably of Norse origin]

⁵**bore** *n* : an uninteresting person or thing [origin unknown]

\ə\ abut	\aù\ out	\i\ tip	\ȯ\ saw	\ù\ foot
\ər\ further	\ch\ chin	\ī\ life	\ȯi\ coin	\y\ yet
\a\ mat	\e\ pet	\j\ job	\th\ thin	\yü\ few
\ā\ take	\ē\ easy	\ŋ\ sing	\th\ this	\yù\ cure
\ä\ cot, cart	\g\ go	\ō\ bone	\ü\ food	\zh\ vision

⁶bore *vb* **bored; bor·ing** : to make weary and restless by being dull or monotonous

bo·re·al \'bō(ə)r-ē-əl, 'bȯ(ə)r-\ *adj* : of, relating to, or located or growing in northern or mountainous regions

bore·dom \'bō(ə)rd-əm, 'bȯ(ə)rd-\ *n* : the state of being bored

bor·er \'bōr-ər, 'bȯr-\ *n* **1** : one that bores; *esp* : a tool used for boring **2 a** : SHIPWORM **b** : an insect that bores in the woody parts of plants

bo·ric acid \,bōr-ik-, ,bȯr-\ *n* : a white boron-containing weak acid that is used as a mild antiseptic

bor·ing \'bō(ə)r-iŋ, 'bȯ(ə)r-\ *adj* : causing boredom : UN-INTERESTING, TEDIOUS — **bor·ing·ly** \-iŋ-lē\ *adv*

born \'bȯ(ə)rn\ *adj* **1 a** : brought into life by or as if by birth **b** : ¹NATIVE 2 ⟨American-*born*⟩ **2** : having from birth a certain ability or characteristic ⟨a *born* leader⟩ **3** : meant from or as if from birth ⟨*born* to rule⟩

borne *past participle of* BEAR

born·ite \'bȯ(ə)r-,nīt\ *n* : a brittle metallic-looking mineral consisting of a sulfide of copper and iron and making up a valuable ore of copper

bo·ron \'bō(ə)r-,än, 'bȯ(ə)r-\ *n* : a metalloid element found in nature only in combination (as in borax) — see ELEMENT table

bor·ough \'bər-ō\ *n* **1 a** : a town or urban area in Great Britain that sends a member to Parliament **b** : a self-governing urban area in Great Britain **2** : a self-governing town or village in some states **3** : one of the five political divisions of New York City

bor·row \'bär-ō, 'bȯr-\ *vb* **1** : to take or receive something with the promise or intention of returning it **2** : to take for one's own use something begun or thought up by another : ADOPT ⟨*borrow* an idea⟩ **3** : to take 1 from the digit in a minuend and add it as 10 to the digit in the next lower place — **bor·row·er** \'bär-ə-wər, 'bȯr-\ *n*

bor·row·ing \'bär-ə-wiŋ, 'bȯr-\ *n* : something borrowed; *esp* : a word or phrase adopted from one language into another

borscht *or* **borsch** \'bȯ(ə)rsh(t)\ *n* : a beet soup often served with sour cream [from Yiddish *borsht* and Ukrainian and Russian *borshch* "beet soup"]

bor·zoi \'bȯr-,zȯi\ *n* : any of a breed of large long-haired dogs developed in Russia especially for hunting wolves [from Russian *borzoĭ* "borzoi dog, swift"]

bos'n *or* **bosun** *variant of* BOATSWAIN

¹bos·om \'bùz-əm\ *n* **1** : the front of the human chest; *esp* : a woman's breasts **2** : the chest thought of as the center of secret thoughts and feelings **3** : a close and comforting relationship ⟨in the *bosom* of her family⟩ **4** : the part of a garment covering the breast — **bos·omed** \-əmd\ *adj*

²bosom *adj* : ²INTIMATE 3a, CLOSE ⟨*bosom* friends⟩

¹boss \'bȯs, 'bäs\ *n* : a raised rounded part often used ornamentally (as on a shield or a ceiling) : STUD [Middle English *boce* "raised rounded part," from early French *boce* (same meaning)]

²boss *vb* : to ornament with bosses : EMBOSS

³boss \'bȯs\ *n* **1** : the person (as an employer or supervisor) who tells workers what to do **2** : the head of a group; *esp* : a powerful politician who controls party business [from Dutch *baas* "master"] — **boss** *adj*

⁴boss \'bȯs\ *vb* **1** : to be in charge of ⟨*boss* a job⟩ **2** : to give orders to ⟨don't *boss* me around⟩

⁵boss \'bȯs\ *adj, slang* : EXCELLENT, FIRST-RATE

bossy \'bȯ-sē\ *adj* **boss·i·er; -est** : fond of ordering people around : DOMINEERING — **boss·i·ness** *n*

Bos·ton ivy \,bȯ-stən-\ *n* : a woody Asian vine that is related to the grape, has leaves with three lobes, and often grows over walls

Boston terrier *n* : any of a U.S. breed of small short-haired dogs having erect ears and a broad flat face — called also *Boston bull*

bot \'bät\ *n* : the larva of a botfly

¹bo·tan·i·cal \bə-'tan-i-kəl\ *adj* **1** : of or relating to plants or botany **2** : made or obtained from plants ⟨*botanical* drugs⟩ — **bo·tan·i·cal·ly** \-i-k(ə-)lē\ *adv*

Boston terrier

²botanical *n* : a usually cosmetic or medicinal product prepared from or containing a plant part or extract; *also* : the plant part or extract used in such a product

bot·a·nist \'bät-ᵊn-əst, 'bät-nəst\ *n* : a person who specializes in botany or in a branch of botany

bot·a·ny \'bät-ᵊn-e, 'bät-ne\ *n* **1** : a branch of biology dealing with plant life **2 a** : plant life (as of a given region) **b** : the biology of a plant or plant group

¹botch \'bäch\ *vb* : to make or do something in a clumsy or unskillful way : SPOIL, BUNGLE

²botch *n* : a botched job : MESS — **botchy** \-ē\ *adj*

bot·fly \'bät-,flī\ *n* : any of various stout two-winged flies whose larvae are parasitic in various mammals

¹both \'bōth\ *adj* : the two : the one and the other ⟨*both* feet⟩

²both *pron* : the one as well as the other ⟨*both* of us⟩ ⟨we are *both* well⟩

³both *conj* — used before two words or phrases connected with *and* to stress that each is included ⟨*both* New York and London⟩

¹both·er \'bäth-ər\ *vb* **both·ered; both·er·ing** \-(ə-)riŋ\ **1 a** : to upset often with minor details : ANNOY **b** : to intrude upon : INTERRUPT **2 a** : to cause to be worried or concerned **b** : to become concerned **3** : to take the trouble : make an effort ⟨don't *bother* to knock⟩

²bother *n* **1 a** : the state of being bothered **b** : someone or something that bothers in a small way ⟨what a *bother* a cold can be⟩ **2** : COMMOTION 2, FUSS

both·er·some \'bäth-ər-səm\ *adj* : causing bother : TROUBLESOME

¹bot·tle \'bät-ᵊl\ *n* **1 a** : a container (as of glass or plastic) with a narrow neck and mouth and usually no handle **b** : a bag made of skin used to hold a liquid **2** : the quantity held by a bottle **3** : a bottle with a rubber or plastic nipple for feeding an infant — **bot·tle·ful** \-,fùl\ *n*

²bottle *vb* **bot·tled; bot·tling** \'bät-liŋ, -ᵊl-iŋ\ **1** : to put into a bottle **2** : to shut up as if in a bottle : RESTRAIN ⟨*bottled* up their anger⟩ — **bot·tler** \-lər, -ᵊl-ər\ *n*

bottled gas *n* : gas under pressure in portable cylinders

bot·tle-feed \'bät-ᵊl-,fēd\ *vb* **-fed; -feed·ing** : to feed (as an infant) with a bottle

bot·tle·neck \'bät-ᵊl-,nek\ *n* **1** : a narrow passageway **2** : someone or something that holds up progress ⟨a traffic *bottleneck*⟩

bot·tle-nosed dolphin \,bät-ᵊl-,nōzd-\ *n* : BOTTLENOSE DOLPHIN

bot·tle·nose dolphin \,bät-ᵊl-,nōz-\ *n* : a medium-sized stout-bodied whale with teeth and a short snout

¹bot·tom \'bät-əm\ *n* **1 a** : the undersurface of something **b** : a supporting surface or part : BASE **c** : BUTTOCK 2a, RUMP **2** : the surface on which a body of water lies **3 a** : the part of a ship's hull lying below the water **b** : ¹BOAT 1, SHIP **4** : the lowest part, place, or point ⟨the *bottom* of the page⟩ **5** : the part of a garment worn on the lower part of the body; *esp* : the trousers of pajamas — usually used in plural **6** : lowland along a river ⟨the Mississippi River *bottoms*⟩ **7** : the most basic or central part : HEART ⟨get to the *bottom* of the problem⟩ **8** : the last half of an inning of baseball — **bot·tomed** \-əmd\ *adj* — **at bottom** : REALLY 1 ⟨no manners, but good-hearted *at bottom*⟩

²**bottom** vb **1** : to provide a foundation for **2** : to rest on, bring to, or reach the bottom

bottom dollar n : one's last dollar ⟨you can bet your *bottom dollar*⟩

bot·tom·land \'bät-əm-ˌland\ n : ¹BOTTOM 6

bot·tom·less \'bät-əm-ləs\ adj **1** : having no bottom **2** : very deep ⟨a *bottomless* pit⟩

bot·u·lism \'bäch-ə-ˌliz-əm\ n : poisoning caused by eating food containing a toxin made by a spore-forming bacterium

bou·clé or **bou·cle** \bü-'klā\ n **1** : an uneven yarn of three fibers one of which forms evenly spaced loops **2** : a fabric of bouclé yarn [from French *bouclé* "curly"]

bou·doir \'büd-ˌwär, 'bud-\ n : a woman's dressing room, bedroom, or private sitting room [from French *boudoir* "lady's dressing room," literally, "a place to sulk," from *bouder* "to sulk"]

bough \'bau\ n : a branch of a tree; esp : a main branch — **boughed** \'baud\ adj

bought past and past participle of BUY

bouil·la·baisse \ˌbü-yə-'bäs, 'bü-yə-ˌbäs\ n : a spicy stew made from a variety of fish and shellfish

bouil·lon \'bü(l)-ˌyän, 'bu(l)-yən\ n : a clear seasoned soup made usually from beef [from French *bouillon* "clear soup," derived from early French *boillir* "to boil," derived from Latin *bulla* "a bubble" — related to ²BOIL]

boul·der \'bōl-dər\ n : a large detached and rounded or worn mass of rock

bou·le·vard \'bul-ə-ˌvärd, 'bül-\ n : a wide avenue often having grass strips with trees along its center or sides [from French *boulevard* "walkway lined with trees," derived from early Dutch *bolwerc* "bulwark, rampart"; so called because the earliest boulevards were at sites of razed fortifications — related to BULWARK]

¹**bounce** \'baun(t)s\ vb **bounced; bounc·ing 1 a** : to cause to rebound ⟨*bounce* a ball⟩ **b** : to spring back or up after striking a surface **2** : to remove from a place by force **3** : to recover quickly from a blow or defeat ⟨*bounced* back after the loss⟩ **4** : to leap suddenly : BOUND **5** of a check : to be returned by a bank because of lack of funds in a checking account

²**bounce** n **1 a** : a sudden leap or bound **b** : a bouncing back : REBOUND **2** : ENTHUSIASM 1, SPIRIT — **bouncy** adj

bounc·er \'baun(t)-sər\ n : one that bounces; esp : someone employed in a public place to remove troublemakers

bounc·ing \'baun(t)-siŋ\ adj : HEALTHY 1a, LIVELY ⟨a *bouncing* baby⟩ — **bounc·ing·ly** \-siŋ-lē\ adv

¹**bound** \'baund\ adj : going or intending to go ⟨*bound* for home⟩ ⟨college-*bound*⟩ [Middle English *boun* "ready"; of Norse origin]

²**bound** n **1** : a boundary line **2** : a point or line beyond which one cannot go : LIMIT ⟨out of *bounds*⟩ **3** : the land within a boundary — usually used in plural [Middle English *bound* "boundary," from early French *bodne* (same meaning), from Latin *bodina* "boundary"]

³**bound** vb **1** : to set limits to : CONFINE **2 a** : to form the boundary of : ENCLOSE **b** : to lie next to **3** : to name the boundaries of

⁴**bound** past and past participle of BIND

⁵**bound** adj **1** : fastened by or as if by bands : CONFINED ⟨desk-*bound*⟩ **2** : required by law or duty **3** : having a binding ⟨*bound* notebook⟩ **4** : firmly determined ⟨we were *bound* we would succeed⟩ **5** : very likely to do something : CERTAIN, SURE **6** : always found in combination with another word or word part (as *un-* in *unknown* and *-er* in *speaker*) [Middle English *bounden* "fastened, tied," from *binden* "bind"]

⁶**bound** n **1** : a long easy leap **2** : ²BOUNCE 1b, REBOUND [from early French *bond* "a leap," from *bondir* "to leap"]

⁷**bound** vb **1** : to move by leaping **2** : ¹REBOUND 1, BOUNCE

bound·ary \'baun-d(ə-)rē\ n, pl **-aries** : something that points out or shows a limit or end : dividing line

bound·en \'baun-dən\ adj **1** archaic : INDEBTED **2** : required as if by law : NECESSARY ⟨our *bounden* duty⟩

bound·less \'baund-ləs\ adj : having no boundaries or limits : VAST ⟨the *boundless* sky⟩ — **bound·less·ly** adv — **bound·less·ness** n

boun·te·ous \'baunt-ē-əs\ adj **1** : giving freely or generously ⟨a *bounteous* host⟩ **2** : given in plenty ⟨*bounteous* gifts⟩ — **boun·te·ous·ly** adv — **boun·te·ous·ness** n

boun·ti·ful \'baunt-i-fəl\ adj **1** : GENEROUS 1 **2** : PLENTIFUL 2 ⟨a *bountiful* supply⟩ — **boun·ti·ful·ly** \-f(ə-)lē\ adv — **boun·ti·ful·ness** \-fəl-nəs\ n

boun·ty \'baunt-ē\ n, pl **bounties 1 a** : GENEROSITY 1 **b** : something given generously **2** : money given as a reward (as for killing a harmful animal or capturing a criminal) [Middle English *bounte* "goodness," from early French *bunté* (same meaning), derived from Latin *bonus* "good" — related to BONUS]

bou·quet \bō-'kā, bü-\ n **1** : a bunch of flowers **2** : FRAGRANCE, AROMA

¹**bour·geois** \'bu(ə)rzh-ˌwä, burzh-'wä\ adj **1** : of or relating to townspeople or members of the middle class **2** : marked by a concern for comfort, wealth, and what is respectable

²**bourgeois** n, pl **bour·geois** \-ˌwä(z), -'wä(z)\ : a person of the middle class of society [from early French *bourgeois* "a resident of a town," from earlier *burgeis* (same meaning), from *burc* "town," from Latin *burgus* "fortified place" — related to BURGESS]

bour·geoi·sie \ˌburzh-ˌwä-'zē\ n : the middle class of society

bourne also **bourn** \'bōrn, 'born, 'bu(ə)rn\ n **1** : BOUNDARY, LIMIT **2** : GOAL 2, DESTINATION

bour·rée \bu-'rā\ n : a lively 17th century French dance

bout \'baut\ n **1** : a spell of activity ⟨nonstop *bout* of reading⟩ **2** : an athletic match ⟨wrestling *bout*⟩ **3** : ²ATTACK 3 ⟨a *bout* of measles⟩

bou·tique \bü-'tēk\ n : a small fashionable store [from French *boutique* "shop"]

bou·ton·niere \ˌbüt-ᵊn-'i(ə)r, ˌbü-tən-'ye(ə)r\ n : a flower or bouquet worn in a buttonhole

¹**bo·vine** \'bō-ˌvīn, -ˌvēn\ adj **1** : of, relating to, or resembling the bovines and especially the ox or cow **2** : slow-moving or patient like an ox or cow

²**bovine** n : any of a group of ruminant mammals including the oxen, bison, and buffalo that have hollow horns and are related to the sheep and goats

¹**bow** \'bau\ vb **1** : to bend the head, body, or knee in greeting, respect, agreement, or obedience **2** : ¹YIELD 1 ⟨*bow* to authority⟩ **3** : ¹BEND 6 ⟨*bowed* with age⟩ **4** : to express by bowing ⟨*bow* one's thanks⟩ [Middle English *bowen* "to bend, yield," from Old English *būgan* "to bend in obedience"]

²**bow** n : a bending of the head or body expressing respect, agreement, obedience, or greeting

³**bow** \'bō\ n **1** : RAINBOW **2** : a weapon used for shooting arrows that is usually made of a strip of wood bent by a cord connecting the two ends **3** : something that is curved like a bow **4** : a wooden rod with horsehairs stretched from end to end used for playing a violin or similar instrument **5** : a knot made with two or more loops ⟨tie the ribbon in a *bow*⟩ [Middle English *bowe* "something curved," from Old English *boga* (same meaning)]

\ə\ **abut**	\au\ **out**	\i\ **tip**	\o\ **saw**	\u\ **foot**
\ər\ **further**	\ch\ **chin**	\ī\ **life**	\oi\ **coin**	\y\ **yet**
\a\ **mat**	\e\ **pet**	\j\ **job**	\th\ **thin**	\yü\ **few**
\ā\ **take**	\ē\ **easy**	\ŋ\ **sing**	\th\ **this**	\yu\ **cure**
\ä\ **cot, cart**	\g\ **go**	\ō\ **bone**	\ü\ **food**	\zh\ **vision**

[4]**bow** \'bō\ vb **1** : to bend into a curve **2** : to play a stringed instrument with a bow

[5]**bow** \'bau̇\ n : the forward part of a ship [Middle English bowe (same meaning), probably from early Dutch boech "bow, shoulder"]

bow·el \'bau̇(-ə)l\ n **1 a** : [2]INTESTINE, GUT — usually used in plural **b** : a division of the intestine **2** pl : the interior parts ⟨the bowels of the earth⟩ **3** archaic : supply of mercy or courage — usually used in plural

bowel movement n : an act of passing usually solid waste through the rectum and anus; also : fecal matter expelled at one passage : STOOL

bow·er \'bau̇(-ə)r\ n **1** : a safe and private place for rest **2** : a shelter in a garden made of tree boughs or vines twisted together — **bow·ery** \-ē\ adj

bow·er·bird \'bau̇(-ə)r-,bərd\ n : any of various birds of Australia and New Guinea of which the male builds a chamber or passage arched over with twigs and branches and often ornamented with bright-colored objects especially to attract the female

bowerbird

bow·ie knife \'bü-ē-, 'bō-ē-\ n : a large hunting knife with a single-edged blade [named for James Bowie]

[1]**bowl** \'bōl\ n **1** : a rounded dish generally deeper than a basin and larger than a cup **2** : the contents of a bowl **3** : the bowl-shaped part of something (as a spoon) **4 a** : a rounded valley or geographical region ⟨the dust bowl⟩ **b** : a bowl-shaped stadium or theater **5** : BOWL GAME [Old English bolla "bowl"] — **bowled** \'bōld\ adj

[2]**bowl** n **1 a** : a ball shaped to roll in a curved path for use in lawn bowling **b** pl : LAWN BOWLING **2** : a cast of the ball in bowling or bowls [Middle English boule "a weighted ball," from early French boule (same meaning), from Latin bulla "bubble" — related to [2]BOIL]

[3]**bowl** vb **1** : to roll a ball in bowling or bowls **2** : to move smoothly and rapidly

bow·leg·ged \'bō-'leg(-ə)d\ adj : having legs that bow outward at or below the knee

[1]**bowl·er** \'bō-lər\ n : a person who bowls

[2]**bow·ler** \'bō-lər\ n : DERBY 3

bowl game n : a football game played after the regular season between specially invited teams

bow·line \'bō-lən, -,līn\ n **1** : a rope used to keep the edge of a sail pulled forward **2** : a knot used for making a loop that will not slip or get stuck

bowl·ing \'bō-liŋ\ n **1** : a game played by rolling balls so as to knock down pins set up at the far end of an alley **2** : LAWN BOWLING

bowl over vb **1** : to hit and knock down while quickly moving past **2** : to greatly surprise or impress

bow·man \'bō-mən\ n : ARCHER

bow·sprit \'bau̇-,sprit\ n : a large pole for sails sticking out from the bow of a ship

bow·string \'bō-,striŋ\ n : the cord connecting the two ends of a bow

bow tie n : a short necktie tied in a bow

bow window \'bō-\ n : a usually curved window that sticks out from the side of a building

[1]**box** \'bäks\ n, pl **box** or **box·es** : an evergreen shrub or small tree used especially for hedges [Old-English box "box (shrub)," from Latin buxus (same meaning), from Greek pyxos "box tree"]

[2]**box** n **1 a** : a container usually having four sides, a bottom, and a cover **b** : the amount held by a box ⟨ate a whole box of popcorn⟩ **2** : a small compartment for a group of spectators in a theater **3** : the driver's seat on a carriage **4** : a shed that protects **5** : a container (as for a car transmission) that resembles a box **6** : a rectangle which encloses and draws attention to something printed **7** : a space on a baseball diamond where a batter, coach, pitcher, or catcher stands **8** : the limits of ordinariness ⟨thinking outside the box⟩ [Old English box "container," from Latin buxis (same meaning), from Greek pyxis, literally, "a container made from boxwood"]

[3]**box** vb : to enclose in or as if in a box

[4]**box** n : a punch or slap especially on the ear [Middle English box "a blow or slap on the ear"]

[5]**box** vb **1** : to strike with the hand **2** : to engage in boxing : fight with the fists

box camera n : a camera of simple box shape with a simple lens and shutter

box·car \'bäk-,skär\ n : a roofed freight car usually with sliding doors in the sides

box cutter n : a small cutting tool used especially for opening cardboard boxes

box elder n : a North American maple with compound leaves

[1]**box·er** \'bäk-sər\ n : one that engages in the sport of boxing

[2]**boxer** n : any of a German breed of medium-sized dogs with a smooth coat and a short square face

boxer shorts n pl : men's or boys' underwear shorts characterized by loose fit

box·ing \'bäk-siŋ\ n : the sport of fighting with the fists

Box·ing Day \'bäk-siŋ-\ n : the first weekday after Christmas observed as a legal holiday in parts of the Commonwealth of Nations and celebrated by the giving of Christmas gifts in boxes (as to postal workers)

boxing glove n : one of a pair of padded leather mittens worn in boxing

box office n : an office in a public place (as a theater or stadium) where admission tickets are sold

box score n : a printed table giving the score of a game (as baseball), a record of how it was played, and the names and positions of the players

box seat n : a seat in a box of a theater or stadium

box stall n : a four-sided enclosure within a barn or stable in which an animal can move around freely

box turtle n : any of several North American land turtles able to withdraw completely into the shell and to close it by hinged joints in the lower shell

box turtle

box·wood \'bäk-,swu̇d\ n : the tough hard wood of the box; also : the box tree

boy \'bȯi\ n **1** : a male child from birth to young manhood **2** : SON 1a — **boy·hood** \-,hu̇d\ n — **boy·ish** \-ish\ adj — **boy·ish·ly** adv — **boy·ish·ness** n

[1]**boy·cott** \'bȯi-,kät\ vb : to join with others in refusing to deal with a person, organization, or country usually to express disapproval or to force acceptance of terms

Word History In the autumn of 1880 there was much unrest in the Irish countryside as the result of a depression. Many farmers who did not own the land they worked were unable to pay their rent. A Land League was formed to fight eviction of tenants, and the first victim of their campaign was one Charles S. Boycott, a retired English army captain who worked as an agent for an absentee landlord in County Mayo. When this landlord's tenants refused to pay their rents unless they received a reduction, Boycott attempted to serve eviction notices. As a result, he was shunned by the community, his laborers and servants quit, and the crops on his own farm began to rot. Fifty volunteers from northern Ireland were sent to Mayo to harvest his crops, guarded by hundreds of troops and police. The new tactic of shunning a person to assert a grievance needed a name, and Boycott's name was at hand. Though the British government banned the Irish Land League, the word *boycott* is still part of English. [named for Charles *Boycott* 1832–1897 estate manager in Ireland]

²**boycott** *n* : the process or an instance of boycotting

boy·friend \'bòi-ˌfrend\ *n* **1** : a male friend **2** : a frequent or regular male companion in a romantic relationship

Boy Scout *n* **1** : a member of any of various national scouting programs (as Boy Scouts of América) for boys usually 11 to 17 years of age **2** : a person whose values or actions are characteristic of a Boy Scout

boy·sen·ber·ry \'bóiz-ᵊn-ˌber-ē, 'bóis-\ *n* **1** : a large berry like a blackberry with the flavor of a raspberry **2** : the trailing bramble that produces boysenberries and was developed by crossing blackberry and raspberry plants

bra \'brä\ *n* : BRASSIERE

¹**brace** \'brās\ *vb* **braced; brac·ing** **1 a** : to make firm or tight **b** : to get ready : PREPARE ⟨*braced* herself for the test⟩ **2** : to furnish or support with a brace **3** : to give life or energy to : FRESHEN **4** : to place firmly **5** : to regain one's courage ⟨*brace* up, all is not lost⟩ [Middle English *bracen* "to fasten, bind," from early French *bracer* "to embrace," from *brace* "pair of arms," derived from Latin *bracchium* "arm" — related to BRACELET, BRASSIERE, EMBRACE; see *Word History* at EMBRACE]

²**brace** *n, pl* **brac·es** *or* **brace** **1** : two of a kind : PAIR ⟨several *brace* of quail⟩ **2** : something that connects, fastens, or tightens **3** : a tool with a U-shaped bend that is used to turn wood-boring bits **4 a** : something that transfers, resists, or supports weight or pressure; *esp* : a slanted timber used as a support in a structure **b** *pl* : SUSPENDER **2 c** : a device for supporting a body part (as the shoulders) **d** *pl* : a usually wire device attached to the teeth to make them straight and pull them into position **5 a** : a mark { or } used to connect words or items or musical staffs that are to be considered together **b** : one of a pair of such marks enclosing words or symbols [Middle English *brace* "pair, clasp," from early French *brace* "pair of arms," derived from Latin *bracchium* "arm" — related to PRETZEL; see *Word History* at PRETZEL]

brace·let \'brā-slət\ *n* **1** : an ornamental band or chain worn around the wrist **2** : something (as handcuffs) resembling a bracelet [Middle English *bracelet* "band for the arm," from early French *bracelet*, literally, "little arm," from *bras* "arm," derived from Latin *bracchium* "arm" — related to BRACE, BRASSIERE]

bra·chio·pod \'brā-kē-ə-ˌpäd\ *n* : any of a phylum of invertebrate marine animals that have bivalve shells and a pair of arms bearing tentacles — called also *lampshell* — **brachiopod** *adj*

brack·en \'brak-ən\ *n* : a large coarse branching fern; *also* : a growth of such ferns

¹**brack·et** \'brak-ət\ *n* **1** : a support for a shelf or other weight usually attached to a wall **2** : a short wall shelf **3 a** : one of a pair of marks [ ] used to enclose words or mathematical symbols to be taken together — called also *square bracket* **b** : one of a pair of marks ⟨ ⟩ — used to enclose written or printed matter; called also *angle bracket* **4** : ¹CLASS 3a, GROUP; *esp* : one of a series of groups sorted according to income **5** : a pairing of opponents in an elimination tournament

²**bracket** *vb* **1** : to place within or as if within brackets **2** : to put into the same class : ASSOCIATE

bracket fungus *n* : a fungus that forms shelflike fruiting bodies

brack·ish \'brak-ish\ *adj* : somewhat salty ⟨*brackish* water⟩

bract \'brakt\ *n* : a small leaf or leaflike structure at the base of a flower or flower cluster

brad \'brad\ *n* : a thin nail with a small cylindrical head

¹**brag** \'brag\ *n* **1** : a boastful statement **2** : overly proud talk or manner **3** : BRAGGART

²**brag** *vb* **bragged; brag·ging** : to praise oneself or one's possessions or achievements   **synonyms** *see* BOAST — **brag·ger** \'brag-ər\ *n*

brag·ga·do·cio \ˌbrag-ə-'dō-shē-ˌō, -sē-ˌō, -shō\ *n, pl* **-cios** **1** : BRAGGART **2** : loud and empty boasting [from *Braggadochio*, a boasting character in literature]

brag·gart \'brag-ərt\ *n* : a person who brags a lot — **braggart** *adj*

Brah·man *or* **Brah·min** *n* **1** \'bräm-ən\ : a member of the highest priestly class of Hindu society **2** \'brām-ən, 'bräm-ən, 'bram-ən\ : a large silvery gray ox that is resistant to heat and was developed in the U.S. from the zebu

¹**braid** \'brād\ *vb* **1** : to form strands into a braid **2** : to ornament especially with ribbon or braid — **braid·er** *n*

²**braid** *n* : a length of cord, ribbon, or hair formed of three or more strands woven together

braille \'brā(ə)l\ *n, often cap* : a system of writing for the blind in which letters are represented by raised dots [named for Louis *Braille* who developed the system]

a	b	c	d	e	f	g	h	i	j
1	2	3	4	5	6	7	8	9	0

k	l	m	n	o	p	q	r	s	t

u	v	w	x	y	z	Capital Sign	Numeral Sign

braille alphabet

¹**brain** \'brān\ *n* **1 a** : the portion of the central nervous system of vertebrate animals that is the organ of thought and the central control point for the nervous system, is enclosed within the skull, and is continuous with the spinal cord **b** : the main nervous center in an invertebrate animal **2 a** : INTELLIGENCE 1 — often used in plural ⟨plenty of *brains* in that family⟩ **b** : a very intelligent person — **brain·like** *adj*

²**brain** *vb* **1** : to kill by smashing the skull **2** : to hit on the head

brain·case \'brān-ˌkās\ *n* : the cranium enclosing the brain

brain death *n* : the final stopping of activity in the central nervous system as indicated by an electroencephalogram showing no brain waves for a set length of time that is

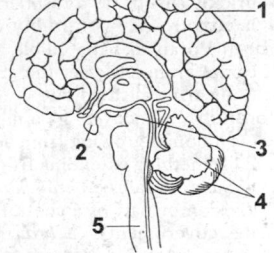

¹brain 1a: *1* cerebrum, *2* pituitary gland, *3* midbrain, *4* cerebellum, *5* spinal cord

\ə\ **abut**	\au̇\ **out**	\i\ **tip**	\ò\ **saw**	\u̇\ **foot**
\ər\ **further**	\ch\ **chin**	\ī\ **life**	\òi\ **coin**	\y\ **yet**
\a\ **mat**	\e\ **pet**	\j\ **job**	\th\ **thin**	\yü\ **few**
\ā\ **take**	\ē\ **easy**	\ŋ\ **sing**	\t͟h\ **this**	\yu̇\ **cure**
\ä\ **cot, cart**	\g\ **go**	\ō\ **bone**	\ü\ **food**	\zh\ **vision**

often used as a criterion for human death — **brain–dead** \'brān-,ded\ *adj*

brain freeze *n* : a sudden sharp pain in the head caused by eating or drinking something very cold

brain·less \'brān-ləs\ *adj* : lacking intelligence — **brain·less·ly** *adv*

brain stem *n* : the back and lower part of the brain including the midbrain and medulla oblongata

brain·storm \'brān-,stȯ(ə)rm\ *n* : a sudden inspiration or idea

brain·storm·ing \-stȯrm-iŋ\ *n* : a technique used to solve problems and encourage creativity in which members of a group share their ideas about a subject — **brain·storm** *vb*

brain·teas·er \-,tē-zər\ *n* : something demanding mental effort for its solution : PUZZLE

brain·wash \-,wȯsh, -,wäsh\ *vb* 1 : to try to change someone's ideas by force ⟨terrorists *brainwashed* the prisoners⟩ 2 : to try to influence someone's habits through sly persuading ⟨advertising that *brainwashes* children⟩

brain wave *n* : rhythmic changes in voltage between parts of the brain

brainy \'brā-nē\ *adj* **brain·i·er; -est** : INTELLIGENT 1b — **brain·i·ness** *n*

braise \'brāz\ *vb* **braised; brais·ing** : to cook slowly in fat and little moisture in a covered pot

¹**brake** \'brāk\ *n* : a common bracken fern

²**brake** *n* : a device for slowing or stopping motion (as of a wheel, vehicle, or engine) especially by friction

³**brake** *vb* **braked; brak·ing** 1 : to slow or stop by or as if by a brake 2 : to use or operate the brake on a vehicle

⁴**brake** *n* : rough or marshy overgrown land : THICKET

¹brake

brake·man \'brāk-mən\ *n* : a member of a train crew who inspects the train and assists the conductor

bram·ble \'bram-bəl\ *n* : any of a large genus of usually prickly shrubs (as a raspberry or blackberry) that are related to roses — **bram·bly** \-b(ə-)lē\ *adj*

bran \'bran\ *n* : the edible broken coat of the seed of a cereal grain left after the grain has been ground and the flour or meal sifted out

¹**branch** \'branch\ *n* 1 : a natural division of a plant stem (as a bough growing from a trunk or twig from a bough) 2 : something extending from a main line or source ⟨river *branch*⟩ ⟨a railroad *branch*⟩ 3 : a separate or subordinate division or part of a central system ⟨executive *branch* of the government⟩ ⟨a *branch* of a bank⟩ — **branched** \'brancht\ *adj* — **branch·less** \'branch-ləs\ *adj*

²**branch** *vb* 1 : to send out branches : spread or separate into branches ⟨a great elm *branches* over the yard⟩ 2 : to spring out from a main body or line : DIVERGE ⟨streets *branching* off the highway⟩ 3 : to extend activities ⟨the business is *branching* out all over the state⟩

¹**brand** \'brand\ *n* 1 : a burnt or burning piece of wood 2 **a** : a mark made by burning (as on cattle) to show ownership, maker, or quality **b** : a printed mark made for similar purposes : TRADEMARK 3 **a** : a mark once put on criminals with a hot iron **b** : a mark of disgrace : STIGMA 4 **a** : a class of goods identified as the product of a single maker **b** : a particular kind : VARIETY

²**brand** *vb* 1 : to mark with or as if with a brand 2 : to describe or identify with a word that expresses disapproval ⟨was *branded* a coward⟩

bran·dish \'bran-dish\ *vb* 1 : to shake or wave in a threatening manner ⟨*brandish* a stick at a dog⟩ 2 : to exhibit in a showy or aggressive manner

brand–new \'bran-'n(y)ü\ *adj* : completely new and unused

bran·dy \'bran-dē\ *n, pl* **brandies** : an alcoholic liquor made from wine or fruit juice

brash \'brash\ *adj* 1 : RECKLESS, RASH ⟨a *brash* attack⟩ 2 : rudely bold : IMPUDENT ⟨a *brash* youth⟩ 3 : marked by vivid contrast ⟨*brash* colors⟩ — **brash·ly** *adv* — **brash·ness** *n*

brass \'bras\ *n* 1 : an alloy containing copper and zinc 2 : the reddish yellow color of brass 3 : the brass instruments of a band or orchestra — often used in plural 4 : bright metal ornaments, fixtures, or utensils 5 : bold self-assurance : GALL 6 : high-ranking officers especially in the armed forces — **brass** *adj*

brass band *n* : a band made up of brass and percussion instruments

bras·siere \brə-'zi(ə)r\ *also* ,bras-ē-'e(ə)r\ *n* : a woman's close-fitting undergarment to cover and support the breasts [from obsolete French *brassière* "bodice," from early French *braciere* "arm protector," from *bras* "arm," from Latin *bracchium* (same meaning) — related to BRACE, BRACELET]

brass instrument *n* : any of a group of musical instruments made of curved tubes of brass in various shapes that includes trumpets, trombones, tubas, and French horns — compare PERCUSSION INSTRUMENT, STRINGED INSTRUMENT, WOODWIND 1

brassy \'bras-ē\ *adj* **brass·i·er; -est** 1 **a** : shamelessly bold **b** : UNRULY 2 : resembling brass especially in color 3 : resembling the sound of a brass instrument — **brass·i·ly** \'bras-ə-lē\ *adv* — **brass·i·ness** \'bras-ē-nəs\ *n*

brat \'brat\ *n* : CHILD 2a; *esp* : an ill-mannered annoying child — **brat·tish** \'brat-ish\ *adj* — **brat·ty** \'brat-ē\ *adj*

bra·va·do \brə-'väd-ō\ *n, pl* **-does** *or* **-dos** : a display of reckless or pretended bravery

¹**brave** \'brāv\ *adj* 1 : feeling or displaying no fear : COURAGEOUS 2 : making a fine show : SPLENDID ⟨*brave* banners flying in the wind⟩ — **brave·ly** *adv*

²**brave** *vb* **braved; brav·ing** : to face or bear with courage ⟨pioneers who *braved* the dangers of the frontier⟩

³**brave** *n* : one who is brave; *esp* : a North American Indian warrior

brav·ery \'brāv-(ə-)rē\ *n, pl* **-er·ies** 1 : the quality or state of being brave : FEARLESSNESS 2 **a** : fine clothes **b** : impressive or showy display **synonyms** see COURAGE

¹**bra·vo** \'bräv-ō\ *n, pl* **bravos** *or* **bravoes** : VILLAIN 2, DESPERADO; *esp* : a hired assassin

²**bra·vo** \'bräv-ō, brä-'vō\ *n, pl* **bravos** : a shout of approval — often used to applaud a performance

brawl \'brȯl\ *vb* 1 : to quarrel noisily : WRANGLE 2 : to make a loud confused noise — **brawl** *n* — **brawl·er** *n*

brawn \'brȯn\ *n* 1 : full strong muscles 2 : muscular strength 3 *British* : the meat of a boar — **brawn·i·ness** \'brȯ-nē-nəs\ *n* — **brawny** \'brȯ-nē\ *adj*

bray \'brā\ *vb* 1 : to utter the loud harsh cry of a donkey 2 : to produce a sound like the call of a donkey — **bray** *n*

braze \'brāz\ *vb* **brazed; braz·ing** : to join metals with an alloy that melts at a lower temperature than that of the metals joined

¹**bra·zen** \'brāz-ᵊn\ *adj* 1 : made of brass 2 : sounding harsh and loud like struck brass 3 : not ashamed of or embarrassed by one's bad behavior : IMPUDENT 4 : of the color of polished brass — **bra·zen·ly** *adv* — **bra·zen·ness** \'brāz-ᵊn-(n)əs\ *n*

²**brazen** *vb* **bra·zened; bra·zen·ing** \'brāz-niŋ, -ᵊn-iŋ\ : to face boldly or defiantly ⟨an enemy who'd rather *brazen* it out than surrender⟩

bra·zier \'brā-zhər\ *n* **1** : a pan for holding burning coals **2** : a utensil on which food is grilled

Bra·zil nut \brə-,zil-\ *n* : a. large 3-sided oily edible nut that occurs packed inside the round fruit of a tall tree of tropical South America

Brazil nut

¹**breach** \'brēch\ *n* **1** : violation of a law, duty, or tie ⟨a *breach* of trust⟩ **2 a** : a broken or torn condition or area **b** : a gap (as in a wall) made by breaking through **3** : a break in friendly relations **4** : a leap especially of a whale out of water

²**breach** *vb* **1** : to make a breach in **2** : ¹BREAK 2, VIOLATE ⟨*breach* an agreement⟩ **3** : to leap out of water

¹**bread** \'bred\ *n* **1** : a baked food made of flour or meal **2** : FOOD 1 **3** *slang* : MONEY 1a

²**bread** *vb* : to cover with bread crumbs ⟨*breaded* pork chops⟩

bread–and–butter \,bred-ᵊn-'bət-ər\ *adj* **1 a** : concerned with or being as basic as earning a living ⟨*bread-and-butter* economic issues⟩ **b** : DEPENDABLE ⟨*bread-and-butter* products that always sell⟩ **2** : sent or given as thanks for hospitality ⟨a *bread-and-butter* note⟩

bread·bas·ket \'bred-,bas-kət\ *n* **1** : a major cereal-producing region **2** *slang* : ¹STOMACH 1

bread·fruit \-,früt\ *n* : a round usually seedless fruit that resembles bread in color and texture when baked; *also* : a tall tropical tree that is related to the mulberries and bears this fruit

bread·line \-,līn\ *n* : a line of people waiting to receive free food

bread·stuff \-,stəf\ *n* **1** : a cereal product (as grain or flour) **2** : ¹BREAD 1

breadth \'bredth, 'bretth, 'breth\ *n* **1** : distance from side to side : WIDTH **2 a** : something of full width **b** : a wide area **3** : ¹SCOPE 2 ⟨*breadth* of knowledge⟩

bread·win·ner \'bred-,win-ər\ *n* : a person whose wages provide support for his or her family

¹**break** \'brāk\ *vb* **broke** \'brōk\; **bro·ken** \'brō-kən\; **break·ing 1 a** : to separate into parts suddenly or forcibly ⟨*break* a stick⟩ ⟨glass *breaks* easily⟩ ⟨*break* a bone⟩ **b** : to fracture a bone of ⟨*broke* her arm⟩ **c** : to curl over and fall apart ⟨waves *breaking* against the shore⟩ **2** : to fail to keep : VIOLATE ⟨*broke* the law⟩ ⟨*break* a promise⟩ **3 a** : to force a way ⟨burglars *broke* into the house⟩ ⟨*break* out of jail⟩ **b** : to appear or burst forth suddenly ⟨day was *breaking* in the east⟩ ⟨the storm *broke*⟩ ⟨pandemonium *broke* loose⟩ **c** : to become fair ⟨wait for the weather to *break*⟩ **d** : to run suddenly ⟨*break* for cover⟩ **e** : to penetrate the surface of ⟨fish *breaking* water⟩ **4** : to cut into and turn over the surface of ⟨*break* ground for a new school⟩ **5 a** : to defeat completely : CRUSH ⟨*broke* the revolt⟩ **b** : to lose or cause to lose health, strength, or spirit ⟨*broke* under the strain⟩ ⟨*broken* by grief⟩ **c** : to lose or cause to lose the ability to function because of damage, wear, or strain ⟨the TV set is *broken*⟩ ⟨I *broke* my watch⟩ **6** : to reduce in rank **7 a** : to bring to an end : STOP ⟨*break* a habit⟩ ⟨*broke* silence⟩ **b** : to have or cause an interruption ⟨we'll *break* to let local stations identify themselves⟩ ⟨*broke* in with a comment⟩ **8** : to train an animal ⟨*break* a horse to the saddle⟩ **9** : to make known ⟨*break* the news⟩ **10** : to turn aside or lessen the force of ⟨the bushes *broke* his fall⟩ **11** : to do better than ⟨*broke* the school record⟩ **12** : ²OPEN 1a ⟨*break* an electric circuit⟩ ⟨*broke* the shotgun to load it⟩ **13** : SOLVE ⟨*broke* the code⟩ **14 a** : to curve, drop, or change direction sharply ⟨the pitch *broke* over the plate for a strike⟩

b : to change sharply in tone, pitch, or intensity ⟨her voice *broke*⟩ — **break·able** \'brā-kə-bəl\ *adj* — **break camp** : to pack up and leave a camp or campsite — **break even** : to reach a point (as in running a business) where profits match losses — **break into 1** : to begin suddenly ⟨*broke into* a trot⟩ **2** : to get a start ⟨*break into* show business⟩ — **break the ice** : to make a beginning especially in friendly relations — **break wind** : to expel gas from the intestine

²**break** *n* **1** : an act, action, or result of breaking **2** : a gap in an electric circuit interrupting the flow of current **3 a** : a short rest from or an interruption of work, duty, or studies **b** : a planned interruption in a radio or television program **c** : a noticeable change (as in a surface, course, movement, or direction) **d** : a sudden run : DASH **4** : a place or situation at which a break occurs : GAP **5** : a stroke of luck ⟨a bad *break*⟩; *esp* : a stroke of good luck ⟨got all the *breaks*⟩ **6 a** : a favorable situation ⟨a big *break* in show business⟩ **b** : favorable treatment ⟨a tax *break*⟩

break·age \'brā-kij\ *n* **1 a** : the action of breaking **b** : a quantity broken **2** : an allowance for things broken

break·down \'brāk-,daún\ *n* **1 a** : a failure to function properly **b** : a physical, mental, or nervous collapse **2** : DECOMPOSITION **3** : division into categories : CLASSIFICATION

break down \'brāk-'daún\ *vb* **1** : to stop working properly ⟨the car *broke down* on the highway⟩ **2 a** : to separate (as a chemical compound) into simpler substances : DECOMPOSE **b** : to go through decomposition **3** : to separate or become separated into parts or groups ⟨this report *breaks down* into three sections⟩ **4 a** : to become overwhelmed by strong emotion ⟨*broke down* and cried⟩ **b** : to lose the strength to resist or fight ⟨*broke down* and confessed⟩ **5** : to use force to push (something) to the ground ⟨*break down* a door⟩

break·er \'brā-kər\ *n* **1** : a person or thing that breaks something **2** : a wave breaking into foam against the shore

break·fast \'brek-fəst\ *n* : the first meal of the day — **breakfast** *vb*

break–in \'brā-,kin\ *n* : an act or instance of breaking in

break in \(')brā-'kin\ *vb* **1** : to enter a house or building by force **2 a** : to make used to an activity ⟨*breaking in* a new employee⟩ **b** : to overcome the newness or stiffness of ⟨*breaking in* a new pair of shoes⟩

break·neck \,brāk-,nek\ *adj* : very fast or dangerous ⟨*breakneck* speed⟩

break off *vb* : to stop suddenly

break out *vb* **1** : to develop or erupt suddenly and with force ⟨fire *broke out*⟩ ⟨a riot *broke out*⟩ **2** : to develop a skin rash ⟨*broke out* in hives⟩

break·through \'brāk-,thrü\ *n* : a sudden advance in knowledge or technique ⟨a *breakthrough* in medical science⟩

break·up \'brā-,kəp\ *n* : an act or an instance of breaking up

break up \(')brā-'kəp\ *vb* **1** : to separate into parts ⟨enzymes help *break up* protein molecules⟩ **2** : to bring or come to an end ⟨the police *broke up* the demonstration⟩ ⟨the party began to *break up*⟩ **3** : to end a romance ⟨they dated for a while but *broke up*⟩ **4** : to go or cause to go into a fit of laughter ⟨that joke always *breaks* me *up*⟩

break·wa·ter \'brāk-,wòt-ər, -,wät-\ *n* : an offshore structure (as a wall) to protect a harbor or beach from the force of waves

\ə\ **abut**	\aú\ **out**	\i\ **tip**	\ò\ **saw**	\ú\ **foot**
\ər\ **further**	\ch\ **chin**	\ī\ **life**	\òi\ **coin**	\y\ **yet**
\a\ **mat**	\e\ **pet**	\j\ **job**	\th\ **thin**	\yü\ **few**
\ā\ **take**	\ē\ **easy**	\ŋ\ **sing**	\th\ **this**	\yú\ **cure**
\ä\ **cot, cart**	\g\ **go**	\ō\ **bone**	\ü\ **food**	\zh\ **vision**

bream \'brim, 'brēm\ *n, pl* **bream** *or* **breams** **1** : any of various freshwater fishes; *esp* : any of several sunfishes (as a bluegill) **2** : any of several saltwater fishes related to the porgy

¹breast \'brest\ *n* **1** : either of two milk-producing glands extending from the front of the chest in the human female and some other mammals; *also* : MAMMARY GLAND **2** : the front part of the body between the neck and the abdomen **3** : the center of emotion **4** : something resembling a breast — **breast·ed** \'bres-təd\ *adj*

²breast *vb* : to face or oppose bravely : CONFRONT ⟨*breast*-ed the waves⟩ ⟨*breast* a storm⟩

breast·bone \'bres(t)-ˌbōn, -ˌbōn\ *n* : STERNUM

breast–feed \'brest-ˌfēd\ *vb* **-fed** \-ˌfed\; **-feed·ing** : to feed a baby from a mother's breast

breast·plate \'bres(t)-ˌplāt\ *n* : metal armor for covering the breast

breast·stroke \'bres(t)-ˌstrōk\ *n* : a swimming stroke performed by extending the arms in front of the head while drawing the knees forward and outward and then sweeping the arms back with palms out while kicking backward and outward

breast·work \'brest-ˌwərk\ *n* : a wall thrown together to serve as a defense in battle

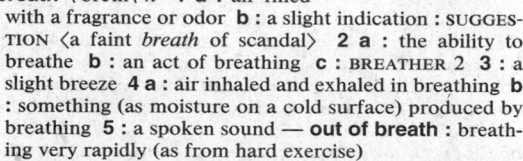
breastplate

breath \'breth\ *n* **1 a** : air filled with a fragrance or odor **b** : a slight indication : SUGGESTION ⟨a faint *breath* of scandal⟩ **2 a** : the ability to breathe **b** : an act of breathing **c** : BREATHER 2 **3** : a slight breeze **4 a** : air inhaled and exhaled in breathing **b** : something (as moisture on a cold surface) produced by breathing **5** : a spoken sound — **out of breath** : breathing very rapidly (as from hard exercise)

breathe \'brēth\ *vb* **breathed; breath·ing** **1** : to draw air into and expel it from the lungs **2** : ¹LIVE 1 **3** : to blow softly **4** : to send out by exhaling ⟨*breathe* a sigh of relief⟩ **5** : to bring by or as if by breathing ⟨*breathe* new life into the movement⟩ **6** : to say quietly or softly ⟨don't *breathe* a word to anybody⟩ **7** : to allow to rest after hard work ⟨*breathe* a horse⟩ **8** : to take in in breathing ⟨*breathe* the scent of roses⟩ **9** : to allow air or moisture to pass through ⟨a fabric that *breathes*⟩ — **breath·able** \'brē-thə-bəl\ *adj*

breath·er \'brē-thər\ *n* **1** : one that breathes **2** : a pause for rest : BREAK

breathing tube *n* **1** : a trachea or bronchial tube of an air-breathing vertebrate **2** : TRACHEA 2 **3** : a usually small plastic tube inserted into the trachea through the mouth or nose to maintain an unobstructed passageway especially to deliver oxygen or anesthesia to the lungs

breath·less \'breth-ləs\ *adj* **1 a** : not breathing **b** : ¹DEAD 1 **2 a** : panting or gasping for breath **b** : BREATHTAKING 1 **3** : difficult to bear because of lack of fresh air or breeze ⟨a hot *breathless* day⟩ — **breath·less·ly** *adv* — **breath·less·ness** *n*

breath·tak·ing \'breth-ˌtā-kiŋ\ *adj* **1** : making one out of breath ⟨*breathtaking* speed⟩ **2** : EXCITING, THRILLING ⟨*breathtaking* beauty⟩ — **breath·tak·ing·ly** \-kiŋ-lē\ *adv*

brec·cia \'brech-(ē-)ə\ *n* : a rock composed of sharp pieces surrounded by a fine-grained material

¹breech \'brēch\ *n* **1** *pl* \'brich-əz *also* 'brē-chəz\ **a** : short trousers fitting snugly at or just below the knee **b** : PANTS 1 **2** : BUTTOCK 2a **3** : the part of a gun at the rear of the barrel

²breech *adj* : involving or being a fetus in which the buttocks or legs rather than the head are situated to emerge first through the birth canal ⟨a *breech* delivery⟩ — **breech** *adv*

breech·cloth \-ˌklôth\ *n* : LOINCLOTH

breech·clout \'brēch-ˌklau̇t\ *n* : LOINCLOTH [from *breech* and *clout* "cloth"]

¹breed \'brēd\ *vb* **bred** \'bred\; **breed·ing** **1** : to produce (plants or animals) by sexual reproduction ⟨*breed* cattle⟩ **2** : to produce offspring by sexual reproduction **3** : BRING UP 1, TRAIN ⟨born and *bred* in this town⟩ **4** : BRING ABOUT, CAUSE ⟨familiarity *breeds* contempt⟩ **5** : to produce (a fissionable element) by bombarding an element that is not fissionable with neutrons from a radioactive element so that more fissionable material is produced than is used up — **breed·er** *n*

²breed *n* **1** : a group of animals or plants usually found only under human care and different from related kinds ⟨a *breed* of cattle⟩ **2** : KIND, CLASS

breed·ing *n* **1** : ANCESTRY 1 **2** : training especially in manners **3** : the producing and raising of plants or animals by sexual reproduction

breeding ground *n* **1** : the place where animals go to breed **2** : a place or situation that helps or allows something to grow or develop ⟨an expanse of warm ocean that is a *breeding ground* for hurricanes⟩

¹breeze \'brēz\ *n* **1** : a gentle wind **2** : something easy to do ⟨the test was a *breeze*⟩

²breeze *vb* **breezed; breez·ing** **1** : to move quickly and lightly ⟨look who just *breezed* in⟩ **2** : to proceed easily ⟨*breezed* through the test⟩

breeze·way \'brēz-ˌwā\ *n* : an open passage connecting two buildings (as a house and garage)

breezy \'brē-zē\ *adj* **breez·i·er; -est** **1** : somewhat windy **2** : lively and somewhat carefree — **breez·i·ly** \-zə-lē\ *adv* — **breez·i·ness** \-zē-nəs\ *n*

breth·ren \'breth-(ə-)rən, 'breth-ərn\ *plural of* BROTHER — used chiefly in formal or solemn address

Bret·on \'bret-ən\ *n* : a person born or living in Brittany

breve \'brēv, 'brev\ *n* : a mark ˘ placed over a vowel to show that the vowel is short [from Latin *breve, brevis* "short, brief" — related to BRIEF]

bre·via·ry \'brē-v(y)ə-rē, -vē-ˌer-ē\ *n, pl* **-ries** : a book containing prayers, hymns, and readings especially for priests for each day of the year

brev·i·ty \'brev-ət-ē\ *n* : the condition of being brief

¹brew \'brü\ *vb* **1** : to make (as beer or ale) from water, malt, and hops **2** : to try to bring about : PLOT, PLAN ⟨*brew* mischief⟩ **3** : to prepare (as tea) by soaking in hot water **4** : to start to form ⟨a storm is *brewing*⟩ — **brew·er** \'brü-ər, 'brü(-ə)r\ *n*

²brew *n* : a brewed beverage

brewer's yeast *n* : a yeast used or suitable for use in brewing; *also* : the dried ground-up cells of such a yeast used as a source of the vitamin B complex

brew·ery \'brü-ə-rē, 'brü(-ə)r-ē\ *n, pl* **-er·ies** : a plant where malt liquors are brewed

¹bri·ar *or* **bri·er** \'brī-(ə)r\ *n* : a plant (as a rose) with a thorny or prickly usually woody stem; *also* : a mass or twig of these [Old English *brēr* "thorny plant"] — **briary** *adj*

²briar *or* **brier** *n* : a pipe for smoking tobacco made from the root or stem of a European heath [short for *briar pipe*, from *briar* "wood of the European heath," from French *bruyère* "heath"]

¹bribe \'brīb\ *n* : something given or promised to a person in order to influence a decision or action dishonestly

²bribe *vb* **bribed; brib·ing** : to influence or try to influence by a bribe — **brib·able** \'brī-bə-bəl\ *adj* — **brib·er** *n*

brib·ery \'brīb-(ə-)rē\ *n, pl* **-er·ies** : the act or practice of bribing

bric–a–brac \'brik-ə-ˌbrak\ *n* : small ornamental articles

¹brick \'brik\ *n* **1 a** *pl* **bricks** *or* **brick** : a building or paving material made from clay molded into blocks and baked **b** : a block made of brick **2** : a block shaped like a brick ⟨a *brick* of ice cream⟩

²brick *vb* : to close, face, or pave with bricks

brick·bat \'brik-ˌbat\ *n* : a piece of a hard material (as a brick)

brick·lay·er \'brik-ˌlā-ər, -ˌle(-ə)r\ *n* : a person who builds with bricks — **brick·lay·ing** \-ˌlā-iŋ\ *n*

brick·work \'brik-ˌwərk\ *n* : work made of bricks and mortar

¹brid·al \'brīd-ᵊl\ *n* : WEDDING

²bridal *adj* : of or relating to a bride or a wedding

bride \'brīd\ *n* : a woman just married or about to be married

bride·groom \-ˌgrüm, -ˌgrum\ *n* : a man just married or about to be married

brides·maid \'brīdz-ˌmād\ *n* : a woman who attends a bride at her wedding

¹bridge \'brij\ *n* **1** : a structure built over something (as a river or a railroad) so people can cross **2** : a platform above and across the deck of a ship for the captain or officer in charge **3 a** : something resembling a bridge (as the upper part of the nose) **b** : music that connects the sections of a song or composition **4** : a curved piece that raises the strings of a musical instrument **5** : an artificial replacement for one or more teeth that is fastened to the remaining nearby teeth [Old English *brycg* "bridge"]

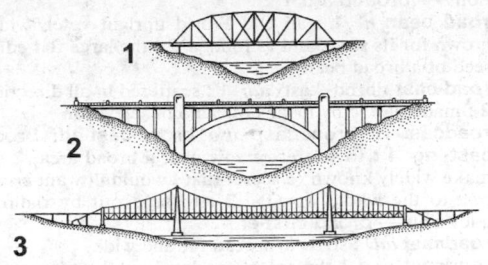

1
2
3

¹bridge 1: *1* truss, *2* arch, *3* suspension

²bridge *vb* **bridged; bridg·ing** : to make a bridge over or across ⟨*bridge* a gap⟩ — **bridge·able** \-ə-bəl\ *adj*

³bridge *n* : a card game for four players in two teams [origin unknown]

bridge·head \'brij-ˌhed\ *n* : a position seized in enemy territory as a place to begin a further advance

¹bri·dle \'brīd-ᵊl\ *n* **1** : a device for controlling a horse made up of a set of straps enclosing the head, a bit, and a pair of reins **2** : something that works or is used like a bridle **3** : RESTRAINT 2 ⟨set a *bridle* on his power⟩

²bridle *vb* **bri·dled; bri·dling** \'brīd-liŋ, -ᵊl-iŋ\ **1** : to put a bridle on **2** : to hold back with or as if with a bridle ⟨*bridled* her anger⟩ **3** : to hold the head high and draw in the chin as an expression of resentment ⟨*bridle* at criticism⟩

bridle path *n* : a path for horseback riding

¹brief \'brēf\ *adj* : not very long : SHORT [Middle English *bref, breve* "short, brief," from early French *brief, bref* (same meaning), from Latin *brevis* "short" — related to BREVE] — **brief·ly** *adv* — **brief·ness** *n*

²brief *n* **1** : a brief statement of the case a lawyer will present in court **2** *pl* : short snug underpants [Middle English *bref* "formal letter," from early French *bref* (same meaning), derived from Latin *brevis* "summary," from earlier *brevis* (adjective) "short, brief"]

³brief *vb* : to give information or instructions to ⟨*brief* the airplane crew⟩

brief·case \'brēf-ˌkās\ *n* : a flat case for carrying papers or books

brier *variant of* BRIAR

¹brig \'brig\ *n* : a square-rigged sailing ship with two masts

²brig *n* : a place (as on a ship) for temporary imprisonment of offenders in the U.S. Navy

bri·gade \brig-'ād\ *n* **1** : a body of soldiers consisting of two or more regiments **2** : a group of people organized for acting together ⟨a fire *brigade*⟩

brig·a·dier general \ˌbrig-ə-'di(ə)r-\ *n* : a military commissioned officer with a rank just below major general

brig·and \'brig-ənd\ *n* : BANDIT

brig·an·tine \'brig-ən-ˌtēn\ *n* : a square-rigged ship with two masts but without a square mainsail

bright \'brīt\ *adj* **1** : giving off or filled with much light **2** : very clear or vivid in color **3** : INTELLIGENT 1b, CLEVER ⟨a *bright* child⟩ ⟨a *bright* idea⟩ **4** : CHEERFUL 1 ⟨a *bright* smile⟩ **5** : full of promise ⟨a *bright* future⟩ — **bright** *adv* — **bright·ly** *adv* — **bright·ness** *n*

synonyms BRIGHT, SHINING, BRILLIANT, RADIANT mean giving off strong light. BRIGHT applies to a light that is strong when compared to other lights from a similar source ⟨a *bright* star⟩. SHINING suggests steady or constant brightness ⟨the *shining* moon⟩. BRILLIANT suggests the giving off of a striking, strong, or sparkling light ⟨a *brilliant* display of fireworks⟩. RADIANT stresses the giving off or the apparent giving off of rays of light ⟨the sun is a *radiant* body⟩ ⟨*radiant* with joy⟩.

bright·en \'brīt-ᵊn\ *vb* **bright·ened; bright·en·ing** \'brīt-niŋ, -ᵊn-iŋ\ : to make or become bright or brighter

bril·liance \'bril-yən(t)s\ *n* : the quality or state of being brilliant

bril·lian·cy \'bril-yən-sē\ *n, pl* **-cies** : BRILLIANCE

¹bril·liant \'bril-yənt\ *adj* **1** : flashing with light : very bright ⟨*brilliant* jewels⟩ **2 a** : very impressive ⟨a *brilliant* career⟩ **b** : very smart or clever ⟨a *brilliant* student⟩ ⟨a *brilliant* idea⟩ — **bril·liant·ly** *adv*

²brilliant *n* : a gem (as a diamond) cut so as to sparkle

¹brim \'brim\ *n* **1** : the edge or rim of something hollow (as a container) ⟨full to the *brim*⟩ **2** : the part of a hat that sticks out around the lower edge — **brim·ful** \-'ful\ *adj* — **brim·less** \-ləs\ *adj* — **brimmed** *adj*

²brim *vb* **brimmed; brim·ming** : to be or become full to overflowing ⟨*brimming* with happiness⟩ ⟨eyes *brimming* with tears⟩ ⟨boats *brimming* with tourists⟩

brim·stone \'brim-ˌstōn\ *n* : SULFUR

brin·dle \'brin-dᵊl\ *n* : a brindled color or animal

brin·dled \'brin-dᵊld\ *or* **brindle** *adj* : having faint dark streaks or spots on a gray or tawny background ⟨a *brindled* cow⟩

brine \'brīn\ *n* **1** : water containing a great deal of salt **2** : the water of a sea or salt lake

brine shrimp *n* : any of a genus of crustaceans found especially in salt lakes

bring \'briŋ\ *vb* **brought** \'brot\; **bring·ing** \'briŋ-iŋ\ **1** : to cause to come with oneself by carrying or leading especially to the place from which the action is viewed ⟨*bring* a lunch⟩ **2** : to cause to reach a certain state or take a certain action ⟨*bring* water to a boil⟩ ⟨couldn't *bring* myself to say it⟩ **3** : to cause to arrive or exist ⟨winter will *bring* snow⟩ ⟨*bring* legal action⟩ **4** : to sell for ⟨will *bring* a good price⟩ — **bring·er** *n* — **bring forth** : to give birth to : PRODUCE — **bring forward 1** : INTRODUCE 3b ⟨*brought* new evidence *forward*⟩ **2** : to carry (a total) to the next line of an account (as in a checkbook) ⟨what is the balance *brought forward*⟩ — **bring to light** : to make known or capable of being seen — **bring to mind** : ¹RECALL 2b — **bring up the rear** : to come last

bring about *vb* : to cause to happen : ACCOMPLISH

bring off *vb* : to bring to a successful conclusion ⟨I knew you could *bring* it *off*⟩

\ə\ **abut**	\au̇\ **out**	\i\ **tip**	\ȯ\ **saw**	\u̇\ **foot**
\ər\ **further**	\ch\ **chin**	\ī\ **life**	\ȯi\ **coin**	\y\ **yet**
\a\ **mat**	\e\ **pet**	\j\ **job**	\th\ **thin**	\yü\ **few**
\ā\ **take**	\ē\ **easy**	\ŋ\ **sing**	\th\ **this**	\yu̇\ **cure**
\ä\ **cot, cart**	\g\ **go**	\ō\ **bone**	\ü\ **food**	\zh\ **vision**

bring out vb 1 : to develop fully ⟨a difficult task seems to *bring out* your best⟩ 2 : to produce and offer for sale ⟨*bring out* a new book⟩

bring to vb : to bring back from unconsciousness : REVIVE

bring up vb 1 : to bring to maturity through care and education ⟨*bring up* a child⟩ 2 : to bring to attention : INTRODUCE ⟨I hate to keep *bringing* this *up*⟩

brink \'briŋk\ n 1 : the edge at the top of a steep place 2 : a point of beginning : VERGE ⟨on the *brink* of war⟩

brink·man·ship \'briŋk-mən-ˌship\ n : the practice of pushing a dangerous situation to the limit of safety before stopping

briny \'brī-nē\ adj **brin·i·er; -est** : of, relating to, or resembling salt water : SALTY — **brin·i·ness** n

bri·quette or **bri·quet** \brik-'et\ n : a compact mass of powdery or ground-up material pressed together and molded ⟨charcoal *briquettes*⟩

bris also **briss** \'bris\ n : the Jewish rite of circumcision

brisk \'brisk\ adj 1 : very active or alert : LIVELY 2 : very refreshing ⟨*brisk* autumn weather⟩ 3 : ENERGETIC, QUICK ⟨a *brisk* pace⟩ — **brisk·ly** adv — **brisk·ness** n

bris·ket \'bris-kət\ n : the breast or lower chest of a four-footed animal; also : a cut of beef from the brisket

¹bris·tle \'bris-əl\ n : a short stiff hair or something like a hair — **bris·tled** \-əld\ adj — **bris·tly** \-(ə-)lē\ adj

²bristle vb **bris·tled; bris·tling** \-(ə-)liŋ\ 1 : to rise up and stiffen like bristles ⟨makes your hair *bristle*⟩ ⟨quills *bristling* in all directions⟩ 2 : to show signs of anger ⟨*bristled* at the insult⟩ 3 : to appear as if covered with bristles ⟨a harbor *bristling* with the masts of ships⟩ — **bris·tly** \-(ə-)lē\ adj

bris·tle·cone pine \ˌbris-əl-ˌkōn-\ n : either of two pines of the western U.S. that include the oldest living trees

Bri·tan·nia metal \bri-ˌtan-yə-\ n : a silver-white alloy that is similar to pewter and consists largely of tin, antimony, and copper

britch·es \'brich-əz\ n pl : ¹BREECH 1, PANTS 1

¹Brit·ish \'brit-ish\ n 1 pl **British** : the people of Great Britain or their descendants 2 : the English language as spoken in England

²British adj 1 : of or relating to the original people of Britain 2 a : of or relating to Great Britain or the British **b** : ¹ENGLISH

Brit·ish·er \'brit-ish-ər\ n : a British person

British thermal unit n : the quantity of heat required to raise the temperature of one pound of water one degree Fahrenheit at a specified temperature (as 39°F or 60°F) and equal to about 1055 joules — called also *Btu*

Brit·on \'brit-ən\ n 1 : a member of one of the peoples living in Britain before the Anglo-Saxon invasions 2 : BRITISHER

Brit·ta·ny spaniel \ˌbrit-ə-nē-\ n : any of a French breed of medium-sized pointers that resemble spaniels

¹brit·tle \'brit-əl\ adj **brit·tler** \'brit-lər, -əl-ər\; **brit·tlest** \-ləst, -əl-əst\ : easily broken, cracked, or snapped ⟨*brittle* glass⟩ — **brit·tle·ness** \'brit-əl-nəs\ n

bristlecone pine

Brittany spaniel

²brittle n : a hard candy made with sugar and nuts and spread in thin sheets ⟨peanut *brittle*⟩

brittle star n : any of a group of sea animals similar to the related starfishes but having slender flexible arms

bro \'brō\ n 1 : BROTHER 1 2 : BROTHER 3

¹broach \'brōch\ n : any of various pointed or narrowed tools or parts; esp : one used for shaping a hole already bored

²broach vb 1 : to make a hole in (as a cask) in order to draw off the contents 2 : to bring up for discussion ⟨*broach* a subject⟩ 3 : to break the surface (as of water) from below ⟨saw a submarine *broaching*⟩

broad \'brȯd\ adj 1 : not narrow : WIDE ⟨a *broad* stripe⟩ 2 : extending far and wide : SPACIOUS ⟨*broad* prairies⟩ 3 : ¹FULL 2c ⟨*broad* daylight⟩ 4 : very clear : OBVIOUS ⟨a *broad* hint⟩ 5 : not limited : large in range or amount ⟨a *broad* choice of subjects⟩ ⟨education in its *broadest* sense⟩ 6 : not covering the fine points : GENERAL ⟨*broad* outlines of a problem⟩ 7 : pronounced like the *a* in *father* — **broad·ly** adv — **broad·ness** n

broad·ax or **broad·axe** \'brȯd-ˌaks\ n : an ax with a broad blade

broad·band adj : of, relating to, or being a high-speed communications network ⟨a *broadband* Internet connection⟩ — **broadband** n

broad bean n 1 : an Old World upright vetch widely grown for its seeds and as fodder 2 : the large flat edible seed of a broad bean

¹broad·cast \'brȯd-ˌkast\ adj 1 : scattered in all directions 2 : made public by means of radio or television

²broadcast vb **broadcast** also **broad·cast·ed; broad·cast·ing** 1 : to scatter or sow over a broad area 2 : to make widely known ⟨a secret that I wouldn't want *broadcast* to the whole world⟩ 3 : to send out by radio or television — **broad·cast·er** n

³broadcast adv : so as to spread far and wide

⁴broadcast n 1 : the act of sending sound or images by radio or television 2 : a single radio or television program

broad·cloth \'brȯd-ˌklȯth\ n : a fine cloth with a firm smooth surface

broad·en \'brȯd-ən\ vb **broad·ened; broad·en·ing** \'brȯd-niŋ, -ən-iŋ\ : to make or become broad or broader ⟨*broaden* your horizons⟩

broad jump n : LONG JUMP — **broad jumper** n

broad–leaved \'brȯd-'lēvd\ or **broad–leaf** \-ˌlēf\ also **broad–leafed** \-'lēft\ adj 1 : having broad leaves; esp : having leaves that are not needles 2 : composed of broad-leaved plants ⟨*broad-leaved* forests⟩

broad·loom \'brȯd-ˌlüm\ adj : woven on a wide loom ⟨*broadloom* rugs⟩ — **broadloom** n

broad–mind·ed \'brȯd-'mīn-dəd\ adj : willing to accept opinions, beliefs, or practices that are unusual or different from one's own — **broad–mind·ed·ly** adv — **broad–mind·ed·ness** n

¹broad·side \'brȯd-ˌsīd\ n 1 : the part of a ship's side above the waterline 2 : a firing of all of the guns that are on the same side of a ship 3 : a sheet of paper printed usually on one side (as an advertisement) 4 : a strongly worded attack ⟨a *broadside* of criticism⟩

²broadside adv 1 : with one side forward : SIDEWAYS ⟨turned *broadside*⟩ 2 : from the side ⟨hit the car *broadside*⟩

broad·sword \'brȯd-ˌsō(ə)rd, -ˌsȯ(ə)rd\ n : a sword with a wide blade

Broad·way \'brȯd-ˌwā, -'wā\ n : the world of the theater in New York City : the New York stage ⟨a big star on *Broadway*⟩ — **Broadway** adj

bro·cade \brō-'kād\ n : a cloth with a raised design woven into it — **bro·cad·ed** \-'kād-əd\ adj

broc·co·li \'bräk-(ə-)lē\ n : an open branching form of cauliflower that bears young flowering shoots used as a vegetable

bro·chure \brō-'shu̇(ə)r\ *n* : a pamphlet containing advertising or descriptive material

bro·gan \'brō-gən, -ˌgan; brō-'gan\ *n* : a heavy shoe

¹brogue \'brōg\ *n* **1** : BROGAN **2** : a low shoe with decorative holes along the seams and often at the toe [from Irish *bróg* and Scottish Gaelic *bròg* "stout shoe," derived from an early Norse word meaning "leg covering"]

²brogue *n* : a dialect or regional pronunciation; *esp* : an Irish accent [Irish *barróg* "accent, speech impediment," literally, "wrestling grip, tight hold"]

broil \'brȯi(ə)l\ *vb* **1** : to cook directly over or under heat **2** : to make or become extremely hot ⟨*broiling* in the sun⟩

broil·er \'brȯi-lər\ *n* **1** : a rack and pan or an oven equipped with a rack and pan for broiling meat **2** : a young chicken suitable for broiling

¹broke *past of* BREAK

²broke *adj* : having no money : PENNILESS

bro·ken \'brō-kən\ *adj* **1** : shattered into pieces ⟨*broken* glass⟩ **2 a** : ¹ROUGH 1a, UNEVEN ⟨*broken* terrain⟩ **b** : having gaps or breaks ⟨a *broken* line⟩ **3** : not kept ⟨a *broken* promise⟩ **4** : subdued completely ⟨a *broken* spirit⟩ **5** : imperfectly spoken ⟨*broken* English⟩ **6** : having undergone fracture ⟨a *broken* leg⟩ **7** : having one parent missing (as because of divorce) ⟨children from *broken* homes⟩ — **bro·ken·ly** *adv* — **bro·ken·ness** \-kən-(n)əs\ *n*

bro·ken–down \ˌbrō-kən-'dau̇n\ *adj* : WORN-OUT 1, WEAK

bro·ken-heart·ed \ˌbrō-kən-'härt-əd\ *adj* : overwhelmed by grief

bro·ker \'brō-kər\ *n* : a person who acts as an agent in the purchase and sale of property

bro·ker·age \'brō-k(ə-)rij\ *n* **1** : the business of a broker **2** : the fee or commission charged by a broker

bro·mide \'brō-ˌmīd\ *n* : any of various compounds of bromine with another element or a chemical group including some used as sedatives

bro·mine \'brō-ˌmēn\ *n* : an element that is a deep red liquid that has two atoms per molecule, gives off an irritating reddish brown vapor of disagreeable odor, and tends to eat into other matter — see ELEMENT table

brom·thy·mol blue \ˌbrōm-ˌthī-ˌmȯl-, -ˌmōl-\ *n* : a dye that is an acid-base indicator — called also *bro·mo·thy·mol blue* \ˌbrō-mō-\

bronc \'bräŋk\ *n* : BRONCO

bron·chi·al \'bräŋ-kē-əl\ *adj* : of, relating to, or involving the bronchi or their branches

bronchial tube *n* : a primary bronchus or any of its branches

bron·chi·ole \'bräŋ-kē-ˌōl\ *n* : a tiny thin-walled branch of a bronchial tube

bron·chi·tis \brän-'kīt-əs, bräŋ-\ *n* : inflammation of the bronchial tubes or a disease marked by this

bron·chus \'bräŋ-kəs\ *n, pl* **bron·chi** \'bräŋ-ˌkī, -ˌkē\ : either of the main divisions of the trachea each leading to a lung

bron·co \'bräŋ-kō\ *n, pl* **broncos 1** : an untamed or partly tamed horse of western North America **2** : MUSTANG 1

bron·to·sau·rus \ˌbränt-ə-'sȯr-əs\ *also* **bron·to·saur** \'bränt-ə-ˌsȯ(ə)r\ *n* : any of several very large four-footed plant-eating dinosaurs [derived from Greek *brontē* "thunder" and Greek *sauros* "lizard"]

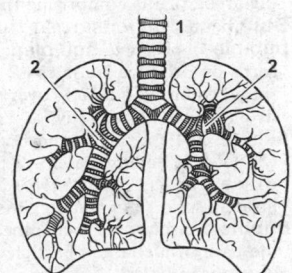

bronchus: *1* trachea, *2* bronchus

¹bronze \'bränz\ *vb* **bronzed; bronz·ing** : to make bronze in color

²bronze *n* **1** : an alloy of copper and tin and sometimes other elements (as zinc) **2** : something (as a medal or a statue) made of bronze **3** : a yellowish brown color **4** : a bronze medal awarded as the third prize in a competition — **bronzy** \'brän-zē\ *adj*

Bronze Age *n* : a period of human culture marked by the use of bronze (as for weapons and tools) that began between 4000 and 3000 B.C.

brooch \'brōch, 'brüch\ *n* : an ornamental pin or clasp worn on clothing

¹brood \'brüd\ *n* : a family of young animals or children; *esp* : the young (as of a bird) hatched or cared for at one time

²brood *vb* **1** : to sit on eggs in order to hatch them **2** : to cover young with the wings **3** : to think long and anxiously about something ⟨*brooded* over his mistake⟩ — **brood·ing·ly** \-iŋ-lē\ *adv*

³brood *adj* : kept for breeding ⟨a *brood* mare⟩ ⟨a *brood* flock⟩

brood·er \'brüd-ər\ *n* **1** : a person or animal that broods **2** : a heated structure for raising young poultry

broody \'brüd-ē\ *adj* : being in a condition to brood eggs ⟨a *broody* hen⟩

¹brook \'bru̇k\ *vb* : TOLERATE 1 ⟨*brooks* no interference⟩ [Old English *brūcan* "to use, enjoy"]

²brook *n* : a small stream [Old English *brōc* "brook, creek"]

brook·let \'bru̇k-lət\ *n* : a small brook

brook trout *n* : a common speckled cold-water char of eastern North America

broom \'brüm, 'bru̇m\ *n* **1** : a plant of the legume family that has long slender branches along which grow many drooping yellow flowers **2** : a brush that has a long handle and is used for sweeping

broom·stick \-ˌstik\ *n* : the handle of a broom

bros *plural of* BRO

broth \'brȯth\ *n, pl* **broths** \'brȯths, 'brȯthz\ **1** : liquid in which food has been cooked **2** : a fluid culture medium

broth·er \'brəth-ər\ *n, pl* **brothers** *also* **breth·ren** \'breth-(ə-)rən, 'breth-ərn\ **1** : a male who has one or both parents in common with another **2** : a male relative **3** : a fellow member of a group

broth·er·hood \'brəth-ər-ˌhu̇d\ *n* **1** : the state of being brothers or a brother **2** : an association of people for a particular purpose **3** : the persons engaged in the same business or profession

broth·er–in–law \'brəth-(ə-)rən-ˌlȯ, 'brəth-ərn-ˌlȯ\ *n, pl* **broth·ers–in–law** \'brəth-ər-zən-\ **1** : the brother of one's husband or wife **2** : the husband of one's sister

broth·er·ly \'brəth-ər-lē\ *adj* **1** : of or relating to brothers **2** : ¹KINDLY 2, AFFECTIONATE — **broth·er·li·ness** *n*

brougham \'brü(-ə)m, 'brō-əm\ *n* : a light closed carriage pulled by horses with the driver outside in front [named for Henry *Brougham* 1778–1868 Scottish judge who designed the carriage]

brought *past and past participle of* BRING

brow \'brau̇\ *n* **1 a** : EYEBROW **b** : FOREHEAD **2** : the upper edge of a steep slope

brow·beat \'brau̇-ˌbēt\ *vb* **-beat; brow·beat·en** \-ˌbēt-ᵊn\; **-beat·ing** : to frighten by a stern manner or threatening speech : BULLY

¹brown \'brau̇n\ *adj* **1** : of the color brown **2** : of dark or tanned complexion

²brown *n* : a color like that of coffee or chocolate that is a blend of red and yellow darkened by black — **brown·ish** \'brau̇-nish\ *adj*

³brown *vb* : to make or become brown

\ə\ **abut**	\au̇\ **out**	\i\ **tip**	\ȯ\ **saw**	\u̇\ **foot**
\ər\ **further**	\ch\ **chin**	\ī\ **life**	\ȯi\ **coin**	\y\ **yet**
\a\ **mat**	\e\ **pet**	\j\ **job**	\th\ **thin**	\yü\ **few**
\ā\ **take**	\ē\ **easy**	\ŋ\ **sing**	\th\ **this**	\yu̇\ **cure**
\ä\ **cot, cart**	\g\ **go**	\ō\ **bone**	\ü\ **food**	\zh\ **vision**

brown alga *n* : any of a group of mostly marine algae with the chlorophyll masked by brown coloring matter

brown–bag *vb* **brown–bagged; brown–bag·ging** : to carry one's lunch usually in a brown paper bag ⟨*brown= bagging* it to the game⟩ — **brown–bag** *adj*

brown bear *n* : any of several bears that are mostly brown in color, are usually lumped together in a single species including the grizzly bear, and at one time inhabited much of North America from Alaska to northern Mexico as well as Europe and Asia

brown coal *n* : LIGNITE

brown dwarf *n* : an object in space that is much smaller and dimmer than a normal star

Brown·ian motion \ˌbraù-nē-ən-\ *n* : a random movement of microscopic particles in liquids or gases that results from collisions with molecules of the fluid surrounding the particles — called also *Brownian movement* [named for Robert *Brown* 1773–1858 Scottish scientist]

brown·ie \ˈbraù-nē\ *n* **1** : a good-natured elf believed to perform helpful services at night **2** *cap* : a member of the Girl Scouts of the United States of America from six through eight years of age **3** : a small square or rectangle of rich usually chocolate cake often containing nuts

brown·out \ˈbraù-ˌnaùt\ *n* : a reduction in the use or availability of electric power; *also* : a period of dimmed lighting resulting from such reduction

brown rat *n* : the common rat that is found about human dwellings

brown recluse spider *n* : a poisonous spider especially of the southern and central U.S. that has a dark violin= shaped mark on the front half of its back

brown·stone \ˈbraùn-ˌstōn\ *n* **1** : a reddish brown sandstone used for building **2** : a dwelling covered with a layer of brownstone

brown sugar *n* : soft sugar whose crystals are covered by a film of purified dark syrup

brown trout *n* : a speckled European trout widely introduced as a game fish

brow·ridge \ˈbraù-ˌrij\ *n* : a prominent ridge on the bone above the eye caused by sinuses in the skull

¹browse \ˈbraùz\ *vb* **browsed; brows·ing 1** : to nibble or feed on leaves and shoots **2** : to read or look over something in a light or careless way

²browse *n* **1** : tender shoots and leaves used by animals for food **2** : an act or instance of browsing

brow·ser \ˈbraù-zər\ *n* **1** : one that browses **2** : a computer program providing access to information on a network and especially to websites

bru·in \ˈbrü-ən\ *n* : ¹BEAR 1 [from *Bruin*, name of a bear in literature, from early Dutch *bruin* "brown"]

¹bruise \ˈbrüz\ *vb* **bruised; bruis·ing 1 a** : to cause a bruise on **b** : to become bruised **2** : to crush (as leaves or berries) by pounding **3** : to hurt the feelings of

²bruise *n* **1** : an injury (as from a blow) in which the skin is not broken but is discolored from the breaking of small blood vessels that lie underneath the skin : CONTUSION **2** : an injury to a plant or fruit that resembles a bruise

bruis·er \ˈbrü-zər\ *n* : a big husky person

¹bruit \ˈbrüt\ *n, archaic* : ¹REPORT 1a, RUMOR

²bruit *vb* : to spread by report or rumor

brunch \ˈbrənch\ *n* : a late breakfast, an early lunch, or a combination of the two [*br*eakfast and l*unch*]

bru·net *or* **bru·nette** \brü-ˈnet\ *adj* : having brown or black hair and dark eyes — **brunet** *or* **brunette** *n*

brung \ˈbrəŋ\ *chiefly dialect past and past participle of* BRING

brunt \ˈbrənt\ *n* : the main force or stress (as of an attack) ⟨the *brunt* of the storm⟩

¹brush \ˈbrəsh\ *n* **1** : BRUSHWOOD 1 **2 a** : short trees or shrubs of poor quality **b** : land covered with brush [Middle English *brusch* "broken or cut twigs or branches," from early French *broce* "small broken branches, brushwood"]

²brush *n* **1** : a tool made of bristles set in a back or handle and used especially for cleaning, smoothing, or painting **2** : a bushy tail (as of a fox or squirrel) **3** : a conductor for an electric current between a moving and a still part of an electric motor or generator **4 a** : an act of brushing **b** : a quick light stroke [Middle English *brusshe* "brush (for sweeping)," derived from early French *broisse*] — **brush·like** \-ˌlīk\ *adj*

³brush *vb* **1 a** : to clean, smooth, scrub, or paint with a brush **b** : to apply with or as if with a brush **2 a** : to remove with or as if with a brush ⟨*brush* the lint off your coat⟩ **b** : to pay no attention to : DISMISS ⟨*brush* off criticism⟩ **3** : to pass lightly across : touch gently against in passing ⟨twigs *brushed* my cheek⟩

⁴brush *n* : a brief fight or meeting ⟨a *brush* with disaster⟩ [Middle English *brusche* "a rush, collision," from *bruschen* "to rush," probably from early French *brosser* "to dash through underbrush," from *broce* "brushwood"]

⁵brush *vb* : to move quickly past without stopping or paying attention ⟨*brushed* by the reporters⟩

brush–off \ˈbrəsh-ˌof\ *n* : rude treatment or behavior by someone who is not interested at all in what another person wants or asks for

brush up *vb* : to refresh one's memory, skill, or knowledge ⟨*brush up* on your Spanish⟩

brush·wood \ˈbrəsh-ˌwùd\ *n* **1** : small branches cut from trees or shrubs **2** : a heavy growth of small trees and shrubs

¹brushy \ˈbrəsh-ē\ *adj* **brush·i·er; -est** : SHAGGY

²brushy *adj* **brush·i·er; -est** : covered with or full of brush or brushwood

brusque \ˈbrəsk\ *adj* : so short and frank in manner or speech as to be impolite ⟨spoke in a *brusque* tone⟩ — **brusque·ly** *adv* — **brusqueness** *n*

brus·sels sprout \ˌbrəs-əl-\ *n, often cap B* : one of the edible small green heads that grow on the stem of a plant related to the cabbage; *also* : this plant

bru·tal \ˈbrüt-ᵊl\ *adj* : being cruel and inhuman : SAVAGE ⟨a *brutal* attack⟩ — **bru·tal·ly** \-ᵊl-ē\ *adv*

bru·tal·i·ty \brü-ˈtal-ət-ē\ *n, pl* **-ties 1** : the quality or state of being brutal **2** : a brutal act or course of action

¹brute \ˈbrüt\ *adj* **1** : of or relating to beasts **2** : typical of beasts : like that of a beast ⟨*brute* force⟩ ⟨*brute* strength⟩

²brute *n* **1** : ¹ANIMAL 2a **2** : a brutal person

brut·ish \ˈbrüt-ish\ *adj* **1** : resembling, befitting, or typical of a brute or beast ⟨lived a short and *brutish* life as a slave⟩ **2 a** : ²ANIMAL 2 **b** : showing little intelligence or sense ⟨*brutish* lack of understanding⟩ — **brut·ish·ly** *adv* — **brut·ish·ness** *n*

bry·o·phyl·lum \ˌbrī-ə-ˈfil-əm\ *n* : KALANCHOE

bry·o·phyte \ˈbrī-ə-ˌfīt\ *n* : any of a division of nonflowering green plants comprising the mosses and liverworts

Btu \ˌbē-ˌtē-ˈyü\ *n* : BRITISH THERMAL UNIT

¹bub·ble \ˈbəb-əl\ *vb* **bub·bled; bub·bling** \-(ə-)liŋ\ **1** : to form or produce bubbles **2** : to flow with a gurgling sound ⟨a brook *bubbling* over rocks⟩ **3** : to be or become lively ⟨*bubbling* with joy⟩

²bubble *n* **1** : a tiny round body of air or gas in a liquid ⟨*bubbles* in boiling water⟩ **2** : a thin film of liquid filled with air or gas ⟨soap *bubbles*⟩ **3** : a round body of air inside a solid ⟨a *bubble* in glass⟩

bubble chamber *n* : a chamber of heated liquid in which the path of a charged particle is made visible by a string of vapor bubbles

bubble gum *n* : a chewing gum that can be blown into large bubbles

bub·bly \ˈbəb-(ə-)lē\ *adj* **bub·bli·er; -est 1** : full of bubbles **2** : showing lively good spirits

bu·bo \ˈb(y)ü-bō\ *n, pl* **buboes** : an inflamed swelling of a lymph node especially in the groin — **bu·bon·ic** \b(y)ü-ˈbän-ik\ *adj*

bubonic plague *n* : a form of plague that is spread especially from rats to humans by fleas and is marked by chills, fever, weakness, and buboes

buc·ca·neer \ˌbək-ə-ˈni(ə)r\ *n* : ¹PIRATE

Word History In the 17th century Frenchmen living off the land on West Indian islands were known as *boucaniers* because they preserved meat by smoking it over a wooden grill. The grill was called a *boucan*, after the Brazilian Indian name for it. When some of these men took to the sea as pirates, the word *boucanier* continued to be applied to them, and was borrowed into English as *buccaneer*. [from French *boucanier* "hunter who smokes meat over a grill"]

¹**buck** \ˈbək\ *n, pl* **bucks 1** *or pl* **buck** : a male animal; *esp* : a male deer or antelope **2 a** : ¹MAN 1a **b** : DANDY 1 **3 a** : DOLLAR 3b **b** : a sum of money especially to be gained ⟨make a quick *buck*⟩

²**buck** *vb* **1 a** : to spring into the air with the back arched ⟨a *bucking* horse⟩ **b** : to throw (as a rider) by bucking **2** : to move or act against the action of ⟨*bucking* a storm⟩ ⟨*buck* a trend⟩ **3** : to move or start jerkily — **buck·er** *n*

³**buck** *n* : an act or instance of bucking

⁴**buck** *n* : RESPONSIBILITY ⟨pass the *buck*⟩ [short for *buckhorn knife*, formerly used in poker to mark the next player to deal]

buck·a·roo \ˌbək-ə-ˈrü, ˈbək-ə-ˌrü\ *n, pl* **-roos** : COWBOY [an altered form of Spanish *vaquero* "cowboy," from *vaca* "cow," from Latin *vacca* "cow" — related to VACCINE, VAQUERO; see *Word History* at VACCINE]

buck·board \ˈbək-ˌbō(ə)rd, -ˌbó(ə)rd\ *n* : a four-wheeled vehicle with a floor made of long springy boards

buckboard

buck·et \ˈbək-ət\ *n* **1 a** : a usually round container for catching, holding, or carrying liquids or solids : PAIL **2** : an object for collecting, scooping, or carrying something **3** : BUCKETFUL

bucket brigade *n* : a chain of persons acting to put out a fire by passing buckets of water from hand to hand

buck·et·ful \ˈbək-ət-ˌfúl\ *n, pl* **buck·et·fuls** \-ət-ˌfúlz\ *or* **buck·ets·ful** \-əts-ˌfúl\ : the amount a bucket holds; *also* : a large quantity

bucket seat *n* : a low seat for one person used chiefly in automobiles and airplanes

buck·eye \ˈbək-ˌī\ *n* : any of several trees or shrubs related to the horse chestnut; *also* : the large nutlike seed of a buckeye

¹**buck·le** \ˈbək-əl\ *n* : a fastening device which is attached to one end of a belt or strap and through which the other end is passed and held

²**buckle** *vb* **buck·led; buck·ling** \-(ə-)liŋ\ **1 a** : to fasten with a buckle ⟨*buckle* your seat belt⟩ **b** : to fasten a buckle ⟨*buckle* up for safety⟩ **2** : to apply oneself ⟨*buckle* down to the job⟩ **3** : to give way : BEND, CRUMPLE ⟨the pavement *buckled* in the heat⟩ ⟨knees *buckled*⟩

³**buckle** *n* : a product of buckling

buck·ler \ˈbək-lər\ *n* : a small round shield worn on the arm

buck·ram \ˈbək-rəm\ *n* : a stiff fabric used in garments, hats, and bookbindings

buck·saw \ˈbək-ˌsò\ *n* : a saw set in a usually H-shaped frame that is used for sawing wood

buck·shot \-ˌshät\ *n, pl* **buckshot** *or* **buckshots** : a large shotgun pellet

buck·skin \-ˌskin\ *n* **1 a** : the skin of a buck **b** : a soft flexible leather **2** *pl* : buckskin breeches **3** : a horse of a dull yellowish color with black mane and tail

buck·tooth \-ˈtüth\ *n* : a large front tooth that sticks out — **buck–toothed** \-ˈtütht\ *adj*

buck·wheat \ˈbək-ˌhwēt, -ˌwēt\ *n* : either of two plants with white or greenish flowers that are grown for their dark triangular seeds which are used as a cereal grain; *also* : the seeds of a buckwheat

bu·col·ic \byü-ˈkäl-ik\ *adj* : ¹PASTORAL 1a, RURAL

¹**bud** \ˈbəd\ *n* **1** : a small growth at the tip or on the side of a plant stem that later develops into a flower, leaf, or new shoot **2** : a flower that has not fully opened **3** : a part that grows out from the body of a plant or animal and develops into a new individual **4** : a stage in which something is not yet fully developed ⟨trees in *bud*⟩ ⟨a plan still in the *bud*⟩

²**bud** *vb* **bud·ded; bud·ding 1** : to set or put forth buds **2** : to be or develop like a bud (as in freshness and promise of growth) ⟨a *budding* diplomat⟩ **3** : to reproduce by the pinching off of a small part of the parent ⟨*budding* yeast cells⟩ **4** : to insert a bud from one plant into an opening cut in the bark of (another plant) in order to grow a desired variety

Bud·dhism \ˈbü-ˌdiz-əm, ˈbúd-ˌiz-\ *n* : a religion of eastern and central Asia growing out of the teaching of Gautama Buddha — **Bud·dhist** \ˈbüd-əst, ˈbúd-\ *n or adj* — **Bud·dhis·tic** \bü-ˈdis-tik, bú-\ *adj*

bud·dy \ˈbəd-ē\ *n, pl* **buddies** : ¹COMPANION 1, PAL

budge \ˈbəj\ *vb* **budged; budg·ing 1** : ¹MOVE 1 **2** : GIVE IN, YIELD ⟨wouldn't *budge* on their opinion⟩

bud·ger·i·gar \ˈbəj-(ə-)ri-ˌgär\ *n* : a small brightly colored Australian parrot often kept as a pet

¹**bud·get** \ˈbəj-ət\ *n* **1** : ²SUPPLY 1a, QUANTITY **2 a** : a statement of estimated income and expenses **b** : a plan for using money **c** : the amount of money available for some purpose [Middle English *bowgette* "small leather pouch," derived from early French *bouge* "leather bag," from Latin *bulga* "leather bag" — related to BULGE] — **bud·get·ary** \ˈbəj-ə-ˌter-ē\ *adj*

²**budget** *vb* **1** : to put on or in a budget ⟨*budget* $50 for entertainment⟩ **2** : to provide funds for in a budget ⟨*budget* a new car⟩ **3** : to plan the use of ⟨*budget* one's time⟩

bud·gie \ˈbəj-ē\ *n* : BUDGERIGAR

bud scale *n* : one of the leaves resembling scales that form the covering of a plant bud

¹**buff** \ˈbəf\ *n* **1** : an orange yellow **2** : a device with a soft absorbent surface (as of cloth) for applying polishing material **3** : ³FAN, ENTHUSIAST ⟨a tennis *buff*⟩

²**buff** *adj* : of the color buff

³**buff** *vb* : to polish with or as if with a buff

buf·fa·lo \ˈbəf-ə-ˌlō\ *n, pl* **-lo** *or* **-loes** : any of several wild mammals related to oxen: as **a** : WATER BUFFALO **b** : CAPE BUFFALO **c** : a large shaggy-maned North American mammal with short horns and heavy forequarters with a large muscular hump

buffalo c

Word History The Greeks traveled over much of the ancient world, and Greek authors gave names to a number of unfamiliar animals. The African gazelle they called *boubalos*, apparently deriving part of the name from the Greek word *bous*, meaning "ox." Later the Romans borrowed this

\ə\ **abut**	\aú\ **out**	\i\ **tip**	\ò\ **saw**	\ú\ **foot**
\ər\ **further**	\ch\ **chin**	\ī\ **life**	\òi\ **coin**	\y\ **yet**
\a\ **mat**	\e\ **pet**	\j\ **job**	\th\ **thin**	\yü\ **few**
\ā\ **take**	\ē\ **easy**	\ŋ\ **sing**	\th\ **this**	\yú\ **cure**
\ä\ **cot, cart**	\g\ **go**	\ō\ **bone**	\ü\ **food**	\zh\ **vision**

Greek word, which they used for "gazelle" and for "wild ox." In Latin the form was first *bubalus* and later *bufalus*. This Latin word for wild ox later passed into Italian as *bufalo* and into Spanish as *búfalo*. From these languages the English picked it up and gave it the spelling *buffalo*. When English settlers arrived in America, they gave the name *buffalo* to the big, shaggy animal that scientists prefer to call *bison*. [from Italian *bufalo* and Spanish *búfalo*, both meaning "wild ox," from Latin *bubalus*, *bufalus* "wild ox, African gazelle," from Greek *boubalos* "African gazelle," probably from *bous* "ox, cow" — related to BUTTER]

buffalo grass *n* : a low-growing grass native to the Great Plains

buffalo wing *n* : a deep-fried chicken wing coated with a spicy sauce and usually served with a blue cheese dressing [named for *Buffalo*, NY]

¹buf·fer \'bəf-ər\ *n* **1** : a device or material for reducing shock resulting from contact **2** : something that serves as a protective barrier **3** : a substance that in solution can neutralize both acids and bases **4** : a temporary storage unit (as in a computer); *esp* : one that accepts information at one rate and delivers it at another

²buffer *vb* **buf·fered; buf·fer·ing** \-(ə-)riŋ\ **1** : to lessen the shock of : CUSHION **2** : to treat (a solution) with a buffer; *also* : to prepare (aspirin) with an antacid **3** : to collect (as data) in a buffer

³buff·er \'bəf-ər\ *n* : one that buffs

buffer state *n* : a small neutral state lying between two larger rival powers

¹buf·fet \'bəf-ət\ *n* : a blow especially with the hand [Middle English *buffet* "a blow with the hand," derived from early French *buffe* "a blow"]

²buffet *vb* : to pound repeatedly : BATTER

³buf·fet \(ˌ)bə-'fā, bü-'fā, 'bü-ˌfā\ *n* **1** : SIDEBOARD **2** : a meal set out on a sideboard, table, or countertop for guests to serve themselves [French]

buf·foon \(ˌ)bə-'fün\ *n* **1** : ¹CLOWN 2 **2** : a crude or stupid person

buf·foon·ery \(ˌ)bə-'fün-(ə-)rē\ *n, pl* **-er·ies** : foolish or playful behavior

¹bug \'bəg\ *n* **1 a** : an insect (as a beetle) or other creeping or crawling invertebrate animal (as a centipede) **b** : any of an order of insects (as bedbugs and stinkbugs) that have sucking mouthparts and the forewings part leathery and part membranous and that undergo incomplete metamorphosis — called also *true bug* **2** : an unexpected mistake or imperfection ⟨a *bug* in a computer program⟩ **3** : a disease-producing germ; *also* : a disease caused by it **4** : ³FAN, ENTHUSIAST ⟨a camera *bug*⟩ **5** : a concealed listening device

²bug *vb* **bugged; bug·ging 1** : to place a concealed microphone in **2** : ¹BOTHER 1, ANNOY **3** : ³FREAK — usually used with *out*

bug·a·boo \'bəg-ə-ˌbü\ *n, pl* **-boos** : BUGBEAR 2, BOGEY

bug·bear \'bəg-ˌba(ə)r, -ˌbe(ə)r\ *n* **1** : an imaginary creature used to frighten children **2** : something one is afraid of **3** : a continuing source of annoyance

bug–eyed \-ˌīd\ *adj* : having the eyes bulging (as in astonishment)

¹bug·gy \'bəg-ē\ *adj* **bug·gi·er; -est** : full of bugs ⟨it's too *buggy* outside⟩ ⟨a *buggy* computer program⟩

²buggy *n, pl* **buggies 1** : a light carriage having a single seat and drawn by one horse **2** : a hand-pushed carriage for a baby

bu·gle \'byü-gəl\ *n* : a brass musical instrument like the trumpet but without valves — **bugle** *vb* — **bu·gler** \-glər\ *n*

Word History In early English the word *bugle*

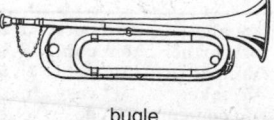
bugle

meant "wild ox." The horns of oxen were made into signaling devices for soldiers and hunters, first called *bugle horns*. Later this was shortened to *bugle*. [Middle English *bugle* "wild ox," from early French *bugle* (same meaning), from Latin *buculus* "young steer"]

¹build \'bild\ *vb* **built** \'bilt\; **build·ing 1** : to make by putting together parts or materials : CONSTRUCT ⟨*build* a house⟩ ⟨*build* a bridge⟩ **2** : to produce or create gradually ⟨*build* a winning team⟩ ⟨*build* up your strength⟩ **3** : to move or grow toward a peak ⟨excitement was *building*⟩

²build *n* : form or kind of structure; *esp* : PHYSIQUE

build·er \'bil-dər\ *n* : one that builds; *esp* : a person whose business is the construction of buildings

build·ing \'bil-diŋ\ *n* **1** : a permanent structure built as a dwelling, shelter, or place for human activity or for storage ⟨an office *building*⟩ **2** : the art, work, or business of assembling materials into a structure

building block *n* : a unit of construction or composition

build·up \'bil-ˌdəp\ *n* **1** : something produced by building up **2** : the act or process of building up

built–in \'bil-'tin\ *adj* **1** : forming a permanent part of a structure or object ⟨*built-in* bookcases⟩ **2** : built into the ground ⟨a *built-in* swimming pool⟩

bulb \'bəlb\ *n* **1 a** : an underground resting stage of a plant (as an onion or tulip) consisting of a short stem base bearing one or more buds enclosed in overlapping leaves **b** : a fleshy structure (as a tuber or corm) resembling a bulb in appearance or function **2** : a rounded object or part shaped more or less like a bulb ⟨a flashlight *bulb*⟩

bulb·ous \'bəl-bəs\ *adj* **1** : having a bulb : growing from or bearing bulbs **2** : resembling a bulb in being rounded or swollen ⟨a *bulbous* nose⟩

Bul·gar·i·an \ˌbəl-'gar-ē-ən, ˌbül-, -'ger-\ *n* **1** : a person born or living in Bulgaria **2** : the Slavic language of the Bulgarians — **Bulgarian** *adj*

¹bulge \'bəlj\ *vb* **bulged; bulg·ing 1** : to swell, curve outward, or stick out ⟨*bulging* eyes⟩ **2** : to be filled to overflowing ⟨a *bulging* notebook⟩

²bulge *n* : a part that swells or sticks out [from early French *boulge, bouge* "leather bag," from Latin *bulga* "leather bag" — related to BUDGET]

bul·gur \'bəl-gər, 'bül-\ *n* : dried cracked wheat [Turkish]

bu·lim·ia \bü-'lē-mē-ə, byü-\ *n* : a serious eating disorder mainly of young women that is characterized by compulsive overeating usually followed by intentional vomiting or laxative abuse — **bu·lim·ic** \-'lē-mik\ *adj*

¹bulk \'bəlk\ *n* **1** : greatness of size or mass : VOLUME **2** : a large body or mass **3** : the main or greater part ⟨did the *bulk* of the work⟩ **4** : FIBER 1f — **in bulk 1** : not divided into parts or packaged in separate units **2** : in large quantities ⟨bought canned goods *in bulk*⟩

²bulk *vb* **1** : to cause to swell or bulge **2** : to appear as a consideration ⟨an issue that *bulks* large in her mind⟩

³bulk *adj* : being in bulk ⟨*bulk* foods⟩

bulk·head \'bəlk-ˌhed\ *n* **1** : a wall separating compartments **2** : an external structure with a sloping door leading to the cellar stairway of a house

bulky \'bəl-kē\ *adj* **bulk·i·er; -est 1** : large in size or mass **2** : being large and hard to handle — **bulk·i·ness** *n*

bull \'bül\ *n* **1 a** : an adult male bovine animal **b** : an adult male of some other large animals (as an elephant, a moose, or a whale) **2** : a person who buys stocks or bonds in the expectation that the price will go up — compare BEAR 3 **3** *slang* : POLICE OFFICER — **bull** *adj* — **bullish** \-ish\ *adj*

¹bull·dog \'bül-ˌdòg\ *n* : any of a breed of stocky short-haired dogs with a broad square head and forelegs set widely apart that was developed in England to fight bulls

²bulldog *adj* : suggestive of a bulldog ⟨*bulldog* courage⟩

³bulldog *vb* : to throw a steer by seizing the horns and twisting the neck

bull·doze \'bul-ˌdōz\ *vb* **bull·dozed; bull·doz·ing** **1** : to move, clear, or level with a bulldozer **2** : to force as if by using a bulldozer ⟨*bulldozed* their way through the crowd⟩

bull·doz·er \'bul-ˌdō-zər\ *n* : a piece of earth-moving equipment that rides on tracks and has a broad blade for pushing (as in clearing land of trees)

¹bulldog

bul·let \'bul-ət\ *n* **1** : a usually cone-shaped lead pellet fixed in the front of a firearms cartridge **2 a** : something like a bullet **b** : a large dot used in print to call attention to a particular passage **3** : a very fast and accurately thrown or hit object (as a ball) [from early French *boulette* "small ball" and *boulet* "something thrown or shot," from *boule* "ball," from Latin *bulla* "bubble" — related to BOIL, BOWL] — **bul·let·ed** \-ət-əd\ *adj*

bul·le·tin \'bul-ət-ᵊn\ *n* : a brief public notice usually from an informed or official source ⟨news *bulletin*⟩

bulletin board *n* **1** : a board for posting notices (as at a school) **2** : a place on a computer network (as the Internet) where people can leave or read public messages

bul·let·proof \'bul-ət-ˌprüf\ *adj* : so made as to prevent the passing through of bullets ⟨*bulletproof* glass⟩

bullet train *n* : a very high-speed passenger train

bull·fight \'bul-ˌfīt\ *n* : a public entertainment in which people excite bulls, display daring in escaping their charges, and finally kill them — **bull·fight·er** *n* — **bull·fight·ing** *n*

bull·frog \-ˌfrȯg, -ˌfräg\ *n* : a large heavy frog that makes a booming or bellowing sound

bull·head \-ˌhed\ *n* : any of various fishes with large heads; *esp* : any of several common freshwater catfishes of the U.S.

bull·head·ed \'bul-'hed-əd\ *adj* : STUBBORN 1 — **bull·head·ed·ness** *n*

bull·horn \'bul-ˌhȯ(ə)rn\ *n* : a handheld combined microphone and loudspeaker

bul·lion \'bul-yən\ *n* : gold or silver especially in bars or blocks

bull·mastiff \'bul-ˌmas-təf\ *n* : any of a breed of large powerful dogs developed by crossing bulldogs with mastiffs

bull·ock \'bul-ək\ *n* **1** : a young bull **2** : ¹STEER 1

bull pen *n* **1** : a large cell where prisoners are held until brought into court **2 a** : a place on a baseball field where relief pitchers warm up **b** : the relief pitchers of a team

bull's–eye \'bul-ˌzī\ *n* **1** : a round hard candy **2 a** : the center of a target **b** : a shot that hits the center of a target

bull snake *n* : any of several large harmless North American snakes feeding chiefly on rodents

bull terrier *n* : any of a breed of short-haired terriers developed in England by crossing the bulldog with terriers

¹**bul·ly** \'bul-ē\ *n, pl* **bullies** : a person who purposely hurts, intimidates, threatens, or ridicules another usually more vulnerable person especially repeatedly

²**bully** *vb* **bul·lied; bul·ly·ing** : to act like a bully toward

bul·rush \'bul-ˌrəsh\ *n* : any of several large sedges or rushes growing in wet land or water

bul·wark \'bul-(ˌ)wərk, -ˌwȯrk; 'bəl-(ˌ)wərk\ *n* **1** : a solid structure like a wall built for defense **2** : a strong support or protection **3** : the side of a ship above the upper deck — usually used in plural [Middle English *bulwerke* "bulwark," from early Dutch *bolwerc* (same meaning) — related to BOULEVARD]

¹**bum** \'bəm\ *n* : BUTTOCK 2a [Middle English *bom*]

²**bum** *adj* **1 a** : INFERIOR 3, WORTHLESS ⟨*bum* advice⟩ **b** : not true or deserved ⟨a *bum* rap⟩ **c** : not enjoyable ⟨a *bum* trip⟩ **2** : unable to work properly : DISABLED ⟨a *bum* knee⟩ [perhaps from ⁴*bum*]

³**bum** *vb* **bummed; bum·ming** **1** : to wander around avoiding work **2** : to obtain by asking or begging ⟨*bum* a ride⟩ [probably from *bummer* "one who avoids work"]

⁴**bum** *n* **1** : a person who avoids work and tries to live off others **2** : ²TRAMP 1, HOBO [probably short for *bummer* "one who avoids work," probably from German *Bummler* "loafer"]

⁵**bum** *vb* : SADDEN — usually used with *out* ⟨the news really *bummed* me out⟩ [probably from *bummer*]

bum·ble·bee \'bəm-bəl-ˌbē\ *n* : any of numerous large hairy social bees

bum·mer \'bəm-ər\ *n* **1** : an unpleasant experience, event, or situation **2** : something that fails : FLOP [²*bum*]

¹**bump** \'bəmp\ *n* **1** : a forceful blow, shock, or jolt **2** : a rounded lump; *esp* : a swelling of tissue (as from a blow)

²**bump** *vb* **1** : to strike or knock against something with force or violence **2** : to move along unevenly : JOLT — **bump into** : to meet especially by chance

¹**bum·per** \'bəm-pər\ *adj* : unusually large or fine ⟨a *bumper* crop⟩

²**bump·er** \'bəm-pər\ *n* : a device for absorbing shock or preventing damage (as in collision); *esp* : a bar at the front or back of a motor vehicle

bumper car *n* : a small electric car made to be driven around in an enclosure and to be bumped into others (as in an amusement park)

bump·kin \'bəm(p)-kən\ *n* : ²RUSTIC, YOKEL

bumpy \'bəm-pē\ *adj* **bump·i·er; -est** : marked by bumps or bumping ⟨a *bumpy* ride⟩ ⟨*bumpy* skin⟩ — **bump·i·ly** \-pə-lē\ *adv* — **bump·i·ness** \-pē-nəs\ *n*

bun \'bən\ *n* **1** : a sweet or plain small bread; *esp* : a round roll **2** : a knot of hair shaped like a bun

¹**bunch** \'bənch\ *n* **1** : a number of things of the same kind ⟨a *bunch* of grapes⟩ **2** : ¹GROUP 1, COLLECTION ⟨a *bunch* of friends⟩ **3** : a large amount : LOT ⟨a *bunch* of money⟩ — **bunchy** \'bən-chē\ *adj*

²**bunch** *vb* : to gather in a bunch

bunch·grass \'bənch-ˌgras\ *n* : any of several grasses chiefly of the western U.S. that grow in bunches

¹**bun·dle** \'bən-dᵊl\ *n* **1 a** : a number of things fastened or wrapped together : PACKAGE, PARCEL **b** : ¹BUNCH **2 a** : a small band of mostly parallel fibers (as of nerve) **b** : VASCULAR BUNDLE

²**bundle** *vb* **bun·dled; bun·dling** \'bən-(d)liŋ, -dᵊl-iŋ\ **1** : to make into a bundle : WRAP **2** : to hurry off : HUSTLE ⟨*bundled* us off to school⟩ — **bun·dler** \-dlər, -dᵊl-ər\ *n*

bundle up *vb* : to dress warmly

¹**bung** \'bəŋ\ *n* **1** : the stopper in the bunghole of a barrel **2** : BUNGHOLE

²**bung** *vb* : to plug with or as if with a bung

bun·ga·low \'bəŋ-gə-ˌlō\ *n* : a house with a single story and a roof with a low slope; *also* : a house having one and a half stories and usually a front porch [from Hindi *baṅglā*, literally, "(house) in the style of Bengal"]

bun·gee \'bən-jē\ *n* : BUNGEE CORD

bungee cord *n* : an elastic cord used especially as a fastening device or to absorb shocks — called also *bungee*

bungee jump *vb* : to jump from a high place while attached to an elastic cord — **bungee jumper** *n*

bung·hole \'bəŋ-ˌhōl\ *n* : a hole for filling or emptying a barrel

\ə\ **abut**	\au̇\ **out**	\i\ **tip**	\ȯ\ **saw**	\u̇\ **foot**
\ər\ **further**	\ch\ **chin**	\ī\ **life**	\ȯi\ **coin**	\y\ **yet**
\a\ **mat**	\e\ **pet**	\j\ **job**	\th\ **thin**	\yü\ **few**
\ā\ **take**	\ē\ **easy**	\ŋ\ **sing**	\th\ **this**	\yu̇\ **cure**
\ä\ **cot, cart**	\g\ **go**	\ō\ **bone**	\ü\ **food**	\zh\ **vision**

bun·gle \'bəŋ-gəl\ *vb* **bun·gled; bun·gling** \-g(ə-)liŋ\ : to act, do, make, or work badly ⟨*bungle* a job⟩ — **bungle** *n* — **bun·gler** \-g(ə-)lər\ *n*

bun·ion \'bən-yən\ *n* : an inflamed swelling on the first joint of the big toe

¹**bunk** \'bəŋk\ *n* **1** : BUNK BED **2** : a built-in bed (as on a ship) **3** : a sleeping place [probably a shortened form of *bunker*]

²**bunk** *vb* **1** : to sleep in a bunk or bed **2** : to provide with a bunk or bed

³**bunk** *n* : NONSENSE 1

> *Word History* The word *bunk* is a shortened form of *bunkum,* which came from the name Buncombe County, North Carolina. Around 1820, the congressman for the district in which this county was located decided to give a very long, boring speech to the Congress. This speech had nothing at all to do with what was under discussion. Still he stubbornly made it, just to please the voters of Buncombe County. The word *buncombe* and its other spelling *bunkum* quickly caught on as a name for empty political nonsense. It didn't take long before its use broadened to include any kind of empty or insincere talk or action. In time it was shortened to the more emphatic *bunk.* [short for *bunkum,* from *Buncombe* County, North Carolina]

bunk bed *n* : one of two single beds placed one above the other

bun·ker \'bəŋ-kər\ *n* **1** : a large bin (as for coal or oil on a ship) **2** : a shelter dug into the ground and made strong against attack **3** : SAND TRAP

bunk·house \'bəŋk-,haùs\ *n* : a simple building providing sleeping quarters

bun·ny \'bən-ē\ *n, pl* **bunnies** : RABBIT

Bun·sen burner \,bən(t)-sən-\ *n* : a gas burner consisting typically of a tube with small holes at the bottom where air enters and mixes with the gas to produce a very hot blue flame [named for Robert *Bunsen* 1811–1899 German chemist]

bunt \'bənt\ *vb* **1** : to strike or push with the horns or head : BUTT **2** : to push or tap a baseball lightly without swinging the bat — **bunt** *n* — **bunt·er** *n*

¹**bun·ting** \'bənt-iŋ\ *n* : any of various finches that are similar to sparrows in size and habits but have stout bills [Middle English *buntynge* "bunting"]

²**bunting** *n* **1** : a thin cloth used chiefly for making flags and patriotic decorations **2** : flags or decorations made of bunting [possibly derived from a dialect word *bunt* "to sift (meal)"]

¹**buoy** \'bü-ē, 'bòi\ *n* **1** : a floating object anchored in a body of water to mark a channel or warn of danger **2** : LIFE BUOY

²**buoy** *vb* **1** : to keep from sinking : keep afloat **2** : to brighten the mood of ⟨the news *buoyed* him up⟩

buoy·an·cy \'bòi-ən-sē, 'bü-yən-\ *n* **1** : the tendency of a body to float or to rise when in a fluid ⟨the *buoyancy* of a cork in water⟩ **2** : the power of a fluid to put an upward force on a body placed in it ⟨the *buoyancy* of seawater⟩

buoy·ant \'bòi-ənt, 'bü-yənt\ *adj* **1** : having buoyancy; *esp* : capable of floating **2** : being in a happy mood : CHEERFUL — **buoy·ant·ly** *adv*

bur *variant of* BURR

burb \'bərb\ *n* : SUBURB 2 — usually used in plural

¹**bur·den** \'bərd-°n\ *n* **1 a** : something carried : LOAD **b** : something taken as a duty or responsibility ⟨tax *burdens*⟩ **2** : something hard to take ⟨a *burden* of sorrow⟩ **3 a** : the carrying of loads ⟨beast of *burden*⟩ **b** : capacity for carrying cargo ⟨a ship of 100 tons *burden*⟩ [Old English *byrthen* "load, burden"] — **burden** *vb*

²**burden** *n* **1** : the refrain or chorus of a song **2** : a main idea : GIST [an altered form of earlier *bourdon* "a refrain or chorus of a song," from Middle English *burdoun* (same meaning), from early French *burdun* "bass horn"]

bur·den·some \'bərd-°n-səm\ *adj* : so heavy or hard to take as to be a burden — **bur·den·some·ness** *n*

bur·dock \'bər-,däk\ *n* : any of a genus of coarse herbs that are related to the daisies and have globe-shaped flower heads surrounded by prickly bracts

bu·reau \'byù(ə)r-ō\ *n, pl* **bu·reaus** *also* **bu·reaux** \-ōz\ **1 a** : a subdivision of a government department ⟨Federal *Bureau* of Investigation⟩ **b** : a business office providing services for the public ⟨a travel *bureau*⟩ **2** : a low chest of drawers for use in a bedroom

burdock

bu·reau·cra·cy \byù-'räk-rə-sē\ *n, pl* **-cies** **1** : a body of government officials **2** : a system of managing an organization (as a government or business) by strictly following a fixed routine or procedure that often results in delay

bu·reau·crat \'byùr-ə-,krat\ *n* : a member of a bureaucracy

bu·reau·crat·ic \,byùr-ə-'krat-ik\ *adj* : of, relating to, or having the characteristics of a bureaucracy or bureaucrat — **bu·reau·crat·i·cal·ly** \-'krat-i-k(ə-)lē\ *adv*

burg \'bərg\ *n* **1** : a fortress or walled town in the Middle Ages **2** : CITY 1, TOWN

bur·geon \'bər-jən\ *vb* **1 a** : to put forth new growth (as buds) **b** : ²BLOOM 1 **2** : EXPAND 3, FLOURISH

bur·ger \'bər-gər\ *n* **1** : HAMBURGER **2** : a sandwich like a hamburger ⟨veggie *burger*⟩

bur·gess \'bər-jəs\ *n* **1** : a citizen of a British borough **2** : a member of the lower house of the legislature of colonial Maryland or Virginia [Middle English *burgeis* "citizen of a borough," from early French *burgeis* "resident of a town," from earlier *burc* "town," from Latin *burgus* "fortified place" — related to BOURGEOIS]

bur·gher \'bər-gər\ *n* : a person who lives in a borough or a town

bur·glar \'bər-glər\ *n* : a person who commits burglary

bur·glar·ize \'bər-glə-,rīz\ *vb* **-ized; -iz·ing** : to break into and steal from ⟨*burglarize* a house⟩

bur·glary \'bər-glə-rē\ *n, pl* **-glar·ies** : the act of breaking into a building (as a house) especially at night to steal

bur·go·mas·ter \'bər-gə-,mas-tər\ *n* : the mayor of a town in some European countries

buri·al \'ber-ē-əl\ *n* : the act of burying

bur·ka *or* **bur·qa** \'bùr-kə\ *n* : a loose garment that covers the head, face, and body and is worn in public by certain Muslim women

bur·lap \'bər-,lap\ *n* : a rough fabric made usually from jute or hemp and used mostly for bags and wrappings

¹**bur·lesque** \(,)bər-'lesk\ *n* **1** : a written or dramatic work that makes fun of something by making it appear ridiculous **2** : theatrical entertainment consisting of comic skits and dance — **burlesque** *adj*

²**burlesque** *vb* **bur·lesqued; bur·lesqu·ing** : to mock or make fun of through burlesque

bur·ly \'bər-lē\ *adj* **bur·li·er; -est** : strongly and heavily built ⟨a *burly* man⟩ — **bur·li·ness** *n*

bur marigold *n* : any of a genus of coarse herbs related to the daisies and having burs that stick to clothing and fur

Bur·mese \,bər-'mēz, -'mēs\ *n, pl* **Burmese** **1** : a person born or living in Burma **2** : the language of the Burmese people — **Burmese** *adj*

¹**burn** \'bərn\ *vb* **burned** \'bərnd, 'bərnt\ *or* **burnt** \'bərnt\; **burn·ing** **1** : to be or set on fire **2 a** : to feel hot or inflamed ⟨the *burning* sand⟩ **b** : to become excited ⟨*burn* with anger⟩ **c** : ¹SCORCH 1 ⟨*burned* the toast⟩ **d** : to appear as if on fire : GLOW ⟨leave a light *burning* in the

window⟩ **e** : to destroy by fire ⟨*burn* trash⟩ **f** : to use as fuel ⟨this furnace *burns* gas⟩ ⟨your body *burns* food⟩ **3 a** : to produce by the action of fire or heat ⟨*burn* a hole in the rug⟩ **b** : to record data or music on a disk using a laser ⟨*burn* a CD⟩ **4** : to injure or change by or as if by fire or heat ⟨*burn* out a bearing⟩ **5** : to suffer sunburn ⟨she *burns* easily⟩ — **burn·able** \'bər-nə-bəl\ *adj* — **burn·ing·ly** \-niŋ-lē\ *adv*

²burn *n* : injury, damage, or effect produced by or as if by burning

burned–out \'bərnd-'aút, 'bərnt-\ *or* **burnt–out** \'bərnt-\ *adj* **1** : WORN-OUT 2 **2** : destroyed by fire ⟨a *burned-out* building⟩

burn·er \'bər-nər\ *n* : one that burns: as **a** : the part of a fuel-burning or heat-producing device (as a furnace or stove) where a flame or heat is produced **b** : a device for recording data on an optical disk

burn–in *n* : the continuous operation of a device (as a computer) as a test for defects or failure prior to putting it to use

bur·nish \'bər-nish\ *vb* : to make shiny especially by rubbing : POLISH — **bur·nish·er** *n*

bur·noose *or* **bur·nous** \(ˌ)bər-'nüs\ *n* : a hooded cloak worn especially in desert areas (as of northern Africa or eastern Mediterranean countries) [derived from Arabic *burnus* "hooded cloak"]

burn·out \'bər-ˌnaút\ *n* **1** : the ending of operation of a jet or rocket engine as a result of the using up or shutting off of fuel **2** : the point in a flight at which burnout occurs **3** : exhaustion of one's bodily or mental strength

burn out *vb* **1** : to drive out or destroy the property of by fire **2** : to cause to wear out or become exhausted

¹burp \'bərp\ *n* : ²BELCH

²burp *vb* **1** : ¹BELCH 1 **2** : to help a baby expel gas from the stomach especially by patting or rubbing the baby's back

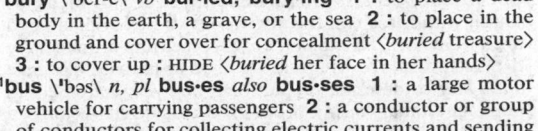

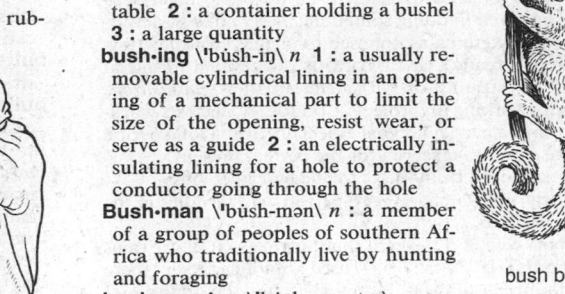

burnoose

burr \'bər\ *n* **1** *usually* **bur** \'bər\ **a** : a rough or prickly envelope of a fruit **b** : a plant that bears burs **2** : roughness left in cutting or shaping metal **3** *usually* **bur** : a bit used on a dentist's drill **4** : a rough trilled \r\ used by some speakers of English especially in northern England and in Scotland — **burred** \'bərd\ *adj*

bur·ri·to \bə-'rēt-ō\ *n, pl* **-tos** : a flour tortilla rolled or folded around a filling (as of meat, beans, and cheese) [American Spanish *burrito* "baked stuffed tortilla," from Spanish *burrito*, literally, "little donkey"]

bur·ro \'bər-ō, 'bùr-; 'bə-rō\ *n, pl* **burros** : a small donkey often used as a pack animal

¹bur·row \'bər-ō, 'bə-rō\ *n* : a hole in the ground made by an animal (as a rabbit or fox) for shelter or protection

²burrow *vb* **1** : to construct by tunneling **2** : to hide oneself in or as if in a burrow **3** : to move or enter by or as if by digging — **bur·row·er** *n*

bur·sa \'bər-sə\ *n, pl* **bursas** *or* **bur·sae** \-ˌsē, -ˌsī\ : a bodily pouch; *esp* : a small fluid-containing pouch between a tendon and a bone

bur·si·tis \(ˌ)bər-'sīt-əs\ *n* : inflammation of a bursa (as of the shoulder or elbow)

¹burst \'bərst\ *vb* **burst; burst·ing** **1 a** : to break open or in pieces (as by an explosion from within) ⟨the balloon *burst*⟩ ⟨buds *bursting* open⟩ **b** : to cause to burst **2 a** : to suddenly show one's feelings ⟨*burst* into tears⟩ **b** : to begin to do something suddenly ⟨*burst* into song⟩ **3** : to come or go suddenly ⟨*burst* into the room⟩ **4** : to be filled to the breaking point ⟨just *bursting* with energy⟩

²burst *n* **1** : a sudden release or effort ⟨a *burst* of speed⟩ **2** : a firing of many shots at the same time

bury \'ber-ē\ *vb* **bur·ied; bury·ing** **1** : to place a dead body in the earth, a grave, or the sea **2** : to place in the ground and cover over for concealment ⟨*buried* treasure⟩ **3** : to cover up : HIDE ⟨*buried* her face in her hands⟩

¹bus \'bəs\ *n, pl* **bus·es** *also* **bus·ses** **1** : a large motor vehicle for carrying passengers **2** : a conductor or group of conductors for collecting electric currents and sending them to outgoing wires

²bus *vb* **bused** *also* **bussed; bus·ing** *also* **bus·sing** : to travel or transport by bus

bus·boy \'bəs-ˌbói\ *n* : a person employed in a restaurant to remove dirty dishes and set tables

bush \'bùsh\ *n* **1** : SHRUB; *esp* : a low densely branched shrub **2** : a stretch of uncleared or lightly settled country **3** : a bushy tuft or mass

bush baby *n* : any of several small African lemurs

bushed \'bùsht\ *adj* : ¹WEARY 1, TIRED

bush·el \'bùsh-əl\ *n* **1** : any of various units of dry capacity — see MEASURE table **2** : a container holding a bushel **3** : a large quantity

bush·ing \'bùsh-iŋ\ *n* **1** : a usually removable cylindrical lining in an opening of a mechanical part to limit the size of the opening, resist wear, or serve as a guide **2** : an electrically insulating lining for a hole to protect a conductor going through the hole

Bush·man \'bùsh-mən\ *n* : a member of a group of peoples of southern Africa who traditionally live by hunting and foraging

bush baby

bush·mas·ter \'bùsh-ˌmas-tər\ *n* : a tropical American pit viper that is the largest New World poisonous snake

bush pilot *n* : a pilot who flies a small plane over remote or lightly settled country where commercial airlines do not go

bushy \'bùsh-ē\ *adj* **bush·i·er; -est** **1** : overgrown with bushes **2** : resembling a bush : being thick and spreading ⟨a *bushy* beard⟩ — **bush·i·ness** *n*

busi·ness \'biz-nəs, -nəz\ *n* **1** : an activity that takes a major part of the time, attention, or effort of a person or group **2 a** : a commercial or industrial activity or organization **b** : the making, buying, and selling of goods and services **3** : something to be dealt with : AFFAIR, MATTER ⟨a strange *business*⟩ **4 a** : personal concern ⟨none of your *business*⟩ **b** : ²RIGHT 2 ⟨you had no *business* saying that⟩

busi·ness·like \'biz-nə-ˌslīk, -nəz-ˌlīk\ *adj* : having or showing qualities desirable in business

busi·ness·man \'biz-nə-ˌsman, -nəz-ˌman\ *n* : a man in business especially as an owner or manager

busi·ness·peo·ple \-ˌspē-pəl\ *n pl* : persons active in business

busi·ness·per·son \-ˌspər-s²n\ *n* : a businessman or businesswoman

busi·ness·wom·an \-ˌswùm-ən\ *n* : a woman in business especially as an owner or manager

¹bust \'bəst\ *n* **1** : a piece of sculpture representing the upper part of the human figure including the human head and neck **2** : the upper part of the human body; *esp* : the breasts of a woman [from French *buste* "head and shoulders sculpture," from Italian *busto* (same meaning), from Latin *bustum* "tomb"]

\ə\ **abut**	\aú\ **out**	\i\ **tip**	\ò\ **saw**	\ù\ **foot**
\ər\ **further**	\ch\ **chin**	\ī\ **life**	\òi\ **coin**	\y\ **yet**
\a\ **mat**	\e\ **pet**	\j\ **job**	\th\ **thin**	\yü\ **few**
\ā\ **take**	\ē\ **easy**	\ŋ\ **sing**	\th\ **this**	\yù\ **cure**
\ä\ **cot, cart**	\g\ **go**	\ō\ **bone**	\ü\ **food**	\zh\ **vision**

²bust *vb* **bust·ed** *also* **bust; bust·ing** **1 a** : to break or smash with force ⟨*busted* my watch⟩ **b** : to bring an end to : BREAK UP **2 c** : to ruin or become ruined financially **d** : ¹EXHAUST 1b, WEAR 3c — used in phrases like *bust one's butt* to describe the act of trying very hard **2** : to tame an animal ⟨*bust* a bronco⟩ **3** : DEMOTE **4** *slang* **a** : ¹ARREST 2 **b** : ²RAID **5** : ¹HIT 1a, PUNCH [an altered form of *burst*] — **bust·er** *n*

³bust *n* **1** : ²PUNCH 1 **2** : a complete failure : FLOP **3** *slang* : a police raid or arrest

¹bus·tle \'bəs-əl\ *vb* **bus·tled; bus·tling** \'bəs-(ə-)liŋ\ : to move about busily or noisily

²bustle *n* : noisy or energetic activity

bust·line \'bəst-ˌlīn\ *n* : a line around a woman's body at the bust; *also* : the length of this line

¹busy \'biz-ē\ *adj* **bus·i·er; -est** **1 a** : involved in action : actively at work ⟨too *busy* to eat⟩ **b** : being in use ⟨the phone line is *busy*⟩ **2** : full of activity ⟨a *busy* street⟩ — **busi·ly** \'biz-ə-lē\ *adv* — **busy·ness** \'biz-ē-nəs\ *n*

synonyms BUSY, INDUSTRIOUS, DILIGENT mean seriously involved in doing something. BUSY stresses actively doing something as opposed to idleness ⟨*busy* getting the house ready⟩. INDUSTRIOUS suggests working at something steadily or with determination ⟨*industrious* students working on projects⟩. DILIGENT suggests working toward a particular goal especially over a long period of time ⟨a *diligent* search for the perfect present⟩.

²busy *vb* **bus·ied; busy·ing** : to make or keep busy

busy·body \'biz-ē-ˌbäd-ē\ *n* : a person who meddles in the affairs of others

¹but \(')bət\ *conj* **1 a** : except that : UNLESS ⟨it never rains *but* it pours⟩ **b** : ³THAT 1b — used after a negative ⟨there is no doubt *but* he won⟩ **2 a** : while just the opposite ⟨I ski *but* you don't⟩ **b** : yet nevertheless ⟨fell *but* wasn't hurt⟩ **c** : EXCEPT 2 ⟨no one *but* you may enter⟩

²but *prep* **1** : with the exception of ⟨no one there *but* me⟩ **2** : other than ⟨this letter is nothing *but* an insult⟩

³but *adv* : no more than : ONLY ⟨we have *but* two weeks to get ready⟩

bu·ta·di·ene \ˌbyüt-ə-ˈdī-ˌēn, -ˌdī-ˈēn\ *n* : a flammable gas that is a hydrocarbon used in making synthetic rubbers

bu·tane \'byü-ˌtān\ *n* : either of two flammable gases that are hydrocarbons obtained usually from petroleum or natural gas and used especially as a fuel

¹butch·er \'bůch-ər\ *n* **1 a** : one whose business is killing animals for sale as food **b** : a dealer in meat **2** : a person who kills in large numbers or in a brutal manner

²butcher *vb* **butch·ered; butch·er·ing** \-(ə-)riŋ\ **1** : to slaughter and prepare for market ⟨*butcher* hogs⟩ **2** : to kill in a barbarous manner : MASSACRE **3** : to make a mess of : BOTCH ⟨*butchered* the performance⟩

butch·ery \'bůch-(ə-)rē\ *n, pl* **-er·ies** : brutal murder : great slaughter

but·ler \'bət-lər\ *n* : a chief male household servant [Middle English *buteler* "household servant in charge of wines," from early French *butiller* (same meaning), from *botele* "bottle," derived from Latin *buttis* "cask"]

¹butt \'bət\ *vb* : to strike or thrust with the head or horns

²butt *n* : a blow or thrust with the head or horns

³butt *n* : a person who is treated badly or is made fun of ⟨the *butt* of a joke⟩

⁴butt *n* **1** : BUTTOCK 2a — often used in idiomatic expressions ⟨saved our *butts*⟩ ⟨get your *butt* over here⟩ **2** : the thicker or bottom end of something ⟨the *butt* of a rifle⟩ **3** : an unused remainder ⟨a cigarette *butt*⟩

butte \'byüt\ *n* : a hill with steep sides standing in a flat area

¹but·ter \'bət-ər\ *n* **1** : a solid yellow fatty food made by churning milk or cream **2** : a substance resembling butter in texture or use ⟨apple *butter*⟩ [Old English *butere* "butter," from Latin *butyrum* (same meaning), from

Greek *boutyron*, from *bous* "ox, cow" and *tyros* "cheese" — related to BUFFALO] — **but·tery** \-ə-rē\ *adj*

²butter *vb* : to spread with or as if with butter

but·ter–and–eggs \ˌbət-ə-rə-ˈnegz, -ˈnägz\ *n sing or pl* : any of several plants related to the snapdragons and having flowers of yellow and orange

butter bean *n* **1** : WAX BEAN **2** : LIMA BEAN **3** : a green shell bean especially as opposed to a snap bean

but·ter·cup \'bət-ər-ˌkəp\ *n* : any of a genus of herbs having cuplike yellow flowers

but·ter·fat \-ˌfat\ *n* : the natural fat of milk from which butter is made

but·ter·fin·gered \-ˌfiŋ-gərd\ *adj* : likely to let things fall or slip through the fingers

but·ter·fish \-ˌfish\ *n* : any of numerous fishes with a slippery coating of mucus

but·ter·fly \-ˌflī\ *n* **1** : any of numerous slender-bodied day-flying insects with large often brightly colored wings — compare MOTH **2** : a swimming stroke performed by moving both arms together in a circular motion while kicking the legs up and down **3** *pl* : a queasy feeling caused by nervousness

butterfly fish *n* : any of various fishes having spots or stripes of several colors, broad fins, or both

butterfly weed *n* : a showy orange-flowered milkweed of eastern North America

but·ter·milk \'bət-ər-ˌmilk\ *n* **1** : the liquid left after the butterfat has been churned from milk or cream **2** : milk from which all or part of the cream has been removed and which has been soured by adding certain bacteria

but·ter·nut \-ˌnət\ *n* : the edible oily nut of a North American tree related to the walnut; *also* : this tree

but·ter·scotch \-ˌskäch\ *n* : a candy or dessert topping made from sugar, corn syrup, and water

butt in *vb* : to meddle in someone else's business

but·tock \'bət-ək\ *n* **1** : the back of the hip which forms one of the fleshy parts on which a person sits **2** *pl* **a** : the seat of the body **b** : RUMP 1a

¹but·ton \'bət-ᵊn\ *n* **1 a** : a small knob or disk used for holding parts of a garment together or as an ornament **b** : a usually round badge bearing a design or slogan ⟨a campaign *button*⟩ **2** : something (as a small or young mushroom) that resembles a button **3** : PUSH BUTTON; *also* : a computer image that resembles a push button in appearance and function

²button *vb* **but·toned; but·ton·ing** \'bət-niŋ, -ᵊn-iŋ\ : to close or fasten with buttons — **but·ton·er** \-nər, -ᵊn-ər\ *n*

¹but·ton·hole \'bət-ᵊn-ˌhōl\ *n* : a slit or loop for fastening a button

²buttonhole *vb* **-holed; -hol·ing** : to detain in conversation by or as if by holding on to the clothes of

but·ton·hol·er \'bət-ᵊn-ˌhō-lər\ *n* : a sewing machine attachment for making buttonholes

but·ton·wood \-ˌwůd\ *n* : SYCAMORE 2

butt out *vb* : to stop meddling in someone else's business

¹but·tress \'bə-trəs\ *n* **1** : a structure built against a wall or building to give support and strength **2** : something that supports, props, or strengthens

²buttress *vb* : to support with or as if with a buttress

bu·tyr·ic acid \byü-ˌtir-ik-\ *n* : an acid with an unpleasant odor found in sweat and spoiling butter

bux·om \'bək-səm\ *adj* : having a healthy plump form — **bux·om·ness** *n*

¹buy \'bī\ *vb* **bought** \'bȯt\; **buy·ing** **1** : to get by paying money for : PURCHASE **2** : to gain control over by bribery ⟨*buy* votes⟩ **3** : BELIEVE 3 ⟨I don't *buy* that nonsense⟩ — **buy·er** \'bī(-ə)r\ *n* — **buy**

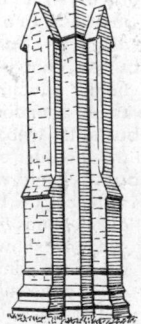

¹buttress 1

it *or* **buy the farm** : to get killed : DIE — **buy time** : to delay an action or decision : STALL

²**buy** *n* : ¹BARGAIN 2

¹**buzz** \'bəz\ *vb* **1** : to make a low continuous humming sound like that of a bee **2** : to be filled with a low hum or murmur ⟨the room *buzzed* with excitement⟩ **3** : to send for or signal by means of a buzzer **4** : to fly an airplane low over

²**buzz** *n* **1** : a sound of buzzing **2 a** : a signal given by a buzzer **b** : a telephone call

buz·zard \'bəz-ərd\ *n* : any of various usually large slow-flying birds of prey — compare TURKEY VULTURE

buzz cut *n* : CREW CUT — **buzz–cut** *adj*

buzz·er \'bəz-ər\ *n* : an electric signaling device that makes a buzzing sound

buzz saw *n* : CIRCULAR SAW

B vitamin *n* : any vitamin of the vitamin B complex

buzzard

¹**by** \(')bī, *especially before consonants* bə\ *prep* **1** : close to : NEAR ⟨*by* the sea⟩ **2 a** : so as to go along or through ⟨*by* a different route⟩ ⟨enter *by* the door⟩ **b** : ²PAST 2 ⟨went right *by* them⟩ **3 a** : AT, DURING ⟨studied *by* night⟩ **b** : not later than ⟨be there *by* 2 p.m.⟩ **4** : through the means or agency of ⟨*by* force⟩ **5** : ACCORDING TO 1 ⟨*by* the rules⟩ ⟨called *by* a different name⟩ **6** : with respect to ⟨a doctor *by* profession⟩ **7** : to or in the amount or length of ⟨win *by* a nose⟩ ⟨sold *by* the pound⟩ **8** : in a series of ⟨walk two *by* two⟩ **9** — used as a function word in multiplication and division and in measurements ⟨divide 6 *by* 2⟩ ⟨a room 15 feet *by* 20 feet⟩ **10** : in the opinion of ⟨it's fine *by* me⟩ — **by oneself** : ²ALONE 2

²**by** \'bī\ *adv* **1 a** : close at hand : NEAR ⟨standing *by*⟩ **b** : at or to another's home ⟨stop *by* for a chat⟩ **2** : ⁴PAST ⟨cars went *by*⟩ **3** : ¹ASIDE 2 ⟨putting some money *by*⟩

³**by** *or* **bye** \'bī\ *n*, *pl* **byes** \'bīz\ : something incidental — **by the by** : by the way : INCIDENTALLY

by–and–by \ˌbī-ən-'bī\ *n* : a future time or occasion

by and by \ˌbī-ən-'bī\ *adv* : BEFORE LONG, SOON

by and large \ˌbī-ən-'lärj\ *adv* : on the whole : in general

bye–bye *or* **by–by** \'bī-ˌbī, ˌbī-'bī\ *interj* — used to express farewell

by·gone \'bī-ˌgon *also* -ˌgän\ *adj* : gone by : PAST ⟨a *bygone* era⟩ — **bygone** *n*

by·law \'bī-ˌlò\ *n* : a rule adopted by an organization for governing its members and regulating its affairs [Middle English *bilawe* "bylaw," probably from an early Norse compound of *bȳr* "town" and *lǫg* "law"]

by·line \'bī-ˌlīn\ *n* : a line at the head of a newspaper or magazine article giving the writer's name

¹**by·pass** \'bī-ˌpas\ *n* : a passage to one side or around a blocked or very crowded area

²**bypass** *vb* : to make a detour around ⟨*bypass* a city⟩

by·path \'bī-ˌpath, -ˌpàth\ *n* : BYWAY

by–prod·uct \'bī-ˌpräd-(ˌ)əkt\ *n* : a product or result produced in addition to the main product or result

by·road \'bī-ˌrōd\ *n* : BYWAY

by·stand·er \-ˌstan-dər\ *n* : a person standing near but taking no part in what is happening

by·street \-ˌstrēt\ *n* : a street off a main street

byte \'bīt\ *n* : a group of eight bits that a computer handles as a unit [possibly an altered form of *bite*]

by·way \'bī-ˌwā\ *n* : a little-traveled side road

by·word \-ˌwərd\ *n* : PROVERB

¹**Byz·an·tine** \'biz-ən-ˌtēn, bə-'zan-, 'bīz-ən-; 'biz-ən-ˌtīn\ *n* : a person born or living in Byzantium or in the Byzantine Empire

²**Byzantine** *adj* **1** : of, relating to, or typical of Byzantium or the Eastern Roman Empire **2** : of or relating to a style of architecture developed in the Byzantine Empire especially in the 5th and 6th centuries characterized by a central dome over a square space and by much use of mosaics

C

c \'sē\ *n*, *often cap* **1** : the third letter of the English alphabet **2** : one hundred in Roman numerals **3** : a musical note referred to by the letter C : the tone on which a C major scale is based **4** : a grade rating a student's work as fair or mediocre

cab \'kab\ *n* **1 a** : a light closed carriage (as a hansom) **b** : a carriage for hire **2** : TAXICAB **3 a** : the covered compartment for the engineer and the controls of a locomotive **b** : a similar compartment on a truck, tractor, or crane [sense 1 from French *cabriolet* "a one-horse carriage"; sense 2 a shortened form of *taxicab*]

ca·bal \kə-'bal, -'bäl\ *n* : a small group of persons working together secretly (as to take over a government)

ca·bana \kə-'ban-(y)ə\ *n* : a shelter usually with an open side facing the sea or a swimming pool

cab·a·ret \ˌkab-ə-'rā, 'kab-ə-ˌrā\ *n* : NIGHTCLUB

cab·bage \'kab-ij\ *n* : a garden plant related to the turnips and mustards that has a round firm head of leaves used as a vegetable

cabbage butterfly *n* : any of several mostly white butterflies whose caterpillars feed on cabbages

cab·bie *or* **cab·by** \'kab-ē\ *n*, *pl* **cabbies** : CABDRIVER

cab·driv·er \'kab-ˌdrī-vər\ *n* : a driver of a cab

cab·in \'kab-ən\ *n* **1 a** : a small private room on a ship **b** : a compartment below deck on a small boat for passen-

gers or crew **c** : a compartment (as in an airplane, airship, or spacecraft) for cargo, crew, or passengers **2** : a small simple dwelling usually having only one story

cabin boy *n* : a boy working as a servant on a ship

cabin cruiser *n* : CRUISER 3

cab·i·net \'kab-(ə-)nət\ *n* **1 a** : a case or cupboard usually having doors and shelves **b** : a case for a radio or television **2** : a group of advisers to the political head of a government ⟨the British *cabinet*⟩ ⟨the president's *cabinet*⟩

cab·i·net·mak·er \-ˌmā-kər\ *n* : a skilled woodworker who makes fine furniture — **cab·i·net·mak·ing** \-kiŋ\ *n*

cab·i·net·work \-ˌwərk\ *n* : the finished work made by a cabinetmaker

¹**ca·ble** \'kā-bəl\ *n* **1** : a very strong thick rope, wire, or chain **2** : a wire or wire rope by which force is applied to operate a piece of machinery ⟨brake *cable*⟩ **3** : a bundle of electrical wires held together usually around a central core **4** : CABLEGRAM **5** : CABLE TELEVISION

\ə\ **abut**	\aú\ **out**	\i\ **tip**	\ò\ **saw**	\ú\ **foot**
\ər\ **further**	\ch\ **chin**	\ī\ **life**	\òi\ **coin**	\y\ **yet**
\a\ **mat**	\e\ **pet**	\j\ **job**	\th\ **thin**	\yü\ **few**
\ā\ **take**	\ē\ **easy**	\ŋ\ **sing**	\th\ **this**	\yú\ **cure**
\ä\ **cot, cart**	\g\ **go**	\ō\ **bone**	\ü\ **food**	\zh\ **vision**

²**cable** *vb* **ca·bled; ca·bling** \'kā-b(ə-)liŋ\ **1** : to fasten or provide with a cable **2** : to telegraph by cable

cable car *n* : a car moved on tracks by an endless cable or along an overhead cable

ca·ble·gram \'kā-bəl-ˌgram\ *n* : a message sent by a submarine cable

cable modem *n* : a modem used to connect a computer to the Internet over a cable television line

cable television *n* : a system of television reception in which signals from distant stations are picked up by a main antenna and sent by cable to the sets of paying subscribers — called also *cable TV*

ca·boo·dle \kə-'büd-ᵊl\ *n* : all of a group of things — used in the phrase *the whole caboodle* or *the whole kit and caboodle*

ca·boose \kə-'büs\ *n* : a car usually at the rear of a freight train for the use of the train crew and railroad workers

cab·ri·ole \'kab-rē-ˌōl\ *n* **1** : a ballet leap in which one leg is extended and the other struck against it **2** : a curved furniture leg ending in an ornamental foot

ca·cao \kə-'kaů, kə-'kā-ō\ *n, pl* **cacaos 1** : a South American tree that bears small yellowish flowers followed by fleshy yellow pods containing many seeds **2** : the dried fatty seeds of the cacao from which cocoa and chocolate are made — called also *cacao bean*

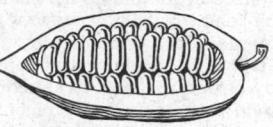
cacao: pod with seeds

¹**cache** \'kash\ *n* **1** : a place for hiding, storing, or preserving treasure or supplies **2** : something hidden or stored in a cache **3** : a computer memory with very short access time

²**cache** *vb* **cached; cach·ing** : to hide or store in a cache

cack·le \'kak-əl\ *vb* **cack·led; cack·ling** \-(ə-)liŋ\ **1** : to make the sharp broken noise or cry that a hen makes especially after laying an egg **2** : to laugh or chatter noisily — **cackle** *n* — **cack·ler** \-(ə-)lər\ *n*

ca·coph·o·ny \ka-'käf-ə-nē\ *n, pl* **-nies** : harsh unpleasant sound — **ca·coph·o·nous** \-ə-nəs\ *adj*

cac·tus \'kak-təs\ *n, pl* **cac·ti** \-ˌtī, -(ˌ)tē\ *or* **cac·tus·es** *also* **cactus** : any of a large family of flowering plants able to live in dry regions and having fleshy stems and branches that bear scales or prickles instead of leaves

cad \'kad\ *n* : a rude and selfish man [from an earlier dialect word *cad* "an unskilled worker," shortened from Scots *caddie* (same meaning) — related to CADDIE, CADET; see *Word History* at CADDIE]

ca·dav·er \kə-'dav-ər\ *n* : a dead body especially of a person : CORPSE

ca·dav·er·ous \kə-'dav-(ə-)rəs\ *adj* : resembling a corpse: as **a** : ¹PALE 1b, GHASTLY **b** : ¹THIN 3, HAGGARD

cad·die *or* **cad·dy** \'kad-ē\ *n, pl* **caddies** : a person who carries a golfer's clubs — **caddie** *or* **caddy** *vb*

> **Word History** In Scotland in the 18th and 19th centuries, a person who made a living by doing odd jobs was called a *cawdy* or *caddie*. The word *caddie* comes from the French word *cadet*, which was borrowed into English in the 17th century. The chief meaning of *cadet* in both French and English is "a student military officer." The first Scottish caddies formed an organized group, and it may be that the somewhat military structure of the group suggested the name. These caddies looked for odd jobs wherever they could, and after a time the name spread from Scotland into England. Some of the caddies lived near the English universities and took jobs working for students. With scorn the students referred to the lower-class caddies as *cads*. Then they used the term for any person they thought of as having poor manners. That is how we get our modern English word *cad* for "a rude and selfish man." Other caddies found jobs carry-

ing clubs for players of golf, which began in Scotland. As the popularity of golf grew, so did use of *caddie* for one who carries a golfer's clubs. [from Scottish *caddie, cawdy* "one who works at odd jobs," from French *cadet* "one training for military service," derived from Latin *caput* "head" — related to CAD, CADET, CAPTAIN]

cad·dis fly \'kad-əs-\ *n* : any of an order of four-winged insects with a larva which lives in water in a silk case covered especially with bits of wood, gravel, sand, or plant matter

cad·dy \'kad-ē\ *n, pl* **caddies** : a small box or chest; *esp* : one to keep tea in

ca·dence \'kād-ᵊn(t)s\ *n* **1 a** : rhythmic flow of sounds : the beat of rhythmic motion or activity **2** : a melodic or rhythmic pattern that serves as the close of a musical phrase or composition — **ca·denced** \-ᵊn(t)st\ *adj*

ca·den·za \kə-'den-zə\ *n* : an impressive solo part usually near the close of a musical composition

ca·det \kə-'det\ *n* **1** : a student military officer **2** : a student at a military school [from French *cadet* "a younger brother or son, one training for military service," derived from Latin *capitellum*, literally, "little (younger) head or chief," from *caput* "head" — related to CAD, CADDIE, CAPITAL, CAPTAIN, CHIEF; see *Word History* at CADDIE] — **ca·det·ship** \-ˌship\ *n*

Ca·dette \kə-'det\ *n* : a member of a program of the Girl Scouts for girls in the sixth through ninth grades

cad·mi·um \'kad-mē-əm\ *n* : a bluish white metallic element used especially in protective coatings — see ELEMENT table

cadmium sulfide *n* : a yellow-brown poisonous salt used especially in electronic parts, in photoelectric cells, and in medicine

ca·du·ceus \kə-'d(y)ü-sē-əs, -shəs\ *n, pl* **-cei** \-sē-ˌī\ **1** : a figure of a staff with two snakes wound around it and two wings at the top **2** : an emblem bearing a caduceus and symbolizing a physician

caecal, caecum *variant of* CECAL, CECUM

Cae·sar \'sē-zər\ *n* : any of the Roman emperors after Caesar Augustus [from Latin *Caesar* (title of a line of emperors after Caesar Augustus, adopted son of Julius Caesar) — see *Word History* at EMPEROR]

caesarean, caesarean section *variant of* CESAREAN, CESAREAN SECTION

cae·su·ra \si-'zùr-ə, -'zhùr-\ *n, pl* **-ras** *or* **-rae** \-'zù(ə)r-(ˌ)ē, -'zhù(ə)r-\ : a break in the flow of sound usually in the middle of a line of verse

ca·fé *also* **ca·fe** \ka-'fā, kə-\ *n* **1** : a usually small restaurant **2** : BARROOM **3** : NIGHTCLUB

caf·e·te·ria \ˌkaf-ə-'tir-ē-ə\ *n* **1** : a restaurant in which the customers serve themselves or are served at a counter but carry their own food to their tables **2** : LUNCHROOM

caf·fein·at·ed \'kaf-ə-ˌnāt-əd\ *adj* **1** : stimulated by or as if by caffeine **2** : containing caffeine 〈*caffeinated* coffee〉

caf·feine \ka-'fēn, 'ka-ˌfēn\ *n* : a bitter stimulating compound found especially in coffee, tea, cacao, and kola nuts

caf·tan *also* **kaf·tan** \kaf-'tan, 'kaf-ˌtan\ *n* : an ankle-length garment with long sleeves that is worn in eastern Mediterranean countries

¹**cage** \'kāj\ *n* **1** : an enclosure that has large openings covered usually with wire net or bars and is used for keeping animals or birds **2** : an enclosure like a cage in form or purpose — **cageful** *n*

²**cage** *vb* **caged; cag·ing** : to put or keep in or as if in a cage

ca·gey *also* **ca·gy** \'kā-jē\ *adj* **ca·gi·er; -est** : very careful of not being trapped or deceived 〈a *cagey* buyer〉 — **ca·gi·ly** \-jə-lē\ *adv* — **ca·gi·ness** \-jē-nəs\ *n*

cai·man *also* **cay·man** \kā-'man, kī-; 'kā-mən\ *n* : any of several Central and South American reptiles closely related to and resembling alligators

ca·ïque \kä-ˈēk\ *n* **1** : a light rowboat used on the Bosporus **2** : a Greek sailing vessel usually equipped with an engine [from Turkish *kayik* "rowboat"]

cairn \ˈka(ə)rn, ˈke(ə)rn\ *n* : a heap of stones piled up as a landmark or as a memorial

cais·son \ˈkā-ˌsän, ˈkā-sᵊn\ *n* **1 a** : a chest for ammunition **b** : a usually two-wheeled vehicle for artillery ammunition **2** : a watertight chamber used in construction work underwater or as a foundation

caisson disease *n* : ²BEND 3

ca·jole \kə-ˈjōl\ *vb* **ca·joled; ca·jol·ing** : to coax or persuade especially by flattery or false promises : WHEEDLE — **ca·jol·ery** \-ˈjōl-(ə-)rē\ *n*

¹Ca·jun \ˈkā-jən\ *n* : a Louisianian whose ancestors were French-speaking immigrants from Acadia, Canada [from an altered form of *Acadian*]

²Cajun *adj* **1** : of or relating to the Cajuns **2** : prepared in a cooking style originating with the Cajuns and marked by the use of hot seasonings (as cayenne pepper)

¹cake \ˈkāk\ *n* **1** : a small piece of food (as dough or batter, meat, or fish) that is baked or fried **2** : a baked food made from a sweet batter or dough **3** : a substance hardened or molded into a solid mass ⟨a *cake* of soap⟩

²cake *vb* **caked; cak·ing** **1** : ENCRUST ⟨*caked* with dust⟩ **2** : to form or harden into a cake

cal·a·bash \ˈkal-ə-ˌbash\ *n* : GOURD 2; *esp* : one whose hard shell is used for a utensil (as a bottle)

cal·a·mari \ˌkä-lə-ˈmär-ē\ *n* : squid used as food

cal·a·mine \ˈkal-ə-ˌmīn, -mən\ *n* : a mixture of zinc oxide and a small amount of ferric oxide used in lotions, liniments, and ointments

cal·am·i·tous \kə-ˈlam-ət-əs\ *adj* : causing or accompanied by calamity ⟨*calamitous* events⟩ — **ca·lam·i·tous·ly** *adv* — **ca·lam·i·tous·ness** *n*

ca·lam·i·ty \kə-ˈlam-ət-ē\ *n, pl* **-ties** **1** : deep distress or misery **2** : an event that causes great harm

calabash

cal·car·e·ous \kal-ˈkar-ē-əs, -ˈker-\ *adj* **1** : resembling calcite or calcium carbonate especially in hardness **2** : consisting of or containing calcium carbonate; *also* : containing calcium

cal·cif·er·ol \kal-ˈsif-ə-ˌrȯl, -ˌrōl\ *n* : a vitamin D that is sometimes added to human and animal diets and is used in medicine to treat rickets and related disorders

cal·cif·er·ous \kal-ˈsif-(ə-)rəs\ *adj* : producing or containing calcium carbonate

cal·ci·fy \ˈkal-sə-ˌfī\ *vb* **-fied; -fy·ing** : to make or become stony by deposit of calcium salts — **cal·ci·fi·ca·tion** \ˌkal-sə-fə-ˈkā-shən\ *n*

cal·cite \ˈkal-ˌsīt\ *n* : a mineral substance made up of calcium carbonate and found in numerous forms including limestone, chalk, and marble — **cal·cit·ic** \kal-ˈsit-ik\ *adj*

cal·ci·um \ˈkal-sē-əm\ *n* : a silver-white soft metallic element that is found only in combination with other elements (as in limestone) and is one of the necessary elements making up the bodies of most plants and animals — see ELEMENT table [derived from Latin *calc-, calx* "lime" — related to CALCULATE, CHALK]

calcium carbonate *n* : a solid substance found in nature as limestone and marble and in plant ashes, bones, and shells and used especially in making lime and portland cement

calcium chloride *n* : a salt that absorbs moisture from the air and is used to dry other substances

calcium hydroxide *n* : a white compound in the form of crystals that is used especially in making mortar and plaster and in softening water

calcium oxide *n* : an oxide of calcium that is white when pure and makes up the major part of lime

calcium phosphate *n* : any of various phosphates of calcium: as **a** : one used as a fertilizer **b** : a naturally occurring phosphate containing other elements (as fluorine) and occurring as an important part of phosphate-bearing rock, bones, and teeth

calcium sulfate *n* : a white odorless compound of calcium that is used especially in building materials and to dry other substances

cal·cu·late \ˈkal-kyə-ˌlāt\ *vb* **-lat·ed; -lat·ing** **1** : to find by performing mathematical operations (as addition, subtraction, multiplication, and division) : COMPUTE ⟨*calculate* the average⟩ **2** : ESTIMATE 1 ⟨*calculate* the risk of losing⟩ **3** : to plan by careful thought ⟨a program *calculated* to succeed⟩ [from Latin *calculatus* "calculate," derived from *calculus* "pebble (used in counting)," from *calc-, calx* "stone used in gambling, lime" — related to CALCIUM, CHALK]

cal·cu·lat·ing \ˈkal-kyə-ˌlāt-iŋ\ *adj* **1** : designed to make calculations ⟨a *calculating* machine⟩ **2 a** : tending to plan or study things with much care and caution **b** : SCHEMING — **cal·cu·lat·ing·ly** *adv*

cal·cu·la·tion \ˌkal-kyə-ˈlā-shən\ *n* **1 a** : the process or an act of calculating **b** : the result obtained by calculation **2** : care in planning : CAUTION

cal·cu·la·tor \ˈkal-kyə-ˌlāt-ər\ *n* **1** : one that calculates **2** : a usually small electronic device for making mathematical calculations

cal·cu·lus \ˈkal-kyə-ləs\ *n, pl* **cal·cu·li** \-ˌlī, -ˌlē\ *also* **-lus·es** **1** : a branch of higher mathematics concerned especially with rates of change and the finding of lengths, areas, and volumes **2 a** : a mass that consists mostly of mineral salts and is formed in a hollow organ or bodily duct **b** : ¹TARTAR 2

cal·de·ra \kal-ˈder-ə, kȯl-, -ˈdir-\ *n* : a large crater formed by the collapse of a volcanic cone or by an explosion

caldron *variant of* CAULDRON

¹cal·en·dar \ˈkal-ən-dər\ *n* **1 a** : an arrangement of time into days, weeks, months, and years **b** : a chart showing the days, weeks, and months of a year **2 a** : a list of items in proper order **b** : a schedule of coming events [Middle English *calender* "calendar," from early French *calender* and Latin *kalendarium* (both, same meaning), derived from Latin *kalendae* "the first day of the (Roman) month"]

²calendar *vb* **-dared; cal·en·dar·ing** \-d(ə-)riŋ\ : to enter in a calendar

¹calf \ˈkaf, ˈkȧf\ *n, pl* **calves** \ˈkavz, ˈkȧvz\ **1 a** : the young of the domestic cow **b** : the young of various other large animals (as the elephant or whale) **2** *pl* **calfs** : CALFSKIN [Old English *cealf* "young cow"]

²calf *n, pl* **calves** : the fleshy or muscular back part of the leg below the knee [Middle English *calf* "part of the leg"; of Norse origin]

calf·skin \ˈkaf-ˌskin, ˈkȧf-\ *n* : leather made from the skin of a calf

cal·i·ber *or* **cal·i·bre** \ˈkal-ə-bər\ *n* **1** : degree of excellence or importance **2** : the diameter of a missile (as a bullet) **3** : the inside diameter of a gun barrel

cal·i·brate \ˈkal-ə-ˌbrāt\ *vb* **-brat·ed; -brat·ing** **1** : to measure the caliber of **2 a** : to determine, correct, or put the measuring marks on (as a thermometer tube) **b** : make standard (as a measuring instrument) by finding out and correcting for the differences from an accepted or ideal value — **cal·i·bra·tion** \ˌkal-ə-ˈbrā-shən\ *n*

cal·i·co \ˈkal-i-ˌkō\ *n, pl* **-coes** *or* **-cos** **1** : cotton cloth especially with a colored pattern printed on one side **2** : a blotched or spotted animal ⟨a *calico* cat⟩ [named for *Calicut,* a city in India, which exported such cloth] — **calico** *adj*

calico bass *n* : BLACK CRAPPIE

Cal·i·for·nia condor \ˌkal-ə-ˌfȯr-nyə-\ *n* : a very large nearly extinct vulture of mountainous southern California that is related to the condor of South America

California condor

California poppy *n* : any of a genus of herbs related to the poppies and including one widely grown for its usually yellow or orange flowers

cal·i·for·ni·um \ˌkal-ə-ˈfȯr-nē-əm\ *n* : an artificially prepared radioactive element — see ELEMENT table

cal·i·per \ˈkal-ə-pər\ *n* : a measuring instrument with two legs or jaws that can be adjusted to determine thickness, diameter, or distance between surfaces — usually used in plural ⟨a pair of *calipers*⟩

ca·liph *also* **ca·lif** \ˈkā-ləf, ˈkal-əf\ *n* : an important Muslim political and religious leader — used as a title

ca·liph·ate \ˈkā-lə-ˌfāt, -fət; ˈkal-ə-\ *n* : the office or dominion of a caliph

cal·is·then·ics \ˌkal-əs-ˈthen-iks\ *n sing or pl* **1** : exercises to develop strength and flexibility that are done without special equipment **2** : the art or practice of calisthenics — **cal·is·then·ic** \-ik\ *adj*

Word History The benefits that exercise can have for both strength and looks are suggested by the origin of the word *calisthenics. Calisthenics* was made by joining the Greek *kalos,* meaning "beautiful," and *sthenos,* meaning "strength." The word was originally used to refer to exercises done by young women, but it later gained the more general meaning that we now know. [from Greek *kalos* "beautiful" and *sthenos* "strength"]

calk *variant of* CAULK

¹call \ˈkȯl\ *vb* **1** : to speak so as to be heard at a distance : SHOUT ⟨*call* for help⟩ **2** : to utter in a loud clear voice ⟨*call* out a command⟩ **3 a** : to announce with authority : PROCLAIM ⟨*call* a halt⟩ **b** : to announce the action of (as a sports game) **4** : SUMMON 1 ⟨*call* a meeting⟩ **5** : to bring into action or discussion ⟨*call* up reserves⟩ **6 a** : to make a request or demand of or for ⟨*call* for an end to war⟩ **b** : to give temporary control of a computer to a particular set of instructions **7** : to make a telephone call to **8** : to make a brief visit ⟨no salesperson will *call*⟩ **9 a** : to give a name to ⟨*called* the cat "Patches"⟩ **b** : to address by a name ⟨what did you *call* me⟩ **10** : to regard as being of a certain kind ⟨you can *call* them generous⟩ **11** : to estimate as being ⟨*call* it an even dollar⟩ **12 a** : to utter a cry ⟨crows *calling*⟩ **b** : to attract game by imitating its cry **13** : ⁴HALT 2, SUSPEND ⟨*call* a game on account of rain⟩ ⟨*call* time⟩ — **call·er** *n* — **call for 1** : to stop by (as at one's house) to get ⟨I'll *call for* you later⟩ **2** : to require as necessary ⟨the job *calls for* computer skills⟩ — **call on 1** : to ask or require : DEMAND **2** : to choose (as a student) to answer ⟨the teacher *called on* her first⟩ — **call the shots** : to be in charge or control — **call upon 1** : ²DEMAND 2 **2** : to depend on

²call *n* **1** : a loud cry : SHOUT **2 a** : a cry of an animal **b** : an imitation of an animal's cry or a device used to make such an imitation **3 a** : ¹SUMMONS 1, INVITATION **b** : ATTRACTION 1 ⟨the *call* of the wild⟩ **4 a** : ¹DEMAND 1a, CLAIM **b** : ¹REQUEST 1 **5** : a brief visit **6** : the act of calling on the telephone **7** : a ruling made by an official of a

sports contest **8** : a temporary transfer of control of computer processing to a particular set of instructions

cal·la lily \ˈkal-ə-\ *n* : a plant often grown for its large white bract surrounding a fleshy spike of small yellow flowers

call·back \ˈkȯl-ˌbak\ *n* **1** : a return call **2** : ²RECALL 5

caller ID \-ˌī-ˈdē\ *n* : a telephone service that identifies the phone number of a caller

cal·lig·ra·phy \kə-ˈlig-rə-fē\ *n* **1 a** : beautiful handwriting **b** : the art of producing such handwriting **2** : PENMANSHIP 2 — **cal·lig·ra·pher** \-rə-fər\ *n*

call·ing \ˈkȯ-liŋ\ *n* : OCCUPATION 1, PROFESSION

cal·li·ope \kə-ˈlī-ə-(ˌ)pē *also* ˈkal-ē-ˌōp\ *n* : a keyboard musical instrument consisting of a set of whistles sounded usually by steam [named for *Calliope,* one of the nine goddesses in Greek mythology who had control over music and poetry]

call number *n* : a combination of numbers and letters assigned to a library book to indicate its location in the library

call off *vb* **1** : to draw away : DIVERT ⟨*call off* a dog⟩ **2** : CANCEL 2a ⟨*call off* a meeting⟩

cal·los·i·ty \ka-ˈläs-ət-ē, kə-\ *n, pl* **-ties** : ¹CALLUS 1

cal·lous \ˈkal-əs\ *adj* **1 a** : being hardened and thickened **b** : having calluses ⟨*callous* hands⟩ **2** : feeling or showing no sympathy for others : UNFEELING ⟨a *callous* refusal to help the poor⟩ — **cal·lous·ly** *adv* — **cal·lous·ness** *n*

cal·low \ˈkal-ō\ *adj* : lacking adult experience : IMMATURE ⟨*callow* youth⟩ — **cal·low·ness** *n*

call–up \ˈkȯ-ˌləp\ *n* : an order to report for military service

¹cal·lus \ˈkal-əs\ *n, pl* **cal·lus·es** **1** : a hard thickened area on skin or bark **2** : a mass of tissue that forms around a break in a bone and is changed into bone in the healing of the break **3** : tissue that forms over an injured plant surface

²callus *vb* : to form callus

call–wait·ing \ˈkȯl-ˈwāt-iŋ\ *n* : a telephone service that signals (as by a click) to the user when an incoming call is received while a call is in progress

¹calm \ˈkäm, ˈkälm\ *n* **1 a** : a period or state of freedom from storm, wind, or rough water **b** : complete lack of wind or the presence of wind of no more than one mile (1.6 kilometers) per hour **2** : a state of freedom from excitement or disturbance : PEACEFULNESS

²calm *vb* : to make or become calm

³calm *adj* **1** : marked by calm : STILL ⟨a *calm* sea⟩ **2** : free from excitement or disturbance ⟨a *calm* manner⟩ — **calm·ly** *adv* — **calm·ness** *n*
    synonyms CALM, TRANQUIL, SERENE, PEACEFUL mean quiet and free from disturbance. CALM may suggest that one is free from disturbance even when there is cause for excitement ⟨stayed *calm* during the fire⟩. TRANQUIL suggests a total or lasting state of rest ⟨led a *tranquil* life in a rural area⟩. SERENE suggests a lofty and dignified kind of tranquillity ⟨the queen looks *serene* on her throne⟩. PEACEFUL suggests a quiet state that follows a period of turmoil ⟨grown *peaceful* in old age⟩.

cal·o·mel \ˈkal-ə-məl, -ˌmel\ *n* : a white tasteless chemical compound of mercury and chlorine that is used especially as a fungicide

ca·lor·ic \kə-ˈlȯr-ik, -ˈlōr-, -ˈlär-; ˈkal-ə-rik\ *adj* **1** : of or relating to heat **2** : relating to or containing calories — **ca·lor·i·cal·ly** \-i-k(ə-)lē\ *adv*

cal·o·rie *also* **cal·o·ry** \ˈkal-(ə-)rē\ *n, pl* **-ries** **1** : a unit of heat: **a** : the heat energy required to raise the temperature of one gram of water one degree Celsius and equal to about 4.19 joules — called also *small calorie* **b** : the amount of energy required to raise the temperature of one kilogram of water one degree Celsius and equal to 1000 small calories — used especially to indicate the value of foods in the production of heat and energy; called also *large calorie, kilocalorie* **2** : an amount of food having an energy-producing value of one large calorie [from French *calorie* "a unit of heat," from Latin *calor* "heat," from *calēre* "to be hot" — related to CAULDRON, NONCHALANT]

cal·o·rif·ic \,kal-ə-'rif-ik\ *adj* : CALORIC

cal·o·rim·e·ter \,kal-ə-'rim-ət-ər\ *n* : a device for measuring quantities of heat given off or taken in

calve \'kav, 'kȧv\ *vb* **calved; calv·ing 1** : to give birth to a calf **2** *of an ice mass* : to break so that a large part becomes separated ⟨a glacier *calving* icebergs⟩

calves *plural of* CALF

ca·lyp·so \kə-'lip-sō\ *n, pl* **-sos** : a folk song or style of singing of West Indian origin having a lively rhythm and words which are usually made up by the singer

ca·lyx \'kā-liks *also* 'kal-iks\ *n, pl* **ca·lyx·es** *or* **ca·ly·ces** \'kā-lə-,sēz *also* 'kal-ə-\ : the usually green or leafy outside part of a flower consisting of sepals

cal·zo·ne \kal-'zōn, -'zō-,nē, -'zō-nā; käl-'zōn-ā\ *n, pl* **calzone** *or* **calzones** : a baked or fried turnover of pizza dough with various fillings usually including cheese

¹**cam** \'kam\ *n* : a device by which circular motion may be transformed into stop-and-start or back-and-forth motion [perhaps from French *came* "cam," from German *Kamm,* literally, "comb"]

²**cam** *n* : CAMERA 2

ca·ma·ra·de·rie \,käm-(ə-)'räd-ə-rē, kam-(ə-)'rad-\ *n* : good feeling existing between comrades

cam·bi·um \'kam-bē-əm\ *n, pl* **cam·bi·ums** *or* **cam·bia** \-bē-ə\ : a thin cell layer between the xylem and phloem of most vascular plants from which new cells (as of wood and bark) develop — **cam·bi·al** \-bē-əl\ *adj*

Cam·bri·an \'kam-brē-ən, 'käm-\ *adj* : of, relating to, or being the earliest period of the Paleozoic era of geological history or the corresponding system of rocks marked by fossils of nearly every major invertebrate animal group — see GEOLOGIC TIME table — **Cambrian** *n*

cam·bric \'kām-brik\ *n* : a fine thin white linen or cotton fabric

cam·cord·er \'kam-,kȯrd-ər\ *n* : a small portable combined camera and VCR

came *past of* COME

cam·el \'kam-əl\ *n* : either of two large cud-chewing mammals used for carrying burdens and for riding in desert regions especially of Africa and Asia: **a** : DROMEDARY **b** : a two-humped camel of central Asia — called also *Bactrian camel*

camel hair *also* **camel's hair** *n* **1** : the hair of a camel or a substitute for it (as hair from squirrels' tails) **2** : a cloth made of camel hair or of camel hair and wool

camel b

ca·mel·lia \kə-'mēl-yə\ *n* : a greenhouse shrub that is related to the tea plant and has glossy evergreen leaves and showy roselike flowers

Ca·mel·o·par·da·lis \kə-,mel-ə-'pärd-ᵊl-əs\ *n* : a northern group of stars between Cassiopeia and Ursa Major

Cam·em·bert \'kam-əm-,be(ə)r\ *n* : a soft cheese with a whitish rind and a yellow inside [named for *Camembert,* a village in France where the cheese is made]

cam·eo \'kam-ē-,ō\ *n, pl* **-eos 1** : a carved gem in which the design is higher than its background **2** : a small role (as in a movie) performed by a well-known actor

cam·era \'kam-(ə-)rə\ *n* **1** : a judge's private office ⟨hearings held in *camera*⟩ **2** : a lightproof box fitted with a lens

through which the image of an object is projected onto a surface that is sensitive to light for recording (as on film) or for converting into electrical signals (as for a live television broadcast) [from Latin *camera* "room, chamber"; sense 2 from the scientific Latin phrase *camera obscura,* literally, "dark chamber" — related to CHAMBER]

camomile *variant of* CHAMOMILE

¹**cam·ou·flage** \'kam-ə-,fläzh, -,fläj\ *n* **1** : the hiding or disguising of something by covering it up or changing the way it looks **2** : the material (as paint or leaves and branches) used for camouflage

²**camouflage** *vb* **-flaged; -flag·ing** : to hide or disguise by camouflage

¹**camp** \'kamp\ *n* **1 a** : a place usually away from cities where tents or buildings are erected for shelter or for living in temporarily **b** : a group of tents, cabins, or huts **c** : a tent or cabin to be lived in temporarily (as during vacation) **d** : a place usually in the country for recreation or instruction often during the summer ⟨summer *camp*⟩; *also* : a program offering access to recreational or educational facilities for a limited period of time ⟨a resort offering boating and hiking *camps*⟩ ⟨computer *camp*⟩ **2** : a body of persons in a camp

²**camp** *vb* **1** : to make or occupy a camp **2** : to live in a camp or outdoors ⟨*camp* out overnight⟩

cam·paign \kam-'pān\ *n* **1** : a series of military operations in a particular area or for a particular purpose as part of a war **2** : a connected series of activities designed to bring about a particular result ⟨an election *campaign*⟩ — **cam·paign** *vb* — **cam·paign·er** *n*

cam·pa·ni·le \,kam-pə-'nē-lē, ,käm-, -(,)lā, *especially of U.S. structures also* ,kam-pə-'nēl\ *n, pl* **-niles** *or* **-nili** : a bell tower; *esp* : one built separate from another building

cam·pan·u·la \kam-'pan-yə-lə\ *n* : BELLFLOWER

camp·er \'kam-pər\ *n* **1** : a person who camps **2** : a portable dwelling or a specially equipped vehicle for use during travel and camping

camp·fire \'kamp-,fī(ə)r\ *n* : a fire built outdoors (as at a camp)

Camp Fire Girl *n* : a member of a national organization for girls from ages 7 to 18

campanile

camp·ground \'kamp-,grau̇nd\ *n* : the area or place used for a camp or for camping

cam·phor \'kam(p)-fər\ *n* : a tough gummy fragrant compound obtained especially from the wood and bark of the camphor tree and used in medicine and as an insect repellent

camphor tree *n* : a large Asian evergreen tree that is related to the laurels and is the source of camphor

camp·o·ree \,kam-pə-'rē\ *n* : a gathering of Boy Scouts or Girl Scouts from a given geographic area

camp·site \'kamp-,sīt\ *n* : a place suitable for or used as the site of a camp

cam·pus \'kam-pəs\ *n, pl* **cam·pus·es** : the grounds of a college or a school

cam·shaft \'kam-,shaft\ *n* : a shaft to which a cam is fastened or of which a cam forms a part

¹**can** \kən, (')kan\ *helping verb, past* **could** \kəd, (')ku̇d\; *pres sing & pl* **can 1 a** : know how to ⟨we *can* read⟩ **b**

\ə\ **abut**	\au̇\ **out**	\i\ **tip**	\ȯ\ **saw**	\u̇\ **foot**
\ər\ **further**	\ch\ **chin**	\ī\ **life**	\ȯi\ **coin**	\y\ **yet**
\a\ **mat**	\e\ **pet**	\j\ **job**	\th\ **thin**	\yü\ **few**
\ā\ **take**	\ē\ **easy**	\ŋ\ **sing**	\t̲h̲\ **this**	\yu̇\ **cure**
\ä\ **cot, cart**	\g\ **go**	\ō\ **bone**	\ü\ **food**	\zh\ **vision**

: be able to ⟨I *can* hear you⟩ **c** : be permitted by conscience or feeling to ⟨they *can* hardly blame you⟩ **d** : have the power or right to **2** : have permission to : MAY ⟨you *can* go now⟩ [Old English *can* "to know, know how to"]

²can \'kan\ *n* **1** : a metal container usually shaped like a cylinder ⟨a soda *can*⟩ **2** : the contents of a can ⟨ate the whole *can* of beans⟩ [Old English *canne* "container"]

³can \'kan\ *vb* **canned; can·ning 1** : to prepare for future use by sealing in an airtight can or jar ⟨*can* tomatoes⟩ **2** : to dismiss from a job : FIRE **3** *slang* : to put a stop or end to — **can·ner** *n*

Can·a·da Day \ˌkan-əd-ə-\ *n* : July 1 observed as a legal holiday in honor of the proclamation of dominion status in 1867

Canada goose *n* : a common wild goose of North America that is mostly gray and brownish with a black head and neck

Ca·na·di·an \kə-'nād-ē-ən\ *adj* : of, relating to, or characteristic of Canada or its people — **Canadian** *n*

Canada goose

Canadian bacon *n* : bacon from the loin of a pig that has little fat and is cut into round or oblong slices for cooking

Canadian lynx *or* **Canada lynx** *n* : LYNX 1

ca·nal \kə-'nal\ *n* **1** : a tube-shaped bodily passage or channel : DUCT **2** : an artificial waterway for boats or for draining or irrigating land **3** : any of various faint narrow lines on the planet Mars seen through telescopes and formerly thought to be canals built by Martians

ca·nary \kə-'ne(ə)r-ē\ *n, pl* **ca·nar·ies** : a small usually yellow or greenish finch native to the Canary Islands that is often kept in a cage

can·cel \'kan(t)-səl\ *vb* **-celed** *or* **-celled; -cel·ing** *or* **-cel·ling** \-s(ə-)liŋ\ **1** : to cross out or strike out with a line : DELETE **2 a** : to destroy the force or effectiveness of ⟨*cancel* an order⟩ ⟨*cancel* an appointment⟩ **b** : to match in force or effect : ²OFFSET ⟨*cancelled* each other out⟩ **3 a** : to divide a numerator and denominator by the same number **b** : to remove something equivalent from both sides of an equation or account **4** : to mark a postage stamp or check so that it cannot be reused — **can·cel·er** *or* **can·cel·ler** \-s(ə-)lər\ *n*

can·cel·la·tion \ˌkan(t)-sə-'lā-shən\ *n* **1** : an act of canceling **2** : a mark made to cancel something

can·cer \'kan(t)-sər\ *n* **1** *cap* : a group of stars between Gemini and Leo usually pictured as a crab **2** *cap* **a** : the fourth sign of the zodiac — see ZODIAC table **b** : a person whose sign of the zodiac is Cancer **3** : a tumor that tends to spread locally and to other parts of the body and often causes death if not treated; *also* : an abnormal state marked by such tumors **4** : a dangerous evil that destroys slowly — **can·cer·ous** \'kan(t)s-(ə-)rəs\ *adj*

Word History The Latin word *cancer,* meaning "crab," was also given as a name to several diseases. One of the diseases was the abnormal, spreading mass of tissue we call a tumor. A possible explanation for this extended use of *cancer* is that the Romans thought some tumors looked like many-legged crabs. A French descendant of this Latin word was borrowed into English as *canker.* It is now applied to several plant and animal disorders. In the 14th century the Latin word *cancer* in the sense of "tumor" was borrowed directly into English, giving us our modern spelling and sense. [Middle English *Cancer* "'Crab' star group," from Latin *cancer* "crab, cancer (disease)"; sense 3 directly from Latin *cancer* "crab, cancer" — related to CANKER, CHANCRE]

can·de·la \kan-'dē-lə, -'del-ə\ *n* : a unit of measurement for the intensity of light

can·de·la·bra \ˌkan-də-'läb-rə *also* -'lab-\ *n* : CANDELABRUM

can·de·la·brum \ˌkan-də-'läb-rəm *also* -'lab-\ *n, pl* **-bra** \-rə\ *also* **-brums** : a candlestick that has several branches for holding candles

can·did \'kan-dəd\ *adj* **1** : marked by or showing sincere honesty : FRANK **2** : relating to photography of people acting naturally without being posed ⟨*candid* picture⟩ [from French *candide* "white" and Latin *candidus* "white, bright," from Latin *candēre* "to shine, be bright" — related to CANDIDATE, CANDLE; see *Word History* at CANDIDATE] — **can·did·ly** *adv* — **can·did·ness** *n*

can·di·da·cy \'kan-dəd-ə-sē, 'kan-əd-\ *n, pl* **-cies** : the state of being a candidate

can·di·date \'kan-də-ˌdāt, 'kan-ə-, -dət\ *n* : one who runs in an election contest or is proposed for an office or honor

Word History In ancient Rome it was the custom for a person who wanted to be elected to public office to wear a toga that had been rubbed with chalk to make it white. The Latin word for "dressed in white" was *candidatus*. In time this word came to be used for the person himself, or the candidate. The Latin word *candidatus* came from *candidus,* meaning "bright, shining white." This in turn came from *candēre,* a verb meaning "to shine, be bright." Latin *candēre* has given us two other English words: *candid,* which at first meant "white, free from prejudice" but now usually means "honest, natural," and *candle,* the mass of wax with a wick that is burned to give off a bright light. [from Latin *candidatus* "candidate," from *candidatus* (adjective) "dressed in white," from *candidus* "shining white," from *candēre* "to be bright, shine" — related to CANDID, CANDLE]

can·di·di·a·sis \ˌkan-də-'dī-ə-səs\ *n, pl* **-a·ses** \-ə-ˌsēz\ : infection with a fungus that resembles a yeast

¹can·dle \'kan-dᵊl\ *n* **1** : a mass of tallow or wax containing a wick that is burned to give light **2** : CANDELA [Old English *candel* "candle," from Latin *candela* "candle," from *candēre* "to shine, be bright" — related to CANDID, CANDIDATE; see *Word History* at CANDIDATE]

²candle *vb* **can·dled; can·dling** \'kan-dliŋ, -dᵊl-iŋ\ : to examine an egg by holding it between the eye and a light — **can·dler** \-dlər, -dᵊl-ər\ *n*

can·dle·light \'kan-dᵊl-ˌ(l)īt\ *n* **1** : the light of a candle **2** : soft artificial light — **can·dle·lit** \-dᵊl-ˌ(l)it\ *adj*

Can·dle·mas \'kan-dᵊl-məs\ *n* : February 2 observed as a Christian festival in honor of the presentation of Christ in the temple and the purification of the Virgin Mary

can·dle·pow·er \'kan-dᵊl-ˌpau̇(-ə)r\ *n* : intensity of light expressed in candelas

can·dle·stick \-ˌstik\ *n* : a holder with a socket for a candle

can·dor \'kan-dər, -dȯ(ə)r\ *n* : sincere and honest expression : FRANKNESS

¹can·dy \'kan-dē\ *n, pl* **candies** : a sweet made of sugar often with flavoring and filling

²candy *vb* **can·died; can·dy·ing** : to coat or become coated with sugar; *esp* : to cook (fruit or fruit peel) in sugar syrup

candy strip·er \-ˌstrī-pər\ *n* : a teenage volunteer hospital worker [so called from the fact that the uniform is traditionally striped like some stick candies]

¹cane \'kān\ *n* **1 a** : a jointed plant stem that is usually slender and more or less flexible **b** : any of various tall woody grasses or reeds; *esp* : SUGARCANE **2 a** : WALKING STICK **b** : a rod for flogging **c** : RATTAN 2

²cane *vb* **caned; can·ing 1** : to beat with a cane **2** : to make with cane ⟨*cane* the seat of a chair⟩

cane·brake \'kān-ˌbrāk\ *n* : a thicket of cane

cane sugar *n* : sugar from sugarcane

¹ca·nine \'kā-ˌnīn\ *adj* : of or relating to dogs or to the family that includes the dogs, wolves, jackals, and foxes [from Latin *caninus* "having to do with dogs," from *canis* "dog"]

²canine *n* **1** : a pointed tooth; *esp* : one located between the outer incisor and the first premolar **2** : ¹DOG 1a, b

can·is·ter *also* **can·nis·ter** \'kan-ə-stər\ *n* : a small box or can for holding a dry product (as coffee, flour, or sugar)

can·ker \'kaŋ-kər\ *n* **1** : an often spreading sore that eats into tissue **2 a** : an area of dead tissue in a plant **b** : a plant disease marked by cankers **3** : any of various animal diseases marked especially by inflammation [Middle English *canker* "spreading sore," from an early French dialect word *cancre* (same meaning), from Latin *cancer* "crab, cancer" — related to CANCER, CHANCRE; see *Word History* at CANCER] — **can·ker·ous** \'kaŋ-k(ə-)rəs\ *adj*

canker sore *n* : a small painful open sore especially of the mouth

can·ker·worm \'kaŋ-kər-ˌwərm\ *n* : a moth larva that injures plants especially by feeding on buds and leaves

can·na \'kan-ə\ *n* : a tall tropical herb with large leaves and bright-colored flowers

can·na·bis \'kan-ə-bəs\ *n* : HEMP 1; *also* : a preparation (as marijuana) made from hemp and affecting the mind

canned \'kand\ *adj* **1** : preserved in a sealed can or jar ⟨*canned* peaches⟩ **2 a** : prepared or recorded in advance; *esp* : prepared in one form for ordinary use or wide distribution ⟨*canned* laughter⟩ **b** : lacking originality as if mass-produced ⟨a *canned* speech⟩

can·nery \'kan-(ə-)rē\ *n, pl* **can·ner·ies** : a factory for the canning of food

can·ni·bal \'kan-ə-bəl\ *n* : a human being or an animal that eats its own kind

> *Word History* On Christopher Columbus's first voyage to the New World the American Indian peoples whom he encountered in Cuba and Hispaniola told him about a people living to their east, who periodically raided them and whom they greatly feared. In his log Columbus recorded a number of phonetically similar names for this people, including *caníbales* and *caribes*. The Spanish court historian Petrus Martyr wrote a Latin account of Columbus's discoveries, first printed in 1516, that used these two words and widely distributed them throughout Europe. In Petrus Martyr's words, "the inhabitants of these islands assert that the *Canibales* or *Caribes* are eaters of human flesh." Later, the meaning of the two words diverged. *Caribes* was applied to the Carib-speaking peoples of the Lesser Antilles and South America who were so feared by their neighbors; it is also ultimately the base of the word *Caribbean*. *Canibales* passed into English as a generic word for any creature that eats the flesh of its own kind. [from New Latin *Canibalis* "Carib," from Spanish *Caníbal* (same meaning), from Taino (American Indian language of the Greater Antilles) *Caniba* (same meaning), of Carib origin]

can·ni·bal·ism \'kan-ə-bə-ˌliz-əm\ *n* **1** : the eating of human flesh by a human being **2** : the eating of the flesh of an animal by another animal of the same kind — **can·ni·bal·is·tic** \ˌkan-ə-bə-'lis-tik\ *adj*

can·ni·bal·ize \'kan-ə-bə-ˌlīz\ *vb* **-ized; -iz·ing** : to take apart a machine for parts to be used as replacements in other machines

can·non \'kan-ən\ *n, pl* **cannons** *or* **cannon** **1** : a large heavy gun usually mounted on wheels **2** : an automatic gun of large caliber on an airplane

cannon 1

can·non·ade \ˌkan-ə-'nād\ *n* : heavy firing of artillery

can·non·ball \'kan-ən-ˌbȯl\ *n* : a usually round solid missile for firing from a cannon

can·non·eer \ˌkan-ə-'ni(ə)r\ *n* : a person who operates artillery

can·not \'kan-(ˌ)ät; kə-'nät, ka-'nät\ : can not — **cannot but** *or* **cannot help but** : to be unable to do something other than

can·ny \'kan-ē\ *adj* **can·ni·er; -est** : watchful of one's own interest — **can·ni·ly** \'kan-ᵊl-ē\ *adv* — **can·ni·ness** \'kan-ē-nəs\ *n*

¹ca·noe \kə-'nü\ *n* : a long light narrow boat with pointed ends and curved sides that is usually moved by someone using a paddle

²canoe *vb* **ca·noed; ca·noe·ing** : to travel or carry in a canoe — **ca·noe·ist** \-'nü-əst\ *n*

ca·no·la \kə-'nō-lə\ *n* **1** : a rape plant of an improved variety having seeds that are the source of canola oil **2** : CANOLA OIL

canola oil *n* : an edible vegetable oil obtained from the seeds of canola that is low in saturated and high in mono-saturated fatty acids

¹can·on \'kan-ən\ *n* **1** : a church law or decree **2** : an official list (as of the books of the Bible) **3** : an accepted standard or rule ⟨*canons* of good taste⟩

²canon *n* : a member of the clergy who is on the staff of a cathedral

cañon *variant of* CANYON

ca·non·i·cal \kə-'nän-i-kəl\ *adj* **1** : relating to or allowed by church law **2** : following a general rule or accepted procedure — **ca·non·i·cal·ly** \-i-k(ə-)lē\ *adv*

can·on·ize \'kan-ə-ˌnīz\ *vb* **-ized; -iz·ing** **1** : to declare to be a saint and worthy of public respect **2** : to treat something as if it were sacred — **can·on·iza·tion** \ˌkan-ə-nə-'zā-shən\ *n*

canon law *n* : the body of religious laws that govern a church

Ca·no·pus \kə-'nō-pəs\ *n* : a very bright star not visible north of 37° latitude

¹can·o·py \'kan-ə-pē\ *n, pl* **-pies** **1 a** : a covering over a bed, throne, or shrine or carried on poles (as over a person of high rank) **b** : AWNING **2** : a shade or shelter that hangs over something; *esp* : the uppermost spreading layer of a forest **3** : the fabric part of a parachute that catches the air

²canopy *vb* **-pied; -py·ing** : to cover with or as if with a canopy

canst \kən(t)st, (')kan(t)st\ *archaic present 2nd singular of* CAN

¹cant \'kant\ *n* **1** : a slanting surface **2** : ³SLOPE 2, INCLINE [Middle English *cant* "corner," from early Dutch *cant* or early French *cant*, both meaning "edge, corner," from Latin *canthus, cantus* "iron rim on a wheel," perhaps of Celtic origin]

²cant *vb* : to give a slant to

³cant *n* **1 a** : ARGOT **b** : JARGON **2** **2** : insincere speech [probably derived from an early French dialect word *canter* "to tell," from Latin *cantare* "to sing," from *canere* "to sing" — related to CANTATA, CHANT, CHANTEY]

can't \'kant, 'kȧnt, *especially Southern* 'kānt\ : can not

can·ta·loupe *also* **can·ta·loup** \'kant-ᵊl-ˌōp\ *n* : a muskmelon with a hard rough skin and reddish orange flesh

can·tan·ker·ous \kan-'taŋ-k(ə-)rəs, kən-\ *adj* : difficult or irritating to deal with — **can·tan·ker·ous·ly** *adv* — **can·tan·ker·ous·ness** *n*

can·ta·ta \kən-'tät-ə\ *n* : a poem, story, or play set to music to be sung by a chorus and soloists [from Italian *cantata* "music for a chorus," from Latin *cantata* (same

\ə\ **abut**	\au̇\ **out**	\i\ **tip**	\ȯ\ **saw**	\u̇\ **foot**
\ər\ **further**	\ch\ **chin**	\ī\ **life**	\ȯi\ **coin**	\y\ **yet**
\a\ **mat**	\e\ **pet**	\j\ **job**	\th\ **thin**	\yü\ **few**
\ā\ **take**	\ē\ **easy**	\ŋ\ **sing**	\t͟h\ **this**	\yu̇\ **cure**
\ä\ **cot, cart**	\g\ **go**	\ō\ **bone**	\ü\ **food**	\zh\ **vision**

meaning), derived from *canere* "to sing" — related to CANTOR, CHANT, CHANTEY]

can·teen \kan-'tēn\ *n* **1** : a store (as in a camp) in which food, drinks, and small supplies are sold **2** : a place of recreation and entertainment for people in military service **3** : a small container for carrying liquids (as on a hike)

[1]can·ter \'kant-ər\ *n* : a three-beat gait of a horse resembling but smoother and slower than the gallop

[2]canter *vb* : to go or cause to go at a canter

Can·ter·bury bell \,kant-ə(r)-,ber-ē\ *n* : a cultivated bellflower

can·ti·cle \'kant-i-kəl\ *n* : a song from the Bible used in church services

Canticle of Canticles : SONG OF SOLOMON

can·ti·le·ver \'kant-ᵊl-,ē-vər *also* -ev-ər\ *n* **1** : a beam or support fastened at only one end **2** : either of two beams or structures that stick out from piers toward each other and when joined form a span in a bridge

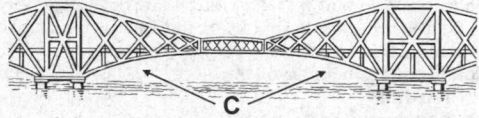

C cantilever 2

can·to \'kan-,tō\ *n, pl* **cantos** : a major division of a long poem

can·ton \'kant-ᵊn, 'kan-,tän\ *n* **1** : a division of a country (as Switzerland) **2** : the top inner quarter of a flag

can·ton·ment \kan-'tōn-mənt, -'tän-\ *n* : a military station in India

can·tor \'kant-ər\ *n* **1** : a choir leader **2** : a synagogue official who sings or chants religious music and leads the congregation in prayer [from Latin *cantor* "singer," from *canere* "to sing" — related to CANTATA, CHANT, CHANTEY]

can·vas \'kan-vəs\ *n* **1 a** : a strong cloth of hemp, flax, or cotton used for clothing and formerly much used for tents and sails **b** : a piece of cloth used as a surface for painting; *also* : a painting on such a surface **2** : something made of canvas **3** : a stiff material (as of coarse cloth or plastic) that has regular meshes for working with a needle (as in needlepoint)

can·vas·back \-,bak\ *n* : a North American wild duck with a reddish brown head and black breast

[1]can·vass \'kan-vəs\ *vb* : to go through (a district) or go to (people) to ask for votes, contributions, or orders or to determine public opinion — **can·vass·er** *n*

[2]canvass *n* : an act of canvassing

can·yon *also* **ca·ñon** \'kan-yən\ *n* : a deep narrow valley with steep sides and often with a stream flowing through it

caou·tchouc \'kaù-,chùk, -,chük, -,chü\ *n* : [1]RUBBER 2a

[1]cap \'kap\ *n* **1** : a head covering; *esp* : one that has a visor and no brim **2** : something that serves as a cover or protection for something ⟨a bottle *cap*⟩ **3** : a natural cover or top: as **a** : the umbrella-shaped part that bears the spores of a mushroom **b** : the top of a bird's head **4** : a paper or metal container holding a small explosive charge (as for a toy pistol) [Middle English *cappe* "cap," from Old English *cæppe* "cap," from Latin *cappa* "head covering, cloak" — related to [2]CAPE, CHAPEL]

[2]cap *vb* **capped; cap·ping 1** : to cover or provide with a cap **2** : to follow with : OUTDO **3** : to bring to a conclusion ⟨*capped* off the show with a song⟩ **4** : to prevent from growing or spreading : set a limit on ⟨*capped* oil prices⟩

ca·pa·ble \'kā-pə-bəl\ *adj* **1** : having the qualities (as physical or mental power) to do or accomplish something

⟨you are *capable* of better work⟩ **2** : having qualities or features permitting ⟨a new train *capable* of very high speeds⟩ **3** : able to do one's job well : generally efficient ⟨tries to hire *capable* people⟩ — **ca·pa·bil·i·ty** \,kā-pə-'bil-ət-ē\ *n* — **ca·pa·bly** \'kā-pə-blē\ *adv*

ca·pa·cious \kə-'pā-shəs\ *adj* : able to contain much or many : ROOMY **synonyms** see SPACIOUS — **ca·pa·cious·ly** *adv* — **ca·pa·cious·ness** *n*

ca·pac·i·tor \kə-'pas-ət-ər\ *n* : a device for storing electric charge — called also *condenser*

ca·pac·i·ty \kə-'pas-ət-ē, -'pas-tē\ *n, pl* **-ties 1** : the ability to hold or contain ⟨the seating *capacity* of a room⟩ **2** : the largest amount or number that can be contained ⟨a jug with a *capacity* of four liters⟩ ⟨the auditorium was filled to *capacity*⟩ **3** : mental or physical ability **4** : [1]POSITION 4a, FUNCTION ⟨in your *capacity* as drama critic⟩

[1]ca·par·i·son \kə-'par-ə-sən\ *n* **1** : an ornamental covering for a horse **2** : fancy clothing or decoration

[2]caparison *vb* : to dress with or as if with fancy clothes

[1]cape \'kāp\ *n* : a point of land that extends out into the sea or a lake [Middle English *cap* "cape, point of land," derived from an early Occitan word *cap* (same meaning), from Latin *caput* "head" — related to CAPITAL]

[2]cape *n* : a sleeveless garment worn so as to hang over the shoulders, arms, and back [probably from Spanish *capa* "cloak," from Latin *cappa* "head covering, cloak" — related to CAP, CHAPEL, CHAPERON, [1]COPE, ESCAPE]

Cape buffalo \'kāp-\ *n* : a large wild buffalo of Africa south of the Sahara

Ca·pel·la \kə-'pel-ə\ *n* : a very bright star in Auriga

[1]ca·per \'kā-pər\ *n* : a pickled flower bud or young berry of a low prickly shrub of the Mediterranean region that is used as a seasoning [from earlier *capers* "caper shrub or berry" (mistaken as a plural), from Middle English *caperis* (same meaning), from Latin *cappeaneris* "caper shrub"]

[2]caper *vb* **ca·pered; ca·per·ing** \-p(ə-)riŋ\ : to leap about in a lively way [probably an altered form of English *capriole* "a playful leap, a leap by a trained horse," from early French *capriole* or early Italian *capriola* (both, same meaning), derived from Latin *capreolus* "goat, male deer"]

[3]caper *n* **1** : a playful bounding leap or spring **2** : a playful or mischievous trick **3** : an illegal or questionable act

cap·il·lar·i·ty \,kap-ə-'lar-ət-ē\ *n* : the action by which the surface of a liquid where (as in a slender tube) it is in contact with a solid is raised or lowered depending upon how much the molecules of the liquid are attracted to one another and to those of the solid

[1]cap·il·lary \'kap-ə-,ler-ē\ *adj* **1** : having a long slender form and a very small inner diameter ⟨a *capillary* tube⟩ **2** : of or relating to capillaries or capillarity

[2]capillary *n, pl* **-lar·ies** : a capillary tube; *esp* : any of the tiny blood vessels connecting the small arteries and veins

[1]cap·i·tal \'kap-ət-ᵊl, 'kap-tᵊl\ *adj* **1 a** : punishable by death ⟨a *capital* crime⟩ **b** : resulting in death ⟨*capital* punishment⟩ **2** : belonging to the series A, B, C, etc. rather than a, b, c, etc. ⟨*capital* letters⟩ **3** : being the location of a government ⟨the *capital* city⟩ **4** : of or relating to capital ⟨*capital* investment⟩ **5** : EXCELLENT ⟨a *capital* idea⟩ [Middle English *capital* "of the head, principal, causing death," from early French (same meaning), from Latin *capitalis* (same meaning); from *caput* "head" — related to ACHIEVE, CADET, [1]CAPE, CAPTAIN, CHIEF]

[2]capital *n* **1 a** : accumulated wealth especially as used to produce more wealth **b** : persons owning or investing capital **2** : profitable use ⟨make *capital* out of another's weakness⟩ **3** : a capital letter **4** : a capital city **5** : a city that is most important for a particular activity or product ⟨the oil *capital* of the country⟩

[3]capital *n* : the top part of an architectural column [Middle English *capitale* (same meaning), from early French (same meaning), from Latin *capitellum* "small head, top of a column," from *caput* "head"]

cap·i·tal·ism \'kap-ət-ᵊl-ˌiz-əm, 'kap-tᵊl-\ *n* : an economic system in which resources and means of production are privately owned and prices, production, and the distribution of goods are determined mainly by competition in a free market — **cap·i·tal·ist** \-əst\ *or* **cap·i·tal·is·tic** \ˌkap-ət-ᵊl-'is-tik, ˌkap-tᵊl-\ *adj* — **cap·i·tal·is·ti·cal·ly** \-ti-k(ə-)lē\ *adv*

cap·i·tal·ist \'kap-ət-ᵊl-əst, 'kap-tᵊl-\ *n* **1** : a person who has capital and especially business capital **2** : a person who supports capitalism

cap·i·tal·ize \'kap-ət-ᵊl-ˌīz, 'kap-tᵊl-\ *vb* **-ized; -iz·ing** **1** : to write or print with a beginning capital letter or in capital letters **2 a** : to supply capital for (as a business or a project) **b** : to use as capital (as in business) **3** : to use to help oneself ⟨*capitalize* on an opponent's mistake⟩ — **cap·i·tal·i·za·tion** \ˌkap-ət-ᵊl-ə-'zā-shən, ˌkap-tᵊl-\ *n*

cap·i·tol \'kap-ət-ᵊl, 'kap-tᵊl\ *n* **1** : the building in which a state legislature meets **2** *cap* : the building in which the U.S. Congress meets in Washington, D.C.

ca·pit·u·late \kə-'pich-ə-ˌlāt\ *vb* **-lat·ed; -lat·ing** : to surrender usually on terms agreed upon in advance — **ca·pit·u·la·tion** \kə-ˌpich-ə-'lā-shən\ *n*

ca·po \'kä-pō\ *n, pl* **capos** : a bar that can be fitted on the fingerboard especially of a guitar to raise the pitch of all the strings

ca·pon \'kā-ˌpän, -pən\ *n* : a castrated male chicken

ca·price \kə-'prēs\ *n* **1** : a sudden change in feeling, opinion, or action **2** : a disposition to change one's mind suddenly

ca·pri·cious \kə-'prish-əs, -'prē-shəs\ *adj* : moved or controlled by caprice : apt to change suddenly ⟨a *capricious* child⟩ ⟨*capricious* weather⟩ — **ca·pri·cious·ly** *adv* — **ca·pri·cious·ness** *n*

Cap·ri·corn \'kap-ri-ˌkȯ(ə)rn\ *n* **1** : a group of stars between Sagittarius and Aquarius that is usually pictured as a goat **2 a** : the 10th sign of the zodiac — see ZODIAC table **b** : a person whose sign of the zodiac is Capricorn

cap·size \'kap-ˌsīz, kap-'sīz\ *vb* **cap·sized; cap·siz·ing** : to become or cause to become upset or overturned : TURN OVER ⟨canoes *capsize* easily⟩

cap·stan \'kap-stən, -ˌstan\ *n* : a device that consists of a drum to which a rope is fastened and that is used especially on ships for moving or raising weights

capstan

¹**cap·sule** \'kap-səl, -(ˌ)sül\ *n* **1** : a surrounding cover of a bodily part (as a knee joint) **2** : a case bearing spores or seeds **3** : a shell usually of gelatin that is used for packaging something (as a drug); *also* : such a shell together with its contents **4** : an envelope of carbohydrate around a microbe and especially a bacterium **5** : a small compartment with nearly normal atmospheric pressure for a pilot or astronaut; *esp* : SPACECRAFT

²**capsule** *adj* : very brief ⟨*capsule* movie reviews⟩

¹**cap·tain** \'kap-tən\ *n* **1 a** : the commanding officer of a military unit **b** : a military commissioned officer with a rank just below that of major **2 a** : the commanding officer of a ship **b** : a naval commissioned officer with a rank just below that of commodore **3** : a fire or police department officer with a rank usually between that of chief and lieutenant **4 a** : the leader of a team or side **b** : a person in charge of several waiters in a restaurant [Middle English *capitane* "military leader," from early French *capitain* (same meaning), from Latin *capitaneus* "chief," from *caput* "head" — related to CADET, CAPITAL, CHIEF] — **cap·tain·cy** \-sē\ *n*

²**captain** *vb* : to be captain of

cap·tion \'kap-shən\ *n* **1** : the heading especially of an article or document **2** : the explanation or description accompanying a pictorial illustration (as a cartoon or photograph) **3** : SUBTITLE 2 — **caption** *vb*

cap·tious \'kap-shəs\ *adj* : quick to find fault especially over small things — **cap·tious·ly** *adv* — **cap·tious·ness** *n*

cap·ti·vate \'kap-tə-ˌvāt\ *vb* **-vat·ed; -vat·ing** : to influence or fascinate by some special charm — **cap·ti·va·tion** \ˌkap-tə-'vā-shən\ *n*

¹**cap·tive** \'kap-tiv\ *adj* **1** : taken and held prisoner especially in war **2** : held or confined so as to prevent escape ⟨a *captive* animal⟩ **3** : in a situation that makes free choice or leaving difficult ⟨the airline passengers were a *captive* audience⟩ — **cap·tiv·i·ty** \kap-'tiv-ət-ē\ *n*

²**captive** *n* : one that is captive : PRISONER

cap·tor \'kap-tər, -ˌtȯ(ə)r\ *n* : one that has captured a person or thing

¹**cap·ture** \'kap-chər, -shər\ *n* **1** : the act of catching or gaining control by force or trickery **2** : something or someone captured [from early French *capture* "capture," from Latin *captura* (same meaning), from *captus* "taken (as a prisoner)," from *capere* "to take" — related to ACCEPT, CATCH, RECEIVE]

²**capture** *vb* **cap·tured; cap·tur·ing** \'kap-chə-riŋ, 'kap-shriŋ\ **1 a** : to take and hold especially by force ⟨*capture* a city⟩ **b** : to gain or win as if by force ⟨*captured* first prize⟩ **2** : ¹PRESERVE 1 ⟨*captured* her smile on film⟩ **synonyms** see CATCH

capture the flag *n* : a game in which players on each of two teams seek to capture the other team's flag and return it to their side without being captured and imprisoned

cap·u·chin \'kap-yə-shən, kə-'p(y)ü-\ *n* : a brown or black monkey of South and Central America with a whitish face, chest, and shoulders

cap·y·bara \ˌkap-i-'bar-ə, -'bär-\ *n* : a tailless South American rodent often exceeding four feet (1.2 meters) in length that is often found in or near water

car \'kär\ *n* **1** : a vehicle (as an automobile or part of a passenger train) moving on wheels **2** : the passenger compartment of an elevator **3** : the part of a balloon or an airship that carries the passengers and equipment

capybara

ca·rafe \kə-'raf, -'räf\ *n* : a bottle that has a lip and is used to hold water or beverages

car·am·bo·la \ˌkar-əm-'bō-lə\ *n* : STAR FRUIT

car·a·mel \'kär-məl; 'kar-ə-məl, -ˌmel\ *n* **1** : burnt sugar used for coloring and flavoring **2** : a firm chewy candy

car·a·pace \'kar-ə-ˌpās\ *n* : a bony or horny case or shield covering all or part of the back of an animal (as a turtle)

¹**carat** *variant of* KARAT

²**car·at** \'kar-ət\ *n* : a unit of weight for precious gems (as diamonds) equal to 200 milligrams

car·a·van \'kar-ə-ˌvan\ *n* **1 a** : a group (as of merchants or pilgrims) traveling together on a long journey through desert or dangerous regions **b** : a group of pack animals or of vehicles traveling together one behind the other **2** : a covered vehicle; *esp* : one equipped as traveling living quarters

\ə\ **abut**	\aů\ **out**	\i\ **tip**	\ȯ\ **saw**	\ů\ **foot**
\ər\ **further**	\ch\ **chin**	\ī\ **life**	\ȯi\ **coin**	\y\ **yet**
\a\ **mat**	\e\ **pet**	\j\ **job**	\th\ **thin**	\yü\ **few**
\ā\ **take**	\ē\ **easy**	\ŋ\ **sing**	\th\ **this**	\yů\ **cure**
\ä\ **cot, cart**	\g\ **go**	\ō\ **bone**	\ü\ **food**	\zh\ **vision**

car·a·van·sa·ry \ˌkar-ə-'van(t)-sə-rē\ *or* **car·a·van·se·rai** \-sə-ˌrī\ *n, pl* **-ries** *or* **-rais** *or* **-rai** **1** : an inn in eastern countries where caravans rest at night **2** : HOTEL, INN

car·a·vel \'kar-ə-ˌvel, -vəl\ *n* : a small 15th and 16th century ship with a broad bow, a high stern, and usually three masts

caravel

car·a·way \'kar-ə-ˌwā\ *n* : a usually white-flowered herb related to the carrot and having fruits used in seasoning and medicine

car·bide \'kär-ˌbīd\ *n* : a compound of carbon with another element

car·bine \'kär-ˌbēn, -ˌbīn\ *n* : a light short-barreled rifle

car·bo·hy·drate \ˌkär-bō-'hī-ˌdrāt, -drət\ *n* : any of various compounds of carbon, hydrogen, and oxygen (as sugars, starches, or celluloses) most of which are formed by plants and are a major animal food

car·bol·ic acid \kär-ˌbäl-ik-\ *n* : PHENOL

car·bon \'kär-bən\ *n* **1** : a nonmetallic element found more or less pure in nature (as in diamond and graphite) or as a part of coal and petroleum and of the bodies of living things or obtained artificially — see ELEMENT table **2 a** : a sheet of carbon paper **b** : CARBON COPY 1

car·bo·na·ceous \ˌkär-bə-'nā-shəs\ *adj* : relating to, containing, or made up of carbon

car·bo·na·do \ˌkär-bə-'näd-ō, -'nad-\ *n, pl* **-dos** : an impure dark-colored fine-grained mass of diamond particles valuable for great strength and hardness

[1]car·bon·ate \'kär-bə-ˌnāt, -nət\ *n* : a compound formed by the reaction of carbonic acid with another substance

[2]car·bon·ate \'kär-bə-ˌnāt\ *vb* **-at·ed; -at·ing** **1** : to change into a carbonate **2** : to saturate with carbon dioxide ⟨a *carbonated* beverage⟩ — **car·bon·ation** \ˌkär-bə-'nā-shən\ *n*

carbon copy *n* **1** : a copy made with carbon paper **2** : [2]DUPLICATE

carbon cycle *n* : the cycle of carbon in living things in which carbon dioxide is used in photosynthesis to form food and growth substances and is later returned to the environment by respiration, decay, and burning

carbon dating *n* : the measurement of age (as of a fossil) by means of the amount of carbon 14 in the material

carbon dioxide *n* : a heavy colorless gas CO_2 that is formed especially by the burning and breaking down of organic substances (as in animal respiration), is absorbed from the air by plants in photosynthesis, and has many industrial uses

carbon disulfide *n* : a colorless flammable poisonous liquid used especially to dissolve rubber and as an insecticide — called also *carbon bisulfide*

carbon footprint *n* : the amount of greenhouse gases and especially carbon dioxide given off by something (as a person's activities or a product's manufacture and transport) during a given period

carbon 14 \-(')fȯr(t)-'tēn, -(')fȯr-\ *n* : a heavy radioactive form of carbon of mass number 14 used especially in finding out the age of very old remains (as bones or charcoal) of formerly living materials

car·bon·ic acid \kär-'bän-ik-\ *n* : a weak acid that is formed from water and carbon dioxide, is found only in mixtures with water, and breaks down easily

car·bon·if·er·ous \ˌkär-bə-'nif-(ə-)rəs\ *adj* **1** : producing or containing carbon or coal **2** *cap* : of, relating to, or being a period of the Paleozoic era of geological history or the corresponding system of rocks that includes coal beds — see GEOLOGIC TIME table — **Carboniferous** *n*

car·bon·ize \'kär-bə-ˌnīz\ *vb* **-ized; -iz·ing** : to change or become changed into carbon — **car·bon·i·za·tion** \ˌkär-bə-nə-'zā-shən\ *n*

carbon monoxide *n* : a colorless odorless very poisonous gas formed by the incomplete burning of carbon

carbon paper *n* : a thin paper coated with a coloring matter and used for making copies of something written or typed

carbon tet·ra·chlo·ride \-ˌte-trə-'klō(ə)r-id, -'klȯ(ə)r-\ *n* : a colorless nonflammable poisonous liquid used to dissolve things (as grease)

car·bun·cle \'kär-ˌbən-kəl\ *n* **1** : a rounded and polished garnet **2** : a painful inflammation of the skin and deeper tissues that releases pus from several openings — compare [1]BOIL

car·bu·re·tor \'kär-b(y)ə-ˌrāt-ər\ *n* : the part of an engine in which fuel (as gasoline) is mixed with air to make it burn easily

car·cass \'kär-kəs\ *n* : a dead body; *esp* : the body of a meat animal prepared for market

car·cin·o·gen \kär-'sin-ə-jən, 'kärs-ᵊn-ə-ˌjen\ *n* : a substance that causes cancer — **car·ci·no·gen·ic** \ˌkärs-ᵊn-ō-'jen-ik\ *adj*

car·ci·no·ma \ˌkärs-ᵊn-'ō-mə\ *n, pl* **-mas** *or* **-ma·ta** \-mət-ə\ : a tumor that consists of epithelial cells and is often fatal if not treated

[1]card \'kärd\ *vb* : to clean and untangle fibers by combing with a card before spinning — **card·er** *n*

[2]card *n* : an instrument usually having bent wire teeth for combing fibers (as wool or cotton) [Middle English *carde* "instrument for combing fibers," from Latin *cardus, carduus* "instrument for combing fibers, thistle," from earlier Latin *carduus* "thistle"]

[3]card *n* **1** : PLAYING CARD **2** *pl* **a** : a game played with cards **b** : card playing **3** : an amusing person : WAG **4** : a flat stiff usually small and rectangular piece of paper, thin cardboard, or plastic: as **a** : POSTCARD **b** : such a card on which computer information is stored **c** : CREDIT CARD **d** : GREETING CARD **5** : a sports program **6** : a removable circuit board (as in a personal computer) [Middle English *carde* "playing card," from early French *carte* (same meaning), probably from early Italian *carta*, literally, "leaf of paper," from Latin *charta* "piece of papyrus" — related to CARTON, CARTOON, CHART]

[4]card *vb* **1** : to provide with a card **2** : to ask for identification

card·board \'kärd-ˌbō(ə)rd, -ˌbȯ(ə)rd\ *n* : a material made from cellulose fiber (as wood pulp) like paper but usually thicker

card catalog *n* : a catalog of library books in which a card for each book is alphabetically filed with its call number usually under the title, author, and subject of the book

car·di·ac \'kärd-ē-ˌak\ *adj* : of, relating to, situated near, or acting on the heart

car·di·gan \'kärd-i-gən\ *n* : a usually collarless sweater opening down the front

Car·di·gan Welsh corgi \'kärd-i-gən-\ *n* : any of a breed of Welsh corgis with rounded ears, a long tail, and forelegs turned slightly outward — called also *Cardigan*

[1]car·di·nal \'kärd-nəl, -ᵊn-əl\ *n* **1** : a high official of the Roman Catholic Church ranking next below the pope **2** : CARDINAL NUMBER **3** : a North American finch of which the male is bright red with a black face and a pointed bunch of feathers on its head

Word History Our word *cardinal* can be traced back to the Latin adjective *cardinalis*, which at first meant "serving as a hinge." The root of this word is the noun *cardo*, meaning "hinge." Since a hinge is the device on which a door turns, the noun *cardo* also came to be used for "something on which a development turns or depends," or in other words, "something very important." Following this, the adjective took on the meaning "very important, chief, principal." Later the Roman Catholic Church applied this adjective in referring to principal churches and priests. By the late Middle Ages *cardinalis* had come to be used for "a clergyman of the highest rank, next to the pope." When borrowed into English, *cardinalis* became *cardinal*. Then other senses of the word developed. A cardinal's robes are a deep red color, and this color influenced the naming of a type of bird whose color was like that of a cardinal's robes. [Middle English *cardinal* "high church official," from Latin *cardinalis* (same meaning), from *cardinalis* (adjective) "principal, most important, of a hinge," from *cardo* "hinge"]

²**cardinal** *adj* **1** : ¹CHIEF 2, PRIMARY ⟨a *cardinal* rule⟩ **2** : very serious ⟨a *cardinal* sin⟩

cardinal flower *n* : a North American plant that bears brilliant red flowers

car·di·nal·i·ty \ˌkärd-ᵊn-ˈal-ət-ē\ *n, pl* **-ties** : the number of elements in a given mathematical set

cardinal number *n* : a number (as 1, 5, 15) that is used in simple counting and that tells how many elements there are in a set but not the order in which they are arranged — compare ORDINAL NUMBER; see NUMBER table

cardinal point *n* : one of the four principal points of the compass: north, south, east, west

car·dio·pul·mo·nary \ˌkärd-ē-ō-ˈpúl-mə-ˌner-ē, -ˈpəl-\ *adj* : of or relating to the heart and lungs

cardiopulmonary resuscitation *n* : a procedure used to restore normal breathing when the heart stops beating that includes clearing the air passages to the lungs, mouth-to-mouth artificial respiration, and applying pressure to the chest to massage the heart

car·dio·vas·cu·lar \ˌkärd-ē-ō-ˈvas-kyə-lər\ *adj* : of, relating to, or involving the heart and blood vessels ⟨*cardiovascular* disease⟩

card table *n* : a table designed for playing cards; *esp* : a square table with folding legs

¹**care** \ˈke(ə)r, ˈka(ə)r\ *n* **1** : a heavy sense of responsibility **2** : serious attention ⟨take *care* in crossing streets⟩ **3** : PROTECTION 1, SUPERVISION ⟨under a doctor's *care*⟩ **4** : an object of one's care

²**care** *vb* **cared; car·ing** **1** : to feel interest or concern ⟨we *care* what happens⟩ **2** : to give care ⟨*care* for the sick⟩ **3** : to have a liking or a desire ⟨would you *care* for some pie?⟩ — **car·er** *n*

ca·reen \kə-ˈrēn\ *vb* **1** : to cause a boat to lean or tilt over on one side for cleaning or repairing **2** : to sway from side to side **3** : ²CAREER

¹**ca·reer** \kə-ˈri(ə)r\ *n* **1 a** : ¹COURSE 1, PROGRESS **b** : full speed or activity ⟨in full *career*⟩ **2** : a course of continued progress or activity **3** : a profession followed as a permanent occupation

²**career** *vb* : to go at top speed ⟨a car *careered* off the road⟩

care·free \ˈke(ə)r-ˌfrē, ˈka(ə)r-\ *adj* : free from care: as **a** : LIGHTHEARTED **b** : IRRESPONSIBLE 2 ⟨*carefree* with money⟩

care·ful \ˈke(ə)r-fəl, ˈka(ə)r-\ *adj* **1** : using care : WATCHFUL ⟨a *careful* driver⟩ **2** : made, done, or said with care ⟨a *careful* examination⟩ — **care·ful·ly** \-f(ə-)lē\ *adv* — **care·ful·ness** \-fəl-nəs\ *n*

synonyms CAREFUL, CAUTIOUS, WARY mean taking care to avoid trouble. CAREFUL suggests that one is alert and thus able to prevent mistakes or accidents ⟨be *careful* not to get paint on the rug⟩. CAUTIOUS suggests that one takes special care to avoid problems ahead of time ⟨a *cautious* driver going slowly around the curve⟩. WARY suggests that one is suspicious of danger and sly in avoiding it ⟨be *wary* of strangers⟩.

care·less \ˈke(ə)r-ləs, ˈka(ə)r-\ *adj* **1** : free from care : not troubled **2** : not taking proper care ⟨a *careless* worker⟩ **3** : done, made, or said without proper care ⟨a *careless* mistake⟩ — **care·less·ly** *adv* — **care·less·ness** *n*

ca·ress \kə-ˈres\ *n* **1** : a tender or loving touch or hug **2** : a light stroking, rubbing, or patting — **caress** *vb*

car·et \ˈkar-ət\ *n* : a mark ^ used to show where something is to be inserted

care·tak·er \ˈke(ə)r-ˌtā-kər, ˈka(ə)r-\ *n* : one that takes care of buildings or land often for an absent owner

care·worn \-ˌwō(ə)rn, -ˌwȯ(ə)rn\ *adj* : showing the effect of grief or worry ⟨a *careworn* face⟩

car·fare \ˈkär-ˌfa(ə)r, -ˌfe(ə)r\ *n* : the fare charged for carrying a passenger (as on a bus)

car·go \ˈkär-ˌgō\ *n, pl* **cargoes** *or* **cargos** : the goods transported in a ship, airplane, or vehicle : FREIGHT

Car·ib \ˈkar-əb\ *n* : a member of an Indian people of northern South America and the Lesser Antilles

car·i·bou \ˈkar-ə-ˌbü\ *n, pl* **-bou** *or* **-bous** : a large animal of the deer family that is found in cold northern regions — used especially for one of the New World; called also *reindeer* [from Canadian French *caribou* "caribou," from Micmac (American Indian language of northeastern Canada) ɣalipu]

caribou

¹**car·i·ca·ture** \ˈkar-i-kə-ˌchù(ə)r, -ˌt(y)ù(ə)r\ *n* **1** : exaggeration of the actions, parts, or features of someone or something usually for comic or satirical effect **2** : something (as a drawing) produced by using caricature **3** : something that seems like a caricature

²**caricature** *vb* **-tured; -tur·ing** : to make or draw a caricature of — **car·i·ca·tur·ist** \-ˌchúr-əst, -ˌt(y)ùr-əst\ *n*

car·ies \ˈka(ə)r-ēz, ˈke(ə)r-\ *n, pl* **caries** : a progressive destruction of bone or tooth; *esp* : tooth decay

car·il·lon \ˈkar-ə-ˌlän, -lən\ *n* : a set of bells sounded by hammers controlled from a keyboard

car·load \ˈkär-ˌlōd\ *n* : a load (as of passengers) that fills a car

car·mine \ˈkär-mən, -ˌmīn\ *n* : a vivid red

car·nage \ˈkär-nij\ *n* : great destruction of life (as in battle) : SLAUGHTER

car·nal \ˈkärn-ᵊl\ *adj* **1** : of or relating to the body **2** : not spiritual : CORPOREAL **3** : SENSUAL 1 — **car·nal·i·ty** \kär-ˈnal-ət-ē\ *n* — **car·nal·ly** \ˈkärn-ᵊl-ē\ *adv*

car·na·tion \kär-ˈnā-shən\ *n* **1** : a moderate red **2** : any of the numerous cultivated herbs of the genus of pinks with reddish, pink, yellow, or white usually double flowers

car·ne·lian \kär-ˈnēl-yən\ *n* : a hard tough reddish quartz used as a gem

car·ni·val \ˈkär-nə-vəl\ *n* **1** : a season or festival of merrymaking before Lent **2** : a noisy merrymaking **3 a** : a traveling group that puts on a variety of amusements **b** : a program of entertainment

car·ni·vore \ˈkär-nə-ˌvō(ə)r, -ˌvȯ(ə)r\ *n* **1** : a flesh-eating animal; *esp* : any of an order of flesh-eating mammals **2** : a plant that traps and digests insects

car·niv·o·rous \kär-ˈniv-(ə-)rəs\ *adj* **1 a** : feeding on animal tissues **b** : trapping and digesting insects ⟨*carnivorous* plants⟩ **2** : of or relating to the carnivores

car·no·tite \ˈkär-nə-ˌtīt\ *n* : a radioactive mineral from which radium and uranium are obtained

\ə\ abut	\aú\ out	\i\ tip	\ȯ\ saw	\ú\ foot
\ər\ further	\ch\ chin	\ī\ life	\ȯi\ coin	\y\ yet
\a\ mat	\e\ pet	\j\ job	\th\ thin	\yü\ few
\ā\ take	\ē\ easy	\ŋ\ sing	\th\ this	\yú\ cure
\ä\ cot, cart	\g\ go	\ō\ bone	\ü\ food	\zh\ vision

car·ob \'kar-əb\ n : the sweet pod of a Mediterranean evergreen tree of the legume family that can be prepared to resemble chocolate and is used in various foods

¹**car·ol** \'kar-əl\ n : a usually religious song of joy

²**carol** vb **-oled** or **-olled; -ol·ing** or **-ol·ling** 1 : to sing especially in a joyful manner 2 : to sing carols and especially Christmas carols — **car·ol·er** or **car·ol·ler** n

¹**car·om** \'kar-əm\ n : a rebounding especially at an angle

²**carom** vb : to strike and rebound at an angle

car·o·tene \'kar-ə-,tēn\ n : any of several orange or red pigments which occur in plants and in the fatty tissues of plant-eating animals and from which vitamin A is formed

ca·rot·id \kə-'rät-əd\ n : one of the pair of arteries that pass up each side of the neck and supply the head — called also *carotid artery* — **carotid** adj

ca·rous·al \kə-'raú-zəl\ n : CAROUSE

ca·rouse \kə-'raúz\ n : a drunken merrymaking — **carouse** vb — **ca·rous·er** n

car·ou·sel also **car·rou·sel** \,kar-ə-'sel also -'zel; 'kar-ə-,sel also -,zel\ n : MERRY-GO-ROUND 1

¹**carp** \'kärp\ vb : to find fault : COMPLAIN — **carp·er** n

²**carp** n, pl **carp** or **carps** : a large Asian freshwater fish often raised for food and widely introduced into U.S. waters; also : any of various related or similar fishes

¹**car·pal** \'kär-pəl\ adj : relating to the wrist or carpus

²**carpal** n : a carpal bone or cartilage

car·pel \'kär-pəl\ n : one of the structures deep inside a flower that together make up the ovary of a flowering plant

car·pen·ter \'kär-pən-tər, 'kärp-ᵊm-tər\ n : a worker who builds or repairs wooden structures — **carpenter** vb

carpenter ant n : any of several ants that nest and gnaw passageways in dead or decaying wood

car·pen·try \'kär-pən-trē, 'kärp-ᵊm-trē\ n : the work or trade of a carpenter

car·pet \'kär-pət\ n 1 : a heavy fabric used especially as a floor covering 2 : a covering like a carpet — **carpet** vb

¹**car·pet·bag** \-,bag\ n : a traveling bag made of carpeting and very popular in the U.S. in the 19th century

²**carpetbag** adj : of or relating to carpetbaggers

car·pet·bag·ger \'kär-pət-,bag-ər\ n : a Northerner in the South after the American Civil War usually seeking private gain under the reconstruction governments

carpet beetle n : a small beetle whose larva damages woolen goods

car·pet·ing \'kär-pət-iŋ\ n : material for carpets; also : CARPET 1 ⟨wall-to-wall *carpeting*⟩

car pool n : an arrangement by a group of automobile owners in which each in turn drives his or her own car and carries the others as passengers usually to and from work — **car·pool** \'kär-,púl\ vb — **car·pool·er** n

car·port \'kär-,pō(ə)rt, -,pò(ə)rt\ n : an automobile shelter with open sides that is usually attached to the side of a building

car·pus \'kär-pəs\ n, pl **car·pi** \-,pī, -,pē\ : the wrist or its bones

car·ra·geen·an or **car·ra·geen·in** \,kar-ə-'gē-nən\ n : a substance obtained from various red algae (as Irish moss) that is used in foods especially to stabilize and thicken them

car·riage \'kar-ij\ n 1 : the act of carrying 2 : manner of holding the body : POSTURE 3 : a horse-drawn wheeled vehicle designed for carrying persons 4 : a wheeled support carrying a load ⟨gun *carriage*⟩ 5 : a movable part of a machine for supporting some other movable object or part ⟨a typewriter *carriage*⟩

car·ri·er \'kar-ē-ər\ n 1 : one that carries ⟨mail *carrier*⟩ 2 : a person or firm engaged in transporting passengers or goods 3 a : a bearer and transmitter of disease germs; *esp* : one who carries germs of a disease (as typhoid fever) in his or her system but is immune to the disease b : one who has a gene for a trait or condition (as sickle-cell ane-

mia) that is not expressed in his or her system 4 : an electric wave or alternating current that is used to send signals (as for radio, television, telephone, and telegraph)

car·ri·on \'kar-ē-ən\ n : dead and decaying flesh

car·rot \'kar-ət\ n : the long orange edible root of a common garden plant that is eaten as a vegetable; *also* : a plant that produces a carrot

¹**car·ry** \'kar-ē\ vb **car·ried; car·ry·ing** 1 : to support and take from one place to another : TRANSPORT ⟨carry a package⟩ 2 : to influence by appeal to the mind or emotions ⟨the speaker *carried* the audience⟩ 3 : ¹WIN 3b, CAPTURE ⟨*carried* off the prize⟩ 4 : to transfer from one place (as a column) to another ⟨carry a number in addition⟩ 5 : to contain and direct the flow of ⟨a pipe *carries* water⟩ 6 a : to wear or have on one's person ⟨*carries* a camera⟩ b : to bear upon or within one ⟨*carries* a scar⟩ ⟨she is *carrying* an unborn child⟩ 7 : IMPLY 1, INVOLVE ⟨the crime *carries* a penalty⟩ 8 : to hold the body or a part of it ⟨*carry* your head high⟩ 9 : to sing in correct pitch ⟨*carry* a tune⟩ 10 : to stock for sale ⟨*carries* three brands of tires⟩ 11 : to keep on a list or record ⟨*carrying* six drivers on the payroll⟩ 12 : ¹SUPPORT 4a ⟨pillars *carry* an arch⟩ 13 a : to succeed in ⟨*carry* an election⟩ b : to win a majority of votes in (as a state) 14 : to present for the public ⟨newspapers *carry* weather reports⟩ 15 : to reach or travel a distance ⟨a voice that *carries* well⟩

²**carry** n, pl **carries** : a quantity that is transferred in addition from one number place to the one of next higher place value

car·ry·all \'kar-ē-,ȯl\ n : a large bag or carrying case

carry away vb : to arouse strong feelings or enthusiasm in

carrying charge n : a charge added to the price of merchandise sold on the installment plan

carry on vb 1 : ²CONDUCT 2, MANAGE ⟨carries on a business⟩ 2 : to continue especially in spite of difficulties ⟨still *carrying on*⟩ 3 : to behave badly ⟨embarrassed at the way you *carried on*⟩

carry out vb : to put into action or effect ⟨*carry out* a plan⟩

car seat n : a portable seat for an infant or a small child that attaches to an automobile seat and holds the child safely

car·sick \'kär-,sik\ adj : having motion sickness associated with riding in a car — **car sickness** n

¹**cart** \'kärt\ n 1 : a heavy two-wheeled wagon usually pulled by a horse 2 : a light usually two-wheeled vehicle ⟨pony *cart*⟩

²**cart** vb : to carry in or as if in a cart — **cart·er** n

car·tel \kär-'tel\ n : a combination of business firms to control world markets and fix prices

car·ti·lage \'kärt-ᵊl-ij, 'kärt-lij\ n 1 : an elastic tissue which composes most of the skeleton of the vertebrate embryo and much of which is changed to bone later in life 2 : a part or structure composed of cartilage

car·ti·lag·i·nous \,kärt-ᵊl-'aj-ə-nəs\ adj : of, relating to, or resembling cartilage

cartilaginous fish n : any of the fishes having the skeleton composed largely of cartilage

car·tog·ra·pher \kär-'täg-rə-fər\ n : a person who makes maps

car·tog·ra·phy \kär-'täg-rə-fē\ n : the making of maps — **car·to·graph·ic** \,kärt-ə-'graf-ik\ adj

car·ton \'kärt-ᵊn\ n : a paperboard box or container [from French *carton* "cardboard box," from Italian *cartone* "pasteboard," from *carta* "sheet of paper," from Latin *charta* "piece of papyrus" — related to ³CARD, CARTOON]

car·toon \kär-'tün\ n 1 : a design, drawing, or painting made as a model for the finished work 2 a : a drawing intended as a humorous comment on public affairs b : COMIC STRIP 3 : ANIMATED CARTOON [from Italian *cartone* "pasteboard, a sketch of a planned drawing or painting done on heavy paper," from *carta* "sheet of paper," from Latin *charta* "piece of papyrus" — related to ³CARD, CARTON] — **car·toon·ist** \-'tü-nəst\ *n*

car·tridge \'kär-trij\ *n* : a case or container that holds a substance or device which is difficult, troublesome, or awkward to handle and that can be easily changed: as **a** : a tube containing a complete charge for a firearm **b** : a holder for photographic film **c** : a device on a phonograph that changes vibrations of the needle into electrical signals **d** : a case for holding a magnetic tape or disk **e** : a case for holding integrated circuits containing a computer program ⟨a video-game *cartridge*⟩

cart·wheel \'kärt-ˌhwēl, -ˌwēl\ *n* **1** : a large coin (as a silver dollar) **2** : a sideways handspring with arms and legs extended

carve \'kärv\ *vb* **carved; carv·ing 1** : to cut with care or exactness **2** : to cut into pieces or slices **3** : to cut up and serve meat — **carv·er** *n*

carv·ing \'kär-viŋ\ *n* **1** : the act or art of a person who carves **2** : a carved object, design, or figure

cary·at·id \ˌkar-ē-'at-əd\ *n, pl* **-atids** *or* **-at·i·des** \-'at-ə-ˌdēz\ : a sculptured figure of a woman in flowing robes used as a column in architecture

ca·sa·ba \kə-'säb-ə\ *n* : any of several muskmelons that have a usually yellow rind and sweet flesh and keep well

¹**cas·cade** \kas-'kād\ *n* : a steep usually small waterfall

²**cascade** *vb* **cas·cad·ed; cas·cad·ing** : to fall in or as if in a cascade

¹**case** \'kās\ *n* **1** : a situation requiring investigation, action, or consideration ⟨a *case* for the police⟩ **2 a** : a form of a noun, pronoun, or adjective showing its grammatical relation to other words ⟨the word "child's" in "a child's shirt" is in the possessive *case*⟩ **b** : such a relation whether shown by change of form or not ⟨the subject of a verb is in the nominative *case*⟩ **3** : what actually exists or happens : FACT ⟨thought he had failed, but that wasn't the *case*⟩ **4** : a question or claim to be settled in a court of law **5** : a convincing argument ⟨made a good *case* for accepting the plan⟩ **6 a** : an instance of disease or injury ⟨a *case* of chicken pox⟩ **b** : ²PATIENT **7** : EXAMPLE 3 ⟨a *case* of injustice⟩ [Middle English *cas* "situation needing action," from early French *cas* (same meaning), from Latin *casus* "fall, chance," from *cadere* "to fall, happen, come by chance"] — **in any case** : no matter what happens ⟨I'll probably go *in any case*⟩ — **in case 1** : IF 1 ⟨*in case* you couldn't figure it out from the first clue, here's a second⟩ **2** : as a precaution ⟨carry an umbrella just *in case*⟩ **3** : as a precaution against the event that ⟨have extra money *in case* we need it⟩ — **in case of** : in the event of ⟨for use *in case of* fire⟩

²**case** *n* **1 a** : a box or container to hold something **b** : a box with its contents **2** : an outer covering or protective shield **3** : CASING 2 [Middle English *cas* "box, container," from early French *case, chase* (same meaning), from Latin *capsa* "chest, box," from *capere* "to take" — related to CAPTURE, CASH]

case–hard·en \'kās-ˌhärd-ᵊn\ *vb* : to harden (an iron alloy) so that the surface layer is harder than the interior — **case–hard·ened** *adj*

ca·sein \'kā-ˌsēn, kā-'sēn\ *n* **1** : a phosphorus-containing protein that is separated from milk especially by the action of acid that is used in making paints and adhesives **2** : a phosphorus-containing protein that is produced when milk is made to form curds by rennet, that makes up a major part of cheese, and that is used in making plastics

case in point : a typical or relevant case

case knife *n* **1** : SHEATH KNIFE **2** : a table knife

case·ment \'kā-smənt\ *n* **1** : a window frame opening on hinges like a door **2** : a window with a casement

caryatid

case·work \'kā-ˌswərk\ *n* : social work involving close study of the problems and needs of a person or family — **case·work·er** \-ˌswər-kər\ *n*

¹**cash** \'kash\ *n* **1** : money in the form of coins or bills **2** : money or its equivalent (as a check) paid for goods at the time of purchase or delivery [from early French *casse* or early Italian *cassa,* both meaning "money box," from Latin *capsa* "chest, box" — related to ²CASE]

²**cash** *vb* : to pay or obtain cash for ⟨*cash* a check⟩

ca·shew \'kash-ü, kə-'shü\ *n* : an edible nut that is shaped like a kidney and comes from a tropical American tree that is related to the sumacs; *also* : the tree that produces cashews

¹**cash·ier** \ka-'shi(ə)r\ *n* **1** : an officer of a bank who is responsible for all money received and paid out **2** : an employee of a store or restaurant who receives and records payments made by customers

²**ca·shier** \ka-'shi(ə)r, kə-\ *vb* : to remove from a job; *esp* : to dismiss in disgrace

cashier's check *n* : a check drawn by a bank upon its own funds and signed by its cashier

cashew

cash in *vb* **1** : to obtain cash for ⟨*cashed in* her bonds⟩ **2** : to benefit financially ⟨souvenir sellers *cashed in* at the fair⟩ ⟨*cashing in* on their brother's fame⟩

cash·mere \'kazh-ˌmi(ə)r, 'kash-\ *n* **1** : fine wool from the undercoat of cashmere goats **2** : a soft yarn or fabric once made from cashmere wool but now often from sheep's wool

cashmere goat *n* : an Indian goat whose fine soft undercoat forms cashmere wool

cash register *n* : a business machine that usually has a money drawer, records the amount of money received, and exhibits the amount of each sale

cash value *n* : the amount paid to the owner of a life insurance policy if it is cashed in before the person named to receive the benefits is due the full amount

cas·ing \'kā-siŋ\ *n* **1** : something that encloses or surrounds **2** : a frame around a door or window opening

ca·si·no \kə-'sē-nō\ *n, pl* **-nos** : a building or room used for gambling

cask \'kask\ *n* **1** : a barrel-shaped container usually for liquids **2** : the quantity contained in a cask

cas·ket \'kas-kət\ *n* **1** : a small chest or box (as for jewels) **2** : COFFIN

casque \'kask\ *n* : HELMET 1

cas·sa·va \kə-'säv-ə\ *n* : any of several tropical plants with a fleshy root that yields a nourishing starch; *also* : the root or its starch — compare TAPIOCA

cas·se·role \'kas-ə-ˌrōl\ *n* **1** : a dish in which food can be baked and served **2** : the food cooked and served in a casserole

cas·sette \kə-'set, ka-\ *n* : a container holding film, photographic plates, or magnetic tape

cas·sia \'kash-ə\ *n* **1** : the dried coarse bark of any of several cinnamons **2** : any of a genus of herbs, shrubs, and trees of the legume family which grow in warm regions

\ə\ **abut**	\aú\ **out**	\i\ **tip**	\ó\ **saw**	\ú\ **foot**
\ər\ **further**	\ch\ **chin**	\ī\ **life**	\ói\ **coin**	\y\ **yet**
\a\ **mat**	\e\ **pet**	\j\ **job**	\th\ **thin**	\yü\ **few**
\ā\ **take**	\ē\ **easy**	\ŋ\ **sing**	\th\ **this**	\yú\ **cure**
\ä\ **cot, cart**	\g\ **go**	\ō\ **bone**	\ü\ **food**	\zh\ **vision**

Cas·si·o·pe·ia \ˌkas-ē-ə-'pē-(y)ə\ *n* : a northern group of stars between Andromeda and Cepheus

cas·sit·er·ite \kə-'sit-ə-ˌrīt\ *n* : a brown or black mineral that consists of tin and oxygen and is the chief source of tin

cas·sock \'kas-ək\ *n* : a close-fitting ankle-length garment worn by clergy (as in the Roman Catholic and Anglican churches)

cas·so·wary \'kas-ə-ˌwer-ē\ *n, pl* **-war·ies** : any of several tall swift-running birds of New Guinea and Australia that are closely related to the emu

cassowary

¹**cast** \'kast\ *vb* **cast; cast·ing 1 a** : ¹THROW 1a, TOSS ⟨*cast* a stone⟩ **b** : to throw a fishing line **c** : ¹DIRECT 3 ⟨*cast* a glance⟩ **d** : to place as if by throwing ⟨*cast* doubt on their honesty⟩ **e** : to deposit formally ⟨*cast* a ballot⟩ **f** : to throw off, out, or away ⟨the horse *cast* a shoe⟩ ⟨a snake *casts* its skin⟩ **2 a** : COMPUTE **b** : to arrange into parts or into a proper form ⟨*cast* the story in the form of a letter⟩ **3** : to assign parts to actors ⟨*cast* a play⟩ **4** : to shape a substance by pouring it in liquid or very soft form into a mold and letting it harden without pressure ⟨*cast* steel⟩ ⟨*cast* machine parts⟩ — **cast lots** : to draw lots to determine a matter by chance

²**cast** *n* **1** : an act of casting **2 a** : the form in which a thing is constructed **b** : the characters or the actors in a story or play **3** : the distance to which a thing can be thrown **4 a** : a glance of the eye **b** : APPEARANCE 1, LOOK **5 a** : CASTING 2 **b** : a rigid casing (as of gauze and plaster of paris) for immobilizing a body part **6** : ²FORECAST **7** : a tinge of color : SHADE **8** : one of the characteristics associated with a person or thing ⟨the humorous *cast* of his stories⟩ ⟨her strict *cast* of mind⟩ **9** : something thrown out or off or shed

cast about *vb* : to look around here and there : SEEK

cas·ta·net \ˌkas-tə-'net\ *n* : a rhythm instrument that consists of two small ivory, wood, or plastic shells fastened together and attached to the thumb and clicked together by the fingers — usually used in plural [from Spanish *castañeta* "castanet," from *castaña* "chestnut"]

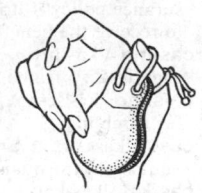

castanet

cast around *vb* : CAST ABOUT

cast·away \'kas-tə-ˌwā\ *adj* **1** : thrown away **2** : cast adrift or ashore — **castaway** *n*

caste \'kast\ *n* **1** : one of the classes into which the Hindu people of India were formerly divided **2 a** : a division of society based upon differences of wealth, rank, or occupation **b** : social rank : PRESTIGE **3** : a specialized form of a social insect that carries out a particular purpose in the colony ⟨the worker *caste* in a colony of honeybees⟩

cas·tel·lat·ed \'kas-tə-ˌlāt-əd\ *adj* : having battlements like a castle

cast·er \'kas-tər\ *n* **1** : one that casts **2** *or* **cas·tor** \'kas-tər\ : a small container (as for salt) with a top having small holes **3** : a small wheel that turns freely and is used for the support and movement of furniture

cas·ti·gate \'kas-tə-ˌgāt\ *vb* **-gat·ed; -gat·ing** : to punish, scold, or criticize harshly — **cas·ti·ga·tion** \ˌkas-tə-'gā-shən\ *n* — **cas·ti·ga·tor** \'kas-tə-ˌgāt-ər\ *n*

cast·ing \'kas-tiŋ\ *n* **1** : the act of one that casts **2** : something cast in a mold **3** : ²CAST 9

cast iron *n* : a hard brittle alloy of iron, carbon, and silicon shaped by being poured into a mold while melted

cas·tle \'kas-əl\ *n* **1 a** : a large building or group of buildings usually having high walls with towers and a surrounding moat for protection **b** : a large or impressive house **2** : ³ROOK [Middle English *castel* "castle," from early French *castel* (same meaning), from Latin *castellum* "castle, fortress" — related to CHÂTEAU]

cast–off \'kas-ˌtȯf\ *adj* : thrown away or aside ⟨*cast-off* clothes⟩ — **castoff** *n*

Cas·tor \'kas-tər\ *n* : the more northern of the two bright stars in Gemini [from Greek *Kastōr* (name of one of the twin heroes in mythology) — see *Word History* at GEMINI]

cas·tor bean \'kas-tər-\ *n* : the very poisonous seed of the castor-oil plant; *also* : CASTOR-OIL PLANT

castor oil *n* : a pale thick oil obtained from castor beans and used chiefly as a lubricant or a laxative

castor–oil plant *n* : a tropical Old World herb widely grown as an ornamental plant or for its oil-rich seeds

cas·trate \'kas-ˌtrāt\ *vb* **cas·trat·ed; cas·trat·ing** : to remove the ovaries or especially the testes of — **cas·tra·tion** \ka-'strā-shən\ *n*

ca·su·al \'kazh-(ə-)wəl, 'kazh-əl\ *adj* **1** : happening unexpectedly or by chance : not planned or foreseen ⟨a *casual* meeting⟩ **2** : happening without regularity : OCCASIONAL ⟨*casual* employment⟩ **3 a** : feeling or showing little concern : NONCHALANT ⟨a *casual* approach to cooking⟩ **b** : designed for ordinary or informal use ⟨*casual* clothes⟩ — **ca·su·al·ly** \-ē\ *adv* — **ca·su·al·ness** *n*

ca·su·al·ty \'kazh-əl-tē, 'kazh-(ə-)wəl-\ *n, pl* **-ties** **1** : a serious or fatal accident : DISASTER **2 a** : a military person lost (as by death or capture) during warfare **b** : a person or thing injured, lost, or destroyed

cat \'kat\ *n* **1 a** : a small domestic meat-eating mammal kept by people as a pet or for catching rats and mice **b** : an animal (as the lion, tiger, leopard, jaguar, cougar, wildcat, lynx, and cheetah) that belongs to the same family as the domestic cat **2** *slang* : ¹MAN 1a, FELLOW

ca·tab·o·lism \kə-'tab-ə-ˌliz-əm\ *n* : metabolism that breaks down complex materials within living plants and animals and usually involves the release of energy and formation of waste products — **cat·a·bol·ic** \ˌkat-ə-'bäl-ik\ *adj*

cat·a·clysm \'kat-ə-ˌkliz-əm\ *n* **1** : a great flood **2** : a violent and destructive natural event (as an earthquake) **3** : a violent social or political change — **cat·a·clys·mal** \ˌkat-ə-'kliz-məl\ *or* **cat·a·clys·mic** \-mik\ *adj*

cat·a·comb \'kat-ə-ˌkōm\ *n* : an underground place of burial — usually used in plural

cat·a·lep·sy \'kat-ᵊl-ˌep-sē\ *n* : a condition in which there is a loss of movement and the arms and legs stay in any position in which they are placed

¹**cat·a·lep·tic** \ˌkat-ᵊl-'ep-tik\ *adj* : of, having, or being like catalepsy ⟨a *cataleptic* state⟩

²**cataleptic** *n* : a person who has catalepsy

¹**cat·a·log** *or* **cat·a·logue** \'kat-ᵊl-ˌȯg, -ˌäg\ *n* **1** : a list of names, titles, or articles arranged according to a system **2** : a book or file containing a catalog

²**catalog** *or* **catalogue** *vb* **-loged** *or* **-logued; -log·ing** *or* **-logu·ing** **1** : to make a catalog of **2** : to enter in a catalog ⟨*catalog* books⟩ — **cat·a·log·er** *or* **cat·a·logu·er** \-ˌȯg-ər, -ˌä-gər\ *n*

ca·tal·pa \kə-'tal-pə, -'tȯl-\ *n* : any of several trees of North America and Asia with broad oval leaves, showy flowers, and long narrow pods [Creek *katȧlpa* "catalpa," from *iká* "head" and *tálpa* "wing"]

ca·tal·y·sis \kə-'tal-ə-səs\ *n* : the change and especially increase in the rate of a chemical reaction caused by a catalyst

cat·a·lyst \'kat-ᵊl-əst\ *n* **1** : a substance that changes the rate of a chemical reaction but is itself unchanged at the end of the process; *esp* : such a substance that speeds up a reaction or enables it to proceed under milder conditions **2** : a person or event that quickly causes change or action ⟨the scandal was a *catalyst* for reform⟩

cat·a·lyt·ic \ˌkat-ᵊl-ˈit-ik\ *adj* : causing, involving, or relating to catalysis ⟨the *catalytic* action of an enzyme⟩

catalytic converter *n* : a device containing a catalyst for changing automobile exhaust into mostly harmless products

cat·a·lyze \ˈkat-ᵊl-ˌīz\ *vb* **-lyzed; -lyz·ing** : to bring about or produce by chemical catalysis

cat·a·ma·ran \ˌkat-ə-mə-ˈran, ˈkat-ə-mə-ˌran\ *n* : a boat with twin hulls

cat·a·mount \ˈkat-ə-ˌmaunt\ *n* : any of various wild cats: as **a** : COUGAR **b** : LYNX

¹cat·a·pult \ˈkat-ə-ˌpəlt, -ˌpùlt\ *n* **1** : an ancient military device for hurling missiles **2** : a device for launching an airplane (as from the deck of an aircraft carrier)

²catapult *vb* **1** : to throw or launch by or as if by a catapult **2** : to become catapulted ⟨he *catapulted* to fame⟩

cat·a·ract \ˈkat-ə-ˌrakt\ *n* **1** : a clouding of the lens of the eye or of the transparent cover around it that blocks the passage of light **2 a** : a large waterfall **b** : a sudden rush like a waterfall

ca·tarrh \kə-ˈtär\ *n* : inflammation of a mucous membrane; *esp* : inflammation of the human nose and air passages that lasts a long time — **ca·tarrh·al** \-ˈtär-əl\ *adj*

ca·tas·tro·phe \kə-ˈtas-trə-(ˌ)fē\ *n* **1** : a sudden disaster **2** : complete failure : FIASCO — **cat·a·stroph·ic** \ˌkat-ə-ˈsträf-ik\ *adj* — **cat·a·stroph·i·cal·ly** \-i-k(ə-)lē\ *adv*

cat·bird \ˈkat-ˌbərd\ *n* : a dark gray American songbird with a black cap and a reddish underside of the base of the tail

cat·boat \-ˌbōt\ *n* : a sailboat with a single mast set far forward and a single large sail with a long boom

cat·call \-ˌkól\ *n* : a sound like the cry of a cat or a noise expressing disapproval — **catcall** *vb*

catbird

¹catch \ˈkach, ˈkech\ *vb* **caught** \ˈkót\; **catch·ing 1 a** : to capture or seize in flight or motion ⟨*catch* butterflies⟩ ⟨*catch* a ball⟩ **b** : ²TRAP 1a **2 a** : to discover unexpectedly ⟨was *caught* in the act⟩ **b** : to stop suddenly ⟨*caught* himself before he gave away the secret⟩ **3** : to take hold of : SNATCH **4 a** : to get entangled ⟨*catch* a sleeve on a nail⟩ **b** : to have the parts connect firmly ⟨this lock will not *catch*⟩ **c** : to attach, join, or fasten tightly **5** : to fall sick with ⟨*catch* a cold⟩ **6** : to take or get for a short time or quickly ⟨*catch* a glimpse of a friend⟩ ⟨*catch* a little sleep⟩ **7 a** : to catch up to ⟨will have to hurry to *catch* the leaders⟩ **b** : to get aboard in time ⟨*catch* the bus⟩ **8** : UNDERSTAND 1a ⟨didn't *catch* what she said⟩ **9** : to play baseball as a catcher [Middle English *cacchen* "to catch," from early French *cacher* "to hunt," derived from Latin *captare* "to chase," from *capere* "to take" — related to CAPTURE] — **catch fire 1** : to begin to burn **2** : to become excited or exciting — **catch one's breath** : to pause or rest long enough to regain normal breathing

synonyms CATCH, CAPTURE, TRAP, SNARE mean to come to possess or control by seizing. CATCH suggests the taking of something that is moving, flying, or hiding ⟨*catch* that dog⟩. CAPTURE suggests taking only after overcoming resistance or difficulty ⟨finally *captured* the fort after many days⟩. TRAP and SNARE suggest the use of a device that catches by surprise and then holds the

prey ⟨*trapped* wild animals⟩ ⟨trying to *snare* fish with nets⟩.

²catch *n* **1 a** : something caught **b** : the quantity caught at one time ⟨a large *catch* of fish⟩ **2 a** : the act of catching **b** : a pastime in which a ball is thrown and caught **3** : something that checks, fastens, or holds immovable ⟨a *catch* on a door⟩ **4** : one worth discovering or finding **5** : a round for three or more voices **6** : a hidden difficulty ⟨there must be a *catch*⟩

catch·all \ˈkach-ˌól, ˈkech-\ *n* : something to hold a variety of odds and ends

catch·er \ˈkach-ər, ˈkech-\ *n* : one that catches; *esp* : a baseball player who plays behind home plate

catching *adj* : INFECTIOUS ⟨the flu is *catching*⟩

catch·ment \ˈkach-mənt, ˈkech-\ *n* **1** : the action of catching water **2** : something that catches water

catch on *vb* **1** : to realize something ⟨they had been teasing me, and I never *caught on*⟩ **2** : to become popular ⟨will the new style *catch on*⟩

catchup *variant of* KETCHUP

catch up *vb* **1** : to pick up suddenly or quickly ⟨*caught* the mouse *up* by the tail⟩ **2** : to go fast enough to get even with someone ahead ⟨trying to *catch up* with the rest of the class⟩ **3** : to bring oneself up to date ⟨have to *catch up* on my homework⟩ ⟨*catch up* on the news⟩

catchy \ˈkach-ē, ˈkech-\ *adj* **catch·i·er; -est 1** : likely to attract attention **2** : easily remembered ⟨*catchy* lyrics⟩ **3** : TRICKY 2 ⟨a *catchy* question⟩

cat·e·chism \ˈkat-ə-ˌkiz-əm\ *n* **1** : a summary of religious doctrine in the form of questions and answers **2** : a set of questions requiring memorized answers put as a test

cat·e·chist \ˈkat-ə-ˌkist, -ə-kəst\ *n* : a person who catechizes

cat·e·chize \ˈkat-ə-ˌkīz\ *vb* **-chized; -chiz·ing** : to instruct by means of a catechism

cat·e·gor·i·cal \ˌkat-ə-ˈgór-i-kəl, -gär-\ *also* **cat·e·gor·ic** \-ik\ *adj* **1** : not restricted or limited in any way : ABSOLUTE ⟨a *categorical* denial⟩ **2** : of, relating to, or being a category — **cat·e·gor·i·cal·ly** \-i-k(ə-)lē\ *adv*

cat·e·go·rize \ˈkat-i-gə-ˌrīz\ *vb* **-rized; -riz·ing** : to put into a category : CLASSIFY — **cat·e·go·ri·za·tion** \ˌkat-i-gə-rə-ˈzā-shən\ *n*

cat·e·go·ry \ˈkat-ə-ˌgōr-ē, -ˌgór-\ *n, pl* **-ries 1** : one of the divisions or groupings used in a system of classification ⟨"species" and "genus" are biological *categories*⟩ **2** : ¹CLASS 3a, KIND

ca·ter \ˈkāt-ər\ *vb* **1** : to provide a supply of food ⟨*cater* for parties⟩ **2** : to supply what is wanted or needed — **ca·ter·er** \-ər-ər\ *n*

cat·er·cor·ner *or* **cat·er–cor·nered** *variant of* KITTY-CORNER

cat·er·pil·lar \ˈkat-ə(r)-ˌpil-ər\ *n* : the long wormlike larva of a butterfly or moth; *also* : any of various similar insect larvae (as of a sawfly)

caterpillar

Word History On looking at a fuzzy caterpillar you might see a resemblance to another animal. One kind of caterpillar must have reminded some people of a bear and was at one time called a *bear worm* and later a *woolly bear*. In France long ago, the fuzzy caterpillars probably made some people think of little dogs. The French word for caterpillar is *chenille,* which comes from a Latin word for "little dog." But our word *caterpillar*

comes from an early French dialect word, *catepelose,*
which is made up of two words meaning "hairy cat."
Pelose, meaning "hairy," was taken from Latin *pilus,*
"hair." This Latin word is the same root that gives us our
modern English word *pile,* meaning "a coat or surface of
short furry hairs." Since many caterpillars are covered
with such a coat, the name is very fitting. [Middle English *catyrpel* "caterpillar," from an early French dialect
word *catepelose* "caterpillar," literally, "hairy cat," from
cate "female cat" and *pelose* "hairy," derived from Latin
pilus "hair" — related to ⁵PILE]

cat·er·waul \'kat-ər-ˌwȯl\ *vb* : to make a harsh cry — **cat-
erwaul** *n*

cat·fish \'kat-ˌfish\ *n* : any of numerous usually freshwater stout-bodied fishes with large heads and long thin feelers about the mouth

cat·gut \-ˌgət\ *n* : a tough cord made from intestines of
animals (as sheep) and used for strings of musical instruments and rackets and for sewing in surgery

ca·thar·tic \kə-'thärt-ik\ *n* : a strong laxative — **cathartic**
adj

ca·the·dral \kə-'thē-drəl\ *n* : the principal church of a district headed by a bishop

cath·ode \'kath-ˌōd\ *n* **1** : the negative electrode of an
electrolytic cell — compare ANODE 1 **2** : the positive
terminal of a battery **3** : the electron-emitting electrode
of an electron tube — **ca·thod·ic** \ka-'thäd-ik\ *adj*

cathode ray *n* **1** : one of the high-speed electrons driven
in a stream from the heated cathode of a vacuum tube
under the force of a strong electric field **2** : a stream of
cathode-ray electrons

cathode–ray tube *n* : a vacuum tube in which a beam of
electrons is projected upon a fluorescent screen and produces a glowing spot

cath·o·lic \'kath-(ə-)lik\ *adj* **1** *cap* **a** : of or relating to the
Christian church as a whole **b** : ROMAN CATHOLIC **2**
: broad in sympathies, tastes, or interests ⟨a *catholic* taste
in music⟩ — **Ca·thol·i·cism** \kə-'thäl-ə-ˌsiz-əm\ *n*

Catholic *n* **1** : ¹CHRISTIAN 2 **2** : a member of the Roman
Catholic church

cat·ion \'kat-ˌī-ən\ *n* : the ion in solution during electrolysis
that travels to the cathode; *also* : a positively charged ion

cat·kin \'kat-kən\ *n* : a flower cluster (as of the willow or
birch) in which the flowers grow in close circular rows
along a slender stalk

cat·like \'kat-ˌlīk\ *adj or adv* : resembling a cat especially
in being quick and silent

cat·nap \-ˌnap\ *n* : a short light nap — **catnap** *vb*

cat·nip \-ˌnip\ *n* : a strong-scented herb of the mint family
that is especially attractive to cats

cat–o'–nine–tails \ˌkat-ə-'nīn-ˌtālz\ *n, pl* **cat–o'–nine–
tails** : a whip made of nine knotted cords fastened to a
handle

CAT scan \'kat-\ *n* : a three-dimensional image of a body
part made by a computer from a series of cross-sectional
images that are formed by exposure to radiation (as
X-rays) [CAT from *computerized axial tomography*]

cat's cradle *n* : a
game played with a
string looped on the
fingers so as to re-
semble a small cradle

cat's–eye \'kats-ˌī\ *n*
: any of various gems
(as chalcedony) with a
changeable luster sug-
gestive of reflections
from the eye of a cat

cat's cradle

catsup *variant of* KETCHUP

cat·tail \'kat-ˌtāl\ *n* : a tall marsh plant that bears very tiny
flowers and fruit in brown furry spikes at the end of long
stalks

cat·tle \'kat-ᵊl\ *n, pl* **cattle** : domestic four-footed animals
held as property or raised for use; *esp* : bovine animals (as
cows, bulls, or steers) kept on a farm or ranch

cat·tle·man \-mən, -ˌman\ *n* : a person who raises cattle

cat·ty \'kat-ē\ *adj* **cat·ti·er; -est** **1** : resembling a cat **2**
: mean in a sly way ⟨*catty* remarks⟩ — **cat·ti·ly** \'kat-ə-lē\
adv — **cat·ti·ness** \'kat-ē-nəs\ *n*

catty–corner *or* **catty–cornered** *variant of* KITTY-COR-
NER

cat·walk \'kat-ˌwȯk\ *n* : a narrow walk or way (as along a
bridge)

Cau·ca·sian \kȯ-'kā-zhən, -'kazh-ən\ *adj* **1** : of or relating
to the Caucasus or persons living there **2** : of, constituting, or characteristic of a race of humankind native to
Europe, North Africa, and southwest Asia and classified
according to physical features — used especially in referring to light-skinned persons of European descent —
Caucasian *n*

cau·cus \'kȯ-kəs\ *n* : a closed meeting of members of a
political party or faction usually to select candidates or
decide policy — **caucus** *vb*

caught *past and past participle of* CATCH

caul·dron *also* **cal·dron** \'kȯl-drən\ *n* **1** : a large kettle **2**
: something resembling a boiling cauldron in intensity or
degree of agitation ⟨a *cauldron* of intense emotion⟩ [Mid-
dle English *caldron, cauldron* "cauldron," from earlier
cauderon (same meaning), derived from an early French
dialect word *caudiere* "basin," derived from Latin *calidus*
"warm," from *calēre* "to be hot"— related to CALORIE,
NONCHALANT]

cau·li·flow·er \'kȯ-li-ˌflaů(-ə)r\ *n* : a garden plant closely
related to the cabbage and grown for its compact edible
head of usually white undeveloped flowers

caulk *or* **calk** \'kȯk\ *vb* : to fill up a crack, seam, or joint
so as to make it watertight — **caulk·er** *n*

caus·al \'kȯ-zəl\ *adj* : of, relating to, or being a cause

caus·a·tive \'kȯ-zə-tiv\ *adj* : making something happen or
exist ⟨a *causative* agent of disease⟩

¹cause \'kȯz\ *n* **1** : something or someone that brings
about a result or condition **2** : a good or adequate reason
⟨a *cause* for celebration⟩ **3 a** : a ground of legal action **b**
: something supported or deserving support ⟨a worthy
cause⟩ — **cause·less** \'kȯz-ləs\ *adj*
synonyms CAUSE, REASON, MOTIVE mean something
that explains an effect or result. CAUSE applies to any
event, circumstance, or condition that brings about or
helps bring about a result ⟨slippery roads were the *cause*
of many accidents⟩. REASON applies to a traceable or
explainable cause of a known effect ⟨too little rain was
the *reason* for the poor harvest⟩. MOTIVE applies to actions explained by a feeling or desire ⟨greater knowledge
was her *motive* for studying so hard⟩ ⟨police are trying
to find a *motive* for the crime⟩.

²cause *vb* **caused; caus·ing** : to be the cause of

cause·way \'kȯz-ˌwā\ *n* : a raised way or road across wet
ground or water

¹caus·tic \'kȯ-stik\ *adj* **1** : capable of eating away by
chemical action : CORROSIVE **2** : likely to offend or hurt
someone's feelings ⟨a *caustic* remark⟩ — **caus·ti·cal·ly**
\-sti-k(ə-)lē\ *adv*

²caustic *n* : a caustic substance (as caustic soda)

caustic potash *n* : POTASSIUM HYDROXIDE

caustic soda *n* : SODIUM HYDROXIDE

cau·ter·ize \'kȯt-ə-ˌrīz\ *vb* **-ized; -iz·ing** : to burn with a
hot iron or a chemical substance usually to destroy infected tissue ⟨*cauterize* a wound⟩ — **cau·ter·i·za·tion**
\ˌkȯt-ə-rə-'zā-shən\ *n*

¹cau·tion \'kȯ-shən\ *n* **1** : ADMONITION, WARNING **2**
: carefulness in regard to danger **3** : someone or something that astonishes or catches one's attention

²caution *vb* **cau·tioned; cau·tion·ing** \'kȯ-sh(ə-)niŋ\ : to
advise caution to : WARN

cau·tion·ary \'kо̇-shə-ˌner-ē\ *adj* : serving as or offering a warning ⟨a *cautionary* tale⟩

cau·tious \'kо̇-shəs\ *adj* : marked by or given to caution ⟨a *cautious* reply⟩ **synonyms** see CAREFUL — **cau·tious·ly** *adv* — **cau·tious·ness** *n*

cav·al·cade \ˌkav-əl-'kād, 'kav-əl-ˌkād\ *n* **1** : a procession especially of riders or carriages **2** : a dramatic series (as of related events)

¹cav·a·lier \ˌkav-ə-'li(ə)r\ *n* **1** : a mounted soldier : KNIGHT **2** : a brave and courteous gentleman [from early French *cavalier* "cavalier," from early Italian *cavaliere* (same meaning), derived from Latin *caballarius* "horseman," from earlier *caballus* "horse" — related to CAVALRY, CHIVALRY; see *Word History* at CHIVALRY]

²cavalier *adj* **1** : lighthearted and charming in manner **2** : having an unconcerned or disdainful attitude about important matters — **cav·a·lier·ly** *adv* — **cav·a·lier·ness** *n*

cav·al·ry \'kav-əl-rē\ *n, pl* **-ries** : troops mounted on horseback or moving in motor vehicles or helicopters [from Italian *cavallerie* "cavalry, chivalry," from *cavaliere* "cavalier, knight," derived from Latin *caballarius* "horseman," from earlier *caballus* "horse" — related to CAVALIER, CHIVALRY; see *Word History* at CHIVALRY]

¹cave \'kāv\ *n* : a natural underground chamber or series of chambers open to the surface

²cave *vb* **caved; cav·ing** : to fall or cause to fall in or down : COLLAPSE — usually used with *in*

cave–in \'kā-ˌvin\ *n* **1** : the action of caving in **2** : a place where earth has caved in

cave·man \'kāv-ˌman\ *n* : a person living in a cave especially during the Stone Age

cav·ern \'kav-ərn\ *n* : a cave often of large or unknown size

cav·ern·ous \'kav-ər-nəs\ *adj* **1** : having caverns or cavities **2** : resembling a cavern in being large and hollow **3** : composed largely of spaces capable of filling with blood to bring about the enlargement of a body part — **cav·ern·ous·ly** *adv*

cav·i·ar *also* **cav·i·are** \'kav-ē-ˌär *also* 'käv-\ *n* : the salted eggs of a large fish (as the sturgeon) usually served as an appetizer

cav·il \'kav-əl\ *vb* **-iled** *or* **-illed; -il·ing** *or* **-il·ling** \-(ə-)liŋ\ : to make objections of little worth or importance : QUIBBLE — **cavil** *n* — **cav·il·er** *or* **cav·il·ler** \-(ə-)lər\ *n*

cav·ing \'kā-viŋ\ *n* : the sport of exploring caves : SPELUNKING

cav·i·ta·tion \ˌkav-ə-'tā-shən\ *n* : the formation of partial vacuums in a liquid by a swiftly moving solid body (as a propeller) or by high-frequency sound waves

cav·i·ty \'kav-ət-ē\ *n, pl* **-ties** **1** : a hollow place; *esp* : an unfilled bodily space ⟨lung *cavity*⟩ **2** : a hole hollowed out in a tooth by decay

ca·vort \kə-'vо̇(ə)rt\ *vb* : to leap or dance about in a lively manner

caw \'kо̇\ *vb* : to utter the harsh call of a crow or a similar cry — **caw** *n*

cay \'kē, 'kā\ *n* : ⁴KEY

cay·enne \ˌkī-'en-, ˌkā-\ *n* : the ground dried fruits and seeds of hot peppers used to add flavor to food — called also *cayenne pepper*

cayman *variant of* CAIMAN

cay·use \'kī-ˌ(y)üs, kī-'(y)üs\ *n* : a small native horse of the western U.S.

CB \ˌsē-'bē\ *n* **1** : CITIZENS BAND **2** : the radio set used for citizens-band communications

cc \ˌsē-'sē\ *vt* **cc'd; cc'·ing** : to send someone a copy of (an e-mail, letter, or memo) ⟨*cc* an e-mail to a coworker⟩ [*carbon copy*]

CCD \ˌsē-ˌsē-'dē\ *n* : CHARGE-COUPLED DEVICE

C–clamp \'sē-ˌklamp\ *n* : a clamp shaped like the letter C

CD \ˌsē-dē\ *n* : a small plastic disk on which information (as music or computer data) is recorded digitally and read by using a laser

CD–ROM \ˌsē-ˌdē-'räm\ *n* : a CD containing computer data that cannot be altered [*compact disc read-only memory*]

cease \'sēs\ *vb* **ceased; ceas·ing** : to come or bring to an end : STOP

cease–fire \'sēs-'fī(ə)r\ *n* : a temporary stopping of warfare

cease·less \'sēs-ləs\ *adj* : ¹CONSTANT 4, CONTINUAL — **cease·less·ly** *adv* — **cease·less·ness** *n*

ce·cro·pia moth \si-ˌkrō-pē-ə-\ *n* : a red and dark brown moth that is the largest moth of North America and has a caterpillar which spins a cocoon of coarse silk

ce·cum *also* **cae·cum** \'sē-kəm\ *n, pl* **ce·ca** *also* **cae·ca** \-kə\ : a cavity open at one end; *esp* : the pouch in which the large intestine begins — **ce·cal** *also* **cae·cal** \-kəl\ *adj*

ce·dar \'sēd-ər\ *n* **1 a** : any of a genus of usually tall trees related to the pines and noted for their fragrant durable wood **b** : any of numerous cone-bearing trees (as some junipers) resembling the true cedars especially in having fragrant long-lasting wood **2** : the wood of a cedar

cedar 1b

cedar waxwing *n* : a brown waxwing of North America that has a yellow band on the tip of the tail

cede \'sēd\ *vb* **ced·ed; ced·ing** : to give up especially by treaty ⟨Russia *ceded* Alaska to the U.S. in 1867⟩

ce·dil·la \si-'dil-ə\ *n* : a mark placed under the letter *c* (as *ç*) to show that it is to be pronounced like *s* [from Spanish *cedilla* "mark under a *c*," originally a name for the obsolete letter *ç*, from *ceda, zeda* "the letter *z*," derived from Greek *zēta* "zeta"]

ceil·ing \'sē-liŋ\ *n* **1** : the overhead inside lining of a room **2** : something that hangs over or is above **3** : the height above the ground of the base of the lowest layer of clouds when over half of the sky is hidden by clouds **4** : the greatest height at which an airplane can operate efficiently **5** : an upper usually prescribed limit ⟨a *ceiling* on prices⟩

cel·an·dine \'sel-ən-ˌdīn, -ˌdēn\ *n* **1** : a yellow-flowered herb related to the poppies **2** : a buttercup with fleshy roots — called also *lesser celandine*

cel·e·brant \'sel-ə-brənt\ *n* : a person who celebrates; *esp* : the priest who is celebrating Mass

cel·e·brate \'sel-ə-ˌbrāt\ *vb* **-brat·ed; -brat·ing** **1** : to perform publicly and according to certain rules ⟨*celebrate* Mass⟩ **2** : to observe in some special way (as by merrymaking or by staying away from work) ⟨*celebrate* a birthday⟩ ⟨*celebrate* Memorial Day⟩ **3** : to praise or make known publicly ⟨her poetry *celebrates* the beauty of nature⟩ **synonyms** see KEEP — **cel·e·bra·tion** \ˌsel-ə-'brā-shən\ *n* — **cel·e·bra·tor** \'sel-ə-ˌbrāt-ər\ *n*

cel·e·brat·ed *adj* : widely known and often mentioned ⟨a *celebrated* writer⟩ **synonyms** see FAMOUS

ce·leb·ri·ty \sə-'leb-rət-ē\ *n, pl* **-ties** **1** : the state of being celebrated : FAME ⟨his short-lived *celebrity*⟩ **2** : a famous or celebrated person

ce·ler·i·ty \sə-'ler-ət-ē\ *n, pl* **-ties** : ¹SPEED 1a

cel·ery \'sel-(ə-)rē\ *n, pl* **-er·ies** : a European herb related to the carrot and widely grown for the thick edible stems; *also* : the stems of celery used for food

ce·les·ta \sə-'les-tə\ *n* : a keyboard instrument with hammers that strike steel plates to make ringing sounds

\ə\ **abut**	\au̇\ **out**	\i\ **tip**	\ȯ\ **saw**	\u̇\ **foot**
\ər\ **further**	\ch\ **chin**	\ī\ **life**	\ȯi\ **coin**	\y\ **yet**
\a\ **mat**	\e\ **pet**	\j\ **job**	\th\ **thin**	\yü\ **few**
\ā\ **take**	\ē\ **easy**	\ŋ\ **sing**	\th\ **this**	\yu̇\ **cure**
\ä\ **cot, cart**	\g\ **go**	\ō\ **bone**	\ü\ **food**	\zh\ **vision**

ce·les·tial \sə-'les-chəl\ *adj* **1** : of, relating to, or suggesting heaven ⟨angels are *celestial* beings⟩ **2** : of or relating to the sky ⟨a star is a *celestial* body⟩ — **ce·les·tial·ly** \-chə-lē\ *adv*

celestial equator *n* : the great circle on the celestial sphere midway between the celestial poles

celestial navigation *n* : navigation by observation of the positions of heavenly bodies

celestial pole *n* : one of two points on the celestial sphere around which the daily rotation of the stars appears to take place

celestial sphere *n* : an imaginary sphere of infinite radius against which the celestial bodies appear to be projected

cel·i·ba·cy \'sel-ə-bə-sē\ *n* : the state of not being married; *esp* : the state of one who has taken a vow not to marry

cel·i·bate \'sel-ə-bət\ *n* : one who lives in celibacy — **celibate** *adj*

cell \'sel\ *n* **1** : a very small room (as in a convent or prison) usually for one person **2** : a small compartment, cavity, or bounded space ⟨the *cells* in a honeycomb often contain honey⟩ **3** : one of the tiny units that are the basic building blocks of living things, that carry on the basic functions of life either alone or in groups, and that include a nucleus and are surrounded by a membrane **4 a** : a container (as a jar) with electrodes and an electrolyte either for generating electricity by chemical action or for use in electrolysis **b** : a single unit in a device for changing radiant energy into electrical energy **5** : CELL PHONE — **celled** \'seld\ *adj*

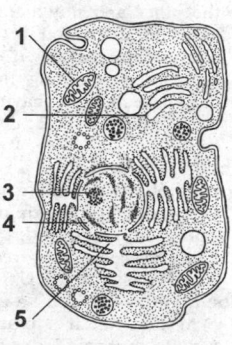

cell 3: *1* mitochondrion, *2* Golgi apparatus, *3* nucleolus, *4* nucleus, *5* endoplasmic reticulum

cel·lar \'sel-ər\ *n* : a room or set of rooms below the surface of the ground : BASEMENT

cell body *n* : the central part of a neuron that includes the nucleus but not the axons and dendrites

cell division *n* : a process by which cells increase in number that usually involves division into similar parts of more or less equal size — compare MEIOSIS, MITOSIS

cel·list \'chel-əst\ *n* : a person who plays the cello

cell membrane *n* : a semipermeable outside layer surrounding the contents of a cell

cel·lo \'chel-ō\ *n, pl* **cellos** : a large musical instrument of the violin family that plays the bass or tenor part [shortened form of *violoncello*]

cel·lo·phane \'sel-ə-,fān\ *n* : a thin transparent material made from cellulose and used as a wrapping

cell phone *n* : a portable cellular telephone

cell sap *n* : a watery solution of food and wastes that fills the vacuole of most plant cells

cell theory *n* : a general statement in biology that all living things consist of cells each of which has come from a previously existing cell

cel·lu·lar \'sel-yə-lər\ *adj* **1** : of, relating to, or consisting of cells **2** : of, relating to, or being a radiotelephone system in which a geographical area (as a city) is divided into small sections each served by a transmitter of limited range ⟨*cellular* phones⟩

cel·lu·loid \'sel-(y)ə-,lȯid\ *n* **1** : a tough flammable plastic **2** : a motion-picture film ⟨watch a western on *celluloid*⟩

cel·lu·lose \'sel-yə-,lōs\ *n* : a complex carbohydrate that is the chief part of the cell walls of plants and is commonly obtained as a white stringy substance from vegetable matter (as wood or cotton) which is used in making various

products (as rayon and paper) — **cel·lu·los·ic** \,sel-yə-'lō-sik\ *adj*

cell wall *n* : the firm nonliving layer that encloses and supports the cells of most plants, bacteria, fungi, and algae

Cel·sius \'sel-sē-əs, 'sel-shəs\ *adj* : relating to or having a scale for measuring temperature on which the interval between the triple point and the boiling point of water is divided into 99.99 degrees with 0.01° representing the triple point and 100.00° the boiling point; *also* : CENTIGRADE — abbreviation *C*

Celt \'kelt, 'selt\ *n* : a member of a division of the early Indo-European peoples spread out from the British Isles and Spain to Asia Minor; *also* : a person whose ancestors were Celts

¹Celt·ic \'kel-tik, 'sel-\ *adj* : of, relating to, or characteristic of the Celts or their languages

²Celtic *n* : a group of languages including Gaelic and Welsh

¹ce·ment \si-'ment\ *n* **1 a** : CONCRETE **b** : a fine powder that is produced from a burned mixture chiefly of clay and limestone and used as an ingredient of mortar and concrete **2 a** : a binding element or substance **b** : an adhesive substance **3 a** : CEMENTUM **b** : a material for filling cavities in teeth

²cement *vb* **1** : to unite by or as if by cement ⟨*cemented* their friendship⟩ **2** : to cover with concrete — **ce·ment·er** *n*

ce·men·tum \si-'ment-əm\ *n* : an outside bony layer that covers the part of the tooth normally within the gum

cem·e·tery \'sem-ə-,ter-ē\ *n, pl* **-ter·ies** : a place where dead people are buried : GRAVEYARD [Middle English *cimitery* "cemetery," from early French *cimiterie* (same meaning), from Latin *coemeterium* "cemetery," from Greek *koimētērion* "sleeping chamber, burial place," from *koiman* "to put to sleep"]

Ce·no·zo·ic \,sē-nə-'zō-ik, ,sen-ə-\ *adj* : of, relating to, or being an era of geological history that extends from the beginning of the Tertiary period to the present time and is marked by a rapid evolution of mammals and birds and of flowering plants and especially grasses; *also* : relating to the corresponding system of rocks — see GEOLOGIC TIME table — **Cenozoic** *n*

cen·ser \'sen(t)-sər\ *n* : a container in which incense is burned

¹cen·sor \'sen(t)-sər\ *n* : an official who checks materials (as publications or movies) to take out things thought to be objectionable

²censor *vb* **cen·sored; cen·sor·ing** \'sen(t)s-(ə-)riŋ\ : to examine in order to prevent publication or take out things thought to be objectionable; *also* : to delete things thought to be objectionable

cen·sor·ship \'sen(t)-sər-,ship\ *n* : the system or practice of censoring

¹cen·sure \'sen-chər\ *n* **1** : the act of blaming or condemning sternly **2** : an official expression of disapproval

²censure *vb* **cen·sured; cen·sur·ing** \'sench-(ə-)riŋ\ **1** : to find fault with **2** : to express formal disapproval of ⟨*censured* the senator for misconduct⟩ — **cen·sur·able** \'sench-(ə-)rə-bəl\ *adj* — **cen·sur·er** \'sen-chər-ər\ *n*

cen·sus \'sen(t)-səs\ *n* : a counting of the population (as of a country, city, or town) and a gathering of related statistics done by a government every so often

cent \'sent\ *n* **1** : a unit of value equal to $\frac{1}{100}$ part of a basic unit of money (as of a dollar or euro) **2** : a coin or bill representing one cent [from early French *cent* "hundred," from Latin *centum* "hundred"]

cen·taur \'sen-,tȯ(ə)r\ *n* : a creature in Greek mythology that is half human and half horse

cen·ta·vo \sen-'täv-ō\ *n, pl* **-vos** **1** : a unit of value equal to $\frac{1}{100}$ part of any of several basic units of money (as the Mexican peso) **2** : a coin representing one centavo

cen·te·nar·i·an \,sent-ᵊn-'er-ē-ən\ *n* : a person 100 years old or older — **centenarian** *adj*

cen·ten·a·ry \sen-'ten-ə-rē, 'sent-ᵊn-ˌer-ē\ *adj or n* : CENTENNIAL

¹**cen·ten·ni·al** \sen-'ten-ē-əl\ *n* : a 100th anniversary or its celebration

²**centennial** *adj* : relating to a period of 100 years — **cen·ten·ni·al·ly** \-ē-ə-lē\ *adv*

¹**cen·ter** \'sent-ər\ *n* **1** : the point inside a circle or sphere that is an equal distance from all the points on the edge **2 a** : a place in or around which an activity takes place or from which something begins ⟨the *center* of the scandal⟩ **b** : a place for a particular activity or service ⟨a day-care *center*⟩ **c** : a group of neurons that have a common purpose ⟨respiratory *center*⟩ **3** : the middle part (as of a stage) **4** : a player occupying a middle position on a team

²**center** *vb* **cen·tered; cen·ter·ing** \'sent-ə-rin, 'sen-trin\ **1** : to place or fix at or around a center or central area **2** : to give a central focus ⟨the story is *centered* on his adventures⟩ **3** : to collect at or around a center

cen·ter·board \'sent-ər-ˌbō(ə)rd, -ˌbȯ(ə)rd\ *n* : a keel that can be raised and is used especially in sailboats

center field *n* **1** : the part of the baseball outfield between right field and left field **2** : the position of the player defending center field — **center fielder** *n*

cen·ter·line \'sen-tər-ˌlīn\ *n* : a real or imaginary line that runs down the middle of something ⟨the *centerline* of the highway⟩

center of gravity : the point at which the entire weight of a body can be thought of as concentrated

center of mass : the point in a body or system of bodies at which the whole mass can be thought of as concentrated

cen·ter·piece \'sent-ər-ˌpēs\ *n* : a piece put in the center of something and especially a decoration (as flowers) for the center of a table

cen·tes·i·mo \sen-'tes-ə-ˌmō\ *n, pl* **-mos 1** : a unit of value equal to ¹⁄₁₀₀ part of a Uruguayan peso **2** : a coin representing one centesimo [Spanish *centésimo*, from Latin *centesimus* "hundredth," from *centum* "hundred"]

centi- *combining form* **1** : hundred ⟨*centi*grade⟩ **2** : one hundredth part of ⟨*centi*meter⟩ — used in terms of the metric system [from Latin *centum* "hundred"]

cen·ti·grade \'sent-ə-ˌgrād, 'sänt-\ *adj* : relating to or having a thermometer scale on which the interval between the freezing point and the boiling point of water is divided into 100 degrees with 0° representing the freezing point and 100° the boiling point — abbreviation *C*; compare CELSIUS

cen·ti·gram \'sent-ə-ˌgram, 'sänt-\ *n* — see METRIC SYSTEM table

cen·ti·li·ter \'sent-ə-ˌlēt-ər, 'sänt-\ *n* — see METRIC SYSTEM table

cen·time \'sän-ˌtēm, 'sen-\ *n* **1** : a unit of value equal to ¹⁄₁₀₀ franc **2** : a coin representing one centime

cen·ti·me·ter \'sent-ə-ˌmēt-ər, 'sänt-\ *n* — see METRIC SYSTEM table

centimeter–gram–second *adj* : of, relating to, or being a system of units based upon the centimeter as the unit of length, the gram as the unit of mass, and the second as the unit of time — abbreviation *cgs*

cen·ti·mo \'sent-ə-ˌmō\ *n, pl* **-mos 1** : a unit of value equal to ¹⁄₁₀₀ part of a basic unit of money (as of a bolivar or sol) **2** : a coin representing one Peruvian centimo [Spanish *céntimo*]

cen·ti·pede \'sent-ə-ˌpēd\ *n* : any of a class of long flattened arthropods that have many segments with each segment having one pair of legs except for the first segment which has a pair of poison fangs — compare MILLIPEDE [from Latin *centipeda* "centipede," from *centi-* "hundred" and *-peda*, from *ped-, pes* "foot" — related to PEDESTRIAN]

cen·tral \'sen-trəl\ *adj* **1** : containing or being a center ⟨the *central* office⟩ **2** : ¹CHIEF 2, PRINCIPAL ⟨the *central*

figure in a story⟩ **3** : situated at, in, or near the center ⟨the store is in a *central* location⟩ **4** : of, relating to, or consisting of the brain and spinal cord; *also* : originating within the central nervous system — **cen·tral·i·ty** \sen-'tral-ət-ē\ *n* — **cen·tral·ly** \'sen-trə-lē\ *adv*

central angle *n* : an angle with its vertex at the center of a circle and with sides that are radii of the circle

cen·tral·ize \'sen-trə-ˌlīz\ *vb* **-ized; -iz·ing** : to bring to a central point or under a single control — **cen·tral·i·za·tion** \ˌsen-trə-lə-'zā-shən\ *n*

central nervous system *n* : the part of the nervous system that in vertebrates consists of the brain and spinal cord

central processing unit *n* : CPU

central tendency *n* : the extent to which statistical values fall around a middle value ⟨the mean, median, and mode are all used to measure *central tendency*⟩

central time *n, often cap C* : the time of the 6th time zone west of Greenwich that includes the central U.S.

cen·tre \'sent-ər\ *chiefly British variant of* CENTER

cen·trif·u·gal \sen-'trif-yə-gəl, -'trif-i-gəl\ *adj* **1** : proceeding or acting in a direction away from a center or axis **2** : using or acting by centrifugal force [from scientific Latin *centrifugus* "centrifugal," literally, "fleeing from the center," from *centri-* "center" and *-fugus*, from Latin *fugere* "to run away, flee" — related to FUGITIVE, REFUGEE]

centrifugal force *n* : the force that tends to cause a thing or parts of a thing to go outward from a center of rotation

cen·tri·fuge \'sen-trə-ˌfyüj\ *n* : a machine using centrifugal force for separating substances of different densities, for removing moisture, or for causing gravitational effects

cen·tri·ole \'sen-trē-ˌōl\ *n* : one of a pair of minute bodies that are located next to the nucleus of a cell, are important in cell division, and consist of a cylinder-shaped central part surrounded by a circle of nine tiny tubes

cen·trip·e·tal \sen-'trip-ət-ᵊl\ *adj* : proceeding or acting in a direction toward a center or axis — **cen·trip·e·tal·ly** \-ət-ᵊl-ē\ *adv*

centripetal force *n* : the force that tends to cause a thing or parts of a thing to go inward toward a center of rotation

cen·tro·mere \'sen-trə-ˌmi(ə)r\ *n* : the point on a chromosome to which the spindle attaches during cell division

cen·tro·some \'sen-trə-ˌsōm\ *n* **1** : CENTRIOLE **2** : the region of a cell that is located next to the nucleus and contains the centrioles

cen·tu·ry \'sench-(ə-)rē\ *n, pl* **-ries 1** : a group of 100 things **2** : a period of 100 years

century plant *n* : a Mexican agave maturing and flowering only once in many years and then dying

CEO \ˌsē-ˌē-'ō\ *n* : the executive with the chief decision-making power in an organization or business [*chief executive officer*]

ceph·a·lo·pod \'sef-ə-lə-ˌpäd\ *n* : any of a class of mollusks that include the squids, cuttlefishes, and octopuses and have a group of muscular sucker-bearing arms, highly developed eyes, and usually a bag of inky fluid which can be released for defense

ceph·a·lo·tho·rax \ˌsef-ə-lə-'thō(ə)r-ˌaks, -'thȯ(ə)r-\ *n* : a combined head and thorax (as of a spider or crab)

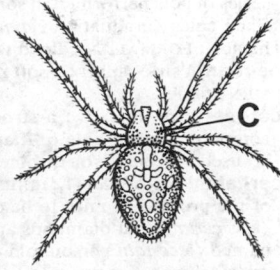

C cephalothorax

\ə\ abut	\au̇\ out	\i\ tip	\ȯ\ saw	\u̇\ foot
\ər\ further	\ch\ chin	\ī\ life	\ȯi\ coin	\y\ yet
\a\ mat	\e\ pet	\j\ job	\th\ thin	\yü\ few
\ā\ take	\ē\ easy	\ŋ\ sing	\t̲h̲\ this	\yu̇\ cure
\ä\ cot, cart	\g\ go	\ō\ bone	\ü\ food	\zh\ vision

Ce·phe·id \'sē-fē-əd\ *n* : one of a class of pulsating stars whose changes in brightness are very regular

Ce·pheus \'sē-ˌfyüs, 'sē-fē-əs\ *n* : a group of stars between Cygnus and the north pole

¹ce·ram·ic \sə-'ram-ik\ *adj* : of or relating to the manufacture of a product (as earthenware, porcelain, or brick) made from a nonmetallic mineral by heating at high temperatures

²ceramic *n* **1** *pl* : the art of making ceramic articles **2** : a product of ceramic manufacture

cer·cus \'sər-kəs\ *n, pl* **cer·ci** \'sər-ˌsī\ : a thin many-jointed part of an insect that sticks out from the hind end of its body

¹ce·re·al \'sir-ē-əl\ *adj* : relating to grain or to the plants that produce it; *also* : made of grain [derived from Latin *cerealis* "of grain," literally, "of Ceres," from *Ceres* (name of Roman goddess of grain)]

²cereal *n* **1** : a plant (as a grass) that produces starchy grain suitable for food; *also* : its grain **2** : a prepared food (as oatmeal or cornflakes) of grain

cer·e·bel·lum \ˌser-ə-'bel-əm\ *n, pl* **-bellums** *or* **-bel·la** \-'bel-ə\ : a large portion of the back part of the brain that is concerned especially with the action of groups of muscles and with bodily balance

cer·e·bral \sə-'rē-brəl, 'ser-ə-\ *adj* **1** : of or relating to the brain **2** : of, relating to, or being the cerebrum **3** : ¹IN-TELLECTUAL 1 〈a *cerebral* novel〉

cerebral hemisphere *n* : either of the two hollow many-ridged right or left halves of the cerebrum

cerebral palsy *n* : a disease resulting from damage to the brain usually before or during birth and resulting in imperfect control of muscles, paralysis, and speech disturbances

ce·re·bro·spi·nal fluid \sə-ˌrē-brō-ˌspīn-ᵊl-\ *n* : a colorless fluid that occupies the cavities of the brain and spinal cord and the space between these and the membranes surrounding them

ce·re·brum \sə-'rē-brəm, 'ser-ə-brəm\ *n, pl* **-brums** *or* **-bra** \-brə\ **1** : ¹BRAIN 1a **2** : the expanded front or upper part of the brain that consists of the cerebral hemispheres and connecting structures and is reported to be the seat of conscious mental processes

¹cer·e·mo·ni·al \ˌser-ə-'mō-nē-əl\ *adj* : of, relating to, or forming a ceremony — **cer·e·mo·ni·al·ism** \-nē-ə-ˌliz-əm\ *n* — **cer·e·mo·ni·al·ist** \-nē-ə-ləst\ *n* — **cer·e·mo·ni·al·ly** \-nē-ə-lē\ *adv* — **cer·e·mo·ni·al·ness** *n*

²ceremonial *n* : a ceremonial act, action, or system

cer·e·mo·ni·ous \ˌser-ə-'mō-nē-əs\ *adj* **1** : ¹CEREMONIAL **2** : careful to observe forms and ceremony : FORMAL — **cer·e·mo·ni·ous·ly** *adv* — **cer·e·mo·ni·ous·ness** *n*

cer·e·mo·ny \'ser-ə-ˌmō-nē\ *n, pl* **-nies** **1** : a formal act or series of acts performed in some regular way according to fixed rules 〈graduation *ceremonies*〉 **2** : very polite behavior : FORMALITY 〈dined without *ceremony*〉

ce·ri·um \'sir-ē-əm\ *n* : a soft metallic element — see ELEMENT table

cer·met \'sər-ˌmet\ *n* : a strong alloy of a heat-resistant compound (as carbide of titanium) and a metal (as nickel) used especially for turbine blades

¹cer·tain \'sərt-ᵊn\ *adj* **1** : FIXED 1b 〈receive a *certain* share of the profits〉 **2** : not to be doubted : known to be true 〈it is *certain* that diamonds are hard〉 **3** : known but not named 〈a *certain* person told me〉 **4** : RELIABLE, SURE 〈a *certain* cure〉 **5 a** : sure to happen : bound to occur : IN-EVITABLE 〈defeat was *certain*〉 **b** : decided in advance by or as if by fate 〈the plan was *certain* to succeed〉 **6** : assured in mind or action 〈feel *certain* they will come〉

²certain *pron* : certain ones 〈*certain* of my classmates are absent〉

cer·tain·ly \'sərt-ᵊn-lē\ *adv* **1** : in a manner that is certain : for certain 〈the earliest voyage of which anything is cer-

tainly known〉 **2** : without doubt : SURELY 〈*certainly* you can do better than that〉

cer·tain·ty \'sərt-ᵊn-tē\ *n, pl* **-ties** **1** : something certain **2** : the quality or state of being or feeling certain

cer·tif·i·cate \(ˌ)sər-'tif-i-kət\ *n* **1** : a document that is proof of some fact; *esp* : one showing that a person has fulfilled the requirements of a school or profession 〈teaching *certificate*〉 **2** : a document showing ownership 〈stock *certificate*〉 〈bond *certificate*〉

certification mark *n* : a mark used to identify a product or service that has been certified to conform to a certain set of standards

certified milk *n* : milk of high quality produced under the rules and regulations of an authorized medical milk commission

cer·ti·fy \'sərt-ə-ˌfī\ *vb* **-fied; -fy·ing** **1** : to guarantee to be true or valid or as claimed or meeting a standard **2** : to recognize as having met special qualifications within a field 〈*certify* teachers〉 — **cer·ti·fi·able** \-ˌfī-ə-bəl\ *adj* — **cer·ti·fi·ca·tion** \ˌsərt-ə-fə-'kā-shən\ *n* — **cer·ti·fi·er** \'sərt-ə-ˌfī(-ə)r\ *n*

cer·ti·tude \'sərt-ə-ˌt(y)üd\ *n* : CERTAINTY

ce·ru·le·an \sə-'rü-lē-ən\ *adj* : colored blue like the sky

cer·vi·cal \'sər-vi-kəl\ *adj* : of or relating to a neck or cervix

cer·vix \'sər-viks\ *n, pl* **cer·vi·ces** \'sər-və-ˌsēz\ *or* **cer·vix·es** : the narrow outer end of the uterus that opens into the cavity of the vagina

ce·sar·e·an *or* **cae·sar·e·an** \si-'zar-ē-ən, -'zer-\ *n, often cap C* : CESAREAN SECTION — **cesarean** *or* **caesarean** *adj*

cesarean section *or* **caesarean section** *n, often cap C* : a surgical operation making an opening in the walls of the abdomen and uterus for delivery of a baby [from *Cesar*, alternate form of *Caesar*, and *-ean* (adjective suffix); from the belief that the original bearer of the name *Caesar* was cut (Latin *caesus*) from his mother's womb]

ce·si·um \'sē-zē-əm\ *n* : a silver-white soft element used especially in photoelectric cells — see ELEMENT table

ces·sa·tion \se-'sā-shən\ *n* : a stopping of action

ces·sion \'sesh-ən\ *n* : a giving over (as of territory or rights) to another

cess·pool \'ses-ˌpül\ *n* : an underground pit or tank for liquid waste (as household sewage)

ce·ta·cean \si-'tā-shən\ *n* : any of an order of aquatic mammals (as a whale, dolphin, or porpoise) — **cetacean** *adj*

Ce·tus \'sēt-əs\ *n* : a group of stars seen above the equator and south of Pisces and Aries [Latin, literally, "whale"]

ce·tyl alcohol \ˌsēt-ᵊl-\ *n* : a waxy crystalline alcohol used especially in cosmetics, drugs, and detergents

cha·dor \'chəd-ər, 'chäd-\ *n* : a large cloth worn as a combination head covering, veil, and shawl usually by Muslim women

chafe \'chāf\ *vb* **chafed; chaf·ing** **1 a** : IRRITATE 1, VEX **b** : to feel irritation, dissatisfaction, or impatience : FRET **2** : to warm by rubbing **3** : to rub so as to wear away or make sore

cha·fer \'chā-fər\ *n* : any of various large beetles

¹chaff \'chaf\ *n* **1** : the seed coverings and other debris separated from the seed in threshing grain **2** : something worthless — **chaffy** \-ē\ *adj*

²chaff *n* : light jesting talk : BANTER

³chaff *vb* : to tease good-naturedly

chaf·fer \'chaf-ər\ *vb* **chaf·fered; chaf·fer·ing** \'chaf-(ə-)riŋ\ : to dispute about a price — **chaf·fer·er** *n*

chafing dish \'chā-fiŋ-\ *n* : a dish for cooking or warming food at the table

¹cha·grin \shə-'grin\ *n* : a feeling of being annoyed by failure or disappointment

²chagrin *vb* **cha·grined** \-'grind\; **cha·grin·ing** \-'grin-iŋ\ : to cause to feel chagrin

chai \'chī\ *n* : a beverage that is a blend of black tea, honey, spices, and milk

¹chain \'chān\ *n* **1 a** : a series of connected links or rings **b** : a measuring instrument of 100 links used in surveying **c** : a unit of length equal to 66 feet (about 20 meters) **2** : something that restricts or binds : BOND **3 a** : a series of things joined together as if by links ⟨a *chain* of mountains⟩ ⟨a *chain* of events⟩ **b** : a number of atoms united like links in a chain

²chain *vb* : to fasten, bind, or connect with or as if with a chain

chain reaction *n* **1** : a series of events so related to each other that each one sets the next one going **2** : a chemical or nuclear reaction producing energy or products that cause further reactions of the same kind

chain saw *n* : a portable power saw that has teeth linked together to form a continuous chain

chain–smoke \'chān-ˌsmōk\ *vb* : to smoke cigarettes one right after another — **chain–smok·er** \-ˌsmō-kər\ *n*

chain store *n* : any of a number of stores under the same ownership selling the same lines of goods

chair \'che(ə)r, 'cha(ə)r\ *n* **1** : a seat with legs and a back for use by one person **2 a** : an official seat or a seat of authority or honor **b** : an office or position of authority or honor **c** : an official who conducts a meeting

chair·man \'che(ə)r-mən, 'cha(ə)r-\ *n* : CHAIR 2c — **chair·man·ship** \-ˌship\ *n*

chair·per·son \-ˌpər-sən\ *n* : CHAIR 2c

chair·wom·an \-ˌwum-ən\ *n* : a woman who conducts a meeting

chaise \'shāz\ *n* : a two-wheeled carriage with a folding top

chaise longue \'shāz-'lȯŋ\ *n* : a long chair that one can lie on [French, literally, "long chair," from *chaise* "chair" and *longue* "long"]

chaise lounge \'shāz-'laȯnj, 'chās-\ *n* : CHAISE LONGUE [from *chaise longue;* the spelling *lounge* influenced by the more familiar English word *lounge* "sofa"]

cha·la·za \kə-'lā-zə, -'laz-ə\ *n, pl* **-zae** \-ˌzē\ *or* **-zas** : either of two twisted bands in the white of a bird's egg that are located at opposite ends of the egg and extend to the yolk

chal·ced·o·ny \kal-'sed-ᵊn-ē, 'chal-sə-ˌdän-ē\ *n, pl* **-nies** : a nearly transparent quartz of various colors and with waxy luster

cha·let \sha-'lā, 'shal-ˌā\ *n* **1** : a herdsman's hut in the Alps away from a town or village **2 a** : a Swiss dwelling with a roof that sticks far out past the walls **b** : a cottage built to look like a chalet

chalet 2a

chal·ice \'chal-əs\ *n* : GOBLET; *esp* : the cup used in the sacrament of Communion

¹chalk \'chȯk\ *n* **1** : a soft white, gray, or buff limestone made up mainly of the shells of tiny saltwater animals and especially foraminifers **2** : chalk or material like chalk especially when used as a crayon [Old English *cealc* "chalk," from Latin *calc-, calx* "lime" — related to CALCIUM] — **chalky** \'chȯ-kē\ *adj*

²chalk *vb* **1** : to rub, mark, write, or draw with chalk **2 a** : to outline roughly ⟨*chalk* out a plan of attack⟩ **b** : to record or add up with or as if with chalk ⟨*chalk* up the totals⟩

chalk·board \'chȯk-ˌbō(ə)rd, -ˌbȯ(ə)rd\ *n* : a dark smooth surface (as of slate) used for writing or drawing on with chalk

¹chal·lenge \'chal-ənj\ *vb* **chal·lenged; chal·leng·ing 1** : to order to stop and prove identity **2 a** : to object to as bad or incorrect : DISPUTE **b** : to demand proof that something is right or legal **3** : to invite or dare to take part in a contest **4** : to arouse or stimulate especially by presenting with difficulties — **chal·leng·er** *n*

²challenge *n* **1 a** : a demand that someone take part in a duel **b** : an invitation or dare for someone to compete in a contest or sport **2** : an objection to something as not being true, genuine, correct, or proper or to a person (as a juror) as not being qualified or approved **3** : a sentry's command to halt and prove identity **4** : a stimulating task or problem

chal·lenged \'chal-ənjd\ *adj* : having a disability or lacking some necessary quality or element ⟨physically *challenged*⟩

chal·lis \'shal-ē\ *n, pl* **chal·lises** \'shal-ēz\ : a lightweight soft clothing fabric

¹cham·ber \'chām-bər\ *n* **1** : a room in a house and especially a bedroom **2** : an enclosed space or compartment ⟨the *chamber* of a pistol⟩ ⟨the *chambers* of the heart⟩ **3 a** : a meeting hall of a government body (as an assembly) **b** : a room where a judge conducts business out of court — usually used in plural **4 a** : a group of people organized into a lawmaking body ⟨the lower *chamber* of the legislature⟩ **b** : a board or council of volunteers (as businesspeople) [Middle English *chambre* "chamber," from early French *chambre* (same meaning), from Latin *camera* "room, chamber" — related to CAMERA] — **cham·bered** \-bərd\ *adj*

²chamber *vb* **cham·bered; cham·ber·ing** \-b(ə-)riŋ\ : to place or hold in or as if in a chamber

chambered nautilus *n* : NAUTILUS 1

cham·ber·lain \'chām-bər-lən\ *n* **1** : a chief officer in the household of a ruler or noble **2** : TREASURER

cham·ber·maid \'chām-bər-ˌmād\ *n* : a maid who takes care of bedrooms (as in a hotel)

chamber music *n* : instrumental music to be performed by a few musicians in a room or small hall

cham·bray \'sham-ˌbrā, -brē\ *n* : a lightweight clothing fabric with colored and white yarns

cha·me·leon \kə-'mēl-yən\ *n* **1** : any of various lizards that can vary the color of their skin **2** : a person who easily or frequently changes attitude or purpose

chameleon 1

Word History The chameleon of the Old World has a fierce look. The Greeks called it *chamaileōn,* combining their words *chamai,* meaning "on the ground," and *leōn* "lion." It may be that the upright ridge of skin behind the head of many of these lizards reminded them of the lion's mane. The Romans borrowed the Greek word for this little creature, and the French later took the Latin word. For a long time after the word was borrowed into Middle English, it was spelled *chamelion,* with the ending like our modern word *lion.* But later writers who knew the form of the word in ancient Greek and Latin changed the spelling to *chameleon,* to match the original form. From its use as the name of a creature able to change color with its mood or the temperature, the word came to be used for a person who is changeable. [Middle English *chamelion*

\ə\ **abut**	\aȯ\ **out**	\i\ **tip**	\ȯ\ **saw**	\ȯ\ **foot**
\ər\ **further**	\ch\ **chin**	\ī\ **life**	\ȯi\ **coin**	\y\ **yet**
\a\ **mat**	\e\ **pet**	\j\ **job**	\th\ **thin**	\yü\ **few**
\ā\ **take**	\ē\ **easy**	\ŋ\ **sing**	\th\ **this**	\yu̇\ **cure**
\ä\ **cot, cart**	\g\ **go**	\ō\ **bone**	\ü\ **food**	\zh\ **vision**

"chameleon," from early French *chamelion* (same meaning), from Latin *chamaeleon* (same meaning), from Greek *chamaileōn*, from *chamai* "on the ground" and *leōn* "lion"]

cham·ois \'sham-ē\ *n, pl* **cham·ois** *also* **cham·oix** \'sham-ē(z)\ **1** : a small goatlike mountain antelope of Europe and the Caucasus **2** : a soft yellowish leather made from the skin of the chamois or from sheepskin

cham·o·mile *or* **cam·o·mile** \'kam-ə-ˌmīl, -ˌmēl\ *n* **1** : an herb related to the daisies with strong-scented leaves and flower heads **2** : the dried flower heads of chamomile often used in making tea

¹champ \'champ\ *vb* **1** : to bite or chew noisily ⟨a horse *champing* its bit⟩ **2** : to show impatience — usually used in the phrase *champing at the bit*

²champ *n* : ¹CHAMPION 2

cham·pagne \sham-'pān\ *n* : a white sparkling wine

¹cham·pi·on \'cham-pē-ən\ *n* **1** : a person who fights or speaks for another person or in favor of a cause **2** : the winner of first prize or first place in a competition; *also* : one showing superior skill or ability

²champion *vb* : to protect or fight for as a champion

cham·pi·on·ship \'cham-pē-ən-ˌship\ *n* **1** : the act of defending as a champion **2** : the position or title of champion **3** : a contest held to find a champion

¹chance \'chan(t)s\ *n* **1** : the uncertain course of events ⟨they met by *chance*⟩ **2** : OPPORTUNITY 1 ⟨had a *chance* to travel⟩ **3** : the possibility of loss or injury ⟨took *chances* driving too fast⟩ **4** : the possibility or probability of something happening ⟨there is a *chance* of rain⟩ **5** : a ticket in a raffle

²chance *vb* **chanced; chanc·ing** **1** : to take place by chance : HAPPEN ⟨it *chanced* to rain that day⟩ **2** : to come unexpectedly — used with *upon* ⟨*chanced* upon a good restaurant⟩ **3** : ²RISK 2 ⟨knew the trip was dangerous but decided to *chance* it⟩

³chance *adj* : happening by chance ⟨a *chance* meeting⟩

chan·cel \'chan(t)-səl\ *n* : the part of a church containing the altar and seats for the clergy and choir

chan·cel·lery *or* **chan·cel·lory** \'chan(t)-s(ə-)lə-rē, -səl-rē\ *n, pl* **-ler·ies** *or* **-lor·ies** **1** : the position or department of a chancellor **2** : the building or office where a chancellor works

chan·cel·lor \'chan(t)-s(ə-)lər\ *n* **1** : the chief minister of state in some European countries **2** : the head of a university

chan·cery \'chan(t)s-(ə-)rē\ *n, pl* **-cer·ies** : a record office for public archives

chan·cre \'shaŋ-kər\ *n* : a sore at the site of entry of an infectious germ (as one causing syphilis) [French *chancre* "a sore," from Latin *cancer* "crab, cancer (disease)" — related to CANCER, CANKER]

chan·de·lier \ˌshan-də-'li(ə)r\ *n* : a branched lighting fixture usually hanging from a ceiling

¹change \'chānj\ *vb* **changed; chang·ing** **1** : to make or become different : ALTER **2** : to give a different position, course, or direction to **3** : to replace with another : SWITCH, EXCHANGE ⟨*change* places⟩ **4** : to give or receive an equal amount of money in usually smaller units of value or in a foreign currency ⟨*change* a $10 bill⟩ **5 a** : to put fresh clothes or covering on ⟨*change* a bed⟩ **b** : to put on different clothes — **chang·er** *n* — **change hands** : to pass from one person's possession to another's

²change *n* **1** : the act, process, or result of changing ⟨a *change* of seasons⟩ ⟨a *change* for the better⟩ **2** : a fresh set of clothes **3 a** : money in small units of value received in exchange for an equal amount in larger units **b** : money returned when a payment is more than the amount due **c** : money in coins **d** : MONEY 1a ⟨cost a large chunk of *change*⟩

change·able \'chān-jə-bəl\ *adj* **1** : likely to change often or suddenly ⟨*changeable* weather⟩ **2** : appearing different

(as in color) from different points of view — **change·abil·i·ty** \ˌchān-jə-'bil-ət-ē\ *n* — **change·able·ness** \'chān-jə-bəl-nəs\ *n* — **change·ably** \-blē\ *adv*

change·ful \'chānj-fəl\ *adj* : CHANGEABLE 1

change·less \'chānj-ləs\ *adj* : UNCHANGEABLE, CONSTANT — **change·less·ly** *adv* — **change·less·ness** *n*

change·ling \'chānj-liŋ\ *n* : a child secretly exchanged for another in infancy

change of life : MENOPAUSE; *also* : a similar period in the male

change·over \'chān-jō-vər\ *n* : ¹TRANSITION 1

¹chan·nel \'chan-ᵊl\ *n* **1** : the bed of a stream **2** : the deeper part of a river, harbor, or strait **3** : a strait or a narrow sea between two close large areas of land ⟨the English *Channel*⟩ **4** : a way of passing something along ⟨negotiating through diplomatic *channels*⟩ **5** : a group of frequencies close enough in value for a single radio or television communication **6** : a closed passage through which something flows **7** : a long gutter, groove, or track

²channel *vb* **-neled** *or* **-nelled; -nel·ing** *or* **-nel·ling** **1** : to form a channel in **2** : to direct into or through a channel

chan·nel·ize \'chan-ᵊl-ˌīz\ *vb* **-ized; -iz·ing** **1** : ²CHANNEL **2** : to straighten by means of a channel ⟨*channelize* a stream⟩ — **chan·nel·i·za·tion** \ˌchan-ᵊl-ə-'zā-shən\ *n*

channel surfing *n* : the action or practice of quickly looking at one television channel after another by use of a remote control — **channel surf** *vb* — **channel surfer** *n*

¹chant \'chant\ *vb* **1** : to sing especially in the way a chant is sung **2** : to recite or speak with no change in tone [Middle English *chaunten* "to chant," from early French *chanter* (same meaning), derived from Latin *canere* "to sing" — related to ³CANT, CANTATA, CHANTEY, CHARM] — **chant·er** *n*

²chant *n* **1** : a melody in which several words or syllables are sung in one tone **2** : something spoken in the style of a chant

chan·tey *or* **chan·ty** \'shant-ē, 'chant-\ *or* **shan·ty** \'shant-\ *n, pl* **chanteys** *or* **chanties** *or* **shanties** : a song sung by sailors in rhythm with their work [from French *chanter* "to sing," derived from Latin *canere* "to sing" — related to CANTATA, CHANT, CHARM]

chan·ti·cleer \ˌchant-ə-'kli(ə)r, ˌshant-\ *n* : ROOSTER

Chanukah *variant of* HANUKKAH

cha·os \'kā-ˌäs\ *n* : complete confusion — **cha·ot·ic** \kā-'ät-ik\ *adj* — **cha·ot·i·cal·ly** \-i-k(ə-)lē\ *adv*

¹chap \'chap\ *n* : a crack or a sore roughening of the skin from exposure especially to wind or cold [Middle English *chappes* "cracks in skin," from *chappen* "to crack"]

²chap *vb* **chapped; chap·ping** : to open in slits or cracks; *also* : to become cracked, roughened, or reddened ⟨*chapped* lips⟩ [Middle English *chappen* "to crack (of skin)"]

³chap *n, chiefly British* : ¹FELLOW 4a [shortened form of *chapman* "merchant," from Old English *cēapman* "merchant," from *cēap* "trade" and *man* "man" — related to CHEAP]

chap·ar·ral \ˌshap-ə-'ral, -'rel\ *n* **1** : a thicket of dwarf evergreen oaks; *also* : a dense thicket **2** : an ecological community that is found especially in parts of southern California and is composed of shrubby plants that grow well in dry sunny summers and moist winters

chap·el \'chap-əl\ *n* **1** : a building or place for prayer or special religious services **2** : a religious service or assembly at a school or college [Middle English *chapel* "chapel," from early French *chapele* (same meaning), from Latin *cappella* "chapel," literally, "little cloak," from *cappa* "cloak, head covering"; so called from the structure built to house a revered cloak of Saint Martin of Tours — related to ²CAPE, CHAPERONE]

¹chap·er·one *or* **chap·er·on** \'shap-ə-ˌrōn\ *n* : a person who goes with and is responsible for a young woman or a group of young people (as at a dance) [from French *chaperon* "chaperone," literally, "hood," derived from early French *chape* "cape," from Latin *cappa* "head covering, cloak" — related to ²CAPE, CHAPEL]

²**chaperone** *or* **chaperon** *vb* **-oned; -on·ing** : to act or go with as a chaperone

chap·lain \'chap-lən\ *n* **1** : a member of the clergy officially attached to a special group (as the army) **2** : a person chosen to conduct religious exercises (as for a club)

chap·pie \'cha-pē\ *n, British* : ¹FELLOW 4a

chaps \'shaps, 'chaps\ *n pl* : leather leggings worn especially by western ranch workers

chap·ter \'chap-tər\ *n* **1** : a main division of a book or of a law code **2** : a local branch of an organization

¹**char** \'chär\ *n, pl* **char** *or* **chars** : any of a genus of trouts that have small scales and include the common brook trout

²**char** *vb* **charred; char·ring** **1** : to change or become changed to charcoal or carbon usually by heat : BURN **2** : to burn or become burned partly or slightly : SCORCH

³**char** *n* : CHARCOAL

char·ac·ter \'kar-ik-tər\ *n* **1 a** : a mark or symbol (as a letter or numeral) used in writing or printing **b** : a symbol (as a letter or number) that represents information; *also* : something standing for such a character that may be accepted by a computer **2 a** : a distinguishing feature : CHARACTERISTIC **b** : the group of qualities that make a person, group, or thing different from others **c** : the bodily expression (as eye color or leaf shape) of the action of a gene or group of genes **3** : an odd or peculiar person **4** : a person in a story, novel, or play **5** : REPUTATION 1 **6** : moral excellence ⟨hard work builds *character*⟩ — **char·ac·ter·less** \-ləs\ *adj*

char·ac·ter·i·sa·tion, char·ac·ter·ise *British variant of* CHARACTERIZATION, CHARACTERIZE

¹**char·ac·ter·is·tic** \ˌkar-ik-tə-'ris-tik\ *n* : a special quality or appearance that makes an individual or group different from others

²**characteristic** *adj* : serving to stress some special quality of an individual or group : TYPICAL — **char·ac·ter·is·ti·cal·ly** \-ti-k(ə-)lē\ *adv*

synonyms CHARACTERISTIC, INDIVIDUAL, PECULIAR, DISTINCTIVE mean indicating a special quality or identity. CHARACTERISTIC applies to something that marks or identifies a person or thing or a class ⟨her *characteristic* attention to detail⟩. INDIVIDUAL stresses qualities that distinguish one from all other members of the same kind or class ⟨an *individual* writing style⟩. PECULIAR applies to qualities possessed only by a particular individual or class and stresses rarity or uniqueness ⟨an accent *peculiar* to people from New England⟩. DISTINCTIVE indicates qualities that are distinguishing and uncommon and often superior or praiseworthy ⟨a *distinctive* singing voice⟩.

char·ac·ter·i·za·tion \ˌkar-ik-tə-rə-'zā-shən\ *n* **1** : the act of characterizing **2** : the creation of characters (as in a book or play)

char·ac·ter·ize \'kar-ik-tə-ˌrīz\ *vb* **-ized; -iz·ing** **1** : to point out the character of an individual or group : DESCRIBE ⟨*characterize* him as ambitious⟩ **2** : to be characteristic of ⟨tragic endings *characterized* her stories⟩

character sketch *n* : a short written piece describing a character

cha·rade \shə-'rād\ *n* **1** *pl* : a game in which some of the players try to guess a word or phrase from the actions of another player who may not speak **2** : an act that is meaningless or is meant to deceive

chaps

char·coal \'chär-ˌkōl\ *n* **1** : a dark or black absorbent carbon made by heating animal or vegetable material in the absence of air **2 a** : a piece or pencil of charcoal used in drawing **b** : a charcoal drawing

chard \'chärd\ *n* : SWISS CHARD

¹**charge** \'chärj\ *n* **1 a** : the amount (as of ammunition or fuel) needed to load or fill something **b** : a quantity of electricity ⟨an electric *charge*⟩ **2 a** : a task, duty, or order given to a person : OBLIGATION **b** : the work or duty of managing ⟨has *charge* of the building⟩ **c** : a person or thing given to another person to look after **3** : an instruction, command, or explanation based on authority ⟨a judge's *charge* to the jury⟩ **4 a** : the price demanded especially for a service **b** : an amount listed as a debt on an account **5** : a claim of wrongdoing : ACCUSATION ⟨a *charge* of burglary⟩ **6 a** : a rush to attack an enemy : ASSAULT ⟨the *charge* of the army⟩ **b** : the signal for attack ⟨sound the *charge*⟩ **c** : a usually illegal rush into an opponent in various sports (as basketball) **synonyms** see PRICE — **in charge** : having control of or responsibility for something ⟨*in charge* of the training program⟩

²**charge** *vb* **charged; charg·ing** **1 a** : ²LOAD 1a, FILL **b** : to give an electric charge to **c** : to restore the active materials in a storage battery by the passage of a direct current through in the opposite direction to that of the flowing out of electricity from the battery **2 a** : to give a task, duty, or responsibility to ⟨*charge* him with the job⟩ **b** : to give an order by right of authority to ⟨I *charge* you not to go⟩ **3** : to accuse formally ⟨*charged* with speeding⟩ **4** : to rush against : make an assault on; *also* : to charge an opponent in sports **5 a** : to enter as a debt or responsibility on a record ⟨*charged* the purchase to my account⟩ ⟨*charge* books on a library card⟩ **b** : to ask or set as a price ⟨they *charge* too much for everything⟩ ⟨*charged* $100 for repairs⟩ **synonyms** see COMMAND — **charge·able** \'chär-jə-bəl\ *adj*

charge account *n* : a customer's account with a creditor (as a store or bank) to which the purchase of goods may be charged

charge card *n* : CREDIT CARD

charged \'chärjd\ *adj* : showing or able to cause strong feelings ⟨an emotionally *charged* book review⟩

charged–coup·led device \'chärj-ˌkə-pəld-\ *n* : an electronic device that is sensitive to light and is used as a sensor (as in a camera) — called also *CCD*

¹**char·ger** \'chär-jər\ *n* : a large flat dish or platter

²**charg·er** \'chär-jər\ *n* **1** : a cavalry horse **2** : a device for charging storage batteries

char·i·ot \'char-ē-ət\ *n* : a two-wheeled horse-drawn vehicle of ancient times used in battle and also in races and parades

char·i·o·teer \ˌchar-ē-ə-'ti(ə)r\ *n* : a driver of a chariot

cha·ris·ma \kə-'riz-mə\ *n* : a special charm or public appeal

chariot

char·i·ta·ble \'char-ət-ə-bəl\ *adj* **1** : freely giving money or help to poor and needy persons : GENEROUS **2** : given for the needy : of service to the needy ⟨*charitable* funds⟩ ⟨a *charitable* institution⟩ **3** : kindly in judging other people — **char·i·ta·ble·ness** *n* — **char·i·ta·bly** \-blē\ *adv*

\ə\ **abut**	\au̇\ **out**	\i\ **tip**	\ȯ\ **saw**	\u̇\ **foot**
\ər\ **further**	\ch\ **chin**	\ī\ **life**	\ȯi\ **coin**	\y\ **yet**
\a\ **mat**	\e\ **pet**	\j\ **job**	\th\ **thin**	\yü\ **few**
\ā\ **take**	\ē\ **easy**	\ŋ\ **sing**	\t̲h̲\ **this**	\yu̇\ **cure**
\ä\ **cot, cart**	\g\ **go**	\ō\ **bone**	\ü\ **food**	\zh\ **vision**

char·i·ty \'char-ət-ē\ *n, pl* **-ties** **1** : love for others **2** : kindliness in judging others **3 a** : the giving of aid to the poor and suffering **b** : public aid for the poor **c** : an institution or fund for aiding the needy

char·la·tan \'shär-lə-tən\ *n* : a person who pretends to have knowledge or ability

Word History In the early 16th century people claiming medical skills they did not really have wandered throughout Italy. They sold medicines of little or no value. Because many of these fakers came from a village called Cerreto, the name *cerretano,* meaning "inhabitant of Cerreto," became a general name for a medical faker. Such people always had a line of talk to help them sell their products. Through the influence of the Italian word *ciarlare,* meaning "to chatter," the word *cerretano,* when used to refer to these fakers, became *ciarlatano.* It is from this word that we get our English *charlatan.* [from Italian *ciarlatano* "charlatan," an altered form of *cerretano* (same meaning), literally, "inhabitant of Cerreto (village in Italy)"]

char·ley horse \'chär-lē-ˌhórs\ *n* : pain and stiffness from muscular strain or bruise especially in a leg

¹charm \'chärm\ *n* **1** : a word, action, or thing believed to have magic power **2** : something worn to keep away evil and bring good luck **3** : a small ornament worn on a chain or bracelet **4** : a quality that attracts and pleases [Middle English *charme* "magic word," from early French *charme* (same meaning), from Latin *carmen* "song," from *canere* "to sing" — related to CHANT, CHANTEY]

²charm *vb* **1** : to affect or influence by or as if by a magic spell ⟨*charm* a snake⟩ **2** : to protect by or as if a charm ⟨a *charmed* life⟩ **3 a** : ²DELIGHT 2, FASCINATE **b** : to attract by grace or beauty — **charm·er** *n*

charm·ing \'chärm-iŋ\ *adj* : pleasant and attractive especially in manner ⟨a *charming* person⟩

char·nel \'chärn-ᵊl\ *n* : a building or chamber in which dead bodies or bones are deposited — **char·nel** *adj*

¹chart \'chärt\ *n* **1 a** : ¹MAP; *esp* : one showing features (as coasts, shoals, and currents) of importance to sailors **b** : an outline map showing something (as differences in climate or magnetism) according to geography **2** : a sheet giving information in the form of a table or of lists or by means of diagrams or graphs [from early French *charte* "map," from Latin *charta* "piece of papyrus" — related to ³CARD]

²chart *vb* **1** : to make a map or chart of **2** : to lay out a plan for

¹char·ter \'chärt-ər\ *n* **1** : an official document granting, guaranteeing, or showing the limits of the rights and duties of the group to which it is given **2** : a contract by which owners of a ship lease it to others **3** : a charter travel arrangement

²charter *vb* **1** : to grant a charter to **2** : to hire (as a ship or a bus) for temporary use — **char·ter·er** \'chärt-ər-ər\ *n*

³charter *adj* : of, relating to, or being a travel arrangement in which transportation (as a bus or plane) is hired by and for a specific group of people ⟨a *charter* flight⟩

charter school *n* : a tax-supported school set up by a charter between an official body (as a state government) and an outside group (as of educators and businesses) to achieve set goals

char·wom·an \'chär-ˌwùm-ən\ *n* : a woman who does cleaning especially in a large building

chary \'cha(ə)r-ē, 'che(ə)r-\ *adj* **char·i·er; -est** **1** : cautious especially to protect something ⟨*chary* of his reputation⟩ **2** : slow to give, accept, or spend ⟨*chary* of praise⟩ — **char·i·ness** *n*

¹chase \'chās\ *n* **1 a** : the hunting of animals — used with *the* **b** : the act of chasing : PURSUIT ⟨saw the thief and gave *chase*⟩ **2** : something pursued **3** : a scene (as in a movie) where the characters chase one another

²chase *vb* **chased; chas·ing** **1** : to follow in order to capture or overtake ⟨*chase* a thief⟩ ⟨*chase* the bus⟩ **2** : ¹HUNT 1 ⟨*chase* the fox⟩ **3** : to drive away or out ⟨*chase* a dog off the lawn⟩ — **chas·er** *n*

synonyms CHASE, PURSUE, FOLLOW, TRAIL mean to go after or on the track of someone or something. CHASE suggests going after something that is fleeing or running and trying to catch up with it ⟨*chased* after the runaway cat⟩. PURSUE suggests an extended effort to catch up ⟨the police *pursued* the robbers all over town⟩. FOLLOW may apply to situations in which there is neither speed nor an effort to catch up ⟨a stray dog *followed* me home⟩. TRAIL applies to a following of tracks or other marks rather than the thing itself ⟨*trail* a deer through the snow⟩.

³chase *vb* **chased; chas·ing** : to decorate (metal) by indenting with a hammer and tools without cutting edges

chasm \'kaz-əm\ *n* : a deep split or gap in the earth

chas·sis \'shas-ē, 'chas-ē\ *n, pl* **chas·sis** \-ēz\ : a supporting frame (as that of the body of an automobile or airplane or the parts of a radio or television receiver)

chaste \'chāst\ *adj* **1** : pure in thought and act : MODEST **2** : simple or plain in design ⟨a *chaste* meal⟩ — **chaste·ly** *adv* — **chaste·ness** \'chās(t)-nəs\ *n*

chas·ten \'chās-ᵊn\ *vb* **chas·tened; chas·ten·ing** \'chās-niŋ, -ᵊn-iŋ\ : to correct by punishment or suffering

chas·tise \(')chas-'tīz\ *vb* **chas·tised; chas·tis·ing** **1** : to punish severely (as by whipping) **2** : to criticize harshly — **chas·tise·ment** \(')chas-'tīz-mənt *also* 'chas-təz-\ *n* — **chas·tis·er** \(')chas-'tī-zər\ *n*

chas·ti·ty \'chas-tət-ē\ *n* : the quality or state of being chaste

cha·su·ble \'chaz-ə-bəl, 'chas-ə-, 'chazh-ə-\ *n* : a sleeveless outer vestment worn by a priest at mass

¹chat \'chat\ *vb* **chat·ted; chat·ting** **1** : to talk in a friendly manner about things that are not serious **2** : to take part in an online discussion in a chat room

²chat *n* **1** : a light friendly conversation **2** : a talk held over the Internet by people using a chat room **3** : any of several songbirds with a chattering call

châ·teau \sha-'tō\ *n, pl* **châ·teaus** \-'tōz\ *or* **châ·teaux** \-'tō(z)\ : a castle or a large country house especially in France [French, from early French *chastel* "castle," from Latin *castellum* "fortress" — related to CASTLE]

chasuble

chat room *n* : an online interactive discussion group on the Internet

chat·tel \'chat-ᵊl\ *n* **1** : a piece of property (as animals, money, or goods) other than real estate **2** : ¹SLAVE 1

chat·ter \'chat-ər\ *vb* **1** : to utter rapid meaningless sounds suggesting speech ⟨squirrels *chattered* angrily⟩ **2** : to talk idly, continually, or rapidly **3** : to click again and again without control ⟨teeth *chattering*⟩ — **chatter** *n* — **chat·ter·er** \'chat-ər-ər\ *n* — **chat·tery** \-ə-rē\ *adj*

chat·ter·box \'chat-ər-ˌbäks\ *n* : a person who talks continually

chat·ty \'chat-ē\ *adj* **chat·ti·er; -est** **1** : fond of chatting ⟨a *chatty* neighbor⟩ **2** : having the style of a chat ⟨a *chatty* letter⟩ — **chat·ti·ly** \'chat-ᵊl-ē\ *adv* — **chat·ti·ness** \'chat-ē-nəs\ *n*

¹chauf·feur \'shō-fər, shō-'fər\ *n* : a person employed to drive people in a car

Word History It seems odd that the word *chauffeur,* meaning "one who drives an automobile for another," should come from the French verb *chauffer,* meaning "to heat." The title comes from the early days of automobiles, when they were still curious, rare, and, to many people, funny. Automobiles were noisy, produced clouds of smoke, and seemed to require a great deal of work to keep them running. To many people they were like the steam engines used to pull trains. *Chauffeur,* the French word for the "stoker," or person who kept the fire going in an engine, was used for anyone driving an automobile. Later the term was used only for a person hired to drive someone else's car. [from French *chauffeur* "driver," literally, "stoker," from *chauffer* "to heat"]

²**chauffeur** *vb* **chauf·feured; chauf·feur·ing** \'shō-f(ə-)riŋ, shō-'fər-iŋ\ **1** : to do the work of a chauffeur **2** : to transport as or as if as a chauffeur 〈*chauffeured* the children to school〉

chau·vin·ism \'shō-və-ˌniz-əm\ *n* **1** : exaggerated or unthinking patriotism **2** : an attitude that the members of one's own sex are always better than those of the opposite sex; *also* : behavior that shows such an attitude [from French *chauvinisme* "chauvinism," named for Nicholas Chauvin, a character in a play] — **chau·vin·ist** \-və-nəst\ *n or adj* — **chau·vin·is·tic** *adj* — **chau·vin·is·ti·cal·ly** *adv*

cheap \'chēp\ *adj* **1 a** : available at low cost or at less than the true value 〈potatoes are *cheap* right now〉 **b** : of low price 〈always buys the *cheapest* brand〉 **c** : charging low prices 〈always wants to go to a *cheap* place〉 **2** : gained with little effort 〈a *cheap* victory〉 **3 a** : of low quality or value 〈*cheap* material wears out quickly〉 〈a *cheap* joke〉 **b** : lowered in one's own opinion 〈feel *cheap*〉 **c** : STINGY 1 〈don't be so *cheap*〉 [from earlier obsolete *cheap* (noun) "bargain," from Old English *cēap* "trade" — related to ³CHAP] — **cheap** *adv* — **cheap·en** \'chē-pən\ *vb* — **cheap·ly** *adv* — **cheap·ness** *n*

cheap·skate \'chēp-ˌskāt\ *n* : a miserly or stingy person; *esp* : one who tries to avoid paying his or her fair share [*-skate* from earlier *skate* "a person," probably from a dialect word *skite,* meaning "an offensive person"]

¹**cheat** \'chēt\ *vb* **1** : to deprive of something valuable by dishonest methods 〈*cheated* them out of their property〉 **2** : to successfully avoid or oppose by or as if by cleverness 〈the daredevil had *cheated* death again〉 **3** : to use unfair or dishonest methods to gain an advantage 〈*cheat* on a test〉 〈*cheat* at cards〉 — **cheat·er** *n*

²**cheat** *n* **1** : an act of cheating **2** : a person who cheats

¹**check** \'chek\ *n* **1** : the exposing of a chess king to attack **2** : a sudden stopping of progress **3** : something that delays, stops, or holds back : RESTRAINT **4** : EXAMINATION 1, INVESTIGATION **5** : a written order telling a bank to pay out money from a person's or company's account to the one named on the order 〈pay a bill by *check*〉 〈cash a *check*〉 **6 a** : a ticket or token that shows that the bearer has a claim to something 〈a baggage *check*〉 **b** : a slip of paper showing the amount due : BILL **7 a** : a pattern of squares **b** : a fabric with such a design **8** : a mark ✓ placed beside an item to show it has been noted [Middle English *chek* "check (in chess), attack," from early French *eschec* (same meaning), from Arabic *shāh* "check (in chess)," from a Persian word meaning literally "king" — related to CHECKER, CHESS] — **in check** : under restraint or control 〈trying to keep his emotions *in check*〉

²**check** *vb* **1** : to put a chess king under attack **2 a** : to bring to a stop 〈to *check* an impulse〉 **b** : to come to a stop **3** : to hold back : RESTRAIN, CURB 〈*checked* her temper〉 **4 a** : to make sure that something is correct or satisfactory 〈*check* your blood pressure〉 〈*check* it out with a teacher〉 **b** : to inspect, examine, or look at 〈*checking* out new cars〉 〈*checked* over the damage〉 **5** : to mark with a check 〈*check* the first item〉 **6** : to mark with squares : CHECKER **7** : to leave or accept for safekeeping or for shipment 〈*check* baggage〉 **8** : to be the same on every point : TALLY — **check into 1** : to check in at 〈*check into* a hotel〉 **2** : INVESTIGATE 〈the police are *checking into* his story〉 — **check up on** : INVESTIGATE

check·book \'chek-ˌbůk\ *n* : a book of blank bank checks

¹**check·er** \'chek-ər\ *n* **1** : a square resembling the markings on a checkerboard **2** : a piece in the game of checkers [Middle English *cheker* "checker (square), board on which chess is played," from early French *checker, escheker* "board for playing chess," from *eschec* "a check (in chess), attack" — related to CHECK, CHESS]

²**checker** *vb* **check·ered; check·er·ing** \-(ə-)riŋ\ : to mark with squares of different colors 〈a *checkered* tablecloth〉

³**checker** *n* : one that checks; *esp* : an employee who checks out purchases in a supermarket

check·er·ber·ry \'chek-ə(r)-ˌber-ē\ *n* : WINTERGREEN 1a; *also* : the spicy red fruit of a checkerberry

check·er·board \-ˌbō(ə)rd, -ˌbò(ə)rd\ *n* : a board used in games and marked with 64 squares in two colors

checkered *adj* : marked by changes of fortune 〈a *checkered* career〉; *esp* : marked by many problems 〈a *checkered* past〉

check·ers \'chek-ərz\ *n* : a game played on a checkerboard by two persons each having 12 pieces

check–in \'chek-'in\ *n* : an act or instance of checking in

check in *vb* **1** : to register at a hotel or motel **2** : to report one's presence or arrival **3** : to bring back : RETURN 〈*checked in* the equipment〉

checking account *n* : an account in a bank from which the depositor can draw money by writing checks

check·list \'chek-ˌlist\ *n* : a list of items to be referred to

¹**check·mate** \'chek-ˌmāt\ *vb* **1** : to block completely : THWART **2** : to check a chess opponent's king so that escape is impossible

²**checkmate** *n* **1 a** : the act of checkmating **b** : the situation of a checkmated king **2** : a complete check

check·out \'chek-ˌaůt\ *n* **1** : the action or an instance of checking out **2** : the time at which a lodger must leave a room (as in a hotel) **3** : a counter at which checking out is done

check out \'chek-'aůt\ *vb* **1** : to pay for one's room and leave (as from a hotel) **2** : to satisfy requirements for taking away 〈*check* a book *out* at the library〉 **3 a** : to add up the cost of purchases and receive payment for them **b** : to have the cost of purchases added up and pay for them

check·point \'chek-ˌpòint\ *n* : a point at which a check is carried out 〈vehicles were inspected at different *checkpoints*〉

check·room \-ˌrüm, -ˌrùm\ *n* : a room at which baggage, parcels, or clothing can be left for safekeeping

checks and balances *n pl* : a system that allows each branch of a government to amend or veto acts of another branch so as to prevent any one branch from having too much power

check·up \'chek-ˌəp\ *n* : EXAMINATION 1 〈a dental *checkup*〉; *esp* : a general physical examination

ched·dar \'ched-ər\ *n, often cap* : a hard yellow or white cheese of smooth texture [named for *Cheddar,* village in England where the cheese was first made]

cheek \'chēk\ *n* **1** : the fleshy side of the face below the eye and above and to the side of the mouth **2** : disrespectful speech or behavior : NERVE

cheek·bone \'chēk-'bōn, -ˌbōn\ *n* : the bone or the bony ridge below the eye

cheeky \'chē-kē\ *adj* **cheek·i·er; -est** : showing disrespect : RUDE, IMPUDENT — **cheek·i·ness** *n*

cheep \'chēp\ *vb* : ¹PEEP 1, CHIRP — **cheep** *n*

¹**cheer** \'chi(ə)r\ *n* **1** : state of mind or heart : SPIRIT 〈be of good *cheer*〉 **2** : good spirits 〈full of *cheer*〉 **3** : something

\ə\ **abut**	\aů\ **out**	\i\ **tip**	\ò\ **saw**	\ů\ **foot**
\ər\ **further**	\ch\ **chin**	\ī\ **life**	\òi\ **coin**	\y\ **yet**
\a\ **mat**	\e\ **pet**	\j\ **job**	\th\ **thin**	\yü\ **few**
\ā\ **take**	\ē\ **easy**	\ŋ\ **sing**	\ṯẖ\ **this**	\yů\ **cure**
\ä\ **cot, cart**	\g\ **go**	\ō\ **bone**	\ü\ **food**	\zh\ **vision**

that gladdens ⟨words of *cheer*⟩ **4** : a shout of praise or encouragement ⟨three *cheers* for our side⟩

²cheer *vb* **1** : to give hope to or make happier : COMFORT ⟨*cheer* up a sick person⟩ **2** : to urge on especially with shouts or cheers ⟨*cheer* the team to victory⟩ **3** : to shout with joy, approval, or enthusiasm ⟨the audience *cheered* loudly⟩ **4** : to grow or be cheerful : REJOICE — usually used with *up* ⟨he *cheered up* at the news⟩

cheer·ful \'chi(ə)r-fəl\ *adj* **1 a** : full of good spirits ⟨a *cheerful* outlook⟩ **b** : WILLING 3 ⟨*cheerful* obedience⟩ **2** : pleasantly bright ⟨a sunny *cheerful* room⟩ — **cheer·ful·ly** \-f(ə-)lē\ *adv* — **cheer·ful·ness** \-fəl-nəs\ *n*

cheer·lead·er \'chi(ə)r-,lēd-ər\ *n* : a person who leads organized cheering (as at a football or basketball game) — **cheer·lead** \-,lēd\ *vb* — **cheer·lead·ing** \-,lē-diŋ\ *n*

cheer·less \'chi(ə)r-ləs\ *adj* : offering no cheer : GLOOMY — **cheer·less·ly** *adv* — **cheer·less·ness** *n*

cheery \'chi(ə)r-ē\ *adj* **cheer·i·er; -est** : merry and bright in manner or effect : CHEERFUL — **cheer·i·ly** \'chir-ə-lē\ *adv* — **cheer·i·ness** \'chir-ē-nəs\ *n*

cheese \'chēz\ *n* : a food made from milk usually by separating out the curd and molding it

cheese·burg·er \'chēz-,bər-gər\ *n* : a hamburger topped with a slice of cheese

cheese·cake \-,kāk\ *n* : a cake made from cream cheese or cottage cheese, eggs, and sugar

cheese·cloth \-,klȯth\ *n* : a thin loosely woven cotton cloth

cheesy \'chē-zē\ *adj* **chees·i·er; -est** **1 a** : resembling or suggesting cheese **b** : containing cheese **2** : CHEAP 3a ⟨a *cheesy* movie⟩ — **chees·i·ness** *n*

chee·tah \'chēt-ə\ *n* : a long-legged spotted African and formerly Asian cat that is the fastest of all animals on land

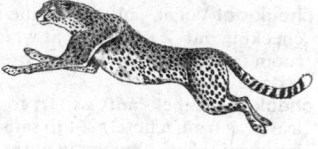
cheetah

chef \'shef\ *n* **1** : a chief cook **2** : ¹COOK

chef's knife *n* : a large kitchen knife with a triangular blade

che·lic·era \ki-'lis-ə-rə\ *n, pl* **-er·as** *or* **-er·ae** \-,rē\ : either of two special front legs of a spider that often function as fangs

¹chem·i·cal \'kem-i-kəl\ *adj* **1** : of, relating to, used in, or produced by chemistry **2** : acting or operated or produced by chemicals — **chem·i·cal·ly** \-i-k(ə-)lē\ *adv*

²chemical *n* : a substance (as an element or compound) obtained from a chemical process or used to get a chemical result

chemical engineering *n* : engineering dealing with the use of chemistry in industry — **chemical engineer** *n*

che·mise \shə-'mēz, -'mēs\ *n* **1** : a woman's one-piece undergarment **2** : a loose dress that hangs straight

chem·is·try \'kem-ə-strē\ *n* **1** : a science that deals with the composition, structure, and properties of substances and with the changes that they go through **2** : chemical composition, properties, or processes ⟨the *chemistry* of gasoline⟩ ⟨the *chemistry* of iron⟩ ⟨the *chemistry* of blood⟩ [an altered form of obsolete *chimistry, chymistry* "alchemy," derived from Latin *alchimista* "alchemist," from *alchymia* "alchemy," from Arabic *al-kīmiyā'* (same meaning), from *al* "the" and *kīmiyā'* "alchemy," from Greek *chēmeia* "alchemy" — related to ALCHEMY, CHE-MO-] — **chem·ist** \-əst\ *n*

chemo- *combining form* : chemical : chemistry ⟨*chemo*taxis⟩ [scientific Latin, from Greek *chēmeia* "alchemy" — related to ALCHEMY, CHEMISTRY]

che·mo·tax·is \,kē-mō-'tak-səs\ *n* : movement or positioning of cells or organisms in relation to a chemical

che·mo·ther·a·py \,ke-mō-'ther-ə-pē\ *n* : the use of chemical agents in the treatment or control of disease (as cancer) — **che·mo·ther·a·peu·tic** \-,ther-ə-'pyüt-ik\ *adj*

che·mot·ro·pism \kē-'mä-trə-,piz-əm, ke-\ *n* : positioning of cells or organisms in relation to a chemical

che·nille \shə-'nē(ə)l\ *n* : a thick fuzzy fabric

cheque \'chek\ *chiefly British variant of* ¹CHECK 5

cher·ish \'cher-ish\ *vb* **1** : to hold dear : feel or show affection for ⟨*cherished* her friends⟩ **2** : to keep with care and affection : NURTURE ⟨*cherishes* her friendship⟩ **3** : to harbor in the mind ⟨*cherish* a hope⟩

Cher·o·kee \'cher-ə-,kē\ *n* : a member of an American Indian people originally from Tennessee and North Carolina

cher·ry \'cher-ē\ *n, pl* **cherries** **1 a** : any of numerous trees and shrubs that are related to the roses and have rather small pale yellow to deep blackish red smooth-skinned fruits **b** : the fruit of a cherry **c** : the reddish brown wood of a cherry **2** : a medium red [Middle English *chery* "a cherry," from early French *cherise* "the cherry" (mistaken as being a plural), derived from Latin *cerasus* "cherry tree"]

chert \'chərt, 'chat\ *n* : a rock resembling flint and consisting mostly of chalcedony that can be separated into fibers and smaller amounts of very fine crystalline quartz and silica that is not crystallized

cher·ub \'cher-əb\ *n* **1** : a painting or drawing of a beautiful child usually with wings **2** : a chubby rosy child — **che·ru·bic** \chə-'rü-bik\ *adj*

Ches·a·peake Bay retriever \,ches-(ə-),pēk-,bā-\ *n* : any of a breed of powerful brown bird dogs developed in Maryland

Chesh·ire cheese \,chesh-ər-\ *n* : a cheese made in England that is similar to cheddar [named for *Cheshire,* county in England where the cheese was first made]

chess \'ches\ *n* : a game for two players each of whom plays with 16 pieces on a checkerboard [Middle English *ches* "game of chess," from early French *eschés* (same meaning), literally, "checks," from *eschec* "check" — related to CHECK, CHECKER]

chess·man \'ches-,man, -mən\ *n* : any of the pieces used in chess

chest \'chest\ *n* **1** : a container (as a box or case) for storing, safekeeping, or shipping ⟨tool *chest*⟩ ⟨linen *chest*⟩ **2** : a public fund ⟨community *chest*⟩ **3** : the part of the body enclosed by the ribs and sternum — **chest·ed** \'ches-təd\ *adj* — **chest·ful** \'chest-,fül\ *n*

ches·ter·field \'ches-tər-,fēld\ *n* **1** : an overcoat with a velvet collar **2** : a sofa with arms [named for a 19th century Earl of *Chesterfield,* English nobleman]

¹chest·nut \'ches-(,)nət\ *n* **1 a** : a sweet edible nut from any of several trees or shrubs related to the beeches **b** : a tree or shrub bearing chestnuts; *esp* : an American tree that was formerly common and grew to large size in eastern forests but has been largely wiped out by the chestnut blight and now grows only to the size of a shrub or sapling **c** : the wood of a chestnut tree **2** : HORSE CHESTNUT **3** : a brown or reddish brown horse

²chestnut *adj* : of a reddish brown color

chestnut blight *n* : a destructive disease of the chestnut of the eastern U.S. caused by a fungus

chest of drawers : a piece of furniture containing drawers (as for storing clothes)

chev·ron \'shev-rən\ *n* **1** : a figure resembling a V or an upside-down V **2** : a sleeve badge indicating rank (as in the armed forces)

¹chew \'chü\ *vb* : to crush or grind with the teeth — **chew·able** \-ə-bəl\ *adj* — **chew·er** *n* — **chewy** \'chü-ē\ *adj* — **chew on** : to think about ⟨*chewing on* the new plans⟩

²chew *n* **1** : the act of chewing **2** : something for chewing ⟨a *chew* of tobacco⟩

chewing gum *n* : a sweetened and flavored soft material (as of chicle) used for chewing

chew out *vb* : [2]REPRIMAND

chew over *vb* : to think over

Chey·enne \shī-'an, -'en\ *n, pl* **Cheyenne** *or* **Cheyennes** : a member of an American Indian people of the western plains of the U.S.

chi \'kī\ *n* : the 22nd letter of the Greek alphabet — X or χ

[1]**chic** \'shēk\ *n* : fashionable style

[2]**chic** *adj* **chic·er; chic·est** : STYLISH, SMART ⟨*chic* clothes⟩

chi·ca·nery \shik-'ān-(ə-)rē\ *n, pl* **-ner·ies** : clever trickery

Chi·ca·no \chi-'kän-ō, shi-\ *n* : an American and especially a man or boy of Mexican ancestry [Mexican Spanish, an altered form of *mexicano* "Mexican"] — **Chicano** *adj*

chick \'chik\ *n* **1 a** : [1]CHICKEN 1; *esp* : one newly hatched **b** : the young of any bird **2** *slang* : GIRL 1b, WOMAN 1

chick·a·dee \'chik-ə-(ˌ)dē\ *n* : any of several small North American birds with the top of the head black or brown

chickadee

Chick·a·saw \'chik-ə-ˌsò\ *n, pl* **-saw** *or* **-saws** : a member of an American Indian people of Mississippi and Alabama

[1]**chick·en** \'chik-ən\ *n* **1** : the common domestic fowl especially when young; *also* : its flesh used as food **2** : any of various birds or their young **3** : COWARD

[2]**chicken** *adj* : COWARDLY 1

[3]**chicken** *vb* **chick·ened; chick·en·ing** \'chik-(ə-)niŋ\ : to lose one's courage — usually used with *out*

chick·en·heart·ed \ˌchik-ən-'härt-əd\ *adj* : COWARDLY 1, TIMID

chicken pox *n* : a contagious virus disease especially of children marked by low fever and a rash or small watery blisters

chicken wire *n* : a light wire fencing with hexagonal openings

chick·pea \'chik-ˌpē\ *n* : an Asian herb of the legume family cultivated for its short pods with one or two edible seeds; *also* : its seed

chick·weed \'chik-ˌwēd\ *n* : any of several low-growing small-leaved weedy plants related to the pinks

chi·cle \'chik-əl, -lē\ *n* : a gum from the latex of a tropical tree that is used as an important part of chewing gum

chic·o·ry \'chik-(ə-)rē\ *n, pl* **-ries** : a thick-rooted usually blue-flowered European herb related to the daisies and grown for its roots and as a salad plant; *also* : its dried ground roasted root that is sometimes added to coffee

chide \'chīd\ *vb* **chid** \'chid\ *or* **chid·ed** \'chīd-əd\; **chid** *or* **chid·den** \'chid-ᵊn\ *or* **chided; chid·ing** \'chīd-iŋ\ : to express mild disapproval of **synonyms** see REBUKE

[1]**chief** \'chēf\ *adj* **1** : highest in rank or authority ⟨*chief* librarian⟩ **2** : most important : MAIN ⟨your *chief* claim to fame⟩

[2]**chief** *n* : the head of a group : LEADER ⟨*chief* of police⟩ [Middle English *chief* "top part, head," from early French *chief* "head, chief," from Latin *caput* "head" — related to CAPITAL, CAPTAIN]

chief executive *n* : a principal executive: as **a** : the president of a republic **b** : the governor of a state **c** : CEO

chief justice *n* : the presiding or principal judge of a court of justice

chief·ly \'chē-flē\ *adv* **1** : above all **2** : for the most part

chief master sergeant *n* : a noncommissioned officer of the highest rank in the air force

chief master sergeant of the air force : a chief master sergeant who advises the chief of staff of the air force

chief of staff **1** : the ranking officer of a staff in the armed forces who advises a commander **2** : the ranking officer of the army or air force

chief of state : the head of a country when not the same person as the head of the country's government

chief petty officer *n* : a naval petty officer with a rank just below that of senior chief petty officer

chief·tain \'chēf-tən\ *n* : a chief especially of a band, tribe, or clan — **chief·tain·cy** \-sē\ *n* — **chief·tain·ship** \-ˌship\ *n*

chief warrant officer *n* : a military or naval warrant officer of senior rank

[1]**chif·fon** \shif-'än, 'shif-ˌän\ *n* : a very thin fabric especially of silk

[2]**chiffon** *adj* : having a light soft texture ⟨a *chiffon* pie⟩

chif·fo·nier \ˌshif-ə-'ni(ə)r\ *n* : a high narrow chest of drawers

chig·ger \'chig-ər, 'jig-\ *n* : a six-legged mite larva that feeds on skin cells and causes itchy red welts

chi·gnon \'shēn-ˌyän\ *n* : a knot of hair worn at the back of the head

Chi·hua·hua \chə-'wä-(ˌ)wä, shə-, -wə\ *n* : any of a breed of very small large-eared dogs that originated in Mexico [named for *Chihuahua,* a state in Mexico]

chil·blain \'chil-ˌblān\ *n* : redness and swelling sometimes with itching and burning especially of the toes, fingers, nose, and ears caused by being exposed to cold

child \'chīld\ *n, pl* **chil·dren** \'chil-drən, -dərn\ **1** : an unborn or recently born person **2 a** : a young person especially between infancy and youth **b** : a childlike or childish person **3** : a son or daughter of human parents — **child·less** \'chīl(d)-ləs\ *adj* — **with child** : PREGNANT 1

child·bear·ing \'chīl(d)-ˌbar-iŋ, -ˌber-\ *adj* : of or relating to the process of becoming and being pregnant with and giving birth to children ⟨women of *childbearing* age⟩ — **childbearing** *n*

child·birth \'chīl(d)-ˌbərth\ *n* : the act or process of giving birth to children — called also *parturition*

child·hood \'chīld-ˌhùd\ *n* : the state or time of being a child

child·ish \'chīl-dish\ *adj* **1** : of, resembling, or suitable to a child ⟨*childish* laughter⟩ **2** : showing the less pleasing qualities (as silliness) often thought to be those of children — **child·ish·ly** *adv* — **child·ish·ness** *n*

child·like \'chīl(d)-ˌlīk\ *adj* **1** : resembling, suggesting, or suitable to a child or childhood **2** : showing the more pleasing qualities (as innocence or trustfulness) often thought to be those of children ⟨*childlike* delight⟩

[1]**child·proof** \'chīl(d)-ˌprüf\ *adj* **1** : made to prevent tampering or opening by children ⟨a *childproof* bottle⟩ **2** : made safe for children (as by safe storage of dangerous materials) ⟨a *childproof* home⟩

[2]**childproof** *vb* : to make childproof

child's play *n* : something that is very easy to do or is unimportant

child support *n* : payment for the support of the children of divorced or separated parents while the children are minors or as otherwise legally required — compare ALIMONY

chili *also* **chile** *or* **chil·li** \'chil-ē\ *n, pl* **chil·ies** *also* **chil·es** *or* **chilis** *or* **chil·lies** **1** : HOT PEPPER 1 **2** : CHILI CON CARNE

chili con car·ne \ˌchil-ē-ˌkän-'kär-nē, ˌchil-ē-kən-\ *n* : a spicy stew made of ground beef, hot peppers or chili pow-

\ə\ **abut**	\aù\ **out**	\i\ **tip**	\ò\ **saw**	\ù\ **foot**
\ər\ **further**	\ch\ **chin**	\ī\ **life**	\òi\ **coin**	\y\ **yet**
\a\ **mat**	\e\ **pet**	\j\ **job**	\th\ **thin**	\yü\ **few**
\ā\ **take**	\ē\ **easy**	\ŋ\ **sing**	\th\ **this**	\yù\ **cure**
\ä\ **cot, cart**	\g\ **go**	\ō\ **bone**	\ü\ **food**	\zh\ **vision**

der, and usually beans [from American Spanish *chile con carne*, literally, "hot pepper with meat"]

chili dog *n* : a hot dog topped with chili

chili powder *n* : a seasoning made of ground hot peppers and other spices

chili sauce *n* : a spiced tomato sauce usually made with red and green peppers

¹**chill** \'chil\ *n* **1** : a feeling of cold accompanied by shivering ⟨*chills* and fever⟩ **2** : a moderate but unpleasant amount of cold ⟨there was a *chill* in the air⟩

²**chill** *adj* **1** : unpleasantly cold : RAW ⟨nights grew *chill*⟩ **2** : not friendly ⟨a *chill* greeting⟩ — **chill·ness** *n*

³**chill** *vb* **1** : to make or become cold or chilly **2** : to cool without freezing ⟨*chill* the pudding for dessert⟩ **3** : to affect as if with cold ⟨we were *chilled* by the ghost story⟩ **4** : CHILL OUT — **chill·er** *n*

chill·ing \'chil-iŋ\ *adj* : very disturbing or frightening ⟨a *chilling* case of abuse⟩ — **chill·ing·ly** *adv*

chill out *vb, slang* : to calm down : go easy

chilly \'chil-ē\ *adj* **chill·i·er; -est** **1** : noticeably cold **2** : unpleasantly affected by cold **3** : not friendly ⟨a *chilly* response⟩ — **chill·i·ness** *n*

¹**chime** \'chīm\ *n* **1** : a set of bells tuned to play music **2** : the sound of a set of bells — usually used in plural

²**chime** *vb* **chimed; chim·ing** **1** : to make the sounds of a chime **2** : to call or indicate by chiming

chime in *vb* : to break into or join in a conversation or discussion

chi·me·ra \kī-'mir-ə, kə-\ *n* **1** *cap* : a fire-breathing female monster in Greek mythology with a lion's head, a goat's body, and a serpent's tail **2** : something made up by or existing only in the mind — **chi·mer·i·cal** \-'mer-i-kəl, -'mir-\ *adj*

chi·mi·chan·ga \ˌchim-ē-'chäng-gə\ *n* : a tortilla wrapped around a filling (as of meat) and deep-fried

chim·ney \'chim-nē\ *n, pl* **chimneys** **1** : a vertical structure extending above the roof of a building for carrying off smoke **2** : a tube usually of glass around a flame (as of a lamp) **3** : something resembling a chimney

chimney pot *n* : a pipe usually made of clay placed at the top of a chimney

chimney sweep *n* : a person who cleans soot from chimneys

chimney swift *n* : a small sooty-gray bird with long narrow wings that often builds its nest inside an unused chimney

chimp \'chimp, 'shimp\ *n* : CHIMPANZEE

chim·pan·zee \ˌchim-ˌpan-'zē, ˌshim-; chim-'pan-zē, shim-\ *n* : an African ape that is related to the gorilla but is smaller and spends more of its time in trees

chin \'chin\ *n* : the lower portion of the face lying below the lower lip and including the pointed part of the lower jaw

chi·na \'chī-nə\ *n* **1** : PORCELAIN **2** : dishes of pottery or porcelain for use as tableware

chi·na·ber·ry \'chī-nə-ˌber-ē\ *n* : a small Asian tree that is related to the mahoganies and that is planted in the southern U.S. for shade or ornament

china clay *n* : KAOLIN

Chi·na·town \'chī-nə-ˌtaùn\ *n* : an area of a city where many people of Chinese ancestry live

Chi·na tree \'chī-nə-\ *n* : CHINA-BERRY

chi·na·ware \'chī-nə-ˌwa(ə)r, -ˌwe(ə)r\ *n* : CHINA 2

chinch bug \'chinch-\ *n* : a small black-and-white bug that is very destructive to cereal grasses

chin·chil·la \chin-'chil-ə\ *n* : a South American rodent that is the size of a large squirrel and is

chinchilla

widely bred in captivity for its very soft fur of a pearly gray color; *also* : its fur

chine \'chīn\ *n* : BACKBONE 1, SPINE; *also* : a cut of meat including the backbone or part of it and the surrounding flesh

Chi·nese \chī-'nēz, -'nēs\ *n, pl* **Chinese** **1 a** : a person born or living in China **b** : a person of Chinese ancestry **2** : a group of related languages used in China — **Chinese** *adj*

Chinese cabbage *n* : either of two Asian garden plants related to the cabbage and widely used as green leafy vegetables

Chinese checkers *n* : a game in which each player seeks to be the first to transfer a set of marbles from a home point to the opposite point of a 6-pointed star by means of single moves and jumps

Chinese lantern *n* : a collapsible nearly transparent covering for a light

¹**chink** \'chiŋk\ *n* : a narrow slit or crack

²**chink** *vb* : to fill the chinks of ⟨*chinked* a log hut with mud⟩

³**chink** *n* : a short sharp sound

⁴**chink** *vb* : to make or cause to make a short sharp sound

chi·no \'chē-nō, 'shē-\ *n, pl* **chinos** **1** : a usually khaki cotton fabric **2** : an article of clothing made of chino — usually used in plural

Chi·nook \shə-'nùk, chə-\ *n, pl* **Chinook** *or* **Chinooks** : a member of an American Indian people of Oregon

Chinook salmon *n* : a large salmon of the northern Pacific Ocean that has red flesh and is used as food

chintz \'chin(t)s\ *n* : a shiny cotton fabric with a flowery pattern printed on it

chintzy \'chin(t)-sē\ *adj* **chintz·i·er; -est** **1** : decorated with or as if with chintz **2 a** : not tasteful or stylish **b** : of low quality **3** : STINGY — **chintz·i·ness** *n*

¹**chip** \'chip\ *n* **1** : a small thin flat piece (as of wood, stone, or glass) broken off : FLAKE **2** : a small piece of food ⟨chocolate *chip*⟩: as **a** : POTATO CHIP **b** : ¹FRENCH FRY ⟨fish and *chips*⟩ **3 a** : a counter used in poker **b** *pl* : MONEY 1c ⟨in the *chips*⟩ **4** : a flaw left after a small piece has been broken off ⟨a cup with a *chip* in it⟩ **5** : a very small slice of silicon containing electronic circuits (as for a computer) — **chip off the old block** : a child that resembles his or her parent — **chip on one's shoulder** : an attitude of being eager to fight or quarrel

²**chip** *vb* **chipped; chip·ping** **1** : to cut or break a chip from something ⟨*chip* a cup⟩ **2** : to break off in small pieces

chip in *vb* : CONTRIBUTE 1

chip·munk \'chip-ˌməŋk\ *n* : any of numerous small striped animals of North America and Asia related to the squirrels

chipped beef \'chip(t)-\ *n* : smoked dried beef sliced thin

chip·per \'chip-ər\ *adj* : being in good health or spirits

Chip·pe·wa \'chip-ə-ˌwò, -ˌwä, -ˌwä\ *n* : OJIBWA

chip·ping sparrow \'chip-iŋ-\ *n* : a small North American sparrow whose song is a fast trill

chi·rop·o·dist \kə-'räp-əd-əst\ *n* : PODIATRIST

chi·rop·o·dy \kə-'räp-əd-ē\ *n* : PODIATRY [from Latin *chir-, chiro-* "hand" and Greek *pod-* "foot"; from the fact that this medical practice originally dealt with hands and feet]

chi·ro·prac·tic \'kī-rə-ˌprak-tik\ *n* : a system of therapy that mostly involves realignment of the spinal column especially by touching or pressing the hands on the back near the spinal column — **chiropractic** *adj* — **chi·ro·prac·tor** \-tər\ *n*

chirp \'chərp\ *vb* : to make a short sharp sound like a small bird or cricket — **chirp** *n*

chirr \'chər\ *vb* : to make a vibrating sound like some insects (as a grasshopper or cicada) — **chirr** *n*

chir·rup \'chər-əp, 'chir-\ *vb* : CHIRP — **chirrup** *n*

¹chis·el \'chiz-əl\ *n* : a metal tool with a cutting edge at the end of a blade used to shape or chip away a solid material (as stone, wood, or metal)

²chisel *vb* **-eled** *or* **-elled; -el·ing** *or* **-el·ling** \'chiz-(ə-)liŋ\ **1** : to cut or work with or as if with a chisel **2** : to use unfair or dishonest methods — **chis·el·er** \'chiz-(ə-)lər\ *n*

chit·chat \'chit-ˌchat\ *n* : SMALL TALK, GOSSIP

chi·tin \'kīt-ᵊn\ *n* : a horny substance that forms part of the hard outer body covering especially of insects and crustaceans — **chi·tin·ous** \'kīt-ᵊn-əs, 'kīt-nəs\ *adj*

chi·ton \'kīt-ᵊn, 'kī-ˌtän\ *n* **1** : any of a class of marine mollusks with a shell of calcium-containing plates **2** : a draped garment worn by the ancient Greeks

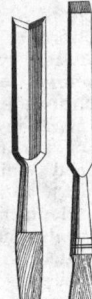

¹chisel

chit·ter·lings *or* **chit·lins** \'chit-lənz\ *n pl* : the intestines of hogs especially prepared as food

chi·val·ric \shə-'val-rik\ *adj* : CHIVALROUS 1

chiv·al·rous \'shiv-əl-rəs\ *adj* **1** : of or relating to chivalry **2 a** : having or showing honor, generosity, and courtesy **b** : showing special courtesy and regard to women — **chiv·al·rous·ly** *adv* — **chiv·al·rous·ness** *n*

chiv·al·ry \'shiv-əl-rē\ *n* **1** : a body of knights **2** : the system, spirit, ways, or customs of knighthood **3** : chivalrous conduct

Word History In the Middle Ages the French referred to a knight as a *chevalier*. This word is derived from the Latin word for "horseman," *caballarius,* which in turn comes from Latin *caballus,* meaning "horse." Knights were supposed to follow a code of conduct which required them to be brave, devoted to duty, and kind to the weak. The French word for these qualities was *chevalerie.* When this noun was borrowed into English, it became *chivalry.* Its adjective forms are *chivalrous* and *chivalric.* The Latin word for "horseman," *caballarius,* has also given us two other common English words. One is *cavalry,* meaning "troops mounted on horseback," and the other is *cavalier,* which as a noun means "mounted knight, gentleman" and as an adjective means "tending to ignore the rights of others." *Cavalier* may be traced back through French and Italian to its Latin source. In English, *cavalier* was used especially to refer to a mounted soldier who was colorful in dress and gallant in manner. During the English Civil War (1641–1649), those who backed the king were called Cavaliers, probably because of their vivid look and stylish manners. Some cavaliers, however, became proud and rude. They showed scorn for people of lower social rank. The result was that the adjective *cavalier* came to be used to describe such a scornful person. [Middle English *chivalrie* "group of knights, qualities of knighthood," from early French *chevalerie* (same meaning), from *chevalier* "knight, noble horseman," from Latin *caballarius* "horseman," from earlier *caballus* "horse" — related to CAVALIER, CAVALRY]

chive \'chīv\ *n* : an herb related to the onion and having leaves used as a seasoning

chivy \'chiv-ē\ *vb* **chiv·ied; chivy·ing** : to annoy or bother again and again about little things : PESTER

chlor·dane \'klȯ(ə)r-ˌdān\ *n* : a poisonous liquid insecticide formerly used in the U.S.

chlo·rel·la \klə-'rel-ə\ *n* : any of a genus of single-celled green algae that have been grown as a possible source of food

chlo·ride \'klō(ə)r-ˌīd, 'klȯ(ə)r-\ *n* : a chemical compound of chlorine with another element, group, or substance

chloride of lime : a white powder used as a bleach, disinfectant, and deodorant

chlo·ri·nate \'klōr-ə-ˌnāt, 'klȯr-\ *vb* **-nat·ed; -nat·ing** : to treat or cause to combine with chlorine or a chlorine

compound — **chlo·ri·na·tion** \ˌklōr-ə-'nā-shən, ˌklȯr-\ *n* — **chlo·ri·na·tor** \'klōr-ə-ˌnāt-ər, 'klȯr-\ *n*

chlo·rine \'klō(ə)r-ˌēn, 'klȯ(ə)r-, -ən\ *n* : a nonmetallic element that is found alone as a heavy greenish yellow irritating gas having two atoms per molecule and a strong odor and that is used especially as a bleach, oxidizing agent, and disinfectant in water purification — see ELEMENT table

chlo·rite \'klō(ə)r-ˌīt, 'klȯ(ə)r-\ *n* : a usually green mineral associated with and resembling the micas

chlo·ro·flu·o·ro·car·bon \ˌklōr-ō-ˌflu̇(-ə)r-ō-'kär-bən, ˌklȯr-\ *n* : a compound that contains carbon, chlorine, fluorine, and sometimes hydrogen and that is used to help refrigerate things, dissolve other compounds, or make aerosol sprays work and is believed to cause ozone loss in the stratosphere

¹chlo·ro·form \'klōr-ə-ˌfȯrm, 'klȯr-\ *n* : a colorless heavy poisonous liquid that smells like ether and is used especially to dissolve other compounds

²chloroform *vb* : to treat with chloroform especially so as to produce anesthesia or death

chlo·ro·phyll \'klōr-ə-ˌfil, 'klȯr-, -fəl\ *n* : the green coloring matter that is found chiefly in the chloroplasts of plants and is necessary for photosynthesis

chlo·ro·plast \'klōr-ə-ˌplast, 'klȯr-\ *n* : a cellular part that contains chlorophyll and is the location of photosynthesis

¹chock \'chäk\ *n* : a wedge or block for steadying or stopping a body (as a barrel), for filling in an unwanted space, or for blocking the movement of a wheel

²chock *vb* : to stop or make steady with or as if with chocks

chock–full *or* **chock·ful** \'chäk-'fu̇l, 'chäk-\ *adj* : full to the limit ⟨hotels *chock-full* of tourists⟩

choc·o·late \'chäk-(ə-)lət, 'chȯk-\ *n* **1** : a beverage of chocolate in water or milk **2** : a food prepared from ground roasted cacao beans **3** : a candy made of or coated with chocolate **4** : a brownish gray — **chocolate** *adj*

Choc·taw \'chäk-ˌtȯ\ *n, pl* **Choctaw** *or* **Choctaws** : a member of an American Indian people of Mississippi, Alabama, and Louisiana

¹choice \'chȯis\ *n* **1** : the act of choosing : SELECTION ⟨finding it hard to make a *choice*⟩ **2** : the power of choosing : OPTION ⟨you have no *choice*⟩ **3 a** : a person or thing chosen ⟨our *choice* for mayor⟩ **b** : the best part **4** : a number and variety to choose among ⟨a wide *choice* of options⟩ — **of choice** : to be preferred

²choice *adj* **1** : very fine ⟨*choice* fruits⟩ **2** : of a grade between prime and good ⟨*choice* meat⟩ — **choice·ly** *adv* — **choice·ness** *n*

choir \'kwī(-ə)r\ *n* **1** : an organized group of singers especially in a church **2** : the part of a church where the choir sits

choir·boy \'kwī(-ə)r-ˌbȯi\ *n* : a boy member of a church choir

choir·mas·ter \-ˌmas-tər\ *n* : the director of a choir

¹choke \'chōk\ *vb* **choked; chok·ing** **1** : to keep from breathing in a normal way by cutting off the supply of air ⟨*choked* by smoke⟩ **2** : to have the windpipe blocked entirely or partly ⟨*choke* on a bone⟩ **3** : to slow or prevent the growth or action of ⟨*choke* back tears⟩ **4** : to block by clogging ⟨leaves *choked* the drain⟩ **5** : to decrease or shut off the air intake of a carburetor to make the fuel mixture richer **6** : to grip (as a baseball bat) some distance from the end of the handle — usually used with *up*

²choke *n* **1** : the act of choking **2** : a portion of a shotgun bore that narrows toward the muzzle; *also* : a device at-

\ə\ **abut**	\au̇\ **out**	\i\ **tip**	\ȯ\ **saw**	\u̇\ **foot**
\ər\ **further**	\ch\ **chin**	\ī\ **life**	\ȯi\ **coin**	\y\ **yet**
\a\ **mat**	\e\ **pet**	\j\ **job**	\th\ **thin**	\yü\ **few**
\ā\ **take**	\ē\ **easy**	\ŋ\ **sing**	\th\ **this**	\yu̇\ **cure**
\ä\ **cot, cart**	\g\ **go**	\ō\ **bone**	\ü\ **food**	\zh\ **vision**

tached to the muzzle that narrows the bore **3** : a device for choking a gasoline engine

choke·cher·ry \'chōk-ˌcher-ē, -'cher-\ *n* : a wild cherry of the U.S. and Canada with a bitter fruit that is nearly black when ripe; *also* : this fruit

chok·er \'chō-kər\ *n* **1** : one that chokes **2** : something (as a necklace) that fits closely around the neck

choky \'chō-kē\ *adj* **chok·i·er; -est** : tending to cause choking or become choked

chol·era \'käl-ə-rə\ *n* : any of several diseases usually marked by severe vomiting and diarrhea

chol·er·ic \'käl-ə-rik, kə-'ler-ik\ *adj* : easily made angry : hot tempered [from earlier *choler* "yellow bile," from Middle English *coler* (same meaning), from early French *colere* (same meaning), from Latin *cholera* "cholera," from Greek *cholē* (same meaning), taken by ancient authors as caused by bile (Greek *cholē*) — see *Word History* at HUMOR]

cho·les·ter·ol \kə-'les-tə-ˌrōl, -ˌról\ *n* : a waxy substance that is present in animal cells and tissues, is important in bodily processes, and may be related to the abnormal thickening and hardening of arteries when too much is present

cho·line \'kō-ˌlēn\ *n* : a vitamin of the vitamin B complex that is widely distributed in animal and plant products (as eggs and beans) and is necessary for the activities of the liver

chomp \'chämp, 'chómp\ *vb* **1** : to chew or bite on something **2** : [1]CHAMP 2 — usually used in the phrase *chomping at the bit* — **chomp** *n*

choose \'chüz\ *vb* **chose** \'chōz\; **cho·sen** \'chōz-ᵊn\; **choos·ing** \'chü-ziŋ\ **1** : to select freely and after consideration ⟨*choose* a leader⟩ **2** : to make a choice : DECIDE ⟨*chose* to go by train⟩ **3** : to see fit ⟨take them if you *choose*⟩ — **choos·er** *n*

choosy *or* **choos·ey** \'chü-zē\ *adj* **choos·i·er; -est** : very careful in choosing : PARTICULAR ⟨*choosy* shoppers⟩

[1]chop \'chäp\ *vb* **chopped; chop·ping** **1** : to cut by striking especially over and over with something sharp ⟨*chop* down a tree⟩ **2** : to cut into small pieces ⟨*chop* onions⟩ **3** : to strike quickly or again and again [Middle English *chappen, choppen* "to cut, crack"]

[2]chop *n* **1** : a sharp downward blow or stroke (as with an ax) **2** : a small cut of meat often including a part of a rib **3** : a short quick motion (as of a wave)

[3]chop *vb* **chopped; chop·ping** : to change direction [Middle English *choppen, chappen* "to trade, barter"]

chop·per \'chäp-ər\ *n* **1** : one that chops **2** : HELICOPTER

[1]chop·py \'chäp-ē\ *adj* **chop·pi·er; -est** : CHANGEABLE 1, VARIABLE ⟨*choppy* wind⟩

[2]choppy *adj* **chop·pi·er; -est** **1** : rough with small waves ⟨the lake was *choppy*⟩ **2** : marked by sudden stops and starts : not connected smoothly ⟨short *choppy* sentences⟩ — **chop·pi·ness** *n*

chops \'chäps\ *n pl* **1** : [1]MOUTH 1 **2** : the fleshy covering of the jaws

chop shop *n* : a place where stolen automobiles are stripped for salable parts

chop·stick \'chäp-ˌstik\ *n* : one of a pair of slender sticks used chiefly in Asian countries to lift food to the mouth

chop su·ey \chäp-'sü-ē\ *n* : a dish made chiefly from bean sprouts, bamboo shoots, water chestnuts, onions, mushrooms, and meat or fish and served with rice and soy sauce [from Chinese (dialect of Guangzhou and Hong Kong) *jaahp seui*, literally, "odds and ends"]

cho·ral \'kōr-əl, 'kór-\ *adj* **1** : of or relating to a chorus or choir ⟨a *choral* group⟩ **2** : sung or recited by a chorus or choir ⟨a *choral* arrangement⟩ — **cho·ral·ly** \-ə-lē\ *adv*

cho·rale \kə-'ral, -'räl\ *n* **1** : a sacred song sung by the choir or congregation or both at a church service : HYMN **2** : [1]CHORUS 1b, CHOIR

[1]chord \'kórd\ *n* : a group of three or more tones sounded together to form harmony — **chord·al** \-əl\ *adj*

[2]chord *vb* : to play chords

[3]chord *n* : a straight line between two points on a curve

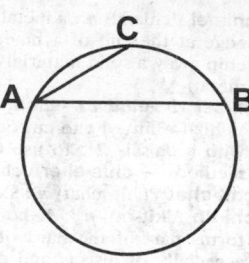

[3]chord: *AC* and *AB*

chor·date \'kór-ˌdāt, 'kórd-ət\ *n* : any of a major group of animals (as vertebrates and tunicates) having at least at some stage of development a notochord, a central nervous system located in the back, and openings for water to pass over the gills — **chordate** *adj*

chord organ *n* : an electronic organ with buttons to play simple chords

chore \'chō(ə)r, 'chó(ə)r\ *n* **1** *pl* : the regular light work of a household or farm **2** : an ordinary task **3** : a dull, unpleasant, or difficult task **synonyms** see TASK

cho·re·og·ra·phy \ˌkōr-ē-'äg-rə-fē, ˌkór-\ *n* : the art of arranging dances especially for ballet — **cho·re·o·graph** \'kōr-ē-ə-ˌgraf, 'kór-\ *vb* — **cho·re·og·ra·pher** \ˌkōr-ē-'äg-rə-fər, ˌkór-\ *n* — **cho·re·o·graph·ic** \-ē-ə-'graf-ik\ *adj*

cho·ri·on \'kōr-ē-ˌän, 'kór-\ *n* : the outer membrane that surrounds the embryo of reptiles, birds, and mammals and that in mammals with a placenta contributes to the formation of the placenta — **cho·ri·on·ic** \ˌkōr-ē-'än-ik, ˌkór-\ *adj*

cho·ris·ter \'kōr-ə-stər, 'kór-, 'kär-\ *n* : a singer in a choir

cho·roid \'kōr-ˌóid, 'kór-\ *also* **cho·ri·oid** \-ē-ˌóid\ *n* : the middle layer of the eye of vertebrates that contains pigment and is located between the sclera and the retina — **choroid** *adj*

choroid coat *n* : CHOROID

chor·tle \'chórt-əl\ *vb* **chor·tled; chor·tling** \'chórt-(ə-)liŋ\ : to chuckle especially in satisfaction — **chortle** *n* — **chor·tler** \'chórt-lər, -(ə)lər\ *n*

[1]cho·rus \'kōr-əs, 'kór-\ *n* **1 a** : a group of singers and dancers in Greek drama who take part in or comment on the action **b** : an organized group of singers : CHOIR **c** : a group of dancers and singers (as in a musical comedy) **2 a** : a part of a song or hymn that is repeated every so often : REFRAIN **b** : a song to be sung by a chorus **3** : something uttered by a number of persons or animals all at the same time ⟨a *chorus* of boos⟩ — **in chorus** : in unison ⟨answering *in chorus*⟩

[2]chorus *vb* : to sing or utter in chorus

chorus girl *n* : a young woman who sings or dances in a chorus (as of a musical)

chose *past of* CHOOSE

[1]chosen *past participle of* CHOOSE

[2]chosen *adj* : selected or marked for favor or special privilege ⟨a *chosen* few⟩

[1]chow \'chaú\ *n* : [1]MEAL 1, FOOD

[2]chow *vb* : EAT 1 ⟨*chowing* down on pizza⟩

chow chow \'chaú-ˌchaú\ *n* : any of a breed of thick-coated muscular dogs with a blue-black tongue and a short tail curled close to the back — called also *chow*

chow chow

chow·der \'chaúd-ər\ *n* : a soup or stew made of seafood with potatoes and onions and milk or tomatoes; *also* : a soup similar to chowder ⟨corn *chowder*⟩

chow mein \'chaú-'mān\ *n* : a thick stew of shredded

meat, mushrooms, and vegetables served with fried noodles

chris·ten \'kris-ᵊn\ *vb* **chris·tened; chris·ten·ing** \'kris-niŋ, -ᵊn-iŋ\ **1** : BAPTIZE 1 **2 a** : to name at baptism 〈*christened* the baby Robin〉 **b** : to name or dedicate in a ceremony like that of baptism 〈*christen* a ship〉

Chris·ten·dom \'kris-ᵊn-dəm\ *n* **1** : the entire body of Christians **2** : the part of the world where Christianity is most common

christening *n* : the ceremony of baptizing and naming a child

¹**Chris·tian** \'kris-chən, 'krish-\ *n* **1** : a person who believes in Jesus Christ and follows his teachings **2** : a member of a Christian church

²**Christian** *adj* **1** : of or relating to Jesus Christ or the religion based on his teachings **2** : of or relating to Christians 〈a *Christian* nation〉 **3** : being what a Christian should be or do 〈*Christian* behavior〉

Christian Era *n* : the period dating from the birth of Christ

Chris·ti·an·i·ty \,kris-chē-'an-ət-ē, ,krish-, -chan-; ,kris-tē-'an-\ *n* **1** : the religion of Christians **2** : the practice of Christianity

Chris·tian·ize \'kris-chə-,nīz, 'krish-\ *vb* **-ized; -iz·ing** : to make Christian — **Chris·tian·i·za·tion** \,kris-chə-nə-'zā-shən, 'krish-\ *n*

Christian name *n* : the personal name given to a person at birth or christening

Christ·mas \'kris-məs\ *n* **1** : December 25 celebrated in honor of the birth of Christ **2** : CHRISTMASTIME

Christmas cactus *n* : a branching Brazilian cactus with flat stems and showy flowers

Christmas club *n* : a savings account into which deposits are put throughout the year to provide money for Christmas shopping

Christmas fern *n* : a North American evergreen fern often used for winter decorations

Christmas rose *n* : a European herb that is related to the buttercups and produces usually white flowers in winter

Christ·mas·tide \'kris-mə-,stīd\ *n* : CHRISTMASTIME

Christ·mas·time \'kris-mə-,stīm\ *n* : the season of Christmas

Christmas tree *n* : a usually evergreen tree decorated at Christmas

¹**chro·mat·ic** \krō-'mat-ik\ *adj* **1** : of or relating to color; *esp* : being a shade other than black, gray, or white **2** : of or relating to the chromatic scale [from Greek *chrōmatikos* "relating to color," from *chrōma* "color"] — **chro·mat·i·cal·ly** \-i-k(ə-)lē\ *adv*

²**chromatic** *n* : ²ACCIDENTAL

chromatic aberration *n* : error caused by the differences in refraction of the colored rays into which light can be separated

chromatic scale *n* : a musical scale that has all half steps

chro·ma·tin \'krō-mə-tən\ *n* : a material present in chromosomes that is made up of DNA and protein and stains deeply with certain biological stains

chro·mato·graph \krō-'mat-ə-,graf, krə-\ *n* : an instrument used in chromatography

chro·ma·tog·ra·phy \,krō-mə-'täg-rə-fē\ *n* : separation and detection of chemical compounds as a result of their having traveled at different rates according to their different attractions to matter that carries them (as flowing liquid or gas) and matter that is not moving (as a liquid coating a solid) — **chro·mato·graph·ic** \krō-,mat-ə-'graf-ik, krə-\ *adj*

chrome \'krōm\ *n* **1 a** : CHROMIUM **b** : a chromium pigment **2** : something plated with an alloy of chromium

chro·mite \'krō-,mīt\ *n* : a black mineral that consists of an oxide of iron and chromium

chro·mi·um \'krō-mē-əm\ *n* : a blue-white metallic element found in nature only in combination and used espe-

cially in alloys and in chrome plating — see ELEMENT table

chro·mo·some \'krō-mə-,sōm, -,zōm\ *n* : one of the rod-shaped or threadlike DNA-containing bodies of a cell nucleus that contain all or most of the genes of an organism and can be seen especially during cell division — **chro·mo·som·al** \,krō-mə-'sō-məl, -'zō-\ *adj*

chromosome number *n* : the number of chromosomes in a cell that is usually constant in the cells making up the body of a particular kind of plant or animal

chro·mo·sphere \'krō-mə-,sfi(ə)r\ *n* : the part of the atmosphere of the sun or a star between the photosphere and corona

chron·ic \'krän-ik\ *adj* **1** : continuing or occurring again and again for a long time 〈a *chronic* disease〉 **2** : HABITUAL **2** 〈a *chronic* complainer〉 [from French *chronique* "chronic," from Greek *chronikos* "of time," from *chronos* "time" — related to ANACHRONISM, CHRONICLE, SYNCHRONOUS] — **chron·i·cal·ly** \-i-k(ə-)lē\ *adv*

¹**chron·i·cle** \'krän-i-kəl\ *n* : an account of events in the order of their happening : HISTORY [Middle English *cronicle* "chronicle," from early French *chronique* (same meaning), derived from Greek *chronikos*, "of time," from *chronos* "time" — related to ANACHRONISM, CHRONIC, SYNCHRONOUS]

²**chronicle** *vb* **chron·i·cled; chron·i·cling** \-k(ə-)liŋ\ : to present a record of in or as if in a chronicle 〈*chronicle* the major events of last year〉 — **chron·i·cler** \-k(ə-)lər\ *n*

Chron·i·cles \'krän-i-kəlz\ *n* — see BIBLE table

chro·no·graph \'krän-ə-,graf, 'krō-nə-\ *n* : an instrument for measuring and recording stretches of time with exactness — **chro·no·graph·ic** \,krän-ə-'graf-ik, ,krō-nə-\ *adj* — **chro·nog·ra·phy** \krə-'näg-rə-fē\ *n*

chro·no·log·i·cal \,krän-ə-'läj-i-kəl, ,krō-nə-\ *adj* : arranged in or according to the order of time 〈*chronological* order〉 〈a *chronological* table〉 — **chron·o·log·i·cal·ly** \-i-k(ə-)lē\ *adv*

chro·nol·o·gy \krə-'näl-ə-jē\ *n, pl* **-gies** **1** : the science that deals with measuring time and dating events **2** : a chronological table or list — **chro·nol·o·gist** \-jəst\ *n*

chro·nom·e·ter \krə-'näm-ət-ər\ *n* : an instrument for measuring time; *esp* : one intended to keep time with great exactness — **chro·no·met·ric** \,krän-ə-'me-trik, ,krō-nə-\ *also* **chro·no·met·ri·cal** \-tri-kəl\ *adj*

chro·no·scope \'krän-ə-,skōp, 'krō-nə-\ *n* : an instrument for exact measurement of small stretches of time

chrys·a·lid \'kris-ə-ləd\ *n* : CHRYSALIS

chrys·a·lis \'kris-ə-ləs\ *n, pl* **chry·sal·i·des** \kris-'al-ə-,dēz\ *or* **chrys·a·lis·es** \'kris-ə-lə-səz\ : the pupa of a butterfly or moth; *also* : the hardened outer layer of such a pupa — compare COCOON 1

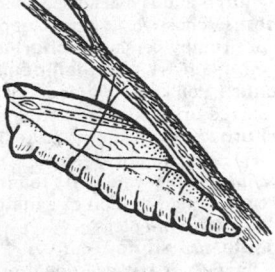

chrysalis

chry·san·the·mum \kris-'an(t)-thə-məm\ *n* **1** : any of a genus of plants that are related to the daisies and include weeds, ornamental plants grown for their brightly colored often double flower heads, and others important as sources of substances used in medicine and as insecticides **2** : a flower head of an ornamental chrysanthemum

\ə\ **abut**	\aú\ **out**	\i\ **tip**	\ò\ **saw**	\ú\ **foot**
\ər\ **further**	\ch\ **chin**	\ī\ **life**	\òi\ **coin**	\y\ **yet**
\a\ **mat**	\e\ **pet**	\j\ **job**	\th\ **thin**	\yü\ **few**
\ā\ **take**	\ē\ **easy**	\ŋ\ **sing**	\t̲h̲\ **this**	\yu̇\ **cure**
\ä\ **cot, cart**	\g\ **go**	\ō\ **bone**	\ü\ **food**	\zh\ **vision**

chryso·phyte \'kris-ə-ˌfīt\ *n* : GOLDEN-BROWN ALGA

chub·by \'chəb-ē\ *adj* **chub·bi·er; -est** : ⁵PLUMP ⟨a *chub*-by baby⟩ — **chub·bi·ness** *n*

¹**chuck** \'chək\ *vb* **1** : to give a pat or a tap to ⟨*chucked* the child under the chin⟩ **2** : TOSS 2 ⟨let's *chuck* the ball around⟩ [origin unknown]

²**chuck** *n* **1** : a pat or nudge under the chin **2** : an easy throw : TOSS

³**chuck** *n* **1** : a portion of a side of dressed beef including most of the neck and the parts around the shoulder blade and the first three ribs **2** : a device for holding work or a tool in a machine [English dialect *chuck* "lump"]

chuck·le \'chək-əl\ *vb* **chuck·led; chuck·ling** \'chək-(ə-)liŋ\ : to laugh in a quiet way — **chuckle** *n*

chuck wagon *n* : a wagon carrying a stove and food for cooking (as on a ranch)

chuck·wal·la \'chək-ˌwäl-ə\ *n* : a large plant-eating lizard of the desert regions of the southwestern U.S.

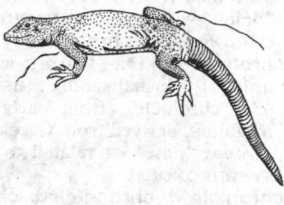
chuckwalla

¹**chug** \'chəg\ *n* : a dull explosive sound made by or as if by a steam engine pulling a heavy load

²**chug** *vb* **chugged; chug·ging** : to move or go with chugs ⟨a locomotive *chugging* along⟩

¹**chum** \'chəm\ *n* : a close friend [probably a shortened and altered form of earlier *chamber fellow* "roommate"]

²**chum** *vb* **chummed; chum·ming** : to be chums

chum·my \'chəm-ē\ *adj* **chum·mi·er; -est** : quite friendly — **chum·mi·ly** \'chəm-ə-lē\ *adv* — **chum·mi·ness** \'chəm-ē-nəs\ *n*

chump \'chəmp\ *n* : ¹FOOL 1, DUPE

chunk \'chəŋk\ *n* **1** : a short thick piece or lump **2** : a large amount or part ⟨a *chunk* of money⟩

chunky \'chəŋ-kē\ *adj* **chunk·i·er; -est 1 a** : STOCKY **b** : ⁵PLUMP **2** : full of chunks ⟨*chunky* peanut butter⟩

chup·pah *or* **hup·pah** *also* **chup·pa** \'kü-pə\ *n* : a canopy under which the bride and groom stand during a Jewish wedding ceremony [Yiddish; of Hebrew origin]

church \'chərch\ *n* **1** : a building for public worship and especially Christian worship **2** *often cap* : an organized body of religious believers **3** : public worship — **church·ly** \-lē\ *adj*

church·yard \'chərch-ˌyärd\ *n* : a yard that belongs to a church and is often used as a burial ground

churl \'chərl\ *n* **1** : a peasant of the Middle Ages **2** : a rude or grumpy person — **churl·ish** \'chər-lish\ *adj* — **churl·ish·ly** *adv* — **churl·ish·ness** *n*

¹**churn** \'chərn\ *n* : a container in which milk or cream is stirred or shaken in making butter

²**churn** *vb* **1** : to stir or shake in a churn (as in making butter) **2 a** : to stir or shake violently ⟨the boat's propeller *churning* the water⟩ **b** : to produce, move with, or experience violent motion or agitation ⟨her stomach was *churning*⟩ ⟨*churning* legs⟩

chute *also* **shute** \'shüt\ *n* **1** : an inclined plane, sloping channel, or passage down or through which things may pass ⟨a coal *chute*⟩ ⟨a mail *chute*⟩ **2** : ¹PARACHUTE 1

chutz·pah *also* **chutz·pa** *or* **hutz·pah** *or* **hutz·pa** \'hùt-spə, 'kút-, -(ˌ)spä\ *n* : NERVE 3c [Yiddish; of Hebrew origin]

chyle \'kī(ə)l\ *n* : lymph that is milky from bits of fat and is found especially in the lymphatic vessels surrounding the small intestine and carrying the digested fat to the blood

chyme \'kīm\ *n* : the partly fluid and partly solid mass of incompletely digested food that passes from the stomach into the first part of the small intestine

ci·ca·da \sə-'kād-ə, -'käd-\ *n* : any of a family of stout-bodied insects that have a wide blunt head, large transparent wings, and the males of which make a loud buzzing noise

-cide \ˌsīd\ *n combining form* **1** : killer ⟨pesti*cide*⟩ **2** : killing ⟨sui*cide*⟩ [derived from Latin *-cida* "killer"]

ci·der \'sīd-ər\ *n* : the juice pressed out of fruit (as apples) and used especially as a drink and in the making of vinegar

cig \'sig\ *n, slang* : CIGARETTE

ci·gar \sig-'är\ *n* : a roll of tobacco leaf for smoking

cig·a·rette \ˌsig-ə-'ret, 'sig-ə-ˌret\ *n* : a small roll of cut tobacco wrapped in paper for smoking [from French *cigarette,* literally, "little cigar"]

cil·i·ary \'sil-ē-ˌer-ē\ *adj* **1** : of or relating to cilia ⟨*ciliary* movement⟩ **2** : of, relating to, or being the muscular body supporting the lens of the eye ⟨*ciliary* muscles⟩

cil·i·ate \'sil-ē-ət, -ˌāt\ *n* : any of a group of protozoans that have cilia

cil·i·at·ed \'sil-ē-ˌāt-əd\ *or* **cil·i·ate** \'sil-ē-ət, -ˌāt\ *adj* : possessing cilia ⟨a *ciliated* cell⟩

cil·i·um \'sil-ē-əm\ *n, pl* **cil·ia** \-ē-ə\ **1** : one of the tiny hairlike structures of many cells that make lashing movements **2** : EYELASH

¹**cinch** \'sinch\ *n* **1** : a strong girth for a pack or saddle **2** : an easy thing to do **3** : something sure to happen

²**cinch** *vb* **1** : to put a cinch on **2** : to make certain ⟨the goal that *cinched* the victory⟩

cin·cho·na \sin-'kō-nə, sin-'chō-\ *n* : any of a genus of South American trees and shrubs with bark containing substances (as quinine) that are used in treating malaria

Cinco de Mayo \ˌsiŋ-kō-də-'mī-ō, ˌsēŋ-kō-thä-'mä-yō\ *n* : a Mexican and Mexican-American celebration held on May 5 in honor of the Mexican victory over the French at Puebla in 1862 [Spanish, "fifth of May"]

cinc·ture \'siŋ(k)-chər\ *n* : ¹GIRDLE 1, BELT

cin·der \'sin-dər\ *n* **1** : SLAG **2 a** : a piece of partly burned coal or wood **b** : a hot coal without flame **3** : a piece of lava from an erupting volcano — **cin·dery** \-d(ə-)rē\ *adj*

cinder block *n* : a building block made of cement and coal cinders

cin·e·ma \'sin-ə-mə\ *n* **1 a** : MOVIE 2a ⟨a *cinema* director⟩ **b** : a theater for showing movies ⟨went to the *cinema*⟩ **2 a** : the business of making movies ⟨worked in *cinema*⟩ **b** : the art or technique of making movies ⟨a student of French *cinema*⟩ [derived from French *cinématographe* "motion picture," from Greek *kinēma* "movement" and *graphe* "picture," from *kinein* "to move" — related to KINETIC] — **cin·e·mat·ic** \ˌsin-ə-'mat-ik\ *adj* — **cin·e·mat·i·cal·ly** \-i-k(ə-)lē\ *adv*

cin·e·ma·tog·ra·phy \ˌsin-ə-mə-'täg-rə-fē\ *n* : the art or science of motion-picture photography — **cin·e·ma·tog·ra·pher** \-fər\ *n* — **cin·e·mat·o·graph·ic** \-ˌmat-ə-'graf-ik\ *adj*

cin·na·bar \'sin-ə-ˌbär\ *n* : a red mineral that consists of a sulfide of mercury and is the only important ore of mercury

cin·na·mon \'sin-ə-mən\ *n* **1 a** : a spice consisting of the pleasant-smelling bark of any of several Asian trees related to the laurels **b** : a tree that yields cinnamon **2 a** : light yellowish brown — **cin·na·mony** \-mə-nē\ *adj*

cinque·foil \'siŋk-ˌfóil, 'saŋk-\ *n* : any of a group of plants that have leaves with five lobes and are related to the roses

cion *variant of* SCION

¹**ci·pher** \'sī-fər\ *n* **1** : the symbol 0 meaning the absence of all magnitude or quantity : ZERO — see NUMBER table **2 a** : a method of changing a message so as to conceal its meaning **b** : a message in code [Middle English *cipher* "zero," from Latin *cifra* (same meaning), from Arabic *ṣifr* "empty"]

²**cipher** *vb* **ci·phered; ci·pher·ing** \-f(ə-)riŋ\ **1** : to use figures in calculating **2** : to change (a message) into cipher

cir·ca \'sər-kə, 'ki(ə)r-ˌkä\ *prep* : in about ⟨born *circa* 1600⟩

¹**cir·cle** \'sər-kəl\ *n* **1 a** : ¹RING 3 **b** : a line segment that is curved so that its ends meet and every point on the line is equally far away from a single point inside **c** : the flat surface enclosed by a circle **2** : something in the form of a circle ⟨a traffic *circle*⟩ **3** : ¹CYCLE 2a, ROUND ⟨the wheel had come full *circle*⟩ **4** : a group of people sharing a common interest ⟨our *circle* of friends⟩ [Middle English *cercle* "circle," from early French *cercle* (same meaning), derived from Latin *circus* "circle, ring, arena"]

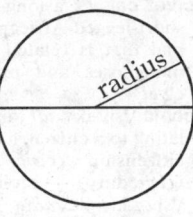

¹circle 1b

²**circle** *vb* **cir·cled; cir·cling** \-k(ə-)liŋ\ **1** : to enclose in or as if in a circle ⟨*circle* the correct answer⟩ ⟨the trees *circling* our little house⟩ **2** : to move or revolve around ⟨the pilot *circled* the field⟩ ⟨satellites *circling* the earth⟩ **3** : to move in or as if in a circle ⟨the quarterback *circled* to the left⟩ — **cir·cler** \-k(ə-)lər\ *n*

circle graph *n* : PIE CHART

cir·clet \'sər-klət\ *n* : an ornament in the form of a circle

cir·cuit \'sər-kət\ *n* **1 a** : a boundary around an enclosed space **b** : an enclosed space **2** : a moving or revolving around ⟨the *circuit* of the earth around the sun⟩ **3** : a traveling from place to place in an area (as by a judge) so as to stop in each place at a certain time; *also* : the route so traveled **4 a** : the complete path of an electric current **b** : a group of electronic elements : HOOKUP **5 a** : ²LEAGUE 2 **b** : a number or chain of theaters at which stage shows are shown in turn

circuit breaker *n* : a switch that automatically stops the flow of electric current in an overloaded circuit

cir·cu·itous \(ˌ)sər-'kyü-ət-əs\ *adj* **1** : not saying what one means in simple and sincere language **2** : having a circular or winding course ⟨a *circuitous* route⟩ — **cir·cu·itous·ly** *adv* — **cir·cu·itous·ness** *n*

cir·cuit·ry \'sər-kə-trē\ *n, pl* **-ries** : the plan or the elements of an electric circuit

¹**cir·cu·lar** \'sər-kyə-lər\ *adj* **1** : having the form of a circle : ROUND ⟨a *circular* driveway⟩ **2** : passing or going around in a circle ⟨*circular* motion⟩ **3** : CIRCUITOUS 1 **4** : sent around to a number of persons ⟨a *circular* letter⟩ — **cir·cu·lar·i·ty** \ˌsər-kyə-'lar-ət-ē\ *n* — **cir·cu·lar·ly** \'sər-kyə-lər-lē\ *adv*

²**circular** *n* : a printed notice or advertisement given or sent to many people

circular cylinder *n* : a cylinder with bases that are circles

circular saw *n* : a power saw with a round cutting blade

cir·cu·late \'sər-kyə-ˌlāt\ *vb* **-lat·ed; -lat·ing** **1** : to move or cause to move in a circle or course; *esp* : to follow a course that returns to the starting point ⟨blood *circulates* through the body⟩ **2** : to pass or be passed from person to person or place to place ⟨*circulate* a rumor⟩ — **cir·cu·la·tive** \-ˌlāt-iv\ *adj* — **cir·cu·la·tor** \-ˌlāt-ər\ *n*

cir·cu·la·tion \ˌsər-kyə-'lā-shən\ *n* **1** : orderly movement through a circuit; *esp* : the movement of blood through the vessels of the body caused by the pumping action of the heart **2 a** : passage from person to person or place to place ⟨coins in *circulation*⟩ **b** : the average number of copies (as of a newspaper) sold over a given period

cir·cu·la·to·ry \'sər-kyə-lə-ˌtōr-ē, -ˌtȯr-\ *adj* : of or relating to circulation or the circulatory system

circulatory system *n* : the bodily system of blood, vessels, and heart concerned with the circulation of the blood and lymph

cir·cum·cen·ter \'sər-kəm-ˌsen-tər\ *n* : the point at which the three perpendicular bisectors of the sides of a triangle intersect and which is the same distance from each of the three vertices of the triangle

cir·cum·cise \'sər-kəm-ˌsīz\ *vb* **-cised; -cis·ing** : to cut off the foreskin of

cir·cum·ci·sion \ˌsər-kəm-'sizh-ən, 'sər-kəm-ˌsizh-\ *n* **1** : the act of circumcising or being circumcised; *esp* : a Jewish rite performed on male infants as a sign of inclusion in the covenant between God and Abraham **2** *cap* : January 1 observed as a festival in some churches in honor of the circumcision of Jesus

cir·cum·fer·ence \sə(r)-'kəm(p)-fərn(t)s, -f(ə-)rən(t)s\ *n* **1** : a line that goes around or encloses a circle **2** : the outer boundary of a figure or area **3** : the distance around something ⟨the *circumference* of the earth at the equator⟩

cir·cum·flex \'sər-kəm-ˌfleks\ *n* : a mark ˆ over a vowel

cir·cum·lo·cu·tion \ˌsər-kəm-lō-'kyü-shən\ *n* **1** : the use of many words to express an idea that could be expressed in few **2** : evasion in speech — **cir·cum·loc·u·to·ry** \-'läk-yə-ˌtōr-ē, -ˌtȯr-\ *adj*

cir·cum·lu·nar \ˌsər-kəm-'lü-nər\ *adj* : revolving about or surrounding the moon ⟨a *circumlunar* orbit⟩

cir·cum·nav·i·gate \ˌsər-kəm-'nav-ə-ˌgāt\ *vb* : to go completely around especially by water ⟨*circumnavigate* the earth⟩; *also* : to go around instead of through : BYPASS — **cir·cum·nav·i·ga·tion** \-ˌnav-ə-'gā-shən\ *n*

cir·cum·po·lar \ˌsər-kəm-'pō-lər\ *adj* **1** : continually visible above the horizon ⟨a *circumpolar* star⟩ **2** : surrounding or found near a pole of the earth

cir·cum·scribe \'sər-kəm-ˌskrīb\ *vb* **-scribed; -scrib·ing** **1 a** : to limit the range or activity of definitely and clearly **b** : to define or set limits for carefully **2 a** : to draw a line around **b** : to put a boundary around [from Latin *circumscribere* "to draw a line around, set limits to," from *circum* "around" and *scribere* "to write, draw" — related to SCRIBE]

cir·cum·spect \'sər-kəm-ˌspekt\ *adj* : careful to consider everything that might happen — **cir·cum·spec·tion** \ˌsər-kəm-'spek-shən\ *n* — **cir·cum·spect·ly** *adv*

cir·cum·stance \'sər-kəm-ˌstan(t)s\ *n* **1 a** : a fact or event that must be considered along with another fact or event **b** : a fact or detail in a chain of events **2** *pl* : conditions at a certain time or place ⟨impossible under the *circumstances*⟩ **3 a** : the way things happen to be : CHANCE — often used in plural ⟨a victim of *circumstances*⟩ **b** *pl* : financial condition ⟨in easy *circumstances*⟩

cir·cum·stan·tial \ˌsər-kəm-'stan-chəl\ *adj* **1** : consisting of, relating to, or depending on circumstances ⟨*circumstantial* evidence⟩ **2** : containing full details ⟨a *circumstantial* account of what happened⟩ — **cir·cum·stan·tial·ly** \-'stanch-(ə-)lē\ *adv*

cir·cum·vent \ˌsər-kəm-'vent\ *vb* **1** : to go around : ²BYPASS **2** : to get the better of or avoid the force or effect of by cleverness ⟨*circumvented* the rules⟩ — **cir·cum·ven·tion** \-'ven-chən\ *n*

cir·cus \'sər-kəs\ *n* **1** : a large arena enclosed by rows of seats (as in ancient Rome) **2 a** : a show that usually travels from place to place and that has a variety of exhibitions including acrobatic feats, wild animal displays, and performances by clowns **b** : a circus performance **c** : the performers and equipment of such a circus **d** : something that suggests a circus [from Latin *circus* "circle, arena"]

ci·ré \sə-'rā\ *n* : a shiny fabric that looks wet [French, literally, "waxed"]

\ə\ abut	\au̇\ out	\i\ tip	\ȯ\ saw	\u̇\ foot
\ər\ further	\ch\ chin	\ī\ life	\ȯi\ coin	\y\ yet
\a\ mat	\e\ pet	\j\ job	\th\ thin	\yü\ few
\ā\ take	\ē\ easy	\ŋ\ sing	\t͟h\ this	\yu̇\ cure
\ä\ cot, cart	\g\ go	\ō\ bone	\ü\ food	\zh\ vision

cirque \'sərk\ *n* : a deep basin on a mountain that is shaped like half a bowl [French, from Latin *circus* "circle, arena"]

cir·rho·sis \sə-'rō-səs\ *n* : an increase in fiber-containing tissue and hardening of the liver

cir·ro·cu·mu·lus \ˌsir-ō-'kyü-myə-ləs\ *n* : a cloud form of small white rounded masses at a high altitude usually in regular groups

cir·ro·stra·tus \ˌsir-ō-'strāt-əs, -'strat-\ *n* : a fairly even high cloud layer that is darker than cirrus

cir·rus \'sir-əs\ *n, pl* **cir·ri** \'si(ə)r-ˌī\ : a thin white cloud usually of tiny ice crystals formed at altitudes about 20,000 to 40,000 feet (6,000 to 12,000 meters)

cis·lu·nar \(')sis-'lü-nər\ *adj* : lying between the earth and the moon or the moon's orbit

cis·tern \'sis-tərn\ *n* : an artificial reservoir or tank for storing water usually underground

cit·a·del \'sit-əd-ᵊl, -ə-ˌdel\ *n* 1 : a fortress that sits high above a city 2 : a strong fortress

ci·ta·tion \sī-'tā-shən\ *n* 1 : an official order to appear (as before a court) 2 a : an act or instance of quoting b : QUOTATION 1 3 : a formal statement of what a person did to be chosen to receive an award

cite \'sīt\ *vb* **cit·ed; cit·ing** 1 : to summon to appear before a court 2 : to quote as an example, authority, or proof 3 : to refer to especially in praise

cit·i·fy \'sit-i-ˌfī\ *vb* **-fied; -fy·ing** : URBANIZE

cit·i·zen \'sit-ə-zən\ *n* 1 : a person who lives in a city or town 2 a : a member of a state b : a person who owes allegiance to a government and is protected by it [Middle English *citizein*, "citizen, resident of a town," derived from early French *citeien* (same meaning), from *cité* "town," derived from Latin *civitas* "state of being a resident of a town, citizenship," from *civis* "citizen" — related to CITY, CIVIL]

cit·i·zen·ry \'sit-ə-zən-rē\ *n, pl* **-ries** : the whole body of citizens

citizens band *n* : a range of radio frequencies set aside for private radio communications

cit·i·zen·ship \'sit-ə-zən-ship\ *n* 1 : possession of the rights and privileges of a citizen 2 : the quality of a person's response to membership in a community

ci·trate \'si-ˌtrāt\ *n* : a salt or ester of citric acid

cit·ric acid \ˌsi-trik-\ *n* : a pleasantly sour-tasting organic acid obtained especially from lemon and lime juices or by the chemical breakdown of sugars and used as a flavoring

cit·ron \'si-trən\ *n* 1 a : a fruit like the lemon in appearance and structure but larger; *also* : the citrus tree producing this fruit b : the preserved rind of the citron used especially in fruitcake 2 : a small watermelon with hard flesh that is used especially in pickles and preserves

cit·ro·nel·la \ˌsi-trə-'nel-ə\ *n* : a lemon-scented oil obtained from a grass of southern Asia and used in perfumes and as an insect repellent

cit·rus \'si-trəs\ *n, pl* **citrus** *or* **cit·rus·es** : any of a genus of often thorny trees and shrubs (as the orange, grapefruit, or lemon) grown in warm regions for their fruits; *also* : the fruit of a citrus — **citrus** *adj*

city \'sit-ē\ *n, pl* **cit·ies** 1 : a place in which people live that is larger or more important than a town 2 : the people of a city [Middle English *citie* "large or small town," from early French *cité* (same meaning), derived from Latin *civitas* "state of being a resident of a town, citizenship," from *civis* "citizen" — related to CITIZEN, CIVIL]

city hall *n* 1 : the main administrative building of a city 2 a : a municipal government b : city officialdom or bureaucracy ⟨you can't fight *city hall*⟩

city manager *n* : an official employed by an elected council to direct the administration of a city government

city–state \'sit-ē-ˌstāt, -ˌstāt\ *n* : a self-governing state consisting of a city and surrounding territory

city·wide \'sit-ē-ˌwīd\ *adj* : including or involving all parts of a city ⟨a *citywide* blackout⟩

civ·et \'siv-ət\ *n* 1 : a thick yellowish strong-smelling substance obtained from the civet cat and used in perfume 2 : CIVET CAT

civet cat *n* : a long-bodied short-legged African mammal that is related to the mongooses and produces civet

civet cat

civ·ic \'siv-ik\ *adj* : of or relating to a citizen, a city, or citizenship ⟨*civic* pride⟩ ⟨*civic* duty⟩ — **civ·i·cal·ly** \'siv-i-k(ə-)lē\ *adv*

civ·ics \'siv-iks\ *n* : the study of the rights and duties of citizens

civ·il \'siv-əl\ *adj* 1 : of or relating to citizens ⟨*civil* liberties⟩ 2 : of or relating to the state ⟨*civil* institutions⟩ 3 : of or relating to ordinary or government affairs rather than to those of the military or the church 4 : polite without being friendly ⟨gave a *civil* answer⟩ 5 : relating to court action between individuals having to do with private rights rather than criminal action ⟨a *civil* suit⟩ [Middle English *civil* "relating to a citizen," from early French *civil* (same meaning), from Latin *civilis* "relating to a citizen," from *civis* "citizen" — related to CITIZEN, CITY]

civil defense *n* : protective actions and emergency relief activities carried on by civilians in case of enemy attack or natural disaster

civil engineer *n* : an engineer whose training or occupation is in the designing and construction of public works (as roads or harbors) and of various private works — **civil engineering** *n*

ci·vil·ian \sə-'vil-yən\ *n* : a person not on active duty in the armed services or not on a police or firefighting force — **civilian** *adj*

ci·vil·i·ty \sə-'vil-ət-ē\ *n, pl* **-ties** 1 : civilized conduct; *esp* : COURTESY 1, POLITENESS 2 : a polite act or expression

civ·i·li·za·tion \ˌsiv-ə-lə-'zā-shən\ *n* 1 a : an advanced stage (as in art, science, and government) of social development b : the way of life of a people ⟨ancient Egyptian *civilization*⟩ 2 : the series of changes involved in becoming civilized 3 : improvement of thought, manners, or taste

civ·i·lize \'siv-ə-ˌlīz\ *vb* **-lized; -liz·ing** : to raise out of a primitive state; *esp* : to bring to an advanced stage (as in art, science, and government) of social development — **civ·i·lized** *adj*

civ·il·ly \'siv-ə(l)-lē\ *adv* : in a civil manner : POLITELY

civil rights *n pl* : the nonpolitical rights of a citizen; *esp* : the rights of personal liberty guaranteed to U.S. citizens by the 13th and 14th amendments to the Constitution and by acts of Congress

civil service *n* : the branch of a government that takes care of the business of running a state but that does not include the lawmaking branch, the military, or the court system

civil war *n* : a war between opposing groups of citizens of the same country or nation

clab·ber \'klab-ər\ *n, chiefly dialect* : sour milk that has thickened or curdled

clab·bered \'klab-ərd\ *adj, of milk or cream* : being thickened or curdled

clack \'klak\ *vb* : to make or cause to make a clattering or clicking sound — **clack** *n* — **clack·er** *n*

¹**clad** *past and past participle of* CLOTHE

²**clad** \'klad\ *adj* : being covered : wearing clothes

¹**claim** \'klām\ *vb* 1 a : to ask for as rightfully belonging to oneself ⟨*claim* an inheritance⟩ b : to call for : REQUIRE ⟨business that *claims* attention⟩ 2 : to put an end to life : TAKE ⟨an accident *claimed* his life⟩ 3 a : to state as a

fact : MAINTAIN ⟨*claimed* to have been cheated⟩ **b** : to make a claim ⟨*claimed* to know nothing about it⟩ [Middle English *claimen* "to ask for as a right, claim," from early French *clamer* (same meaning), from Latin *clamare* "to shout" — related to ACCLAIM, CLAMOR] — **claim·able** \ˈklā-mə-bəl\ *adj* — **claim·er** *n*

²claim *n* **1** : a demand for something due or believed to be due ⟨an insurance *claim*⟩ **2 a** : a right or title to something **b** : a statement that may be doubted ⟨a *claim* of authenticity⟩ **3** : something claimed; *esp* : an area of land marked out by a settler or prospector

claim·ant \ˈklā-mənt\ *n* : a person who claims to have a right to something

clair·voy·ance \kla(ə)r-ˈvȯi-ən(t)s, kle(ə)r-\ *n* : the power of seeing or knowing about things that are not present to the senses [from French *clairvoyance* "clairvoyance," from *clair* "clear" (from Latin *clarus* "clear") and *voyant* "seeing" (derived from Latin *vidēre* "to see") — related to CLEAR, VISION]

¹clair·voy·ant \kla(ə)r-ˈvȯi-ənt, kle(ə)r-\ *adj* : of, relating to, or having clairvoyance

²clairvoyant *n* : a person who has clairvoyance

¹clam \ˈklam\ *n* **1** : any of numerous edible marine mollusks that have two hinged shells and live in sand or mud **2** : a freshwater mussel

²clam *vb* **clammed; clam·ming** : to dig or gather clams

clam·bake \ˈklam-ˌbāk\ *n* : an outdoor party; *esp* : an outing at which food is cooked usually on heated rocks covered by seaweed

clam·ber \ˈklam-bər\ *vb* **clam·bered; clam·ber·ing** \-b(ə-)riŋ\ : to climb awkwardly

clam·my \ˈklam-ē\ *adj* **clam·mi·er; -est** : being damp, soft, sticky, and usually cool — **clam·mi·ness** *n*

clam·or \ˈklam-ər\ *n* **1 a** : a noisy shouting **b** : a loud continuous noise **2** : strong and active protest or demand [Middle English *clamor* "noisy shouting," from early French *clamour* (same meaning), derived from Latin *clamare* "to shout" — related to ACCLAIM, CLAIM] — **clamor** *vb* — **clam·or·ous** \-(ə-)rəs\ *adj* — **clam·or·ous·ly** *adv*

¹clamp \ˈklamp\ *n* : a device that holds or presses parts together firmly

²clamp *vb* : to fasten or tighten with or as if with a clamp

clamp down *vb* : to act in a strict and forceful manner to stop something ⟨police are *clamping down* on drunk driving⟩

clam·shell \ˈklam-ˌshel\ *n* : the shell of a clam

clam up *vb* : to become silent ⟨they *clammed up* when asked for more information⟩

clam worm *n* : any of several large burrowing marine worms related to the earthworms and often used as bait

¹clamp

clan \ˈklan\ *n* **1 a** : a group (as in the Scottish Highlands) made up of households whose heads claim to have a common ancestor **b** : a group of people having a common ancestor : FAMILY **2** : a group of persons united by a common interest ⟨the whole *clan* of actors⟩

clan·des·tine \klan-ˈdes-tən\ *adj* : done in secret ⟨a *clandestine* meeting⟩ **synonyms** see SECRET — **clan·des·tine·ly** *adv*

¹clang \ˈklaŋ\ *vb* : to make or cause to make a loud ringing sound

²clang *n* : a loud ringing sound like that made by pieces of metal striking together

clan·gor \ˈklaŋ-(g)ər\ *n* : a loud clanging noise — **clan·gor·ous** \-(g)ə-rəs\ *adj*

¹clank \ˈklaŋk\ *vb* : to make or move with a clank or series of clanks

²clank *n* : a sharp short ringing sound

clan·nish \ˈklan-ish\ *adj* : tending to associate only with a group of persons like oneself — **clan·nish·ness** *n*

clans·man \ˈklanz-mən\ *n* : a member of a clan

¹clap \ˈklap\ *vb* **clapped; clap·ping** **1** : to strike noisily : BANG ⟨*clap* two boards together⟩ ⟨the door *clapped* shut⟩ **2** : to strike the hands together over and over in applause **3** : to strike with the open hand ⟨*clap* a friend on the shoulder⟩ **4** : to place, put, or set especially energetically ⟨*clap* him into jail⟩ ⟨since I first *clapped* eyes on it⟩ **5** : to make or build hastily ⟨*clap* together a shelter⟩

²clap *n* **1** : a sound made by or as if by clapping ⟨a *clap* of thunder⟩ **2** : a friendly slap ⟨a *clap* on the shoulder⟩

³clap *n* : GONORRHEA — often used with *the*

clap·board \ˈklab-ərd; ˈkla(p)-ˌbō(ə)rd, -ˌbȯ(ə)rd\ *n* : a narrow board thicker at one edge than at the other used to cover the sides of wooden buildings — **clapboard** *vb*

clap·per \ˈklap-ər\ *n* **1** : the tongue of a bell **2** : one that makes a clapping sound

clap·trap \ˈklap-ˌtrap\ *n* : NONSENSE 1

clar·et \ˈklar-ət\ *n* **1** : a dry red table wine **2** : a dark purplish red — **claret** *adj*

clar·i·fy \ˈklar-ə-ˌfī\ *vb* **-fied; -fy·ing** **1** : to make or become pure or clear ⟨*clarify* a liquid⟩ **2** : to make or become easier to understand ⟨*clarify* a statement⟩ — **clar·i·fi·ca·tion** \ˌklar-ə-fə-ˈkā-shən\ *n* — **clar·i·fi·er** \ˈklar-ə-ˌfī(-ə)r\ *n*

C clapper 1

clar·i·net \ˌklar-ə-ˈnet, ˈklar-ə-nət\ *n* : a woodwind musical instrument in the shape of a cylindrical tube having a single-reed mouthpiece — **clar·i·net·ist** *or* **clar·i·net·tist** \ˌklar-ə-ˈnet-əst\ *n*

clar·i·on \ˈklar-ē-ən\ *adj* : brilliantly clear ⟨a *clarion* call to action⟩

clar·i·ty \ˈklar-ət-ē\ *n* : the quality or state of being clear ⟨the *clarity* of their voices⟩

¹clash \ˈklash\ *vb* **1** : to make a clash ⟨*clashing* cymbals⟩ **2 a** : to come into conflict ⟨pickets *clashed* with the police⟩ **b** : to not match well ⟨our ideas *clashed*⟩ ⟨some colors *clash*⟩ — **clash·er** *n*

²clash *n* **1** : a loud sharp sound usually of metal striking metal ⟨the *clash* of swords⟩ **2** : a sharp fight or strong disagreement

¹clasp \ˈklasp\ *n* **1** : a device for holding together objects or parts of something **2** : a holding or embracing with or as if with the hands or arms

²clasp *vb* **1** : to fasten with or as if with a clasp **2** : to enclose and hold with the arms; *esp* : EMBRACE **3** : to seize with or as if with the hand : GRASP — **clasp·er** *n*

¹class \ˈklas\ *n* **1 a** : a group of students meeting regularly to study the same subject **b** : the period during which such a group meets **c** : a course of instruction **d** : a group of students who graduate together ⟨*class* of 1990⟩ **2 a** : a group or rank of society ⟨the working *class*⟩ **b** : high social rank **c** : high quality : ELEGANCE **2** ⟨a hotel with *class*⟩ **3 a** : a group or set alike in some way **b** : a major category in biological classification that is above the order and below the phylum or division **c** : a group-

\ə\ abut	\au̇\ out	\i\ tip	\ȯ\ saw	\u̇\ foot
\ər\ further	\ch\ chin	\ī\ life	\ȯi\ coin	\y\ yet
\a\ mat	\e\ pet	\j\ job	\th\ thin	\yü\ few
\ā\ take	\ē\ easy	\ŋ\ sing	\t͟h\ this	\yu̇\ cure
\ä\ cot, cart	\g\ go	\ō\ bone	\ü\ food	\zh\ vision

ing or standing (as of goods or services) based on quality
— **class·less** \-ləs\ *adj*

²class *vb* : CLASSIFY

¹clas·sic \'klas-ik\ *adj* **1 a** : serving as a standard of excellence ⟨a *classic* literature⟩ **b** : fashionable year after year : TRADITIONAL, ENDURING ⟨a *classic* design⟩ **2** : of or relating to the ancient Greeks or Romans or their culture **3 a** : notable as the best of its kind ⟨a *classic* film⟩ **b** : notable as the most basic or typical of its kind ⟨a *classic* example⟩

²classic *n* **1** : a literary work of ancient Greece or Rome **2** : a great work of art; *also* : its author **3** : something regarded as perfect of its kind **4** : an event that has become a tradition ⟨a football *classic*⟩

clas·si·cal \'klas-i-kəl\ *adj* **1** : ¹CLASSIC 1a **2** : of or relating to the classics of literature or art; *esp* : of or relating to the ancient Greek and Roman classics ⟨*classical* studies⟩ **3** : of or relating to serious music in the European tradition **4** : of or relating to tradition : AUTHENTIC **5** : concerned with a general study of the arts and sciences and not specializing in technical studies ⟨*classical* high school⟩

clas·si·cal·ly \'klas-i-k(ə-)lē\ *adv* : in a classic or classical manner

clas·si·cism \'klas-ə-ˌsiz-əm\ *n* **1** : the principles or style of the literature, art, or architecture of ancient Greece and Rome **2** : a following of the standards of tradition (as in music or art)

clas·si·fi·ca·tion \ˌklas-(ə-)fə-'kā-shən\ *n* **1** : the act or process of classifying **2 a** : systematic arrangement in groups : TAXONOMY **b** : ¹CLASS 3a, CATEGORY — **clas·si·fi·ca·to·ry** \'klas-(ə-)fə-kə-ˌtōr-ē, -ˌtòr-\ *adj*

¹clas·si·fied \'klas-ə-ˌfīd\ *adj* **1** : divided into classes or placed in a class ⟨*classified* ads⟩ **2** : withheld from the knowledge of the general public for reasons of national security ⟨*classified* information⟩

²classified *n* : an advertisement grouped with others of the same kind — usually used in plural

clas·si·fy \'klas-ə-ˌfī\ *vb* **-fied; -fy·ing** : to arrange in or assign to classes ⟨*classify* books by subjects⟩ — **clas·si·fi·able** \-ˌfī-ə-bəl\ *adj* — **clas·si·fi·er** \-ˌfī-(ə)r\ *n*

class·mate \'klas-ˌmāt\ *n* : a member of the same class in a school or college

class·room \-ˌrüm, -ˌrùm\ *n* : a room in a school or college in which classes meet

classy \'klas-ē\ *adj* **class·i·er; -est** : having or showing class: as **a** : ELEGANT 1, STYLISH **b** : having or showing refined behavior ⟨a *classy* guy⟩ **c** : very skillful and graceful ⟨a *classy* player⟩ — **class·i·ness** *n*

¹clat·ter \'klat-ər\ *vb* **1** : to make or cause to make a rattling sound **2** : to move with a clatter — **clat·ter·er** \-ər-ər\ *n* — **clat·ter·ing·ly** \'klat-ə-riŋ-lē\ *adv*

²clatter *n* **1** : a rattling sound (as of hard objects striking together) ⟨the *clatter* of pots and pans⟩ **2** : COMMOTION **3** : noisy chatter — **clat·tery** \'klat-ə-rē\ *adj*

clause \'klòz\ *n* **1** : a separate distinct part of an article or document ⟨a *clause* in a will⟩ **2** : a group of words having its own subject and predicate but forming only part of a compound or complex sentence (as "when it rained" or "they went inside" in the sentence "when it rained, they went inside")

claus·tro·pho·bia \ˌklò-strə-'fō-bē-ə\ *n* : abnormal fear of being in closed or narrow spaces — **claus·tro·pho·bic** \-'fō-bik\ *adj*

clav·i·chord \'klav-ə-ˌkò(ə)rd\ *n* : an early keyboard instrument in use before the piano

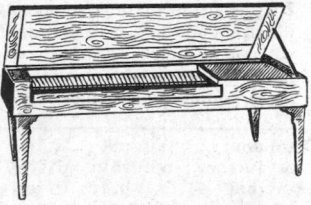

clavichord

clav·i·cle \'klav-i-kəl\ *n* : a bone of the shoulder that joins the breastbone and the shoulder blade — called also *collarbone*

¹claw \'klò\ *n* **1 a** : a sharp usually slender and curved nail on the toe of an animal (as a cat or bird) **b** : a sharp curved extension especially if at the end of a limb (as of an insect); *also* : one of the pincerlike organs on some limbs of arthropods (as a lobster or scorpion) **2** : something that resembles a claw in shape or use — **clawed** \'klòd\ *adj* — **claw·like** \'klò-ˌlīk\ *adj*

²claw *vb* : to scratch, seize, or dig with or as if with claws

clay \'klā\ *n* **1** : an earthy material that is sticky and easily molded when wet and hard when baked **2** : a plastic substance used like clay for modeling

clay·ey \'klā-ē\ *adj* **clay·i·er; -est** : resembling clay or containing much clay ⟨a *clayey* soil⟩

clay pigeon *n* : a saucer-shaped object made of baked clay and used as a target in trapshooting

¹clean \'klēn\ *adj* **1** : free from dirt or pollution ⟨*clean* clothes⟩ **2** : free of objectionable behavior or language ⟨led a *clean* life⟩ ⟨a *clean* joke⟩ **3** : being such to the fullest degree : COMPLETE ⟨made a *clean* sweep⟩ **4** : being precise or distinct : TRIM ⟨a ship with *clean* lines⟩ ⟨a *clean* writing style⟩ **5** : ¹SMOOTH 1a ⟨a sharp knife makes a *clean* cut⟩ — **clean·ness** \'klēn-nəs\ *n*

²clean *adv* **1 a** : so as to clean ⟨a new broom sweeps *clean*⟩ **b** : in a clean manner ⟨fight *clean*⟩ **2** : all the way ⟨trout leaping *clean* out of the water⟩

³clean *vb* **1** : to make or become clean ⟨*clean* your room⟩ ⟨*cleaned* up for supper⟩ **2** : to take or use up the contents or resources of ⟨tourists *cleaned* out the shops⟩

clean–cut \'klēn-'kət\ *adj* : neat and wholesome looking

clean·er \'klē-nər\ *n* **1** : one whose work is cleaning **2** : a substance used for cleaning **3** : a device or machine for cleaning

¹clean·ly \'klēn-lē\ *adv* : in a clean manner

²clean·ly \'klen-lē\ *adj* **clean·li·er; -est** **1** : careful to keep clean ⟨a *cleanly* animal⟩ **2** : being kept clean by habit ⟨*cleanly* surroundings⟩ — **clean·li·ness** *n*

cleanse \'klenz\ *vb* **cleansed; cleans·ing** : to make clean

cleans·er \'klen-zər\ *n* : a substance (as a scouring powder or cold cream) used for cleaning

clean·up \'klē-ˌnəp\ *n* : an act or instance of cleaning ⟨helped with the *cleanup* after the meal⟩

¹clear \'kli(ə)r\ *adj* **1 a** : shining brightly : LUMINOUS ⟨*clear* sunlight⟩ **b** : free from clouds, haze, dust, or mist ⟨a *clear* day⟩ **c** : free from trouble : SERENE ⟨a *clear* gaze⟩ **2 a** : free of blemishes ⟨a *clear* complexion⟩ **b** : easily seen through : TRANSPARENT ⟨*clear* glass⟩ **3** : easily heard, seen, or understood ⟨a *clear* voice⟩ ⟨the meaning was *clear*⟩ **4** : free from doubt : SURE ⟨a *clear* understanding of the issue⟩ **5** : free from guilt : INNOCENT ⟨a *clear* conscience⟩ **6** : free from restriction or entanglement ⟨a *clear* profit⟩ ⟨the coast is *clear*⟩ [Middle English *clere* "clear, bright," from early French *cler* (same meaning), from Latin *clarus* "clear, bright" — related to CLAIRVOYANCE, DECLARE] — **clear·ness** *n*

²clear *adv* **1** : in a clear manner ⟨shout loud and *clear*⟩ **2** : all the way : COMPLETELY ⟨can see *clear* to the mountains⟩ ⟨the hole goes *clear* through⟩

³clear *vb* **1 a** : to make or become clear ⟨*clear* the water by filtering⟩ ⟨the sky is *clearing*⟩ **b** : to go away : VANISH ⟨clouds *cleared* away after the rain⟩ **2** : to free from blame ⟨*cleared* my name⟩ **3** : to make understandable : EXPLAIN ⟨*cleared* the matter up for me⟩ **4 a** : to free from things blocking ⟨*clear* land for crops⟩ ⟨*clear* a path⟩ **b** : to remove stored or displayed data from (as a computer or calculator) **5** : to give or get approval ⟨the proposal *cleared* the committee⟩ **6** : to pay in full : SETTLE ⟨*clear* an account⟩ **7** : to go through customs **8** : ⁴NET ⟨*cleared* a profit⟩ **9** : to get rid of : REMOVE ⟨*clear* the dishes from the table⟩ **10** : to go over or by without

touching ⟨*cleared* the fence⟩ — **clear·able** \-ə-bəl\ *adj* —
clear·er \-ər\ *n* — **clear the air** : to remove tension or
confusion ⟨*cleared the air* by discussing their differences⟩
⁴**clear** *n* : a clear space or part — **in the clear** **1** : free of
something blocking **2** : free from suspicion or guilt
clear·ance \'klir-ən(t)s\ *n* **1 a** : an act or process of clearing **b** : the act of clearing a ship at the customhouse **c**
: the papers showing that a ship has cleared **d** : authorization for an airplane to proceed **2** : a sale to clear out
stock **3** : the distance by which one object keeps from
hitting or touching another or the clear space between them
clear–cut \'kli(ə)r-'kət\ *adj* : free from doubt or uncertainty : DEFINITE ⟨a *clear-cut* victory⟩
clear·head·ed \-'hed-əd\ *adj* : able to think clearly
clear·ing \'kli(ə)r-iŋ\ *n* **1** : the act or process of making or
becoming clear **2** : an area of land cleared of wood and brush
clear·ing·house \-ˌhaus\ *n* **1** : an institution run by banks
for the exchanging of checks and claims **2** : a central
agency for collecting and giving out information
clear·ly \'kli(ə)r-lē\ *adv* **1** : in a clear manner ⟨was *clearly*
visible⟩ **2** : without doubt or question ⟨*clearly* something
had to be done⟩
clear off *vb, chiefly British* : to go away : DEPART 1a
clear out *vb* **1** : to go or run away often suddenly or secretly ⟨a horse broke loose and *cleared out*⟩ ⟨*cleared out*
without paying me back⟩ **2** : to drive out or away usually with force ⟨police *cleared out* the demonstrators⟩
clear–sight·ed \'kli(ə)r-'sīt-əd\ *adj* **1** : having good vision
2 : having a clear understanding
cleat \'klēt\ *n* **1** : a wooden
or metal device around
which a rope may be made
fast **2** : a strip or projection fastened on or across
something (as a shoe) to
give strength or a place to
hold or to prevent slipping

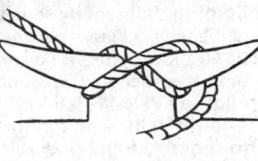

cleat 1

cleav·age \'klē-vij\ *n* **1**
: the quality of a crystal-
lized substance or rock of splitting in definite directions
2 : the action of cleaving : the state of being cleaved **3**
: the series of mitotic cell divisions of a fertilized egg that
changes the single cell into a many-celled embryo
¹**cleave** \'klēv\ *vb* **cleaved** \'klēvd\ *or* **clove** \'klōv\;
cleaved; cleav·ing : to cling to a person or thing closely
[Middle English *clevien* "adhere," from Old English *clifian*
"adhere"]
²**cleave** *vb* **cleaved** \'klēvd\ *also* **cleft** \'kleft\ *or* **clove**
\'klōv\; **cleaved** *also* **cleft** *or* **clo·ven** \'klō-vən\; **cleaving** : to split by or as if by a cutting blow ⟨the bow of the
ship *cleaving* the water⟩ [Middle English *cleven* "divide,"
from Old English *clēofan* "divide"]
cleav·er \'klē-vər\ *n* : a heavy knife with a wide blade
clef \'klef\ *n* : a sign placed on the staff in writing music to
show what pitch is represented by each line and space
¹**cleft** \'kleft\ *n* **1** : a space or opening made by splitting
: CREVICE **2** : a hollow resembling a cleft
²**cleft** *adj* : partially split or divided ⟨a *cleft* wood⟩
cleft lip *n* : one or more splits in the upper lip that occur
as a birth defect
cleft palate *n* : a split in the roof of the mouth that occurs
as a birth defect
clem·a·tis \'klem-ət-əs, kli-'mat-əs\ *n* : a vine or herb related to the buttercups that has leaves with three leaflets
and is widely grown for its showy usually white, red, pink,
or purple flowers
clem·en·cy \'klem-ən-sē\ *n, pl* **-cies** **1** : disposition to be
merciful **2** : an act or instance of mercy **synonyms** see
MERCY
clem·ent \'klem-ənt\ *adj* **1** : inclined to be merciful : LE-
NIENT ⟨a *clement* judge⟩ **2** : not too hot or too cold
: MILD ⟨*clement* weather⟩ — **clem·ent·ly** *adv*

clench \'klench\ *vb* **1** : to hold fast : CLUTCH **2** : to set or
close tightly ⟨*clench* one's teeth⟩ ⟨*clench* one's fist⟩
clere·sto·ry \'kli(ə)r-ˌstōr-
ē, -ˌstȯr-\ *n, pl* **-ries** : an
outside wall of a room or
building that rises above a
roof next to it and con-
tains windows
cler·gy \'klər-jē\ *n, pl* **cler-
gies** : the group of religious officials (as priests,
ministers, or rabbis) specially prepared and authorized to conduct religious
services
cler·gy·man \'klər-ji-mən\
n : a member of the clergy
cler·gy·per·son \-ˌpər-sᵊn\
n : a member of the clergy
cler·gy·wom·an \-ˌwum-
ən\ *n* : a woman who is a
member of the clergy

clerestory

cler·ic \'kler-ik\ *n* : a member of the clergy
cler·i·cal \'kler-i-kəl\ *adj* **1** : of, relating to, or characteristic of the clergy **2** : of or relating to a clerk or office
worker — **cler·i·cal·ly** \-i-k(ə-)lē\ *adv*
clerical collar *n* : a narrow stiffly upright white collar
worn by members of the clergy
¹**clerk** \'klərk\ *n* **1** : a person whose job is to keep records
and accounts ⟨town *clerk*⟩ ⟨a stock *clerk*⟩ **2** : a salesperson in a store
²**clerk** *vb* : to act or work as a clerk
clev·er \'klev-ər\ *adj* **1** : showing skill especially in using
one's hands ⟨*clever* fingers⟩ **2** : quick in learning ⟨a *clever*
pupil⟩ **3** : showing wit or imagination ⟨a *clever* idea⟩ **synonyms** see INTELLIGENT — **clev·er·ish** \-(ə-)rish\ *adj* —
clev·er·ly \-ər-lē\ *adv* — **clev·er·ness** \-ər-nəs\ *n*
¹**clew** \'klü\ *n* **1** : ¹CLUE **2** : a metal loop attached to the
lower corner of a sail
²**clew** *vb* **1** : ²CLUE **2** : to haul (a sail) up or down by ropes
through the clews
cli·ché \klē-'shā, 'klē-ˌshā, kli-'shā\ *n* : a phrase or expression used so often that it becomes stale; *also* : the idea
expressed by it [French, literally, "metal printing plate"]
¹**click** \'klik\ *vb* **1** : to make or cause to make a click **2 a**
: to fit together ⟨they did not *click* as friends⟩ **b** : to work
smoothly **3** : SUCCEED 2 ⟨the idea *clicked*⟩ **4** : to select
by pressing a button on a control device (as a computer
mouse) ⟨*click* on the icon⟩
²**click** *n* **1** : a slight sharp sound **2** : an instance of clicking
⟨a mouse *click*⟩
click beetle *n* : any of a family of beetles that are able
when turned over to flip into the air by a sudden movement that produces a distinct click
click·er \'klik-ər\ *n* : REMOTE CONTROL 2
cli·ent \'klī-ənt\ *n* **1** : a person who uses the professional
advice or services of another **2** : CUSTOMER 1
cli·en·tele \ˌklī-ən-'tel\ *n* : a group of clients
cliff \'klif\ *n* : a high steep surface of rock, earth, or ice
cli·mac·tic \klī-'mak-tik, klə-\ *adj* : of, relating to, or being a climax ⟨the movie's *climactic* scene⟩
cli·mate \'klī-mət\ *n* **1 a** : a region with specified weather
conditions **b** : the average weather conditions of a particular place or region over a period of years **2** : the
usual or most widespread mood or conditions ⟨a *climate*
of fear⟩ — **cli·mat·ic** \klī-'mat-ik, klə-\ *adj*

\ə\ **abut**	\au̇\ **out**	\i\ **tip**	\ȯ\ **saw**	\u̇\ **foot**
\ər\ **further**	\ch\ **chin**	\ī\ **life**	\ȯi\ **coin**	\y\ **yet**
\a\ **mat**	\e\ **pet**	\j\ **job**	\th\ **thin**	\yü\ **few**
\ā\ **take**	\ē\ **easy**	\ŋ\ **sing**	\t͟h\ **this**	\yu̇\ **cure**
\ä\ **cot, cart**	\g\ **go**	\ō\ **bone**	\ü\ **food**	\zh\ **vision**

Word History If you stand at the equator and look up at the sky, the celestial pole (the point in the sky directly above earth's North and South Poles) lies on the horizon. As you move northward, the celestial pole gradually rises above the horizon, so that the sky is in effect tilted. This tilt or inclination was called by the ancient Greeks *klima* (literally, "slope," "inclination"). Because the angle of inclination is determined by your latitude on earth, *klima* came to mean "latitude," and the earth was divided into seven latitudinal regions, called *klimata* (the plural of *klima*). This word was borrowed into modern European languages as *clime* or *climate*, and the weather characteristic of a particular region was also called *climate*. [Middle English *climat* "climate," from Latin *climat-, clima* (same meaning), from Greek *klimat-, klima* "slope, latitude, climate," from *klinein* "to lean, recline" — related to CLIMAX, CLINIC]

cli·ma·tol·o·gy \ˌklī-mə-ˈtäl-ə-jē\ *n* : a science that deals with climates — **cli·ma·tol·o·gist** \-jəst\ *n*

¹cli·max \ˈklī-ˌmaks\ *n* **1 a** : the highest point ⟨the storm had reached its *climax*⟩ **b** : the point of highest dramatic interest or a major turning point in the action (as of a play) **c** : ORGASM **2** : a relatively stable ecological stage or community especially when it is the final one in a series of ecological stages or communities [from Latin *climax* "arrangement of words or phrases in increasing forcefulness," from Greek *klimax* "ladder," from *klinein* "to lean, recline" — related to CLIMATE, CLINIC]

²climax *vb* : to come or bring to a climax

¹climb \ˈklīm\ *vb* **1 a** : to rise gradually to a higher point ⟨*climb* from poverty to wealth⟩ **b** : to slope upward ⟨the road *climbs* steeply to the summit⟩ **2 a** : to go up or down often with the help of the hands in holding or pulling **b** : to go upward in growing (as by winding around something) ⟨a *climbing* vine⟩ — **climb·able** \ˈklī-mə-bəl\ *adj* — **climb·er** \-mər\ *n*

²climb *n* **1** : a place where climbing is necessary **2** : the act of climbing

clime \ˈklīm\ *n* : CLIMATE 1a

¹clinch \ˈklinch\ *vb* **1 a** : to turn over or flatten the end of something sticking out ⟨*clinch* a nail⟩ **b** : to fasten by clinching **2 a** : to make final : SETTLE ⟨the evidence *clinched* the case⟩ **b** : to assure the winning of ⟨a touchdown that *clinched* the game⟩

²clinch *n* **1** : a fastening by means of a clinched nail, rivet, or bolt **2** : the clinched part of a nail, bolt, or rivet

clinch·er \ˈklin-chər\ *n* : one that clinches; *esp* : a decisive fact or argument

cling \ˈkliŋ\ *vb* **clung** \ˈkləŋ\; **cling·ing** \ˈkliŋ-iŋ\ **1** : to stick to as if glued **2** : to hold or hold on tightly ⟨*clung* desperately to the ladder⟩ **3** : to remain close : be dependent ⟨*clings* to the family⟩

cling peach *n* : a clingstone peach

cling·stone \ˈkliŋ-ˌstōn\ *n* : a fruit (as a peach) whose flesh sticks strongly to the pit

clin·ic \ˈklin-ik\ *n* **1** : a class of medical instruction in which patients are examined and discussed **2** : a group meeting for teaching a certain skill and working on individual problems ⟨a reading *clinic*⟩ **3** : a place for the treatment of people needing medical help who do not stay overnight [from French *clinique* "medical instruction at a hospital bed," from Greek *klinikē* "medical practice at a sickbed," derived from *klinē* "bed," from *klinein* "to lean, recline" — related to CLIMATE, CLIMAX]

clin·i·cal \ˈklin-i-kəl\ *adj* **1** : of, relating to, or conducted in or as if in a clinic ⟨*clinical* examination⟩ **2** : involving or based on direct observation of the patient ⟨*clinical* studies⟩ — **clin·i·cal·ly** \-i-k(ə-)lē\ *adv*

clinical thermometer *n* : a thermometer used to measure body temperature that continues to show the highest temperature reached by a column of liquid until the thermometer is reset by shaking

clink \ˈkliŋk\ *vb* : to make or cause to make a slight sharp short sound like that of metal being struck ⟨glasses *clinked*⟩ — **clink** *n*

clin·ker \ˈkliŋ-kər\ *n* : a mass of stony matter fused together (as in a furnace) : SLAG

cli·nom·e·ter \klī-ˈnäm-ət-ər\ *n* : an instrument for measuring angles of elevation or slope

¹clip \ˈklip\ *vb* **clipped; clip·ping** : to fasten with a clip ⟨*clip* the papers together⟩ [Old English *clyppan* "to clasp"]

²clip *n* **1** : a device that grips, clasps, or hooks **2** : a device for loading cartridges into a firearm; *also* : MAGAZINE 4a **3** : a piece of jewelry held by a clip

³clip *vb* **clipped; clip·ping 1** : to cut or cut off with or as if with shears ⟨*clip* a hedge⟩ ⟨*clip* out a news item⟩ **2** : to cut off or trim the hair or wool of ⟨have the dog *clipped*⟩ [Middle English *clippen* "to cut," of Norse origin]

⁴clip *n* **1** : a two-bladed instrument for cutting especially the nails **2** : a section of filmed, videotaped, or recorded material **3** : an act of clipping **4** : a sharp blow **5** : a rapid pace ⟨move along at a good *clip*⟩

clip art *n* : ready-made illustrations sold in books or as software from which they may be taken for use in a printed work

clip·board \ˈklip-ˌbō(ə)rd, -ˌbȯ(ə)rd\ *n* **1** : a small board with a clip at the top for holding papers **2** : a part of computer memory used to store data temporarily

clip·per \ˈklip-ər\ *n* **1** : one that clips **2** *pl* : a device for clipping ⟨hair *clippers*⟩ **3** : a fast sailing ship with usually three tall masts and large square sails

clip·ping \ˈklip-iŋ\ *n* : something cut out or off ⟨a newspaper *clipping*⟩ ⟨grass *clippings*⟩

clique \ˈklēk, ˈklik\ *n* : a small group of people who spend time together and are not friendly to other people — **cliqu·ey** \ˈklē-kē, ˈkli-\ *adj*

cli·to·ris \ˈklit-ə-rəs, kli-ˈtȯr-əs\ *n, pl* **cli·to·ris·es** *also* **cli·to·ri·des** \kli-ˈtȯr-ə-ˌdēz\ : a small structure in the sex organs of the female mammal that corresponds to the penis in the male — **cli·to·ral** \ˈklit-ə-rəl\ *adj*

clo·aca \klō-ˈā-kə\ *n, pl* **clo·a·cae** \-ˌkē, -ˌsē\ : a chamber into which the intestinal, urinary, and reproductive canals empty in birds, reptiles, amphibians, and some fishes; *also* : a chamber like this in an invertebrate animal that serves the same purpose — **clo·acal** \-ˈā-kəl\ *adj*

¹cloak \ˈklōk\ *n* **1** : a long loose outer garment **2** : something that conceals or covers ⟨a *cloak* of secrecy surrounded the talks⟩ [Middle English *cloke* "cloak," from early French *cloque* "cloak, bell," so named because a cloak resembled a bell in shape — related to CLOCK]

²cloak *vb* : to cover or hide with a cloak

cloak·room \ˈklō-ˌkrüm, -ˌkru̇m\ *n* : CHECKROOM

clob·ber \ˈkläb-ər\ *vb* **1** : to hit with force **2** : to defeat by a wide margin

¹clock \ˈkläk\ *n* **1** : a device for measuring or telling the time and especially one not meant to be worn or carried about by a person **2** : a registering device with a dial that is attached to a machine to measure or record what it is doing **3** : a device (as in a computer) that sends out signals at regular spaces of time so that other events can happen in the correct order [Middle English *clok* "clock," from early Dutch *clocke* "bell, clock," from early French *cloque* "bell" or Latin *clocca* "bell"; of Celtic origin — related to CLOAK] — **against the clock** : with or within a set time ⟨working *against the clock*⟩ — **around the clock** *also* **round the clock 1** : continuously for 24 hours : day and night continuously **2** : without relaxing or paying attention to time

²clock *vb* **1** : to time (as a person or a piece of work) by a timing device **2** : to show (as time or speed) on a recording device ⟨he *clocked* in late⟩

clock radio *n* : a clock and radio combined in which the clock can be set to turn on the radio at a certain time

clock·wise \'kläk-ˌwīz\ *adv or adj* : in the direction in which the hands of a clock turn

clock·work \'kläk-ˌwərk\ *n* : machinery (as in a mechanical toy) containing a set of small cogwheels

clod \'kläd\ *n* **1** : a lump or mass especially of earth or clay **2** : a person who is dull or not sensitive : OAF — **clod·dish** \'kläd-ish\ *adj* — **clod·dy** \'kläd-ē\ *adj*

clod·hop·per \'kläd-ˌhäp-ər\ *n* **1** : a person who is living or raised in the country **2** : a large heavy shoe

¹clog \'kläg, 'klȯg\ *n* **1** : something that hinders or holds back ⟨a *clog* in the drain⟩ **2** : a shoe or sandal having a thick usually wooden sole

²clog *vb* **clogged; clog·ging 1** : to get in the way of **2** : to block passage through **3** : to fill or become filled beyond capacity ⟨heavy traffic *clogged* the roads⟩

clog dance *n* : a dance in which the dancers wear clogs and beat out a rhythm on the floor — **clog dancer** *n* — **clog dancing** *n*

¹clois·ter \'klȯi-stər\ *n* **1 a** : MONASTERY, CONVENT **b** : monastic life **2** : a covered usually arched passage along or around a court

²cloister *vb* **1** : to shut away from the world in or as if in a cloister ⟨leads a *cloistered* life⟩ **2** : to surround with a cloister ⟨*cloistered* gardens⟩

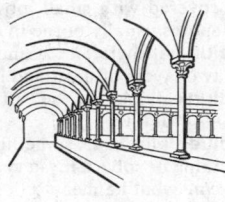

¹cloister 2

clomp \'klämp, 'klȯmp\ *vb* : ²CLUMP 1

¹clone \'klōn\ *n* **1** : the whole collection of offspring produced asexually from an individual (as a plant increased by grafting) **2** : an individual grown from a single body cell of its parent and having the same genes as its parent — **clon·al** \'klōn-ᵊl\ *adj*

²clone *vb* **cloned; clon·ing** : to make a clone from

clop \'kläp\ *n* : a sound like that of a hoof or wooden shoe against pavement — **clop** *vb*

¹close \'klōz\ *vb* **closed; clos·ing 1 a** : to move so as to prevent passage through something ⟨*close* the gate⟩ **b** : to block against passage ⟨*close* a street⟩ **2** : to stop the operations of ⟨*close* school early⟩ — often used with *down* **3** : to bring or come to an end or conclusion ⟨*close* a deal⟩ ⟨the meeting *closed* with a song⟩ ⟨*close* the computer program⟩ **4** : to bring together the parts or edges of ⟨a *closed* fist⟩ ⟨*close* the book⟩ **5 a** : to draw near ⟨the second-place runner was *closing* fast⟩ **b** : to engage in a struggle at close quarters ⟨*close* with the enemy⟩ — **clos·er** *n*

²close \'klōz\ *n* : the point at which something ends

³close \'klōs\ *n* : an enclosed area

⁴close \'klōs\ *adj* **clos·er; clos·est 1** : having no openings : CLOSED **2 a** : hidden from sight **b** : not open or frank : SECRETIVE **3** : RIGOROUS 1 ⟨keep *close* watch⟩ **4** : hot and stuffy **5** : not generous : STINGY ⟨*close* with money⟩ **6** : having little space between items or units ⟨flying in *close* formation⟩ **7** : fitting tightly or exactly **8** : very short or near the surface ⟨a *close* haircut⟩ **9** : being near in time, space, effect, or degree **10** : having a strong liking each one for the other ⟨a *close* friend⟩ **11** : very precise and attentive to details ⟨*close* measurements⟩ ⟨a *close* observer⟩ **12** : decided by a narrow margin ⟨a *close* race⟩ — **close·ly** *adv* — **close·ness** *n*

⁵close \'klōs\ *adv* : in a close position or manner

close call *n* : a narrow escape

closed \'klōzd\ *adj* **1 a** : not open : ENCLOSED **b** : made up entirely of closed tubes or vessels ⟨a *closed* circulatory system⟩ **2** : formed by a line that returns to its starting point ⟨a *closed* curve⟩ **3** : having elements that when a mathematical operation (as addition) is performed on them produce only other elements of the same set ⟨the set of whole numbers is *closed* under addition⟩ **4** : not ad-

mitting or not easily admitting new members ⟨a *closed* meeting⟩ ⟨a *closed* society⟩

closed–cir·cuit \'klōz(d)-ˈsər-kət\ *n* : a television installation in which the signal is sent by wire to a limited number of receivers

close·fist·ed \'klōs-ˈfis-təd\ *adj* : STINGY 1

close in \(ˈ)klō-ˈzin\ *vb* : to gather in close all around with an oppressing effect ⟨despair *closed in* on her⟩

close–knit \'klō-ˈsnit\ *adj* : bound together by feelings of very close association ⟨a *close-knit* family⟩

close·mouthed \-ˈmauҭhd, -ˈmautht\ *adj* : not saying very much

close·out \'klōz-ˌaut\ *n* : a sale of leftover merchandise

¹clos·et \'kläz-ət\ *n* **1** : a small private room **2** : a cabinet or small room for china, household utensils, or clothing

²closet *vb* **1** : to shut up in or as if in a closet **2** : to take into a private room for an interview

close–up \'klōs-ˌəp\ *n* : a photograph or movie shot taken at close range

clos·ing \'klō-zin\ *n* : a concluding part

clo·sure \'klō-zhər\ *n* **1 a** : an act of closing **b** : the condition of being closed **2** : something that closes ⟨a pocket with zipper *closure*⟩ **3** : the property of being closed under a mathematical operation ⟨the set of whole numbers does not have *closure* under division⟩

¹clot \'klät\ *n* : a mass or lump made by a liquid (as blood) that thickens and sticks together

²clot *vb* **clot·ted; clot·ting** : to become or cause to become a clot : form clots

cloth \'klȯth\ *n, pl* **cloths** \'klȯthz, 'klȯths\ **1** : a woven or knitted material (as of cotton or nylon) **2** : a piece of cloth used for a particular purpose ⟨a polishing *cloth*⟩ **3** : TABLECLOTH

clothe \'klōth\ *vb* **clothed** *or* **clad** \'klad\; **cloth·ing 1 a** : to cover with or as if with clothing : DRESS **b** : to provide with clothes **2** : to express in a certain way ⟨*clothe* your thoughts clearly⟩

clothes \'klō(th)z\ *n pl* **1** : CLOTHING 1 **2** : BEDCLOTHES

clothes·horse \'klō(th)z-ˌhȯrs\ *n* : a person who dresses well enough to be noticed

clothes·line \-ˌlīn\ *n* : a line (as of cord) on which clothes may be hung to dry

clothes moth *n* : any of several small moths whose caterpillars eat wool, fur, or feathers

clothes·pin \'klō(th)z-ˌpin\ *n* : a peg (as of wood) with the lower part slit or a clamp for holding clothes in place on a line

clothes·press \-ˌpres\ *n* : something (as a tall piece of furniture) in which clothes may be hung

cloth·ier \'klȯth-yər, 'klō-thē-ər\ *n* : a person who makes or sells cloth or clothing

cloth·ing \'klō-thiŋ\ *n* **1** : covering for the human body **2** : something that covers or conceals

¹cloud \'klaud\ *n* **1 a** : a visible mass of particles of water or ice in the form of fog, mist, or haze usually high in the air **2 a** : a usually visible mass of tiny particles in the

¹cloud 1: *1* cirrus, *2* cirrostratus, *3* cirrocumulus, *4* altostratus, *5* stratocumulus, *6* nimbostratus, *7* cumulus, *8* cumulonimbus, *9* stratus

\ə\ **abut**	\au\ **out**	\i\ **tip**	\ȯ\ **saw**	\u̇\ **foot**
\ər\ **further**	\ch\ **chin**	\ī\ **life**	\ȯi\ **coin**	\y\ **yet**
\a\ **mat**	\e\ **pet**	\j\ **job**	\th\ **thin**	\yü\ **few**
\ā\ **take**	\ē\ **easy**	\ŋ\ **sing**	\th\ **this**	\yu̇\ **cure**
\ä\ **cot, cart**	\g\ **go**	\ō\ **bone**	\ü\ **food**	\zh\ **vision**

air or bits of matter between stars **b** : a group of charged particles (as electrons) **3** : something resembling or thought to be like a cloud ⟨a *cloud* of mosquitoes⟩ ⟨under a *cloud* of suspicion⟩ **4** : something that appears dark or threatening ⟨*clouds* of war⟩ **5** : the computers and connections that support cloud computing ⟨storing files in the *cloud*⟩ — **cloud·less** \-ləs\ *adj*

²**cloud** *vb* **1** : to make or become cloudy **2** : to darken or hide with or as if by a cloud ⟨smog *clouded* our view⟩

cloud·burst \'klaud-ˌbərst\ *n* : a sudden heavy rainfall

cloud chamber *n* : a container of air saturated with water vapor whose sudden cooling reveals the path of an ionizing particle (as an electron) by a trail of visible droplets

cloud computing *n* : the practice of storing regularly used computer data on multiple servers that can be accessed through the Internet

cloud forest *n* : a wet mountain forest of very warm areas that usually has many clouds

cloud·let \'klaud-lət\ *n* : a small cloud

cloudy \'klaud-ē\ *adj* **cloud·i·er; -est** **1** : darkened by gloom or anxiety ⟨a *cloudy* mood⟩ **2** : covered over by clouds ⟨a *cloudy* sky⟩ **3** : dimmed or dulled as if by clouds ⟨a *cloudy* mirror⟩ **4** : uneven in color or texture **5** : having visible material in suspension ⟨the water from the faucet was *cloudy*⟩ — **cloud·i·ly** \'klaud-ᵊl-ē\ *adv* — **cloud·i·ness** \'klaud-ē-nəs\ *n*

clout \'klaut\ *n* **1** : a blow especially with the hand or with a baseball bat **2** : ¹INFLUENCE 1 ⟨political *clout*⟩ — **clout** *vb*

¹**clove** \'klōv\ *n* : one of the small bulbs that grows at the base of the scales of a large bulb ⟨a *clove* of garlic⟩ [Old English *clufu* "clove, bulb"]

²**clove** *past of* CLEAVE

³**clove** *n* : the dried flower bud of a tropical tree related to the myrtle that is used as a spice and is the source of an oil; *also* : this tree [Middle English *clowe* "clove bud," from early French *clou*, shortened form of the phrase *clou de girofle*, literally, "nail of clove," from Latin *clavus* "nail"]

clo·ven \'klō-vən\ *past participle of* CLEAVE

cloven foot *n* : a foot (as of a sheep) that has the front part divided into two parts — **clo·ven–foot·ed** \ˌklō-vən-'fut-əd\ *adj*

cloven hoof *n* : CLOVEN FOOT — **clo·ven–hoofed** \ˌklō-vən-'huft, -'huft, -'huvd, -'huvd\ *adj*

clo·ver \'klō-vər\ *n* : any of a genus of herbs of the legume family that have leaves with three leaflets and flowers in dense heads and that include many plants valuable for forage and as a source of nectar for bees; *also* : any of various related plants

clo·ver·leaf \-ˌlēf\ *n, pl* **-leafs** \-ˌlēfs\ *or* **-leaves** \-ˌlēvz\ : a road plan that resembles a four-leaf clover in shape and is used for passing one highway over another and turning traffic onto connecting roadways which branch only to the right and lead around in a circle to enter the other highway from the right

clover

¹**clown** \'klaun\ *n* **1** : a rude and often stupid person **2** : a performer (as in a play or circus) who usually wears funny clothes and makeup and tries to make people laugh — **clown·ish** \'klau-nish\ *adj* — **clown·ish·ly** *adv* — **clown·ish·ness** *n*

²**clown** *vb* : to act like a clown

cloy \'kloi\ *vb* : to supply with too much of something that was originally pleasing — **cloy·ing·ly** \-iŋ-lē\ *adv*

¹**club** \'kləb\ *n* **1 a** : a heavy usually wooden stick used as a weapon **b** : a stick or bat used for hitting a ball in a game ⟨a golf *club*⟩ **2 a** : a black figure resembling a clo-

ver leaf used to distinguish a suit of playing cards **b** : a card of the suit bearing clubs **3 a** : a group of people associated because of a common interest **b** : the meeting place of a club **c** : NIGHTCLUB

²**club** *vb* **clubbed; club·bing** **1** : to beat or strike with or as if with a club **2** : to unite or combine for a common cause ⟨*club* together to buy a boat⟩

club·foot \'kləb-ˌfut\ *n* : a misshapen foot twisted out of position from birth; *also* : this deformed condition — **club·foot·ed** \- əd\ *adj*

club fungus *n* : any of a group of fungi that have the hyphae divided by partitions and a special cell for forming spores and that include rusts, smuts, and mushrooms

club·house \'kləb-ˌhaus\ *n* **1** : a meeting place (as a house) used by a club for club activities **2** : locker rooms used by an athletic team

club moss *n* : any of an order of low often trailing evergreen plants (as the ground pine) having branching stems covered with small mosslike leaves and reproducing by spores usually borne in club-shaped cones

club sandwich *n* : a sandwich of three slices of bread with two layers of meat and lettuce, tomato, and mayonnaise

cluck \'klək\ *n* : the call of a hen especially to her chicks — **cluck** *vb*

¹**clue** \'klü\ *n* **1** : something that helps a person find something or solve a mystery **2** : IDEA 2, CONCEPTION ⟨had no *clue* what he meant⟩

²**clue** *vb* **clued; clue·ing** *or* **clu·ing** **1** : to provide with a clue **2** : to give information to ⟨*clue* me in on the news⟩

clue·less \'klü-ləs\ *adj* : having or providing no clue

¹**clump** \'kləmp\ *n* **1** : a group of things clustered together ⟨a *clump* of bushes⟩ **2** : a cluster or lump of something **3** : a heavy tramping sound — **clumpy** \'kləm-pē\ *adj*

²**clump** *vb* **1** : to walk or move clumsily and noisily **2** : to form or cause to form clumps

clum·sy \'kləm-zē\ *adj* **clum·si·er; -est** **1 a** : lacking skill or grace in movement ⟨*clumsy* fingers⟩ **b** : showing social awkwardness or a lack of tact ⟨a *clumsy* attempt at a joke⟩ **2** : awkwardly or poorly made : hard to use ⟨a *clumsy* tool⟩ — **clum·si·ly** \-zə-lē\ *adv* — **clum·si·ness** \-zē-nəs\ *n*

clung *past and past participle of* CLING

¹**clus·ter** \'kləs-tər\ *n* : a number of similar things growing, collected, or grouped together : BUNCH ⟨a *cluster* of houses⟩ ⟨a flower *cluster*⟩

²**cluster** *vb* **clus·tered; clus·ter·ing** \-t(ə-)riŋ\ : to grow, collect, or gather in a cluster

¹**clutch** \'kləch\ *vb* **1** : to grip with or as if with the hand or claws : GRASP **2** : to make a grab ⟨*clutch* at a swinging rope⟩ [Old English *clyccan* "to grasp, hold"]

²**clutch** *n* **1 a** : the claws or a hand in the act of grasping **b** : an often cruel or stern power or control ⟨had the enemy in their *clutches*⟩ **2** : a device for gripping an object **3 a** : a coupling used to connect and disconnect a driving and a driven part in machinery **b** : a lever or pedal operating a clutch **4** : a tight or critical situation : PINCH ⟨he came through in the *clutch*⟩

³**clutch** *adj* : done or doing well in a tight or critical situation ⟨a *clutch* play⟩ ⟨a *clutch* player⟩

⁴**clutch** *n* : a nest or batch of eggs or a brood of chicks [altered form of dialect word *cletch* "a hatching, brood"]

¹**clut·ter** \'klət-ər\ *vb* : to fill or cover with a disorderly scattering of things ⟨*clutter* up a room⟩

²**clutter** *n* : a crowded or confused collection

Clydes·dale \'klīdz-ˌdāl\ *n* : any of a breed of heavy draft horses originally from Clydesdale, Scotland, with long silky hair on the legs

cni·dar·i·an \ni-'der-ē-ən\ *n* : COELENTERATE — **cnidari·an** *adj*

co- *prefix* **1** : with : together : joint : jointly ⟨*co*exist⟩ ⟨*co*author⟩ **2** : in or to the same degree ⟨*co*extensive⟩ **3**

: fellow : partner ⟨*co*worker⟩ [derived from Latin *com-* "with, together"]

¹coach \'kōch\ *n* **1 a** : a large usually closed four-wheeled carriage that has a raised seat in front for the driver and is drawn by horses **b** : a railroad passenger car without berths **c** : ¹BUS 1 **d** : a class of passenger air transportation at a lower fare than first class **2 a** : a private tutor **b** : a person who instructs or trains a performer or team ⟨a football *coach*⟩

²coach *vb* : to act as a coach

coach dog *n* : DALMATIAN

coach·man \'kōch-mən\ *n* : a person whose business is driving a coach or carriage

co·ad·ju·tor \ˌkō-ə-'jüt-ər, kō-'aj-ət-ər\ *n* **1** : one who works together with another : ASSISTANT **2** : a bishop assisting a diocesan bishop and often having the right of succession — **coadjutor** *adj*

co·ad·ju·trix \ˌkō-ə-'jü-triks, kō-'aj-ə-ˌtriks\ *n, pl* **co·ad·ju·tri·ces** \ˌkō-ə-'jü-trə-ˌsēz, kō-ˌaj-ə-'trī-ˌsēz\ : a woman who is a coadjutor

co·ag·u·late \kō-'ag-yə-ˌlāt\ *vb* **-lat·ed; -lat·ing** : to become or cause to become thickened into a compact mass : CLOT [from Latin *coagulatus,* past participle of *coagulare* "to curdle," derived from *cogere* "to drive together" — related to ²QUAIL] — **co·ag·u·la·tion** \kō-ˌag-yə-'lā-shən\ *n*

¹coal \'kōl\ *n* **1** : a piece of glowing or charred wood : EMBER **2** : a black or brownish black solid substance that is formed by the partial decay of vegetable matter under the influence of moisture and often increased pressure and temperature within the earth and that is widely used as a fuel

²coal *vb* **1** : to supply with coal **2** : to take in coal

co·alesce \ˌkō-ə-'les\ *vb* **co·alesced; co·alesc·ing** **1** : to grow together ⟨the ends of the broken bones *coalesced*⟩ **2** : to unite into a whole : FUSE **synonyms** see MIX — **co·ales·cence** \-'les-ᵊn(t)s\ *n*

coal gas *n* : gas from coal; *esp* : gas made from bituminous coal and used for heating and lighting

co·ali·tion \ˌkō-ə-'lish-ən\ *n* : a temporary union of persons, parties, or countries for a common purpose

coal oil *n* **1** : petroleum or a refined oil prepared from it **2** : KEROSENE

coal tar *n* : tar obtained from bituminous coal and used especially in making drugs and dyes

coarse \'kō(ə)rs, 'ko(ə)rs\ *adj* **coars·er; coars·est** **1** : of ordinary or poor quality **2** : made up of large parts or particles ⟨*coarse* sand⟩ **3** : being harsh or rough ⟨*coarse* cloth⟩ **4** : not precise or detailed : roughly approximate **5** : crude in taste, manners, or language — **coarse·ly** *adv* — **coars·en** \'kōrs-ᵊn, 'kors-\ *vb* — **coarse·ness** *n*

¹coast \'kōst\ *n* **1** : the land near a shore : SEASHORE **2** : a slide down a slope (as on a sled) **3** : the present area in view ⟨the *coast* is clear⟩ — **coast·al** \'kōst-ᵊl\ *adj*

²coast *vb* **1** : to sail along the shore of **2 a** : to slide downhill by the force of gravity **b** : to move along (as on a bicycle when not pedaling) without applying power **3** : to succeed without special effort ⟨*coasted* through school⟩

coast·er \'kō-stər\ *n* **1** : one that coasts; *esp* : a ship engaged in coastal trade **2 a** : a round tray usually of silver and sometimes on wheels **b** : a shallow container or a plate or a mat to protect a surface **3** : a small vehicle (as a sled or wagon) for coasting

coast guard *n* **1** : a seagoing force for protecting a coast and people and property at sea **2** *usually* **coast·guard** *chiefly British* : COASTGUARDSMAN

coast·guards·man \'kōs(t)-ˌgärdz-mən\ *or* **coast·guard·man** \-ˌgärd-mən\ *n* : a member of a coast guard

coast·line \'kōst-ˌlīn\ *n* : the outline or shape of a coast

coast redwood *n* : REDWOOD

coast·wise \'kōst-ˌwīz\ *adv* : by way of or along the coast — **coastwise** *adj*

¹coat \'kōt\ *n* **1** : an outer garment varying in length and style according to fashion and use **2** : the outer covering (as of fur) of an animal **3** : a layer of material covering a surface ⟨a *coat* of paint⟩ — **coat·ed** \-əd\ *adj*

²coat *vb* : to cover with a coat or covering

co·ati \kə-'wät-ē, kwä-'tē\ *n* : a tropical American mammal related to the raccoon but with a longer body and tail and a long flexible snout

co·a·ti·mun·di \kə-ˌwät-ē-'mən-dē, ˌkwä-, -'mùn-\ *n* : COATI

coat·ing \'kōt-iŋ\ *n* : ¹COAT 3, COVERING ⟨a *coating* of ice on the pond⟩

coat of arms : the heraldic arms belonging to a person, family, or group or a representation of these (as on a shield)

coati

coat of mail : a garment of metal scales or rings worn long ago as armor

coat·room \'kōt-ˌrüm, -ˌrùm\ *n* : CHECKROOM

coat·tail \'kōt-ˌtāl\ *n* **1** : the rear flap of a man's coat **2** *pl* : the influence of a popular movement or person ⟨politicians riding into office on the president's *coattails*⟩

co·au·thor \(')kō-'o-thər\ *n* : an author who works with another author

coax \'kōks\ *vb* **1** : to influence by gentle urging, special attention, or flattering **2** : to get or win by means of gentle urging or flattery ⟨*coaxed* a raise from the boss⟩

co·ax·i·al cable \kō-ˌak-sē-əl-\ *n* : a cable that consists of a tube of electrically conducting material surrounding a central conductor and is used to send telegraph, telephone, and television signals

cob \'käb\ *n* **1** : a male swan **2** : CORNCOB **3** : a short-legged stocky horse

co·bal·a·min \kō-'bal-ə-mən\ *n* : VITAMIN B_{12}

co·balt \'kō-ˌbolt\ *n* : a tough shiny silver-white magnetic metallic element that is found with iron and nickel and is used especially in alloys — see ELEMENT table [from German *Kobalt* "cobalt," an altered form of *Kobold,* literally, "goblin"; so called because its appearance in silver ore was thought to have been the work of goblins who left it in place of silver which they stole]

cobalt chloride *n* : a chloride of cobalt; *esp* : one that has two atoms of chlorine per molecule, is blue when dry and deep pink when combined with water, and is used to indicate humidity

cobalt 60 *n* : a heavy radioactive form of cobalt of the mass number 60 made in nuclear reactors and used to produce gamma rays

¹cob·ble \'käb-əl\ *vb* **cob·bled; cob·bling** \-(ə-)liŋ\ : to make roughly or hastily — often used with *together* or *up*

²cobble *n* : a rounded stone larger than a pebble and smaller than a boulder

cob·bler \'käb-lər\ *n* **1** : a mender or maker of shoes **2** : a deep-dish fruit pie with a thick top crust

cob·ble·stone \'käb-əl-ˌstōn\ *n* : ²COBBLE — **cob·ble·stoned** \-ˌstōnd\ *adj*

CO·BOL *or* **Co·bol** \'kō-ˌbol\ *n* : a computer programming language used especially in business [*c*ommon *b*usiness *o*riented *l*anguage]

\ə\ abut	\au̇\ out	\i\ tip	\o̅\ saw	\u̇\ foot
\ər\ further	\ch\ chin	\ī\ life	\oi\ coin	\y\ yet
\a\ mat	\e\ pet	\j\ job	\th\ thin	\yü\ few
\ā\ take	\ē\ easy	\ŋ\ sing	\th\ this	\yu̇\ cure
\ä\ cot, cart	\g\ go	\ō\ bone	\ü\ food	\zh\ vision

co·bra \'kō-brə\ *n* : any of several poisonous Asian and African snakes that when excited expand the skin of the neck into a hood; *also* : any of several related African snakes

cobra

Word History During the early part of the 16th century, Portuguese traders took control of cities along India's western coast. During this period of contact, the Portuguese became familiar with some of India's animal life. One animal they noticed was a poisonous snake that could expand the skin of its neck to form a hood. The Portuguese called this snake *cobra de capello,* meaning "snake with a hood." The Portuguese name was first borrowed into English in the 17th century. By the 19th century the name had become shortened to *cobra.* [from Portuguese *cobra (de capello)* "snake (with a hood)," from Latin *colubra* "snake"]

cob·web \'käb-ˌweb\ *n* **1** : SPIDERWEB **2** : tangles of the silken threads of a spiderweb usually covered with dirt and dust — **cob·webbed** \-ˌwebd\ *adj* — **cob·web·by** \-ˌweb-ē\ *adj*

co·ca \'kō-kə\ *n* : a South American shrub with leaves that are the source of cocaine; *also* : its dried leaves

co·caine \kō-'kān, 'kō-ˌkān\ *n* : a bitter habit-forming drug obtained from coca leaves and used in medicine to deaden pain and illegally to stimulate the central nervous system

coc·cus \'käk-əs\ *n, pl* **coc·ci** \'käk-ˌ(s)ī, 'käk-ˌ(ˌ)s)ē\ : a bacterium shaped like a sphere — **coc·cal** \'käk-əl\ *adj*

coc·cyx \'käk-siks\ *n, pl* **coc·cy·ges** \'käk-sə-ˌjēz\ *also* **coc·cyx·es** \'käk-sik-səz\ : the bone at the end of the spinal column that is composed of four vertebrae combined into one bone

co·chi·neal \'käch-ə-ˌnēl, 'kō-chə-\ *n* : a red dye consisting of the dried bodies of female cochineal insects

cochineal insect *n* : a small bright red insect that is related to and resembles the mealybug, feeds on cacti, and yields cochineal

co·chlea \'kō-klē-ə, 'käk-lē-\ *n, pl* **co·chle·as** *or* **co·chle·ae** \-klē-ˌē, -lē-ˌē, -ˌī\ : a hollow tube of the inner ear of higher vertebrates that is usually coiled like a snail shell and contains the endings of the nerve which carries information about sound to the brain — **coch·le·ar** \'kō-klē-ər, 'käk-lē-\ *adj*

¹cock \'käk\ *n* **1** : the adult male of a bird and especially the domestic chicken **2** : a device (as a faucet or valve) for controlling the flow of a liquid **3** : the cocked position of the hammer of a firearm ⟨a rifle at half *cock*⟩ [Old English *cocc* "cock, rooster"; probably in imitation of the sound it makes]

²cock *vb* **1 a** : to draw back the hammer of (a gun) in readiness for firing ⟨*cock* a pistol⟩ **b** : to set or draw back in readiness for some action ⟨*cock* your arm to throw⟩ **2** : to turn, tip, or tilt upward or to one side ⟨*cock* one's head⟩

³cock *n* : ²TILT 4, SLANT ⟨a *cock* of the head⟩

⁴cock *n* : a small pile (as of hay) [Middle English *cok* "small pile"]

cock·ade \kä-'kād\ *n* : an ornament (as a rosette) worn on the hat as a badge

cock·a·too \'käk-ə-ˌtü\ *n, pl* **-toos** : any of various large noisy usually

cockatoo

showy chiefly Australasian parrots that have a bunch of feathers on the head

cock·crow \'käk-ˌkrō\ *n* : early morning

cock·er·el \'käk-(ə-)rəl\ *n* : a young male domestic chicken

cock·er spaniel \ˌkäk-ər-\ *n* : any of a breed of small spaniels with long drooping ears and long silky coat

cock·eyed \'käk-ˌīd\ *adj* **1** : having a squinting eye **2 a** : turned or tilted to one side **b** : slightly crazy : FOOLISH

cock·fight \'käk-ˌfīt\ *n* : a fight between roosters usually fitted with metal spurs

¹cock·le \'käk-əl\ *n* : any of several weeds of grain fields [Old English *coccel* "weed"]

²cockle *n* **1** : an edible mollusk with a ribbed two-valved shell **2** : COCKLESHELL [Middle English *cokille* "cockle, cockleshell," from early French *coquille* "shell," from Latin *conchylia* "shells," derived from Greek *konchylion,* literally, "little shell"]

cock·le·bur \'käk-əl-ˌbər, 'käk-\ *n* : any of a genus of plants that have prickly fruits and are related to the thistles; *also* : one of its fruits

cock·le·shell \'käk-əl-ˌshel\ *n* **1 a** : a shell or shell valve of a cockle **b** : a shell (as a scallop) that looks like a cockleshell **2** : a light flimsy boat

cock·ney \'käk-nē\ *n, pl* **cockneys** *often cap* **1** : a native of London and especially of the East End of London **2** : the dialect spoken by the cockneys — **cockney** *adj*

cock·pit \'käk-ˌpit\ *n* : a space or compartment in a usually small vehicle (as a boat, airplane, or automobile) from which it is steered, piloted, or driven

cock·roach \-ˌrōch\ *n* : any of an order of quick-moving insects that have long antennae and leathery forewings, are mainly nocturnal, and include pests of human dwellings

cock·sure \'käk-'shu̇(ə)r\ *adj* **1** : perfectly sure : CERTAIN **2** : COCKY 1

cock·tail \'käk-ˌtāl\ *n* **1** : an iced drink of distilled liquor mixed with flavoring ingredients **2** : an appetizer (as tomato juice) served as a first course at a meal

cocky \'käk-ē\ *adj* **cock·i·er; -est** **1** : being too sure of oneself **2** : JAUNTY — **cock·i·ly** \'käk-ə-lē\ *adv* — **cock·i·ness** \'käk-ē-nəs\ *n*

co·coa \'kō-kō\ *n* **1** : a cacao tree **2 a** : powdered ground cacao beans from which some of the fat has been removed **b** : a beverage made from heating cocoa with water or milk

cocoa butter *n* : a pale fat obtained from cacao beans

co·co·nut \'kō-kə-(ˌ)nət\ *n* : the large egg-shaped husk-covered fruit of the coconut palm

coconut oil *n* : a nearly colorless oil or soft white fat that comes from coconuts and is used especially in soaps and foods

coconut palm *n* : a tall palm that grows along tropical coasts and produces coconuts

co·coon \kə-'kün\ *n* **1** : an envelope usually of silk which the larva of some insects (as moths) forms about itself and in which it passes the pupa stage — compare CHRYSALIS **2** : a covering suggesting a cocoon

cod \'käd\ *n, pl* **cod** *also* **cods** : a soft-finned fish of the colder parts of the North Atlantic that is a major food fish; *also* : any of several related fishes

co·da \'kōd-ə\ *n* : a closing section in a musical composition [Italian, literally, "tail," from Latin *coda, cauda* "tail" — related to COWARD, ³CUE, QUEUE; see *Word History* at COWARD, QUEUE]

coconut palm

cod·dle \'käd-ᵊl\ *vb* **cod·dled; cod·dling** \'käd-liŋ, -ᵊl-iŋ\ **1 :** to cook slowly in water below the boiling point ⟨*coddle* eggs⟩ **2 :** to treat with extreme care or kindness **:** PAMPER

¹code \'kōd\ *n* **1 :** a collection of laws arranged in some orderly way ⟨criminal *code*⟩ **2 :** a system of principles or rules ⟨moral *code*⟩ **3 a :** a system of signals for communicating **b :** a system of symbols (as letters or numbers) used to represent assigned and often secret meanings **4 :** GENETIC CODE **5 :** a set of instructions for a computer

²code *vb* **cod·ed; cod·ing :** to put into the form or symbols of a code — **cod·er** *n*

co·deine \'kō-ˌdēn, 'kōd-ē-ən\ *n* **:** a drug that is obtained from opium, is weaker than morphine, and is used as a pain reliever and in cough remedies

cod·fish \'käd-ˌfish\ *n* **:** COD

cod·ger \'käj-ər\ *n* **:** an odd or cranky fellow

cod·i·fy \'käd-ə-ˌfī, 'kōd-\ *vb* **-fied; -fy·ing :** to arrange (as a collection of laws) in an orderly form — **cod·i·fi·ca·tion** \ˌkäd-ə-fə-'kā-shən, ˌkōd-\ *n*

cod·ling moth \'käd-liŋ-\ *n* **:** a small moth whose larva lives in fruit and nuts and is a serious pest of orchard-grown crops (as apples, pears, plums, and walnuts)

cod-liver oil *n* **:** an oil obtained from the liver of the cod and closely related fishes and used as a source of vitamins A and D

¹co·ed \'kō-ˌed\ *n* **:** a female student in a coeducational institution

²coed *adj* **1 :** COEDUCATIONAL **2 :** open to or used by both men and women

co·ed·u·ca·tion·al \ˌ(ˌ)kō-ˌej-ə-'kā-shnəl, -shən-ᵊl\ *adj* **:** having both male and female students

co·ef·fi·cient \ˌkō-ə-'fish-ənt\ *n* **1 :** a number or symbol by which another number or symbol (as a mathematical variable) is multiplied ⟨3 is the *coefficient* of x in the expression $3x$⟩ **2 :** a number that serves as a measure of some property (as of a substance or device) ⟨the metal's *coefficient* of expansion⟩

coel·acanth \'sē-lə-ˌkan(t)th\ *n* **:** a fish or fossil of a group of mostly extinct fishes — **coelacanth** *adj*

coel·en·ter·ate \si-'lent-ə-ˌrāt, -rət\ *n* **:** any of a phylum of invertebrate animals including the corals, sea anemones, sea fans, jellyfishes, and hydras and usually have a body with radial symmetry — called also *cnidarian* — **coelenterate** *adj*

coe·lom \'sē-ləm\ *n* **:** the fluid-filled body cavity of an animal that contains the internal organs (as the heart, lungs, and kidneys)

co·equal \(')kō-'ē-kwəl\ *adj* **:** equal with one another — **co·equal·i·ty** \ˌkō-ē-'kwäl-ət-ē\ *n* — **co·equal·ly** \ˌkō-'ē-kwə-lē\ *adv*

co·erce \kō-'ərs\ *vb* **co·erced; co·erc·ing :** to cause someone to do something by force or threat — **co·er·cion** \-'ər-zhən, -shən\ *n* — **co·er·cive** \-'ər-siv\ *adj*

co·eval \kō-'ē-vəl\ *adj* **:** of the same age or duration — **co·eval** *n*

co·evo·lu·tion \ˌkō-ˌev-ə-'lü-shən, -ˌē-və-\ *n* **:** evolution occurring in two interdependent species (as a flowering plant and a pollinator) in which long-term adaptive changes are influenced by their close interactions

co·ex·ist \ˌkō-ig-'zist\ *vb* **1 :** to exist together or at the same time **2 :** to live in peace with each other — **co·ex·is·tence** \-'zis-tən(t)s\ *n* — **co·ex·is·tent** \-tənt\ *adj*

co·ex·ten·sive \ˌkō-ik-'sten(t)-siv\ *adj* **:** having the same length or boundaries in space or time — **co·ex·ten·sive·ly** *adv*

cof·fee \'kò-fē, 'käf-ē\ *n* **1 :** a drink made from the roasted and ground seeds of a tropical tree or shrub related to the madder **2 :** coffee seeds or a plant producing them **3 :** a cup of coffee ⟨two *coffees*⟩ [from Italian *caffè* "coffee" and Turkish *kahve* "coffee," both from Arabic *qaḥwa* "coffee"]

coffee break *n* **:** a short period of time for rest and refreshments

cof·fee·house \'kò-fē-ˌhaús, 'käf-ē-\ *n* **:** a business that sells coffee and usually other refreshments and that often serves as an informal club for its regular customers

cof·fee·mak·er \-ˌmā-kər\ *n* **:** a utensil or appliance in which coffee is brewed

cof·fee·pot \-ˌpät\ *n* **:** a pot for brewing or serving coffee

coffee table *n* **:** a low table usually placed in front of a sofa

cof·fer \'kò-fər, 'käf-ər\ *n* **1 :** a box used especially to store money and valuables **2 :** TREASURY 1, FUNDS — usually used in plural

cof·fin \'kò-fən\ *n* **:** a box or case to hold a dead body

cog \'käg\ *n* **1 :** a tooth on the rim of a wheel adjusted to fit notches in another wheel or bar and to give or receive motion **2 :** a person whose job is of low rank but still important

co·gen·cy \'kō-jən-sē\ *n* **:** the quality or state of being cogent

co·gent \'kō-jənt\ *adj* **1 :** appealing forcibly to the mind **:** CONVINCING ⟨*cogent* evidence⟩ ⟨a *cogent* argument⟩ **2 :** being to the point **:** PERTINENT ⟨some *cogent* remarks on the situation⟩ — **co·gent·ly** \'kō-jənt-lē\ *adv*

cog·i·tate \'käj-ə-ˌtāt\ *vb* **-tat·ed; -tat·ing :** to think over **:** PONDER — **cog·i·ta·tion** \ˌkäj-ə-'tā-shən\ *n*

co·gnac \'kōn-ˌyak\ *n, often cap* **:** a French brandy [named for *Cognac,* town in France in and near which it is made]

cog·ni·tion \käg-'nish-ən\ *n* **:** the act or process of knowing

cog·ni·tive \'käg-nət-iv\ *adj* **:** of, relating to, or being conscious mental activities (as thinking, reasoning, remembering, imagining, learning words, and using language)

cog·ni·zance \'käg-nə-zən(t)s\ *n* **1 :** particular knowledge ⟨had no *cognizance* of the crime⟩ **2 :** the act or power of fixing one's mind on something **:** NOTICE, HEED ⟨take *cognizance* of what is happening⟩ — **cog·ni·zant** \-zənt\ *adj*

cog·no·men \käg-'nō-mən, 'käg-nə-mən\ *n, pl* **-nomens** *or* **-no·mi·na** \-'näm-ə-nə, -'nō-mə-\ **1 :** a person's last name **:** SURNAME **2 :** ¹NAME 1; *esp* : ¹NICKNAME

cog·wheel \'käg-ˌhwēl, -ˌwēl\ *n* **:** a wheel with cogs

co·hab·it \kō-'hab-ət\ *vb* **:** to live together as or as if husband and wife — **co·hab·i·ta·tion** \kō-ˌhab-ə-'tā-shən\ *n*

co·here \kō-'hi(ə)r\ *vb* **co·hered; co·her·ing 1 a :** to hold together firmly as parts of the same mass **b :** to consist of parts that cohere **2 a :** to become united in principles, relationships, or interests **b :** to be in agreement between parts — **co·her·ence** \-'hir-ən(t)s, -'her-\ *n* — **co·her·ent** \-ənt\ *adj* — **co·her·ent·ly** *adv*

co·he·sion \kō-'hē-zhən\ *n* **1 :** the action or state of sticking together **2 :** molecular attraction by which the particles of a body are united throughout the mass — **co·he·sive** \kō-'hē-siv, -ziv\ *adj* — **co·he·sive·ness** *n*

co·hort \'kō-ˌhòrt\ *n* **1 a :** one of 10 divisions of an ancient Roman legion **b :** a group of warriors or followers **2 :** COMPANION 1, ACCOMPLICE

¹coif \'kòif, *in sense 2 usually* 'kwäf\ *n* **1 :** a close-fitting cap **2 :** COIFFURE

²coif \'kòif, 'kwäf\ *vb* **coiffed** *or* **coifed; coif·fing** *or* **coif·ing :** to cover or dress with a coif

coif·fure \kwä-'fyú(ə)r\ *n* **:** a style or manner of arranging the hair

¹coil \'kòil\ *vb* **1 :** to wind into or lie in loops, rings, or a spiral **2 :** to move in a circular, spiral, or winding direction

\ə\ **abut**	\aú\ **out**	\i\ **tip**	\ò\ **saw**	\ú\ **foot**
\ər\ **further**	\ch\ **chin**	\ī\ **life**	\òi\ **coin**	\y\ **yet**
\a\ **mat**	\e\ **pet**	\j\ **job**	\th\ **thin**	\yü\ **few**
\ā\ **take**	\ē\ **easy**	\ŋ\ **sing**	\th\ **this**	\yú\ **cure**
\ä\ **cot, cart**	\g\ **go**	\ō\ **bone**	\ü\ **food**	\zh\ **vision**

²**coil** *n* **1 a** : a series of loops : SPIRAL **b** : a single loop of a coil **2 a** : a number of turns of wire wound around a core (as of iron) to create a magnetic field for an electromagnet or an induction coil **b** : INDUCTION COIL **3** : a series of connected pipes (as in water-heating apparatus) in rows, layers, or windings

¹**coin** \ˈkȯin\ *n* **1** : a piece of metal put out by a government authority as money **2** : metal money ⟨three dollars in *coin*⟩

²**coin** *vb* **1 a** : to make (a coin) especially by stamping : MINT **b** : to convert (metal) into coins **2** : CREATE, INVENT ⟨*coin* a phrase⟩ — **coin·er** *n*

³**coin** *adj* **1** : of or relating to coins ⟨a *coin* show⟩ **2** : operated by coins ⟨a laundromat's *coin* washers⟩

coin·age \ˈkȯi-nij\ *n* **1** : the act or process of coining **2** : ¹COIN 2 **3** : something (as a word) made up or invented

co·in·cide \ˌkō-ən-ˈsīd\ *vb* **-cid·ed; -cid·ing 1** : to occupy the same place in space or time **2** : to occupy the same positions on a scale **3** : to agree exactly

co·in·ci·dence \kō-ˈin(t)-səd-ən(t)s\ *n* **1** : the act or condition of coinciding **2 a** : two things that happen at the same time by accident but seem to have some connection **b** : either one of these happenings

co·in·ci·dent \kō-ˈin(t)-səd-ənt\ *adj* **1** : of similar nature : HARMONIOUS ⟨a theory *coincident* with the facts⟩ **2** : occupying the same space or time ⟨*coincident* events⟩ — **co·in·ci·dent·ly** *adv*

co·in·ci·den·tal \(ˌ)kō-ˌin(t)-sə-ˈdent-ᵊl\ *adj* **1** : resulting from a coincidence ⟨a *coincidental* resemblance⟩ **2** : occurring or existing at the same time — **co·in·ci·den·tal·ly** \-ˈdent-lē, -ᵊl-ē\ *adv*

coir \ˈkȯi(-ə)r\ *n* : a stiff coarse fiber from the outer husk of a coconut

co·i·tus \ˈkō-ət-əs, kō-ˈēt-\ *n* : SEXUAL INTERCOURSE

¹**coke** \ˈkōk\ *n* : gray lumps of fuel with pores made by heating soft coal in a closed chamber until some of its gases have passed off

²**coke** *n* : COCAINE

Coke \ˈkōk\ *trademark* — used for a cola drink

coke·head \ˈkōk-ˌhed\ *n* : a compulsive user of cocaine

col- — see COM-

co·la \ˈkō-lə\ *n* : a sweet usually caffeinated carbonated soft drink typically colored with caramel and having a flavoring from kola nuts

col·an·der \ˈkəl-ən-dər, ˈkäl-\ *n* : a utensil with small holes for draining food

col·chi·cine \ˈkäl-chə-ˌsēn, ˈkäl-kə-\ *n* : a poisonous substance that is obtained from the corms or seeds of a plant resembling a crocus and that is used on cells to cause changes in chromosome numbers and to produce new varieties of plants

colander

¹**cold** \ˈkōld\ *adj* **1** : having a low temperature or one much below normal ⟨a *cold* day⟩ ⟨a *cold* drink⟩ **2** : lacking warmth of feeling : UNFRIENDLY ⟨a *cold* stare⟩ **3** : suffering or uncomfortable from lack of warmth ⟨they feel *cold*⟩ **4 a** : marked by the loss of normal body heat ⟨*cold* hands⟩ **b** : giving the appearance of being dead : UNCONSCIOUS ⟨passed out *cold*⟩ — **cold·ly** *adv* — **cold·ness** \ˈkōl(d)-nəs\ *n* — **in cold blood** : with planning beforehand : DELIBERATELY ⟨was killed *in cold blood*⟩

²**cold** *n* **1 a** : a condition of low temperature **b** : cold weather **2** : bodily sensation produced by loss or lack of heat : CHILL **3** : a bodily disorder popularly associated with chilling; *esp* : COMMON COLD

cold–blood·ed \ˈkōl(d)-ˈbləd-əd\ *adj* **1** : lacking or showing a lack of natural human feelings ⟨a *cold-blooded* criminal⟩ **2** : having a body temperature not regulated by the body and close to that of the environment **3** : sensitive to cold — **cold–blood·ed·ly** *adv*

cold chisel *n* : a strong steel chisel for chipping and cutting cold metal

cold cream *n* : a soothing and cleansing cosmetic

cold cuts *n pl* : sliced cold cooked meats

cold frame *n* : a usually glass- or plastic-covered frame without artificial heat used to protect plants and seedlings

cold front *n* : an advancing edge of a cold air mass

cold frame

cold shoulder *n* : treatment that is purposely unfriendly — **cold–shoulder** *vb*

cold sore *n* : a group of blisters about or within the mouth caused by a herpes virus — called also *fever blister*

cold sweat *n* : perspiration and chill occurring together and usually associated with fear, pain, or shock

cold war *n* : a struggle over political differences (as of two nations) carried on by methods short of war and usually without breaking off diplomatic relations

cole \ˈkōl\ *n* : any of several closely related crop plants (as broccoli, kale, brussels sprouts, and cabbage) related to the mustards

co·le·op·tera \ˌkō-lē-ˈäp-tə-rə\ *n pl* : insects that are beetles

cole·slaw \ˈkōl-ˌslȯ\ *n* : a salad made of sliced or chopped raw cabbage

co·le·us \ˈkō-lē-əs\ *n* : any of a large genus of herbs related to the mints and often grown for their leaves of various colors

col·ic \ˈkäl-ik\ *n* **1** : sharp sudden pain in the abdomen **2** : a condition marked by periods of prolonged and uncontrollable crying and irritability in an otherwise healthy infant — **col·icky** \-i-kē\ *adj*

col·i·se·um \ˌkäl-ə-ˈsē-əm\ *n* : a large structure (as a stadium) for athletic contests or public entertainment [from the Latin spelling used in the Middle Ages for the *Colosseum*, a great outdoor arena in ancient Rome]

col·lab·o·rate \kə-ˈlab-ə-ˌrāt\ *vb* **-rat·ed; -rat·ing 1** : to work with others (as in writing a book) **2** : to cooperate with an enemy force that has taken over one's country — **col·lab·o·ra·tion** \kə-ˌlab-ə-ˈrā-shən\ *n* — **col·lab·o·ra·tion·ist** \-sh(ə-)nəst\ *n* — **col·lab·o·ra·tor** \kə-ˈlab-ə-ˌrāt-ər\ *n*

col·lage \kə-ˈläzh, kȯ-, kō-\ *n* : a work of art made by gluing pieces of different materials to a flat surface [from French *collage* "gluing," from *coller* "to glue"]

col·la·gen \ˈkäl-ə-jən\ *n* : a protein that occurs in the form of fibers, does not dissolve, is found in connective tissue, and forms glue and gelatin upon boiling with water

¹**col·lapse** \kə-ˈlaps\ *vb* **col·lapsed; col·laps·ing 1** : to fall or shrink together abruptly ⟨a blood vessel that *collapsed*⟩ **2** : to break down completely ⟨the opponent's resistance *collapsed*⟩ **3** : to cave or fall in or give way ⟨the tunnel *collapsed*⟩ **4** : to suddenly lose value or effectiveness ⟨the country's currency *collapsed*⟩ **5** : to break down physically or mentally because of exhaustion or disease **6** : to fold together ⟨a chair that *collapses*⟩ — **col·laps·ible** \kə-ˈlap-sə-bəl\ *adj*

²**collapse** *n* : the act or an instance of collapsing : BREAKDOWN

¹**col·lar** \ˈkäl-ər\ *n* **1 a** : a band, strip, or chain worn around the neck or the neckline of a garment **b** : a part of the harness of draft animals fitted over the shoulders **2** : something (as a ring to hold something in place) resembling a collar — **col·lared** \-ərd\ *adj* — **col·lar·less** \-ər-ləs\ *adj*

²collar *vb* **1 a :** to seize by the collar **b :** to take possession of : GRAB **2 :** to put a collar on

col·lar·bone \'käl-ər-,bōn, ,käl-ər-'bōn\ *n* : CLAVICLE

col·lard \'käl-ərd\ *n* : a kale with smooth leaves that grow at the top of a short thick stalk

¹col·lat·er·al \kə-'lat-ə-rəl, -'la-trəl\ *adj* **1 :** associated but of secondary importance **2 :** descended from common ancestors but not in the same line ⟨cousins are *collateral* relatives⟩ — **col·lat·er·al·ly** \-ə-rə-lē, -trə-lē\ *adv*

²collateral *n* : property (as stocks, bonds, or a mortgage) pledged as security for a loan

col·league \'käl-,ēg\ *n* : an associate in a profession or office

¹col·lect \'käl-ikt *also* -,ekt\ *n* : an opening prayer in the Communion service or the Mass [Middle English *collecte* "prayer," from early French *collecte* (same meaning), from Latin *collecta* "prayer, collect," shortened form of *oratio ad collectam* "prayer upon assembly," derived from earlier *collectus* "collected," derived from *colligere* "to gather together," from *col-, com-* "together" and *legere* "to gather" — related to LEGEND]

²col·lect \kə-'lekt\ *vb* **1 a :** to bring or come together into one body or place **b :** to gather from a number of sources ⟨*collect* stamps⟩ **2 :** to gain or regain control of ⟨*collecting* my thoughts⟩ **3 :** to demand and take payment for ⟨*collect* a bill⟩ **4 :** to form in a heap or mass : ACCUMULATE ⟨junk *collecting* in the attic⟩ [from Latin *collectus* "collected," from *colligere* "to gather together," from *col-, com-* "together" and *legere* "to gather" — related to LEGEND] **synonyms** see GATHER — **col·lect·ible** *or* **col·lect·able** \kə-'lek-tə-bəl\ *adj*

³col·lect \kə-'lekt\ *adv or adj* : to be paid for by the receiver ⟨a *collect* phone call⟩ ⟨call *collect*⟩

col·lect·ed \kə-'lek-təd\ *adj* : being calm and in control of oneself — **col·lect·ed·ly** *adv* — **col·lect·ed·ness** *n*

col·lec·tion \kə-'lek-shən\ *n* **1 :** the act or process of collecting **2 a :** something collected; *esp* : an accumulation of objects gathered for study, comparison, or exhibition or as a hobby **b :** ²SET 7 **3 :** a gathering of money ⟨take up a *collection*⟩

¹col·lec·tive \kə-'lek-tiv\ *adj* **1 :** having to do with a number of persons or things considered as one group ⟨"flock" is a *collective* noun⟩ **2 :** formed by collecting **3 :** of, relating to, or involving all members of a group ⟨the *collective* feelings of the team⟩ ⟨*collective* legal action⟩ **4 :** shared or done by a number of persons as a group ⟨a *collective* effort⟩ — **col·lec·tive·ly** *adv*

²collective *n* **1 :** a collective body : GROUP **2 :** a cooperative unit or organization

collective bargaining *n* : discussion between an employer and union representatives over wages, hours, and working conditions

collective farm *n* : a farm operated by a group; *esp* : one under supervision of the government in a communist country

collective mark *n* : a trademark or a service mark of a group (as a cooperative association)

col·lec·tor \kə-'lek-tər\ *n* **1 :** a person whose job is to collect money due ⟨tax *collector*⟩ ⟨bill *collector*⟩ **2 :** one that makes a collection ⟨stamp *collector*⟩ **3 :** an object or device that collects ⟨the ornament was just a dust *collector*⟩

col·lege \'käl-ij\ *n* **1 :** a building used for an educational or religious purpose **2 a :** a self-governing body of a university offering living quarters and instruction but not granting degrees ⟨Balliol *College* at Oxford⟩ **b :** a school higher than a high school **c :** an independent institution offering a course of general studies leading to a bachelor's degree; *also* : a university division offering this **3 :** an organized body of persons having common interests or duties ⟨the *college* of cardinals⟩

col·le·gian \kə-'lē-jən, -jē-ən\ *n* : a college student

col·le·giate \kə-'lē-jət, -jē-ət\ *adj* **1 :** of or relating to a college **2 :** of, relating to, or characteristic of college students ⟨*collegiate* sports⟩

col·lide \kə-'līd\ *vb* **col·lid·ed; col·lid·ing 1 :** to come together with solid impact ⟨the football players *collided*⟩ **2 :** ¹CLASH 2a ⟨their different outlooks *collided*⟩

col·lie \'käl-ē\ *n* : any of a breed of large dogs developed in Scotland for herding sheep

col·lier \'käl-yər\ *n* **1 :** a coal miner **2 :** a ship for carrying coal

col·liery \'käl-yə-rē\ *n, pl* **-lier·ies :** a coal mine and the buildings connected with it

col·li·mate \'käl-ə-,māt\ *vb* **-mat·ed; -mat·ing :** to make (as rays of light) parallel

collie

col·li·sion \kə-'lizh-ən\ *n* : an act or instance of colliding

col·lo·ca·tion \,käl-ə-'kā-shən\ *n* : the act or result of placing together

col·loid \'käl-,oid\ *n* : a very finely divided substance which is scattered throughout another substance; *also* : a mixture consisting of such a substance together with the substance in which it is scattered (as in smoke, gelatin, or marshmallow) — **col·loi·dal** \kə-'loid-ᵊl, kä-\ *adj*

col·lo·qui·al \kə-'lō-kwē-əl\ *adj* **1 :** used in or suited to familiar and informal conversation ⟨a *colloquial* word⟩ **2 :** using conversational style ⟨a *colloquial* writer⟩ — **col·lo·qui·al·ly** \-kwē-ə-lē\ *adv*

col·lo·qui·al·ism \kə-'lō-kwē-ə-,liz-əm\ *n* **1 :** a colloquial expression **2 :** colloquial style

col·lo·quy \'käl-ə-kwē\ *n, pl* **-quies :** CONVERSATION; *esp* : a formal conversation or conference

col·lu·sion \kə-'lü-zhən\ *n* : secret agreement or cooperation for an illegal or dishonest purpose — **col·lu·sive** \-'lü-siv, -ziv\ *adj*

co·logne \kə-'lōn\ *n* : a liquid similar to perfume but not as strongly scented or as long-lasting [named for *Cologne*, city in Germany where it was first made]

¹co·lon \'kō-lən\ *n* : the part of the large intestine between the cecum and the rectum [from Latin *colon* "part of the intestine," from Greek *kolon* (same meaning)] — **co·lon·ic** \kō-'län-ik\ *adj*

²colon *n* : a punctuation mark : used chiefly to direct attention to what follows (as a list, explanation, quotation, or amplification) [from earlier *colon* "rhythmic unit in verse," from Latin *colon* "part of a poem," from Greek *kōlon* "limb, part of a poem"]

col·o·nel \'kərn-ᵊl\ *n* : a military commissioned officer with a rank just below that of brigadier general [an altered form of earlier *coronel* "colonel," from early French *coronel* (same meaning), from early Italian *colonnello* "colonel, column of soldiers," derived from Latin *columna* "column" — related to COLUMN] — **col·o·nel·cy** \-sē\ *n*

¹co·lo·nial \kə-'lō-nē-əl, -nyəl\ *adj* **1 :** of, relating to, or characteristic of a colony **2** *often cap* : of or relating to the original 13 colonies forming the U.S. **3 :** forming or existing in a colony ⟨*colonial* organisms⟩ **4 :** possessing or composed of colonies ⟨a *colonial* empire⟩

²colonial *n* : COLONIST 1

\ə\ **abut**	\aủ\ **out**	\i\ **tip**	\ȯ\ **saw**	\ủ\ **foot**
\ər\ **further**	\ch\ **chin**	\ī\ **life**	\ȯi\ **coin**	\y\ **yet**
\a\ **mat**	\e\ **pet**	\j\ **job**	\th\ **thin**	\yü\ **few**
\ā\ **take**	\ē\ **easy**	\ŋ\ **sing**	\th\ **this**	\yủ\ **cure**
\ä\ **cot, cart**	\g\ **go**	\ō\ **bone**	\ü\ **food**	\zh\ **vision**

co·lo·nial·ism \kə-'lō-nē-ə-ˌliz-əm, -nyə-ˌliz-\ *n* : control by one nation over a dependent area or people; *also* : a policy that favors or is based on such control — **co·lo·nial·ist** \-ləst\ *n or adj*

col·o·nist \'käl-ə-nəst\ *n* **1** : a person who lives in a colony **2** : a person who takes part in founding a colony

col·o·nize \'käl-ə-ˌnīz\ *vb* **-nized; -niz·ing 1** : to establish a colony in or on ⟨England *colonized* Australia⟩ **2** : to establish in a colony ⟨the rights of *colonized* people⟩ **3** : to settle in a colony — **col·o·ni·za·tion** \ˌkäl-ə-nə-'zā-shən\ *n* — **col·o·niz·er** \'käl-ə-ˌnī-zər\ *n*

col·on·nade \ˌkäl-ə-'nād\ *n* : an evenly spaced row of columns usually supporting the base of a roof structure — **col·on·nad·ed** \-'nād-əd\ *adj*

colonnade

col·o·ny \'käl-ə-nē\ *n, pl* **-nies 1 a** : a group of people sent out by a state to a new territory **b** : the territory in which such colonists live **c** : a distant territory belonging to or under the control of a nation **2 a** : a population of plants or animals in a particular place that belong to one species **b** : a mass of microbes usually growing in or on a solid food source (as agar) **3** : a group of people with common qualities or interests located in close association ⟨an artist *colony*⟩

¹**col·or** \'kəl-ər\ *n* **1 a** : an aspect of light (as red, brown, or gray) or sight that allows one to tell otherwise identical objects apart from each other ⟨the *color* of blood is red⟩ **b** : the property of objects and light sources that may be described in terms of hue, lightness, and chromatic purity for objects and hue, brightness, and chromatic purity for light sources ⟨the sky's changing *color*⟩ **c** : a particular combination of hue, lightness or brightness, and chromatic purity ⟨the car comes in six *colors*⟩ **d** : a color other than black, white, or gray **2** : an outward and often deceiving appearance ⟨her story has the *color* of truth⟩ **3 a** : the color of a person's skin especially other than white as a mark of race ⟨a person of *color*⟩ ⟨does not discriminate on the basis of *color*⟩ **b** : a pink or red tone in a person's face especially because of good health, excitement, or embarrassment **4** : the use or combination of colors ⟨a painter who is a master of *color*⟩ **5** *pl* **a** : an identifying flag, badge, or pennant ⟨a ship sailing under Swedish *colors*⟩ **b** : service in the armed forces ⟨a call to the *colors*⟩ **c** : a person's nature or character ⟨showed his true *colors* during the crisis⟩ **6** : VITALITY 3b, ¹INTEREST 4b ⟨her comments added *color* to the broadcast⟩ **7** : something used to give color : PIGMENT

²**color** *vb* **1 a** : to give color to ⟨the wind *colored* our cheeks⟩ **b** : to change the color of (as by dyeing, staining, or painting) **2** : MISREPRESENT, DISTORT ⟨his story is *colored* by his prejudices⟩ **3** : to take on or change color; *esp* : BLUSH — **col·or·er** *n*

Col·o·ra·do potato beetle \ˌkäl-ə-'rad-ō-, -'räd-\ *n* : a black-and-yellow striped beetle that feeds on the leaves of the potato — called also *potato beetle, potato bug*

col·or·ation \ˌkəl-ə-'rā-shən\ *n* **1** : use or arrangement of colors or shades : COLORING ⟨study the *coloration* of a flower⟩ **2** : the state of having color

col·or–blind \'kəl-ər-ˌblīnd\ *adj* : being partly or totally unable to recognize one or more colors — **color blindness** *n*

col·ored \'kəl-ərd\ *adj* **1** : having color ⟨*colored* pictures⟩ **2 a** *sometimes offensive* : of a race other than the white race; *esp* : ¹BLACK 2b **b** *sometimes offensive* : of or relating to persons of a mixed race or a race other than the white race

col·or·fast \'kəl-ər-ˌfast\ *adj* : having color that does not fade or run — **col·or·fast·ness** \-ˌfas(t)-nəs\ *n*

color filter *n* : ¹FILTER 3

col·or·ful \'kəl-ər-fəl\ *adj* **1** : having noticeable colors **2** : full of variety or interest ⟨a *colorful* personality⟩ — **col·or·ful·ly** \-f(ə-)lē\ *adv* — **col·or·ful·ness** \-fəl-nəs\ *n*

color guard *n* : an honor guard for the colors of an organization

col·or·im·e·ter \ˌkəl-ə-'rim-ət-ər\ *n* : a device for determining and specifying colors; *esp* : one used for chemical analysis by comparison of a liquid's color with standard colors

col·or·ing \'kəl-(ə-)riŋ\ *n* **1** : the act of applying colors **2** : something that produces color ⟨food *coloring*⟩ **3** : the effect produced by applying or combining colors **4** : COMPLEXION 1, COLORATION **5** : change of appearance (as by adding color)

coloring book *n* : a book of line drawings for coloring (as with crayons)

col·or·less \'kəl-ər-ləs\ *adj* **1** : lacking color ⟨a *colorless* liquid⟩ **2** : ¹DULL 8 ⟨*colorless* writing⟩ — **col·or·less·ly** *adv* — **col·or·less·ness** *n*

co·los·sal \kə-'läs-əl\ *adj* **1** : of, relating to, or resembling a colossus; *esp* : of very great size ⟨a *colossal* office building⟩ **2** : EXTRAORDINARY, EXCEPTIONAL ⟨*colossal* growth⟩ ⟨a *colossal* failure⟩ **synonyms** see MONSTROUS — **co·los·sal·ly** \-ə-lē\ *adv*

col·os·se·um \ˌkäl-ə-'sē-əm\ *n* **1** *cap* : an outdoor arena built in Rome in the first century A.D. **2** : COLISEUM [Latin, from *colosseus* "colossal," derived from *colossus* "colossus"]

Co·los·sians \kə-'läsh-ənz *also* -'läs-ē-ənz, -'läsh-ē-ənz\ *n* — see BIBLE table

co·los·sus \kə-'läs-əs\ *n, pl* **-los·si** \-'läs-ˌī\ **1** : a huge statue **2** : a person or thing of great size or power [from Latin *colossus* "huge statue, colossus"]

co·los·trum \kə-'läs-trəm\ *n* : milk secreted for a few days after giving birth and having a high protein and antibody content

col·our \'kəl-ər\ *chiefly British variant of* COLOR

colt \'kōlt\ *n* **1** : ¹FOAL; *esp* : a young male horse **2** : an inexperienced young person

colt·ish \'kōl-tish\ *adj* : FRISKY, PLAYFUL

col·um·bine \'käl-əm-ˌbīn\ *n* : any of a genus of plants that are related to the buttercups and have showy flowers with five petals of which each usually has a long hollow spur

co·lum·bi·um \kə-'ləm-bē-əm\ *n* : NIOBIUM

Co·lum·bus Day \kə-'ləm-bəs-\ *n* : the second Monday in October observed as a legal holiday in many states of the U.S. in honor of the landing of Columbus in the Bahamas in 1492

col·umn \'käl-əm\ *n* **1 a** : a printed or written vertical arrangement of items ⟨add together the *column* of numbers⟩ **b** : one of two or more vertical sections of a printed page separated by a rule or blank space **c** : a special regular feature in a newspaper or magazine ⟨a sports *column*⟩ **2** : a supporting pillar; *esp* : one consisting of a usually round shaft, a capital, and a base **3** : something

columbine

resembling a column in form, position, or function ⟨a *column* of water⟩ **4** : a long row (as of soldiers) [Middle English *columne* "column," from early French *colompne* (same meaning), from Latin *columna* "column" — related to COLONEL] — **col·umned** *adj*

co·lum·nar \kə-'ləm-nər\ *adj* **1** : of, relating to, or being columns **2** : of, relating to, being, or composed of somewhat cylinder-shaped or prism-shaped epithelial cells

col·um·nist \'käl-əm-(n)əst\ *n* : a person who writes a newspaper or magazine column

com- *or* **col-** *or* **con-** *prefix* : with : together : jointly — usually *com-* before *b, p,* or *m* ⟨*com*mingle⟩, *col-* before *l* ⟨*col*lateral⟩, and *con-* before other sounds ⟨*con*centrate⟩ [derived from Latin *com-, col-, con-* "together, with"]

¹**co·ma** \'kō-mə\ *n* : a sleeplike state of unconsciousness caused by disease, injury, or poison [scientific Latin, from Greek *kōma* "deep sleep"]

²**coma** *n, pl* **co·mae** \-,mē, -,mī\ : the head of a comet made up of a cloud of gas and dust and usually containing a nucleus [from Latin *coma* "hair," from Greek *komē* "hair" — related to COMET]

Co·man·che \kə-'man-chē\ *n, pl* **Comanche** *or* **Comanches** **1** : a member of an American Indian people ranging from Wyoming and Nebraska south into New Mexico and northwestern Texas **2** : the Aztec-related language of the Comanche people

¹**comb** \'kōm\ *n* **1 a** : a toothed implement used to smooth and arrange the hair or worn in the hair to hold it in place **b** : a toothed instrument used for separating fibers (as of wool or flax) **2** : a fleshy crest on the head of the domestic chicken and some related birds **3** : ¹HONEYCOMB — **combed** \'kōmd\ *adj*

²**comb** *vb* **1** : to smooth, arrange, or untangle with a comb ⟨*comb* one's hair⟩ ⟨*comb* wool⟩ **2** : to go over or through carefully in search of something or someone ⟨we *combed* the beach for shells⟩

¹**com·bat** \'käm-,bat\ *n* **1** : a fight or contest between individuals or groups **2** : ¹CONFLICT 2 **3** : active fighting in a war : ACTION ⟨soldiers experienced in *combat*⟩

²**com·bat** \kəm-'bat, 'käm-,bat\ *vb* **-bat·ed** *or* **-bat·ted;** **-bat·ing** *or* **-bat·ting** **1** : to fight with : BATTLE **2** : to struggle against; *esp* : to strive to reduce or eliminate ⟨*combat* disease⟩

com·bat·ant \kəm-'bat-ᵊnt *also* 'käm-bət-\ *n* : one that is engaged in or ready to engage in combat — **combatant** *adj*

com·bat·ive \kəm-'bat-iv\ *adj* : eager to fight : PUGNACIOUS — **com·bat·ive·ness** *n*

comb·er \'kō-mər\ *n* **1** : one that combs fibers **2** : a long curling wave of the sea

com·bi·na·tion \,käm-bə-'nā-shən\ *n* **1** : a result or product of combining; *esp* : a number of persons or groups joined together to achieve some end **2 a** : a connected series of letters or numbers chosen in setting a lock **b** : any of the possible subsets of a set without regard to the order of their elements **3** : the act or process of combining; *esp* : that of uniting to form a chemical compound

¹**com·bine** \kəm-'bīn\ *vb* **com·bined; com·bin·ing** **1** : to bring into close relationship : UNIFY **2** : to mix together so that the identity of each part is lost ⟨*combine* the ingredients of a recipe⟩ **3 a** : to become one **b** : to unite to form a chemical compound *synonyms* see JOIN — **com·bin·able** \-'bī-nə-bəl\ *adj* — **com·bin·er** *n*

²**com·bine** \'käm-,bīn\ *n* **1** : a union of persons or groups especially for business or political benefits **2** : a machine that harvests, threshes, and cleans grain while moving over a field

comb·ings \'kō-miŋz\ *n pl* : loose hairs or fibers removed by a comb

combining form \kəm-,bī-niŋ-\ *n* : a linguistic form that occurs only in compounds or derivatives (as *electro-* in *electromagnetic* or *mal-* in *malodorous*)

com·bo \'käm-,bō\ *n, pl* **combos** **1** : a small jazz or dance band **2** : COMBINATION

com·bust \kəm-'bəst\ *vb* : to be or set on fire : BURN

com·bus·ti·ble \kəm-'bəs-tə-bəl\ *adj* **1** : capable of being burned **2** : catching fire or burning easily — **com·bus·ti·bil·i·ty** \-,bəs-tə-'bil-ət-ē\ *n* — **combustible** *n*

com·bus·tion \kəm-'bəs-chən\ *n* **1** : an act or instance of burning **2** : a chemical process in which substances combine with oxygen

com·bus·tor \kəm-'bəs-tər\ *n* : a chamber (as in a jet engine) in which combustion takes place

come \(')kəm\ *vb* **came** \'kām\; **come; com·ing** \'kəm-iŋ\ **1** : to move toward or journey to something : APPROACH ⟨*come* here⟩ ⟨*come* see us⟩ **2** : to arrive at or enter a scene of action ⟨the police *came* to our rescue⟩ **3 a** : to reach the point of being or becoming ⟨the rope *came* untied⟩ **b** : to add up : AMOUNT ⟨the bill *came* to $10⟩ **4** : to take place ⟨the holiday *came* on Thursday⟩ **5** : ORIGINATE 2, ARISE ⟨*comes* from a fine family⟩ ⟨honey *comes* from bees⟩ **6** : to be available ⟨the dress *comes* in three colors⟩ **7** : EXTEND 4, REACH ⟨a coat that *comes* to the knees⟩ **8 a** : to arrive at a place, end, result, or conclusion ⟨*came* to their senses⟩ ⟨we now *come* to the next chapter⟩ **b** : HAPPEN 5 ⟨no harm will *come* to you⟩ **9** : to fall within the range or limits of something ⟨*comes* under the terms of the treaty⟩ **10** : to turn out to be : BECOME ⟨her dreams have *come* true⟩ — **com·er** \'kəm-ər\ *n* — **come across** : to meet or find by chance — **come into one's own** : to reach one's appropriate level of importance, skill, or recognition — **come over** : to affect suddenly and strangely ⟨what's *come over* you⟩ — **come to pass** : HAPPEN 2 — **come upon** : to meet or find by chance — **to come** : existing or arriving in the future ⟨in days *to come*⟩

come about *vb* **1** : HAPPEN 2 **2** : to change direction ⟨the wind has *come about* into the north⟩

come along *vb* **1** : to go with as a companion **2** : to make progress ⟨work is *coming along* well⟩ **3** : to make an appearance ⟨won't take the first offer that *comes along*⟩

come around *vb* : COME ROUND

come·back \'kəm-,bak\ *n* **1** : ²RETORT **2** : a return to a former position or condition (as of health, power, popularity, or prosperity) : RECOVERY

come by *vb* **1** : to make a visit ⟨*come by* after dinner⟩ **2** : ACQUIRE ⟨good help is hard to *come by*⟩

co·me·di·an \kə-'mēd-ē-ən\ *n* **1** : an actor who plays in comedy **2** : a comical individual; *esp* : a humorous professional entertainer

co·me·di·enne \kə-,mēd-ē-'en\ *n* : a female comedian

come·down \'kəm-,daun\ *n* : a falling in status, position, or reputation

come down \(,)kəm-'daun\ *vb* : to fall sick ⟨*came down* with the flu⟩

com·e·dy \'käm-əd-ē\ *n, pl* **-dies** **1** : a light amusing play with a happy ending **2** : a comic literary work **3 a** : an amusing or ridiculous event **b** : humorous entertainment

come·ly \'kəm-lē\ *adj* **come·li·er; -est** : pleasing to the eye : PRETTY, ATTRACTIVE — **come·li·ness** *n*

come out *vb* **1** : to come into public view **2** : to turn out to be ⟨everything *came out* all right⟩

come round *vb* **1** : COME TO **2** : to change direction or opinion ⟨you'll *come round* to our side soon⟩

com·et \'käm-ət\ *n* : a bright heavenly body that develops a cloudy tail as it moves closer to the sun in its orbit [Old English *cometa* "comet," from Latin *cometa* (same mean-

\ə\ **abut**	\au̇\ **out**	\i\ **tip**	\ȯ\ **saw**	\u̇\ **foot**
\ər\ **further**	\ch\ **chin**	\ī\ **life**	\ȯi\ **coin**	\y\ **yet**
\a\ **mat**	\e\ **pet**	\j\ **job**	\th\ **thin**	\yü\ **few**
\ā\ **take**	\ē\ **easy**	\ŋ\ **sing**	\th\ **this**	\yu̇\ **cure**
\ä\ **cot, cart**	\g\ **go**	\ō\ **bone**	\ü\ **food**	\zh\ **vision**

ing), from Greek *kométēs,* literally, "long-haired," derived from *komē* "hair" — related to ²COMA]

come to *vb* : to recover consciousness

come up *vb* **1** : ¹RISE 4 ⟨the sun *comes up* in an hour⟩ **2** : to come near or approach ⟨*came up* and introduced himself⟩ **3** : to come to attention : INTRODUCE 4 ⟨the question *came up* again⟩ — **come up with** : to produce especially in dealing with a problem or challenge ⟨*came up* with a solution⟩

¹**com·fort** \'kəm(p)-fərt\ *vb* **1** : to give strength and hope to : CHEER **2** : to ease the grief or trouble of : CONSOLE — **com·fort·ing·ly** \'kəm(p)-fər-tiŋ-lē\ *adv*

²**comfort** *n* **1** : acts or words that comfort **2** : the feeling of the one that is comforted ⟨find *comfort* in a mother's love⟩ **3** : something that makes a person comfortable ⟨the *comforts* of home⟩ — **com·fort·less** \-ləs\ *adj*

com·fort·able \'kəm(p)(f)-tə(r)-bəl, 'kəm(p)-fərt-ə-bəl\ *adj* **1** : giving comfort; *esp* : providing physical comfort ⟨a *comfortable* chair⟩ **2** : more than adequate ⟨a *comfortable* income⟩ **3** : enjoying comfort : at ease ⟨you *comfortable*?⟩ — **com·fort·able·ness** *n* — **com·fort·ably** \-blē\ *adv*

com·fort·er \'kəm(p)-fə(r)t-ər\ *n* **1** : one that gives comfort **2** : a long narrow neck scarf **3** : ¹QUILT

¹**com·ic** \'käm-ik\ *adj* **1** : of or relating to comedy ⟨a *comic* actor⟩ **2** : causing laughter or amusement : FUNNY **3** : of or relating to comic strips

²**comic** *n* **1** : COMEDIAN 2 **2 a** : COMIC STRIP **b** *pl* : the part of a newspaper devoted to comic strips

com·i·cal \'käm-i-kəl\ *adj* : LAUGHABLE, FUNNY — **com·i·cal·ly** \-i-k(ə-)lē\ *adv*

comic book *n* : a magazine made up of a series of comic strips

comic strip *n* : a series of cartoons that tell a story or part of a story

com·ing \'kəm-iŋ\ *adj* **1** : immediately following : NEXT ⟨in the *coming* year⟩ **2** : gaining importance ⟨recognized as a *coming* young star⟩

co·mi·ty \'käm-ət-ē, 'kō-mət-\ *n, pl* **-ties** : courteous behavior : CIVILITY

com·ma \'käm-ə\ *n* : a punctuation mark , used chiefly to show separation of words or word groups within a sentence

¹**com·mand** \kə-'mand\ *vb* **1 a** : to issue orders by right of authority **b** : to have authority and control over : be commander of ⟨*command* an army⟩ **2** : to have for one's use ⟨*commands* many resources⟩ **3** : to demand or receive as one's due : EXACT ⟨*commands* a high fee⟩ **4** : to look down on especially from a militarily strong position ⟨the hill *commands* the town⟩

synonyms COMMAND, DIRECT, INSTRUCT, CHARGE mean to issue orders. COMMAND suggests the use of authority and usually some degree of formality ⟨the troops were *commanded* to march forward⟩. DIRECT suggests that obedience is expected and usually applies to specific procedures or methods ⟨we were *directed* to write with pencils only⟩. INSTRUCT is similar to DIRECT but sometimes implies greater detail or formality ⟨the judge *instructed* the jury to ignore the remark⟩. CHARGE suggests the assigning of a duty or responsibility ⟨the principal is *charged* with keeping the school running smoothly⟩.

²**command** *n* **1** : the act of commanding ⟨march on *command*⟩ **2** : an order given ⟨obey a *command*⟩ **3 a** : the ability to control : MASTERY ⟨a good *command* of French⟩ **b** : the authority, right, or power to command **4** : the people, area, or unit under a commander **5** : a position from which military operations are directed

com·man·dant \'käm-ən-ˌdant, -ˌdänt\ *n* : an officer in command

com·man·deer \ˌkäm-ən-'di(ə)r\ *vb* : to take possession of by force especially for military purposes

com·mand·er \kə-'man-dər\ *n* **1** : one in official command especially of a military force or base **2** : a naval commissioned officer with a rank just below that of captain — **com·mand·er·ship** \-ˌship\ *n*

commander in chief : one who holds the supreme command of an armed force

commanding officer *n* : an officer having charge of a military or naval unit, organization, or base

com·mand·ment \kə-'man(d)-mənt\ *n* : something commanded; *esp* : one of the biblical Ten Commandments

command module *n* : part of a space vehicle designed to carry the crew, the chief communications equipment, and the equipment for return to Earth's atmosphere

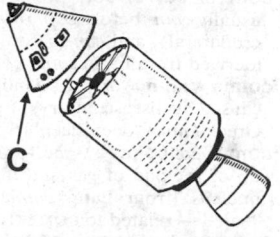

C command module separating from service module

com·man·do \kə-'man-dō\ *n, pl* **-dos** *or* **-does 1** : a military unit trained and organized for surprise raids **2** : a member of a commando

comma splice *n* : the error of using a comma between coordinate main clauses not connected by a conjunction — called also **comma fault**

com·mem·o·rate \kə-'mem-ə-ˌrāt\ *vb* **-rat·ed; -rat·ing 1** : to call to remembrance **2** : to mark by a ceremony **3** : to be a memorial of ⟨a plaque that *commemorates* the battle⟩ **synonyms** see KEEP — **com·mem·o·ra·tor** \-ˌrāt-ər\ *n*

com·mem·o·ra·tion \kə-ˌmem-ə-'rā-shən\ *n* **1** : the act of commemorating **2** : a ceremony that commemorates

com·mem·o·ra·tive \kə-'mem-ə-rət-iv, -ˌrāt-\ *adj* : intended to commemorate a person, thing, or event ⟨a *commemorative* postage stamp⟩ — **commemorative** *n*

com·mence \kə-'men(t)s\ *vb* **com·menced; com·menc·ing** : to bring or come into activity, being, or operation : BEGIN, START ⟨*commence* firing⟩ [Middle English *comencen* "to begin," from early French *comencer* (same meaning), probably from a Latin word *cominitiare* "to begin," from *com-* "with, together" and *initiare* "to begin" — related to INITIATE] — **com·menc·er** *n*

com·mence·ment \kə-'men(t)s-mənt\ *n* **1** : an act, instance, or time of commencing **2** : the ceremonies or the day for presenting degrees or diplomas to graduates of a school or college

com·mend \kə-'mend\ *vb* **1** : to give into another's care : ENTRUST **2** : to speak of someone or something with approval : PRAISE ⟨*commended* her for her honesty⟩ — **com·mend·able** \-'men-də-bəl\ *adj* — **com·mend·ably** \-blē\ *adv*

com·men·da·tion \ˌkäm-ən-'dā-shən, -ˌen-\ *n* **1** : an act of commending **2** : something that commends ⟨was awarded a *commendation* for bravery⟩ — **com·men·da·to·ry** \kə-'men-də-ˌtōr-ē, -ˌtor-\ *adj*

com·men·sal \kə-'men(t)-səl\ *adj* : relating to or living in a state of commensalism

com·men·sal·ism \kə-'men(t)-sə-ˌliz-əm\ *n* : a relation between two kinds of plants or animals in which one obtains a benefit (as food) from the other without damaging or benefiting it

com·men·su·rate \kə-'men(t)s-(ə-)rət, -'mench-(ə-)rət\ *adj* **1** : equal in measure or extent **2** : PROPORTIONAL 1 ⟨an income *commensurate* with one's needs⟩ — **com·men·su·rate·ly** *adv* — **com·men·su·ra·tion** \kə-ˌmen(t)s-ə-'rā-shən, -ˌmench-ə-\ *n*

¹**com·ment** \'käm-ˌent\ *n* **1** : an expression of opinion or attitude in speech or writing **2** : a remark that explains or criticizes **synonyms** see REMARK

²**comment** *vb* : to make a comment : REMARK

com·men·tary \'käm-ən-ˌter-ē\ *n, pl* **-tar·ies** : a series of comments or notes; *also* : a book made up of such material — usually used in plural

com·men·tate \'käm-ən-ˌtāt\ *vb* : to give a commentary on : to act as a commentator

com·men·ta·tor \'käm-ən-ˌtāt-ər\ *n* : a person who gives a commentary; *esp* : a person who reports and discusses news on radio or television

com·merce \'käm-(ˌ)ərs\ *n* : buying and selling of goods especially on a large scale and between different places : TRADE [from early French *commerce* "exchange of ideas or opinions, commerce," from Latin *commercium* (same meaning), from *com-* "with" and *merc-, merx* "merchandise" — related to MARKET, MERCHANT]

¹**com·mer·cial** \kə-'mər-shəl\ *adj* **1** : of or relating to commerce **2** : designed mainly for profit; *esp* : designed for mass appeal ⟨the *commercial* theater⟩ **3** : paid for by advertisers ⟨*commercial* TV⟩ — **com·mer·cial·ly** \-'mərsh-(ə-)lē\ *adv*

²**commercial** *n* : an advertisement broadcast on radio or television

commercial bank *n* : a bank that accepts deposits that can be withdrawn without notice and creates credit through loans mainly to businesses

com·mer·cial·ize \kə-'mər-shə-ˌlīz\ *vb* **-ized; -iz·ing** **1** : to manage for the sake of making a profit **2** : to use for profit ⟨*commercialize* Christmas⟩ — **com·mer·cial·i·za·tion** \-ˌmər-shə-lə-'zā-shən\ *n*

com·min·gle \kə-'miŋ-gəl\ *vb* : to mix together : MINGLE

com·mis·er·ate \kə-'miz-ə-ˌrāt\ *vb* **-at·ed; -at·ing** : to feel or express sorrow or sympathy : SYMPATHIZE — **com·mis·er·a·tion** \-ˌmiz-ə-'rā-shən\ *n*

com·mis·sar \'käm-ə-ˌsär\ *n* : the head of a government department in the U.S.S.R. before 1946

com·mis·sar·i·at \ˌkäm-ə-'ser-ē-ət\ *n* **1** : a system for supplying an army with food **2** : a government department headed by a commissar

com·mis·sary \'käm-ə-ˌser-ē\ *n, pl* **-sar·ies** **1** : a person to whom a duty or office is entrusted by someone of higher rank **2** : a store that provides supplies (as food) especially to members of the military and their families

¹**com·mis·sion** \kə-'mish-ən\ *n* **1 a** : an order granting the power to perform various acts or duties **b** : a certificate that gives military rank and authority; *also* : the rank and authority so given **2 a** : authority to act as agent for another **b** : a matter entrusted to an agent **3** : a group of persons directed to perform some duty **4** : an act of committing ⟨*commission* of a theft⟩ **5** : a fee paid to an agent or employee for taking care of a piece of business ⟨a 5% sales *commission*⟩ — **in commission** : in use or ready for use ⟨put a ship *in commission*⟩ — **out of commission** **1** : out of service or use **2** : out of working order ⟨the doorbell was *out of commission*⟩

²**commission** *vb* **-mis·sioned; -mis·sion·ing** \-'mish-(ə-)niŋ\ **1** : to give a commission to ⟨was *commissioned* lieutenant⟩ ⟨*commissioned* to write the biography⟩ **2** : to order to be made ⟨*commissioned* a portrait of himself⟩ **3** : to put (a ship) in commission

com·mis·sion·aire \kə-ˌmish-ə-'na(ə)r, -'ne(ə)r\ *n, chiefly British* : a uniformed attendant

commissioned officer *n* : a military or naval officer holding by a commission a rank of second lieutenant or ensign or a higher rank

com·mis·sion·er \kə-'mish-(ə-)nər\ *n* **1** : a member of a commission **2** : an official in charge of a government department ⟨Police *Commissioner*⟩

com·mit \kə-'mit\ *vb* **com·mit·ted; com·mit·ting** **1 a** : to make secure or put in safekeeping : ENTRUST ⟨*commit* the poem to memory⟩ **b** : to place in a prison or mental institution **2** : BRING ABOUT, PERFORM ⟨*commit* a crime⟩ **3** : to pledge or assign to some particular course or use

⟨*committed* myself to a meeting on Thursday⟩ — **com·mit·ta·ble** \-'mit-ə-bəl\ *adj*

com·mit·ment \kə-'mit-mənt\ *n* **1** : an act of committing **2 a** : an agreement or pledge to do something in the future **b** : something pledged ⟨financial *commitments*⟩

com·mit·tee \kə-'mit-ē\ *n* : a group of persons appointed or elected to consider or take action on some matter ⟨a legislative *committee*⟩

com·mit·tee·man \-mən, -ˌman\ *n* : a member of a committee

com·mit·tee·wom·an \-ˌwùm-ən\ *n* : a woman who is a member of a committee

com·mode \kə-'mōd\ *n* **1 a** : a low chest of drawers **b** : a movable washstand with a cupboard underneath **2** : TOILET 2b

com·mo·di·ous \kə-'mōd-ē-əs\ *adj* : having a comfortable amount of space **synonyms** see SPACIOUS — **com·mo·di·ous·ly** *adv* — **com·mo·di·ous·ness** *n*

com·mod·i·ty \kə-'mäd-ət-ē\ *n, pl* **-ties** **1** : a product of agriculture or mining **2** : an article that is bought and sold in commerce

com·mo·dore \'käm-ə-ˌdō(ə)r, -ˌdò(ə)r\ *n* **1** : a naval commissioned officer with a rank just below that of rear admiral **2** : the senior captain of a line of merchant ships

¹**com·mon** \'käm-ən\ *adj* **1** : relating or belonging to or used by everyone : PUBLIC ⟨work for the *common* good⟩ **2** : belonging to or shared by two or more individuals or by the members of a group or set ⟨a *common* ancestor⟩ **3 a** : WIDESPREAD 1, GENERAL ⟨facts of *common* knowledge⟩ **b** : ADEQUATE ⟨*common* decency⟩ **4** : occurring or appearing frequently : FAMILIAR ⟨a *common* sight⟩ **5** : not above the average in rank, merit, or social position ⟨a *common* soldier⟩ ⟨the *common* people⟩ **6 a** : falling below ordinary standards : SECOND-RATE **b** : COARSE 5, VULGAR — **com·mon·ly** *adv* — **com·mon·ness** \-ən-nəs\ *n*

²**common** *n* **1** *pl* : the common people **2** : a piece of land that is open to common use especially for pasture — often used in plural — **in common** : shared together ⟨intersecting lines have one point *in common*⟩

common cold *n* : a contagious viral illness of the structures used in breathing which causes the nose and throat to be sore, swollen, and inflamed and in which there is usually much mucus and coughing and sneezing

common denominator *n* : a number or expression that is a multiple of each of the denominators in a set of fractions ⟨12 is a *common denominator* of ¼ and ⅓⟩

common divisor *n* : a number that divides two or more numbers without remainder ⟨4 is a *common divisor* of 12, 24, and 36⟩ — called also *common factor*

com·mon·er \'käm-ə-nər\ *n* : one of the common people : a person who is not of noble rank

Common Era *n* : CHRISTIAN ERA

common law *n* : a group of legal practices and traditions originating in judges' decisions in earlier cases and in social customs and having the same force in most of the U.S. as if passed into law by a legislative body

common multiple *n* : a number that is a multiple of each of two or more numbers ⟨20 is a *common multiple* of 5 and 4⟩

common noun *n* : a noun (as *chair* or *fear*) that names a class of persons or things or any individual of a class

¹**com·mon·place** \'käm-ən-ˌplās\ *n* : something that is often seen, heard, or met with

²**commonplace** *adj* : very common or ordinary

common salt *n* : ¹SALT 1a

\ə\ abut	\au̇\ out	\i\ tip	\ȯ\ saw	\u̇\ foot
\ər\ further	\ch\ chin	\ī\ life	\ȯi\ coin	\y\ yet
\a\ mat	\e\ pet	\j\ job	\th\ thin	\yü\ few
\ā\ take	\ē\ easy	\ŋ\ sing	\th\ this	\yu̇\ cure
\ä\ cot, cart	\g\ go	\ō\ bone	\ü\ food	\zh\ vision

common sense *n* : ordinary good sense and judgment — **commonsense** \ˌkäm-ən-ˌsen(t)s\ *adj*

com·mon·weal \ˈkäm-ən-ˌwēl\ *n* **1** *archaic* : COMMONWEALTH **2** : the general good

com·mon·wealth \-ˌwelth\ *n* **1** : a political unit (as a nation or state) **2** : a state of the U.S. — used officially of Kentucky, Massachusetts, Pennsylvania, and Virginia

com·mo·tion \kə-ˈmō-shən\ *n* **1** : irregular or violent motion **2** : noisy excitement and confusion : TUMULT

com·mu·nal \kə-ˈmyün-ᵊl, ˈkäm-yən-ᵊl\ *adj* **1** : of or relating to a commune or community **2** : shared or used in common by members of a group or community

¹com·mune \kə-ˈmyün\ *vb* **com·muned; com·mun·ing 1** : to receive Communion **2** : to be in close communication with someone or something ⟨*commune* with nature⟩

²com·mune \ˈkäm-ˌyün, kə-ˈmyün\ *n* **1** : the smallest administrative district of many countries especially in Europe **2** : a small group of people that live together and share property and duties

com·mu·ni·ca·ble \kə-ˈmyü-ni-kə-bəl\ *adj* : capable of being transferred or carried from one person or thing to another ⟨*communicable* diseases⟩ — **com·mu·ni·ca·bil·i·ty** \-ˌmyü-ni-kə-ˈbil-ət-ē\ *n*

com·mu·ni·cant \kə-ˈmyü-ni-kənt\ *n* **1** : a person who takes Communion : a church member **2** : a person who communicates

com·mu·ni·cate \kə-ˈmyü-nə-ˌkāt\ *vb* **-cat·ed; -cat·ing 1 a** : to make known ⟨*communicate* the news⟩ **b** : to pass from one to another : TRANSMIT ⟨*communicate* a disease⟩ **2** : to transmit information, thought, or feeling so that it is satisfactorily received or understood ⟨the pilot *communicated* with the airport⟩ **3** : to open into each other : CONNECT ⟨the rooms *communicate*⟩ — **com·mu·ni·ca·tor** \-ˌkāt-ər\ *n*

com·mu·ni·ca·tion \kə-ˌmyü-nə-ˈkā-shən\ *n* **1** : an act or instance of transmitting **2** : information communicated : MESSAGE ⟨received an important *communication*⟩ **3** : an exchange of information **4** *pl* **a** : a system (as of telephones) for sending and receiving messages **b** : a system of routes for moving troops, supplies, and vehicles

com·mu·ni·ca·tive \kə-ˈmyü-nə-ˌkāt-iv, -ni-kət-iv\ *adj* : tending to communicate : TALKATIVE **2** : of or relating to communication — **com·mu·ni·ca·tive·ness** *n*

com·mu·nion \kə-ˈmyü-nyən\ *n* **1** *cap* **a** : a Christian sacrament in which bread and wine are partaken of as a commemoration of the last supper of Jesus **b** : the part of the Mass in which the Eucharist is received **2** : friendly communication **3** : a body of Christians having a common faith and discipline

com·mu·ni·qué \kə-ˈmyü-nə-ˌkā, -ˌmyü-nə-ˈkā\ *n* : BULLETIN [French, literally, "something communicated"]

com·mu·nism \ˈkäm-yə-ˌniz-əm\ *n* **1** : a social system in which property and goods are owned in common; *also* : a theory that favors such a system **2** *cap* : a system of government in which a single party controls state-owned means of production with the aim of establishing a stateless society

com·mu·nist \ˈkäm-yə-nəst\ *n* **1** : a person who believes in communism **2** *cap* : a member or follower of a Communist party or movement — **communist** *adj, often cap* — **com·mu·nis·tic** \ˌkäm-yə-ˈnis-tik\ *adj, often cap*

com·mu·ni·ty \kə-ˈmyü-nət-ē\ *n, pl* **-ties 1 a** : the people living in an area; *also* : the area itself **b** : a group of living things that belong to one or more species, interact ecologically, and are located in one place (as a bog or pond) **c** : a group of people with common interests especially when living together ⟨a *community* of monks⟩ **2 a** : shared ownership or participation ⟨*community* of goods⟩ **b** : SIMILARITY 1, LIKENESS ⟨a *community* of ideas⟩ **c** : shared activity : FELLOWSHIP

community center *n* : a building or group of buildings for a community's educational and recreational activities

community college *n* : a public junior college that fits its instruction to the community's needs

com·mu·ta·tion \ˌkäm-yə-ˈtā-shən\ *n* **1** : ¹EXCHANGE 2, REPLACEMENT **2** : a reduction of a legal penalty **3** : an act of commuting **4** : the process of reversing the direction of an electric circuit

com·mu·ta·tive \ˈkäm-yə-ˌtāt-iv, kə-ˈmyüt-ət-iv\ *adj* : of, relating to, having, or being the property of giving the same mathematical result no matter in which order two numbers are used with an operation ⟨addition is *commutative* because $a + b = b + a$⟩ — **com·mu·ta·tiv·i·ty** \kə-ˌmyüt-ə-ˈtiv-ət-ē, ˌkäm-yə-tə-\ *n*

com·mu·ta·tor \ˈkäm-yə-ˌtāt-ər\ *n* : a device for reversing the direction of an electric current so that the alternating currents made in a dynamo are changed to direct current

¹com·mute \kə-ˈmyüt\ *vb* **com·mut·ed; com·mut·ing 1** : ²EXCHANGE; *esp* : to change a penalty to another one that is less severe ⟨*commute* a death sentence to life imprisonment⟩ **2** : to travel back and forth regularly — **com·mut·able** \-ˈmyüt-ə-bəl\ *adj* — **com·mut·er** *n*

²commute *n* **1** : an act or instance of commuting ⟨the morning *commute* to work⟩ **2** : the distance covered in commuting ⟨a long *commute*⟩

¹com·pact \kəm-ˈpakt, ˈkäm-ˌpakt\ *adj* **1** : closely united or packed : SOLID, FIRM **2** : arranged so as to save space ⟨a *compact* house⟩ **3** : not wordy : BRIEF [Middle English *compact* "firmly put together," from Latin *compactus* (same meaning), from *compingere* "to join," from *com-* "together" and *pangere* "to fasten"] — **com·pact·ly** *adv* — **com·pact·ness** \kəm-ˈpak(t)-nəs, ˈkäm-ˌpak(t)-\ *n*

²compact *vb* **1** : to draw together : COMBINE, CONSOLIDATE **2** : to make or become compact : COMPRESS — **compac·tor** *also* **com·pact·er** \kəm-ˈpak-tər, ˈkäm-ˌpak-\ *n*

³com·pact \ˈkäm-ˌpakt\ *n* **1** : a small cosmetic case **2** : a somewhat small automobile

⁴com·pact \ˈkäm-ˌpakt\ *n* : AGREEMENT 2a, CONTRACT [from Latin *compactum* "agreement," derived from *compacisci* "to make an agreement," from *com-* "with, together" and *pacisci* "to agree"]

compact disc *n* : CD

com·pa·dre \kəm-ˈpäd-rā\ *n* : a close friend

¹com·pan·ion \kəm-ˈpan-yən\ *n* **1** : one that often accompanies another : COMRADE **2 a** : one of a pair of matching things **b** : a person employed to live with and serve another [Middle English *compainoun* "companion," from early French *cumpaignun* (same meaning), from Latin *companion-, companio* "companion," literally, "one who eats with another," from *com-* "with, together" and *panis* "food, bread" — related to ACCOMPANY, COMPANY, PANTRY]

²companion *n* : COMPANIONWAY

com·pan·ion·able \kəm-ˈpan-yə-nə-bəl\ *adj* : FRIENDLY — **com·pan·ion·ably** \-blē\ *adv*

com·pan·ion·ship \kəm-ˈpan-yən-ˌship\ *n* : the good feeling that comes from being with someone else

com·pan·ion·way \-ˌwā\ *n* : a ship's stairway from one deck to another

com·pa·ny \ˈkəmp-(ə-)nē\ *n, pl* **-nies 1 a** : association with another : FELLOWSHIP ⟨enjoy a person's *company*⟩ **b** : a person's companions or associates ⟨known by the *company* you keep⟩ **c** : guests or visitors especially at one's home ⟨we have *company*⟩ **2 a** : a group of persons or things **b** : a body of soldiers; *esp* : a unit consisting of two or more platoons **c** : an organization of musical or dramatic performers ⟨an opera *company*⟩ **d** : the officers and crew of a ship **e** : a firefighting unit **3 a** : an association of persons carrying on a business **b** : those members of a partnership whose names do not appear in the firm name ⟨Doe and *Company*⟩ [Middle English *companie* "company, fellowship," from early French *cumpaingie* (same meaning), derived from Latin *companio* "companion" — related to ACCOMPANY, COMPANION]

com·pa·ra·ble \'käm-p(ə-)rə-bəl\ *adj* **1** : capable of being compared **2** : SIMILAR, LIKE ⟨cloth *comparable* to the best⟩ — **com·pa·ra·bly** \-blē\ *adv*

¹com·par·a·tive \kəm-'par-ət-iv\ *adj* **1** : of, relating to, or constituting the degree of grammatical comparison that denotes increase in the quality, quantity, or relation expressed by an adjective or adverb **2** : measured by comparison : RELATIVE ⟨a *comparative* stranger⟩ **3** : involving the study of things that are alike by comparing them ⟨*comparative* anatomy⟩ — **com·par·a·tive·ly** *adv*

²comparative *n* : the comparative degree or a word form expressing it ⟨"taller" is the *comparative* of "tall"⟩

¹com·pare \kəm-'pa(ə)r, -'pe(ə)r\ *vb* **com·pared; com·par·ing** **1** : to describe as similar ⟨*compare* an anthill to a town⟩ **2** : to examine in order to discover likenesses or differences ⟨*compare* two bicycles⟩ **3 a** : to be worthy of comparison ⟨roller-skating does not *compare* with ice-skating⟩ **b** : to appear in comparison to others ⟨*compares* well with the rest of the class⟩ **4** : to inflect or modify (an adjective or adverb) according to the degrees of comparison [Middle English *comparen* "to show to be similar, examine for points of likeness," from early French *comparer* (same meaning), from Latin *comparare* "to couple, compare," from *compar* (adjective) "like, similar," from *com-* "with, together" and *par* "equal" — related to PAIR, PAR, PEER, UMPIRE; see *Word History* at UMPIRE]

²compare *n* : the possibility of comparing ⟨beauty beyond *compare*⟩

com·par·i·son \kəm-'par-ə-sən\ *n* **1** : the act of comparing : the state of being compared **2** : change in the form of an adjective or an adverb (as by having *-er* or *-est* added or *more* or *most* prefixed) to show different levels of quality, quantity, or relation

com·part·ment \kəm-'pärt-mənt\ *n* **1** : a separate division or section **2** : one of the parts into which an enclosed space is divided

¹com·pass \'kəm-pəs *also* 'käm-\ *vb* **1** : to travel entirely around ⟨*compass* the earth⟩ **2** : ACCOMPLISH, ACHIEVE

²compass *n* **1 a** : BOUNDARY, CIRCUMFERENCE **b** : an enclosed space **c** : ¹RANGE 6, SCOPE ⟨within the *compass* of my voice⟩ **2 a** : a device for determining directions by means of a magnetic needle pointing to the magnetic north **b** : any of various other devices that indicate direction **3** : an instrument for drawing circles or transferring measurements that consists of two pointed branches joined at the top — usually used in plural

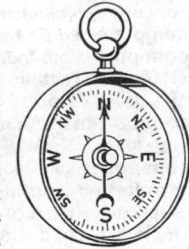

²compass 2a

com·pas·sion \kəm-'pash-ən\ *n* : sorrow or pity caused by the suffering or misfortune of another : SYMPATHY — **com·pas·sion·ate** \-'pash-(ə-)nət\ *adj* — **com·pas·sion·ate·ly** *adv*

com·pat·i·ble \kəm-'pat-ə-bəl\ *adj* **1** : capable of existing together in harmony ⟨*compatible* colors⟩ ⟨*compatible* devices⟩ **2** : able to cross-fertilize freely ⟨*compatible* plants⟩ — **com·pat·i·bil·i·ty** \-,pat-ə-'bil-ət-ē\ *n*

com·pa·tri·ot \kəm-'pā-trē-ət, käm-, -trē-,ät\ *n* : a person from one's own country : COUNTRYMAN

com·pel \kəm-'pel\ *vb* **com·pelled; com·pel·ling** **1** : to cause to do something by the use of physical, moral, or mental pressure : FORCE ⟨illness *compelled* him to stay in bed⟩ **2** : ¹EXACT, EXTORT ⟨*compel* obedience⟩ — **com·pel·ler** *n* — **com·pel·ling·ly** \-'pel-iŋ-lē\ *adv*

com·pen·di·ous \kəm-'pen-dē-əs\ *adj* : marked by a brief presentation of a broad subject : CONCISE ⟨a *compendious* book⟩

com·pen·sate \'käm-pən-,sāt\ *vb* **-sat·ed; -sat·ing** **1** : to be equal in value or effect : COUNTERBALANCE **2** : to

make up for ⟨effort that *compensates* for lack of skill⟩ **3** : to make equal return to : PAY ⟨*compensate* workers for their labor⟩ — **com·pen·sa·to·ry** \kəm-'pen(t)-sə-,tōr-ē, -,tȯr-\ *adj*

com·pen·sa·tion \,käm-pən-'sā-shən\ *n* **1** : the act of compensating : the state of being compensated **2 a** : something that compensates; *esp* : payment to an unemployed or injured worker **b** : payment in the form of salary or wages

com·pete \kəm-'pēt\ *vb* **com·pet·ed; com·pet·ing** : to strive for something (as a prize or reward) for which another is also striving : CONTEST

com·pe·tence \'käm-pət-ən(t)s\ *n* **1** : a supply (as of money or property) that is enough to provide for the necessities of life **2** : the quality or state of being competent

com·pe·ten·cy \'käm-pət-ən-sē\ *n* : COMPETENCE

com·pe·tent \'käm-pət-ənt\ *adj* : having the necessary ability or qualities : CAPABLE ⟨a *competent* musician⟩ — **com·pe·tent·ly** *adv*

com·pe·ti·tion \,käm-pə-'tish-ən\ *n* **1** : the act or process of competing **2 a** : a contest between rivals **b** : RIVALRY **c** : an individual or group one is competing against ⟨look over the *competition*⟩ **3** : the effort of persons or firms to attract business by offering the most favorable terms **4** : the active seeking after and use of an environmental resource (as food) in limited supply by two or more plants or animals or kinds of plants and animals

com·pet·i·tive \kəm-'pet-ət-iv\ *adj* : relating to, characterized by, or based on competition ⟨*competitive* sports⟩ ⟨*competitive* bidding⟩ — **com·pet·i·tive·ly** *adv* — **com·pet·i·tive·ness** *n*

com·pet·i·tor \kəm-'pet-ət-ər\ *n* : one that competes especially in the selling of goods or services : RIVAL

com·pi·la·tion \,käm-pə-'lā-shən\ *n* **1** : the act or process of compiling **2** : something compiled; *esp* : a book of materials gathered from other books

com·pile \kəm-'pīl\ *vb* **com·piled; com·pil·ing** **1** : to collect into a volume or list ⟨*compile* a book of poems⟩ **2** : to put together in a new form out of materials from other books or documents ⟨*compile* a history of India⟩ **3** : to translate (as a computer program) with a compiler

com·pil·er \kəm-'pī-lər\ *n* **1** : one that compiles **2** : a computer program that automatically translates an entire set of instructions written in a computer programming language (as BASIC) into machine language

com·pla·cence \kəm-'plās-ᵊn(t)s\ *n* : a calm or satisfied feeling about one's self : SELF-SATISFACTION

com·pla·cen·cy \kəm-'plās-ᵊn-sē\ *n* : COMPLACENCE

com·pla·cent \kəm-'plās-ᵊnt\ *adj* **1** : marked by complacency : SELF-SATISFIED ⟨a *complacent* smile⟩ **2** : feeling or showing complaisance — **com·pla·cent·ly** *adv*

com·plain \kəm-'plān\ *vb* **1** : to express grief, pain, or discontent : find fault ⟨*complaining* about the weather⟩ **2** : to accuse someone of wrongdoing — **com·plain·er** *n* — **com·plain·ing·ly** \-'plā-niŋ-lē\ *adv*

com·plain·ant \kəm-'plā-nənt\ *n* **1** : one who makes a legal complaint **2** : one who complains

com·plaint \kəm-'plānt\ *n* **1** : expression of grief, pain, or resentment **2 a** : a cause or reason for complaining ⟨the noise was her biggest *complaint*⟩ **b** : a pain or sickness in the body **3** : a charge of illegal wrongdoing against a person

com·plai·sance \kəm-'plās-ᵊn(t)s, -'plāz-; ,käm-plā-'zan(t)s\ *n* : a desire or willingness to please — **com·plai·sant** \-ᵊnt, -'zant\ *adj*

¹com·ple·ment \'käm-plə-mənt\ *n* **1** : something that fills up, completes, or makes perfect **2** : full quantity, number, or amount ⟨a ship's *complement* of officers and crew⟩ **3 a :** the angle that when added to a given angle equals 90 degrees **b :** the set of all elements not included in a given mathematical set **4 :** an added word or group of words by which the predicate of a sentence is made complete ⟨"president" in "they elected her president" and "to work" in "he wants to work" are different kinds of *complements*⟩ **5 :** a heat-sensitive substance in normal blood that in combination with antibodies destroys antigens (as bacteria and foreign blood corpuscles)

²**com·ple·ment** \'käm-plə-ˌment\ *vb* : to form or serve as a complement to ⟨a shirt that *complements* a suit⟩

com·ple·men·ta·ry \ˌkäm-plə-'ment-ə-rē, -'men-trē\ *adj* : forming or serving as a complement

complementary angles *n pl* : two angles whose sum is 90 degrees

complementary colors *n pl* : a pair of colors that when mixed in proper proportions produce a neutral color

¹**com·plete** \kəm-'plēt\ *adj* **com·plet·er; com·plet·est 1 :** possessing all necessary parts : ENTIRE ⟨a *complete* set of books⟩ ⟨a *complete* diet⟩ **2 :** brought to an end : having been completed ⟨five *complete* days⟩ **3 :** being such to the fullest degree : THOROUGH, ABSOLUTE ⟨*complete* freedom⟩ ⟨a *complete* failure⟩ **4** *of a football pass* : legally caught — **com·plete·ly** *adv* — **com·plete·ness** *n*

²**complete** *vb* **com·plet·ed; com·plet·ing 1 :** to bring to an end : accomplish or achieve fully ⟨*complete* a job⟩ **2 :** to make whole or perfect ⟨the shoes *complete* the outfit⟩

complete metamorphosis *n* : insect metamorphosis (as of a butterfly) in which there is a pupal stage between the immature stage and the adult and in which the young insect is very different in form from the adult — compare INCOMPLETE METAMORPHOSIS

complete protein *n* : protein (as in meat, fish, milk, and eggs) supplying all the amino acids that are needed by the human body but cannot be made by it

com·ple·tion \kəm-'plē-shən\ *n* : the act or process of completing : the state of being complete ⟨a job near *completion*⟩

¹**com·plex** \'käm-ˌpleks\ *n* **1 :** a whole made up of many complicated or related parts **2 :** a system of thoughts, feelings, and memories that exist in one's mind but of which one is not aware and which influence one's behavior **3 :** a building or group of buildings housing related units ⟨an apartment *complex*⟩

²**com·plex** \käm-'pleks, kəm-; 'käm-ˌpleks\ *adj* **1 a :** composed of two or more parts ⟨a *complex* mixture⟩ **b :** consisting of a main clause and one or more subordinate clauses ⟨a *complex* sentence⟩ **c :** formed by union of simpler substances **2 :** having many parts, details, ideas, or functions often related in a complicated way ⟨a *complex* problem⟩ ⟨a *complex* machine⟩ — **com·plex·ly** *adv*

complex fraction *n* : a fraction with a fraction or mixed number in the numerator or denominator or both

com·plex·ion \kəm-'plek-shən\ *n* **1 :** the hue or appearance of the skin and especially of the face ⟨has a dark *complexion*⟩ **2 :** general appearance : CHARACTER ⟨information that changes the whole *complexion* of a situation⟩ — **com·plex·ioned** \-shənd\ *adj*

com·plex·i·ty \kəm-'plek-sət-ē, käm-\ *n, pl* **-ties 1 :** something complex ⟨the *complexities* of the English language⟩ **2 :** the quality or state of being complex

com·pli·ance \kəm-'plī-ən(t)s\ *n* **1 :** the act or process of complying **2 :** a readiness or willingness to yield to others — **in compliance with :** in agreement with : in obedience to ⟨*in compliance with* a court order⟩

com·pli·ant \kəm-'plī-ənt\ *adj* : ready or willing to comply : SUBMISSIVE — **com·pli·ant·ly** *adv*

com·pli·cate \'käm-plə-ˌkāt\ *vb* **-cat·ed; -cat·ing :** to make or become complex or difficult

com·pli·cat·ed \'käm-plə-ˌkāt-əd\ *adj* **1 :** consisting of many combined parts ⟨*complicated* machinery⟩ **2 :** difficult to analyze, understand, or explain : COMPLEX — **com·pli·cat·ed·ly** *adv* — **com·pli·cat·ed·ness** *n*

com·pli·ca·tion \ˌkäm-plə-'kā-shən\ *n* **1 a :** an act or instance of complicating something **b :** a situation or detail of character that complicates a plot **c :** a complex feature or element **d :** something that makes a situation more complicated or difficult ⟨we were unable to agree when *complications* arose⟩ **2 :** a disease or bodily condition existing at the same time as and affecting the course or severity of another disease or condition

com·plic·i·ty \kəm-'plis-ət-ē\ *n, pl* **-ties :** association or participation in a wrongful act

¹**com·pli·ment** \'käm-plə-mənt\ *n* **1 :** an expression of respect, affection, or admiration; *esp* : an admiring remark **2** *pl* : best wishes : REGARDS

 synonyms COMPLIMENT, FLATTERY mean praise directed to someone. COMPLIMENT suggests that one is sincere in admiring someone or giving credit ⟨received many *compliments* on his appearance⟩. FLATTERY is more likely to suggest that one is insincere and appealing to another's vanity especially for selfish reasons ⟨the king received much *flattery* from his servants⟩.

²**com·pli·ment** \'käm-plə-ˌment\ *vb* : to pay a compliment to ⟨was *complimented* on his performance⟩

com·pli·men·ta·ry \ˌkäm-plə-'ment-ə-rē, -'men-trē\ *adj* **1 :** expressing or containing a compliment ⟨a *complimentary* remark⟩ **2 :** given free as a courtesy or favor ⟨*complimentary* tickets⟩

com·ply \kəm-'plī\ *vb* **com·plied; com·ply·ing :** to act in agreement with another's wishes or in obedience to a rule ⟨*comply* with a request⟩ — **com·pli·er** \-'plī(-ə)r\ *n*

¹**com·po·nent** \kəm-'pō-nənt, käm-; 'käm-ˌpō-nənt\ *n* : a part or element of something ⟨*components* of an electric circuit⟩ ⟨*components* of a meal⟩

²**component** *adj* : being or forming a part : CONSTITUENT

com·port \kəm-'pōrt, -'pȯrt\ *vb* **1 :** to be in agreement : ACCORD ⟨actions that *comport* with the rules⟩ **2 :** BEHAVE 1, CONDUCT ⟨*comport* yourself with dignity⟩

com·port·ment \kəm-'pōrt-mənt, -'pȯrt-\ *n* : BEHAVIOR 1, BEARING

com·pose \kəm-'pōz\ *vb* **com·posed; com·pos·ing 1 a :** to form by putting together : FASHION **b :** to form the substance of : CONSTITUTE ⟨a stew *composed* of many ingredients⟩ **c :** to arrange type in order for printing : SET **2 :** to create by mental or artistic labor ⟨*compose* a song⟩ **3 :** to arrange in proper form **4 a :** to make (oneself) calm **b :** to gain control of ⟨try to *compose* your feelings⟩

com·posed \kəm-'pōzd\ *adj* : being calm and in control : SELF-POSSESSED — **com·pos·ed·ly** \-'pō-zəd-lē\ *adv*

com·pos·er \kəm-'pō-zər\ *n* : one that composes; *esp* : a person who writes music

¹**com·pos·ite** \käm-'päz-ət, kəm-\ *adj* **1 :** made up of various parts or elements ⟨a *composite* photograph⟩ **2 :** of or relating to a very large family of dicotyledonous plants (as a daisy or aster) that are characterized by flowers arranged in dense heads that resemble single flowers **3** : able to be factored into two or more prime factors other than 1 and itself ⟨12 is a *composite* number since $2 \times 2 \times 3 = 12$⟩

²**composite** *n* **1 :** something that is made up of different parts : COMPOUND **2 :** a composite plant

com·po·si·tion \ˌkäm-pə-'zish-ən\ *n* **1 :** the act or process of composing **2 :** the manner in which the parts of a thing are put together : MAKEUP ⟨the *composition* of a painting⟩ **3 :** the elements of a compound ⟨the *composition* of

complementary angles: *ACD* and *DCB*

rubber⟩ **4** : a product of combining ingredients : COMBI-NATION ⟨a *composition* made of several different metals⟩ **5** : a literary, musical, or artistic production; *esp* : a short piece of writing done as a school exercise

com·pos·i·tor \kəm-'päz-ət-ər\ *n* : one who arranges type for printing

com·post \'käm-ˌpōst\ *n* : a mixture largely of decayed matter of once living things (as grass) or their products (as coffee grinds) and used for fertilizing and conditioning land

com·po·sure \kəm-'pō-zhər\ *n* : calmness especially of mind, manner, or appearance ⟨she kept her *composure*⟩

com·pote \'käm-ˌpōt\ *n* **1** : fruits cooked in syrup **2** : a bowl usually with a base and stem from which compotes, fruits, nuts, or sweets are served

¹**com·pound** \käm-'paund, kəm-; 'käm-ˌpaund\ *vb* **1** : to put together or be joined to form a whole : COMBINE **2** : to form by combining parts ⟨*compound* a medicine⟩ **3** : to settle or adjust by agreement ⟨*compound* a debt⟩ **4 a** : to pay in the form of compound interest ⟨interest *compounded* quarterly⟩ **b** : to add to ⟨*compounded* our errors⟩ [Middle English *compounen* "combine, compound," from early French *compondre* (same meaning), from Latin *componere* "compound, combine," from *com-* "with, together" and *ponere* "to place, put" — related to POSITION] — **com·pound·able** \-'paun-də-bəl, -ˌpaun-\ *adj* — **com·pound·er** *n*

²**com·pound** \'käm-ˌpaund; käm-'paund, kəm-\ *adj* **1** : made of or by the union of separate elements or parts ⟨a *compound* substance⟩ **2** : made up of two or more parts that are alike and form a common whole ⟨a raspberry is a *compound* fruit⟩ **3 a** : being a word that is a compound ⟨the *compound* noun "steamboat"⟩ **b** : consisting of two or more main clauses ⟨"I told him to leave and he left" is a *compound* sentence⟩

³**com·pound** \'käm-ˌpaund\ *n* **1** : a word consisting of parts that are words ⟨"rowboat," "high school," and "light-year" are *compounds*⟩ **2** : something formed by a union of elements or parts; *esp* : a distinct substance formed by the union of two or more chemical elements in definite proportion by weight

⁴**com·pound** \'käm-ˌpaund\ *n* : an enclosed area containing a group of buildings [from a word in Malay, the language of the people of the Malay Peninsula, *kampung* "enclosure around a building"; both spelling and pronunciation influenced by the more familiar English word *compound*]

compound–complex *adj* : having two or more main clauses and one or more subordinate clauses ⟨*compound-complex* sentence⟩

compound eye *n* : an eye (as of an insect) made up of many separate visual units

compound fracture *n* : a breaking of a bone in such a way as to produce an open wound through which bone fragments stick out — compare SIMPLE FRACTURE

compound interest *n* : interest paid or to be paid both on the principal and on accumulated unpaid interest

compound leaf *n* : a leaf in which the blade is divided to the middle several times forming two or more leaflets

compound microscope *n* : a microscope having an objective and an eyepiece in a tube that can be adjusted in length

com·pre·hend \ˌkäm-pri-'hend\ *vb* **1** : to grasp the meaning of : UNDERSTAND **2** : INCLUDE — **com·pre·hend·ible** \-'hen-də-bəl\

compound leaf

adj — **com·pre·hen·si·bil·i·ty** \-ˌhen(t)-sə-'bil-ət-ē\ *n* — **com·pre·hen·si·ble** \-'hen(t)-sə-bəl\ *adj* — **com·pre·hen·si·bly** \-'hen(t)-sə-blē\ *adv*

com·pre·hen·sion \ˌkäm-pri-'hen-chən\ *n* **1** : the act of comprehending **2** : knowledge gained by comprehending **3** : the capacity for understanding

com·pre·hen·sive \ˌkäm-pri-'hen(t)-siv\ *adj* : including much or all : FULL ⟨a *comprehensive* course of study⟩ ⟨a *comprehensive* list⟩ — **com·pre·hen·sive·ness** *n*

¹**com·press** \kəm-'pres\ *vb* **1** : to press or become pressed together **2** : to reduce the size, amount, or volume of by or as if by pressure — **com·press·ibil·i·ty** \-ˌpres-ə-'bil-ət-ē\ *n* — **com·press·ible** \-'pres-ə-bəl\ *adj*

²**com·press** \'käm-ˌpres\ *n* **1** : a folded cloth or pad applied so as to press upon a body part ⟨a cold *compress*⟩ **2** : a machine for compressing

com·pressed air \kəm-ˌprest-\ *n* : air under pressure greater than that of the atmosphere

com·pres·sion \kəm-'presh-ən\ *n* **1** : the act, process, or result of compressing : the state of being compressed **2** : the process of compressing the fuel mixture in the cylinders of an internal-combustion engine — **com·pres·sion·al** \-(ə-)nəl\ *adj*

com·pres·sor \kəm-'pres-ər\ *n* : a person or machine that compresses ⟨an air *compressor*⟩

com·prise \kəm-'prīz\ *vb* **com·prised; com·pris·ing** **1** : INCLUDE, CONTAIN ⟨the test *comprised* two essay questions⟩ **2** : to be made up of ⟨the play *comprises* three acts⟩ **3** : COMPOSE 1b, CONSTITUTE ⟨nine players *comprise* a baseball team⟩

¹**com·pro·mise** \'käm-prə-ˌmīz\ *n* **1** : a settlement of a dispute by each party giving up some demands **2** : a giving up to something that is wrong or degrading : SURRENDER ⟨a *compromise* of one's principles⟩ **3** : the thing agreed upon as a result of a compromise

²**compromise** *vb* **-mised; -mis·ing** **1** : to adjust or settle differences by means of a compromise **2** : to expose to disgrace, suspicion, or danger ⟨*compromised* his reputation⟩ ⟨*compromise* security⟩ — **com·pro·mis·er** *n*

comp·trol·ler \kən-'trō-lər, käm(p)-; 'käm(p)-ˌtrō-lər\ *n* : a public official who examines financial accounts

com·pul·sion \kəm-'pəl-shən\ *n* **1** : an act of compelling : the state of being compelled **2** : a force that compels **3** : an irresistible persistent urge ⟨felt a *compulsion* to eat⟩

com·pul·sive \kəm-'pəl-siv\ *adj* : caused by or subject to an irresistible urge ⟨*compulsive* behavior⟩ — **com·pul·sive·ly** *adv*

com·pul·so·ry \kəm-'pəls-(ə-)rē\ *adj* **1** : required by or as if by law ⟨*compulsory* education⟩ **2** : having the power of forcing someone to do something ⟨a *compulsory* law⟩

com·punc·tion \kəm-'pəŋ(k)-shən\ *n* **1** : sharp uneasiness caused by a sense of guilt : REMORSE **2** : a passing feeling of regret for some slight wrong **synonyms** see QUALM

com·pu·ta·tion \ˌkäm-pyù-'tā-shən\ *n* **1** : the act or action of computing : CALCULATION **2** : a system of calculating especially by mathematical means **3** : an amount computed — **com·pu·ta·tion·al** \-shnəl, -shən-ᵊl\ *adj*

com·pute \kəm-'pyüt\ *vb* **com·put·ed; com·put·ing** : to determine or calculate especially by mathematical means; *also* : to determine or calculate by means of a computer [from Latin *computare* "to count, compute" — related to ACCOUNT, ¹COUNT] — **com·put·able** \-'pyüt-ə-bəl\ *adj*

computed tomography *n* : the process by which a CAT scan is produced — called also *computerized tomography*

\ə\ abut	\aú\ out	\i\ tip	\ò\ saw	\ú\ foot
\ər\ further	\ch\ chin	\ī\ life	\òi\ coin	\y\ yet
\a\ mat	\e\ pet	\j\ job	\th\ thin	\yü\ few
\ā\ take	\ē\ easy	\ŋ\ sing	\th\ this	\yù\ cure
\ä\ cot, cart	\g\ go	\ō\ bone	\ü\ food	\zh\ vision

com·put·er \-'pyüt-ər\ *n* : one that computes; *esp* : a programmable usually electronic machine that can store, get back again, and work with data

com·put·er·ize \kəm-'pyüt-ə-ˌrīz\ *vb* **-ized; -iz·ing** **1** : to carry out, control, or produce through the use of a computer **2** : to provide with computers **3 a** : to store in a computer **b** : to put into a form that a computer can use

computer science *n* : a branch of science that deals with the theory of computing or the design of computers

com·rade \'käm-ˌrad, -rəd\ *n* : a close friend or associate — **com·rade·ly** *adj* — **com·rade·ship** \-ˌship\ *n*

¹con \'kän\ *vb* **conned; con·ning** **1** : MEMORIZE **2** : to study carefully [Middle English *connen* "to know, learn," derived from *can* (auxiliary verb) "to know, know how to"]

²con *adv* : on the negative side : in opposition ⟨argue pro and *con*⟩ [Middle English *con* "on the negative side, against"; a shortened form of *contra* "against, contrary"]

³con *n* : an opposing argument, person, or position ⟨the pros and *cons* of the question⟩

⁴con *adj* : ²CONFIDENCE ⟨a *con* game⟩

con- — see COM-

con·cat·e·nate \kän-'kat-ə-ˌnāt, kən-\ *vb* **-nat·ed; -nat·ing** : to link together in a series or chain — **con·cat·e·na·tion** \(ˌ)kän-ˌkat-ə-'nā-shən, kən-\ *n*

con·cave \kän-'kāv, 'kän-ˌkāv\ *adj* : hollowed or rounded inward like the inside of a bowl ⟨*concave* lens⟩ — **con·cav·i·ty** \kän-'kav-ət-ē\ *n*

con·ceal \kən-'sē(ə)l\ *vb* **1** : to keep secret ⟨*conceal* a fact⟩ **2** : to hide from sight ⟨carry a *concealed* weapon⟩ — **con·ceal·able** \-'sē-lə-bəl\ *adj* — **con·ceal·er** *n*

con·ceal·ment \kən-'sē(ə)l-mənt\ *n* **1** : the act of hiding : the state of being hidden **2** : a hiding place ⟨attacked from *concealment*⟩

con·cede \kən-'sēd\ *vb* **con·ced·ed; con·ced·ing** **1** : to grant as a right or privilege **2** : to admit the truth or existence of something ⟨*concede* defeat⟩ [from French *concéder* or Latin *concedere,* both meaning "to yield, grant, concede," from Latin *con-, com-* "together, with" and *cedere* "to go, withdraw, yield" — related to ANCESTOR, NECESSARY, PREDECESSOR, SUCCEED] — **con·ced·er** *n*

con·ceit \kən-'sēt\ *n* **1** : too much pride in one's own worth or virtue **2 a** : an idea showing imagination **b** : a complicated way of expressing something

con·ceit·ed \kən-'sēt-əd\ *adj* : having or showing too high an opinion of oneself — **con·ceit·ed·ly** *adv* — **con·ceit·ed·ness** *n*

con·ceive \kən-'sēv\ *vb* **con·ceived; con·ceiv·ing** **1** : to become pregnant or pregnant with ⟨*conceive* a child⟩ **2 a** : to take into the mind ⟨*conceived* a liking for the singer⟩ **b** : to form an idea of : IMAGINE ⟨*conceive* a new design⟩ **3** : to have as an opinion : THINK ⟨*conceived* of her as a genius⟩ — **con·ceiv·able** \-'sē-və-bəl\ *adj* — **con·ceiv·ably** \-blē\ *adv* — **con·ceiv·er** *n*

¹con·cen·trate \'kän(t)-sən-ˌtrāt, -sen-\ *vb* **-trat·ed; -trat·ing** **1 a** : to bring, direct, or come toward or meet in a common center or objective ⟨*concentrate* one's efforts⟩ **b** : to gather into one body, mass, or force **2** : to increase the amount of a substance in a space by removing other substances with which it is mixed or in which it is dissolved ⟨*concentrate* syrup⟩ ⟨*concentrate* ore⟩ **3** : to fix one's powers, efforts, or attention on one thing ⟨*concentrate* on a problem⟩ — **con·cen·tra·tor** \-ˌtrāt-ər\ *n*

²concentrate *n* : something concentrated ⟨frozen orange juice *concentrate*⟩

con·cen·tra·tion \ˌkän(t)-sən-'trā-shən, -sen-\ *n* **1** : the act or process of concentrating : the state of being concentrated; *esp* : direction of attention on a single object ⟨don't disturb my *concentration*⟩ **2** : a concentrated mass **3** : the amount of an ingredient or part in relation to that of others : STRENGTH ⟨the *concentration* of salt in a solution⟩

concentration camp *n* : a camp where persons (as prisoners of war, political prisoners, or refugees) are detained

con·cen·tric \kən-'sen-trik, (')kän-\ *adj* : having a common center ⟨*concentric* circles⟩

con·cept \'kän-ˌsept\ *n* **1** : something conceived in the mind : THOUGHT, NOTION **2** : a general idea ⟨arrived at the *concept* of a flower by studying many different kinds of flowers⟩ — **con·cep·tu·al** \kən-'sep-chə(-wə)l, -'sepsh-wəl\ *adj*

con·cep·tion \kən-'sep-shən\ *n* **1** : the beginning of pregnancy involving formation of a zygote **2 a** : the function or process of conceiving ideas **b** : a general idea : CONCEPT ⟨had no *conception* of what he was saying⟩ **3** : the originating of an idea ⟨the *conception* of a new device⟩

¹con·cern \kən-'sərn\ *vb* **1** : to relate to : be about ⟨the novel *concerns* three soldiers⟩ **2** : to be the business or affair of ⟨the problem *concerns* us all⟩ **3** : to make worried or disturbed ⟨our mother's illness *concerns* us⟩ **4** : INVOLVE 1, ENGAGE ⟨*concerned* himself in the matter⟩

²concern *n* **1** : something that concerns one : AFFAIR ⟨the *concerns* of the day⟩ **2** : a state of interest and uncertainty : ANXIETY ⟨deep *concern* for their friend's health⟩ ⟨public *concern* over pollution⟩ **3** : a business or manufacturing establishment ⟨a banking *concern*⟩

con·cerned \kən-'sərnd\ *adj* : being worried and disturbed ⟨*concerned* for our safety⟩

con·cern·ing \kən-'sər-niŋ\ *prep* : relating to : ABOUT ⟨news *concerning* friends⟩

¹con·cert \'kän(t)-sərt, 'kän-ˌsərt\ *n* **1** : agreement in design or plan **2** : a musical performance usually by several voices or instruments or both — **in concert** : TOGETHER 4a ⟨acting *in concert* with others⟩

²con·cert \kən-'sərt\ *vb* : to plan or arrange together : settle by agreement ⟨*concerted* their differences⟩

con·cert·ed \kən-'sərt-əd\ *adj* **1 a** : mutually planned or agreed on ⟨*concerted* effort⟩ **b** : performed at the same time ⟨*concerted* artillery fire⟩ **2** : being music written to be performed by several voices or instruments

con·cer·ti·na \ˌkän(t)-sər-'tē-nə\ *n* : a small musical instrument resembling an accordion

con·cert·mas·ter \'kän(t)-sərt-ˌmas-tər\ *or* **con·cert·meis·ter** \-ˌmī-stər\ *n* : the leader of the first violins and assistant conductor of an orchestra

con·cer·to \kən-'chert-ō\ *n, pl* **-ti** \-(ˌ)ē\ *or* **-tos** : a piece for one or more soloists and orchestra usually in three movements

con·ces·sion \kən-'sesh-ən\ *n* **1** : the act or an instance of conceding **2** : something conceded or granted **3** : a special right or privilege given by an authority ⟨a *concession* to sell souvenirs⟩ ⟨a mining *concession*⟩

concertina

con·ces·sion·aire \kən-ˌsesh-ə-'na(ə)r, -'ne(ə)r\ *n* : one that has been given a concession (as to sell something)

conch \'käŋk, 'känch\ *n, pl* **conchs** \'käŋks\ *or* **conch·es** \'kän-chəz\ : a large marine gastropod mollusk having a spiral shell; *also* : its shell

con·cil·i·ate \kən-'sil-ē-ˌāt\ *vb* **-at·ed; -at·ing** **1** : to bring into agreement : RECONCILE **2** : to gain the goodwill or favor of ⟨*conciliate* the opposition⟩ — **con·cil·i·a·tion** \-ˌsil-ē-'ā-shən\ *n* — **con·cil·i·a·tor** \-'sil-ē-ˌāt-ər\ *n* — **con·cil·ia·to·ry** \-'sil-yə-ˌtōr-ē, -'sil-ē-ə-, -ˌtòr-\ *adj*

conch

con·cise \kən-'sīs\ *adj* : being brief and to the point ⟨a *concise* summary⟩ — **con·cise·ly** *adv* — **con·cise·ness** *n*

con·clave \'kän-ˌklāv\ *n* : a private or secret meeting or assembly

con·clude \kən-'klüd\ *vb* **con·clud·ed; con·clud·ing** **1** : to bring or come to an end : FINISH ⟨*conclude* a speech⟩ **2** : to form an opinion : decide by reasoning ⟨*conclude* that they are right⟩ **3** : to bring about as a result : ARRANGE ⟨*conclude* an agreement⟩ — **con·clud·er** *n*

con·clu·sion \kən-'klü-zhən\ *n* **1** : a final decision reached by reasoning ⟨came to the *conclusion* that we couldn't go⟩ **2 a** : the last part of something : END **b** : a final result : OUTCOME **c** : a final summing up ⟨the *conclusion* of a speech⟩ **3** : an act or instance of concluding

con·clu·sive \kən-'klü-siv, -ziv\ *adj* : DECISIVE 1, CONVINCING ⟨*conclusive* proof⟩ — **con·clu·sive·ly** *adv* — **con·clu·sive·ness** *n*

con·coct \kən-'käkt, kän-\ *vb* **1** : to prepare by combining various ingredients ⟨*concoct* a stew⟩ **2** : to think up : INVENT ⟨*concoct* a likely story⟩ — **con·coc·tion** \-'käk-shən\ *n*

con·com·i·tant \kən-'käm-ə-tənt, kän-\ *adj* : accompanying especially as something of less importance — **con·comitant** *n* — **con·com·i·tant·ly** *adv*

con·cord \'kän-kȯ(ə)rd, 'käŋ-\ *n* : a state of agreement : HARMONY

con·cord·ance \kən-'kȯrd-ᵊn(t)s, kän-\ *n* **1** : an alphabetical index of the principal words in a book or in the works of an author **2** : CONCORD

con·cord·ant \kən-'kȯrd-ᵊnt\ *adj* : being in agreement : CONSONANT — **con·cord·ant·ly** *adv*

con·course \'kän-kȯ(ə)rs, 'käŋ-, -kȯ(ə)rs\ *n* **1** : a flocking, moving, or flowing together : GATHERING **2** : a place (as a boulevard, open area, or hall) where many people pass or gather ⟨the *concourse* of the bus terminal⟩

¹con·crete \(')kän-'krēt, kən-; 'kän-ˌkrēt\ *adj* **1** : naming a real thing or class of things : not abstract ⟨"book" is a *concrete* noun but "goodness" is not⟩ **2 a** : belonging to or based on actual experience ⟨*concrete* examples⟩ **b** : ¹MATERIAL 1, REAL ⟨*concrete* evidence⟩ **3** \'kän-ˌkrēt, kän-'krēt\ : relating to or made of concrete ⟨a *concrete* wall⟩ — **con·crete·ly** *adv* — **con·crete·ness** *n*

²con·crete \'kän-ˌkrēt, (')kän-'krēt\ *vb* **con·cret·ed; con·cret·ing** **1** : SOLIDIFY **2** : to cover with, form of, or set in concrete

³con·crete \'kän-ˌkrēt, (')kän-'krēt\ *n* : a hard strong building material made by mixing cement, sand, and gravel or broken rock with water

con·cre·tion \kän-'krē-shən, kən-\ *n* **1** : a hard usually inorganic mass formed in a living body **2** : a lump or egg-shaped mass of mineral matter found in rock of different composition

con·cu·bine \'käŋ-kyu̇-ˌbīn, 'kän-\ *n* : a woman who lives with a man and among some peoples has a legally recognized position in his household less than that of a wife

con·cur \kən-'kər, kän-\ *vb* **con·curred; con·cur·ring** **1** : to act together : COMBINE ⟨several events *concurred* to mark the occasion as special⟩ **2** : to be in agreement : ACCORD ⟨*concur* with an opinion⟩ **3** : to happen together : COINCIDE

con·cur·rence \kən-'kər-ən(t)s, -'kə-rən(t)s, kän-\ *n* **1** : agreement in action, opinion, or intent : COOPERATION **2** : ²CONSENT **3** : a coming together : CONJUNCTION

con·cur·rent \kən-'kər-ənt, -'kə-rənt, kän-\ *adj* **1** : operating or occurring at the same time ⟨*concurrent* expeditions to the Antarctic region⟩ **2** : coming together : meeting in a point ⟨*concurrent* lines⟩ **3** : acting together — **con·cur·rent·ly** *adv*

con·cus·sion \kən-'kəsh-ən\ *n* **1** : a violent uneven motion **2** : a hard blow or collision **3** : bodily injury especially of the brain resulting from a sudden sharp jar (as from a blow) — **con·cus·sive** \-'kəs-iv\ *adj*

con·demn \kən-'dem\ *vb* **1** : to declare to be wrong : CENSURE ⟨*condemned* their behavior⟩ **2 a** : to pronounce guilty : CONVICT **b** : ²SENTENCE 1 **3** : to declare to be unfit for use or consumption ⟨a *condemned* building⟩ — **con·dem·na·tion** \ˌkän-ˌdem-'nā-shən, -dəm-\ *n* — **con·demn·er** or **con·demn·or** \-'dem-ər\ *n*

con·den·sate \'kän-dən-ˌsāt, -ˌden-; kən-'den-\ *n* : a product of condensation ⟨steam *condensate*⟩

con·den·sa·tion \ˌkän-ˌden-'sā-shən, -dən-\ *n* **1** : the act or process of condensing **2** : the quality or state of being condensed **3** : a product of condensing; *esp* : a shortened literary work

con·dense \kən-'den(t)s\ *vb* **con·densed; con·dens·ing** **1** : to make or become more close, compact, concise, or dense : CONCENTRATE ⟨*condense* a paragraph into a sentence⟩ **2** : to change from a less dense to a denser form ⟨steam *condenses* into water⟩

con·densed milk \kən-'den(t)st-\ *n* : evaporated milk with sugar added

con·dens·er \kən-'den(t)-sər\ *n* **1** : one that condenses **2** : CAPACITOR

con·de·scend \ˌkän-di-'send\ *vb* **1** : to lower oneself to a level considered less dignified or humbler than one's own **2** : to act in a way that suggests that one considers oneself better than other people — **con·de·scend·ing·ly** \-'sen-diŋ-lē\ *adv*

con·de·scen·sion \ˌkän-di-'sen-chən\ *n* : the attitude or behavior of a person who condescends

con·di·ment \'kän-də-mənt\ *n* : something used to give food a good taste; *esp* : a tangy seasoning

¹con·di·tion \kən-'dish-ən\ *n* **1** : something on which the carrying out of an agreement depends ⟨*conditions* of employment⟩ **2** : something essential to the appearance or occurrence of something else **3** : something that limits or restricts : QUALIFICATION **4 a** : a state of being **b** : position in life ⟨people of humble *condition*⟩ **c** *pl* : state of affairs ⟨poor living *conditions*⟩ **5 a** : a bodily state in which something is wrong ⟨a serious heart *condition*⟩ **b** : a state of physical fitness or readiness for use ⟨an athlete in good *condition*⟩ ⟨the car was in poor *condition*⟩

²condition *vb* **-di·tioned; -di·tion·ing** \-'dish-(ə-)niŋ\ **1** : to put into a proper or desired condition **2 a** : to adapt, modify, or mold to respond in a particular way **b** : to change the behavior of (an organism) in such a way that a response to a given stimulus becomes connected with a different and formerly unrelated stimulus ⟨dogs can be *conditioned* to salivate at the sound of a bell⟩

con·di·tion·al \kən-'dish-nəl, -ən-ᵊl\ *adj* **1** : depending on a condition ⟨a *conditional* sale⟩ **2** : expressing, containing, or implying something supposed ⟨"if we go" is a *conditional* clause⟩ — **con·di·tion·al·ly** \-nə-lē, -ən-ᵊl-ē\ *adv*

con·di·tioned \kən-'dish-ənd\ *adj* : caused or established by conditioning ⟨a *conditioned* reflex to a stimulus⟩

con·di·tion·er \kən-'dish-(ə-)nər\ *n* : something that conditions; *esp* : a preparation used to improve the condition of hair

con·do \'kän-dō\ *n, pl* **condos** : CONDOMINIUM

con·dole \kən-'dōl\ *vb* **con·doled; con·dol·ing** : to express sympathetic sorrow ⟨*condole* with them in their grief⟩ — **con·do·lence** \kən-'dō-lən(t)s, 'kän-də-\ *n*

con·dom \'kən-dəm, 'kän-\ *n* : a usually rubber covering worn over the penis during sexual intercourse especially to prevent pregnancy or venereal disease

con·do·min·i·um \ˌkän-də-'min-ē-əm\ *n* : an individually

\ə\ **abut**	\au̇\ **out**	\i\ **tip**	\ȯ\ **saw**	\u̇\ **foot**
\ər\ **further**	\ch\ **chin**	\ī\ **life**	\ȯi\ **coin**	\y\ **yet**
\a\ **mat**	\e\ **pet**	\j\ **job**	\th\ **thin**	\yü\ **few**
\ā\ **take**	\ē\ **easy**	\ŋ\ **sing**	\th\ **this**	\yu̇\ **cure**
\ä\ **cot, cart**	\g\ **go**	\ō\ **bone**	\ü\ **food**	\zh\ **vision**

owned unit in a structure (as an apartment building) with many units [derived from Latin *condominium* "joint rule or ownership," from earlier *con-, com-* "together" and *dominium* "ownership, rule," from *dominus* "master, owner" — related to DOMAIN, DOMINATE]

con·done \kən-'dōn\ *vb* **con·doned; con·don·ing** : to regard or treat (something bad) as acceptable, forgivable, or harmless ⟨*condones* his friend's faults⟩ *synonyms* see EXCUSE — **con·do·na·tion** \ˌkän-də-'nā-shən, -dō-\ *n* — **con·don·er** \kən-'dō-nər\ *n*

con·dor \'kän-dər, -ˌdȯ(ə)r\ *n* **1** : a very large South American vulture of the high Andes having the head and neck bare and the plumage dull black with a ring of white down behind the head **2** : CALIFORNIA CONDOR

con·duce \kən-'d(y)üs\ *vb* **con·duced; con·duc·ing** : to lead or tend to a usually desirable result — **con·du·cive** \-'d(y)ü-siv\ *adj* — **con·du·cive·ness** *n*

¹con·duct \'kän-(ˌ)dəkt\ *n* **1** : the act, manner, or process of carrying on : MANAGEMENT ⟨the *conduct* of foreign affairs⟩ **2** : personal behavior ⟨scolded for bad *conduct*⟩

²con·duct \kən-'dəkt\ *vb* **1** : ²GUIDE 1, ESCORT ⟨*conducted* tourists through the museum⟩ **2** : to carry on or direct from a position of command : LEAD ⟨*conduct* a business⟩ ⟨*conduct* a band⟩ **3 a** : to carry in a channel **b** : to act as a substance through which something is carried ⟨copper *conducts* electricity⟩ **4** : to cause (oneself) to act in a particular manner ⟨*conducted* themselves well at the party⟩

con·duc·tance \kən-'dək-tən(t)s\ *n* **1** : conducting power **2** : the readiness with which a conductor carries an electric current that is expressed as the reciprocal of electrical resistance

con·duc·tion \kən-'dək-shən\ *n* **1** : the act of conducting or conveying **2 a** : passage through a conductor **b** : CONDUCTIVITY **3** : the passage of a reaction to a stimulus through living and especially nerve tissue

con·duc·tive \kən-'dək-tiv\ *adj* : having conductivity : relating to conduction (as of electricity)

con·duc·tiv·i·ty \ˌkän-ˌdək-'tiv-ət-ē, kən-\ *n, pl* **-ties** : the quality or power of conducting or transmitting

con·duc·tor \kən-'dək-tər\ *n* **1** : a person who collects fares in a public means of transportation (as a bus or railroad train) **2** : the leader of a musical group **3** : a substance or body that can allow electricity, heat, or sound to pass through it

con·duc·tress \kən-'dək-trəs\ *n* : a woman who is a conductor

con·duit \'kän-ˌd(y)ü-ət *also* -d(w)ət\ *n* **1** : a channel through which water or other fluid is carried **2** : a pipe, tube, or tile for protecting electric wires or cables

cone \'kōn\ *n* **1** : a mass of overlapping woody scales that especially in the pines and other conifers are arranged on a structure like a stem and produce seeds between them; *also* : any of several flower or fruit clusters resembling such cones **2 a** : a solid figure formed by rotating a right triangle about one of its legs — called also *right circular cone* **b** : a solid figure that slopes evenly to a point from a usually circular base **3** : something shaped like a cone: as **a** : any of the cells of the retina that are sensitive to light and function in color vision **b** : the tip of a volcano **c** : ICE-CREAM CONE

Con·es·to·ga \ˌkän-ə-'stō-gə\ *n* : a broad-wheeled covered wagon formerly used to carry freight across the prairies — called also *Conestoga wagon* [named for *Conestoga*, town in Pennsylvania where the wagons were first made]

Conestoga

co·ney *or* **co·ny** \'kō-nē\ *n* **1 a** : RABBIT; *esp* : the common European rabbit **b** : rabbit fur **2** : PIKA

con·fec·tion \kən-'fek-shən\ *n* : a fancy dish or sweet [Middle English *confectioun* "mixture, candy," from early French *confection* "mixture," derived from Latin *conficere* "to prepare," from *con-, com-* "together" and *-ficere*, from *facere* "to make, do" — related to FASHION]

con·fec·tion·er \kən-'fek-sh(ə-)nər\ *n* : a manufacturer of or dealer in confections

confectioners' sugar *n* : finely powdered sugar

con·fec·tion·ery \kən-'fek-shə-ˌner-ē\ *n, pl* **-er·ies** **1** : confectioner's art or business **2** : sweet things to eat (as candy) **3** : a confectioner's shop

con·fed·er·a·cy \kən-'fed-(ə-)rə-sē\ *n, pl* **-cies** : a league of persons, parties, or states : ALLIANCE

¹con·fed·er·ate \kən-'fed-(ə-)rət\ *adj* **1** : united in a league : ALLIED **2** *cap* : of or relating to the Confederate States of America ⟨*Confederate* money⟩

²confederate *n* **1** : ²ALLY 2a, ACCOMPLICE **2** *cap* : a soldier, citizen, or supporter of the Confederate States of America

³con·fed·er·ate \kən-'fed-ə-ˌrāt\ *vb* **-at·ed; -at·ing** : to unite in a confederacy

Confederate Memorial Day *n* : any of several days observed in the South in honor of the soldiers of the Confederate States of America

con·fed·er·a·tion \kən-ˌfed-ə-'rā-shən\ *n* **1** : an act of confederating : a state of being confederated : ALLIANCE **2** : ²LEAGUE

con·fer \kən-'fər\ *vb* **con·ferred; con·fer·ring** **1** : to compare views especially in studying a problem ⟨*confer* with the committee⟩ **2** : to give or grant publicly ⟨*confer* knighthood on him⟩ — **con·fer·ment** \-'fər-mənt\ *n* — **con·fer·ra·ble** \-'fər-ə-bəl\ *adj* — **con·fer·ral** \-'fər-əl\ *n* — **con·fer·rer** \-'fər-ər\ *n*

con·fer·ee \ˌkän-fə-'rē\ *n* : one taking part in a conference

con·fer·ence \'kän-f(ə-)rən(t)s, -fərn(t)s\ *n* **1** : a meeting for discussion or exchange of opinions; *also* : the discussion itself **2** : a meeting of members of the two branches of a legislature to settle differences **3** : an association of athletic teams ⟨a football *conference*⟩

con·fess \kən-'fes\ *vb* **1** : to make known (as something wrong) **2 a** : to admit one's sins to God or to a priest **b** : to hear the confession of ⟨the priest *confessed* the penitents⟩ *synonyms* see ACKNOWLEDGE

con·fess·ed·ly \kən-'fes-əd-lē, -'fest-lē\ *adv* : by confession : ADMITTEDLY

con·fes·sion \kən-'fesh-ən\ *n* **1 a** : an act of confessing; *esp* : a telling of one's sins to a priest **b** : a meeting for the confessing of sins ⟨go to *confession*⟩ **2** : a statement admitting guilt ⟨the thief signed a *confession*⟩ **3** : a formal statement of religious beliefs : CREED

con·fes·sion·al \kən-'fesh-(ə-)nəl\ *n* **1** : the enclosed place in which a priest sits and hears confessions **2** : the practice of confessing to a priest

con·fes·sor \kən-'fes-ər\ *n* **1** : one that confesses **2** : a priest who hears confessions

con·fet·ti \kən-'fet-ē\ *n* : small bits of brightly colored paper made for throwing (as at weddings) [from Italian *confetti*, plural of *confetto* "a little candy or bonbon"; so named because the paper bits were originally imitations of the candies thrown at festivals]

con·fi·dant \'kän-fə-ˌdant, -ˌdänt\ *n* : a person to whom secrets are entrusted : a close friend

con·fi·dante \'kän-fə-ˌdant, -ˌdänt\ *n* : CONFIDANT; *esp* : one who is a woman

con·fide \kən-'fīd\ *vb* **con·fid·ed; con·fid·ing** **1** : to have confidence : TRUST ⟨*confide* in a doctor's skill⟩ **2** : to show confidence by telling secrets ⟨*confided* in her mother⟩ **3** : to tell in confidence ⟨*confide* a secret to a friend⟩ **4** : ENTRUST 1 ⟨*confide* one's safety to the police⟩ [Middle English *confiden* "to confide, trust," from early French *confider* or Latin *confidere* (both, same meaning), from Latin *con-*, *com-* "with, together" and *fidere* "to trust" — related to FAITH] — **con·fid·er** *n*

¹con·fi·dence \'kän-fəd-ən(t)s, -fə-ˌden(t)s\ *n* **1** : a feeling of trust or belief ⟨had *confidence* in our coach⟩ **2** : a feeling of certainty : ASSURANCE ⟨spoke with great *confidence*⟩ **3 a** : reliance on another's secrecy or loyalty ⟨told us in *confidence*⟩ **b** : legislative support ⟨vote of *confidence*⟩ **4** : something told in confidence : SECRET

²confidence *adj* : of, relating to, or skilled at swindling by false promises ⟨a *confidence* game⟩ ⟨a *confidence* man⟩

con·fi·dent \'kän-fəd-ənt, -fə-ˌdent\ *adj* : having or showing confidence : SURE, SELF-ASSURED ⟨*confident* of winning⟩ ⟨a *confident* manner⟩ — **con·fi·dent·ly** *adv*

con·fi·den·tial \ˌkän-fə-'den-chəl\ *adj* **1** : ¹SECRET 1a, PRIVATE ⟨*confidential* information⟩ **2** : indicating or suggesting closeness : INTIMATE ⟨a *confidential* tone of voice⟩ **3** : trusted with secret matters ⟨a *confidential* secretary⟩ — **con·fi·den·tial·ly** \-'dench-(ə-)lē\ *adv*

con·fid·ing \kən-'fīd-iŋ\ *adj* : tending to confide : TRUSTFUL ⟨a *confiding* friend⟩ — **con·fid·ing·ly** \-iŋ-lē\ *adv*

con·fig·u·ra·tion \kən-ˌfig-(y)ə-'rā-shən, kän-\ *n* : arrangement of parts or the pattern produced by such arrangement

con·fig·ure \kən-'fig-yər\ *vb* **-ured; -ur·ing** : to set up for operation especially in a particular way ⟨ships *configured* for observation⟩

con·fine \kən-'fīn\ *vb* **con·fined; con·fin·ing** **1** : to keep within limits : RESTRICT ⟨*confined* the message to twenty words⟩ **2 a** : to shut up : IMPRISON ⟨*confined* for life⟩ **b** : to keep indoors ⟨*confined* with a cold⟩ — **con·fine·ment** \kən-'fīn-mənt\ *n* — **con·fin·er** *n*

con·fines \'kän-ˌfīnz\ *n pl* : the boundary or limits of something ⟨within the *confines* of the city⟩

con·firm \kən-'fərm\ *vb* **1** : to make firm or firmer (as in habit, faith, or intention) : STRENGTHEN **2** : APPROVE 2, RATIFY ⟨*confirm* a treaty⟩ **3** : to administer confirmation to **4** : to make sure of the truth of : VERIFY ⟨*confirm* a suspicion⟩ — **con·firm·able** \-'fər-mə-bəl\ *adj*

con·fir·ma·tion \ˌkän-fər-'mā-shən\ *n* **1** : an act or process of confirming **2** : a religious ceremony admitting a person to full privileges in a church or synagogue **3** : something that confirms : PROOF — **con·firm·a·to·ry** \kən-'fər-mə-ˌtōr-ē, -ˌtȯr-\ *adj*

con·firmed \kən-'fərmd\ *adj* **1** : deeply established ⟨a *confirmed* habit⟩ **2** : unlikely to change : HABITUAL, CHRONIC ⟨a *confirmed* optimist⟩

con·fis·cate \'kän-fə-ˌskāt\ *vb* **-cat·ed; -cat·ing** : to seize by or as if by public authority ⟨smuggled goods may be *confiscated* by the police⟩ — **con·fis·ca·tion** \ˌkän-fə-'skā-shən\ *n* — **con·fis·ca·tor** \'kän-fə-ˌskāt-ər\ *n* — **con·fis·ca·to·ry** \kən-'fis-kə-ˌtōr-ē, -ˌtȯr-\ *adj*

con·fla·gra·tion \ˌkän-flə-'grā-shən\ *n* : a large disastrous fire

¹con·flict \'kän-ˌflikt\ *n* **1** : an extended struggle : FIGHT, BATTLE **2 a** : a clashing or sharp disagreement (as between ideas, interests, or purposes) **b** : mental struggle resulting from needs, drives, wishes, or demands that are in opposition or are not compatible

²con·flict \kən-'flikt, 'kän-ˌflikt\ *vb* : to be in opposition : CLASH ⟨duty and desire often *conflict*⟩

con·flu·ence \'kän-ˌflü-ən(t)s, kən-'flü-\ *n* **1** : a coming together to one place **2** : a flowing together or place of meeting especially of streams

con·flu·ent \'kän-ˌflü-ənt, kən-'flü-\ *adj* : flowing or coming together ⟨*confluent* rivers⟩

con·form \kən-'fó(ə)rm\ *vb* **1** : to bring into harmony ⟨*conform* my behavior to the circumstances⟩ **2** : to be similar or identical ⟨the data *conforms* to the pattern⟩ **3** : to act in obedience or agreement; *esp* : to adapt oneself to accepted standards or customs — **con·form·er** *n* — **con·form·ist** \-'fȯr-məst\ *n*

con·form·able \kən-'fȯr-mə-bəl\ *adj* **1** : similar in form or character ⟨*conformable* to established practice⟩ **2** : SUBMISSIVE, COMPLIANT — **con·form·ably** \-blē\ *adv*

con·for·mal \kən-'fȯr-məl, (')kän-\ *adj* : representing small areas in their true shape ⟨a *conformal* map⟩

con·for·ma·tion \ˌkän-(ˌ)fȯr-'mā-shən, -fər-\ *n* **1** : the act of conforming or producing conformity : ADAPTATION **2** : a shaping or putting into form **3 a** : ¹STRUCTURE **3 b** : the form or outline especially of an animal

con·for·mi·ty \kən-'fȯr-mət-ē\ *n, pl* **-ties** **1** : agreement in form, manner, or character ⟨behaved in *conformity* with their beliefs⟩ **2** : action in accordance with a standard or authority : OBEDIENCE ⟨*conformity* to social custom⟩

con·found \kən-'faund, kän-\ *vb* **1** : ¹DAMN 1 **2** : to throw into disorder : mix up : CONFUSE ⟨our clever tactics *confounded* our opponents⟩ — **con·found·ed·ly** *adv*

con·front \kən-'frənt\ *vb* **1** : to face especially in challenge : OPPOSE ⟨*confront* an enemy⟩ **2** : to bring face-to-face : cause to meet ⟨*confronted* with difficulties⟩ — **con·fron·ta·tion** \ˌkän-(ˌ)frən-'tā-shən\ *n*

Con·fu·cian \kən-'fyü-shən\ *adj* : of or relating to the Chinese philosopher Confucius or his teachings or followers — **Confucian** *n* — **Con·fu·cian·ism** \-shə-ˌniz-əm\ *n* — **Con·fu·cian·ist** \-shə-nəst\ *n or adj*

con·fuse \kən-'fyüz\ *vb* **con·fused; con·fus·ing** **1 a** : to make mentally foggy or uncertain : PERPLEX ⟨the complicated problem *confused* us⟩ **b** : to cause to be embarrassed or upset : DISCONCERT **2** : to make unclear : BLUR ⟨stop *confusing* the issue⟩ **3** : to make disordered : JUMBLE ⟨his motives were hopelessly *confused*⟩ **4** : to fail to tell apart ⟨teachers always *confused* the twins⟩ — **con·fused·ly** \-'fyüz(-ə)d-lē\ *adv* — **con·fus·ing·ly** \-'fyü-ziŋ-lē\ *adv*

con·fu·sion \kən-'fyü-zhən\ *n* **1** : an act or instance of confusing **2** : the quality or state of being confused ⟨her *confusion* was obvious⟩

con·fute \kən-'fyüt\ *vb* **con·fut·ed; con·fut·ing** : to overwhelm in argument : REFUTE — **con·fu·ta·tion** \ˌkän-fyü-'tā-shən\ *n*

con·ga \'käŋ-gə\ *n* **1** : a Cuban dance of African origin performed by a group usually in single file **2** : a tall narrow drum that is played with the hands

con·geal \kən-'jē(ə)l\ *vb* **1** : to change from a fluid to a solid state by or as if by cold **2** : to make or become stiff, thick, or lumpy : COAGULATE

con·ge·nial \kən-'jē-nyəl\ *adj* **1** : having the same disposition, interests, or tastes **2** : suited to one's nature or tastes : AGREEABLE — **con·ge·ni·al·i·ty** \-ˌjē-nē-'al-ət-ē, -ˌjēn-'yal-\ *n* — **con·ge·nial·ly** \-'jē-nyə-lē\ *adv*

con·gen·i·tal \kən-'jen-ə-tᵊl\ *adj* : existing at or dating from birth ⟨*congenital* heart disease⟩

con·gest \kən-'jest\ *vb* **1** : to cause an excessive accumulation especially of blood or mucus in (as an organ or body part) **2** : to block by filling too full : CLOG, OVERCROWD ⟨*congested* streets⟩ — **con·ges·tion** \-'jes-chən, -'jesh-\ *n*

con·ges·tive heart failure \kən-'jes-tiv-\ *n* : heart failure in which the heart is unable to keep enough blood circulating in the tissues or is unable to pump out the blood returned to it by the veins

¹con·glom·er·ate \kən-'gläm-(ə-)rət\ *adj* : made up of parts from various sources or of various kinds

²con·glom·er·ate \kən-'gläm-ə-ˌrāt\ *vb* **-at·ed; -at·ing** : to collect or form into a mass — **con·glom·er·a·tion** \-ˌgläm-ə-'rā-shən, kän-\ *n*

\ə\ **abut**	\au̇\ **out**	\i\ **tip**	\ȯ\ **saw**	\u̇\ **foot**
\ər\ **further**	\ch\ **chin**	\ī\ **life**	\ȯi\ **coin**	\y\ **yet**
\a\ **mat**	\e\ **pet**	\j\ **job**	\th\ **thin**	\yü\ **few**
\ā\ **take**	\ē\ **easy**	\ŋ\ **sing**	\t̲h̲\ **this**	\yu̇\ **cure**
\ä\ **cot, cart**	\g\ **go**	\ō\ **bone**	\ü\ **food**	\zh\ **vision**

³**con·glom·er·ate** \kən-'gläm-(ə-)rət\ *n* **1** : a composite mass or mixture; *esp* : rock made up of rounded pieces varying from small pebbles to large boulders in a cement (as of hardened clay) **2** : a corporation engaging in many different kinds of business

Con·go red \ˌkäŋ-ˌgō-\ *n* : a dye that is red in alkaline and blue in acid solution [named for *Congo*, territory in Africa]

con·grat·u·late \kən-'grach-ə-ˌlāt\ *vb* **-lat·ed; -lat·ing** : to express pleasure to on account of success or good fortune ⟨*congratulate* the winner⟩ [from Latin *congratulatus* "has wished joy," derived from Latin *con-, com-* "with, together" and *gratulari* "to wish joy," from *gratus* "pleasing, agreeable, thankful" — related to GRACE, GRATITUDE]

con·grat·u·la·tion \kən-ˌgrach-ə-'lā-shən\ *n* **1** : the act of congratulating **2** : an expression of joy or pleasure at another's success or good fortune — usually used in plural

con·grat·u·la·to·ry \kən-'grach-(ə-)lə-ˌtōr-ē, -ˌtȯr-\ *adj* : expressing congratulations

con·gre·gate \'käŋ-gri-ˌgāt\ *vb* **-gat·ed; -gat·ing** : to come together into a group or crowd [Middle English *congregaten* "to collect or assemble together," derived from Latin *congregare* "to assemble, gather," from *con-, com-* "with, together" and *gregare* "to gather into a flock or herd," from *greg-, grex* "flock, herd" — related to AGGREGATE, GREGARIOUS, SEGREGATE] **synonyms** see GATHER — **con·gre·ga·tor** \-ˌgāt-ər\ *n*

con·gre·ga·tion \ˌkäŋ-gri-'gā-shən\ *n* **1** : a gathering or collection of persons or things **2 a** : an assembly of persons gathered especially for religious worship **b** : the members of a church or synagogue

con·gre·ga·tion·al \ˌkäŋ-gri-'gā-shnəl, -shən-ᵊl\ *adj* **1** : of or relating to a congregation **2** : of or relating to church government placing final authority in the local congregation

con·gress \'käŋ-grəs\ *n* **1** : a formal meeting of delegates for discussion and action **2** : the chief lawmaking body of a nation and especially of a republic that in the U.S. is made up of the Senate and the House of Representatives **3** : an association of organizations having a common interest — **con·gres·sion·al** \kən-'gresh-nəl, -ən-ᵊl\ *adj* — **con·gres·sion·al·ly** \-ē\ *adv*

con·gress·man \'käŋ-grəs-mən\ *n* : a member of a congress; *esp* : a member of the U.S. House of Representatives

con·gress·wom·an \-ˌwu̇m-ən\ *n* : a woman who is a member of a congress; *esp* : a woman who is a member of the U.S. House of Representatives

con·gru·ence \kən-'grü-ən(t)s, 'käŋ-grə-wən(t)s\ *n* : the quality or state of having the same size and shape

con·gru·en·cy \kən-'grü-ən-sē, 'käŋ-grə-wən-sē\ *n* : CONGRUENCE

con·gru·ent \kən-'grü-ənt, 'käŋ-grə-wənt\ *adj* : having the same size and shape : capable of being placed over another figure and exactly matching ⟨*congruent* triangles⟩ — **con·gru·ent·ly** *adv*

con·gru·ity \kən-'grü-ət-ē, kän-\ *n, pl* **-ities** **1** : the quality or state of being congruous : AGREEMENT **2** : a point of agreement

con·gru·ous \'käŋ-grə-wəs\ *adj* **1** : being in agreement or harmony **2** : SUITABLE 2, APPROPRIATE ⟨a *congruous* place to work⟩ — **con·gru·ous·ly** *adv*

con·ic \'kän-ik\ *adj* : of, relating to, or shaped like a cone

con·i·cal \'kän-i-kəl\ *adj* : shaped like a cone ⟨a *conical* cap⟩ — **con·i·cal·ly** \-i-k(ə-)lē\ *adv*

conic section *n* : a curve formed by the intersection of a plane and a cone

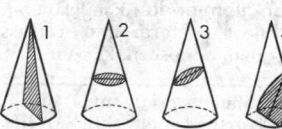

conic section: *1* straight lines, *2* circle, *3* ellipse, *4* parabola

con·i·fer \'kän-ə-fər *also* 'kō-nə-\ *n* : any of an order of mostly evergreen trees and shrubs having leaves resembling needles or scales in shape and including forms (as pines) with true cones

co·nif·er·ous \kō-'nif-(ə-)rəs, kə-\ *adj* : of, relating to, or being a conifer or conifers ⟨a *coniferous* tree⟩ ⟨*coniferous* forests⟩

con·jec·tur·al \kən-'jek-chə-rəl, -'jeksh-rəl\ *adj* : being, involving, or based on conjecture ⟨a *conjectural* interpretation⟩ — **con·jec·tur·al·ly** \-rə-lē\ *adv*

¹**con·jec·ture** \kən-'jek-chər\ *n* : an opinion or judgment based on little or no evidence

²**conjecture** *vb* **-jec·tured; -jec·tur·ing** \-'jek-chə-riŋ, -'jek-shriŋ\ : GUESS 1 — **con·jec·tur·er** \-'jek-chər-ər\ *n*

con·join \kən-'jȯin, kän-\ *vb* : to join together for a common purpose

con·joint \kən-'jȯint, kän-\ *adj* : made up of or carried on by two or more in combination : JOINT — **con·joint·ly** *adv*

con·ju·gal \'kän-ji-gəl, kən-'jü-\ *adj* : of or relating to marriage — **con·ju·gal·ly** \-gə-lē\ *adv*

¹**con·ju·gate** \'kän-ji-gət, -jə-ˌgāt\ *adj* : joined together especially in pairs : COUPLED

²**con·ju·gate** \'kän-jə-ˌgāt\ *vb* **-gat·ed; -gat·ing** **1** : to give the various forms of a verb in order **2** : to join together **3** : to pair and unite in conjugation

con·ju·ga·tion \ˌkän-jə-'gā-shən\ *n* **1** : the act of conjugating : the state of being conjugated **2** : a class of verbs having the same type of inflectional forms **3 a** : the union of sex cells that are usually of the same size and shape and that in most fungi and some algae serves as a simple form of sexual reproduction **b** : a method of reproduction in ciliated protozoans (as a paramecium) that involves the formation of a bridge of cytoplasm between two individuals, the exchange of material in their nuclei, and the division of each individual after they separate

con·junc·tion \kən-'jəŋ(k)-shən\ *n* **1** : a joining together **2** : a word or expression that joins together sentences, clauses, phrases, or words

con·junc·ti·va \ˌkän-jəŋk-'tī-və, -'tē-\ *n, pl* **-vas** *or* **-vae** \-(ˌ)vē\ : the mucous membrane that lines the inner surface of the eyelids and is continued over the front part of the eyeball

con·junc·tive \kən-'jəŋ(k)-tiv\ *adj* **1** : ¹CONNECTIVE **2** : done or existing in combination : JOINT **3** : being or used like a conjunction ⟨*conjunctive* adverbs such as "however" and "therefore"⟩

con·junc·ti·vi·tis \kən-ˌjəŋ(k)-ti-'vīt-əs\ *n* : inflammation of the conjunctiva

con·ju·ra·tion \ˌkän-jə-'rā-shən, ˌkän-\ *n* **1** : the act of conjuring : INCANTATION **2** : an expression or trick used in conjuring

con·jure \'kän-jər, 'kən-; *in sense 1* kən-'ju̇(ə)r\ *vb* **conjured; con·jur·ing** **1** : to beg earnestly or solemnly : BESEECH **2 a** : to call forth (as a spirit or a devil) by magical words **b** : to produce as if by magic ⟨her imagination *conjured* up a splendid scene⟩ ⟨managed to *conjure* up something for lunch⟩ **3** : to practice magic or magical tricks — **con·jur·er** *or* **con·ju·ror** \'kän-jər-ər, 'kən-\ *n*

conk \'käŋk, 'kȯŋk\ *vb* **1** : BREAK DOWN 1 ⟨the motor suddenly *conked* out⟩ **2** : to go to sleep ⟨*conked* out after lunch⟩

con·nect \kə-'nekt\ *vb* **1** : to join or link together directly or by something coming between : UNITE ⟨towns *connected* by a railroad⟩ ⟨the two bones *connect* at the elbow⟩ **2** : to attach by personal relationship ⟨*connected* by marriage⟩ **3** : to bring together in thought ⟨*connect* the smell of burning leaves with childhood⟩ **4** : to be related ⟨an event *connected* with our success⟩ **5** : to establish a means of communication ⟨*connect* to the Internet⟩ **synonyms** see JOIN — **con·nec·tor** *also* **con·nect·er** \-'nek-tər\ *n*

con·nec·tion \kə-'nek-shən\ *n* **1** : the act of connecting **2** : the fact or condition of being connected : RELATIONSHIP ⟨the *connection* between dirt and disease⟩ **3 a** : a thing that connects **b** : a means of communication ⟨a bad telephone *connection*⟩ **c** : a means of continuing a trip (as by train) **4 a** : a person connected with others (as by kinship) **b** : a social, professional, or commercial relationship

¹**con·nec·tive** \kə-'nek-tiv\ *adj* : connecting or tending to connect — **con·nec·tive·ly** *adv*

²**connective** *n* : something that connects; *esp* : a word or expression (as a conjunction or a relative pronoun) that connects words or word groups

connective tissue *n* : a tissue (as bone, cartilage, or tendon) that forms a supporting framework for the body or its parts and has protein fibers between the cells composing it

conn·ing tower \'kän-iŋ-\ *n* : a raised structure on a submarine used especially for navigation and to direct attacks [from earlier *conn* "to give directions for steering," probably from still earlier *cond* (same meaning), from Middle English *condien*, *conduen* "to conduct"]

conning tower

con·niv·ance \kə-'nī-vən(t)s\ *n* : the act of conniving; *esp* : knowledge that something wrong is going on without trying to stop it

con·nive \kə-'nīv\ *vb* **con·nived; con·niv·ing** : to cooperate secretly or have a secret understanding — **con·niv·er** *n*

con·nois·seur \,kän-ə-'sər, -'su̇(ə)r\ *n* : a person qualified to act as a judge in matters of taste and appreciation [from obsolete French *connoisseur* "expert," from early French *connoisseor* (same meaning), from *connoistre* "to know," from Latin *cognoscere* "to know" — related to INCOGNITO, RECOGNIZE] — **con·nois·seur·ship** \-ˌship\ *n*

con·no·ta·tion \,kän-ə-'tā-shən\ *n* : a meaning suggested by a word or an expression in addition to its exact meaning

con·note \kə-'nōt, kä-\ *vb* **con·not·ed; con·not·ing** : to suggest in addition to the exact meaning

con·nu·bi·al \kə-'n(y)ü-bē-əl\ *adj* : of or relating to marriage — **con·nu·bi·al·ly** \-bē-ə-lē\ *adv*

con·quer \'käŋ-kər\ *vb* **con·quered; con·quer·ing** \-k(ə)riŋ\ **1** : to get or gain by force of arms ⟨*conquer* a country⟩ **2** : to defeat by force of arms ⟨*conquered* all their enemies⟩ **3** : OVERCOME 1, SUBDUE ⟨*conquer* a habit⟩ **4** : to be victorious — **con·quer·or** \-kər-ər\ *n*
    synonyms CONQUER, VANQUISH, OVERCOME, OVERTHROW mean to defeat by force or planning. CONQUER suggests gaining control over another after a lengthy struggle and then more or less permanently ⟨ancient Rome *conquered* most of southern Europe⟩. VANQUISH stresses a complete overpowering ⟨the *vanquished* people lost many basic rights⟩. OVERCOME suggests defeating with difficulty or after a hard struggle ⟨try to *overcome* your fear of flying⟩. OVERTHROW stresses the bringing down and eventual destruction of those already in power ⟨used violence to *overthrow* the dictator⟩.

con·quest \'kän-ˌkwest, 'käŋ-\ *n* **1** : the act or process of conquering **2** : something conquered

con·quis·ta·dor \kȯn-'kēs-tə-ˌdȯ(ə)r, kän-'k(w)is-, kən-\ *n, pl* **con·quis·ta·do·res** \kȯn-ˌkēs-tə-'dȯr-ēz, -'dȯr-ˌās; -'dȯr-; kän-k(w)is-, 'kən-\ *or* **con·quis·ta·dors** : a leader

in the Spanish conquest of America in the 16th century [Spanish, derived from Latin *conquirere* "to search for"]

con·science \'kän-chən(t)s\ *n* : knowledge of right and wrong and a feeling one should do what is right

con·sci·en·tious \,kän-chē-'en-chəs\ *adj* **1** : guided by or agreeing with one's conscience : SCRUPULOUS **2** : using or done with careful attention — **con·sci·en·tious·ly** *adv* — **con·sci·en·tious·ness** *n*

conscientious objector *n* : a person who refuses to serve in the armed forces or to bear arms because of his or her moral or religious beliefs

con·scious \'kän-chəs\ *adj* **1** : aware of facts or feelings ⟨was *conscious* of the cold⟩ **2** : known or felt by one's inner self ⟨*conscious* guilt⟩ **3** : mentally alert or active ⟨became *conscious* again⟩ **4** : done with awareness or purpose ⟨a *conscious* effort to improve⟩ [from Latin *conscius* "knowing or being aware of something, knowing something along with another person," derived from *con-*, *com-* "with" and *scire* "to know" — related to SCIENCE] — **con·scious·ly** *adv*

con·scious·ness \'kän-chəs-nəs\ *n* **1** : the condition of being conscious **2** : the normal state of conscious life in contrast to sleep or an insensible state **3** : the part of mental life that involves conscious thought and awareness

¹**con·script** \'kän-ˌskript\ *adj* **1** : enrolled into service by force **2** : made up of conscripted persons

²**con·script** \kən-'skript\ *vb* : to enroll into service by force : DRAFT ⟨was *conscripted* into the army⟩ — **con·scrip·tion** \kən-'skrip-shən\ *n*

³**con·script** \'kän-ˌskript\ *n* : a conscripted person (as a military recruit)

con·se·crate \'kän(t)-sə-ˌkrāt\ *vb* **-crat·ed; -crat·ing** **1** : to make or declare sacred : to set apart to the service of God **2** : to devote to a purpose in a very sincere manner [Middle English *consecraten* "to consecrate," derived from Latin *consecrare* "to make holy," from *con-*, *com-* "together" and *sacrare* "to consecrate," from *sacr-*, *sacer* "sacred" — related to SACRED] **synonyms** see DEVOTE

con·se·cra·tion \,kän(t)-sə-'krā-shən\ *n* **1** : the act or ceremony of consecrating **2** : the state of being consecrated

con·sec·u·tive \kən-'sek-(y)ət-iv\ *adj* : following one after the other in order [from French *consécutif* "following in a series, consecutive," from Latin *consecutus*, past participle of *consequi* "to follow," from *con*, *com-* "with, together" and *sequi* "to follow" — related to SEQUEL] — **con·sec·u·tive·ly** *adv*

con·sen·su·al \kən-'sench-(ə-)wəl, -'sen-shəl\ *adj* : involving, made by, or based on shared agreement ⟨a *consensual* contract⟩

con·sen·sus \kən-'sen(t)-səs\ *n, pl* **-sus·es** **1** : general agreement ⟨the *consensus* of opinion⟩ **2** : the judgment arrived at by most of those concerned ⟨the *consensus* was to go ahead⟩

¹**con·sent** \kən-'sent\ *vb* : to express willingness or approval : AGREE — **con·sent·er** *n*

²**consent** *n* : approval of what is done or suggested

con·se·quence \'kän(t)-sə-ˌkwen(t)s, -si-kwən(t)s\ *n* **1** : ²RESULT 1, ¹EFFECT 1 **2** : importance that comes from the power to produce an effect ⟨a mistake of no *consequence*⟩ **synonyms** see IMPORTANCE

con·se·quent \'kän(t)-si-kwənt, -sə-ˌkwent\ *adj* : following as a result or effect

con·se·quen·tial \,kän(t)-sə-'kwen-chəl\ *adj* **1** : CONSEQUENT **2** : having important consequences

\ə\ **abut**	\au̇\ **out**	\i\ **tip**	\ȯ\ **saw**	\u̇\ **foot**
\ər\ **further**	\ch\ **chin**	\ī\ **life**	\ȯi\ **coin**	\y\ **yet**
\a\ **mat**	\e\ **pet**	\j\ **job**	\th\ **thin**	\yü\ **few**
\ā\ **take**	\ē\ **easy**	\ŋ\ **sing**	\th\ **this**	\yu̇\ **cure**
\ä\ **cot, cart**	\g\ **go**	\ō\ **bone**	\ü\ **food**	\zh\ **vision**

con·se·quent·ly \'kän(t)-sə-ˌkwent-lē, -si-kwənt-\ *adv* : as a result : ACCORDINGLY

con·ser·va·tion \ˌkän(t)-sər-'vā-shən\ *n* : a careful preservation and protection of something; *esp* : planned management of a natural resource to prevent exploitation, pollution, destruction, or neglect

con·ser·va·tion·ist \ˌkän(t)-sər-'vā-sh(ə-)nəst\ *n* : a person who is in favor of conservation especially of natural resources (as forests)

conservation of energy : a principle in physics that states that energy can neither be created nor destroyed and that the total energy of a system by itself remains constant

conservation of mass : a principle in physics that states that mass can neither be created nor destroyed and that the total mass of any material system is neither increased nor decreased by reactions between the parts — called also *conservation of matter*

con·ser·va·tism \kən-'sər-və-ˌtiz-əm\ *n* 1 : a political belief supporting established institutions and customs and preferring gradual development to sudden change 2 : a desire to preserve an existing situation or existing ways

¹**con·ser·va·tive** \kən-'sər-vət-iv\ *adj* 1 : tending to conserve or preserve 2 : of or relating to conservatism 3 : tending to preserve existing views, conditions, or institutions : TRADITIONAL 4 : CAUTIOUS, MODERATE ⟨a *conservative* estimate⟩ 5 : being in agreement with the usual standards of taste or manners ⟨a *conservative* suit⟩ ⟨a *conservative* dresser⟩ — **con·ser·va·tive·ly** *adv* — **con·ser·va·tive·ness** *n*

²**conservative** *n* : a person who is conservative especially in politics

Conservative Judaism *n* : Judaism as practiced especially among some U.S. Jews that keeps to the Torah and Talmud but makes allowance for some changes suitable for different times and circumstances

con·ser·va·to·ry \kən-'sər-və-ˌtōr-ē, -ˌtȯr-\ *n, pl* **-ries** 1 : a greenhouse for growing or displaying plants 2 : a place of instruction in some special study (as music)

¹**con·serve** \kən-'sərv\ *vb* **con·served; con·serv·ing** 1 a : to keep in a safe or sound state b : to avoid wasteful or destructive use of : use carefully ⟨*conserve* natural resources⟩ ⟨*conserve* energy⟩ 2 : to preserve with sugar 3 : to keep (a quantity) constant during a process of change (as chemical change) — **con·serv·er** *n*

²**con·serve** \'kän-ˌsərv\ *n* 1 : a candied fruit 2 : ²PRESERVE 1

con·sid·er \kən-'sid-ər\ *vb* **-ered; -er·ing** \-(-ə-)riŋ\ 1 a : to think about carefully ⟨*consider* your options⟩ b : to think about with the idea of taking some action ⟨we are *considering* you for the job⟩ 2 : to treat in a kind or thoughtful way ⟨you never *consider* my feelings⟩ 3 : to think of in a certain way ⟨*consider* the price too high⟩

con·sid·er·able \kən-'sid-ər(-ə)-bəl, -'sid-rə-bəl\ *adj* : large in size, amount, or quantity ⟨a *considerable* number⟩ ⟨was in *considerable* pain⟩ — **con·sid·er·ably** \-blē\ *adv*

con·sid·er·ate \kən-'sid-(ə-)rət\ *adj* 1 : tending to consider things carefully 2 : thoughtful of the rights and feelings of others — **con·sid·er·ate·ly** *adv* — **con·sid·er·ate·ness** *n*

con·sid·er·ation \kən-ˌsid-ə-'rā-shən\ *n* 1 : careful thought : DELIBERATION 2 : thoughtfulness for other people 3 : something that needs to be considered before deciding or acting 4 : a payment made in return for something

con·sid·er·ing \kən-'sid-(ə-)riŋ\ *prep* : in view of : taking into account

con·sign \kən-'sīn\ *vb* 1 : to give over to another's care : ENTRUST 2 : to give, transfer, or deliver to another 3 : to send or address (as goods) to an agent to be cared for or sold

con·sign·ment \kən-'sīn-mənt\ *n* 1 : the act or process of consigning 2 : something consigned especially in a single shipment

con·sist \kən-'sist\ *vb* : to be made up or composed ⟨breakfast *consisted* of cereal, milk, and fruit⟩ ⟨coal *consists* mostly of carbon⟩

con·sis·ten·cy \kən-'sis-tən-sē\ *n, pl* **-cies** 1 : the degree of thickness, firmness, or stickiness ⟨dough of the right *consistency*⟩ 2 : agreement or harmony between parts or elements 3 : a sticking with one way of thinking or acting

con·sis·tent \kən-'sis-tənt\ *adj* 1 : being in agreement or harmony ⟨actions *consistent* with our policy⟩ 2 : being unchanging in behavior or beliefs ⟨a *consistent* supporter⟩ — **con·sis·tent·ly** *adv*

con·so·la·tion \ˌkän-sə-'lā-shən\ *n* 1 : the act or an instance of consoling : the state of being consoled 2 : something that consoles — **con·sol·a·to·ry** \kən-'sōl-ə-ˌtōr-ē, -sä-lə-, -ˌtȯr-\ *adj*

¹**con·sole** \'kän-ˌsōl\ *n* 1 a : the part of an organ at which the organist sits and which contains the keyboard and controls b : a panel or cabinet with dials and switches for controlling an electronic or mechanical device 2 : a cabinet (as for a phonograph or television set) that stands on the floor 3 : an electronic system that connects to a display (as a TV set) and is used to play video games

²**con·sole** \kən-'sōl\ *vb* **con·soled; con·sol·ing** : to comfort in times of grief, distress, or suffering

con·sol·i·date \kən-'säl-ə-ˌdāt\ *vb* **-dat·ed; -dat·ing** 1 : to join together into one whole : UNITE 2 : to make firm or safe : STRENGTHEN ⟨*consolidate* a beachhead⟩ — **con·sol·i·da·tion** \kən-ˌsäl-ə-'dā-shən\ *n*

consolidated school *n* : a public school that is formed by joining other schools together

con·som·mé \ˌkän(t)-sə-'mā\ *n* : a clear soup made chiefly of meat stock [French]

con·so·nance \'kän(t)-s(ə-)nən(t)s\ *n* : harmony or agreement especially of musical tones or speech sounds

¹**con·so·nant** \'kän(t)-s(ə-)nənt\ *adj* : being in harmony or agreement — **con·so·nant·ly** *adv*

²**consonant** *n* 1 : a speech sound (as \p\, \n\, or \s\) produced by narrowing or closing the breath channel at one or more points 2 : a letter representing a consonant; *esp* : any letter of the English alphabet except *a, e, i, o,* and *u* — **con·so·nan·tal** \ˌkän(t)-sə-'nant-ᵊl\ *adj*

¹**con·sort** \'kän-ˌsȯ(ə)rt\ *n* : a wife or husband : SPOUSE

²**con·sort** \kən-'sȯ(ə)rt\ *vb* : to go together as companions : ASSOCIATE ⟨*consorting* with criminals⟩

con·spic·u·ous \kən-'spik-yə-wəs\ *adj* 1 : easily seen 2 : attracting attention : STRIKING *synonyms* see NOTICEABLE — **con·spic·u·ous·ly** *adv* — **con·spic·u·ous·ness** *n*

con·spir·a·cist \kən-'spir-ə-sist\ *n* : one who believes or promotes a conspiracy theory

con·spir·a·cy \kən-'spir-ə-sē\ *n, pl* **-cies** 1 : the act of conspiring together 2 a : an agreement among conspirators b : a group of conspirators

conspiracy theory *n* : a theory that explains an event or situation as being the result of a secret plot — **conspiracy theorist** *n*

con·spir·a·tor \kən-'spir-ət-ər\ *n* : a person who conspires

con·spir·a·to·ri·al \kən-ˌspir-ə-'tōr-ē-əl, -'tȯr-\ *adj* : of or relating to a conspiracy — **con·spir·a·to·ri·al·ly** \-ē-ə-lē\ *adv*

con·spire \kən-'spī(ə)r\ *vb* **con·spired; con·spir·ing** 1 : to agree secretly to do an unlawful act : PLOT ⟨*conspiring* to overthrow the dictator⟩ 2 : to act together ⟨measles and the weather *conspired* to spoil our vacation⟩

con·sta·ble \'kän(t)-stə-bəl, 'kən(t)-\ *n* 1 : a high officer of a royal court or noble household in the Middle Ages 2 : the person in charge of a royal castle or a town 3 : a police officer usually of a village or small town

Word History A constable in the Middle Ages was a very important official in a court, even though the title meant "officer of the stable." Early French *conestable* came from the Latin phrase *comes stabuli,* meaning "officer of the stable." Being in charge of a ruler's horses in those days was something like being in charge of all the vehicles — tanks, trucks, airplanes, helicopters — of a modern army. As time went on, the title remained, but it came to describe the person in charge of guarding a castle or fortified city. From this idea came the modern sense: "a police officer." [Middle English *conestable* "chief military or police officer of a court or royal domain," from early French *conestable* (same meaning), from Latin *comes stabuli,* literally, "officer of the stables," from *comes* "companion, member of a royal court" and *stabuli,* genitive of *stabulum* "stable" — related to ³COUNT, ¹STABLE]

con·stab·u·lary \kən-'stab-yə-ˌler-ē\ *n, pl* **-lar·ies** 1 : an organized body of constables or of police officers 2 : a police force organized like the military

con·stan·cy \'kän(t)-stən-sē\ *n, pl* **-cies** 1 : firmness and loyalty in one's beliefs or personal relationships 2 : freedom from change

¹**con·stant** \'kän(t)-stənt\ *adj* 1 : always faithful and true ⟨*constant* friends⟩ 2 : remaining steady and unchanged ⟨a *constant* temperature⟩ 3 : occurring over and over again ⟨*constant* headaches⟩ — **con·stant·ly** *adv*

²**constant** *n* : something unchanging; *esp* : a quantity whose value does not change under given mathematical conditions — compare VARIABLE 1

con·stel·la·tion \ˌkän(t)-stə-'lā-shən\ *n* : any of 88 groups of stars forming patterns [Middle English *constellacioun* "the position of the stars in the sky at the time of a person's birth," from early French *constellation* (same meaning), from Latin *con-, com-* "with" and *stella* "star"]

con·ster·na·tion \ˌkän(t)-stər-'nā-shən\ *n* : amazement or dismay that makes one feel helpless or confused

con·sti·pate \'kän(t)-stə-ˌpāt\ *vb* **-pat·ed; -pat·ing** : to cause constipation in

constipated *adj* : affected with constipation

con·sti·pa·tion \ˌkän(t)-stə-'pā-shən\ *n* : abnormally difficult or infrequent bowel movements

con·stit·u·en·cy \kən-'stich-(ə-)wən-sē\ *n, pl* **-cies** 1 : a body of citizens having the right to elect a representative to a legislature 2 : the people living in an electoral district 3 : an electoral district

¹**con·stit·u·ent** \kən-'stich-(ə-)wənt\ *n* 1 : one of the parts of which a thing is made up : ELEMENT, INGREDIENT 2 : any of the voters who elect a person to represent them

²**constituent** *adj* 1 : forming a part of a whole : COMPONENT 2 : having the power to create a government or make or change a constitution ⟨a *constituent* assembly⟩

con·sti·tute \'kän(t)-stə-ˌt(y)üt\ *vb* **-tut·ed; -tut·ing** 1 : to appoint to an office or duty ⟨*constituted* authorities⟩ 2 : SET UP 4, ESTABLISH ⟨a fund was *constituted* to help needy students⟩ 3 : MAKE UP 2, FORM ⟨twelve months *constitute* a year⟩

con·sti·tu·tion \ˌkän(t)-stə-'t(y)ü-shən\ *n* 1 : the act of establishing, making, or setting up 2 a : the physical makeup of an individual b : the structure, composition, or basic qualities of something 3 a : the basic beliefs and laws of a nation, state, or social group that establish the powers and duties of the government and guarantee certain rights to the people in it b : a document containing a constitution

¹**con·sti·tu·tion·al** \'kän(t)-stə-'t(y)ü-shnəl, -shən-ᵊl\ *adj* 1 : of or relating to a person's physical or mental makeup 2 : of, relating to, or in agreement with a constitution ⟨a *constitutional* amendment⟩ ⟨*constitutional* rights⟩ — **con·sti·tu·tion·al·ly** \-shnə-lē, -shən-ᵊl-ē\ *adv*

²**constitutional** *n* : exercise (as a walk) taken for one's health

con·sti·tu·tion·al·i·ty \ˌkän(t)-stə-ˌt(y)ü-shə-'nal-ət-ē\ *n* : the quality or state of being in agreement with a constitution

con·strain \kən-'strān\ *vb* 1 : COMPEL 1 2 : CONFINE 1 3 : RESTRAIN 1

con·straint \kən-'strānt\ *n* 1 : the act of constraining : the state of being constrained 2 : something that constrains : CHECK 3 : a holding back of one's feelings, actions, or behavior

con·strict \kən-'strikt\ *vb* : to make or become narrower or smaller by drawing together : SQUEEZE, TIGHTEN — **con·stric·tive** \-'strik-tiv\ *adj*

con·stric·tion \kən-'strik-shən\ *n* 1 : an act or instance of constricting 2 : something that constricts : a part that is constricted

con·stric·tor \kən-'strik-tər\ *n* : a snake that kills its prey by coiling around and crushing it

con·struct \kən-'strəkt\ *vb* 1 : to make or form by combining or arranging parts : BUILD 2 : to draw (a geometrical figure) with suitable instruments and under given conditions — **con·struct·able** *or* **con·struct·ible** \-'strək-tə-bəl\ *adj* — **con·struc·tor** \-'strək-tər\ *n*

con·struc·tion \kən-'strək-shən\ *n* 1 : INTERPRETATION 1 ⟨strict *construction* of the law⟩ 2 : the process, art, or manner of constructing 3 : something built or put together : STRUCTURE 4 : the arrangement and connection of words or groups of words in a sentence

construction paper *n* : a thick paper available in many colors and used especially for school art work

con·struc·tive \kən-'strək-tiv\ *adj* : helping to develop or improve something ⟨*constructive* suggestions⟩ — **con·struc·tive·ly** *adv* — **con·struc·tive·ness** *n*

con·strue \kən-'strü\ *vb* **con·strued; con·stru·ing** 1 : to explain the grammatical relationships of the words in a sentence, clause, or phrase 2 : to understand or explain the sense or intention of : INTERPRET — **con·stru·able** \-'strü-ə-bəl\ *adj*

con·sul \'kän(t)-səl\ *n* 1 : either of two chief officials of the ancient Roman republic who were elected each year 2 : an official appointed by a government to live in a foreign country to look after the commercial interests of citizens of the appointing country — **con·sul·ar** \-s(ə-)lər\ *adj* — **con·sul·ship** \-səl-ˌship\ *n*

con·sul·ate \'kän(t)-s(ə-)lət\ *n* : the residence or office of a consul

con·sult \kən-'səlt\ *vb* 1 : to seek the opinion or advice of ⟨*consult* a doctor⟩ 2 : to seek information from ⟨*consult* a dictionary⟩ 3 : to talk something over ⟨have to *consult* with my lawyer⟩ — **con·sult·er** *n*

con·sult·ant \kən-'səlt-ᵊnt\ *n* 1 : a person who consults another 2 : a person who gives professional advice or services

con·sul·ta·tion \ˌkän(t)-səl-'tā-shən\ *n* 1 : a discussion between doctors on a case or its treatment 2 : the act of consulting

con·sume \kən-'süm\ *vb* **con·sumed; con·sum·ing** 1 : to destroy by or as if by fire 2 : USE UP, SPEND ⟨the search *consumed* most of our time⟩ 3 : to eat or drink up ⟨*consumed* a whole gallon of ice cream⟩ 4 : to take up the interest or attention of ⟨was *consumed* with curiosity⟩ 5 : to use as a customer ⟨*consume* goods and services⟩ **synonyms** see EAT — **con·sum·able** \-'sü-mə-bəl\ *adj*

con·sum·er \kən-'sü-mər\ *n* 1 : one that consumes; *esp* : a person who buys and uses up goods 2 : a plant or animal that requires complex organic compounds for

\ə\ **abut**	\aů\ **out**	\i\ **tip**	\ò\ **saw**	\ů\ **foot**
\ər\ **further**	\ch\ **chin**	\ī\ **life**	\òi\ **coin**	\y\ **yet**
\a\ **mat**	\e\ **pet**	\j\ **job**	\th\ **thin**	\yü\ **few**
\ā\ **take**	\ē\ **easy**	\ŋ\ **sing**	\t̲h̲\ **this**	\yů\ **cure**
\ä\ **cot, cart**	\g\ **go**	\ō\ **bone**	\ü\ **food**	\zh\ **vision**

food which it obtains by preying on other living things or eating particles of organic matter — compare PRODUCER 3

con·sum·er·ism \kən-'sü-mə-ˌriz-əm\ *n* : the promotion of the consumer's interests

¹**con·sum·mate** \kən-'səm-ət, 'kän(t)-sə-mət\ *adj* : of the highest degree, quality, or skill ⟨a *consummate* politician⟩ — **con·sum·mate·ly** *adv*

²**con·sum·mate** \'kän(t)-sə-ˌmāt\ *vb* **-mat·ed; -mat·ing** : to make perfect or complete — **con·sum·ma·tion** \ˌkän(t)-sə-'mā-shən\ *n*

con·sump·tion \kən-'səm(p)-shən\ *n* **1 a** : the act or process of consuming **b** : the amount consumed **2 a** : a gradual and continuous wasting away of the body especially from tuberculosis of the lungs **b** : TUBERCULOSIS

¹**con·sump·tive** \kən-'səm(p)-tiv\ *adj* : of, relating to, or affected with consumption

²**consumptive** *n* : a person who has consumption

¹**con·tact** \'kän-ˌtakt\ *n* **1** : a meeting or touching of surfaces **2** : the connection of two electrical conductors through which a current passes or a part made for such a connection **3** : a person one knows who has influence especially in the business or political world ⟨our *contacts* in Los Angeles may be able to assist you⟩ **4** : an establishing of communication especially with someone or something distant ⟨make *contact* by radio⟩ **5** : CONTACT LENS [from French *contact* or Latin *contactus*, both meaning "a touching of body surfaces," from Latin *contingere* "to have contact with, affect, happen," from *con-, com-* "with, together" and *tangere* "to touch" — related to CONTAGIOUS, CONTINGENT, TANGENT, TANGIBLE]

²**con·tact** \'kän-ˌtakt, kən-'takt\ *vb* **1** : to bring or come into contact **2** : to get in touch or communication with ⟨*contact* your local dealer for details⟩

³**con·tact** \'kän-ˌtakt\ *adj* : involving or acting upon contact ⟨football and ice hockey are *contact* sports⟩ ⟨*contact* insecticides⟩

contact lens \ˌkän-ˌtak(t)-\ *n* : a thin lens used to correct bad eyesight and worn right over the cornea of the eye

con·ta·gion \kən-'tā-jən\ *n* **1** : the passing of a disease from one individual to another by direct or indirect contact **2** : a contagious disease or something (as a virus) that causes a contagious disease

con·ta·gious \kən-'tā-jəs\ *adj* **1 a** : able to be passed on by contact between individuals ⟨colds are *contagious*⟩ ⟨*contagious* diseases⟩ **b** : capable of passing on a contagious disease to another ⟨he is *contagious*⟩ **2** : so pleasantly irresistible as to be picked up by one person after another ⟨your enthusiasm is *contagious*⟩ [Middle English *contagious* "likely to be passed on through contact," from early French *contagieus* (same meaning), derived from Latin *contingere* "to have contact with, affect, happen" — related to CONTACT, CONTINGENT]

con·tain \kən-'tān\ *vb* **1** : to keep within limits : RESTRAIN, CHECK ⟨tried to *contain* my laughter⟩ ⟨the forest fire was finally *contained*⟩ **2** : to have within **3** : to consist of : INCLUDE **4** : to be divisible by especially without a remainder ⟨20 *contains* 5⟩ — **con·tain·ment** \-'tān-mənt\ *n*

synonyms CONTAIN, HOLD, ACCOMMODATE mean to have or be capable of having within. CONTAIN suggests the actual presence of a particular thing or quantity within something ⟨a bottle *containing* a liter of liquid⟩. HOLD suggests the capacity of something or its usual or permanent purpose ⟨that cooler will *hold* 12 cartons of milk⟩. ACCOMMODATE stresses holding without crowding or inconvenience ⟨the ballroom can *accommodate* 500 people easily⟩.

con·tain·er \kən-'tā-nər\ *n* : one that contains; *esp* : something into which other things can be put (as for storage)

con·tain·er·ship \kən-'tā-nər-ˌship\ *n* : a ship designed or equipped to carry very large containers of cargo

con·tam·i·nant \kən-'tam-ə-nənt\ *n* : something that contaminates

con·tam·i·nate \kən-'tam-ə-ˌnāt\ *vb* **-nat·ed; -nat·ing 1** : to soil, stain, or infect by contact or association **2** : to make impure or unfit for use by adding something harmful or unpleasant ⟨wells *contaminated* by chemicals⟩ — **con·tam·i·na·tion** \-ˌtam-ə-'nā-shən\ *n* — **con·tam·i·na·tor** \-'tam-ə-ˌnāt-ər\ *n*

con·tem·plate \'känt-əm-ˌplāt, 'kän-ˌtem-\ *vb* **-plat·ed; -plat·ing 1** : to view or consider with careful and thoughtful attention **2** : to have in mind : plan on ⟨*contemplating* a trip⟩ — **con·tem·pla·tor** \-ˌplāt-ər\ *n*

con·tem·pla·tion \ˌkänt-əm-'plā-shən, ˌkän-ˌtem-\ *n* **1** : the act of thinking about spiritual things : MEDITATION **2** : the act of looking at or thinking about something steadily **3** : a looking ahead to some future event : ANTICIPATION

con·tem·pla·tive \kən-'tem-plət-iv; 'känt-əm-ˌplāt-, 'kän-ˌtem-\ *adj* : involving or devoted to contemplation : MEDITATIVE ⟨the *contemplative* life⟩ — **con·tem·pla·tive·ly** *adv* — **con·tem·pla·tive·ness** *n*

con·tem·po·ra·ne·ous \kən-ˌtem-pə-'rā-nē-əs\ *adj* : existing, occurring, or beginning during the same time — **con·tem·po·ra·ne·ous·ly** *adv* — **con·tem·po·ra·ne·ous·ness** *n*

¹**con·tem·po·rary** \kən-'tem-pə-ˌrer-ē\ *adj* **1** : living or occurring at the same period of time **2** : of the present time : MODERN, CURRENT

²**contemporary** *n, pl* **-rar·ies** : a person who lives at the same time or is about the same age as another

con·tempt \kən-'tem(p)t\ *n* **1** : the act of despising : the state of mind of one who despises **2** : the state of being despised **3** : disobedience or disrespect to a court, judge, or legislature

con·tempt·ible \kən-'tem(p)-tə-bəl\ *adj* : deserving contempt ⟨a *contemptible* lie⟩ — **con·tempt·ibly** \-blē\ *adv*

con·temp·tu·ous \kən-'tem(p)-ch(ə-w)əs, -'tem(p)sh-wəs\ *adj* : feeling or showing contempt — **con·temp·tu·ous·ly** *adv* — **con·temp·tu·ous·ness** *n*

synonyms CONTEMPTUOUS, SCORNFUL, DISDAINFUL mean feeling or showing a lack of respect or concern. CONTEMPTUOUS suggests a lofty attitude toward whatever one hates ⟨*contemptuous* of cowards⟩. SCORNFUL suggests anger and disgust often expressed in mockery ⟨*scornful* of their customs and traditions⟩. DISDAINFUL suggests proudly considering someone or something as not worthy of one's notice ⟨*disdainful* of people who were not as rich as they were⟩.

con·tend \kən-'tend\ *vb* **1** : COMPETE **2** : to try hard to deal with ⟨many problems to *contend* with⟩ **3** : to argue or state earnestly ⟨*contend* that my opinion is right⟩ — **con·tend·er** *n*

¹**con·tent** \kən-'tent\ *adj* : pleased and satisfied with what one has or is

²**content** *vb* : to make content : SATISFY

³**content** *n* : CONTENTMENT; *esp* : freedom from care or discomfort

⁴**con·tent** \'kän-ˌtent\ *n* **1 a** : something contained — usually used in plural ⟨the *contents* of a jar⟩ **b** : the subject matter or topics treated (as in a book) ⟨table of *contents*⟩ **2** : the essential meaning ⟨I enjoy the rhythm of the poem but I don't understand its *content*⟩ **3** : an amount that is contained or can be contained ⟨oil with a high *content* of sulfur⟩ ⟨the jug has a *content* of four liters⟩

con·tent·ed \kən-'tent-əd\ *adj* : satisfied with one's possessions or situation in life — **con·tent·ed·ly** *adv* — **con·tent·ed·ness** *n*

con·ten·tion \kən-'ten-chən\ *n* **1** : an act or instance of contending **2** : an idea or point for which a person argues (as in a debate or argument)

con·ten·tious \kən-'ten-chəs\ *adj* : inclined to argue **synonyms** see BELLIGERENT — **con·ten·tious·ness** *n*

con·tent·ment \kən-'tent-mənt\ *n* : freedom from worry or restlessness : peaceful satisfaction

¹con·test \kən-'test, 'kän-ˌtest\ *vb* : to make (something) a cause of dispute or fighting ⟨*contest* a claim⟩

²con·test \'kän-ˌtest\ *n* : a struggle for victory : COMPETITION

con·test·ant \kən-'tes-tənt *also* 'kän-ˌtes-\ *n* : a person who takes part in a contest

con·text \'kän-ˌtekst\ *n* : the parts of something written or spoken that are near a certain word or group of words and that help to explain its meaning — **con·tex·tu·al** \kän-'teks-chə-(-wə)l, kən-\ *adj* — **con·tex·tu·al·ly** \-ē\ *adv*

con·ti·gu·ity \ˌkänt-ə-'gyü-ət-ē\ *n* : the quality or state of being contiguous

con·tig·u·ous \kən-'tig-yə-wəs\ *adj* **1** : being in contact : ADJOINING **2** : very near though not in contact **3** : touching or connected in an unbroken series ⟨the 48 *contiguous* states of the U.S.⟩ — **con·tig·u·ous·ly** *adv*

con·ti·nent \'känt-ᵊn-ənt, 'känt-nənt\ *n* **1** : one of the great divisions of land (as North America, South America, Europe, Asia, Africa, Australia, or Antarctica) on the globe **2** *cap* : the continent of Europe

¹con·ti·nen·tal \ˌkänt-ᵊn-'ent-ᵊl\ *adj* **1** : of or relating to a continent ⟨*continental* waters⟩; *esp, often cap* : of or relating to the continent of Europe **2** *often cap* : of or relating to the colonies later forming the U.S. ⟨*Continental* Congress⟩

²continental *n* **1 a** *often cap* : a soldier in the Continental army **b** : a piece of paper money issued by the Continental Congress **2** : ²EUROPEAN

continental drift *n* : the slow movement of the continents on a fluid layer that extends to deep within the earth

continental shelf *n* : a shallow submarine plain of varying width forming a border to a continent and typically ending at the continental slope

continental slope *n* : a usually steep slope from a continental shelf to the ocean floor

con·tin·gen·cy \kən-'tin-jən-sē\ *n, pl* **-cies** : something (as an emergency) that might or might not happen or that might happen if something else occurs ⟨prepared for every *contingency*⟩

¹con·tin·gent \kən-'tin-jənt\ *adj* : depending on something else ⟨plans *contingent* on the weather⟩ [Middle English *contingent* "uncertain," from early French *contingent* "touching, happening," derived from Latin *contingere* "to have contact with, affect, happen" — related to CONTACT, CONTAGIOUS] — **con·tin·gent·ly** *adv*

²contingent *n* : a number of persons representing or drawn from an area or group

con·tin·u·al \kən-'tin-yə(-wə)l\ *adj* **1** : continuing without interruption ⟨days of *continual* sunshine⟩ **2** : occurring again and again within short intervals ⟨*continual* interruptions⟩ — **con·tin·u·al·ly** \-ē\ *adv*

con·tin·u·ance \kən-'tin-yə-wən(t)s\ *n* **1** : the act of continuing **2** : the extent of continuing : DURATION **3** : postponement of a case in a law court

con·tin·u·a·tion \kən-ˌtin-yə-'wā-shən\ *n* **1** : the act or fact of continuing in or extending the time of a state or activity **2** : a beginning again after an interruption **3** : a thing or part by which something is continued

con·tin·ue \kən-'tin-yü\ *vb* **-tin·ued; -tin·u·ing** **1** : to do or cause to do the same thing without stopping ⟨I *continue* to work hard⟩ ⟨the weather *continued* hot and sunny⟩ **2** : to go on or carry on after an interruption : RESUME ⟨to be *continued* next week⟩ — **con·tin·u·er** \-yə-wər\ *n*

continued fraction *n* : a fraction whose numerator is a whole number and whose denominator is a

$$a$$
$$b + c$$
$$d + e$$
$$f + \ldots$$

continued fraction

whole number plus a fraction whose numerator is a whole number and whose denominator is a whole number plus a fraction and so on

con·ti·nu·ity \ˌkänt-ᵊn-'(y)ü-ət-ē\ *n, pl* **-ities** **1** : the quality or state of being continuous **2** : something that has or provides continuity

con·tin·u·ous \kən-'tin-yə-wəs\ *adj* : continuing without a stop — **con·tin·u·ous·ly** *adv* — **con·tin·u·ous·ness** *n*

con·tin·u·um \kən-'tin-yə-wəm\ *n, pl* **-ua** \-yə-wə\ *also* **-uums** : something that is continuous and the same throughout and that is often thought of as a series of elements or values which differ by only tiny amounts ⟨"light" and "dark" stand at opposite ends of a *continuum*⟩

con·tort \kən-'tȯ(ə)rt\ *vb* : to twist into an unusual appearance or unnatural shape

con·tor·tion \kən-'tȯr-shən\ *n* **1** : a twisting or being twisted out of shape **2** : a contorted shape or thing

con·tor·tion·ist \kən-'tȯr-sh(ə-)nəst\ *n* : an acrobat able to twist the body into unusual positions

¹con·tour \'kän-ˌtu̇(ə)r\ *n* **1** : the outline of a figure, body, or surface **2** : a line or drawing showing an outline

²contour *adj* **1** : following contour lines or forming furrows or ridges along them ⟨*contour* farming⟩ ⟨*contour* flooding⟩ **2** : made to fit the contour of something ⟨*contour* bedsheets⟩

³contour *vb* **1** : to shape the contour of **2** : to shape to fit contours

contour line *n* : a line (as on a map) connecting the points that have the same elevation on a land surface

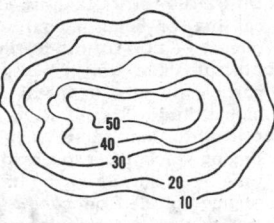

contour line

contra- *prefix* **1** : against : contrary : contrasting **2** : pitched below normal bass ⟨*contra*bassoon⟩ [from Latin *contra* "against, opposite"]

con·tra·band \'kän-trə-ˌband\ *n* **1** : goods forbidden by law to be owned or to be brought into or out of a country **2** : smuggled goods [from Italian *contrabbando* "smuggling," from Latin *contrabannum*, literally, "against the decree or command," from *contra* "against" and *bannum, bannus* "decree"; of Germanic origin] — **contra·band** *adj*

con·tra·bas·soon \ˌkän-trə-bə-'sün, -ba-\ *n* : a musical instrument that is similar to a bassoon but has a longer body with more turns and is pitched an octave lower

con·tra·cep·tion \ˌkän-trə-'sep-shən\ *n* : deliberate prevention of conception and pregnancy especially by using a drug or a device (as a condom)

¹con·tra·cep·tive \ˌkän-trə-'sep-tiv\ *adj* : relating to or used for contraception

²contraceptive *n* : a contraceptive drug or device

¹con·tract \'kän-ˌtrakt\ *n* **1** : a legally binding agreement between two or more parties **2** : a document stating the terms of a contract **synonyms** see AGREEMENT

²con·tract \kən-'trakt, *sense 2 usually* 'kän-ˌtrakt\ *vb* **1 a** : to bring on oneself ⟨*contract* debts⟩ **b** : to become affected with ⟨*contract* a cold⟩ **2** : to agree by contract ⟨*contract* to build a house⟩ **3 a** : to draw or squeeze together so as to make or become smaller or shorter and broader ⟨brows *contracting* in puzzlement⟩ ⟨*contract* a muscle⟩ **b** : to make or become smaller ⟨metal *contracts*

\ə\ **abut**	\au̇\ **out**	\i\ **tip**	\ȯ\ **saw**	\u̇\ **foot**
\ər\ **further**	\ch\ **chin**	\ī\ **life**	\ȯi\ **coin**	\y\ **yet**
\a\ **mat**	\e\ **pet**	\j\ **job**	\th\ **thin**	\yü\ **few**
\ā\ **take**	\ē\ **easy**	\ŋ\ **sing**	\th\ **this**	\yu̇\ **cure**
\ä\ **cot, cart**	\g\ **go**	\ō\ **bone**	\ü\ **food**	\zh\ **vision**

when cold⟩ **4** : to shorten (a word) by leaving out one or more sounds or letters

con·trac·tile \kən-'trak-t²l, -₁tīl\ *adj* : having the power or property of contracting ⟨a *contractile* cell⟩ ⟨a *contractile* fiber⟩ — **con·trac·til·i·ty** \₁kän-₁trak-'til-ət-ē\ *n*

contractile vacuole *n* : a vacuole in a single-celled organism that contracts regularly to discharge water from the cell

con·trac·tion \kən-'trak-shən\ *n* **1 a** : the act or process of contracting : the state of being contracted **b** : the shortening and thickening of a working muscle or muscle fiber **2 a** : a shortening of a word, syllable, or word group by leaving out a sound or letter **b** : a form (as *don't* or *they've*) produced by such shortening

con·trac·tor \'kän-₁trak-tər, kən-'trak-\ *n* : one that enters into a contract; *esp* : a person who contracts to perform work or provide supplies at a certain price or within a certain time ⟨building *contractor*⟩

con·trac·tu·al \kən-'trak-chə(-wə)l, kän-, -'traksh-wəl\ *adj* : of, relating to, or being a contract ⟨*contractual* agreements⟩ — **con·trac·tu·al·ly** \-ē\ *adv*

con·tra·dict \₁kän-trə-'dikt\ *vb* **1** : to say the opposite of what someone else has said : deny the truth of **2** : to be opposed or contrary to : go against ⟨your actions *contradict* your words⟩ — **con·tra·dic·tor** \-'dik-tər\ *n*

con·tra·dic·tion \₁kän-trə-'dik-shən\ *n* **1** : something (as a statement) that contradicts something else **2** : a condition in which things oppose each other

con·tra·dic·to·ry \₁kän-trə-'dik-t(ə-)rē\ *adj* : involving, causing, or being a contradiction ⟨*contradictory* statements⟩ — **con·tra·dic·to·ri·ness** \-t(ə-)rē-nəs\ *n*

con·trail \'kän-₁trāl\ *n* : a stream of visible water or ice particles created in the air by an airplane or rocket at high altitudes

con·tral·to \kən-'tral-tō\ *n, pl* **-tos** **1 a** : the lowest female singing voice **b** : a singer with such a voice **2** : the part sung by a contralto [from Italian *contralto* "lowest female singing voice," from *contra-* "having a lower pitch than" and *alto* "a female singing voice"]

con·trap·tion \kən-'trap-shən\ *n* : DEVICE 1c, GADGET

con·trari·wise \'kän-₁trer-ē-₁wīz, kən-'trer-\ *adv* **1** : just the opposite : on the contrary **2** : VICE VERSA, CONVERSELY

¹con·trary \'kän-₁trer-ē\ *n, pl* **-trar·ies** : something opposite or contrary — **on the contrary** : just the opposite

²con·trary \'kän-₁trer-ē, sense 4 is often kən-'tre(ə)r-ē\ *adj* **1** : exactly opposite : entirely different ⟨*contrary* opinions⟩ **2** : being against or opposed : in violation ⟨actions *contrary* to the law⟩ **3** : not favorable or helpful ⟨a *contrary* wind⟩ **4** : unwilling to obey or behave well ⟨a *contrary* child⟩ — **con·trar·i·ly** \-₁trer-ə-lē, -'trer-\ *adv* — **con·trar·i·ness** \-₁trer-ē-nəs, -'trer-\ *n*

¹con·trast \kən-'trast, 'kän-₁trast\ *vb* **1** : to show noticeable differences **2** : to compare two persons or things so as to show the differences between them

²con·trast \'kän-₁trast\ *n* **1** : a person or thing that shows differences when compared to another **2** : difference or unlikeness (as in color or brightness) between related things especially when very plain

con·trib·ute \kən-'trib-yət, -(₁)yüt\ *vb* **-ut·ed; -ut·ing** **1** : to give along with others ⟨*contribute* money to a cause⟩ **2** : to have a part in bringing about something ⟨everybody *contributed* to the success of the show⟩ **3** : to supply (as an article) for publication especially in a magazine — **con·trib·u·tor** \-yət-ər\ *n*

con·tri·bu·tion \₁kän-trə-'byü-shən\ *n* **1** : the act of contributing **2** : a sum or a thing contributed — **con·trib·u·tive** \kən-'trib-yət-iv\ *adj*

con·trib·u·to·ry \kən-'trib-yə-₁tōr-ē, -₁tȯr-ē\ *adj* : serving to contribute; *esp* : helping to accomplish a result

con·trite \'kän-₁trīt, kən-'trīt\ *adj* : feeling or showing sorrow and remorse for a wrong that one has done ⟨a con-

trite criminal⟩ ⟨a *contrite* apology⟩ — **con·trite·ly** *adv* — **con·trite·ness** *n*

con·tri·tion \kən-'trish-ən\ *n* : the state of being contrite

con·triv·ance \kən-'trī-vən(t)s\ *n* : something (as a scheme or mechanical device) produced with skill and cleverness

con·trive \kən-'trīv\ *vb* **con·trived; con·triv·ing** **1** : ²PLAN 1, PLOT ⟨*contrive* a way to escape⟩ **2** : to form or make in a skillful or clever way : INVENT **3** : BRING ABOUT, MANAGE ⟨*contriving* to make ends meet⟩ — **con·triv·er** *n*

¹con·trol \kən-'trōl\ *vb* **con·trolled; con·trol·ling** **1 a** : to keep within limits : RESTRAIN ⟨*control* your temper⟩ **b** : to direct the action of ⟨*control* a plane⟩ **2** : to have power over : RULE **3** : to reduce the number of individuals or cases especially to a level that is not dangerous ⟨*control* insects⟩ ⟨*control* a disease⟩ — **con·trol·la·bil·i·ty** \-₁trō-lə-'bil-ət-ē\ *n* — **con·trol·la·ble** \-'trō-lə-bəl\ *adj*

²control *n* **1** : the power or authority to control **2** : ability to control ⟨the car went out of *control*⟩ ⟨keep *control* of a situation⟩ **3 a** : a means for controlling ⟨the *controls* of an airplane⟩ ⟨price *controls*⟩ **b** : an organization that directs a flight beyond the earth's atmosphere ⟨mission *control*⟩ **4 a** : CONTROLLED EXPERIMENT **b** : an individual or group in a controlled experiment that is not subject to the factor being tested and functions as a standard of comparison **5** : reduction in or regulation of the number of individuals or cases in an area ⟨disease *control*⟩

controlled experiment *n* : an experiment in which all the variables in a control group and an experimental group are the same except for one — called also *control, control experiment*

con·trol·ler \kən-'trō-lər, 'kän-₁trō-lər\ *n* **1** : the chief accounting officer of a business or institution **2** : a person who controls ⟨an air traffic *controller*⟩

controlling *adj* : tending to control the behavior of other people

con·tro·ver·sial \₁kän-trə-'vər-shəl, -'vər-sē-əl\ *adj* : relating to or causing controversy ⟨a *controversial* movie⟩ — **con·tro·ver·sial·ly** \-ē\ *adv*

con·tro·ver·sy \'kän-trə-₁vər-sē\ *n, pl* **-sies** **1** : an often long or heated discussion of something about which there is great difference of opinion : DISPUTE **2** : ¹QUARREL 2, STRIFE [Middle English *controversie*, from early French (same meaning), from Latin *controversia* "act or cause of disagreeing, dispute," literally, "something turned against or to the contrary," from *contro-, contra-* "against, contrary" and *versus* "turned," from *vertere* "to turn" — related to ANNIVERSARY, CONVERSE, DIVERT, VERSATILE]

con·tu·sion \kən-'t(y)ü-zhən\ *n* : an injury to tissue that usually does not break the skin : BRUISE — **con·tuse** \-'t(y)üz\ *vb*

co·nun·drum \kə-'nən-drəm\ *n* : ¹RIDDLE 1, PUZZLE

con·ur·ba·tion \₁kän-(₁)ər-'bā-shən\ *n* : a number of cities or towns that come one right after the other with no countryside in between

con·va·lesce \₁kän-və-'les\ *vb* **-lesced; -lesc·ing** : to regain health and strength gradually after illness or weakness

con·va·les·cence \₁kän-və-'les-ᵊn(t)s\ *n* : the process or period of convalescing

¹con·va·les·cent \₁kän-və-'les-ᵊnt\ *adj* : going through convalescence

²convalescent *n* : a person who is convalescing

con·vec·tion \kən-'vek-shən\ *n* : motion in a fluid in which the warmer portions rise and the colder portions sink; *also* : the transfer of heat by this motion — **con·vec·tion·al** \-shnəl, -shən-ᵊl\ *adj* — **con·vec·tive** \-'vek-tiv\ *adj*

convection oven *n* : an oven with a fan that circulates hot air evenly and continuously around the food as it cooks

con·vene \kən-'vēn\ *vb* **con·vened; con·ven·ing 1** : to come together in a group : ASSEMBLE **2** : to cause to convene : call together ⟨*convened* a meeting⟩

¹**con·ve·nience** \kən-'vēn-yən(t)s\ *n* **1** : the quality or state of being convenient **2** : personal comfort : freedom from trouble **3** : a convenient time : OPPORTUNITY ⟨come at your earliest *convenience*⟩ **4** : something that gives comfort or advantage ⟨a house with all the modern *conveniences*⟩

²**convenience** *adj* : designed for quick and easy preparation ⟨*convenience* foods⟩

convenience store *n* : a small market that is open many hours

con·ve·nient \kən-'vēn-yənt\ *adj* **1** : suited to a person's comfort or easy use ⟨a *convenient* time⟩ ⟨a *convenient* location⟩ **2** : easy to get to ⟨schools, churches, and stores are all *convenient*⟩ — **con·ve·nient·ly** *adv*

con·vent \'kän-vənt, -,vent\ *n* **1** : a community of nuns living together **2** : a house or set of buildings occupied by nuns

con·ven·tion \kən-'ven-chən\ *n* **1** : AGREEMENT 2a, COVENANT ⟨an international *convention* banning the spread of nuclear weapons⟩ **2** : a meeting of persons for a common purpose ⟨a constitutional *convention*⟩ ⟨teachers' *convention*⟩ **3** : a custom or a way of acting or doing things that is widely accepted and followed ⟨the *conventions* of punctuation⟩

con·ven·tion·al \kən-'vench-nəl, -'ven-chən-ᵊl\ *adj* : following, agreeing with, or based on convention ⟨*conventional* people⟩ ⟨*conventional* remarks⟩ ⟨a *conventional* detective story⟩ — **con·ven·tion·al·ly** \-ē\ *adv*

con·ven·tion·al·i·ty \kən-,ven-chə-'nal-ət-ē\ *n, pl* **-ties 1** : the quality or state of being conventional **2** : a conventional practice, custom, or rule

con·verge \kən-'vərj\ *vb* **con·verged; con·verg·ing 1** : to tend or move toward one point or one another **2** : to come together and unite in a common interest

con·ver·gence \kən-'vər-jən(t)s\ *n* : the act or condition of converging

con·ver·gent \kən-'vər-jənt\ *adj* : tending to converge

con·ver·sant \kən-'vərs-ᵊnt\ *adj* : having knowledge or experience : FAMILIAR ⟨*conversant* with the issues⟩

con·ver·sa·tion \,kän-vər-'sā-shən\ *n* : talking or a talk between two or more people — **con·ver·sa·tion·al** \-'sā-shnəl, -shən-ᵊl\ *adj* — **con·ver·sa·tion·al·ly** \-ē\ *adv*

con·ver·sa·tion·al·ist \,kän-vər-'sā-shnə-ləst, -shən-ᵊl-əst\ *n* : a person who is fond of or good at conversation

¹**con·verse** \kən-'vərs\ *vb* **con·versed; con·vers·ing** : to engage in conversation : TALK [Middle English *conversen* "to live with," from early French *converser* (same meaning), from Latin *conversari* "to pass one's life, be associated with," derived from *convertere* "to turn around, change," from *con-* "with, together" and *vertere* "to turn" — related to ANNIVERSARY, ³CONVERSE, CONTROVERSY, DIVERT, REVERSE, UNIVERSE, VERTICAL, VERSATILE, VICE VERSA] — **con·vers·er** *n*

²**con·verse** \'kän-,vərs\ *n* : something that is the opposite of something else

³**con·verse** \kən-'vərs, 'kän-,vərs\ *adj* : reversed in order, relation, or action [from Latin *conversus*, past participle of *convertere* "to turn around, change," from *con-* "with, together" and *vertere* "to turn" — related to ¹CONVERSE] — **con·verse·ly** *adv*

con·ver·sion \kən-'vər-zhən\ *n* **1** : the act of converting : the state of being converted **2** : a change in nature, form, or units **3** : a change of religion

¹**con·vert** \kən-'vərt\ *vb* **1** : to change from one belief, view, or party to another **2 a** : to change from one substance, form, use, or unit to another ⟨*convert* pounds to grams⟩ **b** : to exchange for something equal in value ⟨*convert* francs into dollars⟩ — **con·vert·er** *n*

²**con·vert** \'kän-,vərt\ *n* : a person who has been converted

converted rice \kən-'vert-əd-\ *n* : rice that has been treated to retain its natural mineral and vitamin content, to improve its texture, and to keep for a longer time

¹**con·vert·ible** \kən-'vərt-ə-bəl\ *adj* : capable of being converted : able to be changed in form or use ⟨a sofa *convertible* into a bed⟩ — **con·vert·ibil·i·ty** \-,vərt-ə-'bil-ət-ē\ *n*

²**convertible** *n* **1** : something convertible **2** : an automobile with a top that can be raised, lowered, or removed

con·vex \kän-'veks, kən-; 'kän-,veks\ *adj* : curved or rounded like the outside of a sphere or circle ⟨a *convex* lens⟩ — **con·vex·i·ty** \kən-'vek-sət-ē, kän-\ *n*

con·vey \kən-'vā\ *vb* **con·veyed; con·vey·ing 1** : to carry from one place to another : TRANSPORT **2** : to serve as a way of carrying ⟨pipes *convey* water⟩ **3** : to make known : COMMUNICATE ⟨using words to *convey* ideas⟩

con·vey·ance \kən-'vā-ən(t)s\ *n* **1** : the act of conveying **2** : something used to carry goods or passengers

con·vey·or \kən-'vā-ər\ *n* : a mechanical device for carrying packages or bulk material from place to place (as by an endless moving belt)

¹**con·vict** \kən-'vikt\ *vb* : to find or prove guilty

²**con·vict** \'kän-,vikt\ *n* : a person serving a prison sentence

con·vic·tion \kən-'vik-shən\ *n* **1** : the act of convicting : the state of being convicted **2 a** : a strong belief or opinion ⟨has deep *convictions*⟩ **b** : the state of mind of a person who is sure that what he or she believes or says is true ⟨spoke with *conviction*⟩ **synonyms** see OPINION

con·vince \kən-'vin(t)s\ *vb* **con·vinced; con·vinc·ing** : to make a person agree or believe by arguing or showing evidence ⟨*convinced* me it was true⟩ — **con·vinc·er** *n*

con·vinc·ing \kən-'vin(t)-siŋ\ *adj* : causing one to believe or agree — **con·vinc·ing·ly** \-siŋ-lē\ *adv*

con·viv·i·al \kən-'viv-yəl, -'viv-ē-əl\ *adj* : of, relating to, or fond of food, drink, merrymaking, and good company — **con·viv·i·al·i·ty** \-,viv-ē-'al-ət-ē\ *n* — **con·viv·i·al·ly** \-'viv-yə-lē, -'viv-ē-ə-lē\ *adv*

con·vo·ca·tion \,kän-və-'kā-shən\ *n* : an assembly of persons called together to a meeting

con·voke \kən-'vōk\ *vb* **con·voked; con·vok·ing** : to call together to a meeting

con·vo·lut·ed \'kän-və-,lüt-əd\ *adj* **1** : folded or curved in twisted windings; *esp* : having convolutions **2** : complicated in form : INTRICATE ⟨*convoluted* phrasing⟩

con·vo·lu·tion \,kän-və-'lü-shən\ *n* : one of the uneven ridges on the surface of the brain and especially of the cerebrum of higher mammals

con·vol·vu·lus \kən-'väl-vyə-ləs, -'vol-\ *n, pl* **-lus·es** *or* **-li** \-,lī, -,lē\ : any of a genus of trailing or twining herbs and shrubs that are related to the morning glories

¹**con·voy** \'kän-,voi, kən-'voi\ *vb* : to go with to protect

²**con·voy** \'kän-,voi\ *n* **1** : one that convoys **2** : the act of convoying **3** : a group convoyed

con·vulse \kən-'vəls\ *vb* **con·vulsed; con·vuls·ing** : to shake violently; *esp* : to shake with usually uncontrolled jerky movements ⟨*convulsed* with laughter⟩

con·vul·sion \kən-'vəl-shən\ *n* **1** : an abnormal violent contraction or series of contractions of the muscles that is not under control of the will **2** : a violent disturbance

con·vul·sive \-'vəl-siv\ *adj* **1 a** : being or producing a convulsion **b** : caused by or having convulsions **2** : resembling a convulsion especially in being sudden or violent — **con·vul·sive·ly** *adv*

cony *variant of* CONEY

coo \'kü\ *vb* **1** : to make the low soft cry of a dove or pigeon or a similar sound **2** : to talk fondly or lovingly — **coo** *n*

\ə\ **abut**	\au̇\ **out**	\i\ **tip**	\o̅\ **saw**	\u̇\ **foot**
\ər\ **further**	\ch\ **chin**	\ī\ **life**	\oi\ **coin**	\y\ **yet**
\a\ **mat**	\e\ **pet**	\j\ **job**	\th\ **thin**	\yü\ **few**
\ā\ **take**	\ē\ **easy**	\ŋ\ **sing**	\th\ **this**	\yu̇\ **cure**
\ä\ **cot, cart**	\g\ **go**	\ō\ **bone**	\ü\ **food**	\zh\ **vision**

¹**cook** \'kùk\ *n* : one who prepares food for eating [Old English *cōc* "person who prepares food," from Latin *coquus* (same meaning), from *coquere* "to cook" — related to KITCHEN; see *Word History* at KITCHEN]

²**cook** *vb* **1** : to prepare food for eating especially by the use of heat **2** : to go through the process of being cooked ⟨the rice is *cooking* now⟩ **3** : to think up : DEVISE ⟨*cook* up a scheme⟩

cook·book \'kùk-ˌbùk\ *n* : a book of cooking recipes and cooking directions

cook·er \'kùk-ər\ *n* : one that cooks; *esp* : a utensil, device, or piece of equipment for cooking

cook·ery \'kùk-(ə-)rē\ *n* : the art or practice of cooking

cook·ie *or* **cooky** \'kùk-ē\ *n, pl* **cook·ies 1** : a small sweet flat or slightly raised cake **2** *cookie* : a small computer file that contains information relating to websites a person has visited

cooking spray *n* : an aerosol that contains vegetable oil and that is sprayed on cookware (as frying pans) to prevent food from sticking

cook·out \'kùk-ˌaút\ *n* : an outing at which a meal is cooked and served outdoors

cook·stove \-ˌstōv\ *n* : a stove for cooking

cook·ware \-ˌwa(ə)r, -ˌwe(ə)r\ *n* : utensils used in cooking

¹**cool** \'kül\ *adj* **1** : somewhat cold : lacking in warmth **2** : not letting in or keeping in heat ⟨*cool* clothes⟩ **3** : marked by steady calmness and self-control **4** : not friendly or interested ⟨was *cool* toward strangers⟩ **5** : producing an impression of being cool ⟨blue is a *cool* color⟩ **6** *slang* **a** : very good : EXCELLENT **b** : FASHIONABLE 1 — **cool·ish** \'kü-lish\ *adj* — **cool·ly** \'kül-(l)ē\ *adv* — **cool·ness** \'kül-nəs\ *n*

²**cool** *vb* **1** : to make or become cool **2** : to make or become less excited : CALM ⟨allow tempers to *cool*⟩ — **cool it** : to calm down

³**cool** *n* : a cool time or place ⟨the *cool* of the night⟩

cool·ant \'kü-lənt\ *n* : a usually fluid cooling substance

cool·er \'kü-lər\ *n* : a container for keeping food or drink cool

cool·head·ed \'kül-'hed-əd\ *adj* : not easily excited — **cool·head·ed·ness** \-'hed-əd-nəs\ *n*

coo·lie \'kü-lē\ *n* : a low-paid unskilled Asian worker

coon \'kün\ *n* : RACCOON

coon·hound \'kün-ˌhaúnd\ *n* : a sporting dog trained to hunt raccoons

coon·skin \-ˌskin\ *n* : the fur or pelt of the raccoon

¹**coop** \'küp, 'kùp\ *n* : a cage or small enclosure or building for housing poultry or small animals

²**coop** *vb* : to place or keep in or as if in a coop

co–op \'kō-ˌäp, kō-'äp\ *n* : ²COOPERATIVE

coo·per \'kü-pər, 'kùp-ər\ *n* : a worker who makes or repairs wooden casks, tubs, or barrels

coo·per·age \'kü-p(ə-)rij, 'kùp-(ə-)rij\ *n* **1** : a cooper's work or products **2** : a cooper's place of business

co·op·er·ate \kō-'äp-(ə-)ˌrāt\ *vb* **-at·ed; -at·ing** : to act, work, or associate with others so as to get something done

co·op·er·a·tion \kō-ˌäp-ə-'rā-shən\ *n* : the act or process of cooperating

¹**co·op·er·a·tive** \kō-'äp-(ə-)rət-iv, -'äp-ə-ˌrāt-\ *adj* **1** : willing to cooperate ⟨*cooperative* neighbors⟩ **2** : of, relating to, or organized as a cooperative ⟨a *cooperative* store⟩ ⟨*cooperative* apartments⟩ — **co·op·er·a·tive·ly** *adv* — **co·op·er·a·tive·ness** *n*

²**cooperative** *n* : an association owned by and operated for the benefit of those using its services

Coo·per's hawk \'kü-pərz-, 'kùp-ərz-\ *n* : an American hawk that has a rounded tail and is slightly smaller than a crow

co–opt \kō-'äpt\ *vb* **co–opt·ed; co–opt·ing 1** : to take into a group (as a faction, movement, or culture) : ASSIMILATE **2** : TAKE OVER, APPROPRIATE 1 ⟨a style *co-opted* by advertisers⟩

¹**co·or·di·nate** \kō-'ôrd-nət, -ᵊn-ət\ *adj* **1** : equal in rank **2** : being of equal rank in a compound sentence ⟨*coordinate* clauses⟩ — **co·or·di·nate·ly** *adv*

²**co·or·di·nate** \kō-'ôrd-ᵊn-ˌāt\ *vb* **-nat·ed; -nat·ing 1** : to make or become coordinate **2** : to work or cause to work together smoothly — **co·or·di·na·tor** \-ˌāt-ər\ *n*

³**co·or·di·nate** \kō-'ôrd-nət, -ᵊn-ət\ *n* **1** : one that is coordinate with another **2** : any of a set of numbers used to locate a point on a line or surface or in space

coordinate axis *n* : a number line (as an x-axis or a y-axis) that is part of a coordinate system and along or parallel to which coordinates are measured

coordinate system *n* : any of various systems for locating points with coordinates and coordinate axes; *esp* : one consisting of a plane in which points are located by pairs of coordinates each of which gives the distance of a point from one of two perpendicular axes

coordinating *adj* : joining words or word groups of the same grammatical rank ⟨*or* and *and* are *coordinating* conjunctions⟩

coordinating conjunction *n* : a conjunction (as *and*, *or*, or *but*) that joins together words or word groups of the same grammatical importance

co·or·di·na·tion \(ˌ)kō-ˌôrd-ᵊn-'ā-shən\ *n* **1** : the act of coordinating **2** : smooth working together (as of parts) ⟨good muscular *coordination*⟩

coot \'küt\ *n* **1** : a slaty-black bird of the rail family that somewhat resembles a duck **2** : any of several North American scoters **3** : a harmless simple person

coo·tie \'küt-ē\ *n* : BODY LOUSE

¹**cop** \'käp\ *vb* **copped; cop·ping 1** *slang* : to get hold of : ²CAPTURE 1a **2** *slang* : ¹STEAL 2a **3** : ADOPT 2 ⟨*cop* an attitude⟩ [probably from Dutch *kapen* "to steal"] — **cop a plea** : to plead guilty to a lesser charge in order to avoid standing trial for a more serious one

²**cop** *n* : POLICE OFFICER

co·pa·cet·ic *also* **co·pa·set·ic** *or* **co·pe·set·ic** \ˌkō-pə-'set-ik\ *adj* : very satisfactory

¹**cope** \'kōp\ *n* : a long vestment that is worn like a cape by a priest or bishop [Old English *-cap* "long vestment, cope," from Latin *cappa* "head covering" — related to ²CAPE]

²**cope** *vb* **coped; cop·ing** : to struggle or try to manage especially with some success ⟨*cope* with a situation⟩ [from earlier *cope* "to strike, fight, engage in a struggle," from Middle English *copen* "to strike, fight," from early French *couper* "to strike, cut," from earlier *cop* "a blow" — related to COUP, COUPON]

co·pe·pod \'kō-pə-ˌpäd\ *n* : any of a large group of usually tiny freshwater and saltwater crustaceans — **co·pepod** *adj*

¹*cope*

Co·per·ni·can \kō-'pər-ni-kən, kə-\ *adj* : of or relating to Copernicus or his theory that the earth rotates daily on its axis and the planets revolve in orbits around the sun

co·per·nic·i·um \ˌkō-pər-'nis-ē-əm\ *n* : a short-lived artificially produced radioactive element that has 112 protons — see ELEMENT table

cop·i·er \'käp-ē-ər\ *n* : one that copies; *esp* : a machine that makes copies (as of letters or drawings)

co·pi·lot \'kō-ˌpī-lət\ *n* : a pilot who assists the pilot or commander of a flight of an aircraft or spacecraft

cop·ing \'kō-piŋ\ *n* : the top or covering layer of a wall that is usually sloped to carry off water

co·pi·ous \'kō-pē-əs\ *adj* : very plentiful **synonyms** see PLENTIFUL — **co·pi·ous·ly** *adv* — **co·pi·ous·ness** *n*

co·pol·y·mer \(ˌ)kō-'päl-ə-mər\ *n* : a product of copolymerization

co·po·lym·er·i·za·tion \ˌkō-pə-ˌlim-ə-rə-'zā-shən, ˌkō-ˌpäl-ə-mə-rə-\ *n* : the repeated chemical combination of two different molecules to form a usually much larger molecule — **co·po·lym·er·ize** \ˌkō-pə-'lim-ə-ˌrīz, ˌkō-'päl-ə-mə-\ *vb*

cop–out \'käp-ˌaut\ *n* **1** : an act or instance of copping out **2** : something that provides a way for someone to cop out **3** : a person who cops out

cop out \(')käp-'aut\ *vb* **1** : to back out of something one does not want to do ⟨said I was *copping out* of the race because I was afraid I'd lose⟩ **2** : to avoid or take the easy way out of something one ought to do ⟨*cop out* on a promise⟩ ⟨*cop out* on a cause⟩

¹cop·per \'käp-ər\ *n* **1** : a reddish metallic element that is one of the best conductors of heat and electricity — see ELEMENT table **2** : a copper or bronze coin **3** *chiefly British* : a large copper kettle or boiler **4** : any of various small butterflies with usually copper-colored wings — **cop·pery** \'käp-(ə-)rē\ *adj*

²copper *n* : POLICE OFFICER

cop·per·head \'käp-ər-ˌhed\ *n* **1** : a common largely coppery brown poisonous snake of the pit viper family that occurs in the eastern and central U.S. **2** : a person in the northern states who sympathized with the South during the American Civil War

copper sulfate *n* : a usually blue crystalline compound that is used to destroy algae and fungi

cop·pice \'käp-əs\ *n* : a thicket, grove, or growth of small trees

co·pra \'kō-prə\ *n* : dried coconut meat

co·pro·ces·sor \kō-'präs-ˌes-ər, -'prōs-\ *n* : an extra processor in a computer that is designed to perform specialized tasks

copse \'käps\ *n* : COPPICE

cop·ter \'käp-tər\ *n* : HELICOPTER

cop·u·late \'käp-yə-ˌlāt\ *vb* **-lat·ed; -lat·ing** : to engage in sexual intercourse — **cop·u·la·tion** \ˌkäp-yə-'lā-shən\ *n* — **cop·u·la·to·ry** \'käp-yə-lə-ˌtōr-ē, -ˌtȯr-\ *adj*

¹copy \'käp-ē\ *n, pl* **cop·ies** **1** : something that is made to look exactly like something else : DUPLICATE ⟨a *copy* of a letter⟩ ⟨a *copy* of a painting⟩ **2** : one of the total number of books, magazines, or papers printed at one time **3** : written or printed material to be set in type

²copy *vb* **cop·ied; copy·ing** **1** : to make a copy : DUPLICATE **2** : IMITATE **1**

copy·cat \'käp-ē-ˌkat\ *n* : one who imitates or adopts the behavior or practices of another

copy editor *n* **1** : an employee of a publishing house who corrects manuscript copy **2** : a person who edits and writes headlines for newspaper copy — **copy·ed·it** \'käp-ē-ˌed-ət\ *vb*

copy·ist \'käp-ē-əst\ *n* **1** : a person who makes copies **2** : one who imitates

copy·read·er \'käp-ē-ˌrēd-ər\ *n* **1** : COPY EDITOR **1** **2** : COPY EDITOR **2** — **copy·read** \-ˌrēd\ *vb*

¹copy·right \-ˌrīt\ *n* : the legal right to be the only one to reproduce, publish, or sell the contents and form of a literary, musical, or artistic work — **copyright** *adj*

²copyright *vb* : to get a copyright on

copy·writ·er \'käp-ē-ˌrīt-ər\ *n* : a writer of advertising or publicity copy

co·que·try \'kō-kə-trē, kō-'ke-trē\ *n, pl* **-tries** : the behavior of a coquette

co·quette \kō-'ket\ *n* : a woman who tries without sincere affection to gain the attention and admiration of men : FLIRT — **co·quett·ish** \-'ket-ish\ *adj* — **co·quett·ish·ly** *adv* — **co·quett·ish·ness** *n*

co·qui·na \kō-'kē-nə\ *n* **1** : a soft whitish limestone formed of broken shells and corals cemented together and used for building **2** : a small marine clam used especially to make broth or chowder

cor·a·cle \'kȯr-ə-kəl, 'kär-\ *n* : a boat made of a wicker frame covered with horsehide or canvas

cor·al \'kȯr-əl, 'kär-\ *n* **1 a** : the stony or horny deposit that is composed of the skeletons of various polyps; *esp* : a richly red coral used in jewelry **b** : a polyp or polyp colony together with its membranes and skeleton **2** : a deep pink — **coral** *adj*

coracle

coral reef *n* : a reef made up of corals, other organic substances, and limestone

coral snake *n* : any of several poisonous chiefly tropical New World snakes brilliantly banded in red, black, and yellow or white; *also* : any of several harmless snakes resembling the coral snakes

¹cord \'kȯ(ə)rd\ *n* **1** : material like a small thin rope that is used mostly for tying things **2** : a bodily structure (as a tendon or nerve) resembling a cord; *esp* : UMBILICAL CORD **3** : a small flexible insulated electrical cable with a plug at one or both ends used for connecting an appliance to an outlet **4** : an amount of firewood equal to a pile of wood 4 × 4 × 8 feet or 128 cubic feet (about 3.6 cubic meters) **5 a** : a rib like a cord on a fabric **b** : a fabric with such ribs

²cord *vb* **1** : to supply, bind, or connect with a cord **2** : to pile up wood in cords

cord·age \'kȯrd-ij\ *n* **1** : ropes or cords; *esp* : the ropes in the rigging of a ship **2** : the number of cords of wood on a specified area

cord·ed \'kȯrd-əd\ *adj* **1 a** : having ridges or cords ⟨*corded* cloth⟩ **b** *of a muscle* : TAUT **1a**, TENSE **2** : bound or wound about with cords

¹cor·dial \'kȯr-jəl\ *n* **1** : a stimulating medicine or drink **2** : LIQUEUR

²cordial *adj* **1** : tending to refresh or cheer **2** : being warm and friendly ⟨*cordial* greeting⟩ [Middle English *cordial* "of the heart, vital," from Latin *cordialis* (same meaning), from *cor* "heart" — related to COURAGE] **synonyms** see GRACIOUS — **cor·di·al·i·ty** \ˌkȯr-jē-'al-ət-ē\ *n* — **cordial·ly** \'kȯrj-(ə-)lē\ *adv*

cord·less \'kȯrd-ləs\ *adj* : having no cord; *esp* : powered by a battery ⟨a *cordless* telephone⟩

cor·don \'kȯrd-ⁿn, 'kȯ(ə)r-ˌdän\ *n* **1** : an ornamental cord used especially on costumes **2** : a line of persons or things around a person or place ⟨a *cordon* of police⟩ **3** : a cord or ribbon worn as a badge or decoration

cor·do·van \'kȯrd-ə-vən\ *n* **1** : a soft fine-grained colored leather **2** : thick leather tanned from the inner layer of horsehide — **cordovan** *adj*

cor·du·roy \'kȯrd-ə-ˌrȯi\ *n, pl* **-roys** **1 a** : a strong ribbed usually cotton cloth **b** *pl* : pants of corduroy **2** : a road built of logs laid side by side

cord·wood \'kȯ(ə)rd-ˌdwu̇d\ *n* : wood piled or sold in cords

¹core \'kō(ə)r, 'kȯ(ə)r\ *n* **1** : a central or most important part **2** : the usually inedible central part of some fruits (as a pineapple or apple) **3** : a part removed from the interior of a mass especially to find out the interior composition or a hidden condition ⟨took a *core* of rock⟩ **4 a** : a mass of iron used to concentrate and strengthen the magnetic field resulting from a current in a surrounding coil **b** : the memory of a computer **5** : the central part of the

\ə\ **abut**	\au̇\ **out**	\i\ **tip**	\ȯ\ **saw**	\u̇\ **foot**
\ər\ **further**	\ch\ **chin**	\ī\ **life**	\ȯi\ **coin**	\y\ **yet**
\a\ **mat**	\e\ **pet**	\j\ **job**	\th\ **thin**	\yü\ **few**
\ā\ **take**	\ē\ **easy**	\ŋ\ **sing**	\th\ **this**	\yu̇\ **cure**
\ä\ **cot, cart**	\g\ **go**	\ō\ **bone**	\ü\ **food**	\zh\ **vision**

earth having different properties from those of the surrounding parts; *also* : the central part of a heavenly body **6** : an arrangement of studies that brings together material from subjects that are usually taught separately **7** : the place in a nuclear reactor where fission takes place

²**core** *vb* **cored; cor·ing** : to remove a core from ⟨*core* an apple⟩ — **cor·er** *n*

co·ri·an·der \'kȯr-ē-,an-dər\ *n* : the ripened dried tiny fruit of an herb related to the carrot that is used as a flavoring; *also* : the herb that produces coriander

Co·rin·thi·an \kə-'rin(t)-thē-ən\ *adj* : of or relating to a style of Greek architecture characterized by a bell-shaped capital covered with sculptured leaves [named for *Corinth*, region and city in ancient Greece]

Co·rin·thi·ans \kə-'rin(t)-thē-ənz\ *n* — see BIBLE table

Co·ri·o·lis effect \,kȯr-ē-,ō-ləs-, ,kȯr-\ *n* : the deflection of a moving object that is a result of the Coriolis force

Coriolis force *n* : a force that as a result of the earth's rotation acts on a body in motion (as a projectile)

¹**cork** \'kȯ(ə)rk\ *n* **1 a** : the elastic tough outer tissue of the cork oak used especially for stoppers and insulation **b** : the tissue of a woody plant making up most of the bark and arising from an inner cambium **2** : a usually cork stopper for a bottle or jug **3** : a fishing float

²**cork** *vb* **1** : to furnish, fit, or seal with a cork ⟨*cork* a bottle⟩ **2** : to blacken with burnt cork ⟨*corked* faces⟩

cork·er \'kȯr-kər\ *n* **1** : one that corks containers **2** : an outstanding person or thing

cork oak *n* : an oak of southern Europe and northern Africa that is the source of the cork used especially for stoppers and insulation

¹**cork·screw** \'kȯrk-,skrü\ *n* : a pointed spiral tool with a handle for pulling corks from bottles

²**corkscrew** *adj* : resembling a corkscrew : SPIRAL

corky \'kȯr-kē\ *adj* **cork·i·er; -est** : resembling cork especially in dry porous quality

corm \'kȯrm\ *n* : a solid underground part of a stem (as of the crocus) that is shaped like a bulb — compare BULB 1a, TUBER 1

cor·mo·rant \'kȯrm-(ə-)rənt, 'kȯr-mə-,rant\ *n* : any of various dark-colored web-footed seabirds with a long neck, a hooked bill, and a patch of bare often brightly colored skin under the mouth

cormorant

¹**corn** \'kȯ(ə)rn\ *n* **1** : a tall American cereal grass plant widely grown for its large ears of starchy grain which come in many varieties **2** : the seeds of a corn plant that are used especially as food for humans and livestock and are typically yellow or whitish **3** : an ear of corn with or without its leafy outer covering ⟨spent the afternoon picking *corn*⟩ **4** : corny actions or speech [Old English *corn* "seeds of a cereal plant"]

²**corn** *vb* : to preserve by packing with salt or by soaking in salty water ⟨*corned* beef⟩

³**corn** *n* : a local hardening and thickening of skin (as on a toe) [Middle English *corne* "thickening of the skin," from early French *corne* "horn," from Latin *cornu* "horn, point" — related to UNICORN]

corn belt *n* : an area (as the central portion of the U.S.) in which more land is used for growing corn than any other single crop

corn borer *n* : any of several insects that bore in corn; *esp* : a moth whose larva is a major pest in the stems and fruits of crop plants and especially corn

corn bread *n* : bread made with cornmeal

corn chip *n* : a piece of a dry crisp snack food prepared from a seasoned cornmeal batter

corn·cob \'kȯ(ə)rn-,käb\ *n* : the woody core on which the kernels of corn are arranged

corncob pipe *n* : a tobacco pipe with a bowl made by hollowing out a piece of corncob

corn·crib \-,krib\ *n* : a crib for storing ears of corn

corn dog *n* : a frankfurter dipped in cornmeal batter, fried, and served on a stick

cor·nea \'kȯr-nē-ə\ *n* : the transparent part of the coat of the eyeball that covers the iris and pupil and lets light through to the interior — **cor·ne·al** \-nē-əl\ *adj*

corn ear·worm \-'i(ə)r-,wərm\ *n* : a moth whose striped yellow-headed larva is especially destructive to ears of corn

¹**cor·ner** \'kȯr-nər\ *n* **1 a** : the point or place where edges or sides meet : ANGLE **b** : the place where two streets or roads meet **c** : a piece designed to form, mark, or protect a corner **2** : a place far away from ordinary affairs or life ⟨a quiet *corner* of the town⟩ **3** : a position from which escape or retreat is difficult or impossible ⟨was backed into a *corner*⟩ **4** : control or ownership of enough of the available supply of something to control its price — **cornered** \-nərd\ *adj* — **around the corner** : being about to happen : near in time or place ⟨good times are just *around the corner*⟩

²**corner** *adj* **1** : situated at a corner ⟨the *corner* drugstore⟩ **2** : used or fitted for use in or on a corner ⟨a *corner* cupboard⟩

³**corner** *vb* **cor·nered; cor·ner·ing** \'kȯr(r)n-(ə-)riŋ\ **1** : to drive into a corner ⟨the police *cornered* the criminal⟩ **2** : to get a corner on ⟨*corner* the wheat market⟩ **3** : to turn a corner ⟨a car that *corners* well⟩

corner kick *n* : a free kick from a corner of a soccer field awarded to an offensive player when a defender plays the ball out-of-bounds over the end line

cor·ner·stone \'kȯr-nər-,stōn\ *n* **1** : a stone forming part of a corner in a wall **2** : something of basic importance ⟨the *cornerstone* of our foreign policy⟩

cor·net \kȯr-'net\ *n* **1** : a brass instrument like the trumpet but having a shorter tube and a softer tone **2** : something shaped like a cone [Middle English *cornet* "cornet," from early French *cornet*, literally, "little horn," from Latin *cornu* "horn" — related to ³CORN] — **cor·net·ist** *or* **cor·net·tist** \-'net-əst\ *n*

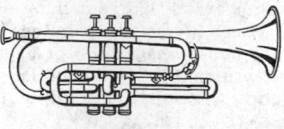

cornet 1

corn·field \'kȯ(ə)rn-,fēld\ *n* : a field in which corn is grown

corn·flakes \-,flāks\ *n pl* : toasted flakes made from hulled kernels of corn and used as a breakfast cereal

corn·flow·er \-,flaù(-ə)r\ *n* : BACHELOR'S BUTTON

cor·nice \'kȯr-nəs\ *n* **1** : the decorative piece that forms the top edge of a building or column and extends beyond it **2** : an ornamental molding where the walls meet the ceiling of a room **3** : a decorative band of metal or wood to conceal curtain fixtures

Cor·nish \'kȯr-nish\ *n* : any of an English breed of sturdy compact chickens

Cor·nish·man \-mən\ *n* : a person born or living in Cornwall, England

corn·meal \'kȯ(ə)rn-'mē(ə)l, -,mēl\ *n* : meal ground from corn

corn oil *n* : a yellow fatty oil obtained from the germ of corn kernels and used chiefly in salad oil, in soft soap, and in margarine

corn pone *n, Southern & Midland* : corn bread often made without milk or eggs and baked or fried

corn·stalk \'kȯ(ə)rn-,stȯk\ *n* : a stalk of corn

corn·starch \-ˌstärch\ *n* : a fine starch made from corn and used in foods for thickening, in making corn syrup and sugars, and in making adhesives and sizes for papers and textiles

corn syrup *n* : a syrup obtained from cornstarch and used in baked goods and candy

cor·nu·co·pia \ˌkȯr-n(y)ə-ˈkō-pē-ə\ *n* **1** : a horn-shaped container overflowing with fruits and flowers used as a symbol of plenty **2** : a container shaped like a horn or a cone

corny \ˈkȯr-nē\ *adj* **corn·i·er; -est** : tastelessly old-fashioned : tiresomely simple or sentimental ⟨*corny* music⟩ ⟨*corny* jokes⟩

co·rol·la \kə-ˈräl-ə, -ˈrōl-\ *n* : the part of a flower that consists of the petals and encloses the stamens and pistil

cor·ol·lary \ˈkȯr-ə-ˌler-ē, ˈkär-\ *n, pl* **-lar·ies** **1** : something that follows directly from something that has been proved **2** : something that naturally follows : RESULT

co·ro·na \kə-ˈrō-nə\ *n* **1** : a usually colored circle often seen around and close to a shining body (as the sun or moon) **2** : the outermost part of the atmosphere of a star (as the sun) **3** : a faint glow next to the surface of an electrical conductor at high voltage — **co·ro·nal** \ˈkȯr-ən-ᵊl, ˈkär-; kə-ˈrōn-\ *adj*

¹cor·o·nary \ˈkȯr-ə-ˌner-ē, ˈkär-\ *adj* : of, relating to, or being the vessels that carry blood to or away from the heart; *also* : of or relating to the heart

²coronary *n, pl* **-nar·ies** **1** : a coronary blood vessel **2** : CORONARY THROMBOSIS; *also* : HEART ATTACK

coronary artery *n* : either of the two arteries that arise from the aorta and supply the tissues of the heart

coronary heart disease *n* : a condition (as coronary thrombosis) that reduces the blood flow through the coronary arteries to the heart — called also *coronary artery disease*

coronary occlusion *n* : the partial or complete blocking (as by a blood clot) of a coronary artery

coronary thrombosis *n* : the blocking of an artery of the heart by a thrombus

cor·o·na·tion \ˌkȯr-ə-ˈnā-shən, ˌkär-\ *n* : the act or ceremony of crowning a king or queen

cor·o·ner \ˈkȯr-ə-nər, ˈkär-\ *n* : a public officer whose chief duty is to discover the causes of any death possibly not due to natural causes

cor·o·net \ˌkȯr-ə-ˈnet, ˌkär-\ *n* **1** : a small crown worn by a noble **2** : an ornamental wreath or band worn around the head ⟨a *coronet* of flowers⟩

coronet 1

¹cor·po·ral \ˈkȯr-p(ə-)rəl\ *adj* : of or relating to the body ⟨*whipping* and other *corporal* punishments⟩ — **cor·po·ral·ly** \-ē\ *adv*

²corporal *n* : a noncommissioned officer in the army or marines with a rank just below that of sergeant

corpora lutea *plural of* CORPUS LUTEUS

cor·po·rate \ˈkȯr-p(ə-)rət\ *adj* **1 a** : formed into a corporation **b** : of, relating to, or being a corporation ⟨take *corporate* action⟩ **2** : of, relating to, or being a whole composed of individuals ⟨united together and took *corporate* action⟩ — **cor·po·rate·ly** *adv*

cor·po·ra·tion \ˌkȯr-pə-ˈrā-shən\ *n* : a group that is authorized by law to carry on an activity (as a business enterprise) with the rights and duties of a single person

cor·po·re·al \kȯr-ˈpōr-ē-əl, -ˈpȯr-\ *adj* : having, consisting of, or relating to a physical material body — **cor·po·re·al·ly** \-ˈpōr-ē-ə-lē, -ˈpȯr-\ *adv*

corps \ˈkō(ə)r, ˈkȯ(ə)r\ *n, pl* **corps** \ˈkō(ə)rz, ˈkȯ(ə)rz\ **1 a** : an organized branch of the military establishment ⟨Marine *Corps*⟩ ⟨*Corps* of Engineers⟩ **b** : a military unit

consisting of two or more divisions **2** : a group of persons acting under one authority ⟨diplomatic *corps*⟩ [from French *corps* "part of a military organization," derived from Latin *corpus* "body" — related to CORPSE]

corpse \ˈkȯ(ə)rps\ *n* : a dead body [Middle English *corps* "human body," from early French *corps* (same meaning), from Latin *corpus* "body"]

corps·man \ˈkō(ə)r(z)-mən, ˈkȯ(ə)r(z)-\ *n* : an enlisted man trained to give first aid

cor·pu·lence \ˈkȯr-pyə-lən(t)s\ *n* : the state of being corpulent : OBESITY

cor·pu·lent \ˈkȯr-pyə-lənt\ *adj* : very fat : OBESE

Cor·pus Chris·ti \ˌkȯr-pəs-ˈkris-tē\ *n* : the Thursday after Trinity Sunday observed as a Roman Catholic festival in honor of the Eucharist [Middle English *Corpus Christi* "church festival of Corpus Christi," from Latin *Corpus Christi,* literally, "body of Christ"]

cor·pus·cle \ˈkȯr-(ˌ)pəs-əl\ *n* **1** : a very small particle **2** : one of the very small cells (as a red blood cell) that float freely in the blood — **cor·pus·cu·lar** \kȯr-ˈpəs-kyə-lər\ *adj*

cor·pus lu·te·um \ˌkȯr-pəs-ˈlüt-ē-əm\ *n, pl* **cor·po·ra lu·tea** \ˌkȯr-p(ə)rə-ˈlüt-ē-ə\ : a yellowish mass of tissue formed in a graafian follicle in the ovary of a mammal after the egg is released

¹cor·ral \kə-ˈral\ *n* **1** : a pen for keeping or capturing livestock **2** : an enclosure made with wagons for defense of a camp

²corral *vb* **cor·ralled; cor·ral·ling** **1** : to keep in or as if in a corral **2** : ¹SURROUND, CAPTURE **3** : to arrange wagons so as to form a corral

¹cor·rect \kə-ˈrekt\ *vb* **1 a** : to make or set right **b** : COUNTERACT, NEUTRALIZE **c** : to alter or adjust so as to bring to some standard or required condition **2 a** : ¹REBUKE, PUNISH **b** : to indicate the faults or errors of and show how they can be made right ⟨*correct* a student's composition⟩ — **cor·rect·able** \-ˈrek-tə-bəl\ *adj* — **cor·rec·tor** \-ˈrek-tər\ *n*

synonyms CORRECT, RECTIFY, AMEND mean to make right. CORRECT suggests doing something that removes mistakes or merely points them out ⟨teachers *correct* tests⟩. RECTIFY suggests changing something to make it accurate or to bring it under proper control ⟨*rectified* the crowded conditions by building a new school⟩. AMEND suggests improving or restoring by making changes ⟨*amend* the sentence so that it makes sense⟩.

²correct *adj* **1** : meeting or agreeing with a particular standard ⟨*correct* behavior⟩ **2** : agreeing with fact or known truth ⟨the *correct* pronunciation⟩ — **cor·rect·ly** \-ˈrek-(t)lē\ *adv* — **cor·rect·ness** \-ˈrek(t)-nəs\ *n*

synonyms CORRECT, ACCURATE, EXACT, PRECISE mean brought into agreement with truth, a fact, or a standard. CORRECT stresses the notion that something is free from error ⟨a *correct* answer⟩. ACCURATE stresses that great care has been taken to make sure that something agrees with the facts ⟨an *accurate* description of the meeting⟩. EXACT stresses that something agrees very closely with fact or truth ⟨the *exact* number of people present at the meeting⟩. PRECISE suggests an even closer or more careful agreement with fact or with a certain standard ⟨the *precise* measurements of the room⟩.

cor·rec·tion \kə-ˈrek-shən\ *n* **1** : the action or an instance of correcting **2** : a change that makes something right **3** : punishment or scolding intended to correct faults of character or behavior — **cor·rec·tion·al** \-shnəl, -shən-ᵊl\ *adj*

\ə\ **abut**	\aú\ **out**	\i\ **tip**	\ȯ\ **saw**	\ú\ **foot**
\ər\ **further**	\ch\ **chin**	\ī\ **life**	\ȯi\ **coin**	\y\ **yet**
\a\ **mat**	\e\ **pet**	\j\ **job**	\th\ **thin**	\yü\ **few**
\ā\ **take**	\ē\ **easy**	\ŋ\ **sing**	\th\ **this**	\yú\ **cure**
\ä\ **cot, cart**	\g\ **go**	\ō\ **bone**	\ü\ **food**	\zh\ **vision**

correction fluid *n* : a liquid used to paint over typing or writing errors

cor·rec·tive \kə-'rek-tiv\ *adj* : serving to correct : having the power of making right, normal, or regular ⟨*corrective* lenses⟩ ⟨*corrective* action⟩ — **corrective** *n*

cor·re·late \'kȯr-ə-ˌlāt, 'kär-\ *vb* **-lat·ed; -lat·ing** : to connect or relate in a systematic way ⟨*correlate* history and literature lessons⟩

cor·re·la·tion \ˌkȯr-ə-'lā-shən, ˌkär-\ *n* **1** : the act or process of correlating **2** : the state of being correlated; *esp* : a mutual relation discovered to exist between things ⟨the *correlation* between smoking and lung cancer⟩ — **cor·re·la·tion·al** \-shnəl, -shən-ᵊl\ *adj*

¹cor·rel·a·tive \kə-'rel-ət-iv\ *adj* **1** : mutually related **2** : having a mutual grammatical relation and regularly used together ⟨"either" and "or" are *correlative* conjunctions⟩ — **cor·rel·a·tive·ly** *adv*

²correlative *n* : either of two correlative things

cor·re·spond \ˌkȯr-ə-'spänd, ˌkär-\ *vb* **1** : to be alike **2** : to be equivalent (as in meaning, position, purpose, or structure) : MATCH **3** : to communicate by means of letters — **cor·re·spond·ing·ly** \-'spän-diŋ-lē\ *adv*

cor·re·spon·dence \ˌkȯr-ə-'spän-dən(t)s\ *n* **1 a** : agreement between certain things **b** : a point of similarity **c** : a relation between sets in which each member of one set is matched to one or more members of the other set **2 a** : communication by letters **b** : the letters exchanged

¹cor·re·spon·dent \ˌkȯr-ə-'spän-dənt\ *adj* **1** : SIMILAR 1 **2** : being in agreement : FITTING

²correspondent *n* **1** : something that corresponds to something else **2 a** : one who communicates with another by letter **b** : one who contributes news to a newspaper or newscast often from a distant place

corresponding angles *n pl* : any pair of angles each of which is on the same side of one of two lines cut by another line and on the same side of that other line

cor·ri·dor \'kȯr-əd-ər, 'kär-, -ə-ˌdȯ(ə)r\ *n* **1** : a passageway (as in a school) into which compartments or rooms open **2** : a narrow strip of land especially through territory held by an enemy [from early French *corridor* "passageway," from early Italian *corridore* (same meaning), from *correre* "to run," from Latin *currere* "to run" — related to COURSE, CURRENT]

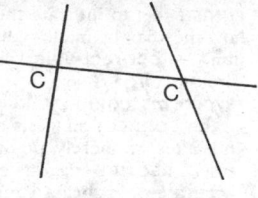

C corresponding angles

cor·rob·o·rate \kə-'räb-ə-ˌrāt\ *vb* **-rat·ed; -rat·ing** : to support with evidence or authority ⟨*corroborated* my brother's story⟩ — **cor·rob·o·ra·tion** \-ˌräb-ə-'rā-shən\ *n* — **cor·rob·o·ra·tive** \-'räb-ə-ˌrāt-iv, -'räb-(ə-)rət-iv\ *adj* — **cor·rob·o·ra·tor** \-'räb-ə-ˌrāt-ər\ *n* — **cor·rob·o·ra·to·ry** \-'räb-(ə-)rə-ˌtōr-ē, -ˌtȯr-\ *adj*

cor·rode \kə-'rōd\ *vb* **cor·rod·ed; cor·rod·ing** : to eat or be eaten away by degrees as if by gnawing ⟨a bridge *corroded* by rust⟩

cor·ro·sion \kə-'rō-zhən\ *n* : the action, process, or effect of corroding

cor·ro·sive \kə-'rō-siv, -ziv\ *adj* : tending or having the power to corrode ⟨*corrosive* acids⟩ — **corrosive** *n* — **cor·ro·sive·ly** *adv* — **cor·ro·sive·ness** *n*

corrosive sublimate *n* : a poisonous chloride of mercury used to kill germs and fungi and in photography

cor·ru·gate \'kȯr-ə-ˌgāt, 'kär-\ *vb* **-gat·ed; -gat·ing** : to form or shape into wrinkles or folds : FURROW ⟨*corrugated* paper⟩

cor·ru·ga·tion \ˌkȯr-ə-'gā-shən, ˌkär-\ *n* **1** : the act of corrugating : the state of being corrugated **2** : a ridge or groove of a corrugated surface

¹cor·rupt \kə-'rəpt\ *vb* **1** : to change from good to bad in morals, manners, or actions; *esp* : to influence a public official improperly **2** : ¹ROT 1a, SPOIL **3** : to change from the original or correct form or version ⟨*corrupt* a text⟩ **4** : to become debased [Middle English *corrupten* "change from good to bad, corrupt," from Latin *corruptus* "corrupted," from *corrumpere* "to corrupt," from *cor-*, *com-* "with" and *rumpere* "to break" — related to ABRUPT, RUPTURE] — **cor·rupt·er** *also* **cor·rup·tor** \-'rəp-tər\ *n*

²corrupt *adj* **1** : morally corrupted : DEPRAVED **2** : characterized by improper conduct ⟨a *corrupt* government⟩ — **cor·rupt·ly** \-'rəp(t)-lē\ *adv* — **cor·rupt·ness** \-'rəp(t)-nəs\ *n*

cor·rupt·ible \kə-'rəp-tə-bəl\ *adj* : capable of being corrupted — **cor·rupt·ibil·i·ty** \-ˌrəp-tə-'bil-ət-ē\ *n*

cor·rup·tion \kə-'rəp-shən\ *n* **1** : physical decay or rotting **2** : dishonest or evil behavior **3** : the causing of someone else to do wrong (as by bribery) **4** : a change from the original or for the worse

cor·sage \kȯr-'säzh, -'säj; 'kȯr-ˌsäzh, -ˌsäj\ *n* : a bouquet of flowers usually worn at the shoulder

cor·sair \'kȯr-ˌsa(ə)r, -ˌse(ə)r\ *n* : ¹PIRATE

corse \'kȯ(ə)rs\ *n, archaic* : CORPSE

corse·let *or* **cors·let** \'kȯr-slət\ *n* : armor worn on the upper part of the body

¹cor·set \'kȯr-sət\ *n* : a woman's tight stiff undergarment worn to support or give shape to waist and hips

²corset *vb* : to dress in or fit with a corset

cor·tege *also* **cor·tège** \kȯr-'tezh, 'kȯr-ˌtezh\ *n* **1** : a group of attendants : RETINUE **2** : PROCESSION 2; *esp* : a funeral procession

cor·tex \'kȯr-ˌteks\ *n, pl* **cor·ti·ces** \'kȯrt-ə-ˌsēz\ *or* **cor·tex·es** **1** : an outer or surrounding layer of an organ or body part ⟨the *cortex* of the kidney⟩; *esp* : the outer layer of gray matter of the cerebrum **2** : the layer of tissue outside the xylem and phloem and inside the corky or epidermal tissues of a vascular plant; *also* : all tissues external to the xylem

cor·ti·sone \'kȯrt-ə-ˌsōn, -ˌzōn\ *n* : a hormone of the adrenal glands that is used especially to reduce inflammation (as in the treatment of arthritis)

co·run·dum \kə-'rən-dəm\ *n* : a very hard mineral of aluminum oxide used for grinding, smoothing, or polishing or in some crystalline forms as a gem (as ruby or sapphire)

cor·vette \kȯr-'vet\ *n* **1** : an armed naval sailing ship **2** : an armed escort ship that is small and fast

co·si·ly, co·si·ness *chiefly British variant of* COZILY, COZINESS

co·sine \'kō-ˌsīn\ *n* : a trigonometric function that is the ratio between the side next to an acute angle in a right triangle and the hypotenuse

¹cos·met·ic \käz-'met-ik\ *n* : a preparation (as a cream, lotion, or powder) used to improve a person's appearance

²cosmetic *adj* : intended to improve a person's appearance

cos·me·tol·o·gist \ˌkäz-mə-'täl-ə-jəst\ *n* : a person who gives beauty treatments (as to skin and hair) — **cos·me·tol·o·gy** \-jē\ *n*

cos·mic \'käz-mik\ *adj* **1** : of or relating to the cosmos ⟨*cosmic* theories⟩ **2** : extremely vast : GRAND ⟨*cosmic* dimensions⟩

cosmic dust *n* : very fine particles of solid matter found in any part of the universe

cosmic ray *n* : a stream of atomic nuclei of extremely penetrating character that enter the earth's atmosphere from outer space at speeds approaching that of light

cos·mol·o·gy \käz-'mäl-ə-jē\ *n, pl* **-gies** : a branch of astronomy that deals with the beginning, structure, and space-time relationships of the universe — **cos·mol·o·gist** \-jəst\ *n*

cos·mo·naut \'käz-mə-ˌnȯt, -ˌnät\ *n* : a Soviet or Russian astronaut

cos·mo·pol·i·tan \ˌkäz-mə-ˈpäl-ət-ᵊn\ *adj* **1** : having a worldwide scope or outlook : not limited or narrow ⟨*cosmopolitan* world travelers⟩ **2** : composed of persons or elements from many parts of the world ⟨a *cosmopolitan* city⟩ **3** : found in most parts of the world and in many kinds of ecological conditions ⟨a *cosmopolitan* herb⟩ — **cosmopolitan** *n*

cos·mos \ˈkäz-məs, *senses 1 & 2 also* -ˌmōs, -ˌmäs\ *n* **1** : the orderly universe **2** : a complex harmonious system **3** : a tall garden plant that is related to the daisies and has showy white, pink, or rose-colored flower heads with usually yellow centers

Cos·sack \ˈkäs-ˌak, -ək\ *n* **1** : a member of any of the groups that formed in Ukraine, southern Russia, the Caucasus, and Siberia after 1400 and were included in czarist Russia during the 18th and 19th centuries **2** : a mounted soldier serving in a unit drafted from Cossack communities

¹**cost** \ˈkost\ *n* **1** : the amount paid or charged for something : PRICE **2** : the loss or penalty involved in achieving a goal ⟨won the battle at the *cost* of many lives⟩ **3** *pl* : legal expenses given to the winning side against the losing side ⟨fined $50 and *costs*⟩ — **at all costs** : without care of the cost or consequences ⟨wanted to win *at all costs*⟩

²**cost** *vb* **cost; cost·ing 1** : to have a price of : require payment of ⟨each ticket *costs* one dollar⟩ **2** : to cause one to pay, spend, or lose ⟨mistakes *cost* him his job⟩

cos·tal \ˈkäs-tᵊl\ *adj* : of, relating to, or located near the ribs

cos·ter \ˈkäs-tər\ *n, British* : COSTERMONGER

cos·ter·mon·ger \ˈkäs-tər-ˌmən-gər, -ˌmäŋ-\ *n, British* : a person who sells fruit or vegetables in the street from a stand or cart

cos·tive \ˈkäs-tiv\ *adj* **1** : affected with constipation **2** : causing constipation ⟨a *costive* diet⟩

cost·ly \ˈkos(t)-lē\ *adj* **cost·li·er; -est 1** : of great cost or value ⟨*costly* furs⟩ **2** : gained at great expense or sacrifice ⟨a *costly* victory⟩ — **cost·li·ness** *n*

¹**cos·tume** \ˈkäs-ˌt(y)üm\ *n* **1** : the style of clothing, ornaments, and hair characteristic of a certain period, region, or class ⟨ancient Roman *costume*⟩ ⟨peasant *costume*⟩ **2** : special or fancy dress (as for wear on the stage or at a masquerade party) **3** : a person's outer clothing — **costume** *adj*

²**costume** *vb* **cos·tumed; cos·tum·ing** : to provide with a costume

cos·tum·er \ˈkäs-ˌt(y)ü-mər\ *n* : one who makes, sells, or rents costumes

co·sy *chiefly British variant of* COZY

¹**cot** \ˈkät\ *n* : COTTAGE 1 [Old English *cot* "cottage"]

²**cot** *n* : a narrow bed often made of fabric stretched over a folding frame [from Hindi and Urdu *khāt* "frame of a bed"]

cote \ˈkōt, ˈkät\ *n* : a shed or coop for small domestic animals (as pigeons)

co·te·rie \ˈkōt-ə-(ˌ)rē, ˌkōt-ə-ˈrē\ *n* : a small close group of people with a shared interest

co·til·lion \kō-ˈtil-yən, kə-\ *n* **1** : a complicated formal dance with frequent changing of partners **2** : a formal ball

cot·tage \ˈkät-ij\ *n* **1** : a small one-family house **2** : a small house for vacation use

cottage cheese *n* : a very soft cheese made from soured skim milk

cot·tag·er \ˈkät-ij-ər\ *n* : one who lives in a cottage; *esp* : one occupying a private house at a vacation resort

cot·tar *or* **cot·ter** \ˈkät-ər\ *n* : a peasant or farm laborer occupying a cottage usually in return for services

cot·ter \ˈkät-ər\ *n* : a wedge-shaped piece used to fasten parts together

cotter pin *n* : a half-round metal strip bent into a pin whose ends can be spread apart after insertion through a slot or hole

¹**cot·ton** \ˈkät-ᵊn\ *n* **1 a** : a soft usually white fluffy material that is made up of the hairs around the seeds of a tall plant related to the mallows and that is spun into yarn **b** : any plant that produces cotton **2 a** : fabric made of cotton **b** : yarn spun from cotton — **cotton** *adj*

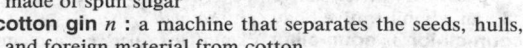

²**cotton** *vb* **cot·toned; cot·ton·ing** \ˈkät-niŋ, -ᵊn-iŋ\ : to take a liking ⟨*cottoned* to them at our first meeting⟩

cotton candy *n* : a candy made of spun sugar

¹cotton 1a

cotton gin *n* : a machine that separates the seeds, hulls, and foreign material from cotton

cot·ton·mouth \ˈkät-ᵊn-ˌmauth\ *n* : WATER MOCCASIN

cottonmouth moccasin *n* : WATER MOCCASIN

cot·ton·seed \ˈkät-nē, -ᵊn-ˌsēd\ *n* : the seed of the cotton plant

cottonseed oil *n* : a pale yellow oil that is obtained from cottonseed and is used chiefly in salad and cooking oils and in shortenings and margarine

cot·ton·tail \ˈkät-ᵊn-ˌtāl\ *n* : any of several small brownish gray rabbits with a fluffy tail that is white on the underside

cot·ton·wood \-ˌwud\ *n* : a poplar with a small bunch of cottony hairs on the seed; *esp* : one of the eastern and central U.S. that grows rapidly and produces many leaves

cot·tony \ˈkät-nē, -ᵊn-ē\ *adj* **1** : covered with soft hairs : DOWNY **2** : ¹SOFT 1d

cot·y·le·don \ˌkät-ᵊl-ˈēd-ᵊn\ *n* : the first leaf or one of the first leaves developed by the embryo of a seed plant that is usually folded within the seed until germination and serves as a storehouse of food — called also *seed leaf*

¹**couch** \ˈkauch\ *vb* **1** : to lie down for rest or sleep **2** : to bring down : LOWER ⟨a knight charging with *couched* lance⟩ **3** : to phrase in a specified manner ⟨a letter *couched* in polite terms⟩

²**couch** *n* : a piece of furniture (as a sofa) that one can sit or lie on

couch potato *n* : someone who spends a lot of time sitting and watching television

cou·gar \ˈkü-gər *also* -ˌgär\ *n, pl* **cougars** *also* **cougar** : a large powerful brownish yellow cat formerly widespread in the Americas but no longer found in many areas — called also *catamount, mountain lion, panther, puma*

cougar

¹**cough** \ˈkof\ *vb* **1** : to force air from the lungs with a sharp short noise or series of noises **2** : to get rid of by coughing ⟨*cough* up mucus⟩ **3** : to make a noise like that of coughing ⟨an engine *coughing* and sputtering⟩

²**cough** *n* **1** : a condition marked by repeated or frequent coughing **2** : an act or sound of coughing

\ə\ **abut**	\au̇\ **out**	\i\ **tip**	\ȯ\ **saw**	\u̇\ **foot**
\ər\ **further**	\ch\ **chin**	\ī\ **life**	\ȯi\ **coin**	\y\ **yet**
\a\ **mat**	\e\ **pet**	\j\ **job**	\th\ **thin**	\yü\ **few**
\ā\ **take**	\ē\ **easy**	\ŋ\ **sing**	\th\ **this**	\yu̇\ **cure**
\ä\ **cot, cart**	\g\ **go**	\ō\ **bone**	\ü\ **food**	\zh\ **vision**

cough drop *n* : a small piece of candy or a tablet that contains medicine and is used to relieve coughing

cough syrup *n* : any of various sweet liquids that contain medicine and are used to relieve coughing

could \kəd, (')kud\ *past of* CAN — used as a helping verb in the past ⟨we found we *could* go⟩ ⟨we said we would go if we *could*⟩ and as a polite or less forceful alternative to *can* ⟨*could* you do this for me⟩

couldn't \'kud-²nt\ : could not

couldst \kədst, (')kudst\ *archaic past 2nd singular of* CAN

cou·lee \'ku-lē\ *n* **1 a** : a dry creek bed **b** : a usually small or shallow ravine **2** : a thick sheet or stream of lava

cou·lomb \'ku-,läm, -,lōm; ku-'läm, -'lōm\ *n* : the practical meter-kilogram-second unit of electric charge equal to the quantity of electricity transferred by a current of one ampere in one second [named for Charles-Augustin de *Coulomb* 1736–1806, French scientist]

coun·cil \'kaun(t)-səl\ *n* **1** : a meeting for consultation **2** : an advisory or legislative body ⟨the governor's *council*⟩ **3** : an administrative body ⟨city *council*⟩

coun·cil·lor *or* **coun·cil·or** \'kaun(t)-s(ə-)lər\ *n* : a member of a council

coun·cil·man \'kaun(t)-səl-mən\ *n* : a member of a council (as of a town or city)

coun·cil·wom·an \'kaun(t)-səl-,wum-ən\ *n* : a woman who is a member of a council

¹coun·sel \'kaun(t)-səl\ *n* **1** : advice given **2** : the act of deliberating or consulting ⟨took *counsel* together⟩ **3** *pl* **counsel** : a lawyer who represents a person or group in a court of law

²counsel *vb* **-seled** *or* **-selled**; **-sel·ing** *or* **-sel·ling** \-s(ə-)liŋ\ **1** : to give advice to ⟨*counsel* a student on a choice of studies⟩ **2** : to seek advice : CONSULT ⟨*counsel* with friends⟩

coun·sel·or *or* **coun·sel·lor** \'kaun(t)-s(ə-)lər\ *n* **1** : a person who gives advice ⟨guidance *counselor*⟩ **2** : LAWYER **3** : a supervisor of campers or activities at a summer camp

¹count \'kaunt\ *vb* **1 a** : to add one by one so as to find the total number of a group of things ⟨*count* the apples in a box⟩ **b** : to name the consecutive numbers up to and including ⟨*count* ten⟩ **c** : to recite the numbers one by one or by groups ⟨*count* to one hundred by fives⟩ **d** : to include in a tally ⟨forty present, *counting* children⟩ **2 a** : CONSIDER **3** ⟨*count* myself lucky⟩ **b** : to include or leave out by or as if by counting ⟨*count* me in⟩ ⟨*count* me out⟩ **3 a** : to have value or importance ⟨every vote *counts*⟩ **b** : to deserve to be regarded or considered ⟨a job so easy it hardly *counts* as work⟩ [Middle English *counten* "to add one by one," from early French *counter* (same meaning), derived from Latin *computare* "to count, compute" — related to ACCOUNT, COMPUTE] — **count·able** \-ə-bəl\ *adj* — **and counting** : with more to come ⟨in business for 50 years *and counting*⟩ — **count on 1** : to rely or depend on (someone) **2** : to expect (something) to happen ⟨*counted* on winning⟩

²count *n* **1 a** : the act or process of counting **b** : a total obtained by counting : TALLY **2** : a charge of wrongdoing; *esp* : a separate item in a legal accusation ⟨guilty on all *counts*⟩ **3** : the number of balls and strikes charged to a baseball batter during one turn

³count *n* : a European nobleman whose rank is equal to that of a British earl [from early French *cunte* "nobleman," derived from Latin *comes* "companion, member of a royal court," literally, "one who goes with another," from *com-* "with" and *-es*, a form of *ire* "to go" — related to COUNTY, ITINERARY]

count·down \'kaunt-,daun\ *n* : the process of counting off backward in fixed units (as seconds) the time remaining before an event (as the launching of a rocket)

¹coun·te·nance \'kaunt-³n-ənts, 'kaunt-nənts\ *n* **1 a** : calm expression **b** : calmness of mind **2 a** : ¹FACE 1 **b** : an expression on the face; *esp* : a facial expression as a sign of mood, emotion, or character **3** : a show of approval ⟨gave no *countenance* to the plan⟩

²countenance *vb* **-nanced**; **-nanc·ing** : TOLERATE 1, ENCOURAGE ⟨refused to *countenance* their behavior⟩

¹count·er \'kaunt-ər\ *n* **1** : a piece (as of metal or plastic) used in counting or in games **2** : a level surface (as a table) over which business is done or food is served or on which goods are displayed [Middle English *countour* "something used in counting," from early French *countour* (same meaning), from Latin *computatorium* "a place for counting or keeping accounts," from earlier *computare* "to count, compute" — related to ¹COUNT, COMPUTE]

²count·er *n* : one that counts; *esp* : a device for indicating a number or amount

³coun·ter \'kaunt-ər\ *vb* **coun·tered**; **coun·ter·ing** \'kaunt-ə-riŋ, 'kaun-triŋ\ **1** : to act in opposition to : OPPOSE ⟨*countering* the claim for damages⟩ **2** : to give a blow in return ⟨*counter* with a left hook⟩ [Middle English *countren* "to oppose," from early French *contre* "against" — related to CONTRA-, COUNTER-]

⁴coun·ter *adv* : in another or opposite direction ⟨acting *counter* to advice⟩

⁵coun·ter *n* **1** : the act of giving a return blow **2** : the blow given

⁶coun·ter *adj* **1** : moving in an opposite direction ⟨the ship slowed by *counter* tides⟩ **2** : designed to oppose ⟨a *counter* opinion⟩

coun·ter- *prefix* **1 a** : contrary : opposite ⟨*counter*clockwise⟩ **b** : opposing : retaliatory ⟨*counter*offensive⟩ **2** : like : matching ⟨*counter*part⟩ [derived from Latin *contra* "against, opposite" — related to CONTRA-]

coun·ter·act \,kaunt-ə-'rakt\ *vb* : to lessen the force, action, or influence of : OFFSET ⟨a drug that *counteracts* a poison⟩ — **coun·ter·ac·tion** \-'rak-shən\ *n*

coun·ter·at·tack \'kaunt-ə-rə-,tak\ *n* : an attack made to counter an enemy's attack — **counterattack** *vb*

¹coun·ter·bal·ance \'kaunt-ər-,bal-ən(t)s, ,kaunt-ər-'bal-\ *n* **1** : a weight that balances another **2** : a force or influence that checks an opposing force

²counterbalance *vb* : to oppose or balance with an equal weight or force

counter check *n* : a blank check available at a bank and usually to be cashed only at the bank by the person writing the check

coun·ter·claim \'kaunt-ər-,klām\ *n* : an opposing claim — **counterclaim** *vb* — **coun·ter·claim·ant** \-,klā-mənt\ *n*

coun·ter·clock·wise \,kaunt-ər-'kläk-,wīz\ *adv* : in a direction opposite to that in which the hands of a clock rotate — **counterclockwise** *adj*

coun·ter·cur·rent \'kaunt-ər-,kər-ənt, -,kə-rənt\ *n* : a current flowing in a direction opposite to that of another current

¹coun·ter·feit \'kaunt-ər-,fit\ *vb* **1** : to imitate or copy especially in order to deceive ⟨*counterfeiting* money⟩ **2** : ¹PRETEND 1, FEIGN ⟨*counterfeit* enthusiasm to mask boredom⟩ — **coun·ter·feit·er** *n*

²counterfeit *adj* **1** : made in exact imitation of something else with the intention of deceiving : FORGED ⟨*counterfeit* money⟩ **2** : not sincere : SHAM

³counterfeit *n* : something counterfeit : FORGERY

coun·ter·foil \'kaunt-ər-,foil\ *n* : a detachable stub (as on a check or ticket) usually serving as a record or receipt

coun·ter·in·tel·li·gence \,kaunt-ə-rin-'tel-ə-jən(t)s\ *n* : activities of an intelligence service meant to hide the truth from an enemy or to prevent the enemy from learning secret information

coun·ter·mand \'kaunt-ər-,mand, ,kaunt-ər-'mand\ *vb* **1** : to cancel a previous command **2** : to recall or order back by a contrary order

coun·ter·march \'kaùnt-ər-ˌmärch\ n : a marching back; *esp* : a maneuver by which a marching unit reverses direction but keeps the same order — **countermarch** vb

coun·ter·mea·sure \'kaùnt-ər-ˌmezh-ər, -ˌmäzh-\ n : an action or device designed to counteract another

coun·ter·mel·o·dy \'kaùnt-ər-ˌmel-əd-ē\ n : a secondary melody that goes along with and often contrasts with a main melody

coun·ter·of·fen·sive \'kaùnt-ə-rə-ˌfen(t)-siv\ n : a large-scale counterattack

coun·ter·pane \'kaùnt-ər-ˌpān\ n : BEDSPREAD

coun·ter·part \'kaùnt-ər-ˌpärt\ n 1 : a part or thing that matches another ⟨the left arm is the *counterpart* of the right⟩ 2 : something that serves to complete something else : COMPLEMENT 3 : a person closely resembling another

coun·ter·point \'kaùnt-ər-ˌpòint\ n 1 : one or more independent melodies added as accompaniment to a principal melody 2 : combination of two or more melodies into a harmony in which each keeps its own identity

coun·ter·poise \'kaùnt-ər-ˌpòiz\ vb : ²COUNTERBALANCE — **counterpoise** n

coun·ter·rev·o·lu·tion \ˌkaùnt-ə(r)-ˌrev-ə-'lü-shən\ n : a revolution intended to overthrow a government established by an earlier revolution — **coun·ter·rev·o·lu·tion·ary** \-'lü-shə-ˌner-ē\ adj or n — **coun·ter·rev·o·lu·tion·ist** \-'lü-sh(ə-)nəst\ n

¹**coun·ter·sign** \'kaùnt-ər-ˌsīn\ n : a sign used in reply to another; *esp* : PASSWORD

²**countersign** vb : to add one's signature to a document after another has already signed it in order to confirm its genuineness — **coun·ter·sig·na·ture** \ˌkaùnt-ər-'sig-nə-ˌchù(ə)r, -chər\ n

¹**coun·ter·sink** \'kaùnt-ər-ˌsiŋk\ vb **-sunk** \-ˌsəŋk\; **-sink·ing** 1 : to make a countersink on (a hole) 2 : to set the head of (as a screw) at or below the surface

²**countersink** n 1 : a bit or drill for making a countersink 2 : a funnel-shaped enlargement at the end of a drilled hole

coun·ter·spy \'kaùnt-ər-ˌspī\ n : a spy employed in counterintelligence

coun·ter·ten·or \'kaùnt-ər-ˌten-ər\ n : a tenor with an unusually high range

coun·ter·top \'kaùnt-ər-ˌtäp\ n : the surface of waist-level kitchen cabinets used as a work area

coun·ter·weight \'kaùnt-ər-ˌwāt\ n : ¹COUNTERBALANCE 1

count·ess \'kaùnt-əs\ n 1 : the wife or widow of a count or an earl 2 : a woman holding the rank of count or earl

count·ing·house \'kaùnt-iŋ-ˌhaùs\ n : a building, room, or office used for keeping books and carrying on business

counting number n : NATURAL NUMBER

count·less \'kaùnt-ləs\ adj : too numerous to be counted : INNUMERABLE

count noun n : a noun (as *bean* or *sheet*) that forms a plural and that can be used with a numeral, with words such as *many* or *few*, or with the indefinite article *a* or *an*

coun·tri·fied also **coun·try·fied** \'kən-tri-ˌfīd\ adj : looking or acting like a person from the country : RUSTIC

¹**coun·try** \'kən-trē\ n, pl **countries** 1 : an indefinite usually large stretch of land : REGION ⟨hill *country*⟩ 2 a : the land of a person's birth, residence, or citizenship b : a nation or its territory 3 : the people of a state or district : POPULACE 4 : the open rural area outside of big towns and cities ⟨lives out in the *country*⟩

²**country** adj : of, relating to, or characteristic of the country : RURAL, RUSTIC

country and western n : COUNTRY MUSIC

country club n : a suburban club for social life and recreation

coun·try·man \'kən-trē-mən, *sense 3 is often* -ˌman\ n 1 : a person born or living in a particular country 2 : a

person born or living in the same country as another 3 : one living in the country or marked by country ways : RUSTIC

country music n : music coming from or imitating the folk style of the Southern U.S. or the Western cowboy

coun·try·seat \ˌkən-trē-'sēt\ n : a mansion or estate in the country

coun·try·side \'kən-trē-ˌsīd\ n : a rural area or its people

coun·try·wom·an \-ˌwùm-ən\ n 1 : a woman born or living in the same country as another 2 : a woman who is a resident of the country

coun·ty \'kaùnt-ē\ n, pl **counties** 1 : the area owned by a count 2 : a division of a state or of a country for local government [Middle English *counte* "division of the country for the purposes of government," from early French *counté* "region under control of a count," derived from Latin *comes* count — related to ³COUNT]

county agent n : a government agent employed to provide information about agriculture and home economics in rural areas

county seat n : a town that is the seat of county administration

coup \'kü\ n, pl **coups** \'küz\ 1 : a brilliant, sudden, and usually highly successful action 2 : COUP D'ÉTAT [from French *coup* "blow, stroke"]

coup d'é·tat \ˌküd-ā-'tä, ˌküd-ə-\ n, pl **coups d'é·tat** \-'tä(z)\ : a sudden overthrowing of a government by a small group [from French *coup d'état*, literally, "stroke of state (the government)," from *coup* "blow, stroke" and *de* "of" and *état* "state"]

cou·pé or **coupe** \kü-'pā, *sense 2 is often* 'küp\ n 1 : a four-wheeled closed carriage pulled by horses for two persons with an outside seat for the driver 2 *usually* coupe a : a closed two-door automobile for usually two persons b : a usually closed two-door automobile with a full-width rear seat

coupé 1

¹**cou·ple** \'kəp-əl\ n 1 : two persons romantically paired or associated together (as by marriage or on a date) 2 : two persons or things paired together 3 : an indefinite small number : FEW ⟨a *couple* of days ago⟩

²**couple** vb **cou·pled; cou·pling** \'kəp-(ə-)liŋ\ 1 : to join together : CONNECT 2 : to join in pairs — **cou·pler** \-p(ə-)lər\ n

³**couple** adj : TWO 1; *also* : ¹SEVERAL 2 ⟨a *couple* days ago⟩

cou·plet \'kəp-lət\ n : two lines of verse that follow in order and form a unit; *esp* : two rhyming lines of the same length

cou·pling \'kəp-liŋ (*usual for sense 2*), -ə-liŋ\ n 1 : the act of bringing or coming together 2 : something that connects two parts or things

cou·pon \'k(y)ü-ˌpän\ n 1 : a statement of due interest to be cut from a bond and presented for payment on a stated date 2 a : one of a series of tickets to be detached and presented as needed b : a ticket or form allowing the bearer to purchase rationed articles c : a certificate or other evidence of a purchase that may be exchanged for premiums d : a part of an advertisement to be cut off to use as an order blank or inquiry form or to obtain a discount on the price of something [from French *coupon* "a

\ə\ **abut**	\aú\ **out**	\i\ **tip**	\ȯ\ **saw**	\ú\ **foot**
\ər\ **further**	\ch\ **chin**	\ī\ **life**	\ȯi\ **coin**	\y\ **yet**
\a\ **mat**	\e\ **pet**	\j\ **job**	\th\ **thin**	\yü\ **few**
\ā\ **take**	\ē\ **easy**	\ŋ\ **sing**	\th\ **this**	\yú\ **cure**
\ä\ **cot, cart**	\g\ **go**	\ō\ **bone**	\ü\ **food**	\zh\ **vision**

part of a bill to be cut off and turned in with payment," from early French *coupon* "a piece (cut off)," from *couper* "to cut" — related to ²COPE, COUP]

cour·age \'kər-ij, 'kə-rij\ *n* : strength of mind to carry on in spite of danger or difficulty [Middle English *corage* "the heart as a source of feelings, spirit, confidence," from early French *curage* (same meaning), from *coer* "heart," from Latin *cor* "heart" — related to CORDIAL]

synonyms COURAGE, BRAVERY, VALOR, HEROISM mean greatness of spirit in facing danger or difficulty. COURAGE suggests strength in overcoming fear and carrying on against difficulties ⟨the *courage* of the pioneers⟩. BRAVERY stresses bold and daring defiance of danger ⟨the *bravery* shown by the firefighters⟩. VALOR applies especially to bravery in fighting a dangerous enemy ⟨honored for *valor* in battle⟩. HEROISM suggests bravery and boldness in accepting risk or sacrifice for a noble or generous purpose ⟨the *heroism* shown by many in the early struggle for women's rights⟩.

cou·ra·geous \kə-'rā-jəs\ *adj* : having or marked by courage : BRAVE — **cou·ra·geous·ly** *adv* — **cou·ra·geous·ness** *n*

cou·ri·er \'kůr-ē-ər, 'kər-ē-, 'kə-rē\ *n* : a messenger especially in the diplomatic service [Middle English *courrier* "a person who carries (runs) messages from one place to another quickly," from early Italian *corriere* (same meaning), derived from Latin *currere* "to run" — related to CURRENT]

¹**course** \'kō(ə)rs, 'kó(ə)rs\ *n* **1** : the act or action of moving in a path from point to point ⟨the planets in their *courses*⟩ **2** : the direction or route of motion or progress ⟨the *course* of a river⟩ ⟨a ship's *course*⟩ **3** : land laid out for golf **4 a** : normal or accustomed process or procedure ⟨the disease ran its *course*⟩ **b** : manner of proceeding : CONDUCT ⟨a wise *course*⟩ **c** : progression through a period of time or a series of acts or events ⟨was built in the *course* of a year⟩ **5 a** : an ordered process or series **b** : a series of classes in a subject; *also* : a group of such courses ⟨a four-year *course* in chemistry⟩ **6** : a part of a meal served at one time ⟨had salad for the first *course*⟩ **7** : a layer of brick or other building material in a wall [Middle English *cours, course* "action of moving in a certain path, path of movement, progress," from early French *curs, course* (same meaning), derived from Latin *currere* "to run" — related to CORRIDOR, CURRENT] — **of course 1** : following the ordinary way or procedure ⟨did it as a matter *of course*⟩ **2** : as might be expected

²**course** *vb* **coursed; cours·ing 1** : to run through or over ⟨buffalo *coursed* the plains⟩ **2** : to move rapidly : RACE ⟨blood *coursing* through the veins⟩

cours·er \'kōr-sər, 'kór-\ *n* : a swift or spirited horse

¹**court** \'kō(ə)rt, 'kó(ə)rt\ *n* **1 a** : the residence of a ruler and especially a king or queen **b** : a ruler's formal assembly of advisers and officers as a governing body **c** : the family and followers of a ruler **2 a** : an open space completely or partly surrounded by buildings **b** : a space for playing a ball game ⟨a tennis *court*⟩ **c** : a wide alley with only one opening onto a street **3 a** : an assembly for carrying out judicial business **b** : a session of a judicial assembly ⟨*court* is now adjourned⟩ **c** : a building or room where legal cases are heard **d** : a judge in session **4** : attention designed to win favor ⟨pay *court* to the king⟩

²**court** *vb* **1 a** : to try to gain ⟨*court* favor⟩ **b** : to act so as to invite or provoke ⟨*court* disaster⟩ **2** : to seek the affections or favor of ⟨the candidate *courted* the voters⟩ **3 a** : to engage in a social relationship usually leading to marriage **b** : to engage in activity leading to mating ⟨a pair of robins *courting*⟩

cour·te·ous \'kərt-ē-əs\ *adj* **1** : marked by good manners suitable to a court **2** : marked by respect for and consideration of others — **cour·te·ous·ly** *adv* — **cour·te·ous·ness** *n*

cour·te·sy \'kərt-ə-sē\ *n, pl* **-sies 1** : courtly politeness **2** : a favor courteously performed **3** : a favor as distinguished from a right ⟨a title by *courtesy* only⟩

court·house \'kō(ə)rt-ˌhaůs, 'kó(ə)rt-\ *n* : a building in which courts of law are held or county offices are located

court·ier \'kōrt-ē-ər, 'kórt-\ *n* **1** : a person in attendance to a ruler at a royal court **2** : a person who practices flattery

court·ly \'kō(ə)rt-lē, 'kó(ə)rt-\ *adj* : suitable to a royal court : ELEGANT ⟨*courtly* manners⟩ — **court·li·ness** *n*

¹**court–mar·tial** \'kōrt-ˌmär-shəl, 'kórt-, -'mär-\ *n, pl* **courts–martial** *also* **court–martials 1** : a military court **2** : a trial by court-martial

²**court–martial** *vb* **-mar·tialed** *also* **-mar·tialled; -mar·tial·ing** *also* **-mar·tial·ling** \-ˌmärsh-(ə)-liŋ, -'märsh-\ : to try by court-martial

court plaster *n* : an adhesive plaster especially of silk coated with isinglass and glycerin

court·room \'kō(ə)rt-ˌrüm, 'kó(ə)rt-, -ˌrům\ *n* : a room in which a court of law is held

court·ship \-ˌship\ *n* : the act or process of courting

court·yard \-ˌyärd\ *n* : a court or enclosure next to a building

cous·in \'kəz-ᵊn\ *n* **1 a** : a child of one's uncle or aunt **b** : a relative descended from a common ancestor **2** : a person of a race or people ethnically or culturally related ⟨our English *cousins*⟩

cove \'kōv\ *n* **1** : a small sheltered inlet or bay **2** : a level area sheltered by hills or mountains

cov·en \'kəv-ən\ *n* : a meeting or band of witches

¹**cov·e·nant** \'kəv-(ə-)nənt\ *n* : a solemn agreement : CONTRACT

²**cov·e·nant** \'kəv-(ə-)nənt, -ə-ˌnant\ *vb* **1** : to promise by a covenant : PLEDGE **2** : to enter into a covenant

¹**cov·er** \'kəv-ər\ *vb* **cov·ered; cov·er·ing** \'kəv-(ə-)riŋ\ **1 a** : to guard from attack **b** : to have within range of one's guns **c** : to provide protection to or against : INSURE ⟨insurance that *covers* the traveler in any accident⟩ ⟨the policy *covered* water damage⟩ **d** : to maintain a check on especially by patrolling ⟨state police *covering* the highways⟩ **2 a** : to hide something from sight or knowledge ⟨*cover* up a scandal⟩ **b** : to conceal something dishonest or embarrassing from notice ⟨*cover* for a friend in an investigation⟩ **c** : to act as a substitute or replacement ⟨*covered* for me during my vacation⟩ **3 a** : to spread or lie over or on ⟨*covered* the child with a blanket⟩ ⟨water *covered* the floor⟩ **b** : to put something protective or concealing over ⟨*cover* the mouth while coughing⟩ **4 a** : to deal with ⟨a text *covering* two chapters⟩ **b** : to provide or plan for ⟨plans *covering* an emergency⟩ **5 a** : to have as one's territory or field of activity ⟨one salesperson *covers* the whole state⟩ **b** : to report news about ⟨*covered* the trial⟩ **6** : to pass over or through ⟨*covered* 10 miles a day⟩ **7** : to pay or provide for the payment of ⟨*cover* expenses⟩ — **cov·er·able** \'kəv-(ə-)rə-bəl\ *adj* — **cov·er·er** \-ər-ər\ *n*

²**cover** *n* **1** : something that protects, shelters, or conceals (as a natural shelter for an animal or natural features that shelter or conceal) **2 a** : something that is placed over or about another thing (as the lid of a box or a sheet or blanket on a bed) **b** : a binding or case for a book or the front or back of such a binding **c** : something (as plants or snow) that covers the ground **3** : an envelope or wrapper for mail — **under cover** : under concealment : in secret

cov·er·age \'kəv-(ə-)rij\ *n* **1** : the act or fact of covering or something that covers ⟨insurance *coverage*⟩ ⟨news *coverage*⟩ **2** : the number or amount covered : SCOPE

cov·er·all \'kəv-ə-ˌról\ *n* : a one-piece outer garment worn to protect clothes — usually used in plural

cover charge *n* : a charge made by a restaurant or nightclub in addition to the charge for food and drink

cover crop *n* : a crop planted to prevent soil erosion and to provide humus

covered wagon *n* : a wagon with an arched canvas top

cover glass *n* : a piece of very thin glass or plastic used to cover something mounted on a microscope slide

cov·er·ing \'kəv-(ə-)riŋ\ *n* : something that covers or conceals

cov·er·let \'kəv-ər-lət\ *n* : BEDSPREAD

cov·er·slip \'kəv-ər-ˌslip\ *n* : COVER GLASS

¹**co·vert** \'kō-(ˌ)vərt, kō-'vərt, 'kəv-ərt\ *adj* **1** : not openly made or done ⟨*covert* military operations⟩ **2** : covered over : SHELTERED ⟨a *covert* nook⟩ **synonyms** see SE-CRET — **cov·ert·ly** *adv* — **cov·ert·ness** *n*

²**co·vert** \'kəv-ərt, 'kō-vərt\ *n* **1** : hiding place : SHELTER **2** : a thicket giving cover to game

cov·er–up \'kəv-ə-ˌrəp\ *n* : a planned effort to conceal a wrongful act or situation

cov·et \'kəv-ət\ *vb* : to wish for greatly or with envy ⟨*covet* another's success⟩ ⟨*covet* a friend's possessions⟩ — **cov·et·er** \-ər\ *n* — **cov·et·ing·ly** \-iŋ-lē\ *adv*

cov·et·ous \'kəv-ət-əs\ *adj* : marked by a too eager desire especially for another's possessions — **cov·et·ous·ly** *adv* — **cov·et·ous·ness** *n*

cov·ey \'kəv-ē\ *n, pl* **coveys** **1** : a small flock (as of quail) **2** : COMPANY 2a, GROUP

¹**cow** \'kaù\ *n* **1** : the adult female of cattle or of any of various usually large animals (as elephants, whales, or seals) **2** : any domestic bovine animal regardless of sex or age [Old English *cū* "cow"]

²**cow** *vb* : to lessen the spirits or courage of : FRIGHTEN ⟨were *cowed* into silence by threats⟩ [probably of Scandinavian origin]

cow·ard \'kaù(-ə)rd\ *n* : one who shows shameful fear or timidity — **coward** *adj*

Word History A frightened animal may put its tail between its hind legs, and if it is very frightened it may run away. In an animal like the hare, the white flash of the fleeing tail is especially obvious. This action gives us the phrase *turn tail*, meaning "to run away, flee." But even tailless animals like people can turn tail and run when frightened. It is in the "tail end" of an army that you might expect to find the cowards. We do not know whether the word *coward* developed from the idea of an animal's tail or an army's, but we do know the word comes from an early French word that meant "tail." [Middle English *coward* "coward," from early French *cuard* "coward," from *cue, coe* "tail," from Latin *cauda* "tail" — related to CODA, ²CUE, QUEUE; see *Word History* at QUEUE]

cow·ard·ice \'kaù(-ə)rd-əs\ *n* : lack of courage to face danger : shameful fear

cow·ard·ly \'kaù(-ə)rd-lē\ *adj* **1** : lacking courage : disgracefully timid ⟨a *cowardly* rascal⟩ **2** : characteristic of a coward ⟨a *cowardly* attack from behind⟩ — **cowardly** *adv* — **cow·ard·li·ness** *n*

cow·bell \'kaù-ˌbel\ *n* : a bell hung about the neck of a cow to indicate its whereabouts

cow·bird \-ˌbərd\ *n* : a small North American blackbird that lays its eggs in the nests of other birds

cow·boy \-ˌbòi\ *n* : one who tends cattle or horses; *esp* : a mounted cattle-ranch worker

cow·catch·er \-ˌkach-ər, -ˌkech-\ *n* : a strong frame on the front of a locomotive for throwing obstacles off the track

cow·er \'kaù(-ə)r\ *vb* : to shrink away or crouch down (as from fear)

cow·girl \'kaù-ˌgər(-ə)l\ *n* : a girl or woman who tends cattle or horses

cow·hand \-ˌhand\ *n* : COWBOY

cow·herd \-ˌhərd\ *n* : one who tends cows

¹**cow·hide** \-ˌhīd\ *n* **1** : the hide of a cow or leather made from it **2** : a whip of rawhide or braided leather

²**cowhide** *vb* **cow·hid·ed; cow·hid·ing** : to whip with a cowhide

cowl \'kaù(ə)l\ *n* **1** : a monk's hood or long hooded cloak **2** : the top part of an automobile body forward of the two front doors to which are attached the windshield and in-strument panel **3** : COWLING — **cowled** \'kaùld\ *adj*

cow·lick \'kaù-ˌlik\ *n* : a lock or bunch of hair that grows in a different direction from the rest of the hair and cannot be made to lie flat

cowl·ing \'kaù-liŋ\ *n* : a removable metal covering for the engine and sometimes a part of the fuselage of an airplane; *also* : a metal cover for an engine

cow·man \'kaù-mən, -ˌman\ *n* **1** : COWBOY **2** : a cattle owner or rancher

co·work·er \'kō-ˌwər-kər\ *n* : a fellow worker

cow·pea \'kaù-ˌpē\ *n* : a sprawling herb related to the bean and grown in the southern U.S. especially as food for livestock and for green manure; *also* : its edible seed — called also *black-eyed pea*

Cow·per's gland \ˌkaù-pərz-, ˌkü-pərz-, ˌkúp-ərz-\ *n* : either of two small glands that empty into the male urethra

cow·poke \'kaù-ˌpōk\ *n* : COWBOY

cow pony *n* : a strong and active saddle horse trained for herding cattle

cow·pox \'kaù-ˌpäks\ *n* : a mild disease of the cow that is caused by a virus and that when passed on to human beings produces a temporary rash and protects against smallpox

cow·punch·er \-ˌpən-chər\ *n* : COWBOY

cow·rie *also* **cow·ry** \'kaù(ə)r-ē\ *n, pl* **cowries** : any of numerous usually small snails of warm seas with glossy often brightly colored shells

cow·slip \'kaù-ˌslip\ *n* : MARSH MARIGOLD

cox \'käks\ *n* : COXSWAIN 2 — **cox** *vb*

cox·comb \'käks-ˌkōm\ *n* : a conceited foolish person

cox·swain \'käk-sən, -ˌswān\ *n* **1** : a sailor who has charge of a ship's boat and its crew **2** : a person who steers a racing shell

coy \'kòi\ *adj* **1** : BASHFUL, SHY **2** : marked by cute or sly playfulness or pretended shyness ⟨using *coy* tricks to attract attention⟩ — **coy·ly** *adv* — **coy·ness** *n*

coy·ote \kī-'ōt-ē, 'kī-ˌōt\ *n, pl* **coyotes** *or* **coyote** : a tannish gray to reddish gray North American mammal related to but smaller than the wolf

coy·pu \'kòi-(ˌ)pü\ *n* : NUTRIA

coz·en \'kəz-ᵊn\ *vb* **coz·ened; coz·en·ing** \'kəz-niŋ, -ᵊn-iŋ\ : to deceive by skillful trickery — **coz·en·er** \'kəz-nər, -ᵊn-ər\ *n*

¹**co·zy** \'kō-zē\ *adj* **co·zi·er; -est** : ²SNUG 2, COMFORTABLE — **co·zi·ly** \-zə-lē\ *adv* — **co·zi·ness** \-zē-nəs\ *n*

²**cozy** *n, pl* **cozies** : a padded cover for a teapot used to keep the contents hot

cpu \ˌsē-ˌpē-'yü\ *n, often cap C&P&U* : the part of a computer that does most of the data processing [*central processing unit*]

¹**crab** \'krab\ *n* **1** : any of various crustaceans with a short broad usually flattened shell of chitin, a small abdomen curled forward beneath the body, and a front pair of limbs with strong pincers; *also*

C cowl 1

¹crab 1

: any of various other crustaceans resembling the true crabs in having an abdomen much reduced in size **2** *cap* : CANCER 1 **3** : any of various machines for raising or hauling heavy weights **4** *pl* : the state of being infested with crab lice

2crab *vb* **crabbed; crab·bing** : to fish for crabs — **crab·ber** *n*

3crab *vb* **crabbed; crab·bing** : to find fault : COMPLAIN

4crab *n* **1** : CRAB APPLE **2** : a sour ill-tempered person

crab apple *n* : any of several cultivated or wild trees related to the apple tree and producing a small sour fruit; *also* : the fruit

crab·bed \'krab-əd\ *adj* **1** : 3CROSS 3 **2** : difficult to read or understand ⟨*crabbed* handwriting⟩ — **crab·bed·ness** *n*

crab·by \'krab-ē\ *adj* **crab·bi·er; -est** : 3CROSS 3, ILL-NATURED

crab·grass \'krab-,gras\ *n* : a weedy grass with creeping or sprawling stems that root freely at the nodes

crab louse *n* : a louse infesting the human pubic region

1crack \'krak\ *vb* **1 a** : to break or cause to break with a sudden sharp sound : SNAP **b** : to make or cause to make such a sound ⟨*crack* a whip⟩ **2** : to break with or without complete separation of parts ⟨the ice *cracked* in several places⟩ **3** : to tell especially in a clever or witty way ⟨*crack* jokes⟩ **4 a** : to lose control under pressure — often used with *up* **b** : to fail in tone ⟨her voice *cracked*⟩ **c** : to give or receive a sharp blow ⟨*cracked* my head⟩ **5 a** : to puzzle out : SOLVE ⟨*crack* a code⟩ **b** : to break into or through ⟨*crack* a safe⟩ ⟨*crack* the sound barrier⟩ **6 a** : to put hydrocarbons through cracking ⟨*crack* petroleum⟩ **b** : to produce by cracking ⟨*cracked* gasoline⟩

2crack *n* **1** : a sudden sharp noise **2** : a sharp witty remark : QUIP **3** : a narrow break or opening ⟨a *crack* in the glass⟩ ⟨open the window a *crack*⟩ **4 a** : WEAKNESS 2, FLAW **b** : a broken tone of the voice **5** : the beginning moment ⟨the *crack* of dawn⟩ **6** : a sharp resounding blow **7** : 2TRY ⟨take a *crack* at it⟩ **8** : highly purified cocaine in small chips used illegally usually for smoking

3crack *adj* : of high quality or ability ⟨*crack* troops⟩

crack·brain \'krak-,brān\ *n* : CRACKPOT — **crack·brained** \-'brānd\ *adj*

crack down \'krak-'daun\ *vb* : to take strong action especially to control or put down ⟨*crack down* on crime⟩ — **crack·down** \-,daun\ *n*

cracked \'krakt\ *adj* **1** : broken into coarse pieces ⟨*cracked* corn⟩ **2** : mentally disturbed : CRAZY

crack·er \'krak-ər\ *n* **1** : something (as a firecracker) that makes a cracking noise **2** : a dry thin crisp baked food made of flour and water **3** : the equipment in which cracking (as of petroleum) is carried out

crack·er·jack \'krak-ər-,jak\ *n* : a person or thing of special excellence ⟨she's a *crackerjack* at solving crossword puzzles⟩ — **crackerjack** *adj*

crack·ing \'krak-iŋ\ *n* : a process in which heavy hydrocarbons (as oils from petroleum) are broken up by heat into lighter products (as gasoline)

crack·le \'krak-əl\ *vb* **crack·led; crack·ling** \-(ə-)liŋ\ : to make small sharp sudden repeated noises — **crackle** *n*

crack·ling *n* **1** \'krak-(ə-)liŋ\ : a series of small sharp crackling sounds **2** \'krak-lən, 'krak-liŋ\ : the crisp remainder left after the fat has been separated from the meat or skin (as of pork) — usually used in plural

crack·pot \'krak-,pät\ *n* : a crazy or very strange person — **crackpot** *adj*

crack–up \'krak-,əp\ *n* : COLLISION, WRECK

crack up \'krak-'əp\ *vb* **1** : PRAISE 1, TOUT ⟨it's not all it's *cracked up* to be⟩ **2** : to cause or have a crack-up ⟨*crack up* a car⟩

1cra·dle \'krād-³l\ *n* **1** : a bed for a baby usually on rockers **2 a** : a place of origin ⟨the *cradle* of civilization⟩ **b** : the earliest period of life **3** : a framework or support resembling a baby's cradle in appearance or use **4** : a tool with

rods like fingers attached to a scythe and used formerly for harvesting grain **5** : a rocking tool used in panning for gold **6** : a support for a telephone handset

2cradle *vb* **cra·dled; cra·dling** \'krād-liŋ, -³l-iŋ\ **1 a** : to place or keep in or as if in a cradle **b** : to protect and cherish lovingly **2** : to cut grain with a cradle **3** : to wash in a miner's cradle

1craft \'kraft\ *n* **1** : skill in planning, making, or doing **2 a** : an occupation requiring skill in using the hands : TRADE **b** *pl* : articles made by craftspeople ⟨a store selling *crafts*⟩ **3** : skill in deceiving to gain an end **4** : the members of a trade **5** *pl usually* **craft a** : a boat especially of small size **b** : AIRCRAFT **c** : SPACECRAFT

2craft *vb* : to make by or as if by hand ⟨*crafted* a sculpture⟩ ⟨a carefully *crafted* story⟩ — **craft·er** *n*

crafts·man \'kraf(t)-smən\ *n* **1** : one who practices a trade or handicraft : ARTISAN **2** : a highly skilled worker — **crafts·man·ship** \-,ship\ *n*

crafts·peo·ple \-,spē-pəl\ *n* : workers who practice a trade or craft

crafts·per·son \-,spər-s³n\ *n* : a craftsman or craftswoman

crafts·wom·an \-,swum-ən\ *n* **1** : a woman who is an artisan **2** : a woman who is skilled in a craft

crafty \'kraf-tē\ *adj* **craft·i·er; -est** : skillful at deceiving others **synonyms** see CUNNING — **craft·i·ly** \-tə-lē\ *adv* — **craft·i·ness** \-tē-nəs\ *n*

crag \'krag\ *n* : a steep rugged rock or cliff — **crag·gy** \'krag-ē\ *adj*

cram \'kram\ *vb* **crammed; cram·ming** **1** : to stuff or crowd in ⟨*cram* clothes into a bag⟩ **2** : to fill full ⟨barns *crammed* with hay⟩ **3** : to study hard just before a test **synonyms** see PACK — **cram·mer** *n*

1cramp \'kramp\ *n* **1** : a sudden painful involuntary tightening of muscle **2** : sharp pain in the abdomen — usually used in plural — **crampy** \'kram-pē\ *adj*

2cramp *vb* **1** : to affect with or as if with cramps **2 a** : to hold back from free movement : CONFINE ⟨felt *cramped* in the tiny room⟩ **b** : to hold back from free action or expression : HAMPER — used especially in the phrase *cramp one's style*

cram·pon \'kram-,pän\ *n* : a set of steel spikes that fit on the bottom of a climbing boot to give a better grip on slopes of hard ice or snow — usually used in plural

cran·ber·ry \'kran-,ber-ē, -b(ə-)rē\ *n* : the bright red sour berry of any of several trailing plants related to the blueberry; *also* : a plant producing these

1crane \'krān\ *n* **1** : any of a family of tall wading birds related to the rails **2** : any of several herons **3 a** : a machine with a swinging arm for lifting and carrying heavy weights **b** : a mechanical arm that swings freely from a center and is used to support or carry a weight

2crane *vb* **craned; cran·ing** **1** : to raise or lift by or as if by a crane **2** : to stretch out one's neck to see better

crane fly *n* : any of numerous long-legged slender two-winged flies that resemble large mosquitoes but do not bite

1crane 1

crania *plural of* CRANIUM

cra·ni·al \'krā-nē-əl\ *adj* **1** : of, relating to, or directed toward the skull or cranium

cranial nerve *n* : any of the paired nerves that arise from the lower surface of the brain and pass through openings in the skull

cra·ni·um \'krā-nē-əm\ *n, pl* **-ni·ums** *or* **-nia** \-nē-ə\ : SKULL 1; *esp* : the part that encloses the brain

¹crank \'kraŋk\ *n* **1** : a bent part of an axle or shaft or an armlike part at right angles to the end of a shaft that gives or receives circular motion **2 a** : a person with strange ideas **b** : a cross or irritable person

²crank *vb* : to move, run, or start by or as if by turning a crank ⟨*crank* up the window⟩ ⟨you had to *crank* the old car⟩ ⟨the engine isn't *cranking* right⟩

crank·case \'kraŋk-ˌkās\ *n* : the covering of a crankshaft

crank·shaft \-ˌshaft\ *n* : a shaft turning or driven by a crank or made up of a series of cranks

cranky \'kraŋ-kē\ *adj* **crank·i·er; -est 1** : easily angered or irritated **2** : hard to handle ⟨a *cranky* boat⟩ — **crank·i·ness** \-kē-nəs\ *n*

cran·ny \'kran-ē\ *n, pl* **crannies** : a small break or slit (as in a cliff)

crape \'krāp\ *n* **1** : CREPE 1 **2** : a band of crepe worn on a hat or sleeve as a sign of mourning

crape myrtle *n* : an Asian shrub widely grown in warm regions for its showy flowers

crap·pie \'kräp-ē\ *n* **1** : BLACK CRAPPIE **2** : WHITE CRAP-PIE

craps \'kraps\ *n pl* : a gambling game played with two dice

crap·shoot·er \'krap-ˌshüt-ər\ *n* : a person who plays craps — **crap·shoot·ing** \-ˌshüt-iŋ\ *n*

¹crash \'krash\ *vb* **1 a** : to break with violence and much noise : SMASH **b** : to damage (an airplane) in landing **2 a** : to make or cause to make a loud noise ⟨*crash* cymbals together⟩ ⟨waves *crashing* on the shore⟩ **b** : to move or force a way roughly or with loud crashing noises ⟨we went *crashing* through the underbrush⟩ **3** : to enter or attend without an invitation or without paying ⟨*crash* a party⟩ ⟨tried to *crash* the gates⟩ **4** : to go bad or go out of order suddenly ⟨the computer system *crashed*⟩ **5** *slang* : to go to bed or fall asleep; *also* : to stay for a short time ⟨*crashing* with friends for the week⟩ [Middle English *crasschen* "crash"] — **crash·er** *n*

²crash *n* **1** : a loud sound (as of things smashing) **2 a** : a breaking to pieces by or as if by hitting something : COLLISION, SMASHUP **b** : an instance of crashing ⟨was hurt in the *crash*⟩ ⟨a computer *crash*⟩ **3** : a sudden weakening or failure (as of a business or prices) ⟨a stock-market *crash*⟩

³crash *adj* : designed to do what it is supposed to do in a big hurry ⟨a *crash* program⟩ ⟨went on a *crash* diet⟩

⁴crash *n* : a coarse fabric used for draperies and clothing [probably from Russian *krashenina* "colored linen"]

crash–land \'krash-ˈland\ *vb* : to land (an airplane or spacecraft) in an emergency usually with damage to it — **crash landing** *n*

crass \'kras\ *adj* : showing no interest in the finer things : INSENSITIVE — **crass·ly** *adv* — **crass·ness** *n*

¹crate \'krāt\ *n* : a box or frame of wooden slats or boards for packing or protecting something in shipment

²crate *vb* **crat·ed; crat·ing** : to pack in a crate

cra·ter \'krāt-ər\ *n* **1** : a hollow shaped like a bowl around the opening of a volcano **2** : a hole made by an impact (as of a meteorite) or by the explosion of a bomb or shell

cra·vat \krə-ˈvat\ *n* : NECKTIE

crave \'krāv\ *vb* **craved; crav·ing 1** : to ask earnestly : BEG ⟨*crave* a person's pardon⟩ **2** : to have a strong desire for ⟨*crave* a glass of water⟩ ⟨*crave* affection⟩

¹cra·ven \'krā-vən\ *adj* : COWARDLY — **cra·ven·ly** *adv* — **cra·ven·ness** \-vən-(n)əs\ *n*

²craven *n* : COWARD

crav·ing \'krā-viŋ\ *n* : a great desire or longing

craw \'krȯ\ *n* **1** : the crop of a bird or insect **2** : the stomach especially of a lower animal

craw·dad \'krȯ-ˌdad\ *n, dialect* : CRAYFISH 1

craw·fish \'krȯ-ˌfish\ *n* **1** : CRAYFISH 1 **2** : SPINY LOBSTER

¹crawl \'krȯl\ *vb* **1** : to move slowly with the body close to the ground : move on hands and knees **2** : to move along slowly ⟨the bus *crawled* along⟩ **3** : to be covered with or have the feeling of being covered with creeping things ⟨the floor was *crawling* with ants⟩ — **crawl·er** *n*

²crawl *n* **1** : the act or motion of crawling **2** : a swimming method in which the swimmer lies facing down in the water and moves with overarm strokes and a thrashing kick

crawl·way \'krȯl-ˌwā\ *n* : a low passage (as in a cave) that one must crawl through

cray·fish \'krā-ˌfish\ *n* **1** : any of numerous freshwater crustaceans that are related to but usually much smaller than the lobster **2** : SPINY LOBSTER

¹cray·on \'krā-ˌän, -ən; 'kran\ *n* : a stick of white or colored chalk or of colored wax used for writing or drawing

²crayon *vb* : to draw or color with a crayon

crayfish 1

¹craze \'krāz\ *vb* **crazed; craz·ing 1** : to make or become insane or as if insane **2** : to develop a network of fine cracks ⟨*crazed* glass⟩

²craze *n* **1** : something that is very popular for a short time ⟨the latest *craze* in music⟩ **2** : a tiny crack in a surface or coating (as of glaze or enamel)

cra·zy \'krā-zē\ *adj* **cra·zi·er; -est 1** : having a diseased or abnormal mind : INSANE **2** : not sensible or logical ⟨that's a *crazy* idea⟩ **3** : very excited or pleased ⟨*crazy* about the new car⟩ — **cra·zi·ly** \-zə-lē\ *adv* — **cra·zi·ness** \-zē-nəs\ *n*

crazy bone *n* : FUNNY BONE

crazy quilt *n* : a patchwork quilt without a regular design

creak \'krēk\ *vb* : to make a long scraping or squeaking sound; *also* : to go slowly with or as if with creaking wheels — **creak** *n*

creaky \'krē-kē\ *adj* **creak·i·er; -est** : making or likely to make a creaking sound — **creak·i·ly** \-kə-lē\ *adv*

¹cream \'krēm\ *n* **1** : the yellowish part of milk containing butterfat **2 a** : a food prepared with cream ⟨*cream* soup⟩ **b** : something having about the same thickness as cream ⟨hand *cream*⟩ **3** : the best part ⟨the *cream* of the crop⟩ **4** : a pale yellow

²cream *vb* **1** : to skim the cream from **2** : to put cream into ⟨*cream* tea⟩ **3** : to stir or blend until soft and smooth

cream cheese *n* : a soft white cheese made from whole milk enriched with cream

cream·er \'krē-mər\ *n* **1** : a device for separating cream from milk **2** : a small container for serving cream **3** : a substitute for cream (as in coffee)

cream·ery \'krēm-(ə-)rē\ *n, pl* **-er·ies** : a place where butter and cheese are made or where milk and cream are sold or prepared

cream of tartar : a white salt used especially in baking powder and in some ways to prepare metals

cream puff *n* : a round shell of light pastry filled with whipped cream or a cream filling

creamy \'krē-mē\ *adj* **cream·i·er; -est 1** : full of or containing cream **2** : resembling cream in appearance, color, or taste — **cream·i·ness** \-mē-nəs\ *n*

¹crease \'krēs\ *n* **1** : a line or mark made by or as if by folding or wrinkling **2** : a specially marked area around the goal in various sports (as hockey or lacrosse)

\ə\ abut	\au̇\ **out**	\i\ **tip**	\ȯ\ **saw**	\u̇\ **foot**
\ər\ **further**	\ch\ **chin**	\ī\ **life**	\ȯi\ **coin**	\y\ **yet**
\a\ **mat**	\e\ **pet**	\j\ **job**	\th\ **thin**	\yü\ **few**
\ā\ **take**	\ē\ **easy**	\ŋ\ **sing**	\th\ **this**	\yu̇\ **cure**
\ä\ **cot, cart**	\g\ **go**	\ō\ **bone**	\ü\ **food**	\zh\ **vision**

²**crease** vb **creased; creas·ing 1** : to make a crease in or on **2** : to become creased

cre·ate \krē-ˈāt, ˈkrē-ˌāt\ vb **cre·at·ed; cre·at·ing** : to bring into existence : MAKE, PRODUCE

cre·ation \krē-ˈā-shən\ n **1** : the act of creating; esp : the bringing of the world into existence out of nothing **2** : something created **3** : all created things : WORLD

cre·ative \krē-ˈāt-iv\ adj **1** : able to create especially new and original things **2** : showing or requiring imagination ⟨creative writing⟩ — **cre·ative·ly** adv — **cre·ative·ness** n — **cre·ativ·i·ty** \ˌkrē-ā-ˈtiv-ət-ē, ˌkrē-ə-\ n

cre·ator \krē-ˈāt-ər\ n **1** : one that creates or produces : MAKER **2** cap : GOD 1

crea·ture \ˈkrē-chər\ n **1** : a created being **2 a** : a lower animal **b** : INDIVIDUAL 2

crèche \ˈkresh\ n : a scene representing the Nativity in the stable at Bethlehem

cre·dence \ˈkrēd-ᵊn(t)s\ n **1** : a ready acceptance of something as true or real ⟨give credence to gossip⟩ **2** : CREDIBILITY 1 ⟨lends credence to the theory⟩ **synonyms** see BELIEF

cre·den·tials \kri-ˈden-chəlz\ n pl : documents showing that a person has a right to perform certain official acts [derived from Latin credentialis (adjective) "showing one is entitled to credit or confidence," from credentia "promise, credit," derived from earlier credere "to believe, trust, entrust" — related to CREDIT, CREED, INCREDIBLE]

cred·i·bil·i·ty \ˌkred-ə-ˈbil-ət-ē\ n **1** : the quality or power of inspiring belief ⟨a story without much credibility⟩ **2** : capacity for belief ⟨an excuse that strained the teacher's credibility⟩

cred·i·ble \ˈkred-ə-bəl\ adj : offering reasonable grounds for being believed ⟨a credible story⟩ — **cred·i·bly** \ˈkred-ə-blē\ adv

¹**cred·it** \ˈkred-ət\ n **1** : a balance in an account in a person's favor ⟨debits and credits⟩ **2** : an amount or sum that a bank or company will let a person use **3 a** : trust given to a customer for future payment for goods purchased ⟨extended them credit⟩ ⟨buy on credit⟩ **b** : reputation for paying one's bills ⟨check on a person's credit⟩ **c** : the providing of money or goods with the expectation of payment in the future ⟨long-term credit⟩; also : money or goods so provided ⟨used up their credit⟩ **4** : CREDENCE, BELIEF ⟨a story that deserves little credit⟩ **5** : reputation for honesty or integrity : good name **6** : a source of honor ⟨a credit to her school⟩ **7** : something that adds to a person's reputation or honor ⟨got credit for the discovery⟩ **8 a** : official certification of the completion of a course of study **b** : a unit of academic work for which such certification is made [from early French credit "reputation, permission to buy without paying immediately," from early Italian credito (same meaning), from Latin creditum "loan," derived from credere "to believe, trust, entrust" — related to CREDENTIALS, CREED, INCREDIBLE]

²**credit** vb **1** : BELIEVE 3 **2** : to enter a sum on the credit side of ⟨we'll credit your account with $10⟩ **3 a** : to think of as the source or performer of an action or having a quality ⟨they credit you with quite a sense of humor⟩ **b** : to give the credit for to somebody or something ⟨credited the rescue to her quick thinking⟩

cred·it·able \ˈkred-ət-ə-bəl\ adj : good enough to deserve praise — **cred·it·abil·i·ty** \ˌkred-ət-ə-ˈbil-ət-ē\ n — **cred·it·ably** \ˈkred-ət-ə-blē\ adv

credit card n : a card with which one can buy things on credit

cred·i·tor \ˈkred-ət-ər\ n : a person to whom a debt is owed

credit union n : a cooperative association that makes small loans to its members at low interest rates and offers other banking services (as savings and checking accounts)

cre·do \ˈkrēd-ō, ˈkrād-\ n, pl **credos** : CREED

cre·du·li·ty \kri-ˈd(y)ü-lət-ē\ n : a willingness to believe statements especially on little or no evidence

cred·u·lous \ˈkrej-ə-ləs\ adj : ready to believe especially on little evidence — **cred·u·lous·ly** adv — **cred·u·lous·ness** n

Cree \ˈkrē\ n, pl **Cree** or **Crees** : a member of an American Indian people of Quebec, Ontario, Manitoba, and Saskatchewan

creed \ˈkrēd\ n **1** : a statement of the basic beliefs of a religious faith **2** : a set of guiding principles or beliefs [Middle English crede "creed," from Old English crēda (same meaning), from Latin credo, literally, "I believe" (used as the first words in many creeds), from credere "to believe, trust, entrust" — related to CREDENTIALS, CREDIT, INCREDIBLE]

creek \ˈkrēk, ˈkrik\ n **1** chiefly British : a small narrow inlet or bay **2** : a stream of water usually smaller than a river

Creek \ˈkrēk\ n : a member of a confederacy of American Indian peoples formerly occupying most of Alabama and Georgia

creel \ˈkrē(ə)l\ n : a basket for holding a catch of fish

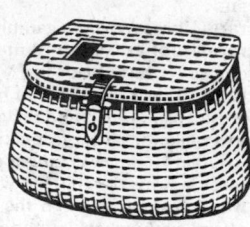

creel

¹**creep** \ˈkrēp\ vb **crept** \ˈkrept\; **creep·ing 1** : to move along with the body close to the ground : move slowly on hands and knees **2** : to advance slowly, timidly, or quietly ⟨the tide crept up the beach⟩ **3** : to spread or grow over the ground or a surface ⟨a creeping vine⟩ **4** : to slip or gradually shift position **5** : to feel as though insects were crawling on the body ⟨the shriek made my flesh creep⟩

²**creep** n **1** : a creeping movement **2 a** : a sensation like that of insects creeping over one's flesh **b** : a feeling of horror — usually used in plural with the ⟨the story gave me the creeps⟩ **3** : an unpleasant or hateful person

creep·er \ˈkrē-pər\ n : one that creeps: as **a** : a creeping plant **b** : a bird that creeps about on trees or bushes searching for insects

creepy \ˈkrē-pē\ adj **creep·i·er; -est** : having or producing a sensation as of insects creeping on the skin; esp : EERIE — **creep·i·ly** \-pə-lē\ adv — **creep·i·ness** n

cre·mate \ˈkrē-ˌmāt, kri-ˈmāt\ vb **cre·mat·ed; cre·mat·ing** : to burn (as a dead body) to ashes — **cre·ma·tion** \kri-ˈmā-shən\ n

cre·ma·to·ri·um \ˌkrē-mə-ˈtōr-ē-əm, ˌkrem-ə-, -ˈtor-\ n, pl **-ri·ums** or **-ria** \-ē-ə\ : ¹CREMATORY

¹**cre·ma·to·ry** \ˈkrē-mə-ˌtōr-ē, ˈkrem-ə-, -ˌtor-\ n, pl **-ries** : a furnace for cremating or a building containing such a furnace

²**crematory** adj : of, relating to, or used in cremation

cren·el·lat·ed or **cren·el·at·ed** \ˈkren-ᵊl-ˌāt-əd\ adj : having battlements ⟨a crenellated tower⟩

cre·ole \ˈkrē-ˌōl\ adj **1** often cap : of or relating to the Creoles or their language **2** often cap : relating to or being the traditional spicy food of the Creoles

Cre·ole \ˈkrē-ˌōl\ n **1** : a white person descended from early French or Spanish settlers in the U.S. Gulf states **2** : a person of mixed French or Spanish and black descent speaking a dialect of French or Spanish **3 a** : a language evolved from a pidgin based on French that is spoken by blacks in southern Louisiana **b** not cap : a language that has evolved from a pidgin and serves as the native language of a group of people

¹**cre·o·sote** \ˈkrē-ə-ˌsōt\ n **1** : a brownish oily liquid obtained from coal tar and used especially to preserve wood

2 : a dark flammable tar left in a chimney especially from the smoke of a wood fire **3** : CREOSOTE BUSH

²creosote vb **-sot·ed; -sot·ing** : to treat with creosote

creosote bush n : a desert shrub of the southwestern U.S. and Mexico with small yellow flowers

crepe or **crêpe** \'krāp\ n **1** : a thin crinkled fabric (as of silk or wool) **2** : a small very thin pancake

crepe de chine \ˌkrāp-də-'shēn\ n : a soft thin crepe made especially of silk and used for clothing

crepe myrtle or **crêpe myrtle** n : CRAPE MYRTLE

crepe paper n : paper with a crinkled or puckered look and feel

crepe su·zette \ˌkrāp-sù-'zet\ n, pl **crepes suzette** \ˌkrāp(s)-sù-'zet\ or **crepe suzettes** \ˌkrāp-sù-'zets\ : a crepe rolled or folded in a hot orange-butter sauce that is sprinkled with a liqueur and set ablaze for serving

crept past and past participle of CREEP

cre·pus·cu·lar \kri-'pəs-kyə-lər\ adj **1** : resembling twilight : DIM ⟨a faint *crepuscular* light⟩ **2** : occurring or active during twilight ⟨*crepuscular* insects⟩

cre·scen·do \kri-'shen-dō\ n, pl **-dos** or **-does 1** : a gradual increase especially in the loudness of music **2** : the peak of a gradual increase — **crescendo** adv or adj

cres·cent \'kres-ᵊnt\ n **1** : the shape of the visible moon during about the first week after a new moon or the last week before the next new moon **2** : a curved figure that tapers to two points like a crescent moon **3** : something shaped like a crescent

cress \'kres\ n : any of various plants related to the mustards and having leaves that are used especially in salads

¹crest \'krest\ n **1 a** : a showy growth (as of flesh or feathers) on the head of an animal **b** : an emblem or design on a helmet (as of a knight) or over a coat of arms **2** : an upper part, edge, or limit ⟨the *crest* of a hill⟩ ⟨the *crest* of a wave⟩ — **crest·ed** \'kres-təd\ adj

²crest vb **1** : to give a crest to **2** : to reach the crest of ⟨*crest* the hill⟩ **3** : to rise to a crest ⟨waves *cresting* in the storm⟩

crest·fall·en \'krest-ˌfȯ-lən\ adj : very sad and disappointed

Cre·ta·ceous \kri-'tā-shəs\ adj : of, relating to, or being the last period of the Mesozoic era of geological history marked by the extinction of the dinosaurs at the close of the period; *also* : relating to the corresponding system of rocks — see GEOLOGIC TIME table — **Cretaceous** n

cre·tin \'krēt-ᵊn\ n **1** : one having cretinism **2** : DOLT

cre·tin·ism \'krēt-ᵊn-ˌiz-əm\ n : an abnormal condition that is usually present from birth, is marked by physical stunting and mental retardation, and is caused by a lack of the secretion of the thyroid gland

cre·tonne \'krē-ˌtän, kri-'tän\ n : a cotton or linen cloth

cre·vasse \kri-'vas\ n : a deep crevice (as in a glacier)

crev·ice \'krev-əs\ n : a narrow opening caused by a split or crack : FISSURE

crew \'krü\ n **1** : a group or gathering of people ⟨a happy *crew*⟩ **2** : a group of people working together ⟨the kitchen *crew*⟩ **3** : a group of people who operate a ship, train, or airplane **4** : the rowers and coxswain of a racing shell

crew cut n : a very short haircut in which the hair resembles the surface of a brush

crew·el \'krü-əl\ n : a loosely twisted wool yarn used for embroidery; *also* : embroidery made with this yarn

crew·man \'krü-mən\ n : a member of a crew

¹crib \'krib\ n **1** : a manger for feeding animals **2** : a small bed frame with high sides for a child **3** : a bin or building for storing grain **4** : the cards discarded in cribbage for the dealer to use in scoring **5 a** : PONY 2 **b** : something used for cheating on a test

crescent 2

²crib vb **cribbed; crib·bing 1** : to copy (as an idea or piece of writing) and use as one's own : PLAGIARIZE **2** : to use a translation or notes dishonestly — **crib·ber** n

crib·bage \'krib-ij\ n : a card game in which each player tries to form various counting combinations of cards

crick \'krik\ n : a painful spasm of muscles (as of the neck or back)

¹crick·et \'krik-ət\ n : any of a family of leaping insects related to the grasshoppers and having leathery forewings used by the males to produce a chirping sound [Middle English *criket* "cricket (insect)," from early French *criquet* (same meaning); probably an imitation of the insect's sound]

¹cricket

²cricket n **1** : a game played on a large field with bats, ball, and wickets by two teams of 11 players each **2** : fair play [from early French *criquet* "goal stake in an old bowling game"] — **crick·et·er** n

cri·er \'krī-(ə)r\ n : one who calls out orders or announcements

crime \'krīm\ n **1** : the doing of an act forbidden by law or the failure to do an act required by law especially when serious **2** : criminal activity ⟨the war on *crime*⟩ **3** : an act that is sinful, foolish, or disgraceful ⟨it's a *crime* to waste good food⟩ *synonyms* see OFFENSE

¹crim·i·nal \'krim-ən-ᵊl, 'krim-nəl\ adj **1** : being or guilty of a crime ⟨a *criminal* act⟩ **2** : relating to crime or its punishment ⟨*criminal* court⟩ — **crim·i·nal·i·ty** \ˌkrim-ə-'nal-ət-ē\ n — **crim·i·nal·ly** \'krim-ən-ᵊl-ē, -nə-lē\ adv

²criminal n : a person who has committed a crime

crim·i·nol·o·gy \ˌkrim-ə-'näl-ə-jē\ n : a scientific study of crime, of criminals, and of their punishment or correction — **crim·i·no·log·i·cal** \ˌkrim-ən-ᵊl-'äj-i-kəl\ adj — **crim·i·nol·o·gist** \ˌkrim-ə-'näl-ə-jəst\ n

¹crimp \'krimp\ vb **1** : to make wavy or bent **2** : to pinch or press together ⟨*crimp* the edges of a pie crust⟩

²crimp n **1** : something produced by or as if by crimping **2** : something that holds back

¹crim·son \'krim-zən\ n : a deep purplish red — **crimson** adj

²crimson vb : to make or become crimson

cringe \'krinj\ vb **cringed; cring·ing** \'krin-jiŋ\ **1** : to shrink in fear or distaste : COWER ⟨*cringed* at the sight of blood⟩ **2** : to behave in a too humble or cowardly way — **cring·er** n

¹crin·kle \'kriŋ-kəl\ vb **crin·kled; crin·kling** \-k(ə-)liŋ\ **1** : to form or cause little waves or wrinkles on the surface **2** : ¹RUSTLE 1

²crinkle n : ¹WRINKLE 1, RIPPLE — **crin·kly** \-k(ə-)lē\ adj

cri·noid \'krī-ˌnȯid\ n : any of a large class of invertebrates that are echinoderms and usually have a cup-shaped body with five or more feathery arms — **crinoid** adj

crin·o·line \'krin-ᵊl-ən\ n **1** : a cloth used for stiffening and lining **2** : a full stiff skirt; *esp* : one lined with crinoline **3** : HOOPSKIRT — **crinoline** adj

¹crip·ple \'krip-əl\ n, *sometimes offensive* : a lame or disabled person

²cripple vb **crip·pled; crip·pling** \'krip-(ə-)liŋ\ **1** : to take away the use of a limb and especially a leg ⟨was *crippled* by the accident⟩ **2** : to make useless or imperfect ⟨loss of power *crippled* the city⟩ — **crip·pler** \-(ə-)lər\ n

cri·sis \'krī-səs\ n, pl **cri·ses** \'krī-ˌsēz\ **1** : the turning point for better or worse in a disease **2** : a turning point (as in a person's life or in the plot of a story) **3 a** : an unstable or difficult time or state of affairs ⟨a financial *crisis*⟩ **b** : a situation that has become very serious ⟨the energy *crisis*⟩

¹crisp \'krisp\ *adj* **1 a** : being thin and hard and easily crumbled ⟨*crisp* crackers⟩ **b** : pleasantly firm and crunchy ⟨*crisp* lettuce⟩ **2 a** : having sharp distinct outlines ⟨a *crisp* illustration⟩ **b** : being clear and brief ⟨a *crisp* reply⟩ **c** : fresh and neat ⟨a *crisp* housedress⟩ **d** : being quick and lively ⟨a *crisp* performance⟩ ⟨a *crisp* tale of adventure⟩ **3** : pleasantly cool and invigorating ⟨a *crisp* autumn day⟩ — **crisp·ly** *adv* — **crisp·ness** *n*

²crisp *vb* : to make or become crisp — **crisp·er** *n*

³crisp *n* : something crisp or brittle ⟨burned to a *crisp*⟩

crispy \'kris-pē\ *adj* **crisp·i·er; -est** : CRUNCHY — **crisp·i·ness** *n*

¹criss·cross \'kris-ˌkrós\ *vb* **1** : to mark with lines that cross each other **2** : to go or cross back and forth ⟨*criss-crossing* the state⟩

²crisscross *n* : a pattern formed by crossed lines — **criss·cross** *adj or adv*

cri·te·ri·on \krī-'tir-ē-ən\ *n, pl* **-ria** \-ē-ə\ : a standard on which a judgment or decision may be based

crit·ic \'krit-ik\ *n* **1** : a person who makes or gives a judgment of the value, worth, beauty, or excellence of something **2** : FAULTFINDER

crit·i·cal \'krit-i-kəl\ *adj* **1 a** : inclined to criticize in an unfavorable way ⟨you're always so *critical*⟩ **b** : consisting of or involving criticism or the judgments of critics ⟨*critical* writings⟩ **c** : using or involving careful judgment ⟨a *critical* examination of a patient⟩ **2 a** : of, relating to, or being a turning point ⟨the *critical* phase of a fever⟩; *also* : being at a critical stage of illness ⟨listed the patient as *critical*⟩ **b** : being or relating to a state or point at which a definite change occurs ⟨the *critical* temperature⟩ **c** : CRUCIAL 1 ⟨a *critical* test⟩ **3** : INDISPENSABLE, VITAL ⟨provides *critical* services⟩ **4** : of big enough size to keep a chain reaction going — used of a mass of material that can go through fission — **crit·i·cal·ly** \-i-k(ə-)lē\ *adv* — **crit·i·cal·ness** \-kəl-nəs\ *n*

crit·i·cism \'krit-ə-ˌsiz-əm\ *n* **1** : the act of criticizing and especially of finding fault **2** : a critical remark or comment **3** : a careful judgment or review especially by a critic

crit·i·cize \'krit-ə-ˌsīz\ *vb* **-cized; -ciz·ing** **1** : to examine and judge as a critic **2** : to find fault with

crit·ter \'krit-ər\ *n* : CREATURE

croak \'krōk\ *vb* **1 a** : to make a deep harsh sound **b** : to speak in a hoarse throaty voice **2** : GRUMBLE 1, COMPLAIN **3** *slang a* : ¹DIE 1 **b** : ¹KILL 1 — **croak** *n*

croak·er \'krō-kər\ *n* **1** : one (as a frog) that croaks **2** : any of various fishes that produce croaking or grunting noises

Croat \'krō-ˌat, 'krō-(ə)t\ *n* : CROATIAN — **Croat** *adj*

Cro·a·tian \krō-'ā-shən\ *n* **1** : a person born or living in Croatia **2** : a Slavic language spoken by the Croatian people — **Croatian** *adj*

croc \'kräk\ *n* : CROCODILE

¹cro·chet \krō-'shā\ *n* : needlework done by forming and weaving loops in a thread with a hooked needle

²crochet *vb* **crocheted; crochet·ing** : to make of or work with crochet — **cro·chet·er** \-'shā-ər\ *n*

¹crock \'kräk\ *n* : a pot or jar made of baked clay

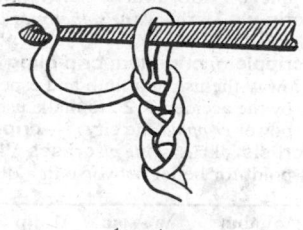
¹crochet

²crock *n* : one that is broken-down or useless ⟨an old *crock* who needs an afternoon nap⟩

crock·ery \'kräk-(ə-)rē\ *n* : EARTHENWARE

Crock–Pot \'kräk-ˌpät\ *trademark* — used for an electric cooking pot

croc·o·dile \'kräk-ə-ˌdīl\ *n* **1** : any of several large thick-skinned long-bodied reptiles of tropical and subtropical waters — compare ALLIGATOR **2** : the skin or hide of a crocodile

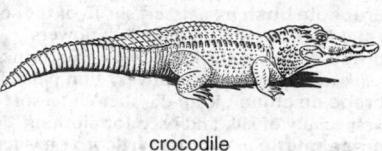
crocodile

Word History The word *crocodile* is taken from Greek *krokodeilos,* which is probably modified from a compound of *krokē,* "pebble, stone," and an obscure word *drilos,* which may have meant "worm." According to the ancient Greek writer Herodotus, some Greeks gave this name to the lizards that lived among the stone walls of their houses. When these Greeks visited Egypt, the enormous reptiles of the Nile River reminded them of the lizards and they applied the same name to them. (The more usual ancient Greek word for "lizard" was *sauros,* which we see in the Latin scientific names of many dinosaurs, such as *Tyrannosaurus,* and in the word *dinosaur* itself.) The Romans took Greek *krokodeilos* into Latin as *crocodilus.* However, later speakers shifted the *r* from the first to the third syllable, giving *cocodrilus* or *cocodrillus.* It was this form that was taken into medieval French and later into Middle English as *cocodrille.* Later, as Englishmen became better acquainted with the classical Latin of ancient Rome, the English word was changed to better reflect Latin *crocodilus,* and *cocodrille* was eventually forgotten. [from Middle English *cocodrille* "crocodile," from early French *cocodrille* (same meaning), from Latin *cocodrillus* and earlier *crocodilus* "crocodile," from Greek *krokodeilos* "crocodile, lizard"]

crocodile tears *n pl* : pretended tears or sorrow

Word History An ancient fable tells of a crocodile that sheds tears while eating its prey. Of course, a crocodile is not really sorry for killing and eating another animal because that's how it survives. So when someone is said to shed *crocodile tears,* it refers to a show of pretended sorrow usually by someone who has done something cruel.

croc·o·dil·ian \ˌkräk-ə-'dil-ē-ən, -'dil-yən\ *n* : any of an order of reptiles that includes the crocodiles, alligators, caimans, and related extinct forms — **crocodilian** *adj*

cro·cus \'krō-kəs\ *n, pl* **cro·cus·es** **1** *pl also* **crocus** or **cro·ci** \-ˌkē, -ˌkī, -ˌsī\ : any of a genus of small herbs that are related to the irises and have showy solitary long-tubed flowers and slender grasslike leaves **2** : SAFFRON 1

croft \'króft\ *n* **1** *chiefly British* : a small enclosed field **2** *chiefly British* : a small farm worked by a tenant — **croft·er** *n, chiefly British*

crois·sant \krò-'sänt, krə-\ *n, pl* **croissants** : a flaky rich crescent-shaped roll

Cro–Mag·non \krō-'mag-nən, -'man-yən\ *n* : any of a tall erect race of people that lived approximately 35,000 to 10,000 years ago and are often placed in the same species as the human beings that live on the earth today [from *Cro-Magnon,* name of a cave in France where remains of the people were found] — **Cro–Magnon** *adj*

crone \'krōn\ *n* : WITCH 1

cro·ny \'krō-nē\ *n, pl* **cronies** : a close companion : PAL ⟨politicians who get jobs for their *cronies*⟩

¹crook \'krůk\ *vb* : ¹BEND 2, CURVE

²crook *n* **1** : a shepherd's staff with one end curved into a hook **2** : a dishonest person (as a thief or swindler) **3** : a curved or hooked part of a thing : BEND

crook·ed \'krůk-əd\ *adj* **1** : having bends and curves ⟨a *crooked* path⟩ **2** : not set or placed straight ⟨the picture

is *crooked*⟩ **3** : DISHONEST ⟨a *crooked* card game⟩ —
crook·ed·ly *adv* — **crook·ed·ness** *n*
crook·neck \'krük-,nek\ *n* : a squash with a long curved
neck
croon \'krün\ *vb* : to hum or sing in a low soft voice
⟨*croon* a lullaby⟩ — **croon** *n* — **croon·er** *n*
¹**crop** \'kräp\ *n* **1 a** : the handle of a whip **b** : a short riding
whip **2** : an enlargement of the gullet of a bird or insect
that forms a pouch to receive food and prepare it for digestion **3 a** : a plant or animal or plant or animal product
that can be grown and harvested **b** : the product or yield
especially of a harvested crop **c** : BATCH 2, LOT ⟨a new
crop of kindergartners⟩
²**crop** *vb* **cropped; crop·ping 1 a** : to remove the upper or
outer parts of ⟨*crop* a hedge⟩ ⟨*crop* a dog's ears⟩ **b** : to
cut off short : CLIP ⟨*crop* a photograph⟩ **2 a** : to cause
land to bear a crop **b** : to grow as a crop ⟨*crop* cotton⟩ **3**
: to produce or make a crop ⟨the apple trees *cropped*
well⟩ **4** : to come or appear when not expected ⟨prob-
lems *crop* up daily⟩
crop duster *n* : a person who sprays crops from an airplane especially with preparations to control insects or
fungi; *also* : the airplane used for such spraying
crop·land \'kräp-,land\ *n* : land on which crops are grown
¹**crop·per** \'kräp-ər\ *n* : one that crops; *esp* : SHARECROP-
PER
²**cropper** *n* **1** : a severe fall **2** : a sudden or violent failure
or collapse
crop rotation *n* : the practice of growing first one and
then another crop on the same land especially to preserve
the ability of the soil to produce crops
cro·quet \krō-'kā\ *n* : a game in which the players use
mallets to drive wooden balls through a series of wickets
set out on a lawn
cro·quette \krō-'ket\ *n* : a roll or ball of hashed meat, fish,
or vegetables fried in deep fat
cro·sier *or* **cro·zier** \'krō-zhər\ *n* : a staff like a
shepherd's crook carried by bishops and ab-
bots as a symbol of office
¹**cross** \'krós\ *n* **1 a** : a structure consisting of
one bar crossing another at right angles **b** *often cap* : the cross on which Jesus was crucified used as a symbol of Christianity and the
Christian religion **2** : sorrow or suffering as a
test of patience or virtue ⟨had their *crosses* to
bear⟩ **3** : an object or mark shaped like a cross
⟨a stone *cross*⟩ ⟨put a *cross* next to the name⟩
4 a : an act of crossing unlike individuals **b** : a
crossbred individual or kind **5** : a punch that
crosses over an opponent's punch in boxing
[Old English *cros,* probably from an early
Norse or an early Irish word derived from
Latin *crux* "cross" — related to CRUCIAL,
CRUISE, CRUSADE, CRUX, EXCRUCIATING]
²**cross** *vb* **1 a** : to lie or be situated across ⟨put
a nail where the boards *cross* each other⟩ **b**
: INTERSECT 1 ⟨where two lines *cross*⟩ **c** : to
move, pass, or extend across ⟨a bridge *crossing* the river⟩
⟨*cross* the street⟩ **2** : to make the sign of the cross on or
over (as in prayer) **3** : to cancel by marking a cross on or
drawing a line through ⟨*cross* names off a list⟩ ⟨*cross* out
a mistake⟩ **4** : to place one over the other ⟨*cross* the
arms⟩ **5** : to act against : OPPOSE ⟨don't *cross* me⟩ **6** : to
draw a line across ⟨*cross* your *t*'s⟩ **7** : INTERBREED, HY-
BRIDIZE **8** : to pass in opposite directions ⟨our letters
crossed in the mail⟩ **9** : to occur to ⟨it never *crossed* my
mind⟩ **10** : to turn (the eyes) inward toward the nose ⟨his
eyes were *crossed*⟩
³**cross** *adj* **1** : lying or moving across ⟨*cross* traffic⟩ **2**
: ²CONTRARY 1 **3** : marked by bad temper : GRUMPY —
cross·ly *adv* — **cross·ness** *n*

crosier

cross·bar \'krós-,bär\ *n* : a bar, piece, or stripe placed
crosswise or across something
cross·bill \-,bil\ *n* : any of a genus of finches with the upper and lower parts of the bill curved so that they cross
each other when the bill is closed
cross·bones \-,bōnz\ *n pl* : two leg or arm bones placed
or pictured as lying across each other ⟨skull and *crossbones*⟩
cross·bow \-,bō\ *n* : a short bow
mounted crosswise near the end
of a wooden stock that shoots
short arrows
cross·bred \'krós-'bred\ *adj* : ²HY-
BRID; *esp* : produced by crossing
two pure but different breeds,
strains, or varieties
¹**cross·breed** \'krós-,brēd, -'brēd\
vb **-bred** \-,bred, -'bred\; **-breed-
ing** : HYBRIDIZE; *esp* : to cross
two varieties or breeds of the
same species
²**cross·breed** \-,brēd\ *n* : ¹HYBRID 1
¹**cross–coun·try** \'kró-'skən-trē\
adj **1** : extending or moving
across a country ⟨a *cross-country*
railroad⟩ ⟨a *cross-country* concert
tour⟩ **2** : going over the countryside rather than by roads **3** : deal-
ing with or being racing or skiing over the countryside
instead of over a track or run — **cross–country** *adv*
²**cross–country** *n* : cross-country skiing or racing
¹**cross·cut** \'kró-,skət, -'skət\ *vb* **-cut; -cut·ting** : to cut or
saw across the grain of wood
²**crosscut** *adj* **1** : made or used for cutting across the grain
of wood ⟨a *crosscut* saw⟩ **2** : cut across ⟨a *crosscut* inci-
sion⟩
³**cross·cut** \'kró-,skət\ *n* **1** : something that cuts across or
through **2** : a crosscut saw
cross–dress·ing \'krós-,dres-iŋ\ *n* : the wearing of
clothes made for the opposite sex — **cross–dress·er**
\-ər\ *n*
crosse \'krós\ *n* : a stick with a small net at one end that
is used in lacrosse
cross–ex·am·ine \,kró-sig-'zam-ən\ *vb* : to question (a
person) in an effort to show that statements or answers
given earlier were false or not credible — **cross–ex·am-
i·na·tion** \-,zam-ə-'nā-shən\ *n* — **cross–ex·am·in·er**
\-'zam-(ə-)nər\ *n*
cross–eyed \'kró-,sīd\ *adj* : having one or both eyes
turned inward toward the nose
cross–fer·til·i·za·tion \'krós-,fərt-ᵊl-ə-'zā-shən\ *n* **1** : fertilization between sex cells produced by separate individuals or sometimes by individuals of different kinds **2**
: CROSS-POLLINATION — **cross–fer·tile** \-'fərt-ᵊl\ *adj* —
cross–fer·til·ize \-'fərt-ᵊl-,īz\ *vb*
cross fire *n* **1** : gunfire from two or more places so that
the lines of fire cross **2** : a rapid or angry exchange (as of
words)
cross hair *n* : one of the very thin wires or threads in the
eyepiece of an optical instrument (as a microscope) used
as a reference line
cross·hatch \'krós-,hach\ *vb* : to mark with sets of parallel lines that cross — **crosshatch** *n*
cross·ing \'kró-siŋ\ *n* **1 a** : the act of one that crosses **b**
: a voyage across water **c** : the act or process of interbreeding or hybridizing **2** : a place where a street or

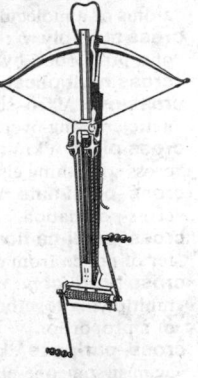

crossbow

\ə\ **abut**	\au̇\ **out**	\i\ **tip**	\ȯ\ **saw**	\u̇\ **foot**
\ər\ **further**	\ch\ **chin**	\ī\ **life**	\ȯi\ **coin**	\y\ **yet**
\a\ **mat**	\e\ **pet**	\j\ **job**	\th\ **thin**	\yu̇\ **few**
\ā\ **take**	\ē\ **easy**	\ŋ\ **sing**	\th\ **this**	\yü\ **cure**
\ä\ **cot, cart**	\g\ **go**	\ō\ **bone**	\ü\ **food**	\zh\ **vision**

stream is crossed **3** : a place where two things (as a street and a railroad track) cross

cross·ing–over \,krò-siŋ-'ō-vər\ *n* : an exchange of genes or chromosome segments between corresponding parts of similar but usually not identical chromosomes during meiosis

cross–legged \'krò-'sleg-(ə)d\ *adv* : with the legs crossed and the knees spread wide

cross–link \'krò-,sliŋk\ *n* : an atom or group of atoms that is a crosswise connection between two long series of atoms of a molecule — **cross–link** *vb*

cross multiply *vb* : to multiply the numerator of each side of a proportion by the denominator of the other side — **cross multiplication** *n*

cross·over \'krò-,sō-vər\ *n* : an instance or product of genetic crossing-over

cross·piece \'krò-,spēs\ *n* : something placed so as to cross something else

cross–pol·li·nate \,krò-'späl-ə-,nāt\ *vb* : to subject to cross-pollination

cross–pol·li·na·tion \,krò-,späl-ə-'nā-shən\ *n* : the transfer of pollen from one flower to the stigma of another

cross product *n* : either of the two products obtained by multiplying together the two means or the two extremes of a proportion

cross–pur·pose \'krò-'spər-pəs\ *n* : a purpose that works against someone else's purpose usually without meaning to ⟨the two were always at *cross-purposes*⟩

cross–ref·er·ence \'kròs-'ref-ərn(t)s, -'ref-(ə-)rən(t)s\ *n* : a reference made from one place to another (as in a dictionary)

cross·road \'kròs-,rōd, -'rōd\ *n* **1** : a road that crosses a main road or runs across country between main roads **2 a** : a place where roads cross — usually used in plural **b** : a small community at a crossroads **3** : a place or time at which a decision must be made

cross section *n* **1 a** : a cutting made across something (as a log or an apple) **b** : a representation of a cross section ⟨a *cross section* of a blood vessel⟩ **2** : a number of persons or things selected from a group to stand for the whole ⟨a *cross section* of society⟩ — **cross–sec·tion·al** \'kròs-'sek-sh(ə-)nəl\ *adj*

cross–stitch \'kròs-,(s)tich\ *n* : a needlework stitch that forms an X; *also* : needlework having cross-stitches

cross·town \'krò-'staún\ *adj* **1** : being on different sides of a town ⟨the two schools were *crosstown* rivals in football⟩ **2** : going across a town ⟨a *crosstown* bus⟩ ⟨*crosstown* streets⟩ — **crosstown** *adv*

cross–train \'kròs-,trān\ *vb* : to engage in various sports or exercises especially for well-rounded health and muscular development

cross–train·er \'kròs-,trā-nər\ *n* : a sports shoe designed for cross-training

cross–walk \'krò-,swòk\ *n* : a specially paved or marked path for people walking across a street or road

cross·ways \-,swāz\ *adv* : CROSSWISE

cross·wise \-,swīz\ *adv* : so as to cross something : ACROSS ⟨logs laid *crosswise*⟩ — **crosswise** *adj*

cross·word puzzle \,krò-,swərd-\ *n* : a puzzle in which words are filled into a pattern of numbered squares in answer to clues so that they read across and down

crotch \'kräch\ *n* : an angle formed by the spreading apart of two legs or branches or of a limb from its trunk

crotch·et \'kräch-ət\ *n* : an unusual personal opinion or habit

crotch·ety \'kräch-ət-ē\ *adj* **1** : having crochets **2** : being cranky or having an ill temper ⟨a *crotchety* old man⟩ — **crotch·et·i·ness** \-ē-nəs\ *n*

crouch \'kraúch\ *vb* : to stoop or bend low with the arms and legs close to the body — **crouch** *n*

¹**croup** \'krüp\ *n* : the rump of a four-footed animal [Middle English *croupe* "rump," from early French *croupe* (same meaning), of Germanic origin]

²**croup** *n* : a laryngitis especially of infants marked by periods of difficult breathing and a hoarse cough [from an English dialect word *croup* "to cry or cough"; probably originally an imitation of the sound] — **croupy** \'krü-pē\ *adj*

crou·pi·er \'krü-pē-ər, -pē-,ā\ *n* : an employee of a gambling casino who collects and pays bets

crou·ton \'krü-,tän, krü-'tän\ *n* : a small cube of bread toasted or fried crisp

¹**crow** \'krō\ *n* **1** : any of various large usually entirely glossy black birds related to the jays **2** *cap* : a member of an American Indian people of Montana — **as the crow flies** : in a straight line

¹crow 1

²**crow** *vb* **crowed** \'krōd\; **crow·ing 1** : to make the loud shrill sound that a rooster makes **2** : to make sounds of delight **3** : to brag loudly or joyfully *synonyms* see BOAST

³**crow** *n* **1** : the cry of the rooster **2** : a cry of triumph

crow·bar \'krō-,bär\ *n* : a metal bar used as a lever (as for prying things apart)

¹**crowd** \'kraúd\ *vb* **1** : to press forward or close ⟨*crowd* into an elevator⟩ ⟨*crowded* around the speaker⟩ **2** : to push or press into a small space ⟨*crowd* clothes into a closet⟩ **3** : to fill or pack by pressing together ⟨cars *crowded* the roads⟩ **4** : to push or force by or as if by a crowd ⟨we were *crowded* off the sidewalk⟩ ⟨don't let soft drinks *crowd* milk out of your diet⟩

²**crowd** *n* **1** : a large number of persons or things crowded or crowding together **2** : the population as a whole : ordinary people ⟨books that appeal to the *crowd*⟩ **3** : a large number of things close together **4** : a group of people having a common interest ⟨running around with the wrong *crowd*⟩ *synonyms* see MULTITUDE

crowd·ed·ness \'kraúd-əd-nəs\ *n* : the state of being crowded

¹**crown** \'kraún\ *n* **1 a** : a wreath or band for the head especially as a mark of victory or honor **b** : the title representing a sports championship ⟨the heavyweight *crown*⟩ **2** : a royal headdress **3 a** : the top of the head **b** : the highest part (as of a mountain or tree) **c** : the part of a hat covering the crown of the head **d** : the part of a tooth outside of the gum **4** : something resembling a crown **5** *often cap* **a** : royal power or authority **b** : the executive part of the British government **6** : any of various coins (as an old British coin worth five shillings) — **crowned** \'kraúnd\ *adj* — **crown·like** \'kraún-,līk\ *adj*

²**crown** *vb* **1 a** : to place a crown on; *esp* : to make sovereign **b** : to declare officially to be ⟨was *crowned* champion⟩ **2 a** : ²TOP 2 ⟨snow *crowned* the mountain's peak⟩ **b** : to top a checker with a checker to make a king **3** : to bring to a successful conclusion : finish off : COMPLETE **4** *of a forest fire* : to burn rapidly through the tops of trees

crown glass *n* : a very clear glass that is used for optical instruments

crown prince *n* : the prince next in line for a crown or throne

crown princess *n* **1** : the wife of a crown prince **2** : the princess next in line for a crown or throne

crow's–foot \'krōz-,fút\ *n, pl* **crow's–feet** \-,fēt\ : any of the wrinkles around the outer corners of the eyes — usually used in plural

crow's nest *n* : a partly enclosed platform high on a ship's mast for use as a lookout

crozier *variant of* CROSIER

cruces *plural of* CRUX

cru·cial \'krü-shəl\ *adj* **1** : being a final or very important test or decision : DECISIVE ⟨the *crucial* game of a series⟩

2 : very important : SIGNIFICANT ⟨water is a *crucial* element in our weather⟩ [from French *crucial* "having the form of a cross, being or involving a crisis," from Latin *cruc-, crux* "cross, trouble, torture" — related to CROSS, CRUCIFY, CRUX] — **cru·cial·ly** \'krüsh-(ə-)lē\ *adv*

cru·ci·ble \'krü-sə-bəl\ *n* **1** : a pot made of a substance not easily damaged by fire that is used for holding something to be treated under great heat **2** : a severe test

cru·ci·fix \'krü-sə-ˌfiks\ *n* : a cross with a figure of Jesus crucified on it [Middle English *crucifix* "crucifix," from Latin *crucifixus* (same meaning), derived from earlier Latin *crucifigere* "to crucify," from *cruc-, crux* "cross" and *figere* "to fasten, fix" — related to CROSS, CRUCIFY, FIX]

cru·ci·fix·ion \ˌkrü-sə-'fik-shən\ *n* **1** *cap* : the crucifying of Jesus **2** : an act of crucifying

cru·ci·form \'krü-sə-ˌfòrm\ *adj* : forming or arranged in a cross — **cruciform** *n*

cru·ci·fy \'krü-sə-ˌfī\ *vb* **-fied; -fy·ing** **1** : to put to death by nailing or binding the hands and feet to a cross **2** : to treat cruelly : TORTURE, PERSECUTE ⟨were *crucified* in the newspapers⟩ [Middle English *crucifien* "to crucify," from early French *crucifier* "to crucify," from Latin *crucifigere* "to crucify," from *cruc-, crux* "cross" and *figere* "to fasten, fix" — related to CROSS, CRUCIFIX, EXCRUCIATING, FIX] — **cru·ci·fi·er** \-ˌfī-ər\ *n*

¹crude \'krüd\ *adj* **crud·er; crud·est** **1** : being in a natural state and not changed by cooking or refining : RAW ⟨*crude* oil⟩ **2** : not having or showing good manners : VULGAR **3** : planned or done in a rough or unskilled way ⟨a *crude* drawing⟩ — **crude·ly** *adv* — **crude·ness** *n*

²crude *n* : crude oil

cru·di·ty \'krüd-ət-ē\ *n, pl* **-ties** **1** : the quality or state of being crude **2** : something that is crude

cru·el \'krü-əl\ *adj* **cru·el·er** *or* **cru·el·ler; cru·el·est** *or* **cru·el·lest** **1** : ready to hurt others : without humane feelings ⟨a *cruel* ruler⟩ **2 a** : causing or helping to cause suffering ⟨a *cruel* joke⟩ **b** : showing no mercy ⟨*cruel* punishment⟩ — **cru·el·ly** \'krü-ə-lē\ *adv* — **cru·el·ness** *n*

cru·el·ty \'krü-əl-tē\ *n, pl* **-ties** **1** : the quality or state of being cruel **2** : cruel treatment

cru·et \'krü-ət\ *n* : a small glass bottle for holding vinegar, oil, or sauce for use at the table

cruise \'krüz\ *vb* **cruised; cruis·ing** **1** : to travel by boat often stopping at a series of ports **2** : to travel for enjoyment **3** : to travel at the best operating speed ⟨the *cruising* speed of an airplane⟩ [from Dutch *kruisen* "to cruise, move crosswise," from early Dutch *crūce* "cross," from Latin *crux* "cross" — related to CROSS, CRUCIAL] — **cruise** *n*

cruis·er \'krü-zər\ *n* **1** : SQUAD CAR **2** : a large fast warship smaller than a battleship **3** : a motorboat equipped for living aboard

cruet

crul·ler \'krəl-ər\ *n* : a small twisted oblong cake made like a doughnut

¹crumb \'krəm\ *n* **1** : a small piece especially of something baked (as bread) **2** : a little bit ⟨a *crumb* of good news⟩

²crumb *vb* **1** : to break into crumbs : CRUMBLE **2** : to cover or thicken with crumbs

crum·ble \'krəm-bəl\ *vb* **crum·bled; crum·bling** \-b(ə-)liŋ\ **1** : to break into small pieces ⟨*crumble* bread⟩ **2** : to fall into ruin ⟨relationships *crumble*⟩

crum·bly \-b(ə-)lē\ *adj* **crum·bli·er; -est** : easily crumbled

crum·my \'krəm-ē\ *adj* **crum·mi·er; -est** : very poor : LOUSY ⟨*crummy* weather⟩

crum·pet \'krəm-pət\ *n* : a small round unsweetened bread cooked on a griddle

crum·ple \'krəm-pəl\ *vb* **crum·pled; crum·pling** \-p(ə-)liŋ\ **1** : to press, bend, or crush out of shape **2** : to become crumpled **3** : ¹COLLAPSE 1

¹crunch \'krənch\ *vb* **1** : to chew, press, or grind with a crushing noise **2** : to move with a crushing sound

²crunch *n* **1** : an act or sound of crunching **2** : CRISIS 3 ⟨the energy *crunch*⟩ **3** : an exercise done by lying on the back and rising up without reaching a sitting position by bending forward at the waist

crunchy \'krən-chē\ *adj* **crunch·i·er; -est** : making a crunching sound (as when bitten or chewed)

crup·per \'krəp-ər, 'krüp-\ *n* **1** : a leather strap passing under a horse's tail to keep a saddle or harness in place **2** : the rump of a horse : CROUP

¹cru·sade \krü-'sād\ *n* **1** *cap* : any of the military expeditions made by Christian countries in the 11th, 12th, and 13th centuries to recover the Holy Land from the Muslims **2** : a campaign to get things changed for the better ⟨a *crusade* against crime⟩ [derived from early French *croisade* and Spanish *cruzada*, both meaning literally "an expedition of persons marked with or bearing the sign of the cross" and both derived from Latin *cruc-, crux* "cross" — related to CROSS]

²crusade *vb* **cru·sad·ed; cru·sad·ing** : to take part in a crusade — **cru·sad·er** *n*

cruse \'krüz, 'krüs\ *n* : a jar or pot for holding a liquid

¹crush \'krəsh\ *vb* **1** : to squeeze together so as to break or destroy the natural shape or condition ⟨*crush* grapes⟩ **2** : HUG 1 **3** : to break into fine pieces by pressing, pounding, or grinding ⟨*crush* stone⟩ **4 a** : OVERWHELM 2 ⟨*crushed* the enemy⟩ **b** : OPPRESS 2 — **crush·er** *n*

²crush *n* **1** : an act of crushing **2** : a crowding together of many people **3** : a strong but often temporary liking : INFATUATION ⟨have a *crush* on someone⟩

crust \'krəst\ *n* **1 a** : the hardened outside surface of bread **b** : a piece of dry hard bread **2** : the pastry cover of a pie **3 a** : a hard surface layer ⟨a *crust* of snow⟩ **b** : the outer part of the earth — **crust·al** \'krəs-təl\ *adj*

crus·ta·cea \ˌkrəs-'tā-sh(ē-)ə\ *n pl* : arthropods that are crustaceans

crus·ta·cean \ˌkrəs-'tā-shən\ *n* : any of a large class of mostly water-dwelling arthropods (as lobsters, shrimps, crabs, wood lice, water fleas, and barnacles) having an exoskeleton of chitin or chitin and a compound of calcium — **crustacean** *adj*

crusty \'krəs-tē\ *adj* **crust·i·er; -est** **1** : having or being a crust **2** : ³CROSS 3 — **crust·i·ness** *n*

crutch \'krəch\ *n* **1** : a support usually made with a piece at the top to fit under the armpit for use by a disabled or injured person as an aid in walking **2** : something (as a support or prop) like a crutch in shape or use

crux \'krəks, 'krúks\ *n, pl* **crux·es** *also* **cru·ces** \'krü-ˌsēz\ : the most important point ⟨the *crux* of the problem⟩ [from Latin *crux* "cross, torture, trouble" — related to CROSS, CRUCIAL, CRUCIFY]

cru·zei·ro \krü-'ze(ə)r-ō, -ü\ *n, pl* **-ros** : the former basic unit of money of Brazil

¹cry \'krī\ *vb* **cried; cry·ing** **1** : to call loudly : SHOUT **2** : to shed tears often noisily : WEEP, BAWL **3** : to utter a special sound or call **4** : to make known to the public **5** : to suggest strongly a need ⟨the situation *cries* out for action⟩ — **cry havoc** : to sound an alarm — **cry over spilled milk** : to express regret over something that cannot be helped — **cry wolf** : to give alarm without a reason

²cry *n, pl* **cries** **1** : a loud call or shout (as of pain, fear, or joy) **2** : ¹APPEAL 2, PLEA ⟨hear my *cry*⟩ **3** : a fit of weep-

\ə\ **abut**	\au̇\ **out**	\i\ **tip**	\ȯ\ **saw**	\u̇\ **foot**
\ər\ **further**	\ch\ **chin**	\ī\ **life**	\ȯi\ **coin**	\y\ **yet**
\a\ **mat**	\e\ **pet**	\j\ **job**	\th\ **thin**	\yü\ **few**
\ā\ **take**	\ē\ **easy**	\ŋ\ **sing**	\t̲h̲\ **this**	\yu̇\ **cure**
\ä\ **cot, cart**	\g\ **go**	\ō\ **bone**	\ü\ **food**	\zh\ **vision**

ing ⟨had a good *cry*⟩ **4** : the special sound of an animal (as a bird) **5** : SLOGAN 2 **6 a** : a pack of hounds **b** : PURSUIT — used in the phrase *in full cry* ⟨hounds in full *cry*⟩ **c** : a peak of activity or excitement — used in the phrase *in full cry* ⟨a campaign in full *cry*⟩

cry·ba·by \'krī-ˌbā-bē\ *n* : a person who cries easily or complains often

cry down *vb* : DISPARAGE 2, BELITTLE

cry·ing \'krī-iŋ\ *adj* **1** : calling for attention and correction ⟨a *crying* need⟩ **2** : NOTORIOUS ⟨a *crying* shame⟩

cryo·gen·ics \ˌkrī-ə-'jen-iks\ *n* : a branch of physics that deals with the production and effects of very low temperatures

cryo·lite \'krī-ə-ˌlīt\ *n* : a mineral consisting of sodium, aluminum, and fluorine that is used especially in making aluminum

crypt \'kript\ *n* : an underground chamber; *also* : a chamber for burial

cryp·tic \'krip-tik\ *adj* **1** : meant to be puzzling or mysterious ⟨a *cryptic* remark⟩ **2** : serving to conceal ⟨*cryptic* coloring of an animal⟩ — **cryp·ti·cal·ly** \-ti-k(ə-)lē\ *adv*

cryp·to·gram \'krip-tə-ˌgram\ *n* : something written in cipher or code

cryp·to·graph \'krip-tə-ˌgraf\ *n* : CRYPTOGRAM — **cryp·to·graph·ic** \ˌkrip-tə-'graf-ik\ *adj*

cryp·tog·ra·phy \krip-'täg-rə-fē\ *n* : the coding and decoding of secret messages — **cryp·tog·ra·pher** \-fər\ *n*

¹**crys·tal** \'kris-tᵊl\ *n* **1** : a quartz that is transparent or nearly so **2** : something transparent like crystal **3** : a solid form of a substance or mixture that has a regularly repeating internal arrangement of its atoms and often external plane faces ⟨a *crystal* of quartz⟩ ⟨a snow *crystal*⟩ ⟨a salt *crystal*⟩ **4** : a clear colorless glass of very good quality; *also* : things made of this glass **5** : the transparent cover over a watch or clock dial

²**crystal** *adj* **1** : made of or resembling crystal **2** : using a crystal as a detector ⟨a *crystal* radio receiver⟩

crystal ball *n* : a clear ball especially of quartz crystal used by a fortune-teller to predict the future

crys·tal·line \'kris-tə-lən\ *adj* **1** : clear or sparkling like crystal ⟨*crystalline* drops of honey⟩ **2** : made of crystal or crystals **3** : of or relating to a crystal

crystalline lens *n* : the lens of the vertebrate eye

crys·tal·lize \'kris-tə-ˌlīz\ *vb* **-lized; -liz·ing 1 a** : to cause to form crystals or assume crystalline form **b** : to become crystallized **2** : to take or cause to take definite form ⟨the plan *crystallized* slowly⟩ — **crys·tal·li·za·tion** \ˌkris-tə-lə-'zā-shən\ *n*

crys·tal·log·ra·phy \ˌkris-tə-'läg-rə-fē\ *n* : a science that deals with the form and structure of crystals — **crys·tal·log·ra·pher** \-fər\ *n*

crys·tal·loid \'kris-tə-ˌlȯid\ *n* : a substance that forms a true solution and is capable of being crystallized

CT scan \ˌsē-'tē-\ *n* : CAT SCAN

cub \'kəb\ *n* **1 a** : a young flesh-eating mammal (as a bear, fox, or lion) **b** : a young shark **2** : a young person **3** : a person just learning a job : APPRENTICE ⟨a *cub* reporter⟩ ⟨a *cub* pilot⟩ **4** : CUB SCOUT

cub·by·hole \'kəb-ē-ˌhōl\ *n* : a snug place (as for storing things)

¹**cube** \'kyüb\ *n* **1** : the solid body having six equal square sides **2** : the result of raising a number to the third power ⟨the *cube* of 2 is 8⟩

²**cube** *vb* **cubed; cub·ing 1** : to raise to the third power **2** : to form into a cube **3** : to cut a checkered pattern into ⟨*cube* a steak⟩

cube root *n* : a number whose cube is a given number ⟨the *cube root* of 27 is 3⟩

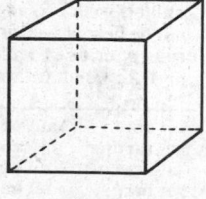

¹cube 1

cu·bic \'kyü-bik\ *also* **cu·bi·cal** \-bi-kəl\ *adj* **1** : having the form of a cube **2 a** : having length, width, and height **b** : relating to volume **3** : being or having the volume of a cube whose edge is a specified unit ⟨*cubic* centimeter⟩ ⟨*cubic* inch⟩ — **cu·bi·cal·ly** \-bi-k(ə-)lē\ *adv*

cu·bi·cle \'kyü-bi-kəl\ *n* : a small separate space (as for sleeping, studying, or working) usually having removable partitions

cubic measure *n* : a unit (as a cubic inch or cubic centimeter) for measuring volume — see MEASURE table, METRIC SYSTEM table

cub·ism \'kyü-ˌbiz-əm\ *n* : a style of art in which natural forms are broken up into geometric shapes (as squares, triangles, or circles) — **cub·ist** \-bist\ *adj or n*

cu·bit \'kyü-bət\ *n* : an ancient unit of length based on the length of the forearm from the elbow to the tip of the middle finger and usually equal to about 18 inches (46 centimeters)

cu·boi·dal \kyü-'bȯid-ᵊl\ *adj* : made of parts (as cells) that are shaped somewhat like cubes ⟨*cuboidal* epithelium⟩

Cub Scout *n* : a member of the Boy Scouts of America program for boys in the first through fifth grades in school

¹**cuck·oo** \'kük-ü, 'kúk-\ *n, pl* **cuckoos 1** : a largely grayish brown European bird that lays its eggs in the nests of other birds for them to hatch; *also* : any of various related birds **2** : the call of a cuckoo

²**cuckoo** *adj* : short on sense or intelligence

cuckoo clock *n* : a clock that announces the hours with sounds like a cuckoo's call

cu·cum·ber \'kyü-(ˌ)kəm-bər\ *n* : the long fleshy usually many-seeded green-skinned fruit of a vine of the gourd family that is grown as a garden vegetable; *also* : this vine

cud \'kəd, 'kúd\ *n* : food brought up into the mouth by some animals (as a cow) from the rumen to be chewed again

cud·dle \'kəd-ᵊl\ *vb* **cud·dled; cud·dling** \'kəd-liŋ, -ᵊl-iŋ\ **1** : to hold close for warmth or comfort or in affection **2** : to lie close : NESTLE, SNUGGLE — **cuddle** *n* — **cud·dly** \'kəd-lē, -ᵊl-ē\ *adj*

cucumber

¹**cud·gel** \'kəj-əl\ *n* : a short heavy club

²**cudgel** *vb* **-geled** *or* **-gelled; -gel·ing** *or* **-gel·ling** \-(ə-)liŋ\ : to beat with or as if with a cudgel — **cudgel one's brains** : to think hard

¹**cue** \'kyü\ *n* **1** : a word, phrase, or action in a play serving as a signal for the next actor to speak or do something **2** : something serving as a signal or suggestion : HINT [probably from *q* or *qu*, abbreviations for Latin *quando* "when," formerly used in actors' copies of scripts of plays]

²**cue** *vb* **cued; cu·ing** : to give a cue to

³**cue** *n* **1** : a tapering rod used in playing billiards or pool **2** : ¹QUEUE 2 [from French *queue* "tail, a line of people," from early French *cue, coe* "tail," from Latin *cauda* "tail" — related to COWARD, QUEUE, CODA; see *Word History* at COWARD, QUEUE]

cue ball *n* : the ball a player strikes with the cue in billiards or pool

¹**cuff** \'kəf\ *n* **1** : a part of a sleeve or glove that goes around the wrist **2** : the turned-back hem of a trouser leg **3** : a band that is capable of being inflated and is wrapped around an arm or leg to control the flow of blood through the part when measuring blood pressure

²**cuff** *vb* : to strike with or as if with the palm of the hand

³**cuff** *n* : a blow with the hand especially when open : SLAP

cuff link *n* : an ornamental device for fastening the cuffs of a shirt — usually used in plural

cui·rass \kwi-'ras, kyu̇-\ *n* : a piece of armor covering the body from neck to waist; *also* : the breastplate of such a piece

cuir·as·sier \ˌkwir-ə-'si(ə)r, ˌkyu̇r-\ *n* : a mounted soldier wearing a cuirass

cui·sine \kwi-'zēn, kwē-\ *n* : style of cooking ⟨Mexican *cuisine*⟩ ⟨Chinese *cuisine*⟩; *also* : the food cooked

cu·lex \'kyü-ˌleks\ *n* : any of a large genus of mosquitoes that includes the common house mosquito of Europe and North America

cul·i·nary \'kəl-ə-ˌner-ē, 'kyü-lə-\ *adj* : of or relating to the kitchen or cooking ⟨*culinary* workers⟩ ⟨*culinary* skills⟩

¹cull \'kəl\ *vb* **1** : to select from a group : CHOOSE **2** : to reduce or control the size of (as a herd) by removal of usually weaker animals ⟨a hunt to *cull* the growing deer population⟩ — **cull·er** *n*

²cull *n* : something rejected from a group or lot as being not as good as the rest

cul·mi·nate \'kəl-mə-ˌnāt\ *vb* **-nat·ed; -nat·ing** : to reach the highest point — **cul·mi·na·tion** \ˌkəl-mə-'nā-shən\ *n*

cu·lotte \'k(y)ü-ˌlät, k(y)ü-'lät\ *n* : a divided skirt or a garment with a divided skirt — often used in plural

cul·pa·ble \'kəl-pə-bəl\ *adj* : deserving blame — **cul·pa·bil·i·ty** \ˌkəl-pə-'bil-ət-ē\ *n* — **cul·pa·ble·ness** \'kəl-pə-bəl-nəs\ *n* — **cul·pa·bly** \'kəl-pə-blē\ *adv*

cul·prit \'kəl-prət, -ˌprit\ *n* **1** : one accused of or charged with a crime or fault **2** : one guilty of a crime or fault

cult \'kəlt\ *n* **1** : a system of religious worship **2 a** : enthusiastic but often temporary devotion to a person, idea, or thing **b** : the object of such devotion **c** : a group of persons who belong to or show devotion to a cult — **cult·ist** \'kəl-təst\ *n*

cul·ti·gen \'kəl-tə-jən\ *n* : a cultivated animal or plant (as the kidney bean) of a variety or species for which a wild ancestor is unknown or uncertain

cul·ti·vate \'kəl-tə-ˌvāt\ *vb* **-vat·ed; -vat·ing** **1 a** : to prepare land for the raising of crops **b** : to loosen or break up the soil around (growing plants) **2 a** : to raise or assist the growth of by tilling or by labor and care ⟨*cultivate* vegetables⟩ ⟨*cultivate* oysters⟩ **b** : ²CULTURE **3** : to improve or develop by careful attention, training, or study : devote time and thought to ⟨*cultivate* one's mind⟩ ⟨*cultivate* the arts⟩ **4** : to seek the company and friendship of

cultivated *adj* **1** : raised or produced under cultivation ⟨*cultivated* fruits⟩ **2** : having or showing good education and elegant taste, speech, and manners : REFINED ⟨*cultivated* speech⟩

cul·ti·va·tion \ˌkəl-tə-'vā-shən\ *n* **1** : the act or art of cultivating especially the soil **2** : REFINEMENT 2

cul·ti·va·tor \'kəl-tə-ˌvāt-ər\ *n* : one that cultivates; *esp* : a tool or machine to loosen the soil while crops are growing

cul·tur·al \'kəlch-(ə-)rəl\ *adj* : of or relating to culture — **cul·tur·al·ly** \-rə-lē\ *adv*

¹cul·ture \'kəl-chər\ *n* **1** : CULTIVATION 1, TILLAGE **2** : the raising or development of a product or crop by careful attention ⟨bee *culture*⟩ ⟨the *culture* of grapes⟩ **3** : improvement of the mind, tastes, and manners through careful training **4 a** : a particular stage, form, or kind of civilization ⟨ancient Greek *culture*⟩ **b** : the beliefs, social practices, and characteristics of a racial, religious, or social group **c** : the characteristic features of everyday life shared by people in a particular place or time ⟨southern *culture*⟩ **5** : cultivation of living material (as bacteria) in a special usually liquid or jellylike nutrient preparation; *also* : a product of such cultivation

²culture *vb* **cul·tured; cul·tur·ing** \'kəlch-(ə-)riŋ\ : to grow in a prepared medium

cultured *adj* **1** : CULTIVATED 2 **2** : produced under artificial conditions ⟨*cultured* viruses⟩ ⟨*cultured* pearls⟩

cul·vert \'kəl-vərt\ *n* : a drain or waterway crossing under a road or railroad

cum \(ˌ)ku̇m, (ˌ)kəm\ *conj* : along with being : in addition to ⟨worked as cook-*cum*-dishwasher⟩ [from Latin *cum* "with"]

cum·ber·some \'kəm-bər-səm\ *adj* : hard to handle or manage because of size or weight — **cum·ber·some·ly** *adv* — **cum·ber·some·ness** *n*

cum·brous \'kəm-b(ə-)rəs\ *adj* : CUMBERSOME — **cum·brous·ly** *adv*

cum laude \ˌku̇m-'lau̇d-ē, -ə; ˌkəm-'lȯd-ē\ *adv or adj* : with distinction : with honors ⟨graduated *cum laude*⟩ [Latin, "with praise"]

cum·mer·bund \'kəm-ər-ˌbənd\ *n* : a wide sash worn around the waist

cu·mu·la·tive \'kyü-myə-lət-iv, -ˌlāt-\ *adj* : increasing (as in force, strength, or amount) by additions one after another ⟨*cumulative* effects⟩ — **cu·mu·la·tive·ly** *adv* — **cu·mu·la·tive·ness** *n*

cu·mu·lo·nim·bus \ˌkyü-myə-lō-'nim-bəs\ *n* : a cumulus cloud that has a low base and that is often spread out in the shape of an anvil extending to great heights

cu·mu·lus \'kyü-myə-ləs\ *n, pl* **cu·mu·li** \-ˌlī, -ˌlē\ : a dense puffy cloud form having a flat base and rounded outlines often piled up like a mountain

¹cu·ne·i·form \kyu̇-'nē-ə-ˌfȯrm, 'kyü-n(ē-)ə-\ *adj* **1** : having the shape of a wedge **2** : made up of or written with marks or letters shaped like wedges

²cuneiform *n* : cuneiform writing

cun·ner \'kən-ər\ *n* : a small American food fish that is common along the rocky shores of New England

¹cun·ning \'kən-iŋ\ *adj* **1** : very good or very clever at using special knowledge or skills or at getting something done ⟨a *cunning* detective⟩ **2** : showing keen understanding ⟨a *cunning* observation⟩ **3** : marked by deception and trickery **4** : CUTE 2, PRETTY — **cun·ning·ly** \-iŋ-lē\ *adv* — **cun·ning·ness** *n*

²cuneiform

synonyms CUNNING, CRAFTY, SLY, WILY mean skillful at trickery. CUNNING suggests cleverness or skill in using sometimes limited intelligence to deal with dangers or difficulties ⟨a *cunning* prisoner making an escape⟩. CRAFTY suggests skill in deceiving with shrewd devices and schemes ⟨a *crafty* peddler known for successful bargaining⟩. SLY often suggests secret or sneaky deceiving ⟨a *sly* thief⟩. WILY suggests cleverness in setting or avoiding traps ⟨the *wily* fox⟩.

²cunning *n* **1** : SKILL 1, DEXTERITY **2** : cleverness in getting what one wants often by tricks or deceiving

¹cup \'kəp\ *n* **1 a** : something to drink out of in the shape of a bowl usually with a handle ⟨a coffee *cup*⟩ **b** : a similar container used to measure amounts (as in cooking) ⟨a measuring *cup*⟩ **2 a** : the contents of a cup : CUPFUL ⟨drank two *cups* of cocoa⟩ **b** : a half pint : eight fluid ounces (about 237 milliliters) **3** : a large ornamental cup offered as a prize **4** : something (as the corolla of a flower) resembling a cup **5** : a food served in a cup-shaped container ⟨fruit *cup*⟩ — **cup·like** *adj*

²cup *vb* **cupped; cup·ping** **1** : to curve into the shape of a cup ⟨*cupped* his hands around his mouth⟩ **2** : to place in or as if in a cup ⟨*cupped* her mouth with her hands⟩

\ə\ **abut**	\au̇\ **out**	\i\ **tip**	\ȯ\ **saw**	\u̇\ **foot**
\ər\ **further**	\ch\ **chin**	\ī\ **life**	\ȯi\ **coin**	\y\ **yet**
\a\ **mat**	\e\ **pet**	\j\ **job**	\th\ **thin**	\yü\ **few**
\ā\ **take**	\ē\ **easy**	\ŋ\ **sing**	\th\ **this**	\yu̇\ **cure**
\ä\ **cot, cart**	\g\ **go**	\ō\ **bone**	\ü\ **food**	\zh\ **vision**

cup·bear·er \'kəp-ˌbar-ər, -ˌber-\ *n* : a person whose duty is to serve cups of wine

cup·board \'kəb-ərd\ *n* : a closet with shelves for cups, dishes, or food

cup·cake \'kəp-ˌkāk\ *n* : a small cake baked in a cup-shaped mold

cup·ful \'kəp-ˌfùl\ *n, pl* **cup·fuls** \-ˌfùlz\ *also* **cups·ful** \'kəps-ˌfùl\ **1** : the amount held by a cup **2** : ¹CUP 2b **3** : ¹CUP 2c

cu·pid \'kyü-pəd\ *n* : a picture or statue of Cupid the Roman god of love often as a winged naked child with a bow and arrow

cu·pid·i·ty \kyù-'pid-ət-ē\ *n* : excessive desire for wealth : GREED

cu·po·la \'kyü-pə-lə\ *n* **1** : a rounded roof or ceiling : DOME **2** : a small structure built on top of a roof

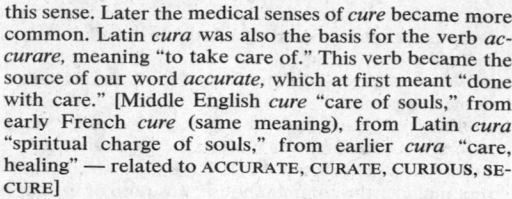
cupola 2

cu·prite \'k(y)ü-ˌprīt\ *n* : a red mineral that is an oxide of copper and an ore of copper

cur \'kər\ *n* **1** : a mongrel dog **2** : ¹HEEL 4, CAD

cur·able \'kyùr-ə-bəl\ *adj* : capable of being cured

cu·ra·re \k(y)ù-'rär-ē\ *n* : a dried product in water especially of a tropical American vine used to poison arrow tips and in medicine to relax muscles

cu·rate \'kyùr-ət\ *n* : a member of the clergy who assists the rector, pastor, or vicar of a church [Middle English *curate* "member of the clergy," from Latin *curatus* (same meaning), from *cura* "spiritual charge of souls," from earlier *cura* "care, healing" — related to ACCURATE, CURE]

cu·ra·tive \'kyùr-ət-iv\ *adj* : relating to or used in the cure of diseases ⟨*curative* treatments⟩

cu·ra·tor \'kyù(ə)r-ˌāt-ər, kyù-'rāt-, 'kyùr-ət-\ *n* : a person in charge of a museum or zoo — **cu·ra·tor·ship** \-ˌship\ *n*

¹**curb** \'kərb\ *n* **1** : a chain or strap on a horse's bit used to control the horse by pressing against the lower jaw **2** : ¹CHECK 3 ⟨price *curbs*⟩ **3** : an enclosing border (as of stone or concrete) often along the edge of a street

²**curb** *vb* **1** : to control by or furnish with or as if with a curb ⟨legislation to *curb* price and wage increases⟩ ⟨*curb* your appetite⟩ **2** : to lead (a dog) to a suitable place (as a gutter) for defecation

curb·ing \'kər-biŋ\ *n* **1** : the material for a curb **2** : ¹CURB 3

curd \'kərd\ *n* **1** : the thickened or solid part of sour or partly digested milk — compare WHEY **2** : something resembling the curd of milk — **curdy** \-ē\ *adj*

cur·dle \'kərd-ᵊl\ *vb* **cur·dled; cur·dling** \'kərd-liŋ, -ᵊl-iŋ\ **1** : to form curds **2** : to cause curds to form in ⟨high heat *curdled* the custard⟩ **3** — used in expressions such as *make one's blood curdle* to indicate a feeling of terror ⟨a ghost story that will make your blood *curdle*⟩

¹**cure** \'kyù(ə)r\ *n* **1 a** : recovery or relief from a disease **b** : something that cures a disease : REMEDY **c** : a method or period of medical treatment **2** : something that corrects or heals a bad situation ⟨a *cure* for unemployment⟩

Word History In Latin the noun *cura* had the general sense of "the care, concern, or attention given to something or someone." Often it referred to "medical care or healing." The Roman Christians, however, used the word chiefly in regard to "the care of souls," since that was one of their main concerns. The word passed into French as *cure* and then into English with this spiritual sense. The English noun *curate*, meaning "one who takes care of souls, a member of the clergy," developed from this sense. Later the medical senses of *cure* became more common. Latin *cura* was also the basis for the verb *accurare*, meaning "to take care of." This verb became the source of our word *accurate*, which at first meant "done with care." [Middle English *cure* "care of souls," from early French *cure* (same meaning), from Latin *cura* "spiritual charge of souls," from earlier *cura* "care, healing" — related to ACCURATE, CURATE, CURIOUS, SECURE]

²**cure** *vb* **cured; cur·ing** **1 a** : to make or become healthy or sound again **b** : to bring about recovery from **2** : ²REMEDY **3 a** : to prepare by a chemical or physical process for use or storage ⟨*cure* bacon⟩ **b** : to go through a curing process ⟨hay *curing* in the sun⟩ — **cur·er** *n*

cure-all \'kyù(ə)r-ˌol\ *n* : a remedy for everything wrong

cu·ret·tage \ˌkyùr-ə-'täzh\ *n* : a surgical cleaning or scraping of a body part (as the uterus)

cur·few \'kər-ˌfyü\ *n* **1** : an order or law requiring certain or all people to be off the streets at a stated time **2** : a signal (as the ringing of a bell) formerly given to announce the beginning of a curfew **3** : the time when a curfew is sounded

Word History During the Middle Ages, houses in European towns were often made of wood, and they were built very close together. A fire burning out of control could quickly spread from house to house. To prevent this disaster, people were required to put out or cover their hearth fires by a certain time in the evening. A bell was rung as a signal when the time had come. In early French this signal was called *coverfeu*, a compound of *covrir*, meaning "to cover," and *feu*, "fire." Even when hearth fires were no longer regulated, many towns had other rules that called for the ringing of an evening bell, and this signal was still called *coverfeu*. A common *coverfeu* regulation required that certain people be off the streets by a given time. This is the meaning taken when the word *coverfeu* was borrowed from early French into Middle English as *curfew*. [Middle English *curfew* "an order to be off the streets at a certain time," from early French *coverfeu* "signal to cover a hearth fire, curfew," from *covrir* "to cover" and *feu* "fire"]

cu·rie \'kyù(ə)r-(ˌ)ē, kyù-'rē\ *n* : a unit of radioactivity equal to 37 billion disintegrations per second

cu·rio \'kyùr-ē-ˌō\ *n, pl* **cu·ri·os** : an object or article valued because it is strange or rare

cu·ri·os·i·ty \ˌkyùr-ē-'äs-ət-ē\ *n, pl* **-ties** **1** : an eager desire to learn and often to learn what does not concern one : INQUISITIVENESS **2 a** : something strange or unusual ⟨the *curiosities* of nature⟩ **b** : CURIO

cu·ri·ous \'kyùr-ē-əs\ *adj* **1** : eager to learn ⟨a cat *curious* about its new surroundings⟩ **2** : INQUISITIVE **2 3** : attracting attention by being strange or unusual : ODD ⟨a *curious* old coin⟩ ⟨that's *curious*—they were here yesterday⟩ [Middle English *curious* "made carefully, skillful, eager to learn," from early French *curios* (same meaning), from Latin *curiosus* "careful, inquisitive," from *cura* "care, healing" — related to ACCURATE, CURE] — **cu·ri·ous·ly** *adv* — **cu·ri·ous·ness** *n*

synonyms CURIOUS, INQUISITIVE, PRYING mean interested in what is not one's own business. CURIOUS in general suggests an active desire to learn or to know ⟨children are *curious* about everything⟩. INQUISITIVE suggests annoying and regular curiosity along with steady quizzing ⟨dreaded the visits of their *inquisitive* relatives⟩. PRYING suggests truly bothersome meddling ⟨*prying* neighbors who refuse to mind their own business⟩.

cu·ri·um \'kyùr-ē-əm\ *n* : a metallic radioactive element artificially produced — see ELEMENT table

¹**curl** \'kərl\ *vb* **1** : to form into or grow in coils or ringlets ⟨*curled* her hair⟩ **2** : to take or move in a curved form ⟨smoke *curling* from the chimney⟩

²curl *n* **1** : a lock of hair that coils : RINGLET **2** : a spiral or winding form : COIL **3** : the state of being curled **4** : a hollow place under the crest of a breaking wave

curl·er \'kər-lər\ *n* **1** : one that curls; *esp* : a device for putting a curl into hair **2** : a player in the game of curling

cur·lew \'kərl-ˌ(y)ü\ *n, pl* **curlews** *or* **curlew** : any of various largely brownish birds which are related to the woodcocks and are distinguished by long legs and a long slender bill that curves downward

curlew

curli·cue *also* **curly·cue** \'kər-li-ˌkyü\ *n* : a fancifully curved or spiral figure (as a flourish in handwriting)

curl·ing \'kər-liŋ\ *n* : a game in which two teams of four players slide special stones over ice toward a target circle

curling iron *n* : a rod-shaped device that is heated and used to curl hair

curl up *vb* : to arrange oneself in or as if in a curl or ball ⟨*curl up* with a good book⟩

curly \'kər-lē\ *adj* **curl·i·er; -est** : tending to curl; *also* : having curls ⟨*curly* hair⟩ — **curl·i·ness** *n*

cur·mud·geon \kər-'məj-ən\ *n* : a grumpy and usually old man

cur·ragh \'kə-rə(k)\ *n* : CORACLE

cur·rant \'kər-ənt, 'kə-rənt\ *n* **1** : a small seedless raisin used in baking and cooking **2** : the acid edible fruit of several shrubs related to the gooseberries; *also* : a plant bearing currants [from Middle English *raison of Coraunte,* literally, "raisin of Corinth," from *Corinth,* city in Greece from which it was exported]

cur·ren·cy \'kər-ən-sē, 'kə-rən-\ *n, pl* **-cies** **1** : common use or acceptance **2** : money in circulation

¹cur·rent \'kər-ənt, 'kə-rənt\ *adj* **1 a** : now passing ⟨the *current* month⟩ **b** : occurring in or belonging to the present time ⟨*current* events⟩ **2** : generally accepted, used, or practiced ⟨*current* customs⟩ [Middle English *curraunt, coraunt* "moving, flowing, running," from early French *corant, curant* "running," derived from Latin *currere* "to run" — related to CORRIDOR, COURIER, COURSE, EXCURSION, INCUR, OCCUR] — **cur·rent·ly** *adv* — **cur·rent·ness** *n*

²current *n* **1 a** : the part of a fluid body moving continuously in a certain direction **b** : the swiftest part of a stream **2** : general course or movement : TREND **3** : a stream of electric charge; *also* : the rate of such movement

cur·ric·u·lum \kə-'rik-yə-ləm\ *n, pl* **-la** \-lə\ *also* **-lums** : all the courses of study offered by a school — **cur·ric·u·lar** \-lər\ *adj*

¹cur·ry \'kər-ē, 'kə-rē\ *vb* **cur·ried; cur·ry·ing** : to rub and clean the coat of ⟨*curry* a horse⟩ [Middle English *currayen* "to comb the coat of (a horse)," from early French *correier* "to prepare," probably from a Latin word of Germanic origin] — **cur·ri·er** *n* — **curry fa·vor** \-'fā-vər\ : to try to win approval by flattering or doing favors

²cur·ry \'kər-ē, 'kə-rē\ *n, pl* **curries** **1** : CURRY POWDER **2** : a food seasoned with curry powder [from Tamil (a language of southern India) *ka i* "a spiced dish of food"]

³curry *vb* **cur·ried; cur·ry·ing** : to flavor or cook with curry powder

cur·ry·comb \'kər-ē-ˌkōm, 'kə-rē-\ *n* : a comb with rows of metallic teeth or ridges used to curry horses — **cur·rycomb** *vb*

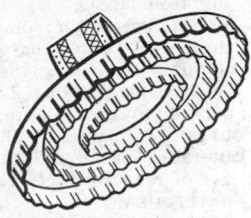
currycomb

curry powder *n* : a sharp seasoning made of ground spices

¹curse \'kərs\ *n* **1** : a calling for harm or injury to come to someone **2** : a word or an expression used in cursing or swearing **3** : evil or misfortune that comes as if in answer to a curse **4** : a cause of great harm or evil

²curse *vb* **cursed; curs·ing** **1** : to call upon divine power to send harm or evil upon **2** : SWEAR **5** **3** : to bring unhappiness or evil upon : AFFLICT

cursed \'kər-səd, 'kərst\ *also* **curst** \'kərst\ *adj* : being under or deserving a curse — **cursed·ly** *adv* — **cursed·ness** *n*

cur·sive \'kər-siv\ *adj* : written or formed with the strokes of the letters joined together and the angles rounded ⟨*cursive* handwriting⟩ — **cursive** *n* — **cur·sive·ly** *adv*

cur·sor \'kər-sər\ *n* : a mark (as a bright blinking spot) on a computer display screen that shows the place where the user is working

cur·so·ry \'kərs(-ə)-rē\ *adj* : rapid and usually careless : HASTY ⟨a *cursory* glance⟩ — **cur·so·ri·ly** \-rə-lē\ *adv* — **cur·so·ri·ness** \-rē-nəs\ *n*

curt \'kərt\ *adj* : rudely abrupt or brief in speech ⟨a *curt* reply⟩ **synonyms** see BLUFF — **curt·ly** *adv* — **curt·ness** *n*

cur·tail \(ˌ)kər-'tā(ə)l\ *vb* : to make less by or as if by cutting off part of — **cur·tail·er** \-'tā-lər\ *n* — **cur·tail·ment** \-'tāl-mənt\ *n*

cur·tain \'kərt-³n\ *n* **1** : a piece of material (as cloth) hung up to darken, hide, divide, or decorate **2** : the opening or closing of the curtain in front of the stage of a theater **3** : something that covers, hides, or separates like a curtain — **curtain** *vb*

curtain call *n* : an appearance by a performer (as after the final curtain of a play) in response to the applause of the audience

¹curt·sy *also* **curt·sey** \'kərt-sē\ *n, pl* **curtsies** *also* **curtseys** : a bow made especially by women that consists of a slight lowering of the body and bending of the knees

²curtsy *also* **curtsey** *vb* **curt·sied** *also* **curt·seyed; curt·sy·ing** *also* **curt·sey·ing** : to make a curtsy

cur·va·ture \'kər-və-ˌchü(ə)r, -chər\ *n* **1** : the act of curving : the state of being curved **2** : an abnormal curving ⟨*curvature* of the spine⟩

¹curve \'kərv\ *vb* **curved; curv·ing** **1** : to turn or change from a straight line or course ⟨the road *curved* to the left⟩ **2** : to cause to curve

²curve *n* **1 a** : a line especially when curved **b** : a line connecting points on a graph or in a coordinate system **2** : something that bends or turns without angles ⟨a *curve* in the road⟩ **3** : a ball thrown so that it moves away from a straight course

¹cur·vet \(ˌ)kər-'vet\ *n* : a leap of a horse in which first the forelegs and then the hind are raised so that for an instant all the legs are in the air

²curvet *vb* **cur·vet·ted** *or* **cur·vet·ed; cur·vet·ting** *or* **cur·vet·ing** **1** : to make a curvet **2** : ²CAPER, PRANCE

¹cush·ion \'kush-ən\ *n* **1** : a soft pillow or pad to rest on or against **2** : something resembling a cushion in use, shape, or softness **3** : a rubber pad along the inner rim of a billiard table **4** : something serving to lessen the effects of something bad or unpleasant

²cushion *vb* **cush·ioned; cush·ion·ing** \-(ə-)niŋ\ **1** : to place on or as if on a cushion **2** : to furnish with a cushion **3** : to soften or lessen the force or shock of

cusp \'kəsp\ *n* : a point or pointed end or part: as **a** : either of the pointed ends of a crescent moon **b** : a point

\ə\ **abut**	\aú\ **out**	\i\ **tip**	\ó\ **saw**	\ú\ **foot**
\ər\ **further**	\ch\ **chin**	\ī\ **life**	\ói\ **coin**	\y\ **yet**
\a\ **mat**	\e\ **pet**	\j\ **job**	\th\ **thin**	\yü\ **few**
\ā\ **take**	\ē\ **easy**	\ŋ\ **sing**	\t̲h̲\ **this**	\yú\ **cure**
\ä\ **cot, cart**	\g\ **go**	\ō\ **bone**	\ü\ **food**	\zh\ **vision**

on the grinding surface of a tooth **c** : a fold or flap of a heart valve

cus·pid \'kəs-pəd\ *n* : ²CANINE 1

¹**cuss** \'kəs\ *n* **1** : ¹CURSE 2 **2** : ¹FELLOW 4a ⟨an ornery *cuss*⟩

²**cuss** *vb* : SWEAR 5

cus·tard \'kəs-tərd\ *n* : a sweetened mixture of milk and eggs baked, boiled, or frozen

cus·to·di·an \ˌkəs-'tōd-ē-ən\ *n* **1** : someone who guards and protects or takes care of something for another person **2** : someone who cleans and takes care of a building : JANITOR 2

cus·to·dy \'kəs-təd-ē\ *n* **1** : direct responsibility for care and control **2** : the state of being arrested or held by the police

¹**cus·tom** \'kəs-təm\ *n* **1** : the usual way of doing things : the usual practice of a person or group **2** *pl* : duties or taxes paid on imports or exports **3** : support given a business by its customers **synonyms** see HABIT

²**custom** *adj* **1** : made or done to order ⟨*custom* clothes⟩ **2** : specializing in custom work ⟨a *custom* tailor⟩

cus·tom·ary \'kəs-tə-ˌmer-ē\ *adj* **1** : based on or established by custom ⟨*customary* rent⟩ **2** : commonly done, observed, or used ⟨my *customary* evening stroll⟩ ⟨*customary* units of weight like the pound⟩ — **cus·tom·ar·i·ly** \ˌkəs-tə-'mer-ə-lē\ *adv*

cus·tom·er \'kəs-tə-mər\ *n* **1** : one that buys a product or service **2** : ²INDIVIDUAL 2, FELLOW ⟨he's a real tough *customer*⟩

cus·tom·house \'kəs-təm-ˌhaủs\ *also* **cus·toms·house** \-təmz-\ *n* : a building where customs are paid or collected and where ships are entered and cleared at a port

cus·tom·ize \'kəs-tə-ˌmīz\ *vb* **-ized; -iz·ing** : to build, fit, or change to suit a specific customer ⟨a *customized* van⟩

cus·tom—made \ˌkəs-təm-'(m)ād\ *adj* : made for a specific customer ⟨*custom-made* clothing⟩

¹**cut** \'kət\ *vb* **cut; cut·ting 1 a** : to penetrate or divide with or as if with an edged tool (as a knife) ⟨*cut* my finger⟩ ⟨*cutting* and pasting colored paper⟩ ⟨*cut* the pie⟩ **b** : to function as an edged tool ⟨be careful — that glass will *cut*⟩ ⟨this old knife won't *cut* anymore⟩ **c** : to be able to be cut ⟨cheese *cuts* easily⟩ **2** : to experience the growth of through the gum ⟨the baby is *cutting* teeth⟩ **3** : to hurt the feelings of ⟨the remark *cut* me⟩ **4 a** : ¹TRIM 3a ⟨*cut* your hair⟩ **b** : ²MOW 1 ⟨*cut* the grass⟩ **c** : DISSOLVE 2 ⟨a detergent *cuts* grease⟩ **5** : to make smaller ⟨*cut* costs⟩ **6** : to remove with or as if with a knife ⟨*cut* a piece of ham⟩ ⟨*cut* two players from the team⟩ **7** : to remove (something) from a computer document in such a way that it can be moved to another part of the document or to another document **8 a** : to go straight rather than around ⟨*cut* across the backyard⟩ **b** : INTERSECT 1, CROSS ⟨lines *cutting* other lines⟩ **c** : to make a quick change of direction ⟨go out 10 steps, then *cut* right and I'll throw you a pass⟩ ⟨the camera *cuts* to the crowd in the street⟩ **9** : to divide a deck of cards **10** : to cause to stop ⟨*cut* the nonsense⟩ ⟨*cut* the engine⟩ **11** : ¹SNUB 2 ⟨*cut* a former friend⟩ **12** : to fail to attend ⟨*cut* a class⟩ **13 a** : to make or shape with or as if with an edged tool ⟨farmers *cut* clearings out of the wilderness⟩ ⟨*cut* a diamond⟩ **b** : to record sounds on ⟨*cut* a record⟩ **14** : to give the appearance of ⟨*cuts* a fine figure⟩ **15** : to advance by skipping or going around another ⟨*cut* to the front of the line⟩ — **cut both ways** : to have good and bad implications — **cut corners** : to do something the easiest or cheapest way — **cut ice** : to be important ⟨that's not going to *cut* any *ice* with the kids⟩ — **cut it** : to meet the necessary requirements for success

²**cut** *n* **1 a** : something cut or cut off ⟨a *cut* of beef⟩ **b** : ¹SHARE 1 ⟨your *cut* of the winnings⟩ **2 a** : a product of cutting **b** : a wound made by something sharp **c** : a passage made by cutting ⟨a railroad *cut*⟩ **d** : a grade or step

especially in a social scale ⟨a *cut* above the ordinary⟩ **e** : a pictorial illustration **3 a** : an act or instance of cutting **b** : something done or said that hurts the feelings ⟨an unkind *cut*⟩ **c** : an act of removing a part ⟨a *cut* in pay⟩ **d** : an act or turn of cutting cards ⟨it's your *cut*⟩ **4** : a voluntary absence from a class ⟨too many *cuts* in gym⟩ **5** : a swing by a batter at the ball ⟨took a good *cut*⟩ **6** : a sudden switch from one sound or image to another in movies, radio, or television **7** : the shape and style in which a thing is cut, formed, or made ⟨clothes of the latest *cut*⟩

cut·abil·i·ty \ˌkət-ə-'bil-ət-ē\ *n* : the proportion of lean edible meat (as in a side of beef)

cu·ta·ne·ous \kyủ-'tā-nē-əs\ *adj* : of, relating to, or affecting the skin ⟨a *cutaneous* infection⟩

¹**cut·away** \'kət-ə-ˌwā\ *adj* : showing the top or outside cut away so the inside parts can be seen ⟨a *cutaway* view of a flower⟩

²**cutaway** *n* **1** : a coat with skirts cut from the front waistline to form tails at the back **2** : a cutaway illustration

cut·back \'kət-ˌbak\ *n* : an act or instance of cutting something back

cut back \'kət-'bak\ *vb* **1 a** : ²PRUNE 2 **b** : ²PRUNE 2a **2** : to reduce something in amount ⟨*cut back* on smoking⟩

cut down *vb* **1** : to knock down and kill or wound **2** : to make over in a smaller size ⟨*cutting down* an older sister's outfit⟩ **3** : to reduce something in amount ⟨*cut down* on energy use⟩

cute \'kyüt\ *adj* **cut·er; cut·est 1** : CLEVER 3, SHREWD ⟨they're not *cute* enough to fool me⟩ **2** : attractive especially in looks or actions ⟨a *cute* baby⟩ ⟨a *cute* outfit⟩ **3 a** : clever in an appealing way ⟨a *cute* idea⟩ **b** : clever in an annoying way ⟨don't get *cute* with me⟩ — **cute·ly** *adv* — **cute·ness** *n*

cut glass *n* : glass ornamented by cutting and polishing

cu·ti·cle \'kyüt-i-kəl\ *n* **1** : an outer layer (as of skin or a leaf) often produced by the cells beneath **2** : a dead or horny layer of skin especially around a fingernail

cu·tin \'kyüt-ᵊn\ *n* : a substance that contains waxes, fatty acids, soaps, and resins and forms a continuous layer on the outer wall of the epidermis of a plant

cut in *vb* **1** : to join in suddenly ⟨*cut in* on a conversation⟩ **2** : to interrupt a dancing couple and take one partner's place **3** : to mix with cutting motions ⟨add the shortening to the flour and *cut* it *in*⟩ **4** : to include among those who get a cut ⟨I'll *cut* you *in* on the profits⟩

cut·lass \'kət-ləs\ *n* : a short curved sword

cut·ler \'kət-lər\ *n* : one who makes, sells, or repairs cutlery

cut·lery \'kət-lə-rē\ *n* **1** : the business of a cutler **2** : cutting tools (as knives and scissors) **3** : utensils for cutting, serving, and eating food

cut·let \'kət-lət\ *n* **1** : a small slice of meat ⟨veal *cutlets*⟩ **2** : a piece of food shaped like a cutlet

cut·off \'kət-ˌof\ *n* **1** : the action of cutting off **2** : a device for cutting off **3** *pl* : shorts made from jeans with the legs cut off short — **cutoff** *adj*

cut off \ˌkət-'of\ *vb* **1** : to stop the flow or movement of ⟨*cut off* a supply⟩ **2** : ISOLATE ⟨*cut off* from the world⟩ **3** : DISCONTINUE 2 ⟨they *cut off* relations with us⟩ **4** : to stop from talking

cut·out \'kət-ˌaủt\ *n* : something cut out or off from something else — **cutout** *adj*

¹**cut out** *vb* **1** : to assign through necessity ⟨you've got your work *cut out* for you⟩ **2** : to put an end to ⟨now *cut* that *out*⟩ **3** : to come to a stop ⟨the engines *cut out*⟩

²**cut out** *adj* : naturally suited ⟨not *cut out* for teaching⟩

cut—rate \'kət-'rāt\ *adj* **1** : marked by, offering, or making use of reduced prices ⟨a *cut-rate* store⟩ **2** : SECOND= RATE, CHEAP

cut·ter \'kət-ər\ *n* **1** : one that cuts ⟨a diamond *cutter*⟩ ⟨a cookie *cutter*⟩ **2 a** : a ship's boat for carrying supplies or

passengers **b** : a small sailing boat with one mast **c**
: a small armed boat in government service **3** : a small
sleigh

¹cut·throat \'kət-ˌthrōt\ *n* **1**
: a person likely to cut
someone's throat **2** : a cruel person with no scruples

²cutthroat *adj* : RUTHLESS
⟨*cutthroat* competition⟩

¹cut·ting \'kət-iŋ\ *n* : something cut or cut off or out;
esp : a section of a plant capable of developing into a
new individual

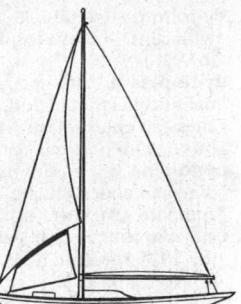

cutter 2b

²cutting *adj* **1** : designed for
cutting : SHARP ⟨a *cutting*
blade⟩ **2** : marked by piercing cold ⟨a *cutting* wind⟩ **3**
: likely to hurt the feelings of others ⟨*cutting* remarks⟩ —
cut·ting·ly \-iŋ-lē\ *adv*

cutting board *n* : a board on which something (as cloth or
food) is placed for cutting

cutting edge *n* **1** : the sharp edge of a cutting tool **2** : the
newest and most advanced area of an activity — **cutting–
edge** *adj*

cut·tle·bone \'kət-ᵊl-ˌbōn\ *n* : the shell of a cuttlefish used
for making polishing powder or for supplying birds in
cages with calcium and salts

cut·tle·fish \-ˌfish\ *n* : a marine mollusk having eight short
arms and two longer tentacles and differing from the related squid in having an internal shell composed of compounds of calcium

cut·up \'kət-ˌəp\ *n* : a person who clowns or acts noisily

cut up \'kət-'əp\ *vb* : to act like a clown

cut·worm \'kət-ˌwərm\ *n* : any of various smooth-bodied
nocturnal moth caterpillars that usually feed on plants

-cy \sē\ *n suffix, pl* **-cies** **1** : action : practice ⟨prophe*cy*⟩
⟨pira*cy*⟩ **2** : rank : office ⟨captain*cy*⟩ **3** : state : quality
⟨accura*cy*⟩ ⟨bankrupt*cy*⟩ ⟨normal*cy*⟩ [derived from Latin *-tia* "action, quality"]

cy·an \'sī-ˌan, -ən\ *n* : a greenish blue

cy·a·nide \'sī-ə-ˌnīd, -nəd\ *n* : a very poisonous compound
consisting of carbon and nitrogen with either sodium or
potassium

cy·a·no·bac·te·ri·um \ˌsī-ə-nō-bak-'tir-ē-əm, sī-ˌan-ō-\ *n*
: BLUE-GREEN ALGA

cy·ano·gen \sī-'an-ə-jən\ *n* : a colorless flammable poisonous gas consisting of carbon and nitrogen

cy·ber \'sī-bər\ *adj* : relating to computers or computer
networks

cyber- *combining form* : computer : computer network
⟨*cyber*space⟩ [*cybernetic*]

cy·ber·bul·ly·ing \'sī-bər-'bùl-ē-iŋ\ *n* : the electronic posting of mean-spirited messages about a person (as a student) often done anonymously — **cy·ber·bul·ly** \-'bùl-ē\
n or vb

cy·ber·net·ics \ˌsī-bər-'net-iks\ *n* : a science concerned
especially with studies comparing automatic control systems (as that of the nervous system and brain and me-
chanical-electrical communication systems) — **cy·ber-
net·ic** \-'net-ik\ *adj*

cy·ber·space \'sī-bər-ˌspās\ *n* : the online world of computer networks

cy·cad \'sī-kəd\ *n* : a tropical palmlike evergreen plant
that is a gymnosperm

cy·cla·men \'sī-klə-mən, 'sik-lə-\ *n* : any of a genus of
plants related to the primroses and often grown in pots
for their showy nodding flowers

¹cy·cle \'sī-kəl\ *n* **1** : a period of time taken up by a series
of events or actions that repeat themselves regularly and
in the same order ⟨the *cycle* of the seasons⟩ **2 a** : a series

of events or operations that happen again and again regularly and usually lead back to the starting point ⟨the *cycle*
of blood from the heart, through the blood vessels, and
back again⟩ ⟨the drying *cycle* of a dishwasher⟩ **b** : one
complete occurrence of a cycle ⟨a *cycle* of alternating
current⟩ ⟨the *cycle* of a vibration⟩ **3** : a long period of
time : AGE — **cy·clic** \'sī-klik *also* 'sik-lik\ *or* **cy·cli·cal**
\'sī-kli-kəl, 'sik-li-\ *adj* — **cy·cli·cal·ly** \-k(ə-)lē\ *adv*

²cy·cle \'sī-kəl, 'sik-əl\ *vb* **cy·cled; cy·cling** \'sī-k(ə-)liŋ,
'sik-(ə-)liŋ\ : to ride a bicycle or motorcycle

cy·clist \'sī-k(ə-)ləst, 'sik-(ə-)ləst\ *n* : a person who rides a
bicycle or motorcycle

cy·cloid \'sī-ˌklòid\ *n*
: a curve that is
traced by a point on
the circumference of
a circle that is roll-
ing along a straight
line

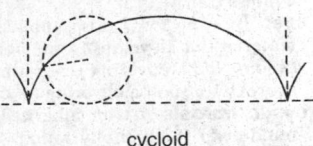

cycloid

cy·clone \'sī-ˌklōn\ *n*
1 : a storm or system of winds that rotates about a center
of low atmospheric pressure counterclockwise in the
northern hemisphere, advances at a speed of 20 to 30
miles (30 to 50 kilometers) an hour, and often brings a
great deal of rain **2** : TORNADO — **cy·clon·ic** \sī-'klän-
ik\ *adj*

cy·clo·pe·dia *or* **cy·clo·pae·dia** \ˌsī-klə-'pēd-ē-ə\ *n* : EN-
CYCLOPEDIA — **cy·clo·pe·dic** \-'pēd-ik\ *adj*

cy·clops \'sī-ˌkläps\ *n* **1** *pl* **cy·clo·pes** \sī-'klō-ˌpēz\ *cap*
: one of a race of giants in Greek legend with a single eye
in the middle of the forehead **2** *pl* **cyclops** : a water flea
with a single eye

cy·clo·tron \'sī-klə-ˌträn\ *n* : a device in which charged
particles are propelled to high speeds by an alternating
electric field in a constant magnetic field

cyg·net \'sig-nət\ *n* : a young swan

Cyg·nus \'sig-nəs\ *n* : a northern group of stars near Pegasus in the Milky Way [from Latin *cygnus*, literally, "swan"]

cyl·in·der \'sil-ən-dər\ *n* **1** : a geometric shape composed
of two parallel faces of identical size and shape (as circles)
and a curved surface that completely connects their borders **2** : a body (as the piston chamber of an engine, the
barrel of a pump, or the part of a revolver which holds
the cartridges) shaped like a cylinder — **cy·lin·dri·cal**
\sə-'lin-dri-kəl\ *adj* — **cy·lin·dri·cal·ly** \-dri-k(ə-)lē\ *adv*

cym·bal \'sim-bəl\ *n* : a brass plate that is struck with a
drumstick or is used in pairs struck together to make a
clashing sound — **cym·bal·ist** \-bə-ləst\ *n*

cyn·ic \'sin-ik\ *n* : a person who distrusts people; *esp* : one
who believes that people act only in self-interest

Word History In ancient Greece a certain philosopher
taught that moral excellence was the only goal in life
worth striving for. He and his followers lived a simple
life, and they sometimes offended other Greeks with
their open scorn of wealth and pleasure. Such a philosopher was called *kynikos*, which literally means "like a
dog." One likely reason for this name is that the leader
of the group taught at a school with a name that began
with the same letters as in the Greek word for dog. It is
also likely that many Greeks who used *kynikos* for these
philosophers had been bothered by their rudeness. *Cynic*
has been used in English since the 16th century for such
philosophers. Once the word had appeared in English, it
wasn't long before *cynic* was applied to any faultfinding
critic. Later it was used chiefly of one who doubts the

\ə\ **abut**	\au̇\ **out**	\i\ **tip**	\o̅\ **saw**	\u̇\ **foot**
\ər\ **further**	\ch\ **chin**	\ī\ **life**	\o̅i\ **coin**	\y\ **yet**
\a\ **mat**	\e\ **pet**	\j\ **job**	\th\ **thin**	\yü\ **few**
\ā\ **take**	\ē\ **easy**	\ŋ\ **sing**	\th\ **this**	\yu̇\ **cure**
\ä\ **cot, cart**	\g\ **go**	\ō\ **bone**	\ü\ **food**	\zh\ **vision**

sincerity of all human motives except selfishness. [from early French *cynique* or Latin *cynicus,* both meaning "cynic," from Greek *kynikos,* literally, "like a dog"]

cyn·i·cal \'sin-i-kəl\ *adj* : having the attitude of a cynic : not trusting human nature — **cyn·i·cal·ly** \-k(ə-)lē\ *adv*

cyn·i·cism \'sin-ə-,siz-əm\ *n* : a cynical attitude or quality; *also* : an expression of cynical quality

cy·no·sure \'sī-nə-,shů(ə)r, 'sin-ə-\ *n* : a center of attraction or attention ⟨the *cynosure* of all eyes⟩

cy·press \'sī-prəs\ *n* **1** : any of a genus of evergreen trees and shrubs that are related to the pines and have overlapping scalelike leaves **2** : BALD CYPRESS **3** : the wood of a cypress tree

cyst \'sist\ *n* **1** : a closed pouch or sac of fluid or solid material that develops in the body in some diseased conditions **2** : a covering resembling a cyst or a body (as a spore) with such a covering — **cys·tic** \'sis-tik\ *adj*

cystic fibrosis *n* : an inherited disease marked by the buildup of thick sticky mucus chiefly in the lungs and pancreas leading to recurrent lung infections and digestive problems

cy·to·chrome \'sīt-ə-,krōm\ *n* : any of several iron-containing pigments that transfer electrons to molecules of oxygen in the living cell

cy·tol·o·gist \sī-'täl-ə-jəst\ *n* : a person who specializes in cytology

cy·tol·o·gy \sī-'täl-ə-jē\ *n* : a branch of biology dealing with cells — **cy·to·log·i·cal** \,sīt-ᵊl-'äj-i-kəl\ *or* **cy·to·log·ic** \-'äj-ik\ *adj*

cy·to·plasm \'sīt-ə-,plaz-əm\ *n* : the part of a cell outside the nucleus that includes a fluidlike substance and organelles (as chloroplasts and mitochondria) — **cy·to·plas·mic** \,sīt-ə-'plaz-mik\ *adj*

cy·to·sine \'sīt-ə-,sēn\ *n* : a chemical base that is a pyrimidine and codes genetic information in DNA and RNA — compare ADENINE, GUANINE, THYMINE, URACIL

czar *also* **tsar** *or* **tzar** \'zär\ *n* **1** : the ruler of Russia until the 1917 revolution **2** : one having great power or authority ⟨a baseball *czar*⟩ [Latin *czar* "czar," from Russian *tsar'* (same meaning), from early Russian *tsĭsarĭ, tsĕsarĭ* "emperor," from a Germanic word *kaisar* "emperor," derived from Latin *Caesar* (title of a line of Roman emperors after Augustus Caesar) — see *Word History* at EMPEROR] — **czar·dom** *also* **tsar·dom** *or* **tzar·dom** \'zärd-əm\ *n*

cza·ri·na *also* **tsa·ri·na** *or* **tza·ri·na** \zä-'rē-nə\ *n* : the wife of a czar

czar·ist *also* **tsar·ist** *or* **tzar·ist** \'zär-əst\ *adj* : of, relating to, or ruled by a czar ⟨*czarist* Russia⟩

Czech \'chek\ *n* **1** : a person born or living in western Czechoslovakia (including Bohemia and Moravia) or the Czech Republic **2** : the Slavic language of the Czechs — **Czech** *adj*

D

d \'dē\ *n, pl* **d's** *or* **ds** *often cap* **1** : the fourth letter of the English alphabet **2** : five hundred in Roman numerals — see NUMBER table **3** : the musical note referred to by the letter D : the second tone of the C-major scale **4** : a grade rating a student's work as poor

'd \d, əd\ *vb* **1** : HAD ⟨they'*d* gone⟩ **2** : WOULD ⟨we'*d* go⟩ **3** : DID ⟨where'*d* they go?⟩

¹dab \'dab\ *n* **1** : a quick blow or thrust : POKE **2** : a gentle touch or stroke : PAT

²dab *vb* **dabbed; dab·bing 1** : to strike or touch lightly ⟨*dabs* at her eyes with a handkerchief⟩ **2** : to apply with quick light strokes : DAUB — **dab·ber** *n*

³dab *n* **1** : ¹SMEAR 1, DAUB **2** : a small amount ⟨just a *dab* more ice cream⟩

dab·ble \'dab-əl\ *vb* **dab·bled; dab·bling** \-(ə-)liŋ\ **1** : to wet by splashing : SPATTER **2 a** : to paddle or play in or as if in water **b** : to reach with the bill to the bottom of shallow water to obtain food ⟨ducks *dabbled* in the pond⟩ **3** : to work or concern oneself lightly or without deep involvement ⟨they *dabble* in poetry⟩ — **dab·bler** \-(ə-)lər\ *n*

da ca·po \dä-'käp-ō, də-\ *adv or adj* : from the beginning — used as a direction in music to repeat

dace \'dās\ *n, pl* **dace** : any of various North American freshwater fishes related to the carp

dachs·hund \'däks-,hůnt, 'däk-sənt\ *n* : any of a breed of dogs of German origin with a long body, very short legs, and long drooping ears

Word History The dachshund is a dog with short legs and a long history. The breed was developed in Germany more than a thousand years ago to hunt burrowing animals such as badgers. With its short legs and long, powerful body, the dachshund could follow a badger right down into its hole. It could even fight

dachshund

with the badger underground. The German name for the breed was *dachshund,* a compound of *dachs,* meaning "badger," and *hund,* "dog." This German name was borrowed directly into English. [from German *Dachshund* "dachshund," literally, "badger dog," from *Dachs* "badger" and *Hund* dog]

Da·cron \'dā-,krän, 'dak-,rän\ *trademark* — used for a synthetic textile fiber

dac·tyl \'dak-tᵊl\ *n* : a metrical foot consisting of one accented syllable followed by two unaccented syllables (as in *tenderly*) — **dac·tyl·ic** \dak-'til-ik\ *adj*

dad \'dad\ *n* : ¹FATHER 1a

dad·dy \'dad-ē\ *n, pl* **daddies** : ¹FATHER 1a

dad·dy long·legs \,dad-ē-'löŋ-,legz\ *n* **1** : CRANE FLY **2** : any of various invertebrates that are arachnids which resemble true spiders but have a small rounded body and very long slender legs — called also *harvestman*

da·do \'dād-ō\ *n, pl* **dadoes** : the part of a pedestal of a column above the base

daemon *variant of* DEMON

daf·fo·dil \'daf-ə-,dil\ *n* : any of various herbs that produce long slender leaves and flowers from an overwintering bulb in the spring; *esp* : one with petals whose inner parts are arranged to form a trumpet-shaped tube — compare JONQUIL, NARCISSUS

daf·fy \'daf-ē\ *adj* **daf·fi·er; -est** : silly, odd, or peculiar usually in an amusing way ⟨a *daffy* spy story⟩; *also* : attracted to or fascinated with ⟨*daffy* over cars⟩ ⟨*daffy* about stamp collecting⟩

daffodil

daft \'daft\ *adj* **1** : FOOLISH, SILLY **2** : INSANE, CRAZY — **daft·ly** *adv* — **daft·ness** \'daf(t)-nəs\ *n*

dag·ger \'dag-ər\ *n* **1** : a short weapon for stabbing **2** : a symbol † used in printing as a reference mark to indicate a death date

da·guerre·o·type \də-'ger-(ē-)ō-ˌtīp\ *n* : an early photograph produced on a metal plate [named for L. J. M. *Daguerre* 1789–1851 French painter and inventor]

dahl·ia \'dal-yə, 'däl-\ *n* : any of a genus of American herbs related to the daisies and having brightly colored flower heads and a root that is a tuber

¹dai·ly \'dā-lē\ *adj* **1 a** : occurring, done, produced, or used every day or every weekday ⟨a *daily* newspaper⟩ **b** : of or relating to every day ⟨*daily* visitor⟩ **2** : figured in terms of one day ⟨*daily* wages⟩ — **daily** *adv*

²daily *n, pl* **dailies** : a newspaper published every weekday

¹dain·ty \'dānt-ē\ *n, pl* **dainties** : something delicious to the taste : DELICACY

²dainty *adj* **dain·ti·er; -est** **1** : TASTY 1, DELICIOUS **2** : delicately pretty ⟨a *dainty* flower⟩ **3** : having or showing delicate or finicky taste ⟨a *dainty* eater⟩ — **dain·ti·ly** \'dān-tə-lē\ *adv* — **dain·ti·ness** \'dānt-ē-nəs\ *n*

dai·qui·ri \'dak-ə-rē, 'dī-kə-\ *n* : a cocktail made usually of rum, lime juice, and sugar

dairy \'de(ə)r-ē, da(ə)r-\ *n, pl* **dair·ies** **1** : a place where milk is kept and butter or cheese is made **2** : a farm devoted to the production of milk **3** : a company that sells milk and milk products **4** : milk from a cow or other domestic animal (as a goat); *also* : food (as ice cream, cheese, or yogurt) made primarily of or from milk

dairy cattle *n* : cattle raised especially to produce milk

dairy·ing \'der-ē-iŋ\ *n* : the business of operating a dairy

dairy·maid \'der-ē-ˌmād\ *n* : a woman employed in a dairy

dairy·man \-mən, -ˌman\ *n* : a person who operates a dairy farm or works in a dairy

da·is \'dā-əs\ *n* : a raised platform (as in a large room)

dai·sy \'dā-zē\ *n, pl* **daisies** **1** : any of numerous plants of the composite family having flower heads with well-developed ray flowers: as **a** : a low-growing European herb with white or pink ray flowers **b** : a tall leafy-stemmed wildflower introduced into America from Europe and having a flower head with a yellow disk in the center surrounded by long white ray flowers **2** : the flower head of a daisy **3** *cap* : a member of the Girl Scouts of the United States of America program for girls in kindergarten and first grade [Old English *dægesēage* "daisy," literally, "day's eye," from *dæg* "day" and *ēage* "eye"]

daisy wheel *n* : a disk having spokes with type on the end that is the printing part of a typewriter or printer

Da·ko·ta \də-'kōt-ə\ *n, pl* **Dakotas** *also* **Dakota** : a member of an American Indian people of the northern Mississippi valley

dale \'dā(ə)l\ *n* : VALLEY

dal·li·ance \'dal-ē-ən(t)s\ *n* **1** : ¹PLAY 2; *esp* : the act of flirting **2** : action lacking in importance or seriousness ⟨a short *dalliance* with politics⟩

dal·ly \'dal-ē\ *vb* **dal·lied; dal·ly·ing** **1** : to act playfully : TRIFLE **2 a** : to waste time ⟨*dally* at one's work⟩ **b** : LINGER 1, DAWDLE ⟨*dally* on the way home⟩ — **dal·li·er** *n*

dal·ma·tian \dal-'mā-shən\ *n, often cap* : any of a breed of dogs that have a white short-haired coat with many black or brown spots

dal se·gno \däl-'sān-yō\ *adv* — used as a direction in music to return to the sign that marks the beginning of a passage to be repeated

dalmatian

¹dam \'dam\ *n* : the female parent especially of a domestic animal [Middle English *dam, dame* "lady, female parent"]

²dam *n* **1** : a barrier preventing the flow of water **2** : a body of water held back by a dam [Middle English *dam* "barrier to hold back water"]

³dam *vb* **dammed; dam·ming** **1** : to provide or restrain with a dam ⟨*dam* a stream⟩ **2** : to stop up : BLOCK ⟨*dammed*-up feelings⟩

¹dam·age \'dam-ij\ *n* **1** : a loss or harm caused by injury to one's person or property **2** *pl* : payment in money ordered by a court for loss or injury ⟨collected *damages* for his broken arm in the accident claim⟩ **synonyms** see INJURY

²damage *vb* **dam·aged; dam·ag·ing** : to cause damage to

dam·ask \'dam-əsk\ *n* **1** : a firm shiny reversible fabric used especially for household linen **2** : a tough steel having decorative wavy lines [Middle English *damaske* "damask," derived from Latin *Damascus*, city in Syria where the fabrics were originally made] — **damask** *adj*

dame \'dām\ *n* : a woman of rank, station, or authority: as **a** *archaic* : the mistress of a household **b** : the wife or daughter of a lord **c** : a female member of an order of knighthood — used as a title before a given name [Middle English *dame* "a woman of rank or authority, lady," from early French *dame* (same meaning), from Latin *domina* "mistress, lady," feminine form of *dominus* "master, owner" — related to DAMSEL, DOMINATE, ²DON, MADAM, MADONNA, PRIMA DONNA]

¹damn \'dam\ *vb* **1** : to condemn to a punishment or fate; *esp* : to condemn to hell **2** : to condemn as bad or as a failure **3** : to swear at : CURSE

²damn *n* **1** : the saying of the word *damn* as a curse **2** : the least bit ⟨not worth a *damn*⟩

dam·na·ble \'dam-nə-bəl\ *adj* **1** : deserving condemnation ⟨*damnable* conduct⟩ **2** : very bad : TERRIBLE ⟨*damnable* weather⟩ — **dam·na·bly** \-blē\ *adv*

dam·na·tion \dam-'nā-shən\ *n* **1** : the act of damning **2** : the state of being damned

¹damp \'damp\ *n* **1** : a harmful gas especially in a coal mine **2** : MOISTURE, HUMIDITY **3** : DISCOURAGEMENT 2

²damp *vb* : DAMPEN

³damp *adj* : slightly wet **synonyms** see MOIST — **damp·ness** *n*

damp·en \'dam-pən\ *vb* **damp·ened; damp·en·ing** \'damp-(ə-)niŋ\ **1** : to check or lessen in activity or vigor : DEADEN **2** : to make or become damp — **damp·en·er** \'damp-(ə-)nər\ *n*

damp·er \'dam-pər\ *n* : one that damps: as **a** : a valve or plate (as in the flue of a furnace) for regulating the draft **b** : a device (as one of the felt-covered pieces of wood in a piano) used to deaden vibrations or oscillations **c** : a dulling or deadening influence ⟨put a *damper* on the celebration⟩

dam·sel \'dam-zəl\ *also* **dam·o·sel** *or* **dam·o·zel** \'dam-ə-ˌzel\ *n* : GIRL 1b, MAIDEN [Middle English *damesel* "damsel," from early French *dameisele* (same meaning), from Latin *domina* "lady, mistress" — related to DAME]

dam·sel·fish \'dam-zəl-ˌfish\ *n* : any of numerous often brilliantly colored marine fishes that live especially along coral reefs

dam·sel·fly \-ˌflī\ *n* : any of a group of insects that are closely related to the dragonflies, have eyes which stick out on the sides, and fold the wings above the body when at rest — compare DRAGONFLY

¹dance \'dan(t)s\ *vb* **danced; danc·ing** **1** : to engage in or perform a dance **2** : to move quickly up and down or about **3** : to perform or take part in as a dancer — **dance·able** \'dan(t)-sə-bəl\ *adj* — **danc·er** *n*

\ə\ **abut**	\au̇\ **out**	\i\ **tip**	\ȯ\ **saw**	\u̇\ **foot**
\ər\ **further**	\ch\ **chin**	\ī\ **life**	\ȯi\ **coin**	\y\ **yet**
\a\ **mat**	\e\ **pet**	\j\ **job**	\th\ **thin**	\yü\ **few**
\ā\ **take**	\ē\ **easy**	\ŋ\ **sing**	\th\ **this**	\yu̇\ **cure**
\ä\ **cot, cart**	\g\ **go**	\ō\ **bone**	\ü\ **food**	\zh\ **vision**

²dance *n* **1** : an act or instance of dancing **2** : a series of rhythmic and patterned bodily movements usually performed to music **3** : a social gathering for dancing **4** : a piece of music by which dancing may be guided **5** : the art of dancing

dan·de·li·on \'dan-də-ˌlī-ən\ *n* : any of a genus of yellow-flowered weedy plants related to the daisies; *esp* : one with long deeply toothed stemless leaves sometimes grown as a potherb

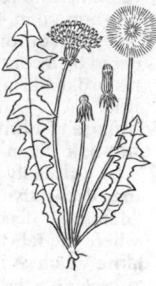

dandelion

Word History Sometimes plants are named for their resemblance, real or imagined, to animal shapes. The dandelion might not be a plant we would be quick to connect with a lion's teeth. And yet, in early French this common plant with its yellow flowers was called *dent de lion*, meaning literally "tooth of the lion." The dandelion leaves have deep notches along the edges. These make the leaves appear to have a row of sharp triangular teeth. In time the French name came to be spelled and pronounced as one word when it came into English, giving us *dandelion* today. [from early French *dent de lion* "dandelion," literally, "tooth of the lion"; *dent* derived from Latin *dens* "tooth" — related to DENTAL]

dan·der \'dan-dər\ *n* **1** : minute scales from hair, feathers, or skin that may cause allergy **2** : ¹ANGER, TEMPER ⟨the insults got my *dander* up⟩

dan·dle \'dan-dᵊl\ *vb* **dan·dled; dan·dling** \-dliŋ, -dᵊl-iŋ\ **1** : to move up and down in one's arms or on one's knee in affectionate play **2** : PAMPER, PET

dan·druff \'dan-drəf\ *n* : scaly white or grayish flakes of dead skin cells especially of the scalp; *also* : the condition marked by the excessive shedding of such flakes

¹dan·dy \'dan-dē\ *n, pl* **dandies 1** : a man who is too interested in his clothing and personal appearance **2** : a very good example of something — **dan·dy·ish** \-dē-ish\ *adj*

²dandy *adj* **dan·di·er; -est** : very good : SPLENDID, EXCELLENT

Dane \'dān\ *n* **1** : a person born or living in Denmark **2** : a person of Danish ancestry

dan·ger \'dān-jər\ *n* **1** : the state of not being protected from injury, harm, or evil **2** : something that may cause injury or harm ⟨the *dangers* of the jungle⟩

synonyms DANGER, HAZARD, PERIL, RISK mean a threat of loss, injury, or death. DANGER suggests possible harm that may or may not be avoided ⟨an animal in *danger* of becoming extinct⟩. HAZARD suggests danger from something beyond one's control ⟨the *hazards* of mining coal⟩. PERIL suggests immediate danger and a cause for fear ⟨during the tornado their lives were in *peril*⟩. RISK suggests danger that may result from a chance freely taken ⟨the *risks* that come with flying a plane⟩.

dan·ger·ous \'dānj-(ə-)rəs\ *adj* **1** : exposing to or involving danger ⟨a *dangerous* mission⟩ **2** : able or likely to cause injury ⟨*dangerous* weapons⟩ — **dan·ger·ous·ly** *adv* — **dan·ger·ous·ness** *n*

dan·gle \'daŋ-gəl\ *vb* **dan·gled; dan·gling** \-g(ə-)liŋ\ **1** : to hang loosely especially with a swinging motion **2** : to be left without proper grammatical connection in a sentence ⟨a *dangling* participle⟩ **3** : to cause to dangle : SWING — **dan·gler** \-g(ə-)lər\ *n*

Dan·iel \'dan-yəl\ *n* — see BIBLE table

¹Dan·ish \'dā-nish\ *adj* : of, relating to, or characteristic of Denmark, the Danes, or Danish

²Danish *n* **1** : the Germanic language of the Danes **2** *pl* **Danish** : a piece of Danish pastry

Danish pastry *n* : a pastry made of a rich raised dough

dank \'daŋk\ *adj* : unpleasantly moist or wet **synonyms** see MOIST — **dank·ly** *adv* — **dank·ness** *n*

dan·seur \dän-'sər\ *n* : a male ballet dancer

dan·seuse \dän-'sə(r)z, -'süz\ *n* : a female ballet dancer

daph·nia \'daf-nē-ə\ *n* : any of a genus of tiny water fleas with antennae used for movement

dap·per \'dap-ər\ *adj* **1** : being neat and trim in dress or appearance : SPRUCE **2** : being alert and lively in movement and manners

¹dap·ple \'dap-əl\ *n* **1** : any spot or patch of a dappled pattern **2** : a dappled state **3** : a dappled animal (as a horse)

²dapple *vb* **dap·pled; dap·pling** \-(ə-)liŋ\ : to mark or become marked with a dappled pattern ⟨daisies *dappled* the field⟩

dap·pled \'dap-əld\ *also* **dapple** *adj* : marked with numerous usually cloudy and rounded spots or patches of a color or shade different from their background ⟨a *dappled* fawn⟩ ⟨rested in the *dappled* shade⟩

¹dare \'da(ə)r, 'de(ə)r\ *vb* **dared; dar·ing 1 a** : to have enough courage : be bold enough to ⟨try it if you *dare*⟩ **b** — used as a helping verb ⟨no one *dared* say a word⟩ **2** : to challenge to perform an action especially as a proof of courage ⟨I *dare* you⟩ **3** : to face boldly ⟨*dared* the dangerous crossing⟩

²dare *n* : an act or instance of daring : CHALLENGE ⟨dived from the bridge on a *dare*⟩

dare·dev·il \'da(ə)r-ˌdev-əl, 'de(ə)r-\ *n* : a recklessly bold person — **daredevil** *adj*

¹dar·ing \'da(ə)r-iŋ, 'de(ə)r-\ *adj* : ready to take risks **synonyms** see ADVENTUROUS — **dar·ing·ly** \-iŋ-lē\ *adv*

²daring *n* : fearless boldness

¹dark \'därk\ *adj* **1 a** : being without light or without much light ⟨in winter it gets *dark* early⟩ **b** : not giving off light ⟨the *dark* side of the moon⟩ **2** : not light in color ⟨a *dark* suit⟩ ⟨*dark* blue⟩ **3** : not bright and cheerful : GLOOMY ⟨look on the *dark* side of things⟩ **4** : being without knowledge and culture : IGNORANT ⟨a *dark* period in history⟩ **5** : ¹SECRET 1a ⟨kept their plans *dark*⟩ **6** : not clear to the understanding ⟨puzzled us with his *dark* sayings⟩ — **dark·ish** \'där-kish\ *adj* — **dark·ly** \-klē\ *adv* — **dark·ness** \'därk-nəs\ *n*

²dark *n* **1 a** : absence of light : DARKNESS **b** : a place or time of little or no light : NIGHT, NIGHTFALL ⟨get home before *dark*⟩ **2** : a dark or deep color

Dark Ages *n pl* : the period from about A.D. 476 to about 1000; *also* : MIDDLE AGES

dark·en \'där-kən\ *vb* **dark·ened; dark·en·ing** \'därk-(ə-)niŋ\ **1** : to make or grow dark or darker ⟨the sky *darkened*⟩ **2** : to make or become gloomy or forbidding ⟨her face *darkened* in anger⟩ — **dark·en·er** \'därk-(ə-)nər\ *n*

dark horse *n* : a contestant or a political figure whose abilities and chances of winning are not known ⟨the convention nominated a *dark horse*⟩

dark lantern *n* : a lantern with an opening that can be closed to hide the light

dark·ling \'där-kliŋ\ *adj* **1** : ¹DARK 1a ⟨a *darkling* plain⟩ **2** : done or taking place in the dark

dark·room \'därk-ˌrüm, -ˌrùm\ *n* : a lightproof room used in developing photographic materials (as film and prints)

dark·some \'därk-səm\ *adj* : gloomily somber : DARK

¹dar·ling \'där-liŋ\ *n* **1** : a dearly loved person **2** : ¹FAVORITE 1

²darling *adj* **1** : dearly loved : FAVORITE **2** : very pleasing : CHARMING

darm·stadt·i·um \ˌdärm-'stat-ē-əm\ *n* : a short-lived radioactive element produced artificially — see ELEMENT table

¹darn \'därn\ *vb* : to mend with interlacing stitches ⟨*darn* socks⟩

²darn *n* : a place that has been darned

³darn *vb* : ¹DAMN 1 — **darn** \'därn\ *or* **darned** \'därn(d)\ *adj or adv*

⁴darn *n* : ²DAMN 2 ⟨not worth a *darn*⟩

darning needle *n* **1** : a long needle with a large eye for use in darning **2** : DRAGONFLY, DAMSELFLY

¹dart \'därt\ *n* **1 a** : a small pointed object that is meant to be thrown **b** *pl* : a game in which darts are thrown at a target **2** : something causing a sudden pain **3** : a stitched fold in a garment **4** : a quick movement ⟨made a *dart* for the door⟩

²dart *vb* : to move or shoot out suddenly and quickly ⟨the toad *darted* its tongue at a fly⟩ ⟨*darted* through the traffic⟩

Dar·win·ian \där-'win-ē-ən\ *adj* : of or relating to Charles Darwin, his theories especially of evolution, or his followers — **Darwinian** *n*

Dar·win·ism \'där-wə-,niz-əm\ *n* : a theory explaining the origin and continued existence of new kinds of animals and plants by means of natural selection acting on chance variations

Dar·win's finches \,där-wənz-\ *n pl* : finches of the Galápagos Islands that differ strikingly in bill shape among the various species and that were studied by Darwin

¹dash \'dash\ *vb* **1** : to knock, hurl, or thrust violently ⟨the storm *dashed* the boat against a reef⟩ **2** : to break by striking or knocking ⟨*dashed* a plate against the wall⟩ **3** : ¹SPLASH 1b, SPATTER **4** : DESTROY 1, RUIN ⟨*dash* one's hopes⟩ **5** : to affect by mixing in something different ⟨the sauce was *dashed* with vinegar⟩ **6** : to perform or finish hastily ⟨*dash* off a letter⟩ **7** : to move with sudden speed ⟨*dashed* upstairs⟩ — **dash·er** *n*

²dash *n* **1** : a sudden burst or splash ⟨a *dash* of cold water⟩ **2 a** : a stroke of a pen **b** : a punctuation mark — that is used chiefly to indicate a break in the thought or structure of a sentence **3** : a small usually special and noticeable addition ⟨add a *dash* of salt⟩ **4** : liveliness in style and action ⟨a leader of *dash* and vigor⟩ **5 a** : a sudden rush or attempt ⟨made a *dash* for the exit⟩ **b** : a short fast race **6** : a long click or buzz forming a letter or part of a letter (as in Morse code) **7** : DASHBOARD 2

dash·board \'dash-,bō(ə)rd, -,bȯ(ə)rd\ *n* **1** : a screen on the front of a usually horse-pulled vehicle to keep out water, mud, or snow **2** : a panel across an automobile or airplane below the windshield usually containing dials and controls

dashed \'dasht\ *adj* : made up of a series of dashes

da·shi·ki \də-'shē-kē\ *n* : a usually brightly colored one-piece pullover garment [derived from *danshiki,* a native word for this garment in a language of western Africa]

dash·ing \'dash-iŋ\ *adj* **1** : noticeably bold and forceful ⟨a *dashing* attack⟩ **2** : showy and stylish especially in dress and manners ⟨made a *dashing* appearance⟩ — **dash·ing·ly** *adv*

das·tard \'das-tərd\ *n* : COWARD; *esp* : one who sneakily commits harmful acts — **das·tard·li·ness** \-lē-nəs\ *n* — **das·tard·ly** \-lē\ *adj*

da·ta \'dāt-ə, 'dat- *also* 'dät-\ *n sing or pl* **1** : facts about something that can be used in calculating, reasoning, or planning **2** : information in numerical form for use especially in a computer

data bank *n* : DATABASE

da·ta·base \'dāt-ə-,bās, 'dat- *also* 'dät-\ *n* : a collection of data that is organized especially to be used by a computer

data processing *n* : the action or process of putting data into a computer and having the computer use it to produce a desired result

¹date \'dāt\ *n* **1** : the oblong edible fruit of a tall Old World palm **2** : the palm that produces dates — called also *date palm*

dashiki

Word History The word *date* that means "the fruit of the palm" and the word *date* that means "the time of an event" look alike. They are not related to each other, though. And neither one is related to the word *day.* The word for the fruit can be traced back to the Greek word *daktylos,* originally meaning "finger" and "toe." No one knows just how the fruit came to be called by the word for finger. It may be because of its small size and shape or because of the long slender shape of the palm leaves. Or it may be that this word *daktylos* was the closest Greek word to the sound of a word for the fruit borrowed from another language. The word for "the time of an event" comes to us from Latin, but the Latin word did not mean either "day" or "time." *Date* derives from the Latin phrase *data Romae,* meaning "given at Rome," an expression used just before the date on letters and documents. The word *data* is from the Latin word *dare* "to give." In later Latin, the word *data* came to be used alone to stand for the date, and it came into English as *date.* [Middle English *date* "fruit of the palm," from early French *date* (same meaning), derived from Latin *dactylus* "date," from Greek *daktylos* "date," literally, "finger"]

²date *n* **1 a** : the time at which an event occurs **b** : a statement giving the time of doing or making (as of a coin or check) **2** : DURATION **3** : the period of time to which something belongs **4 a** : APPOINTMENT 3; *esp* : a social engagement between two persons that often has a romantic character **b** : a person with whom one has a social engagement [Middle English *date* "time of an event," from early French *date* (same meaning), derived from Latin *data (Romae)* "given (at Rome)," a phrase used in putting the date on documents, derived from *dare* "to give" — see *Word History* at ¹DATE] — **to date** : up to the present moment ⟨have received no complaints *to date*⟩

³date *vb* **dat·ed; dat·ing** **1** : to record the date of or on ⟨*date* a letter⟩ **2** : to show or find out the date, age, or period of ⟨the architecture *dates* the house⟩ ⟨*dating* geological periods⟩ **3** : to make or have a date with **4 a** : to come into existence : ORIGINATE ⟨*dates* from the sixth century⟩ **b** : to go as far back : EXTEND ⟨*dating* back to childhood⟩ **5** : to show qualities typical of a past period ⟨such formality is *dated*⟩ — **dat·able** *also* **date·able** \'dāt-ə-bəl\ *adj* — **dat·er** *n*

date·less \'dāt-ləs\ *adj* **1** : ENDLESS 1 **2** : having no date **3** : too ancient to be dated **4** : not restricted to a particular time or date

date line *n* : INTERNATIONAL DATE LINE

date rape *n* : rape committed by the victim's date

da·tive \'dāt-iv\ *adj* : of, relating to, or being the grammatical case that marks typically the indirect object of a verb or the object of some prepositions — **dative** *n*

da·tum \'dāt-əm, 'dat-, 'dät-\ *n, pl* **da·ta** \-ə\ *or* **datums** : something used as a basis for reasoning or arriving at a conclusion or for calculating or measuring

¹daub \'dȯb, 'däb\ *vb* **1** : to cover with soft sticky matter : PLASTER **2** : to coat with a dirty substance **3** : to apply coloring material thickly and heavily to — **daub·er** *n*

²daub *n* **1** : something daubed on **2** : a quickly and carelessly done picture

¹daugh·ter \'dȯt-ər\ *n* **1 a** : a female offspring especially of parents that are human beings **b** : a female adopted child **2** : something considered as a daughter **3** : a form of an element that is the product of the radioactive decay of another element — **daugh·ter·ly** \-lē\ *adj*

\ə\ **abut**	\au̇\ **out**	\i\ **tip**	\ȯ\ **saw**	\u̇\ **foot**
\ər\ **further**	\ch\ **chin**	\ī\ **life**	\ȯi\ **coin**	\y\ **yet**
\a\ **mat**	\e\ **pet**	\j\ **job**	\th\ **thin**	\yü\ **few**
\ā\ **take**	\ē\ **easy**	\ŋ\ **sing**	\th\ **this**	\yu̇\ **cure**
\ä\ **cot, cart**	\g\ **go**	\ō\ **bone**	\ü\ **food**	\zh\ **vision**

²**daughter** adj **1** : having the characteristics or relationship of a daughter ⟨daughter cities⟩ **2** : being first generation offspring ⟨daughter cells⟩

daugh·ter–in–law \'dȯt-ə-rən-ˌlȯ, -ərn-ˌlȯ\ n, pl **daughters–in–law** \-ər-zən-\ : the wife of one's son

daunt \'dȯnt, 'dänt\ vb : to lessen the courage of : make afraid

daunt·ing \'dȯnt-iŋ\ adj : tending to overwhelm or intimidate ⟨a daunting task⟩ — **daunt·ing·ly** adv

daunt·less \'dȯnt-ləs, 'dänt-\ adj : FEARLESS, UNDAUNTED — **daunt·less·ly** adv — **daunt·less·ness** n

dau·phin \'dȯ-fən\ n, often cap : the eldest son of a king of France

dav·en·port \'dav-ən-ˌpō(ə)rt, 'dav-ᵊm-, -pȯ(ə)rt\ n : a large upholstered sofa

da·vit \'dā-vət, 'dav-ət\ n : one of a pair of posts with curved arms having ropes and pulleys attached and used especially on ships to raise and lower small boats

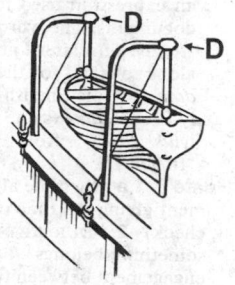

D davit

Da·vy Jones's locker \ˌdā-vē-ˌjōnz(-əz)-\ n : the bottom of the sea [from *Davy Jones,* a name used by sailors to represent the spirit of the sea]

daw \'dȯ\ n : JACKDAW

daw·dle \'dȯd-ᵊl\ vb **daw·dled**; **daw·dling** \'dȯd-liŋ, -ᵊl-iŋ\ **1** : to spend time wastefully or idly : LINGER ⟨dawdled over her homework⟩ **2** : to move slowly and aimlessly : LOITER ⟨dawdled on the way back⟩ **3** : ²IDLE 1 ⟨dawdle the time away⟩ — **daw·dler** \'dȯd-lər, -ᵊl-ər\ n

¹**dawn** \'dȯn, 'dän\ vb **1** : to begin to grow light as the sun rises ⟨waited for the day to dawn⟩ **2** : to begin to appear or develop ⟨a smile dawned on her face⟩ **3** : to begin to be understood ⟨the solution dawned on him⟩

²**dawn** n **1** : the first appearance of light in the morning **2** : a first appearance : BEGINNING ⟨the dawn of a new age⟩

day \'dā\ n **1 a** : the time of light between one night and the next **b** : DAYLIGHT **2 a** : the time the earth takes to make one turn on its axis **b** : the time required for a heavenly body to turn once on its axis ⟨a lunar day⟩ **3** : a period of 24 hours beginning at midnight **4** : a specified day or date ⟨the day of the picnic⟩ ⟨their wedding day⟩ **5** : a specified time or period : AGE ⟨in grandmother's day⟩ **6** : the conflict or dispute of the day ⟨fought hard and won the day⟩ **7** : the time set apart by custom or law for work ⟨the eight-hour day⟩

day·bed \'dā-ˌbed\ n : a couch that can be converted into a bed

day·break \-ˌbrāk\ n : ²DAWN 1

day care n **1** : supervision of and care for children or disabled adults that is provided during the day by a person or organization **2** : a program, facility, or organization offering day care

¹**day·dream** \'dā-ˌdrēm\ n : a dreamy sequence of usually happy or pleasant imaginings

²**daydream** vb : to have a daydream — **day·dream·er** n

day laborer n : one who works by the day or for daily wages especially as an unskilled laborer

day·light \'dā-ˌlīt\ n **1** : the light of day **2** : DAYTIME **3** : ²DAWN 1 **4** : knowledge or understanding of something that has been unclear ⟨began to see daylight on the problem⟩

daylight saving time n : time usually one hour ahead of standard time

day·lily \'dā-ˌlil-ē\ n : any of various plants related to the lilies that have short-lived flowers and are widespread in cultivation and in the wild after escaping from cultivation

Day of Atonement : YOM KIPPUR

day·time \'dā-ˌtīm\ n : the period of daylight

day-to-day \'dāt-ə-ˌdā\ adj **1** : taking place, made, or done in the course of days ⟨day-to-day problems⟩ **2** : providing for a day at a time with little thought of the future ⟨a day-to-day existence⟩

¹**daze** \'dāz\ vb **dazed**; **daz·ing** **1** : to stun especially by a blow ⟨the boxer was dazed by blows to the head⟩ **2** : to dazzle with light

²**daze** n : the state of being dazed

daz·zle \'daz-əl\ vb **daz·zled**; **daz·zling** \-(ə-)liŋ\ **1** : to overpower with light ⟨the desert sunlight dazzled us⟩ **2** : to impress greatly or confuse with brilliance ⟨dazzled the crowds with fiery speeches⟩ — **dazzle** n — **daz·zler** \-(ə-)lər\ n — **daz·zling·ly** \-(ə-)liŋ-lē\ adv

DDT \ˌdēd-(ˌ)ē-'tē\ n : a colorless formerly used insecticide that is poisonous to many animals with backbones

de- prefix **1** : do the opposite of ⟨decode⟩ **2 a** : remove a specified thing) from ⟨delouse⟩ **b** : remove from (a specified thing) ⟨dethrone⟩ **3** : reduce ⟨degrade⟩ [derived from Latin de- "from, down, away" and Latin dis-, literally, "apart"]

dea·con \'dē-kən\ n **1** : a member of the Christian clergy next below a priest **2** : a church member in various Christian churches who has special duties

dea·con·ess \'dē-kə-nəs\ n : a woman in various Christian churches who is chosen to assist in the church ministry

de·ac·ti·vate \(')dē-'ak-tə-ˌvāt\ vb : to make inactive or ineffective — **de·ac·ti·va·tion** \(ˌ)dē-ˌak-tə-'vā-shən\ n

¹**dead** \'ded\ adj **1** : deprived of life : no longer alive **2 a** : having the appearance of death : DEATHLY ⟨in a dead faint⟩ **b** : ¹NUMB 1 **c** : very tired ⟨the trip was really tiring; I'm dead⟩ **d** : not reacting : INSENSITIVE ⟨dead to pity⟩ **e** : burned out : grown cold ⟨dead coals⟩ **3 a** : not naturally having life : INANIMATE ⟨dead matter⟩ **b** : no longer producing or functioning ⟨dead battery⟩ **4 a** : no longer in use or effect : OBSOLETE ⟨dead language⟩ **b** : no longer active : EXTINCT ⟨dead volcano⟩ **c** : not lively ⟨a dead party⟩ **d** : lacking in commercial activity : QUIET **e** : lacking spring ⟨dead tennis ball⟩ **f** : being out of action or out of use ⟨a dead telephone line⟩ **g** : being out of play ⟨a dead ball⟩ **5** : not running or circulating : STAGNANT ⟨dead air⟩ **6 a** : absolutely uniform ⟨the dead level of the prairie⟩ **b** : UNERRING, EXACT ⟨a dead shot⟩ ⟨dead center of the target⟩ **c** : being sudden and complete ⟨a dead stop⟩ — **dead·ness** n — **over one's dead body** : only by overcoming one's utter and determined resistance

²**dead** n, pl **dead** **1** pl : those that are dead ⟨the living and the dead⟩ **2** : the time of greatest quiet or least activity ⟨dead of night⟩ ⟨dead of winter⟩

³**dead** adv **1** : to the highest degree ⟨dead right⟩ **2** : suddenly and completely ⟨stopped dead⟩ **3** : ²STRAIGHT ⟨dead ahead⟩

dead·beat \'ded-ˌbēt\ n : one who fails to pay his or her debts

dead bolt n : a lock bolt that is moved by turning a knob or key

dead·en \'ded-ᵊn\ vb **dead·ened**; **dead·en·ing** \'ded-niŋ, -ᵊn-iŋ\ : to reduce or weaken in strength or feeling : DULL ⟨deaden pain with drugs⟩

dead–end \ˌded-ˌend\ adj **1 a** : having no opportunities for advancement ⟨a dead-end job⟩ **b** : lacking an exit ⟨dead-end street⟩ **2** : UNRULY ⟨dead-end kids⟩

dead end n : an end (as of a street) without an exit

dead heat n : a contest in which two or more competitors tie

dead letter n **1** : something that has lost its force or authority without being abolished **2** : a letter that cannot be delivered or returned by the post office

dead·line \'ded-ˌlīn\ n : a date or time before which something must be done

dead·lock \-ˌläk\ n : a stopping of action because both sides in a struggle are equally powerful and neither will give in — **deadlock** vb

¹**dead·ly** \'ded-lē\ adj **dead·li·er; -est** **1** : likely to cause or capable of causing death ⟨a *deadly* weapon⟩ **2 a** : aiming to kill or destroy ⟨a *deadly* enemy⟩ **b** : very accurate : UNERRING ⟨a *deadly* marksman⟩ **3** : very great : EXTREME ⟨a *deadly* bore⟩ — **dead·li·ness** n

synonyms DEADLY, MORTAL, FATAL, LETHAL mean causing or capable of causing death. DEADLY applies to known or likely causes of death ⟨a *deadly* disease⟩. MORTAL suggests that death has occurred or will certainly occur ⟨a *mortal* wound⟩. FATAL stresses the necessity of what has in fact resulted in death or destruction ⟨the *fatal* consequence of their error⟩. LETHAL applies especially to something that is bound to cause death or exists for the destruction of life ⟨*lethal* gas⟩.

²**deadly** adv **1** : suggesting death ⟨*deadly* pale⟩ **2** : to a very great degree ⟨*deadly* dull⟩

deadly nightshade n : BELLADONNA 1

deadly sin n : one of seven sins of pride, covetousness, lust, anger, gluttony, envy, and sloth considered in Christianity to be very serious and believed to cause other sins

dead march n : a solemn march for a funeral

dead·pan \'ded-ˌpan\ n : a face that shows no emotion — **deadpan** adj or adv

dead reckoning n : calculation of the position of a ship or aircraft from the distance it has covered and the direction it has traveled without taking observations of the sun, stars, or moon

dead·weight \'ded-ˈwāt\ n : the full weight of a mass that is not moving

dead·wood \-ˌwu̇d\ n **1** : wood that is dead on a tree **2** : useless material or unproductive persons

deaf \'def\ adj **1** : wholly or partly unable to hear **2** : unwilling to hear or listen ⟨*deaf* to all suggestions⟩ — **deaf·ness** n

deaf·en \'def-ən\ vb **deaf·ened; deaf·en·ing** \-(ə-)niŋ\ : to make deaf — **deaf·en·ing·ly** \-(ə-)niŋ-lē\ adv

deaf–mute \'def-ˌmyüt\ n, often offensive : a deaf person who cannot speak or has not been taught to speak

¹**deal** \'dē(ə)l\ n **1** : a large or indefinite amount or extent ⟨means a great *deal*⟩ **2 a** : the act or right of passing out cards to players in a card game **b** : ¹HAND 11b

²**deal** vb **dealt** \'delt\; **deal·ing** \'dē-liŋ\ **1** : to give as one's portion : DISTRIBUTE ⟨*deal* out sandwiches⟩ ⟨*deal* the cards⟩ **2** : ¹GIVE 9a ⟨*dealt* him a blow⟩ **3** : to have to do : TREAT ⟨the book *deals* with education⟩ **4** : to take action ⟨*deal* with offenders⟩ **5 a** : to engage in bargaining : TRADE **b** : to sell or distribute something as a business ⟨*deals* in insurance⟩ — **deal·er** \'dē-lər\ n

³**deal** n **1 a** : an act of dealing : TRANSACTION **b** : the result of bargaining : a mutual agreement ⟨make a *deal* for a used car⟩ **2** : treatment received ⟨a dirty *deal*⟩ **3** : an arrangement for the advantage of all involved

dealing n **1** pl : friendly or business relations ⟨*dealings* with an automobile agency⟩ **2** : a way of acting or of doing business ⟨fair *dealing*⟩

dean \'dēn\ n **1** : the head of the chapter of a cathedral church **2 a** : the head of a division, faculty, college, or school of a university **b** : a college or secondary school administrator in charge of counseling or disciplining students **3** : the senior member of a group ⟨the *dean* of the diplomatic corps⟩ — **dean·ship** \-ˌship\ n

¹**dear** \'di(ə)r\ adj **1** : highly valued : PRECIOUS **2** — used as a form of address in letters and sometimes in speech ⟨*Dear* Sir⟩ **3** : high-priced : EXPENSIVE **4** : deeply and earnestly felt ⟨my *dearest* wish⟩ — **dear** adv — **dear·ly** adv — **dear·ness** n

²**dear** n : a loved one : DARLING

dearth \'dərth\ n : SCARCITY, LACK

death \'deth\ n **1** : the permanent stopping of all the vital bodily activities (as the beating of the heart and working of the brain) : the end of life **2** : the cause of loss of life ⟨drinking was the *death* of him⟩ **3** cap : the destroyer of life represented usually as a skeleton with a scythe **4** : the state of being dead **5** : DESTRUCTION 1, EXTINCTION — **death·like** \-ˌlīk\ adj

death·bed \-ˌbed\ n **1** : the bed in which a person dies **2** : the last hours of life

death·blow \-ˌblō\ n : a destructive or killing stroke or event

death cap n : a very poisonous mushroom that varies in color from pure white to olive to yellow and has an obvious swollen covering about the base — called also *death cup*

death·less \'deth-ləs\ adj : ¹IMMORTAL, IMPERISHABLE ⟨*deathless* fame⟩ — **death·less·ness** n

death·ly \'deth-lē\ adj **1** : causing death or destruction **2** : of, relating to, or suggestive of death ⟨a *deathly* paleness⟩ — **deathly** adv

death rate n : the proportion of deaths in a population that is often expressed as the number of individuals that die in a year per thousand individuals in the population at the beginning of the year

death cap

death ray n : a weapon that generates an intense beam of particles or radiation by which it destroys its target

death's–head \'deths-ˌhed\ n : a human skull representing death

death trap n : an object or situation likely to cause death ⟨that old elevator is a *death trap*⟩

¹**death·watch** \'deth-ˌwäch\ n : a small insect (as a beetle) that makes a ticking sound

²**deathwatch** n : a watch kept over the dead or dying

deb \'deb\ n : DEBUTANTE

de·ba·cle also **dé·bâ·cle** \di-'bäk-əl, -'bak-\ n : a great disaster or complete failure ⟨the army's retreat was a *debacle*⟩

de·bar \di-'bär\ vb **de·barred; de·bar·ring** : to prevent from having or doing something — **de·bar·ment** \-mənt\ n

de·bark \di-'bärk\ vb : to go or put ashore from a ship — **de·bar·ka·tion** \ˌdē-ˌbär-'kā-shən\ n

de·base \di-'bās\ vb **de·based; de·bas·ing** : to lower in character, dignity, quality, or value — **de·base·ment** \-mənt\ n — **de·bas·er** n

de·bat·able \di-'bāt-ə-bəl\ adj : open to question or dispute ⟨a *debatable* decision⟩ — **de·bat·ably** \-blē\ adv

¹**de·bate** \di-'bāt\ n : a verbal argument: as **a** : the discussion of a motion before a legislature **b** : a regulated discussion of a problem between two matched sides

²**debate** vb **de·bat·ed; de·bat·ing** **1** : to discuss or examine a question often publicly by presenting and considering arguments on both sides **2** : to take part in a debate **3** : to present or consider the reasons for and against : CONSIDER **synonyms** see DISCUSS — **de·bat·er** n

¹**de·bauch** \di-'bȯch, -'bäch\ vb : to lead away from virtue or morality : CORRUPT — **de·bauch·er** n

²**debauch** n : an act, occasion, or period of debauchery

de·bauch·ery \di-'bȯch-(ə-)rē, -'bäch-\ n, pl **-er·ies** : extreme and unreasonable involvement in physical pleasures

\ə\ **abut**	\au̇\ **out**	\i\ **tip**	\ȯ\ **saw**	\u̇\ **foot**
\ər\ **further**	\ch\ **chin**	\ī\ **life**	\ȯi\ **coin**	\y\ **yet**
\a\ **mat**	\e\ **pet**	\j\ **job**	\th\ **thin**	\yü\ **few**
\ā\ **take**	\ē\ **easy**	\ŋ\ **sing**	\th\ **this**	\yu̇\ **cure**
\ä\ **cot, cart**	\g\ **go**	\ō\ **bone**	\ü\ **food**	\zh\ **vision**

de·bil·i·tate \di-'bil-ə-ˌtāt\ *vb* **-tat·ed; -tat·ing** : to reduce the strength of : WEAKEN — **de·bil·i·ta·tion** \-ˌbil-ə-'tā-shən\ *n*

de·bil·i·ty \di-'bil-ət-ē\ *n, pl* **-ties** : a weakened state

¹**deb·it** \'deb-ət\ *vb* : to enter as a debit : charge with or as a debt

²**debit** *n* : an entry in an account representing an amount paid out or owed

debit card *n* : a card like a credit card but by which money is withdrawn from the holder's bank account immediately at the time of a transaction (as a purchase)

deb·o·nair \ˌdeb-ə-'na(ə)r, -'ne(ə)r\ *adj* : gracefully charming ⟨a *debonair* manner⟩ [Middle English *debonere* "courteous, debonair," from early French *deboneire* (same meaning), from earlier phrase *de bon aire* "of good family"] — **deb·o·nair·ly** *adv* — **deb·o·nair·ness** *n*

de·brief \di-'brēf, 'dē-\ *vb* : to question (as an astronaut) on return from a mission or assignment in order to obtain useful information

de·bris \də-'brē, dā-; 'dā-ˌbrē\ *n, pl* **de·bris** \-'brēz, -ˌbrēz\ **1** : the remains of something broken down or destroyed : RUINS **2** : an accumulation of fragments of rock **3** : something discarded : RUBBISH

debt \'det\ *n* **1** : ¹SIN 1, TRESPASS **2** : something owed to another : a thing or amount due ⟨pay a *debt* of $10⟩ **3** : a condition of owing ⟨hopelessly in *debt*⟩

debt·or \'det-ər\ *n* **1** : SINNER **2** : one that owes a debt

de·bug \(')dē-'bəg\ *vb* : to remove mistakes from ⟨*debug* a computer program⟩

de·bunk \(')dē-'bəŋk\ *vb* : to expose the falseness in ⟨*debunk* popular myths⟩ — **de·bunk·er** *n*

¹**de·but** \'dā-ˌbyü, dā-'byü\ *n* **1** : a first public appearance ⟨my *debut* as a pianist⟩ **2** : a formal entrance into society

²**debut** *vb* **1** : to make a debut **2** : to present to society for the first time ⟨*debut* a new product⟩

deb·u·tante \'deb-yu̇-ˌtänt\ *n* : a young woman making her debut

deca- *or* **dec-** *or* **deka-** *or* **dek-** *combining form* : ten [derived from Greek *deka* "ten"]

de·cade \'dek-ˌād, -əd; de-'kād; *sense 3 is usually* 'dek-əd\ *n* **1** : a group or set of 10 **2** : a period of 10 years **3** : a part of the rosary made up mainly of 10 Hail Marys

dec·a·dence \'dek-əd-ən(t)s *also* di-'kād-ᵊn(t)s\ *n* **1** : a falling off in quality or strength : a sinking to a lower state or level **2** : the tendency to give in to one's desires for comfort and pleasure — **dec·a·dent** \'dek-əd-ənt *also* di-'kād-ᵊnt\ *adj* — **decadent** *n* — **dec·a·dent·ly** *adv*

de·caf \'dē-ˌkaf\ *n* : decaffeinated coffee

de·caf·fein·at·ed \(')dē-'kaf-(ē-)ə-ˌnāt-əd\ *adj* : having the caffeine removed ⟨*decaffeinated* coffee⟩

deca·gon \'dek-ə-ˌgän\ *n* : a polygon of 10 angles and 10 sides

deca·gram \-ˌgram\ *n* : DEKAGRAM

de·cal \'dē-ˌkal, di-'kal, 'dek-əl\ *n* : a picture, design, or label made to be transferred (as to glass) from specially prepared paper [a shortened form of earlier *decalcomania* "the art of transferring pictures," from French *décalcomanie* (same meaning), from *décalquer* "to copy by tracing" and *manie* "mania, craze"]

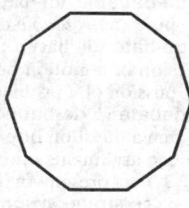
decagon

deca·li·ter \'dek-ə-ˌlēt-ər\ *n* : DEKALITER

dec·a·logue \'dek-ə-ˌlóg, -ˌläg\ *n* **1** *cap* : TEN COMMANDMENTS **2** : a basic set of rules that must be obeyed

deca·me·ter \'dek-ə-ˌmēt-ər\ *n* : DEKAMETER

de·camp \di-'kamp\ *vb* **1** : to pack up gear and leave a camp **2** : to depart suddenly : ABSCOND ⟨*decamped* with the funds⟩ — **de·camp·ment** \-mənt\ *n*

de·cant \di-'kant\ *vb* : to pour from one container into another — **de·can·ta·tion** \ˌdē-ˌkan-'tā-shən\ *n*

de·cant·er \di-'kant-ər\ *n* : an ornamental glass bottle used especially for serving wine

de·cap·i·tate \di-'kap-ə-ˌtāt\ *vb* **-tat·ed; -tat·ing** : to cut off the head of : BEHEAD [derived from Latin *decapitare* "to cut off the head of," from *de-* "from, away" and *caput* "head" — related to CAPITAL] — **de·cap·i·ta·tion** \-ˌkap-ə-'tā-shən\ *n*

de·cath·lon \di-'kath-lən, -ˌlän\ *n* : an athletic contest in which each competitor takes part in each of a series of 10 track-and-field events

¹**de·cay** \di-'kā\ *vb* **1** : to lose soundness, health, strength, or vigor **2** : to go through or cause to go through decomposition ⟨a radioactive element *decays*⟩ ⟨apples that *decayed* in storage⟩

²**decay** *n* **1** : gradual loss of strength, soundness, health, or vigor **2** : ²ROT 1 **3** : a natural decrease in the number of radioactive atoms in radioactive material

de·cease \di-'sēs\ *n* : DEATH 1 — **decease** *vb*

¹**de·ceased** \di-'sēst\ *n, pl* **deceased** : a dead person ⟨the will of the *deceased*⟩

²**deceased** *adj* : no longer living ⟨his *deceased* grandparents⟩

de·ce·dent \di-'sēd-ᵊnt\ *n* : a deceased person — used chiefly in law

de·ceit \di-'sēt\ *n* **1** : the act or practice of deceiving : DECEPTION **2** : an attempt or scheme to deceive : TRICK **3** : the quality of being deceitful

de·ceit·ful \di-'sēt-fəl\ *adj* **1** : practicing or tending to practice trickery **2** : showing or containing deceit or fraud : DECEPTIVE ⟨a *deceitful* answer⟩ — **de·ceit·ful·ly** \-fə-lē\ *adv* — **de·ceit·ful·ness** \-fəl-nəs\ *n*

de·ceive \di-'sēv\ *vb* **de·ceived; de·ceiv·ing** **1** : to cause to believe what is untrue : MISLEAD ⟨*deceived* the customer about the condition of the car⟩ **2** : to use or practice deceit — **de·ceiv·er** *n* — **de·ceiv·ing·ly** \-'sē-viŋ-lē\ *adv*

de·cel·er·ate \(')dē-'sel-ə-ˌrāt\ *vb* **-at·ed; -at·ing** : to move or cause to move at decreasing speed : slow down — **de·cel·er·a·tion** \(ˌ)dē-ˌsel-ə-'rā-shən\ *n* — **de·cel·er·a·tor** \(')dē-'sel-ə-ˌrāt-ər\ *n*

De·cem·ber \di-'sem-bər\ *n* : the twelfth month of the year

Word History In the first calendar used by the ancient Romans, the year began with the month of March. The Romans called the tenth month of the year *December*, using the Latin word *decem*, meaning "ten." When the word was borrowed into early French, it became *decembre*. That was also how it was first spelled when it came into Middle English. In time, however, the English word was changed to match the original Latin in spelling and in having a capital letter. [Middle English *Decembre, December* "last month of the year," from early French *decembre* (same meaning), from Latin *December*, literally, "tenth month," from *decem* "ten" — related to DECIMAL, DIME]

de·cen·cy \'dēs-ᵊn-sē\ *n, pl* **-cies** **1 a** : the quality or state of being decent : PROPRIETY **b** : agreement with standards of taste, quality, or proper behavior ⟨*decency*, not fear of punishment, made them behave⟩ **2** : a standard of proper behavior — usually used in plural ⟨had been taught to observe the ordinary *decencies*⟩

de·cen·ni·al \di-'sen-ē-əl\ *adj* **1** : consisting of 10 years **2** : happening every 10 years ⟨*decennial* census⟩ — **de·cen·ni·al·ly** \-ē-ə-lē\ *adv*

de·cent \'dēs-ᵊnt\ *adj* **1 a** : agreeing with standards of proper behavior, good taste, or morality **b** : clothed in a proper and suitable manner and style **2** : free from poor taste or bad manners ⟨our conversations were always *decent*, never obscene⟩ **3** : fairly good : ADEQUATE ⟨*decent* housing⟩ — **de·cent·ly** *adv*

de·cen·tral·ize \(')dē-'sen-trə-ˌlīz\ *vb* **1** : to scatter or spread out among various regional or local authorities

⟨*decentralize* the operations of the school system⟩ **2** : to cause to withdraw from urban centers to outlying areas ⟨*decentralize* industries⟩ — **de·cen·tral·i·za·tion** \(ˌ)dē-ˌsen-trə-lə-ˈzā-shən\ *n*

de·cep·tion \di-ˈsep-shən\ *n* **1 a** : the act of deceiving **b** : the fact or condition of being deceived **2** : something that deceives : TRICK

de·cep·tive \di-ˈsep-tiv\ *adj* : tending or having power to deceive : MISLEADING ⟨a *deceptive* appearance⟩ — **de·cep·tive·ly** *adv* — **de·cep·tive·ness** *n*

deci- *combining form* : tenth part ⟨*deci*gram⟩ [derived from Latin *decimus* "tenth," from *decem* "ten"]

deci·bel \ˈdes-ə-ˌbel, -bəl\ *n* : a unit for measuring the relative loudness of sounds — abbreviation *dB*

de·cide \di-ˈsīd\ *vb* **de·cid·ed; de·cid·ing** **1** : to give a judgment on ⟨*decided* the case in favor of the person accused⟩ **2** : to bring to a final end ⟨one blow *decided* the fight⟩ **3** : to cause to come to a choice or judgment ⟨their appeals *decided* me to give generously⟩ **4** : to make a choice or judgment ⟨*decided* to go⟩ — **de·cid·able** \-ˈsīd-ə-bəl\ *adj* — **de·cid·er** *n*

decided *adj* **1** : UNMISTAKABLE, CLEAR ⟨a *decided* advantage⟩ **2** : free from doubt : ¹FIRM ⟨a *decided* tone of voice⟩ — **de·cid·ed·ly** *adv* — **de·cid·ed·ness** *n*

de·cid·u·ous \di-ˈsij-ə-wəs\ *adj* **1** : falling off (as at the end of a growing period or stage of development) ⟨antlers are *deciduous*⟩ ⟨*deciduous* leaves⟩ **2** : having deciduous parts or members with deciduous parts ⟨*deciduous* trees⟩ ⟨a *deciduous* forest⟩

deciduous tooth *n* : MILK TOOTH

deci·gram \ˈdes-ə-ˌgram\ *n* — see METRIC SYSTEM table

deci·li·ter \ˈdes-ə-ˌlēt-ər\ *n* — see METRIC SYSTEM table

de·cil·lion \di-ˈsil-yən\ *n* — see NUMBER table

¹dec·i·mal \ˈdes-(ə-)məl\ *adj* **1** : based on the number 10; *esp* : expressed in, used in, or using a number system with a base of 10 especially with the decimal point ⟨a *decimal* system of writing numerals⟩ ⟨¼ in *decimal* form is .25⟩ **2** : divided into 10th or 100th units ⟨switched to a *decimal* money system⟩ [derived from Latin *decimalis* "of a tenth part," from *decimus* "a tenth part," from *decem* "ten" — related to DECEMBER, DIME]

²decimal *n* **1** : any real number expressed in base 10 **2** : a fraction in which the denominator is a power of 10 and that is expressed in decimal form ⟨the *decimal* .25 is equivalent to the common fraction $^{25}/_{100}$⟩ — called also *decimal fraction*

decimal fraction *n* : ²DECIMAL 2

decimal notation *n* : expression of a number in base 10 that uses one of the digits from 0 to 9 for each place

decimal place *n* : any of the places to the right of the decimal point in a number expressed in decimal notation ⟨5.732 has three *decimal places*⟩

decimal point *n* : the dot at the left of a decimal (as .678) or between the decimal and whole parts of a mixed number (as 3.678)

decimal system *n* **1** : a system of numbers that uses a base of 10 **2** : a system of measurement or money in which each basic unit is 10 times larger than the next smaller unit ⟨the metric system is a *decimal system*⟩

dec·i·mate \ˈdes-ə-ˌmāt\ *vb* **-mat·ed; -mat·ing** **1** : to pick by lot and kill every tenth man of ⟨the Roman army would *decimate* a legion for cowardice⟩ **2** : to destroy a large part of ⟨a population *decimated* by an epidemic⟩ — **dec·i·ma·tion** \ˌdes-ə-ˈmā-shən\ *n*

deci·me·ter \ˈdes-ə-ˌmēt-ər\ *n* — see METRIC SYSTEM table

de·ci·pher \di-ˈsī-fər\ *vb* **1** : to convert into understandable form; *esp* : DECODE **2** : to make out the meaning of despite lack of clearness ⟨*decipher* sloppy handwriting⟩ — **de·ci·pher·able** \-f(ə-)rə-bəl\ *adj* — **de·ci·pher·ment** \-fər-mənt\ *n*

de·ci·sion \di-ˈsizh-ən\ *n* **1** : the act or result of deciding ⟨the *decision* of the court⟩ **2** : promptness and firmness in deciding : DETERMINATION ⟨a leader of courage and *decision*⟩

de·ci·sive \di-ˈsī-siv\ *adj* **1** : having the power to decide ⟨the *decisive* vote⟩ **2** : UNMISTAKABLE, UNQUESTIONABLE ⟨a *decisive* victory⟩ **3** : marked by or showing decision ⟨a *decisive* manner⟩ — **de·ci·sive·ly** *adv* — **de·ci·sive·ness** *n*

¹deck \ˈdek\ *n* **1** : a platform extending from side to side in a ship and forming a floor **2 a** : a flat structure resembling the deck of a ship **b** : a flat floored roofless area adjoining a house **3** : a pack of playing cards — **on deck** : next in line

²deck *vb* **1 a** : to clothe in a fine and impressive way : ARRAY ⟨*decked* out in a new suit⟩ **b** : DECORATE 1 **2** : to provide (as a ship) with a deck

deck·hand \ˈdek-ˌhand\ *n* : a sailor who performs manual duties

de·claim \di-ˈklām\ *vb* : to speak or deliver in the manner of a formal speech — **de·claim·er** *n* — **dec·la·ma·tion** \ˌdek-lə-ˈmā-shən\ *n* — **de·clam·a·to·ry** \di-ˈklam-ə-ˌtōr-ē, -ˌtȯr-\ *adj*

dec·la·ra·tion \ˌdek-lə-ˈrā-shən\ *n* **1** : the act of declaring : ANNOUNCEMENT **2** : something declared or a document containing such a declaration ⟨the *Declaration* of Independence⟩

de·clar·a·tive \di-ˈklar-ət-iv, -ˈkler-\ *adj* : making a declaration or statement ⟨*declarative* sentence⟩

de·clare \di-ˈkla(ə)r, -ˈkle(ə)r\ *vb* **de·clared; de·clar·ing** **1** : to make known openly or officially ⟨*declare* war⟩ **2** : to state strongly ⟨*declared* his innocence⟩ **3** : to make a full statement of (taxable property or items on which duty must be paid) [Middle English *declaren* "to make clear, make known," from early French *declarer* (same meaning), from Latin *declarare* "to make clear," from *de-* "from" and *clarare* "to make clear," from *clarus* "clear, bright" — related to CLEAR] *synonyms* see ASSERT — **de·clar·a·to·ry** \-ˈklar-ə-ˌtōr-ē, -ˌtȯr-\ *adj* — **de·clar·er** *n*

de·clen·sion \di-ˈklen-chən\ *n* **1 a** : the giving of noun, adjective, or pronoun inflections especially in a specified order **b** : a class of nouns or adjectives having the same type of inflectional forms **2** : ²DECLINE 1, DETERIORATION **3** : DESCENT 4a, SLOPE — **de·clen·sion·al** \-ˈklench-nəl, -ˈklen-chən-ᵊl\ *adj*

dec·li·na·tion \ˌdek-lə-ˈnā-shən\ *n* **1** : angular distance north or south from the celestial equator measured along a great circle passing through the celestial poles ⟨the *declination* of a star⟩ **2** : a bending downward : INCLINATION **3** : the angle that the magnetic needle makes with a true north and south line

¹de·cline \di-ˈklīn\ *vb* **de·clined; de·clin·ing** **1 a** : to slope downward : DESCEND **b** : to bend down ⟨*declined* his head⟩ **2** : to pass toward a lower state or level ⟨his health *declined*⟩ ⟨their enthusiasm *declined*⟩ **3** : to draw toward a close : WANE ⟨the day *declined*⟩ **4** : to become less in amount ⟨prices *declined*⟩ **5 a** : to show unwillingness to accept, do, engage in, or agree to ⟨*declined* to run for a second term⟩ **b** : to refuse especially courteously ⟨*declined* the offer⟩ **6** : to give the declension of a noun, pronoun, or adjective — **de·clin·able** \-ˈklī-nə-bəl\ *adj* *synonyms* DECLINE, REFUSE, REJECT mean to express unwillingness to go along with a demand or request. DECLINE suggests a polite negative response ⟨*decline* an invitation to a party⟩. REFUSE suggests a forceful or absolute denial ⟨*refused* to see him at all⟩. REJECT may suggest an unwillingness even to consider a demand or request ⟨*rejected* her plan before she could explain it⟩.

\ə\ **abut**	\aú\ **out**	\i\ **tip**	\ó\ **saw**	\ú\ **foot**
\ər\ **further**	\ch\ **chin**	\ī\ **life**	\ói\ **coin**	\y\ **yet**
\a\ **mat**	\e\ **pet**	\j\ **job**	\th\ **thin**	\yü\ **few**
\ā\ **take**	\ē\ **easy**	\ŋ\ **sing**	\th\ **this**	\yú\ **cure**
\ä\ **cot, cart**	\g\ **go**	\ō\ **bone**	\ü\ **food**	\zh\ **vision**

²**decline** *n* **1** : the process of declining: **a** : a gradual sinking and wasting away **b** : a change to a lower state or level **2** : the time when something is approaching its end ⟨an empire in *decline*⟩ **3** : a downward slope

de·cliv·i·ty \di-'kliv-ət-ē\ *n, pl* **-ties 1** : downward inclination **2** : a descending slope

de·code \(')dē-'kōd\ *vb* : to change (as a secret message) from code into ordinary language — **de·cod·er** *n*

de·col·or·ize \(')dē-'kəl-ə-ˌrīz\ *vb* **-ized; -iz·ing** : to remove color from — **de·col·or·i·za·tion** \(ˌ)dē-ˌkəl-ə-rə-'zā-shən\ *n* — **de·col·or·iz·er** \(')dē-'kəl-ə-ˌrī-zər\ *n*

de·com·mis·sion \ˌdē-kə-'mish-ən\ *vb* : to remove (as a ship) from use or service

de·com·pose \ˌdē-kəm-'pōz\ *vb* **1** : to separate a thing into its parts or into simpler compounds ⟨*decompose* water into hydrogen and oxygen⟩ **2** : to break down through chemical change : ROT — **de·com·pos·able** \-'pō-zə-bəl\ *adj*

de·com·pos·er \ˌdē-kəm-'pō-zər\ *n* : an organism (as a bacterium or a fungus) that feeds on and breaks down dead plant or animal matter

de·com·po·si·tion \(ˌ)dē-ˌkäm-pə-'zish-ən\ *n* : the action or process of decomposing: as **a** : the separation of a chemical substance into simpler chemical substances and especially the elements of which it is made up ⟨*decomposition* of water into hydrogen and oxygen⟩ **b** : the breakdown of plant or animal matter ⟨*decomposition* of a dead body⟩

de·com·press \ˌdē-kəm-'pres\ *vb* **1** : to release from pressure or compression **2** : to convert (as a computer file) from compressed form to an expanded or original size — **de·com·pres·sion** \-'presh-ən\ *n*

decompression sickness *n* : ²BEND 3

de·con·tam·i·nate \ˌdē-kən-'tam-ə-ˌnāt\ *vb* : to rid of something (as radioactive material) that contaminates — **de·con·tam·i·na·tion** \-ˌtam-ə-'nā-shən\ *n*

dec·o·rate \'dek-ə-ˌrāt\ *vb* **-rat·ed; -rat·ing 1** : to make more attractive by adding something that is beautiful or becoming ⟨*decorate* a room⟩ **2** : to award a decoration of honor to ⟨*decorate* a soldier for bravery⟩ **synonyms** see ADORN

dec·o·ra·tion \ˌdek-ə-'rā-shən\ *n* **1** : the act or action of decorating **2** : something that decorates or beautifies : ORNAMENT ⟨holiday *decorations*⟩ **3** : a badge of honor (as a medal, cross, or ribbon)

Decoration Day *n* : MEMORIAL DAY

dec·o·ra·tive \'dek-(ə-)rət-iv, 'dek-ə-ˌrāt-\ *adj* : serving to decorate : ORNAMENTAL — **dec·o·ra·tive·ly** *adv* — **dec·o·ra·tive·ness** *n*

dec·o·ra·tor \'dek-ə-ˌrāt-ər\ *n* : one that decorates; *esp* : a person who decorates the interiors of buildings

dec·o·rous \'dek-ə-rəs *also* di-'kōr-əs, -'kór-\ *adj* : noticeable for proper behavior and good taste : CORRECT ⟨*decorous* conduct⟩ — **dec·o·rous·ly** *adv* — **dec·o·rous·ness** *n*

de·co·rum \di-'kōr-əm, -'kór-\ *n* **1** : agreement with accepted standards of conduct : proper behavior ⟨social *decorum*⟩ **2** : the state or condition of being calm, orderly, and well-regulated ⟨the *decorum* of the meeting⟩

¹**de·coy** \'dē-ˌkói, di-'kói\ *n* **1** : something intended to lure into a trap; *esp* : an artificial bird used to attract live birds within shooting range **2** : a person used to lead another into a trap

²**decoy** \di-'kói, 'dē-ˌkói\ *vb* : to attract by or as if by a decoy : ENTICE **synonyms** see LURE

¹**de·crease** \di-'krēs, 'dē-ˌkrēs\ *vb* **de·creased; de·creas·ing** : to make or become smaller ⟨*decrease* speed⟩ ⟨*decrease* 6 by 2⟩

²**de·crease** \'dē-ˌkrēs, di-'krēs\ *n* **1** : a process of decreasing ⟨a *decrease* in accidents⟩ **2** : the amount by which a thing decreases ⟨a *decrease* of three dollars⟩

¹**de·cree** \di-'krē\ *n* : an order or decision given by one in authority

²**decree** *vb* **de·creed; de·cree·ing** : to command or order by decree

dec·re·ment \'dek-rə-mənt\ *n* : a gradual loss or the amount lost

de·crep·it \di-'krep-ət\ *adj* : broken down with age : WORN-OUT

de·crep·i·tude \di-'krep-ə-ˌt(y)üd\ *n* : the quality or state of being decrepit : loss of strength or sturdiness especially from old age

¹**de·cre·scen·do** \ˌdā-krə-'shen-dō\ *n, pl* **-dos** : a lessening in volume of sound

²**decrescendo** *adv or adj* : with diminishing volume — used as a direction in music

de·cry \di-'krī\ *vb* **1** : to express disrespect and scorn for : BELITTLE ⟨*decry* a hero's deeds⟩ **2** : to find fault with : CONDEMN ⟨*decried* the waste of resources⟩ — **de·cri·er** \-'krī(-ə)r\ *n*

ded·i·cate \'ded-i-ˌkāt\ *vb* **-cat·ed; -cat·ing 1** : to set apart for some purpose and especially a sacred or serious purpose **2** : to address or inscribe as a compliment ⟨*dedicated* her book to her mother⟩ **synonyms** see DEVOTE — **ded·i·ca·tor** \-ˌkāt-ər\ *n*

ded·i·ca·tion \ˌded-i-'kā-shən\ *n* **1 a** : an act or rite of dedicating to a divine being or to a sacred use **b** : a setting aside for a particular purpose **2** : the inscription dedicating a literary, musical, or artistic work to a person or cause **3** : self-sacrificing devotion — **ded·i·ca·to·ry** \'ded-i-kə-ˌtōr-ē, -ˌtór-\ *adj*

de·duce \di-'d(y)üs\ *vb* **de·duced; de·duc·ing 1 a** : to draw a conclusion about particular facts or examples by applying them to a general rule or principle **b** : to determine by reasoning from a general rule or principle **2** : to trace the course or origin of — **de·duc·ible** \-'d(y)ü-sə-bəl\ *adj*

de·duct \di-'dəkt\ *vb* : to take away (an amount) from a total : SUBTRACT — **de·duct·ible** \-'dək-tə-bəl\ *adj*

de·duc·tion \di-'dək-shən\ *n* **1 a** : an act of taking away **b** : something that is or may be subtracted ⟨*deductions* from taxable income⟩ **2 a** : the drawing of a conclusion by reasoning; *esp* : reasoning in which the conclusion follows necessarily from a general rule or principle **b** : a conclusion reached by such reasoning — **de·duc·tive** \-'dək-tiv\ *adj* — **de·duc·tive·ly** *adv*

¹**deed** \'dēd\ *n* **1** : something that is done : ACT ⟨we are judged by our *deeds*⟩ **2** : a legal document by which one person transfers land or buildings to another

²**deed** *vb* : to transfer by deed

dee·jay \'dē-ˌjā\ *n* : DISC JOCKEY

deem \'dēm\ *vb* : to have an opinion : BELIEVE, SUPPOSE ⟨*deemed* it wise to go slow⟩

¹**deep** \'dēp\ *adj* **1 a** : extending far downward ⟨a *deep* well⟩ **b** : having a great distance between the top and bottom surfaces : not shallow ⟨*deep* water⟩ **c** : extending well inward from an outer or front surface ⟨a *deep* gash⟩ **d** : extending far outward from a center ⟨*deep* space⟩ **e** : occurring or located near the outer limits ⟨*deep* right field⟩ **2** : having a specified extension downward or backward ⟨a shelf 40 centimeters *deep*⟩ **3 a** : difficult to understand ⟨a *deep* book⟩ **b** : MYSTERIOUS, OBSCURE ⟨a *deep* dark secret⟩ **c** : PROFOUND 1 ⟨a *deep* thinker⟩ **d** : completely absorbed ⟨*deep* in thought⟩ **e** : being to an extreme degree : HEAVY ⟨*deep* sleep⟩ **4 a** : dark and rich in color ⟨a *deep* red⟩ **b** : having a low musical pitch or range ⟨a *deep* voice⟩ **5 a** : coming from or located well within ⟨a *deep* sigh⟩ ⟨a house *deep* in the forest⟩ **b** : covered, enclosed, or filled often to a specified degree ⟨knee-*deep* in water⟩ ⟨a road *deep* with snow⟩ — **deep·ly** *adv*

²**deep** *adv* **1** : to a great depth : DEEPLY **2** : far on : LATE ⟨read *deep* into the night⟩ **3** : near the outer limits ⟨the shortstop was playing *deep*⟩

³deep *n* **1 a :** an extremely deep place or part (as of the ocean) **b :** OCEAN 1 **2 :** the middle or most intense part ⟨the *deep* of night⟩

deep–dish \-ˌdish\ *adj* **:** baked in a deep dish ⟨a *deep-dish* pizza⟩; *esp* **:** baked in a deep dish with usually a fruit filling and no bottom crust ⟨a *deep-dish* apple pie⟩

deep·en \'dē-pən\ *vb* **deep·ened; deep·en·ing** \'dēp-(ə-)niŋ\ **:** to make or become deep or deeper

deep fat *n* **:** hot fat or oil deep enough in a cooking utensil to cover the food to be fried

deep–fry \'dēp-'frī\ *vb* **:** to cook in deep fat

deep–root·ed \'dēp-'rüt-əd, -'rüt-\ *adj* **:** deeply fixed or established ⟨a *deep-rooted* loyalty⟩

deep–sea \ˌdēp-ˌsē\ *adj* **:** of, relating to, or occurring in the deeper parts of the sea ⟨*deep-sea* fishing⟩

deep–seat·ed \'dēp-'sēt-əd\ *adj* **1 :** set or located far below the surface **2 :** firmly established ⟨a *deep-seated* tradition⟩

deep–set \-'set\ *adj* **:** set far in ⟨*deep-set* eyes⟩

deep–sky \ˌdēp-ˌskī\ *adj* **:** relating to or existing in space outside the solar system ⟨*deep-sky* objects⟩

deep space *n* **:** space outside the earth's atmosphere and especially that part lying beyond the earth-moon system

deep·wa·ter \ˌdēp-ˌwȯt-ər, -ˌwät-\ *adj* **:** of or relating to water of great depth; *esp* **:** DEEP-SEA ⟨*deepwater* sailors⟩

deer \'di(ə)r\ *n, pl* **deer :** any of a family of cloven-hoofed cud-chewing mammals (as an elk, a caribou, or a white-tailed deer) of which the males of almost all species have antlers while the females of only a few species do

Word History The meaning of a word often develops from the general to the specific. For instance, *deer* is used in modern English to mean several related forms, including white-tailed deer, mule deer, elk, and moose. The Old English *dēor*, however, could refer to any animal, tame or wild, or to wild animals in general. In time, *deer* came to be used only for wild animals that were hunted and then for the red deer, once widely hunted in England. From that usage the term has spread to related animals, becoming somewhat more general again. [Old English *dēor* "wild animal, beast"]

deer fly *n* **:** any of numerous small horseflies that are about the size of houseflies and have a painful bite

deer mouse *n* **:** any of numerous North American mice of fields and woodlands

deer·skin \'di(ə)r-ˌskin\ *n* **1 :** leather made from the skin of a deer **2 :** a garment of deerskin

deer mouse

deer tick *n* **:** a tick that transmits the bacterium causing Lyme disease

de–es·ca·late \(')dē-'es-kə-ˌlāt\ *vb* **:** to decrease in extent, volume, or scope ⟨*de-escalate* the war⟩ — **de–es·ca·la·tion** \(ˌ)dē-ˌes-kə-'lā-shən\ *n*

de·face \di-'fās\ *vb* **:** to destroy or damage the face or surface of — **de·face·ment** \-'fās-mənt\ *n* — **de·fac·er** *n*

de·fame \di-'fām\ *vb* **de·famed; de·fam·ing :** to injure or destroy the reputation of **:** speak evil of **:** LIBEL — **def·a·ma·tion** \ˌdef-ə-'mā-shən\ *n* — **de·fam·a·to·ry** \di-'fam-ə-ˌtōr-ē, -ˌtȯr-\ *adj* — **de·fam·er** *n*

¹de·fault \di-'fȯlt\ *n* **1 :** failure to take action ⟨lost a great opportunity by *default*⟩ ⟨a decision made by *default*, not by deciding⟩ **2 :** failure to do something required (as make a payment or appear in court) ⟨in *default* on a loan⟩ ⟨lost a court case by *default*⟩ **3 :** a selection to be made automatically according to a computer program when the user does not specify a choice

²default *vb* **:** to fail to carry out a contract, obligation, or duty — **de·fault·er** *n*

¹de·feat \di-'fēt\ *vb* **1 :** to destroy the value or effect of ⟨the lawyers *defeated* the will⟩ **2 :** to win a victory over ⟨*defeated* their team⟩ — **de·feat·able** \-'fēt-ə-bəl\ *adj*

²defeat *n* **1 :** the act or an instance of making ineffective by prevention of success ⟨the bill suffered *defeat* by Congress⟩ ⟨the *defeat* of one's hopes⟩ **2 a :** an overthrow of an army in battle **b :** loss of a contest (as by a team)

de·feat·ism \di-'fēt-ˌiz-əm\ *n* **:** an attitude of expecting defeat or of accepting defeat with the belief that further effort would be useless — **de·feat·ist** \-'fēt-əst\ *n or adj*

def·e·cate \'def-i-ˌkāt\ *vb* **-cat·ed; -cat·ing :** to expel feces from the bowels — **def·e·ca·tion** \ˌdef-i-'kā-shən\ *n*

¹de·fect \'dē-ˌfekt, di-'fekt\ *n* **:** a lack of something necessary for completeness or perfection **synonyms** see BLEMISH

²de·fect \di-'fekt\ *vb* **:** to desert a cause or party often in order to take up another — **de·fec·tion** \-'fek-shən\ *n* — **de·fec·tor** \-'fek-tər\ *n*

de·fec·tive \di-'fek-tiv\ *adj* **:** lacking something essential **:** FAULTY ⟨*defective* brakes⟩ — **de·fec·tive·ly** *adv* — **de·fec·tive·ness** *n*

de·fence, de·fence·man *chiefly British variant of* DEFENSE, DEFENSEMAN

de·fend \di-'fend\ *vb* **1 :** to repel danger or attack ⟨*defending* their own country⟩ **2 :** to act as attorney for **3 :** to oppose the claim of another in a lawsuit **:** CONTEST **4 :** to uphold against opposition ⟨*defended* the freedom of the press⟩

de·fend·ant \di-'fen-dənt\ *n* **:** a person who is being sued or accused in a legal action

de·fend·er \-'fen-dər\ *n* **1 :** one that defends **2 :** a player in a sport (as football) who plays a defensive position

de·fense \di-'fen(t)s; *as antonym of* "offense" *often* 'dē-ˌfen(t)s\ *n* **1 :** the act of defending **:** resistance against attack **2 :** capability of resisting attack **3 a :** means or method of defending **b :** an argument in support **4 a :** a defending party or group **b :** a defensive team **5 :** the answer made by the defendant in a legal action — **de·fense·less** \di-'fen(t)s-ləs\ *adj* — **de·fense·less·ly** *adv* — **de·fense·less·ness** *n* — **de·fen·si·bil·i·ty** \di-ˌfen(t)-sə-'bil-ət-ē\ *n* — **de·fen·si·ble** \-'fen(t)-sə-bəl\ *adj* — **de·fen·si·bly** \-blē\ *adv*

de·fense·man \-mən, -ˌman\ *n* **:** a player in a sport who is assigned to a defensive zone or position

¹de·fen·sive \di-'fen(t)-siv, 'dē-ˌfen(t)-\ *adj* **1 :** serving or intended to defend or protect ⟨a *defensive* alliance⟩ **2 :** resisting or preventing attack ⟨*defensive* behavior⟩ **3 :** of or relating to the attempt to keep an opponent from scoring in a game or contest ⟨a player with good *defensive* skills⟩ — **de·fen·sive·ly** *adv* — **de·fen·sive·ness** *n*

²defensive *n* **:** a defensive position ⟨put on the *defensive* by an attack⟩

¹de·fer \di-'fər\ *vb* **de·ferred; de·fer·ring :** POSTPONE, PUT OFF ⟨*defer* payment⟩ [Middle English *deferren, differren* "to put off, delay," from early French *differer* (same meaning), from Latin *differre* "to postpone, be different," from *dif-, dis-* "apart" and *ferre* "to bear, carry, yield" — related to ²DEFER, FERTILE, OFFER, REFER, TRANSFER] — **de·fer·ra·ble** \-'fər-ə-bəl\ *adj* — **de·fer·rer** *n*

²defer *vb* **de·ferred; de·fer·ring :** to give in or yield to another's wish or opinion ⟨*deferred* to their guest's choice of TV shows⟩ [Middle English *deferren, differren* "to entrust to another person," from early French *deferer, defferer* (same meaning), derived from Latin *deferre* "to bring down," from *de-* "down, from, away" and *ferre* "to bear, carry" — related to ¹DEFER]

\ə\ **abut**	\aú\ **out**	\i\ **tip**	\ȯ\ **saw**	\ú\ **foot**
\ər\ **further**	\ch\ **chin**	\ī\ **life**	\ȯi\ **coin**	\y\ **yet**
\a\ **mat**	\e\ **pet**	\j\ **job**	\th\ **thin**	\yü\ **few**
\ā\ **take**	\ē\ **easy**	\ŋ\ **sing**	\th\ **this**	\yú\ **cure**
\ä\ **cot, cart**	\g\ **go**	\ō\ **bone**	\ü\ **food**	\zh\ **vision**

def·er·ence \'def-(ə-)rən(t)s\ *n* : courteous, respectful, or flattering regard for another's wishes

def·er·en·tial \ˌdef-ə-'ren-chəl\ *adj* : showing or expressing deference — **def·er·en·tial·ly** \-'rench-(ə-)lē\ *adv*

de·fer·ment \di-'fər-mənt\ *n* : the act of delaying

de·fi·ance \di-'fī-ən(t)s\ *n* **1** : the act or an instance of defying : CHALLENGE **2** : a tendency to resist : contempt of opposition

de·fi·ant \di-'fī-ənt\ *adj* : full of or showing defiance : IMPUDENT, INSOLENT — **de·fi·ant·ly** *adv*

de·fi·cien·cy \di-'fish-ən-sē\ *n, pl* **-cies 1** : the quality or state of being deficient **2** : the quality or state of being inadequate; *esp* : a shortage of substances necessary to health

deficiency disease *n* : a disease (as scurvy or beriberi) caused by a lack of one or more essential substances (as a vitamin or mineral) in the diet

de·fi·cient \di-'fish-ənt\ *adj* : lacking something necessary for completeness : not up to a given or normal standard ⟨a diet *deficient* in proteins⟩ ⟨*deficient* in their knowledge of history⟩ — **de·fi·cient·ly** *adv*

def·i·cit \'def-ə-sət\ *n* : a deficiency in amount; *esp* : an excess of expenses over income

¹**de·file** \di-'fī(ə)l\ *vb* **de·filed; de·fil·ing 1** : to make filthy : DIRTY ⟨stored grain *defiled* by rats⟩ **2** : to corrupt the purity or perfection of ⟨*defile* buildings with posters⟩ **3** : DESECRATE ⟨a shrine *defiled* by the invaders⟩ **4** : ²DISHONOR 1 ⟨*defiled* our good name⟩ — **de·file·ment** \-fī(ə)l-mənt\ *n* — **de·fil·er** \-'fī-lər\ *n*

²**de·file** \di-'fī(ə)l, 'dē-ˌfīl\ *n* : a narrow passage or gorge

de·fine \di-'fīn\ *vb* **de·fined; de·fin·ing 1 a** : to determine the essential qualities of ⟨*define* the idea of loyalty⟩ ⟨*define* a circle⟩ **b** : to set forth the meaning of ⟨*define* a word⟩ **c** : to specify (as a programming task) for a computer to use ⟨*define* a procedure⟩ **2 a** : to fix or mark the limits of ⟨the boundary was clearly *defined*⟩ **b** : to make distinct, clear, or detailed especially in outline ⟨the tree was well *defined* against the sky⟩ ⟨your argument is not well *defined*⟩ [Middle English *definen* "to define, mark the limits of," Latin *definire* (same meaning), from Latin *de-* "from, away" and *finire* "to limit," from *finis* "end, limit" — related to FINAL, FINISH, INFINITY] — **de·fin·able** \-'fī-nə-bəl\ *adj* — **de·fin·er** *n*

def·i·nite \'def-(ə-)nət\ *adj* **1** : having certain or distinct limits : FIXED ⟨a *definite* period of time⟩ **2 a** : clear in meaning : EXPLICIT, EXACT ⟨a *definite* answer⟩ **b** : UNQUESTIONABLE ⟨a *definite* improvement⟩ **3** : typically designating an identified or immediately identifiable person or thing ⟨the *definite* article "the"⟩ — **def·i·nite·ly** *adv* — **def·i·nite·ness** *n*

def·i·ni·tion \ˌdef-ə-'nish-ən\ *n* **1** : an act of determining or settling the limits **2 a** : a statement of the meaning of a word or word group or a sign or symbol **b** : the action or process of defining **3 a** : the action or the power of making definite and clear **b** : CLARITY, DISTINCTNESS — **def·i·ni·tion·al** \-'nish-nəl, -ən-ᵊl\ *adj*

de·fin·i·tive \di-'fin-ət-iv\ *adj* **1** : serving to provide a final solution : DECISIVE ⟨a *definitive* victory⟩ **2** : being the most accurate and thorough ⟨the *definitive* book on the subject⟩ **3** : serving to define or specify precisely ⟨*definitive* laws⟩ — **de·fin·i·tive·ly** *adv* — **de·fin·i·tive·ness** *n*

de·flate \di-'flāt, 'dē-\ *vb* **de·flat·ed; de·flat·ing 1** : to release air or gas from **2** : to cause to move from a higher to a lower level : reduce from a state of inflation ⟨*deflate* the national economy⟩ **3** : to become deflated : COLLAPSE — **de·fla·tor** \-'flāt-ər\ *n*

de·fla·tion \di-'flā-shən, 'dē-\ *n* **1** : an act or instance of deflating : the state of being deflated **2** : a reduction in the volume of available money or credit resulting in a decline of the general price level — **de·fla·tion·ary** \-shə-ˌner-ē\ *adj*

de·flect \di-'flekt\ *vb* : to turn or cause to turn aside (as from a course, direction, or position) ⟨a bullet *deflected* by striking a wall⟩ — **de·flec·tion** \-'flek-shən\ *n*

de·fo·li·ant \(ˌ)dē-'fō-lē-ənt\ *n* : a chemical that is applied to plants and causes their leaves to drop off

de·fo·li·ate \(ˌ)dē-'fō-lē-ˌāt\ *vb* **-at·ed; -at·ing** : to deprive of leaves — **de·fo·li·a·tion** \(ˌ)dē-ˌfō-lē-'ā-shən\ *n* — **de·fo·li·a·tor** \(ˌ)dē-'fō-lē-ˌāt-ər\ *n*

de·for·es·ta·tion \(ˌ)dē-ˌfȯr-ə-'stā-shən, -ˌfär-\ *n* : the action or process of clearing an area of forests; *also* : the state of having been cleared of forests — **de·for·est** \(ˈ)dē-'fȯr-əst, -'fär-\ *vb*

de·form \di-'fȯrm, 'dē-\ *vb* : to make or become misshapen or changed in shape — **de·for·ma·tion** \ˌdē-ˌfȯr-'mā-shən, ˌdef-ər-\ *n*

de·formed *adj* : distorted in form : MISSHAPEN

de·for·mi·ty \di-'fȯr-mət-ē\ *n, pl* **-ties 1** : the state of being deformed **2** : a physical blemish or twisting out of a natural shape or condition **3** : a morally disgusting or artistically ugly imperfection

de·frag·ment \(ˌ)dē-'frag-mənt\ *vb* : to reorganize fragments of computer data on (a computer disk) into a continuous series ⟨*defragment* the hard drive⟩

de·fraud \di-'frȯd\ *vb* : to deprive of something by trickery, deception, or fraud — **de·fraud·er** \di-'frȯd-ər\ *n*

de·fray \di-'frā\ *vb* : to pay or provide for the payment of ⟨more money to *defray* expenses⟩

de·frost \di-'frȯst, 'dē-\ *vb* **1** : to free from a frozen state : thaw out ⟨*defrost* meat⟩ **2** : to free from ice ⟨*defrost* a refrigerator⟩ **3** : to remove fog or condensed moisture from ⟨*defrost* the windshield⟩

deft \'deft\ *adj* : quick and skillful in action ⟨knitting with *deft* fingers⟩ — **deft·ly** *adv* — **deft·ness** \'def(t)-nəs\ *n*

de·funct \di-'fəŋ(k)t\ *adj* : having finished the course of life or existence : DEAD, EXTINCT ⟨a *defunct* organization⟩

de·fy \di-'fī\ *vb* **de·fied; de·fy·ing 1** : to challenge to do something considered impossible : DARE ⟨the magician *defied* the audience to explain the trick⟩ **2** : to refuse boldly to obey or to yield to : DISREGARD ⟨*defy* public opinion⟩ **3** : to resist attempts at : WITHSTAND, BAFFLE ⟨a scene that *defies* description⟩ — **de·fi·er** \-'fī-(ə)r\ *n*

de·gas \(ˈ)dē-'gas\ *vb* : to free from gas

de·gen·er·a·cy \di-'jen-(ə-)rə-sē\ *n, pl* **-cies** : the state of being or process of becoming degenerate : DEGRADATION, DEBASEMENT

¹**de·gen·er·ate** \di-'jen-(ə-)rət\ *adj* : having degenerated : DEBASED, DEGRADED — **de·gen·er·ate·ly** *adv*

²**de·gen·er·ate** \di-'jen-ə-ˌrāt\ *vb* **1** : to pass from a higher to a lower type or condition : DETERIORATE ⟨the meeting *degenerated* into noisy chatter⟩ **2** : to undergo evolution toward an earlier or less highly organized biological form

³**de·gen·er·ate** \di-'jen-(ə-)rət\ *n* : a degenerate person

de·gen·er·a·tion \di-ˌjen-ə-'rā-shən, ˌdē-\ *n* **1** : a lowering of power, vitality, or essential quality to a feebler and poorer kind or state **2 a** : a change in a tissue or an organ resulting in lessened activity or usefulness ⟨kidney *degeneration* in old age⟩ **b** : a condition marked by degeneration of physical parts (as organs) present in related forms ⟨tapeworms exhibit extreme *degeneration*⟩

de·gen·er·a·tive \di-'jen-ə-ˌrāt-iv, -'jen-(ə-)rət-iv\ *adj* : of, relating to, or tending to cause degeneration ⟨a *degenerative* disease⟩

deg·ra·da·tion \ˌdeg-rə-'dā-shən\ *n* **1 a** : a reduction in rank, dignity, or standing **b** : removal from office **2** : loss of honor or reputation **3** : DEGENERATION 1, DETERIORATION

de·grade \di-'grād\ *vb* **1** : to reduce from a higher to a lower rank or degree : deprive of an office or position **2** : to lower the character of : DEBASE **3** : to reduce the complexity of a chemical compound : DECOMPOSE — **de·grad·able** \-'grād-ə-bəl\ *adj* — **de·grad·er** *n*

de·gree \di-'grē\ *n* **1** : a step or stage in a process or series ⟨advance by *degrees*⟩ **2 a** : the intensity of something as measured by degrees ⟨murder in the first *degree*⟩ **b** : one of the forms used in the comparison of an adjective or adverb **3** : a rank or grade of official or social position ⟨persons of high *degree*⟩ **4 a** : a grade of membership in an order or society **b** : a title given a student by a college, university, or professional school upon completion of a program of study ⟨a *degree* of doctor of medicine⟩ **c** : an academic title granted to honor a person who is not a student **5** : one of the divisions marked on a measuring instrument (as a thermometer) **6** : a unit of measure for angles and arcs that for angles is equal to an angle with its vertex at the center of a circle and its sides cutting off $\frac{1}{360}$ of the circumference and that for an arc of a circle is equal to $\frac{1}{360}$ of the circumference **7 a** : a line or space of the musical staff **b** : a step, note, or tone of a musical scale — **to a degree 1** : to a remarkable extent **2** : in a small way

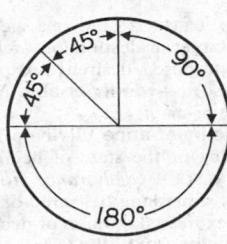

degree 6

de·hu·mid·i·fy \,dē-hyü-'mid-ə-,fī, ,dē-yü-\ *vb* : to remove moisture from (as the air) — **de·hu·mid·i·fi·er** \-,fī-(ə)r\ *n* — **de·hu·mid·i·fi·ca·tion** \-,mid-ə-fə-'kā-shən\ *n*

de·hy·drate \(')dē-'hī-,drāt\ *vb* **1** : to remove water from (as foods) **2** : to lose water or body fluids — **de·hy·dra·tion** \,dē-,hī-'drā-shən\ *n*

de·hy·dro·ge·nase \,dē-(,)hī-'dräj-ə-,nās, (')dē-'hī-drə-jə-\ *n* : an enzyme that speeds up the removal and transfer of hydrogen

de·hy·dro·ge·na·tion \,dē-(,)hī-,dräj-ə-'nā-shən, (,)dē-,hī-drə-jə-\ *n* : the process of removing hydrogen from a chemical compound

de·ice \(')dē-'īs\ *vb* : to keep free or rid of ice — **de·ic·er** *n*

de·i·fy \'dē-ə-,fī\ *vb* **-fied; -fy·ing 1 a** : to make a god of ⟨Roman emperors were often *deified*⟩ **b** : to take as an object of worship ⟨Druids *deified* oak trees⟩ **2** : to glorify as of supreme worth ⟨*deify* money⟩ — **de·i·fi·ca·tion** \,dē-ə-fə-'kā-shən\ *n*

deign \'dān\ *vb* : to think proper to one's dignity ⟨did not *deign* to reply to the rude remark⟩

de·ion·ize \(')dē-'ī-ə-,nīz\ *vb* : to remove ions from

de·i·ty \'dē-ət-ē\ *n, pl* **-ties 1 a** : DIVINITY **2 b** *cap* : GOD 1 ⟨the *Deity*⟩ **2 a** : GOD **2 b** : GODDESS 1 [Middle English *deitee* "the nature of being divine," from early French *deité* (same meaning), derived from Latin *deus* "god" — related to ADIEU, ADIOS]

dé·jà vu \,dā-,zhä-'vü, -'vue\ *n* : a feeling that one has seen or heard something before [French, literally, "already seen"]

de·ject·ed \di-'jek-təd\ *adj* : low in spirits : SAD, DEPRESSED — **de·ject·ed·ly** *adv* — **de·ject·ed·ness** *n*

de·jec·tion \di-'jek-shən\ *n* : lowness of spirits

deka- *or* **dek-** — see DECA-

deka·gram \'dek-ə-,gram\ *n* — see METRIC SYSTEM table

deka·li·ter \'dek-ə-,lēt-ər\ *n* — see METRIC SYSTEM table

deka·me·ter \'dek-ə-,mēt-ər\ *n* — see METRIC SYSTEM table

Del·a·ware \'del-ə-,wa(ə)r, -,we(ə)r, -wər\ *n, pl* **Delaware** *or* **Delawares** : a member of an American Indian people originally of the Delaware River valley

¹de·lay \di-'lā\ *n* **1** : the act of delaying : the state of being delayed ⟨start without *delay*⟩ **2** : the time during which something is delayed ⟨a *delay* of 30 minutes⟩

²delay *vb* **1** : POSTPONE, PUT OFF ⟨*delay* a trip⟩ **2** : to stop, detain, or hinder for a time ⟨*delayed* by a storm⟩ **3** : to move or act slowly — **delay·er** *n*

de·lec·ta·ble \di-'lek-tə-bəl\ *adj* **1** : highly pleasing : DELIGHTFUL **2** : DELICIOUS — **de·lec·ta·bly** \-blē\ *adv*

de·lec·ta·tion \,dē-,lek-'tā-shən, di-; ,del-ək-\ *n* **1** : ¹DELIGHT 1 **2** : something that gives pleasure : DIVERSION

¹del·e·gate \'del-i-gət, -,gāt\ *n* : a person sent with power to act for another : REPRESENTATIVE

²del·e·gate \'del-i-,gāt\ *vb* **-gat·ed; -gat·ing 1** : to entrust to another ⟨*delegate* authority⟩ **2** : to appoint as one's delegate

del·e·ga·tion \,del-i-'gā-shən\ *n* **1** : the act of delegating power or authority to another **2** : one or more persons chosen to represent others

de·lete \di-'lēt\ *vb* **de·let·ed; de·let·ing** : to eliminate especially by blotting out, cutting out, or erasing ⟨*delete* a part of the story⟩ ⟨*delete* a computer file⟩ — **de·le·tion** \di-'lē-shən\ *n*

del·e·te·ri·ous \,del-ə-'tir-ē-əs\ *adj* : HARMFUL, NOXIOUS — **del·e·te·ri·ous·ly** *adv* — **del·e·te·ri·ous·ness** *n*

delft \'delft\ *n* : a Dutch pottery with a white glaze and blue decoration [named for *Delft*, an area in the Netherlands where the pottery was first made]

delft·ware \'delf-,twa(ə)r, -,twe(ə)r\ *n* : DELFT

deli \'del-ē\ *n, pl* **del·is** : DELICATESSEN 2

¹de·lib·er·ate \di-'lib-ə-,rāt\ *vb* **-at·ed; -at·ing** : to think about carefully : consider problems and decisions carefully ⟨*deliberate* before answering⟩

Word History To weigh a decision is to think about it carefully, comparing one fact or idea with another as if by balancing them on a scale. The notion that slow and careful thought is like using a scale has given us the word *deliberate*. *Deliberate* can be traced back to the Latin verb *deliberare*, meaning "to weigh in the mind." The core of this word is the noun *libra*, meaning "a scale." A deliberate decision, therefore, is one that has been carefully weighed. [from Latin *deliberatus*, past participle of *deliberare* "to weigh in the mind," derived from *de-* "from, away" and *libra* "scale, pound" — related to EQUILIBRIUM, LIBRA]

²de·lib·er·ate \di-'lib-(ə-)rət\ *adj* **1** : decided on as a result of careful thought : carefully considered ⟨a *deliberate* judgment⟩ **2** : done or said on purpose ⟨a *deliberate* lie⟩ **3** : considering facts and arguments carefully : careful and slow in deciding ⟨a *deliberate* speaker⟩ **4** : slow in action : not hurried ⟨*deliberate* movements⟩ **synonyms** see VOLUNTARY — **de·lib·er·ate·ly** *adv* — **de·lib·er·ate·ness** *n*

de·lib·er·a·tion \di-,lib-ə-'rā-shən\ *n* **1** : the act of deliberating **2** : a discussion and consideration of the reasons for and against something **3** : the quality of being deliberate : DELIBERATENESS

de·lib·er·a·tive \di-'lib-ə-,rāt-iv, -'lib-(ə-)rət-iv\ *adj* : of, relating to, or engaged in deliberation

del·i·ca·cy \'del-i-kə-sē\ *n, pl* **-cies 1** : something pleasing to eat because it is rare or a luxury **2 a** : fineness of structure : DAINTINESS ⟨lace of great *delicacy*⟩ **b** : weakness of body : FRAILTY ⟨the *delicacy* of his health⟩ **3** : the ability to express very slight degrees of feeling (as in painting or music) **4** : consideration for the feelings of others **5** : the ability to sense or indicate very slight differences : PRECISION **6** : the tendency to be or state of being squeamish **7** : the quality or state of requiring careful treatment ⟨the *delicacy* of a situation⟩

del·i·cate \'del-i-kət\ *adj* **1** : satisfying or pleasing because of fineness or mildness ⟨a *delicate* flavor⟩ ⟨*delicate* blossoms⟩ **2** : having fineness of structure, workmanship, or texture ⟨*delicate* lace⟩ **3** : FASTIDIOUS ⟨a person of *deli-*

\ə\ abut	\au̇\ out	\i\ tip	\ȯ\ saw	\u̇\ foot
\ər\ further	\ch\ chin	\ī\ life	\ȯi\ coin	\y\ yet
\a\ mat	\e\ pet	\j\ job	\th\ thin	\yü\ few
\ā\ take	\ē\ easy	\ŋ\ sing	\th\ this	\yu̇\ cure
\ä\ cot, cart	\g\ go	\ō\ bone	\ü\ food	\zh\ vision

cate tastes⟩ **4** : easily torn or hurt; *also* : WEAK 1, SICKLY ⟨was too *delicate* to play football⟩ **5** : easily unsettled or upset ⟨a *delicate* balance⟩ **6** : resulting from or requiring skill or careful treatment ⟨*delicate* handling of a difficult situation⟩ ⟨a *delicate* operation⟩ **7** : able to sense or indicate very slight differences ⟨a *delicate* instrument⟩ — **del·i·cate·ly** *adv* — **del·i·cate·ness** *n*

del·i·ca·tes·sen \ˌdel-i-kə-ˈtes-ᵊn\ *n pl* **1** : ready-to-eat food products (as cooked meats and prepared salads) **2** *sing, pl* **delicatessens** : a store where delicatessen are sold

Word History We owe both the word *delicatessen* and the special food it represents to the German immigrants who came to this country toward the end of the 19th century. But although the food was originally German, the word was not. The Germans borrowed the word from the French. The obsolete German word *delicatessen* is a plural form of *delicatesse* and means "delicacies, ready-to-eat foods." This word was borrowed from the French word *délicatesse,* meaning "delicacy." In English, *delicatessen* originally meant only the specially-prepared food. In time, the delicatessen store where this food was sold came to be called a *delicatessen,* and a new meaning for the word was born. Now the word is often shortened to *deli.* [from obsolete German *Delicatessen* (now spelled *Delikatessen*) "specially prepared ready-to-eat foods," plural of *Delicatesse* "delicacy," from French *délicatesse* (same meaning), derived from Latin *delicatus* "delicate"]

de·li·cious \di-ˈlish-əs\ *adj* : giving great pleasure : DELIGHTFUL; *esp* : very pleasing to the taste — **de·li·cious·ly** *adv* — **de·li·cious·ness** *n*

De·li·cious \di-ˈlish-əs\ *n, pl* **De·li·cious·es** *or* **Delicious** : a sweet red or yellow apple of U.S. origin that has five bumps arranged around the end opposite the stem

¹de·light \di-ˈlīt\ *n* **1** : extreme pleasure or satisfaction : JOY **2** : something that gives great pleasure

²delight *vb* **1** : to take great pleasure ⟨*delighted* in playing guitar⟩ **2** : to give joy or satisfaction to : please greatly ⟨a book sure to *delight*⟩

de·light·ed \di-ˈlīt-əd\ *adj* : highly pleased : GRATIFIED, JOYOUS — **de·light·ed·ly** *adv* — **de·light·ed·ness** *n*

de·light·ful \di-ˈlīt-fəl\ *adj* : highly pleasing : giving delight — **de·light·ful·ly** \-fə-lē\ *adv* — **de·light·ful·ness** *n*

de·lim·it \di-ˈlim-ət\ *vb* : to fix or mark the limits of : BOUND — **de·lim·i·ta·tion** \-ˌlim-ə-ˈtā-shən\ *n*

de·lin·eate \di-ˈlin-ē-ˌāt\ *vb* **-eat·ed; -eat·ing** **1** : to indicate by lines : SKETCH **2** : to describe in sharp or vivid detail ⟨*delineate* the characters in a story⟩ — **de·lin·ea·tion** \-ˌlin-ē-ˈā-shən\ *n* — **de·lin·ea·tor** \-ˈlin-ē-ˌāt-ər\ *n*

¹de·lin·quent \di-ˈlin-kwənt\ *n* : a delinquent person

²delinquent *adj* **1** : offending by neglect or violation of duty or of law **2** : being overdue in payment ⟨a *delinquent* charge account⟩ — **de·lin·quen·cy** \-kwən-sē\ *n* — **de·lin·quent·ly** *adv*

del·i·quesce \ˌdel-ə-ˈkwes\ *vb* **-quesced; -quesc·ing** : to dissolve or melt away; *esp* : to exhibit the behavior of a deliquescent substance

del·i·ques·cent \ˌdel-ə-ˈkwes-ᵊnt\ *adj* **1** : tending to melt or dissolve; *esp* : tending to dissolve gradually by absorbing moisture from the air **2** : having repeated division into branches ⟨elms are *deliquescent* trees⟩ — **del·i·ques·cence** \-ᵊn(t)s\ *n*

de·lir·i·ous \di-ˈlir-ē-əs\ *adj* **1** : affected with, marked by, or characteristic of delirium **2** : wildly excited ⟨*delirious* fans⟩ — **de·lir·i·ous·ly** *adv* — **de·lir·i·ous·ness** *n*

de·lir·i·um \di-ˈlir-ē-əm\ *n* **1** : a mental disturbance marked by confusion, disturbed speech, and hallucinations **2** : wild excitement

de·liv·er \di-ˈliv-ər\ *vb* **de·liv·ered; de·liv·er·ing** \-(ə-)riŋ\ **1** : to set free : SAVE ⟨*deliver* us from evil⟩ **2** : HAND OVER, TRANSFER ⟨*deliver* a letter⟩ **3 a** : to assist in giving birth; *also* : to aid in the birth of **b** : to give birth to **4**

: ²UTTER 2 ⟨*deliver* a speech⟩ **5** : to send to an intended target or destination ⟨*deliver* a pitch⟩ **6** : to produce the promised, desired, or expected results ⟨*deliver* on a promise⟩ — **de·liv·er·able** \-(-ə-)rə-bəl\ *adj* — **de·liv·er·er** \-ər-ər\ *n*

de·liv·er·ance \di-ˈliv-(ə-)rən(t)s\ *n* **1** : an act of delivering or the state of being delivered; *esp* : SALVATION 3, RESCUE ⟨*deliverance* from the hands of the enemy⟩ **2** : something delivered or communicated; *esp* : a publicly expressed opinion or decision

de·liv·ery \di-ˈliv-(ə-)rē\ *n, pl* **-er·ies 1** : a delivering from something that restricts or burdens **2 a** : the act of handing over **b** : a legal transfer of right or title **c** : something delivered at one time or in one unit **3** : the action of giving birth **4** : a delivering especially of a speech **5** : manner or style of delivering

de·liv·ery·man \di-ˈliv-(ə-)rē-mən, -ˌman\ *n* : a person who delivers goods to customers usually over a regular local route

dell \ˈdel\ *n* : a secluded small valley

de·louse \(ˈ)dē-ˈlaús, -ˈlaúz\ *vb* **de·loused; de·lous·ing** : to remove lice from

del·phin·i·um \del-ˈfin-ē-əm\ *n* : any of a large genus of herbs related to the buttercups and widely grown for their flowers in showy spikes

del·ta \ˈdel-tə\ *n* **1** : the 4th letter of the Greek alphabet — Δ or δ **2** : something shaped like a capital Δ; *esp* : the triangular or fan-shaped piece of land made by deposits of mud and sand at the mouth of a river — **del·ta·ic** \del-ˈtā-ik\ *adj*

de·lude \di-ˈlüd\ *vb* **de·lud·ed; de·lud·ing** : to lead into error : mislead the judgment of : ¹DECEIVE, TRICK ⟨*deluded* by false promises⟩ — **de·lud·er** *n*

¹del·uge \ˈdel-yüj\ *n* **1 a** : an overflowing of the land by water : FLOOD **b** : a drenching rain **2** : an overwhelming amount or number ⟨a *deluge* of Christmas mail⟩

delphinium

²deluge *vb* **del·uged; del·ug·ing 1** : to overflow with water : INUNDATE, FLOOD **2** : to overwhelm as if with a deluge ⟨*deluged* with inquiries⟩

de·lu·sion \di-ˈlü-zhən\ *n* **1** : the act of deluding : the state of being deluded **2 a** : a mistaken or misleading belief **b** : a false belief that persists despite evidence proving it false and occurs especially in some mentally disturbed states — **de·lu·sion·al** \-ˈlüzh-nəl, -ən-ᵊl\ *adj*

de·lu·sive \di-ˈlü-siv, -ziv\ *adj* : deluding or likely to delude — **de·lu·sive·ly** *adv*

de·lu·so·ry \di-ˈlü-sə-rē, -zə-\ *adj* : DECEPTIVE, DELUSIVE

de·luxe \di-ˈlúks, -ˈləks, -ˈlüks\ *adj* : very luxurious or elegant ⟨a *deluxe* edition⟩

delve \ˈdelv\ *vb* **delved; delv·ing 1** : to dig or labor with a spade **2** : to make a careful or thorough search for information — **delv·er** *n*

Dem \ˈdem\ *n* : DEMOCRAT 2

de·mag·ne·tize \(ˈ)dē-ˈmag-nə-ˌtīz\ *vb* : to cause to lose magnetic properties — **de·mag·ne·ti·za·tion** \(ˌ)dē-ˌmag-nət-ə-ˈzā-shən\ *n*

dem·a·gogue *also* **dem·a·gog** \ˈdem-ə-ˌgäg\ *n* : a person who appeals to the emotions and prejudices of people in order to arouse discontent and advance his or her own political purposes — **dem·a·gog·ic** \ˌdem-ə-ˈgäg-ik *also* -ˈgäj-\ *adj* — **dem·a·gog·uery** \ˈdem-ə-ˌgäg-(ə-)rē\ *n* — **dem·a·gogy** \-ˌgäg-ē, -ˌgäj-, -ˌgō-jē\ *n*

¹de·mand \di-ˈmand\ *n* **1 a** : an act of demanding ⟨a *demand* for obedience⟩ **b** : something claimed as due ⟨a list of *demands*⟩ **2 a** : the ability and desire to purchase goods or services at a specified time and price **b** : the quantity of an article or service that is wanted at a specified price ⟨the *demand* for quality education⟩ ⟨supply and *demand*⟩ **3** : a seeking or state of being sought after ⟨tickets are in great *demand*⟩ **4** : an urgent need or requirement ⟨*demands* on her energy⟩ — **on demand** : upon request for payment; *also* : when requested or needed ⟨video *on demand*⟩

²demand *vb* **1** : to ask or call for with authority : claim as one's right ⟨*demand* payment of a debt⟩ ⟨*demand* an apology⟩ **2** : to ask earnestly or in the manner of a command ⟨the guard *demanded* the password⟩ **3** : ²NEED 2, REQUIRE ⟨an illness that *demands* constant care⟩ — **de·mand·able** \-ˈman-də-bəl\ *adj* — **de·mand·er** *n*

de·mand·ing \di-ˈman-diŋ\ *adj* : making many or difficult demands : EXACTING ⟨a *demanding* job⟩ — **de·mand·ing·ly** *adv*

de·mar·cate \di-ˈmär-ˌkāt, ˈdē-ˌmär-\ *vb* **-cat·ed; -cat·ing** **1** : to mark the limits or boundaries of **2** : to set apart : DISTINGUISH **4** — **de·mar·ca·tion** \ˌdē-ˌmär-ˈkā-shən\ *n*

¹de·mean \di-ˈmēn\ *vb* **de·meaned; de·mean·ing** : to conduct or behave (oneself) usually in a proper manner ⟨he *demeans* himself like a true gentleman⟩

²demean *vb* **de·meaned; de·mean·ing** : DEGRADE 2, DEBASE ⟨*demeaned* themselves by dishonesty⟩

de·mean·or \di-ˈmē-nər\ *n* : outward manner or behavior : CONDUCT, BEARING

de·ment·ed \di-ˈment-əd\ *adj* : MAD 1, INSANE — **de·ment·ed·ly** *adv*

de·men·tia \di-ˈmen-chə\ *n* **1** : a condition of the brain that is marked especially by a deterioration in the ability to think, reason, or remember **2** : a condition of deteriorating mental functioning

de·mer·it \di-ˈmer-ət\ *n* **1** : a quality that deserves blame : FAULT **2** : a mark placed against a person's record for some fault or offense

de·mesne \di-ˈmān, -ˈmēn\ *n* **1** : REALM 2, DOMAIN **2** : land actually possessed by the lord of an estate and not held by tenants **3 a** : the land attached to a mansion **b** : property that is land : ESTATE **c** : REGION 2a, TERRITORY

demi- *prefix* : one that partly belongs to (a specified type or class) ⟨*demi*god⟩ [derived from Latin *dimidius* "half"]

demi·god \ˈdem-i-ˌgäd\ *n* **1** : one who is partly divine and partly human **2** : an outstanding person who seems godlike

demi·john \ˈdem-i-ˌjän\ *n* : a large bottle of glass or stoneware enclosed in a basket of the same shape

de·mil·i·ta·rize \ˌdē-ˈmil-ə-tə-ˌrīz\ *vb* : to strip of military forces, weapons, or fortification ⟨a *demilitarized* zone⟩ — **de·mil·i·ta·ri·za·tion** \ˌdē-ˌmil-ə-tə-rə-ˈzā-shən\ *n*

de·mise \di-ˈmīz\ *n* **1** : DEATH 1 **2** : an ending of existence or activity ⟨the *demise* of a newspaper⟩

demi·tasse \ˈdem-i-ˌtas, -ˌtäs\ *n* : a small cup of black coffee; *also* : the cup used to serve it

demo \ˈdem-ō\ *n, pl* **dem·os** : DEMONSTRATOR 2

de·mo·bi·lize \di-ˈmō-bə-ˌlīz, (ˈ)dē-\ *vb* **1** : to dismiss from military service ⟨*demobilize* an army⟩ **2** : to change from a state of war to a state of peace — **de·mo·bi·li·za·tion** \di-ˌmō-bə-lə-ˈzā-shən, (ˈ)dē-\ *n*

de·moc·ra·cy \di-ˈmäk-rə-sē\ *n, pl* **-cies 1 a** : government by the people; *esp* : rule of the majority **b** : government in which the supreme power is held by the people and used by them directly or indirectly through representation **2** : a political unit (as a nation) that has a democratic government **3** : belief in or practice of the idea that all people are socially equal [from early French *democratie* "democracy," from Latin *democratia* (same meaning), from Greek *demokratia* "democracy," from *dēmos*

demijohn

"people, the masses" and *-kratia* "rule, government," from *kratos* "strength, power, authority" — related to EPIDEMIC]

dem·o·crat \ˈdem-ə-ˌkrat\ *n* **1** : one who believes in or practices democracy **2** *cap* : a member of the Democratic party of the U.S.

dem·o·crat·ic \ˌdem-ə-ˈkrat-ik\ *adj* **1** : of, relating to, or favoring political, social, or economic democracy **2** *cap* : of or relating to a major U.S. political party associated with policies of helping the common people and encouraging cooperation between nations **3** : of, relating to, or appealing to the common people ⟨*democratic* art⟩ **4** : favoring social equality : not snobbish — **dem·o·crat·i·cal·ly** \-i-k(ə-)lē\ *adv*

Democratic–Republican *adj* : of or relating to an early 19th century American political party preferring strict interpretation of the constitution and emphasizing states' rights

de·moc·ra·tize \di-ˈmäk-rə-ˌtīz\ *vb* **-tized; -tiz·ing** : to make democratic — **de·moc·ra·ti·za·tion** \-ˌmäk-rət-ə-ˈzā-shən\ *n*

de·mod·u·late \(ˈ)dē-ˈmäj-ə-ˌlāt\ *vb* : to get the information from (a modulated radio, laser, or computer signal) — **de·mod·u·la·tor** \-ˌlāt-ər\ *n*

de·mog·ra·phy \di-ˈmäg-rə-fē\ *n* : the statistical study of human populations — **de·mog·ra·pher** \-fər\ *n* — **de·mo·graph·ic** \ˌdē-mə-ˈgraf-ik, ˌdem-ə-\ *adj*

de·mol·ish \di-ˈmäl-ish\ *vb* **1 a** : TEAR DOWN, RAZE **b** : to break to pieces : SMASH **2** : to do away with : put an end to — **de·mol·ish·er** *n* — **de·mol·ish·ment** \-ish-mənt\ *n*

de·mo·li·tion \ˌdem-ə-ˈlish-ən, ˌdē-mə-\ *n* : the act of demolishing; *esp* : destruction by means of explosives

de·mon *or* **dae·mon** \ˈdē-mən\ *n* **1** : an evil spirit **2** *usually* daemon : an accompanying power or spirit : GENIUS **3** *usually* daemon : DEMIGOD 1 **4** : one that has a lot of energy ⟨a *demon* for work⟩ — **de·mon·ic** \di-ˈmän-ik\ *adj*

¹de·mo·ni·ac \di-ˈmō-nē-ˌak\ *also* **de·mo·ni·a·cal** \ˌdē-mə-ˈnī-ə-kəl\ *adj* **1** : possessed or influenced by a demon **2** : of, relating to, or suggestive of a demon : DEVILISH, FIENDISH ⟨*demoniac* cruelty⟩ — **de·mo·ni·a·cal·ly** \ˌdē-mə-ˈnī-ə-k(ə-)lē\ *adv*

²demoniac *n* : one possessed by a demon

de·mon·stra·ble \di-ˈmän(t)-strə-bəl\ *adj* : capable of being demonstrated or proved — **de·mon·stra·bly** \-blē\ *adv*

dem·on·strate \ˈdem-ən-ˌstrāt\ *vb* **-strat·ed; -strat·ing 1** : to show clearly **2 a** : to prove or make clear by reasoning or evidence **b** : to illustrate and explain especially with examples **3** : to show publicly the good qualities of a product ⟨*demonstrate* a new car⟩ **4** : to make a public display (as of feeling or military force) ⟨citizens *demonstrated* in protest⟩

dem·on·stra·tion \ˌdem-ən-ˈstrā-shən\ *n* **1** : an act, process, or means of demonstrating the truth of something: **a** : convincing evidence **b** : an explanation (as of a theory) by experiment **c** : a course of reasoning intended to prove that a conclusion must be true when certain conditions are accepted **d** : a showing or using of a product for sale to display its good points **2** : an outward expression or display ⟨a *demonstration* of joy⟩ **3** : a show of armed force **4** : a public display of group feelings toward a person or cause

¹de·mon·stra·tive \di-ˈmän(t)-strət-iv\ *adj* **1** : characterized or established by demonstration ⟨*demonstrative* reasoning⟩ **2** : indicating the one referred to and pointing it

\ə\ abut	\au̇\ out	\i\ tip	\ȯ\ saw	\u̇\ foot
\ər\ further	\ch\ chin	\ī\ life	\ȯi\ coin	\y\ yet
\a\ mat	\e\ pet	\j\ job	\th\ thin	\yü\ few
\ā\ take	\ē\ easy	\ŋ\ sing	\t͟h\ this	\yu̇\ cure
\ä\ cot, cart	\g\ go	\ō\ bone	\ü\ food	\zh\ vision

out from others of the same kind ⟨the *demonstrative* pronoun "this" in "this is my hat"⟩ ⟨the *demonstrative* adjective "that" in "that book"⟩ **3** : showing feeling freely ⟨a *demonstrative* greeting⟩ — **de·mon·stra·tive·ly** *adv*

²demonstrative *n* : a demonstrative word; *esp* : a demonstrative pronoun

dem·on·stra·tor \'dem-ən-ˌstrāt-ər\ *n* **1** : a person who makes or takes part in a demonstration **2** : a manufactured article (as an automobile) used for purposes of demonstration

de·mor·al·ize \di-'mȯr-ə-ˌlīz, -'mär-\ *vb* **1** : to make bad or evil **2** : to weaken in spirit or discipline ⟨fear *demoralized* the army⟩ — **de·mor·al·i·za·tion** \-ˌmȯr-ə-lə-'zā-shən, -ˌmär-\ *n* — **de·mor·al·iz·er** \-'mȯr-ə-ˌlī-zər, -'mär-\ *n*

de·mote \di-'mōt, 'dē-\ *vb* **de·mot·ed; de·mot·ing** : to reduce to a lower grade or rank — **de·mo·tion** \di-'mō-shən, 'dē-\ *n*

de·mount \(')dē-'maunt\ *vb* **1** : to remove from an attached position **2** : to take apart : DISASSEMBLE — **de·mount·able** \-ə-bəl\ *adj*

¹de·mur \di-'mər\ *vb* **de·murred; de·mur·ring** : ²OBJECT 2

²demur *n* : the act of objecting : PROTEST ⟨accepted without *demur*⟩

de·mure \di-'myu̇(ə)r\ *adj* **1 a** : quiet and polite ⟨a *demure* young lady⟩ **b** : not showy or flashy ⟨a *demure* gray dress⟩ **2** : falsely modest, reserved, or serious : COY — **de·mure·ly** *adv* — **de·mure·ness** *n*

den \'den\ *n* **1** : the shelter or resting place of a wild animal **2** : a hiding place (as for thieves) **3** : a dirty run-down place in which people live or gather ⟨*dens* of misery⟩ **4** : a comfortable room set apart usually for reading and relaxation **5** : a division of a Cub Scout pack

de·na·ture \(')dē-'nā-chər\ *vb* **de·na·tured; de·na·tur·ing** \-'nāch-(ə-)riŋ\ : to remove the natural qualities of: as **a** : to make (alcohol) unfit for drinking without taking away usefulness for other purposes **b** : to change the structure of (as a protein) so that the original properties are removed or diminished — **de·na·tur·ation** \(ˌ)dē-ˌnā-chə-'rā-shən\ *n*

den·drite \'den-ˌdrīt\ *n* **1** : a branching figure (as in a mineral or stone) resembling a tree **2** : any of the usually branching extensions of a neuron over which impulses travel toward the cell body — compare AXON — **den·drit·ic** \den-'drit-ik\ *adj*

den·drol·o·gy \den-'dräl-ə-jē\ *n* : the study of trees

Den·eb \'den-ˌeb, -əb\ *n* : the brightest star in the group of stars of Cygnus

de·ni·al \di-'nī-(ə)l\ *n* **1** : a refusal to grant something asked for **2** : a refusal to admit the truth of a statement : CONTRADICTION ⟨a flat *denial* of the charges⟩ **3** : a refusal to accept or believe in something ⟨make a public *denial* of political beliefs once held⟩ **4** : a cutting down or limiting of a person's own desires or activity ⟨*denial* of one's appetite⟩ — **in denial** : refusing to accept or believe in something bad ⟨the student was *in denial* about his poor grade⟩

¹de·ni·er \di-'nī-(ə)r\ *n* : one who denies [*deny* and *-er* (noun suffix)]

²den·ier \'den-yər\ *n* : a unit of fineness for silk, rayon, or nylon yarn [Middle English *denere* "small silver coin formerly used in Europe," from early French *denier* (same meaning), from Latin *denarius* "coin valued at 10 asses," derived from *deni* "ten each," from *decem* "ten"]

den·im \'den-əm\ *n* **1** : a firm durable twilled usually cotton fabric **2** *pl* : overalls or trousers of denim

   Word History Many fabrics have been named for the places where they were once made. *Denim* gets its name from Nîmes, a city in France famous for its textiles. But the name came about in an unusual way. The fabric, a heavy serge, was originally called *serge de Nîmes,* literally, "serge from Nîmes." The "s" on *Nîmes* is not pro-

nounced in French, so when the name of the fabric came into English, it was often written *serge de Nim* and later *serge denim.* In time this was shortened to simply *denim.* [from French (*serge*) *de Nîmes* "serge (fabric) from Nîmes (city in France)"]

de·ni·tri·fi·ca·tion \(ˌ)dē-ˌnī-trə-fə-'kā-shən\ *n* : a process by which various nitrogen compounds are changed or broken down and which is usually brought about (as in soil) by bacteria with formation of free nitrogen

de·ni·tri·fy \(')dē-'nī-trə-ˌfī\ *vb* : to change a nitrogen compound to free nitrogen or to a different state especially as a step in the nitrogen cycle

den·i·zen \'den-ə-zən\ *n* : INHABITANT; *esp* : a person, animal, or plant found in a particular region or environment

den mother *n* : a female adult leader of a Cub Scout den

de·nom·i·nate \di-'näm-ə-ˌnāt\ *vb* : to give a name to : DESIGNATE

de·nom·i·nate number \di-ˌnäm-ə-nət-\ *n* : a number (as 7 in 7 *meters*) that specifies a quantity in terms of a unit of measurement

de·nom·i·na·tion \di-ˌnäm-ə-'nā-shən\ *n* **1** : an act of denominating **2** : one of a series of related values each having a special name ⟨a $5 bill and a $10 bill represent two *denominations* of U.S. money⟩ **3** : ¹NAME 1, DESIGNATION; *esp* : a general name for a class of things **4** : a religious body made up of a number of congregations with similar beliefs — **de·nom·i·na·tion·al** \-shnəl, -shən-ᵊl\ *adj*

de·nom·i·na·tor \di-'näm-ə-ˌnāt-ər\ *n* : the part of a fraction that is below the line and that functions as the divisor of the numerator

de·no·ta·tion \ˌdē-nō-'tā-shən\ *n* **1** : an act or process of denoting **2** : MEANING 1a; *esp* : a direct specific meaning as distinct from connotations **3** : a term or label that indicates something : NAME, SIGN — **de·no·ta·tive** \'dē-nō-ˌtāt-iv, di-'nōt-ət-iv\ *adj*

de·note \di-'nōt\ *vb* **1** : to mark out plainly : point out : INDICATE ⟨the hands of a clock *denote* the time⟩ **2** : to make known : SHOW ⟨smiled to *denote* pleasure⟩ **3** : to have the meaning of : MEAN, NAME ⟨the word "derby" can *denote* a horse race or a kind of hat⟩

de·noue·ment \ˌdā-nü-'mäⁿ, dā-'nü-ˌ\ *n* **1** : the final solution or untangling of the conflicts or difficulties that make up the plot of a literary work **2** : a solution or working out especially of a complicated or difficult situation

de·nounce \di-'nau̇n(t)s\ *vb* **de·nounced; de·nounc·ing** **1** : to point out as deserving blame or punishment **2** : to inform against : ACCUSE **3** : to announce formally the ending of (as a treaty) — **de·nounce·ment** \-mənt\ *n* — **de·nounc·er** *n*

dense \'den(t)s\ *adj* **dens·er; dens·est** **1 a** : marked by closeness or crowding together of parts ⟨a *dense* forest⟩ **b** : having a high mass per unit volume ⟨lead is a very *dense* metal⟩ **2** : slow to understand : STUPID 1a **3** : ¹THICK 4 ⟨*dense* fog⟩ **4** : having between any two mathematical elements at least one element ⟨the set of rational numbers is *dense*⟩ — **dense·ly** *adv* — **dense·ness** *n*

den·si·ty \'den(t)-sət-ē\ *n, pl* **-ties** **1** : the quality or state of being dense **2** : the quantity of something per unit volume, unit area, or unit length: as **a** : the mass of a substance per unit volume ⟨*density* expressed in grams per cubic centimeter⟩ **b** : the average number of individuals or units in a unit of area or volume ⟨a population *density* of 500 per square mile⟩ **3** : STUPIDITY 1

¹dent \'dent\ *vb* **1** : to make a dent in or on **2** : to become marked by a dent

²dent *n* **1** : a notch or hollow made by a blow or by pressure **2 a** : an impression or effect made usually against resistance ⟨that purchase made a big *dent* in our savings⟩ **b** : noticeable progress ⟨made a *dent* in our pile of work⟩

den·tal \'dent-ᵊl\ *adj* : of or relating to the teeth or dentistry [from Latin *dentalis* "relating to the teeth," from *dent-, dens* "tooth" — related to DANDELION, INDENT, TRIDENT]

dental floss *n* : a thread used to clean between the teeth

dental hygienist *n* : a person who assists a dentist especially in cleaning teeth

den·ti·frice \'dent-ə-frəs\ *n* : a powder, paste, or liquid for cleaning the teeth

den·tin \'dent-ᵊn\ *or* **den·tine** \'den-ˌtēn, den-'tēn\ *n* : a calcium-containing material that is similar to bone but harder and that makes up the principal mass of a tooth — **den·tin·al** \den-'tēn-ᵊl, 'dent-ᵊn-ᵊl\ *adj*

den·tist \'dent-əst\ *n* : a professional person who is trained in the care, treatment, and repair of the teeth and the fitting of artificial teeth

den·tist·ry \'dent-ə-strē\ *n* : the profession or practice of a dentist

den·ti·tion \den-'tish-ən\ *n* : the number, kind, and arrangement of teeth (as of a person or animal)

den·ture \'den-chər\ *n* : a set of teeth; *esp* : a partial or complete set of false teeth

de·nude \di-'n(y)üd\ *vb* **de·nud·ed; de·nud·ing** : to strip of covering : lay bare ⟨erosion that *denudes* the rocks of soil⟩ — **de·nu·da·tion** \ˌdē-(ˌ)n(y)ü-'dā-shən, ˌden-yu-\ *n*

de·nun·ci·a·tion \di-ˌnən(t)-sē-'ā-shən\ *n* : the act of denouncing; *esp* : a public charge of wrongdoing — **de·nun·ci·a·to·ry** \-'nən(t)-sē-ə-ˌtōr-ē, -ˌtȯr-\ *adj*

de·ny \di-'nī\ *vb* **de·nied; de·ny·ing** 1 : to declare not to be true : CONTRADICT ⟨*deny* a report⟩ 2 : to refuse to grant ⟨*deny* a request⟩ 3 : to refuse to accept the existence or truth of

de·odor·ant \dē-'ōd-ə-rənt\ *n* : a preparation that destroys or masks unpleasant odors — **deodorant** *adj*

de·odor·ize \dē-'ōd-ə-ˌrīz\ *vb* **-ized; -iz·ing** : to eliminate or prevent the unpleasant odor of — **de·odor·iz·er** *n*

de·ox·i·dize \(')dē-'äk-sə-ˌdīz\ *vb* : to remove oxygen from

de·oxy·ri·bo·nu·cle·ic acid \(ˌ)dē-ˌäk-sē-ˌrī-bō-n(y)ü-ˌklē-ik-, -ˌklā-\ *n* : DNA

de·oxy·ri·bose \dē-ˌäk-sē-'rī-ˌbōs\ *n* : a sugar that has five carbon atoms and four oxygen atoms in each molecule and is part of DNA — compare RIBOSE

de·part \di-'pärt\ *vb* 1 a : to go away or go away from : LEAVE b : ¹DIE 1 2 : to turn aside : DEVIATE

de·part·ed *adj* 1 : BYGONE ⟨*departed* days⟩ 2 : no longer living

de·part·ment \di-'pärt-mənt\ *n* 1 : a distinct area of interest or activity ⟨taking care of the cat is not my *department*⟩ 2 a : a major administrative division of a government or business b : a major territorial administrative division c : a division of a college or school giving instruction in a particular subject d : a section of a department store — **de·part·men·tal** \di-ˌpärt-'ment-ᵊl, ˌdē-\ *adj* — **de·part·men·tal·ly** \-ᵊl-ē\ *adv*

department store *n* : a store having separate sections for a wide variety of goods

de·par·ture \di-'pär-chər\ *n* 1 : the act of going away 2 : a setting out (as on a new course) 3 : a change from a usual course or standard ⟨a *departure* from tradition⟩

de·pend \di-'pend\ *vb* 1 : to be determined by or based on ⟨success of the picnic will *depend* on the weather⟩ 2 : ²TRUST 1a, RELY ⟨a person you can *depend* on⟩ 3 : to rely for support ⟨children *depend* on their parents⟩ 4 : to hang down ⟨a vine *depending* from a tree⟩ [Middle En-

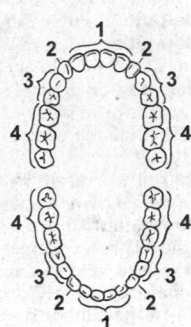

dentition: *top* upper jaw, *bottom* lower jaw, 1 incisors, 2 canines, 3 premolars, 4 molars

glish *dependen* "to exist or result from some other condition," from early French *dependre* (same meaning), derived from Latin *dependēre* "to hang down, hang from," from *de-* "from, down" and *pendēre* "to hang" — related to PENDULUM, PERPENDICULAR]

de·pend·able \di-'pen-də-bəl\ *adj* : capable of being depended on : TRUSTWORTHY, RELIABLE ⟨a *dependable* car⟩ — **de·pend·abil·i·ty** \-ˌpen-də-'bil-ət-ē\ *n* — **de·pend·ably** \-'pen-də-blē\ *adv*

de·pend·ence \di-'pen-dən(t)s\ *n* 1 : the quality or state of being dependent; *esp* : the quality or state of being influenced by or subject to another 2 : RELIANCE 2, TRUST 3 : something on which one relies 4 : a drug addiction

de·pend·en·cy \di-'pen-dən-sē\ *n, pl* **-cies** 1 : DEPENDENCE 1 2 : a territory under the authority of a nation but not formally a part of it

¹de·pend·ent \di-'pen-dənt\ *adj* 1 : hanging down 2 a : determined by something else b : relying on another for support ⟨*dependent* children⟩ c : affected with a drug addiction d : being under another's authority ⟨a *dependent* territory⟩ 3 : ¹SUBORDINATE 3a ⟨a *dependent* clause⟩ — **de·pend·ent·ly** *adv*

²dependent *also* **de·pend·ant** \-dənt\ *n* : a person who relies on another for support

dependent variable *n* : mathematical variable whose value is determined by that of one or more other variables in a function — compare INDEPENDENT VARIABLE

de·pict \di-'pikt\ *vb* 1 : to represent by a picture 2 : to describe in words — **de·pic·tion** \-'pik-shən\ *n*

de·pil·a·to·ry \di-'pil-ə-ˌtōr-ē, -ˌtȯr-\ *n, pl* **-ries** : a preparation for removing hair, wool, or bristles

de·plete \di-'plēt\ *vb* **de·plet·ed; de·plet·ing** : to reduce in amount by using up : exhaust especially of strength or resources ⟨soil *depleted* of minerals⟩ ⟨a *depleted* treasury⟩ — **de·ple·tion** \-'plē-shən\ *n*

de·plor·able \di-'plōr-ə-bəl, -'plȯr-\ *adj* 1 : deserving to be deplored : LAMENTABLE ⟨a *deplorable* accident⟩ 2 : very bad : WRETCHED ⟨*deplorable* conditions⟩ — **de·plor·able·ness** *n* — **de·plor·ably** \-blē\ *adv*

de·plore \di-'plō(ə)r, -'plȯ(ə)r\ *vb* **de·plored; de·plor·ing** 1 a : to feel or express grief for b : to regret strongly 2 : to consider unfortunate or deserving of disapproval — **de·plor·er** *n* — **de·plor·ing·ly** \-iŋ-lē\ *adv*

de·ploy \di-'plȯi\ *vb* : to move, spread out, or place in position for some purpose ⟨troops *deployed* for battle⟩ ⟨*deploy* police to prevent a riot⟩ — **de·ploy·ment** \-mənt\ *n*

de·po·nent \di-'pō-nənt\ *n* : a person who gives evidence

de·pop·u·late \(')dē-'päp-yə-ˌlāt\ *vb* : to reduce greatly the population of (as a city or region) by destroying or driving away the inhabitants ⟨*depopulated* by plague⟩ — **de·pop·u·la·tion** \(ˌ)dē-ˌpäp-yə-'lā-shən\ *n*

de·port \di-'pō(ə)rt, -'pȯ(ə)rt\ *vb* 1 : to cause (oneself) to act in a certain way : CONDUCT ⟨*deported* themselves well in public⟩ 2 : to force (a person who is not a citizen) to leave a country — **de·por·ta·tion** \ˌdē-ˌpōr-'tā-shən, -ˌpȯr-\ *n* — **de·por·tee** \ˌdē-ˌpōr-'tē, -ˌpȯr-\ *n*

de·port·ment \di-'pōrt-mənt, -'pȯrt-\ *n* : manner of conducting oneself : BEHAVIOR

de·pose \di-'pōz\ *vb* **de·posed; de·pos·ing** 1 : to remove from a high office ⟨*deposed* the king⟩ 2 : to testify under oath or by a sworn written statement

¹de·pos·it \di-'päz-ət\ *vb* 1 : to place for safekeeping; *esp* : to put money in a bank 2 : to give as a pledge that a purchase will be made or a service used ⟨*deposit* $10 on a new bicycle⟩ 3 : to lay down : PLACE, PUT ⟨*deposit* a

\ə\ **abut**	\aů\ **out**	\i\ **tip**	\ȯ\ **saw**	\ů\ **foot**	
\ər\ **further**	\ch\ **chin**	\ī\ **life**	\ȯi\ **coin**	\y\ **yet**	
\a\ **mat**	\e\ **pet**	\j\ **job**	\th\ **thin**	\yü\ **few**	
\ā\ **take**	\ē\ **easy**	\ŋ\ **sing**	\th\ **this**	\yů\ **cure**	
\ä\ **cot, cart**	\g\ **go**	\ō\ **bone**	\ü\ **food**	\zh\ **vision**	

parcel on a table⟩ **4** : to let fall or sink ⟨silt *deposited* by a flood⟩ — **de·pos·i·tor** \-'päz-ət-ər, -'päz-tər\ *n*

²**deposit** *n* **1** : the state of being deposited ⟨money on *deposit*⟩ **2 a** : something placed for safekeeping; *esp* : money deposited in a bank **b** : money given as a pledge or down payment **3** : an act of depositing **4** : something laid or thrown down ⟨a *deposit* of silt left by the flood⟩ **5** : an accumulation of mineral matter (as ore, oil, or gas) in nature

de·po·si·tion \ˌdep-ə-'zish-ən, ˌdē-pə-\ *n* **1** : the act of removing a person from high office ⟨the *deposition* of the king⟩ **2** : a statement especially in writing made under oath **3** : the action or process of depositing ⟨the *deposition* of silt by a stream⟩ **4** : something deposited : DEPOSIT — **de·po·si·tion·al** \-'zish-nəl, -ən-ᵊl\ *adj*

de·pos·i·to·ry \di-'päz-ə-ˌtōr-ē, -ˌtor-\ *n, pl* **-ries** : a place where something is deposited especially for safekeeping

de·pot *senses 1 & 2 are* 'dep-ˌō *also* 'dē-ˌpō, *sense 3 is* 'dē-ˌpō *sometimes* 'dep-ˌō\ *n* **1** : a place of deposit for goods : STOREHOUSE **2** : a place where military supplies are kept or where troops are assembled and trained **3** : a building for railroad or bus passengers or freight : STATION

de·prave \di-'prāv\ *vb* **de·praved; de·prav·ing** : to make evil : PERVERT — **de·praved·ly** \-'prā-vəd-lē, -'prāvd-lē\ *adv* — **de·praved·ness** \-'prā-vəd-nəs, -'prāvd-nəs\ *n*

de·prav·i·ty \di-'prav-ət-ē\ *n, pl* **-ties** : a corrupt act or practice **2** : the quality or state of being depraved

dep·re·cate \'dep-ri-ˌkāt\ *vb* **-cat·ed; -cat·ing** **1** : to express disapproval of **2** : to represent as of little value : DEPRECIATE — **dep·re·cat·ing·ly** \-ˌkāt-iŋ-lē\ *adv* — **dep·re·ca·tion** \ˌdep-ri-'kā-shən\ *n*

dep·re·ca·to·ry \'dep-ri-kə-ˌtōr-ē, -ˌtor-\ *adj* : seeking to avoid disapproval : APOLOGETIC

de·pre·ci·ate \di-'prē-shē-ˌāt\ *vb* **-at·ed; -at·ing** **1** : to lower the price or value of ⟨*depreciate* the currency⟩ **2** : to represent as of little value : DISPARAGE **3** : to fall in value ⟨new cars *depreciate* rapidly⟩ — **de·pre·cia·tive** \-'prē-shət-iv, -shē-ˌāt-iv\ *adj* — **de·pre·cia·to·ry** \-shə-ˌtōr-ē, -ˌtor-\ *adj*

de·pre·ci·a·tion \di-ˌprē-shē-'ā-shən\ *n* **1** : a decline in the purchasing power or exchange value of money **2** : the act of making a person or a thing seem little or unimportant : DISPARAGEMENT **3** : a decline (as from age or wear and tear) in the value of something

dep·re·da·tion \ˌdep-rə-'dā-shən\ *n* : the action or an act of looting or laying waste

de·press \di-'pres\ *vb* **1 a** : to press down **b** : to cause to sink to a lower position **2** : to lessen the activity or strength of **3** : SADDEN, DISCOURAGE **4** : to lessen in price or value : DEPRECIATE — **de·press·ible** \-ə-bəl\ *adj* — **de·press·ing·ly** \-iŋ-lē\ *adv*

de·pres·sant \di-'pres-ᵊnt\ *n* : a substance (as a drug) that reduces the activity of bodily systems — **depressant** *adj*

de·pressed *adj* **1 a** : low in spirits : SAD **b** : suffering from mental depression **2** : suffering from economic depression

de·pres·sion \di-'presh-ən\ *n* **1** : an act of depressing : a state of being depressed: as **a** : a pressing down : LOWERING **b** : a state of feeling sad : DEJECTION; *also* : a mental disorder marked by sadness, inactivity, and loss of a sense of one's own worth **c** : a reduction in activity, amount, quality, or force **2** : a depressed place or part : HOLLOW ⟨a *depression* in the road⟩ **3** : a period of low general economic activity with widespread unemployment

de·pres·sor \di-'pres-ər\ *n* : one that depresses; *esp* : a device for pressing a part (as the tongue) down or aside

de·pres·sur·ize \(')dē-'presh-ə-ˌrīz\ *vb* : to release (as an aircraft with near-normal atmospheric pressure) from pressure

de·prive \di-'prīv\ *vb* **de·prived; de·priv·ing** **1** : to take something away from ⟨*deprive* a ruler of power⟩ **2** : to

stop from having something ⟨*deprived* of sleep by street noises⟩ — **dep·ri·va·tion** \ˌdep-rə-'vā-shən\ *n*

deprived *adj* : kept from having the necessities of life or a healthful environment ⟨culturally *deprived* families⟩

depth \'depth\ *n* **1 a** : something that is deep : a deep place or part (as of a body of water) **b** : a part that is far from the outside or surface ⟨the *depths* of the woods⟩ **c** : ABYSS **2 a** : the middle of a time ⟨the *depth* of winter⟩ **b** : an extreme state (as of despair) **3** : distance from top to bottom or from front to back **4** : the quality of being deep ⟨*depth* of understanding⟩ **5** : degree of intensity ⟨the *depth* of a color⟩ — **depth·less** \-ləs\ *adj*

depth charge *n* : an explosive device for underwater use especially against submarines that is designed to detonate at a predetermined depth

dep·u·ta·tion \ˌdep-yə-'tā-shən\ *n* **1** : the act of appointing a deputy **2** : a group of people appointed to represent others

de·pute \di-'pyüt\ *vb* **de·put·ed; de·put·ing** : ²DELEGATE

dep·u·tize \'dep-yə-ˌtīz\ *vb* **-tized; -tiz·ing** **1** : to appoint as deputy **2** : to act as deputy

dep·u·ty \'dep-yət-ē\ *n, pl* **-ties** **1** : a person appointed to act for or in place of another **2** : an assistant who usually takes charge when his or her superior is absent — **deputy** *adj*

de·rail \di-'rā(ə)l\ *vb* : to cause to run off the rails ⟨a train *derailed* by heavy snow⟩ — **de·rail·ment** \-mənt\ *n*

de·rail·leur \di-'rā-lər\ *n* : a device for shifting gears on a bicycle that operates by moving the chain from one set of exposed gears to another [from French *dérailleur* "gear changing device," from *dérailler* "to derail"]

de·range \di-'rānj\ *vb* **de·ranged; de·rang·ing** **1** : to put out of order : DISARRANGE ⟨hair *deranged* by the wind⟩ **2** : to make insane — **de·range·ment** \-mənt\ *n*

der·by \'dər-bē, *especially British* 'där-\ *n, pl* **derbies** **1** : a horse race usually for three-year-olds held annually **2** : a race or contest open to all comers ⟨a fishing *derby*⟩ **3** : a stiff felt hat with dome-shaped top and narrow brim

Word History The first horse race called a *Derby* was named after an English nobleman named Edward Stanley, the Earl of Derby (1752–1834). The Earl instituted the race in 1780, and it continues to be run to the present day on the first Wednesday in June at Epsom Downs, a racetrack south of London. The name *Derby* has become attached to other races usually restricted to three-year-old horses, such as the Kentucky Derby. It is used as well of races that have nothing to do with horses, such as the Pinewood Derby run by the Cub Scouts. In the 1800s *derby* was also the name given in the U.S. to a dome-shaped hat called a *bowler* in England. The reason why the hat was given this name is uncertain, and nothing seems to link it with horse races. [named for Edward Stanley, 12th earl of *Derby* (a county and town in England)]

de·re·cho \də-'rā-(ˌ)chō\ *n, pl* **de·re·chos** : a large fast-moving complex of thunderstorms with powerful winds that move in a straight line and that cause widespread destruction [from Spanish, "straight" (opposed to *tornado*, taken to mean "turned" in Spanish)]

¹**der·e·lict** \'der-ə-ˌlikt\ *adj* **1** : abandoned by the owner or occupant ⟨a *derelict* ship⟩ **2** : NEGLIGENT 2, NEGLECTFUL ⟨*derelict* in one's duty⟩

²**derelict** *n* **1** : something voluntarily abandoned; *esp* : a ship abandoned on the high seas **2** : a person without apparent means of support : BUM

der·e·lic·tion \ˌder-ə-'lik-shən\ *n* **1** : the act of abandoning : the state of being abandoned ⟨the *dereliction* of a cause by its leaders⟩ **2** : neglect of one's duty

de·ride \di-'rīd\ *vb* **de·rid·ed; de·rid·ing** : to laugh at scornfully : make fun of — **de·rid·er** *n* — **de·rid·ing·ly** \-'rīd-iŋ-lē\ *adv*

de·ri·sion \di-'rizh-ən\ *n* : scornful ridicule — **de·ri·sive** \-'rī-siv\ *adj* — **de·ri·sive·ly** *adv* — **de·ri·sive·ness** *n* — **de·ri·so·ry** \-'rī-sə-rē, -zə-\ *adj*

der·i·va·tion \der-ə-'vā-shən\ *n* **1 a** : the formation (as by the addition of a prefix or suffix) of a word from another word or root **b** : an act of finding out or stating how a word was formed **c** : ETYMOLOGY **2 a** : a point of origin : SOURCE **b** : development from a source : DESCENT **c** : an act or process of deriving — **der·i·va·tion·al** \-shnəl, -shən-ᵊl\ *adj*

¹de·riv·a·tive \di-'riv-ət-iv\ *n* **1** : a word formed by derivation ⟨the word "kindness" is a *derivative* of "kind"⟩ **2** : something derived **3** : a substance that can be made from another substance in one or more steps ⟨a *derivative* of coal tar⟩

²derivative *adj* **1** : formed by derivation **2** : made up of or having elements derived from something else ⟨*derivative* poetry⟩

de·rive \di-'rīv\ *vb* **de·rived; de·riv·ing 1** : to receive or obtain from a source **2** : to arrive at by reasoning and observation : INFER, DEDUCE **3** : to trace the origin, descent, or derivation of **4** : to come from a certain source or basis ⟨the tradition *derives* from ancient practices⟩ — **de·riv·able** \-'rī-və-bəl\ *adj*

der·mal \'dər-məl\ *adj* : of or relating to the dermis or epidermis : CUTANEOUS

der·ma·ti·tis \dər-mə-'tīt-əs\ *n, pl* **der·ma·tit·i·des** \-'tit-ə-dēz\ *or* **der·ma·ti·tis·es** : inflammation of the skin

der·ma·tol·o·gist \dər-mə-'täl-ə-jəst\ *n* : a physician who specializes in dermatology and especially in the treatment of the diseases of the skin

der·ma·tol·o·gy \dər-mə-'täl-ə-jē\ *n* : a branch of medicine concerned with the structure, functions, and diseases of the skin

der·mis \'dər-məs\ *n* : the sensitive inner layer of skin directly under the epidermis

de·rog·a·to·ry \di-'räg-ə-tōr-ē, -tor-\ *adj* **1** : intended to lower the reputation of a person or thing **2** : expressing a low opinion ⟨*derogatory* remarks⟩ — **de·rog·a·to·ri·ly** \-räg-ə-'tōr-ə-lē, -'tor-\ *adv*

der·rick \'der-ik\ *n* **1** : any of various machines for moving or hoisting heavy weights by means of a long beam fitted with pulleys and cables **2** : a framework or tower over a deep drill hole (as of an oil well) for supporting machinery

der·ring–do \der-iŋ-'dü\ *n* : daring action : DARING

der·vish \'dər-vish\ *n* : a member of a Muslim religious group noted for its customs (as bodily movements leading to a trance)

de·sa·li·nate \(')dē-'sal-ə-nāt *also* -'sā-lə-\ *vb* **-nat·ed; -nat·ing** : DESALT — **de·sa·li·na·tion** \(,)dē-,sal-ə-'nā-shən *also* -,sā-lə-\ *n*

de·sal·i·ni·za·tion \(,)dē-,sal-ə-nə-'zā-shən\ *n* : removal of salt (as from seawater)

de·salt \(')dē-'sölt\ *vb* : to remove salt from (as seawater)

¹des·cant \'des-,kant\ *n* **1** : a melody sung or played usually above a principal melody **2** : a discussion or comment on a subject

²des·cant \'des-,kant, des-'kant\ *vb* **1 a** : to sing or play a descant **b** : ¹SING 2 **2** : to talk or write at length ⟨*descanted* on foreign films⟩

de·scend \di-'send\ *vb* **1** : to pass from a higher to a lower place or level **2 a** : to originate or come down from a source : DERIVE ⟨*descended* from an ancient family⟩ **b** : to be handed down to an heir or from an earlier time ⟨the mansion *descended* to a son⟩ ⟨a custom *descended* from ancient times⟩ **3 a** : to incline, lead, or extend downward ⟨the road *descends* to the river⟩ **b** : to pass, move, or climb down or down along **4** : to make a sudden

derrick 2

attack by or as if by swooping down **5** : to sink in status, dignity, or condition

¹de·scend·ant *also* **de·scend·ent** \di-'sen-dənt\ *adj* **1** : moving or directed downward **2** : proceeding from an ancestor or source

²descendant *also* **descendent** *n* **1** : one descended from another or from a common stock **2** : one coming directly from an earlier and usually similar type or individual

de·scent \di-'sent\ *n* **1** : one's line of ancestors : BIRTH, LINEAGE **2** : the act or process of descending **3** : a downward step (as in station or value) : DECLINE **4 a** : a downward slant : SLOPE **b** : a descending way (as a stairway) **5** : a sudden raid or assault

de·scribe \di-'skrīb\ *vb* **des·cribed; des·crib·ing 1** : to represent or give an account of in words **2** : to trace the outline of ⟨*describe* a circle⟩ — **de·scrib·able** \-'skrī-bə-bəl\ *adj* — **de·scrib·er** *n*

de·scrip·tion \di-'skrip-shən\ *n* **1** : an account of something; *esp* : an account that presents a picture to a person who reads or hears it **2** : ¹SORT 1a, KIND ⟨people of every *description*⟩ [Middle English *descripcioun* "description," from early French *descripcioun* and Latin *description-, descriptio* (both, same meaning), from Latin *describere* "to describe," from *de-* "down" and *scribere* "to write" — related to SCRIBE]

de·scrip·tive \di-'skrip-tiv\ *adj* : serving to describe ⟨a *descriptive* account⟩ ⟨a *descriptive* adjective⟩ — **de·scrip·tive·ly** *adv* — **de·scrip·tive·ness** *n*

de·scry \di-'skrī\ *vb* **de·scried; de·scry·ing 1** : to catch sight of **2** : to discover or detect by observation or investigation

des·e·crate \'des-i-,krāt\ *vb* **-crat·ed; -crat·ing** : to treat a sacred place or sacred object shamefully or with great disrespect — **des·e·crat·er** *or* **des·e·cra·tor** \-,krāt-ər\ *n* — **des·e·cra·tion** \,des-i-'krā-shən\ *n*

de·seg·re·gate \(')dē-'seg-ri-,gāt\ *vb* : to eliminate segregation in; *esp* : to end by law the isolation of members of a particular race in separate units ⟨*desegregate* city schools⟩ — **de·seg·re·ga·tion** \(,)dē-,seg-ri-'gā-shən\ *n*

de·se·lect \,dē-sə-'lekt\ *vb* **1** : DISMISS 3, REJECT **2** : to cause (something previously selected) to no longer be selected in a software interface

¹des·ert \'dez-ərt\ *n* : dry land with few plants and little rainfall [Middle English *desert* "barren land," from early French *desert* (same meaning), derived from Latin *deserere* "to desert, abandon," from *de-* "from, away" and *serere* "to join together"] — **des·ert·like** \-,līk\ *adj*

²des·ert \'dez-ərt\ *adj* : of, relating to, or resembling a desert; *esp* : being barren and without life ⟨a *desert* island⟩

³de·sert \di-'zərt\ *n* **1** : worthiness of reward or punishment ⟨rewarded according to their *deserts*⟩ **2** : a deserved reward or punishment ⟨got your just *deserts*⟩ [Middle English *deserte* "quality of being worthy of a reward or punishment," from early French *desert* (same meaning), from *deservir* "to deserve," from Latin *deservire* "to devote oneself to"]

⁴de·sert \di-'zərt\ *vb* **1** : to withdraw from : LEAVE ⟨*desert* a town⟩ **2** : to leave someone or something one should stay with ⟨*deserted* a friend in trouble⟩ **3** : to fail one in time of need ⟨my courage *deserted* me⟩ **4** : to quit one's post without permission especially with the intention of remaining away permanently [from French *déserter* "to desert, abandon," from Latin *desertare* (same meaning), derived from earlier *deserere* "to desert, abandon" — related to ¹DESERT] *synonyms* see ABANDON — **de·sert·er** *n* — **de·ser·tion** \di-'zər-shən\ *n*

\ə\ abut	\au̇\ out	\i\ tip	\o̊\ saw	\u̇\ foot
\ər\ further	\ch\ chin	\ī\ life	\o̊i\ coin	\y\ yet
\a\ mat	\e\ pet	\j\ job	\th\ thin	\yü\ few
\ā\ take	\ē\ easy	\ŋ\ sing	\t̲h̲\ this	\yu̇\ cure
\ä\ cot, cart	\g\ go	\ō\ bone	\ü\ food	\zh\ vision

de·serve \di-'zərv\ *vb* **de·served; de·serv·ing** : to be worthy of : MERIT ⟨*deserves* another chance⟩

de·served \-'zərvd\ *adj* : of, relating to, or being that which one deserves ⟨a *deserved* punishment⟩ — **de·served·ly** \-'zər-vəd-lē\ *adv* — **de·served·ness** \-nəs\ *n*

de·serv·ing \di-'zər-viŋ\ *adj* : [1]WORTHY 2; *esp* : worthy of financial help ⟨aid for *deserving* families⟩

de·sex \(')dē-'seks\ *vb* : CASTRATE, SPAY ⟨capons are *de-sexed* male chickens⟩

des·ic·ca·tor \'des-i-ˌkāt-ər\ *n* : a container for drying substances and keeping them free of moisture

[1]de·sign \di-'zīn\ *vb* **1 a** : to think up and plan out in the mind ⟨*designed* the perfect crime⟩ **b** : to have as a purpose : INTEND ⟨*designed* to become a lawyer⟩ **c** : to create for a specific function or end ⟨*design* a training program for auto mechanics⟩ **2 a** : to make a pattern or sketch of ⟨*design* new fashions⟩ **b** : to think up and draw the plans for ⟨*design* an airplane⟩

[2]design *n* **1** : a project or scheme in which means to an end are laid down **2** : deliberate planning : a planned intention ⟨happened by accident rather than by *design*⟩ **3** : a secret project or scheme : PLOT — often used in plural with *on* or *against* ⟨had *designs* on the money⟩ ⟨has no *designs* against friendly governments⟩ **4** : a preliminary sketch, model, or plan **5** : the arrangement of elements that make up a structure or a work of art **6** : a decorative pattern **synonyms** see INTENTION

des·ig·nate \'dez-ig-ˌnāt\ *vb* **-nat·ed; -nat·ing** **1** : to appoint or choose by name for a special purpose ⟨*designate* someone as team captain⟩ **2** : to mark or point out : INDICATE **3** : to call by name or title [from Latin *designatus,* past participle of *designare* "to choose for a purpose," from *de-* "down, from" and *signare* "to mark, mark out, sign, stamp with a seal," from *signum* "mark, sign, image" — related to SIGN]

des·ig·na·tion \ˌdez-ig-'nā-shən\ *n* **1** : the act of indicating or identifying **2** : appointment to or selection for an office, post, or service **3** : a name, sign, or title that identifies something

de·sign·ed·ly \di-'zī-nəd-lē\ *adv* : PURPOSELY

[1]de·sign·er \di-'zī-nər\ *n* : one who designs; *esp* : one who creates and manufactures a new product style

[2]designer *adj* : relating to or produced by a designer and often displaying the name of the designer ⟨*designer* jeans⟩

de·sign·ing \di-'zī-niŋ\ *adj* : CRAFTY, SCHEMING

de·sir·able \di-'zī-rə-bəl\ *adj* **1** : having pleasing qualities or properties : ATTRACTIVE ⟨a *desirable* location⟩ **2** : worth having, seeking, or doing : ADVISABLE ⟨*desirable* legislation⟩ — **de·sir·abil·i·ty** \-ˌzī-rə-'bil-ət-ē\ *n* — **de·sir·able·ness** \-'zī-rə-bəl-nəs\ *n* — **de·sir·ably** \-blē\ *adv*

[1]de·sire \di-'zī(ə)r\ *vb* **de·sired; de·sir·ing** **1** : to long for : wish earnestly ⟨*desire* wealth⟩ ⟨*desire* peace⟩ **2** : to call for : express a wish for : REQUEST ⟨the librarian *desires* us to return all overdue books⟩

[2]desire *n* **1** : a strong wish : LONGING; *also* : the mental power or ability to experience desires **2** : an expressed wish : REQUEST **3** : something desired

de·sir·ous \di-'zī(ə)r-əs\ *adj* : eagerly wishing ⟨*desirous* of an invitation⟩ — **de·sir·ous·ly** *adv* — **de·sir·ous·ness** *n*

de·sist \di-'sist, -'zist\ *vb* : to stop something one is doing

desk \'desk\ *n* **1 a** : a table, frame, or case with a flat or sloping surface especially for writing and reading **b** : a counter at which a person works **2 a** : a specialized division of an organization (as a newspaper) ⟨city *desk*⟩ **b** : a seating position according to rank in an orchestra

[1]desk·top \'desk-ˌtäp\ *n* **1 a** : the top of a desk **b** : an area on a computer screen in which items are arranged as if on top of a desk **2** : a desktop computer

[2]desktop *adj* : of a size that is suitable for use on a desk or table ⟨a *desktop* computer⟩

des·mid \'dez-məd\ *n* : any of numerous single-celled or colonial green algae

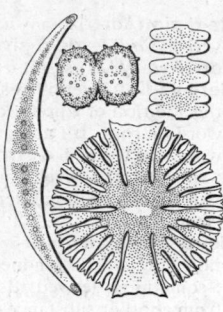
desmid

[1]des·o·late \'des-ə-lət, 'dez-\ *adj* **1** : ABANDONED 1 **2** : having no companionship : LONELY **3 a** : showing the results of abandonment and neglect : DILAPIDATED **b** : lacking signs of life : BARREN ⟨a *desolate* landscape⟩ **c** : CHEERLESS ⟨*desolate* thoughts⟩ [Middle English *desolat* "having no inhabitants or visitors, deserted," from Latin *desolatus,* past participle of *desolare* "to abandon," from *de-* "from, away" and *solus* "alone" — related to [4]SOLE, SOLITUDE, SOLO] — **des·o·late·ly** *adv* — **des·o·late·ness** *n*

[2]des·o·late \'des-ə-ˌlāt, 'dez-\ *vb* **-lat·ed; -lat·ing** : to make or leave desolate

des·o·la·tion \ˌdes-ə-'lā-shən, ˌdez-\ *n* **1** : the action of desolating **2** : sadness resulting from grief or loneliness **3** : the condition of being desolated : RUIN **4** : lifeless land

des·oxy·ri·bo·nu·cle·ic acid \de-ˌzäk-sē-ˌrī-bō-n(y)ù-ˌklē-ik-, -ˌklä-\ *n* : DNA

[1]de·spair \di-'spa(ə)r, -'spe(ə)r\ *vb* : to lose all hope or confidence ⟨*despair* of winning⟩

[2]despair *n* **1** : utter loss of hope : feeling of complete hopelessness **2** : a cause of hopelessness

de·spair·ing \di-'spa(ə)r-iŋ, -'spe(ə)r-\ *adj* : given to, coming from, or marked by despair : not having hope — **de·spair·ing·ly** \-iŋ-lē\ *adv*

des·patch *chiefly British variant of* DISPATCH

des·per·a·do \ˌdes-pə-'räd-ō, -'rād-\ *n, pl* **-does** *or* **-dos** : a bold or reckless criminal

des·per·ate \'des-p(ə-)rət\ *adj* **1** : being beyond or almost beyond hope ⟨a *desperate* illness⟩ **2** : reckless because of despair : RASH ⟨a *desperate* attempt⟩ — **des·per·ate·ly** *adv* — **des·per·ate·ness** *n*

des·per·a·tion \ˌdes-pə-'rā-shən\ *n* **1** : a loss of hope and surrender to misery or dread **2** : a state of hopelessness leading to extreme recklessness

de·spi·ca·ble \di-'spik-ə-bəl, 'des-(ˌ)pik-\ *adj* : deserving to be despised ⟨a *despicable* traitor⟩ — **de·spi·ca·ble·ness** *n* — **de·spi·ca·bly** \-blē\ *adv*

de·spise \di-'spīz\ *vb* **de·spised; de·spis·ing** : to consider as beneath one's notice or respect : feel scorn and dislike for — **de·spis·er** *n* — **de·spis·ing·ly** *adv*

[1]de·spite \di-'spīt\ *n* **1** : CONTEMPT 1 **2** : SPITE, MALICE **3 a** : an act showing scorn and disrespect **b** : DETRIMENT — **in despite of** : in spite of

[2]despite *prep* : in spite of ⟨ran *despite* an injury⟩

de·spite·ful \di-'spīt-fəl\ *adj* : expressing hate or the wish to harm — **de·spite·ful·ly** \-fə-lē\ *adv* — **de·spite·ful·ness** *n*

de·spoil \di-'spȯil\ *vb* : to strip of belongings, possessions, or value : PLUNDER, PILLAGE — **de·spoil·er** *n* — **de·spoil·ment** \-'spȯi(ə)l-mənt\ *n*

de·spo·li·a·tion \di-ˌspō-lē-'ā-shən\ *n* : the action or process of despoiling

de·spond \di-'spänd\ *vb* : to become discouraged

de·spond·en·cy \di-'spän-dən-sē\ *n* : the state of being despondent : DEJECTION, DISCOURAGEMENT

de·spond·ent \di-'spän-dənt\ *adj* : feeling quite discouraged or depressed : being in very low spirits — **de·spond·ent·ly** *adv*

des·pot \'des-pət, -ˌpät\ *n* **1** : a ruler with absolute power and authority **2** : a person who uses power in a cruel, unjust, or harmful way — **des·pot·ic** \des-'pät-ik\ *adj* — **des·pot·i·cal·ly** \-i-k(ə-)lē\ *adv*

des·po·tism \'des-pə-ˌtiz-əm\ *n* **1** : rule by a despot : TYR-ANNY **2** : a state or a system of government in which the ruler has unlimited power

des·sert \di-'zərt\ *n* : a course of usually sweet food, fruit, or cheese usually served at the end of a meal

de·stig·ma·tize \(ˌ)dē-'stig-mə-ˌtīz\ *vb* : to remove shame or disgrace from

des·ti·na·tion \ˌdes-tə-'nā-shən\ *n* **1** : the purpose for which something is destined **2** : an act of appointing, set-ting aside for a purpose, or deciding beforehand **3** : a place which is the goal of a journey or to which some-thing is sent

des·tine \'des-tən\ *vb* **des·tined; des·tin·ing 1** : to settle in advance ⟨a plan *destined* to fail⟩ **2** : to choose, assign, or dedicate in advance ⟨*destined* their child for the study of law⟩ **3** : to be bound or directed ⟨a ship *destined* for New York⟩

des·ti·ny \'des-tə-nē\ *n, pl* **-nies 1** : something to which a person or thing is destined : FORTUNE **2** : the course of events held to be arranged by a superhuman power
synonyms DESTINY, FATE, LOT, DOOM mean a state or end that has been decided beforehand. DESTINY suggests something that has been ordered in advance and often suggests a great or noble course ⟨the *destiny* of this great country⟩. FATE suggests an unavoidable and usually un-fortunate ending ⟨his *fate* was to die unhappy⟩. LOT sug-gests that chance alone decides the handing out of suc-cess or happiness ⟨it was not their *lot* to have children⟩. DOOM suggests an unhappy judgment or end ⟨a sense of *doom* hung over the starving city⟩.

des·ti·tute \'des-tə-ˌt(y)üt\ *adj* **1** : lacking something needed or desirable ⟨*destitute* of the necessities of life⟩ **2** : extremely poor : suffering great want — **des·ti·tu·tion** \ˌdes-tə-'t(y)ü-shən\ *n*

de–stress \'dē-'stres\ *vb* : UNWIND 2

de·stroy \di-'stròi\ *vb* **1** : to put an end to : do away with : RUIN **2** : ¹KILL 1, SLAUGHTER

de·stroy·er \di-'stròi(-ə)r\ *n* **1** : one that destroys **2** : a small fast warship armed with guns, depth charges, torpe-does, and often guided missiles

de·struct \di-'strəkt\ *n* : the deliberate destruction of a rocket after launching

de·struc·ti·ble \di-'strək-tə-bəl\ *adj* : capable of being de-stroyed — **de·struc·ti·bil·i·ty** \-ˌstrək-tə-'bil-ət-ē\ *n*

de·struc·tion \di-'strək-shən\ *n* **1** : the state or fact of be-ing destroyed : RUIN **2** : the action or process of destroy-ing something

de·struc·tive \di-'strək-tiv\ *adj* **1** : causing destruction : RUINOUS ⟨a *destructive* storm⟩ **2** : designed or tending to hurt or destroy ⟨*destructive* criticism⟩ — **de·struc-tive·ly** *adv* — **de·struc·tive·ness** *n*

destructive distillation *n* : the breakup of a substance (as coal, oil, or wood) by heat in a closed container and col-lection of the volatile products produced

des·ul·to·ry \'des-əl-ˌtōr-ē, -ˌtòr-\ *adj* : passing aimlessly from one thing or subject to another ⟨*desultory* conversa-tion⟩ — **des·ul·to·ri·ly** \ˌdes-əl-'tòr-ə-lē, -'tōr-\ *adv* — **des·ul·to·ri·ness** \'des-əl-ˌtōr-ē-nəs, -ˌtòr-\ *n*

de·tach \di-'tach\ *vb* : to separate especially from a larger mass and usually without violence or damage — **de·tach-able** \-'tach-ə-bəl\ *adj* — **de·tach·ably** \-blē\ *adv*

de·tached \di-'tacht\ *adj* **1** : not joined or connected : SEPARATE ⟨a *detached* house⟩ **2** : ²ALOOF, UNCON-CERNED, IMPARTIAL ⟨a *detached* attitude⟩ — **de·tached-ly** \-'tach-əd-lē, -'tach-tlē\ *adv* — **de·tached·ness** \-'tach-əd-nəs, -'tach(t)-nəs\ *n*

de·tach·ment \di-'tach-mənt\ *n* **1** : the action or process of detaching : SEPARATION **2 a** : the sending out of a body of troops or part of a fleet from the main body **b** : a small military unit with a special task or function **3 a** : a lack of interest in worldly concerns **b** : freedom from the influence of emotions : IMPARTIALITY

¹de·tail \di-'tā(ə)l, 'dē-ˌtāl\ *n* **1 a** : a dealing with something item by item ⟨go into *detail* about an event⟩ **b** : a small part or feature : ITEM ⟨the *details* of a story⟩ **2 a** : selec-tion (as of a group of soldiers) for some special service **b** : a soldier or group of soldiers appointed for special duty — **in detail** : item by item leaving out nothing : THOR-OUGHLY ⟨explained the assignment *in detail*⟩

²detail *vb* **1** : to report in detail : SPECIFY ⟨*detailed* their complaints⟩ **2** : to assign to a task — **de·tail·er** *n*

de·tailed \di-'tā(ə)ld, 'dē-ˌtāld\ *adj* **1** : including many de-tails ⟨a *detailed* report⟩ **2** : furnished with finely finished details ⟨beautifully *detailed* hats⟩ — **de·tailed·ly** \di-'tāl(-ə)d-lē, 'dē-ˌtāld-\ *adv* — **de·tailed·ness** \di-'tā-ləd-nəs, -'tāl(d)-nəs, 'dē-ˌtāld-\ *n*

de·tain \di-'tān\ *vb* **1** : to hold or keep in or as if in prison **2** : to prevent from proceeding : STOP ⟨was *detained* by a flat tire⟩ — **de·tain·ment** \-mənt\ *n*

de·tect \di-'tekt\ *vb* : to discover the nature, existence, presence, or fact of ⟨*detect* the approach of an airplane⟩ — **de·tect·able** \-'tek-tə-bəl\ *adj* — **de·tec·tion** \-'tek-shən\ *n*

¹de·tec·tive \di-'tek-tiv\ *adj* : of or relating to detectives or their work ⟨a *detective* story⟩

²detective *n* : a person whose business is solving crimes and catching criminals or gathering information that is not easy to get

de·tec·tor \di-'tek-tər\ *n* **1** : one that detects or warns ⟨a smoke *detector*⟩ **2** : a device in a radio receiver for chang-ing the high-frequency current of radio waves into cur-rent that can vibrate a loudspeaker to reproduce the original sound

de·ten·tion \di-'ten-chən\ *n* : the act of detaining : the state of being detained: as **a** : temporary custody before a trial **b** : the punishment of being kept in after school

de·ter \di-'tər\ *vb* **de·terred; de·ter·ring 1** : to turn aside, discourage, or prevent from acting ⟨wasn't *deterred* by the threats⟩ **2** : INHIBIT 2 ⟨painting to *deter* rust⟩ — **de-ter·ment** \-'tər-mənt\ *n*

¹de·ter·gent \di-'tər-jənt\ *adj* : able to clean : used in cleansing ⟨*detergent* oil for engines⟩

²detergent *n* : a substance that cleanses; *esp* : a chemical product that is like soap in its ability to cleanse

de·te·ri·o·rate \di-'tir-ē-ə-ˌrāt\ *vb* **-rat·ed; -rat·ing 1** : to make or become worse or of less value : DEGENERATE **2** : DISINTEGRATE 1 — **de·te·ri·o·ra·tion** \-ˌtir-ē-ə-'rā-shən\ *n* — **de·te·ri·o·ra·tive** \-'tir-ē-ə-ˌrāt-iv\ *adj*

de·ter·mi·nant \di-'tərm-(ə-)nənt\ *n* : something that de-termines or influences

de·ter·mi·nate \di-'tərm-(ə-)nət\ *adj* **1** : having fixed lim-its : DEFINITE ⟨a *determinate* period of time⟩ **2** : defi-nitely settled ⟨arranged in a *determinate* order⟩ — **de·ter-mi·nate·ly** *adv* — **de·ter·mi·nate·ness** *n*

de·ter·mi·na·tion \di-ˌtər-mə-'nā-shən\ *n* **1** : the act of coming to a decision; *also* : the decision or conclusion reached **2** : a settling or making sure of the position, size, or nature of something ⟨*determination* of the position of a ship⟩ **3** : accurate measurement (as of length or vol-ume) **4** : firm or fixed intention : FIRMNESS

de·ter·mine \di-'tər-mən\ *vb* **de·ter·mined; de·ter·min-ing** \-'tərm-(ə-)niŋ\ **1 a** : to fix exactly or with authority ⟨*determine* who will be president⟩ **b** : to have a strong influence on : GOVERN ⟨demand *determines* the price⟩ **2** : to find out or come to a decision ⟨*determine* the answer to the problem⟩ ⟨she *determined* to do better⟩ **3** : to be the cause of or reason for ⟨a pupil's work *determines* his grade⟩

\ə\ abut	\aů\ out	\i\ tip	\ò\ saw	\ů\ foot
\ər\ further	\ch\ chin	\ī\ life	\òi\ coin	\y\ yet
\a\ mat	\e\ pet	\j\ job	\th\ thin	\yü\ few
\ā\ take	\ē\ easy	\ŋ\ sing	\th\ this	\yů\ cure
\ä\ cot, cart	\g\ go	\ō\ bone	\ü\ food	\zh\ vision

de·ter·mined \di-'tər-mənd\ *adj* **1** : having reached a decision : firmly resolved ⟨*determined* to be a pilot⟩ **2** : not weak or uncertain ⟨a very *determined* opponent⟩ — **de·ter·mined·ly** \-mən-dlē, -mə-nəd-lē\ *adv*

de·ter·min·er \di-'tər-mə-nər\ *n* : a word belonging to a group of noun modifiers that can occur before descriptive adjectives modifying the same noun ⟨"the" in "the red house" is a *determiner*⟩

de·ter·rence \di-'tər-ən(t)s, -'ter-\ *n* : the act, process, or capability of deterring

de·ter·rent \di-'tər-ənt, -'ter-\ *adj* : able or acting to deter — **deterrent** *n*

de·test \di-'test\ *vb* : to dislike very strongly **synonyms** see HATE

de·test·able \di-'tes-tə-bəl\ *adj* : arousing or deserving strong dislike : ABOMINABLE

de·throne \di-'thrōn\ *vb* **de·throned; de·thron·ing** : to remove from a throne : DEPOSE — **de·throne·ment** \-mənt\ *n*

det·o·nate \'det-ᵊn-ˌāt, 'det-ə-ˌnāt\ *vb* **-nat·ed; -nat·ing** : to explode or cause to explode with sudden violence — **det·o·na·tion** \ˌdet-ᵊn-'ā-shən, ˌdet-ə-'nā-\ *n*

det·o·na·tor \'det-ᵊn-ˌāt-ər, -ə-ˌnāt-\ *n* : a device or small quantity of explosive used for detonating another explosive

¹de·tour \'dē-ˌtu̇(ə)r *also* di-'tu̇(ə)r\ *n* : a departure from a direct course or the usual procedure; *esp* : a roundabout way temporarily replacing a regular route

²detour *vb* : to send or proceed by a detour ⟨*detour* traffic around an accident⟩

de·tract \di-'trakt\ *vb* : to take away some of the value or importance ⟨*detract* from a person's reputation⟩ — **de·trac·tion** \-'trak-shən\ *n* — **de·trac·tive** \-'trak-tiv\ *adj* — **de·trac·tive·ly** *adv* — **de·trac·tor** \-'trak-tər\ *n*

det·ri·ment \'de-trə-mənt\ *n* : injury or damage or its cause

det·ri·men·tal \ˌde-trə-'ment-ᵊl\ *adj* : HARMFUL ⟨*detrimental* effects of drug abuse⟩ — **det·ri·men·tal·ly** \-ᵊl-ē\ *adv*

de·tri·tus \di-'trīt-əs\ *n, pl* **detritus** \-'trīt-əs, -'trī-tüs\ **1** : loose material that results directly from the natural breaking up of rocks **2** : a product of disintegration or wearing away

deuce \'d(y)üs\ *n* **1 a** : the face of a die that bears two spots **b** : a playing card bearing the number two **c** : a throw of dice resulting in two points **2** : a tie in tennis after each side has scored 40 **3** : ¹DEVIL 1, DICKENS — used chiefly as a mild oath [from early French *deus* "two," from Latin *duos* (same meaning), from *duo* "two" — related to DUAL]

deu·te·ri·um \d(y)ü-'tir-ē-əm\ *n* : the hydrogen isotope that is twice the mass of ordinary hydrogen — called also *heavy hydrogen*

Deu·ter·on·o·my \ˌd(y)üt-ə-'rän-ə-mē\ *n* — see BIBLE table

deut·sche mark \'dȯich(-ə)-ˌmärk\ *also* **deutsch·mark** \'dȯich-\ *n* **1** : the former basic unit of money of Germany and earlier of West Germany **2** : a coin or bill representing one deutsche mark

dev·as·tate \'dev-ə-ˌstāt\ *vb* **-tat·ed; -tat·ing 1** : to reduce to ruin : lay waste ⟨a country *devastated* by war⟩ **2** : OVERWHELM 2, OVERPOWER ⟨*devastated* by grief⟩ — **dev·as·tat·ing·ly** \-ˌstāt-iŋ-lē\ *adv* — **dev·as·ta·tion** \ˌdev-ə-'stā-shən\ *n*

de·vel·op \di-'vel-əp\ *vb* **1 a** : to make or become clear gradually or in detail ⟨as the story *developed*⟩ **b** : to apply chemicals to exposed photographic material (as a film) in order to bring out the picture ⟨*develop* film⟩; *also* : to make visible by such a method ⟨*develop* pictures⟩ **c** : to make (a musical theme) more complicated by varying the rhythm and harmony **2** : to bring to a more advanced or more nearly perfect state ⟨*develop* an idea⟩ ⟨exercise de-

velops one's muscles⟩ **3** : to create or produce especially by effort ⟨*develop* new ways of doing business⟩ **4** : to make more available or usable ⟨*develop* land⟩ **5** : to acquire gradually ⟨*developed* a taste for olives⟩ **6** : to go through a process of natural growth or evolution in a series of stages ⟨a blossom *develops* from a bud⟩ — **de·vel·op·able** \-'vel-ə-pə-bəl\ *adj*

de·vel·oped \di-'vel-əpt\ *adj* : having a relatively high level of industrialization and standard of living ⟨a *developed* country⟩

de·vel·op·er \di-'vel-ə-pər\ *n* : one that develops: as **a** : a chemical used to develop exposed photographic materials **b** : a person who develops real estate; *esp* : one who divides land and builds and sells houses on it

de·vel·op·ing \di-ˌvel-ə-piŋ\ *adj* : UNDERDEVELOPED 2 ⟨*developing* nations⟩

de·vel·op·ment \di-'vel-əp-mənt\ *n* **1** : the act, process, or result of developing **2** : the state of being developed **3** : a developed piece of land; *esp* : one that has houses built on it

de·vel·op·men·tal \-ˌvel-əp-'ment-ᵊl\ *adj* : of or relating to development — **de·vel·op·men·tal·ly** \-ᵊl-ē\ *adv*

developmentally disabled *adj* : having a physical or mental disability (as mental retardation) that slows down or prevents normal development

de·vi·ance \'dē-vē-ən(t)s\ *n* : quality, state, or behavior that differs from what is normal or accepted

¹de·vi·ant \'dē-vē-ənt\ *adj* : deviating especially from some accepted standard of behavior or morals

²deviant *n* : a person whose behavior or morals differs from accepted or normal standards

de·vi·ate \'dē-vē-ˌāt\ *vb* **-at·ed; -at·ing** : to turn aside from a course, principle, standard, or topic

de·vi·a·tion \ˌdē-vē-'ā-shən\ *n* : an act or instance of deviating: as **a** : the difference found by subtracting some fixed number (as the arithmetic mean of a series of statistical data) from any item of the series **b** : noticeable difference from accepted standards (as of behavior or morals)

de·vice \di-'vīs\ *n* **1 a** : a scheme to deceive : STRATAGEM **b** : something (as a figure of speech) in a written work designed to achieve a particular artistic effect **c** : a piece of equipment to serve a special purpose **2** *pl* : a preferred way of doing or acting : INCLINATION ⟨left to her own *devices*⟩ **3** : a design that is an emblem; *esp* : one used in a coat of arms

¹dev·il \'dev-əl\ *n* **1** *often cap* : the personal supreme spirit of evil often represented as the ruler of hell — often used with *the* as a mild oath or expression of surprise, irritation, or emphasis **2** : DEMON 2 **3 a** : a person who is wicked, mischievous, reckless, or lively **b** : PERSON 1 — usually used in the phrases *poor devil* and *lucky devil*

²devil *vb* **dev·iled** *or* **dev·illed; dev·il·ing** *or* **dev·il·ling** \'dev-(ə-)liŋ\ **1** : to season highly ⟨*deviled* eggs⟩ **2** : ¹TEASE 2a, ANNOY

dev·il·fish \'dev-əl-ˌfish\ *n* **1** : MANTA RAY **2** : OCTOPUS 1

dev·il·ish \'dev-(ə-)lish\ *adj* **1** : characteristic of or resembling the devil ⟨*devilish* tricks⟩ **2** : ¹EXTREME 1, EXCESSIVE ⟨in a *devilish* hurry⟩ — **devilish** *adv* — **dev·il·ish·ly** *adv* — **dev·il·ish·ness** *n*

dev·il–may–care \ˌdev-əl-(ˌ)mā-'ke(ə)r, -'ka(ə)r\ *adj* : EASYGOING, CAREFREE

dev·il·ment \'dev-əl-mənt, -ˌment\ *n* : DEVILRY

devil ray *n* : MANTA RAY

dev·il·ry \'dev-əl-rē\ *or* **dev·il·try** \-əl-trē\ *n, pl* **-ries** *or* **-tries 1** : wicked or cruel behavior **2** : MISCHIEF 3

devil's advocate *n* **1** : a Roman Catholic official whose duty is to point out faults in the evidence when someone is proposed for sainthood **2** : a person who supports the less accepted or approved cause for the sake of argument

devil's darning needle *n* **1** : DRAGONFLY **2** : DAMSELFLY

dev·il's food cake \'dev-əlz-ˌfüd-ˌkāk\ *n* : a rich chocolate cake

devil's paintbrush *n* : any of various hawkweeds found in the eastern U.S.; *esp* : ORANGE HAWKWEED

de·vi·ous \'dē-vē-əs\ *adj* **1** : straying from a straight course : ROUNDABOUT ⟨the *devious* trail that wound along the creek⟩ ⟨leading through *devious* mazes⟩ **2** : SNEAKY, DECEPTIVE ⟨a *devious* plan⟩ ⟨got it by *devious* means⟩ — **de·vi·ous·ly** *adv* — **de·vi·ous·ness** *n*

de·vise \di-'vīz\ *vb* **de·vised; de·vis·ing 1** : to form in the mind by new combinations or applications of ideas or principles : INVENT ⟨*devise* a solution to the problem⟩ **2** : to give (real estate) by will ⟨*devised* the property to his daughter⟩ — **de·vis·er** *n*

de·void \di-'vȯid\ *adj* : not having a usual or expected quality ⟨a book *devoid* of interest⟩

De·vo·ni·an \di-'vō-nē-ən\ *adj* : of, relating to, or being a period of the Paleozoic era of geological history or the corresponding system of rocks — see GEOLOGIC TIME table — **Devonian** *n*

de·vote \di-'vōt\ *vb* **de·vot·ed; de·vot·ing 1** : to set apart for a special purpose ⟨*devote* land to farming⟩ **2** : to give (oneself) up to ⟨*devoted* herself to her career⟩

synonyms DEVOTE, DEDICATE, CONSECRATE mean to set apart for a special and often higher purpose. DEVOTE is likely to suggest strong reasons and often a long-term goal ⟨*devoted* her evenings to studying law⟩. DEDICATE suggests a solemn devotion to a serious or sacred purpose ⟨*dedicated* his life to helping the poor⟩. CONSECRATE suggests the giving of a solemn or sacred quality to something ⟨*consecrate* a church to the worship of God⟩.

devoted *adj* : having strong loyalty, affection, or dedication ⟨her grandchildren were *devoted* to her⟩ ⟨a rock singer's *devoted* fans⟩ — **de·vot·ed·ly** *adv* — **de·vot·ed·ness** *n*

dev·o·tee \ˌdev-ə-'tē, -'tā\ *n* : a keen or earnest follower, supporter, or enthusiast ⟨a *devotee* of sports⟩

de·vo·tion \di-'vō-shən\ *n* **1 a** : strong religious feeling **b** : a religious exercise or practice other than the regular worship of a congregation **2 a** : the act of devoting or the quality of being devoted **b** : strong love, affection, or dedication — **de·vo·tion·al** \-shnəl, -shən-ᵊl\ *adj* — **de·vo·tion·al·ly** \-ē\ *adv*

de·vour \di-'vaȯ(ə)r\ *vb* **1** : to eat up greedily or hungrily ⟨*devoured* everything on his plate⟩ **2** : to use up or destroy as if by eating ⟨fire *devoured* the barn⟩ **3** : to enjoy eagerly ⟨*devour* a book⟩ **synonyms** see EAT

de·vout \di-'vaȯt\ *adj* **1** : devoted to religion or to religious duties or exercises **2** : expressing devotion ⟨a *devout* attitude⟩ **3 a** : devoted to an activity, belief, or type of behavior ⟨a *devout* baseball fan⟩ **b** : ²EARNEST 1, SINCERE ⟨gave them *devout* thanks⟩ — **de·vout·ly** *adv* — **de·vout·ness** *n*

dew \'d(y)ü\ *n* **1** : moisture that collects on the surfaces of cool bodies at night **2** : something resembling dew in purity, freshness, or power to refresh — **dewy** \'d(y)ü-ē\ *adj*

dew·ber·ry \'d(y)ü-ˌber-ē\ *n* : any of several sweet edible berries related to and resembling blackberries; *also* : a plant with trailing stems that bears dewberries

dew·drop \'d(y)ü-ˌdräp\ *n* : a drop of dew

Dew·ey decimal classifica·tion \ˌd(y)ü-ē-\ *n* : a system of library classification in which publications are assigned a number from 0 to 999 according to subject — called also *Dewey decimal system* [named for Melvil *Dewey* 1851–1931 American librarian]

dew·lap \'d(y)ü-ˌlap\ *n* : loose skin hanging under the neck of various animals (as dogs or cattle of some breeds)

D dewlap

dew point *n* : the temperature at which the moisture in the air begins or would begin to collect on surfaces

dex·ter·i·ty \dek-'ster-ət-ē\ *n, pl* **-ties 1** : mental skill or quickness **2** : ease and grace in physical activity; *esp* : skill and ease in using the hands

dex·ter·ous *also* **dex·trous** \'dek-st(ə-)rəs\ *adj* **1** : mentally skillful and clever : EXPERT ⟨her *dexterous* handling of the problem⟩ **2** : done with skill ⟨a *dexterous* maneuver⟩ **3** : skillful with the hands — **dex·ter·ous·ly** *adv* — **dex·ter·ous·ness** *n*

dex·trose \'dek-ˌstrōs\ *n* : the naturally occurring form of glucose found in plants, fruits, and blood

¹DH \ˌdē-'āch\ *n, pl* **DHs** : DESIGNATED HITTER

²DH \ˌdē-'āch, 'dē-ˌāch\ *vb* **DHed; DHing** : to play as a designated hitter in a baseball game

di- *combining form* **1** : twice : twofold : double **2** : containing two atoms, radicals, or groups ⟨*dichloride*⟩ [derived from Greek *di-* "twice, containing two"]

di·a·be·tes \ˌdī-ə-'bēt-ēz, -'bēt-əs\ *n* : any of various bodily conditions in which abnormally large amounts of urine are produced; *esp* : DIABETES MELLITUS

diabetes mel·li·tus \-'mel-ət-əs\ *n* : an abnormal bodily condition in which less than the normal amount of insulin is produced, greater than normal amounts of urine are produced, and large amounts of sugar are contained in the blood and urine and which is marked especially by thirst, hunger, and loss of weight

¹di·a·bet·ic \ˌdī-ə-'bet-ik\ *adj* : of, relating to, or having diabetes ⟨a *diabetic* person⟩

²diabetic *n* : a person who has diabetes

di·a·bol·i·cal \ˌdī-ə-'bäl-i-kəl\ *or* **di·a·bol·ic** \-'bäl-ik\ *adj* : of, relating to, or characteristic of the devil : FIENDISH — **di·a·bol·i·cal·ly** \-i-k(ə-)lē\ *adv* — **di·a·bol·i·cal·ness** \-i-kəl-nəs\ *n*

di·a·crit·ic \ˌdī-ə-'krit-ik\ *n* : DIACRITICAL MARK

di·a·crit·i·cal mark \ˌdī-ə-ˌkrit-i-kəl-\ *n* : a mark used with a letter or group of letters and indicating a sound value different from that given the unmarked or otherwise marked letter or combination of letters

di·a·dem \'dī-ə-ˌdem, -əd-əm\ *n* : a headband or crown worn especially as a symbol of royalty

di·aer·e·sis *or* **di·er·e·sis** \dī-'er-ə-səs\ *n, pl* **di·aer·e·ses** *or* **di·er·e·ses** \-'er-ə-ˌsēz\ : a mark ¨ placed over a vowel to show that it is pronounced in a separate syllable (as in *naïve* or *Brontë*)

di·ag·nose \'dī-ig-ˌnōs, -ˌnōz; ˌdī-ig-'nōs, -'nōz\ *vb* **-nosed; -nos·ing** : to recognize by signs and symptoms : make a diagnosis ⟨*diagnose* a disease⟩ ⟨*diagnose* a play in football⟩

di·ag·no·sis \ˌdī-ig-'nō-səs\ *n, pl* **-no·ses** \-'nō-ˌsēz\ **1 a** : the art or act of identifying a disease from its signs and symptoms **b** : the decision reached by diagnosis **2 a** : a careful study of something especially to determine its nature or importance **b** : the conclusion reached after a study or examination

di·ag·nos·tic \ˌdī-ig-'näs-tik\ *adj* : of, relating to, or used in diagnosis ⟨a *diagnostic* test for heart disease⟩

di·ag·nos·ti·cian \ˌdī-ig-(ˌ)näs-'tish-ən\ *n* : a person who makes diagnoses; *esp* : a specialist in making medical diagnoses

¹di·ag·o·nal \dī-'ag-ən-ᵊl, -'ag-nəl\ *adj* **1** : joining two opposite corners of a four-sided figure **2** : running in a slanting direction — **di·ag·o·nal·ly** \-ən-ᵊl-ē, -nə-lē\ *adv*

²diagonal *n* **1** : a diagonal line or direction **2** : a diagonal row, arrangement, or pattern **3** : ²SLASH 2

\ə\ **abut**	\au̇\ **out**	\i\ **tip**	\ȯ\ **saw**	\u̇\ **foot**
\ər\ **further**	\ch\ **chin**	\ī\ **life**	\ȯi\ **coin**	\y\ **yet**
\a\ **mat**	\e\ **pet**	\j\ **job**	\th\ **thin**	\yü\ **few**
\ā\ **take**	\ē\ **easy**	\ŋ\ **sing**	\th\ **this**	\yu̇\ **cure**
\ä\ **cot, cart**	\g\ **go**	\ō\ **bone**	\ü\ **food**	\zh\ **vision**

¹di·a·gram \'dī-ə-ˌgram\ *n* : a drawing, sketch, plan, or chart that makes something clearer or easier to understand — **di·a·gram·mat·ic** \ˌdī-ə-grə-'mat-ik\ *also* **di·a·gram·mat·i·cal** \-'mat-i-kəl\ *adj* — **di·a·gram·mat·i·cal·ly** \-'mat-i-k(ə-)lē\ *adv*

²diagram *vb* **-grammed** *or* **-gramed** \-ˌgramd\; **-gram·ming** *or* **-gram·ing** \-ˌgram-iŋ\ : to represent by or put into the form of a diagram ⟨*diagram* a sentence⟩ ⟨*diagrammed* a football play⟩

¹di·al \'dī-(-ə)l\ *n* **1 a** : SUNDIAL **b** : the face of a watch or clock **2 a** : a face or scale on which some measurement is registered usually by means of numbers and a pointer ⟨the thermometer *dial* reads 60°⟩ **b** : a disk usually with a knob or slots that may be turned to make electrical connections (as on a telephone) or to regulate the operation of a device (as a radio)

²dial *vb* **di·aled** *or* **di·alled**; **di·al·ing** *or* **di·al·ling** **1** : to turn a dial so as to operate, regulate, or select **2** : to make a telephone call or connection

di·a·lect \'dī-ə-ˌlekt\ *n* **1** : a regional variety of a language differing from the standard language **2** : a variety of a language used by the members of a particular group or class ⟨peasant *dialect*⟩ — **di·a·lec·tal** \ˌdī-ə-'lek-t°l\ *adj* — **di·a·lec·tal·ly** \-t°l-ē\ *adv*

di·a·logue *also* **di·a·log** \'dī-ə-ˌlog, -ˌläg\ *n* **1** : a conversation between two or more persons **2** : conversation given in a written story or play

dial–up \'dī-(-ə)l-ˌəp\ *adj* : relating to or done using an ordinary telephone line ⟨*dial-up* Internet access⟩

di·al·y·sis \dī-'al-ə-səs\ *n, pl* **-y·ses** \-ə-ˌsēz\ **1** : the separation of substances in solution by means of their unequal diffusion through membranes with pores of a specified maximum size; *esp* : such a separation of colloids from dissolved substances **2** : the process of removing blood from an artery (as of a patient with failing kidneys), purifying it by dialysis, and returning it to a vein

di·am·e·ter \dī-'am-ət-ər\ *n* **1** : a straight line passing through the center of a figure or body; *esp* : a line segment through the center of a circle with its ends on the circle's circumference **2** : the length of a diameter

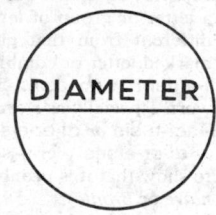

diameter 1

di·a·met·ric \ˌdī-ə-'me-trik\ *or* **di·a·met·ri·cal** \-'me-tri-kəl\ *adj* **1** : of or relating to a diameter **2** : completely opposed or opposite — **di·a·met·ri·cal·ly** \-tri-k(ə-)lē\ *adv*

di·a·mond \'dī-(-ə)mənd\ *n* **1 a** : a very hard stone of crystallized carbon that is used as a precious gem and industrially as a powder for grinding, smoothing, or polishing and in cutting tools **b** : a piece of this stone especially when cut and polished **2** : a shape that is formed by four equal straight lines and has two opposite acute angles and two opposite obtuse angles **3 a** : a playing card marked with a red diamond-shaped figure **b** *pl* : the suit made up of cards marked with diamonds **4 a** : INFIELD 1a **b** : the entire playing field in baseball or softball

Word History Diamond, the hardest substance found in nature, was known to the ancient Greeks. They called the gemstone *adamas,* using the same word they used for any unbreakable or indestructible substance, such as the hardest metal, or for anything unmovable. The stem of this word was *adamant-.* Later, Latin writers borrowed these Greek words, sometimes as *adamant-, adamas* and sometimes *adamant-, adimas.* The forms *adamant-, adamas* in time gave us the English noun *adamant,* meaning "an imaginary stone of great hardness," and the adjective *adamant,* meaning "firmly fixed or decided." The "i" forms in Latin were later changed from *adimant-, adimas* to *diamant-, diamas*

and came to be used only for the gemstone which we now call *diamond.* [Middle English *diamaunde* "diamond," from early French *diamant* (same meaning), derived from Latin *diamant-, diamas,* an altered form of *adimant-, adimas* and *adamant-, adamas* "the hardest metal, diamond," from Greek *adamant-, adamas* (same meaning) — related to ADAMANT]

di·a·mond·back \'dī-(-ə)mən(d)-ˌbak\ *adj* : having marks like diamonds on the back

diamondback rattlesnake *n* : either of two large and deadly rattlesnakes of the southern U.S. — called also *diamondback, diamondback rattler*

diamondback terrapin *n* : any of several edible terrapins of coastal salt marshes of the southeastern U.S.

dia·pause \'dī-ə-ˌpóz\ *n* : a period (as in some insects) in which development slows down or in which bodily activities are decreased

¹di·a·per \'dī-(-ə)pər\ *n* **1** : a usually white linen or cotton fabric woven in a pattern formed by the repetition of a simple design; *also* : the design on such cloth **2** : a garment for infants consisting of a piece of absorbent material drawn up between the legs and fastened about the waist

²diaper *vb* **di·a·pered**; **di·a·per·ing** \-p(ə-)riŋ\ **1** : to decorate with diaper designs **2** : to put a diaper on ⟨*diaper* a baby⟩

di·a·phragm \'dī-ə-ˌfram\ *n* **1** : a sheet of muscle that separates the cavities of the chest and abdomen in mammals **2** : a device that limits the size of an opening in order to control the amount of light passing through a lens (as of a camera or microscope) **3** : a thin flexible disk that vibrates (as in a microphone) **4** : a cup-shaped device usually of thin rubber that fits over the cervix of the uterus and acts to prevent pregnancy by keeping sperm from reaching the egg — **di·a·phrag·mat·ic** \ˌdī-ə-frə(g)-'mat-ik, -ˌfrag-\ *adj*

di·ar·rhea \ˌdī-ə-'rē-ə\ *n* : abnormally frequent and watery bowel movements

di·a·ry \'dī-(-ə)rē\ *n, pl* **-ries** : a daily record especially of personal experiences and thoughts; *also* : a book for keeping such a record [from Latin *diarium* "a record of business dealings or activities during the day," from *dies* "day" — related to MERIDIAN, SUNDAY; see *Word History* at SUNDAY]

di·a·stase \'dī-ə-ˌstās\ *n* : AMYLASE

di·as·to·le \dī-'as-tə-(ˌ)lē\ *n* : the relaxation of the heart during which its cavities expand and fill with blood — compare SYSTOLE

di·a·stol·ic \ˌdī-ə-'stäl-ik\ *adj* : of, relating to, caused by, or occurring during diastole ⟨*diastolic* blood pressure is lower than systolic blood pressure⟩

di·as·tro·phism \dī-'as-trə-ˌfiz-əm\ *n* : TECTONISM — **di·a·stroph·ic** \ˌdī-ə-'sträf-ik\ *adj*

di·a·tom \'dī-ə-ˌtäm\ *n* : any of a class of minute floating single-celled or colonial algae that are common in fresh and salt water and have a cell wall of silica that remains as a skeleton after death — **di·a·to·ma·ceous** \ˌdī-ət-ə-'mā-shəs\ *adj*

diatomaceous earth *n* : a light crumbly material that is made up mostly of the silica-containing skeletons of dead diatoms and is used especially as a filter

di·atom·ic \ˌdī-ə-'täm-ik\ *adj* : having two atoms in the molecule

diatom

di·at·o·mite \dī-'at-ə-ˌmīt\ *n* : DIATOMACEOUS EARTH

dia·ton·ic \ˌdī-ə-'tän-ik\ *adj* : relating to or being a standard major or minor scale of eight tones to the octave — **dia·ton·i·cal·ly** \-'tän-i-k(ə-)lē\ *adv*

di·a·tribe \'dī-ə-ˌtrīb\ *n* : a bitter or angry attack in speech or writing

dib·ble \'dib-əl\ *n* : a small hand tool for making holes in the ground for plants, seeds, or bulbs

¹dice \'dīs\ *n, pl* **dice 1** : ²DIE 1 **2** : a gambling game played with dice — **no dice** : definitely no; *also* : of no use

²dice *vb* **diced; dic·ing 1** : to cut into small cubes ⟨*diced* carrots⟩ **2** : to play games with dice — **dic·er** *n*

di·chot·o·mous \dī-'kät-ə-məs\ *adj* **1** : dividing into two parts or groups **2** : relating to, involving, or resulting from dichotomy

dichotomous key *n* : a series of pairs of phrases or descriptions which are used to classify a group of living things by making choices between the sets of traits and characters described in each pair

di·chot·o·my \-mē\ *n, pl* **-mies** : a division into or distinction between two groups that differ greatly ⟨the *dichotomy* between good and evil⟩

dick·ens \'dik-ənz\ *n* : ¹DEVIL 1, DEUCE — used chiefly as a mild oath ⟨what the *dickens* do you mean?⟩

dick·er \'dik-ər\ *vb* **dick·ered; dick·er·ing** \'dik-(ə-)riŋ\ : ²BARGAIN, HAGGLE — **dicker** *n*

dick·ey *or* **dicky** \'dik-ē\ *n, pl* **dick·eys** *or* **dick·ies 1** : any of various articles of clothing: as **a** : a separate or detachable front of a shirt **b** : a small cloth insert worn to fill in the neckline **2** : a small bird

di·cot \'dī-ˌkät\ *n* : DICOTYLEDON

di·cot·y·le·don \ˌdī-ˌkät-ᵊl-'ēd-ᵊn\ *n* : any of a group of flowering plants (as an aster, an oak, or a bean) having an embryo with two cotyledons, leaves with veins that usually branch and interlace to form a network, and flower parts that occur in groups of four or five — compare MONOCOTYLEDON

di·cot·y·le·don·ous \ˌdī-ˌkät-ᵊl-'ēd-ᵊn-əs\ *adj* : of, relating to, or being plants that are dicotyledons

¹dic·tate \'dik-ˌtāt, dik-'tāt\ *vb* **dic·tat·ed; dic·tat·ing 1** : to speak or read for a person to write down or for a machine to record ⟨*dictate* a letter to a secretary⟩ **2** : to say or state with authority or power : give orders ⟨*dictate* terms of surrender⟩ ⟨few people enjoy being *dictated* to⟩ [from Latin *dictatus*, past participle of *dictare* "to assert, dictate," from *dicere* "to say" — related to DICTIONARY, PREDICT, VERDICT]

²dic·tate \'dik-ˌtāt\ *n* : an order or direction given with authority : COMMAND ⟨the *dictates* of conscience⟩

dic·ta·tion \dik-'tā-shən\ *n* **1** : the act or process of giving commands **2 a** : the dictating of words ⟨write from *dictation*⟩ **b** : something that is dictated or is taken down from dictation

dic·ta·tor \'dik-ˌtāt-ər, dik-'tāt-ər\ *n* **1** : a person who rules with total authority and often in a cruel or brutal manner **2** : one that dictates — **dic·ta·to·ri·al** \ˌdik-tə-'tōr-ē-əl, -tor-\ *adj* — **dic·ta·to·ri·al·ly** \-ē-ə-lē\ *adv* — **dic·ta·to·ri·al·ness** *n*

dic·ta·tor·ship \dik-'tāt-ər-ˌship, 'dik-ˌtāt-\ *n* **1** : the office of a dictator **2** : rule, control, or leadership by one person with total power **3** : a government or country in which total power is held by a dictator or a small group

dic·tion \'dik-shən\ *n* **1** : choice of words especially with regard to correctness, clearness, or effectiveness : WORDING ⟨careless *diction* in the student's essay⟩ **2** : quality of vocal expression : ENUNCIATION ⟨a good singer with excellent *diction*⟩

dic·tio·nary \'dik-shə-ˌner-ē\ *n, pl* **-nar·ies 1** : a reference source in print or electronic form giving information about the meanings, forms, pronunciations, uses, and origins of words listed in alphabetical order **2** : a reference book that lists in alphabetical order terms or names important to a particular subject along with explanations of their meanings and uses ⟨a law *dictionary*⟩ **3** : a reference book giving words of one language and their meanings in another ⟨an English-French *dictionary*⟩ [from Latin *dic-*

tionarium "dictionary," from earlier *diction-, dictio-* "words, speaking," from *dicere* "to say" — related to DICTATE]

dic·tum \'dik-təm\ *n, pl* **dic·ta** \-tə\; *also* **dic·tums** : a statement made with authority : PRONOUNCEMENT

did *past of* DO

di·dac·tic \dī-'dak-tik, də-\ *adj* : intended primarily to teach rather than to entertain ⟨a *didactic* story with a moral lesson⟩ — **di·dac·ti·cal** \-ti-kəl\ *adj* — **di·dac·ti·cal·ly** \-ti-k(ə-)lē\ *adv* — **di·dac·ti·cism** \-tə-ˌsiz-əm\ *n*

didn't \'did-ᵊnt\ : did not

didst \(')didst\ *archaic past 2nd singular of* DO

¹die \'dī\ *vb* **died; dy·ing** \'dī-iŋ\ **1** : to stop living : EXPIRE ⟨*died* of old age⟩ **2 a** : to pass out of existence : come to an end ⟨their anger was *dying* down⟩ **b** : to disappear or lessen gradually ⟨the wind *died* down⟩ **3 a** : to wish eagerly or desperately ⟨*dying* to go⟩ **b** : to be completely overcome with emotion ⟨almost *died* of embarrassment⟩ **4** : to stop functioning ⟨the motor sputtered and *died*⟩ [Middle English *dien* "to die," of Norse origin]

²die \'dī\ *n* **1** *pl* **dice** \'dīs\ : a small cube marked on each side with one to six spots and used usually in pairs in various games — often used figuratively in expressions concerning chance or the absence of possible change in a course of action ⟨the *die* was cast⟩ **2** *pl* **dies** \'dīz\ : any of various devices used for cutting, shaping, or stamping a material or object [Middle English *dee* "small cube marked with spots and thrown in gambling, dice," from early French *dé* (same meaning)]

die–hard \'dī-ˌhärd\ *adj* : strongly or excessively determined or devoted ⟨*die-hard* fans⟩ — **die·hard** *n*

die–off \'dī-ˌof\ *n* : a sudden sharp drop in the numbers of plants or animals in a group

dieresis *variant of* DIAERESIS

die·sel \'dē-zəl, -səl\ *n* **1** : DIESEL ENGINE **2** : a vehicle (as a truck or train) driven by a diesel engine **3** : a fuel designed for use in diesel engines [named for Rudolf *Diesel* 1858–1913 German engineer]

diesel engine *n* : an internal-combustion engine in which air is compressed to make enough heat to ignite the fuel in the cylinder

¹di·et \'dī-ət\ *n* **1 a** : the food and drink that a person, animal, or group usually takes ⟨many birds live on a *diet* of insects⟩ **b** : the kind and amount of food selected for a person or animal for a special reason (as improving health) ⟨a high-protein *diet*⟩ **c** : a plan of eating and drinking less than usual so as to reduce one's weight ⟨going on a *diet*⟩ **2** : something experienced repeatedly ⟨a steady *diet* of television⟩ [Middle English *diete* "regular food, diet," from early French *diete* (same meaning), derived from Greek *diaita*, literally, "manner of living"]

²diet *vb* : to eat or cause to eat less or according to special rules

³diet *adj* : reduced in calories ⟨a *diet* soft drink⟩

⁴diet *n* : a body of lawmakers : LEGISLATURE [Middle English *diete* "day's journey, day set for a meeting," from Latin *dieta*, literally, "daily regimen, diet" (associated with Latin *dies* "day"), derived from Greek *diaita*]

di·etary \'dī-ə-ˌter-ē\ *adj* : of or relating to a diet or to the rules of diet

di·et·er \'dī-ət-ər\ *n* : a person who is on a diet

di·etet·ic \ˌdī-ə-'tet-ik\ *adj* : of or relating to diet or dietetics

di·etet·ics \ˌdī-ə-'tet-iks\ *n* : the science of applying the principles of nutrition to feeding

\ə\ **abut**	\au̇\ **out**	\i\ **tip**	\o̅\ **saw**	\u̇\ **foot**
\ər\ **further**	\ch\ **chin**	\ī\ **life**	\oi\ **coin**	\y\ **yet**
\a\ **mat**	\e\ **pet**	\j\ **job**	\th\ **thin**	\yü\ **few**
\ā\ **take**	\ē\ **easy**	\ŋ\ **sing**	\t̲h̲\ **this**	\yu̇\ **cure**
\ä\ **cot, cart**	\g\ **go**	\ō\ **bone**	\ü\ **food**	\zh\ **vision**

di·eti·tian *or* **di·eti·cian** \ˌdī-ə-'tish-ən\ *n* : a specialist in dietetics

diff \'dif\ *n, slang* : DIFFERENCE

dif·fer \'dif-ər\ *vb* **dif·fered; dif·fer·ing** \'dif-(ə-)riŋ\ **1** : to be not the same : be unlike ⟨brothers who *differ* in looks⟩ **2** : DISAGREE 2 ⟨*differ* only on one issue⟩

dif·fer·ence \'dif-ərn(t)s, 'dif-(ə-)rən(t)s\ *n* **1** : the quality or state of being different ⟨the striking *difference* in the sisters' looks⟩ **2** : the degree or amount by which things differ; *esp* : the number that is obtained by subtracting one number from another ⟨the *difference* between 4 and 6 is 2⟩ **3** : a disagreement in opinion ⟨persons unable to settle their *differences*⟩ **4** : an important change in or effect on a situation ⟨made no *difference* to me⟩

dif·fer·ent \'dif-ərnt, 'dif-(ə-)rənt\ *adj* **1** : not of the same kind : partly or totally unlike another ⟨this apple is *different* from the others in size and color⟩ **2** : not the same : OTHER, SEPARATE ⟨see the same person at *different* times⟩ — **dif·fer·ent·ly** *adv*

¹dif·fer·en·tial \ˌdif-ə-'ren-chəl\ *adj* **1 a** : of, relating to, or being a difference **b** : treating some individuals or classes differently from others : DISCRIMINATORY **2** : acting or proceeding differently or at a different rate ⟨*differential* diffusion of molecules through a membrane⟩ — **dif·fer·en·tial·ly** \-'rench-(ə-)lē\ *adv*

²differential *n* **1** : an amount or degree of difference between comparable things ⟨the price *differential* between a small and large box of popcorn⟩ **2** : an arrangement of gears in an automobile that allows one wheel to turn faster than another (as in going around a curve)

differential gear *n* : ²DIFFERENTIAL 2

dif·fer·en·ti·ate \ˌdif-ə-'ren-chē-ˌāt\ *vb* **-at·ed; -at·ing** **1** : to make or become different in some way ⟨the color of their eyes *differentiates* the twins⟩ **2** : to undergo or cause to undergo differentiation in the course of development **3** : to see or state the difference or differences ⟨*differentiate* between two plants⟩

dif·fer·en·ti·a·tion \ˌdif-ə-ˌren-chē-'ā-shən\ *n* **1** : the act or process of differentiating **2** : the processes by which cells and tissues develop their specialized adult form and function; *also* : the result of these processes

dif·fi·cult \'dif-i-(ˌ)kəlt\ *adj* **1** : hard to do, make, or carry out ⟨a *difficult* climb⟩ **2 a** : hard to deal with, manage, or overcome ⟨a *difficult* child⟩ **b** : hard to understand : PUZZLING ⟨*difficult* reading⟩ — **dif·fi·cult·ly** *adv*

dif·fi·cul·ty \'dif-ə-(ˌ)kəl-tē\ *n, pl* **-ties** **1** : difficult nature ⟨the *difficulty* of a task⟩ **2** : great effort ⟨walked with *difficulty*⟩ **3** : something that is hard to do : OBSTACLE ⟨overcome *difficulties*⟩ **4** : a difficult or trying situation : TROUBLE ⟨in financial *difficulties*⟩ **5** : a disagreement in opinion ⟨we ironed out our *difficulties*⟩

dif·fi·dent \'dif-əd-ənt, -ə-ˌdent\ *adj* **1** : lacking confidence : TIMID **2** : RESERVED 1, UNASSERTIVE **synonyms** see SHY — **dif·fi·dence** \-əd-ən(t)s, -ə-ˌden(t)s\ *n* — **dif·fi·dent·ly** *adv*

dif·fract \dif-'rakt\ *vb* : to cause to go through diffraction

dif·frac·tion \dif-'rak-shən\ *n* : the bending or spreading of a beam of light especially when passing through a narrow opening or by the edge of an object; *also* : similar changes in other waves (as sound waves)

diffraction grating *n* : GRATING 2

¹dif·fuse \dif-'yüs\ *adj* **1** : using too many words : VERBOSE ⟨a *diffuse* writer⟩ **2** : poured or spread out : not concentrated ⟨*diffuse* daylight⟩ — **dif·fuse·ly** *adv* — **dif·fuse·ness** *n*

²dif·fuse \dif-'yüz\ *vb* **dif·fused; dif·fus·ing** **1** : to pour out and permit or cause to spread freely **2** : to go through or cause to go through diffusion

dif·fu·sion \dif-'yü-zhən\ *n* **1** : a diffusing or a being diffused **2** : the mixing of particles of liquids, gases, or solids so that they move from a region of high concentration to one of lower concentration **3** : the scattering of light by

reflection from a rough surface or by passage through a translucent material (as frosted glass)

¹dig \'dig\ *vb* **dug** \'dəg\; **dig·ging** **1 a** : to turn up the soil (as with a spade or hoe) **b** : to hollow out or form by removing earth ⟨*dig* a hole⟩ **2** : to uncover or search by or as if by turning up earth ⟨*dig* potatoes⟩ ⟨*dig* for gold⟩ ⟨*dig* through books for help⟩ **3** : FIND OUT ⟨*dig* up the facts⟩ **4** : ¹PROD 1, POKE ⟨*dug* me in the ribs⟩ **5 a** : to pay attention to : NOTICE ⟨*dig* that hat⟩ **b** : UNDERSTAND 1a ⟨you *dig* me?⟩ **c** : ¹LIKE 1 ⟨I *dig* music⟩ — **dig·ger** *n*

²dig *n* **1** : ³POKE, THRUST **2** : a harsh remark : GIBE **3** : a place where scientists (as archaeologists or paleontologists) try to recover buried objects by digging; *also* : the process of digging for such objects

¹di·gest \'dī-ˌjest\ *n* : a body of information or a literary work in shortened form ⟨a *digest* of the laws⟩

²di·gest \dī-'jest, də-\ *vb* **1** : to think over and arrange in the mind ⟨*digest* the news⟩ **2** : to convert food into simpler forms that can be taken in and used by the body **3** : SUMMARIZE 1 **4** : to become digested

di·gest·ible \dī-'jes-tə-bəl, də-\ *adj* : capable of being digested — **di·gest·ibil·i·ty** \-ˌjes-tə-'bil-ət-ē\ *n*

di·ges·tion \dī-'jes-chən, də-\ *n* : the process by which food is broken down into simpler forms in the body by mechanical and enzymatic means

di·ges·tive \dī-'jes-tiv, də-\ *adj* **1** : of or relating to digestion ⟨*digestive* processes⟩ **2** : having the power to cause or help digestion ⟨*digestive* enzymes⟩

digestive system *n* : the bodily system concerned with the intake, breakdown, and absorption of food and the discharge of wastes and that includes the mouth, pharynx, esophagus, stomach, intestine, anus, and glands (as the salivary glands)

dig·ger wasp \'dig-ər-\ *n* : a burrowing wasp; *esp* : one that digs nests in the soil and stocks them with insects or spiders paralyzed by stinging

dig·gings \'dig-iŋz\ *n pl* **1** : a place where ore, metals, or gems are dug **2** : LODGING 2

dig in *vb* **1** : to dig and take position in a trench ⟨the soldiers *dug in*⟩ **2 a** : to go to work **b** : to begin eating

dig·it \'dij-ət\ *n* **1 a** : any of the arabic numerals 1 to 9 and usually the symbol 0 **b** : one of the elements that are used to form numbers in a system other than the decimal system **2** : a finger or toe [Middle English *digit* "numeral," from Latin *digitus* "finger, toe"]

dig·i·tal \'dij-ət-ᵊl\ *adj* **1** : of, relating to, or done with a finger or toe **2** : of, relating to, or using calculation directly with digits rather than through measurable physical quantities **3** : of or relating to data in the form of numerical digits ⟨*digital* images⟩ ⟨*digital* broadcasting⟩ **4** : providing displayed or recorded information in numerical digits ⟨a *digital* watch⟩ **5** : characterized by electronic and computerized technology ⟨living in a *digital* world⟩ — **dig·i·tal·ly** \-ᵊl-ē\ *adv*

digital camera *n* : a camera that records images as digital data instead of on film

digital computer *n* : a computer that operates with numbers expressed as digits (as in the binary system) — compare ANALOG COMPUTER

dig·i·tal·is \ˌdij-ə-'tal-əs *also* -'tāl-\ *n* **1** : FOXGLOVE **2** : a powerful drug used to stimulate the heart and prepared from the dried leaves of the common foxglove

digital versatile disc *n* : DVD

digital video disc *n* : DVD

digital video recorder *n* : DVR

dig·i·tize \'dij-ə-ˌtīz\ *vb* **-tized; -tiz·ing** : to change (as data or an image) to digital form — **dig·i·tiz·er** *n*

dig·ni·fied \'dig-nə-ˌfīd\ *adj* : having or showing dignity

dig·ni·fy \'dig-nə-ˌfī\ *vb* **-fied; -fy·ing** : to give dignity or importance to : HONOR

dig·ni·tary \'dig-nə-ˌter-ē\ *n, pl* **-tar·ies** : a person of high position or honor ⟨*dignitaries* of the church⟩

dig·ni·ty \'dig-nət-ē\ n, pl **-ties 1** : the quality or state of being worthy, honored, or respected **2** : high rank, office, or position **3** : a look or way of behaving that suggests seriousness and self-control

di·gress \dī-'gres, də-\ vb : to turn aside especially from the main subject in writing or speaking — **di·gres·sion** \-'gresh-ən\ n — **di·gres·sive** \-'gres-iv\ adj

di·he·dral angle \(')dī-,hē-drəl-\ n : the angle between two intersecting planes

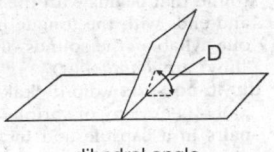

dihedral angle

¹**di·hy·brid** \(,)dī-'hī-brəd\ n : an individual that is hybrid with respect to two different traits or pairs of genes

²**dihybrid** adj : being, involving, or producing individuals that are hybrid with respect to two different traits or pairs of genes

¹**dike** \'dīk\ n **1** : a channel dug in the earth to carry water : DITCH **2** : a bank of earth constructed to control water : LEVEE **3** : a long body of igneous rock that has been forced while molten into a narrow opening or crack

²**dike** vb **diked; dik·ing 1** : to surround or protect with a dike **2** : to drain by a dike — **dik·er** n

di·lap·i·dat·ed \də-'lap-ə-,dāt-əd\ adj : partly ruined or decayed especially from age or lack of care ⟨a dilapidated old house⟩

di·lap·i·da·tion \də-,lap-ə-'dā-shən\ n : a dilapidated condition : partial ruin

di·la·ta·tion \,dil-ə-'tā-shən, ,dī-lə-\ n : DILATION 2

di·late \dī-'lāt, 'dī-,lāt\ vb **di·lat·ed; di·lat·ing** : to make or grow larger or wider ⟨lungs dilated with air⟩ **synonyms** see EXPAND

di·la·tion \dī-'lā-shən\ n **1** : the act of dilating : the state of being dilated : EXPANSION ⟨dilation of the pupils of the eyes⟩ **2** : the action of stretching or enlarging an organ or part of the body

dil·a·to·ry \'dil-ə-,tōr-ē, -,tòr-\ adj **1** : tending or intended to cause delay ⟨dilatory tactics⟩ **2** : tending to be late : TARDY ⟨dilatory in paying her bills⟩ — **dil·a·to·ri·ly** \,dil-ə-'tōr-ə-lē, -'tòr-\ adv — **dil·a·to·ri·ness** \'dil-ə-,tōr-ē-nəs, -,tòr-\ n

di·lem·ma \də-'lem-ə also dī-\ n : a situation in which one has to choose between two or more things, ways, or plans that are equally unsatisfactory : a difficult choice

dil·et·tante \'dil-ə-,tänt, -,tant; ,dil-ə-'tänt(-ē), -'tant(-ē)\ n, pl **-tantes** or **-tan·ti** \-'tänt-ē, -'tant-ē\ **1** : an admirer or lover of the arts **2** : a person who has a shallow interest in an art or area of knowledge — **dilettante** adj — **dil·et·tan·tism** \-,tän-,tiz-əm, -,tan-\ n

dil·i·gence \'dil-ə-jən(t)s\ n : careful and continued work : INDUSTRY

dil·i·gent \'dil-ə-jənt\ adj : showing steady and earnest care and effort : PAINSTAKING ⟨a diligent search⟩ ⟨a diligent worker⟩ **synonyms** see BUSY — **dil·i·gent·ly** adv

dill \'dil\ n : an herb related to the carrot and having aromatic foliage and seeds used especially in flavoring pickles

dill pickle n : a pickle seasoned with dill

dil·ly-dal·ly \'dil-ē-,dal-ē\ vb : to waste time : DAWDLE

¹**di·lute** \dī-'lüt, də-\ vb **di·lut·ed; di·lut·ing** : to make thinner or more liquid by adding in and mixing something ⟨added water to dilute the punch⟩

²**dilute** adj : lacking normal strength especially as a result of being diluted

di·lu·tion \dī-'lü-shən, də-\ n **1** : the action of diluting : the state of being diluted **2** : something (as a solution) that is diluted

¹**dim** \'dim\ adj **dim·mer; dim·mest 1** : not bright or clear : OBSCURE, FAINT ⟨a dim light⟩ **2** : being without luster : DULL ⟨dim colors⟩ **3 a** : not seeing or understanding

clearly ⟨dim eyes⟩ **b** : not seen or understood clearly ⟨had only a dim notion of what was going on⟩ — **dim·ly** adv — **dim·ness** n

²**dim** vb **dimmed; dim·ming 1** : to make or become dim **2** : to reduce the light from

dime \'dīm\ n : a U.S. coin worth ¹/₁₀ dollar [Middle English dime "a tenth part," from early French dime (same meaning), derived from Latin decimus "a tenth part," from decem "ten" — related to DECEMBER, DECIMAL, DOZEN] — **a dime a dozen** : so plentiful or common as to be of little value

di·men·sion \də-'men-chən also dī-\ n **1 a** : extension in one direction ⟨the dimensions of length, width, and height⟩ **b** : measure of extension in one direction or in all directions : SIZE **2** : the range over which something extends : SCOPE — usually used in plural [Middle English dimensioun "dimension," from early French dimension (same meaning), from Latin dimensio "measurement, dimension," from dimetiri "to measure out," from di-, dis- "apart" and metiri "to measure" — related to IMMENSE, MEASURE] — **di·men·sion·al** \-'mench-nəl, -'men-chən-ᵊl\ adj — **di·men·sion·al·ly** \-'mench-nə-lē, -'men-chən-ᵊl-ē\ adv — **di·men·sion·less** \-'men-chən-ləs\ adj

dime store n : a store that sells mainly inexpensive goods

di·min·ish \də-'min-ish\ vb **1** : to make less or cause to appear less **2** : to lessen the authority, dignity, or reputation of : BELITTLE **3** : to become gradually less (as in size or importance) : DWINDLE — **di·min·ish·ment** \-mənt\ n

di·min·u·en·do \də-,min-(y)ə-'wen-dō\ adv or adj : ²DE-CRESCENDO — **diminuendo** n

dim·i·nu·tion \,dim-ə-'n(y)ü-shən\ n : the act, process, or an instance of diminishing : DECREASE

¹**di·min·u·tive** \də-'min-yət-iv\ n **1** : a diminutive word, name, or affix **2** : a diminutive object or individual

²**diminutive** adj **1** : indicating small size and sometimes the state or quality of being lovable or pitiful ⟨the diminutive suffixes "-ette" and "-ling"⟩ ⟨the diminutive noun "duckling"⟩ **2** : extremely small : TINY — **di·min·u·tive·ly** adv — **di·min·u·tive·ness** n

dim·i·ty \'dim-ət-ē\ n, pl **-ties** : a usually corded cotton fabric in checks or stripes

dim·mer \'dim-ər\ n **1** : a device for controlling the amount of light from an electric lighting unit (as the headlights of an automobile or the lights of a room) **2** : LOW BEAM

¹**dim·ple** \'dim-pəl\ n **1** : a slight natural indentation in the surface of some part of the human body (as the chin) **2** : a slight hollow ⟨the dimples on a golf ball⟩

²**dimple** vb **dim·pled; dim·pling** \-p(ə-)liŋ\ : to mark with or form dimples

¹**din** \'din\ n : a loud confused mixture of noises

²**din** vb **dinned; din·ning 1** : to make a loud noise **2** : to repeat again and again in order to impress on someone's mind ⟨dinned into us the consequences of failure⟩

di·nar \di-'när, 'dē-,\ n **1** : a basic unit of money (as of Jordan) **2** : a coin or bill representing one dinar

dine \'dīn\ vb **dined; din·ing 1** : to eat dinner ⟨dine out⟩ **2** : to give a dinner to : FEED ⟨wined and dined their friends⟩

din·er \'dī-nər\ n **1** : one that dines **2 a** : DINING CAR **b** : a restaurant in the shape of a railroad car

di·nette \dī-'net\ n : a separate area or small room used for dining

ding \'diŋ\ vb : to make a ringing sound : CLANG

ding—dong \'diŋ-,dòŋ, -,däŋ\ n : the ringing sound made by repeated strokes especially on a bell

---

\ə\ **abut**	\aú\ **out**	\i\ **tip**	\ò\ **saw**	\ú\ **foot**
\ər\ **further**	\ch\ **chin**	\ī\ **life**	\ói\ **coin**	\y\ **yet**
\a\ **mat**	\e\ **pet**	\j\ **job**	\th\ **thin**	\yü\ **few**
\ā\ **take**	\ē\ **easy**	\ŋ\ **sing**	\th\ **this**	\yú\ **cure**
\ä\ **cot, cart**	\g\ **go**	\ō\ **bone**	\ü\ **food**	\zh\ **vision**

din·ghy \'diŋ-ē, -gē\ *n, pl* **dinghies** **1** : a small rowboat or sailboat; *esp* : one carried on a larger boat **2** : a rubber life raft

din·gle \'diŋ-gəl\ *n* : a small wooded valley

din·go \'diŋ-gō\ *n, pl* **dingoes** : a reddish brown bushy-tailed wild dog of Australia

dingo

din·gy \'din-jē\ *adj* **din·gi·er; -est** : rather dark and dirty : not fresh or clean ⟨a *dingy* room⟩ ⟨*dingy* colors⟩ — **din·gi·ly** \-jə-lē\ *adv* — **din·gi·ness** \-jē-nəs\ *n*

din·ing car \'dī-niŋ-\ *n* : a railroad car in which meals are served

dining room *n* : a room used for eating meals

din·ky \'diŋ-kē\ *adj* **din·ki·er; -est** : very small and unimpressive ⟨a *dinky* room⟩

din·ner \'din-ər\ *n* **1** : the main meal of the day **2** : [1]BANQUET

din·ner·time \-ˌtīm\ *n* : the usual time for dinner

din·ner·ware \-ˌwa(ə)r, -ˌwe(ə)r\ *n* : utensils (as dishes and glasses) used at the dinner table

di·no·flag·el·late \ˌdī-nō-'flaj-ə-lət, -ˌlāt\ *n* : any of an order of chiefly marine single-celled floating organisms that resemble both algae and protozoa and are important in marine food chains

di·no·saur \'dī-nə-ˌsȯr\ *n* : any of a group of extinct often very large mostly land-dwelling long-tailed reptiles of the Mesozoic era [derived from Greek *deinos* "terrible" and Greek *sauros* "lizard"]

[1]**dint** \'dint\ *n* **1** : the force or power of something — used chiefly in the phrase *by dint of* ⟨succeeded by *dint* of hard work⟩ **2** : [2]DENT 1

[2]**dint** *vb* : [1]DENT 1

[1]**di·oc·e·san** \dī-'äs-ə-sən\ *adj* : of or relating to a diocese

[2]**diocesan** *n* : a bishop having authority over a diocese

di·o·cese \'dī-ə-səs, -ˌsēz, -ˌsēs\ *n, pl* **-ces·es** \'dī-ə-ˌsēz, -ˌsē-zēz, -sə-səz\ : the district over which a bishop has authority

di·ode \'dī-ˌōd\ *n* : an electronic device with two electrodes that is used especially for changing alternating current into direct current

di·o·rama \ˌdī-ə-'ram-ə, -'räm-\ *n* : a scenic representation in which lifelike sculptured figures and surrounding details are realistically set against a painted background

di·ox·ide \(')dī-'äk-ˌsīd\ *n* : an oxide containing two atoms of oxygen in the molecule

[1]**dip** \'dip\ *vb* **dipped; dip·ping** **1** : to sink or push briefly into or as if into a liquid ⟨*dip* a towel in water⟩ ⟨*dips* a hand into his pocket⟩ **2** : to lift out with something that holds liquid : LADLE ⟨*dip* water from a pail⟩ **3** : to lower and then raise again ⟨*dip* a flag in salute⟩ **4 a** : to drop down into a liquid and quickly come out ⟨oars *dipping* rhythmically⟩ **b** : to put something for treatment under the surface of a liquid **5 a** : to drop down or out of sight ⟨the road *dipped* below the crest⟩ **b** : to decrease somewhat usually for a short time ⟨prices *dipped*⟩ **6** : to reach down inside or as if inside especially to take out a part of the contents ⟨*dipped* into their savings⟩ **7** : to look at or consider something briefly; *esp* : to read a little of something ⟨*dip* into a book⟩

[2]**dip** *n* **1** : an act of dipping; *esp* : a brief plunge into the water for sport or exercise **2 a** : a downward slope **b** : a sharp or slight downward course : DROP ⟨a *dip* in prices⟩ **3** : the angle formed with the horizon by a magnetic needle free to rotate in a vertical plane **4** : something obtained by or used in dipping ⟨a *dip* of ice cream⟩ **5 a** : a sauce or soft mixture into which food (as raw vegetables)

may be dipped **b** : a liquid into which something may be dipped (as for cleansing or coloring)

diph·the·ria \dif-'thir-ē-ə, dip-\ *n* : a contagious bacterial disease with fever in which the air passages become coated with a membranous layer that often obstructs breathing — **diph·the·rit·ic** \ˌdif-thə-'rit-ik, ˌdip-\ *adj*

diph·thong \'dif-ˌthȯŋ, 'dip-\ *n* : a two-element speech sound that begins with the tongue position for one vowel and ends with the tongue position for another all within one syllable ⟨the sounds of "ou" in "out" and of "oy" in "boy" are *diphthongs*⟩

dip·lo·coc·cus \ˌdip-lō-'käk-əs\ *n, pl* **dip·lo·coc·ci** \-'käk-ˌ(s)ī, -ˌ(s)ē\ : any of various bacteria that occur usually in pairs in a capsule and include some that cause serious diseases

di·plod·o·cus \də-'pläd-ə-kəs, dī-\ *n* : any of a genus of very large plant-eating dinosaurs known from fossils found in several western states of the U.S.

di·plo·ma \də-'plō-mə\ *n* : a document granting a special right, honor, or power; *esp* : a document that shows a person has finished a course or graduated from a school

di·plo·ma·cy \də-'plō-mə-sē\ *n* **1** : the work of keeping up relations between the governments of different countries **2** : skill in dealing with others without causing bad feelings : TACT

dip·lo·mat \'dip-lə-ˌmat\ *n* : a person employed or skilled in diplomacy

dip·lo·mat·ic \ˌdip-lə-'mat-ik\ *adj* **1** : of, relating to, or concerned with diplomacy or diplomats ⟨*diplomatic* relations⟩ **2** : TACTFUL ⟨found a *diplomatic* way to say no⟩ — **dip·lo·mat·i·cal·ly** \-'mat-i-k(ə-)lē\ *adv*

di·plo·ma·tist \də-'plō-mət-əst\ *n* : DIPLOMAT

dip·lo·pod \'dip-lə-ˌpäd\ *n* : MILLIPEDE

dip net *n* : a small bag-shaped net with a handle that is used especially to scoop small fish from the water

di·pole \'dī-ˌpōl\ *n* : a pair of equal and opposite electric charges or magnetic poles of opposite sign separated especially by a small distance

dip·per \'dip-ər\ *n* **1** : one that dips; *esp* : something (as a long-handled cup) used for dipping **2** : any of several birds that dive into streams in search of food — called also *water ouzel* **3** *cap* **a** : the seven major stars of Ursa

dipper 1

Major arranged in a form resembling a dipper — called also *Big Dipper* **b** : the seven major stars in Ursa Minor similarly arranged with the North Star forming the outer end of the handle — called also *Little Dipper* — **dip·per·ful** \-ˌfu̇l\ *n*

dip·stick \'dip-ˌstik\ *n* : a rod with marks for indicating depth (as of the oil in an automobile)

[1]**dip·ter·an** \'dip-tə-rən\ *adj* : of, relating to, or being a two-winged fly

[2]**dipteran** *n* : TWO-WINGED FLY

dip·ter·ous \'dip-tə-rəs\ *adj* : DIPTERAN

dire \'dī(ə)r\ *adj* **dir·er; dir·est** **1** : causing horror : DREADFUL ⟨*dire* suffering⟩ **2** : warning of disaster ⟨a *dire* forecast⟩ **3** : [1]EXTREME 1 ⟨*dire* need⟩ — **dire·ly** *adv* — **dire·ness** *n*

[1]**di·rect** \də-'rekt, dī-\ *vb* **1** : to mark with a name and address ⟨*direct* a letter⟩ **2** : to cause to turn, move, or point or to follow a straight course **3** : to point in a specified line, course, or direction **4** : to show or point out the way for ⟨the signs *directed* us to the museum⟩ **5** : to guide the activities or course of ⟨*direct* the project⟩ ⟨*direct* a play⟩ **6** : to request or instruct with authority ⟨the court *directed* the jury to acquit them⟩ **synonyms** see COMMAND

²direct *adj* **1** : proceeding from one point to another in time or space without turning or stopping : STRAIGHT **2 a** : coming immediately from a source, cause, or reason ⟨*direct* result⟩ **b** : done or working without something else coming in between ⟨*direct* action⟩ ⟨*direct* printing⟩ **c** : being in an unbroken family line : LINEAL ⟨*direct* ancestor⟩ **3** : ¹NATURAL 8, STRAIGHTFORWARD ⟨a *direct* manner⟩ **4** : consisting of or reproducing the exact words of a speaker or writer ⟨a *direct* quotation⟩ — **direct** *adv* — **di·rect·ness** \-'rek(t)-nəs\ *n*

direct current *n* : an electric current flowing in one direction only — abbreviation *DC*

directed *adj* : proceeding or measured in a direction marked as positive or negative ⟨a *directed* line segment⟩

di·rec·tion \də-'rek-shən, dī-\ *n* **1** : guidance of action or conduct : MANAGEMENT ⟨many people working under my *direction*⟩ ⟨*direction* of a play⟩ **2** : an instruction, indication, or order given with authority ⟨follow *directions*⟩ **3** : the line or course along which something moves, lies, or points ⟨headed in a northerly *direction*⟩ **4** : TENDENCY 1, TREND ⟨a new *direction* in literature⟩ — **di·rec·tion·less** \-ləs\ *adj*

di·rec·tion·al \də-'rek-sh(ə-)nəl, dī-\ *adj* **1** : relating to or indicating direction ⟨*directional* signal lights on an automobile⟩ **2** : relating to direction or guidance especially of thought or effort

di·rec·tive \də-'rek-tiv, dī-\ *n* : something that guides or directs; *esp* : a general instruction from a high-level body or official

di·rect·ly \də-'rek-(t)lē, dī-, *in sense 2 also* 'drek-lē\ *adv* **1 a** : in a direct manner ⟨she spoke *directly*⟩ **b** : most closely located ⟨the person *directly* to my left⟩ **2** : without delay : IMMEDIATELY ⟨go *directly* home⟩ **3** : in the manner of direct variation ⟨the perimeter of a square varies *directly* with the length of a side⟩

directly proportional *adj* : related by direct variation ⟨our earnings are *directly proportional* to the number of items we sell⟩ — compare INVERSELY PROPORTIONAL

direct object *n* : a grammatical object that is the main goal or the result of the action of a verb ⟨"me" in "he called me" and "house" in "we built a house" are *direct objects*⟩

di·rec·tor \də-'rek-tər, dī-\ *n* : one that directs: as **a** : one of a group of persons who direct the business of an organized body (as a corporation) ⟨the board of *directors*⟩ **b** : one that guides the making of a show (as for stage or screen) **c** : CONDUCTOR 2 — **di·rec·to·ri·al** \də-,rek-'tōr-ē-əl, (,)dī-, -'tòr-\ *adj* — **di·rec·tor·ship** \də-'rek-tər-,ship, dī-\ *n*

di·rec·to·ry \də-'rek-t(ə-)rē, dī-\ *n, pl* **-ries** : an alphabetical list containing names and addresses

direct variation *n* **1** : mathematical relationship between two variables which can be expressed by an equation in which one variable is equal to a constant times the other **2** : an equation or function expressing direct variation — compare INVERSE VARIATION 2

dire·ful \'dī(ə)r-fəl\ *adj* **1** : causing great fear : DREADFUL **2** : foretelling bad things to come — **dire·ful·ly** \-fə-lē\ *adv*

dirge \'dərj\ *n* : a song or hymn of mourning; *esp* : one intended for funeral or memorial ceremonies

Word History The meaning of English *dirge* is not directly related to the meaning of the Latin word it comes from. *Dirge* and its earlier form *dirige*, meaning "a song or hymn of mourning," come from the first word of a Latin chant used in the church service for the dead: "Dirige, Domine deus meus, in conspectu tuo viam meam" (Direct, O Lord my God, my way in thy sight). Because hymns and chants were often referred to by their first words, *dirge* became the common word for this chant. Later it was used for a slow, solemn hymn of mourning. [Middle English *dirige* "service performed when someone dies," from Latin *dirige* "direct," first word in a prayer for the dead, from earlier *dirigere* "to direct"]

¹dir·i·gi·ble \'dir-ə-jə-bəl, də-'rij-ə-\ *adj* : capable of being steered

²dirigible *n* : AIRSHIP

dirk \'dərk\ *n* : a long dagger with a straight blade — **dirk** *vb*

dirndl \'dərn-dᵊl\ *n* : a full skirt with a tight waistband [a shortened form of German *Dirndlkleid*, literally, "girl's dress," from *Dirndl* "girl" and *Kleid* "dress"]

dirt \'dərt\ *n* **1** : a filthy or soiling substance (as mud, dust, or grime) **2** : loose or packed earth : SOIL ⟨a mound of *dirt*⟩ **3 a** : CORRUPTION 2 **b** : indecent language : OBSCENITY **4** : harmful gossip ⟨stop spreading *dirt* about him⟩

dirt bike *n* : a light motorcycle designed to be used off the road

¹dirty \'dərt-ē\ *adj* **dirt·i·er; -est 1** : not clean ⟨*dirty* clothes⟩ ⟨*dirty* air⟩ **2** : UNFAIR 1, DISHONORABLE ⟨a *dirty* trick⟩ **3** : INDECENT, VULGAR ⟨*dirty* jokes⟩ **4** : disagreeable or objectionable but usually necessary (as in achieving a desired result) ⟨had to scrub the floor and do other *dirty* work⟩ **5** : STORMY 1 ⟨*dirty* weather⟩ **6** : not clear in color : DULL ⟨a *dirty* red⟩ **7** : showing dislike or anger ⟨a *dirty* look⟩ — **dirt·i·ly** \'dərt-ᵊl-ē\ *adv* — **dirt·i·ness** \'dərt-ē-nəs\ *n*

synonyms DIRTY, FILTHY, FOUL, SQUALID mean being especially unclean. DIRTY is a general word used to describe anything covered with dirt ⟨children who were *dirty* after playing⟩. FILTHY stresses the fact that the dirt has been building up and is really unpleasant ⟨a *filthy* kitchen floor covered with grease⟩. FOUL adds to FILTHY the idea that something is rotten or stinking ⟨a *foul* garbage dump⟩. SQUALID suggests that the dirtiness is the result of carelessness and neglect ⟨*squalid* slums⟩.

²dirty *vb* **dirt·ied; dirty·ing** : to make or become dirty

dirty rice *n* : a Cajun dish of white rice cooked with chopped or ground giblets

dis \'dis\ *vb* **dissed; dis·sing 1** *slang* : to treat with disrespect or contempt : INSULT **2** *slang* : to find fault with : CRITICIZE

dis- *prefix* **1 a** : do the opposite of ⟨*disagree*⟩ **b** : deprive of ⟨*disarm*⟩ **c** : exclude or expel from ⟨*disbar*⟩ **2** : opposite or absence of ⟨*disaffection*⟩ ⟨*disfavor*⟩ **3** : not ⟨*discourteous*⟩ [Latin *dis-*, literally, "apart"]

dis·abil·i·ty \,dis-ə-'bil-ət-ē\ *n, pl* **-ties 1** : the condition of being disabled : lack of ability, power, or fitness to do something **2** : something that disables (as a physical injury)

dis·able \dis-'ā-bəl\ *vb* **dis·abled; dis·abling** \-b(ə-)liŋ\ **1** : to disqualify legally **2** : to cause to be unable to do or act ⟨*disable* a computer key⟩; *esp* : to deprive of physical or moral strength ⟨a *disabling* illness⟩ — **dis·able·ment** \-bəl-mənt\ *n*

disabled *adj* : deprived of the power to perform one or more tasks (as climbing stairs or lifting heavy items) by illness or injury; *also* : functioning physically or mentally below normal levels in a way that limits or interferes with one's ability to receive an education or perform a job

dis·abuse \,dis-ə-'byüz\ *vb* : to free from mistakes or false beliefs ⟨*disabuse* us of our errors⟩

¹dis·ad·van·tage \,dis-əd-'vant-ij\ *n* **1** : loss or damage especially to one's good name or finances ⟨the deal worked to our *disadvantage*⟩ **2 a** : a state or condition that favors

\ə\ **abut**	\aú\ **out**	\i\ **tip**	\ò\ **saw**	\ú\ **foot**	
\ər\ **further**	\ch\ **chin**	\ī\ **life**	\òi\ **coin**	\y\ **yet**	
\a\ **mat**	\e\ **pet**	\j\ **job**	\th\ **thin**	\yü\ **few**	
\ā\ **take**	\ē\ **easy**	\ŋ\ **sing**	\th\ **this**	\yù\ **cure**	
\ä\ **cot, cart**	\g\ **go**	\ō\ **bone**	\ü\ **food**	\zh\ **vision**	

someone else ⟨was at a *disadvantage* in educated company⟩ **b** : something not helpful : a cause of difficulty

²dis·ad·van·tage *vb* **-taged; -tag·ing** : to place at a disadvantage : HARM

dis·ad·van·ta·geous \(ₜ)dis-ₜad-ₜvan-ˈtā-jəs, -vən-\ *adj* : making it harder for a person to succeed or do something ⟨in a *disadvantageous* position⟩ — **dis·ad·van·ta·geous·ly** *adv* — **dis·ad·van·ta·geous·ness** *n*

dis·af·fect \ₜdis-ə-ˈfekt\ *vb* : to lose the affection or loyalty of : cause discontent in ⟨the troops were *disaffected*⟩ — **dis·af·fec·tion** \-ˈfek-shən\ *n*

dis·agree \ₜdis-ə-ˈgrē\ *vb* **1** : to fail to agree ⟨the two stories *disagree*⟩ **2** : to differ in opinion ⟨*disagree* over the price⟩ **3** : to have an unpleasant effect ⟨fried foods *disagree* with me⟩

dis·agree·able \ₜdis-ə-ˈgrē-ə-bəl\ *adj* **1** : causing discomfort : UNPLEASANT, OFFENSIVE ⟨a *disagreeable* taste⟩ **2** : having a bad disposition : PEEVISH ⟨a *disagreeable* person⟩ — **dis·agree·able·ness** *n* — **dis·agree·ably** \-blē\ *adv*

dis·agree·ment \ₜdis-ə-ˈgrē-mənt\ *n* **1** : the act of disagreeing **2 a** : the state of being different **b** : a difference of opinion : QUARREL

dis·al·low \ₜdis-ə-ˈlau̇\ *vb* : to refuse to admit or allow : REJECT ⟨*disallow* a claim⟩ — **dis·al·low·ance** \-ˈlau̇-ən(t)s\ *n*

dis·ap·pear \ₜdis-ə-ˈpi(ə)r\ *vb* **1** : to cease to be visible : pass out of sight : VANISH ⟨the moon *disappeared* behind a cloud⟩ **2** : to cease to be ⟨the dinosaur *disappeared* ages ago⟩ — **dis·ap·pear·ance** \-ˈpir-ən(t)s\ *n*

dis·ap·point \ₜdis-ə-ˈpȯint\ *vb* : to fail to meet the expectation or hope of ⟨the team *disappointed* its fans⟩

dis·ap·point·ed *adj* : defeated in expectation or hope ⟨we were *disappointed* that they couldn't go⟩

dis·ap·point·ment \ₜdis-ə-ˈpȯint-mənt\ *n* **1** : the act or an instance of disappointing : the state or emotion of being disappointed **2** : one that disappoints ⟨the play was a *disappointment*⟩

dis·ap·pro·ba·tion \(ₜ)dis-ₜap-rə-ˈbā-shən\ *n* : DISAPPROVAL

dis·ap·prov·al \ₜdis-ə-ˈprü-vəl\ *n* **1** : the act of disapproving : the state of being disapproved ⟨frowned in *disapproval*⟩ **2** : unfavorable opinion or judgment : CRITICISM ⟨the plan met with *disapproval*⟩

dis·ap·prove \ₜdis-ə-ˈprüv\ *vb* **1** : to dislike or be against someone or something ⟨*disapproved* the child's conduct⟩ ⟨*disapproves* of smoking⟩ **2** : to refuse to give approval to : REJECT ⟨*disapproved* the architect's plans⟩ — **dis·ap·prov·ing·ly** \-ˈprü-viŋ-lē\ *adv*

dis·arm \(ˈ)dis-ˈärm\ *vb* **1** : to take weapons from ⟨*disarm* a prisoner⟩ **2** : to reduce the size and strength of the armed forces of a country **3** : to make harmless, peaceable, or friendly : remove dislike or suspicion ⟨a *disarming* smile⟩ — **dis·ar·ma·ment** \-ˈär-mə-mənt\ *n*

dis·ar·range \ₜdis-ə-ˈrānj\ *vb* : to disturb the arrangement or order of ⟨the wind *disarranged* my hair⟩ — **dis·ar·range·ment** \-mənt\ *n*

¹dis·ar·ray \ₜdis-ə-ˈrā\ *n* **1** : a lack of order : CONFUSION, DISORDER ⟨the room was in *disarray*⟩ **2** : disorderly dress

²disarray *vb* : to throw into disorder

dis·as·sem·ble \ₜdis-ə-ˈsem-bəl\ *vb* : to take apart ⟨*disassemble* an engine⟩ — **dis·as·sem·bly** \-ˈsem-blē\ *n*

di·sas·ter \diz-ˈas-tər, dis-\ *n* : a sudden great misfortune; *esp* : something (as a flood or tornado) that happens suddenly and causes much suffering or loss — **di·sas·trous** \-ˈas-trəs\ *adj* — **di·sas·trous·ly** *adv*

Word History People who have bad luck are sometimes said to be "star-crossed." This expression comes from the traditional belief that the positions of the stars and planets can have a direct influence on earthly events. The origins of the word *disaster* can be traced to this belief. *Disaster* comes from *disastro*, an Italian word formed by combining the negative prefix *dis-* and the noun *astro*, meaning "star." *Disaster* at first meant "an unfavorable position of a star or planet." In time it came to be applied to the kind of terrible misfortune which such a position was thought to cause. [from early French *desastre* and early Italian *disastro*, both meaning "an unfavorable position of a star," from early Italian *dis-* (negative prefix) and *astro* "star," from Latin *astrum* "star"]

dis·avow \ₜdis-ə-ˈvau̇\ *vb* : to deny having, knowing, or being responsible for ⟨will *disavow* any knowledge of your activities⟩ — **dis·avow·al** \-ˈvau̇(-ə)l\ *n*

dis·band \dis-ˈband\ *vb* : to break up the organization of a group : DISPERSE ⟨*disband* the club⟩ — **dis·band·ment** \-ˈban(d)-mənt\ *n*

dis·bar \dis-ˈbär\ *vb* **dis·barred; dis·bar·ring** : to deprive (a lawyer) of the right to work in the legal profession — **dis·bar·ment** \-ˈbär-mənt\ *n*

dis·be·lief \ₜdis-bə-ˈlēf\ *n* : the act or state of disbelieving : mental rejection of something as untrue

dis·be·lieve \ₜdis-bə-ˈlēv\ *vb* : to think not to be true or real : fail to believe ⟨*disbelieved* the witness's testimony⟩ — **dis·be·liev·er** *n*

dis·bur·den \(ˈ)dis-ˈbərd-ᵊn\ *vb* : UNBURDEN — **dis·bur·den·ment** \-mənt\ *n*

dis·burse \dis-ˈbərs\ *vb* **dis·bursed; dis·burs·ing** : to pay out : EXPEND ⟨*disburse* money⟩ [from early French *desbourser* "to pay out money," from *des-* "out, away" and *borse* "a purse," from Latin *bursa* "a small leather bag" — related to PURSE, REIMBURSE] — **dis·burs·er** *n*

dis·burse·ment \dis-ˈbər-smənt\ *n* : the act of disbursing; *also* : funds paid out

disc *variant of* DISK

¹dis·card \dis-ˈkärd, ˈdis-ₜkärd\ *vb* **1** : to remove a playing card from one's hand **2** : to get rid of as useless or unwanted ⟨*discard* an old hat⟩ — **dis·card·able** \-ə-bəl\ *adj*

²dis·card \ˈdis-ₜkärd\ *n* **1** : the act of discarding in a card game **2** : a person or thing cast off or rejected

disc brake *n* : a brake that operates by the friction of two plates pressing against the sides of a rotating disc

dis·cern \dis-ˈərn, diz-\ *vb* **1** : to detect with the eyes : DISTINGUISH ⟨*discern* an airplane in the clouds⟩ **2** : to come to know, recognize, or understand ⟨*discern* the basic issue⟩ ⟨*discern* right from wrong⟩ — **dis·cern·ible** \-ˈərn-ə-bəl\ *adj* — **dis·cern·ibly** \-blē\ *adv*

dis·cern·ing *adj* : seeing and understanding clearly and intelligently ⟨a *discerning* critic⟩ — **dis·cern·ing·ly** \-ˈər-niŋ-lē\ *adv*

dis·cern·ment \dis-ˈərn-mənt, diz-\ *n* : the quality of being able to understand clearly

¹dis·charge \dis-ˈchärj, ˈdis-ₜchärj\ *vb* **1** : to relieve of a charge, load, or burden : UNLOAD ⟨*discharge* a ship⟩ **2** : ¹SHOOT 1, ²FIRE 4a ⟨*discharge* a gun⟩ **3** : to set free ⟨*discharge* a prisoner⟩ **4** : to dismiss from service or employment ⟨*discharge* a soldier⟩ **5** : to let go or let off ⟨*discharge* passengers⟩ **6** : to give forth fluid or other contents ⟨this river *discharges* into the ocean⟩ **7** : to get rid of by paying or doing ⟨*discharge* a debt⟩ ⟨*discharge* a function⟩ — **dis·charg·er** *n*

²dis·charge \ˈdis-ₜchärj, dis-ˈchärj\ *n* **1 a** : the act of discharging **b** : something that discharges; *esp* : a certification of release or payment **2** : a firing off **3 a** : a flowing out; *also* : a rate of flow **b** : something that is given forth ⟨a *discharge* of pus from a wound⟩ **4 a** : release or dismissal especially from an office or employment **b** : complete separation from military service ⟨was given an honorable *discharge*⟩ **5** : a flow of electricity (as in lightning or through a gas)

discharge tube *n* : an electron tube which contains gas or vapor at low pressure and through which electrical conduction takes place when a high voltage is applied

dis·ci·ple \dis-'ī-pəl\ *n* **1** : a person who accepts and helps to spread the teachings of another **2** : APOSTLE 1a [Middle English *disciple* "one who follows and spreads the teaching of another," from Old English *discipul* and early French *disciple* (both, same meaning), from Latin *discipulus* "follower of Jesus Christ in his lifetime," from earlier *discipulus* "pupil"] — **dis·ci·ple·ship** \-,ship\ *n*

dis·ci·pli·nar·i·an \,dis-ə-plə-'ner-ē-ən\ *n* : one who disciplines or enforces order — **disciplinarian** *adj*

dis·ci·plin·ary \'dis-ə-plə-,ner-ē\ *adj* : of or relating to discipline : CORRECTIVE ⟨take *disciplinary* action⟩

¹**dis·ci·pline** \'dis-ə-plən\ *n* **1** : a field of study : SUBJECT **2** : strict training that corrects or strengthens mental ability or moral character **3** : PUNISHMENT 1 **4** : control gained by enforcing obedience or order ⟨trying to maintain *discipline*⟩ **5** : a system of rules governing conduct

²**discipline** *vb* **-plined; -plin·ing 1** : to punish or penalize for the sake of discipline **2** : to train or develop by instruction and exercise especially in self-control **3** : to bring under control ⟨*discipline* troops⟩ **synonyms** see PUNISH — **dis·ci·plin·er** *n*

disc jockey *or* **disk jockey** *n* : one who conducts and announces a radio show of popular recorded music; *also* : one who plays recorded music for dancing (as at a party)

dis·claim \dis-'klām\ *vb* : to deny being a part of or responsible for : DISOWN ⟨the student *disclaimed* any part in the prank⟩

dis·claim·er \dis-'klā-mər\ *n* : an act of disclaiming : a statement that denies responsibility : DENIAL

dis·close \dis-'klōz\ *vb* : to make known ⟨*disclose* secrets⟩ **synonyms** see REVEAL — **dis·clos·er** *n*

dis·clos·ing \dis-'klō-ziŋ\ *adj* : being a substance (as a tablet or liquid) containing a usually red dye that is used to stain and make visible dental plaque

dis·clo·sure \dis-'klō-zhər\ *n* **1** : the act or an instance of disclosing : EXPOSURE ⟨full *disclosure* of the facts⟩ **2** : something that is disclosed : REVELATION

dis·co \'dis-kō\ *n, pl* **dis·cos** : a nightclub for dancing to music

dis·col·or \(')dis-'kəl-ər\ *vb* : to change in color especially for the worse ⟨the stain *discolored* the rug⟩ — **dis·col·or·a·tion** \(,)kəl-ə-'rā-shən\ *n*

dis·com·bob·u·late \,dis-kəm-'bäb-yə-,lāt, -ə-\ *vb* : ¹UP-SET 3a, CONFUSE

dis·com·fit \dis-'kəm(p)-fət, *especially Southern* ,dis-kəm-'fit\ *vb* : to make confused or upset ⟨the speaker was *discomfited* by the embarrassing question⟩ — **dis·com·fi·ture** \dis-'kəm(p)-fə-,chů(ə)r, -fə-chər\ *n*

¹**dis·com·fort** \dis-'kəm(p)-fərt\ *vb* : to make uncomfortable or uneasy : DISTRESS

²**discomfort** *n* : physical or mental uneasiness

dis·com·mode \,dis-kə-'mōd\ *vb* **-mod·ed; -mod·ing** : to make things difficult for : TROUBLE

dis·com·pose \,dis-kəm-'pōz\ *vb* **1** : to disturb the calmness or peace of : AGITATE ⟨*discomposed* by the bad news⟩ **2** : DISARRANGE ⟨hair *discomposed* by the wind⟩ — **dis·com·po·sure** \-'pō-zdhər\ *n*

dis·con·cert \,dis-kən-'sərt\ *vb* **1** : to disturb the arrangement of : UPSET ⟨the unexpected event *disconcerted* their plans⟩ **2** : to disturb the self-control of ⟨your frank stare *disconcerted* me⟩ **synonyms** see EMBARRASS — **dis·con·cert·ing·ly** \-iŋ-lē\ *adv*

dis·con·nect \,dis-kə-'nekt\ *vb* : to undo or break the connection of ⟨*disconnect* two pipes⟩ ⟨*disconnect* a telephone⟩ — **dis·con·nec·tion** \-'nek-shən\ *n*

dis·con·nect·ed *adj* **1** : not connected : SEPARATE **2** : impossible to understand : INCOHERENT 2 ⟨a *disconnected* speech⟩ — **dis·con·nect·ed·ly** *adv* — **dis·con·nect·ed·ness** *n*

dis·con·so·late \dis-'kän(t)-sə-lət\ *adj* : very sad : DE-JECTED — **dis·con·so·late·ly** *adv* — **dis·con·so·late·ness** *n*

¹**dis·con·tent** \,dis-kən-'tent\ *adj* : DISCONTENTED

²**discontent** *vb* : to make discontented — **dis·con·tent·ment** \-mənt\ *n*

³**discontent** *n* : the condition of being dissatisfied

dis·con·tent·ed *adj* : not satisfied or pleased — **dis·con·tent·ed·ly** *adv* — **dis·con·tent·ed·ness** *n*

dis·con·tin·ue \,dis-kən-'tin-yü\ *vb* **1** : to cease to operate, use, produce, or take ⟨will *discontinue* that product⟩ **2** : to bring or come to an end : STOP ⟨*discontinued* broadcast of my favorite show⟩ — **dis·con·tin·u·ance** \-'tin-yə-wən(t)s\ *n*

dis·con·tin·u·ous \,dis-kən-'tin-yə-wəs\ *adj* : not continuous : having interruptions or gaps : BROKEN ⟨*discontinuous* sleep⟩ — **dis·con·ti·nu·i·ty** \(,)dis-,känt-°n-'(y)ü-ət-ē\ *n* — **dis·con·tin·u·ous·ly** \,dis-kən-'tin-yə-wəs-lē\ *adv*

dis·cord \'dis-,kó(ə)rd\ *n* **1** : lack of agreement or harmony : CONFLICT ⟨*discord* between political parties⟩ **2 a** : a harsh combination of musical sounds **b** : a harsh or unpleasant sound

dis·cord·ance \dis-'kórd-°n(t)s\ *n* **1** : the state or an instance of being discordant **2** : discordant sounds or noise

dis·cord·ant \dis-'kórd-°nt\ *adj* **1 a** : not being in agreement ⟨*discordant* opinions⟩ **b** : QUARRELSOME ⟨a *discordant* family⟩ **2** : relating to or producing a discord ⟨*discordant* music⟩ — **dis·cord·ant·ly** *adv*

dis·co·theque \'dis-kə-,tek, ,dis-kə-'tek\ *n* : DISCO [from French *discothèque* "nightclub with music for dancing," from *disque* "phonograph record, disk" and *-thèque* (the same ending as in French *bibliothèque* "library")]

¹**dis·count** \'dis-,kaůnt\ *n* : an amount taken off a regular price ⟨a ten percent *discount* for all employees⟩

²**dis·count** \'dis-,kaůnt, dis-'kaůnt\ *vb* **1 a** : to lower the amount of a bill, debt, or charge **b** : to sell or offer for sale at a lowered price **2 a** : MINIMIZE 2b ⟨shouldn't *discount* the importance of studying⟩ **b** : to believe only partly : view with doubt ⟨*discount* the rumors⟩ — **dis·count·able** \-ə-bəl\ *adj*

dis·coun·te·nance \dis-'kaůnt-°n-ən(t)s, -'kaůnt-nən(t)s\ *vb* **1** : EMBARRASS 1, DISCONCERT 2 **2** : to look with disfavor on

dis·cour·age \dis-'kər-ij, -'kə-rij\ *vb* **-aged; -ag·ing 1** : to lessen the courage or confidence of : DISHEARTEN ⟨didn't let losing *discourage* me⟩ **2 a** : to make less likely or appealing : DETER ⟨laws that *discourage* speeding⟩ **b** : to advise against a course of action : DISSUADE ⟨*discouraged* careless work⟩ — **dis·cour·ag·ing·ly** \-iŋ-lē\ *adv*

dis·cour·age·ment \dis-'kər-ij-mənt, -'kə-rij-\ *n* **1** : an act of discouraging : the state of being discouraged **2** : something that discourages

¹**dis·course** \'dis-,kō(ə)rs, -,kó(ə)rs, dis-'\ *n* **1** : CONVERSA-TION **2** : a long talk or composition about a subject

²**dis·course** \dis-'kō(ə)rs, -'kó(ə)rs, 'dis-,\ *vb* **dis·coursed; dis·cours·ing** : to talk especially for a long time

dis·cour·te·ous \(')dis-'kərt-ē-əs\ *adj* : not polite : UN-CIVIL, RUDE — **dis·cour·te·ous·ly** *adv* — **dis·cour·te·ous·ness** *n*

dis·cour·te·sy \dis-'kərt-ə-sē\ *n, pl* **-sies 1** : rude behavior **2** : a rude act

dis·cov·er \dis-'kəv-ər\ *vb* **dis·cov·ered; dis·cov·er·ing** \-'kəv-(ə-)riŋ\ **1** : to make known or visible (as something secret or hidden) **2 a** : to obtain sight or knowledge of for the first time ⟨*discovered* an uncharted island⟩ ⟨*discovered* the law of gravity⟩ **b** : to detect the presence of : FIND ⟨*discovered* a pizza waiting on the table⟩ **c** : FIND OUT ⟨was surprised to *discover* that I had lost my keys⟩ —

\ə\ abut	\au̇\ out	\i\ tip	\ȯ\ saw	\u̇\ foot
\ər\ further	\ch\ chin	\ī\ life	\ȯi\ coin	\y\ yet
\a\ mat	\e\ pet	\j\ job	\th\ thin	\yü\ few
\ā\ take	\ē\ easy	\ŋ\ sing	\th\ this	\yu̇\ cure
\ä\ cot, cart	\g\ go	\ō\ bone	\ü\ food	\zh\ vision

dis·cov·er·able \-ˈkəv-(ə-)rə-bəl\ *adj* — **dis·cov·er·er** \-ˈkəv-ər-ər\ *n*

dis·cov·ery \dis-ˈkəv-(ə-)rē\ *n, pl* **-er·ies 1** : the act or process of discovering **2** : something discovered

¹dis·cred·it \(ˈ)dis-ˈkred-ət\ *vb* **1** : to refuse to accept as true or correct : DISBELIEVE 〈*discredit* a rumor〉 **2** : to cause to seem dishonest or untrue 〈*discredit* a witness〉 **3** : to destroy the good reputation of : ¹DISGRACE 〈involvement in the scandal *discredited* them〉 — **dis·cred·it·able** \-ə-bəl\ *adj* — **dis·cred·it·ably** \-blē\ *adv*

²discredit *n* **1** : loss of good name or respect 〈brought *discredit* on their family〉 **2** : lack or loss of belief or confidence 〈bring a story into *discredit*〉

dis·creet \dis-ˈkrēt\ *adj* : having or showing good judgment especially in conduct or speech — **dis·creet·ly** *adv* — **dis·creet·ness** *n*

dis·crep·an·cy \dis-ˈkrep-ən-sē\ *n, pl* **-cies 1** : the quality or state of being different : DISAGREEMENT 〈a great *discrepancy* between the two reports〉 **2** : something that is different or that disagrees 〈*discrepancies* in the firm's financial statements〉

dis·crep·ant \dis-ˈkrep-ənt\ *adj* : not being in agreement 〈widely *discrepant* conclusions〉 — **dis·crep·ant·ly** *adv*

dis·crete \dis-ˈkrēt, ˈdis-ˌkrēt\ *adj* : DISTINCT 1, SEPARATE 〈several *discrete* sections〉 — **dis·crete·ly** *adv* — **dis·crete·ness** *n*

dis·cre·tion \dis-ˈkresh-ən\ *n* **1** : the quality of being discreet : PRUDENCE **2 a** : individual choice or judgment 〈left the decision to your *discretion*〉 **b** : power of free decision 〈reached the age of *discretion*〉 — **dis·cre·tion·ary** \-ˈkresh-ə-ˌner-ē\ *adj*

dis·crim·i·nant \dis-ˈkrim-(ə-)nənt\ *n* : the expression $b^2 - 4ac$ which is used to find out how many solutions exist for a quadratic equation of the general form $ax^2 + bx + c = 0$ and which indicates that two real solutions exist when it is positive, one solution exists when it is equal to zero, and no solutions exist when it is less than zero

dis·crim·i·nate \dis-ˈkrim-ə-ˌnāt\ *vb* **-nat·ed; -nat·ing 1 a** : to see the special features of 〈*discriminate* the geologic features of an area〉 **b** : DISTINGUISH 1, DIFFERENTIATE 〈*discriminate* hundreds of colors〉 **2** : to be able to tell the difference especially between similar things 〈*discriminate* between a tree and a bush〉 **3** : to treat some people better than others without any fair or proper reason 〈*discriminated* against because of their race〉 — **dis·crim·i·na·ble** \-ə-nə-bəl\ *adj*

dis·crim·i·nat·ing \dis-ˈkrim-ə-ˌnāt-iŋ\ *adj* **1** : showing careful judgment : DISCERNING 〈a *discriminating* taste〉 **2** : DISCRIMINATORY — **dis·crim·i·nat·ing·ly** *adv*

dis·crim·i·na·tion \dis-ˌkrim-ə-ˈnā-shən\ *n* **1** : the act of perceiving distinctions **2** : the ability to make fine distinctions **3** : the treating of some people better than others without any fair or proper reason 〈laws to end racial *discrimination*〉 — **dis·crim·i·na·tion·al** \-shnəl, -shən-ᵊl\ *adj*

dis·crim·i·na·tive \dis-ˈkrim-ə-ˌnāt-iv, -ˈkrim-(ə)nə-tiv\ *adj* **1** : seeing the differences between things **2** : DISCRIMINATORY — **dis·crim·i·na·tive·ly** *adv*

dis·crim·i·na·to·ry \dis-ˈkrim-(ə)nə-ˌtōr-ē, -ˌtȯr-\ *adj* : showing discrimination : being unfair 〈*discriminatory* treatment〉

dis·cur·sive \dis-ˈkər-siv\ *adj* : passing from one topic to another 〈a *discursive* speech〉 — **dis·cur·sive·ly** *adv* — **dis·cur·sive·ness** *n*

dis·cus \ˈdis-kəs\ *n, pl* **dis·cus·es** : a heavy disk that is hurled for distance in a track-and-field event; *also* : the event

dis·cuss \dis-ˈkəs\ *vb* **1** : to consider carefully and openly by reasoning or argument 〈*discuss* a proposal〉 **2** : to talk about 〈*discuss* the weather〉

discus

synonyms DISCUSS, ARGUE, DEBATE mean to talk about something with the intention of reaching agreement or merely of putting forth different points of view. DISCUSS suggests a lively expression of differing opinions in order to clarify a problem 〈*discuss* plans for a new road〉. ARGUE suggests an exchange of opinions by people who disagree often strongly 〈*argued* over who was to blame〉. DEBATE suggests an often public contest between persons taking opposite sides of a question 〈the candidates will *debate* the need for new taxes〉.

dis·cus·sion \dis-ˈkəsh-ən\ *n* : conversation or debate for the purpose of understanding a question or subject

¹dis·dain \dis-ˈdān\ *n* : a feeling of scorn for something or someone regarded as beneath oneself

²disdain *vb* **1** : to look with scorn on 〈*disdained* us for being afraid〉 **2** : to reject or refuse because of disdain 〈*disdained* to answer〉

dis·dain·ful \dis-ˈdān-fəl\ *adj* : full of or expressing disdain **synonyms** see CONTEMPTUOUS — **dis·dain·ful·ly** \-fə-lē\ *adv* — **dis·dain·ful·ness** *n*

dis·ease \diz-ˈēz\ *n* : an abnormal bodily condition of a living plant or animal that interferes with functioning and can usually be recognized by signs and symptoms : ILLNESS — **dis·eased** \-ˈēzd\ *adj*

dis·em·bark \ˌdis-əm-ˈbärk\ *vb* : to go or put ashore from a ship 〈the passengers *disembarked*〉 — **dis·em·bar·ka·tion** \(ˌ)dis-ˌem-ˌbär-ˈkā-shən, -bər-\ *n*

dis·em·body \ˌdis-əm-ˈbäd-ē\ *vb* : to deprive of bodily existence 〈*disembodied* spirits〉

dis·em·bow·el \ˌdis-əm-ˈbau̇-(ə)l\ *vb* **-eled** *or* **-elled; -el·ing** *or* **-el·ling** : to take out the bowels of — **dis·em·bow·el·ment** \-mənt\ *n*

dis·em·pow·er \dis-im-ˈpau̇(-ə)r\ *vb* : to keep one from having authority, power, or influence : make weak or unimportant — **dis·em·pow·er·ment** \-mənt\ *n*

dis·en·chant \ˌdis-ᵊn-ˈchant\ *vb* : to free from illusion — **dis·en·chant·ment** \-mənt\ *n*

dis·en·cum·ber \ˌdis-ᵊn-ˈkəm-bər\ *vb* : to free from a burden

dis·en·fran·chise \ˌdis-ᵊn-ˈfran-ˌchīz\ *vb* : to deprive of a legal right; *esp* : to deprive of the right to vote — **dis·en·fran·chise·ment** \-ˌchīz-mənt, -chəz-\ *n*

dis·en·gage \ˌdis-ᵊn-ˈgāj\ *vb* : to free or release from an engagement, entanglement, or burden 〈*disengage* an automobile clutch〉 — **dis·en·gage·ment** \-mənt\ *n*

dis·en·tan·gle \ˌdis-ᵊn-ˈtaŋ-gəl\ *vb* : to straighten out : UNTANGLE — **dis·en·tan·gle·ment** \-mənt\ *n*

¹dis·fa·vor \(ˈ)dis-ˈfā-vər\ *n* **1** : ¹DISLIKE, DISAPPROVAL 〈practices looked upon with *disfavor*〉 **2** : the state or fact of being disliked or disapproved 〈fell into *disfavor*〉

²disfavor *vb* : ²DISLIKE, DISAPPROVE

dis·fig·ure \dis-ˈfig-yər, *especially British* -ˈfig-ər\ *vb* : to spoil the appearance of 〈*disfigured* by a scar〉 — **dis·fig·ure·ment** \-mənt\ *n*

dis·fran·chise \(ˈ)dis-ˈfran-ˌchīz\ *vb* **-chised; -chis·ing** : DISENFRANCHISE — **dis·fran·chise·ment** \-ˌchīz-mənt, -chəz-\ *n*

dis·gorge \(ˈ)dis-ˈgȯ(ə)rj\ *vb* **1** : ²VOMIT 1 **2** : to cause to come out violently or forcefully 〈the volcano *disgorged* lava〉

¹dis·grace \dis-ˈgrās\ *vb* **dis·graced; dis·grac·ing** : to bring shame to — **dis·grac·er** *n*

²**dis·grace** *n* **1** : the condition of being looked down on : loss of respect ⟨in *disgrace* with one's schoolmates⟩ **2** : ¹DISHONOR 1, SHAME ⟨the *disgrace* of being a coward⟩ **3** : a cause of shame ⟨that person's manners are a *disgrace*⟩ — **dis·grace·ful** \dis-'grās-fəl\ *adj* — **dis·grace·ful·ly** \-fə-lē\ *adv* — **dis·grace·ful·ness** *n*

dis·grun·tle \dis-'grənt-ᵊl\ *vb* **dis·grun·tled; dis·grun·tling** \-'grənt-liŋ, -ᵊl-iŋ\ : to put in a bad mood — **dis·grun·tle·ment** \-ᵊl-mənt\ *n*

¹**dis·guise** \dis-'gīz\ *vb* **dis·guised; dis·guis·ing** **1** : to change the dress or looks of so as to conceal identity ⟨spies *disguised* as tourists⟩ **2** : to keep from showing the existence or true character of : HIDE ⟨*disguised* their true feelings⟩ ⟨tried to *disguise* her voice⟩ — **dis·guised·ly** \-'gīz(-ə)d-lē\ *adv* — **dis·guis·er** *n*

²**disguise** *n* **1** : clothing put on to hide one's true identity or imitate another's **2** : an outward appearance that hides what something really is ⟨a blessing in *disguise*⟩

¹**dis·gust** \dis-'gəst\ *n* : a strong feeling of dislike caused especially by something sickening or evil

²**disgust** *vb* : to cause to feel disgust — **dis·gust·ed** *adj* — **dis·gust·ed·ly** *adv*

dis·gust·ing \dis-'gəs-tiŋ\ *adj* : causing disgust ⟨*disgusting* behavior⟩ — **dis·gust·ing·ly** *adv*

¹**dish** \'dish\ *n* **1 a** : a shallow usually circular vessel for serving food **b** : the food served in a dish ⟨a *dish* of strawberries⟩ **2** : food prepared in a particular way **3 a** : something that is shaped like a dish **b** : a directional receiver having a concave reflector; *esp* : one used as a microwave or radar antenna

²**dish** *vb* **1** : to put into a dish or dishes ⟨*dish* up some soup⟩ **2** : to shape something like a dish

dish·cloth \'dish-ˌklȯth\ *n* : a cloth for washing dishes

dis·heart·en \(')dis-'härt-ᵊn\ *vb* : to deprive of courage and hope : DISCOURAGE — **dis·heart·en·ing** \-'härt-niŋ, -ᵊn-iŋ\ *adj* — **dis·heart·en·ing·ly** \-lē\ *adv* — **dis·heart·en·ment** \-'härt-ᵊn-mənt\ *n*

di·shev·el \dish-'ev-əl\ *vb* **di·shev·eled** *or* **di·shev·elled; di·shev·el·ing** *or* **di·shev·el·ling** \-'ev-(ə-)liŋ\ : to throw into disorder : make untidy ⟨the wind *disheveled* her clothes⟩

disheveled *or* **dishevelled** *adj* : marked by disorder ⟨*disheveled* hair⟩

dis·hon·est \(')dis-'än-əst\ *adj* : not honest or trustworthy : DECEITFUL ⟨*dishonest* people⟩ — **dis·hon·est·ly** *adv*

dis·hon·es·ty \(')dis-'än-ə-stē\ *n* : lack of honesty : the quality of being dishonest

¹**dis·hon·or** \(')dis-'än-ər\ *n* **1** : loss of honor or good name **2** : the state of one who has lost honor **3** : a cause of disgrace

²**dishonor** *vb* **1** : to bring shame on : DISGRACE **2** : to refuse to accept or pay (as a check) — **dis·hon·or·er** *n*

dis·hon·or·able \-'än-(ə-)rə-bəl, -'än-ər-bəl\ *adj* : not honorable : SHAMEFUL ⟨*dishonorable* conduct⟩ — **dis·hon·or·ably** \-blē\ *adv*

dish out *vb* : to give out freely ⟨*dish out* advice⟩

dish·wash·er \'dish-ˌwȯsh-ər, -ˌwäsh-\ *n* : a person or a machine that washes dishes

dish·wa·ter \-ˌwȯt-ər, -ˌwät-\ *n* : water in which dishes have been or are to be washed

dis·il·lu·sion \ˌdis-ə-'lü-zhən\ *vb* **dis·il·lu·sioned; dis·il·lu·sion·ing** \-'lüzh-(ə-)niŋ\ : to free from mistaken beliefs or foolish hopes ⟨a loss that *disillusioned* the fans⟩ — **dis·il·lu·sion·ment** \-'lü-zhən-mənt\ *n*

dis·in·cline \ˌdis-ᵊn-'klīn\ *vb* : to make or be unwilling ⟨was *disinclined* to go⟩ — **dis·in·cli·na·tion** \(ˌ)dis-ˌin-klə-'nā-shən, -ˌiŋ-\ *n*

dis·in·fect \ˌdis-ᵊn-'fekt\ *vb* : to cleanse of germs that might cause disease — **dis·in·fec·tion** \-'fek-shən\ *n*

dis·in·fec·tant \dis-ᵊn-'fek-tənt\ *n* : something (as a chemical) that is able to destroy harmful germs (as bacteria and fungi) — **disinfectant** *adj*

dis·in·her·it \ˌdis-ᵊn-'her-ət\ *vb* : to deprive of the right to inherit

dis·in·te·grate \(')dis-'int-ə-ˌgrāt\ *vb* **1** : to break or decompose into the elements, parts, or small particles making up something **2** : to go through a change in composition ⟨an atomic nucleus that *disintegrates* because of radioactivity⟩ — **dis·in·te·gra·tor** \-ˌgrāt-ər\ *n*

dis·in·te·gra·tion \(ˌ)dis-ˌint-ə-'grā-shən\ *n* : the act or process of disintegrating : the state of being disintegrated

dis·in·ter \ˌdis-ᵊn-'tər\ *vb* **1** : to take out of the grave or tomb **2** : to bring back into awareness : UNEARTH — **dis·in·ter·ment** \-mənt\ *n*

dis·in·ter·est·ed \dis-'int-ə-res-təd, 'dis-; -'in-trəs-, -ˌtres-, -'int-ərs-, -'int-ə-rəs-\ *adj* **1** : not interested ⟨was *disinterested* in sports⟩ **2** : not influenced by personal feelings, opinions, or concerns : UNBIASED ⟨a *disinterested* decision⟩ — **dis·in·ter·est·ed·ly** *adv* — **dis·in·ter·est·ed·ness** *n*

dis·join \(')dis-'jȯin\ *vb* : to end the union of : become separated

¹**dis·joint** \(')dis-'jȯint\ *adj* : having no members in common ⟨*disjoint* mathematical sets⟩

²**disjoint** *vb* **1** : to separate the parts of **2** : to take or come apart at the joints

dis·joint·ed *adj* **1** : separated at or as if at the joint **2** : not clear and orderly : INCOHERENT ⟨*disjointed* conversation⟩ — **dis·joint·ed·ly** *adv* — **dis·joint·ed·ness** *n*

¹**disk** *or* **disc** \'disk\ *n* **1 a** : the central part of the flower head of a typical plant (as a daisy or aster) of the composite family made up of closely packed tube-shaped flowers **b** : any of various rounded and flattened animal anatomical structures; *esp* : INTERVERTEBRAL DISK **2** : a thin circular object: as **a** *usually* **disc** : a phonograph record **b** : a round flat plate coated with a magnetic substance on which data for a computer is stored **c** : CD **3** *usually* **disc** : a tilling implement (as a plow) with sharp-edged circular cutting blades; *also* : one of these blades — **disk·like** \-ˌlīk\ *adj*

²**disk** *or* **disc** *vb* : to cultivate (land) with a disc

disk drive *n* : a device for reading and writing computer data on a magnetic disk

disk flower *n* : any of the tube-shaped flowers in the disk of a plant (as a daisy or aster) of the composite family — compare RAY FLOWER

disk jockey *variant of* DISC JOCKEY

¹**dis·like** \(')dis-'līk\ *n* : a strong feeling of not liking or approving

²**dislike** *vb* : to feel dislike for

dis·lo·cate \'dis-lō-ˌkāt, (')dis-'lō-\ *vb* **1** : to put out of place; *esp* : to displace (a bone) from normal connections with another bone **2** : DISRUPT

dis·lo·ca·tion \ˌdis-(ˌ)lō-'kā-shən\ *n* : the act of dislocating : the state of being dislocated; *esp* : displacement of one or more bones at a joint

dis·lodge \(')dis-'läj\ *vb* : to force out of a place especially of rest, hiding, or defense

dis·loy·al \(')dis-'lȯi-(ə)l\ *adj* : lacking in loyalty — **dis·loy·al·ly** \-'lȯi-ə-lē\ *adv* — **dis·loy·al·ty** \-'lȯi-(ə)l-tē\ *n*

dis·mal \'diz-məl\ *adj* : very gloomy and depressing : DREARY ⟨*dismal* weather⟩ — **dis·mal·ly** \-mə-lē\ *adv*

Word History At the time of the Roman Empire, certain days of each month, called "Egyptian days," were regarded as inauspicious. These days of ill omen were probably a relic of ancient Egyptian belief, but their source had been forgotten by the Middle Ages. People then took them to be anniversaries of the plagues visited

\ə\ abut	\au̇\ out	\i\ tip	\ȯ\ saw	\u̇\ foot
\ər\ further	\ch\ chin	\ī\ life	\ȯi\ coin	\y\ yet
\a\ mat	\e\ pet	\j\ job	\th\ thin	\yü\ few
\ā\ take	\ē\ easy	\ŋ\ sing	\th\ this	\yu̇\ cure
\ä\ cot, cart	\g\ go	\ō\ bone	\ü\ food	\zh\ vision

on Egypt in Moses' time—though there were 24 Egyptian days in the year and only ten biblical plagues. In medieval French the Egyptian days were called collectively *dismal* (from Latin *dies mali,* "evil days"), and this word was borrowed into Middle English. Any day of the 24 was a *dismal day,* but the original sense "evil days" was forgotten, and *dismal* was simply taken as an adjective meaning "disastrous." [Middle English *dismal* "days marked on a calendar as unlucky," from early French (same meaning), from Latin *dies mali,* "evil days"]

dis·man·tle \(')dis-'mant-ᵊl\ *vb* **dis·man·tled; dis·man·tling** \-'mant-liŋ, -ᵊl-iŋ\ **1** : to take to pieces : take apart ⟨*dismantled* the engine to repair it⟩ **2** : to strip of furniture and equipment ⟨*dismantle* an office⟩ — **dis·man·tle·ment** \-'mant-ᵊl-mənt\ *n*

¹dis·may \dis-'mā, diz-\ *vb* **1** : to cause to lose courage or to feel concern : DAUNT ⟨*dismayed* by their opponent's size⟩ **2** : ¹UPSET 2a, PERTURB ⟨*dismayed* by the poor turnout⟩ — **dis·may·ing·ly** \-iŋ-lē\ *adv*

²dismay *n* **1** : loss of courage or determination from alarm or fear **2** : a feeling of alarm or disappointment

dis·mem·ber \(')dis-'mem-bər\ *vb* **dis·mem·ber·ing** \-b(ə-)riŋ\ **1** : to cut off or separate the limbs or parts of **2** : to break up or tear into pieces — **dis·mem·ber·ment** \-bər-mənt\ *n*

dis·miss \dis-'mis\ *vb* **1** : to send away : cause or allow to go ⟨*dismissed* the troops⟩ **2** : to discharge from office, service, or employment **3** : to put aside or out of mind ⟨*dismiss* the thought⟩ **4** : to refuse further judicial hearing or consideration to ⟨the judge *dismissed* the charge⟩ [derived from Latin *dimissus,* past participle of *dimittere* "to send away," from *di-, dis-* "away, apart," and *mittere* "to send, throw" — related to EMIT] — **dis·miss·al** \-'mis-əl\ *n* — **dis·mis·sive** \-'mis-iv\ *adj* — **dis·mis·sive·ly** *adv*

dis·mount \(')dis-'maúnt\ *vb* **1** : to get down from something (as a horse) **2** : to remove or throw down especially from a horse — **dismount** *n*

dis·obe·di·ence \ˌdis-ə-'bēd-ē-ə(n)t)s\ *n* : failure or refusal to obey — **dis·obe·di·ent** \-ənt\ *adj* — **dis·obe·di·ent·ly** *adv*

dis·obey \ˌdis-ə-'bā\ *vb* : to refuse, neglect, or fail to obey

dis·oblige \ˌdis-ə-'blīj\ *vb* **1** : to go against the wishes of **2** : ²INCONVENIENCE

¹dis·or·der \(')dis-'ȯrd-ər\ *vb* **1** : to disturb the order of **2** : to disturb the regular or normal functions of

²disorder *n* **1** : lack of order : a state or condition without order ⟨clothes in *disorder*⟩ **2** : an abnormal physical or mental condition : AILMENT

dis·or·dered *adj* **1** : marked by disorder **2** : not functioning in a normal orderly healthy way

dis·or·der·ly \(')dis-ȯrd-ər-lē\ *adj* **1** : not behaving quietly or well : upsetting public order : UNRULY ⟨*disorderly* persons⟩ ⟨*disorderly* conduct⟩ **2** : not neat or orderly ⟨a *disorderly* mass of papers⟩ — **dis·or·der·li·ness** *n*

dis·or·ga·nize \(')dis-'ȯr-gə-ˌnīz\ *vb* : to break up the regular arrangement of : CONFUSE, DISORDER — **dis·or·ga·ni·za·tion** \(ˌ)dis-ˌȯrg-(ə-)nə-'zā-shən\ *n*

dis·ori·ent \(')dis-'ōr-ē-ˌent, -'ȯr-\ *vb* : to cause to be confused or lost

dis·own \(')dis-'ōn\ *vb* : to refuse to accept any longer as one's own : RENOUNCE, DISCLAIM

dis·par·age \dis-'par-ij\ *vb* **-aged; -ag·ing** **1** : to lower in rank : DEGRADE **2** : to speak of as unimportant or not much good : BELITTLE ⟨*disparaged* the performance⟩ — **dis·par·age·ment** \-mənt\ *n* — **dis·par·ag·ing** *adj* — **dis·par·ag·ing·ly** \-ij-iŋ-lē\ *adv*

dis·par·ate \dis-'par-ət, 'dis-p(ə-)rət\ *adj* : very different : unique in quality or character — **dis·par·ate·ly** *adv* — **dis·par·ate·ness** *n* — **dis·par·i·ty** \dis-'par-ət-ē\ *n*

dis·pas·sion·ate \(')dis-'pash-(ə-)nət\ *adj* : not influenced by strong feeling : CALM, IMPARTIAL ⟨a *dispassionate* judge⟩ — **dis·pas·sion·ate·ly** *adv*

¹dis·patch \dis-'pach\ *vb* **1** : to send away quickly to a particular place or for a particular purpose ⟨*dispatch* a messenger⟩ ⟨*dispatch* a train⟩ **2** : to put to death : KILL **3** : to get done speedily — **dis·patch·er** *n*

²dispatch *n* **1** : MESSAGE 1; *esp* : an important official message **b** : a news story sent in to a newspaper **2** : the sending of a message or messenger **3** : the act of killing **4** : the shipment of goods **5** : promptness in performing a task ⟨did our homework with *dispatch*⟩

dis·pel \dis-'pel\ *vb* **dis·pelled; dis·pel·ling** : to drive away by or as if by scattering : DISSIPATE

dis·pens·able \dis-'pen(t)-sə-bəl\ *adj* : not necessary : NONESSENTIAL — **dis·pens·abil·i·ty** \-ˌpen(t)-sə-'bil-ət-ē\ *n*

dis·pen·sa·ry \dis-'pen(t)s-(ə-)rē\ *n, pl* **-ries** : a place where medical or dental aid is given

dis·pen·sa·tion \ˌdis-pən-'sā-shən, -ˌpen-\ *n* **1 a** : a system of rules for ordering affairs **b** : a particular arrangement especially of nature **2** : release from a rule or from a vow or oath **3 a** : the act of dispensing **b** : something dispensed or distributed — **dis·pen·sa·tion·al** \-shnəl, -shən-ᵊl\ *adj*

dis·pense \dis-'pen(t)s\ *vb* **dis·pensed; dis·pens·ing** **1 a** : to give out in shares ⟨*dispense* charity⟩ **b** : to give out as deserved ⟨*dispense* justice⟩ **2** : to prepare and give out (medicines) *synonyms* see DISTRIBUTE — **dispense with** **1** : to set aside : DISCARD **2** : to do or get along without

dis·pens·er \dis-'pen(t)-sər\ *n* : one that dispenses; *esp* : a container that gives out something a little at a time ⟨a soap *dispenser*⟩

dis·pers·al \dis-'pər-səl\ *n* : the act or result of dispersing

dispenser

dis·perse \dis-'pərs\ *vb* **dis·persed; dis·pers·ing** **1** : to cause to become spread widely : SCATTER ⟨police *dispersed* the crowd⟩ **2** : to subject (as light) to dispersion **3** : to move in different directions ⟨the clouds *dispersed*⟩

dis·per·sion \dis-'pər-zhən\ *n* **1** : the act or process of dispersing : the state of being dispersed **2** : the separation of light (as by a prism) into a series of colors — **dis·per·sive** \-'pər-siv, -ziv\ *adj*

dis·pir·it \(')dis-'pir-ət\ *vb* : to deprive of cheerful spirit : DISHEARTEN — **dis·pir·it·ed·ly** *adv* — **dis·pir·it·ed·ness** *n*

dis·place \(')dis-'plās\ *vb* **1** : to remove from a usual or proper place; *esp* : to expel or force to flee from home or homeland ⟨*displaced* persons⟩ **2 a** : to remove physically out of position ⟨water *displaced* by a floating object⟩ **b** : to take the place of : REPLACE — **dis·place·able** \-ə-bəl\ *adj*

dis·place·ment \-'plā-smənt\ *n* **1** : the act of displacing : the state of being displaced **2 a** : the volume or weight of a fluid (as water) displaced by a floating body (as a ship) of equal weight **b** : the difference between the first position of an object and any later position **c** : the volume displaced by a piston (as in a pump or engine) in a single stroke; *also* : the total volume displaced in this way by all the pistons in an internal-combustion engine (as of an automobile)

¹dis·play \dis-'plā\ *vb* **1** : to put in plain view ⟨*display* the flag⟩ ⟨the results *displayed* on a computer screen⟩ ⟨*display* toys in a store window⟩ **2** : to make clear the existence or presence of : make a display of ⟨*display* anger⟩ *synonyms* see SHOW

²**display** *n* **1 a** : a showing of something **b** : an electronic device (as a cathode-ray tube in a computer or radar receiver) that gives information in visual form; *also* : the visual information **2** : overdone or unnecessary show **3** : an attractive exhibition

dis·please \(')dis-'plēz\ *vb* : to cause to feel disapproval, dislike, or annoyance 〈was *displeased* by the delay〉

dis·plea·sure \(')dis-'plezh-ər, -'plāzh-\ *n* : a feeling of dislike and irritation : DISSATISFACTION

dis·port \dis-'pō(ə)rt, -'pò(ə)rt\ *vb* **1 a** : AMUSE 1, DIVERT 〈*disporting* themselves on the beach〉 **b** : ¹FROLIC **2** : ¹DISPLAY 2 — **dis·port·ment** \-mənt\ *n*

dis·pos·able \dis-'pō-zə-bəl\ *adj* : made to be thrown away after use 〈a *disposable* bottle〉 〈*disposable* diapers〉

dis·pos·al \dis-'pō-zəl\ *n* **1** : the right or power to use or control something : COMMAND 〈funds at our *disposal*〉 **2** : an orderly arrangement 〈the *disposal* of troops for battle〉 **3** : a getting rid of or putting out of the way 〈trash *disposal*〉 **4** : MANAGEMENT 1, ADMINISTRATION **5** : the transfer of something to a new owner 〈a *disposal* of property〉

dis·pose \dis-'pōz\ *vb* **dis·posed; dis·pos·ing** **1** : ¹INCLINE 2 〈I was not *disposed* to go to the meeting〉 **2** : to put in place or in readiness : ARRANGE 〈you'll need more room to *dispose* your legs comfortably〉 — **dis·pos·er** *n* — **dispose of** **1** : to settle or decide the future, condition, or use of 〈King James claimed the right to *dispose of* the whole American continent〉 **2 a** : to transfer to the control of another 〈*disposing of* one's property to another〉 **b** : to get rid of : put out of the way : DISCARD 〈how to *dispose of* radioactive waste〉 **3** : to take care of : deal with 〈I have some business to *dispose of* first〉

dis·po·si·tion \,dis-pə-'zish-ən\ *n* **1** : the act or power of disposing : DISPOSAL **2** : ARRANGEMENT 1 〈the *disposition* of furniture in a room〉 **3 a** : one's usual attitude or mood 〈a cheerful *disposition*〉 **b** : a leaning toward a particular way of thinking or acting : TENDENCY, INCLINATION 〈neither showed a *disposition* to retreat〉

dis·pos·sess \,dis-pə-'zes\ *vb* : to take away the possession of or the right to occupy land or houses — **dis·pos·ses·sion** \-'zesh-ən\ *n*

dis·proof \(')dis-'prüf\ *n* **1** : the action of disproving **2** : evidence that disproves

dis·pro·por·tion \,dis-prə-'pōr-shən, -'pòr-\ *n* : lack of proportion, balance, or proper relation; *also* : an instance of this

dis·pro·por·tion·ate \,dis-prə-'pōr-sh(ə-)nət, -'pòr-\ *adj* : being out of proportion — **dis·pro·por·tion·ate·ly** *adv*

dis·prove \(')dis-'prüv\ *vb* : to prove to be false

dis·put·able \,dis-'pyüt-ə-bəl, 'dis-pyət-\ *adj* : not yet proved : DEBATABLE — **dis·put·ably** \-blē\ *adv*

dis·pu·tant \dis-'pyüt-ᵊnt, 'dis-pyət-\ *n* : a person who takes part in a dispute

dis·pu·ta·tion \,dis-pyə-'tā-shən\ *n* : the act of disputing : DEBATE

dis·pu·ta·tious \,dis-pyə-'tā-shəs\ *adj* : likely to dispute or cause dispute; *also* : marked by disputation — **dis·pu·ta·tious·ness** *n*

¹**dis·pute** \dis-'pyüt\ *vb* **dis·put·ed; dis·put·ing** **1** : to engage in argument : DEBATE **2** : to quarrel angrily : WRANGLE **3** : to question the truth or rightness of 〈*dispute* a statement〉 **4** : to fight over : CONTEST 〈the two nations *disputed* the territory〉 — **dis·put·er** *n*

²**dispute** *n* **1** : ARGUMENT 1b, DEBATE **2** : an angry difference of opinion : QUARREL

dis·qual·i·fi·ca·tion \(,)dis-,kwäl-ə-fə-'kā-shən\ *n* **1** : something that disqualifies **2** : the act of disqualifying : the state of being disqualified

dis·qual·i·fy \(')dis-'kwäl-ə-,fī\ *vb* **-fied; -fy·ing** : to make or declare unfit or not qualified

¹**dis·qui·et** \(')dis-'kwī-ət\ *vb* : to make uneasy or restless : DISTURB — **dis·qui·et·ing·ly** \-iŋ-lē\ *adv*

²**disquiet** *n* : an uneasy feeling

¹**dis·re·gard** \,dis-ri-'gärd\ *vb* : to pay no attention to : treat as unworthy of regard or notice **synonyms** see NEGLECT

²**disregard** *n* : the act of disregarding : the state of being disregarded — **dis·re·gard·ful** \-fəl\ *adj*

dis·re·pair \,dis-ri-'pa(ə)r, -'pe(ə)r\ *n* : the condition of needing repair

dis·rep·u·ta·ble \(')dis-'rep-yət-ə-bəl\ *adj* : not respectable : having a bad reputation — **dis·rep·u·ta·ble·ness** *n* — **dis·rep·u·ta·bly** \-blē\ *adv*

dis·re·pute \,dis-ri-'pyüt\ *n* : loss or lack of good reputation : DISGRACE

¹**dis·re·spect** \,dis-ri-'spekt\ *vb* **1** : to have disrespect for **2** : to show or express disrespect or dislike for : INSULT

²**disrespect** *n* : lack of respect : DISCOURTESY — **dis·re·spect·ful** \-fəl\ *adj* — **dis·re·spect·ful·ly** \-fə-lē\ *adv* — **dis·re·spect·ful·ness** *n*

dis·re·spect·able \,dis-ri-'spek-tə-bəl\ *adj* : not respectable — **dis·re·spect·abil·i·ty** \-,spek-tə-'bil-ət-ē\ *n*

dis·robe \(')dis-'rōb\ *vb* : ¹UNDRESS

dis·rupt \dis-'rəpt\ *vb* : to throw into disorder 〈*disrupted* the class〉 — **dis·rupt·er** *n* — **dis·rup·tion** \-'rəp-shən\ *n* — **dis·rup·tive** \-'rəp-tiv\ *adj* — **dis·rup·tive·ly** *adv* — **dis·rup·tive·ness** *n*

dis·sat·is·fac·tion \(,)dis-(,)sat-əs-'fak-shən\ *n* : the quality or state of being dissatisfied

dis·sat·is·fac·to·ry \-'fak-t(ə-)rē\ *adj* : causing dissatisfaction

dis·sat·is·fy \(')dis-'(s)at-əs-,fī\ *vb* : to fail to satisfy : DISPLEASE

dis·sect \dī-'sekt, 'dī-; 'dī-,sekt\ *vb* **1** : to cut up (as a plant or animal) into separate parts for examination and study **2** : to make a careful examination of 〈*dissect* a problem〉 [from Latin *dissectus,* past participle of *dissecare* "to cut apart," from *dis-* "apart" and *secare* "to cut" — related to INSECT, SECTION]

dis·sec·tion \-'sek-shən, -,sek-\ *n* **1** : the act or process of dissecting : the state of being dissected **2** : a plant or animal or a part of one that has been dissected for study of the anatomy

dis·sem·ble \dis-'em-bəl\ *vb* **-bled; -bling** \-b(ə-)liŋ\ : to hide one's true feelings : put on a false appearance — **dis·sem·bler** \-b(ə-)lər\ *n*

dis·sem·i·nate \dis-'em-ə-,nāt\ *vb* **-nat·ed; -nat·ing** : to spread around as if sowing seed 〈*disseminate* ideas〉 — **dis·sem·i·na·tion** \-,em-ə-'nā-shən\ *n* — **dis·sem·i·na·tor** \-'em-ə-,nāt-ər\ *n*

dis·sen·sion \dis-'en-chən\ *n* : disagreement in opinion : DISCORD

¹**dis·sent** \dis-'ent\ *vb* : to differ in opinion : DISAGREE

²**dissent** *n* : difference of opinion

dis·sent·er \dis-'ent-ər\ *n* **1** : one that dissents **2** *cap* : an English Protestant who is not in agreement with the rules or beliefs of the Church of England

dis·sen·tient \dis-'en-chənt\ *adj* : expressing dissent 〈a *dissentient* opinion〉

dis·ser·ta·tion \,dis-ər-'tā-shən\ *n* : a long usually written treatment of a subject

dis·ser·vice \(')dis-'(s)ər-vəs\ *n* : an unhelpful, unkind, or harmful act 〈behavior that did a *disservice* to the sport〉

dis·sev·er \dis-'ev-ər\ *vb* : to separate completely

dis·si·dence \'dis-əd-ən(t)s\ *n* : DISSENT, DISAGREEMENT

dis·si·dent \'dis-əd-ənt\ *adj* : disagreeing with an opinion or a group — **dissident** *n*

dis·sim·i·lar \(')dis-'(s)im-ə-lər\ *adj* : DIFFERENT 1, UNLIKE — **dis·sim·i·lar·i·ty** \(,)dis-(,)sim-ə-'lar-ət-ē\ *n* — **dis·sim·i·lar·ly** \(')dis-'(s)im-ə-lər-lē\ *adv*

\ə\ abut	\aù\ out	\i\ tip	\ò\ saw	\ù\ foot
\ər\ further	\ch\ chin	\ī\ life	\òi\ coin	\y\ yet
\a\ mat	\e\ pet	\j\ job	\th\ thin	\yü\ few
\ā\ take	\ē\ easy	\ŋ\ sing	\th\ this	\yù\ cure
\ä\ cot, cart	\g\ go	\ō\ bone	\ü\ food	\zh\ vision

dis·sim·u·late \(')dis-'im-yə-ˌlāt\ *vb* **-lat·ed; -lat·ing** : DISSEMBLE — **dis·sim·u·la·tion** \(ˌ)dis-ˌim-yə-'lā-shən\ *n* — **dis·sim·u·la·tor** \(')dis-'im-yə-ˌlāt-ər\ *n*

dis·si·pate \'dis-ə-ˌpāt\ *vb* **-pat·ed; -pat·ing** 1 : to cause to spread out to the point of vanishing : DISSOLVE ⟨the breeze *dissipated* the fog⟩ 2 : to use up wastefully or foolishly : SQUANDER ⟨*dissipated* his fortune⟩ 3 : to separate into parts and scatter or vanish 4 : to be unreasonable or uncontrollable in the pursuit of pleasure; *esp* : to drink alcoholic beverages to excess

dis·si·pat·ed *adj* : affected by or showing the effects of dissipation : DISSOLUTE — **dis·si·pat·ed·ly** *adv* — **dis·si·pat·ed·ness** *n*

dis·si·pa·tion \ˌdis-ə-'pā-shən\ *n* : the action or process of dissipating : the state of being dissipated

dis·so·ci·ate \(')dis-'ō-sē-ˌāt, -shē-\ *vb* **-at·ed; -at·ing** 1 : to separate from association or union with another 2 : ¹DIVIDE 1

dis·so·ci·a·tion \(ˌ)dis-ˌō-sē-'ā-shən, -shē-\ *n* : the act or process of dissociating : the state of being dissociated; *esp* : the process by which a chemical combination breaks up into simpler substances of which it is made

dis·so·lute \'dis-ə-ˌlüt\ *adj* : having or showing bad morals or behavior — **dis·so·lute·ly** *adv* — **dis·so·lute·ness** *n*

dis·so·lu·tion \ˌdis-ə-'lü-shən\ *n* 1 : the action or process of dissolving 2 : the ending or breaking up of an assembly or a partnership or corporation

dis·solve \diz-'älv, -'olv\ *vb* **dis·solved; dis·solv·ing** 1 : to mix or cause to mix with a liquid so that the result is a liquid that is the same throughout ⟨sugar *dissolves* in water⟩ 2 : to bring to an end ⟨*dissolved* their partnership⟩ 3 : to fade away as if by breaking up or melting ⟨his courage *dissolved* in the face of danger⟩ 4 : to be overcome by a strong feeling ⟨*dissolved* into tears⟩ 5 : to appear or fade out gradually so that one scene is replaced by another (as in movies or television) — **dis·solv·er** *n*

dis·so·nance \'dis-ə-nən(t)s\ *n* : an unpleasant combination of musical sounds

dis·so·nant \'dis-ə-nənt\ *adj* : marked by dissonance — **dis·so·nant·ly** *adv*

dis·suade \dis-'wād\ *vb* **dis·suad·ed; dis·suad·ing** : to persuade or advise not to do something

¹dis·taff \'dis-ˌtaf\ *n, pl* **distaffs** \-ˌtafs, -ˌtavz\ 1 : a staff for holding the flax or wool in spinning 2 : the female branch or side of a family

Word History Before the invention of the spinning wheel, the spinning of yarn or thread was traditionally done by women using a spindle and a distaff. A spindle was a long spool to hold and spin the yarn. A distaff was a short rod with an opening or branches at the top for holding the flax or wool. The word *distæf* in Old English meant literally "flax staff," from *dis-* "a bunch of flax" and *stæf* "staff." Because women usually did

D ¹distaff 1

the spinning, the distaff came to be a symbol for women's work. The word *distaff* in time took on the meaning "women's work" and later "woman." The noun *distaff* is rarely used in this way today, but the female members of a family are still referred to as the distaff side. [from earlier *distaff* (noun) "a staff for holding flax or wool for spinning," from Old English *distæf* (same meaning), from *dis-* "bunch of flax" and *stæf* "staff"]

²distaff *adj* : of, relating to, or being a woman ⟨the *distaff* side of the family⟩ ⟨*distaff* skiers⟩

¹dis·tance \'dis-tən(t)s\ *n* 1 **a** : separation in time **b** : the space or amount of space between two points, lines, surfaces, or objects **c** : the full length ⟨go the *distance*⟩ 2

: the quality or state of being not friendly : RESERVE 3 : a distant point or place ⟨a light seen in the *distance*⟩

²distance *vb* **dis·tanced; dis·tanc·ing** : to leave far behind

dis·tant \'dis-tənt\ *adj* 1 : separated in space or time : AWAY **b** : being at a great distance : FAR-OFF ⟨*distant* countries⟩ 2 : not close in relationship ⟨*distant* cousin⟩ 3 : ¹COLD 2, UNFRIENDLY — **dis·tant·ly** *adv* — **dis·tant·ness** *n*

dis·taste \(')dis-'tāst\ *n* : a strong dislike : AVERSION ⟨a *distaste* for work⟩

dis·taste·ful \dis-'tāst-fəl\ *adj* : causing displeasure : UNPLEASANT, DISAGREEABLE — **dis·taste·ful·ly** \-fə-lē\ *adv* — **dis·taste·ful·ness** *n*

dis·tem·per \dis-'tem-pər\ *n* : a highly contagious virus disease especially of dogs marked by fever and by respiratory and sometimes nervous symptoms

dis·tend \dis-'tend\ *vb* : to stretch or bulge out in all directions : SWELL

dis·ten·sion *or* **dis·ten·tion** \dis-'ten-chən\ *n* : the act of distending or the state of being distended

dis·till *also* **dis·til** \dis-'til\ *vb* **dis·tilled; dis·till·ing** : to obtain or purify by distillation

dis·til·late \'dis-tə-ˌlāt, -lət; dis-'til-ət\ *n* : a liquid product cooled from vapor during distillation

dis·til·la·tion \ˌdis-tə-'lā-shən\ *n* : a process of heating a liquid or solid until it sends off a vapor and then cooling the vapor until it becomes liquid

dis·till·er \dis-'til-ər\ *n* : one that distills especially alcoholic liquors

dis·till·ery \dis-'til-(ə-)rē\ *n, pl* **-er·ies** : a place where distilling especially of alchoholic liquors is done

dis·tinct \dis-'tiŋ(k)t\ *adj* 1 : real and different from each other ⟨five *distinct* varieties⟩ ⟨pears as *distinct* from apples⟩ 2 : clearly seen, heard, or understood : PLAIN, UNMISTAKABLE ⟨speaks with a *distinct* accent⟩ ⟨a *distinct* possibility⟩ — **dis·tinct·ly** *adv* — **dis·tinct·ness** *n*

dis·tinc·tion \dis-'tiŋ(k)-shən\ *n* 1 **a** : the seeing or pointing out of a difference **b** : DIFFERENCE 1 ⟨the *distinction* between good and evil⟩ 2 : something that makes a person or thing special or different ⟨the *distinction* of being the oldest house in the city⟩ 3 **a** : ¹HONOR 5b ⟨served with *distinction*⟩ **b** : ¹HONOR 4b

dis·tinc·tive \dis-'tiŋ(k)-tiv\ *adj* 1 : clearly marking a person or a thing as different from others ⟨a *distinctive* walk⟩ 2 : having or giving a special look or way ⟨*distinctive* clothes⟩ — **dis·tinc·tive·ly** *adv* — **dis·tinc·tive·ness** *n*

dis·tin·guish \dis-'tiŋ-(g)wish\ *vb* 1 : to recognize one thing from others by some mark or quality ⟨*distinguish* the sound of a piano in an orchestra⟩ 2 : to hear or see clearly : MAKE OUT, DISCERN ⟨*distinguish* a light in the distance⟩ 3 : to know or point out the difference ⟨*distinguish* between right and wrong⟩ 4 : to set apart as different or special ⟨*distinguished* themselves by heroic actions⟩ — **dis·tin·guish·able** \-ə-bəl\ *adj* — **dis·tin·guish·ably** \-blē\ *adv*

dis·tin·guished *adj* : widely known and admired for excellence ⟨a *distinguished* scientist⟩

dis·tort \dis-'tȯ(ə)rt\ *vb* 1 : to tell in a way that is misleading : MISREPRESENT ⟨*distorted* the facts⟩ 2 : to twist out of a natural, normal, or original shape or condition [from Latin *distortus*, past participle of *distorquēre* "to distort, twist out of proper meaning," from *dis-* "reverse, apart" and *torquēre* "to twist" — related to EXTORT, RETORT, TORTURE] — **dis·tort·er** *n*

dis·tor·tion \dis-'tȯr-shən\ *n* 1 : the act of distorting 2 : the condition of being distorted or a product of distortion — **dis·tor·tion·al** \-shnəl, -shən-ᵊl\ *adj*

dis·tract \dis-'trakt\ *vb* 1 : to draw the attention or mind to something else 2 : to upset or trouble in mind to the point of confusion — **dis·tract·ible** \-'trak-tə-bəl\ *adj*

dis·trac·tion \dis-'trak-shən\ *n* **1** : the act of distracting : the state of being distracted; *esp* : mental confusion **2 a** : something that makes it hard to pay attention **b** : AMUSEMENT 1 — **dis·trac·tive** \-'trak-tiv\ *adj*

dis·traught \dis-'trȯt\ *adj* **1** : disturbed with doubt or painful feelings **2** : INSANE 1 — **dis·traught·ly** *adv*

¹**dis·tress** \dis-'tres\ *n* **1** : great suffering of body or mind : PAIN, ANGUISH **2** : a painful situation : MISFORTUNE **3** : a condition of danger or desperate need ⟨a ship in *distress*⟩

²**distress** *vb* **1** : to cause to experience painful difficulties **2** : to cause to worry or be troubled : UPSET — **dis·tress·ing·ly** \-iŋ-lē\ *adv*

dis·tress·ful \-'tres-fəl\ *adj* : causing distress : full of distress — **dis·tress·ful·ly** \-fə-lē\ *adv* — **dis·tress·ful·ness** *n*

dis·trib·u·tary \dis-'trib-yə-ˌter-ē\ *n, pl* **-tar·ies** : a river branch flowing away from the main stream

dis·trib·ute \dis-'trib-yət\ *vb* **-ut·ed; -ut·ing** **1** : to divide among several or many ⟨*distributed* the food to the needy⟩ **2** : to spread out so as to cover something : SCATTER **3** : to give out or deliver especially to members of a group ⟨*distribute* the directions to the class⟩ ⟨*distribute* newspapers⟩ **4** : to divide or separate especially into kinds

> **synonyms** DISTRIBUTE, DISPENSE, DIVIDE, DOLE mean to give out usually in shares to each member of a group. DISTRIBUTE suggests the giving out of something by separating it into parts, units, or amounts ⟨*distributed* the art supplies to the class⟩. DISPENSE suggests the giving of a carefully measured portion ⟨*dispensed* the medicine to the patients⟩. DIVIDE stresses the separation of a whole into usually equal parts ⟨*divided* the money that they had earned together⟩. DOLE suggests a carefully measured portion of something in short supply ⟨slowly *doled* out the last of the food⟩.

dis·tri·bu·tion \ˌdis-trə-'byü-shən\ *n* **1** : the act or process of distributing **2 a** : the position, arrangement, or numbers (as of the members of a group) over an area or throughout a space or unit of time **b** : the natural geographic range of a living thing ⟨the *distribution* of human beings⟩ **3 a** : something distributed **b** : FREQUENCY DISTRIBUTION ⟨population age *distribution*⟩ **4** : the marketing of goods — **dis·tri·bu·tion·al** \-shnəl, -shən-ᵊl\ *adj*

dis·trib·u·tive \dis-'trib-yət-iv\ *adj* **1** : of or relating to distribution : serving to distribute **2** : of, having, or being the property of giving the same mathematical result when an operation is carried out on a whole expression and when it is carried out on each part of an expression with the results then collected together ⟨the *distributive* property of multiplication means $a(b + c) = ab + ac$⟩ — **dis·trib·u·tive·ly** *adv*

dis·trib·u·tor \dis-'trib-yət-ər\ *n* **1** : one that distributes **2** : an agent or agency for marketing goods **3** : a device that sends electric current to the spark plugs of an engine so that they fire in the proper order

¹**dis·trict** \'dis-(ˌ)trikt\ *n* **1** : an area or section (as of a city or nation) set apart for some purpose ⟨a school *district*⟩ ⟨a judicial *district*⟩ **2** : an area or region having some special feature ⟨a coal-mining *district*⟩

²**district** *vb* : to divide or organize into districts

district attorney *n* : the prosecuting officer of a judicial district

¹**dis·trust** \(')dis-'trəst\ *vb* : to have no trust or confidence in

²**distrust** *n* : a lack of trust or confidence **synonyms** see DOUBT — **dis·trust·ful** \-fəl\ *adj* — **dis·trust·ful·ly** \-fə-lē\ *adv* — **dis·trust·ful·ness** *n*

dis·turb \dis-'tərb\ *vb* **1 a** : to interfere with : INTERRUPT **b** : to change the position, arrangement, or stability of **2 a** : to trouble the mind of : make uneasy **b** : to throw into confusion or disorder **c** : to cause bother to — **dis·turb·er** *n*

dis·turb·ance \dis-'tər-bən(t)s\ *n* **1** : the act of disturbing **2** : mental confusion : UPSET **3** : public commotion : DISORDER

dis·turbed \dis-'tərbd\ *adj* : showing signs of mental or emotional illness

di·sul·fide \(')dī-'səl-ˌfīd\ *n* : a compound containing two atoms of sulfur combined with an element or chemical group

dis·union \dish-'ü-nyən, (')dis-'yü-\ *n* : the ending of union : SEPARATION

dis·unite \ˌdish-ü-'nīt, ˌdis-yü-\ *vb* : ¹DIVIDE 1, SEPARATE

dis·uni·ty \dish-'ü-nət-ē, (')dis-'yü-\ *n* : lack of unity; *esp* : DISSENSION

dis·use \dish-'üs, (')dis-'yüs\ *n* : lack of use

dis·used \-'yüzd\ *adj* : no longer used or occupied ⟨*disused* buildings⟩

¹**ditch** \'dich\ *n* : a long narrow channel or trench dug in the earth

²**ditch** *vb* **1** : to dig a ditch in or around **2 a** : to get rid of : DISCARD ⟨*ditch* an old car⟩ **b** : to end association with : LEAVE ⟨his girlfriend *ditched* him⟩ **3** : to make a forced landing of (an airplane) on water

¹**dith·er** \'dith-ər\ *n* : a highly nervous or excited state ⟨the news had him in a *dither*⟩ — **dith·ery** \-ə-rē\ *adj*

²**dither** *vb* **dith·ered; dith·er·ing** : to act nervously or indecisively

dit·to \'dit-ō\ *n, pl* **dittos** **1** : another of the same thing mentioned before or above — used to avoid repeating a word ⟨lost: one shirt (white); *ditto* (blue)⟩ **2** : a mark composed of a pair of quotation marks or apostrophes used as a symbol for the word *ditto*

dit·ty \'dit-ē\ *n, pl* **ditties** : a short simple song

dit·zy *or* **dit·sy** \'dit-sē\ *adj* **ditz·i·er** *or* **dits·i·er; -est** : unusually silly or giddy — **dit·zi·ness** *or* **dit·si·ness** *n*

di·uret·ic \ˌdī-(y)ə-'ret-ik\ *n* : a substance that increases the amount of urine produced by the body — **diuretic** *adj*

di·ur·nal \dī-'ərn-ᵊl\ *adj* **1** : occurring every day : DAILY ⟨a *diurnal* task⟩ **2 a** : of, relating to, or occurring in the daytime ⟨the city's *diurnal* noises⟩ **b** : active chiefly in the daytime ⟨*diurnal* animals⟩ — **di·ur·nal·ly** \-'ərn-ᵊl-ē\ *adv*

di·va \'dē-və\ *n, pl* **divas** *or* **di·ve** \-ˌvā\ **1 a** : PRIMA DONNA 1 **b** : PRIMA DONNA 2 **2** : a usually glamorous and successful female performer or celebrity ⟨a fashion *diva*⟩; *esp* : a popular female singer ⟨pop *divas*⟩ [from Italian *diva* "goddess," from Latin *diva* (same meaning)]

di·van \di-'van, 'dī-ˌvan\ *n* : a large couch often with no back or arms

¹**dive** \'dīv\ *vb* **dived** \'dīvd\ *or* **dove** \'dōv\; **div·ing** **1 a** : to plunge into water headfirst **b** : SUBMERGE 1 **2 a** : to fall fast ⟨the temperature *dived* at night⟩ **b** : to descend in an airplane at a very steep angle **3 a** : to plunge into some matter or activity **b** : to thrust oneself forward suddenly : LUNGE ⟨*dived* for cover⟩ — **div·er** *n*

²**dive** *n* **1** : the act or an instance of diving: as **a** : a plunge into water done in a specified manner **b** : a steep downward movement of a submarine or an airplane **c** : a sharp drop (as in prices) **2** : a shabby place (as a bar) **3** : a faked knockout in boxing

di·verge \də-'vərj, dī-\ *vb* **di·verged; di·verg·ing** : to move or extend in different directions from a common point : draw apart ⟨*diverging* rays of light⟩ ⟨two roads *diverged*⟩

\ə\ **abut**	\au̇\ **out**	\i\ **tip**	\ȯ\ **saw**	\u̇\ **foot**
\ər\ **further**	\ch\ **chin**	\ī\ **life**	\ȯi\ **coin**	\y\ **yet**
\a\ **mat**	\e\ **pet**	\j\ **job**	\th\ **thin**	\yü\ **few**
\ā\ **take**	\ē\ **easy**	\ŋ\ **sing**	\th\ **this**	\yu̇\ **cure**
\ä\ **cot, cart**	\g\ **go**	\ō\ **bone**	\ü\ **food**	\zh\ **vision**

di·ver·gence \də-'vər-jən(t)s, dī-\
n : the state of diverging : a drawing apart (as of lines extending
from a common center)

di·ver·gent \də-'vər-jənt, dī-\ *adj*
: diverging from each other — **di-
ver·gent·ly** *adv*

di·vers \'dī-vərz\ *adj* : VARIOUS 4

di·verse \dī-'vərs, də-, 'dī-,vərs\
adj : differing from one another
: UNLIKE — **di·verse·ly** *adv* —
di·verse·ness *n*

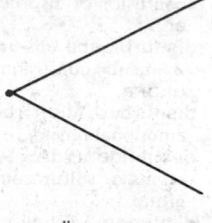

divergence

di·ver·si·fy \də-'vər-sə-,fī, dī-\ *vb* **-fied; -fy·ing** **1** : to
make diverse : give variety to **2** : to increase the variety
of products of ⟨*diversify* a business⟩ — **di·ver·si·fi·ca-
tion** \-,vər-sə-fə-'kā-shən\ *n*

di·ver·sion \də-'vər-zhən, dī-\ *n* **1** : the act or an instance
of diverting or turning aside **2** : something that relaxes,
amuses, or entertains — **di·ver·sion·ary** \-zhə-,ner-ē\ *adj*

di·ver·si·ty \də-'vər-sət-ē, dī-\ *n, pl* **-ties** **1** : the condition
of being different **2** : an instance or a point of difference

di·vert \də-'vərt, dī-\ *vb* **1 a** : to turn aside : turn from one
course or use to another **b** : to turn the attention away
: DISTRACT **2** : to give pleasure to by causing the time to
pass pleasantly [Middle English *diverten* "to turn aside
from a course," from early French *divertir* "to divert" and
Latin *divertere* "to turn in opposite directions," from *dis-*
"away, apart" and *vertere* "to turn" — related to CON-
VERSE, REVERSE, VERSATILE] **synonyms** see AMUSE

di·vest \dī-'vest, də-\ *vb* : to take something off or away
from ⟨*divested* myself of my heavy backpack⟩

1di·vide \də-'vīd\ *vb* **di·vid·ed; di·vid·ing** **1 a** : to separate
into two or more parts or pieces **b** : to separate into
classes or categories **c** : ²CLEAVE, PART **2 a** : to give out
in shares **b** : to own or use in common : SHARE **3** : to
cause to be separate, different, or apart from one another
4 a : to perform or use in mathematical division **b** : to
subject (a number) to the operation of finding how many
times it contains another number ⟨*divide* 42 by 14⟩ **c** : to
use as a divisor ⟨*divide* 14 into 42⟩ **5 a** : to undergo cell
division ⟨the cell *divides*⟩ **b** : ²BRANCH 2, FORK **synonyms** see DISTRIBUTE, SEPARATE

2divide *n* : a dividing ridge between drainage areas : WA-
TERSHED

divided *adj* **1 a** : separated into parts or pieces **b** : having
a barrier (as a guardrail) to separate lanes of traffic going
in opposite directions ⟨a *divided* highway⟩ **2** : disagreeing with each other ⟨*divided* over the issue⟩

div·i·dend \'div-ə-,dend, -əd-ənd\ *n* **1** : a sum to be divided and given out **2** : BONUS **3** : a number to be divided by another

di·vid·er \də-'vīd-ər\ *n* **1** : something that divides
⟨a room *divider*⟩ **2** *pl* : an instrument for measuring or marking

div·i·na·tion \,div-ə-'nā-shən\ *n* : the art or practice of using omens or magic powers to foretell
the future

1di·vine \də-'vīn\ *adj* **1 a** : of, relating to, or coming directly from God or a god **b** : being God or
a god ⟨the *divine* Savior⟩ **c** : directed to God or
a god ⟨*divine* worship⟩ **2 a** : extremely good
: SUPERB **b** : having godlike qualities — **di-
vine·ly** *adv*

2divine *n* : a member of the clergy

3divine *vb* **di·vined; di·vin·ing** **1** : to discover or
understand something without reasoning **2** : to
practice divination : PROPHESY — **di·vin·er** *n*

diving bell *n* : a diving device consisting of a
container open only at the bottom and supplied
with compressed air by a hose

diving board *n* : a flexible board fastened at one end and
used for diving into water

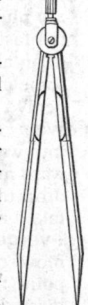

divider
2

divining rod *n* : a forked rod believed to reveal the presence of water or minerals by dipping downward when
held over a vein

di·vin·i·ty \də-'vin-ət-ē\ *n, pl* **-ties** **1** : THEOLOGY 1 **2** : the
quality or state of being divine **3** *often cap* **a** : GOD 1 **b**
: GOD 2 **c** : GODDESS 1 **d** : DEMIGOD 1

di·vis·i·ble \də-'viz-ə-bəl\ *adj* : capable of being divided —
di·vis·i·bil·i·ty \-,viz-ə-'bil-ət-ē\ *n*

di·vi·sion \də-'vizh-ən\ *n* **1 a** : the act or process of dividi-
ing : the state of being divided **b** : DISTRIBUTION 1 **c**
: CELL DIVISION **2** : a part or portion of a whole **3**
: something that divides, separates, or marks off **4** : a
large military unit **5** : a large unit of a governmental,
business, or educational organization **6** : difference in
opinion or interest : DISAGREEMENT **7** : the mathematical operation of dividing something **8** : a category in
most classifications of the plant kingdom that is equal to
a phylum — **di·vi·sion·al** \-'vizh-(ə-)nəl\ *adj*

di·vi·sor \də-'vī-zər\ *n* : the number by which a dividend is
divided

1di·vorce \də-'vōrs, -'vȯrs\ *n* **1** : the action or an instance
of legally ending a marriage **2** : complete separation

2divorce *vb* **di·vorced; di·vorc·ing** **1 a** : to end marriage
with one's spouse by divorce **b** : to cancel the marriage
contract between two spouses **2** : to make or keep separate : SEPARATE, DISUNITE — **di·vorce·ment** \-mənt\ *n*

di·vor·cé \də-,vōr-'sā, -,vȯr-, -'sē\ *n* : a divorced man

di·vor·cée \də-,vōr-'sā, -,vȯr-, -'sē\ *n* : a divorced woman

di·vulge \də-'vəlj, dī-\ *vb* **di·vulged; di·vulg·ing** : to
make public : DISCLOSE — **di·vul·gence** \-'vəl-jən(t)s\ *n*

Dix·ie·land \'dik-sē-,land\ *n* : lively jazz music in a style
developed in New Orleans

DIY \,dē-(,)ī-'wī\ *adj* : DO-IT-YOURSELF

diz·zy \'diz-ē\ *adj* **diz·zi·er; -est** **1 a** : having a feeling of
whirling **b** : mentally confused **2 a** : causing or caused
by a whirling sensation ⟨*dizzy* heights⟩ **b** : extremely
rapid ⟨prices climbing at a *dizzy* rate⟩ — **diz·zi·ly** \'diz-ə-
lē\ *adv* — **diz·zi·ness** \'diz-ē-nəs\ *n*

DJ \'dē-,jā\ *n, often not cap* : DISC JOCKEY

D layer *n* : a layer or region of the lower ionosphere

DNA \,dē-,en-'ā\ *n* : any of various nucleic acids that are
located especially in cell nuclei, are usually the chemical
basis of heredity, and are composed of two nucleotide
chains held together by hydrogen bonds in a pattern resembling a flexible twisted ladder — compare RNA

DNA fingerprinting *n* : a method of identification (as for
forensic purposes) by determining the unique pattern of a
person's DNA — **DNA fingerprint** *n*

1do \(')dü\ *vb* **did** \(')did\; **done** \'dən\; **do·ing** \'dü-iŋ\;
does \(')dəz\ **1 a** : to cause (as an act or action) to hap-
pen : CARRY OUT, PERFORM ⟨*do* me a favor⟩ **b** : ²ACT 3,
BEHAVE ⟨*do* as I say⟩ **2 a** : to work at ⟨what one *does* for
a living⟩ **b** : to take suitable action on ⟨*do* your home-
work⟩ ⟨*do* the dishes⟩ **c** : ¹SET 11 ⟨have my hair *done*⟩ **d**
: DECORATE 1 ⟨*did* the bedroom in blue⟩ **3** : to make
progress ⟨*does* well in school⟩ **4** : to act so as to bring
: RENDER ⟨sleep will *do* you good⟩ **5** : to come to the end
of : FINISH ⟨turn out the light when you are *done*⟩ **6** : to
put forth : EXERT ⟨*did* your best to win⟩ **7 a** : to travel a
distance of ⟨*did* 500 miles that day⟩ **b** : to travel at a
speed of ⟨*doing* 55 miles per hour on the turnpike⟩ **8**
: ¹SERVE 1d ⟨*did* five years for armed robbery⟩ **9 a** : to
serve the purpose ⟨half of that will *do*⟩ **b** : to be fitting
or proper ⟨it won't *do* to be late⟩ **10** — used as a helping
verb (1) before the subject in an interrogative sentence
⟨*do* you play the piano?⟩, (2) in a negative statement ⟨I
do not know⟩, (3) for emphasis ⟨you *do* know⟩, and (4) as
a substitute for a preceding verb ⟨you work harder than I
do⟩ [Old English *dōn* "to cause to happen, perform"] —
do away with **1** : to put an end to : get rid of : ABOLISH
2 : ¹KILL 1 — **do the trick** : to give or have a desired result

²do \'dō\ *n* : the first note of the musical scale [Italian]

do·able \'dü-ə-bəl\ *adj* : capable of being done

Do·ber·man pin·scher \ˌdō-bər-mən-'pin-chər\ *n* : any of a breed of short-haired medium-sized dogs of German origin [from German *Dobermann-pinscher* (breed of dog), from Friedrich Ludwig *Dobermann,* German dog breeder, and *pinscher* "breed of hunting dog"]

dob·son·fly \'däb-sən-ˌflī\ *n* : a large-eyed winged insect with a large flesh-eating water-dwelling larva

doc·ile \'däs-əl\ *adj* : easily taught, led, or managed ⟨a *docile* pet⟩ [from Latin *docilis* "easily taught," from *docēre* "to teach" — related to DOCTOR, DOCTRINE] — **doc·ile·ly** \'däs-ə(l)-lē\ *adv* — **do·cil·i·ty** \dä-'sil-ət-ē, dō-\ *n*

¹dock \'däk\ *n* : any of a genus of coarse weedy plants which are related to the buckwheat and some of which are cooked for food [Old English *docce* "the dock plant"]

²dock *vb* **1** : to cut off the end of : cut short ⟨a *docked* tail⟩ **2** : to take away a part of : make a deduction from **3** : to deprive of something due because of a fault ⟨was *docked* for being late⟩ [Middle English *docken* "to cut off the end of a tail," from *dok, docke* "end of an animal's tail"]

³dock *n* **1** : a usually artificial basin to receive ships that has gates to control the water height **2** : ²SLIP 1b **3** : a wharf or platform for loading and unloading **4** : a usually wooden pier used as a landing place or moorage [probably from early Dutch *docke* "ditch, dock"]

⁴dock *vb* **1** : to bring or come into or alongside a dock **2** : to join (as two spacecraft) mechanically while in space

⁵dock *n* : the place in a court where a prisoner stands or sits during trial [from a Dutch dialect word *docke* "cage"]

¹dock·et \'däk-ət\ *n* **1** : a list of legal cases to be tried **2** : a list of items to be acted on : AGENDA

²docket *vb* : to place on the docket for legal action

dock·side \'däk-ˌsīd\ *n* : the shore or area next to a dock

dock·work·er \-ˌwər-kər\ *n* : LONGSHOREMAN

dock·yard \-ˌyärd\ *n* : SHIPYARD

¹doc·tor \'däk-tər\ *n* **1** : a person holding one of the highest degrees (as a PhD) given by a university **2** : a person (as a physician, dentist, or veterinarian) skilled and specializing in the art of healing [Middle English *doctour* "doctor, teacher," from early French *doctour* and Latin *doctor* (both, same meaning), from earlier Latin *doctor* "teacher," from *docēre* "to teach" — related to DOCILE, DOCTRINE] — **doc·tor·al** \-t(ə-)rəl\ *adj*

²doctor *vb* **doc·tored; doc·tor·ing** \-t(ə-)riŋ\ **1 a** : to give medical treatment to **b** : to practice medicine **c** : to bring back to good condition : REPAIR ⟨*doctor* an old clock⟩ **2** : to tamper with ⟨*doctored* the election returns⟩

doc·tor·ate \'däk-t(ə-)rət\ *n* : the degree, title, or rank of a doctor

doc·trine \'däk-trən\ *n* **1** : something that is taught **2** : a principle or the principles in a system of belief [Middle English *doctrine* "instruction," from early French *doctrine* and Latin *doctrina* (both, same meaning), from earlier Latin *doctor* "teacher," from *docēre* "to teach" — related to DOCILE, DOCTOR] — **doc·tri·nal** \-trən-ᵊl\ *adj* — **doc·tri·nal·ly** \-ᵊl-ē\ *adv*

do·cu·dra·ma \'däk-yə-ˌdräm-ə-ˌdram-\ *n* : a drama (as for television) dealing freely with historical events especially of a recent or controversial nature

¹doc·u·ment \'däk-yə-mənt\ *n* **1** : a written or printed paper giving information about or proof of something **2** : a computer file usually created with an application program (as a word processor)

²doc·u·ment \'däk-yə-ˌment\ *vb* : to give evidence of by a document — **doc·u·ment·able** \'däk-yə-ˌment-ə-bəl, ˌdäk-yə-'ment-\ *adj*

¹doc·u·men·ta·ry \ˌdäk-yə-'ment-ə-rē, -'men-trē\ *adj* **1** : consisting of documents; *also* : being in writing ⟨*documentary* proof⟩ **2** : presenting actual events or facts about something ⟨a *documentary* film⟩ — **doc·u·men·tar·i·ly** \-mən-ˌter-ə-lē, -ˌmen-\ *adv*

²documentary *n, pl* **-ries** : a documentary presentation (as a film or novel)

doc·u·men·ta·tion \ˌdäk-yə-mən-'tā-shən, -ˌmen-\ *n* **1** : the providing of documents as proof **2** : evidence in the form of documents **3** : written instructions for using a computer or computer program

dod·der \'däd-ər\ *vb* **dod·dered; dod·der·ing** \-(ə-)riŋ\ **1** : to tremble or shake from weakness or age **2** : to go in a shaky or feeble way

doddering *adj* : showing signs of old age

do·deca·he·dron \(ˌ)dō-ˌdek-ə-'hē-drən\ *n, pl* **-drons** *or* **-dra** \-drə\ : a polyhedron that has 12 faces

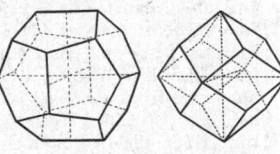

dodecahedron

¹dodge \'däj\ *n* **1** : an act of avoiding by sudden bodily movement **2** : a sly means of avoiding, deceiving, or tricking ⟨just another *dodge* to get out of working⟩ — **dodg·er** *n*

²dodge *vb* **dodged; dodg·ing** **1 a** : to move suddenly aside or to and fro ⟨*dodging* through the crowd⟩ **b** : to avoid by moving quickly aside ⟨*dodge* a blow⟩ **2** : EVADE 1 ⟨*dodged* the question⟩

dodge·ball \'däj-ˌból\ *n* : a game in which players stand in a circle and try to hit other players within the circle with a large inflated ball

do·do \'dōd-ō\ *n, pl* **dodoes** *or* **dodos** **1** : a large heavy flightless extinct bird related to the pigeons and formerly found on some of the islands of the Indian Ocean **2 a** : a person who is hopelessly behind the times **b** : a stupid person [from Portuguese *doudo,* name given by Portuguese sailors to the bird, from *doudo* (adjective) "silly, stupid"]

dodo 1

doe \'dō\ *n, pl* **does** *or* **doe** : the female especially of an adult mammal (as a deer, an antelope, or a rabbit) of which the male is called *buck*

do·er \'dü-ər\ *n* : one that does

does present 3rd singular of DO

doe·skin \'dō-ˌskin\ *n* **1** : the skin of does or leather made of it; *also* : soft leather from sheepskins or lambskins **2** : a soft smooth firm cloth

doesn't \'dəz-ᵊnt\ : does not

doff \'däf, 'dof\ *vb* : to take off (as one's hat as an act of politeness) [Middle English *doffen* "to take off," from *don* "to do" and *of* "off"]

¹dog \'dog\ *n* **1 a** : a domestic mammal that eats meat and is closely related to the gray wolf **b** : any animal of the family to which the dog belongs **c** : a male dog **2 a** : a worthless person **b** : PERSON 1 ⟨you lucky *dog*⟩ **3 a** : any of various devices for holding, gripping, or fastening that consist of a spike, rod, or bar **b** : ANDIRON **4** : a show of being stylish or rich ⟨put on the *dog*⟩ **5** *pl* : FEET — **dog·like** \-ˌlīk\ *adj*

²dog *vb* **dogged; dog·ging** : to hunt, track, or follow like a hound

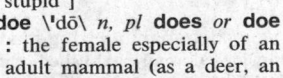

\ə\ abut	\au̇\ out	\i\ tip	\ȯ\ saw	\u̇\ foot
\ər\ further	\ch\ chin	\ī\ life	\ȯi\ coin	\y\ yet
\a\ mat	\e\ pet	\j\ job	\th\ thin	\yü\ few
\ā\ take	\ē\ easy	\ŋ\ sing	\th\ this	\yu̇\ cure
\ä\ cot, cart	\g\ go	\ō\ bone	\ü\ food	\zh\ vision

dog·cart \'dȯg-ˌkärt\ *n* **1** : a cart drawn by a dog **2** : a light one-horse carriage with two seats back to back

dog days *n pl* : the hot and humid period of summer between early July and early September

Word History The brightest star in the sky is Sirius, also known as the Dog Star. Sirius was given this name by the ancients because it was considered the hound of the hunter Orion, whose constellation was nearby; Sirius itself is in a constellation now called Canis Major ("larger dog"). The Dog Star was regarded by the ancient Greeks as the bringer of scorching heat, because its early-morning rising coincided with the hottest summer days of July and August. The Greek writer Plutarch called this time *hēmerai kynades*, literally, "dog days"—the days of the Dog Star—and via Latin this phrase was translated into English as *dog days*. [translation of Latin *dies caniculares*, from *canicula*, literally, "little dog," from *canis* "dog"; so called from the fact that they begin at the time when the Dog Star rises with or near the sun — related to CANINE]

doge \'dōj\ *n* : the chief magistrate in the former republics of Venice and Genoa

dog-ear \'dȯ-ˌgi(ə)r\ *n* : the turned-down corner of a leaf of a book — **dog-ear** *vb*

dog-eared \'dȯ-ˌgi(ə)rd\ *adj* **1** : having dog-ears **2** : worn-out from too much use

dog·face \'dȯg-ˌfās\ *n* : an infantry soldier

dog·fight \-ˌfīt\ *n* : a fight at close range between fighter planes — **dogfight** *vb* — **dog·fight·er** \-ˌfīt-ər\ *n*

dog·fish \-ˌfish\ *n* : any of various small sharks that often appear in schools near shore

dog·ged \'dȯ-gəd\ *adj* : stubbornly determined : TENACIOUS ⟨in *dogged* pursuit of power⟩ *synonyms* see OBSTINATE — **dog·ged·ly** *adv* — **dog·ged·ness** *n*

dog·gie bag *or* **doggy bag** \'dȯ-gē-\ *n* : a container used for carrying home leftover food from a meal eaten at a restaurant

dog·gy *or* **dog·gie** \'dȯ-gē\ *n, pl* **dog·gies** : a small or young dog

dog·house \'dȯg-ˌhau̇s\ *n* : a shelter for a dog — **in the doghouse** : in a state of disfavor

do·gie \'dō-gē\ *n, chiefly Western* : a motherless calf in a range herd

dog·ma \'dȯg-mə, 'däg-\ *n, pl* **dog·mas** *also* **dog·ma·ta** \-mət-ə\ **1** : something considered as an established opinion **2** : a belief or body of beliefs concerning faith or morals laid down by a church

dog·mat·ic \dȯg-'mat-ik, däg-\ *adj* **1** : expressing opinions very strongly or positively as if they were facts **2** : of or relating to dogma — **dog·mat·i·cal·ly** \-'mat-i-k(ə-)lē\ *adv*

dog·ma·tism \'dȯg-mə-ˌtiz-əm, 'däg-\ *n* : positiveness in expressing one's opinions especially when no supporting evidence is given — **dog·ma·tist** \-mət-əst\ *n*

dog paddle *n* : a simple swimming stroke in which the arms paddle in the water and the legs make a kicking motion

dog·sled \'dȯg-ˌsled\ *n* : a sled drawn by dogs — **dogsled** *vb*

Dog Star *n* : SIRIUS

dog tick *n* : a common North American tick especially of dogs and human beings that may transmit the bacterium causing Rocky Mountain spotted fever and tularemia

dog·tooth violet \'dȯg-ˌtüth-\ *n* : any of a genus of wild herbs that are related to the lilies, grow from bulbs, and produce flowers in the spring — called also *adder's-tongue*

dog·trot \-ˌträt\ *n* : a gentle trot — **dogtrot** *vb*

dog watch *n* **1** : a watch on a ship from 4 to 6 or from 6 to 8 p.m. **2** : any of various night shifts; *esp* : the last shift

dog·wood \'dȯg-ˌwu̇d\ *n* : any of various trees and shrubs having clusters of small flowers often surrounded by four showy leaves that look like petals

doi·ly \'dȯi-lē\ *n, pl* **doilies** **1** : a small napkin **2** : a small often decorative cloth or paper used to protect the surface of furniture

do in *vb* **1** : to bring about the defeat or destruction of : RUIN **2** : [1]KILL **3** : to bring almost to the point of exhaustion : WEAR OUT ⟨*done in* at the end of the day⟩

do·ing \'dü-iŋ\ *n* **1** : the act of performing or carrying out : ACTION ⟨it will take some *doing* to beat us⟩ **2** *pl* **a** : things that are done or that occur ⟨everyday *doings*⟩ **b** : social activities ⟨big *doings* tonight⟩

do–it–your·self \ˌdü-ə-chər-'self\ *adj* : of, relating to, or designed for a person without professional training or help to do or make — **do–it–your·self·er** \-'sel-fər\ *n*

dol·drums \'dōl-drəmz, 'dȯl-, 'däl-\ *n pl* **1** : a spell of low spirits **2** : a part of the ocean near the equator known for its calms **3** : a state in which nothing seems to be going on ⟨business is in the *doldrums*⟩

¹dole \'dōl\ *n* **1** : a giving out of food, money, or clothing to the needy **2** : something given out as charity

²dole *vb* **doled; dol·ing** **1** : to give out as charity **2** : to give or deliver in small portions : PARCEL — usually used with *out* *synonyms* see DISTRIBUTE

dole·ful \'dōl-fəl\ *adj* **1** : full of grief : SAD **2** : expressing grief — **dole·ful·ly** \-fə-lē\ *adv* — **dole·ful·ness** *n*

doll \'däl, 'dȯl\ *n* **1** : a small figure of a human being used especially as a child's plaything **2 a** : a pretty young woman **b** : an attractive person

dol·lar \'däl-ər\ *n* **1** : a coin (as a Spanish peso) similar to an earlier German silver coin **2 a** : a basic unit of money (as of the U.S. and Canada) **b** : a coin or bill representing one dollar [from Dutch *daler* "silver coin formerly used in Germany," from German *Taler* (same meaning), shortened from *Joachimstaler* "a coin made in *Sankt Joachimsthal* (Saint Joachim's Valley) in Bohemia (a former kingdom in Europe)"]

dollar sign *n* : a mark $ or $ placed before a number to indicate that it stands for dollars

doll·house \'däl-ˌhau̇s, 'dȯl-\ *n* : a child's small toy house

doll up *vb* : to dress in fine stylish clothing

dolly \'däl-ē, 'dȯl-ē\ *n, pl* **doll·ies** **1** : DOLL 1 **2** : a platform on a roller or on wheels for moving heavy objects; *esp* : a wheeled platform for a television or motion-picture camera

dol·man sleeve \ˌdōl-mən-, 'dȯl-, ˌdäl-\ *n* : a sleeve that is very wide at the armhole and tight at the wrist [from French *dolman* "a woman's coat with dolman sleeves," derived from Turkish *dolama* "a robe (in the Turkish style)"]

do·lo·mite \'dō-lə-ˌmīt, 'däl-ə-\ *n* : a mineral found in broad layers as a compact limestone

do·lor \'dō-lər, 'däl-ər\ *n* : [1]SORROW 1a

do·lor·ous \'dō-lə-rəs, 'däl-ə-\ *adj* : causing, marked by, or expressing sorrow — **do·lor·ous·ly** *adv*

dol·phin \'däl-fən, 'dȯl-\ *n* **1 a** : any of various small whales with teeth and a long nose **b** : PORPOISE 1 **2** : either of two active saltwater food fishes noted for their brilliant coloring

dolphin 1a

dolt \'dōlt\ *n* : a stupid person — **dolt·ish** \'dōlt-ish\ *adj* — **dolt·ish·ly** *adv* — **dolt·ish·ness** *n*

-dom \dəm\ *n suffix* **1** : dignity : office ⟨duke*dom*⟩ **2** : realm : jurisdiction ⟨king*dom*⟩ **3** : state or fact of being ⟨free*dom*⟩ **4** : those having a (specified) office, occupation, interest, or character ⟨official*dom*⟩ [Old English *-dōm* "office, high position or rank, area of authority"]

do·main \dō-'mān, də-\ *n* **1** : a territory over which control is exercised **2** : an area of influence, knowledge, or activity **3** : a small region of a magnetic substance that contains atoms all lined up in the same direction and behaving like a single tiny magnet **4** : the highest category in the scientific classification of living things ranking above the kingdom **5** : a main subdivision of the Internet [from early French *demeine* "land one owns," from Latin *dominium* "rule, ownership," from *dominus* "master, owner" — related to CONDOMINIUM, DOMINATE, DOMINION]

domain name *n* : a name (as Merriam-Webster.com) that is the primary Internet address for a website

¹dome \'dōm\ *n* **1** : a large rounded roof or ceiling shaped like half of a ball **2** : a structure or natural formation that resembles the dome of a building ⟨rock *domes*⟩ [from French *dôme* "mansion, cathedral" and Italian *duomo* "cathedral" and Latin *domus* "church," from earlier Latin *domus* "house" — related to DOMESTIC, DOMICILE]

²dome *vb* **domed; dom·ing 1** : to cover with or as if with a dome **2** : to form into or swell upward or outward like a dome

¹do·mes·tic \də-'mes-tik\ *adj* **1 a** : living near or about the places where human beings live ⟨*domestic* vermin⟩ **b** : living with or under the care of human beings : TAME ⟨a *domestic* cat⟩ **2** : of, relating to, made in, or done in one's own country ⟨*domestic* steel⟩ **3** : of or relating to a household or family ⟨*domestic* chores⟩ [from early French *domestique* "living around humans, domestic," from Latin *domesticus* (same meaning), from *domus* "house" — related to DOME, DOMICILE] — **do·mes·ti·cal·ly** \-ti-k(ə-)lē\ *adv*

²domestic *n* : a household servant

domestic animal *n* : any of various domesticated animals (as the horse or sheep)

do·mes·ti·cate \də-'mes-ti-ˌkāt\ *vb* **-cat·ed; -cat·ing** : to adapt to living with human beings and to serving their purposes — **do·mes·ti·ca·tion** \-ˌmes-ti-'kā-shən\ *n*

do·mes·tic·i·ty \ˌdō-ˌmes-'tis-ət-ē, -məs-, də-\ *n* : the quality or state of being domestic or domesticated

domestic science *n* : instruction and training in household management and arts (as cooking and sewing)

¹dom·i·cile \'däm-ə-ˌsīl, 'dō-mə-; 'däm-ə-səl\ *n* : a place to live : HOME [from early French *domicile* "place where one lives, home," from Latin *domicilium* (same meaning), from *domus* "house" — related to DOME, DOMESTIC]

²domicile *vb* **-ciled; -cil·ing** : to establish in or provide with a place to live

dom·i·nance \'däm-(ə-)nən(t)s\ *n* : the fact or state of being dominant: as **a** : the dominant position of an individual in a series of social ranks or levels **b** : the property of one of a pair of alternate forms of a gene or character that prevents or masks expression of the other when both are present in the heterozygous condition **c** : the control or influence over the environment of an ecological community that a dominant has **d** : greater activity and usage of one of a pair of body parts (as the right hand compared to the left hand)

¹dom·i·nant \'däm-(ə-)nənt\ *adj* **1 a** : commanding, controlling, or having great influence over all others ⟨a *dominant* political figure⟩ **b** : very important, powerful, or successful ⟨a *dominant* industry⟩ **2** : rising high above the surroundings **3** : PREDOMINANT, OUTSTANDING **4** : exhibiting genetic dominance ⟨a *dominant* gene⟩ ⟨*dominant* traits in peas⟩ — compare ¹RECESSIVE 2 **5** : of, relating to, or being an ecological dominant — **dom·i·nant·ly** *adv*

²dominant *n* **1 a** : a dominant gene or a character which it controls **b** : a kind of living thing (as a species) that has a

major influence on the environment of an ecological community **2** : the fifth note of the musical scale

dom·i·nate \'däm-ə-ˌnāt\ *vb* **-nat·ed; -nat·ing 1** : to have a commanding position or controlling power over **2** : to seem to command by rising high above ⟨a volcano *dominates* the island⟩ ⟨the statue *dominates* the square⟩ [derived from Latin *dominari* "to rule, govern, control," from *dominus* "master, owner" — related to CONDOMINIUM, DAME, DOMAIN, DOMINION, ²DON] — **dom·i·na·tion** \ˌdäm-ə-'nā-shən\ *n* — **dom·i·na·tive** \'däm-ə-ˌnāt-iv\ *adj* — **dom·i·na·tor** \-ˌnāt-ər\ *n*

dom·i·neer \ˌdäm-ə-'ni(ə)r\ *vb* : to rule or behave in a bossy way — **dom·i·neer·ing** *adj*

Do·min·i·can \də-'min-i-kən\ *n* : a member of a mendicant order of preaching friars founded in 1215 — **Dominican** *adj*

do·mi·nie *sense 1 usually* 'däm-ə-nē, *sense 2 usually* 'dō-mə-\ *n* **1** *chiefly Scottish* : SCHOOLMASTER **2** : a member of the clergy

do·min·ion \də-'min-yən\ *n* **1** : DOMAIN 1 **2** : supreme authority : SOVEREIGNTY **3** *often cap* : a self-governing nation of the Commonwealth of Nations other than the United Kingdom that accepts the British monarch as chief of state [Middle English *dominioun* "control, rule," from early French *dominion* (same meaning), from Latin *dominium* "rule, ownership," from *dominus* "master, owner" — related to DOMAIN, DOMINATE]

Dominion Day *n* : CANADA DAY

dom·i·no \'däm-ə-ˌnō\ *n, pl* **-noes** *or* **-nos 1** : a long loose hooded cloak usually worn with a half mask as a masquerade costume **2 a** : a flat rectangular block whose face is divided into two equal parts that are blank or bear dots **b** *pl* : any of several games played with dominoes

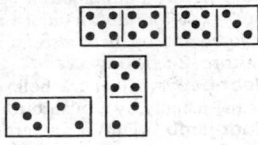

domino 2a

domino theory *n* **1** : a theory that if one nation becomes Communist-controlled the neighboring nations will also become Communist-controlled **2** : the theory that if one act or event is allowed to take place a series of similar acts or events will follow

¹don \'dän\ *vb* **donned; don·ning** : to dress onself in : PUT ON [from a contraction of *do on*]

²don *n* **1** : a Spanish nobleman or gentleman — used as a title **2** : a teacher in a college or university [from Spanish *don* "a nobleman or gentleman," from Latin *dominus* "master, owner" — related to DAME, DOMINATE]

do·ña \'dō-nyə\ *n* : a Spanish woman of rank — used as a title [from Spanish *doña* "a woman of rank," from Latin *domina* (same meaning) — related to DAME]

do·nate \'dō-ˌnāt, dō-'nāt\ *vb* **do·nat·ed; do·nat·ing** : to make a gift of : CONTRIBUTE ⟨*donate* blood⟩ *synonyms* see GIVE — **do·na·tor** \-ˌnāt-ər, -'nāt-\ *n*

do·na·tion \dō-'nā-shən\ *n* : a giving of something without charge; *also* : the thing given (as to charity)

¹done \'dən\ *past participle of* DO

²done *adj* **1** — used to say that something has ended **2** : cooked completely or enough **3** : socially acceptable ⟨divorce just wasn't *done* at the time⟩ — **done for** : doomed to failure, death, or defeat — **done in** : physically exhausted

done·ness \'dən-nəs\ *n* : the condition of being cooked to the desired degree

\ə\ **abut**	\au̇\ **out**	\i\ **tip**	\ȯ\ **saw**	\u̇\ **foot**
\ər\ **further**	\ch\ **chin**	\ī\ **life**	\ȯi\ **coin**	\y\ **yet**
\a\ **mat**	\e\ **pet**	\j\ **job**	\th\ **thin**	\yü\ **few**
\ā\ **take**	\ē\ **easy**	\ŋ\ **sing**	\th̲\ **this**	\yu̇\ **cure**
\ä\ **cot, cart**	\g\ **go**	\ō\ **bone**	\ü\ **food**	\zh\ **vision**

don·jon \\'dän-jən, 'dən-\\ *n* : the main inner tower in a castle [Middle English *donjon* "inner tower of a castle," from early French *donjon* (same meaning) — related to DUNGEON; see *Word History* at DUNGEON]

D donjon

don·key \\'dän-kē, 'dəŋ-, 'dòŋ-\\ *n, pl* **donkeys** 1 : a sturdy domestic mammal that is classified with the asses and is used especially to carry things 2 : a stupid or stubborn person

do·nor \\'dō-nər, -ˌnȯr\\ *n* 1 : one that donates 2 : one used as a source of bodily material or parts ⟨a blood *donor*⟩ ⟨a kidney *donor*⟩

don't \\(')dōnt\\ : do not

¹doo·dle \\'düd-ᵊl\\ *vb* **doo·dled; doo·dling** \\'düd-liŋ, -ᵊl-iŋ\\ : to make a doodle — **doo·dler** \\-lər, -ᵊl-ər\\ *n*

²doodle *n* : a scribble, design, or sketch done while thinking of something else

doo·dle·bug \\'düd-ᵊl-ˌbəg\\ *n* : the larva of an ant lion

¹doom \\'düm\\ *n* 1 : a decision made by a court : SENTENCE 2 a : a usually unhappy end b : DEATH 1, RUIN **synonyms** see DESTINY

²doom *vb* 1 : CONDEMN 2 2 : to set on a fixed course to an unhappy end ⟨the plan was *doomed* to failure⟩

dooms·day \\'dümz-ˌdā\\ *n* : JUDGMENT DAY

door \\'dō(ə)r, 'dȯ(ə)r\\ *n* 1 : a barrier by which an entry is closed and opened; *also* : a similar part of a piece of furniture 2 : DOORWAY

door·bell \\-ˌbel\\ *n* : a bell, gong, or set of chimes to be rung usually by a push button at an outside door

door·jamb \\-ˌjam\\ *n* : a vertical piece that forms a side of a doorway

door·keep·er \\-ˌkē-pər\\ *n* : a person who tends a door

door·knob \\-ˌnäb\\ *n* : a knob that when turned releases a door latch

door·man \\-ˌman, -mən\\ *n* : a person who tends a door (as of a hotel) and assists people (as by calling taxis)

door·mat \\-ˌmat\\ *n* : a mat placed before or inside a door for wiping dirt from the shoes

door·post \\-ˌpōst\\ *n* : DOORJAMB

door·step \\-ˌstep\\ *n* : a step or series of steps before an outer door

door-to-door \\ˌdȯrt-ə-'dō(ə)r, ˌdȯrt-ə-'dȯ(ə)r\\ *adj* : being or making a call (as to sell something) at every house in an area — **door-to-door** *adv*

door·way \\-ˌwā\\ *n* 1 : the opening or passage that a door closes 2 : a means of reaching or gaining something ⟨the *doorway* to success⟩

door·yard \\-ˌyärd\\ *n* : a yard right outside the door of a house

¹dope \\'dōp\\ *n* 1 : a thick sticky material (as one used to make pipe joints tight) 2 : an illegal, habit-forming, or narcotic drug; *esp* : MARIJUANA 3 : a stupid person 4 : information especially from a reliable source

²dope *vb* **doped; dop·ing** 1 : to treat or affect with dope; *esp* : to give a narcotic to 2 : FIND OUT — usually used with *out*

dop·er \\'dō-pər\\ *n* : a person who regularly uses drugs especially illegally

dop·ey \\'dō-pē\\ *adj* **dop·i·er; -est** 1 : dulled by or as if by alcohol or a narcotic 2 : mentally slow or silly : STUPID ⟨your *dopey* friends⟩ ⟨a *dopey* TV show⟩ — **dop·i·ness** *n*

Dopp·ler effect \\'däp-lər-\\ *n* : a change in the frequency with which waves (as of sound or light) from a source reach an observer when the source and the observer are moving rapidly toward or away from each other [named for Christian J. *Doppler* 1803–1853 Austrian physicist]

Doppler radar *n* : a radar system using the Doppler effect for measuring speed

do–rag \\'dü-ˌrag\\ *n* : a kerchief worn to cover the hair [from hair*do*]

Dor·ic \\'dȯr-ik, 'där-\\ *adj* : belonging to the simplest Greek architectural order [derived from Greek *Dōris*, name of a kingdom in ancient Greece]

dork \\'dȯrk\\ *n, slang* : JERK 3

dorky \\'dȯr-kē\\ *adj* **dork·i·er; -est** *slang* : foolishly stupid

dorm \\'dȯ(ə)rm\\ *n* : DORMITORY

dor·man·cy \\'dȯr-mən-sē\\ *n* : the quality or state of being dormant

dor·mant \\'dȯr-mənt\\ *adj* 1 : not active but capable of becoming active ⟨a *dormant* volcano⟩ 2 a : sleeping or appearing to be asleep : SLUGGISH b : having growth or other biological activity much reduced or suspended ⟨a *dormant* bud⟩ 3 : of, relating to, or used during a period of no or greatly reduced activity or growth ⟨a *dormant* spray for fruit trees⟩

dor·mer \\'dȯr-mər\\ *n* : a window placed upright in a sloping roof; *also* : the structure containing a dormer window

dor·mi·to·ry \\'dȯr-mə-ˌtōr-ē, -ˌtȯr-\\ *n, pl* **-ries** 1 : a sleeping room especially for several people 2 : a residence hall having many sleeping rooms

dor·mouse \\'dȯ(ə)r-ˌmau̇s\\ *n, pl* **dor·mice** \\-ˌmīs\\ : any of numerous Old World rodents that resemble small squirrels

dor·sal \\'dȯr-səl\\ *adj* : relating to or situated near or on the back (as of an animal) — **dor·sal·ly** \\-sə-lē\\ *adv*

dormouse

dorsal fin *n* : a fin on the ridge along the middle of the back of a fish or sea mammal (as a whale)

do·ry \\'dōr-ē, 'dȯr-\\ *n, pl* **dories** : a boat with a flat bottom, high sides that curve upward and outward, and a sharp bow

dos·age \\'dō-sij\\ *n* 1 a : the giving of medicine in doses b : the amount of a single dose 2 : the addition or application of a substance in a measured dose

¹dose \\'dōs\\ *n* 1 a : the measured amount of a medicine to be taken at one time b : the quantity of radiation given or absorbed 2 : a portion of a substance added during a process 3 : an experience to which one is exposed ⟨a *dose* of hard work⟩

²dose *vb* **dosed; dos·ing** 1 : to give medicine to 2 : to treat with something

do·sim·e·ter \\ˌdō-'sim-ət-ər\\ *n* : an instrument for measuring doses of X-rays or of radioactivity

dos·sier \\'dȯs-ˌyā, 'dȯs-ē-ˌā, 'däs-\\ *n* : a file of papers containing a detailed report

dost \\(')dəst\\ *archaic present 2nd singular of* DO

¹dot \\'dät\\ *n* 1 : a small spot : SPECK 2 : a small round mark made with or as if with a pen: as a : a point after a note or rest in music indicating increase of the time value by one half b : a centered dot · used as a sign of multiplication 3 : an exact point in time or space ⟨arrived at six on the *dot*⟩ 4 : a short click or buzz forming a letter or part of a letter (as in the Morse code)

²dot *vb* **dot·ted; dot·ting** 1 : to mark with a dot ⟨*dot* an "i"⟩ 2 : to cover with or as if with dots ⟨green buds *dotted* the branches⟩ — **dot·ter** *n*

dote \\'dōt\\ *vb* **dot·ed; dot·ing** : to be excessive in one's attention or fondness — usually used with *on* ⟨*doted on* their grandchild⟩ — **dot·ing·ly** \\'dōt-iŋ-lē\\ *adv*

doth \\(')dəth\\ *archaic present 3rd singular of* DO

dot matrix *n* : a rectangular arrangement of dots from which letters, numbers, and symbols can be formed (as by a computer printer or on a display screen)

dot·ty \\'dät-ē\\ *adj* **dot·ti·er; -est** : a little crazy

Dou·ay Version \dü-ˈā-\ *n* : an English translation of the Vulgate used by Roman Catholics [named for *Douay*, city in France where part of this translation was published in 1609–1610]

¹**dou·ble** \ˈdəb-əl\ *adj* **1** : DUAL 1 ⟨a *double* role⟩ **2** : consisting of two members or parts ⟨an egg with a *double* yolk⟩ **3** : being twice as great or as many ⟨had *double* the number of expected sales⟩ **4** : folded in two **5** : having more than the usual number of floral parts and especially petals ⟨*double* roses⟩ [Middle English *double* "double, dual," from early French *double* (same meaning), from Latin *duplus* "double," from *duo* "two" and *-plus* "multiplied by" — related to DUAL] — **dou·ble·ness** *n*

²**double** *vb* **dou·bled; dou·bling** \ˈdəb-(ə-)liŋ\ **1** : to make, be, or become twice as great or as many ⟨*double* a recipe⟩ **2 a** : to bend or fold (as a sheet of paper) usually in the middle so that one part lies directly against the other part **b** : to close tightly the fingers of : CLENCH ⟨*doubled* his fist⟩ **c** : to cause to bend at the waist **d** : to become bent or folded usually in the middle ⟨she *doubled* up in pain⟩ **3** : to have an additional use or job ⟨the cook *doubles* as dishwasher⟩ **4** : to make a double in baseball **5** : to turn sharply and go back on the same path first taken ⟨the rabbit *doubled* back on its tracks⟩

³**double** *adv* **1** : DOUBLY 1 **2** : two together ⟨sleep *double*⟩

⁴**double** *n* **1 a** : something twice another ⟨12 is the *double* of 6⟩ **b** : a hit in baseball that allows a batter to reach second base **2** : ³DUPLICATE; *esp* : a person who closely resembles another **3** : a sharp turn : REVERSAL **4** : ⁴FOLD 2 **5** *pl* : a game between two pairs of players ⟨tennis *doubles*⟩ — **on the double** : very quickly : RIGHT AWAY

double bass *n* : the largest instrument of the violin family

double boiler *n* : a kitchen utensil consisting of two saucepans fitting together so that the contents of the upper can be cooked or heated by boiling water in the lower

double bond *n* : a chemical bond in which two atoms in a molecule share two pairs of electrons — compare SINGLE BOND, TRIPLE BOND

dou·ble–breast·ed \ˌdəb-əl-ˈbres-təd\ *adj* : having one half of the front lapped over the other and usually two rows of buttons ⟨a *double-breasted* jacket⟩

dou·ble–check \ˌdəb-əl-ˈchek, ˈdəb-əl-ˌchek\ *vb* : to make a careful check (as for accuracy) of something already checked — **double check** *n*

double cross *n* : an act of betraying or cheating especially an associate — **dou·ble–cross** \ˌdəb-əl-ˈkròs\ *vb* — **dou·ble–cross·er** *n*

dou·ble–deal·ing \ˌdəb-əl-ˈdē-liŋ\ *n* : DUPLICITY — **dou·ble–deal·er** *n* — **double–dealing** *adj*

dou·ble–deck·er \ˌdəb-əl-ˈdek-ər\ *n* : something (as a bus or sandwich) having two decks, levels, or layers

dou·ble–head·er \ˌdəb-əl-ˈhed-ər\ *n* : two games played one after the other on the same day

double helix *n* : the arrangement in space of DNA that resembles a spirally twisted ladder with the sides made up of the sugar and phosphate units of the two nucleotide strands and the rungs made up of the pyrimidine and purine bases extending into the center and joined by hydrogen bonds

double hyphen *n* : a punctuation mark ⸗ that is used in place of a hyphen in a word divided at the end of a line to show that the word is usually hyphenated at that place

dou·ble–joint·ed \ˌdəb-əl-ˈjòint-əd\ *adj* : having one or more joints that permit the parts joined to be bent freely to unusual angles ⟨a *double-jointed* finger⟩

double knit *n* : a knitted fabric made with a double set of needles to produce a double thickness of fabric with each thickness joined by interlocking stitches; *also* : an article of clothing made of such fabric

double negative *n* : a now nonstandard grammatical construction that contains two negatives and has a negative meaning (as in "I didn't hear nothing" instead of "I didn't hear anything")

double play *n* : a play in baseball in which two base runners are put out

double pneumonia *n* : pneumonia involving both lungs

dou·ble–space \ˌdəb-əl-ˈspās\ *vb* : to type something leaving every other line blank

double standard *n* : a set of standards that applies differently and usually more harshly to one group of people or circumstances than to another

double star *n* : two stars that appear very near each other; *esp* : BINARY STAR

dou·blet \ˈdəb-lət\ *n* **1** : a close-fitting jacket worn by men of western Europe chiefly in the 16th century **2** : one of two similar or identical things

dou·ble take \ˈdəb-əl-ˌtāk\ *n* : a delayed reaction to a surprising or unusual situation after first failing to notice anything unusual

dou·ble–talk \ˈdəb-əl-ˌtòk\ *n* **1** : language that seems to make sense but is actually a mixture of sense and nonsense : GIBBERISH **2** : language that is purposely ambiguous

dou·ble–time \ˈdəb-əl-ˌtīm\ *vb* : to move at double time

D doublet 1

double time *n* **1** : a marching rate of 180 steps per minute **2** : payment of a worker at twice the regular wage rate

double vision *n* : vision in which an object is seen as double (as from unequal action of the eye muscles)

dou·bloon \ˌdə-ˈblün\ *n* : an old gold coin of Spain and Spanish America [from Spanish *doblón* "doubloon"]

dou·bly \ˈdəb-lē\ *adv* : to twice the amount or degree ⟨*doubly* glad⟩

¹**doubt** \ˈdaút\ *vb* **1** : to be uncertain about ⟨*doubts* her sincerity⟩ **2** : to lack confidence in ⟨*doubted* his own abilities⟩ **3** : to consider unlikely ⟨*doubt* if I can go⟩ — **doubt·able** \-ə-bəl\ *adj* — **doubt·er** *n* — **doubt·ing·ly** \-iŋ-lē\ *adv*

²**doubt** *n* **1** : uncertainty of belief or opinion **2** : the state of being uncertain ⟨the outcome is in *doubt*⟩ **3 a** : a lack of confidence **b** : an inclination not to believe or accept

synonyms DOUBT, UNCERTAINTY, DISTRUST, SUSPICION mean a feeling that one is not sure about someone or something. DOUBT may suggest a lack of certainty that results in an inability to make a decision ⟨so filled with *doubt* that she didn't know what to do⟩. UNCERTAINTY may range from a feeling just short of certainty to almost complete lack of knowledge about something ⟨there is still *uncertainty* about what caused the accident⟩. DISTRUST suggests lack of trust or confidence on vague or general grounds ⟨long-standing *distrust* of strangers⟩. SUSPICION stresses lack of faith in the truth, reality, fairness, or reliability of someone or something ⟨my *suspicion* is that he is lying⟩.

doubt·ful \ˈdaút-fəl\ *adj* **1** : not clear or certain as to fact ⟨a *doubtful* claim⟩ **2** : QUESTIONABLE 2 ⟨*doubtful* intentions⟩ **3** : undecided in opinion **4** : not certain in outcome — **doubt·ful·ly** \-fə-lē\ *adv* — **doubt·ful·ness** *n*

¹**doubt·less** \ˈdaút-ləs\ *adv* **1** : CERTAINLY **2** : PROBABLY

²**doubtless** *adj* : free from doubt : CERTAIN — **doubt·less·ly** *adv*

\ə\ abut	\aú\ out	\i\ tip	\ò\ saw	\ú\ foot
\ər\ further	\ch\ chin	\ī\ life	\òi\ coin	\y\ yet
\a\ mat	\e\ pet	\j\ job	\th\ thin	\yü\ few
\ā\ take	\ē\ easy	\ŋ\ sing	\th\ this	\yú\ cure
\ä\ cot, cart	\g\ go	\ō\ bone	\ü\ food	\zh\ vision

douche \'düsh\ *n* **1** : a cleansing of a part or cavity of the body by means of a jet of liquid (as water) **2** : a device for giving douches — **douche** *vb*

dough \'dō\ *n* **1** : a soft mass of moistened flour or meal thick enough to knead or roll **2** : something resembling dough especially in consistency **3** : MONEY 1a — **doughy** \'dō-ē\ *adj*

dough·boy \'dō-,bòi\ *n* : an American infantryman especially in World War I

dough·nut *also* **do·nut** \-(,)nət\ *n* **1** : a small ring of sweet dough fried in fat **2** : something resembling a doughnut especially in shape

dough·ty \'daùt-ē\ *adj* **dough·ti·er; -est** : very strong and brave — **dough·ti·ly** \'daùt-ᵊl-ē\ *adv* — **dough·ti·ness** \'daùt-ē-nəs\ *n*

Doug·las fir \,dəg-ləs-\ *n* : a tall evergreen cone-bearing timber tree of the western U.S.

dour \'dù(ə)r, 'daù(ə)r\ *adj* : looking or being stern or sullen — **dour·ly** *adv* — **dour·ness** *n*

douse *also* **dowse** \'daùs *also* 'daùz\ *vb* **doused** *also* **dowsed; dous·ing** *also* **dows·ing** **1 a** : to stick into water **b** : to throw a liquid on **2** : to put out : EXTINGUISH *douse* the lights\

¹**dove** \'dəv\ *n* **1** : any of numerous pigeons; *esp* : a small wild pigeon **2** : a person who opposes war or warlike policies — **dov·ish** \-ish\ *adj*

²**dove** \'dōv\ *past and past participle of* DIVE

dove·cote \'dəv-,kōt, -,kät\ *also* **dove·cot** \-,kät\ *n* : a small raised house or box with compartments for domestic pigeons

¹dove 1

¹**dove·tail** \-,tāl\ *n* : something shaped like a dove's tail; *esp* : a joint between two pieces (as of wood) formed by a wedge-shaped part that sticks out from one piece fitting tightly into a wedge-shaped slot in the other piece

²**dovetail** *vb* **1 a** : to join by means of dovetails **b** : to cut to a dovetail **2** : to fit skillfully together to form a whole

dow·a·ger \'daù-i-jər\ *n* : a dignified elderly woman

dowdy \'daùd-ē\ *adj* **dowd·i·er; -est** **1** : not neatly or well dressed or cared for **2** : not stylish — **dowd·i·ly** \'daùd-ᵊl-ē\ *adv* — **dowd·i·ness** \'daùd-ē-nəs\ *n*

¹**dow·el** \'daù(-ə)l\ *n* : a pin or peg used for fastening together two pieces of wood; *also* : a round rod or stick used especially for cutting up into dowels

²**dowel** *vb* **-elled** *also* **-eled; -el·ling** *also* **-el·ing** : to fasten by dowels

¹**down** \'daùn\ *n* : a rolling grassy upland — usually used in plural [Old English *dūn* "hill"]

²**down** *adv* **1 a** : toward or in a lower position **b** : to a lying or sitting position **c** : toward or to the ground, floor, or bottom **2** : as a down payment \paid $10 *down*\ **3** : in a direction opposite to up \add the numbers across and *down*\ **4** : to or in a lower or worse condition \Parliament could tax them *down* to their last penny\ **5** : from a past time \heirlooms that have been handed *down*\ **6** : to or in a state of less activity \excitement died *down*\ [Old English *dūne* "down," shortened from *adūne*, literally, "off the hill," from *a-* "off" and *dūne*, form of *dūn* "hill"]

³**down** *adj* **1 a** : being in a low position; *esp* : lying on the ground **b** : directed or going downward \a *down* escalator\ **c** : being at a lower level \sales are *down*\ **2 a** : low in spirits : DOWNCAST \feeling a bit *down*\ **b** : SICK 1a *down* with flu\ **3** : being finished, completed, or come to an end \eight *down* and two to go\ — **down on** : having a low opinion of or dislike for — **down on one's**

luck : experiencing bad luck and especially money trouble

⁴**down** *prep* : down along : down through : down toward : down in : down into : down on *down* the road\

⁵**down** *n* **1** : a low or falling period \the ups and *downs* of life\ **2** : one of a series of four plays that a football team gets to advance the ball ten yards

⁶**down** *vb* **1** : to go or cause to go or come down **2** : ²SWALLOW 1a, CONSUME *downing* slices of pizza\ **3** : to cause (a football) to be out of play

⁷**down** *n* **1** : a covering of soft fluffy feathers **2** : something soft and fluffy like down [Middle English *doun* "down, feathers"; of Norse origin]

down·beat \'daùn-,bēt\ *n* : the downward stroke of a conductor indicating the principally accented note of a measure of music

down·cast \-,kast\ *adj* **1** : being in a state of lowered confidence or courage : DEJECTED **2** : directed down \a *downcast* glance\

down·draft \-,draft, -,dràft\ *n* : a downward current of gas (as air in a chimney or during a thunderstorm)

down·er \'daùn-ər\ *n* **1** : a depressant drug; *esp* : BARBITURATE **2** : something that is depressing, disagreeable, or unsatisfactory

down·fall \'daùn-,fòl\ *n* : a sudden fall (as from power, happiness, or high position) or a cause of such a fall — **down·fall·en** \-,fò-lən\ *adj*

¹**down·grade** \-,grād\ *n* **1** : a downward slope **2** : a lowering toward a worse condition \a neighborhood on the *downgrade*\ — **downgrade** *adv*

²**downgrade** *vb* : to lower in grade, rank, or standing

down·heart·ed \'daùn-'härt-əd\ *adj* : DOWNCAST 1 — **down·heart·ed·ly** *adv* — **down·heart·ed·ness** *n*

¹**down·hill** \'daùn-'hil\ *adv* **1** : toward the bottom of a hill \sleds speeding *downhill*\ **2** : toward a worsened or lower state or level \her health went *downhill* quickly\

²**down·hill** \-,hil\ *adj* : sloping downhill \a *downhill* path\

³**down·hill** \-,hil\ *n* **1** : the sport of skiing on downhill trails *downhill* skiing\ **2** : a skiing race against time down a trail \finished second in the *downhill*\

down·load \'daùn-,lōd\ *vb* : to transfer (data) from a usually large computer to the memory of another device (as a smaller computer) — **down·load·able** \-,lōd-ə-bəl\ *adj*

down payment *n* : a part of the full price paid at the time of purchase or delivery with the remainder to be paid later

down·pour \-,pōr, -,pòr\ *n* : a heavy rain

¹**down·right** \-,rīt\ *adv* : in a complete and absolute manner \that was *downright* stupid\

²**downright** *adj* **1** : ABSOLUTE 3, UTTER \a *downright* lie\ **2** : OUTSPOKEN, BLUNT *downright* country people\ — **down·right·ly** *adv* — **down·right·ness** *n*

down·size \'daùn-,sīz\ *vb* : to reduce in size \the company *downsized* its staff to cut costs\

down·stage \'daùn-'stāj\ *adv or adj* : toward or at the part of a theatrical stage or set closest to the audience or the motion-picture or television camera

¹**down·stairs** \'daùn-'sta(ə)rz, -'ste(ə)rz\ *adv* : down the stairs : on or to a lower floor

²**down·stairs** \-,sta(ə)rz, -,ste(ə)rz\ *adj* : situated on a lower level or on the main or first floor

³**down·stairs** \'sta(ə)rz, -'ste(ə)rz, -,sta(ə)rz, -,ste(ə)rz\ *n sing or pl* : the lower floor of a building

down·stream \'daùn-'strēm\ *adv or adj* : in the direction a stream is flowing

down·stroke \-,strōk\ *n* : a downward stroke

Down syndrome \'daùn-\ *or* **Down's syndrome** \'daùn(z)-\ *n* : a birth defect marked by moderate to severe mental retardation, by distinctive physical characteristics (as slanted eyes and broad hands with short fingers), and by the presence of three chromosomes numbered 21 in human beings [named for J.L.H. *Down,* 1828–1896, English doctor]

down‑to‑earth \ˌdau̇n-tə-'(w)ərth\ *adj* **1** : PRACTICAL 3 〈*down-to-earth* advice〉 **2** : UNPRETENTIOUS 〈a *down-to‑earth* person〉 — **down‑to‑earthness** *n*

¹down·town \ˌdau̇n-'tau̇n\ *adv* : to, toward, or in the main business district

²downtown \-ˌtau̇n\ *adj* : situated downtown

down·trod·den \'dau̇n-'träd-ᵊn\ *adj* : crushed by superior power

¹down·ward \'dau̇n-wərd\ *or* **down·wards** \-wərdz\ *adv* **1** : from a higher place or condition to a lower one **2** : from an earlier time

²downward *adj* : moving or reaching down

down·wind \'dau̇n-'wind\ *adv or adj* : in the direction that the wind is blowing

downy \'dau̇-nē\ *adj* **down·i·er; -est 1** : resembling a bird's down **2** : covered with or made of down

downy woodpecker *n* : a small black-and-white woodpecker of North America that has a white back

dow·ry \'dau̇(ə)r-ē\ *n, pl* **dowries** : the property that a woman brings to her husband in marriage in some cultures

¹dowse *variant of* DOUSE

²dowse \'dau̇z\ *vb* : to use a divining rod especially to find water — **dows·er** \'dau̇-zər\ *n*

dox·ol·o·gy \däk-'säl-ə-jē\ *n, pl* **-gies** : an expression of praise to God

doze \'dōz\ *vb* **dozed; doz·ing** : to sleep lightly — **doze** *n* — **doz·er** *n*

doz·en \'dəz-ᵊn\ *n, pl* **dozens** *or* **dozen** : a group of twelve [Middle English *dozeine* "dozen," from early French *dozeyne* (same meaning), derived from Latin *duodecim* "twelve," from *duo* "two" and *decem* "ten" — related to DECIMAL, DIME, DUAL] — **dozen** *adj* — **doz·enth** \-ᵊn(t)th\ *adj*

doz·er \'dō-zər\ *n* : BULLDOZER

DP \'dē-'pē\ *n, pl* **DP's** *or* **DPs 1** : a displaced person **2** : DOUBLE PLAY

¹drab \'drab\ *n* : a light olive brown

²drab *adj* **drab·ber; drab·best 1** : of the color drab **2** : lacking variety and interest : DULL 〈a *drab* life〉 — **drab·ly** *adv* — **drab·ness** *n*

dra·cae·na \drə-'sē-nə\ *n* : any of a genus of trees or shrubs that are related to the lilies, have branches with bunches of sword-shaped leaves at the ends, and bear clusters of small greenish white flowers

drach·ma \'drak-mə\ *n, pl* **drach·mas** *or* **drach·mai** \-ˌmī\ *or* **drach·mae** \-(ˌ)mē, -ˌmī\ **1** : any of various ancient Greek units of weight **2 a** : an ancient Greek silver coin **b** : the former basic unit of money of Greece; *also* : a coin representing this unit

Dra·co \'drā-kō\ *n* : a group of stars between the Big Dipper and Little Dipper [from Latin *Draco,* literally, "dragon"]

¹draft \'draft, 'dráft\ *n* **1 a** : the act of pulling or hauling **b** : the thing or amount pulled **2** : the act or an instance of drinking or inhaling; *also* : the portion drunk or inhaled at one time **3 a** : something represented in words or lines : DESIGN, PLAN **b** : a quick sketch, outline, or version from which a final work is produced 〈a rough *draft* of the essay〉 **4 a** : the act of drawing out liquid (as from a barrel) **b** : a portion of liquid drawn out **5** : the depth of water required for a ship to float when loaded **6** : a picking of persons for required military service **7** : an order (as a check) issued by one party to another (as a bank) to pay money to a third party **8 a** : a current of air **b** : a device to regulate an air supply (as in a stove) — **on draft** : ready to be drawn from a container

²draft *adj* **1** : used for pulling loads 〈*draft* animals〉 **2** : being a version to be finished later 〈a *draft* treaty〉 **3** : being or having been on draft 〈*draft* beer〉

³draft *vb* **1** : to pick especially for required military service **2 a** : to make a draft of : OUTLINE 〈*draft* a plan〉 **b** : to put into written form 〈*draft* an essay〉 — **draft·er** *n*

draft·ee \draf-'tē, dráf-\ *n* : a person who is drafted especially into the armed forces

drafts·man \'draf(t)s-mən, 'dráf(t)s-\ *n* : a person who draws plans (as for machinery) — **drafts·man·ship** \-ˌship\ *n*

drafty \'draf-tē, 'dráf-\ *adj* **draf·ti·er; -est** : exposed to a draft or current of air 〈a *drafty* hall〉 — **draft·i·ly** \-tə-lē\ *adv* — **draft·i·ness** \-tē-nəs\ *n*

¹drag \'drag\ *n* **1** : a device for dragging under water to detect or gather objects **2** : something without wheels (as a sledge for carrying heavy loads) that is dragged, pulled, or drawn along or over a surface **3 a** : the act or an instance of dragging or drawing **b** : a draw on a pipe, cigarette, or cigar : PUFF; *also* : a drink of liquid **4 a** : something that slows down motion **b** : the force acting on a body (as an airplane) to slow it down as the body moves through a fluid (as air) **c** : something that hinders or obstructs progress **5** : someone or something boring **6** : STREET 1, ROAD 〈the main *drag*〉

²drag *vb* **dragged; drag·ging 1 a** : to haul slowly or heavily 〈*dragging* the suitcase across the room〉 **b** : to move with slowness or difficulty 〈*dragged* myself up the stairs〉 **c** : to bring by or as if by force 〈*dragged* them to the opera〉 **d** : to pass or cause to pass slowly 〈the day *dragged* on〉 **2** : to hang or lag behind **3** : to trail along on the ground **4** : to search or fish with a drag **5** : to take part in a drag race **6** : to move (an item on a computer screen) using a mouse — **drag·ging·ly** *adv* — **drag one's feet** *also* **drag one's heels** : to act in a slow manner or in a manner intended to cause delay

drag·ger \'dra-gər\ *n* : one that drags; *esp* : a fishing boat using a trawl or dragnet

drag·gle \'drag-əl\ *vb* **drag·gled; drag·gling** \-(ə-)liŋ\ **1** : to make or become wet and dirty by dragging **2** : to follow slowly : STRAGGLE

drag·net \'drag-ˌnet\ *n* **1** : a net dragged along the bottom of a body of water **2** : a series of planned actions for catching a criminal

drag·on \'drag-ən\ *n* **1** : an imaginary animal usually pictured as a huge serpent or lizard with wings and large claws **2** *cap* : DRACO [Middle English *dragon* "dragon," from early French *dragun* (same meaning), from Latin *dracon-, draco* "serpent, dragon," from Greek *drakōn* "serpent" — related to RANKLE]

drag·on·fly \-ˌflī\ *n* : any of a group of large harmless insects that have four long wings held horizontal and sticking out instead of folded to the side next to the body when at rest and that feed especially on flies, gnats, and mosquitoes — compare DAMSEL-FLY

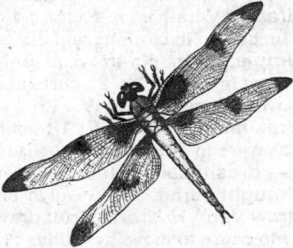

dragonfly

¹dra·goon \drə-'gün, dra-\ *n* : a mounted infantry soldier

²dragoon *vb* : to get (someone) to do something by force

drag race *n* : a race between two vehicles to see which can accelerate faster — **drag racer** *n* — **drag racing** *n*

drag·ster \'drag-stər\ *n* : a vehicle (as an automobile) made for drag racing

drag strip *n* : a place for drag races that is paved and usually at least a quarter mile long

¹**drain** \'drān\ *vb* **1 a** : to draw off or flow off gradually or completely ⟨*drain* water from a tank⟩ **b** : to exhaust physically or emotionally **2** : to make or become gradually dry or empty ⟨*drain* a swamp⟩ ⟨*drained* the country of its resources⟩ — **drain·er** *n*

²**drain** *n* **1** : a means (as a pipe, channel, or sewer) of draining **2 a** : the act of draining **b** : a gradual using up **3** : something that causes a using up ⟨a *drain* on our resources⟩ — **down the drain** : to a state of being wasted or lost

drain·age \'drā-nij\ *n* **1 a** : the act of draining **b** : something drained off **2** : a method of draining; *also* : a system of drains

drain·pipe \'drān-,pīp\ *n* : a pipe for drainage

drake \'drāk\ *n* : a male duck

dram \'dram\ *n* — see MEASURE table

dra·ma \'dräm-ə, 'dram-\ *n* **1 a** : a written work that tells a story through action and speech and is meant to be acted on a stage : PLAY **b** : a play, movie, or television production with a serious tone or subject **2** : dramatic art, literature, or affairs **3 a** : an exciting event or series of events ⟨the *drama* of the basketball playoffs⟩ **b** : dramatic effect or quality ⟨used colored lighting for *drama*⟩

dra·mat·ic \drə-'mat-ik\ *adj* **1** : of or relating to drama ⟨a *dramatic* actor⟩ **2 a** : suitable to or resembling that of drama ⟨a *dramatic* escape⟩ **b** : attracting attention ⟨made a *dramatic* entrance⟩ — **dra·mat·i·cal·ly** \-'mat-i-k(ə-)lē\ *adv*

dra·mat·ics \drə-'mat-iks\ *n sing or pl* **1** : the study or practice of theatrical arts **2** : dramatic behavior or expression

dra·ma·tis per·so·nae \,dram-ət-əs-pər-'sō-(,)nē, ,dräm-, -,nī\ *n pl* : the characters or actors in a play [modern Latin]

dram·a·tist \'dram-ət-əst, 'dräm-\ *n* : PLAYWRIGHT

dram·a·tize \'dram-ə-,tīz, 'dräm-\ *vb* **1** : to make into a drama **2** : to present or represent in a dramatic manner — **dram·a·ti·za·tion** \,dram-ət-ə-'zā-shən, ,dräm-\ *n*

drank *past of* DRINK

¹**drape** \'drāp\ *n* **1** *pl* : DRAPERY 2 **2** : arrangement in or of folds **3** : the cut or hang of clothing

²**drape** *vb* **draped; drap·ing 1** : to cover or decorate with or as if with folds of cloth **2** : to arrange in flowing lines or folds ⟨a beautifully *draped* satin dress⟩

drap·er \'drā-pər\ *n, British* : a dealer in cloth and sometimes also in clothing and dry goods

drap·ery \'drā-p(ə-)rē\ *n, pl* **-er·ies 1** : a decorative fabric hung in loose folds **2** : curtains of heavy fabric often used over thinner curtains

dras·tic \'dras-tik\ *adj* **1** : acting rapidly or violently **2** : severe in effect : HARSH ⟨had to take *drastic* measures⟩ — **dras·ti·cal·ly** \-ti-k(ə-)lē\ *adv*

draught \'draft, 'dråft\ *chiefly British variant of* DRAFT

¹**draw** \'dró\ *vb* **drew** \'drü\; **drawn** \'drón\; **draw·ing 1 a** : to cause to move by pulling : cause to follow **b** : to pull up or to one side ⟨*draw* the curtains⟩ **c** : to pull up or out ⟨*drew* water from the well⟩ ⟨*draw* a gun⟩ **d** : to cause to come out of a container or source ⟨*draw* water for a bath⟩ **2** : to move or go steadily or gradually ⟨day was *drawing* to a close⟩ **3 a** : ATTRACT, ENTICE ⟨*drew* a crowd⟩ **b** : PROVOKE 2 ⟨*drew* criticism⟩ **c** : to bring on as a response ⟨*drew* cheers from the crowd⟩ **4** : INHALE 1 ⟨*drew* a deep breath⟩ **5 a** : to cause (as the contents or essence) to come forth ⟨brine *draws* moisture and sugars from the cucumbers⟩ **b** : EVISCERATE ⟨*drawn* and plucked chickens⟩ **6** : to need (a specified depth) to float in ⟨the boat *draws* three feet of water⟩ **7 a** : ACCUMULATE 1, GAIN ⟨*drawing* interest⟩ **b** : to take money from

a place of deposit : WITHDRAW **c** : to receive regularly from a source ⟨*draw* a salary⟩ **8 a** : to take (cards) from a stack or from the dealer **b** : to receive or take at random ⟨*drew* a winning number⟩ **9** : to bend (a bow) by pulling back the string **10** : to cause to shrink or pucker **11** : to leave (a contest) undecided : TIE **12 a** : to produce a likeness of by making lines on a surface ⟨*draw* a picture⟩ ⟨the computer can *draw* a graph on the screen⟩ **b** : to write out in proper form ⟨*draw* up a will⟩ **c** : to describe in words ⟨a writer who *draws* characters well⟩ **13** : DEDUCE 1a ⟨*draw* a conclusion⟩ **14** : to stretch or spread by or as if by pulling ⟨some metals can be *drawn* out to form wire⟩ **15** : to produce a draft of air ⟨the chimney *draws* well⟩ — **draw·able** \-ə-bəl\ *adj* — **draw a blank** : to be unable to think of something — **draw on** *or* **draw upon** : to use as a source of supply ⟨what experiences can you *draw on* for a story⟩ — **draw straws** : to decide or assign something by lottery in which straws of unequal length are used — **draw the line** *or* **draw a line 1** : to set a dividing line between two things **2** : to set a limit that points out what one will not tolerate or do

²**draw** *n* **1** : the act or result of drawing **2** : a tie contest or game **3** : something that draws attention **4** : a gully shallower than a ravine

draw·back \'dró-,bak\ *n* : an undesirable feature : ¹DISADVANTAGE

draw·bar \-,bär\ *n* : a beam across the rear of a tractor to which tools are hitched

draw·bridge \-,brij\ *n* : a bridge made to be wholly or partly raised up, let down, or drawn aside so as to permit or prevent passage

draw·er \'dró(-ə)r\ *n* **1** : one that draws **2** : a sliding boxlike compartment (as in a desk) **3** *pl* : an undergarment for the lower part of the body

draw·ing \'dró-iŋ\ *n* **1** : an act or instance of drawing lots **2** : the act or art of making a figure, plan, or sketch by means of lines **3** : a picture made by drawing

drawbridge

drawing board *n* **1** : a board on which paper for drawing can be fastened **2** : a planning stage ⟨his project was still on the *drawing board*⟩

drawing room *n* : a formal room for entertaining company [shortened from *withdrawing room* "a room one can go to to be alone"]

¹**drawl** \'dról\ *vb* : to speak slowly with vowels drawn out beyond their usual length

²**drawl** *n* : a drawling way of speaking

drawn butter \'drón-\ *n* : melted butter

draw on *vb* : to come closer : APPROACH ⟨as night *drew on*⟩

draw out *vb* **1** : to cause to last longer than usual **2** : to cause or encourage to speak freely ⟨tried to *draw* the shy child *out*⟩

draw·string \'dró-,striŋ\ *n* : a string, cord, or tape used to close a bag, control fullness in clothes, or open or close curtains

draw up *vb* **1** : to arrange (as troops) in order **2** : to prepare a draft or version of ⟨*draw up* plans⟩ **3** : to straighten (oneself) to an erect posture ⟨*drew* himself *up* angrily and left the room⟩ **4** : to bring or come to a stop ⟨the car *drew up* at the door⟩

dray \'drā\ *n* : a strong low cart or wagon without sides for hauling heavy loads

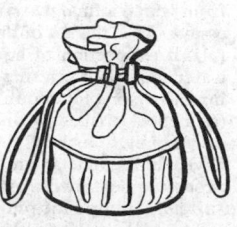

drawstring

1dread \'dred\ *vb* **1** : to fear greatly **2** : to be very unwilling to meet or face

2dread *n* **1 a** : great fear especially in the face of approaching harm **b** *archaic* : **1AWE 2** : one causing fear or awe **synonyms** see FEAR

3dread *adj* : causing great fear or anxiety ⟨a *dread* disease⟩

dread·ful \'dred-fəl\ *adj* **1** : causing dread or awe ⟨a *dreadful* storm⟩ **2** : very disagreeable, unpleasant, or shocking ⟨a *dreadful* cold⟩ ⟨*dreadful* news⟩ — **dread·ful·ly** \-f(ə-)lē\ *adv* — **dread·ful·ness** \-fəl-nəs\ *n*

dread·locks \'dred-ˌläks\ *n pl* : hair that is twisted together into long pieces that hang down around the shoulders

dread·nought \'dred-ˌnȯt, -ˌnät\ *n* : BATTLESHIP

1dream \'drēm\ *n* **1** : a series of thoughts, pictures, or feelings occurring during sleep **2** : a vision created in the imagination : DAYDREAM **3** : something notable for its beauty or pleasing quality **4** : a goal that is longed for : IDEAL — **dream·like** \-ˌlīk\ *adj*

2dream \'drēm\ *vb* **dreamed** \'drem(p)t, 'drēmd\ *or* **dreamt** \'drem(p)t\; **dream·ing** \'drē-miŋ\ **1** : to have a dream ⟨*dreamed* about my dog⟩ **2** : to spend time having daydreams **3** : to think of as happening or possible : IMAGINE ⟨never *dreamed* I'd win⟩ — **dream·er** *n*

dream·land \'drēm-ˌland\ *n* : an unreal delightful country existing only in imagination or in dreams

dream·less \'drēm-ləs\ *adj* : having no dreams ⟨a *dreamless* sleep⟩ — **dream·less·ly** *adv* — **dream·less·ness** *n*

dreamy \'drē-mē\ *adj* **dream·i·er; -est 1** : full of dreams **2** : tending to spend time in dreaming **3 a** : suggesting a dream **b** : being quiet and soothing ⟨*dreamy* music⟩ **c** : DELIGHTFUL, PLEASING — **dream·i·ly** \-mə-lē\ *adv* — **dream·i·ness** \-mē-nəs\ *n*

drear \'dri(ə)r\ *adj* : DREARY

drea·ry \'dri(ə)r-ē\ *adj* **drea·ri·er** \'drir-ē-ər\; **-est** : having nothing that provides cheer, comfort, or interest — **drea·ri·ly** \'drir-ə-lē\ *adv* — **drea·ri·ness** \'drir-ē-nəs\ *n*

1dredge \'drej\ *vb* **dredged; dredg·ing 1 a** : to dig, gather, or pull out with or as if with a dredge ⟨*dredged* up scallops from the sea bottom⟩ **b** : to deepen (as a waterway) with a dredge **2** : to bring to light by deep searching ⟨*dredging* up memories⟩

2dredge *n* **1** : an iron frame with an attached net used especially to catch fish or shellfish **2** : a machine for removing earth usually by buckets on a continuous chain or by a suction tube [probably from Old English *dragan* "to pull, drag"]

3dredge *vb* **dredged; dredg·ing** : to coat (food) by sprinkling (as with flour) [from obsolete *dredge* (noun) "a candied fruit," derived from early French *dragee* (same meaning), from Latin *tragemata* (plural) "candied fruits," from Greek *tragemata* (same meaning), derived from *trōgein* "to gnaw"]

dregs \'dregz\ *n pl* **1** : sediment contained in a liquid or precipitated from it : LEES **2** : the most undesirable part ⟨the *dregs* of humanity⟩

drench \'drench\ *vb* : to wet thoroughly **synonyms** see SOAK

1dress \'dres\ *vb* **1** : to make or set straight **2 a** : to put clothes on **b** : to provide with clothing **c** : to put on or wear formal or fancy clothes **3** : to trim or decorate for display **4** : to put in order **5 a** : to apply dressings or medicine to ⟨*dress* a wound⟩ **b** : to arrange (as the hair) by combing, brushing, or curling **c** : **2GROOM 1 d** : to kill and prepare for market ⟨*dress* a chicken⟩ **e** : to apply manure or fertilizer to **6** : **2SMOOTH 2, FINISH**

2dress *n* **1** : CLOTHING **1 2** : an outer garment with a skirt for a woman or child **3** : clothing appropriate to a particular time or occasion ⟨Roman *dress*⟩ ⟨evening *dress*⟩

3dress *adj* **1** : suitable or required for a formal occasion ⟨*dress* clothes⟩ **2** : relating to or used for a dress

dress down *vb* **1** : to criticize severely **2** : to dress casually

1dress·er \'dres-ər\ *n* : a piece of furniture (as a chest or bureau) with a mirror

2dresser *n* : one that dresses ⟨a fashionable *dresser*⟩

dress·ing \'dres-iŋ\ *n* **1 a** : the act or process of one that dresses **b** : an instance of dressing **2 a** : a sauce for adding to a dish **b** : a seasoned mixture used as a stuffing (as for poultry) or baked and served separately **3 a** : material (as ointment or gauze) used to cover an injury **b** : fertilizing material (as manure or compost)

dres·sing–down \ˌdres-iŋ-'daún\ *n* : a severe criticism

dressing gown *n* : a loose robe worn indoors

dressing room *n* : a room (as in a theater) used for dressing

dressing table *n* : a table often with drawers and a mirror in front of which one sits while dressing and grooming oneself

dress·mak·ing \'dres-ˌmā-kiŋ\ *n* : the process or occupation of making dresses — **dress·mak·er** \-kər\ *n*

dress rehearsal *n* : a rehearsal of a play in costume and with stage properties shortly before the first performance

dress up *vb* **1** : to put on one's best or formal clothes **2** : to put on strange or fancy clothes ⟨*dress up* for Halloween⟩

dressy \'dres-ē\ *adj* **dress·i·er; -est 1** : showy in dress **2** : suitable for formal occasions ⟨*dressy* clothes⟩

drew *past of* DRAW

1drib·ble \'drib-əl\ *vb* **drib·bled; drib·bling** \-(ə-)liŋ\ **1** : to fall or flow or let fall in small drops : TRICKLE **2** : DROOL 2 **3** : to move forward by tapping, bouncing, or kicking ⟨*dribble* a basketball⟩ ⟨*dribble* a puck⟩ — **drib·bler** \-(ə-)lər\ *n*

2dribble *n* **1** : a small trickling flow **2** : an act or instance of dribbling a ball or puck

drib·let \'drib-lət\ *n* **1** : a small amount **2** : a falling drop

1drier *comparative of* DRY

2dri·er *or* **dry·er** \'drī-(ə)r\ *n* **1** : something that dries **2** : a substance used (as in paints or varnishes) to speed up drying **3** *usually dryer* : a device for drying something by heat or air

driest *superlative of* DRY

1drift \'drift\ *n* **1 a** : a drifting motion or course **b** : the flow or the velocity of a river or ocean stream **2 a** : wind-driven snow, rain, cloud, dust, or smoke usually near the ground **b** : a mass of matter (as sand) deposited by or as if by wind or water **c** : a deposit of clay, sand, gravel, and boulders transported by a glacier or by running water from a glacier **3 a** : a course something appears to be taking **b** : the underlying meaning of what is said or written ⟨following the *drift* of the conversation⟩

2drift *vb* **1** : to become or cause to be driven or carried along by a current of water, wind, or air **2** : to move along without effort **3** : to be piled up in heaps by wind or water — **drift·ing·ly** \'drif-tiŋ-lē\ *adv*

drift·er \'drif-tər\ *n* : one that drifts; *esp* : a person who travels about without purpose

drift·wood \'drift-ˌwúd\ *n* : wood drifted or floated by water

1drill \'dril\ *n* **1** : a tool for making holes in hard substances **2** : the training of soldiers in military skill and discipline **3** : a physical or mental exercise regularly practiced **4** : a marine snail that

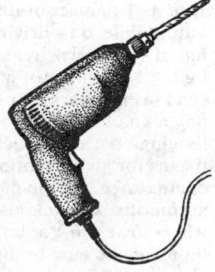
¹drill 1

\ə\ abut	\aú\ out	\i\ tip	\ȯ\ saw	\ú\ foot
\ər\ further	\ch\ chin	\ī\ life	\ȯi\ coin	\y\ yet
\a\ mat	\e\ pet	\j\ job	\th\ thin	\yü\ few
\ā\ take	\ē\ easy	\ŋ\ sing	\th\ this	\yú\ cure
\ä\ cot, cart	\g\ go	\ō\ bone	\ü\ food	\zh\ vision

bores through oyster shells and feeds on the soft parts [probably from Dutch *dril* "a tool for drilling holes," derived from early Dutch *drillen* (verb) "to drill"]

²**drill** *vb* 1 : to instruct or train by repetition ⟨*drill* a child in multiplication⟩ ⟨*drill* troops⟩ 2 : to bore or make a hole in with or as if with a drill ⟨*drill* a tooth⟩ ⟨*drill* a hole⟩ — **drill·er** *n*

³**drill** *n* 1 : a shallow furrow or trench into which seed is sown 2 : a planting machine that makes holes or furrows, drops in seed, and covers it with earth [perhaps from earlier *drill* "a trickling stream"]

⁴**drill** *vb* : to sow with or as if with a drill

⁵**drill** *n* : a strong cotton fabric in twill weave [shortened from *drilling* "heavy cotton fabric," from German *Drillich* (same meaning)]

dril·ling \'dril-iŋ\ *n* : ⁵DRILL

drill·mas·ter \'dril-,mas-tər\ *n* : an instructor in military drill

¹**drink** \'driŋk\ *vb* **drank** \'draŋk\; **drunk** \'drəŋk\ *or* **drank; drink·ing** 1 a : to swallow liquid b : ABSORB 1 c : to take in through the senses ⟨*drink* in the scenery⟩ 2 : to drink alcoholic beverages — **drink·er** *n*

²**drink** *n* 1 a : BEVERAGE b : alcoholic liquor 2 : a draft or portion of liquid

drink·able \'driŋ-kə-bəl\ *adj* : suitable or safe for drinking ⟨*drinkable* water⟩

¹**drip** \'drip\ *vb* **dripped; drip·ping** 1 : to fall or let fall in or as if in drops 2 : to let fall drops of liquid ⟨a *dripping* faucet⟩ — **drip·per** *n*

²**drip** *n* 1 a : a falling in drops b : liquid that drips 2 : the sound made by drops

drip–dry \'drip-'drī\ *vb* : to dry with few or no wrinkles when hung dripping wet — **drip–dry** \-,drī\ *adj*

drip·pings \'drip-iŋz\ *n pl* : fat and juices drawn from meat during cooking

¹**drive** \'drīv\ *vb* **drove** \'drōv\; **driv·en** \'driv-ən\; **driv·ing** \'drī-viŋ\ 1 a : to urge, push, or force onward ⟨*drive* cattle⟩ ⟨waves *drove* the boat ashore⟩ b : to cause to penetrate with force ⟨*drive* a nail⟩ 2 a : to direct the movement or course of (as a vehicle or animals drawing a vehicle) b : to move or transport in a vehicle ⟨his father *drove* me home⟩ 3 : to set or keep in motion ⟨*drive* machinery by electricity⟩ 4 : to carry through strongly ⟨*drive* a bargain⟩ 5 a : to force to act ⟨*driven* by hunger to steal⟩ b : to project, inject, or impress forcefully ⟨his last example *drove* the lesson home⟩ 6 : to bring into a specified condition ⟨noise enough to *drive* a person crazy⟩ 7 : to force (a passage) by pressing or digging 8 : to move ahead rapidly or with great force ⟨the rain was *driving* hard⟩ 9 a : to hit (a ball or puck) with force b : to cause (a run or runner) to be scored in baseball — usually used with *in* ⟨*drove* in two runs⟩

²**drive** *n* 1 : an act of driving: as a : a trip in a carriage or automobile b : a driving together of animals c : the guiding of logs downstream to a mill d : the act of driving a ball e : the flight of a ball 2 a : DRIVEWAY b : a public road (as in a park) for driving 3 : a long or forceful campaign ⟨a charity *drive*⟩ 4 a : an urgent or basic need or longing b : energetic quality ⟨full of *drive*⟩ 5 a : the means for giving motion to a machine or machine part ⟨a chain *drive*⟩ b : the means by which the movement of an automotive vehicle is controlled and directed ⟨front wheel *drive*⟩ 6 : a device for reading or writing data (as on magnetic tape or disks)

drive–in \'drī-,vin\ *n* : a business (as a movie theater or restaurant) set up so that customers can be served or provided for while remaining in their automobiles — **drive–in** *adj*

¹**driv·el** \'driv-əl\ *vb* **driv·eled** *or* **driv·elled; driv·el·ing** *or* **driv·el·ling** \-(ə-)liŋ\ 1 : to let saliva dribble from the mouth : SLOBBER 2 : to talk stupidly — **driv·el·er** *or* **driv·el·ler** \-(ə-)lər\ *n*

²**drivel** *n* : NONSENSE 1

driv·er \'drī-vər\ *n* 1 : one that drives: as a : the operator of a motor vehicle b : a tool for driving ⟨a nail *driver*⟩ c : a golf club having a usually wooden head with a nearly straight face

drive shaft *n* : a shaft that transmits mechanical power

drive–through \'drīv-,thrü\ *adj* : DRIVE-UP

drive–up \'drīv-,əp\ *adj* : designed to allow customers to be served while remaining in their automobiles ⟨a bank's *drive-up* window⟩

drive·way \'drīv-,wā\ *n* : a short private road from the street to a house, garage, or parking lot

driving range *n* : an area equipped for practicing golf shots

¹**driz·zle** \'driz-əl\ *vb* **driz·zled; driz·zling** \-(ə-)liŋ\ : to rain in very small drops

²**drizzle** *n* : a fine misty rain — **driz·zly** \'driz-(ə-)lē\ *adj*

drogue \'drōg\ *n* : a parachute for slowing down or stabilizing something (as an astronaut's capsule) or for pulling out a larger parachute

droll \'drōl\ *adj* : having an odd or amusing quality — **droll·ness** *n* — **drol·ly** \'drō(l)-lē\ *adv*

-drome \,drōm\ *n combining form* 1 : racecourse 2 : large specially prepared place ⟨aero*drome*⟩ [derived from Greek *dromos* "course for running"]

drom·e·dary \'dräm-ə-,der-ē\ *also* 'drəm-\ *n, pl* **-dar·ies** : the one-humped camel of western Asia and northern Africa — called also *Arabian camel*

dromedary

¹**drone** \'drōn\ *n* 1 : a stingless male bee (as of the honeybee) whose only function is to mate with the queen bee 2 : a lazy person 3 : an aircraft or ship without a pilot that is controlled by radio signals

²**drone** *vb* **droned; dron·ing** : to make or speak with a continuous low humming sound ⟨a plane *droning* overhead⟩ ⟨*droned* on about himself⟩

³**drone** *n* 1 : one of the pipes on a bagpipe that sound fixed continuous tones 2 : a deep monotonous sound : HUM

drool \'drül\ *vb* 1 : to water at the mouth 2 : to let saliva or some other substance flow from the mouth : DRIVEL

¹**droop** \'drüp\ *vb* 1 : to sink, bend, or hang down 2 : to become depressed or weak — **droop·ing·ly** \'drü-piŋ-lē\ *adv* — **droopy** \'drü-pē\ *adj*

²**droop** *n* : the condition or appearance of drooping

¹**drop** \'dräp\ *n* 1 a : the quantity of fluid that falls naturally in one rounded mass b *pl* : a dose of medicine measured by drops ⟨eye *drops*⟩ c : a small quantity of drink d : the smallest practical unit of liquid measure 2 : something (as a hanging ornament on jewelry or a round candy) shaped like a drop 3 a : the act or an instance of dropping : FALL b : a decline in quantity or quality ⟨a *drop* in water pressure⟩ ⟨a *drop* in prices⟩ c : a descent by parachute d : a place where something (as mail or goods) is left to be picked up 4 : the distance through which something drops 5 : an unframed piece of cloth scenery in a theater 6 : ADVANTAGE 1 ⟨we've got the *drop* on them⟩

²**drop** *vb* **dropped; drop·ping** 1 : to fall or let fall in drops 2 a : to let fall : cause to fall ⟨*dropped* the book⟩ b : to reduce to a lower level or stage ⟨*dropped* his speed⟩ 3 : SEND 1 ⟨*drop* me a line⟩ 4 : to stop doing, using, or considering ⟨*drop* the subject⟩ ⟨*dropped* everything and ran to the door⟩ ⟨you can *drop* that idea⟩ 5 : to knock or shoot down 6 : to go lower ⟨prices *dropped*⟩ 7 : to make a brief visit ⟨*drop* in for a chat⟩ 8 : to pass into a less active state ⟨*drop* off to sleep⟩ 9 : to move downward or with a current 10 : to leave (a letter standing for a speech

sound) unsounded ⟨*drop* the "g" in "running"⟩ **11** : to give birth to ⟨the cow *dropped* her calf⟩

drop–down \-ˌdau̇n\ *adj* : PULL-DOWN

drop-kick \'dräp-ˈkik\ *n* : a kick made by dropping a ball to the ground and kicking it as it bounces — **drop–kick** *vb* — **drop–kick·er** *n*

drop·let \'dräp-lət\ *n* : a very small drop

drop·out \'dräp-ˌau̇t\ *n* : a person who drops out especially from a school or a training program

drop out \'dräp-ˈau̇t\ *vb* : to withdraw from taking part or membership : QUIT ⟨*dropped out* of school⟩

drop·per \'dräp-ər\ *n* **1** : one that drops **2** : a short glass or plastic tube with a rubber bulb used to measure out liquids by drops — called also *eyedropper, medicine dropper* — **drop·per·ful** \-ˌfu̇l\ *n*

dropping bottle *n* : a bottle designed to supply liquid in drops; *esp* : a bottle with a dropper

drop·pings \'dräp-iŋz\ *n pl* : DUNG

drop·sy \'dräp-sē\ *n* : EDEMA — **drop·si·cal** \-si-kəl\ *adj*

dro·soph·i·la \drō-ˈsäf-ə-lə\ *n* : any of a genus of fruit flies used especially in genetics research

dross \'dräs, 'drȯs\ *n* **1** : the scum that forms on molten metal **2** : waste or foreign matter

dropper 2

drought *also* **drouth** \'drau̇t, 'drau̇th\ *n* : a long period of dry weather — **droughty** \-ē\ *adj*

¹drove \'drōv\ *n* **1** : a group of animals driven or moving in a body **2** : a crowd of people moving or acting together [Old English *drāf* "group of animals moving together," from *drīfan* "to drive"]

²drove *past of* DRIVE

drov·er \'drō-vər\ *n* : a person who drives cattle or sheep

drown \'drau̇n\ *vb* **1 a** : to suffocate in a liquid and especially in water **b** : to become drowned **2** : to cover with water : INUNDATE **3** : to overpower especially with noise — usually used with *out* ⟨the music was *drowned* out by shouting⟩

drowse \'drau̇z\ *vb* **drowsed; drows·ing** : DOZE — **drowse** *n*

drowsy \'drau̇-zē\ *adj* **drows·i·er; -est** **1** : ready to fall asleep **2** : making one sleepy ⟨a *drowsy* afternoon⟩ **syn·onyms** see SLEEPY — **drows·i·ly** \-zə-lē\ *adv* — **drows·i·ness** \-zē-nəs\ *n*

drub \'drəb\ *vb* **drubbed; drub·bing** **1** : to beat severely **2** : to defeat completely ⟨*drubbed* her opponent in the tennis match⟩

¹drudge \'drəj\ *vb* **drudged; drudg·ing** : to do hard or dull work — **drudg·er** *n*

²drudge *n* : a person who drudges

drudg·ery \'drəj-(ə-)rē\ *n, pl* **-er·ies** : hard or dull work

¹drug \'drəg\ *n* **1** : a substance used as a medicine or in making medicines **2** : something for which there is no demand — used in the phrase *drug on the market* **3** : a usually illegal substance (as heroin, LSD, or cocaine) that affects bodily activities often in a harmful way and is taken for other than medical reasons

²drug *vb* **drugged; drug·ging** **1** : to affect or treat with a drug; *esp* : to make dull or numb by a narcotic drug **2** : to lull or make dull or numb as if with a drug

drug·gist \'drəg-əst\ *n* : a person who sells drugs and medicines; *also* : PHARMACIST

drug·store \'drəg-ˌstō(ə)r, -ˌstȯ(ə)r\ *n* : a retail store where medicines and miscellaneous articles are sold — called also *pharmacy*

dru·id \'drü-əd\ *n, often cap* : a member of an ancient Celtic priesthood appearing in sagas and legends as magicians and wizards — **dru·id·ic** \drü-ˈid-ik\ *or* **dru·id·i·cal**

\-i-kəl\ *adj, often cap* — **dru·id·ism** \'drü-ə-ˌdiz-əm\ *n, often cap*

¹drum \'drəm\ *n* **1** : a musical percussion instrument consisting of a hollow cylinder with a thin layer of material (as animal skin or plastic) stretched over one or both ends that is beaten with a stick or with the hands **2** : the sound of a drum; *also* : a similar sound **3** : a drum-shaped object: as **a** : a cylindrical mechanical device or part **b** : a cylindrical container ⟨oil *drums*⟩ **c** : a disk-shaped ammunition container that may be attached to a firearm

²drum *vb* **drummed; drum·ming** **1** : to beat or play on or as if on a drum **2** : to sound rhythmically : THROB, BEAT **3** : to call or gather together by or as if by beating a drum ⟨*drum* up business⟩ **4** : to dismiss in shame : EXPEL ⟨*drummed* out of the army⟩ **5** : to drive or force by steady effort or repetition ⟨*drummed* the lesson into their heads⟩ **6** : to strike or tap repeatedly so as to produce rhythmic sounds ⟨*drummed* the table with his fingers⟩

drum·beat \'drəm-ˌbēt\ *n* : a stroke on a drum or its sound

drum·lin \'drəm-lən\ *n* : a long or oval hill of material left by a glacier

drum major *n* : the leader of a marching band

drum ma·jor·ette \ˌdrəm-ˌmā-jə-ˈret\ *n* : a girl or woman who leads a marching band

drum·mer \'drəm-ər\ *n* **1** : one that plays a drum **2** : TRAVELING SALESMAN

drum·stick \'drəm-ˌstik\ *n* **1** : a stick for beating a drum **2** : the lower part of a fowl's leg

¹drunk *past participle of* DRINK

²drunk \'drəŋk\ *adj* **1** : having consumed alcohol to the point that normal thinking or acting becomes difficult or impossible **2** : controlled by some feeling as if under the influence of alcohol ⟨*drunk* with power⟩ **3 a** : DRUNKEN 2a **b** : occurring while drunk ⟨*drunk* driving⟩

³drunk *n* **1 a** : a person who is drunk **b** : DRUNKARD **2** : a period of drinking too much : SPREE

drunk·ard \'drəŋ-kərd\ *n* : a person who makes a habit of getting drunk

drunk·en \'drəŋ-kən\ *adj* **1 a** : ²DRUNK 1 **b** : having a habit of drinking too much alcohol **2 a** : resulting from being drunk ⟨a *drunken* brawl⟩ **b** : ²DRUNK 3b — **drunk·en·ly** *adv* — **drunk·en·ness** \-kən-nəs\ *n*

drupe \'drüp\ *n* : a fleshy fruit (as the plum, cherry, or peach) having one seed enclosed in a hard stony material

¹dry \'drī\ *adj* **dri·er** \'drī(-ə)r\; **dri·est** \'drī-əst\ **1** : free or nearly free from liquid and especially water ⟨*dry* weight⟩ ⟨*dry* steam⟩ **2** : characterized by loss or lack of water: as **a** : lacking precipitation and humidity ⟨a *dry* climate⟩ **b** : lacking freshness : STALE **c** : low in or deprived of natural juices or moisture ⟨*dry* hay⟩ ⟨a *dry* fruit⟩ **3** : not being in or under water ⟨*dry* land⟩ **4 a** : THIRSTY **1 b** : marked by the absence of alcoholic beverages ⟨a *dry* party⟩ **c** : no longer damp or sticky ⟨the paint is *dry*⟩ **5** : containing or using no liquid (as water) ⟨a *dry* creek⟩ ⟨*dry* heat⟩ **6** : not giving milk ⟨a *dry* cow⟩ **7** : not producing phlegm ⟨*dry* cough⟩ **8** : not producing or yielding what is expected or wanted ⟨a *dry* oil well⟩ **9** : marked by a matter-of-fact, ironic, or terse manner of expression ⟨*dry* humor⟩ **10** : failing to arouse interest or enthusiasm ⟨a *dry* lecture⟩ **11** : not sweet ⟨*dry* wines⟩ **12** : relating to, favoring, or practicing prohibition of alcoholic beverages ⟨a *dry* county⟩ — **dry·ly** *or* **dri·ly** *adv* — **dry·ness** *n*

²dry *vb* **dried; dry·ing** : to make or become dry

³dry *n, pl* **drys** \'drīz\ : PROHIBITIONIST

dry·ad \'drī-əd, -ˌad\ *n* : a nymph living in woods

\ə\ **abut**	\au̇\ **out**	\i\ **tip**	\ȯ\ **saw**	\u̇\ **foot**
\ər\ **further**	\ch\ **chin**	\ī\ **life**	\ȯi\ **coin**	\y\ **yet**
\a\ **mat**	\e\ **pet**	\j\ **job**	\th\ **thin**	\yü\ **few**
\ā\ **take**	\ē\ **easy**	\ŋ\ **sing**	\th\ **this**	\yu̇\ **cure**
\ä\ **cot, cart**	\g\ **go**	\ō\ **bone**	\ü\ **food**	\zh\ **vision**

dry cell *n* : a small battery whose contents cannot be spilled ⟨a *dry cell* for a flashlight⟩

dry–clean \'drī-ˌklēn\ *vb* : to clean (fabrics) with chemical solvents — **dry–clean·able** \-ˈklē-nə-bəl\ *adj* — **dry cleaner** *n* — **dry cleaning** *n*

dry dock \'drī-ˌdäk\ *n* : a dock that can be kept dry during the construction or repair of ships

dryer *variant of* DRIER

dry–erase board *n* : WHITEBOARD

dry farmer *n* : a person who engages in dry farming

dry farming *n* : farming on dry land without irrigation using moisture-conserving methods and drought-resistant crops — **dry–farm** *vb* — **dry farm** *n*

dry fly *n* : a fishing fly designed to float on the water

dry goods \'drī-ˌgu̇dz\ *n pl* : cloth goods (as fabrics, lace, and ribbon)

dry ice *n* : solid carbon dioxide

dry measure *n* : a series of units of capacity for dry products — see MEASURE table, METRIC SYSTEM table

dry·point \'drī-ˌpȯint\ *n* : a picture made by engraving a metal plate with a tool and not using acid

dry rot *n* : decay of dried timber in which the cellulose of wood is used for food by fungi leaving a soft skeleton that easily crumbles to powder

dry run *n* **1** : a practice firing without ammunition **2** : a practice exercise

dry–shod \'drī-ˈshäd\ *adj* : having dry shoes or feet

dry·wall \'drī-ˌwȯl\ *n* : a board made of layers of fiberboard, paper, or felt bonded to a plaster core

du·al \'d(y)ü-əl\ *adj* **1** : consisting of two parts or elements : having two parts alike ⟨*dual* headphone jacks⟩ **2** : having a double character or nature ⟨a *dual* function⟩ ⟨*dual* citizenship⟩ [from Latin *dualis* "dual," from *duo* "two" — related to DEUCE, DOUBLE, DOZEN] — **du·al·i·ty** \d(y)ü-ˈal-ət-ē\ *n* — **du·al·ly** \'d(y)ü-ə-lē\ *adv*

¹dub \'dəb\ *vb* **dubbed**; **dub·bing 1** : to make a knight of **2** : ²NAME 1

²dub *vb* **dubbed**; **dub·bing** : to add sound effects or new dialogue to a film or broadcast

du·bi·ous \'d(y)ü-bē-əs\ *adj* **1** : causing doubt : UNCERTAIN ⟨a *dubious* honor⟩ **2** : feeling doubt : UNDECIDED ⟨*dubious* about our chances in the race⟩ **3** : of uncertain outcome ⟨a *dubious* struggle⟩ **4** : questionable in value, quality, or origin ⟨won by *dubious* means⟩ — **du·bi·ous·ly** *adv* — **du·bi·ous·ness** *n*

dub·ni·um \'düb-nē-əm, 'dəb-\ *n* : a short-lived radioactive element produced artificially — see ELEMENT table [from scientific Latin, from *Dubna*, a city in Russia where the element is produced and studied]

du·cal \'d(y)ü-kəl\ *adj* : of or relating to a duke or duchy

duc·at \'dək-ət\ *n* : a former gold coin of various European countries

duch·ess \'dəch-əs\ *n* **1** : the wife or widow of a duke **2** : a woman holding the rank of duke in her own right

duchy \'dəch-ē\ *n, pl* **duch·ies** : the territory of a duke or duchess

¹duck \'dək\ *n, pl* **duck** or **ducks** : any of various typically web-footed swimming birds with the neck and legs short, the body heavy, the bill often broad and flat, and the males and females usually differing in color; *also* : the flesh of a duck used as food [Old English *dūce* "duck"]

¹duck

²duck *vb* **1** : to thrust or plunge underwater **2** : to lower the head or body suddenly **3** : to move quickly : disappear suddenly ⟨he *ducked* around the corner to escape detection⟩ **4** : to evade a duty, question, or responsibility

: ²DODGE ⟨*ducked* our question⟩ [Middle English *douken* "thrust under water"] — **duck·er** *n*

³duck *n* **1** : a coarse usually cotton cloth **2** *pl* : clothes made of duck [from Dutch *doek* "cloth"]

⁴duck *n* : an amphibious truck [altered form of *DUKW*, military code name for this vehicle]

duck·bill \'dək-ˌbil\ *n* : PLATYPUS — called also *duck-billed platypus* \ˌdək-ˌbil(d)-\

duck·ling \'dək-liŋ\ *n* : a young duck

duck sauce *n* : a thick sweet sauce made mostly of fruits (as plums or apricots), sweeteners, and vinegar and used especially with Chinese food

duck soup *n* : something easy to do : CINCH

duck·weed \'dək-ˌwēd\ *n* : a tiny stemless plant that floats without attachment on the surface of a body of still water (as a pond)

duct \'dəkt\ *n* **1** : a tube or vessel carrying a bodily fluid (as the secretion of a gland) **2** : a pipe, tube, or channel through which a fluid (as air or water) flows [from scientific Latin *ductus* "tube or vessel from a gland," from Latin *ductus* "aqueduct," from earlier *ductus* "act of leading" — related to AQUEDUCT, ³DOCK] — **duct·less** \'dək-tləs\ *adj*

duc·tile \'dək-t°l, -ˌtīl\ *adj* : capable of being drawn out (as into a wire) or hammered thin ⟨*ductile* metal⟩ — **duc·til·i·ty** \ˌdək-ˈtil-ət-ē\ *n*

ductless gland *n* : ENDOCRINE GLAND

duct tape *n* : a wide cloth adhesive tape

dud \'dəd\ *n* **1** *pl* **a** : CLOTHES 1 **b** : personal belongings **2** : a complete failure ⟨the movie was a *dud*⟩ **3** : a missile (as a bomb or shell) that fails to explode

dude \'d(y)üd\ *n* **1** : a man who pays excessive attention to his dress : DANDY **2** : an Easterner in the West **3** : ¹MAN 1a, GUY — **dud·ish** \'d(y)üd-ish\ *adj*

dude ranch *n* : a vacation resort offering horseback riding and other activities typical of western ranches

dud·geon \'dəj-ən\ *n* : ill humor ⟨stomped off in high *dudgeon*⟩

¹due \'d(y)ü\ *adj* **1** : owed or owing as a debt or right ⟨respect *due* to the court⟩ **2** : according to accepted beliefs or procedures : ²APPROPRIATE ⟨treat the judge with *due* respect⟩ **3 a** : SUFFICIENT, ADEQUATE ⟨arrived in *due* time⟩ **b** : ¹REGULAR 2a, LAWFUL ⟨*due* process of law⟩ **4** : being a result — used with *to* ⟨accidents *due* to carelessness⟩ **5** : having reached the date at which payment is required ⟨bills are *due*⟩ **6** : required or expected to happen ⟨*due* to arrive any minute now⟩

²due *n* **1** : something owed : DEBT **2** *pl* : a regular or legal charge or fee ⟨membership *dues*⟩

³due *adv* : ¹DIRECTLY 1, EXACTLY ⟨*due* north⟩

¹du·el \'d(y)ü-əl\ *n* **1** : a combat between two persons; *esp* : one fought with weapons in the presence of witnesses **2** : a conflict between two opponents [from Latin *duellum* "duel," from an archaic form of earlier *bellum* "war"; revived in the Middle Ages to mean combat between two persons because the *du-* suggested Latin *duo* "two"]

²duel *vb* **du·eled** or **du·elled**; **du·el·ing** or **du·el·ling** : to fight in a duel — **du·el·er** or **du·el·ler** *n* — **du·el·ist** or **du·el·list** \'d(y)ü-ə-ləst\ *n*

du·en·na \d(y)ü-ˈen-ə\ *n* **1** : an elderly woman in charge of the younger ladies in a Spanish or Portuguese family **2** : ¹CHAPERONE

du·et \d(y)ü-ˈet\ *n* : a composition for two performers

due to *prep* : because of

duff \'dəf\ *n* : the partly decayed plant and animal matter on the floor of a forest

duf·fel \'dəf-əl\ *n* : an outfit of supplies (as for camping) : KIT

duffel bag *n* : a soft oblong bag for personal belongings

dug *past and past participle of* DIG

du·gong \'dü-ˌgäŋ, -ˌgȯŋ\ *n* : a mammal that lives in water, eats plants, and is related to the manatees but has a two-lobed tail and tusks in the male

dug·out \'dəg-ˌau̇t\ *n* **1** : a boat made by hollowing out a log **2** : a shelter dug in a hillside or in the ground **3** : a low shelter facing a baseball diamond and containing the players' bench

dui·ker \'dī-kər\ *n* : any of several small African antelopes

duke \'d(y)ük\ *n* **1** : a supreme and independent ruler of a duchy **2** : a nobleman of the highest rank especially of the British nobility

duke·dom \'d(y)ük-dəm\ *n* : DUCHY

dul·cet \'dəl-sət\ *adj* : sweet to the ear : MELODIOUS ⟨*dulcet* voices⟩

dul·ci·mer \'dəl-sə-mər\ *n*
1 : a stringed instrument played with light hammers held in the hands **2** *or* **dul·ci·more** \-ˌmōr, -ˌmȯr\ : an American folk instrument with three or four strings held on the lap and played by plucking or strumming

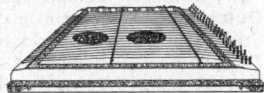
dulcimer 1

¹dull \'dəl\ *adj* **1** : mentally slow : STUPID **2** : LISTLESS **3** : slow in action : SLUGGISH **4** : lacking sharpness of edge or point **5** : lacking brilliance or luster **6** : not ringing, sharp, or intense ⟨a *dull* roar⟩ **7** : CLOUDY 2, OVERCAST **8** : TEDIOUS, UNINTERESTING ⟨a *dull* lecture⟩ **9** : slightly grayish ⟨a *dull* blue⟩ — **dull·ness** *also* **dul·ness** \'dəl-nəs\ *n* — **dul·ly** \'dəl-(l)ē\ *adv*

²dull *vb* : to make or become dull

du·ly \'d(y)ü-lē\ *adv* : in a due manner, time, or degree

dumb \'dəm\ *adj* **1 a** : lacking the human power of speech ⟨*dumb* animals⟩ **b** *of a person, often offensive* : lacking the ability to speak **2** : not willing to speak **3** : STUPID 1a, UNTHINKING — **dumb·ly** \'dəm-lē\ *adv* — **dumb·ness** *n*

dumb·bell \'dəm-ˌbel\ *n* **1** : a bar with weights at the ends that is usually used for exercise or building strength **2** : a stupid person : ¹DUMMY

dumb·found *also* **dum·found** \ˌdəm-'fau̇nd\ *vb* : to cause to become speechless with astonishment : AMAZE — **dumb·found·ing·ly** \-'fau̇n-diŋ-lē\ *adv*

dumb·wait·er \'dəm-'wāt-ər\ *n* : a small elevator for carrying food or goods from one story to another

¹dum·my \'dəm-ē\ *n, pl* **dummies** **1** : a person who lacks or seems to lack the power of speech **2** : a stupid person **3** : an imitation used as a substitute for something: as **a** : MANNEQUIN 2 **b** : a large puppet usually having movable features (as mouth and arms) controlled by a ventriloquist **4 a** : the bridge hand of the partner of the player who wins the bid that is placed face up and played by the bid winner **b** : a bridge player whose hand is a dummy

²dummy *adj* **1** : having the appearance of being real but lacking ability to function ⟨*dummy* hinges for ornament⟩ **2** : existing in name only : FICTITIOUS ⟨a *dummy* corporation⟩

¹dump \'dəmp\ *vb* **1** : to let fall in a heap or mass ⟨*dump* the coats on the bed⟩ **2** : to get rid of quickly or without concern ⟨*dumped* us at the party and went home⟩ ⟨got *dumped* by his girlfriend⟩ **3** : to dump trash or garbage ⟨no *dumping* allowed⟩ **4** : to send a copy of (data in a computer's internal storage) to an external storage device (as a flash drive) or to an output device (as a printer) — **dump·er** *n*

²dump *n* **1** : a place where discarded materials (as trash) are dumped **2** : a place where reserve military supplies are stored ⟨an ammunition *dump*⟩ **3** : a disorderly or undesirable place **4** : the dumping of data stored in a computer

dump·ling \'dəm-pliŋ\ *n* **1** : a portion of dough cooked by boiling or steaming **2** : a dessert of fruit baked in biscuit dough

dumps \'dəm(p)s\ *n pl* : a dull gloomy state of mind : low spirits ⟨in the *dumps*⟩

dump truck *n* : a truck for carrying and dumping loose material

dumpy \'dəm-pē\ *adj* **dump·i·er; -est** **1** : short and thick in build : SQUAT **2** : SHABBY 2b — **dump·i·ness** *n*

¹dun \'dən\ *n* **1** : a light tan horse with a black mane and tail **2** : a slightly brownish dark gray [Old English *dunn* (adjective) "having the color of brownish dark gray"] — **dun** *adj*

²dun *vb* **dunned; dun·ning** : to make repeated demands upon for payment ⟨an organization that *duns* its members for dues⟩ [origin unknown]

³dun *n* **1** : a person who duns another **2** : a demand for payment

dunce \'dən(t)s\ *n* : a mentally dull or stupid person [an altered form of earlier *duns,* from the name John *Duns* Scotus 1266?–1308 a Scottish religious teacher whose writings came to be ridiculed in the 16th century]

dune \'d(y)ün\ *n* : a hill or ridge of sand piled up by the wind

dune buggy *n* : a motor vehicle with oversize tires for use on sand

dung \'dəŋ\ *n* : waste matter of an animal : MANURE

dun·ga·ree \ˌdəŋ-gə-'rē\ *n* **1** : blue denim **2** *pl* : trousers or work clothes made of blue denim

dung beetle *n* : a beetle (as a tumblebug) that rolls balls of dung in which to lay eggs and on which the larvae feed

dun·geon \'dən-jən\ *n* **1** : DONJON **2** : a dark usually underground prison

Word History The word *dungeon,* in use in English since the 1300s, originally referred to the keep of a castle—the massive inner tower detached from the rest of the structure that was its most securely located and protected part. During its early history this word had about a dozen different spellings, but nowadays, in the sense of a castle's keep, the usual form is *donjon.* The donjon was the stronghold to which the residents of the castle retreated if the outer walls had been scaled or breached in a siege. The subterranean part of a donjon was called by the same word in the form *dungeon,* the usual spelling for this sense. This dark, damp chamber was used as a cell for the confinement of prisoners. Both *donjon* and *dungeon* are borrowed from medieval French *donjon,* most likely the descendant of an unrecorded spoken Latin form *domnio,* ultimately a derivative of Latin *dominus,* "lord." The underlying sense of *domnio* would have been "dominating tower," reflecting the relation between the keep and the rest of the castle. [Middle English *donjon* "tower in a castle, dungeon," from early French *donjon* "castle tower" — related to DONJON]

dung·hill \'dəŋ-ˌhil\ *n* : a manure pile

dunk \'dəŋk\ *vb* **1** : to dip (as a doughnut) into liquid (as coffee) **2** : to plunge oneself into water

dunk shot *n* : a shot in basketball made by jumping high in the air and throwing the ball down through the basket

duo \'d(y)ü-ō\ *n, pl* **du·os** **1** : DUET **2** : a group of two : ¹PAIR

¹duo·dec·i·mal \ˌd(y)ü-ə-'des-ə-məl\ *adj* : of, relating to, or being a system of numbers with a base of 12

²duodecimal *n* : a number or digit in the duodecimal system of numbers

du·o·de·num \ˌd(y)ü-ə-'dē-nəm, d(y)u̇-'äd-ᵊn-əm\ *n, pl* **-de·na** \-'dē-nə, -ᵊn-ə\ *or* **-denums** : the first part of the small intestine extending from the opening from the stomach into the small intestine to the jejunum — **du·o·de·nal** \-'dēn-ᵊl, -ᵊn-əl\ *adj*

¹dupe \'d(y)üp\ *n* : one who is easily deceived or cheated

\ə\ **abut**	\au̇\ **out**	\i\ **tip**	\ȯ\ **saw**	\u̇\ **foot**
\ər\ **further**	\ch\ **chin**	\ī\ **life**	\ȯi\ **coin**	\y\ **yet**
\a\ **mat**	\e\ **pet**	\j\ **job**	\th\ **thin**	\yü\ **few**
\ā\ **take**	\ē\ **easy**	\ŋ\ **sing**	\th\ **this**	\yu̇\ **cure**
\ä\ **cot, cart**	\g\ **go**	\ō\ **bone**	\ü\ **food**	\zh\ **vision**

²**dupe** *vb* **duped; dup·ing** : DECEIVE 1, CHEAT — **dup·er** *n*

du·ple \'d(y)ü-pəl\ *adj* **1** : taken by twos : TWOFOLD **2** : having two beats or a multiple of two beats to the measure ⟨*duple* time⟩

¹**du·plex** \'d(y)ü-‚pleks\ *adj* **1** : being or consisting of two parts : TWOFOLD **2** : allowing communication at a distance (as by telephone or television) in opposite directions at the same time

²**duplex** *n* : something duplex: as **a** : a two-family house **b** : an apartment with rooms on two floors

¹**du·pli·cate** \'d(y)ü-pli-kət\ *adj* **1** : having two parts exactly the same or alike **2** : being the same as another

²**du·pli·cate** \'d(y)ü-pli-‚kāt\ *vb* **-cat·ed; -cat·ing** **1** : to make double **2** : to make a duplicate of — **du·pli·ca·tive** \-‚kāt-iv\ *adj*

³**duplicate** \'d(y)ü-pli-kət\ *n* : a thing that is exactly like another

du·pli·ca·tion \‚d(y)ü-pli-'kā-shən\ *n* **1 a** : an act or process of duplicating **b** : the state of being duplicated **2** : ³DUPLICATE

du·pli·ca·tor \'d(y)ü-pli-‚kāt-ər\ *n* : one that duplicates; *esp* : COPIER

du·plic·i·ty \d(y)ù-'plis-ət-ē\ *n, pl* **-ties** : deception by pretending to feel and act one way while feeling and acting another

du·ra·ble \'d(y)ùr-ə-bəl\ *adj* : able to last a long time ⟨*durable* clothing⟩ ⟨*durable* goods⟩ **synonyms** see LASTING — **du·ra·bil·i·ty** \‚d(y)ùr-ə-'bil-ət-ē\ *n* — **du·ra·bly** \'d(y)ùr-ə-blē\ *adv*

durable press *n* : PERMANENT PRESS

du·rance \'d(y)ùr-ən(t)s\ *n* : the state of being restrained by or as if by physical force

du·ra·tion \d(y)ù-'rā-shən\ *n* : the time during which something exists or lasts

du·ress \d(y)ù-'res\ *n* : the use of force or threats

dur·ing \‚d(y)ùr-iŋ\ *prep* **1** : throughout the course of ⟨swims every day *during* the summer⟩ **2** : at some time in the course of ⟨you may call me *during* the day⟩

dur·ra \'dùr-ə\ *n* : any of several sorghums widely grown for their grain in warm dry regions

du·rum wheat \‚d(y)ùr-əm-\ *n* : a wheat that yields a flour used especially in pasta

dusk \'dəsk\ *n* **1** : the darker part of twilight especially at night **2** : partial darkness

dusky \'dəs-kē\ *adj* **dusk·i·er; -est** **1** : somewhat dark in color **2** : somewhat dark : DIM ⟨a *dusky* room⟩ — **dusk·i·ly** \-kə-lē\ *adv* — **dusk·i·ness** \-kē-nəs\ *n*

¹**dust** \'dəst\ *n* **1 a** : fine dry powdery particles (as of earth) **b** : a fine powder **2** : the powdery remains of bodies once alive **3** : something worthless **4** : the surface of the ground

²**dust** *vb* **1** : to make free of dust : brush or wipe away dust ⟨*dusted* the living room⟩ **2** : to sprinkle with dust or as a dust ⟨*dust* a pan with flour⟩ ⟨*dust* insecticide on plants⟩

dust bowl *n* : a region that suffers from long droughts and dust storms

dust devil *n* : a small whirlwind containing sand or dust

dust·er \'dəs-tər\ *n* **1** : one that dusts **2 a** : a loose-fitting usually lightweight long coat — called also *duster coat* **b** : a dress-length housecoat **3** : one that scatters fine particles; *esp* : a device for applying insecticidal or fungicidal dusts to crops — compare CROP DUSTER

dust jacket *n* : a removable usually decorative paper cover for a book

dust·pan \'dəs(t)-‚pan\ *n* : a pan shaped like a shovel for sweepings

dust storm *n* : a violent wind carrying dust across a dry region

dusty \'dəs-tē\ *adj* **dust·i·er; -est** **1** : filled or covered with dust **2** : resembling dust ⟨*dusty* soil⟩ — **dust·i·ly** \-tə-lē\ *adv* — **dust·i·ness** \-tē-nəs\ *n*

dutch \'dəch\ *adv, often cap* : with each person paying his or her own way ⟨went *dutch* to the movies⟩

¹**Dutch** \'dəch\ *adj* : of or relating to the Netherlands, its inhabitants, or their language

²**Dutch** *n* **1** : the Germanic language of the Netherlands **2** **Dutch** *pl* : the people of the Netherlands **3** : ¹DISFAVOR **2** ²TROUBLE ⟨was in *Dutch* with the teacher⟩

Dutch door *n* : a door divided so that the lower part can be shut while the upper part remains open

Dutch elm disease *n* : a disease of elms caused by a fungus carried from one tree to another by bark beetles and marked by yellowing of the foliage, loss of leaves, and death

Dutch·man \'dəch-mən\ *n* **1** : a person born or living in the Netherlands **2** : a person of Dutch ancestry

Dutch·man's-breech·es \‚dəch-mənz-'brich-əz\ *n pl* : a delicate spring-flowering herb of the eastern U.S. resembling the related bleeding heart but having cream⹀white flowers with two spurs

Dutchman's-breeches

Dutch oven *n* **1** : a brick oven for cooking **2 a** : a kettle with a tight cover used for baking in an open fire **b** : a large pot

Dutch treat *n* : a meal or other entertainment for which each person pays his or her own way

du·ti·able \'d(y)üt-ē-ə-bəl\ *adj* : subject to a tax

du·ti·ful \'d(y)üt-i-fəl\ *adj* : having or showing a sense of duty — **du·ti·ful·ly** \-f(ə-)lē\ *adv* — **du·ti·ful·ness** \-fəl-nəs\ *n*

du·ty \'d(y)üt-ē\ *n, pl* **duties** **1** : conduct due to parents and superiors : RESPECT **2** : the action required by one's position or occupation **3 a** : a moral or legal obligation **b** : the force of moral obligation **4** : ²TAX 1; *esp* : a tax on imports **5** : the service required (as of an electric machine) ⟨withstands heavy *duty*⟩ **synonyms** see TASK

DVD \‚dē-‚vē-'dē\ *n* : a high-capacity plastic disk on which information (as computer data or a movie) is recorded digitally and read by using a laser [from *d*igital *v*ideo *disc*]

DVR \‚dē-‚vē-'är\ *n, pl* **DVRs** : a machine that is used to make and watch recordings of television programs [from *d*igital *v*ideo *r*ecorder]

¹**dwarf** \'dwò(ə)rf\ *n, pl* **dwarfs** \'dwò(ə)rfs\ *also* **dwarves** \'dwò(ə)rvz\ **1** : a person, animal, or plant much below normal size or height **2** : a small legendary being usually pictured as a deformed and ugly person **3** : a star (as the sun) that in comparison to other stars gives off an ordinary or small amount of energy and has small mass and size — **dwarf** *adj* — **dwarf·ish** \'dwòr-fish\ *adj* — **dwarf·ness** *n*

²**dwarf** *vb* **1** : to restrict the growth or development of : STUNT **2** : to cause to appear smaller

dwarf planet *n* : a celestial object similar to a planet but too small to clear other objects from its orbit

dwell \'dwel\ *vb* **dwelled** \'dweld, 'dwelt\ *or* **dwelt** \'dwelt\; **dwell·ing** **1** : to stay for a while **2** : to live in a place : RESIDE **3** : to keep the attention directed ⟨*dwelled* on their mistakes⟩ — **dwell·er** *n*

dwell·ing \'dwel-iŋ\ *n* : a shelter in which people live : HOUSE

dwin·dle \'dwin-dᵊl\ *vb* **dwin·dled; dwin·dling** \'dwin-dliŋ, -dᵊliŋ\ : to make or become less

¹**dye** \'dī\ *n* **1** : color produced by dyeing **2** : a material used for dyeing or staining

²**dye** *vb* **dyed; dye·ing** : to stain or color usually permanently — **dy·er** \'dī(-ə)r\ *n*

dye·stuff \ˈdī-ˌstəf\ *n* : ¹DYE 2

dying *present participle of* DIE

dyke *variant of* DIKE

dy·nam·ic \dī-ˈnam-ik\ *adj* **1** *also* **dy·nam·i·cal** \-ˈnam-i-kəl\ **a** : of or relating to physical force or energy **b** : of or relating to dynamics **2 a** : marked by continuous usually productive activity or change ⟨a *dynamic* city⟩ **b** : marked by energy : FORCEFUL ⟨a *dynamic* personality⟩ — **dy·nam·i·cal·ly** \-ˈnam-i-k(ə-)lē\ *adv*

dy·nam·ics \dī-ˈnam-iks\ *n sing or pl* **1** : the science of the motion of bodies and the action of forces in producing or changing their motion **2** : physical, moral, or intellectual forces or the laws relating to them **3** : the pattern of change or growth **4** : variation in force or intensity (as in music)

¹**dy·na·mite** \ˈdī-nə-ˌmīt\ *n* : a blasting explosive that is made chiefly of nitroglycerin absorbed in another substance; *also* : a blasting explosive that contains no nitroglycerin

²**dynamite** *vb* **-mit·ed; -mit·ing** : to blow up with dynamite — **dy·na·mit·er** *n*

dy·na·mo \ˈdī-nə-ˌmō\ *n, pl* **-mos** **1** : GENERATOR a **2** : a forceful energetic person

dy·nas·ty \ˈdī-nə-stē *also* -ˌnas-tē\ *n, pl* **-ties** : a succession of rulers of the same line of descent — **dy·nas·tic** \dī-ˈnas-tik\ *adj* — **dy·nas·ti·cal·ly** \-ti-k(ə-)lē\ *adv*

dyne \ˈdīn\ *n* : the unit of force in the centimeter-gram-second system equal to the force that would give a free mass of one gram an acceleration of one centimeter per second squared

dys·en·tery \ˈdis-ən-ˌter-ē\ *n* **1** : a disease characterized by severe diarrhea with passage of mucus and blood from the bowels **2** : DIARRHEA

dys·func·tion \dis-ˈfəŋ(k)-shən\ *n* : impaired or abnormal functioning ⟨liver *dysfunction*⟩ — **dys·func·tion·al** \-shnəl, -shən-ᵊl\ *adj*

dys·lex·ia \dis-ˈlek-sē-ə\ *n* : a learning disability that is usually marked by problems in reading, spelling, and writing

¹**dys·lex·ic** \dis-ˈlek-sik\ *adj* : having dyslexia

²**dyslexic** *n* : a person who has dyslexia

dys·pep·sia \dis-ˈpep-shə, -sē-ə\ *n* : INDIGESTION

¹**dys·pep·tic** \dis-ˈpep-tik\ *adj* **1** : relating to or having indigestion **2** : showing or having a sour disposition — **dys·pep·ti·cal·ly** \-ti-k(ə-)lē\ *adv*

²**dyspeptic** *n* : a person having indigestion

dys·pnea \ˈdis(p)-nē-ə\ *n* : difficult or labored breathing

dys·pro·si·um \dis-ˈprō-zē-əm, -zh(ē-)əm\ *n* : a chemical element that forms very magnetic compounds — see ELEMENT table

E

e \ˈē\ *n, pl* **e's** *or* **es** *often cap* **1** : the fifth letter of the English alphabet **2** : the musical note referred to by the letter E : the third tone of a C-major scale **3** : a grade rating a student's work as poor or failing

e– *combining form* : electronic ⟨*e*-book⟩

¹**each** \ˈēch\ *adj* : being one of two or more individuals ⟨read *each* book⟩

²**each** *pron* : each one ⟨*each* of us took a turn⟩

³**each** *adv* : to or for each one : APIECE ⟨cost 50 cents *each*⟩

each other *pron* : each of two or more participating in a shared action or relation ⟨they turned and looked at *each other*⟩

ea·ger \ˈē-gər\ *adj* : having or showing an impatient or enthusiastic desire or interest ⟨was *eager* to get going⟩ [Middle English *egre* "sharp, sour, keen," from early French *aigre* (same meaning), from Latin *acer* (same meaning) — related to VINEGAR] — **ea·ger·ly** *adv* — **ea·ger·ness** *n*

> **synonyms** EAGER, KEEN, ANXIOUS mean moved by a strong and urgent desire or interest. EAGER suggests great enthusiasm and sometimes impatience at delay or restriction ⟨*eager* passengers waiting for the tour to start⟩. KEEN suggests strong interest and readiness to act ⟨the new members are *keen* and willing to learn⟩. ANXIOUS stresses fear of failure or disappointment ⟨I'm *anxious* to see the test scores⟩.

ea·gle \ˈē-gəl\ *n* **1** : any of various large day-flying sharp-eyed birds of prey with a powerful flight that are related to the hawks **2** : a seal or standard shaped like or bearing an eagle **3** : a 10-dollar gold coin of the U.S. **4** : a golf score of two strokes less than par on a hole

Eagle Scout *n* : a Boy Scout who has reached the highest level of achievement in scouting

ea·glet \ˈē-glət\ *n* : a young eagle

-ean — see -AN

¹**ear** \ˈi(ə)r\ *n* **1 a** : the organ of hearing and balance of vertebrates that in the typical mammal consists of a sound-collecting outer ear separated by an eardrum from a sound-carrying middle ear that in turn is separated from

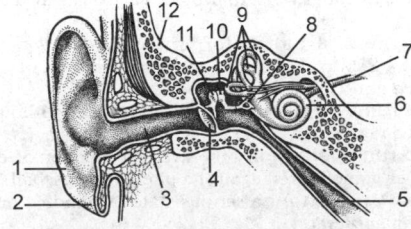

¹ear 1a: *1* pinna, *2* lobe, *3* auditory canal, *4* eardrum, *5* eustachian tube, *6* cochlea, *7* auditory nerve, *8* stirrup, *9* semicircular canals, *10* anvil, *11* malleus, *12* bones of skull

an inner ear containing neurons that receive sound and send nerve impulses to the brain **b** : OUTER EAR **2 a** : the sense or act of hearing **b** : an ability to understand and appreciate something heard ⟨an *ear* for languages⟩ **3** : willing or sympathetic attention ⟨lend an *ear*⟩ **4** : something resembling an ear in shape or position [Old English *ēare* "organ of hearing"] — **eared** \ˈi(ə)rd\ *adj* — **ear·less** \ˈi(ə)r-ləs\ *adj* — **all ears** : listening eagerly — **by ear** : relying on what one has heard rather than reading music ⟨play a song *by ear*⟩

²**ear** *n* : the seed-bearing head of a cereal (as corn) including both the seeds and protective structures [Old English *ēar* "seed part of a plant"] — **ear** *vb*

ear·ache \ˈi(ə)r-ˌāk\ *n* : an ache or pain in the ear

ear·bud \ˈi(ə)r-ˌbəd\ *n* : a small earphone inserted into the ear

\ə\ **abut**	\au̇\ **out**	\i\ **tip**	\ȯ\ **saw**	\u̇\ **foot**
\ər\ **further**	\ch\ **chin**	\ī\ **life**	\ȯi\ **coin**	\y\ **yet**
\a\ **mat**	\e\ **pet**	\j\ **job**	\th\ **thin**	\yü\ **few**
\ā\ **take**	\ē\ **easy**	\ŋ\ **sing**	\t̶h\ **this**	\yu̇\ **cure**
\ä\ **cot, cart**	\g\ **go**	\ō\ **bone**	\ü\ **food**	\zh\ **vision**

ear canal *n* : AUDITORY CANAL

ear·drum \-ˌdrəm\ *n* : the thin membrane that separates the outer and middle ear and carries sound waves as vibrations to the chain of tiny bones in the middle ear — called also *tympanic membrane, tympanum*

eared seal *n* : any of a family of seals including the sea lions and fur seals and having small well-developed ears on the outside of the head

earl \ˈərl\ *n* : a member of the British nobility ranking below a marquess and above a viscount [Old English *eorl* "nobleman"] — **earl·dom** \-dəm\ *n*

ear·less seal \ˌi(ə)r-ləs-\ *n* : HAIR SEAL

ear·lobe \ˈi(ə)r-ˌlōb\ *n* : a part hanging down from the ear of human beings and some domestic chickens

¹**ear·ly** \ˈər-lē\ *adv* **ear·li·er; -est** **1** : near the beginning of a period of time or of a process or series ⟨woke up *early*⟩ **2** : before the usual or expected time ⟨arrived *early*⟩

²**early** *adj* **ear·li·er; -est** **1 a** : of, relating to, or occurring near the beginning of a period of time, a development, or a series ⟨in the *early* evening⟩ **b** : PRIMITIVE ⟨*early* art forms⟩ **2 a** : occurring before the usual or expected time ⟨had an *early* winter⟩ **b** : maturing or producing sooner than related forms ⟨an *early* peach⟩ — **ear·li·ness** *n*

early on *adv* : at or during an early point or stage ⟨had decided *early on* not to accept⟩

¹**ear·mark** \ˈi(ə)r-ˌmärk\ *n* **1** : a mark of identification on the ear of an animal **2** : a mark or quality by which something can be identified ⟨the *earmarks* of success⟩

²**earmark** *vb* **1** : to mark with or as if with an earmark **2** : to set aside for a special purpose ⟨money *earmarked* for a vacation⟩

ear·muff \ˈi(ə)r-ˌməf\ *n* : one of a pair of pads joined by a flexible band and worn to protect the ears against cold or noise

earn \ˈərn\ *vb* **1** : to get for services given ⟨*earn* a good salary⟩ **2** : to deserve as a result of labor or service ⟨*earned* good grades⟩ — **earn·er** *n*

earned run *n* : a run in baseball that scores without benefit of an error

earned run average *n* : the average number of earned runs per game scored against a pitcher in baseball

¹**ear·nest** \ˈər-nəst\ *n* : a serious state of mind ⟨a promise made in *earnest*⟩

²**earnest** *adj* **1** : having or showing a serious attitude : not light or playful ⟨made an *earnest* request⟩ **2** : IMPORTANT 1 **synonyms** see SERIOUS — **ear·nest·ly** *adv* — **ear·nest·ness** \-nəs(t)-nəs\ *n*

earn·ings \ˈər-niŋz\ *n pl* : something earned; *esp* : money received as wages or gained as profit

ear·phone \ˈi(ə)r-ˌfōn\ *n* : a device that changes electrical energy into sound waves and is worn over or inserted into the ear

ear·piece \-ˌpēs\ *n* : a part of an instrument (as a telephone) that is placed against or in the ear; *esp* : EARPHONE

ear·ring \-ˌriŋ\ *n* : an ornament for the earlobe

ear·shot \-ˌshät\ *n* : the range within which a person can hear another's unaided voice ⟨waited until he was out of *earshot*⟩

ear·split·ting \-ˌsplit-iŋ\ *adj* : unbearably loud or shrill

earth \ˈərth\ *n* **1** : the soft or granular material composing part of the surface of the globe; *esp* : soil that can be cultivated **2** : the place of mortal life as distinguished from heaven and hell **3** : land as distinguished from sea and air : GROUND **4** *often cap* : the planet on which we live — see PLANET table

earth·en \ˈər-thən, -thən\ *adj* : made of earth or of baked clay ⟨an *earthen* floor⟩ ⟨*earthen* dishes⟩

earth·en·ware \-ˌwa(ə)r, -ˌwe(ə)r\ *n* : articles (as dishes or ornaments) made of baked clay

earth·light \ˈərth-ˌlīt\ *n* : EARTHSHINE

earth·ling \ˈərth-liŋ\ *n* : one who lives on the planet earth

earth·ly \ˈərth-lē\ *adj* **1** : belonging to or having to do with the earth ⟨*earthly* joys⟩ **2** : IMAGINABLE, POSSIBLE ⟨that tool is of no *earthly* use⟩ — **earth·li·ness** *n*

earth·quake \ˈərth-ˌkwāk\ *n* : a shaking or trembling of a portion of the earth

earth science *n* : any of the sciences (as geology, meteorology, or oceanography) that deal with the earth or with one or more of its parts — **earth scientist** *n*

earth·shine \ˈərth-ˌshīn\ *n* : sunlight reflected by the earth that lights up the dark part of the moon

earth·work \-ˌwərk\ *n* : something (as a raised bank or wall) constructed out of earth especially for protection

earth·worm \-ˌwərm\ *n* : a long slender annelid worm that lives in damp earth, moves with the aid of bristles, and feeds on decaying organic matter

earthy \ˈər-thē, -thē\ *adj* **earth·i·er; -est** **1** : consisting of or resembling earth ⟨an *earthy* flavor⟩ **2 a** : suggestive of plain or poor people or their ways : PRACTICAL **4**, DOWN-TO-EARTH ⟨*earthy* problems of everyday life⟩ **b** : not polite : CRUDE ⟨*earthy* humor⟩ — **earth·i·ness** *n*

ear·wax \ˈi(ə)r-ˌwaks\ *n* : a brownish yellow or orange waxlike substance produced by the glands of the external ear

ear·wig \-ˌwig\ *n* : any of numerous insects with slender many-jointed antennae and a large forcepslike organ at the end of the body

Word History Centuries ago it was thought that a certain insect, whose body ended in what looked like a pair of pincers, crawled into people's ears. The Old English name for this insect was *ēarwicga*, a compound of *ēare,* meaning "ear," and *wicga,* meaning "insect." *Earwig,* our modern English name for the insect, comes from the Old English word, even though we know that the old belief is not true. [Old English *ēarwicga,* from *ēare* "ear" and *wicga* "insect"]

¹**ease** \ˈēz\ *n* **1** : freedom from pain or trouble : comfort of body or mind ⟨a life of *ease*⟩ **2** : freedom from any feeling of difficulty or embarrassment ⟨speak with *ease*⟩ **3** : skill that does not require a lot of hard work ⟨rides a horse with *ease*⟩ — **at ease** **1** : free from pain, discomfort, or difficulty **2** : free to act in a way one feels comfortable ⟨feels *at ease* with old friends⟩

²**ease** *vb* **eased; eas·ing** **1** : to free from discomfort or worry : RELIEVE ⟨*ease* one's pain⟩ **2** : to make less tight or difficult : LOOSEN ⟨*ease* up on the rope⟩ **3** : to move slowly or gently ⟨*eased* herself into the chair⟩

ea·sel \ˈē-zəl\ *n* : a frame for supporting something (as an artist's canvas)

Word History An easel is a frame for holding up such things as an artist's painting or a chalkboard. In the 17th century the Dutch had become famous throughout Europe for their oil painting. Thus it was their word *ezel,* which they used to refer to this piece of equipment, that was borrowed into English at that time. This sense of *ezel* was an extension of the original meaning "donkey," probably because an easel, like a beast of burden, is used to hold things. [from Dutch *ezel* "a frame to hold an artist's canvas," literally, "donkey"]

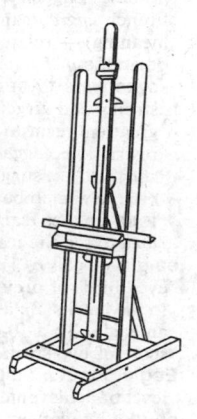

easel

eas·i·ly \ˈēz-(ə-)lē\ *adv* **1** : without difficulty ⟨won the game *easily*⟩ **2 a** : by a large margin ⟨*easily* the best player⟩ **b** : at least ⟨costs *easily* twice as much⟩

¹**east** \ˈēst\ *adv* : to or toward the east

²**east** *adj* **1** : located toward or at the east ⟨the *east* door of the school⟩ **2** : coming from the east ⟨an *east* wind⟩

³**east** *n* **1 a** : the general direction of sunrise **b** : the compass point directly opposite to west **2** *cap* : regions or countries east of a specific place

east·bound \'ēs(t)-ˌbau̇nd\ *adj* : going east

Eas·ter \'ē-stər\ *n* : a Christian holiday celebrating Christ's resurrection that is observed on the first Sunday following the first full moon on or after March 21

Easter lily *n* : any of several white cultivated lilies that bloom in early spring

east·er·ly \'ē-stər-lē\ *adv or adj* **1** : toward the east ⟨they sailed *easterly*⟩ **2** : from the east ⟨an *easterly* storm⟩

east·ern \'ē-stərn\ *adj* **1** *cap* : of, relating to, or like that of the East ⟨*Eastern* religion⟩ **2** : lying toward or coming from the east — **east·ern·most** \-ˌmōst\ *adj*

East·ern·er \'ē-stə(r)-nər\ *n* : a person born or living in the East (as of the U.S.)

eastern hemisphere *n, often cap E&H* : the half of the earth to the east of the Atlantic ocean including Europe, Asia, Australia, and Africa

Eastern Orthodox *adj* : of or consisting of the Christian churches that originated in the church of the Eastern Roman Empire and do not recognize the authority of the pope

eastern time *n, often cap E* : the time of the fifth time zone west of Greenwich that includes the eastern U.S.

¹**east·ward** \'ēs-twərd\ *adv or adj* : toward the east — **east·ward·ly** *adv or adj* — **east·wards** \-twərdz\ *adv*

²**eastward** *n* : eastward direction or part

¹**easy** \'ē-zē\ *adj* **eas·i·er; -est** **1** : not hard to do or get : not difficult ⟨an *easy* lesson⟩ **2 a** : not hard to please : LENIENT ⟨an *easy* teacher⟩ **b** : not steep ⟨*easy* slopes⟩ **3 a** : free from pain, trouble, or worry **b** : not hurried : LEISURELY ⟨an *easy* pace⟩ **4** : not false or strained : NATURAL ⟨an *easy* manner⟩ **5** : giving relaxation and comfort ⟨an *easy* chair⟩ — **eas·i·ness** *n*

²**easy** *adv* **eas·i·er; -est** **1** : EASILY 1 ⟨take life *easy*⟩ **2** : with slow care : CAUTIOUSLY ⟨go *easy*⟩

easy·go·ing \ˌē-zē-'gō-iŋ\ *adj* : taking life easy : CAREFREE — **easy·go·ing·ness** *n*

eat \'ēt\ *vb* **ate** \'āt\; **eat·en** \'ēt-ᵊn\; **eat·ing** **1** : to take into the mouth and swallow food : chew and swallow in turn **2** : to have a meal ⟨*eat* at home⟩ **3** : to destroy as if by eating : wear away ⟨rocks *eaten* away by waves⟩ **4** : to affect something by destroying or using up bit by bit ⟨acid *eating* into metal⟩ **5** : to enjoy with excitement ⟨the audience *ate* the show up⟩ — **eat·er** *n*

synonyms EAT, CONSUME, DEVOUR mean to swallow usually after chewing. EAT is a general word that can apply to any manner of taking in food ⟨*eat* your dinner⟩. CONSUME suggests eating up something completely ⟨by noon they had *consumed* all of their food supplies⟩. DEVOUR suggests eating quickly and greedily ⟨the hungry children *devoured* the grapes⟩.

¹**eat·able** \'ēt-ə-bəl\ *adj* : fit to be eaten

²**eatable** *n* **1** : something to eat **2** *pl* : FOOD

eating disorder *n* : any of several disorders (as bulimia) marked by abnormal eating behaviors

eave \'ēv\ *n* : the lower edge of a roof that sticks out beyond the wall of a building — usually used in plural

eaves·drop \'ēvz-ˌdräp\ *vb* : to listen secretly to private conversation — **eaves·drop·per** *n*

eaves trough *n* : GUTTER 1a

¹**ebb** \'eb\ *n* **1** : the flow away from the shore of seawater brought in by the tide **2** : a passing from a high to a low point ⟨our spirits were at a low *ebb*⟩; *also* : the time of such a passing

²**ebb** *vb* **1** : to recede from the flood **2** : to fall from a higher level or better state : WEAKEN ⟨her strength *ebbed*⟩

ebb tide *n* **1** : the tide while ebbing **2** : ¹EBB 2

EBCDIC \'eps-ə-ˌdik, 'ebs-\ *n* : a computer code for representing numbers, letters of the alphabet, and symbols [*ex*tended *b*inary *c*oded *d*ecimal *i*nterchange *c*ode]

Ebo·la \ē-'bō-lə\ *n* : a serious often deadly disease that is caused by a virus found in Africa and is marked by fever, muscle aches, and bleeding inside the body

¹**eb·o·ny** \'eb-ə-nē\ *n, pl* **-nies** **1** : a hard heavy blackish wood of various tropical chiefly southeast Asian trees related to the persimmon **2** : a tree that produces ebony

²**ebony** *adj* **1** : made of or resembling ebony **2** : ¹BLACK 1

e–book \'ē-ˌbu̇k\ *n* : a book composed in or converted to a digital format for display on a computer screen or handheld device

¹**ec·cen·tric** \ik-'sen-trik, ek-\ *adj* **1 a** : acting or thinking in an unusual way **b** : not of the usual or normal kind **2** : not following a truly circular path ⟨an *eccentric* orbit⟩ — **ec·cen·tri·cal·ly** \-tri-k(ə-)lē\ *adv*

²**eccentric** *n* : a strange or eccentric person

ec·cen·tric·i·ty \ˌek-ˌsen-'tris-ət-ē\ *n, pl* **-ties** **1 a** : the quality or state of being eccentric **b** : something that does not follow an established pattern, norm, or rule; *esp* : unusual behavior **2** : the amount by which a nearly circular path is not circular ⟨an orbit's *eccentricity*⟩

Ec·cle·si·as·tes \ik-ˌlē-zē-'as-(ˌ)tēz, e-ˌklē-\ *n* — see BIBLE table

ec·cle·si·as·tic \ik-ˌlē-zē-'as-tik, e-ˌklē-\ *n* : CLERGYMAN

ec·cle·si·as·ti·cal \ik-ˌlē-zē-'as-ti-kəl, e-ˌklē-\ *or* **ec·cle·si·as·tic** \-tik\ *adj* : of or relating to a church ⟨*ecclesiastical* history⟩ — **ec·cle·si·as·ti·cal·ly** \-ti-k(ə-)lē\ *adv*

Ec·cle·si·as·ti·cus \ik-ˌlē-zē-'as-ti-kəs, e-ˌklē-\ *n* — see BIBLE table

ech·e·lon \'esh-ə-ˌlän\ *n* **1** : a formation of units (as troops or airplanes) resembling a series of steps; *also* : a unit in such a formation **2** : one of a series of levels especially of authority ⟨involved officials at every *echelon*⟩; *also* : the people who are at such a level ⟨the upper *echelons* of the government⟩

echid·na \i-'kid-nə\ *n* : a spiny-coated toothless burrowing egg-laying mammal of Australia with a tapering snout and long tongue for eating ants — called also *spiny anteater*

echi·no·derm \i-'kī-nə-ˌdərm\ *n* : any of a phylum of marine invertebrate animals (as starfishes, sea urchins, and sea cucumbers) that have a number of similar body parts (as the arms of a starfish) arranged around a central axis, a calcium-containing inner skeleton, and a water-vascular system

echidna

¹**echo** \'ek-ō\ *n, pl* **ech·oes** **1** : the repeating of a sound caused by reflection of sound waves **2 a** : a repetition or imitation of another **b** : REPERCUSSION 2, RESULT ⟨environmental *echoes* of oil spills⟩ **3** : one who closely imitates or repeats another — **echo·ic** \i-'kō-ik, e-\ *adj*

²**echo** *vb* **ech·oed; echo·ing** **1** : to be filled with echoes ⟨the stadium *echoed* with cheers⟩ **2 a** : to produce an echo : send back or repeat a sound ⟨shouts *echoing* off the wall⟩ **3 a** : ¹REPEAT 1c, IMITATE ⟨*echoing* the teacher's words⟩ **b** : to state again in support or agreement ⟨*echoed* his opinion⟩

echo·lo·ca·tion \ˌek-ō-lō-'kā-shən\ *n* : a process for locating distant or invisible objects by means of sound waves reflected back to the sender from the objects

\ə\ **abut**	\au̇\ **out**	\i\ **tip**	\ȯ\ **saw**	\u̇\ **foot**
\ər\ **further**	\ch\ **chin**	\ī\ **life**	\ȯi\ **coin**	\y\ **yet**
\a\ **mat**	\e\ **pet**	\j\ **job**	\th\ **thin**	\yü\ **few**
\ā\ **take**	\ē\ **easy**	\ŋ\ **sing**	\th\ **this**	\yu̇\ **cure**
\ä\ **cot, cart**	\g\ **go**	\ō\ **bone**	\ü\ **food**	\zh\ **vision**

echo sounder *n* : an instrument used to find out the depth of a body of water or of an object below the surface by means of sound waves

éclair \ā-ˈkla(ə)r, i-, -ˈkle(ə)r; ˈā-ˌkla(ə)r, -ˌkle(ə)r, ˈē-\ *n* : an oblong pastry with whipped cream or custard filling ***Word History*** The English word *éclair* comes directly from a French word whose chief meaning is "lightning" or "flash of lightning." No one is sure why a pastry was named after lightning. Some say the lightness of the cream puff and its soft filling is the reason for the name. Perhaps more likely its richness and oblong shape, easily held in one hand, compel a person to eat it in a flash. [French, literally, "lightning"]

eclec·tic \e-ˈklek-tik, i-\ *adj* **1** : selecting what appears to be best from various styles, doctrines, or methods ⟨*eclectic* taste in music⟩ **2** : composed of elements drawn from various sources ⟨an *eclectic* guest list⟩

¹eclipse \i-ˈklips\ *n* **1 a** : the total or partial hiding of a planet, star, or moon by another **b** : the passing into the shadow of a planet, star, or moon **2** : a falling into disgrace or out of use or public favor

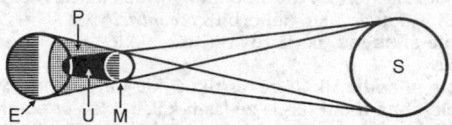

¹eclipse 1a: *E* earth, *M* moon in solar eclipse, *P* penumbra, *S* sun, *U* umbra

²eclipse *vb* **eclipsed; eclips·ing 1** : to cause an eclipse of **2 a** : to reduce in importance **b** : to do or be much better than : OUTSHINE

eclip·tic \i-ˈklip-tik\ *n* : the great circle of the celestial sphere on which the sun appears to move among the stars

eco- *combining form* : habitat or environment ⟨*eco*system⟩ [Greek *oikos* "house, household"]

E. coli \ˌē-ˈkō-ˌlī\ *n, pl* **E. coli** : a bacterium in the shape of a short rod that may cause intestinal illness [short for *Escherichia coli,* the taxonomic name in biology]

ecol·o·gist \i-ˈkäl-ə-jəst, e-\ *n* : a person who specializes in ecology

ecol·o·gy \i-ˈkäl-ə-jē, e-\ *n* **1** : a branch of science concerned with the relationships between living things and their environment **2** : the pattern of relationships between a group of living things and their environment — **eco·log·i·cal** \ˌē-kə-ˈläj-i-kəl, ˌek-ə-\ *also* **eco·log·ic** \-ˈläj-ik\ *adj* — **eco·log·i·cal·ly** \-ˈläj-i-k(ə-)lē\ *adv*

ec·o·nom·ic \ˌek-ə-ˈnäm-ik, ˌē-kə-\ *adj* **1 a** : of or relating to the science of economics ⟨*economic* theories⟩ **b** : of, relating to, or based on the production, distribution, and consumption of goods and services ⟨*economic* growth⟩ **2** : having practical or industrial uses : affecting material resources ⟨*economic* pests⟩

ec·o·nom·i·cal \ˌek-ə-ˈnäm-i-kəl, ˌē-kə-\ *adj* **1** : using resources with care and without waste **2** : operating with little waste or at a savings ⟨an *economical* car⟩ — ***syn·onyms*** see FRUGAL — **ec·o·nom·i·cal·ly** \-i-k(ə-)lē\ *adv*

ec·o·nom·ics \ˌek-ə-ˈnäm-iks, ˌē-kə-\ *n sing or pl* **1** : a social science concerned with description and analysis of the production, distribution, and consumption of goods and services **2** : financial considerations ⟨the *economics* of buying a house⟩ — **econ·o·mist** \i-ˈkän-ə-məst\ *n*

econ·o·mize \i-ˈkän-ə-ˌmīz\ *vb* **-mized; -miz·ing 1** : to practice economy : be thrifty ⟨*economize* on fuel⟩ **2** : to use less of : SAVE ⟨*economize* fuel⟩ — **econ·o·miz·er** *n*

econ·o·my \i-ˈkän-ə-mē\ *n, pl* **-mies 1** : careful use of money and goods : THRIFT **2** : a special arrangement or system : ORGANIZATION **3** : the way an economic system (as of a country or a period in history) is arranged [de-

rived from Greek *oikonomos* "household manager," from *oikos* "house" and *nemein* "to manage"]

eco·sys·tem \ˈē-kō-ˌsis-təm, ˈek-ō-\ *n* : a system made up of an ecological community of living things interacting with their environment especially under natural conditions

ec·ru \ˈek-rü, ˈā-krü\ *n* : BEIGE — **ecru** *adj*

ec·sta·sy \ˈek-stə-sē\ *n, pl* **-sies 1** : a state of being beyond reason and self-control **2** : a state of overwhelming emotion ⟨an *ecstasy* of fear⟩; *esp* : very great joy **3** : a drug used illegally to stimulate the central nervous system and to cause hallucinations — **ec·stat·ic** \ek-ˈstat-ik, ik-\ *adj* — **ec·stat·i·cal·ly** \-i-k(ə-)lē\ *adv*

ecto- *combining form* : outside : outer ⟨*ecto*derm⟩ [scientific Latin *ect-, ecto-* "outside," from Greek *ekto-* (same meaning), from *ex* "out"]

ec·to·derm \ˈek-tə-ˌdərm\ *n* **1** : the outer layer of cells of a two-layered animal (as a jellyfish) **2** : the outermost of the three basic layers of an embryo from which skin, nerves, and certain other structures develop — **ec·to·der·mal** \ˌek-tə-ˈdər-məl\ *adj*

ec·to·plasm \ˈek-tə-ˌplaz-əm\ *n* : the firm outer layer of the cytoplasm of a cell

ec·to·therm \ˈek-tə-ˌthərm\ *n* : a cold-blooded animal : POIKILOTHERM

ec·u·men·i·cal \ˌek-yə-ˈmen-i-kəl\ *adj* **1** : worldwide or general in extent, influence, or application **2** : of, relating to, or representing the whole of a body of churches **3** : leading toward agreement or cooperation among Christians [from Latin *oecumenicus* "worldwide," from Greek *oikoumenē* "the inhabited world," from *oikein* "to inhabit," from *oikos* "house"] — **ec·u·men·i·cal·ly** \-i-k(ə-)lē\ *adv*

ec·ze·ma \ig-ˈzē-mə, ˈeg-zə-mə, ˈek-sə-\ *n* : a skin disease marked by redness, itching, and scaly or crusty lesions

¹-ed \d *after a vowel or* b, g, j, l, m, n, ŋ, r, th, v, z, zh; əd, id *after* d, t; t *after other sounds; exceptions are pronounced at their subentries or entries*\ *vb suffix or adj suffix* **1** — used to form the past participle of regular weak verbs ⟨end*ed*⟩ ⟨fad*ed*⟩ ⟨tri*ed*⟩ ⟨patt*ed*⟩ **2 a** : having : characterized by ⟨cultur*ed*⟩ ⟨two-legg*ed*⟩ **b** : having the characteristics of ⟨bigot*ed*⟩ [Old English *-ed, -od, -ad* (mark of the past participle of certain verbs)]

²-ed *vb suffix* — used to form the past tense of regular weak verbs ⟨judg*ed*⟩ ⟨deni*ed*⟩ ⟨dropp*ed*⟩ [Old English *-de, -ede, -ode, -ade* (mark of the past tense of certain verbs)]

Edam \ˈēd-əm, ˈē-ˌdam\ *n* : a Dutch cheese of yellow color and mild flavor [named for *Edam,* seaport in the Netherlands, where the cheese was first sold]

edaph·ic \i-ˈdaf-ik\ *adj* : of, relating to, or influenced by the soil

¹ed·dy \ˈed-ē\ *n, pl* **eddies** : a current of air or water running against the main current or in a circle

²eddy *vb* **ed·died; ed·dy·ing** : to move in an eddy or in a way that forms an eddy

eddy current *n* : an electric current caused by an alternating magnetic field

edel·weiss \ˈād-ᵊl-ˌwīs\ *n* : a small woolly herb that is related to the thistles and grows high in the Alps

ede·ma \i-ˈdē-mə\ *n* : an abnormal collection of watery fluid in a bodily tissue or cavity

Eden \ˈēd-ᵊn\ *n* **1** : PARADISE 3 **2** : the garden where according to the Bible Adam and Eve first lived

eden·tate \(ˈ)ē-ˈden-ˌtāt\ *n* : any of a group of mammals having few or no teeth and

edelweiss

including the sloths, armadillos, and New World anteaters — **edentate** *adj*

¹**edge** \'ej\ *n* **1 a** : the cutting side of a blade ⟨a knife's *edge*⟩ **b** : the sharpness of a blade ⟨a razor with no *edge*⟩ **c** : a harsh or sharp quality ⟨his voice had a sarcastic *edge*⟩ **2 a** : the line where an object or surface begins or ends; *also* : the narrow part next to it ⟨the *edge* of the deck⟩ **b** : the line where two plane faces of a solid meet ⟨an *edge* of the cube⟩ **3** : ADVANTAGE 3 ⟨our experience gave us an *edge*⟩ **synonyms** see BORDER — **edged** \'ejd\ *adj* — **on edge** : ANXIOUS 1, NERVOUS

²**edge** *vb* **edged; edg·ing** **1** : to give an edge to ⟨*edge* a sleeve with lace⟩ **2** : to advance slowly or by short moves ⟨*edged* my chair closer⟩

edge·wise \'ej-ˌwīz\ *adv* **1** : with the edge in front : SIDE-WAYS **2** : as if by an edge : BARELY ⟨couldn't get a word in *edgewise*⟩

edg·ing \'ej-iŋ\ *n* : something that forms an edge or border ⟨a lace *edging*⟩

edgy \'ej-ē\ *adj* **edg·i·er; -est** **1** : having an edge : SHARP **2** : ²TENSE 2, IRRITABLE ⟨spoke with an *edgy* tone⟩ — **edg·i·ly** \'ej-ə-lē\ *adv* — **edg·i·ness** \'ej-ē-nəs\ *n*

ed·i·ble \'ed-ə-bəl\ *adj* : fit or safe to be eaten ⟨*edible* fruit⟩ — **ed·i·bil·i·ty** \ˌed-ə-'bil-ət-ē\ *n* — **edible** *n*

edict \'ē-ˌdikt\ *n* : a law or order made or given by an authority (as a ruler) — **edic·tal** \i-'dik-t²l\ *adj*

ed·i·fice \'ed-ə-fəs\ *n* : BUILDING 1; *esp* : a large or impressive building (as a church)

ed·i·fy \'ed-ə-ˌfī\ *vb* **-fied; -fy·ing** : to instruct and improve especially in moral and religious knowledge ⟨an *edifying* sermon⟩ — **ed·i·fi·ca·tion** \ˌed-ə-fə-'kā-shən\ *n*

ed·it \'ed-ət\ *vb* **1 a** : to correct, revise, and prepare for publication ⟨*edit* a book of poems⟩ **b** : to assemble (as a film or tape recording) by cutting and rearranging **2** : to direct the publication of ⟨*edit* a daily newspaper⟩

edi·tion \i-'dish-ən\ *n* **1** : the form in which a book is published ⟨an illustrated *edition*⟩ **2** : the whole number of copies printed or published at one time ⟨a third *edition*⟩ **3** : one of the several issues of a newspaper for a single day ⟨the late *edition*⟩

ed·i·tor \'ed-ət-ər\ *n* **1** : a person who edits especially as an occupation **2** : a computer program that permits the user to create or change data (as text or graphics) in a computer system — **ed·i·tor·ship** \-ˌship\ *n*

¹**ed·i·to·ri·al** \ˌed-ə-'tōr-ē-əl, -'tȯr-\ *adj* **1** : of or relating to an editor or editing ⟨an *editorial* office⟩ **2** : being or resembling an editorial ⟨an *editorial* statement⟩ — **ed·i·to·ri·al·ly** \-ē-ə-lē\ *adv*

²**editorial** *n* : a newspaper or magazine article that gives the opinions of its editors or publishers

ed·u·ca·ble \'ej-ə-kə-bəl\ *adj* : capable of being educated

ed·u·cate \'ej-ə-ˌkāt\ *vb* **-cat·ed; -cat·ing** **1** : to provide schooling for **2 a** : to develop the mind and morals of especially by instruction **b** : ²TRAIN 2a — **ed·u·ca·tor** \-ˌkāt-ər\ *n*

educated *adj* **1** : having an education; *esp* : having an education beyond the average **2** : showing education ⟨*educated* speech⟩ **3** : based on some knowledge of fact ⟨an *educated* guess⟩

ed·u·ca·tion \ˌej-ə-'kā-shən\ *n* **1 a** : the action or process of educating or of being educated **b** : knowledge, skill, and development gained from study or practice **2** : the field of study that deals mainly with methods and problems of teaching — **ed·u·ca·tion·al** \-shnəl, -shən-²l\ *adj* — **ed·u·ca·tion·al·ly** \-ē\ *adv*

synonyms EDUCATION, TRAINING mean an action or process of learning. EDUCATION suggests a general course of instruction in a school with the stress on mental development ⟨much *education* is needed in order to become a lawyer⟩. TRAINING suggests practical and usu-

ally specific instruction for learning certain skills (as in a craft or trade) ⟨six months of *training* for a clerk⟩.

ed·u·ca·tive \'ej-ə-ˌkāt-iv\ *adj* : helping to educate : IN-STRUCTIVE ⟨an *educative* experience⟩

educe \i-'d(y)üs\ *vb* **educed; educ·ing** : to bring out : ELICIT ⟨*educe* a response⟩ — **educ·i·ble** \-'d(y)ü-sə-bəl\ *adj*

¹**-ee** \'ē, (ˌ)ē\ *n suffix* **1** : one that receives or benefits from (a specified action or thing) ⟨appoint*ee*⟩ ⟨grant*ee*⟩ ⟨pat-ent*ee*⟩ **2** : a person who does (a specified action) ⟨es-cap*ee*⟩ [derived from Latin *-atus* (past participle ending of certain verbs)]

²**-ee** *n suffix* **1** : a particular especially small kind of ⟨boot*ee*⟩ **2** : one resembling or suggestive of ⟨goat*ee*⟩ [probably an altered form of *-y* (noun suffix)]

eek \'ēk\ *interj* — used to express surprise and fear

eel \'ē(ə)l\ *n, pl* **eels** *or* **eel** : any of numerous long snake-like fishes that have a smooth slimy skin and the fins in the middle of the back and bottom continuous around the tail — **eel·like** \'ē(ə)l-ˌlīk\ *adj*

eel·grass \'ē(ə)l-ˌgras\ *n* : a saltwater plant that is a mono-cotyledon and has long ribbonlike leaves

e'en \(')ēn\ *adv* : ³EVEN

-eer \'i(ə)r\ *n suffix* : one who is connected with or who operates or produces ⟨auction*eer*⟩ ⟨puppet*eer*⟩ ⟨pam-phlet*eer*⟩ [derived from Latin *-arius* (noun suffix)]

e'er \(')e(ə)r, (')a(ə)r\ *adv* : EVER

ee·rie *also* **ee·ry** \'i(ə)r-ē\ *adj* **ee·ri·er; -est** : causing fear or uneasiness because of strangeness or gloominess ⟨an *eerie* shadow⟩ — **ee·ri·ly** \'ir-ə-lē\ *adv* — **ee·ri·ness** \'ir-ē-nəs\ *n*

ef·face \i-'fās, e-\ *vb* **ef·faced; ef·fac·ing** **1** : WIPE OUT 1, OBLITERATE **2** : to make unclear by or as if by rubbing out — **ef·face·able** \-'fā-sə-bəl\ *adj* — **ef·face·ment** \-'fās-mənt\ *n* — **ef·fac·er** *n*

¹**ef·fect** \i-'fekt\ *n* **1** : an event, condition, or state of affairs that is produced by a cause **2** : ¹INFLUENCE 1 ⟨the *effect* of climate on growth⟩ **3** *pl* : personal property or posses-sions ⟨household *effects*⟩ **4** : the act of making a particu-lar impression ⟨talked merely for *effect*⟩ **5** : EXECUTION 1, OPERATION ⟨the law went into *effect* today⟩ — **in ef-fect** : in actual fact ⟨the suggestion was *in effect* an order⟩

²**effect** *vb* : BRING ABOUT, ACCOMPLISH ⟨*effect* a change⟩ — **ef·fect·er** *n*

ef·fec·tive \i-'fek-tiv\ *adj* **1 a** : producing or able to pro-duce a desired effect ⟨*effective* treatment of a disease⟩ **b** : IMPRESSIVE, STRIKING ⟨an *effective* performance⟩ **2** : being in actual operation ⟨the law becomes *effective* next year⟩ — **ef·fec·tive·ly** *adv* — **ef·fec·tive·ness** *n*

ef·fec·tor \i-'fek-tər, -ˌtȯ(ə)r\ *n* : a bodily part (as a gland or muscle) that becomes active in response to stimulation (as by a nerve)

ef·fec·tu·al \i-'fek-chə-(wə)l, -'feksh-wəl\ *adj* : producing or able to produce the desired result ⟨an *effectual* reme-dy⟩ — **ef·fec·tu·al·ly** \-ē\ *adv* — **ef·fec·tu·al·ness** *n*

ef·fec·tu·ate \i-'fek-chə-ˌwāt\ *vb* **-at·ed; -at·ing** : BRING ABOUT

ef·fem·i·na·cy \ə-'fem-ə-nə-sē\ *n* : the quality of being ef-feminate

ef·fem·i·nate \ə-'fem-ə-nət\ *adj* : having or showing quali-ties that are considered more suited to women than to men : not manly — **ef·fem·i·nate·ly** *adv* — **ef·fem·i·nate·ness** *n*

ef·fer·ent \'ef-ə-rənt; 'ef-ˌer-ənt, 'ē-ˌfer-\ *adj* : conducting outward from a part or organ; *esp* : conveying nerve im-pulses to an effector ⟨*efferent* nerve fibers⟩

\ə\ **abut**	\au̇\ **out**	\i\ **tip**	\ȯ\ **saw**	\u̇\ **foot**
\ər\ **further**	\ch\ **chin**	\ī\ **life**	\ȯi\ **coin**	\y\ **yet**
\a\ **mat**	\e\ **pet**	\j\ **job**	\th\ **thin**	\yü\ **few**
\ā\ **take**	\ē\ **easy**	\ŋ\ **sing**	\th\ **this**	\yu̇\ **cure**
\ä\ **cot, cart**	\g\ **go**	\ō\ **bone**	\ü\ **food**	\zh\ **vision**

ef·fer·vesce \,ef-ər-'ves\ *vb* **-vesced; -vesc·ing 1 :** to bubble, hiss, and foam as gas escapes **2 :** to show liveliness or excitement ⟨*effervesced* at the good news⟩ — **ef·fer·ves·cence** \-'ves-ᵊn(t)s\ *n* — **ef·fer·ves·cent** \-ᵊnt\ *adj* — **ef·fer·ves·cent·ly** *adv*

ef·fete \e-'fēt, i-\ *adj* **1 :** no longer productive **2 a :** WORN=OUT 2, EXHAUSTED **b :** having lost strength, courage, or spirit : DECADENT ⟨*effete* snobs⟩ — **ef·fete·ly** *adv* — **ef·fete·ness** *n*

ef·fi·ca·cious \,ef-ə-'kā-shəs\ *adj* **:** having the power to produce a desired result ⟨an *efficacious* remedy⟩ — **ef·fi·ca·cious·ly** *adv* — **ef·fi·ca·cious·ness** *n*

ef·fi·ca·cy \'ef-i-kə-sē\ *n, pl* **-cies :** the power to produce a desired result

ef·fi·cien·cy \i-'fish-ən-sē\ *n, pl* **-cies 1 :** the quality or degree of being efficient **2 :** efficient operation **3 :** the ratio of the useful energy delivered by a machine to the energy supplied to it

ef·fi·cient \i-'fish-ənt\ *adj* **:** capable of producing desired results especially without waste (as of time or energy) ⟨an *efficient* worker⟩ ⟨*efficient* machinery⟩ — **ef·fi·cient·ly** *adv*

ef·fi·gy \'ef-ə-jē\ *n, pl* **-gies :** a likeness especially of a person; *esp* : a crude figure meant to represent a hated person ⟨hanged their cruel ruler in *effigy*⟩

ef·flu·ent \'ef-,lü-ənt\ e-'flü-, ə-\ *n* **:** liquid (as sewage or industrial by-products) discharged as waste — **effluent** *adj*

ef·fort \'ef-ərt, -,ȯrt\ *n* **1 :** hard work of mind or body ⟨requires time and *effort*⟩ **2 :** a serious attempt : TRY ⟨made a good *effort*⟩ **3 :** something produced by work ⟨this painting was one of my best *efforts*⟩ **4 :** the force applied to a simple machine (as a lever) in contrast to the force applied by it against a load

ef·fort·less \'ef-ərt-ləs\ *adj* **:** showing or requiring little or no effort : EASY — **ef·fort·less·ly** *adv* — **ef·fort·less·ness** *n*

ef·fron·tery \i-'frənt-ə-rē, e-\ *n, pl* **-ter·ies :** shameless display of boldness : NERVE 3c ⟨had the *effrontery* to deny any guilt⟩

ef·ful·gence \i-'fu̇l-jən(t)s, e-, -'fəl-\ *n* **:** shining brightness — **ef·ful·gent** \-jənt\ *adj*

ef·fu·sion \i-'fyü-zhən, e-\ *n* **1 :** free expression of words or feelings **2 a :** escape of a fluid from containing vessels **b :** the fluid that escapes

ef·fu·sive \i-'fyü-siv, e-, -ziv\ *adj* **:** expressing or showing much emotion ⟨*effusive* thanks for their anniversary present⟩ — **ef·fu·sive·ly** *adv* — **ef·fu·sive·ness** *n*

eft \'eft\ *n* **:** NEWT

eft·soons \eft-'sünz\ *adv, archaic* **:** soon afterward

egad \i-'gad\ *interj* — used as a mild oath

¹**egg** \'eg\ *vb* **:** to incite to action : URGE — usually used with *on* ⟨*egged* us on to fight⟩ [Old Norse *eggja* "to incite"]

²**egg** *n* **1 a :** a hard-shelled reproductive body produced by a bird and especially by domestic poultry; *also* : its contents used as food **b :** a reproductive body produced by an animal and consisting of an ovum with its food=containing and protecting envelopes and being capable of development into a new individual **c :** a germ cell produced by a female — called also *ovum* **2 :** something shaped like an egg ⟨darning *egg*⟩ [Middle English *egge* "egg," from early Norse *egg* (same meaning)]

egg·beat·er \'eg-,bēt-ər\ *n* **:** a device used for beating eggs or liquids (as cream)

egg case *n* **:** a case that encloses and protects eggs (as of an insect)

egg cell *n* **:** ²EGG 1c

egg·head \'eg-,hed\ *n* **:** HIGHBROW, INTELLECTUAL

egg·nog \-,näg\ *n* **:** a drink made of eggs beaten with sugar, milk or cream, and often alcoholic liquor

egg·plant \-,plant\ *n* **1 :** a widely cultivated herb that is related to the potato and yields edible fruit **2 :** the usually glossy blackish purple egg-shaped fruit of an eggplant

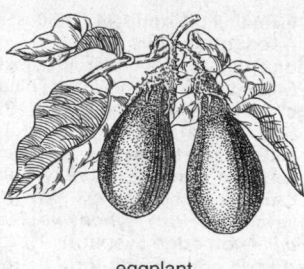
eggplant

egg roll *n* **:** a thin egg=dough casing filled with minced vegetables and often bits of meat (as shrimp or pork) and usually deep-fried

¹**egg·shell** \-,shel\ *n* **:** the shell of an egg

²**eggshell** *adj* **1 :** being thin and fragile ⟨*eggshell* china⟩ **2 :** slightly glossy

egg white *n* **:** the clear fluid mass of material surrounding the yolk of an egg

eg·lan·tine \'eg-lən-,tīn, -,tēn\ *n* **:** SWEETBRIER

ego \'ē-gō\ *n, pl* **egos 1 :** ²SELF 1; *esp* : the conscious self **2 a :** CONCEIT 1 ⟨has a big *ego*⟩ **b :** SELF-RESPECT 1

ego·cen·tric \,ē-gō-'sen-trik\ *adj* **:** overly concerned with oneself : SELF-CENTERED

ego·ism \'ē-gə-,wiz-əm\ *n* **:** excessive interest in oneself : a self-centered attitude — **ego·ist** \-wəst\ *n* — **ego·is·tic** \,ē-gə-'wis-tik\ *adj* — **ego·is·ti·cal·ly** \-'wis-ti-k(ə-)lē\ *adv*

ego·tism \'ē-gə-,tiz-əm\ *n* **1 :** the practice of talking about oneself too much **2 :** an overly high opinion of one's own importance : CONCEIT — **ego·tist** \-təst\ *n* — **ego·tis·tic** \,ē-gə-'tis-tik\ *or* **ego·tis·ti·cal** \-'tis-ti-kəl\ *adj* — **ego·tis·ti·cal·ly** \-'tis-ti-k(ə-)lē\ *adv*

egre·gious \i-'grē-jəs\ *adj* **:** very noticeable; *esp* : glaringly bad ⟨*egregious* errors⟩ — **egre·gious·ly** *adv* — **egre·gious·ness** *n*

egress \'ē-,gres\ *n* **1 :** the act or right of going or coming out **2 :** a way out : EXIT

egret \'ē-grət, i-'gret, 'ē-,gret, 'eg-rət\ *n* **:** any of various herons that bear long feathers during the breeding season

egret

Egyp·tian \i-'jip-shən\ *n* **1 :** a person born or living in Egypt **2 :** the language spoken by the ancient Egyptians — **Egyptian** *adj*

ei·der \'īd-ər\ *n* **1 :** a large duck that is found in northern coastal regions, is mostly white above and black below, and has very soft down — called also *eider duck* **2 :** EIDERDOWN 1

ei·der·down \-,daun\ *n* **1 :** the down of the eider **2 :** a quilt filled with eiderdown

eight \'āt\ *n* **1 :** — see NUMBER table **2 :** the eighth in a set or series **3 :** something having eight units or members — **eight** *adj or pron*

eigh·teen \(,)ā(t)-'tēn\ *n* — see NUMBER table — **eigh·teen** *adj or pron* — **eigh·teenth** \-'tēn(t)th\ *adj or n*

eighth \'ātth, 'āth\ *n, pl* **eighths** \'āt(th)s\ — see NUMBER table — **eighth** *adj or adv*

eighth note *n* **:** a musical note equal in time to ⅛ of a whole note

eighth rest *n* **:** a musical rest equal in time to an eighth note

eighty \'āt-ē\ *n, pl* **eight·ies** — see NUMBER table — **eight·i·eth** \-ē-əth\ *adj or n* — **eighty** *adj or pron*

ein·stei·ni·um \īn-'stī-nē-əm\ *n* **:** a radioactive element produced artificially — see ELEMENT table

¹**ei·ther** \'ē-thər *also* 'ī-\ *adj* **1 :** being the one and the other of two : EACH ⟨signs on *either* side of the walk⟩ **2 :** being the one or the other of two ⟨take *either* road⟩

²**either** *pron* : the one or the other 〈tell *either* of my sisters〉

³**either** *conj* — used before the first of two or more words or word groups the last of which follows *or* to show that they are choices or possibilities 〈a statement is *either* true or false〉

⁴**either** *adv* **1** : LIKEWISE 2, MOREOVER — used after a negative 〈not wise or handsome *either*〉 **2** : so far as that is concerned — used after a choice or possibility following a question or conditional clause 〈if your father had come or your mother *either* all would have gone well〉

ejac·u·late \i-'jak-yə-ˌlāt\ *vb* **-lat·ed; -lat·ing 1** : to eject a fluid and especially semen **2** : to utter suddenly and forcefully — **ejac·u·la·to·ry** \-yə-lə-ˌtōr-ē, -ˌtòr-\ *adj*

ejac·u·la·tion \i-ˌjak-yə-'lā-shən\ *n* **1** : an act of ejaculating; *esp* : a sudden emptying of a fluid from a duct **2** : something ejaculated; *esp* : a short sudden exclamation

eject \i-'jekt\ *vb* **1 a** : to throw out especially by physical force or authority 〈*ejected* from the game〉 **b** : to force off property **2** : to throw out or off from within 〈*ejects* the cassette〉 — **ejec·tion** \-'jek-shən\ *n* — **ejec·tor** \-'jek-tər\ *n*

eke out \'ēk-\ *vb* **1 a** : ²SUPPLEMENT 〈*eked* out their small income by working for neighbors〉 **b** : to make (a supply) last by careful use **2** : to get with great difficulty 〈*eked* out a living from the poor soil of the family's farm〉

el \'el\ *n, often cap* : a railroad operating chiefly on elevated tracks

¹**elab·o·rate** \i-'lab-(ə-)rət\ *adj* : made or done with great care or with much detail 〈*elaborate* plans〉 〈an *elaborate* design〉 — **elab·o·rate·ly** *adv* — **elab·o·rate·ness** *n*

²**elab·o·rate** \i-'lab-ə-ˌrāt\ *vb* **-rat·ed; -rat·ing 1** : to work out in detail : DEVELOP 〈*elaborate* an idea〉 **2** : to give more details 〈*elaborate* on a story〉 — **elab·o·ra·tion** \-ˌlab-ə-'rā-shən\ *n* — **elab·o·ra·tive** \-'lab-ə-ˌrāt-iv\ *adj*

eland \'ē-lənd, -ˌland\ *n* : either of two large African antelopes resembling oxen and having short spirally twisted horns in both sexes

elapse \i-'laps\ *vb* **elapsed; elaps·ing** : to slip or glide away : PASS 〈weeks *elapsed* before I found time to write〉

¹**elas·tic** \i-'las-tik\ *adj* **1 a** : capable of returning to original shape or size after being stretched, pressed, or squeezed together 〈sponges are *elastic*〉 **b** : capable of indefinite expansion 〈gases are *elastic* substances〉 **2** : able to recover quickly especially from sadness or disappointment 〈youthful, *elastic* spirit〉 **3** : capable of being changed : FLEXIBLE 〈an *elastic* plan〉 — **elas·tic·i·ty** \i-ˌlas-'tis-ət-ē, ˌē-ˌlas-\ *n*

²**elastic** *n* **1** : RUBBER BAND **2 a** : an elastic fabric usually made of yarns containing rubber **b** : something made from elastic fabric

elas·ti·cized \i-'las-tə-ˌsīzd\ *adj* : made with elastic threads or inserts 〈an *elasticized* waistband〉

elas·tin \i-'las-tən\ *n* : a protein that is similar to collagen and helps make up the elastic fibers of connective tissue

elate \i-'lāt\ *vb* **elat·ed; elat·ing** : to fill with joy or pride 〈*elated* over the team's victory〉 — **elat·ed·ly** *adv* — **elat·ed·ness** *n*

ela·tion \i-'lā-shən\ *n* : the quality or state of being elated

E layer *n* : a layer of the ionosphere that occurs at about 65 miles (110 kilometers) above the earth's surface during daylight hours and is capable of reflecting radio waves

¹**el·bow** \'el-ˌbō\ *n* **1 a** : the joint of the arm; *also* : the outer curve of a bent arm **b** : a corresponding joint in the front limb of an animal **2** : a part (as of a pipe) bent like an elbow

²**elbow** *vb* **1** : to push or shove with the elbow : JOSTLE **2** : to advance by or as if by pushing with the elbow 〈*elbowed* his way to the front〉

¹elbow 2

elbow grease *n* : forceful effort in doing physical labor

el·bow·room \'el-ˌbō-ˌrüm, -ˌrùm\ *n* **1** : room for moving the elbows freely **2** : enough space for work or operation

eld \'eld\ *n* **1** : old age **2** *archaic* : ancient times

¹**el·der** \'el-dər\ *n* : ELDERBERRY 2 [Old English *ellærn* "elder tree"]

²**elder** *adj* : of greater age 〈the *elder* cousin〉 [Old English *ieldra,* comparative form of *eald* "old"]

³**elder** *n* **1** : one who is older : SENIOR **2** : a person having authority because of age and experience 〈the village *elders*〉 **3** : any of various church officers — **el·der·ship** \-ˌship\ *n*

el·der·ber·ry \'el-də(r)-ˌber-ē\ *n* **1** : the edible black or red fruit of any of a genus of shrubs or trees of the same family as the honeysuckles that produce flat clusters of small white or pink flowers **2** : any tree or shrub that produces elderberries

el·der·ly \'el-dər-lē\ *adj* **1** : rather old; *esp* : past middle age **2** : of or relating to later life or elderly persons — **el·der·li·ness** *n*

elder statesman *n* : a respected older member of a group or organization; *esp* : a retired statesman who gives advice to current leaders

el·dest \'el-dəst\ *adj* : of the greatest age : OLDEST

¹**elect** \i-'lekt\ *adj* **1** : carefully selected **2** : chosen for office but not yet holding office 〈president-*elect*〉

²**elect** *n pl* : a carefully chosen group — used with *the*

³**elect** *vb* **1** : to select by vote for an office, position, or membership 〈*elect* a senator〉 **2** : ¹SELECT, CHOOSE 〈we *elected* to stay home〉

elec·tion \i-'lek-shən\ *n* **1** : an act or process of electing; *esp* : the process of voting to choose a person for office 〈the *election* of a new governor〉 **2** : the fact of being elected 〈her *election* to the presidency〉

elec·tion·eer \i-ˌlek-shə-'ni(ə)r\ *vb* : to work for a candidate or party in an election

¹**elec·tive** \i-'lek-tiv\ *adj* **1** : chosen by election 〈an *elective* official〉 **2** : held by a person who is elected 〈the presidency is an *elective* office〉 **3** : followed or taken by choice : not required 〈an *elective* subject in school〉 — **elec·tive·ly** *adv* — **elec·tive·ness** *n*

²**elective** *n* : an elective course or subject in school

elec·tor \i-'lek-tər, -ˌtò(ə)r\ *n* **1** : one qualified to vote in an election **2** : a member of the electoral college in the U.S.

elec·tor·al \i-'lek-t(ə-)rəl\ *adj* : of or relating to an election or electors

electoral college *n* : a body of electors; *esp* : one that elects the president and vice president of the U.S.

elec·tor·ate \i-'lek-t(ə-)rət\ *n* : a body of people entitled to vote

electr- *or* **electro-** *combining form* : electricity : electric

¹**elec·tric** \i-'lek-trik\ *adj* **1** *or* **elec·tri·cal** \-tri-kəl\ : of, relating to, operated by, or produced by electricity 〈an *electric* current〉 〈an *electric* charge〉 〈an *electric* stove〉 **2** : having a thrilling effect 〈an *electric* performance〉 [from scientific Latin *electricus* "produced from amber by friction," derived from earlier Latin *electrum* "amber," derived from Greek *ēlektron* (same meaning); so called because static electricity was first discovered by the friction produced by rubbing a piece of amber] — **elec·tri·cal·ly** \-tri-k(ə)lē\ *adv* — **elec·tri·cal·ness** \-kəl-nəs\ *n*

²**electric** *n* : something (as a light, automobile, or train) operated by electricity

electrical engineering *n* : engineering dealing with the practical applications of electricity — **electrical engineer** *n*

electrical storm *n* : THUNDERSTORM — called also *electric storm*

\ə\ **abut**	\aù\ **out**	\i\ **tip**	\ò\ **saw**	\ù\ **foot**
\ər\ **further**	\ch\ **chin**	\ī\ **life**	\òi\ **coin**	\y\ **yet**
\a\ **mat**	\e\ **pet**	\j\ **job**	\th\ **thin**	\yü\ **few**
\ā\ **take**	\ē\ **easy**	\ŋ\ **sing**	\th\ **this**	\yù\ **cure**
\ä\ **cot, cart**	\g\ **go**	\ō\ **bone**	\ü\ **food**	\zh\ **vision**

electric eel *n* : a large South American eel-shaped fish able to give a severe electric shock

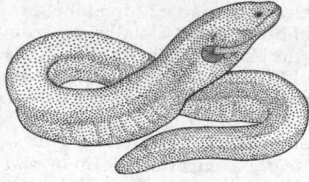

electric eel

electric eye *n* : PHOTOELECTRIC CELL

electric field *n* : a region associated with a distribution of electric charge or a varying magnetic field in which forces due to that charge or field act upon other electric charges

elec·tri·cian \i-ˌlek-ˈtrish-ən\ *n* : a person who installs, operates, or repairs electrical equipment

elec·tric·i·ty \i-ˌlek-ˈtris-ət-ē, -ˈtris-tē\ *n* 1 : a form of energy that is found in nature but that can be artificially produced by rubbing together two unlike things (as glass and silk), by the action of chemicals, or by means of a generator 2 : electric current 3 : great excitement ⟨felt the *electricity* in the theater⟩

electric ray *n* : any of various round-bodied short-tailed rays of warm seas able to give a severe electric shock

elec·tri·fy \i-ˈlek-trə-ˌfī\ *vb* **-fied; -fy·ing** 1 a : to charge with electricity b : to equip for use of electric power or supply with electric power 2 : to cause to feel great or sudden excitement : THRILL ⟨*electrified* the audience⟩ — **elec·tri·fi·ca·tion** \-ˌlek-trə-fə-ˈkā-shən\ *n*

elec·tro·chem·i·cal \i-ˌlek-trō-ˈkem-i-kəl\ *adj* : of or relating to electrochemistry ⟨an *electrochemical* cell⟩

elec·tro·chem·is·try \i-ˌlek-trō-ˈkem-ə-strē\ *n* : a science that deals with the relation of electricity to chemical changes and with the change of chemical to electrical energy or vice versa

elec·tro·cute \i-ˈlek-trə-ˌkyüt\ *vb* **-cut·ed; -cut·ing** 1 : to execute (a criminal) by electricity 2 : to kill by electric shock — **elec·tro·cu·tion** \-ˌlek-trə-ˈkyü-shən\ *n*

elec·trode \i-ˈlek-ˌtrōd\ *n* : a conductor (as a metal or carbon) used to make electrical contact with a part of an electrical circuit that is not metallic

elec·tro·en·ceph·a·lo·gram \i-ˌlek-trō-en-ˈsef-ə-lə-ˌgram\ *n* : the tracing of brain waves that is made by an electroencephalograph

elec·tro·en·ceph·a·lo·graph \i-ˌlek-trō-en-ˈsef-ə-lə-ˌgraf\ *n* : an apparatus for detecting and recording brain waves — **elec·tro·en·ceph·a·lo·graph·ic** \-en-ˌsef-ə-lə-ˈgraf-ik\ *adj* — **elec·tro·en·ceph·a·log·ra·phy** \-ˌsef-ə-ˈläg-rə-fē\ *n*

elec·trol·y·sis \i-ˌlek-ˈträl-ə-səs\ *n* 1 : the producing of chemical changes by passage of an electric current through an electrolyte 2 : the destruction of hair roots with an electric current

elec·tro·lyte \i-ˈlek-trə-ˌlīt\ *n* 1 : a conductor in which electric current is carried by the movement of ions that are not metallic 2 a : a substance that when dissolved in a suitable solvent or when melted becomes an ionic conductor b : an ion (as of sodium) that regulates or affects metabolic processes of the body (as the movement of waste products out of a cell)

elec·tro·lyt·ic \i-ˌlek-trə-ˈlit-ik\ *adj* : of or relating to electrolysis or an electrolyte — **elec·tro·lyt·i·cal·ly** \-ˈlit-i-k(ə-)lē\ *adv*

elec·tro·mag·net \i-ˌlek-trō-ˈmag-nət\ *n* : a core of magnetic material (as soft iron) surrounded by a coil of wire through which an electric current is passed to magnetize the core

elec·tro·mag·net·ic \i-ˌlek-trō-mag-ˈnet-ik\ *adj* : of, relating to, or produced by electromagnetism

electromagnetic radiation *n* : energy in the form of electromagnetic waves; *also* : a series of electromagnetic waves

electromagnetic spectrum *n* : the entire range of wavelengths or frequencies of electromagnetic waves extending from gamma rays to the longest radio waves and including visible light

electromagnetic wave *n* : a wave (as a radio wave, wave of visible light, or X-ray) that consists of an associated electric and magnetic effect and travels at the speed of light

elec·tro·mag·ne·tism \i-ˌlek-trō-ˈmag-nə-ˌtiz-əm\ *n* 1 : magnetism developed by a current of electricity 2 : a natural force arising from interactions between charged particles

elec·tro·me·chan·i·cal \i-ˌlek-trō-mə-ˈkan-i-kəl\ *adj* : of, relating to, or being a mechanical process or device put into motion or controlled electrically

elec·tro·mo·tive force \i-ˌlek-trə-ˈmōt-iv-\ *n* : the work per unit charge required to carry a positive charge around a closed circuit in an electric field — abbreviation *emf*

elec·tron \i-ˈlek-ˌträn\ *n* : an elementary particle that has a negative charge of electricity and travels around the nucleus of an atom

electron gun *n* : the part of a cathode-ray tube that produces, accelerates, and focuses a stream of electrons

elec·tron·ic \i-ˌlek-ˈträn-ik\ *adj* 1 : of or relating to electrons 2 : of, relating to, or using devices constructed or working by principles of electronics 3 a : producing music by electronic means ⟨an *electronic* organ⟩ b : of, relating to, or being music produced electronically 4 : of, relating to, or being a medium (as television) by which information is transmitted electronically ⟨*electronic* journalism⟩ — **elec·tron·i·cal·ly** \-ˈträn-i-k(ə-)lē\ *adv*

electronic mail *n* : E-MAIL

elec·tron·ics \i-lek-ˈträn-iks\ *n* 1 : a branch of physics that deals with the giving off, action, and effects of electrons and with electronic devices 2 : electronic circuits, devices, and equipment

electron microscope *n* : an instrument in which a beam of electrons is used to produce an enlarged image of a very small object

electron tube *n* : a device in which conduction of electricity by electrons takes place through a vacuum or a gas within a sealed glass or metal container and which has various common uses (as in radio and television)

elec·tro·plate \i-ˈlek-trə-ˌplāt\ *vb* : to cover with a coating (as of metal or rubber) by means of electrolysis

elec·tro·scope \i-ˈlek-trə-ˌskōp\ *n* : any of various instruments for detecting the presence of an electric charge on a body, for finding out whether the charge is positive or negative, or for indicating and measuring intensity of radiation

elec·tro·stat·ic \i-ˌlek-trə-ˈstat-ik\ *adj* : of or relating to static electricity or electrostatics

electrostatic generator *n* : VAN DE GRAAFF GENERATOR

electrostatic precipitator *n* : an electrostatic device in chimneys that removes particles from escaping gases

elec·tro·stat·ics \i-ˌlek-trə-ˈstat-iks\ *n* : physics that deals with happenings resulting from attractions or repulsions of electric charges but not dependent on their motion

elec·trum \i-ˈlek-trəm\ *n* : a natural pale yellow alloy of gold and silver

el·e·gance \ˈel-i-gən(t)s\ *n* 1 : gracefulness of style or movement 2 : decoration or design that is rich but in good taste

el·e·gan·cy \ˈel-i-gən-sē\ *n, pl* **-cies** : ELEGANCE

el·e·gant \ˈel-i-gənt\ *adj* 1 : having or showing elegance 2 : of excellent quality : SPLENDID — **el·e·gant·ly** *adv*

el·e·gy \ˈel-ə-jē\ *n, pl* **-gies** : a poem or song expressing sorrow especially for one who is dead — **el·e·gi·ac** \ˌel-ə-ˈjī-ak\ *adj* — **el·e·gize** \ˈel-ə-ˌjīz\ *vb*

el·e·ment \ˈel-ə-mənt\ *n* 1 a : one of the four substances air, water, fire, or earth formerly believed to make up the physical universe b *pl* : forces of nature; *esp* : stormy or cold weather c : the state or place natural or suited to a person or thing ⟨at school she was in her *element*⟩ 2 : one of the parts of which something is made up: as a *pl* : the simplest principles of a subject of study b : one of the basic individual things that belong to a mathematical set or class — called also *member* c : any of more than 100 fundamental substances that consist of atoms of only one kind and that cannot be separated by ordinary chemical means into simpler substances **d** : a distinct part of a device used in the composing of print matter **3** *pl* : the bread and wine used in the sacrament of Communion

CHEMICAL ELEMENTS

ELEMENT	SYMBOL	ATOMIC NUMBER	ATOMIC WEIGHT[1]
actinium	Ac	89	(227)
aluminum	Al	13	26.98154
americium	Am	95	(243)
antimony	Sb	51	121.760
argon	Ar	18	39.948
arsenic	As	33	74.92160
astatine	At	85	(210)
barium	Ba	56	137.33
berkelium	Bk	97	(247)
beryllium	Be	4	9.012182
bismuth	Bi	83	208.98040
bohrium	Bh	107	(264)
boron	B	5	10.81
bromine	Br	35	79.904
cadmium	Cd	48	112.41
calcium	Ca	20	40.078
californium	Cf	98	(251)
carbon	C	6	12.011
cerium	Ce	58	140.116
cesium	Cs	55	132.90545
chlorine	Cl	17	35.453
chromium	Cr	24	51.996
cobalt	Co	27	58.93320
copernicium	Cn	112	(285)
copper	Cu	29	63.546
curium	Cm	96	(247)
darmstadtium	Ds	110	(269)
dubnium	Db	105	(262)
dysprosium	Dy	66	162.50
einsteinium	Es	99	(252)
erbium	Er	68	167.259
europium	Eu	63	151.964
fermium	Fm	100	(257)
fluorine	F	9	18.998403
francium	Fr	87	(223)
gadolinium	Gd	64	157.25
gallium	Ga	31	69.723
germanium	Ge	32	72.64
gold	Au	79	196.96657
hafnium	Hf	72	178.49
hassium	Hs	108	(277)
helium	He	2	4.002602
holmium	Ho	67	164.93032
hydrogen	H	1	1.0079
indium	In	49	114.818
iodine	I	·53	126.90447
iridium	Ir	77	192.217
iron	Fe	26	55.845
krypton	Kr	36	83.80
lanthanum	La	57	138.90547
lawrencium	Lr	103	(262)
lead	Pb	82	207.2
lithium	Li	3	6.941
lutetium	Lu	71	174.967
magnesium	Mg	12	24.305
manganese	Mn	25	54.93805
meitnerium	Mt	109	(268)
mendelevium	Md	101	(258)
mercury	Hg	80	200.59
molybdenum	Mo	42	95.94
neodymium	Nd	60	144.242
neon	Ne	10	20.180
neptunium	Np	93	(237)
nickel	Ni	28	58.6934
niobium	Nb	41	92.90638
nitrogen	N	7	14.0067
nobelium	No	102	(259)
osmium	Os	76	190.23
oxygen	O	8	15.9994
palladium	Pd	46	106.42
phosphorus	P	15	30.973762
platinum	Pt	78	195.084
plutonium	Pu	94	(244)
polonium	Po	84	(209)
potassium	K	19	39.0983
praseodymium	Pr	59	140.90765
promethium	Pm	61	(145)
protactinium	Pa	91	(231)
radium	Ra	88	(226)
radon	Rn	86	(222)
rhenium	Re	75	186.207
rhodium	Rh	45	102.90550
roentgenium	Rg	111	(280)
rubidium	Rb	37	85.4678
ruthenium	Ru	44	101.07
rutherfordium	Rf	104	(261)
samarium	Sm	62	150.36
scandium	Sc	21	44.95591
seaborgium	Sg	106	(266)
selenium	Se	34	78.96
silicon	Si	14	28.0855
silver	Ag	47	107.8682
sodium	Na	11	22.989769
strontium	Sr	38	87.62
sulfur	S	16	32.07
tantalum	Ta	73	180.9479
technetium	Tc	43	(98)
tellurium	Te	52	127.60
terbium	Tb	65	158.92535
thallium	Tl	81	204.3833
thorium	Th	90	(232)
thulium	Tm	69	168.93421
tin	Sn	50	118.71
titanium	Ti	22	47.867
tungsten	W	74	183.84
uranium	U	92	(238)
vanadium	V	23	50.9415
xenon	Xe	54	131.29
ytterbium	Yb	70	173.04
yttrium	Y	39	88.90585
zinc	Zn	30	65.39
zirconium	Zr	40	91.224

[1] Weights are based on the naturally occurring isotope compositions and scaled to $^{12}C = 12$. For elements lacking stable isotopes, the mass number of the most stable nuclide is shown in parentheses.

el·e·men·tal \ˌel-ə-ˈment-ᵊl\ *adj* **1 a** : of, relating to, or being an element; *esp* : existing as an uncombined chemical element **b** : ELEMENTARY 1 **2** : of, relating to, or resembling a force of nature — **el·e·men·tal·ly** \-ˈment-ᵊl-ē\ *adv*
el·e·men·ta·ry \ˌel-ə-ˈment-ə-rē, -ˈmen-trē\ *adj* **1** : of or relating to the simplest principles of a subject **2** : of, relating to, or teaching the basic subjects of education
elementary particle *n* : any of the particles (as electrons or photons) of matter and energy that are smaller than atoms and do not appear to be made up of a combination of more basic things
el·e·phant \ˈel-ə-fənt\ *n* : any of a family of huge thickset nearly hairless mammals that have the snout lengthened into a trunk and two incisors in the upper jaw developed into long outward-curving pointed ivory tusks and that include two living forms: **a** : one with large ears that occurs in tropical Africa **b** : one with relatively small ears that occurs in forests of southeastern Asia

elephant: *left* African, *right* Asian

elephant grass *n* : an Old World cattail used especially in making baskets
el·e·phan·ti·a·sis \ˌel-ə-fən-ˈtī-ə-səs, -ˌfan-\ *n* : the enormous enlargement of an arm or a leg or of the scrotum that is caused by blocking of the vessels carrying lymph by nematode worms

\ə\ **abut**	\au̇\ **out**	\i\ **tip**	\ȯ\ **saw**	\u̇\ **foot**
\ər\ **further**	\ch\ **chin**	\ī\ **life**	\ȯi\ **coin**	\y\ **yet**
\a\ **mat**	\e\ **pet**	\j\ **job**	\th\ **thin**	\yü\ **few**
\ā\ **take**	\ē\ **easy**	\ŋ\ **sing**	\th\ **this**	\yu̇\ **cure**
\ä\ **cot, cart**	\g\ **go**	\ō\ **bone**	\ü\ **food**	\zh\ **vision**

el·e·phan·tine \ˌel-ə-ˈfan-ˌtēn, -ˌtīn, ˈel-ə-fən-\ *adj* **1 a** : very big : HUGE, MASSIVE **b** : lacking grace **2** : of or relating to an elephant

el·e·vate \ˈel-ə-ˌvāt\ *vb* **-vat·ed; -vat·ing 1** : to lift up or make higher : RAISE **2** : to raise in rank or importance **3** : to improve the mind or spirits of [Latin *elevatus,* past participle of *elevare* "to lift up," from *e-* "away" and *levare* "to raise" — related to LEVER]

¹el·e·vat·ed \ˈel-ə-ˌvāt-əd\ *adj* **1** : raised especially above the ground ⟨*elevated* highway⟩ **2 a** : being on a high level ⟨an *elevated* mind⟩ **b** : DIGNIFIED, FORMAL ⟨*elevated* language⟩

²elevated *n* : EL

el·e·va·tion \ˌel-ə-ˈvā-shən\ *n* **1 a** : the height to which something is raised **b** : the height above sea level : ALTITUDE **2** : an act or instance of elevating **3** : an elevated place (as a hill) **4** : the quality or state of being elevated **synonyms** see HEIGHT

el·e·va·tor \ˈel-ə-ˌvāt-ər\ *n* **1 a** : a continuous belt or chain conveyor for raising material **b** : a cage or platform and its hoisting machinery for carrying things or people to different levels **c** : a building for elevating, storing, unloading, and sometimes grinding grain — called also *grain elevator* **2** : a movable device shaped like a wing that is usually attached to the tail of an airplane for producing motion up or down

elev·en \i-ˈlev-ən\ *n* **1** — see NUMBER table **2** : the eleventh in a set or series **3** : something having 11 units or members — **eleven** *adj or pron* — **elev·enth** \-ən(t)th\ *n* — **eleventh** *adj or adv*

elf \ˈelf\ *n, pl* **elves** \ˈelvz\ : a small and often mischievous fairy — **elf·ish** \ˈel-fish\ *adj* — **elf·ish·ly** *adv*

elf·in \ˈel-fən\ *adj* **1** : of or relating to elves **2** : resembling an elf; *esp* : having a strange beauty or charm

elf owl *n* : a very small insect-eating owl that rests, sleeps, and nests in the holes of trees and saguaro cacti of desert areas of the southwestern U.S. and northern Mexico

elic·it \i-ˈlis-ət\ *vb* : to draw out often by skillful questioning or discussion ⟨*elicit* the truth from an unwilling witness⟩ — **elic·i·ta·tion** \i-ˌli-sə-ˈtā-shən\ *n* — **elic·i·tor** \i-ˈli-sə-tər\ *n*

el·i·gi·ble \ˈel-ə-jə-bəl\ *adj* : qualified to be chosen or to participate ⟨*eligible* to be president⟩ ⟨*eligible* to retire⟩ — **el·i·gi·bil·i·ty** \ˌel-ə-jə-ˈbil-ət-ē\ *n* — **eligible** *n* — **el·i·gi·bly** \ˈel-ə-jə-blē\ *adv*

elim·i·nate \i-ˈlim-ə-ˌnāt\ *vb* **-nat·ed; -nat·ing 1 a** : to get rid of : REMOVE ⟨*eliminate* the causes of an epidemic⟩ **b** : to remove from further competition by defeating ⟨a team *eliminated* in the first round⟩ **2** : to expel from the living body — **elim·i·na·tive** \-ˌnāt-iv\ *adj* — **elim·i·na·tor** \-ˌnāt-ər\ *n*

elim·i·na·tion \i-ˌlim-ə-ˈnā-shən\ *n* : the act or process of eliminating or emptying: as **a** : the act of excreting or emptying waste products from the body **b** : the act or process of excluding from a match, game, or contest the losers of any round or heat

elite \ā-ˈlēt, i-\ *n* **1** : the part or group having the highest quality or importance **2** : a small powerful group of people — **elite** *adj*

elix·ir \i-ˈlik-sər\ *n* **1 a** : a substance held to be capable of changing metals into gold **b** : a substance held to be capable of extending life **c** : CURE-ALL **2** : a sweetened usually alcoholic liquid containing medicine

Eliz·a·be·than \i-ˌliz-ə-ˈbē-thən\ *adj* : of, relating to, or suggesting Elizabeth I of England or her time — **Elizabethan** *n*

elk \ˈelk\ *n, pl* **elk** *or* **elks 1** : MOOSE — used for one of Europe or Asia **2** : a large deer of North Amer-

elk 2

ica, Europe, Asia, and northwestern Africa that has large curved antlers with many branches and that lives in herds — called also *red deer, wapiti*

¹ell \ˈel\ *n* : a former English unit of length for cloth equal to 45 inches (1.1 meters)

²ell *n* : a part of a building that extends at right angles to the main part

el·lipse \i-ˈlips, e-\ *n* : an oval shape that is a conic section

el·lip·sis \i-ˈlip-səs, e-\ *n, pl* **-lip·ses** \-ˈlip-ˌsēz\ **1** : the leaving out of one or more words that are not necessary for a phrase to be understood ⟨"begin when ready" for "begin when you are ready" is an example of *ellipsis*⟩ **2** : marks or a mark (as . . .) used to indicate that something (as words) has been left out

el·lip·tic \i-ˈlip-tik, e-\ *or* **el·lip·ti·cal** \-ti-kəl\ *adj* **1** : having the shape of an ellipse **2** : of, relating to, or marked by ellipsis — **el·lip·ti·cal·ly** \-ti-k(ə-)lē\ *adv*

elm \ˈelm\ *n* **1** : any of a genus of large deciduous trees that have toothed leaves and nearly circular one-seeded winged fruits and are often grown as shade trees; *esp* : AMERICAN ELM **2** : the wood of an elm

El Ni·ño \el-ˈnē-nyō\ *n, pl* **El Niños** : an irregularly occurring flow of unusually warm surface water along the western coast of South America that disrupts the normal regional and global weather patterns — compare LA NIÑA [Spanish, "the child" (referring to the Christ child); from the appearance of the flow at the Christmas season]

el·o·cu·tion \ˌel-ə-ˈkyü-shən\ *n* **1** : a style of speaking especially in public **2** : the art of effective public speaking — **el·o·cu·tion·ary** \-shə-ˌner-ē\ *adj* — **el·o·cu·tion·ist** \-sh(ə-)nəst\ *n*

elo·dea \i-ˈlōd-ē-ə\ *n* : any of a small genus of American herbs with leafy stems that live underwater

¹elon·gate \i-ˈlȯn-ˌgāt\ *vb* **-gat·ed; -gat·ing** : to make or grow longer — **elon·ga·tion** \(ˌ)ē-ˌlȯn-ˈgā-shən\ *n*

²elongate *or* **elon·gat·ed** \i-ˈlȯn-ˌgāt-əd\ *adj* : stretched out; *esp* : being much greater in length than in width

elope \i-ˈlōp\ *vb* **eloped; elop·ing** : to run away secretly especially to get married without parental consent — **elope·ment** \-mənt\ *n* — **elop·er** *n*

el·o·quence \ˈel-ə-kwən(t)s\ *n* : speech or writing that is forceful and convincing; *also* : the art or power of speaking or writing in a forceful and convincing way

el·o·quent \ˈel-ə-kwənt\ *adj* **1** : having or showing clear and forceful expression ⟨an *eloquent* speaker⟩ ⟨an *eloquent* essay⟩ **2** : clearly showing some feeling or meaning ⟨an *eloquent* look⟩ — **el·o·quent·ly** *adv*

¹else \ˈels\ *adv* **1** : in a different or additional manner or place or at a different time ⟨how *else* could it be done⟩ ⟨where *else* can we meet⟩ **2** : if the facts are or were different : if not : OTHERWISE ⟨leave or *else* you'll be sorry⟩

²else *adj* **1** : being different in identity ⟨somebody *else*⟩ **2** : being in addition ⟨what *else*⟩

else·where \ˈels-ˌ(h)we(ə)r, -ˌ(h)wa(ə)r\ *adv* : in or to another place ⟨took my buiness *elsewhere*⟩

elu·ci·date \i-ˈlü-sə-ˌdāt\ *vb* **-dat·ed; -dat·ing** : to make clear or plain : EXPLAIN — **elu·ci·da·tion** \i-ˌlü-sə-ˈdā-shən\ *n* — **elu·ci·da·tive** \i-ˈlü-sə-ˌdāt-iv\ *adj* — **elu·ci·da·tor** \-ˌdāt-ər\ *n*

elude \ē-ˈlüd\ *vb* **elud·ed; elud·ing 1** : to avoid or escape by being quick, skillful, or tricky **2** : to escape the understanding or grasp of ⟨the explanation *eludes* me⟩

elu·sive \ē-ˈlü-siv, -ziv\ *adj* **1** : hard to find or capture : EVASIVE ⟨*elusive* prey⟩ **2** : hard to understand or define ⟨an *elusive* idea⟩ — **elu·sive·ly** *adv* — **elu·sive·ness** *n*

el·ver \ˈel-vər\ *n* : a young eel

elves *plural of* ELF

elv·ish \ˈel-vish\ *adj* : MISCHIEVOUS 2, 3

Ely·si·um \i-ˈlizh-ē-əm, -ˈliz-\ *n* : a place or condition of ideal happiness : PARADISE [derived from Greek *Ēlysion,* name in mythology of a place for the dead] — **Ely·sian** \-ˈlizh-ən\ *adj*

el·y·tron \'el-ə-ˌträn\ *also* **el·y·trum** \-trəm\ *n, pl* **-tra** \-trə\ : one of the thick modified front wings in beetles and some other insects that protect the hind pair of wings that are used for flying

em- — see EN-

ema·ci·ate \i-'mā-shē-ˌāt\ *vb* **-at·ed; -at·ing** : to cause to lose flesh so as to become very thin — **ema·ci·a·tion** \-ˌmā-shē-'ā-shən, -sē-\ *n*

e-mail \'ē-ˌmāl\ *n* **1** : a system for sending messages between computers **2 a** : messages sent through an e-mail system ⟨receives a lot of *e-mail*⟩ **b** : an e-mail message ⟨sent him an *e-mail*⟩ — **e-mail** *vb* — **e-mail·er** \-ˌmāl-ər\ *n*

em·a·nate \'em-ə-ˌnāt\ *vb* **-nat·ed; -nat·ing** **1** : to come out from a source ⟨a scent *emanating* from the flowers⟩ **2** : EMIT 1a, GIVE OUT ⟨seems to *emanate* confidence⟩ — **em·a·na·tion** \ˌem-ə-'nā-shən\ *n* — **em·a·na·tion·al** \-shnəl, -shən-ᵊl\ *adj* — **em·a·na·tive** \'em-ə-ˌnāt-iv\ *adj*

eman·ci·pate \i-'man(t)-sə-ˌpāt\ *vb* **-pat·ed; -pat·ing** : to free from someone else's control or power; *esp* : to free from slavery — **eman·ci·pa·tion** \-ˌman(t)-sə-'pā-shən\ *n* — **eman·ci·pa·tor** \-'man(t)-sə-ˌpāt-ər\ *n* — **eman·ci·pa·tory** \-'man(t)-sə-pə-ˌtōr-ē, -ˌtòr-ē\ *adj*

emas·cu·late \i-'mas-kyə-ˌlāt\ *vb* **-lat·ed; -lat·ing** **1** : to deprive of masculine strength or spirit : WEAKEN **2** : CASTRATE — **emas·cu·la·tion** \-ˌmas-kyə-'lā-shən\ *n* — **emas·cu·la·tor** \-'mas-kyə-ˌlāt-ər\ *n*

em·balm \im-'bä(l)m\ *vb* : to treat a dead body with special preparations to preserve it from decay — **em·balm·er** *n* — **em·balm·ment** \-mənt\ *n*

em·bank \im-'baŋk\ *vb* : to enclose by an embankment

em·bank·ment \im-'baŋk-mənt\ *n* : a raised bank or wall to carry a roadway, prevent floods, or hold back water

em·bar·go \im-'bär-gō\ *n, pl* **-goes** **1** : an order of a government prohibiting commercial ships from leaving its ports **2** : legal prohibition or restriction of trade **3** : an informal or unofficial stoppage : IMPEDIMENT; *esp* : PROHIBITION **2** — **embargo** *vb*

em·bark \im-'bärk\ *vb* **1** : to go or put on board a ship or airplane **2** : to begin some task or project ⟨*embark* on a career⟩ — **em·bar·ka·tion** \ˌem-ˌbär-'kā-shən\ *n* — **em·bark·ment** \im-'bärk-mənt\ *n*

em·bar·rass \im-'bar-əs\ *vb* **1** : to cause to feel self-consciously confused or distressed ⟨unexpected laughter *embarrassed* the speaker⟩ **2** : to restrict the movement of : HINDER, IMPEDE **3** : to involve in financial difficulties — **em·bar·rass·ing·ly** \-'bar-ə-siŋ-lē\ *adv*

synonyms EMBARRASS, DISCONCERT, ABASH mean to make upset, uncomfortable, or confused in one's emotions. EMBARRASS suggests a feeling of uneasiness or discomfort ⟨*embarrassed* to see my relatives in the audience⟩. DISCONCERT suggests emotional upset or confusion from a strong and direct source ⟨street noises *disconcert* me during piano practice⟩. ABASH suggests a complete loss of self-control (as from feelings of guilt or inferiority) ⟨was *abashed* by their haughty behavior⟩.

em·bar·rass·ment \im-'bar-əs-mənt\ *n* **1 a** : something that embarrasses ⟨the scandal was a terrible *embarrassment*⟩ **b** : an overly large quantity from which to select — used especially in the phrase *embarrassment of riches* **2** : the state of being embarrassed ⟨blushed with *embarrassment*⟩

em·bas·sy \'em-bə-sē\ *n, pl* **-sies** **1** : a group of representatives headed by an ambassador **2** : the position, role, or business of an ambassador **3** : the residence or office of an ambassador

em·bat·tle \im-'bat-ᵊl\ *vb* **em·bat·tled; em·bat·tling** \-'bat-liŋ, -ᵊl-iŋ\ **1** : to arrange in order of battle : prepare for battle **2** : FORTIFY a

embattled *adj* : engaged in battle or conflict

em·bed *also* **im·bed** \im-'bed\ *vb* **em·bed·ded** *also* **im·bed·ded; em·bed·ding** *also* **im·bed·ding** **1** : to enclose in or as if in a surrounding mass : set solidly in or as if in

a bed ⟨*embed* a post in concrete⟩ **2** : to prepare (material for use under a microscope) for cutting by infiltrating with and enclosing in a supporting substance (as paraffin)

em·bel·lish \im-'bel-ish\ *vb* : to make beautiful with ornamentation : DECORATE ⟨a book *embellished* with pictures⟩ **synonyms** see ADORN — **em·bel·lish·ment** \-mənt\ *n*

em·ber \'em-bər\ *n* : a glowing piece of coal or wood from a fire; *esp* : such a piece smoldering in ashes

em·bez·zle \im-'bez-əl\ *vb* **-bez·zled; -bez·zling** \-(ə-)liŋ\ : to take (property entrusted to one's care) dishonestly for one's own use ⟨*embezzled* thousands of dollars⟩ — **em·bez·zle·ment** \-əl-mənt\ *n* — **em·bez·zler** \-(ə-)lər\ *n*

em·bit·ter \im-'bit-ər\ *vb* : to make bitter; *esp* : to cause bitter feeling in — **em·bit·ter·ment** \-mənt\ *n*

em·bla·zon \im-'blāz-ᵊn\ *vb* **1** : to inscribe or decorate with markings or emblems used in heraldry **2** : CELEBRATE **3**, EXTOL ⟨a name *emblazoned* in history⟩

em·blem \'em-bləm\ *n* **1** : an object or likeness used to suggest a thing that cannot be pictured ⟨the flag is the *emblem* of our nation⟩ **2** : a device, symbol, design, or figure used as an identifying mark ⟨the club's *emblem*⟩ **synonyms** EMBLEM, TOKEN, SYMBOL mean a sign for something else. EMBLEM applies to an object or picture that is commonly understood to stand for an idea ⟨the bald eagle is an *emblem* of the United States⟩. TOKEN applies to an act, gesture, or object that is taken as a sign of sentiment ⟨please accept this watch as a *token* of our appreciation⟩. SYMBOL applies to anything that is understood as a sign of something else ⟨the lion is the *symbol* of courage⟩.

em·blem·at·ic \ˌem-blə-'mat-ik\ *also* **em·blem·at·i·cal** \-'mat-i-kəl\ *adj* : of, relating to, or serving as an emblem : SYMBOLIC

em·bod·i·ment \im-'bäd-i-mənt\ *n* **1** : the act of embodying : the state of being embodied **2** : one that embodies something

em·body \im-'bäd-ē\ *vb* **-bod·ied; -body·ing** **1** : to give definite form to ⟨*embodied* her ideas in suitable words⟩ **2** : to cause to become a body or a part of a body or system ⟨the Constitution *embodies* the fundamental laws of the United States⟩ **3** : to represent in visible form ⟨a leader who *embodies* courage⟩ — **em·bod·i·er** *n*

em·bold·en \im-'bōl-dən\ *vb* : to make bold

em·bo·lism \'em-bə-ˌliz-əm\ *n* **1** : the sudden blocking of a blood vessel by an embolus **2** : EMBOLUS

em·bo·lus \'em-bə-ləs\ *n, pl* **-li** \-ˌlī\ : an abnormal particle (as an air bubble) circulating in the blood — compare THROMBUS

em·bos·om \im-'bùz-əm\ *vb* : to shelter closely : ENCLOSE

em·boss \im-'bäs, -'bòs\ *vb* : to decorate with a raised pattern or design — **em·boss·er** *n* — **em·boss·ment** \-mənt\ *n*

em·bow·er \im-'baù(-ə)r\ *vb* : to shelter or enclose in or as if in a shelter of tree branches

¹**em·brace** \im-'brās\ *vb* **em·braced; em·brac·ing** **1** : to clasp in the arms : HUG **2** : to enclose on all sides ⟨low hills *embraced* the valley⟩ **3 a** : to take up readily or gladly ⟨*embrace* a cause⟩ **b** : to make use of : WELCOME ⟨*embrace* an opportunity⟩ **4** : TAKE IN 4, INCLUDE — **em·brace·able** \-'brā-sə-bəl\ *adj* — **em·brac·er** *n*

Word History One of the meanings of the English word *brace* is "two of a kind," as in "a brace of quail." In early French, however, the word *brace*, from which we get our English words *brace* and *embrace*, had a more limited meaning of "two arms." The early French *brace* came from the plural form of the Latin word *bracchium*,

\ə\ **abut**	\aù\ **out**	\i\ **tip**	\ò\ **saw**	\ù\ **foot**
\ər\ **further**	\ch\ **chin**	\ī\ **life**	\òi\ **coin**	\y\ **yet**
\a\ **mat**	\e\ **pet**	\j\ **job**	\th\ **thin**	\yü\ **few**
\ā\ **take**	\ē\ **easy**	\ŋ\ **sing**	\th\ **this**	\yù\ **cure**
\ä\ **cot, cart**	\g\ **go**	\ō\ **bone**	\ü\ **food**	\zh\ **vision**

meaning "arm." When combined with the early French prefix *em-*, meaning "to put into," the word formed the verb *embracer*, which meant literally "to put into the two arms"; in other words, "to hug." In time the word was borrowed into English and became *embrace*. [early French *embracer* "to hug, embrace," literally, "to put into the two arms," from *em-* "into" and *brace* "two arms," derived from Latin *bracchium* "arm" — related to ¹BRACE, BRACELET]

²**embrace** *n* : a close encircling with the arms : HUG

em·bra·sure \im-'brā-zhər\ *n* **1** : an opening with sides slanting outward in a wall or parapet for the firing of cannon **2** : an opening in a wall for a door or window

em·broi·der \im-'bròid-ər\ *vb* **em·broi·dered; em·broi·der·ing** \-(ə-)riŋ\ **1** : to make or fill in a design with needlework **2** : to decorate with needlework **3** : to add to the interest of (as a story) with details or by exaggerating — **em·broi·der·er** \-ər-ər\ *n*

em·broi·dery \im-'bròid-(ə-)rē\ *n, pl* **-der·ies 1** : the process or art of embroidering **2** : needlework done to decorate cloth

E embrasure 2

em·broil \im-'bròi(ə)l\ *vb* **1** : to throw into disorder or confusion **2** : to involve in conflict or difficulties ⟨*embroiled* in a lawsuit⟩ — **em·broil·ment** \-mənt\ *n*

em·bryo \'em-brē-‚ō\ *n, pl* **-bry·os 1** : an animal in the early stages of development that are marked by cleavage, the laying down of the basic tissues, and the formation of primitive organs and organ systems — compare FETUS **2** : a tiny young plant within a seed **3** : a beginning or undeveloped stage — used especially in the phrase *in embryo*

em·bry·ol·o·gist \‚em-brē-'äl-ə-jəst\ *n* : a person who specializes in embryology

em·bry·ol·o·gy \‚em-brē-'äl-ə-jē\ *n* **1** : a branch of biology dealing with embryos and their development **2** : the facts and events characteristic of the development of an embryo — **em·bry·o·log·i·cal** \‚em-brē-ə-'läj-i-kəl\ *adj* — **em·bry·o·log·i·cal·ly** \-i-k(ə-)lē\ *adv*

em·bry·on·ic \‚em-brē-'än-ik\ *adj* **1** : of or relating to an embryo **2** : being in an early or undeveloped stage : being in embryo ⟨an *embryonic* plan⟩ — **em·bry·on·i·cal·ly** \-i-k(ə-)lē\ *adv*

embryo sac *n* : the individual that produces female germ cells in the sexually reproducing generation of a seed plant and that consists of a thin-walled sac containing the egg nucleus and other nuclei which form tissue used for food upon fertilization

¹**em·cee** \'em-'sē\ *n* : MASTER OF CEREMONIES [an altered form of *M.C.*, from *m*aster of *c*eremonies]

²**emcee** *vb* **em·ceed; em·cee·ing** : to act as master of ceremonies for something : HOST ⟨*emcee* a television show⟩

emend \ē-'mend\ *vb* : to correct usually by changing the wording of ⟨*emend* a text⟩ — **emen·da·tion** \‚ē-‚men-'dā-shən, ‚em-ən-\ *n*

¹**em·er·ald** \'em-(ə-)rəld\ *n* : a rich green gem

²**emerald** *adj* : brightly or richly green

emerge \i-'mərj\ *vb* **emerged; emerg·ing 1** : to become known or apparent ⟨the facts *emerged*⟩ **2** : to rise from or as if from a fluid : come out into view ⟨a diver *emerging* from the ocean⟩

emer·gence \i-'mər-jən(t)s\ *n* : the act or an instance of emerging

emer·gen·cy \i-'mər-jən-sē\ *n, pl* **-cies 1** : an unexpected situation that calls for immediate action **2** : an urgent need for help ⟨a state of *emergency*⟩

emergency room *n* : a hospital room or area with doctors, nurses, and medical equipment for treating persons needing immediate medical care

emer·i·tus \i-'mer-ət-əs\ *adj* : retired with an honorary title from an office or position ⟨professor *emeritus*⟩ — **emeritus** *n*

em·ery \'em-(ə-)rē\ *n, pl* **em·er·ies** : a dark mineral used in the form of powder or grains for polishing and grinding

emery board *n* : a nail file made of cardboard covered with powdered emery

emet·ic \i-'met-ik\ *n* : something (as a chemical) that causes vomiting — **emetic** *adj*

em·i·grant \'em-i-grənt\ *n* **1** : one that emigrates **2** : a migrant plant or animal — **emigrant** *adj*

em·i·grate \'em-ə-‚grāt\ *vb* **-grat·ed; -grat·ing** : to leave a country or region to live elsewhere — **em·i·gra·tion** \‚em-ə-'grā-shən\ *n*

émi·gré *also* **emi·gré** \'em-i-‚grā, ‚em-i-'grā\ *n* : EMIGRANT 1; *esp* : a person forced to emigrate for political reasons [French]

em·i·nence \'em-ə-nən(t)s\ *n* **1** : the condition of being eminent **2 a** : a person of high rank or achievements — often used as a title for a cardinal **b** : an area of high ground : HEIGHT

em·i·nent \'em-ə-nənt\ *adj* : standing above others especially in rank, worth, or achievement ⟨an *eminent* physician⟩ — **em·i·nent·ly** *adv*

eminent domain *n* : a right of a government to take private property for public use

emir \i-'mi(ə)r, ā-\ *n* : a ruler, chief, or commander in Islamic countries [from Arabic *amīr* "commander"]

emir·ate \'em-ə-rət, -‚rāt\ *n* : the state or jurisdiction of an emir

em·is·sary \'em-ə-‚ser-ē\ *n, pl* **-sar·ies** : a person sent on a mission to represent another

emis·sion \ē-'mish-ən\ *n* **1** : an act or instance of emitting **2** : something emitted or discharged — **emis·sive** \ē-'mis-iv\ *adj*

emit \ē-'mit\ *vb* **emit·ted; emit·ting 1 a** : to throw or give off or out ⟨*emit* light⟩ **b** : to send out : EJECT **2** : ²UTTER 1 ⟨*emit* a groan⟩ [from Latin *emittere* "to send out," from *e-, ex-* "out, forth" and *mittere* "to send, throw" — related to DISMISS, MESSAGE, MISSILE, TRANSMIT]

em·mer \'em-ər\ *n* : an ancient wheat having spikelets with two hard red kernels

emol·u·ment \i-'mäl-yə-mənt\ *n* : profit from one's job or from an office held : SALARY, WAGES

emote \i-'mōt\ *vb* **emot·ed; emot·ing** : to give expression to emotion in or as if in a play — **emot·er** \-'mōt-ər\ *n*

emo·ti·con \i-'mō-ti-‚kän\ *n* : a group of characters (as :-) for a smile) that suggests an attitude or facial expression

emo·tion \i-'mō-shən\ *n* **1** : strong feeling : EXCITEMENT **2** : a mental reaction (as anger or fear) marked by strong feeling and usually causing physical effects

emo·tion·al \i-'mō-shnəl, -shən-əl\ *adj* **1** : of or relating to the emotions ⟨an *emotional* upset⟩ **2** : likely to show or express emotion : easily moved ⟨an *emotional* person⟩ **3** : causing one to feel emotion ⟨an *emotional* speech⟩ — **emo·tion·al·ly** \-ē\ *adv*

empanel *variant of* IMPANEL

em·pa·thy \'em-pə-thē\ *n* : a being aware of and sharing another person's feelings, experiences, and emotions; *also* : the ability for this

em·per·or \'em-pər-ər, -prər\ *n* : the ruler of an empire

Word History The word *emperor* is a general word for a ruler having total control of a country or region. There are similar words for such all-powerful rulers in various countries: the *Caesars* in ancient Rome, the *czars* in Russia, the *kaisers* in Germany. All these terms go back to one source: the first of the emperors of the Roman lands, known as Imperator Caesar Augustus. Augustus (whose name was really a title, meaning "honorable") was the adopted son of the great Roman general and ruler Julius Caesar. Augustus took the family name Caesar as part of his official name. Later emperors of Rome also used the name *Caesar* to show that they were heirs to the throne. This is how the word *Caesar* came to be used to mean "an emperor of Rome." The word *Caesar* was spelled *kaisar* and later *kaiser* in the Germanic languages of Europe. It is from this word that we got our English word *kaiser* for "a ruler in Germany." Through the Russian word *tsar'*, which also came from the Germanic word *kaisar*, we got our English word *czar*, meaning "a ruler in Russia." Use of the word *emperor* itself can also be traced back to Imperator Caesar Augustus. The Latin word *imperator* was originally a title given to great Roman generals. The word meant "commander," and it was derived from the verb *imperare* "to command." It is because Augustus, the first Roman emperor, used *imperator* as a title that we use *emperor* as we do today. [Middle English *emperour* "emperor," from early French *emperur* (same meaning), from Latin *imperator* "commander" (title assumed by Caesar Augustus), from *imperare* "to command"]

em·pha·sis \'em(p)-fə-səs\ *n, pl* **-pha·ses** \-fə-,sēz\ **1 a** : forcefulness of expression ⟨spoke with *emphasis*⟩ **b** : the act or fact of giving stress to a word or syllable when speaking **2** : special attention or importance given to something ⟨put great *emphasis* on cleanliness⟩

em·pha·size \'em(p)-fə-,sīz\ *vb* **-sized; -siz·ing** : to place emphasis on : stress as being important or so as to stand out

em·phat·ic \im-'fat-ik, em-\ *adj* **1** : uttered with or marked by emphasis **2** : tending to express oneself in forceful speech or action **3** : attracting special attention ⟨an *emphatic* design⟩ — **em·phat·i·cal·ly** \-'fat-i-k(ə-)lē\ *adv*

em·phy·se·ma \,em(p)-fə-'zē-mə, -'sē-\ *n* : a condition marked by abnormal enlargement of the air spaces of the lungs, shortness of breath, and often by faulty heart action

em·pire \'em-,pī(ə)r\ *n* **1 a** : a major political unit with a large territory or a number of territories or peoples under one ruler with total authority; *esp* : one having an emperor as chief of state **b** : the territory of such a unit **c** : something resembling an empire; *esp* : a large group of businesses under one control **2** : the state of being under or of having complete rule or control

em·pir·i·cal \im-'pir-i-kəl, em-\ *also* **em·pir·ic** \-'pir-ik\ *adj* **1** : relying on experience or observation usually without regard for a system and theory ⟨*empirical* medicine⟩ **2** : based on observation or experience ⟨*empirical* data⟩ **3** : capable of being proved or disproved by observation or experiment ⟨*empirical* laws⟩ — **em·pir·i·cal·ly** \-'pir-i-k(ə-)lē\ *adv*

empirical formula *n* : a chemical formula showing the simplest ratio of elements in a compound rather than the total number of atoms in the molecule

em·pir·i·cism \im-'pir-ə-,siz-əm, em-\ *n* **1** : the practice of relying on observation and experiment in the natural sciences **2** : a theory that knowledge begins with experience — **em·pir·i·cist** \-səst\ *n or adj*

em·place \im-'plās\ *vb* : to put into place

em·place·ment \im-'plās-mənt\ *n* **1** : a prepared position for weapons **2** : a putting into position : PLACEMENT

¹em·ploy \im-'plȯi\ *vb* **1** : to make use of : USE **2 a** : to use or obtain the services of ⟨*employ* a lawyer to draw up a will⟩ **b** : to provide with a job that pays wages or a salary ⟨*employ* a staff of twenty⟩ **3** : to use or direct toward a particular goal ⟨*employ* all of your energies to getting the job done⟩ — **em·ploy·able** \-ə-bəl\ *adj*

²employ *n* : employment especially for wages or a salary ⟨generous to people in their *employ*⟩

em·ploy·ee \im-,plȯi-'ē, (,)em-; im-'plȯi-,ē, em-\ *n* : one who works for another for wages or a salary

em·ploy·er \im-'plȯi(-ə)r\ *n* : one that employs others

em·ploy·ment \im-'plȯi-mənt\ *n* **1** : ¹USE 1a, PURPOSE; *also* : the act of using **2 a** : the act of hiring a person for work **b** : the job for which one is hired : OCCUPATION **c** : the state of being employed ⟨*employment* in the machine trade⟩ **d** : the relative number of persons in a labor force who are employed ⟨*employment* is high⟩

employment agency *n* : a company whose business is to find jobs for certain people and to find people suitable for certain jobs

em·po·ri·um \im-'pōr-ē-əm, em-, -'pȯr-\ *n, pl* **-ri·ums** *also* **-ria** \-ē-ə\ **1 a** : MARKETPLACE **b** : a center of business activity **2** : a store carrying a wide variety of merchandise

em·pow·er \im-'pau̇(-ə)r\ *vb* : to give official authority or legal power to

em·press \'em-prəs\ *n* **1** : the wife or widow of an emperor **2** : a woman who is the ruler of an empire

¹emp·ty \'em(p)-tē\ *adj* **emp·ti·er; -est** **1** : containing nothing ⟨an *empty* box⟩ **2** : not being lived in ⟨an *empty* house⟩ **3** : having no reality or importance ⟨*empty* dreams⟩ **4** : lacking in value, sense, effect, or sincerity ⟨*empty* threats⟩ **5** : HUNGRY 1 ⟨feel *empty* before dinner⟩ **6** : having no members ⟨*empty* set⟩ — **emp·ti·ly** \-tə-lē\ *adv* — **emp·ti·ness** \-tē-nəs\ *n*

²empty *vb* **emp·tied; emp·ty·ing** **1** : to make empty : remove the contents of ⟨*empty* a barrel⟩ **2** : to remove all of from a container ⟨*empty* flour from a bag⟩ **3** : to become empty ⟨the theater *emptied* quickly⟩ **4** : to give forth contents (as fluid) : DISCHARGE ⟨the river *empties* into the ocean⟩

³empty *n, pl* **emp·ties** : an empty container

emp·ty–hand·ed \,em(p)-tē-'han-dəd\ *adj* **1** : having nothing in the hands **2** : having acquired or gained nothing ⟨came back *empty-handed*⟩

em·pur·ple \im-'pər-pəl\ *vb* **em·pur·pled; em·pur·pling** \-'pər-p(ə-)liŋ\ : to tinge or color purple

em·py·re·an \,em-,pī-'rē-ən, -pə-; em-'pir-ē-ən, -'pī-rē-ən\ *n* **1** : the highest heaven or heavenly sphere **2** : SKY 1, HEAVENS — **em·py·re·al** \-əl\ *adj* — **empyrean** *adj*

EMT \,ē-(,)em-'tē\ *n* : a person specially trained to provide basic emergency medical care before and during the trip to a hospital [*emergency medical technician*]

emu \'ē-myü\ *n* : a swift-running Australian bird with undeveloped wings that is related to but smaller than the ostrich

em·u·late \'em-yə-,lāt\ *vb* **-lat·ed; -lat·ing** : to try to be like or better than — **em·u·la·tor** \-,lāt-ər\ *n*

em·u·la·tion \,em-yə-'lā-shən\ *n* : the ambition or effort to emulate — **em·u·la·tive** \'em-yə-,lāt-iv\ *adj*

em·u·lous \'em-yə-ləs\ *adj* : eager or ambitious to emulate someone or something — **em·u·lous·ly** *adv* — **em·u·lous·ness** *n*

emu

emul·si·fi·er \i-'məl-sə-,fī(-ə)r\ *n* : a substance (as a soap) that helps to form and stabilize an emulsion

emul·si·fy \i-'məl-sə-,fī\ *vb* **-fied; -fy·ing** : to change (as an oil) into an emulsion — **emul·si·fi·able** \-,fī-ə-bəl\ *adj* — **emul·si·fi·ca·tion** \i-,məl-sə-fə-'kā-shən\ *n*

emul·sion \i-'məl-shən\ *n* : a material consisting of a mixture of liquids that do not dissolve in each other and having droplets of one liquid scattered throughout the other ⟨an *emulsion* of oil in water⟩

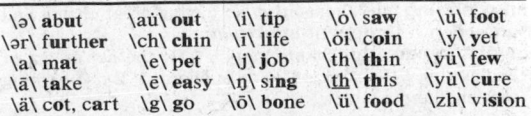

\ə\ abut	\au̇\ out	\i\ tip	\ȯ\ saw	\u̇\ foot	
\ər\ further	\ch\ chin	\ī\ life	\ȯi\ coin	\y\ yet	
\a\ mat	\e\ pet	\j\ job	\th\ thin	\yü\ few	
\ā\ take	\ē\ easy	\ŋ\ sing	\th\ this	\yu̇\ cure	
\ä\ cot, cart	\g\ go	\ō\ bone	\ü\ food	\zh\ vision	

en- *also* **em-** \e *also occurs in these prefixes although only* i *may be shown as in "engage"*\ *prefix* **1** : put into or onto ⟨en*code*⟩ ⟨en*throne*⟩ : go into or onto ⟨en*plane*⟩ **2** : cause to be ⟨en*slave*⟩ **3** : provide with ⟨em*power*⟩ **4** : so as to cover ⟨en*wrap*⟩ : thoroughly ⟨en*tangle*⟩ — in all senses usually *em-* before *b, m,* or *p* [derived from Latin *in-* "in, into, put into"]

¹**-en** \ən\ *also* **-n** \n\ *adj suffix* : made of : consisting of ⟨earth*en*⟩ ⟨wool*en*⟩ [Old English *-en* (adjective suffix)]

²**-en** *vb suffix* **1** : become or cause to be ⟨sharp*en*⟩ **2** : cause or come to have ⟨length*en*⟩ [Old English *-nian* (verb suffix)]

en·able \in-'ā-bəl\ *vb* **en·abled; en·abling** \-b(ə-)liŋ\ **1 a** : to make able ⟨glasses *enable* you to read⟩ **b** : to make possible, practical, or easy **2** : to give legal power or permission to

en·act \in-'akt\ *vb* **1** : to make (as a bill) into law ⟨*enact* legislation⟩ **2** : to act out ⟨*enact* a scene from a play⟩ — **en·ac·tor** \-'ak-tər\ *n*

en·act·ment \in-'ak(t)-mənt\ *n* **1** : the act of enacting : the state of being enacted **2** : LAW 1a, STATUTE

¹**enam·el** \in-'am-əl\ *vb* **-eled** *or* **-elled; -el·ing** *or* **-el·ling** \-'am-(ə-)liŋ\ : to cover or decorate with enamel

²**enamel** *n* **1** : a glassy substance used to coat the surface of metal, glass, or pottery **2** : a surface that resembles enamel **3** : a very hard outer layer covering the crown of a tooth **4** : a paint that turns to a smooth hard coat when applied and dries with a glossy appearance

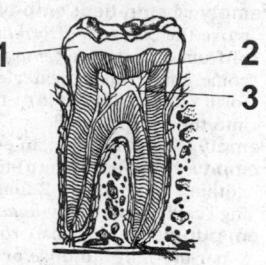

²enamel 3: *1* enamel, *2* dentin, *3* pulp

enam·el·ware \in-'am-əl-,wa(ə)r, -,we(ə)r\ *n* : metal utensils (as pots and pans) coated with enamel

en·am·or \in-'am-ər\ *vb* **-ored; -or·ing** \-(ə-)riŋ\ : to cause to feel love

en·camp \in-'kamp\ *vb* **1** : to set up and occupy a camp : CAMP **2** : to place or establish in a camp ⟨*encamp* troops⟩

en·camp·ment \in-'kamp-mənt\ *n* **1** : the act of encamping : the state of being encamped **2** : the site of a camp

en·cap·su·late \in-'kap-sə-,lāt\ *vb* **-lat·ed; -lat·ing** **1** : to enclose in a capsule **2** : to tell or relate (as a report) in a few words — **en·cap·su·la·tion** \-,kap-sə-'lā-shən\ *n*

en·case \in-'kās\ *vb* : to enclose in or as if in a case — **en·case·ment** \-mənt\ *n*

-ence \ən(t)s, ²n(t)s\ *n suffix* **1** : action or process ⟨emer*gence*⟩ : instance of an action or process ⟨refer*ence*⟩ **2** : quality or state ⟨exist*ence*⟩ [derived from Latin *-entia* "action or process"]

encephal- *or* **encephalo-** *combining form* : brain ⟨*encephal*itis⟩ [derived from Greek *en-* "in" and *kephalē* "head"]

en·ceph·a·li·tis \in-,sef-ə-'līt-əs, (,)en-\ *n* : inflammation of the brain; *also* : a disease marked by encephalitis

en·chain \in-'chān\ *vb* : to bind with or as if with chains — **en·chain·ment** \-mənt\ *n*

en·chant \in-'chant\ *vb* **1** : to influence by charms and magic : BEWITCH **2** : ¹THRILL 1, FASCINATE

en·chant·ed \in-'chant-əd\ *adj* : being or appearing to be under a magic spell ⟨an *enchanted* forest⟩

en·chant·er \in-'chant-ər\ *n* : one that enchants; *esp* : SORCERER

en·chant·ing \in-'chant-iŋ\ *adj* : having great charm and attraction — **en·chant·ing·ly** *adv*

en·chant·ment \in-'chant-mənt\ *n* **1** : the act or art of enchanting : the state of being enchanted **2** : something that enchants : SPELL

en·chant·ress \in-'chan-trəs\ *n* **1** : a woman who practices magic : SORCERESS **2** : a fascinating or beautiful woman

en·chi·la·da \,en-chə-'läd-ə\ *n* : a tortilla rolled around a meat or cheese filling and covered with a chili sauce [American Spanish, derived from earlier *enchilar* "to season with chili"]

en·ci·pher \in-'sī-fər, en-\ *vb* : to change (a message) from ordinary language into cipher

en·cir·cle \in-'sər-kəl\ *vb* **1** : to form a circle around : SURROUND **2** : to go completely around — **en·cir·cle·ment** \-mənt\ *n*

en·clave \'en-,klāv, 'än-, 'äŋ-\ *n* : a distinct territorial, cultural, or social group within a foreign region or community [from French *enclave* "enclave," derived from early French *enclaver* "to enclose"]

en·close *also* **in·close** \in-'klōz\ *vb* **1 a** : to close in : SURROUND ⟨*enclose* a porch with glass⟩ **b** : to hold in : CONFINE ⟨*enclose* animals in a pen⟩ **2** : to place in a parcel or envelope ⟨*enclose* a card with the present⟩

en·clo·sure *also* **in·clo·sure** \in-'klō-zhər\ *n* **1** : the act of enclosing : the state of being enclosed **2** : an enclosed space **3** : something (as a fence) that encloses **4** : something enclosed ⟨a letter with two *enclosures*⟩

en·code \in-'kōd, en-\ *vb* : to change (as a body of information) from one system of communication into another; *esp* : to change (a message) into code — **en·cod·er** *n*

en·co·mi·um \en-'kō-mē-əm\ *n, pl* **-mi·ums** *also* **-mia** \-mē-ə\ : warm or high praise especially when formally expressed : EULOGY

en·com·pass \in-'kəm-pəs, -'käm-\ *vb* **1** : to form a circle about : SURROUND **2 a** : to cover or surround especially so as to hide or protect **b** : to take in as a part : INCLUDE — **en·com·pass·ment** \-mənt\ *n*

en·core \'än-,kō(ə)r, -,kò(ə)r\ *n* : a demand made by an audience for a repeat or an additional performance; *also* : a further performance in response to such a demand — **encore** *vb*

¹**en·coun·ter** \in-'kaůnt-ər\ *vb* **en·coun·tered; en·coun·ter·ing** \-'kaůnt-ə-riŋ, -'kaůn-triŋ\ **1** : to engage in a struggle with as an enemy or rival **2** : to come upon face=to-face : MEET **3** : to come upon unexpectedly ⟨*encountered* problems⟩

²**encounter** *n* **1** : a clash between enemies or rivals; *also* : a very unfriendly meeting ⟨had an *encounter* with the boss⟩ **2 a** : a chance meeting **b** : a meeting face-to-face

en·cour·age \in-'kər-ij, -'kə-rij\ *vb* **-aged; -ag·ing** **1 a** : to cause to feel courage, spirit, or hope ⟨*encouraged* by her kind words⟩ **b** : to try to persuade ⟨*encouraged* him to go back to school⟩ **2** : to spur on : STIMULATE **3** : to give help to : FOSTER ⟨government grants to *encourage* young artists⟩ ⟨warm weather *encourages* plant growth⟩ — **en·cour·age·ment** \-mənt\ *n* — **en·cour·ag·ing·ly** \-ij-iŋ-lē, -rij-\ *adv*

en·croach \in-'krōch\ *vb* **1** : to enter or force oneself on another's property or rights little by little **2** : to advance beyond the usual or desirable limits ⟨the gradually *encroaching* sea⟩ — **en·croach·ment** \-mənt\ *n*

en·crust *also* **in·crust** \in-'krəst\ *vb* **1** : to cover with a crust **2** : to form a crust

encrustation *variant of* INCRUSTATION

en·cum·ber \in-'kəm-bər\ *vb* **en·cum·bered; en·cum·ber·ing** \-b(ə-)riŋ\ **1** : to place an excessive burden on **2** : to make problems for the work or activity of

en·cum·brance \in-'kəm-brən(t)s\ *n* **1** : something that encumbers : BURDEN **2** : a legal claim (as a mortgage) against property

-en·cy \ən-sē, ²n-\ *n suffix, pl* **-encies** : quality or state ⟨despond*ency*⟩ [derived from Latin *-entia* (noun suffix)]

en·cyc·li·cal \in-'sik-li-kəl, en-\ *n* : a letter addressed to a whole group; *esp* : a letter from the pope to the bishops of the church — **encyclical** *adj*

en·cy·clo·pe·dia *also* **en·cy·clo·pae·dia** \in-ˌsī-klə-ˈpēd-ē-ə\ *n* : a work that contains information on all subjects or one that covers a certain subject thoroughly usually with articles arranged alphabetically [from Latin *encyclopedia* "course of general education," from Greek *enkyklios* "general, all-around," literally, "circular" and Greek *paideia* "education, child rearing"]

en·cy·clo·pe·dic *also* **en·cy·clo·pae·dic** \in-ˌsī-klə-ˈpēd-ik\ *adj* **1** : of or relating to an encyclopedia **2** : covering a wide range of subjects ⟨*encyclopedic* knowledge⟩

en·cyst \in-ˈsist, en-\ *vb* : to form or become enclosed in a cyst — **en·cyst·ment** \-ˈsis(t)-mənt\ *n*

¹end \ˈend\ *n* **1 a** : the part at the boundary of an area **b** : a point that marks the limit of something or the point where something no longer exists ⟨no *end* to her generosity⟩ ⟨the *end* of the month⟩ **c** : the last part lengthwise : TIP **2 a** : the stopping of a process or activity **b** : DEATH **1**, DESTRUCTION **3** : something left over : REMNANT **4** : GOAL **2**, PURPOSE **5** : a football lineman whose position is at the end of the line **6** : a phase of an undertaking ⟨the sales *end* of the business⟩ — **end·ed** \ˈen-dəd\ *adj* — **in the end** : AFTER ALL ⟨will succeed *in the end*⟩ — **on end** : without interruption ⟨rained for days *on end*⟩

²end *vb* : to bring or come to an end : STOP

end- *or* **endo-** *combining form* **1** : within : inside ⟨*endo*skeleton⟩ — compare EXO- **2** : taking in ⟨*endo*thermic⟩ [derived from Greek *end-, endo-* "inside, within"]

en·dan·ger \in-ˈdān-jər\ *vb* **en·dan·gered; en·dan·ger·ing** \-ˈdānj-(ə-)riŋ\ : to bring into danger or peril — **en·dan·ger·ment** \-mənt\ *n*

en·dan·gered *adj* : threatened with extinction ⟨an *endangered* species⟩

en·dear \in-ˈdi(ə)r\ *vb* : to cause to become dear or beloved ⟨her generosity has *endeared* her to the public⟩

en·dear·ment \in-ˈdi(ə)r-mənt\ *n* : a word or an act (as a caress) showing love or affection

en·deav·or \in-ˈdev-ər\ *vb* **en·deav·ored; en·deav·or·ing** \-(ə-)riŋ\ **1** : to make an effort : TRY **2** : to work for a particular goal or result — **endeavor** *n*

en·dem·ic \en-ˈdem-ik, in-\ *adj* : originating or growing or found especially and often only in a certain locality or region ⟨*endemic* diseases⟩ ⟨an *endemic* plant⟩

end·ing \ˈen-diŋ\ *n* : the final part : CONCLUSION, END ⟨a novel with a happy *ending*⟩

en·dive \ˈen-ˌdīv\ *n* **1** : an herb closely related to chicory and widely grown as a salad plant — called also *escarole* **2** : the developing shoot of chicory when it is made pale or white by growing in the dark for use in salads

endive 1

end·less \ˈen-(d)ləs\ *adj* **1** : being or seeming to be without end **2** : joined at the ends : CONTINUOUS ⟨an *endless* belt⟩ — **end·less·ly** *adv* — **end·less·ness** *n*

end line *n* : a line marking an end or boundary (as on a playing field)

end·most \ˈen(d)-ˌmōst\ *adj* : situated at the very end

en·do·crine \ˈen-də-krən, -ˌkrīn, -ˌkrēn\ *adj* **1** : producing secretions that are distributed in the body by way of the bloodstream or lymph **2** : of, relating to, or resembling an endocrine gland or secretion

endocrine gland *n* : any of various glands that have no duct and release their secretions directly into the lymph or blood circulating through them — called also *ductless gland*

endocrine system *n* : the bodily system of glands and cells that release their secretions and especially hormones directly into the bloodstream or lymph and includes the thyroid, pituitary gland, adrenal glands, and islets of Langerhans

en·do·cy·to·sis \ˌen-də-sī-ˈtō-səs\ *n* : the process by which a cell takes in material by engulfing it with a portion of the cell membrane to form a vesicle that pinches off into the cell's interior

en·do·derm \ˈen-də-ˌdərm\ *n* **1** : the innermost of the three basic layers of an embryo that forms the epithelium of the digestive tract and the parts of the body formed from it **2** : the inner layer of cells of an animal (as a jellyfish or hydra) whose body is composed of two layers of cells — **en·do·der·mal** \ˌen-də-ˈdər-məl\ *adj*

en·do·me·tri·um \ˌen-dō-ˈmē-trē-əm\ *n, pl* **-tria** \-trē-ə\ : the mucous membrane lining the uterus

en·do·plasm \ˈen-də-ˌplaz-əm\ *n* : the inner relatively fluid part of the cytoplasm

en·do·plas·mic reticulum \ˌen-də-ˈplaz-mik-\ *n* : a system of cavities and tiny connecting canals that occupy much of the cytoplasm of the cell and functions especially in the movement of materials within the cell

en·dorse *also* **in·dorse** \in-ˈdȯ(ə)rs\ *vb* **en·dorsed; en·dors·ing** **1** : to sign the back of (a check, bank note, or bill) especially to receive payment, to indicate method of payment, or to transfer to someone else **2** : to show support or approval of ⟨*endorse* a candidate⟩ — **en·dors·ee** \in-ˌdȯ(ə)r-ˈsē\ *n* — **en·dors·er** *n*

en·dorse·ment *also* **in·dorse·ment** \in-ˈdȯr-smənt\ *n* **1** : the act or process of endorsing **2** : a signature endorsing a check or note **3** : official approval and support

en·do·scope \ˈen-də-ˌskōp\ *n* : a tubular medical instrument that allows the interior of a hollow organ or body part to be seen — **en·do·scop·ic** \ˌen-də-ˈskäp-ik\ *adj*

en·do·skel·e·ton \ˌen-dō-ˈskel-ət-ᵊn\ *n* : an inside skeleton or supporting framework in an animal

en·do·sperm \ˈen-də-ˌspərm\ *n* : a food-containing tissue formed within the seed in seed plants

en·do·therm \ˈen-dō-ˌthərm\ *n* : a warm-blooded animal

en·do·ther·mic \ˌen-dō-ˈthər-mik\ *adj* : characterized by or formed with absorption of heat

en·dow \in-ˈdaů\ *vb* **1** : to provide with money for support or maintenance **2** : to furnish with something freely or naturally ⟨humans are *endowed* with reason⟩

en·dow·ment \in-ˈdaů-mənt\ *n* **1** : the providing of a permanent fund for support; *also* : the fund provided ⟨a college's *endowment*⟩ **2** : a person's natural ability

end·point \ˈen(d)-ˌpȯint\ *n* : either of two points that mark the ends of a line segment; *also* : a point that marks the end of a ray

end rhyme *n* : a rhyme of the last word or the last syllable of two or more lines of verse

end run *n* : a football play in which the ballcarrier attempts to run wide around the end

end table *n* : a small table used beside a sofa or chair

en·due \in-ˈd(y)ü\ *vb* **en·dued; en·du·ing** : to provide with a quality or power ⟨*endued* with grace⟩

en·dur·ance \in-ˈd(y)ůr-ən(t)s\ *n* **1** : the quality of lasting or of being permanent **2** : the ability to withstand hardship, adversity, or stress ⟨athletes need to develop *endurance*⟩ **3** : SUFFERING **1** ⟨*endurance* of many hardships⟩

en·dure \in-ˈd(y)ů(ə)r\ *vb* **en·dured; en·dur·ing** **1** : to continue in the same state : LAST **2** : to bear patiently : SUFFER **3** : to allow to happen or continue : TOLERATE — **en·dur·able** \-ˈd(y)ůr-ə-bəl\ *adj* — **en·dur·ing** \in-ˈd(y)ůr-iŋ\ *adj* — **en·dur·ing·ly** *adv*

end user *n* : the ultimate consumer of a finished product

\ə\ **abut**	\aů\ **out**	\i\ **tip**	\ȯ\ **saw**	\ů\ **foot**
\ər\ **further**	\ch\ **chin**	\ī\ **life**	\ȯi\ **coin**	\y\ **yet**
\a\ **mat**	\e\ **pet**	\j\ **job**	\th\ **thin**	\yü\ **few**
\ā\ **take**	\ē\ **easy**	\ŋ\ **sing**	\th\ **this**	\yů\ **cure**
\ä\ **cot, cart**	\g\ **go**	\ō\ **bone**	\ü\ **food**	\zh\ **vision**

end·ways \'en-ˌdwāz\ *adv or adj* **1** : with the end forward **2** : LENGTHWISE **3** : on end ⟨boxes set *endways*⟩

end·wise \'end-ˌwīz\ *adv or adj* : ENDWAYS

end zone *n* : the area where points are scored beyond the goal line at each end of a football field

-ene \ˌēn\ *n suffix* : unsaturated carbon compound ⟨benzene⟩; *esp* : carbon compound with one double bond ⟨ethylene⟩ [derived from Greek *-ēnos* (adjective suffix)]

en·e·ma \'en-ə-mə\ *n* : the injection of liquid into the rectum by way of the anus usually to cause the intestines to empty; *also* : the material injected

en·e·my \'en-ə-mē\ *n, pl* **-mies** **1** : one that tries to hurt or overthrow or that seeks the failure of another **2** : something that harms **3 a** : a nation with which a country is at war **b** : a military force or a person belonging to such a nation [Middle English *enemi* "enemy," from early French *enemi* (same meaning), from Latin *inimicus* (same meaning), from *in-* "not" and *amicus* "friend"]

en·er·get·ic \ˌen-ər-'jet-ik\ *adj* : having or showing energy : ACTIVE ⟨an *energetic* salesperson⟩ *synonyms* see VIGOROUS — **en·er·get·i·cal·ly** \-'jet-i-k(ə-)lē\ *adv*

en·er·gize \'en-ər-ˌjīz\ *vb* **-gized; -giz·ing** **1** : to put forth energy : ACT **2 a** : to give energy to ⟨sunlight *energizes* the chemical reactions⟩ **b** : to make energetic **3** : to apply voltage to — **en·er·giz·er** *n*

en·er·gy \'en-ər-jē\ *n, pl* **-gies** **1** : power or ability to be active : strength of body or mind to do things or to work ⟨a teacher of great intellectual *energy*⟩ **2** : natural power exerted with force : lively action ⟨work with *energy*⟩ **3** : the capacity (as of heat, light, or running water) for doing work **4 a** : usable power (as heat or electricity) **b** : a source of energy; *esp* : a resource (as oil) used to provide energy *synonyms* see POWER

energy level *n* : one of the stable states of constant energy that may be assumed by a physical system — used especially of the states of electrons in atoms

energy pyramid *n* : a triangle-shaped diagram that represents the amount of energy in an ecosystem that is transferred from one level of a food chain or food web to the next

en·er·vate \'en-ər-ˌvāt\ *vb* **-vat·ed; -vat·ing** : to cause to decline in strength or vigor : WEAKEN — **en·er·vat·ing·ly** *adv* — **en·er·va·tion** \ˌen-ər-'vā-shən\ *n*

en·fee·ble \in-'fē-bəl\ *vb* **en·fee·bled; en·fee·bling** \-b(ə-)liŋ\ : to make feeble

en·fold \in-'fōld\ *vb* **1** : to cover with folds : enclose in the folds of something **2** : ¹EMBRACE 1, HUG

en·force \in-'fō(ə)rs, -'fȯ(ə)rs\ *vb* **1** : to bring about by force : COMPEL ⟨*enforce* obedience⟩ **2** : to carry out effectively ⟨*enforce* the law⟩ — **en·force·able** \-'fȯr-sə-bəl, -fȯr-\ *adj* — **en·force·ment** \-'fȯr-smənt, -fȯr-\ *n* — **en·forc·er** *n*

en·fran·chise \in-'fran-ˌchīz\ *vb* **-chised; -chis·ing** **1** : to set free (as from slavery) **2** : to give full privileges of citizenship to; *esp* : to give the right to vote — **en·fran·chise·ment** \-ˌchīz-mənt, -chəz-\ *n*

en·gage \in-'gāj\ *vb* **en·gaged; en·gag·ing** **1** : to commit oneself to do something; *esp* : to bind by a pledge to marry **2** : to arrange for the use or services of : HIRE ⟨*engage* a lawyer⟩ **b** : to keep fixed or concentrated ⟨the task *engaged* our attention⟩ **3 a** : to cause to take part ⟨*engaged* the stranger in conversation⟩ **b** : PARTICIPATE ⟨she *engages* in sports⟩ **4** : to enter into contest or battle with ⟨*engage* the enemy⟩ **5** : to come together or cause to come together and mesh ⟨the gears *engaged*⟩

en·gaged \in-'gājd\ *adj* **1** : being occupied with some activity ⟨they were *engaged* in conversation⟩ **2** : pledged to be married : BETROTHED ⟨an *engaged* couple⟩

en·gage·ment \in-'gāj-mənt\ *n* **1 a** : a promise to be present at a specified place and time **b** : employment especially for a stated time ⟨the band had *engagements* in different towns⟩ **2** : ¹PLEDGE 5, OBLIGATION **3 a** : the act

of engaging : the state of being engaged **b** : an agreement to marry; *also* : the period during which one is pledged to be married **4** : the state of being meshed in a working arrangement in which one part drives another **5** : the state of being in conflict, opposition, or battle

en·gag·ing \in-'gā-jiŋ\ *adj* : having a very pleasing appearance or manner : ATTRACTIVE — **en·gag·ing·ly** *adv*

en·gen·der \in-'jen-dər\ *vb* **-dered; -der·ing** \-d(ə-)riŋ\ **1** : to reproduce offspring **2** : to be the source or cause of : PRODUCE ⟨tensions that *engender* emotional conflicts⟩

en·gine \'en-jən\ *n* **1** : a mechanical device **2** : a machine that changes energy (as heat from burning fuel) into mechanical motion **3** : a railroad locomotive [Middle English *engin* "natural talent or skill, mechanical device," from early French *engin* (same meaning), from Latin *ingenium* "natural ability or desire to do something," from *in* "in" and *-genium*, from *gignere* "to father, beget" — related to GENIUS, ¹GIN, INGENIOUS]

¹en·gi·neer \ˌen-jə-'ni(ə)r\ *n* **1** : a member of a military group devoted to engineering work **2 a** : a designer or builder of engines **b** : a person who is trained in or follows as a profession a branch of engineering **3** : a person who runs or supervises an engine or technical machinery

²engineer *vb* **1** : to plan, build, or manage as an engineer **2** : to guide the course of ⟨*engineer* a rally⟩

en·gi·neer·ing \ˌen-jə-'ni(ə)r-iŋ\ *n* : the science or profession of developing and using nature's power and resources in ways that are useful to people (as in designing and building roads, bridges, dams, or machines and in creating new products)

¹En·glish \'iŋ-glish\ *adj* : of, relating to, or characteristic of England, the English people, or the English language [Old English *englisc* "English," from *Engle* "the Angles (Germanic people who invaded England in the 5th century along with the Saxons and with them formed the Anglo-Saxon peoples)"]

²English *n* **1 a** : the language of the people of England and the U.S. and many areas now or formerly under British control **b** : English language, literature, or writing technique that is a subject of study **2 English** *pl* : the people of England **3** : a sideways spin given to a ball when it is struck or bowled

English horn *n* : a woodwind instrument similar to the oboe but lower in pitch

English ivy *n* : IVY 1

En·glish·man \'iŋ-glish-mən\ *n* : a person born or living in England

English saddle *n* : a rather flat saddle without a horn and high seat back

English setter *n* : any of a breed of bird dogs with a long flat silky coat of white usually with flecks or patches of black or brown

English sonnet *n* : a sonnet in which the rhyme pattern is in three groups of four lines each and one group of two lines

English sparrow *n* : HOUSE SPARROW

English springer spaniel *n* : any of a breed of springer spaniels with a flat silky coat of white with large patches of usually black or brown

English horn

English system *n* : a system of weights and measures in which the foot is the principal unit of length and the pound is the principal unit of weight

En·glish·wom·an \'iŋ-glish-ˌwùm-ən\ *n* : a woman born or living in England

en·gorge \in-'gȯ(ə)rj\ *vb* **1** : to eat greedily : GORGE **2** : to fill with blood : CONGEST — **en·gorge·ment** \-mənt\ *n*

en·grave \in-ˈgrāv\ *vb* **en·graved; en·grav·ing 1** : to impress deeply ⟨the incident was *engraved* in my memory⟩ **2 a** : to cut or carve (as letters or designs) on a hard surface **b** : to cut lines, letters, figures, or designs on or into (a hard surface) often for use in printing **c** : to print from a cut surface ⟨an *engraved* wedding invitation⟩ — **en·grav·er** *n*

en·grav·ing \in-ˈgrā-viŋ\ *n* **1** : the art of cutting something especially into the surface of wood, stone, or metal **2** : a print made from an engraved surface

en·gross \in-ˈgrōs\ *vb* : to take up the whole interest or attention of : ABSORB — **en·gross·er** *n* — **en·gross·ment** \-mənt\ *n*

en·gulf \in-ˈgəlf\ *vb* : to flow over and enclose : OVERWHELM — **en·gulf·ment** \-mənt\ *n*

en·hance \in-ˈhan(t)s\ *vb* **en·hanced; en·hanc·ing** : to increase or improve in value, desirability, or attractiveness — **en·hance·ment** \-mənt\ *n* — **en·hanc·er** *n*

enig·ma \i-ˈnig-mə\ *n* : something hard to understand or explain **synonyms** see MYSTERY — **en·ig·mat·ic** \ˌen-ig-ˈmat-ik, ˌē-nig-\ *also* **en·ig·mat·i·cal** \-ˈmat-i-kəl\ *adj* — **en·ig·mat·i·cal·ly** \-i-k(ə-)lē\ *adv*

en·join \in-ˈjȯin\ *vb* **1** : to direct or demand (an action) by authoritative order (as from a court of law) **2** : FORBID 1, PROHIBIT

en·joy \in-ˈjȯi\ *vb* **1** : to have or experience as a benefit or for one's use ⟨*enjoy* great success⟩ ⟨*enjoying* the freedom to pursue one's interests⟩ **2** : to take pleasure from ⟨I didn't *enjoy* the movie⟩ — **en·joy·able** \-ə-bəl\ *adj* — **en·joy·able·ness** *n* — **en·joy·ably** \-blē\ *adv*

en·joy·ment \in-ˈjȯi-mənt\ *n* **1** : the condition of enjoying something : possession and use of something that gives satisfaction ⟨the *enjoyment* of good health⟩ **2** : satisfaction taken in something ⟨find *enjoyment* in skating⟩ **3** : something that gives pleasure ⟨the poorest life has its *enjoyments*⟩ **synonyms** see PLEASURE

en·large \in-ˈlärj\ *vb* **en·larged; en·larg·ing 1** : to make or grow larger : INCREASE, EXPAND **2** : to give more details : ELABORATE ⟨*enlarge* on a story⟩ — **en·larg·er** *n*

en·large·ment \in-ˈlärj-mənt\ *n* **1** : an act or instance of enlarging : the state of being enlarged **2** : a photographic print made larger than the negative

en·light·en \in-ˈlīt-ᵊn\ *vb* **en·light·ened; en·light·en·ing** \-ˈlīt-niŋ, -ᵊn-iŋ\ : to give knowledge or understanding to : INSTRUCT ⟨*enlightened* us about the problem⟩ — **en·light·en·ment** \-ᵊn-mənt\ *n*

en·list \in-ˈlist\ *vb* **1 a** : to enroll for military or naval service; *esp* : to join one of the armed services voluntarily **b** : to participate heartily (as in a cause or drive) **2** : to obtain the help or support of ⟨*enlisted* their friends in the campaign⟩ — **en·list·ment** \-ˈlis(t)-mənt\ *n*

en·list·ed \in-ˈlis-təd\ *adj* : of, relating to, or forming the part of a military or naval force in the ranks below commissioned or warrant officers

en·liv·en \in-ˈlī-vən\ *vb* : to give life, action, or spirit to : ANIMATE ⟨*enliven* the party with dance music⟩

en masse \än-ˈmas\ *adv* : in a body : as a whole

en·mesh \in-ˈmesh\ *vb* : to entangle in or as if in meshes ⟨was *enmeshed* in a series of disputes⟩

en·mi·ty \ˈen-mət-ē\ *n, pl* **-ties** : a very deep unfriendly feeling : HATRED

en·no·ble \in-ˈō-bəl\ *vb* **-bled; -bling** \-b(ə-)liŋ\ **1** : to make noble : ELEVATE ⟨seemed *ennobled* by his hardship⟩ **2** : to raise to the rank of nobility — **en·no·ble·ment** \-bəl-mənt\ *n*

en·nui \ˈän-ˌwē\ *n* : a lack of spirit, enthusiasm, or satisfaction : BOREDOM

enor·mi·ty \i-ˈnȯr-mət-ē\ *n, pl* **-ties 1** : great wickedness ⟨the *enormity* of the crime⟩ **2** : an outrageous or immoral act or offense **3** : very large size **4** : the quality of great impact or importance

enor·mous \i-ˈnȯr-məs\ *adj* : extraordinarily great in size, number, or degree — **enor·mous·ly** *adv* — **enor·mous·ness** *n*

   synonyms ENORMOUS, IMMENSE, HUGE, VAST mean unusually large. ENORMOUS suggests going beyond the usual limits in size, amount, or degree ⟨the *enormous* cost of the project⟩. IMMENSE suggests size far beyond ordinary measurements or ideas ⟨an *immense* waste of resources⟩. HUGE suggests greatness of bulk, size, or capacity ⟨*huge* barrels of oil⟩. VAST suggests greatness or broadness of extent ⟨*vast* stretches of desert⟩.

¹**enough** \i-ˈnəf\ *adj* : equal to the demands or needs : SUFFICIENT

²**enough** *adv* **1** : in or to a sufficient amount or degree : SUFFICIENTLY ⟨ran fast *enough*⟩ **2** : FULLY 1, QUITE ⟨qualified *enough* for the job⟩ **3** : so as to be moderately good : TOLERABLY ⟨sang well *enough*⟩

³**enough** *n* : a sufficient quantity ⟨*enough* to meet our needs⟩

enow \i-ˈnau̇\ *adv or adj, archaic* : ENOUGH

en·plane \in-ˈplān\ *vb* : to board an airplane

enquire, enquiry *chiefly British variant of* INQUIRE, INQUIRY

en·rage \in-ˈrāj\ *vb* : to fill with rage : MADDEN

en·rap·ture \in-ˈrap-chər\ *vb* **en·rap·tured; en·rap·tur·ing** \-ˈrap-chə-riŋ, -ˈrap-shriŋ\ : to fill with delight

en·rich \in-ˈrich\ *vb* **1** : to make rich or richer ⟨*enrich* the mind⟩ **2** : ADORN, ORNAMENT **3 a** : to make (soil) more fertile **b** : to improve the value of (food) for nutrition by adding vitamins and minerals in processing **c** : to increase the proportion of a desirable ingredient ⟨*enriched* uranium⟩ ⟨*enriched* natural gas⟩ — **en·rich·ment** \-mənt\ *n*

en·roll *also* **en·rol** \in-ˈrōl\ *vb* **en·rolled; en·roll·ing 1** : to enter in a list or roll : REGISTER **2 a** : to take into membership **b** : to become a member : JOIN, ENTER ⟨*enroll* in the army⟩ ⟨*enroll* in school⟩ — **en·roll·ment** \-mənt\ *n*

en route \än-ˈrüt, en-, in-\ *adv* : on or along the way

en·sconce \in-ˈskän(t)s\ *vb* **en·sconced; en·sconc·ing 1** : to place or hide securely : CONCEAL ⟨*ensconced* myself behind a tree⟩ **2** : to establish comfortably : settle snugly ⟨*ensconced* in a new house⟩

en·sem·ble \än-ˈsäm-bəl\ *n* : a group of people or things making up a complete unit: as **a** : musicians that perform music in several parts; *also* : the music itself **b** : a set of clothes that look nice together [from French *ensemble* "group, ensemble," from *ensemble* (adverb) "together," from Latin *insimul* (same meaning), from *in-* "in, into" and *simul* "at the same time, together" — related to ASSEMBLE, SIMULTANEOUS]

en·shrine \in-ˈshrīn\ *vb* **en·shrined; en·shrin·ing 1** : to enclose in or as if in a shrine **2** : to preserve or cherish as sacred

en·shroud \in-ˈshraud\ *vb* : to cover or enclose with or as if with a shroud

en·sign \ˈen(t)-sən, *in senses 1 & 2 also* ˈen-ˌsīn\ *n* **1** : a flag flown as the symbol of nationality (as on a ship) **2** : a badge of office, rank, or power **3** : a naval commissioned officer of the lowest rank

en·si·lage \ˈen(t)-sə-lij\ *n* : the process of converting feed crops into silage; *also* : SILAGE

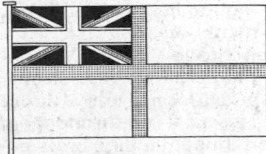

ensign 1 (British Royal Navy ensign)

en·slave \in-'slāv\ *vb* : to make a slave of — **en·slave·ment** \-mənt\ *n* — **en·slav·er** *n*

en·snare \in-'sna(ə)r, -'sne(ə)r\ *vb* : ²SNARE 1, ENTRAP

en·sue \in-'sü\ *vb* **en·sued; en·su·ing** : to come at a later time or as a result : FOLLOW ⟨*ensuing* effects⟩

en·sure \in-'shù(ə)r\ *vb* **en·sured; en·sur·ing** : to make sure, certain, or safe : GUARANTEE

¹**en·tail** \in-'tā(ə)l\ *vb* **1** : to limit the inheritance of (property) to the owner's direct descendants or to a certain group of them **2** : to have as a necessary part or result ⟨the essay *entails* a lot of research⟩ — **en·tail·ment** \-mənt\ *n*

²**en·tail** \'en-ˌtāl, in-'tā(ə)l\ *n* **1 a** : an entailing of property **b** : an entailed estate **2** : the rule fixing descent by entailment

en·tan·gle \in-'taŋ-gəl\ *vb* **1** : to make tangled or confused **2** : to involve in a tangle or a confusing or difficult situation — **en·tan·gle·ment** \-mənt\ *n*

en·ter \'ent-ər\ *vb* **en·tered; en·ter·ing** \'ent-ə-riŋ, 'en-triŋ\ **1** : to go or come in or into ⟨*enter* a room⟩ **2** : PENETRATE 1b, PIERCE ⟨the needle *enters* the skin at an angle⟩ **3** : to cause to be admitted to : ENROLL ⟨*enter* a child in kindergarten⟩ **4 a** : to become a member of **b** : to take part in : JOIN ⟨*enter* a race⟩ ⟨*enter* into a discussion⟩ **5** : to make a beginning ⟨*enter* into business⟩ **6** : to take possession ⟨*entered* upon their inheritance⟩ **7 a** : to set down in a book or list ⟨*entered* my name on the roster⟩ **b** : to put in or into : INSERT ⟨*enter* data into the computer program⟩ **8** : to place formally before a legal authority (as a court) ⟨*enter* a complaint⟩ — **en·ter·able** \'ent-ə-rə-bəl, 'en-trə-bəl\ *adj*

en·ter·i·tis \ˌent-ə-'rīt-əs\ *n* : inflammation of the intestines; *also* : a disease marked by this

en·ter·prise \'ent-ə(r)-ˌprīz\ *n* **1** : a difficult, complicated, or risky project or undertaking **2** : readiness to engage in daring or difficult action ⟨showed great *enterprise* in the face of danger⟩ **3** : a business organization — **en·ter·pris·er** \-ˌprī-zər\ *n*

en·ter·pris·ing \'ent-ə(r)-ˌprī-ziŋ\ *adj* : bold, active, and energetic in undertaking or experimenting

en·ter·tain \ˌent-ər-'tān\ *vb* **1** : to receive and provide for as host : have as a guest ⟨*entertain* friends over the weekend⟩ **2 a** : to provide entertainment **b** : to be a source of entertainment for ⟨*entertained* us with stories⟩ **3** : to have in mind : CONSIDER ⟨*entertained* thoughts of quitting⟩ **synonyms** see AMUSE — **en·ter·tain·er** \ˌen-tər-'tā-nər\ *n*

en·ter·tain·ing \ˌen-tər-'tān-iŋ\ *adj* : providing amusement, diversion, or recreation ⟨an *entertaining* book⟩ — **en·ter·tain·ing·ly** *adv*

en·ter·tain·ment \ˌen-tər-'tān-mənt\ *n* **1** : the act or process of providing pleasure, recreation, or amusement **2** : a means of amusement or recreation; *esp* : a public performance

en·thrall *or* **en·thral** \in-'thrȯl\ *vb* **en·thralled; en·thrall·ing** : to hold by or as if by a spell : CHARM — **en·thrall·ment** \-mənt\ *n*

en·throne \in-'thrōn\ *vb* **en·throned; en·thron·ing** **1 a** : to install in office or in a position of authority **b** : to install formally on a throne **2** : to place high value on : EXALT — **en·throne·ment** \-mənt\ *n*

en·thuse \in-'th(y)üz\ *vb* **en·thused; en·thus·ing** **1** : to make enthusiastic **2** : to show enthusiasm

en·thu·si·asm \in-'th(y)ü-zē-ˌaz-əm\ *n* **1** : strong excitement and active interest **2** : something causing a feeling of excitement and active interest

en·thu·si·ast \in-'th(y)ü-zē-ˌast, -əst\ *n* : a person filled with enthusiasm

en·thu·si·as·tic \in-ˌth(y)ü-zē-'as-tik\ *adj* : filled with or marked by enthusiasm ⟨an *enthusiastic* welcome⟩ — **en·thu·si·as·ti·cal·ly** \-ti-k(ə-)lē\ *adv*

en·tice \in-'tīs\ *vb* **en·ticed; en·tic·ing** : to attract by arousing hope or desire : TEMPT — **en·tice·ment** \-mənt\ *n* — **en·tic·ing·ly** \-iŋ-lē\ *adv*

en·tire \in-'tī(ə)r, 'en-ˌtī(ə)r\ *adj* **1** : having no element or part left out : COMPLETE **2** : being to the fullest degree : TOTAL ⟨her *entire* devotion⟩ **3** : having the margin continuous and free from indentations ⟨an *entire* leaf⟩ — **entire** *adv* — **en·tire·ly** *adv* — **en·tire·ness** *n*

en·tire·ty \in-'tī-rət-ē, -'tī(ə)rt-ē\ *n* : the state of being entire or complete — **in its entirety** : taking or involving the whole of something

en·ti·tle \in-'tīt-ᵊl\ *vb* **en·ti·tled; en·ti·tling** \-'tīt-liŋ, -ᵊl-iŋ\ **1** : to give a title to **2** : to give a right to : QUALIFY ⟨the card *entitles* us to a discount⟩ — **en·ti·tle·ment** \-ᵊl-mənt\ *n*

en·ti·ty \'ent-ət-ē\ *n, pl* **-ties** : something existing or thought of as existing as a separate and independent thing

en·tomb \in-'tüm\ *vb* : to place in a tomb : BURY — **en·tomb·ment** \-'tüm-mənt\ *n*

en·to·mol·o·gist \ˌent-ə-'mäl-ə-jəst\ *n* : a person who specializes in entomology

en·to·mol·o·gy \ˌent-ə-'mäl-ə-jē\ *n* : a branch of zoology that deals with insects — **en·to·mo·log·i·cal** \-'läj-i-kəl\ *adj*

en·trails \'en-trəlz, -ˌtrālz\ *n pl* : internal organs : VISCERA; *esp* : the part of the digestive system composed of the intestines

en·train \in-'trān\ *vb* : to put or go aboard a train

¹**en·trance** \'en-trən(t)s\ *n* **1** : the act of entering ⟨made an *entrance*⟩ **2 a** : the means or place of entry **b** : a point in a play where a character comes on stage ⟨watch for your *entrance*⟩ **3** : the right to enter : ADMISSION ⟨gained *entrance* to the club⟩ ⟨an *entrance* exam⟩

²**en·trance** \in-'tran(t)s\ *vb* **en·tranced; en·tranc·ing** **1** : to put into a trance **2** : to fill with delight, wonder, or overwhelming emotion — **en·trance·ment** \-mənt\ *n*

en·trant \'en-trənt\ *n* : one that enters; *esp* : one that enters a contest

en·trap \in-'trap\ *vb* : to catch in or as if in a trap — **en·trap·ment** \-mənt\ *n*

en·treat \in-'trēt\ *vb* : to ask in a serious and urgent manner : PLEAD, BEG — **en·treat·ing·ly** \-iŋ-lē\ *adv*

en·treaty \in-'trēt-ē\ *n, pl* **-treat·ies** : earnest request : APPEAL, PLEA

en·trée *or* **en·tree** \'än-ˌtrā\ *n* **1** : the main dish of a meal **2 a** : ¹ENTRANCE 1 **b** : freedom of entry [from French *entrée* "act or manner of entering"]

en·trench \in-'trench\ *vb* **1 a** : to dig, place within, surround with, or occupy a trench especially for defense **b** : to establish solidly **2** : ENCROACH 1 — used with *on* or *upon*

en·trench·ment \in-'trench-mənt\ *n* **1** : the act of entrenching : the state of being entrenched **2** : DEFENSE 3a; *esp* : a defensive work consisting of a trench and a wall of earth

en·tre·pre·neur \ˌän-trə-p(r)ə-'nər, -'n(y)ùr\ *n* : one who organizes, manages, and takes on the risks of a business or enterprise

en·trust \in-'trəst\ *vb* **1** : to give into the care of another ⟨*entrust* your savings to a bank⟩ **2** : to give custody, care, or charge of something to ⟨*entrust* a bank with your savings⟩ — **en·trust·ment** \-'trəs(t)-mənt\ *n*

en·try \'en-trē\ *n, pl* **entries** **1** : the act or opportunity of entering : ENTRANCE ⟨gained *entry* through a back window⟩ **2** : a place through which entrance is made : HALL 2a, VESTIBULE **3 a** : the act of making a written record of something (as in a book or list) **b** : the thing recorded (as in a book or list) ⟨dictionary *entries*⟩ **4** : a person or thing entered into something (as a contest)

en·try·way \in-trē-ˌwā\ *n* : ENTRY 2

entry word *n* : a word entered in a list or book; *esp* : a word in boldface type that is being explained in a dictionary

en·twine \in-'twīn\ *vb* : to twine together or around

enu·mer·ate \i-'n(y)ü-mə-ˌrāt\ *vb* **-at·ed; -at·ing** **1** : to find out the number of : COUNT **2** : to list one after another — **enu·mer·a·tion** \-ˌn(y)ü-mə-'rā-shən\ *n*

enun·ci·ate \ē-'nən(t)-sē-ˌāt\ *vb* **-at·ed; -at·ing** **1** : to make known publicly : PROCLAIM **2** : to pronounce clearly : ARTICULATE — **enun·ci·a·ble** \-ə-bəl\ *adj* — **enun·ci·a·tion** \-ˌnən(t)-sē-'ā-shən\ *n* — **enun·ci·a·tor** \-'nən(t)-sē-ˌāt-ər\ *n*

en·vel·op \in-'vel-əp\ *vb* : to surround and enclose completely with or as if with a covering — **en·vel·op·ment** \-mənt\ *n*

en·ve·lope \'en-və-ˌlōp, 'än-\ *n* **1** : a flat usually paper container (as for a letter) **2** : something that envelops **3** : the bag containing the gas in a balloon or airship **4** : a natural enclosing covering (as a membrane)

en·ven·om \in-'ven-əm\ *vb* **1** : to poison with venom **2** : to cause to feel bitterness or hatred

en·vi·able \'en-vē-ə-bəl\ *adj* : likely to be the object of envy : highly desirable — **en·vi·able·ness** *n* — **en·vi·ably** \-blē\ *adv*

en·vi·ous \'en-vē-əs\ *adj* : feeling or showing envy ⟨*envious* of a neighbor's good luck⟩ ⟨an *envious* look⟩ — **en·vi·ous·ly** *adv* — **en·vi·ous·ness** *n*

en·vi·ron \in-'vī-rən, -'vī(-ə)rn\ *vb* : ENCIRCLE 1, SURROUND

en·vi·ron·ment \in-'vī-rən-mənt, -'vī(-ə)rn-\ *n* **1** : SURROUNDINGS ⟨living in a rural *environment*⟩ **2** : the surrounding conditions or forces that influence or modify: as **a** : the whole complex of factors (as soil, climate, and living things) that influence the form and the ability to survive of a plant or animal or ecological community **b** : the social and cultural conditions that influence the life of a person or human community ⟨an unhappy home *environment*⟩ — **en·vi·ron·men·tal** \-ˌvī-rən-'ment-ᵊl, -ˌvī(-ə)rn-\ *adj* — **en·vi·ron·men·tal·ly** \-ᵊl-ē\ *adv*

en·vi·ron·men·tal·ism \-ˌvī-rən-'ment-ᵊl-ˌi-zəm, -ˌvī(-ə)rn-\ *n* : the act or process of preserving, restoring, or improving the natural environment

en·vi·ron·men·tal·ist \-ˌvī-rən-'ment-ᵊl-əst, -ˌvī(-ə)rn-\ *n* : a person concerned about environmental quality and especially with controlling pollution

en·vi·rons \in-'vī-rənz, -'vī(-ə)rnz\ *n pl* **1** : the districts around a city **2** : SURROUNDINGS

en·vis·age \in-'viz-ij\ *vb* **-aged; -ag·ing** : to have a mental picture of : VISUALIZE

en·vi·sion \in-'vizh-ən\ *vb* : to picture to oneself ⟨*envisions* herself as a doctor⟩ ⟨could not *envision* the building from the description⟩

en·voy \'en-ˌvȯi, 'än-\ *n* **1 a** : a diplomatic representative who ranks between an ambassador and a minister **b** : a representative sent by one government to another ⟨ambassadors and other *envoys*⟩ **2** : ²REPRESENTATIVE 2, MESSENGER

¹en·vy \'en-vē\ *n, pl* **envies** **1** : painful or resentful awareness of an advantage or possession enjoyed by another and the desire to possess the same thing **2** : an object of envy ⟨she was the *envy* of all her friends⟩

²envy *vb* **en·vied; en·vy·ing** : to feel envy toward or on account of — **en·vi·er** *n* — **en·vy·ing·ly** \-iŋ-lē\ *adv*

en·wrap \in-'rap\ *vb* : ENFOLD 1, ENVELOP

en·zyme \'en-ˌzīm\ *n* : any of various complex proteins produced by living cells that bring about or speed up reactions (as in the digestion of food) without being permanently altered — **en·zy·mat·ic** \ˌen-zə-'mat-ik\ *adj* — **en·zy·mat·i·cal·ly** \-'mat-i-k(ə)lē\ *adv*

Eo·cene \'ē-ə-ˌsēn\ *adj* : of, relating to, or being an epoch of the Tertiary period of geological history or the corresponding series of rocks — see GEOLOGIC TIME table — **Eocene** *n*

eo·hip·pus \ˌē-ō-'hip-əs\ *n* : any of a genus of small primitive horses from the Eocene epoch of the western U.S. and Europe with four toes on each front leg and three toes on each rear leg

eo·lian *also* **ae·o·lian** \ē-'ō-lē-ən, -'ōl-yən\ *adj* : carried, deposited, produced, or eroded by the wind ⟨*eolian* sand⟩

Eo·lith·ic \ˌē-ə-'lith-ik\ *adj* : of or relating to the earliest period of the Stone Age marked by the use of very crudely chipped flint tools

eon *variant of* AEON

eo·sin·o·phil \ˌē-ə-'sin-ə-ˌfil\ *n* : a white blood cell with a granule-containing cytoplasm that is found in the body at sites of allergic reactions and parasitic infections

-eous *adj suffix* : resembling : being : having the form or qualities of ⟨gas*eous*⟩ [from Latin *-eus* (adjective suffix)]

ep·au·let *also* **ep·au·lette** \ˌep-ə-'let, 'ep-ə-ˌlet\ *n* : a shoulder ornament on a uniform especially of a military or naval officer

ephed·rine \i-'fed-rən\ *n* : a basic substance obtained from Chinese woody plants or made artificially and used as a salt in relieving hay fever, asthma, and nasal congestion

E epaulet

ephem·er·al \i-'fem-(ə-)rəl\ *adj* **1** : lasting one day only ⟨an *ephemeral* fever⟩ **2** : lasting a very short time ⟨*ephemeral* pleasures⟩ — **ephem·er·al·ly** \-rə-lē\ *adv*

Ephe·sians \i-'fē-zhənz\ *n* — see BIBLE table

epi- *prefix* : over : upon ⟨*epi*phyte⟩ [derived from Greek *epi* "on, at"]

¹ep·ic \'ep-ik\ *adj* **1** : of, relating to, or being like an epic ⟨an *epic* poem⟩ **2** : unusually long or great in size or scope ⟨*epic* genius⟩

²epic *n* : a long poem telling of the deeds of a hero and often centering on the ideals of a nation or culture

epi·cen·ter \'ep-i-ˌsent-ər\ *n* : the part of the earth's surface directly above the starting point of an earthquake

epi·cure \'ep-i-ˌkyu̇(ə)r\ *n* : a person with carefully improved tastes in food or wine [named for *Epicurus,* an ancient Greek philosopher who believed pleasure to be the chief aim of life] — **ep·i·cu·re·an** \ˌep-i-kyu̇-'rē-ən, -'kyu̇r-ē-\ *adj or n*

epi·cy·cle \'ep-ə-ˌsī-kəl\ *n* : a circle according to an early astronomy theory in which a planet moves and which has a center that is itself carried around at the same time on the circumference of a larger circle

¹ep·i·dem·ic \ˌep-ə-'dem-ik\ *adj* : spreading widely and affecting many individuals at one time [derived from Greek *epidēmia* "an epidemic, visit," from *epidēmos* "visiting, epidemic," from *epi-* "on, at" and *dēmos* "people, the masses" — related to DEMOCRACY]

²epidemic *n* **1** : an outbreak of epidemic disease **2** : a sudden rapidly spreading outbreak or growth ⟨a crime *epidemic*⟩

ep·i·de·mi·ol·o·gist \ˌep-ə-ˌdē-mē-'äl-ə-jəst\ *n* : a person who specializes in epidemiology

ep·i·de·mi·ol·o·gy \ˌep-ə-ˌdē-mē-'äl-ə-jē\ *n* **1** : a branch of medical science that deals with the occurrence, distribu-

\ə\ abut	\au̇\ out	\i\ tip	\ȯ\ saw	\u̇\ foot
\ər\ further	\ch\ chin	\ī\ life	\ȯi\ coin	\y\ yet
\a\ mat	\e\ pet	\j\ job	\th\ thin	\yü\ few
\ā\ take	\ē\ easy	\ŋ\ sing	\th\ this	\yu̇\ cure
\ä\ cot, cart	\g\ go	\ō\ bone	\ü\ food	\zh\ vision

tion, and control of disease in a population **2** : the sum of the factors controlling the presence or absence of a particular disease — **ep·i·de·mi·o·log·i·cal** \-mē-ə-'läj-i-kəl\ *also* **ep·i·de·mi·o·log·ic** \-'läj-ik\ *adj*

epi·der·mal \ˌep-ə-'dər-məl\ *adj* : of, relating to, or arising from the epidermis ⟨*epidermal* tissues⟩

epi·der·mis \ˌep-ə-'dər-məs\ *n* **1** : the thin outer layer of the animal body that in vertebrates forms an insensitive covering over the dermis **2** : a thin surface layer of protecting cells in seed plants and ferns

ep·i·did·y·mis \ˌep-ə-'did-ə-məs\ *n, pl* **-mi·des** \-mə-ˌdēz\ : a mass at the back of the testis composed of coiled tubes in which sperms are stored

epi·glot·tis \ˌep-ə-'glät-əs\ *n* : a thin plate of flexible cartilage in front of the glottis that folds back over and protects the glottis during swallowing — **epi·glot·tal** \-'glät-ᵊl\ *adj*

ep·i·gram \'ep-ə-ˌgram\ *n* **1** : a short poem ending with a clever or witty expression **2** : a brief witty saying — **ep·i·gram·ma·tist** \ˌep-ə-'gram-ət-əst\ *n*

ep·i·gram·mat·ic \ˌep-ə-grə-'mat-ik\ *adj* **1** : of, relating to, or resembling an epigram **2** : marked by or given to the use of epigrams — **ep·i·gram·mat·i·cal** \-'mat-i-kəl\ *adj* — **ep·i·gram·mat·i·cal·ly** \-i-k(ə-)lē\ *adv*

ep·i·lep·sy \'ep-ə-ˌlep-sē\ *n* : a disorder marked by abnormal electrical discharges in the brain, by attacks of convulsions, and by loss of consciousness

¹ep·i·lep·tic \ˌep-ə-'lep-tik\ *adj* : of, relating to, or having epilepsy ⟨an *epileptic* seizure⟩

²epileptic *n* : a person who has epilepsy

ep·i·logue *also* **ep·i·log** \'ep-ə-ˌlòg, -ˌläg\ *n* **1** : a final section that brings to an end and summarizes or comments on the action or characters of a story **2** : a speech often in verse addressed to the audience by an actor at the end of a play

ep·i·neph·rine \ˌep-ə-'nef-rən\ *n* : a hormone of the adrenal gland acting especially on smooth muscle, causing narrowing of blood vessels, and raising blood pressure — called also *adrenaline*

Epiph·a·ny \i-'pif-ə-nē\ *n* : January 6 observed as a Christian festival in honor of the coming of the three kings to the infant Jesus or in the Eastern church in commemoration of Jesus' baptism

ep·i·phyte \'ep-ə-ˌfīt\ *n* : a plant that gets moisture and the materials needed to make its food from the air and rain and that usually grows on another plant

ep·i·phyt·ic \ˌep-ə-'fit-ik\ *adj* **1** : of, relating to, or being an epiphyte **2** : living on the surface of plants

epis·co·pa·cy \i-'pis-kə-pə-sē\ *n, pl* **-cies** **1** : government of a church by bishops **2** : EPISCOPATE 2

epis·co·pal \i-'pis-kə-pəl\ *adj* **1** : of or relating to a bishop or episcopacy **2** *cap* : of or relating to

epiphyte

the Protestant Episcopal Church [derived from Latin *episcopus* "bishop," from Greek *episkopos,* literally, "overseer," from *epi-* "over" and *skopos* "watcher, goal, object" — related to BISHOP, HOROSCOPE, SCOPE; see *Word History* at BISHOP] — **epis·co·pal·ly** \-p(ə-)lē\ *adv*

Epis·co·pa·lian \i-ˌpis-kə-'pāl-yən\ *n* : a member of the Protestant Episcopal Church — **Episcopalian** *adj* — **Epis·co·pa·lian·ism** \-yə-ˌniz-əm\ *n*

epis·co·pate \i-'pis-kə-pət\ *n* **1** : the rank or office of or term of office of as a bishop **2** : the whole body of bishops

epis·i·ot·o·my \i-ˌpiz-ē-'ät-ə-mē\ *n, pl* **-mies** : an operation to enlarge the opening of the vagina at the time of childbirth to make delivery easier

ep·i·sode \'ep-ə-ˌsōd\ *n* : an event that is part of a longer story or of history or a life but which is viewed as complete by itself — **ep·i·sod·ic** \ˌep-ə-'säd-ik\ *adj*

epis·tle \i-'pis-əl\ *n* **1** *cap* : any of the letters to the early Christians that are part of the New Testament **2** : a formal letter

epis·to·lary \i-'pis-tə-ˌler-ē\ *adj* : of, relating to, or suitable to a letter

ep·i·taph \'ep-ə-ˌtaf\ *n* : something written (as on a gravestone) in memory of a dead person

ep·i·the·li·um \ˌep-ə-'thē-lē-əm\ *n, pl* **-lia** \-lē-ə\ **1** : a tissue like a membrane that is made up of cells and covers a free surface or lines a tube or cavity of an animal body **2** : a usually thin layer of cells of a plant that is part of the parenchyma and lines a cavity or tube — **ep·i·the·li·al** \-lē-əl\ *adj*

ep·i·thet \'ep-ə-ˌthet\ *n* **1 a** : a word or phrase (as *Lionhearted* in "Richard the Lionhearted") that expresses a quality thought to be characteristic of a person or thing **b** : a word or name used as a term of abuse **2** : the part of a taxonomic name identifying a subordinate unit within a genus — **ep·i·thet·ic** \ˌep-ə-'thet-ik\ *or* **ep·i·thet·i·cal** \-'thet-i-kəl\ *adj*

epit·o·me \i-'pit-ə-mē\ *n* **1 a** : a summary of a written work **b** : a brief statement of the main points or facts **2** : something thought to represent a basic quality or an ideal example ⟨your response was the *epitome* of good sense⟩

epit·o·mize \i-'pit-ə-ˌmīz\ *vb* **-mized; -miz·ing** : to make or serve as an epitome of

ep·och \'ep-ək, -ˌäk *also* 'ē-ˌpäk\ *n* **1** : an event or a time that begins a new period of development **2** : a memorable event, date, or period **3** : a division of geologic time less than a period and greater than an age — **ep·och·al** \-əl\ *adj* — **ep·och·al·ly** \-ə-lē\ *adv*

¹ep·oxy \i-'päk-sē\ *n, pl* **epoxies** : EPOXY RESIN

²epoxy *vb* **epoxied** *or* **epoxyed; epoxying** : to glue, fill, or coat with epoxy resin

epoxy resin *n* : a synthetic resin used chiefly in coatings and adhesives

ep·si·lon \'ep-sə-ˌlän, -lən\ *n* : the 5th letter of the Greek alphabet — E or ε

Ep·som salt \ˌep-səm-\ *n* : a bitter colorless or white salt of magnesium used especially as a strong laxative — usually used in plural

equa·ble \'ek-wə-bəl, 'ē-kwə-\ *adj* : not varying or changing; *esp* : free from extremes or sudden or harsh changes ⟨an *equable* temper⟩ ⟨an *equable* climate⟩ — **eq·ua·bly** \-blē\ *adv*

¹equal \'ē-kwəl\ *adj* **1 a** : exactly the same in number, amount, degree, rank, or quality ⟨an *equal* number of apples and oranges⟩ ⟨officers of *equal* rank⟩ ⟨of *equal* importance⟩ **b** : identical in mathematical value : EQUIVALENT **2** : not varying from one person or part to another ⟨*equal* job opportunities⟩ ⟨*equal* pressure throughout the system⟩ **3** : IMPARTIAL ⟨*equal* laws⟩ **4** : capable of meeting requirements : SUFFICIENT ⟨*equal* to the task⟩ **synonyms** see SAME — **equal·ly** *adv*

²equal *n* **1** : one that is equal ⟨has no *equal* at chess⟩ **2** : an equal quantity

³equal *vb* **equaled** *or* **equalled; equal·ing** *or* **equal·ling** **1** : to be equal to **2** : to produce something equal to : MATCH ⟨see if you can *equal* that!⟩

equal·i·ty \i-'kwäl-ət-ē\ *n, pl* **-ties** : the quality, fact, or state of being equal

equal·ize \'ē-kwə-ˌlīz\ *vb* **-ized; -iz·ing** **1** : to make equal **2** : to make uniform; *esp* : to distribute evenly — **equal·i·za·tion** \ˌē-kwə-lə-'zā-shən\ *n* — **equal·iz·er** \'ē-kwə-ˌlī-zər\ *n*

equal sign *n* : a sign = meaning mathematical or logical equality — called also *equality sign, equals sign*

equa·nim·i·ty \ˌē-kwə-ˈnim-ət-ē, ˌek-wə-\ *n, pl* **-ties** : evenness of emotions or temper : COMPOSURE ⟨accept misfortunes with *equanimity*⟩

equate \i-ˈkwāt\ *vb* **equat·ed; equat·ing** : to make or treat as equal or equivalent

equa·tion \i-ˈkwā-zhən *also* -shən\ *n* **1** : the act or process of equating : the state of being equated **2 a** : a statement of the equality of two mathematical expressions **b** : an expression involving chemical symbols for a chemical reaction

equa·tor \i-ˈkwāt-ər, ˈē-ˌkwāt-\ *n* : an imaginary circle around the earth everywhere equally distant from the north pole and the south pole

equa·to·ri·al \ˌē-kwə-ˈtōr-ē-əl, ˌek-wə-, -ˈtòr-\ *adj* **1** : of, relating to, or located at the equator **2** : of, originating in, or suggesting the region around the equator ⟨*equatorial* heat⟩

equer·ry \ˈek-wə-rē, i-ˈkwer-ē\ *n, pl* **equerries 1** : an officer in charge of the horses of a prince or nobleman **2** : a personal attendant of a member of the British royal family

¹**eques·tri·an** \i-ˈkwes-trē-ən\ *adj* : of or relating to horses, horseback riding, or people who ride horses

²**equestrian** *n* : one who rides on horseback

eques·tri·enne \i-ˌkwes-trē-ˈen\ *n* : a girl or woman who rides on horseback

equi- *combining form* : equal ⟨*equi*poise⟩ : equally ⟨*equi*angular⟩ [derived from Latin *aequi-* "equal"]

equi·an·gu·lar \ˌē-kwi-ˈaŋ-gyə-lər, ˌek-wi-\ *adj* : having all or corresponding angles equal

equi·dis·tant \ˌē-kwə-ˈdis-tənt, ˌek-wə-\ *adj* : equally distant ⟨the two points are *equidistant* from the line⟩

equi·lat·er·al \ˌē-kwə-ˈlat-ə-rəl, ˌek-wə-, -ˈla-trəl\ *adj* : having all sides or faces equal ⟨an *equilateral* triangle⟩

equi·lib·ri·um \ˌē-kwə-ˈlib-rē-əm, ˌek-wə-\ *n, pl* **-ri·ums** *or* **-ria** \-rē-ə\ **1** : a state of balance between opposing forces or actions **2** : the normal balanced state of the body of an animal that is maintained in relation to the forces (as gravity) acting on it and to things in the environment (as the surface on which life is lived) and that is sensed and checked by the inner ear of vertebrates including human beings [from Latin *aequilibrium* "state of being in balance," from *aequus* "equal" and *libra* "weight, balance, scales" — related to DELIBERATE, LIBRA]

equine \ˈē-ˌkwīn, ˈek-ˌwīn\ *adj* : of, relating to, or resembling a horse or a closely related animal — **equine** *n*

equi·noc·tial \ˌē-kwə-ˈnäk-shəl, ˌek-wə-\ *adj* **1** : of, relating to, or occurring at or near an equinox **2** : of or relating to the regions or climate near the equator : EQUATORIAL

equi·nox \ˈē-kwə-ˌnäks, ˈek-wə-\ *n* : either of the two times each year about March 21 and September 23 when the sun appears overhead at the equator and day and night are everywhere of equal length [Latin *equinoxium* (same meaning), derived from earlier Latin *aequi-* "equal" and *noct-, nox* "night" — related to NOCTURNAL]

equip \i-ˈkwip\ *vb* **equipped; equip·ping 1** : to provide with the necessary materials or supplies for service or action **2** : to make ready : PREPARE

eq·ui·page \ˈek-wə-pij\ *n* **1** : things that serve as equipment **2** : a horse-drawn carriage with or without attendants

equip·ment \i-ˈkwip-mənt\ *n* **1 a** : the act of equipping a person or thing **b** : the state of being equipped **2** : the articles serving to equip a person or thing

equi·poise \ˈek-wə-ˌpòiz, ˈē-kwə-\ *n* **1** : a state of balance : EQUILIBRIUM **2** : a weight used to balance another weight

equi·se·tum \ˌek-wə-ˈsēt-əm\ *n, pl* **-se·tums** *or* **-se·ta** \-ˈsēt-ə\ : HORSETAIL

eq·ui·ta·ble \ˈek-wət-ə-bəl\ *adj* : being fair or just ⟨reached an *equitable* settlement of their dispute⟩ — **eq·ui·ta·ble·ness** *n* — **eq·ui·ta·bly** \-blē\ *adv*

eq·ui·ta·tion \ˌek-wə-ˈtā-shən\ *n* : the action or art of riding on horseback

eq·ui·ty \ˈek-wət-ē\ *n, pl* **-ties 1** : fairness or justice in dealings between persons **2** : a system of law that is a more flexible addition to ordinary common and statute law and is designed to protect rights and achieve just settlements in cases where ordinary legal settlements may be too strict **3** : the value of an owner's interest in a property in excess of claims against it (as the amount of a mortgage)

equiv·a·lence \i-ˈkwiv-(ə-)lən(t)s\ *n* : the quality or state of being equivalent

equiv·a·len·cy \i-ˈkwiv-(ə-)lən-sē\ *n, pl* **-cies** : EQUIVALENCE

¹**equiv·a·lent** \i-ˈkwiv-(ə-)lənt\ *adj* **1 a** : alike or equal in number, value, or meaning ⟨*equivalent* statements⟩ **b** : having the same numerical value ⟨*equivalent* fractions⟩ ⟨*equivalent* numerals⟩ **c** : having the same solution set ⟨y = 2 and 2y = 4 are *equivalent* equations⟩ **2** : having the same effect or function ⟨*equivalent* methods⟩ **3** : capable of being placed in a one-to-one correspondence ⟨*equivalent* sets⟩ **synonyms** see IDENTICAL — **equiv·a·lent·ly** *adv*

²**equivalent** *n* : one that is equivalent; *esp* : a number (as a decimal) that is equivalent to another (as a fraction)

equiv·o·cal \i-ˈkwiv-ə-kəl\ *adj* **1** : having two or more possible meanings : AMBIGUOUS ⟨an *equivocal* answer⟩ **2** : not easily or definitely understood : UNCERTAIN, DOUBTFUL ⟨an *equivocal* result⟩ **3** : SUSPICIOUS 1, QUESTIONABLE ⟨*equivocal* behavior⟩ — **equiv·o·cal·ly** \-k(ə-)lē\ *adv* — **equiv·o·cal·ness** \-kəl-nəs\ *n*

equiv·o·cate \i-ˈkwiv-ə-ˌkāt\ *vb* **-cat·ed; -cat·ing** : to use equivocal language especially to deceive; *also* : to avoid giving a definite answer — **equiv·o·ca·tion** \-ˌkwiv-ə-ˈkā-shən\ *n* — **equiv·o·ca·tor** \-ˈkwiv-ə-ˌkāt-ər\ *n*

¹**-er** \ər; *after some vowels, often* r; *after* ŋ, *usually* gər\ *adj suffix or adv suffix* — used to form the comparative degree of adjectives and adverbs of one syllable ⟨hott*er*⟩ ⟨dri*er*⟩ and of some adjectives and adverbs of two or more syllables ⟨complet*er*⟩ ⟨beautiful*er*⟩ [Old English *-ra* (adjective suffix) or Old English *-or* (adverb suffix)]

²**-er** \ər; *after some vowels, often* r\ *also* **-ier** \ē-ər, yər\ *or* **-yer** \yər\ *n suffix* **1 a** : person connected with a particular job or occupation ⟨furri*er*⟩ ⟨lawy*er*⟩ **b** : person or thing belonging to or associated with ⟨old-tim*er*⟩ **c** : native of ⟨New York*er*⟩ : resident of ⟨cottag*er*⟩ **d** : one that has ⟨double-deck*er*⟩ **e** : one that produces or yields ⟨pork*er*⟩ **2 a** : one that does or performs (a specified action) ⟨report*er*⟩ **b** : one that is a suitable object of (a specified action) ⟨broil*er*⟩ **3** : one that is ⟨foreign*er*⟩ [derived from Old English *-ere* and Latin *-arius* (both noun suffixes)]

era \ˈir-ə, ˈer-ə, ˈē-rə\ *n* **1** : a period of time beginning with some special date or event ⟨the Christian *era*⟩ **2** : an important or outstanding period of history ⟨the Revolutionary *era*⟩ **3** : one of the five major divisions of geologic time ⟨Paleozoic *era*⟩ **synonyms** see PERIOD

erad·i·cate \i-ˈrad-ə-ˌkāt\ *vb* **-cat·ed; -cat·ing** : to remove by or as if by uprooting : ELIMINATE, DESTROY ⟨*eradicate* weeds⟩ ⟨*eradicating* a disease⟩ [from Latin *eradicatus*, past participle of *eradicare* "to root out, pull up by the roots," from *e-, ex-* "out, forth" and *radic-, radix* "root" — related to RADICAL, RADISH; see *Word History* at RADICAL] — **erad·i·ca·tion** \-ˌrad-ə-ˈkā-shən\ *n*

\ə\ **abut**	\aủ\ **out**	\i\ **tip**	\ò\ **saw**	\ủ\ **foot**
\ər\ **further**	\ch\ **chin**	\ī\ **life**	\òi\ **coin**	\y\ **yet**
\a\ **mat**	\e\ **pet**	\j\ **job**	\th\ **thin**	\yü\ **few**
\ā\ **take**	\ē\ **easy**	\ŋ\ **sing**	\th\ **this**	\yủ\ **cure**
\ä\ **cot, cart**	\g\ **go**	\ō\ **bone**	\ü\ **food**	\zh\ **vision**

erad·i·ca·tor \i-'rad-ə-ˌkāt-ər\ *n* : something that eradicates; *esp* : a chemical preparation for removing ink marks or stains by bleaching

erase \i-'rās\ *vb* **erased; eras·ing 1 a** : to rub out (as something written) **b** : to remove written or drawn marks from ⟨*erase* a chalkboard⟩ **c** : to remove recorded matter from ⟨*erase* a videotape⟩ **d** : to delete from a computer storage device ⟨*erase* a file⟩ **2** : to remove as if by erasing ⟨*erase* an event from one's memory⟩ — **eras·abil·i·ty** \-ˌrā-sə-'bil-ə-tē\ *n* — **eras·able** \-'rā-sə-bəl\ *adj*

eras·er \i-'rā-sər\ *n* : one that erases; *esp* : a piece of rubber or a felt pad used to erase marks (as from a pencil or chalk)

era·sure \i-'rā-shər *also* -zhər\ *n* : an act or instance of erasing

er·bi·um \'ər-bē-əm\ *n* : a soft rare metallic element — see ELEMENT table

¹ere \(ˌ)e(ə)r, (ˌ)a(ə)r\ *prep* : ²BEFORE 3

²ere *conj* : ³BEFORE 2

e–read·er \'ē-ˌrē-dər\ *n* : a handheld electronic device designed to be used for reading e-books and similar material

¹erect \i-'rekt\ *adj* **1** : straight up and down : UPRIGHT ⟨an *erect* pole⟩ ⟨*erect* poplars⟩ **2** : straight in posture ⟨sit *erect*⟩ **3** : directed upward : RAISED ⟨a tree with *erect* branches⟩ **4** : being in a state of physiological erection — **erect·ly** \-'rek-(t)lē\ *adv* — **erect·ness** \-'rek(t)-nəs\ *n*

²erect *vb* **1** : to put up or together by fitting together materials : BUILD, ASSEMBLE ⟨*erect* a building⟩ ⟨*erect* a playground slide⟩ **2** : to set upright ⟨*erect* a flagpole⟩ **3** : to construct (as a perpendicular) on a given base — **erec·tor** \i-'rek-tər\ *n*

erec·tile \i-'rek-t⁹l, -ˌtīl\ *adj* : capable of becoming erect ⟨*erectile* tissue⟩ ⟨*erectile* feathers of a bird⟩

erec·tion \i-'rek-shən\ *n* **1** : the process of erecting : the state of being erected **2 a** : the state marked by firm swollen form and erect position of a previously limp or flabby bodily part whose tissue becomes dilated with blood **b** : an occurrence of such a state (as in the penis) **3** : something erected

ere·long \e(ə)r-'lȯŋ, a(ə)r-\ *adv* : before long : SOON

erep·sin \i-'rep-sən\ *n* : a mixture of peptidases from the intestinal juice

erg \'ərg\ *n* : a centimeter-gram-second unit of work equal to the work done by a force of one dyne acting through a distance of one centimeter and equal to one ten-millionth joule

er·go \'e(ə)r-gō, 'ər-\ *adv* : THEREFORE, HENCE

er·go·nom·ics \ˌər-gə-'näm-iks\ *n sing or pl* : a science concerned with designing and arranging things people use so that the people and things interact most efficiently and safely — **er·go·nom·ic** \-ik\ *adj* — **er·go·nom·i·cal·ly** \-i-k(ə-)lē\ *adv*

Er·len·mey·er flask \ˌər-lən-ˌmī(-ə)r-, ˌer-lən-\ *n* : a flat=bottomed laboratory flask that tapers upward to a straight neck [named for Emil *Erlenmeyer* 1825–1909 German chemist]

er·mine \'ər-mən\ *n, pl* **ermine** *or* **ermines 1** : any of several weasels with black on the tail and a brown coat of fur which usually becomes white in the winter **2** : the white fur of an ermine

ermine 1

erne \'ərn, 'e(ə)rn\ *n* : EAGLE 1; *esp* : one with a white tail

erode \i-'rōd\ *vb* **erod·ed; erod·ing 1 a** : to destroy gradually by chemical means : CORRODE **b** : to wear away by or as if by the action of water, wind, or glacial ice **2** : to

undergo erosion [from Latin *erodere* "to eat away," from *e-* "away" and *rodere* "to gnaw" — related to RODENT]

ero·sion \i-'rō-zhən\ *n* : the action or process of eroding : the state of being eroded — **ero·sion·al** \-'rōzh-nəl, -'rō-zhən-⁹l\

ero·sive \i-'rō-siv, -ziv\ *adj* : tending to erode or to bring about or permit erosion ⟨the *erosive* effect of water⟩ — **ero·sive·ness** *n*

erot·ic \i-'rät-ik\ *adj* : of, relating to, or marked by sexual love or desire — **erot·i·cal·ly** \-'rät-i-k(ə-)lē\ *adv* — **erot·i·cism** \-'rät-ə-ˌsiz-əm\ *n*

err \'e(ə)r, 'ər\ *vb* **1** : to make a mistake ⟨*erred* in my calculations⟩ **2** : to do wrong : SIN

er·rand \'er-ənd\ *n* : a short trip taken to do or get something especially for someone else; *also* : the object or purpose of such a trip

er·rant \'er-ənt\ *adj* **1 a** : moving around from place to place without apparent purpose or goal **b** : wandering in search of adventure ⟨an *errant* knight⟩ **2 a** : straying outside proper bounds ⟨an *errant* calf⟩ **b** : behaving or having behaved badly or wrongfully — **er·rant·ry** \-ən-trē\ *n*

er·rat·ic \ir-'at-ik\ *adj* **1** : marked by lack of consistency or regularity ⟨*erratic* dieting⟩ **2** : not of the usual or normal kind : ECCENTRIC ⟨*erratic* behavior⟩ — **er·rat·i·cal·ly** \-'at-i-k(ə-)lē\ *adv*

er·ro·ne·ous \ir-'ō-nē-əs, e-'rō-\ *adj* : being wrong or inaccurate; *esp* : being or containing an error ⟨an *erroneous* report⟩ — **er·ro·ne·ous·ly** *adv* — **er·ro·ne·ous·ness** *n*

er·ror \'er-ər\ *n* **1 a** : departure from a code of behavior ⟨the *error* of their ways⟩ **b** : an unintentional departure from truth, accuracy, or a goal ⟨made an *error* in my adding⟩ **c** : a misplay made by a fielder in baseball **2** : the quality or state of erring **3** : a false belief or a set of false beliefs **4** : something produced by mistake **5** : the difference between an observed or calculated value and a true value; *esp* : variation in measurements, calculations, or observations of a quantity as a result of mistakes or uncontrollable conditions **6** : the amount of error — **er·ror·less** \-ləs\ *adj*

synonyms ERROR, MISTAKE, BLUNDER mean a failure to speak or act according to truth, accuracy, or good judgment. ERROR suggests that one fails to follow a model correctly ⟨an *error* in subtraction⟩. MISTAKE suggests that one misunderstands something and does not mean to do wrong ⟨took someone else's coat by *mistake*⟩. BLUNDER suggests a bad mistake made because of a lack of knowledge, intelligence, caution, or care ⟨the actors made several *blunders* during the play⟩.

¹erst·while \'ərst-ˌ(h)wīl\ *adv* : in the past : ONCE, FORMERLY

²erstwhile *adj* : FORMER 3, PREVIOUS

er·u·dite \'er-(y)ə-ˌdīt\ *adj* : having or showing erudition — **er·u·dite·ly** *adv*

er·u·di·tion \ˌer-(y)ə-'dish-ən\ *n* : a wide amount of knowledge gained chiefly from books : LEARNING

erupt \i-'rəpt\ *vb* **1** : to burst forth or cause to burst forth : EXPLODE **2** : to break through a surface ⟨teeth *erupting* from the gum⟩ **3** : to break out with or as if with a skin eruption — **erup·tive** \-'rəp-tiv\ *adj*

erup·tion \i-'rəp-shən\ *n* **1** : an act, process, or instance of erupting **2** : a product (as a skin rash) of erupting

-ery \(ə-)rē\ *n suffix, pl* **-er·ies 1** : qualities considered as a group : character ⟨snobb*ery*⟩ **2** : place of doing, keeping, producing, or selling (the thing specified) ⟨fish*ery*⟩ ⟨bak*ery*⟩ **3** : collection : aggregate ⟨fin*ery*⟩ **4** : state or condition ⟨slav*ery*⟩ [derived from early French *-erie* (noun suffix)]

eryth·ro·blas·to·sis fe·ta·lis \i-ˌrith-rə-ˌblas-'tō-səs-fi-'tal-əs\ *n* : a disease of fetuses and newborn babies that occurs when the system of an Rh-negative mother produces antibodies which destroy the red blood cells of an Rh₌ positive fetus

eryth·ro·cyte \i-ˈrith-rə-ˌsīt\ *n* : RED BLOOD CELL

eryth·ro·my·cin \i-ˌrith-rə-ˈmī-sᵊn\ *n* : an antibiotic produced by a streptomyces and active against various bacteria

eryth·ro·poi·e·tin \i-ˌrith-rō-ˈpȯi-ət-ən\ *n* : a hormone that stimulates red blood cell formation and is formed especially in the kidney

¹-es \əz, iz *after* s, z, sh, ch; z *after* v *or a vowel*\ *n pl suffix* — used to form the plural of most nouns that end in *s* ⟨glass*es*⟩, *z* ⟨fuzz*es*⟩, *sh* ⟨bush*es*⟩, *ch* ⟨peach*es*⟩, or a final *y* that changes to *i* ⟨lad*ies*⟩ and of some nouns ending in *f* that changes to *v* ⟨loa*ves*⟩ [derived from Old English *-as* (plural suffix)]

²-es *adv suffix* : ²-s

³-es *vb suffix* — used to form the third person singular present of most verbs that end in *s* ⟨bless*es*⟩, *z* ⟨fizz*es*⟩, *sh* ⟨hush*es*⟩, *ch* ⟨catch*es*⟩, or a final *y* that changes to *i* ⟨def*ies*⟩ [derived from Old English *-es, -as* (verb suffix)]

es·ca·late \ˈes-kə-ˌlāt\ *vb* **-lat·ed; -lat·ing** : to increase in extent, volume, or scope : EXPAND ⟨*escalate* prices⟩ — **es·ca·la·tion** \ˌes-kə-ˈlā-shən\ *n*

es·ca·la·tor \ˈes-kə-ˌlāt-ər\ *n* : a moving set of stairs arranged like a continuous belt

es·ca·pade \ˈes-kə-ˌpād\ *n* : a mischievous adventure

¹es·cape \is-ˈkāp\ *vb* **es·caped; es·cap·ing 1 a** : to get away ⟨*escape* from the daily routine⟩ ⟨*escape* from a burning building⟩ **b** : to leak out from some enclosed place ⟨gas is *escaping*⟩ **c** : to grow in the wild after being in cultivation **2** : to get out of the way of : AVOID ⟨*escape* punishment⟩ **3** : to fail to be noticed or recalled by ⟨the name *escapes* me⟩ **4** : to come out from or be uttered by unexpectedly or almost uncontrollably ⟨a sigh of relief *escaped* us⟩ — **es·cap·er** *n*

Word History If you were being held captive by someone gripping your coat or cloak, you might be able to get away by slipping out of it. This is the idea on which the word *escape* is based. *Escape* is made up of the Latin prefix *ex-,* which means "out of," and the Latin word *cappa,* which means "head covering" or "cloak." [early French *escaper* "to escape," from assumed Latin *excappare* (same meaning), from Latin *ex-* "out, out of" and *cappa* "head covering, cloak" — related to ²CAPE]

²escape *n* **1** : an act or instance of escaping **2** : a means of escaping **3** : a cultivated plant growing in the wild

es·cap·ee \is-ˌkāp-ˈē\ *n* : one that has escaped; *esp* : an escaped prisoner

escape velocity *n* : the lowest velocity that a moving body (as a rocket) must have to escape from the field of gravity of the earth or of a heavenly body and move outward into space

es·cap·ism \is-ˈkā-ˌpiz-əm\ *n* : a habit of thinking or a form of entertainment about purely imaginary or amusing things that provides an escape from reality or everyday matters — **es·cap·ist** \-pəst\ *adj or n*

es·car·got \ˌes-ˌkär-ˈgō\ *n, pl* **-gots** \-ˈgō(z)\ : a snail prepared for use as food

es·ca·role \ˈes-kə-ˌrōl\ *n* : endive with broad flat leaves used especially cooked as a vegetable

es·carp·ment \is-ˈkärp-mənt\ *n* **1** : a steep slope in front of a fort or defensive area **2** : a long cliff

es·chew \is-ˈchü\ *vb* : SHUN, AVOID

¹es·cort \ˈes-ˌkȯ(ə)rt\ *n* **1** : a person or group of persons accompanying another to give protection or show courtesy **2** : the man who goes on a date with a woman **3** : a protective screen of vehicles, warships, or planes ⟨motorcycle *escort*⟩ ⟨fighter *escort*⟩

²es·cort \is-ˈkȯ(ə)rt, es-ˈ, ˈes-ˌ\ *vb* : to go along with as an escort **synonyms** see ACCOMPANY

es·cu·do \is-ˈküd-ō\ *n, pl* **-dos 1** : the former basic unit of money of Portugal **2** : a coin representing one escudo [Portuguese, literally, "shield"]

es·cu·lent \ˈes-kyə-lənt\ *adj* : fit to eat

es·cutch·eon \is-ˈkəch-ən\ *n* : the shield-shaped surface on which a coat of arms is shown

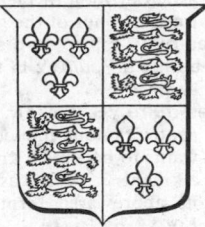

Es·dras \ˈez-drəs\ *n* — see BIBLE table

¹-ese \ˈēz, ˈēs\ *adj suffix* : of, relating to, or originating in (a specified place or country) ⟨Japan*ese*⟩ [derived from Latin *-ensis* (adjective suffix)]

escutcheon

²-ese *n suffix, pl* **-ese 1** : one born or living in (a specified place or country) ⟨Chin*ese*⟩ **2 a** : language of (a specified place, country, or nationality) ⟨Vietnam*ese*⟩ **b** : speech or literary style of (a specified place, person, group subject, or activity) ⟨journal*ese*⟩ [from ¹-ese]

es·ker \ˈes-kər\ *n* : a long narrow mound of material (as sand or gravel) deposited by a stream flowing on, within, or beneath a melting glacier

Es·ki·mo \ˈes-kə-ˌmō\ *n, pl* **Eskimo** *or* **Eskimos 1** : a member of a group of peoples of northern North America and eastern Siberia **2** : any of the languages of the Eskimo people — **Es·ki·mo·an** \ˌes-kə-ˈmō-ən\ *adj*

Eskimo dog *n* : any of an American breed of spitz dogs with a thick white coat; *also* : any of a breed of Canadian sled dogs

esoph·a·gus \i-ˈsäf-ə-gəs\ *n, pl* **-gi** \-ˌgī, -ˌjī\ : a muscular tube that leads from the cavity behind the mouth to the stomach — **esoph·age·al** \-ˌsäf-ə-ˈjē-əl\ *adj*

es·o·ter·ic \ˌes-ə-ˈter-ik\ *adj* **1** : taught to or understood by members of a special group ⟨*esoteric* knowledge⟩ **2** : hard to understand ⟨*esoteric* subjects⟩ **3** : of special or unusual interest ⟨*esoteric* colors⟩ — **es·o·ter·i·cal·ly** \-ˈter-i-k(ə-)lē\ *adv*

ESP \ˌē-ˌes-ˈpē\ *n* : EXTRASENSORY PERCEPTION

es·pa·drille \ˈes-pə-ˌdril\ *n* : a lightweight shoe with a cloth upper and flexible sole often with a rope braid around the edge

es·pal·ier \is-ˈpal-yər, -ˌyā\ *n* : a plant (as a fruit tree) trained to grow flat against a support (as a wall or trellis) — **espalier** *vb*

es·par·to \is-ˈpärt-ō\ *n, pl* **-tos** : either of two Spanish and Algerian grasses from which rope, shoes, baskets, and paper are made — called also *esparto grass*

es·pe·cial \is-ˈpesh-əl\ *adj* **1** : UNUSUAL, NOTABLE ⟨put *especial* emphasis on this point⟩ **2** : relating to or unique to a certain person or thing : PARTICULAR ⟨each has its own *especial* qualities⟩ — **es·pe·cial·ly** \-ˈpesh-(ə-)lē\ *adv*

es·pi·o·nage \ˈes-pē-ə-ˌnäzh, -näj, -nij\ *n* : the practice of spying : the use of spies

es·pla·nade \ˈes-plə-ˌnäd, ˌes-plə-ˈ\ *n* : a level open stretch or area; *esp* : one for walking or driving along a shore

es·pous·al \is-ˈpau̇-zəl *also* -səl\ *n* **1 a** : WEDDING **b** : the act of becoming engaged : state of being engaged **2** : a taking up of a cause or belief as a supporter

es·pouse \is-ˈpau̇z, -ˈpau̇s\ *vb* **es·poused; es·pous·ing 1 a** : ¹MARRY 2 **b** : ¹MARRY 3 **2** : to take up the cause of : SUPPORT — **es·pous·er** *n*

\ə\ abut	\au̇\ out	\i\ tip	\ȯ\ saw	\u̇\ foot
\ər\ further	\ch\ chin	\ī\ life	\ȯi\ coin	\y\ yet
\a\ mat	\e\ pet	\j\ job	\th\ thin	\yü\ few
\ā\ take	\ē\ easy	\ŋ\ sing	\th\ this	\yu̇\ cure
\ä\ cot, cart	\g\ go	\ō\ bone	\ü\ food	\zh\ vision

espres·so \e-'spres-ō\ *also* **ex·pres·so** \ik-'spres-ō\ *n, pl* **-sos** : coffee brewed by forcing steam or hot water through finely ground darkly roasted coffee beans

es·prit \is-'prē\ *n* : lively cleverness or wit [from French *esprit*, literally, "spirit"]

es·prit de corps \is-,prēd-ə-'kō(ə)r, -'kȯ(ə)r\ *n* : enthusiastic devotion of members to a group and strong regard for the honor of the group

es·py \is-'pī\ *vb* **es·pied; es·py·ing** : to catch sight of

-esque *adj suffix* : in the manner or style of : like 〈statu-*esque*〉

es·quire \'es-,kwī(ə)r, is-'\ *n* **1** : a member of the English gentry ranking immediately below a knight **2** : one who wants to become a knight and who works as a servant to a knight **3** — used as a title of courtesy usually placed in its abbreviated form after the surname 〈John Smith, *Esq.*〉

-ess \əs, is *also* ,es\ *n suffix* : female 〈priest*ess*〉 [derived from Greek *-issa* (feminine noun suffix)]

¹es·say \e-'sā, 'es-,ā\ *vb* : ¹ATTEMPT 1, TRY 〈again *essayed* to ride on the camel〉

²es·say \'es-,ā, *in sense 1 also* e-'sā\ *n* **1** : ²ATTEMPT 1, TRY; *esp* : an uncertain or hesitant effort **2** : a usually short written work giving a personal view or opinion on a subject

es·say·ist \'es-,ā-əst\ *n* : a writer of essays

es·sence \'es-ən(t)s\ *n* **1** : the basic nature of a thing : the quality or qualities that make a thing what it is 〈the *essence* of love is unselfishness〉 **2** : a substance physically or chemically separated from another substance (as a plant or drug) and having the special qualities (as odor) of the original substance 〈*essence* of peppermint〉 **3** : ¹PERFUME 1, SCENT

¹es·sen·tial \i-'sen-chəl\ *adj* **1** : forming or belonging to the essence 〈free speech is an *essential* right of citizenship〉 **2** : containing or having the character of an easily evaporated essence 〈*essential* oils〉 **3** : important in the highest degree : NECESSARY 〈food is *essential* to life〉 — **es·sen·ti·al·i·ty** \-,sen-chē-'al-ət-ē\ *n* — **es·sen·tial·ly** \-'sench-(ə-)lē\ *adv* — **es·sen·tial·ness** \-'sen-chəl-nəs\ *n*

²essential *n* : something basic, necessary, or indispensable 〈the *essentials* for success〉

essential amino acid *n* : an amino acid that is necessary for proper growth of the animal body and that cannot be made by the body in sufficient amounts but must be obtained from food containing proteins

¹-est \əst, ist\ *adj suffix or adv suffix* — used to form the superlative degree of adjectives and adverbs of one syllable 〈fatt*est*〉 〈lat*est*〉 and of some adjectives and adverbs of two or more syllables 〈lucki*est*〉 〈often*est*〉 [Old English *-est, -ost* (adjective or adverb suffix)]

²-est \əst, ist\ *or* **-st** \st\ *vb suffix* — used to form the archaic second person singular of verbs (with *thou*) 〈gett*est*〉 〈did*st*〉 〈can*st*〉 [Old English *-est, -ast* (verb suffix)]

es·tab·lish \is-'tab-lish\ *vb* **1** : to make a permanent part of a nation's laws 〈*establish* a constitution〉 **2** : to make firm or stable 〈*establish* a statue on its base〉 **3 a** : to bring into existence : FOUND 〈*establish* a republic〉 〈*establish* a school〉 **b** : to cause to exist 〈*establish* good relations〉 〈*establish* radio contact〉 **4** : to set on a firm basis 〈*establish* their children in business〉 **5** : to gain full recognition or acceptance of 〈*establish* a claim〉 〈a film that *established* her as a star〉 〈*established* his innocence〉 **6** : PROVE **7** : FIND OUT 1 〈*establish* the cause of the fire〉 — **es·tab·lish·er** *n*

established church *n* : a church recognized by law as the official church of a nation

es·tab·lish·ment \is-'tab-lish-mənt\ *n* **1** : the act of establishing : the state or fact of being established 〈*establishment* of a church〉 〈*establishment* of a scientific fact〉 **2** : a place for residence or business 〈a dry-cleaning *establishment*〉 **3** : an established order of society; *also, often*

cap : the social, economic, and political leaders of such an order 〈rebelling against the *establishment*〉

es·tate \is-'tāt\ *n* **1** : the condition or circumstances of one's existence **2** : a social or political class **3 a** : the possessions or property of a person; *esp* : a person's property in land **b** : the assets and liabilities left by a person at death **c** : a large country house on a large piece of land

¹es·teem \is-'tēm\ *n* : the degree of respect or liking one has for something or someone; *esp* : a very favorable opinion

²esteem *vb* **1** : to think of in a particular way : CONSIDER 〈*esteem* it a privilege〉 **2** : to think very highly or favorably of

es·ter \'es-tər\ *n* : an organic compound formed by the reaction between an acid and an alcohol

Es·ther \'es-tər\ *n* — see BIBLE table

esthetic, esthetics *variant of* AESTHETIC, AESTHETICS

¹es·ti·mate \'es-tə-,māt\ *vb* **-mat·ed; -mat·ing** **1** : to judge the approximate value, size, or cost of on the basis of experience or observation rather than actual measurement 〈*estimate* the distance〉 〈*estimate* a painting job〉 **2** : CONCLUDE 2, DETERMINE 〈*estimated* that the fire started in the kitchen〉 — **es·ti·ma·tor** \-,māt-ər\ *n*

²es·ti·mate \'es-tə-mət\ *n* **1** : the act of estimating **2** : an opinion or judgment of the nature, character, or quality of a thing **3** : a rough or approximate calculation **4** : a statement by a contractor of the probable cost for a job

es·ti·ma·tion \,es-tə-'mā-shən\ *n* **1** : JUDGMENT 3, OPINION **2** : ²ESTIMATE 3 **3** : ¹ESTEEM

es·ti·vate *also* **aes·ti·vate** \'es-tə-,vāt\ *vb* **-vat·ed; -vat·ing** : to pass the summer in an inactive or resting state — **es·ti·va·tion** *also* **aes·ti·va·tion** \,es-tə-'vā-shən\ *n*

Es·to·nian \e-'stō-nē-ən, -nyən\ *n* **1** : a member of a people chiefly of Estonia **2** : the language of the Estonians — **Estonian** *adj*

es·trange \is-'trānj\ *vb* **es·tranged; es·trang·ing** : to cause to change from friendly or loving to unfriendly or uncaring : ALIENATE 〈*estranged* from their children〉 — **es·trange·ment** \-mənt\ *n*

es·tro·gen \'es-trə-jən\ *n* : a substance that tends to cause the development of secondary sex characteristics in the female and promote the growth and normal functioning of the female reproductive system — **es·tro·gen·ic** \,es-trə-'jen-ik\ *adj*

estrous cycle *n* : the cycle of changes in the endocrine and reproductive systems of a female mammal from the beginning of one period of estrus to the beginning of the next

es·trus \'es-trəs\ *n* **1** : a periodic state during which the female of most mammals is willing to mate with the male and is capable of becoming pregnant **2** : ESTROUS CYCLE — **es·trous** \-trəs\ *adj*

es·tu·ary \'es-chə-,wer-ē\ *n, pl* **-ar·ies** : a passage where the tide meets a river current; *esp* : an arm of the sea at the lower end of a river — **es·tu·a·rine** \'es-chə-wə-,rīn\ *adj*

¹-et \'et, ,et, ət, it\ *n suffix* : small one : lesser one 〈baron*et*〉 〈cellar*et*〉 [derived from Latin *-itus, -ita* (noun suffix) "small one"]

²-et *n suffix* : group 〈oct*et*〉 [from du*et*]

eta \'āt-ə\ *n* : the seventh letter of the Greek alphabet — H or η

éta·gère *or* **eta·gere** \,ā-tä-'zhe(ə)r, ,āt-ə-\ *n* : a piece of furniture that consists of a set of open shelves [French]

et cet·era \et-'set-ə-rə, -'se-trə\ : and others especially of the same kind [Latin]

etch \'ech\ *vb* **1 a** : to produce (as a pattern or design) on a hard material by lines eaten into the material's surface (as by acid or laser beam) **b** : to produce a pattern or design on by such etching 〈*etched* glass〉 〈an *etched* silicon chip〉 **2** : to outline or impress clearly 〈migrating ducks *etched* against the sky〉 — **etch·er** *n*

etch·ing \'ech-in\ *n* **1 a** : the act or process of etching a hard material **b** : the art of printing from an etched metal plate **2 a** : a product of etching **b** : a print made from an etched metal plate

eter·nal \i-'tərn-ᵊl\ *adj* **1** : having no beginning and no end : lasting forever ⟨*eternal* bliss⟩ **2** : continuing without interruption ⟨that dog's *eternal* barking⟩ — **eter·nal·ly** \-ᵊl-ē\ *adv* — **eter·nal·ness** *n*

eter·ni·ty \i-'tər-nət-ē\ *n, pl* **-ties** **1** : the quality or state of being eternal **2** : endless time **3** : the state after death : IMMORTALITY **4** : time that seems to be endless

¹-eth \əth, ith\ *or* **-th** \th\ *vb suffix* — used to form the archaic third person singular present of verbs ⟨do*th*⟩ [Old English *-eth, -ath, -th* (verb suffix)]

²-eth — see **²-TH**

eth·ane \'eth-ˌān\ *n* : a colorless odorless gas that consists of carbon and hydrogen, is found in natural gas, and is used especially as a fuel

eth·a·nol \'eth-ə-ˌnȯl, -ˌnōl\ *n* : a colorless flammable easily evaporated liquid that is used to dissolve things and that is the substance in fermented and distilled liquors that can make one drunk — called also *ethyl alcohol, grain alcohol*

eth·ene \'eth-ˌēn\ *n* : ETHYLENE

ether \'ē-thər\ *n* **1 a** : an invisible substance once believed to fill the upper regions of space **b** : the upper regions of space : HEAVENS **2** : an easily evaporated flammable liquid used chiefly to dissolve other substances and especially formerly as an anesthetic

ethe·re·al \i-'thir-ē-əl\ *adj* **1** : of or relating to the heavens : HEAVENLY **2** : being light and airy : DELICATE — **ethe·re·al·ly** \-ē-ə-lē\ *adv* — **ethe·re·al·ness** *n*

ether·ize \'ē-thə-ˌrīz\ *vb* **-ized; -iz·ing** : to treat or anesthetize with ether

eth·i·cal \'eth-i-kəl\ *adj* **1** : of or relating to ethics **2 a** : following accepted rules of conduct **b** : following professional standards of conduct **3** : sold only on a doctor's prescription ⟨*ethical* drugs⟩ — **eth·i·cal·ly** \-i-k(ə-)lē\ *adv*

eth·ics \'eth-iks\ *n sing or pl* **1** : a branch of philosophy dealing with what is good and bad and with moral duty and obligation **2** : the rules of moral conduct governing an individual or a group

Ethi·op·ic \ˌē-thē-'äp-ik, -'ō-pik\ *n* : a language formerly spoken in Ethiopia and still used in church services there

¹eth·nic \'eth-nik\ *n* : a member of an ethnic group; *esp* : a member of a minority group who keeps customs, language, or social ideas of the group

²ethnic *adj* **1** : of or relating to groups of people with common traits and customs and a sense of shared identity ⟨*ethnic* minorities⟩ **2** : of or relating to ethnics ⟨*ethnic* neighborhoods⟩ — **eth·ni·cal·ly** \-ni-k(ə-)lē\ *adv*

eth·no·cen·tric \ˌeth-nō-'sen-trik\ *adj* : favoring one's own ethnic group

eth·nol·o·gist \eth-'näl-ə-jəst\ *n* : a specialist in the science or study of ethnology

eth·nol·o·gy \eth-'näl-ə-jē\ *n* : a science that studies and compares human cultures — **eth·no·log·i·cal** \ˌeth-nə-'läj-i-kəl\ *adj*

ethol·o·gist \ē-'thäl-ə-jəst\ *n* : a specialist in ethology

ethol·o·gy \ē-'thäl-ə-jē\ *n* : the scientific study of animal behavior

ethyl alcohol *n* : ETHANOL

eth·yl·ene \'eth-ə-ˌlēn\ *n* : a colorless flammable gas found in coal gas or obtained from petroleum and used to ripen fruits or as an anesthetic

ethylene gly·col \-'glī-ˌkȯl, -ˌkōl\ *n* : a thick liquid alcohol used especially as an antifreeze and in making polyester fibers

eth·yne \'ē-ˌthīn, e-'thīn\ *n* : ACETYLENE

eti·o·lat·ed \ˌēt-ē-ə-'lāt-əd\ *adj* **1** : bleached because of having grown in the absence of light ⟨*etiolated* bean seedlings⟩ **2** : pale and sickly

eti·ol·o·gy \ˌēt-ē-'äl-ə-jē\ *n* : the cause or origin especially of a disease

et·i·quette \'et-i-kət, -ˌket\ *n* : the rules governing the proper way to behave [from French *étiquette* "etiquette," literally, "ticket," from earlier *etiquet* "ticket" — related to TICKET]

Etrus·can \i-'trəs-kən\ *n* **1** : a person born or living in ancient Etruria **2** : the language of the Etruscans — **Etruscan** *adj*

-ette \'et, ˌet, ət, it\ *n suffix* **1** : little one ⟨kitchen*ette*⟩ **2** : female ⟨major*ette*⟩ [derived from early French *-ette,* feminine form of *-et* "small one"]

étude \'ā-ˌt(y)üd\ *n* : a piece of music for practice [from French *étude,* literally, "study"]

et·y·mol·o·gy \ˌet-ə-'mäl-ə-jē\ *n, pl* **-gies** : the history of a word shown by tracing it or its parts back to the earliest known forms and meanings both in its own language and any other language from which it or its parts may have been taken [Latin *etymologia* "etymology," from Greek *etymon* "true meaning of a word" and Greek *-logia* "study, science," from *etymos* "true" and *logos* "word, reason"] — **et·y·mo·log·i·cal** \-mə-'läj-i-kəl\ *adj* — **et·y·mo·log·i·cal·ly** \-'läj-i-k(ə-)lē\ *adv* — **et·y·mol·o·gist** \-'mäl-ə-jəst\ *n*

eu·ca·lypt \'yü-kə-ˌlipt\ *n* : EUCALYPTUS

eu·ca·lyp·tus \ˌyü-kə-'lip-təs\ *n, pl* **-ti** \-ˌtī, -ˌtē\ *or* **-tus·es** : any of a genus of mostly Australian evergreen trees of the myrtle family including many that are widely cultivated for their gums, resins, oils, and useful woods

Eu·cha·rist \'yü-k(ə-)rəst\ *n* : COMMUNION 1a [derived from Greek *eucharistia* "Eucharist, gratitude," from *eu-* "good" and *charizesthai* "to show favor or gratitude"] — **eu·cha·ris·tic** \ˌyü-kə-'ris-tik\ *adj, often cap*

Eu·clid·e·an \yu̇-'klid-ē-ən\ *adj* : of or relating to the geometry of Euclid

eu·di·om·e·ter \ˌyüd-ē-'äm-ət-ər\ *n* : an instrument used to analyze and measure the volume of gases

eu·gen·ic \yu̇-'jen-ik\ *adj* **1** : relating to or fitted for the production of good offspring **2** : of or relating to eugenics

eu·gen·ics \yu̇-'jen-iks\ *n* : a science that deals with the improvement of inherited qualities of a race or breed and especially of human beings

eu·gle·na \yu̇-'glē-nə\ *n* : any of a large genus of green freshwater flagellates often classified with the algae

eu·gle·noid \yu̇-'glē-ˌnȯid\ *n* : any of a group of varied flagellates that are typically green or colorless, live alone, and have one or two flagella coming out of a food-intake opening — **euglenoid** *adj*

euglenoid movement *n* : wriggly movement typical of some euglenoid flagellates

eu·kary·ote \(ˌ)yü-'ke(ə)r-ē-ˌōt, 'ka(ə)r-\ *n* : an organism composed of one or more cells with clearly viewable nuclei

eu·lo·gize \'yü-lə-ˌjīz\ *vb* **-gized; -giz·ing** : to speak or write high praise of — **eu·lo·gist** \-jəst\ *n*

eu·lo·gy \'yü-lə-jē\ *n, pl* **-gies** **1** : a formal speech or writing especially in honor of a dead person **2** : high praise

eu·lo·gis·tic \ˌyü-lə-'jis-tik\ *adj* — **eu·lo·gis·ti·cal·ly** \-ti-k(ə-)lē\ *adv*

euglena

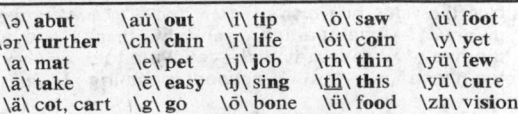

\ə\ abut	\au̇\ out	\i\ tip	\ȯ\ saw	\u̇\ foot
\ər\ further	\ch\ chin	\ī\ life	\ȯi\ coin	\y\ yet
\a\ mat	\e\ pet	\j\ job	\th\ thin	\yü\ few
\ā\ take	\ē\ easy	\ŋ\ sing	\th\ this	\yu̇\ cure
\ä\ cot, cart	\g\ go	\ō\ bone	\ü\ food	\zh\ vision

eu·phe·mism \\'yü-fə-ˌmiz-əm\\ *n* : the substitution of a mild or pleasant expression for one that is too strong or unpleasant; *also* : a mild or pleasant expression so substituted 〈"pass away" is a widely used *euphemism* for die〉 — **eu·phe·mis·tic** \\ˌyü-fə-'mis-tik\\ *adj* — **eu·phe·mis·ti·cal·ly** \\-ti-k(ə-)lē\\ *adv*

eu·pho·ni·um \\yu̇-'fō-nē-əm\\ *n* : a brass musical instrument resembling a tuba but playing in a higher pitch range

eu·pho·ny \\'yü-fə-nē\\ *n, pl* **-nies** : pleasing or sweet sound; *esp* : the pleasant sound of words combined together [from French *euphonie* "pleasing sound," from Latin *euphonia* (same meaning), derived from Greek *eu-* "good" and Greek *phōnē* "voice, sound" — related to PHONETIC, SYMPHONY] — **eu·pho·ni·ous** \\yu̇-'fō-nē-əs\\ *adj*

eu·pho·ria \\yu̇-'fōr-ē-ə, -'fȯr-\\ *n* : a strong feeling of happiness — **eu·phor·ic** \\-'fȯr-ik, -'fär-\\ *adj*

euphonium

Eur·asian \\yu̇-'rā-zhən, -shən\\ *adj* **1** : of or relating to Eurasia **2** : of mixed European and Asian origin — **Eurasian** *n*

eu·re·ka \\yu̇-'rē-kə\\ *interj* — used to express the thrill of discovery [from Greek *heurēka* "I have found it"]

eu·ro \\'yu̇r-(ˌ)ō\\ *n, pl* **euros** *also* **euro** : the common basic unit of money of most countries of the European Union

Eu·ro-Amer·i·can \\ˌyu̇r-ō-ə-'mer-ə-kən\\ *adj* **1** : of or relating to Europe and America **2** : of mixed European and American origin — **Euro-American** *n*

¹**Eu·ro·pe·an** \\ˌyu̇r-ə-'pē-ən\\ *adj* : of or relating to Europe or its people

²**European** *n* **1** : a person born or living in Europe **2** : a person of European ancestry

Eu·ro·pe·an·ism \\ˌyu̇r-ə-'pē-ə-niz-əm\\ *n* : loyalty to the traditions, interests, or standards of Europeans

Eu·ro·pe·an·ize \\yu̇r-ə-'pē-ə-ˌnīz\\ *vb* **-ized; -iz·ing** : to make or become European (as in customs, habits, dress, or speech) — **Eu·ro·pe·an·i·za·tion** \\-ˌpē-ə-nə-'zā-shən\\ *n*

eu·ro·pi·um \\yu̇-'rō-pē-əm\\ *n* : a soft rare metallic chemical element — see ELEMENT table

eu·ro·zone \\'yu̇r-ō-ˌzōn\\ *n* : the geographical area comprising the countries that use the euro as the official currency

eu·sta·chian tube \\yu̇-ˌstā-sh(ē)ən-, -ˌstā-kē-ən-\\ *n, often cap E* : a tube connecting the middle ear with the upper pharynx and equalizing air pressure on both sides of the eardrum

eu·tha·na·sia \\ˌyü-thə-'nā-zh(ē-)ə\\ *n* : the act or practice of killing or permitting the death of hopelessly sick or injured persons or animals with as little pain as possible for reasons of mercy — called also *mercy killing*

evac·u·ate \\i-'vak-yə-ˌwāt\\ *vb* **-at·ed; -at·ing** **1** : to make empty **2** : to discharge waste matter from the body **3** : to remove something (as a gas) from especially by pumping **4 a** : to remove troops or people from a place of danger **b** : VACATE 〈*evacuate* the building〉 — **evac·u·a·tion** \\-ˌvak-yə-'wā-shən\\ *n*

evac·u·ee \\i-ˌvak-yə-'wē\\ *n* : an evacuated person

evade \\i-'vād\\ *vb* **evad·ed; evad·ing** **1** : to get away from or avoid by skill or trickery 〈*evade* a question〉 〈*evade* capture〉 **2** : to escape the understanding of 〈the meaning of the message *evaded* them〉 — **evad·able** \\-'vād-ə-bəl\\ *adj* — **evad·er** *n*

eval·u·ate \\i-'val-yə-ˌwāt\\ *vb* **-at·ed; -at·ing** **1** : to find the value of 〈*evaluate* a mathematical expression〉 **2** : to decide the value or worth of after study 〈*evaluate* a new program〉 — **eval·u·a·tion** \\-ˌval-yə-'wā-shən\\ *n* — **eval·u·a·tive** \\-'val-yə-ˌwāt-iv\\ *adj* — **eval·u·a·tor** \\-ˌwāt-ər\\ *n*

ev·a·nesce \\ˌev-ə-'nes\\ *vb* **-nesced; -nesc·ing** : to vanish like vapor

ev·a·nes·cence \\ˌev-ə-'nes-ᵊn(t)s\\ *n* : evanescent quality

ev·a·nes·cent \\ˌev-ə-'nes-ᵊnt\\ *adj* : tending to vanish like vapor : not lasting 〈*evanescent* pleasures〉

evan·gel·i·cal \\ˌē-ˌvan-'jel-i-kəl, ˌev-ən-\\ *adj* **1** : of, relating to, or being in agreement with the Christian gospel especially as given in the four Gospels **2** : stressing salvation by faith in Jesus, the authority of the Bible, and the importance of preaching

evan·ge·lism \\i-'van-jə-ˌliz-əm\\ *n* : the winning or reawakening of personal commitments to Jesus — **evan·ge·lis·tic** \\-ˌvan-jə-'lis-tik\\ *adj*

evan·ge·list \\i-'van-jə-ləst\\ *n* : a Christian preacher who goes about from place to place trying to change or increase people's religious feelings [Middle English *evangelist* "one of the writers of the four Gospels," from early French and Latin *evangelista* (same meaning), from Greek *euangelizein* "to preach the gospel," from *euangelion* "good news, gospel," from *eu-* "good" and *angelos* "messenger, angel"]

evap·o·rate \\i-'vap-ə-ˌrāt\\ *vb* **-rat·ed; -rat·ing** **1** : to pass off or cause to pass off into vapor from a liquid state **2** : to pass off or away : DISAPPEAR 〈felt the excitement *evaporate*〉 **3** : to remove some of the water from (as by heating) — **evap·o·ra·tor** \\-ˌrāt-ər\\ *n*

evaporated milk *n* : unsweetened canned milk from which much of the water has been evaporated

evap·o·ra·tion \\i-ˌvap-ə-'rā-shən\\ *n* : the process of evaporating

evap·o·rite \\i-'vap-ə-ˌrīt\\ *n* : a sedimentary rock (as gypsum) that forms from evaporation of seawater in an enclosed basin

eva·sion \\i-'vā-zhən\\ *n* **1** : a means of evading **2** : the act or an instance of evading : ESCAPE 〈tax *evasion*〉

eva·sive \\i-'vā-siv, -ziv\\ *adj* : tending or meant to evade 〈gave an *evasive* answer〉 — **eva·sive·ly** *adv* — **eva·sive·ness** *n*

eve \\'ēv\\ *n* **1** : EVENING **2** : the evening or the day before a special day 〈New Year's *Eve*〉 **3** : the period just before an important event

¹**even** \\'ē-vən\\ *n, archaic* : EVENING

²**even** *adj* **1 a** : having a horizontal surface : FLAT 〈*even* ground〉 **b** : being without breaks or bumps : SMOOTH 〈an *even* line〉 **c** : being on the same line or level 〈houses *even* with each other〉 **2 a** : equal in size, number, or amount 〈*even* distances apart〉 **b** : staying the same over a period of time 〈*even* breathing〉 **3 a** : without advantage on either side : FAIR 〈start out *even*〉 〈an *even* trade〉 **b** : leaving nothing due on either side 〈now we're *even*〉 **c** : showing neither profit nor loss **4 a** : being any number that can be divided by two without remainder 〈2, 4, 6, 8, . . . are *even* numbers〉 **b** : marked by an even number 〈an *even* page of a book〉 **5** : being whole or exact without a remainder or fractional part 〈an *even* dollar〉 〈an *even* dozen〉 *synonyms* see LEVEL — **even·ly** *adv* — **even·ness** \\-vən-nəs\\ *n*

³**even** *adv* **1 a** : EXACTLY 1, PRECISELY 〈believes *even* as we do〉 **b** : to a degree that extends : FULLY 〈faithful *even* to death〉 **c** : at the very same time 〈raining *even* as the sun came out〉 **2** : INDEED 〈willing, *even* eager, to help〉 **3** — used to stress an extreme or highly unlikely condition or instance 〈so simple *even* a child can do it〉 **4** : to a greater extent or degree 〈*even* better〉 **5** — used to stress the smallness of an amount or effort 〈didn't *even* offer to help〉 〈gave it not *even* a glance〉

⁴**even** *vb* **evened; even·ing** \\'ēv-(ə-)nin̈\\ : to make or become even — **even·er** \\'ēv-(ə-)nər\\ *n*

even·hand·ed \\ˌē-vən-'han-dəd\\ *adj* : not favoring one over another : FAIR, IMPARTIAL 〈an *evenhanded* decision〉

eve·ning \\'ēv-nin̈\\ *n* **1** : the final part of the day and early part of the night **2** : a late part 〈the *evening* of life〉

evening primrose *n* **1** : a coarse herb that lives two years and produces yellow flowers that open in the evening **2** : any of several plants related to the evening primrose

evening star *n* : a bright planet (as Venus) seen especially in the western sky at or after sunset

even·song \'ē-vən-ˌsȯŋ\ *n, often cap* : VESPERS

event \i-'vent\ *n* **1 a** : something usually of importance that happens **b** : a social occasion or activity (as a party) **2** : EVENTUALITY ⟨in the *event* of rain the ceremony will be held indoors⟩ **3** : any of the contests in a program of sports ⟨track-and-field *events*⟩ **4** : a possible result in an experiment in probability or statistics ⟨rolling a 7 is an *event* in the throwing of two dice⟩

event·ful \i-'vent-fəl\ *adj* **1** : full of events ⟨an *eventful* day⟩ **2** : very important : MOMENTOUS — **event·ful·ly** \-fə-lē\ *adv* — **event·ful·ness** *n*

even·tide \'ē-vən-ˌtīd\ *n* : EVENING 1

even·tu·al \i-'vench-(ə-)wəl, -'ven-chəl\ *adj* : coming at some later time ⟨our *eventual* success⟩

even·tu·al·i·ty \i-ˌven-chə-'wal-ət-ē\ *n, pl* **-ties** : something that might happen : POSSIBILITY

even·tu·al·ly \i-'vench-(ə-)wəl-ē, -'ven-chəl-ē\ *adv* : at some later time : in the end

ev·er \'ev-ər\ *adv* **1** : at all times : ALWAYS ⟨*ever* faithful⟩ **2 a** : at any time ⟨has this *ever* been done before⟩ **b** : in any way : AT ALL ⟨how can I *ever* thank you⟩ **3** — used especially with *so* to give more force to a word ⟨thank you *ever* so much⟩

ev·er·glade \'ev-ər-ˌglād\ *n* : a low-lying tract of swampy or marshy land

¹ev·er·green \'ev-ər-ˌgrēn\ *adj* : having leaves that remain green and functional through more than one growing season ⟨most conifers are *evergreen* trees⟩ — compare DECIDUOUS

²evergreen *n* **1** : an evergreen plant; *also* : CONIFER **2** *pl* : twigs and branches of evergreen plants used for decoration

¹ev·er·last·ing \ˌev-ər-'las-tiŋ\ *adj* **1** : lasting forever : ETERNAL **2 a** : going on for a long time or for too long ⟨*everlasting* complaints⟩ **b** : keeping form or color for a long time when dried ⟨*everlasting* flowers⟩ — **ev·er·last·ing·ly** \-tiŋ-lē\ *adv* — **ev·er·last·ing·ness** *n*

²everlasting *n* **1** : a plant with everlasting flowers **2** : an everlasting flower

ev·er·more \ˌev-ər-'mō(ə)r, -'mȯ(ə)r\ *adv* : FOREVER

ev·ery \'ev-rē\ *adj* **1** : being each one of a group or series without leaving out any ⟨heard *every* word you said⟩ **2** : ¹COMPLETE 3, ENTIRE ⟨have *every* confidence in you⟩

ev·ery·body \'ev-ri-ˌbäd-ē, -ˌbəd-ē\ *pron* : EVERYONE

ev·ery·day \ˌev-rē-ˌdā\ *adj* : used, suitable for, or seen every day : ORDINARY ⟨*everyday* clothes⟩

ev·ery·one \'ev-rē-(ˌ)wən\ *pron* : every person : EVERYBODY

ev·ery·place \-ˌplās\ *adv* : EVERYWHERE

ev·ery·thing \-ˌthiŋ\ *pron* **1 a** : every thing there is : ALL **b** : all that relates to the subject ⟨tell *everything*⟩ **2** : the most important thing ⟨to some people money is *everything*⟩

ev·ery·where \-ˌ(h)we(ə)r, -ˌ(h)wa(ə)r\ *adv* : in or to every place

evict \i-'vikt\ *vb* : to put (a person) out from property by legal action — **evic·tion** \-'vik-shən\ *n* — **evic·tor** \-'vik-tər\ *n*

¹ev·i·dence \'ev-əd-ən(t)s, -ə-ˌden(t)s\ *n* **1** : an outward sign : INDICATION ⟨*evidence* of the life of ancient people⟩ ⟨gave no *evidence* that he was going to bunt⟩ **2** : material presented to a court to help find the truth in a matter — **in evidence** : to be easily seen : CONSPICUOUS

²evidence *vb* **-denced; -denc·ing** : to be or give evidence of : PROVE

ev·i·dent \'ev-əd-ənt, -ə-ˌdent\ *adj* : clear to the sight or mind : PLAIN ⟨was *evident* that they were twins⟩ [Middle English *evident* "clearly seen or understood," from early French *evident* (same meaning), from Latin *evident-*, *evidens* (same meaning), from *e-*, *ex-* "out, away" and *vident-*, *videns*, a form of *vidēre* "to see" — related to VISION]

ev·i·dent·ly \'ev-əd-ənt-lē, -ə-ˌdent-; ˌev-ə-'dent-lē\ *adv* : in an evident manner : OBVIOUSLY ⟨a document *evidently* forged⟩

¹evil \'ē-vəl\ *adj* **evil·er** *or* **evil·ler; evil·est** *or* **evil·lest 1** : morally bad : WICKED **2 a** : causing harm : tending to injure **b** : marked by misfortune ⟨*evil* days⟩ — **evil·ly** \-vəl-(l)ē\ *adv*

²evil *n* **1** : something that brings sorrow, trouble, or destruction **2** : the fact of suffering or wrongdoing

evil·do·er \ˌē-vəl-'dü-ər\ *n* : a person who does evil — **evil·do·ing** \-'dü-iŋ\ *n*

evil eye *n* : an eye or glance thought to be able to do harm

evil–mind·ed \ˌē-vəl-'mīn-dəd\ *adj* : having an evil character or evil thoughts

evince \i-'vin(t)s\ *vb* **evinced; evinc·ing** : to give evidence of : show clearly ⟨*evinced* an interest in music at an early age⟩

evis·cer·ate \i-'vis-ə-ˌrāt\ *vb* **-at·ed; -at·ing** : to take out the internal organs of — **evis·cer·a·tion** \-ˌvis-ə-'rā-shən\ *n*

evo·ca·tion \ˌē-vō-'kā-shən, ˌev-ə-\ *n* : an act or instance of evoking

evoc·a·tive \i-'väk-ət-iv\ *adj* : having the power to evoke an especially emotional response ⟨an *evocative* photograph⟩

evoke \i-'vōk\ *vb* **evoked; evok·ing** : to call forth or up : SUMMON ⟨the song *evoked* memories of summer⟩

evo·lu·tion \ˌev-ə-'lü-shən, ˌē-və-\ *n* **1 a** : a process of change in a certain direction; *esp* : a process of constant change from a lower or simple state to a higher or more complex state : GROWTH **b** : something evolved **2** : the process of working out or developing **3 a** : the process by which new species or populations of living things develop from preexisting forms through successive generations **b** : the scientific theory explaining the appearance of new species and varieties through the action of various biological mechanisms (as natural selection or genetic mutation) — **evo·lu·tion·ary** \-shə-ˌner-ē\ *adj*

evo·lu·tion·ist \ˌev-ə-'lü-sh(ə-)nəst\ *n* : a student of or a follower of a theory of evolution

evolve \i-'välv, -'vȯlv\ *vb* **evolved; evolv·ing** **1** : to develop or work out from something else ⟨*evolved* a new plan⟩ ⟨*evolved* a safer design from the old one⟩ **2** : to produce by a process of evolution **3** : to change by a process of evolution — **evolv·able** \i-'väl-və-bəl, -'vȯl-\ *adj*

ewe \'yü\ *n* : a female of the sheep or a related animal especially when mature

ew·er \'yü-ər, 'yu̇(-ə)r\ *n* : a vase-shaped pitcher or jug

¹ex- \(ˌ)eks,'eks\ *prefix* : former ⟨*ex*-president⟩ [from earlier *ex-* (prefix), from Latin *ex-* "out of, from"]

²ex- — see EXO-

¹ex·act \ig-'zakt\ *vb* **1** : to demand and get by force or threat ⟨*exact* burdensome concessions⟩ **2** : to call for as necessary or desirable ⟨*exact* a high price⟩ — **ex·ac·tion** \-'zak-shən\ *n*

²exact *adj* **1** : fully and completely in agreement with fact, a standard, or

ewer

\ə\ abut	\au̇\ out	\i\ tip	\ȯ\ saw	\u̇\ foot
\ər\ further	\ch\ chin	\ī\ life	\ȯi\ coin	\y\ yet
\a\ mat	\e\ pet	\j\ job	\th\ thin	\yü\ few
\ā\ take	\ē\ easy	\ŋ\ sing	\ṯh\ this	\yu̇\ cure
\ä\ cot, cart	\g\ go	\ō\ bone	\ü\ food	\zh\ vision

an original ⟨the *exact* time⟩ ⟨an *exact* rhyme⟩ ⟨an *exact* replica⟩ **2** : providing great accuracy ⟨*exact* instruments⟩ **synonyms** see CORRECT — **exact·ness** \-ˈzak(t)-nəs\ *n*

ex·act·ing \ig-ˈzak-tiŋ\ *adj* : making many or difficult demands upon a person ⟨an *exacting* task⟩ ⟨an *exacting* teacher⟩ — **ex·act·ing·ly** \-tiŋ-lē\ *adv* — **ex·act·ing·ness** *n*

ex·ac·ti·tude \ig-ˈzak-tə-ˌt(y)üd\ *n* : the quality or state of being exact

ex·act·ly \ig-ˈzak-(t)lē\ *adv* **1 a** : in an exact manner ⟨do *exactly* as you're told⟩ **b** : so as to match fact or a state ⟨at *exactly* three o'clock⟩ ⟨*exactly* the same size⟩ **c** : in every way : ALTOGETHER ⟨that was *exactly* the wrong thing to do⟩ ⟨not *exactly* what I had in mind⟩ **2** : quite so : just as you say — used to express agreement

ex·ag·ger·ate \ig-ˈzaj-ə-ˌrāt\ *vb* **-at·ed; -at·ing** : to enlarge a fact or statement beyond what is actual or true [from Latin *exaggeratus* "exaggerate," from *exaggerare,* literally, "to heap up"] — **ex·ag·ger·at·ed·ly** \-ˌrāt-əd-lē\ *adv* — **ex·ag·ger·at·ed·ness** \-nəs\ *n* — **ex·ag·ger·a·tion** \-ˌzaj-ə-ˈrā-shən\ *n* — **ex·ag·ger·a·tor** \-ˈzaj-ə-ˌrāt-ər\ *n*

ex·alt \ig-ˈzȯlt\ *vb* **1** : to raise in rank, power, or character **2** : to praise highly : GLORIFY — **ex·alt·er** *n*

ex·al·ta·tion \ˌeg-ˌzȯl-ˈtā-shən\ *n* **1** : the act of exalting : the state of being exalted **2** : a greatly heightened sense of personal well-being, power, or importance

ex·am \ig-ˈzam\ *n* : EXAMINATION

ex·am·i·na·tion \ig-ˌzam-ə-ˈnā-shən\ *n* **1** : the act or process of examining : the state of being examined **2** : a test to determine progress, fitness, or knowledge

ex·am·ine \ig-ˈzam-ən\ *vb* **-ined; -in·ing** **1** : to look at or check carefully ⟨*examine* a company's books⟩ ⟨have your eyes *examined*⟩ **2** : to question closely ⟨*examine* a witness⟩ — **ex·am·in·er** *n*

ex·am·ple \ig-ˈzam-pəl\ *n* **1** : one that serves as a pattern to be followed or not followed ⟨set a good *example*⟩ ⟨a bad *example*⟩ **2 a** : punishment given to someone as a warning to others **b** : the person so punished ⟨we'll make an *example* of you⟩ **3** : one of a group or collection that shows what the whole is like : SAMPLE ⟨a fine *example* of the silversmith's art⟩ **4** : a problem to be solved to show how a rule works ⟨*examples* in arithmetic⟩ **synonyms** see PATTERN — **for example** : as an example

ex·as·per·ate \ig-ˈzas-pə-ˌrāt\ *vb* **-at·ed; -at·ing** : to make angry : ANNOY, IRRITATE

ex·as·per·a·tion \ig-ˌzas-pə-ˈrā-shən\ *n* **1** : extreme annoyance : ANGER **2** : a source of annoyance

Ex·cal·i·bur \ek-ˈskal-ə-bər\ *n* : King Arthur's sword

ex·ca·vate \ˈek-skə-ˌvāt\ *vb* **-vat·ed; -vat·ing** **1** : to hollow out : form a hole in ⟨*excavate* the side of a hill⟩ **2** : to make by hollowing out ⟨*excavate* a tunnel⟩ **3** : to dig out and remove ⟨*excavate* sand⟩ **4** : to uncover by digging away covering earth ⟨*excavate* an ancient city⟩ — **ex·ca·va·tor** \-ˌvāt-ər\ *n*

ex·ca·va·tion \ˌek-skə-ˈvā-shən\ *n* **1** : the act or process of excavating **2** : a hollowed-out place formed by excavating

ex·ceed \ik-ˈsēd\ *vb* **1** : to be greater than ⟨the cost must not *exceed* ten dollars⟩ **2** : to go or be beyond the limit **synonyms** EXCEED, SURPASS, EXCEL, OUTDO mean to go beyond a certain limit, measure, or degree. EXCEED suggests going beyond a limit set by authority, custom, or earlier achievement ⟨*exceed* the speed limit⟩. SURPASS suggests being greater in worth, merit, or skill ⟨the book *surpassed* our hopes⟩. EXCEL suggests supremacy in achievement or value ⟨*excels* in science⟩. OUTDO suggests bettering one's previous work ⟨the chef really *outdid* herself this time⟩.

ex·ceed·ing \ik-ˈsēd-iŋ\ *adj* : EXCEPTIONAL 2, EXTRAORDINARY ⟨*exceeding* darkness⟩

ex·ceed·ing·ly \ik-ˈsēd-iŋ-lē\ *also* **ex·ceed·ing** *adv* : to a very great degree : EXTREMELY ⟨an *exceedingly* fine job⟩

ex·cel \ik-ˈsel\ *vb* **ex·celled; ex·cel·ling** : to do or be better than others : SURPASS ⟨a student who *excels* in sports⟩ ⟨*excels* her brother at tennis⟩ **synonyms** see EXCEED

ex·cel·lence \ˈek-s(ə-)lən(t)s\ *n* **1** : high quality **2** : an excellent quality : VIRTUE **3** : EXCELLENCY 2

ex·cel·len·cy \ˈek-s(ə-)lən-sē\ *n, pl* **-cies** **1** : EXCELLENCE **2** — used as a title for some high government and church officials ⟨your *Excellency*⟩

ex·cel·lent \ˈek-s(ə-)lənt\ *adj* : very good of its kind : FIRST-CLASS — **ex·cel·lent·ly** *adv*

ex·cel·si·or \ik-ˈsel-sē-ər\ *n* : fine curled wood shavings used especially for packing fragile items

¹ex·cept \ik-ˈsept\ *also* **ex·cept·ing** \ik-ˈsept-iŋ\ *prep* **1** : not including ⟨daily *except* Sundays⟩ **2** : with the exception of ⟨take no orders *except* from me⟩

²except *vb* : to leave out from a number or a whole : EXCLUDE, OMIT [Middle English *excepten* "to take or leave out," from early French *excepter* (same meaning), derived from Latin *excipere* "to take out," from *ex-* "out" and *capere* "to take" — related to ACCEPT, CAPTURE, INTERCEPT]

³except *also* **excepting** *conj* **1** : if it were not for the fact that : ONLY ⟨I'd go, *except* it's too far⟩ **2** : with this exception, namely ⟨was impossible to get to *except* by boat⟩

except for *prep* : with the exception of : but for ⟨all A's *except for* a B in Latin⟩

ex·cep·tion \ik-ˈsep-shən\ *n* **1** : the act of excepting : EXCLUSION ⟨it's all here, with the *exception* of the sweater⟩ **2** : a case where a rule does not apply ⟨we'll make an *exception* this time⟩ **3** : an objection or a ground for objection ⟨took *exception* to the remark⟩

ex·cep·tion·able \ik-ˈsep-sh(ə-)nə-bəl\ *adj* : OBJECTIONABLE — **ex·cep·tion·ably** \-blē\ *adv*

ex·cep·tion·al \ik-ˈsep-shnəl, -shən-ᵊl\ *adj* **1** : forming an exception : being unusual ⟨an *exceptional* amount of rain⟩ **2** : better than average : SUPERIOR ⟨an *exceptional* student in math⟩ — **ex·cep·tion·al·ly** \-ē\ *adv* — **ex·cep·tion·al·ness** *n*

¹ex·cerpt \ek-ˈsərpt, eg-ˈzərpt; ˈek-ˌsərpt, ˈeg-ˌzərpt\ *vb* **1** : to select for quoting **2** : to take excerpts from

²ex·cerpt \ˈek-ˌsərpt, ˈeg-ˌzərpt\ *n* : a part taken from a longer work ⟨read an *excerpt* from the play⟩

¹ex·cess \ik-ˈses, ˈek-ˌses\ *n* **1** : a state of being more than enough **2 a** : an amount beyond what is usual, needed, or asked **b** : the amount by which one thing or quantity exceeds another

²excess *adj* : more than what is usual, acceptable, or needed ⟨*excess* baggage⟩ ⟨an outlet for their *excess* energy⟩

ex·ces·sive \ik-ˈses-iv\ *adj* : showing excess : too much — **ex·ces·sive·ly** *adv* — **ex·ces·sive·ness** *n*

¹ex·change \iks-ˈchānj, ˈeks-ˌchānj\ *n* **1** : a giving or taking of one thing in return for another : TRADE **2 a** : the act of substituting one thing for another **3 a** : a place where things or services are exchanged ⟨a stock *exchange*⟩ **b** : a central office in which telephone lines are connected to permit communication

²exchange *vb* **ex·changed; ex·chang·ing** : to give in exchange : TRADE, SWAP — **ex·change·abil·i·ty** \iks-ˌchānj-ə-ˈbil-ət-ē\ *n* — **ex·change·able** \iks-ˈchān-jə-bəl\ *adj* — **ex·chang·er** *n*

exchange student *n* : a student from one country received into a school in another country in exchange for one sent to a school in the home country of the first student

ex·che·quer \ˈeks-ˌchek-ər, iks-ˈchek-\ *n* **1** : a department of the British government concerned with funds to run the government **2** : money available : FUNDS

¹ex·cise \ˈek-ˌsīz, -ˌsīs\ *n* : a tax on the manufacture, sale, or use of certain goods within a country [from obsolete Dutch *excijs* "tax," probably derived from early French *assise* "assessment"]

²**ex·cise** \ek-'sīz\ *vb* **ex·cised; ex·cis·ing** : to remove by cutting out ⟨*excise* a tumor⟩ [from Latin *excisus,* past participle of *excidere* "to cut out," from *ex-* "out, out of" and *caedere* "to cut"] — **ex·ci·sion** \-'sizh-ən\ *n*

ex·cit·able \ik-'sīt-ə-bəl\ *adj* **1** : easily excited **2** : capable of being excited — **ex·cit·abil·i·ty** \-ˌsīt-ə-'bil-ət-ē\ *n*

ex·ci·ta·tion \ˌek-ˌsī-'tā-shən, ˌek-sə-\ *n* : EXCITEMENT 1; *esp* : the activity or change in condition resulting from stimulation of an individual, organ, tissue, or cell

ex·cite \ik-'sīt\ *vb* **ex·cit·ed; ex·cit·ing** **1** : to stir up feeling in ⟨ideas that *excite* young people⟩ **2** : to cause to be felt or done ⟨*excite* admiration⟩ ⟨posters *excited* interest in the show⟩ **3 a** : ENERGIZE 2a **b** : to produce a magnetic field in **4** : to increase the activity of (as nervous tissue) : STIMULATE **5** : to raise (as an atom) to a higher energy level **synonyms** *see* PROVOKE — **ex·cit·er** *n*

excited *adj* : having or showing strong feeling ⟨*excited* about the trip⟩ — **ex·cit·ed·ly** *adv*

ex·cite·ment \ik-'sīt-mənt\ *n* **1** : something that excites **2** : the state of being excited : AGITATION

ex·cit·ing \ik-'sīt-iŋ\ *adj* : causing excitement ⟨*exciting* news⟩ — **ex·cit·ing·ly** \-iŋ-lē\ *adv*

ex·claim \iks-'klām\ *vb* : to cry out or speak suddenly or with strong feeling ⟨*exclaimed* in delight⟩

ex·cla·ma·tion \ˌeks-klə-'mā-shən\ *n* **1** : a sharp or sudden cry of strong feeling **2** : a strong expression of anger or complaint

exclamation mark *n* : EXCLAMATION POINT

exclamation point *n* : a punctuation mark ! used chiefly after an exclamation to show a forceful way of speaking or a strong feeling

ex·clam·a·to·ry \iks-'klam-ə-ˌtōr-ē, -ˌtȯr-\ *adj* : containing or using exclamation ⟨an *exclamatory* sentence⟩

ex·clude \iks-'klüd\ *vb* **ex·clud·ed; ex·clud·ing** : to shut or keep out — **ex·clud·able** \-'klüd-ə-bəl\ *adj* — **ex·clu·sion** \-'klü-zhən\ *n*

ex·clu·sive \iks-'klü-siv, -ziv\ *adj* **1** : excluding or trying to exclude others ⟨an *exclusive* neighborhood⟩ **2** : ⁴SOLE 2a ⟨we have *exclusive* use of the beach⟩ **3** : ¹FULL 2c, COMPLETE ⟨gave their *exclusive* attention to the job⟩ — **ex·clu·sive·ly** *adv* — **ex·clu·sive·ness** *n*

exclusive of *prep* : not taking into account ⟨for five days *exclusive of* today⟩

ex·clu·siv·i·ty \ˌeks-ˌklü-'siv-ət-ē, iks-, -'ziv-\ *n, pl* **-ties** **1** : the quality or state of being exclusive **2** : exclusive rights or services

ex·com·mu·ni·cate \ˌeks-kə-'myü-nə-ˌkāt\ *vb* **-cat·ed; -cat·ing** : to shut off officially from the rights of church membership — **ex·com·mu·ni·ca·tion** \-ˌmyü-nə-'kā-shən\ *n* — **ex·com·mu·ni·ca·tor** \-'myü-nə-ˌkāt-ər\ *n*

ex·co·ri·ate \ek-'skōr-ē-ˌāt, -'skȯr-\ *vb* **-at·ed; -at·ing** : to criticize very severely — **ex·co·ri·a·tion** \(ˌ)ek-ˌskōr-ē-'ā-shən, -ˌskȯr-\ *n*

ex·cre·ment \'ek-skrə-mənt\ *n* : waste matter discharged from the body and especially from the anus

ex·cres·cence \ek-'skres-ᵊn(t)s\ *n* : OUTGROWTH 1; *esp* : an abnormal outgrowth (as a wart) on the body

ex·cre·ta \ek-'skrēt-ə\ *n pl* : waste matter eliminated or separated from the body

ex·crete \ik-'skrēt\ *vb* **ex·cret·ed; ex·cret·ing** : to separate and remove (waste produced by cellular activity) from the living body ⟨urea is *excreted* by the kidneys in urine⟩

ex·cre·tion \ik-'skrē-shən\ *n* **1** : the act or process of excreting ⟨the skin and lungs function in *excretion*⟩ **2** : cellular waste (as carbon dioxide and urea) excreted from the body

ex·cre·to·ry \'ek-skrə-ˌtōr-ē, -ˌtȯr-\ *adj* : of, relating to, or functioning in excretion ⟨kidneys are *excretory* organs⟩

ex·cru·ci·at·ing \ik-'skrü-shē-ˌāt-iŋ\ *adj* **1** : causing great mental or physical pain : AGONIZING ⟨*excruciating* torture⟩ ⟨an *excruciating* decision to leave⟩ **2** : very severe ⟨*excruciating* pain⟩ [derived from Latin *excruciatus,* past participle of *excruciare* "to torture," from *ex-* "out of, from" and *cruciare* "to torment, crucify," from *cruc-, crux* "cross" — related to CROSS, CRUCIAL, CRUCIFY] — **ex·cru·ci·at·ing·ly** \-iŋ-lē\ *adv*

ex·cul·pate \'ek-(ˌ)skəl-ˌpāt, ek-'skəl-\ *vb* **-pat·ed; -pat·ing** : to clear from a charge of fault or guilt — **ex·cul·pa·tion** \ˌek-(ˌ)skəl-'pā-shən\ *n* — **ex·cul·pa·to·ry** \ek-'skəl-pə-ˌtōr-ē, -ˌtȯr-\ *adj*

ex·cur·rent \ek-'skər-ənt, -'skə-rənt\ *adj* : marked by a current that flows outward ⟨a clam's *excurrent* siphon⟩

ex·cur·sion \ik-'skər-zhən\ *n* **1 a** : a short trip for pleasure **b** : a trip at special reduced rates **2** : a wandering off from the subject : DIGRESSION [from Latin *excursio, excursion-* "a going out," from *excurrere* "to run out, make an excursion, extend," from *ex-* "out, forth" and *currere* "to run" — related to CURRENT]

ex·cur·sion·ist \ik-'skərzh-(ə-)nəst\ *n* : a person who goes on an excursion

¹**ex·cuse** \ik-'skyüz\ *vb* **ex·cused; ex·cus·ing** **1** : to make apology for ⟨*excused* myself for being late⟩ **2** : to overlook or dismiss as of little importance ⟨*excuse* a mistake⟩ **3 a** : to release from doing something ⟨*excused* the class from homework⟩ **b** : to allow to leave ⟨*excused* the sick student from class⟩ **4** : to be an acceptable reason for : JUSTIFY ⟨nothing *excuses* bad manners⟩ — **ex·cus·able** \-'skyü-zə-bəl\ *adj* — **ex·cus·ably** \-blē\ *adv* — **ex·cus·er** *n*

synonyms EXCUSE, CONDONE, PARDON, FORGIVE mean to demand neither punishment nor payment in return for a loss or wrong. EXCUSE suggests overlooking a fault or error by not criticizing or punishing the one responsible ⟨*excused* them for being late⟩. CONDONE suggests accepting without protest a blameworthy act or condition ⟨does not *condone* cheating on taxes⟩. PARDON suggests the freeing from a penalty that is due ⟨the governor *pardoned* the convicted criminals⟩. FORGIVE suggests giving up feelings of resentment and the desire for revenge ⟨*forgave* those who had hurt her⟩.

²**ex·cuse** \ik-'skyüs\ *n* **1** : the act of excusing **2 a** : something offered as a reason for being excused **b** : a note that explains an absence **3** : something that excuses or is a reason for excusing

ex·e·cra·ble \'ek-si-krə-bəl\ *adj* : very bad ⟨living conditions in the slums were *execrable*⟩ — **ex·e·cra·ble·ness** *n* — **ex·e·cra·bly** \-blē\ *adv*

ex·e·crate \'ek-sə-ˌkrāt\ *vb* **-crat·ed; -crat·ing** **1** : to declare to be evil **2** : to dislike very strongly : ABHOR — **ex·e·cra·tion** \ˌek-sə-'krā-shən\ *n*

ex·e·cute \'ek-sə-ˌkyüt\ *vb* **-cut·ed; -cut·ing** **1** : to put into effect : CARRY OUT, PERFORM ⟨*execute* a plan⟩ ⟨*execute* a dance step⟩ **2** : to do what is required by ⟨the computer *executed* the first line of the program⟩ **3** : to put to death according to a legal order **4** : to make or produce by carrying out a design ⟨a statue *executed* in bronze⟩

ex·e·cu·tion \ˌek-sə-'kyü-shən\ *n* **1** : the act or process of executing : a carrying through of something to its finish ⟨put a plan into *execution*⟩ **2** : a putting to death as a legal penalty **3** : the way in which something is executed

\ə\ **abut**	\au̇\ **out**	\i\ **tip**	\ȯ\ **saw**	\u̇\ **foot**
\ər\ **further**	\ch\ **chin**	\ī\ **life**	\ȯi\ **coin**	\y\ **yet**
\a\ **mat**	\e\ **pet**	\j\ **job**	\th\ **thin**	\yü\ **few**
\ā\ **take**	\ē\ **easy**	\ŋ\ **sing**	\th\ **this**	\yu̇\ **cure**
\ä\ **cot, cart**	\g\ **go**	\ō\ **bone**	\ü\ **food**	\zh\ **vision**

ex·e·cu·tion·er \,ek-sə-'kyü-sh(ə-)nər\ *n* : a person who carries out a sentence of death

¹ex·ec·u·tive \ig-'zek-(y)ət-iv\ *adj* **1** : of or relating to the carrying out of laws and the conduct of public and national affairs ⟨the *executive* branch of government⟩ **2** : fitted for or relating to the managing or directing of things ⟨*executive* skills⟩ ⟨an *executive* program for a computer⟩ **3** : of or relating to an executive ⟨the *executive* offices⟩

²executive *n* **1** : the executive branch of a government **2** : a person who manages or directs

ex·ec·u·tor \ig-'zek-(y)ət-ər, *in sense 1 also* 'ek-sə-,kyüt-\ *n* **1** : a person who executes something **2** : the person named in a will to carry it out

ex·ec·u·trix \ig-'zek-(y)ə-(,)triks\ *n, pl* **ex·ec·u·tri·ces** *or* **ex·ec·u·trix·es** \-,zek-(y)ə-'trī-,sēz\ : a woman who is an executor

ex·em·plar \ig-'zem-,plär, -plər\ *n* **1** : one that serves as a model or pattern; *esp* : an ideal model **2** : a typical example

ex·em·pla·ry \ig-'zem-plə-rē\ *adj* : deserving to be imitated : COMMENDABLE ⟨*exemplary* behavior⟩ — **ex·em·plar·i·ly** \,eg-,zem-'pler-ə-lē\ *adv*

ex·em·pli·fy \ig-'zem-plə-,fī\ *vb* **-fied; -fy·ing** **1** : to show by example ⟨the story *exemplifies* the virtue of generosity⟩ **2** : to serve as an example of ⟨she *exemplifies* a good leader⟩ — **ex·em·pli·fi·ca·tion** \-,zem-plə-fə-'kā-shən\ *n*

ex·em·plum \ig-'zem-pləm\ *n, pl* **-pla** \-plə\ : a story used to point out a moral or support an argument

¹ex·empt \ig-'zem(p)t\ *adj* : free or released from some requirement that others must meet or deal with

²exempt *vb* : to make exempt

ex·emp·tion \ig-'zem(p)-shən\ *n* **1** : the act of exempting : the state of being exempt **2** : something that is exempted

¹ex·er·cise \'ek-sər-,sīz\ *n* **1** : the act of putting into use, action, or practice ⟨the *exercise* of power⟩ **2** : bodily activity for the sake of physical fitness ⟨get plenty of fresh air and *exercise*⟩ **3** : something done to develop skill ⟨arithmetic *exercises*⟩ ⟨finger *exercises*⟩ **4** *pl* : a program of songs, speeches, and announcements of awards and honors ⟨graduation *exercises*⟩

²exercise *vb* **-cised; -cis·ing** **1** : to put into use : EXERT ⟨*exercise* patience⟩ ⟨*exercise* authority⟩ **2 a** : to use again and again in order to strengthen or develop ⟨*exercise* a muscle⟩ **b** : to put through exercises : give exercise to ⟨*exercise* the dog⟩ **3** : to worry, alarm, or annoy about something ⟨the people were *exercised* about pollution⟩ **4** : to take exercise ⟨*exercises* every day⟩ — **ex·er·cis·able** \-,sī-zə-bəl\ *adj* — **ex·er·cis·er** *n*

ex·ert \ig-'zərt\ *vb* **1** : to put forth (as strength) ⟨the force *exerted* by a machine⟩ : bring into use or action ⟨*exert* influence⟩ **2** : to put (oneself) into action or to tiring effort ⟨don't *exert* yourself too much⟩

ex·er·tion \ig-'zər-shən\ *n* : the act or an instance of exerting

ex·e·unt \'ek-sē-(,)ənt\ — used as a stage direction to indicate that all or some characters leave the stage

ex·fo·li·a·tion \(,)eks-,fō-lē-'ā-shən\ *n* : the action or process of shedding or removing in thin layers or scales — **ex·fo·li·ate** \(')eks-'fō-lē-,āt\ *vb*

ex·ha·la·tion \,eks-(h)ə-'lā-shən\ *n* **1** : something exhaled or given off **2** : the act of exhaling

ex·hale \eks-'hāl\ *vb* **ex·haled; ex·hal·ing** **1** : to breathe out **2** : to send forth (as gas or odor)

¹ex·haust \ig-'zȯst\ *vb* **1 a** : to use up completely ⟨*exhausted* our funds⟩ **b** : to use up all of the mental or physical energy of : TIRE, WEAR OUT **2 a** : to draw off or let out completely ⟨*exhaust* the air from the jar⟩ **b** : to empty by drawing something from **3** : to try out all of ⟨they *exhausted* all possibilities⟩ **synonyms** see TIRE —

ex·haust·er *n* — **ex·haust·ibil·i·ty** \-,zȯ-stə-'bil-ət-ē\ *n* — **ex·haust·ible** \-'zȯ-stə-bəl\ *adj*

²exhaust *n* **1** : the gas that escapes from an engine **2** : a system of pipes through which exhaust escapes

ex·haus·tion \ig-'zȯs-chən\ *n* **1** : the act of exhausting **2** : the state of being exhausted

ex·haus·tive \ig-'zȯ-stiv\ *adj* : trying all possibilities : THOROUGH ⟨an *exhaustive* search⟩ — **ex·haus·tive·ly** *adv* — **ex·haus·tive·ness** *n*

¹ex·hib·it \ig-'zib-ət\ *vb* **1** : to show by outward signs : REVEAL ⟨*exhibit* an interest in music⟩ **2** : to put on display ⟨*exhibit* a collection of paintings⟩ **synonyms** see SHOW — **ex·hib·i·tor** \-ət-ər\ *n*

²exhibit *n* **1** : an article or a collection shown in an exhibition **2** : an article presented as evidence in a court of law

ex·hi·bi·tion \,ek-sə-'bish-ən\ *n* **1** : an act or instance of exhibiting **2** : a public showing (as of works of art, manufactured goods, or athletic skill)

ex·hil·a·rate \ig-'zil-ə-,rāt\ *vb* **-rat·ed; -rat·ing** : to cause to feel cheerful or lively : put into high spirits ⟨the fresh air *exhilarated* us⟩ — **ex·hil·a·ra·tive** \-,rāt-iv\ *adj*

ex·hil·a·ra·tion \ig-,zil-ə-'rā-shən\ *n* **1** : the action of exhilarating **2** : the state or the feeling of being exhilarated : high spirits

ex·hort \ig-'zȯrt\ *vb* : to urge strongly ⟨*exhorted* all citizens to vote⟩ — **ex·hort·er** *n*

ex·hor·ta·tion \,eks-ȯr-'tā-shən, ,egz-\ *n* : an act or instance of exhorting

ex·hume \igz-'(y)üm, iks-'(h)yüm\ *vb* **ex·humed; ex·hum·ing** : to remove from a place of burial — **ex·hu·ma·tion** \,eks-(h)yü-'mā-shən, ,egz-(y)ü-\ *n*

ex·i·gence \'ek-sə-jən(t)s\ *n* : EXIGENCY

ex·i·gen·cy \'ek-sə-jən-sē, ig-'zij-ən-\ *n, pl* **-cies** : a situation requiring immediate action

¹ex·ile \'eg-,zīl, 'ek-,sīl\ *n* **1 a** : an act or instance of being forced to leave one's country or home; *also* : voluntary absence from one's country or home **b** : the state of one so absent **2** : a person who is in exile

²exile *vb* **ex·iled; ex·il·ing** : to force to leave one's own country or home

ex·ist \ig-'zist\ *vb* **1** : to have actual being : be real ⟨do unicorns *exist*?⟩ **2** : to continue to be ⟨as long as doubt *exists*⟩ **3** : to continue to live : stay alive ⟨earned barely enough to *exist* on⟩

ex·ist·ence \ig-'zis-tən(t)s\ *n* **1** : the fact or the state of having being or of being real ⟨the largest animal in *existence*⟩ **2** : the state of being alive : LIFE ⟨owed my *existence* to a doctor's skill⟩

ex·ist·ent \ig-'zis-tənt\ *adj* **1** : having being **2** : existing now : EXTANT

¹ex·it \'eg-zət, 'ek-sət\ — used as a stage direction to indicate who goes off the stage [from Latin *exit* "he or she goes out," from *exire* "to go out," from *ex-* "out of, from" and *ire* "to go" — related to ISSUE, ITINERARY]

²exit *n* **1** : a departure from a stage **2** : the act of going out or away **3** : a way to go out of a place

³exit *vb* : to go out : LEAVE, DEPART

exo- *or* **ex-** *combining form* : outside ⟨*exurb*⟩ : outer ⟨*exoskeleton*⟩ — compare END- 1 [from Greek *exō* "out, outside"]

exo·crine \'ek-sə-krən, -,krīn, -,krēn\ *adj* : producing, being, or relating to a secretion that is released outside its source ⟨*exocrine* cells of the pancreas⟩

exocrine gland *n* : a gland (as a sweat gland or pancreas) that releases a secretion outside of or at the surface of an organ or part by means of a duct or canal

exo·cy·to·sis \,ek-sō-sī-'tō-səs\ *n* : the process by which a cell discharges material by enclosing it in a vesicle which fuses with the cell membrane

ex·o·dus \'ek-səd-əs\ *n* **1** *cap* — see BIBLE table **2** : a mass departure [from Latin *Exodus* "a book of the Bible," derived from Greek *exodos* "a road or journey out," from *ex-* "out" and *hodos* "road"]

ex·of·fi·cio \ˌeks-ə-ˈfish-ē-ˌō, -ˈfis-\ *adv or adj* : because of an office ⟨the Vice President serves *ex officio* as president of the Senate⟩

ex·on·er·ate \ig-ˈzän-ə-ˌrāt\ *vb* **-at·ed; -at·ing** : to clear from a charge of wrongdoing or from blame : declare innocent — **ex·on·er·a·tion** \ig-ˌzän-ə-ˈrā-shən\ *n*

ex·or·bi·tant \ig-ˈzór-bət-ənt\ *adj* : going beyond the limits of what is fair, reasonable, or expected ⟨*exorbitant* prices⟩ — **ex·or·bi·tant·ly** *adv*

ex·or·cise \ˈek-ˌsór-ˌsīz, -sər-\ *vb* **-cised; -cis·ing** : to drive (as an evil spirit) off by calling upon some holy name or by spells

ex·or·cism \ˈek-ˌsór-ˌsiz-əm, -sər-\ *n* : the act or practice of exorcising — **ex·or·cist** \-ˌsist, -səst\ *n*

exo·skel·e·ton \ˌek-sō-ˈskel-ət-ᵊn\ *n* : a hard supporting or protective structure (as of an insect, spider, or crustacean) on the outside of the body

exo·sphere \ˈek-sō-ˌsfi(ə)r\ *n* : the outermost region of the atmosphere of the earth or a planet

exo·ther·mic \ˌek-sō-ˈthər-mik\ *adj* : characterized by or formed by the giving off of heat ⟨an *exothermic* chemical reaction⟩

exoskeleton

¹**ex·ot·ic** \ig-ˈzät-ik\ *adj* **1** : introduced from another country ⟨*exotic* plants⟩ **2** : very different or unusual ⟨*exotic* colors⟩ — **ex·ot·i·cal·ly** \-ˈzät-i-k(ə-)lē\ *adv* — **ex·ot·ic·ness** \-ik-nəs\ *n*

²**exotic** *n* : something (as a plant) that is exotic

ex·pand \ik-ˈspand\ *vb* **1** : to open wide : UNFOLD ⟨a bird with wings *expanded*⟩ **2** : to increase in size, number, or amount ⟨substances *expand* when heated⟩ ⟨the *expanding* universe⟩ ⟨their work *expanded*⟩ **3** : to work out in greater detail ⟨*expand* an argument⟩ **4** : to perform the indicated mathematical operations of : write out in full ⟨*expand* both sides of an equation⟩ — **ex·pand·able** \-ˈspan-də-bəl\ *adj* — **ex·pand·er** *n*

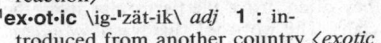

synonyms EXPAND, SWELL, INFLATE, DILATE mean to increase in size or volume. EXPAND may apply to increases coming from both inside and outside ⟨bread *expands* as it bakes⟩ ⟨*expanded* the house by adding a room⟩. SWELL suggests a gradual enlargement beyond the original or normal limits of a thing ⟨the injury caused her leg to *swell*⟩. INFLATE suggests expanding by the addition of air or something that lacks substance ⟨*inflate* a tire⟩. DILATE applies especially to the expansion of an outer boundary ⟨the pupils of your eyes *dilate* in dim light⟩.

expanded notation *n* : the writing of a number in terms of powers of the base in which it is expressed ⟨123 in base 10 when written in *expanded notation* is $1(10^2) + 2(10^1) + 3(10^0)$⟩

ex·panse \ik-ˈspan(t)s\ *n* : a wide space, area, or stretch ⟨the vast *expanse* of the ocean⟩

ex·pan·sion \ik-ˈspan-chən\ *n* **1** : the act of expanding **2** : the state of being expanded **3** : something expanded or a result of expanding **4** : the result of carrying out indicated mathematical operations ⟨the *expansion* of $(a + b)^2$ is $a^2 + 2ab + b^2$⟩

ex·pan·sive \ik-ˈspan(t)-siv\ *adj* **1** : having a capacity or a tendency to expand ⟨gases are *expansive*⟩ **2** : causing or tending to cause expansion ⟨an *expansive* force⟩ **3** : being in a good or talkative mood **4** : having considerable extent : BROAD — **ex·pan·sive·ly** *adv* — **ex·pan·sive·ness** *n*

ex·pa·ti·ate \ek-ˈspā-shē-ˌāt\ *vb* **-at·ed; -at·ing** : to speak or write in a full or lengthy manner — **ex·pa·ti·a·tion** \(ˌ)ek-ˌspā-shē-ˈā-shən\ *n*

¹**ex·pa·tri·ate** \ek-ˈspā-trē-ˌāt\ *vb* **-at·ed; -at·ing** : ²EXILE — **ex·pa·tri·a·tion** \(ˌ)ek-ˌspā-trē-ˈā-shən\ *n*

²**ex·pa·tri·ate** \ek-ˈspā-trē-ˌāt, -trē-ət\ *adj* : living in a foreign country

³**ex·pa·tri·ate** \ek-ˈspā-trē-ˌāt, -trē-ət\ *n* : a person living in a foreign country; *esp* : one who has renounced his or her native country

ex·pect \ik-ˈspekt\ *vb* **1** : to believe that something will occur and wait for it to happen ⟨*expect* rain⟩ ⟨*expect* her home soon⟩ **2** : SUPPOSE **3**, THINK ⟨who do you *expect* will win?⟩ **3 a** : to consider reasonable, due, or necessary ⟨*expect* an honest day's work⟩ **b** : to consider obligated ⟨*expected* you to pay your debts⟩ [from Latin *expectare*, *exspectare* "to look forward to," from *ex-* "out, forth" and *spectare* "to watch, look at," derived from *specere* "to look, look at" — related to AUSPICE, SPECTACLE] — **ex·pect·able** \-ˈspek-tə-bəl\ *adj*

ex·pect·an·cy \ik-ˈspek-tən-sē\ *n, pl* **-cies** **1** : EXPECTATION 1 **2** : the expected amount (as of years of life) based on statistical probability ⟨life *expectancy*⟩

ex·pect·ant \ik-ˈspek-tənt\ *adj* **1** : characterized by or being in a state of expectation **2** : expecting the birth of a child ⟨*expectant* mothers⟩ — **ex·pect·ant·ly** *adv*

ex·pec·ta·tion \ˌek-ˌspek-ˈtā-shən, ik-\ *n* **1** : the act or state of expecting : a looking forward to or waiting for something **2** : chances of good or bad fortune — usually used in plural **3** : something expected

ex·pec·to·rant \ik-ˈspek-t(ə-)rənt\ *n* : an agent that promotes the discharge of mucus from the respiratory tract — **expectorant** *adj*

ex·pec·to·rate \ik-ˈspek-tə-ˌrāt\ *vb* **-rat·ed; -rat·ing** : to discharge (as phlegm) from the throat or lungs by coughing and spitting; *also* : ²SPIT 1a — **ex·pec·to·ra·tion** \-ˌspek-tə-ˈrā-shən\ *n*

ex·pe·di·ence \ik-ˈspēd-ē-ən(t)s\ *n* : EXPEDIENCY

ex·pe·di·en·cy \ik-ˈspēd-ē-ən-sē\ *n, pl* **-cies** : the use of expedient means and methods

¹**ex·pe·di·ent** \ik-ˈspēd-ē-ənt\ *adj* : suitable for bringing about a desired result often without regard to what is fair or right — **ex·pe·di·ent·ly** *adv*

²**expedient** *n* : a means to accomplish an end; *esp* : one used in place of a better means that is not available

ex·pe·dite \ˈek-spə-ˌdīt\ *vb* **-dit·ed; -dit·ing** : to speed up the process or progress of

ex·pe·di·tion \ˌek-spə-ˈdish-ən\ *n* **1 a** : a journey or trip undertaken for a specific purpose (as war or exploring) **b** : a group making such a journey **2** : prompt handling of what needs to be done — **ex·pe·di·tion·er** \-ˈdish-(ə-)nər\ *n*

ex·pe·di·tion·ary \ek-spə-ˈdish-ə-ˌner-ē\ *adj* : sent on military service abroad ⟨an *expeditionary* force⟩

ex·pe·di·tious \ˌek-spə-ˈdish-əs\ *adj* : marked by or acting with promptness ⟨*expeditious* service⟩ — **ex·pe·di·tious·ly** *adv* — **ex·pe·di·tious·ness** *n*

ex·pel \ik-ˈspel\ *vb* **ex·pelled; ex·pel·ling** **1** : to drive or force out ⟨*expel* air from the lungs⟩ **2** : to force to leave usually by official action ⟨*expelled* from school⟩

ex·pend \ik-ˈspend\ *vb* **1** : to pay out : SPEND ⟨*expend* state funds⟩ **2** : USE UP ⟨*expend* energy⟩

ex·pend·able \ik-ˈspen-də-bəl\ *adj* : normally used up in service ⟨*expendable* supplies like pencils and paper⟩ — **ex·pend·abil·i·ty** \-ˌspen-də-ˈbil-ət-ē\ *n* — **expendable** *n* — **ex·pend·ably** \-ˈspen-də-blē\ *adv*

\ə\ abut	\aú\ out	\i\ tip	\ó\ saw	\ú\ foot
\ər\ further	\ch\ chin	\ī\ life	\ói\ coin	\y\ yet
\a\ mat	\e\ pet	\j\ job	\th\ thin	\yü\ few
\ā\ take	\ē\ easy	\ŋ\ sing	\th\ this	\yú\ cure
\ä\ cot, cart	\g\ go	\ō\ bone	\ü\ food	\zh\ vision

ex·pen·di·ture \ik-'spen-di-chər, -də-ˌchu̇(ə)r\ *n* **1** : the act of spending (as money, time, or energy) **2** : something that is spent

ex·pense \ik-'spen(t)s\ *n* **1** : something spent or required to be spent : COST **2** : a cause of spending ⟨a car is a great *expense*⟩

ex·pen·sive \ik-'spen(t)-siv\ *adj* **1** : COSTLY **2** ⟨an *expensive* hobby⟩ **2 a** : having a high price ⟨*expensive* gifts⟩ **b** : marked by high prices ⟨*expensive* shops⟩ — **ex·pen·sive·ly** *adv* — **ex·pen·sive·ness** *n*

¹**ex·pe·ri·ence** \ik-'spir-ē-ən(t)s\ *n* **1** : the actual living through an event or series of events ⟨learn by *experience*⟩ **2 a** : skill or knowledge gained by actually doing or feeling a thing ⟨a job that requires someone with *experience*⟩ ⟨had gained a lot of *experience* by the end of the season⟩ **b** : the amount of such skill or knowledge ⟨has five years' *experience*⟩ **3** : something one has actually done or lived through ⟨my *experiences* as a riverboat pilot⟩

²**experience** *vb* **-enced; -enc·ing** : to have experience of : UNDERGO ⟨*experienced* many hardships as a child⟩

ex·pe·ri·enced \ik-'spir-ē-ən(t)st\ *adj* : made skillful or wise through experience ⟨an *experienced* driver⟩

¹**ex·per·i·ment** \ik-'sper-ə-mənt\ *n* : ¹TEST 1, ¹TRIAL 1; *esp* : a procedure or operation carried out under controlled conditions in order to discover something, to test a hypothesis, or to serve as an example

²**ex·per·i·ment** \ik-'sper-ə-ˌment\ *vb* : to make experiments — **ex·per·i·men·ta·tion** \ik-ˌsper-ə-mən-'tā-shən, -ˌmen-\ *n*

ex·per·i·men·tal \ik-ˌsper-ə-'ment-ᵊl\ *adj* **1 a** : of, relating to, or based on experience or experiment ⟨*experimental* evidence⟩ **b** : subjected to the condition that is different from normal for a factor being tested in an experiment ⟨the *experimental* group⟩ **2** : relating to or having the characteristics of experiment : TENTATIVE 1 ⟨still in the *experimental* stage⟩ — **ex·per·i·men·tal·ly** \-'ment-ᵊl-ē\ *adv*

ex·per·i·ment·er \ik-'sper-ə-ˌment-ər\ *n* : a person who experiments or conducts an experiment

experiment station *n* : a place specifically designed for scientific research and experimentation (as in agriculture) of practical importance and for the giving out of information

¹**ex·pert** \'ek-ˌspərt, ik-'spərt\ *adj* : showing special skill or knowledge gained from training or experience ⟨*expert* advice⟩ **synonyms** see SKILLFUL — **ex·pert·ly** *adv* — **ex·pert·ness** *n*

²**ex·pert** \'ek-ˌspərt\ *n* : a person with special skill in or knowledge of a subject

ex·per·tise \ˌek-(ˌ)spər-'tēz, -'tēs\ *n* : the skill of an expert

ex·pi·ate \'ek-spē-ˌāt\ *vb* **-at·ed; -at·ing** : to make up for : ATONE — **ex·pi·a·tion** \ˌek-spē-'ā-shən\ *n*

ex·pi·ra·tion \ˌek-spə-'rā-shən\ *n* **1 a** : the expelling of air from the lungs in breathing **b** : air or vapor expelled from the lungs **2** : the fact of coming to an end

expiration date *n* **1** : the date on which something (as a credit card) is no longer of use **2** : the last date on which a product (as food or medicine) can be safely used

ex·pi·ra·to·ry \ik-'spī-rə-ˌtōr-ē, ek-, -ˌtȯr-; 'ek-sp(ə)rə-\ *adj* : of, relating to, or used in breathing air out of the lungs

ex·pire \ik-'spī(ə)r, *usually for sense 3* ek-\ *vb* **ex·pired; ex·pir·ing** **1** : to breathe one's last breath : DIE **2** : to come to an end : be no longer in force ⟨this offer *expires* March 1⟩ ⟨my driver's license has *expired*⟩ **3 a** : to let the breath out **b** : to breathe out from or as if from the lungs

ex·plain \ik-'splān\ *vb* **1** : to make plain or understandable **2** : to give the reason for or cause of — **ex·plain·able** \-'splā-nə-bəl\ *adj* — **ex·plain·er** *n*

explain away *vb* : to cause to seem less important by explaining ⟨*explained away* her mistake⟩

ex·pla·na·tion \ˌek-splə-'nā-shən\ *n* **1** : the act or process of explaining **2** : a statement that makes something clear

ex·plan·a·to·ry \ik-'splan-ə-ˌtōr-ē, -ˌtȯr-\ *adj* : serving to explain ⟨*explanatory* notes⟩ — **ex·plan·a·to·ri·ly** \-ˌsplan-ə-'tōr-ə-lē, -ˌtȯr-\ *adv*

ex·ple·tive \'ek-splət-iv\ *n* : an exclamatory word or phrase; *esp* : SWEARWORD

ex·pli·ca·ble \ek-'splik-ə-bəl, 'ek-(ˌ)splik-\ *adj* : able to be explained — **ex·pli·ca·bly** \-blē\ *adv*

ex·pli·cate \'ek-splə-ˌkāt\ *vb* **-cat·ed; -cat·ing** : to give a complete explanation of — **ex·pli·ca·tion** \ˌek-splə-'kā-shən\ *n*

ex·plic·it \ik-'splis-ət\ *adj* : so clear in statement that there is no doubt about the meaning ⟨*explicit* instructions⟩ — **ex·plic·it·ly** *adv* — **ex·plic·it·ness** *n*

ex·plode \ik-'splōd\ *vb* **ex·plod·ed; ex·plod·ing** **1** : to cause to be given up or rejected ⟨science has *exploded* many old theories⟩ **2 a** : to burst or cause to burst with violence and noise ⟨the boiler *exploded*⟩ **b** : to go through a rapid chemical or nuclear reaction with the production of noise, heat, and violent expansion of gases ⟨the bomb *exploded*⟩ **3** : to burst forth ⟨*exploded* with laughter⟩ ⟨zoomed out of the alley and *exploded* into the street⟩

Word History Theatergoers in ancient Rome could be noisy in showing both their enjoyment and their dislike of a performance. One of the ways they made noise was by clapping their hands loudly. The Latin verb *plaudere* meant "to make a noise by loud clapping." When the Romans were showing their approval of a performance, the word used was *applaudere,* from which we get our English word *applaud.* When the Romans did not like a performance, they often drove the performer from the stage by loud claps. The word for this was *explaudere,* from the prefix *ex-,* meaning "out, away," and *plaudere.* It is from this word that we get our English word *explode.* In the beginning, the English word *explode* had the meaning "to drive from the stage by a noisy expression of dislike." But this sense has all but disappeared. Other meanings that have either the idea of disapproval or the idea of violent noise have since come into wide use. [from Latin *explaudere* "to drive off the stage by clapping," from *ex-* "out, away" and *plaudere* "to clap" — related to APPLAUD, PLAUDIT, PLAUSIBLE; see *Word History* at PLAUSIBLE]

exploded *adj* : showing the parts separated but in correct relationship to each other ⟨an *exploded* view of a machine⟩

¹**ex·ploit** \'ek-ˌsplȯit, ik-'splȯit\ *n* : a brave or daring act

²**ex·ploit** \ik-'splȯit, 'ek-ˌsplȯit\ *vb* **1** : to get value or use from ⟨*exploit* your talents⟩ ⟨*exploit* an opponent's weaknesses⟩ **2** : to make use of unfairly for one's own advantage ⟨*exploiting* migrant farm workers⟩ — **ex·ploit·able** \-ə-bəl\ *adj* — **ex·ploi·ta·tion** \ˌek-ˌsplȯi-'tā-shən\ *n* — **ex·ploit·er** \ik-'splȯit-ər, 'ek-ˌsplȯit-\ *n*

ex·plo·ra·tion \ˌek-splə-'rā-shən\ *n* : the act or an instance of exploring

ex·plor·a·to·ry \ik-'splōr-ə-ˌtōr-ē, -ˌtȯr-\ *adj* : of, relating to, or being exploration ⟨*exploratory* drilling for oil⟩ ⟨an *exploratory* trip⟩ ⟨*exploratory* surgery⟩

ex·plore \ik-'splō(ə)r, -'splȯ(ə)r\ *vb* **ex·plored; ex·plor·ing** **1 a** : to search through : look into ⟨*exploring* new ideas⟩ **b** : to go into or travel over for purposes of discovery or adventure ⟨*explore* a cave⟩ ⟨*explore* the moon⟩ **c** : to examine carefully and in detail especially in order to make a diagnosis ⟨*explore* a wound⟩ **2** : to make a careful search ⟨*explore* for oil⟩

ex·plor·er \ik-'splōr-ər, -'splȯr-\ *n* **1** : one that explores ⟨a vehicle called the lunar *explorer*⟩; *esp* : a person who travels in search of new geographical or scientific information **2** *cap* : a member of the scouting program of the Boy Scouts of America for young people 14 to 20 years old

ex·plo·sion \ik-'splō-zhən\ *n* **1** : the act or an instance of exploding **2** : a violent outburst of feeling

¹ex·plo·sive \ik-'splō-siv, -ziv\ *adj* **1** : able to cause explosion ⟨the *explosive* power of gunpowder⟩ **2** : likely to explode ⟨an *explosive* temper⟩ — **ex·plo·sive·ly** *adv* — **ex·plo·sive·ness** *n*

²explosive *n* : an explosive substance

ex·po·nent \ik-'spō-nənt, 'ek-ˌspō-\ *n* **1** : a symbol written above and to the right of a mathematical expression to mean raising that expression to the power of the symbol ⟨in the expression a^3, the *exponent 3* indicates that a is to be raised to the third power⟩ **2** : a person who supports or favors a cause

ex·po·nen·tial \ˌek-spə-'nen-chəl\ *adj* : of, relating to, or involving an exponent ⟨x^n is an *exponential* expression⟩ — **ex·po·nen·tial·ly** \-'nench-(ə-)lē\ *adv*

ex·po·nen·ti·a·tion \ˌek-spə-ˌnen-chē-'ā-shən\ *n* : the mathematical operation of raising a quantity to a power

¹ex·port \ek-'spō(ə)rt, -'spó(ə)rt, 'ek-ˌspō(ə)rt, 'ek-ˌspó(ə)rt\ *vb* : to carry or send abroad especially for sale in another country — **ex·port·able** \-'spōrt-ə-bəl, -'spórt-\ *adj* — **ex·por·ta·tion** \ˌek-ˌspōr-'tā-shən, -ˌspór-, -spər-\ *n* — **ex·port·er** \ek-'spōrt-ər, -'spórt-, 'ek-ˌ\ *n*

²ex·port \'ek-ˌspō(ə)rt, -ˌspó(ə)rt\ *n* **1** : something that is exported **2** : an act of exporting — **export** *adj*

ex·pose \ik-'spōz\ *vb* **ex·posed; ex·pos·ing** **1 a** : to leave without shelter, protection, or care **b** : to make open to an action or influence ⟨*expose* students to good books⟩ ⟨had been *exposed* to measles⟩; *esp* : to let light fall on (photographic film) **2** : to make known ⟨*expose* a dishonest scheme⟩ **3** : to put on display — **ex·pos·er** *n*

ex·po·sé \ˌek-spō-'zā\ *n* : an exposing of something disgraceful

ex·po·si·tion \ˌek-spə-'zish-ən\ *n* **1** : an explanation of something **2** : a piece of writing that explains **3** : the first part of a piece of music in which the theme is presented **4** : a public exhibition — **ex·pos·i·tor** \ik-'späz-ət-ər\ *n* — **ex·pos·i·to·ry** \ik-'späz-ə-ˌtōr-ē, -ˌtór-\ *adj*

¹ex post fac·to \ˌek-ˌspōst-'fak-tō\ *adv* : after the fact ⟨an explanation given *ex post facto*⟩ [Latin, literally, "from a thing done afterward"]

²ex post facto *adj* : made, done, or formulated after the fact ⟨got *ex post facto* approval⟩

ex·pos·tu·late \ik-'späs-chə-ˌlāt\ *vb* **-lat·ed; -lat·ing** : REMONSTRATE — **ex·pos·tu·la·tion** \-ˌspäs-chə-'lā-shən\ *n*

ex·po·sure \ik-'spō-zhər\ *n* **1** : the fact or condition of being exposed ⟨*exposure* to cold⟩ **2 a** : the act or an instance of exposing **b** : the act of letting light expose photographic film; *also* : the amount or length of time of such exposure **3** : a position with respect to direction ⟨a southern *exposure*⟩ **4** : a section of a film for a single picture ⟨36 *exposures* per roll of film⟩

ex·pound \ik-'spaúnd\ *vb* **1** : to make known (as one's ideas or beliefs) : set forth **2** : to explain clearly : INTERPRET — **ex·pound·er** *n*

¹ex·press \ik-'spres\ *adj* **1** : EXPLICIT ⟨my *express* orders⟩ ⟨*express* written consent⟩ **2** : of a particular sort : SPECIFIC ⟨came for that *express* purpose⟩ **3** : sent or traveling at high speed ⟨*express* mail⟩; *esp* : making few or no stops ⟨an *express* train⟩

²express *adv* : by express ⟨send a package *express*⟩

³express *n* **1 a** : a system for the special transportation of goods **b** : a company operating such a service **c** : the goods or shipments so transported **2** : an express vehicle (as an elevator or train)

⁴express *vb* **1 a** : to represent or give expression to especially in words : STATE **b** : to make one's opinions, feelings, or abilities known **c** : to represent especially by a mathematical sign or symbol : SYMBOLIZE **2** : to press or squeeze out **3** : to send by express — **ex·press·er** *n* — **ex·press·ible** \-ə-bəl\ *adj*

ex·pres·sion \ik-'spresh-ən\ *n* **1** : the act or process of expressing especially in words **2 a** : a meaningful word or phrase **b** : a mathematical or logical symbol or a combination of symbols and signs representing a quantity or operation **3** : a way of speaking or singing or of playing an instrument so as to show mood or feeling ⟨sing with *expression*⟩ **4** : the way one's face looks or one's voice sounds that shows one's feelings ⟨a pleased *expression*⟩ **5** : the detectable effect of a gene — **ex·pres·sion·less** \-ləs\ *adj* — **ex·pres·sion·less·ly** *adv* — **ex·pres·sion·less·ness** *n*

ex·pres·sive \ik-'spres-iv\ *adj* **1** : of or relating to expression **2** : serving to express **3** : full of expression; *also* : openly expressing one's feelings ⟨an *expressive* face⟩ — **ex·pres·sive·ly** *adv* — **ex·pres·sive·ness** *n*

ex·press·ly \ik-'spres-lē\ *adv* **1** : so as to be absolutely clear : EXPLICITLY ⟨was *expressly* forbidden to smoke⟩ **2** : for the express purpose : ESPECIALLY ⟨came *expressly* to congratulate her⟩

expresso *variant of* ESPRESSO

ex·press·way \ik-'spres-ˌwā\ *n* : a divided superhighway that may be entered and left only at special places

ex·pro·pri·ate \ek-'sprō-prē-ˌāt\ *vb* **-at·ed; -at·ing** **1** : to deprive of ownership or the right of ownership **2** : to take over the property of another especially by government action — **ex·pro·pri·a·tion** \(ˌ)ek-ˌsprō-prē-'ā-shən\ *n*

ex·pul·sion \ik-'spəl-shən\ *n* : the act of expelling : the state of being expelled

ex·punge \ik-'spənj\ *vb* **ex·punged; ex·pung·ing** : to blot or rub out : ERASE — **ex·pung·er** *n*

ex·pur·gate \'ek-spər-ˌgāt\ *vb* **-gat·ed; -gat·ing** : to remove objectionable parts from (as a book) — **ex·pur·ga·tion** \ˌek-spər-'gā-shən\ *n* — **ex·pur·ga·tor** \'ek-spər-ˌgāt-ər\ *n*

ex·quis·ite \ek-'skwiz-ət, 'ek-(ˌ)skwiz-\ *adj* **1** : finely done or made ⟨an *exquisite* lacy handkerchief⟩ ⟨an *exquisite* painting⟩ **2** : showing fine discrimination, deep sensitivity, or clear understanding ⟨*exquisite* taste⟩ **3** : pleasing through beauty, fitness, or perfection ⟨*exquisite* flowers⟩ **4** : very severe : INTENSE ⟨*exquisite* pain⟩ — **ex·quis·ite·ly** *adv* — **ex·quis·ite·ness** *n*

ex·tant \'ek-stənt, ek-'stant\ *adj* : existing at the present time : not destroyed or lost

ex·tem·po·ra·ne·ous \(ˌ)ek-ˌstem-pə-'rā-nē-əs\ *adj* : made up or done on the spur of the moment : IMPROMPTU — **ex·tem·po·ra·ne·ous·ly** *adv* — **ex·tem·po·ra·ne·ous·ness** *n*

ex·tem·po·re \ik-'stem-pə-(ˌ)rē\ *adv or adj* : in an extemporaneous manner ⟨speaking *extempore*⟩

ex·tem·po·rize \ik-'stem-pə-ˌrīz\ *vb* **-rized; -riz·ing** : to do, make, or speak extempore : IMPROVISE

ex·tend \ik-'stend\ *vb* **1** : to straighten out or stretch forth ⟨*extended* both arms⟩ **2 a** : to offer to someone ⟨*extend* an apology⟩ **b** : to make available ⟨*extend* credit⟩ **3 a** : to stretch out : make longer ⟨an *extended* visit⟩ **b** : to make larger ⟨*extend* the meaning of a word⟩ **4** : to stretch out or reach across a distance, space, or time ⟨the woods *extend* for miles to the west⟩ ⟨the bridge *extends* across the river⟩ — **ex·tend·able** *also* **ex·tend·ible** \-'sten-də-bəl\ *adj*

extended family *n* : a family that includes parents and children and other relatives (as grandparents, aunts, or uncles) in the same household

ex·tend·er \ik-'sten-dər\ *n* : something added to something else especially to make it go farther ⟨meat *extenders*⟩

ex·ten·si·ble \ik-'sten(t)-sə-bəl\ *adj* : able to be extended — **ex·ten·si·bil·i·ty** \-ˌsten(t)-sə-'bil-ət-ē\ *n*

\ə\ abut	\aú\ out	\i\ tip	\ó\ saw	\ú\ foot
\ər\ further	\ch\ chin	\ī\ life	\ói\ coin	\y\ yet
\a\ mat	\e\ pet	\j\ job	\th\ thin	\yü\ few
\ā\ take	\ē\ easy	\ŋ\ sing	\th\ this	\yú\ cure
\ä\ cot, cart	\g\ go	\ō\ bone	\ü\ food	\zh\ vision

ex·ten·sion \ik-'sten-chən\ *n* **1** : the act of extending : the state of being extended **2** : an increase in time ⟨was given an *extension* to finish his project⟩ **3** : education by special programs at a distance from a school **4 a** : a part forming an addition or increase **b** : an extra telephone connected to the main line

extension agent *n* : COUNTY AGENT

ex·ten·sive \ik-'sten(t)-siv\ *adj* : having wide or large extent — **ex·ten·sive·ly** *adv* — **ex·ten·sive·ness** *n*

ex·ten·sor \ik-'sten(t)-sər\ *n* : a muscle serving to extend a bodily part (as a leg or arm)

ex·tent \ik-'stent\ *n* **1** : the range, distance, or space over or through which something extends ⟨the *extent* of the Roman empire⟩ **2** : the point, degree, or limit to which something extends ⟨the *extent* of her knowledge⟩

ex·ten·u·ate \ik-'sten-yə-ˌwāt\ *vb* **-at·ed; -at·ing** : to try to make less serious by partial excuses — **ex·ten·u·a·tion** \-ˌsten-yə-'wā-shən\ *n*

¹ex·te·ri·or \ek-'stir-ē-ər\ *adj* **1** : situated on the outside **2** : ¹EXTERNAL 1 **3** : suitable for use on outside surfaces ⟨*exterior* paint⟩ — **ex·te·ri·or·ly** *adv*

²exterior *n* **1** : an exterior part or surface : OUTSIDE **2** : visible manner or appearance ⟨a calm *exterior*⟩

exterior angle *n* : any of the four angles formed by a line cutting across two other lines and located on the outside of those lines

ex·ter·mi·nate \ik-'stər-mə-ˌnāt\ *vb* **-nat·ed; -nat·ing** : to get rid of completely ⟨*exterminate* termites⟩ — **ex·ter·mi·na·tion** \-ˌstər-mə-'nā-shən\ *n* — **ex·ter·mi·na·tor** \-'stər-mə-ˌnāt-ər\ *n*

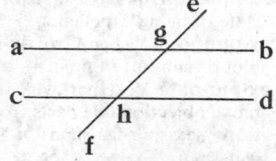

exterior angle: *ega, egb, fhc, fhd*

¹ex·ter·nal \ek-'stərn-ᵊl\ *adj* **1** : outwardly visible ⟨*external* signs of relief⟩ **2 a** : of, relating to, or connected with the outside or an outer part ⟨the building's *external* features⟩ **b** : applied or applicable to the outside ⟨for *external* use only⟩ **3** : arising or acting from outside ⟨*external* pressures⟩ **4** : of or relating to relationships with foreign countries ⟨*external* affairs⟩ — **ex·ter·nal·ly** \-ᵊl-ē\ *adv*

²external *n* : something external — usually used in plural

external–combustion engine *n* : a heat engine (as a steam engine) that gets its heat from fuel burned outside the engine cylinder

external ear *n* : the outer part of the ear consisting of the projecting sound-collecting part composed of cartilage and the canal leading from this to the eardrum

ex·tinct \ik-'stiŋ(k)t, 'ek-ˌ\ *adj* **1** : no longer active ⟨an *extinct* volcano⟩ **2** : no longer existing ⟨an *extinct* species of animal⟩

ex·tinc·tion \ik-'stiŋ(k)-shən\ *n* **1** : an act of extinguishing or an instance of being extinguished **2 a** : the state of being extinct **b** : the process of becoming extinct **3** : the process of eliminating or reducing a conditioned response by not providing the stimulus with which it has become associated by conditioning

ex·tin·guish \ik-'stiŋ-gwish\ *vb* **1** : to cause to stop burning **2** : to cause to die out — **ex·tin·guish·able** \-ə-bəl\ *adj* — **ex·tin·guish·er** *n*

ex·tir·pate \'ek-stər-ˌpāt\ *vb* **-pat·ed; -pat·ing** **1** : to pull up by the roots **2** : to destroy completely — **ex·tir·pa·tion** \ˌek-(ˌ)stər-'pā-shən\ *n*

ex·tol *also* **ex·toll** \ik-'stōl\ *vb* **ex·tolled; ex·tol·ling** : to praise highly — **ex·tol·ler** *n* — **ex·tol·ment** \-mənt\ *n*

ex·tort \ik-'stȯ(ə)rt\ *vb* : to get (as money) from a person by the use of force or threats [from Latin *extortus*, past participle of *extorquēre* "to twist out, extort," from *ex-* "out, away" and *torquēre* "to twist" — related to DISTORT, RETORT, TORTURE] — **ex·tort·er** *n*

ex·tor·tion \ik-'stȯr-shən\ *n* : the practice or crime of extorting (as money) — **ex·tor·tion·er** \-sh(ə-)nər\ *n* — **ex·tor·tion·ist** \-sh(ə-)nəst\ *n*

ex·tor·tion·ate \ik-'stȯr-sh(ə-)nət\ *adj* **1** : marked by extortion **2** : extremely high : EXORBITANT ⟨*extortionate* prices⟩ — **ex·tor·tion·ate·ly** *adv*

¹ex·tra \'ek-strə\ *adj* : more than is due, usual, or necessary

²extra *n* : something extra: as **a** : a special edition of a newspaper **b** : a person hired to act in a group scene (as in a movie)

³extra *adv* : beyond the usual size, extent, or degree ⟨*extra* long⟩ ⟨*extra* large eggs⟩

extra- *prefix* : outside : beyond ⟨*extra*curricular⟩ [derived from Latin *extra* "outside, beyond" — related to STRANGE]

ex·tra·cel·lu·lar \ˌek-strə-'sel-yə-lər\ *adj* : situated or occurring outside a cell or the cells of the body

¹ex·tract \ik-'strakt, *usually in sense 4* ek-ˌstrakt\ *vb* **1** : to remove by pulling ⟨*extract* a tooth⟩ **2** : to get out by pressing, distilling, or by a chemical process ⟨*extract* juice from apples⟩ **3** : to calculate a mathematical root **4** : to choose and take out for separate use ⟨*extract* a few lines from a poem⟩ — **ex·tract·able** \ik-'strak-tə-bəl, 'ek-ˌ\ *adj* — **ex·trac·tor** \-tər\ *n*

²ex·tract \'ek-ˌstrakt\ *n* **1** : a selection from a writing **2** : a product obtained by extracting ⟨vanilla *extract*⟩

ex·trac·tion \ik-'strak-shən\ *n* **1** : the act or process of extracting **2** : the origin of a person ⟨of Italian *extraction*⟩

ex·tra·cur·ric·u·lar \ˌek-strə-kə-'rik-yə-lər\ *adj* : of or relating to those activities (as athletics) that are offered by a school but are not part of the course of study

ex·tra·dite \'ek-strə-ˌdīt\ *vb* **-dit·ed; -dit·ing** : to cause to be delivered by extradition — **ex·tra·dit·able** \-ˌdīt-ə-bəl\ *adj*

ex·tra·di·tion \ˌek-strə-'dish-ən\ *n* : the delivery of an accused criminal from one place (as a U.S. state) to another where the trial will be held

ex·tra·le·gal \ˌek-strə-'lē-gəl\ *adj* : not regulated or sanctioned by law — **ex·tra·le·gal·ly** \-gə-lē\ *adv*

ex·tra·mar·i·tal \ˌek-strə-'mar-ət-ᵊl\ *adj* : of or relating to sexual intercourse between a married person and someone other than his or her spouse

ex·tra·ne·ous \ek-'strā-nē-əs\ *adj* **1** : not forming a necessary part **2** : IRRELEVANT — **ex·tra·ne·ous·ly** *adv* — **ex·tra·ne·ous·ness** *n*

ex·traor·di·nary \ik-'strȯrd-ᵊn-ˌer-ē, ˌek-strə-'ȯrd-\ *adj* : so unusual as to be remarkable — **ex·traor·di·nar·i·ly** \ik-ˌstrȯrd-ᵊn-ˌer-ə-lē, ˌek-strə-'ȯrd-\ *adv* — **ex·traor·di·nar·i·ness** \ik-'strȯrd-ᵊn-ˌer-ē-nəs, ˌek-strə-'ȯrd-\ *n*

extra point *n* : a point scored in football after a touchdown by kicking the ball between the goalposts or advancing it a short distance into the end zone

ex·trap·o·late \ik-'strap-ə-ˌlāt\ *vb* **-lat·ed; -lat·ing** : to work out unknown facts from known facts — **ex·trap·o·la·tion** \-ˌstrap-ə-'lā-shən\ *n* — **ex·trap·o·la·tor** \-'strap-ə-ˌlāt-ər\ *n*

ex·tra·sen·so·ry \ˌek-strə-'sen(t)s-(ə-)rē\ *adj* : not acting or occurring through use of the known senses ⟨*extrasensory* experience⟩

extrasensory perception *n* : an awareness of events or facts that cannot be explained by communication using any of the known senses

ex·tra·ter·res·tri·al \ˌek-strə-tə-'res-trē-əl\ *adj* : coming from or existing outside the earth or its atmosphere ⟨*extraterrestrial* life⟩ — **extraterrestrial** *n*

ex·trav·a·gance \ik-'strav-i-gən(t)s\ *n* **1 a** : the wasteful or careless spending of money **b** : something that is extravagant **2** : the quality or fact of being extravagant

ex·trav·a·gant \ik-'strav-i-gənt\ *adj* **1** : going beyond what is reasonable or suitable ⟨*extravagant* praise⟩ **2** : wasteful especially of money ⟨*extravagant* spending⟩

[Middle English *extravagaunt* "wandering away, going beyond the usual limits," from early French *extravagant* (same meaning), from Latin *extravagant-*, *extravagans* (same meaning), from earlier *extra-* "outside, beyond" and *vagari* "to wander away" — related to VAGABOND] — **ex·trav·a·gant·ly** *adv*

ex·trav·a·gan·za \ik-ˌstrav-ə-ˈgan-zə\ *n* : a spectacular show

ex·tra·ve·hic·u·lar \ˌek-strə-vē-ˈhik-yə-lər\ *adj* : taking place outside a vehicle (as a spacecraft)

¹ex·treme \ik-ˈstrēm\ *adj* **1** : existing to a very great degree ⟨*extreme* heat⟩ ⟨*extreme* poverty⟩ **2** : farthest from a center **3** : most advanced or thorough ⟨the *extreme* political right⟩ **4** : relating to a form of a sport that involves an unusually high degree of risk ⟨*extreme* skiing⟩ — **ex·treme·ly** *adv* — **ex·treme·ness** *n*

²extreme *n* **1** : something situated as far away as possible from another ⟨*extremes* of heat and cold⟩ **2** : the first term or the last term of a mathematical proportion **3** : a very pronounced or excessive degree **4** : an extraordinary measure ⟨going to *extremes*⟩

$$\frac{a}{b} = \frac{c}{d}$$

²extreme 2: *a* and *d*

ex·trem·ism \ik-ˈstrē-ˌmiz-əm\ *n* **1** : the quality or state of being extreme **2** : belief in and support for extreme ideas especially in politics — **ex·trem·ist** \-məst\ *n or adj*

ex·trem·i·ty \ik-ˈstrem-ət-ē\ *n, pl* **-ties** **1** : the farthest limit, point, or part **2** : an end part of a limb of the body (as a hand or foot) **3** : an extreme degree (as of emotion or pain)

ex·tri·cate \ˈek-strə-ˌkāt\ *vb* **-cat·ed; -cat·ing** : to free or remove from entanglement or difficulty — **ex·tri·ca·ble** \ek-ˈstrik-ə-bəl, ˈek-(ˌ)strik-\ *adj* — **ex·tri·ca·tion** \ˌek-strə-ˈkā-shən\ *n*

ex·trin·sic \ek-ˈstrin-zik, -ˈstrin(t)-sik\ *adj* : not being part of or belonging to a thing : EXTRANEOUS — **ex·trin·si·cal·ly** \-zi-k(ə-)lē, -si-\ *adv*

ex·tro·vert *also* **ex·tra·vert** \ˈek-strə-ˌvərt\ *n* **1** : a person who is interested only or mostly in things outside the self **2** : a gregarious and unreserved person — **ex·tro·ver·sion** \ˌek-strə-ˈvər-zhən, -shən\ *n* — **ex·tro·vert·ed** \ˈek-strə-ˌvərt-əd\ *adj*

ex·trude \ik-ˈstrüd\ *vb* **ex·trud·ed; ex·trud·ing** **1** : to force, press, or push out **2** : to shape by forcing through a die

ex·tru·sion \ik-ˈstrü-zhən\ *n* : the act or process of extruding; *also* : a form or product produced by this process

ex·tru·sive \ik-ˈstrü-siv, -ziv\ *adj* : relating to or formed by geological extrusion from the earth in a melted state or as volcanic ash ⟨*extrusive* rock⟩

ex·u·ber·ant \ig-ˈzü-b(ə-)rənt\ *adj* : joyfully enthusiastic — **ex·u·ber·ance** \-b(ə-)rən(t)s\ *n* — **ex·u·ber·ant·ly** *adv*

ex·ude \ig-ˈzüd\ *vb* **ex·ud·ed; ex·ud·ing** **1** : to discharge slowly through pores or cuts : OOZE ⟨*exude* sweat⟩ **2** : to give forth ⟨brown eyes *exuding* confidence⟩

ex·ult \ig-ˈzəlt\ *vb* : to be very joyful : REJOICE — **ex·ult·ing·ly** \-ˈzəl-tiŋ-lē\ *adv*

ex·ult·ant \ig-ˈzəlt-ᵊnt\ *adj* : full of or expressing joy or triumph — **ex·ult·ant·ly** *adv*

ex·ul·ta·tion \ˌek-(ˌ)səl-ˈtā-shən, ˌeg-(ˌ)zəl-\ *n* : the act of exulting : the state of being exultant

ex·urb \ˈek-ˌsərb, ˈeg-ˌzərb\ *n* : a region or district outside a city and its suburbs where many well-to-do people live

ex·ur·ban·ite \ek-ˈsər-bə-ˌnīt, eg-ˈzər-\ *n* : a person living in an exurb

ex·ur·bia \ek-ˈsər-bē-ə, eg-ˈzər-\ *n* : the region of exurbs

-ey — see ¹-Y

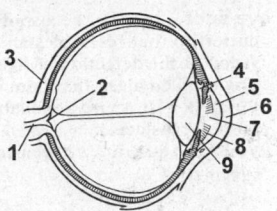

¹eye 1a: *1* optic nerve, *2* blind spot, *3* sclera, *4* posterior chamber, *5* anterior chamber, *6* cornea, *7* pupil, *8* iris, *9* lens

¹eye \ˈī\ *n* **1 a** : an organ of sight; *esp* : a rounded hollow organ that is filled with a jellylike material, is lined with a sensitive retina, and is located in a bone-lined cavity in the skull of a vertebrate **b** : all the visible parts (as the eyelids) within and surrounding the bone-lined cavity **2 a** : ability to see or appreciate ⟨a good *eye* for painting⟩ **b** : ²GLANCE 3 ⟨cast an eager *eye*⟩ **c** : close attention or observation ⟨keep an *eye* on it⟩ **d** : JUDGMENT 1 ⟨guilty in the *eyes* of the law⟩ **3** : something like or suggestive of an eye: as **a** : the hole through the head of a needle **b** : a loop to catch or receive a hook **c** : an undeveloped bud (as on a potato) **d** : a device (as a photoelectric cell) that functions somewhat like human vision **4** : the center of something ⟨the *eye* of a hurricane⟩ — **eyed** \ˈīd\ *adj* — **eye·less** \ˈī-ləs\ *adj* — **eye·like** \-ˌlīk\ *adj*

²eye *vb* **eyed; eye·ing** *or* **ey·ing** : to watch or study closely

eye·ball \ˈī-ˌból\ *n* : the eye of a vertebrate

eye·brow \ˈī-ˌbrau̇\ *n* : the ridge over the eye or hair growing usually in a line or arch on the skin over it

eye–catching \ˈī-ˌkach-iŋ, -ˌkech-\ *adj* : attractive to the eye

eye chart *n* : a chart with rows of letters or objects of decreasing size that is read at a fixed distance for purposes of testing sight

eye contact *n* : the act of looking another person straight in the eye

eye·cup \ˈī-ˌkəp\ *n* : a small oval cup with a rim curved to fit the orbit of the eye and used for applying liquid medicine to the eyes

eye doctor *n* : a specialist (as an optometrist or ophthalmologist) in the examination, treatment, or care of the eyes

eye·drop·per \ˈī-ˌdräp-ər\ *n* : DROPPER 2

eye·ful \-ˌfu̇l\ *n* : something attractive to look at

eye·glass \-ˌglas\ *n* **1** : a glass lens used to help one see clearly **2** *pl* : ¹GLASS 2b

eye·hole \-ˌhōl\ *n* : EYELET 1

eye·lash \-ˌlash\ *n* : a single hair of the fringe on the eyelid

eye lens *n* : the lens nearest the eye in an eyepiece

eye·let \ˈī-lət\ *n* **1** : a small hole (as in cloth or leather) for a lace or rope **2** : GROMMET

eye·lid \ˈī-ˌlid\ *n* : one of the movable lids of skin and muscle that can be closed over the eyeball

eye·lin·er \ˈī-ˌlī-nər\ *n* : makeup used to emphasize the outline of the eye

eye–open·ing \ˈī-ˌōp(-ə)-niŋ\ *adj* : being surprising or startling

eye·piece \ˈī-ˌpēs\ *n* : the lens or combination of lenses at the eye end of an optical instrument (as a microscope or telescope)

eye shadow *n* : a colored cosmetic applied to the eyelids

eye·sight \ˈī-ˌsīt\ *n* : SIGHT 3, VISION ⟨keen *eyesight*⟩

eye socket *n* : ¹ORBIT

eye·sore \ˈī-ˌsór, -ˌsȯr\ *n* : something displeasing to the sight

\ə\ abut	\au̇\ out	\i\ tip	\ȯ\ saw	\u̇\ foot
\ər\ further	\ch\ chin	\ī\ life	\ȯi\ coin	\y\ yet
\a\ mat	\e\ pet	\j\ job	\th\ thin	\yü\ few
\ā\ take	\ē\ easy	\ŋ\ sing	\th\ this	\yu̇\ cure
\ä\ cot, cart	\g\ go	\ō\ bone	\ü\ food	\zh\ vision

eye·spot \-ˌspät\ *n* **1** : a spot of color (as on the wing of a butterfly) that resembles an eye **2 a** : a simple organ for vision or the detection of light **b** : a small body in various single-celled algae that contains pigment
eye·stalk \-ˌstók\ *n* : a movable stalk bearing an eye at the tip in a crustacean
eye·strain \-ˌsträn\ *n* : weariness or a strained state of the eye

eye·tooth \-ˈtüth\ *n* : a canine tooth of the upper jaw
eye·wash \-ˌwȯsh, -ˌwäsh\ *n* : an eye lotion
eye·wit·ness \-ˈwit-nəs\ *n* : a person who sees an occurrence and is able to give a report of it
ey·rie *chiefly British variant of* AERIE
Eze·chiel \i-ˈzē-kyəl, -kē-əl\ *n* : EZEKIEL
Eze·kiel \i-ˈzē-kyəl, -kē-əl\ *n* — see BIBLE table
Ez·ra \ˈez-rə\ *n* — see BIBLE table

F

f \ˈef\ *n, pl* **f's** *or* **fs** *often cap* **1** : the sixth letter of the English alphabet **2** : a musical note referred to by the letter F : the fourth tone of a C-major scale **3** : a grade rating a student's work as failing
fa \ˈfä\ *n* : the fourth note of the musical scale
fa·ble \ˈfā-bəl\ *n* : a short fictitious story; *esp* : one intended to teach a lesson and in which animals speak and act like human beings
fa·bled \ˈfā-bəld\ *adj* : told about in fables ⟨a *fabled* mountain of gold⟩
fab·ric \ˈfab-rik\ *n* **1** : the basic structure ⟨the *fabric* of society⟩ **2** : CLOTH 1
fab·ri·cate \ˈfab-ri-ˌkāt\ *vb* **-cat·ed; -cat·ing 1** : INVENT 2, CREATE **2** : to make up in order to deceive ⟨*fabricated* evidence to support her claim⟩ **3** : CONSTRUCT 1, MANUFACTURE — **fab·ri·ca·tion** \ˌfab-ri-ˈkā-shən\ *n* — **fab·ri·ca·tor** \ˈfab-ri-ˌkāt-ər\ *n*
fab·u·lous \ˈfab-yə-ləs\ *adj* **1 a** : resembling a fable especially in being marvelous or beyond belief ⟨*fabulous* wealth⟩ **b** : very good : MARVELOUS ⟨had a *fabulous* time⟩ **2** : told in or based on fable ⟨*fabulous* animals⟩ — **fab·u·lous·ly** *adv* — **fab·u·lous·ness** *n*
fa·cade *also* **fa·çade** \fə-ˈsäd\ *n* **1** : the face or front of a building **2** : a false or misleading appearance ⟨a *facade* of wealth⟩

facade 1

¹**face** \ˈfās\ *n* **1** : the front part of the head **2 a** : an expression of the face ⟨a friendly *face*⟩ **b** : GRIMACE ⟨make a *face*⟩ **3 a** : outward appearance ⟨on the *face* of it⟩ **b** : DIGNITY 1, PRESTIGE ⟨lose *face*⟩ **4 a** : a front, upper, or outer surface ⟨the *face* of a cliff⟩ **b** : any of the flat surfaces that form the boundary of a solid in geometry ⟨every cube has six *faces*⟩ **c** : a surface or side that is marked or specially prepared ⟨the *face* of a certificate⟩ **d** : an exposed surface of rock **5** : the end (as of a mine tunnel) at which work is going on **6** : PERSON ⟨a lot of new *faces* around here⟩ — **in one's face** : directly and aggressively ⟨made the dunk shot *in her face*⟩ — **in the face of** : face-to-face with : DESPITE ⟨brave *in the face of* danger⟩
²**face** *vb* **faced; fac·ing 1 a** : to line near the edge especially with a different material ⟨*face* a hem⟩ **b** : to cover the front or surface of ⟨*faced* the building with marble⟩ **2** : to meet face-to-face ⟨*faced* the opposing team⟩ ⟨*face* one's accusers⟩ **3 a** : to stand or sit with the face toward ⟨*face* the class⟩ **b** : to have the front oriented toward ⟨a house *facing* the park⟩ **4 a** : to recognize and deal with ⟨*face* facts⟩ **b** : to oppose by confronting with determination ⟨*face* down their critics⟩ **5** : to turn toward ⟨*face* the

east⟩ — **face the music** : to meet a danger or something unpleasant (as punishment)
face card *n* : a king, queen, or jack in a deck of cards
-faced *adj combining form* : having (such) a face or (so many) faces ⟨rosy-*faced*⟩ ⟨two-*faced*⟩
face·down \ˈfās-ˈdaún\ *adv* : with the face down ⟨floated *facedown*⟩
face–first \ˌfās-ˈfərst\ *adv* : with the face leading the body ⟨hit the ground *face-first*⟩ — **face–first** *adj*
face·less \ˈfās-ləs\ *adj* **1** : not able to be identified **2** : lacking a face — **face·less·ness** *n*
face–lift \ˈfā-ˌslift\ *n* **1** : plastic surgery on the face and neck to remove defects and imperfections (as wrinkles or sagging skin) **2** : an alteration, restoration, or remodeling (as of a building) intended especially to make more modern — **face–lift** *vb*
face–off \ˈfā-ˌsóf\ *n* **1** : a method of putting a puck in play in ice hockey by dropping it between two opposing players **2** : a meeting of opposing forces : CONFRONTATION
face off *vb* : to be in or come into opposition or competition ⟨politicians *facing off* each other in a debate⟩
face·plate \ˈfā-ˌsplāt\ *n* : a protective plate or cover (as for protecting the face of a diver)
fac·et \ˈfas-ət\ *n* **1** : a small plane surface (as on a cut gem) **2** : a definable aspect of something ⟨explained all *facets* of the company⟩ **3** : the surface of a functional unit of vision of a compound eye — **fac·et·ed** \ˈfas-ət-əd\ *adj*

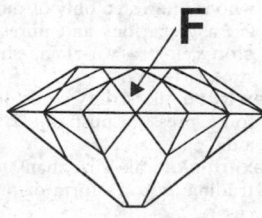

F facet 1

fa·ce·tious \fə-ˈsē-shəs\ *adj* **1** : joking or kidding often inappropriately ⟨just being *facetious*⟩ **2** : meant to be funny : not serious ⟨a *facetious* remark⟩ — **fa·ce·tious·ly** *adv* — **fa·ce·tious·ness** *n*
face–to–face \ˌfās-tə-ˈfās\ *adv or adj* **1** : within each other's close presence ⟨met *face-to-face*⟩ **2** : in or into direct contact or confrontation ⟨*face-to-face* with a crisis⟩
face·up \ˈfā-ˌsəp\ *adv* : with the face up ⟨the card fell *faceup*⟩
face value *n* **1** : the value indicated on the face of something (as a coin, bill, bond, or insurance policy) **2** : the apparent worth or significance ⟨can't take what he says at *face value*⟩
¹**fa·cial** \ˈfā-shəl\ *adj* : of or relating to the face — **fa·cial·ly** \-shə-lē\ *adv*
²**facial** *n* : a treatment to improve the condition of the skin of the face
fac·ile \ˈfas-əl\ *adj* **1 a** : easily done, handled, or achieved **b** : overly simple : ¹SHALLOW 2 **c** : easily experienced or displayed and often insincere **2** : working, moving, or performing with skill and ease : FLUENT ⟨a *facile* writer⟩ — **fac·ile·ly** \-ə(l)-lē\ *adv*

fa·cil·i·tate \fə-'sil-ə-ˌtāt\ *vb* **-tat·ed; -tat·ing** : to make easier — **fa·cil·i·ta·tion** \-ˌsil-ə-'tā-shən\ *n*

fa·cil·i·ty \fə-'sil-ət-ē\ *n, pl* **-ties** **1** : freedom from difficulty : EASE ⟨handled with *facility*⟩ **2** : skill and ease in doing something ⟨a great *facility* for writing well⟩ **3 a** : something that makes an action, operation, or activity easier — usually used in plural ⟨*facilities* for study⟩ **b** : something (as a hospital) that is put up for a particular purpose

fac·ing \'fā-siŋ\ *n* **1** : a lining at the edge especially of a garment **2** : an ornamental or protective layer ⟨a house with brick *facing*⟩ **3** : material for facing

fac·sim·i·le \fak-'sim-ə-lē\ *n* **1** : an exact copy **2** : a system of transmitting and reproducing printed matter or pictures by means of signals sent over telephone lines

fact \'fakt\ *n* **1 a** : a thing done **b** : CRIME 1 ⟨accessory after the *fact*⟩ **2** : the quality of being actual **3** : something that actually exists or occurs ⟨space travel is now a *fact*⟩ ⟨prove the *fact* of damage⟩ **4** : a piece of information about something presented as true and accurate ⟨a book filled with *facts*⟩ — **in fact** : in truth : ACTUALLY

fac·tion \'fak-shən\ *n* : a group acting together within a larger body (as a government) : CLIQUE — **fac·tion·al** \-shnəl, -shən-ᵊl\ *adj* — **fac·tion·al·ism** \-ˌiz-əm\ *n*

fac·ti·tious \fak-'tish-əs\ *adj* : not natural or genuine : ARTIFICIAL ⟨a *factitious* display of grief⟩ — **fac·ti·tious·ly** *adv* — **fac·ti·tious·ness** *n*

fact of life *n* **1** : something that exists and must be taken into consideration ⟨tests are a *fact of life* for students⟩ **2** *pl* : the basic bodily processes and behavior involved in sex and reproduction

fac·toid \'fak-ˌtòid\ *n* **1** : a made-up piece of information thought to be true due to its appearance in print **2** : a brief often trivial news item

¹fac·tor \'fak-tər\ *n* **1** : one that buys or sells property for another : AGENT **2** : something that contributes to the production of a result ⟨price wasn't a *factor* in our decision⟩ **3** : GENE **4** : any of the numbers or symbols in mathematics that when multiplied together form a product; *esp* : a number that divides another number without leaving a remainder ⟨the *factors* of 6 are 1, 2, 3, and 6⟩

²factor *vb* **fac·tored; fac·tor·ing** \-t(ə-)riŋ\ **1** : to find the mathematical factors of and especially the prime mathematical factors **2** : to act as a factor ⟨attendance will *factor* into your grade⟩ — **fac·tor·able** \-t(ə-)rə-bəl\ *adj*

¹fac·to·ri·al \fak-'tōr-ē-əl, -'tòr-\ *n* **1** : the product of all the positive whole numbers from 1 to the number given — symbol **!** **2** : the quantity 0! that is defined as equal to 1

²factorial *adj* : of, relating to, or being a factor or factorial

fac·tor·i·za·tion \ˌfak-tə-rə-'zā-shən\ *n* : the act or process or an instance or result of factoring

factor tree *n* : a branching diagram that shows the prime factors of a number

fac·to·ry \'fak-t(ə-)rē\ *n, pl* **-ries** : a building or set of buildings equipped for manufacturing [from early French *factorie* "a place where business is carried on," derived from Latin *factor* "one that does or makes," from *factus*, past participle of *facere* "to make, do" — related to FASHION, MANUFACTURE]

fac·tu·al \'fak-chə-(-wə)l, 'faksh-wəl\ *adj* **1** : of or relating to facts ⟨a *factual* error⟩ **2** : restricted to or based on fact ⟨a *factual* statement⟩ — **fac·tu·al·i·ty** \ˌfak-chə-'wal-ət-ē\ *n* — **fac·tu·al·ly** \'fak-chə-(-wə)-lē, 'faksh-wə-lē\ *adv* — **fac·tu·al·ness** *n*

fac·ul·ty \'fak-əl-tē\ *n, pl* **-ties** **1** : ability to do something : TALENT ⟨a *faculty* for making friends⟩ **2** : one of the powers of the mind or body ⟨the *faculty* of hearing⟩ **3** : the teachers in a school or college

fad \'fad\ *n* : a practice or interest followed for a time with exaggerated zeal : CRAZE — **fad·dish** \'fad-ish\ *adj* — **fad·dist** \'fad-əst\ *n* — **fad·dy** \'fad-ē\ *adj*

¹fade \'fād\ *vb* **fad·ed; fad·ing** **1** : to lose freshness or health ⟨*fading* flowers⟩ **2** : to lose or cause to lose brightness of color **3** : to disappear gradually ⟨a *fading* memory⟩ **4** : to change gradually in loudness or visibility — used of a motion-picture image or of an electronics signal and usually with *in* or *out*

²fade *n* : a gradual changing of one picture to another in a motion-picture or television sequence

fa·er·ie *also* **fa·ery** \'fā-(ə)rē, 'fa(ə)r-ē, 'fe(ə)r-ē\ *n, pl* **fa·er·ies** : FAIRY — **faery** *adj*

¹fag \'fag\ *vb* **fagged; fag·ging** **1** : to work hard : TOIL **2** : to act as a fag in an English public school **3** : to tire by hard work [from obsolete *fag* "to droop"]

²fag *n* **1** : an English public-school boy who acts as a servant to another **2** : ²DOMESTIC, ²DRUDGE

³fag *n* : CIGARETTE [from *fag end*]

fag end *n* **1 a** : a poor or worn-out end : REMNANT **b** : the extreme end **2 a** : the last part or coarser end of a piece of cloth **b** : the untwisted end of a rope

fag·ot *or* **fag·got** \'fag-ət\ *n* : a bundle of sticks or twigs

fag·ot·ing *or* **fag·got·ing** \'fag-ət-iŋ\ *n* : embroidery done by tying threads in hourglass-shaped bunches

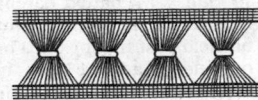
fagoting

Fahr·en·heit \'far-ən-ˌhīt\ *adj* : relating or conforming to or having a thermometer scale on which under standard atmospheric pressure the boiling point of water is at 212 degrees above the zero of the scale and the freezing point is at 32 degrees above zero — abbreviation *F* [named for Gabriel *Fahrenheit* 1686–1736 German physicist]

¹fail \'fā(ə)l\ *vb* **1 a** : to lose strength : WEAKEN ⟨*failing* eyesight⟩ **b** : to stop functioning ⟨the engine *failed*⟩ **2 a** : to fall short ⟨*failed* in their duty⟩ **b** : to become absent or lacking ⟨the power *failed*⟩ **c** : to be unsuccessful (as in passing an examination) **d** : to grade as not passing ⟨*fail* a student⟩ **e** : to become bankrupt **3** : DISAPPOINT, DESERT ⟨*fail* a friend in need⟩ **4** : to leave undone : NEGLECT ⟨*fail* to answer the telephone⟩

²fail *n* : FAILURE 1 — usually used in the phrase *without fail*

¹fail·ing \'fā-liŋ\ *n* : WEAKNESS 2, SHORTCOMING

²failing *prep* : in the absence or lack of ⟨*failing* specific instructions, use your own judgment⟩

fail·ure \'fā(ə)l-yər\ *n* **1 a** : a failing to do or perform ⟨*failure* to pass the test⟩ **b** : neglect of an assigned or expected action ⟨*failure* to pay on time⟩ **c** : inability to perform a normal function well enough ⟨heart *failure*⟩ **2 a** : a lack of success ⟨*failure* in the campaign⟩ **b** : BANKRUPTCY ⟨a business *failure*⟩ **3 a** : a falling short : DEFICIENCY ⟨crop *failure*⟩ **b** : a breaking down ⟨a *failure* of memory⟩ **4** : one that has failed ⟨the scheme was a complete *failure*⟩

¹fain \'fān\ *adj* **1** *archaic* : GLAD, HAPPY **2** *archaic* : DESIROUS **3** : FORCED 1

²fain *adv* **1** : in a willing manner : GLADLY **2** : RATHER 1

¹faint \'fānt\ *adj* **1** : TIMID, COWARDLY ⟨*faint* heart⟩ **2** : being weak, dizzy, and likely to collapse ⟨feel *faint*⟩ **3** : lacking strength : WEAK ⟨*faint* praise⟩ **4 a** : not clear or plain : DIM ⟨*faint* cries for help⟩ **b** : VAGUE 2 ⟨haven't the *faintest* idea⟩ — **faint·ly** *adv* — **faint·ness** *n*

²faint *vb* : to lose consciousness

³faint *n* : an act or condition of fainting

faint·heart·ed \'fānt-'härt-əd\ *adj* : TIMID — **faint·heart·ed·ly** *adv* — **faint·heart·ed·ness** *n*

\ə\ **abut**	\aú\ **out**	\i\ **tip**	\ò\ **saw**	\ú\ **foot**
\ər\ **further**	\ch\ **chin**	\ī\ **life**	\òi\ **coin**	\y\ **yet**
\a\ **mat**	\e\ **pet**	\j\ **job**	\th\ **thin**	\yü\ **few**
\ā\ **take**	\ē\ **easy**	\ŋ\ **sing**	\th\ **this**	\yú\ **cure**
\ä\ **cot, cart**	\g\ **go**	\ō\ **bone**	\ü\ **food**	\zh\ **vision**

¹fair \'fa(ə)r, 'fe(ə)r\ *adj* **1** : attractive in appearance : BEAUTIFUL ⟨our *fair* city⟩ **2 a** : ¹CLEAN 2, PURE ⟨*fair* sparkling water⟩ **b** : ¹CLEAR 3, LEGIBLE ⟨make a *fair* copy⟩ **3** : not stormy or cloudy ⟨*fair* weather⟩ **4 a** : UNBIASED, JUST ⟨wanted *fair* treatment⟩ **b** : observing the rules : ALLOWED ⟨*fair* play⟩ **c** : open to lawful pursuit or attack ⟨*fair* game⟩ **5 a** : PROMISING, LIKELY ⟨a *fair* chance of winning⟩ **b** : favorable to a ship's course ⟨a *fair* wind⟩ **6** : not dark ⟨*fair* skin⟩ **7** : neither good nor bad ⟨did a *fair* job⟩ [Old English *fæger* "pleasing to the eye or mind"] — **fair·ness** *n*

²fair *adv* : in a fair manner ⟨play *fair*⟩

³fair *n* **1** : a gathering of buyers and sellers for trade **2** : an exhibition (as of farm products) usually with accompanying entertainment, amusements, and competitions **3** : a sale of articles usually for a charitable purpose [Middle English *feire* "a gathering of buyers and sellers," from early French *feire* (same meaning), from Latin *feria* "weekday, fair," derived from earlier *feriae* (plural) "holidays"]

fair ball *n* : a batted baseball that lands within the foul lines or that is within the foul lines when bounding to the outfield past first or third base or when going beyond the outfield for a home run

fair·ground \'fa(ə)r-ˌgrau̇nd, 'fe(ə)r-\ *n* : an area set aside for fairs, circuses, and exhibitions

fair·ly \'fa(ə)r-lē, 'fe(ə)r-\ *adv* **1** : in a favorable manner ⟨*fairly* situated⟩ **2** : in a manner of speaking : NEARLY ⟨*fairly* bursting with pride⟩ **3** : in a fair manner : JUSTLY ⟨treat each person *fairly*⟩ **4** : for the most part : RATHER ⟨a *fairly* easy job⟩

fair trade *n* **1** : trade conforming to a fair trade agreement **2** : a movement that aims to help producers in developing countries get a fair price for their products so as to reduce poverty, provide for ethical treatment of workers and farmers, and promote environmentally sustainable practices — **fair trade** *vb*

fair–trade agreement *n* : an agreement between a producer and a seller that products bearing a trademark, label, or brand name belonging to the producer be sold at or above a specified price

fair·way \'fa(ə)r-ˌwā, 'fe(ə)r-\ *n* : the mowed part of a golf course between a tee and a green

fairy \'fa(ə)r-ē, 'fe(ə)r-\ *n, pl* **fair·ies** : an imaginary being usually having a small human form and magic powers — **fairy** *adj* — **fairy·like** \-ē-ˌlīk\ *adj*

fairy·land \-ˌland\ *n* **1** : the land of fairies **2** : a place of delicate beauty or magical charm

fairy ring *n* : a ring of mushrooms in a lawn or meadow that is produced at the edge of a mass of mycelium which is growing outward from a central point

fairy shrimp *n* : any of several very small translucent freshwater crustaceans

fairy tale *n* **1** : a simple children's story about imaginary beings — called also *fairy story* **2** : a made-up story usually meant to mislead

faith \'fāth\ *n* **1 a** : devotion to duty or a person : LOYALTY **b** : the quality of keeping one's promises **2 a** : belief and trust in and loyalty to God **b** : belief in the doctrines of a religion **c** : firm belief even in the absence of proof **d** : complete confidence **3** : something that is firmly believed; *esp* : a system of religious beliefs [Middle English *feith* "loyalty," from early French *feid, foi* (same meaning), from Latin *fides* "faith," from *fidere* "to trust" — related to BONA FIDE, CONFIDE, FIANCÉ] **synonyms** see BELIEF

¹faith·ful \'fāth-fəl\ *adj* **1** : LOYAL 1b ⟨a *faithful* friend⟩ **2** : firm in keeping promises or in fulfilling duties ⟨a *faithful* worker⟩ **3** : true to the facts : ACCURATE ⟨*faithful* copy⟩ — **faith·ful·ly** \-fə-lē\ *adv* — **faith·ful·ness** *n*

synonyms FAITHFUL, LOYAL, STAUNCH, STEADFAST mean firm in one's allegiance to someone or something.

FAITHFUL suggests that one has a firm and constant allegiance that is based on or as if on a pledge ⟨always be *faithful* to your duty⟩. LOYAL suggests that one firmly refuses to desert or betray ⟨citizens who are *loyal* to their country⟩. STAUNCH suggests courage and determination in one's allegiance ⟨*staunch* supporters of the senator⟩. STEADFAST suggests a steady and unfailing course in love, allegiance, or deeply held belief ⟨a *steadfast* fighter for civil rights⟩.

²faithful *n, pl* **faithful** *or* **faithfuls** : one that has faith or is faithful

faith·less \'fāth-ləs\ *adj* **1** : not true to allegiance or duty : DISLOYAL **2** : not worthy of being trusted or relied upon — **faith·less·ly** *adv* — **faith·less·ness** *n*

¹fake \'fāk\ *adj* : not genuine : PHONY

²fake *n* **1** : an imitation that is passed off as genuine : COUNTERFEIT **2** : IMPOSTOR ⟨a medical *fake*⟩

³fake *vb* **faked; fak·ing** **1** : to change or treat so as to make false ⟨*faked* the results⟩ **2** : ¹COUNTERFEIT 1 ⟨*fake* a rare first edition⟩ **3** : ¹PRETEND 1, SIMULATE ⟨*fake* surprise⟩ — **fak·er** *n* — **fak·ery** \'fā-k(ə-)rē\ *n*

fa·kir \fə-'ki(ə)r, fä-, fa-; 'fā-kər\ *n* **1** : a Muslim beggar : DERVISH **2** : a wandering Hindu holy person who performs feats of magic [from Arabic *faqir*, literally, "poor man"]

fal·con \'fal-kən, 'fȯl- *also* 'fȯ-kən\ *n* **1** : a hawk trained for use in falconry **2** : any of various swift hawks with long pointed wings, a long tail, and a notch on the upper half of the beak for killing prey

fal·con·er \'fal-kə-nər, 'fȯl- *also* 'fȯ-\ *n* : one who hunts with hawks or trains hawks for hunting

fal·con·ry \'fal-kən-rē, 'fȯl- *also* 'fȯ-\ *n* **1** : the art of training hawks to hunt in cooperation with a person **2** : the sport of hunting with hawks

¹fall \'fȯl\ *vb* **fell** \'fel\; **fall·en** \'fȯ-lən\; **fall·ing** **1 a** : to come or go down freely by the force of gravity **b** : to hang freely ⟨hair *falling* over her shoulders⟩ **c** : to drop oneself to a lower position ⟨*fell* to their knees⟩ **d** : to come as if by dropping down ⟨night *fell*⟩ **2 a** : to become of lower degree or level ⟨the temperature *fell* 10°⟩ **b** : to become lowered ⟨his eyes *fell*⟩ **3 a** : to topple from an upright position suddenly ⟨slipped and *fell* on the ice⟩ **b** : to enter blindly : STRAY ⟨*fell* into a trap⟩ **c** : to drop down wounded or dead ⟨soldiers who have *fallen* in battle⟩ **d** : to become captured or defeated ⟨the fortress *fell*⟩ **e** : to experience ruin or failure ⟨our plans *fell* through⟩ **4** : to fail to live up to a standard of conduct **5 a** : to move or extend downward ⟨the ground *falls* away to the east⟩ **b** : to become less in amount or degree : DIMINISH ⟨the tide is *falling*⟩ **c** : to become less in quality, activity, quantity, or value ⟨prices *fell*⟩ **d** : to take on a look of shame or low spirits ⟨my face *fell* when I lost⟩ **6 a** : to occur at a certain time ⟨my birthday *falls* on a Tuesday⟩ **b** : to come by chance **c** : to pass (as a responsibility) from one person to another ⟨it *fell* to us to break the news⟩ **d** : to have the proper place or station ⟨the accent *falls* on the second syllable⟩ **7** : to come within the range of something ⟨*falls* under her responsibilities⟩ **8** : to pass from one condition of body or mind to another ⟨*fall* ill⟩ ⟨*fall* asleep⟩ **9** : to set about with enthusiasm or activity ⟨*fell* to work⟩ — **fall flat** : to produce no response or result — **fall for** **1** : to fall in love with **2** : to become a victim of ⟨we *fell for* the trick⟩ — **fall from grace** : to lapse morally : SIN, BACKSLIDE — **fall short** **1** : to be lacking **2** : to fail to reach a desired goal

²fall *n* **1** : the act of falling by the force of gravity ⟨a *fall* from a horse⟩ **2 a** : a falling out, off, or away ⟨the *fall* of the leaves⟩ **b** : AUTUMN 1 **c** : a thing or quantity that falls or has fallen ⟨a heavy *fall* of snow⟩ **3 a** : loss of greatness : COLLAPSE **b** : the surrender or capture of a place under attack **c** : departure from innocence or goodness **4 a** : the downward slope of a hill **b** : WATER-

FALL — usually used in plural **5** : a decrease in size, quantity, degree, activity, or value **6** : the distance which something falls **7** : an act of forcing a wrestler's shoulders to the mat

¹**fal·la·cious** \fə-ˈlā-shəs\ *adj* **1** : containing a fallacy ⟨a *fallacious* argument⟩ **2** : leading in a wrong direction or into a mistaken action or belief — **fal·la·cious·ly** *adv* — **fal·la·cious·ness** *n*

fal·la·cy \ˈfal-ə-sē\ *n, pl* **-cies 1** : a false or mistaken idea **2** : the quality or state of being false

fall back *vb* : ²RETREAT 1 — **fall back on** *or* **fall back upon** : to turn for help to ⟨*falls back on* her best friend⟩

fall guy *n* : a person on whom something is blamed : SCAPEGOAT

fal·li·ble \ˈfal-ə-bəl\ *adj* : capable of making a mistake or being wrong — **fal·li·bil·i·ty** \ˌfal-ə-ˈbil-ət-ē\ *n* — **fal·li·bly** \ˈfal-ə-blē\ *adv*

fall·ing–out \ˌfó-liŋ-ˈaút\ *n, pl* **fallings–out** *or* **falling–outs** : ¹QUARREL 2 ⟨had a *falling-out* with his parents⟩

falling star *n* : METEOR

fal·lo·pi·an tube \fə-ˌlō-pē-ən-\ *n, often cap F* : either of the pair of tubes that carry eggs from the ovary to the uterus

fall·out \ˈfó-ˌlaút\ *n* : the often radioactive particles that are stirred up by or result from a nuclear explosion and descend through the atmosphere

fall out \(ˈ)fó-ˈlaút\ *vb* **1** : to have a quarrel **2** : HAPPEN 1

¹**fal·low** \ˈfal-ō\ *n* **1** : land for crops allowed to lie idle during the growing season **2** : the tilling of land without sowing it for a season

²**fallow** *vb* : to till (land) without seeding

³**fallow** *adj* **1** : left untilled or unsown **2** : DORMANT 1, INACTIVE

fallow deer *n* : a small European deer with broad antlers and a pale yellow coat spotted white in the summer [from earlier *fallow* "a pale yellowish brown color"]

fall to *vb* : to begin doing something (as eating or working) especially energetically

fallow deer

¹**false** \ˈfóls\ *adj* **fals·er; fals·est 1** : not genuine ⟨*false* documents⟩ ⟨*false* teeth⟩ **2 a** : intentionally untrue ⟨*false* testimony⟩ **b** : intended or tending to mislead ⟨*false* promise⟩ **3** : not true : INCORRECT ⟨*false* information⟩ **4** : not faithful or loyal : TREACHEROUS **5** : not necessary to structure ⟨a *false* ceiling⟩ **6** : inaccurate in pitch ⟨a *false* note⟩ **7** : based on mistaken ideas ⟨*false* pride⟩ — **false·ly** *adv* — **false·ness** *n*

false·hood \ˈfóls-ˌhúd\ *n* **1** : an untrue statement : LIE **2** : the habit of lying

fal·set·to \fól-ˈset-ō\ *n, pl* **-tos** : an artificially high voice

fal·si·fy \ˈfól-sə-ˌfī\ *vb* **-fied; -fy·ing** : to make false : change so as to deceive ⟨*falsify* financial accounts⟩ — **fal·si·fi·ca·tion** \ˌfól-sə-fə-ˈkā-shən\ *n* — **fal·si·fi·er** \ˈfól-sə-ˌfī-(ə)r\ *n*

fal·si·ty \ˈfól-sət-ē\ *n, pl* **-ties 1** : something false : LIE **2** : the quality or state of being false

fal·ter \ˈfól-tər\ *vb* **fal·tered; fal·ter·ing** \ˈfól-t(ə-)riŋ\ **1** : to move unsteadily : WAVER **2** : to stumble or hesitate in speech : ¹STAMMER ⟨her voice *faltered*⟩ **3** : to hesitate in purpose or action ⟨courage that never *falters*⟩ — **falter** *n* — **fal·ter·er** \-tər-ər\ *n* — **fal·ter·ing·ly** \-t(ə-)riŋ-lē\ *adv*

fame \ˈfām\ *n* : the fact or condition of being known to the public : RENOWN — **famed** \ˈfāmd\ *adj*

fa·mil·ial \fə-ˈmil-yəl\ *adj* : of, relating to, or typical of a family

¹**fa·mil·iar** \fə-ˈmil-yər\ *n* **1** : a close associate : COMPANION **2** : a spirit believed to serve or guard a person — called also *familiar spirit*

²**familiar** *adj* **1** : closely acquainted : INTIMATE **2 a** : INFORMAL 1 ⟨spoke in a *familiar* way⟩ **b** : too friendly or bold : FORWARD **3 a** : frequently seen or experienced **b** : of everyday occurrence **4** : having a good knowledge ⟨*familiar* with the rules⟩ — **fa·mil·iar·ly** *adv*

fa·mil·iar·i·ty \fə-ˌmil-ˈyar-ət-ē, -ˌmil-ē-ˈar-\ *n, pl* **-ties 1** : close friendship : INTIMACY **2** : lack of formality : freedom and ease in personal relations **3** : close acquaintance with or knowledge of something **4** : an overly bold act or expression

fa·mil·iar·ize \fə-ˈmil-yə-ˌrīz\ *vb* **-ized; -iz·ing** : to make familiar ⟨*familiarize* yourself with the place⟩ — **fa·mil·iar·i·za·tion** \-ˌmil-yə-rə-ˈzā-shən\ *n*

fam·i·ly \ˈfam-(ə-)lē\ *n, pl* **-lies 1** : a group of individuals living under one roof and under one head **2** : a group of persons who come from the same ancestor **3** : a group of things having common characteristics; *esp* : a closely related series of elements or chemical compounds **4 a** : a social group composed of one or two parents and their children **b** : a social group different from but considered equal to the traditional family **5** : a group of related plants or animals ranking in biological classification above a genus and below an order

family name *n* : SURNAME 2

family planning *n* : planning that is intended to determine the number and spacing of one's children by using effective methods of birth control

family tree *n* **1** : GENEALOGY 1 **2** : a diagram showing family relationships

fam·ine \ˈfam-ən\ *n* **1** : an extreme general shortage of food **2** : a great shortage

fam·ish \ˈfam-ish\ *vb* **1** : to suffer or cause to suffer from extreme hunger **2** : to suffer from a lack of something necessary — **fam·ish·ment** \-mənt\ *n*

fa·mous \ˈfā-məs\ *adj* **1** : much talked about : very well-known ⟨*famous* explorer⟩ **2** : EXCELLENT ⟨*famous* weather for a picnic⟩

    synonyms FAMOUS, RENOWNED, CELEBRATED, NOTORIOUS mean known far and wide. FAMOUS suggests simply that one is popularly known and sometimes only for a short time ⟨a *famous* actor⟩. RENOWNED stresses glory and honor ⟨heroes *renowned* in story and song⟩. CELEBRATED stresses frequent public notice and mention especially in print ⟨a *celebrated* murder trial⟩. NOTORIOUS suggests that one is famous for wrongdoing ⟨one of the most *notorious* traitors in history⟩.

fa·mous·ly \ˈfā-məs-lē\ *adv* : in a splendid or excellent manner ⟨got along *famously* together⟩

¹**fan** \ˈfan\ *n* **1** : an instrument for producing a current of air: as **a** : a device that is often in the shape of a section of a circle and is waved back and forth by hand **b** : a device with a set of rotating blades driven by a motor **2** : something shaped like a hand fan [Old English *fann* "fan," from Latin *vannus* "fan"] — **fan·like** \-ˌlīk\ *adj*

²**fan** *vb* **fanned; fan·ning 1** : to move air with a fan **2 a** : to direct a current of air upon with a fan **b** : to stir up to activity as if by fanning **3** : to spread out or move like a fan **4** : to strike out in baseball — **fan·ner** *n*

³**fan** *n* : an enthusiastic follower or admirer [probably a shortened form of *fanatic*]

\ə\ **abut**	\aú\ **out**	\i\ **tip**	\ó\ **saw**	\ú\ **foot**
\ər\ **further**	\ch\ **chin**	\ī\ **life**	\ói\ **coin**	\y\ **yet**
\a\ **mat**	\e\ **pet**	\j\ **job**	\th\ **thin**	\yü\ **few**
\ā\ **take**	\ē\ **easy**	\ŋ\ **sing**	\th\ **this**	\yú\ **cure**
\ä\ **cot, cart**	\g\ **go**	\ō\ **bone**	\ü\ **food**	\zh\ **vision**

fa·nat·ic \fə-'nat-ik\ *or* **fa·nat·i·cal** \-'nat-i-kəl\ *adj* : overly enthusiastic or devoted — **fanatic** *n* — **fa·nat·i·cal·ly** \-i-k(ə-)lē\ *adv* — **fa·nat·i·cism** \-'nat-ə-,siz-əm\ *n*

fan·ci·er \'fan(t)-sē-ər\ *n* : a person with a special liking or interest ⟨a cat *fancier*⟩

fan·ci·ful \'fan(t)-si-fəl\ *adj* **1** : having or showing free imagination rather than reason ⟨a *fanciful* person⟩ ⟨a *fanciful* tale⟩ **2** : existing in fancy only ⟨a *fanciful* notion⟩ — **fan·ci·ful·ly** \-f(ə-)lē\ *adv* — **fan·ci·ful·ness** \-fəl-nəs\ *n*

¹fancy *vb* **fan·cied; fan·cy·ing** **1** : to have a fancy for : LIKE **2** : to form a mental image of : IMAGINE

²fan·cy \'fan(t)-sē\ *n, pl* **fancies** **1** : LIKING ⟨took a *fancy* to the stray dog⟩ **2** : NOTION, WHIM ⟨a passing *fancy*⟩ **3** : IMAGINATION

³fancy *adj* **fan·ci·er; -est** **1** : based on fancy : UNPREDICTABLE **2 a** : not plain : ORNAMENTAL **b** : of particular excellence **c** : bred especially for a showy appearance ⟨a *fancy* goldfish⟩ **3** : done with great skill and grace ⟨*fancy* footwork⟩ — **fan·ci·ly** \'fan(t)-sə-lē\ *adv* — **fan·ci·ness** \-sē-nəs\ *n*

fan·cy–free \'fan(t)-sē-'frē\ *adj* : not in love

fan·cy·work \-,wərk\ *n* : ornamental needlework (as embroidery)

fan·dan·go \fan-'daŋ-gō\ *n, pl* **-gos** : a lively Spanish or Spanish-American dance

fan·fare \'fan-,fa(ə)r, -,fe(ə)r\ *n* : a short stirring tune played by trumpets

fang \'faŋ\ *n* **1 a** : one of the long sharp teeth which are used by an animal to seize, hold, and tear apart its prey **b** : one of the long hollow or grooved teeth of a poisonous snake **2** : a root of a tooth — **fanged** \'faŋd\ *adj*

fan·light \'fan-,līt\ *n* : a semicircular window having bars extending from the center that is placed over a door or window

fan·ny \'fan-ē\ *n, pl* **fannies** : BUTTOCKS

fanny pack *n* : a pack that straps to the waist and is used for carrying personal items

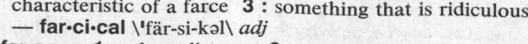

F fang 1b

fan·ta·sia \fan-'tā-zhə, ,fant-ə-'zē-ə\ *n* : a musical composition written without following a particular style

fan·tas·tic \fan-'tas-tik, fən-\ *adj* **1** *also* **fan·tas·ti·cal** \-ti-kəl\ : produced by the imagination or like something produced by the imagination ⟨a *fantastic* scheme⟩ **2** : extremely high or great ⟨*fantastic* speeds⟩ **3** : EXCELLENT, GREAT ⟨a *fantastic* meal⟩ — **fan·tas·ti·cal·ly** \-ti-k(ə-)lē\ *adv* — **fan·tas·ti·cal·ness** \-kəl-nəs\ *n*

fan·ta·sy *also* **phan·ta·sy** \'fant-ə-sē, -ə-zē\ *n, pl* **-sies** **1** : IMAGINATION 3, FANCY **2** : something imagined: as **a** : ILLUSION 2 **b** : FANTASIA **c** : a work of literature set in an unreal world often with superhuman characters and monsters

¹far \'fär\ *adv* **far·ther** \-thər\ *or* **fur·ther** \'fər-\; **far·thest** *or* **fur·thest** \-thəst\ **1** : at or to a great distance in space or time ⟨*far* from home⟩ **2** : to a great extent : MUCH ⟨*far* better⟩ **3** : to or at a definite distance, point, or degree ⟨as *far* as I know⟩ **4** : to an advanced point or extent : a long way ⟨a smart student can go *far*⟩ — **by far** : FAR AND AWAY, GREATLY ⟨*by far* our best runner⟩

²far *adj* **farther** *or* **further; farthest** *or* **furthest** **1** : very distant in space or time **2** : ¹LONG 3 ⟨a *far* journey⟩ **3** : the more distant of two ⟨the *far* side of the lake⟩

far and away *adv* : by a great extent or degree ⟨was *far and away* the better team⟩

far·away \,fär-ə-,wā\ *adj* **1** : ¹REMOTE 1, DISTANT ⟨*faraway* lands⟩ **2** : PREOCCUPIED 1, DREAMY ⟨a *faraway* look⟩

farce \'färs\ *n* **1** : a play about ridiculous and absurd situations that is intended to make people laugh **2** : humor characteristic of a farce **3** : something that is ridiculous — **far·ci·cal** \'fär-si-kəl\ *adj*

far cry *n* **1** : a long distance **2** : something notably different ⟨her completed project was a *far cry* from what she had envisioned⟩

¹fare \'fa(ə)r, 'fe(ə)r\ *vb* **fared; far·ing** **1** : ¹GO 1, TRAVEL **2** : to proceed toward a goal : SUCCEED ⟨*fared* well on the test⟩ **3** : EAT 1, DINE

²fare *n* **1** : FOOD 1 ⟨a café serving light *fare*⟩ **2 a** : the money a person pays to travel by public transportation (as a bus) **b** : a person paying a fare : PASSENGER

¹fare·well \fa(ə)r-'wel, fe(ə)r-\ *imperative verb* : get along well — used to or by one departing

²farewell *n* **1** : an expression of good wishes at parting : GOOD-BYE **2** : an act of departure

³fare·well \,fa(ə)r-,wel, ,fe(ə)r-\ *adj* : of or relating to a time or act of leaving : FINAL ⟨a *farewell* concert⟩

far–fetched \'fär-'fecht\ *adj* : not easily or naturally thought of : IMPROBABLE ⟨gave some *far-fetched* excuse⟩

far–flung \'fär-'fləŋ\ *adj* : covering great areas : having wide range

fa·ri·na \fə-'rē-nə\ *n* : a fine meal made chiefly from cereal grains used especially as a breakfast cereal

¹farm \'färm\ *n* **1 a** : a piece of land used for growing crops or raising livestock **b** : a body of water used for the cultivation of aquatic animals ⟨an oyster *farm*⟩ **2** : a minor-league baseball team

²farm *vb* **1** : to turn over to another usually for an agreed payment — usually used with *out* ⟨*farm* out the electrical work⟩ **2 a** : to devote to agriculture ⟨*farm* 60 acres⟩ **b** : to engage in raising crops or animals

farm·er \'fär-mər\ *n* : a person who cultivates land or crops or raises animals

farm·hand \'färm-,hand\ *n* : a farm laborer

farm·house \-,haùs\ *n* : a dwelling on a farm

farm·ing \'fär-miŋ\ *n* : the occupation or business of a person who farms

farm·land \'färm-,land\ *n* : land used or suitable for farming

farm·stead \-,sted\ *n* : the buildings and nearby service areas of a farm

farm·yard \-,yärd\ *n* : space around or enclosed by farm buildings

far–off \'fär-'öf\ *adj* : remote in time or space

far–out \-'aùt\ *adj* : very strange or unusual ⟨*far-out* clothes⟩

far–reach·ing \-'rē-chiŋ\ *adj* : having a wide range, influence, or effect ⟨a *far-reaching* decision⟩

¹far·row \'far-ō\ *vb* : to give birth to pigs

²farrow *n* : a litter of pigs

Far·si \'fär-sē\ *n* : PERSIAN 2

far·sight·ed \'fär-'sīt-əd\ *adj* **1** : having foresight **2** : able to see distant things more clearly than near ones — **far·sight·ed·ly** *adv*

far·sight·ed·ness \-'sīt-əd-nəs\ *n* **1** : the condition of having foresight **2** : a visual condition in which a person can see distant things more clearly than near ones

¹far·ther \'fär-thər\ *adv* **1** : at or to a greater distance or more advanced point **2** : more completely

²farther *adj* **1** : more distant : REMOTER **2** : ³FURTHER 2, ADDITIONAL

far·ther·most \'fär-thər-,mōst\ *adj* : ¹FARTHEST

¹far·thest \'fär-thəst\ *adj* : most distant in space or time

²farthest *adv* **1** : to or at the greatest distance in space or time : REMOTEST **2** : to the most advanced point or extent **3** : by the greatest degree or extent : MOST

far·thing \'fär-thiŋ\ *n* : a former British unit of money equal to ¼ of a penny; *also* : a coin representing this unit

fas·ci·nate \'fas-³n-,āt\ *vb* **-nat·ed; -nat·ing** **1** : to grip the attention of especially so as to take away the power to move, act, or think for oneself ⟨the belief that serpents can *fascinate* their prey⟩ **2** : to cause (someone) to be very interested in something or someone — **fas·ci·na·tion** \ˌfas-ᵊn-ˈā-shən\ *n* — **fas·ci·na·tor** \ˈfas-ᵊn-ˌāt-ər\ *n*

fas·ci·nat·ing \ˈfas-ə-ˌnāt-iŋ\ *adj* : extremely interesting or charming — **fas·ci·nat·ing·ly** *adv*

fas·cism \ˈfash-ˌiz-əm\ *n, often cap* : a political system headed by a dictator in which the government controls business and labor and opposition is not permitted — **fas·cist** \ˈfash-əst\ *n or adj, often cap*

¹**fash·ion** \ˈfash-ən\ *n* **1** : the shape or form of something **2** : MANNER 2, WAY ⟨behave in a strange *fashion*⟩ **3** : a common style especially of dress during a particular time or among a certain group ⟨an idea that is out of *fashion*⟩ [Middle English *facioun* "shape, manner," from early French *façon* (same meaning), from Latin *faction-, factio* "action of making," from *facere* "to make, do" — related to ARTIFICIAL, BENEFIT, CONFECTION, FACTORY, MANUFACTURE, PERFECT, SATISFY]

²**fashion** *vb* **fash·ioned; fash·ion·ing** \ˈfash-(ə-)niŋ\ : to give shape or form to — **fash·ion·er** \-(ə-)nər\ *n*

fash·ion·able \ˈfash-(ə-)nə-bəl\ *adj* **1** : following the fashion : STYLISH ⟨*fashionable* clothes⟩ **2** : of or relating to the world of fashion : popular among those who set fashions ⟨*fashionable* stores⟩ — **fash·ion·able·ness** *n* — **fash·ion·ably** \-blē\ *adv*

¹**fast** \ˈfast\ *adj* **1 a** : firmly fixed or bound **b** : tightly shut **c** : sticking firmly **2** : firmly loyal ⟨became *fast* friends⟩ **3 a** : moving or able to move rapidly **b** : taking a short time **c** : giving quickness of motion (as to a thrown ball) **d** : favorable to speed ⟨the *faster* route⟩ **4** : indicating ahead of the correct time ⟨my clock is *fast*⟩ **5** : tricky and unfair ⟨pulled a *fast* one⟩ **6** : not likely to fade ⟨*fast* colors⟩ [Old English *fæst* "firmly fixed"]

synonyms FAST, RAPID, SWIFT, HASTY mean moving, proceeding, or acting with great speed. FAST usually applies to things that move ⟨a *fast* horse⟩. RAPID usually applies to the movement itself ⟨a river with a *rapid* current⟩. SWIFT suggests great rapidity combined with ease of movement ⟨returned the ball with one *swift* stroke⟩. HASTY suggests rashness and often carelessness ⟨a *hasty* inspection of the damage⟩.

²**fast** *adv* **1** : in a fixed manner ⟨stuck *fast*⟩ **2** : in a complete manner : SOUNDLY, DEEPLY ⟨*fast* asleep⟩ **3** : with great speed ⟨a building *fast* going to ruin⟩

³**fast** *vb* **1** : to go without eating **2** : to eat in small amounts or only certain foods [Old English *fæstan* "to go without eating"]

⁴**fast** *n* **1** : the act of fasting **2** : a time of fasting

fast·back \ˈfas(t)-ˌbak\ *n* **1** : an automobile roof with a long curving downward slope to the rear **2** : an automobile having a fastback

fast·ball \ˈfas(t)-ˌból\ *n* : a baseball pitch thrown at full speed

fas·ten \ˈfas-ᵊn\ *vb* **fas·tened; fas·ten·ing** \ˈfas-niŋ, -ᵊn-iŋ\ **1** : to attach or join by or as if by pinning, tying, or nailing ⟨*fasten* clothes on a line⟩ **2** : to make fast : fix securely ⟨*fasten* a door⟩ **3** : to fix or set steadily ⟨*fastened* their eyes on the distant ship⟩ **4** : to become fixed or joined ⟨the shoes *fasten* with a buckle⟩ — **fas·ten·er** \ˈfas-nər, -ᵊn-ər\ *n*

fas·ten·ing *n* : something that fastens

fast–food \ˌfas(t)-ˈfüd\ *adj* : specializing in food that can be prepared and served quickly ⟨a *fast-food* restaurant⟩

¹**fast–for·ward** \ˌfast-ˈfór-wərd\ *n* **1** : a function of an electronic device that advances a recording at a higher than normal speed **2** : a state of rapid advancement

²**fast–forward** *vb* **1** : to advance (a tape) at a high speed **2** : to advance rapidly especially in time ⟨*fast-forward* to the future⟩

fas·tid·i·ous \fa-ˈstid-ē-əs\ *adj* : hard to please : very particular — **fas·tid·i·ous·ly** *adv* — **fas·tid·i·ous·ness** *n*

fast lane *n* **1** : a traffic lane used by vehicles moving at higher speeds **2** : a way of life marked by a fast pace and the attempt to get everything one wants quickly **3** : FAST TRACK

fast·ness \ˈfas(t)-nəs\ *n* **1** : the quality or state of being fast **2** : a fortified or secure place

¹**fast–track** \ˈfas(t)-ˌtrak\ *adj* : of, relating to, or moving along a fast track ⟨*fast-track* executives⟩

²**fast–track** *vb* : to speed up the processing or production of in order to meet a goal — **fast–track·er** *n*

fast track *n* : a course leading to rapid advancement or success

¹**fat** \ˈfat\ *adj* **fat·ter; fat·test** **1 a** : ⁵PLUMP, FLESHY **b** : OILY 1, GREASY **2 a** : ¹THICK 1 ⟨a *fat* book⟩ **b** : well stocked : ABUNDANT **3** : PROFITABLE ⟨accepted a *fat* contract⟩ **4** : PRODUCTIVE 1, FERTILE **5** : being swollen ⟨got a *fat* lip in the fight⟩ — **fat·ness** *n*

²**fat** *vb* **fat·ted; fat·ting** : to make fat : FATTEN

³**fat** *n* **1** : animal tissue consisting chiefly of cells containing much greasy or oily matter **2 a** : any of numerous compounds of carbon, hydrogen, and oxygen that make up most of plant and animal fat, are a major class of energy-rich food, and can be dissolved by ether but not by water **b** : a solid or semisolid fat (as lard) as distinguished from an oil **3** : the best or richest part ⟨the *fat* of the land⟩ **4** : an amount beyond what is usual or needed : EXCESS

fa·tal \ˈfāt-ᵊl\ *adj* **1** : deciding one's fate : FATEFUL ⟨on that *fatal* day⟩ **2** : causing death or ruin ⟨a *fatal* accident⟩ **synonyms** see DEADLY — **fa·tal·ly** \-ᵊl-ē\ *adv*

fa·tal·ism \ˈfāt-ᵊl-ˌiz-əm\ *n* : the belief or attitude that events are decided in advance by powers beyond one's control — **fa·tal·ist** \-əst\ *n* — **fa·tal·is·tic** \ˌfāt-ᵊl-ˈis-tik\ *adj* — **fa·tal·is·ti·cal·ly** \-ti-k(ə-)lē\ *adv*

fa·tal·i·ty \fā-ˈtal-ət-ē, fə-\ *n, pl* **-ties** : a death resulting from a disaster or accident

fat·back \ˈfat-ˌbak\ *n* : the strip of fat from the back of a hog carcass

fat cell *n* : any of the fat-containing cells that make up the connective tissue in which bodily fat is stored

¹**fate** \ˈfāt\ *n* **1** : a power beyond one's control that is believed to decide what happens **2** : something that happens as though decided by fate **3** : a final result **4** *pl, cap* : the three goddesses in classical mythology who decide the course of human life **synonyms** see DESTINY

²**fate** *vb* **fat·ed; fat·ing** **1** : DESTINE 1 **2** : ²DOOM 2

fate·ful \ˈfāt-fəl\ *adj* **1** : foretelling usually bad things to come ⟨a *fateful* remark⟩ **2** : having serious results : IMPORTANT ⟨a *fateful* decision⟩ — **fate·ful·ly** \-fə-lē\ *adv* — **fate·ful·ness** *n*

fat·head \ˈfat-ˌhed\ *n* : a stupid person

¹**fa·ther** \ˈfäth-ər, ˈfȧth-\ *n* **1 a** : a male parent **b** *cap* : GOD 1 **c** *cap* : the first person of the Christian Trinity **2** : ANCESTOR 1 **3** : a man who cares for another as a father might **4** : a man who invents or begins something ⟨the *father* of modern science⟩ **5** : PRIEST — used especially as a title — **fa·ther·hood** \-ˌhùd\ *n* — **fa·ther·less** \-ləs\ *adj*

²**father** *vb* **fa·thered; fa·ther·ing** \ˈfäth-(ə-)riŋ, ˈfȧth-\ **1 a** : BEGET 1 **b** : to be the founder, producer, or author of **2** : to treat or care for someone as a father

fa·ther–in–law \ˈfäth-(ə-)rən-ˌló, ˈfȧth-, -ərn-ˌló\ *n, pl* **fa·thers–in–law** \ˈfäth-ər-zən-, ˈfȧth-\ : the father of one's husband or wife

fa·ther·land \ˈfäth-ər-ˌland, ˈfȧth-\ *n* **1** : the native land of one's ancestors **2** : one's native land

fa·ther·ly \ˈfäth-ər-lē, ˈfȧth-\ *adj* **1** : of or resembling a father ⟨*fatherly* responsibilities⟩ **2** : showing the affection or concern of a father ⟨*fatherly* advice⟩ — **fa·ther·li·ness** *n*

Fa·ther's Day \'fäth-ərz-, 'fäth-\ *n* : the third Sunday in June set aside for the honoring of fathers

[1]**fath·om** \'fath-əm\ *n* : a unit of length equal to six feet (about 1.83 meters) used especially for measuring the depth of water

[2]**fathom** *vb* 1 : to measure by a sounding line 2 : to come to understand ⟨can't *fathom* why⟩ — **fath·om·able** \'fath-ə-mə-bəl\ *adj*

[1]**fa·tigue** \fə-'tēg\ *n* 1 *pl* : the uniform worn by members of the armed forces for physical labor 2 a : tiredness from work or stress b : the condition of a part of the body (as a sense organ or gland) that temporarily loses the power to respond after a long period of stimulation 3 : the tendency of a material (as metal) to break under repeated stress (as bending)

[2]**fatigue** *vb* **fa·tigued; fa·tigu·ing** 1 : to cause to become very tired ⟨pulling weeds *fatigues* me⟩ 2 : to cause a condition of fatigue in ⟨running *fatigues* my legs⟩ **synonyms** see TIRE

fat·ten \'fat-ᵊn\ *vb* **fat·tened; fat·ten·ing** \'fat-niŋ, -ᵊn-iŋ\ : to make or become fat — **fat·ten·er** \-(ə-)nər\ *n*

fat·ty \'fat-ē\ *adj* **fat·ti·er; -est** 1 : containing fat especially in unusual amounts 2 : GREASY 2 — **fat·ti·ness** *n*

fatty acid *n* : any of numerous acids that contain only carbon, hydrogen, and oxygen and occur naturally in fats and various oils

fa·tu·ity \fə-'t(y)ü-ət-ē, fa-\ *n, pl* **-ities** 1 : something foolish or stupid 2 : STUPIDITY 1

fat·u·ous \'fach-(ə-)wəs\ *adj* : FOOLISH, SILLY — **fat·u·ous·ly** *adv*

fau·cet \'fò-sət, 'fäs-ət\ *n* : a fixture for controlling the flow of a liquid (as from a pipe)

[1]**fault** \'fòlt\ *n* 1 a : a weakness in character : FAILING b : a physical or mental flaw 2 a : a wrongful act b : [2]MISTAKE 2 3 : responsibility for wrongdoing or failure ⟨it's all my *fault*⟩ 4 : a break in the earth's crust accompanied by a displacement of rock masses parallel to the break —

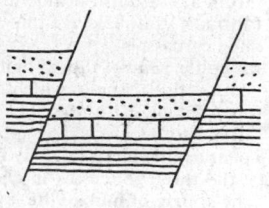

[1]fault 4

fault·less \-ləs\ *adj* — **fault·less·ly** *adv* — **fault·less·ness** *n* — **at fault** : deserving blame : RESPONSIBLE — **to a fault** : to the point of being or doing too much ⟨generous *to a fault*⟩

[2]**fault** *vb* 1 : to fracture so as to produce a geologic fault 2 : to find a fault in

fault·find·er \'fòlt-,fīn-dər\ *n* : a person who tends to find fault — **fault·find·ing** \-diŋ\ *n or adj*

faulty \'fòl-tē\ *adj* **fault·i·er; -est** : having a fault or weakness : IMPERFECT — **fault·i·ly** \-tə-lē\ *adv* — **fault·i·ness** \-tē-nəs\ *n*

faun \'fòn, 'fän\ *n* : a figure in Roman mythology dwelling in the country and represented as part goat and part man

fau·na \'fòn-ə, 'fän-\ *n, pl* **faunas** *also* **fau·nae** \-,ē, -,ī\ : animals or animal life especially of a region, period, or environment — **fau·nal** \-ᵊl\ *adj*

faux \'fō\ *adj* : [2]IMITATION ⟨*faux* marble⟩ [from French, "false," from Latin *falsus*]

fa·va bean \'fä-və-\ *n* : BROAD BEAN

[1]**fa·vor** \'fā-vər\ *n* 1 a : friendly regard shown toward another ⟨enjoyed the *favor* of the king⟩ b : APPROVAL ⟨look with *favor* on a project⟩ c : PARTIALITY 1, PREFERENCE ⟨the judge showed *favor* to one side⟩ d : the quality or state of being popular ⟨lose *favor*⟩ 2 : an act of kindness ⟨do a friend a *favor*⟩ 3 : a small gift given out at a party — **in favor of** 1 : in agreement or sympathy with 2 : in support of

[2]**favor** *vb* **fa·vored; fa·vor·ing** \'fāv-(ə-)riŋ\ 1 a : to look upon or treat with favor b : to do a kindness for : OBLIGE

c : to treat gently or carefully : SPARE ⟨*favor* a sore leg⟩ 2 : PREFER 1 3 : to make possible or easy : help to succeed ⟨darkness *favored* the attack⟩ 4 : to look like : RESEMBLE ⟨*favors* his mother⟩ — **fa·vor·er** \'fā-vər-ər\ *n*

fa·vor·able \'fāv-(ə-)rə-bəl, 'fā-vər-bəl\ *adj* 1 : showing favor : APPROVING ⟨a *favorable* reply⟩ 2 : PROMISING, ADVANTAGEOUS ⟨*favorable* weather for the fair⟩ — **fa·vor·able·ness** *n* — **fa·vor·ably** \-blē\ *adv*

[1]**fa·vor·ite** \'fāv-(ə-)rət\ *n* 1 : a person or a thing that is preferred more than others 2 : the contestant considered as having the best chance to win

[2]**favorite** *adj* : being a favorite ⟨our *favorite* show⟩

fa·vor·it·ism \'fāv-(ə-)rət-,iz-əm\ *n* : unfairly favorable treatment of some while neglecting others

[1]**fawn** \'fòn, 'fän\ *vb* 1 : to show affection — used especially of a dog 2 : to try to win favor by behavior that shows lack of self-respect [Old English *fagnian* "to rejoice," from *fægen* "glad, fain"] — **fawn·er** *n* — **fawn·ing·ly** \-iŋ-lē\ *adv*

[2]**fawn** *n* 1 : a young deer; *esp* : one in its first year 2 : a light grayish brown [early French *feen, foon* "young of an animal," derived from Latin *fetus* "offspring"]

fax \'faks\ *n* 1 : FACSIMILE 2 2 : a machine used to send or receive facsimile communications 3 : a facsimile communication — **fax** *vb*

fay \'fā\ *n* : FAIRY, ELF — **fay** *adj*

faze \'fāz\ *vb* **fazed; faz·ing** : to disturb the self-control or courage of : DAUNT ⟨didn't *faze* her⟩

F clef *n* : BASS CLEF 1

fe·al·ty \'fē(-ə)l-tē\ *n, pl* **-ties** : LOYALTY, ALLEGIANCE

[1]**fear** \'fi(ə)r\ *n* 1 a : an unpleasant often strong emotion caused by expectation or awareness of danger b : an instance of fear or a state marked by fear 2 : concern about what may happen : WORRY 3 : [1]AWE

synonyms FEAR, DREAD, ALARM, FRIGHT mean painful emotion experienced in the presence or expectation of danger. FEAR is the most general word and suggests great worry and usually loss of courage ⟨*fear* of the unknown⟩. DREAD suggests strong unwillingness to face something ⟨the *dread* felt by people awaiting bad news⟩. ALARM may suggest strong emotional upset caused by an unexpected or immediate danger ⟨viewed the worsening food shortage with *alarm*⟩. FRIGHT suggests the shock of something startling and often suggests a short-lived emotion ⟨the creaking door caused them *fright*⟩.

[2]**fear** *vb* 1 : to feel great awe of ⟨*fear* God⟩ 2 : to be afraid of : have fear 3 : to be worried ⟨*feared* they would miss the train⟩ — **fearer** *n*

fear·ful \'fi(ə)r-fəl\ *adj* 1 : causing fear ⟨the *fearful* roar of a lion⟩ 2 : filled with fear ⟨*fearful* of danger⟩ 3 : showing or caused by fear ⟨a *fearful* glance⟩ 4 : extremely bad, large, or intense ⟨*fearful* cold⟩ — **fear·ful·ly** \-fə-lē\ *adv* — **fear·ful·ness** *n*

fear·less \'fi(ə)r-ləs\ *adj* : free from fear : BRAVE — **fear·less·ly** *adv* — **fear·less·ness** *n*

fear·some \'fi(ə)r-səm\ *adj* 1 : causing fear 2 : TIMID — **fear·some·ly** *adv* — **fear·some·ness** *n*

fea·si·ble \'fē-zə-bəl\ *adj* : possible to do or carry out — **fea·si·bil·i·ty** \,fē-zə-'bil-ət-ē\ *n* — **fea·si·ble·ness** \'fē-zə-bəl-nəs\ *n* — **fea·si·bly** \-blē\ *adv*

[1]**feast** \'fēst\ *n* 1 : a meal with plenty of food and drink : BANQUET 2 : a religious festival or observance [Middle English *feste* "feast, festival," from early French *feste* (same meaning), from Latin *festa,* plural of *festum* "festival, feast" — related to FESTIVAL, FIESTA]

[2]**feast** *vb* 1 : to eat plentifully : take part in a feast 2 : to entertain with a feast 3 : [2]DELIGHT 2 ⟨*feast* your eyes on the view⟩ — **feast·er** *n*

feat \'fēt\ *n* 1 : [1]ACT 1, DEED 2 a : a deed notable especially for courage b : an act or product of skill, strength, or cleverness

¹feath·er \ˈfeth-ər\ *n* **1** : one of the light horny growths that make up the outer covering of the body of a bird **2 a** : ¹KIND 1, NATURE ⟨birds of a *feather*⟩ **b** : CLOTHING 1, DRESS ⟨in full *feather*⟩ **c** : ¹CONDITION 5b, MOOD ⟨in fine *feather*⟩ — **feath·ered** \-ərd\ *adj* — **feath·er·less** \-ər-ləs\ *adj* — **feath·ery** \-(ə-)rē\ *adj* — **a feather in one's cap** : an accomplishment deserving praise

²feather *vb* **feath·ered; feath·er·ing** \ˈfeth-(ə-)riŋ\ **1 a** : to provide (as an arrow) with a feather **b** : to cover, clothe, or adorn with feathers **2 a** : to turn (an oar blade) parallel to the water when lifting from the water at the end of a stroke **b** : to change the angle of (airplane propeller blades) to reduce air resistance; *also* : to change the angle of airplane propeller blades of (an engine) in such a manner **3** : to grow feathers **4** : to move, spread, or grow like feathers — **feather one's nest** : to get richer in a dishonest or improper way

¹feather 1: *1* quill, *2* vane

feather bed *n* : a mattress filled with feathers; *also* : a bed with such a mattress

feath·er·brain \ˈfeth-ər-ˌbrān\ *n* : a foolish scatterbrained person — **feath·er·brained** \-ˌbrānd\ *adj*

feath·er·weight \-ˌwāt\ *n* **1** : a very light weight **2** : one that weighs little; *esp* : a boxer in a weight division having an upper limit of about 126 pounds

¹fea·ture \ˈfē-chər\ *n* **1 a** : the shape or appearance of the face **b** : a single part of the face (as the nose or the mouth) **2** : a part or detail that stands out **3 a** : the principal motion picture on a program **b** : a special column or section in a newspaper or magazine — **fea·ture·less** \-ləs\ *adj*

²feature *vb* **fea·tured; fea·tur·ing** \ˈfēch-(ə-)riŋ\ **1** : to play an important part **2 a** : to have as a feature ⟨a menu *featuring* seafood⟩ **b** : to give special prominence to

Feb·ru·ary \ˈfeb-(y)ə-ˌwer-ē, ˈfeb-rə-\ *n* : the second month of the year

> **Word History** Every winter the ancient Romans would celebrate a festival of spiritual cleansing. The name of the festival was *Februa.* Because of its importance the Romans named the month in which it fell *Februarius,* which means "of Februa." The English name *February* comes from the Latin *Februarius.* [Old English *Februarius* "February," from Latin *Februarius* "February," literally, "of Februa," from *Februa* "feast of cleansing"]

fe·ces \ˈfē-(ˌ)sēz\ *n pl* : bodily waste discharged through the anus : EXCREMENT — **fe·cal** \ˈfē-kəl\ *adj*

fe·cund \ˈfek-ənd, ˈfē-kənd\ *adj* **1** : producing many offspring or much vegetation : PROLIFIC **2** : mentally productive or inventive — **fe·cun·di·ty** \fi-ˈkən-dət-ē\ *n*

fed·er·al \ˈfed-(ə-)rəl\ *adj* **1 a** : formed by an agreement between political units that surrender supreme authority to a central authority but keep certain powers **b** : of or being a form of government in which power is distributed between a central authority and individual units **2** *often cap* : of, relating to, or loyal to the U.S. federal government during the American Civil War — **fed·er·al·ly** \-rə-lē\ *adv*

Fed·er·al \ˈfed-(ə-)rəl\ *n* **1** : a supporter of the government of the U.S. in the American Civil War; *esp* : a soldier in the federal armies **2** : a federal agent or officer

fed·er·al·ist \ˈfed-(ə-)rə-ləst\ *n* **1** : a supporter of federal government; *esp, often cap* : a supporter of the adoption of the U.S. Constitution **2** *cap* : a member of a major political party in the early years of the U.S. favoring a strong central national government — **fed·er·al·ism** \-ˌliz-əm\ *n, often cap* — **federalist** *adj, often cap*

fed·er·al·ize \ˈfed-(ə-)rə-ˌlīz\ *vb* **-ized; -iz·ing** : to unite in or under a federal system of authority — **fed·er·al·i·za·tion** \ˌfed-(ə-)rə-lə-ˈzā-shən\ *n*

fed·er·ate \ˈfed-ə-ˌrāt\ *vb* **-at·ed; -at·ing** : to join in a federation

fed·er·a·tion \ˌfed-ə-ˈrā-shən\ *n* **1** : a political body formed by uniting smaller bodies; *esp* : a federal government **2** : the act of creating or becoming a federation

fe·do·ra \fi-ˈdōr-ə, -ˈdȯr-\ *n* : a low soft felt hat with the crown creased lengthwise

fedora

fed up *adj* : utterly worn-out and disgusted

fee \ˈfē\ *n* **1** : a set charge ⟨admission *fee*⟩ ⟨license *fee*⟩ **2** : a charge for a professional service ⟨a doctor's *fees*⟩ **synonyms** see PRICE

fee·ble \ˈfē-bəl\ *adj* **fee·bler** \-b(ə-)lər\; **-blest** \-b(ə-)ləst\ **1** : lacking in strength or endurance **2** : not forceful or loud ⟨a *feeble* cry⟩ ⟨a *feeble* attempt⟩ **synonyms** see WEAK — **fee·ble·ness** \-bəl-nəs\ *n* — **fee·bly** \-blē\ *adv*

fee·ble·mind·ed \ˌfē-bəl-ˈmīn-dəd\ *adj* : not having normal intelligence : mentally deficient — **fee·ble·mind·ed·ly** *adv* — **fee·ble·mind·ed·ness** *n*

¹feed \ˈfēd\ *vb* **fed** \ˈfed\; **feed·ing** **1 a** : to give food to **b** : to give as food **c** : EAT 1 ⟨cattle *feeding* in the barn⟩ **d** : ²PREY 1a — used with *on, upon,* or *off* ⟨*feeds* on insects⟩ **2 a** : to supply with something necessary **b** : to supply (material to be operated on) to a machine **c** : to nourish or become nourished as if by food **3 a** : to supply for use **b** : to supply (a signal) to an electronic circuit or to a transmitter for broadcast

²feed *n* **1** : ¹MEAL; *esp* : a large meal **2** : food for livestock **3** : a mechanism by which feeding is carried out **4** : a signal fed to a transmitter

feed·back \ˈfēd-ˌbak\ *n* **1 a** : the return to the input of a part of the output of a machine, system, or process **b** : noise resulting from the feedback of an amplified or broadcast signal **2** : the giving or sending of information or of something from which information can be obtained about the value, effect, or result of an action or process to the controlling source; *also* : the information or information-containing material so given or sent

feed·er \ˈfēd-ər\ *n* **1** : a device for supplying food ⟨bird *feeder*⟩ **b** : a branch (as of a river or a transportation system) that supplies or connects to another **2** : one that eats; *esp* : an animal being fattened or suitable for fattening

feed·lot \ˈfēd-ˌlät\ *n* : a plot of land on which livestock are fattened for market

feed·stuff \-ˌstəf\ *n* : ²FEED 2

¹feel \ˈfēl\ *vb* **felt** \ˈfelt\; **feel·ing** **1 a** : to sense through direct contact **b** : to examine or test by touching : HANDLE **2 a** : ²EXPERIENCE **b** : to suffer from **3** : to discover by trying carefully — often used with *out* **4 a** : to be aware of ⟨*feel* trouble brewing⟩ **b** : to be conscious of a physical or mental state ⟨*feel* happy⟩ ⟨*feel* sick⟩ **c** : BELIEVE 5, THINK **5** : to search for something with the fingers **6** : to seem especially to the touch ⟨*feels* like wool⟩ **7** : to have sympathy or pity ⟨I *feel* for you⟩

²feel *n* **1** : the sense of touch **2** : SENSATION 1c, FEELING **3** : the quality of a thing as indicated through touch **4** : intuitive knowledge or ability ⟨a *feel* for languages⟩

\ə\ **abut**	\au̇\ **out**	\i\ **tip**	\ȯ\ **saw**	\u̇\ **foot**
\ər\ **further**	\ch\ **chin**	\ī\ **life**	\ȯi\ **coin**	\y\ **yet**
\a\ **mat**	\e\ **pet**	\j\ **job**	\th\ **thin**	\yü\ **few**
\ā\ **take**	\ē\ **easy**	\ŋ\ **sing**	\th\ **this**	\yu̇\ **cure**
\ä\ **cot, cart**	\g\ **go**	\ō\ **bone**	\ü\ **food**	\zh\ **vision**

feel·er \'fē-lər\ *n* **1** : one that feels; *esp* : a movable organ (as an antenna) of an animal that is usually an organ of touch **2** : a suggestion or remark made to find out the views of other people

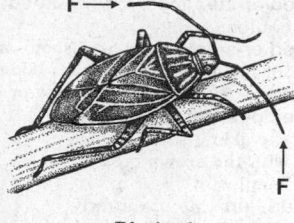

F feeler 1

feel–good \'fēl-ˌgu̇d\ *adj* **1** : relating to or promoting an often false sense of satisfaction or well-being **2** : cheerfully sentimental ⟨a *feel-good* movie⟩

¹feel·ing \'fē-liŋ\ *n* **1 a** : a sense by which the hardness or softness, hotness or coldness, or heaviness or lightness of things is found out; *esp* : ²TOUCH **3 b** : a sensation experienced through this sense **2 a** : a state of mind ⟨a *feeling* of loneliness⟩ **b** *pl* : general emotional condition : SENSIBILITIES ⟨hurt their *feelings*⟩ **3** : an opinion or belief often when not based on evidence ⟨a *feeling* that it will rain⟩ **4** : SYMPATHY 3 **5** : FEEL 4

²feeling *adj* : SENSITIVE 2 — **feel·ing·ly** \'fē-liŋ-lē\ *adv* — **feel·ing·ness** *n*

feet *plural of* FOOT

feet-first \'fēt-'fərst\ *adv* : with both feet or all four feet going first ⟨fell *feetfirst*⟩

Feh·ling's solution \'fā-liŋ(z)-\ *n* : a blue solution prepared by mixing solutions of Rochelle salt and copper sulfate and used especially in a test for sugars

feign \'fān\ *vb* **1** : to give a false appearance of : FAKE ⟨*feign* illness⟩ **2** : to state as if true ⟨*feign* an excuse⟩

feint \'fānt\ *n* : a pretended blow or attack at one point in order to distract attention from the point one really intends to attack — **feint** *vb*

feld·spar \'fel(d)-ˌspär\ *n* : any of a group of crystalline minerals that consist of silicates of aluminum with potassium, sodium, calcium, or barium and that are a basic part of nearly all crystalline rocks

fe·lic·i·tate \fi-'lis-ə-ˌtāt\ *vb* **-tat·ed; -tat·ing** : CONGRATULATE — **fe·lic·i·ta·tion** \-ˌlis-ə-'tā-shən\ *n*

fe·lic·i·tous \fi-'lis-ət-əs\ *adj* **1** : very well suited or expressed ⟨*felicitous* wording⟩ **2** : PLEASANT 1, DELIGHTFUL — **fe·lic·i·tous·ly** *adv* — **fe·lic·i·tous·ness** *n*

fe·lic·i·ty \fi-'lis-ət-ē\ *n, pl* **-ties 1** : great happiness : BLISS **2** : something that causes happiness **3** : a pleasing manner or quality especially in art or language ⟨a *felicity* with words⟩ **4** : a suitable expression

¹fe·line \'fē-ˌlīn\ *adj* **1 a** : belonging to the family of flesh-eating mammals with soft fur that includes the cats, lions, tigers, leopards, pumas, and lynxes **b** : of or resembling a cat : characteristic of cats **2** : SLY 1, STEALTHY

²feline *n* : a feline animal : CAT

¹fell \'fel\ *vb* **1 a** : to cut, beat, or knock down ⟨*fell* trees⟩ **b** : ¹KILL 1 **2** : to sew (a seam) by folding one edge under the other [Old English *fellan* "to knock down"]

²fell *past of* ¹FALL

³fell *adj* : FIERCE 1, CRUEL; *also* : ¹DEADLY 1, ¹DEADLY 2a [Middle English *fel* "fierce, terrible," from early French *fel* (same meaning), from *fel, felon* "villain, evildoer" — related to FELON]

fel·lah \'fel-ə, fə-'lä\ *n, pl* **fel·la·hin** \ˌfel-ə-'hēn, fə-ˌlä-'hēn\ : a peasant or farm worker in an Arab country (as Egypt or Syria)

¹fel·low \'fel-ō\ *n* **1** : COMRADE, ASSOCIATE **2 a** : an equal in rank, power, or character : PEER **b** : one of a pair : MATE **3** : a person holding any of various positions at a university **4 a** : a male person **b** : BOYFRIEND 2 **5** : a person granted funds for advanced study

²fellow *adj* : being a companion, mate, or associate

fellow man *n* : a human being of similar nature

fel·low·ship \'fel-ō-ˌship\ *n* **1** : a friendly relationship among people **2** : a sharing of interest or feeling **3** : a group with similar interests **4 a** : the position of a fellow (as of a university) **b** : the funds granted a fellow

fel·on \'fel-ən\ *n* : ²CRIMINAL; *esp* : one who has committed a felony [Middle English *felon* "one who has committed a felony," from early French *felon* "villain, evildoer," of Germanic origin — related to ³FELL]

fel·o·ny \'fel-ə-nē\ *n, pl* **-nies** : a serious crime punishable by a heavy sentence — **fe·lo·ni·ous** \fə-'lō-nē-əs\ *adj* — **fe·lo·ni·ous·ly** *adv*

¹felt \'felt\ *n* : a heavy material made by rolling and pressing fibers (as of wool) together

²felt *vb* **1** : to mat together **2** : to make into felt

³felt *past of* FEEL

¹fe·male \'fē-ˌmāl\ *n* : a female plant or animal

Word History In the 14th century, *female* appeared in English with such spellings as *femel, femelle,* and *female.* The word comes from the Latin *femella,* meaning "young woman, girl," which in turn is based on *femina,* meaning "woman." In English, the similarity in form and sound between the words *female* and *male* led people to use only the *female* spelling. This closeness also led to the belief that *female* comes from or is somehow related to *male.* However, apart from the influence of *male* on the modern spelling of *female,* there is no link between the origins of the two words. [Middle English *female* "a girl or woman," an altered form of *femel, femelle* (same meaning), from early French *femelle* and Latin *femella,* both meaning "a girl or woman," from earlier Latin *femella* "a young woman, girl," from *femina* "woman" — related to FEMININE]

²female *adj* **1 a** : of, relating to, or being the sex that bears young or produces eggs **b** : having only seed-producing flowers ⟨a *female* holly⟩ **2 a** : of, relating to, or characteristic of the female sex **b** : made up of females — **fe·male·ness** *n*

¹fem·i·nine \'fem-ə-nən\ *adj* **1** : of the female sex **2** : characteristic of or belonging to women : WOMANLY **3** : of, relating to, or making up the class of words that ordinarily includes most of those referring to females ⟨a *feminine* noun in Latin⟩ [Middle English *feminine* "female," from early French *feminin* (same meaning), derived from Latin *femina* "woman" — related to FEMALE; see *Word History* at FEMALE] — **fem·i·nine·ly** *adv* — **fem·i·nine·ness** *n* — **fem·i·nin·i·ty** \ˌfem-ə-'nin-ət-ē\ *n*

²feminine *n* **1** : a word or form of the feminine gender **2** : the feminine gender

fem·i·nism \'fem-ə-ˌniz-əm\ *n* **1** : the theory supporting the political, economic, and social equality of the sexes **2** : organized activity on behalf of women's rights and interests — **fem·i·nist** \-nəst\ *n or adj* — **fem·i·nis·tic** \ˌfem-ə-'nis-tik\ *adj*

fe·mur \'fē-mər\ *n, pl* **fe·murs** *or* **fem·o·ra** \'fem-(ə-)rə\ **1** : the long bone of the hind or lower limb extending from the hip to the knee — called also *thighbone* **2** : the segment of an insect's leg that is third from the body — **fem·o·ral** \'fem-(ə-)rəl\ *adj*

fen \'fen\ *n* : low land covered wholly or partly by water

¹fence \'fen(t)s\ *n* **1** : a barrier (as of wood or wire) to prevent escape or entry or to mark a boundary **2** : a person who receives stolen goods — **fence·less** \-ləs\ *adj* — **on the fence** : not having one's mind made up

²fence *vb* **fenced; fenc·ing 1 a** : to enclose with a fence **b** : to keep in or out with a fence **2** : to practice fencing **3** : to sell (stolen property) to a fence — **fenc·er** *n*

fenc·ing *n* **1** : the art or practice of attack and defense with a sword **2** : material for fences

fend \'fend\ *vb* **1** : to keep or ward off : REPEL 1 ⟨*fend* off an attack⟩ **2** : to try to get along without help ⟨had to *fend* for themselves⟩

fend·er \'fen-dər\ *n* : a device that protects: as **a** : a frame in front of a locomotive or streetcar to catch or throw off anything that is hit **b** : a guard over a wheel of an automobile, motorcycle, or bicycle **c** : a low metal frame or screen placed on the hearth before an open fireplace

feng shui \'fəŋ-'shwē, -'shwā\ *n* : a Chinese system for positioning a building and objects within a building in a way that is thought to agree with spiritual forces and to bring health and happiness [from Chinese *fēng* "wind" and *shŭi* "water"]

fen·nec \'fen-ik\ *n* : a small African fox with large ears

fen·nel \'fen-ᵊl\ *n* : a garden plant related to the carrot that is grown for its fragrant seeds and needle-shaped leaflets

fe·ral \'fir-əl, 'fer-\ *adj* : having escaped from domestication and become wild ⟨*feral* cats⟩

fer–de–lance \,ferd-ᵊl-'än(t)s, -'än(t)s\ *n, pl* **fer–de–lance** : a large extremely poisonous pit viper of Central and South America [from French *fer-de-lance,* literally, "iron (point) of a lance"]

¹fer·ment \(ˌ)fər-'ment\ *vb* **1** : to undergo or cause to undergo fermentation **2** : to be or cause to be in a state of unrest or excitement — **fer·ment·able** \-'ment-ə-bəl\ *adj* — **fer·ment·er** *n*

²fer·ment \'fər-ˌment\ *n* **1** : an agent (as a yeast) that is capable of causing fermentation **2** : a state of unrest or excitement

fer·men·ta·tion \,fər-mən-'tā-shən, -ˌmen-\ *n* : chemical breaking down of a substance (as in the souring of milk or the formation of alcohol from sugar) produced by an enzyme and often accompanied by the formation of a gas — **fer·men·ta·tive** \(ˌ)fər-'ment-ət-iv\ *adj*

fer·mi·um \'fer-mē-əm, 'fər-\ *n* : a radioactive metallic element artificially produced (as by bombardment of plutonium with neutrons) — see ELEMENT table

fern \'fərn\ *n* : any of an order of vascular plants resembling seed plants in having root, stem, and leaflike fronds but reproducing by spores instead of by flowers and seeds — **fern·like** \-ˌlīk\ *adj* — **ferny** \'fər-nē\ *adj*

fe·ro·cious \fə-'rō-shəs\ *adj* **1** : FIERCE 1, SAVAGE **2** : very great : EXTREME ⟨*ferocious* heat⟩ — **fe·ro·cious·ly** *adv* — **fe·ro·cious·ness** *n* — **fe·roc·i·ty** \fə-'räs-ət-ē\

¹fer·ret \'fer-ət\ *n* **1** : a domesticated usually albino, brownish, or silver-gray mammal closely related to the European polecat **2** : BLACK-FOOTED FERRET

²ferret *vb* **1** : to drive out of a hiding place **2** : to find and bring to light by searching — usually used with *out*

fer·ric \'fer-ik\ *adj* : of, relating to, or containing iron

ferric oxide *n* : the red or black oxide of iron found in nature as hematite and as rust

Fer·ris wheel \'fer-əs-\ *n* : an amusement ride consisting of a large vertical wheel that is driven by a motor and has seats around its rim [named for G. W. G. *Ferris* 1859–1896 American engineer]

fer·ro·mag·net·ic \,fer-ō-mag-'net-ik\ *adj* : of or relating to substances (as iron and nickel) that are easily magnetized

fer·rous \'fer-əs\ *adj* : of, relating to, or containing iron

ferrous sulfate *n* : a salt that consists of iron, sulfur, and oxygen and is used in treating industrial wastes and in medicine

fern

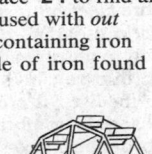

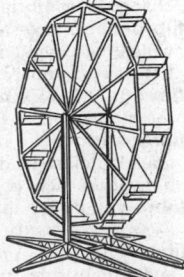

Ferris wheel

fer·rule \'fer-əl\ *n* : a metal ring or cap placed around the end of a wooden shaft or handle to prevent splitting or to provide a strong joint

¹fer·ry \'fer-ē\ *vb* **fer·ried; fer·ry·ing 1 a** : to carry by boat over a body of water **b** : to cross by a ferry **2 a** : to carry (as by aircraft or motor vehicle) from one place to another **b** : to deliver (an airplane) by flying it to its destination

²ferry *n, pl* **ferries 1** : a place where persons or things are ferried **2** : FERRYBOAT

fer·ry·boat \'fer-ē-ˌbōt\ *n* : a boat used to ferry passengers, vehicles, or goods

fer·tile \'fərt-ᵊl\ *adj* **1** : producing vegetation or crops plentifully : RICH ⟨*fertile* farmland⟩ **2** : producing thoughts and ideas abundantly ⟨a *fertile* mind⟩ **3 a** : capable of growing and developing ⟨a *fertile* seed⟩ **b** : capable of reproducing or of producing reproductive cells ⟨a *fertile* bull⟩ ⟨*fertile* fungal hyphae⟩ [Middle English *fertile* "bearing in abundance, productive," from early French *fertile* and Latin *fertilis* (both same meaning), from Latin *ferre* "to bear, carry, yield, produce" — related to ¹DEFER, TRANSFER] — **fer·til·i·ty** \(ˌ)fər-'til-ət-ē\ *n*

synonyms FERTILE, FRUITFUL, PROLIFIC mean producing or capable of producing offspring or fruit. FERTILE suggests having the power to reproduce or helping in reproduction and growth ⟨the *fertile* soil of the farm states⟩. FRUITFUL stresses the yielding of desirable or useful results ⟨*fruitful* methods of increasing the corn harvest⟩. PROLIFIC stresses the power to reproduce and spread rapidly ⟨rabbits are *prolific* animals⟩.

fer·til·i·za·tion \,fərt-ᵊl-ə-'zā-shən\ *n* **1** : an act or process of making fertile; *esp* : the application of fertilizer **2** : the union of male and female germ cells to form a zygote

fer·til·ize \'fərt-ᵊl-ˌīz\ *vb* **-ized; -iz·ing** : to make fertile: as **a** : to cause the fertilization of; *also* : to unite with in the process of fertilization ⟨a sperm *fertilizes* an egg⟩ **b** : to apply a fertilizer to ⟨*fertilize* land⟩

fer·til·iz·er \'fərt-ᵊl-ˌī-zər\ *n* : a substance (as manure or a chemical) used to make soil produce larger or more plant life

fer·vent \'fər-vənt\ *adj* : having or expressing great warmth or depth of feeling ⟨a *fervent* hope⟩ — **fer·ven·cy** \-vən-sē\ *n* — **fer·vent·ly** *adv*

fer·vid \'fər-vəd\ *adj* : filled with passion or eagerness — **fer·vid·ly** *adv* — **fer·vid·ness** *n*

fer·vor \'fər-vər\ *n* : strength of feeling

fes·cue \'fes-(ˌ)kyü\ *n* : a tufted perennial grass

fes·tal \'fest-ᵊl\ *adj* : FESTIVE 1 — **fes·tal·ly** \-ᵊl-ē\ *adv*

¹fes·ter \'fes-tər\ *n* : a pus-filled sore

²fester *vb* **fes·tered; fes·ter·ing** \-t(ə-)riŋ\ **1** : to form pus **2** : ¹ROT 1a **3** : to grow or cause to grow increasingly more irritating ⟨let her jealousy *fester*⟩

fes·ti·val \'fes-tə-vəl\ *n* **1** : a time of celebration in honor of a special occasion **2** : an often regularly occurring program of events or entertainment [from earlier *festival* (adjective), derived from early French *festival* "festive," from Latin *festivus* "festive," from *festum* (noun) "festival, feast" — related to FEAST, FIESTA] — **festival** *adj*

fes·tive \'fes-tiv\ *adj* **1** : of, relating to, or suitable for a feast or festival **2** : JOYOUS, MERRY — **fes·tive·ly** *adv* — **fes·tive·ness** *n*

fes·tiv·i·ty \fes-'tiv-ət-ē\ *n, pl* **-ties 1** : FESTIVAL 1 **2** : the quality or state of being festive **3** : festive activity

¹fes·toon \fes-'tün\ *n* : a decorative chain or strip hanging between two points

\ə\ **abut**	\au̇\ **out**	\i\ **tip**	\ȯ\ **saw**	\u̇\ **foot**
\ər\ **further**	\ch\ **chin**	\ī\ **life**	\ȯi\ **coin**	\y\ **yet**
\a\ **mat**	\e\ **pet**	\j\ **job**	\th\ **thin**	\yü\ **few**
\ā\ **take**	\ē\ **easy**	\ŋ\ **sing**	\th\ **this**	\yu̇\ **cure**
\ä\ **cot, cart**	\g\ **go**	\ō\ **bone**	\ü\ **food**	\zh\ **vision**

[2]**festoon** *vb* : to hang or form festoons on

fe·ta \'fet-ə, 'fe-ˌtä\ *n* : a white Greek cheese made from sheep's or goat's milk and cured in salt water [from modern Greek *pheta* "slice (of cheese)"]

fe·tal \'fēt-ᵊl\ *adj* : of, relating to, or being a fetus

fetal alcohol syndrome *n* : a variable group of birth defects including deficient mental and physical growth that tend to occur in the offspring of women who drink large amounts of alcohol during pregnancy

fetch \'fech\ *vb* **1** : to go after and bring back **2** : to cause to come : bring forth **3** : to bring as a price : sell for — **fetch·er** *n*

fetch·ing \'fech-iŋ\ *adj* : ATTRACTIVE, PLEASING ⟨a *fetching* smile⟩ — **fetch·ing·ly** *adv*

fetch up *vb* : to come to or bring to a stop

[1]**fete** *or* **fête** \'fāt\ *n* **1** : FESTIVAL 1 **2** : a fancy entertainment or party

[2]**fete** *or* **fête** *vb* **fet·ed** *or* **fêt·ed**; **fet·ing** *or* **fêt·ing** **1** : to honor with a fete **2** : to pay high honor to

fet·id \'fet-əd\ *adj* : having a strong unpleasant smell — **fet·id·ly** *adv* — **fet·id·ness** *n*

fe·tish *also* **fe·tich** \'fet-ish *also* 'fēt-\ *n* **1** : an object (as an idol or image) believed to have supernatural or magical powers **2** : an object of unreasonable devotion or concern — **fe·tish·ism** \-ˌiz-əm\ *n*

fet·lock \'fet-ˌläk\ *n* **1** : a projection with a bunch of hair on the back of a horse's leg above the hoof **2** : the bunch of hair growing out of the fetlock

fet·ter \'fet-ər\ *n* **1** : a chain for the feet **2** : something that restricts : RESTRAINT — **fetter** *vb*

fet·tle \'fet-ᵊl\ *n* : a state of fitness or order : CONDITION ⟨in fine *fettle*⟩

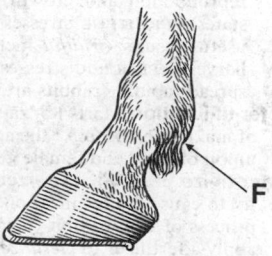

F fetlock 1

fe·tus \'fēt-əs\ *n*, *pl* **fe·tus·es** : a young animal while in the body of its mother or in the egg especially in the later stages of development; *esp* : a developing human being in the uterus from usually two months after pregnancy occurs to birth — compare EMBRYO 1

feud \'fyüd\ *n* : a long lasting quarrel; *esp* : a lasting conflict between families or clans usually having acts of violence and revenge — **feud** *vb*

feu·dal \'fyüd-ᵊl\ *adj* : of or relating to feudalism — **feu·dal·ly** *adv*

feu·dal·ism \'fyüd-ᵊl-ˌiz-əm\ *n* : a system of political organization (as in Europe during the Middle Ages) in which a vassal served a lord and received protection and land in return — **feu·dal·is·tic** \ˌfyüd-ᵊl-'is-tik\ *adj*

fe·ver \'fē-vər\ *n* **1 a** : a rise of body temperature above the normal **b** : a disease of which fever is an important symptom **2** : a state of excited emotion or activity

fever blister *n* : COLD SORE

fe·ver·ish \'fēv-(ə-)rish\ *adj* **1 a** : having a fever **b** : of, relating to, or being fever **c** : tending to cause fever **2** : showing great emotion or activity : HECTIC ⟨*feverish* excitement⟩ — **fe·ver·ish·ly** *adv* — **fe·ver·ish·ness** *n*

[1]**few** \'fyü\ *pron* : not many persons or things — used in plural ⟨*few* were present⟩

[2]**few** *adj* **1** : amounting to only a small number ⟨one of the *few* sports I play⟩ **2** : not many but some ⟨caught a *few* fish⟩ — **few·ness** *n*

[3]**few** *n* **1** : a small number of units or individuals ⟨a *few* of them⟩ **2** : a special limited number ⟨the select *few*⟩

[1]**few·er** \'fyü-ər\ *adj* : not so many : a smaller number of

[2]**fewer** *pron* : a smaller number of persons or things — used in plural ⟨*fewer* are available⟩

fez \'fez\ *n*, *pl* **fez·zes** : a round red felt hat that has a flat top and a tassel but no brim

fi·an·cé \ˌfē-ˌän-'sā, fē-'än-ˌsā\ *n* : a man engaged to be married [from French *fiancé* "man engaged to be married," derived from early French *fiancé*, past participle of *fiancer* "to promise," derived from Latin *fidere* "to trust" — related to FAITH]

fi·an·cée \ˌfē-ˌän-'sā, fē-'än-ˌsā\ *n* : a woman engaged to be married

fi·as·co \fē-'as-kō\ *n*, *pl* **-coes** : a complete failure

fi·at \'fē-ət, -at, -ät; 'fī-ət, -at\ *n* : an order from someone in charge

fib \'fib\ *n* : an unimportant lie — **fib** *vb* — **fib·ber** *n*

fi·ber \'fī-bər\ *n* **1** : a thread or a structure or object resembling a thread: as **a** : a slender root (as of a grass) **b** : a long tapering thick-walled plant cell especially of vascular tissue **c** : a muscle cell **d** : AXON, DENDRITE **e** : a slender and very long natural or synthetic unit of material (as wool, cotton, asbestos, gold, glass, or rayon) usually able to be spun into yarn **f** : mostly indigestible material in food that stimulates the intestine to move its contents along — called also *bulk, roughage* **2** : material made of fibers **3** : basic toughness : STRENGTH ⟨moral *fiber*⟩

fi·ber·board \'fī-bər-ˌbōrd, -ˌbord\ *n* : a material made by pressing fibers (as of wood) into stiff sheets; *also* : CARDBOARD

fi·ber·fill \-ˌfil\ *n* : synthetic fibers used as a filling material (as for pillows)

fi·ber·glass \-ˌglas\ *n* : glass in the form of fibers used in making various products (as yarn, insulation, or boats)

fi·ber–op·tic \'fī-bər-ˌäp-tik\ *adj* : of or relating to fiber optics

fiber optics *n* **1** *pl* : thin transparent enclosed fibers of glass or plastic that carry light by internal reflections; *also* : a bundle of such fibers used in an instrument **2** : the technique of the use of fiber optics

Fi·bo·nac·ci number \ˌfē-bə-'näch-ē-, ˌfib-ə-\ *n* : any of the integers in the infinite sequence 1, 1, 2, 3, 5, 8, 13 . . . of which the first two terms are 1 and 1 and each following term is the sum of the two just before it [named for Leonardo *Fibonacci* about 1170–about 1240 Italian mathematician]

Fibonacci sequence *n* : a mathematical sequence composed of the Fibonacci numbers in order

fi·bre *chiefly British variant of* FIBER

fi·brin \'fī-brən\ *n* : a white fibrous substance that is difficult to dissolve and is formed in the clotting of the blood

fi·brin·o·gen \fī-'brin-ə-jən\ *n* : a protein that is produced in the liver, is present especially in blood plasma, and is changed into fibrin during the clotting of blood

fi·bro·sis \fī-'brō-səs\ *n* : an abnormal bodily condition in which increased amounts of fibrous tissue form in other tissues — compare CYSTIC FIBROSIS

fi·brous \'fī-brəs\ *adj* **1** : containing, consisting of, or resembling fibers **2** : [1]TOUGH 1b, STRINGY

fibrous root *n* : a root (as in most grasses) that is one of many similar slender roots branching directly from the base of the stem of a plant — compare TAPROOT

fi·bro·vas·cu·lar bundle \ˌfīb-rō-ˌvas-kyə-lər-, ˌfib-\ *n* : VASCULAR BUNDLE

fib·u·la \'fib-yə-lə\ *n*, *pl* **-lae** \-ˌlē, -ˌlī\ *or* **-las** : the outer and usually the smaller of the two bones between the knee and ankle of the hind or lower limb — **fib·u·lar** \-lər\ *adj*

fez

fick·le \'fik-əl\ *adj* : likely to change frequently without good reason : INCONSTANT ⟨*fickle* friends⟩ — **fick·le·ness** *n* — **fick·ly** \'fik-(ə-)lē\ *adv*

fic·tion \'fik-shən\ *n* **1** : something told or written that is not fact **2** : a made-up story — **fic·tion·al** \-shnəl, -shən-ᵊl\ *adj* — **fic·tion·al·ly** \-shnə-lē, -shən-ᵊl-ē\ *adv*

fic·tion·al·ize \'fik-shnə-ˌlīz, -shən-ᵊl-ˌīz\ *vb* **-ized; -iz·ing** : to make into fiction ⟨*fictionalize* a biography⟩ — **fic·tion·al·i·za·tion** \ˌfik-shnə-lə-'zā-shən, -shən-ᵊl-ə-\ *n*

fic·tion·ize \'fik-shə-ˌnīz\ *vb* **-ized; -iz·ing** : FICTIONALIZE

fic·ti·tious \fik-'tish-əs\ *adj* : not real : MADE-UP, IMAGINARY ⟨a *fictitious* story⟩ — **fic·ti·tious·ly** *adv* — **fic·ti·tious·ness** *n*

¹fid·dle \'fid-ᵊl\ *n* : VIOLIN 1

²fiddle *vb* **fid·dled; fid·dling** \'fid-liŋ, -ᵊl-iŋ\ **1** : to play on a fiddle **2 a** : to move the hands or fingers restlessly **b** : to spend time in aimless activity **c** : MEDDLE, TAMPER — **fid·dler** \'fid-lər, -ᵊl-ər\ *n*

fid·dle·head \'fid-ᵊl-ˌhed\ *n* : one of the young tightly coiled leaves of some ferns that are often eaten as greens

fiddler crab *n* : a burrowing crab of which the male has one claw much larger than the other

fid·dle·stick \'fid-ᵊl-ˌstik\ *n* **1** : a violin bow **2** *pl* : NONSENSE 1 — used as an interjection

fi·del·i·ty \fə-'del-ət-ē, fī-\ *n, pl* **-ties 1 a** : the quality or state of being faithful **b** : exactness in details **2** : the degree to which an electronic device (as a record player, radio, or television) correctly reproduces its effect (as sound or a picture)

¹fidg·et \'fij-ət\ *n* **1** *pl* : restlessness as shown by nervous movements **2** : one that fidgets — **fidg·ety** \-ət-ē\ *adj*

²fidget *vb* : to move or act nervously or restlessly — **fidget with** : to move or handle (something) in a nervous way

fie \'fī\ *interj* — used to express disgust or disapproval

fief \'fēf\ *n* : a feudal estate

¹field \'fē(ə)ld\ *n* **1 a** : an open land area free of woods and buildings **b** : an area of cleared land used especially for planting crops **c** : a piece of land put to some special use or yielding some special product ⟨an athletic *field*⟩ ⟨a gas *field*⟩ **d** : a place in which military operations are carried on **e** : an open space ⟨a *field* of ice⟩ **2 a** : an area of activity or influence ⟨the *field* of science⟩ **b** : the area of practical activity outside a laboratory, office, or factory ⟨earth scientists working in the *field*⟩ **3** : a background on which something is drawn, painted, or mounted ⟨painted white stars on a blue *field*⟩ **4** : the individuals that make up all or part of a contest ⟨a race with a large *field* of runners⟩ **5** : a region or space in which an effect (as gravity, electricity, or magnetism) exists **6** : the area visible through the lens of an optical instrument

²field *vb* : to catch or stop and throw a ball to a teammate ⟨the shortstop *fielded* the ground ball⟩

³field *adj* : of or relating to a field

field corn *n* : corn with starchy kernels that are used for livestock feed or are processed into food products (as corn oil or corn syrup) or ethanol

field day *n* **1** : a day of outdoor sports and athletic competition **2** : a time of unusual pleasure or unexpected success ⟨newspapers had a *field day* with the story⟩

field·er \'fēl-dər\ *n* : one that fields; *esp* : a baseball player stationed in the outfield while the opposing team is at bat

field event *n* : an event in a track meet other than a race

field glass *n* : a handheld instrument for seeing at a distance that consists of two telescopes, a focusing device, and usually prisms — usually used in plural

field goal *n* **1** : a score of three points in football made by kicking the ball over the crossbar during ordinary play **2** : BASKET 3b

field guide *n* : a small book with words and pictures for identifying plants, animals, or natural objects (as rocks) that are found in nature

field hockey *n* : a game played on a field in which each team uses curved sticks to try to knock a ball into the other team's goal

field magnet *n* : a magnet for producing and maintaining a magnetic field especially in a generator or electric motor

field marshal *n* : an officer (as in the British army) of the highest rank

field mouse *n* : any of various mice that inhabit fields

field of view : ¹FIELD 6

field of vision : VISUAL FIELD

field·stone \'fē(ə)ld-ˌstōn\ *n* : stone (as in building) in usually unchanged form as taken from nature

field trip *n* : a visit (as to a factory, farm, or museum) made by students and usually a teacher for purposes of firsthand observation

fiend \'fēnd\ *n* **1** : DEMON 1, DEVIL **2** : an extremely wicked or cruel person **3 a** : a person enthusiastically devoted to something **b** : ²ADDICT 1 — **fiend·ish** \'fēn-dish\ *adj* — **fiend·ish·ly** *adv* — **fiend·ish·ness** *n*

fierce \'fi(ə)rs\ *adj* **fierc·er; fierc·est 1 a** : violently unfriendly or aggressive in disposition **b** : eager to fight or kill **2** : expressed with extreme force or anger : INTENSE ⟨a *fierce* argument⟩ **3** : furiously active or determined ⟨a *fierce* effort⟩ **4** : wild or threatening in appearance — **fierce·ly** *adv* — **fierce·ness** *n*

fi·ery \'fī-(ə-)rē\ *adj* **fi·er·i·er; -est 1** : being on fire : BLAZING **2** : hot or glowing like a fire **3 a** : full of spirit ⟨a *fiery* speech⟩ **b** : easily set off ⟨a *fiery* temper⟩ — **fi·er·i·ness** *n*

fi·es·ta \fē-'es-tə\ *n* : FESTIVAL 1; *esp* : a saint's day celebrated in Spain and Latin America with parades and dances [from Spanish *fiesta* "a festival, a religious celebration," from Latin *festa*, plural of *festum* "festival, feast" — related to FEAST, FESTIVAL]

fife \'fīf\ *n* : a small high-pitched musical instrument resembling a flute

fif·teen \(')fif-'tēn\ *n* — see NUMBER table — **fifteen** *adj or pron* — **fif·teenth** \-'tēn(t)th\ *adj or n*

fifth \'fifth, 'fif(t)th\ *n* **1** — see NUMBER table **2** : the difference in pitch between the first tone and the fifth tone of a scale — **fifth** *adj or adv* — **fifth·ly** *adv*

fif·ty \'fif-tē\ *n, pl* **fifties** — see NUMBER table — **fif·ti·eth** \-tē-əth\ *adj or n* — **fifty** *adj or pron*

fif·ty–fif·ty \ˌfif-tē-'fif-tē\ *adj* **1** : shared equally **2** : half favorable and half unfavorable ⟨a *fifty-fifty* chance⟩ — **fifty–fifty** *adv*

fig \'fig\ *n* : an oblong or pear-shaped fruit that grows on a tree related to the mulberries; *also* : a tree bearing figs

¹fight \'fīt\ *vb* **fought** \'fot\; **fight·ing 1 a** : to struggle against another in battle or physical combat **b** : ⁵BOX 2 **2** : to try hard ⟨*fighting* to stay awake⟩ **3 a** : to act for or against : STRUGGLE, CONTEND ⟨*fight* for the right⟩ ⟨*fight* a fire⟩ ⟨*fight* discrimination⟩ **b** : to attempt to prevent the success or effectiveness of ⟨*fight* off a cold⟩

²fight *n* **1 a** : a violent struggle between opposing forces : COMBAT, BATTLE **b** : a boxing match **c** : a verbal dis-

fig

\ə\ **abut**	\aú\ **out**	\i\ **tip**	\ȯ\ **saw**	\ú\ **foot**
\ər\ **further**	\ch\ **chin**	\ī\ **life**	\ȯi\ **coin**	\y\ **yet**
\a\ **mat**	\e\ **pet**	\j\ **job**	\th\ **thin**	\yü\ **few**
\ā\ **take**	\ē\ **easy**	\ŋ\ **sing**	\th\ **this**	\yú\ **cure**
\ä\ **cot, cart**	\g\ **go**	\ō\ **bone**	\ü\ **food**	\zh\ **vision**

agreement **2** : a struggle for a goal or an objective ⟨in a *fight* for their lives⟩ **3** : strength or disposition for fighting ⟨full of *fight*⟩

fight·er \'fīt-ər\ *n* : one that fights: **a** : WARRIOR, SOLDIER **b** : ¹BOXER **c** : a fast airplane armed with weapons for destroying enemy aircraft

fig·ment \'fig-mənt\ *n* : something imagined or made up

fig·u·ra·tive \'fig-(y)ə-rət-iv\ *adj* : expressing one thing in terms normally used for another : METAPHORICAL ⟨the *figurative* use of "foot" in "the foot of the mountain"⟩ — **fig·u·ra·tive·ly** *adv* — **fig·u·ra·tive·ness** *n*

¹fig·ure \'fig-yər, *British and often US* 'fig-ər\ **1 a** : NUMERAL 1 **b** *pl* : ARITHMETIC **2** ⟨a good head for *figures*⟩ **c** : ¹PRICE 1 **2 a** : the shape or outline of something **b** : bodily shape or form especially of a person **3 a** : something that represents a form especially of a person **b** : a diagram or pictorial illustration **c** : a combination of points, lines, or surfaces in geometry ⟨a circle is a closed plane *figure*⟩ **4** : ¹PATTERN 3, DESIGN **5** : PERSONALITY 4, PERSONAGE

²figure *vb* **fig·ured; fig·ur·ing** \'fig-yə-riŋ, 'fig(-ə)-\ **1** : to decorate with a pattern **2** : BELIEVE 5, DECIDE ⟨*figured* we might win⟩ **3** : to be or appear important ⟨*figure* in the news⟩ **4** : COMPUTE, CALCULATE — **fig·ur·er** \-(y)ər-ər\ *n* — **figure on 1** : to take into consideration **2** : to rely on **3** : ²PLAN 2

fig·ured \'fig-(y)ərd\ *adj* **1** : adorned with, formed into, or marked with a figure **2** : being represented **3** : indicated by figures

fig·ure·head \'fig-(y)ər-hed\ *n* **1** : a figure, statue, or bust on the bow of a ship **2** : a person who has the title but not the powers of the head of something

figure of speech : a form of expression (as a simile or metaphor) that uses words other than in a plain or literal way

figurehead 1

figure out *vb* **1** : FIND OUT, DISCOVER ⟨try to *figure out* a way to do it⟩ **2** : SOLVE ⟨*figure out* a problem⟩

figure skating *n* : skating in which the skaters move in exact patterns and also perform various jumps and turns

fig·u·rine \,fig-(y)ə-'rēn\ *n* : a small carved or molded figure

fig·wort \'fig-,wərt, -,wó(ə)rt\ *n* : any of a genus of herbs related to the snapdragons and having toothed leaves and clusters of small purple, yellow, or greenish flowers

fil·a·ment \'fil-ə-mənt\ *n* : a single thread or a thin flexible threadlike object, process, or part: as **a** : a wire (as in a light bulb) that is made to glow by the passage of an electric current **b** : a long chain of cells (as of some bacteria or algae) **c** : the anther-bearing stalk of a plant stamen — **fil·a·men·tous** \,fil-ə-'ment-əs\ *adj*

fil·bert \'fil-bərt\ *n* **1** : either of two European hazels **2** : the sweet thick-shelled nut of a filbert; *also* : HAZELNUT **Word History** Hazel trees are common in England, and their sweet nuts become ripe in late summer. The feast day of a French saint named Philibert was celebrated during the time that people picked these nuts. In the form of French spoken in England after the Normans conquered it in 1066, the nut of the hazel tree was called *philber,* after the saint. English borrowed the word as *filbert.* [Middle English *filbert* "filbert," from *philber,* name for the nut in the French language used in England after 1066; named for Saint *Philibert,* French abbot who has a feast day at the time when the nuts ripen]

filch \'filch\ *vb* : to steal something slyly : PILFER

¹file \'fīl\ *n* : a usually steel tool with sharp ridges or teeth on its surface for smoothing hard substances [Old English *fēol* "tool for smoothing rough edges"]

²file *vb* **filed; fil·ing** : to rub, smooth, or cut away with a file

³file *vb* **filed; fil·ing 1** : to arrange in order for keeping or reference **2** : to enter or record as required by law [Middle English *filen* "to arrange (documents) in order," from Medieval Latin *filare* "to thread documents on a string," derived from Latin *filum* "thread" — related to ⁵FILE]

⁴file *n* **1** : a device (as a folder, case, or cabinet) for keeping papers or records in order **2 a** : a collection of papers or records arranged in order **b** : a collection of data considered as a unit (as for a computer)

⁵file *n* : a row of persons, animals, or things arranged one behind the other [from early French *file* "a row of things," from *filer* (verb) "to spin," derived from Latin *filum* "thread" — related to ³FILE]

⁶file *vb* **filed; fil·ing** : to march or proceed in file

file·fish \'fī(ə)l-,fish\ *n* : any of various fishes with rough leathery skin

fi·let mi·gnon \,fil-(,)ā-mēn-'yän, fi-,lā-\ *n, pl* **filets mi·gnons** \-mēn-'yänz\ : a thick slice of beef cut from the narrow end of a tenderloin [French, literally, "dainty fillet"]

fil·i·al \'fil-ē-əl, 'fil-yəl\ *adj* **1** : of, relating to, or befitting a son or daughter ⟨*filial* obedience⟩ **2** : being or having the relation of a child or offspring

¹fil·i·bus·ter \'fil-ə-,bəs-tər\ *n* : the use of delaying tactics (as long speeches) to put off or prevent action especially in a legislative assembly; *also* : an instance of this practice **Word History** One Dutch word has given us two different English words. The Dutch word *vrijbuiter* referred to a pirate or plunderer. The English borrowed this word in the 16th century, translating it as *freebooter.* The word was later picked up by the Spanish, who kept the same meaning but altered it to *filibustero.* Both words stayed in the realm of history until the middle of the 19th century. Then soldiers of fortune went out from the U.S. to try to cause uprisings in Central American countries. The governments there accused these Americans of wanting personal gain more than justice and called them *filibusteros.* English-speaking journalists wrote this word as *filibuster,* making it sound more like an English word. Later in the 19th century, members of Congress who delayed passage of laws by means such as long speeches were compared to the adventurers of Central America, who were trying to overthrow legitimate rule. *Filibuster* then came to mean "the use of delaying tactics to put off or prevent the passage of laws." [from Spanish *filibustero,* literally, "freebooter," probably derived from English *freebooter*]

²filibuster *vb* **-tered; -ter·ing** \-t(ə-)riŋ\ : to engage in a filibuster — **fil·i·bus·ter·er** \-tər-ər\ *n*

fil·i·gree \'fil-ə-,grē\ *n* **1** : ornamental work especially of fine wire applied chiefly to gold and silver surfaces **2 a** : ornamental work of delicate or complicated design done so as to show openings through the material **b** : a pattern or design resembling such work

filigree 2a

fil·ing \'fī-liŋ\ *n* : a small piece scraped off in filing ⟨iron *filings*⟩

Fil·i·pi·na \,fil-ə-'pē-nə\ *n* : a Filipino girl or woman

Fil·i·pi·no \,fil-ə-'pē-nō\ *n, pl* **-nos :** a person born or living in the Philippines [Spanish] — **Filipino** *adj*

¹**fill** \'fil\ *vb* **1 :** to put into as much as can be held or contained ⟨*fill* one's plate⟩ **2 :** to become full ⟨puddles *filling* with rain⟩ **3 :** SATISFY 1a ⟨*fill* all requirements⟩ **4 :** to occupy fully : take up whatever space there is ⟨clothes *filled* the closet⟩ **5 :** to spread through ⟨laughter *filled* the room⟩ **6 :** to stop up (as holes) : PLUG ⟨*fill* a crack with putty⟩ ⟨*fill* a tooth⟩ **7 a :** to perform the duties of : OCCUPY ⟨*fill* the office of president⟩ **b :** to put a person in ⟨*filled* several vacancies⟩ **8 :** to supply according to directions ⟨*fill* a prescription⟩ — **fill one's shoes :** to take one's place or position

²**fill** *n* **1 :** a full supply; *esp* : a quantity that satisfies ⟨eat one's *fill*⟩ **2 :** material used to fill a container, cavity, passage, or low place

fill·er \'fil-ər\ *n* : one that fills: as **a :** a substance added to a product (as to increase size or weight) **b :** a pack of paper to put in a binder **c :** a sound, word, or phrase used to fill pauses in speaking

¹**fil·let** \'fil-ət *also* fi-'lā, 'fil-(,)ā\ *also* **fi·let** \fi-'lā, 'fil-(,)ā\ *n* : a piece or slice of boneless meat or fish

²**fillet** *vb* : to cut into fillets

fill in *vb* **1 :** to furnish with specified information ⟨*fill in* an application⟩ ⟨*filled* us *in* on the latest news⟩ **2 :** to fill a vacancy usually temporarily : SUBSTITUTE ⟨*filled in* during the emergency⟩

fill·ing \'fil-iŋ\ *n* **1 :** material that is used to fill something ⟨a *filling* for a tooth⟩ **2 :** something that completes: as **a** : the yarn crossing over and under the warp in a fabric **b** : a food mixture used to fill pastry or sandwiches

fil·lip \'fil-əp\ *n* : a feature added to attract interest

fill out *vb* **1 :** to put on flesh **2 :** to complete by filling in blanks ⟨*fill out* an application⟩

fil·ly \'fil-ē\ *n, pl* **fillies :** a young female horse usually less than four years old

¹**film** \'film\ *n* **1 :** a thin skin or membrane **2 :** a thin coating or layer **3 :** a roll or strip of thin flexible transparent material coated with a chemical substance sensitive to light and used in taking pictures **4 :** MOTION PICTURE

²**film** *vb* **1 :** to cover or become covered with film **2 :** to make a motion picture of or from

film·strip \'film-,strip\ *n* : a strip of film for projecting still pictures on a screen

filmy \'fil-mē\ *adj* **film·i·er; -est :** of, resembling, suggesting, or made of film — **film·i·ness** *n*

¹**fil·ter** \'fil-tər\ *n* **1 :** a substance with pores through which a gas or liquid is passed to separate out floating matter **2 :** a device containing a filter **3 :** a transparent material (as colored glass) that absorbs light of some wavelengths and is used to change light (as in photography)

²**filter** *vb* **fil·tered; fil·ter·ing** \-t(ə-)riŋ\ **1 :** to expose to the action of a filter **2 :** to remove by means of a filter **3 :** to pass through or as if through a filter

fil·ter·able *also* **fil·tra·ble** \'fil-t(ə-)rə-bəl\ *adj* : capable of being separated by or of passing through a filter — **fil·ter·abil·i·ty** \,fil-t(ə-)rə-'bil-ət-ē\ *n*

filterable virus *n* : any of the infectious agents that remain infectious after passing through a filter with pores too fine for a bacterium to pass through

filter bed *n* : a bed of sand or gravel for filtering water or sewage

filter feeder *n* : an animal (as a clam or baleen whale) that obtains its food by filtering food particles or tiny living things from water

filter paper *n* : porous paper used especially for filtering

filth \'filth\ *n* **1 :** disgusting dirt or waste **2 :** something that tends to disgust, offend, or dirty

filthy \'fil-thē\ *adj* **filth·i·er; -est :** covered with or containing filth : disgustingly dirty **2 a :** ²UNDERHAND 1, EVIL **b :** OBSCENE 2 *synonyms* see DIRTY — **filth·i·ly** \-thə-lē\ *adv* — **filth·i·ness** \-thē-nəs\ *n*

fil·trate \'fil-,trāt\ *n* : the fluid that has passed through a filter

fil·tra·tion \fil-'trā-shən\ *n* : the act or process of filtering

fin \'fin\ *n* **1 :** a thin process on the outside of an aquatic animal (as a fish or whale) used in propelling or guiding the body **2 :** something shaped like a fin — **fin·like** \-,līk\ *adj* — **finned** \'find\ *adj*

fi·na·gle \fə-'nā-gəl\ *vb* **-gled; -gling** \-g(ə-)liŋ\ **:** to use trickery to get what one wants — **fi·na·gler** \-g(ə-)lər\ *n*

¹**fi·nal** \'fīn-əl\ *adj* **1 :** not to be changed or undone ⟨my *final* offer⟩ **2 :** relating to or occurring at the end or conclusion : ULTIMATE ⟨the *final* act of the play⟩ [Middle English *final* "perfect, final, not to be changed," from early French *final* (same meaning), from Latin *finalis* "final, relating to the end" — related to DEFINE, FINISH, INFINITY] — **fi·nal·ly** \'fīn-əl-ē, -lē\ *adv*

²**final** *n* : something final: as **a :** the last match or game of a tournament — usually used in plural **b :** the last examination in a course — often used in plural

fi·na·le \fə-'nal-ē, fi-'näl-\ *n* : the close or end of something (as a musical work)

fi·nal·ist \'fīn-əl-əst\ *n* : a contestant in the finals of a competition

fi·nal·i·ty \fī-'nal-ət-ē, fə-\ *n, pl* **-ties 1 :** the character or state of being final, settled, or complete **2 :** something final

fi·nal·ize \'fīn-əl-,īz\ *vb* **-ized; -iz·ing :** to put in final or finished form

¹**fi·nance** \fə-'nan(t)s, 'fī-,nan(t)s, fī-'nan(t)s\ *n* **1** *pl* **:** resources (as money) available to a government, person, group, or business **2 :** the obtaining or providing of funds or capital **3 :** the system that includes the circulation of money, the providing of banks and credit, and the making of investments — **fi·nan·cial** \fə-'nan-chəl, fī-\ *adj* — **fi·nan·cial·ly** \-'nanch-(ə-)lē\ *adv*

²**finance** *vb* **fi·nanced; fi·nanc·ing :** to provide money for ⟨*finance* a trip⟩

finance charge *n* : a charge for credit that is generally a percentage of the amount of credit given

finance company *n* : a company that specializes in making small loans usually to individuals

fin·an·cier \,fin-ən-'si(ə)r, fə-,nan-, ,fī-nan-\ *n* : a person who specializes in finance and especially in the financing of businesses

fin·back \'fin-,bak\ *n* : FIN WHALE

finch \'finch\ *n* : any of numerous songbirds (as the sparrows, grosbeaks, crossbills, goldfinches, and buntings) that have a short stout bill adapted for crushing seeds

¹**find** \'fīnd\ *vb* **found** \'faund\; **find·ing 1 :** to meet with someone or something by chance ⟨*found* a dime⟩ **2 :** to come upon by searching, study, or effort ⟨finally *found* the answer⟩ **3 :** to obtain by effort or management ⟨*find* time to do it⟩ **4 :** to make a decision ⟨*find* a verdict⟩ **5 :** to know by experience ⟨people *found* it useful⟩ **6 :** to gain or regain the use of ⟨*found* my voice again⟩ — **find fault :** CRITICIZE, COMPLAIN

²**find** *n* : something found; *esp* : a valuable item found

find·er \'fīn-dər\ *n* : one that finds: as **a :** a small telescope attached to a larger one for finding an object **b :** a device on a camera that shows the view being photographed by the camera

find·ing \'fīn-diŋ\ *n* **1 :** ²FIND **2 :** the result of a judicial proceeding or inquiry

find out *vb* **1 :** to learn by study, observation, or search : DISCOVER **2 :** to catch doing something bad ⟨the culprit was *found out*⟩

\ə\ **abut**	\au̇\ **out**	\i\ **tip**	\ȯ\ **saw**	\u̇\ **foot**
\ər\ **further**	\ch\ **chin**	\ī\ **life**	\ȯi\ **coin**	\y\ **yet**
\a\ **mat**	\e\ **pet**	\j\ **job**	\th\ **thin**	\yü\ **few**
\ā\ **take**	\ē\ **easy**	\ŋ\ **sing**	\th\ **this**	\yu̇\ **cure**
\ä\ **cot, cart**	\g\ **go**	\ō\ **bone**	\ü\ **food**	\zh\ **vision**

¹fine \'fīn\ *n* : a sum of money to be paid as a punishment [from earlier *fine* "a final agreement to settle a lawsuit," from Middle English *fine* "end, conclusion," from early French *fin* (same meaning), from Latin *finis* "end, limit" — related to FINAL]

²fine *vb* **fined; fin·ing** : to punish by a fine

³fine *adj* **fin·er; fin·est** **1** : free from impurity **2 a** : not thick, coarse, or dull ⟨*fine* thread⟩ ⟨*fine* sand⟩ **b** : ¹SMALL 1 ⟨*fine* print⟩ **c** : done with extreme care and accuracy ⟨*fine* measurement⟩ **3** : SUBTLE 1b ⟨a *fine* distinction⟩ **4** : excellent in quality or appearance ⟨a *fine* spring day⟩ **5** : to one's liking : AGREEABLE ⟨that's *fine* with me⟩ **6** : very well ⟨feel *fine*⟩ [Middle English *fin* "pure, brought to perfection," from early French *fin* (same meaning), from Latin *finis* (noun) "end, limit" as in *finis honorum* "the height of honor, the highest honor"] — **fine·ly** *adv* — **fine·ness** \'fīn-nəs\ *n*

⁴fine *adv* **1** : in a fine manner **2** : very well ⟨did *fine* on the test⟩ ⟨I liked it *fine*⟩

⁵fi·ne \'fē-(,)nā\ *n* : ¹END 1b — used as a direction in music to mark the closing point after a repeat [Italian, from Latin *finis* "end, limit"]

fine art *n* : art (as painting, sculpture, or music) concerned mainly with the creation of beautiful objects — usually used in plural

fin·ery \'fīn-(ə-)rē\ *n, pl* **-er·ies** : showy clothing and jewels

¹fi·nesse \fə-'nes\ *n* : skillful or delicate handling or artistry

²finesse *vb* **fi·nessed; fi·ness·ing** : to bring about a result by finesse

fin·fish \'fin-,fish\ *n* : ¹FISH 1b

¹fin·ger \'fiŋ-gər\ *n* **1** : one of the five divisions of the end of the hand; *esp* : one other than the thumb **2 a** : something that resembles or does the work of a finger **b** : a part of a glove into which a finger is inserted **3** : the width of a finger — **fin·gered** \-gərd\ *adj* — **fin·ger·like** \-gər-,līk\ *adj*

²finger *vb* **fin·gered; fin·ger·ing** \-g(ə-)riŋ\ **1** : to touch with the fingers : HANDLE **2** : to perform with the fingers or with a certain fingering

fin·ger·board \'fiŋ-gər-,bō(ə)rd, -,bȯ(ə)rd\ *n* : the part of a stringed instrument against which the fingers press the strings to vary the pitch

finger bowl *n* : a small bowl of water for rinsing the fingers at the table

finger food *n* : a food (as a carrot stick) that is meant to be picked up with the fingers and eaten

finger hole *n* : a hole in the tube of a wind instrument that may be covered with the finger or left open to change the tone

fin·ger·ing \'fiŋ-g(ə-)riŋ\ *n* **1 a** : the method of using the fingers in playing an instrument **b** : the marking on a piece of music that shows what fingers are to be used **2** : the act or process of handling or touching with fingers

fin·ger·nail \'fiŋ-gər-,nāl, ,fiŋ-gər-'nā(ə)l\ *n* : the nail of a finger

finger painting *n* **1** : a method of spreading paint on wet paper chiefly with the fingers **2** : a picture produced by finger painting

fin·ger·print \'fiŋ-gər-,print\ *n* : the pattern of marks made by pressing the tip of a finger on a surface; *esp* : a pattern of marks in ink of the lines on the tip of a finger taken for the purpose of identification — **fingerprint** *vb* — **fin·ger·print·ing** \-,prin-tiŋ\ *n*

fin·ger·tip \-,tip\ *n* : the tip of a finger

fin·icky \'fin-i-kē\ *adj* : very hard to please : FUSSY ⟨a *finicky* eater⟩ — **fin·ick·i·ness** *n*

fin·is \'fin-əs, 'fī-nəs\ *n* : ¹END 2a, CONCLUSION

¹fin·ish \'fin-ish\ *vb* **1** : to bring or come to an end : TERMINATE, ²COMPLETE **2** : to put a final coat or surface on

3 : to end a competition in a specified position ⟨*finished* third in the race⟩ **4** : to come to the end of a course, task, or undertaking [Middle English *finisshen* "to finish," from early French *finiss-, finir* (same meaning), derived from Latin *finis* "end, limit" — related to DEFINE, FINAL, INFINITY] — **fin·ish·er** *n*

²finish *n* **1** : ¹END 2a, CONCLUSION **2** : the final coating on a surface or the appearance given by a final coating

finish line *n* : a line marking the end of a racecourse

fi·nite \'fī-,nīt\ *adj* **1** : having certain limits : limited in scope or nature : not infinite **2** : limited in grammatical person and number ⟨a *finite* verb⟩ — **fi·nite·ly** *adv* — **fi·nite·ness** *n*

Finn \'fin\ *n* : a person born or living in Finland

fin·nan had·die \,fin-ən-'had-ē\ *n* : smoked haddock

¹Finn·ish \'fin-ish\ *adj* : of, relating to, or characteristic of Finland, the Finns, or Finnish

²Finnish *n* : a language of the Finns

fin·ny \'fin-ē\ *adj* : resembling or having fins

fin whale *n* : a baleen whale that may reach a length of over 70 feet (21 meters)

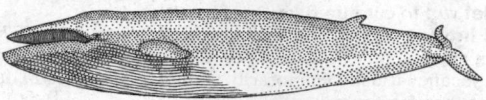

fin whale

fiord *variant of* FJORD

fir \'fər\ *n* **1** : any of various usually large evergreen trees related to the pines some of which yield useful lumber or resins **2** : the wood of a fir

¹fire \'fī(ə)r\ *n* **1** : the light and heat and especially the flame produced by burning **2** : eager liveliness : ENTHUSIASM **3** : fuel that is burning (as in a fireplace or stove) **4** : the destructive burning of something (as a building or a forest) **5** : the shooting of guns — **on fire** **1** : in the process of burning **2** : ARDENT 1, EAGER — **under fire** **1** : exposed to the firing of enemy guns **2** : under attack

²fire *vb* **fired; fir·ing** **1 a** : to set on fire : KINDLE, IGNITE **b** : ¹STIR 3, ENLIVEN ⟨a story to *fire* the imagination⟩ ⟨all *fired* up⟩ **2** : to dismiss from employment **3** : to cause to explode ⟨*fire* dynamite⟩ **4 a** : to cause to be driven from or as if from a gun : LAUNCH ⟨*fire* an arrow⟩ ⟨*fire* a rocket⟩ **b** : to shoot off a firearm : DISCHARGE **c** : to throw with speed : HURL ⟨*fired* the ball to first base⟩ **5 a** : to subject to great heat ⟨*fire* pottery⟩ **b** : to feed the fire of ⟨*fire* a furnace⟩ **6 a** : to begin to burn **b** : to have fuel (as in a cylinder of an engine) ignite at the proper time **7** : to transmit a nerve impulse ⟨the neuron *fired*⟩ — **fir·er** *n*

fire alarm *n* : an alarm sounded to signal the outbreak of a fire; *also* : a device for sounding such an alarm

fire ant *n* : any of a genus of fiercely stinging ants; *esp* : IMPORTED FIRE ANT

fire·arm \'fī(ə)r-,ärm\ *n* : a weapon from which a shot is discharged by gunpowder — usually used only of small arms

fire·ball \-,bȯl\ *n* **1** : a ball of fire **2** : a very bright meteor **3** : the glowing cloud of vapor and dust created by a nuclear explosion

fire·boat \-,bōt\ *n* : a boat equipped for fighting fires

fire·box \-,bäks\ *n* **1** : a chamber (as of a furnace) that contains a fire **2** : a box containing a fire alarm

fire·brand \-,brand\ *n* **1** : a piece of burning wood **2** : AGITATOR 1

fire·break \-,brāk\ *n* : a barrier of cleared or plowed land intended to stop the spread of a forest or grass fire

fire·brick \-,brik\ *n* : a brick capable of resisting great heat and used for lining furnaces or fireplaces

fire·bug \-ˌbəg\ *n* : a person who deliberately sets destructive fires : ARSONIST

fire·clay \-ˌklā\ *n* : clay capable of resisting high temperatures that is used especially for firebrick or heat-resistant containers

fire·crack·er \-ˌkrak-ər\ *n* : a paper tube containing an explosive and set off to make a noise

fired \'fī(ə)rd\ *adj* : using a specified fuel ⟨an oil-*fired* furnace⟩

fire·damp \-ˌdamp\ *n* : a flammable mine gas that consists chiefly of methane; *also* : the explosive mixture of this gas with air

fire·dog \-ˌdòg\ *n* : ANDIRON

fire drill *n* : a practice drill in putting out fires or in getting out of a building in case of fire

fire engine *n* : FIRE TRUCK

fire escape *n* : a stairway or ladder that provides a means of escape from a building in case of fire

fire extinguisher *n* : something used to put out a fire; *esp* : a portable or wheeled device for putting out small fires by spraying fire-extinguishing chemicals

firefighter *n* : a member of a company organized to fight fires — **firefighting** *n*

fire·fly \'fī(ə)r-ˌflī\ *n* : any of numerous night-flying beetles that produce a bright soft flashing light for courtship purposes

fire·house \-ˌhaús\ *n* : FIRE STATION

fire irons *n pl* : tools for tending a fire in a fireplace

fire·light \'fī(ə)r-ˌlīt\ *n* : the light of a fire and especially of one in a fireplace

fire line *n* : FIREBREAK

fire·man \-mən\ *n* **1** : FIREFIGHTER **2** : a person who tends fires : STOKER

fire extinguisher

fire·place \-ˌplās\ *n* **1** : a framed opening in a chimney to hold an open fire **2** : an outdoor structure of brick, stone, or metal for an open fire

fire·plug \-ˌpləg\ *n* : HYDRANT

fire·pow·er \-ˌpaú(-ə)r\ *n* : the ability to deliver gunfire or warheads on a target

¹**fire·proof** \-'prüf\ *adj* : not easily burned : made safe against fire

²**fireproof** *vb* : to make fireproof

fireship *n* : a ship carrying flammable materials or explosives that is sent among the enemy's ships and set on fire to destroy them

fire·side \'fī(ə)r-ˌsīd\ *n* **1** : a place near the hearth **2** : ¹HOME 1a

fire station *n* : a building housing fire trucks and usually firefighters

fire tower *n* : a tower (as in a forest) from which a watch for fires is kept

fire·trap \'fī(ə)r-ˌtrap\ *n* : a building or place that is apt to catch on fire or is difficult to escape from in case of fire

fire truck *n* : an automotive vehicle equipped for fighting fires

fire wall *n* **1** : a wall for preventing the spread of fire **2** *usually* **fire·wall** \'fīr-ˌwòl\ : computer hardware or software that limits access by outside users on a network

fire·weed \'fī(ə)r-ˌwēd\ *n* : a plant with pinkish purple flowers that grows especially in clearings or burned areas

fire·wood \-ˌwúd\ *n* : wood cut for fuel

fire·work \-ˌwərk\ *n* **1** : a device that makes a display of light or noise by the burning of explosive or flammable materials **2** *pl* : a display of fireworks **3** *pl* : a display of temper

fir·ing squad \'fī(ə)r-iŋ-\ *n* **1** : a military unit assigned to fire shots over the grave of one buried with military honors **2** : a military unit assigned to carry out a sentence of death by shooting

firkin

fir·kin \'fər-kən\ *n* : a small wooden container or barrel

¹**firm** \'fərm\ *adj* **1 a** : solidly fixed in place **b** : not weak or uncertain : VIGOROUS **c** : having a solid or compact texture **2 a** : not likely to be changed ⟨a *firm* offer⟩ **b** : not easily moved or disturbed : STEADFAST ⟨a *firm* believer⟩ **3** : indicating firmness or determination [Middle English *ferm* "firm, secure," from early French *ferm* (same meaning), from Latin *firmus* "firm, secure, solid"] **synonyms** see HARD — **firm·ly** *adv* — **firm·ness** *n*

²**firm** *adv* : in a firm manner ⟨stood *firm*⟩

³**firm** *vb* **1 a** : to make secure ⟨*firm* your grip on the racket⟩ **b** : to make solid or compact ⟨*firm* the soil⟩ **2** : to become firm

⁴**firm** *n* : a business organization ⟨law *firm*⟩ [from German *firma* "the name or sign under which a company does business," from Italian *firma* "signature," derived from Latin *firmare* "to make firm, to approve, to sign," from *firmus* "firm, secure"]

fir·ma·ment \'fər-mə-mənt\ *n* : the arch of the sky : HEAVENS

firm·ware \'fərm-ˌwa(ə)r, -ˌwe(ə)r\ *n* : computer programs contained permanently in a hardware device (as a read-only memory)

¹**first** \'fərst\ *adj* **1** — see NUMBER table **2** : coming before all others in time, order, or importance: as **a** : being the earliest **b** : being the lowest forward gear or speed of a motor vehicle **c** : having or playing the principal part of a group of instruments ⟨*first* oboe⟩

²**first** *adv* **1 a** : before any other in time, space, or importance **b** : for the first time **2** : rather than something else ⟨surrender? We will die *first*⟩

³**first** *n* **1** — see NUMBER table **2 a** : the first forward gear or speed of a motor vehicle **b** : the winning place in a competition or contest **3** : FIRST BASE — **at first** : in the beginning

first aid *n* : emergency treatment given to an ill or injured person

first base *n* : the base that must be touched first by a base runner in baseball; *also* : the position of the player defending the area around first base

first baseman *n* : the player defending the area around first base

first·born \'fərs(t)-'bò(ə)rn\ *adj* : born first : ELDEST — **firstborn** *n*

first–class *adj* **1** : of or relating to first class **2** : of the highest quality : EXCELLENT ⟨a *first-class* meal⟩

first class *n* : the best or highest group in a classification

first cousin *n* : COUSIN 1a

first–degree burn *n* : a mild burn marked by heat, pain, and reddening of the burned surface but not showing blistering or charring of tissues

first·hand \'fərst-'hand\ *adj* : coming directly from the original source ⟨a *firsthand* account of the war⟩ — **firsthand** *adv*

first lady *n, often cap F&L* : the wife or hostess of the male chief executive of a state or nation

first lieutenant *n* : a military commissioned officer with a rank just below that of captain

first·ling \'fərst-liŋ\ *n* : one that comes or is produced first

first·ly \'fərst-lē\ *adv* : in the first place

\ə\ abut	\aú\ out	\i\ tip	\ò\ saw	\ú\ foot
\ər\ further	\ch\ chin	\ī\ life	\òi\ coin	\y\ yet
\a\ mat	\e\ pet	\j\ job	\th\ thin	\yü\ few
\ā\ take	\ē\ easy	\ŋ\ sing	\th\ this	\yú\ cure
\ä\ cot, cart	\g\ go	\ō\ bone	\ü\ food	\zh\ vision

first person *n* **1** : a set of words or forms (as pronouns or verb forms) referring to the person speaking or writing them **2** : a writing style making use of pronouns and verbs of the first person ⟨*first person* narration⟩

first–rate \'fərst-'rāt\ *adj* : of the first order of size, importance, or quality — **first–rate** *adv*

first re·spond·er \-ri-'spän-dər\ *n* : a person (as a police officer or an EMT) who is among those responsible for going immediately to the scene of an accident or emergency to provide assistance

first sergeant *n* **1** : a noncommissioned officer who is the chief assistant to a military commander **2** : a noncommissioned officer with the rank just below sergeant major in the army and the marines

firth \'fərth\ *n* : a narrow arm of the sea

fis·cal \'fis-kəl\ *adj* **1** : of or relating to public finances **2** : of or relating to financial matters — **fis·cal·ly** \-kə-lē\ *adv*

¹**fish** \'fish\ *n, pl* **fish** *or* **fish·es** **1 a** : a water-dwelling animal — usually used in combination ⟨star*fish*⟩ ⟨cuttle*fish*⟩ **b** : a cold-blooded vertebrate animal with a typically long scaly tapering body, limbs developed as fins, and a vertical tail fin that lives and breathes in water **2** : the flesh of fish used as food — **fish·like** \-ˌlīk\ *adj*

²**fish** *vb* **1** : to catch or try to catch fish **2 a** : to catch or try to catch fish in ⟨*fish* the stream⟩ **b** : to search for something underwater ⟨*fishing* for pearls⟩ **3** : to seek something by or as if by groping or feeling ⟨*fished* for compliments⟩ ⟨*fished* in his pocket for change⟩

fish–and–chips *n* : fried fish and french fried potatoes

fish·er \'fish-ər\ *n* **1** : one that fishes **2** : a dark brown North American flesh-eating mammal related to the weasels; *also* : its valuable fur or pelt

fish·er·man \'fish-ər-mən\ *n* **1** : a person who fishes **2** : a ship used in commercial fishing

fish·ery \'fish-(ə-)rē\ *n, pl* **-er·ies** **1** : the activity or business of fishing **2** : a place or establishment for catching fish

fish hawk *n* : OSPREY

fish·hook \'fish-ˌhu̇k\ *n* : a usually barbed hook for catching fish

fish ladder *n* : an arrangement of pools by which fish can pass around a dam

fish–liver oil *n* : a fatty oil from fish livers (as of cod, halibut, and sharks) used as a source of vitamin A and formerly of vitamin D

fish·net \'fish-ˌnet\ *n* : a net for catching fish

fish·pond \-ˌpänd\ *n* : a pond stocked with fish

fish protein concentrate *n* : a nearly colorless and tasteless powder that is obtained from ground whole fish, is rich in protein, and is added to food

fish stick *n* : a small elongated breaded fillet of fish

fishy \'fish-ē\ *adj* **fish·i·er; -est** **1** : of, relating to, or resembling fish ⟨a *fishy* odor⟩ **2** : arousing doubt or suspicion : QUESTIONABLE ⟨the story sounds *fishy* to me⟩

¹**fis·sion** \'fish-ən *also* 'fizh-\ *n* **1** : a splitting or breaking up into parts **2** : a method of reproduction in which a living cell or body divides into two or more parts each of which grows into a whole new individual **3** : the splitting of an atomic nucleus resulting in the release of large amounts of energy

²**fission** *vb* **fis·sioned; fis·sion·ing** \'fish-(ə-)niŋ, 'fizh-\ : to go through or cause to go through fission

fis·sion·able \'fish-(ə-)nə-bəl, 'fizh-\ *adj* : capable of going through fission ⟨*fissionable* material⟩

fis·sure \'fish-ər\ *n* **1** : a narrow opening or crack ⟨a *fissure* in rock⟩ **2** : a narrow natural space between body parts (as bones of the skull) or in the material making up an organ — **fissure** *vb*

fist \'fist\ *n* **1** : the hand clenched with fingers doubled into the palm **2** : ¹INDEX 4

fist bump *n* : a gesture in which two people bump their fists together (as in greeting or celebration) — **fist–bump** *vb*

fist·i·cuffs \'fis-ti-ˌkəfs\ *n pl* : a fight with fists

fis·tu·la \'fis-chə-lə\ *n, pl* **fis·tu·las** *or* **fis·tu·lae** \-ˌlē, -ˌlī\ : an abnormal passage leading from an abscess or hollow organ

¹**fit** \'fit\ *adj* **fit·ter; fit·test** **1** : suitable for a particular purpose ⟨water *fit* for drinking⟩; *esp* : so adapted to the environment as to be capable of surviving — often used in the phrase *survival of the fittest* **2** : acceptable from a particular point of view : PROPER ⟨a movie *fit* for the whole family⟩ **3** : ¹READY 1, PREPARED ⟨get the ship *fit* for sea⟩ **4** : QUALIFIED 1, COMPETENT ⟨*fit* for the job⟩ **5** : sound physically and mentally : HEALTHY [Middle English *fit* "suitable to a particular purpose"] — **fit·ness** *n*

synonyms FIT, PROPER, SUITABLE, APPROPRIATE mean right with respect to the nature, condition, or use of the thing referred to. FIT suggests that something has been made right or is qualified for use or action ⟨a rebuilt bike now *fit* for riding⟩. PROPER suggests that something is right because of its basic nature ⟨a *proper* diet⟩ or because it agrees with some custom or rule ⟨*proper* dress is required⟩. SUITABLE suggests that something meets the requirements of the situation ⟨find a *suitable* container for the mixture⟩. APPROPRIATE suggests that something is especially suitable for the purpose ⟨furniture that would be *appropriate* in a large living room⟩.

²**fit** *n* **1** : a sudden violent attack of a disease or condition (as epilepsy) especially when marked by convulsions or loss of consciousness **2** : a sudden outburst (as of laughter or anger) [Old English *fitt* "strife"]

³**fit** *vb* **fit·ted** *or* **fit; fit·ting** **1** : to be suitable for or to : BEFIT **2 a** : to be of the right size and shape ⟨the suit *fits*⟩ **b** : to insert or adjust until correctly in place **c** : to make a place or room for ⟨*fit* another chair⟩ **3** : to be in agreement with ⟨his story *fits* the facts⟩ **4 a** : to make ready : PREPARE **b** : to bring to a required form and size : ADJUST **5** : to supply what is needed for : EQUIP ⟨*fit* out an expedition⟩ **6** : to be in harmony or agreement : BELONG — often used with *in*

⁴**fit** *n* **1** : the way something fits ⟨a tight *fit*⟩ **2** : a piece of clothing that fits

fit·ful \'fit-fəl\ *adj* : not regular : RESTLESS ⟨*fitful* sleep⟩ — **fit·ful·ly** \-fə-lē\ *adv* — **fit·ful·ness** *n*

fitted *adj* **1** : SUITABLE **2** : shaped for a close fit ⟨*fitted* sheets⟩

fit·ter \'fit-ər\ *n* : one that fits; *esp* : a person who adjusts articles of clothing being tried on by a customer

¹**fit·ting** \'fit-iŋ\ *adj* : ²APPROPRIATE, SUITABLE ⟨a *fitting* gift⟩ — **fit·ting·ly** *adv* — **fit·ting·ness** *n*

²**fitting** *n* **1** : a trying on of clothes being made or altered **2** : a small accessory part ⟨a pipe *fitting*⟩

five \'fīv\ *n* **1** — see NUMBER table **2** : the fifth in a set or series **3** : something having five units or members; *esp* : a basketball team **4** : a 5-dollar bill **5** : a slapping of extended hands by two people (as in greeting or celebration) ⟨I slapped him *five* after he scored⟩ — **five** *adj or pron*

five–and–ten \ˌfī-vən-'ten\ *also* **five–and–dime** \-vən-'dīm\ *n* : a store selling inexpensive articles

¹**fix** \'fiks\ *vb* **1 a** : to make firm, stable, or fast **b** : to give a permanent or final form to **c** : to change into a stable or useful form ⟨bacteria that *fix* nitrogen⟩ **d** : ¹AFFIX 1, ATTACH **2** : to hold or direct steadily ⟨*fixed* his eyes on the stage⟩ **3** : to set or place definitely : ESTABLISH ⟨*fix* the date of a meeting⟩ **4** : to get ready : PREPARE ⟨*fix* dinner⟩ **5** : ²REPAIR 1 **6 a** : to get even with **b** : to influence the outcome of (as a sports contest) dishonestly **7** : to get set : be on the verge ⟨we're *fixing* to go⟩ [Middle English *fixen* "to fix, make firm," from Latin *fixus*, past participle of *figere* "to fasten, fix" — related to CRUCIFIX, CRUCIFY] — **fix·able** \'fik-sə-bəl\ *adj*

²**fix** *n* **1** : a position of difficulty or embarrassment : PREDICAMENT **2** : the position (as of a ship) decided upon by calculations and compass, observations, or radio; *also* : a deciding upon of one's position **3 a** : an act of bribery or fraud **b** : a sports contest whose outcome has been ar-

ranged in advance **4** : a dose of something strongly desired or craved ⟨a chocolate *fix*⟩; *esp* : a shot of a narcotic
fix·a·tion \fik-ˈsā-shən\ *n* **1** : the act, process, or result of fixing **2** : a state of concern or attachment especially when abnormal and lasting for a long time
fix·a·tive \ˈfik-sət-iv\ *n* : something that fixes or sets
fixed \ˈfikst\ *adj* **1 a** : firmly placed or fastened ⟨a *fixed* gaze⟩ **b** : not changing : SETTLED ⟨a *fixed* income⟩ **2** : supplied with a definite amount of something needed ⟨well *fixed* for food⟩ — **fix·ed·ly** \ˈfik-səd-lē\ *adv* — **fix·ed·ness** \ˈfik-səd-nəs\ *n*
fixed star *n* : a star so distant that its motion can be measured only by very exact observations over long periods
fix·er \ˈfik-sər\ *n* **1** : one that fixes **2** : SODIUM THIOSULFATE; *also* : a solution of sodium thiosulfate
fix·ing \ˈfik-sing, *sense 2 is often* -sənz\ *n* **1** : a putting in permanent form **2** *pl* : something that decorates or completes ⟨turkey with all the *fixings*⟩
fix·i·ty \ˈfik-sət-ē\ *n, pl* **-ties** **1** : the quality or state of being fixed **2** : something that is fixed
fix·ture \ˈfiks-chər\ *n* **1** : the act of fixing : the state of being fixed **2** : something attached as a permanent part ⟨bathroom *fixtures*⟩ **3** : one firmly established in a place
¹**fizz** \ˈfiz\ *vb* : to make a hissing or sputtering sound
²**fizz** *n* **1** : a hissing sound **2** : a bubbling drink — **fizzy** \ˈfiz-ē\ *adj*
fiz·zle \ˈfiz-əl\ *vb* **fiz·zled; fiz·zling** \-(ə-)ling\ : to fail after a good start — often used with *out* — **fizzle** *n*
fjord *also* **fiord** \fē-ˈôrd\ *n* : a narrow inlet of the sea between cliffs or steep slopes [Norwegian]

fjord

flab·ber·gast \ˈflab-ər-ˌgast\ *vb* : ASTONISH, DUMBFOUND
flab·by \ˈflab-ē\ *adj* **flab·bi·er; -est** : not hard and firm : SOFT — **flab·bi·ly** \ˈflab-ə-lē\ *adv* — **flab·bi·ness** \ˈflab-ē-nəs\ *n*
flac·cid \ˈflas-əd, ˈflak-səd\ *adj* : not firm or stiff
¹**flag** \ˈflag\ *n* : any of various irises; *esp* : a wild iris [Middle English *flagge* "reed"]
²**flag** *n* **1** : a piece of cloth with a special design that is used as a symbol (as of a nation) or for signaling **2** : something used like a flag to signal or attract attention [probably akin to *fag* "end of cloth"]
³**flag** *vb* **flagged; flag·ging** : to signal with or as if with a flag; *esp* : to signal to stop ⟨*flag* a taxi⟩
⁴**flag** *vb* **flagged; flag·ging** **1** : to be limp : DROOP **2** : to become weak ⟨his hope *flagged*⟩ [probably from ²flag]
⁵**flag** *n* **1** : a hard stone that easily splits into flat pieces **2** : a piece of flag used for paving [Middle English *flagge* "a piece of turf, a flat paving stone"]
⁶**flag** *vb* **flagged; flag·ging** : to pave (as a walk) with flags
Flag Day *n* : June 14 observed in some states as the anniversary of the adoption of the U.S. flag in 1777
¹**flag·el·late** \ˈflaj-ə-ˌlāt\ *vb* **-lat·ed; -lat·ing** : ¹WHIP 2 — **flag·el·la·tion** \ˌflaj-ə-ˈlā-shən\ *n*
²**flag·el·late** \ˈflaj-ə-lət, -ˌlāt; flə-ˈjel-ət\ *adj* **1 a** *or* **flag·el·lat·ed** \ˈflaj-ə-ˌlāt-əd\ : having flagella **b** : shaped like a flagellum **2** : of, relating to, or caused by flagellates
³**flagellate** \like ²\ *n* : a protozoan or alga having flagella
fla·gel·lum \flə-ˈjel-əm\ *n, pl* **-gel·la** \-ˈjel-ə\ *also* **-gel·lums** : a long whiplike structure by which some tiny plants and animals move — **fla·gel·lar** \-ˈjel-ər\ *adj*
fla·geo·let \ˌflaj-ə-ˈlet\ *n* : a musical instrument resembling a flute but with a whistle mouthpiece
flag·ging \ˈflag-ing\ *n* : a pavement of flagstones

flag·man \ˈflag-mən\ *n* : a person who signals with or as if with a flag
flag·on \ˈflag-ən\ *n* : a container for liquids usually having a handle, spout, and lid
flag·pole \ˈflag-ˌpōl\ *n* : a pole from which a flag flies
flag rank *n* : any of the ranks in the navy or coast guard above a captain
fla·grant \ˈflā-grənt\ *adj* : so bad as to be impossible to overlook : OUTRAGEOUS ⟨a *flagrant* lie⟩ — **fla·grant·ly** *adv*
flag·ship \ˈflag-ˌship\ *n* **1** : the ship carrying the commander of a group of ships and flying the flag that tells the commander's rank **2** : the best, largest, or most important one of a group of things ⟨the store is the company's *flagship*⟩
flag·staff \-ˌstaf\ *n* : FLAGPOLE
flag·stone \-ˌstōn\ *n* : ⁵FLAG 2

flagon

¹**flail** \ˈflā(ə)l\ *n* : a tool for threshing grain by hand
²**flail** *vb* **1** : to strike with or as if with a flail **2** : to move or wave about as if swinging a flail ⟨*flailed* their arms⟩
flair \ˈfla(ə)r, ˈfle(ə)r\ *n* : natural ability
flak *also* **flack** \ˈflak\ *n, pl* **flak** *also* **flack** **1** : antiaircraft guns or the bursting shells fired from them **2** : severe criticism [derived from the German word for "antiaircraft guns," from the first letters of *Flieger* "flier" and *Abwehr* "defense" and *Kanonen* "cannons"]
¹**flake** \ˈflāk\ *n* : a small thin flat usually loose piece : CHIP
²**flake** *vb* **flaked; flak·ing** : to form or separate into flakes
flaky \ˈflā-kē\ *adj* **flak·i·er; -est** **1** : consisting of flakes **2** : tending to flake ⟨pie with a crisp *flaky* crust⟩ **3** : odd or strange in behavior — **flak·i·ly** \-kə-lē\ *adv* — **flak·i·ness** \-kē-nəs\ *n*
flam·beau \ˈflam-ˌbō\ *n, pl* **flam·beaux** \-ˌbōz\ *or* **flam·beaus** : a flaming torch
flam·boy·ance \flam-ˈbȯi-ən(t)s\ *n* : the quality or state of being flamboyant
flam·boy·ant \flam-ˈbȯi-ənt\ *adj* : tending to make a striking display : SHOWY — **flam·boy·ant·ly** *adv*
¹**flame** \ˈflām\ *n* **1** : the glowing gas that makes up part of a fire **2** : a state of burning brightly ⟨the car burst into *flame*⟩ ⟨a building in *flames*⟩ **3** : a condition or appearance suggesting a flame **4** : the person one is in love with : SWEETHEART ⟨an old *flame*⟩ **5** : a hostile or rude electronic message ⟨sent me a *flame* by e-mail⟩
²**flame** *vb* **flamed; flam·ing** **1** : to burn with a flame : BLAZE **2** : to burst or break out violently ⟨*flaming* with anger⟩ **3** : to shine brightly **4** : to treat or affect by flame or fire; *esp* : to sterilize by a flame **5** : to send a hostile or rude electronic message to or about
fla·min·go \flə-ˈmiŋ-gō\ *n, pl* **-gos** *also* **-goes** : any of several rosy-white birds with scarlet wings, a very long neck and legs, and a broad bill bent down at the end that are often found wading in shallow water [from Portuguese *flamingo* "flamingo," from Spanish *flamenco* "flamingo," derived from Latin *flamma* "flame"; so called from the fiery red feathers on the underside of the wings]
flam·ma·ble \ˈflam-ə-bəl\ *adj* : capable of being easily set on

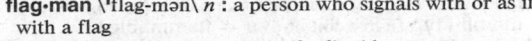

flamingo

\ə\ **abut**	\aú\ **out**	\i\ **tip**	\ȯ\ **saw**	\ú\ **foot**
\ər\ **further**	\ch\ **chin**	\ī\ **life**	\ȯi\ **coin**	\y\ **yet**
\a\ **mat**	\e\ **pet**	\j\ **job**	\th\ **thin**	\yü\ **few**
\ā\ **take**	\ē\ **easy**	\ŋ\ **sing**	\th\ **this**	\yú\ **cure**
\ä\ **cot, cart**	\g\ **go**	\ō\ **bone**	\ü\ **food**	\zh\ **vision**

fire and of burning rapidly ⟨a *flammable* liquid⟩ — **flam-ma·bil·i·ty** \ˌflam-ə-'bil-ət-ē\ *n* — **flammable** *n*

flange \'flanj\ *n* : a rib or rim used for strength, for guiding, or for attachment to another object ⟨the *flange* on a locomotive wheel⟩ — **flanged** \'flanjd\ *adj*

¹**flank** \'flaŋk\ *n* **1 a** : the fleshy part of the side between the ribs and the hip **b** : a cut of meat from this part of an animal **2 a** : ¹SIDE 2 **b** : the right or left of a military formation

²**flank** *vb* **1** : to be located at the side of : BORDER **2** : to protect a flank of **3** : to attack or threaten the flank of (as a body of troops)

flank·er \'flaŋ-kər\ *n* **1** : one that flanks **2** : a football player stationed wide of the formation especially as a pass receiver

flan·nel \'flan-ᵊl\ *n* **1** : a soft cloth made of wool or cotton **2** *pl* : flannel underwear or trousers

flan·nel·ette \ˌflan-ᵊl-'et\ *n* : a cotton flannel

¹**flap** \'flap\ *n* **1** : ²SLAP **1 2** : a broad, limber, or flat piece that hangs loose (as on a pocket or envelope) **3** : the motion or sound of a flap **4** : a movable part of an airplane wing that is attached to the trailing edge of the wing and that is used to increase lift or drag

²**flap** *vb* **flapped; flap·ping 1** : ²SLAP 1a **2** : to move or cause to move with a beating motion ⟨*flapping* its wings⟩

flap·jack \'flap-ˌjak\ *n* : PANCAKE

¹**flare** \'fla(ə)r, 'fle(ə)r\ *n* **1** : a fire or blaze of light used to signal, light up something, or attract attention; *also* : a device or material that produces such a flare **2** : an unsteady glaring light **3** : FLARE-UP **4** : a spreading outward; *also* : a place or part that spreads **5** *pl* : bell-bottom trousers

²**flare** *vb* **flared; flar·ing 1** : to burn with an unsteady flame **2 a** : to shine or blaze suddenly **b** : to become suddenly excited or angry ⟨*flare* up⟩ **3** : to open or spread outward ⟨pants that *flare* at the bottom⟩

flare–up \'fla(ə)r-ˌəp, 'fle(ə)r-\ *n* : a sudden burst (as of flame or anger)

¹**flash** \'flash\ *vb* **1** : to shine in or like a sudden flame ⟨lightning *flashed*⟩ ⟨her eyes *flashed* with excitement⟩ **2** : to send out in or as if in flashes ⟨*flash* a message⟩ **3** : to appear or pass very suddenly ⟨a car *flashed* by⟩ **4** : to gleam or glow in sudden bursts **5** : to expose to view usually briefly ⟨*flash* a badge⟩

Word History The origin of the word *flash* is uncertain, though it rhymes with a number of other verbs that also mean forceful, often violent movement that may come to a quick end: *dash, lash, crash, slash, clash, gash, bash, splash, smash.* These words turn up in English over a fairly long period of time, from *dash*—the only word in the group with a likely foreign source—in the 14th century to *smash* in the 18th century. The element *-ash* has thus provided a kind of model for new words. The initial *fl-* that is added to *-ash* to make *flash* is also heard in words meaning quick movement, as *flee, fly, flicker,* and *flutter.* [Middle English *flaschen*]

²**flash** *n* **1 a** : a sudden burst of light, flame, or heat **b** : a movement of a flag or light in signaling **2** : a sudden and brilliant burst ⟨a *flash* of wit⟩ **3** : a brief time **4** : one that attracts notice; *esp* : an outstanding athlete **5** : a device for producing a brief and very bright flash of light for taking photographs

³**flash** *adj* **1** : beginning suddenly and lasting only a short time ⟨a *flash* fire⟩ **2** : having or using a solid-state data storage technology that retains data even without a connection to a power source

flash·back \'flash-ˌbak\ *n* **1** : the introduction of a past event into a story or motion picture; *also* : this past event **2** : a past incident recurring clearly in the mind

flash·bulb \-ˌbəlb\ *n* : an electric bulb that can be used only once to produce a brief and very bright flash for taking photographs

flash card *n* : a card having words, numbers, or pictures that is held up briefly by a teacher to a class during drills (as in spelling or arithmetic)

flash drive *n* : a data storage device that uses flash memory; *specif* : a small rectangular device that is designed to be plugged into a USB port on a computer and is often used for transferring files from one computer to another — called also *jump drive, thumb drive*

flash·er \'flash-ər\ *n* : BLINKER 1

flash·light \'flash-ˌlīt\ *n* : a small battery-operated portable electric light

flash memory *n* : a computer memory chip that retains its data even without a connection to a power source

flashy \'flash-ē\ *adj* **flash·i·er; -est** : GAUDY, SHOWY — **flash·i·ly** \'flash-ə-lē\ *adv* — **flash·i·ness** \'flash-ē-nəs\ *n*

flask \'flask\ *n* : a container shaped like a flattened bottle

¹**flat** *adj* **flat·ter; flat·test 1** : having a smooth level surface ⟨*flat* ground⟩ **2** : having a smooth even surface **3** : spread out on or along a surface ⟨was *flat* on the ground⟩ **4** : having a broad smooth surface and little thickness ⟨shoes with *flat* heels⟩ **5** : ABSOLUTE 3 ⟨a *flat* refusal⟩ **6** : FIXED 1b, UNCHANGING ⟨charge a *flat* rate⟩ **7** : ²EXACT 1 ⟨in two minutes *flat*⟩ **8 a** : lacking in interest or flavor ⟨a *flat* story⟩ ⟨the stew tastes *flat*⟩ **b** : lacking bubbles or sparkle ⟨*flat* ginger ale⟩ **c** : lacking any rise or decline ⟨sales were *flat*⟩ **9** : being deflated — used of tires **10 a** : lower than the true pitch **b** : lower by a half step ⟨tone of A *flat*⟩ **11** : free from gloss ⟨*flat* paint⟩ *synonyms* see LEVEL — **flat·ly** *adv* — **flat·ness** *n*

²**flat** \'flat\ *n* **1** : a level surface of land : PLAIN **2** : a flat part or surface **3 a** : a musical tone one half step lower than a specified tone **b** : a character ♭ before a note indicating that it is to be a flat **4** : a shallow box in which seedlings are started **5** : a shoe or slipper having a flat heel or no heel **6** *chiefly British* : an apartment on one floor **7** : a deflated tire

³**flat** *adv* **1** : on or against a flat surface ⟨lie *flat*⟩ **2** : as much as possible : COMPLETELY ⟨was *flat* broke⟩ **3** : below the true musical pitch

⁴**flat** *vb* **flat·ted; flat·ting** : to lower in pitch especially by a half step

¹**flat·bed** \'flat-ˌbed\ *adj* : having a horizontal bed on which material rests ⟨a *flatbed* scanner⟩

²**flatbed** *n* : a truck or trailer with a body in the form of a platform or shallow box

flat·boat \-ˌbōt\ *n* : a boat with a flat bottom and square ends used on rivers for carrying freight

flat·car \-ˌkär\ *n* : a railroad freight car without sides or roof

flat·fish \-ˌfish\ *n* : any of a group of marine fishes (as halibuts, flounders, or soles) that as adults swim on one side of the flattened body and have both eyes on the upper side

flatboat

flat·foot \-ˌfüt, -'füt\ *n, pl* **flat·feet** \-ˌfēt, -'fēt\ **1** : a condition in which the main arch of the foot is so flattened that the entire sole rests upon the ground **2** : a foot affected with flatfoot — **flat–foot·ed** \-ˌfüt-əd, -'füt-əd\ *adj*

flat·iron \-ˌī(-ə)rn\ *n* : ¹IRON 2c

flat·ten \'flat-ᵊn\ *vb* **flat·tened; flat·ten·ing** \'flat-niŋ, -ᵊn-iŋ\ : to make or become flat

flat·ter \'flat-ər\ *vb* **1** : to praise too much and not sincerely **2** : to judge oneself as better than another ⟨I *flatter* myself on my skill in dancing⟩ **3** : to represent too attractively ⟨a picture that *flatters* me⟩ — **flat·ter·er** \-ər-ər\ *n* — **flat·ter·ing·ly** \-ə-riŋ-lē\ *adv*

flat·tery \'flat-ə-rē\ *n, pl* **-ter·ies** **1** : the act of flattering **2** : praise that is excessive or not sincere **synonyms** see COMPLIMENT

flat·top \'flat-ˌtäp\ *n* : AIRCRAFT CARRIER

flat·u·lence \'flach-ə-lən(t)s\ *n* : the presence of too much gas or air in the stomach or intestine

flat·ware \'flat-ˌwa(ə)r, -ˌwe(ə)r\ *n* : eating and serving utensils (as forks, spoons, and knives)

flat·worm \-ˌwərm\ *n* : any of a phylum of simple worms (as planarians, flukes, or tapeworms) that have a soft flat body, lack a body cavity, and have bilateral symmetry

flaunt \'flȯnt, 'flänt\ *vb* **1** : to wave or flutter in a showy way ⟨a flag *flaunting* in the breeze⟩ **2** : to make a big show of : PARADE ⟨*flaunting* their knowledge⟩

flau·ta \'flaȯt-ə\ *n* : a usually corn tortilla rolled tightly around a filling (as of meat) and deep-fried

flau·tist \'flȯt-əst, 'flaȯt-\ *n* : FLUTIST

fla·vor \'flā-vər\ *n* **1 a** : the quality of something that affects the sense of taste : SAVOR **b** : the blend of taste and smell sensations caused by a substance in the mouth **2** : a substance added to food or drink to give it a desired taste **3** : characteristic or most noticeable quality — **flavor** *vb* — **fla·vored** \-vərd\ *adj* — **fla·vor·ful** \-vər-fəl\ *adj* — **fla·vor·less** \-ləs\ *adj*

fla·vor·ing \'flā-vər-iŋ\ *n* : FLAVOR 2

¹flaw \'flȯ\ *n* : a small often hidden defect **synonyms** see BLEMISH — **flaw·less** \-ləs\ *adj* — **flaw·less·ly** *adv* — **flaw·less·ness** *n*

²flaw *vb* : to make or become defective

flax \'flaks\ *n* : a slender plant with blue flowers that is grown for its fiber from which linen is made and for its seed from which oil and livestock feed are obtained; *also* : its fiber

flax·en \'flak-sən\ *adj* **1** : made of flax **2** : of a pale yellow color ⟨*flaxen* hair⟩

flax·seed \'flak(s)-ˌsēd\ *n* : the small seed of flax used as a source of linseed oil and in medicinal preparations

flay \'flā\ *vb* **1** : to strip off the skin or surface of : SKIN **2** : to scold severely

F layer *n* : the highest and most highly charged layer of the ionosphere

flea \'flē\ *n* : any of an order of small wingless bloodsucking insects with a hard body and legs used for leaping

flea·bane \'flē-ˌbān\ *n* : any of various plants related to the daisies

flea collar *n* : a collar for dogs and cats that contains insecticide to kill fleas

flea

flea market *n* : a usually outdoor market for secondhand articles and antiques

¹fleck \'flek\ *vb* : ²STREAK 1, SPOT

²fleck *n* **1** : ¹SPOT 2a, MARK **2** : ¹FLAKE, PARTICLE

fledge \'flej\ *vb* **fledged; fledg·ing** **1** : to develop the feathers necessary for flying; *also* : to leave the nest after developing such feathers **2** : to provide with feathers ⟨*fledge* an arrow⟩

fledg·ling \'flej-liŋ\ *n* **1** : a young bird just fledged **2** : an immature or inexperienced person

flee \'flē\ *vb* **fled** \'fled\; **flee·ing** **1 a** : to run away often from danger or evil : FLY **b** : to run away from : SHUN **2** : to pass away swiftly : VANISH ⟨the mist *fled* before the rising sun⟩

¹fleece \'flēs\ *n* **1** : the woolly coat of an animal (as a sheep) **2 a** : any of various soft or woolly coverings **b** : a soft bulky knitted or woven fabric used especially for clothing — **fleecy** \'flē-sē\ *adj*

²fleece *vb* **fleeced; fleec·ing** **1** : to rob by trickery **2** : to remove the fleece from : SHEAR

¹fleet \'flēt\ *n* **1** : a group of warships under one command **2** : a group of ships or vehicles that move together or are under one management ⟨a *fleet* of taxis⟩ ⟨a fishing *fleet*⟩

²fleet *adj* : very swift ⟨*fleet* of foot⟩ — **fleet·ly** *adv* — **fleet·ness** *n*

fleet admiral *n* : an admiral of the highest rank in the navy

fleet–foot·ed \'flēt-ˌfu̇t-əd\ *adj* : able to run fast

fleet·ing \'flēt-iŋ\ *adj* : not lasting : passing swiftly ⟨a *fleeting* glimpse⟩ **synonyms** see TRANSIENT

Flem·ing \'flem-iŋ\ *n* : a member of a people living in northern Belgium

Flem·ish \'flem-ish\ *n* **1** : the Germanic language of the Flemings **2** **Flemish** *pl* : FLEMINGS — **Flemish** *adj*

¹flesh \'flesh\ *n* **1 a** : the soft parts of the body of an animal and especially the muscular parts **b** : sleek plump condition of body ⟨cattle in good *flesh*⟩ **2** : parts of an animal used as food **3** : the physical being of a person as distinguished from the soul **4** : a fleshy plant part (as the pulp of a fruit) — **fleshed** \'flesht\ *adj* — **in the flesh** : in person

²flesh *vb* : to make more complete by adding details ⟨*flesh* out a story⟩

flesh·ly \'flesh-lē\ *adj* **1** : CORPOREAL, BODILY **2** : WORLDLY 1 **3** : SENSUAL 1

fleshy \'flesh-ē\ *adj* **flesh·i·er; -est** **1 a** : resembling or consisting of flesh **b** : ⁵PLUMP, FAT **2** : having or being soft juicy tissue : PULPY ⟨*fleshy* fruits⟩ — **flesh·i·ness** *n*

fleur-de-lis *or* **fleur-de-lys** \ˌflərd-ᵊl-'ē, ˌflu̇rd-\ *n, pl* **fleurs-de-lis** *or* **fleur-de-lis** *or* **fleurs-de-lys** *or* **fleur-de-lys** \ˌflärd-ᵊl-'ē(z), ˌflu̇rd-\ **1** : IRIS 2 **2** : a simple drawing of an iris used in art and heraldry [Middle English *flourdelis* "fleur-de-lis," from early French *flur de lis,* literally, "flower of the lily"]

flew *past of* ¹FLY

flex \'fleks\ *vb* **1** : to bend especially over and over **2 a** : to move muscles so as to cause flexion of **b** : to move or tense (a muscle) by contraction

fleur-de-lis 2

flex·i·ble \'flek-sə-bəl\ *adj* **1** : capable of being bent : PLIANT **2** : readily changed or changing : ADAPTABLE ⟨a *flexible* schedule⟩ — **flex·i·bil·i·ty** \ˌflek-sə-'bil-ət-ē\ *n* — **flex·i·bly** \'flek-sə-blē\ *adv*

flex·ion \'flek-shən\ *n* : a bending movement around a joint (as the knee or elbow) in an arm or leg that lessens the angle between bones of the arm or leg at the joint; *also* : the resulting state

flex·or \'flek-sər, -ˌsȯ(ə)r\ *n* : a muscle that produces flexion

flex·ure \'flek-shər\ *n* **1** : the quality or state of being flexed **2** : ²TURN 2b, FOLD

¹flick \'flik\ *n* **1** : a light sharp jerky stroke or movement ⟨a *flick* of the wrist⟩ **2** : a sound produced by a flick **3** : ²FLICKER 1

²flick *vb* **1** : to strike lightly with a quick sharp motion ⟨*flicked* a speck off the table⟩ **2** : ¹FLICKER 1

¹flick·er \'flik-ər\ *vb* **flick·ered; flick·er·ing** \-(ə-)riŋ\ **1** : to move irregularly or unsteadily : FLUTTER **2** : to burn unsteadily or with a constantly changing light ⟨a *flickering* candle⟩

²flicker *n* **1** : an act of flickering **2** : a brief stirring ⟨a *flicker* of interest⟩ **3** : a flickering light — **flick·ery** \'flik-(ə-)rē\ *adj*

³**flicker** n : a large insect-eating North American wood-pecker with a black crescent on the breast and yellow or red on the underside of the wings and tail — compare RED-SHAFTED FLICKER, YELLOW-SHAFTED FLICKER

fli·er also **fly·er** \'flī-(ə)r\ n 1 : one that flies; esp : ¹PILOT 3 2 : an undertaking (as in business) that involves much risk 3 : an advertising circular

¹**flight** \'flīt\ n 1 : an act or instance of passing through the air by the use of wings ⟨a *flight* in a plane⟩ ⟨the *flight* of birds⟩ 2 a : a passing through the air or through outer space ⟨the *flight* of a bullet⟩ ⟨the *flight* of a rocket to the moon⟩ b : the distance covered in a flight 3 : a scheduled airplane trip 4 : a group of similar things flying through the air together ⟨a *flight* of ducks⟩ 5 : a brilliant, imaginative, or uncontrolled exercise or display ⟨a *flight* of fancy⟩ 6 : a continuous series of stairs from one landing or floor to another

²**flight** n : an act or instance of running away

flight attendant n : a person who provides service to passengers on an airplane

flight control n : the control from a ground station of an airplane or spacecraft especially by radio

flight engineer n : a crew member of an airplane responsible for mechanical operation

flight·less \'flīt-ləs\ adj : unable to fly ⟨*flightless* birds⟩

flight path n : the path in the air or space made or followed by something (as a particle, an airplane, or a spacecraft) in flight

flighty \'flīt-ē\ adj **flight·i·er; -est** 1 : easily excited : SKITTISH ⟨*flighty* horses⟩ 2 : SILLY 3, FRIVOLOUS — **flight·i·ly** \'flīt-ᵊl-ē\ adv — **flight·i·ness** \'flīt-ē-nəs\ n

flim·sy \'flim-zē\ adj **flim·si·er; -est** 1 : not strong or solid ⟨*flimsy* clothes⟩ ⟨a *flimsy* old car⟩ 2 : not likely or convincing ⟨a *flimsy* excuse⟩ ⟨a movie with a *flimsy* plot⟩ — **flim·si·ly** \-zə-lē\ adv — **flim·si·ness** \-zē-nəs\ n

flinch \'flinch\ vb : to draw back from or as if from physical pain : WINCE — **flinch** n — **flinch·er** n

¹**fling** \'fliŋ\ vb **flung** \'fləŋ\; **fling·ing** \'fliŋ-iŋ\ 1 : to move in an abrupt or headlong manner ⟨*flung* out of the room in a huff⟩ 2 : to kick or plunge vigorously ⟨the horse *flung* out at him as he went by⟩ 3 a : to throw or swing with force ⟨*flung* herself down on the couch⟩ b : to cast aside : DISCARD 4 : to put suddenly and unexpectedly into a state or condition ⟨*flung* into confusion⟩ **synonyms** see THROW — **fling·er** \'fliŋ-ər\ n

²**fling** n 1 : an act or instance of flinging 2 : a casual try or involvement 3 : a time of freedom for pleasure

flint \'flint\ n 1 : a hard dark quartz that produces a spark when struck by steel 2 a : a piece of flint b : an alloy (as of iron and cerium) used for producing a spark in lighters 3 : something very hard ⟨a heart of *flint*⟩ — **flint·i·ly** \'flint-ᵊl-ē\ adv — **flint·i·ness** \'flint-ē-nəs\ n — **flinty** \-ē\ adj

flint glass n : heavy glass that contains an oxide of lead and is used in lenses and prisms

flint·lock \'flint-ˌläk\ n 1 : a lock for a gun using a flint to ignite the charge 2 : a gun fitted with a flintlock

flintlock

¹**flip** \'flip\ vb **flipped; flip·ping** 1 : to turn by tossing ⟨*flip* a coin⟩ 2 : to turn over quickly ⟨*flip* the pages of a magazine⟩ 3 : ²FLICK 1 ⟨*flip* a switch⟩ 4 : to get excited or angry ⟨you'll *flip* when you hear this⟩

²**flip** n 1 : an act or instance of flipping 2 : a somersault especially in the air

³**flip** adj : FLIPPANT

flip·pan·cy \'flip-ən-sē\ n, pl **-cies** : an act or instance of being flippant

flip·pant \'flip-ənt\ adj : treating lightly something serious or worthy of respect — **flip·pant·ly** adv

flip·per \'flip-ər\ n 1 : a broad flat limb (as of a seal or whale) used for swimming 2 : a flat rubber shoe with the front widened into a paddle for use in skin diving

¹**flirt** \'flərt\ vb 1 : to show a liking for someone of the opposite sex just for fun 2 : ²TOY ⟨*flirted* with the idea⟩ — **flir·ta·tion** \ˌflər-'tā-shən\ n — **flir·ta·tious** \-shəs\ adj — **flir·ta·tious·ness** n — **flirt·er** \'flərt-ər\ n

²**flirt** n 1 : an act or instance of flirting 2 : a person who flirts a lot

flit \'flit\ vb **flit·ted; flit·ting** : to move or progress in a quick irregular manner — **flit** n

fliv·ver \'fliv-ər\ n : a small cheap old automobile

¹**float** \'flōt\ n 1 : an act or instance of floating 2 : something that floats: as a : a device (as a cork) that holds up the baited end of a fishing line b : a floating platform anchored near a shoreline for use by swimmers or boats c : a hollow ball that controls the flow or level of the liquid it floats on (as in a tank) d : a watertight structure that holds up an airplane on water 3 : a vehicle with a platform used to carry an exhibit in a parade; also : the vehicle and exhibit together 4 : a drink consisting of ice cream floating in a beverage

²**float** vb 1 : to rest on the surface of a fluid 2 : to drift on or through or as if on or through a fluid ⟨dust *floating* through the air⟩ 3 : to cause to float ⟨*float* logs down a river⟩ — **float·er** n

floating–point adj : involving or being a system of representing numbers (as in computer programming) in which a quantity is written as a number multiplied by a power of that number's base ⟨999.9 can be expressed in a *floating-point* system as 9.999×10^2⟩

floating rib n : a rib (as one of the two bottom pairs in human beings) that has no attachment to the sternum

¹**flock** \'fläk\ n 1 : a group of animals (as birds or sheep) assembled or herded together 2 : a group someone keeps watch over 3 : a large number ⟨a *flock* of tourists⟩

²**flock** vb : to gather or move in a crowd ⟨they *flocked* to the beach⟩

floe \'flō\ n : a sheet or mass of floating ice

flog \'fläg\ vb **flogged; flog·ging** : to beat severely with or as if with a rod or whip — **flog·ger** n

¹**flood** \'fləd\ n 1 a : a great flow of water that rises and spreads over the land b cap : a flood described in the Bible as covering the earth in the time of Noah 2 : the flowing in of the tide 3 : an overwhelming quantity or volume ⟨a *flood* of mail⟩

²**flood** vb 1 : to cover or become filled with a flood 2 : to fill as if with a flood ⟨a room *flooded* with light⟩ ⟨*flood* a carburetor⟩ 3 : to pour forth, go, or come in a flood

flood·gate \'fləd-ˌgāt\ n : a gate (as in a canal) for controlling a body of water : SLUICE

flood·light \-ˌlīt\ n 1 : artificial light in a broad beam 2 : a light that gives a broad beam — **floodlight** vb

flood·plain \-ˌplān\ n 1 : low flat land along a stream or river that may flood 2 : a plain built up from earth left by floodwaters

flood tide n 1 : a rising tide 2 a : an overwhelming quantity ⟨a *flood tide* of criticism⟩ b : a high point : PEAK

flood·wa·ter \'fləd-ˌwȯt-ər, -ˌwät-\ n : the water of a flood

¹**floor** \'flō(ə)r, 'flȯ(ə)r\ n 1 : the part of a room on which one stands 2 a : the lower inside surface of a hollow structure ⟨the *floor* of a car⟩ b : a ground surface ⟨the ocean *floor*⟩ 3 : a story of a building ⟨lives on the second *floor*⟩

²**floor** vb 1 : to cover with a floor or flooring 2 a : to knock to the floor b : ³SHOCK 1, OVERWHELM

floor·ing \'flōr-iŋ, 'flȯr-\ n 1 : ¹FLOOR 1 2 : material for floors

¹**flop** \'fläp\ vb **flopped; flop·ping** 1 : to swing or bounce loosely : flap about ⟨a hat brim *flopping*⟩ 2 a : to throw oneself down in a heavy, clumsy, or relaxed manner ⟨*flopped* into the chair⟩ b : to throw or drop suddenly

and heavily or noisily ⟨*flopped* the bundles down with a thud⟩ **3** : to fail completely ⟨the play *flopped*⟩

²**flop** *n* **1** : an act or sound of flopping **2** : a complete failure : DUD

flop·py \'fläp-ē\ *adj* **flop·pi·er; -est** : being soft and flexible

flo·ra \'flōr-ə, 'flȯr-\ *n, pl* **floras** *also* **flo·rae** \'flō(ə)r-ē, 'flō(ə)r-, -ī\ : plants or plant life especially of a region, period, or environment

flo·ral \'flōr-əl, 'flȯr-\ *adj* : of or relating to flowers or a flora ⟨a *floral* pattern in wallpaper⟩

Flor·ence flask \ˌflȯr-ən(t)s-, ˌflär-\ *n* : a round usually flat-bottomed glass laboratory container with a long neck [named for *Florence,* city in Italy; so called from the fact that at one time some Italian wines were sold in bottles of this shape]

flo·ret \'flōr-ət, 'flȯr-\ *n* : a small flower; *esp* : one of the small flowers forming the head of a daisy and related plants

flor·id \'flōr-əd, 'flär-\ *adj* **1** : FLOWERY 2, ORNATE ⟨*florid* writing⟩ **2** : tinged with red : RUDDY ⟨a *florid* complexion⟩ [from Latin *floridus* "blooming, flowery," from *florēre* "to blossom, flourish," from *flor-, flos* "a flower, blossom" — related to FLOUR, FLOURISH, FLOWER] — **flor·id·ly** *adv*

flor·in \'flōr-ən, 'flär-, 'flȯr-\ *n* **1** : an old gold coin first made in Florence in 1252 **2** : any of various coins patterned after the florin

flor·ist \'flōr-əst, 'flȯr-, 'flär-\ *n* : a person who sells flowers and ornamental plants

¹**floss** \'fläs, 'flȯs\ *n* **1 a** : soft silk or cotton thread used for embroidery **b** : DENTAL FLOSS **2** : fluffy material full of fibers

²**floss** *vb* : to use dental floss on (one's teeth)

flo·ta·tion *also* **floa·ta·tion** \flō-'tā-shən\ *n* **1** : the act, process, or state of floating **2** : the separation of the particles of a mass of ground ore according to how they compare in ability to float on a liquid

flo·til·la \flō-'til-ə\ *n* : ¹FLEET 1; *esp* : a fleet of small ships

flot·sam \'flät-səm\ *n* : floating wreckage of a ship or its cargo

¹**flounce** \'flaun(t)s\ *vb* **flounced; flounc·ing** **1** : to move with exaggerated jerky motions **2** : to go with sudden determination ⟨*flounced* out of the room in anger⟩ [perhaps of Scandinavian origin]

²**flounce** *n* : an act or instance of flouncing

³**flounce** *vb* **flounced; flounc·ing** : to trim with flounces [an altered form of earlier *frounce* "to trim with ruffles," from Middle English *frouncen* "to curl"]

⁴**flounce** *n* : a strip of fabric attached by the upper edge

¹**floun·der** \'flaun-dər\ *n, pl* **flounder** *or* **flounders** : FLATFISH; *esp* : any of various important marine food fishes [Middle English *flounder* "a flatfish"; of Scandinavian origin]

²**flounder** *vb* **floun·dered; floun·der·ing** \-d(ə-)riŋ\ : to struggle or go clumsily ⟨*floundering* through the deep snow⟩ [probably an altered form of *founder* "to go lame, collapse"]

¹**flour** \'flau(ə)r\ *n* **1** : finely ground powdery meal of wheat or of any cereal grain or edible seed **2** : a fine soft powder [Middle English *flour* "finely ground wheat meal," from earlier *flour* "best part, flower," from early French *flor, flour* "flower," from Latin *flor-, flow* "flower, blossom" — related to FLORID, FLOURISH, FLOWER]

²**flour** *vb* : to coat with flour

flour beetle *n* : any of several usually flattened brown beetles that are pests especially in flour or meal

¹**flour·ish** \'flər-ish, 'flə-rish\ *vb* **1** : to grow well : THRIVE **2 a** : PROSPER 1, SUCCEED **b** : to be active ⟨*flourished* around 1850⟩ **3** : to make bold sweeping gestures **4** : to shake or wave around ⟨*flourish* a sword⟩ [Middle English *florisshen* "to flourish, thrive," from early French *floriss-,*

florir (same meaning), derived from Latin *florēre* "to blossom, flourish," from *flor-, flos* "a flower, blossom" — related to FLORID, FLOUR, FLOWER]

²**flourish** *n* **1** : a fancy bit of decoration added to something (as handwriting) **2** : a sweeping motion **3** : FANFARE **4** : a period of thriving **5** : a sudden burst ⟨a *flourish* of activity⟩

floury \'flau̇(ə)r-ē\ *adj* **1** : of, relating to, or resembling flour **2** : covered with flour

flout \'flaut\ *vb* : to ignore in a disrespectful way ⟨*flouting* the rules⟩ — **flout·er** *n*

¹**flow** \'flō\ *vb* **1** : to move in a stream **2** : ¹RISE 5a ⟨the tide ebbs and *flows*⟩ **3** : to glide or pass smoothly and readily **4** : to hang loose and waving ⟨her gown *flowed* around her⟩ **5** : to come from as a source ⟨money that *flows* from trade⟩ — **flow·ing·ly** \-iŋ-lē\ *adv*

²**flow** *n* **1** : an act of flowing **2 a** : ¹FLOOD 1 **b** : the flowing in of the tide ⟨the tide's ebb and *flow*⟩ **3 a** : a smooth even movement **b** : a mass of matter that has flowed when melted ⟨a lava *flow*⟩ **4** : the quantity that flows in a certain time ⟨the *flow* of water over a dam⟩

flow·chart \'flō-ˌchärt\ *n* : a diagram that shows step-by-step progression through a process or system by using special symbols and connecting lines

¹**flow·er** \'flau̇(-ə)r\ *n* **1 a** : a specialized plant part that occurs singly or in clusters, possesses often colorful petals or sepals, and bears reproductive organs involved in the development of seeds and fruit : BLOSSOM **b** : a cluster of small flowers growing closely together that resembles and is often viewed as a single flower : INFLORESCENCE ⟨a hydrangea

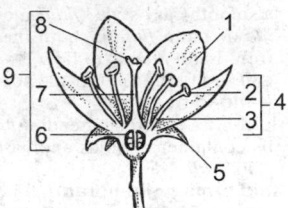

¹flower 1a: *1* petal, *2* anther, *3* filament, *4* stamen, *5* sepal, *6* ovary, *7* style, *8* stigma, *9* pistil

flower⟩ **c** : a plant grown or valued for its flowers ⟨planted *flowers*⟩ **d** : a cut stem of a plant with its flower ⟨a bouquet of *flowers*⟩ **2** : the best part or example ⟨in the *flower* of his youth⟩ [Middle English *flour* "flower, best part," from early French *flor, flour* (same meaning), from Latin *flor-, flos* "flower, blossom" — related to FLORID, FLOUR, FLOURISH] — **flow·er·less** \-ləs\ *adj* — **flow·er·like** \-ˌlīk\ *adj*

²**flower** *vb* **1** : to produce flowers : BLOOM **2** : ¹FLOURISH 1

flow·ered \'flau̇(-ə)rd\ *adj* **1** : having or bearing flowers **2** : decorated with flowers or flowerlike figures ⟨*flowered* wallpaper⟩

flower head *n* : a tight cluster of small flowers without stems that are arranged so that the whole looks like a single flower

flowering plant *n* : any of a major group of higher plants that produce flowers, fruits, and seeds with the seeds in a closed ovary — called also *angiosperm;* compare SEED PLANT

flow·er·pot \'flau̇(-ə)r-ˌpät\ *n* : a pot in which to grow plants

flow·ery \'flau̇(-ə)r-ē\ *adj* **flow·er·i·er; -est** **1** : full of or covered with flowers **2** : full of fine words or phrases ⟨*flowery* language⟩ — **flow·er·i·ness** *n*

flown *past participle of* ¹FLY

\ə\ **abut**	\au̇\ **out**	\i\ **tip**	\ȯ\ **saw**	\u̇\ **foot**
\ər\ **further**	\ch\ **chin**	\ī\ **life**	\ȯi\ **coin**	\y\ **yet**
\a\ **mat**	\e\ **pet**	\j\ **job**	\th\ **thin**	\yü\ **few**
\ā\ **take**	\ē\ **easy**	\ŋ\ **sing**	\th\ **this**	\yu̇\ **cure**
\ä\ **cot, cart**	\g\ **go**	\ō\ **bone**	\ü\ **food**	\zh\ **vision**

flu \'flü\ *n* **1** : INFLUENZA 1 **2** : any of several virus diseases that are something like a cold — **flu–like** \'flü-,līk\ *adj*

flub \'fləb\ *vb* **flubbed; flub·bing** : BOTCH, BUNGLE — **flub** *n*

fluc·tu·ate \'flək-chə-,wāt\ *vb* **-at·ed; -at·ing 1** : to move up and down or back and forth like a wave **2** : to be constantly changing especially up and down — **fluc·tu·a·tion** \,flək-chə-'wā-shən\ *n*

flue \'flü\ *n* : an enclosed passageway for directing a current; *esp* : a channel in a chimney for carrying flame and smoke to the outer air

flu·en·cy \'flü-ən-sē\ *n* : the quality or state of being fluent

flu·ent \'flü-ənt\ *adj* **1** : ¹FLUID 1a **2 a** : able to speak easily and smoothly ⟨*fluent* in Spanish⟩ **b** : done in a smooth easy way [from Latin *fluent-, fluens,* present participle of *fluere* "to flow" — related to FLUID] — **flu·ent·ly** *adv*

¹fluff \'fləf\ *n* **1** : ³NAP, DOWN **2** : something fluffy

²fluff *vb* : to make or become fluffy

fluffy \'fləf-ē\ *adj* **fluff·i·er; -est 1** : having, covered with, or resembling fluff or down ⟨the *fluffy* fur of a kitten⟩ **2** : being light and soft or airy : puffed up ⟨a *fluffy* omelet⟩ — **fluff·i·ness** *n*

¹flu·id \'flü-əd\ *adj* **1 a** : capable of flowing like a liquid or gas **b** : likely or tending to change or move **2** : showing a smooth easy style ⟨*fluid* movements⟩ [from French *fluide* or Latin *fluidus,* both meaning "fluid, able to flow," from Latin *fluere* "to flow" — related to AFFLUENT, FLUENT, ¹FLUSH, INFLUENCE, SUPERFLUOUS] — **flu·id·ly** *adv* — **flu·id·ness** *n*

²fluid *n* : a substance tending to flow or take the shape of its container ⟨liquids and gases are *fluids*⟩ — **flu·id·like** \-,līk\ *adj*

fluid dram *or* **flu·i·dram** \,flü-ə(d)-'dram\ *n* : a unit of liquid capacity equal to ⅛ fluid ounce (about 3.7 milliliters) — see MEASURE table

flu·id·i·ty \flü-'id-ət-ē\ *n* : the quality or state of being fluid

fluid mechanics *n* : a branch of science that deals with the special properties of liquids and gases

fluid ounce *n* : a unit of liquid capacity equal to 1/16 pint (about 29.6 milliliters) — see MEASURE table

¹fluke \'flük\ *n* : any of various trematode flatworms — compare LIVER FLUKE

²fluke *n* **1** : the part of an anchor that digs into the ground **2** : a barbed head (as of a harpoon) **3** : one of the lobes of a whale's tail

³fluke *n* : a stroke of good luck ⟨won by a *fluke*⟩ — **fluky** \'flü-kē\ *adj*

flume \'flüm\ *n* **1** : a sloping channel for carrying water (as for power) **2** : a ravine or gorge with a stream running through it

flung *past and past participle of* FLING

flunk \'fləŋk\ *vb* **1** : ¹FAIL 2c ⟨*flunk* a test⟩ **2** : to give a failing grade to — **flunk** *n*

flunk out *vb* : to dismiss or be dismissed from a school for failing

flun·ky *also* **flun·key** *or* **flun·kie** \'fləŋ-kē\ *n, pl* **flunkies** *also* **flunkeys 1 a** : a servant in livery **b** : a person who has simple or unskilled duties **2** : a person who flatters or constantly agrees with another in the hope of receiving favors

flu·o·resce \,flu(-ə)r-'es\ *vb* **-resced; -resc·ing** : to produce, exhibit, or be exposed to fluorescence

flu·o·res·cence \,flu(-ə)r-'es-ᵊn(t)s\ *n* : the giving off of radiation usually as visible light when exposed to radiation from another source (as ultraviolet light); *also* : the radiation given off

flu·o·res·cent \,flu(-ə)r-'es-ᵊnt\ *adj* **1** : having or relating to fluorescence **2** : very bright in color ⟨*fluorescent* markers⟩

fluorescent lamp *n* : an electric lamp in the form of a tube in which light is produced on the inside fluorescent coating by the action of ultraviolet light

flu·o·ri·date \'flur-ə-,dāt\ *vb* **-dat·ed; -dat·ing** : to add a fluoride to (as drinking water) in order to reduce tooth decay — **flu·o·ri·da·tion** \,flur-ə-'dā-shən\ *n*

flu·o·ride \'flu(-ə)r-,īd\ *n* : a compound of fluorine with another element or chemical group

flu·o·ri·nate \'flur-ə-,nāt\ *vb* **-at·ed; -at·ing** : to treat or cause to combine with fluorine or a compound of fluorine — **flu·o·ri·na·tion** \,flur-ə-'nā-shən\ *n*

flu·o·rine \'flu(-ə)r-,ēn, -ən\ *n* : a nonmetallic element that is normally found alone as a pale yellowish flammable irritating poisonous gas having two atoms per molecule — see ELEMENT table

flu·o·rite \'flu(-ə)r-,īt\ *n* : a transparent or nearly transparent mineral of different colors that consists of a fluoride of calcium and is used as a flux and in making glass

flu·o·ro·car·bon \,flu(-ə)r-ō-'kär-bən\ *n* : any of various compounds of carbon and fluorine used chiefly as lubricants, refrigerants, and nonstick coatings and in making plastics and formerly as the driving force in aerosol cans

¹flu·o·ro·scope \'flur-ə-,skōp\ *n* : an instrument that is used for observing with X-rays the inner structure of objects (as the living body) through which light cannot pass — **flu·o·ro·scop·ic** \,flur-ə-'skäp-ik\ *adj* — **flu·o·ros·co·py** \,flu(-ə)r-'äs-kə-pē\ *n*

²fluoroscope *vb* **-scoped; -scop·ing** : to examine by fluoroscopy

flu·or·spar \'flu(-ə)r-,spär\ *n* : FLUORITE

¹flur·ry \'flər-ē, 'flə-rē\ *n, pl* **flurries 1 a** : a gust of wind **b** : a brief light snowfall **2** : a sudden commotion ⟨a *flurry* of publicity⟩ **3** : a brief outburst of activity ⟨a *flurry* of trading in the stock exchange⟩

²flurry *vb* **flur·ried; flur·ry·ing** : to become or cause to become agitated and confused

¹flush \'fləsh\ *vb* : to take flight or cause to take flight suddenly ⟨*flushed* several quail⟩ [Middle English *flusshen* "to fly up suddenly"]

²flush *n* **1** : a sudden flow (as of water) **2** : a sudden increase (as of emotion) ⟨a *flush* of triumph⟩ **3 a** : ²BLUSH **2 b** : a fresh and vigorous state ⟨the *flush* of youth⟩ **4** : a brief sensation of heat [perhaps from Latin *fluxus,* "flow," from *fluere* "to flow" — related to FLUID]

³flush *vb* **1** : ²BLUSH 1 **2** : to pour liquid over or through; *esp* : to wash out with a rush of liquid ⟨*flush* a toilet⟩ **3** : INFLAME 2, EXCITE ⟨*flushed* with pride⟩ **4** : to make red or hot

⁴flush *adj* **1 a** : of a healthy reddish color **b** : full of life and vigor : LUSTY **2 a** : filled to overflowing **b** : well supplied especially with money **3 a** : having an unbroken surface ⟨*flush* paneling⟩ **b** : even with the neighboring surface ⟨a river *flush* with the top of its bank⟩ — **flush·ness** *n*

⁵flush *adv* **1** : so as to be flush **2** : so as to make solid contact ⟨a blow *flush* on the chin⟩

flus·ter \'fləs-tər\ *vb* **flus·tered; flus·ter·ing** \-t(ə-)riŋ\ : to make nervous and unsure : UPSET ⟨*flustered* by their rudeness⟩ — **fluster** *n*

¹flute \'flüt\ *n* **1** : a woodwind instrument played by blowing across a hole near the closed end **2** : a rounded groove; *esp* : one on an architectural column — **flute·like** \-,līk\ *adj*

²flute *vb* **flut·ed; flut·ing 1** : to play a flute **2** : to make a sound like that of a flute **3** : to form flutes in ⟨*fluted* columns⟩

¹flute 1

flut·ing \'flüt-iŋ\ *n* : fluted decoration

flut·ist \'flüt-əst\ *n* : a flute player

¹**flut·ter** \'flət-ər\ *vb* **1** : to move or cause the wings to move rapidly without flying or in short flights ⟨butterflies *flutter*⟩ **2** : to move with quick wavering or flapping motions ⟨flags *fluttered* in the breeze⟩ **3** : to move about or behave in an excited aimless manner — **flut·tery** \'flət-ə-rē\ *adj*

²**flutter** *n* **1** : an act of fluttering **2** : FLURRY 2, COMMOTION **3** : an unsteadiness of pitch in reproduced sound

¹**flux** \'fləks\ *n* **1 a** : a flowing in ⟨*flux* of the tide⟩ **b** : a series of changes : a state of continuous change **2** : a substance used to aid the melting or joining (as by removing impurities) of metals or minerals

²**flux** *vb* **1** : to become or cause to become fluid : FUSE **2** : to treat with a flux

¹**fly** \'flī\ *vb* **flew** \'flü\; **flown** \'flōn\; **fly·ing** **1 a** : to move in or pass through the air with wings **b** : to move through the air or with the wind; *also* : to move through outer space **c** : to float or cause to float, wave, or soar in the air ⟨flags *flying*⟩ ⟨*fly* a kite⟩ **2** : to take flight : FLEE **3** : to move or pass swiftly ⟨time *flies*⟩ **4 a** : to operate or travel in an aircraft or spacecraft **b** : to journey over or through by flying ⟨*fly* the Atlantic⟩ **c** : to transport by aircraft or spacecraft [Old English *flēogan* "to move through the air, fly"] — **fly at** : to attack suddenly and violently

²**fly** *n*, *pl* **flies** **1 a** : a garment closing concealed by a fold of cloth **b** : the outer fabric of a tent with a double top **c** : the length of an extended flag; *also* : the loose end of a flag **2** : a baseball hit high into the air — **on the fly** **1** : in motion **2** : while still in the air ⟨the home run carried 450 feet *on the fly*⟩

³**fly** *vb* **flied**; **fly·ing** : to hit a fly in baseball

⁴**fly** *n*, *pl* **flies** **1** : a winged insect **2** : TWO-WINGED FLY; *esp* : one (as a housefly) that is large and has a stout body in comparison with others (as a mosquito) **3** : a fishhook covered to look like an insect [Old English *flēoge* "flying insect"] — **fly in the ointment** : an unpleasant feature in something otherwise pleasant

fly ash *n* : fine solid particles consisting of ashes, dust, and soot carried out from burning fuel (as coal or oil) by the draft

fly ball *n* : ²FLY 2

fly·blown \'flī-ˌblōn\ *adj* : not pure : TAINTED, CORRUPT

fly·by \-ˌbī\ *n*, *pl* **fly·bys** **1** : a usually low-altitude flight past a chosen place by one or more aircraft **2 a** : a flight of a spacecraft past a heavenly body (as Mars) close enough to obtain scientific information **b** : a spacecraft that makes a flyby

fly–by–wire *adj* : controlled by electrical signals rather than mechanically

fly·catch·er \-ˌkach-ər, -ˌkech-\ *n* : a small bird that feeds on insects that it captures in the air

flyer *variant of* FLIER

fly·ing \'flī-iŋ\ *adj* **1 a** : moving or made by moving rapidly ⟨a *flying* leap⟩ **b** : HASTY 1a ⟨a *flying* visit⟩ **2** : ready to move or act quickly ⟨a *flying* squad car⟩

flying boat *n* : a seaplane with a hull designed for floating

flying buttress *n* : an arched structure that extends beyond a wall or building and supports it

flying fish *n* : any of numerous sea fishes having long fins that look like wings and are used to glide some distance through the air

flying fish

flying fox *n* : FRUIT BAT

flying machine *n* : AIRCRAFT

flying saucer *n* : any of various unidentified flying objects often reported to be saucer-shaped or disk-shaped

flying squirrel *n* : a squirrel with folds of skin connecting the forelegs and hind legs that enable it to make long gliding leaps

fly·leaf \'flī-ˌlēf\ *n* : a blank leaf at the beginning or end of a book

fly·pa·per \-ˌpā-pər\ *n* : paper coated with a sticky often poisonous substance for killing flies

fly·speck \-ˌspek\ *n* **1** : a speck of waste matter of a fly **2** : something small and of little importance — **flyspeck** *vb*

fly·way \-ˌwā\ *n* : an established air route of birds that migrate

fly·weight \-ˌwāt\ *n* : a boxer in a weight division having an upper limit of 112 pounds

fly·wheel \-ˌhwēl, -ˌwēl\ *n* : a heavy wheel for regulating the speed of machinery

FM \'ef-ˌem\ *n* : a system of broadcasting using frequency modulation; *also* : a receiver of radio waves broadcast by such a system — **FM** *adj*

¹**foal** \'fōl\ *n* : a young animal of the horse family; *esp* : one under one year

²**foal** *vb* : to give birth to a foal

¹**foam** \'fōm\ *n* **1** : a light mass of fine bubbles formed in or on a liquid **2** : a mass of fine bubbles formed (as by a horse) in producing saliva or sweating **3** : a long-lasting mass of bubbles produced chemically and used especially in fighting oil fires **4** : a material (as rubber) in a lightweight cellular form resulting from the presence of gas bubbles during manufacture — **foam·i·ly** \'fō-mə-lē\ *adv* — **foam·i·ness** \'fō-mē-nəs\ *n* — **foamy** \-mē\ *adj*

²**foam** *vb* **1** : to produce or form foam : FROTH **2** : to be angry

foam rubber *n* : rubber prepared in the form of a spongy foam

fob \'fäb\ *n* **1** : a short strap, ribbon, or chain attached especially to a pocket watch **2** : a small ornament worn on a watch chain

fo·cal \'fō-kəl\ *adj* : of, relating to, or having a focus — **fo·cal·ly** \-kə-lē\ *adv*

focal length *n* : the distance of a focus from the surface of a lens or inwardly-curved mirror

focal point *n* : ¹FOCUS 1

fo'c'sle *variant of* FORECASTLE

¹**fo·cus** \'fō-kəs\ *n*, *pl* **fo·ci** \-ˌsī\ *also* **fo·cus·es** **1** : a point at which rays (as of light, heat, or sound) meet or from which they draw apart or appear to draw apart; *esp* : the point at which an image is formed by a mirror, lens, or optical system **2 a** : FOCAL LENGTH **b** : adjustment (as of the eye or binoculars) for clear vision ⟨bring into *focus*⟩ **3** : one of the two points within an ellipse the sum of whose distances from any point on the ellipse is a constant number **4** : a center of activity or interest **5** : the starting point of an earthquake

²**focus** *vb* **fo·cused** *also* **fo·cussed**; **fo·cus·ing** *also* **fo·cus·sing** **1 a** : to bring into focus **b** : to adjust the focus of ⟨*focus* the eyes⟩ ⟨*focus* a telescope⟩ **2** : to cause to be concentrated ⟨*focus* public attention on a problem⟩ **3** : to bring to a focus ⟨*focus* rays of light⟩ **4** : to come to a focus **5** : to adjust one's eye or a camera to a certain range

fod·der \'fäd-ər\ *n* : coarse dry food (as cornstalks) for livestock

foe \'fō\ *n* **1** : one who hates another : ENEMY **2** : an enemy in war

foehn *or* **föhn** \'fə(r)n, 'fān\ *n* : a warm dry wind blowing down the side of a mountain

\ə\ **abut**	\au̇\ **out**	\i\ **tip**	\o̅\ **saw**	\u̇\ **foot**
\ər\ **further**	\ch\ **chin**	\ī\ **life**	\ȯi\ **coin**	\y\ **yet**
\a\ **mat**	\e\ **pet**	\j\ **job**	\th\ **thin**	\yü\ **few**
\ā\ **take**	\ē\ **easy**	\ŋ\ **sing**	\t͟h\ **this**	\yu̇\ **cure**
\ä\ **cot, cart**	\g\ **go**	\ō\ **bone**	\ü\ **food**	\zh\ **vision**

foe·tal, foe·tus *chiefly British variant of* FETAL, FETUS

¹fog \'fȯg, 'fäg\ *n* **1 a** : fine particles of water floating in the atmosphere near the ground **b** : a fine spray or a foam for firefighting **2** : a gloomy condition of the atmosphere or a substance causing it **3** : a state of mental confusion ⟨spent the morning in a *fog*⟩

²fog *vb* **fogged; fog·ging** **1** : to cover or become covered with or as if with fog **2** : to make confused

fog·gy \'fȯg-ē, 'fäg-\ *adj* **fog·gi·er; -est** **1** : filled with fog **2** : VAGUE 2 — **fog·gi·ly** \-ə-lē\ *adv* — **fog·gi·ness** \-ē-nəs\ *n*

fog·horn \'fȯg-ˌhȯ(ə)rn, 'fäg-\ *n* : a horn (as on a ship) sounded in foggy weather to give warning

fo·gy *also* **fo·gey** \'fō-gē\ *n, pl* **fogies** *also* **fogeys** : a person with old-fashioned ideas — usually used with *old*

foi·ble \'fȯi-bəl\ *n* : a minor fault in personal character or behavior : WEAKNESS

¹foil \'fȯi(ə)l\ *vb* : to prevent from achieving a goal : DE-FEAT ⟨*foil* a plot⟩ [Middle English *foilen* "to trample underfoot," from early French *fuller, fouler* "to shrink and thicken (cloth), trample underfoot," from Latin *fullare* "to shrink and thicken (cloth)"] *synonyms* see FRUS-TRATE

²foil *n* **1** : a very thin sheet of metal ⟨tin or aluminum *foil*⟩ **2** : one that serves as a contrast to another ⟨acted as a *foil* for the comedian⟩ [Middle English *foil* "leaf," from early French *fuille, foille* (same meaning), derived from Latin *folium* "leaf" — related to FOLIAGE]

³foil *n* : a fencing weapon having a light flexible blade with a blunt point [origin unknown]

foist \'fȯist\ *vb* : to pass off (something false) as genuine

fo·la·cin \'fō-lə-sən\ *n* : FOLIC ACID

¹fold \'fōld\ *n* **1** : a pen for sheep **2** : a group of people with a common faith or interest [Old English *falod* "pen for sheep"]

²fold *vb* : to shut up in a fold

³fold *vb* **1** : to lay one part over or against another part ⟨*fold* a letter⟩ ⟨birds *folding* their wings⟩ **2** : to clasp together ⟨*fold* the hands⟩ **3** : ¹EM-BRACE 1 **4** : to bend (as a layer of rock) into folds **5** : to add (a food in-gredient) to a mixture by gently and repeatedly lifting one part over another **6** : to become doubled or pleated **7** : to fail completely ⟨the business *folded*⟩ [Old English *fealdan* "to fold, make double thickness"]

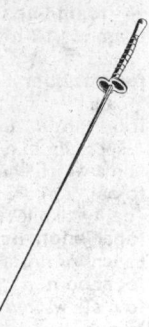
³foil

⁴fold *n* **1** : a doubling or folding over **2** : a part dou-bled or laid over another part **3** : a bend produced in rock

-fold \ˌfōld, 'fōld\ *suffix* **1** : multiplied by (a specified number) : times — in adjectives ⟨a twelve*fold* increase⟩ and adverbs ⟨repay you ten*fold*⟩ **2** : having (so many) parts ⟨a three*fold* problem⟩ [Old English *-feald* (suffix) "being increased (so many) times"]

fold·er \'fōl-dər\ *n* **1** : one that folds **2** : a printed circular of folded sheets **3 a** : a folded cover or large envelope for holding loose papers **b** : an element of a computer oper-ating system used to group and organize files

fo·li·age \'fō-l(ē-)ij *also* 'fōl-yij\ *n* : the mass of leaves of a plant [an altered form of earlier *foillage* "a mass of leaves," from early French *fuellage* (same meaning), from *fuelle, foille* "leaf," derived from Latin *folium* "leaf" — related to ²FOIL, PORTFOLIO] — **fo·li·aged** \-l(ē-)ijd *also* -yijd\ *adj*

fo·li·at·ed \'fō-lē-ˌāt-əd\ *adj* : composed of or capable of being separated into layers ⟨*foliated* metamorphic rocks⟩

fo·lic acid \ˌfō-lik-\ *n* : a crystalline vitamin of the B com-plex used especially in the treatment of anemia resulting from inadequate intake of nutrients

fo·lio \'fō-lē-ˌō\ *n, pl* **fo·li·os** **1** : a leaf of a manuscript or book **2 a** : a book made up of sheets of paper that have been folded to produce two leaves **b** : a very large book

¹folk \'fōk\ *n, pl* **folk** *or* **folks** **1** : a group of people forming a tribe or nation **2** *pl* : a certain kind or class of people ⟨country *folks*⟩ **3** *pl* : people in general **4** *folks pl* : the persons of one's own family; *esp* : PARENTS ⟨visit my *folks*⟩ **5** : folk music

²folk *adj* : of, relating to, or originating among the common people of a country or region ⟨*folk* customs⟩ ⟨*folk* music⟩

folk art *n* : the traditional art of usually untrained people typically created by an unknown artist

folk·lore \'fōk-ˌlō(ə)r, -ˌlȯ(ə)r\ *n* : customs, beliefs, stories, and sayings of a people handed down from generation to generation — **folk·lor·ist** \-ˌlōr-əst, -ˌlȯr-\ *n*

folk medicine *n* : traditional medicine that usually in-volves the use of plant-based remedies especially by peo-ple isolated from modern medical services

folk·sing·er \-ˌsing-ər\ *n* : a singer of folk songs

folk song *n* : a traditional or composed song typically hav-ing stanzas, a refrain, and a simple melody

folk·tale \-ˌtāl\ *n* : a story made up and handed down by the common people

fol·li·cle \'fäl-i-kəl\ *n* **1 a** : a small cavity or a deep bodily depression with a narrow mouth (as one from which a hair grows) **b** : GRAAFIAN FOLLICLE **2** : a dry one-celled fruit (as in the milkweed) that splits open by one seam when ripe — **fol·lic·u·lar** \fə-'lik-yə-lər, fä-\ *adj*

follicle–stimulating hormone *n* : a hormone from the pituitary gland that causes the graafian follicles to grow in females and makes sperm-forming cells active in males

¹follow \'fäl-ō\ *vb* **1** : to go or come after or behind **2** : to be guided by : OBEY ⟨*follow* your conscience⟩ ⟨*follow* in-structions⟩ **3** : to go after or on the track of ⟨*follow* that car⟩ **4** : to go along ⟨*follow* a path⟩ **5** : to work in or at something as a business or way of life ⟨*follow* the sea⟩ **6** : to come after in order of rank or natural sequence ⟨two *follows* one⟩ **7** : to keep one's attention fixed on ⟨*follow* a speech⟩ **8** : to result from something ⟨fame *followed* the captain's success⟩ ⟨from the evidence given, it *follows* that the accused is guilty⟩ *synonyms* see CHASE — **fol-low suit** **1** : to play a card of the same suit as the card led **2** : to follow an example set

²follow *n* : the act or process of following

fol·low·er \'fäl-ə-wər\ *n* **1** : ²ATTENDANT 1 **2** : SUPPORT-ER, ADHERENT **3** : DISCIPLE 1

¹fol·low·ing \'fäl-ə-win\ *adj* **1** : being next in order or time ⟨the *following* day⟩ **2** : listed or shown next ⟨trains will leave at the *following* times⟩

²following *n* : a group of followers

³following *prep* : immediately after ⟨*following* the concert refreshments were served⟩

follow through *vb* **1** : to complete a stroke or swing **2** : to continue in an activity or process especially to a conclu-sion ⟨*follow through* with a study⟩ — **fol·low–through** \'fäl-ō-ˌthrü, ˌfäl-ō-'thrü, -ə-\ *n*

fol·low–up \'fäl-ə-ˌwəp\ *n* **1** : the act or an instance of following up ⟨therapy as a *follow-up* to surgery⟩ **2** : something that follows up — **follow–up** *adj*

follow up \ˌfäl-ə-'wəp\ *vb* **1** : to follow with something similar, related, or additional ⟨*follow up* an idea with ac-tion⟩ **2** : to seek more details about ⟨the police are *fol-lowing up* leads⟩

fol·ly \'fäl-ē\ *n, pl* **follies** **1** : lack of good sense or judg-ment **2** : foolish actions or conduct **3** : a foolish act or idea

fo·ment \'fō-ˌment, fō-'ment\ *vb* : to stir up : ROUSE, IN-STIGATE ⟨*foment* rebellion⟩ — **fo·ment·er** *n*

fo·men·ta·tion \ˌfō-mən-'tā-shən, -ˌmen-\ *n* **1** : a warm or hot moist material (as a hot damp cloth) applied to the body to ease pain **2** : the act of fomenting : INSTIGA-TION

fond \'fänd\ *adj* **1** : having a liking or love ⟨*fond* of praise⟩ ⟨*fond* of music⟩ **2** : LOVING, AFFECTIONATE ⟨a *fond* fam-ily⟩ ⟨a *fond* farewell⟩ **3** : cherished with great affection ⟨their *fondest* hopes⟩ — **fond·ly** \'fän(d)lē\ *adv* — **fond-ness** \'fän(d)-nəs\ *n*

fon·dant \'fän-dənt\ *n* **1** : a creamy preparation of sugar used as a basis for candies or icings **2** : a candy consisting chiefly of fondant

fon·dle \'fän-dᵊl\ *vb* **fon·dled; fon·dling** \-(d)liŋ, -dᵊl-iŋ\ : to touch or handle in a tender or loving manner : CA-RESS, PET — **fon·dler** \-(d)lər, -dᵊl-ər\ *n*

fon·due \fän-'d(y)ü\ *n* : a preparation of melted cheese and flavorings

¹**font** \'fänt\ *n* **1** : a basin for baptismal or holy water **2** : FOUNTAIN 2 [Old English *font* "basin for holy water," derived from Latin *font-, fons* "fountain, spring" — relat-ed to FOUNTAIN]

²**font** *n* : an assortment of type or characters all of one size and style [from early French *fonte* "act of casting metal," derived from Latin *fundere* "to pour melted metal into a mold" — related to ³FOUND, ²FOUNDER]

fon·ta·nel *also* **fon·ta·nelle** \ˌfänt-ə-'nel, 'fänt-ə-ˌ\ *n* : a membrane-covered opening between the bones of the skull of a fetus or infant

food \'füd\ *n* **1** : material containing or consisting of car-bohydrates, fats, and proteins used in the body of an ani-mal to sustain growth, repair, and vital processes and to furnish energy; *also* : such material together with extra substances (as vitamins and minerals) **2 a** : organic sub-stances taken in by green plants and used to build or-ganic nutrients **b** : organic material produced by green plants and used by them as building material and as a source of energy **3** : nourishment in solid form **4** : some-thing that nourishes, supports, or supplies ⟨*food* for thought⟩

food chain *n* : a series of organisms in which each uses the next usually lower member of the series as a food source

foodie *n* : a person having an avid interest in the latest food fads

food poisoning *n* : a digestive sickness caused by bacteria or by chemicals in food

food processor *n* : an electric kitchen appliance that has blades that turn inside a container and is used for cutting and blending food

food pyramid *n* : a series of levels of ecological food rela-tionships arranged by levels in which a chief predator is at the top, each level preys on the next lower level, and green plants are usually at the bottom

food stamp *n* : a coupon issued by the government that is given to low-income persons to be exchanged for food

food·stuff \'füd-ˌstəf\ *n* : a substance with food value; *esp* : a specific nutrient (as protein or fat)

food vacuole *n* : a vacuole (as in an amoeba) in which ingested food is digested

food web *n* : the whole group of interacting food chains in an ecological community

¹**fool** \'fül\ *n* **1** : a person who lacks good sense or judg-ment **2** : a person formerly kept in a noble or royal household to amuse with jests and pranks

²**fool** *vb* **1 a** : to spend time idly ⟨just *fooling* around⟩ **b** : to meddle or tamper thoughtlessly or ignorantly ⟨don't *fool* with that dial⟩ **2** : to speak or act in fun : JOKE ⟨I was only *fooling*⟩ **3** : to make a fool of : TRICK ⟨I *fooled* you⟩

fool·ery \'fül-(ə-)rē\ *n, pl* **-er·ies 1** : a foolish act : HORSE-PLAY **2** : foolish behavior

fool·har·dy \'fül-ˌhärd-ē\ *adj* : foolishly adventurous or bold — **fool·har·di·ly** \-ˌhärd-ᵊl-ē\ *adv* — **fool·har·di-ness** \-ˌhärd-ē-nəs\ *n*

fool·ish \'fü-lish\ *adj* : lacking in good sense or judgment : SENSELESS, SILLY — **fool·ish·ly** *adv* — **fool·ish·ness** *n*

fool·proof \'fül-ˈprüf\ *adj* : done, made, or planned so well that nothing can go wrong ⟨*foolproof* directions⟩

fool's gold *n* : PYRITE

¹**foot** \'fut\ *n, pl* **feet** \'fēt\ *also* **foot 1 a** : the end part of the leg below the ankle of a vertebrate animal **b** : an or-gan upon which an invertebrate animal stands or moves; *esp* : a bottom muscular part of a mollusk **2** : a unit of length equal to ⅓ yard or 12 inches (0.3048 meter) ⟨a 10-*foot* pole⟩ ⟨six *feet* tall⟩ — see MEASURE table **3** : the basic unit of verse meter made up of a group of accented and unaccented syllables **4** : something resembling an animal's foot in position or use or in being opposite the head ⟨the *foot* of a mountain⟩ ⟨the *foot* of a bed⟩ — **on foot 1** : by walking ⟨went *on foot*⟩ **2** : UNDER WAY 2 ⟨an investigation was set *on foot*⟩ — **on one's feet 1** : in a standing position **2** : in an established position or state **3** : in a recovered condition (as from illness) ⟨back *on my feet*⟩ **4** : while in action ⟨good debaters can think *on their feet*⟩

²**foot** *vb* **1 a** : ¹DANCE 1 **b** : ¹WALK 1 **c** : ¹RUN 1a **2 a** : to add up **b** : to pay or provide for paying ⟨*foot* the bill⟩

foot–and–mouth disease *n* : a virus disease especially of cattle that is marked by fever and by ulcers in the mouth, about the hooves, and on the udder — called also *hoof-and-mouth disease*

foot·ball \'fut-ˌbol\ *n* **1** : any of several games in which two teams try to advance a ball to the goals at each end of a large rectangular field: as **a** *British* : SOCCER **b** *British* : RUGBY **c** : an American game played between two teams of 11 players each in which the ball is ad-vanced by running or passing **2** : the ball used in foot-ball

foot·board \-ˌbō(ə)rd, -ˌbo(ə)rd\ *n* : a board forming the foot of a bed

foot·bridge \-ˌbrij\ *n* : a bridge for pedestrians

foot–can·dle \-'kan-dᵊl\ *n* : a unit for measuring illumina-tion that equals one lumen per square foot

foot·ed \'fut-əd\ *adj* : having a foot or feet especially of a certain kind or number ⟨flat-*footed*⟩ ⟨a four-*footed* ani-mal⟩

foot·fall \'fut-ˌfol\ *n* : the sound of a footstep

foot·gear \-ˌgi(ə)r\ *n* : FOOTWEAR

foot·hill \-ˌhil\ *n* : a hill at the foot of higher hills or moun-tains

foot·hold \-ˌhōld\ *n* **1** : a hold for the feet : FOOTING **2** : a position usable as a base for further advance

foot·ing \'fut-iŋ\ *n* **1 a** : the placing of one's feet in a posi-tion to secure a firm or safe stand **b** : a place for the foot to rest securely **2 a** : a place or position providing a base of operations : FOOTHOLD **2 b** : position with respect to one another : STATUS ⟨all started off on an equal *footing*⟩ **c** : BASIS ⟨put the business on a firm *footing*⟩

foot·lights \'fut-ˌlīts\ *n pl* **1** : a row of lights set across the front of a stage floor **2** : acting on the stage as a profes-sion ⟨the attraction of the *footlights*⟩

foot·lock·er \-ˌläk-ər\ *n* : a small trunk designed to be placed at the foot of a bed

\ə\ abut	\au̇\ out	\i\ tip	\o̊\ saw	\u̇\ foot
\ər\ further	\ch\ chin	\ī\ life	\o̊i\ coin	\y\ yet
\a\ mat	\e\ pet	\j\ job	\th\ thin	\yü\ few
\ā\ take	\ē\ easy	\ŋ\ sing	\t͟h\ this	\yu̇\ cure
\ä\ cot, cart	\g\ go	\ō\ bone	\ü\ food	\zh\ vision

foot·loose \-,lüs\ *adj* : having no ties : free to roam

foot·man \-mən\ *n* 1 : an infantry soldier 2 : a male servant who lets in visitors and waits on the table

foot·note \-,nōt\ *n* : a note of reference, explanation, or comment usually placed below the text on a printed page — **footnote** *vb*

foot·pad \-,pad\ *n* : a somewhat flat foot on the leg of a spacecraft for distributing weight to decrease sinking into a surface (as on the moon)

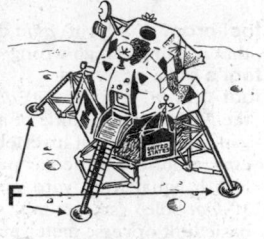

F footpad

foot·path \-,path, -,päth\ *n* : a narrow path for pedestrians

foot–pound \-'pau̇nd\ *n, pl* **foot–pounds** : a unit of work that equals the work done by a force of one pound acting through a distance of one foot and that is equal to about 1.36 joules

foot–pound–second *adj* : being or relating to a system of units based upon the foot as the unit of length, the pound as the unit of weight, and the second as the unit of time — abbreviation *fps*

foot·print \'fu̇t-,print\ *n* : a track left by the foot

foot·race \-,rās\ *n* : a race run on foot

foot·rest \-,rest\ *n* : a support for the feet

foot soldier *n* : INFANTRYMAN

foot·sore \'fu̇t-,sō(ə)r, -,sȯ(ə)r\ *adj* : having sore or tender feet (as from much walking)

foot·step \-,step\ *n* 1 a : a step of the foot b : the distance covered by a step : PACE 2 a : the mark of the foot b : the sound of a footstep 3 : a step on which to go up or down

foot·stool \-,stül\ *n* : a low stool to support the feet

foot·wear \-,wa(ə)r, -,we(ə)r\ *n* : covering (as shoes) for the feet

foot·work \-,wərk\ *n* : the movement of the feet (as in boxing)

foo·zle \'fü-zəl\ *vb* **foo·zled; foo·zling** \'füz-(ə-)liŋ\ : BUNGLE — **foozle** *n*

fop \'fäp\ *n* : [1]DANDY 1 — **fop·pish** \'fäp-ish\ *adj*

[1]**for** \fər, (')fȯ(ə)r\ *prep* 1 — used to indicate a purpose (money *for* lunch), an intended goal (left *for* work), or an object of one's desire (now *for* a good rest) 2 : as being (do you take me *for* a fool) (eggs *for* breakfast) 3 : because of (cried *for* joy) 4 a : in support of (fighting *for* their country) b — used to indicate suitability or fitness (it's not *for* me to say) (medicine *for* an illness) c : so as to bring about a certain state (shouted the news *for* all to hear) 5 a : in place of (go to the store *for* me) b : as the equal or equivalent of in an exchange or loan (paid $10 *for* a hat) 6 : in spite of (unconvinced *for* all the clever arguments) 7 : with respect to : CONCERNING (had an eye *for* news) 8 — used to indicate equality or proportion (point *for* point) (tall *for* your age) 9 — used to indicate length of time or extent of space (waited *for* several hours) 10 : [2]AFTER 3a (named *for* my grandmother)

[2]**for** *conj* : for the reason that : on this ground : BECAUSE (they were certainly there, *for* I saw them)

fora *plural of* FORUM

[1]**for·age** \'fȯr-ij, 'fär-\ *n* 1 : food (as pasture) for browsing or grazing animals 2 : a search for food or supplies

[2]**forage** *vb* **for·aged; for·ag·ing** 1 : [1]BROWSE 1, GRAZE 2 : to make a search especially for food or supplies (*forage* for grain) (*forage* for firewood) 3 : to get by foraging — **for·ag·er** *n*

fo·ra·men mag·num \fə-,rā-mən-'mag-nəm\ *n* : the opening in the skull through which the spinal cord joins the brain

for·a·min·i·fer \,fȯr-ə-'min-ə-fər, ,fär-\ *n* : any of an order of large chiefly marine protozoans that resemble amoebas, usually have perforated shells containing calcium, and are important sources of chalk and limestone

fo·ra·mi·nif·era \fə-,ram-ə-'nif-(ə-)rə, ,fȯr-ə-mə-'nif-, ,fär-\ *n pl* : protozoans that are foraminifers

for·a·mi·nif·er·an \-'nif-(ə-)rən\ *n* : FORAMINIFER

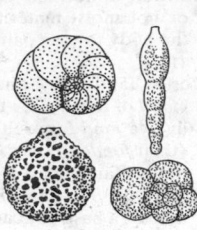

foraminifer shells

for·ay \'fȯr-,ā\ *vb* : to raid especially in order to steal : PILLAGE — **foray** *n*

[1]**for·bear** \fȯr-'ba(ə)r, fər-, -'be(ə)r\ *vb* **-bore** \-'bō(ə)r, -'bȯ(ə)r\; **-borne** \-'bō(ə)rn, -'bȯ(ə)rn\; **-bear·ing** 1 : to hold back or keep from : ABSTAIN 2 : to be patient when annoyed — **for·bear·er** *n*

[2]**forbear** *variant of* FOREBEAR

for·bear·ance \fȯr-'bar-ən(t)s, fər-, -'ber-\ *n* 1 : the act of forbearing 2 : the quality of being forbearing : PATIENCE

for·bid \fər-'bid, fȯr-\ *vb* **-bade** \-'bad, -'bād\ *also* **-bad** \-'bad\; **-bid·den** \-'bid-ᵊn\; **-bid·ding** : to order not to do or to be done or used (I *forbid* you to go) (cameras are *forbidden*) — **for·bid·der** *n*

forbidding *adj* : tending to frighten or discourage (a dark *forbidding* sky) — **for·bid·ding·ly** \-iŋ-lē\ *adv*

forbode *variant of* FOREBODE

[1]**force** \'fō(ə)rs, 'fȯ(ə)rs\ *n* 1 a : strength or energy put forth : active power (*forces* of nature) b : capacity to persuade or convince (the *force* of this argument) c : the state of existing and being enforced : EFFECT (that law is still in *force*) 2 : a group of persons trained and available for action (a police *force*) (the nation's labor *force*) 3 : violence or power used on a person or thing (open a door by *force*) 4 : an influence (as a push or pull) that tends to produce a change in the speed or direction of motion of something (the *force* of gravity) — **force·less** \-ləs\ *adj*

[2]**force** *vb* **forced; forc·ing** 1 : to make (as a person) do something (*forced* them to work) 2 a : to get or make by using force (*forced* their way into the room) b : to break open or through (*force* a lock) 3 : to produce with effort (*forced* a weak smile) 4 : to speed up the development of (*force* flowers) — **forc·er** *n*

forced \'fō(ə)rst, 'fȯ(ə)rst\ *adj* 1 : caused or brought about by force or necessity : INVOLUNTARY (made a *forced* landing) 2 : done or produced with effort (a *forced* laugh)

force–feed \'fō(ə)rs-,fēd, 'fȯ(ə)rs-\ *vb* **-fed** \-,fed\; **-feed·ing** 1 : to feed (an animal or person) by forcefully giving food 2 : to force to take in (*force-feed* the classics to students)

force·ful \'fōrs-fəl, 'fȯrs-\ *adj* : having or done with much force : VIGOROUS (a *forceful* speech) — **force·ful·ly** \-fə-lē\ *adv* — **force·ful·ness** *n*

for·ceps \'fȯr-səps, -,seps\ *n, pl* **forceps** : a tool for grasping or holding objects especially in delicate operations (as by a jeweler or surgeon) — **for·ceps·like** \-,līk\ *adj*

forc·i·ble \'fȯr-sə-bəl, 'fȯr-\ *adj* 1 : got, made, or done by force or violence (a *forcible* entrance) 2 : FORCEFUL — **forc·i·bly** \-blē\ *adv*

[1]**ford** \'fō(ə)rd, 'fȯ(ə)rd\ *n* : a shallow part of a body of water that may be crossed by wading

[2]**ford** *vb* : to cross (a body of water) by wading — **ford·able** \-ə-bəl\ *adj*

¹fore \'fō(ə)r, 'fò(ə)r\ *adv* : in, toward, or near the front : FORWARD

²fore *adj* : being or coming before in time, order, or space

³fore *n* : a front place or position ⟨came to the *fore*⟩

⁴fore *interj* — used by a golfer to warn anyone within range of a hit ball

fore- *combining form* **1 a** : earlier : beforehand ⟨*foresee*⟩ **b** : occurring earlier : occurring beforehand ⟨*forethought*⟩ **2 a** : situated at the front : in front ⟨*foreleg*⟩ **b** : front part of (something specified) ⟨*forearm*⟩ [Old English *fore-* "earlier, beforehand"]

fore–and–aft \ˌfōr-ə-'naft, ˌfòr-\ *adj* **1** : lying, running, or acting along the length of a structure (as of a ship) ⟨*fore-and-aft* sails⟩ **2** : having no square sails

fore–and–aft rig *n* : a sailing-ship rig in which most or all of the sails are set lengthwise along the centerline of the ship rather than across it

fore-and-aft rig

¹fore·arm \(')fōr-ˌärm, (')fòr-\ *vb* : to arm in advance : PREPARE

²fore·arm \'fōr-ˌärm, 'fòr-\ *n* : the part of the human arm between the elbow and the wrist

fore·bear *also* **for·bear** \'fōr-ˌba(ə)r, 'fòr-, -ˌbe(ə)r\ *n* : ANCESTOR 1, FOREFATHER

fore·bode *also* **for·bode** \fōr-'bōd, fòr-\ *vb* **1** : to have a feeling that something especially unfortunate is going to happen **2** : FORETELL, PORTEND ⟨the heavy air *forebodes* a storm⟩ — **fore·bod·er** *n* — **fore·bod·ing** \-'bōd-iŋ\ *n* — **fore·bod·ing·ly** \-iŋ-lē\ *adv*

fore·brain \'fō(ə)r-ˌbrān, 'fò(ə)r-\ *n* : the front division of the embryonic brain of a vertebrate animal or the parts developed from it

¹fore·cast \'fō(ə)r-ˌkast, 'fò(ə)r-\ *vb* **forecast** *also* **fore·cast·ed; fore·cast·ing** : to calculate or predict (a future event or state) usually by study and examination of data ⟨*forecast* the weather⟩ **synonyms** see FORETELL — **fore·cast·er** *n*

²forecast *n* : an estimate or prediction of a future happening or condition ⟨weather *forecasts*⟩

fore·cas·tle \'fōk-səl; 'fōr-ˌkas-əl, 'fòr-\ *or* **fo'·c'sle** \'fōk-səl\ *n* **1** : the forward part of the upper deck of a ship **2** : the living area for the crew in the front part of a ship

fore·close \(')fōr-'klōz, (')fòr-\ *vb* : to take legal measures to end a mortgage and take possession of the mortgaged property because the conditions of the mortgage have not been met — **fore·clo·sure** \-'klō-zhər\ *n*

fore·deck \'fō(ə)r-ˌdek, 'fò(ə)r-\ *n* : the front part of a ship's main deck

fore·doom \(')fōr-'düm, (')fòr-\ *vb* : to doom beforehand

fore·fa·ther \'fō(ə)r-ˌfath̠-ər, 'fò(ə)r-, -ˌfath̠-\ *n* **1** : ANCESTOR 1 **2** : a person of an earlier period and similar culture

fore·fin·ger \-ˌfiŋ-gər\ *n* : INDEX FINGER

fore·foot \-ˌfut\ *n* : one of the front feet of a four-footed animal

fore·front \-ˌfrənt\ *n* : the most important part or place

foregather *variant of* FORGATHER

¹fore·go \fōr-'gō, fòr-\ *vb* **-went** \-'went\; **-gone** \-'gòn *also* -'gän\; **-go·ing** \-'gō-iŋ\ : to go before : PRECEDE — **fore·go·er** \-'gō(-ə)r\ *n*

²forego *variant of* FORGO

fore·go·ing \fōr-'gō-iŋ, fòr-\ *adj* : going before : PRECEDING

fore·gone \ˌfōr-'gòn, ˌfòr- *also* -ˌgän\ *adj* : settled in advance ⟨a *foregone* conclusion⟩

fore·ground \'fō(ə)r-ˌgraùnd, 'fò(ə)r-\ *n* : the part of a scene or picture that is nearest to and in front of the viewer

fore·hand \-ˌhand\ *n* : a stroke made with the palm of the hand turned in the direction in which the hand is moving — **forehand** *adv or adj*

forehand

fore·hand·ed \fōr-'han-dəd, fòr-\ *adj* : thinking of future needs : THRIFTY — **fore·hand·ed·ly** *adv* — **fore·hand·ed·ness** *n*

fore·head \'fär-əd, 'fòr-; 'fō(ə)r-ˌhed, 'fò(ə)r-\ *n* : the part of the face above the eyes

for·eign \'fòr-ən, 'fär-\ *adj* **1** : located outside a place or country and especially outside one's own country ⟨*foreign* nations⟩ **2** : born in, belonging to, or characteristic of a place or country other than the one under consideration ⟨*foreign* language⟩ ⟨*foreign* customs⟩ **3** : related to or dealing with other nations ⟨*foreign* affairs⟩ ⟨*foreign* office⟩ **4** : not normally found in an area or part ⟨a *foreign* body in the eye⟩ — **for·eign·ness** \-ən-nəs\ *n*

for·eign·er \'fòr-ə-nər, 'fär-\ *n* : a person who is from a foreign country

foreign minister *n* : a government minister for foreign affairs

fore·know \(')fōr-'nō, (')fòr-\ *vb* **-knew** \-'n(y)ü\; **-known** \-'nōn\; **-know·ing** : to have earlier knowledge of : know beforehand — **fore·knowl·edge** \-'näl-ij\ *n*

fore·leg \'fōr-ˌleg, 'fòr-\ *n* : a front leg

fore·limb \-ˌlim\ *n* : an arm, fin, wing, or leg that is one of a front pair of limbs or corresponds to one

fore·lock \-ˌläk\ *n* : a lock of hair growing from the front of the head

fore·man \'fōr-mən, 'fòr-\ *n* **1** : a member of a jury who is the leader **2** : a person in charge of a group of workers

fore·mast \-ˌmast, -məst\ *n* : the mast nearest the bow of a ship

fore·most \-ˌmōst\ *adj* : first in time, place, or order : most important — **foremost** *adv*

fore·name \-ˌnām\ *n* : a first name

fore·noon \-ˌnün\ *n* : the early part of the day ending with noon : MORNING

fo·ren·sic \fə-'ren(t)-sik, -'ren-zik\ *adj* : belonging to, used in, or suitable to courts of law or to public discussion and debate [from Latin *forensis* "of a forum, public," from *forum* "market, place of public discussion, court"] — **fo·ren·si·cal·ly** \-si-k(ə-)lē, -zi-\ *adv*

fore·or·dain \ˌfōr-òr-'dān, ˌfòr-\ *vb* : to determine in advance : PREDESTINE

fore·part \'fō(ə)r-ˌpärt, 'fò(ə)r-\ *n* : the part most advanced or first in place or in time

fore·paw \-ˌpò\ *n* : the paw of a foreleg

fore·quar·ter \-ˌkwò(r)t-ər\ *n* : the left or right half of a front half of the body of a four-footed animal

fore·run·ner \-ˌrən-ər\ *n* **1** : one going or sent before to give notice of the approach of others : HARBINGER **2** : PREDECESSOR, ANCESTOR

\ə\ **abut**	\aù\ **out**	\i\ **tip**	\ò\ **saw**	\ù\ **foot**
\ər\ **further**	\ch\ **chin**	\ī\ **life**	\òi\ **coin**	\y\ **yet**
\a\ **mat**	\e\ **pet**	\j\ **job**	\th\ **thin**	\yü\ **few**
\ā\ **take**	\ē\ **easy**	\ŋ\ **sing**	\th̠\ **this**	\yù\ **cure**
\ä\ **cot, cart**	\g\ **go**	\ō\ **bone**	\ü\ **food**	\zh\ **vision**

fore·sail \-,sāl, -səl\ *n* : the lowest and largest sail on the foremast of a square-rigged ship or schooner

F foresail

fore·see \fōr-'sē, fòr-\ *vb* **-saw** \-'sò\; **-seen** \-'sēn\; **-see·ing** : to see or realize beforehand : EXPECT — **fore·see·able** \-'sē-ə-bəl\ *adj* — **fore·se·er** \-'sē-ər\ *n*

fore·shad·ow \-'shad-ō\ *vb* : to give a hint or suggestion of beforehand — **fore·shad·ow·er** *n*

fore·shock \'fō(ə)r-,shäk, 'fò(ə)r-\ *n* : a minor tremor prior to an earthquake

fore·short·en \fōr-'shòrt-ᵊn, fòr-\ *vb* : to shorten (a detail) in a drawing or painting so that it appears to have depth

fore·sight \'fō(ə)r-,sīt, 'fò(ə)r-\ *n* **1** : the act or power of foreseeing **2** : care or preparation for the future ⟨had the *foresight* to invest his money wisely⟩ — **fore·sight·ed** \-,sīt-əd\ *adj* — **fore·sight·ed·ly** *adv* — **fore·sight·ed·ness** *n*

fore·skin \-,skin\ *n* : a fold of skin that covers the end of the penis — called also *prepuce*

for·est \'fòr-əst, 'fär-\ *n* : a dense growth of trees and underbrush covering a large area

fore·stall \fōr-'stòl, fòr-\ *vb* : to keep out, interfere with, or prevent by steps taken in advance — **fore·stall·er** *n* — **fore·stall·ment** \-'stòl-mənt\ *n*

for·es·ta·tion \,fòr-ə-'stā-shən, ,fär-\ *n* : the planting and care of a forest

for·est·ed \'fòr-ə-stəd, 'fär-\ *adj* : covered with trees or forests : WOODED

for·est·er \'fòr-ə-stər, 'fär-\ *n* : a person who practices or is trained in forestry

forest fire *n* : an uncontrolled fire in a wooded area

forest floor *n* : the upper layer of mixed soil and decayed or decaying organic material typical of forested land

forest ranger *n* : a person in charge of the management and protection of a forest

for·est·ry \'fòr-ə-strē, 'fär-\ *n* : the science and practice of caring for forests

foreswear *variant of* FORSWEAR

fore·taste \'fō(ə)r-,tāst, 'fò(ə)r-\ *n* : a sample or partial experience of something that will not be fully experienced until later ⟨the cold day was a *foretaste* of winter⟩

fore·tell \fōr-'tel, fòr-\ *vb* **-told** \-'tōld\; **-tell·ing** : to tell of or describe beforehand — **fore·tell·er** *n*
   synonyms FORETELL, PREDICT, FORECAST mean to tell beforehand. FORETELL applies to the coming of a future event especially through mysterious powers ⟨the fortune-teller *foretold* his future⟩. PREDICT may suggest an exact statement that is the result of the gathering of information and the use of scientific methods ⟨scientists can sometimes *predict* the course of a hurricane⟩. FORECAST suggests the gathering of evidence and a statement of what is most likely to happen ⟨the weather bureau *forecast* that it would snow⟩.

fore·thought \'fō(ə)r-,thòt, 'fò(ə)r-\ *n* : thought or care taken in advance — **fore·thought·ful** \-fəl\ *adj*

fore·top \'fō(ə)r-,täp, 'fò(ə)r-; 'fōrt-əp, 'fòrt-\ *n* : a platform near the top of a ship's foremast

for·ev·er \fə-'rev-ər, fò-\ *adv* **1** : for a limitless time : EVERLASTINGLY ⟨wants to live *forever*⟩ **2** : ALWAYS 1, CONSTANTLY ⟨a dog that was *forever* chasing cars⟩

for·ev·er·more \fə-,rev-ə(r)-'mō(ə)r, -'mò(ə)r, fò-\ *adv* : FOREVER 1

fore·warn \fōr-'wò(ə)rn, fòr-\ *vb* : to warn in advance ⟨*forewarned* of danger⟩

forewent *past of* FOREGO

fore·wing \'fō(ə)r-,wiŋ, 'fò(ə)r-\ *n* : either of the front wings of a four-winged insect

fore·word \'fōr-(,)wərd, 'fòr-\ *n* : ¹PREFACE

¹for·feit \'fòr-fət\ *n* : something forfeited : PENALTY, FINE

²forfeit *vb* : to lose or lose the right to as a punishment for an error, offense, or crime — **for·feit·er** *n*

for·fei·ture \'fòr-fə-,chù(ə)r, -chər\ *n* **1** : the act of forfeiting **2** : something forfeited : PENALTY

for·gath·er *or* **fore·gath·er** \fòr-'gath-ər, fōr-\ *vb* : to come together : ASSEMBLE, MEET

¹forge \'fō(ə)rj, 'fò(ə)rj\ *n* : a furnace or a shop with its furnace where metal is shaped and worked by heating and hammering [Middle English *forge* "workshop where metal is heated and shaped," from early French *forge* (same meaning), from Latin *fabrica* "workshop for making things of metal"]

²forge *vb* **forged; forg·ing** **1 a** : to form (as metal) by heating and hammering **b** : to form (metal) by a press **2** : to make or imitate falsely especially with intent to deceive : COUNTERFEIT ⟨*forge* a check⟩ ⟨*forge* a signature⟩ **3** : to form or shape in any way : FASHION ⟨*forged* an agreement⟩ — **forg·er** *n*

³forge *vb* **forged; forg·ing** : to move forward steadily but gradually ⟨*forged* through the snow⟩ [origin unknown]

forg·ery \'fōrj-(ə)-rē, 'fòrj-\ *n, pl* **-er·ies** **1** : something (as a signature) that has been forged **2** : the crime of falsely making or changing a written paper or signing someone else's name

for·get \fər-'get, fòr-\ *vb* **-got** \-'gät\; **-got·ten** \-'gät-ᵊn\ *or* **-got; -get·ting** **1** : to be unable to think of or recall ⟨*forgot* the address⟩ **2 a** : to fail to remember to do something ⟨*forgot* to call you⟩ ⟨*forgot* about practicing⟩ **b** : ¹NEGLECT 1 ⟨*forget* old friends⟩ **3** : OVERLOOK 3b ⟨I shouldn't have said that, so just *forget* it⟩ **4** : to stop remembering or noticing ⟨forgive and *forget*⟩ — **for·get·ter** *n* — **forget oneself** : to lose one's temper or self-control

for·get·ful \fər-'get-fəl, fòr-\ *adj* : forgetting easily — **for·get·ful·ly** \-fə-lē\ *adv* — **for·get·ful·ness** *n*

for·get–me–not \fər-'get-mē-,nät, fòr-\ *n* : any of a genus of small herbs with bright blue or white flowers

forg·ing \'fōr-jiŋ, 'fòr-\ *n* : a piece of forged work ⟨aluminum *forgings*⟩

forget-me-not

for·give \fər-'giv, fòr-\ *vb* **-gave** \-'gāv\; **-giv·en** \-'giv-ən\; **-giv·ing** **1 a** : to give up resentment of or claim to revenge for ⟨*forgive* an insult⟩ **b** : to stop requiring payment of ⟨*forgive* a debt⟩ **2** : to stop feeling anger toward (an offender) ⟨*forgive* your enemies⟩ **synonyms** see EXCUSE — **for·giv·able** \-'giv-ə-bəl\ *adj* — **for·giv·er** *n*

for·give·ness \fər-'giv-nəs, fòr-\ *n* : the act of forgiving : PARDON

for·giv·ing \fər-'giv-iŋ, fòr-\ *adj* **1** : showing forgiveness : inclined or ready to forgive ⟨a person with a *forgiving* nature⟩ **2** : allowing for human error or weakness ⟨a tennis racket designed to be *forgiving*⟩ — **for·giv·ing·ly** *adv* — **for·giv·ing·ness** *n*

for·go *also* **fore·go** \fòr-'gō, fōr-\ *vb* **-went** \-'went\; **-gone** \-'gòn *also* -'gän\; **-go·ing** \-'gō-iŋ\ : to let pass ⟨*forgo* an opportunity⟩ : go without ⟨*forgo* lunch⟩

¹fork \'fò(ə)rk\ *n* **1** : a tool with two or more prongs used especially for taking up (as in eating), pitching, or digging **2** : a forked part or tool **3 a** : a dividing into branches or the place where something divides into branches ⟨a *fork* in the road⟩ **b** : a branch of a fork ⟨take the left *fork*⟩

²fork *vb* **1** : to divide into two or more branches ⟨the road *forks*⟩ **2** : to raise or pitch with a fork ⟨*fork* hay⟩ **3** : to give the form of a fork to ⟨*forked* her fingers⟩ **4** : ¹PAY 2, CONTRIBUTE ⟨had to *fork* over $100⟩ — **fork·er** *n*

forked \'fò(ə)rkt, 'fòr-kəd\ *adj* : having a fork : shaped like a fork

fork·ful \'fò(ə)rk-,fùl\ *n, pl* **forkfuls** *also* **forks·ful** \'fò(ə)rks-,fùl\ : as much as a fork will hold

fork·lift \'fòr-,klift\ *n* : a machine for lifting heavy objects by means of steel fingers inserted under the load

for·lorn \fər-'lò(ə)rn, fòr-\ *adj* **1** : feeling sad and lonely especially because of being left alone **2** : nearly hopeless ⟨a *forlorn* cause⟩ — **for·lorn·ly** *adv* — **for·lorn·ness** \-'lòrn-nəs\ *n*

¹form \'fò(ə)rm\ *n* **1 a** : the shape and structure of something as distinguished from its material **b** : a body (as of a person) especially in its outward appearance or as distinguished from the face **2 a** : an established manner of doing or saying something ⟨a *form* of worship⟩ **b** : a standard or expectation based on past experience ⟨true to *form*, the champions won again⟩ **3** : a document with blank spaces for inserting information ⟨a tax *form*⟩ **4 a** : conduct determined by custom : CEREMONY, CONVENTION; *also* : display without meaning ⟨the usual *forms* upon being introduced⟩ **b** : manner of behaving according to recognized standards ⟨it's bad *form* not to wait for your turn⟩ **5** : a long seat : BENCH **6 a** : a model of the human figure used for displaying clothes **b** : a mold in which concrete is placed to set **7** : one of the different varieties of a particular thing or substance ⟨coal is a *form* of carbon⟩ **8** : any of the different pronunciations or spellings a word may take in inflection or compounding **9** : a special way of stating a mathematical expression ⟨the number 2.5 can be written in fractional *form* as ⁵⁄₂⟩ **10 a** : orderly method of arrangement; *also* : a kind or instance of such arrangement ⟨painting is an art *form*⟩ **b** : the structural element, plan, or design of a work of art **11** : a surface or space enclosed by mathematical boundaries **12** : a grade in a British secondary school or in some American private schools **13 a** : ability as shown by past performance **b** : condition for performing ⟨in top *form*⟩

²form *vb* **1** : to give form or shape to : FASHION, MAKE ⟨*form* the letter A⟩ **2** : INSTRUCT 1, TRAIN ⟨education *forms* the mind⟩ **3** : MAKE UP 2, CONSTITUTE ⟨a hat *formed* of straw⟩ **4** : DEVELOP 5, ACQUIRE ⟨*form* a habit⟩ **5** : to arrange in order ⟨*form* a line⟩ **6** : to take form : ARISE ⟨fog *forms* in the valleys⟩ **7** : to take a definite form, shape, or arrangement ⟨the customers *formed* in lines⟩ **synonyms** see MAKE — **form·er** *n*

¹for·mal \'fòr-məl\ *adj* **1** : of, relating to, or being the form of something rather than content **2 a** : following or agreeing with established form, custom, or rule ⟨a *formal* education⟩ **b** : relating to, suitable for, or being an event requiring elegant dress and manners ⟨a *formal* ball⟩ ⟨*formal* dress⟩ **3** : done in due or lawful form ⟨a *formal* contract⟩ — **for·mal·ly** \-mə-lē\ *adv* — **for·mal·ness** *n*

²formal *n* : something (as a dance) formal in nature

form·al·de·hyde \fòr-'mal-də-,hīd, fər-\ *n* : a colorless gas that consists of carbon, hydrogen, and oxygen, has a sharp irritating odor, and when dissolved in water is used to disinfect or to prevent decay

for·mal·ism \'fòr-mə-,liz-əm\ *n* : the strict observance of forms or customs — **for·mal·ist** \-ləst\ *n* — **for·mal·is·tic** \,fòr-mə-'lis-tik\ *adj* — **for·mal·is·ti·cal·ly** \-ti-k(ə-)lē\ *adv*

for·mal·i·ty \fòr-'mal-ət-ē\ *n, pl* **-ties** **1** : a going along with formal or customary rules : CEREMONY **2** : the quality or state of being formal **3** : an established form that is required or usual ⟨the interview was just a *formality*⟩

for·mal·ize \'fòr-mə-,līz\ *vb* **-ized; -iz·ing** **1** : to make formal **2** : to give formal rank or approval to — **for·mal·i·za·tion** \,fòr-mə-lə-'zā-shən\ *n* — **for·mal·iz·er** *n*

¹for·mat \'fò(ə)r-,mat\ *n* **1** : the general organization or arrangement of something **2** : a method of organizing data (as for storage) ⟨a file *format*⟩

²format *vb* **for·mat·ted; for·mat·ting** **1** : to produce in a particular format **2** : to prepare for storing computer data ⟨*format* the disk⟩

for·ma·tion \fòr-'mā-shən\ *n* **1** : a forming of something **2** : something formed **3** : the manner in which a thing is formed : STRUCTURE, SHAPE **4** : a bed of rocks or series of beds recognizable as a unit **5** : an arrangement or grouping of persons, ships, or airplanes

for·ma·tive \'fòr-mət-iv\ *adj* **1** : giving or able to give form ⟨a *formative* influence⟩ **2** : of, relating to, or characterized by important growth or formation ⟨*formative* years⟩ — **for·ma·tive·ly** *adv* — **for·ma·tive·ness** *n*

for·mer \'fòr-mər\ *adj* **1** : coming before in time **2** : first mentioned or first of two things mentioned or understood ⟨of the two choices the *former* is better⟩ **3** : having once been ⟨a *former* big-league ballplayer⟩

for·mer·ly \'fòr-mər-lē\ *adv* : at an earlier time : PREVIOUSLY

for·mic acid \,fòr-mik-\ *n* : a colorless strong-smelling acid that irritates the skin, is found in insects (as ants) and in many plants, and is used chiefly in dyeing and finishing woven fabrics

for·mi·da·ble \'fòr-məd-ə-bəl *also* fòr-'mid-\ *adj* **1** : causing fear or dread ⟨a *formidable* foe⟩ **2** : offering serious difficulties ⟨the mountains were a *formidable* barrier⟩ **3** : very impressive ⟨had won a *formidable* number of medals⟩ — **for·mi·da·ble·ness** *n* — **for·mi·da·bly** \-blē\ *adv*

form·less \'fòrm-ləs\ *adj* : having no regular form or shape — **form·less·ly** *adv* — **form·less·ness** *n*

for·mu·la \'fòr-myə-lə\ *n, pl* **-las** *or* **-lae** \-,lē, -,lī\ **1** : a set form of words for use in a ceremony or ritual **2 a** : RECIPE 3, PRESCRIPTION ⟨my *formula* for happiness⟩ **b** : a milk mixture or substitute for feeding a baby **3 a** : a general fact or rule expressed in symbols and especially mathematical symbols **b** : an expression in symbols of the composition of a substance ⟨the *formula* for water is H₂O⟩ **4** : a required or set form or method — **for·mu·la·ic** \,fòr-myə-'lā-ik\ *adj* — **for·mu·la·ical·ly** \-'lā-ə-k(ə-)lē\ *adv*

for·mu·late \'fòr-myə-,lāt\ *vb* **-lat·ed; -lat·ing** **1** : to express in a formula **2** : to put in systematic form : state definitely and clearly ⟨*formulate* a plan⟩ — **for·mu·la·tion** \,fòr-myə-'lā-shən\ *n* — **for·mu·la·tor** \'fòr-myə-,lāt-ər\ *n*

for·ni·cate \'fòr-nə-,kāt\ *vb* **-cat·ed; -cat·ing** : to commit fornication — **for·ni·ca·tor** \-,kāt-ər\ *n*

for·ni·ca·tion \,fòr-nə-'kā-shən\ *n* : sexual intercourse between two people who are not married to each other

for–prof·it \'fòr-'präf-ət\ *adj* : existing or carried on for the purpose of making a profit ⟨*for-profit* business⟩

for·sake \fər-'sāk, fòr-\ *vb* **for·sook** \-'sùk\; **for·sak·en** \-'sā-kən\; **for·sak·ing** : to give up or leave entirely ⟨her friends have *forsaken* her⟩ **synonyms** see ABANDON

for·sooth \fər-'süth\ *adv* : in truth : INDEED

for·swear *also* **fore·swear** \fòr-'swa(ə)r, fōr-, -'swe(ə)r\ *vb* **-swore** \-'swōr(ə)r, -'swò(ə)r\; **-sworn** \-'swō(ə)rn, -'swò(ə)rn\; **-swear·ing** : to make a false statement while under oath : commit perjury

for·syth·ia \fər-'sith-ē-ə\ *n, pl* **-ias** *also* **-ia** : any of a genus of shrubs related to the olive and having yellow bell-shaped flowers appearing before the leaves in early spring

fort \'fō(ə)rt, 'fò(ə)rt\ *n* **1** : a strong or fortified place **2** : a permanent army post

\ə\ **abut**	\aú\ **out**	\i\ **tip**	\ò\ **saw**	\ú\ **foot**
\ər\ **further**	\ch\ **chin**	\ī\ **life**	\òi\ **coin**	\y\ **yet**
\a\ **mat**	\e\ **pet**	\j\ **job**	\th\ **thin**	\yü\ **few**
\ā\ **take**	\ē\ **easy**	\ŋ\ **sing**	\t͟h\ **this**	\yù\ **cure**
\ä\ **cot, cart**	\g\ **go**	\ō\ **bone**	\ü\ **food**	\zh\ **vision**

¹forte \'fō(ə)rt, 'fȯ(ə)rt, 'fȯr-ˌtā\ *n* : something in which a person shows special ability : a strong point ⟨drawing was always your *forte*⟩ [from earlier *fort* "the thing a person does very well, strong point," from early French *fort* (same meaning), derived from Latin *fortis* "strong"]

²for·te \'fȯr-ˌtā, 'fȯrt-ē\ *adv or adj* : LOUD 1 — used as a direction in music [from Italian *forte* "strongly, loudly," from *forte* (adjective) "strong, loud," from Latin *fortis* "strong"]

forth \'fō(ə)rth, 'fȯ(ə)rth\ *adv* 1 : ²FORWARD, ONWARD ⟨from that time *forth*⟩ ⟨back and *forth*⟩ 2 : out into view ⟨plants putting *forth* leaves⟩

forth·com·ing \(')fōrth-'kəm-iŋ, (')fȯrth-\ *adj* 1 a : being about to appear : APPROACHING ⟨the *forthcoming* holidays⟩ ⟨your *forthcoming* novel⟩ b : readily available ⟨supplies will be *forthcoming* soon⟩ 2 a : OUTGOING 2 ⟨a *forthcoming* and courteous man⟩ b : open and candid ⟨not *forthcoming* about her past⟩

forth·right \'fōrth-ˌrīt, 'fȯrth-\ *adj* : going straight to the point clearly and firmly ⟨a *forthright* answer⟩ — **forth·right·ly** *adv* — **forth·right·ness** *n*

forth·with \(')fōrth-'with, (')fȯrth-, -'with\ *adv* : IMMEDIATELY 2 ⟨expect an answer *forthwith*⟩

for·ti·fi·ca·tion \ˌfȯrt-ə-fə-'kā-shən\ *n* 1 : the act of fortifying 2 : a construction built for defense

for·ti·fy \'fȯrt-ə-ˌfī\ *vb* **-fied; -fy·ing** : to make strong: as a : to strengthen by military defenses ⟨*fortify* a town⟩ b : to give strength or endurance to ⟨*fortify* the body against illness⟩ ⟨a team *fortified* by the cheering crowd⟩ c : to add material to for strengthening or improving : ENRICH ⟨*fortify* a soil with fertilizer⟩ ⟨milk *fortified* with vitamin D⟩ — **for·ti·fi·er** \-ˌfī-(ə)r\ *n*

for·tis·si·mo \fȯr-'tis-ə-ˌmō\ *adv or adj* : very loud — used as a direction in music

for·ti·tude \'fȯrt-ə-ˌt(y)üd\ *n* : strength of mind that enables a person to meet danger or bear pain or hardship with courage

fort·night \'fȯrt-ˌnīt, 'fȯrt-\ *n* : a period of 14 days : two weeks [Old English *fēowertȳne niht* "fourteen nights"] — **fort·night·ly** \-lē\ *adv or adj*

FOR·TRAN *or* **For·tran** \'fō(ə)r-ˌtran\ *n* : a language for programming a computer especially to solve mathematical, scientific, and engineering problems [*formula translation*]

for·tress \'fȯr-trəs\ *n* : a fortified place

for·tu·i·tous \fȯr-'t(y)ü-ət-əs, fər-\ *adj* 1 : occurring by chance 2 : FORTUNATE 1 — **for·tu·i·tous·ly** *adv* — **for·tu·i·tous·ness** *n*

for·tu·nate \'fȯrch-(ə-)nət\ *adj* 1 : coming or happening by good luck : bringing good that was not expected 2 : receiving some unexpected or unearned good : LUCKY — **for·tu·nate·ness** *n*

for·tun·ate·ly \'fȯrch-(ə-)nət-lē\ *adv* : it is fortunate : LUCKILY ⟨*fortunately* it landed right side up⟩

for·tune \'fȯr-chən\ *n* 1 a : favorable results that come partly by chance : good luck b : what happens to a person : good or bad luck ⟨follows the *fortunes* of two families through the years⟩ 2 : what is to happen to one in the future ⟨had my *fortune* told⟩; *also* : a prediction of fortune 3 a : the possession of material goods : WEALTH b : a store of material possessions : RICHES ⟨the family *fortune*⟩ c : a large sum of money

fortune cookie *n* : a thin cookie folded to contain a slip of paper on which is written a fortune

for·tune–tell·er \-ˌtel-ər\ *n* : a person who claims to foretell future events — **for·tune–tell·ing** \-ˌtel-iŋ\ *n or adj*

for·ty \'fȯrt-ē\ *n, pl* **forties** — see NUMBER table — **for·ti·eth** \-ē-əth\ *adj or adj* — **forty** *adj or pron* — **for·ty·ish** \-ē-ish\ *adj*

for·ty–five \ˌfȯrt-ē-'fīv\ *n* : a .45 caliber pistol — usually written .45

for·ty–nin·er \ˌfȯrt-ē-'nī-nər\ *n* : a person who went to California in the gold rush of 1849

forty winks *n sing or pl* : a short sleep : NAP

fo·rum \'fōr-əm, 'fȯr-\ *n, pl* **forums** *also* **fo·ra** \-ə\ 1 : the marketplace or public place of an ancient Roman city serving as the center of public business 2 : a means (as a newspaper or online service) of open discussion or expression of ideas 3 : a meeting or program involving discussion

¹for·ward \'fȯr-wərd\ *adj* 1 : near, being at, or belonging to the front part 2 : lacking proper modesty or reserve 3 : moving, tending, or leading to a position in front — **for·ward·ly** *adv* — **for·ward·ness** *n*

²forward *adv* : to or toward what is in front

³forward *vb* 1 : to help onward ⟨*forward* a friend's career⟩ 2 : to send on or forward ⟨*forward* a letter⟩

⁴forward *n* : a player who plays at the front of the team near the opponent's goal

for·ward·er \'fȯr-wərd-ər\ *n* : one that forwards

forward pass *n* : a pass in football thrown in the direction of the opponent's goal

for·wards \'fȯr-wərdz\ *adv* : ²FORWARD

forwent *past of* FORGO

fos·sa \'fäs-ə\ *n* : a slender long-tailed meat-eating mammal of Madagascar that has usually reddish brown short thick fur and is an excellent climber

¹fos·sil \'fäs-əl\ *adj* : being or resembling a fossil

²fossil *n* 1 : a trace or print or the remains of a plant or animal of a past age preserved in earth or rock 2 a : a person whose ideas are out-of-date b : something that has become fixed and cannot be changed

fossil fuel *n* : a fuel (as coal, oil, or natural gas) that is formed in the earth from plant or animal remains

fos·sil·ize \'fäs-ə-ˌlīz\ *vb* **-ized; -iz·ing** : to change or become changed into a fossil — **fos·sil·i·za·tion** \ˌfäs-ə-lə-'zā-shən\ *n*

¹fos·ter \'fȯs-tər, 'fäs-\ *adj* : giving, receiving, or sharing parental care even though not related by blood or legal ties ⟨*foster* parent⟩ ⟨*foster* child⟩

²foster *vb* **fos·tered; fos·ter·ing** \-t(ə-)riŋ\ 1 : to give parental care to 2 : to help the growth or development of — **fos·ter·er** \-tər-ər\ *n*

foster home *n* : a household in which an orphaned, neglected, or delinquent child is placed for care

Fou·cault pendulum \ˌfü-ˌkō-\ *n* : a device that consists of a heavy weight hung by a long wire and that swings in a constant direction which appears to change showing that the earth rotates

fought *past and past participle of* FIGHT

¹foul \'fau̇(ə)l\ *adj* 1 a : disgusting in looks, taste, or smell ⟨*foul* odor⟩ b : full of or covered with dirt ⟨*foul* clothes⟩ 2 a : DETESTABLE ⟨a *foul* crime⟩ b : notably unpleasant or bad ⟨a *foul* mood⟩ c : being vulgar or insulting ⟨*foul* language⟩ 3 : being wet and stormy ⟨*foul* weather⟩ 4 a : very unfair ⟨fair means or *foul*⟩ b : breaking a rule in a game or sport ⟨a *foul* blow in boxing⟩ 5 : being outside the foul lines in baseball ⟨a *foul* grounder⟩ *synonyms* see DIRTY — **foul·ly** \'fau̇(l)-lē\ *adv* — **foul·ness** \'fau̇(ə)l-nəs\ *n*

²foul *n* 1 : an entanglement or collision in fishing or sailing 2 a : a breaking of the rules in a game or sport b : FREE THROW 3 : FOUL BALL

³foul *vb* 1 : to make or become foul or filthy ⟨*foul* the air⟩ ⟨*foul* a stream⟩ 2 a : to make a foul in a game or sport b : to hit a foul ball 3 : to become or cause to become entangled ⟨*foul* the lines⟩

⁴foul *adv* : in a foul manner : so as to be foul

foul ball *n* : a baseball batted into foul territory

foul line *n* 1 : either of two straight lines running from the rear corner of home plate through first and third base on to the boundary of a baseball field 2 : a line across which a player must not step (as when bowling or shooting a free throw)

foul of *prep* : AFOUL OF

foul out *vb* : to be put out of a basketball game for making too many fouls ⟨three of our players *fouled out*⟩

foul play *n* : unfair dealing : dishonest conduct; *esp* : VIOLENCE 1 ⟨a victim of *foul play*⟩

foul shot *n* : a free throw in basketball

foul–up \ˈfau̇-ˌləp\ *n* : an instance of fouling up : a state of being fouled up

foul up \(ˈ)fau̇-ˈləp\ *vb* : to spoil by bad work or stupidity : BOTCH ⟨*fouled up* the surprise attack⟩

¹found \ˈfau̇nd\ *past and past participle of* FIND

²found *vb* : ESTABLISH 3a ⟨*found* a colony⟩ ⟨*founded* the company in 1847⟩ [Middle English *founden* "found, establish," from early French *funder* (same meaning), from Latin *fundare* (same meaning), from *fundus* "bottom, base" — related to FUND, FUNDAMENTAL]

³found *vb* : to melt (metal) and pour into a mold [from early French *fondre* "to pour, melt," from Latin *fundere* (same meaning) — related to ²FONT, ²FOUNDER]

foun·da·tion \fau̇n-ˈdā-shən\ *n* **1** : the act of founding **2** : the support upon which something rests ⟨a house with a cinder-block *foundation*⟩ ⟨suspicions with no *foundation* in fact⟩ **3** : funds given for the permanent support of an institution; *also* : an institution supported by such funds — **foun·da·tion·al** \-shnəl, -shən-ᵊl\ *adj*

¹found·er \ˈfau̇n-dər\ *n* : one that founds or establishes

²foun·der \ˈfau̇n-dər\ *vb* **foun·der·ing** \-d(ə-)riŋ\ **1** : to become lame ⟨the horse *foundered*⟩ **2** : to sink below the surface of the water ⟨a *foundering* ship⟩ [Middle English *foundren* "to fall to the ground, sink," from early French *fondrer* (same meaning), derived from Latin *fundere* "to pour, cast, disperse, lay low" — related to ²FONT, ³FOUND]

³found·er *n* : one that founds metal

found·ing father \ˈfau̇n-diŋ-\ *n* **1** : one that starts or helps to start an institution or a movement **2** *often cap* : a leading figure in the founding of the U.S.

found·ling \ˈfau̇n-(d)liŋ\ *n* : an infant found after being abandoned by unknown parents

found·ry \ˈfau̇n-drē\ *n, pl* **foundries** : a building or factory where metals are cast

fount \ˈfau̇nt\ *n* : FOUNTAIN 2

foun·tain \ˈfau̇nt-ᵊn\ *n* **1** : a spring of water coming from the earth **2** : the source from which something comes ⟨a *fountain* of knowledge⟩ **3** : an artificial stream or spray of water (as for drinking or ornament); *also* : the device from which such a stream or spray rises [Middle English *fountain* "fountain," from early French *funtaine* (same meaning), derived from Latin *font-, fons* "fountain, spring" — related to ¹FONT]

foun·tain·head \ˈfau̇nt-ᵊn-ˌhed\ *n* **1** : a spring that is the source of a stream **2** : an original or primary source : ORIGIN ⟨the *fountainhead* of our liberties⟩

fountain pen *n* : a pen with ink inside that is fed to the writing point as needed

four \ˈfō(ə)r, ˈfȯ(ə)r\ *n* **1** — see NUMBER table **2** : the fourth in a set or series **3** : something having four units or members — **four** *adj or pron*

4x4 \ˈfōr-bī-ˌfōr, ˈfȯr-bī-ˌfȯr\ *also* **four–by–four** *n* : a four-wheel automotive vehicle with four-wheel drive

four·fold \-ˌfōld, -ˈfōld\ *adj* : being four times as great or as many

four–foot·ed \-ˈfu̇t-əd\ *adj* : having four feet : QUADRUPED

4–H \ˈfō(ə)r-ˈāch, ˈfȯ(ə)r-\ *adj* : of or relating to a program set up by the U.S. Department of Agriculture to instruct young people in useful skills (as in agriculture) and in good citizenship ⟨*4-H* club⟩ [so called from the goal of improving a person in *head, heart, hands,* and *health*] — **4–H'·er** \-ˈāch-ər\ *n*

four–in–hand \ˈfōr-ən-ˌhand, ˈfȯr-\ *n* : a necktie tied in a slipknot so that the ends overlap and hang down in front

four–o'clock \ˈfōr-ə-ˌkläk, ˈfȯr-\ *n* : an American garden plant with fragrant yellow, red, or white flowers that open late in the afternoon

four–post·er \-ˈpō-stər\ *n* : a bed with tall posts at each corner

four·score \ˈfōr-ˈskō(ə)r, ˈfȯr-ˈskȯ(ə)r\ *adj* : being four times twenty : EIGHTY

four·some \ˈfōr-səm, ˈfȯr-\ *n* **1** : a group of four persons or things **2** : a golf match between two pairs of partners

four·square \ˈfōr-ˈskwa(ə)r, -ˈskwe(ə)r, ˈfȯr-\ *adj* **1** : ²SQUARE 1a **2** : marked by boldness and firmness : FORTHRIGHT — **foursquare** *adv*

four-poster

four·teen \(ˈ)fōr(t)-ˈtēn, (ˈ)fȯr(t)-\ *n* — see NUMBER table — **fourteen** *adj or pron* — **four·teenth** \-ˈtēn(t)th\ *adj or n*

fourth \ˈfō(ə)rth, ˈfȯ(ə)rth\ *n* **1** — see NUMBER table **2** : the difference in pitch between the first tone and the fourth tone of a scale — **fourth** *adj or adv* — **fourth·ly** *adv*

fourth estate *n, often cap F&E* : the journalists of a country

Fourth of July : INDEPENDENCE DAY

four–wheel \ˌfōr-ˌhwēl, ˌfȯr-, -ˌwēl\ *or* **four–wheeled** \ˈfōr-ˈhwē(ə)ld, ˈfȯr-, -ˈwē(ə)ld\ *adj* **1** : having four wheels **2** : acting on or by means of four wheels ⟨a car with *four-wheel* drive⟩

fo·vea \ˈfō-vē-ə\ *n, pl* **fo·ve·ae** \-vē-ˌē, -vē-ˌī\ : an area in the middle of the retina that gives the sharpest vision of any part of the retina and contains only cones

¹fowl \ˈfau̇(ə)l\ *n, pl* **fowl** *or* **fowls** **1** : ¹BIRD 1: as **a** : a domestic cock or hen; *esp* : a full-grown hen **b** : any of several domesticated or wild birds related to the common domestic chicken **2** : the meat of fowl used as food

²fowl *vb* : to hunt, catch, or kill wildfowl — **fowl·er** *n*

fowling piece *n* : a light shotgun for shooting birds or small animals

¹fox \ˈfäks\ *n, pl* **fox·es** *also* **fox** **1 a** : any of various alert flesh-eating mammals related to the wolves but smaller and with shorter legs and a more pointed muzzle **b** : the fur of a fox **2** : a clever tricky person **3** : an attractive young woman or man

²fox *vb* : OUTWIT

fox fire *n* : an eerie glow seen at night in woods and bogs that is caused by a fungus in decaying wood

fox·glove \ˈfäks-ˌgləv\ *n* : any of a genus of upright herbs related to the snapdragons; *esp* : a tall herb with showy dotted white or purple tube-shaped flowers that is a source of digitalis

fox·hole \-ˌhōl\ *n* : a pit dug usually in a hurry for individual cover against enemy fire

fox·hound \-ˌhau̇nd\ *n* : a large swift powerful hound of any of several breeds often trained to hunt foxes

fox·tail \-ˌtāl\ *n* **1** : the tail of a fox **2** : any of several grasses with spikes that resemble brushes

\ə\ **abut**	\au̇\ **out**	\i\ **tip**	\ȯ\ **saw**	\u̇\ **foot**	
\ər\ **further**	\ch\ **chin**	\ī\ **life**	\ȯi\ **coin**	\y\ **yet**	
\a\ **mat**	\e\ **pet**	\j\ **job**	\th\ **thin**	\yü\ **few**	
\ā\ **take**	\ē\ **easy**	\ŋ\ **sing**	\th\ **this**	\yu̇\ **cure**	
\ä\ **cot, cart**	\g\ **go**	\ō\ **bone**	\ü\ **food**	\zh\ **vision**	

fox terrier *n* : a small lively terrier formerly used to dig out foxes and existing in smooth-haired and wire-haired varieties

fox terrier

foxy \'fäk-sē\ *adj* **fox·i·er; -est 1** : resembling a fox in appearance **2** : cunning and careful in planning and action **3** : physically attractive — **fox·i·ly** \-sə-lē\ *adv* — **fox·i·ness** \-sē-nəs\ *n*

foy·er \'fȯi-(ə)r, 'fȯi-(y)ā\ *n* **1** : a lobby especially in a theater **2** : an entrance hallway : VESTIBULE

fra·cas \'frā-kəs, 'frak-əs\ *n* : a noisy quarrel or fight

frack·ing \'fra-kiŋ\ *n* : the injection of fluid into shale beds at high pressure in order to free up petroleum resources (such as oil or natural gas) [from (*hydraulic*) *fracturing*] — **frack** \'frak\ *vb*

frac·tal \'frak-t³l\ *n* : an irregular shape that looks the same at any scale on which it is examined

frac·tion \'frak-shən\ *n* **1** : a number (as ½, ¾, or 3.323) that represents a number of equal parts of a whole or the division of one number by another **2** : a part of a whole

frac·tion·al \'frak-shnəl, -shən-³l\ *adj* **1** : of, relating to, or being a fraction ⟨*fractional* equivalents of percentages⟩ **2** : fairly small — **frac·tion·al·ly** \-ē\ *adv*

frac·tion·ate \'frak-shə-ˌnāt\ *vb* **-at·ed; -at·ing** : to separate into different portions — **frac·tion·ation** \ˌfrak-shə-'nā-shən\ *n*

frac·ture \'frak-chər, -shər\ *n* **1** : the act or process of breaking : the state of being broken; *esp* : the breaking of a bone **2** : the result of fracturing; *esp* : an injury resulting from fracture of a bone — **fracture** *vb*

frag·ile \'fraj-əl, -ˌīl\ *adj* : easily broken or destroyed : DELICATE — **fra·gil·i·ty** \frə-'jil-ət-ē\ *n*

frag·ment \'frag-mənt\ *n* **1** : a part that is broken off or incomplete **2** : SENTENCE FRAGMENT **synonyms** see PART — **frag·ment** \-ˌment\ *vb*

frag·men·tal \frag-'ment-³l\ *adj* : FRAGMENTARY

frag·men·tary \'frag-mən-ˌter-ē\ *adj* : made up of fragments : INCOMPLETE ⟨a *fragmentary* report⟩

fra·grance \'frā-grən(t)s\ *n* : a sweet, pleasant, and often flowery or fruity smell

fra·grant \'frā-grənt\ *adj* : having a sweet or agreeable smell — **fra·grant·ly** *adv*

frail \'frā(ə)l\ *adj* **1** : easily led into evil ⟨*frail* humanity⟩ **2** : FRAGILE **3** : not having normal strength or force ⟨spoke in a *frail* voice⟩ **synonyms** see WEAK — **frail·ly** \'frā(ə)l-lē\ *adv* — **frail·ness** *n*

frail·ty \'frā(ə)l-tē\ *n, pl* **frailties 1** : the quality or state of being frail **2** : a weakness of character

¹frame \'frām\ *vb* **framed; fram·ing 1 a** : ²PLAN 1 ⟨*framed* a new strategy⟩ **b** : ¹SHAPE 1, CONSTRUCT ⟨*frame* a figure out of clay⟩ **c** : to give expression to ⟨*frame* a reply⟩ **d** : to set down in writing ⟨*frame* a constitution⟩ **2** : to make (an innocent person) appear guilty **3** : to enclose in a frame ⟨*frame* a picture⟩ — **fram·er** *n*

²frame *n* **1** : the bodily structure of an animal and especially a human being : PHYSIQUE **2** : an arrangement of parts that gives form or support to something ⟨the *frame* of a house⟩ **3 a** : an open case or structure for holding or enclosing something ⟨a picture *frame*⟩ ⟨a window *frame*⟩ **b** *pl* : the part of a pair of glasses that holds the lenses **4** : a turn in bowling **5** : an enclosing border: as **a** : one of the drawings in a comic strip **b** : one picture of the series on a length of film or in a television transmission **6** : a particular state or mood ⟨in a good *frame* of mind⟩

³frame *adj* : having a wood frame ⟨*frame* houses⟩

frame—up \'frā-ˌməp\ *n* : a scheme to cause an innocent person to be accused of a crime

frame·work \'frām-ˌwərk\ *n* : a basic supporting part or structure

franc \'fraŋk\ *n* **1** : the former basic unit of money of France and Belgium **2** : a basic unit of money (as of Switzerland) **3** : a coin representing one franc

fran·chise \'fran-ˌchīz\ *n* **1** : the right to vote **2** : the right to sell a company's goods or services in a particular territory

fran·ci·um \'fran(t)-sē-əm\ *n* : a radioactive element obtained artificially by the bombardment of thorium with protons — see ELEMENT table

Franco- \'fraŋ-kō\ *combining form* **1** : French and ⟨*Franco*-German⟩ **2** : French ⟨*Franco*phile⟩ [derived from Latin *Francus* "Frenchman, Frank"]

Fran·co·phile \'fraŋ-kə-ˌfīl\ *or* **Fran·co·phil** \-ˌfil\ *adj* : very friendly to France or French culture — **Francophile** *n*

fran·gi·pa·ni *also* **fran·gi·pan·ni** \ˌfran-jə-'pan-ē, -'pän-\ *n, pl* **-pani** *also* **-panni** : any of several shrubs or small trees that have thick fleshy branches and large fragrant waxy-looking white, yellow, red, or pink flowers and are native to the American tropics but are grown elsewhere for their beauty

frank \'fraŋk\ *adj* : free in speaking one's feelings and opinions — **frank·ness** *n*

Frank \'fraŋk\ *n* : a member of a Germanic people living in ancient Gaul — **Frank·ish** \'fraŋ-kish\ *adj*

frank·furt·er \'fraŋk-fə(r)t-ər\ *or* **frank·furt** \-fərt\ *n* : a seasoned beef or beef and pork sausage [named for *Frankfurt am Main*, city in West Germany]

frank·in·cense \'fraŋ-kən-ˌsen(t)s\ *n* : a fragrant gum resin from African or Arabian trees that is burned as incense

Frank·lin stove \ˌfraŋ-klən-\ *n* : a metal heating stove that looks like a fireplace when its doors are open and is made to be set out in a room [named for Benjamin *Franklin* 1706–1790 American inventor]

Franklin stove

frank·ly \'fraŋ-klē\ *adv* **1** : in a frank manner ⟨you can speak *frankly* to us⟩ **2** : to tell the truth ⟨*frankly,* I don't think it's wise⟩

fran·tic \'frant-ik\ *adj* **1** : wildly excited ⟨*frantic* cries for help⟩ ⟨was *frantic* with fear⟩ **2** : marked by wild and hurried activity ⟨a *frantic* search for the missing child⟩ — **fran·ti·cal·ly** \-i-k(ə-)lē\ *adv* — **fran·tic·ly** \-i-klē\ *adv*

fra·ter·nal \frə-'tərn-³l\ *adj* **1 a** : of or relating to brothers **b** : of, relating to, or being a fraternity **2** : ¹KINDLY 2, FRIENDLY — **fra·ter·nal·ly** \-³l-ē\ *adv*

fraternal twin *n* : either of a pair of twins that are produced from different fertilized eggs and may not have the same sex, appearance, or disposition

fra·ter·ni·ty \frə-'tər-nət-ē\ *n, pl* **-ties 1** : a social, honorary, or professional organization; *esp* : a social club of male college students **2** : BROTHERHOOD 1, BROTHERLINESS

frat·er·nize \'frat-ər-ˌnīz\ *vb* **-nized; -niz·ing** : to associate as friends — **frat·er·ni·za·tion** \ˌfrat-ər-nə-'zā-shən\ *n* — **frat·er·niz·er** \'frat-ər-ˌnī-zər\ *n*

fraud \'frȯd\ *n* **1 a** : TRICKERY, DECEIT; *esp* : the use of dishonest methods to cheat another person of something valuable **b** : an act of deceiving : TRICK **2** : a person who pretends to be what he or she is not

fraud·u·lent \'frȯ-jə-lənt\ *adj* : based on or done by fraud — **fraud·u·lent·ly** *adv* — **fraud·u·lent·ness** *n*

fraught \'frȯt\ *adj* : full of something specified ⟨*fraught* with danger⟩

¹fray \'frā\ *n* : an usually disorderly or long fight, struggle, or dispute [from earlier *fray* "fright," from *affray* "quarrel, fight," derived from early French *affreer* "to attack, disturb, frighten" — related to AFRAID]

²fray *vb* **1 a** : to wear (as an edge of cloth) by or as if by rubbing **b** : to separate the threads at the edge of ⟨cutoff jeans with *frayed* edges⟩ **2** : to show or cause to show signs of strain ⟨nerves were beginning to *fray*⟩ [Middle English *fraien* "to fray," from early French *freier, froier* "to rub," from Latin *fricare* "to rub" — related to FRICTION]

fraz·zle \'fraz-əl\ *n* : a tired or nervous condition ⟨worn to a *frazzle*⟩

¹freak \'frēk\ *n* **1 a** : a sudden strange idea : WHIM **b** : a strange, abnormal, or unusual person, thing, or event **2 a** : ENTHUSIAST ⟨a movie *freak*⟩ **b** : a person who is obsessed with something ⟨a control *freak*⟩ — **freak·ish** \'frē-kish\ *adj* — **freak·ish·ly** *adv* — **freak·ish·ness** *n*

²freak *adj* : being or suggesting a freak : IMPROBABLE ⟨a *freak* accident⟩

³freak *vb* : to disturb one's calmness of mind : UPSET — usually used with *out* ⟨it *freaks* me out to think they would do that⟩

freaky \'frē-kē\ *adj* **freak·i·er; freak·i·est 1** : characterized by caprice **2** : very strange or abnormal ⟨a *freaky* appearance⟩ ⟨a *freaky* coincidence⟩

¹freck·le \'frek-əl\ *n* : a small brownish spot in the skin — **freck·ly** \-(ə-)lē\ *adj*

²freckle *vb* **freck·led; freck·ling** \'frek-(ə-)liŋ\ : to mark or become marked with freckles

¹free \'frē\ *adj* **fre·er** \'frē-ər\; **fre·est** \'frē-əst\ **1 a** : having liberty : not being a slave ⟨*free* citizens⟩ **b** : not controlled by others : INDEPENDENT ⟨a *free* country⟩ ⟨a *free* press⟩ **2 a** : released or not suffering from something unpleasant or painful ⟨*free* from worry⟩ ⟨*free* from disease⟩ **b** : not bound or contained by or as if by force ⟨you are *free* to leave⟩ **3** : having nothing that must be done instead ⟨I'm *free* tomorrow night⟩ **4 a** : not blocked : CLEAR ⟨*free* space⟩ **b** : not being used or occupied ⟨*free* time⟩ ⟨*free* memory in the computer⟩ **5** : not fastened ⟨put the *free* end of the tube in the water⟩ **6** : not cheap : GENEROUS ⟨a *free* spender⟩ **7** : not costing or charging anything ⟨*free* tickets⟩ **8** : not held back by fear or distrust : OPEN ⟨*free* expression of opinion⟩ **9** : not combined with something else ⟨*free* oxygen⟩ **10** : able to be used alone as a meaningful unit of language ⟨the word "hats" is a *free* form⟩ **11** : not restricted by or limited to the usual forms ⟨*free* skating⟩ — **free·ly** *adv*

²free *vb* **freed; free·ing** : to make or set free

³free *adv* **1** : in a free manner **2** : without charge

¹free·base \'frē-ˌbās\ *vb* : to prepare or use cocaine as freebase

²freebase *n* : solid cocaine without impurities that can be heated to produce vapors for inhalation or smoked as crack

free·bie *or* **free·bee** \'frē-bē\ *n* : something given or received without charge

free·board \'frē-ˌbō(ə)rd, -ˌbȯ(ə)rd\ *n* : the distance between the waterline and the upper edge of the side of a ship or boat

free·boo·ter \'frē-ˌbüt-ər\ *n* : ¹PIRATE [partial translation (influenced by English *booty*) of Dutch *vrijbuiter* "one who robs people openly and with force," from *vrijbuit* "plundering," from *vrij* "free" and *buit* "stolen property, booty" — related to FILIBUSTER; see *Word History* at FILIBUSTER]

free·born \'frē-ˈbȯrn\ *adj* : not born in slavery

freed·man \'frēd-mən, -ˌman\ *n* : a person freed from slavery

free·dom \'frēd-əm\ *n* **1 a** : the state of being free : LIBERTY, INDEPENDENCE **b** : ability to move or act freely **c** : the state of being released from something usually unpleasant ⟨*freedom* from care⟩ **d** : the quality of being frank or open ⟨answered with *freedom*⟩ **e** : use without restriction ⟨has the *freedom* of the house⟩ **2** : a political right

freedom fighter *n* : a person who takes part in a movement against an oppressive political or social system

freed·wom·an \'frēd-ˌwum-ən\ *n* : a woman freed from slavery

free enterprise *n* : freedom of private business to operate with little regulation by the government

free–fall \'frē-ˈfȯl\ *n* : a condition of falling freely (as before opening one's parachute)

free–fire zone *n* : a combat area in which any moving thing is considered a target

free–for–all \'frē-fə-ˌrȯl\ *n* : a competition or fight open to all comers usually without rules — **free–for–all** *adj*

free–hand \'frē-ˌhand\ *adj* : done without mechanical aids or devices ⟨*freehand* drawing⟩ — **freehand** *adv*

free hand *n* : freedom to act or decide

free·hand·ed \'frē-ˈhan-dəd\ *adj* : GENEROUS 1

free kick *n* : a kick (as in football or soccer) with which an opponent may not interfere; *also* : such a kick awarded because an opponent has broken the rules

freelance \'frē-ˌlan(t)s\ *n* **1** *usually* **free lance 1** : a knight whose services could be bought by any ruler or state **2** : a person who pursues a profession without being committed to work for one employer for a long time ⟨a *freelance* writer⟩ — **free·lance** \'frē-ˌlan(t)s\ *adj* — **free·lance** *vb* — **free·lanc·er** \-ˌlan(t)-sər\ *n*

free·man \'frē-mən, -ˌman\ *n* : a free person : one who is not a slave

free market *n* : an economic market operating by free competition

free on board *adv or adj* : delivered without charge onto a means of transportation

free–range \'frē-ˌrānj\ *adj* : allowed to roam and forage freely ⟨*free-range* chickens⟩; *also* : of, relating to, or produced by free-range animals ⟨*free-range* eggs⟩

free speech *n* : speech that is protected by the First Amendment to the U.S. Constitution; *also* : the right to such speech

free–spo·ken \'frē-ˈspō-kən\ *adj* : speaking freely : OUTSPOKEN

free·stand·ing \-ˈstan-diŋ\ *adj* : standing alone on its own foundation free of attachment or support

free·stone \-ˌstōn\ *adj* : having or being a fruit stone to which the flesh does not stick when the fruit is split open ⟨*freestone* peaches⟩ — **freestone** *n*

free·style \-ˌstīl\ *n* : a competition (as a swimming race) in which the competitors are not restricted to a certain way of performing

free–swim·ming \-ˌswim-iŋ\ *adj* : able to swim about : not attached

free throw *n* : a basketball shot worth one point that must be made from behind a specfic line and is given because of a foul by an opponent

free trade *n* : trade between nations without restrictions (as high taxes on imports)

free verse *n* : poetry that does not rhyme and does not have a regular rhythm

free·ware \'frē-ˌwa(ə)r, -ˌwe(ə)r\ *n* : software available at no cost

\ə\ abut	\au̇\ out	\i\ tip	\ȯ\ saw	\u̇\ foot
\ər\ further	\ch\ chin	\ī\ life	\ȯi\ coin	\y\ yet
\a\ mat	\e\ pet	\j\ job	\th\ thin	\yü\ few
\ā\ take	\ē\ easy	\ŋ\ sing	\th\ this	\yu̇\ cure
\ä\ cot, cart	\g\ go	\ō\ bone	\ü\ food	\zh\ vision

free·way \'frē-ˌwā\ *n* : a highway that is free of tolls

free·wheel·ing \-'hwē(ə)l-iŋ, -'wē(ə)l-iŋ\ *adj* : free and loose in form or manner; *esp* : not held back by rules, duties, or worries ⟨led a *freewheeling* life in the city⟩

free·will \ˌfrē-ˌwil\ *adj* : of or done by one's own free will : VOLUNTARY ⟨a *freewill* offering⟩

free will \'frē-'wil\ *n* : one's own choice or decision

free·writ·ing \'frē-ˌrīt-iŋ\ *n* : writing done with little or no attention to rules of grammar or sentence structure — **free·write** \-ˌrīt\ *vb*

¹freeze \'frēz\ *vb* **froze** \'frōz\; **fro·zen** \'frōz-ᵊn\; **freez·ing** **1** : to harden into or be hardened into a solid (as ice) by loss of heat ⟨the river *froze* over⟩ ⟨*freeze* the stew for dinner next week⟩ **2** : to be or become uncomfortably cold ⟨turn up the heat—I'm *freezing*⟩ **3 a** : to damage or kill by frost ⟨*froze* the tomato plants⟩ **b** : to anesthetize by cold **4** : to stick by or as if by freezing ⟨the clothes *froze* to the line⟩ ⟨fear *froze* the driver's hands to the wheel⟩ **5** : to clog or become clogged with ice ⟨the water pipes *froze*⟩ **6** : to make or become fixed or motionless ⟨the engine *froze*⟩ ⟨*froze* in their tracks⟩ **7** : to fix at a certain stage or level ⟨*freeze* prices⟩

²freeze *n* **1** : a state of weather marked by low temperature **2 a** : an act or instance of freezing ⟨a wage *freeze*⟩ **b** : the state of being frozen

freeze–dry \'frēz-'drī\ *vb* : to dry in a vacuum while frozen in order to preserve ⟨*freeze-dried* foods⟩

freez·er \'frē-zər\ *n* : a compartment, device, or room for freezing food or keeping it frozen

freezer burn *n* : a dried-out spot on food (as meat) that has been frozen that results from improper wrapping

freezing point *n* : the temperature at which a liquid becomes solid

¹freight \'frāt\ *n* **1** : the amount paid (as to a shipping company) for carrying goods **2 a** : goods or cargo carried by ship, train, truck, or airplane **b** : the carrying of goods from one place to another by vehicle ⟨ship the order by *freight*⟩ **3** : a train that carries freight

²freight *vb* **1** : to load for transportation **2** : to ship by freight

freight·er \'frāt-ər\ *n* **1** : a person who carries or ships freight **2** : a ship or airplane used chiefly to carry freight

¹French \'french\ *adj* : of or relating to France, its people, or their language

²French *n* **1** : the Romance language of the French **2 French** *pl* : the people of France

French bread *n* : a crusty bread usually baked in long thin loaves

French Canadian *n* : a person whose ancestors were French settlers in what is now the province of Quebec — **French–Canadian** *adj*

French cuff *n* : a shirt cuff that folds over and is fastened by cuff links

French door *n* : a door with small panes of glass extending the full length

French dressing *n* **1** : a salad dressing made with oil and vinegar or lemon juice, and spices **2** : a creamy salad dressing flavored with tomatoes

¹french fry *n, often cap 1st F* : a strip of potato fried in deep fat

²french fry *vb, often cap 1st F* : to fry in deep fat until brown

French horn *n* : a circular brass musical instrument with a large opening at one end and a mouthpiece shaped like a small funnel

French·man \'french-mən\ *n* : a person who is French

French provincial *n, often cap P* : a style (as of furniture) based on styles popular in the French provinces in the 17th and 18th centuries

French toast *n* : bread dipped in a mixture of eggs and milk and fried at low heat

French window *n* : a pair of windows with small panes that reach to the floor and open in the middle like doors

French window

French·wom·an \'french-ˌwu̇m-ən\ *n* : a woman who is French

fren·e·my \'fren-ə-mē\ *n, pl* **-mies** : someone who pretends to be a friend but is really an enemy

fre·net·ic \fri-'net-ik\ *adj* : FRENZIED, FRANTIC — **fre·net·i·cal·ly** \-'net-i-k(ə-)lē\ *adv*

fren·zied \'fren-zēd\ *adj* : very excited or upset — **fren·zied·ly** *adv*

fren·zy \'fren-zē\ *n, pl* **frenzies** : great and often wild or disorderly activity

Fre·on \'frē-ˌän\ *trademark* — used for any of various chlorofluorocarbons

fre·quen·cy \'frē-kwən-sē\ *n, pl* **-cies** **1** : the fact or condition of happening often **2** : how often something happens : rate of repetition **3** : the number of repetitions of a periodic process in a unit of time: as **a** : the number of times per second that an electric current flowing in one direction changes direction then changes back ⟨a current having a *frequency* of 60 hertz⟩ **b** : the number of waves (as of sound or electromagnetic energy) that pass a fixed point each second ⟨a sound having a *frequency* of 1500 hertz⟩ ⟨the *frequency* of yellow light⟩ **4** : the number or proportion of one kind of item in a group ⟨the *frequency* of chocolate doughnuts in the box⟩

frequency distribution *n* : a diagram that shows the frequency of different values of a variable in statistics

frequency modulation *n* : variation of the frequency of the carrier wave according to the strength of the audio or video signal; *also* : the system of broadcasting using this method of modulation

¹fre·quent \'frē-kwənt\ *adj* **1** : happening often ⟨made *frequent* trips to town⟩ **2** : ¹REGULAR 3b, HABITUAL ⟨a *frequent* visitor to the museum⟩ — **fre·quent·ly** *adv* — **fre·quent·ness** *n*

²fre·quent \frē-'kwent, 'frē-kwənt\ *vb* : to visit, associate with, or go to often ⟨*frequents* the library⟩ — **fre·quent·er** *n*

fres·co \'fres-kō\ *n, pl* **frescoes** **1** : the art of painting on freshly spread moist plaster **2** : a painting done in fresco [Italian, from *fresco* "fresh"]

fresh \'fresh\ *adj* **1 a** : not frozen, canned, or pickled ⟨*fresh* fish⟩ ⟨*fresh* vegetables⟩ **b** : not stale, sour, or spoiled ⟨*fresh* bread⟩ **c** : not worn, dirty, or wrinkled ⟨a *fresh* shirt⟩ **2 a** : not salt ⟨*fresh* water⟩ **b** : ¹PURE 1, INVIGORATING ⟨*fresh* air⟩ **c** : fairly strong : brisk ⟨*fresh* breeze⟩ **3 a** : newly made or received ⟨a *fresh* wound⟩ **b** : ¹NEW 6 ⟨make a *fresh* start⟩ **c** : remaining clear or vivid ⟨*fresh* in my mind⟩ **4** : behaving or talking in a rude or disrespectful way ⟨don't get *fresh* with me⟩ **synonyms** see NEW — **fresh·ly** *adv* — **fresh·ness** *n*

fresh·en \'fresh-ən\ *vb* **fresh·ened**; **fresh·en·ing** \-(ə-)niŋ\ **1** : to make or become fresh : REFRESH ⟨*freshen* up with a shower⟩ **2** : to become brisk or strong ⟨the wind *freshened*⟩ **3** : to brighten in appearance ⟨*freshen* up a room with some color⟩ — **fresh·en·er** \-(ə-)nər\ *n*

fresh·et \'fresh-ət\ *n* : a sudden overflowing of a stream

fresh·man \'fresh-mən\ *n* **1** : BEGINNER, NEWCOMER **2** : a student in the first year (as of high school or college)

fresh·wa·ter \ˌfresh-ˌwȯt-ər, -ˌwät-\ *adj* : of, relating to, or living in fresh water ⟨a *freshwater* fish⟩

¹fret \'fret\ *vb* **fret·ted**; **fret·ting** **1** : to make or become worried ⟨*fret* over a problem⟩ **2** : to eat into or wear away ⟨adobe *fretted* clean by wind and sand⟩ [Old English *fretan* "to devour"]

²fret *n* : an irritated or worried state ⟨in a *fret*⟩

³fret *n* : an ornamental design of short lines or bars [Middle English *fret, fretted* "interwoven," from early French *fretté*, past participle of *fretter* "to tie"]

³fret

⁴fret *n* : one of a series of ridges fixed across the fingerboard of a stringed musical instrument [perhaps from early French *frete* "connecting sleeve"] —

fret·less \ˈfret-ləs\ *adj* — **fret·ted** \ˈfret-əd\ *adj*

fret·ful \ˈfret-fəl\ *adj* **1** : inclined to worry ⟨a *fretful* child⟩ **2** : not relaxing or restful ⟨a *fretful* sleep⟩ — **fret·ful·ly** \-fə-lē\ *adv* — **fret·ful·ness** *n*

fret·work \ˈfret-ˌwərk\ *n* : decoration consisting of frets

fri·a·ble \ˈfrī-ə-bəl\ *adj* : easily crumbled or broken up ⟨*friable* soil⟩ — **fri·a·bil·i·ty** \ˌfrī-ə-ˈbil-ət-ē\ *n*

fri·ar \ˈfrī-(ə)r\ *n* : a member of a Roman Catholic religious order for men

fri·ary \ˈfrī-(ə-)rē\ *n, pl* **-ar·ies** : a monastery of friars

¹fric·as·see *also* **fric·as·sée** \ˈfrik-ə-ˌsē, ˌfrik-ə-ˈ\ *n* : a dish of meat (as chicken) or vegetables cut into pieces and stewed in a white sauce

²fricassee *vb* **-seed; -see·ing** : to cook as a fricassee

fric·tion \ˈfrik-shən\ *n* **1 a** : the rubbing of one thing against another **b** : the force that resists motion between bodies in contact ⟨the *friction* of a box sliding along the floor⟩ ⟨lubrication reduces *friction*⟩ **2** : disagreement between persons or groups **3** : sound produced by the movement of air through a narrow constriction in the mouth or glottis [Middle English *friction* "a rubbing of two things together, friction," from early French *friction* or Latin *friction-, frictio* (both same meaning), derived from Latin *fricare* "to rub" — related to ²FRAY] — **fric·tion·al** \-shnəl, -shən-ᵊl\ *adj* — **fric·tion·al·ly** \-ē\ *adv* — **fric·tion·less** \-ləs\ *adj*

Fri·day \ˈfrīd-ā, -ē\ *n* : the sixth day of the week

Word History The Germanic people of northern Europe worshipped many gods and goddesses in ancient times. Their most important goddess was one who is now usually known as *Frigga*. Her name in Old English was *Frig*, and the sixth day of the week was called *frīgedæg*, meaning "day of Frig," in her honor. Modern English *Friday* comes from Old English *frīgedæg*. [Old English *frīgedæg*, literally, "day of Frig"]

¹friend \ˈfrend\ *n* **1** : a person who has a strong liking for and trust in another **2** : a person who is not an enemy ⟨are you *friend* or foe⟩ **3** : a person who aids or favors something **4** *cap* : a member of a Christian group that stresses Inner Light, rejects sacraments and an ordained ministry, and opposes war — **friend·less** \-ləs\ *adj* — **friend·less·ness** *n*

²friend *vb* **1** : to act as the friend of : BEFRIEND **2** : to include (a name) in a list of designated friends on one's social networking site

¹friend·ly \ˈfren-dlē\ *adj* **friend·li·er; -est** : of, relating to, or right for a friend: as **a** : showing kindly interest and goodwill ⟨a *friendly* gesture⟩ **b** : not hostile ⟨*friendly* natives⟩ **c** : HELPFUL, FAVORABLE ⟨a *friendly* breeze⟩ **d** : bringing comfort or cheer ⟨the *friendly* glow of the fire⟩ **e** : ACCOMMODATING, COMPATIBLE ⟨environmentally *friendly* packaging⟩ — often used in combination ⟨a kid-*friendly* restaurant⟩ — **friend·li·ness** *n*

²friendly *n, pl* **friend·lies** : a person who is friendly or co-operative

friend·ship \ˈfren(d)-ˌship\ *n* : the state of being friends

frier *variant of* FRYER

frieze \ˈfrēz\ *n* : a sculptured or ornamental band (as around a building)

frig·ate \ˈfrig-ət\ *n* **1** : a medium-sized square-rigged warship **2** : a modern warship that is smaller than a destroyer and that is used for escort and patrol duties

frigate bird *n* : any of several sea-birds noted for their power of flight and the habit of robbing other birds of fish — called also *man-o'-war bird*

F frieze

fright \ˈfrīt\ *n* **1** : fear caused by sudden danger : sudden terror ⟨cry out in *fright*⟩ **2** : something that is strange, ugly, or shocking ⟨your hair looks a *fright*⟩ **synonyms** *see* FEAR

fright·en \ˈfrīt-ᵊn\ *vb* **fright·ened; fright·en·ing** \ˈfrīt-niŋ, -ᵊn-iŋ\ **1** : to make afraid : TERRIFY **2** : to drive away or out by frightening **3** : to become frightened — **fright·en·ing·ly** \-niŋ-lē, -ᵊn-iŋ-\ *adv*

fright·ful \ˈfrīt-fəl\ *adj* **1** : causing fear or alarm **2** : causing shock or horror ⟨a *frightful* novel⟩ **3** : very strong ⟨a *frightful* thirst⟩ — **fright·ful·ly** \-fə-lē\ *adv* — **fright·ful·ness** *n*

frig·id \ˈfrij-əd\ *adj* **1** : freezing cold **2** : not friendly ⟨a *frigid* stare⟩ — **fri·gid·i·ty** \frij-ˈid-ət-ē\ *n* — **frig·id·ly** \ˈfrij-əd-lē\ *adv* — **frig·id·ness** *n*

frigid zone *n* : the area or region between the arctic circle and the north pole or between the antarctic circle and the south pole — compare TEMPERATE ZONE, TORRID ZONE

fri·jo·le \frē-ˈhō-lē\ *n* : any of various beans used in Mexican-style cooking — usually used in plural [Spanish *frijol* "bean"]

frill \ˈfril\ *n* **1** : ²RUFFLE 2a **2** : something added mostly for show **3** : a thick fringe of hair or feathers or projection of bone or cartilage about the neck of an animal

frilly \ˈfril-ē\ *adj* **frill·i·er; -est** : having or resembling frills

¹fringe \ˈfrinj\ *n* **1** : an ornamental border consisting of hanging threads or strips **2** : something suggesting a fringe ⟨lived on the *fringe* of the forest⟩

²fringe *vb* **fringed; fring·ing** **1** : to provide or decorate with a fringe ⟨*fringed* a buckskin jacket⟩ **2** : to serve as a fringe for : BORDER ⟨a jungle *fringed* the shore⟩

fringe benefit *n* : a benefit (as vacation, health insurance, or pension plan) given by an employer to employees in addition to pay

fringy \ˈfrin-jē\ *adj* : decorated with fringes

frip·pery \ˈfrip-(ə-)rē\ *n, pl* **-per·ies** **1** : showy or elegant clothing **2** : something that is not necessary, not serious, or not important

Fris·bee \ˈfriz-bē\ *trademark* — used for a plastic disk for tossing between players

Fri·sian \ˈfrizh-ən, ˈfrē-zhən\ *n* **1** : a member of a people that live mainly in the Netherlands province of Friesland and the Frisian Islands in the North Sea **2** : the Germanic language of the Frisian people

frisk \ˈfrisk\ *vb* **1** : to move around in a lively or playful way **2** : to search (a person) quickly especially for concealed weapons — **frisk·er** *n*

frisky \ˈfris-kē\ *adj* **frisk·i·er; -est** : tending to frisk : PLAYFUL ⟨*frisky* puppies⟩; *also* : LIVELY ⟨a *frisky* performance⟩ — **frisk·i·ly** \-kə-lē\ *adv* — **frisk·i·ness** \-kē-nəs\ *n*

\ə\ **abut**	\au̇\ **out**	\i\ **tip**	\ȯ\ **saw**	\u̇\ **foot**
\ər\ **further**	\ch\ **chin**	\ī\ **life**	\ȯi\ **coin**	\y\ **yet**
\a\ **mat**	\e\ **pet**	\j\ **job**	\th\ **thin**	\yü\ **few**
\ā\ **take**	\ē\ **easy**	\ŋ\ **sing**	\th\ **this**	\yu̇\ **cure**
\ä\ **cot, cart**	\g\ **go**	\ō\ **bone**	\ü\ **food**	\zh\ **vision**

frit·il·lary \'frit-ºl-,er-ē\ *n, pl* **-laries** : any of numerous butterflies that are usually orange with black spots on the upper side of both wings and silver spotted on the underside of the hind wings

¹**frit·ter** \'frit-ər\ *n* : a small lump of fried batter often containing fruit or meat

²**fritter** *vb* : to spend or use up bit by bit especially on worthless things — usually used with *away* ⟨*frittered* away his savings⟩ — **frit·ter·er** \-ər-ər\ *n*

friv·ol \'friv-əl\ *vb* **-oled** *or* **-olled; -ol·ing** *or* **-ol·ling** \-(ə-)liŋ\ : ²TRIFLE 1b

fri·vol·i·ty \friv-'äl-ət-ē\ *n, pl* **-ties** **1** : the quality or state of being frivolous **2** : a frivolous act or thing

friv·o·lous \'friv-(ə-)ləs\ *adj* **1** : of little importance : TRIVIAL ⟨a *frivolous* complaint⟩ **2** : lacking in seriousness ⟨a *frivolous* attitude about a serious matter⟩ — **friv·o·lous·ly** *adv* — **friv·o·lous·ness** *n*

friz·zle \'friz-əl\ *vb* **friz·zled; friz·zling** \-(ə-)liŋ\ : to fry until crisp and curled

frizzy \'friz-ē\ *adj* **frizz·i·er; -est** : tightly curled ⟨*frizzy* hair⟩

fro \'frō\ *adv* : in a direction away — used in the phrase *to and fro*

frock \'fräk\ *n* **1** : a long outer garment worn by monks and friars **2** : a woman's or girl's dress

frock coat *n* : a man's long overcoat

frog \'frôg, 'fräg\ *n* **1** **a** : any of various tailless leaping amphibians that have slender bodies with smooth moist skin and strong long hind legs with webbed feet and that spend more of their time in the water than the related toads **b** : a hoarse condition ⟨have a *frog* in one's throat⟩ **2** : an ornamental fastening for a garment (as a jacket)

frog 2

frog·man \-,man, -mən\ *n* : a swimmer equipped to work underwater for long periods of time

¹**frol·ic** \'fräl-ik\ *vb* **frol·icked; frol·ick·ing** : to play about happily : ROMP — **frol·ick·er** *n*

²**frol·ic** *n* **1** : a playful or mischievous action **2** : a good time : FUN

frol·ic·some \'fräl-ik-səm\ *adj* : full of high spirits : given to frolic : PLAYFUL, FRISKY

from \(')frəm, 'främ\ *prep* **1** — used to show a starting or central point ⟨came here *from* the city⟩ ⟨a letter *from* home⟩ ⟨ran a business *from* home⟩ **2** — used to show removal or separation ⟨the dictator fell *from* power⟩ ⟨subtract 3 *from* 9⟩ ⟨far *from* safe⟩ **3** — used to show a material, source, or cause ⟨a doll made *from* rags⟩ ⟨reading aloud *from* a book⟩ ⟨suffering *from* a cold⟩

frond \'fränd\ *n* : a large leaf especially of a fern or palm tree that often has many divisions

¹**front** \'frənt\ *n* **1** : outer often pretended appearance ⟨put up a good *front*⟩ **2** : a region in which active warfare is taking place **3** : the forward part or surface ⟨the *front* of a shirt⟩ ⟨the *front* of the house⟩ **4** : the boundary between two dissimilar air masses **5** : someone or something that hides the true identity of those who are in control ⟨a *front* for organized crime⟩ — **in front of** : directly ahead of ⟨the car *in front of* ours⟩

²**front** *vb* : to have the front or face toward ⟨the cottage *fronting* on the lake⟩ ⟨the house *fronts* the street⟩

³**front** *adj* : of, relating to, or situated at the front

front·age \'frənt-ij\ *n* : the front boundary line of a lot or its length ⟨a cottage with 200 feet of lake *frontage*⟩

front·al \'frənt-ºl\ *adj* **1** : of, relating to, or next to the forehead **2** : of, relating to, or directed at the front ⟨a *frontal* attack⟩ — **fron·tal·ly** \-ºl-ē\ *adv*

front–end loader *n* : a vehicle with a scoop in front for digging and loading loose material

fron·tier \,frən-'ti(ə)r, frän-\ *n* **1** : a border between two countries **2 a** : a region that forms the edge of the settled part of a country **b** : the outer limits of knowledge or achievement ⟨the *frontiers* of science⟩ — **frontier** *adj*

fron·tiers·man \,frən-'ti(ə)rz-mən, frän-\ *n* : a person living on the frontier

fron·tis·piece \'frənt-ə-,spēs\ *n* : an illustration facing the title page of a book

¹**frost** \'frȯst\ *n* **1** : the temperature that causes freezing **2** : a covering of tiny ice crystals on a cold surface

²**frost** *vb* **1 a** : to cover with or as if with frost; *esp* : to put icing on (as cake) **b** : to give a surface that looks like frost to **2** : to injure or kill by frost : FREEZE

¹**frost·bite** \'frȯs(t)-,bīt\ *vb* **frost·bit** \-,bit\; **frost·bit·ten** \-,bit-ºn\; **-bit·ing** \-,bīt-iŋ\ : to injure by frost or frostbite

²**frostbite** *n* : the freezing of a surface or deeper layer of tissues of some part of the body (as the feet or hands)

frost–free \,frȯs(t)-'frē\ *adj* : needing no defrosting ⟨a *frostfree* refrigerator⟩

frost·ing \'frȯs-tiŋ\ *n* **1** : ¹ICING 1 **2** : a dull finish on metal or glass

frost·work \'frȯs-,twərk\ *n* : the design made by moisture freezing on a surface (as a window)

frosty \'frȯs-tē\ *adj* **frost·i·er; -est** **1** : cold enough to produce frost ⟨a *frosty* night⟩ **2** : covered or appearing to be covered with frost ⟨a *frosty* glass⟩ **3** : cool in manner — **frost·i·ly** \-stə-lē\ *adv* — **frost·i·ness** \-stē-nəs\ *n*

¹**froth** \'frȯth\ *n, pl* **froths** **1 a** : bubbles formed in or on a liquid **b** : the foam produced by saliva in certain diseases or nervous excitement **2** : something of little value — **froth·i·ly** \'frȯ-thə-lē\ *adv* — **froth·i·ness** \-thē-nəs\ *n* — **frothy** \-thē\ *adj*

²**froth** \'frȯth, 'frȯth\ *vb* **1** : to foam at the mouth **2** : to produce or form froth

fro·ward \'frō-(w)ərd\ *adj* : likely to disobey and oppose : WILLFUL — **fro·ward·ly** *adv* — **fro·ward·ness** *n*

¹**frown** \'fraun\ *vb* **1** : to wrinkle the forehead (as in anger or thought) **2** : to show displeasure or disapproval by or as if by facial expression ⟨*frowns* on rudeness⟩ — **frown·er** *n* — **frown·ing·ly** \'frau-niŋ-lē\ *adv*

²**frown** *n* **1** : an expression of displeasure **2** : a wrinkling of the brow in displeasure or thought

frow·sy *or* **frow·zy** \'frau-zē\ *adj* **frow·si·er** *or* **frow·zi·er; -est** : having an untidy appearance

froze *past of* ¹FREEZE

¹**frozen** *past participle of* ¹FREEZE

²**frozen** *adj* **1** : treated, affected, or crusted over by freezing **2 a** : FIXED 1 ⟨*frozen* wages⟩ **b** : not available for present use ⟨*frozen* assets⟩ — **fro·zen·ness** *n*

fruc·tose \'frək-,tōs, 'fruk-\ *n* : a very sweet sugar that dissolves easily and occurs especially in fruit juices and honey

fru·gal \'frü-gəl\ *adj* : careful in spending or using resources — **fru·gal·i·ty** \frü-'gal-ət-ē\ *n* — **fru·gal·ly** \'frü-gə-lē\ *adv*

synonyms FRUGAL, THRIFTY, ECONOMICAL mean careful with money and other resources. FRUGAL suggests a simple lifestyle that is lacking in luxuries ⟨a *frugal* woman who seldom allowed herself even small pleasures⟩. THRIFTY suggests a habit of saving and an avoidance of wastefulness ⟨*thrifty* shoppers looking for bargains⟩. ECONOMICAL suggests the wise management of one's resources ⟨*economical* cooks waste nothing⟩.

¹**fruit** \'früt\ *n* **1** : a usually useful product of plant growth (as grain) ⟨*fruits* of the earth⟩ **2 a** : a product of fertilization in a plant with its coverings or associated parts; *esp* : the ripened ovary of a seed plant (as the pod of a pea, a nut, a grain, or a berry) with or without the attached parts **b** : the ripened ovary of a seed plant (as an apple or raspberry) when sweet and pulpy **c** : a juicy plant part (as the

stalk of a rhubarb) used chiefly as a dessert **3** : ²RESULT 1, PRODUCT ⟨the *fruits* of our labors⟩ — **fruit·ed** \-əd\ *adj*

²fruit *vb* : to bear or cause to bear fruit

fruit bat *n* : any of numerous large Old World fruit-eating bats of warm regions — called also *flying fox*

fruit·cake \'früt-ˌkāk\ *n* : a rich cake containing nuts, dried or candied fruits, and spices

fruit fly *n* : any of various small two-winged flies whose larvae feed on fruit or decaying vegetable matter

fruit·ful \'früt-fəl\ *adj* **1** : yielding or producing fruit **2 a** : very productive ⟨a *fruitful* soil⟩ **b** : bringing results ⟨a *fruitful* idea⟩ **synonyms** see FERTILE — **fruit·ful·ly** \-fə-lē\ *adv* — **fruit·ful·ness** *n*

fruit bat

fruiting body *n* : a plant organ specialized for producing spores

fru·i·tion \frü-'ish-ən\ *n* **1** : the state of bearing fruit **2** : the state of being real or complete : REALIZATION, ACCOMPLISHMENT ⟨brought her dreams to *fruition*⟩

fruit·less \'früt-ləs\ *adj* **1** : not bearing fruit **2** : producing no good results : UNSUCCESSFUL ⟨a *fruitless* attempt⟩ — **fruit·less·ly** *adv* — **fruit·less·ness** *n*

fruit sugar *n* : FRUCTOSE

fruity \'früt-ē\ *adj* **fruit·i·er; -est** : relating to or suggesting fruit ⟨a *fruity* smell⟩

frus·trate \'frəs-ˌtrāt\ *vb* **frus·trat·ed; frus·trat·ing 1** : to prevent from carrying out a purpose ⟨tried to *frustrate* his opponents in their efforts⟩ **2** : to bring to nothing ⟨the accident *frustrated* the plan⟩

    synonyms FRUSTRATE, THWART, FOIL, OUTWIT mean to check or defeat another's plan or prevent achievement of a goal. FRUSTRATE suggests the causing of failure despite determined or repeated efforts ⟨lack of education *frustrated* him in his attempt to find a job⟩. THWART suggests checking another's plan by deliberately opposing it ⟨at every turn they were *thwarted* by the enemy⟩. FOIL suggests checking or defeating that discourages further attempts ⟨her accident *foiled* her dream of becoming a dancer⟩. OUTWIT suggests the use of slyness or cunning to defeat others ⟨*outwitted* the waiting reporters by leaving from the roof in a helicopter⟩.

frustrating *adj* : producing frustration ⟨a *frustrating* delay⟩ — **frus·trat·ing·ly** *adv*

frus·tra·tion \(ˌ)frəs-'trā-shən\ *n* **1 a** : an act of frustrating **b** : a state or an instance of being frustrated **2** : a feeling of being unable to get anything done **3** : something that frustrates

¹fry \'frī\ *vb* **fried; fry·ing** : to cook in fat or oil [Middle English *frien* "to fry," from early French *frire* (same meaning), from Latin *frigere* "to roast"]

²fry *n*, *pl* **fries 1** : something fried; *esp* : ¹FRENCH FRY — usually used in plural ⟨steak and *fries*⟩ **2** : a get-together where fried food is eaten ⟨a fish *fry*⟩

³fry *n*, *pl* **fry 1 a** : recently hatched or young fish **b** : the young of animals other than fish **2** : very small adult fish **3** : members of a group or class : INDIVIDUALS ⟨small *fry*⟩ [Middle English *fry* "recently hatched fish," from early French *frie* (same meaning), from *freier, frier* "to rub, spawn"]

fry bread *n* : quick bread cooked in deep fat

fry·er *also* **fri·er** \'frī-(-ə)r\ *n* **1** : something (as a young chicken) suitable for frying **2** : a deep utensil for frying foods

frying pan *n* : a metal pan with a handle for frying foods

fry pan *n* : FRYING PAN

fuch·sia \'fyü-shə\ *n* **1** : any of a genus of shrubs related to the evening primrose and having showy nodding flow-

ers usually in deep pinks, reds, and purples **2** : a vivid reddish purple

fuch·sin *or* **fuch·sine** \'fyük-sən, -ˌsēn\ *n* : a synthetic dye that yields a brilliant bluish red

fu·cus \'fyü-kəs\ *n* : ROCKWEED

fud·dy–dud·dy \'fəd-ē-ˌdəd-ē\ *n*, *pl* **-dies** : a person who is old-fashioned, very cautious, or fussy

¹fudge \'fəj\ *vb* **fudged; fudg·ing 1** : to change (something) in order to trick people ⟨*fudged* the figures⟩ **2** : to avoid being open or direct : HEDGE ⟨politicians *fudging* on the issues⟩

²fudge *n* **1** : foolish nonsense **2** : a soft creamy candy made typically of milk, sugar, butter, and flavoring

¹fu·el \'fyü(-ə)l\ *n* **1 a** : a material used to produce heat or power by burning **b** : a material from which atomic energy can be produced especially in a reactor **2** : a source of energy

²fuel *vb* **-eled** *or* **-elled; -el·ing** *or* **-el·ling** : to supply with or take in fuel

fuel cell *n* : a device that continuously changes the chemical energy of a fuel (as hydrogen) into electrical energy

fuel oil *n* : an oil that is used for fuel and that usually ignites at a higher temperature than kerosene

¹fu·gi·tive \'fyü-jət-ˌiv\ *adj* **1** : running away or trying to run away ⟨a *fugitive* slave⟩ **2** : lasting a very short time : not fixed or lasting ⟨*fugitive* thoughts⟩ — **fu·gi·tive·ly** *adv*

²fugitive *n* **1** : a person who runs away or tries to escape; *esp* : REFUGEE **2** : something that is hard to find [Middle English *fugitif, fugitive* "one who is running away," from early French *fugitif* and Latin *fugitivus* (both, same meaning), from Latin *fugitus*, past participle of *fugere* "to run away, flee" — related to CENTRIFUGAL, REFUGEE]

fugue \'fyüg\ *n* : a musical composition in which themes are repeated in complex patterns — **fu·gal** \'fyü-gəl\ *adj*

¹-ful \fəl\ *adj suffix* **1** : full of ⟨joy*ful*⟩ **2** : characterized by ⟨peace*ful*⟩ **3** : having the qualities of ⟨master*ful*⟩ **4** : tending, given, or liable to ⟨mourn*ful*⟩ ⟨help*ful*⟩ [Old English *-ful* "full"]

²-ful \ˌfùl\ *n suffix* : number or quantity that fills or would fill ⟨room*ful*⟩

ful·crum \'fùl-krəm, 'fəl-\ *n*, *pl* **fulcrums** *or* **ful·cra** \-krə\ : the support about which a lever turns

ful·fill *or* **ful·fil** \fùl-'fil\ *vb* **ful·filled; ful·fill·ing 1** : ACCOMPLISH ⟨*fulfill* a promise⟩ **2** : to measure up to : SATISFY ⟨*fulfill* requirements⟩ — **ful·fill·er** *n* — **ful·fill·ment** \-mənt\ *n*

¹full \'fùl\ *adj* **1** : containing as much or as many as possible or normal ⟨a bottle *full* of milk⟩ ⟨the disk is *full* and will take no more data⟩ **2 a** : complete in number, amount, or duration ⟨a *full* set of dishes⟩ ⟨for a *full* hour⟩ **b** : not missing any essentials : PERFECT ⟨in *full* control of the car⟩ **c** : being at the highest or greatest degree ⟨in *full* bloom⟩ ⟨at *full* power⟩ ⟨*full* strength⟩ **d** : fully lighted ⟨the moon is *full*⟩ **e** : completely occupied by runners ⟨come to bat with the bases *full*⟩ **f** : having three balls and two strikes ⟨a *full* count⟩ **3 a** : plump and rounded in outline ⟨a *full* face⟩ **b** : having much material ⟨a *full* skirt⟩ **4** : possessing or containing a great number or amount ⟨a room *full* of pictures⟩ ⟨*full* of hope⟩ **5** : satisfied especially with food or drink **6** : having the same parents ⟨*full* sisters⟩ **7** : completely taken up especially with a thought or plan ⟨*full* of one's own concerns⟩ ⟨*full* of oneself⟩ **8** : having a rich quality ⟨a *full* voice⟩ — **full·ness** *n* — **full of it** : not to be believed

\ə\ **abut**	\aù\ **out**	\i\ **tip**	\ò\ **saw**	\ù\ **foot**
\ər\ **further**	\ch\ **chin**	\ī\ **life**	\òi\ **coin**	\y\ **yet**
\a\ **mat**	\e\ **pet**	\j\ **job**	\th\ **thin**	\yü\ **few**
\ā\ **take**	\ē\ **easy**	\ŋ\ **sing**	\th\ **this**	\yù\ **cure**
\ä\ **cot, cart**	\g\ **go**	\ō\ **bone**	\ü\ **food**	\zh\ **vision**

²full *adv* **1 a :** ²VERY 1, EXTREMELY ⟨knew *full* well who they were⟩ **b :** all the way : ENTIRELY ⟨filled *full*⟩ **2 :** ⁵SMACK, SQUARELY ⟨was hit *full* in the face⟩

³full *n* : the highest state, extent, or degree — **in full 1 :** to the complete amount ⟨paid *in full*⟩ **2 :** to the fullest extent : COMPLETELY ⟨read the book *in full*⟩

full·back \'fu̇l-ˌbak\ *n* **1 :** a football back who usually lines up between the halfbacks **2 :** a mainly defensive player (as in soccer or field hockey) who usually plays near the goal to be defended

full blast *adv* : with all power or resources being used ⟨a sawmill running *full blast*⟩ ⟨the stereo was going *full blast*⟩

full–blood·ed \'fu̇l-'bləd-əd\ *adj* : of pure ancestry

full–blown \-'blōn\ *adj* **1 :** fully mature or developed ⟨a *full-blown* theory⟩ **2 :** being at the height of bloom

full–bod·ied \-'bäd-ēd\ *adj* : having a rich strong flavor

full dress *n* : the style of dress required on certain special occasions

ful·ler·ene \ˌfu̇l-ə-'rēn\ *n* : any of various hollow carbon compounds

full·er's earth \'fu̇l-ərz-\ *n* : an earthy substance used for filtering and as an absorbent

full–fledged \'fu̇l-'flejd\ *adj* : fully developed : MATURE

full–grown \-'grōn\ *adj* : having reached full growth or development : MATURE

full–length \-'leŋ(k)th\ *adj* **1 :** made to fit the full length of the human figure ⟨a *full-length* dress⟩ **2 :** having a length that is normal for one of its kind ⟨a *full-length* play⟩

full moon *n* : the moon with its whole disk lighted

full–on \'fu̇l-ˌȯn, -ˌän\ *adj* : ¹COMPLETE 3, FULL-FLEDGED

full–scale \'fu̇l-'skā(ə)l\ *adj* **1 :** identical to an original in size **2 :** not limited in any way : using everything that can be used ⟨a *full-scale* war⟩

full–ser·vice \-'sər-vəs\ *adj* : offering all services of a certain kind ⟨a *full-service* bank⟩

full–size \'fu̇l-'sīz\ *adj* **1 :** having the usual or normal size of its kind **2 :** having a size of 54 inches by 75 inches (about 1.4 meters by 1.9 meters) ⟨a *full-size* bed⟩

full steam ahead *adv* : at full power or speed

full tilt *adv* : at high speed : very fast ⟨running *full tilt*⟩

full–time \'fu̇l-'tīm\ *adj* : working or involving the full number of hours considered normal or standard ⟨a *full-time* job⟩ ⟨*full-time* employees⟩

ful·ly \'fu̇l-(l)ē\ *adv* **1 :** in a full manner : in every way or detail : COMPLETELY **2 :** at least ⟨*fully* 90 percent of us⟩

ful·mi·nate \'fu̇l-mə-ˌnāt, 'fəl-\ *vb* **-nat·ed; -nat·ing :** to utter loud or forceful complaints or strong or violent language — **ful·mi·na·tion** \ˌfu̇l-mə-'nā-shən, ˌfəl-\ *n* — **ful·mi·na·tor** \'fu̇l-mə-ˌnāt-ər, 'fəl-\ *n*

ful·some \'fu̇l-səm\ *adj* **1 :** very full or complete ⟨described in *fulsome* detail⟩ **2 :** very or overly flattering ⟨praised the boss in *fulsome* terms⟩ — **ful·some·ly** *adv* — **ful·some·ness** *n*

¹fum·ble \'fəm-bəl\ *vb* **fum·bled; fum·bling** \-b(ə-)liŋ\ **:** to feel about for or handle something clumsily — **fum·bler** \-b(ə-)lər\ *n*

²fumble *n* **1 :** an act or instance of fumbling **2 :** a fumbled ball

¹fume \'fyüm\ *n* : a disagreeable smoke, vapor, or gas — usually used in plural ⟨acid *fumes*⟩ — **fumy** \'fyü-mē\ *adj*

²fume *vb* **fumed; fum·ing** **1 :** to expose to or treat with fumes **2 :** to give off fumes **3 :** to show bad temper or anger

fu·mi·gant \'fyü-mi-gənt\ *n* : a substance used in fumigating

fu·mi·gate \'fyü-mə-ˌgāt\ *vb* **-gat·ed; -gat·ing :** to apply smoke, vapor, or gas to especially for the purpose of disinfecting or of destroying pests — **fu·mi·ga·tion** \ˌfyü-mə-'gā-shən\ *n* — **fu·mi·ga·tor** \'fyü-mə-ˌgāt-ər\ *n*

¹fun \'fən\ *n* **1 :** someone or something that provides amusement or enjoyment ⟨the twins were *fun* to have around⟩ ⟨picnics are great *fun*⟩ **2 :** a good time : AMUSEMENT, ENJOYMENT ⟨have *fun*⟩ ⟨plays cards just for *fun*⟩ **3 :** words or actions that make someone or something an object of unkind laughter ⟨kids making *fun* of me⟩

²fun *vb* **funned; fun·ning :** to engage in joking or play ⟨I was only *funning*⟩

³fun *adj* **1 :** providing fun ⟨a *fun* party⟩ ⟨a *fun* person⟩ **2 :** full of fun : PLEASANT 1 ⟨have a *fun* time⟩

¹func·tion \'fəŋ(k)-shən\ *n* **1 :** professional job or duties : OCCUPATION **2 a :** the particular purpose for which a person or thing is specially fitted or used or for which a thing exists ⟨the *function* of a knife is cutting⟩ **b :** the natural or proper action of a bodily part in a living thing ⟨the *function* of the heart⟩ **3 :** a large important ceremony or social affair **4 a :** a mathematical relationship that assigns exactly one element of one set to each element of the same or another set **b :** something (as a quality, trait, or measurement) that is determined by or based on something else ⟨height is a *function* of age in children⟩ — **func·tion·less** \-ləs\ *adj*

²function *vb* **func·tioned; func·tion·ing** \-sh(ə-)niŋ\ **:** to serve a certain purpose : WORK

func·tion·al \'fəŋ(k)-shnəl, -shən-ᵊl\ *adj* **1 a :** of, connected with, or being a function **b :** affecting bodily functions but not structure ⟨*functional* heart disease⟩ **2 :** designed or developed chiefly from the point of view of use ⟨*functional* clothes⟩ ⟨*functional* writing⟩ **3 :** performing or able to perform a regular function — **func·tion·al·ly** \-shnə-lē, -shən-ᵊl-ē\ *adv*

func·tion·ary \'fəŋ(k)-shə-ˌner-ē\ *n, pl* **-ar·ies :** a person who works for a government or political party

function word *n* : a word (as a preposition, helping verb, or conjunction) expressing primarily grammatical relationship

¹fund \'fənd\ *n* **1 :** a quantity of available resources : STOCK, SUPPLY ⟨a large *fund* of jokes⟩ **2 a :** a sum of money for a special purpose ⟨the book *fund*⟩ **b :** available money — usually used in plural [Latin *fundus* "bottom, piece of land owned as property" — related to ²FOUND, FUNDAMENTAL]

²fund *vb* : to supply funds for ⟨a program *funded* by the state⟩

¹fun·da·men·tal \ˌfən-də-'ment-ᵊl\ *adj* **1 :** being or forming a foundation : BASIC, ESSENTIAL ⟨a discovery *fundamental* to modern science⟩ ⟨our *fundamental* rights⟩ **2 :** of or relating to essential structure or function : RADICAL ⟨*fundamental* change⟩ **3 :** of, relating to, or produced by the lowest part of a complex vibration **4 :** of central importance : PRINCIPAL ⟨*fundamental* purpose⟩ [Middle English *fundamental* "serving as a base or source of support," from Latin *fundamentalis* "of a foundation," from *fundamentum* "foundation," derived from *fundus* "bottom, base" — related to ²FOUND, FUND] — **fun·da·men·tal·ly** \-ᵊl-ē\ *adv*

²fundamental *n* **1 :** something fundamental : a basic part ⟨*fundamentals* of arithmetic⟩ **2 :** the part of a complex wave that has the lowest frequency and commonly the greatest amplitude

fu·ner·al \'fyün-(ə-)rəl\ *n* : the ceremonies held for a dead person (as before burial) — **funeral** *adj*

funeral director *n* : a person whose profession is the managing of funerals and the preparation of the dead for burial or cremation

funeral home *n* : a place where the dead are prepared for burial or cremation and funerals are held

fu·ne·re·al \fyü-'nir-ē-əl\ *adj* : suggesting a funeral ⟨*funereal* gloom⟩ — **fu·ne·re·al·ly** \-ē-ə-lē\ *adv*

fun·gal \'fəŋ-gəl\ *adj* **1 :** of, relating to, or resembling fungi **2 :** caused by a fungus ⟨a *fungal* skin disease⟩

fun·gi·ble \\'fən-jə-bəl\\ *adj* **1** : having such a nature that one part or quantity may be replaced by another part or quantity to satisfy an obligation **2** : capable of being interchanged **3** : FLEXIBLE 2

fun·gi·cide \\'fən-jə-ˌsīd, 'fəŋ-gə-\\ *n* : a substance that destroys fungi — **fun·gi·cid·al** \\ˌfən-jə-'sīd-ᵊl, ˌfəŋ-gə-\\ *adj*

fun·gous \\'fəŋ-gəs\\ *adj* : FUNGAL

fun·gus \\'fəŋ-gəs\\ *n, pl* **fun·gi** \\'fən-ˌjī, 'fəŋ-ˌgī\\ *also* **fun·gus·es 1** : any of a kingdom of living things (as molds, rusts, mildews, smuts, and mushrooms) that lack chlorophyll, are parasitic or live on dead or decaying organic matter, and were formerly considered plants **2** : infection with a fungus — **fungus** *adj*

fu·nic·u·lar \\fyu̇-'nik-yə-lər, fə-\\ *n* : a cable railway going up a mountain

¹funk \\'fəŋk\\ *n* : a strong bad smell

²funk *vb* **1** : to be or become frightened of **2** : to shrink back from in fear

³funk *n* **1 a** : great fear **b** : a depressed state of mind **2** : COWARD **3** : ²SLUMP ⟨the team went into a *funk*⟩

⁴funk *n* : music that combines forms of blues, gospel, or soul music and has a strong backbeat

funky \\'fəŋ-kē\\ *adj* **1** : having a bad smell **2** : down-to-earth in style and feeling; *esp* : having the style and feeling of funk ⟨a *funky* beat⟩ **3 a** : odd in appearance or feeling **b** : lacking taste or style ⟨wearing a *funky* old hat⟩ **c** : stylish in an untypical way : HIP 1

¹fun·nel \\'fən-ᵊl\\ *n* **1** : a utensil usually shaped like a hollow cone with a tube extending from the point and used to catch and direct a downward flow (as of liquid) **2** : something shaped like a funnel ⟨the *funnel* cloud of a tornado⟩ **3** : a large pipe for the escape of smoke or for ventilation (as on a ship)

¹funnel 1

²funnel *vb* **-neled** *also* **-nelled; -nel·ing** *also* **-nel·ling** : to move or cause to move to a central point or into a central channel

¹fun·ny \\'fən-ē\\ *adj* **fun·ni·er; -est 1** : causing or intended to cause laughter ⟨a *funny* story⟩ **2** : different from ordinary in a way that is odd, curious, or suspicious ⟨it's *funny* you should ask⟩ ⟨that's *funny*—they were here yesterday⟩ ⟨there's something *funny* going on⟩ **3** : involving trickery ⟨don't try anything *funny*⟩ — **fun·ni·ly** \\'fən-ᵊl-ē\\ *adv* — **fun·ni·ness** \\'fən-ē-nəs\\ *n* — **fun·ny** *adv*

²funny *n, pl* **funnies 1** : one that is funny; *esp* : ¹JOKE 1 **2** *pl* : comic strips or the comic section of a newspaper — usually used with *the*

funny bone *n* **1** : a place at the back of the elbow where a blow causes a painful tingling sensation **2** : a sense of humor ⟨it tickled my *funny bone*⟩

funny paper *n* : the comic section of a newspaper

fur \\'fər\\ *n* **1** : a piece of the pelt of an animal **2** : an article of clothing made with fur **3** : the hairy coat of a mammal especially when fine, soft, and thick — **fur·less** \\-ləs\\ *adj* — **furred** \\'fərd\\ *adj*

Word History When the word *fur* first came into English, it was a verb that meant "to line a person's garment with the soft hair of an animal." The noun developed from the verb. First the noun referred to animal hair used for lining and trimming a garment. Then it came to refer to the hairy coat on the animal itself. The verb, not much used anymore, was taken from the early French verb *furrer* meaning "to stuff, fill, line." It was formed from an earlier French word meaning "a sheath." Thus our word *fur* for the coat that covers or encases an animal traces back to a word for a sheath that encases a knife or sword. [Middle English *furre* "a piece of animal skin used to line a garment," from *furren* (verb) "to line a

garment with fur," from early French *furrer*, "to stuff, fill, line," from *fuerre* "sheath," of Germanic origin]

fur·bear·er \\'fər-ˌbar-ər, -ˌber-\\ *n* : an animal that bears fur

fur·be·low \\'fər-bə-ˌlō\\ *n* **1** : ⁴FLOUNCE, RUFFLE **2** : something suggesting a furbelow

fu·ri·ous \\'fyu̇r-ē-əs\\ *adj* **1** : very angry **2** : very active : VIOLENT ⟨a *furious* storm⟩ — **fu·ri·ous·ly** *adv*

¹furl \\'fər(-)l\\ *vb* : to wrap or roll (as a sail or a flag) close to or around something

²furl *n* **1** : a furled coil **2** : the act of furling

fur·long \\'fər-ˌlȯŋ\\ *n* : a unit of distance equal to 220 yards (about 201 meters)

¹fur·lough \\'fər-lō\\ *n* : a leave of absence from duty granted especially to a soldier

²furlough *vb* **1** : to grant a furlough to **2** : to lay off from work

fur·nace \\'fər-nəs\\ *n* : an enclosed structure in which heat is produced (as for heating a house or melting metals)

fur·nish \\'fər-nish\\ *vb* **1** : to provide with what is needed ⟨the cave *furnished* us with shelter⟩; *esp* : to provide with furniture ⟨*furnish* an apartment⟩ **2** : to supply or give to someone or something ⟨we'll *furnish* the food for the guests⟩ — **fur·nish·er** *n*

fur·nish·ings \\'fər-nish-iŋz\\ *n pl* : articles of furniture for a room or building

fur·ni·ture \\'fər-ni-chər\\ *n* : movable articles (as chairs, tables, or beds) used in making a room ready for use

fu·ror \\'fyu̇r-ˌȯr, -ˌōr\\ *n* **1** : FURY 1, RAGE **2** : an outburst of excitement : UPROAR

fu·rore \\'fyu̇r-ˌōr, -ˌȯr\\ *n* : FUROR 2

fur·ri·er \\'fər-ē-ər\\ *n* : a person who deals in furs

¹fur·row \\'fər-ō, 'fə-rō\\ *n* **1** : a trench in the earth made by or as if by a plow **2** : a narrow groove or wrinkle

²furrow *vb* : to make furrows, grooves, wrinkles, or lines in

fur·ry \\'fər-ē\\ *adj* **fur·ri·er; -est 1** : made of or resembling fur **2** : covered with fur

fur seal *n* : any of various eared seals with a dense soft undercoat

fur seal

¹fur·ther \\'fər-thər\\ *adv* **1** : ¹FARTHER 1 **2** : in addition : BESIDES, ALSO **3** : to a greater degree or extent

²further *vb* **fur·thered; fur·ther·ing** \\'fərth-(ə-)riŋ\\ : to help forward : PROMOTE — **fur·ther·er** \\'fər-thər-ər\\ *n*

³further *adj* **1** : ²FARTHER 1 **2** : going or extending beyond : ADDITIONAL ⟨*further* study is needed⟩

fur·ther·ance \\'fərth-(ə-)rən(t)s\\ *n* : the act of furthering : ADVANCEMENT

fur·ther·more \\'fər-thə(r)-ˌmō(ə)r, -ˌmȯ(ə)r\\ *adv* : in addition to what precedes : MOREOVER

fur·ther·most \\'fər-thə(r)-ˌmōst\\ *adj* : most distant : FARTHEST

fur·thest \\'fər-thəst\\ *adv or adj* : FARTHEST

fur·tive \\'fərt-iv\\ *adj* : done in a sneaky or sly manner ⟨a *furtive* look⟩ — **fur·tive·ly** *adv* — **fur·tive·ness** *n*

fu·ry \\'fyu̇(ə)r-ē\\ *n, pl* **furies 1** : violent anger ⟨threw the vase in a *fury*⟩ **2 a** *cap* : one of the avenging spirits of classical mythology **b** : a violently angry person **3** : wild and dangerous force ⟨the *fury* of the storm⟩ **synonyms** see ANGER

\\ə\\ **abut**	\\au̇\\ **out**	\\i\\ **tip**	\\ȯ\\ **saw**	\\u̇\\ **foot**
\\ər\\ **further**	\\ch\\ **chin**	\\ī\\ **life**	\\ȯi\\ **coin**	\\y\\ **yet**
\\a\\ **mat**	\\e\\ **pet**	\\j\\ **job**	\\th\\ **thin**	\\yu̇\\ **few**
\\ā\\ **take**	\\ē\\ **easy**	\\ŋ\\ **sing**	\\th\\ **this**	\\yu̇\\ **cure**
\\ä\\ **cot, cart**	\\g\\ **go**	\\ō\\ **bone**	\\ü\\ **food**	\\zh\\ **vision**

furze \\'fərz\\ *n* : GORSE

¹fuse *vb* **fused; fus·ing** 1 : to change into a liquid or plastic state by heat 2 : to become fluid with heat 3 : to unite by or as if by melting together [from Latin *fusus* past participle of *fundere* "to pour melted metal into a mold" — related to ³FOUND]

²fuse *n* : an electrical safety device having a metal wire or strip that melts and interrupts the circuit when the current becomes too strong

³fuse \\'fyüz\\ *n* 1 : a cord or cable that is set afire to ignite an explosive charge by carrying fire to it 2 *also* **fuze** : a mechanical or electrical device for setting off the explosive charge of an artillery shell, bomb, or torpedo [from Italian *fuso* "a slender tapering rod used for twisting yarn, spindle," from Latin *fusus* "spindle"]

⁴fuse *also* **fuze** *vb* **fused** *also* **fuzed; fus·ing** *also* **fuz·ing** : to equip with a fuse

fu·se·lage \\'fyü-sə-ˌläzh, 'fyü-zə-\\ *n* : the central body portion of an airplane that holds the crew, passengers, and cargo

fus·ible \\'fyü-zə-bəl\\ *adj* : capable of being fused and especially melted by heat — **fus·ibil·i·ty** \\ˌfyü-zə-'bil-ət-ē\\ *n*

fu·sil·lade \\'fyü-sə-ˌläd, -ˌlād, -zə-; ˌfyü-sə-'läd, -'lād, -zə-\\ *n* 1 : a number of shots fired at the same time or rapidly one after another 2 : something like a fusillade of shots ⟨a *fusillade* of rocks⟩ 3 : an outburst especially of criticism

fu·sion \\'fyü-zhən\\ *n* 1 : the act or process of melting or making fluid by heat 2 : union by or as if by melting 3 : the union of light atomic nuclei to form heavier nuclei resulting in the release of enormous quantities of energy

¹fuss \\'fəs\\ *n* 1 : unnecessary activity or excitement often over something unimportant 2 : ¹PROTEST 3 : a great show of interest ⟨made a *fuss* over the baby⟩

²fuss *vb* : to make a fuss — **fuss·er** *n*

fussy \\'fəs-ē\\ *adj* **fuss·i·er; -est** 1 : inclined to complain or whine ⟨a *fussy* child⟩ 2 a : needing or giving much attention to details ⟨a *fussy* job⟩ b : hard to please ⟨*fussy* about food⟩ — **fuss·i·ly** \\'fəs-ə-lē\\ *adv* — **fuss·i·ness** \\'fəs-ē-nəs\\ *n*

fus·tic \\'fəs-tik\\ *n* : the wood of a tropical American tree that is related to the mulberries and is the source of a yellow dye; *also* : a tree that produces this wood

fus·ty \\'fəs-tē\\ *adj* **fus·ti·er; -est** 1 : full of dust and stale odors : MUSTY 2 : very old-fashioned — **fus·ti·ly** \\-tə-lē\\ *adv* — **fus·ti·ness** \\-tē-nəs\\ *n*

fu·tile \\'fyüt-ᵊl, 'fyü-ˌtīl\\ *adj* 1 : having no result or effect : USELESS ⟨all our efforts proved *futile*⟩ ⟨a *futile* and foolish gesture⟩ 2 : concerned with unimportant matters ⟨*futile* pleasures⟩ — **fu·tile·ly** \\-ᵊl-(l)ē, -ˌtīl-lē\\ *adv* — **fu·tile·ness** \\-ᵊl-nəs, -ˌtīl-nəs\\ *n*

fu·til·i·ty \\ˌfyü-'til-ət-ē\\ *n, pl* **-ties** 1 : the quality or state of being futile 2 : a useless act

futon \\'fü-ˌtän\\ *n, pl* **futons** *also* **futon** : a usually cotton-filled mattress used on the floor or in a frame as a bed, couch, or chair [Japanese]

¹fu·ture \\'fyü-chər\\ *adj* 1 : coming after the present ⟨*future* events⟩ 2 : of, relating to, or being a verb form in the future tense [Middle English *future* "future," from early French *futur* (same meaning) and Latin *futurus* "about to be," from the Latin verb *esse* "to be"]

²future *n* 1 a : time that is to come ⟨sometime in the *future*⟩ b : what is going to happen ⟨predict the *future*⟩ 2 : expectation of future success ⟨a promising *future*⟩ 3 : something (as a commodity) bought or sold for delivery at a future time — usually used in plural ⟨grain *futures*⟩ 4 a : FUTURE TENSE b : a verb form in the future tense

fu·ture·less \\'fyü-chər-ləs\\ *adj* : having no expectation of future success ⟨a *futureless* acting career⟩ — **fu·ture·less·ness** *n*

future perfect tense *n* : a verb tense formed in English with *will have* and *shall have* and expressing completion of an action by a specified time that is yet to come

future tense *n* : a verb tense formed in English with *will* or *shall* and expressing an action or state in time yet to come

fu·tur·ist \\'fyü-chə-rəst\\ *n* : a person who tries to tell what the future will be like by studying current trends

fu·tur·is·tic \\ˌfyü-chə-'ris-tik\\ *adj* : being or resembling the style or type predicted for the future ⟨*futuristic* furniture⟩ — **fu·tur·is·ti·cal·ly** \\-ti-k(ə-)lē\\ *adv*

fu·tu·ri·ty \\fyü-'t(y)ùr-ət-ē, -'chùr-\\ *n, pl* **-ties** 1 : ²FUTURE 1a 2 : the quality or state of being future 3 *pl* : future events or possibilities

fuze *variant of* FUSE

fuzz \\'fəz\\ *n* : fine light particles or fibers (as of down or fluff)

fuzzy \\'fəz-ē\\ *adj* **fuzz·i·er; -est** 1 : covered with or resembling fuzz 2 : not clear : INDISTINCT ⟨a *fuzzy* picture⟩ 3 : being, relating to, or causing pleasant and usually emotional feelings ⟨warm and *fuzzy* feelings⟩ — **fuzz·i·ly** \\'fəz-ə-lē\\ *adv* — **fuzz·i·ness** \\'fəz-ē-nəs\\ *n*

-fy \\ˌfī\\ *vb suffix* **-fied; -fy·ing** 1 : cause to become ⟨beautify⟩ 2 : gain or cause to gain qualities related to ⟨citify⟩ [derived from Latin *-ficare*, from *facere* "to make, do"]

G

g \\'jē\\ *n, pl* **g's** *or* **gs** *often cap* 1 : the seventh letter of the English alphabet 2 : the musical note referred to by the letter G 3 : the fifth tone of a C-major scale 3 : ACCELERATION OF GRAVITY; *also* : a unit of force equal to the weight of a body on which the force acts ⟨an astronaut may experience 3 *g's* during liftoff⟩

G *certification mark* — used to certify that a motion picture is of such a nature that persons of all ages may be allowed admission

gab \\'gab\\ *vb* **gabbed; gab·bing** : to talk idly : CHATTER — **gab** *n* — **gab·ber** *n*

gab·ar·dine \\'gab-ər-ˌdēn\\ *n* 1 : a firm cloth with diagonal ribs and a hard smooth finish 2 : a garment of gabardine

gab·ble \\'gab-əl\\ *vb* **gab·bled; gab·bling** \\'gab-(ə-)liŋ\\ 1 : to talk quickly or foolishly : JABBER 2 : to utter sounds that cannot be understood : BABBLE — **gabble** *n* — **gab·bler** \\'gab-(ə-)lər\\ *n*

gab·by \\'gab-ē\\ *adj* **gab·bi·er; -est** : TALKATIVE

gab·fest \\'gab-ˌfest\\ *n* 1 : a gathering for talking 2 : a long conversation

ga·ble \\'gā-bəl\\ *n* 1 : the triangular part of an outside wall of a building that is formed by the sides of the roof sloping down from the ridgepole to the eaves 2 : a triangular structure (as over a door or window) — **ga·bled** \\-bəld\\ *adj*

gable roof *n* : a roof having two sides sloping from a ridge and forming a gable at each end

¹gad \'gad\ *vb* **gad·ded; gad·ding** : to be on the go without specific purpose — usually used with *about* ⟨*gadding* about the city⟩

²gad *interj* — used as a mild oath

gad·about \'gad-ə-ˌbaut\ *n* : a person who goes from place to place in social activity — **gadabout** *adj*

gad·fly \'gad-ˌflī\ *n* **1** : any of various flies (as a horsefly or botfly) that are pests especially of livestock **2** : a person who annoys others especially by persistent criticism

gad·get \'gaj-ət\ *n* : an interesting, unfamiliar, or unusual device with a practical use — **gad·get·ry** \'gaj-ə-trē\ *n*

gad·o·lin·i·um \ˌgad-ᵊl-'in-ē-əm\ *n* : a magnetic metallic chemical element — see ELEMENT table

Gael \'gā(ə)l\ *n* **1** : a Scottish Highlander **2** : a Celtic especially Gaelic-speaking person born or living in Ireland, Scotland, or the Isle of Man

Gael·ic \'gāl-ik, 'gal-, 'gäl-\ *adj* **1** : of or relating to the Gaels and especially the Celtic Highlanders of Scotland **2** : of, relating to, or being the Celtic speech of persons born or living in Ireland, the Isle of Man, and the Scottish Highlands — **Gaelic** *n*

gaff \'gaf\ *n* **1** : a spear or hook for lifting heavy fish **2** : a pole that extends from the back of a mast to support the top of a sail **3** : something hard to take ⟨couldn't stand the *gaff*⟩ **4** : GAFFE — **gaff** *vb*

gaffe \'gaf\ *n* : a noticeable mistake especially of manners

¹gag \'gag\ *vb* **gagged; gag·ging** **1** : to prevent from speaking or crying out by or as if by stopping up the mouth **2 a** : to vomit or cause to feel like vomiting **b** : ¹CHOKE 2 **3** : to be unable to endure something : BALK **4** : to tell jokes

²gag *n* **1 a** : something thrust into the mouth especially to prevent speech or outcry **b** : a check to free speech **2** : something said or done to cause laughter **3** : PRANK

¹gage \'gāj\ *n* **1** : a glove or cap thrown on the ground as a challenge to combat **2** : something given as a pledge of performance : SECURITY

²gage *variant of* GAUGE

gag·gle \'gag-əl\ *n* **1** : ¹FLOCK 1; *esp* : a flock of geese when not in flight **2** : an unorganized group ⟨a *gaggle* of reporters⟩

gai·ety *also* **gay·ety** \'gā-ət-ē\ *n, pl* **-eties** **1** : MERRYMAKING 1 **2** : high spirits

gai·ly *also* **gay·ly** \'gā-lē\ *adv* **1** : in a merry or lively way **2** : in a bright or showy way ⟨*gaily* dressed crowds⟩

¹gain \'gān\ *n* **1** : resources or advantage acquired or increased : PROFIT ⟨financial *gains*⟩ **2** : an increase in amount, size, or degree ⟨a *gain* in weight⟩

²gain *vb* **1 a** : to get possession of often by effort : EARN ⟨*gain* an advantage⟩ **b** : to win in competition or conflict ⟨*gain* a victory⟩ **c** : to get by a natural development or process ⟨*gain* strength⟩ **d** : to arrive at ⟨the swimmer *gained* the shore⟩ **2** : to win to one's side : PERSUADE **3** : to increase in ⟨*gain* momentum⟩ **4** : to run fast ⟨my watch *gains* a minute a day⟩ **5** : to get advantage : PROFIT ⟨hoped to *gain* from the deal⟩ **6 a** : ¹INCREASE 1 ⟨the day was *gaining* in warmth⟩ **b** : to increase in weight **c** : to improve in health — **gain·er** *n* — **gain ground** : to make progress

gain·ful \'gān-fəl\ *adj* : producing gain : making money ⟨*gainful* employment⟩ — **gain·ful·ly** \-fə-lē\ *adv* — **gain·ful·ness** *n*

gain·say \gān-'sā\ *vb* **gain·said** \-'sād, -'sed\; **gain·say·ing** \-'sā-iŋ\ **1** : to declare untrue : DENY **2** : to speak against : CONTRADICT — **gain·say·er** *n*

gait \'gāt\ *n* : a manner of moving on foot; *also* : a particular style of such movement ⟨the *gait* of a horse⟩ — **gait·ed** \-əd\ *adj*

gai·ter \'gāt-ər\ *n* : a leg covering reaching from the instep to above the ankle or to mid-calf or knee

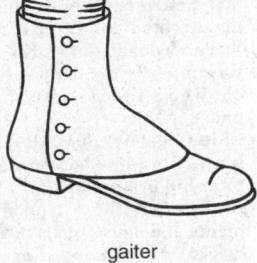
gaiter

gal \'gal\ *n* : GIRL

ga·la \'gā-lə, 'gal-ə\ *n* : a festive celebration — **gala** *adj*

ga·lac·tic \gə-'lak-tik\ *adj* : of or relating to a galaxy

ga·lac·tose \gə-'lak-ˌtōs\ *n* : a sugar that is less easily dissolved and is less sweet than glucose

Ga·la·tians \gə-'lā-shənz\ *n* — see BIBLE table

galavant *variant of* GALLIVANT

gal·axy \'gal-ək-sē\ *n, pl* **gal·ax·ies** **1** : MILKY WAY GALAXY **2** : one of the very large groups of stars and other matter that are found throughout the universe [Middle English *galaxie* "the Milky Way," from Latin *galaxias* (same meaning), from Greek *galaxias* "Milky Way," from *galakt-, gala* "milk"]

gale \'gā(ə)l\ *n* **1** : a strong current of air; *esp* : a wind of from 32 to 63 miles (about 51 to 101 kilometers) per hour **2** : an emotional outburst ⟨*gales* of laughter⟩

ga·le·na \gə-'lē-nə\ *n* : a bluish gray mineral with metallic luster that consists of sulfide of lead and that is the principal ore of lead

¹gall \'gol\ *n* **1 a** : BILE 1 **b** : something hard to endure **c** : ILL WILL **2** : NERVE 3c [Old English *gealla* "bile"]

²gall *n* **1** : a skin sore (as on a horse's back) caused by repeated irritation (as from rubbing by a saddle) **2** : a cause or state of aggravation [Old English *gealla* "skin sore," from Latin *galla* "plant gall"]

³gall *vb* **1** : to make or become sore or worn by rubbing **2** : IRRITATE 1, VEX ⟨sarcasm *galls* her⟩

⁴gall *n* : an abnormal growth of plant tissue usually due to fungi or insect parasites [Middle English *galle* "a swelling on a plant, plant gall," from early French *galle* (same meaning), from Latin *galla* "plant gall"]

¹gal·lant \gə-'lant, gə-'länt, 'gal-ənt\ *n* **1** : a fashionable young man **2** : a man who likes the company of women and is attentive to them **b** : SUITOR 3

²gal·lant \'gal-ənt *(usually in sense 2b)*; gə-'lant, gə-'länt *(usually in sense 3)*\ *adj* **1** : showy in dress or bearing **2 a** : SPLENDID 2, STATELY ⟨a *gallant* ship⟩ **b** : SPIRITED, BRAVE **c** : CHIVALROUS 2a, NOBLE ⟨a *gallant* knight⟩ **3** : polite and attentive to women — **gal·lant·ly** *adv*

gal·lant·ry \'gal-ən-trē\ *n, pl* **-ries** **1 a** : an act of notable courtesy **b** : courteous attention to a woman **2** : notable bravery

gall·blad·der \'gol-ˌblad-ər\ *n* : a muscular sac in which bile from the liver is stored

gal·le·on \'gal-ē-ən\ *n* : a large sailing ship with square sails used from the 1400s to the 1700s especially by the Spanish

gal·lery \'gal(-ə)-rē\ *n, pl* **gal·ler·ies** **1** : an outdoor balcony **2 a** : a long narrow room, hall, or passage **b** : an underground passageway (as in a mine or cave) **c** : a passage (as in earth or wood) made by an ani-

galleon

\ə\ abut	\au\ out	\i\ tip	\o\ saw	\u\ foot
\ər\ further	\ch\ chin	\ī\ life	\oi\ coin	\y\ yet
\a\ mat	\e\ pet	\j\ job	\th\ thin	\yü\ few
\ā\ take	\ē\ easy	\ŋ\ sing	\th\ this	\yu\ cure
\ä\ cot, cart	\g\ go	\ō\ bone	\ü\ food	\zh\ vision

mal and especially an insect **3 a** : a room or building devoted to the exhibition of works of art **b** : a business dealing in works of art **4** : a balcony in an auditorium; *esp* : the highest balcony in a theater or the people who sit there ⟨play to the *gallery*⟩ **5** : a photographer's studio

gal·ley \'gal-ē\ *n, pl* **galleys 1** : a large low ship of olden times moved by oars and sails **2** : the kitchen especially of a ship or airplane

gall·fly \'gȯl-ˌflī\ *n* : an insect that deposits its eggs in plants and causes galls in which the larvae feed

Gal·lic \'gal-ik\ *adj* : of or relating to Gaul or France

gall·ing \'gȯ-liŋ\ *adj* : very irritating : VEXING

gal·li·nule \'gal-ə-ˌn(y)ü(ə)l\ *n* : any of several birds related to the rails that are usually found in or near water

gal·li·um \'gal-ē-əm\ *n* : a bluish white metallic element — see ELEMENT table

gal·li·vant *also* **gal·a·vant** \'gal-ə-ˌvant\ *vb* : to travel or roam about for pleasure

gal·lon \'gal-ən\ *n* — see MEASURE table

¹**gal·lop** \'gal-əp\ *vb* **1** : to go or cause to go at a gallop **2** : to run fast — **gal·lop·er** *n*

²**gallop** *n* **1** : a fast bounding gait of a four-footed animal in which all four feet are off the ground at one time once in each stride; *esp* : a fast gait of the horse with a three-beat or four-beat rhythm **2** : a ride or run at a gallop **3** : a rapid progression or pace

gal·lows \'gal-(ˌ)ōz, -əz\ *n, pl* **gallows** *or* **gal·lows·es 1** : a structure from which criminals are hanged **2** : the punishment of hanging ⟨was sentenced to the *gallows*⟩

gall·stone \'gȯl-ˌstōn\ *n* : a hard mass like a pebble that is formed in the gallbladder or bile passages

gall wasp *n* : a wasp that is a gallfly

ga·lore \gə-'lō(ə)r, -'lȯ(ə)r\ *adj* : ABUNDANT, PLENTIFUL — used after the word it modifies ⟨has charm *galore*⟩

ga·losh \gə-'läsh\ *n* : a high overshoe worn especially in snow and slush

ga·lumph \gə-'ləm(p)f\ *vb* : to move in a loud and clumsy way

gal·va·nize \'gal-və-ˌnīz\ *vb* **-nized; -niz·ing 1 a** : to subject to the action of an electric current ⟨*galvanize* a muscle⟩ **b** : to cause excitement or concern and a desire for action in ⟨an issue that *galvanized* the public⟩ **2** : to coat (as iron) with zinc for protection — **gal·va·ni·za·tion** \ˌgal-və-nə-'zā-shən\ *n*

gal·va·nom·e·ter \ˌgal-və-'näm-ət-ər\ *n* : an instrument for detecting or measuring a small electric current

¹**gam·ble** \'gam-bəl\ *vb* **gam·bled; gam·bling** \-b(ə-)liŋ\ **1 a** : to play a game for money or property **b** : to bet on an uncertain outcome **2** : to bet something on the chance of gain : take a chance ⟨we *gambled* on not being seen⟩ **3** : ²RISK 1, HAZARD — **gam·bler** \-blər\ *n*

²**gamble** *n* **1** : a risky undertaking **2** : a betting on a game of chance

gam·bol \'gam-bəl\ *vb* **-boled** *or* **-bolled; -bol·ing** *or* **-bol·ling** \-bə-liŋ *also* -bliŋ\ : to run or skip about in play : FROLIC — **gambol** *n*

gam·brel roof \ˌgam-brəl-\ *n* : a roof with a lower steeper slope and an upper less steep one on each side

¹**game** \'gām\ *n* **1 a** : activity engaged in for amusement **b** : ¹FUN 1, SPORT ⟨make *game* of a nervous player⟩ **2 a** : a procedure or strategy for gaining an end : TACTIC **b** : a line of work : PROFESSION **3 a** : a contest carried on following set rules for amusement, exercise, or reward **b** : a division of a larger contest **c** : the number of points necessary to win **d** : the manner of playing in a contest **4 a** : animals pursued or taken by hunting **b** : the flesh of game animals **c** : an object of ridicule or attack — often used in the phrase *fair game*

²**game** *vb* **gamed; gam·ing** : ¹GAMBLE 1a

³**game** *adj* **gam·er; gam·est 1 a** : full of spirit or eagerness : DETERMINED ⟨*game* to the end⟩ **b** : willing or ready to go ⟨were *game* for anything⟩ **2** : of or relating to animals that are hunted ⟨*game* laws⟩ — **game·ly** *adv* — **game·ness** *n*

⁴**game** *adj* : ¹LAME 1b ⟨a *game* leg⟩

game·cock \'gām-ˌkäk\ *n* : a rooster trained for fighting

game fish *n* : a fish regularly sought by anglers

game·keep·er \'gām-ˌkē-pər\ *n* : a person in charge of the breeding and protection of game animals or birds on private land

gam·er \'gā-mər\ *n* **1** : a person who plays games and especially video games **2** : a person who is game; *esp* : an athlete who enjoys competition

game show *n* : a television program in which contestants compete for prizes in a game (as a quiz)

ga·mete \gə-'mēt, 'gam-ˌēt\ *n* : a mature sex cell that usually has half of the normal number of chromosomes and is capable of uniting with a gamete of the opposite sex to begin the formation of a new individual — **ga·met·ic** \gə-'met-ik\ *adj* — **ga·met·i·cal·ly** \-'met-i-k(ə-)lē\ *adv*

ga·me·to·phyte \gə-'mēt-ə-ˌfīt\ *n* : the individual or generation of plants or fungi with alternating sexual and asexual generations that produces gametes — compare SPOROPHYTE — **ga·me·to·phyt·ic** \-ˌmēt-ə-'fit-ik\ *adj*

gam·in \'gam-ən\ *n* **1** : a boy who hangs out on the streets **2** : GAMINE 2

ga·mine \ga-'mēn\ *n* **1** : a girl who hangs out on the streets **2** : a small playfully mischievous girl

gam·ing \'gā-miŋ\ *n* **1** : the practice of gambling **2** : the acting out of a situation (as war) for training or testing **3** : the playing of video games

gam·ma \'gam-ə\ *n* : the third letter of the Greek alphabet — Γ or γ

gamma globulin *n* **1** : a part of blood plasma that is rich in antibodies **2** : a solution of gamma globulin made by mixing blood from human blood donors and given to provide immunity against some infectious diseases (as measles and German measles)

gamma radiation *n* : radiation made up of gamma rays

gamma ray *n* : a ray that is like an X-ray but of higher energy and that is given off especially by a radioactive substance

gam·ut \'gam-ət\ *n* : an entire range or series ⟨ran the *gamut* from rich to poor⟩ [probably a contraction of *gamma ut*, a Latin expression in the Middle Ages for "the full range of notes in music," from *gamma* "the lowest note on the staff" and *ut* "the first note of the scale"]

gamy *or* **gam·ey** \'gā-mē\ *adj* **gam·i·er; -est 1** : BRAVE, PLUCKY **2** : having the flavor of wild game especially when slightly spoiled ⟨*gamy* meat⟩ — **gam·i·ly** \'gā-mə-lē\ *adv* — **gam·i·ness** \'gā-mē-nəs\ *n*

¹**gan·der** \'gan-dər\ *n* : a male goose

²**gander** *n* : a look often for judging ⟨take a *gander*⟩

¹**gang** \'gaŋ\ *n* **1** : two or more tools or devices arranged to work together **2** : a group of persons working or going about together **3** : a group of persons associated together to do something illegal **4** : a group of friends

²**gang** *vb* : to form into or move or act as a gang

gang·land \'gaŋ-ˌland, -lənd\ *n* : the world of organized crime

gan·gling \'gaŋ-gliŋ, -glən\ *adj* : GANGLY

gan·gli·on \'gaŋ-glē-ən\ *n, pl* **gan·glia** \-glē-ə\ *also* **-gli·ons** : a mass of nerve tissue lying outside the brain or spinal cord and containing neurons; *also* : NUCLEUS c — **gan·gli·on·ic** \ˌgaŋ-glē-'än-ik\ *adj*

gan·gly \'gaŋ-glē\ *adj* **gan·gli·er; -est** : loosely and awkwardly built : LANKY

gang·plank \'gaŋ-ˌplaŋk\ *n* : a movable bridge from a ship to the shore

¹**gan·grene** \'gaŋ-ˌgrēn, 'gan-; gaŋ-'grēn, gan-\ *n* : the death of soft tissues in a local area of the body due to loss of the blood supply — **gan·gre·nous** \'gaŋgrə-nəs\ *adj*

²**gangrene** *vb* **gan·grened; gan·gren·ing** : to make or become diseased with gangrene

gangplank

gang·ster \'gaŋ-stər\ *n* : a member of a gang of criminals : RACKETEER — **gang·ster·ism** \-stə-ˌriz-əm\ *n*

gang up *vb* : to join together for an often hostile purpose ⟨*ganged up* on their little brother⟩

gang·way \'gaŋ-ˌwā\ *n* **1** : a passage into, through, or out of an enclosed place **2** : GANGPLANK **3** : a clear passage through a crowd — often used as an interjection ⟨*Gangway!* Coming through!⟩

gan·net \'gan-ət\ *n, pl* **gannets** *also* **gannet** : any of several large fish-eating seabirds that breed chiefly on offshore islands

gantlet *variant of* GAUNTLET

gan·try \'gan-trē\ *n, pl* **gantries 1** : a platform made to carry a traveling crane and supported by towers running on parallel tracks **2** : a movable structure used for erecting and servicing rockets before launching **3** : a structure spanning several railroad tracks and displaying signals

gaol, gaol·er *chiefly British variant of* JAIL, JAILER

gap \'gap\ *n* **1** : a break in a barrier **2 a** : a mountain pass **b** : RAVINE **3** : a space or separation : a break in continuity ⟨*gaps* in your story⟩ ⟨a *gap* where the tooth had been⟩ **4** : a wide difference (as in amount, character, or attitude) ⟨a wage *gap*⟩

¹**gape** \'gāp\ *vb* **gaped; gap·ing 1 a** : to open the mouth wide **b** : to open or part widely **2** : to stare with mouth open in surprise or wonder **3** : ¹YAWN 2 **synonyms** *see* GAZE — **gap·er** *n* — **gap·ing·ly** \'gā-piŋ-lē\ *adv*

²**gape** *n* **1** : an act or instance of gaping **2** : an unfilled space

gar \'gär\ *n* : any of various fishes with a long body like that of a pike and long narrow jaws

¹**ga·rage** \gə-'räzh, -'räj\ *n* : a shelter or repair shop for automotive vehicles

²**garage** *vb* **ga·raged; ga·rag·ing** : to keep or put in a garage

garage sale *n* : a sale of used household or personal items (as furniture or clothing) held at the seller's home

garb \'gärb\ *n* **1** : style of dress **2** : outward form : APPEARANCE — **garb** *vb*

gar·bage \'gär-bij\ *n* **1** : food waste **2** : discarded or useless material : REFUSE

gar·bage·man \'gär-bij-ˌman\ *n* : a person who collects and hauls away garbage

gar·ban·zo \gär-'bän-zō\ *n, pl* **-zos** : CHICKPEA — called also *garbanzo bean*

gar·ble \'gär-bəl\ *vb* **gar·bled; gar·bling** \-b(ə-)liŋ\ : to change or twist the meaning or sound of — **gar·bler** \-b(ə-)lər\ *n*

¹**gar·den** \'gärd-ᵊn\ *n* **1** : a plot of ground where herbs, fruits, flowers, or vegetables are grown **2 a** : a public recreation area or park usually ornamented with plants and trees ⟨a botanical *garden*⟩ **b** : an open-air eating or drinking place

²**garden** *vb* **gar·dened; gar·den·ing** \'gärd-niŋ, -ᵊn-iŋ\ **1** : to lay out or work in a garden **2** : to make into a garden

³**garden** *adj* **1** : of, relating to, used in, or frequenting gardens **2** : of a kind grown under cultivation especially in the open ⟨*garden* plants⟩

gar·den·er \'gärd-nər, -ᵊn-ər\ *n* : a person who gardens especially for pay

gar·de·nia \gär-'dē-nyə\ *n* : any of various Old World tropical trees and shrubs with leathery leaves and fragrant white or yellow flowers; *also* : one of the flowers

garden–variety *adj* : ²ORDINARY 2, COMMONPLACE ⟨not the flu, just a *garden-variety* cold⟩

gar·gan·tuan \gär-'ganch-wən, -ə-wən\ *adj* : extraordinary in size, degree, or volume : GIGANTIC [from *Gargantua*, a giant with an enormous appetite in books by the French author François Rabelais]

¹**gar·gle** \'gär-gəl\ *vb* **gar·gled; gar·gling** \-g(ə-)liŋ\ : to cleanse the mouth or throat with a liquid kept in motion by air forced through it from the lungs

²**gargle** *n* **1** : a liquid used in gargling **2** : a gargling sound

gar·goyle \'gär-ˌgȯil\ *n* : a waterspout in the form of a strange or frightening human or animal figure sticking out at the roof or eaves of a building

gargoyle

gar·ish \'ga(ə)r-ish, 'ge(ə)r-\ *adj* : too bright or showy : GAUDY — **gar·ish·ly** *adv* — **gar·ish·ness** *n*

¹**gar·land** \'gär-lənd\ *n* : a wreath or rope of leaves or flowers or of other material

²**garland** *vb* : to form into or decorate with a garland

gar·lic \'gär-lik\ *n* : a European herb related to onion and grown for its bulbs that have a strong smell and taste and are used to flavor foods; *also* : one of the bulbs — **gar·licky** \-li-kē\ *adj*

garlic salt *n* : a seasoning made of ground dried garlic and salt

gar·ment \'gär-mənt\ *n* : an article of clothing — **garment** *vb*

gar·ner \'gär-nər\ *vb* **1** : to gather into storage **2 a** : to acquire by effort : EARN **b** : ACCUMULATE 1, COLLECT

gar·net \'gär-nət\ *n* **1** : a transparent usually red mineral used as a gem or for grinding, smoothing, or polishing **2** : a deep red color

Word History The garnet owes its name to its color. The deep red color of a garnet reminded the French of a red-skinned fruit. In early French the fruit was called *pomme gernete,* which means "seedy apple." This later became *pomegranate* in English. The early French word *gernete,* meaning "seedy," is the source of the adjective *gernet,* meaning "red like a pomegranate." This word was then used as a noun to mean the red gemstone. When borrowed into English, *gernet* became *garnet.* [Middle English *gernet* "garnet," from early French *gernete* (same meaning), from *gernet* (adjective) "red like a pomegranate," from *pomme gernete* "pomegranate," literally, "seedy apple"; *pomme* from earlier *pome* "apple" and *gernete* derived from Latin *granum* "grain, seed" — related to GRAIN, GRENADE, POMEGRANATE]

garnet paper *n* : a paper that has crushed garnet glued on one side and is used for smoothing and polishing

gar·nish \'gär-nish\ *vb* **1** : DECORATE 1, EMBELLISH **2** : to add decorations or seasonings to (food) **3** : ACCESSORIZE — **garnish** *n* — **gar·nish·ment** \-mənt\ *n*

\ə\ **abut**	\au̇\ **out**	\i\ **tip**	\o̤\ **saw**	\u̇\ **foot**
\ər\ **further**	\ch\ **chin**	\ī\ **life**	\o̤i\ **coin**	\y\ **yet**
\a\ **mat**	\e\ **pet**	\j\ **job**	\th\ **thin**	\yü\ **few**
\ā\ **take**	\ē\ **easy**	\ŋ\ **sing**	\th\ **this**	\yu̇\ **cure**
\ä\ **cot, cart**	\g\ **go**	\ō\ **bone**	\ü\ **food**	\zh\ **vision**

gar·ret \'gar-ət\ *n* : a room or unfinished part of a house just under the roof

¹gar·ri·son \'gar-ə-sən\ *n* **1** : a military post; *esp* : a permanent military installation **2** : the troops stationed at a garrison

²garrison *vb* **gar·ri·soned; gar·ri·son·ing** \'gar-əs(ə-)niŋ\ **1** : to station troops in **2** : to send (troops) to a garrison

¹gar·rote *or* **ga·rotte** \gə-'rät, -'rōt; 'gar-ət\ *n* **1 a** : a method of execution by strangling **b** : the apparatus used **2** : an implement (as a wire with a handle at each end) for strangling

²garrote *or* **garotte** *vb* **gar·rot·ed** *or* **ga·rott·ed; gar·rot·ing** *or* **ga·rott·ing** : to strangle with or as if with a garrote — **gar·rot·er** *n*

gar·ru·lous \'gar-ə-ləs\ *adj* : overly talkative **synonyms** see TALKATIVE — **gar·ru·lous·ly** *adv* — **gar·ru·lous·ness** *n*

gar·ter \'gärt-ər\ *n* : a band worn to hold up a stocking or sock

garter snake *n* : any of numerous harmless American snakes with stripes along the back

garter snake

¹gas \'gas\ *n, pl* **gas·es** *also* **gas·ses** **1** : a fluid (as hydrogen or air) that has no fixed shape and tends to expand without limit **2 a** : a gas or mixture of gases used as a fuel or as an anesthetic **b** : a gaseous product of digestion **c** : a fluid substance (as tear gas) that can be used to produce a poisonous or suffocating atmosphere **3** : unimportant talk : BOMBAST **4** : GASOLINE **5** *slang* : something appealing or enjoyable ⟨the party was a *gas*⟩

²gas *vb* **gassed; gas·sing** **1** : to supply with gas ⟨*gas* up the car⟩ **2 a** : to treat with gas **b** : to poison with gas **3** : to talk idly

gas·eous \'gas-ē-əs, 'gash-əs\ *adj* **1** : having the form of or being gas **2** : of or relating to gas **3** : lacking solidity

gas–guz·zler \'gas-'gəz(-ə)-lər\ *n* : a usually large automobile that gets low gas mileage — **gas–guz·zling** \-'gəz(-ə)-liŋ\ *adj*

¹gash \'gash\ *n* : a long deep cut

²gash *vb* : to make a long deep cut in

gas·ket \'gas-kət\ *n* : a material (as rubber) or a part used to prevent a joint from leaking

gas·light \'gas-ˌlīt, -'līt\ *n* **1** : light made by burning gas **2 a** : a gas flame **b** : a gas lighting fixture — **gas·light·ing** \-iŋ\ *n* — **gas·lit** \-ˌlit, -'lit\ *adj*

gas mask *n* : a mask connected to a chemical air filter and used to protect the face and lungs against harmful gases

gas·o·hol \'gas-ə-ˌhȯl\ *n* : a fuel consisting of 10 percent ethanol and 90 percent gasoline [from *gas*oline and alco*hol*]

gas·o·line \'gas-ə-ˌlēn, ˌgas-ə-'lēn\ *n* : a flammable liquid produced usually by blending products from natural gas and petroleum and used especially as a fuel for engines

gasp \'gasp\ *vb* **1** : to draw in a breath sharply (as with shock) **2** : to breathe with difficulty : PANT **3** : to utter with quick difficult breaths — **gasp** *n*

gas station *n* : a place for servicing motor vehicles especially with gasoline and oil

gas·sy \'gas-ē\ *adj* **gas·si·er; -est** **1** : full of or containing gas **2** : having the characteristics of gas — **gas·si·ness** *n*

gas·tric \'gas-trik\ *adj* : of, relating to, or located near the stomach ⟨*gastric* ulcers⟩

gastric juice *n* : a watery acid fluid that helps in digestion and is secreted by glands in the walls of the stomach

gas·tri·tis \ga-'strīt-əs\ *n* : inflammation of the stomach and especially of its mucous membrane

gas·troc·ne·mi·us \ˌgas-(ˌ)träk-'nē-mē-əs, -trək-\ *n, pl* **-mii** \-mē-ˌī\ : the largest muscle of the calf of the leg that points the toe and flexes the leg below the knee

gas·tro·in·tes·ti·nal \ˌgas-trō-in-'tes-tən-ᵊl\ *adj* : of, relating to, or including both stomach and intestine

gas·tron·o·my \ga-'strän-ə-mē\ *n* : the art of appreciating fine food — **gas·tro·nom·ic** \ˌgas-trə-'näm-ik\ *also* **gas·tro·nom·i·cal** \-'näm-i-kəl\ *adj*

gas·tro·pod \'gas-trə-ˌpäd\ *n* : any of a large class of mollusks (as snails) that have a muscular foot at the bottom and usually both a distinct head bearing sense organs and a spiral shell into which the body can be withdrawn — **gastropod** *adj*

gas·tro·trich \'gas-trə-ˌtrik\ *n* : any of a small group of tiny animals that live in water and move by gliding

gas·tru·la \'gas-trə-lə\ *n, pl* **-las** *or* **-lae** \-ˌlē, -ˌlī\ : a cup-shaped three-layered early embryo formed from the blastula by the movement of layers of cells to establish the ectoderm, mesoderm, and endoderm

gas·tru·la·tion \ˌgas-trə-'lā-shən\ *n* : the process of becoming or of forming a gastrula

gas turbine *n* : an engine in which gases produced by burning fuel are used to spin blades connected to a drive shaft

gas·works \'gas-ˌwərks\ *n pl* : a plant for manufacturing gas

gat \'gat\ *n, slang* : HANDGUN

gate \'gāt\ *n* **1** : an opening in a wall or fence **2** : a city or castle entrance often with defensive structures **3** : the frame or door that closes a gate **4** : a means of entrance or exit **5** : a door, valve, or other device for controlling the passage of fluid **6** : the total admission receipts or the number of spectators especially at a sports event

gat·ed \'gāt-əd\ *adj* **1** : having a gate **2** : having guarded or locked gates designed to restrict access ⟨a *gated* community⟩

gate·house \'gāt-ˌhaủs\ *n* : a small building near a gate at an entrance (as to a park or gated community)

gate·keep·er \-ˌkē-pər\ *n* : a person who tends or guards a gate

gate·way \-ˌwā\ *n* **1** : an opening for a gate **2** : a passage into or out of a place or state ⟨knowledge is the *gateway* to wisdom⟩

¹gath·er \'gath-ər *also* 'geth-\ *vb* **gath·ered; gath·er·ing** \'gath-(ə-)riŋ\ **1** : to bring together : COLLECT **2** : ¹PICK 2b, HARVEST **3** : to gain by gradual increase ⟨*gather* speed⟩ **4** : to prepare (as oneself) by calling on strength ⟨*gather* courage to dive⟩ **5** : to draw about or close to something **6** : to pull (cloth) along a line of stitching so as to draw into puckers **7** : GUESS 1, DEDUCE **8** : to come together in a body or around a center of attraction ⟨a crowd *gathered* round⟩ **9** : ¹INCREASE, GROW ⟨a storm *gathered* outside⟩ — **gath·er·er** \-ər-ər\ *n*

synonyms GATHER, COLLECT, ASSEMBLE, CONGREGATE mean to come or bring together into a group, mass, or unit. GATHER applies broadly to the coming or bringing together of things from a spread-out or scattered state ⟨farmers from all over *gathered* at the fair⟩. COLLECT often suggests careful selection or orderly arrangement ⟨she likes to *collect* stamps⟩. ASSEMBLE suggests an ordered gathering or organization of persons or things usually for a purpose ⟨all students will *assemble* in the auditorium to hear the speaker⟩. CONGREGATE suggests an unplanned coming together into a crowd or huddle ⟨people began to *congregate* on street corners⟩.

²gather *n* : the result of gathering cloth : PUCKER

gathering *n* **1** : ASSEMBLY 1, MEETING **2** : a pus-filled swelling (as an abscess) **3** : the collecting of food and raw materials from the wild **4** : COLLECTION 2a **5** : a gather in cloth

ga·tor \ˈgāt-ər\ *n* : ALLIGATOR

gauche \ˈgōsh\ *adj* : lacking social experience or grace [French, literally, "left, on the left hand"; probably so called because for most people the left hand is more awkward to use than the right] — **gauche·ness** *n*

gau·cho \ˈgaù-chō\ *n, pl* **gauchos** : a cowboy of the South American grass-covered plains

gaud \ˈgód, ˈgäd\ *n* : ¹ORNAMENT 1, TRINKET

gaudy \ˈgód-ē, ˈgäd-\ *adj* **gaud·i·er; -est** : overly or tastelessly ornamented — **gaud·i·ly** \ˈgód-ᵊl-ē, ˈgäd-\ *adv* — **gaud·i·ness** \-ēnəs\ *n*

¹gauge *also* **gage** \ˈgāj\ *n* **1** : measurement according to some standard or system: as **a** : the distance between the rails of a railroad **b** : the size of a shotgun expressed as the number of lead balls of the same size as the interior diameter of the barrel required to make a pound ⟨a 12-*gauge* shotgun⟩ **c** : the thickness of sheet metal or the diameter of wire or a screw **d** : the fineness of a knitted fabric in loops per unit of width **2** : an instrument for measuring, testing, or registering

²gauge *also* **gage** *vb* **gauged** *also* **gaged; gaug·ing** *also* **gag·ing 1 a** : to measure exactly **b** : to find out the capacity or contents of **2** : ¹ESTIMATE 1 — **gaug·er** *n*

gaunt \ˈgónt, ˈgänt\ *adj* **1** : being thin and bony (as from hunger or suffering) **2** : grim and forbidding : BARREN, DESOLATE ⟨*gaunt*, leafless trees⟩ — **gaunt·ly** *adv* — **gaunt·ness** *n*

¹gaunt·let \ˈgónt-lət, ˈgänt-\ *n* **1** : a protective glove worn with a suit of armor **2** : a protective glove used in industry — **gaunt·let·ed** \-lət-əd\ *adj*

²gauntlet *also* **gant·let** *n* : a double file of men armed with weapons (as clubs) with which to strike at a person who is made to run between them

gauze \ˈgóz\ *n* **1** : a thin often transparent fabric **2** : a loosely woven cotton surgical bandage **3** : a woven fabric of fine metal or plastic wires — **gauzy** \ˈgó-zē\ *adj*

gave *past of* GIVE

gav·el \ˈgav-əl\ *n* : the mallet of an officer in charge of a meeting or of an auctioneer

ga·votte \gə-ˈvät\ *n* : a French peasant dance in moderately quick 4/4 time — **gavotte** *vb*

gawk \ˈgók\ *vb* : to stare stupidly [probably an altered form of obsolete *gaw* "to stare"]

gawky \ˈgó-kē\ *adj* **gawk·i·er; -est** : AWKWARD 2, CLUMSY — **gawk·i·ly** \-kə-lē\ *adv* — **gawk·i·ness** \-kē-nəs\ *n*

gay \ˈgā\ *adj* **gay·er; gay·est 1** : happily excited : MERRY ⟨a *gay* mood⟩ **2 a** : CHEERFUL 1a, LIVELY ⟨a *gay* meadow⟩ **b** : brilliant in color **3** : given to social pleasures **4** : ¹HOMOSEXUAL — **gay** *adv* — **gay·ness** *n*

gayety *variant of* GAIETY

gayly *variant of* GAILY

gaze \ˈgāz\ *vb* **gazed; gaz·ing** : to fix the eyes in a steady intent look — **gaze** *n* — **gaz·er** *n*

    synonyms GAZE, GAPE, STARE, GLARE mean to fix one's eyes on something for a long time. GAZE suggests looking steadily at something in wonder, admiration, or absentmindedness ⟨*gazing* at the moon⟩. GAPE suggests an open-mouthed, often stupid, wonder ⟨toddlers *gaping* at strangers⟩. STARE suggests a wide-eyed, often curious, rude, or vacant, gaze ⟨people were *staring* at the couple who were arguing⟩. GLARE suggests fierce or angry staring ⟨the speaker *glared* at the people talking⟩.

ga·ze·bo \gə-ˈzē-bō\ *n, pl* **-bos** : a freestanding roofed structure usually open on the sides [perhaps from *gaze* and Latin *-ebo*, as in *videbo* "I shall see"]

ga·zelle \gə-ˈzel\ *n, pl* **ga·zelles** *also* **gazelle** : any of numerous small graceful swift antelopes of Africa and Asia

gazelle

ga·zette \gə-ˈzet\ *n* **1** : NEWSPAPER **2** : an official journal

gaz·et·teer \ˌgaz-ə-ˈti(ə)r\ *n* : a geographical dictionary

ga·zil·lion \gə-ˈzil-yən\ *n* : ZILLION

gaz·pa·cho \gəz-ˈpäch-ō, gəs-\ *n, pl* **-chos** : a spicy soup that is usually made from chopped vegetables (as tomato and cucumber) and is served cold [Spanish]

G clef *n* : TREBLE CLEF

¹gear \ˈgi(ə)r\ *n* **1** : EQUIPMENT **2** ⟨camping *gear*⟩ ⟨electronic *gear*⟩ **2 a** : a mechanism that performs a specific function in a machine ⟨steering *gear*⟩ **b** : a toothed wheel : COGWHEEL **3 a** : working order, relation, or adjustment ⟨got her career in *gear*⟩ **b** : one of the adjustments of a transmission (as of a bicycle or motor vehicle) that determine the direction of travel and the relative speed of the engine and the vehicle — **gear·less** \-ləs\ *adj*

²gear *vb* **1** : to provide or connect with gearing **2** : to prepare for operation ⟨*gear* up for production⟩ **3** : to make suitable ⟨a book *geared* for children⟩

gear·box \ˈgi(ə)r-ˌbäks\ *n* : TRANSMISSION 3

gear·ing \ˈgi(ə)r-iŋ\ *n* **1** : the act or process of providing or fitting with gears **2** : the parts by which motion is transmitted from one portion of machinery to another

gear·shift \ˈgi(ə)r-ˌshift\ *n* : a mechanism by which transmission gears are connected and disconnected

gearwheel \ˈgir-ˌhwēl, -ˌwēl\ *n* : ¹GEAR 2b

gecko \ˈgek-ō\ *n, pl* **geck·os** *or* **geck·oes** : any of numerous small harmless chiefly tropical lizards that eat insects and are active at night

¹gee \ˈjē\ *imperative verb* — used as a direction to turn to the right or move ahead

²gee *interj* — used to show surprise, enthusiasm, or disappointment

geese *plural of* GOOSE

gee·zer \ˈgē-zər\ *n* : an eccentric person; *esp* : an odd old man [probably an altered form of Scots *guiser* "person in disguise"]

Gei·ger counter \ˌgī-gər-\ *n* : an instrument for detecting the presence of cosmic rays or radioactive substances

Geiger–Mül·ler counter \-ˈmyül-ər, -ˈmil-, -ˈməl-\ *n* : GEIGER COUNTER

gei·sha \ˈgā-shə, ˈgē-\ *pl* **geisha** *or* **geishas** : a Japanese woman who is trained to provide entertaining company for men [Japanese, from *gei* "art" and *-sha* "person"]

¹gel \ˈjel\ *n* : a solid jellylike colloid (as gelatin dessert)

²gel *vb* **gelled; gel·ling** : to change into or take on the form of a gel

gel·a·tin *also* **gel·a·tine** \ˈjel-ət-ᵊn\ *n* **1** : gummy or sticky protein obtained by boiling animal tissues and used as food, in photography, and in medicine **2** : an edible jelly formed with gelatin **3** : a thin colored transparent sheet used to color a stage light

ge·lat·i·nous \jə-ˈlat-nəs, -ᵊn-əs\ *adj* **1** : resembling gelatin or jelly **2** : of, relating to, or containing gelatin

\ə\ **abut**	\aù\ **out**	\i\ **tip**	\ò\ **saw**	\ù\ **foot**
\ər\ **further**	\ch\ **chin**	\ī\ **life**	\òi\ **coin**	\y\ **yet**
\a\ **mat**	\e\ **pet**	\j\ **job**	\th\ **thin**	\yü\ **few**
\ā\ **take**	\ē\ **easy**	\ŋ\ **sing**	\th\ **this**	\yù\ **cure**
\ä\ **cot, cart**	\g\ **go**	\ō\ **bone**	\ü\ **food**	\zh\ **vision**

geld \\'geld\\ *vb* : CASTRATE

geld·ing \\'gel-diŋ\\ *n* : a castrated animal; *esp* : a castrated male horse

gem \\'jem\\ *n* **1 a** : ¹JEWEL **b** : a usually valuable stone cut and polished for ornament **2** : something prized as being beautiful or perfect — **gem** *vb*

Gem·i·ni \\'jem-ə-(,)nē, -,nī; 'gem-ə-,nē\\ *n* **1** : a group of stars between Taurus and Cancer usually pictured as twins sitting together **2 a** : the third sign of the zodiac — see ZODIAC table **b** : a person whose sign of the zodiac is Gemini

Word History Among the gods worshipped by the ancient Greeks and Romans were twins named Castor and Pollux. They were believed to be sons of Zeus and Leda. These twins spent most of their lives together. After their deaths, Zeus allowed them to spend eternity together as stars. They were worshipped as protectors of athletes and sailors. The two of them are usually pictured together in the constellation called *Gemini,* the Latin word for "twins." [Latin, literally, "the twins" (Castor and Pollux)]

gem·stone \\'jem-,stōn\\ *n* : a mineral that when cut and polished can be used in jewelry

gen·darme \\'zhän-,därm *also* 'jän-\\ *n* : a member of a police force especially in France [from French *gendarme* "policeman," derived as a singular form from earlier *gensdarmes, gent d'armes,* literally, "armed people"]

gen·der \\'jen-dər\\ *n* **1 a** : SEX 1 **b** : the behavioral, cultural, or emotional traits typically associated with one sex **2** : any of two or more classes of words (as nouns or pronouns) or of forms of words (as adjectives) that are partly based on sex and that determine agreement with other words or grammatical forms

gene \\'jēn\\ *n* : a part of DNA or sometimes RNA that is usually located on a chromosome and that contains chemical information needed to make a particular protein (as an enzyme) controlling or influencing an inherited bodily trait or activity (as eye color or metabolism) or that influences or controls the activity of another gene or genes

ge·ne·al·o·gy \\,jē-nē-'äl-ə-jē, ,jen-ē-, -'al-\\ *n, pl* **-gies** **1** : the line of ancestors of a person or family or a history of such a line of ancestors **2** : the study of family lines of ancestors — **ge·ne·a·log·i·cal** \\,jē-nē-ə-'läj-i-kəl, ,jen-ē-\\ *adj* — **ge·ne·a·log·i·cal·ly** \\-k(ə-)lē\\ *adv* — **ge·ne·al·o·gist** \\-'äl-ə-jəst, -'al-\\ *n*

gene mutation *n* : mutation due to a chemical change in a gene

genera *plural of* GENUS

¹gen·er·al \\'jen-(ə-)rəl\\ *adj* **1** : involving, applying to, or affecting the whole : not local or partial (a *general* election) (the *general* body of citizens) **2** : relating to or covering all instances (a *general* conclusion) **3** : not specific or in detail (a *general* outline) **4** : common to many (the *general* custom here) **5** : not special : not specialized (a *general* store) **6** : of top rank (*general* manager)

²general *n* : a military officer with a rank above that of a colonel; *esp* : an officer with the rank just above that of a lieutenant general — **in general** : for the most part

gen·er·a·lis·si·mo \\,jen-(ə-)rə-'lis-ə-,mō\\ *n, pl* **-mos** : the commander in chief of an army [Italian]

gen·er·al·ist \\'jen-(ə-)rə-ləst\\ *n* : a person whose skills or interests extend to several different fields

gen·er·al·i·ty \\,jen-ə-'ral-ət-ē\\ *n, pl* **-ties** **1** : the quality or state of being general **2 a** : GENERALIZATION 2 **b** : a statement that is unclear or that does not give enough information **3** : the greatest part : BULK

gen·er·al·i·za·tion \\,jen-(ə-)rə-lə-'zā-shən\\ *n* **1** : the act or process of generalizing **2** : a general statement, law, principle, or proposition

gen·er·al·ize \\'jen-(ə-)rə-,līz\\ *vb* **-ized; -iz·ing** : to put in the form of a general rule : draw or state a general conclusion from a number of items or instances

gen·er·al·ly \\'jen-(ə-)rə-lē, 'jen-ər-lē\\ *adv* **1** : for the most part (*generally* speaking) **2** : as a rule : USUALLY

general of the air force : a general of the highest rank in the air force

general of the army : a general of the highest rank in the army

general practitioner *n* : a physician or veterinarian whose practice is not limited to a specialty

general relativity *n* : RELATIVITY 2b

general store *n* : a retail store located usually in a small or rural community that carries a wide variety of goods including groceries but is not divided into departments

gen·er·ate \\'jen-ə-,rāt\\ *vb* **-at·ed; -at·ing** **1** : to bring into existence (*generate* electricity) **2** : to be the cause of or reason for (news that *generated* excitement) — **gen·er·a·tive** \\-ə-,rāt-iv, -(ə-)rət-\\ *adj*

gen·er·a·tion \\,jen-ə-'rā-shən\\ *n* **1 a** : those being a step in a line from one ancestor (a family that has lived in the same house for four *generations*) **b** : a group of individuals born and living at the same time **c** : a type or class of objects developed from an earlier type **2** : the average length of time between the birth of parents and that of their offspring **3** : the action or process of generating — **gen·er·a·tion·al** \\-shnəl, -shən-ᵊl\\ *adj*

gen·er·a·tor \\'jen-ə-,rāt-ər\\ *n* : one that generates: as **a** : a piece of laboratory equipment in which vapor or gas is formed **b** : a machine by which mechanical energy is changed into electrical energy

ge·ner·ic \\jə-'ner-ik\\ *adj* **1 a** : of, relating to, or characteristic of a whole group or class : GENERAL **b** : not protected by a trademark registration (*generic* drugs) **2** : of, relating to, or having the rank of a biological genus — **ge·ner·i·cal·ly** \\-ner-i-k(ə-)lē\\ *adv*

gen·er·os·i·ty \\,jen-ə-'räs-ət-ē\\ *n, pl* **-ties** **1** : freedom in spirit or act; *esp* : readiness in giving **2** : a generous act

gen·er·ous \\'jen-(ə-)rəs\\ *adj* **1** : free in giving or sharing **2** : ¹NOBLE 5, HIGH-MINDED **3** : ABUNDANT (a *generous* supply) — **gen·er·ous·ly** *adv* — **gen·er·ous·ness** *n*

gen·e·sis \\'jen-ə-səs\\ *n, pl* **gen·e·ses** \\-ə-,sēz\\ : the origin or coming into being of something

Genesis — see BIBLE table

gene therapy *n* : the insertion of a functioning gene into cells especially to replace a defective gene in the treatment of genetic disorders

ge·net·ic \\jə-'net-ik\\ *also* **ge·net·i·cal** \\-i-kəl\\ *adj* : of, relating to, or involving genes or genetics (*genetic* research); *also* : caused or controlled by genes (a *genetic* disease) — **ge·net·i·cal·ly** \\-i-k(ə-)lē\\ *adv*

genetic code *n* : the chemical code that is the basis of genetic inheritance and consists of units of three linked chemical groups which specify particular kinds of amino acids used to make proteins or which start or stop the process of making proteins

genetic engineering *n* : the alteration of genetic material and especially the cutting up and piecing together of DNA from one or more species for introduction into a living thing in order to change one or more of its characteristics — **genetically engineered** *adj* — **genetic engineer** *n*

ge·net·i·cist \\jə-'net-ə-səst\\ *n* : a person who specializes in genetics

ge·net·ics \\jə-'net-iks\\ *n* : a branch of biology that deals with the inherited traits and variation of organisms

ge·nial \\'jēn-yəl\\ *adj* **1** : favoring growth or comfort (a *genial* climate) **2** : being cheerful and pleasant **synonyms** see GRACIOUS — **ge·nial·i·ty** \\,jē-nē-'al-ət-ē, jēn-'yal-\\ *n* — **ge·nial·ly** \\'jē-nyə-lē\\ *adv*

ge·nie \ˈjē-nē\ *n* : a magic spirit believed to take human form and serve the person who calls it

gen·i·tal \ˈjen-ə-tᵊl\ *adj* : of or relating to reproduction or the sexual organs

genital herpes *n* : herpes simplex of the type typically affecting the genitalia

gen·i·ta·lia \ˌjen-ə-ˈtāl-yə\ *n pl* : reproductive organs; *esp* : the genital organs on the outside of the body — **gen·i·ta·lic** \-ˈtal-ik, -ˈtāl-\ *adj*

gen·i·tals \ˈjen-ə-tᵊlz\ *n pl* : GENITALIA

gen·i·tive \ˈjen-ət-iv\ *adj* : of, relating to, or being a grammatical case marking typically possession or source — compare POSSESSIVE — **gen·i·ti·val** \ˌjen-ə-ˈtī-vəl\ *adj* — **genitive** *n*

gen·i·to·uri·nary \ˌjen-ə-tō-ˈyu̇r-ə-ˌner-ē\ *adj* : of or relating to the genital and urinary organs or functions

ge·nius \ˈjēn-yəs, ˈjē-nē-əs\ *n, pl* **ge·nius·es** *or* **ge·nii** \-ē-ˌī, -nē-ˌī\ **1** *pl* **genii** : an accompanying spirit of a person or place **2** : a strong leaning or inclination ⟨a *genius* for getting into trouble⟩ **3** : a peculiar, distinctive, or identifying character ⟨the *genius* of a nation⟩ **4** *pl usually* **geniuses a** : great natural ability **b** : extraordinary intelligence **c** : a very gifted person

Word History The ancient Romans believed in special beings or spirits that were not gods or humans but something in between. They believed that from birth each person had one of these spirits to act as a protector. The Latin name for this spirit was *genius*, which came from *gignere*, meaning "to be the father of, beget." Part of such a genius's role was to protect a person's moral character. From this idea in the 16th century came the sense of *genius* meaning "an identifying character." This led to the sense of "a marked aptitude." In time *genius* came to mean "very great intellectual power." [from Latin *genius* "special guardian spirit," from *gignere* "to father, beget" — related to ENGINE, ¹GIN, INGENIOUS]

geno·cide \ˈjen-ə-ˌsīd\ *n* : the deliberate destruction of a racial, political, or cultural group — **geno·cid·al** \ˌjen-ə-ˈsīd-ᵊl\ *adj*

ge·no·type \ˈjē-nə-ˌtīp, ˈjen-ə-\ *n* : the whole set of genes of an individual or group — **ge·no·typ·ic** \ˌjē-nə-ˈtip-ik, ˌjen-ə-\ *adj*

genre \ˈzhän-rə, ˈzhäⁿ-, ˈjän-rə\ *n* : a particular type or category of literary, musical, or artistic composition [French]

gent \ˈjent\ *n* : ¹MAN 1a, FELLOW

gen·teel \jen-ˈtē(ə)l\ *adj* **1** : of or relating to the upper classes **2** : ELEGANT 1, GRACEFUL **3** : free from bad manners or bad taste — **gen·teel·ly** \-ˈtē(ə)l-lē\ *adv* — **gen·teel·ness** *n*

gen·tian \ˈjen-chən\ *n* : any of various herbs with smooth leaves and showy bell-shaped or funnel-shaped usually blue flowers

gentian violet *n* : a violet dye used as a stain in biology and in a cream or liquid as an antiseptic in some infections caused by bacteria and fungi

gentian

gen·tile \ˈjen-ˌtīl\ *n* **1** *often cap* : a person who is not Jewish **2** : a person who does not follow the God of the Bible : HEATHEN, PAGAN **3** *often cap* : a person who is not a Mormon [Middle English *gentil, gentile* "one who is not Jewish," derived from Latin *gentilis* "a member of the same family, clan, or nation," from *gent-, gens* "clan, family, race"; from the fact that the early Christians used the Latin word *genes*, plural of *gens*, as a translation of the Hebrew word *gōyīm*, literally, "the nations," used to refer to all non-Jewish people] — **gentile** *adj, often cap*

gen·til·i·ty \jen-ˈtil-ət-ē\ *n, pl* **-ties 1** : good birth and family **2** : the qualities of a well-bred person **3** : good manners

gen·tle \ˈjent-ᵊl\ *adj* **gen·tler** \ˈjent-lər, -ᵊl-ər\; **gen·tlest** \ˈjent-ləst, -ᵊl-əst\ **1** : belonging or suitable to a family of high social rank **2 a** : easily handled : DOCILE ⟨a *gentle* horse⟩ **b** : not harsh : MILD ⟨*gentle* soap⟩ **c** : not stern or rough ⟨*gentle* words⟩ **3** : ¹SOFT 1, SOOTHING ⟨a *gentle* murmur⟩ **4** : ¹MODERATE 2a ⟨*gentle* slopes⟩ — **gen·tle·ness** *n* — **gent·ly** \ˈjent-lē\ *adv*

²gentle *vb* **gen·tled; gen·tling** \ˈjent-liŋ, ᵊl-iŋ\ **1** : to make gentle or mild **2** : to make calmer : SOOTHE

gen·tle·folk \ˈjent-ᵊl-ˌfōk\ *also* **gen·tle·folks** \-ˌfōks\ *n pl* : persons of gentle or good family and breeding

gen·tle·man \ˈjent-ᵊl-mən\ *n* **1** : a man of good birth and position **2** : a man of good education and social position **3** : a male with very good manners ⟨reminded her young son to be a *gentleman*⟩ **4** : MAN ⟨I can help this gentleman⟩ ⟨ladies and *gentlemen*⟩ — **gen·tle·man·li·ness** \-lē-nəs\ *n* — **gen·tle·man·ly** \-lē\ *adj*

gen·tle·wom·an \ˈjent-ᵊl-ˌwu̇m-ən\ *n* **1 a** : a woman of good birth and position **b** : a woman attending a lady of rank **2** : a woman with very good manners : LADY

gen·try \ˈjen-trē\ *n, pl* **gentries** : people of high social status : ARISTOCRACY

gen·u·flect \ˈjen-yə-ˌflekt\ *vb* : to kneel on one knee and then rise again as an act of deep respect

gen·u·ine \ˈjen-yə-wən, -(ˌ)win\ *adj* **1** : being actually what it seems to be : REAL ⟨*genuine* gold⟩ **2** : not pretended : SINCERE, HONEST ⟨a *genuine* interest⟩ — **gen·u·ine·ly** *adv* — **gen·u·ine·ness** \-wən-(n)əs\ *n*

ge·nus \ˈjē-nəs\ *n, pl* **gen·era** \ˈjen-ə-rə\ : a category of classification in biology that ranks between the family and the species, contains related species, and is named by a capitalized noun formed in Latin

geo *combining form* : earth : ground : soil ⟨*geology*⟩ [Greek *gē* "earth, land"]

geo·cach·ing \ˈjē-ō-ˌka-shiŋ\ *n* : a game in which players use a GPS device to search for a cache of items hidden at given geographical coordinates — **geo·cach·er** \-shər\ *n*

geo·cen·tric \ˌjē-ō-ˈsen-trik\ *adj* **1** : relating to or measured from the earth's center **2** : having or relating to the earth as a center

geo·chem·is·try \ˈjē-ō-ˈkem-ə-strē\ *n* : a science that deals with the chemical composition of and chemical changes in the solid material of the earth or of another body (as the moon) — **geo·chem·i·cal** \-ˈkem-i-kəl\ *adj* — **geo·chem·ist** \-ˈkem-əst\ *n*

ge·ode \ˈjē-ˌōd\ *n* : a stone having a cavity lined with crystals or mineral matter

geo·de·sic \ˌjē-ə-ˈdes-ik, -ˈdēs-, -ˈdez-, -ˈdēz-\ *adj* : made of light short straight structural elements ⟨a *geodesic* dome⟩

geo·det·ic survey \ˌjē-ə-ˈdet-ik-\ *n* : a survey of a large land area in which corrections are made for the curving of the earth's surface

ge·og·ra·phy \jē-ˈäg-rə-fē\ *n, pl* **-phies 1** : a science that deals with the location of living and nonliving things on earth and the way they affect one another **2** : the natural parts of an area ⟨the *geography* of the western U.S.⟩ — **ge·og·ra·pher** \-fər\ *n* — **geo·graph·ic** \ˌjē-ə-ˈgraf-ik\ *or* **geo·graph·i·cal** \-i-kəl\ *adj* — **geo·graph·i·cal·ly** \-i-k(ə-)lē\ *adv*

\ə\ **abut**	\au̇\ **out**	\i\ **tip**	\o̯\ **saw**	\u̇\ **foot**
\ər\ **further**	\ch\ **chin**	\ī\ **life**	\o̯i\ **coin**	\y\ **yet**
\a\ **mat**	\e\ **pet**	\j\ **job**	\th\ **thin**	\yü\ **few**
\ā\ **take**	\ē\ **easy**	\ŋ\ **sing**	\th\ **this**	\yu̇\ **cure**
\ä\ **cot, cart**	\g\ **go**	\ō\ **bone**	\ü\ **food**	\zh\ **vision**

GEOLOGIC TIME

EONS	ERAS	PERIODS AND SYSTEMS	EPOCHS AND SERIES	APPROXIMATE BEGINNING OF INTERVAL (YEARS AGO)	BIOLOGICAL FORMS
Phanerozoic	Cenozoic	Quaternary	Holocene	10,000	
			Pleistocene	1,800,000	Earliest humans
		Tertiary	Pliocene	5,000,000	
			Miocene	24,000,000	Earliest hominids
			Oligocene	34,000,000	
			Eocene	55,000,000	Earliest grasses
			Paleocene	65,000,000	Earliest large mammals
		Cretaceous-Tertiary boundary (65 million years ago): extinction of dinosaurs			
	Mesozoic	Cretaceous	Upper	98,000,000	
			Lower	144,000,000	Earliest flowering plants; dinosaurs dominate the land
		Jurassic		208,000,000	Earliest birds
		Triassic		248,000,000	Earliest dinosaurs & mammals
	Paleozoic	Permian		286,000,000	
		Carboniferous			
		Pennsylvanian		320,000,000	Earliest reptiles
		Mississippian		360,000,000	Earliest winged insects
		Devonian		410,000,000	Earliest amphibians & bony fish
		Silurian		438,000,000	Earliest land plants & insects
		Ordovician		505,000,000	Earliest corals
		Cambrian		544,000,000	Earliest fish
Proterozoic	Precambrian			2,500,000,000	Earliest colonial algae & soft-bodied invertebrates
Archean				3,800,000,000	Earliest surviving fossils of primitive single-celled organisms
Hadean				4,600,000,000	No surviving fossils

geologic time *n* : the long period of time marked by events in the earth's geological history

ge·ol·o·gy \jē-'äl-ə-jē\ *n, pl* **-gies** **1 a** : a science that deals with the history of the earth and its life especially as recorded in rocks **b** : a study of the features of a heavenly body (as the moon) **2** : the geologic features (as mountains or plains) of an area — **geo·log·ic** \ˌjē-ə-'läj-ik\ *or* **geo·log·i·cal** \-i-kəl\ *adj* — **geo·log·i·cal·ly** \-i-k(ə-)lē\ *adv* — **ge·ol·o·gist** \jē-'äl-ə-jəst\ *n*

geo·mag·net·ic \ˌjē-ō-mag-'net-ik\ *adj* : of or relating to the magnetism of the earth — **geo·mag·ne·tism** \-'mag-nə-ˌtiz-əm\ *n*

ge·om·e·ter \jē-'äm-ət-ər\ *n* : a person who specializes in geometry

geo·met·ric \ˌjē-ə-'me-trik\ *or* **geo·met·ri·cal** \-'me-tri-kəl\ *adj* : of, relating to, or based on the methods or principles of geometry — **geo·met·ri·cal·ly** \-tri-k(ə-)lē\ *adv*

ge·om·e·try \jē-'äm-ə-trē\ *n, pl* **-tries** **1** : a branch of mathematics that deals with points, lines, angles, surfaces, and solids **2** : ²SHAPE ⟨the *geometry* of a crystal⟩

geo·phys·ics \ˌjē-ə-'fiz-iks\ *n* : a science that deals with the physical processes occurring in or near the earth — **geo·phys·i·cal** \-i-kəl\ *adj* — **geo·phys·i·cist** \-ə-sist\ *n*

Geor·gian \'jȯr-jən\ *adj* : of, relating to, or characteristic of the reigns of the first four British kings named George 〈*Georgian* architecture〉

geo·sci·ence \ˌjē-ō-'sī-ən(t)s\ *n* : the sciences (as geology or geophysics) dealing with the earth

geo·tax·is \ˌjē-ō-'tak-səs\ *n, pl* **-tax·es** \-'tak-sēz\ : a taxis in which the force of gravity is the cause of the movement

geo·ther·mal \ˌjē-ō-'thər-məl\ *also* **geo·ther·mic** \-mik\ *adj* : of, relating to, or using the heat of the earth's interior; *also* : produced by such heat

ge·ot·ro·pism \jē-'ä-trə-ˌpiz-əm\ *n* : a tropism involving turning or movement toward the earth — **geo·tro·pic** \ˌjē-ə-'trō-pik, -'träp-ik\ *adj*

ge·ra·ni·um \jə-'rā-nē-əm\ *n* **1** : any of a genus of herbs with usually deeply cut leaves and typically white, pink, or purple flowers in which glands alternate with the petals **2** : any of a genus of herbs native to southern Africa with showy flowers of usually red, pink, or white

Word History Many of the plants in the geranium family have long, thin, pointed seedpods or fruits that look like the bills of birds. The ancient Greeks noticed this resemblance. They named the wild geranium *geranion*, literally meaning "little crane," for the long-legged, long-billed wading bird. English borrowed the Latin form *geranium*. English also borrowed the idea that the geranium's seedpod looks like a bird's bill. The common English name of the wild geranium is *cranesbill*. [from Latin *geranium* "geranium," from Greek *geranion*, literally, "little crane," from *geranos* "crane"]

ger·bil \'jər-bəl\ *n* : any of several Old World desert rodents with long hind legs

ge·ri·at·ric \ˌjer-ē-'a-trik, jir-\ *adj* : of or relating to geriatrics, the aged, or the process of aging

ge·ri·at·rics \ˌjer-ē-'a-triks, jir-\ *n* : a branch of medicine that deals with the problems and diseases of old age and aging people

germ \'jərm\ *n* **1 a** : a small mass of living substance capable of developing into a whole individual or one of its parts **b** : the embryo in the seed of a cereal (as corn or wheat) together with its cotyledon that is usually separated from the starchy part of the seed during milling **2** : something that serves as an origin 〈the *germ* of an idea〉 **3** : a microscopic living thing; *esp* : one that causes disease

Ger·man \'jər-mən\ *n* **1** : a person born or living in Germany **2** : the Germanic language of Germany, Austria, and parts of Switzerland — **German** *adj*

German cockroach *n* : a small active cockroach with wings that is probably of African origin but is now common in many city buildings in the U.S.

ger·mane \(ˌ)jər-'mān\ *adj* : both relevant and appropriate 〈a *germane* comment〉 — **ger·mane·ly** *adv*

¹Ger·man·ic \(ˌ)jər-'man-ik\ *adj* **1** : of, relating to, or characteristic of the peoples speaking Germanic languages **2** : of or relating to Germanic

²Germanic *n* : a branch of the Indo-European language family containing English, German, Dutch, Afrikaans, Frisian, Gothic, and the Scandinavian languages

ger·ma·ni·um \(ˌ)jər-'mā-nē-əm\ *n* : a grayish white hard brittle element used especially as a semiconductor — see ELEMENT table

German measles *n sing or pl* : a contagious virus disease that is like the usual kind of measles but is milder and that may cause birth defects or the death of the fetus when it occurs in a pregnant woman — called also *rubella*

German shepherd *n* : any of a breed of large erect-eared intelligent dogs of German origin that are often used in police work and as guide dogs for the blind

German silver *n* : a silver-white blend of copper, zinc, and nickel

germ cell *n* : an egg or sperm cell or one of the cells from which they arise

germ·free \'jərm-ˌfrē\ *adj* : free of germs

ger·mi·cid·al \ˌjər-mə-'sīd-ᵊl\ *adj* : of or relating to a germicide; *also* : destroying germs

ger·mi·cide \'jər-mə-ˌsīd\ *n* : a substance that destroys germs

ger·mi·nate \'jər-mə-ˌnāt\ *vb* **-nat·ed; -nat·ing** **1** : to cause to sprout or develop **2** : to begin to grow : SPROUT **3** : to come into being : EVOLVE — **ger·mi·na·tion** \ˌjər-mə-'nā-shən\ *n*

germ theory *n* : the theory that infectious and contagious disease results from the action of living things

¹ger·ry·man·der \ˌjer-ē-'man-dər, 'jer-ē-ˌman-dər *also* ˌger-, 'ger-\ *n* : the act or result of gerrymandering [from Elbridge *Gerry*, former governor of Massachusetts, and *salamander*; so called from the shape of an election district formed during Gerry's term in office]

²gerrymander *vb* **-dered; -der·ing** \-d(ə-)riŋ\ : to divide (as a state) into election districts so as to give one political party an advantage over its opponents

¹gerrymander

ger·und \'jer-ənd\ *n* : an English noun formed from a verb by the addition of *-ing* that is capable of being modified by adverbs and taking an object

ges·so \'jes-ō\ *n, pl* **ges·soes** : a material like plaster used in art (as for modeling)

ges·ta·tion \je-'stā-shən\ *n* : the carrying of young in the uterus : PREGNANCY

ges·tic·u·late \je-'stik-yə-ˌlāt\ *vb* **-lat·ed; -lat·ing** : to make gestures especially when speaking — **ges·tic·u·la·tion** \-ˌstik-yə-'lā-shən\ *n*

¹ges·ture \'jes-chər, 'jesh-\ *n* **1** : a movement of the body or limbs that expresses or emphasizes an idea or a feeling **2** : something said or done by way of courtesy or for its effect on other people 〈a political *gesture*〉

²gesture *vb* **ges·tured; ges·tur·ing** : to make or direct with a gesture

ge·sund·heit \gə-'zunt-ˌhīt\ *interj* — used to wish good health especially to one who has just sneezed [German *Gesundheit*, literally, "health"]

get \(ˈ)get, *especially when unemphatic also* git\ *vb* **got** \(ˈ)gät\; **got** *or* **got·ten** \'gät-ᵊn\; **get·ting** **1** : to gain possession of (as by receiving, acquiring, earning, buying, or winning) 〈*get* a present〉 〈*got* first prize〉 〈*get* a dog〉 **2 a** : to obtain by request or as a favor 〈*get* your mother's permission〉 **b** : to come to have 〈*get* a good night's sleep〉 **c** : to come down with (an illness) : CATCH 〈*get* the measles〉 **3 a** : to succeed in coming or going 〈*got* out〉 〈*got* home early〉 **b** : to cause to come or go 〈*got* the car to the gas station〉 **4** : to become the father of : BEGET **5 a** : to cause to be in a certain condition 〈*got* his hair cut〉 〈*got* her feet wet〉 **b** : BECOME 1 〈*get* sick〉 〈*get* better〉 〈it's *getting* warmer〉 **c** : PREPARE 2 〈started *getting* dinner〉 **6 a** : ¹BAFFLE 1, PUZZLE 〈the third question *got* ev-

\ə\ **abut**	\au̇\ **out**	\i\ **tip**	\ȯ\ **saw**	\u̇\ **foot**	
\ər\ **further**	\ch\ **chin**	\ī\ **life**	\ȯi\ **coin**	\y\ **yet**	
\a\ **mat**	\e\ **pet**	\j\ **job**	\th\ **thin**	\yü\ **few**	
\ā\ **take**	\ē\ **easy**	\ŋ\ **sing**	\th\ **this**	\yu̇\ **cure**	
\ä\ **cot, cart**	\g\ **go**	\ō\ **bone**	\ü\ **food**	\zh\ **vision**	

erybody⟩ **b** : IRRITATE 1 ⟨don't let it *get* you⟩ **c** : ¹HIT 1c ⟨*got* him in the leg⟩ **d** : ¹KILL 1 ⟨swore to *get* them⟩ **7 a** : to be subjected to or experience ⟨*get* a broken nose⟩ **b** : to receive as punishment ⟨*got* six months for stealing⟩ **8 a** : to find out by calculation ⟨*got* the right answer⟩ **b** : to hear correctly ⟨I didn't *get* your name⟩ **c** : UNDERSTAND 1a ⟨now I've *got* it⟩ ⟨I *get* you⟩ **9** : PERSUADE, INDUCE ⟨couldn't *get* her to agree⟩ **10 a** : ¹HAVE 1 — used in the present perfect form with present meaning ⟨I've *got* no time⟩ **b** : to have to : MUST — used in the present perfect form with present meaning ⟨has *got* to come⟩ **c** : to be able ⟨*got* to go swimming⟩ **11** : DELIVER 6 ⟨the car *gets* 20 miles to the gallon⟩ **12** : to leave immediately ⟨told them to *get*⟩ — **get ahead** : to achieve success (as in business) — **get at 1** : to reach effectively **2** : to try to prove or make clear ⟨what is he *getting at*?⟩ — **get away with** : to avoid criticism or punishment for (as a bad action) — **get even** : to get revenge — **get even with** : to repay in kind — **get into** : to become strongly involved in or deeply interested in — **get it** : to receive a scolding or punishment — **get one's goat** : to make one angry or annoyed — **get over** : to recover from — **get through** : to reach the end of — **get to 1** : BEGIN 1 ⟨*gets* to worrying easily⟩ **2** : to be ready to deal with ⟨I'll *get to* my homework after dinner⟩ **3** : to have an effect on; *esp* : BOTHER — **get together 1** : to bring or come together **2** : to reach agreement — **get wind of** : to become aware of — **get with it** : to become alert or aware

synonyms GET, OBTAIN, PROCURE, SECURE mean to bring into one's possession. GET applies broadly to any manner of gaining possession ⟨*get* me another pencil⟩. OBTAIN may suggest getting by planning or effort ⟨*obtain* a loan from the bank⟩. PROCURE may suggest getting something through a formal or set procedure ⟨*procured* new math textbooks⟩. SECURE may suggest safe or lasting possession ⟨*secured* rights to publish the book⟩.

get across *vb* : to make or become clear ⟨*got* the point *across*⟩

get along *vb* **1 a** : PROGRESS **b** : to approach old age ⟨*getting along* in years⟩ **2** : MANAGE 4 ⟨*get along* on a small paycheck⟩ **3** : to be or remain on pleasant terms

get around *vb* **1** : EVADE **2** : to do or deal with (something not yet done or dealt with) ⟨will *get around* to it⟩ **3** : to go from place to place **4** : to become known ⟨word *got around*⟩

get•away \'get-ə-ˌwā\ *n* **1** : ²ESCAPE 1 **2** : ²START 2 **3** : a short vacation **4** : a place suitable for a vacation

get back *vb* **1** : to return to a person, place, or condition ⟨*getting back* to our first topic⟩ **2** : to get revenge ⟨*get back* at him for the insult⟩ **3** : to regain possession of

get by *vb* **1** : to make ends meet : MANAGE **2** : to succeed with the least possible effort or accomplishment

get off *vb* **1** : SET OUT 2 ⟨*got off* on their camping trip⟩ **2** : to escape or help to escape punishment or harm

get on *vb* **1** : GET ALONG 3 ⟨they *got on* well⟩ **2** : to start dealing with ⟨I'll *get on* it right away⟩ **3** : to criticize (someone) repeatedly **4** : to grow old

get out *vb* **1** : PUBLISH 2a **2** : to escape or help to escape **3** : to become known : leak out ⟨their secret *got out*⟩

get–to•geth•er \'get-tə-ˌgeth-ər\ *n* : MEETING 2; *esp* : an informal social gathering

get•up \'get-ˌəp\ *n* : ¹OUTFIT 1, COSTUME

get up \get-'əp, git-\ *vb* **1 a** : to arise from bed **b** : to rise to one's feet **2** : PREPARE 2, ORGANIZE ⟨*get up* a petition⟩ **3** : to produce in oneself by effort ⟨*get up* the courage⟩

gew•gaw \'g(y)ü-gò\ *n* : a thing of little worth : TRINKET

gey•ser \'gī-zər\ *n* : a spring that now and then shoots out hot water and steam [from Icelandic *Geyser* "a hot spring in Iceland," from *geysa* "to rush forth"]

g–force \'jē-ˌfò(ə)rs, -ˌfó(ə)rs\ *n* : the force of gravity or acceleration on a body

ghast•ly \'gast-lē\ *adj* **ghast•li•er; -est 1 a** : HORRIBLE 1, SHOCKING ⟨a *ghastly* crime⟩ **b** : very unpleasant, disagreeable, or objectionable **2** : resembling a ghost ⟨a *ghastly* face⟩ — **ghast•li•ness** *n* — **ghastly** *adv*

gher•kin \'gər-kən\ *n* : a small young cucumber used to make pickles; *also* : a small prickly fruit of a vine related to the cucumber that is used for the same purpose

ghet•to \'get-ō\ *n, pl* **ghettos** *also* **ghettoes 1** : a part of a city in which Jews were formerly required to live **2** : a part of a city in which members of a minority group live especially because of social, legal, or economic pressure

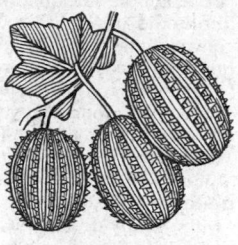

gherkin

ghost \'gōst\ *n* : the soul of a dead person thought of as living in an unseen world or as appearing to living people

ghost•ly \'gōst-lē\ *adj* **ghost•li•er; -est** : of, relating to, or having the characteristics of a ghost — **ghost•li•ness** *n*

ghost town *n* : a town deserted because some natural resource has been used up

ghost•write \'gō-ˌstrīt\ *vb* **-wrote** \-ˌstrōt\; **-writ•ten** \-ˌstrit-ən\; **-writ•ing** \-ˌstrīt-iŋ\ : to write for and in the name of another — **ghost•writ•er** *n*

ghoul \'gül\ *n* **1** : an evil being of legend that robs graves and feeds on corpses **2** : a person (as a grave robber) whose activities suggest those of a ghoul — **ghoul•ish** \'gü-lish\ *adj* — **ghoul•ish•ly** *adv* — **ghoul•ish•ness** *n*

¹GI \(')jē-'ī\ *adj* : of, relating to, or characteristic of U.S. military forces [from the abbreviation for *galvanized iron* used in listing such articles as garbage cans, but mistaken as standing for *government issue*]

²GI *n, pl* **GIs** *or* **GI's** : a member or former member of the U.S. armed forces

¹gi•ant \'jī-ənt\ *n* **1** : a very large and strong being of legend **2** : a person or thing that is very large or powerful

²giant *adj* : much larger or more powerful than ordinary

giant anteater *n* : a large anteater of Central and South America that has shaggy gray fur and a bushy tail

giant cactus *n* : SAGUARO

giant panda *n* : PANDA 2

giant sequoia *n* : a California evergreen tree related to the bald cypresses and sometimes exceeding 270 feet (about 82 meters) in height — called also *big tree, sequoia*

giant squid *n* : any of a group of very large squids up to 60 feet (18 meters) long including the long arms

giant star *n* : a very bright star of large mass

giant tortoise *n* : any of various large plant-eating tortoises of the Galapagos Islands and islands of the western Indian Ocean

gib•ber \'jib-ər\ *vb* **gib•bered; gib•ber•ing** \-(ə-)riŋ\ : to speak rapidly and often foolishly — **gib•ber** *n*

gib•ber•el•lin \ˌjib-ə-'rel-ən\ *n* : any of several chemical substances that regulate the growth of plants

gib•ber•ish \'jib-(ə-)rish, 'gib-\ *n* : confused meaningless talk

gib•bet \'jib-ət\ *n* : GALLOWS 1

gib•bon \'gib-ən\ *n* : any of several tailless apes of southeastern Asia that are smaller and spend more time in trees than the gorilla, chimpanzee, and orangutan

gib•bous \'jib-əs, 'gib-\ *adj* : seen with more than half but not all of the disk lighted ⟨*gibbous* moon⟩

gibe *or* **jibe** \'jīb\ *vb* **gibed** *or* **jibed; gib•ing** *or* **jib•ing** : TAUNT, JEER — **gibe** *n* — **gib•er** *n*

gib•lets \'jib-ləts *also* 'gib-\ *n* : the edible inner organs (as the heart and liver) of a bird — usually used in plural

gid•dy \'gid-ē\ *adj* **gid•di•er; -est 1** : DIZZY **2** : causing dizziness **3** : SILLY 3 — **gid•di•ly** \'gid-əl-ē\ *adv* — **gid•di•ness** \'gid-ē-nəs\ *n*

gid·dy·ap \ˌgid-ē-ˈap\ *or* **gid·dy·up** \-ˈəp\ *imperative verb* — used as a command to a horse to go ahead or go faster

gift \ˈgift\ *n* **1** : a special ability : TALENT **2** : something given : PRESENT

gift card *n* : a card that is worth a certain amount of money and that is given to someone to buy something (as goods or services from a business)

gift certificate *n* : a certificate that is worth a certain amount of money and that is given to someone to buy something (as goods or services from a business)

gift·ed \ˈgif-təd\ *adj* : having great natural ability

¹gig \ˈgig\ *n* **1** : a long light boat **2** : a light two-wheeled one-horse carriage

²gig *n* : GIGABYTE

³gig *n* : an entertainer's job for a specified time

¹gig 2

giga- \ˈjig-ə, ˈgig-ə\ *combining form* : billion ⟨*giga*hertz⟩ [derived from Greek *gigas* "giant"]

giga·byte \-ˌbīt\ *n* : 1,073,741,824 bytes

giga·hertz \-ˌhərts, -ˌhe(ə)rts\ *n* : a unit of frequency equal to one billion hertz

gi·gan·tic \jī-ˈgant-ik\ *adj* : being beyond the ordinary or expected (as in size, weight, or strength)

gig·gle \ˈgig-əl\ *vb* **gig·gled; gig·gling** \-(ə-)liŋ\ : to laugh with repeated short high sounds — **giggle** *n* — **gig·gly** \-(ə-)lē\ *adj*

Gi·la monster \ˌhē-lə-\ *n* : a large orange and black poisonous lizard of the southwestern U.S.; *also* : a related Mexican lizard [from *Gila*, name of a river in Arizona]

¹gild \ˈgild\ *vb* **gild·ed** \ˈgil-dəd\ *or* **gilt** \ˈgilt\; **gild·ing** : to cover with or as if with a coating of gold — **gilder** *n*

²gild *variant of* GUILD

¹gill \ˈjil\ *n* — see MEASURE table

²gill \ˈgil\ *n* **1** : an organ (as of a fish) of thin plates or threadlike processes for obtaining oxygen from water **2** : the flesh under or about the chin or jaws — usually used in plural **3** : one of the plates arranged in a circle and forming the undersurface of the cap of a mushroom

gill arch *n* **1** : one of the several bars of bone or cartilage that occur in pairs with one of each pair on each side of the throat and that support the gills of fishes and amphibians **2** : one of the undeveloped ridges that occur in the embryos of all higher vertebrates and correspond to the gill arches of fishes and amphibians

gill raker *n* : any of the bony spines on the gill arch of a fish that prevent solid particles from entering the gills

gill slit *n* **1** : any of the openings which occur in vertebrates with gills and through which water taken in at the mouth moves to the outside bathing the gills **2** : an undeveloped gill slit that occurs at some time in the development of the embryos of air-breathing vertebrates

¹gilt \ˈgilt\ *adj* : of the color of gold

²gilt *n* : gold or something like gold laid on a surface

³gilt *n* : a young female pig

gim·let \ˈgim-lət\ *n* : a small tool with a screw point and cross handle for boring holes

gim·mick \ˈgim-ik\ *n* **1 a** : an ingenious scheme or device **b** : a trick or device used to attract business or attention ⟨a marketing *gimmick*⟩ **2** : an important feature that is not immediately apparent — **gim·micky** \-i-kē\ *adj*

¹gin \ˈjin\ *n* : COTTON GIN [Middle English *gin* "a mechanical device, skill, trick," from early French *engin* (same meaning), from Latin *ingenium* "natural ability or desire to do something, inborn ability," from *in* "in" and *-genium*, from *gignere* "to father, beget" — related to ENGINE, GENIUS, INGENIOUS]

²gin *vb* **ginned; gin·ning** : to separate (cotton fiber) from seeds and waste material — **gin·ner** *n*

³gin *n* : a clear strong alcoholic liquor flavored with juniper berries [an altered form of earlier *geneva* "gin (liquor)," from obsolete Dutch *genever*, literally, "juniper"]

gin·ger \ˈjin-jər\ *n* **1 a** : a thick underground plant stem that is used especially to make a spice **b** : a spice prepared by drying and grinding ginger **2** : any of a genus of Old World herbs that have thick underground stems and include one supplying most of the ginger used as a spice **3** : high spirit : PEP — **gin·gery** \ˈjinj-(ə-)rē\ *adj*

ginger ale *n* : a soft drink flavored with ginger

gin·ger·bread \ˈjin-jər-ˌbred\ *n* **1** : a cake made with molasses and flavored with ginger **2** : showy ornamentation especially in architecture — **gingerbread** *adj*

gin·ger·ly \ˈjin-jər-lē\ *adv* : very carefully

gin·ger·root \ˈjin-jər-ˌrüt, -ˌ(r)ut\ *n* : GINGER 1a

gin·ger·snap \ˈjin-jər-ˌsnap\ *n* : a thin brittle cookie flavored with ginger

ging·ham \ˈgiŋ-əm\ *n* : a cotton cloth that is often marked with a pattern of colored squares

gin·gi·vi·tis \ˌjin-jə-ˈvīt-əs\ *n* : inflammation of the gums

gink·go *also* **ging·ko** \ˈgiŋ-kō *also* ˈgiŋk-gō\ *n, pl* **ginkgoes** *or* **ginkgos** : a large Chinese tree with fan-shaped leaves and bad-smelling fruit that is often grown as a shade tree

gi·nor·mous \jī-ˈnȯr-məs\ *adj* : GIGANTIC [blend of *gigantic* and *enormous*]

gin·seng \ˈjin-ˌsaŋ, -ˌseŋ, -ˌ(ˌ)siŋ\ *n* **1** : a Chinese herb with small greenish flowers and red berries; *also* : a closely related herb of North America **2** : the forked fragrant root of the ginseng used especially as a medicine in China

Gipsy *chiefly British variant of* GYPSY

gi·raffe \ˈjə-ˈraf\ *n, pl* **giraffes** *or* **gi·raffe** : a large swift cud-chewing spotted African mammal with a very long neck that is the tallest of living four-footed animals

gird \ˈgərd\ *vb* **gird·ed** \ˈgərd-əd\ *or* **girt** \ˈgərt\; **gird·ing** **1** : to encircle or fasten with or as if with a belt or cord **2** : to provide especially with the sword of knighthood **3** : to get ready (as for a fight)

gird·er \ˈgərd-ər\ *n* : a horizontal main supporting beam

¹gir·dle \ˈgərd-ᵊl\ *n* **1** : a belt or sash encircling the waist **2** : a light corset worn below the waist **3** : a bony arch that supports an arm or leg

²girdle *vb* **gir·dled; gir·dling** \ˈgərd-liŋ, -ᵊl-iŋ\ **1** : to bind or encircle with or as if with a girdle : CIRCLE **2** : to cut away the bark and cambium in a ring around (a plant) usually in order to kill by stopping the circulation of water and food

giraffe

girl \ˈgər(-ə)l\ *n* **1 a** : a female child **b** : a young woman **2** *sometimes offensive* : a female servant **3** : SWEETHEART [Middle English *gurle, girle* "a young person of either sex"] — **girl·hood** \-ˌhud\ *n* — **girl·ish** \ˈgər-lish\ *adj* — **girl·ish·ly** *adv* — **girl·ish·ness** *n*

girl·friend \ˈgər(ə)l-ˌfrend\ *n* **1** : a female friend **2** : a regular female companion in a romantic relationship

Girl Scout *n* : a member of the Girl Scouts of the United States of America

girt \ˈgərt\ *vb* **1** : GIRD **2** : to fasten by means of a girth

\ə\ **abut**	\au̇\ **out**	\i\ **tip**	\ȯ\ **saw**	\u̇\ **foot**
\ər\ **further**	\ch\ **chin**	\ī\ **life**	\ȯi\ **coin**	\y\ **yet**
\a\ **mat**	\e\ **pet**	\j\ **job**	\th\ **thin**	\yü\ **few**
\ā\ **take**	\ē\ **easy**	\ŋ\ **sing**	\t̶h̶\ **this**	\yu̇\ **cure**
\ä\ **cot, cart**	\g\ **go**	\ō\ **bone**	\ü\ **food**	\zh\ **vision**

girth \ˈgərth\ *n* **1** : a band around the body of an animal to fasten something (as a saddle) upon its back **2** : a measure around a body ⟨the *girth* of a tree trunk⟩ — **girth** *vb*

gist \ˈjist\ *n* : the main point of a subject : DRIFT

¹give \ˈgiv\ *vb* **gave** \ˈgāv\; **giv·en** \ˈgiv-ən\; **giv·ing** **1** : to make a present of ⟨*gave* me a book⟩ **2 a** : ¹GRANT 2, BESTOW **b** : to make a donation ⟨*give* blood⟩ ⟨we already *gave* at the office⟩ **c** : to grant or yield to another ⟨*gave* her trust to her friend⟩ **3 a** : to put into the possession or keeping of another ⟨*give* me the letter to mail⟩ **b** : to offer to another : PROFFER ⟨*gave* his hand to the visitor⟩ **c** : ¹PAY 1 ⟨wouldn't *give* a penny for that bike⟩ **4 a** : to present in public performance ⟨*give* a concert⟩ **b** : to present to view ⟨*gave* the signal to start⟩ **5** : to provide by way of entertainment ⟨*give* a party⟩ **6** : to point out or set aside as a share or portion ⟨*gave* their daughter half of their estate⟩ **7** : to indicate the source or cause of ⟨*gave* all the glory to her mother⟩ **8** : to form, make, or yield as a product or result ⟨cows *give* milk⟩ ⟨84 divided by 12 *gives* 7⟩ **9 a** : to deliver by some bodily action ⟨*gave* me a push⟩ **b** : to carry out a movement : PERFORM ⟨*gave* a sudden leap⟩ **c** : PRONOUNCE 1 ⟨*give* judgment⟩ **10** : to offer for consideration or acceptance ⟨*gives* no reason for his absence⟩ **11** : to apply fully : DEVOTE ⟨*gave* herself to the cause⟩ **12** : to cause to have ⟨*gave* pleasure to the reader⟩ **13** : to yield or collapse under force or pressure ⟨the box *gave* under his foot⟩ — **giv·er** *n* — **give birth** : to have a baby — **give birth to** : to bring forth : BEAR — **give rise to** : to be the cause or source of : PRODUCE — **give the lie to** : to show to be false — **give way 1** : ²RETREAT 1 **2** : to lose control of oneself ⟨*gave way* to tears at the sad news⟩ **3** : ¹COLLAPSE 3

> **synonyms** GIVE, PRESENT, DONATE mean to hand over to someone without expecting something in return. GIVE can be used of anything that is delivered in any way ⟨*give* me those cups⟩ ⟨*give* a gift to a friend⟩. PRESENT suggests that something is given with some ceremony ⟨*presented* a trophy to the winner⟩. DONATE suggests giving to a charity or for the public good ⟨*donated* new uniforms for the school band⟩.

²give *n* **1** : tendency to yield to force or strain **2** : the quality or state of being springy

give–and–take \ˌgiv-ən-ˈtāk\ *n* **1** : the practice of all sides in a dispute settling for less than they want : COMPROMISE **2** : a good-natured exchange of ideas

give·away \ˈgiv-ə-ˌwā\ *n* **1** : an unintentional act of revealing or betraying ⟨his expression was a dead *giveaway* of his guilt⟩ **2** : something that is given away free **3** : an event at which things are given away

give away \ˌgiv-ə-ˈwā\ *vb* **1** : to present (a bride) to the bridegroom at a wedding **2 a** : to show unintentionally **b** : DISCLOSE, REVEAL

give in *vb* : to yield to demands or pleading ⟨*gave in* to the children's cries for a treat⟩

¹giv·en \ˈgiv-ən\ *adj* **1** : PRONE 1 ⟨*given* to gossiping⟩ **2** : FIXED 1b, PARTICULAR ⟨at a *given* time⟩ **3** : granted as true ⟨*given* that we are all equal⟩

²given *n* : something taken for granted : a basic condition or assumption

given name *n* : FORENAME

give off *vb* : EMIT 1a ⟨*gave off* a sweet smell⟩

give out *vb* **1** : EMIT 1 **2** : to become exhausted : COLLAPSE 3 **3** : BREAK DOWN 1 **4** : to pass out : ISSUE ⟨*give out* the new books⟩

give up *vb* **1** : ¹SURRENDER 1 **2** : to abandon (oneself) to a feeling, influence, or activity **3** : ¹STOP 7a

giz·mo *or* **gis·mo** \ˈgiz-mō\ *n, pl* **gizmos** *or* **gismos** : GADGET

giz·zard \ˈgiz-ərd\ *n* : a large muscular part of the digestive tube (as of a bird or insect) which has a horny lining and in which food is churned and ground into small pieces

gla·cial \ˈglā-shəl\ *adj* **1 a** : extremely cold : FRIGID **b** : lacking warmth of feeling **2 a** : of, relating to, or produced by glaciers **b** : of, relating to, or being any of those parts of geologic time when a large portion of the earth was covered by glaciers **c** *cap* : PLEISTOCENE

gla·ci·ate \ˈglā-shē-ˌāt\ *vb* **-at·ed; -at·ing** **1** : to cover with a glacier **2** : to expose to glacial action; *also* : to produce glacial effects in or on — **gla·ci·a·tion** \ˌglā-shē-ˈā-shən, -sē-\ *n*

gla·cier \ˈglā-shər\ *n* : a large body of ice moving slowly down a slope or valley or spreading outward on a land surface

glad \ˈglad\ *adj* **glad·der; glad·dest** **1 a** : experiencing pleasure, joy, or delight : made happy ⟨*glad* things turned out well⟩ **b** : made pleased, satisfied, or grateful ⟨was *glad* of their help⟩ **c** : very willing ⟨*glad* to do it⟩ **2 a** : marked by, expressive of, or caused by happiness ⟨a *glad* shout⟩ **b** : causing happiness and joy : PLEASANT ⟨*glad* tidings⟩ **3** : full of brightness and cheerfulness ⟨a *glad* spring morning⟩ — **glad·ly** *adv* — **glad·ness** *n*

glad·den \ˈglad-ən\ *vb* **glad·dened; glad·den·ing** \-(ə-)niŋ\ : to make glad

glade \ˈglād\ *n* : a grassy open space in a forest

glad·i·a·tor \ˈglad-ē-ˌāt-ər\ *n* **1** : a person engaged in a fight to the death for public entertainment in ancient Rome **2** : a person engaging in a fierce fight or controversy [from Latin *gladiator*, literally, "swordsman," from *gladius* "sword" — related to GLADIOLUS] — **glad·i·a·to·ri·al** \ˌglad-ē-ə-ˈtōr-ē-əl, -ˈtȯr-\ *adj*

glad·i·o·la \ˌglad-ē-ˈō-lə\ *n* : GLADIOLUS

glad·i·o·lus \ˌglad-ē-ˈō-ləs\ *n, pl* **-o·li** \-ˈō-(ˌ)lē, -ˈō-ˌlī\ *or* **-o·lus** *also* **-o·lus·es** : any of a genus of chiefly African plants related to the irises and having erect sword-shaped leaves and stalks of brilliantly colored flowers [from Latin *gladiolus*, literally, "little sword," from *gladius* "sword" — related to GLADIATOR]

gladiolus

glad·some \ˈglad-səm\ *adj* : giving or showing joy : CHEERFUL ⟨*gladsome* looks and cheerful voice⟩ — **glad·some·ly** *adv* — **glad·some·ness** *n*

glam·or·ize *also* **glam·our·ize** \ˈglam-ə-ˌrīz\ *vb* **-ized; -iz·ing** **1** : to make glamorous **2** : to present so as to seem glamorous

glam·or·ous *also* **glam·our·ous** \ˈglam-(ə-)rəs\ *adj* : excitingly attractive : full of glamour — **glam·or·ous·ly** *adv* — **glam·or·ous·ness** *n*

glam·our *also* **glam·or** \ˈglam-ər\ *n* : romantic, exciting, and often misleading attractiveness

¹glance \ˈglan(t)s\ *vb* **glanced; glanc·ing** **1** : to strike and fly off at an angle ⟨the arrow *glanced* off the shield⟩ **2** : to give a quick or hasty look ⟨*glanced* at my watch⟩ ⟨*glanced* up from a book⟩ **3** : GLINT a — **glanc·ing·ly** \ˈglan(t)-siŋ-lē\ *adv*

²glance *n* **1** : a quick flash or gleam that comes and goes **2** : an impact or blow that is turned aside **3 a** : a swift movement of the eyes **b** : a quick or hasty look

gland \ˈgland\ *n* : a cell or group of cells that makes and secretes a product (as saliva, sweat, bile, or shell) for further use in or for elimination from the plant or animal body

glan·ders \ˈglan-dərz\ *n sing or pl* : an infectious often fatal bacterial disease especially of horses

glan·du·lar \ˈglan-jə-lər\ *adj* **1** : of, relating to, or involving glands, gland cells, or their products ⟨*glandular* activity⟩ **2** : having the traits or activities of a gland ⟨*glandular* tissue⟩ — **glan·du·lar·ly** *adv*

glans \ˈglanz\ *n, pl* **glan·des** \ˈglan-ˌdēz\ : a cone-shaped vascular body forming the end of the penis or clitoris

glare \'gla(ə)r, 'gle(ə)r\ *vb* **glared; glar·ing** **1 a** : to shine with a harsh uncomfortably brilliant light **b** : to stand out annoyingly **2** : to stare angrily or fiercely **synonyms** see GAZE — **glare** *n* — **glary** \'gla(ə)r-ē, 'gle(ə)r-\ *adj*

glar·ing \'gla(ə)r-iŋ, 'gle(ə)r-\ *adj* : painfully obvious ⟨a *glaring* mistake⟩ — **glar·ing·ly** *adv* — **glar·ing·ness** *n*

¹glass \'glas\ *n* **1** : a hard brittle usually transparent substance commonly formed by melting a mixture of sand and chemicals and cooling to hardness **2 a** : something (as a water tumbler, lens, mirror, barometer, or telescope) that is made of glass or has a glass lens **b** *pl* : a pair of glass or plastic lenses held in a frame and used to help one see clearly or to protect the eyes **3** : the quantity held by a glass — **glass·ful** \-,ful\ *n*

²glass *vb* : to fit or protect with glass

glass·blow·ing \-,blō-iŋ\ *n* : the art of shaping a mass of hot glass by blowing air into it through a tube — **glass·blow·er** \-,blō(-ə)r\ *n*

glass ceiling *n* : an informal limit to how high a position women and minorities can earn in a company

glass·mak·er \-,mā-kər\ *n* : a person who makes glass — **glass·mak·ing** \-kiŋ\ *n*

glass snake *n* : a limbless lizard of the southern U.S. resembling a snake and having a fragile tail that easily breaks off from the body often in pieces

glass·ware \'glas-,wa(ə)r, -,we(ə)r\ *n* : articles of glass

glassy \'glas-ē\ *adj* **glass·i·er; -est** **1** : resembling glass **2** : not shiny or bright : DULL ⟨*glassy* eyes⟩ — **glass·i·ly** \'glas-ə-lē\ *adv* — **glass·i·ness** \'glas-ē-nəs\ *n*

glau·co·ma \glaù-'kō-mə, glò-\ *n* : an abnormal condition of the eye marked by increased pressure inside the eye that causes damage to the retina and gradual loss of vision

¹glaze \'glāz\ *vb* **glazed; glaz·ing** **1** : to set glass in ⟨*glaze* a window⟩ **2** : to cover with a glassy surface ⟨*glaze* pottery⟩ **3** : to become shiny in appearance — **glaz·er** *n*

²glaze *n* : a glassy surface or coating

gla·zier \'glā-zhər, -zē-ər\ *n* : a person who sets glass in window frames

gleam \'glēm\ *n* **1** : a small briefly visible light : GLINT **2** : a brief or faint appearance : TRACE ⟨*gleam* of hope⟩ — **gleam** *vb*

glean \'glēn\ *vb* **1** : to gather from a field or vineyard what has been left (as by reapers) **2** : to gather little by little ⟨*glean* knowledge from books⟩ — **glean·er** *n*

glean·ings \'glē-niŋz\ *n pl* : things acquired by gleaning

glee \'glē\ *n* **1** : high-spirited joy **2** : an unaccompanied song for three or more voices — **glee·ful** \-fəl\ *adj* — **glee·ful·ly** \-fə-lē\ *adv* — **glee·ful·ness** *n*

glee club *n* : a group of people who sing together especially as a social activity in a school or college

glen \'glen\ *n* : a narrow hidden valley

gli·a·din \'glī-əd-ən\ *n* : a simple protein that can be obtained from gluten from wheat or rye

glib \'glib\ *adj* **glib·ber; glib·best** : speaking or spoken with careless ease and often with little regard for truth ⟨a *glib* excuse⟩ — **glib·ly** *adv* — **glib·ness** *n*

glide \'glīd\ *vb* **glid·ed; glid·ing** **1** : to move smoothly, silently, and effortlessly **2** : to descend gradually without enough engine power for level flight ⟨*glide* in an airplane⟩ — **glide** *n*

glid·er \'glīd-ər\ *n* **1** : an aircraft without an engine that glides on air currents **2** : a porch seat suspended from a frame

glim·mer \'glim-ər\ *n* **1 a** : a feeble or unsteady light **b** : a soft shimmer **2 a** : a faint idea : INKLING **b** : a small amount : BIT — **glimmer** *vb*

¹glimpse \'glim(p)s\ *vb* **glimpsed; glimps·ing** : to take a brief look : see momentarily or incompletely ⟨*glimpsed* the deer running⟩ — **glimps·er** *n*

²glimpse *n* : a short hurried view ⟨catch a *glimpse* of something rushing by⟩

glint \'glint\ *vb* : to shine by reflection: **a** : to shine with small bright flashes **b** : to shine briefly — **glint** *n*

glis·san·do \gli-'sän-dō\ *n, pl* **-di** \-(,)dē\ *or* **-dos** : a rapid sliding up or down the musical scale

glis·ten \'glis-ᵊn\ *vb* **glis·tened; glis·ten·ing** \'glis-niŋ, -ᵊn-iŋ\ : to shine by reflection with a soft luster or sparkle — **glisten** *n*

glis·ter \'glis-tər\ *vb* **glis·tered; glis·ter·ing** \-t(ə-)riŋ\ : GLISTEN — **glister** *n*

glitch \'glich\ *n* : an unexpected usually minor problem ⟨*glitches* in a new computer program⟩

¹glit·ter \'glit-ər\ *vb* **1** : to shine with brilliant or metallic luster ⟨*glittering* sequins⟩ **2** : to shine with strong emotion ⟨eyes *glittered* cruelly⟩

²glitter *n* **1** : sparkling brilliancy **2** : small glittering objects used for ornamentation — **glit·tery** \'glit-ə-rē\ *adj*

glitz \'glits\ *n* : a great showiness ⟨the *glitz* and glamour of show business⟩ — **glitzy** \'glit-sē\ *adj*

gloam·ing \'glō-miŋ\ *n* : TWILIGHT, DUSK

gloat \'glōt\ *vb* : to gaze at or think about something with great satisfaction or joy ⟨*gloating* over their enemy's loss⟩ — **gloat·er** *n*

glob \'gläb\ *n* : a small drop : BLOB

glob·al \'glō-bəl\ *adj* **1** : SPHERICAL **2** : WORLDWIDE ⟨*global* war⟩ **3** : of, relating to, or applying to the whole of something (as a computer program) ⟨a *global* search through the data⟩ — **glob·al·ly** \-bə-lē\ *adv*

Global Positioning System *n* : GPS

global warming *n* : a warming of the earth's atmosphere and oceans that is predicted to result from an increase in the greenhouse effect caused by air pollution

globe \'glōb\ *n* : a round object: as **a** : a model of the earth or heavens **b** : EARTH 4 — **glob·u·lar** \'gläb-yə-lər\ *adj*

glob·ule \'gläb-(,)yü(ə-)l\ *n* : a tiny globe or ball ⟨*globules* of fat⟩

glob·u·lin \'gläb-yə-lən\ *n* : any of a class of simple proteins that cannot be dissolved in pure water but can be dissolved in weak salt solutions and that occur widely in plant and animal tissues

glock·en·spiel \'gläk-ən-,shpēl, -,spēl\ *n* : a portable musical instrument consisting of a series of metal bars played with two hammers [German, from *Glocke* "bell" and *Spiel* "play"]

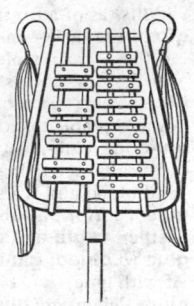

glockenspiel

¹gloom \'glüm\ *vb* **1** : to look sullen, discouraged, or depressed **2** : to be or become overcast

²gloom *n* **1** : partial or total darkness **2** : a sad mood — **gloom·i·ly** \'glü-mə-lē\ *adv* — **gloom·i·ness** \-mē-nəs\ *n* — **gloomy** \-mē\ *adj*

Glo·ria Pa·tri \,glōr-ē-ə-'pä-(,)trē, ,glòr-\ *n* : a Christian hymn of praise to God beginning "Glory be to the Father"

glo·ri·fy \'glōr-ə-,fī, 'glòr-\ *vb* **-fied; -fy·ing** **1** : ²WORSHIP 1, ADORE **2** : to praise highly **3** : to present in a highly often overly favorable light ⟨*glorify* war⟩ — **glo·ri·fi·ca·tion** \,glōr-ə-fə-'kā-shən, ,glòr-\ *n* — **glo·ri·fi·er** \'glōr-ə-fī(-ə)r, 'glòr-\ *n*

glo·ri·ous \'glōr-ē-əs, 'glòr-\ *adj* **1 a** : possessing or deserving glory : ILLUSTRIOUS **b** : bringing glory ⟨*glorious* victory⟩ **2** : having great beauty or splendor ⟨a *glorious*

\ə\ **abut**	\aù\ **out**	\i\ **tip**	\ò\ **saw**	\ú\ **foot**
\ər\ **further**	\ch\ **chin**	\ī\ **life**	\òi\ **coin**	\y\ **yet**
\a\ **mat**	\e\ **pet**	\j\ **job**	\th\ **thin**	\yü\ **few**
\ā\ **take**	\ē\ **easy**	\ŋ\ **sing**	\th\ **this**	\yù\ **cure**
\ä\ **cot, cart**	\g\ **go**	\ō\ **bone**	\ü\ **food**	\zh\ **vision**

sunset⟩ **3** : DELIGHTFUL ⟨had a *glorious* day⟩ **synonyms** see SPLENDID — **glo·ri·ous·ly** *adv* — **glo·ri·ous·ness** *n*

¹glo·ry \'glōr-ē, 'glȯr-\ *n, pl* **glories** **1 a** : praise, honor, or distinction given by common consent **b** : worshipful praise, honor, and thanksgiving **2 a** : something that brings praise or renown **b** : a distinguished quality or brilliant asset ⟨the *glory* of the town was its fountain⟩ **3 a** : great beauty : SPLENDOR 2 **b** : the splendor and bliss of heaven **4** : a height of prosperity or achievement ⟨in her *glory* when she's painting⟩

²glory *vb* **glo·ried; glo·ry·ing** : to rejoice proudly : EXULT ⟨he *gloried* in his fame⟩

¹gloss \'gläs, 'glȯs\ *n* **1** : brightness from a smooth surface : LUSTER, SHEEN **2** : a falsely attractive appearance ⟨a thin *gloss* of good manners⟩

²gloss *vb* **1** : to give a gloss to **2** : to smooth over : make falsely attractive ⟨*gloss* over one's mistakes⟩

glos·sa·ry \'gläs-(ə-)rē, 'glȯs-\ *n, pl* **-ries** **1** : a list of the hard or unusual words found in a book **2** : a dictionary of the special terms in a particular field

glossy \'gläs-ē, 'glȯs-\ *adj* **gloss·i·er; -est** : having a surface luster or brightness — **gloss·i·ness** *n*

glot·tis \'glät-əs\ *n, pl* **glot·tis·es** *or* **glot·ti·des** \'glät-ə-ˌdēz\ : the long opening between the vocal cords in the larynx — **glot·tal** \'glät-ᵊl\ *adj*

glove \'gləv\ *n* **1** : a covering for the hand having separate sections for each finger **2 a** : a padded leather covering for the hand used in baseball **b** : BOXING GLOVE — **gloved** \'gləvd\ *adj*

glove compartment *n* : a small storage cabinet in the dashboard of an automobile

¹glow \'glō\ *vb* **1** : to shine with or as if with great heat : give off light without flame ⟨*glowing* coals⟩ **2** : to have a rich warm usually reddish color **3** : to be or look warm and flushed (as from excitement) ⟨*glow* with pride⟩

²glow *n* **1** : brightness or warmth of color ⟨a rosy *glow* of health⟩ **2 a** : warmth of feeling **b** : a feeling of physical warmth **3** : light such as that given off by something that is very hot but not flaming

glow·er \'glaů(-ə)r\ *vb* : to stare angrily — **glower** *n*

glow-worm \'glō-ˌwərm\ *n* : any of various insect larvae or adults (as of a firefly) that give off light

glox·in·ia \gläk-'sin-ē-ə\ *n* : any of a genus of herbs related to the African violets; *esp* : one from Brazil often grown for its showy bell-shaped or slipper-shaped flowers

gloze \'glōz\ *vb* **glozed; gloz·ing** : to make appear right or acceptable : GLOSS ⟨*gloze* over a person's faults⟩

glu·cose \'glü-ˌkōs\ *n* : a sugar that occurs especially in a naturally occurring form that is found in plants, fruits, and blood and is a source of energy for living things

¹glue \'glü\ *n* : a substance used to stick things tightly together — **glu·ey** \'glu-ē\ *adj*

²glue *vb* **glued; glu·ing** *also* **glue·ing** : to stick with or as if with glue

glum \'gləm\ *adj* **glum·mer; glum·mest** **1** : SULLEN 1a **2** : seeming gloomy and sad ⟨a *glum* expression⟩ — **glum·ly** *adv* — **glum·ness** *n*

¹glut \'glət\ *vb* **glut·ted; glut·ting** **1** : to fill with food to the point of discomfort : STUFF **2** : to flood with more goods than are needed ⟨the market was *glutted* with fruit⟩

²glut *n* : too much of something

glu·tam·ic acid \(ˌ)glü-ˌtam-ik-\ *n* : an amino acid found in many plant and animal proteins and used in the form of a sodium salt as a seasoning

glu·ten \'glüt-ᵊn\ *n* : a tough elastic protein substance in flour especially from wheat that holds together dough and makes it sticky

glu·te·us max·i·mus \ˌglüt-ē-əs-'mak-sə-məs, glü-'tē-\ *n, pl* **glu·tei max·i·mi** \ˌglüt-ē-ˌī-'mak-sə-ˌmī, glü-'tē-\ : the largest and outermost of the three major muscles in each of the human buttocks that extends the thigh and rotates it to the side

glu·ti·nous \'glüt-nəs, -ᵊn-əs\ *adj* : resembling glue : STICKY ⟨*glutinous* rice⟩ — **glu·ti·nous·ly** *adv*

glut·ton \'glət-ᵊn\ *n* **1** : one that eats too much **2** : WOLVERINE — **glut·ton·ous** \'glət-nəs, -ᵊn-əs\ *adj* — **glut·ton·ous·ly** *adv*

glut·tony \'glət-nē, -ᵊn-ē\ *n, pl* **-ton·ies** : the act or habit of eating or drinking too much

glyc·er·in *or* **glyc·er·ine** \'glis-(ə-)rən\ *n* : GLYCEROL

glyc·er·ol \'glis-ə-ˌrȯl, -ˌrōl\ *n* : a sweet colorless syrupy alcohol usually obtained from fats and oils

gly·co·gen \'glī-kə-jən\ *n* : a white tasteless substance that is the chief form in which glucose is stored in animals

G–man \'jē-ˌman\ *n* : a special agent of the Federal Bureau of Investigation [probably a shortened form of *government man*]

gnarl \'närl\ *n* : a large or hard knot in wood or on a tree — **gnarled** \'närld\ *adj* — **gnarly** \'när-lē\ *adj*

gnash \'nash\ *vb* : to strike or grind (as the teeth) together

gnat \'nat\ *n* : any of various small usually biting two-winged flies

gnaw \'nȯ\ *vb* **1 a** : to bite or chew with the teeth; *esp* : to wear away by repeated biting or nibbling ⟨dog *gnawing* a bone⟩ **b** : to make by gnawing ⟨*gnawed* a hole⟩ **2 a** : ANNOY, IRRITATE ⟨worry *gnawed* at me day and night⟩ **b** : to affect like gnawing ⟨*gnawing* hunger⟩ — **gnaw·er** \'nȯ(-ə)r\ *n*

gneiss \'nīs\ *n* : a rock in layers that is similar in composition to granite

gnome \'nōm\ *n* : a small manlike creature of folklore living inside the earth and guarding precious ore or treasure — **gnom·ish** \'nō-mish\ *adj*

gno·mon \'nō-mən, -ˌmän\ *n* : an object (as on a sundial) that by the position or length of its shadow serves to indicate the hour of the day

gnu \'n(y)ü\ *n, pl* **gnu** *or* **gnus** : WILDEBEEST

¹go \'gō\ *vb* **went** \'went\; **gone** \'gȯn *also* 'gän\; **go·ing** \'gō-iŋ\; **goes** \'gōz\ **1** : to move on a course : PROCEED ⟨*go* slow⟩ ⟨*go* by train⟩ **2 a** : to move away from one point to or toward another : LEAVE, DEPART **b** : ¹FOLLOW 4, TRAVERSE ⟨*go* the whole route⟩ ⟨*go* my way⟩ **3 a** : to pass by a process like journeying ⟨the message *went* by wire⟩ ⟨the prize *went* to the winner⟩ **b** : EXTEND 4, RUN ⟨our land *goes* to the river⟩ **c** : ¹LEAD 1d ⟨that door *goes* to the cellar⟩ **4** : to be habitually in a certain state ⟨*goes* bareheaded⟩ **5 a** : to become lost, consumed, or spent ⟨funds *going* for research⟩ **b** : to slip away : ELAPSE ⟨where did the time *go*⟩ **c** : to pass by sale ⟨*went* for a good price⟩ **d** : to become damaged or weakened ⟨my hearing started to *go*⟩ **e** : to give way under force or pressure : BREAK ⟨the dam *went*⟩ **6 a** : to be in general or on an average ⟨cheap, as yachts *go*⟩ **b** : to become especially as the result of a contest ⟨decision *went* against us⟩ **7** : to put or subject oneself ⟨*go* to great expense⟩ **8** : to make use of to settle a dispute : RESORT ⟨*go* to court to recover damages⟩ **9 a** : to begin or continue an action or motion ⟨*go* when the light turns⟩ ⟨drums *going* strong⟩ **b** : to function properly ⟨get the motor to *go*⟩ **10** : to be known ⟨*goes* by a nickname⟩ **11** : to be or act in agreement ⟨a good rule to *go* by⟩ **12** : to contribute to a result ⟨qualities that *go* to make a hero⟩ **13 a** : to be about, intending, or expecting ⟨is *going* to leave town⟩ **b** : to come or arrive at a certain state or condition ⟨*go* to sleep⟩ **c** : to come to be ⟨the tire *went* flat⟩ **14 a** : to be able to be placed ⟨these clothes will *go* in your suitcase⟩ **b** : to have a usual or proper place ⟨these books *go* on the top shelf⟩ **c** : to be capable of being contained in another quantity ⟨5 *goes* into 60 12 times⟩ **15** : to be likely : TEND ⟨*goes* to show they can be trusted⟩ **16** : to be acceptable or satisfactory ⟨any kind of dress *goes*⟩ **17** : ²BET 1, BID ⟨willing to *go* $50⟩ **18 a** : to be as expressed ⟨as the story *goes*⟩ **b** : to be capable of being sung or played ⟨the tune *goes* like this⟩ — **go·er** *n* — **go at** **1** : to make an attack on **2** : to set to work on — **go back on** : BETRAY 2 — **go for** **1** : to pass for or serve as **2** : to have an interest in or liking for — **go in** **1** : to share costs or expenses ⟨*went in* with his friends on a used car⟩ — **go in for** : to take part in out of interest or liking ⟨*go in for* stamp collecting⟩ — **go one better** : EXCEL, SURPASS ⟨*went* him *one better*⟩ — **go over** **1** : [2]STUDY 2, REVIEW **2** : to look over in order to correct or improve ⟨*went over* my term paper twice⟩ — **go places** : to be on the way to success — **go steady** : to have frequent dates with only one person — **go through** **1** : EXAMINE 1, STUDY **2** : [2]EXPERIENCE, UNDERGO **3** : CARRY OUT, PERFORM ⟨*went through* his act perfectly⟩ — **to go** **1** : remaining to pass or be done ⟨five minutes *to go*⟩ **2** : to be taken from a restaurant ⟨lunch *to go*⟩

[2]**go** *n, pl* **goes** **1** : the height of fashion ⟨that dress is all the *go*⟩ **2** : ENERGY 1, VIGOR ⟨full of *go*⟩ **3 a** : [2]ATTEMPT 1, TRY ⟨have a *go* at it⟩ **b** : a spell of activity ⟨did it in one *go*⟩ **c** : SUCCESS 1c ⟨make a *go* of a business⟩ — **no go** : of no help : USELESS — **on the go** : constantly or restlessly active

[3]**go** *adj* : in good and ready condition ⟨all systems are *go*⟩

goad \'gōd\ *n* **1** : a pointed rod used to urge an animal on **2** : something that urges : SPUR — **goad** *vb*

goal \'gōl\ *n* **1 a** : the ending point of a race **b** : an area to be reached safely in children's games **2** : the object toward which effort is directed **3 a** : an area or object into which a ball or puck must be driven to score points in various games **b** : the score resulting from driving a ball or puck into a goal

goal·ie \'gō-lē\ *n* : GOALKEEPER

goal·keep·er \'gōl-ˌkē-pər\ *n* : a player who defends the goal in various games

goal line *n* : a line at either end of a playing area that marks the goal

goal·post \'gōl-ˌpōst\ *n* : one of two upright posts that serve as the goal in various games

goal·tend·er \-ˌten-dər\ *n* : GOALKEEPER

goat \'gōt\ *n, pl* **goat** *or* **goats** **1** : any of various cud-chewing mammals having hollow horns that curve backward, a short tail, and usually straight hair and related to the sheep but of lighter build; *esp* : one raised for its milk, wool, and flesh **2** : SCAPEGOAT — **goat·like** \-ˌlīk\ *adj*

goa·tee \gō-'tē\ *n* : a small trim pointed or tufted beard on a man's chin

goat 1

goat·fish \'gōt-ˌfish\ *n* : any of a family of medium-sized often brightly colored fishes having two stringy feelers under the chin

goat·herd \'gōt-ˌhərd\ *n* : a person who tends goats

goat·skin \-ˌskin\ *n* : the skin of a goat or a leather made from it

[1]**gob** \'gäb\ *n* **1** : [1]LUMP 1, MASS **2** : a large amount — usually used in plural ⟨*gobs* of money⟩

[2]**gob** *n* : SAILOR

gob·bet \'gäb-ət\ *n* : [1]LUMP 1, MASS

[1]**gob·ble** \'gäb-əl\ *vb* **gob·bled**; **gob·bling** \-(ə-)liŋ\ **1** : to swallow or eat greedily **2** : to take eagerly : GRAB ⟨the small country was *gobbled* up by its neighbor⟩

[2]**gobble** *vb* : to make the sound of a male turkey — **gobble** *n*

gob·ble·dy·gook *also* **gob·ble·de·gook** \'gäb-əl-dē-ˌgük\ *n* : wordy and generally meaningless jargon [a playful expansion of *gobble* (noun) "a noise like that of a turkey"]

gob·bler \'gäb-lər\ *n* : a male turkey — called also *tom, turkey-cock*

go–be·tween \'gō-bə-ˌtwēn\ *n* : a person who acts as a messenger or a peacemaker between two persons or groups

gob·let \'gäb-lət\ *n* : a drinking glass with a foot and stem

gob·lin \'gäb-lən\ *n* : an ugly, evil, or mischievous elf

go-by \'gō-bē\ *n, pl* **gobies** *also* **goby** : any of numerous spiny-finned fishes that often have the pelvic fins united to form a sucking disk

god \'gäd *also* 'gȯd\ *n* **1** *cap* : the supreme or almighty reality; *esp* : the Being perfect in power, wisdom, and goodness whom people worship as creator and ruler of the universe **2** : a being believed to have more than human powers ⟨ancient peoples worshiped many *gods*⟩ **3** : a physical object (as an image or idol) worshiped as divine **4** : something held to be the most important thing in existence ⟨make a *god* of money⟩ — **god·hood** \-ˌhu̇d\ *n* — **god·like** \-ˌlīk\ *adj*

god·child \-ˌchīld\ *n* : a person for whom another person acts as sponsor at baptism

god·daugh·ter \-ˌdȯt-ər\ *n* : a female person for whom another person acts as sponsor at baptism

god·dess \'gäd-əs\ *n* **1** : a female god **2** : a woman of great charm or beauty

god·fa·ther \'gäd-ˌfäth-ər *also* 'gȯd-\ *n* : a male sponsor at baptism

god·for·sak·en \-fər-ˌsā-kən\ *adj* : [1]REMOTE 1, DESOLATE ⟨the most *godforsaken* place in the world⟩

god·head \-ˌhed\ *n* **1** : divine nature : DIVINITY **2** *cap* : GOD 1

god·less \'gäd-ləs *also* 'gȯd-\ *adj* : not believing in God or a god — **god·less·ness** *n*

god·ly \'gäd-lē *also* 'gȯd-\ *adj* **god·li·er**; **-est** : PIOUS 1, DEVOUT ⟨a *godly* person⟩ — **god·li·ness** *n*

god·moth·er \'gäd-ˌməth-ər *also* 'gȯd-\ *n* : a female sponsor at baptism

god·par·ent \-ˌpar-ənt, -ˌper-\ *n* : a sponsor at baptism

god·send \-ˌsend\ *n* : a desirable or needed thing or event that comes unexpectedly

god·son \-ˌsən\ *n* : a male person for whom another person acts as sponsor at baptism

God·speed \-'spēd\ *n* : a wish for success given to a person on parting

goes *present 3rd singular of* [1]GO; *plural of* [2]GO

go–get·ter \'gō-ˌget-ər\ *n* : an ambitious person who eagerly goes after what is desired — **go–get·ting** \-ˌget-iŋ\ *adj or n*

[1]**gog·gle** \'gäg-əl\ *vb* **gog·gled**; **gog·gling** \-(ə-)liŋ\ : to stare with goggle eyes — **gog·gler** \-(ə-)lər\ *n*

[2]**goggle** *adj* : being bulging ⟨*goggle* eyes⟩ — **gog·gly** \'gäg-(ə-)lē\ *adj* — **gog·gle–eyed** \ˌgäg-ə-'līd\ *adj*

gog·gles \'gäg-əlz\ *n pl* : protective eyeglasses set in a flexible frame that fits snugly against the face

[1]**go·ing** \'gō-iŋ\ *n* **1** : DEPARTURE 1 **2** : the condition of the ground especially for walking or driving **3** : advance toward an objective : PROGRESS

[2]**going** *adj* **1** : being in existence : ALIVE ⟨best novelist *going*⟩ **2** : [1]CURRENT 1b, PREVAILING ⟨the *going* price⟩ **3** : being successful and likely to continue successfully ⟨a *going* concern⟩ — **going on** : drawing near to : APPROACHING ⟨is six years old *going on* seven⟩

go·ings–on \ˌgō-iŋ-'zȯn, -'än\ *n pl* : actions or events that are taking place

goi·ter \'gȯit-ər\ *n* : a swelling on the front of the neck caused by enlargement of the thyroid gland

\ə\ **abut**	\au̇\ **out**	\i\ **tip**	\ȯ\ **saw**	\u̇\ **foot**
\ər\ **further**	\ch\ **chin**	\ī\ **life**	\ȯi\ **coin**	\y\ **yet**
\a\ **mat**	\e\ **pet**	\j\ **job**	\th\ **thin**	\yü\ **few**
\ā\ **take**	\ē\ **easy**	\ŋ\ **sing**	\th\ **this**	\yu̇\ **cure**
\ä\ **cot, cart**	\g\ **go**	\ō\ **bone**	\ü\ **food**	\zh\ **vision**

go–kart \'gō-ˌkärt\ *n* : a small motorized vehicle used for racing

gold \'gōld\ *n* **1** : a soft yellow metallic element that is used especially in coins and jewelry — see ELEMENT table **2 a** : gold coins **b** : MONEY 1a **3** : a deep yellow **4** : a medal awarded as the first prize in a competition : a gold medal — **gold** *adj*

gold·en \'gōl-dən\ *adj* **1** : consisting of, relating to, or containing gold **2** : having the color of gold ⟨*golden* hair⟩ **3** : PROSPEROUS ⟨a *golden* age⟩ **4** : FAVORABLE 2 ⟨a *golden* opportunity⟩ **5** : having a rich and smooth sound ⟨a *golden* voice⟩ **6** : of or relating to a 50th anniversary

gold·en·ag·er \'gōl-də-ˌnā-jər\ *n* : SENIOR CITIZEN

golden–brown alga *n* : any of a group of algae (as diatoms) that are yellowish green to golden brown in color

golden eagle *n* : a dark brown eagle of the northern regions that has brownish yellow head and neck feathers

Golden Fleece *n* : a treasure in the form of a fleece of gold placed in a grove guarded by dragons and sought and recovered by Jason and the Argonauts

golden hamster *n* : a small brownish yellow hamster that is native chiefly to Syria and often kept as a pet or used as a laboratory animal elsewhere

golden mean *n* : the medium between extremes

golden retriever *n* : any of a breed of medium-sized retrievers that have a coat of golden hair of medium length

gold·en·rod \'gōl-dən-ˌräd\ *n* : any of numerous chiefly North American herbs that are related to the daisies and have tall stiff stems topped with rows of tiny usually yellow flowers on slender branches

golden retriever

golden rule *n* : a rule that one should treat others as one would like to be treated

gold–filled \'gōl(d)-ˈfild\ *adj* : covered with a layer of gold ⟨a *gold-filled* bracelet⟩

gold·finch \-ˌfinch\ *n* **1** : a small largely red, black, and yellow European finch often kept in a cage **2** : any of several small American finches of which the males in their summer coat of feathers are usually yellow with black wings, tail, and top of the head

gold·fish \-ˌfish\ *n* : a small usually golden orange fish that is often kept in aquariums or ponds

gold leaf *n* : a very thin sheet of gold used especially for gilding

gold·smith \'gōl(d)-ˌsmith\ *n* : one who makes or sells articles of gold

golf \'gälf, 'gȯlf, 'gäf, 'gȯf\ *n* : a game in which the player uses specialized clubs to try to hit a small ball with as few strokes as possible into each of 9 or 18 holes — **golf** *vb* — **golf·er** *n*

Gol·gi apparatus \'gȯl-(ˌ)jē-\ *n* : a stack of flattened sacs of membranes in the cytoplasm of a cell that is active in the formation and transport of cell products — called also *Golgi complex*

Golgi body *n* : GOLGI APPARATUS; *also* : any particle that is part of the Golgi apparatus

-gon \ˌgän *also* -gən\ *n combining form* : figure having (so many) angles ⟨deca*gon*⟩ [derived from Greek *gōnia* "angle"]

go·nad \'gō-ˌnad\ *n* : a sperm- or egg-producing gland (as a testis or ovary) — called also *sex gland*

go·nad·o·tro·pin \gō-ˌnad-ə-ˈtrō-pən\ *also* **go·nad·o·tro·phin** \-fən\ *n* : a hormone that acts on or stimulates the gonads

gon·do·la \'gän-də-lə (*usual for sense 1*), gän-ˈdō-\ *n* **1** : a long narrow boat with a high prow and stern used on the canals of Venice **2** : a railroad car with low sides and no top used for hauling loose freight **3** : an enclosure that hangs from something: as **a** : the part of a balloon in which passengers or instruments are carried **b** : a car that hangs from a cable and is used especially as a lift for skiers

gondola 1

gon·do·lier \ˌgän-də-ˈli(ə)r\ *n* : one who drives a gondola

gone \'gȯn *also* 'gän\ *adj* **1** : ¹DEAD 1 **2 a** : being advanced, involved, or absorbed ⟨far *gone* in grief⟩ **b** : being infatuated ⟨*gone* on each other⟩

gon·er \'gȯn-ər *also* 'gän-\ *n* : one whose case is hopeless

gong \'gäŋ, 'gȯŋ\ *n* **1** : a metallic disk that makes a deep ringing sound when struck **2** : a flat saucer-shaped bell

gono·coc·cus \ˌgän-ə-ˈkäk-əs\ *n, pl* **-coc·ci** \-ˈkäk-ˌ(s)ī, -ˈkäk-(ˌ)(s)ē\ : a pus-producing bacterium that causes gonorrhea

gon·or·rhea \ˌgän-ə-ˈrē-ə\ *n* : a contagious inflammatory venereal disease of the genital and urinary organs that is caused by the gonococcus — called also *clap* — **gon·or·rhe·al** \-ˈrē-əl\ *adj*

goo \'gü\ *n* : a sticky substance [perhaps short for *burgoo* "oatmeal gruel"] — **goo·ey** \'gü-ē\ *adj*

goo·ber \'gü-bər, 'gub-ər\ *n, dialect* : PEANUT 1

¹good \'gu̇d\ *adj* **bet·ter** \'bet-ər\; **best** \'best\ **1 a** : of a favorable character or tendency ⟨*good* news⟩ **b** : FERTILE 1 ⟨*good* land⟩ **c** : HANDSOME 3, ATTRACTIVE ⟨*good* looks⟩ **d** : AGREEABLE 1, PLEASANT ⟨a *good* place to live⟩ **e** : SUITABLE 1, FIT ⟨*good* to eat⟩ ⟨a remedy *good* for a cold⟩ **f** : RELIABLE ⟨a *good* friend in a pinch⟩ **g** : ¹SOUND 1a ⟨one *good* arm⟩ **2 a** : certain to last or live ⟨*good* for another year⟩ **b** : certain to provide or produce ⟨always *good* for a laugh⟩ **3 a** : of a noticeably large size or quantity ⟨present in *good* numbers⟩ **b** : ¹FULL 2a ⟨waited a *good* hour⟩ **4 a** : based on sound reasoning, information, judgment, or grounds ⟨*good* reasons⟩ **b** : ¹TRUE 2 ⟨holds *good* for society as a whole⟩ **c** : deserving of respect or honor ⟨a member in *good* standing⟩ **d** : legally valid ⟨has a *good* title⟩ **5 a** : ADEQUATE 1, SATISFACTORY ⟨*good* care⟩ **b** : conforming to a standard ⟨*good* English⟩ **c** : showing or favoring high quality ⟨*good* taste⟩ **6 a** : VIRTUOUS, JUST ⟨a *good* person⟩ **b** : ¹RIGHT 2 ⟨*good* conduct⟩ **c** : ²KIND 1, BENEVOLENT ⟨*good* intentions⟩ **d** : being of the upper class ⟨of *good* family⟩ **e** : SKILLFUL 1 ⟨a *good* doctor⟩ **f** : LOYAL 2 ⟨a *good* party member⟩ — **good·ness** *n* — **as good as** : in effect : VIRTUALLY ⟨as *good* as dead⟩ — **good and** : ²VERY 1, ENTIRELY ⟨was *good and* mad⟩

²good *n* **1** : something good, useful, or desirable ⟨health and prosperity are *goods*⟩ **2** : ¹BENEFIT 1a, WELFARE ⟨the *good* of the community⟩ **3** *pl* : CLOTH 1 **4** *pl* : manufactured articles or products of art or craft **5** : good persons — used with *the* **6** *pl* : proof of wrongdoing ⟨got the *goods* on them⟩

³good *adv* : ³WELL 1

good book *n, often cap G&B* : BIBLE 1a

good–bye *or* **good–by** \gu̇d-ˈbī, gəd-, gə-\ *n* : a concluding remark at parting — often used interjectionally [a shortened and altered form of *God be with you*]

good faith *n* : honesty or lawfulness of purpose ⟨bargained in *good faith*⟩

Good Friday *n* : the Friday before Easter observed by Christians as the anniversary of the crucifixion of Christ

good–heart·ed \'gu̇d-ˈhärt-əd\ *adj* : having a kindly generous disposition — **good–heart·ed·ly** *adv* — **good–heart·ed·ness** *n*

good–hu·mored \-'hyü-mərd, -'yü-\ *adj* : GOOD-NA-
TURED, CHEERFUL — **good–hu·mored·ly** *adv* — **good–
hu·mored·ness** *n*
good·ish \'gùd-ish\ *adj* : fairly good
good·ly \'gùd-lē\ *adj* **good·li·er; -est 1** : of pleasing appearance **2** : LARGE, CONSIDERABLE ⟨a *goodly* number⟩
good·man \'gùd-mən\ *n* **1** *archaic* : the master of a
household **2** *archaic* : MR. 1
good–na·tured \'gùd-'nā-chərd\ *adj* : of a pleasant cheerful disposition — **good–na·tured·ly** *adv* — **good–na-
tured·ness** *n*
good–sized \-'sīzd\ *adj* : fairly large
good–tem·pered \-'tem-pərd\ *adj* : not easily angered or
upset — **good–tem·pered·ly** *adv*
good–wife \-,wīf\ *n* **1** *archaic* : the mistress of a household
2 *archaic* : MRS.
good·will \-'wil\ *n* **1** : kindly feeling : BENEVOLENCE **2**
: the value of the trade a business has built up **3 a** : cheerful consent **b** : willing effort
goody \'gùd-ē\ *n, pl* **good·ies** : something that is particularly good to eat or otherwise attractive
goody–goody \,gùd-ē-'gùd-ē\ *adj* : pretending to be good
in order to impress people — **goody–goody** *n*
Goody Two–shoes \'gùd-ē-'tü-,shüz\ *n, often cap S* : a
person who is a goody-goody; *also* : a person who is un-
commonly good
¹goof \'gùf\ *n* **1** : a silly or stupid person **2** : ²BLUNDER
[probably an altered form of dialect word *goff* "simpleton"]
²goof *vb* **1 a** : to spend time foolishly ⟨*goofing* off instead
of working⟩ **b** : to engage in a playful activity ⟨*goofing*
around after school⟩ **2** : ¹BLUNDER 2 **3** : to make a mess
of : BUNGLE ⟨*goofed* up the assignment⟩
go off *vb* **1** : EXPLODE 2b **2** : to burst forth or break out
suddenly or noisily **3** : to take place : PROCEED ⟨the
dance *went off* as planned⟩
goofy \'gü-fē\ *adj* **goof·i·er; -est** : CRAZY 2, SILLY —
goof·i·ly \-fə-lē\ *adv* — **goof·i·ness** \-fē-nəs\ *n*
goo·gle \'gü-gəl\ *vb* **goo·gled; goo·gling** \-g(ə-)liŋ\ : to
use the Google search engine to obtain information about
(as a person) on the Internet
goo·gol \'gü-,gòl\ *n* : a very large number that is expressed
in numerals as 1 followed by one hundred 0's
　　Word History The term *googol* was invented by a nine-
　　year-old boy. In the late 1930s an American mathemati-
　　cian, Edward Kasner, asked his nephew, Milton Sirotta,
　　to think up a word for a very big number, in particular,
　　the number 1 followed by 100 zeros. The boy came up
　　with the word *googol*. The term was then used by Kasner
　　and other mathematicians and scientists. Such people
　　needed this word, and so it became part of the language.
　　[coined by Milton Sirotta, age 9, and first used by his
　　uncle Edward Kasner 1878–1955 American mathemati-
　　cian]
goon \'gün\ *n* **1** : a stupid person **2** : a person hired to
terrorize or beat up or kill opponents : THUG
　　Word History Some comic strips have had a lasting ef-
　　fect on culture. One such strip, first drawn in the 1920s
　　by Elzie Segar and now known as "Popeye," apparently
　　was responsible for adding the word *goon* to the every-
　　day language. One of the characters Segar created for
　　the comic strip looked a bit like an overgrown pear with
　　legs. This creature, which was not really human, had a
　　big nose, a bald head, and hairy arms and legs. It
　　was called "Alice the goon." Alice was basically good-
　　hearted but not very smart. As a result of the popularity
　　of the comic strip and of Alice, people began to use the
　　word *goon* in the meaning "a stupid person" or "a person
　　with not much common sense." Later, when thugs and
　　criminals were hired to terrorize workers during labor
　　troubles in the 1930s, these thugs, whose actions weren't
　　very "human," were also called *goons*. But even though
　　Alice may have been responsible for making the word

goon popular, the word may not have started with the
comic strip. The word can be traced back to an English
dialect word *gooney*, first used in the 16th century,
meaning "a person lacking in common sense, simpleton."
[probably a shortened form of a dialect word *gooney*
"simpleton"]
go on *vb* **1 a** : to continue on or as if on a journey ⟨life
goes on⟩ **b** : to keep on : CONTINUE ⟨*went on* talking⟩ **2**
: to take place : HAPPEN ⟨what's *going on*⟩
goose \'güs\ *n, pl* **geese**

goose 1a

\'gēs\ **1 a** : any of numerous birds with long
necks that are larger
than the related ducks
and smaller than swans
b : a female goose in
contrast to a gander **2**
: a person lacking in
common sense **3** *pl*
goos·es : an iron with a
gooseneck handle used
by tailors for smoothing
clothes
goose·ber·ry \'güs-,ber-ē, 'güz-\ *n* : the acid usually prickly fruit of any of several shrubs related to the currant
goose bumps *n pl* : a roughening of the skin caused especially from cold, fear, or a sudden feeling of excitement
goose egg *n* : ¹ZERO 1, NOTHING
goose·flesh \'güs-,flesh\ *n* : GOOSE BUMPS
goose·foot \-,fùt\ *n, pl* **goose·foots** : any of numerous
mostly weedy smooth herbs with branched clusters of
small greenish or whitish flowers without petals
goose·neck \'gü-,snek\ *n* : something (as a flexible jointed metal pipe) curved like the neck of a goose or U=
shaped — **goose·necked** \-,snekt\ *adj*
goose pimples *n pl* : GOOSE BUMPS
goose step *n* : a straight-legged stiff-kneed step used by
troops of some armies on parade — **goose–step** \'güs-
,step\ *vb*
go out *vb* **1** : to leave one's home **2** : to stop working **3**
: to stop burning or glowing **4** : to become a candidate
⟨*went out* for the football team⟩
go over *vb* **1** : to make one's way ⟨*going over* to the store⟩
2 : to be favorably received : SUCCEED ⟨the joke *went
over* very well⟩
go·pher \'gō-fər\ *n* **1** : a
burrowing land tortoise
of the southern U.S. **2 a**
: any of several burrow-
ing American rodents
with large cheek pouch-
es — called also *pocket
gopher* **b** : a small
striped ground squirrel
of the prairie region of
the U.S.

gopher 2a

gopher snake *n* : BULL SNAKE
¹gore \'gō(ə)r, 'gò(ə)r\ *n* : a tapering or triangular piece of
cloth (as in a skirt) [Old English *gāre* "triangular piece of
land"]
²gore *vb* **gored; gor·ing 1** : to cut into a tapering triangular form **2** : to provide with a gore
³gore *vb* **gored; gor·ing** : to pierce or wound with something pointed (as a tusk or horn) [Middle English *goren*
"pierce, gore"]

\ə\ **abut**	\aù\ **out**	\i\ **tip**	\ò\ **saw**	\ù\ **foot**
\ər\ **further**	\ch\ **chin**	\ī\ **life**	\òi\ **coin**	\y\ **yet**
\a\ **mat**	\e\ **pet**	\j\ **job**	\th\ **thin**	\yü\ **few**
\ā\ **take**	\ē\ **easy**	\ŋ\ **sing**	\th\ **this**	\yù\ **cure**
\ä\ **cot, cart**	\g\ **go**	\ō\ **bone**	\ü\ **food**	\zh\ **vision**

⁴gore *n* : ¹BLOOD 1a; *esp* : clotted blood [Old English *gor* "filth"]

¹gorge \'gȯ(ə)rj\ *n* : a narrow passage, ravine, or steep-walled canyon

²gorge *vb* **gorged; gorg·ing** : to eat greedily : stuff oneself — **gorg·er** *n*

gor·geous \'gȯr-jəs\ *adj* : having an impressive beauty ⟨a *gorgeous* sunset⟩ **synonyms** see SPLENDID — **gor·geous·ly** *adv* — **gor·geous·ness** *n*

Word History In the late Middle Ages many women wore a type of headdress—called a *wimple* in English—that surrounded the neck and head, leaving only the face uncovered. The word *gorgias,* from *gorge,* meaning "throat," was then the French name for the part of the headdress that covered the throat and shoulders. In time it also came to be used as a name for the entire garment. Perhaps because a beautiful headdress was the mark of a fashionable lady, *gorgias* seems to have become an adjective meaning "elegant" or "fond of dress." Borrowed into English as *gorgayse* and then *gorgeous,* the word gradually took on the meaning of "beautiful" which it has today. [Middle English *gorgeouse* "very showy, splendid," from early French *gorgias* "elegant," from *gorgias* "headdress, wimple," from *gorge* "part of the wimple covering the throat, throat"]

Gor·gon \'gȯr-gən\ *n* : any of three snaky-haired sisters in Greek mythology capable of turning to stone anyone who looked at them

Gor·gon·zo·la \ˌgȯr-gən-'zō-lə\ *n* : a cheese of Italian origin ripened by veins of greenish blue mold [named for *Gorgonzola,* town in Italy where the cheese was first made]

go·ril·la \gə-'ril-ə\ *n* : a typically black ape of equatorial Africa that is much larger but stands less erect than the related chimpanzee [derived from Greek *Gorillai,* a name used by ancient explorers for what they thought was a tribe of hairy women in Africa]

gor·man·dize \'gȯr-mən-ˌdīz\ *vb* **-dized; -diz·ing** : to eat greedily — **gor·man·diz·er** *n*

gorp \'gȯrp\ *n* : a snack consisting of high-energy food (as raisins and nuts)

gorse \'gȯ(ə)rs\ *n* : an evergreen shrub of the legume family that has yellow flowers and leaves reduced to spines — called also *furze*

gory \'gō(ə)r-ē, 'gȯ(ə)r-\ *adj* **gor·i·er; -est** **1** : covered with gore : BLOODSTAINED **2** : BLOODCURDLING

gos·hawk \'gäs-ˌhȯk\ *n* : a hawk of northern forests that has a long tail and short wings and is noted for its powerful flight and vigor

gos·ling \'gäz-liŋ, 'gȯz-, -lən\ *n* : a young goose

¹gos·pel \'gäs-pəl\ *n* **1 a** *often cap* : the Christian message concerning Christ, the kingdom of God, and salvation **b** *cap* : one of the first four New Testament books telling of the life, death, and resurrection of Jesus Christ **2** : something accepted as the truth or as a guiding principle **3** : gospel music [Old English *gōdspel,* a translation of Greek *euangelion* "gospel," literally, "good tidings, good news"; *gōdspel* from *gōd* "good" and *spell* "talk, tale"]

²gospel *adj* **1** : relating to or in accordance with the gospel : EVANGELICAL **2** : of or relating to religious songs associated with evangelism ⟨a *gospel* singer⟩

gos·sa·mer \'gäs-ə-mər *also* 'gäz(-ə)-mər\ *n* **1** : a film of cobwebs floating in air **2** : something light or very delicate — **gossamer** *adj* — **gos·sa·mery** \-mə-rē\ *adj*

gos·sip \'gäs-əp\ *n* **1** : a person who reveals personal or sensational facts **2 a** : rumor or report of a personal nature **b** : chatty talk — **gossip** *vb* — **gos·sip·er** *n* — **gos·sipy** \-ə-pē\ *adj*

got *past and past participle of* GET

Goth·ic \'gäth-ik\ *adj* : relating to or being an old style of architecture (as for churches) having pointed arches, thin tall walls, and large windows

gotten *past participle of* GET

¹gouge \'gauj\ *n* **1** : a chisel with a curved blade for scooping or cutting holes **2** : a hole or groove made with or as if with a gouge

²gouge *vb* **gouged; goug·ing** **1** : to cut holes or grooves in with or as if with a gouge **2** : to force out (an eye) with the thumb **3** : OVERCHARGE — **goug·er** *n*

gou·lash \'gü-ˌläsh, -ˌlash\ *n* : a stew made with meat (as beef), vegetables, and paprika [from Hungarian *gulyás,* short for *gulyáshús,* literally, "herdsman's meat"]

gourd \'gō(ə)rd, 'gȯ(ə)rd, 'gu(ə)rd\ *n* **1** : any of a family of tendril-bearing vines (as the cucumber, melon, squash, and pumpkin) **2** : the usually hard-shell many-seeded fruit of a gourd — **gourd·like** \-ˌlīk\ *adj*

gour·mand \'gu(ə)r-ˌmänd\ *n* **1** : GLUTTON 1 **2** : GOURMET — **gour·mand·ism** \'gu(ə)r-ˌmän-ˌdiz-əm, -mən-\ *n*

gour·met \'gu(ə)r-ˌmā, gur-'mā\ *n* : a person who can enjoy and appreciate fine eating and drinking

gourd 2

gout \'gaut\ *n* : a disease marked by a painful inflammation and swelling of the joints and by the deposit of salts of uric acid in and around the joints — **gouty** \-ē\ *adj*

gov·ern \'gəv-ərn\ *vb* **1** : to exercise authority over : RULE ⟨the queen *governed* wisely⟩ **2** : to control the speed of by automatic means **3 a** : to control, direct, or strongly influence the actions and conduct of ⟨*governed* by his emotions⟩ **b** : to hold in check : RESTRAIN ⟨our income *governs* our spending⟩ **4** : to require a word to be in a certain case or mood ⟨in English a transitive verb *governs* a pronoun in the objective case⟩ **5** : to serve as a rule or law for ⟨etiquette *governing* their behavior⟩ — **gov·ern·able** \-ər-nə-bəl\ *adj*

synonyms GOVERN, RULE mean to use power or authority in controlling others. GOVERN suggests the aim of keeping something running smoothly for the good of both the individual and the whole group ⟨*governed* the country wisely⟩. RULE stresses the laying down of laws and the giving of commands and often suggests the harsh use of power ⟨a king who *ruled* firmly⟩.

gov·er·nance \'gəv-ər-nən(t)s\ *n* : the exercise of control : GOVERNMENT

gov·ern·ess \'gəv-ər-nəs\ *n* : a woman who teaches and trains a child in a private home

gov·ern·ment \'gəv-ər(n)-mənt, 'gəb-ᵊm-ənt, 'gəv-mənt\ *n* **1 a** : the act or process of governing; *esp* : direction of a political unit **b** : the making of policy as distinguished from the administration of policy decisions **2 a** : the agency through which a political unit exercises authority **b** : manner of governing : the institutions, laws, and customs through which a political unit is governed ⟨republican *government*⟩ **3 a** : the officials making up the governing body of a political unit **b** *cap* : the executive branch of the U.S. federal government **4** : POLITICAL SCIENCE — **government** *adj* — **gov·ern·men·tal** \ˌgəv-ər(n)-'ment-ᵊl\ *adj* — **gov·ern·men·tal·ly** \-ᵊl-ē\ *adv*

gov·er·nor \'gəv-(ə-)nər *also* 'gəv-ər-nər\ *n* **1** : one that governs; *esp* : an official elected or appointed to act as ruler, chief executive, or head of a political unit (as a colony, state, or province) **2** : an attachment to a machine for automatic control of speed — **gov·er·nor·ship** \-ˌship\ *n*

gown \'gaun\ *n* **1** : an official robe worn especially by a judge, a member of the clergy, or a teacher **2** : a woman's dress; *esp* : one suitable for afternoon or evening wear **3** : a loose robe (as a dressing gown or a nightgown) — **gown** *vb* — **gowned** \'gaund\ *adj*

GPS \ˌjē-ˌpē-ˈes\ *n* : a navigation system that uses satellite signals to find the location of a radio receiver on or above the earth's surface; *also* : a radio receiver used in a GPS system [*Global Positioning System*]

graaf·ian follicle \ˌgräf-ē-ən-, ˌgraf-\ *n, often cap G* : a small fluid-filled cavity in the ovary of a mammal that encloses a developing egg

¹grab \ˈgrab\ *vb* **grabbed; grab·bing** : to take hastily : CLUTCH, SNATCH — **grab·ber** *n*

²grab *n* **1 a** : a sudden snatch **b** : an unlawful or forceful taking of something ⟨a land *grab*⟩ **c** : something grabbed **2** : a device for clutching an object

¹grace \ˈgrās\ *n* **1 a** : help given to people by God in overcoming temptation **b** : a state of freedom from sin enjoyed through divine grace **2** : a short prayer at a meal **3 a** : APPROVAL, FAVOR ⟨stayed in the boss's good *graces*⟩ **b** : a special favor : PRIVILEGE **c** : a temporary delay granted from the performance of an obligation (as the payment of a debt) **4 a** : a charming trait or quality **b** : ease of movement ⟨walks with *grace*⟩ **5** — used as a title for a duke, a duchess, or an archbishop [Middle English *grace* "help from God," from early French *grace* (same meaning), from Latin *gratia* "favor, charm, thanks," from *gratus* "pleasing, thankful, agreeable" — related to AGREE, CONGRATULATE, GRACIOUS, GRATITUDE] — **grace·ful** \-fəl\ *adj* — **grace·ful·ly** \-fə-lē\ *adv* — **grace·ful·ness** *n*

²grace *vb* **graced; grac·ing** **1** : ²HONOR 1b ⟨deeds that *graced* the town⟩ **2** : ADORN, EMBELLISH

grace·less \ˈgrā-sləs\ *adj* : having no grace, charm, or elegance; *esp* : showing lack of feeling for what is fitting ⟨*graceless* behavior⟩ — **grace·less·ly** *adv* — **grace·less·ness** *n*

grace note *n* : a short musical note added before another as an ornament

gra·cious \ˈgrā-shəs\ *adj* **1** : marked by kindness and courtesy **2** : pleasing or attractive in motion or form ⟨*gracious* ballet steps⟩ **3** : characterized by charm, good taste, and politeness ⟨*gracious* living⟩ [Middle English *gracious* "having received divine grace," from early French *gracieus* (same meaning), from Latin *gratiosus* "enjoying favor, agreeable," from *gratia* "favor, thanks," from *gratus* "pleasing, agreeable, thankful" — related to GRACE, GRATITUDE] — **gra·cious·ly** *adv* — **gra·cious·ness** *n*
synonyms GRACIOUS, CORDIAL, AFFABLE, GENIAL mean very pleasant and relaxed in social situations. GRACIOUS suggests courtesy and kindly consideration ⟨a *gracious* host makes his guests feel comfortable⟩. CORDIAL stresses warmth and heartiness ⟨the *cordial* innkeeper welcomed us⟩. AFFABLE suggests ease and readiness in responding pleasantly to conversation or requests ⟨a principal who is *affable* and friendly⟩. GENIAL stresses cheerfulness and even joyfulness ⟨a *genial* woman with a nice sense of humor⟩.

grack·le \ˈgrak-əl\ *n* : any of several rather large American blackbirds with glossy mostly black feathers

grad \ˈgrad\ *n or adj* : GRADUATE

gra·da·tion \grā-ˈdā-shən, grə-\ *n* **1 a** : a series of grades **b** : ²GRADE 2 **2** : the act or process of grading — **gra·da·tion·al** \-shnəl, -shən-ᵊl\ *adj* — **gra·da·tion·al·ly** \-ē\ *adv*

grackle

¹grade \ˈgrād\ *vb* **grad·ed; grad·ing** **1** : to arrange in grades : SORT ⟨*grade* apples⟩ **2** : to make level or evenly sloping ⟨*grade* a highway⟩ **3** : to give a grade to ⟨*grade* a student's performance⟩ **4** : to assign to a grade **5** : to

form a series having only slight differences ⟨colors that *grade* into one another⟩

²grade *n* **1** : position in a scale of rank, quality, or order ⟨the *grade* of sergeant⟩ ⟨leather of the highest *grade*⟩ **2** : a stage, step, or degree in a series, order, or ranking **3** : a class of things that are of the same rank, quality, or order **4 a** : a division of the school course representing a year's work ⟨finished the fourth *grade*⟩ **b** : the pupils in a school division **c** *pl* : the elementary school system ⟨teach in the *grades*⟩ **5** : a mark or rating especially of accomplishment in school ⟨a *grade* of 90 on a test⟩ **6** : a standard of quality ⟨government *grades* for meat⟩ **7** : the degree of slope (as of a road or railroad track)

grade crossing *n* : a crossing (as of highways, railroad tracks, or pedestrian walks) on the same level

grade point *n* : one of the points assigned to each course credit (as in a college) in accordance with the letter grade earned in the course

grade point average *n* : the average obtained by dividing the total number of grade points earned by the total number of credits taken

grad·er \ˈgrād-ər\ *n* **1** : one that grades **2** : a machine for leveling earth **3** : a pupil in a school grade ⟨a group of sixth *graders*⟩

grade school *n* : a public school including the first six or the first eight grades

gra·di·ent \ˈgrād-ē-ənt\ *n* **1** : ³SLOPE 2, GRADE **2** : a continuous graded change in measure, activity, or substance ⟨vertical temperature *gradient* in a lake⟩ ⟨a *gradient* in developmental activity in a seedling⟩

grad·u·al \ˈgraj-(ə-)wəl, ˈgraj-əl\ *adj* **1** : proceeding by steps or degrees **2** : moving or changing by slight degrees — **grad·u·al·ly** *adv* — **grad·u·al·ness** *n*

grad·u·al·ism \ˈgraj-(ə-)wəl-ˌiz-əm, ˈgraj-əl-\ *n* : the policy of approaching a desired goal by gradual stages — **grad·u·al·ist** \-əst\ *n or adj*

¹grad·u·ate \ˈgraj-(ə-)wət, -ə-ˌwāt\ *n* **1** : a holder of an academic degree or diploma **2** : a graduated cup, cylinder, or flask for measuring

²graduate *adj* **1** : holding an academic degree or diploma **2** : of or relating to studies beyond the bachelor's degree

³grad·u·ate \ˈgraj-ə-ˌwāt\ *vb* **-at·ed; -at·ing** **1** : to grant or receive an academic degree or diploma **2** : to divide into grades, classes, or intervals ⟨*graduated* thermometer⟩ — **grad·u·a·tor** \-ˌwāt-ər\ *n*

graduated cylinder *n* : a tall narrow container with a volume scale used especially for measuring liquids

grad·u·a·tion \ˌgraj-ə-ˈwā-shən\ *n* **1** : a mark or the marks on an instrument or container indicating degrees or quantity **2 a** : an act or process of graduating **b** : the ceremony marking the completion by a student of a course of study at a school or college : COMMENCEMENT **3** : arrangement in degrees or ranks

graf·fi·ti \grə-ˈfēt-ē\ *n* : usually unlawful writing or drawing on a public surface [Italian, plural of *graffito*] — **graffiti** *vb*

graf·fi·to \gra-ˈfēt-ō\ *n, pl* **-ti** \-(ˌ)ē\ : a writing or drawing made on a public surface (as a wall or rock) [Italian, literally, "little scratch," from *graffio* "scratch," derived from Latin *graphium* "pointed device for writing on wax tablets," derived from Greek *graphein* "to write" — related to -GRAM, GRAMMAR, -GRAPH]

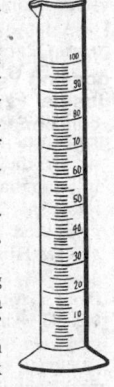
graduated cylinder

\ə\ **abut**	\aú\ **out**	\i\ **tip**	\ȯ\ **saw**	\ú\ **foot**
\ər\ **further**	\ch\ **chin**	\ī\ **life**	\ȯi\ **coin**	\y\ **yet**
\a\ **mat**	\e\ **pet**	\j\ **job**	\th\ **thin**	\yü\ **few**
\ā\ **take**	\ē\ **easy**	\ŋ\ **sing**	\th\ **this**	\yú\ **cure**
\ä\ **cot, cart**	\g\ **go**	\ō\ **bone**	\ü\ **food**	\zh\ **vision**

¹graft \'graft\ *vb* **1 a** : to insert a twig or bud from one plant into another plant so that they are joined and grow together **b** : to join one thing to another as if by grafting ⟨*graft* skin over the burn⟩ **2** : to gain money or advantage by graft — **graft·er** *n*

²graft *n* **1 a** : a grafted plant **b** : the point in a plant where a part that is being grafted is inserted **2** : the act of grafting **3** : something used in grafting: as **a** : SCION 1 **b** : living tissue used in surgical grafting **4 a** : the getting of money or advantage by dishonest means through misuse of an official position ⟨exposed *graft* in the city government⟩ **b** : the money or advantage gained ⟨accused of taking *graft*⟩

gra·ham cracker \'grā-əm-, 'gra(-ə)m-\ *n* : a slightly sweet cracker made chiefly of whole wheat flour

¹grain \'grān\ *n* **1 a** : the edible seed or seedlike fruit of grasses that are cereals (as wheat, corn, or oats) **b** : the threshed seed or fruits of various food plants (as cereal grasses, flax, peas, or sugarcane) **c** : plants producing grain **2 a** : a small hard particle ⟨a *grain* of sand⟩ **b** : the least amount possible ⟨a *grain* of truth⟩ **3** : a unit of weight based on the weight of a grain of wheat — see MEASURE table **4 a** : the arrangement of fibers in wood **b** : appearance or feel due to the particles or fibers of which something is composed ⟨the *grain* of a rock⟩ **c** : the direction of threads in cloth **5** : natural disposition : TEMPER ⟨making excuses goes against my *grain*⟩ [Middle English *grain, grein* "kernel, seed," from early French *grain* "cereal plant" and early French *graine* "seed," both derived from Latin *granum* "grain, seed" — related to GARNET, GRENADE, POMEGRANATE; see *Word History* at GARNET] — **grained** \'grānd\ *adj* — **grainy** \'grā-nē\ *adj*

²grain *vb* **1** : to form into grains : GRANULATE **2** : to paint in imitation of the grain of wood or stone — **grain·er** *n*

grain alcohol *n* : ETHANOL

grain elevator *n* : ELEVATOR 1c

grain sorghum *n* : any of several sorghums cultivated primarily for grain

gram \'gram\ *n* **1** : a metric unit of mass equal to ¹⁄₁₀₀₀ kilogram and nearly equal to the mass of one cubic centimeter of water at its maximum density — see METRIC SYSTEM table **2** : the weight of a gram of mass

-gram \ˌgram\ *n combining form* : drawing : writing : record ⟨tele*gram*⟩ [from Latin *-gramma* "piece of writing, record," derived from Greek *gramma* "letter," derived from *graphein* "to write" — related to GRAFFITO, GRAMMAR, -GRAPH]

grama \'gram-ə\ *n* : any of several pasture grasses of the western U.S. — called also *grama grass*

gra·mer·cy \grə-'mər-sē\ *interj, archaic* — used to express gratitude or astonishment

gram·mar \'gram-ər\ *n* **1** : the study of the classes of words, their inflections, and their functions and relations in a language **2** : the facts of language with which grammar deals **3 a** : a grammar textbook **b** : speech or writing evaluated according to its conformity to grammatical rules ⟨"Him and I went" is bad *grammar*⟩ [Middle English *gramere,* from early French *gramaire* (same meaning), from Latin *grammatica* (same meaning), derived from Greek *gramma* "letter, piece of writing," derived from *graphein* "to write" — related to GRAFFITO, -GRAM, -GRAPH]

gram·mar·i·an \grə-'mer-ē-ən, -'mar-\ *n* : a specialist in or a teacher of grammar

grammar school *n* : an elementary school

gram·mat·i·cal \grə-'mat-i-kəl\ *adj* **1** : of or relating to grammar **2** : conforming to the rules of grammar ⟨a *grammatical* sentence⟩ — **gram·mat·i·cal·i·ty** \-ˌmat-ə-'kal-ət-ē\ *n* — **gram·mat·i·cal·ly** \-'mat-i-k(ə-)lē\ *adv* — **gram·mat·i·cal·ness** \-kəl-nəs\ *n*

grana *plural of* GRANUM

gra·na·ry \'grān-(ə-)rē, 'gran-\ *n, pl* **-ries** **1** : a storehouse for grain **2** : a region producing plenty of grain

¹grand \'grand\ *adj* **1** : higher in rank than others of the same class : FOREMOST, PRINCIPAL ⟨the *grand* champion⟩ ⟨the *grand* prize⟩ **2** : great in size **3** : including all things being considered : COMPLETE ⟨a *grand* total⟩ **4 a** : marked by magnificence : SPLENDID ⟨a *grand* coronation ceremony⟩ **b** : showing wealth or high social standing ⟨the airs of a *grand* lady⟩ **5** : IMPRESSIVE ⟨made *grand* statements about our progress⟩ **6** : very good : FINE ⟨*grand* weather⟩ ⟨have a *grand* time⟩ — **grand·ly** \'gran-(d)lē\ *adv* — **grand·ness** \'gran(d)-nəs\ *n*

synonyms GRAND, MAGNIFICENT, MAJESTIC, GRANDIOSE mean large and impressive. GRAND suggests handsomeness and dignity ⟨the royal wedding was a *grand* affair⟩. MAGNIFICENT suggests an appropriate greatness of size that remains dignified and in good taste ⟨a *magnificent* palace⟩. MAJESTIC suggests awe-inspiring grandeur or great size ⟨a *majestic* waterfall⟩. GRANDIOSE may suggest largeness or greatness but is usually applied to something that is foolishly exaggerated or showy ⟨*grandiose* plans for world conquest⟩.

²grand *n* : GRAND PIANO

gran·dam \'gran-ˌdam, -dəm\ *or* **gran·dame** \-ˌdām, -dəm\ *n* **1** : GRANDMOTHER 1 **2** : an old woman

grand·aunt \'gran-'dant, -'dànt\ *n* : an aunt of one's father or mother

grand·child \'gran(d)-ˌchīld\ *n* : a child of one's son or daughter

grand·daugh·ter \'gran-ˌdȯt-ər\ *n* : a daughter of one's son or daughter

gran·dee \gran-'dē\ *n* : a man of elevated rank or station; *esp* : a high-ranking Spanish or Portuguese nobleman

gran·deur \'gran-jər\ *n* **1** : the quality or state of being grand : awe-inspiring magnificence **2** : something that is grand

grand·fa·ther \'gran(d)-ˌfäth-ər\ *n* **1** : the father of one's father or mother **2** : ANCESTOR 1

grandfather clock *n* : a tall clock standing directly on the floor

gran·dil·o·quence \gran-'dil-ə-kwən(t)s\ *n* : high-sounding or overly impressive language in speech or writing : BOMBAST — **gran·dil·o·quent** \-kwənt\ *adj* — **gran·dil·o·quent·ly** *adv*

gran·di·ose \'gran-dē-ˌōs\ *adj* **1** : impressive because of uncommon largeness, scope, effect, or grandeur **2** : characterized by deliberately assumed grandeur or splendor or by absurd exaggeration ⟨*grandiose* schemes⟩ *synonyms* see GRAND — **gran·di·ose·ly** *adv* — **gran·di·os·i·ty** \ˌgran-dē-'äs-ət-ē\ *n*

grandfather clock

grand jury *n* : a jury that chiefly examines accusations of crime made against persons and if the evidence warrants makes formal charges on which the accused persons are later tried

grand·moth·er \'gran(d)-ˌməth-ər\ *n* **1** : the mother of one's father or mother **2** : a female ancestor

grand·neph·ew \-'nef-(ˌ)yü\ *n* : a grandson of one's brother or sister

grand·niece \-'nēs\ *n* : a granddaughter of one's brother or sister

grand opera *n* : a serious opera in which the entire text is sung

grand·par·ent \'gran(d)-ˌpar-ənt, -ˌper-\ *n* : a parent of one's father or mother

grand piano *n* : a piano in which the frame and strings are in a horizontal rather than an upright position

grand·sire \'gran(d)-ˌsī(ə)r\ *n* **1** *or* **grand·sir** \'gran(t)-sər\ *dialect* : GRANDFATHER 1 **2** *archaic* : an aged man

grand slam *n* : a home run hit with three runners on base

grand·son \'gran(d)-,sən\ *n* : a son of one's son or daughter

grand·stand \-,stand\ *n* : a usually roofed stand for spectators at a racecourse or stadium

grand·un·cle \'gran-'dən-kəl\ *n* : an uncle of one's father or mother

grange \'grānj\ *n* 1 : [1]FARM 1a; *esp* : a farmhouse with its various buildings 2 *cap* : one of the lodges of a national association of farmers; *also* : the association itself

grang·er \'grān-jər\ *n* : a member of a Grange

gran·ite \'gran-ət\ *n* 1 : a very hard rock that can be polished and is used in buildings and monuments 2 : unyielding firmness (as of character, will, or opinion)

gran·ny *or* **gran·nie** \'gran-ē\ *n, pl* **grannies** 1 : GRANDMOTHER 1 2 : an ankle-length dress usually with long sleeves and a high waist

granny glasses *n pl* : metal-rimmed eyeglasses with small lenses

granny knot *n* : an insecure knot often made instead of a square knot — see KNOT illustration

gra·no·la \grə-'nō-lə\ *n* : a mixture of oats and other ingredients (as brown sugar, raisins, coconut, or nuts) that is eaten especially for breakfast or as a snack

[1]grant \'grant\ *vb* **1 a** : to consent to : PERMIT ⟨*grant* your request⟩ **b** : to permit as a right, privilege, or favor ⟨*granted* them a day off for volunteer work⟩ **2** : to give the possession or benefit of formally or legally ⟨the king *granted* land to the settlers⟩ **3** : to admit something not yet proved to be true ⟨*granted* you are right, you must still pay for the damage⟩ — **grant·er** \-ər\ *n* — **grant·or** \'grant-ər, grant-'ȯr\ *n*

[2]grant *n* **1** : the act of granting **2** : something granted: as **a** : a gift (as of money or land) for a particular purpose ⟨a research *grant*⟩ **b** : an area of land granted by a government

grant·ee \grant-'ē\ *n* : one to whom a grant is made

gran·u·lar \'gran-yə-lər\ *adj* **1** : consisting of grains **2** : having a grainy structure, feel, or appearance — **gran·u·lar·i·ty** \,gran-yə-'lar-ət-ē\ *n*

gran·u·late \'gran-yə-,lāt\ *vb* **-lat·ed; -lat·ing** : to form or crystallize into grains or granules

gran·u·la·tion \,gran-yə-'lā-shən\ *n* **1** : the act or process of granulating or the condition of being granulated **2** : one of the small raised places of a granulated surface

gran·ule \'gran-yü(ə)l\ *n* **1** : a small grain or particle ⟨*granules* of sugar⟩ **2** : a small short-lived bright spot on the sun

gra·num \'grā-nəm\ *n, pl* **gra·na** \-nə\ : one of the stacks of chlorophyll-containing material in plant chloroplasts

grape \'grāp\ *n* **1** : a smooth-skinned juicy light green or deep red to purplish black berry eaten dried or fresh as a fruit or fermented to produce wine **2** : any of numerous woody vines widely grown for their bunches of grapes **3** : GRAPESHOT — **grapy** \'grā-pē\ *adj*

grape 1

grape·fruit \'grāp-,früt\ *n* **1** *pl* **grapefruit** *or* **grapefruits** : a large citrus fruit with a bitter yellow rind and a highly flavored somewhat acid juicy pulp **2** : a tree that bears grapefruit

grape hyacinth *n* : any of several small herbs related to the lilies that produce usually blue flowers in the spring

grape·shot \'grāp-,shät\ *n* : small iron balls formerly fired at short range from a cannon against people (as soldiers or rioters)

grape sugar *n* : DEXTROSE

grape·vine \'grāp-,vīn\ *n* **1** : GRAPE 2 **2** : an unofficial means of spreading information or gossip from person to person

[1]graph \'graf\ *n* **1** : the collection of all the points whose coordinates are a solution to an equation ⟨the *graph* of $y = x^2$⟩ **2** : a diagram that shows (as by dots or lines) the change in one variable in comparison with that of one or more other variables ⟨a *graph* of population growth⟩

[2]graph *vb* : to represent by or plot on a graph ⟨*graph* each equation⟩

-graph \,graf\ *n combining form* : something written or drawn ⟨homo*graph*⟩ [derived from Greek *-graphon* "something written," from *-graphos* "written," from *graphein* "to write" — related to GRAFFITO, -GRAM]

[1]graph·ic \'graf-ik\ *also* **graph·i·cal** \-i-kəl\ *adj* **1** : of, relating to, or being arts such as painting, engraving, printing, or photography **2** : of, relating to, or represented by a graph **3** : clearly and impressively told or described — **graph·i·cal·ly** \-i-k(ə-)lē\ *adv*

> **synonyms** GRAPHIC, VIVID, PICTURESQUE mean presenting a picture of something in words. GRAPHIC suggests that the picture is sharp and lifelike ⟨a *graphic* report on hunger in the world⟩. VIVID suggests giving a strong or lasting impression of reality ⟨a *vivid* story about heroes⟩. PICTURESQUE suggests an impressive or effective picture that is the product of many separate pleasing or clear details ⟨a *picturesque* tale about farm life⟩.

[2]graphic *n* **1** : a picture, map, or graph used for illustration **2** *pl* : a display (as of pictures or graphs) generated by a computer on a screen, printer, or plotter

graphical user interface *n* : software that simplifies the use of a computer especially by using icons and menus

graphic equalizer *n* : an electronic device for controlling the response of an audio system to a number of frequency bands

graphic novel *n* : a work of fiction or non-fiction that is presented in comic-strip format and published as a book

graphics tablet *n* : a device by which pictures, graphs, or maps are put into a computer in a manner similar to drawing

graph·ite \'graf-,īt\ *n* : a soft shiny black carbon that is used in making lead pencils and as a dry lubricant

gra·phol·o·gy \gra-'fäl-ə-jē\ *n* : the study of handwriting especially for the purpose of analyzing the writer's personality — **gra·phol·o·gist** \-jəst\ *n*

graph paper *n* : paper ruled (as into small squares) for drawing graphs or making diagrams

-g·ra·phy \g-rə-fē\ *n combining form, pl* **-graphies** : writing or representation in a (specified) manner or by a (specified) means or of a (specified) object ⟨photo*graphy*⟩ ⟨tele*graphy*⟩ [derived from Latin *-graphia* "writing," from Greek *graphein* "to write"]

grap·nel \'grap-nᵊl\ *n* : a small anchor with pointed hooks or claws

[1]grap·ple \'grap-əl\ *n* : the act of grappling : GRIP, HOLD

[2]grapple *vb* **grap·pled; grap·pling** \'grap-(ə-)liŋ\ **1** : to seize or hold with or as if with a hooked instrument **2** : to seize and struggle with one another **3** : to attempt to deal ⟨*grappled* with a problem⟩ — **grap·pler** \-(ə-)lər\ *n*

[1]grasp \'grasp\ *vb* **1** : to make the motion of seizing : CLUTCH ⟨*grasp* at straws⟩ **2** : to clasp or embrace with or as if with the fingers or arms **3** : to lay hold of with the mind : COMPREHEND ⟨failed to *grasp* its importance⟩ — **grasp·able** \'gras-pə-bəl\ *adj* — **grasp·er** *n*

\ə\ abut	\au̇\ out	\i\ tip	\ȯ\ saw	\u̇\ foot
\ər\ **further**	\ch\ **chin**	\ī\ **life**	\ȯi\ **coin**	\y\ **yet**
\a\ **mat**	\e\ **pet**	\j\ **job**	\th\ **thin**	\yü\ **few**
\ā\ **take**	\ē\ **easy**	\ŋ\ **sing**	\th\ **this**	\yu̇\ **cure**
\ä\ **cot, cart**	\g\ **go**	\ō\ **bone**	\ü\ **food**	\zh\ **vision**

²grasp *n* **1** : ²EMBRACE **2** : ²CONTROL 1, HOLD ⟨land in the *grasp* of a tyrant⟩ **3 a** : the reach of the arms ⟨the tree limb was beyond my *grasp*⟩ **b** : the power of seizing and holding ⟨success lies within their *grasp*⟩ **4** : COMPREHENSION 3, UNDERSTANDING

grasp·ing \'gras-piŋ\ *adj* : GREEDY 3, AVARICIOUS — **grasp·ing·ly** *adv* — **grasp·ing·ness** *n*

¹grass \'gras\ *n* **1** : herbs suitable for or eaten by grazing animals **2** : any of a large family of green plants (as wheat, corn, bamboo, or sugarcane) with jointed usually hollow stems, long slender leaves, and small dry one= seeded fruits often in groups **3** : grass-covered land; *esp* : ²LAWN **4** : MARIJUANA — **grass·like** \-,līk\ *adj* — **grassy** \'gras-ē\ *adj*

²grass *vb* **1** : to seed with grass **2** : to provide (as cattle) with grass for food

grass·hop·per \'gras-,häp-ər\ *n* : any of numerous plant-eating insects that have long hind legs used for leaping

grasshopper

grass·land \-,land\ *n* : land covered with herbs (as grasses and clover) rather than shrubs and trees

grass roots *n pl* : society at the local and popular level especially in areas away from political or cultural centers

¹grate \'grāt\ *n* **1** : GRATING 1 **2** : a frame of iron bars for holding burning fuel (as in a fireplace)

²grate *vb* **grat·ed; grat·ing** **1** : to make into small particles by rubbing against something rough ⟨*grate* cheese⟩ **2** : to grind or rub against something with a scratching noise **3** : to have a harsh or irritating effect — **grat·er** *n*

grate·ful \'grāt-fəl\ *adj* **1 a** : appreciative of benefits received **b** : expressing gratitude **2** : giving pleasure or contentment : PLEASING — **grate·ful·ly** \-fə-lē\ *adv* — **grate·ful·ness** *n*

grat·i·fy \'grat-ə-,fī\ *vb* **-fied; -fy·ing** **1** : to give or be a source of pleasure or satisfaction to **2** : to grant a favor to : INDULGE — **grat·i·fi·ca·tion** \,grat-ə-fə-'kā-shən\ *n*

grat·ing \'grāt-iŋ\ *n* **1** : a frame of parallel bars or crossbars **2** : a transparent surface that is ruled with a series of very closely spaced parallel lines or bars and is used to produce spectra by the diffraction of light

gra·tis \'grat-əs, 'grāt-\ *adv or adj* : without charge : FREE

grat·i·tude \'grat-ə-,t(y)üd\ *n* : the state of being grateful [Middle English *gratitude* "gratitude," derived from Latin *gratitudo* (same meaning), from *gratus* "thankful" — related to CONGRATULATE, GRACE]

gra·tu·i·tous \grə-'t(y)ü-ət-əs\ *adj* **1** : done or provided freely with nothing expected in return **2** : not called for by the circumstances : UNWARRANTED ⟨a *gratuitous* insult⟩ — **gra·tu·i·tous·ly** *adv* — **gra·tu·i·tous·ness** *n*

gra·tu·i·ty \grə-'t(y)ü-ət-ē\ *n, pl* **-ties** : something given freely; *esp* : ¹⁰TIP

¹grave \'grāv\ *vb* **graved; grav·en** \'grā-vən\ *or* **graved; grav·ing** **1** : CARVE 1, SCULPTURE **2** : ENGRAVE 1a [Old English *grafan* "dig, carve"]

²grave *n* **1** : a hole dug to bury a body in **2** : TOMB 2

³grave \'grāv, *in sense 3 often* 'gräv\ *adj* **1 a** : deserving serious consideration : IMPORTANT ⟨a *grave* matter⟩ **b** : threatening great harm or danger ⟨received a *grave* injury⟩ **2** : dignified in appearance or manner : SOLEMN, SERIOUS ⟨a *grave* and thoughtful look⟩ **3** : of, marked by, or being an accent mark having the form ` [from early French *grave* "important, serious, weighty," from Latin *gravis* "heavy, serious" — related to AGGRAVATE, GRAVITY, GRIEVE] — **grave·ly** *adv* — **grave·ness** *n*

⁴gra·ve \'gräv-(,)ā\ *adv or adj* : in a slow and solemn manner — used as a direction in music

¹grav·el \'grav-əl\ *n* : small pieces of rock and pebbles larger than grains of sand

²gravel *adj* : GRAVELLY 2

³gravel *vb* **grav·eled** *or* **grav·elled; grav·el·ing** *or* **grav·el·ling** \'grav-(ə-)liŋ\ : to cover or spread with gravel

grav·el·ly \'grav-(ə-)lē\ *adj* **1** : of, containing, or covered with gravel ⟨*gravelly* soil⟩ **2** : having a harsh scratchy sound ⟨a *gravelly* voice⟩

grave·stone \'grāv-,stōn\ *n* : a burial monument

grave·yard \-,yärd\ *n* : CEMETERY

grav·id \'grav-əd\ *adj* : PREGNANT 1

gra·vi·me·ter \gra-'vim-ət-ər, 'grav-ə-,mēt-\ *n* : an instrument for measuring differences in the force of gravity at different places

grav·i·tate \'grav-ə-,tāt\ *vb* **-tat·ed; -tat·ing** : to move or tend to move toward something

grav·i·ta·tion \,grav-ə-'tā-shən\ *n* **1** : a force of attraction that tends to draw particles or bodies together : GRAVITY 3b **2** : the action or process of gravitating — **grav·i·ta·tion·al** \-shnəl, -shən-ᵊl\ *adj* — **grav·i·ta·tion·al·ly** \-ē\ *adv* — **grav·i·ta·tive** \'grav-ə-,tāt-iv\ *adj*

grav·i·ty \'grav-ət-ē\ *n, pl* **-ties** **1 a** : the quality or state of being dignified and proper **b** : the quality or state of being important or serious **2** : WEIGHT **3 a** : the gravitational attraction of the mass of a heavenly body (as the earth) for bodies at or near its surface **b** : a force of attraction between particles or bodies that occurs because of their mass, is stronger as mass is increased, and is weaker as the distance between the objects is increased **c** : ACCELERATION OF GRAVITY [from early French *gravité* or Latin *gravitas,* both meaning "the quality or state of being serious or dignified, the quality of being weighty," from Latin *gravis* "heavy, serious" — related to AGGRAVATE, ³GRAVE, GRIEVE]

gra·vy \'grā-vē\ *n, pl* **gravies** **1** : a sauce made from the thickened and seasoned juices of cooked meat **2** : something additional or unexpected that is pleasing or valuable

¹gray *also* **grey** \'grā\ *adj* **1** : of the color gray; *also* : dull in color **2** : having gray hair **3** : lacking cheer or brightness : DISMAL ⟨a *gray* day⟩ — **gray·ness** *n*

²gray *also* **grey** *n* **1** : one of the series of neutral colors ranging between black and white **2** : something gray — **gray** *vb* — **gray·ish** \'grā-ish\ *adj*

gray·beard \'grā-,bi(ə)rd\ *n* : an old man

gray fox *n* : a gray-haired fox with white underparts that is found from southern Canada to northern South America

gray·ling \'grā-liŋ\ *n, pl* **grayling** *also* **graylings** : any of several freshwater fishes related to the trouts and salmons and valued for food and sport

gray matter *n* **1** : nerve tissue especially of the brain and spinal cord that has a brownish gray color **2** : INTELLIGENCE 1

gray squirrel *n* : a common light gray to black squirrel native to eastern North America and introduced into Europe

gray whale *n* : a large baleen whale of the northern Pacific Ocean

gray wolf *n* : a large wolf of northern regions that is usually gray — called also *timber wolf*

¹graze \'grāz\ *vb* **grazed; graz·ing** **1** : to feed on growing grass or herbs ⟨cattle *grazing* on the hill⟩ **2** : to put to feed on grass or herbs ⟨the farmer *grazed* the cattle⟩

²graze *vb* **grazed; graz·ing** **1** : to rub or touch lightly in passing : touch against and quickly move away from ⟨the car's wheel *grazed* the curb⟩ **2** : to scratch or scrape by rubbing against something ⟨fell and *grazed* her knee⟩

³graze *n* : an act or result of grazing; *esp* : a skin injury caused by grazing : SCRAPE

¹grease \'grēs\ *n* **1** : melted animal fat **2** : oily matter **3** : a thick lubricant

²**grease** \'grēs, 'grēz\ *vb* **greased; greas·ing** **1** : to smear with grease **2** : to lubricate with grease — **greas·er** *n*

grease·paint \'grē-ˌspānt\ *n* : theatrical makeup

grease pencil *n* : a pencil with lead like a soft crayon for marking on hard surfaces (as glass)

grease·wood \'grē-ˌswu̇d\ *n* : a low stiff shrub of the western U.S. that is related to the goosefoots and is common in soils with a high salt content

greasy \'grē-sē, -zē\ *adj* **greas·i·er; -est** **1** : smeared with grease **2** : containing grease ⟨*greasy* food⟩ **3** : resembling grease or oil : SMOOTH, SLIPPERY — **greas·i·ly** \-sə-lē, -zə-\ *adv* — **greas·i·ness** \-sē-nəs, -zē-\ *n*

¹**great** \'grāt, *in South also* 'gre(ə)t\ *adj* **1** : large in size : not small or little **2** : large in number : NUMEROUS ⟨a *great* crowd⟩ **3** : long continued ⟨a *great* while⟩ **4** : beyond the average or ordinary ⟨a *great* weight⟩ ⟨in *great* pain⟩ **5** : DISTINGUISHED, PROMINENT ⟨a *great* artist⟩ **6** : more distant in relationship by one generation **7** : superior in quality or character **8** : remarkable in skill ⟨*great* at tennis⟩ **9** — used as a term of general approval ⟨had a *great* time⟩ — **great·ly** *adv* — **great·ness** *n*

²**great** *adv* : in a great manner : SUCCESSFULLY, WELL

³**great** *n, pl* **great** *or* **greats** : an outstandingly superior or skillful person ⟨the *greats* of baseball⟩

great ape *n* : any of a family of apes that includes the gorilla, orangutan, and chimpanzee

great auk *n* : an extinct large auk that was unable to fly and was formerly common along North Atlantic coasts

great–aunt *n* : GRANDAUNT

Great Bear *n* : URSA MAJOR

great blue heron *n* : a large grayish blue American heron with a crest of dark feathers on its head

great circle *n* : a circle on the surface of a sphere that has the same center as the sphere; *esp* : one on the surface of the earth a portion of which is the shortest travel distance between two points

great·coat \'grāt-ˌkōt\ *n* : a heavy overcoat

Great Dane *n* : any of a breed of very tall powerful smooth-coated dogs

great divide *n* : a watershed located between major drainage systems

greatest common divisor *n* : the largest whole number that is an exact divisor of each of two or more whole numbers — called also *greatest common factor*

great·heart·ed \'grāt-'härt-əd\ *adj* **1** : COURAGEOUS **2** : nobly generous — **great·heart·ed·ly** *adv*

great horned owl *n* : an American owl with two bunches of feathers resembling ears or horns at the top of the head

great–nephew *n* : GRANDNEPHEW

great–niece *n* : GRANDNIECE

great power *n* : one of the nations that have the greatest influence, resources, and military strength in the world

great–uncle *n* : GRANDUNCLE

great white shark *n* : a large and dangerous shark of warm seas that is quick to attack human beings and is bluish when young but becomes whitish with age

grebe \'grēb\ *n* : any of a family of swimming and diving birds closely related to the loons

Gre·cian \'grē-shən\ *adj* : GREEK — **Grecian** *n*

Greco- *or* **Graeco-** \'grek-ō, 'grē-kō\ *combining form* **1** : Greece : Greeks ⟨*Greco*phile⟩ **2** : Greek and ⟨*Greco*-Roman⟩

grebe

greed \'grēd\ *n* : selfish desire for food, money, or possessions over and above one's needs

greedy \'grēd-ē\ *adj* **greed·i·er; -est** **1** : having a keen appetite **2** : having an eager and often selfish desire or longing ⟨*greedy* for praise⟩ **3** : wanting more than one needs or more than one's fair share (as of food) — **greed·i·ly** \'grēd-ᵊl-ē\ *adv* — **greed·i·ness** \'grēd-ē-nəs\ *n*

Greek \'grēk\ *n* **1 a** : a person born or living in Greece **b** : a person of Greek ancestry **2** : the Indo-European language of the Greeks — **Greek** *adj*

¹**green** \'grēn\ *adj* **1** : of the color green **2 a** : covered by green leaves or herbs **b** : consisting of green plants or of the leafy part of a plant ⟨a *green* salad⟩ **3** : not fully grown or ripe **4 a** : marked by a sickly appearance **b** : ENVIOUS — used especially in the phrase *green with envy* **5** : lacking training, knowledge, or experience ⟨*green* troops⟩ **6 a** : concerned with or supporting environmentalism **b** : tending to preserve the quality of the environment ⟨*green* dish soap⟩ — **green·ish** \'grē-nish\ *adj* — **green·ly** \'grēn-lē\ *adv* — **green·ness** \'grēn-nəs\ *n*

²**green** *n* **1** : a color (as that of growing fresh grass) that ranges between blue and yellow **2 a** : green vegetation **b** *pl* : leafy parts of plants used for some purpose (as ornament or food) **3** : a grassy plain or plot; *esp* : a smooth grassy area around the hole into which the ball must be played in golf **4** : MONEY 1a **5** *often cap* : ENVIRONMENTALIST; *esp* : a member of a political party focusing on environmental and social issues — **greeny** \'grē-nē\ *adj*

green alga *n* : any of a group of green-colored algae that occur especially in fresh water

green anole *n* : a long-tailed lizard of the southeastern U.S. that is often found on trees and can change from green to brown

green·back \'grēn-ˌbak\ *n* : a piece of U.S. paper money

green bean *n* : a kidney bean with the pods green when ready for harvest

green·belt \'grēn-ˌbelt\ *n* : a belt of landscaped roads, parks, or farmlands that encircles a community

green·ery \'grēn-(ə-)rē\ *n, pl* **-er·ies** : green leaves or plants : VERDURE

green·gro·cer \'grēn-ˌgrō-sər\ *n, chiefly British* : a person who sells fresh vegetables and fruit to the public — **green·gro·cery** \-ˌgrōs-(ə-)rē\ *n*

green·horn \-ˌhȯrn\ *n* : an inexperienced person; *esp* : one easily tricked or cheated

¹**green·house** \-ˌhau̇s\ *n* : a glassed enclosure for cultivation of plants

²**greenhouse** *adj* : relating to, causing, or caused by the greenhouse effect ⟨*greenhouse* warming⟩ ⟨carbon dioxide is a *greenhouse* gas⟩

greenhouse effect *n* : the warming of the earth's atmosphere that occurs when the sun's radiation passes through the atmosphere, is absorbed by the earth, and is given off as radiation of longer wavelength which can be absorbed by atmospheric gases (as carbon dioxide and water vapor)

green manure *n* : a crop of plants (as clover) that is plowed under while green to enrich the soil

green mold *n* : a mold (as a penicillium) that is green or produces green spores

green onion *n* : a young onion that is pulled from the ground before the bulb has become large

green pepper *n* : a sweet pepper before it turns red at maturity

green snake *n* : either of two bright green harmless largely insect-eating snakes of North America

\ə\ **abut**	\au̇\ **out**	\i\ **tip**	\ȯ\ **saw**	\u̇\ **foot**
\ər\ **further**	\ch\ **chin**	\ī\ **life**	\ȯi\ **coin**	\y\ **yet**
\a\ **mat**	\e\ **pet**	\j\ **job**	\th\ **thin**	\yü\ **few**
\ā\ **take**	\ē\ **easy**	\ŋ\ **sing**	\th\ **this**	\yu̇\ **cure**
\ä\ **cot, cart**	\g\ **go**	\ō\ **bone**	\ü\ **food**	\zh\ **vision**

green soap n : a soft soap made from vegetable oils and used especially to treat skin diseases

green·sward \'grēn-ˌswȯ(ə)rd\ n : turf that is green with growing grass

green thumb n : an unusual ability to make plants grow — **green–thumbed** \'grēn-'thəmd\ adj

green turtle n : a large usually plant-eating sea turtle with a smooth greenish shell

green turtle

green vegetable n : a vegetable that has the edible parts rich in chlorophyll and is an important source of vitamins

Green·wich mean time \'grin-ij-, 'gren-, -ich-\ n : the time of the meridian of Greenwich used as the basis of standard time throughout the world — called also *Greenwich time*

green·wood \'grēn-ˌwu̇d\ n : a forest that is green with leaves

greet \'grēt\ vb 1 : to address upon arrival or meeting with expressions of kind wishes ⟨*greeted* guests at the door⟩ 2 : to meet or react to in a specified manner ⟨*greeted* with cheers⟩ 3 : to appear or present itself to ⟨a surprising sight *greeted* her eyes⟩ — **greet·er** n

greet·ing n 1 : SALUTATION 2 : an expression of good wishes : REGARDS — usually used in plural

greeting card n : a decorated card with a message of goodwill that is sent to or received by a person usually on a special occasion

gre·gar·i·ous \gri-'gar-ē-əs, -'ger-\ adj 1 : tending to associate with others of one's kind : SOCIAL; *also* : tending to live in a flock, herd, or community rather than alone ⟨*gregarious* birds⟩ 2 : marked by a liking for companionship : SOCIABLE [from Latin *gregarius* "relating to a herd or flock," from *greg-, grex* "flock, herd" — related to CONGREGATE] — **gre·gar·i·ous·ly** adv — **gre·gar·i·ous·ness** n

Gre·go·ri·an calendar \gri-ˌgōr-ē-ən-, -ˌgȯr-\ n : a calendar introduced by Pope Gregory XIII in 1582 and adopted in Great Britain and the American colonies in 1752 — compare JULIAN CALENDAR

Gregorian chant n : a simple tune with no regular rhythm that is sung in unison and without accompaniment in services of the Roman Catholic Church

grem·lin \'grem-lən\ n : a small mischievous or troublesome creature

gre·nade \grə-'nād\ n : a small bomb designed to be thrown by hand or launched (as by a rifle) [from early French *grenade, granade* "pomegranate, grenade," from Latin *granata* "pomegranate," derived from Latin *granatus* "seedy," from *granum* "grain, seed" — related to GARNET, GRAIN, POMEGRANATE; see *Word History* at GARNET]

gren·a·dier \ˌgren-ə-'di(ə)r\ n : a soldier who carries and throws grenades

grew *past of* GROW

grey *variant of* GRAY

grey·hound \'grā-ˌhau̇nd\ n : any of a breed of tall slender swift dogs with a smooth coat and narrow head

grid \'grid\ n 1 : GRATING 1 2 : a metal plate used as a conductor in a storage battery 3 : an element of an electron tube consisting of a network of fine wire 4 : a network of horizontal and perpendicular lines (as for locating points on a map using coordinates or for counting a sample of particles or organisms on a microscope slide)

grid·dle \'grid-ᵊl\ n : a flat surface or pan on which food is cooked

griddle cake n : PANCAKE

grid·iron \'grid-ˌī(-ə)rn\ n 1 : a grate for broiling food 2 : something consisting of or covered with a grid 3 : a football field

grief \'grēf\ n 1 a : deep sorrow : SADNESS b : a cause of sorrow 2 a : things that cause problems ⟨enough *grief* for one day⟩ b : an unfortunate happening ⟨the boat came to *grief* on the rocks⟩ **synonyms** see SORROW

griev·ance \'grē-vən(t)s\ n 1 : a cause of distress giving reason for complaint 2 : the formal expression of a grievance : COMPLAINT

grieve \'grēv\ vb **grieved; griev·ing** 1 : to cause grief or suffering to : DISTRESS 2 : to feel or express grief [Middle English *greven* "to distress, grieve," from early French *grever* (same meaning), from Latin *gravare* "to burden," from *gravis* "heavy, serious" — related to AGGRAVATE, ³GRAVE, GRAVITY] — **griev·er** n

griev·ous \'grē-vəs\ adj 1 : ¹HEAVY 2, SEVERE ⟨the *grievous* cost of war⟩ 2 : causing pain, suffering, or sorrow ⟨a *grievous* wound⟩ 3 : SERIOUS 4, GRAVE ⟨a *grievous* mistake⟩ — **griev·ous·ly** adv — **griev·ous·ness** n

grif·fin or **grif·fon** also **gryph·on** \'grif-ən\ n : an imaginary animal that is half eagle and half lion

¹grill \'gril\ vb 1 : to broil on a grill 2 a : to torment as if by broiling b : to question with repeated questions

²grill n 1 : a grate on which food is broiled 2 : broiled food 3 : a restaurant that serves broiled foods

grille or **grill** \'gril\ n 1 : a grating forming a barrier or screen 2 : an opening covered with a grille

grim \'grim\ adj **grim·mer; grim·mest** 1 : CRUEL 2, FIERCE 2 a : stern in action or appearance b : DISMAL ⟨*grim* news⟩ c : DEPRESSED 3 : FRIGHTFUL 1 ⟨a *grim* tale⟩ 4 : UNFLINCHING, UNYIELDING ⟨*grim* determination⟩ — **grim·ly** adv — **grim·ness** n

grim·ace \'grim-əs, grim-'ās\ n : a twisting of the face or features (as in disgust, disapproval, or pain) — **grimace** vb

grime \'grīm\ n : dirt rubbed into or covering a surface; *also* : accumulated dirtiness and disorder — **grime** vb — **grim·i·ness** \'grī-mē-nəs\ n — **grimy** \'grī-mē\ adj

grin \'grin\ vb **grinned; grin·ning** : to draw back the lips so as to show the teeth especially in laughter — **grin** n

¹grind \'grīnd\ vb **ground** \'grau̇nd\; **grind·ing** 1 : to reduce to powder or pieces by friction (as in a mill or with the teeth) 2 : to wear down, polish, or sharpen by friction : WHET 3 : to press with a scraping noise : GRIT 4 : OPPRESS 2, HARASS 5 a : to operate or produce by turning a crank b : to produce by steady hard work ⟨*grind* out an essay⟩ 6 : to move with difficulty or friction especially so as to make a scraping noise ⟨*grind* the gears⟩

²grind n 1 a : an act of grinding b : the sound of grinding 2 a : steady hard work; *esp* : study that takes much effort b : a student who studies too much 3 : the result of grinding; *esp* : the size of particle obtained by grinding

grind·er \'grīn-dər\ n 1 : one that grinds 2 : ²SUBMARINE 2

grind·stone \'grīn-ˌstōn\ n : a stone disk that turns on an axle and is used for grinding or sharpening

gri·ot \'grē-ˌō\ n : any of a class of musician-entertainers of western Africa whose performances include tribal histories and genealogies

grindstone

¹grip \'grip\ vb **gripped; grip·ping** 1 : to seize firmly 2 : to hold strongly the interest of ⟨the story *grips* the reader⟩

²grip n 1 a : a firm grasp b : strength in gripping c : a way of clasping the hand by which members of a secret society recognize or greet one another 2 a : a firm hold giving control ⟨in the *grip* of winter⟩ **b** : COMPREHEN-SION 3, UNDERSTANDING **3** : a part or device for gripping or by which something is grasped; *esp* : ¹HANDLE 1 **4** : SUITCASE

¹gripe \'grīp\ *vb* **griped; grip·ing 1** *archaic* : to seize firmly : GRIP **2 a** : AFFLICT, DISTRESS **b** : IRRITATE 1, VEX ⟨laziness *gripes* our teacher⟩ **3** : to cause or experience spasms of pain in the intestines **4** : COMPLAIN 1 — **grip·er** *n*

²gripe *n* **1** : ²GRIP 1 **2 a** : AFFLICTION 1 **b** : COMPLAINT 1 **3** : a spasm of pain in the intestines

grippe \'grip\ *n* : a virus disease that is the same as or very much like influenza — **grippy** \'grip-ē\ *adj*

gris·ly \'griz-lē\ *adj* **gris·li·er; -est** : HORRIBLE, GRUE-SOME ⟨a *grisly* description of the fire⟩ — **gris·li·ness** *n*

grist \'grist\ *n* : grain to be ground or already ground

gris·tle \'gris-əl\ *n* : tough chewy matter in meat served as food that is composed usually of cartilage — **gris·tly** \'gris-(ə-)lē\ *adj*

grist·mill \'grist-,mil\ *n* : a mill for grinding grain

¹grit \'grit\ *n* **1 a** : a small hard sharp particle (as of sand) **b** : material (as an abrasive) composed of grits **2** : firmness of mind or spirit : unyielding courage — **grit·ty** \'grit-ē\ *adj*

²grit *vb* **grit·ted; grit·ting** : to grind or cause to grind : GRATE ⟨*grit* one's teeth⟩

grits \'grits\ *n pl* : coarsely ground hulled grain ⟨hominy *grits*⟩

griz·zled \'griz-əld\ *adj* : sprinkled, streaked, or mixed with gray ⟨a *grizzled* beard⟩

¹griz·zly \'griz-lē\ *adj* **griz·zli·er; -est** : GRIZZLED

²grizzly *n, pl* **grizzlies** : GRIZZLY BEAR

grizzly bear *n* : a large powerful brown bear found from the north-western U.S. to Alaska

groan \'grōn\ *vb* **1** : to utter a deep moan of pain, grief, or irritation **2** : to make a harsh sound under strain ⟨the chair *groaned* under my weight⟩ — **groan** *n* — **groan·er** *n*

grizzly bear

¹groat \'grōt\ *n* **1** : hulled grain broken into fragments larger than grits — usually used in plural ⟨buckwheat *groats*⟩ **2** : a grain (as of oats) without the hull [Old English *grotan*, plural of *grot*]

²groat *n* : a former British coin worth four pennies [Middle English *groot* "coin"; of Dutch origin]

gro·cer \'grō-sər\ *n* : a dealer in food and household supplies

gro·cery \'grōs-(ə-)rē\ *n, pl* **-cer·ies 1** *pl* : food sold by a grocer ⟨went out to buy the *groceries*⟩ **2** : a grocer's store

grog \'gräg\ *n* : alcoholic liquor; *esp* : liquor (as rum) weakened with water — **grog·gery** \'gräg-ə-rē\ *n*

grog·gy \-'gräg-ē\ *adj* **grog·gi·er; -est** : weak and un-steady on the feet or in action — **grog·gi·ly** \'gräg-ə-lē\ *adv* — **grog·gi·ness** \'gräg-ē-nəs\ *n*

¹groin \'gròin\ *n* **1** : the junction of the lower abdomen and the inner part of the thigh or the part of the body around this junction **2** : the curved line or rib on a ceiling along which two vaults meet

²groin *vb* : to build or equip with groins

grom·met \'gräm-ət, 'grəm-\ *n* : an eyelet of firm material to strengthen or protect an opening

¹groom \'grüm, 'grùm\ *n* **1 a** *archaic* : a male servant **b** : a person in charge of horses **2** : BRIDEGROOM

²groom *vb* **1** : to clean and keep up the appearance of (as the coat of a horse or dog) **2** : to make neat, attractive, or acceptable

grooms·man \'grümz-mən, 'grùmz-\ *n* : a male friend who accompanies a bridegroom at his wedding

¹groove \'grüv\ *n* **1** : a long narrow channel made in a surface **2** : a fixed routine : RUT **3** : top form

²groove *vb* **grooved; groov·ing 1 a** : to form a groove in **b** : to become grooved **2** : to enjoy very much

groovy \'grü-vē\ *adj* **groov·i·er; -est** : very good : EXCEL-LENT

grope \'grōp\ *vb* **groped; grop·ing 1** : to seek by or as if by feeling around uncertainly ⟨*groped* for the light switch⟩ ⟨*grope* for the right word⟩ **2** : to feel one's way by groping ⟨*grope* along a wall⟩

gros·beak \'grōs-,bēk\ *n* : any of several finches (as the rose-breasted grosbeak) of Europe or America having large stout cone-shaped bills

¹gross \'grōs\ *adj* **1 a** : very obvious : GLARING ⟨a *gross* error⟩ **b** : SHAMEFUL 1 ⟨*gross* injustice⟩ **2** : ¹BIG 2a, BULKY; *esp* : excessively fat **3** : consisting of a whole be-fore any deductions ⟨*gross* earnings⟩ **4** : COARSE 5, VUL-GAR ⟨*gross* language⟩ **5** : causing disgust or distaste [Middle English *gros, gross* "large, thick, easy to see or understand," from early French *gros* "thick, coarse," from Latin *grossus* (same meaning)] — **gross·ly** *adv* — **gross·ness** *n*

²gross *n* : a whole before any deductions

³gross *vb* : to earn before deductions ⟨*grossed* $50,000 be-fore taxes⟩

⁴gross *n, pl* **gross** : 12 dozen ⟨a *gross* of pencils⟩ [Middle English *gross* "a group of 12 dozen," probably from early French *grosse* "sum, whole," derived from *gros* "thick"]

gross national product *n* : the total value of the goods and services produced in a nation during a year

grot \'grät\ *n* : GROTTO

gro·tesque \grō-'tesk\ *adj* **1** : combining (as in a painting) details not found together in nature **2** : unnaturally odd or ugly — **gro·tesque·ly** *adv* — **gro·tesque·ness** *n*

Word History Italians exploring the ruins of ancient Rome found strange paintings on the walls of some of the rooms. These paintings were of human and animal forms mixed with those of strange fruits and flowers. The Italians called such a painting *pittura grottesca,* which means "cave painting." The Italian adjective *grot-tesca* came from *grotta,* meaning "cave." We also get English *grotto* from this word. The Italian word *grotta* in turn came from the Latin *crypta,* which meant "cavern, crypt." The French borrowed the word *grottesca* from Italian and spelled it *grotesque,* the form in which it came into English. At first the adjective was used to de-scribe pictures having strange combinations of things not normally found together. Later it came to be used for anything that looked weird or unnatural. [from French *grotesque* "relating to or being a style of art with unusual designs and combinations of figures of animals, humans, and plants," from Italian *(pittura) grottesca* "cave painting," from *grottesca* "of a cave," from *grotta, grotto* "cave," from Latin *crypta* "cavern, crypt" — re-lated to GROTTO]

grot·to \'grät-ō\ *n, pl* **grottoes** *also* **grottos 1** : ¹CAVE **2** : an artificial structure made to resemble a natural cave [from Italian *grotta, grotto* "cave," from Latin *crypta* "cavern, crypt" — related to GROTESQUE]

grouch \'graùch\ *n* **1** : a sudden outburst of bad temper **2** : an irritable or complaining person — **grouch** *vb* — **grouch·i·ly** \'graù-chə-lē\ *adv* — **grouch·i·ness** \-chē-nəs\ *n* — **grouchy** \-chē\ *adj*

\ə\ abut	\aù\ out	\i\ tip	\ò\ saw	\ù\ foot
\ər\ further	\ch\ chin	\ī\ life	\òi\ coin	\y\ yet
\a\ mat	\e\ pet	\j\ job	\th\ thin	\yü\ few
\ā\ take	\ē\ easy	\ŋ\ sing	\th\ this	\yù\ cure
\ä\ cot, cart	\g\ go	\ō\ bone	\ü\ food	\zh\ vision

¹ground \'graund\ *n* **1 a** : the bottom of a body of water ⟨the boat struck *ground*⟩ **b** *pl* : SEDIMENT 1, LEES **2** : BASIS, FOUNDATION ⟨*grounds* for divorce⟩ **3** : a surrounding area : BACKGROUND ⟨a picture on a gray *ground*⟩ **4 a** : the surface of the earth **b** : an area used for a particular purpose ⟨the parade *ground*⟩ ⟨fishing *grounds*⟩ **c** *pl* : the area around and belonging to a building **5** : ³SOIL 1, EARTH **6** : an area to be won or defended in or as if in battle ⟨gaining *ground* on the other runners⟩ **7 a** : an object that makes an electrical connection with the earth **b** : a large conducting body (as the earth) used as a common return for an electric circuit

²ground *vb* **1** : to bring to or place on the ground **2 a** : to provide a reason for **b** : to instruct in fundamentals ⟨well *grounded* in mathematics⟩ **3** : to connect electrically with a ground **4 a** : to restrict to the ground ⟨*ground* a pilot⟩ **b** : to prohibit from taking part in some usual activities ⟨*grounded* her for a week⟩ **5** : to run aground ⟨the ship *grounded* on a reef⟩ **6** : to hit a ground ball ⟨*grounded* to the shortstop⟩

³ground *past and past participle of* GRIND

ground ball *n* : a batted baseball that rolls or bounces along the ground

ground cover *n* : low-growing plants that cover the ground (as in a forest or in place of grass or a lawn); *also* : a plant used as ground cover

ground crew *n* : the mechanics and technicians who maintain and service an aircraft

ground·er \'graun-dər\ *n* : GROUND BALL

ground finch *n* : any of several dull-colored finches with large bills that are found in the Galápagos Islands

ground·hog \'graund-ˌhȯg, -ˌhäg\ *n* : WOODCHUCK

Groundhog Day *n* : February 2 when according to tradition the groundhog comes out of its burrow and if it sees its shadow and is frightened back underground there will be six more weeks of winter

ground·less \'graun-(d)ləs\ *adj* : not justified : having no real basis ⟨*groundless* fears⟩ — **ground·less·ly** *adv* — **ground·less·ness** *n*

ground·ling \'graun-(d)liŋ\ *n* : a spectator who stood in the part of a theater in Shakespeare's time where there were no seats

ground·nut \'graun(d)-ˌnət\ *n, chiefly British* : PEANUT 1

ground pine *n* : any of several club mosses with long creeping stems and upright branches

ground plan *n* **1** : a plan of a floor of a building **2** : a first or basic plan

ground rule *n* : a rule set up for a specified activity

ground squirrel *n* : any of numerous burrowing rodents (as gophers and chipmunks) that differ from true squirrels in having cheek pouches and shorter fur

ground state *n* : the energy level of a physical system (as an atom) having the least energy of all its possible states

ground swell *n* : a broad deep ocean swell caused by a distant storm or earthquake

ground·wa·ter \'graun-ˌdwȯt-ər, -ˌdwät-\ *n* : water within the earth that supplies wells and springs

ground·work \'graun-ˌdwərk\ *n* : FOUNDATION 2, BASIS

ground zero *n* **1** : the site of a nuclear explosion **2** : the center of rapid, intense, or violent activity or change **3** : the very beginning : SQUARE ONE

¹group \'grüp\ *n* **1** : a number of objects or persons considered as a unit **2 a** : a number of living things having some natural relationship **b** : a combination of atoms commonly found together in a molecule ⟨a methyl *group*⟩ **3** : a small band : COMBO ⟨a rock *group*⟩

²group *vb* : to arrange or combine in a group ⟨*group* children by ages⟩

grou·per \'grü-pər\ *n, pl* **groupers** *also* **grouper** : any of various mostly large fishes that live at the bottom of warm seas and are related to the sea basses

group·ie \'grü-pē\ *n* : a fan of a rock group who usually follows the group around on concert tours

¹grouse \'graus\ *n, pl* **grouse** *or* **grouses** : any of various plump-bodied game birds that are usually reddish or grayish brown with feathers on the legs

¹grouse

²grouse *vb* **groused; grous·ing** : COMPLAIN 1, GRUMBLE — **grous·er** *n*

grove \'grōv\ *n* : a small wood; *esp* : a group of trees without underbrush ⟨an orange *grove*⟩

grov·el \'gräv-əl, 'grəv-\ *vb* **-eled** *or* **-elled; -el·ing** *or* **-el·ling** \-(ə-)liŋ\ **1** : to creep or lie face down on the ground (as in fear) **2** : to degrade oneself by behaving like a fearful slave : CRINGE — **grov·el·er** *or* **grov·el·ler** \-(ə-)lər\ *n*

grow \'grō\ *vb* **grew** \'grü\; **grown** \'grōn\; **grow·ing 1 a** : to spring up and develop to maturity **b** : to be able to grow in some place or situation ⟨rice *grows* in water⟩ **c** : to take on some relation through or as if through growth ⟨a tree with limbs *grown* together⟩ **2** : ¹INCREASE 1, EXPAND ⟨the city is *growing* rapidly⟩ ⟨*grows* in wisdom⟩ **3** : ORIGINATE ⟨the project *grew* out of a mere suggestion⟩ **4 a** : to pass into a condition : BECOME ⟨*grew* pale⟩ **b** : to have an increasing influence ⟨habits *grow* on you⟩ **5** : to cause to grow : CULTIVATE, RAISE ⟨*grow* wheat⟩ — **grow·er** \'grō(-ə)r\ *n*

growing pains *n pl* **1** : pains in the legs of growing children having no proven relation to growth **2** : difficulties that accompany something new ⟨a business going through *growing pains*⟩

growing point *n* : the tip of a plant shoot from which additional shoot tissues develop

growing season *n* : the period of the year that is warm enough for growth especially of cultivated plants; *esp* : the period between the last killing frost in the spring and the first one in the fall

growl \'grau(ə)l\ *vb* **1 a** : ¹RUMBLE **b** : to utter a deep threatening sound ⟨the dog *growled*⟩ **2** : COMPLAIN 1 — **growl** *n* — **growl·er** \'grau-lər\ *n*

grown \'grōn\ *adj* : fully grown : ADULT ⟨a job for a *grown* man⟩

grown–up \'grō-ˌnəp\ *adj* : ¹ADULT 2 — **grown–up** *n*

growth \'grōth\ *n* **1 a** : stage or condition reached in growing : SIZE ⟨the dog hasn't reached full *growth*⟩ **b** : a process of growing especially through an increase in size or amount ⟨a *growth* of wealth⟩ ⟨good nutrition promotes *growth*⟩ ⟨*growth* of a crystal⟩ **c** : a process of developing ⟨the *growth* of civilization⟩ **2** : a result or product of growing ⟨covered with a *growth* of mold⟩ ⟨a thick *growth* of underbrush⟩ **3** : an abnormal mass of tissue (as a tumor or wart)

growth hormone *n* : a hormone in plants or animals that regulates growth; *esp* : one produced by the pituitary gland

growth ring *n* : a layer of wood (as an annual ring) produced during a single period of growth

grow up *vb* : to grow toward or reach full mental and physical growth

¹grub \'grəb\ *vb* **grubbed; grub·bing 1** : to clear or root out by digging ⟨*grub* up roots⟩ ⟨*grub* for potatoes⟩ **2** : to work hard : DRUDGE — **grub·ber** *n*

²grub *n* **1** : a soft thick wormlike larva of an insect (as a beetle) **2 a** : ²DRUDGE **b** : an untidy or dirty person **3** : FOOD 1

grub·by \'grəb-ē\ *adj* **grub·bi·er; -est** : ¹DIRTY 1, SLOV-ENLY — **grub·bi·ly** \'grəb-ə-lē\ *adv* — **grub·bi·ness** \'grəb-ē-nəs\ *n*

grub·stake \'grəb-,stāk\ *n* : supplies or funds given to a mining prospector in return for a promise of a share in his finds — **grubstake** *vb* — **grub·stak·er** *n*

¹**grudge** \'grəj\ *vb* **grudged; grudg·ing** : BEGRUDGE — **grudg·er** *n* — **grudg·ing·ly** \-iŋ-lē\ *adv*

²**grudge** *n* : a strong lasting feeling of resentment toward someone for a real or imagined wrong

gru·el \'grü-əl\ *n* : a thin food made by boiling cereal (as oatmeal or cornmeal) in water or milk

gru·el·ing *or* **gru·el·ling** \'grü-ə-liŋ\ *adj* : requiring extreme effort : EXHAUSTING

grue·some \'grü-səm\ *adj* : causing horror or disgust : HORRIBLE — **grue·some·ly** *adv* — **grue·some·ness** *n*

gruff \'grəf\ *adj* **1** : rough or stern in manner, speech, or look ⟨a *gruff* reply⟩ **2** : being deep and harsh : HOARSE ⟨a *gruff* voice⟩ — **gruff·ly** *adv* — **gruff·ness** *n*

grum·ble \'grəm-bəl\ *vb* **grum·bled; grum·bling** \-b(ə-)liŋ\ **1** : to mutter in discontent **2** : ¹RUMBLE — **grumble** *n* — **grum·bler** \-b(ə-)lər\ *n* — **grum·bling·ly** \-b(ə-)liŋ-lē\ *adv*

grump \'grəmp\ *n* : GROUCH 2 — **grump·i·ly** \'grəm-pə-lē\ *adv* — **grump·i·ness** \-pē-nəs\ *n* — **grumpy** \-pē\ *adj*

grun·gy \'grən-jē\ *adj* **grun·gi·er; -est** : being in a shabby or dirty condition

grunt \'grənt\ *n* **1 a** : the deep short sound made by a hog **b** : a similar sound **2** : any of numerous marine fishes related to the snappers — **grunt** *vb* — **grunt·er** *n*

Gru·yère \grü-'ye(ə)r, grē-'(y)e(ə)r\ *n* : a firm cheese of Switzerland that has a nutty flavor [named for *Gruyère,* district in Switzerland where the cheese was first made]

gryphon *variant of* GRIFFIN

G suit *n* : a suit designed to counteract the effects of acceleration on an aviator or astronaut [*gravity suit*]

gua·ca·mo·le \,gwäk-ə-'mō-lē\ *n* : spiced mashed avocado that is often served as a spread or dip

gua·na·co \gwə-'näk-ō\ *n, pl* **-cos** : a South American mammal that has a soft thick light grayish brown coat and is related to the camels but lacks a hump

gua·nine \'gwän-,ēn\ *n* : a purine base that codes genetic information in DNA and RNA — compare ADENINE, CYTOSINE, THYMINE, URACIL

gua·no \'gwän-ō\ *n* : a substance composed chiefly of the excrement of seabirds or bats and used as a fertilizer

guanaco

¹**guar·an·tee** \,gar-ən-'tē, ,gär-\ *n* **1** : GUARANTOR **2** : an agreement by which a person or firm guarantees something **3** : something given as security : PLEDGE

²**guarantee** *vb* **-teed; -tee·ing 1** : to promise to answer for the debt, failure to perform, or faulty performance of another **2** : to promise that some condition holds or will be fulfilled ⟨*guarantee* a car against defects for one year⟩ ⟨*guaranteed* annual wage⟩ **3** : to give security : SECURE

guar·an·tor \,gar-ən-'to(ə)r, 'gar-ən-tər, ,gär-, 'gär-\ *n* : one that gives a guarantee

guar·an·ty \'gar-ən-tē, 'gär-\ *n, pl* **-ties 1** : ¹GUARANTEE 2 **2** : ¹GUARANTEE 3 — **guaranty** *vb*

¹**guard** \'gärd\ *n* **1** : an attitude or state of defense ⟨asked dad for money when his *guard* was down⟩ **2** : the act or duty of protecting or defending **3 a** : a person who guards or a group of persons who guard **b** *pl* : a body of troops whose duties include guarding a head of state **4 a**

: a football player who lines up next to the center **b** : either of two players stationed usually away from the basket in basketball **5** : a protective or safety device (as on a machine) — **off guard** : in an unprepared state — **on guard** : WATCHFUL, ALERT

²**guard** *vb* **1** : to protect from danger : DEFEND **2** : to watch over so as to restrict, control, or check ⟨*guard* a prisoner⟩ ⟨a closely *guarded* secret⟩ ⟨*guard* one's tongue⟩ **3** : to try to keep (an opponent) from scoring **4** : to be on guard : take precautions ⟨*guard* against infection⟩

guard cell *n* : one of two crescent-shaped cells that form the margin of a stoma in the epidermis of a leaf and serve to open and close it

guard·ed \'gärd-əd\ *adj* : CAUTIOUS, NONCOMMITTAL ⟨a *guarded* answer⟩ — **guard·ed·ly** *adv*

guard·house \'gärd-,haús\ *n* **1** : a building occupied by a guard or used as a headquarters by soldiers on guard duty **2** : a military jail

guard·i·an \'gärd-ē-ən\ *n* **1** : one that guards : CUSTODIAN **2** : one who legally has the care of a person or the property of another — **guard·i·an·ship** \-,ship\ *n*

guard·rail \'gär-,drāl\ *n* : a protective railing placed along dangerous areas (as of a road)

guard·room \'gär-,drüm, -,drúm\ *n* **1** : a room used by a military guard while on duty **2** : a room where military prisoners are kept

guards·man \'gärdz-mən\ *n* : a member of a national guard, coast guard, or similar military body

gua·va \'gwäv-ə\ *n* : the sweet acid yellow-skinned fruit of a shrubby tropical American tree of the myrtle family that is used especially for making jelly and jam; *also* : a tree that produces guavas and is widely grown in cultivation

gua·yu·le \(g)wī-'ü-lē\ *n* : a low shrubby plant related to the daisies that is found in Mexico and the southwestern U.S. and has been grown as a source of rubber

gu·ber·na·to·ri·al \,güb-ə(r)-nə-'tōr-ē-əl, ,gyüb-, -'tör-\ *adj* : of or relating to a governor

Guern·sey \'gərn-zē\ *n, pl* **Guernseys** : any of a breed of usually reddish brown and white dairy cattle that are larger than Jerseys and produce rich yellowish milk

Guernsey

guer·ril·la *or* **gue·ril·la** \gə-'ril-ə\ *n* : a member of a band of persons engaged in warfare not as part of a regular army but as an independent unit making surprise raids behind enemy lines [from Spanish *guerrilla,* literally, "small war," from *guerra* "war"] — **guerrilla** *adj*

guess \'ges\ *vb* **1** : to form an opinion from little or no evidence **2** : to solve correctly by or as if by chance ⟨we *guessed* the riddle⟩ **3** : BELIEVE 5, SUPPOSE ⟨I *guess* you're right⟩ — **guess** *n* — **guess·er** *n*

guess·work \-,wərk\ *n* : work performed or results gotten by guessing

guest \'gest\ *n* **1** : a person entertained in one's house **2** : a person to whom hospitality is given ⟨*guests* at a school banquet⟩ **3** : a customer at a hotel, motel, inn, or restaurant **4** : a usually well-known person who appears or performs on a program by invitation ⟨*guests* on a TV show⟩

guf·faw \(,)gə-'fò\ *n* : a loud burst of laughter — **guffaw** *vb*

\ə\ **abut**	\aú\ **out**	\i\ **tip**	\ó\ **saw**	\ú\ **foot**
\ər\ **further**	\ch\ **chin**	\ī\ **life**	\ói\ **coin**	\y\ **yet**
\a\ **mat**	\e\ **pet**	\j\ **job**	\th\ **thin**	\yü\ **few**
\ā\ **take**	\ē\ **easy**	\ŋ\ **sing**	\th\ **this**	\yú\ **cure**
\ä\ **cot, cart**	\g\ **go**	\ō\ **bone**	\ü\ **food**	\zh\ **vision**

guid·ance \\'gīd-ᵊn(t)s\\ *n* **1** : the act or process of guiding **2** : advice given to students to help them make educational or personal decisions **3** : the process of controlling the course (as of a missile) by built-in equipment ⟨*guidance* system⟩

¹guide \\'gīd\\ *n* **1 a** : one that leads or directs another on a course **b** : a person who shows and explains points of interest (as on a tour) **c** : something that provides guiding information ⟨a street *guide*⟩ **2** : a device for steadying or directing the motion of something

²guide *vb* **guid·ed; guid·ing** **1** : to act as a guide : CONDUCT ⟨*guide* a group on a tour⟩ **2 a** : MANAGE 1, DIRECT ⟨*guide* a boat through the rapids⟩ **b** : ²COUNSEL 1, INSTRUCT — **guid·able** \\'gīd-ə-bəl\\ *adj*

guide·book \\'gīd-,bùk\\ *n* : a book of information for travelers

guided missile *n* : a missile whose course may be changed during flight

guide dog *n* : a dog trained to lead the blind

guide·line \\'gīd-,līn\\ *n* **1** : a line by which one is guided **2** : an outline of standards for future policy or action

guide·post \\-,pōst\\ *n* **1** : a post (as at the fork of a road) with directions for travelers **2** : INDICATION 2, SIGN

guide word *n* : either of the terms at the head of a page of an alphabetical reference work (as a dictionary) indicating the alphabetically first and last entries on the page

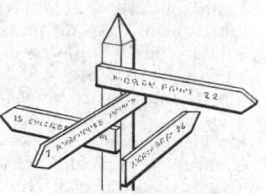

guidepost 1

gui·don \\'gīd-,än, -ᵊn\\ *n* : a small flag (as of a military unit)

guild *also* **gild** \\'gild\\ *n* : an association of persons with common interests or aims; *esp* : an association of merchants or craftsmen in the Middle Ages

guile \\'gī(ə)l\\ *n* : sly trickery : DUPLICITY — **guile·ful** \\-fəl\\ *adj*

guile·less \\'gī(ə)l-ləs\\ *adj* : not sly or tricky : INNOCENT, NAÏVE ⟨a *guileless* person⟩ ⟨a *guileless* smile⟩ — **guile·less·ly** *adv* — **guile·less·ness** *n*

guil·lo·tine \\'gil-ə-,tēn, ,gē-(y)ə-'tēn, 'gē-(y)ə-,tēn\\ *n* : a machine for cutting off a person's head by means of a heavy blade sliding in two upright grooved posts [named for Joseph *Guillotin* 1738–1814 French doctor and public official] — **guillotine** *vb*

guilt \\'gilt\\ *n* **1** : the fact of having done something wrong and especially something that is punishable by law **2** : the state of one who has done something wrong : BLAMEWORTHINESS **3** : a feeling of responsibility for wrongdoing — **guilt·less** \\-ləs\\ *adj*

guilty \\'gil-tē\\ *adj* **guilt·i·er; -est** **1** : having done wrong **2 a** : suggesting or involving guilt ⟨a *guilty* manner⟩ **b** : aware of or suffering from guilt ⟨a *guilty* conscience⟩ — **guilt·i·ly** \\-tə-lē\\ *adv* — **guilt·i·ness** \\-tē-nəs\\ *n*

guin·ea \\'gin-ē\\ *n* **1** : an English gold coin no longer issued worth 21 shillings **2** : a former unit of value equal to 21 shillings

guin·ea fowl \\'gin-ē-\\ *n* : a gray and white spotted African bird related to the pheasants that has a bare neck and head and is widely raised for food

guinea hen *n* : GUINEA FOWL; *esp* : a female guinea fowl

guinea pig *n* **1** : a small stocky rodent with short ears and a very short tail

guinea fowl

that is often kept as a pet and is used in biological research **2** : a person or thing experimented on

guise \\'gīz\\ *n* **1** : a form or style of dress : COSTUME ⟨in the *guise* of a shepherd⟩ **2** : outer or disguised appearance : SEMBLANCE ⟨swindled people under the *guise* of friendship⟩

gui·tar \\gə-'tär\\ *n* : a stringed instrument with a flat body, a long neck with frets, and usually six strings that are played with the fingers or with a pick [from French *guitare* "guitar," derived from Arabic *qītār* (same meaning)] — **gui·tar·ist** \\-əst\\ *n*

gulch \\'gəlch\\ *n* : RAVINE

gul·den \\'gül-dən, 'gùl-\\ *n, pl* **guldens** *or* **gulden** : the basic unit of money of the Netherlands until 2002

gulf \\'gəlf\\ *n* **1** : a part of an ocean or sea extending into the land **2** : a deep hollow in the earth : CHASM, ABYSS **3** : a difference between two people, groups, or things

¹gull \\'gəl\\ *n* : any of numerous mostly white or gray birds that have long wings and webbed feet and are typically found near water [Middle English *gull* "gull"; of Celtic origin]

²gull *vb* : to take advantage of : DECEIVE [from obsolete English *gull* "gullet"]

³gull *n* : a person easily deceived or cheated : DUPE

gul·let \\'gəl-ət\\ *n* **1 a** : the tube that leads from the back of the mouth to the stomach : ESOPHAGUS **b** : THROAT 1 **2** : a tubular structure of various protozoans (as a paramecium) that is used especially to take in food

¹gull

gull·ible \\'gəl-ə-bəl\\ *adj* : easily deceived or cheated — **gull·ibil·i·ty** \\,gəl-ə-'bil-ət-ē\\ *n* — **gull·ibly** \\'gəl-ə-blē\\ *adv*

gul·ly \\'gəl-ē\\ *n, pl* **gullies** : a trench worn in the earth by running water after rains — **gully** *vb*

gully erosion *n* : soil erosion produced by running water

gulp \\'gəlp\\ *vb* **1** : to swallow hurriedly or greedily or in one swallow **2** : to keep back as if by swallowing ⟨*gulp* down a sob⟩ **3** : to catch the breath as if in taking a long drink — **gulp** *n* — **gulp·er** *n*

¹gum \\'gəm\\ *n* : the tissue along the jaws of animals that surrounds the necks of the teeth [Old English *gōma* "roof of the mouth, palate"]

²gum *n* **1** : any of numerous complex sticky colloidal substances (as gum arabic) that are obtained from plants, harden on drying, and are either soluble in water or swell up in contact with water and that are used in preparing some drugs, for adhesives, as food thickeners, and in inks; *also* : any of various gummy plant substances including natural resins, rubber, and rubberlike substances **2** : a substance resembling a plant gum (as in stickiness) **3** : a tree that yields a gum **4** : CHEWING GUM [Middle English *gomme* "plant gum," from early French *gomme* (same meaning), from Latin *cummi, gummi* (same meaning), derived from Egyptian *qmyt* "plant gum"]

³gum *vb* **gummed; gum·ming** **1** : to smear, seal, or clog with or as if with gum **2** : to cause not to work properly ⟨*gum* up the works⟩

gum arabic *n* : a gum that can be dissolved in water, is obtained from several acacias, and is used especially in making adhesives, drugs, and candy

gum·bo \\'gəm-bō\\ *n, pl* **gumbos** **1 a** : OKRA **b** : a soup thickened with okra pods **2** : any of various silty soils that become very sticky when wet

gum·boil \\'gəm-,bòil\\ *n* : an abscess in the gums

gum·drop \-ˌdräp\ *n* : a candy made usually from corn syrup with gelatin or gum arabic and coated with sugar crystals

gum·my \ˈgəm-ē\ *adj* **gum·mi·er; -est** 1 : consisting of, containing, or covered with gum 2 : VISCOUS 1, STICKY — **gum·mi·ness** *n*

gump·tion \ˈgəm(p)-shən\ *n* : courageous or ambitious initiative ⟨lacked the *gumption* to try⟩

¹gun \ˈgən\ *n* 1 a : an artillery piece with a usually long barrel and firing shot or shells in a somewhat flattened curve b : a portable firearm (as a rifle or pistol) 2 a : a firing of a gun ⟨a 21-*gun* salute⟩ b : a signal marking a beginning or ending ⟨the opening *gun* of the campaign⟩ 3 : something suggesting a gun in shape or use ⟨a grease *gun*⟩ 4 : ²THROTTLE 1 — **gunned** \ˈgənd\ *adj*

²gun *vb* **gunned; gun·ning** 1 : to hunt or shoot with a gun ⟨*gunning* for rabbits⟩ 2 : to open up the throttle of so as to increase speed ⟨*gun* the engine⟩

gun·boat \ˈgən-ˌbōt\ *n* : a small lightly armed ship for use in shallow waters

gun·fight \-ˌfīt\ *n* : a fight fought with guns — **gun·fight·er** *n*

gun·fire \-ˌfī(ə)r\ *n* : the firing of guns

gung ho \ˈgəŋ-ˈhō\ *adj* : extremely enthusiastic

Word History Since the war was not going well for the U.S. in 1942, Marine Lt. Col. Evans F. Carlson needed something special to make his troops feel hopeful and excited. He was organizing the Marines' Second Raider Battalion in California and told his men their motto would be *gung ho*. This, he told them, was Chinese for "work together." Since there was a Chinese Industrial Cooperative Society known as *Gōnghé* and since *gōng* does mean "work," and *hé* does mean "join," what he said seemed to make sense. But *gōng* and *hé* cannot be put together in Chinese to mean "work together." The organization known as *Gōnghé* was, in full, *Zhōngguó Gōngyè Hézuò Shè*. The Chinese themselves shortened it to *Gōnghé* just as we abbreviate long names and titles in English. But in English *gung ho* stuck as a motto and went on to become an adjective meaning "extremely enthusiastic." [*Gung ho!* motto (thought to mean "work together") of a U.S. Marine battalion in World War II, from the Chinese (Beijing dialect) phrase *Zhōngguó Gōngyè Hézuò Shè* "Chinese Industrial Cooperative Society"]

gun·man \-mən\ *n* : a person armed with a gun; *esp* : an armed criminal

gun·ner \ˈgən-ər\ *n* 1 : one who operates or aims a gun 2 : one who hunts with a gun

gun·nery \ˈgən-(ə-)rē\ *n* : the use of guns

gunnery sergeant *n* : a noncommissioned officer in the marines with a rank just below that of master sergeant

gun·ny·sack \-ˌsak\ *n* : a sack made of a coarse heavy fabric (as burlap)

gun·point \ˈgən-ˌpȯint\ *n* : the muzzle of a gun — **at gunpoint** : under a threat of death by being shot

gun·pow·der \-ˌpau̇d-ər\ *n* : an explosive mixture used in guns and blasting

gun·ship \-ˌship\ *n* : an aircraft armed with rockets and machine guns for protection of ground troops or helicopters carrying them

gun·shot \-ˌshät\ *n* 1 : shot fired from a gun 2 : the range of a gun ⟨within *gunshot*⟩ 3 : the firing of a gun

gun–shy \-ˌshī\ *adj* 1 : afraid of loud noise (as that of a gun) 2 : being distrustful, afraid, or cautious

gun·sling·er \-ˌsliŋ-ər\ *n* : a person known for speed and skill in handling and shooting a gun especially in the American West

gun·smith \-ˌsmith\ *n* : one who makes or repairs firearms

gun·wale *also* **gun·nel** \ˈgən-ᵊl\ *n* : the upper edge of a ship's side

gup·py \ˈgəp-ē\ *n, pl* **guppies** : a small tropical minnow often kept in aquariums

gur·gle \ˈgər-gəl\ *vb* **gur·gled; gur·gling** \ˈgər-g(ə-)liŋ\ 1 : to flow in a broken bubbling current 2 : to make a sound like that of a gurgling liquid — **gurgle** *n*

gu·ru \gə-ˈrü, ˈgu̇(ə)r-ü\ *n* 1 : a personal religious teacher and spiritual guide in Hinduism 2 a : a person that is generally recognized as a leader or teacher b : a person with knowledge and expertise : EXPERT [from *gurū*, a word in Hindi (the major language in India) meaning "Hindu teacher or spiritual guide," derived from Sanskrit *guru* (adjective) "worthy of respect"]

¹gush \ˈgəsh\ *vb* 1 : to flow out or pour forth in great quantities or violently : SPOUT ⟨oil *gushed* from the new well⟩ 2 : to make an exaggerated display of affection or enthusiasm ⟨*gushed* about their favorite rock star⟩

²gush *n* 1 : a sudden outpouring 2 : an exaggerated display of affection or enthusiasm

gush·er \ˈgəsh-ər\ *n* : one that gushes; *esp* : an oil well with a very plentiful natural flow

gushy \ˈgəsh-ē\ *adj* **gush·i·er; -est** : expressing much sentimentality — **gush·i·ly** \ˈgəsh-ə-lē\ *adv* — **gush·i·ness** \ˈgəsh-ē-nəs\

gus·set \ˈgəs-ət\ *n* : a usually triangular or diamond-shaped insert (as on a bridge) to give width or strength

gust \ˈgəst\ *n* 1 : a sudden brief rush of wind 2 : a sudden outburst ⟨a *gust* of anger⟩ — **gusty** \ˈgəs-tē\ *adj*

gus·ta·to·ry \ˈgəs-tə-ˌtōr-ē, -ˌtȯr-\ *adj* : relating to, associated with, or being the sense or sensation of taste

gus·to \ˈgəs-tō\ *n* : keen enjoyment or appreciation ⟨eat with *gusto*⟩

¹gut \ˈgət\ *n* 1 a : ENTRAILS, VISCERA — usually used in plural b : the alimentary canal or part of it (as the intestine or stomach) c : ABDOMEN 1, BELLY 2 *pl* : the inner essential parts 3 *pl* : COURAGE

²gut *vb* **gut·ted; gut·ting** 1 : to remove the entrails from ⟨scale and *gut* a fish⟩ 2 : to destroy the inside of ⟨fire *gutted* the building⟩

gutsy \ˈgət-sē\ *adj* **guts·i·er; -est** : aggressively tough : COURAGEOUS ⟨a *gutsy* decision⟩ ⟨a *gutsy* hockey player⟩ — **guts·i·ness** *n*

¹gut·ter \ˈgət-ər\ *n* 1 a : a trough along the eaves of a house to catch and carry off water b : a low area (as at a roadside) to carry off surface water 2 : a narrow channel or groove

²gutter *vb* 1 : to form gutters in 2 a : to flow in small streams b : to melt away by having wax stream down in channels ⟨a *guttering* candle⟩ 3 : to flicker in a draft

gut·tur·al \ˈgət-ə-rəl\ *adj* 1 : formed or pronounced in the throat ⟨*guttural* sounds⟩ 2 : formed with the back of the tongue touching or near the palate — **guttural** *n* — **gut·tur·al·ly** \-rə-lē\ *adv*

¹guy \ˈgī\ *n* : a rope, chain, rod, or wire attached to something as a brace or guide [probably from Dutch *gei* "a rope used to control a sail"]

²guy *vb* **guyed; guy·ing** : to steady or strengthen with a guy

³guy *n* : FELLOW 4a, b

Word History November 5 is a holiday in England, and people celebrate it by setting off fireworks and lighting

G ¹gutter 1a

bonfires. Human likenesses made of tattered clothes stuffed with hay or rags are burned on the bonfires. The holiday is called Guy Fawkes Day for a 17th century man who played a leading role in a plot to blow up the British Parliament buildings. Fawkes managed to hide 20 barrels of gunpowder in the cellars of the buildings. However, the plot was discovered before Fawkes could carry out his plans. He was seized and later put to death. The human likenesses burned to celebrate the failure of Guy Fawkes's plot came to be called *guys*. The use of the word was extended to similar figures and then to a person of strange appearance or dress. In the U.S. the word came to mean simply "man" or "fellow" and in time came to be used for a person of either sex. [named for *Guy* Fawkes 1570–1606 English criminal]

guz·zle \'gəz-əl\ *vb* **guz·zled; guz·zling** \-(ə-)liŋ\ 1 : to drink greedily ⟨*guzzled* soft drinks⟩ 2 : to use up : CON-SUME ⟨automobiles *guzzling* a lot of gasoline⟩ — **guz·zler** \-(ə-)lər\ *n*

gybe *variant of* 1JIBE

gym \'jim\ *n* 1 : GYMNASIUM 2 : PHYSICAL EDUCATION

gym·na·si·um \jim-'nā-zē-əm, -zhəm\ *n, pl* **-si·ums** *or* **-sia** \-zē-ə, -zhə\ : a room or building for sports activities [from Latin *gymnasium* "exercise ground, school," from Greek *gymnasion* (same meaning), from *gymnazein* "to exercise naked," from *gymnos* "naked"]

gym·nast \'jim-ˌnast, -nəst\ *n* : a person who is skilled in gymnastics

gym·nas·tics \jim-'nas-tiks\ *n sing or pl* : physical exer-cises for developing skill, strength, and control in the use of the body; *also* : a sport in which such exercises are performed — **gym·nas·tic** \-tik\ *adj*

gym·no·sperm \'jim-nə-ˌspərm\ *n* : any of a group of woody nonflowering vascular plants (as pines, yews, and gingkos) that produce naked seeds not enclosed in a true fruit

gy·ne·col·o·gist \ˌgīn-i-'käl-ə-jəst, ˌjin-\ *n* : a physician who specializes in gynecology

gy·ne·col·o·gy \ˌgīn-i-'käl-ə-jē, ˌjin-\ *n* : a branch of medi-cine that is concerned with the diseases and routine med-ical care of the reproductive system of women

1**gyp** \'jip\ *n* 1 : 2CHEAT 2, SWINDLER 2 : 2SWINDLE, FRAUD

2**gyp** *vb* **gypped; gyp·ping** : 1CHEAT 1, SWINDLE

gyp·sum \'jip-səm\ *n* : a colorless mineral that consists of calcium sulfate occurring in crystals or masses and that is used especially as a soil improver and in making plaster of paris

Gyp·sy \'jip-sē\ *n, pl* **Gypsies** 1 : one of a people coming originally from India to Europe in the 14th or 15th cen-tury and living and maintaining a wandering way of life 2 : ROMANY 2 [a shortened and altered form of *Egyptian;* so called because Gypsies were once believed to have come from Egypt]

gypsy moth *n* : an Old World moth introduced about 1869 into the U.S. and having a grayish hairy caterpillar that is marked with spots and does great damage to trees by eating the leaves

gy·rate \'jī-ˌrāt\ *vb* **gy·rat·ed; gy·rat·ing** 1 : to rotate around a point or axis 2 : 1SPIN 3, WHIRL — **gy·ra·tion** \jī-'rā-shən\ *n* — **gy·ra·tion·al** \-shnəl, -shən-ᵊl\ *adj*

gyr·fal·con \'jər-ˌfal-kən, -ˌfȯl-; -ˌfȯl-kən\ *n* : an arctic fal-con that occurs in shades of white, gray, or dark brown and is the largest of all falcons

1**gy·ro** \'jī-rō\ *n, pl* **gyros** 1 : GYROCOMPASS 2 : GYRO-SCOPE

2**gy·ro** \'yē-ˌrō, 'zhir-ō\ *n, pl* **gyros** : a sandwich especially of lamb and beef, tomato, onion, and yogurt sauce on pita bread [from Greek *gyros* "turn," so called from the rota-tion of the meat on a spit]

gy·ro·com·pass \'jī-rō-ˌkəm-pəs *also* -ˌkäm-\ *n* : a com-pass consisting of a constantly spinning gyroscope whose spin axis is always parallel to the earth's axis of rotation so that the compass always points to true north

gy·ro·scope \'jī-rə-ˌskōp\ *n* : a wheel or disk mounted to spin rapidly about an axis that is free to turn in various directions — **gy·ro·scop·ic** \ˌjī-rə-'skäp-ik\ *adj*

H

h \'āch\ *n, often cap* : the eighth letter of the English alpha-bet

ha *or* **hah** \'hä\ *interj* — used to express surprise, joy, or victory

Ha·ba·cuc \'hab-ə-ˌkək, hə-'bak-ək\ *n* : HABAKKUK

Hab·ak·kuk \'hab-ə-ˌkək, hə-'bak-ək\ *n* — see BIBLE table

ha·be·as cor·pus \ˌhā-bē-ə-'skȯr-pəs\ *n* 1 : a legal order for an inquiry to determine whether a person has been lawfully imprisoned 2 : the right of a citizen to obtain a writ of habeas corpus as a protection against illegal im-prisonment [derived from the Latin phrase, meaning liter-ally "you should have the body," used as the opening words of a legal order to jailers to bring the prisoner to court]

hab·er·dash·er \'hab-ə(r)-ˌdash-ər\ *n* : a dealer in men's clothing and accessories

hab·er·dash·ery \'hab-ə(r)-ˌdash-(ə-)rē\ *n, pl* **-er·ies** 1 : goods sold by a haberdasher 2 : a haberdasher's shop

ha·bil·i·ment \hə-'bil-ə-mənt\ *n* : CLOTHING 1 — usually used in plural

hab·it \'hab-ət\ *n* 1 : a costume characteristic of an oc-cupation, rank, or function ⟨her riding *habit*⟩ ⟨a nun's *habit*⟩ 2 : a usual manner of behavior or thinking ⟨his *habit* of taking a morning walk⟩ 3 : a way of behaving that has become fixed by being repeated often — com-pare 1REFLEX 1 4 : characteristic way of growing or oc-curring ⟨elms have a spreading *habit*⟩

synonyms HABIT, PRACTICE, USAGE, CUSTOM mean a way of acting that has become fixed through repetition. HABIT suggests doing something without thinking about it because one has done it so often ⟨had a *habit* of tap-ping his fingers⟩. PRACTICE suggests an act performed regularly and usually by choice ⟨our *practice* is to go to the park every Sunday⟩. USAGE suggests a practice fol-lowed by so many that it becomes the accepted practice of society ⟨what a word means in common *usage*⟩. CUS-TOM applies to an act so long and continuously associ-ated with an individual or group that in effect it becomes an unofficial rule ⟨the *custom* of many is to eat turkey on Thanksgiving⟩.

hab·it·able \'hab-ət-ə-bəl\ *adj* : suitable or fit to live in ⟨a *habitable* cave⟩ — **hab·it·abil·i·ty** \ˌhab-ət-ə-'bil-ət-ē\ *n*

hab·i·tant \'hab-ət-ənt\ *n* : INHABITANT, RESIDENT

hab·i·tat \'hab-ə-ˌtat\ *n* : the place or type of place where a plant or animal naturally or normally lives or grows

hab·i·ta·tion \ˌhab-ə-'tā-shən\ *n* 1 : the act of inhabiting : OCCUPANCY 2 : a dwelling place : RESIDENCE

hab·it–form·ing \'hab-ət-ˌfȯr-miŋ\ *adj* : causing an addic-tion ⟨heroin is a *habit-forming* drug⟩

ha·bit·u·al \hə-'bich-(ə-)wəl, ha-\ *adj* 1 : being or done by habit ⟨*habitual* tardiness⟩ 2 : doing or acting out of hab-it ⟨*habitual* talkers⟩ 3 : done, followed, or used often or regularly ⟨took our *habitual* path⟩ — **ha·bit·u·al·ly** \-ē\ *adv* — **ha·bit·u·al·ness** *n*

ha·bit·u·ate \hə-'bich-ə-,wāt, ha-\ *vb* **-at·ed; -at·ing** : to make used to something — **ha·bit·u·a·tion** \-,bich-ə-'wā-shən\ *n*

ha·chure \ha-'shú(ə)r\ *n* : a short line used for shading or especially to show different levels or slopes on a map

ha·ci·en·da \,(h)äs-ē-'en-də\ *n* : a large estate in Spanish-speaking countries

¹hack \'hak\ *vb* **1** : to cut or sever with repeated irregular or unskillful blows **2** : to cough in a short dry manner **3 a** : to write computer programs for enjoyment **b** : to gain access to a computer illegally [Old English *-haccian* "to cut with repeated blows"]

²hack *n* **1** : ¹NICK 1, NOTCH **2** : a short dry cough

³hack *n* **1 a** : a horse that can be hired for use by the public **b** : a horse used in all kinds of work **c** : a worn-out horse **d** : a light saddle horse **2 a** : ¹HACKNEY 2 **b** : TAXICAB **c** : a driver of a taxicab **3 a** : a writer who works mainly for reward **b** : one who serves a cause merely for reward ⟨political *hacks*⟩ **c** : HACKER 2 [a shortened form of *hackney*]

⁴hack *adj* **1** : working for hire ⟨a *hack* writer⟩ **2** : done by or characteristic of a hack ⟨*hack* writing⟩

⁵hack *vb* **1** : to ride or drive at an ordinary pace or over the roads rather than across country **2** : to operate a taxicab

hack·ber·ry \'hak-,ber-ē\ *n* **1** : any of a genus of trees and shrubs that are related to the elms and have small often edible berries **2** : the wood of a hackberry

hack·er \'hak-ər\ *n* **1** : one that hacks **2** : a person who is unskilled at a particular activity **3** : an expert at programming and solving problems with a computer **4** : a person who illegally gains access to a computer system

hack·le \'hak-əl\ *n* **1** : a comb for smoothing fibers (as flax or hemp) **2** : one of the long narrow feathers on the neck or lower back of a bird **3** : hairs along the neck and back especially of a dog that can be made to stand up

¹hack·ney \'hak-nē\ *n, pl* **hackneys** **1** : any of a breed of compact high-stepping English horses **2** : a carriage or automobile kept for hire

²hackney *adj* **1** : kept for public hire **2** : HACKNEYED

hack·neyed \'hak-nēd\ *adj* : worn out from too much use : COMMONPLACE ⟨a *hackneyed* expression⟩

hack·saw \'hak-,sò\ *n* : a saw used for cutting hard materials (as metal) that consists of a frame holding a blade with small teeth — **hacksaw** *vb*

hack·work \'hak-,wərk\ *n* : literary, artistic, or professional work done on order usually according to a set standard

had *past and past participle of* HAVE

had·dock \'had-ək\ *n, pl* **haddock** *also* **haddocks** : an important food fish of the Atlantic that is usually smaller than the related common cod

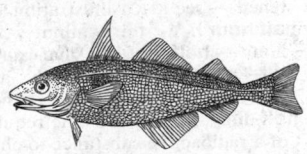

haddock

Ha·de·an \'hā-,dē-ən, hā-'dē-ən\ *adj* : of, relating to, or being the part of the earth's history that came before the formation of the first rocks — see GEOLOGIC TIME table [from *Hades*] — **Hadean** *n*

ha·des \'hād-(,)ēz\ *n* : HELL 1 [Greek *Haidēs*, god of the underworld, abode of the dead in Greek mythology]

hadj *variant of* HAJJ

hadn't \'had-²nt\ : had not

hadst \(')hadst, (h)ədst\ *archaic past 2nd singular of* HAVE

hae \(')hā\ *chiefly Scottish variant of* HAVE

haf·ni·um \'haf-nē-əm\ *n* : a gray metallic element that is useful because of its ready absorption of neutrons — see ELEMENT table

haft \'haft\ *n* : the handle of a weapon or tool

hag \'hag\ *n* **1** : an ugly or evil old woman **2** : WITCH 1

Hag·gai \'hag-ē-,ī, 'hag-,ī\ *n* — see BIBLE table

hag·gard \'hag-ərd\ *adj* : very thin especially from great hunger, worry, or pain

hag·gle \'hag-əl\ *vb* **hag·gled; hag·gling** \-(ə-)liŋ\ : to dispute or argue especially in bargaining — **haggle** *n* — **hag·gler** \-(ə-)lər\ *n*

Hag·i·og·ra·pha \,hag-ē-'äg-rə-fə, ,hā-jē-\ *n sing or pl* : WRITINGS

hah *variant of* HA

hai·ku \'hī-(,)kü\ *n, pl* **haiku** : a verse form of Japanese origin having three lines containing five, seven, and five syllables respectively; *also* : a poem written in this form

¹hail \'hā(ə)l\ *n* **1** : small lumps of ice that fall from clouds sometimes during thunderstorms **2** : something that gives the effect of falling hail ⟨a *hail* of bullets⟩ [Old English *hægl* "lumps of ice, hail"]

²hail *vb* **1** : to fall as hail **2** : to pour down like hail

³hail *interj* **1** — used to express enthusiastic approval **2** *archaic* — used as a greeting [Middle English *hail* (an interjection of approval or greeting), derived from early Norse *heill* "healthy" — related to ¹HALE, WASSAIL]

⁴hail *vb* **1 a** : GREET 1 **b** : to greet with enthusiastic approval : ACCLAIM ⟨*hailed* them as heroes⟩ **2** : to summon by calling ⟨*hail* a taxi⟩ **3** : to call out to ⟨*hail* a passing ship⟩ — **hail from** : to come from ⟨he *hails from* New York⟩

⁵hail *n* **1** : an act or instance of hailing **2** : hearing distance ⟨stayed within *hail*⟩

Hail Mary \-'me(ə)r-ē, -'ma(ə)r-ē, -'mä-rē\ *n* : a Roman Catholic prayer to the Virgin Mary

hail·stone \'hā(ə)l-,stōn\ *n* : a small lump of hail

hail·storm \-,stó(ə)rm\ *n* : a storm accompanied by hail

hair \'ha(ə)r, 'he(ə)r\ *n* **1 a** : a slender threadlike growth from the skin of an animal; *esp* : one that usually contains coloring and forms part of the characteristic coat of a mammal **b** : a covering or growth of hairs of an animal or a body part **2** : a tiny distance or amount ⟨won by a *hair*⟩ **3** : a threadlike structure that resembles hair ⟨leaf *hairs*⟩ — **haired** \'ha(ə)rd, 'he(ə)rd\ *adj* — **hair·less** \'ha(ə)r-ləs, 'he(ə)r-\ *adj* — **hair·like** \-,līk\ *adj* — **in one's hair**

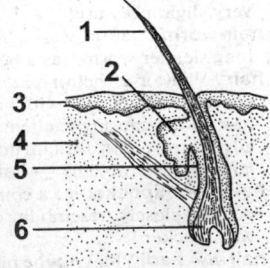

hair 1a: *1* shaft, *2* sebaceous gland, *3* epidermis, *4* dermis, *5* follicle, *6* root

: annoyingly always in one's presence ⟨can't work with you *in my hair* all day⟩ — **out of one's hair** : out of one's way ⟨stayed *out of his hair* while he made dinner⟩

hair·breadth \'ha(ə)r-,bretth, 'he(ə)r-, -,bredth\ *or* **hairs·breadth** \'ha(ə)rz-, 'he(ə)rz-\ *n* : a very small distance or margin — **hairbreadth** *adj*

hair·brush \'ha(ə)r-,brəsh, 'he(ə)r-\ *n* : a brush for the hair

hair·cloth \-,klòth\ *n* : any of various stiff wiry fabrics especially of horsehair or camel hair used for upholstery or stiffening in garments

hair·cut \-,kət\ *n* **1** : the act or process of cutting and shaping the hair **2** : HAIRDO — **hair·cut·ter** \-,kət-ər\ *n* — **hair·cut·ting** \-,kət-iŋ\ *n*

hair·do \-,dü\ *n, pl* **hairdos** : a way of dressing a person's hair : COIFFURE ⟨the very latest in *hairdos*⟩

\ə\ **abut**	\aú\ **out**	\i\ **tip**	\ò\ **saw**	\ù\ **foot**
\ər\ **further**	\ch\ **chin**	\ī\ **life**	\òi\ **coin**	\y\ **yet**
\a\ **mat**	\e\ **pet**	\j\ **job**	\th\ **thin**	\yü\ **few**
\ā\ **take**	\ē\ **easy**	\ŋ\ **sing**	\th\ **this**	\yù\ **cure**
\ä\ **cot, cart**	\g\ **go**	\ō\ **bone**	\ü\ **food**	\zh\ **vision**

hair·dress·er \-,dres-ər\ *n* : a person who dresses or cuts hair — **hair·dress·ing** \-,dres-iŋ\ *n*

hair follicle *n* : the tube-shaped sheath surrounding the lower part of a hair shaft

hair·line \'ha(ə)r-,līn, 'he(ə)r-\ *n* **1 a** : a very slender line **b** : a very thin crack on a surface ⟨a *hairline* bone fracture⟩ **2** : the outline of the hair on the head and especially on the forehead — **hair·line** *adj*

hair·net \-,net\ *n* : a net worn over the hair to keep it in place

hair·pin \-,pin\ *n* **1** : a U-shaped pin to hold the hair in place **2** : something shaped like a hairpin; *esp* : an extremely sharp turn in a road — **hairpin** *adj*

hair–rais·ing \-,rā-ziŋ\ *adj* : very frightening or exciting ⟨a *hair-raising* story⟩ — **hair–rais·ing·ly** \-ziŋ-lē\ *adv*

hair seal *n* : any of a family of seals with hairy coats and no ears on the outside of the head — called also *earless seal, true seal*

hair·split·ter \'ha(ə)r-,split-ər\ *n* : a person who argues about differences too small to be important — **hair·split·ting** \-,split-iŋ\ *adj or n*

hair spray *n* : a liquid sprayed on the hair to keep it in place

hair·spring \-,spriŋ\ *n* : a slender coiled spring that regulates the motion of the balance wheel in a timepiece

hair·streak \-,strēk\ *n* : any of various small butterflies with hairlike tails sticking out from the hind wings

hair·style \-,stī(ə)l\ *n* : HAIRDO

hair·styl·ist \-,stī-list\ *n* : HAIRDRESSER — **hair·styl·ing** \-,stī-liŋ\ *n*

hair–trig·ger \-,trig-ər\ *adj* : immediately responsive : ¹QUICK 2c ⟨a *hair-trigger* temper⟩ [from *hair trigger*, a trigger adjusted so as to permit a firearm to be fired with very slight pressure]

hair·worm \'ha(ə)r-,wərm, 'he(ə)r-\ *n* : any of various very long slender worms (as a horsehair worm)

hairy \'ha(ə)r-ē, 'he(ə)r-\ *adj* **hair·i·er; -est 1** : bearing or covered with or as if with hair **2** : made of or resembling hair **3 a** : causing excitement (as from danger) ⟨a *hairy* adventure⟩ **b** : difficult to deal with or understand ⟨a *hairy* math problem⟩ — **hair·i·ness** *n*

hairy woodpecker *n* : a common North American woodpecker closely resembling but larger than the downy woodpecker

hajj *also* **hadj** \'haj\ *n* : the pilgrimage to Mecca prescribed as a religious duty for Muslims

hake \'hāk\ *n* : any of several marine food fishes related to the cod

ha·lal \hə-'läl\ *adj* **1** : accepted by Islamic law; *esp* : fit for eating under Islamic law ⟨*halal* foods⟩ **2** : selling or serving food fit for eating under Islamic law ⟨a *halal* restaurant⟩ [from Arabic *ḥalāl* "permissible"]

hal·berd \'hal-bərd, 'hȯl-\ *also* **hal·bert** \-bərt\ *n* : a long=handled weapon used both as a spear and as a battle-ax especially in the 15th and 16th centuries

hal·berd·ier \,hal-bər-'di(ə)r, ,hȯl-\ *n* : a person armed with a halberd

¹hal·cy·on \'hal-sē-ən\ *n* **1** : a bird identified with the kingfisher and believed in ancient legend to nest at sea in December and calm the waves **2** : KINGFISHER

Word History According to ancient legend, fourteen days of good weather occurred every year around December 22. This time of clear skies and calm seas was thought to be the result of a magical bird's concern for her nest. The legend explained that the female kingfisher built a floating nest on the sea during this period. She calmed the waves and winds to keep her nest safe. The Greek name for the kingfisher was *halkyōn*. English borrowed the Latin spelling of the bird's name, and today we call any quiet, peaceful period *halcyon days*. [Middle English *alceon* "kingfisher," from Latin *halcyon* (same

meaning), from Greek *halkyōn* "legendary bird that builds a nest at sea"]

²halcyon *adj* : ³CALM 2, PEACEFUL ⟨*halcyon* days⟩

¹hale \'hā(ə)l\ *adj* : ¹SOUND 1a, HEALTHY ⟨grandmother was still *hale* and hearty at eighty⟩ [partly from Middle English *hale* "healthy, unhurt," from Old English *hāl* (same meaning) and partly from Middle English *hail* (an interjection of approval or greeting), derived from early Norse *heill* "healthy" — related to ³HAIL, HEALTH, WASSAIL, WHOLE]

²hale *vb* **haled; hal·ing 1** : ¹HAUL 1, PULL **2** : to force to go ⟨*haled* them into court⟩ [Middle English *halen* "to pull," from early French *haler* (same meaning); of Germanic origin — related to HAUL]

¹half \'haf, 'håf\ *n, pl* **halves** \'havz, 'håvz\ **1** : one of two equal or nearly equal parts that make up something ⟨*half* of an apple⟩ **2** : half an hour ⟨*half* past ten⟩ **3** : one of a pair; *esp* : one of the two equal periods that make up the playing time of some games (as football) — **in half** : into two halves

²half *adj* **1** : being one of two halves ⟨a *half* sheet of paper⟩ **2** : of half the usual size or extent ⟨a *half* smile⟩

³half *adv* **1 a** : to the extent of half ⟨*half* full⟩ **b** : to some degree : not completely ⟨*half* persuaded⟩ **2** : by any means : AT ALL ⟨the song wasn't *half* bad⟩

half·back \'haf-,bak, 'håf-\ *n* **1** : a football back who lines up toward the right or left side of the formation **2** : a player positioned behind the forward line in some games (as soccer or field hockey)

half–baked \-'bākt\ *adj* **1 a** : poorly developed or carried out ⟨a *half-baked* plan⟩ **b** : lacking in judgment or common sense ⟨*half-baked* ideas⟩ **2** : imperfectly baked : UNDERDONE

half–breed \-,brēd\ *n, often offensive* : a person who has parents of different races; *esp* : a person who has an American Indian parent and a white parent — **half–breed** *adj, often offensive*

half brother *n* : a brother by one parent only

half–caste \'haf-,kast, 'håf-\ *n, often offensive* : the offspring of parents of different races — **half–caste** *adj, often offensive*

half–cocked \-'käkt\ *adj* : lacking preparation or planning ⟨went off *half-cocked*⟩

half–dol·lar \-'däl-ər\ *n* **1** : a coin representing one half of a dollar **2** : the sum of fifty cents

half·heart·ed \-'härt-əd\ *adj* : lacking spirit or interest — **half·heart·ed·ly** *adv* — **half·heart·ed·ness** *n*

half hitch *n* : a simple knot so made as to be easily unfastened — see KNOT illustration

half hour *n* **1** : thirty minutes **2** : the middle point of an hour — **half–hour·ly** \'haf-'au̇(ə)r-lē, 'håf-\ *adv or adj*

half–knot \'haf-,nät, 'håf-\ *n* : a knot joining the ends of two cords and used in tying other knots

half–life \-,līf\ *n* : the time required for half of the atoms of a radioactive substance to change composition

half line *n* : a straight line extending from a point in one direction only

half–mast \'haf-,mast, 'håf-\ *n* : a point about halfway down below the top of a mast or staff ⟨flags hanging at *half-mast*⟩

half–moon \-,mün\ *n* : the moon when half its disk appears lighted

half note *n* : a musical note equal in time to ½ of a whole note

half·pen·ny \'hāp-(ə-)nē, *U.S. also* 'haf-,pen-ē, 'håf-\ *n, pl* **half·pence** \'hā-pən(t)s, *U.S. also* 'haf-,pen(t)s, 'håf-\ *or* **halfpennies** : a former British coin representing one half of a penny

half plane *n* : the part of a plane on one side of an indefinitely long straight line drawn in the plane

half rest *n* : a musical rest equal in time to a half note

half sister *n* : a sister by one parent only

half sole *n* : a shoe sole extending from the shank forward

half step *n* : the pitch interval between any two adjacent tones on a keyboard instrument — called also *semitone*

half·time \'haf-₁tīm, 'hȧf-\ *n* : an intermission marking the completion of half of a game (as in football)

half·tone \'haf-₁tōn, 'hȧf-\ *n* : a medium tint or tone in a painting, engraving, or photograph

half–track \-₁trak\ *n* **1** : an endless-chain track used in place of a rear wheel on a heavy-duty vehicle **2** : a motor vehicle moved by half-tracks

half–truth \-₁trüth\ *n* : a statement that is only partly true; *esp* : one that deliberately mixes truth and falsehood

half·way \-'wā\ *adj* **1** : midway between two points ⟨stop at the *halfway* mark⟩ **2** : PARTIAL **3** ⟨*halfway* measures⟩ — **halfway** *adv*

halfway house *n* : a place that provides living quarters and usually counseling to persons who have left an institution (as a prison or mental hospital) but are not ready to live in the community

half–wit \'haf-₁wit, 'hȧf-\ *n* : a foolish or unintelligent person — **half–wit·ted** \-'wit-əd\ *adj*

hal·i·but \'hal-ə-bət, 'häl-\ *n, pl* **halibut** *also* **halibuts** : either of two marine food fishes of the Atlantic or Pacific oceans that are the largest flatfishes reaching several hundred pounds

> ***Word History*** Among the different kinds of fish found in the world's oceans is a group called the flatfish. Flatfish are well named, for they have flattened bodies with both eyes on the upper side of the head. In Middle English the word for flatfish was *butte.* Many of the flatfish are good to eat, and the largest of the flatfish got its name because it was popular as food. During the Middle Ages fish was often eaten on holy days in place of meat. The most popular fish for the holy days was the largest variety of flatfish, or "butte." Thus, this particular fish came to be called in Middle English *halybutte,* meaning literally "holy flatfish," from *haly,* a form of *holy,* and *butte.* In Modern English the spelling has been changed to *halibut.* [Middle English *halybutte,* literally "holy flatfish," from *haly* "holy" and *butte* "flatfish"; so called from the fact it was regularly eaten on holy days]

hal·ite \'hal-₁īt, 'hā-₁līt\ *n* : ROCK SALT

hall \'hȯl\ *n* **1 a** : a large or impressive residence or public building ⟨symphony *hall*⟩ **b** : one of the buildings of a college or university ⟨Science *Hall*⟩ ⟨residence *halls*⟩ **2 a** : the entrance room of a building : LOBBY **b** : a corridor or passage in a building **3** : a large room for assembly : AUDITORIUM **4** : a place used for public entertainment

¹hal·le·lu·jah \₁hal-ə-'lü-yə\ *interj* — used to express praise, joy, or thanks

²hallelujah *n* : a shout or song of praise or thanksgiving

hall·mark \'hȯl-₁märk\ *n* **1** : an official mark stamped on gold and silver articles in England to certify their purity **2** : a distinguishing characteristic or feature ⟨bears the *hallmarks* of genius⟩ [named for Goldsmith's *Hall* in London, England, where gold and silver articles formerly were tested for purity and stamped] — **hallmark** *vb*

hal·low \'hal-ō\ *vb* **1** : to make holy or set apart for holy use : CONSECRATE **2** : to respect greatly : VENERATE — **hal·lowed** \-'hal-ōd, *in the Lord's Prayer also* 'hal-ə-wəd\ *adj*

Hal·low·een \₁hal-ə-'wēn, ₁häl-\ *n* : October 31 celebrated especially by wearing costumes, trick-or-treating, and displaying jack-o'-lanterns

> ***Word History*** Modern-day Christians know the first of November as All Saints' Day. In the Middle Ages it was called All Hallow Day. This was a hallowed or holy day celebrated in honor of all the saints in heaven. Since November 1 was a special holy day with a special name, the day before it had a special name as well. October 31 was called All Hallow Eve or All Hallow Even. The words *eve* and *even* were used both for the evening and the day before a special day. This name was sometimes written *All Hallow E'en* and later shortened to *Halloween.* [an altered form of *All Hallow Even,* the eve of All Saints' Day]

hal·lu·ci·nate \hə-'lüs-ə-₁nāt\ *vb* **-nat·ed; -nat·ing** : to have hallucinations or experience as a hallucination

hal·lu·ci·na·tion \hə-₁lüs-ə-'nā-shən\ *n* : the awareness of something (as a visual image, a sound, or a smell) that seems to be experienced through one of the senses but is not real, cannot be sensed by someone else, and is usually the result of mental disorder or the effect of a drug; *also* : something of which one is aware but which is not real

hal·lu·ci·na·to·ry \hə-'lü-sə-nə-₁tōr-ē, -₁tȯr-\ *adj* **1** : tending to produce hallucinations **2** : resembling, involving, or being a hallucination

hal·lu·ci·no·gen \hə-'lü-sə-nə-jən\ *n* : a drug that causes hallucinations — **hal·lu·ci·no·gen·ic** \-₁lü-sə-nə-'jen-ik\ *adj*

hall·way \'hȯl-₁wā\ *n* **1** : an entrance hall **2** : CORRIDOR 1

ha·lo \'hā-lō\ *n, pl* **halos** *or* **haloes** **1** : a circle of light around the sun or moon caused by the presence of tiny ice crystals in the air **2 a** : NIMBUS 1 **b** : NIMBUS 2 **3** : the atmosphere of glory or sentiment surrounding a person or thing considered perfect

¹hal·o·gen \'hal-ə-jən\ *n* : any of the elements fluorine, chlorine, bromine, iodine, and astatine

²halogen *adj* : containing, using, or being a halogen ⟨a *halogen* lamp⟩

¹halt \'hȯlt\ *adj* : ¹LAME 1a [Old English *healt* "lame"]

²halt *vb* **1** : ¹LIMP 1 **2** : to move unsteadily

³halt *n* : the ending of movement, progress, or action ⟨call a *halt*⟩ [from German *halt* "stop," derived from earlier *halten* "to hold"]

⁴halt *vb* **1** : to stop marching or journeying **2** : to bring to a stop : END

hal·ter \'hȯl-tər\ *n* **1 a** : a rope or strap for leading or tying an animal **b** : a set of straps enclosing an animal's head to which a lead may be attached **2** : a rope for hanging criminals : NOOSE **3** : a woman's blouse or top that is held in place by straps around the neck and across the back and that leaves the back, arms, and midriff bare — **halter** *vb*

hal·tere \'hȯl-₁ti(ə)r, 'hal-\ *n, pl* **hal·teres** \hȯl-'ti(ə)r-(₁)ēz, 'hȯl-₁ti(ə)rz\ : one of a pair of club-shaped organs that are the modified second pair of wings of a two-winged fly and serve to maintain balance in flight

halter 1b

halt·ing \'hȯl-tiŋ\ *adj* : being unsure or hesitant ⟨spoke in a *halting* manner⟩ — **halt·ing·ly** *adv*

halve \'hav, 'hȧv\ *vb* **halved; halv·ing** **1** : to divide into two halves **2** : to reduce to one half ⟨*halving* the cost⟩

halves *plural of* HALF

hal·yard \'hal-yərd\ *n* : a rope or tackle for raising and lowering (as a sail)

¹ham \'ham\ *n* **1** : a buttock with its associated thigh — usually used in plural **2** : a cut of meat consisting of a thigh; *esp* : one from a hog **3 a** : an unskillful but showy

\ə\ abut	\au̇\ out	\i\ tip	\ȯ\ saw	\u̇\ foot
\ər\ further	\ch\ chin	\ī\ life	\ȯi\ coin	\y\ yet
\a\ mat	\e\ pet	\j\ job	\th\ thin	\yü\ few
\ā\ take	\ē\ easy	\ŋ\ sing	\<u>th</u>\ this	\yu̇\ cure
\ä\ cot, cart	\g\ go	\ō\ bone	\ü\ food	\zh\ vision

performer **b** : an operator of an amateur radio station —
ham *adj*

²**ham** *vb* **hammed; ham·ming** : to act with exaggerated
speech or gestures ⟨*ham* it up for the camera⟩

ham·burg·er \'ham-ˌbər-gər\ *or* **ham·burg** \-ˌbərg\ *n* **1 a**
: ground beef **b** : a cooked patty of ground beef **2** : a
sandwich consisting of a patty of hamburger in a split
round bun

> **Word History** It may seem odd that there isn't any ham
> in a hamburger. The origins of the word *hamburger,*
> however, have nothing to do with a type of meat. The
> word really comes from the name of the German city
> Hamburg. *Hamburger,* when capitalized, means "of
> Hamburg." Cakes of ground beef, often served raw,
> were a popular food in northern Germany in the 19th
> century, and so they became known in English as *Ham-
> burger steaks.* The name was later shortened to *hamburg-
> er.* Most people no longer associate the word *hamburger*
> with the city of Hamburg, since the hamburger is now
> usually thought of as an American food. [German *Ham-
> burger* (adjective) "of Hamburg," city in Germany]

ham·let \'ham-lət\ *n* : a small village

¹**ham·mer** \'ham-ər\ *n* **1 a** : a hand tool that consists of a
solid head set crosswise on a handle and is used for
pounding (as in driving nails) **b** : a power tool for pounding **2** : something that resembles a hammer in shape or
action (as the part of a gun whose striking action causes
explosion of the charge) **3** : MALLEUS **4** : a heavy metal
ball with a flexible handle that is thrown for distance in a
track-and-field contest

²**hammer** *vb* **ham·mered; ham·mer·ing** \'ham-(ə-)riŋ\ **1**
: to strike blows with or as if with a hammer : POUND **2**
a : to make repeated efforts ⟨*hammer* away at one's les-
sons⟩ **b** : to emphasize (as an opinion) by repetition
⟨*hammers* his point home⟩ **3** : to fasten, build, drive, or
shape with a hammer — **ham·mer·er** \'ham-ər-ər\ *n*

ham·mer·head \'ham-ər-
ˌhed\ *n* : any of various
active sharks of medium
size that have the eyes at
the ends of sideward ex-
tensions of the flattened
head

hammerhead

hammer out *vb* : to produce or bring about by
persistent effort ⟨*hammered out* an agreement⟩

ham·mock \'ham-ək\ *n* : a swinging couch or bed usually
made of netting or canvas and slung by cords from supports at each end

¹**ham·per** \'ham-pər\ *vb* **ham·pered; ham·per·ing**
\-p(ə-)riŋ\ : to slow the movement, progress, or action of
⟨bad weather *hampered* the search⟩

²**hamper** *n* : a large basket usually with a cover ⟨a clothes
hamper⟩

ham·ster \'ham(p)-stər\ *n* : any of various small Old
World rodents with a short tail and large cheek pouches

¹**ham·string** \'ham-ˌstriŋ\ *n* **1** : either of two groups of
tendons at the back of the human knee **2** : any of three
muscles at the back of the thigh that function to extend
the thigh, rotate the leg, and bend the knee

²**hamstring** *vb* **-strung** \-ˌstrəŋ\; **-string·ing** \-ˌstriŋ-iŋ\ **1**
: to cripple by cutting the leg tendons **2** : to make ineffective or powerless : CRIPPLE ⟨*hamstrung* by restric-
tions⟩

¹**hand** \'hand\ *n* **1 a** : the free end of the arm or forelimb when used (as in human beings) for handling, grasping, and holding **b** : any of various bodily parts (as the
hind foot of an ape or the pincers of a crab) that are like
the hand in structure or function **2** : something resembling a hand: as **a** : a pointer on a dial **b** : a figure of a
hand with index finger extended to point something out
c : a bunch of bananas **3** : personal possession : CON-
TROL ⟨in the *hands* of the enemy⟩ **4 a** : ¹SIDE 2, DIREC-
TION ⟨fighting on either *hand*⟩ **b** : a side or point of view
in an issue or argument ⟨on the one *hand*, we can declare
a tie, or on the other *hand*, keep playing⟩ **5** : a pledge
especially of marriage ⟨asked for her *hand*⟩ **6** : HAND-
WRITING 2 **7** : SKILL 1, ABILITY ⟨try one's *hand* at chess⟩
8 a : assistance or help involving physical effort ⟨lend a
hand⟩ **b** : a part or share in doing something ⟨take a
hand in the work⟩ **9** : a unit of measure equal to 4 inches
(about 10.2 centimeters) used especially for the height of
horses **10** : a round of applause ⟨give him a *hand*⟩ **11 a**
: the cards or pieces held by a player in a game **b** : a
single round in a game **12 a** : one who performs or produces a work ⟨two portraits by the same *hand*⟩ **b** : a
hired worker **c** : a member of a ship's crew ⟨all *hands* on
deck⟩ **d** : one skilled in a particular activity or field ⟨an
old *hand* at foreign affairs⟩ **13** : WORKMANSHIP 2 ⟨the
hand of a master⟩ — **at hand** : near in time or place
: within reach ⟨use whatever ingredients are *at hand*⟩ —
by hand : with the hands — **in hand 1** : in one's possession or control ⟨had matters well *in hand*⟩ ⟨with money
in hand⟩ **2** : in preparation — **on hand 1** : in present
possession ⟨always kept snacks *on hand*⟩ **2** : in attendance : PRESENT — **on one's hands** : in one's possession
or care ⟨too much time *on my hands*⟩ — **out of hand**
: out of control ⟨a crowded meeting that got *out of hand*⟩
— **out of one's hands** : out of one's control

²**hand** *vb* **1** : to guide or assist with the hand **2** : to give or
pass with or as if with the hand ⟨*hand* a person a letter⟩

hand·bag \'han(d)-ˌbag\ *n* **1** : SUITCASE **2** : a woman's
bag for carrying small personal articles and money

hand·ball \-ˌból\ *n* **1** : a game played in a walled court or
against a single wall or board by two or four players who
use their hands to strike a ball **2** : the ball used in handball

hand·bill \-ˌbil\ *n* : a printed sheet to be distributed by
hand

hand·book \-ˌbúk\ *n* : a small book of facts or useful information usually about a particular subject : MANUAL

hand·car \'han(d)-ˌkär\ *n* : a small railroad car powered
by a hand-operated device or by a small motor

¹**hand·craft** \-ˌkraft\ *n* : HANDICRAFT

²**handcraft** *vb* : to make by handicraft

hand·cuff \'han(d)-ˌkəf\ *n* : a metal fastening locking
around a wrist and usually connected by a chain or bar
with another such fastening — usually used in plural —
handcuff *vb*

hand down *vb* **1** : to pass down from older to younger (as
from parent to child) **2** : to form and express a judicial
decision

hand·ed \'han-dəd\ *adj* : having or using such or so many
hands ⟨a right-*handed* person⟩ — **hand·ed·ness** *n*

hand·ful \'han(d)-ˌfúl\ *n, pl* **handfuls** \-ˌfúlz\ *also* **hands-
ful** \'han(d)z-ˌfúl\ **1** : as much or as many as the hand will
grasp ⟨a *handful* of jelly beans⟩ **2** : a small quantity or
number ⟨a *handful* of people⟩ **3** : as much as one can
control or manage ⟨the three babies are quite a *handful*⟩

hand·gun \'han(d)-ˌgən\ *n* : a firearm designed to be held
and fired with one hand

hand·held \-ˌheld\ *adj* : held in the hand; *esp* : designed to
be used while being held in the hand ⟨a *handheld* com-
puter⟩ — **handheld** *n*

¹**hand·i·cap** \'han-di-ˌkap\ *n* **1** : a race or contest in which
competitors with different levels of ability are given an
artificial advantage or disadvantage to equalize chances
of winning; *also* : the advantage or disadvantage given **2**
a : a disadvantage that makes progress or success difficult
⟨being lazy was a *handicap*⟩ **b** *sometimes offensive* : a
physical disability

²**handicap** *vb* **-capped; -cap·ping 1** : to give a handicap
to **2** : to put at a disadvantage

handicapped *adj* **1** *sometimes offensive* : having a physical or mental disability **2** : of or reserved for individuals with a physical disability ⟨*handicapped* parking spaces⟩

hand·i·craft \'han-di-ˌkraft\ *n* **1** : an occupation (as weaving or pottery making) requiring skill with the hands **2** : articles made by one working at a handicraft — **hand·i·craft·er** \-ˌkraf-tər\ *n*

hand·i·ly \'han-də-lē\ *adv* **1** : in a skillful manner **2** : EASILY 1 ⟨won *handily*⟩

hand·i·ness \'han-dē-nəs\ *n* : the quality or state of being handy

hand in hand *adv* **1** : with one's hand clasping another's hand ⟨walked *hand in hand*⟩ **2** : in close association : TOGETHER ⟨hard work and success go *hand in hand*⟩

hand·i·work \'han-di-ˌwərk\ *n* : work done by the hands or by oneself

hand·ker·chief \'haŋ-kər-chəf, -(ˌ)chif, -ˌchēf\ *n, pl* **-chiefs** *also* **-chieves** \-chəfs, -(ˌ)chifs, -ˌchēvz, -ˌchēfs, -ˌchəvz, -ˌchivz\ **1** : a small piece of cloth used for wiping the face, nose, or eyes **2** : KERCHIEF 1

¹han·dle \'han-dᵊl\ *n* **1** : a part that is designed to be grasped by the hand **2** : ¹NAME 1, TITLE **3** — **han·dled** \-dᵊld\ *adj* — **off the handle** : into a state of sudden and violent anger ⟨flew *off the handle* and yelled at my friend⟩

²handle *vb* **han·dled; han·dling** \'han-(d)liŋ, -dᵊl-iŋ\ **1 a** : to touch, feel, hold, or move with the hand **b** : to manage with the hands ⟨*handle* a horse⟩ **2 a** : to deal with or act on ⟨*handle* a problem⟩ **b** : ¹CONTROL 1b, DIRECT ⟨an accountant *handles* my financial concerns⟩ **c** : to put up with : STAND ⟨can't *handle* the heat⟩ **3** : to deal or trade in ⟨a store that *handles* rugs⟩ **4** : to act, behave, or respond in a certain way when managed or directed ⟨a car that *handles* well⟩ — **han·dler** \'han-(d)lər, -dᵊl-ər\ *n*

   synonyms HANDLE, MANIPULATE, WIELD mean to manage skillfully or efficiently. HANDLE suggests applying an acquired skill in order to accomplish something ⟨knows how to *handle* her bike well⟩. MANIPULATE suggests using special skills in order to accomplish a complicated or difficult task ⟨surgeons must be able to *manipulate* delicate instruments⟩. WIELD suggests handling a tool or weapon with power or authority ⟨*wielded* the sword with all his might⟩.

han·dle·bar \'han-dᵊl-ˌbär\ *n* : a bar with a handle (as for steering a bicycle) at each end — usually used in plural

hand lens *n* : a magnifying glass to be held in the hand

hand·made \'han(d)-'mād\ *adj* : made by hand or with hand tools

hand·maid·en \-ˌmād-ᵊn\ *also* **hand·maid** \-ˌmād\ *n* : a female servant or attendant

hand–me–down \'han(d)-mē-ˌdaùn\ *adj* : put in use by one person or group after being used, discarded, or handed down by another — **hand–me–down** *n*

hand–off \'han-ˌdòf\ *n* : the act of handing the ball to a teammate (as in football)

hand organ *n* : a barrel organ operated by a hand crank

hand·out \'han-ˌdaùt\ *n* **1** : food, clothing, or money given to a beggar **2** : an information sheet for free distribution **3** : a prepared statement released to the press

hand over *vb* : to yield control of

hand·pick \'han(d)-'pik\ *vb* : to select personally ⟨a *handpicked* successor⟩

hand·rail \'han-ˌdrāl\ *n* : a narrow rail for grasping as a support (as on a staircase)

hand·saw \'han(d)-ˌsò\ *n* : a saw designed to be used with one hand

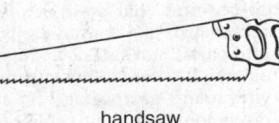

handsaw

hands down *adv* **1** : EASILY 1 ⟨won the race *hands down*⟩ **2** : without question ⟨is *hands down* the best pizza in town⟩

hand·shake \-ˌshāk\ *n* : a clasping of hands by two people especially in greeting or farewell

hand·some \'han(t)-səm\ *adj* **1** : fairly large : SIZABLE ⟨a *handsome* fortune⟩ **2** : marked by generosity or graciousness ⟨a *handsome* contribution⟩ **3** : having a pleasing and usually impressive or dignified appearance ⟨a *handsome* young lad⟩ ⟨*handsome* old buildings⟩ **synonyms** *see* BEAUTIFUL — **hand·some·ly** *adv* — **hand·some·ness** *n*

hand·spring \'han(d)-ˌspriŋ\ *n* : a tumbling feat in which the body turns in a full circle from a standing position and lands first on the hands and then on the feet

hand–to–hand \ˌhan-tə-'hand\ *adj* : involving physical contact ⟨*hand-to-hand* combat⟩

hand–to–mouth \-tə-'maùth\ *adj* : having or providing nothing to spare ⟨a *hand-to-mouth* existence⟩ — **hand to mouth** *adv*

hand·work \'han-ˌdwərk\ *n* : work done with the hands and not by machine

hand·writ·ing \'han-ˌdrīt-iŋ\ *n* **1** : writing done by hand **2** : the form of a particular person's writing **3** : something written by hand

hand·writ·ten \'han-ˌdrit-ᵊn\ *adj* : written by hand ⟨a *handwritten* note⟩

handy \'han-dē\ *adj* **hand·i·er; -est 1 a** : conveniently near **b** : easily handled or used ⟨a *handy* sloop⟩ ⟨a *handy* reference book⟩ **2** : clever in using the hands : DEXTEROUS ⟨*handy* with a needle⟩

handy·man \-ˌman\ *n* : a person who does various small jobs

¹hang \'haŋ\ *vb* **hung** \'həŋ\ *also* **hanged** \'haŋd\; **hang·ing** \'haŋ-iŋ\ **1 a** : to fasten or be fastened to an elevated point without support from below : SUSPEND, DANGLE **b** : to kill or be killed by hanging from a rope tied round the neck ⟨sentenced to be *hanged*⟩ **c** : to fasten so as to allow free motion forward and backward ⟨*hang* a door⟩ **2** : to furnish with hanging decorations (as pictures or curtains) **3** : ¹DROOP 1 ⟨*hung* my head in shame⟩ **4** : to fasten to a wall ⟨*hang* wallpaper⟩ **5** : to display pictures in a gallery **6** : HOVER 1b ⟨clouds *hanging* low overhead⟩ **7** : to stay steadily **8** : DEPEND 1 ⟨election *hangs* on one vote⟩ **9 a** : to take hold for support : CLING ⟨the children *hung* on his arm⟩ **b** : to be hard to bear ⟨worry *hung* on his mind⟩ **10** : to be uncertain ⟨the decision is still *hanging*⟩ **11** : to be in a state of close attention ⟨*hung* on my every word⟩ **12** : to pass time idly especially by relaxing or socializing — often used with *around* or *out* ⟨*hung* out with friends⟩ — **hang·able** \'haŋ-ə-bəl\ *adj*

²hang *n* **1** : the manner in which a thing hangs ⟨the *hang* of a skirt⟩ **2 a** : ¹MEANING 1b ⟨the *hang* of an argument⟩ **b** : a special method : KNACK ⟨get the *hang* of driving⟩ — **give a hang** *or* **care a hang** : to be concerned or worried

hang·ar \'haŋ-ər, 'haŋ-gər\ *n* : a shelter for housing and repairing aircraft [from French *hangar* "shed"]

hang around *vb* : to pass time or stay idly in or at ⟨*hung around* the house all day⟩

hang back *vb* **1** : to linger behind others ⟨*hung back* to wait for the slower children⟩ **2** : to be unwilling to do something : HESITATE ⟨always *hangs back* when everyone else is dancing⟩

hang·dog \'haŋ-ˌdòg\ *adj* **1** : ASHAMED 1, GUILTY ⟨a *hangdog* look⟩ **2** : DEJECTED, COWED

hang·er \'haŋ-ər\ *n* **1** : one that hangs **2** : a device by which something hangs; *esp* : a device for hanging a garment from a hook or rod

hang·er–on \'haŋ-ə-,ròn, -,rän\ *n, pl* **hangers–on** : one that hangs around a person, place, or institution in hope of personal gain

hang glider *n* : a glider which resembles a kite and from which a rider hangs while gliding down from a cliff or hill — **hang glide** *vb* — **hang gliding** *n*

hang in *vb* : to refuse to be discouraged or frightened ⟨*hang in* there, kid! Don't quit⟩

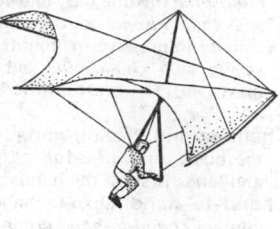
hang glider

¹**hang·ing** \'haŋ-iŋ\ *n* **1** : an execution by strangling or breaking the neck by a suspended noose **2** : something hung (as a curtain or tapestry) — usually used in plural

²**hanging** *adj* **1** : located on steeply sloping ground ⟨*hanging* gardens⟩ **2 a** : sticking out ⟨*hanging* rocks⟩ **b** : supported only by the wall on one side ⟨a *hanging* staircase⟩ **3** : suitable for holding a hanging object **4** : punishable by hanging ⟨a *hanging* offense⟩

hang·man \'haŋ-mən\ *n* **1** : a person who hangs condemned criminals **2** : a game in which the object is for one player to guess the letters of an unknown word before the player who knows the word creates a stick figure of a hanged man by drawing one line for each incorrect guess

hang·nail \-,nāl\ *n* : a bit of skin hanging loose at the side or base of a fingernail

hang on *vb* **1** : to keep hold or possession especially tightly ⟨*hang on* or you'll fall⟩ ⟨*hang on* to your money⟩ **2** : to continue stubbornly ⟨a cold that *hung on* all spring⟩

hang·out \'haŋ-,aùt\ *n* : a favorite place for spending time

hang·over \'haŋ-,ō-vər\ *n* **1** : something (as a surviving custom) that remains from what is past **2** : a sick uncomfortable state that comes from drinking too many drinks of alcoholic beverage

hang·tag \-,tag\ *n* : a tag attached to an article of merchandise giving information about its material and care

hang–up \'haŋ-,əp\ *n* : a source of mental or emotional difficulty

hang up \(')haŋ-'əp\ *vb* **1 a** : to place on a hook or hanger ⟨*hang up* your coat⟩ **b** : to replace a telephone receiver on the cradle so that the connection is broken; *also* : to end a telephone conversation **2** : to snag or cause to snag so as to be immovable ⟨the ship *hung up* on a sandbar⟩

hank \'haŋk\ *n* : ²COIL 1a, SKEIN; *esp* : a coil of yarn

han·ker \'haŋ-kər\ *vb* **han·kered; han·ker·ing** \-k(ə-)riŋ\ : to have an eager or continual desire ⟨*hanker* after fame⟩ — **han·ker·er** \-kər-ər\ *n*

han·ky–pan·ky \,haŋ-kē-'paŋ-kē\ *n* : questionable or sneaky activity : TRICKERY

Han·sen's disease \'han(t)-sənz-\ *n* : LEPROSY

han·som \'han(t)-səm\ *n* : a light two-wheeled covered carriage with the driver's seat elevated behind — called also *hansom cab*

Ha·nuk·kah *also* **Cha·nu·kah** *or* **Ha·nu·kah** \'kän-ə-kə, 'hän-\ *n* : an eight-day Jewish holiday celebrated in November or December in honor of the cleansing and second dedication of the Temple after the Syrians were driven out of Jerusalem in 165 B.C.

hansom

¹**hap** \'hap\ *n* **1** : something that happens : OCCURRENCE **2** : something that happens unexpectedly without intention or observable cause

²**hap** *vb* **happed; hap·ping** **1** : HAPPEN 3 **2** : HAPPEN 4a

hap·haz·ard \(')hap-'haz-ərd\ *adj* : marked by lack of plan, order, or direction — **haphazard** *adv* — **hap·haz·ard·ly** *adv* — **hap·haz·ard·ness** *n*

hap·ki·do \,häp-'kēd-ō\ *n* : a Korean martial art based on kicking motions and using some aikido moves [Korean *hapkido* "a martial art using both kicking and aikido moves," from *hap-* "together, joined" + *ki* "breath, energy" + *to* "way, art"]

hap·less \'hap-ləs\ *adj* : having no luck : UNFORTUNATE — **hap·less·ly** *adv* — **hap·less·ness** *n*

hap·ly \'hap-lē\ *adv* : by chance, luck, or accident

hap·pen \'hap-ən, 'hap-ᵊm\ *vb* **hap·pened; hap·pen·ing** \'hap-(ə-)niŋ\ **1** : to occur or come about by chance **2** : to take place : OCCUR **3** : to have occasion or opportunity ⟨*happened* to overhear⟩ **4 a** : to meet or find something by chance ⟨*happened* upon the right answer⟩ **b** : to appear casually or by chance ⟨*happened* into the room just as the music started⟩ **5** : to come by way of injury or harm ⟨nothing will *happen* to you⟩ [Middle English *happen* "to occur by chance," from *hap* "chance, chance occurrence" — related to HAPPY, MISHAP, PERHAPS]

hap·pen·ing *n* **1** : something that happens : OCCURRENCE **2** : an event that is especially interesting, entertaining, or important

hap·pi·ly \'hap-ə-lē\ *adv* **1** : in a fortunate or lucky manner ⟨*happily*, no one was injured⟩ **2** : in a happy manner or state ⟨lived *happily* ever after⟩ **3** : in a fitting, effective, or successful manner ⟨remarks *happily* worded⟩

hap·pi·ness \'hap-i-nəs\ *n* : a state of well-being and contentment : JOY

hap·py \'hap-ē\ *adj* **hap·pi·er; -est** **1** : FORTUNATE 1, LUCKY **2** : SUITABLE 1 ⟨a *happy* choice for governor⟩ **3 a** : enjoying well-being and contentment ⟨*happy* in my work⟩ **b** : expressing or suggestive of happiness ⟨*happy* laughter⟩ **c** : being pleased or glad ⟨*happy* to accept an invitation⟩ [Middle English *happy* "having or being good luck," a specialized sense of *hap* "chance, chance occurrence" — related to HAPPEN, MISHAP, PERHAPS]

happy camper : one who is content

hap·py–go–lucky \,hap-ē-gō-'lək-ē\ *adj* : cheerfully unconcerned : CAREFREE

ha·rangue \hə-'raŋ\ *n* **1** : a speech addressed to a public assembly **2** : a forceful or scolding speech or writing — **harangue** *vb* — **ha·rangu·er** \-'raŋ-ər\ *n*

ha·rass \hə-'ras, 'har-əs\ *vb* **1 a** : to tire out by continual efforts **b** : to annoy persistently **c** : to create an unpleasant situation for by unwelcome verbal or physical conduct **2** : to worry with repeated attacks — **ha·rass·er** *n* — **ha·rass·ment** \-mənt\ *n*

har·bin·ger \'här-bən-jər\ *n* : one that announces or shows what is coming : FORERUNNER ⟨warm rains that come as *harbingers* of spring⟩ — **harbinger** *vb*

¹**har·bor** \'här-bər\ *n* **1** : a place of safety and comfort : REFUGE **2** : a part of a body of water protected and deep enough to be a place of safety for ships : PORT — **har·bor·less** \-ləs\ *adj*

²**harbor** *vb* **har·bored; har·bor·ing** \-b(ə-)riŋ\ **1** : to give shelter to ⟨*harbor* an escaped convict⟩ **2** : to hold a thought or feeling of ⟨*harbor* a grudge⟩ **3** : to take shelter in or as if in a harbor — **har·bor·er** *n*

har·bor·age \'här-bə-rij\ *n* : ¹SHELTER 1a, HARBOR

¹**hard** \'härd\ *adj* **1** : not easily penetrated, cut, or divided into parts : not soft **2 a** : high in alcoholic content ⟨*hard* cider⟩ **b** : containing substances that prevent lathering with soap ⟨*hard* water⟩ **3** : stable and high in value and often convertible into gold ⟨*hard* currency⟩ **4 a** : physically fit **b** : resistant to stress or disease **c** : free of weakness or defects **5 a** : ¹FIRM 2a, DEFINITE ⟨a *hard* agree-

ment⟩ **b** : based on clear fact ⟨*hard* evidence⟩ **c** : being thorough, intense, and searching ⟨a *hard* look⟩ **d** : lacking sympathy or tender feelings : UNFEELING ⟨a *hard* heart⟩ **6 a** : difficult to endure : HARSH, SEVERE ⟨*hard* words⟩ ⟨a *hard* winter⟩ ⟨*hard* times⟩ **b** : RESENTFUL 2 ⟨*hard* feelings⟩ **c** : STRICT 1, UNRELENTING ⟨drives a *hard* bargain⟩ **d** : physically or mentally difficult ⟨a *hard* problem⟩ ⟨*hard* work⟩ **7** : DILIGENT, ENERGETIC ⟨a *hard* worker⟩ **8 a** : sharply or harshly defined or outlined ⟨*hard* shadows⟩ **b** : sounding as in *cold* and *geese* respectively — used of *c* and *g*

    synonyms HARD, FIRM, SOLID mean having a structure that can stand up against pressure. HARD is used of something that does not easily bend, stretch, or dent ⟨steel is *hard*⟩. FIRM is used of something that is flexible but also tough or compact ⟨*firm* muscles⟩ ⟨a *firm* mattress⟩. SOLID is used of something that has a fixed structure and is heavy and compact all the way through ⟨a *solid* wall of bricks⟩.

²hard *adv* **1 a** : with great effort or energy ⟨work *hard*⟩ ⟨try *hard*⟩ **b** : in a violent manner : FIERCELY ⟨the wind blew *hard*⟩ **2 a** : in such a manner as to cause hardship, bitterness, or pain ⟨the storm hit them *hard*⟩ **b** : with bitterness or grief ⟨took the defeat *hard*⟩ **3** : in a firm manner : TIGHTLY ⟨hold *hard* to something⟩ **4** : to the point of hardness ⟨dry *hard*⟩ **5** : close in time or space ⟨the school stood *hard* by a river⟩

hard–and–fast \ˌhärd-ᵊn-ˈfast\ *adj* : not to be changed : FIXED ⟨a *hard-and-fast* rule⟩

hard·back \ˈhärd-ˌbak\ *n* : a book bound in hard covers

hard·ball \-ˌból\ *n* : BASEBALL

hard–bit·ten \-ˈbit-ᵊn\ *adj* : ¹TOUGH 3 ⟨*hard-bitten* veterans⟩

hard–boiled \-ˈbóild\ *adj* **1** : boiled until both white and yolk have become solid ⟨*hard-boiled* eggs⟩ **2** : lacking tender feelings : TOUGH ⟨a *hard-boiled* prison guard⟩

hard coal *n* : ANTHRACITE

hard copy *n* : a copy of information (as from computer storage) produced on paper in normal size ⟨a *hard copy* of an e-mail message⟩

hard core *n* **1** : an unchanging and lasting central part **2** : a small number of aggressive members of a group — **hard–core** *adj*

hard disk *n* **1** : a small hard metal disk with a magnetic coating on which computer data can be stored **2** : HARD DRIVE

hard drive *n* : a device for storing computer data that consists of one or more hard disks in a sealed case

hard–driv·ing \ˈhärd-ˈdrī-viŋ\ *adj* : extremely ambitious, energetic, or hardworking ⟨a *hard-driving* salesperson⟩

hard·en \ˈhärd-ᵊn\ *vb* **hard·ened; hard·en·ing** \ˈhärd-niŋ, -ᵊn-iŋ\ **1** : to make or become hard or harder **2** : to make unfeeling or unsympathetic ⟨*hardened* his heart⟩ **3** : to make or become hardy or strong ⟨muscles *hardened* by exercise⟩ **4** : to protect from blast, heat, or radiation (as by a thick barrier or by placing underground) ⟨*hardened* missile sites⟩ **5 a** : to become firm, stable, or settled **b** : to express harshness — **hard·en·er** \ˈhärd-nər, -ᵊn-ər\ *n*

hard·en·ing *n* : SCLEROSIS ⟨*hardening* of the arteries⟩

hard·hack \ˈhärd-ˌhak\ *n* : a North American spirea with dense bunches of small usually pink flowers and leaves having a hairy rust-colored underside

hard hat *n* **1** : a protective helmet worn especially by construction workers **2** : a construction worker

hard·head·ed \ˈhärd-ˈhed-əd\ *adj* **1** : STUBBORN 1 **2** : marked by sound judgment : REALISTIC ⟨a *hardheaded* judgment⟩ — **hard·head·ed·ly** *adv* — **hard·head·ed·ness** *n*

hard·heart·ed \-ˈhärt-əd\ *adj* : UNFEELING 2, PITILESS — **hard·heart·ed·ly** *adv* — **hard·heart·ed·ness** *n*

har·di·hood \ˈhärd-ē-ˌhúd\ *n* **1** : BRAVERY 1 **2** : VIGOR 1, ROBUSTNESS

hard–luck \ˈhärd-ˌlək\ *adj* : marked by, relating to, or experiencing bad luck ⟨*hard-luck* stories⟩

hard·ly \ˈhärd-lē\ *adv* **1** : in a severe or harsh manner ⟨deal *hardly* with them⟩ **2** : with difficulty ⟨a *hardly* won victory⟩ **3** : only just : BARELY, SCARCELY ⟨we *hardly* knew them⟩ **4** : certainly not ⟨that news is *hardly* surprising⟩

hard·ness \ˈhärd-nəs\ *n* **1** : the quality or state of being hard **2** : the ability of a substance (as a mineral) to scratch another substance or be itself scratched

hard–of–hearing \ˌhärd-ə(v)-ˈhi(ə)r-iŋ\ *adj* : relating to or having a faulty but functional sense of hearing

hard palate *n* : the bony front part of the roof of the mouth

hard put *adj* : barely able ⟨*hard put* to describe it⟩

hard rubber *n* : a firm rubber or rubber product

hard·ship \ˈhärd-ˌship\ *n* **1** : ¹PAIN 2a, PRIVATION **2** : something that causes pain or loss

hard·tack \-ˌtak\ *n* : a hard biscuit or bread made of flour and water without salt

hard·top \-ˌtäp\ *n* : an automobile having a permanent or removable rigid top

hard up *adj* **1** : short of money **2** : poorly provided ⟨*hard up* for friends⟩

hard·ware \ˈhär-ˌdwa(ə)r, -ˌdwe(ə)r\ *n* **1** : articles (as fittings, cutlery, tools, utensils, or parts of machines) made of metal **2** : the equipment used for a particular purpose ⟨computer *hardware*⟩ ⟨military *hardware*⟩

hard wheat *n* : a wheat with hard kernels that is used to make a flour especially suitable for bread and macaroni

hard–wired \-ˌwī(ə)rd\ *adj* : having or done using or as if using permanent electronic circuits or connections ⟨a *hardwired* phone⟩ ⟨a mother *hardwired* to defend her child⟩

¹hard·wood \ˈhär-ˌdwúd\ *n* **1** : the wood of a tree (as an oak or maple) producing flowers and having usually broad leaves as compared to the wood of a tree bearing cones and having needlelike leaves — compare SOFTWOOD 1 **2** : a tree that yields hardwood

²hardwood *adj* **1** : having or made of hardwood ⟨*hardwood* floors⟩ **2** : consisting of mature woody tissue ⟨a *hardwood* cutting⟩

hard·work·ing \-ˈwər-kiŋ\ *adj* : INDUSTRIOUS, DILIGENT ⟨*hardworking* students⟩

har·dy \ˈhärd-ē\ *adj* **har·di·er; -est** **1** : BOLD 1a, BRAVE **2** : able to stand fatigue or hardships : ROBUST **3** : able to survive unfavorable conditions (as of weather) ⟨a *hardy* rose bush⟩ — **har·di·ly** \ˈhärd-ᵊl-ē\ *adv* — **har·di·ness** \ˈhärd-ē-nəs\ *n*

hare \ˈha(ə)r, ˈhe(ə)r\ *n, pl* **hare** *or* **hares** : any of various swift animals that are like the related rabbits but usually have longer ears and hind legs and have young born with open eyes and a furry coat

hare

hare·bell \-ˌbel\ *n* : a slender herb with bright blue bell-shaped flowers

hare·brained \-ˈbrānd\ *adj* : SILLY 1, GIDDY

hare·lip \-ˈlip\ *n, sometimes offensive* : CLEFT LIP

har·em \ˈhar-əm, ˈher-\ *n* **1 a** : the rooms assigned to the women in a Muslim household **b** : the women of a Mus-

\ə\ **abut**	\aú\ **out**	\i\ **tip**	\ó\ **saw**	\ú\ **foot**
\ər\ **further**	\ch\ **chin**	\ī\ **life**	\ói\ **coin**	\y\ **yet**
\a\ **mat**	\e\ **pet**	\j\ **job**	\th\ **thin**	\yü\ **few**
\ā\ **take**	\ē\ **easy**	\ŋ\ **sing**	\th\ **this**	\yú\ **cure**
\ä\ **cot, cart**	\g\ **go**	\ō\ **bone**	\ü\ **food**	\zh\ **vision**

lim household **2** : a group of female animals (as horses) controlled by and usually mating with one male

hark \'härk\ *vb* : LISTEN 1

hark back *vb* : to recall or cause to recall something earlier ⟨*hark back* to the good old days⟩

har·le·quin \'här-li-k(w)ən\ *n* **1** : ¹CLOWN 2 **2** : a pattern of usually diamond-shaped figures of different colors — **harlequin** *adj*

har·lot \'här-lət\ *n* : ²PROSTITUTE

har·lot·ry \'här-lə-trē\ *n* : PROSTITUTION 1

harm \'härm\ *n* **1** : physical or mental damage : INJURY **2** : MISCHIEF **3**, HURT *synonyms* see INJURY — **harm** *vb*

harm·ful \'härm-fəl\ *adj* : causing damage : INJURIOUS — **harm·ful·ly** \-fə-lē\ *adv* — **harm·ful·ness** *n*

harm·less \'härm-ləs\ *adj* **1** : free from harm **2** : unable to harm ⟨a *harmless* joke⟩ — **harm·less·ly** *adv* — **harm·less·ness** *n*

¹har·mon·ic \här-'män-ik\ *adj* : of or relating to musical harmony as opposed to melody or rhythm — **har·mon·i·cal·ly** \-'män-i-k(ə-)lē\ *adv*

²harmonic *n* : OVERTONE 1

har·mon·i·ca \här-'män-i-kə\ *n* : a small musical instrument that is held in the hand and played by the mouth and that produces a sound through metal reeds which vibrate as air is blown or drawn past them

har·mo·ni·ous \här-'mō-nē-əs\ *adj* **1** : having a pleasing mixture of notes ⟨a *harmonious* song⟩ ⟨*harmonious* voices⟩ **2** : having the parts agreeably related ⟨decorated in *harmonious* colors⟩ **3** : marked by agreement in feeling or action ⟨a *harmonious* family⟩ — **har·mo·ni·ous·ly** *adv* — **har·mo·ni·ous·ness** *n*

har·mo·nize \'här-mə-ˌnīz\ *vb* **-nized; -niz·ing 1** : to play or sing in harmony **2** : to be in harmony **3** : to bring into harmony **4** : to provide or accompany with harmony — **har·mo·ni·za·tion** \ˌhär-mə-nə-'zā-shən\ *n* — **har·mo·niz·er** \'här-mə-ˌnī-zər\ *n*

har·mo·ny \'här-mə-nē\ *n, pl* **-nies 1 a** : the combination of musical notes played together as chords **b** : the structure of music with respect to the way it is written and to the way notes are grouped as chords **c** : the science of harmony **2 a** : pleasing or suitable arrangement of parts **b** : AGREEMENT 1b, ACCORD ⟨lives in *harmony* with her neighbors⟩

¹har·ness \'här-nəs\ *n* **1** : the straps and fastenings by which an animal pulls a load **2** : an arrangement that resembles a harness

²harness *vb* **1** : to put a harness on **2** : to tie together : YOKE **3** : to put to work : UTILIZE ⟨*harness* the sun's energy to heat homes⟩

harness racing *n* : the sport of racing horses that are harnessed to two-wheeled vehicles

¹harp \'härp\ *n* : a musical instrument that has strings stretched across a large open triangular frame and that is plucked with the fingers — **harp·ist** \'här-pəst\ *n*

²harp *vb* **1** : to play on a harp **2** : to dwell on a subject tiresomely ⟨always *harping* on his shortcomings⟩ — **harp·er** *n*

¹har·poon \här-'pün\ *n* : a barbed spear used especially in hunting large fish or whales

²harpoon *vb* : to strike with a harpoon — **har·poon·er** *n*

harp·si·chord \'härp-si-ˌkȯ(ə)rd\ *n* : a keyboard instrument similar to a piano but with strings that are plucked rather than struck

¹harp

har·py \'här-pē\ *n, pl* **harpies 1** *cap* : a foul creature of Greek mythology that is part woman and part bird **2 a** : a greedy person **b** : an evil-tempered woman

har·que·bus \'här-kwi-(ˌ)bəs\ *or* **ar·que·bus** \'är-\ *n* : a portable firearm of the 15th and 16th centuries later replaced by the musket

¹har·ri·er \'har-ē-ər\ *n* : any of a breed of hunting dogs like a large beagle that were originally used for hunting rabbits

²harrier *n* **1** : one that harries **2** : any of various slender long-legged hawks

¹har·row \'har-ō\ *n* : a cultivating tool that has spikes, teeth, or disks and is used for breaking up and smoothing the soil

²harrow *vb* **1** : to cultivate with a harrow **2** : ²TORMENT, VEX — **har·row·er** *n*

har·ry \'har-ē\ *vb* **har·ried; har·ry·ing 1** : ²RAID, PILLAGE **2** : ²TORMENT 2, WORRY

harsh \'härsh\ *adj* **1** : disagreeable to the touch **2** : causing discomfort or pain **3** : making many or difficult demands : SEVERE ⟨*harsh* discipline⟩ **4** : not pleasant to the artistic sense ⟨*harsh* colors⟩ *synonyms* see ROUGH — **harsh·ly** *adv* — **harsh·ness** *n*

hart \'härt\ *n, chiefly British* : a male red deer especially over five years old : STAG

harte·beest \'härt-(ə-)ˌbēst\ *n* : either of two large African antelopes with a long head and ringed horns

har·um–scar·um \ˌhar-əm-'skar-əm, ˌher-əm-'sker-\ *adj* : RECKLESS, IRRESPONSIBLE — **harum–scarum** *adv*

¹har·vest \'här-vəst\ *n* **1** : the season when crops are gathered **2** : the gathering of a crop **3** : a ripe crop (as of grain or fruit); *also* : the quantity of a crop gathered in a single season

²harvest *vb* **1** : to gather in a crop : REAP **2** : to gather as if by harvesting ⟨*harvest* timber⟩

har·vest·er \'här-vəs-tər\ *n* **1** : a person who gathers by or as if by harvesting **2** : a machine for harvesting field crops

har·vest·man \'här-vəs(t)-mən\ *n* : DADDY LONGLEGS 2

harvest moon *n* : the full moon nearest the time of the September equinox

has *present 3rd singular of* HAVE

has–been \'haz-ˌbin\ *n* : one that has passed the peak of ability, power, or popularity

¹hash \'hash\ *vb* **1 a** : to chop into small pieces **b** : CONFUSE 3, MUDDLE **2** : to talk about : DISCUSS ⟨*hashed* over the problem⟩ [from French *hacher* "to chop up into small pieces," from early French *hachier* (same meaning), from *hache* "battle-ax"; of Germanic origin — related to ⁴HATCH, HATCHET]

²hash *n* **1** : chopped meat mixed with potatoes and browned **2** : a mixture of many different things

³hash *n* : HASHISH [a shortened form of *hashish*]

hash·ish \'hash-ˌēsh, ha-'shēsh\ *n* : a drug prepared from the flowering tops of the hemp that is smoked, chewed, or drunk for its intoxicating effect

hash·tag \'hash-ˌtag\ *n* : a word or phrase preceded by the symbol # that classifies or categorizes the accompanying text (such as a tweet)

hasn't \'haz-ᵊnt\ : has not

hasp \'hasp\ *n* : a fastener especially for a door or lid consisting of a hinged metal strap that fits over a staple and is held by a pin or padlock

has·si·um \'has-ē-əm\ *n* : a short-lived radioactive element produced artificially — see ELEMENT table [from *Hassia* "Hesse," name of the German state containing the laboratory that first produced the element]

¹has·sle \'has-əl\ *vb* **has·sled; has·sling** \-(ə-)liŋ\ **1** : ARGUE 2, DISPUTE ⟨*hassled* with the umpire⟩ **2** : to annoy continuously : HARASS

²hassle *n* **1** : ARGUMENT 2 **2** : ²FIGHT 1a **3** : something that is annoying or troublesome

has·sock \'has-ək\ *n* **1** : TUSSOCK **2 a** : a cushion to kneel on in prayer **b** : a cushion that serves as a seat or as a leg rest

hast \(')hast, (h)əst\ *archaic present 2nd singular of* HAVE

has·tate \'has-ˌtāt\ *adj* : shaped like an arrowhead with flaring barbs ⟨a *hastate* leaf⟩

¹**haste** \'hāst\ *n* **1** : rapidity of motion or action **2** : reckless action **3** : eagerness to act that is not proper or suitable

²**haste** *vb* **hast·ed; hast·ing** : HASTEN

has·ten \'hā-sᵊn\ *vb* **has·tened; has·ten·ing** \'hās-niŋ, -ᵊn-iŋ\ **1** : to urge on **2** : to speed up : ACCELERATE ⟨*hastened* my steps⟩ **3** : to move or act quickly : HURRY — **has·ten·er** \'hās-nər, -ᵊn-ər\ *n*

hasty \'hā-stē\ *adj* **hast·i·er; -est 1 a** : done or made in a hurry ⟨made a *hasty* sketch of the scene⟩ **b** : fast and often not thorough ⟨made a *hasty* survey of the problem⟩ **2** : acting or done without forethought : RASH **3** : quick to anger : IRRITABLE ⟨a *hasty* temper⟩ **synonyms** see FAST — **hast·i·ly** \-stə-lē\ *adv* — **hast·i·ness** \-stē-nəs\ *n*

hasty pudding *n* **1** *British* : a porridge of oatmeal or flour boiled in water **2** *New England* **a** : cornmeal mush **b** : INDIAN PUDDING

hat \'hat\ *n* : a covering for the head usually having a shaped crown and brim — **under one's hat** : ¹SECRET 1b ⟨kept the news *under his hat*⟩

hat·box \'hat-ˌbäks\ *n* : a round piece of luggage for carrying hats

¹**hatch** \'hach\ *n* **1** : an opening in a deck, floor, or roof **2** : a small door or opening (as in an airplane) **3** : the covering for a hatch [Old English *hæc* "small door or opening"]

²**hatch** *vb* **1 a** : to produce from eggs ⟨the hen *hatched* chicks⟩ **b** : INCUBATE 1 ⟨the hen *hatched* the eggs⟩ **2 a** : to emerge from an egg, pupa, or chrysalis ⟨the chicks *hatched* today⟩ **b** : to give forth young ⟨the eggs *hatched* today⟩ **3** : to bring into being : ORIGINATE; *esp* : to organize or put together in secret ⟨*hatch* a plot⟩ [Middle English *hacchen* "to cause to be born out of an egg"]

³**hatch** *n* **1** : an act or instance of hatching **2** : a brood of hatched young

⁴**hatch** *vb* : to mark (as the shading in a picture) with hatching [Middle English *hachen* "to mark with a pattern of fine lines," from early French *hacher* "to inlay, chop up," derived from earlier *hache* "battle-ax"; of Germanic origin — related to ¹HASH, HATCHET]

hatch·back \'hach-ˌbak\ *n* **1** : a back on an automobile having an upward-opening hatch **2** : an automobile having a hatchback

hatch·ery \'hach-(ə-)rē\ *n, pl* **-er·ies** : a place for hatching eggs ⟨a fish *hatchery*⟩

hatch·et \'hach-ət\ *n* : a small ax with a short handle [Middle English *hachet* "small ax, hatchet," from early French *hachette*, literally, "small battle-ax," from *hache* "battle-ax"; of Germanic origin — related to ¹HASH, ⁴HATCH]

hatch·ing \'hach-iŋ\ *n* : the engraving or drawing of fine lines close together chiefly to give an effect of shading; *also* : the pattern so created

hatch·ling \'hach-liŋ\ *n* : a recently hatched animal

hatch·way \'hach-ˌwā\ *n* : a hatch usually with a ladder or stairs

¹**hate** \'hāt\ *n* **1** : strong dislike **2** : something or someone that is hated

²**hate** *vb* **hat·ed; hat·ing** **1** : to feel strong dislike toward ⟨*hates* his country's enemies⟩ **2 a** : to have a strong feeling of disgust for ⟨*hate* hypocrisy⟩ **b** : to find distasteful : DISLIKE ⟨*hates* cold weather⟩ — **hat·er** *n* — **hate one's guts** : to hate someone to an extreme degree

synonyms HATE, DETEST, ABHOR, LOATHE mean to have strong feelings against. HATE suggests deep dislike and the wishing of harm to another ⟨they *hated* their enemies⟩. DETEST suggests violent feelings against someone or something but without the desire for harm ⟨I

detest lying and cheating⟩. ABHOR suggests strong distaste ⟨she *abhors* dishonesty⟩. LOATHE suggests complete disgust or rejection ⟨*loathed* the thought of having to move again⟩.

hate·ful \'hāt-fəl\ *adj* **1** : full of hate : MALICIOUS ⟨*hateful* enemies⟩ **2** : causing or deserving hate ⟨a *hateful* crime⟩ — **hate·ful·ly** \-fə-lē\ *adv* — **hate·ful·ness** *n*

hath \(')hath, (h)əth\ *archaic present 3rd singular of* HAVE

ha·tred \'hā-trəd\ *n* : ¹HATE 1

hat·ter \'hat-ər\ *n* : one that makes, sells, or cleans and repairs hats

hau·berk \'hȯ-(ˌ)bərk\ *n* : a tunic of chain mail worn as defensive armor from the 12th to the 14th century

haugh·ty \'hȯt-ē, 'hät-\ *adj* **haugh·ti·er; -est** : rudely proud in a manner that expresses scorn for others : ARROGANT — **haugh·ti·ly** \'hȯt-ə-lē, 'hät-\ *adv* — **haugh·ti·ness** \'hȯt-ē-nəs, 'hät-\ *n*

¹**haul** \'hȯl\ *vb* **1** : to pull or drag with effort : DRAW ⟨*haul* a cart⟩ **2** : to obtain or move by or as if by hauling **3** : to transport in a vehicle [Middle English *halen* "to pull," from early French *haler* (same meaning); of Germanic origin — related to ²HALE] — **haul·er** *n*

²**haul** *n* **1** : the act or process of hauling : PULL **2 a** : an amount collected : TAKE ⟨a burglar's *haul*⟩ **b** : the amount of fish taken in a single drawing of a net **3** : the distance over which a load is hauled ⟨a long *haul*⟩

haunch \'hȯnch, 'hänch\ *n* **1 a** : ²HIP **b** : HINDQUARTER **2** — usually used in plural **2** : HINDQUARTER

¹**haunt** \'hȯnt, 'hänt\ *vb* **1** : to visit often : FREQUENT ⟨they *haunted* the antique shops⟩ **2 a** : to have a disturbing or harmful effect on ⟨problems we ignore now will come back to *haunt* us⟩ **b** : to come back to the mind of again and again ⟨the song *haunted* me all day⟩ **3** : to visit or live in as a ghost ⟨spirits *haunted* the house⟩ — **haunt·er** *n* — **haunt·ing·ly** \-iŋ-lē\ *adv*

²**haunt** \'hȯnt, 'hänt\ *n* : a place repeatedly visited ⟨favorite *haunts* of birds⟩

haut·bois *or* **haut·boy** \'(h)ō-ˌbȯi\ *n, pl* **hautbois** \-ˌbȯiz\ *or* **hautboys** : OBOE

¹**have** \(')hav, (h)əv, v; *in* "have to" *meaning* "must" *usually* 'haf\ *vb, past & past participle* **had** \(')had, (h)əd, d\; *present participle* **hav·ing** \'hav-iŋ\; *present 3rd sing* **has** \(')haz, (h)əz, z, s; *in* "have to" *meaning* "must" *usually* 'has\ **1 a** : POSSESS 1, OWN ⟨*have* a dog⟩ ⟨*have* the right to vote⟩ **b** : to consist of ⟨April *has* 30 days⟩ **2** : to be forced by duty or conscience in regard to : MUST ⟨*have* to go⟩ ⟨*have* a letter to write⟩ **3** : to stand in relationship to ⟨*has* three sisters⟩ **4 a** : OBTAIN 1, GET ⟨the best to be *had*⟩ **b** : RECEIVE 1 ⟨*had* bad news⟩ **c** : ACCEPT 1a; *esp* : to accept in marriage ⟨she wouldn't *have* him⟩ **5 a** : to be marked or characterized by ⟨*has* red hair⟩ **b** : REVEAL 1 ⟨*had* the courage to refuse⟩ **c** : ²USE 3, EXERCISE ⟨*have* mercy⟩ **6 a** : ²EXPERIENCE, UNDERGO ⟨*have* a good time⟩ ⟨I *have* a cold⟩ **b** : to perform an action or engage in an activity ⟨*have* a look at that mess⟩ ⟨*had* a fight⟩ **c** : to hold in the mind ⟨*have* an opinion⟩ ⟨*have* doubts⟩ **7 a** : to cause to do or be done ⟨*had* my hair cut⟩ ⟨please *have* the children stay⟩ **b** : to cause to be ⟨*has* everyone confused⟩ **8** : ¹PERMIT 1 ⟨we'll *have* no more of that⟩ **9 a** : to hold an advantage over ⟨we *have* them now⟩ **b** : ²TRICK 1, FOOL ⟨been *had* by a partner⟩ **10** : ²BEAR 2a ⟨*have* a baby⟩ **11** : to partake of ⟨*have* dinner⟩ **12** : ²BRIBE ⟨can be *had* for a price⟩ **13** — used as a helping verb with the past participle of another verb ⟨*has* gone home⟩ ⟨*had* already eaten⟩ ⟨will *have* finished dinner by then⟩ — **had better** *or* **had best** : would be wise to ⟨you

\ə\ **abut**	\au̇\ **out**	\i\ **tip**	\ȯ\ **saw**	\u̇\ **foot**	
\ər\ **further**	\ch\ **chin**	\ī\ **life**	\ȯi\ **coin**	\y\ **yet**	
\a\ **mat**	\e\ **pet**	\j\ **job**	\th\ **thin**	\yü\ **few**	
\ā\ **take**	\ē\ **easy**	\ŋ\ **sing**	\th\ **this**	\yu̇\ **cure**	
\ä\ **cot, cart**	\g\ **go**	\ō\ **bone**	\ü\ **food**	\zh\ **vision**	

had better start your work⟩ — **have at** : to go at or deal with : ATTACK — **have done** : ¹FINISH 1, STOP — **have coming** : to deserve what one gets, benefits by, or suffers ⟨he *had* that punishment *coming*⟩ — **have it in for** : to intend to do harm to — **have one's eye on** : to watch constantly and attentively — **have to do with 1** : to deal with ⟨the book *has to do with* fish⟩ **2** : to have a specified relationship with or effect on ⟨luck *had* nothing *to do with* winning⟩

²**have** \'hav\ *n* : one that has much material wealth

ha·ven \'hā-vən\ *n* **1** : ¹HARBOR 2, PORT **2** : a place of safety : SHELTER

have–not \'hav-ˌnät, -ˌnät\ *n* : one that is poor in material wealth

haven't \'hav-ənt\ : have not

hav·er·sack \'hav-ər-ˌsak\ *n* : a bag similar to a knapsack but worn over one shoulder

hav·oc \'hav-ək\ *n* **1** : wide and general destruction ⟨*hav-oc* caused by a tornado⟩ **2** : great confusion and disorder

¹**haw** \'hȯ\ *vb* **1** : to make a sound (as \ə\) which is usually written as *haw* ⟨hemmed and *hawed* before answering⟩ **2** : to hesitate in speaking

²**haw** *n* : a pause in speaking filled by the sound which is usually written as *haw*

³**haw** *imperative verb* — used as a direction to turn left

Ha·waii–Aleu·tian time \hə-ˌwä-(y)ē-ə-ˈlü-shən-, -ˈwī-, -ˈwȯ-\ *n* : the time of the 10th time zone west of Greenwich that includes the Hawaiian Islands and the Aleutian Islands west of the Fox group

Ha·wai·ian \hə-ˈwä-yən, -ˈwī(y)ən, -ˈwȯ-yən\ *n* **1** : a person born or living in Hawaii; *esp* : one of Polynesian ancestry **2** : the Polynesian language of the Hawaiians — **Hawaiian** *adj*

¹**hawk** \'hȯk\ *n* **1** : any of numerous birds of prey that have a strong hooked bill and sharp curved claws and are smaller than most eagles **2** : a person who supports war or warlike policies [Old English *hafoc* "hawk"] — **hawk·ish** \'hȯ-kish\ *adj*

¹hawk 1

²**hawk** *vb* : to hunt birds by means of a trained hawk

³**hawk** *vb* : to offer for sale by calling out in the street ⟨*hawk* vegetables⟩ [back-formation from ²*hawker*]

⁴**hawk** *vb* **1** : to make a harsh coughing sound in or as if in clearing the throat **2** : to raise by hawking ⟨*hawk* up phlegm⟩

¹**hawk·er** \'hȯ-kər\ *n* : FALCONER

²**hawker** *n* : a person who hawks wares [Low German *höker*, from *höken* "to peddle"]

hawk moth *n* : any of numerous moths with a stout body, long strong narrow pointed front wings, and small hind wings

hawk·weed \'hȯ-ˌkwēd\ *n* : any of several plants related to the daisies and having usually yellow, red, or orange flowers — compare ORANGE HAWKWEED

haw·ser \'hȯ-zər\ *n* : a large rope for towing or tying up a ship

haw·thorn \'hȯ-ˌthȯ(ə)rn\ *n* : any of a genus of thorny shrubs or small trees that are related to the roses and have glossy leaves, white or pink fragrant flowers that bloom in the spring, and small red fruits

¹**hay** \'hā\ *n* : herbs (as grasses) cut and dried for use as fodder

²**hay** *vb* **1** : to cut, cure, and store plants for hay **2** : to feed with hay

hay·cock \'hā-ˌkäk\ *n* : a cone-shaped pile of hay

hay fever *n* : an allergy to pollen that is usually marked by sneezing, a runny or stuffed nose, and itchy and watering eyes

hay·loft \-ˌlȯft\ *n* : the upper part of a barn where hay is stored

hay·mow \-ˌmau̇\ *n* : HAYLOFT

hay·rack \-ˌrak\ *n* : a frame mounted on a wagon and used especially in hauling hay or straw; *also* : the wagon and frame

hay·rick \-ˌrik\ *n* : a large sometimes thatched outdoor stack of hay

hay·stack \-ˌstak\ *n* : a stack of hay

hay·wire \-ˌwī(ə)r\ *adv or adj* **1** : being out of order : not working ⟨the radio went *haywire*⟩ **2** : CRAZY 1

¹**haz·ard** \'haz-ərd\ *n* **1** : a game of chance played with two dice **2** : ¹CHANCE 1, ACCIDENT **3** : a source of danger ⟨a fire *hazard*⟩ **4** : an obstacle on a golf course **synonyms** see DANGER

Word History *Hazard* was at first a game of chance played with dice. The English word comes from an early form of French, in which the game was called *hasard*. This French word was probably borrowed during the time of the Crusades from Arabic *az-zahr*, meaning "the die (one of the dice)." The game was borrowed from the French by the English, and within a few centuries what had been a chance taken on the outcome of a throw of the dice could be any venture or risk. Now "chance" or "venture" and "risk" or "peril" are the usual meanings of *hazard*. [Middle English *hazard* "game of chance," from early French *hasard* (same meaning), from Arabic *az-zahr* "the die (one of the dice)"]

²**hazard** *vb* : ¹VENTURE 1, RISK ⟨*hazard* a guess⟩

haz·ard·ous \'haz-ərd-əs\ *adj* : DANGEROUS 1, RISKY ⟨a *hazardous* voyage⟩ — **haz·ard·ous·ly** *adv* — **haz·ard·ous·ness** *n*

¹**haze** \'hāz\ *n* **1** : fine dust, smoke, or light vapor causing lack of transparency in the air **2** : unclearness of mind or perception : DAZE [from *hazy*]

²**haze** *vb* **hazed; haz·ing** : to make or become hazy or cloudy

³**haze** *vb* **hazed; haz·ing** : to play unpleasant and humiliating tricks on (as new members of a college fraternity) or force to perform humiliating tasks or stunts [origin unknown] — **haz·er** *n*

ha·zel \'hā-zəl\ *n* **1** : any of a genus of shrubs or small trees related to birches and bearing edible nuts enclosed in a leafy case **2** : a light brown to a strong yellowish brown — **hazel** *adj*

ha·zel·nut \-ˌnət\ *n* : the nut of a hazel

hazy \'hā-zē\ *adj* **haz·i·er; -est 1** : partly hidden or darkened by or as if by haze ⟨*hazy* weather⟩ **2** : VAGUE 2, INDEFINITE ⟨a *hazy* idea⟩ — **haz·i·ly** \-zə-lē\ *adv* — **haz·i·ness** \-zē-nəs\ *n*

hazel 1

H–bomb \'āch-ˌbäm\ *n* : HYDROGEN BOMB

he \(ˈ)hē, ē\ *pron* **1** : that male one who is neither speaker nor hearer ⟨*he* is my father⟩ **2** — used in a general sense or when the sex of the person is unknown ⟨everyone should do the best *he* can⟩ ⟨tell whoever is in there that *he* had better come out⟩

¹**head** \'hed\ *n* **1** : the upper or front part of the body (as of a human being or an insect) that contains the brain, the chief sense organs, and the mouth **2 a** : ¹MIND 2, UNDERSTANDING ⟨a good *head* for figures⟩ **b** : control of the

mind or feelings ⟨kept a level *head* in time of danger⟩ **3** : the side of a coin bearing a head or the major design **4 a** : PERSON 1, INDIVIDUAL ⟨count *heads*⟩ **b** *pl* **head** : one of a number (as of livestock) ⟨100 *head* of cattle⟩ **5 a** : the end that is upper or higher or opposite the foot ⟨the *head* of the bed⟩ **b** : the uppermost part : TOP **c** : a skin or something like a thin piece of skin stretched across one or both ends of a drum **6** : HEADMASTER **7** : a compact mass of plant parts (as leaves or flowers) ⟨a *head* of cabbage⟩ **8 a** : the place where a stream begins **b** : the difference in elevation between two points in a body of fluid **c** : the resulting pressure at the lower point; *also* : pressure of a fluid ⟨a *head* of steam⟩ **9 a** : the place of leadership or command ⟨the person at the *head* of the group⟩ **b** : a person in this place : CHIEF, LEADER **10** : the foam that rises on a foaming liquid **11 a** : the part of a boil, pimple, or abscess at which it is likely to break **b** : CRISIS 2 ⟨events came to a *head*⟩ **12** : a part of a machine, tool, or weapon that performs the main function ⟨*head* of a lance⟩ ⟨a machine with a grinding *head*⟩ — **head·ship** \'hed-ˌship\ *n* — **out of one's head** : DELIRIOUS 1 — **over one's head 1** : beyond one's understanding **2** : so as to bypass one in a higher position ⟨went over the principal's *head* to complain to the school board⟩

²head *adj* **1** : PRINCIPAL, CHIEF ⟨*head* cook⟩ **2** : placed at the head ⟨sat at the *head* table at the banquet⟩ **3** : coming from in front ⟨*head* sea⟩

³head *vb* **1** : to form a head ⟨this cabbage *heads* early⟩ **2** : to be or put oneself at the head of : LEAD ⟨*head* a revolt⟩ ⟨*head* the list of heroes⟩ **3 a** : to get in front of so as to hinder, stop, or turn back ⟨*head* them off at the pass⟩ **b** : to take a lead over (as in a race) **4** : to go or point in a specified course ⟨*head* for home⟩ ⟨*head* the ship north⟩

head·ache \'hed-ˌāk\ *n* **1** : pain in the head **2** : an annoying or baffling situation or problem — **head·achy** \-ˌā-kē\ *adj*

head·band \-ˌband\ *n* : a band worn on or around the head

head·board \-ˌbō(ə)rd, -ˌbȯ(ə)rd\ *n* : a board forming the head (as of a bed)

head cold *n* : a common cold centered in the nasal passages and nearby tissues

head·dress \'hed-ˌdres\ *n* : a covering or ornament for the head

head·ed \'hed-əd\ *adj* : having such a head or so many heads ⟨curly-*headed*⟩ ⟨two-*headed* ax⟩

head·er \'hed-ər\ *n* : a fall or dive headfirst ⟨took a *header* downstairs⟩

head·first \'hed-'fərst\ *adv* : with the head foremost — **headfirst** *adj*

head·gear \-ˌgi(ə)r\ *n* **1** : a covering (as a hat or helmet) for the head **2** : harness for a horse's head

head–hunt·ing \-ˌhənt-iŋ\ *n* : the practice of cutting off and preserving the heads of enemies — **head·hunt·er** *n*

head·ing \'hed-iŋ\ *n* **1** : the direction in which a ship or aircraft points **2** : something (as a title or an address) at the top or beginning (as of a letter or chapter)

head·land \'hed-lənd, -ˌland\ *n* : a point of land sticking out into the sea : PROMONTORY

head·less \'hed-ləs\ *adj* **1** : having no head **2** : having no chief **3** : lacking good sense or prudence : FOOLISH — **head·less·ness** *n*

head·light \'hed-ˌlīt\ *n* : a light on the front of a vehicle

¹head·line \-ˌlīn\ *n* **1** : a line at the top of a page (as in a book) giving a heading **2** : the title over an item or article in a newspaper

²headline *vb* **1** : to provide with a headline **2** : to publicize highly

¹head·long \'hed-'lȯŋ\ *adv* **1** : HEADFIRST **2** : without careful thought : RECKLESSLY

²headlong *adj* **1** : lacking in calmness or restraint : RASH ⟨*headlong* flight⟩ **2** : plunging headfirst ⟨a *headlong* dive⟩

head louse *n* : a sucking louse that lives on the human scalp

head·man \'hed-'man, -ˌman\ *n* : one who is a leader (as of a tribe, clan, or village) : CHIEF

head·mas·ter \-ˌmas-tər, -'mas-\ *n* : a male head of a private school

head·mis·tress \-ˌmis-trəs, -'mis-\ *n* : a female head of a private school

head–on \-'ȯn, -'än\ *adj* : having the head or front facing forward : front to front ⟨a *head-on* collision⟩

head over heels *adv* **1** : in or as if in a somersault ⟨fell *head over heels* down the hill⟩ **2** : very much : DEEPLY ⟨*head over heels* in love⟩

head·phone \'hed-ˌfōn\ *n* : an earphone held over the ear by a band worn on the head — usually used in plural

head·piece \-ˌpēs\ *n* : a protective covering for the head

head·pin \-ˌpin\ *n* : a pin that stands at the front in a triangular arrangement of bowling pins

head·quar·ters \'hed-ˌkwȯ(r)t-ərz, (')hed-'kwȯ(r)t-ərz\ *n sing or pl* **1** : a place from which a commander exercises command **2** : the governing and directing center of an organization

headphone

head·rest \'hed-ˌrest\ *n* : a support for the head

head·set \-ˌset\ *n* : a pair of headphones

head·shrink·er \-ˌshriŋk-ər\ *n, slang* : PSYCHIATRIST

heads·man \'hedz-mən\ *n* : one that beheads

head·stand \'hed-ˌstand\ *n* : the acrobatic feat of standing on one's head usually with support from the hands

head start *n* **1** : an advantage given to a contestant at the beginning of a race ⟨a five-minute *head start*⟩ **2** : a favorable or promising beginning

head·stone \-ˌstōn\ *n* : a memorial stone placed at the head of a grave

head·strong \-ˌstrȯŋ\ *adj* **1** : not easily controlled : wanting one's own way ⟨a *headstrong* child⟩ **2** : directed by uncontrollable will ⟨violent *headstrong* actions⟩ **synonyms** see UNRULY

head·wait·er \-'wāt-ər\ *n* : the head of the dining-room staff of a restaurant or hotel

head·wa·ter \-ˌwȯt-ər, -ˌwät-\ *n* : the beginning and upper part of a stream — usually used in plural

head·way \-ˌwā\ *n* **1** : motion forward **2** : ¹PROGRESS 2

head·wind \-ˌwind\ *n* : a wind blowing in a direction opposite to a course of movement (as of a ship or aircraft)

head·work \'hed-ˌwərk\ *n* : mental work : clever thinking

heady \'hed-ē\ *adj* **head·i·er; -est 1** : WILLFUL 1, RASH **2** : likely to make one giddy ⟨*heady* wine⟩ ⟨a *heady* height⟩ — **head·i·ly** \'hed-ə-lē\ *adv* — **head·i·ness** \'hed-ē-nəs\ *n*

heal \'hē(ə)l\ *vb* : to make or become healthy or whole ⟨*heal* the sick⟩ ⟨a cut that *heals* slowly⟩

heal·er \'hē-lər\ *n* : one that heals

health \'helth\ *n* **1 a** : the condition of being sound in body, mind, or spirit; *esp* : freedom from disease **b** : the overall condition of the body ⟨in poor *health*⟩ **2** : flourishing condition **3** : a toast to someone's health or suc-

\ə\ **abut**	\au̇\ **out**	\i\ **tip**	\ȯ\ **saw**	\u̇\ **foot**
\ər\ **further**	\ch\ **chin**	\ī\ **life**	\ȯi\ **coin**	\y\ **yet**
\a\ **mat**	\e\ **pet**	\j\ **job**	\th\ **thin**	\yü\ **few**
\ā\ **take**	\ē\ **easy**	\ŋ\ **sing**	\th\ **this**	\yu̇\ **cure**
\ä\ **cot, cart**	\g\ **go**	\ō\ **bone**	\ü\ **food**	\zh\ **vision**

cess ⟨drink a *health*⟩ [Old English *hælth* "health," from *hāl* "healthy" — related to ¹HALE]

health food *n* : a food that is said to be especially good for one's health

health·ful \'helth-fəl\ *adj* **1** : good for the health of the body or mind ⟨*healthful* exercise⟩ **2** : HEALTHY 1 — **health·ful·ly** \-fə-lē\ *adv* — **health·ful·ness** *n*
synonyms HEALTHFUL, WHOLESOME mean good for the health of the body or mind. HEALTHFUL suggests a positive contribution to a healthy condition ⟨a *healthful* diet⟩. WHOLESOME applies to whatever benefits, builds up, or maintains one's physical, mental, or spiritual health ⟨*wholesome* foods⟩ ⟨*wholesome* family entertainment⟩.

healthy \'hel-thē\ *adj* **health·i·er; -est 1 a** : being in good health : WELL **b** : indicating good health ⟨*healthy* complexion⟩ **2** : HEALTHFUL 1 **3 a** : enjoying vigorous and rapid growth ⟨a *healthy* economy⟩ **b** : not small or feeble : CONSIDERABLE ⟨a *healthy* crowd in attendance⟩ — **health·i·ly** \-thə-lē\ *adv* — **health·i·ness** \-thē-nəs\ *n*

¹heap \'hēp\ *n* **1** : a collection of things thrown one on another : PILE ⟨a rubbish *heap*⟩ **2** : a great number or large quantity : LOT ⟨*heaps* of money⟩ ⟨a *heap* of fun⟩

²heap *vb* **1** : to throw or lay in a heap : AMASS, PILE ⟨*heap* up leaves⟩ **2** : to toss or give in large quantities ⟨*heaped* scorn on our efforts⟩ **3** : to form a heap on : load heavily ⟨*heaped* the plate with food⟩

hear \'hi(ə)r\ *vb* **heard** \'hərd\; **hear·ing** \'hi(ə)r-iŋ\ **1** : to take in through the ear ⟨*hear* music⟩; *also* : to have the power of taking in sound ⟨doesn't *hear* well⟩ **2** : to gain knowledge of by hearing : LEARN ⟨*heard* you're leaving⟩ **3** : to listen to : HEED ⟨*hear* me out⟩ **4 a** : to give a legal hearing to ⟨*hear* a case⟩ **b** : to take testimony from ⟨*hear* witnesses⟩ **5 a** : to get news ⟨*heard* from them yesterday⟩ **b** : to have knowledge ⟨never *heard* of such a thing⟩ **6** : to consider the idea ⟨wouldn't *hear* of it⟩ — **hear·er** \'hir-ər\ *n*

hear·ing *n* **1 a** : the process or power of taking in sound : the sense by which a person hears **b** : the range within which the normal voice may be heard ⟨stay within *hearing*⟩ **2 a** : a chance to present one's case ⟨demanded a *hearing*⟩ **b** : a listening to arguments or testimony **c** : a session in which testimony is heard ⟨held public *hearings* on the bill⟩

hearing aid *n* : an electronic device usually worn by a person with poor hearing to make sounds louder

hear·ken \'här-kən\ *vb* **hear·kened; hear·ken·ing** \'härk-(ə-)niŋ\ : LISTEN 1, ATTEND

hear·say \'hi(ə)r-,sā\ *n* **1** : something heard from another : RUMOR **2** : HEARSAY EVIDENCE

hearsay evidence *n* : a statement made out of court and not under oath that is offered as proof that what is stated is true

hearse \'hərs\ *n* : a vehicle for conveying the dead to the grave
Word History An early form of French used the word *herce* for a harrow, a farm tool used to break up and smooth the soil. *Herce* was also applied to a triangular frame that was similar in shape to the frame of a harrow and was used for holding candles. *Herce* was borrowed into English as *hearse,* and both the literal sense of "harrow" and the extended sense of "a frame for holding candles" were kept. In those days a large and decorative framework might be raised over the tomb or coffin of an honored person. Because this framework was often decorated with candles, the word *hearse* was applied to it. A series of slightly changed meanings led to the use of *hearse* for a platform for a corpse or coffin, and from that to a vehicle to carry the dead to the grave. [Middle English *herse* "a triangular frame for holding candles," from early French *herce* "frame for holding candles, harrow," from Latin *hirpex* "harrow"]

heart \'härt\ *n* **1 a** : a hollow muscular organ of vertebrates that expands and contracts to move blood through the arteries, veins, and capillaries **b** : a structure in an invertebrate that serves a purpose like that of the heart of a vertebrate **2** : the central or most important part ⟨the *heart* of a forest⟩ ⟨the *heart* of the argument⟩ **3 a** : something resembling a heart in shape **b** : a playing card marked with red simplified patterns of hearts **c** *pl* : a card game whose object is to avoid taking tricks with hearts **4 a** : human feelings : AFFECTION, KINDNESS ⟨a ruler without *heart*⟩ **b** : COURAGE, SPIRIT ⟨take *heart*⟩ **5** : PERSONALITY 2, DISPOSITION **3** ⟨a cold *heart*⟩ — **heart·ed** \-əd\ *adj* — **by heart** : by rote or from memory — **to heart** : with deep concern

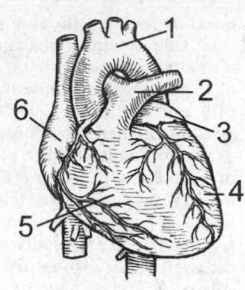

heart 1a: *1* aorta, *2* pulmonary artery, *3* left atrium, *4* left ventricle, *5* right ventricle, *6* right atrium

heart·ache \'härt-,āk\ *n* : ¹SORROW 1a, ANGUISH

heart attack *n* : a sudden severe occurrence of damage to heart muscle caused by too little blood going to the heart usually as a result of the blocking of a coronary artery (as by a bit of fatty matter)

heart·beat \'härt-,bēt\ *n* : a single contracting and expanding of the heart

heart·break \-,brāk\ *n* : crushing grief, anguish, or distress — **heart·break·ing** \-,brā-kiŋ\ *adj* — **heart·break·ing·ly** *adv* — **heart·bro·ken** \-,brō-kən\ *adj*

heart·burn \-,bərn\ *n* : a burning discomfort seeming to occur in the area of the heart and usually due to spasms which pass acid from the stomach into the esophagus

heart disease *n* : an abnormal condition of the heart or of the heart and blood circulation

heart·en \'härt-ᵊn\ *vb* **heart·ened; heart·en·ing** \'härt-niŋ, -ᵊn-iŋ\ : to cheer up : ENCOURAGE

heart·felt \'härt-,felt\ *adj* : deeply felt : EARNEST ⟨*heartfelt* thanks⟩

hearth \'härth\ *n* **1 a** : the area in front of a fireplace **b** : the floor of a fireplace **c** : the lowest section of a blast furnace **2** : ¹HOME 1a

hearth·stone \-,stōn\ *n* **1** : stone forming a hearth **2** : ¹HOME 1a

heart·i·ly \'härt-ᵊl-ē\ *adv* **1** : with sincerity, goodwill, or enthusiasm ⟨set to work *heartily*⟩ ⟨eat *heartily*⟩ **2** : in a cheerful manner ⟨make a guest *heartily* welcome⟩ **3** : in a complete or thorough manner ⟨*heartily* sick of their complaints⟩

H hearth 1a

heart·land \'härt-,land\ *n* : a central land area; *esp* : one of great economic and military importance

heart·less \'härt-ləs\ *adj* : PITILESS, CRUEL — **heart·less·ly** *adv* — **heart·less·ness** *n*

heart·rend·ing \'härt-,ren-diŋ\ *adj* : causing heartbreak ⟨a *heartrending* tragedy⟩

heart·sick \-,sik\ *adj* : very sad and discouraged : DEPRESSED — **heart·sick·ness** *n*

heart·sore \-,sō(ə)r, -,sò(ə)r\ *adj* : HEARTSICK

heart·string \-,striŋ\ *n* : the deepest emotions or affections ⟨touched the *heartstrings* of the audience⟩

heart·throb \-ˌthräb\ *n* **1** : the throb of a heart **2** : a sentimental emotion : PASSION **b** : SWEETHEART; *also* : an attractive and usually famous man

heart–to–heart \ˌhärt-tə-ˌhärt\ *adj* : FRANK, SINCERE ⟨a *heart-to-heart* talk⟩

heart·warm·ing \ˈhärt-ˌwȯr-miŋ\ *adj* : making one feel good inside : cheering to one's emotions

heart·wood \-ˌwu̇d\ *n* : the older harder nonliving and usually darker wood of the central part of a tree trunk — compare SAPWOOD

¹hearty \ˈhärt-ē\ *adj* **heart·i·er; -est 1 a** : WHOLEHEARTED, SINCERE ⟨*hearty* agreement⟩ **b** : enthusiastically friendly ⟨a *hearty* welcome⟩ **c** : UNRESTRAINED 2 ⟨*hearty* laughter⟩ **2 a** : exhibiting very good health ⟨hale and *hearty*⟩ **b** : having a good appetite ⟨a *hearty* eater⟩ **c** : being plentiful and satisfying ⟨a *hearty* meal⟩ **3** : ENERGETIC, VIGOROUS ⟨gave a *hearty* pull⟩ — **heart·i·ness** *n*

²hearty *n, pl* **heart·ies** : COMRADE; *also* : SAILOR

¹heat \ˈhēt\ *vb* **1** : to make or become warm or hot **2** : to make excited

²heat *n* **1 a** : a condition of being hot : WARMTH **b** : a high degree of hotness **c** : a hot place or period ⟨the *heat* of the day⟩ **d** : a form of energy that causes substances to rise in temperature or to go through associated changes (as melting, evaporation, or expansion) **2 a** : strength of feeling ⟨answered with some *heat*⟩ **b** : the height of an action or condition ⟨the *heat* of battle⟩ **c** : ESTRUS 1 **3** : a single race in a contest made up of two or more races — **heat·less** \ˈhēt-ləs\ *adj* — **heat·proof** \-ˈprüf\ *adj*

heat·ed \ˈhēt-əd\ *adj* : marked by excited or angry feelings ⟨a *heated* debate⟩ — **heat·ed·ly** *adv*

heat·er \ˈhēt-ər\ *n* : a device that heats or holds something to be heated

heat exchanger *n* : a device (as an automobile radiator) for transferring heat from one fluid to another without allowing them to mix

heat exhaustion *n* : a condition marked by weakness, nausea, dizziness, and much sweating that results from physical exertion in a hot environment — called also *heat prostration;* compare HEAT STROKE

heath \ˈhēth\ *n* **1** : any of a family of shrubby often evergreen plants that grow well on open barren usually acid and poorly drained soil; *esp* : a low evergreen shrub with needlelike leaves and clusters of small flowers **2** : a usually level area of land overgrown with low shrubs — **heathy** \ˈhē-thē\ *adj*

hea·then \ˈhē-thən\ *n, pl* **heathens** *or* **heathen 1** : a person who does not know about and worship the God of the Bible : PAGAN **2** : an uncivilized person — **heathen** *adj* — **hea·then·dom** \-dəm\ *n* — **hea·then·ish** \-thə-nish\ *adj* — **hea·then·ism** \-ˌniz-əm\ *n*

heath·er \ˈheth-ər\ *n* : HEATH 1; *esp* : a common evergreen heath of northern and alpine regions with very small stemless leaves and tiny usually purplish pink flowers — **heath·ery** \-(ə-)rē\ *adj*

heath hen *n* : an extinct grouse of the northeastern U.S. related to the prairie chicken

heat lightning *n* : flashes of lightning without thunder seen near the horizon

heat pump *n* : a device for heating or cooling a building by transferring heat contained in a fluid to or from the building

heat rash *n* : PRICKLY HEAT

heat shield *n* : a barrier of insulation to protect a space capsule from heat on its return to earth

heat·stroke \ˈhēt-ˌstrōk\ *n* : a condition marked especially by the stopping of sweating, a high body temperature, and exhaustion that results from exposure to high temperature for a long time — compare SUNSTROKE

heat wave *n* : a period of unusually hot weather

¹heave \ˈhēv\ *vb* **heaved** *or* **hove** \ˈhōv\; **heav·ing 1** : to raise with effort ⟨*heave* a trunk onto a truck⟩ **2** : ¹THROW 1a, CAST, HURL ⟨*heave* a rock⟩ **3** : to utter with effort ⟨*heave* a sigh⟩ **4** : to rise and fall repeatedly ⟨the runner's chest was *heaving*⟩ **5** : to be thrown up or raised ⟨the ground *heaved* during the earthquake⟩ **6** : ²VOMIT **1** *synonyms* see RAISE — **heav·er** *n* — **heave to** : to bring a ship to a stop

²heave *n* **1 a** : an effort to heave or raise **b** : a forceful throw : CAST **2** : a rhythmic rising (as of the chest in breathing)

heav·en \ˈhev-ən\ *n* **1** : SKY 1 — usually used in plural **2** *often cap* : the dwelling place of God and of the blessed dead **3** : a place or condition of complete happiness

heav·en·ly \ˈhev-ən-lē\ *adj* **1** : of or relating to heaven or the heavens ⟨*heavenly* bodies such as the stars⟩ **2** : suggesting the blessed state of heaven ⟨*heavenly* grace⟩ **3** : completely delightful ⟨a *heavenly* day⟩ — **heav·en·li·ness** *n*

heav·en·ward \ˈhev-ən-wərd\ *adv or adj* : toward heaven

heavier–than–air *adj* : of greater weight than the air that would occupy the same amount of space

¹heavy \ˈhev-ē\ *adj* **heavi·er; -est 1 a** : having great weight or greater than usual weight **b** : weighty in proportion to bulk : having a high density ⟨gold is a *heavy* metal⟩ **c** : having or being atoms of greater than normal mass ⟨*heavy* isotopes⟩ **2** : very hard to deal with : GRIEVOUS ⟨a *heavy* sorrow⟩ **3** : of weighty importance : SERIOUS ⟨*words heavy* with meaning⟩ **4** : lacking life, gaiety, or charm : DULL **5** : DROWSY 1 **6** : greater in volume, force, or power than the average ⟨*heavy* traffic⟩ ⟨*heavy* seas⟩ ⟨*heavy* infantry⟩ **7** : ²OVERCAST ⟨a *heavy* sky⟩ **8** : LABORIOUS 2, LABORED ⟨*heavy* breathing⟩ **9** : using or consuming much ⟨a *heavy* eater⟩ **10** : rich and not easily digested ⟨*heavy* desserts⟩ **11** : producing goods (as coal or steel) used in the production of other goods ⟨*heavy* industry⟩ — **heavi·ly** \ˈhev-ə-lē\ *adv* — **heavi·ness** \ˈhev-ē-nəs\ *n*

²heavy *adv* : in a heavy manner : HEAVILY ⟨time hung *heavy* on their hands⟩

³heavy *n, pl* **heav·ies 1** : HEAVYWEIGHT 2 **2 a** : a theatrical role or an actor representing a dignified or impressive person **b** : VILLAIN 2

heavy–du·ty \ˌhev-ē-ˈd(y)üt-ē\ *adj* : able or designed to take hard use or great strain ⟨*heavy-duty* vehicles⟩

heavy–hand·ed \ˌhev-ē-ˈhan-dəd\ *adj* **1** : CLUMSY 1 **2** : severe or harsh in dealing with others

heavy hydrogen *n* : DEUTERIUM

heavy·set \ˌhev-ē-ˈset\ *adj* : STOCKY; *also* : ¹STOUT 4

heavy water *n* : water enriched in deuterium

heavy·weight \ˈhev-ē-ˌwāt\ *n* **1** : one above average in weight **2** : one in the heaviest class of contestants; *esp* : a boxer in an unlimited weight division **3** : someone or something that is very important or powerful ⟨a company that is an industry *heavyweight*⟩

He·brew \ˈhē-(ˌ)brü\ *n* **1** : a member of one of a group of northern Semitic peoples including the Israelites; *esp* : ISRAELITE **2** : the Semitic language of the Hebrews — **He·bra·ic** \hi-ˈbrā-ik\ *adj* — **Hebrew** *adj*

He·brews \ˈhē-(ˌ)brüz\ *n* — see BIBLE table

heck·le \ˈhek-əl\ *vb* **heck·led; heck·ling** \-(ə-)liŋ\ : to interrupt with questions or comments usually with the intention of annoying or hindering ⟨were *heckling* the speaker⟩ — **heck·ler** \-(ə-)lər\ *n*

\ə\ **abut**	\au̇\ **out**	\i\ **tip**	\ȯ\ **saw**	\u̇\ **foot**
\ər\ **further**	\ch\ **chin**	\ī\ **life**	\ȯi\ **coin**	\y\ **yet**
\a\ **mat**	\e\ **pet**	\j\ **job**	\th\ **thin**	\yü\ **few**
\ā\ **take**	\ē\ **easy**	\ŋ\ **sing**	\th\ **this**	\yu̇\ **cure**
\ä\ **cot, cart**	\g\ **go**	\ō\ **bone**	\ü\ **food**	\zh\ **vision**

hect- *or* **hecto-** *combining form* : hundred [from French *hect-* "hundred," an altered form of Greek *hekaton* "hundred"]

hect·are \'hek-ˌta(ə)r, -ˌte(ə)r, -ˌtär\ *n* — see METRIC SYSTEM table

hec·tic \'hek-tik\ *adj* **1** : being hot and flushed **2** : filled with excitement, activity, or confusion ⟨a *hectic* day of shopping⟩ — **hec·ti·cal·ly** \-ti-k(ə-)lē\ *adv*

hec·to·gram \'hek-tə-ˌgram\ *n* — see METRIC SYSTEM table

hec·to·li·ter \'hek-tə-ˌlēt-ər\ *n* — see METRIC SYSTEM table

hec·to·me·ter \'hek-tə-ˌmēt-ər\ *n* — see METRIC SYSTEM table

hec·tor \'hek-tər\ *vb* **hec·tored; hec·tor·ing** \-t(ə-)riŋ\ **1** : to act like a bully : SWAGGER **2** : to frighten by threatening or bullying

he'd \(ˌ)hēd, ēd\ : he had : he would

¹hedge \'hej\ *n* **1** : a boundary formed by a dense row of shrubs or low trees **2** : BARRIER 1, LIMIT

²hedge *vb* **hedged; hedg·ing** **1** : to enclose or protect with or as if with a hedge **2** : to block with or as if with a barrier ⟨*hedged* in by restrictions⟩ **3** : to avoid giving a direct or exact answer or promise ⟨*hedged* when asked to support the campaign⟩ — **hedg·er** *n*

hedge·hog \'hej-ˌhòg, -ˌhäg\ *n* **1** : any of several mammals of Europe, Asia, and Africa that eat insects, have sharp spines mixed with the hair on their back, and are able to roll themselves up into a spiny ball when threatened **2** : PORCUPINE

hedgehog 1

hedge·hop \-ˌhäp\ *vb* : to fly an airplane so low that it is necessary to climb to avoid obstacles (as trees) — **hedge·hop·per** *n*

hedge·row \-ˌrō\ *n* : a row of shrubs or trees forming the boundary of or separating fields

¹heed \'hēd\ *vb* **1** : to pay attention **2** : to take notice of : MIND ⟨*heed* my words⟩

²heed *n* : ATTENTION 1, NOTICE

heed·ful \'hēd-fəl\ *adj* : taking heed : ATTENTIVE — **heed·ful·ly** \-fə-lē\ *adv* — **heed·ful·ness** *n*

heed·less \'hēd-ləs\ *adj* : not taking heed : THOUGHTLESS — **heed·less·ly** *adv* — **heed·less·ness** *n*

¹heel \'hē(ə)l\ *n* **1 a** : the back part of the human foot behind the arch and below the ankle; *also* : the corresponding part of a lower vertebrate **b** : the part of the palm of the hand nearest the wrist **2** : a part (as of a shoe) that covers or supports the human heel **3** : a lower, back, or end part; *esp* : one of the crusty ends of a loaf of bread **4** : a despisable person [Old English *hēla* "back part of the foot"] — **heel·less** \'hē(ə)l-ləs\ *adj* — **on the heels of** : close behind

²heel *vb* : to provide with a heel — **heel·er** \'hē-lər\ *n*

³heel *vb* : to tilt to one side : TIP [Old English *hieldan* "to lean to one side"]

⁴heel *n* : a tilt to one side

¹heft \'heft\ *n* : ¹WEIGHT 1a, HEAVINESS

²heft *vb* **1** : to heave up : LIFT **2** : to test the weight of by lifting

hefty \'hef-tē\ *adj* **heft·i·er; -est** : ¹HEAVY 1a, BULKY — **heft·i·ly** \-tə-lē\ *adv* — **heft·i·ness** \-tē-nəs\ *n*

heif·er \'hef-ər\ *n* : a young cow; *esp* : one that has not had a calf

height \'hīt, 'hītth\ *n* **1 a** : the highest part or point : SUMMIT, CLIMAX **b** : the most advanced or extreme point ⟨the *height* of stupidity⟩ **2 a** : the distance from bottom to top of something **b** : the distance above a level **3** : the condition of being tall or high **4 a** : a landmass rising above the surrounding country **b** : a high point or position

synonyms HEIGHT, ALTITUDE, ELEVATION mean distance upward. HEIGHT refers to measuring something from bottom to top ⟨a wall that is three meters in *height*⟩. ALTITUDE is used in measuring the distance of an object above a fixed level or surface ⟨a plane flying at an *altitude* of 5000 feet⟩. ELEVATION is used in measuring vertical height on land especially above sea level ⟨Denver is situated at a high *elevation*⟩.

height·en \'hīt-ᵊn\ *vb* **height·ened; height·en·ing** \'hīt-niŋ, -ᵊn-iŋ\ **1** : to make or become brighter or greater ⟨*heightened* the citizens' awareness⟩ **2** : to raise high or higher : ELEVATE

Heim·lich maneuver \'hīm-lik-\ *n* : a method for forcing an object out the airway of a choking person that involves standing behind the person with arms wrapped about the person's waist and applying sudden upward pressure with the fist to the area directly above the navel [named after Henry J. *Heimlich*, an American surgeon born in 1920]

hei·nous \'hā-nəs\ *adj* : shockingly evil : ABOMINABLE — **hei·nous·ly** *adv* — **hei·nous·ness** *n*

heir \'a(ə)r, 'e(ə)r\ *n* **1** : a person who inherits or has the right to inherit property **2** : a person who has legal claim to a title or a throne when the person holding it dies — **heir·ship** \-ˌship\ *n*

heir apparent *n, pl* **heirs apparent** : an heir whose right to succeed (as to a throne) cannot be taken away if he or she outlives the present holder

heir·ess \'ar-əs, 'er-\ *n* : a girl or woman who is an heir

heir·loom \'a(ə)r-ˌlüm, 'e(ə)r-\ *n* : a piece of personal property handed down from generation to generation

heist \'hīst\ *n* : armed robbery; *also* : THEFT [from a dialect variant of *hoist* "an act of hoisting"]

held *past of* HOLD

he·li·cop·ter \'hel-ə-ˌkäp-tər, 'hē-lə-\ *n* : an aircraft that is supported in the air by propellers revolving on a vertical axis

he·lio·cen·tric \ˌhē-lē-ō-'sen-trik\ *adj* **1** : referred to or measured from the sun's center or appearing as if seen from it **2** : having or relating to the sun as a center

he·lio·sphere \'hē-lē-ə-ˌsfir, -ō-\ *n* : the region of space that is affected by the sun or solar wind

he·lio·trope \'hē-lē-ə-ˌtrōp, 'hēl-yə-\ *n* : any of a genus of herbs or shrubs having small white or purple flowers

he·li·ot·ro·pism \ˌhē-lē-'ä-trə-ˌpiz-əm\ *n* : a turning or curving (as of a sunflower head) toward the sunlight

he·li·port \'hel-ə-ˌpō(ə)rt, 'hē-lə-, -ˌpò(ə)rt\ *n* : a landing and takeoff place for a helicopter

he·li·um \'hē-lē-əm\ *n* : a light colorless nonflammable element that is found in various natural gases and is used especially to blow up balloons — see ELEMENT table

he·lix \'hē-liks\ *n, pl* **he·li·ces** \'hel-ə-ˌsēz, 'hē-lə-\ *also* **he·lix·es** \'hē-lik-səz\ : a curve that is formed by a point rotating around a straight line and moving forward in a direction parallel to that line — compare DOUBLE HELIX — **he·li·cal** \'hel-i-kəl, 'hē-li-\ *adj*

hell \'hel\ *n* **1** : a place where souls are believed to survive after death **2** : the place or state of punishment for the wicked after death : the home of evil spirits **3** : a place or condition of misery or wickedness **4** : a place or state of great confusion, disorder, or destruction : HAVOC, PANDEMONIUM **5** : something that causes torment; *esp* : a severe scolding

he'll \(ˌ)hē(ə)l, hil, ēl, il\ : he shall : he will

hell·ben·der \\'hel-ˌben-dər\\ *n* : a large water-dwelling salamander of streams of the eastern and central U.S.

hellbender

hell–bent \\-ˌbent\\ *adj* : stubbornly and often recklessly determined ⟨*hell-bent* on revenge⟩

hel·le·bore \\'hel-ə-ˌbō(ə)r, -ˌbȯ(ə)r\\ *n* **1** : any of a genus of poisonous herbs related to the buttercups; *also* : its dried root formerly used in medicine **2** : a poisonous herb related to the lilies; *also* : its dried root or a product of this containing chemical substances used in medicine and insecticides

Hel·lene \\'hel-ˌēn\\ *n* : GREEK **1** — **Hel·len·ic** \\he-'len-ik, hə-\\ *adj*

Hel·le·nis·tic \\ˌhel-ə-'nis-tik\\ *adj* : of or relating to the widespread Greek-based culture that developed after the conquests of Alexander the Great

hell·gram·mite \\'hel-grə-ˌmīt\\ *n* : the larva of a dobsonfly that lives in water and is much used as fish bait

hell·ion \\'hel-yən\\ *n* : a troublesome or mischievous person

hell·ish \\'hel-ish\\ *adj* : of, resembling, or suitable to hell : INFERNAL — **hell·ish·ly** *adv* — **hell·ish·ness** *n*

hel·lo \\hə-'lō, he-\\ *n, pl* **hellos** : an expression or gesture of greeting — used in greeting, in answering the telephone, or to express surprise

¹helm \\'helm\\ *n* : HELMET 1

²helm *n* **1** : a lever or wheel controlling the rudder of a ship; *also* : the steering equipment of a ship **2** : a position of control : HEAD ⟨at the *helm* of the business⟩

hel·met \\'hel-mət\\ *n* **1** : a covering or enclosing headpiece of armor **2** : any of various protective head coverings usually made of a hard material — **hel·met·like** \\-ˌlīk\\ *adj*

helms·man \\'helmz-mən\\ *n* : the person at the helm

hel·ot \\'hel-ət\\ *n* : SERF, SLAVE

¹help \\'help\\ *vb* **1** : to provide with what is useful in achieving an end : AID, ASSIST ⟨*helped* me get a job⟩ **2** : ²REMEDY, RELIEVE ⟨rest *helps* a cold⟩ **3 a** : to keep from ⟨couldn't *help* laughing⟩ **b** : PREVENT 1 ⟨it couldn't be *helped*⟩ **4** : to serve with food or drink ⟨*help* yourself⟩

²help *n* **1** : an act or instance of helping : AID, ASSISTANCE ⟨give *help*⟩ ⟨thanked us for our *help*⟩ **2** : the state of being helped : RELIEF ⟨a situation beyond *help*⟩ **3** : a person or a thing that helps ⟨a *help* in time of trouble⟩ **4** : a hired helper or a body of hired helpers ⟨hire new *help*⟩

help·er \\'hel-pər\\ *n* : one that helps; *esp* : a person who helps a more skilled person

helper T cell *n* : a T cell that participates in an immune response by recognizing a foreign antigen and releasing substances which promote an increase in the number of T cells and B cells — called also *helper cell*

help·ful \\'help-fəl\\ *adj* : providing help ⟨a *helpful* neighbor⟩ — **help·ful·ly** \\-fə-lē\\ *adv* — **help·ful·ness** *n*

help·ing \\'hel-pin\\ *n* : a portion of food : SERVING

helping verb *n* : a verb (as *have, be, may, do, shall, will, can, must*) that is used with another verb and expresses such things as person, number, mood, or tense — called also *auxiliary verb*

help·less \\'hel-pləs\\ *adj* **1** : being without defense **2** : POWERLESS — **help·less·ly** *adv* — **help·less·ness** *n*

help·mate \\'help-ˌmāt\\ *n* : one that is a companion and helper; *esp* : WIFE 2

help·meet \\-ˌmēt\\ *n* : HELPMATE

hel·ter–skel·ter \\ˌhel-tər-'skel-tər\\ *adv* **1** : in a confused and reckless manner : PELL-MELL ⟨ran *helter-skelter* down the hill⟩ **2** : in no particular order : HAPHAZARDLY ⟨clothes strewn *helter-skelter* about the room⟩ — **helter–skelter** *adj*

¹hem \\'hem\\ *n* : a border of a garment or cloth made by folding back an edge and sewing it down [Old English *hem* "border on a garment"]

²hem *vb* **hemmed; hem·ming 1** : to finish with or make a hem in sewing **2** : to surround in a confining manner ⟨a town *hemmed* in by mountains⟩ — **hem·mer** *n*

³hem *vb* **hemmed; hem·ming 1** : to make a sound during a pause in speaking which is usually written as *hem* **2** : to hesitate in speaking

⁴hem *a throat-clearing sound; often read as* '*hem*\\ *interj* — often used to indicate a pause in speaking [an imitation of the throat-clearing sound]

hem- *or* **hemo-** *combining form* : blood [derived from Greek *haima* "blood"]

he–man \\'hē-ˌman\\ *n* : a strong active man

he·ma·tite \\'hē-mə-ˌtīt\\ *n* : a mineral that consists of an oxide of iron, is an important iron ore, and is found in crystals or in a red earthy form

he·ma·tol·o·gist \\ˌhē-mə-'täl-ə-jəst\\ *n* : a person who specializes in the study of blood and the blood-forming organs

he·ma·tox·y·lin \\ˌhē-mə-'täk-sə-lən\\ *n* : a compound found in the wood of a tropical American tree and used chiefly as a biological stain

heme \\'hēm\\ *n* : a deep red pigment that contains iron and is obtained from hemoglobin

hemi- *prefix* : half [derived from Greek *hēmi-* "half"]

he·mip·ter·an \\hi-'mip-tə-rən\\ *n* : any of a large order of insects (as the true bugs) having flattened bodies, two pairs of wings, and heads with piercing and sucking organs

hemi·sphere \\'hem-ə-ˌsfi(ə)r\\ *n* **1** : one of the halves of the earth as divided by the equator or by a meridian **2** : one of two halves of a sphere **3** : CEREBRAL HEMISPHERE

hemi·spher·ic \\ˌhem-ə-'sfi(ə)r-ik, -'sfer-\\ *or* **hemi·spher·i·cal** \\-'sfir-i-kəl, -'sfer-\\ *adj* : of or relating to a hemisphere

hem·line \\'hem-ˌlīn\\ *n* : the line formed by the hem of a dress, skirt, or coat

hem·lock \\'hem-ˌläk\\ *n* **1** : any of several poisonous herbs related to the carrot and having finely divided leaves and small white flowers **2** : any of a genus of evergreen trees related to the pines; *also* : the soft light splintery wood of a hemlock

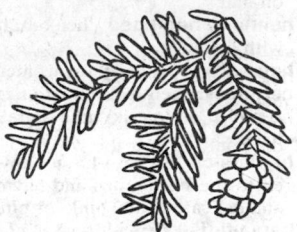

hemlock 2

hemo- — see HEM-

he·mo·glo·bin \\'hē-mə-ˌglō-bən\\ *n* : a protein that contains iron, is the chief means of transporting oxygen in the body of vertebrate animals, occurs in the red blood cells, and is able to combine loosely with oxygen in regions (as the lungs) where it is in high concentration and release it in regions (as the tissues of the internal organs) where it is in low concentration

\\ə\\ **abut**	\\au̇\\ **out**	\\i\\ **tip**	\\ȯ\\ **saw**	\\u̇\\ **foot**	
\\ər\\ **further**	\\ch\\ **chin**	\\ī\\ **life**	\\ȯi\\ **coin**	\\y\\ **yet**	
\\a\\ **mat**	\\e\\ **pet**	\\j\\ **job**	\\th\\ **thin**	\\yü\\ **few**	
\\ā\\ **take**	\\ē\\ **easy**	\\ŋ\\ **sing**	\\th\\ **this**	\\yu̇\\ **cure**	
\\ä\\ **cot, cart**	\\g\\ **go**	\\ō\\ **bone**	\\ü\\ **food**	\\zh\\ **vision**	

he·mo·phil·ia \ˌhē-mə-ˈfil-ē-ə\ *n* : an inherited blood defect that is sex-linked, is found almost always in males, and is marked by delayed clotting of blood and a resulting difficulty in stopping bleeding

he·mo·phil·i·ac \ˌhē-mə-ˈfil-ē-ˌak\ *n* : a person who has hemophilia

¹hem·or·rhage \ˈhem-(ə-)rij\ *n* : a great loss of blood from the blood vessels especially when caused by injury — **hem·or·rhag·ic** \ˌhem-ə-ˈraj-ik\ *adj*

²hemorrhage *vb* **-rhaged; -rhag·ing** : to bleed heavily or uncontrollably

hem·or·rhoid \ˈhem-(ə-)ˌroid\ *n* **1** : a swollen mass of veins located at or just within the anus **2** *pl* : the condition of a person who has hemorrhoids — called also *piles*

hemp \ˈhemp\ *n* **1** : a tall Asian herb widely grown for its tough woody fiber that is used to make rope and for its flowers and leaves from which are obtained various drugs (as hashish and marijuana) that affect the mind or behavior **2** : the fiber of hemp

hemp·en \ˈhem-pən\ *adj* : made of hemp

¹hem·stitch \ˈhem-ˌstich\ *vb* : to embroider fabric by drawing out parallel threads and stitching the exposed threads in groups to form designs — **hem·stitch·er** *n*

²hemstitch *n* **1** : decorative needlework **2** : a stitch used in hemstitching

hen \ˈhen\ *n* **1** : a female chicken especially over a year old **2** : a female of any bird

hence \ˈhen(t)s\ *adv* **1** : from this place or time ⟨a week *hence*⟩ **2** : CONSEQUENTLY, THEREFORE ⟨was a newcomer and *hence* had no close friends in the city⟩

hence·forth \ˈhen(t)s-ˌfō(ə)rth, -ˌfȯ(ə)rth; hen(t)s-ˈfō(ə)rth, -ˈfȯ(ə)rth\ *adv* : from this point on

hence·for·ward \hen(t)s-ˈfȯr-wərd\ *adv* : HENCEFORTH

hench·man \ˈhench-mən\ *n* : a trusted follower or supporter who performs unpleasant, wrong, or illegal tasks for a powerful person

hen·e·quen \ˈhen-i-kən, ˌhen-i-ˈken\ *n* : a strong hard fiber obtained from the leaves of a tropical American agave and used to make twine; *also* : a plant that produces henequen

hen·house \ˈhen-ˌhau̇s\ *n* : a house or shelter for fowl and especially for domestic chickens

¹hen·na \ˈhen-ə\ *n* : a reddish brown dye obtained from the leaves of an Old World tropical shrub and used especially on hair

²henna *vb* **hen·naed** \ˈhen-əd\; **hen·na·ing** : to dye or tint with henna

hen party *n* : a party for women only

hen·peck \ˈhen-ˌpek\ *vb* : to nag and boss one's husband

he·pat·ic \hi-ˈpat-ik\ *adj* : of, relating to, or resembling the liver

he·pat·i·ca \hi-ˈpat-i-kə\ *n* : any of a genus of herbs related to the buttercups and having leaves with three lobes and delicate white, pink, or bluish flowers

hep·a·ti·tis \ˌhep-ə-ˈtīt-əs\ *n, pl* **-tit·i·des** \-ˈtit-ə-ˌdēz\ *also* **-ti·tis·es** \-ˈtīt-ə-səz\ : inflammation of the liver; *also* : any of several virus diseases marked especially by inflammation of the liver

hep·ta·gon \ˈhep-tə-ˌgän\ *n* : a polygon of seven angles and seven sides — **hep·tag·o·nal** \hep-ˈtag-ən-ᵊl\ *adj*

hep·tath·lon \hep-ˈtath-lən, -ˌlän\ *n* : an athletic contest made up of seven different track-and-field events

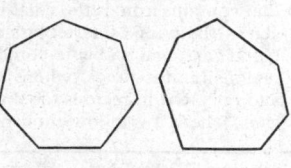

heptagon

¹her \(h)ər, ˌhər\ *adj* : of, relating to, or belonging to her or herself ⟨*her* house⟩ ⟨*her* success⟩

²her \ər, (ˈ)hər\ *pron, objective case of* SHE

¹her·ald \ˈher-əld\ *n* **1** : an official announcer or messenger **2** : an officer responsible for granting and registering coats of arms **3** : one that precedes or foreshadows : HARBINGER

²herald *vb* **1** : to give notice of : ANNOUNCE **2** : to greet with enthusiasm : HAIL

he·ral·dic \he-ˈral-dik, hə-\ *adj* : of or relating to heralds or heraldry — **he·ral·di·cal·ly** \-di-k(ə-)lē\ *adv*

her·ald·ry \ˈher-əl-drē\ *n, pl* **-ries** **1** : the practice of tracing a person's family and finding out the family's coat of arms **2** : COAT OF ARMS

herb \ˈərb *also* ˈhərb\ *n* **1** : a seed-producing plant that does not develop long-lived woody tissue but dies down at the end of a growing season **2** : a plant or plant part used for making medicine and seasonings

her·ba·ceous \ˌ(h)ər-ˈbā-shəs\ *adj* **1** : of, relating to, or resembling an herb **2** : being a stem with little or no woody tissue and lasting usually only for a single growing season

herb·age \ˈ(h)ər-bij\ *n* **1** : vegetation (as grass) composed of herbs especially when used for grazing **2** : the juicy parts of herbs or plants that resemble herbs

herb·al \ˈ(h)ər-bəl\ *adj* : of, relating to, or made of herbs

herbal medicine *n* **1** : the practice of using plants or preparations containing plant products to maintain health and to prevent or treat illness or disease **2** : a preparation consisting of or made from plants that is used medicinally

her·bar·i·um \ˌ(h)ər-ˈbar-ē-əm, -ˈber-\ *n, pl* **her·bar·ia** \-ē-ə\ **1** : a collection of dried plant specimens **2** : a place that houses an herbarium

her·bi·cide \ˈ(h)ər-bə-ˌsīd\ *n* : a chemical substance used to destroy or stop plant growth — **her·bi·cid·al** \ˌ(h)ər-bə-ˈsīd-ᵊl\ *adj*

her·bi·vore \ˈ(h)ər-bə-ˌvō(ə)r, -ˌvȯ(ə)r\ *n* : a plant-eating animal

her·biv·o·rous \ˌ(h)ər-ˈbiv-ə-rəs\ *adj* : eating or living on plants

her·cu·le·an \ˌhər-kyə-ˈlē-ən, hər-ˈkyü-lē-\ *adj* **1** *cap* : of, relating to, or characteristic of Hercules **2** *often cap* : of great power, size, or difficulty ⟨a *herculean* task⟩

¹herd \ˈhərd\ *n* **1** : a number of animals of one kind kept or living together **2** : the common people

²herd *vb* **1** : to assemble or come together into a herd or group **2** : to gather, lead, or drive a herd ⟨*herd* cattle⟩ — **herd·er** *n*

herds·man \ˈhərdz-mən\ *n* : a manager, breeder, or tender of livestock

¹here \ˈhi(ə)r\ *adv* **1** : in or at this place ⟨turn *here*⟩ **2** : at this point ⟨*here* we agree⟩ **3** : to or into this place ⟨come *here*⟩

²here *n* : this place ⟨get away from *here*⟩

here·abouts \ˈhi(ə)r-ə-ˌbau̇ts\ *or* **here·about** \-ˌbau̇t\ *adv* : near or around this place : in this vicinity

¹here·af·ter \hi(ə)r-ˈaf-tər\ *adv* **1** : after this **2** : in some future time or state

²hereafter *n, often cap* **1** : ²FUTURE 1a **2** : life after death ⟨belief in the *hereafter*⟩

here and there *adv* : in one place and another

here·by \hi(ə)r-ˈbī, ˈhi(ə)r-ˌbī\ *adv* : by means of this

he·red·i·tary \hə-ˈred-ə-ˌter-ē\ *adj* **1** : genetically passed or capable of being passed from parent to offspring ⟨*hereditary* traits⟩ **2 a** : received or passing by inheritance ⟨*hereditary* rank⟩ **b** : having title or possession through inheritance ⟨*hereditary* ruler⟩ **3** : of or relating to inheritance or heredity

he·red·i·ty \hə-ˈred-ət-ē\ *n, pl* **-ties** **1** : the genes and the genetic traits whose expression they control that are passed on from one's parents **2** : the passing on of genes and genetic traits from parent to offspring

Her·e·ford \\'hər-fərd\\ *n* : any of an English breed of hardy red cattle with white faces that are widely raised in the western U.S. for beef

Hereford

here·in \\hi(ə)r-'in\\ *adv* : in this

here·of \\-'əv, -'äv\\ *adv* : of this

here·on \\-'ȯn, -'än\\ *adv* : on this

her·e·sy \\'her-ə-sē\\ *n, pl* **-sies** **1** : religious opinion that is opposed to the doctrines of a church **2** : opinion that is opposed to a generally accepted belief

her·e·tic \\'her-ə-ˌtik\\ *n* : a person who believes or teaches something opposed to accepted beliefs

he·ret·i·cal \\hə-'ret-i-kəl\\ *adj* : of, relating to, or characterized by heresy : UNORTHODOX — **he·ret·i·cal·ly** \\-i-k(ə-)lē\\ *adv*

here·to·fore \\'hi(ə)rt-ə-ˌfō(ə)r, -ˌfȯ(ə)r; ˌhirt-ə-'fō(ə)r, -'fȯ(ə)r\\ *adv* : up to this time

here·un·to \\hi(ə)r-'ən-tü\\ *adv* : to this

here·up·on \\'hi(ə)r-ə-ˌpȯn, -ˌpän; ˌhir-ə-'pȯn, -'pän\\ *adv* : on this : immediately after this

here·with \\hi(ə)r-'with, -'with\\ *adv* : with this communication : enclosed in this

her·i·ta·ble \\'her-ət-ə-bəl\\ *adj* : capable of being inherited : HEREDITARY ⟨*heritable* differences in structure⟩

her·i·tage \\'her-ət-ij\\ *n* **1** : property that is handed down to an heir **2** : something acquired from the past ⟨a rich *heritage* of folklore⟩

her·maph·ro·dite \\(ˌ)hər-'maf-rə-ˌdīt\\ *n* : a hermaphroditic plant or animal

her·maph·ro·dit·ic \\(ˌ)hər-ˌmaf-rə-'dit-ik\\ *adj* : having both male and female reproductive organs — **her·maph·ro·dit·ism** \\-'maf-rə-ˌdit-ˌiz-əm\\ *n*

her·met·ic \\(ˌ)hər-'met-ik\\ *adj* : AIRTIGHT 1 — **her·met·i·cal·ly** \\-i-k(ə-)lē\\ *adv*

her·mit \\'hər-mət\\ *n* **1** : one that lives apart from others especially for religious reasons : RECLUSE **2** : a spiced molasses cookie

her·mit·age \\'hər-mət-ij\\ *n* : a hermit's home; *also* : a residence screened or hidden from view : RETREAT

hermit crab *n* : any of various small crabs that occupy empty mollusk shells

her·nia \\'hər-nē-ə\\ *n, pl* **her·ni·as** *or* **her·ni·ae** \\-nē-ˌē, -nē-ˌī\\ : a sticking out of an organ or part through connective tissue or through a wall of the cavity in which it is normally enclosed — called also *rupture*

he·ro \\'hē-rō, 'hi(ə)r-ō\\ *n, pl* **heroes** **1 a** : a mythological or legendary figure of great strength or ability **b** : an outstanding warrior or soldier **c** : a person admired for achievements and qualities **d** : one that shows great courage ⟨the *hero* of a rescue⟩ **2** : the chief male figure in a literary work or in an event or period **3** *pl* **heros** : [2]SUBMARINE 2

he·ro·ic \\hi-'rō-ik *also* her-'ō- *or* hē-'rō-\\ *adj* **1** : of or relating to heroes especially in ancient times ⟨the *heroic* age⟩ ⟨*heroic* legends⟩ **2** : COURAGEOUS, DARING ⟨a *heroic* rescue⟩ **3** : large or impressive in size or range : GRAND — **he·ro·i·cal·ly** \\-i-k(ə-)lē\\ *adv*

he·ro·ics \\hi-'rō-iks *also* her-'ō- *or* hē-'rō-\\ *n pl* : exaggerated display of heroic attitudes in action or expression

her·o·in \\'her-ə-wən\\ *n* : a strongly addictive drug made from the opium poppy and stronger than morphine

her·o·ine \\'her-ə-wən\\ *n* **1** : a woman in legends or myths who has great courage and daring **2** : a woman admired for her achievements and qualities **3** : the chief female figure in a literary work or in an event or period

her·o·ism \\'her-ə-ˌwiz-əm *also* 'hir-\\ *n* : heroic conduct or qualities **synonyms** see COURAGE

her·on \\'her-ən\\ *n, pl* **herons** *also* **heron** : any of various wading birds with a long neck, long legs, a long thin bill and large wings

her·pes \\'hər-(ˌ)pēz\\ *n* : any of several virus diseases (as herpes simplex) marked by the formation of blisters on the skin or mucous membranes and caused by herpesviruses

herpes sim·plex \\-'sim-ˌpleks\\ *n* : either of two kinds of herpes marked in one case by groups of watery blisters on the skin and mucous membranes (as of the mouth and lips) above the waist and in the other by such blisters on the genitalia

her·pes·vi·rus \\ˌhər-(ˌ)pēz-'vī-rəs\\ *n* : any of a group of viruses that contain DNA and cause herpes

her·pe·tol·o·gist \\ˌhər-pə-'täl-ə-jəst\\ *n* : a person who specializes in herpetology

her·pe·tol·o·gy \\ˌhər-pə-'täl-ə-jē\\ *n* : a branch of zoology dealing with reptiles and amphibians

her·ring \\'her-iŋ\\ *n, pl* **herring** *or* **herrings** : a valuable food fish that is very common in the north Atlantic Ocean; *also* : any of various fishes like this one or related to it

her·ring·bone \\'her-iŋ-ˌbōn\\ *n* **1** : a pattern of rows of parallel lines with every other row slanting in the opposite direction **2** : a fabric with a herringbone pattern

herring gull *n* : a common large gull of the northern hemisphere that as an adult is largely white and gray with dark wing tips

hers \\'hərz\\ *pron* : her one : her ones ⟨the book is *hers*⟩

her·self \\(h)ər-'self\\ *pron* **1** : that identical female one — used for emphasis or to show that the subject and object of the verb are the same ⟨she considers *herself* lucky⟩ ⟨she *herself* did it⟩ **2** : her normal, healthy, or sane self ⟨was *herself* again after a good night's sleep⟩

hertz \\'he(ə)rts, 'herts\\ *n* : a unit of frequency equal to one cycle per second — abbreviation *Hz*

he's \\(ˌ)hēz, ēz\\ : he is : he has

hes·i·tance \\'hez-ə-tən(t)s\\ *n* : HESITANCY

hes·i·tan·cy \\'hez-ə-tən-sē\\ *n, pl* **-cies** **1** : a tendency to hesitate **2** : an act or instance of hesitating

hes·i·tant \\'hez-ə-tənt\\ *adj* : tending to hesitate : slow to act or proceed — **hes·i·tant·ly** *adv*

hes·i·tate \\'hez-ə-ˌtāt\\ *vb* **-tat·ed; -tat·ing** **1** : to stop or pause because of uncertainty or indecision ⟨*hesitate* before answering⟩ **2** : to be unwilling ⟨*hesitate* to ask a favor⟩ **3** : [1]STAMMER — **hes·i·tat·er** *n* — **hes·i·tat·ing·ly** \\-ˌtāt-iŋ-lē\\ *adv* — **hes·i·ta·tion** \\ˌhez-ə-'tā-shən\\ *n*

Hes·sian \\'hesh-ən\\ *n* : a German soldier serving in the British forces during the American Revolution [from *Hesse,* a region in Germany]

Hessian fly *n* : a small two-winged fly destructive to wheat in North America

heter- *or* **hetero-** *combining form* : other : different ⟨*het*erosexual⟩ [derived from Greek *heteros* "different, other"]

het·ero·dox \\'het-ə-rə-ˌdäks\\ *adj* **1** : opposed to established opinions, beliefs, or standards : UNORTHODOX **2** : holding or expressing unaccepted beliefs or opinions

het·ero·doxy \\'het-ə-rə-ˌdäk-sē\\ *n, pl* **-dox·ies** **1** : the quality or state of being heterodox **2** : a heterodox opinion or belief

het·er·o·ge·neous \\ˌhet-ə-rə-'jē-nē-əs, -nyəs\\ *adj* : differing in kind : consisting of dissimilar parts : MIXED ⟨a *heterogeneous* population⟩ — **het·er·o·ge·neous·ly** *adv* — **het·er·o·ge·neous·ness** *n*

[1]het·ero·sex·u·al \\ˌhet-ə-rō-'seksh-(ə-)wəl, -'sek-shəl\\ *adj* : of, relating to, or marked by sexual interest in members

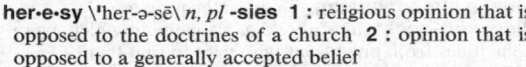

\\ə\\ **abut**	\\au̇\\ **out**	\\i\\ **tip**	\\ȯ\\ **saw**	\\u̇\\ **foot**
\\ər\\ **further**	\\ch\\ **chin**	\\ī\\ **life**	\\ȯi\\ **coin**	\\y\\ **yet**
\\a\\ **mat**	\\e\\ **pet**	\\j\\ **job**	\\th\\ **thin**	\\yü\\ **few**
\\ā\\ **take**	\\ē\\ **easy**	\\ŋ\\ **sing**	\\th\\ **this**	\\yu̇\\ **cure**
\\ä\\ **cot, cart**	\\g\\ **go**	\\ō\\ **bone**	\\ü\\ **food**	\\zh\\ **vision**

of the opposite sex — **het·ero·sex·u·al·i·ty** \-ˌsek-shə-ˈwal-ət-ē\ *n*

²**heterosexual** *n* : a heterosexual individual

het·er·o·sis \ˌhet-ə-ˈrō-səs\ *n* : HYBRID VIGOR

het·ero·troph \ˈhet-ə-rə-ˌtrōf, -ˌträf\ *n* : an organism (as an insect, bird, fish, or human being) that cannot make its own food and must obtain it by eating other animals or plants — **het·ero·tro·phic** \ˌhet-ə-rə-ˈtrōf-ik\ *adj*

het·ero·zy·gos·i·ty \ˌhet-ə-rō-(ˌ)zī-ˈgäs-ət-ē\ *n* : the state of being heterozygous

het·ero·zy·gote \ˌhet-ə-rō-ˈzī-ˌgōt\ *n* : a heterozygous individual

het·ero·zy·gous \ˌhet-ə-rō-ˈzī-gəs\ *adj* : having at least one gene pair that contains different genes ⟨a pea plant *heterozygous* for seed color⟩

het up \ˈhet-ˈəp\ *adj* : highly excited : UPSET

hew \ˈhyü\ *vb* **hewed; hewed** *or* **hewn** \ˈhyün\; **hew·ing** **1** : to chop down ⟨*hew* trees⟩ **2** : to make or shape by cutting with an ax ⟨a cabin built of rough-*hewn* logs⟩ **3** : to stick close to : ADHERE ⟨*hew* to the established rules⟩ — **hew·er** *n*

¹**hex** \ˈheks\ *vb* **1** : to put a hex on **2** : to affect as if by an evil spell : JINX — **hex·er** *n*

²**hex** *n* **1** : ¹SPELL 1b, JINX **2** : WITCH 1

³**hex** *adj or n* : HEXADECIMAL

hexa- *or* **hex-** *combining form* : six [derived from Greek *hex* "six"]

hexa·dec·i·mal \ˌhek-sə-ˈdes-(ə-)məl\ *adj* : of, relating to, or being a number system with a base of 16 ⟨*hexadecimal* numbers⟩ ⟨*hexadecimal* notation⟩ — **hexadecimal** *n*

hexa·gon \ˈhek-sə-ˌgän\ *n* : a polygon of six angles and six sides

hex·ag·o·nal \hek-ˈsag-ən-ᵊl\ *adj* **1** : having six angles and six sides **2** : having a hexagon as a section or base ⟨a *hexagonal* prism⟩

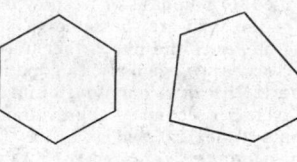

hexagon

hexa·gram \ˈhek-sə-ˌgram\ *n* : a figure consisting of two equilateral triangles forming a 6-pointed star

hex·am·e·ter \hek-ˈsam-ət-ər\ *n* : a line of verse consisting of six metrical feet

hex·ose \ˈhek-ˌsōs\ *n* : a sugar containing six carbon atoms in a molecule

hey \ˈhā\ *interj* — used especially to call attention to or to express surprise or joy

hey·day \ˈhā-ˌdā\ *n* : the time of greatest strength, popularity, or vigor

hi \ˈhī(-ē)\ *interj* — used especially as a greeting

hi·a·tus \hī-ˈāt-əs\ *n*, *pl* **-tus·es** : a gap in space or time; *esp* : a break where a part is missing

hi·ba·chi \hi-ˈbäch-ē\ *n* : a charcoal grill

hi·ber·nate \ˈhī-bər-ˌnāt\ *vb* **-nat·ed; -nat·ing** : to pass the winter in a sleeping or resting state — **hi·ber·na·tion** \ˌhī-bər-ˈnā-shən\ *n* — **hi·ber·na·tor** \ˈhī-bər-ˌnāt-ər\ *n*

hi·bis·cus \hī-ˈbis-kəs, hə-\ *n*, *pl* **-cus·es** : any of a large genus of herbs, shrubs, or small trees related to the mallow and having toothed leaves and large showy flowers

¹**hic·cup** *also* **hic·cough** \ˈhik-(ˌ)əp\ *n* : a sudden drawing in of breath that is followed and stopped by sudden closure of the glottis and accompanied by a gulping sound

²**hiccup** *also* **hiccough** *vb* **hic·cuped** *also* **hic·cupped; hic·cup·ing** *also* **hic·cup·ping** : to make a hiccup or be affected with hiccups

hick \ˈhik\ *n* : an awkward or simple person especially from a small town or the country

hick·o·ry \ˈhik-(ə-)rē\ *n*, *pl* **-ries** **1** : any of a genus of North American trees related to the walnut and having an edible nut with a hard shell **2** : the usually tough pale wood of a hickory

hi·dal·go \hid-ˈal-gō, ē-ˈthäl-\ *n*, *pl* **-gos** : a member of the lower nobility of Spain [Spanish contraction of earlier *hijo de algo, fijo de algo* "a person born into wealth," literally, "son of something"]

¹**hide** \ˈhīd\ *vb* **hid** \ˈhid\; **hid·den** \ˈhid-ᵊn\ *or* **hid; hid·ing** \ˈhīd-iŋ\ **1** : to put or get out of sight : CONCEAL ⟨*hide* a treasure⟩ ⟨*hid* in a closet⟩ **2** : to keep secret ⟨*hide* one's grief⟩ **3** : to screen from view ⟨a house *hidden* by trees⟩ ⟨clouds *hid* the sun⟩ **4** : to seek protection or avoid responsibility [Old English *hȳdan* "to get out of sight"] — **hid·er** \ˈhīd-ər\ *n*

²**hide** *n* : the skin of an animal whether raw or dressed [Old English *hȳd* "skin of an animal"]

³**hide** *vb* **hid·ed; hid·ing** : to give a beating to

hide–and–seek \ˌhīd-ᵊn-ˈsēk\ *n* : a game in which everyone hides from one player who tries to find them

hide·away \ˈhīd-ə-ˌwā\ *n* : ¹RETREAT 2, HIDEOUT

hide·bound \-ˌbaȯnd\ *adj* **1** : having a dry skin adhering closely to the underlying flesh ⟨a *hidebound* horse⟩ **2** : stubbornly unwilling to change

hid·eous \ˈhid-ē-əs\ *adj* : horribly ugly or disgusting : FRIGHTFUL — **hid·eous·ly** *adv* — **hid·eous·ness** *n*

hide·out \ˈhī-ˌdaȯt\ *n* : a secret place for hiding

hie \ˈhī\ *vb* **hied; hy·ing** *or* **hie·ing** : ¹HURRY 1, HASTEN

hi·er·ar·chi·cal \ˌhī-(ə-)ˈrär-ki-kəl\ *or* **hi·er·ar·chic** \-kik\ *adj* : of, relating to, or arranged in a hierarchy — **hi·er·ar·chi·cal·ly** \-ˈrär-ki-k(ə-)lē\ *adv*

hi·er·ar·chy \ˈhī-(ə-)ˌrär-kē\ *n*, *pl* **-chies** **1** : a ruling body especially of clergy organized into ranks **2 a** : an arrangement into a series according to rank **b** : persons or things arranged in ranks or classes

hi·ero·glyph \ˈhī-(ə-)rə-ˌglif\ *n* : a character used in hieroglyphic writing

hi·ero·glyph·ic \ˌhī-(ə-)rə-ˈglif-ik\ *n* **1** : HIEROGLYPH **2** : a system of writing mainly in pictorial characters; *esp* : the picture script of the ancient Egyptian priesthood

hieroglyphic 2

3 : unclear or unreadable signs or writing [derived from early French *hieroglyphique* (adjective) "relating to or being writing that consists of pictures or symbols rather than words," derived from Greek *hieroglyphikos* (same meaning), from *hieros* "sacred, holy" and *glyphikos* "of carving"; so called because it referred to the system of carvings used on ancient Egyptian temples] — **hieroglyphic** *adj*

hi–fi \ˈhī-ˈfī\ *n* **1** : HIGH FIDELITY **2** : equipment for reproduction of sound with high fidelity

hig·gle·dy–pig·gle·dy \ˌhig-əl-dē-ˈpig-əl-dē\ *adv* : in confusion : TOPSY-TURVY — **higgledy–piggledy** *adj*

¹**high** \ˈhī\ *adj* **1 a** : extending to a great distance upward : having greater height than average or usual ⟨rooms with *high* ceilings⟩ **b** : having a specified elevation ⟨six feet *high*⟩ **2** : advanced toward fullness ⟨*high* summer⟩ **3** : ²SHRILL, SHARP ⟨*high* note⟩ **4** : far from the equator ⟨*high* latitude⟩ **5** : ¹NOBLE 5 ⟨a writer of *high* purpose⟩ **6** : of greater degree, size, amount, or content than average or ordinary ⟨*high* pressure⟩ ⟨*high* power of a microscope⟩ **7** : of relatively great importance: as **a** : first in rank or standing ⟨*high* society⟩ **b** : SERIOUS 4, GRAVE ⟨*high* crimes⟩ **8** : STRONG 7 ⟨*high* winds⟩ **9 a** : showing joy or excitement ⟨*high* spirits⟩ **b** : ²DRUNK 1; *also* : affected or impaired by or as if by a drug **10** : advanced or complex in structure or development ⟨*higher* mathematics⟩ ⟨*higher* fungi⟩

synonyms HIGH, TALL, LOFTY mean being above the usual level in height. HIGH is used of height that is measured from the ground or some other standard ⟨a *high* fence surrounded the house⟩. TALL is used of what is considered high when compared to others of the same kind ⟨a *tall* youngster for that age⟩. LOFTY is used of something that rises to a grand or impressive height ⟨*lofty* mountains⟩.

²high *adv* **1** : at or to a high place, altitude, or degree ⟨climbed *high*⟩ **2** : RICHLY 1, LUXURIOUSLY ⟨living *high*⟩

³high *n* **1 a** : ¹HILL 1, KNOLL **b** : SKY 1 ⟨watched the birds on *high*⟩ **c** : HEAVEN 2 ⟨a judgment from on *high*⟩ **2** : a region of high barometric pressure : ANTICYCLONE **3 a** : a high point or level : HEIGHT ⟨prices reached a new *high*⟩ **b** : the arrangement of gears (as in an automobile) that gives the highest speed and consequently the highest speed of travel **4** : a state of good feeling, excitement, or intoxication produced by or as if by a drug

high·ball \'hī-ˌbȯl\ *n* : a drink of alcoholic liquor with water or a carbonated beverage served in a tall glass

high beam *n* : a vehicle headlight beam aimed for long distances

high blood pressure *n* : blood pressure that is abnormally high especially in the arteries or the condition resulting from it — called also *hypertension*

high·born \'hī-'bȯ(ə)rn\ *adj* : of noble birth

high·boy \-ˌbȯi\ *n* : a high chest of drawers set on a base with long legs

high·brow \-ˌbrau̇\ *n* : a person who has or pretends to have more learning or culture than others : INTELLECTUAL — **highbrow** *adj*

high chair *n* : a child's chair with long legs, a feeding tray, and a footrest

high–definition *adj* : relating to or being a television with a more detailed and sharper picture than usual

higher education *n* : education provided by a college or university

high·fa·lu·tin \ˌhī-fə-'lüt-ᵊn\ *adj* : PRETENTIOUS, POMPOUS ⟨*highfalutin* talk⟩ ⟨*highfalutin* people⟩

high fidelity *n* : the reproduction of sound with a high degree of faithfulness to the original

high five *n* : a slapping of upraised right hands by two people (as in celebration) — **high–five** *vb*

high–flown \'hī-'flōn\ *adj* : not plain or simple : FLOWERY, EXTRAVAGANT ⟨*high-flown* language⟩

high frequency *n* : a radio frequency in the range between 3 and 30 megahertz — abbreviation HF

high–grade \'hī-'grād\ *adj* : of a better grade or quality

high–hand·ed \-'han-dəd\ *adj* : having or showing no regard for the rights, concerns, or feelings of others — **high–hand·ed·ly** *adv* — **high–hand·ed·ness** *n*

¹high–hat \-'hat\ *adj* : behaving like a snob

²high–hat *vb* **-hat·ted; -hat·ting** : to treat in a snobbish manner

high horse *n* : an arrogant and stubborn mood or attitude

high jinks \'hī-'jiŋks\ *n pl* : wild or rowdy behavior

high jump *n* : a track-and-field event in which competitors try to jump over a high crossbar — **high–jump** *vb* — **high jumper** *n*

¹high·land \'hī-lənd\ *n* : elevated or mountainous land

²highland *adj* **1** : of or relating to a highland **2** *cap* : of or relating to the Highlands of Scotland

high·land·er \'hī-lən-dər\ *n* **1** : an inhabitant of a highland **2** *cap* : an inhabitant of the Highlands of Scotland

Highland fling *n* : a lively Scottish folk dance

high–lev·el \'hī-'lev-əl\ *adj* **1** : being of high importance or rank ⟨*high-level* officials⟩ **2** : relating to or being a computer programming language that is similar to a natural language (as English) **3** : relating to or being very radioactive nuclear waste

¹high·light \'hī-ˌlīt\ *n* **1** : the brightest spot or area (as in a painting or drawing) **2** : something (as an event or detail) that is of major interest

²highlight *vb* **-light·ed; -light·ing** **1** : to throw a strong light on **2 a** : to center attention on : EMPHASIZE **b** : to be a highlight of **3 a** : to mark (text) with a highlighter

pen **b** : to cause (as text) to stand out on a computer screen

high·light·er *n* : a pen with a broad felt tip and brightly colored transparent ink for marking selected passages in a text

high·ly \'hī-lē\ *adv* **1** : ²VERY 1, EXTREMELY ⟨*highly* pleased⟩ **2** : with approval ⟨speaks *highly* of you⟩

high–mind·ed \'hī-'mīn-dəd\ *adj* : having or expressing noble ideas and feelings — **high–mind·ed·ly** *adv* — **high–mind·ed·ness** *n*

high·ness \'hī-nəs\ *n* **1** : the quality or state of being high **2** — used as a title for persons (as a king or queen) of high rank ⟨Your Royal *Highness*⟩

high noon *n* : exactly noon

high–octane *adj* : having a high octane number and therefore good antiknock properties ⟨*high-octane* gasoline⟩

high–pitched \'hī-'picht\ *adj* : having a high pitch ⟨a *high-pitched* voice⟩

¹high–pressure *adj* **1 a** : having or involving a high pressure especially much higher than that of the atmosphere **b** : having a high atmospheric pressure **2** : using or involving very aggressive sales techniques

²high–pressure *vb* : to sell or influence by high-pressure methods

high–rise \'hī-'rīz\ *adj* : having several stories and being equipped with elevators ⟨*high-rise* apartments⟩ — **high–rise** *n*

high·road \-ˌrōd\ *n* : HIGHWAY

high school *n* : a secondary school usually including the 9th to 12th or 10th to 12th years of study — **high schooler** *n*

high seas *n pl* : the open part of a sea or ocean especially outside territorial waters

high–sound·ing \'hī-'sauṅ-diŋ\ *adj* : POMPOUS 1, IMPOSING

high–speed \-'spēd\ *adj* : going or made for operation at high speed

high–spir·it·ed \-'spir-ət-əd\ *adj* : characterized by a bold or lively spirit : EXUBERANT — **high–spir·it·ed·ly** *adv* — **high–spir·it·ed·ness** *n*

high–strung \-'strəŋ\ *adj* : very nervous or sensitive ⟨a dog too *high-strung* for children⟩

high–tech \-ˌtek\ *adj* : of or relating to high technology

high technology *n* : technology involving complex devices (as electronics or computers)

high–tension *adj* : having or using a high voltage

high–test *adj* : meeting a high standard; *also* : HIGH=OCTANE

high tide *n* : the tide when the water is at its greatest height

high–top \'hī-ˌtäp\ *adj* : extending up over the ankle ⟨*high-top* sneakers⟩ — **high–tops** \-ˌtäps\ *n pl*

high treason *n* : TREASON 2

high–water mark *n* : the highest point of development : PEAK

high·way \'hī-ˌwā\ *n* : a public road; *esp* : a main direct road

high·way·man \-mən\ *n* : a person who robs travelers on a highway

hi·jack *also* **high·jack** \'hī-ˌjak\ *vb* **1** : to stop and steal from a moving vehicle ⟨*hijack* a truck⟩ ⟨*hijack* a load of furs⟩ **2** : to force a pilot to fly an aircraft where one wants — **hi·jack·er** *n*

¹hike \'hīk\ *vb* **hiked; hik·ing** **1** : to move or raise up ⟨*hike* rents⟩ **2** : to go on a long walk — **hik·er** *n*

\ə\ **abut**	\au̇\ **out**	\i\ **tip**	\ȯ\ **saw**	\u̇\ **foot**	
\ər\ **further**	\ch\ **chin**	\ī\ **life**	\ȯi\ **coin**	\y\ **yet**	
\a\ **mat**	\e\ **pet**	\j\ **job**	\th\ **thin**	\yü\ **few**	
\ā\ **take**	\ē\ **easy**	\ŋ\ **sing**	\th\ **this**	\yu̇\ **cure**	
\ä\ **cot, cart**	\g\ **go**	\ō\ **bone**	\ü\ **food**	\zh\ **vision**	

²hike n **1** : a long walk especially for pleasure or exercise **2** : an upward movement : RISE ⟨a price *hike*⟩

hi·lar·i·ous \hil-'ar-ē-əs, -'er-; hī-'lar-, -'ler-\ adj : causing hilarity : wildly funny — **hi·lar·i·ous·ly** adv — **hi·lar·i·ous·ness** n

hi·lar·i·ty \hil-'ar-ət-ē, -'er-; hī-'lar-, -'ler-\ n : noisy fun

¹hill \'hil\ n **1** : a usually rounded height of land lower than a mountain **2** : an artificial heap or mound (as of earth) **3** : several seeds or plants planted in a group rather than a row ⟨a *hill* of beans⟩

²hill vb **1** : to form into a heap **2** : to draw earth around the roots or base of

hill·bil·ly \'hil-,bil-ē\ n, pl **-lies** : a person from a mountainous backwoods area

hillbilly music n : COUNTRY MUSIC

hill·ock \'hil-ək\ n : a small hill — **hill·ocky** \-ə-kē\ adj

hill·side \'hil-,sīd\ n : the side of a hill

hill·top \-,täp\ n : the highest part of a hill

hilly \'hil-ē\ adj **hill·i·er; -est** : having many hills ⟨a *hilly* city⟩

hilt \'hilt\ n : a handle especially of a sword or dagger — **to the hilt** : COMPLETELY

hi·lum \'hī-ləm\ n, pl **hi·la** \-lə\ : a scar on a seed at the point of attachment of the ovule

him \im, (')him\ pron, objective case of HE

¹Hi·ma·la·yan \,him-ə-'lā-ən, him-'äl-(ə-)yən\ adj : of, relating to, or characteristic of the Himalaya Mountains

²Himalayan n : any of a breed of stocky blue-eyed domestic cats that have a long thick coat and a pale body with darker ears, paws, tail, and face

²Himalayan

him·self \(h)im-'self\ pron **1** : that identical male one : that identical one whose sex is unknown or immaterial — used for emphasis or to show that the subject and object of the verb are the same ⟨considers *himself* lucky⟩ ⟨he *himself* did it⟩ **2** : his normal, healthy, or sane self ⟨he's *himself* again⟩

¹hind \'hīnd\ n, pl **hinds** also **hind** chiefly British : a female red deer [Old English *hind* "female red deer"]

²hind adj : located behind : REAR ⟨*hind* legs⟩ [probably from Old English *hinder* (adverb) "behind"]

hind·brain \'hīn(d)-,brān\ n : the third and most posterior division of the embryonic vertebrate brain or the parts that develop from it

hin·der \'hin-dər\ vb **hin·dered; hin·der·ing** \-d(ə-)riŋ\ **1** : to make slow or difficult : HAMPER ⟨progress was *hindered* by bad weather⟩ **2** : to hold back : CHECK

Hin·di \'hin-(,)dē\ n : an official language of northern India — **Hindi** adj

hind·most \'hīn(d)-,mōst\ adj : farthest to the rear

hind·quar·ter \-,kwȯ(r)t-ər\ n **1** : one side of the back half of the body or carcass of a four-footed animal ⟨a *hind-quarter* of beef⟩ **2** pl : the part of a four-footed animal behind the attachment of the hind legs to the trunk

hin·drance \'hin-drən(t)s\ n **1** : the state of being hindered **2** : the action of hindering **3** : something that hinders : IMPEDIMENT

hind·sight \'hīn(d)-,sīt\ n : realization of the meaning or importance of an event only after it has happened

Hin·du \'hin-(,)dü\ n **1** : a follower of Hinduism **2** : a person born or living in India — **Hindu** adj

Hindu–Arabic adj : relating to, being, or composed of Arabic numerals ⟨the *Hindu-Arabic* numeration system⟩

Hin·du·ism \'hin-(,)dü-,iz-əm\ n : a body of social, cultural, and religious beliefs and practices native to the Indian subcontinent

Hin·du·stani \,hin-dù-'stan-ē, -'stän-ē\ n : a group of Indic dialects of northern India

hind wing n : either of the back wings of a four-winged insect located behind the forewings

¹hinge \'hinj\ n **1** : a jointed piece on which a door, lid, or other swinging part turns **2** : the joint between valves of a bivalve's shell

²hinge vb **hinged; hing·ing** **1** : to attach by or provide with hinges **2** : to hang or turn as if on a hinge : DEPEND ⟨our success *hinges* on this decision⟩

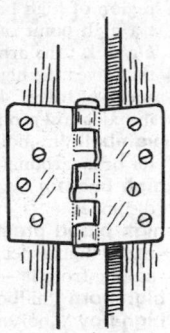

¹hinge 1

hinge joint n : a joint between bones (as at the elbow) that permits motion in only one plane

hin·ny \'hin-ē\ n, pl **hinnies** : a hybrid between a male horse and a female donkey

¹hint \'hint\ n **1** : a slight mention : a suggestion or reminder ⟨a *hint* of winter in the air⟩ **2** : a slight indication of the existence or nature of something : CLUE **3** : a very small amount : TRACE ⟨a *hint* of garlic⟩

²hint vb : to bring to mind by or give a hint — **hint·er** n

hin·ter·land \'hint-ər-,land\ n **1** : a region lying inland from a coast **2** : a region far from cities and towns

¹hip \'hip\ n : ROSE HIP [Old English *hēope* "fruit of a rose"]

²hip n : the part of the body that curves outward below the waist on each side and is formed by the side part of the pelvis and the upper part of the thigh [Old English *hype* "hip of the body"] — **hipped** \'hipt\ adj

³hip adj **hip·per; hip·pest** **1** : keenly aware of or interested in the newest developments **2** : ²WISE 2, ALERT [an altered form of *hep* "keenly aware of and interested in the newest developments"; of unknown origin]

hip·bone \'hip-'bōn, -,bōn\ n : either of two large bones that make up the side halves of the pelvis in mammals and are composed of the ilium, ischium, and pubis which are fused into one bone in the adult

hip–hop \'hip-,häp\ n : the rhythmic music that often accompanies rap; also : the part of the culture especially of inner-city youths who are typically devotees of rap music

hip·po \'hip-ō\ n, pl **hippos** : HIPPOPOTAMUS

hip·po·drome \'hip-ə-,drōm\ n **1** : an oval stadium for horse and chariot races in ancient Greece **2** : an arena for spectacles (as horse shows or circuses)

hip·po·pot·a·mus \,hip-ə-'pät-ə-məs\ n, pl **hip·po·pot·a·mus·es** or **hip·po·pot·a·mi** \-,mī, -(,)mē\ : a very large mammal of Africa south of the Sahara Desert that spends most of its time in the water, feeds on plants, has an extremely large head and mouth, very thick hairless grayish skin, and short legs with four toes on each foot; also : a smaller related mammal of western Africa

hippopotamus

Word History The ancient Greeks gave the name *hippopotamos* to a big, barrel-shaped animal they saw in Africa. English, using the Latin spelling *hippopotamus*, has kept this name. It is a combination of the Greek words *hippos*, meaning "horse" and *potamos*, meaning "river." In fact, the hippopotamus is more closely related to the hog than to the horse. However, the "river" in the name is certainly right for an animal that always lives near water and spends most of its time in it. The eyes, ears, and nostrils of a hippopotamus are placed so that the animal can see, hear, and breathe even if most of its head is underwater. [from Latin *hippopotamus* "hippopotamus," from Greek *hippopotamos* (same meaning), literally, "river horse," from *hippos* "horse" and *potamos* "river"]

¹hire \'hī(ə)r\ *n* **1 a :** payment for temporary use **b :** payment for services : WAGES **2 a :** the act of hiring **b :** the state of being hired : EMPLOYMENT

²hire *vb* **hired; hir·ing 1 :** ¹EMPLOY 2 ⟨*hire* a new crew⟩ **2 :** to get the temporary use of for a set sum ⟨*hire* a hall⟩ **3 :** to take a job ⟨*hired* out as a cook⟩ — **hir·er** *n*

hire·ling \'hī(ə)r-liŋ\ *n :* a person who works for wages and usually for no other reason

hir·sute \'hər-ˌsüt, 'hi(ə)r-\ *adj* **1 :** HAIRY 1 **2 :** covered with coarse stiff hairs ⟨a *hirsute* leaf⟩

¹his \(h)iz, ˌhiz\ *adj* **:** of, relating to, or belonging to him or himself ⟨*his* house⟩ ⟨*his* writings⟩

²his \'hiz\ *pron* **:** his one : his ones ⟨the book is *his*⟩

His·pan·ic \his-'pan-ik\ *adj* **1 :** of or relating to the people, culture, or speech of Spain or of Spain and Portugal **2 :** of, relating to, or being a person living in the U.S. from or whose ancestors were from Latin America — **Hispanic** *n*

hiss \'his\ *vb* **:** to make a long sharp sound like that of the speech sound \s\ or that made by an alarmed animal (as a snake or cat) usually as a sign of disapproval ⟨*hissed* them off the stage⟩ — **hiss** *n* — **hiss·er** *n*

hissy fit \'his-ē-\ *n* **:** TANTRUM

hist \s *often prolonged and usually with* p *preceding and* t *following; often read as* 'hist\ *interj* — used to attract attention

his·ta·mine \'his-tə-ˌmēn, -mən\ *n :* a compound that occurs in many animal tissues and plays an important part in allergic reactions (as in hives, asthma, and hay fever)

his·to·gram \'his-tə-ˌgram\ *n :* a bar graph that uses rectangles of different heights to show how often the different values of a variable in statistics occur

his·tol·o·gist \his-'täl-ə-jəst\ *n :* a person who specializes in histology

his·tol·o·gy \his-'täl-ə-jē\ *n, pl* **-gies 1 :** a branch of anatomy that deals with the structure of animal and plant tissues as seen under a microscope **2 :** tissue structure or organization

his·to·ri·an \his-'tōr-ē-ən, -'tòr-, -'tär-\ *n :* a student or writer of history

his·tor·ic \his-'tòr-ik, -'tär-\ *adj* **1 :** HISTORICAL 1 **2 :** famous in history ⟨*historic* events⟩

his·tor·i·cal \his-'tòr-i-kəl, -'tär-\ *adj* **1 a :** of, relating to, or having the character of history ⟨*historical* fact⟩ **b :** based on history ⟨*historical* novels⟩ **c :** of, relating to, or exhibiting objects from the past ⟨a *historical* museum⟩ **2 :** HISTORIC 2 — **his·tor·i·cal·ly** \-i-k(ə-)lē\ *adv* — **his·tor·i·cal·ness** \-i-kəl-nəs\ *n*

his·to·ry \'his-t(ə-)rē\ *n, pl* **-ries 1 :** a story of real or imaginary events **2 a :** a written record of important events and their causes **b :** a branch of knowledge that records and explains past events **c :** events that form the topics of a history

his·tri·on·ic \ˌhis-trē-'än-ik\ *adj* **1 :** too emotional or dramatic **2 :** of or relating to actors, acting, or the theater — **his·tri·on·i·cal·ly** \-'än-i-k(ə-)lē\ *adv*

his·tri·on·ics \ˌhis-trē-'än-iks\ *n sing or pl* **1 :** theatrical performances **2 :** exaggerated display of feeling

¹hit \'hit\ *vb* **hit; hit·ting 1 a :** to strike usually with force ⟨*hit* a ball⟩ ⟨the ball *hit* the house⟩ **b :** to make or bring into contact with something ⟨tipped over and *hit* the floor⟩ **c :** to strike something aimed at ⟨*hit* the bull's-eye⟩ **2 a :** ¹ATTACK 1 **b :** to affect as if by a blow **3 :** to arrive with a forceful effect ⟨the storm *hit* at sundown⟩ **4**

a : to come upon : DISCOVER ⟨*hit* upon the answer accidentally⟩ **b :** to get to : REACH ⟨*hit* town that night⟩ ⟨prices *hit* a new high⟩ **c :** to reflect accurately ⟨*hits* the right note⟩ **5 :** to fire the charge in the cylinders — **hit·ter** *n* — **hit it off :** to get along well

²hit *n* **1 a :** a blow striking an object aimed at **b :** ⁴BLOW 1, COLLISION **2 a :** a stroke of luck **b :** a great success ⟨the show was a *hit*⟩ **3 :** BASE HIT **4 :** a single dose of a narcotic drug **5 :** an instance of a computer user connecting to a given website ⟨a million *hits* per day⟩ **6 :** a successful match in a computer search

hit–and–miss \ˌhit-ᵊn-'mis\ *adj* **:** sometimes successful and sometimes not : HAPHAZARD

hit–and–run \-'rən\ *adj* **1 :** being or involving a motor-vehicle driver who does not stop after having an accident **2 :** involving or intended for quick action or results

¹hitch \'hich\ *vb* **1 :** to move by jerks **2 :** to catch, fasten, or connect by or as if by a hook or knot ⟨*hitch* a horse to a rail⟩ **3 :** HITCHHIKE — **hitch·er** *n*

²hitch *n* **1 :** a jerky movement or pull **2 :** an unexpected stop or obstacle ⟨the plan went off without a *hitch*⟩ **3 :** the connection between something towed (as a plow or trailer) and its mover (as a tractor, automobile, or animal) **4 :** a knot used for a temporary fastening **5 :** a period usually of military service ⟨do a *hitch* in the army⟩

hitch·hike \'hich-ˌhīk\ *vb* **:** to travel by securing free rides from passing vehicles — **hitch·hik·er** *n*

¹hith·er \'hith-ər\ *adv* **:** to this place ⟨come *hither*⟩

²hither *adj* **:** ³NEAR 3, NEARER ⟨the *hither* side of the hill⟩

hith·er·to \'hith-ər-ˌtü\ *adv* **:** up to this time ⟨*hitherto* unknown facts⟩

hit or miss *adv* **:** without plan, order, or direction : HAPHAZARDLY — **hit–or–miss** \ˌhit-ər-'mis\ *adj*

HIV \ˌāch-ˌī-'vē\ *n :* any of a group of viruses that infect and destroy helper T cells causing the marked reduction in their numbers that is diagnostic of AIDS

¹hive \'hīv\ *n* **1 a :** a container for housing honeybees **b :** the usually aboveground nest of bees **c :** a colony of bees **2 :** a place swarming with busy occupants

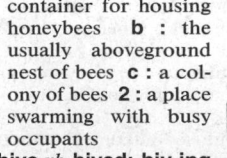

¹hive 1a

²hive *vb* **hived; hiv·ing 1 a :** to collect into a hive ⟨*hive* bees⟩ **b :** to enter and take over a hive or nesting place **2 :** to live or gather in close association

hives \'hīvz\ *n sing or pl* **:** an allergic condition in which the skin or mucous membrane breaks out in large red itching patches

ho \'hō\ *interj* — used especially to attract attention ⟨land *ho*⟩

hoa·gie \'hō-gē\ *n :* ²SUBMARINE 2

¹hoar \'hō(ə)r, 'hò(ə)r\ *adj* **:** HOARY

²hoar *n* **:** ¹FROST 2

hoard \'hō(ə)rd, 'hò(ə)rd\ *n :* a hidden supply or fund stored up — **hoard** *vb* — **hoard·er** *n*

hoar·frost \'hō(ə)r-ˌfròst, 'hò(ə)r-\ *n :* ¹FROST 2

hoarse \'hō(ə)rs, 'hò(ə)rs\ *adj* **hoars·er; hoars·est 1 :** harsh in sound **2 :** having a rough voice ⟨a cold made me *hoarse*⟩ — **hoarse·ly** *adv* — **hoarse·ness** *n*

hoary \'hō(ə)r-ē, 'hò(ə)r-\ *adj* **hoar·i·er; -est 1 :** grayish or whitish especially from age ⟨bowed his *hoary* head⟩ **2 :** very old : ANCIENT ⟨*hoary* legends⟩ — **hoar·i·ness** *n*

\ə\ **abut**	\au̇\ **out**	\i\ **tip**	\ȯ\ **saw**	\u̇\ **foot**
\ər\ **further**	\ch\ **chin**	\ī\ **life**	\ȯi\ **coin**	\y\ **yet**
\a\ **mat**	\e\ **pet**	\j\ **job**	\th\ **thin**	\yü\ **few**
\ā\ **take**	\ē\ **easy**	\ŋ\ **sing**	\t̲h̲\ **this**	\yu̇\ **cure**
\ä\ **cot, cart**	\g\ **go**	\ō\ **bone**	\ü\ **food**	\zh\ **vision**

hoax \'hōks\ *n* **1** : an act intended to trick or deceive **2** : something false passed off or accepted as genuine — **hoax** *vb* — **hoax·er** *n*

hob \'häb\ *n* : ²TROUBLE 1b, MISCHIEF ⟨raise *hob*⟩

¹**hob·ble** \'häb-əl\ *vb* **hob·bled; hob·bling** \-(ə-)liŋ\ **1 a** : to walk with difficulty : LIMP ⟨*hobble* along on crutches⟩ **b** : to make lame ⟨*hobbled* by an ankle injury⟩ **2 a** : to keep from straying by tying two legs together ⟨*hobble* a horse⟩ **b** : ¹HAMPER, IMPEDE

²**hobble** *n* **1** : a hobbling walk **2** : something used to hobble an animal

hob·ble·de·hoy \'häb-əl-di-ˌhoi\ *n* : an awkward youth

hob·by \'häb-ē\ *n, pl* **hobbies** : an interest or activity to which a person devotes time for pleasure — **hob·by·ist** \-ē-əst\ *n*

hob·by·horse \-ˌho(ə)rs\ *n* **1** : a stick with an imitation horse's head at one end that a child pretends to ride **2** : ROCKING HORSE **3** : a toy horse hung by springs from a frame

hob·gob·lin \'häb-ˌgäb-lən\ *n* **1** : a mischievous elf or goblin **2** : BOGEY 2

hob·nail \'häb-ˌnāl\ *n* : a large-headed nail driven into the soles of heavy shoes as a protection against wear — **hob·nailed** \-ˌnāld\ *adj*

hob·nob \'häb-ˌnäb\ *vb* **hob·nobbed; hob·nob·bing** : to associate in a friendly manner ⟨*hobnobbing* with politicians⟩ — **hob·nob·ber** *n*

ho·bo \'hō-bō\ *n, pl* **hoboes** *also* **hobos** : a homeless and usually penniless wanderer : TRAMP — **hobo** *vb*

¹**hock** \'häk\ *n* **1** : the region in the hind limb of a four-footed animal (as the horse) that corresponds to the human ankle **2** : a small cut of meat from either the front or hind leg just above the foot especially of a pig ⟨ham *hocks*⟩ [Old English *hōh* "heel"]

²**hock** *vb* : ³PAWN

³**hock** *n* : ²PAWN 2 ⟨got the ring out of *hock*⟩ [from Dutch *hok* "pen, prison"]

hock·ey \'häk-ē\ *n* **1** : FIELD HOCKEY **2** : ICE HOCKEY

ho·cus–po·cus \ˌhō-kə-ˈspō-kəs\ *n* **1** : a magic trick **2** : nonsense used to deceive

hod \'häd\ *n* **1** : a long-handled tray used to carry mortar or bricks on the shoulder **2** : a bucket for holding or carrying coal

hodge·podge \'häj-ˌpäj\ *n* : a confused mixture : JUMBLE
Word History *Hodgepodge* and its older form *hotchpotch* are part of a group of words that rhyme all by themselves. *Hobnob* and *willy-nilly* are others. In the case of *hodgepodge* and *hotchpotch*, the rhyme is not an accident. These words came to English from early French in the form *hochepot*. The spelling was changed to make the second half of the word rhyme with the first. In French *hochepot* was a stew of many foods cooked together in a pot. Perhaps the pot was shaken instead of stirred since *hochepot* was formed from *hochier*, meaning "to shake," and *pot*, which had the same meaning in early French as it does in English now. Before long *hotchpotch* and *hodgepodge* were used not just for a mixture of foods cooking in a pot but for any mixture of different things. [an altered form of *hotchpotch*, from Middle English *hochepot* "mixed stew," derived from early French *hochepot* (same meaning), from *hochier* "to shake" and *pot* "pot, container"]

¹**hoe** \'hō\ *n* : a farm or garden tool with a thin flat blade at nearly a right angle to a long handle that is used especially for weeding and loosening the earth

²**hoe** *vb* **hoed; hoe·ing** : to use or work with a hoe

hoe·cake \'hō-ˌkāk\ *n* : a small cornmeal cake

hoe·down \'hō-ˌdaun\ *n* **1** : SQUARE DANCE **2** : a gathering featuring square dances

¹**hog** \'hog, 'häg\ *n, pl* **hogs** *also* **hog 1 a** : a domesticated swine especially when weighing more than 120 pounds (54 kilograms) — compare PIG 1a **b** : any of various animals related to the domesticated swine **2** : a selfish, greedy, or filthy person — **hog·gish** \'hog-ish, 'häg-\ *adj* — **hog·gish·ly** *adv* — **hog·gish·ness** *n*

²**hog** *vb* **hogged; hog·ging** : to take more than one's share

ho·gan \'hō-ˌgän\ *n* : a Navajo Indian dwelling usually made of logs and mud with a door traditionally facing east

hogan

hog cholera *n* : a highly infectious often fatal virus disease of swine

hog heaven *n* : a very satisfying state or situation

hog–nose snake \ˌhog-ˌnōz-, ˌhäg-\ *n* : any of several rather small harmless North American snakes that have stout bodies and hiss when disturbed — called also *hog-nosed snake* \-ˌnōzd-\, *puff adder*

hogs·head \'hogz-ˌhed, 'hägz-\ *n* **1** : a large cask or barrel **2** : any of various units of capacity; *esp* : a U.S. unit for liquids equal to 63 gallons (about 238 liters)

hog–tie \'hog-ˌtī, 'häg-\ *vb* **1** : to tie together the feet of ⟨*hog-tie* a calf⟩ **2** : to make helpless

hog·wash \'hog-ˌwosh, 'häg-, -ˌwäsh\ *n* **1** : ²SWILL 1 **2** : NONSENSE 1

hog wild *adj* : lacking control : UNRESTRAINED ⟨went *hog wild* at the sight of all that candy⟩

ho hum \'hō-'həm\ *interj* — used to express weariness, boredom, or disdain [imitative]

¹**hoist** \'hoist\ *vb* : to raise or become raised into position especially by mechanical means **synonyms** see RAISE — **hoist·er** *n*

²**hoist** *n* **1** : an act of hoisting : LIFT **2** : a machine for hoisting heavy loads

hol- *or* **holo-** *combining form* : complete : total [derived from Greek *holos* "whole"]

¹**hold** \'hōld\ *vb* **held** \'held\; **hold·ing 1 a** : to keep in one's possession : POSSESS, HAVE ⟨*hold* this for me⟩ **b** : to have by right ⟨*hold* property⟩ ⟨*hold* a bachelor's degree⟩ ⟨*hold* elective office⟩ **2 a** : to keep or restrict by force ⟨the troops *held* the bridge⟩ **b** : to restrain especially by keeping back ⟨*hold* your temper⟩ **c** : ²DELAY 2 ⟨*held* the train⟩ **d** : to keep back from use ⟨will *hold* the seats for us⟩ **e** : to make accept a legal or moral duty ⟨I'll *hold* you to your word⟩ **3 a** : to have or keep in the grasp ⟨*hold* the pen upright⟩ **b** : to cause to be or remain in a place, position, or situation ⟨*hold* the ladder steady⟩ **c** : to remain fastened ⟨the anchor *held*⟩ **d** : ¹SUPPORT 4a, SUSTAIN ⟨the floor will *hold* 10 metric tons⟩ **e** : to keep as or as if a captive ⟨*held* without bail⟩ **4** : to bear or carry oneself ⟨please *hold* still⟩ **5 a** : to keep up without interruption ⟨*hold* silence⟩ **b** : to keep the interest or devotion of ⟨the play *held* the audience⟩ **6** : to receive and contain ⟨the bottle *holds* two liters⟩ **7 a** : to have in mind : ENTERTAIN ⟨*hold* a theory⟩ **b** : CONSIDER 3, JUDGE ⟨was *held* to be the best⟩ **8** : to carry on as a group ⟨*hold* a meeting⟩ **9 a** : to maintain position ⟨the line *held* under attack⟩ **b** : to continue unchanged : LAST ⟨their interest *held* up⟩ ⟨hope the weather *holds*⟩ **10** : to be true : APPLY ⟨the rule *holds* in most cases⟩ **11** : to refrain from an act : HALT, PAUSE [Old English *healdan* "to hold, own"] **synonyms** see CONTAIN — **hold a candle to** : to compare with ⟨doesn't *hold a candle to* the original⟩ — **hold forth** : to preach or speak in public usually for a long time — **hold good** : to remain true ⟨the rule *holds good* in this case⟩ — **hold hands** : to join one's hand with another's especially as an expression of affection — **hold one's breath 1** : to prevent oneself from breathing

temporarily **2** : to wait in anxious anticipation — **hold one's own** : to maintain one's place or condition especially against opposition — **hold one's tongue** *or* **hold one's peace** : to keep one's thoughts to oneself : keep silent — **hold the bag 1** : to be left empty-handed **2** : to get the blame that should be shared by others — **hold to** : to adhere to strongly ⟨*held to* his promise⟩ — **hold water** : to stand up under criticism or examination ⟨your story doesn't *hold water*⟩ — **hold with** : to agree with : approve of

²hold *n* **1** : FORTRESS, STRONGHOLD **2** : the act or manner of holding : GRIP, GRASP ⟨have a *hold* on the rope⟩ **3** : a manner of grasping the opponent in wrestling **4 a** : full or immediate control ⟨get *hold* of yourself⟩ **b** : TOUCH 4 ⟨trying to get a *hold* of you⟩ **5** : a bond that affects or controls : POWER ⟨the law has no *hold* over this person⟩ **6** : something that may be grasped or held **7** : a note or rest in music that is continued longer than usual **8 a** : an order or indication that something is to be reserved or delayed **b** : STOPPAGE, HALT ⟨a *hold* in a rocket countdown⟩ — **on hold** : in a state of interruption

³hold *n* **1** : the interior of a ship below decks; *esp* : the cargo deck of a ship **2** : the cargo compartment of an airplane [an altered form of *hole*]

hold back *vb* **1** : to make difficult the progress or achievement of **2** : to keep from revealing or giving ⟨*held back* important information⟩

hold·er \ˈhōl-dər\ *n* **1** : a person that holds; *esp* : a legal owner **2** : a device that holds

hold·fast \ˈhōl(d)-ˌfast\ *n* : a part by which a plant (as a seaweed) or animal (as a tapeworm) clings (as to a flat surface or the body of a host)

hold·ing \ˈhōl-diŋ\ *n* **1** : property (as land or stocks) owned — usually used in plural ⟨decided to sell her *holdings*⟩ **2** : a ruling of a court

holding pattern *n* **1** : the course flown (as over an airport) by an aircraft waiting for permission to land **2** : a state of waiting or suspended activity ⟨the project is in a *holding pattern*⟩

hold off *vb* **1** : to keep away : WITHSTAND ⟨*held off* the attack⟩ **2** : POSTPONE, DELAY ⟨decided to *hold off* on the decision⟩ ⟨will *hold off* production for the summer⟩

hold on *vb* **1** : to keep a hold **2** : ¹WAIT 1a — **hold on to** : to keep or adhere to ⟨*hold on to* your dreams⟩

hold out *vb* **1** : to remain in being : LAST ⟨hope the food *holds out*⟩ **2** : to remain unyielding : refuse to surrender or give in ⟨*held out* until help arrived⟩ — **hold·out** \ˈhōl-ˌdau̇t\ *n* — **hold out on** : to keep something (as information) from

hold over *vb* : to continue beyond a normal or planned time ⟨the movie was *held over* for three weeks⟩ — **hold·over** \ˈhōl-ˌdō-vər\ *n*

hold·up *n* **1** : a robbery at gunpoint **2** : ¹DELAY 1

hold up \(ˈ)hōl-ˈdəp\ *vb* **1** : ²DELAY 2, IMPEDE **2** : to rob at gunpoint **3** : to continue without failing or losing effectiveness ⟨*holding up* under the stress⟩ ⟨music that *holds up* twenty years later⟩

hole \ˈhōl\ *n* **1** : an opening into or through a thing **2 a** : a hollow place (as a pit or cave) **b** : a deep place in a body of water ⟨trout *holes*⟩ **3** : an underground habitation : BURROW **4** : FLAW, FAULT **5 a** : the shallow cup into which the ball is played in golf **b** : a part of a golf course from the tee to the putting green **6** : a shabby or dingy place **7** : an awkward position : FIX — **hole** *vb* — **hol·ey** \ˈhō-lē\ *adj* — **in the hole** : in a position of owing or losing money

hole in one : ¹ACE 4

hole up *vb* : to take shelter in or as if in a hole or cave

hol·i·day \ˈhäl-ə-ˌdā\ *n* **1** : HOLY DAY **2** : a day of freedom from work; *esp* : a day of celebration or remembrance fixed by law **3** *chiefly British* : a period of relaxation : VACATION — **holiday** *vb* — **hol·i·day·er** *n*

ho·li·ness \ˈhō-lē-nəs\ *n* **1** : the quality or state of being holy **2** *cap* — used as a title for various high religious officials ⟨His *Holiness* the Pope⟩

ho·lis·tic \hō-ˈlis-tik\ *adj* : relating to or concerned with wholes or with complete systems rather than with the individual parts ⟨*holistic* medicine attempts to treat both the mind and the body⟩ [*hol-* + *-istic*]

hol·ler \ˈhäl-ər\ *vb* **hol·lered; hol·ler·ing** \-(ə-)riŋ\ **1** : to cry or call out : SHOUT **2** : COMPLAIN 1 — **holler** *n*

¹hol·low \ˈhäl-ō\ *n* **1** : an empty space within something : HOLE **2** : a low spot in a surface; *esp* : VALLEY

²hollow *adj* **1** : curved inward : SUNKEN ⟨*hollow* cheeks⟩ **2** : having a hole inside : not solid throughout ⟨*hollow* tree⟩ **3** : lacking value, sincerity, or meaning ⟨*hollow* victory⟩ ⟨*hollow* promises⟩ **4** : being like a sound made in or by beating on a large empty enclosure : MUFFLED ⟨a *hollow* roar⟩ — **hollow** *vb* — **hol·low·ly** \ˈhäl-ō-lē, -ə-lē\ *adv* — **hol·low·ness** *n*

hol·ly \ˈhäl-ē\ *n, pl* **hollies 1** : either of two trees or shrubs of which one is found in the eastern U.S. and the other in Eurasia and which have evergreen leaves with spiny margins and usually bright red berries **2** : the leaves, berries, and branches of the holly

hol·ly·hock \ˈhäl-ē-ˌhäk, -ˌhȯk\ *n* : a widely grown Asian herb related to the mallows and having large coarse rounded leaves and tall stalks bearing showy flowers

hol·mi·um \ˈhō(l)-mē-əm\ *n* : a rare metallic element that forms highly magnetic compounds — see ELEMENT table

holly 2

holo- — see HOL-

ho·lo·caust \ˈhō-lə-ˌkȯst, ˈhäl-ə- *also* -ˌkäst *or* ˈhȯ-lə-ˌkȯst\ *n* **1** : a sacrifice destroyed by fire **2** : a thorough destruction especially by fire **3 a** *often cap* : the killing of European civilians and especially Jews by the Nazis during World War II **b** : GENOCIDE

Ho·lo·cene \ˈhō-lə-ˌsēn, ˈhäl-ə-\ *adj* : of, relating to, or being the present epoch of geological history — see GEOLOGIC TIME table — **Holocene** *n*

ho·lo·gram \ˈhō-lə-ˌgram, ˈhäl-ə-\ *n* : a three-dimensional picture made by a complex pattern of light (as laser light)

ho·lo·graph \ˈhō-lə-ˌgraf, ˈhäl-ə-\ *n* : a document entirely in the handwriting of the author — **holograph** *or* **ho·lo·graph·ic** \ˌhō-lə-ˈgraf-ik, ˌhäl-ə-\ *adj*

ho·log·ra·phy \hō-ˈläg-rə-fē\ *n* : the process of making or using a hologram — **ho·lo·graph·ic** \ˌhō-lə-ˈgraf-ik, ˌhal-ə-\ *adj* — **ho·lo·graph·i·cal·ly** \-i-k(ə-)lē\ *adv*

Hol·stein \ˈhōl-ˌstēn, -ˌstīn\ *n* : any of a breed of large black-and-white dairy cattle producing large quantities of milk that is low in fat compared to the milk of other breeds

Hol·stein–Frie·sian \-ˈfrē-zhən\ *n* : HOLSTEIN

hol·ster \ˈhōl(t)-stər\ *n* : a usually leather case for carrying a pistol

ho·ly \ˈhō-lē\ *adj* **ho·li·er; -est 1** : worthy of complete devotion and trust **2** : DIVINE **3** : set apart to the service of God or a god : SACRED **4** : respected as sacred **5** : COMPLETE, UTTER ⟨he is a *holy* terror⟩ — used in combination as a mild oath ⟨*holy* cow⟩

holy day *n* : a day set aside for special religious observance

Holy Ghost n : HOLY SPIRIT

Holy Grail \-'grā(ə)l\ n : the cup or platter which according to legend was used by Christ and was sought after by knights during the Middle Ages

Holy Saturday n : the Saturday before Easter

Holy Spirit n : the third person of the Christian Trinity

ho·ly·stone \'hō-lē-ˌstōn\ n : a soft sandstone used to scrub a ship's wooden decks — **holystone** vb

Holy Thursday n : MAUNDY THURSDAY

holy war n : a war or violent campaign carried on for what is considered a holy purpose

holy water n : water blessed by a priest and used to purify

Holy Week n : the week before Easter

Holy Writ n : BIBLE 1

hom- or **homo-** combining form : similar : alike ⟨homograph⟩ [derived from Greek homos "same"]

hom·age \'(h)äm-ij\ n **1** : a ceremony in which a person pledged allegiance to a lord and became his vassal **2** : something done or given in fulfilling a vassal's duty to a lord **3** : ¹RESPECT 2a, HONOR ⟨paid homage to her father⟩

hom·bre \'äm-brē, 'əm-, -ˌbrā\ n : ¹MAN 1a, FELLOW [from Spanish hombre "man," from Latin homin-, homo "man"]

hom·burg \'häm-ˌbərg\ n : a man's felt hat with a stiff curled brim and a high crown creased lengthwise

¹home \'hōm\ n **1 a** : the house in which a person or family lives **b** : ¹HOUSE 1 **2** : a family living together in one dwelling **3** : the place where something is usually or naturally found : HABITAT ⟨the home of the elephant⟩ **4 a** : a place of origin ⟨salmon returning to their home to spawn⟩ **b** : the country or place where one lives or where one's ancestors lived **5** : a place for the care of persons unable to care for themselves ⟨old people's home⟩ **6** : the goal in some games; esp : HOME PLATE [Middle English hom, from Old English hām "village, home"] — **home·like** \-ˌlīk\ adj — **at home** : relaxed and comfortable

²home adv **1** : to or at home ⟨went home⟩ **2** : to a final, closed, or standard position ⟨drive a nail home⟩ **3** : deeply and meaningfully ⟨the truth struck home⟩

³home adj **1** : of, relating to, or being a home **2** : prepared, done, or designed for use in a home ⟨home cooking⟩ **3** : happening or operating in a home area ⟨the home team⟩

⁴home vb **homed; hom·ing 1** : to go or return home **2** : to send to or provide with a home

home·body \'hōm-ˌbäd-ē\ n : one whose life centers in the home

¹home·bound \'hōm-ˌbaund\ adj : going or heading for home ⟨homebound travelers⟩

²homebound adj : confined to the home ⟨was homebound with a broken foot⟩

home·boy \-ˌboi\ n **1** : a boy or man from one's neighborhood, hometown, or region **2** : a fellow member of a youth gang

home·com·ing \'hōm-ˌkəm-ing\ n **1** : a return home **2 a** : the return of a group of people usually on a special occasion to a place formerly frequented **b** : a yearly celebration for alumni at a school

home economics n : the study of the care and management of a household — **home economist** n

home·girl \'hōm-ˌgərl\ n **1** : a girl or woman from one's neighborhood, hometown, or region **2** : a girl or woman who is a member of one's peer group

home·grown \'hōm-'grōn\ adj **1** : grown or made at home or nearby ⟨homegrown vegetables⟩ **2** : native to or characteristic of a particular place ⟨the festival will feature homegrown artists⟩

home·land \'hōm-ˌland\ n : native land : FATHERLAND

home·less \-ləs\ adj : having no home or permanent residence — **home·less·ness** n

home·ly \'hōm-lē\ adj **home·li·er; -est 1** : characteristic of home life ⟨homely meals⟩ **2** : not pretty or handsome ⟨a homely person⟩ — **home·li·ness** n

home·made \'hōm-'(m)ād\ adj : made in the home

home·mak·er \'hōm-ˌmā-kər\ n : one who manages a household especially as a wife and mother — **home·mak·ing** \-kiŋ\ n or adj

homeo- also **homoio-** combining form : like : similar ⟨homeostasis⟩ [derived from Greek homoios "like, similar," from homos "same"]

ho·meo·sta·sis \ˌhō-mē-ō-'stā-səs\ n : a tendency for the conditions inside the body of an animal (as a mammal) to stay pretty much the same even when outside environmental conditions (as temperature) change — **ho·meo·stat·ic** \-'stat-ik\ adj

home page n : the page of a World Wide Web site that is usually seen first and that usually contains links to the other pages of the site

home plate n : the base where a baseball batter stands and which a base runner must touch in order to score

hom·er \'hō-mər\ n **1** : HOME RUN **2** : HOMING PIGEON

home·room \'hōm-ˌrüm, -ˌrum\ n : a classroom where pupils report usually at the beginning of each school day

home rule n : self-government in local affairs by the citizens of a local political unit

home run n : a hit in baseball that allows the batter to go completely around the bases and score a run

home·school \'hōm-ˌskül\ vb : to teach school subjects to one's children at home

home·school·er \-ˌskül-ər\ n **1** : a person who homeschools **2** : a child who is homeschooled

home·sick \'hōm-ˌsik\ adj : longing for home and family while away from them — **home·sick·ness** n

¹home·spun \-ˌspən\ adj **1 a** : spun or made at home **b** : made of homespun **2** : not worldly : SIMPLE 3 ⟨homespun ideas⟩

²homespun n : a loosely woven usually woolen or linen fabric

¹home·stead \-ˌsted\ n **1** : a home and surrounding land **2** : a piece of land acquired from U.S. public lands by living on and cultivating it

²homestead vb : to acquire or settle on public land for use as a homestead — **home·stead·er** \-ˌsted-ər\ n

home·stretch \-'strech\ n **1** : the part of a racetrack between the final turn and the finish line **2** : a final stage

home·town \-'taun\ n : the city or town where one was born or grew up

home·ward \'hōm-wərd\ or **home·wards** \-wərdz\ adv : toward or in the direction of home — **homeward** adj

home·work \'hōm-ˌwərk\ n : work and especially school lessons to be done outside the regular class period

hom·ey \'hō-mē\ adj **hom·i·er; -est** : resembling or suggestive of a home : COZY — **hom·ey·ness** or **hom·i·ness** n

ho·mi·cid·al \ˌhäm-ə-'sīd-ᵊl, ˌhō-mə-\ adj : of, relating to, or having tendencies toward the killing of another person : MURDEROUS — **ho·mi·cid·al·ly** \-'sīd-ᵊl-ē\ adv

ho·mi·cide \'häm-ə-ˌsīd, 'hō-mə-\ n : a killing of one human being by another [Middle English homicide "the killing of a person," from early French homicide (same meaning), from Latin homicidium "the act of killing a man," from homo "man" and -cidium "the act of killing," from caedere "to kill, cut"]

hom·i·ly \'häm-ə-lē\ n, pl **-lies** : SERMON 1

homing adj **1** : returning by habit to a known place **2** : guiding or being guided to a goal

homing pigeon n : a racing pigeon trained to return home

hom·i·nid \'häm-ə-nəd, -ˌnid\ n : any of a family of two-footed primate mammals that include the human beings together with their extinct ancestors and related forms — **hominid** adj

hom·i·ny \'häm-ə-nē\ n : kernels of dried corn from which the hulls have been removed by soaking and boiling in water containing lye

ho·mo \ˈhō-mō\ *n, pl* **homos** : any of a genus of primate mammals that includes all human beings alive today and extinct related species

homo- — see HOM-

ho·mog·e·nate \hō-ˈmäj-ə-ˌnāt\ *n* : a product of homogenizing

ho·mo·ge·neous \ˌhō-mə-ˈjē-nē-əs, -nyəs\ *adj* **1** : of the same or a similar kind or nature **2** : being the same throughout ⟨a culturally *homogenous* neighborhood⟩ — **ho·mo·ge·neous·ly** \-jə-ˈnē-ət-ē\ *n* — **ho·mo·ge·neous·ly** \-ˈjē-nē-əs-lē\ *adv*

ho·mog·e·nize \hō-ˈmäj-ə-ˌnīz, hə-\ *vb* **-nized; -niz·ing** **1** : to make homogeneous **2 a** : to reduce to small particles of uniform size and distribute evenly ⟨*homogenize* peanut butter⟩ ⟨*homogenize* paint⟩ **b** : to break up the fat of (milk) into very fine particles — **ho·mog·e·ni·za·tion** \-ˌmäj-ə-nə-ˈzā-shən\ *n* — **ho·mog·e·niz·er** \-ˈmäj-ə-ˌnī-zər\ *n*

ho·mo·graph \ˈhäm-ə-ˌgraf, ˈhō-mə-\ *n* : one of two or more words spelled the same but different in origin or meaning or pronunciation ⟨"row" of seats and "row" (a fight) are *homographs,* as are "fair" (market) and "fair" (beautiful)⟩

homoio- *variant of* HOMEO-

ho·mol·o·gous \hō-ˈmäl-ə-gəs, hə-\ *adj* **1** : showing biological homology ⟨a *homologous* wing and arm⟩ **2** : having the same or allelic genes usually arranged in the same order ⟨a pair of *homologous* chromosomes⟩

ho·mo·logue *or* **ho·mo·log** \ˈhō-mə-ˌlòg, ˈhäm-ə-, -ˌläg\ *n* : either chromosome of a homologous pair

ho·mol·o·gy \hō-ˈmäl-ə-jē, hə-\ *n, pl* **-gies** : a likeness often due to common origin: as **a** : structural likeness between corresponding parts (as the wing of a bat and the arm of a human being) of different plants or animals due to evolution from a common ancestor in the distant past **b** : structural likeness between a series of parts (as vertebrae) in the same individual

hom·onym \ˈhäm-ə-ˌnim, ˈhō-mə-\ *n* **1** : HOMOPHONE **2** : HOMOGRAPH **3** : one of two or more words spelled and pronounced alike but different in meaning ⟨the noun "bear" and the verb "bear" are *homonyms*⟩ [from Latin *homonymum* "homonym," derived from Greek *homonymos* (adjective) "having the same name," from *hom-, homos* "same" and *onyma, onoma* "name"] — **hom·onym·ic** \ˌhäm-ə-ˈnim-ik, ˌhō-mə-\ *adj*

ho·mo·pho·bia \ˌhō-mə-ˈfō-bē-ə\ *n* : irrational fear or dislike of or prejudice against homosexuality or homosexuals — **ho·mo·pho·bic** \-ˈfō-bik\ *adj*

ho·mo·phone \ˈhäm-ə-ˌfōn, ˈhō-mə-\ *n* : one of two or more words pronounced alike but different in meaning, origin, or spelling ⟨"to," "too," and "two" are *homophones*⟩ — **ho·mo·pho·nic** \ˌhäm-ə-ˈfän-ik, ˌhō-mə, -ˈfō-nik\ *adj* — **ho·moph·o·nous** \hō-ˈmäf-ə-nəs\ *adj*

Ho·mo sa·pi·ens \ˌhō-mō-ˈsap-ē-ənz, -ˈsä-pē-ˌenz\ *n* : the human race [scientific Latin, derived from *homo* "human being" and *sapiens* "wise, intelligent"]

¹ho·mo·sex·u·al \ˌhō-mə-ˈseksh-(ə-)wəl, -ˈsek-shəl\ *adj* : of, relating to, or showing sexual desire toward another of the same sex

²homosexual *n* : a homosexual individual

ho·mo·sex·u·al·i·ty \ˌhō-mə-ˌsek-shə-ˈwal-ət-ē\ *n* : the quality or state of being homosexual

ho·mo·zy·gos·i·ty \ˌhō-mə-zī-ˈgäs-ət-ē\ *n* : the state of being homozygous

ho·mo·zy·gote \ˌhō-mə-ˈzī-ˌgōt\ *n* : a homozygous individual

ho·mo·zy·gous \ˌhō-mə-ˈzī-gəs\ *adj* : having at least one gene pair that contains identical genes ⟨a pea plant *homozygous* for yellow seed⟩

hone \ˈhōn\ *vb* **honed; hon·ing** **1** : to sharpen with or as if with a fine abrasive stone **2** : to make more intense or effective ⟨top athletes *honing* their skills⟩

¹hon·est \ˈän-əst\ *adj* **1** : free from fraud or trickery : TRUTHFUL ⟨an *honest* plea⟩ **2** : being just what is indicated : GENUINE, REAL ⟨made an *honest* mistake⟩ **3** : good in the eyes of society : RESPECTABLE ⟨poor but *honest* people⟩ **4** : TRUSTWORTHY **5** : FRANK, OPEN *synonyms* see UPRIGHT

²honest *adv* : to tell the truth : I mean it ⟨I didn't do it, *honest* I didn't⟩

hon·est·ly \ˈän-əst-lē\ *adv* **1** : in an honest manner: as **a** : without cheating ⟨counted the votes *honestly*⟩ **b** : ACTUALLY, GENUINELY ⟨was *honestly* scared⟩ **2** : to be honest : to tell the truth ⟨*honestly,* I don't know how you do it⟩

hon·es·ty \ˈän-ə-stē\ *n* : the quality or state of being honest

hon·ey \ˈhən-ē\ *n, pl* **honeys** **1** : a thick sugary material prepared by bees from the nectar of flowers and stored by them in a honeycomb for food **2 a** : SWEETHEART, DEAR — often used as a term of affection **b** : something very good ⟨a *honey* of a play⟩ **3** : the quality or state of being sweet — **honey** *adj*

hon·ey·bee \-ˌbē\ *n* : a bee that produces honey and lives in colonies; *esp* : a European bee widely kept in hives for the honey it produces

¹hon·ey·comb \-ˌkōm\ *n* **1** : a mass of six-sided wax cells built by honeybees in their nest to contain young bees and stores of honey **2** : something that resembles a honeycomb in structure or appearance

²honeycomb *vb* : to make or become full of holes like a honeycomb

¹honeycomb 1

hon·ey·dew \ˈhən-ē-ˌd(y)ü\ *n* **1** : a sugary substance deposited on the leaves of plants usually by aphids or scale insects or sometimes by a fungus **2** : HONEYDEW MELON

honeydew melon *n* : a pale smooth-skinned muskmelon with greenish sweet flesh

hon·ey·moon \ˈhən-ē-ˌmün\ *n* **1** : a trip or vacation taken by a newly married couple **2** : the time immediately after marriage **3** : a pleasant period after the start of something (as a relationship) — **honeymoon** *vb* — **hon·ey·moon·er** *n*

hon·ey·suck·le \-ˌsək-əl\ *n* : any of a genus of shrubs having fragrant tube-shaped flowers rich in nectar

honk \ˈhäŋk, ˈhòŋk\ *n* : the cry of a goose; *also* : a similar sound (as of a horn) — **honk** *vb*

¹hon·or \ˈän-ər\ *n* **1 a** : a good name or public admiration : REPUTATION **b** : a showing of respect : RECOGNITION ⟨a dinner in *honor* of a new coach⟩ **2** : ¹PRIVILEGE ⟨whom have I the *honor* of addressing⟩ **3 a** *cap* — used especially as a title for an official of high rank (as a judge) ⟨if your *Honor* please⟩ **b** : one whose worth brings respect or fame : CREDIT ⟨an *honor* to your profession⟩ **4 a** : evidence or a symbol of great respect (as a title or medal) **b** *pl* : special credit or recognition given to graduating students for high achievement; *also* : a course of study for advanced students that is in place of or in addition to regular courses **5 a** : CHASTITY, PURITY **b** : high moral standards of behavior : INTEGRITY ⟨a person of *honor*⟩ **6** *pl* : courteous actions of a host or hostess ⟨did the *honors* at the table⟩

\ə\ abut	\aú\ out	\i\ tip	\ò\ saw	\ú\ foot
\ər\ further	\ch\ chin	\ī\ life	\òi\ coin	\y\ yet
\a\ mat	\e\ pet	\j\ job	\th\ thin	\yü\ few
\ā\ take	\ē\ easy	\ŋ\ sing	\th\ this	\yu̇\ cure
\ä\ cot, cart	\g\ go	\ō\ bone	\ü\ food	\zh\ vision

²honor *vb* **hon·ored; hon·or·ing** \'än-(ə-)riŋ\ **1 a** : to treat with honor : RESPECT ⟨*honor* your parents⟩ **b** : to give an honor to **2** : to fulfill the terms of ⟨*honored* the contract⟩

hon·or·able \'än-(ə-)rə-bəl, 'än-ər-bəl\ *adj* **1** : deserving of honor **2** — used as a title especially for various government officials **3** : performed or accompanied with marks of honor ⟨an *honorable* burial⟩ **4** : doing credit to the possessor ⟨*honorable* wounds⟩ **5** : characterized by honesty : ETHICAL — **hon·or·ably** \-blē\ *adv*

hon·or·ary \'än-ə-ˌrer-ē\ *adj* **1** : given or done as a sign of honor ⟨an *honorary* degree⟩ **2** : ¹VOLUNTARY 1, UNPAID ⟨*honorary* president⟩ — **hon·or·ari·ly** \ˌän-ə-ˈrer-ə-lē\ *adv*

honor guard *n* : a guard assigned to a ceremonial duty

honor system *n* : a system (as at a school) where persons are trusted to follow the rules without supervision

¹hood \'hu̇d\ *n* **1** : a soft covering for the head and neck often attached to a coat or cape **2** : a marking, crest, or fold on the head of an animal **3 a** : something resembling a hood in form or use **b** : a cover for parts of mechanisms; *esp* : the movable metal covering over the engine of an automobile **c** : an enclosure provided with a draft for carrying off disagreeable or harmful fumes, sprays, or dust — **hood·ed** \-əd\ *adj* — **hood·like** \-ˌlīk\ *adj*

²hood \'hu̇d, 'hüd\ *n* : HOODLUM

-hood \ˌhu̇d\ *n suffix* **1** : state : condition : quality ⟨hardi*hood*⟩ **2** : time : period ⟨child*hood*⟩ **3** : instance of a state or quality ⟨false*hood*⟩ **4** : individuals sharing a state or character ⟨brother*hood*⟩ [Old English *hād* "condition, quality"]

hood·lum \'hüd-ləm\ *n* **1** : MOBSTER, THUG **2** : a young ruffian

hoo·doo \'hüd-ü\ *n, pl* **hoodoos 1** : VOODOOISM 1 **2** : something that brings bad luck [perhaps an altered form of *voodoo*] — **hoodoo** *vb* — **hoo·doo·ism** \-ˌiz-əm\ *n*

hood·wink \'hu̇d-ˌwiŋk\ *vb* : to deceive by false appearance : TRICK

¹hoof \'hu̇f, 'hüf\ *n, pl* **hooves** \'hu̇vz, 'hüvz\ *or* **hoofs 1** : a covering of horn that protects the front of or encloses the ends of the toes of some mammals (as horses, oxen, and pigs) and that corresponds to a nail or claw **2** : a hoofed foot especially of a horse — **hoofed** \'hu̇ft, 'hüft, 'hu̇vd, 'hüvd\ *adj* — **on the hoof** : LIVING 1a ⟨meat animals bought *on the hoof*⟩

²hoof *vb* **1** : to walk especially with haste ⟨*hoofed* it to class⟩ **2** : to dance especially as a performer ⟨watched the cast *hoofing* on the stage⟩ — **hoof·er** *n*

hoof–and–mouth disease *n* : FOOT-AND-MOUTH DISEASE

hoof·beat \'hu̇f-ˌbēt, 'hüf-\ *n* : the sound of a hoof striking a hard surface (as the ground)

hoof·print \-ˌprint\ *n* : a mark or hollow made by a hoof

¹hook \'hu̇k\ *n* **1** : a curved or bent tool for catching, holding, or pulling **2** : something curved or bent **3** : the flight of a ball curving to the left when hit or thrown by a right=hander or to the right when hit or thrown by a left=hander **4** : a short sweeping punch made with the elbow bent **5** : ¹CRADLE 6 ⟨left the phone off the *hook*⟩ — **by hook or by crook** : by any means — **off the hook** : out of trouble — **on one's own hook** : by oneself : INDEPENDENTLY

²hook *vb* **1** : to form into a hook : CROOK, CURVE **2 a** : to seize, make fast, or connect by or as if by a hook **b** : to become secured or connected by or as if by a hook **3** : PILFER, STEAL **4** : to make by drawing loops of thread, yarn, or cloth through a coarse fabric with a hook ⟨*hook* a rug⟩ **5** : to hit or throw a ball so that a hook results

hook and eye *n* : a fastener (as for clothing) made up of a small hook that catches over a bar or into a loop

hooked \'hu̇kt\ *adj* **1** : shaped like or provided with a hook **2 a** : addicted to narcotics **b** : fascinated by or fond of something ⟨*hooked* on skiing⟩

hook·up \'hu̇k-ˌəp\ *n* **1** : CONNECTION 2, ALLIANCE ⟨a *hookup* between two countries⟩ **2 a** : an arrangement (as

of circuits) used for a specific purpose (as in radio) **b** : the diagram of such an arrangement **3** : an arrangement of mechanical parts

hook·worm \-ˌwərm\ *n* **1** : a parasitic nematode worm having strong hooks or plates about the mouth **2** : a diseased state marked by blood loss, paleness, and weakness due to hookworms in the intestine — called also *hookworm disease*

hooky *also* **hook·ey** \'hu̇k-ē\ *n, pl* **hook·ies** *or* **hookeys** : TRUANT ⟨play *hooky*⟩

hoo·li·gan \'hü-li-gən\ *n* : HOODLUM 2 [perhaps from the name of Patrick *Hooligan*, an Irish hoodlum who lived in London around 1898]

hoop \'hu̇p, 'hüp\ *n* **1** : a circular band used for holding together the strips that make up the sides of a barrel; *also* : a similar band used as a toy **2 a** : a circular figure or object : RING **b** : the rim of a basketball goal; *broadly* : the entire goal **3** : BASKETBALL — usually used in plural **4** : a circle or series of circles of flexible material used to expand a woman's skirt — **hoop** *vb*

hoop·skirt \-ˌskərt\ *n* : a skirt stiffened with or as if with hoops

hoo·ray \hu̇-ˈrā\ *also* **hur·rah** \-ˈrȯ, -ˈrä\ *or* **hur·ray** \-ˈrā\ *interj* — used to express joy, approval, or encouragement

hoose·gow \'hüs-ˌgau̇\ *n* : PRISON 2 [from Spanish *juzgado* "panel of judges, courtroom," derived from *juzgar* "to judge," from Latin *judicare* "to judge" — related to JUDGE]

¹hoot \'hüt\ *vb* **1** : to utter a loud shout usually of scorn **2** : to make the characteristic call of an owl or a similar sound **3** : to drive out by hooting — **hoot·er** *n*

²hoot *n* **1** : a sound of hooting; *esp* : the call of an owl **2** : a very small amount ⟨don't care a *hoot*⟩ **3** : an amusing person or thing

hoo·te·nan·ny \'hüt-ᵊn-ˌan-ē\ *n, pl* **-nies** : a gathering at which folksingers entertain

¹hop \'häp\ *vb* **hopped; hop·ping 1** : to move by a quick springy leap or series of leaps; *esp* : to jump on one foot **2** : to jump over ⟨*hop* a puddle⟩ **3** : to move or get aboard by or as if by hopping ⟨*hop* a train⟩ ⟨*hop* in the car⟩ **4** : to make a quick trip especially by air [Old English *hoppian* "to leap, hop"]

²hop *n* **1 a** : a short brisk leap especially on one leg **b** : ²BOUNCE 1b **2** : ²DANCE 3, BALL ⟨the junior *hop*⟩ **3 a** : a flight in an airplane **b** : a short trip

³hop *n* **1** : a twining vine related to the mulberry and having leaves with lobes and flowers in cone-shaped catkins **2** *pl* : the ripe dried catkins of a hop used especially to give a bitter flavor to malt liquors [Middle English *hoppe* "the hop vine"; of Dutch origin]

³hop 1

⁴hop *vb* **hopped; hop·ping** : to flavor with hops

¹hope \'hōp\ *vb* **hoped; hop·ing** : to desire something and expect that it will happen or be obtained ⟨*hope* to succeed⟩ ⟨*hope* you'll accept the invitation⟩ ⟨*hope* for a bicycle⟩

²hope *n* **1** *archaic* : ¹TRUST 1a, RELIANCE ⟨our *hope* is in the king⟩ **2 a** : desire accompanied by expectation of fulfillment ⟨in *hope* of an early recovery⟩ **b** : someone or something on which hopes are centered ⟨a home run was the only *hope* for victory⟩ **c** : something hoped for

¹hope·ful \'hōp-fəl\ *adj* **1** : having qualities which inspire hope **2** : full of or inclined to hope — **hope·ful·ness** *n*

²hopeful *n* : a person who has hopes or is considered promising

hope·ful·ly \'hōp-fə-lē\ adv **1** : in a hopeful manner ⟨a dog looking *hopefully* for a tidbit⟩ **2** : I hope : we hope ⟨*hopefully* it won't rain tomorrow⟩

hope·less \'hō-pləs\ adj **1 a** : having no expectation of good or success **b** : INCURABLE **2 a** : giving no reason for hope : DESPERATE ⟨a *hopeless* situation⟩ **b** : incapable of solution or accomplishment : IMPOSSIBLE ⟨a *hopeless* task⟩ — **hope·less·ly** adv — **hope·less·ness** n

Ho·pi \'hō-pē\ n, pl **Hopi** or **Hopis** : a member of an American Indian people of northeastern Arizona

hopped–up \'häpt-'əp\ adj **1** : full of excitement or enthusiasm **2** : having more power than usual ⟨put a *hopped-up* engine in his hot rod⟩

hop·per \'häp-ər\ n **1 a** : one that hops **b** : a leaping insect; esp : a young hopping form of an insect **2 a** : a usually funnel-shaped container for delivering material (as grain) **b** : a railroad car with a sloping floor and hinged doors — called also *hopper car* **c** : a tank with a device for releasing its liquid through a pipe

hop·scotch \'häp-ˌskäch\ n : a child's game in which a player hops through a figure drawn on the ground

horde \'hō(ə)rd, 'ho(ə)rd\ n **1** : a wandering people or tribe **2** : a great multitude : THRONG, SWARM ⟨*hordes* of tourists⟩

ho·ri·zon \hə-'rīz-ºn\ n **1** : the line where the earth or sea seems to meet the sky **2** : the limit or range of a person's outlook or experience ⟨reading broadens our *horizons*⟩ **3** : a distinct layer of soil or its underlying material in a vertical section of land — **ho·ri·zon·al** \-'rīz-nəl, -ºn-əl\ adj

¹**hor·i·zon·tal** \ˌhȯr-ə-'zänt-ºl, ˌhär-\ adj **1** : of or relating to the horizon **2** : parallel to the horizon : LEVEL **3** : being on the same level — **hor·i·zon·tal·ly** \-ºl-ē\ adv

²**horizontal** n : a horizontal line or plane

hor·mon·al \hȯr-'mōn-ºl\ adj : of, relating to, or brought about by hormones

hor·mone \'hȯr-ˌmōn\ n : a product of living cells that circulates in body fluids (as blood) or sap and produces a specific and often stimulating effect on cells usually at a distance from the place where it is made

horn \'hȯ(ə)rn\ n **1** : one of the hard bony growths on the head of many hoofed animals (as cattle, goats, or sheep) **2** : a part like an animal's horn **3** : the material of which horns are composed or a similar material **4** : a hollow horn used to hold something ⟨powder *horn*⟩ **5** : something resembling a horn ⟨saddle *horn*⟩ ⟨*horns* of the crescent moon⟩ **6 a** : a brass wind instrument (as a trumpet or French horn) **b** : a device that makes a noise like that of a horn ⟨an automobile *horn*⟩ — **horned** \'hȯ(ə)rnd\ adj — **horn·less** \'hȯ(ə)rn-ləs\ adj — **horn·like** \-ˌlīk\ adj

horn·beam \-ˌbēm\ n : any of a genus of trees related to the birches and having smooth gray bark and hard white wood

horn·bill \-ˌbil\ n : any of a family of large Old World birds having enormous bills

horn·blende \-ˌblend\ n : a dark mineral commonly found as a kind of rock

horned owl n : any of several owls with two bunches of feathers on the head that look like ears; esp : GREAT HORNED OWL

horned pout n : a common bullhead of the eastern U.S.

horned toad n : any of several small harmless insect-eating lizards of the western U.S. and Mexico resembling toads and having hornlike spines

hornbill

hor·net \'hȯr-nət\ n : any of the larger wasps that live in colonies

horn·fels \'hȯ(ə)rn-ˌfelz\ n : a fine-grained rock formed by the action of heat

horn of plenty : CORNUCOPIA

horn·pipe \'hȯ(ə)rn-ˌpīp\ n **1** : a wind instrument made up of a wooden or bone pipe and a bell usually of horn **2** : a lively folk dance originally accompanied by hornpipe playing

horn·wort \-ˌwərt, -ˌwȯ(ə)rt\ n : any of various plants that usually live in water and are related to the liverworts

horny \'hȯr-nē\ adj **horn·i·er; -est** **1** : made of horn or of something resembling horn **2** : ¹HARD 1, CALLOUS ⟨*horny* hands⟩

horo·scope \'hȯr-ə-ˌskōp, 'här-\ n **1** : a diagram of the positions of planets and signs of the zodiac used by astrologers to foretell events of a person's life **2** : an astrological forecast [Middle English *horoscopum* "horoscope," from Latin *horoscopus* (same meaning), from Greek *hōroskopos*, literally, "hour watcher," from *hōra* "hour" and *skopos* "watcher" — related to BISHOP, EPISCOPAL, SCOPE; see *Word History* at BISHOP]

hor·ren·dous \hȯ-'ren-dəs, hä-, hə-\ adj : DREADFUL, HORRIBLE — **hor·ren·dous·ly** adv

hor·ri·ble \'hȯr-ə-bəl, 'här-\ adj **1** : marked by or arousing horror **2** : extremely unpleasant or bad ⟨*horrible* food⟩ — **hor·ri·bly** \-blē\ adv

hor·rid \'hȯr-əd, 'här-\ adj **1** : inspiring horror : SHOCKING **2 a** : arousing disgust : NASTY ⟨a *horrid* man⟩ **b** : HORRIBLE 2 ⟨had *horrid* manners⟩ — **hor·rid·ly** adv — **hor·rid·ness** n

hor·ri·fy \'hȯr-ə-ˌfī, 'här-\ vb **-fied; -fy·ing** : to cause to feel horror

hor·ror \'hȯr-ər, 'här-\ n **1** : strong fear, dread, or dislike **2** : the quality of inspiring horror **3** : something horrible — **horror** adj

hors d'oeuvre \ȯr-'dərv\ n, pl **hors d'oeuvres** also **hors d'oeuvre** \-'dərv(z)\ : any of various tasty foods usually served as appetizers [from French *hors-d'œuvre* "appetizers," from the phrase *hors d'œuvre*, literally, "outside of work"]

¹**horse** \'hȯ(ə)rs\ n, pl **hors·es** also **horse** **1 a** : a large hoofed grazing domestic mammal that is used to carry or draw loads and for riding **b** : a male horse : STALLION **2 a** : a frame that supports something (as wood while being cut) **b** : a piece of gymnasium equipment used for bal-

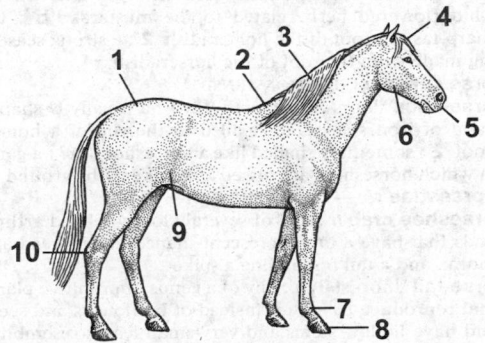

¹horse 1a: *1* croup, *2* withers, *3* mane, *4* forelock, *5* muzzle, *6* cheek, *7* fetlock, *8* hoof, *9* flank, *10* hock

\ə\ **abut**	\au̇\ **out**	\i\ **tip**	\ȯ\ **saw**	\u̇\ **foot**
\ər\ **further**	\ch\ **chin**	\ī\ **life**	\ȯi\ **coin**	\y\ **yet**
\a\ **mat**	\e\ **pet**	\j\ **job**	\th\ **thin**	\yü\ **few**
\ā\ **take**	\ē\ **easy**	\ŋ\ **sing**	\th\ **this**	\yu̇\ **cure**
\ä\ **cot, cart**	\g\ **go**	\ō\ **bone**	\ü\ **food**	\zh\ **vision**

ancing and swinging movements or for vaulting exercises **3** *horse pl* : CAVALRY — **horse** *adj*

²horse *vb* **horsed; hors·ing** : to provide with a horse

horse around *vb* : to engage in horseplay : FOOL ⟨was *horsing around* instead of studying⟩

¹horse·back \\'hȯrs-ˌbak\ *n* : the back of a horse

²horseback *adv* : on horseback

horse-car \\'hȯrs-ˌkär\ *n* : a streetcar drawn by horses

horse chestnut *n* **1** : a large European tree with leaves divided into fingerlike parts and large flower clusters that is widely grown as an ornamental and shade tree **2** : the large glossy brown seed of a horse chestnut

horse·fly \\'hȯrs-ˌflī\ *n* : any of a family of swift usually large two-winged flies with bloodsucking females

horse·hair \-ˌha(ə)r, -ˌhe(ə)r\ *n* **1** : hair of a horse especially from the mane or tail **2** : cloth made from horsehair — **horsehair** *adj*

horsehair worm *n* : any of various long slender worms whose adults live in water and whose larvae are parasites of insects

horse·hide \\'hȯrs-ˌhīd\ *n* : a horse's hide or leather made from it

horse latitudes *n pl* : either of two regions in the neighborhoods of 30° north and 30° south latitude having high pressure, calms, and light changeable winds

horse-laugh \\'hȯr-ˌslaf, -ˌslȧf\ *n* : a loud laugh : GUFFAW

horse·man \\'hȯr-smən\ *n* **1 a** : a rider or driver of horses **b** : one skilled in managing horses **2** : a breeder or raiser of horses — **horse·man·ship** \-ˌship\ *n*

horse opera *n* : ²WESTERN

Word History You have probably noticed that while there may be lots of horses in a cowboy film, there is usually no singing. The word *opera* is used in this term because the exciting stories and the overacting reminded people of operas. *Horse opera,* in reference to a western, dates from the late 1920s. About ten years later the term *soap opera* came to be used for a radio and still later for a television drama that was frequently sponsored by a soap manufacturer. By the late 1940s the term *space opera* came into use for a drama involving space travelers and beings on other planets.

horse·play \\'hȯr-ˌsplā\ *n* : rough or loud play

horse·pow·er \\'hȯr-ˌspau̇(-ə)r\ *n* : a unit of power equal in the U.S. to 746 watts and nearly equal to the English unit of the same name that equals 550 foot-pounds of work per second

horse·rad·ish \\'hȯrs-ˌrad-ish, -ˌred-\ *n* **1 a** : a tall coarse white-flowered herb related to the mustards **b** : the sharp-tasting root of the horseradish **2** : a strong seasoning made from the root of the horseradish

horse sense *n* : COMMON SENSE

horse·shoe \\'hȯrs-ˌshü, 'hȯrsh-\ *n* **1** : a usually U-shaped band of iron shaped and nailed to the rim of a horse's hoof **2** : something shaped like a horseshoe **3** *pl* : a game in which horseshoes are tossed at a stake in the ground — **horseshoe** *vb* — **horse·sho·er** *n*

horseshoe crab *n* : any of several closely related arthropods that have a broad crescent-shaped united head and thorax and a tail resembling a spike

horse·tail \\'hȯr-ˌstāl\ *n* : any of a genus of primitive plants that reproduce by spores instead of by flowers and seeds and have hollow stems and very small leaves resembling scales — called also *equisetum, scouring rush*

horse trade *n* : bargaining marked by clever careful dealing by both sides — **horse–trade** *vb* — **horse trader** *n*

horse·whip \\'hȯr-ˌswip, 'hȯrs-ˌhwip\ *vb* : to beat with or as if with a whip made to be used on a horse

horse·wom·an \\'hȯr-ˌswu̇m-ən\ *n* **1** : a woman who is a rider or driver of horses **2** : a woman skilled in caring for or managing horses **3** : a woman who breeds or raises horses

hors·ey *or* **horsy** \\'hȯr-sē\ *adj* **hors·i·er; -est 1** : of, relating to, or suggesting a horse, horses, or horse racing **2** : characteristic of horsemen or horsewomen — **hors·i·ness** *n*

hor·ti·cul·ture \\'hȯrt-ə-ˌkəl-chər\ *n* : the science of growing fruits, vegetables, flowers, or ornamental plants — **hor·ti·cul·tur·al** \ˌhȯrt-ə-'kəlch-(ə)-rəl\ *adj*

hor·ti·cul·tur·ist \ˌhȯrt-ə-'kəlch-(ə)-rəst\ *also* **hor·ti·cul·tur·al·ist** \-'kəlch-(ə)-rə-list\ *n* : a person who specializes in horticulture

ho·san·na \hō-'zan-ə\ *interj* — used as a cry of praise and adoration

¹hose \\'hōz\ *n* **1** *pl* **hose a** : STOCKING, SOCK **b** : a close-fitting garment covering the legs and waist worn by men in about 1600 **c** : short pants reaching to the knee **2** *pl* **hose** *or* **hos·es** : a flexible tube for carrying fluid

²hose *vb* **hosed; hos·ing** : to spray, water, or wash with a hose

Ho·sea \hō-'zā-ə, -'zē-\ *n* — see BIBLE table

ho·siery \\'hōzh-(ə)-rē, 'hōz-(ə)-\ *n* : stockings or socks in general

hos·pice \\'häs-pəs\ *n* **1** : an inn for travelers; *esp* : one kept by a religious order **2** : a place or program for caring for dying persons

hos·pi·ta·ble \hä-'spit-ə-bəl, 'häs-(ˌ)pit-\ *adj* **1** : generous and friendly in entertaining guests **2 a** : PLEASANT 2, INVITING ⟨a *hospitable* inn⟩ **b** : offering a pleasant or healthful environment ⟨a *hospitable* climate⟩ **3** : ¹OPEN 7 ⟨*hospitable* to new ideas⟩ — **hos·pi·ta·bly** \-blē\ *adv*

hos·pi·tal \\'häs-ˌpit-ᵊl\ *n* : an institution where the sick or injured are given medical or surgical care [Middle English *hospital* "a stopping place for travelers, a place that cares for people too old, sick, or poor to care for themselves," from early French *hospital* (same meaning), derived from Latin *hospitale* "hospice, guest house," from *hospitalis* "of a guest," from *hospit-, hospes* "host, stranger, guest," from *hostis* "stranger, enemy" — related to HOSPITALITY, ¹HOST, ²HOST, HOSTILE, HOTEL]

hos·pi·tal·i·ty \ˌhäs-pə-'tal-ət-ē\ *n, pl* **-ties** : generous and friendly treatment of visitors and guests [Middle English *hospitalite* "hospitality," from early French *hospitalité* (same meaning), derived from Latin *hospitale* "of a guest, showing hospitality," from *hospit-, hospes* "host, stranger, guest" — related to HOSPITAL, ²HOST, HOTEL]

hos·pi·tal·ize \\'häs-ˌpit-ᵊl-ˌīz\ *vb* **-ized; -iz·ing** : to place in a hospital as a patient — **hos·pi·tal·i·za·tion** \ˌhäs-ˌpit-ᵊl-ə-'zā-shən\ *n*

¹host \\'hōst\ *n* **1** : ARMY 1a **2** : a great number [Middle English *host* "army," from early French *ost* (same meaning), from Late Latin *hostis* (same meaning), from earlier *hostis* "stranger, enemy" — related to HOSPITAL, HOSTILE]

²host *n* **1** : one who receives or entertains guests socially or as a business **2** : a living animal or plant on or in which a parasite lives [Middle English *hoste* "host, guest," from early French *hoste* (same meaning), from Latin *hospit-, hospes* "host, stranger, guest" — related to HOSPITAL, HOSPITALITY]

³host *vb* **1** : to serve as host to, for, or at ⟨*host* friends⟩ ⟨*hosting* a dinner⟩ **2** : to serve as master of ceremonies for ⟨*hosted* the awards show⟩

⁴host *n, often cap* : a round thin piece of bread used in the Eucharist

hos·tage \\'häs-tij\ *n* : a person held captive as a pledge that promises will be kept or terms met by another

hos·tel \\'häs-tᵊl\ *n* **1** : INN **2** : an inexpensive lodging for usually young travelers — called also *youth hostel*

hos·tel·er \\'häs-tə-lər\ *n* **1** : one who lodges paying guests **2** : a traveler who stays overnight in hostels

hos·tel·ry \\'häs-tᵊl-rē\ *n, pl* **-ries** : INN, HOTEL

host·ess \ˈhō-stəs\ *n* : a woman who acts as host; *esp* : one who greets and provides service for diners in a restaurant or passengers on an airplane or ship — **hostess** *vb*

hos·tile \ˈhäs-t³l, -ˌtīl\ *adj* **1** : of or relating to an enemy ⟨*hostile* troops⟩ **2** : showing open resistance or opposition ⟨a *hostile* critic⟩ ⟨*hostile* to new things⟩ **3** : not hospitable : FORBIDDING ⟨a *hostile* environment⟩ [from early French *hostile* or Latin *hostilis*, both meaning "hostile," from Latin *hostis* "stranger, enemy" — related to HOSPITAL, ¹HOST] — **hos·tile·ly** \-t³l-(l)ē, -tīl-lē\ *adv*

hos·til·i·ty \hä-ˈstil-ət-ē\ *n, pl* **-ties** **1** : a hostile state, attitude, or action **2** *pl* : acts of warfare

hos·tler \ˈäs-lər, ˈhäs-\ *also* **ost·ler** \ˈäs-\ *n* : one who takes care of horses or mules

hot \ˈhät\ *adj* **hot·ter; hot·test** **1** : having a high temperature **2 a** : easily excited : ARDENT, FIERY ⟨*hot* temper⟩ **b** : VIOLENT 1, RAGING ⟨a *hot* battle⟩ **c** : EAGER ⟨*hot* for reform⟩ **3** : feeling or causing an uncomfortable degree of body heat ⟨my forehead is *hot*⟩ ⟨it's *hot* in here⟩ **4** : newly made : FRESH ⟨*hot* scent⟩; *also* : close to something sought ⟨you're getting *hotter*⟩ **5** : suggestive of heat or of burning or glowing objects ⟨*hot* spicy foods⟩ ⟨*hot* colors⟩ **6 a** : temporarily capable of unusual performance (as in a sport) **b** : currently popular or interesting ⟨a *hot* topic of conversation⟩ ⟨the *hot* fashions for spring⟩ **7 a** : carrying electric current **b** : RADIOACTIVE **c** : dealing with radioactive material **8 a** : recently stolen ⟨*hot* jewels⟩ **b** : wanted by the police — **hot** *adv* — **hot·ly** *adv* — **hot·ness** *n*

hot air *n* : empty talk

hot·bed \ˈhät-ˌbed\ *n* **1** : a heated bed of soil enclosed in glass and used for growing seedlings **2** : an environment that favors rapid growth or development ⟨a *hotbed* of crime⟩

hot–blood·ed \-ˈbləd-əd\ *adj* : easily excited : PASSIONATE — **hot–blood·ed·ness** *n*

hot·box \-ˌbäks\ *n* : a bearing (as of a railroad car) overheated by friction

hot·cake \-ˌkāk\ *n* : PANCAKE

hotch·potch \ˈhäch-ˌpäch\ *n* : HODGEPODGE [Middle English *hochepot* "mixed stew," derived from early French *hochepot* (same meaning), from *hocher* "to shake" and *pot* "pot, container" — see *Word History* at HODGEPODGE]

hot dog \ˈhät-ˌdȯg\ *n* : FRANKFURTER; *esp* : a cooked frankfurter served in a long split roll

ho·tel \hō-ˈtel\ *n* : an establishment that provides lodging and usually meals, entertainment, and personal services for its guests [from French *hôtel* "hotel," from early French *hostel* "a place for travelers to spend the night," derived from Latin *hospitalis* "of a guest, showing hospitality," from *hospit-, hospes* "host, stranger, guest" — related to HOSPITAL, HOSPITALITY]

¹hot·foot \ˈhät-ˌfút\ *adv* : in haste

²hotfoot *vb* : to go quickly : HURRY ⟨*hotfoot* it home⟩

hot·head \ˈhät-ˌhed\ *n* : a hotheaded person

hot·head·ed \-ˈhed-əd\ *adj* : easily angered : RASH, FIERY — **hot·head·ed·ly** *adv* — **hot·head·ed·ness** *n*

hot·house \-ˌhaús\ *n* : a heated greenhouse — **hothouse** *adj*

hot·line \ˈhät-ˌlīn\ *n* : a telephone line for direct emergency use (as between heads of governments or to a counseling service)

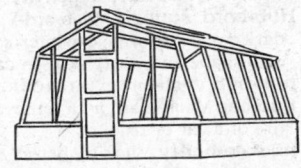
hothouse

hot link *n* : HYPERLINK

hot pepper *n* **1** : an often thin-walled and small pepper with a sharp or biting taste **2** : a pepper plant of the nightshade family that bears hot peppers

hot plate *n* : a small portable appliance for heating or cooking

hot rod *n* : an automobile rebuilt or changed for high speed and fast acceleration

hot–rod·der \ˈhät-ˌräd-ər\ *n* : a hot rod driver, builder, or enthusiast

hot·shot \ˈhät-ˌshät\ *n* : a showily skillful person

hot spot *n* **1** : a place of more than normal interest, activity, or popularity ⟨surfing *hot spots*⟩ **2** : a place where hot magma from the earth's interior rises through the mantle and crust to form a volcanic feature **3** : an area of political, military, or civil unrest usually considered dangerous **4** : a place where a wireless Internet connection is available

hot spring *n* : a spring whose water flows out at a temperature higher than the average temperature of the place where the spring is located

hot war *n* : a conflict involving actual fighting

hot water *n* : a distressing situation : TROUBLE ⟨in *hot water* for not doing my chores⟩

¹hound \ˈhaúnd\ *n* **1** : ¹DOG 1a **2** : a dog of any of various hunting breeds having large drooping ears and a deep voice and following their prey by scent or sight

²hound *vb* : to pursue with or as if with hounds

hour \ˈaú(ə)r\ *n* **1** : a time for or rite of religious worship **2** : one of the 24 divisions of a day : 60 minutes **3** : the time of day ⟨the *hour* is now 10:00 a.m.⟩ **4** : a fixed or particular time ⟨lunch *hour*⟩ ⟨an *hour* of need⟩ **5** : the distance traveled in an hour ⟨lives two *hours* away⟩ **6** : a class session ⟨I have math this *hour*⟩ — **after hours** : after the regular hours of work or operation

hour·glass \ˈaú(ə)r-ˌglas\ *n* : an instrument for measuring time in which usually sand runs from the upper part to the lower part of a glass container in an hour — **hourglass** *adj*

hour hand *n* : the short hand that marks the hours on the face of a watch or clock

hour·ly \ˈaú(ə)r-lē\ *adj* **1** : occurring every hour ⟨*hourly* bus service⟩ **2** : figured in terms of one hour ⟨*hourly* wages⟩ — **hourly** *adv*

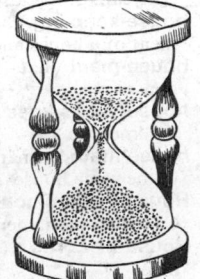
hourglass

¹house \ˈhaús\ *n, pl* **hous·es** \ˈhaú-zəz\ **1** : a building in which one or more families live **2 a** : something (as a nest or den) used by an animal for shelter **b** : a building in which something is stored ⟨carriage *house*⟩ **3 a** : one of the 12 equal sections into which the celestial sphere is divided in astrology **b** : a sign of the zodiac that is the seat of a planet's greatest influence **4 a** : ¹HOUSEHOLD **b** : FAMILY 2; *esp* : a royal or noble family **5** : a residence for a religious community or for students **6** : a body of persons assembled to make and discuss laws **7 a** : a place of business or entertainment ⟨went to a movie *house*⟩ **b** : a business firm ⟨a publishing *house*⟩ **c** : the audience in a theater or concert hall ⟨played to a full *house*⟩ [Old English *hūs* "house, home" — related to HUSBAND]

²house \ˈhaúz\ *vb* **housed; hous·ing** **1 a** : to provide with living quarters or shelter **b** : to store in a house **2** : to encase or enclose as if by putting in a house **3** : to take shelter : LODGE

\ə\ abut	\aú\ out	\i\ tip	\ȯ\ saw	\ú\ foot
\ər\ further	\ch\ chin	\ī\ life	\ȯi\ coin	\y\ yet
\a\ mat	\e\ pet	\j\ job	\th\ thin	\yú\ few
\ā\ take	\ē\ easy	\ŋ\ sing	\th\ this	\yú\ cure
\ä\ cot, cart	\g\ go	\ō\ bone	\ü\ food	\zh\ vision

house·boat \'haús-ˌbōt\ *n* : a roomy usually shallow and flat-bottomed pleasure boat equipped for use as a dwelling or for cruising

house·boy \-ˌbói\ *n* : a boy or man hired as a general household servant

house·break \-ˌbrāk\ *vb* **-broke; -bro·ken; -break·ing** : to make housebroken

house·break·ing \-ˌbrā-kiŋ\ *n* : the act of breaking into a person's house with the intention of committing a crime — **house·break·er** \-kər\ *n*

house·bro·ken \-ˌbrō-kən\ *adj* : trained in habits of eliminating bodily waste that are acceptable in indoor living ⟨a *housebroken* dog⟩

house cat *n* : CAT 1a

house·clean·ing \'haús-ˌklē-niŋ\ *n* : the cleaning of a house and its furniture

house·coat \'haú-ˌskōt\ *n* : a woman's loose and often long garment for wear around the house

house·dress \'haús-ˌdres\ *n* : a dress that is suitable for housework

house·fly \-ˌflī\ *n* : a two-winged fly that is common about human living places and may spread disease (as typhoid fever)

¹house·hold \'haús-ˌhōld, 'haú-ˌsōld\ *n* : those who live as a family in one house; *also* : a social unit made up of those living together in the same house

²household *adj* **1** : of or relating to a household : DOMESTIC **2** : ²FAMILIAR 3a, COMMON ⟨a *household* word⟩

house·hold·er \'haús-ˌhōl-dər, 'haú-ˌsōl-\ *n* : one who lives in a dwelling alone or as the head of a household

house·hus·band \'haús-ˌhəz-bənd\ *n* : a husband who does housework while his wife earns the family income

house·keep·er \'haú-ˌskē-pər\ *n* : a person employed to take care of a house

house·keep·ing \'haú-ˌskē-piŋ\ *n* : the care and management of a house and home affairs

house·maid \'haú-ˌsmād\ *n* : a girl or woman hired to do housework

housemaid's knee *n* : a swelling over the knee in front of the kneecap

house·mate \-ˌsmāt\ *n* : a person who lives with another in the same house

House of Commons : the lower house of the British and Canadian parliaments

House of Lords : the upper house of the British Parliament

house of representatives : the lower house of a legislative body (as the U.S. Congress)

house·plant \'haú-ˌsplant\ *n* : a plant grown or kept indoors

house sparrow *n* : a sparrow native to Europe and Asia that has been introduced into and now occurs widely in the New World — called also *English sparrow*

house·top \'haú-ˌstäp\ *n* : ¹ROOF 1a

house·warm·ing \'haú-ˌswór-miŋ\ *n* : a party to celebrate moving into a new home

house·wife \'haú-ˌswīf, *sense 2 is often* 'həz-əf, 'həs-əf\ *n* **1** : a married woman who manages her own home **2** : a small container for small articles (as thread) — **house·wife·li·ness** \'haú-ˌswī-flē-nəs\ *n* — **house·wife·ly** \-flē\ *adj* — **house·wif·ery** \'haú-ˌswī-fə-rē, -frē\ *n*

house·work \'haú-ˌswərk\ *n* : the work of housekeeping

¹hous·ing \'haú-ziŋ\ *n* **1 a** : the shelter of a temporary or permanent structure (as a tent or house) : LODGING **b** : dwellings provided for people ⟨*housing* for the elderly⟩ **2 a** : something that covers or protects **b** : a support (as a frame) for mechanical parts

²housing *n* : CAPARISON 1

hove *past and past participle of* HEAVE

hov·el \'həv-əl, 'häv-\ *n* **1** : an open shed or shelter **2** : a small poorly built house : HUT

hov·er \'həv-ər, 'häv-\ *vb* **hov·ered; hov·er·ing** \-(ə-)riŋ\ **1 a** : to hang fluttering in the air or on the wing **b** : to remain floating over a place or object **2 a** : to move to and fro near a place ⟨waiters *hovered* about⟩ **b** : to be in an undecided or uncertain state ⟨*hovering* between life and death⟩ — **hover** *n* — **hov·er·er** \-ər-ər\ *n*

hov·er·craft \-ˌkraft\ *n* : a vehicle supported above the surface of land or water by a cushion of air produced by fans blowing downward

¹how \('ˌ)haú\ *adv* **1** : in what manner or way ⟨study *how* plants grow⟩ ⟨*how* was it done⟩ **2** : for what reason : WHY ⟨*how* could you say that⟩ **3** : to what degree or extent ⟨*how* far is Denver⟩ **4** : in what state or condition ⟨*how* are you⟩ — **how about** : what do you say to or think of ⟨*how about* another game⟩ — **how come** : ¹WHY

²how *conj* : in what manner or condition ⟨remember *how* they fought⟩ ⟨asked *how* they were⟩

¹how·be·it \haú-'bē-ət\ *adv* : NEVERTHELESS

²howbeit *conj* : ALTHOUGH

how·dah \'haúd-ə\ *n* : a seat or covered platform on the back of an elephant or camel

¹how·ev·er \haú-'ev-ər\ *conj* : in whatever way or manner ⟨do it *however* you like⟩

²however *adv* **1 a** : in whatever manner or way ⟨I'll get there *however* I can⟩ **b** : to whatever degree or extent ⟨no prank, *however* innocent, was done⟩ **2** : in spite of that : on the other hand : BUT ⟨I'd like to go; *however*, I'd better not⟩

howdah

how·it·zer \'haú-ət-sər\ *n* : a short cannon capable of firing a shell in a high arc [from Dutch *houwitser* "howitzer," derived from a Czechoslovakian word for "catapult"]

howl \'haú(ə)l\ *vb* **1** : to make a long loud mournful sound like that of a dog **2** : to cry out loudly (as with pain, grief, or amusement) ⟨*howled* in protest⟩ ⟨*howling* with laughter⟩ **3** : to drown out or cause to fail by an outcry ⟨*howled* down the opposition⟩ — **howl** *n*

howl·er \'haú-lər\ *n* **1** : one that howls **2** : a stupid and ridiculous blunder

how·so·ev·er \ˌhaú-sə-'wev-ər\ *adv* **1** : in whatever manner **2** : to whatever degree or extent

hoy·den \'hóid-ᵊn\ *n* : a bold rowdy girl or woman — **hoy·den·ish** \-ish\ *adj*

HTML \ˌāch-ˌtē-ˌem-'el\ *n* : a computer language used to create pages for the World Wide Web that can include text, pictures, sound, and hyperlinks [*h*ypertext *m*arkup *l*anguage]

hua·ra·che \wə-'räch-ē, hə-\ *n* : a sandal made of leather thongs woven together [Mexican Spanish]

hub \'həb\ *n* **1** : the central part of a circular object (as a wheel) **2** : a center of activity

Hub·bard squash \'həb-ərd-\ *n* : any of various large dark green to orange winter squashes with a somewhat oval shape and warty skin — called also *Hubbard*

hub·bub \'həb-ˌəb\ *n* : UPROAR, TURMOIL

hub·cap \'həb-ˌkap\ *n* : a removable metal covering on the tire of a car or truck

huck·le·ber·ry \'hək-əl-ˌber-ē\ *n* **1** : an American shrub related to the blueberry; *also* : it's edible dark blue to black usually acid berry **2** : BLUEBERRY

huck·ster \'hək-stər\ *n* **1** : one that peddles : HAWKER **2** : a writer of advertising especially for radio or television

¹hud·dle \ˈhəd-ᵊl\ *vb* **hud·dled; hud·dling** \ˈhəd-liŋ, ᵊl-iŋ\ **1** : to crowd, push, or pile together ⟨people *huddled* in a doorway⟩ **2** : to gather in a huddle in football **3** : CURL UP, CROUCH ⟨a child *huddled* in its crib⟩ — **hud·dler** \ˈhəd-lər, -ᵊl-ər\ *n*

²huddle *n* **1** : a close-packed group : BUNCH **2 a** : CONFERENCE 1 **b** : a brief gathering of football players away from the line of scrimmage to hear instructions for the next play

hue \ˈhyü\ *n* **1** : COLOR 1 **2** : a particular variety of a color : SHADE **3** : an aspect of colors that allows them to be identified as red, yellow, green, blue, or something between any two of these colors

hue and cry \ˌhyü-\ *n* **1** : a loud outcry formerly used in the pursuit of someone suspected of a crime **2** : a loud noise of alarm or protest

¹huff \ˈhəf\ *vb* : ¹PUFF 1a

²huff *n* : a fit of anger or irritation

huffy \ˈhəf-ē\ *adj* **huff·i·er; -est** : easily offended : TOUCHY — **huff·i·ly** \ˈhəf-ə-lē\ *adv* — **huff·i·ness** \ˈhəf-ē-nəs\ *n*

hug \ˈhəg\ *vb* **hugged; hug·ging 1** : to press tightly especially in the arms : EMBRACE **2** : to stay close to ⟨drives along *hugging* the curb⟩ — **hug** *n*

huge \ˈhyüj, ˈyüj\ *adj* **1** : of great size or area **2** : of great scale or degree **3** : great in range or character **synonyms** see ENORMOUS — **huge·ly** *adv* — **huge·ness** *n*

hug·ger–mug·ger \ˈhəg-ər-ˌməg-ər\ *n* **1** : SECRECY 2 **2** : a disorderly jumble — **hugger–mugger** *adj*

hu·la \ˈhü-lə\ *or* **hu·la–hu·la** \ˌhü-lə-ˈhü-lə\ *n* : a Polynesian dance composed of slow rhythmic body movements usually accompanied by chants and drumming [a native word in Hawaii]

¹hulk \ˈhəlk\ *n* **1 a** : a heavy clumsy ship **b** : the body of an old ship unfit for service or of an abandoned wreck **2** : a bulky or clumsy person or thing

²hulk *vb* : to appear impressively large ⟨factories *hulking* along the river⟩ — **hulk·ing** \ˈhəl-kiŋ\ *adj*

¹hull \ˈhəl\ *n* **1 a** : the outer covering of a fruit or seed **b** : the remains of the flower that cling to the base of some fruits (as a strawberry) **2** : the frame or body of a ship, flying boat, or airship

²hull *vb* : to remove the hulls of ⟨*hulling* strawberries⟩ ⟨*hulled* the corn kernels⟩ — **hull·er** *n*

hul·la·ba·loo \ˈhəl-ə-bə-ˌlü\ *n, pl* **-loos** : UPROAR, DIN

hum \ˈhəm\ *vb* **hummed; hum·ming 1 a** : to utter a continuous \m\ sound **b** : to make the natural buzzing sound of an insect in motion or a sound like it : DRONE **c** : to give forth a low continuous blend of sound **2** : to produce musical tones while keeping the lips closed **3** : to be busily active ⟨the place was *humming*⟩ — **hum** *n* — **hum·mer** *n*

¹hu·man \ˈhyü-mən, ˈyü-\ *adj* **1** : relating to or characteristic of human beings; *esp* : showing qualities typical of human beings ⟨a *human* failing⟩ **2** : consisting of human beings ⟨the *human* race⟩ **3** : having human form or characteristics ⟨the dog's expression was almost *human*⟩ — **hu·man·ness** \-mən-nəs\ *n*

²human *n* : a human being — **hu·man·like** \-ˌlīk\ *adj*

human being *n* : an individual of the species of primate mammal that walks on two feet, is related to the great apes, and is distinguished by a greatly developed brain with capacity for speech and abstract reasoning

hu·mane \hyü-ˈmān, yü-\ *adj* : marked by sympathy or consideration for others — **hu·mane·ly** *adv* — **hu·mane·ness** \-ˈmān-nəs\ *n*

human im·mu·no·de·fi·cien·cy virus \-ˌim-yə-nō-di-ˈfish-ən(t)-sē-, -im-ˌyü-nō-\ *n* : HIV

hu·man·i·tar·i·an \hyü-ˌman-ə-ˈter-ē-ən, yü-\ *n* : a person devoted to or working for the health and happiness of other people — **humanitarian** *adj* — **hu·man·i·tar·i·an·ism** \-ē-ə-ˌniz-əm\ *n*

hu·man·i·ty \hyü-ˈman-ət-ē, yü-\ *n, pl* **-ties 1** : the quality or state of being human or of being humane **2** *pl* : studies (as literature, history, and art) concerned primarily with human culture **3** : the whole collection of human beings both past and present

hu·man·ize \ˈhyü-mə-ˌnīz, ˈyü-\ *vb* **-ized; -iz·ing 1** : to make suitable for human nature or use **2** : to make humane : CIVILIZE, REFINE — **hu·man·i·za·tion** \ˌhyü-mə-nə-ˈzā-shən, ˌyü-\ *n*

hu·man·kind \ˈhyü-mən-ˌkīnd, ˈyü-\ *n* : HUMANITY 3

hu·man·ly \ˈhyü-mən-lē, ˈyü-\ *adv* **1** : within the range of human ability ⟨a task not *humanly* possible⟩ **2** : of or concerning human needs or emotions ⟨deal *humanly* with the poor⟩

human nature *n* : the nature of human beings; *esp* : the ways of thinking, acting, and reacting that are common to most or all human beings or that are learned in social situations

hu·man·oid \ˈhyü-mə-ˌnoid, ˈyü-\ *adj* : having human form or characteristics — **humanoid** *n*

human trafficking *n* : organized criminal activity in which human beings are treated as possessions to be controlled and exploited (as by being forced into prostitution or involuntary labor)

¹hum·ble \ˈhəm-bəl, ˈəm-\ *adj* **hum·bler** \-b(ə-)lər\; **hum·blest** \-b(ə-)ləst\ **1** : modest or meek in spirit or manner : not proud or bold ⟨*humble* apology⟩ **2** : low in rank or status ⟨a *humble* position⟩ — **hum·bly** \-blē\ *adv*

²humble *vb* **hum·bled; hum·bling** \-b(ə-)liŋ\ **1** : to make humble in spirit or manner **2** : to destroy the power or influence of ⟨*humbled* the enemy with a crushing attack⟩ — **hum·bler** \-b(ə-)lər\ *n*

hum·bug \ˈhəm-ˌbəg\ *n* **1** : a false or deceiving person or thing : FRAUD **2** : NONSENSE 1, DRIVEL — **hum·bug** *vb* — **hum·bug·gery** \-ˌbəg-(ə-)rē\ *n*

hum·drum \ˈhəm-ˌdrəm\ *adj* : MONOTONOUS 2, DULL

hu·mer·us \ˈhyüm-(ə-)rəs\ *n, pl* **hu·meri** \ˈhyü-mə-ˌrī, -ˌrē\ : the long bone of the upper arm or forelimb that extends from the shoulder to the elbow

hu·mid \ˈhyü-məd, ˈyü-\ *adj* : ³DAMP, MOIST ⟨a *humid* climate⟩ — **hu·mid·ly** *adv*

hu·mid·i·fy \hyü-ˈmid-ə-ˌfī, yü-\ *vb* **-fied; -fy·ing** : to make (as the air of a room) moister : MOISTEN — **hu·mid·i·fi·ca·tion** \-ˌmid-ə-fə-ˈkā-shən\ *n* — **hu·mid·i·fi·er** \-ˈmid-ə-ˌfī(-ə)r\ *n*

hu·mid·i·ty \hyü-ˈmid-ət-ē, yü-\ *n, pl* **-ties** : MOISTURE, DAMPNESS; *esp* : the amount of moisture in the air

hu·mi·dor \ˈhyü-mə-ˌdor, ˈyü-\ *n* : a case in which the air is kept properly humidified for storing usually cigars or tobacco

hu·mil·i·ate \hyü-ˈmil-ē-ˌāt, yü-\ *vb* **-at·ed; -at·ing** : to cause a loss of pride or self-respect : HUMBLE — **hu·mil·i·a·tion** \-ˌmil-ē-ˈā-shən\ *n*

Word History In modern English we sometimes say that a person who has been criticized or humiliated has been *put down*. We speak as though the person had actually been forced to the ground or made to bow down in front of someone else. The origins of the word *humiliate* itself also suggest the idea of physically putting someone down to the ground. *Humiliate* can be be traced back to the Latin *humus*, meaning "earth, ground." From *humus* came the Latin adjective *humilis*, meaning "low, humble," which later gave rise to the verb *humiliare*, meaning "to make low or humble." The English *humiliate* derives from Latin *humiliare*. [from Latin *humiliatus* "made to lose pride or self-respect," from earlier *humili-*

\ə\ **abut**	\au̇\ **out**	\i\ **tip**	\o͗\ **saw**	\u̇\ **foot**
\ər\ **further**	\ch\ **chin**	\ī\ **life**	\o͘i\ **coin**	\y\ **yet**
\a\ **mat**	\e\ **pet**	\j\ **job**	\th\ **thin**	\yü\ **few**
\ā\ **take**	\ē\ **easy**	\ŋ\ **sing**	\t̲h̲\ **this**	\yu̇\ **cure**
\ä\ **cot, cart**	\g\ **go**	\ō\ **bone**	\ü\ **food**	\zh\ **vision**

are "to make low or humble," from *humilis* "low, humble," from *humus* "earth"]

hu·mil·i·ty \hyü-'mil-ət-ē, yü-\ *n* : the quality or state of being humble

hum·ming·bird \'həm-iŋ-ˌbərd\ *n* : any of numerous tiny brightly colored American birds related to the swifts and having narrow swiftly beating wings, a slender bill, and a long tongue for sipping nectar

hum·mock \'həm-ək\ *n* **1** : a rounded mound of earth : KNOLL **2** : a ridge or pile of ice — **hum·mocky** \-ə-kē\ *adj*

¹hu·mor \'hyü-mər, 'yü-\ *n* **1** : a changeable state of mind often influenced by circumstances ⟨in a bad *humor*⟩ **2** : the amusing quality of things ⟨the *humor* of a situation⟩ **3** : the power to see or tell about the amusing or comic side of things **4** : something that is humorous — **hu·mor·less** \-ləs\ *adj* — **hu·mor·less·ness** *n*

Word History In the Middle Ages it was believed that a person's health and disposition were the result of a balance or imbalance of four fluids in the body. These fluids were called "humors," from the Latin word *humor*, meaning "moisture." These fluids were blood, phlegm, yellow bile, and black bile. If a person had a cheerful, confident disposition, it was said to be a result of an excess of blood. Such a person was called "sanguine," from the Latin word *sanguis*, meaning "blood." A sluggish disposition was said to be the result of an excess of phlegm. A person having such a disposition was called "phlegmatic," from the Greek word *phlegma*, meaning "flame, phlegm." A fiery, hot-tempered disposition was said to be caused by an excess of yellow bile. A person with this disposition was said to be "choleric," from the Greek word *cholē*, meaning "bile." The disposition of a gloomy, depressed person was said to be the result of an excess of black bile. Such a person was called "melancholy," from the Greek words *melan-*, meaning "black," and *cholē*, meaning "bile." In time the word *humor* came to be used as a general term for "disposition or temperament." From this developed the sense of "a changeable state of mind" or "mood." More recently *humor* has come to refer to something that is funny. [Middle English *humour* "one of the four bodily fluids thought to affect a person's health," from early French *umor, umour* (same meaning), derived from Latin *humor, umor* "moisture"]

²humor *vb* **hu·mored; hu·mor·ing** \'hyüm-(ə-)riŋ, 'yüm-\ : to go along with the wishes or mood of ⟨*humor* a sick person⟩

hu·mor·ist \'hyüm-(ə-)rəst, 'yüm-\ *n* : a person specializing in or noted for humor

hu·mor·ous \'hyüm-(ə-)rəs, 'yüm-\ *adj* : full of, characterized by, or expressing humor : DROLL ⟨a *humorous* story⟩ — **hu·mor·ous·ly** *adv* — **hu·mor·ous·ness** *n*

¹hump \'həmp\ *n* **1** : a rounded bulge or lump (as on the back of a camel) **2** : a difficult part (as of a task) — **humped** \'həm(p)t\ *adj*

²hump *vb* **1** : to move or work energetically : HUSTLE **2** : to make hump-shaped : HUNCH

hump·back \'həmp-ˌbak\ *n* **1** : a humped or crooked back **2** : HUNCHBACK 1 **3** : HUMPBACK WHALE — **hump·backed** \-'bakt\ *adj*

humpback whale *n* : a large baleen whale that is black above and white below and has very long flippers

hu·mus \'hyü-məs, 'yü-\ *n* : a brown or black product of partial decay of plant or animal matter that forms the organic portion of soil

humpback whale

Hun \'hən\ *n* : a member of a warlike central Asian people gaining control of a large part of Europe about A.D. 450

¹hunch \'hənch\ *vb* **1** : to push oneself forward by jerks ⟨*hunch* nearer the fire⟩ **2** : to bend one's body into an arch or hump ⟨were *hunched* over the table⟩ **3** : to draw up close together or into an arch ⟨*hunched* my shoulders⟩

²hunch *n* **1** : ¹HUMP 1 **2** : a strong feeling about what will happen : INTUITION

hunch·back \'hənch-ˌbak\ *n* **1** : a person with a humpback **2** : HUMPBACK 1 — **hunch·backed** \-'bakt\ *adj*

hun·dred \'hən-drəd, -dərd\ *n, pl* **hundreds** *or* **hundred** **1** — see NUMBER table **2** : a very large number ⟨*hundreds* of times⟩ **3** : a 100-dollar bill ⟨gave me change for a *hundred*⟩ — **hundred** *adj*

hundreds digit *n* : the numeral (as 4 in 456) in the hundreds place

hundreds place *n* : the place three to the left of the decimal point in a number

hun·dredth \'hən-drədth, -drətth\ *n* **1** : one of 100 equal parts of something **2** — see NUMBER table — **hundredth** *adj*

hun·dredths place \'hən-drədths-, -drətths-\ *n* : the second place to the right of a decimal point in a number

hun·dred·weight \'hən-drə-ˌdwāt, -dər-ˌdwāt\ *n, pl* **-weight** *or* **-weights 1** : a unit of weight equal to 100 pounds (about 45.4 kilograms) — called also *short hundredweight;* see MEASURE table **2** *British* : a unit of weight equal to 112 pounds (about 50.8 kilograms) — called also *long hundredweight*

¹hung *past and past participle of* HANG

²hung \'həŋ\ *adj* : unable to reach a decision or verdict ⟨a *hung* jury⟩

Hun·gar·i·an \ˌhəŋ-'ger-ē-ən, -'gar-\ *n* **1 a** : a person born or living in Hungary : MAGYAR **b** : a person of Hungarian descent **2** : the language of the Hungarians — **Hungarian** *adj*

¹hun·ger \'həŋ-gər\ *n* **1 a** : a desire or a need for food **b** : an uneasy feeling or weakened condition resulting from lack of food **2** : a strong desire : CRAVING ⟨a *hunger* for praise⟩ — **hunger** *adj*

²hunger *vb* **hun·gered; hun·ger·ing** \-g(ə-)riŋ\ **1** : to feel or suffer hunger **2** : to have an eager desire ⟨*hungered* for affection⟩

hunger strike *n* : refusal (as by a prisoner) to eat enough to stay alive

hun·gry \'həŋ-grē\ *adj* **hun·gri·er; -est 1** : feeling or showing hunger **2** : EAGER, AVID ⟨*hungry* for all the details⟩ — **hun·gri·ly** \-grə-lē\ *adv*

hung up *adj* **1** : delayed or detained for a time **2** : anxiously nervous **3** : much involved or concerned with something or someone ⟨*hung up* on winning⟩

hunk \'həŋk\ *n* **1** : a large lump or piece **2** : a male who is physically very attractive

hun·ker \'həŋ-kər\ *vb* **hun·kered; hun·ker·ing** \-k(ə-)riŋ\ **1** : CROUCH ⟨*hunker* down under the tent⟩ **2** : to settle in for a long time ⟨*hunkering* down for the winter⟩

¹hunt \'hənt\ *vb* **1 a** : to seek out and chase (game) for food or sport ⟨*hunt* squirrel⟩ **b** : to use in hunting game ⟨*hunts* a pack of dogs⟩ **2 a** : to chase in order to capture **b** : to search out : look for : SEEK ⟨*hunting* for my gloves⟩ **3** : to drive or chase especially by repeated attacks ⟨*hunt* a criminal out of town⟩ **4** : to search through looking for prey ⟨*hunts* the woods⟩ **synonyms** see SEEK

²hunt *n* **1** : the action, the practice, or an instance of hunting **2** : a group of hunters; *esp* : a group of hunters on horseback and their hunting dogs

hunt·er \'hənt-ər\ *n* **1** : a person who hunts; *esp* : one who hunts game **2** : a dog or horse used or trained for hunting

hunt·er-gath·er·er \-'gath-ər-ər, -'geth-\ *n* : a member of a culture in which food is gotten by hunting, fishing, and gathering rather than by agriculture

hunt·ing *n* : the action of one that hunts; *esp* : the chasing of game

Hun·ting·ton's disease \'hənt-iŋ-tənz-\ *n* : an inherited nervous disorder that develops in adult life and leads to severely reduced mental functioning

hunt·ress \'hən-trəs\ *n* : a woman who hunts game

hunts·man \'hən(t)-smən\ *n* **1** : a person who hunts game **2** : a person who manages a hunt and looks after the hounds

huppah *variant of* CHUPPAH

¹hur·dle \'hərd-ᵊl\ *n* **1** : a movable panel used as a fence **2 a** : a barrier to be jumped in a race **b** : a race in which such barriers must be jumped **3** : OBSTACLE

²hurdle *vb* **hur·dled; hur·dling** \'hərd-liŋ, -ᵊl-iŋ\ **1** : to leap over while running ⟨the horse *hurdled* the fence⟩ **2** : OVERCOME 1 — **hur·dler** \'hərd-lər, -ᵊl-ər\ *n*

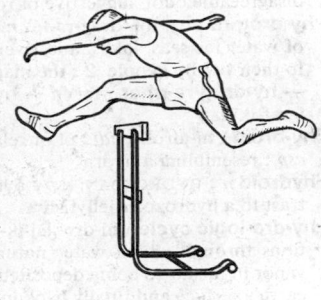

¹hurdle 2a

hur·dy–gur·dy \,hərd-ē-'gərd-ē\ *n, pl* **-gur·dies** : a musical instrument in which the sound is produced by turning a crank; *esp* : BARREL ORGAN

hurl \'hər(-ə)l\ *vb* **hurled; hurl·ing** \'hər-liŋ\ **1** : to throw violently or powerfully **2** : ³PITCH 6a **3** : ²VOMIT **synonyms** see THROW — **hurl·er** \'hər-lər\ *n*

hurling *n* : an Irish game resembling field hockey played between two teams of 15 players each

hur·ly–bur·ly \,hər-lē-'bər-lē\ *n, pl* **-bur·lies** : TUMULT

hurrah, hurray *variant of* HOORAY

hur·ri·cane \'hər-ə-,kān, -i-kən, 'hə-rə-, 'hə-ri-\ *n* : a cyclone formed in the tropics with winds of 74 miles (119 kilometers) per hour or greater that is usually accompanied by rain, thunder, and lightning

hur·ried \'hər-ēd, 'hə-rēd\ *adj* **1** : going or working with speed ⟨a *hurried* waitress⟩ **2** : done in a hurry ⟨a *hurried* meal⟩ — **hur·ried·ly** \'hər-əd-lē, 'hə-rəd-\ *adv*

¹hur·ry \'hər-ē, 'hə-rē\ *vb* **hur·ried; hur·ry·ing** **1 a** : to carry or cause to go with haste ⟨*hurry* the child to the hospital⟩ **b** : to move or act with haste ⟨had to *hurry* to arrive in time⟩ **2 a** : to urge on to greater speed : PROD **b** : to hasten the doing of ⟨*hurry* a repair job⟩ — **hur·ri·er** *n*

²hurry *n, pl* **hurries** **1** : great speed; *esp* : unnecessary haste **2** : a state of eagerness or urgency : RUSH — **in a hurry** : without delay ⟨wanted their tickets *in a hurry*⟩

¹hurt \'hərt\ *vb* **hurt; hurt·ing** **1 a** : to cause physical pain to **b** : to do harm to : DAMAGE **2 a** : to cause mental suffering to : OFFEND ⟨the teasing *hurts* me⟩ **b** : ¹HAMPER ⟨injuries *hurt* our chances of winning⟩ **3** : to feel or cause pain ⟨my tooth *hurts*⟩ — **hurt·er** *n*

²hurt *n* **1** : a cause of injury or damage **2** : a physical injury or wound **3 a** : physical pain **b** : mental distress : SUFFERING **4** : ¹WRONG 1, HARM

hurt·ful \'hərt-fəl\ *adj* : causing injury or suffering : DAMAGING — **hurt·ful·ly** \-fə-lē\ *adv* — **hurt·ful·ness** *n*

hur·tle \'hərt-ᵊl\ *vb* **hur·tled; hur·tling** \'hərt-liŋ, -ᵊl-iŋ\ **1** : to move suddenly or violently ⟨boulders *hurtled* down the hill⟩ **2** : HURL 1, FLING

¹hus·band \'həz-bənd\ *n* : a male partner in a marriage [Old English *hūsbonda* "master of a house," from early Norse *hūsbondi*, literally, "house owner" — related to HOUSE]

²husband *vb* : to manage carefully and economically : CONSERVE ⟨*husbanded* their resources⟩ — **hus·band·er** *n*

hus·band·man \'həz-bən(d)-mən\ *n* : one that plows and cultivates land : FARMER

hus·band·ry \'həz-bən-drē\ *n* **1** : wise management of resources : ECONOMY **2** : FARMING, AGRICULTURE

¹hush \'həsh\ *vb* **1** : to make quiet, calm, or still : SOOTHE ⟨*hush* a baby⟩ **2** : to become quiet **3** : to keep from public knowledge : SUPPRESS ⟨*hush* up the crime⟩

²hush *n* : a silence or calm especially following noise : QUIET

husk \'həsk\ *n* **1** : a usually thin dry outer covering of various seeds or fruits (as barley and corn) : HULL **2** : an outer layer : SHELL

²husk *vb* : to strip the husk from — **husk·er** *n*

¹hus·ky \'həs-kē\ *adj* **hus·ki·er; -est** : HOARSE 2 [probably derived from an obsolete sense of *husk,* meaning "to have a dry cough"] — **hus·ki·ly** \'həs-kə-lē\ *adv* — **hus·ki·ness** \-kē-nəs\ *n*

²hus·ky *n, pl* **huskies** **1** : a heavy-coated working dog especially of the New World arctic region **2** : SIBERIAN HUSKY [probably an altered form of *Huskemaw, Uskemaw* "Eskimo," from Cree *aškimeˑw* (same meaning)]

³hus·ky *adj* **hus·ki·er; -est** : BURLY, ROBUST [probably from *husk* "a hard outer covering"]

hus·sar \(,)hə-'zär, -'sär\ *n* : a member of any of various European originally cavalry military units

hus·sy \'həs-ē, 'həz-\ *n, pl* **hussies** **1** : an immoral woman **2** : a disrespectful or mischievous girl

hus·tings \'həs-tiŋz\ *n pl* : a place where political campaign speeches are made [Old English *hūsting* "local court or assembly," from early Norse *hūsthing* "an assembly of the king's council," literally, "house assembly," from *hūs* "house" and *thing* "assembly"]

hus·tle \'həs-əl\ *vb* **hus·tled; hus·tling** \'həs-(ə-)liŋ\ **1** : to push, crowd, or force forward roughly ⟨*hustled* the prisoner to jail⟩ **2** : to move or work rapidly and tirelessly **3** : to sell something to or get something from by energetic and especially dishonest activity — **hustle** *n* — **hus·tler** \'həs-lər\ *n*

hut \'hət\ *n* : a small and often temporary dwelling or shelter : SHACK

hutch \'həch\ *n* **1 a** : a chest or compartment for storage **b** : a low cupboard topped by usually open shelves **2** : a pen or coop for an animal **3** : SHANTY, SHACK

huz·zah *or* **huz·za** \(,)hə-'zä\ *interj* — used to express joy or approval

hy·a·cinth \'hī-ə-(,)sin(t)th\ *n* **1** : a red or brownish gem **2** : a common garden plant that grows from a bulb, is related to the lilies, and is widely grown for its showy dense spikes of fragrant bell-shaped flowers — compare GRAPE HYACINTH, WATER HYACINTH

¹hy·brid \'hī-brəd\ *n* **1** : an offspring of parents with different genes especially when of different races, breeds, species, or genera **2** : something of mixed origin or composition

²hybrid *adj* : of or relating to a hybrid : of mixed origin

hy·brid·ize \'hī-brə-,dīz\ *vb* **-ized; -iz·ing** : to produce or cause to produce hybrids : INTERBREED — **hy·brid·i·za-**

\ə\ abut	\aú\ out	\i\ tip	\ò\ saw	\ú\ foot
\ər\ further	\ch\ chin	\ī\ life	\òi\ coin	\y\ yet
\a\ mat	\e\ pet	\j\ job	\th\ thin	\yü\ few
\ā\ take	\ē\ easy	\ŋ\ sing	\t̲h̲\ this	\yú\ cure
\ä\ cot, cart	\g\ go	\ō\ bone	\ü\ food	\zh\ vision

tion \ˌhī-brəd-ə-'zā-shən\ *n* — **hy·brid·iz·er** \'hī-brə-ˌdī-zər\ *n*

hybrid vigor *n* : unusual vigor or capacity for growth often shown by hybrid plants or animals

hydr- *or* **hydro-** *combining form* **1** : water ⟨*hydrous*⟩ ⟨*hydro*electricity⟩ **2** : hydrogen : containing or combined with hydrogen ⟨*hydro*carbon⟩ [derived from Greek *hydōr* "water"]

hy·dra \'hī-drə\ *n* **1** *cap* : a many-headed serpent or monster in Greek mythology killed by Hercules **2** : any of numerous small tube-shaped freshwater animals related to the jellyfishes and having a mouth surrounded by tentacles at one end

hy·dran·gea \hī-'drān-jə\ *n* : any of a genus of shrubby plants with showy clusters of usually sterile white, pink, or bluish flowers

hy·drant \'hī-drənt\ *n* : a pipe with a valve and spout at which water may be drawn from the main pipes

¹hy·drate \'hī-ˌdrāt\ *n* : a compound formed by the union of water with some other substance ⟨a *hydrate* of copper sulfate⟩

²hydrate *vb* **hy·drat·ed; hy·drat·ing** **1** : to cause to take up or combine with water or the elements of water **2** : to supply with sufficient amounts of fluid or moisture — **hy·dra·tion** \hī-'drā-shən\ *n*

hy·drau·lic \hī-'dró-lik\ *adj* **1** : operated, moved, or brought about by means of water **2** : of or relating to hydraulics ⟨*hydraulic* engineer⟩ **3** : operated by pressure transmitted when a quantity of liquid is forced through a small hole or through a tube ⟨*hydraulic* brakes⟩ **4** : hardening or setting under water ⟨*hydraulic* cement⟩ — **hy·drau·li·cal·ly** \-'dró-li-k(ə-)lē\ *adv*

hy·drau·lics \hī-'dró-liks\ *n* : a science that deals with uses of liquid (as water) in motion

hy·dra·zine \'hī-drə-ˌzēn\ *n* : a colorless fuming liquid used especially in fuels for rocket engines

hy·dro \'hī-drō\ *n* : hydroelectric power

hy·dro·bro·mic acid \ˌhī-drə-ˌbrō-mik-\ *n* : a strong acid formed by dissolving the bromide of hydrogen in water

hy·dro·car·bon \ˌhī-drə-'kär-bən\ *n* : a compound containing only carbon and hydrogen

hy·dro·ceph·a·lus \ˌhī-drō-'sef-ə-ləs\ *also* **hy·dro·ceph·a·ly** \-'sef-ə-lē\ *n* : an abnormal condition in which an increased amount of cerebrospinal fluid causes an increase in the size of the ventricles of the brain and the size of the skull and the wasting away of the brain

hy·dro·chlo·ric acid \ˌhī-drə-'klōr-ik-, -'klȯr-\ *n* : a strong acid formed by dissolving hydrogen chloride in water that is widely used in industry and in the laboratory

hy·dro·elec·tric \ˌhī-drō-i-'lek-trik\ *adj* : of or relating to production of electricity by waterpower — **hy·dro·elec·tric·i·ty** \-ˌlek-'tris-ət-ē, -'tris-tē\ *n*

hy·dro·flu·or·ic acid \ˌhī-drō-flù-ˌȯr-ik-, -flù-ˌär-ik-\ *n* : a weak poisonous acid that is formed by dissolving hydrogen fluoride in water

hy·dro·foil \'hī-drə-ˌfȯil\ *n* : a boat that has fins attached to the bottom by braces for lifting the hull clear of the water to allow faster speeds

hy·dro·gen \'hī-drə-jən\ *n* : a chemical element that is the simplest and lightest of all chemical elements and is normally found alone as a colorless odorless highly flammable gas having two atoms per molecule — see ELEMENT table [from French *hydrogène* "hydrogen," from *hydr-* "water" and *-gène* "producer"; so called because when hydrogen gas burns, it combines with oxygen to produce water] — **hy·drog·e·nous** \hī-'dräj-ə-nəs\ *adj*

hy·dro·ge·nate \hī-'dräj-ə-ˌnāt, 'hī-drə-jə-\ *vb* **-nat·ed; -nat·ing** : to combine or treat with hydrogen; *esp* : to add hydrogen to a molecule of ⟨*hydrogenate* a vegetable oil to form a fat⟩ — **hy·dro·ge·na·tion** \hī-ˌdräj-ə-'nā-shən, ˌhī-drə-jə-\ *n*

hydrogen bomb *n* : a bomb whose violent explosive power is due to the sudden release of atomic energy when hydrogen nuclei unite

hydrogen chloride *n* : a colorless sharp-smelling poisonous gas that is made up of hydrogen and chlorine and produces hydrochloric acid when dissolved in water

hydrogen fluoride *n* : a colorless poisonous gas that is made up of hydrogen and fluorine and produces hydrofluoric acid when dissolved in water

hydrogen ion *n* : the positive ion of acids that consists of a hydrogen atom whose electron has been transferred to the negative ion of the acid

hydrogen peroxide *n* : an unstable liquid compound containing hydrogen and oxygen and used especially for bleaching and as an antiseptic

hydrogen sulfide *n* : a flammable poisonous gas with a disagreeable odor suggestive of rotten eggs

hy·drog·ra·phy \hī-'dräg-rə-fē\ *n* **1** : the study of bodies of water (as seas, lakes, and rivers) especially in relation to their use by people **2** : the mapping of bodies of water — **hy·drog·ra·pher** \-fər\ *n* — **hy·dro·graph·ic** \ˌhī-drə-'graf-ik\ *adj*

¹hy·droid \'hī-ˌdrȯid\ *adj* : of or relating to the hydrozoans; *esp* : resembling a hydra

²hydroid *n* : HYDROZOAN; *esp* : a hydrozoan polyp in contrast to a hydrozoan jellyfish

hy·dro·log·ic cycle \ˌhī-drə-ˌläj-ik-\ *n* : the series of conditions through which water naturally passes from water vapor in the air to being deposited (as by rain or snow) on earth's surface and finally back into the air especially as a result of evaporation

hy·drol·o·gy \hī-'dräl-ə-jē\ *n* : a science dealing with the characteristics, distribution, and circulation of water on and below the surface of the land and in the atmosphere — **hy·dro·log·ic** \ˌhī-drə-'läj-ik\ *or* **hy·dro·log·i·cal** \-i-kəl\ *adj* — **hy·drol·o·gist** \hī-'dräl-ə-jist\ *n*

hy·drol·y·sis \hī-'dräl-ə-səs\ *n* : a process of breaking down a chemical compound that involves splitting a bond and adding the elements of water to the resulting molecular fragments

hy·dro·lyze \'hī-drə-ˌlīz\ *vb* **-lyzed; -lyz·ing** : to go through or cause to go through hydrolysis

hy·drom·e·ter \hī-'dräm-ət-ər\ *n* : an instrument for finding out the strength of a liquid (as battery acid or an alcohol solution) by measuring its specific gravity

hy·dro·ni·um \hī-'drō-nē-əm\ *n* : an ion formed by the combination of a hydrogen ion with a water molecule

hy·dro·pho·bia \ˌhī-drə-'fō-bē-ə\ *n* **1** : RABIES **2** : an abnormal fear of water — **hy·dro·pho·bic** \-'fō-bik, -'fäb-ik\ *adj*

hy·dro·phone \'hī-drə-ˌfōn\ *n* : an instrument for listening to sound transmitted through water

hy·dro·phyte \'hī-drə-ˌfīt\ *n* : a plant growing in water or in waterlogged soil

hy·dro·plane \'hī-drə-ˌplān\ *n* **1** : a speedboat whose hull is completely or partly out of the water as it skims the water **2** : SEAPLANE

hydroplane 1

hy·dro·pon·ics \ˌhī-drə-'pän-iks\ *n* : the growing of plants in nutrient solutions — **hy·dro·pon·ic** \-ik\ *adj*

hy·dro·pow·er \'hī-drə-ˌpaù(-ə)r\ *n* : hydroelectric power

hy·dro·sphere \'hī-drə-ˌsfi(ə)r\ *n* : the surface waters of the earth and the water vapor in the atmosphere

hy·drot·ro·pism \hī-'drä-trə-ˌpiz-əm\ *n* : a tropism (as in plant roots) in which water or water vapor causes the movement — **hy·dro·tro·pic** \ˌhī-drə-'trō-pik, -'träp-ik\ *adj*

hy·drox·ide \hī-'dräk-ˌsīd\ *n* : a negatively charged ion consisting of one atom of oxygen and one atom of hydrogen

hy·drox·yl \hī-'dräk-səl\ *n* : a chemical group or ion that consists of one atom of hydrogen and one of oxygen

hy·dro·zo·an \ˌhī-drə-'zō-ən\ *n* : any of a class of coelenterates including the jellyfishes and single or colonial polyps (as hydras or corals) — **hydrozoan** *adj*

hy·e·na \hī-'ē-nə\ *n* : any of several large strong Old World mammals that eat flesh and are active at night

hyena

Word History Many pigs have manes of stiff hair that extend down their necks. When the ancient Greeks first saw hyenas, they thought the animals' manes looked like the manes of pigs. They called these strange animals *hyaina*, which comes from the Greek word *hys*, meaning "hog, pig." *Hyaena* is the Latin form, which was borrowed into English and spelled *hyena*. [Middle English *hyene* "hyena," from Latin *hyaena* (same meaning), from Greek *hyaina* (same meaning), from *hys* "hog, pig"]

hy·giene \'hī-ˌjēn\ *n* **1** : a science that deals with the bringing about and keeping up of good health in individuals and groups **2** : conditions or practices (as of cleanliness) that are aids to good health

hy·gien·ic \ˌhī-jē-'en-ik, hī-'jen-, hī-'jēn-\ *adj* : of, relating to, or leading toward good health or hygiene — **hy·gien·i·cal·ly** \-i-k(ə-)lē\ *adv*

hy·gien·ist \hī-'jēn-əst, 'hī-ˌjēn-, hī-'jen-\ *n* : a person skilled in hygiene; *esp* : DENTAL HYGIENIST

hy·gro·graph \'hī-grə-ˌgraf\ *n* : an instrument for automatic recording of changes in the amount of moisture in the air

hy·grom·e·ter \hī-'gräm-ət-ər\ *n* : an instrument for measuring the amount of moisture in the air

hying *present participle of* HIE

hy·men \'hī-mən\ *n* : a fold of mucous membrane partly closing the opening of the vagina — **hy·men·al** \-əl\ *adj*

hy·me·nop·tera \ˌhī-mə-'näp-tə-rə\ *n pl* : insects that are hymenopterans

hy·me·nop·ter·an \ˌhī-mə-'näp-tə-rən\ *n* : any of an order of highly specialized and often colonial insects (as bees, wasps, and ants) that have usually four thin transparent wings and the abdomen on a slender stalk — **hymenopteran** *adj* — **hy·me·nop·ter·ous** \-rəs\ *adj*

hymn \'him\ *n* **1** : a song of praise especially to God **2** : a religious song

hym·nal \'him-nəl\ *n* : a book of hymns

hymn·book \'him-ˌbùk\ *n* : HYMNAL

hyp- — see HYPO-

hyper- *prefix* **1** : above : beyond : SUPER- **2 a** : excessively ⟨*hyper*sensitive⟩ **b** : excessive **3** : being or existing in a space of more than three dimensions ⟨*hyper*space⟩ **4** : connecting things (as in a network) that are not close in a sequence ⟨*hyper*text⟩ [derived from Greek *hyper* "over"]

hy·per·acid·i·ty \ˌhī-pə-rə-'sid-ət-ē\ *n* : the condition of containing more than the normal amount of acid — **hy·per·ac·id** \ˌhī-pə-'ras-əd\ *adj*

hy·per·ac·tive \ˌhī-pər-'ak-tiv\ *adj* : very active especially to an abnormal amount — **hy·per·ac·tiv·i·ty** \-ak-'tiv-ət-ē\ *n*

hy·per·bo·le \hī-'pər-bə-(ˌ)lē\ *n* : extravagant exaggeration used to emphasize a point ⟨"mile-high ice cream cones" is an example of *hyperbole*⟩ — **hy·per·bol·ic** \ˌhī-pər-'bäl-ik\ *adj*

hy·per·cor·rec·tion \ˌhī-pər-kə-'rek-shən\ *n* : a mistaken word or form (as *badly* used for *bad* in "my eyes have gone badly") used especially to avoid what one believes to be a grammatical error but is not — **hy·per·cor·rect** \-'rekt\ *adj* — **hy·per·cor·rect·ly** \-'rek-(t)lē\ *adv* — **hy·per·cor·rect·ness** \-'rek-nəs, -'rekt-\ *n*

hy·per·crit·i·cal \ˌhī-pər-'krit-i-kəl\ *adj* : too critical — **hy·per·crit·i·cal·ly** \-k(ə-)lē\ *adv*

hy·per·in·fla·tion \-in-'flā-shən\ *n* : inflation that increases very quickly over a short period of time

hy·per·link \'hī-pər-ˌliŋk\ *n* : a computerized connector that allows one to move quickly from one place in a document to another place in the same or a different document usually with a single mouse click

hy·per·sen·si·tive \ˌhī-pər-'sen(t)-sət-iv, -'sen(t)-stiv\ *adj* : very sensitive especially to an abnormal degree — **hy·per·sen·si·tive·ness** *n*

hy·per·sen·si·tiv·i·ty \ˌhī-pər-ˌsen(t)-sə-'tiv-ət-ē\ *n* : the state of being hypersensitive; *esp* : an abnormal bodily condition in which certain substances (as pollen or food) cause an extreme reaction (as sneezing, hives, or asthma)

hy·per·space \'hī-pər-ˌspās\ *n* **1** : space of more than three dimensions **2** : a fictional space held to support extraordinary events (as travel faster than the speed of light)

hy·per·ten·sion \'hī-pər-ˌten-chən\ *n* : HIGH BLOOD PRESSURE

hy·per·ten·sive \ˌhī-pər-'ten(t)-siv\ *adj* : having or marked by high blood pressure

hy·per·text \'hī-pər-ˌtekst\ *n* : a database method in which information related to that shown on a display screen can be accessed quickly from the display (as by a mouse click)

hypertext markup language *n* : HTML

hypertext transfer protocol *n* : a method for controlling the exchange of computer data especially on the World Wide Web

hy·per·thy·roid·ism \ˌhī-pər-'thī-ˌróid-ˌiz-əm, -rəd-\ *n* : abnormally high activity of the thyroid gland; *also* : the resulting abnormal state of health — **hy·per·thy·roid** \-ˌróid\ *adj*

hy·per·ven·ti·la·tion \ˌhī-pər-ˌvent-ᵊl-'ā-shən\ *n* : breathing that is very fast and deep and leads to abnormal loss of carbon dioxide from the blood — **hy·per·ven·ti·late** \-'vent-ᵊl-ˌāt\ *vb*

hy·pha \'hī-fə\ *n, pl* **hy·phae** \-(ˌ)fē\ : one of the threads that make up the mycelium of a fungus — **hy·phal** \-fəl\ *adj*

¹hy·phen \'hī-fən\ *n* : a punctuation mark - used to divide or to compound words or word elements

²hyphen *vb* : HYPHENATE

hy·phen·ate \'hī-fə-ˌnāt\ *vb* **-at·ed; -at·ing** : to connect or divide with a hyphen

hyp·no·sis \hip-'nō-səs\ *n, pl* **-no·ses** \-'nō-ˌsēz\ : a trancelike state resembling sleep that is caused in a person by another whose suggestions are readily accepted and acted upon by the person in this state [scientific Latin *hypnosis* "hypnosis," derived from Greek *hypnos* "sleep," from *Hypnos* "the Greek god of sleep"]

\ə\ abut	\aù\ out	\i\ tip	\ò\ saw	\ù\ foot
\ər\ further	\ch\ chin	\ī\ life	\ói\ coin	\y\ yet
\a\ mat	\e\ pet	\j\ job	\th\ thin	\yü\ few
\ā\ take	\ē\ easy	\ŋ\ sing	\th\ this	\yù\ cure
\ä\ cot, cart	\g\ go	\ō\ bone	\ü\ food	\zh\ vision

¹hyp·not·ic \hip-'nät-ik\ *adj* **1** : tending to cause sleep **2** : of or relating to hypnosis or hypnotism — **hyp·not·i·cal·ly** \-i-k(ə-)lē\ *adv*

²hypnotic *n* : an agent (as a drug) that causes or tends to cause sleep

hyp·no·tism \'hip-nə-ˌtiz-əm\ *n* **1** : the study of or act of causing hypnosis **2** : HYPNOSIS

hyp·no·tist \'hip-nə-təst\ *n* : a person who practices hypnotism

hyp·no·tize \'hip-nə-ˌtīz\ *vb* **-tized; -tiz·ing** **1** : to cause hypnosis in **2** : to deaden judgment or resistance by or as if by hypnotic suggestion — **hyp·no·tiz·able** \-ˌtī-zə-bəl\ *adj*

¹hy·po \'hī-ˌpō\ *n* : SODIUM THIOSULFATE; *also* : a solution of sodium thiosulfate

²hypo *n, pl* **hypos** : a hypodermic syringe or injection

hypo- *or* **hyp-** *prefix* **1** : under : beneath : down ⟨*hypo*dermic⟩ **2** : less than normal or normally ⟨*hypo*tension⟩ [derived from Greek *hypo* "under"]

hy·po·chon·dria \ˌhī-pə-'kän-drē-ə\ *n* : an abnormal concern about one's health especially when accompanied by a false belief that one has a physical disease or ailment

hy·po·chon·dri·ac \ˌhī-pə-'kän-drē-ˌak\ *n* : a person who has hypochondria

hy·po·cot·yl \'hī-pə-ˌkät-ᵊl\ *n* : the part of the axis of a plant embryo or seedling below the cotyledons

hy·poc·ri·sy \hip-'äk-rə-sē\ *n, pl* **-sies** : behavior that does not agree with what one claims to believe or feel ⟨the *hypocrisy* of people who say one thing and do another⟩

hyp·o·crite \'hip-ə-ˌkrit\ *n* **1** : a person who pretends to have virtues or qualities that he or she does not have **2** : a person whose actions contradict their stated beliefs or feelings — **hyp·o·crit·i·cal** \ˌhip-ə-'krit-i-kəl\ *adj* — **hyp·o·crit·i·cal·ly** \-i-k(ə-)lē\ *adv*

¹hy·po·der·mic \ˌhī-pə-'dər-mik\ *adj* : of, relating to, or injected into the parts beneath the skin — **hy·po·der·mi·cal·ly** \-mi-k(ə-)lē\ *adv*

²hypodermic *n* **1** : HYPODERMIC INJECTION **2** : HYPODERMIC SYRINGE

hypodermic injection *n* : an injection made into the tissues beneath the skin

hypodermic needle *n* **1** : ¹NEEDLE 1c **2** : a hypodermic syringe complete with needle

hypodermic syringe *n* : a small syringe used with a hollow needle for injection of material into or beneath the skin

hy·po·gly·ce·mia \ˌhī-pō-glī-'sē-mē-ə\ *n* : abnormal decrease of sugar in the blood — **hy·po·gly·ce·mic** \-mik\ *adj or n*

hy·poph·y·sis \hī-'päf-ə-səs\ *n, pl* **-y·ses** \-ə-ˌsēz\ : PITUITARY GLAND

hy·po·ten·sion \'hī-pō-ˌten-chən\ *n* : LOW BLOOD PRESSURE

hy·pot·e·nuse \hī-'pät-ᵊn-ˌ(y)üs, -ˌ(y)üz\ *n* **1** : the side opposite the right angle of a right triangle **2** : the length of a hypotenuse

hy·po·thal·a·mus \ˌhī-pō-'thal-ə-məs\ *n* : a part of the brain that lies beneath the thalamus, produces hormones which pass to the front part of the pituitary gland, and is important in regulating the activities of the autonomic nervous system

hy·po·ther·mia \ˌhī-pō-'thər-mē-ə\ *n* : reduction of the body temperature to an abnormally low level

hy·poth·e·sis \hī-'päth-ə-səs\ *n, pl* **-e·ses** \-ə-ˌsēz\ : something not proved but assumed to be true for purposes of argument or further study or investigation

hy·poth·e·size \hī-'päth-ə-ˌsīz\ *vb* **-sized; -siz·ing** **1** : to make a hypothesis **2** : to adopt as a hypothesis

hy·po·thet·i·cal \ˌhī-pə-'thet-i-kəl\ *adj* **1** : involving a hypothesis or the making of assumptions : ASSUMED **2** : imagined for purposes of example ⟨a *hypothetical* case⟩ — **hy·po·thet·i·cal·ly** \-i-k(ə-)lē\ *adv*

hy·po·thy·roid·ism \ˌhī-pō-'thī-ˌroid-ˌiz-əm\ *n* : too little activity of the thyroid gland; *also* : the abnormal bodily condition that results from this — **hy·po·thy·roid** \-ˌroid\ *adj*

hy·rax \'hī-ˌraks\ *n, pl* **hy·rax·es** \-ˌrak-səz\ *also* **hy·ra·ces** \-rə-ˌsēz\ : any of several small mammals of Africa and the Middle East that have a thickset body with short ears, legs, and tail and feet with soft pads and broad nails

hys·te·ria \his-'ter-ē-ə, -'tir-\ *n* **1** : a nervous disorder marked by excitability of the emotions **2** : unmanageable fear or outburst of emotion — **hys·ter·i·cal** \-'ter-i-kəl\ *adj* — **hys·ter·i·cal·ly** \-i-k(ə-)lē\ *adv*

hys·ter·ics \his-'ter-iks\ *n sing or pl* : a fit of uncontrollable laughter or crying

AC hypotenuse

I

i \'ī\ *n, often cap* **1** : the ninth letter of the English alphabet **2** : one in Roman numerals **3** : a grade rating a student's work as incomplete

I \(')ī, ə\ *pron* : the person speaking or writing ⟨*I* feel fine⟩

-ial *adj suffix* : ¹-AL ⟨financ*ial*⟩

iamb \'ī-ˌam(b)\ *n* : a metrical foot consisting of one unaccented syllable followed by one accented syllable (as in *away*) — **iam·bic** \ī-'am-bik\ *adj or n*

-ian — see -AN

-i·a·sis \'ī-ə-səs\ *n suffix, pl* **-i·a·ses** \-ˌsēz\ : disease produced by (something specified) ⟨ameb*iasis*⟩ [derived from Greek *-iasis* (noun suffix)]

ibex \'ī-ˌbeks\ *n, pl* **ibex** *or* **ibex·es** : any of several wild goats living chiefly in high mountain areas of the Old World and having large horns that curve backward

-ibility — see -ABILITY

ibis \'ī-bəs\ *n, pl* **ibis** *or* **ibis·es** : any of several wading birds that differ from the related herons in having a long slender bill that curves downward

-ible — see -ABLE

IC \(')ī-'sē\ *n* : INTEGRATED CIRCUIT

-ic \ik\ *adj suffix* **1 a** : resembling in form or manner ⟨cherub*ic*⟩ **b** : made up of ⟨run*ic*⟩ **2 a** : of or relating to ⟨chivalr*ic*⟩ **b** : derived from or containing ⟨alcohol*ic*⟩ **3** : in the manner of ⟨autocrat*ic*⟩ **4**

ibis

: making use of ⟨electron*ic*⟩ **5 a** : marked by ⟨nostalg*ic*⟩ **b** : affected with ⟨allerg*ic*⟩ **6** : caused by ⟨amoeb*ic*⟩ [derived from Latin *-icus* (adjective suffix)]

-i·cal \i-kəl\ *adj suffix* : -IC ⟨symmetr*ical*⟩ ⟨geolog*ical*⟩

ICBM \ˌī-ˌsē-(ˌ)bē-'em\ *n* : an intercontinental ballistic missile

¹ice \'īs\ *n* **1 a** : frozen water **b** : a sheet of frozen water ⟨skating on the *ice*⟩ **2** : a state of coldness (as in personal behavior) **3** : a substance resembling ice **4** : a frozen dessert usually made with sweetened fruit juice — **on ice** : set aside for use when needed : in reserve

²ice *vb* **iced; ic·ing 1 a** : to coat or become coated with ice **b** : to chill with ice **2** : to cover with icing

ice age *n* **1** : a time of widespread glaciation **2** *cap I&A* : the most recent such period in the earth's past

ice·berg \'īs-ˌbərg\ *n* : a large floating mass of ice detached from a glacier

iceberg lettuce *n* : a lettuce with a tight round head of light green crisp leaves

ice·boat \-ˌbōt\ *n* : a frame resembling a boat that is driven by sails and glides over the ice on runners

ice·bound \-ˌbaund\ *adj* : surrounded or blocked by ice

ice·box \-ˌbäks\ *n* : REFRIGERATOR

ice·break·er \-ˌbrā-kər\ *n* **1** : a ship equipped to make and keep open a channel through ice **2** : something (as a joke or game) that makes one feel more at ease and less reserved (as at a party or meeting)

iceboat

ice cap *n* : a large glacier forming on level land and flowing outward from its center

ice–cold \'ī-'skōld\ *adj* : very cold

ice cream \(')ī-'skrēm, 'ī-ˌskrēm\ *n* : a frozen food containing sweetened and flavored cream or butterfat

ice–cream cone *n* : a crisp cone-shaped wafer for holding ice cream; *also* : one filled with ice cream

ice field *n* : ICE CAP

ice floe *n* : a flat free mass of floating sea ice

ice hockey *n* : a game played on an ice rink in which two teams of skating players use curved sticks to try to shoot a puck into the opponent's goal

ice·house \'īs-ˌhaus\ *n* : a building in which ice is made or stored

Ice·land·er \'ī-ˌslan-dər, 'ī-slən-\ *n* : a person born or living in Iceland

¹Ice·lan·dic \ī-'slan-dik\ *adj* : of, relating to, or characteristic of Iceland, the Icelanders, or Icelandic

²Icelandic *n* : the Germanic language of the Icelandic people

ice·man \'ī-ˌsman\ *n* : one who sells or delivers ice

ice milk *n* : a sweetened frozen food made of skim milk

ice pack *n* **1** : a large area of pack ice **2** : ice placed in a container or folded in a towel and applied to the body

ice pick *n* : a hand tool ending in a spike for chipping ice

ice sheet *n* : ICE CAP

ice show *n* : a show consisting of exhibitions by ice skaters usually with music

ice–skate \'ī(s)-ˌskāt\ *vb* : to skate on ice — **ice–skater** *n*

ice skate *n* : a shoe with a usually metal blade attached to the sole for ice-skating

ice storm *n* : a storm in which falling rain freezes as it lands

ice water *n* : chilled or iced water especially for drinking

ich·neu·mon wasp \ik-'n(y)ü-mən-\ *n* : any of a large group of insects that are related to wasps and whose larvae are usually parasites inside the bodies of other insect larvae — called also *ichneumon fly*

ichor \'ī-ˌkò(ə)r, -kər\ *n* : a fluid taking the place of blood in the veins of the gods and goddesses of Greek mythology

ich·thy·ol·o·gist \ˌik-thē-'äl-ə-jəst\ *n* : a person who specializes in ichthyology

ich·thy·ol·o·gy \ˌik-thē-'äl-ə-jē\ *n* : a branch of zoology that deals with fishes

ich·thy·o·saur \'ik-thē-ə-ˌsò(ə)r\ *n* : any of an order of extinct marine reptiles with a fish-shaped body and a long snout

-i·cian \'ish-ən\ *n suffix* : one who practices or specializes in a particular field ⟨beaut*ician*⟩ ⟨techn*ician*⟩ [derived from Latin *-ica* (noun suffix) and early French *-ien* (noun suffix)]

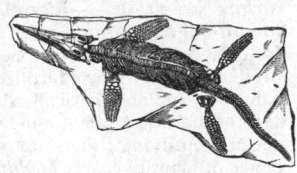

ichthyosaur (fossil)

ici·cle \'ī-ˌsik-əl\ *n* : a hanging mass of ice formed by the freezing of dripping water

¹ic·ing \'ī-siŋ\ *n* **1** : a sweet coating for baked goods (as cakes) — called also *frosting* **2** : something that adds to the interest, value, or appeal of an item or event — often used in the phrase *icing on the cake*

²icing *n* : the shooting of a hockey puck the length of the rink and beyond the opponent's goal line

icon *also* **ikon** \'ī-ˌkän\ *n* **1** : a religious image usually painted on a small wooden panel **2** : EMBLEM 1, SYMBOL **3** : a pictorial symbol on a computer screen

-ics \(ˌ)iks\ *n sing or pl suffix* **1** : study : knowledge : skill : practice ⟨electron*ics*⟩ **2** : characteristic actions or activities ⟨acrobat*ics*⟩ **3** : characteristic qualities or operations ⟨mechan*ics*⟩ [derived from Greek *-ika* "study, skill"]

icy \'ī-sē\ *adj* **ic·i·er; -est 1 a** : covered with, full of, or consisting of ice **b** : very cold ⟨*icy* weather⟩ **2** : UNFRIENDLY 1 — **ic·i·ly** \-sə-lē\ *adv* — **ic·i·ness** \-sē-nəs\ *n*

I'd \(ˌ)īd\ : I had : I should : I would

-ide \ˌīd\ *also* **-id** \əd, (ˌ)id\ *n suffix* : negatively charged atom or chemical group that is usually part of a compound ⟨hydrogen sulf*ide*⟩ [derived from French *-ide* (as in ox*ide*)]

idea \ī-'dē-ə, 'īd-(ˌ)ē-ə\ *n* **1** : a plan of action : INTENTION ⟨my *idea* is to study law⟩ **2** : something imagined or pictured in the mind : NOTION ⟨form an *idea* of a place from reading⟩ **3** : a central meaning or purpose ⟨the *idea* of the game is to score goals⟩ **4** : COMPREHENSION 2 ⟨had no *idea* what he meant⟩ **5** : an opinion or belief ⟨has some strange *ideas*⟩ — **idea·less** \ī-'dē-ə-ləs\ *adj*

¹ide·al \ī-'dē-(ə)l, 'ī-ˌdē(ə)l\ *adj* **1** : existing only in the mind : not real ⟨an *ideal* conception of society⟩ **2** : having no flaw : PERFECT ⟨*ideal* weather⟩

²ideal *n* **1** : a standard of perfection, beauty, or excellence **2** : a perfect type : a model for imitation **synonyms** see PATTERN

ide·al·ism \ī-'dē-(ə-)ˌliz-əm, 'ī-(ˌ)dē-\ *n* : the practice of forming ideals or living under their influence — **ide·al·ist** \-(ə-)ləst\ *n* — **ide·al·is·tic** \(ˌ)ī-ˌdē-(ə-)'lis-tik, ˌī-dē-\ *adj* — **ide·al·is·ti·cal·ly** \-ti-k(ə-)lē\ *adv*

ide·al·ize \ī-'dē-(ə-)ˌlīz\ *vb* **-ized; -iz·ing** : to think of or represent persons or things as one believes they should be

\ə\ **abut**	\au̇\ **out**	\i\ **tip**	\ȯ\ **saw**	\u̇\ **foot**
\ər\ **further**	\ch\ **chin**	\ī\ **life**	\ȯi\ **coin**	\y\ **yet**
\a\ **mat**	\e\ **pet**	\j\ **job**	\th\ **thin**	\yü\ **few**
\ā\ **take**	\ē\ **easy**	\ŋ\ **sing**	\th\ **this**	\yu̇\ **cure**
\ä\ **cot, cart**	\g\ **go**	\ō\ **bone**	\ü\ **food**	\zh\ **vision**

rather than as they are — **ide·al·iza·tion** \-ˌdē-(ə)-lə-ˈzā-shən\ *n* — **ide·al·iz·er** \-ˈdē-(ə-)ˌlī-zər\ *n*

ide·al·ly \ī-ˈdē-ə-lē, -ˈdē(-ə)l-lē\ *adv* **1** : in agreement with an ideal : PERFECTLY ⟨*ideally* suited to the job⟩ **2** : for best results ⟨*ideally*, each student should arrive early⟩

idée fixe \(ˌ)ē-ˌdā-ˈfēks\ *n, pl* **idées fixes** \-ˈfēks(-əz)\ : an idea that takes over a person's mind [French, literally "fixed idea"]

iden·ti·cal \ī-ˈdent-i-kəl, ə-ˈdent-\ *adj* **1** : being one and the same ⟨the *identical* place we stopped at last year⟩ **2** : exactly alike or equal ⟨wearing *identical* coats⟩ **synonyms** see SAME — **iden·ti·cal·ly** \-i-k(ə-)lē\ *adv* — **iden·ti·cal·ness** \-kəl-nəs\ *n*

identical twin *n* : either member of a pair of twins that are produced from a single fertilized egg, usually have identical genes, and are physically similar

iden·ti·fi·ca·tion \ī-ˌdent-ə-fə-ˈkā-shən, ə-ˌdent-\ *n* **1** : an act of identifying : the state of being identified **2** : evidence of identity ⟨carry *identification* at all times⟩

iden·ti·fy \ī-ˈdent-ə-ˌfī, ə-ˈdent-\ *vb* **-fied; -fy·ing** **1** : to think of as united (as in spirit or principle) ⟨groups *identified* with conservation⟩ **2** : to find out or show the identity of ⟨*identified* the dog as her lost pet⟩ **3** : to think of oneself as having the same problems and feelings as someone else ⟨*identify* with a character in a story⟩ — **iden·ti·fi·able** \-ˌfī-ə-bəl\ *adj* — **iden·ti·fi·ably** \-blē\ *adv* — **iden·ti·fi·er** \-ˌfī-(ə)r\ *n*

iden·ti·ty \ī-ˈden(t)-ət-ē, ə-ˈden(t)-\ *n, pl* **-ties** **1** : the condition of being exactly alike : SAMENESS **2** : INDIVIDUALITY 1 **3** : the fact of being the same person or thing as claimed ⟨prove one's *identity*⟩ **4** : IDENTITY ELEMENT

identity element *n* : an element of a set that leaves any other element of the set unchanged when combined with it using a given mathematical operation ⟨0 is the *identity element* of the set of whole numbers under addition⟩

ideo·gram \ˈīd-ē-ə-ˌgram, ˈid-\ *n* **1** : a picture or symbol used in a system of writing to represent a thing or an idea but not a particular word or phrase **2** : a character or symbol (as 3) used in a system of writing to represent an entire word but not its individual sounds

ideo·graph \ˈīd-ē-ə-ˌgraf, ˈid-\ *n* : IDEOGRAM — **ideo·graph·ic** \ˌīd-ē-ə-ˈgraf-ik, ˌid-\ *adj* — **ideo·graph·i·cal·ly** \-ˈgraf-i-k(ə-)lē\ *adv*

ide·ol·o·gy \ˌīd-ē-ˈäl-ə-jē, ˌid-\ *n, pl* **-gies** : ideas characteristic of a person, group, or political party — **ideo·log·i·cal** \-ē-ə-ˈläj-i-kəl\ *adj* — **ideo·log·i·cal·ly** \-i-k(ə-)lē\ *adv* — **ide·ol·o·gist** \-ē-ˈäl-ə-jəst\ *n*

ides \ˈīdz\ *n pl* : the 15th day of March, May, July, or October or the 13th day of any other month in the ancient Roman calendar

id·i·o·cy \ˈid-ē-ə-sē\ *n, pl* **-cies** : something stupid or foolish

id·i·om \ˈid-ē-əm\ *n* **1** : the choice of words and the way they are combined that is characteristic of a language **2** : an expression that cannot be understood from the meanings of its separate words but must be learned as a whole ⟨the expression "give way," meaning "retreat," is an *idiom*⟩ — **id·i·om·at·ic** \ˌid-ē-ə-ˈmat-ik\ *adj* — **id·i·om·at·i·cal·ly** \-i-k(ə-)lē\ *adv*

id·io·syn·cra·sy \ˌid-ē-ə-ˈsiŋ-krə-sē\ *n, pl* **-sies** : a way of behaving or thinking that is characteristic of a person — **id·io·syn·crat·ic** \ˌid-ē-ō-(ˌ)sin-ˈkrat-ik\ *adj* — **id·io·syn·crat·i·cal·ly** \-ˈkrat-i-k(ə-)lē\ *adv*

id·i·ot \ˈid-ē-ət\ *n* : a silly or foolish person — **idiot** *adj*

id·i·ot·ic \ˌid-ē-ˈät-ik\ *adj* : showing complete lack of thought or common sense : FOOLISH — **id·i·ot·i·cal·ly** \-ˈät-i-k(ə-)lē\ *adv*

¹idle \ˈīd-ᵊl\ *adj* **idler** \ˈīd-lər, -ᵊl-ər\; **idlest** \ˈīd-ləst, -ᵊl-əst\ **1** : having no worth or basis ⟨*idle* rumors⟩ ⟨*idle* chatter⟩ **2** : not being used or employed ⟨*idle* workers⟩ ⟨*idle* fac-

tories⟩ ⟨*idle* hours⟩ **3** : LAZY 1 — **idle·ness** \ˈīd-ᵊl-nəs\ *n* — **idly** \ˈīd-lē, -ᵊl-ē\ *adv*

²idle *vb* **idled; idling** \ˈīd-liŋ, -ᵊl-iŋ\ **1** : to spend time doing nothing **2** : to run without being connected for doing useful work ⟨left the engine *idling*⟩ — **idler** \ˈīd-lər, -ᵊl-ər\ *n*

idol \ˈīd-ᵊl\ *n* **1** : an image worshipped as a god **2** : a greatly loved and admired person or thing

idol·a·ter *or* **idol·a·tor** \ī-ˈdäl-ət-ər\ *n* **1** : a worshipper of idols **2** : a person who admires or loves greatly

idol·a·trous \ī-ˈdäl-ə-trəs\ *adj* **1** : of or relating to idolatry **2** : given to idolatry — **idol·a·trous·ly** *adv*

idol·a·try \ī-ˈdäl-ə-trē\ *n, pl* **-tries** **1** : the worship of an idol as a god **2** : very great attachment or devotion to something

idol·ize \ˈīd-ᵊl-ˌīz\ *vb* **-ized; -iz·ing** : to worship as an idol : love or admire too much — **idol·iza·tion** \ˌīd-ᵊl-ə-ˈzā-shən\ *n* — **idol·iz·er** \ˈīd-ᵊl-ˌī-zər\ *n*

idyll *also* **idyl** \ˈīd-ᵊl\ *n* **1** : a simple poetic or prose work that describes peaceful country life **2** : a scene or event one might write an idyll about

idyl·lic \ī-ˈdil-ik\ *adj* : simple and charming ⟨an *idyllic* little town⟩

-ie *also* **-y** \ē\ *n suffix, pl* **-ies** **1** : little one ⟨sonn*y*⟩ ⟨boot*ie*⟩ **2** : one belonging to : one having to do with ⟨cabb*ie*⟩ **3** : one having such a quality ⟨smart*y*⟩ ⟨tough*ie*⟩ [Middle English *-ie* "little one"]

-ier — see ²-ER

¹if \(ˌ)if, əf\ *conj* **1** : in the event that ⟨come *if* you can⟩ **2** : whether it is or was true that ⟨asked *if* the mail had come⟩ **3** — used to introduce a wish ⟨*if* it would only rain⟩ **4** : even though : BUT ⟨an interesting *if* unbelievable excuse⟩

²if \ˈif\ *n* **1** : ¹CONDITION 3, STIPULATION ⟨too many *ifs* make the contract confusing⟩ **2** : SUPPOSITION 1 ⟨a theory full of *ifs*⟩

if·fy \ˈif-ē\ *adj* **1** : having many uncertain or unknown qualities or conditions ⟨an *iffy* situation⟩ **2** : of inconsistent or unreliable quality — **if·fi·ness** *n*

-i·fy \ə-ˌfī\ *vb suffix* **-i·fied; -i·fy·ing** : -FY

ig·loo \ˈig-lü\ *n, pl* **ig·loos** : an Eskimo house usually made of wood, sod, or stone when permanent or of blocks of snow or ice in the form of a dome when built for temporary use

igloo

ig·ne·ous \ˈig-nē-əs\ *adj* : formed by hardening of melted earth ⟨*igneous* rock⟩ — compare METAMORPHIC, SEDIMENTARY 2

ig·nite \ig-ˈnīt\ *vb* **ig·nit·ed; ig·nit·ing** **1 a** : to set on fire : LIGHT **b** : to cause (a fuel mixture) to burn **2** : to catch fire **3** : to set in motion : SPARK ⟨*ignite* a debate⟩ — **ig·nit·able** \-ˈnīt-ə-bəl\ *adj* — **ig·nit·er** *also* **ig·ni·tor** \-ˈnīt-ər\ *n*

ig·ni·tion \ig-ˈnish-ən\ *n* **1** : the act of igniting **2** : the process or means (as an electric spark) of igniting a fuel mixture; *also* : an electrical device for operating an ignition system (as in an automobile) ⟨put the key in the *ignition*⟩

ig·no·ble \ig-ˈnō-bəl\ *adj* **1** : not of noble birth **2** : not noble or honorable ⟨*ignoble* thoughts⟩ ⟨*ignoble* conduct⟩ — **ig·no·bly** \-blē\ *adv*

ig·no·min·i·ous \ˌig-nə-ˈmin-ē-əs\ *adj* : causing disgrace or shame ⟨an *ignominious* defeat⟩ — **ig·no·min·i·ous·ly** *adv*

ig·no·mi·ny \ˈig-nə-ˌmin-ē, ig-ˈnäm-ə-nē\ *n, pl* **-nies** : deep humiliation and disgrace

ig·no·ra·mus \ˌig-nə-ˈrā-məs\ *n, pl* **-mus·es** *also* **-mi** \-mē\ : an ignorant person [from *Ignoramus*, name of a character in a play]

ig·no·rance \'ig-nə-rən(t)s\ *n* : the state or fact of being ignorant : lack of knowledge, education, or awareness

ig·no·rant \'ig-nə-rənt\ *adj* **1 a** : having no knowledge or education **b** : having no knowledge or understanding of a certain thing ⟨*ignorant* of mathematics⟩ **2** : not informed : UNAWARE ⟨*ignorant* of the facts⟩ **3** : resulting from or showing lack of knowledge ⟨an *ignorant* mistake⟩ — **ig·no·rant·ly** *adv*

synonyms IGNORANT, UNEDUCATED, UNLETTERED, ILLITERATE mean not having the kind of knowledge gained from education. IGNORANT suggests a lack of knowledge either in general or in some particular field ⟨*ignorant* about physics⟩. UNEDUCATED suggests a general lack of formal education ⟨there are few jobs for *uneducated* people⟩. UNLETTERED suggests a lack of the kind of knowledge gained from reading ⟨*unlettered* people would not appreciate the play⟩. ILLITERATE suggests either a total or major inability to read and write ⟨countries having large numbers of *illiterate* people⟩.

ig·nore \ig-'nō(ə)r, -'nȯ(ə)r\ *vb* **ig·nored; ig·nor·ing** : to refuse to notice : pay no attention to ⟨*ignored* his advice⟩ **synonyms** see NEGLECT — **ig·nor·able** \-'nō(ə)r-ə-bəl, -'nȯ(ə)r-\ *adj* — **ig·nor·er** *n*

igua·na \i-'gwän-ə\ *n*
: any of various large plant-eating tropical American lizards that have a ridge of tall scales along the middle of the back and loose skin hanging below the neck

iguana

iguan·odon \i-'gwän-ə-ˌdän\ *n* : a large plant-eating dinosaur of the Cretaceous period that usually walked on all four legs [from Spanish *iguana* "iguana" and Greek *odōn* "tooth"]

ike·ba·na \ˌik-ā-'bän-ə, ˌik-i-, ˌēk-\ *n* : the Japanese art of flower arranging [Japanese, from *ikeru* "to keep alive, arrange" and *hana* "flower"]

ikon *variant of* ICON

il- — see IN-

il·e·um \'il-ē-əm\ *n, pl* **il·ea** \-ē-ə\ : the last part of the small intestine between the jejunum and the large intestine — **il·e·al** \-ē-əl\ *adj*

il·i·ac \'il-ē-ˌak\ *adj* : of, relating to, or located on or near the ilium ⟨an *iliac* spine⟩

Il·i·ad \'il-ē-əd, -ē-ˌad\ *n* : an ancient Greek epic poem about the Trojan War that is believed to have been composed by Homer

il·i·um \'il-ē-əm\ *n, pl* **il·ia** \-ē-ə\ : the broad, upper, and largest of the three bones composing either side of the pelvis

ilk \'ilk\ *n* : ¹SORT 1a, KIND ⟨gamers and their *ilk*⟩

¹ill \'il\ *adj* **worse** \'wərs\; **worst** \'wərst\ **1** : meant to do harm or evil ⟨*ill* deeds⟩ **2 a** : causing suffering or distress ⟨*ill* weather⟩ **b** : not normal or sound ⟨*ill* health⟩ **c** : not being in good health ⟨had been *ill* for some years⟩ **d** : affected by nausea **3** : not helpful to one : UNLUCKY ⟨an *ill* omen⟩ **4** : not right or proper ⟨*ill* manners⟩ **5** : not kind or friendly ⟨*ill* feeling⟩ ⟨never said an *ill* word⟩

²ill *adv* **worse; worst 1 a** : with displeasure or anger ⟨the remark was *ill* received⟩ **b** : in a harsh manner ⟨treated me *ill*⟩ **2** : in a way that deserves blame ⟨an *ill*-spent youth⟩ ⟨*ill*-gotten gains⟩ **3** : HARDLY 3, SCARCELY ⟨can *ill* afford it⟩ **4** : in a faulty way : BADLY, POORLY ⟨*ill*-prepared to face the winter⟩

³ill *n* **1** : the opposite of good : EVIL **2 a** : SICKNESS 2 ⟨childhood *ills*⟩ **b** : ²TROUBLE 1a ⟨the *ills* of society⟩

I'll \(ˌ)ī(ə)l\ : I shall : I will

ill–ad·vised \ˌil-əd-'vīzd\ *adj* : showing bad advice or too little thinking ahead ⟨an *ill-advised* decision⟩ — **ill–ad·vis·ed·ly** \-'vī-zəd-lē\ *adv*

ill at ease *adj* : feeling uncomfortable

ill–bred \'il-'bred\ *adj* : badly brought up : IMPOLITE

il·le·gal \(')il-'(l)ē-gəl\ *adj* : contrary to the laws or rules : UNLAWFUL — **il·le·gal·i·ty** \ˌil-i-'gal-ət-ē\ *n* — **il·le·gal·ly** \(')il-'(l)ē-gə-lē\ *adv*

il·leg·i·ble \(')il-'(l)ej-ə-bəl\ *adj* : impossible or very hard to read ⟨*illegible* handwriting⟩ — **il·leg·i·bly** \(')il-'(l)ej-ə-blē\ *adv*

il·le·git·i·ma·cy \ˌil-i-'jit-ə-mə-sē\ *n* : the quality or state of being illegitimate

il·le·git·i·mate \ˌil-i-'jit-ə-mət\ *adj* **1** : born of a father and mother who are not married **2** : ILLEGAL — **il·le·git·i·mate·ly** *adv*

ill–fat·ed \'il-'fāt-əd\ *adj* : doomed to disaster ⟨an *ill-fated* expedition⟩

ill–fa·vored \'il-'fā-vərd\ *adj* : not pretty or handsome

ill–got·ten \-'gät-ᵊn\ *adj* : to get by unlawful or improper means ⟨*ill-gotten* wealth⟩

ill–hu·mored \'il-'hyü-mərd, 'il-'yü-\ *adj* : being in a bad mood : IRRITABLE, CROSS — **ill–hu·mored·ly** *adv*

il·lic·it \(')il-'(l)is-ət\ *adj* : ILLEGAL ⟨*illicit* drug traffic⟩ — **il·lic·it·ly** *adv*

il·lim·it·able \(')il-'(l)im-ət-ə-bəl\ *adj* : not able to be limited or measured

il·lit·er·a·cy \(')il-'(l)it-ə-rə-sē, -'(l)i-trə-sē\ *n, pl* **-cies 1** : the quality or state of being illiterate; *esp* : inability to read or write **2** : a mistake made by or typical of an illiterate person

il·lit·er·ate \(')il-'(l)it-ə-rət, -'(l)i-trət\ *adj* **1** : having little or no education; *esp* : unable to read or write **2** : showing lack of education **synonyms** see IGNORANT — **illiterate** *n* — **il·lit·er·ate·ly** *adv*

ill–man·nered \'il-'man-ərd\ *adj* : showing bad manners : RUDE

ill–na·tured \'il-'nā-chərd\ *adj* : having a bad disposition : SURLY ⟨is usually *ill-natured* in the morning until after breakfast⟩ — **ill–na·tured·ly** *adv*

ill·ness \'il-nəs\ *n* **1** : an unhealthy condition of body or mind **2** : SICKNESS 2

il·log·i·cal \(')il-'(l)äj-i-kəl\ *adj* : not using or following good reasoning — **il·log·i·cal·ly** \-i-k(ə-)lē\ *adv*

ill–starred \'il-'stärd\ *adj* : ILL-FATED, UNLUCKY ⟨*ill-starred* lovers⟩

ill–tem·pered \'il-'tem-pərd\ *adj* : having or showing a bad temper : ILL-NATURED ⟨an *ill-tempered* neighbor⟩ ⟨wrote an *ill-tempered* reply⟩ — **ill–tem·pered·ly** *adv*

ill–treat \'il-'trēt\ *vb* : to treat in a cruel or improper way : MALTREAT ⟨punished for *ill-treating* the neighbor's cat⟩ — **ill–treat·ment** \-mənt\ *n*

il·lu·mi·nate \il-'ü-mə-ˌnāt\ *vb* **-nat·ed; -nat·ing 1** : to supply with light : light up ⟨*illuminate* a room⟩ ⟨the part of the moon *illuminated* by the sun⟩ **2** : to make clear : EXPLAIN ⟨*illuminated* the point with good examples⟩ **3** : to decorate with designs or pictures in gold or colors ⟨*illuminate* a manuscript⟩ — **il·lu·mi·na·tive** \-ˌnāt-iv\ *adj* — **il·lu·mi·na·tor** \-ˌnāt-ər\ *n*

il·lu·mi·na·tion \il-ˌü-mə-'nā-shən\ *n* **1 a** : the action of illuminating or state of being illuminated **b** : amount of light **2** : gold or colored decoration in a manuscript

il·lu·mine \il-'ü-mən\ *vb* **-mined; -min·ing** : ILLUMINATE 1

ill–use \'il-'yüz\ *vb* : ILL-TREAT, MALTREAT — **ill–us·age** \-'yü-sij, -'yü-zij\ *n*

il·lu·sion \il-ˈü-zhən\ *n*
1 : a misleading image presented to the eye **2** : the state or fact of being led to accept as true something unreal or imagined **3** : a mistaken idea

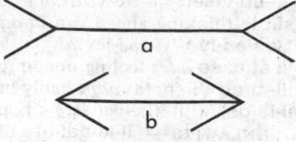
illusion 1: *a* equals *b* in length

il·lu·sion·ist \i-ˈlü-zhə-nist\ *n* : a person who produces illusions; *esp* : a performer of sleight of hand or a magician

il·lu·sive \il-ˈü-siv, -ˈü-ziv\ *adj* : ILLUSORY — **il·lu·sive·ly** *adv*

il·lu·so·ry \il-ˈüs-(ə-)rē, -ˈüz-\ *adj* : based on or producing illusion : DECEPTIVE ⟨an *illusory* hope⟩

il·lus·trate \ˈil-əs-ˌtrāt, il-ˈəs-\ *vb* **-trat·ed; -trat·ing 1** : to make clear by using examples ⟨*illustrated* his point with a personal experience⟩ **2 a** : to provide with pictures or diagrams intended to explain or decorate ⟨*illustrate* a book⟩ **b** : to serve as an illustration — **il·lus·tra·tor** \-ˌtrāt-ər\ *n*

il·lus·tra·tion \ˌil-əs-ˈtrā-shən\ *n* **1** : the action of illustrating : the condition of being illustrated **2** : an example or instance used to make something clear **3** : a picture or diagram that explains or decorates

il·lus·tra·tive \il-ˈəs-strət-iv\ *adj* : serving or meant to illustrate ⟨*illustrative* examples⟩

il·lus·tri·ous \il-ˈəs-trē-əs\ *adj* : very outstanding : EMINENT — **il·lus·tri·ous·ly** *adv*

ill will *n* : unfriendly feeling

il·ly \ˈil-(l)ē\ *adv* : [2]ILL, BADLY

IM \ˈī-ˈem\ *vb* **IM'd; IM'ing 1** : to send an instant message to ⟨*IM'd* my friends⟩ **2** : to communicate by instant message ⟨were *IM'ing* during lunch⟩

im- — see IN-

I'm \(ˌ)īm\ : I am

[1]im·age \ˈim-ij\ *n* **1** : something (as a statue) made to look like a person or thing **2** : a picture of an object formed by a device (as a mirror, lens, or electronic system) **3** : a likeness or picture produced on a photographic material or electronic display screen **4** : a person who looks very much like another **5 a** : a mental picture of something not actually present **b** : a mental picture created by words **c** : a popular idea of what something or someone is that is created especially by advertising and publicity

[2]image *vb* **im·aged; im·ag·ing 1** : to describe in words or pictures **2** : to form an image of **3** : REFLECT 2, MIRROR

im·ag·ery \ˈim-ij-(ə-)rē\ *n, pl* **-er·ies 1** : images that can be seen or that are imagined **2** : language that suggests how someone or something looks, sounds, feels, smells, or tastes

imag·in·able \im-ˈaj-(ə-)nə-bəl\ *adj* : possible to imagine ⟨any *imaginable* place⟩ — **imag·in·ably** \-blē\ *adv*

imag·i·nary \im-ˈaj-ə-ˌner-ē\ *adj* : existing only in imagination : not real ⟨unicorns are *imaginary*⟩

imag·i·na·tion \im-ˌaj-ə-ˈnā-shən\ *n* **1** : the act or power of forming a mental picture of something not present and especially of something one has not known or experienced **2** : creative ability **3** : a creation of the mind

imag·i·na·tive \im-ˈaj-(ə-)nət-iv, -ˈaj-ə-ˌnāt-\ *adj* **1** : of, relating to, or showing imagination **2** : having a lively imagination — **imag·i·na·tive·ly** *adv* — **imag·i·na·tive·ness** *n*

imag·ine \im-ˈaj-ən\ *vb* **imag·ined; imag·in·ing** \-ˈaj-(ə-)niŋ\ **1** : to form a mental picture of : use the imagination **2** : THINK 2, SUPPOSE ⟨I *imagine* it will snow⟩

imag·in·ings \im-ˈaj(ə-)niŋz\ *n pl* : products of the imagination : THOUGHTS, IMAGES

ima·go \im-ˈā-gō, -ˈäg-ō\ *n, pl* **imagoes** *or* **ima·gi·nes** \-ˈā-gə-ˌnēz, -ˈäg-ə-\ : an insect in its final adult, sexually mature, and usually winged state — **ima·gi·nal** \-ˈā-gən-[ə]l, -ˈäg-ən-\ *adj*

im·bal·ance \(ˈ)im-ˈbal-ən(t)s\ *n* : the state of being out of balance or out of proportion

im·be·cile \ˈim-bə-səl, -ˌsil\ *n* : [1]FOOL 1, IDIOT — **imbecile** *or* **im·be·cil·ic** \ˌim-bə-ˈsil-ik\ *adj*

im·be·cil·i·ty \ˌim-bə-ˈsil-ət-ē\ *n, pl* **-ties 1** : complete foolishness **2** : something very foolish

imbed *variant of* EMBED

im·bibe \im-ˈbīb\ *vb* **im·bibed; im·bib·ing 1** : to receive into the mind and retain ⟨*imbibe* knowledge⟩ **2 a** : [1]DRINK 1a **b** : ABSORB 1 — **im·bib·er** *n*

im·bue \im-ˈbyü\ *vb* **im·bued; im·bu·ing 1** : to spread through or influence deeply as if by dyeing ⟨*imbued* with a deep sense of loyalty⟩ **2** : to tinge or dye deeply **3** : ENDOW 2 ⟨the new lighting *imbues* the room with warmth⟩

im·i·ta·ble \ˈim-ət-ə-bəl\ *adj* : able to be imitated or worth imitating

im·i·tate \ˈim-ə-ˌtāt\ *vb* **-tat·ed; -tat·ing 1** : to follow as a pattern, model, or example **2** : to be or appear similar to **3** : to copy exactly — **im·i·ta·tor** \-ˌtāt-ər\ *n*

synonyms IMITATE, APE, MIMIC, MOCK mean to follow the example of another. IMITATE suggests using someone that one admires as a model or pattern ⟨children *imitating* their parents⟩. APE suggests a close and often clumsy imitation of an admired example ⟨she *apes* the behavior of pop stars⟩. MIMIC may suggest imitation of another's personal manner often for humor ⟨the comedian *mimicked* a popular actor⟩. MOCK suggests making fun of someone by imitating that person in his or her presence ⟨*mocked* the dictator's swaggering walk⟩.

[1]im·i·ta·tion \ˌim-ə-ˈtā-shən\ *n* **1** : an act of imitating **2** : something produced as a copy

[2]imitation *adj* : resembling something else especially of better quality ⟨*imitation* pearls⟩ ⟨*imitation* leather⟩

im·i·ta·tive \ˈim-ə-ˌtāt-iv\ *adj* **1** : involving imitation **2** : given to imitating **3** : imitating something better — **im·i·ta·tive·ly** *adv*

im·mac·u·late \im-ˈak-yə-lət\ *adj* **1** : having no stain or blemish : PURE ⟨an *immaculate* record of service⟩ **2** : perfectly clean ⟨*immaculate* linen⟩ — **im·mac·u·late·ly** *adv* — **im·mac·u·late·ness** *n*

Immaculate Conception *n* : December 8 observed as a Roman Catholic festival in honor of the conception of the Virgin Mary as free from original sin

im·ma·te·ri·al \ˌim-ə-ˈtir-ē-əl\ *adj* **1** : not consisting of matter **2** : not important : INSIGNIFICANT

im·ma·ture \ˌim-ə-ˈt(y)ù(ə)r\ *adj* **1** : not mature or fully developed : YOUNG, UNRIPE ⟨an *immature* bird⟩ ⟨*immature* fruit⟩ **2** : showing less than an expected degree of maturity ⟨*immature* behavior⟩ — **im·ma·ture·ly** *adv*

im·ma·tu·ri·ty \ˌim-ə-ˈt(y)ùr-ət-ē\ *n* : the state or quality of being immature

im·mea·sur·able \(ˌ)im-ˈ(m)ezh-(ə-)rə-bəl, -ˈ(m)ezh-ər-bəl, -ˈ(m)āzh-\ *adj* : impossible to measure : VAST, BOUNDLESS — **im·mea·sur·ably** \-blē\ *adv*

im·me·di·a·cy \im-ˈēd-ē-ə-sē\ *n, pl* **-cies 1** : the quality or state of being immediate **2** : something that is of immediate importance ⟨*immediacies* of daily life⟩

im·me·di·ate \im-ˈēd-ē-ət\ *adj* **1** : acting or being without anything else coming between ⟨the *immediate* cause of disease⟩ **2** : being next in line or nearest in relationship ⟨my *immediate* family⟩ **3** : closest in importance ⟨our *immediate* needs⟩ **4** : acting or being without delay ⟨needs *immediate* help⟩ **5** : not far away in time or space

im·me·di·ate·ly \im-ˈēd-ē-ət-lē\ *adv* **1** : with nothing between : DIRECTLY ⟨the person *immediately* to my left⟩ **2** : right away : at once ⟨do it *immediately*⟩

im·me·mo·ri·al \ˌim-ə-ˈmōr-ē-əl, -ˈmòr-\ *adj* : going back beyond the reach of memory or record : very ancient

⟨from time *immemorial*⟩ — **im·me·mo·ri·al·ly** \-ē-ə-lē\ *adv*

im·mense \im-'en(t)s\ *adj* : very great in size or amount; *esp* : not capable of being measured by ordinary means ⟨the *immense* universe⟩ [from early French *immense* "immense, huge," from Latin *immensus* "boundless, too great to be measured," from *im-*, *in-* "not" and *mensus*, past participle of *metiri* "to measure" — related to DI-MENSION, MEASURE] *synonyms* see ENORMOUS — **im·mense·ly** *adv* — **im·mense·ness** *n*

im·men·si·ty \im-'en(t)-sət-ē\ *n, pl* **-ties** **1** : the quality or state of being immense **2** : something immense

im·merse \im-'ərs\ *vb* **im·mersed; im·mers·ing** **1** : to plunge into something (as a fluid) that surrounds or covers **2** : to become completely involved in ⟨*immersed* in a good book⟩ — **im·mer·sion** \-'ər-zhən, -shən\ *n*

im·mers·ible \im-'ər-sə-bəl\ *adj* : able to be completely put under water without damage ⟨an *immersible* electric frying pan⟩

im·mi·grant \'im-i-grənt\ *n* **1** : a person who comes to a country to live there **2** : a plant or animal that becomes established in an area where it did not occur previously — **immigrant** *adj*

im·mi·grate \'im-ə-ˌgrāt\ *vb* **-grat·ed; -grat·ing** : to come into a foreign country to live — **im·mi·gra·tion** \ˌim-ə-'grā-shən\ *n*

im·mi·nence \'im-ə-nən(t)s\ *n* : the quality or state of being imminent

im·mi·nent \'im-ə-nənt\ *adj* : being about to happen ⟨in *imminent* danger⟩ — **im·mi·nent·ly** *adv*

im·mo·bile \(')im-'(m)ō-bəl, -ˌbēl, -ˌbīl\ *adj* : unable to move or be moved — **im·mo·bil·i·ty** \ˌim-(ˌ)ō-'bil-ət-ē\ *n*

im·mo·bi·lize \im-'ō-bə-ˌlīz\ *vb* **-lized; -liz·ing** : to fix in place : make immobile — **im·mo·bi·li·za·tion** \im-ˌō-bə-lə-'zā-shən\ *n* — **im·mo·bi·liz·er** \im-'ō-bə-ˌlī-zər\ *n*

im·mod·er·a·cy \(')im-'(m)äd-(ə-)rə-sē\ *n* : the quality or state of being immoderate

im·mod·er·ate \(')im-'(m)äd-(ə-)rət\ *adj* : going too far or asking too much : EXCESSIVE — **im·mod·er·ate·ly** *adv*

im·mod·est \(')im-'(m)äd-əst\ *adj* : not modest — **im·mod·est·ly** *adv* — **im·mod·es·ty** \-ə-stē\ *n*

im·mo·late \'im-ə-ˌlāt\ *vb* **-lat·ed; -lat·ing** : to kill as a sacrifice — **im·mo·la·tion** \ˌim-ə-'lā-shən\ *n* — **im·mo·la·tor** \'im-ə-ˌlāt-ər\ *n*

im·mor·al \(')im-'(m)ȯr-əl, -'(m)är-\ *adj* : not moral : WICKED, BAD — **im·mor·al·ly** \-ə-lē\ *adv*

im·mo·ral·i·ty \ˌim-(ˌ)ȯ-'ral-ət-ē, ˌim-ə-'ral-\ *n, pl* **-ties** **1** : the quality or state of being immoral **2** : an immoral act or custom

¹**im·mor·tal** \(')im-'ȯrt-ᵊl\ *adj* : living or lasting forever — **im·mor·tal·ly** \-ᵊl-ē\ *adv*

²**immortal** *n* **1** : an immortal being **2** : a person whose fame is lasting ⟨baseball *immortals*⟩

im·mor·tal·i·ty \ˌim-ˌȯr-'tal-ət-ē\ *n* : the quality or state of being immortal: **a** : endless life **b** : lasting fame or glory

im·mor·tal·ize \im-'ȯrt-ᵊl-ˌīz\ *vb* **-ized; -iz·ing** : to make immortal ⟨the battle was *immortalized* in a famous poem⟩ — **im·mor·tal·iza·tion** \-ˌȯrt-ᵊl-ə-'zā-shən\ *n*

im·mov·able \(')im-'(m)ü-və-bəl\ *adj* **1 a** : not able to be moved **b** : not moving : STATIONARY **2** : STEADFAST 1b — **im·mov·abil·i·ty** \(ˌ)im-ˌ(m)ü-və-'bil-ət-ē\ *n* — **im·mov·ably** \(')im-'(m)ü-və-blē\ *adv*

im·mune \im-'yün\ *adj* **1** : ¹EXEMPT ⟨*immune* from punishment⟩ **2 a** : not influenced by something ⟨*immune* to persuasion⟩ **b** : having a high degree of resistance to an illness or disease ⟨*immune* to the chicken pox⟩ **3** : containing or producing antibodies

immune response *n* : a bodily response to a foreign substance, cell, or tissue that involves the formation of antibodies and cells capable of reacting with it and rendering it harmless — called also *immune reaction*

immune system *n* : the bodily system that protects the body from foreign substances, cells, and tissues by producing the immune response and that includes especially the thymus, spleen, lymph nodes, lymphocytes, and antibodies

im·mu·ni·ty \im-'yü-nət-ē\ *n, pl* **-ties** **1** : EXEMPTION 1 **2** : bodily power to resist an infectious disease that usually results from vaccination or inoculation, a previous attack of the disease, or a natural resistance

im·mu·ni·za·tion \ˌim-yə-nə-'zā-shən\ *n* : treatment (as with a vaccine) to produce immunity to a disease

im·mu·nize \'im-yə-ˌnīz\ *vb* **-nized; -niz·ing** : to make immune ⟨have been *immunized* against polio⟩

im·mu·no·de·fi·cien·cy \ˌim-yə-(ˌ)nō-də-'fish-ən-sē, (ˌ)im-'yü-nō-\ *n* : inability to produce the normal number of antibodies or T cells capable of acting in an immune system

im·mu·nol·o·gist \ˌim-yə-'näl-ə-jəst\ *n* : a person who specializes in immunology

im·mu·nol·o·gy \ˌim-yə-'näl-ə-jē\ *n* : a science that deals with immunity to disease — **im·mu·no·log·ic** \-yən-ᵊl-'äj-ik\ *or* **im·mu·no·log·i·cal** \-'äj-i-kəl\ *adj*

im·mure \im-'yu̇(ə)r\ *vb* **im·mured; im·mur·ing** : to enclose within or as if within walls : IMPRISON — **im·mure·ment** \-mənt\ *n*

im·mu·ta·ble \(')im-'(m)yüt-ə-bəl\ *adj* : impossible to change — **im·mu·ta·bil·i·ty** \(ˌ)im-ˌ(m)yüt-ə-'bil-ət-ē\ *n* — **im·mu·ta·bly** \(')im-'(m)yüt-ə-blē\ *adv*

imp \'imp\ *n* **1** : a small demon **2** : a mischievous child

¹**im·pact** \im-'pakt\ *vb* **1** : to have a strong effect on ⟨volcanic ash *impacted* weather conditions worldwide⟩ **2** : to hit or cause to hit with force

²**im·pact** \'im-ˌpakt\ *n* **1** : a striking together of two bodies : COLLISION **2** : a forceful effect ⟨the *impact* of pollution on the environment⟩

im·pact·ed \im-'pak-təd\ *adj* **1** : wedged between the jawbone and another tooth ⟨an *impacted* molar⟩ **2** : packed or wedged in

im·pac·tion \im-'pak-shən\ *n* : the act of becoming or the state of being impacted

impact printer *n* : a printing device in which a printing element directly strikes a surface (as in a typewriter)

im·pair \im-'pa(ə)r, -'pe(ə)r\ *vb* : to damage or make worse by or as if by making smaller, less, or weaker ⟨smoking can *impair* one's health⟩ — **im·pair·ment** \-mənt\ *n*

im·paired \-'pa(ə)rd, -'pe(ə)rd\ *adj* **1 a** : functioning in a defective or less than perfect way ⟨*impaired* heart action⟩ **b** : having a defective physical or mental function — often used in combination ⟨a hearing-*impaired* person⟩ **2** : intoxicated by alcohol or drugs ⟨driving while *impaired*⟩

im·pa·la \im-'pal-ə, -'päl-\ *n* : a large brownish African antelope that in the male has slender curving horns [from the name in Zulu, an African language]

im·pale \im-'pa(ə)l\ *vb* **im·paled; im·pal·ing** : to pierce with or as if with something pointed — **im·pale·ment** \-mənt\ *n* — **im·pal·er** \-ər\ *n*

impala

\ə\ **abut**	\au̇\ **out**	\i\ **tip**	\ȯ\ **saw**	\u̇\ **foot**
\ər\ **further**	\ch\ **chin**	\ī\ **life**	\ȯi\ **coin**	\y\ **yet**
\a\ **mat**	\e\ **pet**	\j\ **job**	\th\ **thin**	\yü\ **few**
\ā\ **take**	\ē\ **easy**	\ŋ\ **sing**	\th\ **this**	\yu̇\ **cure**
\ä\ **cot, cart**	\g\ **go**	\ō\ **bone**	\ü\ **food**	\zh\ **vision**

im·pal·pa·ble \(')im-'pal-pə-bəl\ *adj* 1 : unable to be felt by touch ⟨the *impalpable* excitement of the audience⟩ 2 : not easily seen or understood ⟨*impalpable* evils⟩

im·pan·el *or* **em·pan·el** \im-'pan-°l\ *vb* **-eled** *or* **-elled; -el·ing** *or* **-el·ling** : to enroll in or on a panel ⟨*impanel* a jury⟩

im·part \im-'pärt\ *vb* 1 : to give or grant from or as if from a store ⟨schools *impart* knowledge⟩ 2 : to make known : DISCLOSE ⟨I have a bit of news to *impart*⟩

im·par·tial \(')im-'pär-shəl\ *adj* : treating all equally : not partial — **im·par·ti·al·i·ty** \(,)im-,pär-shē-'al-ət-ē, -,pär-'shal-\ *n* — **im·par·tial·ly** \(')im-'pärsh-(ə-)lē\ *adv*

im·pass·able \(')im-'pas-ə-bəl\ *adj* : impossible to pass, cross, or travel over ⟨roads made *impassable* by the hurricane⟩ — **im·pass·abil·i·ty** \(,)im-,pas-ə-'bil-ət-ē\ *n*

im·passe \'im-,pas, im-'pas\ *n* : a situation from which it seems impossible to escape; *esp* : DEADLOCK

im·pas·sioned \im-'pash-ənd\ *adj* : showing very strong feeling ⟨an *impassioned* speech⟩

im·pas·sive \(')im-'pas-iv\ *adj* : not feeling or not showing emotion — **im·pas·sive·ly** *adv* — **im·pas·siv·i·ty** \,im-,pas-'iv-ət-ē\ *n*

im·pa·tience \(')im-'pā-shən(t)s\ *n* 1 : lack of patience 2 : restless or eager desire

im·pa·tiens \im-'pā-shənz, -shən(t)s\ *n* : any of a large genus of herbs that produce often brightly colored flowers

im·pa·tient \(')im-'pā-shənt\ *adj* 1 : not patient ⟨an *impatient* disposition⟩ 2 : showing or coming from impatience ⟨an *impatient* answer⟩ 3 : restless and eager ⟨*impatient* to get going⟩ — **im·pa·tient·ly** *adv*

im·peach \im-'pēch\ *vb* 1 **a** : to charge a public official formally with misconduct in office **b** : to remove from office especially for misconduct 2 : to cast doubt on ⟨*impeached* the witness's testimony⟩ — **im·peach·able** \-'pē-chə-bəl\ *adj* — **im·peach·ment** \-'pēch-mənt\ *n*

im·pec·ca·ble \(')im-'pek-ə-bəl\ *adj* : free from fault or blame — **im·pec·ca·bil·i·ty** \(,)im-,pek-ə-'bil-ət-ē\ *n* — **im·pec·ca·bly** \(')im-'pek-ə-blē\ *adv*

im·pe·cu·nious \,im-pi-'kyü-nyəs, -nē-əs\ *adj* : having little or no money — **im·pe·cu·nious·ness** *n*

im·pede \im-'pēd\ *vb* **im·ped·ed; im·ped·ing** : to interfere with the movement or progress of [from Latin *impedire* "to hinder, get in the way of," literally, "to bind or hold the feet of," derived from *im-, in-* "in, into" and *ped-, pes* "foot" — related to PEDESTRIAN] — **im·ped·er** *n*

im·ped·i·ment \im-'ped-ə-mənt\ *n* 1 : something that impedes 2 : a defect in speech

im·ped·i·men·ta \(,)im-,ped-ə-'ment-ə\ *n pl* : things (as baggage or equipment) that keep one from moving freely

im·pel \im-'pel\ *vb* **im·pelled; im·pel·ling** : to urge or drive forward or into action — **im·pel·ler** \-'pel-ər\ *n*

im·pend \im-'pend\ *vb* 1 : to threaten to occur immediately ⟨*impending* danger⟩ 2 : to be about to happen ⟨an *impending* trip⟩ 3 *archaic* : to hang out or over

im·pen·e·tra·ble \(')im-'pen-ə-trə-bəl\ *adj* 1 : impossible to get through or into ⟨*impenetrable* walls⟩ ⟨*impenetrable* jungle⟩ 2 : impossible to understand ⟨an *impenetrable* mystery⟩ — **im·pen·e·tra·bil·i·ty** \(,)im-,pen-ə-trə-'bil-ət-ē\ *n* — **im·pen·e·tra·bly** \(')im-'pen-ə-trə-blē\ *adv*

im·pen·i·tence \(')im-'pen-ə-tən(t)s\ *n* : the quality or state of being impenitent

im·pen·i·tent \(')im-'pen-ə-tənt\ *adj* : not sorry for having done wrong — **im·pen·i·tent·ly** *adv*

¹**im·per·a·tive** \im-'per-ət-iv\ *adj* 1 **a** : of, relating to, or being the grammatical mood that expresses a command, request, or encouragement **b** : expressing a command, request, or strong encouragement ⟨an *imperative* sentence⟩ 2 : impossible to avoid or ignore : URGENT — **im·per·a·tive·ly** *adv* — **im·per·a·tive·ness** *n*

²**imperative** *n* 1 : the imperative mood of a verb or a verb in this mood 2 : something that is imperative

im·pe·ra·tor \,im-pə-'rät-ər, -'rä-,tó(ə)r\ *n* : a commander in chief or emperor of the ancient Romans

im·per·cep·ti·ble \,im-pər-'sep-tə-bəl\ *adj* 1 : not noticeable : not perceptible by a sense or by the mind ⟨one whose beauty was *imperceptible* to others⟩ 2 : hardly noticeable : very small or gradual ⟨an *imperceptible* smile⟩ — **im·per·cep·ti·bly** \-blē\ *adv*

¹**im·per·fect** \(')im-'pər-fikt\ *adj* 1 : not perfect: **a** : DEFECTIVE ⟨*imperfect* clothing⟩ **b** : having stamens or pistils but not being a flower with both 2 : of, relating to, or being a verb tense used to express a continuing state or an incomplete action especially in the past — **im·per·fect·ly** \-fik-(t)lē\ *adv*

²**imperfect** *n* : the imperfect tense of a verb or a verb in this tense

im·per·fec·tion \,im-pər-'fek-shən\ *n* 1 : the quality or state of being imperfect 2 : FLAW, FAULT

¹**im·pe·ri·al** \im-'pir-ē-əl\ *adj* : of, relating to, or fine enough for an empire or an emperor — **im·pe·ri·al·ly** \-ē-ə-lē\ *adv*

²**imperial** *n* : a pointed beard growing below the lower lip

im·pe·ri·al·ism \im-'pir-ē-ə-,liz-əm\ *n* : the actions by which one nation is able to control other usually smaller or weaker nations — **im·pe·ri·al·ist** \-ē-ə-ləst\ *n or adj* — **im·pe·ri·al·is·tic** \im-,pir-ē-ə-'lis-tik\ *adj* — **im·pe·ri·al·is·ti·cal·ly** \-ti-k(ə-)lē\ *adv*

²imperial

im·per·il \im-'per-əl\ *vb* **-iled** *or* **-illed; -il·ing** *or* **-il·ling** : to place in great danger : ENDANGER — **im·per·il·ment** \-əl-mənt\ *n*

im·pe·ri·ous \im-'pir-ē-əs\ *adj* 1 : behaving like someone who is a supreme ruler 2 : ¹IMPERATIVE 2, URGENT ⟨the *imperious* problems of a new age⟩ — **im·pe·ri·ous·ly** *adv* — **im·pe·ri·ous·ness** *n*

im·per·ish·able \(')im-'per-ish-ə-bəl\ *adj* : INDESTRUCTIBLE — **im·per·ish·abil·i·ty** \(,)im-,per-ish-ə-'bil-ət-ē\ *n* — **im·per·ish·ably** \(')im-'per-ish-ə-blē\ *adv*

im·per·ma·nence \(')im-'pərm(-ə)-nən(t)s\ *n* : the quality or state of being impermanent

im·per·ma·nent \(')im-'pərm(-ə)-nənt\ *adj* : not permanent : not lasting long — **im·per·ma·nent·ly** *adv*

im·per·me·able \(')im-'pər-mē-ə-bəl\ *adj* : not permitting passage (as of a fluid) through the material of which it is made — **im·per·me·abil·i·ty** \(,)im-,pər-mē-ə-'bil-ət-ē\ *n*

im·per·mis·si·ble \,im-pər-'mis-ə-bəl\ *adj* : not permissible — **im·per·mis·si·bil·i·ty** \-,mis-ə-'bil-ət-ē\ *n* — **im·per·mis·si·bly** \-'mis-ə-blē\ *adv*

im·per·son·al \(')im-'pərs-nəl, -°n-əl\ *adj* 1 : having no expressed subject or no subject other than "it" ⟨"rained" in "it rained" is an *impersonal* verb⟩ 2 : not personal: **a** : not showing or involving personal feelings : DETACHED ⟨an *impersonal* professional attitude⟩ **b** : not caring about individual persons or their feelings ⟨cold *impersonal* cities⟩ ⟨a giant *impersonal* corporation⟩ — **im·per·son·al·i·ty** \(,)im-,pərs-°n-'al-ət-ē\ *n* — **im·per·son·al·ly** \(')im-'pərs-nə-lē, -°n-ə-lē\ *adv*

im·per·son·ate \im-'pərs-°n-,āt\ *vb* **-at·ed; -at·ing** : to pretend to be some other person ⟨*impersonate* a police officer⟩ — **im·per·son·ation** \-,pərs-°n-'ā-shən\ *n* — **im·per·son·ator** \-'pərs-°n-,āt-ər\ *n*

im·per·ti·nence \(')im-'pərt-°n-ən(t)s, -'pərt-nən(t)s\ *n* 1 : the quality or state of being impertinent 2 : a rude act or remark

im·per·ti·nent \(')im-'pərt-°n-ənt, -'pərt-nənt\ *adj* : INSOLENT, RUDE ⟨an *impertinent* reply⟩ — **im·per·ti·nent·ly** *adv*

im·per·turb·able \,im-pər-'tər-bə-bəl\ *adj* : hard to disturb or upset — **im·per·turb·abil·i·ty** \-,tər-bə-'bil-ət-ē\ *n* — **im·per·turb·ably** \-'tər-bə-blē\ *adv*

im·per·vi·ous \(')im-'pər-vē-əs\ *adj* **1** : not letting something enter or pass through ⟨a coat *impervious* to rain⟩ **2** : not disturbed or upset ⟨*impervious* to criticism⟩ — **im·per·vi·ous·ness** *n*

im·pe·ti·go \,im-pə-'tē-gō, -'tī-\ *n* : a contagious skin disease marked by pimples, blisters, and yellowish crusts

im·pet·u·os·i·ty \im-,pech-ə-'wäs-ət-ē\ *n, pl* **-ties 1** : the quality or state of being impetuous : RASHNESS **2** : an impetuous act

im·pet·u·ous \im-'pech-(ə-)wəs\ *adj* **1** : IMPULSIVE, RASH **2** : marked by force of action or movement — **im·pet·u·ous·ly** *adv* — **im·pet·u·ous·ness** *n*

im·pe·tus \'im-pət-əs\ *n* **1 a** : a driving force : IMPULSE **b** : INCENTIVE **2** : MOMENTUM 1

im·pi·ety \(')im-'pī-ət-ē\ *n, pl* **-ties 1** : the quality or state of being impious **2** : an impious act

im·pinge \im-'pinj\ *vb* **im·pinged; im·ping·ing 1** : to strike or dash especially with a sharp collision ⟨sound waves *impinge* on the eardrums⟩ **2** : ENCROACH 1, INFRINGE ⟨*impinge* on another's rights⟩ — **im·pinge·ment** \-mənt\ *n*

im·pi·ous \'im-pē-əs, (')im-'pī-\ *adj* : not pious : IRREVERENT — **im·pi·ous·ly** *adv*

imp·ish \'im-pish\ *adj* : MISCHIEVOUS 3 — **imp·ish·ly** *adv* — **imp·ish·ness** *n*

im·pla·ca·ble \(')im-'plak-ə-bəl, -'plā-kə-\ *adj* : not possible to please, satisfy, or change ⟨an *implacable* enemy⟩ — **im·pla·ca·bil·i·ty** \-,plak-ə-'bil-ət-ē, -,plā-kə-\ *n* — **im·pla·ca·bly** \-'plak-ə-blē, -'plā-kə-\ *adv*

im·plant \im-'plant\ *vb* **1** : to fix or set securely or deeply **2** : to insert in living tissue (as for growth or absorption) — **im·plant** \'im-,plant\ *n* — **im·plant·able** \-ə-bəl\ *adj*

im·plan·ta·tion \,im-,plan-'tā-shən\ *n* **1** : the act of implanting something **2** : the process of becoming implanted or the resulting state

im·plau·si·ble \(')im-'plò-zə-bəl\ *adj* : causing disbelief : not plausible — **im·plau·si·bil·i·ty** \(,)im-,plò-zə-'bil-ət-ē\ *n* — **im·plau·si·bly** \(')im-'plò-zə-blē\ *adv*

¹im·ple·ment \'im-plə-mənt\ *n* : an article intended for use in work

synonyms IMPLEMENT, TOOL, INSTRUMENT, UTENSIL mean a device for doing work. IMPLEMENT may apply to anything needed to complete a task ⟨gardening *implements* such as rakes and hoes⟩. TOOL suggests a device designed for a specific job that may require some skill on the user's part ⟨a carpenter's *tools*⟩. INSTRUMENT suggests a device that can be used for delicate or precise work ⟨one needs great skill to handle the *instruments* of a surgeon⟩. UTENSIL suggests a fairly simple device for jobs around the house ⟨kitchen *utensils* include knives and ladles⟩ or some routine unskilled activity ⟨the pencil was her favorite writing *utensil*⟩.

²im·ple·ment \'im-plə-,ment\ *vb* : to take steps to put into practice : CARRY OUT ⟨*implement* the terms of a treaty⟩ — **im·ple·men·ta·tion** \,im-plə-mən-'tā-shən, -,men-\ *n*

im·pli·cate \'im-plə-,kāt\ *vb* **-cat·ed; -cat·ing** : to show to be connected or involved ⟨evidence that *implicates* him in the robbery⟩

im·pli·ca·tion \,im-plə-'kā-shən\ *n* **1** : the act of implicating : the state of being implicated **2 a** : the act of implying : the state of being implied **b** : something implied

im·plic·it \im-'plis-ət\ *adj* **1** : understood though not put clearly into words ⟨an *implicit* agreement⟩ **2** : being without doubt : ABSOLUTE, COMPLETE ⟨*implicit* trust⟩ — **im·plic·it·ly** *adv* — **im·plic·it·ness** *n*

im·plode \im-'plōd\ *vb* **im·plod·ed; im·plod·ing** : to burst inward

im·plore \im-'plō(ə)r, -'plò(ə)r\ *vb* **im·plored; im·plor·ing** : to call upon with a humble request : BESEECH ⟨*implored*

the manager to give her more responsibility⟩ — **im·plor·ing·ly** *adv*

im·plo·sion \im-'plō-zhən\ *n* : the action of imploding — **im·plo·sive** \-'plō-siv, -ziv\ *adj*

im·ply \im-'plī\ *vb* **im·plied; im·ply·ing 1** : to include or involve as a natural or necessary part even though not put clearly into words ⟨rights *imply* obligations⟩ ⟨an *implied* warranty⟩ **2** : to express indirectly : suggest rather than say plainly ⟨your remark *implies* that I am wrong⟩

im·po·lite \,im-pə-'līt\ *adj* : not polite : RUDE — **im·po·lite·ly** *adv* — **im·po·lite·ness** *n*

im·pon·der·able \(')im-'pän-d(ə-)rə-bəl\ *adj* : not able to have the importance, strength, or value figured out ⟨an *imponderable* mystery⟩ — **imponderable** *n*

¹im·port \im-'pō(ə)rt, -'pó(ə)rt; 'im-,pō(ə)rt, -,pó(ə)rt\ *vb* **1** : ²MEAN 2 **2** : to be important : MATTER **3** : to bring (as goods) into a country from another country usually for selling ⟨*imports* coffee⟩ ⟨*imported* cars⟩ — **im·port·er** *n*

²im·port \'im-,pō(ə)rt, -,pó(ə)rt\ *n* **1** : ¹MEANING 1 **2** : IMPORTANCE **3** : something brought into a country

im·por·tance \im-'pórt-³n(t)s, -ən(t)s\ *n* : the quality or state of being important

synonyms IMPORTANCE, CONSEQUENCE, SIGNIFICANCE mean a quality or condition of something that makes people believe it to be of great value or influence. IMPORTANCE suggests the making of a value judgment regarding something's superior worth ⟨he said nothing of *importance*⟩. CONSEQUENCE suggests that a thing's importance comes from its possible or likely outcome, effects, or results ⟨choosing the right courses will be of great *consequence* for your college career⟩. SIGNIFICANCE may apply to some aspect of a thing that makes it important but may not be immediately obvious ⟨at first people did not realize the *significance* of the invention⟩.

im·por·tant \im-'pórt-³nt, -ənt\ *adj* **1** : having great meaning or influence : SIGNIFICANT ⟨an *important* day to remember⟩ ⟨our most *important* product⟩ ⟨an *important* change⟩ **2** : having power or authority ⟨an *important* leader⟩ **3** : believing or acting as if one's importance is greater than it really is — **im·por·tant·ly** *adv*

im·por·ta·tion \,im-,pōr-'tā-shən, -,pòr-, -pər-\ *n* **1** : the act or practice of importing **2** : something imported : IMPORT

imported fire ant *n* : either of two small South American fire ants that are pests in the southeastern U.S. especially in fields used to grow crops

im·por·tu·nate \im-'pórch-(ə-)nət\ *adj* : making a nuisance of oneself with requests or demands — **im·por·tu·nate·ly** *adv*

im·por·tune \,im-pər-'t(y)ün, im-'pór-chən\ *vb* **-tuned; -tun·ing** : to beg or urge so much as to be a nuisance — **im·por·tun·er** *n*

imported fire ant

im·por·tu·ni·ty \,im-pər-'t(y)ü-nət-ē\ *n, pl* **-ties** : the quality or state of being importunate

im·pose \im-'pōz\ *vb* **im·posed; im·pos·ing 1 a** : to establish or apply as a charge or penalty ⟨*impose* a fine⟩ ⟨*impose* a tax⟩ **b** : to force somebody to accept or put up with ⟨*impose* one's will on another⟩ **2** : to take unfair advantage ⟨*impose* on a friend's good nature⟩ — **im·pos·er** *n*

im·pos·ing \im-'pō-ziŋ\ *adj* : impressive in size, dignity, or magnificence — **im·pos·ing·ly** *adv*

im·po·si·tion \ˌim-pə-'zish-ən\ *n* **1** : the act of imposing **2 a** : something (as a tax) that is imposed **b** : a demand or request that is very troublesome

im·pos·si·bil·i·ty \(ˌ)im-ˌpäs-ə-'bil-ət-ē\ *n, pl* **-ties 1** : the quality or state of being impossible **2** : something impossible

im·pos·si·ble \(')im-'päs-ə-bəl\ *adj* **1 a** : incapable of being or of occurring **b** : very difficult : HOPELESS ⟨an *impossible* situation⟩ **2** : very bad or unpleasant ⟨an *impossible* person⟩ — **im·pos·si·bly** \-blē\ *adv*

im·post \'im-ˌpōst\ *n* : ²TAX 1

im·pos·tor *or* **im·pos·ter** \im-'päs-tər\ *n* : a person who pretends to be someone else in order to deceive

im·pos·ture \im-'päs-chər\ *n* : the act or conduct of an impostor

im·po·tence \'im-pət-ən(t)s\ *n* : the quality or state of being impotent

im·po·tent \'im-pət-ənt\ *adj* **1** : lacking in power or strength **2** : incapable of engaging in sexual intercourse; *also* : STERILE 1 — usually used of males — **im·po·tent·ly** *adv*

im·pound \im-'paůnd\ *vb* **1** : to shut up in or as if in an enclosed place **2** : to seize and hold in the hands of the law ⟨*impound* evidence for a trial⟩ — **im·pound·ment** \-'paůn(d)-mənt\ *n*

im·pov·er·ish \im-'päv-(ə-)rish\ *vb* **1** : to make poor **2** : to use up the strength or richness of ⟨*impoverished* soil⟩ — **im·pov·er·ish·ment** \-mənt\ *n*

im·prac·ti·ca·ble \(')im-'prak-ti-kə-bəl\ *adj* : difficult to put into practice or use ⟨an *impracticable* plan⟩ — **im·prac·ti·ca·bil·i·ty** \(ˌ)im-ˌprak-ti-kə-'bil-ət-ē\ *n*

im·prac·ti·cal \(')im-'prak-ti-kəl\ *adj* : not practical: as **a** : not wise to put into or keep in practice or effect ⟨an *impractical* rule disliked by many⟩ **b** : incapable of dealing sensibly with practical matters **c** : IMPRACTICABLE ⟨the new gadgets were complicated and *impractical*⟩ — **im·prac·ti·cal·i·ty** \(ˌ)im-ˌprak-ti-'kal-ət-ē\ *n* — **im·prac·ti·cal·ly** \(')im-'prak-ti-k(ə-)lē\ *adv*

im·pre·cate \'im-pri-ˌkāt\ *vb* **-cat·ed; -cat·ing** : ²CURSE 1

im·pre·ca·tion \ˌim-pri-'kā-shən\ *n* **1** : ¹CURSE 1 **2** : ²CURSE 2

im·pre·cise \ˌim-pri-'sīs\ *adj* : not precise ⟨an *imprecise* estimate⟩ — **im·pre·cise·ly** *adv* — **im·pre·cise·ness** *n* — **im·pre·ci·sion** \-'sizh-ən\ *n*

im·preg·na·ble \im-'preg-nə-bəl\ *adj* : not able to be captured by assault : UNCONQUERABLE ⟨an *impregnable* fortress⟩ — **im·preg·na·bly** \-blē\ *adv*

im·preg·nate \im-'preg-ˌnāt\ *vb* **-nat·ed; -nat·ing 1 a** : to make pregnant **b** : to introduce sperm cells into **2** : to cause (a material) to be filled or soaked with something ⟨*impregnate* wood with varnish⟩ — **im·preg·na·tion** \(ˌ)im-ˌpreg-'nā-shən\ *n* — **im·preg·na·tor** \im-'preg-ˌnāt-ər\ *n*

im·pre·sa·rio \ˌim-prə-'sär-ē-ˌō, -'sar-, -'zär-\ *n, pl* **-ri·os** : a person who puts on an entertainment (as a concert)

¹im·press \im-'pres\ *vb* **1** : to produce by stamping, pressing, or printing **2 a** : to fix in or on one's mind : produce a vivid impression of ⟨the lesson was *impressed* on their minds⟩ **b** : to affect strongly or deeply ⟨I am *impressed* by what you've done⟩; *also* : to gain the admiration or interest of ⟨tries to *impress* people⟩

²im·press \'im-ˌpres\ *n* **1** : the act of impressing **2** : a mark made by pressure **3** : a characteristic or special mark **4** : IMPRESSION 2b

³im·press \im-'pres\ *vb* : to force into naval service — **im·press·ment** \-mənt\ *n*

im·pres·sion \im-'presh-ən\ *n* **1** : the act or process of impressing **2 a** : something (as a design or a footprint)

made by pressing or stamping **b** : something that impresses or is impressed on one's mind ⟨those words made a strong *impression*⟩ ⟨the candidate made a good *impression*⟩ **3** : a memory or belief that is vague or uncertain ⟨it's my *impression* that you don't have to go⟩ **4** : an imitation of a famous person done for entertainment

im·pres·sion·able \im-'presh-(ə-)nə-bəl\ *adj* : easy to impress or influence — **im·pres·sion·abil·i·ty** \-ˌpresh-(ə-)nə-'bil-ət-ē\ *n*

im·pres·sion·ism \im-'presh-ə-ˌniz-əm\ *n* **1** *often cap* : a style of painting beginning in France around 1870 in which dabs or strokes of primary colors are used to give the effect of light actually reflected from things **2** : a style of musical composition designed to create moods through rich and varied harmonies

im·pres·sion·ist \im-'presh-(ə-)nəst\ *n* **1** *often cap* : a person (as a painter) who practices impressionism **2** : an entertainer who does impressions

im·pres·sion·is·tic \(ˌ)im-ˌpresh-ə-'nis-tik\ *adj* **1** *or* **im·pres·sion·ist** \im-'presh-(ə-)nəst\ *often cap* : of or relating to impressionism ⟨an *impressionistic* style of painting⟩ **2** : based on or involving one's impressions rather than knowledge or facts ⟨*impressionistic* descriptions⟩ — **im·pres·sion·is·ti·cal·ly** \(ˌ)im-ˌpresh-ə-'nis-ti-k(ə-)lē\ *adv*

im·pres·sive \im-'pres-iv\ *adj* : having the power to impress the mind or feelings ⟨an *impressive* speech⟩ — **im·pres·sive·ly** *adv* — **im·pres·sive·ness** *n*

im·pri·ma·tur \ˌim-prə-'mä-tú(ə)r\ *n* : official approval (as to print or publish)

¹im·print \im-'print, 'im-ˌ\ *vb* **1** : to mark by or as if by pressure : STAMP **2** : to fix firmly (as on the memory) **3** : to go through the process of imprinting

²im·print \'im-ˌprint\ *n* **1** : something imprinted or printed : IMPRESSION ⟨the *imprint* of a hippo's foot⟩ **2** : a publisher's name on the title page of a book

im·print·ing \'im-ˌprint-iŋ, im-'print-\ *n* : a rapid learning process that takes place early in the life of a social animal (as a goose) and that results in the formation of a special way of behaving (as knowing and being attracted to one's own kind)

im·pris·on \im-'priz-ᵊn\ *vb* **-pris·oned; -pris·on·ing** \-'priz-(ə-)niŋ\ : to put in or as if in prison — **im·pris·on·ment** \-'priz-ən-mənt\ *n*

im·prob·a·ble \(')im-'präb-(ə-)bəl\ *adj* : not probable : unlikely to be true or to occur — **im·prob·a·bil·i·ty** \(ˌ)im-ˌpräb-ə-'bil-ət-ē\ *n* — **im·prob·a·bly** \(')im-'präb-(ə-)blē\ *adv*

im·promp·tu \im-'präm(p)-t(y)ü\ *adj* : not prepared ahead of time : EXTEMPORANEOUS ⟨an *impromptu* speech⟩ — **im·promptu** *adv or n*

im·prop·er \(')im-'präp-ər\ *adj* : not proper, right, or suitable — **im·prop·er·ly** *adv*

improper fraction *n* : a fraction whose numerator is equal to or larger than the denominator

im·pro·pri·ety \ˌim-prə-'prī-ət-ē\ *n, pl* **-ties 1** : the quality or state of being improper **2** : an improper act or remark

im·prove \im-'prüv\ *vb* **im·proved; im·prov·ing 1** : to make or become better ⟨genetics helps us *improve* plants⟩ ⟨when economic conditions *improve*⟩ **2** : to increase the value of (land or property) by making improvements **3** : to make good use of ⟨*improved* their time by studying German⟩ **4** : to make useful additions or changes — **im·prov·able** \-'prü-və-bəl\ *adj* — **im·prov·er** *n*

im·prove·ment \im-'prüv-mənt\ *n* **1** : the act or process of improving **2 a** : increased value or excellence **b** : something that adds to the value or appearance (as of a house)

im·prov·i·dence \(')im-'präv-əd-ən(t)s, -ə-ˌden(t)s\ *n* : the quality or state of being improvident

im·prov·i·dent \(')im-'präv-əd-ənt, -ə-ˌdent\ *adj* : not providing or saving up for the future — **im·prov·i·dent·ly** *adv*

im·pro·vi·sa·tion \(ˌ)im-ˌpräv-ə-'zā-shən, ˌim-prə-və-\ *n* **1** : the act or art of improvising **2** : something that is improvised — **im·pro·vi·sa·tion·al** \-shnəl, -shən-ᵊl\ *adj*

im·pro·vise \ˌim-prə-'vīz, 'im-prə-ˌvīz\ *vb* **-vised; -vis·ing** **1** : to compose, recite, play, or sing without preparation **2** : to make, invent, or arrange on the spur of the moment or without planning ⟨the quarterback *improvised* a play⟩ **3** : to make out of what is conveniently on hand ⟨*improvise* a bed from leaves and straw⟩ — **im·pro·vis·er** *or* **im·pro·vis·or** \-'vī-zər, -ˌvī-\ *n*

im·pru·dence \(')im-'prüd-ᵊn(t)s\ *n* : the quality or state of being imprudent

im·pru·dent \(')im-'prüd-ᵊnt\ *adj* : not prudent : RASH, UNWISE — **im·pru·dent·ly** *adv*

im·pu·dence \'im-pyəd-ən(t)s\ *n* : impudent behavior or speech : INSOLENCE, DISRESPECT

im·pu·dent \'im-pyəd-ənt\ *adj* : showing scorn for or disregard of others : INSOLENT, DISRESPECTFUL — **im·pu·dent·ly** *adv*

im·pugn \im-'pyün\ *vb* : to attack as false or not to be trusted ⟨*impugn* the honesty of an opponent⟩

im·pulse \'im-ˌpəls\ *n* **1 a** : a force that starts a body into motion **b** : the motion produced by an impulse **2** : a sudden stirring up of the mind and spirit to do something ⟨an *impulse* to run away⟩ ⟨buy something on *impulse*⟩ **3** : NERVE IMPULSE **4** : ²PULSE 3a

im·pul·sive \im-'pəl-siv\ *adj* **1** : acting or tending to act on impulse **2** : resulting from a sudden impulse — **im·pul·sive·ly** *adv* — **im·pul·sive·ness** *n*

im·pu·ni·ty \im-'pyü-nət-ē\ *n* : freedom from punishment, harm, or loss

im·pure \(')im-'pyù(ə)r\ *adj* **1** : not pure : UNCLEAN, DIRTY **2** : mixed with something else that is usually not as good ⟨an *impure* chemical⟩ — **im·pure·ly** *adv*

im·pu·ri·ty \(')im-'pyùr-ət-ē\ *n, pl* **-ties** **1** : the quality or state of being impure **2** : something that is impure or that makes impure ⟨remove *impurities* from water⟩

im·pu·ta·tion \ˌim-pyə-'tā-shən\ *n* : the act or an instance of imputing

im·pute \im-'pyüt\ *vb* **im·put·ed; im·put·ing** : to give the blame or credit for to some person or cause — **im·put·able** \-'pyüt-ə-bəl\ *adj*

¹**in** \(')in\ *prep* **1 a** — used to show enclosing, including, or placing within limits ⟨*in* the lake⟩ ⟨wounded *in* the leg⟩ ⟨*in* the summer⟩ ⟨*in* a minute⟩ **b** : INTO 1a ⟨went *in* the house⟩ ⟨don't come *in* here with those muddy feet⟩ **2** — used to show means or medium ⟨written *in* pencil⟩ ⟨works *in* plastics⟩ ⟨photographs *in* color⟩ **3 a** — used to show a state or condition ⟨we're *in* trouble⟩ ⟨is made *in* three sizes⟩ ⟨*in* power⟩ ⟨*in* love⟩ **b** : INTO 2a ⟨broke *in* pieces⟩ **4** — used to show manner or purpose ⟨said *in* reply⟩ **5** — used to show the larger member of a ratio ⟨one *in* five⟩

²**in** \'in\ *adv* **1 a** : to or toward the inside ⟨went *in* and closed the door⟩ **b** : to or toward a place ⟨flew *in* yesterday⟩ **c** : so as to be or seem near ⟨play close *in*⟩ **d** : into the midst of something ⟨mix *in* the flour⟩ **e** : to or at its proper place ⟨fit a piece *in*⟩ **f** : so as to be in agreement ⟨fell *in* with our plans⟩ **2 a** : on the inner side : WITHIN ⟨everyone is *in*⟩ **b** : on good terms ⟨*in* with the right people⟩ **c** : in fashion ⟨boots are *in* this year⟩ **d** : at hand : on hand ⟨the evidence was *in*⟩ ⟨harvests are *in*⟩ — **in for** : sure to experience ⟨*in* for a surprise⟩

³**in** \'in\ *adj* **1 a** : being inside or within ⟨the *in* part⟩ **b** : being in power ⟨the *in* party⟩ **2** : directed or bound inward : INCOMING ⟨the *in* train⟩ **3 a** : very fashionable ⟨the *in* thing to do⟩ ⟨the *in* place to go⟩ **b** : very aware of and taking part in what is new and fashionable ⟨the *in* crowd⟩

¹**in-** *or* **il-** *or* **im-** *or* **ir-** *prefix* : not : NON-, UN- — usually *il-* before *l* ⟨*il*logical⟩, *im-* before *b, m,* or *p* ⟨*im*balance⟩ ⟨*im*moral⟩ ⟨*im*practical⟩, *ir-* before *r* ⟨*ir*reducible⟩, and

in- before other sounds ⟨*in*conclusive⟩ [derived from Latin *in-* "not"]

²**in-** *or* **il-** *or* **im-** *or* **ir-** *prefix* **1** : in : within : into : toward : on — usually *il-* before *l, im-* before *b, m,* or *p, ir-* before *r,* and *in-* before other sounds ⟨*in*filtrate⟩ **2** : EN- 2 ⟨*im*peril⟩ [derived from Latin *in* "in, into"]

-in \ən\ *n suffix* : chemical compound ⟨stear*in*⟩ ⟨insul*in*⟩ ⟨niac*in*⟩ [derived from Latin *-ina, -inus* (adjective suffixes)]

in·abil·i·ty \ˌin-ə-'bil-ət-ē\ *n* : lack of ability, power, or means ⟨his *inability* to carry a tune⟩

in·ac·ces·si·ble \ˌin-ik-'ses-ə-bəl, (ˌ)in-ˌak-\ *adj* : not accessible ⟨an *inaccessible* area⟩ ⟨an *inaccessible* goal⟩ — **in·ac·ces·si·bil·i·ty** \-ˌses-ə-ə-'bil-ət-ē\ *n* — **in·ac·ces·si·bly** \-'ses-ə-blē\ *adv*

in·ac·cu·ra·cy \(')in-'ak-yə-rə-sē\ *n, pl* **-cies** **1** : the quality or state of being inaccurate **2** : ERROR 1b, MISTAKE

in·ac·cu·rate \(')in-'ak-yə-rət\ *adj* : not accurate : not correct or exact ⟨*inaccurate* information⟩ — **in·ac·cu·rate·ly** *adv*

in·ac·tion \(')in-'ak-shən\ *n* : lack of action or activity : IDLENESS

in·ac·ti·vate \(')in-'ak-tə-ˌvāt\ *vb* : to make inactive — **in·ac·ti·va·tion** \ˌin-ˌak-tə-'vā-shən\ *n*

in·ac·tive \(')in-'ak-tiv\ *adj* : not active: as **a** : slow to move or act : SLUGGISH **b** : being out of use or activity ⟨an *inactive* mine⟩ ⟨an *inactive* volcano⟩ **c** : INERT ⟨argon is chemically *inactive*⟩ — **in·ac·tive·ly** *adv*

in·ac·tiv·i·ty \(ˌ)in-ˌak-'tiv-ət-ē\ *n* : the state of being inactive

in·ad·e·qua·cy \(')in-'ad-i-kwə-sē\ *n, pl* **-cies** **1** : the quality or state of being inadequate **2 a** : an inadequate amount **b** : a failure to meet expectations ⟨feelings of *inadequacy*⟩ ⟨aware of my own *inadequacies*⟩

in·ad·e·quate \(')in-'ad-i-kwət\ *adj* : not adequate : not enough or not good enough ⟨an *inadequate* supply of food⟩ — **in·ad·e·quate·ly** *adv*

in·ad·mis·si·ble \ˌin-əd-'mis-ə-bəl\ *adj* : not admissible ⟨*inadmissible* evidence⟩ — **in·ad·mis·si·bil·i·ty** \-ˌmis-ə-'bil-ət-ē\ *n*

in·ad·ver·tence \ˌin-əd-'vərt-ᵊn(t)s\ *n* **1** : the fact or action of being inattentive **2** : a result of not paying attention : OVERSIGHT

in·ad·ver·ten·cy \ˌin-əd-'vərt-ᵊn-sē\ *n, pl* **-cies** : INADVERTENCE

in·ad·ver·tent \ˌin-əd-'vərt-ᵊnt\ *adj* **1** : not paying attention : INATTENTIVE **2** : not meant, sought, or intended : UNINTENTIONAL ⟨an *inadvertent* violation of the law⟩ — **in·ad·ver·tent·ly** *adv*

in·ad·vis·able \ˌin-əd-'vī-zə-bəl\ *adj* : not wise to do : not advisable : UNWISE ⟨*inadvisable* haste⟩ — **in·ad·vis·abil·i·ty** \-ˌvī-zə-'bil-ət-ē\ *n*

in·alien·able \(')in-'āl-yə-nə-bəl, -'ā-lē-ə-nə-\ *adj* : impossible to take away or give up ⟨*inalienable* rights⟩ — **in·alien·ably** \-blē\ *adv*

inane \in-'ān\ *adj* : lacking meaning or point : SILLY ⟨*inane* remarks about the weather⟩ — **inane·ly** *adv* — **inane·ness** \-'ān-nəs\ *n*

in·an·i·mate \(')in-'an-ə-mət\ *adj* **1** : not having life ⟨stones are *inanimate*⟩ ⟨an *inanimate* object⟩ **2** : not animated or lively : DULL — **in·an·i·mate·ly** *adv*

inan·i·ty \in-'an-ət-ē\ *n, pl* **-ties** **1** : the quality or state of being inane **2** : something inane

in·ap·pli·ca·ble \(')in-'ap-li-kə-bəl *also* ˌin-ə-'plik-ə-\ *adj* : not applicable : IRRELEVANT — **in·ap·pli·ca·bil·i·ty** \(ˌ)in-ˌap-li-kə-'bil-ət-ē *also* ˌin-ə-ˌplik-ə-\ *n*

\ə\ abut	\aú\ out	\i\ tip	\ò\ saw	\ú\ foot
\ər\ further	\ch\ chin	\ī\ life	\òi\ coin	\y\ yet
\a\ mat	\e\ pet	\j\ job	\th\ thin	\yü\ few
\ā\ take	\ē\ easy	\ŋ\ sing	\th\ this	\yù\ cure
\ä\ cot, cart	\g\ go	\ō\ bone	\ü\ food	\zh\ vision

in·ap·pre·cia·ble \ˌin-ə-ˈprē-shə-bəl\ *adj* : very small or slight ⟨an *inappreciable* amount⟩

in·ap·pro·pri·ate \ˌin-ə-ˈprō-prē-ət\ *adj* : not appropriate : UNSUITABLE ⟨*inappropriate* behavior⟩ — **in·ap·pro·pri·ate·ly** *adv* — **in·ap·pro·pri·ate·ness** *n*

in·apt \(ˈ)in-ˈapt\ *adj* : not suitable ⟨an *inapt* comparison⟩ — **in·apt·ly** \-ˈap-(t)lē\ *adv* — **in·apt·ness** \-ˈap(t)-nəs\ *n*

in·ap·ti·tude \(ˈ)in-ˈap-tə-ˌt(y)üd\ *n* : lack of aptitude

in·ar·tic·u·late \ˌin-(ˌ)är-ˈtik-yə-lət\ *adj* **1 a** : not understandable as spoken words ⟨*inarticulate* cries⟩ ⟨*inarticulate* murmurs⟩ **b** : not able to speak **c** : not able to be expressed ⟨*inarticulate* longings⟩ **2** : not able to give clear expression to ideas or feelings ⟨an *inarticulate* speaker⟩ — **in·ar·tic·u·late·ly** *adv* — **in·ar·tic·u·late·ness** *n*

in·ar·tis·tic \ˌin-är-ˈtis-tik\ *adj* : not artistic — **in·ar·tis·ti·cal·ly** \-ti-k(ə-)lē\ *adv*

in·as·much as \ˌin-əz-ˌməch-əz\ *conj* : considering that : ³SINCE 2

in·at·ten·tion \ˌin-ə-ˈten-chən\ *n* : failure to pay attention — **in·at·ten·tive·ly** *adv* — **in·at·ten·tive·ness** *n*

in·at·ten·tive \-ˈtent-iv\ *adj* : not attentive : not paying attention ⟨the student was *inattentive* in class⟩

in·au·di·ble \(ˈ)in-ˈod-ə-bəl\ *adj* : impossible to hear : not audible — **in·au·di·bil·i·ty** \(ˌ)in-ˌod-ə-ˈbil-ət-ē\ *n* — **in·au·di·bly** \(ˈ)in-ˈod-ə-blē\ *adv*

¹in·au·gu·ral \in-ˈo-gyə-rəl, -g(ə-)rəl\ *adj* **1** : of or relating to an inauguration ⟨the *inaugural* address⟩ ⟨an *inaugural* ball⟩ **2** : marking a beginning ⟨the *inaugural* run of a new high-speed train⟩

²inaugural *n* **1** : an inaugural address **2** : INAUGURATION

in·au·gu·rate \in-ˈo-g(y)ə-ˌrāt\ *vb* **-rat·ed; -rat·ing** **1** : to introduce into office with suitable ceremonies : INSTALL ⟨*inaugurate* a president⟩ **2** : to celebrate the opening of ⟨*inaugurate* a new gym⟩ **3** : to bring into being or action ⟨*inaugurate* a new plan⟩ — **in·au·gu·ra·tor** \-ˌrāt-ər\ *n*

in·au·gu·ra·tion \in-ˌo-g(y)ə-ˈrā-shən\ *n* : an act or ceremony of inaugurating

in·aus·pi·cious \ˌin-o-ˈspish-əs\ *adj* : not auspicious : not looking good for future success — **in·aus·pi·cious·ly** *adv* — **in·aus·pi·cious·ness** *n*

¹in–be·tween \ˌin-bi-ˈtwēn\ *adj* : INTERMEDIATE

²in–between *n* : an intermediate term, thing, or class

¹in between *adv* : ²BETWEEN ⟨were neither young nor old but fell somewhere *in between*⟩

²in between *prep* : ¹BETWEEN 2 ⟨a meadow lies *in between* the house and the road⟩

in·board \ˈin-ˌbō(ə)rd, -ˌbȯ(ə)rd\ *adv* **1** : inside the hull of a ship or boat **2** : close or closest to the center line of an aircraft or ship — **inboard** *adj*

in·born \ˈin-ˈbȯ(ə)rn\ *adj* **1** : born in one : not acquired by training or experience : NATURAL, INSTINCTIVE ⟨an *inborn* ability to grow flowers⟩ **2** : HEREDITARY 1, INHERITED ⟨an *inborn* defect in metabolism⟩

in·bound \ˈin-ˌbaȯnd\ *adj* : inward bound ⟨*inbound* traffic⟩

in·bred \ˈin-ˈbred\ *adj* **1** : deeply rooted in a person ⟨an *inbred* love of freedom⟩ **2** : subjected to or produced by inbreeding

in·breed \ˈin-ˈbrēd\ *vb* **in·bred** \-ˈbred\; **in·breed·ing** : to subject to or engage in inbreeding

in·breed·ing \ˈin-ˌbrēd-iŋ\ *n* : the interbreeding of closely related individuals especially to preserve desirable characteristics and eliminate undesirable characteristics from a stock

In·ca \ˈiŋ-kə\ *n* **1** : a noble or a member of the American Indian peoples of Peru maintaining an empire until the Spanish conquest **2** : a member of any people under Inca influence — **In·can** \-kən\ *adj*

in·cal·cu·la·ble \(ˈ)in-ˈkal-kyə-lə-bəl\ *adj* : not able to be calculated: as **a** : very great **b** : not able to be predicted — **in·cal·cu·la·bil·i·ty** \(ˌ)in-ˌkal-kyə-lə-ˈbil-ət-ē\ *n* — **in·cal·cu·la·bly** \(ˈ)in-ˈkal-kyə-lə-blē\ *adv*

in·can·des·cence \ˌin-kən-ˈdes-ᵊn(t)s\ *n* : the glowing of a substance due to its high temperature

¹in·can·des·cent \ˌin-kən-ˈdes-ᵊnt\ *adj* : white or glowing with great heat — **in·can·des·cent·ly** *adv*

²incandescent *n* : LIGHTBULB a

incandescent lamp *n* : LIGHTBULB a

in·can·ta·tion \ˌin-kan-ˈtā-shən\ *n* : a series of words used to produce a magic spell

in·ca·pa·ble \(ˈ)in-ˈkā-pə-bəl\ *adj* : not able to do something ⟨*incapable* of cleaning her room thoroughly⟩ — **in·ca·pa·bil·i·ty** \(ˌ)in-ˌkā-pə-ˈbil-ət-ē\ *n*

in·ca·pac·i·tate \ˌin-kə-ˈpas-ə-ˌtāt\ *vb* **-tat·ed; -tat·ing** : to make incapable : DISABLE — **in·ca·pac·i·ta·tion** \-ˌpas-ə-ˈtā-shən\ *n*

in·ca·pac·i·ty \ˌin-kə-ˈpas-ət-ē, -ˈpas-tē\ *n, pl* **-ties** : lack of ability or power

in·car·cer·ate \in-ˈkär-sə-ˌrāt\ *vb* **-at·ed; -at·ing** : to put in prison : CONFINE — **in·car·cer·a·tion** \(ˌ)in-ˌkär-sə-ˈrā-shən\ *n*

¹in·car·nate \in-ˈkär-nət, -ˌnāt\ *adj* : given bodily or actual form ⟨the devil *incarnate*⟩ ⟨a little tornado *incarnate*⟩

²in·car·nate \in-ˈkär-ˌnāt, ˈin-ˌkär-ˌnāt\ *vb* **-nat·ed; -nat·ing** : to give bodily or actual form to

in·car·na·tion \ˌin-ˌkär-ˈnā-shən\ *n* **1** : the appearance of a god or spirit in an earthly form **2** *cap* : the union of divine and human natures in Jesus Christ **3** : an actual instance of a quality or concept ⟨she was the *incarnation* of goodness⟩

in·cau·tious \(ˈ)in-ˈkȯ-shəs\ *adj* : not cautious : RASH — **in·cau·tious·ly** *adv* — **in·cau·tious·ness** *n*

¹in·cen·di·ary \in-ˈsen-dē-ˌer-ē\ *n, pl* **-ar·ies** **1** : a person who commits arson : ARSONIST **2** : a person who excites quarrels : AGITATOR

²incendiary *adj* **1** : of, relating to, or involving arson **2** : tending to excite quarrels : INFLAMMATORY ⟨an *incendiary* speech⟩ **3** : containing chemicals that burst into flame on contact ⟨an *incendiary* bomb⟩

¹in·cense \ˈin-ˌsen(t)s\ *n* **1 a** : material used to produce a fragrant odor when burned **b** : the odor so produced **2** : a pleasing scent

²in·cense \in-ˈsen(t)s\ *vb* **in·censed; in·cens·ing** : to make very angry

in·cen·ter \ˈin-ˌsent-ər\ *n* : the one and only point in a triangle that is passed through by each of the three lines that divide in half one of its three angles

in·cen·tive \in-ˈsent-iv\ *n* : something that makes a person try or work hard or harder

in·cep·tion \in-ˈsep-shən\ *n* : an act or instance of beginning

in·cer·ti·tude \(ˈ)in-ˈsərt-ə-ˌt(y)üd\ *n* : UNCERTAINTY

in·ces·sant \(ˈ)in-ˈses-ᵊnt\ *adj* : going on and on : not stopping or letting up — **in·ces·sant·ly** *adv*

in·cest \ˈin-ˌsest\ *n* : sexual intercourse between persons so closely related that they are forbidden by law to marry

in·ces·tu·ous \in-ˈses-chə-wəs\ *adj* **1** : being or involving incest **2** : guilty of incest — **in·ces·tu·ous·ly** *adv*

¹inch \ˈinch\ *n* **1** : a unit of length equal to ¹/₃₆ yard (2.54 centimeters) — see MEASURE table **2** : a small amount, distance, or degree ⟨won't budge an *inch*⟩ **3** : a small advantage especially from kind treatment — usually used in the phrase *give an inch* ⟨did not *give an inch* during negotiations⟩ [Old English *ynce* "inch," from Latin *uncia* "a 12th part, ounce," from *unus* "one" — related to OUNCE, UNITE; see *Word History* at OUNCE] — **inch by inch** : very gradually or slowly — **within an inch of** : almost to the point of ⟨came *within an inch of* succeeding⟩

²inch *vb* : to move a little bit at a time

inch·worm \ˈinch-ˌwərm\ *n* : LOOPER 1

in·ci·dence \ˈin(t)-səd-ən(t)s, -sə-ˌden(t)s\ *n* **1** : ANGLE OF INCIDENCE **2** : rate of occurrence ⟨a high *incidence* of illness⟩

¹**in·ci·dent** \'in(t)-səd-ənt, -sə-ˌdent\ *n* : an often unimportant happening that may form part of a larger event

²**incident** *adj* **1** : ¹INCIDENTAL **2** : falling or striking on something ⟨*incident* light rays⟩

¹**in·ci·den·tal** \ˌin(t)-sə-'dent-ᵊl\ *adj* **1** : happening by chance **2** : of minor importance

²**incidental** *n* : something that is incidental

in·ci·den·tal·ly \ˌin(t)-sə-'dent-ᵊl-ē, *especially for sense 2* -'dent-lē\ *adv* **1** : in an incidental manner ⟨discusses the problem only *incidentally*⟩ **2** : apart from that : by the way ⟨a one-room school—still standing, *incidentally*—which was painted red⟩

in·cin·er·ate \in-'sin-ə-ˌrāt\ *vb* **-at·ed; -at·ing** : to burn to ashes — **in·cin·er·a·tion** \-ˌsin-ə-'rā-shən\ *n*

in·cin·er·a·tor \in-'sin-ə-ˌrāt-ər\ *n* : a furnace or a container for burning waste materials

in·cip·i·en·cy \in-'sip-ē-ən-sē\ *n* : the fact or state of being incipient

in·cip·i·ent \in-'sip-ē-ənt\ *adj* : beginning to come into being or to become apparent ⟨the *incipient* light of day⟩ — **in·cip·i·ent·ly** *adv*

in·cise \in-'sīz\ *vb* **in·cised; in·cis·ing** : to cut into : CARVE, ENGRAVE

in·ci·sion \in-'sizh-ən\ *n* **1** : a cut or gash made in something; *esp* : a cut made into the body during surgery ⟨removed the diseased appendix through a small *incision*⟩ **2** : an act of cutting into something ⟨watched the surgeon's skillful *incision*⟩

in·ci·sive \in-'sī-siv\ *adj* : impressively clear and direct ⟨an *incisive* argument⟩ — **in·ci·sive·ly** *adv* — **in·ci·sive·ness** *n*

in·ci·sor \in-'sī-zər\ *n* : a front tooth for cutting; *esp* : one of the cutting teeth between the canines of a mammal

in·cite \in-'sīt\ *vb* **in·cit·ed; in·cit·ing** : to move to action : stir up — **in·cit·er** *n*

in·cite·ment \in-'sīt-mənt\ *n* **1** : the act of inciting : the state of being incited **2** : something that incites

in·ci·vil·i·ty \ˌin(t)-sə-'vil-ət-ē\ *n, pl* **-ties 1** : the quality or state of being impolite **2** : a rude or discourteous act

in·clem·ent \(')in-'klem-ənt\ *adj* : STORMY 1 ⟨*inclement* weather⟩ — **in·clem·ent·ly** *adv*

in·cli·na·tion \ˌin-klə-'nā-shən, iŋ-\ *n* **1** : a feeling of liking or of wanting to do something ⟨an *inclination* for sleeping late⟩ **2** : an act or the action of bending or tilting **3** : a departure from the true vertical or horizontal : SLANT ⟨the *inclination* of the earth's axis⟩; *also* : the amount of such departure **b** : an inclined surface : SLOPE **4** : a quality which leads to some state or action ⟨the door has an *inclination* to stick⟩ — **in·cli·na·tion·al** \-shnəl, -shən-ᵊl\ *adj*

¹**in·cline** \in-'klīn\ *vb* **in·clined; in·clin·ing 1** : to bend the head or body forward : BOW **2** : to be drawn to an opinion or course of action ⟨*inclined* to go swimming⟩ **3** : to turn or move from a line, direction, or course : LEAN, SLOPE **4** : to cause to bend, bow, or slant **5** : to have influence on : PERSUADE ⟨my teacher's example *inclined* me to become a teacher too⟩ — **in·clin·able** \in-'klī-nə-bəl\ *adj*

²**in·cline** \'in-ˌklīn\ *n* : ³SLOPE 2

inclined *adj* : having an inclination, disposition, or tendency ⟨was *inclined* to stay up late⟩

inclined plane *n* : a flat surface that makes an angle with the plane of the horizon

inclose, inclosure *variant of* ENCLOSE, ENCLOSURE

in·clude \in-'klüd\ *vb* **in·clud·ed; in·clud·ing** : to take in or have as part of a whole or group ⟨the recipe *included* many ingredients⟩ — **in·clud·able** *or* **in·clud·ible** \-'klüd-ə-bəl\ *adj*

in·clu·sion \in-'klü-zhən\ *n* **1** : the act of including : the state of being included **2** : something that is included

in·clu·sive \in-'klü-siv, -ziv\ *adj* **1** : including the stated limits and everything in between ⟨pages 10 to 20 *inclu-*

sive⟩ **2** : covering everything or all important points ⟨an *inclusive* tour⟩ ⟨an *inclusive* insurance policy⟩ — **in·clu·sive·ly** *adv* — **in·clu·sive·ness** *n*

in·cog·ni·to \ˌin-ˌkäg-'nēt-ō, in-'käg-nə-ˌtō\ *adv or adj* : with one's identity concealed (as by a false name or title) ⟨was traveling *incognito*⟩ [from Italian *incognito* "so as not to be known or recognized," from Latin *incognitus* "unknown," from *in-* "not" and *cognitus*, past participle of *cognoscere* "to know" — related to CONNOISSEUR, RECOGNIZE]

in·co·her·ence \ˌin-kō-'hir-ən(t)s, -'her-\ *n* **1** : the quality or state of being incoherent **2** : something that is incoherent

in·co·her·ent \ˌin-kō-'hir-ənt, -'her-\ *adj* **1** : not sticking closely or compactly together : LOOSE **2** : not clearly or logically connected ⟨told an *incoherent* story⟩ **3** : not clear or understandable in speech or thought ⟨*incoherent* with grief⟩ — **in·co·her·ent·ly** *adv*

in·com·bus·ti·ble \ˌin-kəm-'bəs-tə-bəl\ *adj* : incapable of being burned

in·come \'in-ˌkəm\ *n* : a gain usually measured in money that comes in from labor, business, or property

income tax \'in-(ˌ)kəm-\ *n* : a tax on the income of a person or business

in·com·ing \'in-ˌkəm-iŋ\ *adj* : coming in: as **a** : taking a place formerly held by another ⟨the *incoming* president⟩ **b** : arriving at a destination ⟨*incoming* mail⟩ **c** : just starting or beginning ⟨the *incoming* year⟩

in·com·men·su·rate \ˌin-kə-'men(t)s-(ə-)rət, -'mench-(ə-)rət\ *adj* : not commensurate: as **a** : INADEQUATE ⟨funds *incommensurate* with need⟩ **b** : DISPROPORTIONATE ⟨a confidence *incommensurate* with his ability⟩

in·com·mode \ˌin-kə-'mōd\ *vb* **-mod·ed; -mod·ing** : ²INCONVENIENCE

in·com·mu·ni·ca·ble \ˌin-kə-'myü-ni-kə-bəl\ *adj* : not capable of being communicated

in·com·mu·ni·ca·do \ˌin-kə-ˌmyü-nə-'käd-ō\ *adv or adj* : without being able to communicate with others ⟨a prisoner held *incommunicado*⟩

in·com·pa·ra·ble \(')in-'käm-p(ə-)rə-bəl\ *adj* **1** : better than any other : MATCHLESS **2** : not suited for comparison — **in·com·pa·ra·bil·i·ty** \(ˌ)in-ˌkäm-p(ə-)rə-'bil-ət-ē\ *n* — **in·com·pa·ra·bly** \(')in-'käm-p(ə-)rə-blē\ *adv*

in·com·pat·i·bil·i·ty \ˌin-kəm-ˌpat-ə-'bil-ət-ē\ *n, pl* **-ties** : the quality or state of being incompatible

in·com·pat·i·ble \ˌin-kəm-'pat-ə-bəl\ *adj* **1** : not able to be brought together in harmony ⟨their personalities were *incompatible*⟩ ⟨*incompatible* colors⟩ **2 a** : not able to be used together ⟨*incompatible* computer systems⟩ **b** : unsuitable for use together because of undesirable chemical or bodily effects ⟨*incompatible* blood types⟩ — **in·com·pat·i·bly** \-blē\ *adv*

in·com·pe·tence \(')in-'käm-pət-ən(t)s\ *n* : the quality, state, or fact of being incompetent

in·com·pe·ten·cy \(')in-'käm-pət-ən-sē\ *n, pl* **-cies** : INCOMPETENCE

¹**in·com·pe·tent** \(')in-'käm-pət-ənt\ *adj* **1** : not legally qualified **2** : lacking qualities (as knowledge, skill, or ability) needed to do something well ⟨an *incompetent* writer⟩ — **in·com·pe·tent·ly** *adv*

²**incompetent** *n* : an incompetent person

in·com·plete \ˌin-kəm-'plēt\ *adj* : not complete : lacking some part ⟨handed in an *incomplete* assignment⟩ — **in·com·plete·ly** *adv* — **in·com·plete·ness** *n*

incomplete metamorphosis *n* : insect metamorphosis (as of a grasshopper) in which there is no pupal stage be-

\ə\ **abut**	\au̇\ **out**	\i\ **tip**	\o̅\ **saw**	\u̇\ **foot**
\ər\ **further**	\ch\ **chin**	\ī\ **life**	\o̅i\ **coin**	\y\ **yet**
\a\ **mat**	\e\ **pet**	\j\ **job**	\th\ **thin**	\yü\ **few**
\ā\ **take**	\ē\ **easy**	\ŋ\ **sing**	\th\ **this**	\yu̇\ **cure**
\ä\ **cot, cart**	\g\ **go**	\ō\ **bone**	\ü\ **food**	\zh\ **vision**

tween the immature stage and the adult and in which the young insect usually resembles the adult — compare COMPLETE METAMORPHOSIS

in·com·pre·hen·si·ble \(ˌ)in-ˌkäm-pri-'hen(t)-sə-bəl\ *adj* : impossible to understand ⟨found their behavior *incomprehensible*⟩ — **in·com·pre·hen·si·bil·i·ty** \-ˌhen(t)-sə-'bil-ət-ē\ *n* — **in·com·pre·hen·si·bly** \-'hen(t)-sə-blē\ *adv*

in·com·pre·hen·sion \(ˌ)in-ˌkäm-pri-'hen-chən\ *n* : lack of understanding

in·com·press·ible \ˌin-kəm-'pres-ə-bəl\ *adj* : impossible or difficult to compress — **in·com·press·ibil·i·ty** \-ˌpres-ə-'bil-ət-ē\ *n*

in·con·ceiv·able \ˌin-kən-'sē-və-bəl\ *adj* : impossible to imagine or believe — **in·con·ceiv·ably** \-blē\ *adv*

in·con·clu·sive \ˌin-kən-'klü-siv, -ziv\ *adj* : not leading to a definite conclusion or result ⟨*inconclusive* evidence⟩ — **in·con·clu·sive·ly** *adv* — **in·con·clu·sive·ness** *n*

in·con·gru·ous \(')in-'käŋ-grə-wəs\ *adj* : not harmonious, suitable, or proper ⟨*incongruous* colors⟩ — **in·con·gru·ity** \ˌin-kən-'grü-ət-ē, -ˌkän-\ *n* — **in·con·gru·ous·ly** \(')in-'kaŋ-grə-wəs-lē\ *adv* — **in·con·gru·ous·ness** *n*

in·con·se·quen·tial \(ˌ)in-ˌkän(t)-sə-'kwen-chəl\ *adj* : not important

in·con·sid·er·able \ˌin-kən-'sid-ər-(ə-)bəl, -'sid-rə-bəl\ *adj* : not worth considering : SLIGHT, TRIVIAL

in·con·sid·er·ate \ˌin-kən-'sid-(ə-)rət\ *adj* : careless of the rights or feelings of others ⟨an *inconsiderate* remark⟩ — **in·con·sid·er·ate·ly** *adv* — **in·con·sid·er·ate·ness** *n* — **in·con·sid·er·ation** \-ˌsid-ə-'rā-shən\ *n*

in·con·sis·ten·cy \ˌin-kən-'sis-tən-sē\ *n, pl* **-cies** 1 : the quality or state of being inconsistent 2 : an example of being inconsistent

in·con·sis·tent \ˌin-kən-'sis-tənt\ *adj* 1 : not being in agreement or harmony : INCOMPATIBLE ⟨an explanation *inconsistent* with the facts⟩ 2 : not logical or regular in thought or actions : CHANGEABLE ⟨a very *inconsistent* person⟩ — **in·con·sis·tent·ly** *adv*

in·con·sol·able \ˌin-kən-'sō-lə-bəl\ *adj* : incapable of being comforted : DISCONSOLATE — **in·con·sol·ably** \-blē\ *adv*

in·con·spic·u·ous \ˌin-kən-'spik-yə-wəs\ *adj* : not easily seen or noticed — **in·con·spic·u·ous·ly** *adv* — **in·con·spic·u·ous·ness** *n*

in·con·stan·cy \(')in-'kän(t)-stən-sē\ *n, pl* **-cies** : the quality or state of being inconstant

in·con·stant \(')in-'kän(t)-stənt\ *adj* : likely to change frequently without apparent reason : CHANGEABLE

in·con·test·able \ˌin-kən-'tes-tə-bəl\ *adj* : not open to doubt : UNQUESTIONABLE ⟨an *incontestable* fact⟩ — **in·con·test·ably** \-'tes-tə-blē\ *adv*

in·con·ti·nence \(')in-'känt-ᵊn-ən(t)s\ *n* : the quality or state of being incontinent

in·con·ti·nent \(')in-'känt-ᵊn-ənt\ *adj* 1 : having or showing a lack of self-restraint or control 2 : unable to control keeping urine or feces in the body — **in·con·ti·nent·ly** *adv*

in·con·tro·vert·ible \(ˌ)in-ˌkän-trə-'vərt-ə-bəl\ *adj* : INDISPUTABLE ⟨*incontrovertible* evidence⟩ — **in·con·tro·vert·ibly** \-blē\ *adv*

¹**in·con·ve·nience** \ˌin-kən-'vē-nyən(t)s\ *n* 1 : something that is inconvenient 2 : the quality or state of being inconvenient

²**inconvenience** *vb* **-nienced; -nienc·ing** : to cause discomfort to : put to trouble ⟨*inconvenienced* by the bad weather⟩

in·con·ve·nient \ˌin-kən-'vē-nyənt\ *adj* : not convenient : causing difficulty, discomfort, or annoyance ⟨an *inconvenient* delay⟩ — **in·con·ve·nient·ly** *adv*

in·cor·po·rate \in-'kȯr-pə-ˌrāt\ *vb* **-rat·ed; -rat·ing** 1 : to unite or combine to form a single whole : BLEND 2 : to give form to : EMBODY 3 : to form, make into, or become

a corporation ⟨*incorporate* a company⟩ — **in·cor·po·ra·tion** \-ˌkȯr-pə-'rā-shən\ *n* — **in·cor·po·ra·tor** \-'kȯr-pə-ˌrāt-ər\ *n*

in·cor·po·re·al \ˌin-(ˌ)kȯr-'pōr-ē-əl, -'pȯr-\ *adj* : having no material body or form : IMMATERIAL

in·cor·rect \ˌin-kə-'rekt\ *adj* : not correct: as **a** : INACCURATE, FAULTY ⟨an *incorrect* copy⟩ **b** : not true : WRONG ⟨an *incorrect* answer⟩ **c** : not proper ⟨*incorrect* behavior⟩ — **in·cor·rect·ly** \-'rek-(t)lē\ *adv* — **in·cor·rect·ness** \-'rek(t)-nəs\ *n*

¹**in·cor·ri·gi·ble** \(')in-'kȯr-ə-jə-bəl, -'kär-\ *adj* : not able to be corrected or reformed ⟨an *incorrigible* gambler⟩

²**incorrigible** *n* : an incorrigible person

in·cor·rupt·ible \ˌin-kə-'rəp-tə-bəl\ *adj* 1 : not subject to decay 2 : incapable of being corrupted : HONEST — **in·cor·rupt·ibil·i·ty** \-ˌrəp-tə-'bil-ət-ē\ *n* — **in·cor·rupt·ibly** \-'rəp-tə-blē\ *adv*

¹**in·crease** \in-'krēs, 'in-ˌkrēs\ *vb* **in·creased; in·creas·ing** 1 : to make or become greater ⟨*increase* speed⟩ ⟨skill *increases* with practice⟩ 2 : to become more numerous by the production of young

²**in·crease** \'in-ˌkrēs, in-'krēs\ *n* 1 : the act of increasing 2 : something added (as by growth) — **on the increase** : becoming greater in size, number, or amount ⟨crime is *on the increase*⟩

in·creas·ing·ly \in-'krē-siŋ-lē, 'in-ˌkrē-\ *adv* : to an increasing degree : more and more ⟨the work became *increasingly* difficult⟩

in·cred·i·ble \(')in-'kred-ə-bəl\ *adj* 1 : UNBELIEVABLE ⟨an *incredible* story⟩ 2 : EXTRAORDINARY ⟨*incredible* skill⟩ [Middle English *incredible* "too unusual to be believed," from Latin *incredibilis* (same meaning), from *in-* "not" and *credibilis* "believable," from *credere* "to believe, trust, entrust" — related to CREDENTIALS, CREDIT, CREED] — **in·cred·ibil·i·ty** \(ˌ)in-ˌkred-ə-'bil-ət-ē\ *n* — **in·cred·i·bly** \(')in-'kred-ə-blē\ *adv*

in·cre·du·li·ty \ˌin-kri-'d(y)ü-lət-ē\ *n* : the quality or state of being incredulous : DISBELIEF

in·cred·u·lous \(')in-'krej-ə-ləs\ *adj* : feeling or showing an inability to believe something : SKEPTICAL ⟨listened with an *incredulous* smile⟩ — **in·cred·u·lous·ly** *adv*

in·cre·ment \'iŋ-krə-mənt, 'in-\ *n* 1 : a growth especially in quantity or value : INCREASE 2 **a** : something gained or added **b** : one of a series of additions — **in·cre·men·tal** \ˌiŋ-krə-'ment-ᵊl, ˌin-\ *adj*

in·crim·i·nate \in-'krim-ə-ˌnāt\ *vb* **-nat·ed; -nat·ing** 1 : to charge with or show evidence or proof of involvement in a crime or fault : ACCUSE 2 : to cause to appear guilty of or responsible for something ⟨evidence that tends to *incriminate* the defendant⟩ — **in·crim·i·na·tion** \(ˌ)in-ˌkrim-ə-'nā-shən\ *n* — **in·crim·i·na·to·ry** \in-'krim-(ə-)nə-ˌtōr-ē, -ˌtȯr-\ *adj*

incrust *variant of* ENCRUST

in·crus·ta·tion \ˌin-ˌkrəs-'tā-shən\ *n* 1 : the act of encrusting : the state of being encrusted 2 : a hard coating : CRUST

in·cu·bate \'iŋ-kyə-ˌbāt, 'in-\ *vb* **-bat·ed; -bat·ing** 1 : to sit on eggs to hatch them by warmth 2 : to maintain (as bacteria or a chemically active system) under conditions good for development or reaction 3 : to go through the process of incubation

in·cu·ba·tion \ˌiŋ-kyə-'bā-shən, ˌin-\ *n* 1 : the act or process of incubating 2 : INCUBATION PERIOD

incubation period *n* 1 : the period of brooding or incubating required to bring an egg to hatching 2 : the period between infection with a germ and the appearance of the disease or illness it causes

in·cu·ba·tor \'iŋ-kyə-ˌbāt-ər, 'in-\ *n* : one that incubates; *esp* : a piece of equipment providing suitable conditions (as of warmth and moisture) for incubating something ⟨an *incubator* for premature babies⟩

in·cu·bus \'iŋ-kyə-bəs, 'in-\ *n, pl* **in·cu·bi** \-ˌbī, -ˌbē\ *also* **-bus·es** **1** : an evil spirit once believed to lie upon persons in their sleep **2** : NIGHTMARE 1

in·cul·cate \in-'kəl-ˌkāt, 'in-(ˌ)kəl-\ *vb* **-cat·ed; -cat·ing** : to teach by frequent repetition ⟨*inculcated* a deep sense of responsibility in their children⟩ — **in·cul·ca·tion** \ˌin-(ˌ)kəl-'kā-shən\ *n*

in·cum·ben·cy \in-'kəm-bən-sē\ *n, pl* **-cies** : the time during which a person holds an office or position

¹in·cum·bent \in-'kəm-bənt\ *n* : the holder of an office or position

²incumbent *adj* **1** : given as a duty : OBLIGATORY ⟨*incumbent* on us to take action⟩ **2** : being an incumbent ⟨an *incumbent* president⟩ **3** : lying or resting on something else

in·cur \in-'kər\ *vb* **in·curred; in·cur·ring** **1** : to meet with (as an inconvenience) ⟨*incur* expenses⟩ **2** : to bring upon oneself ⟨*incur* punishment⟩ [from Latin *incurrere* "to meet with," literally, "to run into," from *in-* "in, into" and *currere* "to run" — related to CURRENT, OCCUR]

in·cur·able \(ˈ)in-'kyùr-ə-bəl\ *adj* : not capable of being cured — **in·cur·ably** \-blē\ *adv*

in·cu·ri·ous \(ˈ)in-'kyùr-ē-əs\ *adj* : showing no interest or concern : INDIFFERENT — **in·cu·ri·ous·ly** *adv*

in·cur·sion \in-'kər-zhən\ *n* : a sudden usually temporary invasion : RAID

in·cus \'iŋ-kəs\ *n, pl* **in·cu·des** \iŋ-'kyüd-(ˌ)ēz\ : ANVIL 2

in·debt·ed \in-'det-əd\ *adj* : being in debt : owing something (as money or gratitude)

in·debt·ed·ness *n* **1** : the condition of being indebted **2** : something that is owed

in·de·cen·cy \(ˈ)in-'dēs-ən-sē\ *n, pl* **-cies** **1** : lack of decency **2** : an indecent act or word

in·de·cent \(ˈ)in-'dēs-ənt\ *adj* : not decent or proper : COARSE, VULGAR ⟨*indecent* language⟩ — **in·de·cent·ly** *adv*

in·de·ci·sion \ˌin-di-'sizh-ən\ *n* : slowness or trouble in making up one's mind

in·de·ci·sive \ˌin-di-'sī-siv\ *adj* **1** : not decisive or final ⟨an *indecisive* battle⟩ **2** : finding it hard to make decisions ⟨an *indecisive* person⟩ — **in·de·ci·sive·ly** *adv* — **in·de·ci·sive·ness** *n*

in·de·co·rous \(ˈ)in-'dek-ə-rəs; ˌin-di-'kōr-əs, -'kòr-\ *adj* : not proper or in good taste : UNBECOMING ⟨*indecorous* behavior⟩ — **in·de·co·rous·ly** *adv* — **in·de·co·rous·ness** *n*

in·deed \in-'dēd\ *adv* : without any question : TRULY, CERTAINLY — often used interjectionally to express disbelief or surprise

in·de·fat·i·ga·ble \ˌin-di-'fat-i-gə-bəl\ *adj* : capable of working a long time without tiring : TIRELESS ⟨an *indefatigable* teacher⟩ — **in·de·fat·i·ga·bly** \-blē\ *adv*

in·de·fea·si·ble \ˌin-di-'fē-zə-bəl\ *adj* : impossible to abolish ⟨*indefeasible* rights⟩ — **in·de·fea·si·bly** \-'fē-zə-blē\ *adv*

in·de·fen·si·ble \ˌin-di-'fen(t)-sə-bəl\ *adj* : impossible to defend ⟨an *indefensible* position⟩

in·de·fin·able \ˌin-di-'fī-nə-bəl\ *adj* : incapable of being exactly described or analyzed — **in·de·fin·ably** \-blē\ *adv*

in·def·i·nite \(ˈ)in-'def-(ə-)nət\ *adj* **1** : not clear or fixed in meaning or details : VAGUE ⟨an *indefinite* answer⟩ **2** : not certain or limited (as in amount or length) ⟨an *indefinite* period⟩ **3** : typically designating a person or thing that is unidentified or cannot be immediately identified ⟨the *indefinite* articles "a" and "an"⟩ — **indefinite** *n* — **in·def·i·nite·ly** *adv* — **in·def·i·nite·ness** *n*

in·del·i·ble \in-'del-ə-bəl\ *adj* **1** : impossible to erase, remove, or blot out ⟨an *indelible* impression⟩ **2** : making or leaving marks not easily erased ⟨an *indelible* pencil⟩ ⟨*indelible* ink⟩ — **in·del·i·bly** \-blē\ *adv*

in·del·i·ca·cy \(ˈ)in-'del-i-kə-sē\ *n, pl* **-cies** **1** : the quality or state of being indelicate : COARSENESS **2** : something (as an act or word) that is indelicate

in·del·i·cate \(ˈ)in-'del-i-kət\ *adj* : having or showing bad manners or taste : IMMODEST, COARSE — **in·del·i·cate·ly** *adv* — **in·del·i·cate·ness** *n*

in·dem·ni·fy \in-'dem-nə-ˌfī\ *vb* **-fied; -fy·ing** **1** : to insure or protect against loss, damage, or injury **2** : to give something in order to make up for loss, damage, or injury ⟨*indemnify* victims of a disaster⟩ — **in·dem·ni·fi·ca·tion** \-ˌdem-nə-fə-'kā-shən\ *n*

in·dem·ni·ty \in-'dem-nət-ē\ *n, pl* **-ties** **1** : protection from loss, damage, or injury : INSURANCE **2** : freedom from penalty for past offenses **3** : something given to make up for loss, damage, or injury

¹in·dent \in-'dent\ *vb* **1** : to notch the edge of : make jagged ⟨*indented* leaves⟩ **2** : to set in from the margin ⟨*indent* the first line of a paragraph⟩ [Middle English *indenten* "indent," from early French *endenter* (same meaning), from earlier *en-* "to provide with" and *dent* "tooth," from Latin *dent-, dens* "tooth" — related to DENTAL]

²indent *vb* : to form a dent in — **in·dent·er** *n*

in·den·ta·tion \ˌin-ˌden-'tā-shən\ *n* **1 a** : an angular cut in an edge : NOTCH **b** : a deep recess (as in a coastline) **2 a** : the action of indenting : the state of being indented **b** : a blank or empty space produced by indenting **3** : ²DENT 1

in·den·tion \in-'den-chən\ *n* : INDENTATION 2b

¹in·den·ture \in-'den-chər\ *n* **1** : a written agreement : CONTRACT **2** : a contract by which one person is made to work for another for a stated period — often used in plural

²indenture *vb* **-tured; -tur·ing** : to bind by indentures ⟨*indenture* an apprentice⟩

in·de·pen·dence \ˌin-də-'pen-dən(t)s\ *n* : the quality or state of being independent : freedom from outside control or support

Independence Day *n* : a holiday celebrating the beginnings of a nation's independence; *esp* : July 4 observed as a legal holiday in the U.S. in honor of the adoption of the Declaration of Independence in 1776

¹in·de·pen·dent \ˌin-də-'pen-dənt\ *adj* **1** : not being controlled or ruled by another : FREE ⟨an *independent* nation⟩ **2** : not having connections with another : SEPARATE ⟨the same story told by *independent* witnesses⟩ **3** : having or providing enough money to live on without anyone else's help; *also* : not having to work for a living ⟨a person of *independent* means⟩ **4** : not easily influenced ⟨an *independent* mind⟩ **5** : having full meaning in itself and capable of standing alone as a simple sentence : ²MAIN ⟨an *independent* clause⟩ **6** : not belonging to a political party **7** : having probabilities such that whether or not one event takes place does not influence whether or not another event takes place ⟨the outcomes of the tossing of two dice are *independent*⟩ — **in·de·pen·dent·ly** *adv*

²independent *n* : one that is independent; *esp* : a voter who doesn't belong to a political party

independent variable *n* : a variable whose values are specified first or before an experiment is performed and are used to find values of an expression, another variable, or a function that depends on the first variable — compare DEPENDENT VARIABLE

in–depth \(ˌ)in-ˌdepth\ *adj* : covering many or all important points : THOROUGH ⟨an *in-depth* investigation⟩

\ə\ **abut**	\aú\ **out**	\i\ **tip**	\ò\ **saw**	\ú\ **foot**
\ər\ **further**	\ch\ **chin**	\ī\ **life**	\òi\ **coin**	\y\ **yet**
\a\ **mat**	\e\ **pet**	\j\ **job**	\th\ **thin**	\yü\ **few**
\ā\ **take**	\ē\ **easy**	\ŋ\ **sing**	\th\ **this**	\yù\ **cure**
\ä\ **cot, cart**	\g\ **go**	\ō\ **bone**	\ü\ **food**	\zh\ **vision**

in·de·scrib·able \ˌin-di-ˈskrī-bə-bəl\ *adj* : impossible to describe ⟨*indescribable* beauty⟩ — **in·de·scrib·ably** \-blē\ *adv*

in·de·struc·ti·ble \ˌin-di-ˈstrək-tə-bəl\ *adj* : impossible to destroy — **in·de·struc·ti·bil·i·ty** \-ˌstrək-tə-ˈbil-ət-ē\ *n* — **in·de·struc·ti·ble·ness** \-ˈstrək-tə-bəl-nəs\ *n* — **in·de·struc·ti·bly** \-blē\ *adv*

in·de·ter·min·able \ˌin-di-ˈtərm-(ə-)nə-bəl\ *adj* : impossible to decide or find out — **in·de·ter·min·ably** \-blē\ *adv*

in·de·ter·mi·na·cy \ˌin-di-ˈtərm-(ə-)nə-sē\ *n* : the quality or state of being indeterminate

in·de·ter·mi·nate \ˌin-di-ˈtərm-(ə-)nət\ *adj* **1** : not clearly or exactly decided : VAGUE ⟨*indeterminate* plans⟩ **2** : not leading to a clear end or result — **in·de·ter·mi·nate·ly** *adv* — **in·de·ter·mi·nate·ness** *n*

¹in·dex \ˈin-ˌdeks\ *n, pl* **in·dex·es** \-ˌdek-səz\ *or* **in·di·ces** \-də-ˌsēz\ **1 a** : a device (as the pointer on a scale) used to indicate a value or quantity **b** : INDICATION 2 ⟨the price of goods is an *index* of business conditions⟩ **2** : an alphabetical list in a printed work that gives with each item listed the page number where it may be found **3** *pl usually* **indices** : a mathematical figure, letter, or expression (as the exponent *3* in *a³*) showing a power or root of another **4** : a symbol ☞ used to direct attention

²index *vb* **1 a** : to provide with an index ⟨*index* a book⟩ **b** : to list in an index **2** : to serve as an index of — **in·dex·er** *n*

index finger *n* : the finger next to the thumb

index fossil *n* : a fossil that is found over a relatively short span of geological time and can be used in dating formations in which it is found

index of refraction *n* : REFRACTIVE INDEX

in·dia ink \ˌin-dē-ə-\ *n, often cap 1st I* **1** : a black pigment (as lampblack) used in drawing and lettering **2** : a fluid made from india ink

In·di·an \ˈin-dē-ən\ *n* **1 a** : a person born or living in the country of India or the East Indies **b** : a person of Indian ancestry **2 a** : AMERICAN INDIAN **b** : an American Indian language — **Indian** *adj*

Word History Once the name India was applied not only to the region we now call India, but also to an ill-defined area south and west of China. Trade with the distant East brought valuable gold, gems, spices, and silk back to Europe. However, the overland journey to eastern Asia by way of the caravan routes was long and difficult. Christopher Columbus, in the late 15th century, believed that he knew an easier way of reaching the wealth of the East. According to his calculations, the westward distance by sea was less than one-third of the eastward overland route. Columbus was able to test his theory in 1492. He was delighted to find land just about where he had said it would be. He decided that he must have reached the outer islands of "India," although in fact he had landed in the Bahamas. Because of Columbus's mistake, the newly discovered lands were called *India* or the *Indies*. They were still called this even after people realized that they were not the same as the *India* or *Indies* of Asia. Later the islands in the New World came to be called the West Indies in order to tell them apart from the East Indies. But *Indian,* the incorrect name given to the people living in the new "India," remained.

Indian corn *n* **1** : ¹CORN 1 **2** : ¹CORN 2 **3** : ¹CORN 3 **4** : corn that is of a variety having seeds of various colors (as reddish brown, dark purple, and yellow) and is typically used for ornamental purposes

Indian elephant *n* : ELEPHANT b

Indian giver *n, sometimes offensive* : a person who gives something to another and then takes it back or expects something of equal value in return — **Indian giving** *n*

Indian paintbrush *n* **1** : any of a large genus of mostly American herbs that have spikes of flowers with brightly colored bracts **2** : ORANGE HAWKWEED

Indian pipe *n* : a waxy white leafless woodland herb with a single nodding bell-shaped flower on each stem that does not make its own food but lives on dead or decaying organic matter

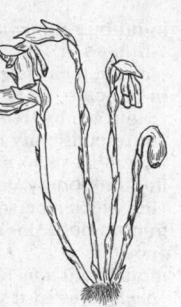

Indian pipe

Indian pudding *n* : a pudding made chiefly of cornmeal, milk, and molasses

Indian summer *n* : a period of mild weather in late autumn or early winter

In·dia paper \ˌin-dē-ə-\ *n* : a thin tough printing paper

india rubber *n, often cap I* : ¹RUBBER 2a

In·dic \ˈin-dik\ *adj* : of, relating to, or being the Indian branch of the Indo-European languages

in·di·cate \ˈin-də-ˌkāt\ *vb* **-cat·ed; -cat·ing** **1 a** : to point out or point to **b** : to be a sign of ⟨flowers *indicating* the arrival of spring⟩ **2** : to state or express briefly : SUGGEST

in·di·ca·tion \ˌin-də-ˈkā-shən\ *n* **1** : the action of indicating **2** : something that indicates : SIGN, SUGGESTION

¹in·dic·a·tive \in-ˈdik-ət-iv\ *adj* **1** : of, relating to, or being the grammatical mood that represents an act or state as a fact that can be known or proved ⟨in "I am here," the verb "am" is in the *indicative* mood⟩ **2** : indicating something ⟨remarks *indicative* of jealousy⟩ — **in·dic·a·tive·ly** *adv*

²indicative *n* : the indicative mood of a verb or a verb in this mood

in·di·ca·tor \ˈin-də-ˌkāt-ər\ *n* **1** : one that indicates: as **a** : a pointer on a dial or scale **b** : ¹GAUGE 2a **2** : a substance used to show visually (as by change of color) the presence of acid or base in a solution

indices *plural of* INDEX

in·dict \in-ˈdīt\ *vb* : to charge with an offense or crime : ACCUSE — **in·dict·able** \-ə-bəl\ *adj*

in·dict·ment \in-ˈdīt-mənt\ *n* **1** : the act or process of indicting **2** : an official written statement charging a person with a crime

in·dif·fer·ence \in-ˈdif-ərn(t)s, -ˈdif-(ə-)rən(t)s\ *n* **1** : lack of feeling for or against something **2** : lack of importance ⟨a matter of *indifference* to them⟩

in·dif·fer·ent \in-ˈdif-ərnt, -ˈdif-(ə-)rənt\ *adj* **1 a** : having or showing no special liking for or dislike of something ⟨the audience was *indifferent*⟩ **b** : not interested or concerned ⟨*indifferent* to the troubles of others⟩ **2** : neither good nor bad : MEDIOCRE ⟨*indifferent* health⟩ **3** : of no special influence or value : not important ⟨that fact is *indifferent* to the argument⟩ — **in·dif·fer·ent·ly** *adv*

in·di·gence \ˈin-di-jən(t)s\ *n* : POVERTY 1

in·dig·e·nous \in-ˈdij-ə-nəs\ *adj* : produced, growing, or living naturally in a particular region or environment ⟨*indigenous* plants⟩ ⟨*indigenous* tribes⟩ — **in·dig·e·nous·ly** *adv*

in·di·gent \ˈin-di-jənt\ *adj* : ¹POOR 1, NEEDY

in·di·gest·ible \ˌin-dī-ˈjes-tə-bəl, -də-\ *adj* : not digestible or easily digested

in·di·ges·tion \ˌin-dī-ˈjes-chən, -də-\ *n* **1** : inability to digest or difficulty in digesting something **2** : a case or attack of indigestion marked especially by a burning or uncomfortable feeling in the upper stomach

in·dig·nant \in-ˈdig-nənt\ *adj* : filled with or expressing indignation — **in·dig·nant·ly** *adv*

in·dig·na·tion \ˌin-dig-ˈnā-shən\ *n* : anger caused by something unjust, unworthy, or mean

in·dig·ni·ty \in-ˈdig-nət-ē\ *n, pl* **-ties** **1** : an act that injures a person's dignity or self-respect : INSULT **2** : humiliating treatment

in·di·go \'in-di-ˌgō\ *n, pl* **-gos** *or* **-goes** **1** : a blue dye made artificially and formerly obtained from plants and especially indigo plants **2** : a deep reddish blue [from an Italian dialect word *indigo* "a blue dye from indigo plants," from Latin *indicum* (same meaning), derived from Greek *indikos* (adjective) "of or relating to India"; so called because the plant dye was first widely produced in India]

indigo plant *n* : any of a genus of plants of the legume family that are a source of indigo

indigo snake *n* : a very large harmless blue-black or brownish snake of the southern U.S. and Texas

in·di·rect \ˌin-də-'rekt, -dī-\ *adj* **1** : not straight or direct ⟨an *indirect* route⟩ **2** : not straightforward ⟨*indirect* methods⟩ ⟨an *indirect* answer⟩ **3** : not having a plainly seen connection ⟨an *indirect* cause⟩ **4** : stating what an original speaker said with changes in wording that make the statement fit grammatically with the rest of the sentence ⟨"that he would call" in "He said that he would call" is in *indirect* discourse⟩ — **in·di·rect·ly** *adv* — **in·di·rect·ness** \-'rek(t)-nəs\ *n*

indirect object *n* : a grammatical object representing the secondary goal of the action of its verb ⟨"me" in "gave me the book" is an *indirect object*⟩

in·dis·creet \ˌin-dis-'krēt\ *adj* : not discreet : IMPRUDENT — **in·dis·creet·ly** *adv*

in·dis·cre·tion \ˌin-dis-'kresh-ən\ *n* **1** : lack of discretion : IMPRUDENCE **2** : an indiscreet act or remark

in·dis·crim·i·nate \ˌin-dis-'krim-(ə-)nət\ *adj* : showing lack of discrimination : not choosing carefully ⟨an *indiscriminate* reader⟩ ⟨*indiscriminate* enthusiasm⟩ — **in·dis·crim·i·nate·ly** *adv*

in·dis·pens·able \ˌin-dis-'pen(t)-sə-bəl\ *adj* : absolutely necessary : ESSENTIAL ⟨an *indispensable* employee⟩ — **in·dis·pens·abil·i·ty** \-ˌpen(t)-sə-'bil-ət-ē\ *n*

in·dis·posed \ˌin-dis-'pōzd\ *adj* **1** : slightly ill **2** : UNWILLING ⟨was *indisposed* to help⟩

in·dis·po·si·tion \(ˌ)in-ˌdis-pə-'zish-ən\ *n* **1** : a slight illness **2** : lack of willingness

in·dis·put·able \ˌin-dis-'pyüt-ə-bəl, (')in-'dis-pyət-\ *adj* : not disputable : UNQUESTIONABLE ⟨*indisputable* proof⟩ — **in·dis·put·ably** \-blē\ *adv*

in·dis·sol·u·ble \ˌin-dis-'äl-yə-bəl\ *adj* : impossible to dissolve, do away with, break up, or decompose ⟨an *indissoluble* contract⟩ — **in·dis·sol·u·bil·i·ty** \-dis-ˌäl-yə-'bil-ət-ē\ *n* — **in·dis·sol·u·bly** \-dis-'äl-yə-blē\ *adv*

in·dis·tinct \ˌin-dis-'tiŋ(k)t\ *adj* : not distinct or clear ⟨*indistinct* figures in the fog⟩ ⟨a far-off *indistinct* light⟩ — **in·dis·tinct·ly** *adv* — **in·dis·tinct·ness** *n*

in·dis·tin·guish·able \ˌin-dis-'tiŋ-gwish-ə-bəl\ *adj* : impossible to distinguish clearly

in·di·um \'in-dē-əm\ *n* : a soft silvery metallic element — see ELEMENT table

¹in·di·vid·u·al \ˌin-də-'vij-(ə-)wəl, -'vij-əl\ *adj* **1** : of or relating to an individual ⟨*individual* traits⟩ **2** : intended for one person ⟨*individual* servings⟩ **3** : ¹PARTICULAR 1, SEPARATE ⟨*individual* copies⟩ **4** : having a special quality : DISTINCT ⟨an *individual* style⟩ **synonyms** *see* CHARACTERISTIC — **in·di·vid·u·al·ly** \-ē\ *adv*

²individual *n* **1** : a single member of a class, species, or collection **2** : a single human being

in·di·vid·u·al·ism \ˌin-də-'vij(ə-)wə-ˌliz-əm, -'vij-ə-ˌliz-\ *n* **1** : a belief that the interests of the individual are of the greatest importance **2** : a belief that the individual has political or economic rights with which the state must not interfere

in·di·vid·u·al·ist \ˌin-də-'vij-(ə-)wə-ləst, -'vij-əl-əst\ *n* **1** : a person who thinks or behaves in an individual or independent way **2** : a supporter of individualism — **individualist** *or* **in·di·vid·u·al·is·tic** \-ˌvij-(ə-)wə-'lis-tik, -ˌvij-ə-'lis-tik\ *adj* — **in·di·vid·u·al·is·ti·cal·ly** \-'lis-ti-k(ə-)lē\ *adv*

in·di·vid·u·al·i·ty \ˌin-də-ˌvij-ə-'wal-ət-ē\ *n, pl* **-ties** **1** : the qualities that make one person or thing different from all others **2** : the quality or state of being an individual

in·di·vid·u·al·ize \ˌin-də-'vij-(ə-)wə-līz, -'vij-ə-ˌliz\ *vb* **-ized; -iz·ing** **1** : to make individual in character **2** : to treat or notice individually **3** : to change to fit the needs of an individual — **in·di·vid·u·al·iza·tion** \-ˌvij-(ə-)wə-lə-'zā-shən, -ˌvij-ə-lə-\ *n*

in·di·vis·i·ble \ˌin-də-'viz-ə-bəl\ *adj* : impossible to divide or separate — **in·di·vis·i·bly** \-blē\ *adv*

In·do-Ar·y·an \ˌin-dō-'ar-ē-ən, -'er-, -'är-yən\ *n* **1** : a member of one of the peoples of the Indian subcontinent speaking an Indo-European language **2** : a branch of the Indo-European language family that includes Hindi and other languages spoken primarily in India, Pakistan, Bangladesh, and Sri Lanka

in·doc·tri·nate \in-'däk-trə-ˌnāt\ *vb* **-nat·ed; -nat·ing** **1** : INSTRUCT 1, TEACH **2** : to teach the ideas, opinions, or beliefs of a particular group — **in·doc·tri·na·tion** \(ˌ)in-ˌdäk-trə-'nā-shən\ *n* — **in·doc·tri·na·tor** \in-'däk-trə-ˌnāt-ər\ *n*

¹In·do-Eu·ro·pe·an \ˌin-dō-ˌyùr-ə-'pē-ən\ *adj* : of, relating to, or being a family of languages including those spoken in most of Europe and in the parts of the world colonized by Europeans since 1500 and also in Persia, the subcontinent of India, and some other parts of Asia

²Indo-European *n* **1** : the Indo-European languages **2** : a member of a people who originally spoke an Indo-European language

in·dole·ace·tic acid \'in-ˌdōl-ə-ˌsēt-ik-\ *n* : a plant hormone that promotes growth and rooting of plants

in·do·lence \'in-də-lən(t)s\ *n* : the quality or state of being indolent : LAZINESS

in·do·lent \'in-də-lənt\ *adj* : disliking effort or activity : LAZY ⟨the heat made us *indolent*⟩ — **in·do·lent·ly** *adv*

in·dom·i·ta·ble \in-'däm-ət-ə-bəl\ *adj* : UNCONQUERABLE ⟨*indomitable* courage⟩ — **in·dom·i·ta·bil·i·ty** \(ˌ)in-ˌdäm-ət-ə-'bil-ət-ē\ *n* — **in·dom·i·ta·ble·ness** \in-'däm-ət-ə-bəl-nəs\ *n* — **in·dom·i·ta·bly** \-blē\ *adv*

In·do·ne·sian \ˌin-də-'nē-zhən, -shən\ *n* **1** : a person born or living in Indonesia **2** : the language based on Malay that is the national language of Indonesia — **Indonesian** *adj*

in·door \ˌin-ˌdō(ə)r, -ˌdȯ(ə)r\ *adj* **1** : of or relating to the interior of a building **2** : done, living, used, or belonging within a building ⟨an *indoor* sport⟩

in·doors \(ˌ)in-'dō(ə)rz, -'dȯ(ə)rz\ *adv* : in or into a building ⟨games to be played *indoors*⟩

indorse, indorsement *variant of* ENDORSE, ENDORSEMENT

in·du·bi·ta·ble \(')in-'d(y)ü-bət-ə-bəl\ *adj* : impossible to doubt : beyond question — **in·du·bi·ta·bly** \-blē\ *adv*

in·duce \in-'d(y)üs\ *vb* **in·duced; in·duc·ing** **1** : to lead on to do something : PERSUADE **2** : BRING ABOUT, CAUSE ⟨an illness *induced* by overwork⟩ **3** : to reach (a general conclusion) based on particular facts or examples **4** : to produce (as an electric current) by induction — **in·duc·er** *n* — **in·duc·ible** \-'d(y)ü-sə-bəl\ *adj*

in·duce·ment \in-'d(y)ü-smənt\ *n* **1** : the act of inducing **2** : something that induces ⟨a money-back guarantee is an *inducement* to buy⟩

in·duct \in-'dəkt\ *vb* **1** : to place in office : INSTALL **2** : to draft into military service — **in·duct·ee** \(ˌ)in-ˌdək-'tē\ *n*

in·duc·tion \in-'dək-shən\ *n* **1 a** : the act or process of inducting (as into office) **b** : a first experience of something : INITIATION **c** : the procedure by which a civilian is inducted into military service **2** : reasoning from particular examples to a general conclusion **3 a** : the act of causing or bringing on or about **b** : the process of producing an electrical or magnetic effect through the influence of a nearby magnet, electric current, or electrically charged body

in·duc·tion coil *n* : a device that changes a low steady voltage into a repeating high voltage by induction

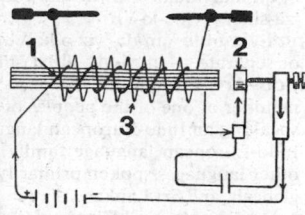

in·duc·tive \in-'dək-tiv\ *adj* : relating to, using, or based on induction — **in·duc·tive·ly** *adv*

in·duc·tor \in-'dək-tər\ *n* **1** : one that inducts **2** : a part of an electrical device that acts upon another or is itself acted upon by induction

induction coil: *1* primary coil, *2* interrupter, *3* secondary coil

in·dulge \in-'dəlj\ *vb* **in·dulged; in·dulg·ing 1** : to give in to one's own or another's desires : HUMOR ⟨*indulged* their grandchildren's whims⟩ **2** : to allow oneself the pleasure of having or doing something ⟨decided to *indulge* in ice cream⟩ — **in·dulg·er** *n*

in·dul·gence \in-'dəl-jən(t)s\ *n* **1** : the act of indulging : the state of being indulgent **2** : an indulgent act **3** : something indulged in

in·dul·gent \in-'dəl-jənt\ *adj* : indulging or showing indulgence : LENIENT ⟨an *indulgent* parent⟩ — **in·dul·gent·ly** *adv*

in·du·rat·ed \'in-d(y)ə-ˌrāt-əd\ *adj* : having become firm or hard ⟨*indurated* tissue⟩ ⟨*indurated* clay⟩

in·dus·tri·al \in-'dəs-trē-əl\ *adj* **1** : of, relating to, or engaged in industry **2** : having highly developed industries ⟨an *industrial* nation⟩ **3** : coming from or used in industry ⟨*industrial* diamonds⟩ — **in·dus·tri·al·ly** \-trē-ə-lē\ *adv*

industrial arts *n sing or pl* : a subject taught in elementary and secondary schools that aims at developing skills necessary for working with tools and machines

industrial engineering *n* : engineering that deals with the design, improvement, and installation of systems of people, materials, equipment, and energy — **industrial engineer** *n*

in·dus·tri·al·ist \in-'dəs-trē-ə-ləst\ *n* : an owner or manager of an industry : MANUFACTURER

in·dus·tri·al·ize \in-'dəs-trē-ə-ˌlīz\ *vb* **-ized; -iz·ing** : to make or become industrial ⟨*industrialize* an agricultural region⟩ — **in·dus·tri·al·i·za·tion** \-ˌdəs-trē-ə-lə-'zā-shən\ *n*

industrial revolution *n* : a rapid major change in an economy (as in England in the late 18th century) marked by the general introduction of power-driven machinery

in·dus·tri·ous \in-'dəs-trē-əs\ *adj* : constantly or regularly active or occupied ⟨an *industrious* farmer⟩ **synonyms** see BUSY — **in·dus·tri·ous·ly** *adv* — **in·dus·tri·ous·ness** *n*

in·dus·try \'in-(ˌ)dəs-trē\ *n, pl* **-tries 1** : the habit of working hard and steadily : DILIGENCE **2** : steady labor ⟨lived by their own *industry*⟩ **3 a** : the businesses that provide a particular product or service ⟨the steel *industry*⟩ ⟨the tourist *industry*⟩ **b** : manufacturing activity ⟨commerce and *industry*⟩

¹**ine·bri·ate** \in-'ē-brē-ət\ *n* : a person who is drunk; *esp* : DRUNKARD

²**ine·bri·ate** \in-'ē-brē-ət, -ˌāt\ *adj* : INEBRIATED

ine·bri·at·ed \in-'ē-brē-ˌāt-əd\ *adj* : affected by or as if by alcohol : being intoxicated — **ine·bri·a·tion** \-ˌē-brē-'ā-shən\ *n*

in·ed·i·ble \(')in-'ed-ə-bəl\ *adj* : not fit or safe for eating ⟨*inedible* mushrooms⟩

in·ef·fa·ble \(')in-'ef-ə-bəl\ *adj* : impossible to express : INEXPRESSIBLE ⟨*ineffable* joy⟩ — **in·ef·fa·bil·i·ty** \(ˌ)in-ˌef-ə-'bil-ət-ē\ *n* — **in·ef·fa·bly** \(')in-'ef-ə-blē\ *adv*

in·ef·fec·tive \ˌin-ə-'fek-tiv\ *adj* **1** : not producing the desired effect ⟨an *ineffective* law⟩ **2** : not performing as well as expected or needed ⟨an *ineffective* leader⟩ — **in·ef·fec·tive·ly** *adv* — **in·ef·fec·tive·ness** *n*

in·ef·fec·tu·al \ˌin-ə-'fek-chə(-wə)l, -'feksh-wəl\ *adj* **1** : not producing the proper or usual effect ⟨an *ineffectual* attempt⟩ **2** : INEFFECTIVE 2 — **in·ef·fec·tu·al·ly** \-'fek-chə(-wə)-lē, -'feksh-wə-\ *adv* — **in·ef·fec·tu·al·ness** *n*

in·ef·fi·cien·cy \ˌin-ə-'fish-ən-sē\ *n, pl* **-cies 1** : the quality or state of being inefficient **2** : something that is inefficient

in·ef·fi·cient \ˌin-ə-'fish-ənt\ *adj* **1** : not producing the effect expected or desired ⟨*inefficient* regulations⟩ **2** : wasteful of time or energy ⟨*inefficient* procedures⟩; *esp* : accomplishing little relative to the time spent or effort expended ⟨an *inefficient* worker⟩ — **in·ef·fi·cient·ly** *adv*

in·elas·tic \ˌin-ə-'las-tik\ *adj* : not elastic : slow to respond to changing conditions — **in·elas·tic·i·ty** \ˌin-i-ˌlas-'tis-ət-ē\ *n*

in·el·e·gant \(')in-'el-i-gənt\ *adj* : lacking in grace or good taste — **in·el·e·gant·ly** *adv*

in·el·i·gi·ble \(')in-'el-ə-jə-bəl\ *adj* : not qualified to be chosen or used — **in·el·i·gi·bil·i·ty** \(ˌ)in-ˌel-ə-jə-'bil-ət-ē\ *n* — **ineligible** *n*

in·ept \in-'ept\ *adj* **1** : not suited for the occasion : INAPPROPRIATE ⟨an *inept* remark⟩ **2** : lacking in skill or ability : INCOMPETENT — **in·ep·ti·tude** \-'ep-tə-ˌt(y)üd\ *n* — **in·ept·ly** \-'ep-(t)lē\ *adv* — **in·ept·ness** \-'ep(t)-nəs\ *n*

in·equal·i·ty \ˌin-i-'kwäl-ət-ē\ *n, pl* **-ties 1** : the quality of being unequal **2** : an instance of being unequal (as an irregularity in a surface) **3** : a statement in mathematics or logic that two quantities usually separated by a special sign (as <, >, or ≠ respectively meaning "is less than," "is greater than," or "is not equal to") are not equal

in·eq·ui·ta·ble \(')in-'ek-wət-ə-bəl\ *adj* : not equitable : UNFAIR — **in·eq·ui·ta·bly** \-blē\ *adv*

in·eq·ui·ty \(')in-'ek-wət-ē\ *n, pl* **-ties 1** : INJUSTICE 1, UNFAIRNESS **2** : an instance of injustice or unfairness

in·ert \in-'ərt\ *adj* : unable or slow to move, act, or react ⟨*inert* ingredients in cough medicine⟩ ⟨*inert* gas⟩ — **in·ert·ly** *adv* — **in·ert·ness** *n*

in·er·tia \in-'ər-shə, -shē-ə\ *n* **1** : a property of matter by which it remains at rest or in unchanging motion unless acted on by some external force **2** : a tendency not to move or change — **in·er·tial** \-shəl\ *adj*

inertial guidance *n* : guidance (as of an aircraft) by automatic devices that respond to changes in speed or direction

in·es·cap·able \ˌin-ə-'skā-pə-bəl\ *adj* : impossible to escape or avoid — **in·es·cap·ably** \-blē\ *adv*

in·es·ti·ma·ble \(')in-'es-tə-mə-bəl\ *adj* **1** : impossible to estimate ⟨*inestimable* damage⟩ **2** : too valuable or excellent to be measured or appreciated — **in·es·ti·ma·bly** \-blē\ *adv*

in·ev·i·ta·ble \in-'ev-ət-ə-bəl\ *adj* : impossible to avoid or evade : sure to happen : CERTAIN ⟨the *inevitable* result⟩ — **in·ev·i·ta·bil·i·ty** \(ˌ)in-ˌev-ət-ə-'bil-ət-ē\ *n* — **in·ev·i·ta·ble·ness** \(')in-'ev-ət-ə-bəl-nəs\ *n*

in·ev·i·ta·bly \-blē\ *adv* **1** : in an inevitable way ⟨the hero *inevitably* defeats the enemy⟩ **2** : as is to be expected ⟨*inevitably*, it rained⟩

in·ex·act \ˌin-ig-'zakt\ *adj* : not exactly correct or true : INACCURATE ⟨*inexact* measurements⟩ — **in·ex·act·ly** \-'zak-(t)lē\ *adv* — **in·ex·act·ness** \-'zak(t)-nəs\ *n*

in·ex·cus·able \ˌin-ik-'skyü-zə-bəl\ *adj* : too bad to be excused : not justifiable ⟨*inexcusable* rudeness⟩ — **in·ex·cus·ably** \-blē\ *adv*

in·ex·haust·ible \ˌin-ig-ˈzȯ-stə-bəl\ *adj* **1** : impossible to use up ⟨an *inexhaustible* supply⟩ **2** : impossible to tire out ⟨an *inexhaustible* worker⟩ — **in·ex·haust·ibil·i·ty** \-ˌzȯ-stə-ˈbil-ət-ē\ *n* — **in·ex·haust·ibly** \-ˈzȯ-stə-blē\ *adv*

in·ex·o·ra·ble \(ˈ)in-ˈeks-(ə-)rə-bəl\ *adj* : RELENTLESS — **in·ex·o·ra·bil·i·ty** \(ˌ)in-ˌeks-(ə-)rə-ˈbil-ət-ē\ *n* — **in·ex·o·ra·ble·ness** \(ˈ)in-ˈeks-(ə-)rə-bəl-nəs\ *n* — **in·ex·o·ra·bly** \-blē\ *adv*

in·ex·pe·di·ent \ˌin-ik-ˈspēd-ē-ənt\ *adj* : not suited to bring about a desired result : UNWISE ⟨an *inexpedient* decision⟩ — **in·ex·pe·di·ent·ly** *adv*

in·ex·pen·sive \ˌin-ik-ˈspen(t)-siv\ *adj* : not high in price : CHEAP — **in·ex·pen·sive·ly** *adv* — **in·ex·pen·sive·ness** *n*

in·ex·pe·ri·ence \ˌin-ik-ˈspir-ē-ən(t)s\ *n* : lack of experience — **in·ex·pe·ri·enced** \-ən(t)st\ *adj*

in·ex·pert \(ˈ)in-ˈek-ˌspərt, ˌin-ik-ˈspərt\ *adj* : not expert : UNSKILLED — **in·ex·pert·ly** *adv* — **in·ex·pert·ness** *n*

in·ex·pli·ca·ble \ˌin-ik-ˈsplik-ə-bəl, (ˈ)in-ˈek-(ˌ)splik-\ *adj* : impossible to explain ⟨an *inexplicable* mystery⟩ — **in·ex·pli·ca·bil·i·ty** \ˌin-ik-ˌsplik-ə-ˈbil-ət-ē, (ˌ)in-ˌek-(ˌ)splik-\ *n* — **in·ex·pli·ca·bly** \-blē\ *adv*

in·ex·press·ible \ˌin-ik-ˈspres-ə-bəl\ *adj* : impossible to express : INDESCRIBABLE ⟨*inexpressible* joy⟩ — **in·ex·press·ibly** \-blē\ *adv*

in·ex·pres·sive \ˌin-ik-ˈspres-iv\ *adj* : lacking expression or meaning ⟨an *inexpressive* face⟩ — **in·ex·pres·sive·ly** *adv* — **in·ex·pres·sive·ness** *n*

in·ex·tin·guish·able \ˌin-ik-ˈstiŋ-(g)wish-ə-bəl\ *adj* : impossible to extinguish ⟨an *inextinguishable* desire⟩

in·ex·tri·ca·ble \ˌin-ik-ˈstrik-ə-bəl, (ˈ)in-ˈek-(ˌ)strik-\ *adj* : impossible to untangle or to get free from ⟨an *inextricable* knot⟩ — **in·ex·tri·ca·bly** \-blē\ *adv*

in·fal·li·ble \(ˈ)in-ˈfal-ə-bəl\ *adj* **1** : not capable of being wrong : UNERRING ⟨an *infallible* memory⟩ **2** : not likely to fail : SURE ⟨an *infallible* remedy⟩ — **in·fal·li·bil·i·ty** \(ˌ)in-ˌfal-ə-ˈbil-ət-ē\ *n* — **in·fal·li·bly** \(ˈ)in-ˈfal-ə-blē\ *adv*

in·fa·mous \ˈin-fə-məs\ *adj* **1** : having an evil reputation ⟨an *infamous* traitor⟩ **2** : causing or bringing an evil reputation : DETESTABLE ⟨an *infamous* crime⟩ — **in·fa·mous·ly** *adv*

in·fa·my \ˈin-fə-mē\ *n, pl* **-mies** **1** : an evil reputation **2 a** : an infamous act **b** : the state of being infamous

in·fan·cy \ˈin-fən-sē\ *n, pl* **-cies** **1** : early childhood **2** : a beginning or early period of existence

in·fant \ˈin-fənt\ *n* : a child in the first period of life — **infant** *adj*

in·fan·tile \ˈin-fən-ˌtīl, -tᵊl, -ˌtēl\ *adj* : of, relating to, or resembling infants or infancy; *also* : CHILDISH

infantile paralysis *n* : POLIOMYELITIS

in·fan·til·ism \ˈin-fən-ˌtīl-ˌiz-əm, -tə-ˌliz-; in-ˈfan-tᵊl-ˌiz-\ *n* : childish qualities or behavior in an adult

in·fan·try \ˈin-fən-trē\ *n, pl* **-tries** : a branch of an army made up of soldiers trained, armed, and equipped to fight on foot

> **Word History** In the Middle Ages in France, a young soldier from a good family who was not yet a knight was called *enfant,* which means "child." Likewise, in Italy a soldier moving on foot behind a knight riding a horse was an *infante.* Later, Italian foot soldiers as a group became known as *infanteria,* which was borrowed into French as *infanterie* and into English as *infantry.* [from early French *infanterie* and early Italian *infanteria,* both meaning "infantry," from early Italian *infante* "infant, boy, foot soldier," from Latin *infans* "infant"]

in·fan·try·man \-mən\ *n* : a soldier of the infantry

in·fat·u·ate \in-ˈfach-ə-ˌwāt\ *vb* **-at·ed; -at·ing** : to fill with a foolish or excessive love or admiration — **in·fat·u·a·tion** \in-ˌfach-ə-ˈwā-shən\ *n*

in·fect \in-ˈfekt\ *vb* **1** : to contaminate with a disease-producing substance or germ ⟨*infected* bedding⟩ **2 a** : to pass a germ or disease to ⟨coughing people who *infect*

others⟩ **b** : to enter and cause disease in ⟨bacteria that *infect* wounds⟩ **c** : to become copied to ⟨a virus has *infected* the computer⟩ **3** : to cause to share one's feelings ⟨*infected* everyone with his enthusiasm⟩ — **in·fec·tor** \-ˈfek-tər\ *n*

in·fec·tion \in-ˈfek-shən\ *n* **1** : an act or process of infecting **2 a** : the state produced by something infectious (as a germ or parasite) living in or on a suitable host **b** : a disease resulting from infection : INFECTIOUS DISEASE **3 a** : something (as a bacterium or virus) infectious **b** : material contaminated with something infectious

in·fec·tious \in-ˈfek-shəs\ *adj* **1 a** : capable of causing infection ⟨*infectious* viruses⟩ **b** : capable of being spread by infection ⟨*infectious* arthritis⟩ **2** : capable of being easily spread ⟨*infectious* laughter⟩ — **in·fec·tious·ly** *adv*

infectious disease *n* : a disease caused by the presence, growth, and increase in numbers of germs in the body

in·fec·tive \in-ˈfek-tiv\ *adj* : producing or able to produce infection — **in·fec·tiv·i·ty** \(ˌ)in-ˌfek-ˈtiv-ət-ē\ *n*

in·fe·lic·i·tous \ˌin-fi-ˈlis-ət-əs\ *adj* : not appropriate : not suitably chosen for the occasion ⟨an *infelicitous* remark⟩ — **in·fe·lic·i·tous·ly** *adv*

in·fe·lic·i·ty \ˌin-fi-ˈlis-ət-ē\ *n, pl* **-ties** **1** : a lack of suitability **2** : an inappropriate act or expression

in·fer \in-ˈfər\ *vb* **in·ferred; in·fer·ring** **1** : to arrive at as a conclusion **2** : ¹GUESS 1, SURMISE **3** : IMPLY 2 — **in·fer·able** \-ə-bəl\ *adj*

in·fer·ence \ˈin-f(ə-)rən(t)s\ *n* **1** : the act or process of inferring **2** : something inferred

¹**in·fe·ri·or** \in-ˈfir-ē-ər\ *adj* **1** : situated lower down **2** : of low or lower degree or rank **3** : of little or less importance, value, or merit

²**inferior** *n* : an inferior person or thing

in·fe·ri·or·i·ty \(ˌ)in-ˌfir-ē-ˈȯr-ət-ē, -ˈär-\ *n, pl* **-ties** **1** : the state of being inferior **2** : a sense of being inferior

inferiority complex *n* : a personal sense of being inferior that may be expressed by behavior that is either timid or aggressive

inferior planet *n* : a planet (as Venus) whose orbit is closer to the sun than that of Earth

inferior vena cava *n* : a large vein that is a branch of the vena cava and returns blood to the heart from the lower parts of the body including the legs and the internal organs below the lungs

in·fer·nal \in-ˈfərn-ᵊl\ *adj* **1** : of or relating to hell **2** : very bad or unpleasant ⟨an *infernal* nuisance⟩ — **in·fer·nal·ly** \-ᵊl-ē\ *adv*

in·fer·no \in-ˈfər-nō\ *n, pl* **-nos** : a place or state that resembles or suggests hell especially in great heat or raging fire [from Italian *inferno* "underworld, hell," from Latin *infernus* (same meaning), from earlier *infernus* (adjective) "lying beneath, in the lower regions"]

in·fer·tile \(ˈ)in-ˈfərt-ᵊl\ *adj* : not fertile or productive : BARREN — **in·fer·til·i·ty** \ˌin-(ˌ)fər-ˈtil-ət-ē\ *n*

in·fest \in-ˈfest\ *vb* **1** : to spread or swarm in or over in a troublesome manner ⟨a neighborhood *infested* with crime⟩ ⟨shark-*infested* waters⟩ **2** : to live in or on as a parasite ⟨horses *infested* with worms⟩ — **in·fes·ta·tion** \ˌin-ˌfes-ˈtā-shən\ *n*

in·fi·del \ˈin-fəd-ᵊl, -fə-ˌdel\ *n* : a person who does not believe in a particular religion — **infidel** *adj*

in·fi·del·i·ty \ˌin-fə-ˈdel-ət-ē, -(ˌ)fī-\ *n, pl* **-ties** **1** : lack of faith in a religion **2** : unfaithfulness especially to one's husband or wife

\ə\ **abut**	\au̇\ **out**	\i\ **tip**	\ȯ\ **saw**	\u̇\ **foot**
\ər\ **further**	\ch\ **chin**	\ī\ **life**	\ȯi\ **coin**	\y\ **yet**
\a\ **mat**	\e\ **pet**	\j\ **job**	\th\ **thin**	\yü\ **few**
\ā\ **take**	\ē\ **easy**	\ŋ\ **sing**	\th\ **this**	\yu̇\ **cure**
\ä\ **cot, cart**	\g\ **go**	\ō\ **bone**	\ü\ **food**	\zh\ **vision**

in·field \'in-ˌfēld\ *n* **1 a** : the area of a baseball field enclosed by the three bases and home plate **b** : the players positioned in the infield **2** : the area enclosed by a racetrack or running track — **in·field·er** \-ˌfēl-dər\ *n*

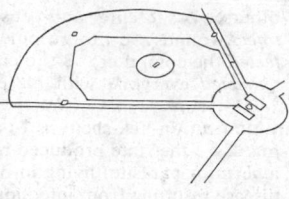

infield 1a

in·fil·trate \in-'fil-ˌtrāt, 'in-(ˌ)fil-\ *vb* **-trat·ed; -trat·ing** **1** : to pass into or through by filtering **2** : to enter or become established gradually or secretly — **in·fil·tra·tion** \ˌin-(ˌ)fil-'trā-shən\ *n* — **in·fil·tra·tor** \in-'fil-ˌtrāt-ər, 'in-(ˌ)fil-\ *n*

¹in·fi·nite \'in-fə-nət\ *adj* **1** : being without limits of any kind : ENDLESS ⟨*infinite* space⟩ **2** : seeming to be without limits : VAST ⟨*infinite* patience⟩ ⟨*infinite* wealth⟩ **3 a** : lying or being beyond or being larger than any number no matter how large ⟨the number of positive numbers is *infinite*⟩ **b** : having an infinite number of elements or terms ⟨an *infinite* set⟩ — **in·fi·nite·ly** *adv*

²infinite *n* : something that is infinite (as in number)

in·fin·i·tes·i·mal \(ˌ)in-ˌfin-ə-'tes-ə-məl\ *adj* : too small to be measurable — **in·fin·i·tes·i·mal·ly** \-mə-lē\ *adv*

in·fin·i·tive \in-'fin-ət-iv\ *n* : a verb form serving as a noun or as a modifier and at the same time taking objects and adverbial modifiers ⟨"carry" in "help them carry it" and "to do" in "they have nothing to do" are *infinitives*⟩ — **infinitive** *adj*

in·fin·i·ty \in-'fin-ət-ē\ *n, pl* **-ties** **1 a** : the quality of being infinite **b** : a space, quantity, or period of time that is without limit **2** : an indefinitely great number or amount **3** : a point infinitely far away [Middle English *infinite* "the quality of having no limit," from early French *infinité* (same meaning), derived from Latin *infinitus* (adjective) "having no limit," from *in-* "not" and *finitus,* past participle of *finire* "to limit, bring to an end," from *finis* "end, limit" — related to DEFINE, FINAL, FINISH]

in·firm \in-'fərm\ *adj* : weak or frail in body (as from age or disease)

in·fir·ma·ry \in-'fərm-(ə-)rē\ *n, pl* **-ries** : a place (as in a school or camp) for the care of sick or injured people; *also* : HOSPITAL

in·fir·mi·ty \in-'fər-mət-ē\ *n, pl* **-ties** **1** : the quality or state of being infirm **2** : AILMENT, DISEASE

in·flame \in-'flām\ *vb* **in·flamed; in·flam·ing** **1** : to set on fire : KINDLE **2** : to excite to too much action or feeling; *esp* : to make angry **3** : to cause to redden or grow hot from anger or excitement **4** : to cause inflammation in (bodily tissue) **5** : to become affected with inflammation

in·flam·ma·ble \in-'flam-ə-bəl\ *adj* **1** : FLAMMABLE **2** : easily inflamed : EXCITABLE — **in·flam·ma·bil·i·ty** \-ˌflam-ə-'bil-ət-ē\ *n* — **in·flam·ma·bly** \-'flam-ə-blē\ *adv*

in·flam·ma·tion \ˌin-flə-'mā-shən\ *n* **1** : the act of inflaming : the state of being inflamed **2** : a bodily response to injury in which heat, redness, pain, swelling, and more than the usual amount of blood are present in the area affected

in·flam·ma·to·ry \in-'flam-ə-ˌtōr-ē, -ˌtȯr-\ *adj* **1** : stirring up anger, disorder, or rebellion ⟨*inflammatory* speeches⟩ **2** : causing or accompanied by inflammation ⟨*inflammatory* diseases⟩

in·flate \in-'flāt\ *vb* **in·flat·ed; in·flat·ing** **1** : to swell or fill with air or gas ⟨*inflate* a balloon⟩ **2** : to increase abnormally ⟨*inflated* prices⟩ **synonyms** see EXPAND — **in·flat·able** \-ə-bəl\ *adj*

in·flat·ed \in-'flāt-əd\ *adj* : hollow and stretched or swelled ⟨*inflated* pods of a plant⟩

in·fla·tion \in-'flā-shən\ *n* **1** : an act of inflating : the state of being inflated **2** : a continual increase in the price of goods and services

in·fla·tion·ary \in-'flā-shə-ˌner-ē\ *adj* : of, relating to, or causing inflation ⟨an *inflationary* policy⟩

in·flect \in-'flekt\ *vb* **1** : to change a word by inflection **2** : to change the pitch of the voice

in·flec·tion \in-'flek-shən\ *n* **1** : a change in the pitch or tone of a person's voice **2** : the change in the form of a word showing its case, gender, number, person, tense, mood, voice, or comparison — **in·flec·tion·al** \-shnəl, -shən-ᵊl\ *adj*

in·flex·i·ble \(')in-'flek-sə-bəl\ *adj* **1** : not easily bent or twisted : RIGID, STIFF **2** : not easily influenced or persuaded : FIRM **3** : incapable of change : UNALTERABLE ⟨*inflexible* laws⟩ — **in·flex·i·bil·i·ty** \(ˌ)in-ˌflek-sə-'bil-ət-ē\ *n* — **in·flex·i·bly** \(')in-'flek-sə-blē\ *adv*

in·flict \in-'flikt\ *vb* **1** : to give by or as if by striking ⟨*inflict* a wound⟩ **2** : to cause (something damaging or painful) to be endured ⟨*inflict* punishment⟩ — **in·flic·tion** \-'flik-shən\ *n*

in·flo·res·cence \ˌin-flə-'res-ᵊn(t)s\ *n* **1 a** : the pattern of development and arrangement of flowers on a stalk **b** : a flowering stalk with all its parts; *also* : a flower cluster or sometimes a flower that grows alone **2** : the forming and unfolding of blossoms

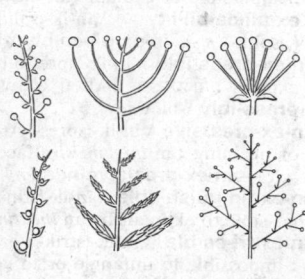

inflorescence 1a

in·flow \'in-ˌflō\ *n* **1** : the act of flowing in **2** : something that flows in

¹in·flu·ence \'in-ˌflü-ən(t)s\ *n* **1** : the act or power of producing an effect indirectly or without apparent use of force or exercise of command **2** : dishonest interference with authority for personal gain **3** : a person or thing that influences [Middle English *influence* "a fluid formerly believed to flow from the stars to cause people to act a certain way," from early French *influence* (same meaning), derived from Latin *influere* "to flow in," from *in-* "in" and *fluere* "to flow" — related to FLUID] — **under the influence** : affected by alcohol

²influence *vb* **-enced; -enc·ing** : to have an influence on : affect by influence — **in·flu·enc·er** *n*

in·flu·en·tial \ˌin-(ˌ)flü-'en-chəl\ *adj* : having influence — **in·flu·en·tial·ly** \-'ench-(ə-)lē\ *adv*

in·flu·en·za \ˌin-(ˌ)flü-'en-zə\ *n* **1** : a very contagious virus disease with fever, exhaustion, severe aches and pains, and inflammation of the respiratory tract **2** : any of various diseases of human beings or domestic animals that are usually caused by viruses and are typically marked by fever and respiratory symptoms

Word History Originally the Italian word *influenza* meant what the similar-sounding word in English, *influence,* means: "the act or power of producing an effect indirectly." But it also had the Latin meaning of "an invisible fluid through which the stars and planets control and direct the earth and things and people on it." When epidemics raged through Europe, no one knew what the real cause was. People blamed them on evil stars working through the invisible fluid, or influence. For this reason the Italians called the disease *influenza.* In 1743 an epidemic very much like our modern flu began in Rome and spread. That was when the Italian word was borrowed into English. *Flu* is a shortened form of *influenza.* [from Italian *influenza,* literally "influence," from Latin *influentia* "influence," derived from earlier *influere* "to flow in," from *in-* "in, into" and *fluere* "to flow"]

in·flux \'in-ˌfləks\ *n* : a flowing or coming in : INFLOW

in·form \in-'fȯ(ə)rm\ *vb* **1** : to let a person know something : TELL **2** : to give information so as to accuse or cause suspicion ⟨*inform* against them to the police⟩

in·for·mal \(')in-'fȯr-məl\ *adj* **1** : not formal ⟨an *informal* party⟩ **2** : suited for ordinary or everyday use ⟨*informal* clothes⟩ — **in·for·mal·i·ty** \ˌin-(ˌ)fȯr-'mal-ət-ē, -fər-\ *n* — **in·for·mal·ly** \(')in-'fȯr-mə-lē\ *adv*

in·for·mant \in-'fȯr-mənt\ *n* : INFORMER

in·for·ma·tion \ˌin-fər-'mā-shən\ *n* **1** : the giving or receiving of knowledge or intelligence **2 a** : knowledge obtained from investigation, study, or instruction **b** : knowledge of a particular event or situation : NEWS **c** : a characteristic or quality (as of DNA or a computer program) that stands for, expresses, or tells about one group of things or ways of doing things instead of others **3** : the quality of something (as DNA or a computer program) that represents a specific choice between a number of possible choices — **in·for·ma·tion·al** \-shnəl, -shən-°l\ *adj*

information superhighway *n* : INTERNET

information technology *n* : the technology involving the development, maintenance, and use of computer systems, software, and networks for the processing and distribution of data

in·for·ma·tive \in-'fȯr-mət-iv\ *adj* : providing knowledge : INSTRUCTIVE ⟨an *informative* book⟩ — **in·for·ma·tive·ly** *adv* — **in·for·ma·tive·ness** *n*

in·formed \in-'fȯ(ə)rmd\ *adj* : having or based on information ⟨*informed* sources⟩ ⟨an *informed* decision⟩

in·form·er \in-'fȯr-mər\ *n* : someone who informs; *esp* : a person who informs against someone else

infra- *prefix* : below in a scale or series ⟨*infra*red⟩ [from Latin *infra* "below, underneath"]

in·frac·tion \in-'frak-shən\ *n* : an act of violating something : VIOLATION

in·fra·red \ˌin-frə-'red, -(ˌ)frä-\ *adj* : being, relating to, producing, or using rays like light but lying outside the visible spectrum at its red end ⟨*infrared* radiation⟩ — **infrared** *n*

in·fra·struc·ture \'in-frə-ˌstrək-chər\ *n* **1** : the underlying foundation or basic framework (as of a system or organization) **2** : the system of public works of a country, state, or region; *also* : the resources (as people, buildings, or equipment) required for an activity

in·fre·quent \(')in-'frē-kwənt\ *adj* **1** : seldom happening or occurring **2** : not placed, made, or done at frequent intervals ⟨made *infrequent* stops⟩ — **in·fre·quent·ly** *adv*

in·fringe \in-'frinj\ *vb* **in·fringed; in·fring·ing 1** : to fail to obey or act in agreement with : VIOLATE ⟨*infringe* a treaty⟩ **2** : ENCROACH 1 ⟨*infringe* on a person's rights⟩ — **in·fringe·ment** \-mənt\ *n* — **in·fring·er** *n*

in·fu·ri·ate \in-'fyu̇r-ē-ˌāt\ *vb* **-at·ed; -at·ing** : to make furious : ENRAGE — **in·fu·ri·at·ing·ly** \-ˌāt-iŋ-lē\ *adv* — **in·fu·ri·a·tion** \-ˌfyu̇r-ē-'ā-shən\ *n*

in·fuse \in-'fyüz\ *vb* **in·fused; in·fus·ing 1** : to put in as if by pouring ⟨*infused* courage into her followers⟩ **2** : to steep without boiling ⟨*infuse* tea⟩

in·fu·sion \in-'fyü-zhən\ *n* **1** : the act or process of infusing ⟨an *infusion* of new ideas⟩ **2** : a product obtained by infusing ⟨a strong *infusion* of tea⟩

¹-ing \iŋ, ēŋ; *in some dialects usually & in other dialects informally* in, ēn, ən\ *vb suffix or adj suffix* — used to form the present participle ⟨sail*ing*⟩ and sometimes to form an adjective not derived from a verb ⟨swashbuckl*ing*⟩ [Middle English *-ing* "-ing," probably from the noun suffix *-ing*]

²-ing *n suffix* **1** : action or process ⟨runn*ing*⟩ ⟨meet*ing*⟩ **2** : product or result of an action or process ⟨an engrav*ing*⟩ ⟨earn*ings*⟩ **3** : something used in or connected with making or doing ⟨bedd*ing*⟩ ⟨roof*ing*⟩ [Old English *-ing, -ung* "one belonging to or of a (specified) kind"]

in·ge·nious \in-'jēn-yəs\ *adj* : having or showing ingenuity : very clever ⟨an *ingenious* plan⟩ [from early French *ingenieus* "calling for or showing special intelligence or cleverness," from Latin *ingeniosus* (same meaning), from *ingenium* "natural ability or desire to do something, inborn ability," from *in* "in" and *-genium*, from *gignere* "to father, beget" — related to ENGINE, GENIUS, ¹GIN] — **in·ge·nious·ly** *adv* — **in·ge·nious·ness** *n*

in·ge·nue *or* **in·gé·nue** \'an-jə-ˌnü, 'än-\ *n* : an innocent girl or young woman or an actress playing such a person

in·ge·nu·ity \ˌin-jə-'n(y)ü-ət-ē\ *n, pl* **-ities 1** : skill or cleverness in discovering, inventing, or planning **2** : an ingenious device

in·gen·u·ous \in-'jen-yə-wəs\ *adj* : showing innocent or childlike simplicity and straightforwardness — **in·gen·u·ous·ly** *adv* — **in·gen·u·ous·ness** *n*

in·gest \in-'jest\ *vb* : to take in for or as if for digestion — **in·ges·tion** \-'jes-chən\ *n*

in·gle·nook \'iŋ-(g)əl-ˌnu̇k\ *n* : a corner by the fire or chimney

in·glo·ri·ous \(')in-'glōr-ē-əs, -'glȯr-\ *adj* **1** : not glorious : not bringing honor or glory **2** : bringing disgrace : SHAMEFUL ⟨*inglorious* defeat⟩ — **in·glo·ri·ous·ly** *adv*

in·got \'iŋ-gət\ *n* : a mass of metal cast into a shape that is easy to handle or store

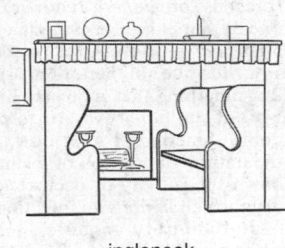

inglenook

¹in·grain \(')in-'grān\ *vb* : to work deeply into the texture of something or into the mental or moral nature of someone ⟨*ingrain* young children with responsibility⟩

²in·grain \'in-ˌgrān\ *adj* **1** : made of fiber that is dyed before being spun into yarn **2** : made of yarn that is dyed before being woven or knitted ⟨*ingrain* carpet⟩

in·grained \'in-ˌgrānd, (')in-'grānd\ *adj* **1** : worked into the grain or fiber **2** : forming a part of the inmost being : DEEP-SEATED ⟨*ingrained* attitudes⟩

in·grate \'in-ˌgrāt\ *n* : an ungrateful person

in·gra·ti·ate \in-'grā-shē-ˌāt\ *vb* **-at·ed; -at·ing** : to gain favor or acceptance for by deliberate effort ⟨quickly *ingratiated* herself with her new pupils⟩ — **in·gra·ti·a·tion** \-ˌgrā-shē-'ā-shən\ *n*

in·gra·ti·at·ing \in-'grā-shē-ˌāt-iŋ\ *adj* **1** : PLEASING ⟨an *ingratiating* smile⟩ **2** : intended to gain favor ⟨*ingratiating* manners⟩ — **in·gra·ti·at·ing·ly** *adv*

in·grat·i·tude \(')in-'grat-ə-ˌt(y)üd\ *n* : lack of gratitude

in·gre·di·ent \in-'grēd-ē-ənt\ *n* : one of the substances that make up a mixture ⟨*ingredients* of a salad⟩

in·gress \'in-ˌgres\ *n* **1** : the act of entering **2** : the power or liberty of entering

in·ground \'in-ˌgrau̇nd\ *adj* : built into the ground ⟨an *inground* pool⟩

in·grown \'in-ˌgrōn\ *adj* : grown in; *esp* : having the free tip or edge grown back into the flesh ⟨an *ingrown* toenail⟩

in·hab·it \in-'hab-ət\ *vb* : to live or dwell in — **in·hab·it·able** \-ət-ə-bəl\ *adj*

in·hab·it·ant \in-'hab-ət-ənt\ *n* : one who lives permanently in a place

in·hal·ant \in-'hā-lənt\ *n* : something (as a medicine-containing spray) that is inhaled — **inhalant** *adj*

in·ha·la·tion \ˌin-(h)ə-'lā-shən\ *n* : the act or instance of inhaling

\ə\ **abut**	\au̇\ **out**	\i\ **tip**	\ȯ\ **saw**	\u̇\ **foot**
\ər\ **further**	\ch\ **chin**	\ī\ **life**	\ȯi\ **coin**	\y\ **yet**
\a\ **mat**	\e\ **pet**	\j\ **job**	\th\ **thin**	\yü\ **few**
\ā\ **take**	\ē\ **easy**	\ŋ\ **sing**	\th\ **this**	\yu̇\ **cure**
\ä\ **cot, cart**	\g\ **go**	\ō\ **bone**	\ü\ **food**	\zh\ **vision**

in·ha·la·tor \'in-(h)ə-ˌlāt-ər, 'in-ᵊl-ˌāt-\ *n* : a device used in inhaling something (as a mixture of oxygen and carbon dioxide); *esp* : INHALER 1

in·hale \in-'hā(ə)l\ *vb* **in·haled; in·hal·ing** **1** : to draw in by breathing **2** : to breathe in

in·hal·er \in-'hā-lər\ *n* **1** : a device used in inhaling medicines (as those to treat asthma) **2** : one that inhales

in·har·mo·ni·ous \ˌin-(ˌ)här-'mō-nē-əs\ *adj* : not harmonious : DISCORDANT ⟨*inharmonious* sounds⟩ ⟨*inharmonious* ideas⟩

in·here \in-'hi(ə)r\ *vb* **in·hered; in·her·ing** : to be inherent : BELONG

in·her·ent \in-'hir-ənt, -'her-\ *adj* : belonging to or being a part of the nature of a person or thing ⟨an *inherent* sense of fair play⟩ ⟨fluidity is an *inherent* quality of gas⟩ — **in·her·ent·ly** *adv*

in·her·it \in-'her-ət\ *vb* **1** : to receive by legal right from a person at the person's death **2** : to receive by genetic transmission ⟨*inherit* red hair⟩ **3** : to have handed on to one by someone else ⟨*inherit* a job⟩ — **in·her·it·able** \-ət-ə-bəl\ *adj* — **in·her·i·tor** \-ət-ər\ *n*

in·her·i·tance \in-'her-ət-ən(t)s\ *n* **1** : the act of inheriting **2** : something that is or may be inherited

in·hib·it \in-'hib-ət\ *vb* **1** : to prevent or hold back from doing something : RESTRAIN, REPRESS ⟨fear can *inhibit* the natural expression of feelings⟩ **2** : to prevent or slow down the activity or occurrence of ⟨oil *inhibits* rust⟩ ⟨a drug which *inhibits* an infection⟩ — **in·hib·i·tor** \-ət-ər\ *n* — **in·hib·i·to·ry** \-ə-ˌtōr-ē, -ˌtȯr-\ *adj*

in·hib·it·ed \in-'hib-ət-əd\ *adj* : finding it hard to show desires, feelings, and thoughts

in·hi·bi·tion \ˌin-(h)ə-'bish-ən\ *n* **1 a** : the act of inhibiting : the state of being inhibited **b** : something that inhibits **2** : an inner force that prevents or makes difficult the free expression of thoughts, emotions, or desires

in·hos·pi·ta·ble \ˌin-(ˌ)häs-'pit-ə-bəl, (')in-'häs-(ˌ)pit-\ *adj* **1** : not friendly or generous : not showing hospitality **2** : providing no shelter or food : BARREN ⟨an *inhospitable* desert⟩ — **in·hos·pi·ta·bly** \-blē\ *adv* — **in·hos·pi·tal·i·ty** \(ˌ)in-ˌhäs-pə-'tal-ət-ē\ *n*

in·hu·man \(')in-'hyü-mən, -'yü-\ *adj* **1 a** : lacking pity or kindness : SAVAGE **b** : lacking human warmth : IMPERSONAL **c** : not fit for human needs ⟨*inhuman* conditions⟩ **2** : unlike what is typically human ⟨an *inhuman* cry⟩ — **in·hu·man·ly** *adv* — **in·hu·man·ness** *n*

in·hu·mane \ˌin-(ˌ)hyü-'mān, -(ˌ)yü-\ *adj* : not humane : INHUMAN 1 ⟨*inhumane* treatment of prisoners⟩ — **in·hu·mane·ly** *adv*

in·hu·man·i·ty \ˌin-(ˌ)hyü-'man-ət-ē, -(ˌ)yü-\ *n, pl* **-ties** : a cruel or barbarous act or attitude

in·im·i·cal \in-'im-i-kəl\ *adj* **1** : not friendly : HOSTILE **2** : having a harmful effect ⟨habits *inimical* to health⟩

in·im·i·ta·ble \(')in-'im-ət-ə-bəl\ *adj* : not capable of being imitated : MATCHLESS ⟨her own *inimitable* style⟩

in·iq·ui·tous \in-'ik-wət-əs\ *adj* : UNJUST, WICKED

in·iq·ui·ty \in-'ik-wət-ē\ *n, pl* **-ties** **1** : complete injustice or wickedness **2** : something that is unjust or wicked : SIN

¹ini·tial \in-'ish-əl\ *adj* **1** : of, relating to, or existing at the beginning : EARLIEST ⟨*initial* stages of a disease⟩ **2** : placed or standing at the beginning : FIRST ⟨the *initial* letter of a word⟩ — **ini·tial·ly** \-'ish-(ə-)lē\ *adv*

²initial *n* **1** : a first letter of a name **2** : a large letter beginning a text or paragraph

³initial *vb* **ini·tialed** *or* **ini·tialled; ini·tial·ing** *or* **ini·tial·ling** \-'ish-(ə-)liŋ\ : to mark with initials or an initial ⟨*initial* a handkerchief⟩

¹ini·ti·ate \in-'ish-ē-ˌāt\ *vb* **-at·ed; -at·ing** **1** : to set going : BEGIN ⟨*initiate* a new policy⟩ **2** : to instruct in the basics of something : INTRODUCE ⟨*initiate* tourists into the local customs⟩ **3** : to admit into membership by special ceremonies [from Latin *initiatus*, past participle of *initiare*

"to begin" — related to COMMENCE] — **ini·ti·a·tor** \-ˌāt-ər\ *n* — **ini·tia·to·ry** \-'ish-(ē-)ə-ˌtōr-ē, -ˌtȯr-\ *adj*

²ini·ti·ate \in-'ish-(ē-)ət\ *n* **1** : a person who is undergoing or has passed an initiation **2** : an expert in a special field

ini·ti·a·tion \in-ˌish-ē-'ā-shən\ *n* **1** : the act of initiating : the process of being initiated : INTRODUCTION **2** : the ceremonies with which a person is made a member of a club or society

ini·tia·tive \in-'ish-ət-iv\ *n* **1** : a first step or movement ⟨take the *initiative* in becoming acquainted⟩ **2** : energy shown in initiating something ⟨has ability but lacks *initiative*⟩ **3** : a plan or program intended to solve a problem

in·ject \in-'jekt\ *vb* **1 a** : to throw, drive, or force into something ⟨*inject* fuel into an engine⟩ **b** : to force a fluid into (a part of the body) especially for medical reasons **2** : to introduce as an additional element ⟨*injected* humor into her speech⟩ — **in·ject·able** \-'jek-tə-bəl\ *adj* — **in·jec·tor** \-'jek-tər\ *n*

in·jec·tion \in-'jek-shən\ *n* **1** : an act or instance of injecting **2** : something (as a medical drug) that is injected

in·ju·di·cious \ˌin-jù-'dish-əs\ *adj* : not judicious : UNWISE ⟨*injudicious* outbursts⟩ — **in·ju·di·cious·ly** *adv* — **in·ju·di·cious·ness** *n*

in·junc·tion \in-'jəŋ(k)-shən\ *n* : a court order commanding or forbidding the doing of some act ⟨an *injunction* against the strike⟩

in·jure \'in-jər\ *vb* **in·jured; in·jur·ing** \'inj-(ə-)riŋ\ **1** : to do an injustice to : WRONG **2** : to cause pain or harm to ⟨*injured* her arm⟩ ⟨*injured* his pride⟩ **3** : to cause to suffer damage or loss ⟨a tax that *injured* business⟩ ⟨houses *injured* by the storm⟩

in·ju·ri·ous \in-'jùr-ē-əs\ *adj* : causing injury : HARMFUL ⟨*injurious* to health⟩ — **in·ju·ri·ous·ly** *adv*

in·ju·ry \'inj-(ə-)rē\ *n, pl* **-ries** **1** : an act that damages or hurts : WRONG **2** : hurt, damage, or loss received
synonyms INJURY, HARM, DAMAGE mean an act that causes loss or pain. INJURY suggests an act that results in the loss or lessening of one's rights, health, freedom, property, or success ⟨the accident caused both physical and emotional *injuries*⟩. HARM applies to any evil that injures and often suggests suffering, pain, or bother ⟨promised that no one would receive *harm* of any kind⟩. DAMAGE applies especially to an injury that results in a loss ⟨the pests did much *damage* to the crop⟩.

in·jus·tice \(')in-'jəs-təs\ *n* **1** : violation of the rights of another : UNFAIRNESS **2** : an unjust act

¹ink \'iŋk\ *n* **1** : a usually liquid material for writing or printing **2** : the black protective secretion of a cephalopod

²ink *vb* **1** : to put ink on **2** : to write or draw in ink — **ink·er** *n*

ink·horn \'iŋk-ˌhȯ(ə)rn\ *n* : a portable container for ink

ink–jet \'iŋk-ˌjet\ *adj* : of, relating to, or being a printer in which droplets of ink are sprayed onto the paper

in·kling \'iŋ-kliŋ\ *n* : a vague notion : HINT ⟨didn't have an *inkling* of what it all meant⟩

ink·stand \'iŋk-ˌstand\ *n* : INKWELL

ink·well \'iŋ-ˌkwel\ *n* : a container for ink

inky \'iŋ-kē\ *adj* **ink·i·er; -est** : of, resembling, or covered with ink ⟨*inky* blackness of the sea⟩ ⟨*inky* hands⟩

in·laid \'in-'lād\ *adj* **1** : set into a surface in a decorative design ⟨tables with *inlaid* marble⟩; *also* : decorated with an inlaid design ⟨a table with an *inlaid* top⟩ **2** : having a design that goes all the way through ⟨*inlaid* linoleum⟩

¹in·land \'in-ˌland, -lənd\ *adj* : of or relating to the part of a country away from the coast or boundaries

²inland *n* : the part of a country away from the coast or boundaries : INTERIOR — **in·land·er** \-ˌlan-dər, -lən-\ *n*

³inland *adv* : into or toward the area away from a coast ⟨traveled *inland*⟩

in–law \'in-ˌlȯ\ *n* : a relative by marriage

¹**in·lay** \\(')in-'lā\ *vb* **in·laid** \-'lād\; **in·lay·ing** : to set into a surface for decoration or strengthening — **in·lay·er** *n*

²**in·lay** \'in-,lā\ *n* **1** : inlaid work or material used in inlaying **2** : a tooth filling shaped to fit a cavity and then cemented into place

in·let \'in-,let, -lət\ *n* **1** : a small or narrow bay **2** : an opening for intake especially of fluids

in–line skate \'in-'līn-\ *n* : a roller skate whose wheels are set in a straight line one behind the other — **in–line skat·er** *n* — **in–line skating** *n*

in·mate \'in-,māt\ *n* : a member of a group living in a single residence; *esp* : a person kept in an institution (as a hospital or prison)

in·most \'in-,mōst\ *adj* : INNERMOST

inn \'in\ *n* : a public house that provides lodging and food for travelers : HOTEL

in·nards \'in-ərdz\ *n pl* **1** : the internal organs of a human being or animal; *esp* : VISCERA **2** : the internal parts of a structure or machine

in·nate \in-'āt, 'in-,āt\ *adj* **1** : existing in or belonging to an individual from birth ⟨an *innate* ability⟩ **2** : INHERENT ⟨*innate* defects in the plan⟩ [Middle English *innat* "belonging from birth," from Latin *innatus,* past participle of *innasci* "to be born in, be a native," from *in-* "in" and *nasci* "to be born" — related to NATIVE, NATURE] — **in·nate·ly** *adv* — **in·nate·ness** *n*

in·ner \'in-ər\ *adj* **1 a** : situated farther in ⟨*inner* room⟩ **b** : being near a center especially of influence ⟨an *inner* circle of advisors⟩ **2** : of or relating to the mind or spirit ⟨*inner* peace⟩ — **in·ner·ly** *adv*

inner city *n* : the usually older and more heavily populated central section of a city — **inner–city** *adj*

inner ear *n* : the part of the ear that is most important for hearing, is located in a cavity in the temporal bone, and contains the ends of the nerves which send nerve impulses concerned with hearing and balance to the brain

inner light *n, often cap I&L* : a divine presence held (as in Quaker doctrine) to enlighten and guide the soul

in·ner·most \'in-ər-,mōst\ *adj* **1** : farthest inward **2** : most intimate : DEEPEST ⟨one's *innermost* feelings⟩

inner tube *n* : an inflatable ring-shaped rubber tube used inside a tire to hold air under pressure

in·ning \'in-iŋ\ *n* : a division of a baseball game consisting of a turn at bat for each team; *also* : a baseball team's turn at bat

inn·keep·er \'in-,kē-pər\ *n* : the person who runs an inn

in·no·cence \'in-ə-sən(t)s\ *n* : the quality or state of being innocent

in·no·cent \'in-ə-sənt\ *adj* **1** : free from sin : PURE **2** : free from guilt or blame : GUILTLESS ⟨*innocent* of the crime⟩ **3** : free from harmful influence or effect : HARMLESS ⟨*innocent* fun⟩ **4** : NAIVE 1, UNSOPHISTICATED — **innocent** *n* — **in·no·cent·ly** *adv*

in·noc·u·ous \in-'äk-yə-wəs\ *adj* **1** : producing no injury : HARMLESS ⟨an *innocuous* gas⟩ **2** : not likely to bother anyone : INOFFENSIVE ⟨made a few *innocuous* jokes⟩ — **in·noc·u·ous·ly** *adv* — **in·noc·u·ous·ness** *n*

in·no·vate \'in-ə-,vāt\ *vb* **-vat·ed; -vat·ing** : to introduce something new ⟨*innovate* a new website⟩ : do something in a new way — **in·no·va·tive** \-,vāt-iv\ *adj* — **in·no·va·tor** \-,vāt-ər\ *n*

in·no·va·tion \,in-ə-'vā-shən\ *n* **1** : the introduction of something new **2** : a new idea, method, or device

in·nu·en·do \,in-yə-'wen-dō\ *n, pl* **-dos** *or* **-does** : a slight suggestion or hint; *esp* : a suggestion that hurts someone's reputation

in·nu·mer·a·ble \in-'(y)üm-(ə-)rə-bəl\ *adj* : too many to be numbered : COUNTLESS ⟨*innumerable* stars in the sky⟩ — **in·nu·mer·a·bly** \-blē\ *adv*

in·oc·u·late \in-'äk-yə-,lāt\ *vb* **-lat·ed; -lat·ing** **1** : to introduce a microscopic living thing into ⟨beans *inoculated* with nitrogen-fixing bacteria⟩ **2** : to introduce material

(as a vaccine) into the body especially by injection to protect against or treat a disease ⟨*inoculate* children against the measles⟩ — **in·oc·u·la·tor** \-,lāt-ər\ *n*

in·oc·u·la·tion \in-,äk-yə-'lā-shən\ *n* **1** : the act or an instance of inoculating **2** : material used in inoculating

in·of·fen·sive \,in-ə-'fen(t)-siv\ *adj* : not offensive or harmful — **in·of·fen·sive·ly** *adv*

in·op·er·a·ble \(')in-'äp-(ə-)rə-bəl\ *adj* **1** : not treatable by surgery ⟨an *inoperable* cancer⟩ **2** : not in working order : INOPERATIVE

in·op·er·a·tive \(')in-'äp-(ə-)rət-iv, -'äp-ə-,rāt-\ *adj* : not functioning : producing no effect ⟨an *inoperative* law⟩

in·op·por·tune \(,)in-,äp-ər-'t(y)ün\ *adj* : INCONVENIENT ⟨an *inopportune* time⟩ — **in·op·por·tune·ly** *adv*

in order that *conj* : ³THAT 2

in·or·di·nate \in-'ord-ᵊn-ət, -'ord-nət\ *adj* : going beyond reasonable limits : IMMODERATE ⟨an *inordinate* curiosity⟩ — **in·or·di·nate·ly** *adv*

in·or·gan·ic \,in-,ȯr-'gan-ik\ *adj* **1** : being or composed of matter that does not come from plants or animals either alive or dead : MINERAL **2** : of or relating to a branch of chemistry concerned with substances that contain little or no carbon — **in·or·gan·i·cal·ly** \-i-k(ə-)lē\ *adv*

in·pa·tient \'in-,pā-shənt\ *n* : a hospital patient who receives lodging and food as well as treatment — compare OUTPATIENT

¹**in·put** \'in-,pùt\ *n* **1** : power, energy, a signal, or information put into a machine or system **2** : ADVICE, COMMENT **3** : a point at which an input is put in **4** : the act or process of putting in

²**input** *vb* **in·put·ted** *or* **input; in·put·ting** : to enter (as data) into a computer

in·quest \'in-,kwest\ *n* : a judicial or official investigation

in·quire \in-'kwī(ə)r\ *vb* **in·quired; in·quir·ing** **1** : to ask about ⟨*inquired* the way to the train station⟩ **2** : to make an investigation ⟨*inquire* into the accident⟩ **3** : to ask a question ⟨*inquired* about the weather⟩ — **in·quir·er** *n* — **in·quir·ing·ly** \-'kwī-riŋ-lē\ *adv*

in·qui·ry \in-'kwī(ə)r-ē, 'in-,kwī(ə)r-; 'in-kwə-rē, 'iŋ-; 'in-,kwi(ə)r-ē\ *n, pl* **-ries** **1 a** : the act of inquiring ⟨learn by *inquiry*⟩ **b** : a request for information ⟨make *inquiries* at the station⟩ **2** : a search for truth or knowledge **3** : a careful examination : INVESTIGATION

in·qui·si·tion \,in-kwə-'zish-ən\ *n* **1** : the act of inquiring **2** : INQUEST **3 a** *cap* : a former Roman Catholic court for the discovery and punishment of heresy **b** : an investigation conducted with little concern for individual rights **c** : a severe questioning — **in·qui·si·tion·al** \-'zish-nəl, -ᵊn-ᵊl\ *adj*

in·quis·i·tive \in-'kwiz-ət-iv\ *adj* **1** : tending to inquire or investigate **2** : asking many questions; *esp* : too curious about other people's affairs ***synonyms*** see CURIOUS — **in·quis·i·tive·ly** *adv* — **in·quis·i·tive·ness** *n*

in·quis·i·tor \in-'kwiz-ət-ər\ *n* : one who conducts an inquisition — **in·quis·i·to·ri·al** \-,kwiz-ə-'tȯr-ē-əl, -'tȯr-\ *adj*

in·road \'in-,rōd\ *n* **1** : a sudden hostile invasion : RAID **2** : an important advance often at the expense of someone or something ⟨making *inroads* against the competition⟩

in·rush \'in-,rəsh\ *n* : a crowding or flooding in ⟨an *inrush* of holiday shoppers⟩ ⟨an *inrush* of air⟩

in·sane \(')in-'sān\ *adj* **1** : having or showing a very abnormal and very sick state of mind : not sane ⟨an *insane* person⟩ ⟨an *insane* look⟩ **2** : used by or for insane persons ⟨an *insane* ward in a hospital⟩ **3** : extremely foolish or unreasonable ⟨an *insane* attempt⟩ — **in·sane·ly** *adv*

\ə\ abut	\aú\ out	\i\ tip	\ȯ\ saw	\ú\ foot
\ər\ further	\ch\ chin	\ī\ life	\ȯi\ coin	\y\ yet
\a\ mat	\e\ pet	\j\ job	\th\ thin	\yü\ few
\ā\ take	\ē\ easy	\ŋ\ sing	\th\ this	\yú\ cure
\ä\ cot, cart	\g\ go	\ō\ bone	\ü\ food	\zh\ vision

in·san·i·tary \(')in-'san-ə-ˌter-ē\ *adj* : so unclean as to endanger health : UNHEALTHY

in·san·i·ty \in-'san-ət-ē\ *n, pl* **-ties** **1** : the condition of being insane especially when serious enough to keep one from being convicted of a crime or from performing duties required by law **2 a** : extreme foolishness or unreasonableness **b** : senseless conduct

in·sa·tia·ble \(')in-'sā-shə-bəl\ *adj* : impossible to satisfy ⟨*insatiable* thirst⟩ ⟨an *insatiable* desire for knowledge⟩ — **in·sa·tia·bly** \-blē\ *adv*

in·scribe \in-'skrīb\ *vb* **in·scribed; in·scrib·ing** **1 a** : to write, engrave, or print as a lasting record ⟨*inscribe* a name on a monument⟩ **b** : to enter on a list : ENROLL **2** : to write, engrave, or print something on or in ⟨*inscribe* a locket⟩ **3** : to dedicate to someone ⟨*inscribe* a poem⟩ **4** : to draw within a figure so as to touch in as many places as possible ⟨a hexagon *inscribed* in a circle⟩ — **in·scrib·er** *n*

in·scrip·tion \in-'skrip-shən\ *n* : something that is inscribed

in·scru·ta·ble \in-'skrüt-ə-bəl\ *adj* : not easily understood : MYSTERIOUS ⟨an *inscrutable* expression⟩ — **in·scru·ta·bly** \-blē\ *adv*

in·seam \'in-ˌsēm\ *n* : the seam on the inside of the leg of a pair of pants; *also* : the length of this seam

in·sect \'in-ˌsekt\ *n* **1** : any of numerous small invertebrate animals (as spiders or centipedes) that are more or less obviously made up of segments — not used technically **2** : any of a class of arthropods (as butterflies, true bugs, two-winged flies, bees, and grasshoppers) with the body clearly divided into a head, thorax, and abdomen, with three pairs of jointed legs, and usually with one or two pairs of wings

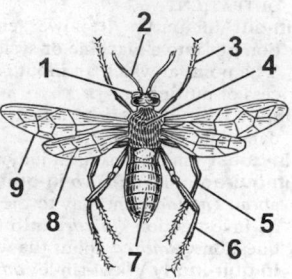

insect 2: 1 compound eye, 2 antenna, 3 front leg, 4 thorax, 5 middle leg, 6 back leg, 7 abdomen, 8 hind wing, 9 forewing

Word History The bodies of insects have segments, or divisions. Thus they seem to have a series of notches cut into them. This appearance led the Greek philosopher Aristotle to give insects the name *entomon* "a thing cut into." *Entomon* comes from the prefix *en-* "in," combined with the verb *temnein* "to cut." Later, when the Romans wanted a word for this kind of creature, they did not simply borrow the Greek word. Instead they translated it into the Latin word *insectum*, from the verb *insecare* "to cut into." *Insectum* was borrowed into English as *insect*. [from Latin *insectum* "insect," derived from *insecare* "to cut into," from *in-* "in" and *secare* "to cut" — related to DISSECT, SECTION]

in·sec·ti·cide \in-'sek-tə-ˌsīd\ *n* : a chemical used to kill insects — **in·sec·ti·cid·al** \(ˌ)in-ˌsek-tə-'sīd-ᵊl\ *adj*

in·sec·ti·vore \in-'sek-tə-ˌvō(ə)r, -ˌvȯ(ə)r\ *n* **1** : any of an order of small mammals (as the moles, shrews, and hedgehogs) that are mostly insect-eating and active at night **2** : an insect-eating plant or animal

in·sec·tiv·o·rous \ˌin-ˌsek-'tiv-(ə-)rəs\ *adj* : feeding on insects as food

in·se·cure \ˌin(t)-si-'kyu̇(ə)r\ *adj* **1** : not confident or sure : UNCERTAIN ⟨felt *insecure* about their response⟩ **2** : not well protected : not safe ⟨*insecure* property⟩ **3** : not firmly fastened : LOOSE ⟨an *insecure* hinge⟩ **4** : lacking self-assurance ⟨*insecure* people⟩ — **in·se·cure·ly** *adv* — **in·se·cu·ri·ty** \-'kyu̇r-ət-ē\ *n*

in·sem·i·nate \in-'sem-ə-ˌnāt\ *vb* **-nat·ed; -nat·ing** : to introduce semen into the genital tract of (a female) — **in·sem·i·na·tion** \-ˌsem-ə-'nā-shən\ *n*

in·sen·sate \(')in-'sen-ˌsāt\ *adj* **1** : lacking awareness or sensation : INANIMATE **2** : lacking sense or understanding **3** : lacking humane feelings : BRUTAL — **in·sen·sate·ly** *adv*

in·sen·si·ble \(')in-'sen(t)-sə-bəl\ *adj* **1** : IMPERCEPTIBLE 1 ⟨*insensible* motion⟩ **2 a** : not endowed with life or spirit : INANIMATE 1 **b** : ¹UNCONSCIOUS 2 ⟨knocked *insensible* by the accident⟩ **c** : not able to feel or be aware of using a sense or senses ⟨*insensible* to pain⟩ **3** : not aware of or caring about something ⟨*insensible* to fear⟩ ⟨*insensible* of their danger⟩ — **in·sen·si·bil·i·ty** \(ˌ)in-ˌsen(t)-sə-'bil-ət-ē\ *n* — **in·sen·si·bly** \-'sen(t)-sə-blē\ *adv*

in·sen·si·tive \(')in-'sen(t)-sət-iv, -'sen(t)-stiv\ *adj* : not sensitive; *esp* : lacking feeling — **in·sen·si·tive·ly** *adv* — **in·sen·si·tiv·i·ty** \(ˌ)in-ˌsen(t)-sə-'tiv-ət-ē\ *n*

in·sep·a·ra·ble \(')in-'sep-(ə-)rə-bəl\ *adj* **1** : impossible to separate ⟨*inseparable* issues⟩ **2** : seemingly always together ⟨*inseparable* friends⟩ — **in·sep·a·ra·bil·i·ty** \(ˌ)in-ˌsep-(ə-)rə-'bil-ət-ē\ *n* — **in·sep·a·ra·bly** \(')in-'sep-(ə-)rə-blē\ *adv*

¹in·sert \in-'sərt\ *vb* **1** : to put or place in ⟨*inserted* the key in the lock⟩ ⟨*insert* a word in a sentence⟩ **2** : to set in and make fast ⟨*insert* the tab into the slot⟩ — **in·sert·er** *n*

²in·sert \'in-ˌsərt\ *n* : something that is or is meant to be inserted; *esp* : printed sheets inserted (as in a newspaper)

in·ser·tion \in-'sər-shən\ *n* **1** : the act or process of inserting **2 a** : something inserted **b** : the part of a muscle that is attached to a part to be moved **3** : the mode or place of attachment of an organ or part

¹in·set \'in-ˌset\ *n* : something that is inset: as **a** : a small map or picture set within a larger one **b** : a piece of cloth set into a garment for decoration

²in·set \'in-ˌset, in-'set\ *vb* **inset** *or* **in·set·ted; in·set·ting** : ¹INSERT 2

¹in·shore \'in-ˌshō(ə)r, -'shȯ(ə)r\ *adj* **1** : situated or carried on near shore ⟨*inshore* fishing⟩ **2** : moving toward shore ⟨an *inshore* wind⟩

²inshore *adv* : to or toward shore

¹in·side \(')in-'sīd, 'in-ˌsīd\ *n* **1** : an inner side or surface **2 a** : an interior or internal part **b** : inward nature, thoughts, or feeling **c** : ENTRAILS — usually used in plural

²inside *adj* **1** : of, relating to, or being on or near the inside ⟨an *inside* wall⟩ **2** : relating or known to a special group of people ⟨*inside* information⟩

³inside *prep* **1 a** : in or into the interior of ⟨they are *inside* the house⟩ **b** : on the inner side of ⟨put the dot *inside* the curve⟩ **2** : before the end of : WITHIN ⟨*inside* an hour⟩

⁴inside *adv* **1** : on the inside ⟨the car is clean *inside*⟩ **2** : in or into the interior ⟨went *inside*⟩

inside of *prep* : ³INSIDE

inside out *adv* **1** : in such a way that the inner surface becomes the outer **2** : to a thorough degree ⟨knows the family history *inside out*⟩

in·sid·er \(')in-'sīd-ər\ *n* : a person who is a member of a special group or organization

in·sid·i·ous \in-'sid-ē-əs\ *adj* **1 a** : awaiting a chance to trap : TREACHEROUS ⟨an *insidious* foe⟩ **b** : harmful but attractive ⟨an *insidious* habit⟩ **2** : having an effect that develops gradually ⟨an *insidious* disease⟩ — **in·sid·i·ous·ly** *adv* — **in·sid·i·ous·ness** *n*

in·sight \'in-ˌsīt\ *n* : the power or act of seeing into or understanding a situation

in·sig·nia \in-'sig-nē-ə\ *n, pl* **-nia** *or* **-ni·as** : an emblem of a special authority, office, or honor : BADGE

in·sig·nif·i·cance \ˌin(t)-sig-ˈnif-i-kən(t)s\ *n* : the quality or state of being insignificant

in·sig·nif·i·cant \ˌin(t)-sig-ˈnif-i-kənt\ *adj* : not significant : UNIMPORTANT — **in·sig·nif·i·cant·ly** *adv*

in·sin·cere \ˌin(t)-sin-ˈsi(ə)r\ *adj* : not sincere : HYPOCRITICAL — **in·sin·cere·ly** *adv* — **in·sin·cer·i·ty** \-ˈser-ət-ē *also* -ˈsir-\ *n*

in·sin·u·ate \in-ˈsin-yə-ˌwāt\ *vb* **-at·ed; -at·ing** **1** : to introduce in a gradual, secret, or clever way ⟨*insinuated* herself into his confidence⟩ **2** : to suggest in an indirect way : IMPLY ⟨*insinuated* that I had cheated⟩ — **in·sin·u·a·tion** \ˌ(ˌ)in-ˌsin-yə-ˈwā-shən\ *n* — **in·sin·u·a·tor** \in-ˈsin-yə-ˌwāt-ər\ *n*

in·sip·id \in-ˈsip-əd\ *adj* **1** : lacking taste or flavor : TASTELESS **2** : not interesting or exciting : DULL, FLAT ⟨*insipid* fiction⟩ [from French *insipide* and Latin *insipidus,* both meaning "insipid, tasteless," from earlier Latin *in-* "not" and *sapidus* "having good flavor," from *sapere* "to taste" — related to ¹SAGE, SAVANT] — **in·si·pid·i·ty** \ˌin(t)-sə-ˈpid-ət-ē\ *n* — **in·sip·id·ly** \in-ˈsip-əd-lē\ *adv*

in·sist \in-ˈsist\ *vb* **1** : to place special stress or great importance ⟨*insists* on punctuality⟩ **2** : to make a demand : request urgently ⟨*insisted* that I come⟩

in·sis·tence \in-ˈsis-tən(t)s\ *n* **1** : the act or an instance of insisting **2** : the quality or state of being insistent

in·sis·tent \in-ˈsis-tənt\ *adj* : demanding attention : PERSISTENT — **in·sis·tent·ly** *adv*

in si·tu \(ˈ)in-ˈsī-t(y)ü, -ˈsi-\ *adv or adj* : in the natural or original position ⟨the cancer cells remained *in situ*⟩ [Latin, "in position"]

in·so·far as \ˌin(t)-sə-ˌfär-əz\ *conj* : to the extent or degree that ⟨helped us *insofar as* she was able⟩

in·so·la·tion \ˌin(t)-(ˌ)sō-ˈlā-shən\ *n* : solar radiation that has been received (as by the earth)

in·sole \ˈin-ˌsōl\ *n* **1** : an inside sole of a shoe **2** : a loose thin strip placed inside a shoe for warmth or comfort

in·so·lence \ˈin(t)-s(ə-)lən(t)s\ *n* **1** : the quality or state of being insolent **2** : an instance of insolent conduct or treatment

in·so·lent \ˈin(t)-s(ə-)lənt\ *adj* **1** : disrespectful or rude in speech or conduct ⟨an *insolent* child⟩ **2** : showing boldness or rudeness ⟨an *insolent* act⟩ — **in·so·lent·ly** *adv*

in·sol·u·bil·i·ty \(ˌ)in-ˌsäl-yə-ˈbil-ət-ē\ *n* : the quality or state of being insoluble

in·sol·u·ble \(ˈ)in-ˈsäl-yə-bəl\ *adj* **1** : impossible to solve ⟨an *insoluble* problem⟩ **2** : impossible or difficult to dissolve ⟨a substance *insoluble* in water⟩

in·sol·ven·cy \(ˈ)in-ˈsäl-vən-sē\ *n, pl* **-cies** : the quality or state of being insolvent

in·sol·vent \(ˈ)in-ˈsäl-vənt\ *adj* : not having or providing enough money to pay debts ⟨an *insolvent* company⟩ ⟨an *insolvent* estate⟩

in·som·nia \in-ˈsäm-nē-ə\ *n* : prolonged inability to sleep : SLEEPLESSNESS

in·som·ni·ac \in-ˈsäm-nē-ˌak\ *n* : a person who has insomnia

in·sou·ci·ance \in-ˈsü-sē-ən(t)s\ *n* : a lighthearted lack of concern — **in·sou·ci·ant** \-ənt\ *adj*

in·spect \in-ˈspekt\ *vb* **1** : to examine closely (as for judging quality or condition) ⟨*inspect* meat⟩ **2** : to view and examine officially ⟨*inspect* the troops⟩

in·spec·tion \in-ˈspek-shən\ *n* : the act or an instance of inspecting

in·spec·tor \in-ˈspek-tər\ *n* **1** : a person who makes inspections ⟨meat *inspector*⟩ **2** : a police officer ranking just below a superintendent or deputy superintendent — **in·spec·tor·ship** \-ˌship\ *n*

in·spi·ra·tion \ˌin(t)-spə-ˈrā-shən\ *n* **1** : the drawing of air into the lungs in breathing **2 a** : the act or power of moving the mind or the emotions ⟨the *inspiration* of music⟩ **b** : the quality or state of being inspired ⟨the artist's *inspiration* came from many sources⟩ **c** : something that is inspired ⟨a scheme that was an *inspiration*⟩ **d** : someone or something that inspires ⟨his wife was his greatest *inspiration*⟩ — **in·spi·ra·tion·al** \-shnəl, -shən-ᵊl\ *adj* — **in·spi·ra·tion·al·ly** \-ē\ *adv*

in·spire \in-ˈspī(ə)r\ *vb* **in·spired; in·spir·ing** **1** : to move or guide by divine influence ⟨prophets *inspired* by God⟩ **2 a** : to stimulate to greater or higher activity : make spirited ⟨*inspired* by his parents⟩ **b** : to cause to have a particular thought or feeling ⟨the old house *inspired* her with longing for the past⟩ **c** : to cause a feeling of : AROUSE ⟨*inspires* confidence in her followers⟩ **3** : INHALE **4** : BRING ABOUT ⟨studies that *inspired* several inventions⟩ — **in·spir·er** *n*

in·sta·bil·i·ty \ˌin(t)-stə-ˈbil-ət-ē\ *n* : the quality or state of being unstable

in·stall \in-ˈstȯl\ *vb* **in·stalled; in·stall·ing** **1** : to place in an office or rank ⟨*installed* the new president⟩ **2** : to put in an indicated place or condition ⟨*installed* himself in the best chair⟩ **3** : to set up for use or service ⟨*install* a TV set⟩ ⟨*installed* the software⟩ — **in·stall·er** *n*

in·stal·la·tion \ˌin(t)-stə-ˈlā-shən\ *n* **1** : the act of installing : the state of being installed **2** : something installed for use **3** : a military base **4** : a work of art that consists of multiple pieces arranged in a large space

¹in·stall·ment *also* **in·stal·ment** \in-ˈstȯl-mənt\ *n* : INSTALLATION 1

²installment *also* **instalment** *n* **1** : one of the parts into which a debt is divided when payments are made over a period of time **2** : one of several parts (as of a publication) presented over a period of time — **installment** *adj*

installment plan *n* : a system of paying for goods or services in installments

¹in·stance \ˈin(t)-stən(t)s\ *n* **1** : ¹REQUEST 1 ⟨entered the writing contest at the *instance* of her teacher⟩ **2** : EXAMPLE 3 ⟨an *instance* of rare courage⟩ **3** : a particular point or step in an action or process ⟨in the first *instance*⟩ — **for instance** : as an example ⟨big dogs, like German shepherds, *for instance*⟩

²instance *vb* **in·stanced; in·stanc·ing** : to mention as an example : CITE

¹in·stant \ˈin(t)-stənt\ *n* : a very small space of time : MOMENT

²instant *adj* **1** : PRESSING, URGENT ⟨in *instant* need⟩ **2** : happening or done at once ⟨an *instant* response⟩ **3** : partially prepared by the manufacturer to make final preparation easy ⟨*instant* cake mix⟩; *esp* : made to dissolve quickly in water ⟨*instant* coffee⟩

in·stan·ta·neous \ˌin(t)-stən-ˈtā-nē-əs, -nyəs\ *adj* **1** : happening in an instant **2** : done without delay — **in·stan·ta·neous·ly** *adv* — **in·stan·ta·neous·ness** *n*

in·stan·ter \in-ˈstant-ər\ *adv* : IMMEDIATELY 2

in·stant·ly \ˈin(t)-stənt-lē\ *adv* : without delay : IMMEDIATELY ⟨came *instantly* when I called⟩

instant mes·sag·ing \-ˈmes-ə-jiŋ\ *n* : a means or system for transmitting electronic messages instantly — **instant message** *n*

in·state \in-ˈstāt\ *vb* **in·stat·ed; in·stat·ing** : to install in a rank or office

in·stead \in-ˈsted\ *adv* : as a substitute ⟨was going to write but called *instead*⟩

instead of \in-ˌsted-ə(v), -ˌstid-\ *prep* : in place of : as a substitute for ⟨had milk *instead of* juice⟩

\ə\ abut	\aú\ out	\i\ tip	\ȯ\ saw	\ú\ foot
\ər\ further	\ch\ chin	\ī\ life	\ȯi\ coin	\y\ yet
\a\ mat	\e\ pet	\j\ job	\th\ thin	\yü\ few
\ā\ take	\ē\ easy	\ŋ\ sing	\<u>th</u>\ this	\yú\ cure
\ä\ cot, cart	\g\ go	\ō\ bone	\ü\ food	\zh\ vision

in·step \'in-ˌstep\ *n* **1** : the arched middle part of the human foot **2** : the part of a shoe or stocking that fits over the instep

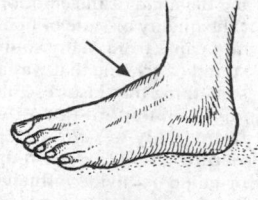

instep 1

in·sti·gate \'in(t)-stə-ˌgāt\ *vb* **-gat·ed; -gat·ing** : INCITE, PROVOKE — **in·sti·ga·tion** \ˌin(t)-stə-'gā-shən\ *n* — **in·sti·ga·tor** \'in(t)-stə-ˌgāt-ər\ *n*

in·still \in-'stil\ *vb* : to gradually cause to feel or have ⟨*instill* a love of music⟩ — **in·stil·la·tion** \ˌin(t)-stə-'lā-shən\ *n* — **in·still·er** *n*

in·stinct \'in-ˌstiŋ(k)t\ *n* **1** : a natural ability or inclination **2 a** : an act or course of action in response to a stimulus that is usually inherited and is automatic rather than learned **b** : behavior that is based on automatic actions

in·stinc·tive \in-'stiŋ(k)-tiv\ *adj* **1** : of, relating to, or being instinct **2** : resulting from or caused by instinct — **in·stinc·tive·ly** *adv*

in·stinc·tu·al \in-'stiŋ(k)-chə(-wə)l, -'stiŋ(k)sh-wəl\ *adj* : of, relating to, or based on instinct : INSTINCTIVE

¹in·sti·tute \'in(t)-stə-ˌt(y)üt\ *vb* **-tut·ed; -tut·ing** **1** : to set up : ESTABLISH ⟨*instituted* a new policy⟩ **2** : to set going : BEGIN ⟨*institute* an investigation⟩ — **in·sti·tut·er** *or* **in·sti·tu·tor** \-ˌt(y)üt-ər\ *n*

²institute *n* **1** : a basic principle **2 a** : an organization for the support of a cause : ASSOCIATION ⟨an *institute* for scientific research⟩ **b** : a place for study usually in a special field ⟨an art *institute*⟩

in·sti·tu·tion \ˌin(t)-stə-'t(y)ü-shən\ *n* **1** : the act of instituting : ESTABLISHMENT **2** : an established custom, practice, or law in a society or culture ⟨the *institution* of marriage⟩ ⟨turkey dinner is a Thanksgiving *institution*⟩ **3 a** : an established organization or corporation and especially one of a public nature ⟨educational *institutions*⟩ ⟨a financial *institution*⟩ **b** : ASYLUM 3 — **in·sti·tu·tion·al** \-shnəl, -shən-ᵊl\ *adj* — **in·sti·tu·tion·al·ly** \-ē\ *adv*

in·sti·tu·tion·al·ize \ˌin(t)-stə-'t(y)ü-shnə-ˌlīz, -shən-ᵊl-ˌīz\ *vb* **-ized; -iz·ing** **1** : to make into or treat like an institution ⟨*institutionalized* housing⟩ **2** : to put into an institution

in·struct \in-'strəkt\ *vb* **1** : to give knowledge to : TEACH ⟨the tutor *instructs* him in math⟩ **2** : to give information to : INFORM ⟨*instructed* us that the cafeteria was downstairs⟩ **3** : to give directions or commands to ⟨*instructed* her to arrive promptly⟩ **synonyms** see COMMAND

in·struc·tion \in-'strək-shən\ *n* **1 a** : PRECEPT ⟨*instructions* of ethical behavior⟩ **b** : ²COMMAND 2, ORDER ⟨had *instructions* not to talk to strangers⟩ **c** *pl* : an outline or set of procedures to be followed : DIRECTIONS ⟨*instructions* for assembling a rocking chair⟩ **d** : a code that tells a computer to perform a particular operation **2** : the action or practice of an instructor or teacher — **in·struc·tion·al** \-shnəl, -shən-ᵊl\ *adj*

in·struc·tive \in-'strək-tiv\ *adj* : giving knowledge : helping to instruct or inform ⟨an *instructive* experience⟩ — **in·struc·tive·ly** *adv*

in·struc·tor \in-'strək-tər\ *n* : one that instructs : TEACHER — **in·struc·tor·ship** \-ˌship\ *n*

in·stru·ment \'in(t)-strə-mənt\ *n* **1** : a device used to produce music **2** : a means of getting something done ⟨curiosity is an *instrument* of discovery⟩ **3** : a tool or implement designed especially for precision work ⟨a surgical *instrument*⟩ **4** : an official legal document (as a deed, bond, or agreement) **5 a** : a measuring device for finding out the present value of a quantity under observation **b** : an electrical or mechanical device used in navigating an airplane; *esp* : such a device used as the only way of navigating **synonyms** see IMPLEMENT

in·stru·men·tal \ˌin(t)-strə-'ment-ᵊl\ *adj* **1 a** : acting as an instrument or means ⟨was *instrumental* in organizing the club⟩ **b** : of, relating to, or done with an instrument ⟨*instrumental* error⟩ **2** : relating to, composed for, or performed on a musical instrument ⟨an unusual *instrumental* arrangement⟩ — **in·stru·men·tal·ly** \-ᵊl-ē\ *adv*

in·stru·men·tal·ist \ˌin(t)-strə-'ment-ᵊl-əst\ *n* : a person who plays a musical instrument

in·stru·men·tal·i·ty \ˌin(t)-strə-mən-'tal-ət-ē, -ˌmen-\ *n, pl* **-ties** **1** : the quality or state of being instrumental **2** : something by which an end is achieved : MEANS ⟨order was restored through the *instrumentality* of rules⟩

in·stru·men·ta·tion \ˌin(t)-strə-mən-'tā-shən, -ˌmen-\ *n* **1** : the arrangement or composition of music for instruments **2** : instruments for a particular purpose ⟨the *instrumentation* of an aircraft⟩

instrument panel *n* : DASHBOARD 2

in·sub·or·di·nate \ˌin(t)-sə-'bȯrd-ᵊn-ət, -'bȯrd-nət\ *adj* : not obeying authority : DISOBEDIENT — **in·sub·or·di·nate·ly** *adv* — **in·sub·or·di·na·tion** \-ˌbȯrd-ᵊn-'ā-shən\ *n*

in·sub·stan·tial \ˌin(t)-səb-'stan-chəl\ *adj* : not substantial: as **a** : not real : IMAGINARY ⟨*insubstantial* differences⟩ **b** : not firm or solid ⟨a flimsy *insubstantial* shelf⟩ — **in·sub·stan·ti·al·i·ty** \-ˌstan-chē-'al-ət-ē\ *n*

in·suf·fer·able \(')in-'səf-(ə-)rə-bəl\ *adj* : impossible to endure : INTOLERABLE ⟨*insufferable* boredom⟩ — **in·suf·fer·able·ness** *n* — **in·suf·fer·ably** \-blē\ *adv*

in·suf·fi·cien·cy \ˌin(t)-sə-'fish-ən-sē\ *n, pl* **-cies** **1** : the quality or state of being insufficient **2** : a lack of something : DEFICIENCY

in·suf·fi·cient \ˌin(t)-sə-'fish-ənt\ *adj* : not sufficient : INADEQUATE — **in·suf·fi·cient·ly** *adv*

in·su·lar \'in(t)s-(y)ə-lər, 'in-shə-lər\ *adj* **1** : of, relating to, or forming an island **2** : being isolated or detached ⟨an *insular* building⟩ **3** : not open to new or different ideas : NARROW ⟨an *insular* viewpoint⟩ — **in·su·lar·i·ty** \ˌin(t)s-(y)ə-'lar-ət-ē, ˌin-shə-'lar-\ *n*

in·su·late \'in(t)-sə-ˌlāt\ *vb* **-lat·ed; -lat·ing** : to place in a detached situation : ISOLATE; *esp* : to separate from conducting bodies by means of nonconductors so as to prevent transfer of electricity, heat, or sound [from Latin *insula* "island" — related to ISLE, ISOLATE, PENINSULA]

in·su·la·tion \ˌin(t)-sə-'lā-shən\ *n* **1** : the act of insulating : the state of being insulated **2** : material used in insulating

in·su·la·tor \'in(t)-sə-ˌlāt-ər\ *n* : one that insulates; *esp* : a material that is a poor conductor of heat or electricity or a device made of such material

in·su·lin \'in(t)-s(ə-)lən\ *n* : a hormone that is produced by the pancreas and is necessary for the normal use of glucose by the body

insulin shock *n* : a condition of too little blood sugar that is associated with too much insulin in the system and that if left untreated may result in coma

¹in·sult \in-'səlt\ *vb* : to treat or speak to with disrespect or scorn — **in·sult·er** *n*

Word History The phrase "to jump on" is used informally today to mean "to criticize or insult severely." The origin of the word *insult* also suggests the idea of jumping. *Insult* comes from the Latin verb *insultare*, literally meaning "to leap upon." It is made up of the prefix *in-*, meaning "on, upon," and a form of the verb *salire* "to leap." One of the first meanings of *insult* in English was "to make a military attack." That sense became obsolete, and *insult* now means to attack or "jump on" someone only with words of scorn or disrespect rather than with weapons. [from early French *insulter* "to insult," from Latin *insultare* "to insult, attack," literally "to leap upon," derived from *in-* "on, upon" and *salire* "to leap, spring" — related to ASSAULT, RESILIENT]

²in·sult \'in-ˌsəlt\ *n* : an act or expression showing disrespect or scorn

in·su·per·a·ble \(')in-'sü-p(ə-)rə-bəl\ *adj* : impossible to overcome ⟨*insuperable* difficulties⟩ — **in·su·per·a·bly** \-blē\ *adv*

in·sup·port·able \,in(t)-sə-'pȯrt-ə-bəl, -'pȯrt-\ *adj* **1** : too bad to be endured ⟨*insupportable* pain⟩ **2** : impossible to justify ⟨*insupportable* charges⟩

in·sur·able \in-'shùr-ə-bəl\ *adj* : capable of being insured — **in·sur·abil·i·ty** \-,shùr-ə-'bil-ət-ē\ *n*

in·sur·ance \in-'shùr-ən(t)s\ *n* **1 a** : the business of insuring persons or property **b** : a contract by which someone guarantees for a fee to pay someone else for the value of property if it is lost or damaged (as through theft or fire) or to pay usually a specified amount for injury or death **c** : the amount for which something is insured **2** : a means of guaranteeing protection ⟨take an umbrella as *insurance* against rain⟩

in·sure \in-'shù(ə)r\ *vb* **in·sured; in·sur·ing 1** : to give or get insurance on or for **2** : to make certain : ENSURE — **in·sur·er** \-'shùr-ər\ *n*

in·sur·gen·cy \in-'sər-jən-sē\ *n, pl* **-cies** : REBELLION 2

¹in·sur·gent \in-'sər-jənt\ *n* : a person who revolts : REBEL

²insurgent *adj* : REBELLIOUS 1

in·sur·mount·able \,in(t)-sər-'maùnt-ə-bəl\ *adj* : incapable of being surmounted

in·sur·rec·tion \,in(t)-sə-'rek-shən\ *n* : REBELLION 2 — **in·sur·rec·tion·ary** \-shə-,ner-ē\ *adj or n* — **in·sur·rec·tion·ist** \-sh(ə-)nəst\ *n*

in·tact \in-'takt\ *adj* : untouched especially by anything that harms : not damaged or lessened

in·ta·glio \in-'tal-yō, -'tag-lē-,ō\ *n, pl* **-glios** : an engraving cut deeply into the surface of a hard material (as stone)

in·take \'in-,tāk\ *n* **1** : a place where liquid or air is taken into something (as a pump) **2** : the act of taking in ⟨an *intake* of breath⟩ **3** : something taken in ⟨inadequate food *intake*⟩

intaglio

in·tan·gi·ble \(')in-'tan-jə-bəl\ *adj* **1** : impossible to touch ⟨light is *intangible*⟩ **2** : impossible to think of as matter or substance ⟨goodwill is an *intangible* asset⟩ — **in·tan·gi·bil·i·ty** \(,)in-,tan-jə-'bil-ət-ē\ *n* — **intangible** *n* — **in·tan·gi·ble·ness** \(')in-'tan-jə-bəl-nəs\ *n* — **in·tan·gi·bly** \-blē\ *adv*

in·te·ger \'int-i-jər\ *n* : a number that is a natural number (as 1, 2, or 3), the negative of a natural number, or 0 — called also *whole number*

in·te·gral \'int-i-grəl (*usually so in mathematics*); in-'teg-rəl *also* -'tēg-\ *adj* **1** : needed for completeness ⟨a lens is an *integral* part of a camera⟩ **2** : of or relating to an integer ⟨9 is an *integral* factor of 72⟩ **3** : made up of components that together make a whole ⟨an *integral* locking system⟩ **4** : lacking nothing essential : ENTIRE — **in·te·gral·ly** \'int-i-grə-lē; in-'teg-rə- *also* -'tēg-\ *adv*

in·te·grate \'int-ə-,grāt\ *vb* **-grat·ed; -grat·ing 1** : to form or unite into a whole **2** : to form or unite into a larger unit; *esp* : to end the segregation of and bring into common and equal membership in society **3** : DESEGREGATE ⟨*integrate* school districts⟩ **4** : to become integrated

integrated circuit *n* : a tiny group of electronic devices and their connections that is produced in or on a small slice of material (as silicon)

in·te·gra·tion \,int-ə-'grā-shən\ *n* : the act, the process, or an instance of integrating; *esp* : acceptance as equals into society of persons of different groups (as races)

in·te·gra·tion·ist \,int-ə-'grā-sh(ə-)nəst\ *n* : a person who favors integration

in·teg·ri·ty \in-'teg-rət-ē\ *n* **1** : the condition of being free from damage or defect **2** : total honesty and sincerity **3** : the quality or state of being complete or undivided

in·teg·u·ment \in-'teg-yə-mənt\ *n* : something that covers or encloses; *esp* : an outer enclosing layer (as a skin, membrane, or cuticle) of a living thing or one of its parts — **in·teg·u·men·ta·ry** \(,)in-,teg-yə-'ment-ə-rē, -'men-trē\ *adj*

in·tel·lect \'int-ᵊl-,ekt\ *n* **1 a** : the power of knowing **b** : the capacity for thought especially when highly developed **2** : a person of notable intellect

¹in·tel·lec·tu·al \,int-ᵊl-'ek-ch(ə-w)əl\ *adj* **1** : relating to the intellect or understanding **2** : having intellect to a high degree : engaged in or given to learning and thinking ⟨an *intellectual* person⟩ **3** : requiring study and thought ⟨*intellectual* games⟩ — **in·tel·lec·tu·al·i·ty** \-,ek-chə-'wal-ət-ē\ *n* — **in·tel·lec·tu·al·ly** \-'ek-chə-(wə-)lē\ *adv*

²intellectual *n* : an intellectual person

intellectual disability *n* : a significant impairment in intellectual ability accompanied by deficits in skills necessary for independent daily functioning : MENTAL RETARDATION

intellectual property *n* : property (as an idea, method, or written work) that derives from the work of the mind

in·tel·li·gence \in-'tel-ə-jən(t)s\ *n* **1** : the ability to learn and understand or to deal with problems : REASON **2 a** : NEWS 1a **b** : information concerning an enemy or possible enemy; *also* : an agency engaged in obtaining such information

intelligence quotient *n* : IQ

intelligence test *n* : a test designed to measure a person's intelligence compared to others

in·tel·li·gent \in-'tel-ə-jənt\ *adj* **1 a** : possessing intelligence ⟨humans are *intelligent* beings⟩ **b** : showing a higher than average degree of intelligence ⟨an *intelligent* student⟩ **c** : revealing or reflecting good judgment or sound thought ⟨an *intelligent* decision⟩ **2** : able to perform computing tasks : controlled by a computer ⟨an *intelligent* terminal⟩ — **in·tel·li·gent·ly** *adv*

synonyms INTELLIGENT, CLEVER, ALERT, QUICK-WITTED mean having a sharp mind. INTELLIGENT stresses the ability to deal with new situations and solve problems ⟨*intelligent* people are needed for police work⟩. CLEVER suggests a natural ability to find solutions but it may also suggest shallow thinking ⟨*clever* enough to get by without studying⟩. ALERT stresses quickness in seeing and understanding something ⟨an *alert* student saw that there was a catch to the question⟩. QUICK-WITTED suggests coming up with quick replies in conversation or finding solutions in emergencies ⟨a *quick-witted* debater⟩ ⟨a *quick-witted* babysitter put out the fire⟩.

in·tel·li·gen·tsia \in-,tel-ə-'jen(t)-sē-ə, -'gen(t)-\ *n* : intellectuals as a group : educated people

in·tel·li·gi·ble \in-'tel-ə-jə-bəl\ *adj* : able to be understood — **in·tel·li·gi·bil·i·ty** \-,tel-ə-jə-'bil-ət-ē\ *n* — **in·tel·li·gi·ble·ness** \-'tel-ə-jə-bəl-nəs\ *n* — **in·tel·li·gi·bly** \-blē\ *adv*

in·tem·per·ance \(')in-'tem-p(ə-)rən(t)s\ *n* : lack of moderation or self-restraint; *esp* : excessive use of alcoholic beverages

in·tem·per·ate \(,)in-'tem-p(ə-)rət\ *adj* **1** : not moderate or mild : SEVERE ⟨*intemperate* weather⟩ **2** : lacking or showing lack of restraint ⟨*intemperate* language⟩ **3** : given to excessive use of alcoholic beverages — **in·tem·per·ate·ly** *adv* — **in·tem·per·ate·ness** *n*

in·tend \in-'tend\ *vb* : to have in mind as a purpose or aim : PLAN ⟨*intends* to travel abroad next year⟩

\ə\ abut	\aù\ out	\i\ tip	\ȯ\ saw	\ù\ foot
\ər\ further	\ch\ chin	\ī\ life	\ȯi\ coin	\y\ yet
\a\ mat	\e\ pet	\j\ job	\th\ thin	\yü\ few
\ā\ take	\ē\ easy	\ŋ\ sing	\th\ this	\yù\ cure
\ä\ cot, cart	\g\ go	\ō\ bone	\ü\ food	\zh\ vision

¹in·tend·ed \in-'ten-dəd\ *adj* **1** : expected to be such in the future ⟨your *intended* career⟩ **2** : INTENTIONAL ⟨an *intended* insult⟩

²intended *n* : the person to whom another is engaged to be married

in·tense \in-'ten(t)s\ *adj* **1** : existing in an extreme degree ⟨*intense* pain⟩ **2** : done or performed with great zeal, energy, or eagerness ⟨*intense* study⟩ **3** : feeling deeply ⟨an *intense* actor⟩ — **in·tense·ly** *adv* — **in·tense·ness** *n*

in·ten·si·fy \in-'ten(t)-sə-ˌfī\ *vb* **-fied; -fy·ing** : to make or become intense or more intensive — **in·ten·si·fi·ca·tion** \-ˌten(t)-sə-fə-'kā-shən\ *n* — **in·ten·si·fi·er** \-'ten(t)-sə-ˌfī(-ə)r\ *n*

in·ten·si·ty \in-'ten(t)-sət-ē\ *n, pl* **-ties** **1** : the quality or state of being intense; *esp* : extreme strength, force, or feeling **2** : the degree or amount of a quality or condition ⟨the *intensity* of an electric field⟩

¹in·ten·sive \in-'ten(t)-siv\ *adj* **1** : marked by special effort ⟨an *intensive* campaign⟩ **2** : serving to give emphasis ⟨an *intensive* adverb, as "dreadfully" in "it was dreadfully cold"⟩ — **in·ten·sive·ly** *adv* — **in·ten·sive·ness** *n*

²intensive *n* : an intensive word ⟨"quite" is an *intensive* in "quite a guy"⟩

intensive care *n* : continuous monitoring and treatment of seriously ill patients using special medical equipment and services; *also* : a unit in a hospital providing intensive care

¹in·tent \in-'tent\ *n* **1** : PURPOSE 1, INTENTION ⟨with *intent* to injure⟩ **2** : ¹MEANING 1a ⟨the *intent* of the law⟩

²intent *adj* **1** : directed with strained or eager attention ⟨an *intent* gaze⟩ **2 a** : having the mind, attention, or will concentrated on something **b** : set on some end or purpose ⟨*intent* on going⟩ — **in·tent·ly** *adv* — **in·tent·ness** *n*

in·ten·tion \in-'ten-chən\ *n* **1** : a determination to act in a certain way **2** : an intended goal : AIM **3** : a person or purpose that is especially prayed for **4** : ¹MEANING 3, SIGNIFICANCE

    synonyms INTENTION, PURPOSE, DESIGN, OBJECTIVE mean what one will try to accomplish or reach. INTENTION suggests only that one has something in mind to do ⟨our *intention* to visit Alaska someday⟩. PURPOSE suggests a fixed determination to accomplish something ⟨have the finding of happiness as one's *purpose* in life⟩. DESIGN suggests a carefully calculated plan ⟨a coach with great *designs* for her star athlete⟩. OBJECTIVE stresses a definite goal and one that is within reach ⟨our *objective* is to cross the river before dark⟩.

in·ten·tion·al \in-'tench-nəl, -'ten-chən-ᵊl\ *adj* : done by intention : not accidental **synonyms** see VOLUNTARY — **in·ten·tion·al·ly** \-'tench-nə-lē, -'ten-chən-ᵊl-ē\ *adv*

in·ter \in-'tər\ *vb* **in·terred; in·ter·ring** : BURY 1 [from the Latin phrase *in terra* "in the earth"]

inter- *prefix* **1** : between : among : in the midst ⟨*inter*lock⟩ ⟨*inter*stellar⟩ **2** : reciprocal ⟨*inter*relate⟩ : reciprocally ⟨*inter*act⟩ **3** : located or occurring between ⟨*inter*lining⟩ **4** : carried on between ⟨*inter*national⟩ **5** : shared by or involving two or more ⟨*inter*racial⟩ [derived from Latin *inter* "between, among"]

in·ter·act \ˌint-ə-'rakt\ *vb* : to act on one another

in·ter·ac·tion \ˌint-ə-'rak-shən\ *n* : the action or influence of people, groups, or things on one another — **in·ter·ac·tion·al** \-shnəl, -shən-ᵊl\ *adj*

in·ter·ac·tive \ˌint-ə-'rak-tiv\ *adj* **1** : active between people, groups, or things **2** : involving the actions or input of a user ⟨an *interactive* museum exhibit⟩; *esp* : allowing two-way electronic communications (as between a person and a computer) — **in·ter·ac·tive·ly** *adv* — **in·ter·ac·tiv·i·ty** \-ˌrak-'tiv-ət-ē\ *n*

in·ter·atom·ic \ˌint-ə-rə-'täm-ik\ *adj* : located or acting between atoms

in·ter·breed \ˌint-ər-'brēd\ *vb* **in·ter·bred** \-'bred\; **-breed·ing** : to breed or cause to breed together: as **a** : CROSSBREED **b** : to breed within a population

in·ter·cede \ˌint-ər-'sēd\ *vb* **-ced·ed; -ced·ing** **1** : to act as a go-between for hostile parties **2** : to plead in behalf of another

in·ter·cel·lu·lar \ˌint-ər-'sel-yə-lər\ *adj* : lying between cells ⟨*intercellular* spaces⟩

¹in·ter·cept \ˌint-ər-'sept\ *vb* **1** : to take or seize on the way to or before arrival ⟨*intercept* a letter⟩ ⟨*intercept* a pass⟩ **2** : to include (part of a line, surface, or solid) between two points, curves, or surfaces ⟨a line *intercepted* between points A and B⟩ [from Latin *interceptus,* past participle of *intercipere* "to take or hinder in the course of," from *inter-* "between, in the course of" and *cipere,* a form of *capere* "to take, seize" — related to CAPTURE, EXCEPT] — **in·ter·cep·tion** \-'sep-shən\ *n*

²in·ter·cept \'int-ər-ˌsept\ *n* : the distance from the origin of a coordinate system to a point where a graph (as of a line) crosses a coordinate axis

in·ter·cep·tor \ˌint-ər-'sep-tər\ *n* : one that intercepts; *esp* : a fast fighter plane designed for defense against bombers

in·ter·ces·sion \ˌint-ər-'sesh-ən\ *n* : the act of interceding — **in·ter·ces·sor** \-'ses-ər\ *n*

¹in·ter·change \ˌint-ər-'chānj\ *vb* **1** : to put each in the place of the other **2** : ²EXCHANGE **3** : to change places mutually — **in·ter·change·abil·i·ty** \-ˌchān-jə-'bil-ət-ē\ *n* — **in·ter·change·able** \-'chān-jə-bəl\ *adj* — **in·ter·change·ably** \-blē\ *adv* — **in·ter·chang·er** *n*

²in·ter·change \'int-ər-ˌchānj\ *n* **1** : the act or process of interchanging **2** : a joining of two or more highways by a system of separate levels that permit streams of traffic to pass from one to another without crossing

in·ter·col·le·giate \ˌint-ər-kə-'lē-j(ē-)ət\ *adj* : existing or carried on between colleges ⟨*intercollegiate* sports⟩

in·ter·com \'int-ər-ˌkäm\ *n* : a two-way communication system with microphone and loudspeaker at each end

in·ter·com·mu·ni·cate \ˌint-ər-kə-'myü-nə-ˌkāt\ *vb* : to exchange communication with one another — **in·ter·com·mu·ni·ca·tion** \-ˌmyü-nə-'kā-shən\ *n*

intercommunication system *n* : INTERCOM

in·ter·con·nect \ˌint-ər-kə-'nekt\ *vb* : to connect with one another — **in·ter·con·nec·ted** *adj* — **in·ter·con·nec·tion** \-'nek-shən\ *n*

in·ter·con·ti·nen·tal \ˌint-ər-ˌkänt-ᵊn-'ent-ᵊl\ *adj* **1** : extending among or carried on between continents ⟨*intercontinental* trade⟩ **2** : capable of traveling from one continent to another ⟨an *intercontinental* ballistic missile⟩

in·ter·course \'int-ər-ˌkō(ə)rs, -ˌko(ə)rs\ *n* **1** : dealings between persons or groups : RELATIONS **2** : physical sexual contact between individuals that involves the genitalia of at least one individual; *esp* : SEXUAL INTERCOURSE

in·ter·crop \ˌint-ər-'kräp\ *vb* : to grow two or more crops at one time on the same piece of land

in·ter·de·pend \ˌint-ər-di-'pend\ *vb* : to depend on one another — **in·ter·de·pen·dence** \-'pen-dən(t)s\ *n* — **in·ter·de·pen·den·cy** \-dən-sē\ *n* — **in·ter·de·pen·dent** \-dənt\ *adj* — **in·ter·de·pen·dent·ly** *adv*

¹in·ter·dict \'int-ər-ˌdikt\ *n* **1** : a Roman Catholic ecclesiastical withdrawal of sacraments and Christian burial from a person or district **2** : PROHIBITION 2

²in·ter·dict \ˌint-ər-'dikt\ *vb* : to prohibit or forbid especially by an interdict — **in·ter·dic·tion** \-'dik-shən\ *n*

¹in·ter·est \'in-trəst; 'int-ə-rəst, -ə-rəst; 'in-ˌtərst; 'in-ˌtrəst\ *n* **1** : a right, title, or legal share in something **2** : something that promotes well-being : BENEFIT; *also* : SELF-INTEREST 2 **3 a** : a charge for borrowed money that is generally a percentage of the amount borrowed **b** : the profit in goods or money that is made on invested capital **4 a** : readiness to be concerned with or moved by something **b** : a quality that arouses interest ⟨modern art holds no *interest* for him⟩

²interest *vb* **1** : to persuade to participate or take part ⟨couldn't *interest* her in joining us⟩ **2** : to arouse or hold the interest of ⟨the movie does not *interest* me⟩

in·ter·est·ing \\'in-trəst-iŋ; 'int-ə-,rest-iŋ, -ə-rəst-, -ərst-\\ *adj* : holding the attention : arousing interest

in·ter·est·ing·ly \\'in-trəst-iŋ-lē; 'int-ə-,rest-iŋ-le, -ə-rəst-, -ərst-\\ *adv* **1** : in an interesting manner ⟨a story *interestingly* told⟩ **2** : it is interesting ⟨*interestingly* enough, that was the first one⟩

¹in·ter·face \\'int-ər-,fās\\ *n* **1** : a surface forming a common boundary of two bodies, spaces, or phases ⟨an *interface* between oil and water⟩ **2 a** : the place at which independent systems meet and act on or communicate with each other **b** : the ways by which interaction or communication is brought about at an interface — **in·ter·fa·cial** \\,int-ər-'fā-shəl\\ *adj*

²interface *vb* **1** : to connect or become connected through an interface **2** : to serve as an interface for

in·ter·fac·ing \\-,fā-siŋ\\ *n* : fabric attached especially between the facing and the outside of a garment (as in a collar) for stiffening or reinforcing

in·ter·fere \\,int-ə(r)-'fi(ə)r\\ *vb* -**fered; -fer·ing** **1** : to come in collision or be in opposition : CLASH ⟨his arrival *interfered* with our plans⟩ **2** : to take part in the concerns of others ⟨don't *interfere* with our negotiations⟩ **3** : to act on one another ⟨*interfering* light waves⟩ **synonyms** see MEDDLE — **in·ter·fer·er** *n*

in·ter·fer·ence \\,int-ə(r)-'fir-ən(t)s\\ *n* **1 a** : the act or process of interfering **b** : something that interferes **2** : the shared effect on meeting of two waves (as of light or sound) whereby the waves cancel each other at some points and strengthen each other at other points **3 a** : the act of legally blocking an opponent in football **b** : the act of illegally getting in the way of an opponent in sports **4 a** : confusion of received radio signals due to undesired signals **b** : something that produces such confusion

in·ter·fer·om·e·ter \\,int-ə(r)-fə-'räm-ət-ər, -,fir-'äm-\\ *n* : an instrument that uses the interference of waves (as of light) for making exact measurements (as of wavelength)

in·ter·fer·on \\,int-ə(r)-'fi(ə)r-,än\\ *n* : any of a group of proteins produced by cells that keep viruses attacking the cells from multiplying

in·ter·ga·lac·tic \\,int-ər-gə-'lak-tik\\ *adj* : located in or relating to the spaces between galaxies

¹in·ter·gla·cial \\,int-ər-'glā-shəl\\ *adj* : occurring or relating to the time between glaciations

²interglacial *n* : a period of time of warm climate between glaciations

in·ter·gov·ern·men·tal \\-,gəv-ər(n)-'ment-ᵊl\\ *adj* : existing or occurring between two or more governments or levels of government ⟨*intergovernmental* meetings⟩

in·ter·im \\'in-tə-rəm\\ *n* : a time intervening : INTERVAL — **interim** *adj*

¹in·te·ri·or \\in-'tir-ē-ər\\ *adj* **1** : existing or occurring within the limits : INNER **2** : remote from the border or shore — **in·te·ri·or·ly** *adv*

²interior *n* **1** : the internal or inner part of something : INSIDE ⟨the *interior* of a house⟩ **2** : the inland part (as of a country or island) ⟨traveled to the *interior* of Australia⟩ **3** : the internal affairs of a state or nation ⟨department of the *Interior*⟩

interior angle *n* : any of the four angles formed in the area between a pair of lines when a third line cuts them

interior decoration *n* : INTERIOR DESIGN

interior decorator *n* : INTERIOR DESIGNER

interior design *n* : the art of decorating and furnishing the interior of a building ⟨the college offers a good program in *interior design*⟩

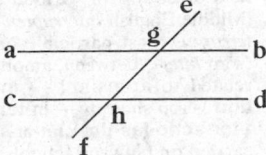

interior angle: *agh, bgh, ghd, ghc*

interior designer *n* : a person who specializes in interior design

in·ter·ject \\,int-ər-'jekt\\ *vb* : to throw in between or among other things ⟨*interject* a remark⟩ — **in·ter·jec·tor** \\-'jek-tər\\ *n* — **in·ter·jec·to·ry** \\-t(ə-)rē\\ *adj*

in·ter·jec·tion \\,int-ər-'jek-shən\\ *n* **1** : an interjecting of something **2** : something interjected **3** : a word or cry expressing sudden or strong feeling — **in·ter·jec·tion·al** \\-shnəl, -shən-ᵊl\\ *adj* — **in·ter·jec·tion·al·ly** \\-shnəl-ē, -shən-ᵊl-ē\\ *adv*

in·ter·lace \\,int-ər-'lās\\ *vb* : to unite or cross by or as if by lacing together : INTERWEAVE ⟨*interlaced* fibers⟩ ⟨*interlacing* branches⟩ — **in·ter·lace·ment** \\-'lā-smənt\\ *n*

¹in·ter·line \\,int-ər-'līn\\ *vb* : to write between lines already written

²interline *vb* : to provide a garment with an interlining

in·ter·lin·ear \\,int-ər-'lin-ē-ər\\ *adj* **1** : written between lines already written or printed **2** : printed in different languages in alternate lines ⟨an *interlinear* translation⟩ — **in·ter·lin·ear·ly** *adv*

in·ter·lin·ing \\'int-ər-,lī-niŋ\\ *n* : a lining between the ordinary lining and the outside fabric

in·ter·lock \\,int-ər-'läk\\ *vb* : to lock together : interlace firmly ⟨a series of rings *interlocking* to form a chain⟩

in·ter·lop·er \\,int-ər-'lō-pər, 'int-ər-,lō-pər\\ *n* : a person who intrudes or interferes wrongly or meddlesomely

in·ter·lude \\'int-ər-,lüd\\ *n* **1** : a performance between the acts of a play **2** : an intervening period, space, or event : INTERVAL **3** : a musical composition inserted between the parts of a longer one, a drama, or a religious service

in·ter·mar·riage \\,int-ər-'mar-ij\\ *n* : marriage between members of different racial, social, or religious groups

in·ter·mar·ry \\,int-ər-'mar-ē\\ *vb* **1** : to marry each other **2** : to become connected by intermarriage

in·ter·me·di·ary \\,int-ər-'mēd-ē-,er-ē\\ *adj* **1** : INTERMEDIATE ⟨an *intermediary* stage⟩ **2** : acting as a mediator ⟨*intermediary* agent⟩ — **intermediary** *n*

in·ter·me·di·ate \\,int-ər-'mēd-ē-ət\\ *adj* : being or occurring in the middle or between extremes [Middle Latin *intermediatus* "intermediate," derived from Latin *inter-* "among, in the midst" and *medius* "middle" — related to ¹MEDIAN] — **intermediate** *n* — **in·ter·me·di·ate·ly** *adv*

intermediate host *n* : a host that is normally used by a parasite in the course of its life cycle and that may actively carry it from one living thing to another

in·ter·ment \\in-'tər-mənt\\ *n* : BURIAL

in·ter·mesh \\,int-ər-'mesh\\ *vb* : to mesh with one another : INTERLOCK

in·ter·mez·zo \\,int-ər-'mets-ō, -'medz-ō\\ *n, pl* -**zi** \\-ē\\ *or* -**zos** **1** : a short light piece between the acts of a serious drama or opera **2 a** : a short movement connecting parts of a longer musical work **b** : a short independent instrumental composition

in·ter·mi·na·ble \\(')in-'tərm-(ə-)nə-bəl\\ *adj* : having or seeming to have no end; *esp* : tiresomely long — **in·ter·mi·na·ble·ness** *n* — **in·ter·mi·na·bly** \\-blē\\ *adv*

in·ter·min·gle \\,int-ər-'miŋ-gəl\\ *vb* : INTERMIX

in·ter·mis·sion \\,int-ər-'mish-ən\\ *n* **1** : ¹PAUSE 1, INTERRUPTION ⟨work without *intermission*⟩ **2** : a pause or interval between the parts of an entertainment (as the acts of a play)

in·ter·mit \\,int-ər-'mit\\ *vb* -**mit·ted; -mit·ting** : to stop for a time and then continue

in·ter·mit·tence \\,int-ər-'mit-ᵊn(t)s\\ *n* : the quality or state of being intermittent

\ə\ abut	\au̇\ out	\i\ tip	\o̊\ saw	\u̇\ foot
\ər\ further	\ch\ chin	\ī\ life	\o̊i\ coin	\y\ yet
\a\ mat	\e\ pet	\j\ job	\th\ thin	\yü\ few
\ā\ take	\ē\ easy	\ŋ\ sing	\<u>th</u>\ this	\yu̇\ cure
\ä\ cot, cart	\g\ go	\ō\ bone	\ü\ food	\zh\ vision

in·ter·mit·tent \,int-ər-'mit-ᵊnt\ *adj* : starting, stopping, and starting again ⟨an *intermittent* fever⟩ — **in·ter·mit·tent·ly** *adv*

in·ter·mix \,int-ər-'miks\ *vb* : to mix together — **in·ter·mix·ture** \-'miks-chər\ *n*

in·ter·mo·lec·u·lar \,int-ər-mə-'lek-yə-lər\ *adj* : existing or acting between molecules

¹in·tern \'in-,tərn, in-'tərn\ *vb* : to confine especially during a war ⟨*interned* enemy aliens⟩

²in·tern *also* **in·terne** \'in-,tərn\ *n* : an advanced student or graduate in a special field (as medicine or teaching) who is gaining supervised practical experience (as in a hospital or classroom)

³in·tern \'in-,tərn\ *vb* : to work as an intern

in·ter·nal \in-'tərn-ᵊl\ *adj* **1** : existing or lying within : IN-NER ⟨*internal* structure⟩ **2** : relating to or occurring or located in the interior of the body ⟨*internal* organs⟩ ⟨*internal* pain⟩ **3** : of or relating to the domestic affairs of a state ⟨*internal* revenue⟩ — **in·ter·nal·ly** \-ē\ *adv*

internal combustion engine *n* : an engine in which the fuel is ignited within the engine cylinder instead of in an external furnace

internal medicine *n* : a branch of medicine that deals with diseases not requiring surgery

internal rhyme *n* : a rhyme between a word within a line and another either at the end of the same line or within another line

internal secretion *n* : HORMONE

¹in·ter·na·tion·al \,int-ər-'nash-nəl, -ən-ᵊl\ *adj* **1** : of, relating to, affecting, or involving two or more nations ⟨*international* trade⟩ **2** : active, known, or reaching beyond national boundaries ⟨an *international* reputation⟩ — **in·ter·na·tion·al·ly** \-'nash-nə-lē, -ən-ᵊl-ē\ *adv*

²international *n* : an organization having branches in more than one country

international date line *n* : an imaginary line along the 180th meridian named as the place where each calendar day begins

in·ter·na·tion·al·ism \,int-ər-'nash-nəl-,iz-əm, -'nash-ən-ᵊl-\ *n* : a policy of cooperation among nations or an attitude favoring such a policy — **in·ter·na·tion·al·ist** \-əst\ *n or adj*

in·ter·na·tion·al·ize \-'nash-nəl-,īz, -ən-ᵊl-\ *vb* : to make international ⟨*internationalized* the company's business⟩ — **in·ter·na·tion·al·i·za·tion** \-,nash-nəl-ə-'zā-shən, -ən-ᵊl-\ *n*

International System of Units *n* : a system of units based on the metric system and used by international agreement especially for scientific work

in·ter·ne·cine \'int-ər-'nes-,ēn, -'nē-,sīn; in-'tər-nə-,sēn\ *adj* **1** : marked by slaughter : DEADLY **2** : of, relating to, or involving conflict within a group ⟨*internecine* feuds⟩

in·tern·ee \,(,)in-,tər-'nē\ *n* : an interned person

In·ter·net \'int-ər-,net\ *n* : a communications system that connects computers and computer networks all over the world

in·ter·neu·ron \,int-ər-'n(y)ü-,rän, -'n(y)ú(ə)r-,än\ *n* : a neuron that carries a nerve impulse from one neuron to another

in·ter·nist \'in-,tər-nəst\ *n* : a physician who specializes in internal medicine

in·tern·ment \in-'tərn-mənt, 'in-,tərn-\ *n* : the act of interning : the state of being interned

in·ter·node \'int-ər-,nōd\ *n* : a part between two nodes (as of a plant stem)

in·tern·ship \-ship\ *n* **1** : the state or position of being an intern **2** : a period of service as an intern

in·ter·pen·e·trate \,int-ər-'pen-ə-,trāt\ *vb* **1** : to penetrate between, within, or throughout **2** : to penetrate mutually — **in·ter·pen·e·tra·tion** \-,pen-ə-'trā-shən\ *n*

in·ter·per·son·al \-'pərs-nəl, -ᵊn-əl\ *adj* : being, relating to, or including relations between persons — **in·ter·per·son·al·ly** \-'pərs-nə-lē, -ᵊn-ə-\ *adv*

in·ter·phase \'int-ər-,fāz\ *n* : the period between the end of one mitotic or meiotic cell division and the beginning of the next

in·ter·plan·e·tary \,int-ər-'plan-ə-,ter-ē\ *adj* : between planets ⟨*interplanetary* space⟩ ⟨*interplanetary* travel⟩

in·ter·play \'int-ər-,plā\ *n* : mutual action or influence : INTERACTION — **in·ter·play** \,int-ər-'plā, 'int-ər-,plā\ *vb*

in·ter·po·late \in-'tər-pə-,lāt\ *vb* **-lat·ed; -lat·ing 1** : to alter (as a text) by inserting new matter **2** : to insert between other things or parts — **in·ter·po·la·tion** \-,tər-pə-'lā-shən\ *n* — **in·ter·po·la·tive** \-'tər-pə-,lāt-iv\ *adj* — **in·ter·po·la·tor** \-,lāt-ər\ *n*

in·ter·pose \,int-ər-'pōz\ *vb* **-posed; -pos·ing 1 a** : to place in an intervening position **b** : INTRUDE 1, INTER-RUPT **2** : to introduce in between the parts of a conversation or argument **3** : to step in between opposing parties — **in·ter·pos·er** *n* — **in·ter·po·si·tion** \-pə-'zish-ən\ *n*

in·ter·pret \in-'tər-prət\ *vb* **1** : to explain the meaning of ⟨*interpret* a dream⟩ **2** : to understand according to one's own belief or judgment ⟨*interpret* an act as unfriendly⟩ **3** : to bring out the meaning of by performing ⟨an actor *interprets* a role⟩ **4** : to translate for speakers of different languages — **in·ter·pret·able** \-prət-ə-bəl\ *adj*

in·ter·pre·ta·tion \in-,tər-prə-'tā-shən\ *n* **1** : the act or the result of interpreting : EXPLANATION **2** : an instance of artistic interpretation in performance or adaptation — **in·ter·pre·ta·tive** \-'tər-prə-,tāt-iv\ *adj* — **in·ter·pre·ta·tive·ly** *adv*

in·ter·pret·er \in-'tər-prət-ər\ *n* **1** : one that interprets; *esp* : a person who translates orally for people speaking different languages **2** : a computer program that translates an instruction into machine language and executes it before going to the next instruction

in·ter·pre·tive \in-'tər-prət-iv\ *adj* **1** : of, relating to, or based on interpretation ⟨*interpretive* errors⟩ **2** : designed to interpret : EXPLANATORY ⟨*interpretive* exhibits⟩ — **in·ter·pre·tive·ly** *adv*

in·ter·ra·cial \,int-ər-'rā-shəl\ *adj* : of, involving, or designed for members of different races

in·ter·reg·num \,int-ə-'reg-nəm\ *n, pl* **-nums** *or* **-na** \-nə\ : a period between two successive reigns or regimes

in·ter·re·late \,int-ə(r)-ri-'lāt\ *vb* : to bring into or have a shared relationship — **in·ter·re·la·tion** \-'lā-shən\ *n* — **in·ter·re·la·tion·ship** \-,ship\ *n*

in·ter·ro·gate \in-'ter-ə-,gāt\ *vb* **-gat·ed; -gat·ing** : to question formally and thoroughly ⟨*interrogate* a prisoner of war⟩ — **in·ter·ro·ga·tion** \-,ter-ə-'gā-shən\ *n* — **in·ter·ro·ga·tor** \-'ter-ə-,gāt-ər\ *n*

interrogation point *n* : QUESTION MARK

¹in·ter·rog·a·tive \,int-ə-'räg-ət-iv\ *adj* **1** : having the form or force of a question ⟨an *interrogative* phrase⟩ **2** : used in a question ⟨an *interrogative* pronoun⟩ — **in·ter·rog·a·tive·ly** *adv*

²interrogative *n* : a word (as *who, what, which*) used in asking questions

in·ter·rog·a·to·ry \,int-ə-'räg-ə-,tōr-ē, -,tòr-\ *adj* : containing, expressing, or implying a question

in·ter·rupt \,int-ə-'rəpt\ *vb* **1** : to stop or hinder by breaking in ⟨*interrupt* a conversation⟩ **2** : to break the sameness or course of ⟨a loud crash *interrupted* the silence⟩ [Middle English *interrupten* "to interrupt," from Latin *interruptus,* past participle of *interrumpere* "to interrupt," from *inter-* "between, among" and *rumpere* "to break" — related to RUPTURE] — **in·ter·rupt·er** *n* — **in·ter·rup·tion** \-'rəp-shən\ *n* — **in·ter·rup·tive** \-'rəp-tiv\ *adj*

in·ter·scho·las·tic \,int-ər-skə-'las-tik\ *adj* : existing or carried on between schools

in·ter·sect \,int-ər-'sekt\ *vb* **1** : to divide by passing through or across : CROSS ⟨one line *intersecting* another⟩ **2** : to meet and cross at one or more points ⟨lines *intersecting* at right angles⟩ ⟨overlapping circles *intersect* at two points⟩

in·ter·sec·tion \,int-ər-'sek-shən\ *n* **1** : the act or process of intersecting **2** : the place or point where two or more things and especially streets intersect ⟨a busy *intersection*⟩ **3** : the set of mathematical elements shared by two or more sets; *esp* : the set of points shared by two geometric figures

in·ter·sex \'int-ər-,seks\ *n* : an individual that is intermediate in sexual characters between a typical male and a typical female

intersection 3

¹in·ter·space \'int-ər-,spās\ *n* : an intervening space

²in·ter·space \,int-ər-'spās\ *vb* : to occupy or fill the space between

in·ter·spe·cif·ic \,int-ər-spi-'sif-ik\ *or* **in·ter·spe·cies** \-'spē-(,)shēz, -(,)sēz\ *adj* : existing or arising between species ⟨an *interspecific* hybrid⟩

in·ter·sperse \,int-ər-'spərs\ *vb* **-spersed; -spers·ing 1** : to set here and there among other things ⟨*intersperse* pictures in a book⟩ **2** : to vary with things inserted here and there ⟨*interspersed* the photo album with her poetry⟩ — **in·ter·sper·sion** \-'spər-zhən\ *n*

¹in·ter·state \,int-ər-'stāt\ *adj* : of, connecting, or existing between states especially of the U.S. ⟨*interstate* highways⟩

²in·ter·state \'int-ər-,stāt\ *n* : an interstate highway

in·ter·stel·lar \,int-ər-'stel-ər\ *adj* : located or taking place among the stars ⟨*interstellar* space⟩

in·ter·stice \in-'tər-stəs\ *n, pl* **in·ter·stic·es** \-stə-,sēz, -stə-səz\ : a little space between two things

in·ter·sti·tial \,int-ər-'stish-əl\ *adj* : relating to or located in the interstices — **in·ter·sti·tial·ly** \-'stish-ə-lē\ *adv*

in·ter·tid·al \,int-ər-'tīd-ᵊl\ *adj* : of, relating to, or being the area that is above low-tide mark but exposed to flooding by the tide

in·ter·twine \,int-ər-'twīn\ *vb* : to twine or cause to twine about one another : INTERLACE

in·ter·ur·ban \,int-ər-'ər-bən\ *adj* : connecting cities or towns ⟨*interurban* transportation⟩

in·ter·val \'int-ər-vəl\ *n* **1** : a period of time between events or states : PAUSE ⟨a three-month *interval*⟩ ⟨the *interval* between elections⟩ **2** : a space between things ⟨the *interval* between two desks⟩ **3** : difference in pitch between tones

in·ter·vene \,int-ər-'vēn\ *vb* **-vened; -ven·ing 1** : to happen as an unrelated event ⟨rain *intervened* and we canceled the game⟩ **2** : to come between points of time or between events ⟨barely one minute *intervened* between the two phone calls⟩ **3** : to come between in order to stop, settle, or change ⟨*intervene* to stop a fight⟩ **4** : to be or lie between ⟨*intervening* hills⟩ — **in·ter·ven·tion** \-'ven-chən\ *n*

in·ter·ver·te·bral disk \,in-tər-'vər-tə-brəl-, -(,)vər-'tē-\ *n* : any of the tough disks situated between adjacent vertebrae of the backbone

in·ter·view \'int-ər-,vyü\ *n* **1** : a meeting usually face to face especially for the purpose of talking or consulting ⟨an *interview* to evaluate a prospective student's qualifications⟩ **2** : a meeting at which information is obtained (as by a reporter) from a person; *also* : the account of such a meeting — **interview** *vb* — **in·ter·view·er** *n*

in·ter·weave \,int-ər-'wēv\ *vb* **1** : to weave together **2** : to blend or cause to blend together — **in·ter·wo·ven** \-'wō-vən\ *adj*

in·tes·tate \in-'tes-,tāt, -'tes-tət\ *adj* **1** : not having made a will ⟨he died *intestate*⟩ **2** : not disposed of by will ⟨*intestate* personal property⟩ — **in·tes·ta·cy** \-'tes-tə-sē\ *n*

in·tes·ti·nal \in-'tes-tən-ᵊl\ *adj* : of or relating to the in-

testine **2** : affecting or occurring in the intestine — **in·tes·ti·nal·ly** \-ē\ *adv*

in·tes·tine \in-'tes-tən\ *n* : the part of the alimentary canal that is a long tube composed of the small intestine and the large intestine, that extends from the stomach to the anus, that helps to digest food and absorb nutrients and water, and that carries waste matter to be discharged

in·ti·fa·da \,int-ə-'fäd-ə\ *n* : UPRISING, REBELLION [Arabic *intifāda*, literally, "the act of shaking off"]

in·ti·ma·cy \'int-ə-mə-sē\ *n, pl* **-cies 1** : the state of being intimate **2** : something of a personal or private nature ⟨shared little *intimacies* in their letters⟩

¹in·ti·mate \'int-ə-,māt\ *vb* **-mat·ed; -mat·ing 1** : ANNOUNCE 1 **2** : to communicate indirectly : HINT — **in·ti·mat·er** *n* — **in·ti·ma·tion** \,int-ə-'mā-shən\ *n*

²in·ti·mate \'int-ə-mət\ *adj* **1** : belonging to or characterizing one's deepest nature ⟨her *intimate* reflections⟩ **2** : marked by very close association or contact ⟨an *intimate* familiarity with the rules⟩ **3 a** : marked by a warm friendship developing through long association ⟨*intimate* friends⟩ **b** : suggesting informal warmth or privacy ⟨*intimate* clubs⟩ **4** : of a very personal or private nature ⟨*intimate* secrets⟩ — **in·ti·mate·ly** *adv* — **in·ti·mate·ness** *n*

³in·ti·mate \'int-ə-mət\ *n* : an intimate friend : CONFIDANT

in·tim·i·date \in-'tim-ə-,dāt\ *vb* **-dat·ed; -dat·ing** : to make timid or fearful by or as if by threats — **in·tim·i·da·tion** \-,tim-ə-'dā-shən\ *n* — **in·tim·i·da·tor** \-'tim-ə-,dāt-ər\ *n*

in·to \'in-tə, -tü\ *prep* **1** — used to indicate entry, introduction, or inclusion ⟨came *into* the room⟩ ⟨enter *into* an agreement⟩ **2 a** : to the state, condition, or form of ⟨got *into* trouble⟩ ⟨divide *into* four parts⟩ **b** : to the occupation, action, or possession of ⟨go *into* farming⟩ **3** : AGAINST 4 ⟨ran *into* a wall⟩ **4** : involved with or interested in ⟨was never *into* abstract art⟩

in·tol·er·a·ble \(')in-'täl-(ə)rə-bəl, -'täl-ər-bəl\ *adj* : not tolerable : UNBEARABLE ⟨*intolerable* pain⟩ — **in·tol·er·a·bil·i·ty** \(,)in-,täl-(ə-)rə-'bil-ət-ē\ *n* — **in·tol·er·a·bly** \(')in-'täl-(ə-)rə-blē, -'täl-ər-blē\ *adv*

in·tol·er·ance \(')in-'täl-(ə-)rən(t)s\ *n* **1** : the quality or state of being intolerant **2** : exceptional sensitivity (as to a drug or food)

in·tol·er·ant \(')in-'täl-(ə-)rənt\ *adj* **1** : unable or unwilling to endure **2** : unwilling to grant equality, freedom, or other social rights — **in·tol·er·ant·ly** *adv*

in·to·na·tion \,in-tə-'nā-shən\ *n* **1** : the act of intoning; *also* : something intoned **2** : the ability to play or sing music in tune **3** : the rise and fall in pitch of the voice in speech — **in·to·na·tion·al** \-shnəl, -shən-ᵊl\ *adj*

in·tone \in-'tōn\ *vb* **in·toned; in·ton·ing** : to utter in musical or prolonged tones : CHANT — **in·ton·er** *n*

in·tox·i·cant \in-'täk-si-kənt\ *n* : something that intoxicates; *esp* : an alcoholic drink — **intoxicant** *adj*

in·tox·i·cate \in-'täk-sə-,kāt\ *vb* **-cat·ed; -cat·ing 1** : to affect by alcohol or a drug especially to the point where physical and mental control is much reduced **2** : to excite to enthusiasm or frenzy

Word History The Greek word *toxon* means "bow" or "arrow." From this came the Greek *toxikon*, meaning "a poison in which arrows are dipped." *Toxikon* was borrowed into Latin as *toxicum*, which gave rise to the Latin verb *intoxicare*, "to poison." The English word *intoxicate* comes from this Latin verb. *Intoxicate* originally meant "to poison" in English, but now it is almost never used with this meaning. It is related to the words *toxic*, meaning "poisonous," and *toxin*, meaning "a poison." Both of

\ə\ abut	\au̇\ **out**	\i\ **tip**	\ȯ\ **saw**	\u̇\ **foot**
\ər\ **further**	\ch\ **chin**	\ī\ **life**	\ȯi\ **coin**	\y\ **yet**
\a\ **mat**	\e\ **pet**	\j\ **job**	\th\ **thin**	\yü\ **few**
\ā\ **take**	\ē\ **easy**	\ŋ\ **sing**	\t̲h̲\ **this**	\yu̇\ **cure**
\ä\ **cot, cart**	\g\ **go**	\ō\ **bone**	\ü\ **food**	\zh\ **vision**

these words can also be traced to the Greek *toxon*. [from Latin *intoxicatus,* past participle of *intoxicare* "to poison," from earlier *in-* "put into" and *toxicum* "poison," from Greek *toxikon* "arrow poison," from *toxon* "bow, arrow" — related to TOXIC, TOXIN]

in·tox·i·ca·tion \in-ˌtäk-sə-'kā-shən\ *n* **1 a** : an unhealthy state that is or is like a poisoning ⟨carbon monoxide *intoxication*⟩ **b** : the condition of being drunk **2** : a strong excitement or elation ⟨the *intoxication* of success⟩

in·tra- \in-trə, ˌin-(ˌ)trä\ *prefix* **1 a** : within ⟨*intramural*⟩ **b** : between layers of ⟨*intradermal*⟩ **2** : INTRO- 1 ⟨*intravenous*⟩ [derived from Latin *intra* "within, between"]

in·tra·cel·lu·lar \ˌin-trə-'sel-yə-lər\ *adj* : being or occurring within a cell — **in·tra·cel·lu·lar·ly** *adv*

in·trac·ta·ble \(ˈ)in-'trak-tə-bəl\ *adj* **1** : not easily managed or controlled ⟨an *intractable* child⟩ **2** : not easily relieved or cured ⟨*intractable* pain⟩ — **in·trac·ta·bil·i·ty** \(ˌ)in-ˌtrak-tə-'bil-ət-ē\ *n* — **in·trac·ta·bly** \(ˈ)in-'trak-tə-blē\ *adv*

in·tra·der·mal \ˌin-trə-'dər-məl, ˌin-(ˌ)trä-\ *adj* : situated or done within or between the layers of the skin — **in·tra·der·mal·ly** \-mə-lē\ *adv*

in·tra·mu·ral \ˌin-trə-'myùr-əl, ˌin-(ˌ)trä-\ *adj* : being, occurring, or undertaken within the limits usually of a school ⟨*intramural* sports⟩

in·tra·mus·cu·lar \ˌin-trə-'məs-kyə-lər, ˌin-(ˌ)trä-\ *adj* : located in, occurring in, or injected into a muscle

in·tran·si·tive \(ˈ)in-'tran(t)s-ət-iv, -'tranz-\ *adj* : not transitive; *esp* : not having or containing a direct object ⟨an *intransitive* verb⟩ — **in·tran·si·tive·ly** *adv*

in·tra·spe·cif·ic \ˌin-trə-spi-'sif-ik\ *adj* : occurring within a species or involving members of one species ⟨*intraspecific* competition⟩

in·tra·state \ˌin-trə-'stāt\ *adj* : existing or occurring within a state

in·tra·uter·ine \ˌin-trə-'yüt-ə-rən, -ˌrīn\ *adj* : located, used, or occurring within the uterus ⟨*intrauterine* growth⟩

intrauterine device *n* : a small plastic or metal device inserted into the uterus and left there to prevent pregnancy — called also *IUD*

in·tra·ve·nous \ˌin-trə-'vē-nəs\ *adj* : being within or entering by way of the veins ⟨*intravenous* feeding⟩ — **in·tra·ve·nous·ly** *adv*

in·trep·id \in-'trep-əd\ *adj* : feeling no fear : BOLD — **in·tre·pid·i·ty** \ˌin-trə-'pid-ət-ē\ *n* — **in·trep·id·ly** \in-'trep-əd-lē\ *adv* — **in·trep·id·ness** *n*

in·tri·ca·cy \'in-tri-kə-sē\ *n, pl* **-cies** **1** : the quality or state of being intricate **2** : something intricate ⟨the *intricacies* of the plot⟩

in·tri·cate \'in-tri-kət\ *adj* : having many complexly interrelating parts, elements, or considerations : COMPLICATED ⟨an *intricate* design⟩ ⟨difficult to solve the *intricate* puzzle⟩ — **in·tri·cate·ly** *adv* — **in·tri·cate·ness** *n*

¹in·trigue \in-'trēg\ *vb* **in·trigued; in·tri·gu·ing** **1** : to get or accomplish by secret plotting ⟨*intrigued* their way into the party⟩ **2** : ²PLOT 2, SCHEME **3** : to arouse the interest or curiosity of ⟨*intrigued* by the tale⟩ — **in·tri·gu·er** *n*

²in·trigue \'in-ˌtrēg, in-'trēg\ *n* **1** : a secret and complicated scheme : PLOT **2** : a secret love affair

in·trin·sic \in-'trin-zik, -'trin(t)-sik\ *adj* : belonging to the essential nature of a thing ⟨the *intrinsic* value of a gem⟩ ⟨the *intrinsic* simplicity of Quaker crafts⟩ — **in·trin·si·cal·ly** \-k(ə-)lē\ *adv*

in·tro- \in-trə, ˌin-(ˌ)trō\ *prefix* **1** : in : into ⟨*introduce*⟩ **2** : inward ⟨*introvert*⟩ [derived from Latin *intro* "inside"]

in·tro·duce \ˌin-trə-'d(y)üs\ *vb* **-duced; -duc·ing** **1** : to bring into practice or use ⟨*introduce* a new fashion⟩ **2** : to lead or bring in ⟨*introduce* nonnative species⟩ ⟨*introduced* a new topic into the conversation⟩ **3 a** : to cause to become acquainted ⟨*introduce* two strangers⟩ **b** : to present or announce officially ⟨*introduce* a legislative bill⟩ **c** : to make preliminary remarks about ⟨*introduced*

the star of the show⟩ **4** : to bring to a knowledge of something ⟨*introduced* them to new ideas⟩ **5** : to put in : INSERT — **in·tro·duc·er** *n*

in·tro·duc·tion \ˌin-trə-'dək-shən\ *n* **1 a** : the action of introducing **b** : something introduced **2** : the part of a book that leads up to and explains what will be found in the main part **3** : a book for beginners in a subject

in·tro·duc·to·ry \ˌin-trə-'dək-t(ə-)rē\ *adj* : serving to introduce — **in·tro·duc·to·ri·ly** \-t(ə-)rə-lē\ *adv*

in·tro·spec·tion \ˌin-trə-'spek-shən\ *n* : an examination of one's own thoughts or feelings — **in·tro·spec·tive** \-'spek-tiv\ *adj* — **in·tro·spec·tive·ly** *adv*

in·tro·vert \'in-trə-ˌvərt\ *n* **1** : a person who is concerned or interested mostly in one's own thoughts and ideas **2** : a person who is shy or restrained in speaking and behavior — **in·tro·ver·sion** \ˌin-trə-'ver-zhən, -shən\ *n* — **in·tro·vert·ed** \-ˌvərt-əd\ *adj*

in·trude \in-'trüd\ *vb* **in·trud·ed; in·trud·ing** **1** : to bring or force in unasked **2** : to come or go in without invitation — **in·trud·er** *n*

in·tru·sion \in-'trü-zhən\ *n* **1** : the act of intruding : the state of being intruded **2** : the entry by force of melted rock into or between other rock formations

in·tru·sive \in-'trü-siv, -ziv\ *adj* **1 a** : characterized by intrusion ⟨*intrusive* memories⟩ **b** : intruding where one is not welcome or invited ⟨*intrusive* neighbors⟩ **2** : having been forced while in a melted state into cavities or between layers ⟨*intrusive* rocks⟩ — **intrusive** *n* — **in·tru·sive·ly** *adv* — **in·tru·sive·ness** *n*

in·tu·ition \ˌin-t(y)ù-'ish-ən\ *n* **1** : the power of knowing immediately and without conscious reasoning **2** : something known or understood at once — **in·tu·ition·al** \-'ish-nəl, -ən-ᵊl\ *adj*

in·tu·itive \in-'t(y)ü-ət-iv\ *adj* **1** : knowing or understanding by intuition ⟨an *intuitive* person⟩ **2** : having or characterized by intuition ⟨an *intuitive* mind⟩ **3** : known or understood by intuition ⟨*intuitive* knowledge⟩ — **in·tu·itive·ly** *adj* — **in·tu·itive·ness** *n*

in·un·date \'in-(ˌ)ən-ˌdāt\ *vb* **-dat·ed; -dat·ing** **1** : to cover with a flood : ²DELUGE 1 ⟨a tidal wave *inundated* the island⟩ **2** : ²DELUGE 2, OVERWHELM ⟨*inundated* with phone calls⟩ — **in·un·da·tion** \ˌin-(ˌ)ən-'dā-shən\ *n*

Inu·pi·at \in-'ü-pē-ˌät, in-'yü-\ *n* **1** *pl* **Inupiat** *or* **Inupiats** : a member of the Eskimo people of northern Alaska **2** : the language of the Inupiat people

in·ure \in-'(y)ù(ə)r\ *vb* **in·ured; in·ur·ing** **1** : to make less sensitive : HARDEN ⟨*inured* to cold⟩ **2** : ACCRUE 1

in·vade \in-'vād\ *vb* **in·vad·ed; in·vad·ing** **1** : to enter for conquest or plunder ⟨*invade* a country⟩ **2** : to disturb or intrude upon ⟨*invaded* their privacy⟩ **3** : to spread over or into usually harmfully ⟨bacteria *invading* tissue⟩ — **in·vad·er** *n*

¹in·val·id \(ˈ)in-'val-əd\ *adj* : having no force or effect : not valid ⟨an *invalid* parking sticker⟩ ⟨an *invalid* assumption⟩ [from earlier *invalid* "not having a sound basis in fact or reason, not valid," from Latin *invalidus* "weak"] — **in·va·lid·i·ty** \ˌin-və-'lid-ət-ē\ *n* — **in·val·id·ly** \(ˈ)in-'val-əd-lē\ *adv*

²in·va·lid \'in-və-ləd\ *adj* **1** : suffering from disease or disability : SICKLY **2** : of, relating to, or suited to an invalid [from French *invalide* "suffering from a disease, sickly," from Latin *invalidus* "weak"]

³invalid *like*²\ *n* : one who is sickly or disabled

⁴in·va·lid \'in-və-ləd, -ˌlid\ *vb* : to make sickly or disabled

in·val·i·date \(ˈ)in-'val-ə-ˌdāt\ *vb* : to weaken or destroy the effect of ⟨evidence *invalidating* their claim⟩ — **in·val·i·da·tion** \(ˌ)in-ˌval-ə-'dā-shən\ *n*

in·valu·able \(ˈ)in-'val-yə-(wə)-bəl\ *adj* : having value too great to be estimated ⟨*invaluable* help⟩ — **in·valu·ably** \-blē\ *adv*

in·vari·able \(ˈ)in-'ver-ē-ə-bəl, -'var-\ *adj* : not changing or capable of change ⟨an *invariable* routine⟩ — **in·vari·abil·i·ty** \(ˌ)in-ˌver-ē-ə-'bil-ət-ē, -ˌvar-\ *n* — **invariable** *n*

in·vari·ably \(ˈ)in-ˈver-ē-ə-blē, -ˈvar-\ *adv* : on every occasion : ALWAYS ⟨*invariably* late⟩

in·vari·ant \(ˈ)in-ˈver-ē-ənt, -ˈvar-\ *adj* : not changing or altering — **invariant** *n*

in·va·sion \in-ˈvā-zhən\ *n* : an act of invading; *esp* : entrance of an army into a country for conquest

in·va·sive \in-ˈvā-siv, -ziv\ *adj* : tending to spread; *esp* : tending to invade healthy tissue ⟨*invasive* cancer cells⟩

in·vec·tive \in-ˈvek-tiv\ *n* : harsh or insulting words

in·veigh \in-ˈvā\ *vb* : to protest or complain bitterly

in·vei·gle \in-ˈvā-gəl\ *vb* **in·vei·gled; in·vei·gling** \-g(ə-)liŋ\ **1** : to win over by flattery : ENTICE ⟨was *inveigled* into helping out⟩ **2** : to acquire by cleverness or flattery : WANGLE ⟨*inveigled* a new bike from my father⟩

in·vent \in-ˈvent\ *vb* **1** : to think up : MAKE UP ⟨*invent* an excuse⟩ **2** : to create or produce for the first time ⟨*invented* a new game⟩ — **in·ven·tor** \-ˈvent-ər\ *n*

in·ven·tion \in-ˈven-chən\ *n* **1** : something invented; *esp* : an original device or process **2** : an imaginary story **3** : the act, process, or power of inventing

in·ven·tive \in-ˈvent-iv\ *adj* : gifted with the skill and imagination to invent — **in·ven·tive·ly** *adv* — **in·ven·tive·ness** *n*

¹in·ven·to·ry \ˈin-vən-ˌtōr-ē, -ˌtòr-\ *n, pl* **-ries** **1** : a complete list of items (as of goods on hand) **2** : the stock of goods on hand **3** : the act or process of making an inventory

²inventory *vb* **-ried; -ry·ing** : to make an inventory of

¹in·verse \(ˈ)in-ˈvərs, ˈin-vərs\ *adj* **1** : opposite in order, nature, or effect ⟨an *inverse* relationship between interest rates and houses sold⟩ **2** : being a mathematical operation opposite in effect to another ⟨addition and subtraction are *inverse* operations⟩

²in·verse \ˈin-ˌvərs, (ˈ)in-ˈvərs\ *n* : something inverse or resulting in or from inversion

in·verse·ly \ˈin-ˌvərs-lē, (ˈ)in-ˈvərs-lē\ *adv* **1** : in an inverse order or manner **2** : in the manner of inverse variation

inversely proportional *adj* : related by inverse variation — compare DIRECTLY PROPORTIONAL

inverse square law *n* : a statement in physics: a physical quantity (as illumination) varies as the reciprocal of the square of the distance of the quantity from its source

inverse variation *n* **1** : mathematical relationship between two variables which can be expressed by an equation in which the product of two variables is equal to a constant **2** : an equation or function expressing inverse variation — compare DIRECT VARIATION 2

in·ver·sion \in-ˈvər-zhən, -shən\ *n* **1** : a reversal of position, order, or relationship **2** : the act or process of inverting **3** : increase of temperature of the air with increasing altitude

in·vert \in-ˈvərt\ *vb* **1** : to reverse the position, order, or relationship of **2 a** : to turn inside out or upside down **b** : to turn inward **3** : to find the mathematical reciprocal of ⟨to divide using fractions, *invert* the divisor and multiply⟩

¹in·ver·te·brate \(ˈ)in-ˈvərt-ə-brət, -ˌbrāt\ *adj* : lacking a backbone ⟨an *invertebrate* animal⟩; *also* : of or relating to invertebrate animals ⟨*invertebrate* fossils⟩

²invertebrate *n* : an animal (as a worm, clam, spider, or butterfly) that lacks a backbone

¹in·vest \in-ˈvest\ *vb* **1 a** : INSTALL **1 b** : to furnish with power or authority : to cover completely **3** : CLOTHE 1a, ADORN **4** : to surround with troops or ships : BESIEGE **5** : to supply with a quality or characteristic

²invest *vb* **1** : to lay out money so as to return a profit ⟨*invest* in bonds and real estate⟩ **2** : to expend for future benefits or advantages ⟨*invest* time and effort in a project⟩ **3** : to involve or engage especially emotionally ⟨were deeply *invested* in their children's lives⟩ — **in·ves·tor** \-ˈves-tər\ *n*

in·ves·ti·gate \in-ˈves-tə-ˌgāt\ *vb* **-gat·ed; -gat·ing** : to

study by close examination and systematic inquiry — **in·ves·ti·ga·tion** \-ˌves-tə-ˈgā-shən\ *n* — **in·ves·ti·ga·tive** \-ˈves-tə-ˌgāt-iv\ *adj* — **in·ves·ti·ga·tor** \-ˌgāt-ər\ *n* — **in·ves·ti·ga·to·ry** \-ˈves-ti-gə-ˌtōr-ē, -ˌtòr-\ *adj*

Word History A detective investigating a crime may find the criminal by following clues. In much the same way, a hunter may find game by following tracks. The origins of the word *investigate* show how fitting it is to compare the detective to the hunter. The Latin word *vestigium* meant "footprint, track." Joined with the prefix *in-*, the noun *vestigium* gave rise to the verb *investigare*. This word meant both "to track or trace by footprints" and "to study or examine closely." Only the second meaning was kept when the verb was borrowed into English as *investigate*. [from Latin *investigare* "to track, investigate," from *in-* "in, toward" and *vestigium* "footprint" — related to VESTIGE]

in·ves·ti·ture \in-ˈves-tə-ˌchùr, -chər\ *n* : a person in an office, rank, or order ⟨*investiture* of the prince⟩ : the act of establishing

¹in·vest·ment \in-ˈves(t)-mənt\ *n* **1** : INVESTITURE 1 **2** : BLOCKADE, SIEGE

²investment *n* **1** : the outlay of money for income or profit **2** : a sum of money invested or a property purchased

in·vet·er·ate \in-ˈvet-ə-rət, -ˈve-trət\ *adj* **1** : firmly established by age or by long continuation ⟨*inveterate* habits⟩ **2** : HABITUAL 2 ⟨an *inveterate* complainer⟩ — **in·vet·er·ate·ly** *adv*

in·vid·i·ous \in-ˈvid-ē-əs\ *adj* **1** : of an unpleasant or objectionable kind ⟨*invidious* criticism⟩ **2** : of a kind to cause resentment ⟨an *invidious* comparison⟩ — **in·vid·i·ous·ly** *adv* — **in·vid·i·ous·ness** *n*

in·vig·o·rate \in-ˈvig-ə-ˌrāt\ *vb* **-rat·ed; -rat·ing** : to give life and energy to — **in·vig·o·ra·tion** \-ˌvig-ə-ˈrā-shən\ *n* — **in·vig·o·ra·tor** \-ˈvig-ə-ˌrāt-ər\ *n*

in·vin·ci·ble \(ˈ)in-ˈvin(t)-sə-bəl\ *adj* : incapable of being defeated, overcome, or subdued ⟨an *invincible* army⟩ — **in·vin·ci·bil·i·ty** \(ˌ)in-ˌvin(t)-sə-ˈbil-ət-ē\ *n* — **in·vin·ci·bly** \(ˈ)in-ˈvin(t)-sə-blē\ *adv*

in·vi·o·la·ble \(ˈ)in-ˈvī-ə-lə-bəl\ *adj* **1** : too sacred to be violated ⟨an *inviolable* oath⟩ **2** : incapable of being harmed or destroyed by violence ⟨an *inviolable* fortress⟩ — **in·vi·o·la·bil·i·ty** \(ˌ)in-ˌvī-ə-lə-ˈbil-ət-ē\ *n* — **in·vi·o·la·bly** \(ˈ)in-ˈvī-ə-lə-blē\ *adv*

in·vi·o·late \(ˈ)in-ˈvī-ə-lət\ *adj* : not violated; *esp* : PURE — **in·vi·o·late·ly** *adv* — **in·vi·o·late·ness** *n*

in·vis·i·ble \(ˈ)in-ˈviz-ə-bəl\ *adj* **1** : impossible to see ⟨sound is *invisible*⟩ **2** : being so small or slight as to be hardly noticeable ⟨an *invisible* error⟩ — **in·vis·i·bil·i·ty** \(ˌ)in-ˌviz-ə-ˈbil-ət-ē\ *n* — **in·vis·i·bly** \(ˈ)in-ˈviz-ə-blē\ *adv*

in·vi·ta·tion \ˌin-və-ˈtā-shən\ *n* **1** : the act of inviting **2** : the written, printed, or spoken expression by which a person is invited — **in·vi·ta·tion·al** \-shnəl, -shən-ᵊl\ *adj*

¹in·vite \in-ˈvīt\ *vb* **in·vit·ed; in·vit·ing** **1** : to make more likely ⟨behavior that *invites* criticism⟩ ⟨*invite* disaster by speeding⟩ **2 a** : to request the presence or participation of **b** : to request formally or politely — **in·vit·er** *n*

²in·vite \ˈin-ˌvīt\ *n* : INVITATION

in·vit·ing \in-ˈvīt-iŋ\ *adj* : ATTRACTIVE, TEMPTING ⟨an *inviting* prospect⟩ — **in·vit·ing·ly** \-iŋ-lē\ *adv*

in vi·tro \in-ˈvē-(ˌ)trō\ *adv or adj* : outside the living body and in an artificial environment ⟨an egg fertilized *in vitro*⟩ [Latin, literally, "in glass"]

in vi·vo \in-ˈvē-(ˌ)vō, -ˈwē-(ˌ)wō\ *adv or adj* : inside the living body of a plant or animal ⟨*in vivo* activity⟩ [Latin, literally, "in the living"]

\ə\ abut	\au̇\ out	\i\ tip	\ȯ\ saw	\u̇\ foot
\ər\ further	\ch\ chin	\ī\ life	\ȯi\ coin	\y\ yet
\a\ mat	\e\ pet	\j\ job	\th\ thin	\yü\ few
\ā\ take	\ē\ easy	\ŋ\ sing	\t͟h\ this	\yu̇\ cure
\ä\ cot, cart	\g\ go	\ō\ bone	\ü\ food	\zh\ vision

in·vo·ca·tion \ˌin-və-ˈkā-shən\ *n* **1 a** : the act or process of asking for help or support **b** : a prayer for blessing or guidance (as at the beginning of a religious service) **2** : a formula for calling forth spirits or performing magic : IN-CANTATION — **in·vo·ca·tion·al** \-shnəl, -shən-ᵊl\ *adj*

¹**in·voice** \ˈin-ˌvȯis\ *n* : an itemized statement of goods or services with their prices and the terms of sale

²**invoice** *vb* **in·voiced; in·voic·ing** : to submit an invoice for : BILL

in·voke \in-ˈvōk\ *vb* **in·voked; in·vok·ing** **1** : to call on for aid or protection (as in prayer) **2** : to call forth by magic : CONJURE ⟨*invoke* spirits⟩ **3** : to appeal to as an authority or for support ⟨*invoke* a law⟩

in·vol·un·tary \(ˈ)in-ˈväl-ən-ˌter-ē\ *adj* **1** : not made or done willingly or from choice : UNWILLING **2** : being enforced or required : MANDATORY **3** : not normally under the control of the will ⟨an *involuntary* response to a stimulus⟩ — **in·vol·un·tari·ly** \(ˌ)in-ˌväl-ən-ˈter-ə-lē\ *adv*

involuntary muscle *n* : SMOOTH MUSCLE

in·vo·lu·tion \ˌin-və-ˈlü-shən\ *n* : INTRICACY 1, COMPLEX-ITY

in·volve \in-ˈvälv, -ˈvȯlv\ *vb* **in·volved; in·volv·ing** **1** : to take part in as a participant ⟨*involved* in bird watching⟩ **2** : to occupy absorbingly ⟨so *involved* in the book, she didn't hear the doorbell⟩ **3** : to have within or as a part of itself : INCLUDE ⟨one problem *involves* others⟩ **4** : to call for : REQUIRE ⟨the job *involved* building 10 bridges⟩ **5** : to have an effect on : AFFECT ⟨the renovations *involved* the whole school⟩ — **in·volve·ment** \-mənt\ *n* — **in·volv·er** *n*

in·volved *adj* : very complicated ⟨a long and *involved* story⟩

in·vul·ner·a·ble \(ˈ)in-ˈvəln-(ə-)rə-bəl, -ˈvəl-nər-bəl\ *adj* **1** : impossible to wound, injure, or damage **2** : immune to or proof against attack : IMPREGNABLE — **in·vul·ner·a·bil·i·ty** \(ˌ)in-ˌvəln-(ə-)rə-ˈbil-ət-ē\ *n* — **in·vul·ner·a·bly** \-ˈvəln-(ə-)rə-blē, -ˈvəl-nər-blē\ *adv*

¹**in·ward** \ˈin-wərd\ *adj* **1** : situated on the inside : INNER **2** : of or relating to the mind or spirit ⟨an *inward* peace⟩ **3** : directed toward the interior ⟨an *inward* flow⟩

²**inward** *or* **in·wards** \ˈin-wərdz\ *adv* **1** : toward the inside, center, or interior **2** : toward the mind or spirit

in·ward·ly \ˈin-wərd-lē\ *adv* **1** : in the mind or spirit **2 a** : on the inside ⟨bled *inwardly*⟩ **b** : to oneself : PRIVATELY ⟨chuckled *inwardly*⟩

in—your—face \ˌin-yər-ˌfās\ *adj* : characterized by bold and often defiant aggressiveness ⟨*in-your-face* basketball⟩

io·dide \ˈī-ə-ˌdīd\ *n* : a compound of iodine with another element or chemical group

io·dine \ˈī-ə-ˌdīn, -əd-ᵊn, -ə-ˌdēn\ *also* **io·din** \ˈī-əd-ᵊn\ *n* **1** : a nonmetallic element that is obtained usually as heavy shining blackish gray crystals and is used especially in medicine and photography — see ELEMENT table **2** : a solution of iodine in alcohol used to kill germs

io·dize \ˈī-ə-ˌdīz\ *vb* **io·dized; io·diz·ing** : to treat with iodine or an iodide ⟨*iodized* salt⟩

Io moth \ˈī-ō-\ *n* : a large North American moth with a large eyelike spot on each yellowish hind wing

ion \ˈī-ən, ˈī-ˌän\ *n* : an atom or group of atoms that carries a positive or negative electric charge as a result of having lost or gained one or more electrons

-ion *n suffix* **1 a** : act or process ⟨valida*tion*⟩ **b** : result of an act or process ⟨regu-

Io moth

la*tion*⟩ **2** : state or condition ⟨hydra*tion*⟩ [derived from Latin *-ion* (suffix) "act or process"]

ion·ic \ī-ˈän-ik\ *adj* : of, relating to, or existing in the form of ions

Ion·ic \ī-ˈän-ik\ *adj* : belonging to or resembling a style of Greek architecture characterized especially by decoration resembling scrolls in the capitals of its columns

ionic bond *n* : a chemical bond formed between ions of opposite charge

ion·ize \ˈī-ə-ˌnīz\ *vb* **ion·ized; ion·iz·ing** **1** : to convert wholly or partly into ions **2** : to become ionized — **ion·iz·able** \-ˌnī-zə-bəl\ *adj* — **ion·i·za·tion** \ˌī-ə-nə-ˈzā-shən\ *n* — **ion·iz·er** \ˈī-ə-ˌnī-zər\ *n*

ion·o·sphere \ī-ˈän-ə-ˌsfi(ə)r\ *n* : the part of the earth's atmosphere beginning at an altitude of about 30 miles (50 kilometers) and extending outward that contains free electrically charged particles — **ion·o·spher·ic** \ī-ˌän-ə-ˈsfi(ə)r-ik, -ˈsfer-\ *adj*

io·ta \ī-ˈōt-ə\ *n* **1** : the ninth letter of the Greek alphabet — I or ι **2** : a tiny amount : JOT ⟨didn't show an *iota* of interest⟩

IOU \ˌī-(ˌ)ō-ˈyü\ *n* : a paper that has on it the letters IOU, a stated sum, and a signature and that is given to acknowledge a debt

-ious *adj suffix* : -OUS ⟨capac*ious*⟩ [derived from Latin *-iosus* and *-ius* (adjective suffixes)]

IP address \ˈī-ˈpē-\ *n* : the address of a computer on the Internet that consists of a series of numbers [*IP* short for *Internet protocol*]

ip·e·cac \ˈip-i-ˌkak\ *or* **ipe·ca·cu·a·nha** \ē-ˌpek-ə-kü-ˈan-yə\ *n* **1** : either of two South American creeping plants **2** : the dried roots or rhizome of an ipecac that are the source of a medicinal syrup used to cause vomiting in the treatment of accidental poisoning; *also* : the medicinal syrup

IQ \ˈī-ˈkyü\ *n* : a number that is often used as a measure of a person's intelligence and is found by dividing the mental age of the person as given by a score on a special test by the age in years and multiplying by 100 [*intelligence quotient*]

ir- — see IN-

Ira·ni·an \ir-ˈā-nē-ən\ *n* **1** : a person born or living in Iran **2** : a branch of the Indo-European family of languages that includes Persian — **Iranian** *adj*

iras·ci·ble \ir-ˈas-ə-bəl\ *adj* : having a hot temper and easily angered — **iras·ci·bil·i·ty** \ir-ˌas-ə-ˈbil-ət-ē\ *n* — **iras·ci·bly** \ir-ˈas-ə-blē\ *adv*

irate \ī-ˈrāt\ *adj* : ANGRY 1a — **irate·ly** *adv* — **irate·ness** *n*

ire \ˈī(ə)r\ *n* : ¹ANGER — **ire** *vb* — **ire·ful** \-fəl\ *adj* — **ire·ful·ly** \-fə-lē\ *adv*

ir·i·des·cence \ˌir-ə-ˈdes-ᵊn(t)s\ *n* : a play of colors producing rainbow effects (as in a soap bubble)

ir·i·des·cent \ˌir-ə-ˈdes-ᵊnt\ *adj* : having or showing iridescence — **ir·i·des·cent·ly** *adv*

irid·i·um \ir-ˈid-ē-əm\ *n* : a rare silver-white hard brittle very heavy metallic element — see ELEMENT table

iris \ˈī-rəs\ *n, pl* **iris·es** \-rə-səz\ *or* **iri·des** \ˈī-rə-ˌdēz, ˈir-ə-\ **1** : the colored part around the pupil of the eye that changes in size to control the amount of light entering the pupil **2** *also pl* **iris** : any of a large genus of plants with long pointed leaves and large usually brightly colored flowers **3** : IRIS DIAPHRAGM

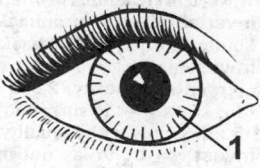

1 iris 1

iris diaphragm *n* : an adjustable diaphragm of thin plates used for changing the diameter of a central opening to control the amount of light passing (as into a microscope or camera)

Irish \ˈī(ə)r-ish\ n **1** Irish pl : the people of Ireland **2** : the Celtic language of Ireland — **Irish** adj

Irish·man \ˈī-rish-mən\ n : a person born or living in Ireland

Irish moss n : either of two red algae; also : these algae when dried and bleached for use especially as thickeners or soothing agents (as in food or lotions)

Irish potato n : POTATO 2b

Irish setter n : any of a breed of bird dogs having a mahogany-red coat

Irish terrier n : any of a breed of active medium-sized terriers having a dense short usually reddish stiff coat

Irish wolfhound n : any of a breed of very tall heavily built hounds having a rough stiff somewhat short coat

Irish·wom·an \ˈī-rish-ˌwum-ən\ n : a woman born or living in Ireland

Irish wolfhound

irk \ˈərk\ vb : to make weary, irritated, or bored : ANNOY

irk·some \ˈərk-səm\ adj : annoying because of length or dullness ⟨an irksome task⟩ — **irk·some·ly** adv — **irk·some·ness** n

¹**iron** \ˈī(-ə)rn\ n **1** : a heavy magnetic silver-white metallic element that quickly rusts in moist air, occurs in meteorites and rocks, and is widely used — see ELEMENT table **2** : something made of iron: as **a** pl : handcuffs or chains used to bind or hinder movement **b** : a heated metal tool used for branding **c** : a household device with a flat metal base that is heated to smooth or press cloth **3** : STRENGTH 1, HARDNESS ⟨muscles of iron⟩

²**iron** adj **1** : of, relating to, or made of iron **2** : resembling iron **3** : being strong and healthy : ROBUST ⟨an iron constitution⟩ **4** : INFLEXIBLE 3, UNRELENTING ⟨iron determination⟩

³**iron** vb : to smooth or press clothes with a heated iron ⟨iron a shirt⟩ — **iron·er** n

Iron Age n : the period of human culture characterized by the smelting and use of iron and beginning somewhat before 1000 B.C. in western Asia and Egypt

iron·bound \ˈī(-ə)rn-ˈbaund\ adj **1** : RUGGED 1 ⟨ironbound coasts⟩ **2** : ¹STERN 1a ⟨ironbound traditions⟩

¹**iron·clad** \-ˈklad\ adj **1** : covered by iron armor **2** : RIGOROUS 1, EXACTING ⟨ironclad laws⟩

²**iron·clad** \-ˌklad\ n : an armored naval vessel

iron curtain n : a political and military barrier that isolates an area from outside contact

iron horse n : ²LOCOMOTIVE

iron·ic \ˈī-ˈrän-ik\ also **iron·i·cal** \-i-kəl\ adj : relating to, containing, or being irony ⟨an ironic turn of events⟩ ⟨an ironic laugh⟩ — **iron·i·cal·ly** \-i-k(ə-)lē\ adv

iron lung n : a device for artificial respiration in which the air pressure in a chamber surrounding a patient's chest changes in a rhythm and forces air into and out of the lungs

iron out vb **1** : to make smooth or flat by or as if by ironing **2** : to work out a solution to ⟨ironed out their differences⟩

iron oxide n : any of the oxides of iron; esp : FERRIC OXIDE

iron·stone \ˈī(-ə)rn-ˌstōn\ n : a hard white pottery first made in England — called also ironstone china

iron sulfide n : a compound (as a pyrite) of iron and sulfur

iron·ware \ˈī(-ə)rn-ˌwa(ə)r, -ˌwe(ə)r\ n : articles made of iron

iron·weed \-ˌwēd\ n : any of several mostly weedy plants related to the daisies and bearing clusters of red, purple, or white flowers

iron·wood \-ˌwud\ n **1** : any of numerous trees and shrubs with very tough hard wood **2** : the wood of an ironwood

iron·work \-ˌwərk\ n **1** : work in iron **2** pl : a mill or building where iron or steel is smelted or heavy iron or steel products are made — **iron·work·er** \-ˌwər-kər\ n

iro·ny \ˈī-rə-nē\ n, pl **-nies** **1 a** : the use of words that mean the opposite of what one really intends **b** : an ironic expression or utterance **2 a** : inconsistency between an actual and an expected result of a sequence of events **b** : a result marked by this inconsistency **3** : the contradiction between the situation developed in a drama and the words or actions of the characters that is understood by the audience but not by the characters themselves

ironwood 1

Ir·o·quois \ˈir-ə-ˌkwoi\ n, pl **Iroquois** \-ˌkwoi(z)\ : a member of any of the peoples of an American Indian confederacy that existed originally in central New York state

ir·ra·di·ate \ir-ˈād-ē-ˌāt\ vb **-at·ed; -at·ing** **1 a** : to cast rays of light on : ILLUMINATE **b** : to affect or treat by exposure to radiation (as of ultraviolet light, X-rays, or gamma rays) **2** : to give off like rays of light : RADIATE — **ir·ra·di·a·tion** \-ˌād-ē-ˈā-shən\ n

ir·ra·tio·nal \(ˈ)ir-ˈ(r)ash-nəl, -ən-ᵊl\ adj **1** : unable to reason ⟨irrational beasts⟩ ⟨irrational from fever⟩ **2** : not based on reason ⟨irrational fear⟩ **3** : being an irrational number ⟨an irrational root of an equation⟩ — **ir·ra·tio·nal·i·ty** \(ˌ)ir-ˌ(r)ash-ə-ˈnal-ət-ē\ n — **ir·ra·tio·nal·ly** \(ˈ)ir-ˈ(r)ash-nə-lē, -ən-ᵊl-ē\ adv

irrational number n : a number (as $\sqrt{2}$) that cannot be expressed as the quotient of two whole numbers

ir·rec·on·cil·able \(ˌ)ir-ˌ(r)ek-ən-ˈsī-lə-bəl, (ˈ)ir-ˈ(r)ek-ən-ˌsī-\ adj : impossible to reconcile, adjust, or harmonize ⟨ended the partnership because of irreconcilable differences⟩ — **ir·rec·on·cil·ably** \-blē\ adv

ir·re·cov·er·able \ˌir-i-ˈkəv-(ə-)rə-bəl\ adj : not capable of being recovered or made right ⟨an irrecoverable loss⟩ — **ir·re·cov·er·ably** \-blē\ adv

ir·re·deem·able \ˌir-i-ˈdē-mə-bəl\ adj **1** : not redeemable **2** : being beyond remedy : HOPELESS — **ir·re·deem·ably** \-blē\ adv

ir·re·duc·ible \ˌir-i-ˈd(y)ü-sə-bəl\ adj : not reducible — **ir·re·duc·ibil·i·ty** \-ˌd(y)ü-sə-ˈbil-ət-ē\ n — **ir·re·duc·ibly** \-ˈd(y)ü-sə-blē\ adv

ir·re·fut·able \ˌir-i-ˈfyüt-ə-bəl, (ˈ)ir-ˈ(r)ef-yət-\ adj : not capable of being proved wrong : INDISPUTABLE ⟨irrefutable proof⟩ — **ir·re·fut·ably** \-blē\ adv

¹**ir·reg·u·lar** \(ˈ)ir-ˈ(r)eg-yə-lər\ adj **1 a** : not following custom or rule **b** : not belonging to a recognized or organized body ⟨irregular troops⟩ **2 a** : not following the normal or usual manner of inflection ⟨the irregular verb "sell"⟩ **b** : STRONG 12 ⟨the irregular verb "write"⟩ **3 a** : having one or more like parts unequal in size, form, or the way they are arranged ⟨irregular flowers⟩ **b** : UNEVEN **4** : not continuous or regular in occurrence ⟨at irregular intervals⟩ — **ir·reg·u·lar·ly** adv

\ə\ abut	\au̇\ out	\i\ tip	\o̅\ saw	\u̇\ foot
\ər\ further	\ch\ chin	\ī\ life	\o̅i\ coin	\y\ yet
\a\ mat	\e\ pet	\j\ job	\th\ thin	\yü\ few
\ā\ take	\ē\ easy	\ŋ\ sing	\t͟h\ this	\yu̇\ cure
\ä\ cot, cart	\g\ go	\ō\ bone	\ü\ food	\zh\ vision

²**irregular** *n* **1** : an irregular soldier **2** : merchandise that is slightly imperfect

ir·reg·u·lar·i·ty \(ͺ)ir-ͺ(r)eg-yə-'lar-ət-ē\ *n, pl* **-ties 1** : the quality or state of being irregular **2** : something (as dishonest conduct) that is irregular **3** : CONSTIPATION

ir·rel·e·vant \(')ir-'(r)el-ə-vənt\ *adj* : not relevant : not applicable or pertinent ⟨the evidence presented was judged *irrelevant* to the case⟩ — **ir·rel·e·vance** \-vən(t)s\ *or* **ir·rel·e·van·cy** \-vən-sē\ *n* — **ir·rel·e·vant·ly** *adv*

ir·re·li·gious \ͺir-i-'lij-əs\ *adj* : lacking religious emotions, principles, or practices — **ir·re·li·gious·ly** *adv*

ir·re·me·di·a·ble \ͺir-i-'mēd-ē-ə-bəl\ *adj* : not remediable; *also* : INCURABLE — **ir·re·me·di·a·bly** \-blē\ *adv*

ir·re·mov·able \ͺir-i-'mü-və-bəl\ *adj* : not removable — **ir·re·mov·abil·i·ty** \-ͺmü-və-'bil-ət-ē\ *n* — **ir·re·mov·ably** \-'mü-və-blē\ *adv*

ir·rep·a·ra·ble \(')ir-'(r)ep-(ə-)rə-bəl\ *adj* : not capable of being repaired or regained ⟨an *irreparable* loss⟩ — **ir·rep·a·ra·bly** \-blē\ *adv*

ir·re·place·able \ͺir-i-'plā-sə-bəl\ *adj* : not replaceable ⟨a museum full of *irreplaceable* works of art⟩

ir·re·press·ible \ͺir-i-'pres-ə-bəl\ *adj* : impossible to repress or control ⟨*irrepressible* curiosity⟩ — **ir·re·press·ibil·i·ty** \-ͺpres-ə-'bil-ət-ē\ *n* — **ir·re·press·ibly** \-'pres-ə-blē\ *adv*

ir·re·proach·able \ͺir-i-'prō-chə-bəl\ *adj* : not reproachable : BLAMELESS — **ir·re·proach·ably** \-blē\ *adv*

ir·re·sist·ible \ͺir-i-'zis-tə-bəl\ *adj* : impossible to resist ⟨an *irresistible* attraction⟩ — **ir·re·sist·ibil·i·ty** \-ͺzis-tə-'bil-ət-ē\ *adj* — **ir·re·sist·ibly** \-'zis-tə-blē\ *adv*

ir·res·o·lute \(')ir-'(r)ez-ə-ͺlüt, -lət\ *adj* : not resolute : HESITANT — **ir·res·o·lute·ly** *adv* — **ir·res·o·lute·ness** *n* — **ir·res·o·lu·tion** \(ͺ)ir-ͺ(r)ez-ə-'lü-shən\ *n*

ir·re·spec·tive of \ͺir-i-'spek-tiv-\ *prep* : without regard to

ir·re·spon·si·ble \ͺir-i-'spän(t)-sə-bəl\ *adj* **1** : not legally responsible **2** : having or showing no sense of responsibility ⟨*irresponsible* behavior⟩ **3** : unable to bear responsibility — **ir·re·spon·si·bil·i·ty** \-ͺspän(t)-sə-'bil-ət-ē\ *n* — **ir·re·spon·si·bly** \-'spän(t)-sə-blē\ *adv*

ir·re·triev·able \ͺir-i-'trē-və-bəl\ *adj* : not capable of being recovered, regained, or remedied — **ir·re·triev·ably** \-blē\ *adv*

ir·rev·er·ent \(')ir-'(r)ev-(ə-)rənt, -ərnt\ *adj* : showing lack of reverence ⟨*irreverent* joking and giggling in church⟩ — **ir·rev·er·ence** \-'(r)ev-(ə-)rən(t)s, -'(r)ev-ərn(t)s\ *n* — **ir·rev·er·ent·ly** *adv*

ir·re·vers·ible \ͺir-i-'vər-sə-bəl\ *adj* : impossible to reverse ⟨an *irreversible* chemical reaction⟩ ⟨*irreversible* damage⟩ — **ir·re·vers·ibil·i·ty** \-ͺvər-sə-'bil-ət-ē\ *n* — **ir·re·vers·ibly** \-'vər-sə-blē\ *adv*

ir·rev·o·ca·ble \(')ir-'(r)ev-ə-kə-bəl\ *adj* : not capable of being revoked ⟨an *irrevocable* decision⟩ — **ir·rev·o·ca·bil·i·ty** \(ͺ)ir-ͺ(r)ev-ə-kə-'bil-ət-ē\ *n* — **ir·rev·o·ca·bly** \(')ir-'(r)ev-ə-kə-blē\ *adv*

ir·ri·gate \'ir-ə-ͺgāt\ *vb* **-gat·ed; -gat·ing 1** : to supply with water by artificial means ⟨*irrigate* a field⟩ ⟨*irrigate* crops⟩ **2** : to flush with a liquid ⟨*irrigate* a wound⟩

ir·ri·ga·tion \ͺir-ə-'gā-shən\ *n* : an act or process of irrigating

ir·ri·ta·bil·i·ty \ͺir-ət-ə-'bil-ət-ē\ *n, pl* **-ties 1** : the quality or state of being irritable; *esp* : readiness to become annoyed or angry **2** : the property of living tissue and living things that permits them to react to stimuli

ir·ri·ta·ble \'ir-ət-ə-bəl\ *adj* : capable of being irritated; *esp* : easily irritated ⟨gets *irritable* when he's tired⟩ — **ir·ri·ta·ble·ness** *n* — **ir·ri·ta·bly** \-blē\ *adv*

¹**ir·ri·tant** \'ir-ə-tənt\ *adj* : tending to produce anger, annoyance, impatience, soreness, or inflammation; *esp* : tending to produce physical irritation

²**irritant** *n* : something that irritates

ir·ri·tate \'ir-ə-ͺtāt\ *vb* **-tat·ed; -tat·ing 1** : to cause impatience, anger, or displeasure in : ANNOY ⟨were *irritated* by the child's rudeness⟩ **2** : to make sore or inflamed ⟨harsh soaps can *irritate* the skin⟩

ir·ri·ta·tion \ͺir-ə-'tā-shən\ *n* **1** : the act of irritating : the state of being irritated **2** : ²IRRITANT

ir·rupt \(')i(ə)r-'(r)əpt\ *vb* : to rush in violently : burst in — **ir·rup·tion** \-'(r)əp-shən\ *n*

is *present 3rd singular of* BE

is- *or* **iso-** *combining form* : equal : uniform ⟨*iso*bar⟩ [derived from Greek *isos* "equal"]

Isa·iah \ī-'zā-ə\ *n* — see BIBLE table

Isa·ias \ī-'zā-əs\ *n* : ISAIAH

is·chi·um \'is-kē-əm\ *n, pl* **-chia** \-kē-ə\ : the one of the three bones making up each side of the pelvis that is lowermost and in back

-ish \ish\ *adj suffix* **1** : of, relating to, or being ⟨Finn*ish*⟩ **2 a** : characteristic of ⟨boy*ish*⟩ ⟨mul*ish*⟩ **b** : somewhat ⟨purpl*ish*⟩ **c** : having the approximate age of ⟨forty*ish*⟩ **d** : being or occurring at the approximate time of ⟨arrive around eight*ish*⟩ [Old English *-isc* (adjective suffix)]

isin·glass \'iz-ᵊn-ͺglas, 'ī-ziŋ-\ *n* : mica in thin sheets

Is·lam \is-'läm, iz-, -'lam; 'is-ͺläm, 'iz-ͺläm, -ͺlam\ *n* **1** : a religion marked by belief in Allah as the sole deity, in Muhammad as his prophet, and in the Koran **2 a** : the civilization erected upon Islamic faith **b** : the modern nations in which Islam is the dominant religion — **Is·lam·ic** \is-'läm-ik, iz-, -'lam-\ *adj*

is·land \'ī-lənd\ *n* **1** : an area of land surrounded by water and smaller than a continent **2** : something suggestive of an island in its isolation [an altered form of earlier *iland* "island," derived from Old English *īgland* "island"; the spelling *island* was influenced by the word *isle,* which is not related]

is·land·er \'ī-lən-dər\ *n* : a person born or living on an island

island universe *n* : a galaxy other than the Milky Way

isle \'ī(ə)l\ *n* **1** : ISLAND 1; *esp* : ISLET [from early French *isle* "isle, island," from Latin *insula* "island" — related to INSULATE, ISOLATE, PENINSULA]

is·let \'ī-lət\ *n* **1** : a little island **2** : ISLET OF LANGERHANS

islet of Lang·er·hans \-'läŋ-ər-ͺhänz, -ͺhän(t)s\ *n, pl* **islets of Langerhans** : one of the groups of small endocrine cells in the pancreas that produce and give off insulin

ism \'iz-əm\ *n* **1** : a distinctive belief, cause, or theory **2** : an oppressive and especially discriminatory attitude or belief

-ism \ͺiz-əm\ *n suffix* **1 a** : act : practice : process ⟨criti*cism*⟩ ⟨plagiar*ism*⟩ **b** : manner of action or behavior ⟨hero*ism*⟩ **2 a** : state : condition : property ⟨skeptic*ism*⟩ **b** : abnormal state or condition ⟨alcohol*ism*⟩ **3** : doctrine : theory : cult ⟨Buddh*ism*⟩ ⟨social*ism*⟩ **4** : characteristic or peculiar feature ⟨colloquial*ism*⟩ [derived from Greek *-isma* and Greek *-ismos* (noun suffixes)]

isn't \'iz-ᵊnt\ : is not

iso·bar \'ī-sə-ͺbär\ *n* : a line drawn on a map to indicate areas having the same atmospheric pressure at a given time or for a given period — **iso·bar·ic** \ͺī-sə-'bär-ik, -'bar-\ *adj*

iso·late \'ī-sə-ͺlāt *also* 'is-ə-\ *vb* **-lat·ed; -lat·ing** : to set or keep apart from others [derived from French *isolé* (adjective) "isolated, set off from others," from Italian *isola* "island," from Latin *insula* "island" — related to INSULATE, ISLE, PENINSULA]

isobar

iso·la·tion \ˌī-sə-ˈlā-shən *also* ˌis-ə-\ *n* **1** : the act of isolating : the condition of being isolated **2** : separation of a population of living things from related forms in such a manner as to prevent crossbreeding

iso·la·tion·ism \ˌī-sə-ˈlā-shə-ˌniz-əm\ *n* : a national policy of avoiding international political and economic relations — **iso·la·tion·ist** \-sh(ə-)nəst\ *n or adj*

iso·mer \ˈī-sə-mər\ *n* : one of two or more chemical compounds or groups that have the same numbers of atoms of the same elements but differ in structure — **iso·mer·ic** \ˌī-sə-ˈmer-ik\ *adj* — **isom·er·ism** \ī-ˈsäm-ə-ˌriz-əm\ *n*

iso·met·ric \ˌī-sə-ˈme-trik\ *adj* : of, relating to, or being muscular contraction of the kind that takes place in doing isometrics

iso·met·rics \ˌī-sə-ˈme-triks\ *n sing or pl* : exercise or a system of exercises in which force is applied to an unmoving object (as a wall) so that opposing muscles are contracted with little shortening of muscle fibers and no movements of joints

iso·pod \ˈī-sə-ˌpäd\ *n* : any of a large order of small crustaceans (as a wood louse) with a thorax made up of seven segments of which each bears a pair of legs — **isopod** *adj*

iso·prene \ˈī-sə-ˌprēn\ *n* : a compound used especially in making synthetic rubber

iso·pro·pyl alcohol \ˌī-sə-ˈprō-pəl-\ *n* : a flammable liquid used especially to dissolve things and as rubbing alcohol

isos·ce·les \ī-ˌsäs-(ə-)ˌlēz\ *adj* **1** : being a triangle with two equal sides **2** : being a trapezoid whose two nonparallel sides are equal

isos·ta·sy \ī-ˈsäs-tə-sē\ *n* : the state of balance that exists between the earth's crust and the denser rock material beneath — **iso·stat·ic** \ˌī-sə-ˈstat-ik\ *adj*

iso·therm \ˈī-sə-ˌthərm\ *n* : a line on a map connecting points having the same temperature

iso·tope \ˈī-sə-ˌtōp\ *n* : any of the forms of an element that differ in the number of neutrons in an atom — **iso·to·pic** \ˌī-sə-ˈtäp-ik, -ˈtō-pik\ *adj* — **iso·to·pi·cal·ly** \-ˈtäp-i-k(ə-)lē, -ˈtō-pi-\ *adv*

Is·rae·li \iz-ˈrā-lē\ *adj* : of, relating to, or characteristic of the republic of Israel or its people — **Israeli** *n*

Is·ra·el·ite \ˈiz-r(ē-)ə-ˌlīt\ *n* : a descendant of the Hebrew patriarch Jacob; *esp* : a person born or living in the ancient kingdom of Israel — **Israelite** *adj*

is·su·ance \ˈish-ú-wən(t)s\ *n* : the act of issuing especially officially

¹**is·sue** \ˈish-ü\ *n* **1** : the action of going, coming, or flowing out **2** : a means or place of going out : EXIT, OUTLET **3** : OFFSPRING, PROGENY **4** : final outcome : RESULT **5** : a point of debate or controversy **6** : a giving off (as of blood) from the body **7** : something issued or issuing; *esp* : the copies of a publication published at one time

²**issue** *vb* **is·sued; is·su·ing** **1** : to go, come, or flow out : EMERGE ⟨water *issuing* from a pipe⟩ **2 a** : to cause to come forth **b** : to distribute officially **c** : to send out for sale or circulation : PUBLISH **3** : to come as an effect : RESULT [Middle English *issuen* "to go out, flow out," derived from early French *issir* "to come or go out," from Latin *exire* "to go out," from *ex-* "out of, from" and *ire* "to go" — related to EXIT, ITINERARY, TRANSIT] — **is·su·er** *n*

-ist \əst\ *n suffix* **1 a** : one that performs a (specified) action ⟨cyclist⟩ : one that makes or produces ⟨novelist⟩ **b** : one that plays a (specified) musical instrument ⟨harpist⟩ **c** : one that operates a (specified) machine ⟨automobilist⟩ **2** : one that specializes in a (specified) art or science or skill ⟨geologist⟩ **3** : one that believes in or favors a (specified) doctrine or system or code of behavior ⟨socialist⟩ or that of a (specified) individual ⟨Buddhist⟩ [derived from Greek *-istēs* (noun suffix)]

isth·mus \ˈis-məs\ *n* : a narrow strip of land connecting two larger land areas

-is·tic \ˈis-tik\ *or* **-is·ti·cal** \ˈis-ti-kəl\ *adj suffix* : of, relating to, or characteristic of [derived from Greek *-istikos* (adjective suffix), from *-istēs* (noun suffix) "-ist"]

¹**it** \(ˈ)it, ət\ *pron* **1** : that one — used usually to refer to a lifeless thing ⟨caught the ball and threw *it* back⟩, a living thing whose sex is unknown or disregarded ⟨don't know who *it* is⟩, a group, or an abstract entity **2** — used as subject of a verb that expresses a condition or action without a doer ⟨*it* is raining⟩ **3 a** — used in the usual place of a noun, phrase, or clause not in its ordinary place ⟨*it* is necessary to repeat the whole thing⟩ ⟨*it* was here that I lost my way⟩ **b** — used as a direct object with little or no meaning ⟨footed *it* back to camp⟩ **4** : the general state of affairs ⟨how is *it* going⟩

²**it** \ˈit\ *n* : the player in a game (as tag) who has to catch the others

Ital·ian \ə-ˈtal-yən, i-\ *n* **1 a** : a person born or living in Italy **b** : a person of Italian ancestry **2** : the Romance language of the Italians — **Italian** *adj*

Italian sandwich *n* : ²SUBMARINE 2

¹**ital·ic** \ə-ˈtal-ik, i-, ī-\ *adj* **1** *cap* : of or relating to ancient Italy, its peoples, or their Indo-European languages **2** : of, relating to, or being a type style with characters that slant upward to the right (as in "*these words are italic*")

²**italic** *n* : an italic character or type

ital·i·cize \ə-ˈtal-ə-ˌsīz, i-, ī-\ *vb* **-cized; -ciz·ing** : to print in italics or underline with a single line

¹**itch** \ˈich\ *vb* **1** : to have or produce an itch **2** : to cause to itch **3** : to have a strong desire ⟨*itching* to get going⟩

²**itch** *n* **1 a** : an uneasy irritating feeling in the skin usually held to result from exciting cells or groups of cells which sense pain **b** : a skin disorder accompanied by an itch; *esp* : SCABIES **2** : a restless usually constant desire — **itch·i·ness** \ˈich-ē-nəs\ *n* — **itchy** \-ē\ *adj*

it'd \ˈit-əd\ : it had : it would

-ite \ˌīt\ *n suffix* **1 a** : one who is from or lives in a (specified) area ⟨suburbanite⟩ ⟨New Jerseyite⟩ **b** : descendant ⟨Israelite⟩ **2** : product **3** : fossil ⟨ammonite⟩ **4** : mineral ⟨halite⟩ : rock ⟨quartzite⟩ [derived from Greek *-itēs* (noun and adjective suffix)]

item \ˈīt-əm\ *n* **1** : a separate part in a list, account, or series **2** : a brief piece of news or an article reporting it

item·ize \ˈīt-ə-ˌmīz\ *vb* **-ized; -iz·ing** : to set down one by one : LIST ⟨*itemize* expenses⟩ — **item·i·za·tion** \ˌīt-ə-mə-ˈzā-shən\ *n*

it·er·a·tion \ˌit-ə-ˈrā-shən\ *n* : REPETITION; *esp* : a computational process in which a series of operations is repeated a number of times

itin·er·ant \ī-ˈtin-ə-rənt, ə-ˈtin-\ *adj* : traveling from place to place ⟨an *itinerant* preacher⟩

itin·er·ary \ī-ˈtin-ə-ˌrer-ē, ə-\ *n, pl* **-ar·ies** **1** : the route of a journey **2** : a travel diary **3** : a traveler's guidebook [Middle English *itinerarie* "route of a journey," from Latin *itinerarium* (same meaning), derived from earlier *itiner-, iter* "journey, passage," from *ire* "to go" — related to EXIT, ISSUE, TRANSIT] — **itinerary** *adj*

-i·tis \ˈīt-əs\ *n suffix, pl* **-i·tis·es** \ˈīt-ə-səz\ *also* **-it·i·des** \ˈit-ə-ˌdēz\ *or* **-i·tes** \ˈīt-(ˌ)ēz, ˈēt-\ : inflamed state of or disorder with inflammation of ⟨bronch*itis*⟩ [derived from Greek *-itis* (noun and adjective suffix)]

it'll \ˌit-ᵊl\ : it shall : it will

its \(ˌ)its, əts\ *adj* : of or relating to it or itself especially as possessor ⟨*its* kennel⟩, agent ⟨a child proud of *its* first drawings⟩, or object of an action ⟨*its* enactment into law⟩

it's \(ˌ)its, əts\ **1** : it is **2** : it has

\ə\ **abut**	\aú\ **out**	\i\ **tip**	\ó\ **saw**	\ú\ **foot**
\ər\ **further**	\ch\ **chin**	\ī\ **life**	\ói\ **coin**	\y\ **yet**
\a\ **mat**	\e\ **pet**	\j\ **job**	\th\ **thin**	\yü\ **few**
\ā\ **take**	\ē\ **easy**	\ŋ\ **sing**	\t͟h\ **this**	\yú\ **cure**
\ä\ **cot, cart**	\g\ **go**	\ō\ **bone**	\ü\ **food**	\zh\ **vision**

it·self \it-'self, ət-\ *pron* **1** : that identical one — used to show that the subject and object of the verb are the same ⟨the cat gave *itself* a bath⟩ or for emphasis ⟨the letter *itself* was missing⟩ **2** : its normal, healthy, or sane self

-i·ty \ət-ē\ *n suffix, pl* **-i·ties** : quality : state : degree ⟨alkali*nity*⟩ [derived from Latin *-itat-, -itas* "quality, state"]

IUD \ˌī-ˌyü-'dē\ *n* : INTRAUTERINE DEVICE

-ive \iv\ *adj suffix* : that performs or tends toward an indicated action ⟨exhaust*ive*⟩ [derived from Latin *-ivus* (adjective suffix)]

I've \(ˌ)īv\ : I have

ivied \'ī-vēd\ *adj* : covered with ivy

ivo·ry \'īv-(ə-)rē\ *n, pl* **-ries** **1** : the hard creamy-white substance of which the tusks of a tusked mammal (as an elephant or walrus) are formed **2** : a pale whitish yellow

ivo·ry–billed woodpecker \ˌīv-(ə-)rē-ˌbild-\ *n* : a large black-and-white woodpecker of the southeastern U.S. that has a large whitish bill and in the male a pointed bunch of red feathers on the head and that is thought to be extinct

ivy \'ī-vē\ *n, pl* **ivies** **1** : a climbing woody vine with glossy evergreen leaves, small yellowish flowers, and black berries that is often grown on the outside of buildings — called also *English ivy* **2** : any of several climbing plants (as Virginia creeper or poison ivy) resembling ivy

ivy 1

-ize \ˌīz\ *vb suffix* **1** : cause to be or conform to or resemble ⟨american*ize*⟩ : form or cause to be formed into ⟨crystall*ize*⟩ ⟨union*ize*⟩ **2 a** : subject to a specified action ⟨satir*ize*⟩ **b** : saturate, treat, or combine with ⟨oxid*ize*⟩ ⟨macadam*ize*⟩ **3** : treat like ⟨idol*ize*⟩ **4** : engage in a (specified) activity ⟨philosoph*ize*⟩ [derived from Greek *-izein* (verb suffix)]

J

j \'jā\ *n, often cap* : the 10th letter of the English alphabet

jab \'jab\ *vb* **jabbed; jab·bing** : to poke quickly or suddenly with or as if with something sharp — **jab** *n*

¹jab·ber \'jab-ər\ *vb* **jab·bered; jab·ber·ing** \-(ə-)riŋ\ : to speak too fast or not clearly enough to be understood — **jab·ber·er** \'jab-ər-ər\ *n*

²jabber *n* : GIBBERISH, CHATTER

jab·ber·wocky \'jab-ər-ˌwäk-ē\ *n* : meaningless speech or writing

ja·bot \zha-'bō, 'jab-ˌō\ *n* : a ruffle of cloth or lace that falls from the collar down the front of a dress or shirt

¹jack \'jak\ *n* **1 a** : ¹MAN 1a **b** *often cap* : SAILOR **2 a** : a device for turning a spit (as in roasting meat) **b** : any of various portable devices for applying pressure or lifting a heavy body (as an automobile or a building) a short distance **3** : any of various animals: as **a** : a male donkey **b** : JACKRABBIT **4 a** : a small national flag flown by a ship **b** : a small six-pointed metal object used in a game **c** *pl* : a game played with jacks **5** : a playing card bearing the figure of a soldier or servant **6** *slang* : MONEY 1a **7** : a socket used with a plug to connect one electric circuit with another

jabot

²jack *vb* **1** : to move or lift by or as if by a jack **2** : ¹INCREASE 1, RAISE ⟨*jack* up prices⟩ — **jack·er** *n*

jack·al \'jak-əl, -ˌȯl\ *n* : any of several wild dogs of Africa and Asia like but smaller than the related wolves

jack·ass \'jak-ˌas\ *n* **1** : DONKEY 1; *esp* : a male donkey **2** : a stupid person : FOOL

jack·boot \-ˌbüt\ *n* : a heavy military boot; *esp* : one reaching above the knee

jack·daw \-ˌdȯ\ *n* : a common black and gray Eurasian bird related to but smaller than the crows

jack·et \'jak-ət\ *n* **1** : a garment for the upper body usually having a front opening, collar, and sleeves **2** : an outer covering or casing: as **a** : a tough metal covering on a bullet or projectile **b** : a coating or covering of a nonconducting material used to prevent heat radiation **c** : an outer paper wrapper on a bound book — **jack·et·ed** \-ət-əd\ *adj*

jack·ham·mer \'jak-ˌham-ər\ *n* : a tool driven by compressed air that is used for drilling or breaking up hard substances (as rock or pavement) by a repeated pounding action

jack–in–the–box \'jak-ən-thə-ˌbäks\ *n, pl* **jack–in–the–box·es** *or* **jacks–in–the–box** : a small box out of which a figure (as of a clown's head) springs when the lid is raised

jack–in–the–pul·pit \ˌjak-ən-thə-'pùl-ˌpit\ *n, pl* **jack–in–the–pulpits** *also* **jacks–in–the–pulpit** : a North American spring-flowering herb that grows in moist shady places and bears an upright club-shaped flower cluster over which arches a green and purple bract like a hood

¹jack·knife \'jak-ˌnīf\ *n* **1** : a large strong pocketknife **2** : a dive in which the diver bends from the waist and touches the ankles before straightening out

²jackknife *vb* : to double up like a jackknife ⟨the trailer truck *jackknifed*⟩

jack–of–all–trades \ˌjak-ə-'vȯl-ˌtrādz\ *n, pl* **jacks–of–all–trades** : a person who can work at various trades

jack–o'–lan·tern \'jak-ə-ˌlant-ərn\ *n* : a lantern made of a pumpkin usually cut to look like a face

jack pine *n* : a North American pine with twisted needles in bundles of two and wood used especially to make pulp for paper

jack·pot \'jak-ˌpät\ *n* **1** : a large poker pot formed by the accumulation of stakes from previous play **2 a** : a combination on a slot machine that wins a top prize or all the coins in the machine **b** : the sum so won **3** : a great often unexpected success or reward

jack·rab·bit \-ˌrab-ət\ *n* : any of several large hares of western North America with very long ears and long hind legs

jack·screw \-ˌskrü\ *n* : a jack operated by a screw for lifting or for applying pressure

jack·stone \-ˌstōn\ *n* **1** : ¹JACK 4b **2** *pl* : ¹JACK 4c

jackrabbit

jack·straw \-ˌstrȯ\ *n* **1** : one of the pieces used in the game jackstraws **2** *pl* : a game in which straws or thin strips are let fall in a heap and each player in turn tries to remove one at a time without disturbing the rest

jack–tar \-ˈtär\ *n, often cap* : SAILOR

¹jade \ˈjād\ *n* : a broken-down, bad-tempered, or worthless horse [Middle English *jade* "a broken-down or worthless horse"]

²jade *vb* **jad·ed; jad·ing** **1 a** : WEAR OUT 1, TIRE **b** : to become weary **2** : to make dull or uninterested by too much of something

³jade *n* : a tough usually green gemstone that takes a high polish

> **Word History** Gemstones were once thought to cure sickness as well as to work magic. Jade was supposed to be especially good at curing kidney problems. In the 16th century the Spanish brought jade back home from the New World. They called the gemstone *piedra de la ijada,* meaning "loin stone," because of their belief that jade could cure kidney disease. Spain was not the only country to value this gemstone. Jade became popular throughout western Europe both for wearing as jewelry and for curing or preventing disease. Our English word comes from French, which had borrowed the last word in the Spanish name, spelling it *jade.* [from French *jade* "the gemstone jade," from obsolete Spanish (*piedra de la*) *ijada,* literally "stone of the loin"; *ijada* derived from Latin *ileum* "groin, ileum"]

jade green *n* : a light bluish green

¹jag \ˈjag\ *n* : a sharp pointed part

²jag *n* : SPREE ⟨a crying *jag*⟩

jag·ged \ˈjag-əd\ *adj* : having a sharp uneven edge or surface ⟨*jagged* mountains⟩ — **jag·ged·ly** *adv* — **jag·ged·ness** *n*

jag·uar \ˈjag(-yə)-ˌwär\ *n* : a large yellowish brown black-spotted cat of tropical America that is larger and has a more solid build than the leopard

jaguar

jai alai \ˈhī-ˌlī, ˌhī-ə-ˈlī\ *n* : a court game somewhat like handball played usually by two or four players using a ball and a long curved basket strapped to the wrist

jail \ˈjā(ə)l\ *n* : PRISON — **jail** *vb*

jail·bird \-ˌbərd\ *n* : a person who is or is often in jail

jail·break \-ˌbrāk\ *n* : an escape from jail by use of force

jail·er *or* **jail·or** \ˈjā-lər\ *n* : a keeper of a jail

ja·lopy \jə-ˈläp-ē\ *n, pl* **-lop·ies** : a worn-out old automobile

jal·ou·sie \ˈjal-ə-sē\ *n* **1** : a blind with adjustable horizontal strips (as of wood, plastic, or glass) to admit light and air and shut out sun and rain **2** : a window made of adjustable glass louvers

¹jam \ˈjam\ *vb* **jammed; jam·ming** **1 a** : to press or push into a close or tight position ⟨*jam* a book into a bookcase⟩ **b** : to be or cause to be wedged so as to be unworkable ⟨*jam* the typewriter keys⟩ **c** : to crowd into : PACK ⟨2000 people *jammed* the hall⟩ **2** : to push suddenly and with force ⟨*jam* on the brakes⟩ **3** : to squeeze or crush painfully ⟨*jammed* my finger in the door⟩ **4** : to make impossible to understand by sending out interfering signals or messages ⟨*jam* a radio broadcast⟩ **5** : to take part in a jam session — **jam·mer** *n*

²jam *n* **1 a** : an act or instance of jamming **b** : a crowded mass that slows or prevents movement ⟨traffic *jam*⟩ **2** : a difficult state of affairs

³jam *n* : a food made of fruit and sugar thickened by boiling

jamb \ˈjam\ *n* : an upright piece forming the side of an opening (as of a door)

jam·ba·laya \ˌjəm-bə-ˈlī-ə\ *n* : rice cooked with ham, sausage, chicken, shrimps, or oysters and seasoned with herbs

jam·bo·ree \ˌjam-bə-ˈrē\ *n* **1** : a large festive gathering **2** : a national or international camping assembly of Boy Scouts

James \ˈjāmz\ *n* — see BIBLE table

jam–pack \ˈjam-ˈpak\ *vb* : to pack tightly : CRAM ⟨cars *jam-packed* the highway⟩ ⟨*jam-packs* her books with interesting facts⟩

jam session *n* : an informal performance by a group of musicians (as jazz musicians) who often invite visitors to join in

Jane Doe \ˈjān-ˈdō\ *n* : a woman who is a party to legal proceedings and whose true name is unknown or withheld

Jane Roe \-ˈrō\ *n* : a woman who is a party to legal proceedings and whose true name is unknown or withheld

jan·gle \ˈjaŋ-gəl\ *vb* **jan·gled; jan·gling** \-g(ə-)liŋ\ **1** : to make or cause to make a harsh ringing sound **2** : to excite to tense irritation ⟨*jangled* nerves⟩ — **jangle** *n*

jan·i·tor \ˈjan-ət-ər\ *n* **1** : DOORKEEPER **2** : a person who has the care of a building — **jan·i·to·ri·al** \ˌjan-ə-ˈtōr-ē-əl, -ˈtȯr-\ *adj*

Jan·u·ary \ˈjan-yə-ˌwer-ē\ *n* : the first month of the year

> **Word History** Among the many gods worshiped by the ancient Romans was one named Janus. He was believed to have two faces, one looking forward and one looking back. Janus was associated with doors, gates, and all beginnings. Because of that, when the Romans changed their calendar and added two months to the beginning of the year, they named the first one *Januarius* to honor Janus. The English *January* comes from Latin *Januarius.* [from Latin *Januarius* "first month of the year," from *Janus,* a Roman god]

Jap·a·nese \ˌjap-ə-ˈnēz, -ˈnēs\ *n, pl* **Japanese** **1 a** : a person born or living in Japan **b** : a person of Japanese ancestry **2** : the language of the Japanese — **Japanese** *adj*

Japanese beetle *n* : a small glossy green and brown beetle introduced into America from Japan that as a grub feeds on the roots of grasses and on decaying vegetation and as an adult eats leaves, flowers, and fruits

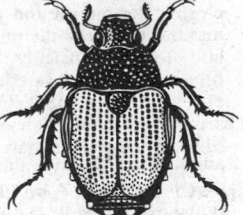

Japanese beetle

Japanese maple *n* : a maple native to Japan, China, and Korea with usually green, red, or purplish leaves

¹jar \ˈjär\ *vb* **jarred; jar·ring** **1 a** : to make a harsh or disagreeable sound **b** : to have a harsh or disagreeable effect ⟨noise that *jars* the nerves⟩ **2** : to cause to vibrate : SHAKE **3** : ¹CLASH 2b, CONFLICT ⟨*jarring* opinions⟩ [probably an imitation of the sound made]

²jar *n* **1** : a harsh sound **2** : ²JOLT **3** : ¹QUARREL 2, DISPUTE **4** : a painful effect : SHOCK

³jar *n* **1** : a usually glass or pottery container having a wide mouth **2** : the quantity held by a jar [from early French *jarre* "a container with a wide mouth," derived from Arabic *jarrah* "a pottery water container"]

jar·di·niere \ˌjärd-ᵊn-ˈi(ə)r\ *n* : an ornamental stand or pot for plants or flowers

\ə\ **abut**	\au̇\ **out**	\i\ **tip**	\ȯ\ **saw**	\u̇\ **foot**
\ər\ **further**	\ch\ **chin**	\ī\ **life**	\ȯi\ **coin**	\y\ **yet**
\a\ **mat**	\e\ **pet**	\j\ **job**	\th\ **thin**	\yü\ **few**
\ā\ **take**	\ē\ **easy**	\ŋ\ **sing**	\t͟h\ **this**	\yu̇\ **cure**
\ä\ **cot, cart**	\g\ **go**	\ō\ **bone**	\ü\ **food**	\zh\ **vision**

jar·gon \\'jär-gən, -ˌgän\\ *n* **1** : a mixed language used for communication between peoples whose native languages are different **2** : the special language of a particular activity or group ⟨*legal jargon*⟩ **3** : language that is not clear and is full of long important-sounding words

jas·mine \\'jaz-mən\\ *or* **jes·sa·mine** \\'jes-(ə-)mən\\ *n* : any of numerous often climbing shrubs that are related to the olive and have extremely fragrant flowers; *also* : any of various plants noted for sweet-scented flowers

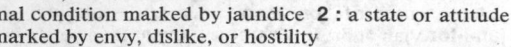

jas·per \\'jas-pər\\ *n* : an opaque mineral that occurs in several colors and is used for making ornamental objects (as vases); *esp* : green chalcedony — **jas·pery** \\-pə-rē\\ *adj*

jaun·dice \\'jȯn-dəs, 'jän-\\ *n* **1** : yellowish discoloring of the skin, tissues, and body fluids caused by the presence of coloring matter from the bile; *also* : a disease or abnormal condition marked by jaundice **2** : a state or attitude marked by envy, dislike, or hostility

jasmine

jaun·diced \\'jȯn-dəst\\ *adj* **1** : affected with or as if with jaundice **2** : showing or influenced by envy, dislike, or hostility ⟨a *jaundiced* eye⟩

jaunt \\'jȯnt, 'jänt\\ *n* : a short trip for pleasure — **jaunt** *vb*

jaun·ty \\'jȯnt-ē, 'jänt-\\ *adj* **jaun·ti·er; -est** : perky in manner or appearance : LIVELY ⟨*jaunty* marching tunes⟩ — **jaun·ti·ly** \\'jȯnt-ᵊl-ē, 'jänt-\\ *adv* — **jaun·ti·ness** \\'jȯnt-ē-nəs, 'jänt-\\ *n*

Ja·va man \\ˌjäv-ə-, ˌjav-\\ *n* : a small-brained prehistoric human being known chiefly from parts of skeletons found in Java and now classified with the direct ancestor of modern human beings

jav·e·lin \\'jav-(ə-)lən\\ *n* **1** : a light spear **2** : a slender usually metal shaft that is thrown for distance in a track-and-field event

¹jaw \\'jȯ\\ *n* **1 a** : either of two structures of bone or cartilage of vertebrate animals that support the soft parts enclosing the mouth and usually bear teeth **b** : the parts making up the walls of the mouth and serving to open and close it — usually used in plural **c** : any of various organs of invertebrate animals that serve the same purpose as the jaws of vertebrate animals **2** : something resembling the jaw of an animal in form or action; *esp* : one of a set of opposing parts that open and close for holding or crushing something between them — **jawed** \\'jȯd\\ *adj*

²jaw *vb* **1** : to talk for a long time **2** : ²SCOLD 1

jaw·bone \\'jȯ-ˌbōn, -ˌbōn\\ *n* : one of the bones of an animal's jaw; *esp* : MANDIBLE 1a

jaw·break·er \\-ˌbrā-kər\\ *n* : a round hard candy

jaw·less fish \\ˌjȯ-ləs-\\ *n* : any of a group of primitive fishes that do not have jaws and include the lampreys and their relatives

jay \\'jā\\ *n* : any of several noisy birds that are related to the crow but are smaller and usually more brightly colored

jay·walk \\'jā-ˌwȯk\\ *vb* : to cross a street carelessly without paying attention to traffic regulations — **jay·walk·er** *n*

¹jazz \\'jaz\\ *n* **1** : American music marked by lively rhythms with unusual accents and often by melodies made up by musicians as they play **2** : empty talk ⟨don't give me any of that *jazz*⟩ **3** : similar but unspecified things : STUFF

²jazz *vb* **1** : ENLIVEN — usually used with *up* **2** : to play in the manner of jazz

jazzy \\'jaz-ē\\ *adj* **jazz·i·er; -est** **1** : resembling jazz **2** : LIVELY **3**, FLASHY — **jazz·i·ness** \\'jaz-ē-nəs\\ *n*

jeal·ous \\'jel-əs\\ *adj* **1** : demanding complete devotion **2** : feeling mean resentment toward a rival or competitor **3** : fearful of the loss of a loved one's devotion **4** : WATCHFUL, CAREFUL — **jeal·ous·ly** *adv*

jeal·ou·sy \\'jel-ə-sē\\ *n, pl* **-sies** : a jealous disposition, attitude, or feeling

jean \\'jēn\\ *n* **1** : a heavy cotton cloth used especially for sportswear and work clothes **2** *pl* : pants made of jean, denim, or corduroy [a shortened form of earlier *jean fustian,* literally "a fustian (heavy cotton cloth) from Genoa," from Middle English *Gene* "Genoa, Italy"]

jeep \\'jēp\\ *n* : a small general-purpose motor vehicle with four-wheel drive used by the U.S. Army in World War II

Word History In March 1936 in newspapers across the country, Popeye's girlfriend, Olive Oyl, was delivered a box labeled "Eugene the Jeep." The contents of the box turned out to be a friendly little animal that made the sound "jeep." Elzie Segar, the creator of the comic strip, went on with the story of Eugene the Jeep through much of 1936. In 1937 work began on the development of an all-purpose vehicle for the military. When this vehicle was ready for use, it was apparently called *g.p.* for "general purpose." Probably because of the popularity of Eugene the Jeep, the pronunciation of *g.p.* was shortened to one syllable, and the spelling *jeep* became normal. [an altered form of *g.p.,* an abbreviation for "general purpose," influenced by the name Eugene the Jeep, a comic strip character]

jeer \\'ji(ə)r\\ *vb* : to laugh at or criticize someone in a loud and angry way — **jeer** *n*

Je·ho·vah \\ji-'hō-və\\ *n* : GOD 1

je·ju·num \\ji-'jü-nəm\\ *n* : the section of the small intestine between the duodenum and the ileum

jell \\'jel\\ *vb* **1** : to make or become jelly **2** : to take shape : FORM ⟨an idea *jelled*⟩

¹jel·ly \\'jel-ē\\ *n, pl* **jellies** **1** : a food with a soft elastic consistency due usually to gelatin or pectin; *esp* : a fruit product made by boiling sugar and the juice of fruit **2** : a substance resembling jelly — **jel·ly·like** \\-ē-ˌlīk\\ *adj*

²jelly *vb* **jel·lied; jel·ly·ing** : JELL 1

jelly bean *n* : a sugar-glazed bean-shaped candy

jel·ly·fish \\'jel-ē-ˌfish\\ *n* **1** : any of numerous free-swimming coelenterate animals that reproduce sexually and have a jellylike, saucer-shaped, and usually nearly transparent body and tentacles with stinging cells **2** : any of various sea animals that resemble a jellyfish

jen·net \\'jen-ət\\ *n* : a small Spanish horse

jen·ny \\'jen-ē\\ *n, pl* **jennies** **1 a** : a female bird ⟨a *jenny* wren⟩ **b** : a female donkey **2** : SPINNING JENNY

jeop·ar·dize \\'jep-ər-ˌdīz\\ *vb* **-dized; -diz·ing** : to expose to danger

jeop·ar·dy \\'jep-ərd-ē\\ *n* : DANGER 1

jer·boa \\jər-'bō-ə\\ *n* : any of several social jumping rodents of dry regions of Asia and northern Africa with long hind legs and a long tail that are active at night

Jer·e·mi·ah \\ˌjer-ə-'mī-ə\\ *n* — see BIBLE table

Jer·e·mi·as \\ˌjer-ə-'mī-əs\\ *n* : JEREMIAH

¹jerk \\'jərk\\ *n* **1** : a short quick pull or twist : TWITCH **2** : an involuntary muscular movement or spasm **3** : an annoyingly stupid or foolish person

²jerk *vb* **1** : to give a short quick push, pull, or twist to **2** : to move in jerks or with a jerk [probably an altered form of earlier *yerk* "to beat or thrash"]

jerboa

³jerk *vb* : to preserve (meat) in long strips dried in the sun [from ¹*jerky*]

jer·kin \\'jər-kən\\ *n* : a close-fitting hip-length sleeveless jacket

jerk·wa·ter \\'jər-ˌkwȯt-ər, -ˌkwät-\\ *adj* : small, rural, and unimportant ⟨*jerkwater* towns⟩

¹jer·ky \\'jər-kē\\ *n* : jerked meat [from Spanish *charqui* "jerky," from Quechua *ch'arki*]

²jerky \\'jər-kē\\ *adj* **jerk·i·er; -est** **1** : marked by jerks ⟨a *jerky* ride on a dirt road⟩ **2** : STUPID, FOOLISH [*jerk* (noun) and *-y* (adjective suffix)] — **jerk·i·ly** \\-kə-lē\\ *adv* — **jerk·i·ness** \\-kē-nəs\\ *n*

jer·ry–rigged \\'jer-ē-ˌrigd\\ *adj* : organized or constructed in a crude or improvised manner

jer·sey \\'jər-zē\\ *n, pl* **jerseys** **1** : a plain knitted fabric **2** : a close-fitting knitted garment (as a shirt) **3** *cap* : any of a breed of small usually light tan dairy cattle having short horns and noted for their rich milk

jessamine *variant of* JASMINE

jest \\'jest\\ *n* **1** : a comic act or remark : JOKE **2** : a playful mood or manner ⟨spoken in *jest*⟩ — **jest** *vb*

jest·er \\'jes-tər\\ *n* **1** : ¹FOOL 2 ⟨court *jester*⟩ **2** : a person given to jests

¹jet \\'jet\\ *n* **1** : a compact black coal that takes a good polish and is often used for jewelry **2** : a very dark black [Middle English *jet* "black mineral," from early French *jaiet* (same meaning), derived from Greek *gagatēs* (same meaning), from *Gagas*, a town and river in Asia Minor]

²jet *vb* **jet·ted; jet·ting** : ¹SPOUT 1, SPURT [from early French *jeter*, literally "to throw," from Latin *jactare* "to throw"]

³jet *n* **1 a** : a forceful rush of liquid, gas, or vapor especially through a narrow opening or a nozzle **b** : a nozzle for a jet of fluid (as gas or water) **2 a** : JET ENGINE **b** : JET AIRPLANE

⁴jet *vb* **jet·ted; jet·ting** : to travel by jet airplane

jet airplane *n* : an airplane powered by one or more jet engines — called also *jet plane*

jet airplane

jet engine *n* : an engine that produces motion as a result of the rearward discharge of a jet of fluid; *esp* : an aircraft engine that uses atmospheric oxygen to burn fuel and produces a rearward discharge of heated air and exhaust gases

jet lag *n* : a condition that is marked by physical and mental symptoms (as tiredness and bad temper) and occurs following a long flight through several time zones

jet–pro·pelled \\ˌjet-prə-'peld\\ *adj* : propelled by a jet engine

jet propulsion *n* : forward motion of a body produced by the forces resulting from the rearward discharge of a jet of fluid; *esp* : propulsion of an airplane by jet engines

jet·sam \\'jet-səm\\ *n* : goods thrown overboard to lighten a ship in distress; *esp* : such goods when washed ashore

jet set *n* : an international group of wealthy people who often travel to fashionable resorts

jet stream *n* : a long narrow wandering current of high-speed winds blowing from a generally westerly direction several miles above the earth's surface

jet·ti·son \\'jet-ə-sən, -ə-zən\\ *vb* **1** : to throw goods overboard from a ship or aircraft especially to lighten it in distress **2** : ¹DISCARD 2 — **jettison** *n*

jet·ty \\'jet-ē\\ *n, pl* **jetties** **1** : a pier built out into the water to influence the current or protect a harbor **2** : a landing wharf

Jew \\'jü\\ *n* **1** : one of the ancient Hebrews or a descendant of the ancient Hebrews **2** : one whose religion is Judaism — **Jew·ish** \\'jü-ish\\ *adj*

¹jew·el \\'jü-əl, 'jül\\ *n* **1** : an ornament of precious metal often set with stones and worn as an accessory of dress **2** : one that is highly valued or prized **3** : a precious stone

: GEM **4** : a bearing in a watch made of a crystal or a precious stone

²jewel *vb* **-eled** *or* **-elled; -el·ing** *or* **-el·ling** : to adorn or equip with jewels

jewel box *n* : a thin plastic case for a CD or DVD

jew·el·er *or* **jew·el·ler** \\'jü-ə-lər, 'jül-ər\\ *n* : a person who makes or deals in jewelry and related articles

jew·el·ry \\'jü-əl-rē, 'jül-rē\\ *n* : ornamental pieces (as rings and necklaces) worn on the person : JEWELS

jew·el·weed \\'jü-əl-ˌwēd, 'jül-\\ *n* : TOUCH-ME-NOT

Jew·ry \\'jü(ə)r-ē, 'jü-rē\\ *n* **1** *pl* **Jewries** : a district in which Jews lived : GHETTO **2** : the Jewish people

Jew's harp *or* **Jews' harp** \\'jüz-ˌhärp\\ *n* : a small simple musical instrument that consists of a flexible metal strip attached at one end to a flat pear-shaped frame and that is played by plucking the strip while holding the frame between the teeth

jib \\'jib\\ *n* : a triangular sail set on a line running from the bow to the head of the foremast

¹jibe *or* **gybe** *vb* **jibed** *or* **gybed; jib·ing** *or* **gyb·ing** **1** : to shift suddenly from one side to the other **2** : to cause a sail to jibe [perhaps a modified form of Dutch *gijben* "to shift suddenly from one side to another"]

²jibe *variant of* GIBE

³jibe *vb* **jibed; jib·ing** : to be in agreement ⟨the two reports *jibed*⟩ [origin unknown]

J jib

ji·ca·ma \\'hē-kə-mə\\ *n* : a starchy root of a tropical American vine related to the pea and eaten raw or cooked [Mexican Spanish *jícama* "a starchy root of a tropical American vine"]

jif·fy \\'jif-ē\\ *n, pl* **jiffies** : MOMENT 1, INSTANT ⟨in a *jiffy*⟩

¹jig \\'jig\\ *n* **1** : a lively springy dance **2** : ¹TRICK 1, GAME — used chiefly in the phrase *the jig is up*

²jig *vb* **jigged; jig·ging** **1** : to dance a jig **2** : to jerk up and down or to and fro

¹jig·ger \\'jig-ər\\ *n* **1** : one that jigs **2** : DEVICE 1c, GADGET **3** : a measure used in mixing drinks that usually holds 1 to 2 ounces (30 to 60 milliliters) [*jig* (verb) and *-er* (noun suffix)]

²jigger *n* : CHIGGER [perhaps from Wolof (an African language) *jiga* "insect"]

jig·gle \\'jig-əl\\ *vb* **jig·gled; jig·gling** \\-(ə-)liŋ\\ : to move or cause to move with quick little jerks — **jiggle** *n*

jig·saw \\'jig-ˌsȯ\\ *n* : an electric saw with a narrow blade for cutting curved and irregular lines

jigsaw puzzle *n* : a puzzle consisting of small pieces of various shapes that are to be fitted together to form a picture

¹jilt \\'jilt\\ *vb* : to cast a lover aside unfeelingly

²jilt *n* : a person who jilts a lover

jim crow \\'jim-'krō\\ *n, often cap J&C* : discrimination against blacks

jim–dan·dy \\'jim-'dan-dē\\ *n* : something very good — **jim–dandy** *adj*

¹jim·my \\'jim-ē\\ *n, pl* **jimmies** : a short crowbar used by burglars

\ə\ **abut**	\aú\ **out**	\i\ **tip**	\ȯ\ **saw**	\ú\ **foot**	
\ər\ **further**	\ch\ **chin**	\ī\ **life**	\ȯi\ **coin**	\y\ **yet**	
\a\ **mat**	\e\ **pet**	\j\ **job**	\th\ **thin**	\yü\ **few**	
\ā\ **take**	\ē\ **easy**	\ŋ\ **sing**	\th\ **this**	\yú\ **cure**	
\ä\ **cot, cart**	\g\ **go**	\ō\ **bone**	\ü\ **food**	\zh\ **vision**	

²jimmy *vb* **jim·mied; jim·my·ing** : to force open with or as if with a jimmy

jim·son·weed \ˈjim(p)-sən-ˌwēd\ *n, often cap* : a tall poisonous weed that is related to the potato and has bad-smelling leaves, large white or violet trumpet-shaped flowers, and a prickly fruit

¹jin·gle \ˈjiŋ-gəl\ *vb* **jin·gled; jin·gling** \-g(ə-)liŋ\ : to make or cause to make a light clinking sound ⟨coins *jingled* in their pockets⟩ — **jin·gler** \-g(ə-)lər\ *n*

²jingle *n* **1** : a light clinking sound **2** : a catchy repetition of sounds in a poem **3** : a verse or song marked by catchy repetition — **jin·gly** \-g(ə-)lē\ *adj*

jin·go \ˈjiŋ-gō\ *n, pl* **jingoes** : a person who favors a warlike policy toward other countries — **jin·go·ism** \-ˌiz-əm\ *n* — **jin·go·is·tic** \ˌjiŋ-gō-ˈis-tik\ *adj*

jin·ni \ˈjē-ˈnē, ˈjin-ē, jə-ˈnē\ *or* **jinn** \ˈjin\ *n, pl* **jinn** *or* **jinns** : GENIE

jin·rick·sha \jin-ˈrik-ˌshò\ *n* : RICKSHAW

¹jinx \ˈjiŋ(k)s\ *n* : someone or something that brings bad luck

²jinx *vb* : to bring bad luck to

jit·ney \ˈjit-nē\ *n, pl* **jitneys** : a small bus that carries passengers over a regular route

jit·ter·bug \ˈjit-ər-ˌbəg\ *n* **1** : a dance in which couples swing, balance, and twirl with lively acrobatics **2** : a person who dances the jitterbug — **jitterbug** *vb*

jit·ters \ˈjit-ərz\ *n pl* : extreme nervousness — **jit·tery** \-ə-rē\ *adj*

jiujitsu *or* **jiujutsu** *variant of* JUJITSU

¹jive \ˈjīv\ *n* **1** : swing music or dancing performed to it **2 a** : glib, deceptive, or foolish talk **b** : a special jargon of difficult or slang terms

²jive *vb* **jived; jiv·ing** **1** : ²KID **2** : to dance or play jive

job \ˈjäb\ *n* **1 a** : a piece of work; *esp* : one done at a specified rate **b** : something produced by or as if by work ⟨did a good *job*⟩ **2** : a special duty or function : TASK ⟨your *job* is to mow the lawn⟩ **3** : a position at which one regularly works for pay ⟨lost my *job*⟩ **synonyms** see TASK — **job·less** \-ləs\ *adj* — **job·less·ness** *n*

Job \ˈjōb\ *n* — see BIBLE table

job·ber \ˈjäb-ər\ *n* : a person who buys goods and then sells them to usually smaller dealers

job·hold·er \ˈjäb-ˌhōl-dər\ *n* : one having a regular job

¹jock \ˈjäk\ *n* **1** : ¹JOCKEY **2** : DISC JOCKEY

²jock *n* **1** : ATHLETIC SUPPORTER **2** : ATHLETE

¹jock·ey \ˈjäk-ē\ *n, pl* **jockeys** **1** : one who rides a horse especially as a professional in a race **2** : one who operates something ⟨a gas-pump *jockey*⟩

²jockey *vb* **jock·eyed; jock·ey·ing** **1** : to ride a horse as a jockey **2** : to move or manage skillfully or cleverly or so as to gain advantage ⟨*jockey* a truck into position⟩ ⟨*jockeying* for position⟩

jock itch *n* : a skin infection of the groin and upper thigh that is caused by a fungus and is marked by itchy, red, and flaking skin [from ²jock "athletic supporter, athlete"]

jock strap *n* : ATHLETIC SUPPORTER

jo·cose \jō-ˈkōs\ *adj* : MERRY 1, MIRTHFUL — **jo·cose·ly** *adv* — **jo·cose·ness** *n*

joc·u·lar \ˈjäk-yə-lər\ *adj* **1** : fond of jesting **2** : said or done in jest — **joc·u·lar·i·ty** \ˌjäk-yə-ˈlar-ət-ē\ *n* — **joc·u·lar·ly** \ˈjäk-yə-lər-lē\ *adv*

jo·cund \ˈjäk-ənd *also* ˈjōk-(ˌ)ənd\ *adj* : MERRY, JOLLY — **jo·cund·ly** *adv*

jodh·pur \ˈjäd-pər\ *n* **1** *pl* : riding breeches loose above the knee and tight-fitting below **2** : an ankle-high boot fastened with a strap that is buckled at the side

Jo·el \ˈjō-əl\ *n* — see BIBLE table

¹jog \ˈjäg, ˈjòg\ *vb* **jogged; jog·ging** **1** : to give a slight shake or push to : NUDGE **2** : ¹ROUSE 2, STIR ⟨jog one's memory⟩ **3** : to move up and down or about with a short heavy motion **4 a** : to go or cause to go at a jog **b** : to run slowly especially for exercise [probably an altered form of a dialect word *shog* "jolt, jostle"] — **jog·ger** *n*

²jog *n* **1** : a slight shake : PUSH **2** : a slow steady jolting gait especially of a horse **3** : an instance of jogging

³jog *n* **1** : an unevenness (as a bulge or a dent) in a line or surface **2** : a short change in direction [probably an altered form of *jag* "a sharp projecting edge"]

jog·gle \ˈjäg-əl\ *vb* **jog·gled; jog·gling** \-(ə-)liŋ\ : to shake slightly

John \ˈjän\ *n* **1** : the fourth Gospel in the New Testament — see BIBLE table **2** : any of three short didactic letters addressed to early Christians and included in the New Testament — see BIBLE table

John Doe \ˈjän-ˈdō\ *n* : a person in legal proceedings whose true name is unknown or withheld

john·ny·cake \ˈjän-ē-ˌkāk\ *n* : a bread made with cornmeal, flour, eggs, and milk

John·ny–jump–up \ˌjän-ē-ˈjəm-ˌpəp\ *n* : any of various pansies or violets with small flowers

join \ˈjòin\ *vb* **1 a** : to bring or fasten together in close contact ⟨*join* hands⟩ **b** : to connect (as points) by a line **c** : to become joined ⟨place where two roads *join*⟩ **2** : to come or bring into close association ⟨*join* a club⟩ ⟨*join* in marriage⟩ **3** : to come into the company of ⟨*join* friends for lunch⟩ **4** : ADJOIN 2 ⟨the two farms *join*⟩ **5** : to take part with others in an activity ⟨*join* in singing⟩ — **join·able** \ˈjòi-nə-bəl\ *adj*

　　synonyms JOIN, CONNECT, COMBINE, UNITE mean to bring or come together into some kind of union. JOIN suggests a bringing together of any degree of closeness including actual touching ⟨*joined* forces in an effort to win⟩ ⟨*join* the ends with glue⟩. CONNECT suggests a loose or outside attachment with little or no loss of separate identity ⟨the treaty *connects* the two nations⟩. COMBINE suggests some blending of the things coming together and some loss of separate identity ⟨*combining* jazz and rock to create a new kind of music⟩. UNITE suggests an even more complete coming together that turns two or more things into one ⟨the colonies *united* to form a republic⟩.

join·er \ˈjòi-nər\ *n* **1** : a woodworker who constructs articles by joining pieces of wood **2** : a person who joins many organizations

¹joint \ˈjòint\ *n* **1 a** : the point of contact of two bones in the animal body often including the surrounding and supporting parts **b** : NODE 2 **c** : a part or space included between two joints, knots, or nodes ⟨the upper *joint* of the arm⟩ **2** : a large piece of meat for roasting **3** : a place where two things or parts are joined ⟨a *joint* in a pipe⟩ **4 a** : a cheap or shabby place of entertainment **b** : ¹PLACE 2b, ESTABLISHMENT **5** : a marijuana cigarette — **joint·ed** \-əd\ *adj* — **out of joint** **1** : being a dislocated bone with its head slipped from its socket **2** : out of harmony : in an unsuitable relationship or arrangement **3** : in bad humor : DISGRUNTLED ⟨losing put her *out of joint*⟩

²joint *adj* **1** : UNITED 1, COMBINED ⟨a *joint* effort⟩ **2** : done by or shared by two or more persons ⟨a *joint* account⟩ : sharing with another ⟨*joint* owner⟩ — **joint·ly** *adv*

³joint *vb* **1 a** : to fit together **b** : to provide with a joint **2** : to separate the joints of — **joint·er** *n*

joist \ˈjòist\ *n* : a small beam laid crosswise to support a floor or ceiling

J joist

¹joke \ˈjōk\ *n* **1 a** : something said or done to cause laughter; *esp* : a brief story with a humorous twist **b** : the humorous element in something **c** : good-natured kidding ⟨can't take a *joke*⟩ **2** : something not to be taken seriously ⟨that exam was a *joke*⟩

²joke *vb* **joked; jok·ing** : to make jokes : JEST — **jok·ing·ly** \ˈjō-kiŋ-lē\ *adv*

jok·er \\'jō-kər\ *n* **1** : a person who jokes **2** : an extra card used in some card games **3** : a hidden or misleading part of an agreement that works to one party's disadvantage : CATCH **4** : HUMAN BEING, FELLOW; *esp* : an obnoxious or incompetent person

joke·ster \\'jōk-stər\ *n* : JOKER 1

jol·li·fi·ca·tion \ˌjäl-i-fə-'kā-shən\ *n* : MERRYMAKING 1

jol·li·ty \\'jäl-ət-ē\ *n, pl* **-ties** : MERRYMAKING 1, GAIETY

¹jol·ly \\'jäl-ē\ *adj* **jol·li·er; -est** **1 a** : MERRY 1, CHEERFUL **b** : JOVIAL **2** : very pleasant or agreeable : SPLENDID

²jolly *adv* : ²VERY 1 〈a *jolly* good time〉

Jol·ly Rog·er \ˌjäl-ē-'räj-ər\ *n* : a black flag with a white skull and crossbones formerly used by pirates

¹jolt \\'jōlt\ *vb* **1** : to give a quick hard blow to : JAR **2** : to move jerkily — **jolt·er** *n*

²jolt *n* **1** : a sudden jarring blow or movement **2** : a sudden shock or surprise

Jo·nah \\'jō-nə\ *n* — see BIBLE table

Jo·nas \\'jō-nəs\ *n* : JONAH

Jon·a·than \\'jän-ə-thən\ *n* : any of a variety of red-skinned apple

jon·quil \\'jän-kwəl, 'jäŋ-\ *n* : a Mediterranean daffodil that bears clusters of fragrant yellow or white flowers having a short central tube

josh \\'jäsh\ *vb* : to joke with : TEASE

Josh·ua \\'jäsh(ə-)wə\ *n* — see BIBLE table

Joshua tree *n* : a tall branched yucca of the southwestern U.S. with short leaves and clusters of greenish white flowers

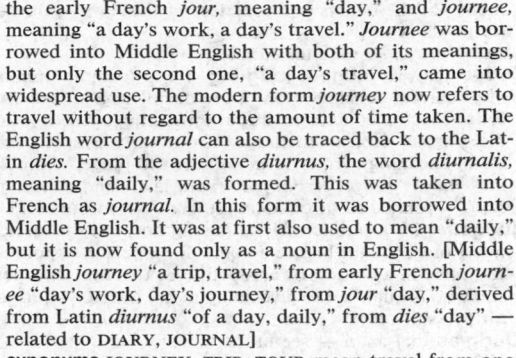

Joshua tree

¹jos·tle \\'jäs-əl\ *vb* **jos·tled; jos·tling** \-(ə-)liŋ\ **1** : to run or knock against so as to jar : push roughly **2** : to make one's way by jostling

²jostle *n* : a jostling blow : SHOVE

Jos·ue \\'jäsh-ə-wē\ *n* : JOSH-UA

¹jot \\'jät\ *n* : the least bit

²jot *vb* **jot·ted; jot·ting** : to make a brief note of 〈*jot* this down〉

joule \\'jü(ə)l\ *n* : a unit of work or energy equal to the work done by a force of one newton acting through a distance of one meter

jounce \\'jaun(t)s\ *vb* **jounced; jounc·ing** : to move or cause to move in an up-and-down manner — **jounce** *n*

jour·nal \\'jərn-ᵊl\ *n* **1 a** : a brief account of daily events : DIARY **b** : a record of the happenings of a conference or a legislative body **2 a** : a daily newspaper **b** : a magazine that reports on things of special interest to a particular group [Middle English *journal* "a religious service book containing the day hours," from early French *jurnal* (same meaning), from *jurnal* (adjective) "daily," derived from Latin *diurnus* "of the day, daily," from *dies* "day" — related to DIARY, JOURNEY; see *Word History* at JOURNEY]

jour·nal·ese \ˌjərn-ᵊl-'ēz, -'ēs\ *n* : a way of writing said to be similar to that of newspapers

jour·nal·ism \\'jərn-ᵊl-ˌiz-əm\ *n* **1** : the collecting and editing of news to be presented in newspapers or magazines or over television or radio **2** : writing designed for or characteristic of newspapers or magazines — **jour·nal·is·tic** \ˌjərn-ᵊl-'is-tik\ *adj*

jour·nal·ist \\'jərn-ᵊl-əst\ *n* : an editor of or writer for a newspaper or magazine or radio and television news

¹jour·ney \\'jər-nē\ *n, pl* **journeys** : travel from one place to another

Word History The Latin word *dies* means "day," and *diurnus* means "of a day." From the word *diurnus* came

the early French *jour,* meaning "day," and *journee,* meaning "a day's work, a day's travel." *Journee* was borrowed into Middle English with both of its meanings, but only the second one, "a day's travel," came into widespread use. The modern form *journey* now refers to travel without regard to the amount of time taken. The English word *journal* can also be traced back to the Latin *dies*. From the adjective *diurnus,* the word *diurnalis,* meaning "daily," was formed. This was taken into French as *journal*. In this form it was borrowed into Middle English. It was at first also used to mean "daily," but it is now found only as a noun in English. [Middle English *journey* "a trip, travel," from early French *journee* "day's work, day's journey," from *jour* "day," derived from Latin *diurnus* "of a day, daily," from *dies* "day" — related to DIARY, JOURNAL]

synonyms JOURNEY, TRIP, TOUR mean travel from one place to another. JOURNEY usually suggests that one travels a long distance and often that the traveling may be dangerous or difficult 〈a long *journey* across the desert〉. TRIP suggests that the traveling is brief, swift, or ordinary 〈our weekly *trip* to the supermarket〉. TOUR suggests a journey with several stopping places and an end at the place where one began 〈the sightseers took a *tour* of the city〉.

²journey *vb* **jour·neyed; jour·ney·ing** : to go on a journey — **jour·ney·er** *n*

jour·ney·man \\'jər-nē-mən\ *n* **1** : a worker who has learned a trade and works for another person usually by the day **2** : an experienced reliable worker

joust \\'jaust\ *n* : a combat on horseback between two knights with lances especially as part of a tournament — **joust** *vb* — **joust·er** *n*

jo·vi·al \\'jō-vē-əl\ *adj* : full of or expressing good humor — **jo·vi·al·i·ty** \ˌjō-vē-'al-ət-ē\ *n* — **jo·vi·al·ly** \\'jō-vē-ə-lē\ *adv*

¹jowl \\'jau(ə)l\ *n* **1** : ¹JAW 1; *esp* : the lower jaw **2** : CHEEK 1

²jowl *n* : loose flesh associated with the cheeks, lower jaw, or throat — **jowly** \\'jau-lē\ *adj*

¹joy \\'jȯi\ *n* **1** : a feeling of great pleasure or happiness that comes from success, good fortune, or a sense of well-being : GLADNESS **2** : something that gives joy 〈a *joy* to behold〉 **synonyms** see PLEASURE — **joy·less** \-ləs\ *adj* — **joy·less·ness** *n*

²joy *vb* : to experience joy : REJOICE

joy·ful \\'jȯi-fəl\ *adj* : feeling, causing, or showing joy 〈a *joyful* family reunion〉 — **joy·ful·ly** \-fə-lē\ *adv* — **joy·ful·ness** *n*

joy·ous \\'jȯi-əs\ *adj* : feeling, causing, or showing joy : JOYFUL — **joy·ous·ly** *adv* — **joy·ous·ness** *n*

joy·ride \\'jȯi-ˌrīd\ *n* : a ride taken for pleasure and often marked by reckless driving — **joy·rid·er** \-ˌrīd-ər\ *n*

joy·stick \-ˌstik\ *n* : a control lever for a device (as a computer display or an airplane) that allows motion in two or more directions

ju·bi·lant \\'jü-bə-lənt\ *adj* : feeling or expressing great joy : EXULTANT 〈*jubilant* teammates celebrating their victory〉 — **ju·bi·lant·ly** *adv*

ju·bi·la·tion \ˌjü-bə-'lā-shən\ *n* : an act of rejoicing : the state of being jubilant

ju·bi·lee \\'jü-bə-ˌlē, ˌjü-bə-'lē\ *n* **1** : a special anniversary; *esp* : a 50th anniversary **2** : a celebration especially of an anniversary

Ju·da·ism \\'jüd-ə-ˌiz-əm, 'jüd-ē-\ *n* **1** : a religion developed among the ancient Hebrews that stresses belief in one God and faithfulness to the laws of the Old Testa-

\ə\ abut	\au\ out	\i\ tip	\ȯ\ saw	\u̇\ foot
\ər\ further	\ch\ chin	\ī\ life	\ȯi\ coin	\y\ yet
\a\ mat	\e\ pet	\j\ job	\th\ thin	\yü\ few
\ā\ take	\ē\ easy	\ŋ\ sing	\th\ this	\yu̇\ cure
\ä\ cot, cart	\g\ go	\ō\ bone	\ü\ food	\zh\ vision

ment **2** : the beliefs and practices of the Jews — **Ju·da·ic** \jü-'dā-ik\ *adj*

Jude \'jüd\ *n* — see BIBLE table

¹judge \'jəj\ *vb* **judged; judg·ing** **1** : to form an opinion after careful consideration **2** : to decide as a judge : TRY **3** : to reach a conclusion about something : THINK [Middle English *juggen* "to judge," from early French *juger* (same meaning), from Latin *judicare* "to judge," from *judic-, judex* "judge," from *jus* "right, law," and *dicere* "to say" — related to HOOSEGOW, JURY, JUST, PREJUDICE]

²judge *n* **1** : a public official having authority to decide questions brought before a court **2** : a person appointed to decide in a contest or competition : UMPIRE **3** : a person who is qualified to give an opinion : CRITIC — **judge·ship** \-ˌship\ *n*

Judg·es \'jəj-əz\ *n* — see BIBLE table

judg·ment *or* **judge·ment** \'jəj-mənt\ *n* **1** : the act of judging **2** : a decision given by a court **3 a** : the process of forming an opinion by examining and comparing **b** : an opinion so formed **4** : the ability to judge : DISCERNMENT

judgment call *n* : a subjective decision, ruling, or opinion

Judgment Day *n* : the day of the final judging of all human beings by God

ju·di·cial \ju-'dish-əl\ *adj* **1** : of or relating to courts or judges **2** : ordered or enforced by a court ⟨a *judicial* decision⟩ — **ju·di·cial·ly** \-(ə-)lē\ *adv*

ju·di·cia·ry \ju-'dish-ē-ˌer-ē, -'dish-ə-rē\ *n* **1 a** : a system of courts of law **b** : the judges of these courts **2** : a branch of government in which judicial power is vested — **judiciary** *adj*

ju·di·cious \ju-'dish-əs\ *adj* : having, exercising, or characterized by sound judgment — **ju·di·cious·ly** *adv*

Ju·dith \'jüd-əth\ *n* — see BIBLE table

ju·do \'jüd-ō\ *n, pl* **judos** : a sport developed from jujitsu in which opponents attempt to throw each other by using quick movements and leverage

¹jug \'jəg\ *n* **1 a** : a large deep container with a narrow mouth and a handle **b** : the amount held by a jug **2** : PRISON 2, JAIL

²jug *vb* **jugged; jug·ging** : IMPRISON

jug·ful \'jəg-ˌful\ *n* : ¹JUG 1b

jug·gle \'jəg-əl\ *vb* **jug·gled; jug·gling** \-(ə-)liŋ\ **1** : to keep several objects in motion in the air at the same time **2** : to do several things at the same time ⟨*juggling* three jobs⟩ **3** : make changes to (something) in order to achieve a desired result ⟨had to *juggle* my schedule⟩ — **jug·gler** \-(ə-)lər\ *n*

¹jug 1a

jug·glery \'jəg-lə-rē\ *n, pl* **-gler·ies** **1** : the art or practice of a juggler **2** : TRICKERY

jug·u·lar \'jəg-yə-lər\ *adj* **1** : of, relating to, or situated in or on the throat or neck **2** : of or relating to the jugular vein

jugular vein *n* : any of several veins on each side of the neck that return blood from the head — called also *jugular*

juice \'jüs\ *n* **1 a** : the liquid part that can be squeezed out of vegetables and fruits ⟨orange *juice*⟩ **b** : the fluid part of meat **2 a** : the natural fluids (as blood, lymph, and secretions) of an animal body **b** : the liquid or moisture contained in something **3** : something (as electricity or gasoline) that supplies power — **juiced** \'jüst\ *adj*

juic·er \'jü-sər\ *n* : an appliance for squeezing juice from fruits or vegetables

juicy \'jü-sē\ *adj* **juic·i·er; -est** **1** : having much juice : SUCCULENT **2 a** : rich in interest : COLORFUL **b** : ¹RACY 2 ⟨a *juicy* scandal⟩ — **juic·i·ly** \-sə-lē\ *adv* — **juic·i·ness** \-sē-nəs\ *n*

ju·jit·su *or* **ju·jut·su** *or* **jiu·jit·su** *or* **jiu·jut·su** \ju-'jit-sü\ *n* : the Japanese art of unarmed fighting using holds, throws, and paralyzing blows

juke·box \'jük-ˌbäks\ *n* : a coin-operated phonograph or compact-disc player that automatically plays recordings selected from its list

ju·lep \'jü-ləp\ *n* : a drink of bourbon, sugar, and mint served with crushed ice

Ju·lian calendar \ˌjül-yən-\ *n* : a calendar introduced in Rome in 46 B.C. establishing the 12-month year of 365 days with each fourth year having 366 days and the months each having 31 or 30 days except for February which has 28 or in leap years 29 days — compare GREGORIAN CALENDAR

Ju·ly \ju-'lī\ *n* : the seventh month of the year

Word History The first ancient Roman calendar began the year with March. The original name of the fifth month of the year was *Quintilis,* a Latin word meaning "fifth." In order to honor the statesman Gaius Julius Caesar, however, the Roman senate changed *Quintilis* to *Julius.* The name *Julius* was borrowed into Old English and eventually became Modern English *July.* [Old English *Julius* "July," from Latin *Julius* "the fifth month of the old Roman calendar," named for Gaius *Julius* Caesar 100–44 B.C.]

jum·ble \'jəm-bəl\ *vb* **jum·bled; jum·bling** \-b(ə-)liŋ\ : to mix in a confused mass — **jumble** *n*

jum·bo \'jəm-bō\ *n, pl* **jumbos** : something very large of its kind [from *Jumbo,* name of a huge elephant shown by circus owner P. T. Barnum] — **jumbo** *adj*

¹jump \'jəmp\ *vb* **1 a** : to spring into the air : LEAP **b** : to give a sudden movement : START **c** : to begin to move — usually used with *off* **2** : to rise or raise suddenly in rank, status, or condition ⟨prices *jumped*⟩ **3** : to make a sudden attack ⟨*jumped* on us for being late⟩ **4** : to become lively with activity ⟨the woods were *jumping*⟩ **5 a** : to pass over or cause to pass over by a leap ⟨*jump* a hurdle⟩ **b** : ²BYPASS ⟨*jump* electrical connections⟩ **c** : to leap aboard ⟨*jump* a freight⟩ **6** : to run away and hide while at liberty under (bail) **7** : to depart from a normal course ⟨*jump* the track⟩ **8** : to occupy illegally ⟨*jump* a mining claim⟩ — **jump the gun** : to start too soon

²jump *n* **1 a** : an act of jumping : LEAP **b** : any of several sports competitions that involve jumping **c** : a space covered by a leap **d** : a sudden involuntary movement : START **e** : a move made in a board game by jumping **2 a** : a sharp sudden increase **b** : one in a series of moves ⟨keep one *jump* ahead⟩ **3** : an advantage at the start

jump drive *n* : a small usually rectangular device used for storing and transferring computer data : FLASH DRIVE

¹jump·er \'jəm-pər\ *n* **1** : one that jumps **2** : JUMP SHOT

²jum·per \'jəm-pər\ *n* **1** : a loose blouse or jacket worn by workers **2** : a sleeveless dress worn usually with a blouse

jumping bean *n* : a seed of any of several Mexican shrubs that tumbles about because of the movements of the larva of a small moth inside it

jumping jack *n* **1** : a toy figure of a man jointed and made to jump or dance by means of strings or a sliding stick **2** : an exercise that involves jumping from a standing position to one with legs spread and arms raised and then back to the original standing position

jump shot *n* : a basketball shot made while jumping

jump·suit \'jəmp-ˌsüt\ *n* **1** : a uniform worn by parachutists for jumping **2** : a one-piece garment consisting of a blouse or shirt with attached trousers or shorts

jumpy \'jəm-pē\ *adj* **jump·i·er; -est** : NERVOUS 2a, JITTERY ⟨after a long restless night, the soldiers were *jumpy*⟩ — **jump·i·ness** *n*

jun·co \'jəŋ-kō\ *n, pl* **juncos** *or* **juncoes** : any of a genus of small North American finches usually with a pink bill, ashy gray head and back, and white tail feathers

junc·tion \'jəŋ(k)-shən\ *n* **1** : an act of joining : the state of being joined **2** : a place or point of meeting ⟨a railroad *junction*⟩

junc·ture \ˈjəŋ(k)-chər\ *n* **1** : an instance of joining : UNION **2** : ¹JOINT 3a, CONNECTION **3** : an important point of time ⟨they feel they must make a decision at this *juncture*⟩ — **junc·tur·al** \-chə-rəl\ *adj*

June \ˈjün\ *n* : the sixth month of the year

Word History The English word *June* comes from the Latin *Junius,* the name given to the first month of summer by the ancient Romans. It isn't known for certain why the Romans named it as they did. *Junius* was also the name of a large Roman family group, and maybe the month was named in honor of the family. Or perhaps it was named for the Roman goddess *Juno.* [from Latin *Junius,* probably from *Junius,* name of a family group, or from *Juno,* a Roman goddess]

June·ber·ry \ˈjün-ˌber-ē\ *n* : SERVICEBERRY

june bug *n, often cap J* : any of various large leaf-eating beetles which fly chiefly in late spring and whose larvae are white grubs that live in soil and feed on roots — called also *june beetle*

jun·gle \ˈjəŋ-gəl\ *n* **1** : a thick tangled mass of tropical vegetation **2** : an area overgrown with jungle or other vegetation

jungle gym *n* : a structure of upright and crosswise bars for use by children at play

¹ju·nior \ˈjün-yər\ *adj* **1 a** : being the younger one — used chiefly to distinguish a son with the same given name as his father **b** : designed for young teenagers **2** : lower in standing or rank ⟨*junior* partner⟩ **3** : of or relating to juniors in a school

²junior *n* **1** : a person who is younger or of lower rank than another **2** : a student in the next-to-last year in a high school, college, or university

junior college *n* : a school that offers two years of studies similar to those in the first two years of a four-year college

junior high school *n* : a school usually including the seventh, eighth, and ninth grades

junior varsity *n* : a team for players who lack the experience or qualifications for the varsity

ju·ni·per \ˈjü-nə-pər\ *n* **1 a** : any of numerous evergreen shrubs and trees that are related to the pines but produce female cones resembling berries **b** : the berrylike cone or fruit of a juniper **2** : any of various evergreen trees resembling true junipers

¹junk \ˈjəŋk\ *n* **1** : articles discarded as worthless **2** : something of poor quality : TRASH **3** *slang* : ¹NARCOTIC 1; *esp* : HEROIN [Middle English *jonke* "piece of old or worn-out rope"] — **junky** \ˈjəŋ-kē\ *adj*

²junk *vb* : to get rid of as worthless : SCRAP

³junk *n* : a ship of eastern Asia with a high stern and four-cornered sails [from Portuguese *junco* "a Chinese ship"]

junk e–mail *n* : SPAM

¹jun·ket \ˈjəŋ-kət\ *n* **1** : a dessert of sweetened flavored milk set in a jelly **2** : ¹TRIP 2a; *esp* : a trip made by an official at public expense

³junk

²junket *vb* **1** : ²FEAST 1, BANQUET **2** : to go on a junket

junk food *n* : food that is high in calories but low in nutritional value

junk·ie *also* **junky** \ˈjəŋ-kē\ *n, pl* **junk·ies** **1** : a person who sells or is addicted to narcotics **2** : a person who gets an unusual amount of pleasure from or is dependent on something ⟨a sugar *junkie*⟩

junk mail *n* : mail that consists mostly of advertising circulars and is often addressed to "occupant" or "resident"

jun·ta \ˈhùn-tə, ˈjənt-ə, ˈhən-tə\ *n* **1** : a group of persons controlling a government especially after a revolution **2** : JUNTO

jun·to \ˈjənt-ō\ *n, pl* **juntos** : a group of persons joined for a common purpose

Ju·pi·ter \ˈjü-pət-ər\ *n* : the largest of the planets and fifth in order of distance from the sun — see PLANET table

Ju·ras·sic \jù-ˈras-ik\ *adj* : of, relating to, or being a period of the Mesozoic era of geological history marked by the presence of dinosaurs and the first appearance of birds; *also* : relating to the corresponding system of rocks — see GEOLOGIC TIME table [from French *jurassique* "Jurassic," from *Jura,* a range of mountains between France and Switzerland formed from the limestone characteristic of this period] — **Jurassic** *n*

ju·ris·dic·tion \ˌjùr-əs-ˈdik-shən\ *n* **1** : the power, right, or authority to interpret and apply the law **2** : the authority of a sovereign power to govern or legislate **3** : the limits or territory within which authority may be exercised

ju·ris·pru·dence \ˌjùr-ə-ˈsprüd-ᵊn(t)s\ *n* **1** : a system of laws **2** : the science of law **3** : a department of law ⟨medical *jurisprudence*⟩

ju·rist \ˈjù(ə)r-əst\ *n* : one (as a lawyer or judge) having a thorough knowledge of law

ju·ris·tic \jù-ˈris-tik\ *adj* **1** : of or relating to a jurist or jurisprudence **2** : relating to law

ju·ror \ˈjùr-ər, -ˌôr\ *n* : a member of a jury

ju·ry \ˈjù(ə)r-ē\ *n, pl* **juries** **1** : a body of persons sworn to inquire into a matter of fact and give their verdict **2** : a committee that judges and awards prizes at an exhibition or contest [Middle English *jure* "jury," derived from early French *jurer* "to swear," from Latin *jurare* (same meaning), from *jur-, jus* "right, law" — related to JUDGE, JUST]

¹just \ˈjəst\ *adj* **1 a** : WELL-FOUNDED, REASONABLE ⟨a *just* comment⟩ **b** : being in agreement with a standard of correctness : PROPER ⟨a *just* price⟩ **2 a** : morally right or good : RIGHTEOUS ⟨a *just* cause for war⟩ **b** : being deserved ⟨*just* punishment⟩ **3** : legally right ⟨a *just* title⟩ [Middle English *just* "reasonable, proper," from early French *juste* and Latin *justus* (same meaning), from *jus* "right, law" — related to JUDGE, JURY, PREJUDICE] **synonyms** see UPRIGHT — **just·ly** *adv*

²just \(ˌ)jəst, (ˌ)jist, (ˌ)jest\ *adv* **1 a** : EXACTLY 1, PRECISELY ⟨*just* right⟩ **b** : very recently ⟨the bell *just* rang⟩ **2 a** : by a small amount : BARELY ⟨*just* over the line⟩ **b** : IMMEDIATELY 1, DIRECTLY ⟨*just* west of here⟩ **3 a** : nothing more than : ONLY ⟨*just* a note⟩ **b** : QUITE 1, VERY ⟨*just* wonderful⟩

jus·tice \ˈjəs-təs\ *n* **1** : just conduct, management, or treatment ⟨do *justice* to a book⟩ **2 a** : ²JUDGE 1 **b** : the administration of law ⟨received *justice* in court⟩ **3 a** : the quality of being fair or just **b** : basis in morality, the right, or the law

justice of the peace : a local official having the authority to try minor cases, to administer oaths, and to perform marriages

jus·ti·fi·ca·tion \ˌjəs-tə-fə-ˈkā-shən\ *n* **1** : the act or an instance of justifying or of being justified **2** : something that justifies : DEFENSE

jus·ti·fy \ˈjəs-tə-ˌfī\ *vb* **-fied; -fy·ing** **1** : to prove or show to be just, right, legal, or reasonable **2** : to release from the guilt of sin — **jus·ti·fi·able** \ˈjəs-tə-ˌfī-ə-bəl\ *adj* — **jus·ti·fi·ably** \-blē\ *adv* — **jus·ti·fi·er** \-ˌfī-(ə)r\ *n*

jut \ˈjət\ *vb* **jut·ted; jut·ting** : to stick out, up, or forward : PROJECT — **jut** *n*

\ə\ **abut**	\aù\ **out**	\i\ **tip**	\ò\ **saw**	\ù\ **foot**
\ər\ **further**	\ch\ **chin**	\ī\ **life**	\òi\ **coin**	\y\ **yet**
\a\ **mat**	\e\ **pet**	\j\ **job**	\th\ **thin**	\yü\ **few**
\ā\ **take**	\ē\ **easy**	\ŋ\ **sing**	\th\ **this**	\yù\ **cure**
\ä\ **cot, cart**	\g\ **go**	\ō\ **bone**	\ü\ **food**	\zh\ **vision**

jute \'jüt\ *n* : a glossy fiber from either of two Asian plants that is used chiefly for making sacks and twine

Jute \'jüt\ *n* : a member of a Germanic people invading England from Jutland and settling in Kent in the 5th century A.D.

¹**ju·ve·nile** \'jü-və-ˌnīl, -vən-ᵊl\ *adj* **1** : showing incomplete development : IMMATURE, CHILDISH **2** : of, relating to, or characteristic of children or young people — **ju·ve·nil·i·ty** \ˌjü-və-'nil-ət-ē\ *n*

²**juvenile** *n* **1** : a young person, animal, or plant **2** : a book for young people **3** : an actor who plays youthful parts

juvenile delinquency *n* : violation of the law (as stealing) or antisocial behavior (as playing hooky from school) by a young person

juvenile delinquent *n* : a person whose behavior or conduct is considered juvenile delinquency

jux·ta·pose \'jək-stə-ˌpōz\ *vb* **-posed; -pos·ing** : to place side by side — **jux·ta·po·si·tion** \ˌjək-stə-pə-'zish-ən\ *n*

K

k \'kā\ *n, often cap* **1** : the 11th letter of the English alphabet **2 a** : THOUSAND **b** : a unit of computer memory equal to 1024 bytes **3** *cap* : STRIKEOUT

Kaa·ba \'käb-ə\ *n* : a small stone building in the court of the Great Mosque at Mecca that contains a sacred black stone and is the point toward which Muslims turn in praying

Ka·bu·ki \kə-'bü-kē, 'käb-ü-(ˌ)kē\ *n* : traditional popular Japanese drama with singing and dancing

kaftan *variant of* CAFTAN

kai·ser \'kī-zər\ *n* : the ruler of Germany from 1871 to 1918 [Middle English *caisere* "emperor," from Old Norse *keisari,* derived from a Germanic word *kaisar* "emperor," derived from Latin *Caesar* (title of a line of Roman emperors after Caesar Augustus) — see *Word History* at EMPEROR]

ka·lan·choe \ˌkal-ən-'kō-ē\ *n* : any of various chiefly African plants with juicy leaves including some grown indoors for their tiny colorful flowers

kale \'kā(ə)l\ *n* : a hardy cabbage with curly leaves that do not form a head

ka·lei·do·scope \kə-'līd-ə-ˌskōp\ *n* **1** : a tube containing loose bits of colored glass or plastic and two mirrors at one end that shows many different patterns as it is turned **2** : a changing pattern or scene **3** : a diverse collection ⟨a *kaleidoscope* of subjects⟩ [from Greek *kalos* "beautiful" and Greek *eidos* "form, shape" and English *-scope*] — **ka·lei·do·scop·ic** \-ˌlīd-ə-'skäp-ik\ *adj* — **ka·lei·do·scop·i·cal·ly** \-'skäp-i-k(ə)lē\ *adv*

kame \'kām\ *n* : a short ridge or mound of material deposited by water from a melting glacier

kan·ga·roo \ˌkaŋ-gə-'rü\ *n, pl* **-roos** : any of numerous leaping marsupial mammals of Australia, New Guinea, and adjacent islands that feed on plants and have a small head, long powerful hind legs, a long thick tail used as a support in standing or walking, and in the female a pouch on the abdomen in which the young are carried

kangaroo

kangaroo court *n* : a court that uses unfair methods or is not a proper court of law

kangaroo rat *n* : a burrowing rodent of dry regions of the western U.S. that travels by hopping on its long hind legs

ka·olin \'kā-ə-lən\ *n* : a fine usually white clay used in making porcelain, in paper, and in medicines that treat diarrhea

ka·olin·ite \'kā-ə-lə-ˌnīt\ *n* : a mineral that consists of a silicate of aluminum and is the principal mineral in kaolin

ka·pok \'kā-ˌpäk\ *n* : a mass of silky fibers that cover the seeds of a large tropical tree and are used as a filling for mattresses, life preservers, and sleeping bags

kap·pa \'kap-ə\ *n* : the 10th letter of the Greek alphabet — K or κ

kar·a·kul \'kar-ə-kəl\ *n* **1** *often cap* : any of a breed of hardy Asian sheep with coarse fur **2** : the usually curly glossy black coat of a young karakul lamb valued as fur

kar·a·o·ke \ˌkar-ē-ˌō-kē, kə-'rō-kē\ *n* : a device that plays music to which the user sings along and that records the user's singing with the music

kar·at *or* **car·at** \'kar-ət\ *n* : a unit of fineness for gold equal to $\frac{1}{24}$ part of pure gold in a blend with one or more other metals

ka·ra·te \kə-'rät-ē\ *n* : a Japanese art of self-defense without a weapon [from Japanese *karate,* literally, "empty hand"]

kart \'kärt\ *n* : GO-KART — **kart·ing** *n*

kar·yo·type \'ka-rē-ə-ˌtīp\ *n* : a photographic image or other representation of all the chromosomes in a cell usually arranged in pairs from largest to smallest

ka·ty·did \'kāt-ē-ˌdid\ *n* : any of various large green American grasshoppers with very long antennae and males that make a high-pitched noise using sound-producing organs on the forewings

> *Word History* Some animal names have been created through imitation of the sounds the animals make. The name *katydid* is an example of this process. These insects were given this name because the noise they make was thought of as sounding like "Katy-did, Katy-didn't" repeated over and over. [imitation]

kay·ak \'kī-ˌak\ *n* **1** : an Eskimo canoe made of a frame covered with skins except for a small opening in the center **2** : a small canvas-covered canoe resembling a kayak

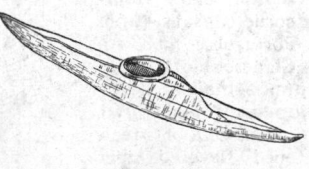
kayak 1

¹**kayo** \(')kā-'ō, 'kā-ō\ *n, pl* **kay·os** : KNOCKOUT 1

²**kayo** *vb* **kay·oed; kayo·ing** : KNOCK OUT

ka·zoo \kə-'zü\ *n, pl* **kazoos** : a toy musical instrument containing a membrane which produces a buzzing tone when one hums into the mouth hole

¹**keel** \'kē(ə)l\ *n* **1** : a timber or plate that runs lengthwise along the center of the bottom of a ship and usually sticks out from the bottom **2** : something (as the breastbone of a bird or the lower two petals of a pea flower) that is like a ship's keel in form or use

²**keel** *vb* : to turn (a ship or boat) over

keel·boat \'kē(ə)l-ˌbōt\ *n* : a shallow covered riverboat with a keel that is usually rowed, poled, or towed and is used to carry freight

keel·haul \-ˌhȯl\ *vb* **1** : to haul under the keel of a ship as punishment or torture **2** : to scold severely

keel over *vb* : to fall suddenly (as in a faint)

¹keen \'kēn\ *adj* **1** : having a sharp edge or point ⟨a *keen* knife⟩ **2** : seeming to cut or sting ⟨a *keen* wind⟩ **3** : full of enthusiasm ⟨*keen* about baseball⟩ **4 a** : having or showing mental sharpness ⟨*keen* mind⟩ **b** : very sensitive (as in seeing or hearing) ⟨*keen* eyesight⟩ **5** : very nice : WONDERFUL ⟨gee, that's *keen*⟩ **synonyms** see EAGER, SHARP — **keen·ly** *adv* — **keen·ness** \'kēn-nəs\ *n*

²keen *vb* : to mourn in a loud wailing voice

³keen *n* : a mourning for the dead with loud wails

¹keep \'kēp\ *vb* **kept** \'kept\; **keep·ing** **1 a** : to be faithful to : FULFILL ⟨*keep* a promise⟩ **b** : to act properly in relation to ⟨*keep* the Sabbath⟩ **2 a** : PROTECT ⟨*keep* us from harm⟩ **b** : to take care of : TEND ⟨*keep* a garden⟩ **3** : to continue doing something : MAINTAIN ⟨*keep* silence⟩ ⟨*keep* on working⟩ ⟨*keep* that up and you'll get into trouble⟩ **4** : to have in one's service or at one's disposal ⟨*keep* a car⟩ **5** : to preserve a record in ⟨*keep* a diary⟩ **6** : to have on hand regularly for sale ⟨*keep* neckties⟩ **7** : to continue to have in one's possession or power ⟨*kept* the marbles I won⟩ **8 a** : to prevent from leaving : DETAIN ⟨*keep* a person in jail⟩ ⟨was *kept* after school⟩ **b** : to place for storage ⟨*keeps* the catsup in the refrigerator⟩ ⟨*keep* my socks in a drawer⟩ **9** : to hold back ⟨*keep* a secret⟩ **10 a** : to remain or cause to remain in a place, situation, or condition ⟨*keep* off the grass⟩ ⟨*keep* him waiting⟩ **b** : to continue in an unspoiled condition ⟨food that *keeps* well⟩ **11** : ¹REFRAIN ⟨*keep* from talking⟩ **12** : to take charge of (as a business) : MANAGE ⟨*kept* an inn⟩

synonyms KEEP, OBSERVE, CELEBRATE, COMMEMORATE mean to notice or honor a day, occasion, or deed. KEEP stresses the idea of not neglecting or violating ⟨*keep* the Sabbath⟩. OBSERVE suggests the holding of formal ceremonies ⟨not all holidays are *observed* across the nation⟩. CELEBRATE suggests honoring an occasion by festivity ⟨*celebrate* Labor Day with a parade⟩. COMMEMORATE suggests having customs or ceremonies that call to mind what the occasion means ⟨*commemorate* Memorial Day with the laying of wreaths on gravestones⟩.

²keep *n* **1** : the strongest part of a castle in the Middle Ages **2** : the necessities of life ⟨earn one's *keep*⟩ — **for keeps** **1** : with the understanding that one may keep what is won ⟨play marbles *for keeps*⟩ **2** : for a long time : PERMANENTLY

keep·er \'kē-pər\ *n* : one that keeps ⟨they are *keepers* of their word⟩; *esp* : a person who watches, guards, or takes care of something or someone ⟨the *keeper* of a shop⟩

keep·ing \'kē-piŋ\ *n* **1** : watchful attention : CARE **2 a** : proper or fitting relationship : HARMONY ⟨in *keeping* with good taste⟩

keep·sake \'kēp-ˌsāk\ *n* : something kept or given to be kept in memory of a person, place, or happening

keep up *vb* **1** : MAINTAIN 1 ⟨*keep* standards *up*⟩ **2** : to keep well informed about something ⟨*keep up* on the news⟩ **3** : to continue without interruption ⟨rain *kept up* all night⟩ **4** : to stay even with others (as in a race)

keg \'keg, 'kag, 'kāg\ *n* **1** : a small cask or barrel holding 30 gallons (about 114 liters) or less **2** : the contents of a keg

kelp \'kelp\ *n* : any of various large brown seaweeds; *also* : a mass of these

kel·vin \'kel-vən\ *n* : a unit of temperature equal to ¹/273.16 of the Kelvin scale temperature of the triple point of water

Kelvin *adj* : relating to or having a temperature scale on which the unit of measurement is the same size as the Celsius degree and according to which absolute zero is 0 K (-273.15°C) — abbreviation *K* [named for William Thomson, Lord Kelvin (1824–1907), British mathematician and physicist]

¹ken \'ken\ *vb* **kenned**; **ken·ning** *chiefly Scottish* : ¹KNOW

²ken *n* **1** : range of vision : SIGHT **2** : range of understanding ⟨miracles beyond human *ken*⟩

¹ken·nel \'ken-ᵊl\ *n* **1** : a shelter for a dog **2** : a place where dogs or cats are bred or housed

²kennel *vb* **-neled** *or* **-nelled**; **-nel·ing** *or* **-nel·ling** : to put or keep in a kennel

Ken·tucky bluegrass \kən-ˌtək-ē-\ *n* : a pasture, lawn, and meadow grass that has tall stalks and slender bright green leaves and is native to Europe but is widely grown in North America

Kentucky rifle *n* : a long flintlock rifle loaded through the muzzle that was developed in the 18th century

ker·a·tin \'ker-ət-ᵊn\ *n* : a sulfur-containing protein that makes up hair and horny tissues (as nails)

ker·chief \'kər-chəf, -ˌchēf\ *n, pl* **kerchiefs** \-chəfs, -ˌchēfs\ *also* **ker·chieves** \-ˌchēvz\ **1** : a square of cloth worn as a head covering or as a scarf **2** : HANDKERCHIEF 1

kerf \'kərf\ *n* : a slit or notch made by a saw or a cutting torch

ker·nel \'kərn-ᵊl\ *n* **1 a** : the inner softer part of a seed, fruit stone, or nut **b** : a whole grain or seed of a cereal (as wheat or corn) **2** : a central or basic part ⟨a *kernel* of truth in what they say⟩

ker·o·sene *also* **ker·o·sine** \'ker-ə-ˌsēn, ker-ə-'sēn, 'kar-, ˌkar-\ *n* : a thin oil obtained from petroleum and used as a fuel and solvent

Ker·ry blue terrier \ˌker-ē-\ *n* : any of an Irish breed of medium-sized terriers with a long head, deep chest, and silky bluish coat

ketch \'kech\ *n* : a two-masted fore-and-aft-rigged ship

ketch·up *also* **catch·up** \'kech-əp, 'kach-\ *or* **cat·sup** \'kech-əp, 'kach-; 'kat-səp\ *n* : a thick seasoned sauce usually made from tomatoes

ket·tle \'ket-ᵊl\ *n* **1** : a pot for boiling liquids **2** : TEAKETTLE

ket·tle·drum \-ˌdrəm\ *n* : a large brass or copper drum that has a rounded bottom and can be varied in pitch

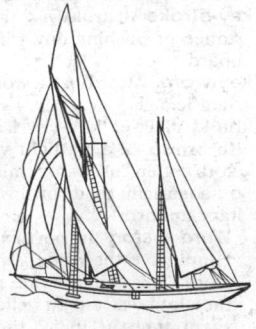
ketch

¹key \'kē\ *n, pl* **keys** **1 a** : a small device that is used to open a lock or start an automobile **b** : a device having the form or function of a key ⟨a *key* for winding a clock⟩ **2** : a means of gaining or preventing entrance, possession, or control **3 a** : something that provides an explanation, solution, or means of identifying ⟨the *key* to a riddle⟩ **b** : a series of phrases or statements that describe characteristics by which plants or animals of a particular group differ and are used to aid in identification **c** : a map legend **4** : one of the levers with a flat surface that is pressed by a finger in operating a machine or playing an instrument **5** : a system of seven musical tones arranged in relation to a keynote from which the system is named ⟨the *key* of C⟩ **6** : a characteristic style or tone **7** : a small switch for opening or closing an electric circuit [Old English *cæg* "key"]

²key *vb* **keyed**; **key·ing** **1** : to adjust the musical pitch of **2** : to bring into harmony **3** : to make nervous, tense, or excited — usually used with *up* ⟨all *keyed* up about the test⟩ **4** : to record by operating the keys of a machine ⟨*key* each price into the cash register⟩

\ə\ **abut**	\au̇\ **out**	\i\ **tip**	\ȯ\ **saw**	\u̇\ **foot**
\ər\ **further**	\ch\ **chin**	\ī\ **life**	\ȯi\ **coin**	\y\ **yet**
\a\ **mat**	\e\ **pet**	\j\ **job**	\th\ **thin**	\yü\ **few**
\ā\ **take**	\ē\ **easy**	\ŋ\ **sing**	\th\ **this**	\yu̇\ **cure**
\ä\ **cot, cart**	\g\ **go**	\ō\ **bone**	\ü\ **food**	\zh\ **vision**

³key *adj* : of great importance ⟨the *key* people in the organization⟩ ⟨the *key* question is "Can we afford it?"⟩ ⟨use *key* words in an outline⟩

⁴key *n* : a low island or reef ⟨the Florida *Keys*⟩ [from Spanish *cayo* "a low island or reef"]

key·board \'kē-ˌbō(ə)rd, -ˌbȯ(ə)rd\ *n* **1** : a row or set of keys by which a musical instrument (as a piano) is played **2** : the whole arrangement of keys by which a machine (as a typewriter or computer) is operated

key deer *n, often cap K* : a very small rare white-tailed deer native to the Florida Keys

key·hole \'kē-ˌhōl\ *n* : a hole for receiving a key

keyhole saw *n* : a narrow pointed handsaw

¹key·note \'kē-ˌnōt\ *n* **1** : the first and harmonically fundamental tone of a scale **2** : the fundamental or central fact, idea, or mood ⟨humor is the *keynote* of the play⟩

²keynote *vb* **1** : to set the keynote of **2** : to give the keynote address at ⟨*keynoted* the convention⟩ — **key·not·er** *n*

keynote address *n* : the main speech given at a gathering (as a political convention)

key·pad \'kē-ˌpad\ *n* : a small keyboard (as on a pocket calculator)

key·punch \-ˌpənch\ *n* : a machine with a keyboard for punching cards to be used in data processing — **key·punch** *vb*

key signature *n* : the sharps or flats placed after a clef in music to indicate the key

key·stone \'kē-ˌstōn\ *n* **1** : the wedge-shaped piece at the top of an arch that locks the other pieces in place **2** : something on which other things depend

key·stroke \-ˌstrōk\ *n* : the act or an instance of pushing down a key on a keyboard

key·word \-ˌwərd\ *n* : a word of interest or significance

kha·ki \'kak-ē, 'käk-\ *n* **1** : a light yellowish brown **2 a** : a light yellowish brown cloth often used for military uniforms **b** : a garment made of this cloth (as a military uniform)

key signature

Word History In northern India a language known as Hindi gave the name *khākī* to a certain kind of strong cloth. This Hindi name meant "dust-colored," because the cloth was a light yellowish brown. When the British spent time in India, they discovered that the strong brown material made good military uniforms. Now the word *khaki* is used in English for a uniform, as well as for the cloth used to make it. [from Hindi *khākī* "dust= colored," from *khāk* "dust"; of Persian origin]

khan \'kän, 'kan\ *n* **1** : a Mongolian leader **2** : a local chieftain or man of rank in some countries of central Asia

khe·dive \kə-'dēv\ *n* : a governor of Egypt from 1867 to 1914

Khmer \kə-'me(ə)r\ *n* : a member of a native people of Cambodia

Khoi·khoi \'kȯi-ˌkȯi\ *n, pl* **Khoikhoi 1** : a member of a group of pastoral peoples who lived in far southern Africa when first encountered by Europeans and who now live mainly in Namibia **2** : the languages spoken by the Khoikhoi

kib·butz \kib-'ùts, -'üts\ *n, pl* **kib·but·zim** \-ˌùt-'sēm, -ˌüt-\ : a farming settlement in Israel that is owned and shared equally by the people who live there and run it

ki·bitz·er \'kib-ət-sər, kə-'bit-\ *n* : a person who looks on and often offers unwanted advice especially at a card game — **ki·bitz** \'kib-əts, kə-'bits\ *vb*

ki·bosh \'kī-ˌbäsh\ *n* : ¹END 2a, STOP — used in the phrase *put the kibosh on*

¹kick \'kik\ *vb* **1** : to strike out or hit with the foot **2** : to object strongly : PROTEST ⟨*kicked* about their low grades⟩ **3** : to spring back ⟨a shotgun *kicks* when fired⟩ **4** : to be full of pep and energy ⟨still alive and *kicking*⟩ **5** : to score by kicking a ball ⟨*kick* a field goal⟩ **6** *slang* : to free oneself of ⟨*kick* the habit⟩ — **kick·er** *n* — **kick up one's heels** : to have a good lively time

²kick *n* **1 a** : a blow with the foot **b** : the movement of the legs in swimming **2 a** : a sudden moving (as of a ball) with the foot **b** : the sudden move backward of a gun when fired **3** : a feeling of or cause for objection **4** : a feeling or source of pleasure

kick·back \'kik-ˌbak\ *n* : a secret return of part of a sum of money received

kick back *vb* : RELAX 4

kick·ball \'kik-ˌbȯl\ *n* : a game resembling baseball played with a large rubber ball that is kicked instead of batted

kick in *vb* **1** : CONTRIBUTE 1 **2** : START 2

kick·off \'kik-ˌȯf\ *n* : a kick that puts the ball into play (as in soccer or football)

kick off \(')kik-'ȯf\ *vb* **1** : to make a kickoff **2** : BEGIN 1

kick·stand \'kik-ˌstand\ *n* : a metal bar or rod attached to a 2-wheeled vehicle (as a bicycle) and used to prop up the vehicle when it is not in use

¹kid \'kid\ *n* **1** : the young of a goat or of a related animal **2 a** : the flesh, fur, or skin of a kid **b** : something (as leather) made of kid **3** : a young person : CHILD, YOUNGSTER — **kid·dish** \'kid-ish\ *adj*

²kid *vb* **kid·ded; kid·ding 1** : to deceive or trick as a joke **2** : ¹TEASE 2a — **kid·der** *n*

kid·do \'kid-(ˌ)ō\ *n* : CHILD 2, KID

kid·nap \'kid-ˌnap\ *vb* **kid·napped** *also* **kid·naped** \-ˌnapt\; **kid·nap·ping** *also* **kid·nap·ing** \-ˌnap-iŋ\ : to carry away a person by unlawful force or by fraud and against his or her will — **kid·nap·per** *also* **kid·nap·er** \-ˌnap-ər\ *n*

kid·ney \'kid-nē\ *n, pl* **kidneys 1** : either of a pair of oval to bean-shaped organs located in the back part of the abdomen near the spine that give off waste products in the form of urine **2** : an organ of an invertebrate animal that gives off waste

kidney bean *n* : an edible seed and especially a large dark red seed of any of several varieties of cultivated bean plants; *also* : a plant that produces kidney beans

kid·skin \'kid-ˌskin\ *n* : the skin of a kid or leather made from or resembling it

¹kill \'kil\ *vb* **1** : to deprive of life : cause the death of **2 a** : to put an end to : RUIN ⟨that *killed* our chances⟩ **b** : ¹DEFEAT 1 ⟨the committee *killed* the bill⟩ **c** : to stop the use or functioning of ⟨*kill* the lights⟩ **d** : DELETE ⟨*kill* the last line⟩ **3** : to cause to pass ⟨just *killing* time⟩ **4** : to use up completely ⟨*killed* two cartons of milk⟩

synonyms KILL, MURDER, ASSASSINATE mean to take the life of. KILL suggests nothing about the manner of death and can apply to the death of anything ⟨frost *killed* the plants⟩ ⟨a person *killed* in an accident⟩. MURDER applies to the deliberate and unlawful killing of a person ⟨convicted of *murdering* a rival⟩. ASSASSINATE usually suggests the murder of an important person often for political reasons ⟨terrorists *assassinated* the Senator⟩.

²kill *n* **1** : an act of killing **2** : an animal killed ⟨a lion devouring its *kill*⟩

kill·deer \'kil-ˌdi(ə)r\ *n, pl* **killdeers** *or* **killdeer** : a North American plover that has two black bands on its breast and a distinctive high-pitched loud cry

Word History Killdeers are not vicious birds. They have no special hatred of deer, and they do not eat venison. This attractive, dark-eyed bird has a loud, rather sad cry that to some people sounds like "Kill deer! Kill deer!" So the killdeer is an animal that got its name from human interpretation of its call. [imitation]

¹killer \'kil-ər\ *n* **1** : one that kills **2** : KILLER WHALE

²killer *adj* **1** : strikingly impressive or effective ⟨a *killer* smile⟩ **2** : extremely difficult ⟨a *killer* exam⟩; *also* : causing death or devastation ⟨a *killer* tornado⟩

killer T cell *n* : a T cell that binds to and destroys cells (as one infected by a virus) which display specific antigens on their surface

kill·er whale \'kil-ər-\ *n* : a flesh-eating mostly black toothed whale 20 to 30 feet (about 6 to 9 meters) long that travels in groups

killer whale

kill·ing \'kil-iŋ\ *n* : a sudden large profit

kill·joy \'kil-ˌjȯi\ *n* : a person who spoils the pleasure of others

kiln \'kiln, 'kil\ *n* : an oven or furnace for hardening, burning, or drying something ⟨brick *kilns*⟩ — **kiln** *vb*

ki·lo \'kē-(ˌ)lō\ *n, pl* **kilos** : KILOGRAM

kilo- *combining form* : thousand ⟨*kilo*ton⟩ [derived from Greek *chilioi* "thousand"]

ki·lo·byte \'kē-lə-ˌbīt, 'kil-ə-\ *n* : 1024 bytes

ki·lo·cal·o·rie \'kē-lə-ˌkal-(ə-)rē, 'kil-ə-\ *n* : CALORIE 1b

kilo·cy·cle \'kil-ə-ˌsī-kəl\ *n* : 1000 cycles; *esp* : KILOHERTZ

ki·lo·gram \'kē-lə-ˌgram, 'kil-ə-\ *n* **1** : the basic unit of mass in the metric system that has been accepted by international agreement and is nearly equal to the mass of 1000 cubic centimeters of water at its highest density — see METRIC SYSTEM table **2** : the weight of a kilogram mass on the earth ⟨he weighs 80 *kilograms*⟩ — see METRIC SYSTEM table

ki·lo·hertz \'kil-ə-ˌhərts, 'kē-lə-, -ˌhe(ə)rts\ *n* : 1000 hertz

kilo·joule \'kil-ə-ˌjül\ *n* : 1000 joules

kilo·li·ter \'kil-ə-ˌlēt-ər\ *n* — see METRIC SYSTEM table

ki·lo·me·ter \kə-'läm-ət-ər, kil-'äm-; 'kil-ə-ˌmēt-ər\ *n* — see METRIC SYSTEM table

kilo·pas·cal \ˌkil-ə-pas-'kal\ *n* : 1000 pascals

ki·lo·ton \'kil-ə-ˌtən, 'kē-lə- *also* -ˌtän\ *n* **1** : 1000 tons **2** : an explosive force equivalent to that of 1000 tons of TNT

ki·lo·volt \'kē-lə-ˌvōlt, 'kil-ə-\ *n* : 1000 volts

kilo·watt \'kil-ə-ˌwät\ *n* : 1000 watts

kilowatt–hour *n* : a unit of work or energy equal to that expended by one kilowatt in one hour and equal to 3.6 million joules

kilt \'kilt\ *n* : a knee-length pleated skirt usually of tartan worn by men in Scotland — **kilt·ed** \'kil-təd\ *adj*

kil·ter \'kil-tər\ *n* : proper condition ⟨the TV is out of *kilter*⟩

ki·mo·no \kə-'mō-nō\ *n, pl* **-nos 1** : a loose robe with wide sleeves that is traditionally worn with a broad sash as an outer garment by the Japanese **2** : a loose dressing gown worn chiefly by women

¹**kin** \'kin\ *n* **1** : a person's relatives **2** : KINSMAN

²**kin** *adj* : being related : KINDRED

-kin \kən\ *also* **-kins** \kənz\ *n suffix* : little — often used in affectionate nicknames ⟨baby*kins*⟩ [Middle English *-kin* "little," from early Dutch *-kin* "little"]

¹**kind** \'kīnd\ *n* **1 a** : a group united by common traits or interests : CATEGORY ⟨hawks and other birds of their *kind*⟩ **b** : VARIETY 3a ⟨all *kinds* of people⟩ ⟨what *kind* of car do you have⟩ **c** : one that is barely a member of a category ⟨a *kind* of gray⟩ **2** : essential quality or character ⟨differences in *kind*⟩ **3 a** : goods as distinguished from money ⟨payment in *kind* rather than in cash⟩ **b** : something equal to what has been offered or received ⟨returned the favor in *kind*⟩

²**kind** *adj* **1** : wanting and liking to do good and to bring

kimono 1

happiness to others **2** : showing or growing out of gentleness or goodness of heart ⟨a *kind* act⟩

kin·der·gar·ten \'kin-də(r)-ˌgärt-ᵊn, -ˌgärd-\ *n* : a school or class for very young children [from German *kindergarten* "a school for very young children," from *kinder* "children" and *garten* "garden"]

kin·der·gart·ner \'kin-der-ˌgärt-nər, -ˌgärd-\ *n* : a kindergarten pupil

kind·heart·ed \'kīnd-'härt-əd\ *adj* : having or showing a kind and sympathetic nature — **kind·heart·ed·ly** *adv* — **kind·heart·ed·ness** *n*

kin·dle \'kin-dᵊl\ *vb* **kin·dled; kin·dling** \-(d)liŋ, -dᵊl-iŋ\ **1** : to set on fire or take fire : LIGHT **2** : to stir up : EXCITE ⟨trying to *kindle* their interest⟩

kin·dling \'kin-(d)liŋ\ *n* : material that burns easily and is used to start a fire

¹**kind·ly** \'kīn-(d)lē\ *adj* **kind·li·er; -est 1** : pleasant or wholesome in nature ⟨a *kindly* climate⟩ **2** : of a sympathetic or generous nature ⟨*kindly* men⟩ — **kind·li·ness** *n*

²**kindly** *adv* **1** : in a willing manner ⟨does not take *kindly* to criticism⟩ **2 a** : in a kind manner ⟨treat animals *kindly*⟩ **b** : in an appreciative manner ⟨I would take it *kindly* if you would put in a good word for us⟩ **c** : in an obliging manner ⟨they *kindly* asked us to go along⟩ **d** : as a matter of courtesy : PLEASE ⟨*kindly* pass the salt⟩

kind·ness \'kīn(d)-nəs\ *n* **1** : a kind deed : FAVOR ⟨returned his *kindness*⟩ **2** : the quality or state of being kind ⟨treat others with *kindness*⟩

kind of \ˌkīn-də(v)\ *adv* : to a moderate degree : SOMEWHAT ⟨it's *kind of* cold in here⟩ ⟨he *kind of* likes me⟩

¹**kin·dred** \'kin-drəd\ *n* **1** : a group of related individuals **2** : a person's relatives

²**kindred** *adj* : alike in nature or character ⟨a *kindred* spirit⟩

kine \'kīn\ *archaic plural of* COW

ki·ne·sics \kə-'nē-siks, kī-, -ziks\ *n* : the study of body motions (as blushes, shrugs, or eye movement) that communicate

ki·net·ic \kə-'net-ik, kī-\ *adj* : of or relating to the motions of material bodies and the forces and energy associated with them [from Greek *kinētikos* "relating to motion," derived from *kinein* "to move" — related to CINEMA]

kinetic energy *n* : energy associated with motion

kinetic theory *n* : a theory that states that all matter is composed of particles in motion and that the rate of motion varies directly with the temperature

kin·folk \'kin-ˌfōk\ *n pl* : ¹KINDRED 2

king \'kiŋ\ *n* **1** : a male ruler of a country who usually inherits his position and rules for life **2** : a chief among competitors ⟨an oil *king*⟩ **3** : the chief piece in the game of chess **4** : a playing card bearing the figure of a king **5** : a piece in the game of checkers that has reached the opponent's back row and has been crowned

king·bird \-ˌbərd\ *n* : any of several American tyrant flycatchers

king cobra *n* : a large very poisonous snake of southeastern Asia and the Philippines

king crab *n* **1** : HORSESHOE CRAB **2** : any of several very large crabs

king·dom \'kiŋ-dəm\ *n* **1** : a country whose ruler is a king or queen **2** : a region in which something or someone has very strong influence ⟨the cotton *kingdom*⟩ **3 a** : one of the three primary divisions into which natural objects are classified — compare ANIMAL KINGDOM, MINERAL KINGDOM, PLANT KINGDOM **b** : a major category in the scientific classification of living things that ranks above the phylum and below the domain

\ə\ **abut**	\au̇\ **out**	\i\ **tip**	\ȯ\ **saw**	\u̇\ **foot**
\ər\ **further**	\ch\ **chin**	\ī\ **life**	\ȯi\ **coin**	\y\ **yet**
\a\ **mat**	\e\ **pet**	\j\ **job**	\th\ **thin**	\yü\ **few**
\ā\ **take**	\ē\ **easy**	\ŋ\ **sing**	\th\ **this**	\yu̇\ **cure**
\ä\ **cot, cart**	\g\ **go**	\ō\ **bone**	\ü\ **food**	\zh\ **vision**

kingdom come *n* : the next world (as heaven)

king·fish \'kiŋ-ˌfish\ *n* : any of various sea fishes (as a king mackerel)

king·fish·er \-ˌfish-ər\ *n* : any of various bright-colored birds with a short tail, a long stout sharp bill, and usually a crest on the head

kingfisher

King James Version \kiŋ-ˈjämz-\ *n* : AU-THORIZED VERSION

king·let \'kiŋ-lət\ *n* : any of several small insect-eating birds

king·ly \'kiŋ-lē\ *adj* **king·li·er; -est** **1** : having royal rank **2** : of, relating to, or worthy of a king — **king·li·ness** *n* — **kingly** *adv*

king mackerel *n* : a mackerel of the warmer waters of the Atlantic Ocean that is a food and sport fish

king·pin \'kiŋ-ˌpin\ *n* **1** : a pin that stands in the middle of a triangular arrangement of bowling pins; *also* : HEADPIN **2** : the chief person in a group or undertaking

Kings \'kiŋz\ *n* — see BIBLE table

king·ship \'kiŋ-ˌship\ *n* **1** : the position, office, or dignity of a king **2** : the personality of a king : MAJESTY **3** : government by a king

king–size \'kiŋ-ˌsīz\ *or* **king–sized** \-ˌsīzd\ *adj* **1** : unusually long or large **2** : having a size of 76 inches by 80 inches (about 1.9 meters by 2.0 meters) ⟨a *king-size* bed⟩

king snake *n* : any of numerous harmless brightly marked large snakes chiefly of the southern and central U.S.

king's ransom *n* : a very large sum of money

¹kink \'kiŋk\ *n* **1** : a short tight twist or curl (as in a thread, rope, or hose) **2** : ¹CRAMP 1 ⟨a *kink* in my back⟩ **3** : an imperfection that makes something hard to use or work

²kink *vb* : to form or cause to form a kink

kin·ka·jou \'kiŋ-kə-ˌjü\ *n* : a slender long-tailed mammal of Central and South America that is related to the raccoon, is active at night, lives in trees, and has large eyes and soft woolly yellowish brown fur

kinky \'kiŋ-kē\ *adj* **kink·i·er; -est** **1** : tightly twisted or curled **2** : very strange or odd — **kink·i·ness** *n*

-kins — see -KIN

kins·folk \'kinz-ˌfōk\ *n pl* : ¹KINDRED 2, RELATIVES

kin·ship \'kin-ˌship\ *n* : the quality or state of being kin : RELATIONSHIP

kins·man \'kinz-mən\ *n* : a relative usually by birth; *esp* : a male relative

kins·wom·an \'kinz-ˌwum-ən\ *n* : a woman who is a relative usually by birth

kinkajou

ki·osk \'kē-ˌäsk, kē-ˈäsk\ *n* **1** : a small light structure with one or more open sides used especially to sell merchandise or services **2** : a small structure that provides information and services on a computer screen

Ki·o·wa \'kī-ə-ˌwò, -ˌwä\ *n, pl* **Kiowa** *or* **Kiowas** : a member of an American Indian people of what are now Colorado, Kansas, New Mexico, Oklahoma, and Texas

¹kip·per \'kip-ər\ *n* : a kippered herring or salmon

²kipper *vb* **kip·pered; kip·per·ing** \-(ə-)riŋ\ : to cure by splitting, cleaning, salting, and smoking

kirk \'ki(ə)rk, 'kərk\ *n, chiefly Scottish* : CHURCH 1

¹kiss \'kis\ *vb* **1** : to touch with the lips as a mark of love or greeting **2** : to touch gently or lightly ⟨wind gently *kissing* the trees⟩ — **kiss·able** \-ə-bəl\ *adj*

²kiss *n* **1** : a loving touch with the lips **2** : a gentle touch or contact **3 a** : a small cookie made of meringue **b** : a bite-size candy ⟨a chocolate *kiss*⟩

kiss·er \'kis-ər\ *n* **1** : one that kisses **2** *slang* **a** : ¹MOUTH 1a **b** : ¹FACE 1

¹kit \'kit\ *n* **1 a** : a collection of articles for personal use ⟨a shaving *kit*⟩ **b** : a set of tools or supplies ⟨a first-aid *kit*⟩ **c** : a set of parts to be put together ⟨model-airplane *kit*⟩ **2** : a container (as a bag or case) for a kit **3** : a group of persons or things — used in the phrase *the whole kit and caboodle* [Middle English *kit* "a wooden tub"]

²kit *n* : a small narrow violin [origin unknown]

³kit *n* **1** : KITTEN **2** : a young or small fur-bearing animal (as a fox) [a shortened form of *kitten*]

kitch·en \'kich-ən\ *n* : a place (as a room) in which cooking is done

> ***Word History*** Although a room where food is cooked is called a kitchen, the words *cook* and *kitchen* are so different that it is surprising to learn that they both come from the same source. Both words can be traced to the Latin verb *coquere,* meaning "to cook." The connection between *coquere* and *cook* is easy to see, but *kitchen* has a more involved history. From the verb *coquere* came the later Latin noun *coquina,* meaning "a kitchen." With some changes in pronunciation, *coquina* came into Old English as *cycene.* Further changes over the course of many years gave us *kichene* and finally the Modern English *kitchen.* [Middle English *kichene* "kitchen," from Old English *cycene* (same meaning), from Latin *coquina* "a place where food is cooked," from earlier *coquere* "to cook" — related to COOK]

kitch·en·ette \ˌkich-ə-ˈnet\ *n* : a small kitchen

kitchen garden *n* : a piece of land where vegetables are grown for household use

kitchen police *n* : KP

kitch·en·ware \'kich-ən-ˌwa(ə)r, -ˌwe(ə)r\ *n* : utensils and appliances for use in a kitchen

kite \'kīt\ *n* **1** : any of various usually small hawks with long narrow wings and a deeply forked tail **2** : a light covered frame for flying in the air at the end of a long string

kith \'kith\ *n* : familiar friends and neighbors or relatives ⟨*kith* and kin⟩

kit·ten \'kit-ᵊn\ *n* : a young cat; *also* : a young individual of various other small mammals

kit·ten·ish \'kit-nish, -ᵊn-ish\ *adj* : resembling a kitten — **kit·ten·ish·ly** *adv* — **kit·ten·ish·ness** *n*

kit·ti·wake \'kit-ē-ˌwāk\ *n* : either of two gulls that nest on cliffs and winter on the open ocean

kite 1

¹kit·ty \'kit-ē\ *n, pl* **kitties** : CAT 1a; *esp* : KITTEN

²kitty *n, pl* **kitties** : a sum of money or collection of goods often made up of small contributions

kit·ty–cor·ner *also* **cat·ty–cor·ner** *or* **cat·er·cor·ner** \'kit-ē-ˌkòr-nər, 'kat-, 'kat-ə-\ *or* **kit·ty–cor·nered** *or* **cat·ty–cor·nered** *or* **cat·er·cor·nered** \-nərd\ *adv or adj* : in a crosswise position : on a diagonal line ⟨the house stood *kitty-corner* across the square⟩

ki·va \'kē-və\ *n* : a Pueblo Indian ceremonial structure that is usually round and partly underground

ki·wi \'kē-(ˌ)wē\ *n* **1** : a flightless New Zealand bird with weak and undeveloped wings, stout legs, a long bill, and grayish brown hairlike feathers **2** : KIWIFRUIT

ki·wi·fruit \-ˌfrüt\ *n* : the edible fruit of a Chinese vine having a fuzzy brown skin and slightly tart green flesh

Klee·nex \'klē-ˌneks\ *trademark* — used for a cleansing tissue

klep·to·ma·nia \ˌklep-tə-ˈmā-nē-ə, -nyə\ *n* : a continuous abnormal desire to steal

klep·to·ma·ni·ac \ˌklep-tə-ˈmā-nē-ˌak\ *n* : a person who exhibits kleptomania

klez·mer \ˈklez-mər\ *n, pl* **klez·mo·rim** \klez-ˈmȯr-əm\ **1** : a Jewish instrumentalist especially of traditional eastern European music **2** : the music played by klezmorim

klieg light *or* **kleig light** \ˈklēg-\ *n* : a very bright lamp used in taking motion pictures

klutz \ˈkləts\ *n* : a clumsy person — **klutz·i·ness** \ˈklət-sē-nəs\ *n* — **klutzy** \ˈklət-sē\ *adj*

knack \ˈnak\ *n* **1** : a clever or skillful way of doing something : TRICK **2** : a natural ability : TALENT ⟨has a *knack* for making friends⟩

knap·sack \ˈnap-ˌsak\ *n* : a carrying case or pouch slung from the shoulders over the back

knave \ˈnāv\ *n* **1** : RASCAL 1 **2** : ¹JACK 5 [from earlier *knave* "a boy servant, a person of humble birth," from Old English *cnafa* "boy"] — **knav·ish** \ˈnā-vish\ *adj* — **knav·ish·ly** *adv*

knav·ery \ˈnāv-(ə-)rē\ *n, pl* **-er·ies** : the practices of a knave : RASCALITY

knead \ˈnēd\ *vb* **1** : to work and press into a mass with or as if with the hands **2** : to treat as if by kneading : MASSAGE — **knead·er** *n*

¹knee \ˈnē\ *n* **1** : the joint or region in the middle part of the human leg in which the femur, tibia, and kneecap come together; *also* : a corresponding part of a four-footed mammal **2** : something resembling the knee; *esp* : a cone-shaped upward growth from the roots of a few swamp-growing trees (as a cypress of the southern U.S.) that extends above the surrounding water **3** : the part of a garment covering the knee — **kneed** \ˈnēd\ *adj*

²knee *vb* **kneed; knee·ing** : to strike with the knee

knee·cap \ˈnē-ˌkap\ *n* : a thick flat movable bone forming the front part of the knee — called also *patella*

knee–deep \-ˈdēp\ *adj* : being up to one's knees ⟨*knee-deep* in mud⟩ ⟨*knee-deep* snowdrifts⟩

knee–hole \-ˌhōl\ *n* : a space (as under a desk) for the knees

knee–jerk \ˈnē-ˌjərk\ *adj* : readily predictable : AUTOMATIC ⟨a *knee-jerk* reaction to the proposal⟩

knee jerk *n* : an involuntary forward kick produced by a light blow on the tendon below the kneecap

kneel \ˈnē(ə)l\ *vb* **knelt** \ˈnelt\ *or* **kneeled** \ˈnē(ə)ld\; **kneel·ing** : to bend the knee : support oneself on the knees — **kneel·er** *n*

¹knell \ˈnel\ *vb* **1** : to ring slowly and solemnly especially for a death, funeral, or disaster : TOLL **2** : to summon, announce, or warn by a knell

²knell *n* **1** : a stroke or sound of a bell especially when rung slowly for a death, funeral, or disaster **2** : an indication (as a sound) of the end or failure of something

knew *past of* KNOW

knick·er·bock·ers \ˈnik-ə(r)-ˌbäk-ərz\ *n pl* : KNICKERS [named for Diedrich *Knickerbocker,* made-up name for the author of *History of New York,* which was really written by Washington Irving]

knick·ers \ˈnik-ərz\ *n pl* **1** : loose-fitting short pants gathered just below the knee **2** *chiefly British* : UNDERPANTS

knick·knack \ˈnik-ˌnak\ *n* : a small ornamental object

¹knife \ˈnīf\ *n, pl* **knives** \ˈnīvz\ **1** : a cutting instrument consisting of a sharp blade fastened to a handle **2** : a cutting blade in a machine

²knife *vb* **knifed; knif·ing** **1** : to stab, slash, or wound with a knife **2** : to move like a knife ⟨ships *knifing* through the sea⟩

knife–edge \ˈnī-ˌfej\ *n* : a sharp

knickers

wedge usually of steel used as a support for a lever beam in a very exact instrument (as a balance)

¹knight \ˈnīt\ *n* **1 a** : a warrior of olden times who fought on horseback, served a king, held a special military rank, and swore to behave in a noble way **b** : a man honored by a sovereign for merit and in Great Britain ranking below a baronet **2** : a chess piece that makes an L-shaped move [Old English *cniht* "boy, attendant, warrior"] — **knight·ly** \-lē\ *adj or adv*

²knight *vb* : to make a knight of

knight–er·rant \ˈnīt-ˈer-ənt\ *n, pl* **knights–errant** : a knight traveling in search of adventures — **knight–er·rant·ry** \ˈnīt-ˈer-ən-trē\ *n*

knight·hood \ˈnīt-ˌhu̇d\ *n* **1** : the rank, dignity, or profession of a knight **2** : the qualities that a knight should have **3** : knights as a class or body

knish \kə-ˈnish\ *n* : a small round or square piece of dough stuffed with a filling and baked or fried [Yiddish]

¹knit \ˈnit\ *vb* **knit** *or* **knit·ted; knit·ting** **1** : to form a fabric or garment by interlacing yarn or thread in connected loops with needles ⟨*knit* a sweater⟩ **2** : to draw or come together closely as if knitted : unite firmly ⟨wait for a broken bone to *knit*⟩ **3** : ²WRINKLE ⟨*knit* her brow⟩ — **knit·ter** *n*

²knit *n* : a knit fabric or garment

knit·ting *n* **1** : the action or method of one that knits **2** : work done or being done by one that knits

knit·wear \ˈnit-ˌwa(ə)r, -ˌwe(ə)r\ *n* : knitted clothing

knob \ˈnäb\ *n* **1 a** : a rounded lump **b** : a small rounded handle **2** : a rounded hill — **knobbed** \ˈnäbd\ *adj* — **knob·by** \ˈnäb-ē\ *adj*

¹knock \ˈnäk\ *vb* **1 a** : to strike with a sharp blow **b** : to set in motion with a sharp blow **2** : to bump against something **3** : WANDER 1 ⟨*knocked* about the country last summer⟩ **4** : to have engine knock **5** : to find fault with ⟨don't *knock* it — there are worse jobs⟩ — **knock cold** : KNOCK OUT — **knock for a loop** : to cause to be overwhelmed : SHOCK, BEWILDER — **knock together** : to make or build hastily or carelessly

²knock *n* **1** : a sharp blow **2** : a severe misfortune or hardship **3 a** : a pounding noise ⟨heard a *knock* on the door⟩ **b** : a sharp rattling noise caused by abnormal ignition in an automobile engine

knock·about \ˈnäk-ə-ˌbau̇t\ *adj* : being noisy and rough : BOISTEROUS

knock down *vb* **1** : to strike to the ground with or as if with a sharp blow **2** : to sell to the highest bidder at an auction **3** : to take apart

knock·er \ˈnäk-ər\ *n* : a device made like a hinge and fastened to a door for use in knocking

knock–kneed \ˈnäk-ˈnēd\ *adj* : having the legs bowed inward

knock–knock joke \ˈnäk-ˈnäk-\ *n* : a punning joke beginning with the lines "Knock, knock." "Who's there?"

knock off *vb* : to stop doing something

knock·out \ˈnäk-ˌau̇t\ *n* **1** : the act of knocking out : the condition of being knocked out **2** : something or someone very striking or attractive — **knockout** *adj*

knock out \ˈnäk-ˈau̇t, näk-ˈau̇t\ *vb* : to make unconscious

knock·wurst \ˈnäk-(ˌ)wərst\ *n* : a short thick sausage [from German *Knackwurst* "knockwurst," from *knacken* "to crackle (when being fried)" and *Wurst* "sausage"]

\ə\ abut	\au̇\ out	\i\ tip	\ȯ\ saw	\u̇\ foot
\ər\ further	\ch\ chin	\ī\ life	\ȯi\ coin	\y\ yet
\a\ mat	\e\ pet	\j\ job	\th\ thin	\yü\ few
\ā\ take	\ē\ easy	\ŋ\ sing	\th\ this	\yu̇\ cure
\ä\ cot, cart	\g\ go	\ō\ bone	\ü\ food	\zh\ vision

knoll \'nōl\ *n* : a small round hill

¹knot \'nät\ *n* **1** : an interlacing (as of string or ribbon)
that forms a lump or knob
2 : something hard to solve
: PROBLEM **3** : a bond of
union; *esp* : the marriage
bond **4 a** : a lump or swelling in bodily tissue **b** : the
base of a woody branch enclosed in the stem from
which it arises; *also* : a section of a knot in lumber **5**
: a cluster of persons or
things **6** : one nautical mile
per hour

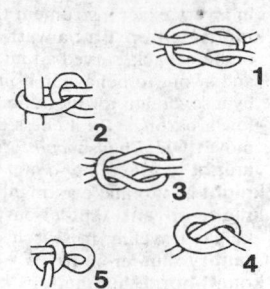

¹knot 1: *1* granny knot, *2*
half hitch, *3* square knot, *4*
overhand knot, *5* slipknot

²knot *vb* **knot·ted; knot·ting**
1 : to tie in or with a knot **2**
: to unite closely

knot·hole \-ˌhōl\ *n* : a hole in a board or tree trunk where
a knot has come out

knot·ted \'nät-əd\ *adj* **1** : tied in or with a knot **2** : KNOT-
TY **3** : ornamented with knots or knobs

knot·ty \'nät-ē\ *adj* **knot·ti·er; -est 1** : full of knots ⟨*knotty* wood⟩ **2** : DIFFICULT 2b ⟨a *knotty* problem⟩

knout \'naút, 'nüt\ *n* : a whip for beating criminals as punishment

¹know \'nō\ *vb* **knew** \'n(y)ü\; **known** \'nōn\; **know·ing 1**
a : to have understanding of ⟨*know* yourself⟩ **b** : to recognize the nature of ⟨*knew* them to be honest⟩ **2 a** : to
recognize the identity of ⟨*knew* me by my walk⟩ **b** : to be
acquainted or familiar with ⟨*knows* the city very well⟩ **3**
a : to be aware of the truth of ⟨*know* that the earth is
round⟩ **b** : to have a practical understanding of ⟨*knows*
how to write⟩ **4** : to have information or knowledge ⟨ask
someone who *knows*⟩ **5** : to be or become aware ⟨*knew*
about the problem⟩ — **know·able** \'nō-ə-bəl\ *adj* —
know·er \'nō(-ə)r\ *n*

²know *n* : the fact of knowing : KNOWLEDGE — **in the**
know : well-informed

know–how \'nō-ˌhaú\ *n* : knowledge of how to get things
done : EXPERTISE

know·ing \'nō-iŋ\ *adj* **1** : having or showing special
knowledge ⟨a *knowing* smile⟩ **2** : shrewdly and keenly
alert **3** : INTENTIONAL — **know·ing·ly** *adv*

know–it–all \'nō-ət-ˌól\ *n* : a person who always claims to
know everything

knowl·edge \'näl-ij\ *n* **1** : understanding or skill gained
by experience ⟨a *knowledge* of carpentry⟩ **2 a** : the state
of being aware of something or of having information **b**
: the range of one's information or understanding ⟨an-
swered to the best of my *knowledge*⟩ **3** : something
learned and kept in the mind : LEARNING ⟨has a vast
knowledge of history⟩

   synonyms KNOWLEDGE, LEARNING, SCHOLARSHIP
mean what is known or can be known by a person or by
human beings in general. KNOWLEDGE applies to facts
or ideas acquired by study, observation, or experience
⟨gained a *knowledge* of horses in growing up on a
ranch⟩. LEARNING applies to knowledge gained usually
through formal schooling especially at an advanced level
⟨a college professor of great *learning*⟩. SCHOLARSHIP
suggests the learning of an advanced scholar in a specialized field of study ⟨a book that shows the author's *scholarship*⟩.

knowl·edge·able \'näl-ij-ə-bəl\ *adj* : having or showing
knowledge or intelligence

known \'nōn\ *adj* : generally recognized ⟨a *known* expert
on art⟩

know–noth·ing \'nō-ˌnəth-iŋ\ *n* : a person who is ignorant
: IGNORAMUS

¹knuck·le \'nək-əl\ *n* **1** : the rounded lump formed by the
ends of two bones where they come together in a joint;
esp : such a lump at a finger joint **2** : any of several parts
(as the hock or shank or a tarsal joint) of the leg of a four-
footed animal as used for food

²knuckle *vb* **knuck·led; knuck·ling** \'nək-(ə-)liŋ\ : to
place the knuckles on the ground in shooting a marble

knuck·le·ball \'nək-əl-ˌból\ *n* : a baseball pitch gripped
with the knuckles or fingertips and thrown with very little
spin

knuckle down *vb* : to apply oneself in an earnest manner

knuckle under *vb* : SUBMIT 4, GIVE IN

¹KO \(')kā-'ō, 'kā-ō\ *n, pl* **KO's** : a knockout in boxing

²KO *vb* **KO'd** \kā-'ōd, 'kā-ōd\; **KO'·ing** \-'ō-iŋ, -ō-\ : to
knock out in boxing

ko·ala \kō-'äl-ə, kə-'wäl-ə\ *n* : an Australian tree-dwelling
marsupial mammal that has large hairy ears, thick gray
fur, sharp claws for climbing, and no tail and feeds on
eucalyptus leaves — called also *koala bear*

Koch's postulates \'kóks-\ *n pl* : a statement of the
four steps required to identify a germ as the cause of a
disease

kohl \'kōl\ *n* : a cosmetic used by women especially in
Arabia and Egypt to darken the edges of the eyelids

kohl·ra·bi \kōl-'räb-ē\ *n, pl* **-bies**
: a cabbage that does not form a
head but has a swollen fleshy edible stem

koi \'kói\ *n* : a carp that has been
bred to be of various bright colors
and is often stocked in ornamental
ponds

ko·la nut \'kō-lə-\ *n* : the bitter seed
of an African tree containing
much caffeine and used in beverages and medicine for its stimulating effect

Ko·mo·do dragon \kə-'mōd-ō-\ *n*
: a lizard of Indonesia that is the
largest of all known lizards and
may grow to be 10 feet (3 meters)
long

kohlrabi

koodoo *variant of* KUDU

kook \'kük\ *n* : a person who acts in a strange or insane
way : NUT — **kooky** \'kü-kē\ *adj*

kook·a·bur·ra \'kùk-ə-ˌbər-ə, 'kük-, -ˌbə-rə\ *n* : an Australian kingfisher that is about the size of a crow and has a
call resembling loud laughter

ko·peck *or* **ko·pek** \'kō-ˌpek\ *n* **1** : a unit of money
equal to $\frac{1}{100}$ ruble **2** : a coin representing one ko-
peck

Ko·ran \kə-'ran, -'rän; 'kō(ə)r-ˌan, 'kó(ə)r-\ *n* : a book of
sacred writings accepted by Muslims as revealed to Muhammad by Allah

Ko·re·an \kə-'rē-ən\ *n* **1** : a person born or living in Korea **2** : the language of the Korean people — **Korean**
adj

ko·ru·na \'kór-ə-ˌnä\ *n, pl* **ko·ru·ny** \-nē\ *or* **korunas** *or*
ko·run \'kór-ən\ **1** : the basic unit of money of Czech
Republic and Slovakia **2** : a coin representing one koru-
na

ko·sher \'kō-shər\ *adj* **1 a** : accepted by Jewish law; *esp*
: ritually fit for use ⟨*kosher* meat⟩ **b** : selling or serving food ritually fit according to Jewish law ⟨a *kosher*
restaurant⟩ **2** : PROPER 4 ⟨made sure the deal was *kosher*⟩

kow·tow \'kaú-'taú, 'kaú-ˌtaú\ *vb* : to show overly respectful attention [from Chinese *kòutóu*, literally, "to bump the
head (in bowing to the ground)"]

KP \(')kā-'pē\ *n* **1** : the military duty of helping to prepare,
serve, and clean up after meals **2** : a person on KP

kraal \'kröl, 'kräl\ *n* **1** : a village of southern African natives **2** : an enclosure for tame animals especially in southern Africa

krait \'krīt\ *n* : any of several brightly banded extremely poisonous Asian snakes

kra·ken \'kräk-ən\ *n* : a sea monster of Scandinavian legend

Krebs cycle \'krebz-\ *n* : a series of chemical reactions in living things in which acetic acid or a related substance is oxidized to produce energy which is stored in ATP

krill \'kril\ *n* : small crustaceans and their larvae that make up plankton and form a major food of baleen whales

¹kro·na \'krō-nə\ *n, pl* **kro·nor** \-ˌnó(ə)r, -nər\ **1** : the basic unit of money of Sweden **2** : a coin representing one krona

²kro·na \'krō-nə\ *n, pl* **kro·nur** \-nər\ **1** : the basic unit of money of Iceland **2** : a coin representing one krona

¹kro·ne \'krō-nə\ *n, pl* **kro·ner** \-nər\ **1** : the basic unit of money of Denmark and Norway **2** : a coin representing one krone

²kro·ne \'krō-nə\ *n, pl* **kro·nen** \-nən\ : the basic unit of money of Austria from 1892 to 1925

kryp·ton \'krip-ˌtän\ *n* : a colorless gaseous element found in air and used especially in electric lamps — see ELEMENT table

K–T \'kā-'tē\ *adj* : of, relating to, or occurring at the K–T boundary ⟨*K-T* extinctions⟩

K–T boundary *n* : the transition between the Cretaceous and Tertiary periods of geologic time marked especially by the extinction of the dinosaurs; *also* : a layer of rock marking this boundary

ku·du *also* **koo·doo** \'küd-(ˌ)ü\ *n, pl* **kudu** *or* **kudus** *also* **koodoo** *or* **koodoos** : a large grayish brown African antelope with long twisted horns

kudu

kud·zu \'kud-zü\ *n* : a fast=growing trailing Asian vine that is related to the pea, is grown for grazing and for erosion control, and is often a serious weed in the southeastern U.S.

kum·quat \'kəm-ˌkwät\ *n* **1** : a small yellowish orange fruit related to the citruses with sweet spongy skin and somewhat tart pulp used especially for preserves **2** : a tree or shrub that bears kumquats

kung fu \ˌkəŋ-'fü, ˌkùŋ-\ *n* : a Chinese art of self-defense resembling karate

Kurd \'kù(ə)rd, 'kərd\ *n* : a member of a nomadic people who live in a region that is partly in Turkey, Iran, Iraq, Syria, Armenia, and Azerbaijan — **Kurd·ish** \-ish\ *adj*

Kwan·zaa \'kwän-zə\ *n* : an African-American cultural festival held from December 26 to January 1 [Swahili *kwanza* "first," in the phrase *matunda ya kwanza* "first fruits"]

kwash·i·or·kor \ˌkwäsh-ē-'ór-kər\ *n* : a disease of young children resulting from not getting enough protein to eat

L

l \'el\ *n, often cap* **1** : the 12th letter of the English alphabet **2** : fifty in Roman numerals

la \'lä\ *n* : the sixth note of the musical scale

lab \'lab\ *n* : LABORATORY

lab coat *n* : a loose-fitting usually white coat with deep pockets that is worn by personnel in a laboratory, medical office, or hospital

¹la·bel \'lā-bəl\ *n* **1** : a slip (as of paper or cloth) that is attached to something to identify or describe it **2 a** : a descriptive or identifying word or phrase **b** : the brand name of a commercial product

²label *vb* **la·beled** *or* **la·belled; la·bel·ing** *or* **la·bel·ling** \-b(ə-)liŋ\ **1** : to attach a label to **2** : to name or describe with or as if with a label **3** : to make (as an element, compound, or cell) traceable by inclusion of a detectable part (as a radioactive isotope or a dye)

la·bi·al \'lā-bē-əl\ *adj* : of or relating to the lips or labia

la·bi·um \'lā-bē-əm\ *n, pl* **la·bia** \-bē-ə\ **1** : any of the folds at the margin of the vulva **2** : the lower mouthpart of an insect

¹la·bor \'lā-bər\ *n* **1** : physical or mental effort especially when hard or required : TOIL, WORK **2 a** : the services performed by workers for wages **b** : those who do labor for wages **3** : the physical efforts and pain of giving birth; *also* : the period of such labor **4** : something that requires work : TASK

²labor *vb* **la·bored; la·bor·ing** \-b(ə-)riŋ\ **1** : to work hard **2** : to move with great effort ⟨the truck *labored* up the hill⟩ **synonyms** see WORK

lab·o·ra·to·ry \'lab-(ə-)rə-ˌtōr-ē, -ˌtor-\ *n, pl* **-ries** : a place equipped for making scientific experiments and tests

Labor Day *n* : the first Monday in September observed in the U.S. and Canada as a legal holiday in honor of working people

la·bored \'lā-bərd\ *adj* : produced or done with labor ⟨*labored* breathing⟩

la·bor·er \'lā-bər-ər\ *n* : one that works; *esp* : a person who does unskilled physical work for wages

la·bo·ri·ous \lə-'bōr-ē-əs, -'bor-\ *adj* **1** : devoted to work : INDUSTRIOUS **2** : requiring hard effort — **la·bo·ri·ous·ly** *adv* — **la·bo·ri·ous·ness** *n*

la·bor·sav·ing \'lā-bər-ˌsā-viŋ\ *adj* : designed to replace or decrease human labor and especially physical labor

labor union *n* : an organization of workers formed to protect the rights and advance the interests of its members concerning wages, benefits, and working conditions

Lab·ra·dor retriever \ˌlab-rə-ˌdór-\ *n* : any of a breed of strongly built retrievers having a broad head, a short dense black, yellow, or chocolate coat, and a thick rounded tail

Labrador retriever

la·brum \'lā-brəm\ : the upper mouthpart of an arthropod in front of or above the mandibles

lab·y·rinth \'lab-ə-ˌrin(t)th\ *n* **1** : a place full of passageways and blind alleys

\ə\ abut	\aů\ out	\i\ tip	\ó\ saw	\ů\ foot
\ər\ further	\ch\ chin	\ī\ life	\ói\ coin	\y\ yet
\a\ mat	\e\ pet	\j\ job	\th\ thin	\yü\ few
\ā\ take	\ē\ easy	\ŋ\ sing	\th\ this	\yů\ cure
\ä\ cot, cart	\g\ go	\ō\ bone	\ü\ food	\zh\ vision

so arranged as to make it difficult to find one's way around : MAZE **2** : something extremely complicated or twisting ⟨the cockpit was a *labyrinth* of instruments and controls⟩ **3** : the internal ear or its bony or membranous part — **lab·y·rin·thine** \ˌlab-ə-ˈrin(t)-thən\ *adj*

lac \ˈlak\ *n* : a substance given off by a scale insect and used in the manufacture of shellac, lacquers, and sealing wax

¹**lace** \ˈlās\ *vb* **laced; lac·ing** **1** : to fasten or join with or as if with a lace ⟨*laced* her shoes⟩ **2** : to adorn with or as if with lace **3** : INTERTWINE, THREAD ⟨*lace* the ribbon through the holes⟩ **4** : ¹BEAT 1a, LASH

²**lace** *n* **1** : a cord or string for drawing together two edges (as of a shoe) **2** : an ornamental braid for trimming coats or uniforms **3** : a fine open-worked fabric of thread or cord used chiefly for ornament of dress — **laced** \ˈlāst\ *adj* — **lace·like** \ˈlā-ˌslīk\ *adj*

Word History When the ancient Romans wanted to trap a small animal, such as a rabbit, they used a loop of light rope laid on the ground in its path. A triggering device was used to tighten the loop around the animal. They called such a loop or noose *laqueus,* which became *laz* in early French. The English borrowed it as *las* in the 14th century. They used it to refer to a cord that holds something together by weaving, as a shoelace. Finally, it came to mean the delicate fabric made by weaving and knotting thin strands of material. [Middle English *las, lace* "a string used to draw together two edges of material," from early French *laz* (same meaning), from Latin *laqueus* "noose, snare" — related to ³LASH, ¹LAS-SO]

lac·er·ate \ˈlas-ə-ˌrāt\ *vb* **-at·ed; -at·ing** : to tear roughly : injure by tearing ⟨a *lacerated* knee⟩

lac·er·a·tion \ˌlas-ə-ˈrā-shən\ *n* **1** : an act or instance of lacerating **2** : a torn and ragged wound

lace·wing \ˈlā-ˌswiŋ\ *n* : any of various insects that have delicate lacelike wings, long antennae, and often bright eyes

lach·ry·mal *or* **lac·ri·mal** \ˈlak-rə-məl\ *adj* **1** *usually lacrimal* : of, relating to, or being the glands that produce tears **2** : of, relating to, or marked by tears

lach·ry·mose \ˈlak-rə-ˌmōs\ *adj* **1** : tending to weep : TEARFUL **2** : tending to cause tears : MOURNFUL ⟨a *lachrymose* drama⟩ — **lach·ry·mose·ly** *adv*

lac·ing \ˈlā-siŋ\ *n* **1** : the action of one that laces **2** : ²LACE

¹**lack** \ˈlak\ *vb* **1** : to be missing **2** : to need, want, or be short of ⟨*lacks* money⟩

²**lack** *n* **1** : the fact or state of being absent or in short supply **2** : something that is lacking or is needed

lack·a·dai·si·cal \ˌlak-ə-ˈdā-zi-kəl\ *adj* : lacking spirit or enthusiasm : LANGUID, LISTLESS — **lack·a·dai·si·cal·ly** \-k(ə-)lē\ *adv*

lack·ey \ˈlak-ē\ *n, pl* **lackeys** **1** : FOOTMAN 2 **2** : an overly respectful follower : TOADY

lack·lus·ter \ˈlak-ˌləs-tər\ *adj* : lacking in brightness, radiance, or interest : DULL ⟨a *lackluster* performance⟩

la·con·ic \lə-ˈkän-ik\ *adj* : using few words : TERSE ⟨a *laconic* reply⟩ — **la·con·i·cal·ly** \-ˈkän-i-k(ə-)lē\ *adv*

lac·quer \ˈlak-ər\ *n* : a material like varnish that dries quickly into a shiny layer (as on wood or metal) — **lacquer** *vb*

la·crosse \lə-ˈkrös\ *n* : a game played on a field in which players use long-handled sticks with shallow nets for catching, throwing, and carrying the ball

lac·tase \ˈlak-ˌtās\ *n* : an enzyme that breaks down lactose and related compounds and occurs especially in the intestines of young mammals and in yeasts

lac·tate \ˈlak-ˌtāt\ *vb* **lac·tat·ed; lac·tat·ing** : to give off milk — **lac·ta·tion** \lak-ˈtā-shən\ *n*

lac·te·al \ˈlak-tē-əl\ *n* : one of the lymphatic vessels that begin in the villi of the small intestine and carry chyle

lac·tic acid \ˌlak-tik-\ *n* : an organic acid present especially in muscle tissue as a result of the breakdown of carbohydrates (as glycogen), is made from carbohydrates usually by fermentation by bacteria, and is used especially in food and medicine

lac·tose \ˈlak-ˌtōs\ *n* : a sugar present in milk that breaks down to give glucose and galactose and on fermentation gives especially lactic acid — called also *milk sugar*

la·cus·trine \lə-ˈkəs-trən\ *adj* : of, relating to, formed in, or growing in lakes

lacy \ˈlā-sē\ *adj* **lac·i·er; -est** : resembling or consisting of lace

lad \ˈlad\ *n* **1** : BOY 1, YOUTH **2** : ¹FELLOW 4a, CHAP

lad·der \ˈlad-ər\ *n* **1** : a structure for climbing that consists of two long pieces (as of wood, rope, or metal) joined at short distances by crosspieces on which one may step **2** : something that suggests a ladder in form or use **3** : a series of steps or stages : SCALE ⟨the corporate *ladder*⟩

lad·die \ˈlad-ē\ *n* : a young lad

lade \ˈlād\ *vb* **lad·ed; lad·ed** *or* **lad·en** \ˈlād-ᵊn\; **lad·ing** **1** : ²LOAD 1a ⟨*lade* a ship⟩ ⟨a truck *laden* with gravel⟩ **2** : to burden heavily ⟨*laden* with cares⟩ **3** : ²LADLE

¹**la·dle** \ˈlād-ᵊl\ *n* : a spoon or dipper with a long handle and a deep bowl used for dipping — **la·dle·ful** \-ˌfu̇l\ *n*

²**ladle** *vb* **la·dled; la·dling** \ˈlād-liŋ, -ᵊl-iŋ\ : to take up and carry in or as if in a ladle

la·dy \ˈlād-ē\ *n, pl* **ladies** **1** : a woman of property, rank, or authority; *esp* : one having a standing equivalent to that of a lord — used as a title **2** *cap* : VIRGIN MARY — usually used with *Our* **3** : a woman of high social position **4** : WOMAN 1 **5** : WIFE 2

Word History The word *lady* is nowadays generally used as a polite term for a woman. In the past, however, *lady* was used primarily for "a woman of a high social class." The Old English ancestor of *lady* was *hlæfdige,* which came from two other words. One was *hlāf,* meaning "loaf of bread." The other was *-dīge,* a form of a root word meaning "to knead dough." But the word *hlæfdige* was not used in Old English for an actual bread maker. It was used instead to refer to the woman in charge of maids and of a household. Only very rich and powerful women, members of the nobility, had maids and large households, so a lady was owed much respect. The title *lady* is still used in Great Britain for a woman who is a member of the nobility. [Old English *hlæfdige,* from *hlāf* "loaf of bread" and *-dīge,* a form of a root word meaning "to knead dough" — related to LOAF, LORD; see *Word History* at LORD]

lady beetle *n* : LADYBUG

la·dy·bird \ˈlād-ē-ˌbərd\ *n* : LADYBUG

la·dy·bug \-ˌbəg\ *n* : any of numerous small roundish-backed often brightly colored and spotted beetles that usually feed both when young and adult on other insects (as aphids)

la·dy–in–wait·ing \ˌlād-ē-in-ˈwāt-iŋ\ *n, pl* **ladies–in–waiting** : a lady appointed to attend or wait on a queen or princess

la·dy·like \ˈlād-ē-ˌlīk\ *adj* **1** : resembling a lady in appearance or manners **2** : suitable to a lady ⟨*ladylike* behavior⟩

ladybug

la·dy·love \ˈlād-ē-ˌləv, ˌlād-ē-ˈləv\ *n* : a woman with whom one is in love : SWEETHEART

la·dy·ship \ˈlād-ē-ˌship\ *n* : the rank or dignity of a lady — used as a title ⟨her *Ladyship* is not at home⟩

lady's slipper *or* **lady slipper** \'lād-ē(z)-ˌslip-ər\ *n* : any of several North American orchids whose large drooping flowers suggest a slipper in shape

¹**lag** \'lag\ *n* **1** : the action or condition of lagging **2 a** : amount of lagging **b** : a time during which lagging continues

²**lag** *vb* **lagged; lag·ging 1** : to stay or fall behind : LINGER, LOITER **2** : to move, function, or develop too slowly ⟨production *lagged* behind schedule⟩ **3** : to slacken little by little : FLAG *synonyms* see LINGER — **lag·ger** *n*

lag·gard \'lag-ərd\ *adj* : lagging or tending to lag : SLOW — **laggard** *n* — **lag·gard·ly** *adv or adj*

la·gniappe \'lan-ˌyap, lan-'yap\ *n* : something given free especially with a customer's purchase [American French]

lago·morph \'lag-ə-ˌmȯrf\ *n* : any of an order of plant-eating gnawing mammals having two pairs of incisor teeth in the upper jaw one behind the other and including the rabbits, hares, and pikas

la·goon \lə-'gün\ *n* : a shallow channel or pond near or connected with a larger body of water

laid *past and past participle of* LAY

laid–back \'lād-'bak\ *adj* : relaxed in style or manner

lain *past participle of* ¹LIE

lair \'la(ə)r, 'le(ə)r\ *n* **1** : the den or resting place of a wild animal **2** : REFUGE 1, HIDEAWAY

laird \'la(ə)rd, 'le(ə)rd\ *n, chiefly Scottish* : LANDOWNER

lais·sez–faire \ˌle-ˌsā-'fa(ə)r, ˌlā-, -ˌzā-, -'fe(ə)r\ *n* : a doctrine opposing governmental interference in economic affairs [from the French phrase *laissez faire* "let (people) do (as they choose)"] — **laissez–faire** *adj*

la·ity \'lā-ət-ē\ *n, pl* **-ities 1** : the people of a religious faith who are not members of its clergy **2** : persons not of a particular profession

lake \'lāk\ *n* : a large inland body of standing water; *also* : a pool of liquid (as oil or pitch)

lake trout *n* : any of various trout and salmon found in lakes; *esp* : MACKINAW TROUT

¹**lam** \'lam\ *vb* **lammed; lam·ming 1** : ¹STRIKE 2a, THRASH **2** : to flee hastily

²**lam** *n* : a sudden or hurried flight especially from the law ⟨on the *lam*⟩

la·ma \'läm-ə\ *n* : a Lamaist monk

La·ma·ism \'läm-ə-ˌiz-əm\ *n* : the Buddhism of Tibet and Mongolia having a ruling body of monks organized into ranks — **La·ma·ist** \'läm-ə-əst\ *n or adj* — **La·ma·is·tic** \ˌläm-ə-'is-tik\ *adj*

La·marck·ism \lə-'mär-ˌkiz-əm\ *n* : a theory of evolution holding that changes in the environment cause changes in the structure of animals and plants that are passed on to offspring — **La·marck·i·an** \-kē-ən\ *adj*

la·ma·sery \'läm-ə-ˌser-ē\ *n, pl* **-ser·ies** : a monastery of lamas

¹**lamb** \'lam\ *n* **1 a** : a young sheep especially less than one year old or without permanent teeth **b** : the flesh of a lamb used as food **2** : an innocent, weak, or gentle person

²**lamb** *vb* : to give birth to a lamb

lam·baste *or* **lam·bast** \(')lam-'bāst, -'bast\ *vb* **lam·bast·ed; lam·bast·ing 1** : ¹STRIKE 2a, BEAT **2** : to scold roughly

lamb·da \'lam-də\ *n* : the eleventh letter of the Greek alphabet — Λ or λ

lam·bent \'lam-bənt\ *adj* **1** : playing lightly over a surface : FLICKERING **2** : softly radiant

lamb·kin \'lam-kən\ *n* : a little lamb

lamb's ears *n sing or pl* : a widely grown Asian herb of the mint family having leaves covered with fuzzy silver-white hairs

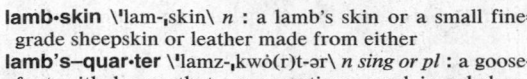
lady's slipper

lamb·skin \'lam-ˌskin\ *n* : a lamb's skin or a small fine-grade sheepskin or leather made from either

lamb's–quar·ter \'lamz-ˌkwȯ(r)t-ər\ *n sing or pl* : a goosefoot with leaves that are sometimes used in salads or cooked as a vegetable — called also *lamb's-quarters*

¹**lame** \'lām\ *adj* **lam·er; lam·est 1 a** : having a body part and especially an arm or a leg disabled enough so as to be unable to get around without pain or difficulty **b** : being stiff and sore ⟨a *lame* shoulder⟩ **2** : not very convincing : WEAK ⟨a *lame* excuse⟩ — **lame·ly** *adv* — **lame·ness** *n*

²**lame** *vb* **lamed; lam·ing** : to make lame

lame duck *n* : an elected official continuing to hold office until a successor takes office

la·mel·la \lə-'mel-ə\ *n, pl* **la·mel·lae** \-'mel-(ˌ)ē, -ˌī\ *also* **-mellas** : a thin flat scale, layer, or membrane

¹**la·ment** \lə-'ment\ *vb* **1** : to mourn aloud : WAIL **2** : to express sorrow for : BEWAIL — **lam·en·ta·tion** \ˌlam-ən-'tā-shən\ *n*

²**lament** *n* **1** : a crying out in grief **2** : a mournful song or poem

la·men·ta·ble \'lam-ən-tə-bəl, lə-'ment-ə-\ *adj* **1** : that is to be regretted or lamented **2** : SORROWFUL 2 — **la·men·ta·ble·ness** *n* — **la·men·ta·bly** \-blē\ *adv*

Lam·en·ta·tions \ˌlam-ən-'tā-shənz\ *n* — see BIBLE table

lam·i·na \'lam-ə-nə\ *n, pl* **lam·i·nae** \-ˌnē, -ˌnī\ *or* **-nas** : a thin plate or scale

lam·i·nar·ia \ˌlam-ə-'ner-ē-ə, -'nar-\ *n* : any of various large kelps with an unbranched cylinder-shaped or flattened stalk and a smooth or wavy blade

lam·i·nate \'lam-ə-ˌnāt\ *vb* **-nat·ed; -nat·ing 1** : to roll or compress into a thin plate **2** : to make by uniting layers of one or more materials — **lam·i·nate** \-nət, -ˌnāt\ *n* — **lam·i·na·tion** \ˌlam-ə-'nā-shən\ *n* — **lam·i·na·tor** \'lam-ə-ˌnāt-ər\ *n*

lamp \'lamp\ *n* : a device for producing light or heat

lamp·black \-ˌblak\ *n* : a fine black soot made by incomplete burning of carbon-containing material and used to color things black

lamp·light \'lam-ˌplīt\ *n* : the light of a lamp

lamp·light·er \'lam-ˌplīt-ər\ *n* : one that lights a lamp; *esp* : a person employed to light gas streetlights

¹**lam·poon** \lam-'pün\ *n* : a writing or drawing that makes fun of a person

²**lampoon** *vb* : to make fun of by a lampoon : RIDICULE — **lam·poon·er** *n*

lamp·post \'lam(p)-ˌpōst\ *n* : a post supporting a usually outdoor lamp or lantern

lam·prey \'lam-prē, -ˌprā\ *n, pl* **lampreys** : any of a family of jawless fishes that resemble eels and have a large sucking mouth with horny teeth

lamprey

lamp·shell \'lamp-ˌshel\ *n* : BRACHIOPOD

LAN \'lan, ˌel-ˌā-'en\ *n* : LOCAL AREA NETWORK

¹**lance** \'lan(t)s\ *n* **1** : a weapon consisting of a long shaft with a sharp steel head that was used by knights on horseback **2** : a sharp instrument; *esp* : LANCET

²**lance** *vb* **lanced; lanc·ing** : to pierce or cut with a lance or lancet

lance corporal *n* : an enlisted person with a rank just below that of corporal in the marines

lance·let \'lan(t)-slət\ *n* : any of various small translucent marine animals that are related to the vertebrates, resem-

ble fish, and usually live partly buried on the ocean floor
— called also *amphioxus*

lan·cet \'lan(t)-sət\ *n* : a sharp-pointed and usually two=
edged surgical instrument

¹land \'land\ *n* **1** : the solid part of the surface of the earth
2 : a portion of the earth's surface ⟨fenced *land*⟩ ⟨marshy
land⟩ **3** : ¹COUNTRY 2b, NATION **4** : REAL ESTATE ⟨owns
land in Alaska⟩ — **land·less** \'lan-dləs\ *adj*

²land *vb* **1 a** : to set or go ashore from a ship : DISEM-
BARK **b** : to stop at or near a place on shore **2** : to come
down or bring down and settle on a surface ⟨*land* a
plane⟩ **3** : to bring to or arrive at a destination or a position or condition ⟨*land* in jail⟩ **4 a** : to catch and bring in
⟨*land* a fish⟩ **b** : ²SECURE 3, GAIN ⟨*land* a job⟩ — **land·**
er *n*

land·ed \'lan-dəd\ *adj* **1** : owning land **2** : consisting of
real estate

land·fall \'lan(d)-ˌfȯl\ *n* **1** : a sighting or making of land
after a voyage or flight **2** : the land first sighted on a voyage or flight

land·fill \-ˌfil\ *n* **1** : a system of trash and garbage disposal
in which the waste is buried between layers of earth **2**
: an area built up by landfill

land·form \-ˌfȯrm\ *n* : a natural feature of a land surface

land·hold·er \'land-ˌhōl-dər\ *n* : LANDOWNER — **land·**
hold·ing \-diŋ\ *n*

land·ing \'lan-diŋ\ *n* **1** : the
action of one that lands **2** : a
place (as a wharf) for unloading or taking on passengers
and cargo **3** : the level part of
a staircase (as between flights
of stairs)

landing craft *n* : any of numerous naval craft designed
for putting troops and equipment ashore

landing field *n* : a field where
aircraft may land and take off

landing gear *n* : the part that
supports the weight of an aircraft or spacecraft when on the ground

landing strip *n* : AIRSTRIP

land·la·dy \'lan-ˌ(d)lād-ē\ *n* **1** : a woman who owns land
or houses that she rents **2** : a woman who runs an inn or
rooming house

land·line \-ˌ(d)līn\ *n* : a line of communication (as by telephone) consisting of a cable laid on land

land·locked \-(d)läkt\ *adj* **1** : enclosed or nearly enclosed
by land ⟨a *landlocked* country⟩ **2** : kept from leaving
fresh water by some barrier ⟨*landlocked* salmon⟩

land·lord \-ˌ(d)lȯ(ə)rd\ *n* **1** : the owner of land or houses
that is rented to another **2** : a person who runs an inn or
rooming house

land·lub·ber \-ˌ(d)ləb-ər\ *n* : LANDSMAN

land·mark \'lan(d)-ˌmärk\ *n* **1** : an object that marks
the boundary of land **2 a** : a usually large object on land
that is easy to see and can help a person find the way to a
place near it **b** : an important building or monument
⟨historical *landmarks*⟩ **3** : an event that marks a turning
point

land·mass \-ˌmas\ *n* : a large area of land

land mine *n* : a mine placed just below the surface of the
ground and designed to be exploded by the weight of the
vehicles or troops passing over it

land·own·er \'lan-ˌdō-nər\ *n* : an owner of land — **land·**
own·ing \-niŋ\ *adj*

¹land·scape \'lan(d)-ˌskāp\ *n* **1** : a picture of natural scenery **2** : the land that can be seen in one glance

²landscape *vb* **land·scaped; land·scap·ing** : to improve

the natural beauties of a piece of land by grading, clearing, or gardening

land·slide \'lan(d)-ˌslīd\ *n* **1** : the slipping down of a mass
of rocks or earth on a steep slope; *also* : the mass of material that slides **2** : an overwhelming victory especially in
a political contest ⟨won by a *landslide*⟩

lands·man \'lan(d)z-mən\ *n* : a person who lives or works
on land; *esp* : one who knows little or nothing of the sea
and ships

land·ward \'lan-dwərd\ *adj or adv* : lying or being toward
the land or on the side toward the land

lane \'lān\ *n* **1** : a narrow way or road usually between
fences, hedges, or buildings **2** : a somewhat narrow way
or track: as **a** : an ocean route for ships; *also* : AIR LANE
b : a strip of roadway for a single line of vehicles **c** : a
bowling alley

lan·guage \'laŋ-gwij\ *n* **1 a** : the words, their pronunciation, and the methods of combining them used and understood by a large group of people **b** : a means of comu-
nicating ideas ⟨sign *language*⟩ **2** : the means by which
animals communicate or are thought to communicate
with each other ⟨*language* of the bees⟩ **3** : a system of
signs and symbols and rules for using them that is used to
carry information ⟨BASIC is a computer *language*⟩ **4**
: the way in which words are used ⟨strong *language*⟩ **5**
: the words and expressions of a particular group or field
⟨the *language* of medicine⟩ **6** : the study of language

Word History The tongue plays an important part in human speech. Different sounds are made by different positions of the tongue. The tongue and speech are so
closely connected that in many languages the word that
means "tongue" also means "language." This is true in
English, as when we say "she spoke a foreign tongue." It
was also true in Latin, where the word *lingua* meant
both "tongue" and "language." From the Latin *lingua*
came the early French *langue,* meaning "tongue,
language," which gave rise to the early French word *lan-*
guage. The English word *language* comes directly from
this early French word. [Middle English *language*
"language," from early French *language* (same meaning), from *langue* "language, tongue," from Latin *lingua*
"tongue, language"]

language arts *n pl* : the subjects (as reading, spelling, and
composition) that aim at developing the student's understanding and skills for using language

lan·guid \'laŋ-gwəd\ *adj* **1** : weak from or as if from exhaustion **2** : lacking spirit : LISTLESS **3** : lacking force or
quickness of movement : SLOW — **lan·guid·ly** *adv*

lan·guish \'laŋ-gwish\ *vb* **1** : to become weak or languid
: waste away ⟨*languish* in prison⟩ **2** : to suffer neglect ⟨a
bill *languishing* in the Senate⟩ — **lan·guish·ment** \-mənt\
n

lan·guor \'laŋ-(g)ər\ *n* **1** : weakness or weariness of body
or mind **2** : a state of dreamy idleness — **lan·guor·ous**
\-(g)ə-rəs\ *adj* — **lan·guor·ous·ly** *adv*

La Ni·ña \lä-'nē-nyə, -nyä\ *n* : an irregularly occurring
movement of deep cold water to the ocean surface along
the western coast of South America that often occurs after an El Niño and that disrupts weather patterns especially in a manner opposite that of an El Niño

lank \'laŋk\ *adj* **1** : not well filled out : THIN ⟨*lank* cattle⟩
2 : hanging straight and limp without spring or curl ⟨*lank*
hair⟩ — **lank·ly** *adv* — **lank·ness** *n*

lanky \'laŋ-kē\ *adj* **lank·i·er; -est** : being tall, thin, and
usually loose-jointed ⟨a *lanky* teenager⟩ — **lank·i·ly** \-kə-
lē\ *adv* — **lank·i·ness** \-kē-nəs\ *n*

lan·o·lin \'lan-ᵊl-ən\ *n* : the fatty coating of sheep's wool
especially when purified for use in ointments and cosmetics

lan·ta·na \lan-'tän-ə\ *n* : any of a genus of tropical shrubs
and herbs that have showy heads of small bright flowers

L landing 3

lan·tern \\'lant-ərn\ *n* **1** : a usually portable light with a protective covering **2** : PROJECTOR

lantern fish *n* : any of numerous small fishes mostly of deep seas that have a large mouth, large eyes, and spots on the body that give off light

lantern fly *n* : any of several large brightly marked insects that are related to the cicadas and aphids and have the front of the head lengthened into a hollow structure

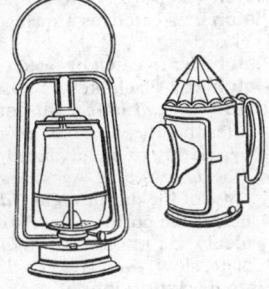

lantern 1

lan·tha·num \\'lan(t)-thə-nəm\ *n* : a white soft metallic element — see ELEMENT table

la·nu·go \lə-'nü-gō, -'nyü-\ *n* : a growth of hair resembling cotton or down; *esp* : the soft hair that covers the fetus of some mammals including humans

lan·yard \\'lan-yərd\ *n* **1** : a rope or line for fastening something in ships **2** : a cord worn around the neck or shoulder to hold a knife or whistle **3** : a strong cord used in firing a cannon

Lao \\'laú\ *n, pl* **Lao** *or* **Laos** **1** : a member of a people living in Laos and northeastern Thailand **2** : the language of the Lao people which is closely related to Thai — **Lao** *adj*

Lao·tian \lā-'ō-shən, 'laú-shən\ *n* **1** : a person born or living in Laos; *also* : LAO 1 **2** : LAO 2 — **Laotian** *adj*

¹lap \\'lap\ *n* **1** : a loose panel in a garment : FLAP **2 a** : the clothing that lies on the knees and thighs when one sits **b** : the front part of a person between the waist and the knees when seated [Old English *læppa* "flap of a garment"]

²lap *vb* **lapped; lap·ping** **1** : ³FOLD 1 **2** : ¹WRAP 1a **3** : to lay or lie over or near something else so as to partly cover it ⟨*lap* one shingle over another⟩

³lap *n* **1** : the amount by which one object overlaps another **b** : the part of an object that overlaps another **2 a** : one time around a racetrack **b** : one part of a journey

⁴lap *vb* **lapped; lap·ping** **1** : to scoop up food or drink with the tongue **2** : to wash or splash gently [Old English *lapian* "to take into the mouth by means of the tongue"]

⁵lap *n* : an act or sound of lapping

lap·dog \\'lap-ˌdȯg\ *n* : a dog small enough to be held in the lap

la·pel \lə-'pel\ *n* : the fold of the front of a coat that is usually a part of the collar

lap·i·dary \\'lap-ə-ˌder-ē\ *n, pl* **-dar·ies** : a person who cuts and polishes precious stones — **lapidary** *adj*

la·pis la·zu·li \ˌlap-ə-'slazh-ə-lē, -'slaz-\ *n* : a deep blue gemstone

Lapp \\'lap\ *n, sometimes offensive* : SAMI

¹lapse \\'laps\ *n* **1 a** : a slight error or slip ⟨*lapse* of memory⟩ **b** : a temporary fall especially from a higher to a lower state ⟨*lapse* into bad habits⟩ **2** : the ending of a right or privilege through failure to meet requirements **3** : a passage of time; *also* : INTERVAL 1

²lapse *vb* **lapsed; laps·ing** **1** : to slip, pass, or fall gradually ⟨*lapse* into silence⟩ **2** : to come to an end : CEASE

¹lap·top \-ˌtäp\ *adj* : of a size and design that makes use on one's lap convenient

²laptop *n* : a portable computer that is small enough to use on one's lap, has its main components (as keyboard and display screen) combined in one unit, and can run on battery power

lar·board \\'lär-bərd\ *n* : ³PORT — **larboard** *adj*

lar·ce·ny \\'lärs-nē, -ᵊn-ē\ *n, pl* **-nies** : the unlawful taking of personal property with the intention of depriving the rightful owner of it permanently : THEFT — **lar·ce·nous** \-nəs, -ᵊn-əs\ *adj*

larch \\'lärch\ *n* : any of a genus of trees related to the pines that shed their short needles each fall

¹lard \\'lärd\ *vb* **1** : to insert strips of usually pork fat into meat before cooking **2** : to smear with lard, fat, or grease **3** : to add something extra and unnecessary to

larch

²lard *n* : a soft white fat from the fatty tissue of the hog

lar·der \\'lärd-ər\ *n* : a place where foods are kept

large \\'lärj\ *adj* **larg·er; larg·est** : greater, bigger, more extended, or more powerful than usual — **large·ness** *n* — **at large** **1** : not locked up : FREE ⟨the criminal is still *at large*⟩ **2** : as a whole ⟨the public *at large*⟩ **3** : representing a whole state or area rather than one of its divisions ⟨delegate-*at-large*⟩

large calorie *n* : CALORIE 1b

large intestine *n* : the last part of the intestine which is wider and shorter than the small intestine, which consists of the cecum, colon, and rectum, and which absorbs water from the material left over from digestion and prepares the feces for release from the body

large·ly \\'lärj-lē\ *adv* **1** : GENERALLY 1 ⟨the story is *largely* true⟩ **2** : in a great amount ⟨tipped the waiter *largely*⟩

large·mouth bass \ˌlärj-ˌmaúth-\ *n* : a large North American bass of warm slow-moving waters that is blackish green above and lighter or whitish below — called also *largemouth black bass*

large–scale integration \ˌlärj-'skäl-\ *n* : the process of placing a large number of circuits on a small chip

lar·gesse *also* **lar·gess** \lär-'zhes, lär-'jes\ *n* **1** : generous giving **2** : a generous gift

larg·ish \\'lär-jish\ *adj* : rather large

¹lar·go \\'lär-gō\ *adv or adj* : in a very slow and broad manner — used as a direction in music

²largo *n, pl* **largos** : a largo movement

lar·i·at \\'lar-ē-ət\ *n* : a rope with a noose used to catch livestock or to tie up grazing animals : LASSO

¹lark \\'lärk\ *n* : any of numerous Old World singing birds that are usually brownish in color and live on the ground; *esp* : ¹SKYLARK — compare MEADOWLARK

²lark *n* : something done for fun or adventure — **lark** *vb*

lark·spur \\'lärk-ˌspər\ *n* : DELPHINIUM; *esp* : a cultivated delphinium grown for its stalks of showy blue, pink, or white flowers

lar·va \\'lär-və\ *n, pl* **lar·vae** \-(ˌ)vē, -ˌvī\ *also* **larvas** **1** : a young wingless often wormlike form (as a grub or caterpillar) that hatches from the egg of many insects **2** : an early form of any animal that at birth or hatching is very different from its parents ⟨the tadpole is the *larva* of the frog⟩ — **lar·val** \-vəl\ *adj*

lar·vi·cide \\'lär-və-ˌsīd\ *n* : a chemical substance used for killing larvae that are pests

lar·yn·gi·tis \ˌlar-ən-'jīt-əs\ *n* : inflammation of the larynx

lar·ynx \\'lar-iŋ(k)s\ *n, pl* **la·ryn·ges** \lə-'rin-(ˌ)jēz\ *or* **lar·ynx·es** : the upper part of the trachea that in human beings and most mammals contains the vocal cords — called also *voice box*

\ə\ **abut**	\aú\ **out**	\i\ **tip**	\ȯ\ **saw**	\ú\ **foot**
\ər\ **further**	\ch\ **chin**	\ī\ **life**	\ȯi\ **coin**	\y\ **yet**
\a\ **mat**	\e\ **pet**	\j\ **job**	\th\ **thin**	\yü\ **few**
\ā\ **take**	\ē\ **easy**	\ŋ\ **sing**	\th\ **this**	\yú\ **cure**
\ä\ **cot, cart**	\g\ **go**	\ō\ **bone**	\ü\ **food**	\zh\ **vision**

la·sa·gna \lə-ˈzän-yə\ n : broad flat noodles baked with a sauce usually of tomatoes, cheese, and meat or vegetables

las·civ·i·ous \lə-ˈsiv-ē-əs\ adj : LEWD 1, LUSTFUL — **las·civ·i·ous·ly** adv — **las·civ·i·ous·ness** n

¹la·ser \ˈlā-zər\ n : a device that uses the natural vibrations of atoms or molecules to generate a narrow beam of light having a small frequency range [*light amplification by stimulated emission of radiation*]

²laser vb : to subject to the action of a laser

laser printer n : a high-quality computer printer that uses a laser to form the image to be printed

¹lash \ˈlash\ vb 1 : to move violently or suddenly 2 : to strike with or as if with a whip 3 : to attack with strong language ⟨*lashed* out at his sister, starting an argument⟩ [Middle English *lassen* "to move violently or suddenly"]

²lash n 1 a : a stroke with a whip or switch b : the flexible part of a whip; *also* : ²WHIP 1 2 : a beating, whipping, or driving force 3 : EYELASH

³lash vb : to tie down with a rope, cord, or chain [Middle English *lasschen* "to lace," from early French *lacer* (same meaning), derived from Latin *laqueare* "to snare, catch in a noose," from *laqueus* "noose, snare" — related to LACE, ¹LASSO; see *Word History* at LACE] — **lash·er** n

lash·ing \ˈlash-iŋ\ n : something used for tying, wrapping, or fastening

lass \ˈlas\ n : a young woman : GIRL

lass·ie \ˈlas-ē\ n : LASS, GIRL

las·si·tude \ˈlas-ə-ˌt(y)üd\ n 1 : a condition of weariness : FATIGUE 2 : a state of dreamy idleness : LANGUOR

¹las·so \ˈlas-ō, la-ˈsü\ n, pl lassos or lassoes : a rope or long leather thong with a noose used especially for catching livestock [from Spanish *lazo* "lasso," from Latin *laqueus* "noose, snare" — related to LACE, ²LASH; see *Word History* at LACE]

²lasso vb : to catch with a lasso

¹last \ˈlast\ vb 1 : to continue in being or operation ⟨*lasted* three hours⟩ 2 : to be enough for the needs of ⟨supplies to *last* a week⟩ [Old English *læstan* "to last, follow"]

²last n : a form which is shaped like the human foot and on which a shoe is shaped or repaired [Old English *læste*]

³last vb : to shape with a last

⁴last adj 1 a : following all the rest in time, place, or rank ⟨*last* one out⟩ b : being the only remaining ⟨*last* dollar⟩ 2 : belonging to the final stage 3 : next before the present : LATEST ⟨*last* week⟩ 4 : least likely ⟨the *last* thing we'd want⟩ [Old English *latost* "latest," from *læt* "late" — related to ¹LATE]

⁵last adv 1 : at the end ⟨ran *last*⟩ 2 : most lately ⟨saw them *last* at school⟩ 3 : in conclusion ⟨and *last*, I'd like to talk about success⟩

⁶last n : something that is last — **at last** or **at long last** : at the end of a period of time : FINALLY

last·ing \ˈlas-tiŋ\ adj : existing or continuing a long while — **last·ing·ly** adv — **last·ing·ness** n

synonyms LASTING, PERMANENT, DURABLE mean going on for so long as to seem fixed. LASTING suggests an ability to continue endlessly ⟨a book that left a *lasting* impression on me⟩. PERMANENT usually adds the suggestion of being intended to stand or continue without limit ⟨a *permanent* living arrangement⟩. DURABLE suggests the ability to withstand forces that tend to wear down or destroy ⟨*durable* furniture⟩.

last·ly \ˈlast-lē\ adv : in conclusion : in the last place

last straw n : the last of a series (as of events or troubles) that causes one to give up or lose patience

Last Supper n : the supper eaten by Jesus and his disciples on the night of his betrayal

last word n 1 : the final remark in a discussion 2 : the power of final decision 3 : the most modern or fashionable one of its kind ⟨the *last word* in sportswear⟩

¹latch \ˈlach\ vb 1 : to get hold 2 : to attach oneself

²latch n : a catch (as a spring bolt) that holds a door or gate closed

³latch vb : to catch or fasten by means of a latch

latch·key \ˈlach-ˌkē\ n : a key for opening a door latch

¹late \ˈlāt\ adj lat·er; lat·est 1 a : coming or remaining after the due, usual, or proper time ⟨a *late* spring⟩ b : of or relating to an advanced stage in time or development ⟨the *late* Middle Ages⟩; *esp* : far advanced toward the close of the day or night ⟨*late* hours⟩ 2 a : having died or held some position or relationship recently ⟨the *late* president⟩ b : RECENT 1b ⟨a *late* discovery⟩ [Old English *læt* "late, slow" — related to ⁴LAST] — **late·ness** n

²late adv lat·er; lat·est 1 a : after the usual or proper time ⟨came in *late*⟩ b : at or to an advanced point in time ⟨*later* in the day⟩ 2 : not long ago : RECENTLY ⟨a musician *late* of Chicago⟩ — **of late** : during a recent period : LATELY

late·com·er \ˈlāt-ˌkəm-ər\ n : one who arrives late; *also* : one who has recently arrived

la·teen \lə-ˈtēn\ adj : of, relating to, or being a sailing rig used especially along the north coast of Africa having a triangular sail extended by a long pole attached to a short mast

late·ly \ˈlāt-lē\ adv : not long ago

la·tent \ˈlāt-ᵊnt\ adj : present but not visible or active ⟨the car's *latent* defects⟩ ⟨a *latent* infection⟩ — **la·ten·cy** \-ᵊn-sē\ n — **la·tent·ly** adv

¹lat·er·al \ˈlat-ə-rəl, ˈla-trəl\ adj 1 : of or relating to the side : located on, directed toward, or coming from the side 2 : being a part of the boundary of a solid in geometry that is not a base or completely included in a base ⟨a *lateral* edge of a prism⟩ ⟨a *lateral* face⟩ — **lat·er·al·ly** \-ē\ adv

²lateral n : a pass in football thrown to the side or to the rear

late·wood \ˈlāt-ˌwu̇d\ n : SUMMERWOOD

la·tex \ˈlā-ˌteks\ n, pl la·ti·ces \ˈlāt-ə-ˌsēz, ˈlat-\ or la·tex·es 1 : a milky juice produced by the cells of various plants (as milkweeds, poppies, and the rubber tree) 2 : a mixture of water and fine particles of rubber or plastic used especially in paints and adhesives

lath \ˈlath also ˈlath\ n, pl laths or lath : a thin narrow strip of wood used especially as a base for plaster — **lath** vb

lathe \ˈlāth\ n : a machine in which a piece of material is held and turned while being shaped by a tool

¹lath·er \ˈlath-ər\ n 1 a : foam formed when a detergent (as soap) is stirred or shaken in water b : foam from sweating (as on a horse) 2 : a highly nervous or excited state : DITHER ⟨worked himself into a *lather*⟩

²lather vb lath·ered; lath·er·ing \ˈlath-(ə-)riŋ\ 1 : to spread lather over 2 : to form lather or a froth like lather

¹Lat·in \ˈlat-ᵊn\ adj 1 a : of, relating to, or composed in Latin ⟨*Latin* grammar⟩ b : ROMANCE ⟨*Latin* languages⟩ 2 : of or relating to that part of the Catholic Church that formerly used a Latin rite 3 : of, relating to, or characteristic of the countries or peoples of Latin America

²Latin n 1 : the Italic language of ancient Rome 2 : an ancient Roman 3 : a member of one of the peoples speaking Romance languages; *esp* : a person born or living in Latin America

La·ti·na \lə-ˈtē-nə\ n 1 : a girl or woman born or living in Latin America 2 : a girl or woman of Latin-American origin living in the U.S. — **Latina** adj

Latin alphabet n : an alphabet that was used for writing Latin and that has been modified for writing many modern languages (as English)

La·ti·no \la-ˈtē-ˌnō\ n, pl -nos often cap 1 : a person born or living in Latin America 2 : a person of Latin-American origin living in the U.S. — **Latino** adj

lat·ish \ˈlāt-ish\ adj or adv : somewhat late

lat·i·tude \'lat-ə-ˌt(y)üd\ *n* **1 a** : distance north or south from the equator measured in degrees **b** : a region or locality as marked by its latitude **2** : freedom from narrow restrictions ⟨were allowed *latitude* in picking report topics⟩ — **lat·i·tu·di·nal** \ˌlat-ə-'t(y)üd-nəl, -ᵊn-əl\ *adj* — **lat·i·tu·di·nal·ly** \-ē\ *adv*

latitude 1a: parallels of latitude

la·trine \lə-'trēn\ *n* : BATHROOM, TOILET

lat·ter \'lat-ər\ *adj* **1 a** : more recent : LATER **b** : of or relating to the end : FINAL **2** : of, relating to, or being the second of two things referred to

lat·ter·ly \'lat-ər-lē\ *adv* : during a recent period

lat·tice \'lat-əs\ *n* **1 a** : a framework or structure of crossed wood or metal strips **b** : a window, door, or gate having a lattice **2** : an arrangement of points or objects that is evenly spaced over an area or throughout a volume ⟨the *lattice* of atoms in a crystal⟩ — **lat·ticed** \-əst\ *adj*

¹Lat·vi·an \'lat-vē-ən\ *adj* : of, relating to, or characteristic of Latvia, the Latvians, or Latvian

²Latvian *n* **1** : a person born or living in Latvia **2** : the Baltic language of the Latvian people

laud \'lȯd\ *vb* : PRAISE 1

laud·able \'lȯd-ə-bəl\ *adj* : PRAISEWORTHY — **laud·able·ness** \-nəs\ *n* — **laud·ably** \'lȯd-ə-blē\ *adv*

lau·da·num \'lȯd-nəm, -ᵊn-əm\ *n* : a formerly used preparation of opium

lau·da·to·ry \'lȯd-ə-ˌtȯr-ē, -ˌtȯr-\ *adj* : expressing praise

¹laugh \'laf, 'låf\ *vb* **1 a** : to show emotion (as mirth, joy, or scorn) with a chuckle or explosive vocal sound **b** : to become amused **2** : to utter with a laugh ⟨she *laughed*, "What fun!"⟩ — **laugh·er** *n*

²laugh *n* **1** : the act or sound of laughing **2 a** : something funny ⟨that game was a real *laugh*⟩ **b** : something deserving scorn ⟨He's an expert? That's a *laugh*⟩

laugh·able \'laf-ə-bəl, 'låf-\ *adj* : causing laughter or scorn : RIDICULOUS — **laugh·able·ness** *n* — **laugh·ably** \-blē\ *adv*

laughing gas *n* : NITROUS OXIDE

laughing jackass *n* : KOOKABURRA

laugh·ing·ly \'laf-iŋ-lē, 'låf-\ *adv* : with laughter

laugh·ing·stock \'laf-iŋ-ˌstäk, 'låf-\ *n* : a person or thing that is made fun of

laugh·ter \'laf-tər, 'låf-\ *n* : the action or sound of laughing

¹launch \'lȯnch, 'länch\ *vb* **1 a** : to throw or spring forward : HURL ⟨*launch* a spear⟩ **b** : to send off an object especially with force ⟨*launch* a rocket⟩ **c** : to set a ship afloat **2 a** : to put in operation : BEGIN ⟨*launch* an attack⟩ **b** : to give a person a start **c** : to make a start especially energetically [Middle English *launchen* "to launch, hurl," from an early French dialect word *launcher* (same meaning), from Latin *lanceare* "to use a lance"] — **launch·er** *n*

²launch *n* : an act of launching

³launch *n* : a small motorboat that is open or that has the front part of the hull covered [from Spanish or Portuguese *lancha* "a boat used to go to and from a large ship"]

launch·pad \'lȯnch-ˌpad, 'länch-\ *n* : a nonflammable platform from which a rocket can be launched — called also *launching pad*

laun·der \'lȯn-dər, 'län-\ *vb* **laun·dered; laun·der·ing** \-d(ə-)riŋ\ **1** : to wash or wash and iron clothing or household linens **2** : to undergo washing and ironing — **laun·der·er** \-dər-ər\ *n*

Laun·dro·mat \'lȯn-drə-ˌmat, 'län-\ *service mark* — used for a self-service laundry

laun·dry \'lȯn-drē, 'län-\ *n, pl* **-dries** **1** : clothes or linens that have been or are to be laundered **2** : a place where laundering is done [from an obsolete word *launder* (noun) "one who washes clothes," derived from early French *lavandier* (or *lavandiere*) "a man (or woman) who washes clothes," from Latin *lavandus* "needing to be washed," from *lavare* "to wash" — related to LAVATORY, LAVISH, LOTION]

lau·re·ate \'lȯr-ē-ət, 'lär-\ *n* : a person honored for achievement in an art or science; *esp* : POET LAUREATE — **laureate** *adj*

lau·rel \'lȯr-əl, 'lär-\ *n* **1** : an evergreen shrub or tree of southern Europe related to the sassafras and cinnamon with shiny pointed leaves used by the ancient Greeks to crown victors in various contests **2** : a tree or shrub (as a mountain laurel) that resembles the true laurel **3 a** : a crown of laurel **b** : ¹HONOR 1, FAME — usually used in plural

laurel 1

la·va \'läv-ə, 'lav-\ *n* : melted rock coming from a volcano; *also* : such rock that has cooled and hardened

la·va·liere *also* **la·val·liere** \ˌläv-ə-'li(ə)r, ˌlav-\ *n* : an ornament hanging from a chain that is worn around the neck

lav·a·to·ry \'lav-ə-ˌtȯr-ē, -ˌtȯr-\ *n, pl* **-ries** **1** : a basin for washing; *esp* : a small sink with running water and drainpipe **2** : a room with lavatories and usually with toilets **3** : TOILET 2b [Middle English *lavatorie* "basin for washing," from Latin *lavatorium* (same meaning), derived from earlier *lavare* "to wash" — related to LAUNDRY, LAVISH, LOTION]

lave \'lāv\ *vb* **laved; lav·ing** **1 a** : ¹WASH 1 **b** *archaic* : to wash oneself : BATHE **2** : to flow along or against

lav·en·der \'lav-ən-dər\ *n* **1 a** : a Mediterranean mint widely cultivated for its narrow somewhat woolly leaves and stalks of small sweet-smelling pale violet flowers — compare SEA LAVENDER **b** : the dried leaves and flowers of lavender used to perfume clothes and bed linen **2** : a pale purple

¹lav·ish \'lav-ish\ *adj* **1** : spending or giving more than is necessary : EXTRAVAGANT ⟨*lavish* with praise⟩ **2** : spent, produced, or given freely ⟨*lavish* gifts⟩ [Middle English *lavas* "an abundance," probably from early French *lavasse, lavache* "a downpour of rain," derived from Latin *lavare* "to wash" — related to LAUNDRY, LAVATORY, LOTION] — **lav·ish·ly** *adv* — **lav·ish·ness** *n*

²lavish *vb* : to spend or give freely

law \'lȯ\ *n* **1 a** : a rule of conduct or action laid down and enforced by the supreme governing authority (as the legislature) of a community or established by custom **b** : the whole collection of such rules ⟨the *law* of the land⟩ **c** : the control brought about by enforcing rules ⟨forces of *law* and order⟩ **d** : trial in a court to decide what is just and right according to the laws ⟨go to *law*⟩ **e** : an agent or agency for enforcing laws **2** *cap* : the first part of the Jewish scriptures — compare HAGIOGRAPHA, PROPHETS **3** : a basic rule or principle ⟨the *laws* of poetry⟩ **4 a** : the profession of a lawyer **b** : the branch of knowledge that deals with laws and their interpretation and application ⟨study *law*⟩ **5** : a rule or principle stating something that

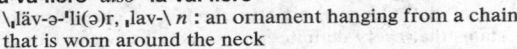

\ə\ abut	\au̇\ out	\i\ tip	\ȯ\ saw	\u̇\ foot
\ər\ further	\ch\ chin	\ī\ life	\ȯi\ coin	\y\ yet
\a\ mat	\e\ pet	\j\ job	\th\ thin	\yü\ few
\ā\ take	\ē\ easy	\ŋ\ sing	\th\ this	\yu̇\ cure
\ä\ cot, cart	\g\ go	\ō\ bone	\ü\ food	\zh\ vision

always works in the same way under the same conditions ⟨the *law* of gravity⟩

law–abid·ing \'lȯ-ə-ˌbīd-iŋ\ *adj* : obedient to the law

law·break·er \'lȯ-ˌbrā-kər\ *n* : a person who breaks the law — **law·break·ing** \-kiŋ\ *adj or n*

law·ful \'lȯ-fəl\ *adj* **1** : permitted by law ⟨*lawful* conduct⟩ **2** : recognized by law : RIGHTFUL ⟨the *lawful* owner⟩ — **law·ful·ly** \-f(ə)-lē\ *adv* — **law·ful·ness** \-fəl-nəs\ *n*

law·giv·er \'lȯ-ˌgiv-ər\ *n* **1** : one who gives a code of laws to a people **2** : LEGISLATOR

law·less \'lȯ-ləs\ *adj* **1** : not based on or regulated by law ⟨the *lawless* society of the frontier⟩ **2** : not controlled by law : UNRULY, DISORDERLY ⟨*lawless* mob⟩ — **law·less·ly** *adv* — **law·less·ness** *n*

law·mak·er \'lȯ-ˌmā-kər\ *n* : LEGISLATOR — **law·mak·ing** \-kiŋ\ *adj or n*

law·man \'lȯ-mən\ *n* : a law-enforcement officer (as a sheriff or marshall)

¹lawn \'lȯn, 'län\ *n* : ground covered with grass that is kept mowed [Middle English *launde* "an open space between woods," from early French *lande* "land overgrown with shrubs"; of Celtic origin]

²lawn *n* : a fine sheer linen or cotton fabric [Middle English *lawn* "a sheer fabric," probably from *Laon,* a town in France where linen was made]

lawn bowling *n* : a game played on a green in which balls are rolled at a small target ball

lawn mower *n* : a machine for cutting grass on lawns

law of definite proportions : a law of chemistry that states that every definite compound always contains the same elements in the same proportions by mass

law of dominance : MENDEL'S LAW 3

law of independent assortment : MENDEL'S LAW 2

law of segregation : MENDEL'S LAW 1

law·ren·ci·um \lȯ-'ren(t)-sē-əm\ *n* : a short-lived radioactive element produced artificially — see ELEMENT table

law·suit \'lȯ-ˌsüt\ *n* : a suit in law : a case before a court

law·yer \'lȯ-yər, 'lȯi-ər\ *n* : a person whose profession is to conduct lawsuits for clients or to advise about legal rights and obligations

lax \'laks\ *adj* **1** : not firm or tight : LOOSE **2** : not strict — **lax·ly** *adv* — **lax·ness** *n*

¹lax·a·tive \'lak-sət-iv\ *adj* : tending to relieve constipation

²laxative *n* : a usually mild drug that helps relieve constipation — compare PURGATIVE

lax·i·ty \'lak-sət-ē\ *n* : the quality or state of being lax

¹lay \'lā\ *vb* **laid** \'lād\; **lay·ing** **1** : to beat or strike down ⟨wheat *laid* flat by the wind and rain⟩ **2 a** : to put or set on or against a surface or in order ⟨*lay* the book on the table⟩ **b** : to place for rest or sleep; *esp* : BURY 1 **3** : to produce and deposit eggs **4** *nonstandard* : ¹LIE **5** : to cause to settle ⟨a shower *laid* the dust⟩; *also* : to make calm : ALLAY ⟨*laid* his fears⟩ **6** : to spread over a surface ⟨*lay* plaster⟩ **7** : to make ready : PREPARE ⟨*lay* plans⟩ ⟨*lay* a table⟩ **8** : to deposit as a wager : BET ⟨I'll *lay* you $10 on that⟩ **9** : IMPOSE 1a ⟨*lay* a tax⟩ **10** : to place or assign in one's scheme of things ⟨*lays* great stress on manners⟩ **11** : to bring to a specified condition ⟨*lay* waste to the land⟩ **12** : to put forward : SUBMIT ⟨*lay* claim to an estate⟩ [Old English *lecgan* "to beat down"] — **lay eyes on** : to catch sight of : SEE — **lay into** : to attack especially verbally

²lay *n* : the way in which a thing lies in relation to something else ⟨*lay* of the land⟩

³lay *past of* ¹LIE

⁴lay *n* **1** : a simple poem that tells a story : BALLAD **2** : MELODY 2, SONG [Middle English *lay* "ballad," from early French *lai* (same meaning)]

⁵lay *adj* : of or relating to laymen or the laity [Middle English *lay* "of the people other than priests and clergy," from early French *lai* (same meaning), from Latin *laicus* "of the people," derived from Greek *laos* "people"]

lay·away \'lā-ə-ˌwā\ *n* : a purchasing agreement by which a seller agrees to hold merchandise on which a deposit has been made until the price is paid in full by the buyer

lay away \ˌlā-ə-'wā\ *vb* : to put aside for future use or delivery

lay down *vb* **1** : ESTABLISH 1, PRESCRIBE ⟨*lay down* standards⟩ **2** : to state or declare forcefully ⟨*lay down* the law⟩

¹lay·er \'lā-ər, 'le(-ə)r\ *n* **1** : one that lays ⟨their hens were poor *layers*⟩ **2** : one thickness or fold over or under another ⟨a *layer* or rock⟩ — **lay·ered** \'lā-ərd, 'le(-ə)rd\ *adj*

²layer *vb* **1** : to separate into layers **2** : to form by adding layers

lay·er·ing \'lā-ə-riŋ, 'le(-ə)-riŋ\ *n* : a method of treating a shoot or branch of a plant to cause rooting (as by bending to the ground and covering with soil) while it is still attached to the parent plant

lay·ette \lā-'et\ *n* : an outfit of clothing and equipment for a newborn infant

lay·man \'lā-mən\ *n* : a person who is not a member of the clergy or a member of a particular profession

lay·off \'lā-ˌȯf\ *n* **1** : the act of laying off an employee or a work force **2** : a period during which there is no activity

lay off \(')lā-'ȯf\ *vb* **1** : to mark or measure off **2** : to stop employing (a person) often temporarily ⟨*lay off* workers⟩ **3** : to stop doing or taking something ⟨*lay off* of that stuff⟩

lay on *vb* : ¹ATTACK 1, BEAT

lay·out \'lā-ˌaut\ *n* **1** : ¹PLAN 1, ARRANGEMENT **2** : something laid out **3** : a set or outfit especially of tools

lay out \(')lā-'aut\ *vb* **1** : ²PLAN 1 ⟨*lay out* a campaign⟩ **2** : to arrange for display or for working on ⟨*lay out* an exhibit⟩ **3** : SPEND 2

lay·over \'lā-ˌō-vər\ *n* : STOPOVER 1

lay over \(')lā-'ō-vər\ *vb* : to make a temporary halt or stop

lay·peo·ple \'lā-ˌpē-pəl\ *n* : LAYPERSONS

lay·per·son \'lā-ˌpərs-³n\ *n* : a member of the laity

lay·up \'lā-ˌəp\ *n* : a basketball shot made from near the basket usually by bouncing the ball off the backboard

lay up *vb* **1** : to store up **2** : to disable or confine with illness or injury ⟨a knee injury *laid* her *up* for a week⟩ **3** : to take out of active service

la·zy \'lā-zē\ *adj* **la·zi·er; -est 1** : not willing to act or work : INDOLENT **2** : moving slowly : SLUGGISH ⟨a *lazy* stream⟩ — **la·zi·ly** \-zə-lē\ *adv* — **la·zi·ness** \-zē-nəs\ *n*

la·zy·bones \-ˌbōnz\ *n* : a lazy person

lazy eye *n* : AMBLYOPIA; *also* : an eye affected with amblyopia

la·zy·ish \'lā-zē-ish\ *adj* : somewhat lazy

LCD \ˌel-ˌsē-'dē\ *n* : a type of electronic display screen [*l*iquid *c*rystal *d*isplay]

lea \'lē, 'lā\ *n* : MEADOW, PASTURE

leach \'lēch\ *vb* : to pass a liquid through to carry off the soluble components; *also* : to dissolve out by such means ⟨*leach* minerals from rocks⟩

¹lead \'lēd\ *vb* **led** \'led\; **lead·ing** \'lēd-iŋ\ **1 a** : to guide especially by going in advance : CONDUCT **b** : to direct on a course or in a direction **c** : to serve as a channel for **d** : to lie, go, or open in a specified direction ⟨the path *leads* uphill⟩ ⟨study *leading* to a degree⟩ **2** : to go through : LIVE ⟨*lead* a quiet life⟩ **3 a** : to direct the activity of : MANAGE, DIRECT ⟨*lead* an orchestra⟩ ⟨*lead* a campaign⟩ **b** : to be first or best in ⟨*lead* the league⟩; *also* : BEGIN 1, OPEN **c** : to be ahead of ⟨*led* their opponents by 20 points at the end of the third quarter⟩ [Old English *lǣdan* "to lead"]

²lead *n* **1 a** : position at the front : LEADERSHIP **b** : EXAMPLE 1, PRECEDENT **c** : an amount or distance ahead **2** : INDICATION 2, CLUE **3** : a principal role in a play; *also* : one who plays such a role **4** : a beginning section of a news story; *also* : a news story of chief importance **5** : the first in a series; *also* : the right to be first **6** : an insulated electrical conductor **7** : a position taken by a base runner off a base toward the next

³lead *adj* : acting or serving as a lead or leader ⟨*lead* guitarist⟩

⁴lead \'led\ *n* **1 a** : a soft bluish white heavy metallic element that is found mostly in combination with other elements, is easily shaped, and is used especially in pipes, cable coverings, batteries, solder, and radiation shields — see ELEMENT table **2 a** : a mass of lead used on a line for finding the depth of water (as in the ocean) **b** *pl* : lead framing for glass (as in windows) **3** : a thin stick of marking substance (as graphite) in or for a pencil **4** : bullets in quantity **5** : TETRAETHYL LEAD [Old English *lēad* "the metal lead"]

⁵lead \'led\ *vb* **lead·ed; lead·ing 1** : to cover, line, or weight with lead **2** : to fix (window glass) in position with lead **3** : to treat or mix with lead or a lead compound ⟨*leaded* gasoline⟩

lead·en \'led-³n\ *adj* **1 a** : made of lead **b** : of the color of lead : dull gray **2** : low in quality : POOR **3 a** : heavy and difficult to move ⟨*leaden* feet⟩ **b** : lacking spirit : DULL

lead·er \'lēd-ər\ *n* **1** : something that leads: as **a** : a short line for attaching the end of a fishing line to a lure or hook **b** : a pipe for conducting fluid **2** : a person that leads: as **a** : ¹GUIDE 1a **b** : COMMANDER 1 **c** : CONDUCTOR 2 **d** : a person in charge or in control : BOSS, CHIEF **3** : a horse placed in front of the other horses of a team — **lead·er·less** \-ləs\ *adj* — **lead·er·ship** \-,ship\ *n*

lead-in \'lēd-,in\ *n* : something (as a television show or segment) that leads into something else — **lead-in** *adj*

lead·ing \'lēd-iŋ\ *adj* **1** : coming or ranking first or among the first : FOREMOST **2** : exercising leadership **3** : providing direction or guidance ⟨a *leading* question⟩

leading lady *n* : an actress who plays the leading female role in a play or movie

leading light *n* : a prominent and influential member (as of a field of study or political movement)

leading man *n* : an actor who plays the leading male role in a play or movie

leading tone *n* : the seventh musical degree of a major or minor scale — called also *subtonic*

lead-off \'lēd-,óf\ *n* **1** : a beginning action **2** : one that begins something — **leadoff** *adj*

lead on *vb* : to persuade to take up or continue in a course of action or belief when unwise or mistaken ⟨*led on* by the promise of wealth⟩

lead pencil \'led-\ *n* : a pencil using graphite as the marking material

lead poisoning *n* : an abnormal condition that is caused by absorption of lead into the body and results in various bodily symptoms (as tiredness, nausea, loss of appetite, and paralysis or weakness of the muscles)

lead up \(')lēd-'əp\ *vb* : to make a gradual approach to a topic

¹leaf \'lēf\ *n, pl* **leaves** \'lēvz\ **1 a** : one of the green usually flat parts that grow from a stem or twig of a plant and that function mainly in making food by photosynthesis **b** : FOLIAGE ⟨trees in full *leaf*⟩ **2 a** : a part of a book or folded sheet containing a page on each side **b** : a part (as of window shutters) that slides or is hinged **c** : the movable or additional part of a table top **d** : a thin sheet (as of metal) — **leaf·less** \'lē-fləs\ *adj* — **leaf·like** \'lē-,flīk\ *adj*

²leaf *vb* **1** : to produce leaves **2** : to turn the pages of a book

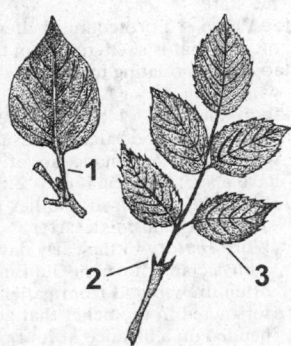

¹leaf 1a: *1* petiole, *2* stipule, *3* leaflet

leaf·age \'lē-fij\ *n* : FOLIAGE

leaf bud *n* : a bud that develops into a leafy shoot and does not produce flowers

leaf·hop·per \'lēf-,häp-ər\ *n* : any of numerous small leaping insects that are related to the cicadas and aphids and suck the juices of plants

leaf·let \'lē-flət\ *n* **1 a** : one of the divisions of a compound leaf — see LEAF illustration **b** : a small or young leaf **2** : a usually folded printed sheet intended for free distribution

leaf miner *n* : any of various small insects that as larvae burrow in and eat the tissue of leaves

leaf mold *n* : a compost or layer composed chiefly of decayed leaves

leaf·stalk \'lēf-,stók\ *n* : PETIOLE

leafy \'lē-fē\ *adj* **leaf·i·er; -est 1 a** : having or full of leaves ⟨*leafy* woodlands⟩ **b** : consisting mostly of leaves ⟨*leafy* vegetables⟩ **2** : resembling a leaf

¹league \'lēg\ *n* : any of various units of distance from about 2.4 to 4.6 statute miles (3.9 to 7.4 kilometers)

²league *n* **1** : an association or alliance of nations **2** : an association of persons or groups united for common interests or goals ⟨a softball *league*⟩ — **league** *vb*

leagu·er \'lē-gər\ *n* : a member of a league

¹leak \'lēk\ *vb* **1** : to enter or escape or permit to enter or escape accidentally or by mistake ⟨fumes *leaked* in⟩ ⟨the secret *leaked* out⟩ **2** : to give out information secretly ⟨*leaked* the story to the press⟩

²leak *n* **1** : something and especially a crack or hole that lets something in or out usually accidentally **2** : LEAKAGE

leak·age \'lē-kij\ *n* **1 a** : the act, process, or an instance of leaking **b** : loss of electricity due especially to faulty insulation **2** : something or the amount that is lost in a leak

leaky \'lē-kē\ *adj* **leak·i·er; -est** : permitting fluid to leak in or out ⟨a *leaky* boat⟩ — **leak·i·ness** *n*

¹lean \'lēn\ *vb* **leaned** \'lēnd, *chiefly British* 'lent\; **lean·ing** \'lē-niŋ\ **1 a** : to slant or cause to slant or bend from an upright position ⟨the tree *leans* to one side⟩ ⟨*lean* a ladder against a wall⟩ **b** : to cast one's weight to one side for support ⟨*lean* on me⟩ **2** : to depend for support ⟨*lean* on one's family in a crisis⟩ **3** : to tend in opinion, taste, or desire ⟨*lean* toward simplicity⟩ [Old English *hleonian* "to slant to one side"]

²lean *n* : the act or an instance of leaning

³lean *adj* **1 a** : having little body fat ⟨*lean* cattle⟩ **b** : containing little or no fat ⟨*lean* meat⟩ **2** : lacking richness or fullness ⟨a *lean* fuel-air mixture⟩ [Old English *hlǣne* "having very little body flesh"] — **lean·ness** \'lēn-nəs\ *n*

synonyms LEAN, THIN, SKINNY mean not having a great amount of flesh. LEAN suggests a lack of unnecessary flesh and may also suggest the tough muscular frame of an athlete ⟨the hard *lean* body of a runner⟩. THIN applies to a person having not much flesh or fat and often having an amount less than is desirable for good health ⟨a *thin* and sickly child⟩. SKINNY suggests a bony, noticeably thin appearance that may indicate a lack of proper nourishment ⟨*skinny* and malnourished⟩.

⁴lean *n* : the part of meat that consists mainly of fat-free muscle

lean·ing \'lē-niŋ\ *n* : TENDENCY 2, INCLINATION

¹lean-to \'lēn-,tü\ *n, pl* **lean-tos 1** : a wing of a building having a lean-to roof **2** : a rough shed or shelter having a lean-to roof

²lean-to *adj* : having only one slope or pitch ⟨*lean-to* roof⟩

¹leap \'lēp\ *vb* **leapt** \'lēpt *also* 'lept\ *or* **leaped; leap·ing**

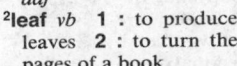

\ə\ abut	\au̇\ out	\i\ tip	\ȯ\ saw	\u̇\ foot
\ər\ further	\ch\ chin	\ī\ life	\ȯi\ coin	\y\ yet
\a\ mat	\e\ pet	\j\ job	\th\ thin	\yü\ few
\ā\ take	\ē\ easy	\ŋ\ sing	\th\ this	\yu̇\ cure
\ä\ cot, cart	\g\ go	\ō\ bone	\ü\ food	\zh\ vision

\\'lē-piŋ\ **1** : to spring or cause to spring free from or as if from the ground : JUMP ⟨*leap* over a fence⟩ **2 a** : to pass suddenly from one state or topic to another **b** : to act hastily ⟨I'd *leap* at the chance⟩ — **leap·er** \\'lē-pər\ *n*

²**leap** *n* **1 a** : an act of leaping : SPRING, BOUND **b** : a place leaped over or from **c** : the distance covered by a leap **2** : a sudden change of state — **by leaps and bounds** : very rapidly

leap·frog \\'lēp-ˌfróg, -ˌfräg\ *n* : a game in which the first player bends down and another leaps over

leap year *n* : a year in the Gregorian calendar containing 366 days with February 29 as the extra day

learn \\'lərn\ *vb* **learned** \\'lərnd, 'lərnt\; **learn·ing** **1** : to gain knowledge or understanding of or skill in by study, instruction, or experience **2** : MEMORIZE ⟨*learn* the lines of a play⟩ **3 a** : to come to be able to ⟨*learn* to swim⟩ **b** : to come to realize **4** *substandard* : to cause to learn : TEACH **5** : FIND OUT, ASCERTAIN **6** : to acquire knowledge ⟨never too late to *learn*⟩ — **learn·able** \\'lər-nə-bəl\ *adj* — **learn·er** *n*

learn·ed \\'lər-nəd\ *adj* : having or showing learning : SCHOLARLY — **learn·ed·ly** *adv* — **learn·ed·ness** *n*

learn·ing \\'lər-niŋ\ *n* **1** : the act or experience of one that learns **2** : knowledge or skill acquired by instruction or study **synonyms** see KNOWLEDGE

learning disability *n* : any of various conditions (as attention deficit disorder and dyslexia) that interfere with a person's ability to learn basic academic skills — **learning disabled** *adj*

¹**lease** \\'lēs\ *n* **1** : an agreement to hand over real estate for a period of time usually for a specified rent; *also* : the act of leasing real estate **2** : property that is leased

²**lease** *vb* **leased; leas·ing** **1** : to grant by lease : LET **2** : to hold under a lease

leash \\'lēsh\ *n* : a line for leading or controlling an animal — **leash** *vb*

¹**least** \\'lēst\ *adj* **1** : lowest in importance or position **2** : smallest in size or degree

²**least** *n* : one that is least : something of the lowest possible value or importance — **at least** **1** : at the minimum ⟨*at least* once a week⟩ **2** : in any case ⟨*at least* you have a choice⟩

³**least** *adv* : in the smallest or lowest degree

least common denominator *n* : the least common multiple of the denominators of two or more fractions — called also *lowest common denominator*

least common multiple *n* : the smallest number that is a multiple of each of two or more numbers

least·wise \\'lēs-ˌtwīz\ *adv* : at least ⟨*leastwise*, that's what I heard⟩

leath·er \\'leth-ər\ *n* **1** : animal skin prepared for use **2** : something entirely or partly made of leather

leath·er·back \\'leth-ər-ˌbak\ *n* : the largest existing sea turtle with a shell composed of small bones embedded in a thick leathery skin

leath·ern \\'leth-ərn\ *adj* : made of or resembling leather

leath·er·neck \\'leth-ər-ˌnek\ *n* : a member of the U.S. Marine Corps

leath·ery \\'leth-(ə-)rē\ *adj* : resembling leather in appearance or quality : TOUGH ⟨a *leathery* face⟩ ⟨*leathery* leaves⟩

¹**leave** \\'lēv\ *vb* **left** \\'left\; **leav·ing** **1 a** : to give by will : BEQUEATH ⟨*left* a fortune to his daughter⟩ **b** : to have remaining after one's death ⟨*leaves* a widow and two children⟩ **c** : to cause to remain as a trace or aftereffect ⟨oil *leaves* a stain⟩; *also* : to cause to remain behind ⟨*leave* your money at home⟩ **2 a** : to cause or allow to be or remain in a specified condition ⟨*leave* the door open⟩ **b** : to fail to include or take along ⟨*left* my notes at home⟩ ⟨the movie *leaves* a lot out⟩ **c** : to have as a remainder ⟨taking 4 from 7 *leaves* 3⟩ **d** : to permit to be or remain subject to another's action or control ⟨just *leave* everything to me⟩ **e** : ²LET 3 **f** : to cause or allow to be or re-

main available ⟨*leave* room for more⟩ **3 a** : to go away from : DEPART ⟨*leave* the room⟩ **b** : to terminate association with : withdraw from ⟨*left* school before graduation⟩ **4** : to put, deposit, or deliver especially before or in the process of departing ⟨*left* a package on your doorstep⟩ [Old English *lǣfan* "to give to one's heirs"] — **leave alone** : to refrain from bothering, disturbing, or using ⟨*leave* him *alone*⟩

²**leave** *n* **1 a** : PERMISSION **2 b** : authorized absence from duty or employment **2** : an act of leaving [Old English *lēaf* "permission"]

³**leave** *vb* **leaved; leav·ing** : ²LEAF 1 [Middle English *leven* "to produce leaves," from *leef* "a leaf"]

leaved \\'lēvd\ *adj* : having leaves ⟨broad-*leaved*⟩

¹**leav·en** \\'lev-ən\ *n* **1 a** : a substance (as yeast) used to produce a gaseous fermentation (as in dough) **b** : a material (as baking powder) used to produce a gas that makes dough or batter rise and become light **2** : something that changes slightly or lightens a mass or whole

²**leaven** *vb* **leav·ened; leav·en·ing** \\'lev-(ə-)niŋ\ **1** : to raise (dough) with a leaven **2** : to mix or spread throughout with leaven

leavening *n* : ¹LEAVEN 1

leave off *vb* : ¹STOP 7a, CEASE

leaves *plural of* LEAF

leave–tak·ing \\'lēv-ˌtā-kiŋ\ *n* : an act of going away : FAREWELL

leav·ings \\'lē-viŋz\ *n pl* : things remaining

lec·i·thin \\'les-ə-thən\ *n* : any of several waxy phosphorus-containing substances that are common in animals and plants and are used especially in foods (as mayonnaise), medicine, and industrial processes

lec·tern \\'lek-tərn\ *n* : a desk to read from while standing; *esp* : one from which scripture lessons are read in a church service

¹**lec·ture** \\'lek-chər, -shər\ *n* **1** : a talk given before an audience or class especially for instruction **2** : ¹REPRIMAND, SCOLDING

²**lecture** *vb* **lec·tured; lec·tur·ing** \\'lek-chə-riŋ, 'lek-shriŋ\ **1** : to give a lecture or a series of lectures **2** : to instruct by lectures **3** : ²REPRIMAND, SCOLD — **lec·tur·er** \-chər-ər, -shrər\ *n*

led *past and past participle of* LEAD

LED \ˌel-ˌē-'dē\ *n* : an electronic device that emits light when a voltage is applied to it [*light-emitting diode*]

ledge \\'lej\ *n* **1** : a projecting ridge or raised edge along a surface **2** : an underwater ridge or reef especially near the shore **3** : a narrow flat surface or shelf; *esp* : one that sticks out from a wall of rock

led·ger \\'lej-ər\ *n* : a book in which accounts are kept in final form

ledger line *n* : a short line added above or below a musical staff for notes that are too high or too low to be placed on the staff

¹**lee** \\'lē\ *n* **1** : protecting shelter **2** : the side (as of a ship) or area that is sheltered from the wind

²**lee** *adj* : of, relating to, or being the side sheltered from the wind

leech \\'lēch\ *n* **1** : any of numerous flesh-eating or bloodsucking usually flattened worms that are made up of segments and have a sucker at each end **2** : a person who clings like a leech to another person for advantage or gain : PARASITE

Word History In the early days of medicine, a physician, known in Old English as a *lǣce*, often drew blood from patients. These doctors acted in the belief that good health depended on a balance of four controlling fluids in the body. These four fluids were called *humors*, and one of them was blood. In those days physicians believed that a per-

leech 1

son became ill if there was too much blood or too little of any of the other humors in the body. Thus they used a controlled bleeding of the patient, or *bloodletting* as it was called, to balance the humors. An easy way to do this was to attach bloodsucking worms to the body. These worms are common in all parts of the world and especially in marshes and swamps. Today we call these sucking worms *leeches,* taking the name from those ancient doctors who used them so often. [Old English *lǣce* "doctor, physician"]

leek \'lēk\ *n* : a garden herb closely related to the onion and grown for its mildly sharp-tasting leaves and thick stalk

leer \'li(ə)r\ *vb* : to give a nasty or sexually suggestive look — **leer** *n*

leery \'li(ə)r-ē\ *adj* : SUSPICIOUS 2, WARY ⟨*leery* of strangers⟩

lees \'lēz\ *n pl* : the settlings of liquor (as wine) during fermentation and aging : DREGS

¹lee·ward \'lē-wərd, *especially among sailors* 'lü-ərd\ *n* : the lee side

²leeward *adj* : located away from the wind : DOWNWIND ⟨the *leeward* side of the ship⟩

lee·way \'lē-ˌwā\ *n* **1** : sideways movement of a ship when under way **2** : an extra amount (as of room or time) that allows some freedom or variation

¹left \'left\ *adj* **1** : of, relating to, or being the side of the body in which the heart is mostly located ⟨the *left* leg⟩ **2** : located nearer to the left side of the body than to the right ⟨the *left* arm of a chair⟩ — **left** *adv*

²left *n* **1** : the left side or the part on the left side **2** : the members of a European legislative body sitting to the left of the presiding officer and holding more radical views than other members **3** *cap* : political liberals or radicals; *also* : their beliefs

³left *past and past participle of* LEAVE

left field *n* **1** : the part of the baseball outfield to the left looking out from home plate **2** : the position of the player defending left field — **left fielder** *n*

left–hand \ˌleft-ˌhand\ *adj* **1** : located on the left **2 a** : LEFT-HANDED 1 **b** : LEFT-HANDED 2

left–hand·ed \'left-'han-dəd\ *adj* **1** : using the left hand more easily than the right **2** : relating to, designed for, or done with the left hand **3** : BACKHANDED 2 **4** : going in or involving a counterclockwise direction ⟨a *left-handed* screw⟩ — **left–handed** *adv* — **left–hand·ed·ly** *adv* — **left–hand·ed·ness** *n* — **left–hand·er** \-'han-dər\ *n*

left·ist \'lef-təst\ *n* : a liberal or radical in politics — **leftist** *adj*

left·over \'lef-ˌtō-vər\ *n* : something remaining; *esp* : food left over from one meal and served at another — usually used in plural — **leftover** *adj*

left·ward \'lef-twərd\ *adv or adj* : toward or on the left

¹leg \'leg\ *n* **1** : a limb of an animal used especially for supporting the body and for walking and running; *also* : the part of a leg of a vertebrate animal between the knee and the foot **2** : something resembling an animal leg in shape or use ⟨*legs* of a table⟩ **3** : the part of an article of clothing that covers the leg **4** : a side of a right triangle that is not the hypotenuse; *also* : a side of an isosceles triangle that is not the base **5 a** : a portion of a trip : STAGE **b** : one section of a relay race

²leg *vb* **legged; leg·ging** : to use the legs in walking or especially in running

leg·a·cy \'leg-ə-sē\ *n, pl* **-cies** : something left to a person by or as if by will

le·gal \'lē-gəl\ *adj* **1** : of or relating to law or lawyers **2** : based on law ⟨a *legal* right⟩ **3** : permitted by law or established rules — **le·gal·ly** \-gə-lē\ *adv*

legal holiday *n* : a holiday established by legal authority

le·gal·i·ty \li-'gal-ət-ē\ *n, pl* **-ties 1** : the quality or state of

being legal : LAWFULNESS **2** : something that is required by law

le·gal·ize \'lē-gə-ˌlīz\ *vb* **-ized; -iz·ing** : to make legal ⟨wanted to *legalize* gambling in their city⟩ — **le·gal·i·za·tion** \ˌlē-gə-lə-'zā-shən\ *n*

legal tender *n* : money that the law authorizes for paying debts

le·gate \'leg-ət\ *n* : an official representative (as an ambassador or envoy)

leg·a·tee \ˌleg-ə-'tē\ *n* : a person to whom a legacy is left

le·ga·tion \li-'gā-shən\ *n* **1** : a group of representatives sent to a foreign country; *esp* : one headed by a minister **2** : the official residence and office of such a group

le·ga·to \li-'gät-ō\ *adv or adj* : in a manner that is smooth and connected — used as a direction in music

leg·end \'lej-ənd\ *n* **1** : a story coming down from the past whose truth is popularly accepted but cannot be checked **2 a** : writing or a title on an object **b** : CAPTION 2 **c** : an explanatory list of the symbols on a map or chart

Word History The Latin verb *legere* originally meant "to gather." In time the verb came to mean "to gather with the eye, to see," and that led to the sense "to read." From this verb came the Latin noun *legenda,* used in the Middle Ages to mean "a thing to be read." *Legenda* was used to refer in particular to stories about the lives of saints. Many such stories were written in the Middle Ages, and they often included fiction along with fact. Because of that, when *legenda* was borrowed into English as *legend,* it came to mean "a story coming down from the past which may or may not be entirely true." [Middle English *legende* "a legend," derived from Latin *legenda* "something to be read," derived from earlier *legere* "to gather, read"]

leg·end·ary \'lej-ən-ˌder-ē\ *adj* **1** : of or resembling a legend **2** : WELL-KNOWN, FAMOUS

leg·er·de·main \ˌlej-ərd-ə-'mān\ *n* **1** : SLEIGHT OF HAND **2** : a display of trickery

legged \'leg-əd, 'legd\ *adj* : having legs especially of a certain kind or number ⟨four-*legged*⟩

leg·ging *or* **leg·gin** \'leg-ən, 'leg-iŋ\ *n* : a covering for the leg

leg·gy \'leg-ē\ *adj* **1** : having unusually long legs **2** : having long and attractive legs **3** : SPINDLY ⟨a *leggy* plant⟩

leg·horn \'leg-ˌ(h)ȯ(ə)rn, 'leg-ərn\ *n* **1 a** : a fine plaited straw made from an Italian wheat **b** : a hat of this straw **2** : any of a Mediterranean breed of small hardy domestic chickens noted for their ability to produce many white eggs

leg·i·ble \'lej-ə-bəl\ *adj* : capable of being read : PLAIN ⟨*legible* handwriting⟩ — **leg·i·bil·i·ty** \ˌlej-ə-'bil-ət-ē\ *n* — **leg·i·bly** \'lej-ə-blē\ *adv*

leghorn 2

le·gion \'lē-jən\ *n* **1** : the chief unit of the Roman army consisting of 3000 to 6000 foot soldiers with cavalry **2** : ARMY 1a **3** : a very large number : MULTITUDE

¹le·gion·ary \'lē-jə-ˌner-ē\ *adj* : of, relating to, or forming a legion

²legionary *n, pl* **-ar·ies** : LEGIONNAIRE

\ə\ **abut**	\au̇\ **out**	\i\ **tip**	\ȯ\ **saw**	\u̇\ **foot**
\ər\ **further**	\ch\ **chin**	\ī\ **life**	\ȯi\ **coin**	\y\ **yet**
\a\ **mat**	\e\ **pet**	\j\ **job**	\th\ **thin**	\yü\ **few**
\ā\ **take**	\ē\ **easy**	\ŋ\ **sing**	\th\ **this**	\yu̇\ **cure**
\ä\ **cot, cart**	\g\ **go**	\ō\ **bone**	\ü\ **food**	\zh\ **vision**

le·gion·naire \ˌlē-jə-'na(ə)r, -'ne(ə)r\ *n* : a member of a legion

leg·is·late \'lej-ə-ˌslāt\ *vb* **-lat·ed; -lat·ing** **1** : to make laws ⟨the constitutional power to *legislate*⟩ **2** : to cause, establish, or regulate by legislation ⟨*legislating* foreign trade⟩

leg·is·la·tion \ˌlej-ə-'slā-shən\ *n* **1** : the action of making laws **2** : the laws made by a legislator or legislative body

leg·is·la·tive \'lej-ə-ˌslāt-iv\ *adj* **1** : having the power of legislating ⟨the *legislative* branch⟩ **2** : of or relating to a legislature or legislation — **leg·is·la·tive·ly** *adv*

leg·is·la·tor \'lej-ə-ˌslā-ˌtó(ə)r, -ˌslāt-ər\ *n* : a person who makes laws; *esp* : a member of a legislature

leg·is·la·ture \'lej-ə-ˌslā-chər\ *n* : an organized body of persons having the authority to make laws

le·git·i·ma·cy \li-'jit-ə-mə-sē\ *n* : the quality or state of being legitimate

¹le·git·i·mate \li-'jit-ə-mət\ *adj* **1** : born of parents who are married ⟨*legitimate* children⟩ **2** : LAWFUL ⟨a *legitimate* claim⟩ **3** : being in keeping with what is right or with standards ⟨a *legitimate* excuse⟩ — **le·git·i·mate·ly** *adv*

²le·git·i·mate \li-'jit-ə-ˌmāt\ *vb* **-mat·ed; -mat·ing** : to make lawful or legal — **le·git·i·ma·tion** \-ˌjit-ə-'mā-shən\ *n*

le·git·i·mize \li-'jit-ə-ˌmīz\ *vb* **-mized; -miz·ing** : ²LEGITI-MATE

leg·less \'leg-ləs\ *adj* : having no legs

leg·man \'leg-ˌman\ *n* **1** : a reporter assigned usually to gather information **2** : an assistant who gathers information and runs errands

leg·ume \'leg-ˌyüm, li-'gyüm\ *n* **1 a** : any of a large family of herbs, shrubs, and trees that have fruits which are dry single-celled pods that split into two pieces when ripe, that bear nodules on the roots that contain nitrogen-fixing bacteria, and that include important food plants (as peas, beans, or clovers) **b** : the part (as seeds or pods) of a legume used as food **2** : the pod of a legume

le·gu·mi·nous \li-'gyü-mə-nəs, le-\ *adj* : of, relating to, or consisting of plants that are legumes

leg·work \'leg-ˌwərk\ *n* : the work involved in gathering information

lei \'lā, 'la-ē\ *n* : a wreath or necklace usually of flowers [Hawaiian]

legume 2

lei·sure \'lēzh-ər, 'lezh-, 'lāzh-\ *n* **1** : freedom from work or duties **2** : ¹EASE 1 **3** : time at one's command : CONVENIENCE ⟨has the *leisure* to pursue a hobby⟩ — **leisure** *adj*

lei·sure·ly \'lēzh-ər-lē, 'lezh-, 'lāzh-\ *adj* : characterized by leisure : UNHURRIED ⟨a *leisurely* pace⟩ — **lei·sure·li·ness** *n* — **leisurely** *adv*

lek \'lek\ *n* : an area where animals (as the prairie chicken) assemble and carry on display and courtship behavior; *also* : a group of animals assembled in such an area

lem·ming \'lem-iŋ\ *n* : any of several small short-tailed northern rodents with furry feet and small ears; *esp* : a European rodent that takes part in periodic mass migrations which often continue into the sea where large numbers are drowned

lem·on \'lem-ən\ *n* **1 a** : a yellow oblong fruit with sour juice and a thick rind from which a fragrant oil is obtained **b** : a small thorny citrus tree that bears lemons **2** : the color of ripe lemons **3** : one that turns out to be unsatisfactory or disappointing ⟨our new car is a *lemon*⟩ — **lemon** *adj*

lem·on·ade \ˌlem-ə-'nād\ *n* : a drink made of lemon juice, sugar, and water

lemon shark *n* : a dangerous medium-sized shark of warm waters that is yellowish brown to gray above with yellow or greenish sides

le·mur \'lē-mər\ *n* : any of various tree-dwelling primates that are active at night, usually have large eyes, very soft woolly fur, and a long furry tail and were formerly widespread but are now found mainly in Madagascar

lemur

Word History The large island of Madagascar off the southeast coast of Africa is home to many unusual animals. Some of these animals live in trees and are active at night. Their big eyes give them an eerie look, especially when the animals are moving through the trees at night. When 18th century scientists saw these mammals for the first time, they thought the creatures looked like ghosts. They named the animals *lemurs*. This name comes from the Latin word *lemures*, meaning "ghosts." In Roman legend *lemures* were the spirits of people left unburied, who returned by night from the dead to haunt the living. [from Latin *lemures* (plural) "ghosts"]

lend \'lend\ *vb* **lent** \'lent\; **lend·ing** **1 a** : to give to another for temporary use with the understanding that it or a like thing will be returned ⟨*lend* a book⟩ **b** : to let out (money) for temporary use with the understanding that it will be paid back with interest ⟨banks and other *lending* institutions⟩ **2** : to give usually for a time ⟨*lend* assistance⟩ **3** : to have the quality or nature that makes suitable ⟨a voice that *lends* itself to opera⟩ — **lend·er** *n*

length \'leŋ(k)th, 'len(t)th\ *n* **1 a** : the measured distance from one end to the other of the longer or longest side of an object; *also* : any measured distance **b** : the quality or state of being long **2 a** : the amount of time something takes ⟨the *length* of a visit⟩ **b** : the sound of a vowel or syllable as it is affected by the time needed to pronounce it **3** : a piece of something long ⟨a *length* of pipe⟩ **4** : the distance from top to bottom of an article of clothing — **at length 1** : very fully ⟨praised her *at length*⟩ **2** : at the end : FINALLY ⟨*at length* we decided to join⟩

length·en \'leŋ(k)-thən, 'len(t)-\ *vb* **length·ened; length·en·ing** \'leŋ(k)th-(ə-)niŋ, 'len(t)th-\ : to make or become longer — **length·en·er** \'leŋ(k)th-(ə-)nər, 'len(t)th-\ *n*

length·ways \'leŋ(k)th-ˌwāz, 'len(t)th-\ *adv* : in the direction of the length

length·wise \'leŋ(k)th-ˌwīz, 'len(t)th-\ *adv or adj* : in the direction of the length ⟨fold the paper *lengthwise*⟩ ⟨a *lengthwise* crease⟩

lengthy \'leŋ(k)-thē, 'len(t)-\ *adj* **length·i·er; -est** : very long — **length·i·ly** \-thə-lē\ *adv* — **length·i·ness** \-thē-nəs\ *n*

le·nience \'lē-nyən(t)s, -nē-ən(t)s\ *n* : LENIENCY

le·nien·cy \'lē-nē-ən-sē, -nyən-sē\ *n* : the quality or state of being lenient **synonyms** see MERCY

le·nient \'lē-nē-ənt, -nyənt\ *adj* : being kind and patient — **le·nient·ly** *adv*

len·i·ty \'len-ət-ē\ *n* : LENIENCY

lens \'lenz\ *n* **1 a** : a clear curved piece of material (as glass) used to bend rays of light to form an image especially to correct vision or magnify an object **b** : a piece of glass or plastic used (as in protective goggles or sunglasses) to protect the eye **2** : a clear part of the eye that focuses rays of light so as to form an image (as upon the retina)

Lent \'lent\ *n* : a period of fasting and regret for one's sins that is observed on the 40 weekdays from Ash Wednesday to Easter by many churches — **Lent·en** \'lent-ᵊn\ *adj*

len·ti·cel \'lent-ə-ˌsel\ *n* : a pore in a stem of a woody plant through which gases are exchanged between the atmosphere and the stem tissues

len·til \'lent-ᵊl\ *n* : a Eurasian plant of the legume family widely grown for its flattened edible seeds and leafy stalks used as food for cattle; *also* : its seed

len·to \'len-ˌtō\ *adv or adj* : in a slow manner — used as a direction in music

Leo \'lē-ō\ *n* **1** : a group of stars between Cancer and Virgo usually pictured as a lion **2 a** : the fifth sign of the zodiac — see ZODIAC table **b** : a person whose sign of the zodiac is Leo

le·o·nine \'lē-ə-ˌnīn\ *adj* : of, relating to, or resembling a lion

leop·ard \'lep-ərd\ *n* : a large strong cat of southern Asia and Africa that has a brownish buff coat with black spots arranged in broken rings — called also *panther*

leopard

leop·ard·ess \'lep-ərd-əs\ *n* : a female leopard

leopard frog *n* : a common spotted frog of the eastern U.S.

le·o·tard \'lē-ə-ˌtärd\ *n* : a tight one-piece garment worn especially by dancers, gymnasts, and acrobats

lep·er \'lep-ər\ *n* : a person who has leprosy

lep·i·dop·tera \ˌlep-ə-'däp-tə-rə\ *n pl* : insects that are lepidopterans

lep·i·dop·ter·an \ˌlep-ə-'däp-tə-rən\ *n* : any of a large order of insects that include the butterflies, moths, and skippers and that as adults have four wings usually covered with minute overlapping often brightly colored scales and as larvae are caterpillars — **lepidopteran** *adj* — **lep·i·dop·ter·ous** \-tə-rəs\ *adj*

lep·re·chaun \'lep-rə-ˌkän, -ˌkȯn\ *n* : a mischievous elf of Irish folklore that some believe will reveal where treasure is hidden if caught

lep·ro·sy \'lep-rə-sē\ *n* : a disease caused by a bacterium and marked by slow-growing spreading swellings accompanied by loss of sensation, wasting away of muscles, and by deformities — called also *Hansen's disease*

lep·rous \'lep-rəs\ *adj* : infected with, relating to, or resembling leprosy

les·bi·an \'lez-bē-ən\ *n* : a woman who is a homosexual — **lesbian** *adj* — **les·bi·an·ism** \-bē-ə-ˌniz-əm\ *n*

le·sion \'lē-zhən\ *n* : a change in the structure of a bodily organ or part due to injury or disease; *esp* : an injured or diseased spot or area clearly marked off from healthy tissue around it

les·pe·de·za \ˌles-pə-'dē-zə\ *n* : any of a genus of plants of the legume family including some widely used to improve soil and for hay

¹less \'les\ *adj* **1** : being a smaller number : FEWER ⟨8 times 2 is *less* than 6 times 3⟩ ⟨*less* than six hours⟩ **2** : of lower rank, degree, or importance ⟨no *less* a person than the president⟩ **3** : not so much : being a smaller amount ⟨we need *less* talk and more work⟩ ⟨finished in *less* time⟩

²less *adv* : not so much or so well ⟨*less* difficult⟩ ⟨liked the second book *less*⟩

³less *prep* : ¹MINUS 1 ⟨the regular price *less* a discount⟩

⁴less *n, pl* **less** **1** : a smaller number or amount ⟨we have *less* than before⟩ **2** : something that is poorer or less important than another ⟨could be arrested for *less*⟩

-less \ləs\ *adj suffix* **1** : not having ⟨child*less*⟩ **2** : not able to be acted on or to act in a specified way ⟨cease*less*⟩ [Old English *-lēas* (suffix) "not having," from *lēas* "false"]

les·see \le-'sē\ *n* : a person holding or occupying property under a lease

less·en \'les-ᵊn\ *vb* **less·ened; less·en·ing** \'les-niŋ, -ᵊn-iŋ\ : to make or become less

¹less·er \'les-ər\ *adj* : of smaller size or importance

²lesser *adv* : ²LESS

lesser celandine *n* : CELANDINE 2

lesser panda *n* : RED PANDA

les·son \'les-ᵊn\ *n* **1** : a part of the Scripture read in a church service **2 a** : a reading or exercise assigned to be studied **b** : something learned by study or experience

les·sor \'les-ˌȯ(ə)r, le-'sȯ(ə)r\ *n* : one that leases property to another

lest \(ˌ)lest\ *conj* : for fear that ⟨tied the dog *lest* it should escape⟩

¹let \'let\ *n* : something that interferes : OBSTACLE ⟨without *let* or hindrance⟩

²let *vb* **let; let·ting** **1** : to cause to : MAKE ⟨*let* it be known⟩ **2** *chiefly British* : to give use of in return for payment ⟨rooms to *let*⟩ **3 a** : to allow or permit to ⟨*let* them go⟩ **b** — used to introduce a request ⟨*let* us hope for the best⟩ **4** : to allow to go or pass ⟨*let* them through⟩ — **let alone** : to leave undisturbed ⟨*let* the flowers *alone*⟩; *also* : to leave to oneself ⟨wanted to be *let alone*⟩ — **let go** **1** : to dismiss from employment ⟨the company *let* him go at the end of the week⟩ **2** : to relax or release one's hold — used with *of* ⟨*let go* of my arm⟩ **3** : to fail to take care of : NEGLECT ⟨stopped exercising and *let* himself *go*⟩ — **let one's hair down** : to act without self-restraint — **let the cat out of the bag** : to give away a secret

-let \lət\ *n suffix* **1** : small one ⟨book*let*⟩ **2** : something worn on ⟨ank*let*⟩ [derived from early French *-elet* "small one," from *-el* and *-et*, both suffixes meaning "small"]

let alone *conj* : to say nothing of : not to mention ⟨lacked the courage, *let alone* the know-how⟩

let·down \'let-ˌdaun\ *n* **1** : DISAPPOINTMENT 2 **2** : a slackening of effort

let down \(')let-'daun\ *vb* **1** : to fail to help or support ⟨*let down* a friend in a crisis⟩ **2** : to fail to come up to expectations : DISAPPOINT ⟨the end of the story *lets* the reader *down*⟩

¹le·thal \'lē-thəl\ *adj* : causing or capable of causing death ⟨*lethal* chemicals⟩ **synonyms** see DEADLY — **le·thal·ly** \'lē-thə-lē\ *adv*

²lethal *n* : LETHAL GENE

lethal gene *n* : a gene capable of preventing development or causing the death of a living thing or its germ cells

leth·ar·gy \'leth-ər-jē\ *n* **1** : abnormal drowsiness **2** : the quality or state of being slow, lazy, or not caring — **le·thar·gic** \lə-'thär-jik, le-\ *adj*

let on *vb* **1** : ADMIT 1b, REVEAL ⟨don't *let on* that I told you⟩ **2** : ¹PRETEND 2 ⟨he's not as happy as he *lets on*⟩

let's \(ˌ)lets, (ˌ)les\ : let us

Lett \'let\ *n* : a member of a people closely related to the Lithuanians and mainly living in Latvia

¹let·ter \'let-ər\ *n* **1** : one of the marks that are symbols for speech sounds in writing or print and that make up the alphabet **2** : a written or printed communication **3** *pl* : LITERATURE 2a **4** : the strict or outward meaning ⟨the *letter* of the law⟩ **5** : the initial of a school awarded to a student especially for athletic achievement

²letter *vb* : to mark with letters — **let·ter·er** \-ər-ər\ *n*

letter carrier *n* : a person who delivers mail

let·ter·head \'let-ər-ˌhed\ *n* : stationery having a printed or engraved heading; *also* : the heading itself

let·ter·ing \'let-ə-riŋ\ *n* : letters used in an inscription

let·ter–per·fect \ˌlet-ər-'pər-fikt\ *adj* : correct to the smallest point

Lett·ish \'let-ish\ *adj* : of or relating to the Latvians or their language — **Lettish** *n*

\ə\ abut	\au̇\ **out**	\i\ **tip**	\ȯ\ **saw**	\u̇\ **foot**
\ər\ **further**	\ch\ **chin**	\ī\ **life**	\ȯi\ **coin**	\y\ **yet**
\a\ **mat**	\e\ **pet**	\j\ **job**	\th\ **thin**	\yü\ **few**
\ā\ **take**	\ē\ **easy**	\ŋ\ **sing**	\th\ **this**	\yu̇\ **cure**
\ä\ **cot, cart**	\g\ **go**	\ō\ **bone**	\ü\ **food**	\zh\ **vision**

let·tuce \'let-əs\ *n* : a common garden vegetable related to the daisies that has crisp juicy leaves used especially in salads

let·up \'let-ˌəp\ *n* : a lessening of effort or force

let up *vb* **1** : to slow down : SLACKEN **2** : to come to a stop : CEASE ⟨the rain *let up*⟩ **3** : to ease off : be less severe — used with *on*

leu·cine \'lü-ˌsēn\ *n* : an amino acid that is very important in the nutrition of human beings

leu·co·plast \'lü-kə-ˌplast\ *n* : a colorless plastid of a plant cell usually concerned with starch formation and storage

leu·ke·mia \lü-'kē-mē-ə\ *n* : a disease of warm-blooded animals including human beings that is a kind of cancer in which there is an abnormal increase in the number of white blood cells in the tissues and often in the blood — **leu·ke·mic** \-mik\ *adj*

leu·ko·cyte \'lü-kə-ˌsīt\ *n* : WHITE BLOOD CELL

le·va·tor \li-'vāt-ər\ *n, pl* **lev·a·to·res** \ˌlev-ə-'tōr-(ˌ)ēz\ *or* **le·va·tors** \li-'vāt-ərz\ : a muscle that serves to raise a body part

lev·ee \'lev-ē\ *n* **1** : a bank built along a river to prevent flooding **2** : a landing place along a river

¹lev·el \'lev-əl\ *n* **1** : a device used (as by a carpenter) to establish a horizontal line or surface **2** : a horizontal line or surface usually at a named height ⟨placed at eye *level*⟩ **3** : a step or stage in a scale or rank (as of achievement, significance, importance, or value) ⟨rose to the *level* of manager⟩ **4 a** : an amount of something especially in comparison with typical or expected amounts ⟨production is at a low *level* this year⟩ **b** : the amount of a substance especially per unit volume of a body fluid (as blood) ⟨a high *level* of sugar in the blood⟩ — **on the level** : BONA FIDE 1, HONEST ⟨find out if the offer is *on the level*⟩

²level *vb* **lev·eled** *or* **lev·elled; lev·el·ing** *or* **lev·el·ling** \'lev-(ə-)liŋ\ **1** : to make or become horizontal, flat, or even **2** : ¹AIM 1, DIRECT **3** : to knock flat ⟨the explosion *leveled* the house⟩ **4** : to reach or come to a level ⟨the plane *leveled* off at 10,000 feet⟩ — **lev·el·er** *or* **lev·el·ler** \-(ə-)lər\ *n*

³level *adj* **1** : having a flat even surface ⟨a *level* lawn⟩ **2** : being on a line with the horizon : HORIZONTAL ⟨in a *level* position⟩ **3** : of the same height or rank : EVEN ⟨the water is *level* with my waist⟩ **4** : steady and cool in judgment ⟨a *level* head⟩ — **lev·el·ly** *adv* — **lev·el·ness** *n* — **level best** : very best

synonyms LEVEL, FLAT, EVEN mean having a surface without bends, curves, or interruptions. LEVEL applies especially to a surface or a line that does not slant up or down ⟨a *level* road between two hills⟩. FLAT applies to a surface that is free from curves or bumps or hollows but may not be parallel to the ground ⟨a room with *flat* walls⟩. EVEN stresses the lack of breaks or bumps in a line or surface but need not suggest that the object is level or straight ⟨trimmed the top of the hedge to make it *even*⟩.

lev·el·head·ed \ˌlev-əl-'hed-əd\ *adj* : having or showing good judgment : SENSIBLE — **lev·el·head·ed·ness** *n*

¹le·ver \'lev-ər, 'lē-vər\ *n* **1** : a bar used to pry or move something **2** : a stiff bar for applying a force (as for lifting a weight) at one point of its length by effort at a second point and turning at a third point on a fulcrum **3** : a bar or rod used to run or adjust something ⟨a gearshift *lever*⟩ [Middle English *lever* "bar for prying," from early French *levier* (same

¹lever 2: *L* lever, *F* fulcrum

meaning), from *lever* (verb) "to raise," from Latin *levare* "to raise" — related to ELEVATE]

²lever *vb* **le·vered; le·ver·ing** \'lev-(ə-)riŋ, 'lēv-\ : to pry, raise, or move with a lever

le·ver·age \'lev-(ə-)rij, 'lēv-\ *n* : the action of a lever or the increase in force gained by using a lever

le·vi·a·than \li-'vī-ə-thən\ *n* **1** *often cap* : a sea monster often standing for evil in the Old Testament and Christian literature **2** : something very large or powerful of its kind

Le·vi's \'lē-ˌvīz\ *trademark* — used especially for blue denim jeans

lev·i·tate \'lev-ə-ˌtāt\ *vb* : to rise or cause to rise in the air in seeming defiance of gravity

lev·i·ta·tion \ˌlev-ə-'tā-shən\ *n* : the act or process of levitating; *esp* : the rising or lifting of a person or thing as if by magic

Le·vit·i·cus \li-'vit-i-kəs\ *n* — see BIBLE table

lev·i·ty \'lev-ət-ē\ *n, pl* **-ties** : a lack of seriousness often at an improper time : FRIVOLITY

lev·u·lose \'lev-yə-ˌlōs\ *n* : FRUCTOSE

¹levy \'lev-ē\ *n, pl* **lev·ies** **1 a** : the laying or collection especially of a tax **b** : an amount levied **2** : the calling of troops into service

²levy *vb* **lev·ied; levy·ing** **1** : to establish or collect by legal authority ⟨*levy* a tax⟩ ⟨*levy* a fine⟩ **2** : to raise or collect troops for military service

lewd \'lüd\ *adj* **1** : showing interest in sex in a rude manner ⟨*lewd* behavior⟩ **2** : INDECENT ⟨*lewd* remarks⟩ — **lewd·ly** *adv* — **lewd·ness** *n*

lex·i·cal \'lek-si-kəl\ *adj* : of or relating to words, a vocabulary, or a dictionary

lex·i·cog·ra·pher \ˌlek-sə-'käg-rə-fər\ *n* : an author or editor of a dictionary

lex·i·cog·ra·phy \ˌlek-sə-'käg-rə-fē\ *n* : the editing or making of a dictionary — **lex·i·co·graph·i·cal** \-kō-'graf-i-kəl\ *or* **lex·i·co·graph·ic** \-'graf-ik\ *adj*

lex·i·con \'lek-sə-ˌkän, -si-kən\ *n* : DICTIONARY 1

Ley·den jar \ˌlīd-ᵊn-\ *n* : a device for storing electric charge consisting of a glass jar coated inside and outside with metal foil and having the inner coating connected to a conducting rod passed through an insulating stopper

Leyden jar

li·a·bil·i·ty \ˌlī-ə-'bil-ət-ē\ *n, pl* **-ties** **1** : the state of being liable ⟨*liability* for his debts⟩ ⟨*liability* to disease⟩ **2** *pl* : that for which a person is liable : DEBTS **3** : something that works as a disadvantage : DRAWBACK

li·a·ble \'lī-ə-bəl, *especially in senses 2 & 3 often* 'lī-bəl\ *adj* **1** : forced by law or by what is right to make good ⟨we are *liable* for damage that we do⟩ **2** : not sheltered or protected (as from danger or accident) ⟨*liable* to diseases⟩ **3** : exposed to or likely to experience something that usually is undesirable ⟨you're *liable* to slip there⟩ ⟨it's *liable* to rain before we're done⟩

li·ai·son \'lē-ə-ˌzän, lē-'ā-\ *n* **1** : a close connection **2** : communication especially between parts of an armed force **3** : a person who sets up or keeps up liaison

li·a·na \lē-'än-ə, -'an-ə\ *n* : any of various usually woody vines especially of tropical rain forests that root in the ground

li·ar \'lī(-ə)r\ *n* : a person who tells lies

lib \'lib\ *n* : LIBERATION 2

li·ba·tion \lī-'bā-shən\ *n* **1 a** : the act of pouring a liquid in honor of a god **b** : a liquid (as wine) poured as a libation **2** : a drink poured or taken as if to honor a god

¹li·bel \'lī-bəl\ *n* **1** : something spoken, written, or drawn that injures a person's good name **2** : the act or crime of publishing a libel

Word History The ancient Romans used the Latin noun *liber* to refer to the inner bark of a tree. Because this material was used to write on before the introduction of papyrus to Rome from Egypt, *liber* came to be applied to a written document, especially a lengthy one. After papyrus became common, a *liber* was usually an entire papyrus scroll, hence a "book." *Libellus*, the diminutive form of *liber*, was borrowed into French as *libelle*, which was in turn borrowed into English as *libel*. Originally *libel* was used in the sense "little book," but in the 1500s handbills and leaflets, being likened to little books, were also called libels. Because they were a popular means of spreading gossip about famous people, the meaning of *libel* was extended to such injurious statements as well as to the crime of writing them. [Middle English *libel* "a written statement, little book" from early French *libel* (same meaning), from Latin *libellus*, "little book," from *liber* "book" — related to LIBRARY]

²**libel** *vb* **li·beled** *or* **li·belled; li·bel·ing** *or* **li·bel·ling** : to hurt by a libel — **li·bel·er** *or* **li·bel·ler** \-b(ə-)lər\ *n*

li·bel·ous *or* **li·bel·lous** \'lī-b(ə-)ləs\ *adj* : being a libel

¹**lib·er·al** \'lib-(ə-)rəl\ *adj* **1** : of, relating to, or based on the liberal arts ⟨a *liberal* education⟩ **2 a** : not stingy : GENEROUS ⟨a *liberal* giver⟩ **b** : more than enough ⟨a *liberal* allowance⟩ **3** : not strict; *esp* : not bound by traditional forms or beliefs **4** : of or relating to liberalism : not conservative — **lib·er·al·ly** \-rə-lē\ *adv*

²**liberal** *n* : a person who is liberal especially in politics

liberal arts *n pl* : the studies (as literature, philosophy, languages, or history) in a college or university intended to develop the mind in a general way rather than give professional or vocational skills

lib·er·al·ism \'lib-(ə-)rə-,liz-əm\ *n* : a political belief stressing progress, the essential goodness of humankind, and individual freedom

lib·er·al·i·ty \,lib-ə-'ral-ət-ē\ *n, pl* **-ties 1** : the quality or state of being liberal **2** : a generous act

lib·er·al·ize \'lib-(ə-)rə-,līz\ *vb* **-ized; -iz·ing** : to make or become liberal or more liberal — **lib·er·al·i·za·tion** \,lib-(ə-)rə-lə-'zā-shən\ *n*

lib·er·ate \'lib-ə-,rāt\ *vb* **-at·ed; -at·ing** : to set free — **lib·er·a·tor** \-,rāt-ər\ *n*

lib·er·at·ed *adj* : freed from or opposed to traditional social and sexual attitudes or roles

lib·er·a·tion \,lib-ə-'rā-shən\ *n* **1** : the act of liberating : the state of being liberated **2** : a movement seeking equal rights for a group

lib·er·tar·i·an \,lib-ər-'ter-ē-ən\ *n* : a person who believes in liberty of thought and action — **libertarian** *adj* — **lib·er·tar·i·an·ism** \-ē-ə-,niz-əm\ *n*

lib·er·tine \'lib-ər-,tēn\ *n* : a person who leads an immoral life — **libertine** *adj*

lib·er·ty \'lib-ərt-ē\ *n, pl* **-ties 1** : the condition of those who are free and independent : FREEDOM **2** : power to do what one pleases ⟨give the child some *liberty*⟩ **3** : an action that goes beyond normal limits (as of proper behavior or good sense) ⟨took *liberties* with the truth⟩ **4 a** : a short authorized absence from naval duty — **at liberty 1** : not held back : FREE ⟨you are *at liberty* to go or stay⟩ **2** : not busy ⟨I'm *at liberty* this afternoon⟩

Li·bra \'lē-brə, 'lī-\ *n* **1** : a group of stars between Virgo and Scorpio usually pictured as a balance scale **2 a** : the seventh sign of the zodiac — see ZODIAC table **b** : a person whose sign of the zodiac is Libra [Middle English *Libra* "a group of stars between Virgo and Scorpio," from Latin *libra*, literally, "balance, scales" — related to DELIBERATE, EQUILIBRIUM]

li·brar·i·an \lī-'brer-ē-ən\ *n* : a person in charge of a library — **li·brar·i·an·ship** \-,ship\ *n*

li·brary \'lī-,brer-ē\ *n, pl* **-brar·ies 1 a** : a place where books, magazines, and records are kept for use but not for sale **b** : a collection of books, magazines, or records

2 : a collection resembling or suggesting a library ⟨a *library* of computer programs⟩ [Middle English *library, librarie* "a place where books are kept," from Latin *librarium* (same meaning), from earlier *librarius* "of books," from *liber* "book" — related to LIBEL; see *Word History* at LIBEL]

library paste *n* : a thick white adhesive paste

li·bret·tist \lə-'bret-əst\ *n* : the writer of a libretto

li·bret·to \lə-'bret-ō\ *n, pl* **-tos** *or* **-ti** \-ē\ : the text of an opera or musical

lice *plural of* LOUSE

¹**li·cense** *or* **li·cence** \'līs-ᵊn(t)s\ *n* **1 a** : permission granted by qualified authority to do something **b** : a document, plate, or tag showing that such permission has been granted **2** : liberty of action that is carried too far

²**license** *also* **licence** *vb* **li·censed** *also* **licenced; li·cens·ing** *also* **licencing** : to permit or authorize by license — **li·cens·able** \'līs-ᵊn-sə-bəl\ *adj*

licensed practical nurse *n* : a person who has been trained and has been given a license (as by a state) to perform routine care of the sick — called also *LPN*

license plate *n* : a plate or tag (as of metal) showing that a license has been gotten and usually bearing a registration number

li·cen·tious \lī-'sen-chəs\ *adj* : marked by immoral or lawless behavior — **li·cen·tious·ly** *adv* — **li·cen·tious·ness** *n*

lichee *variant of* LYCHEE

li·chen \'lī-kən\ *n* : any of numerous plantlike living things made up of an alga and a fungus growing together on a solid surface (as a rock or a tree)

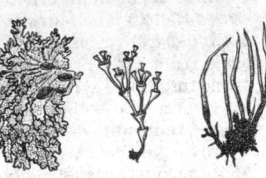

lichen

¹**lick** \'lik\ *vb* **1 a** : to pass the tongue over ⟨*licked* the bowl⟩ **b** : to touch or pass over like a tongue ⟨flames were already *licking* the ceiling⟩ **2** : to take up with the tongue ⟨kittens *licking* milk⟩ **3 a** : to hit again and again : BEAT **b** : to get the better of — **lick·ing** *n*

²**lick** *n* **1 a** : an act or instance of licking **b** : a small amount : BIT ⟨hasn't done a *lick* of work⟩ **c** : a hasty careless effort **2** : a sharp hit : BLOW ⟨got in a few *licks* of my own⟩ **3** : a place (as a spring) having a deposit of salt that animals regularly lick — called also *salt lick*

lic·o·rice \'lik-(ə-)rish, -rəs\ *n* **1 a** : a European plant of the legume family with spikes of blue flowers **b** : the dried root of licorice; *also* : a preparation made from the root **2** : a candy flavored with licorice or a substitute (as anise) [Middle English *licorice* "licorice," from early French *licoris* (same meaning), from Latin *liquiritia* (same meaning), derived from Greek *glykyrrhiza*, literally, "sweet root"]

lid \'lid\ *n* **1** : a movable cover (as for a box or jar) **2** : EYELID **3** *slang* : HAT **4** : a force that holds back ⟨tried to keep a *lid* on the news⟩ — **lid·ded** \'lid-əd\ *adj*

¹**lie** \'lī\ *vb* **lay** \'lā\; **lain** \'lān\; **ly·ing** \'lī-iŋ\ **1 a** : to be in, stay in, or take up a horizontal position ⟨*lay* fast asleep⟩ ⟨*lie* down⟩ **b** : to stay in hiding or in ambush ⟨*lie* low⟩ ⟨*lie* in wait⟩ **2** : to be spread flat so as to cover ⟨snow *lying* on the ground⟩ **3** : to have direction : EXTEND ⟨our route *lay* to the west⟩ **4** : to be located ⟨Ohio *lies* east of

\ə\ **abut**	\au̇\ **out**	\i\ **tip**	\ȯ\ **saw**	\u̇\ **foot**
\ər\ **further**	\ch\ **chin**	\ī\ **life**	\ȯi\ **coin**	\y\ **yet**
\a\ **mat**	\e\ **pet**	\j\ **job**	\th\ **thin**	\yü\ **few**
\ā\ **take**	\ē\ **easy**	\ŋ\ **sing**	\t̲h̲\ **this**	\yu̇\ **cure**
\ä\ **cot, cart**	\g\ **go**	\ō\ **bone**	\ü\ **food**	\zh\ **vision**

Indiana⟩ [Old English *licgan* "to get into or be in a horizontal position"]

²lie *n* **1** : the position in which something lies **2** *chiefly British* : ²LAY

³lie *vb* **lied; ly·ing** \'lī-iŋ\ **1** : to make a statement one knows to be untrue **2** : to give a false idea ⟨statistics sometimes *lie*⟩ [Old English *lēogan* "to say something that is not true"]

⁴lie *n* : something said or done in the hope of deceiving

lie detector *n* : an instrument for detecting bodily changes (as an increase in heart rate) that are considered to go along with lying

lief \'lēv, 'lēf\ *adv* : SOON 4, WILLINGLY ⟨I would as *lief* go as not⟩

¹liege \'lēj\ *adj* **1** : having the right to receive service and loyalty ⟨*liege* lord⟩ **2** : owing or giving service to a lord

²liege *n* **1** : VASSAL **2** : a feudal lord

lien \'lēn, 'lē-ən\ *n* : a legal claim on the property of another person until he or she has met a certain obligation (as a debt)

lieu \'lü\ *n*, *archaic* : ¹PLACE 7b, STEAD — **in lieu of** : in the place of : INSTEAD OF

lieu·ten·an·cy \lü-'ten-ən-sē\ *n*, *pl* **-cies** : the office, rank, or commission of a lieutenant

lieu·ten·ant \lü-'ten-ənt\ *n* **1** : an official who acts for a higher official **2 a** : FIRST LIEUTENANT **b** : SECOND LIEUTENANT **c** : a naval commissioned officer with a rank just below that of lieutenant commander **d** : a fire or police department officer ranking below a captain

Word History The phrase *in lieu of* means the same thing as *in place of* or *instead of*. The word *lieu* came into English from early French, in which it meant "place, position, function." Another English word that came from early French is *tenant*. In early French, this word was an adjective meaning "holding." Joined together, these two words gave the early French word *lieutenant*. It originally meant "a person holding another person's place" or "a person acting in place of another." In English, *lieutenant* is best known as a military title, but the word is still sometimes used in its original meaning to refer to a person who acts in *lieu* of someone else. [Middle English *lieutenant* "lieutenant," from early French *lieutenant* (same meaning), literally, "one holding the place for another," from *lieu* "place, position" and *tenant* "holding"]

lieutenant colonel *n* : a military commissioned officer with a rank just below that of colonel

lieutenant commander *n* : a naval commissioned officer with a rank just below that of commander

lieutenant general *n* : a military commissioned officer with a rank just below that of general

lieutenant governor *n* **1** : an elected official serving as deputy to the governor of an American state **2** : the formal head of the government of a Canadian province appointed to represent the crown

lieutenant junior grade *n* : a naval commissioned officer with a rank just below that of lieutenant

¹life \'līf\ *n*, *pl* **lives** \'līvz\ **1 a** : the quality that separates plants and animals from such things as water or rock : the quality that plants and animals lose when they die **b** : a state of a living thing marked especially by capacity for metabolism, growth, reaction to stimuli, and reproduction **2 a** : all the experiences that make up the existence of a person ⟨never heard of such a thing in all my *life*⟩ **b** : BIOGRAPHY **3 a** : the period during which a person, animal, or plant lives **b** : a specific part of living ⟨adult *life*⟩ **c** : the period from an event until death ⟨remained friends for *life*⟩ **4** : a way or manner of living ⟨the *life* of the ant⟩ **5** : a living being ⟨many *lives* were saved⟩ **6** : energy or spirit in action or expression ⟨eyes full of *life*⟩ ⟨still some *life* left in the coals⟩ **7** : the form or pattern of something that exists in actual fact ⟨painted from *life*⟩

⟨looks larger than *life*⟩ **8** : the period of usefulness, popularity, or existence of something ⟨battery *life*⟩ ⟨the *life* of an insurance policy⟩ **9** : living beings (as of a kind or place) ⟨forest *life*⟩ **10** : living activity and movement ⟨stirrings of *life*⟩ ⟨streets humming with *life*⟩ **11** : one providing interest and vigor ⟨the *life* of the party⟩

²life *adj* **1** : of or relating to living existence ⟨the *life* force⟩ **2** : LIFELONG ⟨a *life* member⟩

life–and–death *adj* : ending in life or death : deciding which will survive ⟨a *life-and-death* struggle⟩

life belt *n* : a life preserver worn like a belt

life·blood \'līf-‚bləd\ *n* : something that gives strength and energy

life·boat \-‚bōt\ *n* : a sturdy boat (as one carried by a ship) for use in an emergency and especially for saving lives at sea

life buoy *n* : a ring-shaped life preserver

life cycle *n* **1** : the series of stages of form and activity through which a living thing passes from a beginning stage (as an egg) in one individual to the same stage in its offspring **2** : LIFE HISTORY 1

life expectancy *n* : the number of years that an individual or group of a certain age can expect to live on the average based on experience in the past for individuals or groups of the same kind

life·guard \'līf-‚gärd\ *n* : a usually expert swimmer employed at a beach or swimming pool to protect swimmers from drowning

life history *n* **1** : a history of the changes through which a living thing passes in its development from the first stage to its natural death **2** : LIFE CYCLE 1

life insurance *n* : insurance providing for a specified sum to be paid when the insured person dies

life jacket *n* : a life preserver that is worn like a jacket or vest

life·less \'lī-fləs\ *adj* : having no life — **life·less·ly** *adv* — **life·less·ness** *n*

life·like \'lī-‚flīk\ *adj* : accurately representing or imitating an actual living thing ⟨a *lifelike* statue⟩ — **life·like·ness** *n*

life·line \'lī-‚flīn\ *n* **1** : a line persons may hang on to for safety or rescue **2** : something providing help or support that is needed for success or survival

life·long \'lī-‚flȯŋ\ *adj* : continuing or lasting through life ⟨a *lifelong* love for trees⟩ ⟨a *lifelong* friendship⟩

life jacket

life preserver *n* : a device designed to save a person from drowning by holding up the body while in the water

life raft *n* : a raft designed for use by people forced into the water

life·sav·er \'līf-‚sā-vər\ *n* **1** : a person trained to save the lives of drowning persons **2** : something that relieves distress when most needed

¹life·sav·ing \'līf-‚sā-viŋ\ *adj* : designed for or used in saving lives ⟨*lifesaving* devices⟩

²lifesaving *n* : the methods that can be used to save lives especially of drowning persons

life science *n* : a branch of science (as biology, medicine, and sometimes anthropology or sociology) that deals with living things and life processes — usually used in plural

life scientist *n* : a person who specializes in one or more of the life sciences

life–size \'līf-'sīz\ *or* **life–sized** \-'sīzd\ *adj* : of natural size : having the same size as the original

life span *n* : the average length of life of a living thing or of the persistence of a material object under specified circumstances or in a particular environment

life·style \'līf-'stī(ə)l\ *n* : the usual way of life of a person, group, or society : the way we live

life–support system *n* : a system that provides all or some of the items (as oxygen, food, water, proper temperature and air pressure, elimination of carbon dioxide and body wastes) necessary for maintaining life or health

life·time \'līf-ˌtīm\ *n* **1** : ¹LIFE 3a **2** : ¹LIFE 8

life·work \-'wərk\ *n* : the entire or chief work of one's lifetime

¹lift \'lift\ *vb* **1** : to move to a higher position, rate, or amount **2** : to rise from the ground ⟨planes *lifting* from the runway⟩ ⟨the rocket *lifted* off⟩ **3** : to stop or remove often temporarily ⟨*lift* a blockade⟩ ⟨*lift* a ban⟩ **4** : to move upward and disappear or become scattered ⟨when the fog *lifts*⟩ **synonyms** see RAISE — **lift·er** *n*

²lift *n* **1** : the amount that may be lifted at one time : LOAD **2** : the action or an instance of lifting **3** : help especially in the form of a ride ⟨can I give you a *lift*?⟩ **4 a** *chiefly British* : ELEVATOR 1b **b** : a device for carrying people up or down a mountain **5** : a raising of the spirits ⟨their visit gave me a *lift*⟩ **6** : an upward force (as on an airplane wing) that opposes the pull of gravity

lift·gate \'lift-ˌgāt\ *n* : a rear panel (as on a station wagon) that opens upward

lift·off \'lif-ˌtȯf\ *n* : a vertical takeoff (as by a rocket)

lig·a·ment \'lig-ə-mənt\ *n* : a tough band of tissue that holds bones together or keeps an organ in place in the body [Middle English *ligament* "connecting tissue, ligament," derived from Latin *ligamentum* "band, something used for tying," from *ligare* "to bind, tie" — related to ALLY]

li·ga·tion \lī-'gā-shən\ *n* : the act of tying a bodily part (as a blood vessel) with a ligature

lig·a·ture \'lig-ə-ˌchü(ə)r, -chər\ *n* **1** : a binding or tying of something **2** : something that binds or connects : BAND, BOND **3** : a thread used in surgery especially for tying blood vessels

¹light \'līt\ *n* **1 a** : something that makes vision possible **b** : the sensation aroused by stimulation of the visual sense organs **c** : electromagnetic radiation of any wavelength (as infrared, visible, ultraviolet, and X-rays) and traveling in a vacuum with a speed of about 186,000 miles (300,000 kilometers) per second; *esp* : such radiation that is visible to the human eye **2** : DAYLIGHT 1 ⟨by dawn's early *light*⟩ **3** : a source (as a lamp) of light ⟨turn on the *light*⟩ **4 a** : public knowledge ⟨facts brought to *light*⟩ **b** : a particular appearance presented to view ⟨were shown in a bad *light* by the lawyer⟩ ⟨I see the matter in a different *light* now⟩ **5** : a particular illumination ⟨by the *light* of the moon⟩ **6** : something that helps one to know or understand ⟨shed *light* on a problem⟩ **7** : a noted person : LEADING LIGHT **8 a** : LIGHTHOUSE, BEACON **b** : TRAFFIC SIGNAL ⟨turn left at the next *light*⟩ **9** : a flame for lighting something [Old English *lēoht* "light, that which makes seeing possible"] — **in light of** : with respect to ⟨consider their advice *in light of* your own needs⟩

²light *adj* **1** : having light : BRIGHT ⟨a *light* room⟩ **2** : not dark or deep in color : PALE ⟨*light* blue⟩ — **light·ness** *n*

³light *vb* **light·ed** *or* **lit** \'lit\; **light·ing** **1** : to make or become bright — often used with *up* **2** : to cause to burn or begin to burn — often used with *up* **3** : to lead with a light ⟨*light* a guest up the stairs⟩

⁴light *adj* **1 a** : having little or less than usual weight : not heavy **b** : designed to carry a small load ⟨*light* truck⟩ **2 a** : of little importance **b** : not abundant : SCANTY ⟨*light* rain⟩ **c** : not strong or violent : MODERATE ⟨*light* breezes⟩ **3 a** : easily disturbed ⟨a *light* sleeper⟩ **b** : putting forth little force or pressure : GENTLE ⟨a *light* touch⟩ **4** : not hard to bear, do, pay, or digest ⟨*light* punishment⟩ ⟨*light* exercise⟩ ⟨*light* food⟩ **5** : capable of moving swiftly or nimbly ⟨*light* on one's feet⟩ **6** : intended chiefly to entertain ⟨*light* reading⟩ ⟨*light* verse⟩ **7** : made with a lower calorie content or with less of some ingredient (as fat) ⟨*light* salad dressing⟩ **8** : having a spongy or fluffy quality ⟨*light* pastry⟩ **9** : producing goods that will be sold to the people who use them rather than to another manufacturer ⟨*light* industry⟩ [Old English *lēoht* "not heavy"] — **light·ly** *adv* — **light·ness** *n*

⁵light *adv* **1** : in a light manner **2** : with little baggage ⟨traveling *light*⟩

⁶light *vb* **light·ed** *or* **lit** \'lit\; **light·ing** **1** : to come down out of the air and settle : ALIGHT ⟨birds *lit* on the lawn⟩ **2** : to come by chance ⟨*lit* upon a solution⟩ [Old English *līhtan* "to come down off something or out of the air"]

light·bulb \'līt-ˌbəlb\ *n* : an electric lamp: as **a** : one in which a filament gives off light when heated by an electric current — called also *incandescent lamp* **b** : FLUORESCENT LAMP

light–emitting diode *n* : LED

¹light·en \'līt-ᵊn\ *vb* **light·ened**; **light·en·ing** \'līt-niŋ, -ᵊn-iŋ\ **1** : to make or become light, lighter, or clear : BRIGHTEN **2** : to give out flashes of lightning — **light·en·er** \'līt-nər, -ᵊn-ər\

²lighten *vb* **light·ened**; **light·en·ing** \'līt-niŋ, -ᵊn-iŋ\ : to make or become less heavy or less difficult ⟨*lighten* a load⟩ ⟨*lightened* her duties⟩ — **light·en·er** \'līt-nər, -ᵊn-ər\ *n*

¹light·er \'līt-ər\ *n* : a large barge used especially in unloading or loading ships [Middle English *lighter* "boat"; of Dutch origin]

²lighter *vb* : to carry by a lighter

³light·er \'līt-ər\ *n* : one that lights; *esp* : a device for lighting ⟨a cigarette *lighter*⟩ [from ³*light* and -er]

lighter–than–air *adj* : able to fly by the use of a gas (as helium or hot air) less dense than the air that would occupy the same amount of space

light·face \'līt-ˌfās\ *n* : the style of printing type used for ordinary text (as in books) — **light·faced** \-'fāst\ *adj*

light–foot·ed \-'fu̇t-əd\ *adj* : having a light and springy step or movement

light–head·ed \-'hed-əd\ *adj* **1** : feeling confused or dizzy **2** : not showing maturity or seriousness : FRIVOLOUS — **light–head·ed·ness** *n*

light–heart·ed \-'härt-əd\ *adj* : free from worry — **light–heart·ed·ly** *adv* — **light–heart·ed·ness** *n*

light heavyweight *n* : a boxer in a weight division having an upper limit of about 175 pounds

light·house \-ˌhau̇s\ *n* : a tower with a powerful light at the top that is built on or near the shore to guide sailors at night

light·ing \'līt-iŋ\ *n* **1** : supply of light : ILLUMINATION **2** : artificial light (as for a play) or the apparatus providing it

light meter *n* **1** : a small portable device for measuring the amount of light in an area **2** : a device for indicating correct photographic exposure for varying amounts of light

¹light·ning \'līt-niŋ\ *n* : the flashing of light produced by a discharge of atmospheric electricity from one cloud to another or between a cloud and the earth; *also* : the discharge itself

lighthouse

²lightning *adj* : moving or done with or as if with the speed of lightning

\ə\ **abut**	\au̇\ **out**	\i\ **tip**	\ȯ\ **saw**	\u̇\ **foot**
\ər\ **further**	\ch\ **chin**	\ī\ **life**	\ȯi\ **coin**	\y\ **yet**
\a\ **mat**	\e\ **pet**	\j\ **job**	\th\ **thin**	\yü\ **few**
\ā\ **take**	\ē\ **easy**	\ŋ\ **sing**	\th\ **this**	\yu̇\ **cure**
\ä\ **cot, cart**	\g\ **go**	\ō\ **bone**	\ü\ **food**	\zh\ **vision**

lightning arrester n : a device for protecting electrical equipment from damage by lightning

lightning bug n : FIREFLY

lightning rod n : a metal rod set up on a building or a ship and connected with the earth or water below to decrease the chances of damage from lightning

light opera n : OPERETTA

light out vb : to leave in a hurry ⟨lit out for home⟩

light pen n : a pen-shaped device that senses light signals and is used to work with information on a computer display screen

light-proof \'līt-'prüf\ adj : not letting in light

light-ship \-,ship\ n : a ship equipped to work like a lighthouse and anchored at a place dangerous to sailors

light-some \'līt-səm\ adj 1 : free from care : CHEERFUL 2 : marked by a light or springy quality

light trap n : a device for collecting or destroying insects by attracting them to a light and trapping or killing them

¹**light-weight** \'līt-,wāt\ n 1 : one of less than average weight; esp : a boxer in a weight division having an upper limit of about 135 pounds 2 : a person of little importance

²**lightweight** adj : having less than the usual or expected weight

light–year \'līt-,yi(ə)r\ n 1 : a unit of length in astronomy equal to the distance that light travels in one year or 5,880,000,000,000 miles (9,460,000,000,000 kilometers) 2 : a very great distance especially in progress ⟨light-years ahead in design⟩

lig-nin \'lig-nən\ n : a substance related to cellulose that occurs in the woody cell walls of plants and in the cementing material between them

lig-nite \'lig-,nīt\ n : a usually brownish black coal between peat and bituminous coal in age and heating ability; esp : one in which the texture of the original wood is distinct

lik-able or **like-able** \'lī-kə-bəl\ adj : easily liked — **lik-able-ness** n

¹**like** \'līk\ vb **liked; lik-ing** 1 : to have a liking for : ENJOY ⟨likes baseball⟩ 2 : to feel toward : REGARD ⟨how do you like this weather?⟩ 3 : to wish to have : WANT ⟨would like a drink⟩ 4 : to feel inclined : CHOOSE ⟨you can leave any time you like⟩ [Old English līcian "to take pleasure in"]

²**like** n : LIKING, PREFERENCE ⟨my likes and dislikes⟩

³**like** adj : being the same or very nearly the same ⟨two like magnetic poles⟩ ⟨suits of like design⟩ [Old English gelīc "alike"]

⁴**like** prep **1 a** : similar to ⟨the house looks like a barn⟩ **b** : typical of ⟨it would be just like you to do that⟩ **2** : similarly to ⟨acting like a fool⟩ ⟨blow it up like a balloon⟩ **3** : likely to ⟨looks like rain⟩ **4** : such as ⟨a subject like physics⟩

⁵**like** n : ²EQUAL 1 ⟨may never see its like again⟩; also : ¹KIND 1a ⟨I'd keep him and his like from causing any more trouble⟩

⁶**like** adv **1** : ²LIKELY, PROBABLY ⟨like enough, you will⟩ ⟨like as not the cat's under the porch⟩ **2** : in some amount : SOMEWHAT, SEEMINGLY ⟨it moves stiff like⟩ **3** : close to : within a little : NEARER ⟨the rate is more like 18 percent⟩

⁷**like** conj **1** : AS IF ⟨the plane looked like it would crash⟩ ⟨pedaling like mad⟩ **2** : in the same way that : AS ⟨you sound just like I do⟩ ⟨does it look like it used to?⟩

⁸**like** or **liked** \'līkt\ helping verb, chiefly dialect : came near : was near ⟨I like to have died laughing⟩

-like \,līk\ adj combining form : resembling or characteristic of ⟨bell-like⟩ ⟨ladylike⟩

like-li-hood \'lī-klē-,hud\ n : PROBABILITY 1

like-li-ness \'lī-klē-nəs\ n : PROBABILITY 1

¹**like-ly** \'lī-klē\ adj **like-li-er; -est** **1** : very possibly going to happen ⟨that bomb is likely to expode any time⟩ **2** : seeming to be the truth : BELIEVABLE ⟨a likely story⟩ **3**

: giving hope of turning out well : PROMISING ⟨a likely spot for a picnic⟩ ⟨a likely looking customer⟩

²**likely** adv : without great doubt : PROBABLY ⟨the first loaves of bread people made were likely hard and flat⟩

lik-en \'lī-kən\ vb **lik-ened; lik-en-ing** \'līk-(ə-)niŋ\ : ¹COMPARE 1

like-ness \'līk-nəs\ n **1** : a picture especially of a person : PORTRAIT **2** : the quality or state of being like : RESEMBLANCE

like-wise \'lī-,kwīz\ adv **1** : in like manner : SIMILARLY ⟨go and do likewise⟩ **2** : in addition : ALSO

lik-ing \'lī-kiŋ\ n : a being pleased with someone or something : FONDNESS, TASTE

li-lac \'lī-lək, -,lak, -,läk\ n **1** : any of a genus of shrubs and trees related to the olive; esp : a European shrub widely grown for its showy clusters of fragrant pink, purple, or white flowers **2** : a medium purple

¹**lilt** \'lilt\ vb : to sing or play in a lively cheerful manner — **lilt-ing-ly** \'lil-tiŋ-lē\ adv

²**lilt** n : a lively and cheerful sound or expression ⟨a tune with a lilt⟩ ⟨a lilt in her voice⟩

lilac 1

lily \'lil-ē\ n, pl **lil-ies** : any of a genus of herbs with leafy stems that grow from bulbs and have funnel-shaped flowers; also : any of various related plants

lily–liv-ered \,lil-ē-'liv-ərd\ adj : COWARDLY 1

Word History In the Middle Ages the study of anatomy, or the cutting up and examining of human corpses, was illegal. Most of what was thought about the body thus was based on the theory of humors. The humor, or body fluid, that was supposed to control anger, spirit, and courage was bile, produced by the liver. A person who lacked courage was supposed to have a white liver, because it had no yellow bile to color it. Thus a cowardly person was called white-livered or, more poetically, lily=livered.

lily of the valley : a low herb that is related to the lilies and has usually two large oblong leaves and a stalk of fragrant flowers shaped like bells

lily pad n : a floating leaf of a water lily

lily–white \,lil-ē-'hwīt, -'wīt\ adj **1** : white as a lily **2** : free from fault or blame : FAULTLESS, PURE

li-ma bean \,lī-mə-\ n : a tropical American bean plant widely grown for its flat edible usually pale green or whitish seeds; also : the seed of a lima bean

¹**limb** \'lim\ n **1** : any of the paired parts (as an arm, wing, or leg) of an animal that stick out from the body and are used mostly in moving and grasping; esp : a leg or arm of a human being **2** : a large branch of a tree — **limb-less** \'lim-ləs\ adj

²**limb** vb : to cut off the limbs of (a felled tree)

¹**lim-ber** \'lim-bər\ adj : bending easily : FLEXIBLE, SUPPLE — **lim-ber-ly** adv — **lim-ber-ness** n

²**limber** vb **lim-bered; lim-ber-ing** \'lim-b(ə-)riŋ\ : to make or become limber ⟨limbered up with exercises⟩

¹**lim-bo** \'lim-bō\ n, pl **limbos** **1** often cap : a place for souls (as of unbaptized infants) believed to be barred from heaven through no fault of their own **2 a** : a place or state of being held or forgotten **b** : a middle place or state [Middle English limbo "a place for souls," derived from Latin limbus (same meaning), from earlier limbus "border"]

²**limbo** n : a dance or contest that involves bending backward and passing under a horizontal pole [from the En-

glish of Trinidad and Barbados *limbo* "a dance that involves bending backwards under a pole," related to Jamaican English *limba* "to bend," from English *limber* "flexible"]

¹lime \'līm\ *n* **1** : a white substance that is primarily an oxide of calcium, is made by heating limestone or shells, and is used in making plaster and cement and in farming **2** : a dry white powder consisting chiefly of the hydroxide of calcium that is made by treating lime with water [Old English *lim* "substance from limestone"]

²lime *vb* **limed; lim·ing** : to treat or cover with lime ⟨*lime* a garden⟩

³lime *adj* : of, relating to, or containing lime or limestone

⁴lime *n* : a European linden tree [Old English *lind* "linden tree"]

⁵lime *n* : a fruit like the lemon but smaller and with a yellowish green skin; *also* : the tropical Asian citrus tree that bears limes [from French *lime* "the fruit lime"; of Arabic origin]

lime·light \'līm-,līt\ *n* : the center of public attention

lim·er·ick \'lim-(ə-)rik\ *n* : a humorous poem five lines long in which the first, second, and fifth lines have one rhyme and the third and fourth another

lime·stone \'līm-,stōn\ *n* : a rock that is formed chiefly from animal remains (as shells or coral), consists mainly of calcium carbonate, is used in building, and gives lime when burned

lime·wa·ter \-,wȯt-ər, -,wät-\ *n* : a water solution of the hydroxide of calcium that is used as an antacid

¹lim·it \'lim-ət\ *n* **1** : a boundary line ⟨within the city *limits*⟩ **2** : a point beyond which a person or thing cannot go — **lim·it·less** \-ləs\ *adj*

²limit *vb* : to set limits to : keep within limits ⟨*limit* expenses⟩ ⟨management reserves the right to *limit* quantities⟩ ⟨an adjective *limits* the meaning of a noun⟩

synonyms LIMIT, RESTRICT, CIRCUMSCRIBE, CONFINE mean to set boundaries for. LIMIT implies setting a point or line (as in time, space, or speed) beyond which something cannot or is not permitted to go ⟨visits are *limited* to 30 minutes⟩. RESTRICT suggests a narrowing or restraining within or as if within an encircling boundary ⟨laws intended to *restrict* the freedom of the press⟩. CIRCUMSCRIBE stresses a restriction on all sides and by clearly defined boundaries ⟨the authority of the investigating committee was carefully *circumscribed*⟩. CONFINE suggests severe restraint and a resulting cramping or hampering ⟨our options were *confined* by our budget⟩.

lim·i·ta·tion \,lim-ə-'tā-shən\ *n* **1** : the act or an instance of limiting **2** : the quality or state of being limited **3** : something that limits

lim·it·ed *adj* **1** : held within limits **2** : having constitutional limitations placed on the exercise of power ⟨a *limited* monarchy⟩ — **lim·it·ed·ly** *adv* — **lim·it·ed·ness** *n*

limited war *n* : a war whose goal is less than the total defeat of the enemy

lim·it·ing *adj* : being an environmental factor (as food) that limits the size of a population of living things

lim·nol·o·gist \lim-'näl-ə-jist\ *n* : a person specializing in limnology

lim·nol·o·gy \lim-'näl-ə-jē\ *n* : the scientific study of bodies of fresh water (as lakes) [from Greek *limnē* "pool, marshy lake" and English *-logy* "science"]

li·mo·nite \'lī-mə-,nīt\ *n* : an ore of iron consisting of oxides of iron

lim·ou·sine \'lim-ə-,zēn, ,lim-ə-'zēn\ *n* **1** : a large luxurious automobile often driven by a chauffeur **2** : a large vehicle for passengers going to and from an airport

¹limp \'limp\ *vb* **1** : to walk lamely **2** : to go slowly or with difficulty

²limp *n* : a limping movement or gait ⟨walked with a *limp*⟩

³limp *adj* **1** : not firm or stiff **2** : ¹WEARY 1, EXHAUSTED — **limp·ly** *adv* — **limp·ness** *n*

lim·pa \'lim-pə\ *n* : rye bread made with molasses or brown sugar

lim·pet \'lim-pət\ *n* : a marine mollusk that has a low cone-shaped shell, moves over rocks or timbers feeding on food found there, and clings very tightly when disturbed

lim·pid \'lim-pəd\ *adj* : perfectly clear : TRANSPARENT ⟨*limpid* streams⟩ — **lim·pid·i·ty** \lim-'pid-ət-ē\ *n* — **lim·pid·ly** \'lim-pəd-lē\ *adv* — **lim·pid·ness** *n*

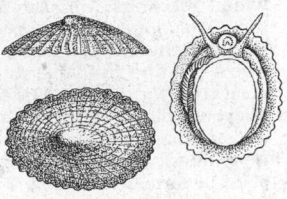

limpet

limy *or* **lim·ey** \'lī-mē\ *adj* **lim·i·er; -est** : containing lime or limestone

linch·pin \'linch-,pin\ *n* : a pin inserted crosswise through something (as the end of an axle or shaft) to keep things in place

Lin·coln's Birthday \,liŋ-kənz-\ *n* : February 12 or the first Monday in February observed as a legal holiday in many of the states of the U.S.

lin·den \'lin-dən\ *n* **1** : any of a genus of trees with large heart-shaped leaves and drooping clusters of yellowish flowers that are often planted as ornamental or shade trees **2** : the light white wood of a linden

¹line \'līn\ *n* **1** : a long thin cord ⟨a fishing *line*⟩ **2** : a cord, wire, or tape used in measuring and leveling **3 a** : a pipe for carrying a fluid ⟨gas *line*⟩ ⟨water *line*⟩ ⟨steam *line*⟩ **b** : a wire or set of wires carrying electricity ⟨a power *line*⟩ ⟨telegraph *lines*⟩ ⟨a telephone *line*⟩ **4 a** : a row of words, letters, numbers, or symbols that are written, printed, or displayed (as on a page or TV screen); *also* : space for such a line **b** : a structural unit of something written (as a poem or a computer program) **c** : a short letter : NOTE ⟨drop me a *line*⟩ **d** *pl* : the words of a part in a play ⟨forgot her *lines*⟩ **5 a** : something (as a ridge, seam, or wrinkle) that is long and narrow **b** : the direction followed by something in motion ⟨the *line* of flight of a bullet⟩ **c** : the boundary or limit of a place or lot ⟨town *line*⟩ ⟨property *line*⟩ **d** : the difference known or pointed out ⟨the fine *line* between love and hate⟩ **e** : the track of a railway **6** : a state of agreement ⟨the red one is more in *line* with what I had in mind⟩ **7 a** : a course of behavior or thinking; *esp* : an official or public position ⟨the party *line*⟩ **b** : what one does or is interested in ⟨is medicine your *line?*⟩ **c** : smooth or interesting talk that is often insincere **8** : FAMILY 2 ⟨descended from a royal *line*⟩ **9 a** : the position of military forces facing the enemy ⟨on the front and behind the *lines*⟩ ⟨our first *line* of defense⟩ **b** : an arrangement of persons or things in a series ⟨waiting in *line*⟩ **10** : goods for sale of one general kind ⟨a *line* of clothing⟩ **11** : a system of transportation or the route over which it travels ⟨a bus *line*⟩ ⟨a steamship *line*⟩ ⟨military supply *lines*⟩ **12 a** : a long narrow mark (as one made by a pencil) **b** : one of the horizontal lines on a music staff **c** : the football players whose positions are along the line of scrimmage **d** : a group of three players who play together as a unit in hockey **13** : a geometric element that is formed by a moving point and that has length but no width or thickness; *esp* : such an element that is straight **14 a** : ¹OUTLINE 1, CONTOUR ⟨a ship's *lines*⟩ **b** : a general plan ⟨a story along these *lines*⟩ [Middle English *line* "thread," partly from Old English *līne* (same meaning) and partly from early French *lingne* (same meaning), derived from Latin *linum* "flax"] — **between the lines** : in such a way as to learn or reveal something not expressed openly ⟨read *between the lines*⟩ — **down the line 1** : all the way : FULLY **2** : in the future — **in line for** : due to receive — **on the line** : at great risk ⟨the champ's title is *on the line*⟩ — **out of line** : beyond what is reasonable to put up with ⟨your behavior is getting *out of line*⟩ ⟨these prices are way *out of line*⟩

²**line** *vb* **lined; lin·ing 1** : to mark with a line or lines **2** : to place or form a line along **3** : to form a line : form into lines **4** : to hit a line drive

³**line** *vb* **lined; lin·ing** : to cover the inner surface of ⟨*line* a box with paper⟩ ⟨tapestries *lined* the walls⟩ [Old English *līn* "flax"]

lin·eage \\'lin-ē-ij\\ *n* **1** : the ancestors from whom a person is descended **2** : the people descended from the same ancestor

lin·eal \\'lin-ē-əl\\ *adj* **1** : LINEAR ⟨*lineal* measure⟩ **2 a** : consisting of or being in a direct line of descent **b** : HEREDITARY **3** — **lin·eal·ly** \\-ē-ə-lē\\ *adv*

lin·ea·ment \\'lin-ē-ə-mənt\\ *n* : an outline or contour of a body or figure and especially of the face

lin·ear \\'lin-ē-ər\\ *adj* **1 a** : relating to, consisting of, or resembling a line : STRAIGHT **b** : involving a single dimension **c** : of, relating to, based on, or being linear equations or linear functions **2** : long and uniformly narrow ⟨the *linear* leaf of the hyacinth⟩ — **lin·ear·i·ty** \\,lin-ē-'ar-ət-ē\\ *n* — **lin·ear·ly** \\'lin-ē-ər-lē\\ *adv*

linear accelerator *n* : a device in which charged particles are accelerated in a straight line by successive pushes from a series of electric fields

linear equation *n* : an equation in which each term is either a constant or contains only one variable, in which each variable has an exponent of 1, and which always has a straight line as a graph ⟨$y = mx + b$ is the general form of a *linear equation* where m and b are any real numbers⟩

linear function *n* : a function whose graph is a straight line and which is represented by an equation of the form $y = ax + b$ where a and b are constants, a does not equal zero, and x is any real number

linear measure *n* **1** : a measure of length **2** : a system of measures of length

linear programming *n* : a mathematical method for solving practical problems (as the distribution of resources) with linear functions whose variables are given specific limitations

line·back·er \\'līn-,bak-ər\\ *n* : a football player on the defending team whose usual position is a short distance in back of the line of scrimmage

line drawing *n* : a drawing made in solid lines

line drive *n* : a batted baseball hit not far above the ground in a nearly straight line

line graph *n* : a graph in which line segments join points representing different values

line·man \\'līn-mən\\ *n* **1** : one who sets up or repairs power or telephone lines **2** : a football player whose position is on the line of scrimmage

lin·en \\'lin-ən\\ *n* **1** : smooth strong cloth or yarn made from flax **2** : household articles (as tablecloths or sheets) or clothing (as shirts or underwear) that were once often made of linen — **linen** *adj*

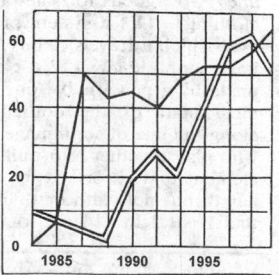

line graph

line of force : an imaginary line that shows the direction in space in which a force (as from a magnetic or electric field) acts

line of scrimmage : an imaginary line in football parallel to the goal lines and running through the place the ball is laid before each play begins

line printer *n* : a very fast printing device for a computer that prints whole lines at once instead of one letter at a time

¹**lin·er** \\'lī-nər\\ *n* **1** : a ship or airplane of a regular transportation line ⟨an ocean *liner*⟩ **2** : something with which lines are made or drawn ⟨use a cosmetic *liner* to make the eyes more attractive⟩

²**liner** *n* : one that lines or is used to line something

line segment *n* : ¹SEGMENT 2b

lines·man \\'līnz-mən\\ *n* : an official who assists a referee in a game (as football or hockey)

line·up \\'līn-,nəp\\ *n* **1** : a line of persons arranged especially for identification by police **2 a** : a list of players taking part in a game (as baseball) **b** : the players on such a list

line up \\(')lī-'nəp\\ *vb* **1** : to come together or arrange in a line or rows ⟨*line up* for inspection⟩ **2** : to put into alignment ⟨*line up* the edges so they are even⟩ ⟨*line up* the decimal points before adding or subtracting⟩ **3** : to arrange for ⟨*lined up* support for the candidate⟩ ⟨*lined up* a summer job⟩

-ling \\liŋ\\ *n suffix* **1** : one connected with or having the quality of ⟨hire*ling*⟩ **2** : young, small, or minor one ⟨duck*ling*⟩ [Old English *-ling* (noun suffix) "one having the quality of . . ."]

lin·ger \\'liŋ-gər\\ *vb* **lin·gered; lin·ger·ing** \\-g(ə-)riŋ\\ **1** : to be slow in quitting a place or activity ⟨*lingered* in bed⟩ **2** : to be slow to act — **lin·ger·er** \\-gər-ər\\ *n* — **lin·ger·ing·ly** \\-g(ə-)riŋ-lē\\ *adv*

synonyms LINGER, LOITER, LAG mean to pause often without good reason or explanation. LINGER suggests an unwillingness to leave a pleasant place ⟨*lingered* in the park after the concert⟩. LOITER suggests aimless wandering or waiting in a place ⟨restless youths *loitering* in the town square⟩. LAG suggests an inability or unwillingness to keep up with others ⟨two of the hikers *lagged* behind the rest of us⟩.

lin·ge·rie \\,län-jə-'rā, ,lan-zhə-, -'rē\\ *n* : women's nightclothes or underwear [French, derived from early French *linge* "linen"]

lin·go \\'liŋ-gō\\ *n, pl* **lingoes** : language that is strange or hard to understand

lin·gual \\'liŋ-g(yə-)wəl\\ *adj* **1** : of, relating to, or resembling a tongue **2** : produced by the tongue ⟨*lingual* sounds such as \\t\\ or \\l\\⟩ — **lin·gual·ly** \\-ē\\ *adv*

lin·guist \\'liŋ-gwəst\\ *n* **1** : a person skilled in languages **2** : a person who specializes in linguistics

lin·guis·tic \\liŋ-'gwis-tik\\ *adj* : of or relating to language or linguistics — **lin·guis·ti·cal·ly** \\-ti-k(ə-)lē\\ *adv*

linguistic form *n* : a meaningful unit of speech (as a part of a word, a word, or a sentence)

lin·guis·tics \\liŋ-'gwis-tiks\\ *n* : the study of human speech including the units, nature, structure, and development of language, languages, or a language

lin·i·ment \\'lin-ə-mənt\\ *n* : a liquid medicine rubbed on the skin especially to relieve pain

lin·ing \\'lī-niŋ\\ *n* : something that lines especially an inner surface of something (as a garment)

¹**link** \\'liŋk\\ *vb* : to join by or as if by a link — **link·er** *n*

²**link** *n* **1** : a connecting structure: as **a** : a single ring of a chain **b** : CUFF LINK **c** : ¹BOND 2b **d** : an intermediate rod or piece for transmitting force or motion **2** : something resembling a link of chain: as **a** : a piece of sausage in a series of connected pieces **b** : a connecting element or factor ⟨found a *link* between smoking and cancer⟩ **c** : HYPERLINK

link·age \'liŋ-kij\ *n* **1** : the manner or style of being united: as **a** : the manner in which atoms or radicals are linked in a molecule **b** : ¹BOND 2b **2** : the quality or state of being linked; *esp* : the occurring together of genes on the same chromosome with the result that the traits they control are not inherited independently of each other but tend to be found together **3** : a system of links; *esp* : a system of links or bars jointed together by means of which lines or curves may be traced

linked \'liŋ(k)t\ *adj* : exhibiting genetic linkage : tending to be inherited together

linking verb *n* : an intransitive verb (as *be* or *seem*) that links a subject with a word or words in the predicate 〈"look" in "you look happy" and "are" in "my favorite fruits are apples and oranges" are *linking verbs*〉 — compare ACTION VERB

links \'liŋ(k)s\ *n pl* : a golf course

link·up \'liŋ-ˌkəp\ *n* **1** : a getting together : MEETING 〈the *linkup* of two spacecraft〉 **2** : something that serves as a link

Lin·nae·an *or* **Lin·ne·an** \lə-'nē-ən, -'nā-; 'lin-ē-\ *adj* : of, relating to, or following the method of the Swedish botanist Linné who established the system of binomial nomenclature used in classifying plants and animals

lin·net \'lin-ət\ *n* : a common small Old-World brownish finch of which the male has red on the breast and top of the head during breeding season

Word History Many birds eat seeds. One small songbird, known as the linnet, seems especially fond of seeds of the flax plant, a fondness that appears to have earned the bird its name. The Latin word for flax is *linum,* which is also the source of the English word *linen,* a cloth made from flax. When *linum* was borrowed from Latin into early French, it became *lin.* The songbird that feeds on the flax seeds came to be called *linette* in early French and later *linnet* in English. [from early French *linette* "linnet," from *lin* "flax," from Latin *linum* "flax"]

li·no·leum \lə-'nō-lē-əm, -'nōl-yəm\ *n* : a floor covering with a canvas back and a surface of hardened linseed oil and usually cork dust

Li·no·type \'lī-nə-ˌtīp\ *trademark* — used for a machine that sets type in whole lines as a solid piece of metal

lin·seed \'lin-ˌsēd\ *n* : FLAXSEED

linseed oil *n* : a yellowish oil obtained from flaxseed and used especially in paint, varnish, printing ink, and linoleum

lin·sey–wool·sey \ˌlin-zē-'wul-zē\ *n* : a coarse fabric made of wool and linen or cotton

lint \'lint\ *n* **1** : loose fibers or bits of thread **2** : ¹COTTON 1a — **lint·less** \-ləs\ *adj* — **linty** \-ē\ *adj*

lin·tel \'lint-ᵊl\ *n* : a horizontal piece across the top of an opening (as of a door) that carries the weight of the structure above it

li·on \'lī-ən\ *n, pl* **lion** *or* **lions** : a large flesh‐eating mammal of the cat family that has a brownish buff coat, a tufted tail, and in the male a shaggy mane and that lives in open or rocky areas of Africa and formerly southern Asia — **li·on·like** \-ˌlīk\ *adj*

lion

li·on·ess \'lī-ə-nəs\ *n* : a female lion

li·on·heart·ed \ˌlī-ən-ˌhärt-əd\ *adj* : COURAGEOUS, BRAVE

lion's share *n* : the largest portion

¹lip \'lip\ *n* **1** : either of the two fleshy folds that surround the mouth **2** *slang* : BACK TALK **3 3 a** : a fleshy edge or margin 〈*lips* of a wound〉 **b** : a part or structure of a plant or animal that resembles a lip (as the protruding part of an orchid's corolla) **4** : the edge of a hollow container especially where it is slightly spread out — **lip·less** \-ləs\ *adj* — **lip·like** \-ˌlīk\ *adj*

²lip *adj* : spoken with the lips only : not sincere 〈*lip* service〉

li·pase \'lī-ˌpās, -ˌpāz\ *n* : an enzyme that functions especially in the breakdown or digestion of fats

lip·id \'lip-əd\ *n* : any of various substances (as fats and waxes) that with proteins and carbohydrates make up the principal structural parts of living cells

li·po·suc·tion \'lip-ə-ˌsək-shən, 'lī-pə-\ *n* : the surgical removal of fat from deposits beneath the skin (as of the thighs) [from *lipid* "fat" and *suction*]

lipped \'lipt\ *adj* : having a lip or lips especially of a certain kind or number — often used in combination 〈tight=lipped〉

lip–read \'lip-ˌrēd\ *vb* **-read** \-ˌred\; **-read·ing** \-ˌrēd-iŋ\ : to use lipreading to understand a speaker's words — **lip–read·er** \-ˌrēd-ər\ *n*

lip–read·ing \-ˌrēd-iŋ\ *n* : the getting of the meaning of a speaker's words without hearing the voice by watching lip and face movements

lip·stick \-ˌstik\ *n* : a waxy solid colored cosmetic for the lips usually in stick form

liquefied petroleum gas *n* : a compressed gas consisting of flammable light hydrocarbons and used especially as fuel or as a starting material for making other chemicals

liq·ue·fy \'lik-wə-ˌfī\ *vb* **-fied; -fy·ing** : to make or become liquid — **liq·ue·fi·able** \-ˌfī-ə-bəl\ *adj*

li·queur \li-'kər, -'k(y)ù(ə)r\ *n* : a flavored and usually sweetened alcoholic beverage

¹liq·uid \'lik-wəd\ *adj* **1** : flowing freely like water **2** : neither solid nor gaseous 〈*liquid* mercury〉 **3** : resembling liquid in clearness or smoothness 〈large *liquid* eyes〉 〈*liquid* notes of a bird〉 **4** : capable of being pronounced without friction and longer than usual like a vowel 〈the *liquid* consonant \l\〉 **5** : made up of or easily changed into cash 〈*liquid* assets〉 — **li·quid·i·ty** \lik-'wid-ət-ē\ *n* — **liq·uid·ly** \'lik-wəd-lē\ *adv*

²liquid *n* **1** : a liquid consonant **2** : a liquid substance

liq·ui·date \'lik-wə-ˌdāt\ *vb* **-dat·ed; -dat·ing** **1** : PAY OFF 1 〈*liquidate* a debt〉 **2** : to put an end to : do away with — **liq·ui·da·tion** \ˌlik-wə-'dā-shən\ *n*

liquid crystal display *n* : LCD

liquid measure *n* : a unit or series of units for measuring liquid capacity — see MEASURE table, METRIC SYSTEM table

li·quor \'lik-ər\ *n* **1** : a liquid substance or solution 〈dye *liquor*〉 **2** : a strong alcoholic beverage

li·ra \'lir-ə\ *n* **1** *pl* **li·re** \'lē-ˌrā\ *also* **liras** : the basic unit of money of Italy until 2002 **2** *pl* **liras** : the basic unit of money of Turkey **3** : a coin or bill representing one lira

lisle \'lī(ə)l\ *n* : a smooth tightly twisted thread usually made of cotton

¹lisp \'lisp\ *vb* : to pronounce the sounds \s\ and \z\ in an imperfect way by giving them the sounds of \th\ and \t͟h\ — **lisp·er** *n*

²lisp *n* : the act or habit of lisping

lis·some *also* **lis·som** \'lis-əm\ *adj* **1** : bending easily : FLEXIBLE, LITHE **2** : quick and light in action : NIMBLE

¹list \'list\ *vb, archaic* : CHOOSE **3** [Old English *lystan* "to please, suit, be desirable"]

²list *vb, archaic* : to listen to : HEAR [Old English *hlystan* "to listen"]

³list *n* **1** : a band or strip of material **2** *pl* **a** : an arena for jousting **b** : a field of competition or dispute [Old English *līste* "strip"]

\ə\ abut	\au̇\ out	\i\ tip	\ȯ\ saw	\u̇\ foot
\ər\ further	\ch\ chin	\ī\ life	\ȯi\ coin	\y\ yet
\a\ mat	\e\ pet	\j\ job	\th\ thin	\yü\ few
\ā\ take	\ē\ easy	\ŋ\ sing	\t͟h\ this	\yu̇\ cure
\ä\ cot, cart	\g\ go	\ō\ bone	\ü\ food	\zh\ vision

⁴list *n* : a leaning to one side : TILT

⁵list *vb* : to lean to one side : TILT ⟨a *listing* ship⟩ [origin unknown]

⁶list *n* : a record or catalog of names or items ⟨guest *list*⟩ ⟨grocery *list*⟩ [from French *liste* "a series of names or numbers," from Italian *lista* (same meaning); of Germanic origin]

⁷list *vb* **1** : to make a list of **2** : to put on a list **3** : to have a list price ⟨a car that *lists* at $20,000⟩

lis·ten \'lis-ᵊn\ *vb* **lis·tened; lis·ten·ing** \'lis-niŋ, -ᵊn-iŋ\ **1** : to pay attention in order to hear ⟨*listen* for a signal⟩ ⟨*listen* to a new CD⟩ **2** : to give heed : follow advice ⟨*listen* to a warning⟩ — **lis·ten·er** \'lis-nər, -ᵊn-ər\ *n*

listen in *vb* **1** : to listen to a broadcast **2** : EAVESDROP

list·ing *n* **1** : ⁴LIST **2** : something listed

list·less \'list-ləs\ *adj* : too tired or too little interested to want to do things [Middle English *listles* "having a lack of desire to act or move," from earlier *list* "desire, liking"] — **list·less·ly** *adv* — **list·less·ness** *n*

list price *n* : the retail price of an item as published in a catalog, price list, or advertisement

lit *past and past participle of* LIGHT

lit·a·ny \'lit-ᵊn-ē, 'lit-nē\ *n, pl* **-nies** : a prayer consisting of a series of lines spoken alternately by a leader and the congregation

litchi *variant of* LYCHEE

li·ter *or* **li·tre** \'lēt-ər\ *n* : a metric unit of capacity equal to one cubic decimeter — see METRIC SYSTEM table

lit·er·a·cy \'lit-ə-rə-sē, 'li-trə-sē\ *n* : the quality or state of being literate ⟨computer *literacy*⟩; *esp* : ability to read and write

lit·er·al \'lit-ə-rəl, 'li-trəl\ *adj* **1 a** : following the ordinary or usual meaning of the words ⟨*literal* and figurative meanings⟩ **b** : true to fact : PLAIN, UNADORNED ⟨took the television drama to be the *literal* truth⟩ **c** : concerned mainly with facts ⟨a *literal*-minded person⟩ **2** : of, relating to, or expressed in letters ⟨*literal* equations⟩ **3** : done word for word : EXACT, VERBATIM ⟨a *literal* translation⟩ — **lit·er·al·ness** *n*

lit·er·al·ly \'lit-ər-(ə-)lē, 'li-trə-lē\ *adv* **1** : in a literal sense or manner : ACTUALLY ⟨the flying machine *literally* never got off the ground⟩ **2** : PRACTICALLY 2, VIRTUALLY ⟨*literally* poured out new ideas⟩

lit·er·ary \'lit-ə-,rer-ē\ *adj* **1 a** : of or relating to literature **b** : BOOKISH 2 **2** : of or relating to writers or writing as a profession — **lit·er·ari·ly** \,lit-ə-'rer-ə-lē\ *adv* — **lit·er·ari·ness** \'lit-ə-,rer-ē-nəs\ *n*

¹lit·er·ate \'lit-ə-rət, 'li-trət\ *adj* **1** : EDUCATED 1, CULTURED **2** : able to read and write **3** : having knowledge or experience in a particular area ⟨computer *literate*⟩ — **lit·er·ate·ly** *adv* — **lit·er·ate·ness** *n*

²literate *n* **1** : an educated person **2** : a person who can read and write

lit·er·a·ture \'lit-ə-rə-,chu̇(ə)r, 'li-trə-, -chər\ *n* **1** : written works having excellence of form or expression and ideas of lasting and widespread interest **2** : written material (as of a period or on a subject)

-lith \,lith\ *n combining form* : structure or implement of stone ⟨mono*lith*⟩ [derived from Greek *lithos* "stone"]

lithe \'līth, 'līth\ *adj* **1** : easily bent : FLEXIBLE ⟨long *lithe* stems⟩ **2** : light and graceful in movement ⟨*lithe* dancers⟩ — **lithe·ly** *adv* — **lithe·ness** *n*

lithe·some \'līth-səm, 'līth-\ *adj* : LITHE 2

lith·i·um \'lith-ē-əm\ *n* : a soft silver-white element that is the lightest metal known — see ELEMENT table

litho- *combining form* : stone ⟨*litho*logy⟩ [derived from Greek *lithos* "stone"]

¹lith·o·graph \'lith-ə-,graf\ *vb* : to print by lithography — **lith·o·gra·pher** \lith-'äg-rə-fər, 'lith-ə-,graf-ər\ *n*

²lithograph *n* : a print made by lithography — **lith·o·graph·ic** \,lith-ə-'graf-ik\ *adj* — **lith·o·graph·i·cal·ly** \-'graf-i-k(ə-)lē\ *adv*

li·thog·ra·phy \lith-'äg-rə-fē\ *n* : a method of printing from a flat surface (as a smooth stone or metal plate) that has been prepared in such a way that only the areas meant to print will take ink

li·thol·o·gy \lith-'äl-ə-jē\ *n* : the study of rocks

litho·sphere \'lith-ə-,sfi(ə)r\ *n* : the outer part of the solid earth consisting of the crust and part of the mantle

Lith·u·a·nian \,lith-(y)ə-'wā-nē-ən, -nyən\ *n* **1** : a person born or living in Lithuania **2** : the Baltic language of the Lithuanian people — **Lithuanian** *adj*

lit·i·gant \'lit-i-gənt\ *n* : a person taking part in a lawsuit

lit·i·gate \'lit-ə-,gāt\ *vb* **-gat·ed; -gat·ing** : to carry on a lawsuit — **lit·i·ga·tion** \,lit-ə-'gā-shən\ *n* — **lit·i·ga·tor** \'lit-ə-,gāt-ər\ *n*

lit·mus paper \'lit-məs-\ *n* : paper treated with coloring matter that turns red in acid solutions and blue in alkaline solutions

litre *variant of* LITER

¹lit·ter \'lit-ər\ *n* **1 a** : a covered and curtained couch with poles to use for handles that is used for carrying a single passenger **b** : a device (as a stretcher) for carrying a sick or injured person **2** : material spread in areas where farm animals (as cows or chickens) are kept especially to absorb their urine and feces **3** : the young born to an animal at a single time ⟨a *litter* of puppies⟩ **4** : a messy collection of things scattered about : RUBBISH

¹litter 1a

²litter *vb* **1** : to give birth to young **2 a** : to cover with litter **b** : to scatter about in disorder **c** : to lie about in disorder

lit·ter·bug \'lit-ər-,bəg\ *n* : a person who litters a public area

lit·ter·mate \-,māt\ *n* : one of a litter of offspring considered in relation to the other members of the litter

¹lit·tle \'lit-ᵊl\ *adj* **lit·tler** \'lit-ᵊl-ər, 'lit-lər\ *or* **less** \'les\ *or* **less·er** \'les-ər\; **lit·tlest** \'lit-ᵊl-əst, 'lit-ləst\ *or* **least** \'lēst\ **1 a** : small in size **b** : ¹YOUNG 1a ⟨was too *little* to remember⟩ **c** : small in comparison with related forms ⟨*little* blue heron⟩ **d** : ¹NARROW 3, MEAN ⟨people with *little* minds⟩ **2 a** : small in quantity ⟨there was *little* food to feed them⟩ **b** : short in duration ⟨*little* time left⟩ **3** : small in importance ⟨life's *little* problems⟩ **4** : being younger ⟨my *little* brother⟩ — **lit·tle·ness** \'lit-ᵊl-nəs\ *n*

²little *adv* **less** \'les\; **least** \'lēst\ **1** : in a very small quantity or degree : SLIGHTLY ⟨had *little* more than we needed⟩ ⟨a *little* known fact⟩ **2** : not very often ⟨travels *little*⟩

³little *n* **1** : a small amount or quantity **2** : a short time or distance

Little Bear *n* : URSA MINOR

little by little *adv* : by small steps or amounts : GRADUALLY

Little Dipper *n* : DIPPER 3b

little finger *n* : the fourth and smallest finger of the hand counting the index finger as the first

little toe *n* : the outermost and smallest digit of the foot

¹lit·to·ral \'lit-ə-rəl; ,lit-ə-'ral, -'räl\ *adj* : of, relating to, or situated or growing on or near a shore (as of the sea)

²littoral *n* : a coastal region

lit·ur·gy \'lit-ər-jē\ *n, pl* **-gies** : a religious rite or body of rites — **li·tur·gi·cal** \lə-'tər-ji-kəl, li-\ *adj*

liv·able *also* **live·able** \'liv-ə-bəl\ *adj* : suitable for living in or with — **liv·able·ness** *n*

¹live \'liv\ *vb* **lived; liv·ing** **1 a** : to be alive **b** : to continue alive **2** : to keep oneself alive : SUBSIST ⟨*lived* on berries the whole time⟩ ⟨courtiers *living* off the king⟩ **3** : to have a home : DWELL ⟨*lives* next door⟩ **4** : to pass one's life ⟨*live* peacefully⟩ **5** : to show great enthusiasm or excitement in ⟨*lived* life to the fullest⟩ **6** : to experience firsthand ⟨*living* a dream⟩ — **live it up** : to carry on an activity or one's life with great enthusiasm and excitement — **live up to** : to act in keeping with : KEEP ⟨*live up to* one's promises⟩ — **live with** : to put up with : TOLERATE ⟨had to *live with* their decision⟩

²**live** \'līv\ *adj* **1 a** : having life : LIVING **b** : existing in fact or reality : ACTUAL ⟨spoke to a real *live* celebrity⟩ **2 a** : burning usually without flame ⟨*live* coals⟩ **b** : carrying an electric current ⟨a *live* wire⟩ **c** : not exploded ⟨a *live* bomb⟩ **3** : of present or continuing interest ⟨a *live* issue⟩ **4 a** : being present at the performance ⟨a *live* audience⟩ **b** : broadcast at the time of production ⟨a *live* television program⟩ **5** : being in play ⟨a *live* ball⟩

live—bear·er \'līv-ˌbar-ər, -ˌber-\ *n* : a fish that brings forth living young rather than eggs; *esp* : any of a family of numerous small fishes (as a molly or swordtail) that feed at the surface of the water

-lived \'līvd, 'livd\ *adj combining form* : having a life of a specified kind or length ⟨long-*lived*⟩ [Middle English *-lived* "having life," from *lif* "life"]

live down *vb* : to live so as to wipe out the memory of ⟨*live down* a mistake⟩

live·li·hood \'līv-lē-ˌhùd\ *n* : ²LIVING 3

live·long \ˌliv-ˌlȯŋ\ *adj* : during the whole of : ENTIRE ⟨worked all the *livelong* day⟩

live·ly \'līv-lē\ *adj* **live·li·er; -est** **1** : full of life : ACTIVE ⟨a *lively* puppy⟩ **2** : ¹KEEN 3 ⟨a *lively* interest⟩ **3** : full of spirit or feeling ⟨a *lively* debate⟩ **4** : showing activity or spirit ⟨a *lively* manner⟩ — **live·li·ness** *n* — **lively** *adv*
synonyms LIVELY, ANIMATED, VIVACIOUS mean very much alive and spirited. LIVELY suggests briskness, alertness, or energy ⟨a *lively* debate⟩. ANIMATED suggests great spirit and activity ⟨an *animated* discussion of current events⟩. VIVACIOUS suggests attractive cheerfulness and a quick wit ⟨a *vivacious* singer⟩.

liv·en \'lī-vən\ *vb* **liv·ened; liv·en·ing** \'līv-(ə-)niŋ\ : to make or become lively — often used with *up*

live oak \'lī-ˌvōk\ *n* : any of several American oaks with evergreen leaves and hard durable wood; *esp* : one of the southeastern U.S. that is grown for its shelter and shade and formerly much used in building ships

¹**liv·er** \'liv-ər\ *n* **1 a** : a large glandular organ of vertebrates that secretes bile and causes changes in the blood (as by changing sugars into glycogen and by forming urea) **b** : any of various large probably digestive glands of invertebrate animals **2** : the liver of an animal (as of a calf or chicken) eaten as food

²**liv·er** \'liv-ər\ *n* : one that lives especially in a specified way

-liv·ered \'liv-ərd\ *adj combining form* : expressing courage or spirit that suggests a person having (such) a liver ⟨lily-*livered*⟩

liver fluke *n* : any of various trematode worms that invade the liver of mammals

liv·er·ied \'liv-(ə-)rēd\ *adj* : wearing a livery

liv·er·wort \'liv-ər-ˌwərt, -ˌwȯ(ə)rt\ *n* : any of a class of flowerless plants related to and resembling the mosses but differing especially in their reproduction and development

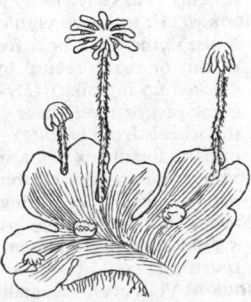

liverwort

liv·er·wurst \'liv-ər(r)-ˌwərst, -ˌwu̇rst; 'liv-ər-ˌwu̇st\ *n* : a sausage made chiefly of cooked liver

liv·ery \'liv-(ə-)rē\ *n, pl* **-er·ies** **1** : a special uniform worn by the servants of a wealthy household ⟨a footman in *livery*⟩ **2** : the clothing worn to distinguish an association of persons ⟨the *livery* of a school⟩ **3 a** : the

feeding, care, and stabling of horses for pay **b** : the keeping of horses and vehicles for hire **c** : LIVERY STABLE

livery stable *n* : a stable where horses and vehicles are kept for hire and where horses may be stabled

lives *plural of* LIFE

live·stock \'līv-ˌstäk\ *n* : animals kept or raised; *esp* : farm animals kept for use and profit

live wire *n* : an alert, active, or forceful person — **live–wire** *adj*

liv·id \'liv-əd\ *adj* **1** : discolored by bruising **2** : pale as ashes **3** : very angry ⟨was *livid* at his son's disobedience⟩ — **liv·id·ly** *adv*

¹**liv·ing** \'liv-iŋ\ *adj* **1 a** : not dead : ALIVE ⟨*living* authors⟩ **b** : ACTIVE 4b ⟨a *living* faith⟩ **2** : naturally giving life ⟨*living* waters⟩ **3 a** : true to life ⟨the *living* image of your mother⟩ **b** : fit for living ⟨the *living* area⟩

²**living** *n* **1** : the condition of being alive **2** : conduct or manner of life **3** : what one has to have to meet one's needs ⟨earned a *living* as a cook⟩

living fossil *n* : an animal or plant (as the horseshoe crab or the ginkgo tree) that has remained almost unchanged from earlier geologic times and whose close relatives are usually all extinct

living room *n* : a room in a house for general family use

liz·ard \'liz-ərd\ *n* : any of a group of reptiles that can be told apart from the related snakes by their lower jaw which has the two halves joined and inseparable, by their ears which are outside the body, by eyes with movable lids, and usually by two pairs of well-formed limbs which function in movement

'**ll** \l, əl, ᵊl\ *vb* : WILL ⟨you'*ll* be late⟩

lla·ma \'läm-ə\ *n* : any of several wild and domesticated long-necked South American hoofed mammals that chew the cud and are related to the camels but smaller and without a hump

lla·no \'län-ō, 'lan-\ *n, pl* **llanos** : an open grassy plain in Spanish America or the southwestern U.S.

lo \'lō\ *interj* — used to call attention or show wonder or surprise

llama

¹**load** \'lōd\ *n* **1 a** : something taken up and carried **b** : the amount that can be carried at one time ⟨10 *loads* of sand⟩ — often used in combination ⟨a boat*load* of tourists⟩ **2** : a mass or weight supported by something ⟨the *load* on a column⟩ **3** : something that depresses the mind or spirits ⟨a *load* of care⟩ **4** : a large quantity : LOT — usually used in plural ⟨had *loads* of fun⟩ **5** : a charge for a firearm **6 a** : amount of work done or expected to be done **b** : the demand upon the ability of a system to produce what it is meant to produce ⟨the *load* on an engine⟩ **7** *slang* : a good look : a full view — used in the phrase *get a load of*

²**load** *vb* **1 a** : to put a load in or on ⟨*load* a truck⟩ ⟨*load* a gun⟩ ⟨*loaded* my arms with books⟩ **b** : to place a weight or burden on ⟨vines *loaded* down with grapes⟩ ⟨*load* more work on him⟩ **c** : to supply abundantly ⟨*load* a person with honors⟩ **d** : to put runners on (first, second, and third base) in baseball ⟨the pitcher *loaded* the bases by walking three batters⟩ **e** : to fill with an often unfair appeal to the emotions ⟨*load* a question⟩ ⟨*loaded* words⟩ **f** : to put something like a load into ⟨*load* a camera with film⟩ ⟨*load* a disk drive⟩ **2 a** : to put or place in, on, or

\ə\ **abut**	\aú\ **out**	\i\ **tip**	\ȯ\ **saw**	\ú\ **foot**
\ər\ **further**	\ch\ **chin**	\ī\ **life**	\ȯi\ **coin**	\y\ **yet**
\a\ **mat**	\e\ **pet**	\j\ **job**	\th\ **thin**	\yü\ **few**
\ā\ **take**	\ē\ **easy**	\ŋ\ **sing**	\th\ **this**	\yu̇\ **cure**
\ä\ **cot, cart**	\g\ **go**	\ō\ **bone**	\ü\ **food**	\zh\ **vision**

into something as or as if a load ⟨*load* wood on a truck⟩ ⟨*load* film into a camera⟩ **b** : to copy or transfer into a computer's memory ⟨*load* a program⟩ — **load·er** *n* —
load up on 1 : to ingest in usually large amounts ⟨*loaded up on* his favorite food⟩ **2** : to acquire in usually large amounts ⟨*loaded up on* dry goods⟩
load·ed \'lōd-əd\ *adj* **1** *slang* : ²DRUNK 1 **2** : WEALTHY 1, RICH
load line *n* : a line on a ship showing the depth to which it sinks in the water when properly loaded
loadstar *variant of* LODESTAR
loadstone *variant of* LODESTONE
¹**loaf** \'lōf\ *n, pl* **loaves** \'lōvz\ **1** : a usually oblong mass of bread **2** : a dish (as of meat) baked in the form of a loaf [Old English *hlāf* "loaf of bread" — related to LADY, LORD; see *Word Histories* at LADY, LORD]
²**loaf** *vb* : to spend time idly or lazily
loaf·er \'lō-fər\ *n* **1** : a person who loafs **2** : a low shoe with no laces
loam \'lōm\ *n* : ³SOIL 2; *esp* : a soil consisting of a loose easily crumbled mixture of varying amounts of clay, silt, and sand — **loamy** \'lō-mē\ *adj*
¹**loan** \'lōn\ *n* **1 a** : money lent at interest **b** : something lent for a limited time **2** : permission to use something for a time
²**loan** *vb* : LEND 1
loan shark *n* : a person who lends money at very high rates of interest
loan·word \'lōn-,wərd\ *n* : a word that is taken into one language from another
loath *also* **loth** \'lōth, 'lōth *or* **loathe** \'lōth, 'lōth\ *adj* : unwilling to do something : RELUCTANT ⟨seems *loath* to trust anyone⟩
loathe \'lōth\ *vb* **loathed; loath·ing** : to feel extreme disgust for or at ⟨*loathe* the smell of burning rubber⟩ **syn·onyms** see HATE — **loath·er** *n*
loath·ing \'lō-thin\ *n* : very great dislike : extreme disgust
loath·some \'lōth-səm, 'lōth-\ *adj* : very unpleasant : OFFENSIVE — **loath·some·ly** *adv* — **loath·some·ness** *n*
¹**lob** \'läb\ *vb* **lobbed; lob·bing** : to send (as a ball) in a high arc by hitting or throwing easily
²**lob** *n* : a lobbed throw or shot (as in tennis)
¹**lob·by** \'läb-ē\ *n, pl* **lobbies** **1** : a hall or entry especially when large enough to serve as a waiting room ⟨a hotel *lobby*⟩ **2** : a group of persons engaged in lobbying ⟨the oil *lobby*⟩
²**lobby** *vb* **lob·bied; lob·by·ing** : to try to influence public officials and especially members of a legislative body — **lob·by·ist** \'läb-ē-əst\ *n*
lobe \'lōb\ *n* : a curved or rounded part; *esp* : one that is part of a bodily organ or part — **lobed** \'lōbd\ *adj*
lobe—finned fish *n* : any of a group of mostly extinct fishes that have paired fins suggesting limbs and may be closely related to or closely resemble the ancestors of the land-dwelling vertebrates — called also *lobe-fin, lobe-fin fish*
lo·be·lia \lō-'bēl-yə\ *n* : any of a genus of widely distributed herbs (as the cardinal flower) often grown for their clusters of showy flowers
lob·lol·ly pine \'läb-,läl-ē-\ *n* : a pine of the southeastern U.S. with thick flaky bark, long needles in groups of three, and spiny-tipped cones; *also* : its coarse-grained wood — called also *loblolly*
lob·ster \'läb-stər\ *n* : any of several large edible marine crustaceans with stalked eyes, a pair of large claws, and a long abdomen; *also* : SPINY LOBSTER

lobelia

lobster pot *n* : a trap for catching lobsters
¹**lo·cal** \'lō-kəl\ *adj* **1** : of or relating to position in space **2** : relating to a particular place ⟨*local* news⟩ ⟨a *local* custom⟩ **3** : serving the needs of a certain district ⟨*local* government⟩ **4** : involving or affecting only a small part of the body ⟨a *local* infection⟩ — **lo·cal·ly** \-kə-lē\ *adv*
²**local** *n* **1** : a public vehicle (as a bus or train) that makes all of the stops or most of the stops along its route **2** : a local branch (as of a lodge or labor union)
local area network *n* : a computer network that spans a small area (as an office building)
local color *n* : the presentation in a story or play of the peculiarities of a particular place and the people who live there
lo·cale \lō-'kal\ *n* : a place where something happens or is supposed to happen ⟨the *locale* of the accident⟩ ⟨the *locale* of a play⟩
lo·cal·ism \'lō-kə-,liz-əm\ *n* : a local peculiarity of speech or acting
lo·cal·i·ty \lō-'kal-ət-ē\ *n, pl* **-ties** : a place and its surroundings
lo·cal·ize \'lō-kə-,līz\ *vb* **-ized; -iz·ing** **1** : to assign to or keep in a definite place or locality **2** : to be restricted to or accumulate in a limited area ⟨pain *localized* in a joint⟩ — **lo·cal·i·za·tion** \,lō-kə-lə-'zā-shən\ *n*
lo·cate \'lō-,kāt, lō-'kāt\ *vb* **lo·cat·ed; lo·cat·ing** **1** : to set oneself or one's business up in a particular place **2** : to state and fix exactly the place, limits, or position of ⟨*locate* property lines⟩ ⟨*locate* point B⟩ **3 a** : to look for and find the position of ⟨trying to *locate* the problem with the engine⟩ **b** : to find or fix the place of in a series ⟨*locate* an event in history⟩
lo·ca·tion \lō-'kā-shən\ *n* **1 a** : a place fit for or having some particular use ⟨a lovely *location* for a house⟩ ⟨each *location* in a computer memory has its own address⟩ **b** : a place outside a studio where a motion picture is filmed ⟨on *location* in the desert⟩ **2** : the act or process of locating
lo·ca·tor *also* **lo·cat·er** \'lō-,kāt-ər, lō-'kāt-\ *n* : one that locates something (as a mining claim or the course of a road)
loch \'läk, 'läk\ *n* **1** *Scottish* : LAKE **2** *Scottish* : an arm of the sea especially when it is nearly surrounded by land
loci *plural of* LOCUS
¹**lock** \'läk\ *n* **1** : a small bunch of hair or fiber (as cotton or wool) **2** *pl* : the hair of the head [Old English *locc* "small bunch of hair"]
²**lock** *n* **1 a** : a fastening (as for a door) in which a bolt is operated (as by a key) **b** : a device for exploding the charge or cartridge of a firearm **2** : an enclosure (as in a canal) with gates at each end used in raising or lowering boats as they pass from level to level **3** : a wrestling hold that prevents any movement of the part of the body that is being held ⟨a leg *lock*⟩ [Old English *loc* "fastener"]
³**lock** *vb* **1** : to fasten with or as if with a lock ⟨*lock* up the house⟩ ⟨the door *locks* from the inside⟩ **2 a** : to shut in or out or make secure by or as if by means of a lock ⟨*locked* up my bike⟩ ⟨*locked* in jail⟩ **b** : to make or become fast or motionless ⟨pump the brake pedal to keep the wheels from *locking*⟩ **3** : to make fast by the linking of parts together ⟨*lock* arms⟩
lock·er \'läk-ər\ *n* : a cabinet, compartment, or chest for personal use or for storing food at a low temperature
locker room *n* : a room for changing clothes and for storing clothes and equipment in lockers; *esp* : one for use by sports players
lock·et \'läk-ət\ *n* : a small ornamental case usually worn on a chain or necklace
lock·jaw \'läk-,jȯ\ *n* : a symptom of tetanus marked by spasms of the jaw muscles and inability to open the jaws; *also* : TETANUS 1

lock·out \-,aut\ *n* : the stopping of work or closing of a plant by an employer during a labor dispute in order to make the employees come to terms

lock·smith \-,smith\ *n* : a person who makes or repairs locks

lock·step \-,step\ *n* : a way of marching in step in which the marchers are very close one behind the other

lock·stitch \-,stich\ *n* : a sewing machine stitch in which a thread on the bottom of the material is looped over a thread pushed through from the top and then both are pulled tight

lock·up \-,əp\ *n* : PRISON 2, JAIL

lo·co \'lō-kō\ *adj, slang* : not sane : CRAZY

lo·co·mo·tion \,lō-kə-'mō-shən\ *n* : the act or power of moving from place to place

¹lo·co·mo·tive \,lō-kə-'mōt-iv\ *adj* **1** : of or relating to locomotion **2** : of, relating to, or being a locomotive

²locomotive *n* : an engine that moves under its own power; *esp* : one that hauls cars on a railroad

lo·co·mo·tor \,lō-kə-'mōt-ər\ *adj* : of, relating to, or used in locomotion

lo·co·weed \'lō-kō-,wēd\ *n* : any of several plants of the legume family that occur in western North America and cause poisoning in livestock

lo·cus \'lō-kəs\ *n, pl* **lo·ci** \'lō-,sī, -,kī, -,kē\ **1** : ¹PLACE 3a, LOCALITY **2** : the set of all points whose location is determined by stated conditions **3** : the position in a chromosome of a particular gene or allele

lo·cust \'lō-kəst\ *n* **1 a** : SHORT-HORNED GRASSHOPPER; *esp* : a grasshopper that often migrates in vast swarms and eats up the plants in its course **b** : CICADA **2 a** : any of various trees of the legume family with hard wood **b** : the wood of a locust

locust 1a

lo·cu·tion \lō-'kyü-shən\ *n* **1** : a particular form of expression ⟨complicated *locutions* in legal documents⟩ **2** : style of expression or speaking

lode \'lōd\ *n* : an ore deposit

lode·star *also* **load·star** \'lōd-,stär\ *n* : a star that leads or guides; *esp* : NORTH STAR

lode·stone *also* **load·stone** \'lōd-,stōn\ *n* **1** : a rock having magnetic properties **2** : something that strongly attracts

¹lodge \'läj\ *vb* **lodged; lodg·ing 1 a** : to provide or serve as especially temporary quarters for ⟨*lodged* their guests overnight⟩ **b** : to establish or settle oneself in a place **c** : to settle or live in as a residence **d** : to rent lodgings to **2** : to serve as a receptacle for : CONTAIN **3** : to bring or come to a rest and remain ⟨the bone *lodged* in the throat⟩ ⟨the bullet *lodged* in a tree⟩ **4** : to lay before a proper authority : FILE ⟨*lodge* a complaint⟩

²lodge *n* **1 a** : a house set apart for residence in a special season ⟨a hunting *lodge*⟩ **b** : a resort hotel ⟨ski *lodge*⟩ **c** : a house for an employee on an estate ⟨the gamekeeper's *lodge*⟩ **2** : a den or lair of wild animals (as beavers) **3** : the meeting place of a branch (as of a fraternal organization); *also* : the members of such a branch **4 a** : WIGWAM **b** : a family of North American Indians

lodge·pole pine \,läj-,pōl-\ *n* : any of several western North American pines with needles in pairs and short cones

lodg·er \'läj-ər\ *n* : one that lodges; *esp* : one that occupies a rented room in another's house

lodg·ing \'läj-iŋ\ *n* **1** : DWELLING; *esp* : a temporary dwelling or sleeping place **2** : a room or suite of rooms in another's house rented as a dwelling — usually used in plural

lodging house *n* : ROOMING HOUSE

lodg·ment *or* **lodge·ment** \'läj-mənt\ *n* **1 a** : a lodging place : SHELTER **b** : LODGING 2 **2 a** : the act, fact, or manner of lodging ⟨a hut for temporary *lodgment* of travelers⟩ **b** : a placing, depositing, or coming to rest **3** : an accumulation of something deposited in a place ⟨a *lodgment* of leaves in a gutter⟩

loess \'les, 'lə(r)s, 'lō-əs\ *n* : a fine usually yellowish brown soil found in North America, Europe, and Asia and believed to be chiefly deposited by the wind

¹loft \'lȯft\ *n* **1** : an upper room or floor : ATTIC **2 a** : a gallery in a church or hall ⟨organ *loft*⟩ **b** : an upper floor of a warehouse or business building when not partitioned **c** : HAYLOFT **3** : the backward slant of the face of a golf-club head

²loft *vb* **1** : to place, house, or store in a loft **2** : to strike or throw a ball so that it rises high in the air ⟨*lofted* a high fly to center field⟩

lofty \'lȯf-tē\ *adj* **loft·i·er; -est 1** : PROUD 1a, HAUGHTY ⟨a *lofty* manner⟩ **2 a** : of high, noble, or excellent quality ⟨*lofty* ideals⟩ **b** : of high rank : SUPERIOR **3** : rising to a great height ⟨*lofty* redwood trees⟩ **synonyms** see HIGH — **loft·i·ly** \-tə-lē\ *adv* — **loft·i·ness** \-tē-nəs\ *n*

¹log \'lȯg, 'läg\ *n* **1** : a large piece of a cut or fallen tree; *esp* : a long piece of a tree trunk trimmed and ready for sawing **2** : a device for measuring the speed of a ship **3 a** : the daily record of a ship's speed and progress **b** : the full record of a ship's voyage or of an aircraft's flight **4** : a record of performance, events, or day-to-day activities ⟨a computer *log*⟩

²log *vb* **logged; log·ging 1** : to cut trees for lumber or to clear land of trees in lumbering **2** : to put details of or about in a log **3 a** : to move a distance or reach a speed as noted in a log **b** : to sail a ship or fly an aircraft for an indicated distance or time ⟨the pilot *logged* thousands of miles and hundreds of hours⟩

³log *n* : LOGARITHM

lo·gan·ber·ry \'lō-gən-,ber-ē\ *n* : a dewberry that grows upright and produces red fruit; *also* : its berry

log·a·rithm \'lȯg-ə-,rith-əm, 'läg-\ *n* : the exponent that indicates the power to which a base number is raised to produce a given number ⟨the *logarithm* of 100 to the base 10 is 2⟩ — **log·a·rith·mic** \,lȯg-ə-'rith-mik, ,läg-\ *adj*

log·book \'lȯg-,buk, 'läg-\ *n* **1** : ¹LOG 3 **2** : ¹LOG 4

loge \'lōzh\ *n* **1** : a box in a theater **2** : the forward section of a theater mezzanine **3** : a raised section or level of seats in a sports stadium

log·ger \'lȯg-ər, 'läg-\ *n* : one whose work is logging

log·ger·head \'lȯg-ər-,hed, 'läg-\ *n* : any of several very large turtles; *esp* : a flesh-eating sea turtle of the warmer parts of the western Atlantic — **at loggerheads** : in or into a state of quarrelsome disagreement

loggerhead

log·ic \'läj-ik\ *n* **1** : the study of the rules and tests of sound reasoning **2** : REASONING 1; *esp* : sound reasoning ⟨no *logic* in that remark⟩ **3** : connection (as of facts or events) in a way that seems reasonable ⟨the *logic* of a situation⟩ **4** : the arrangement of circuit elements (as in a computer) needed for computation

\ə\ abut	\au̇\ out	\i\ tip	\ȯ\ saw	\u̇\ foot
\ər\ further	\ch\ chin	\ī\ life	\ȯi\ coin	\y\ yet
\a\ mat	\e\ pet	\j\ job	\th\ thin	\yü\ few
\ā\ take	\ē\ easy	\ŋ\ sing	\th\ this	\yu̇\ cure
\ä\ cot, cart	\g\ go	\ō\ bone	\ü\ food	\zh\ vision

log·i·cal \ˈläj-i-kəl\ *adj* **1** : of or relating to logic : used in logic **2** : according to the rules of logic ⟨a *logical* argument⟩ **3** : skilled in logic ⟨a *logical* thinker⟩ **4** : being in agreement with what may be reasonably expected ⟨a *logical* result of an action⟩ — **log·i·cal·ly** \-k(ə-)lē\ *adv* — **log·i·cal·ness** \-kəl-nəs\ *n*

lo·gi·cian \lō-ˈjish-ən\ *n* : a person who is skilled in logic

log in *vb* : LOG ON — **log–in** \ˈlȯg-ˌin, ˈläg-\ *n*

lo·gis·tics \lō-ˈjis-tiks\ *n sing or pl* : a branch of military science that deals with the transporting, housing, and supplying of troops — **lo·gis·tic** \-tik\ *or* **lo·gis·ti·cal** \-ti-kəl\ *adj*

logo \ˈlō-gō; ˈlȯg-ō, ˈläg-\ *n, pl* **log·os** \-gōz, -ōz\ : an identifying symbol or motto ⟨T-shirts with company *logos*⟩

Lo·go \ˈlō-gō\ *n* : a simplified language for programming and communicating with a computer that uses drawing on a display screen as a tool for teaching programming principles

log on *vb* : to make a connection with a computer or network ⟨*logged on* to the Internet⟩ — **log–on** \ˈlȯg-ˌȯn, ˈläg-ˌän\ *n*

log·roll·ing \ˈlȯg-ˌrō-liŋ, ˈläg-\ *n* **1** : the rolling of logs in water by treading **2** : the trading of votes by two legislators to secure favorable action on projects of interest to each

log·wood \ˈlȯg-ˌwu̇d, ˈläg-\ *n* : a Central American and West Indian tree of the legume family that has hard brown or brownish red heartwood used in dyeing; *also* : the heartwood or a preparation made from it

lo·gy \ˈlō-gē\ *adj* **lo·gi·er; -est** : SLUGGISH, TIRED — **lo·gi·ness** \-gē-nəs\ *n*

-l·o·gy \l-ə-jē\ *n combining form* : doctrine : theory : science ⟨bio*logy*⟩ [derived from Greek *logos* "word"]

loin \ˈlȯin\ *n* **1 a** : the part of the body on each side of the spinal column between the hip and the lower ribs **b** : a cut of meat (as beef) from the loin of an animal **2** *pl* **a** : the pubic region **b** : the organs of reproduction

loin·cloth \-ˌklȯth\ *n* : a cloth worn as a garment about the loins

loi·ter \ˈlȯit-ər\ *vb* **1** : to interrupt or delay an errand or a journey with pointless stops **2 a** : to remain in an area for no good reason **b** : to lag behind *synonyms* see LINGER — **loi·ter·er** *n*

loll \ˈläl\ *vb* **1** : to hang or let hang loosely : DROOP **2** : to recline, lean, or move in a loose or lazy manner : LOUNGE ⟨*loll* around in the sun⟩

lol·li·pop *or* **lol·ly·pop** \ˈläl-i-ˌpäp\ *n* : a lump of hard candy on the end of a stick

lone \ˈlōn\ *adj* **1** : having no company : SOLITARY ⟨a *lone* traveler⟩ **2** : situated by itself ⟨a *lone* outpost⟩

lone·ly \ˈlōn-lē\ *adj* **lone·li·er; -est** **1** : LONE 1 **2** : not visited by human beings : DESOLATE ⟨a *lonely* spot⟩ **3** : LONESOME 1 ⟨feeling *lonely*⟩ — **lone·li·ness** *n*

lon·er \ˈlō-nər\ *n* : one that avoids others; *esp* : INDIVIDUALIST 1

lone·some \ˈlōn(t)-səm\ *adj* **1** : sad from lack of companionship or separation from others **2** : not often visited or traveled over ⟨a *lonesome* highway⟩ ⟨the *lonesome* frontier⟩ — **lone·some·ness** *n*

lone wolf *n* : a person who prefers to act, live, or work alone : LONER

¹long \ˈlȯŋ\ *adj* **lon·ger** \ˈlȯŋ-gər\; **lon·gest** \ˈlȯŋ-gəst\ **1** : of great extent from end to end : not short **2 a** : having a specified length ⟨a meter *long*⟩ **b** : forming the chief linear dimension ⟨the *long* side of the table⟩ **3** : lasting for a considerable or specified time ⟨a *long* friendship⟩ ⟨two hours *long*⟩ **4** : overly long or lasting too long ⟨a *long* look⟩ ⟨a *long* explanation⟩ **5** : containing many or a specified number of units ⟨a *long* series of wins⟩ **6** : being a syllable or speech sound of relatively great duration **7**

: extending far into the future **8** : strong in or well supplied with something ⟨*long* on golf⟩ ⟨*long* on wisdom⟩ [Old English *long, lang* "extending a great distance"] — **at long last** : after a long wait : FINALLY

²long *adv* **1** : for or during a long time ⟨*long* a popular hangout⟩ **2** : for the length of a specified period ⟨all summer *long*⟩ **3** : at a distant point of time ⟨*long* before we arrived⟩ — **as long as** *or* **so long as** **1** : in view of the fact that : SINCE **2** : provided that : IF — **so long** : GOOD-BYE

³long *vb* **longed; long·ing** \ˈlȯŋ-iŋ\ : to feel a strong desire or wish ⟨*longing* to return home⟩ [Old English *langian* "to feel a strong desire for something"] *synonyms* see YEARN

long·boat \ˈlȯŋ-ˌbōt\ *n* : a large boat carried on a ship

long bone *n* : one of the bones supporting a limb of a vertebrate and consisting of a long nearly cylinder-shaped shaft that contains bone marrow and has enlarged ends

long·bow \ˈlȯŋ-ˌbō\ *n* : a wooden bow drawn by hand

¹long–dis·tance \-ˈdis-tən(t)s\ *adj* **1** : of or relating to telephone communication with a distant point **2 a** : situated a long distance away **b** : going or covering a long distance ⟨*long-distance* roads⟩ ⟨a *long-distance* runner⟩ **c** : conducted or effective over a long distance ⟨a *long-distance* relationship⟩ ⟨*long-distance* listening devices⟩

²long–distance *adv* : by long-distance telephone

long distance *n* **1** : communication by long-distance telephone **2** : a telephone operator or exchange that gives long-distance connections

long division *n* : arithmetical division in which the several steps involved in the division are shown in detail

lon·gev·i·ty \län-ˈjev-ət-ē, lȯn-\ *n* **1** : long life or continuance **2** : length of life

long–haired \ˈlȯŋ-ˌha(ə)rd, -ˌhe(ə)rd\ *or* **long–hair** \-ˌha(ə)r, -ˌhe(ə)r\ *adj* : having long hair or fur ⟨a *long-haired* dog⟩

long·hand \ˈlȯŋ-ˌhand\ *n* **1** : the characters or words written out fully by hand **2** : cursive writing

long·horn \-ˌhȯ(ə)rn\ *n* : any of the cattle with long horns that were formerly common in the southwestern U.S.

long–horned \-ˌhȯrn(d)\ *adj* : having long horns or antennae ⟨*long-horned* beetles⟩

long·house \-ˌhau̇s\ *n* : a long dwelling especially of the Iroquois for several families

long hundredweight *n, British* : HUNDREDWEIGHT 2

long·ing \ˈlȯŋ-iŋ\ *n* : an eager desire : CRAVING — **long·ing·ly** \-iŋ-lē\ *adv*

long·ish \ˈlȯŋ-ish\ *adj* : somewhat long

lon·gi·tude \ˈlän-jə-ˌt(y)üd\ *n* : distance measured by degrees or time east or west from the prime meridian ⟨the *longitude* of New York is 74 degrees or about five hours west of Greenwich⟩

lon·gi·tu·di·nal \ˌlän-jə-ˈt(y)üd-nəl, -ᵊn-əl\ *adj* **1** : of or relating to length **2** : placed or running lengthwise — **lon·gi·tu·di·nal·ly** \-ē\ *adv*

longitude: meridians of longitude

long johns \ˈlȯŋ-ˌjänz\ *n pl* : long underwear

long jump *n* : a jump for distance in track-and-field competition — **long jumper** *n*

long·leaf pine \ˌlȯŋ-ˌlēf-\ *n* : a tall pine of the southeastern U.S. that has long needles in clusters of three and long cones and is a major timber tree; *also* : its tough coarse-grained reddish orange wood

long–leaved pine \ˌlȯŋ-ˌlēv(d)-\ *n* : LONGLEAF PINE

long–lived \ˈlȯŋ-ˈlīvd, -ˈlivd\ *adj* : living or lasting long

long–play·ing \'lȯṅ-'plā-iṅ\ *adj* : of, relating to, or being a phonograph record designed to be played at 33⅓ revolutions per minute

long–range \-'rānj\ *adj* **1** : relating to or fit for long distances ⟨a *long-range* gun⟩ **2** : LONG-TERM ⟨*long-range* planning⟩

long–ship \-,ship\ *n* : a long sail and oar ship used by the Vikings

long–shore·man \'lȯn-'shōr-mən, -'shȯr-\ *n* : one who loads and unloads ships at a port : STEVEDORE

long shot \'lȯṅ-,shät\ *n* **1** : a great risk that promises a great reward if successful **2** : an entry (as in a horse race) given little chance of winning — **by a long shot** : by a great deal

long–stand·ing \'lȯṅ-'stan-diṅ\ *adj* : of long duration ⟨a *long-standing* dispute⟩

long–suf·fer·ing \-'səf(-ə)-riṅ\ *adj* : patiently enduring lasting offense or hardship — **long–suffering** *n* — **long–suf·fer·ing·ly** *adv*

long–term \-'tərm\ *adj* : extending over or involving a long period of time

long–wind·ed \'lȯṅ-'win-dəd\ *adj* : boringly long in speaking or writing — **long–wind·ed·ly** *adv* — **long–wind·ed·ness** *n*

loof·ah *also* **luf·fa** \'lü-fə\ *n* : any of various Old World tropical plants of the gourd family with large fruits; *also* : a sponge consisting of the fiber-containing skeleton of its fruit [derived from Arabic *lūf* "loofah"]

¹**look** \'lu̇k\ *vb* **1** : to exercise the power of vision : SEE **2** : to express by the eyes or by an expression of the face **3 a** : to have an appearance that is suitable for ⟨*looks* her age⟩ **b** : SEEM 1 ⟨it *looks* dangerous⟩ **4** : to direct one's attention or eyes ⟨*look* in the mirror⟩ **5** : ²POINT 4, FACE ⟨the house *looks* east⟩ — **look after** : to attend to — **look at 1** : CONSIDER 1 ⟨*looking at* the possibility of moving⟩ **2** : meet face-to-face : FACE ⟨*looking at* detention after school⟩ — **look daggers** : to look threateningly — **look down on** : to treat as an inferior : DISDAIN — **look for 1** : EXPECT 2 **2** : to search for : SEEK — **look forward to** : to expect with pleasure — **look into** : to examine carefully — **look on** *or* **look upon 1** : CONSIDER 3, REGARD ⟨*looked upon* me as a friend⟩ **2** : to observe as a spectator — **look out for 1** : to be on guard against ⟨*look out for* cars⟩ **2** : to care for : PROTECT ⟨*look out for* our interests⟩ — **look to 1** : to direct one's attention to ⟨*looking to* the future⟩ **2** : to take care of **3** : to rely on ⟨*looks to* reading for relaxation⟩

²**look** *n* **1 a** : the act of looking **b** : ²GLANCE 3 **2 a** : the expression of the face **b** : physical appearance; *esp* : attractive physical appearance — usually used in plural **3** : the state or form in which something appears : ASPECT

look·er–on \,lu̇k-ə-'rȯn, -'rän\ *n, pl* **lookers–on** : SPECTATOR, ONLOOKER

looking glass *n* : ¹MIRROR 1

look·out \'lu̇k-,au̇t\ *n* **1** : a person who keeps watch **2** : a high place or structure from which a wide view is possible **3** : a careful looking or watching **4** : OUTLOOK 1b **5** : a matter of care or concern ⟨the plants are wilting, but that's not my *lookout*⟩

look over *vb* : to inspect or examine usually in a hurried or careless way

look–up \'lu̇k-,əp\ *n* : the process or an instance of looking something up; *esp* : the process of matching by computer the words of a text with material stored in memory

look up *vb* : to seek for or out ⟨*look up* a word in the dictionary⟩ ⟨*look up* a friend⟩

¹**loom** \'lüm\ *n* : a frame or machine for weaving threads or yarns to produce cloth

²**loom** *vb* **1** : to appear suddenly and often with a large, dim, or strange form ⟨*loomed* out of the fog⟩ **2** : to be about to happen

loon \'lün\ *n* : any of several large diving birds that eat fish, have a long pointed bill and webbed feet, and usually nest on the banks of lakes and ponds

loon

loo·ny *also* **loo·ney** \'lü-nē\ *adj* **loo·ni·er; -est** : CRAZY, FOOLISH [an altered form of *lunatic* (adjective)] — **loo·ni·ness** *n* — **loony** *n*

¹**loop** \'lüp\ *n* **1** : a fold or doubling of a line through which another line can be passed or into which a hook may be hooked **2** : a loop-shaped ornament, figure, bend, course, or device ⟨a *loop* in a river⟩ **3** : a circular airplane maneuver involving flying upside down **4** : a complete electric circuit **5** : a piece of motion-picture film or magnetic tape whose ends are joined together to project or play back the same things continuously **6** : a series of instructions (as for a computer) that is repeated usually until a requirement for ending is met — **for a loop** : into a state of amazement, confusion, or distress ⟨the news knocked me *for a loop*⟩

²**loop** *vb* **1** : to make or form a loop **2 a** : to make a loop in, on, or about **b** : to fasten with a loop **3** : to perform a loop in an airplane

loop·er \'lü-pər\ *n* **1** : any of numerous small caterpillars that are mostly larvae of moths, move with a looping movement, and have little or no hair — called also *inch-worm, measuring worm* **2** : one that loops

loop·hole \'lüp-,hōl\ *n* **1** : a small opening; *esp* : one in a wall through which firearms may be discharged **2** : a way of escaping something; *esp* : a way of avoiding a law or regulation

loop of Hen·le \-'hen-lē\ *n* : a U-shaped part of the nephron of birds and mammals that plays a part in removing water during the formation of urine [from the name F. G. J. *Henle*, died 1885, German pathologist]

¹**loose** \'lüs\ *adj* **loos·er; loos·est 1 a** : not firmly fastened or securely attached ⟨a *loose* tooth⟩ **b** : no longer attached ⟨a boat *loose* from its moorings⟩ **c** : not tight-fitting **2 a** : not shut in, tied up, or held back ⟨a lion *loose* in the streets⟩ **b** : not brought together in a bundle, container, or binding ⟨*loose* sheets of pages⟩ **3** : not dense or compact ⟨*loose* dirt⟩ ⟨cloth of *loose* weave⟩ **4** : not respectable : IMMORAL ⟨*loose* conduct⟩ **5** : not tightly drawn or stretched : SLACK **6** : not exact or careful ⟨a *loose* guess⟩ — **loose** *adv* — **loose·ly** *adv* — **loose·ness** *n*

²**loose** *vb* **loosed; loos·ing 1** : LOOSEN 1 **2** : ¹SHOOT 1, FIRE ⟨*loose* a volley⟩

loose end *n* **1** : something left hanging loose **2** : a piece of unfinished business ⟨tying up *loose ends*⟩

loose–joint·ed \'lüs-'jȯint-əd\ *adj* **1** : having flexible joints **2** : moving with unusual freedom or ease

loose–leaf \'lü-'slēf\ *adj* **1** : designed so that sheets (as of paper) can be removed or inserted by opening a locking device ⟨*loose-leaf* notebook⟩ **2** : of, relating to, or used with a loose-leaf binding ⟨*loose-leaf* paper⟩

loos·en \'lüs-ᵊn\ *vb* **loos·ened; loos·en·ing** \'lüs-niṅ, -ᵊn-iṅ\ **1** : to set free **2** : to make or become loose or looser **3** : to cause or permit to become less strict ⟨*loosened* the rules⟩

loose·strife \'lü(s)-,strīf\ *n* **1** : any of a genus of herbs that are related to the primroses and have leafy stems and yel-

\ə\ abut	\au̇\ out	\i\ tip	\ȯ\ saw	\u̇\ foot
\ər\ further	\ch\ chin	\ī\ life	\ȯi\ coin	\y\ yet
\a\ mat	\e\ pet	\j\ job	\th\ thin	\yü\ few
\ā\ take	\ē\ easy	\ṅ\ sing	\t͟h\ this	\yu̇\ cure
\ä\ cot, cart	\g\ go	\ō\ bone	\ü\ food	\zh\ vision

low or white flowers **2** : any of a genus of herbs including some with showy spikes of purple flowers

[1]loot \'lüt\ *n* : something stolen or taken by force

[2]loot *vb* : [1]PLUNDER, STEAL — **loot·er** *n*

lop \'läp\ *vb* **lopped; lop·ping 1** : to cut branches or twigs from a tree **2** : to remove unnecessary or undesirable parts from something — usually used with *off* — **lop·per** *n*

lope \'lōp\ *n* : an easy leaping way of moving — **lope** *vb* — **lop·er** *n*

lop–eared \'läp-ˌi(ə)rd\ *adj* : having ears that droop ⟨a *lop-eared* rabbit⟩

lop·sid·ed \'läp-ˈsīd-əd\ *adj* : leaning to one side : UNBALANCED — **lop·sid·ed·ness** *n*

lo·qua·cious \lō-ˈkwā-shəs\ *adj* : very talkative **synonyms** see TALKATIVE — **lo·qua·cious·ly** *adv* — **lo·qua·cious·ness** *n* — **lo·quac·i·ty** \-ˈkwas-ət-ē\ *n*

lo·quat \'lō-ˌkwät\ *n* : a small Asian tree related to the roses and bearing yellow fruits resembling plums; *also* : its fruit used especially in preserves [Chinese *làuhgwāt* "small tree related to the roses"]

[1]lord \'lo(ə)rd\ *n* **1 a** : a person who has power and authority; *esp* : a ruler to whom service and obedience are due **b** : a person from whom a feudal estate is held **2** *cap* **a** : GOD **1 b** : JESUS **3** : a man of rank or high position: as **a** : a feudal tenant holding his estate directly from the king **b** : a British nobleman or a bishop entitled to sit in the House of Lords — used as a title **c** *pl, cap* : HOUSE OF LORDS

Word History The word *lord* comes from the Old English word *hlāford*. This word was formed from the words *hlāf*, meaning "loaf of bread," and *weard*, meaning "keeper, guard." This "bread keeper," however, actually had no more to do with bread than our modern "breadwinner." The *hlāford* was much more important than his title suggests. He was the head of a great household and had power and authority over many people. The related word *lady* developed in much the same way. [Old English *hlāford* "lord," literally, "bread keeper," from *hlāf* "loaf of bread" and *weard* "keeper, guard" — related to LADY, LOAF; see *Word History* at LADY]

[2]lord *vb* : to act as if having the rank or power of a lord : DOMINEER — used with *it* ⟨*lording* it over her younger brothers⟩

lord·ly \'lo(ə)rd-lē\ *adj* **lord·li·er; -est 1** : of, relating to, or having the characteristics of a lord : NOBLE **2** : PROUD 1a, HAUGHTY — **lord·li·ness** *n* — **lordly** *adv*

lor·do·sis \lor-ˈdō-səs\ *n* : abnormal curving of the lower part of the spine inward

lord·ship \'lo(ə)rd-ˌship\ *n* **1** : the rank or dignity of a lord — used as a title ⟨his *lordship* is not at home⟩ **2** : the authority, power, or territory of a lord

Lord's Prayer *n* : the prayer with different versions in Matthew and Luke that according to Luke Jesus taught his disciples

Lord's Supper *n* : COMMUNION 1a

lore \'lō(ə)r, 'lo(ə)r\ *n* : KNOWLEDGE 1; *esp* : a particular body of knowledge or tradition ⟨forest *lore*⟩

lo·ris \'lōr-əs, 'lor-\ *n* : any of several small slow-moving primates that are active at night and do not have tails

lorn \'lor(ə)rn\ *adj* : having been abandoned or forsaken

lor·ry \'lor-ē, 'lär-\ *n, pl* **lorries** *chiefly British* : a large open truck

lose \'lüz\ *vb* **lost** \'lost\; **los·ing** \'lü-ziŋ\ **1** : [2]RUIN 1, DESTROY ⟨the ship was *lost* on the reef⟩ **2** : to

loris

be unable to find or have at hand : MISLAY ⟨*lose* a billfold⟩ **3** : to become deprived of especially accidentally or by death ⟨*lose* his eyesight⟩ ⟨*lost* her son by drowning⟩ **4 a** : to fail to use to advantage : WASTE ⟨no time to *lose*⟩ **b** : to fail to win, gain, or obtain ⟨*lose* a contest⟩ **c** : to fail to catch with the senses or the mind ⟨*lost* part of what was said⟩ **5** : to cause the loss of ⟨one careless statement *lost* her the election⟩ **6** : to fail to keep, sustain, or maintain ⟨*lost* his balance⟩ **7 a** : to miss or cause to miss one's way or bearings ⟨*lost* herself in the woods⟩ **b** : to make oneself completely absorbed by one specific thing ⟨*lost* himself in the music⟩ **8** : to leave behind by going faster or farther ⟨*lost* their pursuers⟩ **9** : to free oneself from : get rid of ⟨dieting to *lose* some weight⟩ — **los·er** *n* — **lose ground** : to fail to advance or improve — **lose it 1** : to lose touch with reality; *also* : to go crazy **2** : to be filled with strong emotion : lose one's composure ⟨so angry I almost *lost it*⟩ — **lose one's heart** : to fall in love

losing *adj* **1** : resulting in or likely to result in defeat ⟨a *losing* battle⟩ **2** : marked by many losses or more losses than wins ⟨a *losing* record⟩

loss \'los\ *n* **1 a** : the act or an instance of losing ⟨the *loss* of a ship⟩ **b** : the harm or distress resulting from losing ⟨her death was a *loss* to the community⟩ **2 a** : a person, thing, or amount lost **b** *pl* : killed, wounded, or captured soldiers **3** : failure to gain, win, obtain, or use; *esp* : an amount by which the cost of something is above its selling price **4** : decrease in amount, size, or degree — **at a loss 1** : uncertain as to how to proceed ⟨was *at a loss* to explain the problem⟩ **2** : unable to produce what is needed ⟨was *at a loss* for a cure⟩

lost \'lost\ *adj* **1** : not used, won, or claimed ⟨*lost* opportunities⟩ **2** : no longer possessed or known ⟨a long *lost* uncle⟩ **3** : ruined or destroyed physically or morally **4** : unable to find the way ⟨a *lost* puppy⟩ **5** : having the mind absorbed and not aware of surroundings ⟨*lost* in daydreams⟩ **6** : FUTILE ⟨a *lost* cause⟩

lot \'lät\ *n* **1** : an object used as a counter in determining a question by chance **2 a** : the use of lots as a means of deciding something ⟨choose by *lot*⟩ **b** : the choice resulting from deciding by lot **3 a** : something that comes to one by or as if by lot **b** : one's course in life especially as decided by chance **4 a** : a piece or plot of land ⟨owns the corner *lot*⟩ ⟨a building *lot*⟩ **b** : a motion-picture studio and its surrounding property **5** : a number of articles offered (as at an auction) for sale as one item **6** : a number of associated persons : SET ⟨the *lot* that hangs around the arcade⟩ **7** : a large amount, quantity, or number ⟨a *lot* of space⟩ ⟨a *lot* of books⟩ ⟨*lots* of food⟩ ⟨had been there *lots* of times⟩ **synonyms** see DESTINY

loth *variant of* LOATH

lo·tion \'lō-shən\ *n* : a liquid preparation for use as a cosmetic or as a medicine on the outside of the body [from Latin *lotion-, lotio* "act of washing," from *lotus,* past participle of *lavere* "to wash" — related to LAUNDRY, LAVATORY, LAVISH]

lots \'läts\ *adv* : MUCH ⟨feeling *lots* better⟩

lot·tery \'lät-ə-rē, 'lä-trē\ *n, pl* **-ter·ies** : a drawing of lots in which prizes are given to the winning names or numbers

lo·tus \'lōt-əs\ *n* : any of various water lilies including several represented in ancient Egyptian and Hindu art

loud \'laud\ *adj* **1 a** : marked by a high volume of sound **b** : producing a loud sound **2** : NOISY 1 **3** : unpleasantly bold or bright in color or

lotus

pattern ⟨a *loud* plaid⟩ — **loud** *adv* — **loud·ly** *adv* — **loud·ness** *n*

loud·mouth \-ˌmaủth\ *n* : a person given to loud unpleasant talk — **loud-mouthed** \-ˈmaủthd, -ˈmaủtht\ *adj*

loud·speak·er \-ˈspē-kər\ *n* : a device that changes electrical signals into sound

¹**lounge** \ˈlaủnj\ *vb* **lounged; loung·ing** 1 : to move or act in a lazy, slow, or tired way : LOAF 2 : to stand, sit, or lie in a lazy relaxed manner — **loung·er** *n*

²**lounge** *n* 1 **a** : a room with comfortable furniture for lounging **b** : a room in a public building or vehicle furnished for lounging and often with toilets and smoking facilities 2 : a long couch

lour, louring *variant of* ¹LOWER, ²LOWER, LOWERING

louse \ˈlaủs\ *n* 1 *pl* **lice** \ˈlīs\ **a** : any of various small wingless usually flat insects that live as parasites on the bodies of warm-blooded animals **b** : any of several other small arthropods (as a book louse or wood louse) that are not parasites 2 *pl* **lous·es** \ˈlaủ-səz\ : a mean person

louse up \(ˈ)laủ-ˈsəp\ *vb* : BUNGLE

lousy \ˈlaủ-zē\ *adj* **lous·i·er; -est** 1 : infested with lice 2 **a** : totally disgusting : CONTEMPTIBLE **b** : of very poor quality ⟨got *lousy* grades⟩ **c** : somewhat ill ⟨felt *lousy* after dinner⟩ **d** : well supplied ⟨*lousy* with money⟩ — **lous·i·ness** \-zē-nəs\ *n*

lout \ˈlaủt\ *n* : a stupid, rude, or awkward person — **lout·ish** \-ish\ *adj* — **lout·ish·ly** *adv* — **lout·ish·ness** *n*

lou·ver *or* **lou·vre** \ˈlü-vər\ *n* 1 : an opening provided with one or more slanted strips to allow flow of air or light but to exclude rain or sun or to provide privacy 2 : one of the slanted strips of a louver — **lou·vered** \-vərd\ *adj*

lov·able *also* **love·able** \ˈləv-ə-bəl\ *adj* : having qualities that tend to make one loved — **lov·able·ness** *n* — **lov·ably** \-blē\ *adv*

¹**love** \ˈləv\ *n* 1 : a quality or feeling of strong or constant affection for and dedication to another ⟨motherly *love*⟩ 2 **a** : attraction based on sexual desire : the strong affection and tenderness felt by lovers **b** : a beloved person : DARLING 3 **a** : warm attachment, enthusiasm, or devotion ⟨*love* of the sea⟩ **b** : the object of attachment or devotion 4 : a score of zero in tennis — **in love** : feeling love for and devotion toward someone

²**love** *vb* **loved; lov·ing** 1 : to hold dear : CHERISH 2 **a** : to feel a lover's passion, devotion, or tenderness for **b** : to touch or stroke lightly 3 : to like or desire actively : take pleasure in ⟨*loved* to play the violin⟩ 4 : to grow well in ⟨the rose *loves* sunlight⟩

love affair *n* : a romantic relationship or incident between lovers

love·bird \ˈləv-ˌbərd\ *n* : any of various small usually gray or green parrots that are noted for the expression of caring behavior for their mates

love knot *n* : a decorative knot sometimes used as an emblem of love

love·lorn \ˈləv-ˌló(ə)rn\ *adj* : deprived of or deserted by one's lover

love·ly \ˈləv-lē\ *adj* **love·li·er; -est** 1 : gracefully or delicately attractive ⟨a *lovely* dress⟩ 2 : beautiful in character 3 : highly pleasing : FINE ⟨a *lovely* view⟩ *synonyms* see BEAUTIFUL — **love·li·ness** *n*

lovebird

lov·er \ˈləv-ər\ *n* 1 **a** : a person in love **b** *pl* : two persons in love with each other 2 : DEVOTEE ⟨a *lover* of music⟩ 3 **a** : PARAMOUR **b** : a person with whom one has sexual relations

love seat *n* : a sofa for two persons

love·sick \ˈləv-ˌsik\ *adj* 1 : weak with love 2 : expressing a lover's desire ⟨*lovesick* poems⟩ — **love·sick·ness** *n*

lov·ing \ˈləv-in\ *adj* : feeling or showing love : AFFECTIONATE ⟨*loving* care⟩ ⟨a *loving* glance⟩ — **lov·ing·ly** *adv*

¹**low** \ˈlō\ *n* : the deep sound of a cow — **low** *vb*

²**low** \ˈlō\ *adj* **low·er** \ˈlō(-ə)r\; **low·est** \ˈlō-əst\ 1 **a** : not high or tall ⟨a *low* wall⟩ ⟨a *low* bridge⟩ **b** : cut far down at the neck **c** : not extending as high as the ankle 2 **a** : placed or passing below the normal level ⟨*low* ground⟩ **b** : marking a bottom ⟨a *low* point of his career⟩ 3 : STRICKEN 1, PROSTRATE ⟨laid *low*⟩ 4 **a** : not loud : SOFT ⟨a *low* whisper⟩ **b** : deep in pitch ⟨a *low* note⟩ 5 **a** : being near the equator ⟨*low* northern latitudes⟩ **b** : being near the horizon ⟨the sun is *low*⟩ 6 : ¹POOR 1, LOWER-CLASS ⟨*low* birth⟩ 7 **a** : FEEBLE 1, WEAK ⟨*low* with fever⟩ **b** : not cheerful or lively ⟨in *low* spirits⟩ 8 : less than usual (as in number, amount, degree, or rank) ⟨a *low* price⟩ ⟨*low* pressure⟩ 9 **a** : lacking dignity ⟨a *low* style of writing⟩ **b** : morally deserving of criticism : BASE ⟨a *low* trick⟩ **c** : COARSE 5, VULGAR ⟨*low* language⟩ 10 : being less complex in structure and development than others ⟨*low* animals⟩ 11 : not favorable ⟨a *low* opinion of their work⟩ — **low** *adv* — **low·ness** *n*

³**low** *n* 1 : something low; *esp* : a region of low barometric pressure 2 : the arrangement of gears in an automobile that gives the lowest speed of travel

low beam *n* : a vehicle headlight beam used for short distances

low blood pressure *n* : blood pressure that is abnormally low especially in the arteries — called also *hypotension*

low·boy \ˈlō-ˌbói\ *n* : a chest of drawers about three feet (one meter) high with long legs

low·bred \-ˈbred\ *adj* : disgusting in manner or action : RUDE, VULGAR

low·brow \-ˌbraủ\ *adj* : of, relating to, or suitable for a person without intellectual interests or culture — **lowbrow** *n*

low·down \ˈlō-ˌdaủn\ *n* : reliable information

lowboy

¹**low·er** *also* **lour** \ˈlaủ(-ə)r\ *vb* 1 : to look angry or threatening : FROWN 2 : to become dark, gloomy, and threatening [Middle English *louren* "frown"]

²**lower** *also* **lour** *n* : a wrinkling of the brow in displeasure

³**low·er** \ˈlō(-ə)r\ *adj* 1 : being below another or others in position, rank, or order ⟨a *lower* court⟩ ⟨the *lower* house of Congress⟩ 2 : less advanced in the scale of development through evolution ⟨*lower* animals⟩ 3 *cap* : of, relating to, or being an earlier geologic period or formation ⟨*Lower* Cretaceous⟩ [comparative form of *low*]

⁴**low·er** \ˈlō(ə)r\ *vb* 1 : ²DROP 2b, DIMINISH ⟨*lowered* my voice⟩ 2 **a** : to let fall ⟨*lower* a flag⟩ **b** : to make the aim or goal lower ⟨*lower* your aim⟩ **c** : to reduce the height of ⟨*lower* a wall⟩ 3 **a** : to reduce in value or amount ⟨*lower* the price⟩ **b** : to bring down : DEGRADE ⟨*lowered* himself by lying⟩ **c** : to reduce in rank or position : HUMBLE

low·er·case \ˌlō-(ə)r-ˈkās\ *adj* : being a letter having as its typical form a, b, c rather than A, B, C — **lowercase** *n*

low·er–class \-ˈklas\ *adj* : of, relating to, or being the social class ranking below the middle class

\ə\ abut	\aủ\ out	\i\ tip	\ó\ saw	\ủ\ foot
\ər\ further	\ch\ chin	\ī\ life	\ói\ coin	\y\ yet
\a\ mat	\e\ pet	\j\ job	\th\ thin	\yü\ few
\ā\ take	\ē\ easy	\n\ sing	\th\ this	\yủ\ cure
\ä\ cot, cart	\g\ go	\ō\ bone	\ü\ food	\zh\ vision

low·er·ing *also* **lour·ing** \ˈlau̇-(ə-)riŋ\ *adj* **1** : looking angry or threatening **2** : ²OVERCAST, GLOOMY ⟨a *lowering* sky⟩

low·er·most \ˈlō-(ə)r-ˌmōst\ *adj* : being the lowest

lowest common denominator *n* : LEAST COMMON DENOMINATOR

lowest common multiple *n* : LEAST COMMON MULTIPLE

lowest terms *n pl* : the form of a fraction in which the numerator and denominator have no factor in common except 1

low frequency *n* : a radio frequency in the range between 30 and 300 kilohertz — abbreviation *LF*

Low German *n* : the German dialects of northern Germany especially since the end of the Middle Ages

low–grade \ˈlō-ˈgrād\ *adj* **1** : of poor grade or quality **2** : being near that end of a range which is lowest, weakest, or least able ⟨a *low-grade* fever⟩

low·land \-lənd, -ˌland\ *n* : low and usually level country — **lowland** *adj*

low·land·er \-lən-dər, -ˌlan-\ *n* : a person born or living in a lowland region

low–lev·el \-ˈlev-əl\ *adj* **1** : occurring, done, or placed at a low level **2** : being of low importance or rank ⟨a *low-level* job⟩ **3** : being or relating to nuclear waste of relatively low radioactivity ⟨*low-level* waste⟩

¹low·ly \ˈlō-lē\ *adv* **1** : in a humble or meek manner **2** : in a low position, manner, or degree **3** : not loudly

²lowly *adj* **low·li·er; -est 1** : ¹HUMBLE 1, MEEK **2** : of low rank or position — **low·li·ness** *n*

low–ly·ing \ˈlō-ˈlī-iŋ\ *adj* : having little upward extension or elevation ⟨*low-lying* clouds⟩

low–pres·sure \ˈlō-ˈpresh-ər\ *adj* **1** : having or operating under a relatively small pressure **2** : EASYGOING

low–spir·it·ed \-ˈspir-ət-əd\ *adj* : DEJECTED, DEPRESSED

low tide *n* : the tide when the water is at its lowest point

¹lox \ˈläks\ *n* : liquid oxygen [*l*iquid *ox*ygen]

²lox *n, pl* **lox** *or* **lox·es** : salmon that has been cured in brine and sometimes smoked [from Yiddish *laks* "lox," from an old German word *lahs* "salmon"]

loy·al \ˈlȯi-(ə)l\ *adj* **1 a** : faithful to one's lawful government **b** : faithful to a person to whom allegiance or affection is due **2** : faithful to a cause or ideal **synonyms** see FAITHFUL — **loy·al·ly** \ˈlȯi-ə-lē\ *adv*

loy·al·ist \ˈlȯi-ə-ləst\ *n* : one who is or remains loyal to a political cause, government, or sovereign especially in times of revolt

loy·al·ty \ˈlȯi-(ə)l-tē\ *n, pl* **-ties** : the quality or state of being loyal

loz·enge \ˈläz-ᵊnj\ *n* **1** : a diamond-shaped figure **2 a** : something shaped like a lozenge **b** : a small disk or tablet that usually contains medicine

LP \ˈel-ˈpē\ *n* : a phonograph record designed to be played at 33⅓ revolutions per minute [*l*ong-*p*laying]

LPN \ˌel-ˌpē-ˈen\ *n* : LICENSED PRACTICAL NURSE

LSD \ˌel-ˌes-ˈdē\ *n* : an illegal drug that causes abnormal sensations, extreme and changeable states of emotion, unnatural changes in the way time and space are experienced, and hallucinations and that may sometimes cause panic in response to the effects experienced

lu·au \ˈlü-ˌau̇\ *n* : a Hawaiian feast

lub·ber \ˈləb-ər\ *n* **1** : a big clumsy person **2** : an unskilled seaman — **lub·ber·ly** \-lē\ *adj or adv*

lube \ˈlüb\ *n* : LUBRICANT

lu·bri·cant \ˈlü-bri-kənt\ *n* : something (as a grease or oil) capable of reducing friction when applied between moving parts — **lubricant** *adj*

lu·bri·cate \ˈlü-brə-ˌkāt\ *vb* **-cat·ed; -cat·ing 1** : to make smooth or slippery **2** : to apply a lubricant to ⟨*lubricate* a car⟩ **3** : to act as a lubricant — **lu·bri·ca·tion** \ˌlü-brə-ˈkā-shən\ *n* — **lu·bri·ca·tor** \ˈlü-brə-ˌkāt-ər\ *n*

lu·cent \ˈlüs-ᵊnt\ *adj* **1** : LUMINOUS 1, BRIGHT **2** : ¹CLEAR 2b, LUCID

lu·cid \ˈlü-səd\ *adj* **1 a** : bright with light : LUMINOUS **b**

: TRANSLUCENT 2 **2** : having full use of one's reasoning ability : clear-minded **3** : clear to the understanding : PLAIN ⟨*lucid* writing⟩ — **lu·cid·i·ty** \lü-ˈsid-ət-ē\ *n* — **lu·cid·ly** \ˈlü-səd-lē\ *adv* — **lu·cid·ness** *n*

Lu·ci·fer \ˈlü-sə-fər\ *n* : ¹DEVIL 1

Word History What we sometimes call "the morning star" is really the planet Venus. The Romans called it *Lucifer,* meaning "bearer of light," because it appeared in the sky just before sunrise. But, in the Old Testament, the prophet Isaiah says, in describing the downfall of the king of Babylon, "How are you fallen from heaven, O Morning Star, son of dawn," the "Morning Star" became *Lucifer* in the Latin translation. Early Christians thought that Isaiah was also referring to the devil, who had likewise "fallen from heaven." Thus the word *Lucifer* came to be applied to the devil. [Old English *Lucifer* "the morning star, a fallen angel, the Devil," from Latin *Lucifer* "the morning star, bearer of light," derived from *luc-, lux* "light" and *-fer* "bearing"]

luck \ˈlək\ *n* **1** : whatever happens to a person apparently by chance ⟨have good *luck* fishing⟩ **2** : the accidental way events occur ⟨happening by pure *luck*⟩ **3** : good fortune : SUCCESS ⟨have *luck*⟩ ⟨be out of *luck*⟩ — **luck·less** \-ləs\ *adj*

luck·i·ly \ˈlək-ə-lē\ *adv* : by good luck ⟨*luckily* no one was hurt⟩

lucky \ˈlək-ē\ *adj* **luck·i·er; -est 1** : favored by luck : FORTUNATE **2** : producing a good result apparently by chance ⟨a *lucky* hit⟩ **3** : seeming to bring good luck ⟨a *lucky* coin⟩ — **luck·i·ness** *n*

lu·cra·tive \ˈlü-krət-iv\ *adj* : producing wealth : PROFITABLE — **lu·cra·tive·ly** *adv* — **lu·cra·tive·ness** *n*

lu·cre \ˈlü-kər\ *n* : gain in money : PROFIT; *also* : MONEY 1a

lu·di·crous \ˈlüd-ə-krəs\ *adj* : laughable because of being ridiculous — **lu·di·crous·ly** *adv* — **lu·di·crous·ness** *n*

luff \ˈləf\ *vb* : to sail toward the wind — **luff** *n*

luffa *variant of* LOOFAH

¹lug \ˈləg\ *vb* **lugged; lug·ging** : to pull or carry especially with great effort

²lug *n* **1** : a part (as a handle) that projects like an ear **2** : a nut used to hold a wheel on an automotive vehicle **3 a** : a big clumsy fellow **b** : an ordinary commonplace person

lug·gage \ˈləg-ij\ *n* : something that is lugged; *esp* : suitcases or traveling bags for a traveler's belongings : BAGGAGE

lug·ger \ˈləg-ər\ *n* : a boat that carries one or more lugsails

Lu·gol's solution \ˈlü-ˌgȯlz-, -ˌgȧlz-\ *n* : any of several deep brown solutions of iodine and the iodide of potassium in water or alcohol that are used in medicine or as microscopic stains — called also *Lugol's iodine solution*

lug·sail \ˈləg-ˌsāl, -səl\ *n* : a four-sided sail fastened at the top to a yard that hangs at a slant and is raised and lowered with the sail

lugger

lu·gu·bri·ous \lu̇-ˈgü-brē-əs *also* -ˈgyü-\ *adj* : MOURNFUL 1; *esp* : exaggeratedly or insincerely mournful — **lu·gu·bri·ous·ly** *adv* — **lu·gu·bri·ous·ness** *n*

Luke \ˈlük\ *n* — see BIBLE table

luke·warm \ˈlü-ˈkwȯ(ə)rm\ *adj* **1** : mildly warm : TEPID ⟨a *lukewarm* bath⟩ **2** : not enthusiastic : INDIFFERENT ⟨our plan got a *lukewarm* reception⟩ — **luke·warm·ly** *adv* — **luke·warm·ness** *n*

¹lull \ˈləl\ *vb* **1** : to cause to sleep or rest **2** : to cause to relax vigilance ⟨were *lulled* into a false sense of security⟩

²**lull** *n* **1** : a temporary calm before or during a storm **2** : a temporary drop in activity

lul·la·by \'ləl-ə-ˌbī\ *n, pl* **-bies** : a song to quiet children or lull them to sleep

lum·ba·go \ˌləm-'bā-gō\ *n* : pain (as that caused by straining the muscles) in the lower part of the back

lum·bar \'ləm-bər, -ˌbär\ *adj* : of, relating to, or near the loins or the bony regions of the lower spinal column ⟨the *lumbar* region⟩

¹**lum·ber** \'ləm-bər\ *vb* **lum·bered; lum·ber·ing** \-b(ə-)riŋ\ : to move heavily or clumsily; *also* : ¹RUMBLE [Middle English *lomeren* "to move heavily or clumsily"] — **lum·ber·ing·ly** *adv*

²**lumber** *n* **1** : extra or unused household articles (as furniture) that are stored away **2** : timber or logs especially when sawed and trimmed for use [perhaps derived from the name *Lombard,* originally associated with bankers and pawnbrokers, and so called from the use of pawnshops for storing unwanted or excess property]

³**lumber** *vb* **lum·bered; lum·ber·ing** \-b(ə-)riŋ\ **1** : ¹CLUTTER, ENCUMBER **2 a** : to cut logs **b** : to saw logs into lumber — **lum·ber·er** \-bər-ər\ *n*

lum·ber·jack \'ləm-bər-ˌjak\ *n* : LOGGER

lum·ber·man \-mən\ *n* : a person involved in the business of cutting, trimming, and selling lumber

lum·ber·yard \-ˌyärd\ *n* : a place where lumber is kept for sale

lu·men \'lü-mən\ *n, pl* **lumens** *also* **lu·mi·na** \-mə-nə\ : a unit of light quantity equal to the light on a unit surface all points of which are at a unit distance from a point source of light having a strength of one candle

lumin- *combining form* : light ⟨*lumin*escence⟩ [derived from Latin *lumen* "light"]

lu·mi·nary \'lü-mə-ˌner-ē\ *n, pl* **-nar·ies** **1** : a very famous person **2** : a source of light; *esp* : one of the heavenly bodies — **luminary** *adj*

lu·mi·nes·cence \ˌlü-mə-'nes-°n(t)s\ *n* : the giving off of light at low temperatures especially as part of a chemical process (as of the body); *also* : such light

lu·mi·nes·cent \ˌlü-mə-'nes-°nt\ *adj* : relating to, exhibiting, or suitable for the production of luminescence ⟨*luminescent* paint⟩

lu·mi·nos·i·ty \ˌlü-mə-'näs-ət-ē\ *n, pl* **-ties** **1** : the quality or state of being luminous : BRIGHTNESS **2** : something luminous

lu·mi·nous \'lü-mə-nəs\ *adj* **1** : giving off light : SHINING **2** : being lighted ⟨a public square *luminous* with sunlight⟩ **3** : ¹CLEAR 3 ⟨*luminous* writing⟩ — **lu·mi·nous·ly** *adv* — **lu·mi·nous·ness** *n*

¹**lump** \'ləmp\ *n* **1** : a small uneven mass **2** : a collection or sum of units or parts : TOTAL ⟨taken in the *lump*⟩ **3** : an abnormal swelling or growth

²**lump** *adj* : not divided into parts : WHOLE ⟨a *lump* sum⟩

³**lump** *vb* **1** : to group together **2** : to move noisily and clumsily **3** : to form into a lump

lump·ish \'ləm-pish\ *adj* **1** : ¹DULL 1, STUPID **2** : ¹HEAVY 1a, AWKWARD — **lump·ish·ly** *adv* — **lump·ish·ness** *n*

lumpy \'ləm-pē\ *adj* **lump·i·er; -est** : having or full of lumps — **lump·i·ness** *n*

lu·na·cy \'lü-nə-sē\ *n, pl* **-cies** : INSANITY

lu·na moth \ˌlü-nə-\ *n* : a large mostly pale green American moth with long tails on the hind wings

lu·nar \'lü-nər\ *adj* **1** : of, relating to, or resembling the moon ⟨*lunar* craters⟩ ⟨a *lu-*

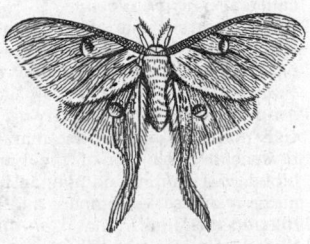

luna moth

nar landscape⟩ **2** : measured by the moon's revolution ⟨*lunar* month⟩

lunar eclipse *n* : an eclipse in which the moon passes partially or entirely through the umbra of the earth's shadow

lunar module *n* : a part of a space vehicle designed to carry astronauts from the command module to the surface of the moon and back — called also *lunar excursion module*

¹**lu·na·tic** \'lü-nə-ˌtik\ *adj* **1 a** : INSANE 1 **b** : designed for insane persons ⟨*lunatic* asylum⟩ **2** : wildly foolish ⟨a *lunatic* idea⟩

²**lunatic** *n* : an insane person

Word History A lunatic now tends to be thought of as a person who usually acts in an insane or wild manner. But until the middle of the 19th century, the word *lunatic* was used for people who were insane some of the time yet had periods of normal behavior. This was a common meaning of the term in courts of law until recent times. The ancient belief was that changes in the moon affected such people. They were thought to be at their worst during a full moon but normal during a new moon. The Latin word for such a person was *lunaticus,* which was based on the noun *luna,* meaning "moon." *Lunaticus* came into Middle English as *lunatik.* Then it passed into Modern English as *lunatic,* meaning "one driven mad by the moon." [Middle English *lunatik* "a person driven mad by the changes in the moon," derived from Latin *lunaticus* (same meaning), from earlier *luna* "moon"]

¹**lunch** \'lənch\ *n* **1** : a light meal; *esp* : one eaten in the middle of the day **2** : the food prepared for a lunch

²**lunch** *vb* : to eat or treat to lunch — **lunch·er** *n*

lun·cheon \'lən-chən\ *n* : a light meal at midday; *esp* : a formal lunch

lun·cheon·ette \ˌlən-chə-'net\ *n* : a place where light lunches are sold

lunch·room \'lənch-ˌrüm, -ˌrüm\ *n* **1** : LUNCHEONETTE **2** : a room (as in a school) where lunches may be eaten

lung \'ləŋ\ *n* **1 a** : one of the usually paired organs forming the special breathing structure of vertebrates that breathe air **b** : any of various respiratory organs of invertebrates **2** : a device (as an iron lung) to promote breathing and make it easier

¹**lunge** \'lənj\ *n* **1** : a sudden stretching thrust or pass (as with a sword) **2** : a sudden forward rush or reach

²**lunge** *vb* **lunged; lung·ing** **1** : to move with or as if with a lunge **2** : to make a lunge (as with a sword)

lung·fish \'ləŋ-ˌfish\ *n* : any of various fishes that breathe with structures resembling lungs as well as with gills

lu·pine *also* **lu·pin** \'lü-pən\ *n* : any of a genus of herbs of the legume family including some poisonous ones and others grown for their showy spikes of colorful flowers or for green manure, fodder, or their edible seeds

¹**lurch** \'lərch\ *n* : an overwhelming defeat in a game (as cribbage) — **in the lurch** : in a helpless or defenseless position

²**lurch** *n* **1** : a sudden roll of a ship to one side **2** : a sudden jerking, swaying, or tipping movement ⟨the car gave a *lurch*⟩; *also* : a staggering gait

³**lurch** *vb* **1** : to roll or tip suddenly **2** : to move with a lurch ⟨suddenly *lurched* forward⟩; *also* : ¹STAGGER 1

¹**lure** \'lu̇(ə)r\ *n* **1 a** : something that persuades one to perform an action for pleasure or gain : TEMPTATION **b** : ¹APPEAL 3, ATTRACTION **2** : a decoy for attracting animals to capture; *esp* : an artificial bait used for catching fish

²**lure** vb **lured; lur·ing** : to tempt or lead away by offering some pleasure or advantage : ENTICE

synonyms LURE, ENTICE, DECOY, TEMPT, SEDUCE mean to lead astray from one's true or usual course. LURE implies an attraction that may be harmless ⟨the resort *lured* skiers from around the world⟩ or may suggest a drawing into danger, evil, or difficulty through deception ⟨*lured* naive investors with get-rich-quick schemes⟩. ENTICE suggests luring by artful or clever means ⟨advertising designed to *entice* new customers⟩. DECOY implies luring and trapping by trickery or false appearances ⟨attempting to *decoy* the enemy into an ambush⟩. TEMPT implies arousing a desire that may be contrary to one's conscience or better judgment ⟨*tempted* by the offer of more money⟩. SEDUCE implies leading astray especially from a proper or responsible course by persuasion or false promises ⟨was *seduced* into breaking the law⟩.

lu·rid \ˈlu̇r-əd\ *adj* **1 a** : causing horror or disgust : GRUESOME ⟨*lurid* tales of murder⟩ **b** : SENSATIONAL **2** ⟨*lurid* book covers⟩ **2** : lifelessly pale : WAN **3** : shining with the red glow of fire seen through smoke — **lu·rid·ly** *adv* — **lu·rid·ness** *n*

lurk \ˈlərk\ *vb* **1 a** : to stay in or about a place secretly **b** : to move quietly and secretly **2** : to lie concealed; *esp* : to be a hidden threat — **lurk·er** *n*

lus·cious \ˈləsh-əs\ *adj* **1** : having a delicious taste or smell ⟨*luscious* berries⟩ **2** : appealing to the senses : DELIGHTFUL — **lus·cious·ly** *adv* — **lus·cious·ness** *n*

lush \ˈləsh\ *adj* **1** : being juicy and fresh ⟨*lush* grass⟩ **2** : covered with thick healthy growth ⟨*lush* pastures⟩ — **lush·ly** *adv* — **lush·ness** *n*

¹**lust** \ˈləst\ *n* **1** : sexual desire especially if strong or uncontrolled **2** : a strong longing : CRAVING

²**lust** *vb* : to have a strong desire : CRAVE; *esp* : to have a strong sexual desire

lus·ter *or* **lus·tre** \ˈləs-tər\ *n* **1** : a shine or sheen especially from reflected light : GLOSS **2** : sparkling brilliance **3** : ¹GLORY 1a, SPLENDOR ⟨the *luster* of a famous name⟩ — **lus·ter·less** \-tər-ləs\ *adj* — **lus·trous** \-trəs\ *adj*

lust·ful \ˈləst-fəl\ *adj* : excited by lust — **lust·ful·ly** \-fə-lē\ *adv* — **lust·ful·ness** *n*

lusty \ˈləs-tē\ *adj* **lust·i·er; -est** : full of vitality : VIGOROUS, ROBUST — **lust·i·ly** \-tə-lē\ *adv* — **lust·i·ness** \-tē-nəs\ *n*

lute \ˈlüt\ *n* : a musical instrument resembling a guitar but with a pear-shaped body

lu·tein·iz·ing hormone \ˈlüt-ē-ə-ˌnī-ziŋ-\ *n* : a hormone produced by the pituitary gland that in the female stimulates ovulation and the development of the corpora lutea and in the male stimulates production of testosterone by certain cells in the testis

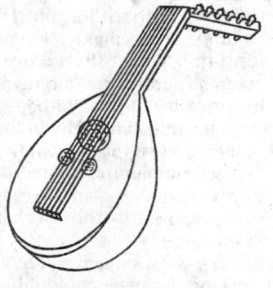
lute

lu·te·tium \lü-ˈtē-sh(ē-)əm\ *n* : a soft metallic chemical element — see ELEMENT table

Lu·ther·an \ˈlü-th(ə-)rən\ *adj* **1** : of or relating to Martin Luther or his religious doctrines **2** : of or relating to the Protestant churches following Lutheran doctrines — **Lutheran** *n* — **Lu·ther·an·ism** \-ˌiz-əm\ *n*

lux \ˈləks\ *n, pl* **lux** *or* **lux·es** : a unit that is used for measuring the amount of light falling on a surface and that is equal to one lumen per square meter

lux·u·ri·ant \(ˌ)ləg-ˈzhu̇r-ē-ənt, (ˌ)lək-ˈshu̇r-\ *adj* **1 a** : producing large crops ⟨*luxuriant* valleys⟩ **b** : characterized by heavy growth : LUSH **2** : ¹LAVISH 2 — **lux·u·ri·ance** \-ē-ən(t)s\ *n* — **lux·u·ri·ant·ly** *adv*

lux·u·ri·ate \(ˌ)ləg-ˈzhu̇r-ē-ˌāt, (ˌ)lək-ˈshu̇r-\ *vb* **-at·ed; -at·ing** **1** : to grow in great numbers or quantity **2** : to enjoy oneself in a luxurious manner

lux·u·ri·ous \(ˌ)ləg-ˈzhu̇r-ē-əs, (ˌ)lək-ˈshu̇r-\ *adj* **1** : fond of luxury **2** : of, relating to, or marked by luxury — **lux·u·ri·ous·ly** *adv* — **lux·u·ri·ous·ness** *n*

lux·u·ry \ˈləksh-(ə-)rē, ˈləgzh-\ *n, pl* **-ries** **1 a** : free use or possession of costly food, dress, or anything that pleases a person **b** : great ease or comfort : rich surroundings ⟨live in *luxury*⟩ **2 a** : something desirable but costly or hard to get **b** : something adding to pleasure or comfort but not absolutely necessary — **luxury** *adj*

¹**-ly** \lē\ *adj suffix* **1** : resembling in appearance, manner, or nature : having the characteristics of ⟨queen*ly*⟩ ⟨father*ly*⟩ **2** : happening in a regular pattern at (specified) time periods ⟨hour*ly*⟩ [Old English *-lic, -lic* "like"]

²**-ly** *adv suffix* **1** : in a (specified) manner ⟨slow*ly*⟩ **2** : from a (specified) point of view ⟨grammatical*ly*⟩ [Old English *-lice, -lice* "in a (specified) manner," from *-lic* "like"]

ly·ce·um \lī-ˈsē-əm, ˈlī-sē-\ *n* **1** : a hall for public lectures or discussions **2** : an association providing public lectures, concerts, and entertainments

ly·chee *or* **li·tchi** *also* **li·chee** \ˈlē-(ˌ)chē, ˈlī-\ *n* **1** : the oval fruit of a Chinese tree related to the soapberries and having a hard reddish outer covering and sweet whitish edible flesh surrounding a single large seed — called also *lychee nut* **2** : a tree bearing lychees [from Chinese *lìzhī* "lychee"]

ly·co·po·di·um \ˌlī-kə-ˈpōd-ē-əm\ *n* : any of a large genus of club mosses that grow upward or creep on the ground and have small or scalelike evergreen leaves

lye \ˈlī\ *n* **1** : a strong alkaline liquid obtained from wood ashes and used especially in making soap and in washing **2** : any of various strong alkaline liquids; *esp* : SODIUM HYDROXIDE **3** : a solid compound (as caustic soda) that causes chemical burns

¹**ly·ing** \ˈlī-iŋ\ *present participle of* LIE

²**lying** *adj* : UNTRUTHFUL, FALSE ⟨a *lying* account of the accident⟩

Lyme disease \ˈlīm-\ *n* : a serious disease that is caused by a bacterium transmitted by some ticks, that is often characterized at first by a spreading red patch on the skin, and that may result in joint pain and disorders of the heart and nervous system if left untreated [from *Lyme*, Connecticut, where the disease was first reported]

lymph \ˈlim(p)f\ *n* : a usually clear fluid that circulates in lymphatic vessels, bathes the cells of the body, and consists of white blood cells and a liquid portion resembling blood plasma

¹**lym·phat·ic** \lim-ˈfat-ik\ *adj* **1** : of, relating to, or produced by lymph **2** : lacking physical or mental energy

²**lymphatic** *n* : a vessel that contains or transports lymph — called also *lymph vessel*

lymphatic system *n* : the part of the circulatory system that consists of special tissue (as of the lymph nodes and tonsils), lymph, lymph-transporting vessels, and the thymus and spleen and is concerned especially with returning fluids and proteins back to the blood and with destroying material (as bacteria) foreign to the body — called also *lymph system*

lymph node *n* : one of the rounded masses of tissue occurring along the lymphatic vessels and containing lymphocytes which filter the flow of lymph — called also *lymph gland*

lym·pho·cyte \ˈlim(p)-fə-ˌsīt\ *n* : any of the white blood cells that arise in the bone marrow, are found especially in special tissue (as of the lymph nodes and spleen), blood, and lymph, and play an important role in the immune response — compare B CELL, T CELL

lym·pho·ma \lim-ˈfō-mə\ *n, pl* **-mas** *or* **-ma·ta** \-mət-ə\ : a tumor composed of the same type of tissue making up lymph nodes

lynch \'linch\ *vb* : to put to death (as by hanging) by mob action without legal authority — **lynch·er** *n*

lynx \'liŋ(k)s\ *n, pl* **lynx** *or* **lynx·es** **1** : a large North American wildcat with rather long legs, a short stubby black-tipped tail, a coat marked with spots and blotches, soft fur, ears with small bunches of long fur at the tip, and large padded feet — called also *Canada lynx* **2** : any of several related wildcats (as the bobcat)

lynx–eyed \'liŋ(k)-'sīd\ *adj* : having sharp sight

lyre \'lī(ə)r\ *n* : a small harp held in the hands for playing

lyre·bird \-,bərd\ *n* : either of two Australian birds of which the males have very long tail feathers displayed during courtship in the shape of a lyre

¹lyr·ic \'lir-ik\ *n* **1** : a lyric poem or song **2** *pl* : the words of a song

²lyric *adj* **1 a** : resembling a song in form, feeling, or liter-ary quality **b** : expressing a poet's own feeling : not narrative or dramatic ⟨*lyric* poetry⟩ **2** : having or involving a light singing style

lyr·i·cal \'lir-i-kəl\ *adj* : ²LYRIC — **lyr·i·cal·ly** \-i-k(ə-)lē\ *adv*

ly·sine \'lī-,sēn\ *n* : an essential amino acid obtained from various proteins

ly·sis \'lī-səs\ *n, pl* **ly·ses** \'lī-,sēz\ : a process of breaking up especially of cells

ly·so·some \'lī-sə-,sōm\ *n* : a saclike organelle that contains enzymes which can break down materials (as food particles and waste) within a cell

lyre

M

m \'em\ *n, often cap* **1** : the 13th letter of the English alphabet **2** : one thousand in Roman numerals

'm \m\ *vb* : AM ⟨*I'm* going⟩

ma \'mä, 'mò\ *n, pl* **mas** : MOTHER

ma'am \'mam, *after "yes" often* əm\ *n* : MADAM

ma·ca·bre \mə-'käb(-rə), -'käb-ər, -'käbrᵊ\ *adj* **1** : having death as a subject **2** : marked by or arousing horror

mac·ad·am \mə-'kad-əm\ *n* : a roadway or pavement constructed by compacting a layer of small broken stone along with a binder (as cement or asphalt) [named for John L. *McAdam* 1756–1836 Scottish engineer who invented the paving process] — **mac·ad·am·ize** \-ə-,mīz\ *vb*

mac·a·da·mia nut \,mak-ə-'dä-mē-ə-\ *n* : a hard-shelled nut of an Australian evergreen tree widely grown in Hawaii — called also *macadamia* [John *Macadam*, died 1865, Australian chemist]

ma·caque \mə-'kak, -'käk\ *n* : any of various monkeys mostly from Asia that includes some with either short or no tails; *esp* : RHESUS MONKEY [French, from Portuguese *macaco*, from *makaku*, plural of *kaku*, name for an African monkey in one or more Bantu languages of Gabon and Congo]

mac·a·ro·ni \,mak-ə-'rō-nē\ *n* : a food made chiefly of wheat flour paste dried in the form of slender tubes

mac·a·roon \,mak-ə-'rün\ *n* : a cookie or small cake made of egg whites, sugar, and ground almonds or coconut

ma·caw \mə-'kò\ *n* : any of numerous parrots of South and Central America that have a long tail, a harsh voice, and bright feathers

Mac·ca·bees \'mak-ə-bēz\ *n* — see BIBLE table

¹mace \'mās\ *n* **1** : a heavy spiked club used as a weapon in the Middle Ages **2** : an ornamental staff carried as a symbol of authority [Middle English *mace* "a heavy spiked club," from early French *mace* (same meaning); probably of Latin origin]

²mace *n* : a spice made from the dried outer covering of the nutmeg [Middle English *mace* "the spice mace," from early French *mascie, macis* (same meaning), from Latin *macis* "an East Indian spice"]

macaw

Mac·Guf·fin *or* **Mc·Guf·fin** \mə-'gəf-ən\ *n* : something (as an object) in a film or story that serves to set and keep the plot in motion despite usually lacking intrinsic importance [coined by Alfred Hitchcock, died 1980, British film director]

Mach \'mäk\ *n* : MACH NUMBER

Mach·a·bees \'mak-ə-bēz\ *n, pl* : MACCABEES

ma·chete \mə-'shet-ē, -'chet-ē; mə-'shet\ *n* : a large heavy knife used especially for cutting sugarcane and underbrush and as a weapon

Ma·chi·a·vel·lian \,mak-ē-ə-'vel-ē-ən, -'vel-yən\ *adj* **1** : of or relating to the belief that a ruler is justified in using any means to stay in power **2** : characterized by dishonesty or trickery [named for Niccolo *Machiavelli* 1469–1527 an Italian political leader] — **Machiavellian** *n* — **Ma·chi·a·vel·lian·ism** \-,iz-əm\ *n*

mach·i·nate \'mak-ə-,nāt, 'mash-ə-\ *vb* **-nat·ed; -nat·ing** : ²PLOT 2; *esp* : to scheme to do harm — **mach·i·na·tion** \,mak-ə-'nā-shən, ,mash-ə-\ *n* — **mach·i·na·tor** \'mak-ə-,nāt-ər, 'mash-\ *n*

¹ma·chine \mə-'shēn\ *n* **1 a** : VEHICLE 2; *esp* : ²AUTOMOBILE **b** : a combination of parts that transmit forces, motion, and energy to do some desired work ⟨a sewing *machine*⟩ **c** : an instrument (as a lever or pulley) designed to transmit or change slightly the application of power, force, or motion **2** : an organized group that controls a political party — **ma·chine·like** \-,līk\ *adj*

²machine *vb* **ma·chined; ma·chin·ing** : to shape or finish by machine-operated tools — **ma·chin·able** \mə-'shē-nə-bəl\ *adj*

machine gun *n* : an automatic gun capable of continuous firing — **machine–gun** *vb* — **machine gunner** *n*

machine language *n* **1** : the set of symbolic instruction codes used to represent operations and data in a machine (as a computer) that are usually expressed in binary form **2** : ASSEMBLY LANGUAGE

ma·chine–read·able *adj* : directly usable by a computer ⟨*machine-readable* text⟩

\ə\ **abut**	\aú\ **out**	\i\ **tip**	\ò\ **saw**	\ù\ **foot**
\ər\ **further**	\ch\ **chin**	\ī\ **life**	\òi\ **coin**	\y\ **yet**
\a\ **mat**	\e\ **pet**	\j\ **job**	\th\ **thin**	\yü\ **few**
\ā\ **take**	\ē\ **easy**	\ŋ\ **sing**	\th\ **this**	\yù\ **cure**
\ä\ **cot, cart**	\g\ **go**	\ō\ **bone**	\ü\ **food**	\zh\ **vision**

ma·chin·ery \mə-'shēn-(ə-)rē\ *n, pl* **-er·ies** **1** : machines in general **2** : the working parts of a machine or instrument **3** : the organization or system by which something is done or carried on ⟨*machinery* of government⟩

machine shop *n* : a workshop in which metal articles are machined and assembled

machine tool *n* : a machine (as a lathe or drill) that is driven by power and is designed for shaping solid work

ma·chin·ist \mə-'shē-nəst\ *n* : a person who makes or works on machines and engines

Mach number \'mäk-\ *n* : a number representing the comparison of the speed of a body to the speed of sound in the surrounding atmosphere ⟨a *Mach number* of 2 indicates a speed that is twice the speed of sound⟩

mack·er·el \'mak-(ə-)rəl\ *n, pl* **-el** *or* **-els** **1** : a North Atlantic food fish that is green with blue bars above and silvery below **2** : any of various usually small or medium-sized fishes related to the mackerel

mackerel sky *n* : a sky covered with rows of clouds resembling the patterns on a mackerel's back

mack·i·naw \'mak-ə-ˌnȯ\ *n* : a short heavy woolen often plaid coat

mackinaw trout *n, often cap M* : a large dark North American char that is an important sport and food fish in northern lakes — called also *lake trout*

mack·in·tosh *or* **mac·in·tosh** \'mak-ən-ˌtäsh\ *n, chiefly British* : RAINCOAT

Mac·Pher·son strut \mək-'fir-sᵊn-, -'fər-\ *n* : a component of an automobile suspension consisting of a shock absorber mounted within a coil spring [named after Earle S. *MacPherson*, 1891–1960, American engineer who designed the strut]

mac·ra·mé *also* **mac·ra·me** \'mak-rə-ˌmā\ *n* : a coarse lace or fringe made by knotting threads or cords; *also* : the art of tying knots in patterns

mac·ro \'mak-rō\ *n, pl* **macros** : a single computer instruction that represents a series of operations

mac·ro·cosm \'mak-rə-ˌkäz-əm\ *n* : the world as a whole : UNIVERSE

macro lens *n* : a camera lens designed to focus at very short distances and producing up to life-size images

ma·cron \'māk-ˌrän, 'mak-, -rən\ *n* : a mark ¯ placed over a vowel (as in \māk\) to show that the vowel is long

mac·ro·phage \'mak-rə-ˌfāj\ *n* : a large phagocyte of the immune system

mac·ro·scop·ic \ˌmak-rə-'skäp-ik\ *adj* : large enough to be observed by the naked eye ⟨*macroscopic* animals⟩

mad \'mad\ *adj* **mad·der; mad·dest** **1** : disordered in mind : INSANE **2** : done or made without thinking ⟨a *mad* promise⟩ **3 a** : extremely angry : FURIOUS ⟨make a bull *mad*⟩ **b** : very displeased **4** : ENTHUSIASTIC ⟨*mad* about dancing⟩ **5** : affected with rabies : RABID ⟨a *mad* dog⟩ **6** : wildly festive ⟨a *mad* party⟩ **7** : wildly excited : FRANTIC ⟨*mad* with pain⟩ **8** : marked by intense and often chaotic activity ⟨a *mad* scramble for the ball⟩ — **mad·ly** *adv* — **mad·ness** *n* — **like mad** : at a high rate

mad·am \'mad-əm\ *n, pl* **mes·dames** \mā-'däm, -'dam\ **1** — used as a form of polite address to a woman **2** *cap* — used as a title especially before the name of rank or office of a high-ranking woman ⟨*Madam* President⟩ [Middle English *madam* "woman of rank or authority, lady," from early French *ma dame*, literally "my lady," from Latin *domina* "mistress, lady," feminine form of *dominus* "master, owner" — related to DAME, DOMINATE, MADONNA]

ma·dame \mə-'dam, ma-'dam, *before a surname also* ˌmad-əm\ *n, pl* **mes·dames** \mā-'däm, -'dam\ — used as a title equivalent to *Mrs.* for a married woman not of English-speaking nationality

mad·cap \'mad-ˌkap\ *adj* : RECKLESS, WILD — **madcap** *n*

mad·den \'mad-ᵊn\ *vb* : to make mad : ENRAGE

mad·den·ing \'mad-niŋ, -ᵊn-iŋ\ *adj* : that irritates or angers ⟨a *maddening* habit⟩ — **mad·den·ing·ly** *adv*

mad·der \'mad-ər\ *n* **1 a** : a Eurasian herb with spear-shaped leaves, small yellowish flowers followed by dark berries, and red fleshy roots used to make a dye **b** : any of several plants related to the madder **2** : the root of a madder or a dye prepared from it

made *past and past participle of* MAKE

ma·de·moi·selle \ˌmad-(ə-)mə-'zel, -mwə-'zel; mam-'zel\ *n, pl* **ma·de·moi·selles** \-'zelz\ *or* **mes·de·moi·selles** \ˌmād-(ə-)mə-'zel, -mwə-'zel\ — used by or to French-speaking people as a title equivalent to *Miss*

made–up \'mā-ˌdəp\ *adj* **1** : created from the imagination ⟨a *made-up* story⟩ **2** : marked by the use of makeup ⟨*made-up* eyelids⟩

madder 1a

mad·house \'mad-ˌhau̇s\ *n* **1** : a place where insane persons are kept **2** : a place of uproar or confusion

mad·man \'mad-ˌman, -mən\ *n* : a man who is or who acts as if insane

Ma·don·na \mə-'dän-ə\ *n* **1** : the Virgin Mary **2** : a painting or statue representing the Virgin Mary [from Italian *madonna* "lady, Virgin Mary," from earlier *ma donna*, literally "my lady," from Latin *domina* "mistress, lady," feminine form of *dominus* "master, owner" — related to DAME, DOMINATE, MADAM]

ma·dras \'mad-rəs; mə-'dras, -'dräs\ *n* : a fine plain-woven fabric usually of cotton with various designs (as plaid)

mad·ri·gal \'mad-ri-gəl\ *n* **1** : a short poem common in the Middle Ages **2 a** : a complex vocal piece developed especially in the 16th and 17th centuries **b** : a song usually not accompanied by musical instruments and consisting of two or more voice parts : PART-SONG — **mad·ri·gal·ist** \-gə-ləst\ *n*

mad·wom·an \'mad-ˌwu̇m-ən\ *n* : a woman who is or who acts as if insane

mael·strom \'mā(ə)l-strəm, -ˌsträm\ *n* **1** : a strong violent whirlpool dangerous to ships **2** : a great confusion ⟨a *maelstrom* of emotions⟩

mae·sto·so \mī-'stō-sō, -zō\ *adv or adj* : so as to be majestic and stately — used as a direction in music

mae·stro \'mī-strō\ *n, pl* **maestros** *or* **mae·stri** \-ˌstrē\ : a master of an art and especially of music [from Italian *maestro*, literally "master," from Latin *magister* "master, one who holds a higher political office" — related to MAGISTRATE, MASTER]

Ma·fia \'mäf-ē-ə, 'maf-\ *n* **1** : a secret criminal society of Sicily or Italy **2** : a similar criminal organization in the U.S. or elsewhere

ma·fi·o·so \ˌmäf-ē-'ō-sō, ˌmaf-, -zō\ *n, pl* **-si** \-sē, -zē\ : a member of the Mafia

mag·a·zine \'mag-ə-ˌzēn, ˌmag-ə-'zēn\ *n* **1** : a storehouse or warehouse especially for military supplies **2** : a place for keeping explosives in a fort or ship **3** : a publication containing different pieces (as stories, articles, or poems) and issued at regular intervals (as weekly or monthly) **4** : a supply chamber: as **a** : a container in a gun for holding cartridges **b** : a container for film on a camera or motion-picture projector

Word History *Magazine* originally meant "storehouse" or "granary" or "cellar." It came into an early French dialect and then English from the Arabic word *makhzan* (plural *makhāzin*). *Makhzan* had all these meanings. In military and naval use *magazine* came to mean a storage place for gunpowder or weapons or a place on a warship where the powder was kept. Later it came to mean either a place where valuable things were stored or the stored things themselves. A new sense of *magazine* appeared in 1731 with the first issue of a monthly publication called *The Gentleman's Magazine*, a collection or storehouse of short stories and articles about things of interest to the general reader. This use of *magazine* caught on and was used for similar publications. [from early French *magazine* "storehouse, warehouse," derived from Arabic *makhāzin*, plural of *makhzan* "storehouse, granary, cellar"]

Ma·gen Da·vid *or* **Mo·gen David** \'mȯ-gən-'dȯ-vid, 'mō-gən-'dā-vəd\ *n* : a hexagram used as a symbol of Judaism [Hebrew *māghēn Dāwīdh*, literally, "shield of David"]

ma·gen·ta \mə-'jent-ə\ *n* **1** : a deep red dye **2** : a deep purplish red

mag·got \'mag-ət\ *n* : a soft-bodied legless larva of a two-winged fly (as the housefly)

mag·goty \'mag-ət-ē\ *adj* : infested with maggots

ma·gi \'mā-,jī\ *n pl, often cap* : the three wise men from the East who paid respect to the infant Jesus [from Latin *magi*, plural of *magus* "Persian priest or wise man," from Greek *magos* "Persian priest, sorcerer" — related to MAGIC]

mag·ic \'maj-ik\ *n* **1** : the power to control natural forces that is possessed by certain persons (as wizards and witches) in folktales and fiction **2 a** : a power that seems mysterious ⟨the *magic* of a great name⟩ **b** : something that charms ⟨the *magic* of their singing⟩ **3** : the art or skill of performing tricks or illusions as if by magic for entertainment [Middle English *magique* "use of supernatural powers," from early French *magique* (same meaning), from Latin *magice* (same meaning), derived from Greek *magikos* "magical, relating to magi," from *magos* "Persian priest, sorcerer" — related to MAGI] **magic** *adj* — **mag·i·cal** \'maj-i-kəl\ *adj* — **mag·i·cal·ly** \-i-k(ə-)lē\ *adv*

ma·gi·cian \mə-'jish-ən\ *n* **1** : a person skilled in magic; *esp* : SORCERER **2** : a performer of tricks of illusion

magic lantern *n* : an early type of slide projector

magic square *n* : a square that contains rows of numbers arranged so that the sum of the numbers in each row, column, and diagonal is always the same

4	9	2
3	5	7
8	1	6

6	3	10	15
9	16	5	4
7	2	11	14
12	13	8	1

magic square

mag·is·te·ri·al \,maj-ə-'stir-ē-əl\ *adj* **1** : of, relating to, or having the characteristics of a master or teacher **2** : of or relating to a magistrate or the office or duties of a magistrate — **mag·is·te·ri·al·ly** \-ē-ə-lē\ *adv*

mag·is·tra·cy \'maj-ə-strə-sē\ *n, pl* **-cies 1** : the state of being a magistrate **2** : the office, power, or dignity of a magistrate **3** : a body of magistrates

mag·is·trate \'maj-ə-,strāt, -strət\ *n* **1** : a chief officer of government (as over a nation) ⟨the president is the chief *magistrate*⟩ **2** : a local official with some judicial power [Middle English *magestrat* "magistrate," from Latin *magistratus* (same meaning), from *magister* "master, one who holds a higher political office" — related to MAESTRO, MASTER]

mag·ma \'mag-mə\ *n* : molten rock material within the earth — **mag·mat·ic** \mag-'mat-ik\ *adj*

mag·na cum lau·de \,mäg-nə-(,)kùm-'laùd-ə, -'laùd-ē; ,mag-nə-,kəm-'lȯd-ē\ *adv* : with great distinction : with great honors ⟨graduated *magna cum laude*⟩ [Latin]

mag·na·nim·i·ty \,mag-nə-'nim-ət-ē\ *n, pl* **-ties 1** : nobility of character : HIGH-MINDEDNESS **2** : a magnanimous act

mag·nan·i·mous \mag-'nan-ə-məs\ *adj* **1** : having or showing a noble and courageous spirit **2** : being generous and forgiving — **mag·nan·i·mous·ly** *adv*

mag·nate \'mag-,nāt, -nət\ *n* : a person of rank, power, or influence (as in an industry)

mag·ne·sia \mag-'nē-shə, -'nē-zhə\ *n* : MAGNESIUM OXIDE — compare MILK OF MAGNESIA

mag·ne·sium \mag-'nē-zē-əm, -zhəm\ *n* : a silver-white metallic element that is light and easily worked, burns with a dazzling light, and is used in making lightweight alloys — see ELEMENT table

magnesium chloride *n* : a bitter salt that occurs dissolved in seawater and is used in producing magnesium metal

magnesium hydroxide *n* : a weak alkaline compound used especially as a laxative and against acid in the stomach

magnesium oxide *n* : a white earthy solid that consists of magnesium and oxygen and is used especially in fertilizers and rubber, as a mild laxative, and against acid in the stomach

magnesium sulfate *n* : any of several sulfates of magnesium; *esp* : EPSOM SALT

mag·net \'mag-nət\ *n* **1** : a piece of some material (as the mineral iron oxide) that is able to attract iron; *esp* : a mass of iron or steel so treated that it has this property **2** : something that attracts ⟨the *magnet* of fame⟩

mag·net·ic \mag-'net-ik\ *adj* **1** : having great power to attract ⟨a *magnetic* personality⟩ **2 a** : of or relating to a magnet or magnetism **b** : of or relating to the earth's magnetism ⟨the *magnetic* meridian⟩ **c** : capable of being magnetized **d** : working by magnetic attraction or repulsion — **mag·net·i·cal·ly** \-i-k(ə-)lē\ *adv*

magnetic disk *n* : ¹DISK 2c

magnetic field *n* : the portion of space near a magnetic body or a body carrying an electric current within which magnetic forces due to the body or current can be detected

magnetic north *n* : the northerly direction in the earth's magnetic field indicated by the north-seeking pole of a compass needle

magnetic pole *n* **1** : either of two small regions of the earth which are located near the North and South Poles and toward which a compass needle points **2** : either of the poles of a magnet

magnetic resonance imaging *n* : a technique that produces computerized images of internal body tissues using a powerful magnetic field and pulses of radio waves — called also *MRI*

magnetic tape *n* : a thin ribbon (as of plastic) coated with a magnetic material on which information (as sound or television images) may be stored

mag·ne·tism \'mag-nə-,tiz-əm\ *n* **1 a** : the property of attracting certain metals or producing a magnetic field as shown by a magnet, a magnetized material, or a conductor carrying an electric current **b** : the science that deals with magnetic occurrences or conditions **2** : the power to attract or charm others

mag·ne·tite \'mag-nə-,tīt\ *n* : a black mineral that is an oxide of iron, is strongly attracted by a magnet, and is an important iron ore

mag·ne·tize \'mag-nə-,tīz\ *vb* **-tized; -tiz·ing 1** : to cause to be magnetic **2** : to attract like a magnet : CHARM — **mag·ne·tiz·able** \-,tī-zə-bəl\ *adj* — **mag·ne·ti·za·tion** \,mag-nət-ə-'zā-shən\ *n*

mag·ne·to \mag-'nēt-ō\ *n, pl* **-tos** : a small electric generator using permanent magnets; *esp* : one used to produce sparks in an internal-combustion engine

mag·ne·tom·e·ter \,mag-nə-'täm-ət-ər\ *n* : an instrument used to detect the presence of a metallic object or to measure the strength of a magnetic field

\ə\ **abut**	\aù\ **out**	\i\ **tip**	\ȯ\ **saw**	\ù\ **foot**	
\ər\ **further**	\ch\ **chin**	\ī\ **life**	\ȯi\ **coin**	\y\ **yet**	
\a\ **mat**	\e\ **pet**	\j\ **job**	\th\ **thin**	\yü\ **few**	
\ā\ **take**	\ē\ **easy**	\ŋ\ **sing**	\t̲h̲\ **this**	\yù\ **cure**	
\ä\ **cot, cart**	\g\ **go**	\ō\ **bone**	\ü\ **food**	\zh\ **vision**	

mag·ne·to·sphere \mag-ˈnēt-ə-ˌsfi(ə)r, -ˈnet-\ *n* : a region of space around an object (as a planet or star) that is dominated by the object's magnetic field

mag·ni·fi·ca·tion \ˌmag-nə-fə-ˈkā-shən\ *n* **1** : the act of magnifying **2 a** : the state of being magnified **b** : the apparent enlargement of an object by an optical instrument — called also *power*

mag·nif·i·cence \mag-ˈnif-ə-sən(t)s\ *n* : the quality or state of being magnificent

mag·nif·i·cent \mag-ˈnif-ə-sənt\ *adj* **1** : having impressive beauty ⟨the *magnificent* cathedrals of Europe⟩ **2** : [1]NOBLE 5 ⟨a *magnificent* character⟩ **synonyms** see GRAND — **mag·nif·i·cent·ly** *adv*

mag·ni·fy \ˈmag-nə-ˌfī\ *vb* **-fied; -fy·ing 1** : EXTOL, PRAISE **2 a** : to increase in importance **b** : EXAGGERATE **3** : to enlarge in fact or in appearance ⟨a microscope *magnifies* an object seen through it⟩ — **mag·ni·fi·er** \-ˌfī(-ə)r\ *n*

mag·ni·fy·ing glass *n* : a lens that magnifies an object seen through it

mag·ni·tude \ˈmag-nə-ˌt(y)üd\ *n* **1 a** : great size or extent : BIGNESS **b** : [1]SIZE 1 **2** : the importance of something in influence or effect **3** : degree of brightness; *esp* : a number representing the brightness of a star **4** : the intensity of an earthquake represented by a number on a scale

mag·no·lia \mag-ˈnōl-yə\ *n* : any of a genus of North American and Asian trees or tall shrubs having usually showy white, yellow, rose, or purple flowers that appear before or sometimes with the leaves in the spring

mag·num opus \ˌmag-nə-ˈmō-pəs\ *n* : a great work and especially the greatest achievement of an artist or writer

mag·pie \ˈmag-ˌpī\ *n* **1** : any of various noisy birds related to the jays but having a long tail and black-and-white feathers **2** : a person who chatters constantly

magpie 1

ma·guey \mə-ˈgā\ *n, pl* **magueys 1** : any of various agaves (as the century plant) with fleshy leaves **2** : any of several hard fibers obtained from magueys

Mag·yar \ˈmag-ˌyär, ˈmäg-; ˈmäj-ˌär\ *n* **1** : a member of the dominant people of Hungary **2** : HUNGARIAN 2 — **Magyar** *adj*

ma·ha·ra·ja *or* **ma·ha·ra·jah** \ˌmä-hə-ˈräj-ə, -ˈräzh-ə\ *n* : a Hindu prince ranking above a raja [from Sanskrit (ancient language of India) *mahārāja* "maharaja," from *mahat* "great" and *rājan* "king, raja"]

ma·ha·ra·ni *or* **ma·ha·ra·nee** \ˌmä-hə-ˈrän-ē\ *n* **1** : the wife of a maharaja **2** : a Hindu princess ranking above a rani

ma·hat·ma \mə-ˈhät-mə, -ˈhat-\ *n* : a person respected for being noble, wise, and unselfish — used as a title of honor especially by Hindus [from Sanskrit (ancient language of India) *mahātman* "great-souled," from *mahat* "great" and *ātman* "self, soul"]

Ma·hi·can \mə-ˈhē-kən\ *or* **Mo·hi·can** \mō-, mə-\ *n, pl* **-can** *or* **-cans** : a member of an American Indian people of the upper Hudson River Valley

ma·hog·a·ny \mə-ˈhäg-ə-nē\ *n, pl* **-nies 1** : the wood of any of various chiefly tropical trees: as **a** : the strong usually reddish brown and heavy wood of a West Indian tree that is widely used to make furniture **b** : any of several African woods that vary in color from pinkish to deep reddish brown **2** : any of various woods resembling or substituted for true mahogany **3** : a tree from which mahogany is obtained **4** : a moderate reddish brown

maid \ˈmād\ *n* **1** : an unmarried girl or woman; *esp* : [1]MAIDEN **2** : a female servant

[1]maid·en \ˈmād-ᵊn\ *n* : a young unmarried girl or woman — **maid·en·hood** \-ˌhúd\ *n* — **maid·en·ly** \-lē\ *adj*

[2]maiden *adj* **1 a** : not married ⟨*maiden* aunt⟩ **b** : [2]VIRGIN 1 **2** : of or relating to a maiden **3** : coming before all others : FIRST, EARLIEST ⟨*maiden* voyage⟩

maid·en·hair fern \ˈmād-ᵊn-ˌha(ə)r-, -ˌhe(ə)r-\ *n* : any of a genus of ferns with slender stems and delicate much-divided often feathery leaves — called also *maidenhair*

maiden name *n* : a woman's family name before she is married

maid of honor 1 : an unmarried woman usually of noble birth who attends a queen or princess **2** : a bride's principal unmarried wedding attendant

maid·ser·vant \ˈmād-ˌsər-vənt\ *n* : a female servant

[1]mail \ˈmā(ə)l\ *n* **1** : letters or parcels sent from one person to another especially through the post office **2** : something that comes in the mail and especially in a single delivery **3** : a vehicle (as a train, truck, or boat) that carries mail **4** : the system used in the public sending and delivery of letters and parcels ⟨do business by *mail*⟩ **5** : E-MAIL 2 [Middle English *male* "a wallet or traveling bag," from early French *male* (same meaning); of Germanic origin]

[2]mail *vb* : to send by mail : POST — **mail·able** \ˈmā-lə-bəl\ *adj* — **mail·er** *n*

[3]mail *n* : armor made of small metal links or sometimes plates ⟨a coat of *mail*⟩ [Middle English *maille* "metal plates used on armor," from early French *maille* (same meaning), derived from Latin *macula* "spot, mesh of a net"] — **mailed** \ˈmā(ə)ld\ *adj*

mail·box \ˈmā(ə)l-ˌbäks\ *n* **1** : a public box in which to place outgoing mail **2** : a private box (as on a house) for the delivery of incoming mail **3** : a computer file in which e-mail is collected

mail carrier *n* : LETTER CARRIER

mail·man \ˈmā(ə)l-ˌman\ *n* : LETTER CARRIER

mail order *n* : an order for goods that is received and filled by mail — **mail-order** *adj*

[3]mail

maim \ˈmām\ *vb* : to injure or disfigure badly

[1]main \ˈmān\ *n* **1** : physical strength : FORCE — used in the phrase *with might and main* **2 a** : MAINLAND **b** : HIGH SEAS **3** : the chief part : essential point ⟨they are in the *main* well trained⟩ **4** : a principal pipe or circuit of a utility system ⟨gas *main*⟩ ⟨water *main*⟩

[2]main *adj* **1** : [1]CHIEF 2, PRINCIPAL ⟨the *main* idea⟩ **2** : PURE 3, SHEER ⟨by *main* force⟩ **3** : being a clause that is capable of standing alone as a simple sentence but is part of a larger sentence that includes a subordinate clause or another main clause — **main·ly** *adv*

main·frame \ˈmān-ˌfrām\ *n* : a large fast computer that can do many jobs at once

main·land \ˈmān-ˌland, -lənd\ *n* : a continent or the main part of a continent as distinguished from an offshore island or sometimes from a cape or peninsula — **main·land·er** *n*

main·mast \ˈmān-ˌmast, -məst\ *n* : the principal mast of a sailing ship

main·sail \ˈmān-ˌsāl, ˈmān(t)-səl\ *n* : the principal sail on the mainmast

main sequence *n* : a group of stars that form a band on a graph of their color versus their brightness

main·spring \ˈmān-ˌspriŋ\ *n* **1** : the principal spring in a mechanical device (as a watch or clock) **2** : the chief or most powerful motive or cause

main·stay \-ˌstā\ *n* **1** : a large strong rope running from the maintop of a ship usually to the foot of the foremast **2** : a chief support ⟨the *mainstay* of the family⟩

main·stream \-ˌstrēm\ *n* : the principal current or direction of activity or influence

main·tain \mān-ˈtān, mən-\ *vb* **1** : to keep in an existing state; *esp* : to keep in good condition ⟨*maintain* one's health⟩ ⟨*maintain* machinery⟩ **2** : to defend by argument ⟨*maintain* a position⟩ **3** : to continue in : CARRY ON, KEEP UP ⟨*maintain* your balance⟩ ⟨*maintain* a correspondence⟩ **4** : to provide for : SUPPORT ⟨*maintain* my family by working⟩ **5** : to insist to be true ⟨*maintained* that all men are equal⟩ — **main·tain·able** \-ˈtā-nə-bəl\ *adj* — **main·tain·er** *n*

main·te·nance \ˈmānt-nən(t)s, -ᵊn-ən(t)s\ *n* **1** : the act of maintaining : the state of being maintained ⟨*maintenance* of law and order⟩ ⟨money for the family's *maintenance*⟩ **2** : something that maintains **3** : the care of property or equipment ⟨workers in charge of *maintenance*⟩

main·top \ˈmān-ˌtäp\ *n* : a platform at the head of the mainmast of a square-rigged ship

maize \ˈmāz\ *n* **1** : ¹CORN 1 **2** ¹CORN 2 **3** ¹CORN 3

ma·jes·tic \mə-ˈjes-tik\ *adj* : being stately and dignified : NOBLE **synonyms** see GRAND — **ma·jes·ti·cal·ly** \-ti-k(ə-)lē\ *adv*

maj·es·ty \ˈmaj-ə-stē\ *n, pl* **-ties** **1** : royal power, authority, or dignity **2** — used as a title for a king, queen, emperor, or empress ⟨Your *Majesty*⟩ **3 a** : royal manner or quality **b** : greatness of quality or character

¹ma·jor \ˈmā-jər\ *adj* **1 a** : greater in dignity, rank, or importance ⟨a *major* poet⟩ **b** : greater in number, quantity, or extent ⟨received the *major* part of the blame⟩ **2 a** : notable in effect or scope ⟨a *major* improvement⟩ **b** : significant in size, amount, or degree ⟨made some *major* cash⟩ **3** : of or relating to an academic major **4 a** : having half steps between the third and fourth and the seventh and eighth degrees ⟨*major* scale⟩ **b** : based on a major scale ⟨*major* key⟩ ⟨*major* chord⟩

²major *n* **1** : a military commissioned officer with a rank just below that of lieutenant colonel **2 a** : the chief subject studied by a student ⟨chose history as his *major*⟩ **b** : a student specializing in a field ⟨a French *major*⟩

³major *vb* **ma·jored; ma·jor·ing** \ˈmāj-(ə-)riŋ\ : to study an academic major ⟨*major* in English⟩

ma·jor·do·mo \ˌmā-jər-ˈdō-mō\ *n, pl* **-mos** : a person in charge of a great and especially of a royal household

ma·jor·ette \ˌmā-jə-ˈret\ *n* : DRUM MAJORETTE

major general *n* : a military commissioned officer with a rank just below that of lieutenant general

ma·jor·i·ty \mə-ˈjȯr-ət-ē, -ˈjär-\ *n, pl* **-ties** **1 a** : the age at which one is given full civil rights **b** : the status of one who has reached this age **2 a** : a number or percentage greater than half of a total **b** : the amount by which such a number exceeds the smaller number ⟨won by a *majority* of seven⟩ **3** : the group or party that makes up the greater part of a whole body of persons ⟨the *majority* in the senate⟩ **4** : the military office or rank of a major

major league *n* : a league in the highest class of U.S. professional sports

¹make \ˈmāk\ *vb* **made** \ˈmād\; **mak·ing** **1 a** : to begin or seem to begin an action ⟨she *made* as if to go⟩ **b** : to act so as to appear ⟨*make* merry⟩ **2 a** : to cause to exist or occur : CREATE ⟨*make* a noise⟩ ⟨*make* trouble⟩ **b** : to create for some purpose or goal ⟨she was *made* to be a surgeon⟩ **3 a** : to form or shape out of material or parts : FASHION, CONSTRUCT ⟨*make* a dress⟩ ⟨*make* a car⟩ **b** : to combine to produce ⟨2 and 2 *make* 4⟩ **4** : to frame in the mind ⟨*make* plans⟩ **5** : to put together from parts ⟨houses *made* of stone⟩ **6** : to estimate to be : COMPUTE ⟨I *make* it an even $5⟩ **7 a** : to set in order ⟨*make* a bed⟩ **b** : PREPARE, FIX ⟨*make* dinner⟩ **8** : to cut and spread for drying ⟨*make* hay⟩ **9 a** : to cause to be or become ⟨*made*

herself useful⟩ **b** : APPOINT ⟨*made* him her assistant⟩ **10 a** : ENACT 1, ESTABLISH ⟨*make* laws⟩ **b** : to prepare in an appropriate manner ⟨*make* a will⟩ **11 a** : UNDERSTAND 1a ⟨unable to *make* anything of the story⟩ **b** : to regard as being : CONSIDER ⟨he is not the fool you *make* him⟩ **12** : ¹DO 1a, PERFORM ⟨*make* war⟩ ⟨*make* a bow⟩ **13** : to produce or acquire by or as if by action or effort ⟨*made* a mess of the job⟩ ⟨*make* good money⟩ ⟨*make* friends⟩ **14** : to force to act in some manner ⟨*made* her return home⟩ **15** : to cause or assure the success of ⟨the first case *made* the new lawyer⟩ **16** : to develop into ⟨she will *make* a fine judge⟩ **17 a** : ¹REACH 2c, ATTAIN ⟨the ship *makes* port tonight⟩ ⟨he *made* corporal in 10 months⟩ ⟨they *made* it to the other side of the bridge⟩ **b** : to gain a place on or in ⟨*made* the track team⟩ ⟨the story *made* the papers⟩ **18** : ¹CATCH 7b ⟨*make* the train⟩ **19** : to set out in pursuit ⟨*made* after the fox⟩ **20** : to provide the most satisfying experience of ⟨meeting the star of the show really *made* our day⟩ — **make away with** : to carry off — **make believe** : to act as if something known to be imaginary is real or true : PRETEND — **make ends meet** : to keep one's expenses within one's income — **make fun of** : to make the target of one's laughter : RIDICULE ⟨*made fun* of the way they talked⟩ — **make good 1** : to make complete : FULFILL ⟨*make good* a promise⟩ **2** : to make up for a deficiency ⟨*make good* the loss⟩ **3** : SUCCEED 2 ⟨*make good* as a reporter⟩ — **make it 1** : to be successful ⟨tried to *make it* in the world of sports⟩ — **make sail 1** : to raise or spread sail **2** : to set out on a voyage — **make shift** : to manage with difficulty — **make time** : to travel fast ⟨can really *make time* on the new highway⟩ — **make use of** : to put to use : EMPLOY — **make way** : to open a path or passage ⟨the crowd *made way* for the injured person⟩

synonyms MAKE, FORM, MANUFACTURE mean to cause to come into being. MAKE is a word that can be used of many kinds of creation ⟨*make* soup⟩ ⟨*made* many friends⟩. FORM suggests that the thing brought into being has a design or structure ⟨the colonies *formed* a new nation⟩. MANUFACTURE suggests making something in a fixed way and usually by machinery ⟨a company that *manufactures* cars⟩.

²make *n* **1** : the way in which a thing is made : STRUCTURE **2** : a particular kind of manufactured goods : BRAND ⟨looked at several *makes* of car before deciding⟩

¹make–be·lieve \ˈmāk-bə-ˌlēv\ *n* : a pretending to be another person or character (as in the play of children)

²make–believe *adj* : IMAGINARY ⟨was only a *make-believe* lion⟩

make out *vb* **1** : to draw up in writing ⟨*make out* a shopping list⟩ **2** : UNDERSTAND 1a ⟨how do you *make* that *out*⟩ **3** : to represent as being ⟨*made* her *out* a hero⟩ **4** : to see and identify with difficulty ⟨*make out* a form in the fog⟩ **5** : SUCCEED 2 ⟨*make out* well in business⟩ **6** : to engage in kissing and petting

make over *vb* **1** : to transfer the title of ⟨*made* the estate *over* to his sister⟩ **2** : REMAKE, REMODEL ⟨*made* the whole house *over*⟩ **3** : ¹REFORM 1

mak·er \ˈmā-kər\ *n* : one that makes: as **a** *cap* : GOD 1 **b** : a person who signs a promissory note

make·shift \ˈmāk-ˌshift\ *n* : a temporary replacement : SUBSTITUTE — **makeshift** *adj*

make·up \ˈmā-ˌkəp\ *n* **1** : the way the parts or elements of something are put together : COMPOSITION ⟨the *makeup* of a newspaper⟩ **2 a** : any of various cosmetics (as lipstick or powder) **b** : materials (as wigs or cosmetics) used

\ə\ **abut**	\au̇\ **out**	\i\ **tip**	\ȯ\ **saw**	\u̇\ **foot**
\ər\ **further**	\ch\ **chin**	\ī\ **life**	\ȯi\ **coin**	\y\ **yet**
\a\ **mat**	\e\ **pet**	\j\ **job**	\th\ **thin**	\yü\ **few**
\ā\ **take**	\ē\ **easy**	\ŋ\ **sing**	\t͟h\ **this**	\yu̇\ **cure**
\ä\ **cot, cart**	\g\ **go**	\ō\ **bone**	\ü\ **food**	\zh\ **vision**

in making up ⟨put on *makeup* for a play⟩ ⟨too young to wear *makeup*⟩

make up \(ˈ)mā-ˈkəp\ *vb* **1** : to form by fitting together or assembling ⟨*make up* a suit⟩ ⟨*make up* a train⟩ **2** : COMPOSE 1b ⟨chapters *make up* a book⟩ **3** : to make good for something lacking or for a loss or injury **4** : DECIDE 3, SETTLE ⟨*made up* my mind to go⟩ **5 a** : to create from the imagination : INVENT ⟨*make up* a story⟩ **b** : to set in order ⟨rooms are *made up* daily⟩ **6** : to become friendly again ⟨they fought and *made up*⟩ **7 a** : to put on costumes or makeup (as for a play) ⟨*made up* as a clown⟩ **b** : to apply cosmetics to

mak·ing \ˈmā-kiŋ\ *n* **1** : the act of forming, causing, doing, or coming into being ⟨spots problems in the *making*⟩ **2** : a process or means of advancement or success **3** : material from which something can be developed : POTENTIALITY ⟨there is the *making* of a racehorse in this colt⟩ — often used in plural ⟨has the *makings* of a great quarterback⟩ **4** *pl* : the materials from which something can be made

mal- *combining form* **1 a** : bad ⟨*mal*practice⟩ **b** : badly ⟨*mal*odorous⟩ **2 a** : abnormal ⟨*mal*formation⟩ **b** : abnormally ⟨*mal*formed⟩ [derived from Latin *malus* "bad, evil"]

Mal·a·chi \ˈmal-ə-ˌkī\ *n* — see BIBLE table

mal·a·chite \ˈmal-ə-ˌkīt\ *n* : a green mineral that contains copper and is used especially for ornamental objects

mal·ad·just·ed \ˌmal-ə-ˈjəs-təd\ *adj* : not well adjusted especially to one's environment ⟨socially *maladjusted* persons⟩

mal·ad·just·ment \ˌmal-ə-ˈjəs(t)-mənt\ *n* : poor or faulty adjustment

mal·adroit \ˌmal-ə-ˈdrȯit\ *adj* : AWKWARD 2, CLUMSY — **mal·adroit·ly** *adv* — **mal·adroit·ness** *n*

mal·a·dy \ˈmal-əd-ē\ *n, pl* **-dies** : a disease or disorder of the body or mind : AILMENT

Mal·a·gasy \ˌmal-ə-ˈgas-ē\ *n, pl* **-gasy**; *also* **-gas·ies** **1** : a person born or living in Madagascar **2** : the language of the Malagasy people — **Malagasy** *adj*

mal·aise \mə-ˈlāz, ma-, -ˈlez\ *n* : a hazy feeling of not being well

mal·a·mute *also* **mal·e·mute** \ˈmal-ə-ˌmyüt\ *n* : a sled dog of northern North America; *esp* : ALASKAN MALAMUTE

ma·lar·ia \mə-ˈler-ē-ə\ *n* : a disease caused by protozoan parasites in the red blood cells, passed from one individual to another by the bite of mosquitoes, and marked by periodic attacks of chills and fever — **ma·lar·i·al** \-ē-əl\ *adj*

mal·a·thi·on \ˌmal-ə-ˈthī-ən, -ˌän\ *n* : a poisonous insecticide that is broken down in nature

Ma·lay \mə-ˈlā, ˈmā-ˌlā\ *n, pl* **Malays** **1** : a member of a people of the Malay Peninsula and neighboring islands **2** : the language of the Malay people — **Malay** *adj* — **Ma·lay·an** \mə-ˈlā-ən, ˈmā-ˌlā\ *adj or n*

mal·con·tent \ˌmal-kən-ˈtent\ *adj* : not satisfied with the existing state of affairs : DISCONTENTED — **malcontent** *n*

¹male \ˈmā(ə)l\ *adj* **1 a** : of, relating to, or being the sex that produces gametes which fertilize the eggs of females **b** : bearing only stamens; *esp* : having only stamens and not producing fruit or seeds ⟨a *male* holly⟩ **2** : made up or consisting of males ⟨a *male* choir⟩ — **male·ness** *n*

²male *n* : a male individual

male·dic·tion \ˌmal-ə-ˈdik-shən\ *n* : a prayer for harm to come to someone : CURSE

male·fac·tion \ˌmal-ə-ˈfak-shən\ *n* : an evil deed : CRIME

male·fac·tor \ˈmal-ə-ˌfak-tər\ *n* **1** : one who is guilty of a crime or offense **2** : one who does evil

ma·lev·o·lence \mə-ˈlev-ə-lən(t)s\ *n* **1** : the quality or state of being malevolent **2** : malevolent behavior

ma·lev·o·lent \mə-ˈlev-ə-lənt\ *adj* : having or showing ill will : SPITEFUL — **ma·lev·o·lent·ly** *adv*

mal·fea·sance \(ˈ)mal-ˈfēz-ᵊn(t)s\ *n* : wrongful conduct especially by a public official

mal·for·ma·tion \ˌmal-fȯr-ˈmā-shən, -fər-\ *n* : a misshapen, abnormal, or faulty formation or structure ⟨*malformation* of the knee joint⟩

mal·formed \(ˈ)mal-ˈfȯ(ə)rmd\ *adj* : marked by malformation : badly or imperfectly formed : MISSHAPEN

mal·func·tion \(ˈ)mal-ˈfəŋ(k)-shən\ *vb* : to fail to function or operate properly — **malfunction** *n*

mal·ice \ˈmal-əs\ *n* : ILL WILL; *esp* : the intention of doing harm for the satisfaction of doing it

ma·li·cious \mə-ˈlish-əs\ *adj* **1** : doing mean things for pleasure **2** : done just to be mean ⟨*malicious* gossip⟩ — **ma·li·cious·ly** *adv* — **ma·li·cious·ness** *n*

¹ma·lign \mə-ˈlīn\ *adj* **1** : evil in influence or effect **2** : showing strong ill will : MALEVOLENT

²malign *vb* : to say evil things about : SLANDER

ma·lig·nan·cy \mə-ˈlig-nən-sē\ *n, pl* **-cies** **1** : the quality or state of being malignant **2** : a malignant tumor

ma·lig·nant \mə-ˈlig-nənt\ *adj* **1** : evil in influence or effect : INJURIOUS **2** : MALICIOUS 1 **3** : tending to produce death ⟨*malignant* tumors⟩ — **ma·lig·nant·ly** *adv*

ma·lig·ni·ty \mə-ˈlig-nət-ē\ *n, pl* **-ties** **1** : the quality or state of being malignant **2** : something (as an act or event) that is malignant

ma·lin·ger \mə-ˈliŋ-gər\ *vb* **-gered; -ger·ing** \-g(ə-)riŋ\ : to pretend to be sick or injured so as to avoid duty or work — **ma·lin·ger·er** \-gər-ər\ *n*

mall \ˈmȯl\ *n* **1** : a shaded walk : PROMENADE **2** : a usually paved or grassy strip between two roadways **3 a** : a group of stores and often restaurants arranged about an often covered way for pedestrians **b** : a usually large suburban building or group of buildings containing shops and often restaurants with connecting passageways

Word History In Italy in the 1500s a popular alley game similar to croquet was known as *pallamaglio*, from *palla* "ball," and *maglio* "mallet." The game (and word) was adopted by the French as *pallemalle* and in the 1600s by the English as *pall-mall*. The alley on which the game was played came to be known as a *mall*. One of the best known of these alleys, covered with sand and crushed shells, was located in London's St. James Park and was known as "The Mall." After the game lost favor, the Mall at St. James, as it continued to be called, was turned into a fashionable walkway with trees and flowers. Similar open-air places came to be called *malls* also. In the 20th century the word was applied to other public spaces, including the shopping complexes we now know as *malls*. [a shortened form of *pall-mall* "a game similar to croquet formerly played in England," literally "ball-mallet"]

mal·lard \ˈmal-ərd\ *n, pl* **mallard** *or* **mallards** : a common and widely distributed wild duck of the northern hemisphere the males of which have a green head and white ring around the neck and that is the source of the domestic ducks

mal·lea·ble \ˈmal-ē-ə-bəl, ˈmal-(y)ə-bəl\ *adj* **1** : capable of being extended or shaped by beating with a hammer or by the pressure of rollers ⟨a *malleable* metal⟩ **2** : capable of being changed so as to fit new uses or situations : FLEXIBLE, ADAPTABLE — **mal·lea·bil·i·ty** \ˌmal-ē-ə-ˈbil-ət-ē, ˌmal-(y)ə-ˈbil-\ *n*

mal·let \ˈmal-ət\ *n* : a hammer usually with a barrel-shaped head: as **a** : one with a large head used for driving a tool (as a chisel) or for striking a surface without damaging it **b** : a club for striking a ball (as in croquet or polo)

mallet a

mal·le·us \ˈmal-ē-əs\ *n, pl* **mal·lei** \ˈmal-ē-ˌī, -ē-ˌē\ : the outermost bone of the three small bones of the middle ear of a mammal

mal·low \\'mal-ō\ *n* : any of a group of herbs with lobed leaves, usually showy flowers, and a disk-shaped fruit

mal·nour·ished \(')mal-'nər-isht, -'nə-risht\ *adj* : poorly nourished : UNDERNOURISHED

mal·nu·tri·tion \,mal-n(y)ù-'trish-ən\ *n* : faulty nutrition especially due to inadequate intake of nutrients

mal·odor·ous \(')mal-'ōd-ə-rəs\ *adj* : having a bad smell — **mal·odor·ous·ly** *adv* — **mal·odor·ous·ness** *n*

Mal·pi·ghi·an tubule \mal-,pig-ē-ən-, -,pē-gē-ən-\ *n* : any of a group of long vessels opening into the intestine in various arthropods (as insects) and functioning in excretion

mal·prac·tice \(')mal-'prak-təs\ *n* : violation of professional standards especially by carelessness or improper conduct

¹malt \'mȯlt\ *n* **1** : grain and especially barley steeped in water and used chiefly in brewing and distilling **2** : MALTED MILK 2 — **malt** *adj*

²malt *vb* **1** : to convert into malt **2** : to make or treat with malt or malt extract

malt·ase \'mȯl-,tās\ *n* : an enzyme that accelerates the breakdown of maltose to glucose

malted milk *n* **1** : a soluble powder prepared from dried milk and malted cereals **2** : a beverage made by dissolving malted milk in a liquid (as milk)

Mal·tese \mȯl-'tēz\ *n, pl* **Maltese** **1** : a person born or living in Malta **2** : the Semitic language of the Maltese people **3** : any of a breed of toy dogs with a long silky white coat, a black nose, and dark eyes — **Maltese** *adj*

Maltese cross *n* : a cross with four arms of equal size that increase in width toward the ends

malt liquor *n* : a fermented liquor (as beer) made with malt

malt·ose \'mȯl-,tōs\ *n* : a sugar formed especially from starch by the action of enzymes and used in brewing and distilling

mal·treat \(')mal-'trēt\ *vb* : to treat unkindly or roughly : ABUSE — **mal·treat·ment** \-mənt\ *n*

ma·ma *also* **mam·ma** *or* **mom·ma** \'mäm-ə\ *n* : ¹MOTHER 1a

mam·ba \'mäm-bə, 'mam-\ *n* : any of several African poisonous snakes related to the cobras but lacking a hood

mam·bo \'mäm-bō\ *n, pl* **mambos** : a dance of Haitian origin related to the rumba — **mambo** *vb*

mam·mal \'mam-əl\ *n* : any of a class of warm-blooded vertebrates that include human beings and all other animals that nourish their young with milk produced by mammary glands and have the skin usually more or less covered with hair

mam·ma·li·an \mə-'mā-lē-ən, ma-'mā-\ *adj* : of, relating to, or characteristic of mammals

mam·ma·ry \'mam-ə-rē\ *adj* : of, relating to, lying near, or affecting the mammary glands

mammary gland *n* : one of the large glands that in female mammals produce milk and in males are usually underdeveloped, are located in pairs on the abdominal side of the animal body, and usually end in a nipple

¹mam·moth \'mam-əth\ *n* **1** : any of various large hairy extinct mammals of the elephant family with very long tusks that curve upward **2** : something very large of its kind ⟨a company that is a *mammoth* of the industry⟩

²mammoth *adj* : very large : HUGE

mam·my \'mam-ē\ *n, pl* **mammies** **1**

¹mammoth 1

: ¹MOTHER 1a **2** : a black woman serving as a nurse to white children especially in the past in the southern states of the U.S.

¹man \'man\ *n, pl* **men** \'men\ **1 a** : a human being; *esp* : an adult male human **b** : the human race : HUMANKIND **c** : ¹HUSBAND, LOVER **d** : a primate mammal that walks on two legs and is the only living member of the hominid family; *also* : any living or extinct hominid **e** — used as an interjection to express strong feeling ⟨*man*, what a game⟩ **2 a** : a tenant in the Middle Ages : VASSAL **b** : an adult male servant **c** *pl* : workers as a group **3** : ²INDIVIDUAL 2, PERSON ⟨a *man* could be killed there⟩ **4** : one of the pieces in a game (as chess) [Old English *man* "person, male person"]

²man *vb* **manned; man·ning** **1** : to supply with people (as for service) ⟨*man* a ship⟩ **2** : to station members of a ship's crew at ⟨*man* the ropes⟩ **3** : to serve in the force of ⟨*man* the ticket counter⟩

man·a·cle \'man-i-kəl\ *n* **1** : a shackle for the hand or wrist : HANDCUFF **2** : something that prevents free action — **manacle** *vb*

man·age \'man-ij\ *vb* **man·aged; man·ag·ing** **1** : to look after and make decisions about : DIRECT ⟨*manage* a factory⟩ **2** : to make and keep under one's control : HANDLE ⟨*manages* her skis well⟩ ⟨skill in *managing* horses⟩ **3** : to treat with care : HUSBAND ⟨there's enough food if it's *managed* well⟩ **4** : to succeed in one's purpose : GET ALONG ⟨*manages* despite a heavy schedule⟩ ⟨always *manages* to win somehow⟩ [from Italian *maneggiare* "to handle, direct, manage," from *mano* "hand," from Latin *manus* "hand" — related to MANEUVER, MANUAL, MANUFACTURE; see *Word History* at MANEUVER] — **man·age·abil·i·ty** \,man-ij-ə-'bil-ət-ē\ *n* — **man·age·able** \'man-ij-ə-bəl\ *adj*

man·age·ment \'man-ij-mənt\ *n* **1** : the act or art of managing : CONTROL, DIRECTION **2** : skill in managing **3** : the people who manage ⟨the company's *management*⟩

man·ag·er \'man-ij-ər\ *n* **1** : a person who manages especially a business or household affairs **2** : a person who directs a team or an athlete — **man·a·ge·ri·al** \,man-ə-'jir-ē-əl\ *adj*

man–at–arms \,man-ət-'ärmz\ *n, pl* **men–at–arms** \,men-\ : ¹SOLDIER 1; *esp* : a heavily armed mounted soldier

man·a·tee \'man-ə-,tē\ *n* : any of several chiefly tropical water-dwelling mammals that eat plants and differ from the related dugong especially in having the tail broad and rounded

Man·chu \'man-chü, man-'chü\ *n* **1** : a member of the native people of Manchuria who conquered China in 1644 **2** : the language of the Manchu people — **Manchu** *adj*

man·da·mus \man-'dā-məs\ *n* : a writ from a superior court ordering the performance of an act or duty

man·da·rin \'man-d(ə-)rən\ *n* **1** : a public official under the Chinese Empire **2** *cap* : the chief dialect of China centering about Beijing **3** : a small spiny Chinese orange tree with yellow to reddish orange fruits having loose rinds; *also* : its fruit

mandarin orange *n* : MANDARIN 3

¹man·date \'man-,dāt\ *n* **1** : an order from a higher court to a lower court **2 a** : an authoritative command, instruction, or direction **b** : authorization or approval given to a representative especially by voters ⟨accepted the *mandate* of the people⟩ **3 a** : a commission granted by the

\ə\ abut	\aù\ out	\i\ tip	\ȯ\ saw	\ù\ foot
\ər\ further	\ch\ chin	\ī\ life	\ȯi\ coin	\y\ yet
\a\ mat	\e\ pet	\j\ job	\th\ thin	\yü\ few
\ā\ take	\ē\ easy	\ŋ\ sing	\th\ this	\yù\ cure
\ä\ cot, cart	\g\ go	\ō\ bone	\ü\ food	\zh\ vision

League of Nations to a member nation to administer a territory on its behalf **b** : a mandated territory

²**mandate** *vb* **man·dat·ed; man·dat·ing 1** : to administer or assign a territory under a mandate **2** : to make mandatory : ORDER, COMMAND

man·da·to·ry \'man-də-ˌtȯr-ē, -ˌtȯr-\ *adj* **1** : containing or constituting a command : OBLIGATORY ⟨the assembly was *mandatory* for all students⟩ **2** : of, relating to, or holding a League of Nations mandate

man·di·ble \'man-də-bəl\ *n* **1 a** (1) : a lower jaw of a vertebrate consisting of a single bone or of bones that are completely united (2) : the lower jaw with its surrounding soft parts **b** : either the upper or lower part of the bill of a bird **2** : either of the first pair of mouthparts of some invertebrates and especially arthropods (as an insect or crustacean) that often form biting organs

man·do·lin \ˌman-də-'lin, 'man-dᵊl-ən\ *also* **man·do·line** \ˌman-də-'lēn, 'man-dᵊl-ən\ *n* : a stringed instrument with a pear-shaped body and four to six pairs of strings played by plucking

man·drake \'man-ˌdrāk\ *n* **1** : a Mediterranean herb of the nightshade family that has a large forked root resembling a human being in form and was once thought to have magical properties; *also* : the root itself **2** : MAYAPPLE

mandrake 1

man·drill \'man-drəl\ *n* : a large baboon of western Africa with a red rump and in the male with blue ridges on the sides of the nose

mane \'mān\ *n* **1** : long heavy hair growing about the neck and head of some mammals (as horses and lions) **2** : long heavy hair on a person's head — **maned** \'mānd\ *adj*

man–eat·er \'man-ˌēt-ər\ *n* : one (as a cannibal, shark, or tiger) that has or is thought to have an appetite for human flesh — **man–eat·ing** \-ˌēt-iŋ\ *adj*

¹**ma·neu·ver** \mə-'n(y)ü-vər\ *n* **1 a** : a planned movement of troops or ships **b** : a training exercise by armed forces **2** : a clever or skillful move or action ⟨avoided an accident by a quick *maneuver*⟩

Word History Strange as it seems, we owe both *maneuver* and *manure* to the same French source. The medieval French verb *manovrer*, meaning "to work" or "to place with the hand," developed from *manuoperare*, literally, "to work by hand," in the spoken Latin of ancient Gaul. From *meinourer*, a variant of *manovrer* used in England, Middle English adopted *maynouren* or *manouren*, which had the senses "to take in hand, manage," and "to cultivate (land)." In the 1500s English derived from the latter sense the noun *manure*, "material that fertilizes land." In the 1700s English adopted *maneuver* from French *manœuvrer* (the descendant of medieval French *manovrer*) which in the intervening centuries had developed a new sense "to perform a movement in military tactics." [from French *manœuvre* "a military movement," from early French *maneuvre* "work done by hand," from Latin *manuopera* (same meaning), from earlier Latin *manu operare* "to perform manual labor," from *manu*, a form of *manus* "hand," and *operare* "to work" — related to MANAGE, MANUAL, MANURE, OPERATE]

²**maneuver** *vb* **ma·neu·vered; ma·neu·ver·ing** \-'n(y)üv-(ə-)riŋ\ **1** : to move (as troops or ships) in a maneuver **2** : to perform a maneuver **3** : to manage skillfully **4** : to use trickery : SCHEME — **ma·neu·ver·abil·i·ty** \-ˌn(y)üv-(ə-)rə-'bil-ət-ē\ *n* — **ma·neu·ver·able** \-'n(y)üv-(ə-)rə-bəl\ *adj*

man·ful \'man-fəl\ *adj* : having or showing courage — **man·ful·ly** \-fə-lē\ *adv* — **man·ful·ness** *n*

man·ga \'mäŋ-gə\ *n* : a Japanese comic book or graphic novel

man·ga·nese \'maŋ-gə-ˌnēz, -ˌnēs\ *n* : a grayish white usually hard and brittle metallic element that resembles iron but is not magnetic — see ELEMENT table

manganese dioxide *n* : a dark compound of manganese and oxygen that is used especially in making glass and ceramics

mange \'mānj\ *n* : any of several contagious skin diseases of domestic animals and sometimes human beings that are marked especially by itching and loss of hair and are caused by tiny mites

man·ger \'mān-jər\ *n* : a trough or open box in which food for farm animals is placed

¹**man·gle** \'maŋ-gəl\ *vb* **man·gled; man·gling** \-g(ə-)liŋ\ **1** : to cut, bruise, or hack with repeated blows or strokes **2** : to spoil or injure in making or performing : BOTCH ⟨*mangle* a speech⟩ — **man·gler** \-g(ə-)lər\ *n*

²**mangle** *n* : a machine for ironing laundry by passing it between heated rollers

³**mangle** *vb* **man·gled; man·gling** \-g(ə-)liŋ\ : to press or smooth with a mangle — **man·gler** \-g(ə-)lər\ *n*

man·go \'maŋ-gō\ *n, pl* **mangoes** *also* **mangos** : a yellowish red tropical fruit with a firm skin, hard central stony seed, and juicy mildly tart pulp; *also* : an evergreen tree related to the cashew that bears this fruit

man·grove \'man-ˌgrōv, 'maŋ-\ *n* : any of various tropical trees or shrubs that grow many prop roots and form dense masses in somewhat salty marshes or shallow salt water

mangy \'mān-jē\ *adj* **mang·i·er; -est 1** : affected with or resulting from mange **2** : SHABBY 1, SEEDY ⟨a *mangy* old rug⟩ — **mang·i·ness** \'mān-jē-nəs\ *n*

man·han·dle \'man-ˌhan-dᵊl\ *vb* **1** : to handle roughly **2** : to move or manage by human force

man·hole \'man-ˌhōl\ *n* : a covered hole (as in a pavement, tank, or boiler) through which a worker may go

man·hood \'man-ˌhùd\ *n* **1** : COURAGE, MANLINESS **2** : the condition of being an adult male **3** : adult human males ⟨the *manhood* of a nation⟩

man–hour \'man-'aù(-ə)r\ *n* : a unit of one hour's work by one worker used especially as a basis for wages and in accounting

man·hunt \-ˌhənt\ *n* : an organized hunt for a person and especially for one charged with a crime

ma·nia \'mā-nē-ə, -nyə\ *n* **1** : excitement that is expressed through excessive physical and mental activity and extreme cheerfulness **2** : excessive enthusiasm : CRAZE ⟨had a *mania* for saving things⟩

ma·ni·ac \'mā-nē-ˌak\ *n* **1** : MADMAN, LUNATIC **2** : a person wildly enthusiastic about something

ma·ni·a·cal \mə-'nī-ə-kəl\ *also* **ma·ni·ac** \'mā-nē-ˌak\ *adj* : affected with or suggestive of madness — **ma·ni·a·cal·ly** \mə-'nī-ə-k(ə-)lē\ *adv*

man·i·cot·ti \ˌman-ə-'kät-ē\ *n, pl* **manicotti** : pasta in the shape of tubes often stuffed with meat or cheese

¹**man·i·cure** \'man-ə-ˌkyù(ə)r\ *n* : a beauty treatment for the hands and nails [from French *manicure* "one who gives a beauty treatment for the hands," derived from Latin *manus* "hand" and Latin *cura* "care"]

²**manicure** *vb* **-cured; -cur·ing 1** : to give a manicure to **2** : to trim closely and evenly ⟨*manicured* their lawn⟩

man·i·cur·ist \'man-ə-ˌkyùr-əst\ *n* : a person who gives manicures

¹**man·i·fest** \'man-ə-ˌfest\ *adj* : clear to the senses or mind : OBVIOUS ⟨their relief was *manifest*⟩ — **man·i·fest·ly** *adv*

²**manifest** *vb* : to show plainly : DISPLAY

³**manifest** *n* : a list of cargo or passengers especially for a ship or plane

man·i·fes·ta·tion \ˌman-ə-fə-ˈstā-shən, -ˌfes-ˈtā-\ *n*   **1 a** : the act or an instance of manifesting : EXPRESSION **b** : something that manifests : EVIDENCE **2** : a public demonstration of power and purpose

man·i·fes·to \ˌman-ə-ˈfes-tō\ *n, pl* **-tos** *or* **-toes** : a public declaration of intentions or views

¹**man·i·fold** \ˈman-ə-ˌfōld\ *adj* **1** : of many and various kinds ⟨*manifold* excuses⟩ **2** : including or uniting various features ⟨a *manifold* personality⟩ **3** : consisting of or operating many of one kind joined together ⟨a *manifold* pipe⟩ — **man·i·fold·ly** \-ˌfōl-(d)lē\ *adv*

²**manifold** *n* : something manifold; *esp* : a pipe fitting having several outlets for connecting one pipe with others

³**manifold** *vb* : to make several copies ⟨*manifold* a manuscript⟩

man·i·kin *or* **man·ni·kin** \ˈman-i-kən\ *n* : MANNEQUIN

ma·ni·la \mə-ˈnil-ə\ *adj, often cap* : made of manila paper or from Manila hemp ⟨*manila* folder⟩ ⟨*manila* rope⟩

Manila hemp *n* : ABACA

manila paper *n, often cap M* : a tough brownish paper made originally from Manila hemp and used especially as a wrapping paper

man in the street : a typical or ordinary person

man·i·oc \ˈman-ē-ˌäk\ *n* : CASSAVA

ma·nip·u·late \mə-ˈnip-yə-ˌlāt\ *vb* **-lat·ed; -lat·ing** **1** : to treat or operate with or as if with the hands or by mechanical means especially with skill ⟨*manipulate* the trackball⟩ **2** : to manage or use skillfully ⟨*manipulate* masses of statistics⟩ **3** : to manage especially with intent to deceive ⟨*manipulate* accounts⟩ ⟨*manipulate* public opinion⟩ **synonyms** see HANDLE — **ma·nip·u·la·tion** \-ˌnip-yə-ˈlā-shən\ *n* — **ma·nip·u·la·tor** \-ˈnip-yə-ˌlāt-ər\ *n*

man·kind *n* **1** \ˈman-ˈkīnd, -ˌkīnd\ : the human race : all human beings **2** \-ˌkīnd\ : men rather than women

man·like \ˈman-ˌlīk\ *adj* : resembling or characteristic of a man : MANNISH

man·ly \ˈman-lē\ *adj* **man·li·er; -est** **1** : having qualities usually expected of a man : STRONG **2** : appropriate in character to a man ⟨*manly* sports⟩ — **man·li·ness** *n*

man–made \ˈman-ˈmād\ *adj* : made by people rather than nature ⟨*man-made* satellites⟩; *esp* : ¹SYNTHETIC 2 ⟨*man-made* fibers⟩

man·na \ˈman-ə\ *n* **1** : food miraculously supplied to the Israelites in the wilderness **2** : a usually sudden and unexpected source of pleasure or gain

manned \ˈmand\ *adj* : carrying or performed by a person ⟨*manned* spaceflight⟩

man·ne·quin \ˈman-i-kən\ *n* **1** : an artist's, tailor's, or dressmaker's jointed figure of the human body **2** : a form representing the human figure used especially for displaying clothes **3** : a person employed to model clothing

man·ner \ˈman-ər\ *n* **1 a** : ¹SORT 1a, KIND ⟨what *manner* of fools are they⟩ **b** : various kinds — usually used in the phrase *all manner of* **2 a** : normal behavior : HABIT, CUSTOM ⟨spoke bluntly as was her *manner*⟩ **b** : a way of acting or proceeding ⟨worked in a brisk *manner*⟩ **c** : ¹STYLE 1 ⟨painted in the artist's early *manner*⟩ **3** *pl* **a** : social conduct or rules of conduct as shown in the prevailing customs **b** : characteristic or habitual conduct : BEHAVIOR ⟨taught the child good *manners*⟩; *esp* : polite behavior

man·nered \ˈman-ərd\ *adj* : having manners of a specified kind ⟨well-*mannered*⟩ ⟨mild-*mannered*⟩

man·ner·ism \ˈman-ə-ˌriz-əm\ *n* : a characteristic and often unconscious way of acting ⟨the *mannerism* of constantly adjusting her glasses⟩

man·ner·ly \ˈman-ər-lē\ *adj* : showing good manners : POLITE — **man·ner·li·ness** *n* — **mannerly** *adv*

manning *present participle of* MAN

man·nish \ˈman-ish\ *adj* : resembling, suggesting, suitable to, or characteristic of a man rather than a woman ⟨a *mannish* voice⟩ ⟨her *mannish* clothes⟩ — **man·nish·ly** *adv* — **man·nish·ness** *n*

ma·noeu·vre \mə-ˈn(y)ü-vər\ *chiefly British variant of* MANEUVER

man of the world : a practical or worldly man of much experience

man–of–war \ˌman-ə(v)-ˈwȯ(ə)r\ *n, pl* **men–of–war** \ˌmen-\ : WARSHIP

ma·nom·e·ter \mə-ˈnäm-ət-ər\ *n* : an instrument for measuring pressure (as of gases and vapors)

man·or \ˈman-ər\ *n* : a usually large estate; *esp* : one granted to a feudal lord — **ma·no·ri·al** \mə-ˈnōr-ē-əl, -ˈnȯr-\ *adj*

manor house *n* : the house of the lord of a manor

man–o'–war bird \ˌman-ə-ˈwȯr-\ *n* : FRIGATE BIRD

man power *n* **1** : power available from or supplied by the physical effort of human beings **2** *usually* **man·pow·er** : the total supply of persons available and fitted for service ⟨military *manpower*⟩

man·sard \ˈman-ˌsärd, -sərd\ *n* : a roof having two slopes on all sides with the lower slope steeper than the upper one

manse \ˈman(t)s\ *n* : the residence of a member of the clergy : PARSONAGE

man·ser·vant \ˈman-ˌsər-vənt\ *n, pl* **men·ser·vants** \ˈmen-ˌsər-vən(t)s\ : a male servant

man·sion \ˈman-chən\ *n* : a large impressive residence

man–size \ˈman-ˌsīz\ *or* **man–sized** \-ˌsīzd\ *adj* **1** : suitable for or requiring a man ⟨a *man-sized* job⟩ **2** : larger than others of its kind

man·slaugh·ter \ˈman-ˌslȯt-ər\ *n* : the unlawful killing of a person without the intention to do so

man·ta ray \ˈmant-ə-\ *n* : any of several extremely large rays that are widely distributed in warm seas and have enlarged pectoral fins resembling wings — called also *devilfish, manta*

man·tel \ˈmant-ᵊl\ *n* : the beam, stone, arch, or shelf above a fireplace

man·tel·piece \-ˌpēs\ *n* **1** : a mantel with its side elements **2** : the shelf of a mantel

man·tid \ˈmant-əd\ *n* : MANTIS

man·til·la \man-ˈtē-(y)ə, -ˈtil-ə\ *n* **1** : a light scarf worn over the head and shoulders especially by Spanish and Latin American women **2** : a short light cape or cloak

man·tis \ˈmant-əs\ *n, pl* **man·tis·es** *also* **man·tes** \ˈman-ˌtēz\ : any of various large usually green insects related to the grasshoppers and cockroaches that feed upon other insects and hold their prey in the stout spiny first pair of legs

¹**man·tle** \ˈmant-ᵊl\ *n* **1** : a loose sleeveless garment worn over other clothes : CLOAK **2 a** : something that covers or surrounds ⟨a *mantle* of snow⟩ ⟨a *mantle* of secrecy⟩ **b** : a fold or lobe or pair of lobes of the body wall of a mollusk or brachiopod that lines and produces the shell **3** : the portion of the earth lying between the crust and the core

²**mantle** *vb* **man·tled; man·tling** \ˈmant-liŋ, -ᵊl-iŋ\ : to cover or surround with or as if with a mantle

¹**man·u·al** \ˈman-yə-(wə)l\ *adj* **1** : of, relating to, or involving the hands ⟨*manual* skill⟩ **2** : worked or operated by hand ⟨a car with a *manual* transmission⟩ **3** : requiring or

\ə\ abut	\au̇\ out	\i\ tip	\ȯ\ saw	\u̇\ foot
\ər\ further	\ch\ chin	\ī\ life	\ȯi\ coin	\y\ yet
\a\ mat	\e\ pet	\j\ job	\th\ thin	\yü\ few
\ā\ take	\ē\ easy	\ŋ\ sing	\th\ this	\yu̇\ cure
\ä\ cot, cart	\g\ go	\ō\ bone	\ü\ food	\zh\ vision

using physical skill and energy ⟨*manual* labor⟩ [Middle English *manuel* "relating to the hands, manual," from early French *manuel* (same meaning), from Latin *manualis* (same meaning), from *manus* "hand" — related to MANAGE, MANEUVER, MANUFACTURE; see *Word History* at MANEUVER] — **man·u·al·ly** \-ē\ *adv*

²manual *n* **1** : a small book; *esp* : HANDBOOK **2** : the set movements in the handling of a weapon during a military drill ⟨the *manual* of arms⟩

manual training *n* : training to develop skill in using the hands (as in woodworking)

man·u·fac·to·ry \ˌman-(y)ə-ˈfak-t(ə-)rē\ *n, pl* **-ries** : FACTORY

¹man·u·fac·ture \ˌman-(y)ə-ˈfak-chər\ *n* **1** : something made from raw materials **2** : the making of products by hand or machinery **3** : PRODUCTION 2 ⟨the *manufacture* of blood in the body⟩ [from early French *manufacture* "something made," from Latin *manufactus* "made by hand," from earlier *manu* "by hand" (from *manus* "hand") and *factus*, past participle of *facere* "to make, do" — related to FACTORY, FASHION, MANAGE, MANUAL]

²manufacture *vb* **-tured; -tur·ing** \-ˈfak-chə-riŋ, -ˈfak-shriŋ\ **1** : to make into a product suitable for use ⟨*manufacture* wool⟩ **2** : to make from raw materials by hand or by machinery **3** : to make up sometimes with the intention of misleading **synonyms** see MAKE — **man·u·fac·tur·ing** *n*

man·u·fac·tur·er \ˌman-(y)ə-ˈfak-chər-ər\ *n* : one that manufactures; *esp* : an employer of workers in manufacturing

man·u·mis·sion \ˌman-yə-ˈmish-ən\ *n* : a setting free from slavery : EMANCIPATION

man·u·mit \ˌman-yə-ˈmit\ *vb* **-mit·ted; -mit·ting** : to set free; *esp* : to release from slavery

¹ma·nure \mə-ˈn(y)u̇(ə)r\ *vb* **ma·nured; ma·nur·ing** : to enrich by applying manure ⟨*manure* a field⟩

²manure *n* : material that fertilizes land; *esp* : bodily waste from birds and animals in stables and barnyards with or without litter

¹manu·script \ˈman-yə-ˌskript\ *adj* : written by hand or typed ⟨*manuscript* letters⟩

²manuscript *n* **1** : a written or typewritten composition or document **2** : writing as opposed to print

Manx cat \ˈmaŋ(k)s-\ *n* : any of a breed of tailless domestic cats with short or long hair

¹many \ˈmen-ē\ *adj* **more** \ˈmō(ə)r, ˈmȯ(ə)r\; **most** \ˈmōst\ **1** : amounting to a large number ⟨worked for *many* years⟩ **2** : being one of a large but indefinite number ⟨told *many* a tale⟩ — **as many** : the same in number ⟨saw three plays in *as many* days⟩

²many *pron* : a large number ⟨*many* of the students were late⟩

³many *n* : a large but indefinite number ⟨a good *many* of them⟩

man·za·ni·ta \ˌman-zə-ˈnēt-ə\ *n* : any of various evergreen shrubs of western North America that belong to the heath family

Mao·ri \ˈmau̇(ə)r-ē\ *n, pl* **Maori** *or* **Maoris** **1** : a member of a Polynesian people native to New Zealand **2** : the language of the Maori

¹map \ˈmap\ *n* **1** : a drawing or picture showing selected features of an area (as the surface of the earth or the moon or a section of the brain) and usually drawn to a given scale **2** : a drawing or picture of the sky showing the position of stars and planets [from Latin *mappa* "map," from earlier *mappa* "napkin, towel" — related to APRON, NAPKIN]

²map *vb* **mapped; map·ping** **1** : to make a map of ⟨*map* the heavens⟩ **2** : to chart the course of : plan in detail — often used with *out* ⟨*map* out a campaign⟩ — **map·per** *n*

ma·ple \ˈmā-pəl\ *n* : any of a group of trees having deeply notched opposite leaves, dry fruits with two wings, and hard light-colored wood and including some from which maple syrup and maple sugar are obtained; *also* : the wood of a maple

maple sugar *n* : a sugar made by boiling maple syrup

maple syrup *n* : syrup made by thickening the sap of maples and especially the sugar maple by boiling

map·mak·er \ˈmap-ˌmā-kər\ *n* : CARTOGRAPHER

maple

mar \ˈmär\ *vb* **marred; mar·ring** : to make a blemish on : SPOIL

ma·ra·ca \mə-ˈräk-ə, -ˈrak-\ *n* : a dried gourd or a rattle like a gourd that contains dried seeds or pebbles and is used as a musical rhythm instrument usually played in pairs by shaking

mar·a·schi·no \ˌmar-ə-ˈskē-nō, -ˈshē-\ *n, pl* **-nos** *often cap* **1** : a sweet alcoholic drink made from the juice of a bitter wild cherry **2** : a cherry preserved in true or imitation maraschino

mar·a·thon \ˈmar-ə-ˌthän\ *n* **1 a** : a long-distance footrace of 26 miles 385 yards (42.2 kilometers) that is run on an open course **b** : a race other than a footrace (as for swimmers) marked especially by great distance **2** : a long hard contest ⟨a dance *marathon*⟩ — **marathon** *adj*

Word History *Marathon* is the name of a plain in Greece located about 26 miles (42 kilometers) from the city of Athens. It was the scene of a great victory by the Greeks over the Persians in 490 B.C. According to legend a Greek soldier named Pheidippides ran all the way from the battlefield to Athens to deliver the news. He reached the city, gasped out his message, and fell dead. When the modern Olympic Games began in 1896, one of the events was a footrace of 26 miles 385 yards (42.2 kilometers), called a *marathon*, in honor of the legendary run by Pheidippides. [named for *Marathon*, site of a battlefield in ancient Greece]

mar·a·thon·er \ˈmar-ə-ˌthän-ər\ *n* : one (as a runner) who takes part in a marathon

ma·raud \mə-ˈrȯd\ *vb* : to roam about and raid in search of things to steal — **ma·raud·er** *n*

¹mar·ble \ˈmär-bəl\ *n* **1 a** : a limestone that takes a high polish and is used in architecture and sculpture **b** : something made from marble; *esp* : a piece of sculpture **2 a** : a little ball (as of glass) used in various games **b** *pl* : a children's game played with these little balls — **marble** *adj*

²marble *vb* **mar·bled; mar·bling** \ˈmär-b(ə-)liŋ\ : to give a streaked, spotted, or blotched appearance to (as by staining) ⟨*marble* the edges of a book⟩

mar·bled \ˈmär-bəld\ *adj* **1** : made from or decorated with marble **2** : having markings or color similar to marble **3** : having lines of fat throughout ⟨*marbled* meat⟩

mar·bling *n* : a mixture of fat and lean in a cut of meat

¹march \ˈmärch\ *n* **1** : a border region : FRONTIER **2** : a district originally set up to defend a boundary — usually used in plural ⟨the Welsh *marches*⟩

²march *vb* **1** : to move along with a steady regular stride especially in step with others **2** : to move in a direct purposeful manner : PROGRESS — **march·er** *n*

³march *n* **1 a** : the action of marching **b** : the distance covered within a period of time by marching **c** : a regular even step used in marching **2** : forward movement

: PROGRESS ⟨the *march* of time⟩ **3** : a musical piece with a strong regular rhythm that is suitable to march to

March \'märch\ *n* : the third month of the year

Word History One of the gods worshipped by the ancient Romans was a war god named Mars. In his honor they named one of the months of the year *martius,* which means "of Mars" or "belonging to Mars." The Latin *martius* later became *march* in early French, and it was from early French that the word came into English. [Middle English *March* "the third month," from early French *march* (same meaning), derived from Latin *martius* "of (the god) Mars"]

mar·chio·ness \'mär-sh(ə-)nəs\ *n* **1** : the wife or widow of a marquess **2** : a woman holding the rank of marquess

Mar·di Gras \'märd-ē-ˌgrä\ *n* : the Tuesday before Ash Wednesday often observed with parades and merrymaking

Word History The Christian period of fasting known as Lent begins every year on Ash Wednesday. The day before Lent begins is a time of celebration and feasting in many places. One of the original reasons for such feasting was probably to use up the last supplies of foods, such as meat and fat, which were not eaten during Lent. The eating of such foods may be why the day became known in France as *Mardi Gras,* which means "fat Tuesday." It is also possible that the name comes from a former custom of parading a fattened ox through Paris on this day. [French, literally "fat Tuesday"]

¹mare \'ma(ə)r, 'me(ə)r\ *n* : an adult female of the horse or a related animal (as a zebra or donkey) [Old English *mere* "a mature female horse"]

²ma·re \'mär-ā\ *n, pl* **ma·ria** \'mär-ē-ə\ : any of several large dark areas on the surface of the moon or Mars [scientific Latin, from Latin *mare* "sea"]

mar·ga·rine \'märj-(ə-)rən, 'märj-ə-ˌrēn\ *n* : a food product made from usually vegetable oils and skim milk and used as a spread and a cooking fat

¹mar·gin \'mär-jən\ *n* **1** : the part of a page outside the main body of printed or written matter **2** : boundary area **3** : an extra amount (as of time) allowed for use if needed **synonyms** see BORDER — **mar·gined** \-jənd\ *adj*

²margin *vb* **1** : to provide with a margin **2** : to form a margin to : BORDER

mar·gin·al \'märj-nəl, -ən-ᵊl\ *adj* **1** : written or printed in the margin ⟨*marginal* notes⟩ **2** : of, relating to, or situated at a margin or border **3** : close to the lower limit of quality ⟨*marginal* ability⟩ ⟨*marginal* land⟩ — **mar·gin·al·ly** \-nə-lē, -ən-ᵊl-ē\ *adv*

mar·gin·al·ize \'märj-nəl-ˌīz, -ən-ᵊl-\ *vb* **-ized; -iz·ing** : to remove to or keep in a position without influence in a society or group — **mar·gin·al·i·za·tion** \ˌmärj-nəl-ə-'zā-shən, -ən-ᵊl-\ *n*

mari·gold \'mar-ə-ˌgōld, 'mer-\ *n* : any of a genus of tropical American herbs related to the daisies and grown for their showy yellow or red and yellow flower heads

mar·i·jua·na *also* **mar·i·hua·na** \ˌmar-ə-'wän-ə *also* -'hwän-\ *n* : any of various preparations of the dried leaves and flowering tops of the female hemp plant that are used as a drug usually illegally especially by smoking

ma·rim·ba \mə-'rim-bə\ *n* : a musical instrument resembling a xylophone but with tubes under each bar to help increase the sound

ma·ri·na \mə-'rē-nə\ *n* : a dock or basin providing a place to anchor motorboats and yachts

¹mar·i·nade \ˌmar-ə-'nād\ *n* : a sauce in which meat or fish is soaked to enrich its flavor

²marinade *vb* **-nad·ed; -nad·ing** : MARINATE

mar·i·nate \'mar-ə-ˌnāt\ *vb* **-nat·ed; -nat·ing** : to soak in a marinade

¹ma·rine \mə-'rēn\ *adj* **1 a** : of or relating to the sea ⟨*marine* life⟩ **b** : of or relating to the navigation of the sea

: NAUTICAL, MARITIME ⟨a *marine* chart⟩ ⟨*marine* insurance⟩ **2** : of or relating to marines ⟨*marine* barracks⟩

²marine *n* **1** : the commercial and naval shipping of a country **2** : one of a class of soldiers serving aboard ship or in association with a naval force; *esp* : a member of the U.S. Marine Corps

mar·i·ner \'mar-ə-nər\ *n* : one who navigates or assists in navigating a ship : SAILOR

mar·i·o·nette \ˌmar-ē-ə-'net, ˌmer-\ *n* : a puppet moved by attached strings or wires

mar·i·tal \'mar-ət-ᵊl\ *adj* : of or relating to marriage : CONJUGAL — **mar·i·tal·ly** \-ət-ᵊl-ē\ *adv*

mar·i·time \'mar-ə-ˌtīm\ *adj* **1** : of, relating to, or bordering on the sea ⟨*maritime* nations⟩ **2** : of or relating to navigation or commerce on the sea ⟨*maritime* law⟩

mar·jo·ram \'märj-(ə-)rəm\ *n* : any of various usually fragrant mints often used as seasoning

marionette

¹mark \'märk\ *n* **1 a** : a noticeable object serving as a guide for travelers **b** : something (as a line, notch, or fixed object) designed to record position ⟨high-water *mark*⟩ **c** : something aimed at : TARGET **d** : the starting line or position in a track event **e** : an object of ridicule **f** : a standard of performance, quality, or condition ⟨not up to the *mark*⟩ **2 a** : something that gives evidence of something else : SIGN, INDICATION ⟨a *mark* of friendship⟩ **b** : an impression (as a scar, scratch, or stain) made on a surface **c** : a characteristic or distinguishing trait or quality **d** : a cross made in place of a signature **e** : a written or printed symbol **f** : a symbol (as a brand or label) used for identification (as of ownership or quality) **g** : a symbol (as a number or letter) representing a teacher's estimation of the quality of work or conduct : GRADE **3 a** : IMPORTANCE, DISTINCTION ⟨stands out as a person of *mark*⟩ **b** : a lasting or strong impression ⟨worked at several jobs but didn't make much of a *mark*⟩ [Old English *mearc* "boundary"] **synonyms** see ¹SIGN

²mark *vb* **1 a** : to fix or trace out the bounds of by or as if by a mark **b** : to set apart by a boundary ⟨*mark* off a tennis court⟩ **2 a** : to designate as if by a mark ⟨*marked* for greatness⟩ **b** : to make a mark or notation on **c** : to furnish with natural marks ⟨wings *marked* with white⟩ **d** : to label so as to indicate price or quality **3 a** : to make note of in writing : JOT ⟨*marking* the date in a journal⟩ **b** : to indicate by a mark or symbol ⟨*mark* an accent⟩ **c** : to determine the value of by means of marks : GRADE ⟨*mark* exam papers⟩ **4** : to be an important characteristic of : CHARACTERIZE, DISTINGUISH ⟨a disease *marked* by fever⟩ **5** : to take notice of : OBSERVE ⟨*mark* my words⟩ —

mark time 1 : to keep the time of a marching step by moving the feet one after another without advancing **2** : to function or operate without making progress

³mark *n* : DEUTSCHE MARK [Old English *marc* "a unit of weight"; probably of Scandinavian origin]

Mark \'märk\ *n* — see BIBLE TABLE

mark·down \'märk-ˌdau̇n\ *n* **1** : a lowering of price **2** : the amount by which an original selling price is reduced

mark down \(')märk-'dau̇n\ *vb* : to put a lower price on ⟨*marked down* all the books for the sale⟩

marked \'märkt\ *adj* **1** : having an identifying mark ⟨*marked* card⟩ **2** : NOTICEABLE, CONSPICUOUS ⟨speaks

\ə\ abut	\au̇\ out	\i\ tip	\o̅\ saw	\u̇\ foot
\ər\ further	\ch\ chin	\ī\ life	\oi\ coin	\y\ yet
\a\ mat	\e\ pet	\j\ job	\th\ thin	\yü\ few
\ā\ take	\ē\ easy	\ŋ\ sing	\th\ this	\yu̇\ cure
\ä\ cot, cart	\g\ go	\ō\ bone	\ü\ food	\zh\ vision

with a *marked* accent⟩ **3 a** : being a person on whom attention is focused **b** : being an object of attack or suspicion ⟨a *marked* man⟩ — **mark·ed·ly** \'mär-kəd-lē\ *adv*

mark·er \'mär-kər\ *n* **1** : one that marks **2** : something used for marking

¹**mar·ket** \'mär-kət\ *n* **1 a** : a meeting together of people to buy and sell **b** : the people at such a meeting **c** : a public place where a market is held; *esp* : a place where provisions are sold at wholesale **2** : a store where foods are sold to the public ⟨a meat *market*⟩ **3 a** : a geographic region in which things may be sold ⟨*markets* for American cotton⟩ **b** : a particular category of people who might buy ⟨the youth *market*⟩ **4** : an opportunity for selling ⟨a good *market* for used cars⟩ [Middle English *market* "market," derived from Latin *mercatus* "trade, marketplace," derived from *mercari* "to trade," from *merc-, merx* "merchandise" — related to COMMERCE, MERCHANT] — **in the market** : in the position of being a potential buyer ⟨*in the market* for a new house⟩ — **on the market** : available to buy : up for sale ⟨put their house *on the market*⟩

²**market** *vb* **1** : to deal in a market **2** : to offer for sale in a market : SELL — **mar·ket·ing** \-iŋ\ *n*

mar·ket·able \'mär-kət-ə-bəl\ *adj* **1** : fit to be offered for sale ⟨food that has gone bad is not *marketable*⟩ **2** : wanted by purchasers or employers ⟨*marketable* skills⟩ — **mar·ket·abil·i·ty** \ˌmär-kət-ə-'bil-ət-ē\ *n*

mar·ket·place \'mär-kət-ˌplās\ *n* **1** : an open square or place in a town where markets are held **2** : the world of trade

market value *n* : a price at which both buyers and sellers are willing to do business

mark·ing \'mär-kiŋ\ *n* **1** : the act, process, or an instance of making or giving a mark ⟨the teacher's *marking* was considered to be fair⟩ **2** : a mark made **3** : an arrangement or pattern of marks (as on the coat of an animal)

mark·ka \'mär-ˌkä\ *n* **1** : the former basic unit of money of Finland **2** : a coin representing one markka

marks·man \'märk-smən\ *n* : a person skilled in shooting at a mark or target — **marks·man·ship** \-ˌship\ *n*

mark·up \'mär-ˌkəp\ *n* : an amount added to the cost price of an article to set the selling price

mark up \(')mär-'kəp\ *vb* : to put a higher price on

markup language *n* : a system (as HTML) for marking or tagging a document that indicates its logical structure (as paragraphs) and gives instructions for its layout on the page especially for electronic transmission and display

marl \'märl\ *n* : a crumbling earthy deposit (as of sand or clay) that contains a lot of calcium carbonate

mar·lin \'mär-lən\ *n* : any of several large saltwater sport fishes related to sailfishes

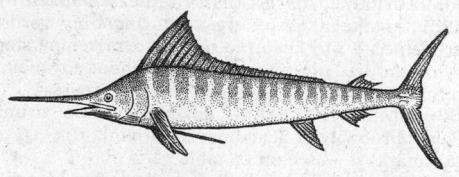

marlin

mar·ma·lade \'mär-mə-ˌlād\ *n* : a clear jelly containing pieces of fruit and fruit rind ⟨orange *marmalade*⟩

Word History Many of us have eaten orange marmalade, but marmalade can be made from any of several fruits. The Portuguese made such a jelly from the quince, a fruit that looks a bit like a yellow apple. The Portuguese word for the quince is *marmelo*, which is based on the Latin word *melimelum*, meaning "a sweet apple." The Portuguese called the jelly they made from the quince

marmelada. English borrowed this word as *marmalade*. [from Portuguese *marmelada* "jelly made from quince," from *marmelo* "quince," from Latin *melimelum* "sweet apple," from Greek *melimēlon* (same meaning), from *meli* "honey" and *mēlon* "apple"]

mar·mo·set \'mär-mə-ˌset, -mə-ˌzet\ *n* : any of numerous South and Central American monkeys that have soft fur, a bushy tail, and claws instead of nails except on the big toe

mar·mot \'mär-mət\ *n* : any of a genus of burrowing rodents with a stout body, short legs, coarse fur, a short bushy tail, and very small ears — compare WOODCHUCK

¹**ma·roon** \mə-'rün\ *vb* **1** : to put ashore and abandon on a lonely island or coast **2** : to leave isolated and helpless

²**maroon** *n* : a dark red

mar·quee \mär-'kē\ *n* **1** : a large tent set up for an outdoor party or exhibition **2** : a rooflike structure sticking out over an entrance ⟨a theater *marquee*⟩

marmot

mar·quess \'mär-kwəs\ *n* **1** : a nobleman of hereditary rank in Europe and Japan **2** : a British nobleman ranking below a duke and above an earl

mar·quis \'mär-kwəs, mär-'kē\ *n, pl* **mar·quis·es** \-kwə-səz, -'kēz\ : MARQUESS 2

mar·quise \mär-'kēz\ *n, pl* **mar·quises** \-'kēz(-əz)\ : MARCHIONESS

mar·qui·sette \ˌmär-k(w)ə-'zet\ *n* : a sheer meshed fabric used for clothing, curtains, and mosquito nets

marred *past and past participle of* MAR

mar·riage \'mar-ij\ *n* **1 a** : the state of being united as spouses in a consensual and contractual relationship recognized by law **b** : the mutual relation of married persons : WEDLOCK **c** : the institution whereby individuals are joined in a marriage **2** : an act of marrying; *esp* : a wedding ceremony **3** : a close union ⟨a *marriage* of music and verse⟩

mar·riage·able \-ə-bəl\ *adj* : fit for or capable of marriage ⟨of *marriageable* age⟩

¹**mar·ried** \'mar-ēd\ *adj* **1** : united in marriage ⟨a *married* couple⟩ **2** : of or relating to marriage

²**married** *n, pl* **marrieds** *or* **married** : a married person ⟨young *marrieds* starting their first home⟩

marring *present participle of* MAR

mar·row \'mar-ō\ *n* **1 a** : BONE MARROW **b** : the substance of the spinal cord **2** : the innermost, best, or essential part : CORE

¹**mar·ry** \'mar-ē\ *vb* **mar·ried; mar·ry·ing** **1** : to join in marriage according to law or custom ⟨they were *married* by a priest⟩ **2** : to give in marriage ⟨*married* their children off⟩ **3** : to take as husband or wife ⟨*married* a singer⟩ **4** : to enter into a marriage relationship : WED ⟨decided to *marry*⟩ **5** : to enter into a close union ⟨working long hours, she is *married* to her job⟩ [Middle English *marien* "to marry," from early French *marier* (same meaning), derived from Latin *maritus* "married"]

²**marry** *interj, archaic* — used to express amused or surprised agreement [Middle English *marie*, an interjection, from *Marie* "the Virgin Mary"]

Mars \'märz\ *n* : the planet fourth in order from the sun — see PLANET table

marsh \'märsh\ *n* : an area of soft wet land usually overgrown by grasses and sedges — **marshy** \'mär-shē\ *adj*

¹**mar·shal** \'mär-shəl\ *n* **1 a** : a high official in a royal household in the Middle Ages **b** : a person who arranges and directs ceremonies or parades **2** : an officer of the

highest rank in some military forces **3 a :** a federal official having duties similar to those of a sheriff **b :** the head of a division of a city government ⟨fire *marshal*⟩

Word History Although most French words come from Latin, some are the result of the Germanic occupation of France in the third century A.D. In early French the word *mareschal,* literally meaning "horse servant," was such a word. By the Middle English period, a mareschal in French was a high royal official. English borrowed the word to name a similar position in England. Much later, *marshal* was used in England as the title of a high-ranking military officer. It is because of this use that many people think the word is related to the word *martial,* meaning "relating to military affairs." But *martial* derives from the Latin name *Mars,* the god of war. It is only an accident that these two words came to be linked many centuries after they had entered English from different languages. [Middle English *marshal* "a high officer in the king's household," from early French *mareschal* (same meaning), literally "horse servant"; of Germanic origin]

²mar·shal *vb* **-shaled** *or* **-shalled; -shal·ing** *or* **-shal·ling** \\ˈmärsh-(ə-)liŋ\ **1 :** to arrange in order ⟨*marshal* troops⟩ **2 :** to lead with ceremony : USHER ⟨*marshaling* the group of children down the street⟩

marsh gas *n* : METHANE

marsh hawk *n* : NORTHERN HARRIER

marsh·land \\ˈmärsh-ˌland\ *n* : a marshy area : MARSH

marsh·mal·low \\ˈmärsh-ˌmel-ō, -ˌmal-\ *n* **1 :** a pink-flowered herb related to the mallows that has a root sometimes used in sweets and in medicine **2 :** a soft spongy sweet formerly made from the root of the marshmallow but now usually prepared from corn syrup, sugar, albumen, and gelatin

marsh marigold *n* : a swamp herb related to the buttercups and having bright yellow flowers and round shiny leaves — called also *cowslip*

¹mar·su·pi·al \\mär-ˈsü-pē-əl\ *adj* : of, relating to, or being a marsupial

²marsupial *n* : any of an order of mammals (as kangaroos and opossums) that have a pouch on the abdomen of the female containing the teats and serving to carry the young

mart \\ˈmärt\ *n* : a trading place : MARKET

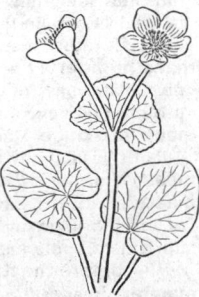
marsh marigold

mar·ten \\ˈmärt-ᵊn\ *n, pl* **marten** *or* **martens :** a slender flesh-eating mammal that is larger than the related weasels and has soft gray or brown fur; *also* : its fur

mar·tial \\ˈmär-shəl\ *adj* **1 :** of, relating to, or suited for war or a warrior ⟨*martial* music⟩ **2 :** of or relating to an army or to military life ⟨*martial* discipline⟩ [Middle English *martial* "relating to or suited for war," from Latin *martialis* "of Mars," from *Mars* "god of war"] — **mar·tial·ly** \\-shə-lē\ *adv*

martial art *n* : any of several arts of combat and self-defense (as karate and judo) that are widely practiced as a sport — **martial artist** *n*

martial law *n* : the law applied by military forces in occupied territory or in an emergency

Mar·tian \\ˈmär-shən\ *adj* : of or relating to the planet Mars or its supposed inhabitants — **Martian** *n*

mar·tin \\ˈmärt-ᵊn\ *n* : a small Eurasian swallow with a forked tail, bluish black head and back, a white underside, and a large white patch on the back at the base of the tail; *also* : any of various related birds

mar·ti·net \\ˌmärt-ᵊn-ˈet\ *n* : a person who demands strict obedience

mar·ti·ni \\mär-ˈtē-nē\ *n* : a cocktail consisting of gin and dry vermouth

Mar·tin·mas \\ˈmärt-ᵊn-məs, -ˌmas\ *n* : November 11 celebrated as the feast day of St. Martin

¹mar·tyr \\ˈmärt-ər\ *n* **1 :** a person who suffers death rather than give up his or her religion **2 :** one who sacrifices life or something of great value for a principle or cause **3 :** a person who suffers greatly

²martyr *vb* **1 :** to put to death for refusing to give up a belief **2 :** ²TORTURE

mar·tyr·dom \\ˈmärt-ərd-əm\ *n* **1 :** the sufferings and death of a martyr **2 :** ¹TORMENT 1

¹mar·vel \\ˈmär-vəl\ *n* : one that causes wonder or astonishment

²marvel *vb* **mar·veled** *or* **mar·velled; mar·vel·ing** *or* **mar·vel·ling** \\ˈmärv-(ə-)liŋ\ : to become filled with surprise or astonishment ⟨*marveled* at the magician's skill⟩

mar·vel·ous *or* **mar·vel·lous** \\ˈmärv-(ə-)ləs\ *adj* **1 :** causing wonder or astonishment **2 :** having the characteristics of a miracle **3 :** of the highest kind or quality : SPLENDID ⟨we had a *marvelous* time⟩ — **mar·vel·ous·ly** *adv* — **mar·vel·ous·ness** *n*

mar·zi·pan \\ˈmärt-sə-ˌpän, ˈmär-zə-ˌpan\ *n* : a candy or icing of almond paste, sugar, and whites of eggs

ma·sa \\ˈmä-sə\ *n* : a dough used in Mexican cuisine (as for tortillas and tamales) that is made from ground corn soaked in a lime and water solution; *also* : MASA HARINA

masa ha·ri·na \\-ä-ˈrē-nä\ *n* : a flour made from dried masa

mas·cara \\ma-ˈskar-ə\ *n* : a cosmetic especially for darkening the eyelashes

mas·cot \\ˈmas-ˌkät *also* -kət\ *n* : a person, animal, or object supposed to bring good luck

Word History The word *mascot* is an example of words that come to have a more pleasant meaning as they develop through the years and through many languages. The ancestor of *mascot* is the Latin word *masca,* used in the Middle Ages to mean "witch." *Masca* passed into the Romance speech of southern France as *masco.* Later it developed a derivative *mascoto,* literally meaning "little witch" but actually used to mean "charm" or "magic spell." A magic spell can be used for good as well as bad. Already, then, we have the beginnings of a change to a nicer idea in the basic use of the word. The word *mascoto* came to be *mascotte* in modern French, meaning a "good luck charm." It was made popular by the operetta *La Mascotte* in 1880. In this operetta "la mascotte" is the lovely young woman Bettina, whose influence brings victories to the army of the prince of Pisa. English later borrowed the word as *mascot,* with the meaning "a person or thing thought to bring good luck." Today the word is often used to refer to an animal chosen by a school or college as a good luck symbol for its sports teams. [from French *mascotte* "mascot," from a Romance word *mascoto* "charm," literally "little witch," from *masco* "witch," from Latin *masca* "witch"]

¹mas·cu·line \\ˈmas-kyə-lən\ *adj* **1 :** of the male sex **2 :** characteristic of or belonging to mèn : MANLY ⟨a *masculine* voice⟩ **3 :** of, relating to, or making up the class of words that ordinarily includes most of those referring to males ⟨a *masculine* noun⟩ ⟨*masculine* gender⟩ — **mas·cu·lin·i·ty** \\ˌmas-kyə-ˈlin-ət-ē\ *n*

\ə\ **abut**	\au̇\ **out**	\i\ **tip**	\ȯ\ **saw**	\u̇\ **foot**
\ər\ **further**	\ch\ **chin**	\ī\ **life**	\ȯi\ **coin**	\y\ **yet**
\a\ **mat**	\e\ **pet**	\j\ **job**	\th\ **thin**	\yü\ **few**
\ā\ **take**	\ē\ **easy**	\ŋ\ **sing**	\th\ **this**	\yu̇\ **cure**
\ä\ **cot, cart**	\g\ **go**	\ō\ **bone**	\ü\ **food**	\zh\ **vision**

²masculine *n* **1** : a word or form of the masculine gender **2** : the masculine gender

ma·ser \'mā-zər\ *n* : a device that uses the natural vibrations of atoms or molecules for generating electromagnetic radiation at a single microwave frequency

¹mash \'mash\ *n* **1** : crushed malt or grain meal soaked and stirred in hot water **2** : a mixture of ground feeds for livestock **3** : a soft pulpy mass

²mash *vb* **1** : to make into a soft pulpy mass by beating or pressure **2** : to expose crushed malt to the action of water with heating and stirring — **mash·er** *n*

mash–up \'mash-,əp\ *n* : something created by combining elements from two or more sources: as **a** : a piece of music created by digitally overlaying an instrumental track with a vocal track from a different recording **b** : a movie or video having characters or situations from other sources **c** : a Web service or application that integrates data and functions from various online sources

¹mask \'mask\ *n* **1 a** : a cover or partial cover for the face used for disguise ⟨a Halloween *mask*⟩ **b** : MASKER **c** : a sculptured face made by a mold in plaster or wax **2** : something

¹mask 1a

that disguises or conceals : CLOAK **3 a** : a covering used to protect the face ⟨a baseball catcher's *mask*⟩ **b** : GAS MASK **c** : a device covering the nose and mouth to make it easier to inhale something ⟨an oxygen *mask*⟩ **d** : a covering (as of gauze) over the nose and mouth to prevent infectious droplets from being exhaled into the air **4** : the head or face of a mammal (as a fox or dog) **5** : MASQUE 2

²mask *vb* **1** : to put on or wear a mask **2 a** : CONCEAL, DISGUISE ⟨*masked* their real purpose⟩ **b** : to make impossible to perceive or distinguish ⟨*masks* undesirable flavors⟩ **3** : to cover for protection

masked \'maskt\ *adj* : marked by the use of masks ⟨a *masked* ball⟩

mask·er \'mas-kər\ *n* : a person who wears a mask; *esp* : one taking part in a masquerade

masking tape *n* : a tape that is sticky on one side and that has many uses (as to cover an area when painting near it)

ma·son \'mās-ᵊn\ *n* : a skilled worker who builds or works with stone, brick, or cement

ma·son·ry \'mās-ᵊn-rē\ *n, pl* **-ries** **1** : something built of stone, brick, or concrete **2** : the art, trade, or occupation of a mason **3** : the work done by a mason

masque \'mask\ *n* **1** : ¹MASQUERADE 1 **2** : an old type of play performed by masked actors

masqu·er \'mas-kər\ *n* : MASKER

¹mas·quer·ade \,mas-kə-'rād\ *n* **1** : a party (as a dance) at which people wear masks and often fantastic costumes **2** : an action or appearance that is only a disguise or outward show : POSE

²masquerade *vb* **-ad·ed; -ad·ing** **1** : to take part in a masquerade **2** : to assume the appearance of something one is not : POSE — **mas·quer·ad·er** *n*

¹mass \'mas\ *n* **1** *cap* : a series of prayers and ceremonies forming the eucharistic service especially of the Roman Catholic Church **2** *often cap* : a celebration of the Eucharist **3** : a musical setting for parts of the Mass [Old English *mæsse* "religious service," from Latin *missa*, literally "dismissal at the end of a religious service," derived from earlier *missus*, past participle of *mittere* "to send"]

²mass *n* **1 a** : a quantity of matter or the form of matter that holds or clings together in one body ⟨a *mass* of metal⟩ **b** : large size : BULK **c** : the principal part : main body **2** : the quantity of matter in a body ⟨weight is the

force on a *mass* due to gravity⟩ **3** : a large amount or number **4** *pl* : the common people [Middle English *masse* "a large body or quantity of material," from early French *masse* (same meaning), from Latin *massa* (same meaning), from Greek *maza* "mass"]

³mass *vb* : to form or collect into a mass

⁴mass *adj* **1** : of, relating to, or designed for the mass of the people ⟨*mass* market⟩ **2** : participated in by or affecting a large number of individuals ⟨*mass* demonstrations⟩

¹mas·sa·cre \'mas-i-kər\ *vb* **-cred; -cring** \-k(ə-)riŋ\ : to kill in a massacre : SLAUGHTER — **mas·sa·crer** \-i-kər-ər, -i-krər\ *n*

²massacre *n* : the violent and cruel killing of a number of persons

¹mas·sage \mə-'säzh, -'säj\ *n* : treatment (as of the body) by rubbing, stroking, kneading, or tapping

²massage *vb* **mas·saged; mas·sag·ing** : to give massage to

mas·sa·sau·ga \,mas-ə-'sȯ-gə\ *n* : a small North American rattlesnake

mas·seur \ma-'sər, mə-\ *n* : a man who practices massage

mas·seuse \ma-'sə(r)z, mə-, -'süz\ *n* : a woman who practices massage

mas·sive \'mas-iv\ *adj* **1** : WEIGHTY 1, HEAVY ⟨*massive* walls⟩ **2 a** : large, solid, or heavy in structure ⟨a *massive* jaw⟩ **b** : large in extent or degree ⟨a *massive* effort⟩ **3** : having mass — **mas·sive·ly** *adv* — **mas·sive·ness** *n*

mass medium *n, pl* **mass media** : a medium of communication (as newspapers, radio, or television) that is designed to reach many people — usually used in plural

mass noun *n* : a noun (as *sand, butter,* or *accuracy*) that indicates something that cannot be counted, that is used in English only in the singular, and that usually has *some* before it rather than *a* or *an*

mass number *n* : a whole number that expresses the approximate mass of an atom in terms of the number of protons and neutrons in the atom

mass–pro·duce \,mas-prə-'d(y)üs\ *vb* : to produce in quantity usually by machinery — **mass production** *n*

massy \'mas-ē\ *adj* **mass·i·er; -est** : MASSIVE 2a

mast \'mast\ *n* **1** : a long pole that rises from the bottom of a ship or boat and supports the sails and rigging **2** : an upright tall pole (as on a crane) — **mast·ed** \'mas-təd\ *adj* — **before the mast** : as a common sailor

¹mas·ter \'mas-tər\ *n* **1 a** : a male teacher **b** : a person holding an academic degree between a bachelor's and a doctor's **2 a** : an independent skilled worker; *esp* : one qualified to teach apprentices **b** : an artist or performer of great skill **3 a** : one having authority : RULER **b** : one that conquers or masters **c** : the captain of a merchant ship **d** : an owner especially of a slave or animal **e** : the employer especially of a servant **4** — used as a title for a boy too young to be called mister **5** : a master machine or device [Middle English *master* "master," from Old English *magister* and early French *meistre*, both meaning "master" and both from Latin *magister* "master, teacher, one who holds political or military office" — related to MAESTRO, MAGISTRATE, MISTRESS] — **mas·ter·ship** \-,ship\ *n*

²master *adj* **1** : being a master ⟨a *master* carpenter⟩ **2** : being the main or guiding one ⟨a *master* plan⟩ **3** : controlling the operation of other devices ⟨a *master* clock⟩

³master *vb* **mas·tered; mas·ter·ing** \-t(ə-)riŋ\ **1** : OVERCOME 1, SUBDUE ⟨*master* an enemy⟩ ⟨*master* a desire⟩ **2** : to become skilled at ⟨*master* arithmetic⟩

master chief petty officer *n* : an enlisted man in the navy or coast guard ranking above a senior chief petty officer

master chief petty officer of the coast guard *n* : a master chief petty officer in the coast guard who advises the commandant

master chief petty officer of the navy *n* : a master chief petty officer in the navy who advises the chief of naval operations

mas·ter·ful \'mas-tər-fəl\ *adj* **1** : inclined to take control or dominate **2** : having or showing the technical or artistic skill of a master — **mas·ter·ful·ly** \-fə-lē\ *adv* — **mas·ter·ful·ness** *n*

master gunnery sergeant *n* : a noncommissioned officer of the highest rank in the marines

mas·ter·ly \'mas-tər-lē\ *adj* : suitable to or resembling a master especially in superior knowledge or skill — **masterly** *adv*

mas·ter·mind \'mas-tər-ˌmīnd, ˌmas-tər-'mīnd\ *n* : a person who invents or directs a project — **mastermind** *vb*

master of ceremonies : a person who acts as host at a formal event or on an entertainment program (as on television)

mas·ter·piece \'mas-tər-ˌpēs\ *n* : a work done with great skill; *esp* : a supreme intellectual or artistic achievement

master sergeant *n* : a military noncommissioned officer with the rank just below that of sergeant major in the army, below that of master gunnery sergeant in the marines, and below that of senior master sergeant in the air force

mas·tery \'mas-t(ə-)rē\ *n, pl* **-ter·ies** **1** : the position or authority of a master **2** : VICTORY **3** : skill or knowledge that makes one master of something : COMMAND ⟨a *mastery* of French⟩

mast·head \'mast-ˌhed\ *n* **1** : the top of a mast **2** : the name of a newspaper displayed on the top of the first page

mas·tic \'mas-tik\ *n* : a yellow or greenish substance that oozes from cuts in the bark of a southern European tree and is used in varnish

mas·ti·cate \'mas-tə-ˌkāt\ *vb* **-cat·ed; -cat·ing** : to grind or crush with the teeth before swallowing : CHEW — **mas·ti·ca·tion** \ˌmas-tə-'kā-shən\ *n*

mas·tiff \'mas-təf\ *n* : any of a breed of large powerful smooth-coated dogs often used as watchdogs and guard dogs

mast·odon \'mas-tə-ˌdän, -dən\ *n* : any of various huge extinct mammals related to the mammoths and existing elephants

mastiff

¹mas·toid \'mas-ˌtȯid\ *adj* : of, relating to, or being the mastoid process; *also* : occurring in the region of the mastoid process

²mastoid *n* : a mastoid bone or process

mastoid process *n* : a somewhat cone-shaped part of a bone of the skull that points downward behind the ear

mas·tur·ba·tion \ˌmas-tər-'bā-shən\ *n* : sexual stimulation of especially one's own genital organs by bodily contact apart from sexual intercourse and usually by use of the hand — **mas·tur·bate** \'mas-tər-ˌbāt\ *vb*

¹mat \'mat\ *n* **1 a** : a piece of coarse fabric of rush, straw, or wool **b** : a piece of material in front of a door to wipe dirty shoe soles on **c** : a decorative piece of material used under a dish or vase **d** : a pad or cushion for gymnastics or wrestling **2** : something made up of many tangled strands ⟨a thick *mat* of vegetation⟩ [Old English *meatte*

"mat," from Latin *matta* (same meaning); of Semitic origin]

²mat *vb* **mat·ted; mat·ting** **1** : to provide with a mat or matting **2** : to become or cause to become a tangled mass

³mat \'mat\ *vb* **mat·ted; mat·ting** **1** *also* **matte** *or* **matt** : to give a dull effect to **2** : to border (a picture) with a mat

⁴mat *variant of* ²MATTE

⁵mat *n* **1** : a border of stiff paper (as cardboard) going around a picture between picture and frame or serving as the frame **2** : a dull finish

mat·a·dor \'mat-ə-ˌdȯr\ *n* : the bullfighter who plays the major human part in a bullfight [Spanish, literally "killer"]

¹match \'mach\ *n* **1 a** : a person or thing that is equal or similar to or exactly like another **b** : one that can compete or fight successfully with another ⟨a *match* for the enemy⟩ **2** : two persons or things that go well together ⟨curtains and carpet are a good *match*⟩ **3** : a contest between two or more parties ⟨a tennis *match*⟩ **4 a** : MARRIAGE 1b **b** : a person to be considered as a marriage partner [Old English *gemæcca* "mate, equal"]

²match *vb* **1** : to meet successfully as a competitor **2 a** : to place in competition ⟨*matched* my strength with my friend's⟩ **b** : to provide with a worthy competitor **3** : to join or give in marriage **4 a** : to make or find the equal or the like of **b** : to make correspond **c** : to be the same as or suitable to one another ⟨do these colors *match*?⟩ **5** : to flip or toss coins and compare upper surfaces — **match·er** *n*

³match *n* **1** : an evenly burning wick or cord formerly used to ignite a charge of powder **2** : a short slender piece of material (as wood) tipped with a mixture that ignites when scratched against something else [Middle English *macche* "a wick," from early French *meiche* (same meaning)]

match·book \'mach-ˌbu̇k\ *n* : a small folder containing rows of paper matches

match·box \-ˌbäks\ *n* : a box for matches

match·less \'mach-ləs\ *adj* : having no equal : better than any other — **match·less·ly** *adv*

match·lock \'mach-ˌläk\ *n* : a firearm in which the charge is ignited by a slow match in a movable holder attached to the breech

match·mak·er \-ˌmā-kər\ *n* : one that arranges marriages — **match·mak·ing** \-kiŋ\ *n*

¹mate \'māt\ *n* **1 a** : ²ASSOCIATE 1, COMPANION **b** : an assistant worker : HELPER ⟨plumber's *mate*⟩ **2** : a deck officer on a merchant ship ranking below the captain **3 a** : either member of a married couple **b** : one of a breeding pair of animals ⟨a dove and its *mate*⟩ **c** : either of two matched objects ⟨the *mate* to a glove⟩

²mate *vb* **mat·ed; mat·ing** **1** : to join or fit together **2 a** : to bring or come together as mates; *esp* : ¹MARRY 1 **b** : to provide a mate for **3** : COPULATE — **mate with** : to take as a mate

ma·té *or* **ma·te** \'mä-ˌtā\ *n* : a fragrant beverage made from the leaves and shoots of a South American shrub or tree related to the hollies; *also* : this shrub or tree or its leaves and shoots

¹ma·te·ri·al \mə-'tir-ē-əl\ *adj* **1** : relating to or consisting of matter : PHYSICAL ⟨the *material* world⟩ ⟨*material* comforts⟩ **2 a** : IMPORTANT 1 ⟨food is *material* to health⟩ **b** : RELEVANT ⟨is that information *material* to the problem?⟩ **3** : physical rather than spiritual or intellectual

\ə\ abut	\au̇\ out	\i\ tip	\ȯ\ saw	\u̇\ foot
\ər\ further	\ch\ chin	\ī\ life	\ȯi\ coin	\y\ yet
\a\ mat	\e\ pet	\j\ job	\th\ thin	\yü\ few
\ā\ take	\ē\ easy	\ŋ\ sing	\<u>th</u>\ this	\yu̇\ cure
\ä\ cot, cart	\g\ go	\ō\ bone	\ü\ food	\zh\ vision

⟨*material* needs⟩ — **ma·te·ri·al·i·ty** \-ˌtir-ē-'al-ət-ē\ *n* — **ma·te·ri·al·ly** \-'tir-ē-ə-lē\ *adv*

²**material** *n* **1** : the elements or substance of which something is made or can be made ⟨building *materials*⟩ **2** : equipment and supplies for doing or making something ⟨writing *materials*⟩

ma·te·ri·al·ism \mə-'tir-ē-ə-ˌliz-əm\ *n* **1** : a theory that everything can be explained as being or coming from matter **2** : a tendency to attach too much importance to physical comfort and well-being — **ma·te·ri·al·ist** \-ē-ə-ləst\ *n or adj* — **ma·te·ri·al·is·tic** \-ˌtir-ē-ə-'lis-tik\ *adj*

ma·te·ri·al·ize \mə-'tir-ē-ə-ˌlīz\ *vb* **-ized; -iz·ing 1** : to give material form and substance to **2** : to assume or cause to assume bodily form ⟨a ghost *materialized* out of nowhere⟩ **3 a** : to come into existence ⟨a promise that never *materialized*⟩ **b** : to appear suddenly

ma·té·ri·el *or* **ma·te·ri·el** \mə-ˌtir-ē-'el\ *n* : equipment and supplies used by a group or organization [French]

ma·ter·nal \mə-'tərn-ᵊl\ *adj* **1** : of or relating to a mother : MOTHERLY **2 a** : related through a mother ⟨*maternal* grandparents⟩ **b** : obtained or received from a female parent ⟨*maternal* chromosomes⟩ [Middle English *maternal* "maternal, or of like a mother," from early French *maternel* (same meaning), from Latin *maternus* "maternal," from *mater* "mother" — related to ALMA MATER] — **ma·ter·nal·ly** \-ᵊl-ē\ *adv*

¹**ma·ter·ni·ty** \mə-'tər-nət-ē\ *n, pl* **-ties 1** : the state of being a mother : MOTHERHOOD **2** : motherly character or qualities : MOTHERLINESS

²**maternity** *adj* **1** : designed for wear during pregnancy ⟨*maternity* clothes⟩ **2** : effective for the time around childbirth ⟨*maternity* leave⟩

math \'math\ *n* : MATHEMATICS

math·e·mat·i·cal \ˌmath-ə-'mat-i-kəl, math-'mat-\ *adj* **1** : of, relating to, or according with mathematics **2** : very exact ⟨*mathematical* precision⟩ — **math·e·mat·i·cal·ly** \-i-k(ə-)lē\ *adv*

math·e·ma·ti·cian \ˌmath-(ə-)mə-'tish-ən\ *n* : a specialist or expert in mathematics

math·e·mat·ics \ˌmath-ə-'mat-iks, math-'mat-\ *n* : the science that is concerned with numbers and their properties, relations, and operations and with shapes in space and their structure and measurement

mat·i·nee *or* **mat·i·née** \ˌmat-ᵊn-'ā\ *n* : a theatrical performance held in the daytime and especially in the afternoon

mat·ins \'mat-ᵊnz\ *n pl, often cap* **1** : special prayers said between midnight and 4 a.m. **2** : a service of morning prayer

ma·tri·arch \'mā-trē-ˌärk\ *n* : a woman who rules a family, group, or state; *esp* : a mother who is head of her family and descendants — **ma·tri·ar·chal** \ˌmā-trē-'är-kəl\ *adj*

ma·tri·ar·chy \'mā-trē-ˌär-kē\ *n, pl* **-chies 1** : a family, group, or state headed by a matriarch **2** : a system of social organization in which descent and inheritance are traced through the female line

ma·tri·cide \'ma-trə-ˌsīd, 'mā-\ *n* **1** : murder of a mother by her child **2** : one that murders his or her mother — **ma·tri·cid·al** \ˌma-trə-'sīd-ᵊl, ˌmā-\ *adj*

ma·tric·u·late \mə-'trik-yə-ˌlāt\ *vb* **-lat·ed; -lat·ing** : to enroll especially in a college or university — **ma·tric·u·la·tion** \-ˌtrik-yə-'lā-shən\ *n*

mat·ri·mo·ny \'ma-trə-ˌmō-nē\ *n, pl* **-nies** : the union of two people as spouses : MARRIAGE — **mat·ri·mo·ni·al** \ˌma-trə-'mō-nē-əl, -nyəl\ *adj* — **mat·ri·mo·ni·al·ly** \-ē\ *adv*

ma·trix \'mā-triks\ *n, pl* **ma·tri·ces** \'mā-trə-ˌsēz, 'ma-\ *or* **ma·trix·es** \'mā-trik-səz\ : something (as a mold) that gives material, foundation, or origin to something else enclosed in it

ma·tron \'mā-trən\ *n* **1** : a usually mature and dignified married woman **2** : a woman in charge of the household

affairs of an institution **3** : a woman who supervises women prisoners in a police station or jail

ma·tron·ly \'mā-trən-lē\ *adj* : of, resembling, or suitable for a matron

matron of honor : a married woman serving as the principal wedding attendant of a bride — compare MAID OF HONOR

¹**matte** *or* **matt** *variant of* ³MAT 1

²**matte** *also* **mat** *or* **matt** \'mat\ *adj* : lacking luster or gloss

matted *past and past participle of* MAT

¹**mat·ter** \'mat-ər\ *n* **1 a** : a subject of interest or concern ⟨a *matter* of dispute⟩ **b** : something to be dealt with : AFFAIR ⟨personal *matters* to take care of⟩ **2 a** : the substance of which a physical object is composed; *esp* : the material substance that occupies space, has mass, and makes up the observable universe **b** : material substance of a particular kind or function ⟨vegetable *matter*⟩ **c** : PUS **3** : a more or less definite amount or quantity ⟨cooks in a *matter* of minutes⟩ **4** : something written or printed **5** : ¹MAIL 1 ⟨first-class *matter*⟩ — **as a matter of fact** : in fact : ACTUALLY — **for that matter** : so far as that is concerned — **no matter** : without regard to ⟨do it *no matter* how unpleasant it seems⟩ — **no matter what** : regardless of the costs, consequences, or results ⟨have to win the race, *no matter what*⟩ — **the matter** : ²WRONG 5 ⟨nothing's *the matter* with me⟩

²**matter** *vb* : to be of importance : SIGNIFY

matter of course : something that may be expected as a result of something else

mat·ter-of-fact \ˌmat-ə-rə(v)-'fakt\ *adj* : sticking to fact ⟨a *matter-of-fact* account⟩; *also* : being plain, straightforward, or unemotional ⟨described the accident in a *matter-of-fact* way⟩ — **mat·ter-of-fact·ly** \-'fak-(t)lē\ *adv*

Mat·thew \'math-yü\ *n* — see BIBLE table

mat·ting \'mat-iŋ\ *n* : material for mats; *also* : mats or a supply of mats

mat·tock \'mat-ək\ *n* : a tool for digging made of a long wooden handle and a steel head one end of which comes to a point or to a cutting edge

mat·tress \'ma-trəs\ *n* **1** : a fabric case filled with springy material used as a bed or on a bedstead **2** : a sack that can be filled with air or water and used as a mattress

mat·u·ra·tion \ˌmach-ə-ə-'rā-shən\ *n* **1** : the process of becoming mature **2** : the process involving meiosis by which body cells having two sets of chromosomes form gametes with one set of chromosomes

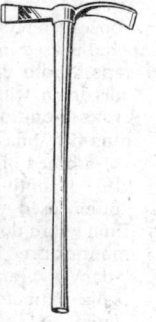

mattock

¹**ma·ture** \mə-'t(y)ů(ə)r\ *adj* **ma·tur·er; -est 1** : fully thought out ⟨a *mature* plan⟩ **2 a** : fully grown or developed : ADULT, RIPE ⟨*mature* fruit⟩ **b** : having reached a final or desired state ⟨*mature* wine⟩ **3** : of or relating to a condition of full development ⟨a *mature* outlook⟩ **4** : due for payment ⟨the note becomes *mature* in 90 days⟩ — **ma·ture·ly** *adv*

²**mature** *vb* **ma·tured; ma·tur·ing 1** : to bring to maturity or completion ⟨*matured* my plans⟩ **2** : to become fully developed or ripe

ma·tu·ri·ty \mə-'t(y)ùr-ət-ē\ *n* **1** : the quality or state of being mature; *esp* : full development **2** : the date when a note becomes due

mat·zo *or* **mat·zoh** \'mät-sə, -ˌsō\ *n, pl* **mat·zoth** \-ˌsōth, -ˌsōt, -sōs\ *or* **mat·zos** *or* **mat·zohs** \-səs, -səs, -ˌsōz\ : unleavened bread eaten at the Passover

maud·lin \'mȯd-lən\ *adj* **1** : drunk enough to be tearfully silly **2** : weakly and overly sentimental

Word History The word *maudlin* can be traced back to the name of a town in ancient Palestine, *Magdala*. But the meaning of *maudlin* is associated with a person in the Christian Bible. In the Gospels, Mary Magdalene was so called because she was thought to have come from Magdala. She was a devoted follower of Jesus and was present at his crucifixion. Yet her name was not always spelled as it is today. Our modern English translations of the Bible have gone back to the Latin text for the form *Magdalene*. But in early French, the *g* dropped out and the word became *Madelaine*. When the name was taken into Middle English from the early French texts, its form was *Maudeleyn* and later *Maudlin*. In the Middle Ages, religious artists painting scenes of the crucifixion and burial of Jesus showed Mary as weeping. In time her name became an adjective for a tearful show of emotion and later especially for an exaggerated display of emotion from a drunken person. [Middle English *Maudeleyn* "Mary Magdalene," from early French *Madeleine* (same meaning), from Latin *Magdalene* (same meaning), from Greek *Magdalēnē* "(Mary) of Magdala (town on the Sea of Galilee)"; so called because Mary was frequently shown in religious paintings as weeping]

¹**maul** \'mȯl\ *n* : a heavy hammer often with a wooden head used especially for driving wedges or posts

²**maul** *vb* **1** : to beat and bruise severely **2** : ¹MANGLE 1 **3** : to handle roughly — **maul·er** *n*

maun·der \'mȯn-dər, 'män-\ *vb* **maun·dered; maun·der·ing** \-d(ə-)riŋ\ **1** : to wander slowly and idly **2** : to speak in a disconnected or aimless way — **maun·der·er** \-dər-ər\ *n*

Maun·dy Thursday \,mȯn-dē-, ,män-\ *n* : the Thursday before Easter [Middle English *maunde* "ceremony of washing the feet of the poor on the Thursday before Easter," from early French *mandé* (same meaning), from Latin *mandatum* "command"; so called from Jesus' words "A new Commandment I give to you . . ." in John 13:34 (RSV) after he washed the feet of his disciples at the Last Supper]

mau·so·le·um \,mȯ-sə-'lē-əm, ,mȯ-zə-\ *n, pl* **-le·ums** *or* **-lea** \-'lē-ə\ : a large or fancy tomb [from Latin *mausoleum* "a large tomb," from Greek *Mausōleion* "the magnificent tomb of Mausolus (ruler of Caria, an ancient country in Asia Minor)," considered one of the seven wonders of the ancient world]

mauve \'mōv, 'mȯv\ *n* : a medium purple, violet, or lilac

mav·er·ick \'mav-(ə-)rik\ *n* **1** : an unbranded range animal; *esp* : a motherless calf **2** : an independent person who refuses to follow the usual standards or customs of the group

Word History A lawyer named Samuel A. Maverick lived in southern Texas in the middle of the 19th century. In 1847 he acquired a farm with about 450 cattle that were left in charge of a single slave with no experience as a cowboy. The cattle were never branded and were left to roam free. Eventually, the term *maverick* came to be used to name any unbranded cattle. Now *maverick* is most often used to speak of a person who acts in an individual way and refuses to be "branded" as a member of any particular group. [named for Samuel A. *Maverick* 1803–1870 American pioneer]

maw \'mȯ\ *n* **1** : a body part (as a stomach or a crop) that receives swallowed food **2** : the throat, gullet, or jaws especially of a flesh-eating animal

mawk·ish \'mȯ-kish\ *adj* **1** : having a weak often unpleasant taste **2** : MAUDLIN 2 — **mawk·ish·ly** *adv* — **mawk·ish·ness** *n*

max \'maks\ *n* **1** : MAXIMUM 1 **2** : MAXIMUM 2 — **max** *adj* — **to the max** : to the greatest extent possible

maxi \'mak-sē\ *n* : a long skirt, dress, or coat

max·il·la \mak-'sil-ə\ *n, pl* **max·il·lae** \-'sil-ē, -'sil-,ī\ *or* **maxillas** **1 a** : an upper jaw especially of a mammal in which the bony parts are closely united **b** : either of the two bones of the upper jaw in higher vertebrates including human beings that bear most of the teeth **2** : one of the first or second pair of mouth appendages behind the mandibles in various arthropods — **max·il·lary** \'mak-sə-,ler-ē\ *adj or n*

max·im \,mak-səm\ *n* **1** : a general truth or rule of conduct **2** : a proverbial saying

max·i·mal \'mak-s(ə-)məl\ *adj* **1** : being an upper limit : HIGHEST ⟨*maximal* growth⟩ **2** : most comprehensive : COMPLETE ⟨*maximal* recovery⟩

max·i·mize \'mak-sə-,mīz\ *vb* **-mized; -miz·ing** **1** : to increase to a maximum ⟨*maximize* profits⟩ **2** : to make the most of ⟨*maximize* your opportunities⟩ **3** : to increase the size of (a window) to fill an entire computer screen

max·i·mum \'mak-s(ə-)məm\ *n, pl* **max·i·ma** \-sə-mə\ *or* **maximums** **1** : the highest quantity, value, or development **2** : an upper limit allowed — **maximum** *adj*

may \(')mā\ *helping verb, past* **might** \(')mīt\; *present sing & pl* **may** **1 a** : have permission to ⟨you *may* go now⟩ **b** : be in some degree likely to ⟨you *may* be right⟩ **2** — used to express a wish or desire ⟨long *may* she reign⟩ ⟨*may* the best man win⟩ **3** — used to express purpose ⟨we exercise so that we *may* be strong⟩ or possibility of happening ⟨he'll do his duty come what *may*⟩

May \'mā\ *n* : the fifth month of the year

Word History Among the gods and goddesses worshipped by the ancient Romans was one known as Maia, a goddess of spring. In spring the Romans would make offerings to her on the first day of a month they called *Maius*, meaning "of Maia." The name of the Roman month was borrowed into early French as *mai* and later into English as *May*. For the early Romans Maius was the third month of the year; but after January and February were added, May became the fifth month. [from Middle English *May* (fifth month), from early French *mai* (same meaning), from Latin *Maius*, originally, "third month," from *Maia* "Roman goddess of spring"]

Ma·ya \'mī-ə\ *n, pl* **Maya** *or* **Mayas** : a member of a group of Indian peoples of the Yucatán Peninsula and neighboring areas — **Ma·yan** \'mī-ən\ *adj*

may·ap·ple \'mā-,ap-əl\ *n* : a North American large-leaved woodland herb related to the barberries that produces a single large waxy white flower followed by a yellow egg-shaped fruit; *also* : its edible fruit

may·be \'mā-bē, 'meb-ē\ *adv* : PERHAPS

May·day \mā-'dā, 'mā-,dā\ — an international radio signal word used as a distress call

May Day \'mā-,dā\ *n* : May 1 celebrated as a springtime festival and in some countries as Labor Day

may·flow·er \'mā-,flaů(-ə)r\ *n* : any of various spring-blooming plants; *esp* : TRAILING ARBUTUS

may·fly \-,flī\ *n* : any of a group of insects that as adults live only a short time and have fragile wings

may·hap \'mā-,hap, mā-'hap\ *adv* : PERHAPS

may·hem \'mā-,hem, 'mā-əm\ *n* **1** : deliberate permanent crippling or injury of any part of the body **2** : needless or willful damage or violence

mayfly

mayn't \'mā-ənt, (')mānt\ : may not

\ə\ abut	\aů\ out	\i\ tip	\ȯ\ saw	\ů\ foot	
\ər\ further	\ch\ chin	\ī\ life	\ȯi\ coin	\y\ yet	
\a\ mat	\e\ pet	\j\ job	\th\ thin	\yü\ few	
\ā\ take	\ē\ easy	\ŋ\ sing	\th\ this	\yů\ cure	
\ä\ cot, cart	\g\ go	\ō\ bone	\ü\ food	\zh\ vision	

may·on·naise \ˈmā-ə-ˌnāz, ˌmā-ə-ˈnāz\ n : a dressing consisting chiefly of egg yolk, vegetable oil, and vinegar or lemon juice

may·or \ˈmā-ər, ˈme(-)ər\ n : an official elected to act as head of a city or borough — **may·or·al** \ˈmā-ə-rəl, ˈme-ə-\ adj

may·or·al·ty \ˈmā-ə-rəl-tē, ˈmer-əl-\ n, pl **-ties** : the office or term of office of a mayor

may·pole \ˈmā-ˌpōl\ n, often cap : a tall pole decorated with ribbons and flowers that forms a center for May Day sports and dances

maze \ˈmāz\ n 1 : a confusing complicated network of passages 2 : something complicated or elaborate ⟨a confusing maze of regulations⟩

ma·zur·ka \mə-ˈzər-kə, -ˈzūr-\ n 1 : a fast Polish folk dance 2 : music for the mazurka

mazy \ˈmā-zē\ adj : resembling a maze in confusing turns and windings

McCoy n : something that is neither imitation nor substitute — often used in the phrase the real McCoy

Mc·In·tosh \ˈmak-ən-ˌtäsh\ n : a juicy bright red eating apple with a thin skin, white flesh, and slightly tart flavor

Mc·Man·sion \mək-ˈman-chən\ n : a very large house usually built in a suburban neighborhood or development; esp : one thought of as too big or showy

me \(ˈ)mē\ pron, objective case of I

¹**mead** \ˈmēd\ n : an alcoholic drink made of water, honey, malt, and yeast [Old English medu "the beverage mead"]

²**mead** n, archaic : MEADOW [Old English mæd "meadow"]

mead·ow \ˈmed-ō\ n : an area of moist low usually level grassland

mead·ow·lark \-ˌlärk\ n : any of several North American songbirds that are largely brown and buff above with a yellow breast having a black V-shaped mark across it

mea·ger or **mea·gre** \ˈmē-gər\ adj 1 : having little flesh : THIN 2 a : lacking desirable qualities (as richness or strength) ⟨led a meager life⟩ b : deficient in quality or quantity ⟨a meager serving of meat⟩ — **mea·ger·ly** adv — **mea·ger·ness** n

synonyms MEAGER, SCANTY, SPARSE mean falling short of what is normal, necessary, or desirable. MEAGER suggests a lack of fullness, richness, or plenty ⟨a meager diet⟩. SCANTY stresses that something is not enough in amount, degree, or range ⟨a scanty supply of fuel⟩. SPARSE suggests a scattering of a small number of units ⟨a big country with a sparse population⟩.

¹**meal** \ˈmēl\ n 1 : the food eaten or prepared for eating at one time 2 : the act or time of eating a meal [Old English mæl "appointed time, meal"]

²**meal** n 1 : ground seeds of a cereal grass; esp : CORNMEAL 2 : something like meal especially in texture [Old English melu "ground grain"]

meal·time \ˈmēl-ˌtīm\ n : the usual time at which a meal is served

meal·worm \-ˌwərm\ n : any of various small brownish larvae of various beetles that live in grain products and are often raised as food for insect-eating animals or as bait

mealy \ˈmē-lē\ adj **meal·i·er; -est** 1 : containing meal 2 : being soft, dry, and crumbly 3 : covered with fine grains or with flecks (as of color) 4 : MEALYMOUTHED

mealy·bug \ˈmē-lē-ˌbəg\ n : any of numerous scale insects that have a white cottony or waxy covering and are destructive pests especially of fruit trees

mealy·mouthed \ˌmē-lē-ˈmau̇t̲h̲d, -ˈmau̇tht\ adj : not plain and sincere in speech ⟨a mealymouthed speaker⟩

¹**mean** \ˈmēn\ adj 1 : lacking distinction or prominence : HUMBLE 2 : of poor, shabby, or inferior quality or status ⟨lives in mean surroundings⟩ 3 : worthy of little regard : INFERIOR — often used in negative constructions as a term of praise ⟨a person of no mean ability⟩ 4 : deliberately unkind 5 : STINGY 1, MISERLY 6 : SPITEFUL,

MALICIOUS ⟨a mean remark⟩ 7 : causing trouble or bother ⟨a mean horse⟩ 8 : EXCELLENT ⟨plays a mean trumpet⟩ [Middle English mene, imene "held in common, inferior," from Old English gemǣne "held in common"] — **mean·ly** adv — **mean·ness** \ˈmēn-nəs\ n

²**mean** \ˈmēn\ vb **meant** \ˈment\; **mean·ing** \ˈmē-niŋ\ 1 a : to have as a purpose : INTEND ⟨I mean to go⟩ b : to intend for a particular purpose or use ⟨a book meant for children⟩ 2 : to serve to communicate, show, or indicate : SIGNIFY ⟨what do these words mean⟩ ⟨those clouds mean rain⟩ 3 : to be important to a specified degree ⟨health means everything to us⟩ [Old English mǣnan "to have in mind, intend"] — **mean business** : to be serious about

³**mean** adj 1 : holding a middle position : INTERMEDIATE 2 a : lying about midway between extremes b : being the mean of a set of values : AVERAGE ⟨mean temperature⟩ [Middle English mene "being in a middle position," from early French meiene (same meaning), from Latin medianus "being in the middle" — related to ¹MEDIAN]

⁴**mean** n 1 : a middle point between extremes 2 a : a value that represents a range of values; esp : ARITHMETIC MEAN b : either of the middle two terms of a proportion 3 pl : something by which a desired result is achieved or furthered ⟨means of production⟩ ⟨use any means you can⟩ 4 pl : WEALTH 1 ⟨a person of means⟩ — **by all means** : without fail : CERTAINLY — **by means of** : through the use of — **by no means** : not at all : certainly not

¹**me·an·der** \mē-ˈan-dər\ n 1 : a turn or winding of a stream 2 : a winding path or course

²**meander** vb **-dered; -der·ing** \-d(ə-)riŋ\ 1 : to follow a winding or complicated course 2 : to wander without a goal or purpose **synonyms** see WANDER

¹**mean·ing** \ˈmē-niŋ\ n 1 a : the sense one intends to communicate especially by language ⟨do not mistake my meaning⟩ b : the sense that is communicated ⟨the poem's meaning is clear⟩ 2 : PURPOSE 1, INTENTION 3 : intent to communicate information : SIGNIFICANCE ⟨a glance full of meaning⟩

²**meaning** adj : conveying or intended to convey meaning : SIGNIFICANT ⟨a meaning look⟩

mean·ing·ful \ˈmē-niŋ-fəl\ adj 1 : having a meaning or purpose ⟨meaningful work⟩ 2 : full of meaning : SIGNIFICANT ⟨a meaningful experience⟩ — **mean·ing·ful·ly** \-fə-lē\ adv

mean·ing·less \ˈmē-niŋ-ləs\ adj 1 : having no meaning or significance ⟨meaningless chatter⟩ 2 : lacking motive ⟨a meaningless murder⟩ — **mean·ing·less·ly** adv — **mean·ing·less·ness** n

mean–spir·it·ed \ˈmēn-ˈspir-ət-əd, ˌmēn-\ adj : feeling or showing a cruel desire to cause pain or harm ⟨a mean-spirited person⟩ ⟨a mean-spirited remark⟩

¹**mean·time** \ˈmēn-ˌtīm\ n : the time between two events

²**meantime** adv : in the meantime

¹**mean·while** \ˈmēn-ˌhwīl, -ˌwīl\ n : ¹MEANTIME

²**meanwhile** adv : ²MEANTIME 2 : at the same time

mea·sles \ˈmē-zəlz\ n sing or pl : a contagious disease caused by a virus and marked by fever and red spots on the skin; also : any of several diseases (as German measles) that resemble measles

mea·sly \ˈmēz-(ə-)lē\ adj **mea·sli·er; -est** : so small or unimportant as to deserve scorn ⟨left a measly nickel tip⟩

mea·sur·able \ˈmezh-(ə-)rə-bəl, ˈmāzh-\ adj : capable of being measured — **mea·sur·ably** \-blē\ adv

¹**mea·sure** \ˈmezh-ər, ˈmāzh-\ n 1 a : an adequate, fixed, or suitable limit or amount ⟨surprised beyond measure⟩ b : ²AMOUNT, EXTENT, DEGREE ⟨gained a large measure of freedom⟩ 2 a : the

¹measure 2b

MEASURES AND WEIGHTS[1]

UNIT	ABBREVIATION OR SYMBOL	EQUIVALENTS IN OTHER UNITS OF SAME SYSTEM	METRIC EQUIVALENT
WEIGHT			
Avoirdupois[2]			
ton			
short ton		2000 pounds, 20 short hundredweight	0.907 metric ton
long ton		2240 pounds, 20 long hundredweight	1.016 metric tons
hundredweight	cwt		
short hundredweight		100 pounds, 0.05 short ton	45.359 kilograms
long hundredweight		112 pounds, 0.05 long ton	50.802 kilograms
pound	lb *or* lb avdp *also* #	16 ounces, 7000 grains	0.454 kilogram
ounce	oz *or* oz avdp	16 drams, 437.5 grains, 0.0625 pound	28.350 grams
dram	dr *or* dr avdp	27.344 grains, 0.0625 ounce	1.772 grams
grain	gr	0.037 dram, 0.002286 ounce	0.0648 gram
Troy			
pound	lb t	12 ounces, 240 pennyweight, 5760 grains	0.373 kilogram
ounce	oz t	20 pennyweight, 480 grains, 0.083 pound	31.103 grams
pennyweight	dwt *also* pwt	24 grains, 0.05 ounce	1.555 grams
grain	gr	0.042 pennyweight, 0.002083 ounce	0.0648 gram
Apothecaries'			
pound	lb ap	12 ounces, 5760 grains	0.373 kilogram
ounce	oz ap *or* ʒ	8 drams, 480 grains, 0.083 pound	31.103 grams
dram	dr ap *or* ʒ	3 scruples, 60 grains	3.888 grams
scruple	s ap *or* ∋	20 grains, 0.333 dram	1.296 grams
grain	gr	0.05 scruple, 0.002083 ounce, 0.0166 dram	0.0648 gram
CAPACITY			
U.S. liquid measure			
gallon	gal	4 quarts (231 cubic inches)	3.785 liters
quart	qt	2 pints (57.75 cubic inches)	0.946 liter
pint	pt	4 gills (28.875 cubic inches)	0.473 liter
gill	gi	4 fluid ounces (7.219 cubic inches)	118.294 milliliters
fluid ounce	fl oz *or* f ʒ	8 fluid drams (1.805 cubic inches)	29.573 milliliters
fluid dram	fl dr *or* f ʒ	60 minims (0.226 cubic inch)	3.697 milliliters
minim	min *or* ♍	⅟₆₀ fluid dram (0.003760 cubic inch)	0.061610 milliliter
U.S. dry measure			
bushel	bu	4 pecks (2150.42 cubic inches)	35.239 liters
peck	pk	8 quarts (537.605 cubic inches)	8.810 liters
quart	qt	2 pints (67.201 cubic inches)	1.101 liters
pint	pt	½ quart (33.600 cubic inches)	0.551 liter
LENGTH			
mile	mi	5280 feet, 1760 yards, 320 rods	1.609 kilometers
rod	rd	5.50 yards, 16.5 feet	5.029 meters
yard	yd	3 feet, 36 inches	0.9144 meter
foot	ft *or* '	12 inches, 0.333 yard	30.48 centimeters
inch	in *or* "	0.083 foot, 0.028 yard	2.54 centimeters
AREA			
square mile	sq mi *or* mi^2	640 acres, 102,400 square rods	2.590 square kilometers
acre	ac	4840 square yards, 43,560 square feet	0.405 hectare
square rod	sq rd *or* rd^2	30.25 square yards, 0.00625 acre	25.293 square meters
square yard	sq yd *or* yd^2	9 square feet, 1296 square inches	0.836 square meter
square foot	sq ft *or* ft^2	144 square inches, 0.111 square yard	0.093 square meter
square inch	sq in *or* in^2	0.0069 square foot, 0.00077 square yard	6.452 square centimeters
VOLUME			
cubic yard	cu yd *or* yd^3	27 cubic feet, 46,656 cubic inches	0.765 cubic meter
cubic foot	cu ft *or* ft^3	1728 cubic inches, 0.0370 cubic yard	0.028 cubic meter
cubic inch	cu in *or* in^3	0.00058 cubic foot, 0.000021 cubic yard	16.387 cubic centimeters

[1]For U.S. equivalents of the metric units see Metric System table.
[2]The U.S. uses the avoirdupois units as the common system of measuring weight.

size, capacity, or quantity of something as fixed by measuring ⟨use equal *measures* of ingredients⟩ **b** : something (as a yardstick or cup) used in measuring **c** : a unit used in measuring ⟨the foot is a *measure* of length⟩ **d** : a system of measuring ⟨metric *measure*⟩ **3** : the act or process of measuring **4 a** : ²DANCE 2; *esp* : a slow and stately dance **b** : rhythm or movement in music or poetry : METER, CADENCE **c** : the part of a musical staff between two bars or the group of beats between these bars **5** : an action planned or taken to achieve a desired result; *esp* : a legislative bill or act [Middle English *mesure* "measure," from early French *mesure* (same meaning), from Latin *mensura* "measure," from *mensus,* past participle of *me-*

tiri "to measure" — related to DIMENSION, IMMENSE] — **for good measure** : in addition to what is required : as an extra

²measure *vb* **mea·sured; mea·sur·ing** \'mezh-(ə-)riŋ, 'māzh-\ **1** : to mark or fix in multiples of a specific unit ⟨*measure* out two cups⟩ **2** : to find out the size, extent, or amount of ⟨*measure* the piece of paper⟩ **3** : ¹ESTIMATE

\ə\ abut	\aů\ out	\i\ tip	\ȯ\ saw	\ů\ foot
\ər\ further	\ch\ chin	\ī\ life	\ȯi\ coin	\y\ yet
\a\ mat	\e\ pet	\j\ job	\th\ thin	\yü\ few
\ā\ take	\ē\ easy	\ŋ\ sing	\th\ this	\yů\ cure
\ä\ cot, cart	\g\ go	\ō\ bone	\ü\ food	\zh\ vision

1 ⟨*measured* the distance with my eye⟩ 4 : to bring into comparison ⟨*measure* your skill against an opponent's⟩ 5 : to serve as a measure of ⟨a thermometer *measures* temperature⟩ 6 : to have as its measurement ⟨the room *measures* 12 by 12 feet⟩ — **mea·sur·er** \-ər-ər\ *n*

mea·sured \'mezh-ərd, 'māzh-\ *adj* 1 a : regulated or determined by a standard b : marked by rhythm : EVEN ⟨walk with *measured* steps⟩ 2 : ²DELIBERATE 1, CALCULATED ⟨speak with *measured* rudeness⟩

mea·sure·less \'mezh-ər-ləs, 'māzh-\ *adj* : being without or beyond measure : IMMEASURABLE ⟨the *measureless* universe⟩

mea·sure·ment \'mezh-ər-mənt, 'māzh-\ *n* 1 : the act or process of measuring 2 : a figure, extent, or amount obtained by measuring 3 : a system of measures

measure up *vb* 1 : to have necessary or fitting qualifications 2 : to be the equal (as in ability) — used with *to*

measuring worm *n* : LOOPER 1

meat \'mēt\ *n* 1 a : something eaten for nourishment; *esp* : solid food as distinguished from drink b : the edible part of something as distinguished from the covering (as a shell or husk) ⟨walnut *meat*⟩ 2 : animal and especially mammal flesh used as food

meat·ball \-,bȯl\ *n* : a small ball of chopped or ground meat

meat loaf *n* : ground meat seasoned and baked in the form of a loaf

meaty \'mēt-ē\ *adj* **meat·i·er; -est** 1 : full of meat : FLESHY 2 : rich in matter for thought : SUBSTANTIAL ⟨a *meaty* book⟩ — **meat·i·ness** *n*

mec·ca \'mek-ə\ *n, often cap* : a place regarded as a center for a specified group, activity, or interest ⟨a *mecca* for tourists⟩ [named for *Mecca*, city in Arabia, the birthplace of Muhammad and the goal of Muslim pilgrimages]

¹**me·chan·ic** \mi-'kan-ik\ *adj* : of or relating to work performed by hand or skill at such work ⟨*mechanic* arts⟩

²**mechanic** *n* : a person who works with his or her hands; *esp* : a repairer of machines

me·chan·i·cal \mi-'kan-i-kəl\ *adj* 1 a : of or relating to machinery ⟨*mechanical* skill⟩ b : made or operated by a machine or machinery ⟨a *mechanical* toy⟩ 2 : done as if by machine : IMPERSONAL ⟨gave a *mechanical* reply⟩ 3 : relating to or according to the principles of mechanics — **me·chan·i·cal·ly** \-i-k(ə-)lē\ *adv*

mechanical advantage *n* : the ratio of the force that performs the useful work of a machine to the force that is applied to the machine

mechanical drawing *n* 1 : drawing done with the aid of instruments (as compasses and squares) 2 : a drawing made with instruments

mechanical engineering *n* : engineering that deals with tools, machinery, and the application of mechanics in industry — **mechanical engineer** *n*

me·chan·ics \mi-'kan-iks\ *n sing or pl* 1 : a science that deals with energy and forces and their effect on bodies 2 : the application of mechanics to the making or operation of machines 3 : the details of the way something works or is done ⟨the *mechanics* of running⟩

mech·a·nism \'mek-ə-,niz-əm\ *n* 1 : a piece of machinery 2 a : the parts by which a machine operates b : the process, way, or system for achieving a goal ⟨the *mechanism* of government⟩ 3 : the processes involved in or responsible for a natural occurrence (as evolution or an action or reaction)

mech·a·nize \'mek-ə-,nīz\ *vb* **-nized; -niz·ing** 1 : to make mechanical; *esp* : to make automatic 2 a : to equip with machinery especially to replace human or animal labor b : to equip with armed and armored motor vehicles ⟨*mechanized* infantry⟩ — **mech·a·ni·za·tion** \,mek-ə-nə-'zā-shən\ *n* — **mech·a·niz·er** \'mek-ə-,nī-zər\ *n*

med·al \'med-ᵊl\ *n* : a piece of metal often in the form of a coin with design and words in honor or of a special event, a person, or an achievement

medal

med·al·ist *or* **med·al·list** \'med-ᵊl-əst\ *n* : a person who receives a medal

me·dal·lion \mə-'dal-yən\ *n* 1 : a large medal 2 : something resembling a large medal (as in shape)

med·dle \'med-ᵊl\ *vb* **med·dled; med·dling** \'med-liŋ, -ᵊl-iŋ\ : to interest oneself in what is not one's concern ⟨*meddle* in another's business⟩ — **med·dler** \'med-lər, -ᵊl-ər\ *n*

synonyms MEDDLE, INTERFERE, TAMPER mean to concern oneself with something that is not one's own business. MEDDLE stresses intruding in a thoughtless and annoying fashion ⟨*meddling* in a friend's personal problems⟩. INTERFERE suggests getting in the way of or disturbing someone or something whether intentionally or not ⟨building the dam *interfered* with nature⟩ ⟨your noise is *interfering* with my studying⟩. TAMPER suggests intruding or experimenting that is wrong or uncalled-for and likely to be harmful ⟨*tampered* with the lock while trying to get into the building⟩.

med·dle·some \'med-ᵊl-səm\ *adj* : inclined to meddle — **med·dle·some·ly** *adv*

med·fly \'med-,flī\ *n* : MEDITERRANEAN FRUIT FLY

media *plural of* MEDIUM

me·dia \'mēd-ē-ə\ *n* 1 : a medium of cultivation, conveyance, or expression; *esp* : MEDIUM 3 2 a *sing or pl* : forms or systems of communication designed to reach a large number of people : MASS MEDIA b *pl* : members of the mass media

mediaeval *variant of* MEDIEVAL

me·di·al \'mēd-ē-əl\ *adj* 1 : ²MEDIAN 1 2 : ²ORDINARY 2, AVERAGE — **me·di·al·ly** \-ə-lē\ *adv*

¹**me·di·an** \'mēd-ē-ən\ *n* 1 : a value in a series arranged from smallest to largest below and above which there are an equal number of values or which is the average of the two middle values if there is no one middle value ⟨the *median* of the set 1, 3, 7, 12, 19 is 7 and the *median* of the set 2, 5, 7, 15 is 6⟩ 2 : a line drawn from the vertex of a triangle to the midpoint of the opposite side [from Latin *mediana vena* "median vein (a large vein in the arm)," from earlier Latin *medianus* "being in the middle," from *medius* "middle" — related to INTERMEDIATE, ³MEAN, MERIDIAN]

²**median** *adj* 1 : being in the middle or in an intermediate position 2 : relating to or making up a median

me·di·ant \'mēd-ē-ənt\ *n* : the third tone above the tonic

me·di·ate \'mēd-ē-,āt\ *vb* **-at·ed; -at·ing** 1 : to work with opposing sides in an argument in order to bring about an agreement ⟨*mediate* a settlement⟩ ⟨*mediate* a dispute⟩ 2 : to pass on or act as a mechanism or agency that is between others — **me·di·a·tion** \,mēd-ē-'ā-shən\ *n*

me·di·a·tor \'mēd-ē-,āt-ər\ *n* : one that mediates — **me·di·a·to·ry** \-ē-ə-,tōr-ē, -,tȯr-\ *adj*

med·ic \'med-ik\ *n* : a person engaged in medical work; *esp* : CORPSMAN

Med·ic·aid \'med-i-,kād\ *n* : a program of medical aid designed for those unable to afford regular medical service and paid for by the state and federal governments

med·i·cal \'med-i-kəl\ *adj* 1 : of, relating to, or concerned with the science or practice of medicine ⟨a *medical* education⟩ **2** : requiring, providing, or used in medical treatment ⟨*medical* emergencies⟩ ⟨a *medical* device⟩ — **med·i·cal·ly** \-k(ə-)lē\ *adv*

Medi·care \'med-i-ˌke(ə)r, -ˌka(ə)r\ *n* : a government program of medical care especially for the aged

med·i·cat·ed \'med-ə-ˌkāt-əd\ *adj* : treated with or containing a medicine ⟨*medicated* soap⟩

med·i·ca·tion \ˌmed-ə-'kā-shən\ *n* : MEDICINE 1

me·dic·i·nal \mə-'dis-nəl, -ᵊn-əl\ *adj* : tending or used to cure disease or relieve pain — **me·dic·i·nal·ly** \-ē\ *adv*

med·i·cine \'med-ə-sən\ *n* **1** : a substance or preparation used in treating disease **2** : the science or art that deals with the prevention, cure, or easing of disease; *esp* : the practice of the physician as it differs from that of the surgeon **3** : an object, power, or ceremony held to give control over natural or magical forces

medicine ball *n* : a heavy usually large ball used especially for strengthening exercises

medicine dropper *n* : DROPPER 2

medicine man *n* : a person especially among the American Indians that is believed to have magic powers that can cure illnesses and keep away evil spirits by potions and charms

medicine show *n* : a traveling show using entertainers to attract a crowd that may buy cures, remedies, and medicines whose benefits are often much exaggerated

me·di·eval *also* **me·di·ae·val** \ˌmēd-ē-'ē-vəl, ˌmed-; mē-'dē-vəl, med-'ē-\ *adj* : of, relating to, or characteristic of the Middle Ages

me·di·o·cre \ˌmēd-ē-'ō-kər\ *adj* : of medium or low quality : ORDINARY ⟨a *mediocre* performance⟩

me·di·oc·ri·ty \ˌmēd-ē-'äk-rət-ē\ *n, pl* **-ties 1** : the quality or state of being mediocre **2** : a mediocre person

med·i·tate \'med-ə-ˌtāt\ *vb* **-tat·ed; -tat·ing 1 a** : to consider or think over carefully : CONTEMPLATE **b** : to spend time in quiet thinking : REFLECT **2** : INTEND, PLAN ⟨*meditate* a trip abroad⟩

med·i·ta·tion \ˌmed-ə-'tā-shən\ *n* : the act or an instance of meditating

med·i·ta·tive \'med-ə-ˌtāt-iv\ *adj* : having the habit of meditating — **med·i·ta·tive·ly** *adv*

Med·i·ter·ra·nean \ˌmed-ə-tə-'rā-nē-ən, -'rā-nyən\ *adj* : of or relating to the Mediterranean Sea or to the lands or peoples around it

Mediterranean fruit fly *n* : a small widely distributed yellowish brown two-winged fly whose larva lives and feeds in ripening fruit — called also *medfly*

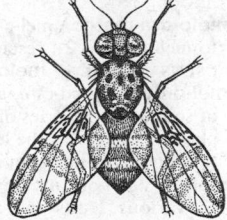

Mediterranean fruit fly

¹me·di·um \'mēd-ē-əm\ *n, pl* **me·diums** *or* **me·dia** \'mēd-ē-ə\ **1 a** : something that is between or in the middle **b** : a middle condition or degree **2** : the thing by which or through which something is done ⟨money is a *medium* of exchange⟩; *esp* : a substance through which a force acts or by which something is carried ⟨air is the common *medium* of sound⟩ **3** *pl usually* **media** : a form or system (as newspapers, radio, or television) of communication, information, or entertainment **4** *pl* **mediums** : a person through whom others seek to communicate with the spirits of the dead **5** : a surrounding substance or condition : ENVIRONMENT ⟨marine fish live in a *medium* of salt water⟩ **6** *pl* **media a** : a nourishing system for the artificial cultivation of microorganisms (as bacteria) or cells **b** : a fluid or solid in which animal or plant parts are placed (as for mounting or preserving)

²medium *adj* : intermediate in amount, quality, position, or degree

med·ley \'med-lē\ *n, pl* **medleys 1** : MIXTURE 2; *esp* : a confused mixture **2** : a musical composition made up of a series of songs or short musical pieces

me·dul·la \mə-'dəl-ə\ *n, pl* **-dul·las** *or* **-dul·lae** \-'dəl-ē, -ˌī\ **1** : MEDULLA OBLONGATA **2** : the inner or deep part of an animal or plant structure (as the adrenal gland or kidney) — **med·ul·lary** \'med-ᵊl-ˌer-ē, 'mej-ə-ˌler-ē\ *adj*

medulla ob·lon·ga·ta \-ˌäb-ˌlòŋ-'gät-ə\ *n* : the somewhat pyramid-shaped bottom part of the vertebrate brain that joins the spinal cord and is concerned with the control of involuntary activities (as breathing and beating of the heart) necessary for life

me·du·sa \mi-'d(y)ü-sə, -zə\ *n, pl* **-sae** \-ˌsē, -ˌzē\ *also* **-sas** : JELLYFISH 1

meek \'mēk\ *adj* **1** : putting up with wrongs patiently and without complaint : MILD **2** : lacking spirit or self-assurance : HUMBLE — **meek·ly** *adv* — **meek·ness** *n*

meer·kat \'mir-ˌkat\ *n* : a burrowing mammal of southern Africa that feeds chiefly on insects, is grayish with faint black markings, and lives in usually large colonies

meer·schaum \'mi(ə)r-shəm, -ˌshòm\ *n* **1** : a soft white lightweight mineral resembling a very fine clay used especially for tobacco pipes **2** : a tobacco pipe made of meerschaum [German, literally, "sea foam"]

¹meet \'mēt\ *vb* **met** \'met\; **meet·ing 1** : to come by chance into the presence of : ENCOUNTER ⟨*met* an old friend⟩ **2 a** : to approach from the opposite direction ⟨when you *meet* another car, keep to the right⟩ **b** : to touch and join or cross ⟨a fork where two roads *meet*⟩ **3** : to go where a person or thing is or will be ⟨agreed to *meet* me at school⟩ **4 a** : to become acquainted ⟨the couple *met* at a dance⟩ **b** : to make the acquaintance of ⟨*met* interesting people there⟩ **5 a** : to come together as opponents ⟨the teams *met* in the finals⟩ **b** : to struggle against : OPPOSE ⟨was chosen to *meet* the champion⟩ **6** : ²MATCH 4a ⟨tries to *meet* the competitor's price⟩ **7** : ENDURE 2 ⟨*meet* defeat bravely⟩ **8** : to come together : ASSEMBLE ⟨*meet* for discussion⟩ **9** : to become noticed by ⟨sounds that *meet* the ears⟩ **10 a** : to fulfill the requirements of : SATISFY ⟨*met* all our demands⟩ **b** : to pay fully : DISCHARGE ⟨*meet* a financial obligation⟩ [Old English *mētan* "to meet"] — **meet halfway** : to compromise with — **meet with** : to be subjected to : ENCOUNTER ⟨the plan *met with* opposition⟩

²meet *n* : a meeting for sports competition ⟨a track *meet*⟩

³meet *adj* : SUITABLE 2, PROPER [Old English *gemǣte* "proper"] — **meet·ly** *adv*

meet·ing \'mēt-iŋ\ *n* **1** : the act of persons or things that meet ⟨a chance *meeting*⟩ **2** : a coming together of a number of persons for a definite purpose ⟨the club *meeting*⟩ **3** : an assembly for religious worship ⟨a Quaker *meeting*⟩ **4** : the place where two things come together : JUNCTION

meet·ing·house \-ˌhaús\ *n* : a building used for public assembly and especially for Protestant worship

meg \'meg\ *n* : MEGABYTE

mega- *or* **meg-** *combining form* **1** : great ⟨*mega*spore⟩ **2** : million : multiplied by one million ⟨*mega*hertz⟩ **3** : to the highest or greatest degree ⟨*mega*-successful⟩ [from Greek *megas* "large"]

mega·bit \'meg-ə-ˌbit\ *n* : one million bits

mega·byte \'meg-ə-ˌbīt\ *n* : 1,048,576 bytes; *also* : one million bytes

mega·cy·cle \'meg-ə-ˌsī-kəl\ *n* : one million cycles; *esp* : MEGAHERTZ

mega·dose \-ˌdōs\ *n* : a large dose (as of a vitamin)

\ə\ **abut**	\aú\ **out**	\i\ **tip**	\ò\ **saw**	\ú\ **foot**
\ər\ **further**	\ch\ **chin**	\ī\ **life**	\òi\ **coin**	\y\ **yet**
\a\ **mat**	\e\ **pet**	\j\ **job**	\th\ **thin**	\yü\ **few**
\ā\ **take**	\ē\ **easy**	\ŋ\ **sing**	\th\ **this**	\yú\ **cure**
\ä\ **cot, cart**	\g\ **go**	\ō\ **bone**	\ü\ **food**	\zh\ **vision**

mega·hertz \\'meg-ə-ˌhərts, -ˌhe(ə)rts\\ *n* : a unit of frequency equal to one million hertz

mega·hit \\'meg-ə-ˌhit\\ *n* : something (as a movie) that is extremely successful

meg·a·lop·o·lis \\ˌmeg-ə-'läp-ə-ləs\\ *n* **1** : a very large city **2** : a thickly populated region centering in a large city or including several large cities

mega·phone \\'meg-ə-ˌfōn\\ *n* : a cone-shaped device used to direct the voice and increase its loudness

mega·pix·el \\-ˌpik-səl\\ *n* : one million pixels ⟨a two-*megapixel* digital camera⟩

mega·plex \\-ˌpleks\\ *n* : a large multiplex typically housing 16 or more movie theaters

mega·spore \\'meg-ə-ˌspō(ə)r, -ˌspȯ(ə)r\\ *n* : a plant spore that produces a female gametophyte

mega·ton \\'meg-ə-ˌtən\\ *n* : an explosive force equal to that of one million tons of TNT

megaphone

mei·o·sis \\mī-'ō-səs\\ *n, pl* **-o·ses** \\-'ō-ˌsēz\\ : the process by which the number of chromosomes in a cell that produces sex cells is reduced to one half and that involves a reduction division in which one of each pair of homologous chromosomes passes to each daughter cell followed by a mitotic division — compare MITOSIS 1 — **mei·ot·ic** \\mī-'ät-ik\\ *adj* — **mei·ot·i·cal·ly** \\-'ät-i-k(ə-)lē\\ *adv*

meit·ner·i·um \\mīt-'nir-ē-əm, -'ner-\\ *n* : a short-lived radioactive element produced artificially — see ELEMENT table

mel·an·cho·lia \\ˌmel-ən-'kō-lē-ə\\ *n* : a mental condition marked especially by extreme depression

¹mel·an·choly \\'mel-ən-ˌkäl-ē\\ *n, pl* **-chol·ies** : a sad or gloomy mood or condition [Middle English *malencolie* "melancholy," from early French *melancolie* (same meaning), from Latin *melancholia* (same meaning), from Greek *melancholia* "melancholy," literally, "black bile," from *melan-*, *melas* "black" and *cholē* "bile"; so called from the ancient belief that the condition was caused by an excess of what was thought to be black bile in the body — related to CHOLERIC, MELANIN; see *Word History* at HUMOR]

²melancholy *adj* **1** : depressed in spirits : DEJECTED, SAD **2** : seriously thoughtful **3** : causing sadness : DISMAL ⟨a *melancholy* thought⟩

Mel·a·ne·sian \\ˌmel-ə-'nē-zhən, -shən\\ *n* : a member of the most numerous native group of Melanesia — **Melanesian** *adj*

mé·lange \\mā-'länzh, -'länj\\ *n* : a mixture often of dissimilar elements

mel·a·nin \\'mel-ə-nən\\ *n* : a dark brown or black animal or plant pigment that in human beings makes some skins darker than others [derived from Greek *melan-*, *melas* "black" — related to MELANCHOLY]

mel·a·nism \\'mel-ə-ˌniz-əm\\ *n* : an exceptionally dark coloring (as of skin, feathers, or hair) of an individual or kind of living thing

me·la·no·cyte \\mə-'lan-ə-ˌsīt, 'mel-ə-nō-\\ *n* : a body cell (as in the skin) that produces or contains melanin

mel·a·no·ma \\ˌmel-ə-'nō-mə\\ *n, pl* **-mas** *also* **-ma·ta** \\-mət-ə\\ : a usually malignant tumor containing dark pigment

mel·a·to·nin \\ˌmel-ə-'tō-nən\\ *n* : a hormone that is secreted by the pineal gland especially in response to darkness and has been linked to the regulation of bodily functions or activities (as sleep) that occur in approximately 24 hour cycles

¹meld \\'meld\\ *vb* : MERGE 1, BLEND ⟨the vocals *meld* perfectly with the instrumental accompaniment⟩

²meld *n* : ²BLEND 1, MIXTURE ⟨a *meld* of new and old ideas⟩

me·lee \\'mā-ˌlā, mā-'lā\\ *n* : a confused struggle; *esp* : a hand-to-hand fight among several people

me·lio·rate \\'mēl-yə-ˌrāt, 'mē-lē-ə-\\ *vb* **-rat·ed; -rat·ing** : to make or become better : IMPROVE — **me·lio·ra·tion** \\ˌmēl-yə-'rā-shən, ˌmē-lē-ə-\\ *n* — **me·lio·ra·tive** \\'mēl-yə-ˌrāt-iv, 'mē-lē-ə-\\ *adj*

mel·lif·lu·ous \\me-'lif-lə-wəs, mə-\\ *adj* : smoothly flowing ⟨*mellifluous* speech⟩ — **mel·lif·lu·ous·ly** *adv* — **mel·lif·lu·ous·ness** *n*

mel·lo·phone \\'mel-ə-ˌfōn\\ *n* : an althorn in circular form

¹mel·low \\'mel-ō\\ *adj* **1 a** : tender and sweet because of ripeness ⟨*mellow* peaches⟩ **b** : well aged and pleasingly mild ⟨a *mellow* wine⟩ **2 a** : made gentle by age or experience ⟨developed a *mellow* disposition from caring for his grandchildren⟩ **b** : PLEASANT 1, AGREEABLE ⟨*mellow* sounds⟩ **c** : LAID-BACK ⟨a *mellow* personality⟩ **3** : being soft and crumbly ⟨*mellow* soil⟩ **4** : being clear, full, and pure ⟨spoke in *mellow* tones⟩ — **mel·low·ly** *adv* — **mel·low·ness** *n*

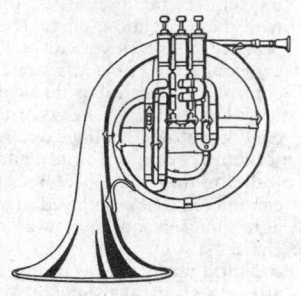

mellophone

²mellow *vb* : to make or become mellow ⟨old houses, weather-beaten and *mellowed* by time⟩

me·lo·de·on \\mə-'lōd-ē-ən\\ *n* : a small reed organ in which a bellows draws air inward through the reeds

me·lod·ic \\mə-'läd-ik\\ *adj* : of or relating to melody : MELODIOUS — **me·lod·i·cal·ly** \\-i-k(ə-)lē\\ *adv*

me·lo·di·ous \\mə-'lōd-ē-əs\\ *adj* **1** : pleasing to the ear because of melody ⟨*melodious* music⟩ **2** : of, relating to, or producing melody ⟨*melodious* birds⟩ — **me·lo·di·ous·ly** *adv* — **me·lo·di·ous·ness** *n*

melo·dra·ma \\'mel-ə-ˌdräm-ə, -ˌdram-\\ *n* **1 a** : a work (as a movie or play) marked by the exaggerated emotions of the characters and the importance of action and plot **b** : such works as a group **2** : melodramatic events or behavior

melo·dra·mat·ic \\ˌmel-ə-drə-'mat-ik\\ *adj* **1** : of or relating to melodrama **2** : resembling or suitable for melodrama : SENSATIONAL — **melo·dra·mat·i·cal·ly** \\-i-k(ə-)lē\\ *adv*

mel·o·dy \\'mel-əd-ē\\ *n, pl* **-dies** **1** : a pleasing succession of sounds **2** : a series of musical tones arranged to give a pleasing effect **3** : the leading part in a musical composition involving harmony

mel·on \\'mel-ən\\ *n* : any of various fruits (as a cantaloupe, honeydew melon, or watermelon) of the gourd family that have juicy and usually sweet flesh eaten raw and a firm rind

¹melt \\'melt\\ *vb* **1** : to change from a solid to a liquid state usually through heat ⟨*melt* butter⟩ ⟨snow *melts*⟩ **2** : DISSOLVE 1 ⟨the sugar *melted* in the coffee⟩ **3** : to grow less : DISAPPEAR ⟨clouds *melting* away⟩ **4** : to make or become gentle : SOFTEN ⟨a warm smile *melts* the heart⟩ **5** : to lose clear outline or shape : BLEND, MERGE — **melt·er** *n*

melon: *1* watermelon, *2* cantaloupe

²melt *n* : a melted substance

melt·down \'melt-ˌdaun\ *n* **1** : the accidental melting of the core of a nuclear reactor **2** : a rapid or disastrous decline or collapse ⟨a financial *meltdown*⟩ **3** : a breakdown of self-control (as from fatigue or overstimulation)

melting point *n* : the temperature at which a solid melts

melting pot *n* **1** : a container in which something is melted : CRUCIBLE **2** : a place (as a city or country) in which various nationalities or races live together and gradually blend into one community

mel·ton \'melt-ᵊn\ *n* : a smooth heavy woolen cloth used for overcoats

melt·wa·ter \'melt-ˌwȯt-ər, -ˌwät-\ *n* : water that comes from the melting of ice and snow

mem·ber \'mem-bər\ *n* **1** : a part (as an arm, leg, leaf, or branch) of an animal or plant **2** : one of the individuals or units of a group or organization ⟨a club *member*⟩ **3** : a part of a whole and especially of a structure ⟨a horizontal *member* of a bridge⟩ **4 a** : the whole expression on one side or the other of a mathematical equation or inequality **b** : ELEMENT 2b

mem·ber·ship \'mem-bər-ˌship\ *n* **1** : the state or status of being a member **2** : all the members of an organization

mem·brane \'mem-ˌbrān\ *n* : a thin soft flexible sheet or layer especially of a plant or animal part (as a cell, tissue, or organ) — **mem·bra·nous** \'mem-brə-nəs\ *adj*

me·men·to \mi-'ment-ō\ *n, pl* **-tos** *or* **-toes** : something that serves to warn or remind; *also* : SOUVENIR ⟨*mementos* of a trip⟩

memo \'mem-ō\ *n, pl* **mem·os** : MEMORANDUM

mem·oir \'mem-ˌwär, -ˌwȯ(ə)r\ *n* **1 a** : a story of a personal experience **b** : AUTOBIOGRAPHY — usually used in plural **c** : BIOGRAPHY **2** : ¹REPORT 2

mem·o·ra·bil·ia \ˌmem-ə-rə-'bil-ē-ə, -'bil-yə\ *n pl* **1** : things worth remembering **2** : things valued or collected for their relation to a particular field or interest ⟨baseball *memorabilia*⟩

mem·o·ra·ble \'mem-(ə-)rə-bəl\ *adj* : worth remembering : NOTABLE — **mem·o·ra·bly** \-blē\ *adv*

mem·o·ran·dum \ˌmem-ə-'ran-dəm\ *n, pl* **-dums** *or* **-da** \-də\ **1** : an informal record or communication **2** : a brief written reminder

¹me·mo·ri·al \mə-'mōr-ē-əl, -'mȯr-\ *adj* : serving to preserve the memory of a person or an event ⟨a *memorial* service⟩ — **me·mo·ri·al·ly** \-ē-ə-lē\ *adv*

²memorial *n* : something that keeps alive the memory of a person or event; *esp* : MONUMENT 1

Memorial Day *n* **1** : May 30 once observed as a legal holiday in honor of those who died in war **2** : the last Monday in May observed as a legal holiday in most states of the U.S. **3** : CONFEDERATE MEMORIAL DAY

me·mo·ri·al·ize \mə-'mōr-ē-ə-ˌlīz, -'mȯr-\ *vb* **-ized; -iz·ing** : COMMEMORATE 1 — **me·mo·ri·al·i·za·tion** \-ˌmōr-ē-ə-lə-'zā-shən, -ˌmȯr-\ *n*

mem·o·rize \'mem-ə-ˌrīz\ *vb* **-rized; -riz·ing** : to learn by heart — **mem·o·ri·za·tion** \ˌmem-(ə-)rə-'zā-shən\ *n*

mem·o·ry \'mem-(ə-)rē\ *n, pl* **-ries** **1 a** : the power or process of recalling what has been learned **b** : the store of things learned and kept in the mind ⟨recite from *memory*⟩ **2** : COMMEMORATION 1 ⟨a monument in *memory* of a hero⟩ **3** : something remembered ⟨has pleasant *memories* of the trip⟩ **4** : the time within which past events can be remembered ⟨within the *memory* of people living today⟩ **5 a** : a device (as in a computer) into which information can be inserted and stored and from which it may be taken when needed **b** : capacity for storing information ⟨a computer with 512 megabytes of *memory*⟩

synonyms MEMORY, REMEMBRANCE, RECOLLECTION, REMINISCENCE mean something remembered. MEMORY applies both to the power of remembering and to what is remembered ⟨had a remarkable *memory*⟩ ⟨had many fond *memories* of her grandfather⟩. REMEMBRANCE stresses the act of remembering or the fact of being remembered ⟨a vivid *remembrance* of their adventure⟩. RECOLLECTION suggests that something is deliberately brought back to mind and often with some effort ⟨to the best of my *recollection* he never said that⟩. REMINISCENCE suggests the remembering of usually pleasant events, experiences, or feelings from a distant past ⟨the author's *reminiscences* of a childhood in Scotland⟩.

men *plural of* MAN

¹men·ace \'men-əs\ *n* **1** : someone or something that represents a threat : DANGER **2** : an annoying person : NUISANCE

²menace *vb* **men·aced; men·ac·ing** **1** : to make a show of intention to harm : THREATEN **2** : ENDANGER — **men·ac·ing·ly** \'men-ə-siŋ-lē\ *adv*

mé·nage \mā-'näzh\ *n* : ¹HOUSEHOLD

me·nag·er·ie \mə-'naj-(ə-)rē *also* -'nazh-\ *n* **1** : a place where animals are kept and trained especially for exhibition **2** : a collection of wild or foreign animals kept especially for exhibition

¹mend \'mend\ *vb* **1** : to improve in manners or morals : REFORM **2** : to put into good shape or working order again **3** : to improve in health; *also* : HEAL — **mend·able** \'men-də-bəl\ *adj* — **mend·er** *n*

synonyms MEND, PATCH, REPAIR mean to take something that has been damaged and make it usable again. MEND suggests making something that has been broken or damaged once again whole or fit for use ⟨*mend* the torn dress⟩. PATCH refers to mending a hole or break by using new material ⟨*patched* the hole with concrete⟩ and it may also suggest a hurried careless job ⟨just *patch* the roof for now⟩. REPAIR applies to the fixing of something that has been damaged considerably ⟨the mechanic *repaired* our car⟩.

²mend *n* **1** : an act of mending : REPAIR **2** : a mended place — **on the mend** : getting better (as in health)

men·da·cious \men-'dā-shəs\ *adj* : apt to tell lies — **men·da·cious·ly** *adv* — **men·dac·i·ty** \men-'das-ət-ē\ *n*

men·de·le·vi·um \ˌmen-də-'lē-vē-əm\ *n* : a radioactive element that is produced artificially — see ELEMENT table

Men·de·lian \men-'dē-lē-ən, -'dēl-yən\ *adj* : of, relating to, or according to Mendel's laws or the operation of Mendel's laws — **Mendelian** *n*

Men·del's law \ˌmen-dᵊlz-\ *n* **1** : a principle in genetics: paired inherited units that control the expression of a character (as height or seed color) separate during germ cell formation so that each sperm or egg receives only one member of each pair — called also *law of segregation* **2** : a principle in genetics that has exceptions due to the discovery of linkage: the members of two or more different pairs of inherited units are passed on to a germ cell independently of each other and the various sperms and eggs unite according to the laws of chance sometimes resulting in new combinations of inherited units and of the characters they control — called also *law of independent assortment* **3** : a principle in genetics that has many exceptions: when the two members of a pair of inherited units are different, the dominant one controls the expression of the character — called also *law of dominance*

men·di·cant \'men-di-kənt\ *n* **1** : one who lives by begging **2** : a member of a religious order originally owning neither personal nor community property and living mostly on charitable donations : FRIAR — **men·di·can·cy** \-kən-sē\ *n* — **mendicant** *adj*

\ə\ **abut**	\au̇\ **out**	\i\ **tip**	\ȯ\ **saw**	\u̇\ **foot**
\ər\ **further**	\ch\ **chin**	\ī\ **life**	\ȯi\ **coin**	\y\ **yet**
\a\ **mat**	\e\ **pet**	\j\ **job**	\th\ **thin**	\yü\ **few**
\ā\ **take**	\ē\ **easy**	\ŋ\ **sing**	\t͟h\ **this**	\yu̇\ **cure**
\ä\ **cot, cart**	\g\ **go**	\ō\ **bone**	\ü\ **food**	\zh\ **vision**

men·folk \'men-ˌfōk\ *or* **men·folks** \-ˌfōks\ *n pl* **1** : men in general **2** : the men of a family or community

men·ha·den \men-'hād-ᵊn, mən-\ *n, pl* **-den** *also* **-dens** : a fish of the Atlantic coast of the U.S. that is related to the herring and is a source of oil and fertilizer

¹**me·nial** \'mē-nē-əl, -nyəl\ *adj* **1** : of, relating to, or suitable for servants **2** : lacking interest or dignity ⟨a *menial* task⟩ — **me·nial·ly** \-ē\ *adv*

²**menial** *n* : ²DOMESTIC

meninges *plural of* MENINX

men·in·gi·tis \ˌmen-ən-'jīt-əs\ *n* : a disease in which a membrane of the brain or spinal cord becomes inflamed

me·ninx \'mē-niŋ(k)s, 'men-iŋ(k)s\ *n, pl* **me·nin·ges** \mə-'nin-jēz\ : any of the three membranes surrounding the brain and spinal cord

me·nis·cus \mə-'nis-kəs\ *n, pl* **me·nis·ci** \-'nis-ˌ(k)ī, -ˌkē\ *also* **me·nis·cus·es** : the curved upper surface of a liquid column

Men·no·nite \'men-ə-ˌnīt\ *n* : a member of one of the Protestant groups founded in Holland in the 16th century and noted for dressing plainly and living simply

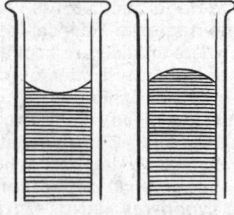

meniscus

meno·pause \'men-ə-ˌpȯz\ *n* : the period of life when menstruation permanently stops naturally that usually occurs between the ages of 45 and 55 — **meno·paus·al** \ˌmen-ə-'pȯ-zəl\ *adj*

me·no·rah \mə-'nōr-ə, -'nȯr-\ *n* : a holder for candles used in Jewish worship

menservants *plural of* MANSERVANT

men·ses \'men-ˌsēz\ *n sing or pl* : the menstrual flow

men·stru·al \'men(t)-strə-(wə)l\ *adj* : of or relating to menstruation

menstrual cycle *n* : the complete cycle of bodily changes from the beginning of one menstrual period to the beginning of the next

men·stru·ate \'men(t)-strə-ˌwāt, 'men-ˌstrāt\ *vb* : to undergo menstruation

men·stru·a·tion \ˌmen(t)-strə-'wā-shən, men-'strā-shən\ *n* : a discharging of blood, secretions, and tissue debris from the uterus at periods of approximately one month in female primates of breeding age that are not pregnant; *also* : PERIOD 3c

men·su·ra·tion \ˌmen(t)-sə-'rā-shən, ˌmen-chə-\ *n* **1** : the process or art of measuring : MEASUREMENT **2** : the branch of mathematics that deals with the measurement of lengths, areas, and volumes

mens·wear \'menz-ˌwer\ *n* : clothing for men

-ment \mənt\ *n suffix* **1** : result, object, or means of a (specified) action ⟨attach*ment*⟩ ⟨govern*ment*⟩ **2 a** : action : process ⟨improve*ment*⟩ ⟨develop*ment*⟩ **b** : place of a (specified) action ⟨encamp*ment*⟩ **3** : state : condition ⟨amaze*ment*⟩ [from Latin *-mentum* (noun suffix)]

men·tal \'ment-ᵊl\ *adj* **1 a** : of or relating to the mind ⟨*mental* powers⟩ **b** : carried on in the mind ⟨*mental* arithmetic⟩ **2 a** : relating to or affected by a disorder of the mind ⟨a *mental* illness⟩ **b** : intended for the care of persons affected by mental disorders ⟨*mental* hospitals⟩ — **men·tal·ly** \-ᵊl-ē\ *adv*

mental age *n* : a measure of a child's mental development in terms of the number of years from birth it takes an average child to reach the same level

men·tal·i·ty \men-'tal-ət-ē\ *n, pl* **-ties** **1** : mental power : INTELLIGENCE **2** : a particular way of thinking : OUTLOOK

mental retardation *n* : a development disability usually present from birth or infancy that is marked by mental ability that is below average and by limitations in those abilities (as in communication or care of oneself) necessary for independent daily functioning : INTELLECTUAL DISABILITY

men·thol \'men-ˌthȯl, -ˌthōl\ *n* : a white soothing substance from oils of mint

¹**men·tion** \'men-chən\ *n* : a brief or passing reference to something

²**mention** *vb* **men·tioned; men·tion·ing** \'mench-(ə-)niŋ\ : to refer to or speak about briefly — **men·tion·able** \'mench-(ə-)nə-bəl\ *adj* — **not to mention** : not even yet counting or considering : and notably in addition ⟨a plan that's risky, *not to mention* expensive⟩

¹**men·tor** \'men-ˌtȯ(ə)r, 'ment-ər\ *n* : a wise and faithful adviser or teacher

²**mentor** *vb* : to serve as a mentor for : TUTOR

menu \'men-yü, 'mān-\ *n* **1** : a list of dishes served at or available for a meal; *also* : a similar list of offerings ⟨a *menu* of TV programs⟩ **2** : the dishes served at a meal **3** : a list of computer operations shown on the display screen for a user to select from ⟨a *menu* of printing options⟩

Word History Many restaurants boast of having large menus, but the origin of the word *menu* actually suggests the idea of smallness. *Menu* can be traced to the Latin adjective *minutus*, meaning "small." *Minutus* is also the source of our word *minute*. From *minutus* came the French adjective *menu*, which has several meanings including "small" and "detailed." The use of *menu* as a noun meaning "a list of food" probably came from the "detailed" sense of the adjective, since a menu is most often a detailed list. [from French *menu* "a list of food dishes," from *menu* (adjective) "small, detailed," from Latin *minutus* "small" — related to MINUTE]

menu–driv·en \-ˌdriv-ən\ *n* : relating to or being computer software in which options are shown to the user on menus

me·ow \mē-'aù\ *n* : the characteristic sound of a cat — **meow** *vb*

mer·can·tile \'mər-kən-ˌtēl, -ˌtīl\ *adj* : of or relating to merchants, trade, or commerce

¹**mer·ce·nary** \'mərs-ᵊn-ˌer-ē\ *n, pl* **-nar·ies** : one that serves only for wages; *esp* : a soldier hired by a foreign country to fight in its army

²**mercenary** *adj* **1** : serving only for the pay or reward **2** : greedy for money

mer·cer \'mər-sər\ *n, British* : a dealer in textile fabrics

mer·cer·ize \'mər-sə-ˌrīz\ *vb* **-ized; -iz·ing** : to treat cotton fiber or fabrics with a chemical so that the fibers are strengthened, take dyes better, and often acquire a soft shine — **mer·cer·i·za·tion** \ˌmərs-(ə-)rə-'zā-shən\ *n*

¹**mer·chan·dise** \'mər-chən-ˌdīz, -ˌdīs\ *n* : the goods that are bought and sold in trade

²**merchandise** \'mər-chən-ˌdīz\ *vb* **-dised; -dis·ing** : to buy and sell : TRADE; *esp* : to try to improve sales of goods or services by attractive presentation and publicity — **mer·chan·dis·er** *n*

¹**mer·chant** \'mər-chənt\ *n* **1** : a buyer and seller of goods for profit; *esp* : one who carries on trade on a large scale or with foreign countries **2** : STOREKEEPER 2 [Middle English *marchant* "merchant," from early French *marcheant* (same meaning), derived from Latin *mercari* "to trade," from *merc-, merx* "merchandise" — related to COMMERCE, MARKET]

²**merchant** *adj* **1** : of, relating to, or used in trade ⟨a *merchant* ship⟩ **2** : of or relating to a merchant marine

mer·chant·man \'mər-chənt-mən\ *n* : a ship used in trade

merchant marine *n* **1** : the commercial ships of a nation **2** : the persons who work in a merchant marine

merchant ship *n* : MERCHANTMAN

mer·ci·ful \'mər-si-fəl\ *adj* : having or showing mercy : COMPASSIONATE ⟨a *merciful* ruler⟩ — **mer·ci·ful·ly** \-f(ə-)lē\ *adv* — **mer·ci·ful·ness** \-fəl-nəs\ *n*

mer·ci·less \'mər-si-ləs\ *adj* : having no mercy : PITILESS ⟨*merciless* slaughter⟩ — **mer·ci·less·ly** *adv* — **mer·ci·less·ness** *n*

mer·cu·ri·al \(ˌ)mər-'kyùr-ē-əl\ *adj* **1** : characterized by rapid and unpredictable change of mood **2** : MERCURIC — **mer·cu·ri·al·ly** \-ē-ə-lē\ *adv*

mer·cu·ric \(ˌ)mər-'kyù(ə)r-ik\ *adj* : of, relating to, or containing mercury

Mer·cu·ro·chrome \(ˌ)mər-'kyùr-ə-ˌkrōm\ *trademark* — used for a red solution of an antiseptic and germicide

mer·cu·ry \'mər-kyə-rē, -k(ə-)rē\ *n* **1 a** : a heavy silver-white poisonous metallic element that is liquid at ordinary temperatures — called also *quicksilver;* see ELEMENT table **b** : the column of mercury in a thermometer or barometer **2** *cap* : the planet nearest the sun — see PLANET table

mer·cy \'mər-sē\ *n, pl* **mercies 1 a** : kind and gentle treatment of someone (as a wrongdoer or opponent) having no right to it **b** : a disposition to show mercy **2 a** : a blessing as an act of divine love ⟨the *mercies* of God⟩ **b** : a fortunate happening ⟨it's a *mercy* the weather cooled off⟩ **3** : kindness shown to victims of misfortune ⟨works of *mercy* among the poor⟩ — **at the mercy of** : wholly in the power of : with no way to protect oneself against ⟨was *at the mercy of* the weather⟩

Word History To the ancient Romans, the Latin word *merces* meant "price paid for something, wages, reward." The early Christians of Rome used the word in a slightly different way. For them it meant the spiritual reward one receives for doing a kindness in response to an unkindness. The word came into early French as *mercit* or *merci* with much the same meaning as was later passed on to our Modern English word *mercy*. But while *mercy* in English now has the meaning "kindness or pity shown to someone," the word *merci* in French has lost much of that meaning and is chiefly used today to mean "thank you." [Middle English *merci, mercy* "mercy," from early French *merci, mercit* (same meaning), from Latin *merces* "price paid for something, wages, reward"]

synonyms MERCY, CLEMENCY, LENIENCY mean the disposition not to be harsh in one's dealings with others. MERCY suggests feeling pity and withholding punishment even when justice demands it ⟨pleaded guilty and asked for *mercy* from the court⟩. CLEMENCY suggests a mild or merciful disposition in the person having the power to punish ⟨the judge refused to show *clemency*⟩. LENIENCY suggests the repeated overlooking of mistakes by one not inclined to be severe ⟨their parents' *leniency* was well-known among the children⟩.

mercy killing *n* : EUTHANASIA

¹mere \'mi(ə)r\ *n* : a sheet of still water : POOL [Old English *mere* "lake, pool"]

²mere *adj, superlative* **mer·est** : being only this and nothing else : nothing more than ⟨a *mere* whisper⟩ ⟨a *mere* child⟩ [Middle English *mere* "nothing more or less than," from Latin *merus* "pure"] — **mere·ly** *adv*

mer·e·tri·cious \ˌmer-ə-'trish-əs\ *adj* : falsely attractive — **mer·e·tri·cious·ly** *adv* — **mer·e·tri·cious·ness** *n*

mer·gan·ser \(ˌ)mər-'gan(t)-sər\ *n, pl* **-sers** *or* **-ser** : any of various fish-eating wild ducks with a slender bill hooked at the end and usually with a bunch of feathers on the head that point backward

merge \'mərj\ *vb* **merged; merg·ing 1** : to be or cause to be swallowed up or absorbed in something

merganser

else : MINGLE, BLEND ⟨*merging* traffic⟩ **2** : COMBINE 3a, UNITE ⟨*merge* two business firms into one⟩

merg·er \'mər-jər\ *n* : the combination of two or more businesses into one

me·rid·i·an \mə-'rid-ē-ən\ *n* **1** : the highest point reached **2 a** : an imaginary circle on the earth's surface passing through the north and south poles **b** : the half of such a circle included between the poles **c** : a line on a globe or map representing such a circle or half circle and numbered by degrees of longitude [Middle English *meridien* "midday," from early French *meridien* (same meaning), derived from Latin *meridies* "noon," from *meri-* (altered form of *medius* "middle") and *dies* "day" — related to DIARY, ¹MEDIAN]

me·ringue \mə-'raŋ\ *n* **1** : a mixture of beaten egg white and sugar put on pies or cakes and browned **2** : a shell of baked meringue filled with fruit or ice cream

me·ri·no \mə-'rē-nō\ *n, pl* **-nos 1** : any of a breed of sheep that produce a heavy fleece of fine white wool **2** : a fine soft wool or wool and cotton fabric resembling cashmere **3** : a fine wool and cotton yarn — **merino** *adj*

mer·i·stem \'mer-ə-ˌstem\ *n* : a plant tissue made up of cells that are not specialized for a particular purpose, are capable of dividing any number of times, and can produce cells that specialize to form the fully developed plant tissues and organs — **mer·i·ste·mat·ic** \ˌmer-ə-stə-'mat-ik\ *adj*

¹mer·it \'mer-ət\ *n* **1** : the qualities or actions that determine one's worthiness of reward or punishment ⟨were rewarded according to *merit*⟩ **2** : a quality worthy of praise : VIRTUE ⟨the *merit* of honesty⟩ **3** : ²WORTH 2, VALUE ⟨your idea has great *merit*⟩ **4** : individual significance or justification ⟨the accusation is without *merit*⟩ — **mer·it·less** *adj*

²merit *vb* : to earn by service or performance : DESERVE

mer·i·to·ri·ous \ˌmer-ə-'tōr-ē-əs, -'tȯr-\ *adj* : deserving reward or honor : PRAISEWORTHY — **mer·i·to·ri·ous·ly** *adv* — **mer·i·to·ri·ous·ness** *n*

mer·maid \'mər-ˌmād\ *n* : an imaginary sea creature usually represented with a woman's body and a fish's tail [Middle English *mermayde* "mermaid," from *mere* "lake, pool, sea" and *mayde* "maid"]

mer·man \'mər-ˌman, -mən\ *n, pl* **mer·men** \-ˌmen, -mən\ : an imaginary sea creature usually represented with a man's body and a fish's tail

mer·ri·ment \'mer-i-mənt\ *n* : MIRTH, FUN

mer·ry \'mer-ē\ *adj* **mer·ri·er; -est 1** : full of good humor and good spirits : MIRTHFUL **2** : marked by gaiety or festivity ⟨a *merry* Christmas⟩ — **mer·ri·ly** \'mer-ə-lē\ *adv* — **mer·ri·ness** \'mer-ē-nəs\ *n*

mer·ry–go–round \'mer-ē-gō-ˌraùnd, -gə-\ *n* **1** : a circular revolving platform fitted with seats and figures of animals on which people sit for a ride **2** : a rapid round of activities : WHIRL ⟨a *merry-go-round* of parties⟩

mer·ry·mak·ing \'mer-ē-ˌmā-kiŋ\ *n* **1** : festive activity : MERRIMENT **2** : a festive occasion — **mer·ry·mak·er** \-kər\ *n*

me·sa \'mā-sə\ *n* : a flat-topped hill or small plateau with steep sides [Spanish, literally, "table"]

mes·cal \me-'skal, mə-\ *n* **1** : PEYOTE 2 **2 a** : a usually colorless Mexican liquor distilled especially from the central leaves of maguey plants **b** : a plant from which this liquor is produced

mes·ca·line \'mes-kə-lən, -ˌlēn\ *n* : a drug that is obtained from the peyote cactus and causes hallucinations

\ə\ **abut**	\aù\ **out**	\i\ **tip**	\ȯ\ **saw**	\ù\ **foot**
\ər\ **further**	\ch\ **chin**	\ī\ **life**	\ȯi\ **coin**	\y\ **yet**
\a\ **mat**	\e\ **pet**	\j\ **job**	\th\ **thin**	\yü\ **few**
\ā\ **take**	\ē\ **easy**	\ŋ\ **sing**	\th\ **this**	\yù\ **cure**
\ä\ **cot, cart**	\g\ **go**	\ō\ **bone**	\ü\ **food**	\zh\ **vision**

mesdames *plural of* MADAM *or of* MADAME *or of* MRS.

mesdemoiselles *plural of* MADEMOISELLE

me·seems \mi-'sēmz\ *impersonal verb, past* **me·seemed** \-'sēmd\ *archaic* : it seems to me

mes·en·tery \'mez-ᵊn-ˌter-ē, 'mes-\ *n, pl* **-ter·ies** : membranous tissue or one of the membranes that enclose the organs (as the intestines) making up the guts and connect them to the wall of the abdominal cavity

¹**mesh** \'mesh\ *n* **1** : one of the spaces formed by the threads of a net or the wires of a sieve or screen **2 a** : a loosely woven fabric with evenly spaced holes **b** : ¹NET 1 **3** : an arrangement of elements that are linked together : NETWORK **4** : the coming or fitting together of the teeth of two gears — **meshed** \'mesht\ *adj*

²**mesh** *vb* **1** : to catch in or as if in a mesh : ENTANGLE **2** : to fit together : INTERLOCK ⟨*mesh* gears⟩

mes·mer·ism \'mez-mə-ˌriz-əm *also* 'mes-\ *n* : HYPNOTISM

mes·mer·ize \'mez-mə-ˌrīz *also* 'mes-\ *vb* **-ized; -iz·ing 1** : HYPNOTIZE **2** : FASCINATE 1, SPELLBIND

me·so·derm \'mez-ə-ˌdərm, 'mēz-, 'mēs-, 'mes-\ *n* : the middle layer of cells of an embryonic animal from which most of the muscular, skeletal, and connective tissues develop; *also* : tissue derived from this layer — **me·so·der·mal** \ˌmez-ə-'dər-məl, ˌmēz-, ˌmēs-, ˌmes-\ *adj*

me·so·glea \ˌmez-ə-'glē-ə, ˌmes-\ *n* : a jellylike material between the endoderm and ectoderm of sponges and coelenterates

me·son \'mez-ˌän, 'mes-; 'mā-ˌzän, 'mē-, -ˌsän\ *n* : any of a group of elementary particles that act strongly on one another and are among the products of nuclear collisions

me·so·pause \'mez-ə-ˌpòz, 'mēz-, 'mēs-, 'mes-\ *n* : the upper boundary of the mesosphere at which the temperature of the atmosphere reaches its lowest point

me·so·phyll \'mez-ə-ˌfil, 'mēz-, 'mēs-, 'mes-\ *n* : the tissue of a leaf that lies between the surface layers and contains cells used for storage and carrying on photosynthesis

me·so·sphere \'mez-ə-ˌsfi(ə)r, 'mēz-, 'mēs-, 'mes-\ *n* : a layer of the atmosphere extending from the top of the stratosphere to an altitude of about 50 miles (80 kilometers)

me·so·tho·rax \ˌmez-ə-'thō(ə)r-ˌaks, ˌmēz-, ˌmēs-, ˌmes-, -'thò(ə)r-\ *n* : the middle of the three segments of the thorax of an insect

Me·so·zo·ic \ˌmez-ə-'zō-ik, ˌmēz-, ˌmēs-, ˌmes-\ *adj* : of, relating to, or being an era of geological history between the Paleozoic and Cenozoic eras or the corresponding system of rocks — see GEOLOGIC TIME table — **Mesozoic** *n*

mes·quite \mə-'skēt, me-\ *n* : a thorny deep-rooted tree or shrub of the southwestern U.S. and Mexico that belongs to the legume family, produces pods rich in sugar, and is important as food for livestock; *also* : the wood of the mesquite used especially in grilling food

¹**mess** \'mes\ *n* **1 a** : a quantity of food **b** : a dish of soft food ⟨a *mess* of porridge⟩ **2 a** : a group of people who regularly eat together; *also* : the meal they eat **b** : a place where meals are regularly served to a group : MESS HALL **3** : a state or condition of confusion, disorder, or unpleasantness ⟨left things in a *mess*⟩; *also* : one that is in such a state or condition ⟨his life was a *mess*⟩ **4** : a large quantity or number ⟨a *mess* of problems⟩

mesquite: *1* flower and leaves, *2* pods

²**mess** *vb* **1 a** : to supply with meals **b** : to take meals with a mess **2 a** : to make dirty or untidy : DISARRANGE ⟨don't *mess* up your room⟩ **b** : to do incorrectly ⟨*messed* up the job⟩ **c** : to become confused or

make an error ⟨tried again and *messed* up again⟩ **3** : to interfere with ⟨the storm *messed* up our plans⟩ **4 a** : to work without a serious goal : PUTTER ⟨likes to *mess* around with paints⟩ **b** : to handle or play with something especially carelessly ⟨don't *mess* with the camera⟩ **c** : INTERFERE 2, MEDDLE ⟨don't *mess* with me⟩ **5** : to rough up : MANHANDLE

mes·sage \'mes-ij\ *n* **1** : a communication in writing, in speech, or by signals **2** : a messenger's errand or function **3** : an underlying theme or idea [Middle English *message* "job or function of a messenger," from early French *message* (same meaning), from Latin *missaticum* "something given to a messenger to deliver," from earlier *missus* (past participle of *mittere* "to send, throw") and *-aticum* "action, result" — related to EMIT, MISSION, PROMISE, SUBMISSIVE]

message board *n* : BULLETIN BOARD 2

messeigneurs *plural of* MONSEIGNEUR

mes·sen·ger \'mes-ᵊn-jər\ *n* : one that carries a message or does an errand

messenger RNA *n* : an RNA that carries the code for a particular protein from DNA in the nucleus to a ribosome and that acts as a pattern for the formation of that protein — compare TRANSFER RNA

mess hall *n* : a hall or building (as on an army post) in which mess is served

mes·si·ah \mə-'sī-ə\ *n* **1** *cap* **a** : the expected king and deliverer of the Jews **b** : Jesus Christ regarded as the savior of the world by Christians **2** : a leader of some hope or cause : DELIVERER

messieurs *plural of* MONSIEUR

mess·mate \'mes-ˌmāt\ *n* : a member of a mess (as on a ship)

Messrs. \ˌmes-ərz\ *plural of* MR.

messy \'mes-ē\ *adj* **mess·i·er; -est 1** : marked by confusion, disorder, or dirt : UNTIDY **2** : extremely unpleasant or trying ⟨*messy* lawsuits⟩ — **mess·i·ly** \'mes-ə-lē\ *adv* — **mess·i·ness** \'mes-ē-nəs\ *n*

mes·ti·za \me-'stē-zə\ *n* : a woman who is a mestizo

mes·ti·zo \me-'stē-zō\ *n, pl* **-zos** : a person having mixed European and American Indian ancestors

met *past and past participle of* MEET

met·a·bol·ic \ˌmet-ə-'bäl-ik\ *adj* : of, relating to, or based on metabolism ⟨*metabolic* activity⟩ ⟨a *metabolic* disorder⟩ — **met·a·bol·i·cal·ly** \-i-k(ə-)lē\ *adv*

me·tab·o·lism \mə-'tab-ə-ˌliz-əm\ *n* **1** : the processes essential for life by which the complex substances in the cells of living things are built up or broken down **2** : the processes by which a particular substance (as iodine) is handled in the living body

me·tab·o·lite \mə-'tab-ə-ˌlīt\ *n* **1** : a substance produced by metabolism **2** : a substance essential to a process of metabolism

me·tab·o·lize \mə-'tab-ə-ˌlīz\ *vb* **-lized; -liz·ing** : to break down by metabolism ⟨food is *metabolized* by the body⟩

¹**meta·car·pal** \ˌmet-ə-'kär-pəl\ *adj* : of, relating to, or being the part of the hand or front foot or a bone of this part that is between the carpal bones and the bones of the fingers or toes

²**metacarpal** *n* : a metacarpal bone

met·al \'met-ᵊl\ *n* **1** : any of various substances (as gold, tin, or copper) that have a more or less shiny appearance, are good conductors of electricity and heat, can be melted, and are usually capable of being shaped; *esp* : one that is a chemical element rather than an alloy **2** : METTLE 2 — **metal** *adj*

me·tal·lic \mə-'tal-ik\ *adj* **1** : of, relating to, or being a metal **2** : containing or made of metal **3** : having a harsh or rasping sound ⟨a *metallic* voice⟩

met·al·loid \'met-ᵊl-ˌòid\ *n* : an element that has some characteristics of metals and some of nonmetals — **metalloid** *adj*

met·al·lur·gy \'met-ᵊl-ˌər-jē\ *n* : the science of obtaining metals from their ores and preparing them for use — **met·al·lur·gi·cal** \ˌmet-ᵊl-'ər-ji-kəl\ *adj* — **met·al·lur·gist** \'met-ᵊl-ˌər-jəst\ *n*

met·al·work \'met-ᵊl-ˌwərk\ *n* : the product of metalworking — **met·al·work·er** \-ˌwər-kər\ *n*

met·al·work·ing \'met-ᵊl-ˌwər-kiŋ\ *n* : the act or process of shaping things out of metal

meta·mor·phic \ˌmet-ə-'mȯr-fik\ *adj* : changed into a more compact form by the action of pressure, heat, and water ⟨a *metamorphic* rock⟩ — compare IGNEOUS, SEDIMENTARY 2

meta·mor·phose \ˌmet-ə-'mȯr-ˌfōz, -ˌfōs\ *vb* **-phosed; -phos·ing** : to change or cause to change in form : go through metamorphosis

meta·mor·pho·sis \ˌmet-ə-'mȯr-fə-səs\ *n, pl* **-pho·ses** \-fə-ˌsēz\ **1** : a change of form, structure, or substance especially by witchcraft or magic **2** : an extraordinary change in appearance, character, or circumstances **3** : the process of basic and usually rather sudden change in the form and habits of some animals during transformation from an immature stage (as a tadpole or a caterpillar) to an adult stage (as a frog or a butterfly) — compare COMPLETE METAMORPHOSIS, INCOMPLETE METAMORPHOSIS

meta·phase \'met-ə-ˌfāz\ *n* : the stage of mitosis or meiosis in which the chromosomes are arranged in the center of the dividing cell prior to their separation or splitting and movement to the poles of the cell

met·a·phor \'met-ə-ˌfȯ(ə)r *also* -fər\ *n* : a figure of speech in which a word or phrase meaning one kind of object or idea is used in place of another to suggest a similarity between them (as in *the ship plows the sea*) — compare SIMILE — **met·a·phor·ic** \ˌmet-ə-'fȯr-ik, -'fär-\ *or* **met·a·phor·i·cal** \ˌmet-ə-'fȯr-i-kəl, -'fär-\ *adj* — **met·a·phor·i·cal·ly** \-i-k(ə-)lē\ *adv*

meta·phys·i·cal \ˌmet-ə-'fiz-i-kəl\ *adj* **1** : of, relating to, or based on metaphysics **2** : SUPERNATURAL 1 **3** : difficult to understand : ABSTRACT — **meta·phys·i·cal·ly** \-i-k(ə-)lē\ *adv*

meta·phys·ics \ˌmet-ə-'fiz-iks\ *n* : the part of philosophy concerned with the ultimate causes and basic nature of things [from Latin *Metaphysica*, title given to a work by Aristotle on the subject, from Greek *(ta) meta (ta) physika*, literally, "the (works) after the physical (works)"; so called because this section came after the section on physics and physical nature in a collection of Aristotle's collected writings]

me·tas·ta·sis \mə-'tas-tə-səs\ *n, pl* **-ta·ses** \-ˌsēz\ **1** : the spread of something that produces disease (as cancer cells) from the original location of disease to another part of the body **2** : a growth of a malignant tumor in another part of the body resulting from metastasis

me·tas·ta·size \mə-'tas-tə-ˌsīz\ *vb* : to spread or grow by or as if by metastasis

¹meta·tar·sal \ˌmet-ə-'tär-səl\ *adj* : of, relating to, or being the part of the foot in human beings or of the hind foot in a four-footed animal that is located between the tarsal bones and the toes

²metatarsal *n* : any of the metatarsal bones of which there are five in human beings

meta·tho·rax \ˌmet-ə-'thō(ə)r-ˌaks, -'thȯ(ə)r-\ *n* : the hindmost of the three segments of the thorax of an insect that is next to the abdomen

meta·zo·an \ˌmet-ə-'zō-ən\ *n* : any of the great group of animals with a body composed of cells forming tissues and organs — **metazoan** *adj*

mete \'mēt\ *vb* **met·ed; met·ing** : to distribute in a fair or proper manner ⟨*mete* out rewards⟩

me·te·or \'mēt-ē-ər, -ē-ˌȯ(ə)r\ *n* : one of the small bodies of matter in the solar system observable when it falls into the earth's atmosphere where the heat of friction may cause it to glow brightly for a short time; *also* : the streak of light produced by the passage of a meteor

me·te·or·ic \ˌmēt-ē-'ȯr-ik, -'är-\ *adj* **1** : of or relating to a meteor ⟨a *meteoric* shower⟩ **2** : resembling a meteor in speed or in sudden and temporary brilliance ⟨a *meteoric* rise to fame⟩ — **me·te·or·i·cal·ly** \-i-k(ə-)lē\ *adv*

me·te·or·ite \'mēt-ē-ə-ˌrīt\ *n* : a meteor that reaches the surface of the earth

me·te·or·oid \'mēt-ē-ə-ˌrȯid\ *n* : a meteor revolving around the sun

me·te·o·rol·o·gy \ˌmēt-ē-ə-'räl-ə-jē\ *n* : a science that deals with the atmosphere, weather, and weather forecasting — **me·te·o·ro·log·ic** \ˌmēt-ē-ə-rə-'läj-ik\ *or* **me·te·o·ro·log·i·cal** \-'läj-i-kəl\ *adj* — **me·te·o·rol·o·gist** \-'räl-ə-jəst\ *n*

¹me·ter \'mēt-ər\ *n* **1** : a systematic rhythm in poetry that is usually repeated **2** : the repeated pattern of musical beats in a measure

²meter *n* : the basic unit of length of the metric system equal to about 39.37 inches — see METRIC SYSTEM table

³meter *n* : an instrument for measuring and sometimes recording the amount of something ⟨a gas *meter*⟩

meter–kilogram–second *adj* : of, relating to, or being a system of units based on the meter as the unit of length, the kilogram as the unit of mass, and the second as the unit of time

me·ter·stick \'mēt-ər-ˌstik\ *n* : a measuring stick one meter long that is marked off in centimeters and usually millimeters

meth·a·done \'meth-ə-ˌdōn\ *also* **meth·a·don** \-ˌdän\ *n* : a narcotic drug $C_{21}H_{27}NO$ that is used to replace heroin in the treatment of heroin addiction

meth·am·phet·amine \ˌmeth-am-'fet-ə-ˌmēn\ *n* : a drug derived from amphetamine that is often used illegally as a stimulant of the central nervous system

meth·ane \'meth-ˌān\ *n* : a colorless odorless flammable gas that consists of carbon and hydrogen and is produced by decay of organic matter

meth·a·nol \'meth-ə-ˌnȯl, -ˌnōl\ *n* : a light flammable poisonous liquid alcohol that consists of carbon, hydrogen, and oxygen and is used especially as antifreeze and to dissolve things

meth·i·cil·lin \ˌmeth-ə-'sil-ən\ *n* : a form of penicillin used especially against certain forms of staphylococcus bacteria

me·thinks \mi-'thiŋ(k)s\ *impersonal verb, past* **methought** \-'thȯt\ *archaic* : it seems to me

meth·od \'meth-əd\ *n* **1** : a way, plan, or procedure for doing something **2** : orderly arrangement

me·thod·i·cal \mə-'thäd-i-kəl\ *adj* **1** : marked by or performed or arranged by method or order ⟨a *methodical* search⟩ **2** : being in the habit of following a method : SYSTEMATIC ⟨a *methodical* teacher⟩ — **me·thod·i·cal·ly** \-i-k(ə-)lē\ *adv* — **me·thod·i·cal·ness** \-i-kəl-nəs\ *n*

Meth·od·ist \'meth-əd-əst\ *adj* : of or relating to any of several Protestant denominations following the teachings of John Wesley — **Meth·od·ism** \-ə-ˌdiz-əm\ *n* — **Methodist** *n*

meth·yl \'meth-əl\ *n* : a chemical group consisting of carbon and hydrogen

methyl alcohol *n* : METHANOL

meth·y·lene blue \ˌmeth-ə-ˌlēn-\ *n* : a dye used as a biological stain and to reverse the effects of cyanide poisoning

\ə\ **abut**	\au̇\ **out**	\i\ **tip**	\ȯ\ **saw**	\u̇\ **foot**
\ər\ **further**	\ch\ **chin**	\ī\ **life**	\ȯi\ **coin**	\y\ **yet**
\a\ **mat**	\e\ **pet**	\j\ **job**	\th\ **thin**	\yü\ **few**
\ā\ **take**	\ē\ **easy**	\ŋ\ **sing**	\th\ **this**	\yu̇\ **cure**
\ä\ **cot, cart**	\g\ **go**	\ō\ **bone**	\ü\ **food**	\zh\ **vision**

METRIC SYSTEM[1]

UNIT	ABBREVIATION	EQUIVALENT IN BASE UNIT	APPROXIMATE U.S. EQUIVALENT		
LENGTH					
kilometer	km	1,000 meters	0.62 mile		
hectometer	hm	100 meters	328.08 feet		
dekameter	dam	10 meters	32.81 feet		
meter	m		39.37 inches		
decimeter	dm	0.1 meter	3.94 inches		
centimeter	cm	0.01 meter	0.39 inch		
millimeter	mm	0.001 meter	0.039 inch		
micrometer	μm	0.000001 meter	0.000039 inch		
AREA					
square kilometer	sq km *or* km^2	1,000,000 square meters	0.39 square mile		
hectare	ha	10,000 square meters	2.47 acres		
are	a	100 square meters	119.60 square yards		
square centimeter	sq cm *or* cm^2	0.0001 square meter	0.16 square inch		
VOLUME					
cubic meter	m^3		1.31 cubic yards		
cubic decimeter	dm^3	0.001 cubic meter	61.02 cubic inches		
cubic centimeter	cu cm *or* cm^3 *also* cc	0.000001 cubic meter	0.061 cubic inch		
CAPACITY			*cubic*	*dry*	*liquid*
kiloliter	kl	1,000 liters	1.31 cubic yards	28.38 bushels	264.17 gallons
hectoliter	hl	100 liters	3.53 cubic feet	2.84 bushels	26.42 gallons
dekaliter	dal	10 liters	0.35 cubic foot	1.14 pecks	2.64 gallons
liter	l		61.02 cubic inches	0.91 quart	1.06 quarts
cubic decimeter	dm^3	1 liter	61.02 cubic inches	0.91 quart	1.06 quarts
deciliter	dl	0.1 liter	6.10 cubic inches	0.18 pint	0.21 pint
centiliter	cl	0.01 liter	0.61 cubic inch		0.34 fluid ounce
milliliter	ml	0.001 liter	0.061 cubic inch		0.27 fluid dram
MASS AND WEIGHT					
metric ton	t	1,000,000 grams	1.10 short tons		
kilogram	kg	1,000 grams	2.20 pounds		
hectogram	hg	100 grams	3.53 ounces		
dekagram	dag	10 grams	0.35 ounce		
gram	g		0.035 ounce		
decigram	dg	0.1 gram	1.54 grains		
centigram	cg	0.01 gram	0.15 grain		
milligram	mg	0.001 gram	0.015 grain		

[1]For metric equivalents of U.S. units, see Measures and Weights table.

methyl orange *n* : an alkaline liquid mixture used as a dye to indicate the presence of acid

me·tic·u·lous \mə-'tik-yə-ləs\ *adj* : extremely or overly careful in thinking about or dealing with small details ⟨a *meticulous* researcher⟩ — **me·tic·u·lous·ly** *adv* — **me·tic·u·lous·ness** *n*

me·tre \'mēt-ər\ *chiefly British variant of* METER

met·ric \'me-trik\ *adj* **1** : of, relating to, or based on the metric system **2** : METRICAL 1

met·ri·cal \'me-tri-kəl\ *adj* **1** : of, relating to, or arranged in meter **2** : METRIC 1 — **met·ri·cal·ly** \-k(ə-)lē\ *adv*

met·ri·cize \'me-trə-ˌsīz\ *vb* **-cized; -ciz·ing** : to change into or express in the metric system

metric system *n* : a system of weights and measures based on the meter and on the kilogram

metric ton *n* — see METRIC SYSTEM table

met·ro \'me-trō\ *n, pl* **metros** : SUBWAY 2

met·ro·nome \'me-trə-ˌnōm\ *n* : an instrument that ticks regularly to help a music student play in exact time

me·trop·o·lis \mə-'träp-(ə-)ləs\ *n* **1** : the chief or capital city of a country, state, or region **2** : a large important city

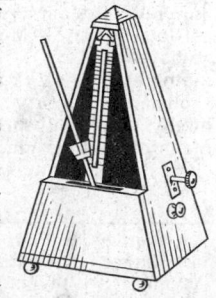

metronome

[1]met·ro·pol·i·tan \ˌme-trə-'päl-ət-ᵊn\ *n* **1** : the head of a church province **2** : one who lives in a metropolis or who has metropolitan manners or customs

[2]metropolitan *adj* **1** : of, relating to, or characteristic of a metropolis **2** : of or relating to a city and the densely populated surrounding areas

met·tle \'met-ᵊl\ *n* **1** : quality of temperament or disposition **2** : strength of spirit **3** : ability to keep going : STAYING POWER — **on one's mettle** : aroused to do one's best

met·tle·some \'met-ᵊl-səm\ *adj* : full of mettle : SPIRITED

[1]mew \'myü\ *n* : [1]GULL; *esp* : a small gull of Eurasia and western North America [Old English *mæw* "gull"]

[2]mew *n* : MEOW [Middle English *mewen* (verb) "meow"; a word imitating the sound of a cat] — **mew** *vb*

[3]mew *n* **1** : a cage for hawks **2** *pl, chiefly British* : stables usually with living quarters built around a court [Middle English *mewe* "a cage for hawks," from early French *mue* (same meaning), from *muer* "to change, molt," from Latin *mutare* "to change"]

mewl \'myü(ə)l\ *vb* : to cry weakly : WHIMPER

Mex·i·can \'mek-si-kən\ *n* **1** : a person born or living in Mexico **2** : a person of Mexican ancestry — **Mexican** *adj*

Mexican bean beetle *n* : a spotted ladybug that feeds on the leaves of beans

Mexican jumping bean *n* : JUMPING BEAN

me·zu·zah *or* **me·zu·za** \mə-'zůz-ə\ *n, pl* **-zahs** *or* **-zas** *or* **-zot** \-,ōt\ : a small scroll of parchment inscribed with two passages from Deuteronomy and the name Shaddai (the Almighty) and placed in a case that is attached to the doorjamb by some Jewish families as a sign and reminder of their faith; *also* : such a scroll and case

mez·za·nine \'mez-ᵊn-,ēn, ,mez-ᵊn-'ēn\ *n* **1** : a story between two main stories of a building often in the form of a balcony **2** : the lowest balcony in a theater or its first few rows

mez·zo for·te \,met-sō-'fôr-,tā, ,med-zō-, -'fôrt-ē\ *adj or adv* : played or sung with medium loudness — used as a direction in music [Italian, from *mezzo* "half, medium" and *forte* "strong"]

mez·zo pia·no \-pē-'än-ō\ *adj or adv* : played or sung with medium softness — used as a direction in music

mez·zo–so·pra·no \,met-sō-sə-'pran-ō, ,med-zō-, -'prän-\ *n* : a woman's voice between that of the soprano and contralto; *also* : a singer having such a voice

mi \mē\ *n* : the third note of the musical scale

mi·as·ma \mī-'az-mə, mē-\ *n, pl* **-mas** *or* **-ma·ta** \-mət-ə\ **1** : a vapor from a swamp formerly believed to cause disease **2** : a harmful influence or atmosphere — **mi·as·mal** \-məl\ *adj* — **mi·as·mat·ic** \,mī-əz-'mat-ik\ *adj*

mi·ca \'mī-kə\ *n* : any of various minerals that contain silicon and can be separated easily into thin often transparent sheets

Mi·cah \'mī-kə\ *n* — see BIBLE table

mice *plural of* MOUSE

Mich·ael·mas \'mik-əl-məs\ *n* : September 29 celebrated as the feast of St. Michael the Archangel

Mi·che·as \'mī-kē-əs, mī-'kē-\ *n* : MICAH

micr- *or* **micro-** *combining form* **1 a** : small : minute ⟨*microfilm*⟩ **b** : making a sound, image, or signal larger or stronger ⟨*microphone*⟩ **2** : one millionth part of a (specified) unit ⟨*microsecond*⟩ [derived from Greek *mikros* "small, short"]

mi·cro \'mī-krō\ *adj* : MICROSCOPIC 3

mi·crobe \'mī-,krōb\ *n* : MICROORGANISM, GERM — **mi·cro·bi·al** \mī-'krō-bē-əl\ *also* **mi·cro·bic** \-bik\ *adj*

mi·cro·bi·ol·o·gist \,mī-krō-bī-'äl-ə-jəst\ *n* : a specialist in microbiology

mi·cro·bi·ol·o·gy \,mī-krō-bī-'äl-ə-jē\ *n* : a branch of biology concerned especially with microscopic forms of life (as bacteria, protozoans, and viruses) — **mi·cro·bi·o·log·i·cal** \'mī-krō-,bī-ə-'läj-i-kəl\ *also* **mi·cro·bi·o·log·ic** \-'läj-ik\ *adj* — **mi·cro·bi·o·log·i·cal·ly** \-i-k(ə-)lē\ *adv*

mi·cro·blog·ging \'mī-krō-,blŏ-giŋ, -,blä-\ *n* : blogging done with severe space or size constraints typically by posting frequent brief messages about personal activities — **mi·cro·blog** \-,blŏg, -,bläg\ *n*

mi·cro·chip \'mī-krō-,chip\ *n* : INTEGRATED CIRCUIT

mi·cro·coc·cus \,mī-krō-'käk-əs\ *n* : a small bacterium that is shaped like a ball

mi·cro·com·put·er \'mī-krō-kəm-,pyüt-ər\ *n* **1** : PERSONAL COMPUTER **2** : MICROPROCESSOR

mi·cro·cosm \'mī-krə-,käz-əm\ *n* : an individual or community thought of as a miniature universe or a world in itself

mi·cro·fiber \'mī-krō-,fī-bər\ *n* : a thin soft polyester fiber

mi·cro·fiche \'mī-krō-,fēsh, -,fish\ *n* : a sheet of microfilm containing rows of images usually of printed pages

mi·cro·film \'mī-krə-,film\ *n* : a film carrying a photographic record (as of printing or a drawing) on a reduced scale — **microfilm** *vb*

mi·cro·grav·i·ty \,mī-krə-'grav-ət-ē\ *n* : the condition of being weightless or of the near absence of gravity

mi·cro·me·te·or·ite \,mī-krō-'mēt-ē-ə-,rīt\ *n* : a very small particle in space

¹mi·crom·e·ter \mī-'kräm-ət-ər\ *n* **1** : an instrument used with a telescope or microscope for measuring very small distances **2** : MICROMETER CALIPER — **mi·crom·e·try** \-'kräm-ə-trē\ *n*

²mi·cro·me·ter \'mī-krō-,mēt-ər\ *n* : a unit of length equal to one millionth of a meter

micrometer caliper *n* : a caliper having a spindle moved by a finely threaded screw for making precise measurements

mi·cro·min·ia·ture \,mī-krō-'min-ē-ə-,chù(ə)r, -'min-i-,chů(ə)r, -'min-yə-, -chər\ *adj* : reduced to or produced in a very small size and especially in a size smaller than one considered miniature

mi·cron \'mī-,krän\ *n* : ²MICROMETER

mi·cro·or·gan·ism \,mī-krō-'ôr-gə-,niz-əm\ *n* : an organism (as a bacterium) of microscopic or less than microscopic size

mi·cro·phone \'mī-krə-,fōn\ *n* : an instrument in which sound energy is changed into electrical energy usually for the purpose of transmitting or recording sound (as speech or music)

mi·cro·pho·to·graph \,mī-krō-'fōt-ə-,graf\ *n* : PHOTOMICROGRAPH

mi·cro·pro·ces·sor \,mī-krō-'präs-,es-ər, -'prōs-\ *n* : a cpu contained on an integrated-circuit chip

mi·cro·scope \'mī-krə-,skōp\ *n* **1** : an optical instrument consisting of a lens or a combination of lenses for making enlarged or magnified images of minute objects **2** : an instrument using radiation other than light for making enlarged images of very small objects

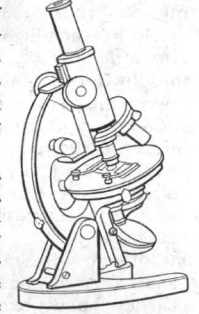

microscope 1

mi·cro·scop·ic \,mī-krə-'skäp-ik\ *also* **mi·cro·scop·i·cal** \-'skäp-i-kəl\ *adj* **1** : of, relating to, or conducted with the microscope or microscopy ⟨a *microscopic* examination⟩ **2** : resembling a microscope : able to see very tiny objects ⟨some insects have *microscopic* vision⟩ **3** : able to be seen only through a microscope : very small ⟨a *microscopic* plant⟩ — **mi·cro·scop·i·cal·ly** \-i-k(ə-)lē\ *adv*

mi·cros·co·pist \mī-'kräs-kə-pəst\ *n* : a person specializing in microscopy

mi·cros·co·py \mī-'kräs-kə-pē\ *n* : the use of the microscope : investigation with the microscope

mi·cro·sec·ond \,mī-krō-'sek-ənd, -ənt\ *n* : one millionth of a second

¹mi·cro·wave \'mī-krō-,wāv\ *n* **1** : a radio wave between one millimeter and one meter in wavelength **2** : MICROWAVE OVEN

²microwave *vb* : to cook or heat in a microwave oven — **mi·cro·wav·able** *or* **mi·cro·wave·able** \,mī-krə-'wā-və-bəl\ *adj*

microwave oven *n* : an oven in which food is cooked by the heat produced from microwave penetration of the food

¹mid \'mid\ *adj* **1** : being the part in the middle or midst ⟨in *mid* ocean⟩ ⟨*mid*-August⟩ **2** : occupying a middle position ⟨the *mid* finger⟩

²mid \(,)mid\ *prep* : AMID

mid·af·ter·noon \'mid-,af-tər-'nün\ *n* : the middle part of the afternoon — **midafternoon** *adj*

mid·air \'mid-'a(ə)r, -'e(ə)r\ *n* : a point or region in the air not very close to the ground ⟨planes collided in *midair*⟩

mid·brain \'mid-,brān\ *n* : the middle division of the three primary divisions of the developing brain of a vertebrate animal or the parts of the adult brain that develop from it that contains the optic lobes and is situated between the forebrain and the hindbrain

mid·day \'mid-,dā, -'dā\ *n* : the middle of the day — **midday** *adj*

mid·den \'mid-ᵊn\ *n* : a refuse heap; *esp* : a mound (as of shells and bones) marking the place where prehistoric humans once lived

¹mid·dle \'mid-ᵊl\ *adj* **1** : equally distant from the ends or sides **2** : being at neither extreme : INTERMEDIATE ⟨of *middle* size⟩ **3** *cap* : constituting an intermediate division or period ⟨*Middle* Paleozoic⟩

²middle *n* **1** : a middle part, point, or position : CENTER **2** : WAIST 1a **3** : the position of being among or in the midst of something ⟨in the *middle* of the crowd⟩ — **middle of nowhere** : an extremely secluded and out-of-the-way place ⟨ran out of gas in the *middle of nowhere*⟩

middle age *n* : the period of life from about 45 to about 64 — **mid·dle–aged** \,mid-ᵊl-'ājd\ *adj*

Middle Ages *n pl* : the period of European history from about A.D. 500 to about 1500

mid·dle·brow \'mid-ᵊl-,braú\ *n* : a person who is moderately but not highly educated and refined — **middlebrow** *adj*

middle C *n* : a note that is printed on a line midway between the treble staff and the bass staff in written music; *also* : the tone made in playing this note

middle class *n* : a social class that occupies a position between the upper class and the lower class and is composed mainly of business and professional people, government officials, farmers, and skilled workers — **middle–class** *adj*

middle ear *n* : a small cavity that is lined with membrane and separated from the outer ear by the eardrum and that carries sound waves from the eardrum to the inner ear through a chain of tiny bones

Middle English *n* : the English language of the 12th to 15th centuries

middle finger *n* : the third finger of the hand if the thumb is counted as the first

middle ground *n* : a position midway between extreme or opposing points of view, choices, or objectives

mid·dle·man \'mid-ᵊl-,man\ *n* : GO-BETWEEN; *esp* : a dealer between the producer of goods and the consumer

mid·dle·most \'mid-ᵊl-,mōst\ *adj* : MIDMOST

middle name *n* **1** : a name between one's first name and last name **2** : a term that names a notable quality of a person ⟨patience is her *middle name*⟩

mid·dle–of–the–road \,mid-ᵊl-əv-thə-'rōd\ *adj* : standing for or following a course of action midway between extremes; *esp* : being neither liberal nor conservative in politics — **mid·dle–of–the–road·er** \-'rōd-ər\ *n*

Middle Passage *n* : the forced voyage of enslaved Africans across the Atlantic Ocean to the Americas

middle school *n* : a school usually including grades 5 to 8 or 6 to 8

mid·dle·weight \'mid-ᵊl-,wāt\ *n* : one of average weight; *esp* : a boxer in a weight division having an upper limit of about 160 pounds

¹mid·dling \'mid-liŋ, -lən\ *adj* : of medium size, degree, or quality — **middling** *adv*

²middling *n* **1** : any of various products of medium quality or size **2** *pl* : a product produced by milling grain; *esp* : a product of wheat milling that is used in animal feeds

mid·dy \'mid-ē\ *n, pl* **middies** **1** : MIDSHIPMAN **2** : a loose blouse for women and children with a wide collar

midge \'mij\ *n* : a very small fly : GNAT

midg·et \'mij-ət\ *n* **1** : something much smaller than usual **2** *often offensive* : a very small person and especially one who is well-proportioned — **midget** *adj*

mid·land \'mid-lənd, -,land\ *n* : the central region of a country — **midland** *adj*

mid·life \'mid-'līf\ *n* : MIDDLE AGE — **midlife** *adj*

middy 2

mid·line \'mid-,līn\ *n* : a line through the middle of something; *esp* : a line through a body or one of its parts that lies in a plane dividing it into halves that are mirror images of each other

mid·most \'mid-,mōst\ *adj* **1** : being in or near the exact middle **2** : INNERMOST 2 — **midmost** *adv or n*

mid·night \'mid-,nīt\ *n* : 12 o'clock at night — **midnight** *adj*

mid·point \'mid-,pöint\ *n* : a point at or near the center or middle

mid·rib \'mid-,rib\ *n* : the central vein or ridge of a leaf or a leaflike part

mid·riff \'mid-,rif\ *n* : the middle region of the human body

mid·ship·man \'mid-,ship-mən, (')mid-'ship-\ *n* : a student naval officer

mid·ships \'mid-,ships\ *adv* : AMIDSHIPS

mid·size \'mid-,sīz\ *adj* : of intermediate size ⟨a *midsize* car⟩

¹midst \'midst\ *n* **1** : the middle part or period ⟨in the *midst* of the forest⟩ **2** : a condition of being near or among the members of a group ⟨a traitor in our *midst*⟩ **3** : the condition of being surrounded ⟨in the *midst* of our troubles⟩

²midst \(,)midst\ *prep* : AMID

mid·stream \'mid-'strēm\ *n* : the middle of a stream

mid·sum·mer \'mid-'səm-ər\ *n* **1** : the middle of summer **2** : the summer solstice

¹mid·way \'mid-,wā, -'wā\ *adv or adj* : in the middle of the way or distance : HALFWAY

²mid·way \'mid-,wā\ *n* : an avenue at a fair, carnival, or amusement park for food stands, games of chance or skill, and amusement rides

mid·week \'mid-,wēk\ *n* : the middle of the week — **midweek** *adj*

mid·wife \'mid-,wīf\ *n* : a woman who helps other women in childbirth

mid·wife·ry \,mid-'wif-(ə-)rē, -'wīf-; 'mid-,wīf-\ *n* : the art or act of assisting at childbirth; *also* : OBSTETRICS

mid·win·ter \'mid-'wint-ər\ *n* **1** : the middle of winter **2** : the winter solstice

mid·year \'mid-,yi(ə)r\ *n* **1** : the middle of a calendar year or academic year **2** : a midyear examination — **midyear** *adj*

mien \'mēn\ *n* : look, appearance, or manner especially as showing mood or personality ⟨a kindly *mien*⟩

¹might \(')mīt\ *past of* MAY — used as a helping verb to express permission ⟨asked if I *might* leave⟩, possibility ⟨we *might* go, if asked⟩ ⟨thought you *might* try⟩, or a present condition that does not in fact exist ⟨if you were older, you *might* understand⟩ [Old English *meahte, mihte* (an auxiliary verb)]

²might \'mīt\ *n* : power to do something : FORCE ⟨with all my *might*⟩ [Old English *miht* "power, might"]

might·i·ly \'mīt-ᵊl-ē\ *adv* **1** : in a mighty manner : VIGOR-

OUSLY ⟨fought *mightily*⟩ **2** : very much ⟨contributed *mightily* to the cause⟩

mightn't \'mīt-ᵊnt\ : might not

¹**mighty** \'mīt-ē\ *adj* **might·i·er; -est 1** : having might : POWERFUL, STRONG ⟨a *mighty* army⟩ **2** : done by might : showing great power ⟨*mighty* deeds⟩ **3** : very great ⟨a *mighty* famine⟩ — **might·i·ness** *n*

²**mighty** *adv* : ²VERY 1, EXTREMELY ⟨*mighty* proud of you⟩

mi·graine \'mī-ˌgrān\ *n* : a severe headache often restricted to one side of the head and accompanied by nausea and vomiting

mi·grant \'mī-grənt\ *n* : a person, animal, or plant that migrates — **migrant** *adj*

mi·grate \'mī-ˌgrāt\ *vb* **mi·grat·ed; mi·grat·ing 1** : to move from one country, place, or locality to another **2** : to pass from one region or climate to another usually on a regular schedule for feeding or breeding **3** : to change position or location in a living thing or substance ⟨parasitic worms *migrating* from the lungs to the liver⟩

mi·gra·tion \mī-'grā-shən\ *n* **1** : the act or an instance of migrating **2** : a group of individuals that are migrating

mi·gra·to·ry \'mī-grə-ˌtōr-ē, -ˌtȯr-\ *adj* : having a way of life that includes making migrations ⟨*migratory* workers⟩

mi·ka·do \mə-'käd-ō\ *n, pl* **-dos** : an emperor of Japan

mike \'mīk\ *n* : MICROPHONE

mil \'mil\ *adj* : a unit of length equal to ¹⁄₁₀₀₀ inch (about .025 millimeter) used especially in measuring thickness

milch \'milk, 'milch, 'milks\ *adj* : ³MILK

mild \'mī(ə)ld\ *adj* **1** : gentle in nature or behavior ⟨a *mild* person⟩ **2 a** : not strong in action or effect ⟨a *mild* drug⟩ **b** : not sharp, spicy, or bitter ⟨a *mild* cheese⟩ **3** : not severe : TEMPERATE **5** ⟨*mild* weather⟩ — **mild·ly** \'mī(ə)l-(d)lē\ *adv* — **mild·ness** \'mī(ə)l(d)-nəs\ *n*

¹**mil·dew** \'mil-ˌd(y)ü\ *n* : a usually whitish growth produced on decaying material or living plants by fungi; *also* : a fungus producing mildew — **mil·dewy** \-ˌd(y)ü-ē\ *adj*

²**mildew** *vb* : to affect with or become affected with mildew

mile \'mī(ə)l\ *n* **1** : a unit of measure equal to 5280 feet (about 1609 meters) — called also *statute mile;* see MEASURE table **2** : NAUTICAL MILE

mile·age \'mī-lij\ *n* **1** : an allowance for traveling expenses at a certain rate per mile **2** : distance or distance covered in miles **3** : the number of miles that something (as a tire) will travel before wearing out **4** : the average number of miles a vehicle will travel on a gallon of gasoline

mile·post \'mī(ə)l-ˌpōst\ *n* : a post indicating the distance in miles to a stated place

mil·er \'mī-lər\ *n* : one that competes in races a mile long

mile·stone \'mī(ə)l-ˌstōn\ *n* **1** : a milepost made of stone **2** : an important point in progress or development

mi·lieu \mēl-'yə(r), -'yü; 'mēl-ˌyü\ *n* : SURROUNDINGS, SETTING

mil·i·tan·cy \'mil-ə-tən-sē\ *n* : the quality or state of being militant

mil·i·tant \'mil-ə-tənt\ *adj* **1** : being at war **2** : aggressively active especially in a cause ⟨*militant* protesters⟩ — **militant** *n* — **mil·i·tant·ly** *adv* — **mil·i·tant·ness** *n*

mil·i·tari·ly \ˌmil-ə-tə-'ter-ə-lē\ *adv* **1** : in a military manner **2** : from a military standpoint

mil·i·ta·rism \'mil-ə-tə-ˌriz-əm\ *n* **1** : control or rule by a military class **2** : extreme admiration and praise of military virtues and ideals **3** : a policy of aggressive military readiness — **mil·i·ta·rist** \-rəst\ *n* — **mil·i·ta·ris·tic** \ˌmil-ə-tə-'ris-tik\ *adj*

milestone 1

mil·i·ta·rize \'mil-ə-tə-ˌrīz\ *vb* **-rized; -riz·ing 1** : to equip with military forces and defenses **2** : to give a military character to — **mil·i·ta·ri·za·tion** \ˌmil-ə-t(ə-)rə-'zā-shən\ *n*

¹**mil·i·tary** \'mil-ə-ˌter-ē\ *adj* **1** : of, relating to, or characteristic of soldiers, arms, or war ⟨*military* discipline⟩ **2** : carried on or supported by armed force ⟨a *military* government⟩ **3** : of or relating to the army ⟨*military* and naval affairs⟩

²**military** *n, pl* **military 1** : ARMED FORCES **2** : military persons; *esp* : army officers

military police *n* : a branch of an army that exercises guard and police functions

mil·i·tate \'mil-ə-ˌtāt\ *vb* **-tat·ed; -tat·ing** : to have weight or effect : OPERATE ⟨factors *militating* against success⟩

mi·li·tia \mə-'lish-ə\ *n* : a body of citizens with some military training who are called to active duty only in an emergency

mi·li·tia·man \mə-'lish-ə-mən\ *n* : a member of a militia

¹**milk** \'milk\ *n* **1** : a whitish liquid secreted by the mammary glands of female mammals as food for their young; *esp* : cow's milk used as food by human beings **2** : a liquid (as the juice of a coconut) like milk

²**milk** *vb* **1** : to draw milk from the breasts or udder of (as by pressing or sucking) ⟨*milk* a cow⟩ **2** : to draw or yield milk ⟨return in time for *milking*⟩ **3** : to draw something from as if by milking — **milk·er** *n*

³**milk** *adj* : giving milk; *esp* : bred for milk production ⟨a *milk* cow⟩

milk chocolate *n* : chocolate containing ground cacao beans, cocoa butter, and milk from which no solids (as of sugar or fat) have been removed

milk·maid \'milk-ˌmād\ *n* : DAIRYMAID

milk·man \-ˌman, -mən\ *n* : a person who sells or delivers milk

milk of magnesia : a milky white liquid preparation of magnesium hydroxide in water used as a laxative and antacid

milk shake *n* : a thoroughly shaken or blended drink made of milk, a flavoring syrup, and often ice cream

milk snake *n* : a common harmless gray or tan snake with black-bordered brown blotches and an arrow-shaped spot on the head; *also* : KING SNAKE

milk sugar *n* : LACTOSE

milk tooth *n* : one of the first temporary teeth of a young mammal that in human beings number 20 — called also *baby tooth, deciduous tooth*

milk·weed \'mil-ˌkwēd\ *n* : any of various herbs with milky juice and flowers usually in dense clusters

milky \'mil-kē\ *adj* **milk·i·er; -est 1** : resembling milk especially in color **2** : consisting of or containing milk — **milk·i·ness** *n*

Milky Way *n* **1** : a broad band of light that stretches across the sky and is caused by the light of a very great number of faint stars **2** : MILKY WAY GALAXY

Milky Way galaxy *n* : the galaxy of which the solar system is a part and which contains the stars that create the light of the Milky Way

milkweed

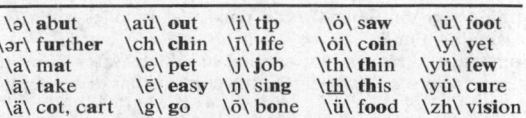

\ə\ **abut**	\au̇\ **out**	\i\ **tip**	\ȯ\ **saw**	\u̇\ **foot**
\ᵊr\ **further**	\ch\ **chin**	\ī\ **life**	\ȯi\ **coin**	\y\ **yet**
\a\ **mat**	\e\ **pet**	\j\ **job**	\th\ **thin**	\yü\ **few**
\ā\ **take**	\ē\ **easy**	\ŋ\ **sing**	\th\ **this**	\yu̇\ **cure**
\ä\ **cot, cart**	\g\ **go**	\ō\ **bone**	\ü\ **food**	\zh\ **vision**

¹mill \'mil\ *n* **1** : a building with machinery for grinding grain into flour **2** : a machine used in treating (as by grinding, crushing, stamping, cutting, or finishing) raw material **3** : FACTORY [Old English *mylen* "mill" from Latin *molina* (same meaning), derived from earlier *mola* "mill, millstone" — related to MOLAR; see *Word History* at MOLAR]

²mill *vb* **1** : to process in a mill (as by grinding into flour, meal, or powder or by shaping with a cutter) **2** : to give a raised rim or a grooved edge to ⟨*mill* a coin⟩ **3** : to move about in a disorderly mass ⟨people were *milling* about the entrance to the theater⟩

³mill *n* : one tenth of a cent [from Latin *mille* "thousand"; so called because it is one one-thousandth of a dollar]

mill·dam \'mil-ˌdam\ *n* **1** : the dam of a millpond **2** : MILLPOND

mil·len·ni·um \mə-'len-ē-əm\ *n, pl* **-nia** \-ē-ə\ *or* **-ni·ums** **1 a** : a period of 1000 years **b** : a 1000th anniversary or its celebration **2** : a period of great happiness — **mil·len·ni·al** \-ē-əl\ *adj*

mill·er \'mil-ər\ *n* **1** : a person who operates a mill; *esp* : a person who grinds grain into flour **2** : any of various moths whose wings have scales like powdery dust

mil·let \'mil-ət\ *n* **1** : a grass cultivated for its small shiny whitish seeds used as human and bird food and sometimes grown for hay **2** : the seed of a millet

milli- *combining form* : thousandth ⟨*milli*meter⟩ [derived from Latin *mille* "thousand"]

mil·li·amp \'mil-ē-ˌamp\ *n* : MILLIAMPERE

mil·li·am·pere \ˌmil-ē-'am-ˌpi(ə)r\ *n* : one thousandth of an ampere

mil·liard \'mil-ˌyärd, 'mil-ē-ˌärd\ *n, British* : a thousand millions — see NUMBER table

mil·li·bar \'mil-ə-ˌbär\ *n* : a unit used in measuring atmospheric pressure equal to $\frac{1}{1000}$ bar

mil·li·gram \'mil-ə-ˌgram\ *n* : a weight equal to $\frac{1}{1000}$ gram — see METRIC SYSTEM table

mil·li·li·ter \'mil-ə-ˌlēt-ər\ *n* : a measure of capacity equal to $\frac{1}{1000}$ liter — see METRIC SYSTEM table

mil·li·me·ter \'mil-ə-ˌmēt-ər\ *n* : a measure of length equal to $\frac{1}{1000}$ meter — see METRIC SYSTEM table

mil·li·ner \'mil-ə-nər\ *n* : a person who designs, makes, trims, or sells women's hats

mil·li·nery \'mil-ə-ˌner-ē\ *n* **1** : women's hats **2** : the business or work of a milliner

mil·lion \'mil-yən\ *n, pl* **millions** *or* **million 1** — see NUMBER table **2** : a very great number ⟨*millions* of mosquitoes⟩ — **million** *adj* — **mil·lionth** \-yən(t)th\ *adj or n*

mil·lion·aire \ˌmil-yə-'na(ə)r, -'ne(ə)r, 'mil-yə-ˌna(ə)r, -ˌne(ə)r\ *n* : one whose wealth is estimated at a million or more (as of dollars)

mil·li·pede \'mil-ə-ˌpēd\ *n* : any of a class of arthropods having a long segmented body with a hard covering, two pairs of legs on most segments, and unlike the related centipedes no poison fangs [from

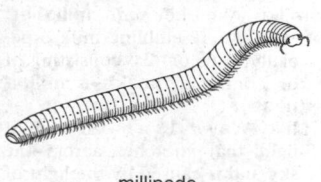

millipede

Latin *millepeda* "a small crawling animal," literally "a thousand-footed animal," from *mille* "thousand" and *ped-, pes* "foot"]

mil·li·sec·ond \'mil-ə-ˌsek-ənd *also* -ənt\ *n* : one thousandth of a second

mill·pond \'mil-ˌpänd\ *n* : a pond that supplies water for running a mill

mill·race \-ˌrās\ *n* **1** : a canal in which water flows to and from a mill wheel **2** : the current that drives a mill wheel

mill·stone \-ˌstōn\ *n* **1** : either of two circular stones used for grinding a substance (as grain) **2** : a heavy burden

mill·stream \-ˌstrēm\ *n* **1** : a stream whose flow is used to run a mill **2** : the stream in a millrace

mill wheel *n* : a waterwheel that drives a mill

mill·wright \'mil-ˌrīt\ *n* : one who builds mills or sets up their machinery

milt \'milt\ *n* : the sperm-containing liquid of a male fish

¹mime \'mīm, 'mēm\ *n* **1 a** : an actor in a mime **b** : a person who practices mime **2** : MIMIC **3** : an ancient play or skit representing scenes from life usually in a ridiculous manner **4** : the art of showing a character or telling a story by body movements

²mime *vb* **mimed; mim·ing 1** : to act in a mime **2** : to imitate closely : MIMIC **3** : to act out in the manner of a mime

mim·eo·graph \'mim-ē-ə-ˌgraf\ *n* : a machine for making copies of typewritten or written matter using a stencil — **mimeograph** *vb*

mi·met·ic \mə-'met-ik, mī-\ *adj* : relating to, characterized by, or exhibiting mimicry ⟨*mimetic* coloring of a butterfly⟩

¹mim·ic \'mim-ik\ *n* **1** : ¹MIME 1 **2** : one that mimics

²mimic *adj* **1** : IMITATIVE 2 **2** : ²IMITATION, MOCK

³mimic *vb* **mim·icked** \'mim-ikt\; **mim·ick·ing 1** : to imitate closely **2** : to make fun of by imitating **3** : to resemble by biological mimicry ⟨an insect that *mimics* a leaf⟩ **synonyms** see IMITATE

mim·ic·ry \'mim-i-krē\ *n, pl* **-ries 1** : the action, art, or an instance of mimicking **2** : a resemblance of one living thing to another or to natural objects among which it lives that gives it an advantage (as concealment or protection from predators)

mi·mo·sa \mə-'mō-sə, mī-, -zə\ *n* : any of a genus of trees, shrubs, and herbs of the legume family that are found in warm regions and have small white or pink flowers in ball-shaped heads

min·a·ret \ˌmin-ə-'ret, 'min-ə-ˌret\ *n* : a tall slender tower of a mosque with a balcony from which the people are called to prayer

¹mince \'min(t)s\ *vb* **minced; minc·ing 1** : to cut into very small pieces **2** : to act, walk, or speak in an unnaturally dainty way ⟨*mince* no words⟩ — **minc·ing·ly** \'min(t)-siŋ-lē\ *adv*

²mince *n* : small bits into which something is chopped; *esp* : MINCEMEAT

mince·meat \'min(t)-ˌsmēt\ *n* **1** : minced meat **2** : a finely chopped mixture (as of raisins, apples, and spices) with or without meat

¹mind \'mīnd\ *n* **1** : the state of remembering or of being remembered : MEMORY, RECOLLECTION ⟨call to *mind*⟩ **2** : the part of a person that feels, perceives, thinks, wills, and especially reasons **3** : INTENTION 1, DESIRE ⟨changed my *mind*⟩ **4** : the normal or healthy condition of the mental abilities ⟨lose one's *mind*⟩ **5** : one's view or opinion about something : VIEW ⟨speak your *mind*⟩

²mind *vb* **1** *chiefly dialect* : REMEMBER 1 **2** : to pay attention to : HEED ⟨*mind* what you're doing⟩ ⟨*mind* your own business⟩ **3** : OBEY 1a ⟨*mind* one's parents⟩ **4** : to be bothered by ⟨never *mind* your mistake⟩ ⟨*minds* the cold⟩ **5** : to be careful about : watch out for ⟨*mind* the broken glass⟩ **6** : to take charge of ⟨*minding* the children⟩

mind·ed \'mīn-dəd\ *adj* **1** : having a specified kind of mind ⟨narrow-*minded*⟩ **2** : greatly interested in something specified ⟨bargain-*minded* customers⟩

mind·ful \'mīn(d)-fəl\ *adj* : keeping in mind : AWARE ⟨*mindful* of the time⟩ — **mind·ful·ly** \-fə-lē\ *adv*

mind·less \'mīn-(d)ləs\ *adj* **1 a** : lacking the ability to think, feel, or respond ⟨a *mindless* killer⟩ **b** : showing no use of the intelligence ⟨*mindless* violence⟩ **2** : not mindful : HEEDLESS ⟨*mindless* of danger⟩ — **mind·less·ly** *adv* — **mind·less·ness** *n*

¹**mine** \(ʹ)mīn\ *adj, archaic* : MY — used before a word beginning with a vowel or *h* or after a noun [Middle English *min* "my," from Old English *mīn*]

²**mine** \ʹmīn\ *pron* : my one : my ones

³**mine** \ʹmīn\ *n* **1** : a pit or tunnel from which minerals (as coal, gold, or diamonds) are **2** : a deposit of ore **3** : an underground passage dug beneath an enemy position **4** : an explosive device placed in the ground or water and set to explode when disturbed **5** : a rich source ⟨a *mine* of information⟩ [Middle English *mine* "a pit or tunnel for digging out coal, gold, or diamonds," from early French *mine* (same meaning)]

⁴**mine** \ʹmīn\ *vb* **mined; min·ing 1** : to dig or form mines under a place **2** : to obtain from a mine ⟨*mine* coal⟩ **3** : to lay military mines in or under ⟨*mine* a harbor⟩ **4** : to work in a mine — **min·er** *n*

¹**min·er·al** \ʹmin-(ə-)rəl\ *n* **1** : a solid chemical element or compound (as diamond or quartz) that occurs naturally in the form of crystals and results from inorganic processes **2** : a naturally occurring substance (as ore, petroleum, or water) obtained usually from the ground

²**mineral** *adj* **1** : of, relating to, or having the characteristics of a mineral : INORGANIC **2** : containing mineral salts or gases ⟨*mineral* water⟩

mineral kingdom *n* : a basic group of natural objects that includes inorganic objects — compare ANIMAL KINGDOM, PLANT KINGDOM

min·er·al·o·gy \ˌmin-ə-ʹräl-ə-jē, -ʹral-\ *n* : a science dealing with the characteristics and classification of minerals — **min·er·al·og·i·cal** \ˌmin-(ə-)rə-ʹläj-i-kəl\ *adj* — **min·er·al·og·i·cal·ly** \-ʹläj-i-k(ə-)lē\ *adv* — **min·er·al·o·gist** \ˌmin-ə-ʹräl-ə-jəst, -ʹral-\ *n*

mineral oil *n* : an oil (as petroleum) of mineral origin; *esp* : a purified petroleum oil having no color, odor, or taste that is used especially as a laxative

mineral water *n* : water containing mineral salts (as of calcium) or gases (as carbon dioxide) which are present naturally or added artificially

min·e·stro·ne \ˌmin-ə-ʹstrō-nē, -ʹstrōn\ *n* : a thick vegetable soup usually made with dried beans and macaroni

mine·sweep·er \ʹmīn-ˌswē-pər\ *n* : a warship for removing or destroying mines

min·gle \ʹmiŋ-gəl\ *vb* **min·gled; min·gling** \-g(ə-)liŋ\ **1** : to bring or combine together or with something else ⟨*mingled* fact with fiction⟩ **2** : to come in contact : ASSOCIATE ⟨*mingles* with all sorts of people⟩ **3** : to move about (as at a party) ⟨*mingled* with the guests⟩ **synonyms** see MIX

mini \ʹmin-ē\ *n* : something small of its kind: as **a** : MINISKIRT **b** : MINICOMPUTER

mini- *combining form* : very small or short : MINIATURE ⟨*mini*bike⟩ ⟨*mini*skirt⟩ [derived by shortening from *miniature*]

¹**min·ia·ture** \ʹmin-ē-ə-ˌchủ(ə)r, ʹmin-i-ˌchủ(ə)r, ʹmin-yə-, -chər\ *n* **1** : something much smaller than the usual size; *esp* : a copy on a much reduced scale **2** : a very small portrait or painting (as on ivory) **3** : the art of painting miniatures [from Italian *miniatura* "a fancy big letter or small picture used to decorate a page of a book copied by hand," derived from Latin *miniare* "to color with red pigment"; so called because the first fancy letters on books were done in red to stand out from the black ink of the rest of the page] — **min·ia·tur·ist** \-ˌchủr-əst, -chər-\ *n*

²**miniature** *adj* : very small : represented on a small scale ⟨collects *miniature* books⟩

min·ia·tur·ize \ʹmin-ē-ə-chə-ˌrīz, ʹmin-i-chə-, ʹmin-yə-chə-\ *vb* **-ized; -iz·ing** : to design or construct in small size — **min·ia·tur·i·za·tion** \ˌmin-ē-ə-ˌchủr-ə-ʹzā-shən, ˌmin-i-, ˌmin-yə-, -chər-\ *n*

mini·bike \ʹmin-i-ˌbīk\ *n* : a small one-passenger motorcycle having a low frame and raised handlebars

mini·bus \ʹmin-i-ˌbəs\ *n* : a small bus

mini·com·put·er \ˌmin-i-kəm-ʹpyüt-ər\ *n* : a small computer that is between a mainframe and a personal computer in size and speed

mini·course \ʹmin-ē-ˌkō(ə)rs, -ˌkȯ(ə)rs\ *n* : a short course of study usually lasting less than a semester

min·im \ʹmin-əm\ *n* — see MEASURE table

min·i·mal \ʹmin-ə-məl\ *adj* : relating to or being a minimum : LEAST — **min·i·mal·ly** \-mə-lē\ *adv*

min·i·mize \ʹmin-ə-ˌmīz\ *vb* **-mized; -miz·ing 1** : to make as small as possible ⟨*minimize* the chance of error⟩ **2 a** : to place a low estimate on ⟨*minimized* their losses⟩ **b** : to make (something) seem little or unimportant : BELITTLE ⟨*minimized* their opponent's victory⟩ **3** : to replace (a window) on a computer display with a small button or icon which will restore the window when selected

min·i·mum \ʹmin-ə-məm\ *n, pl* **-i·ma** \-ə-mə\ *or* **-i·mums 1** : the least quantity possible or allowable **2** : the lowest degree or amount reached or recorded — **minimum** *adj*

minimum wage *n* : a wage fixed (as by law) as the least that may be paid to employed persons

min·ing \ʹmī-niŋ\ *n* : the process or business of working mines

min·ion \ʹmin-yən\ *n* **1** : a person who obediently serves or works for a usually powerful person or organization **2** : ¹FAVORITE 1

mini·skirt \ʹmin-i-ˌskərt\ *n* : a woman's very short skirt

¹**min·is·ter** \ʹmin-ə-stər\ *n* **1 a** : one who performs religious ceremonies in church services **b** : a member of the clergy of a Protestant church **2** : a high official who heads a department of the government **3** : a government representative in a foreign country

²**minister** *vb* **-tered; -ter·ing** \-st(ə-)riŋ\ : to give aid : SERVE ⟨*minister* to the sick⟩ — **min·is·tra·tion** \ˌmin-ə-ʹstrā-shən\ *n*

min·is·te·ri·al \ˌmin-ə-ʹstir-ē-əl\ *adj* : of or relating to a minister or ministry

min·is·try \ʹmin-ə-strē\ *n, pl* **-tries 1** : the action of ministering **2** : the office, duties, or work of a minister **3 a** : the body of ministers governing a nation or state **b** : a government department headed by a minister **c** : the building in which a ministry is housed

mini·van \ʹmin-ē-ˌvan\ *n* : a small passenger van

mink \ʹmiŋk\ *n, pl* **mink;** *or* **minks** : either of two flesh-eating mammals that resemble the related weasels, have a slender body, partly webbed feet, and a somewhat bushy tail, and live near water; *also* : the soft normally dark brown fur of a mink

mink

min·now \ʹmin-ō\ *n, pl* **minnows** *also* **min·now** : any of various small freshwater fishes (as a dace or shiner) related to the carps; *also* : any of various small fishes that resemble minnows

¹**mi·nor** \ʹmī-nər\ *adj* **1** : less in size, importance, or value ⟨a *minor* poet⟩ ⟨a *minor* injury⟩ **2** : not having reached the age to have full civil rights **3 a** : relating to or being a musical scale in which the third tone is lowered a half step **b** : based on a minor scale ⟨*minor* key⟩

²**minor** *n* : a person who has not reached the age to have full civil rights

mi·nor·i·ty \mə-ʹnȯr-ət-ē, mī-, -ʹnär-\ *n, pl* **-ties 1** : the state or period of being a legal minor **2** : the smaller

\ə\ **abut**	\aủ\ **out**	\i\ **tip**	\ȯ\ **saw**	\ủ\ **foot**
\ər\ **further**	\ch\ **chin**	\ī\ **life**	\ȯi\ **coin**	\y\ **yet**
\a\ **mat**	\e\ **pet**	\j\ **job**	\th\ **thin**	\yü\ **few**
\ā\ **take**	\ē\ **easy**	\ŋ\ **sing**	\th\ **this**	\yủ\ **cure**
\ä\ **cot, cart**	\g\ **go**	\ō\ **bone**	\ü\ **food**	\zh\ **vision**

number; *esp* : a group having less than the number of votes necessary for control **3** : a part of a population that differs from other groups in some characteristics and is often given unfair treatment

minor league *n* : a professional sports league (as in baseball) that is not one of the major leagues

minor party *n* : a political party whose electoral strength is so small as to prevent its gaining control of a government except in rare and exceptional circumstances

min·strel \'min(t)-strəl\ *n* **1** : a medieval musical entertainer; *esp* : a singer of verses accompanied by music **2 a** : MUSICIAN **b** : POET **3 a** : one of a group of performers giving a program of black American melodies and jokes usually with faces blackened with makeup **b** : a performance by a group of minstrels

min·strel·sy \'min(t)-strəl-sē\ *n, pl* **-sies** **1** : the singing and playing of a minstrel **2** : a body of minstrels **3** : a collection of songs or verse

¹mint \'mint\ *n* **1** : any of a family of herbs and shrubs (as basil or catnip) with square stems and opposite leaves; *esp* : one (as peppermint or spearmint) that is fragrant and is the source of a flavoring oil **2** : a mint-flavored piece of candy [Old English *minte* "the herb mint," from Latin *mentha, menta* "mint"]

²mint *n* **1** : a place where coins, medals, and tokens are made **2** : a great amount ⟨worth a *mint*⟩ [Middle English *mynt* "coin, money," from Old English *mynet* (same meaning), from Latin *moneta* "coin, place where coins are made," from *Moneta* "a special name for the goddess Juno"; so called because the ancient Romans made coins at the temple of Juno Moneta — related to MONEY; see *Word History* at MONEY]

³mint *vb* : to make (as coins) out of metal — **mint·er** *n*

min·u·end \'min-yə-ˌwend\ *n* : a number from which another number is to be subtracted

min·u·et \ˌmin-yə-'wet\ *n* **1** : a slow graceful dance **2** : music for or in the rhythm of a minuet

¹mi·nus \'mī-nəs\ *prep* **1** : with the subtraction of : LESS ⟨7 *minus* 4 is 3⟩ **2** : ¹WITHOUT 3a ⟨*minus* his hat⟩

²minus *n* **1** : a negative quantity **2** : a negative quality; *esp* : ¹DISADVANTAGE 2b

³minus *adj* **1** : mathematically negative ⟨4 plus *minus* 3⟩ **2** : falling low in a specified range ⟨a grade of C *minus*⟩

mi·nus·cule \'mi-nəs-ˌkyül\ *adj* : very small ⟨*minuscule* amounts⟩

minus sign *n* : a sign – used to show subtraction (as in 8 – 6 = 2) or a quantity less than zero (as in –10°)

¹min·ute \'min-ət\ *n* **1 a** : the 60th part of an hour of time **b** : the 60th part of a degree of angular measure **2** : the distance one can cover in a minute **3** : MOMENT 1 **4** *pl* : a brief record of what went on in a meeting [Middle English *minute* "¹/₆₀ part of an hour," from early French *minute* (same meaning), from Latin *minuta* (same meaning), from *minutus* "small" — related to MENU; see *Word History* at MENU]

²mi·nute \mī-'n(y)üt, mə-\ *adj* **1** : very small : TINY **2** : of small importance : PETTY **3** : marked by close attention to details — **mi·nute·ly** *adv* — **mi·nute·ness** *n*

minute hand *n* : the long hand that marks the minutes on the face of a watch or clock

min·ute·man \'min-ət-ˌman\ *n* : a member of an armed group pledged to take the field at a minute's notice during and immediately before the American Revolution

Mio·cene \'mī-ə-ˌsēn\ *adj* : of, relating to, or being an epoch of the Tertiary period of geological history or the corresponding series of rocks — see GEOLOGICAL TIME table — **Miocene** *n*

mir·a·cle \'mir-i-kəl\ *n* **1** : an extraordinary event taken as a sign of the supernatural power of God **2** : an extremely outstanding or unusual event, thing, or accomplishment [Middle English *miracle* "a miracle," from early French *miracle* (same meaning), derived from Latin *miraculum*

"a wonder," from *mirari* "to wonder at" — related to ADMIRE]

miracle drug *n* : WONDER DRUG

miracle play *n* **1** : MYSTERY PLAY **2** : a medieval play showing events from the life of a saint or martyr

mi·rac·u·lous \mə-'rak-yə-ləs\ *adj* **1** : of the nature of a miracle : SUPERNATURAL **2** : suggesting a miracle : MARVELOUS **3** : working or able to work miracles — **mi·rac·u·lous·ly** *adv*

mi·rage \mə-'räzh\ *n* : an illusion that gives the appearance of a pool of water or a mirror in which distant objects are seen inverted, that is sometimes seen at sea, in the desert, or over a hot pavement, and that is caused by the bending or reflection of light passing through layers of air having different temperatures

Mi·ran·da \mə-'ran-də\ *adj* : of, relating to, or being the legal rights of an arrested person to have an attorney and to remain silent so as to avoid self-incrimination ⟨the suspect was given a *Miranda* warning⟩ [from *Miranda v. Arizona*, the U.S. Supreme Court ruling establishing such rights]

¹mire \'mī(ə)r\ *n* **1** : wet spongy ground (as of a bog or marsh) **2** : heavy often deep mud or slush — **miry** \'mī(ə)r-ē\ *adj*

²mire *vb* **mired; mir·ing** **1 a** : to sink or stick fast in mire **b** : ENTANGLE 2, INVOLVE **2** : to soil with mud or slush

¹mir·ror \'mir-ər\ *n* **1** : a smooth or polished surface (as of glass) that forms images by reflection **2** : something that gives a true likeness or description

²mirror *vb* **1** : to reflect in or as if in a mirror **2** : RESEMBLE ⟨her presentation *mirrored* that of her classmates⟩

mirror image *n* : something that has its parts joined together in much the same way as those of something else except that each part of one thing is directly opposite to the corresponding part of the other thing and located on the opposite side of, the same distance away from, and facing in the same way toward or away from an axis or plane between the two things ⟨the two sides of an animal with bilateral symmetry are *mirror images* of each other⟩

mirth \'mərth\ *n* : gaiety accompanied by laughter

mirth·ful \'mərth-fəl\ *adj* : full of, expressing, or producing mirth — **mirth·ful·ly** \-fə-lē\ *adv* — **mirth·ful·ness** *n*

mis- *prefix* **1** : badly : wrongly ⟨*mis*judge⟩ **2** : bad : wrong ⟨*mis*deed⟩ **3** : opposite or lack of ⟨*mis*trust⟩ [partly from Old English *mis-* "badly, wrongly," and partly from early French *mes-* (same meaning)]

mis·ad·ven·ture \ˌmis-əd-'ven-chər\ *n* : MISFORTUNE 2

mis·an·thrope \'mis-ᵊn-ˌthrōp\ *n* : a person who dislikes and distrusts other people

mis·an·thro·py \mis-'an(t)-thrə-pē\ *n* : a dislike or hatred of all human beings — **mis·an·throp·ic** \ˌmis-ᵊn-'thräp-ik\ *adj* — **mis·an·throp·i·cal·ly** \-'thräp-i-k(ə-)lē\ *adv*

mis·ap·ply \ˌmis-ə-'plī\ *vb* : to apply wrongly — **mis·ap·pli·ca·tion** \ˌmis-ˌap-lə-'kā-shən\ *n*

mis·ap·pre·hend \(ˌ)mis-ˌap-ri-'hend\ *vb* : MISUNDERSTAND — **mis·ap·pre·hen·sion** \-'hen-chən\ *n*

mis·ap·pro·pri·ate \ˌmis-ə-'prō-prē-ˌāt\ *vb* : to appropriate wrongly; *esp* : to take dishonestly for one's own use — **mis·ap·pro·pri·a·tion** \-ˌprō-prē-'ā-shən\ *n*

mis·be·got·ten \ˌmis-bi-'gät-ᵊn\ *adj* **1** : ILLEGITIMATE 1 **2** : wrongfully or improperly created

mis·be·have \ˌmis-bi-'hāv\ *vb* : to behave in a wrong or improper manner — **mis·be·hav·ior** \-'hā-vyər\ *n*

mis·be·lief \ˌmis-bə-'lēf\ *n* : a mistaken or false belief — **mis·be·liev·er** \-'lē-vər\ *n*

mis·cal·cu·late \(')mis-'kal-kyə-ˌlāt\ *vb* : to calculate wrongly : make a mistake in calculation — **mis·cal·cu·la·tion** \ˌmis-ˌkal-kyə-'lā-shən\ *n*

mis·call \(')mis-'kol\ *vb* : to call by a wrong name

mis·car·riage \mis-'kar-ij\ *n* **1** : bad management; *esp* : a failure in the administration of justice **2** : the accidental separation of an unborn child from the body of its mother before it is capable of living independently : loss of an unborn child through premature birth

mis·car·ry \(')mis-'kar-ē\ *vb* **1** : to have a miscarriage : give birth prematurely **2** : to go wrong ⟨the plan *miscarried*⟩

mis·cast \(')mis-'kast\ *vb* : to cast in an unsuitable role

mis·ce·ge·na·tion \(ₐ)mis-ₐej-ə-'nā-shən, ₐmis-i-jə-'nā-\ *n* : marriage or interbreeding between persons of different races

mis·cel·la·neous \ₐmis-ə-'lā-ne-əs, -nyəs\ *adj* : consisting of many things of different sorts — **mis·cel·la·neous·ly** *adv* — **mis·cel·la·neous·ness** *n*

mis·cel·la·ny \'mis-ə-ₐlā-nē\ *n, pl* **-nies** **1** : a mixture of various things **2** : a collection of writings

mis·chance \(')mis-'chan(t)s\ *n* **1** : bad luck that is not of a serious nature **2** : a piece of bad luck : MISHAP *synonyms* see MISFORTUNE

mis·chief \'mis-chəf, 'mish-\ *n* **1** : INJURY 2, HARM **2** : a person or animal who causes mischief **3** : mischievous conduct or quality ⟨a child gets into *mischief*⟩ ⟨had *mischief* in their eyes⟩

mis·chie·vous \'mis-chə-vəs, 'mish-\ *adj* **1** : harming or intended to do harm ⟨*mischievous* gossip⟩ **2** : causing or tending to cause minor injury or annoyance ⟨a *mischievous* puppy⟩ **3** : showing a spirit of mischief ⟨*mischievous* behavior⟩ — **mis·chie·vous·ly** *adv* — **mis·chie·vous·ness** *n*

mis·con·ceive \ₐmis-kən-'sēv\ *vb* : to form a wrong or mistaken idea of

mis·con·cep·tion \ₐmis-kən-'sep-shən\ *n* : a wrong or mistaken idea

mis·con·duct \(')mis-'kän-(ₐ)dəkt\ *n* **1** : bad management **2** : improper or unlawful behavior — **mis·con·duct** \ₐmis-kən-'dəkt\ *vb*

mis·con·struc·tion \ₐmis-kən-'strək-shən\ *n* : the act, the process, or an instance of misconstruing

mis·con·strue \ₐmis-kən-'strü\ *vb* : to construe wrongly : MISINTERPRET

mis·count \(')mis-'kaunt\ *vb* : to count incorrectly — **miscount** *n*

mis·cre·ant \'mis-krē-ənt\ *n* : VILLAIN 2, SCOUNDREL — **miscreant** *adj*

¹**mis·cue** \(')mis-'kyü\ *n* **1** : a faulty stroke in billiards in which the cue slips **2** : ²MISTAKE 2, SLIP

²**miscue** *vb* **1** : to make a miscue **2 a** : to miss a stage cue **b** : to answer a wrong cue

mis·deal \(')mis-'dē(ə)l\ *vb* **-dealt** \-'delt\; **-deal·ing** \-'dē-liŋ\ : to deal cards incorrectly — **misdeal** *n*

mis·deed \(')mis-'dēd\ *n* : an evil or illegal deed

mis·de·mean·or \ₐmis-di-'mē-nər\ *n* **1** : a crime less serious than a felony **2** : MISDEED

mis·di·rect \ₐmis-də-'rekt, -(ₐ)dī-\ *vb* : to direct incorrectly — **mis·di·rec·tion** \-'rek-shən\ *n*

mis·do·ing \(')mis-'dü-iŋ\ *n* : MISDEED — **mis·do·er** \-'dü-ər\ *n*

mi·ser \'mī-zər\ *n* : a mean grasping person; *esp* : one who lives poorly in order to store away money

mis·er·a·ble \'miz-ər-bəl, 'miz-(ə)rə-bəl\ *adj* **1 a** : shabby in condition or quality ⟨a *miserable* place to live⟩ **b** : causing great discomfort or unhappiness ⟨a *miserable* cold⟩ **2** : extremely poor or unhappy : WRETCHED **3** : PITIFUL 1, LAMENTABLE — **mis·er·a·ble·ness** *n* — **mis·er·a·bly** \-blē\ *adv*

mi·ser·ly \'mī-zər-lē\ *adj* : of, relating to, or characteristic of a miser — **mi·ser·li·ness** *n*

mis·ery \'miz-(ə-)rē\ *n, pl* **-er·ies** **1** : a state of great suffering and want due to poverty or misfortune **2** : a source of misery **3** : a state of unhappiness

mis·file \(')mis-'fī(ə)l\ *vb* : to file in an incorrect place

mis·fire \(')mis-'fī(ə)r\ *vb* **1** : to have the explosive or driving charge fail to ignite at the proper time ⟨the engine *misfired*⟩ **2** : to fail to fire ⟨the gun *misfired*⟩ **3** : to miss an intended effect ⟨the plan *misfired*⟩ — **misfire** *n*

mis·fit \'mis-ₐfit, (')mis-'fit\ *n* **1** : something that fits badly **2** : a person poorly adjusted to his or her environment

mis·for·tune \(')mis-'fȯr-chən\ *n* **1** : bad luck especially for a long period of time **2** : an unfortunate condition or event : DISASTER

synonyms MISFORTUNE, MISCHANCE, MISHAP mean an unlucky turn of events. MISFORTUNE stresses the state of unhappiness that follows an unlucky event ⟨it was her *misfortune* to change jobs unwisely⟩. MISCHANCE usually suggests a situation involving no more than a minor trouble or bother ⟨by *mischance* he took the wrong road⟩. MISHAP suggests an example of bad luck of no real importance ⟨in one of the show's *mishaps* the winner's name was mispronounced⟩.

mis·give \(')mis-'giv\ *vb* **-gave** \-'gāv\; **-giv·en** \-'giv-ən\; **-giv·ing** : to suggest doubt or fear to

mis·giv·ing \(')mis-'giv-iŋ\ *n* : a feeling of doubt or suspicion especially concerning a future event

mis·gov·ern \(')mis-'gəv-ərn\ *vb* : to govern badly — **mis·gov·ern·ment** \'gəv-ər(n)-mənt, -ə-mənt; 'gəb-ºm-ənt, 'gəv-\ *n*

mis·guide \(')mis-'gīd\ *vb* : to lead astray : MISLEAD — **mis·guid·ance** \-'gīd-ºn(t)s\ *n*

mis·han·dle \(')mis-'han-dºl\ *vb* **1** : to treat roughly : MALTREAT **2** : to manage wrongly

mis·hap \'mis-ₐhap, mis-'hap\ *n* **1** *archaic* : bad luck **2** : an unfortunate accident [Middle English *mishap* "bad luck," from *mis-* "bad, unfavorable," and *hap* "chance, chance occurrence" — related to HAPPEN, HAPPY, PERHAPS] *synonyms* see MISFORTUNE

mish·mash \'mish-ₐmash, -ₐmäsh\ *n* : HODGEPODGE, JUMBLE

mis·in·form \ₐmis-ən-'fȯ(ə)rm\ *vb* : to give false or misleading information to — **mis·in·for·ma·tion** \ₐmis-ₐin-fər-'mā-shən\ *n*

mis·in·ter·pret \ₐmis-ºn-'tər-prət, -pət\ *vb* : to understand or explain wrongly — **mis·in·ter·pre·ta·tion** \-ₐtər-prə-'tā-shən, -pə-'tā-\ *n*

mis·judge \(')mis-'jəj\ *vb* : to judge wrongly or unfairly — **mis·judg·ment** \-'jəj-mənt\ *n*

mis·lay \(')mis-'lā\ *vb* **-laid** \-'lād\; **-lay·ing** : to put in a place later forgotten : LOSE ⟨*mislaid* the car keys⟩

mis·lead \(')mis-'lēd\ *vb* **-led** \-'led\; **-lead·ing** : to lead in a wrong direction or into a mistaken action or belief — **misleading** *adj*

mis·man·age \(')mis-'man-ij\ *vb* : to manage badly or improperly — **mis·man·age·ment** \-mənt\ *n*

mis·match \(')mis-'mach\ *vb* : to match unsuitably or badly — **mismatch** *n*

mis·mate \(')mis-'māt\ *vb* : to mate unsuitably

mis·name \(')mis-'nām\ *vb* : to name incorrectly : MISCALL

mis·no·mer \(')mis-'nō-mər\ *n* : a wrong or unsuitable name

mi·sog·a·mist \mə-'säg-ə-məst\ *n* : one who hates marriage — **mi·sog·a·my** \-'säg-ə-mē\ *n*

mi·sog·y·nist \mə-'säj-ə-nəst\ *n* : one who hates or distrusts women — **mi·sog·y·ny** \-ə-nē\ *n*

mis·place \(')mis-'plās\ *vb* **1** : to put in a wrong place **2** : MISLAY — **mis·place·ment** *n*

mis·play \(')mis-'plā\ *n* : a wrong or unskillful play — **misplay** \'mis-ₐplā, (')mis-'plā\ *vb*

mis·print \(')mis-'print\ *vb* : to print incorrectly — **misprint** \'mis-ₐprint, (')mis-'print\ *n*

\ə\ abut	\au\ out	\i\ tip	\o\ saw	\u\ foot
\ər\ further	\ch\ chin	\ī\ life	\oi\ coin	\y\ yet
\a\ mat	\e\ pet	\j\ job	\th\ thin	\yü\ few
\ā\ take	\ē\ easy	\ŋ\ sing	\th\ this	\yu\ cure
\ä\ cot, cart	\g\ go	\ō\ bone	\ü\ food	\zh\ vision

mis·pro·nounce \ˌmis-prə-ˈnaún(t)s\ *vb* : to pronounce in a way considered incorrect

mis·pro·nun·ci·a·tion \ˌmis-prə-ˌnən(t)-sē-ˈā-shən\ *n* : an act or an instance of mispronouncing

mis·quote \(ˈ)mis-ˈkwōt\ *vb* : to quote incorrectly — **mis·quo·ta·tion** \ˌmis-kwō-ˈtā-shən\ *n*

mis·read \(ˈ)mis-ˈrēd\ *vb* **-read** \-ˈred\; **-read·ing** \-ˈrēd-iŋ\ **1** : to read incorrectly **2** : to misinterpret in or as if in reading

mis·rep·re·sent \(ˌ)mis-ˌrep-ri-ˈzent\ *vb* : to give a false or misleading idea of — **mis·rep·re·sen·ta·tion** \(ˌ)mis-ˌrep-ri-ˌzen-ˈtā-shən\ *n*

¹mis·rule \(ˈ)mis-ˈrül\ *vb* : to rule or govern badly

²misrule *n* **1** : the action of misruling : the state of being misruled **2** : ²DISORDER 1, ANARCHY

¹miss \ˈmis\ *vb* **1** : to fail to hit, catch, reach, or get ⟨*miss* a target⟩ ⟨*miss* the ball⟩ **2** : ¹ESCAPE 2, AVOID ⟨just *missed* being hurt⟩ **3 a** : to leave out : OMIT ⟨*missed* their lunch⟩ **b** : to fail to attend ⟨*missed* three days of school⟩ **4** : to discover or feel the absence of ⟨*missed* our old friends⟩ **5** : to fail to understand, sense, or experience ⟨*missed* the main point of the story⟩ **6** : MISFIRE 1 ⟨the engine *missed*⟩ [Old English *missan* "to fail to reach or get"]

²miss *n* **1** : a failure to reach a desired goal or result **2** : a failure to fire

³miss *sense 1 is* (ˌ)mis, məs; *sense 2 is* ˈmis\ *n* **1 a** — used as a title before the name of an unmarried woman or girl **b** — used before the name of a place, an activity, an epithet, or a quality to form a title for a girl who represents the thing indicated ⟨*Miss* America⟩ ⟨*Miss* Punctuality⟩ **2** : a young woman or girl — used as a term of address ⟨this way, *Miss*⟩ **3** *pl* : a clothing size for women of average height and build [a shortened form of *mistress*]

mis·sal \ˈmis-əl\ *n* : a book containing the prayers to be said or sung in the Mass during the year

mis·send \(ˈ)mis-ˈsend\ *vb* **-sent** \-ˈsent\; **-send·ing** : to send to the wrong place

mis·shap·en \(ˈ)mis-ˈshā-pən, (ˈ)mish-\ *adj* : badly shaped : having an ugly shape

mis·sile \ˈmis-əl\ *n* : an object (as a stone, arrow, artillery shell, bullet, or rocket) that is thrown, shot, or launched usually so as to strike something at a distance [from Latin *missile* "a weapon that is thrown or shot rather than held in the hand," derived from *missus*, past participle of *mittere* "to send, throw" — related to EMIT]

miss·ing \ˈmis-iŋ\ *adj* : ¹ABSENT 1, LOST ⟨*missing* persons⟩ ⟨*missing* in action⟩

missing link *n* : a form of animal believed to have existed that shares characteristics with one animal group and the ancestors from which the group is thought to have evolved but has not been discovered in the fossil record ⟨find the *missing link* between humans and apes⟩

mis·sion \ˈmish-ən\ *n* **1 a** : a group of missionaries **b** : the work of a missionary **c** : a place where a mission or missionary works **2 a** : a group sent to a foreign country to carry on discussions or to provide training or assistance ⟨trade *mission*⟩ ⟨military *mission*⟩ **b** : a group of diplomats who stay in a foreign country **3 a** : a task or job that is assigned ⟨our *mission* was to recover the stolen plans⟩ **b** : a definite military, naval, or aerospace task ⟨a space *mission*⟩ [from modern Latin *mission-, missio* "a group sent out by a religious organization," derived from earlier Latin *missus*, past participle of *mittere* "to send, throw" — related to MESSAGE]

¹mis·sion·ary \ˈmish-ə-ˌner-ē\ *adj* **1** : relating to, engaged in, or devoted to missions **2** : characteristic of a missionary : ZEALOUS

²missionary *n, pl* **-ar·ies** : one sent to spread a religious faith among unbelievers or to engage in charitable work with religious support

Mis·sis·sip·pi·an \ˌmis-(ə-)ˈsip-ē-ən\ *adj* **1** : of or relating to Mississippi, its people, or the Mississippi River **2** : of, relating to, or being the earlier part of the Carboniferous period of the Paleozoic era of geological history in North America or the corresponding system of rocks — see GEOLOGIC TIME table — **Mississippian** *n*

mis·sive \ˈmis-iv\ *n* : ¹LETTER 2, MESSAGE

mis·spell \(ˈ)mis-ˈspel\ *vb* : to spell incorrectly

mis·spell·ing \(ˈ)mis-ˈspel-iŋ\ *n* : an incorrect spelling

mis·spend \(ˈ)mis-ˈspend\ *vb* **-spent** \-ˈspent\; **-spend·ing** : ²WASTE 3, SQUANDER ⟨a misspent youth⟩

mis·state \(ˈ)mis-ˈstāt\ *vb* : to state incorrectly — **mis·state·ment** \-mənt\ *n*

mis·step \(ˈ)mis-ˈstep\ *n* **1** : a wrong step **2** : ²MISTAKE 2, BLUNDER

¹mist \ˈmist\ *n* **1** : water in the form of particles floating in the air or falling as fine rain **2** : something that keeps one from seeing or understanding clearly

²mist *vb* **1** : to be or become misty **2** : to become dim or blurred **3** : to cover with a mist

¹mis·take \mə-ˈstāk\ *vb* **mis·took** \-ˈstúk\; **mis·tak·en** \-ˈstā-kən\; **mis·tak·ing 1** : to understand wrongly : MISINTERPRET ⟨*mistook* my meaning⟩ **2** : to estimate incorrectly ⟨*mistook* the strength of the enemy⟩ **3** : to identify wrongly ⟨*mistook* me for her⟩ — **mis·tak·en·ly** *adv*

²mistake *n* **1** : a wrong judgment : MISUNDERSTANDING **2** : a wrong action or statement **synonyms** see ERROR

¹mis·ter \ˈmis-tər, *for sense 1* ˌmis-tər\ *n* **1** — used sometimes in writing instead of *Mr.* : SIR **2** — used without a name as a term of direct address of a man who is a stranger ⟨hey, *mister*, do you want to buy a paper?⟩ [an altered form of *master*]

²mist·er \ˈmis-tər\ *n* : a device for spraying a mist [²*mist* "cover with a mist" and ²*-er* "one that does (a specified action)"]

mis·time \(ˈ)mis-ˈtīm\ *vb* : to time wrongly

mis·tle·toe \ˈmis-əl-ˌtō\ *n* : a European plant with yellowish flowers and waxy white berries that grows on the branches and trunks of trees; *also* : any of various related plants that resemble the mistletoe

mist net *n* : a large finely woven net that is set up to capture birds or bats as they fly into it

mis·treat \(ˈ)mis-ˈtrēt\ *vb* : to treat badly : ABUSE — **mis·treat·ment** \-mənt\ *n*

mis·tress \ˈmis-trəs\ *n* **1** : a woman who has control or authority like that of a master ⟨the *mistress* of the household⟩ **2** : something considered as a female that rules or directs **3** : a woman to whom a man is not married and with whom he has a sexual relationship **4** — used formerly as a title before the name of a woman [Middle English *maistresse* "mistress," from early French *mestresse* (same meaning), a feminine form of *mestre* "master" — related to MASTER]

mistletoe

mis·tri·al \ˈmis-ˌtrī-(ə)l\ *n* : a trial that is cancelled because of an error in the proceedings

¹mis·trust \(ˈ)mis-ˈtrəst\ *n* : ²DISTRUST — **mis·trust·ful** \-fəl\ *adj* — **mis·trust·ful·ly** \-fə-lē\ *adv* — **mis·trust·ful·ness** *n*

²mistrust *vb* : ¹DISTRUST

misty \ˈmis-tē\ *adj* **mist·i·er; -est 1** : full of mist ⟨a *misty* valley⟩ **2** : VAGUE 3, INDISTINCT ⟨a *misty* memory⟩ — **mist·i·ly** \-tə-lē\ *adv* — **mist·i·ness** \-tē-nəs\ *n*

mis·un·der·stand \(ˌ)mis-ˌən-dər-ˈstand\ *vb* **-stood** \-ˈstúd\; **-stand·ing 1** : to fail to understand **2** : to interpret incorrectly

mis·un·der·stand·ing \(ˌ)mis-ˌən-dər-ˈstan-diŋ\ *n* **1** : a failure to understand **2** : DISAGREEMENT 2b, QUARREL

¹mis·use \mish-'üz, (')mish-'yüz, (')mis-'yüz\ *vb* **1** : to use incorrectly : MISAPPLY **2** : ¹ABUSE 2, MISTREAT — **mis·us·age** \-'(y)ü-sij, -zij\ *n*

²mis·use \mish-'üs, (')mish-'yüs, (')mis-'yüs\ *n* : incorrect or improper use

mite \'mīt\ *n* **1** : any of various invertebrates that are tiny arachnids closely related to the ticks, that often live on plants, animals, and stored foods, and that include important carriers of disease **2** : a very small coin or sum of money **3 a** : a very little amount : BIT **b** : a very small object or creature

¹mi·ter *or* **mi·tre** \'mīt-ər\ *n* **1** : a high pointed headdress worn by a bishop or abbot in church ceremonies **2** : MITER JOINT

²miter *or* **mitre** *vb* **mi·tered** *or* **mi·tred**; **mi·ter·ing** *or* **mi·tring** \'mīt-ə-riŋ\ : to match or fit together in a miter joint

miter joint *n* : the joint or corner made by cutting the edges of two boards at an angle and fitting them together

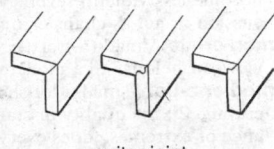

miter joint

mit·i·gate \'mit-ə-ˌgāt\ *vb* **-gat·ed**; **-gat·ing** : to make less severe ⟨*mitigate* a punishment⟩ — **mit·i·ga·tion** \ˌmit-ə-'gā-shən\ *n*

mi·to·chon·dri·on \ˌmīt-ə-'kän-drē-ən\ *n, pl* **-dria** \-drē-ə\ : one of the round or long bodies found in the cytoplasm of cells outside the nucleus that are rich in fats, proteins, and enzymes and are important centers of metabolic processes which use oxygen and produce energy

mi·to·sis \mī-'tō-səs\ *n, pl* **-to·ses** \-'tō-ˌsēz\ **1** : a process that takes place in the nucleus of a dividing cell and that results in the formation of two new nuclei with the same number of chromosomes as the parent nucleus — compare MEIOSIS **2** : a cell division in which mitosis occurs — **mi·tot·ic** \-'tät-ik\ *adj*

mitt \'mit\ *n* **1** : MITTEN **2** : a baseball catcher's or first baseman's glove

mit·ten \'mit-ᵊn\ *n* : a covering for the hand and wrist having a separate section for the thumb only — **mit·tened** \'mit-ᵊnd\ *adj*

¹mix \'miks\ *vb* **1** : to make into one mass by stirring together : BLEND **2** : to make by combining different things **3** : to become one mass through blending ⟨oil will not *mix* with water⟩ **4** : to associate with others on friendly terms ⟨*mixes* well in any company⟩ **5** : CONFUSE 3 ⟨*mix* up facts⟩

synonyms MIX, MINGLE, BLEND, COALESCE mean to combine into a whole that is more or less the same throughout. MIX suggests a fairly complete combining in which the elements may or may not lose their individual identities ⟨*mix* several vegetables for a salad⟩ ⟨*mix* water and frozen orange juice⟩. MINGLE suggests that the different elements can still be identified to some degree ⟨the author *mingled* comic and tragic events in her story⟩. BLEND suggests a complete uniting of things so that the original parts cannot be separated or recognized ⟨*blend* milk and canned tomato soup⟩. COALESCE stresses the action or process of similar things growing into a natural union ⟨the two groups slowly *coalesced* into one⟩.

²mix *n* : MIXTURE; *esp* : a prepared mixture of ingredients for use in preparing foods ⟨a muffin *mix*⟩

mixed \'mikst\ *adj* **1 a** : made of mingled or blended elements ⟨*mixed* nuts⟩ **b** : combining features of more than one kind ⟨a *mixed* economy⟩ **2 a** : involving persons differing in race, national origin, or religion ⟨a *mixed* marriage⟩ **b** : made up of or involving individuals of both sexes ⟨*mixed* company⟩ ⟨a *mixed* chorus⟩ **3** : including or accompanied by different or opposing elements ⟨a *mixed* blessing⟩ ⟨a *mixed* reaction⟩ **4** : resulting from the crossing or breeding of individuals of different races or breeds ⟨a stallion of *mixed* blood⟩

mixed media *n* : ²MULTIMEDIA

mixed nerve *n* : a nerve that carries nerve impulses toward the central nervous system from a sense organ and also away from the central nervous system to cause movement in muscles

mixed number *n* : a number (as $5\frac{2}{3}$) composed of a whole number and a fraction

mix·er \'mik-sər\ *n* **1** : one that mixes; *esp* : a device or machine for mixing **2** : a party to give members of a group an opportunity to get acquainted

mix·ture \'miks-chər\ *n* **1** : the act or process or an instance of mixing **2 a** : something mixed or being mixed ⟨add eggs to the *mixture*⟩ **b** : a preparation consisting of two or more ingredients or kinds **3** : two or more substances that are mixed together but not chemically combined and that may vary in proportion

mix–up \'mik-ˌsəp\ *n* : an instance of confusion

¹miz·zen *also* **miz·en** \'miz-ᵊn\ *n* **1** : a fore-and-aft sail set on the mizzenmast **2** : MIZZENMAST

²mizzen *also* **mizen** *adj* : of or relating to the mizzenmast

miz·zen·mast \'miz-ᵊn-ˌmast, -məst\ *n* : the mast just behind the mainmast in a ship

mne·mon·ic \ni-'män-ik\ *adj* : assisting or intended to assist memory

moa \'mō-ə\ *n* : any of various usually very large extinct birds of New Zealand that were not able to fly

M mizzenmast

¹moan \'mōn\ *n* **1** : a long low sound indicating pain or grief **2** : a sound like a moan

²moan *vb* **1** : to utter a moan **2** : COMPLAIN 1 **3** : to utter with moans

moat \'mōt\ *n* : a deep wide trench around the walls of a castle or fortress that is usually filled with water

¹mob \'mäb\ *n* **1** : the common people : MASSES **2** : a large rowdy crowd : RABBLE **3** : a criminal gang **synonyms** see MULTITUDE

²mob *vb* **mobbed**; **mob·bing** : to crowd about and attack or annoy

¹mo·bile \'mō-bəl, -ˌbēl, -ˌbīl\ *adj* **1** : capable of moving or being moved : ¹MOVABLE **2** : changing quickly in expression ⟨a *mobile* face⟩ **3** : easily moved ⟨*mobile* troops⟩ **4** : tending to travel or migrate from place to place : MIGRATORY ⟨*mobile* workers⟩ **5** : characterized by movement from one social class to another ⟨a *mobile* society⟩ **6** : CELLULAR 2 — **mo·bil·i·ty** \mō-'bil-ət-ē\ *n*

²mo·bile \'mō-ˌbēl\ *n* : an artistic structure that is moved easily or that has parts easily moved (as by a current of air)

mobile home *n* : a trailer that is used as a dwelling at a permanent site

mobile phone *n* : CELL PHONE

mo·bi·lize \'mō-bə-ˌlīz\ *vb* **-lized**; **-liz·ing** : to assemble and make ready for action : MARSHAL — **mo·bi·li·za·tion** \ˌmō-bə-lə-'zā-shən\ *n*

Mö·bi·us strip \ˌmə(r)-bē-əs-, ˌmō-\ *n* : a one-sided surface made by holding one end of a rectangle in place, twisting

\ə\ abut	\aú\ out	\i\ tip	\ȯ\ saw	\ú\ foot
\ər\ further	\ch\ chin	\ī\ life	\ȯi\ coin	\y\ yet
\a\ mat	\e\ pet	\j\ job	\th\ thin	\yü\ few
\ā\ take	\ē\ easy	\ŋ\ sing	\t̲h̲\ this	\yu̇\ cure
\ä\ cot, cart	\g\ go	\ō\ bone	\ü\ food	\zh\ vision

the rectangle to turn over the other end, and joining the two ends together

mob·ster \'mäb-stər\ *n* : a member of a criminal gang

moc·ca·sin \'mäk-ə-sən\ *n* **1 a** : a soft leather shoe without a heel and with the sole and sides made of one piece **b** : a similar shoe with a separate sole **2** : WATER MOCCASIN

moccasin flower *n* : any of several lady's slippers; *esp* : a woodland orchid of eastern North America with usually pink or white flowers

mo·cha \'mō-kə\ *n* **1** : coffee of high quality grown in Arabia **2** : a mixture of coffee and chocolate

¹mock \'mäk, 'mȯk\ *vb* **1** : to treat with scorn : RIDICULE ⟨*mocked* his ideas⟩ **2** : DEFY 2 ⟨don't *mock* the rules⟩ **3** : to make fun of by mimicking ⟨*mocked* the statue's pose⟩ **synonyms** see IMITATE — **mock·er** *n* — **mock·ing·ly** \-iŋ-lē\ *adv*

²mock *n* **1** : an act of mocking : JEER **2** : someone or something that is made fun of

³mock *adj* : not real : IMITATION

mock·ery \'mäk-(ə-)rē, 'mȯk-\ *n, pl* **-er·ies** **1** : insulting action or speech **2** : someone or something that is laughed at **3** : a ridiculous or poor imitation

mock·ing·bird \'mäk-iŋ-,bərd, 'mȯk-\ *n* : a common grayish North American songbird that is closely related to the catbirds and thrashers and is noted for the sweetness of its song and for its imitations of the notes of other birds

mockingbird

mock orange *n* : any of several shrubs widely grown for their showy white flowers

mock·up \'mäk-,əp, 'mȯk-\ *n* : a full-sized model built for study, testing, or display ⟨a *mock-up* of a car⟩

mod \'mäd\ *adj* : MODERN

mod·acryl·ic fiber \,mäd-ə-,kril-ik-\ *n* : a synthetic fiber used for clothing that dries quickly and resists burning

mod·al \'mōd-ᵊl\ *adj* : relating to or being a modal auxiliary

modal auxiliary *n* : a verb (as *can, must, might, should*) that is typically used with another verb to indicate that the state or action expressed is something other than a simple fact (as a possibility or a necessity) ⟨in "we may go tomorrow" "may" is a *modal auxiliary*⟩

¹mode \'mōd\ *n* **1** : ²MOOD **2** : a form or manner of expression or acting : WAY ⟨a *mode* of travel⟩ **3** : a particular operating arrangement or condition **4** : the most frequent value of a set of values (as data)

²mode *n* : a popular fashion or style

¹mod·el \'mäd-ᵊl\ *n* **1 a** : a small but exact copy of something ⟨a ship *model*⟩ **b** : a pattern or figure of something to be made ⟨clay *models* for a statue⟩ **2** : a person who sets a good example ⟨a *model* of politeness⟩ **3 a** : a person or thing that serves as an artist's pattern; *esp* : a person who poses for an artist or photographer **b** : a person who wears in the presence of customers garments that are for sale or who poses for ads for merchandise (as clothes) **4** : ¹TYPE 2b, KIND ⟨our car is a late *model*⟩ **5 a** : a description or construction used to help form a picture of something (as an atom) that cannot be seen directly ⟨a *model* of a DNA molecule⟩ **b** : a computer simulation ⟨climate *models*⟩ **synonyms** see PATTERN

²model *vb* **mod·eled** *or* **mod·elled**; **mod·el·ing** *or* **mod·el·ling** \'mäd-liŋ, -ᵊl-iŋ\ **1** : to plan or shape after a pattern **2** : to make a model : MOLD **3** : to act or serve as a model — **mod·el·er** *or* **mod·el·ler** \'mäd-lər, -ᵊl-ər\ *n*

³model *adj* **1** : serving as or worthy of being a pattern ⟨a *model* student⟩ **2** : being a miniature copy of something ⟨a *model* airplane⟩

mo·dem \'mō-,dem\ *n* : a device that changes signals from one form to a form which can be used by another kind of equipment ⟨computer information is sent over telephone lines using a *modem*⟩

¹mod·er·ate \'mäd-(ə-)rət\ *adj* **1 a** : avoiding or lacking extremes (as in behavior or temperature) ⟨a *moderate* eater⟩ ⟨*moderate* climates⟩ **b** : ³CALM 2, REASONABLE ⟨his demands were *moderate*⟩ **2 a** : neither very much nor very little : average in size or amount ⟨a *moderate* rain⟩ **b** : neither very good nor very bad : MEDIOCRE ⟨met with only *moderate* success⟩ **3** : opposed to major social change or extreme political ideas ⟨a *moderate* candidate⟩ **4** : not expensive : reasonable or low in price ⟨*moderate* rates⟩ — **mod·er·ate·ly** *adv* — **mod·er·ate·ness** *n*

²mod·er·ate \'mäd-ə-,rāt\ *vb* **-at·ed; -at·ing** **1** : to make or become less violent, severe, or intense **2** : to guide a discussion or act as chairperson of a meeting

³mod·er·ate \'mäd-(ə-)rət\ *n* : one who holds moderate views or belongs to a moderate group (as in politics)

mod·er·a·tion \,mäd-ə-'rā-shən\ *n* **1** : the action of moderating **2** : the quality or state of being moderate : avoidance of extremes ⟨does everything in *moderation*⟩

mo·der·a·to \,mäd-ə-'rät-ō\ *adv or adj* : at a moderate tempo — used as a direction in music

mod·er·a·tor \'mäd-ə-,rāt-ər\ *n* **1** : one that moderates: as **a** : the leader of a Presbyterian governing body **b** : the chairperson of a town meeting **c** : the chairperson of a discussion group (as on television) **2** : a substance (as graphite) used for slowing down neutrons in a nuclear reactor

¹mod·ern \'mäd-ərn\ *adj* **1** : of, relating to, or characteristic of the present or the recent past : CONTEMPORARY **2** : of or relating to the period from about 1500 to the present ⟨*modern* history⟩ ⟨*Modern* English⟩ — **mo·der·ni·ty** \mə-'dər-nət-ē, mä-\ *n* — **mod·ern·ness** \'mäd-ərn-nəs\ *n*

²modern *n* : a person of modern times or with modern ideas

mod·ern·ism \'mäd-ər-,niz-əm\ *n* : a modern custom, expression, style, or idea — **mod·ern·ist** \-nəst\ *n or adj* — **mod·ern·is·tic** \,mäd-ər-'nis-tik\ *adj*

mod·ern·ize \'mäd-ər-,nīz\ *vb* **-ized; -iz·ing** : to make or become modern, *esp* : to change to suit present styles, tastes, or needs ⟨*modernize* an old house⟩ — **mod·ern·i·za·tion** \,mäd-ər-nə-'zā-shən\ *n* — **mod·ern·iz·er** \'mäd-ər-,nī-zər\ *n*

mod·est \'mäd-əst\ *adj* **1 a** : having a limited and not overly high opinion of oneself and one's abilities **b** : not boastful : somewhat shy ⟨a *modest* winner⟩ **2** : moderate in amount, size, or extent ⟨a *modest* request⟩ ⟨a *modest* cottage⟩ **3** : clean and proper in thought, conduct, and dress : DECENT — **mod·est·ly** *adv*

mod·es·ty \'mäd-ə-stē\ *n* : the quality of being modest

mo·di·cum \'mäd-i-kəm, 'mōd-\ *n* : a small amount ⟨anyone with a *modicum* of intelligence would understand⟩

mod·i·fi·ca·tion \,mäd-ə-fə-'kā-shən\ *n* **1 a** : the act of modifying **b** : the state of being modified **2** : the limiting of a statement : QUALIFICATION **3** : the result of modifying : partial change ⟨*modification* of plans⟩

mod·i·fi·er \'mäd-ə-,fī(-ə)r\ *n* : a word (as an adjective or adverb) or group of words (as a phrase or clause) used with another word or group of words to limit its meaning

mod·i·fy \'mäd-ə-,fī\ *vb* **-fied; -fy·ing** **1** : to make changes in : ALTER ⟨*modify* a plan⟩ **2** : to lower or reduce in amount or degree : MODERATE **3** : to limit in meaning : QUALIFY ⟨in the phrase "green gloves," "green" *modifies* "gloves"⟩ — **mod·i·fi·able** \-,fī-ə-bəl\ *adj*

mod·ish \'mōd-ish\ *adj* : FASHIONABLE 1, STYLISH — **mod·ish·ly** *adv* — **mod·ish·ness** *n*

mod·u·lar \'mäj-ə-lər\ *adj* **1** : of, relating to, or based on a module or modulus **2** : constructed in similar sizes or with similar units for flexibility and variety in use

modular arithmetic *n* : arithmetic that deals with whole numbers in such a way that all numbers are replaced by their remainders after division by a modulus ⟨5 hours after 10 o'clock is 3 o'clock because clocks follow a *modular arithmetic* with modulus 12⟩

mod·u·late \'mäj-ə-ˌlāt\ *vb* **-lat·ed; -lat·ing 1** : to tune to a key or pitch **2** : to adjust or regulate to the proper proportion; *esp* : to tone down : SOFTEN ⟨*modulated* his voice⟩ **3** : to vary a quality (as frequency or amplitude) of an electromagnetic wave for the transmission of information (as by radio) — **mod·u·la·tor** \-ˌlāt-ər\ *n* — **mod·u·la·to·ry** \-lə-ˌtōr-ē, -ˌtȯr-\ *adj*

mod·u·la·tion \ˌmäj-ə-'lā-shən\ *n* **1** : an action of modulating **2** : the extent or degree by which something is modulated **3** : a change from one musical key to another by using a chord that is found in both keys **4** : the process of modulating a carrier wave or signal (as in radio); *also* : the result of this process

mod·ule \'mäj-ü(ə)l\ *n* **1 a** : any in a series of similar units for use together **b** : a usually packaged collection of parts (as for an electronic device) **2** : an independent unit of a space vehicle ⟨a propulsion *module*⟩

mod·u·lo \'mäj-ə-ˌlō\ *prep* : with respect to a modulus of

mod·u·lus \'mäj-ə-ləs\ *n, pl* **-li** \-ˌlī, -ˌlē\ : a fixed whole number by which all the numbers in a system of modular arithmetic are divided ⟨using the *modulus* 5, the product of 3 times 4 equals 2 because 12 divided by 5 has remainder 2⟩

Mogen David *variant of* MAGEN DAVID

¹mo·gul \'mō-(ˌ)gəl, mō-'gəl\ *n* **1** *also* **mo·ghul** *or* **mu·ghal** *cap* : an Indian Muslim of or descended from a family of Turkish and Mongolian origin that ruled India from the 16th to the 18th century **2** : an important person : MAGNATE [Persian *Mughul* "mogul," from Mongolian *mongyol* "Mongol"] — **mogul** *adj, often cap*

²mo·gul \'mō-gəl\ *n* : a bump on a ski slope [from German dialect]

mo·hair \'mō-ˌha(ə)r, -ˌhe(ə)r\ *n* : a fabric or yarn made of or with the long silky hair of the Angora goat; *also* : the hair of the Angora goat

Mo·ham·med·an *also* **Mu·ham·mad·an** \mō-'ham-əd-ən\ *adj* : of or relating to Muhammad or Islam — **Mohammedan** *n* — **Mo·ham·med·an·ism** \-ˌiz-əm\ *n*

Mo·hawk \'mō-ˌhȯk\ *n, pl* **Mohawk** *or* **Mohawks** : a member of an American Indian people of the Mohawk River valley in New York state

Mo·he·gan \mō-'hē-gən, mə-\ *or* **Mo·hi·can** \-kən\ *n, pl* **Mohegan** *or* **Mohegans** *or* **Mohican** *or* **Mohicans** : a member of an American Indian people of southeastern Connecticut

Mohican *variant of* MAHICAN, MOHEGAN

Mohs' scale \'mōz-, 'mōs-, 'mō-səz-\ *n* : a scale of hardness for minerals that ranges from a value of 1 for talc to 10 for diamond [named after Friedrich *Mohs*, 1773–1839, German mineralogist who introduced the scale]

moi·ety \'mȯi-ət-ē\ *n, pl* **-eties 1** : one of two equal or approximately equal parts : HALF **2** : one of the parts making up something

moil \'mȯi(ə)l\ *vb* : to work hard : DRUDGE

moi·ré \mȯ-'rā, mwä-\ *or* **moire** *same, or* '\mȯi(-ə)r, 'mȯ)r, 'mwär\ *n* : a fabric (as silk) that has a shiny wavy-patterned surface — **moiré** *adj*

moist \'mȯist\ *adj* **1** : slightly or moderately wet ⟨*moist* earth⟩ **2** : characterized by high humidity — **moist·ly** *adv* — **moist·ness** \'mȯis(t)-nəs\ *n*

    synonyms MOIST, DAMP, DANK mean somewhat wet. MOIST suggests a wetness that is just noticeable ⟨grass just *moist* with dew⟩. DAMP suggests that something is wet to the point where it is disagreeable to touch ⟨those clothes are too *damp* to wear⟩. DANK suggests a cold unpleasant wetness ⟨a *dank* cellar⟩.

moist·en \'mȯis-ᵊn\ *vb* **moist·ened; moist·en·ing** \'mȯis-niŋ, -ᵊn-iŋ\ : to make or become moist — **moist·en·er** \'mȯis-nər, -ᵊn-ər\ *n*

mois·ture \'mȯish-chər, 'mȯis-\ *n* : a small amount of liquid that causes moistness : DAMPNESS

mois·tur·ize \'mȯish-chə-ˌrīz, 'mȯis-\ *vb* **-ized; -iz·ing** : to add moisture to ⟨*moisturize* the air⟩ — **mois·tur·iz·er** *n*

mo·jo \'mō-jō\ *n, pl* **mojoes** *or* **mojos** : a magic spell, hex, or charm; *also* : magical power [probably of African origin]

¹mo·lar \'mō-lər\ *n* : a tooth with a rounded or flattened surface adapted for grinding; *esp* : one behind the premolars of a mammal

    Word History Food is crushed in the mouth by the grinding of teeth, especially the molars. In much the same manner, grain may be ground into flour between two rough circular millstones. The Latin word for millstone is *mola,* and it seemed fitting to the English in the late Middle Ages that a tooth which acted like a millstone be called a *molar.* [from Latin *molaris* "a grinding tooth," from *mola* "millstone" — related to ¹MILL]

²molar *adj* **1** : adapted for grinding **2** : of or relating to a molar

mo·las·ses \mə-'las-əz\ *n* : a thick brown syrup that is separated from raw sugar in sugar manufacture

¹mold \'mōld\ *n* : light rich crumbly earth that contains decaying matter (as leaves) [Old English *molde* "rich soil"]

²mold *n* **1** : the frame on, around, or in which something is constructed or shaped ⟨a candle *mold*⟩ **2** : something shaped in a mold ⟨a *mold* of gelatin⟩ [Middle English *mold* "special nature of something, frame on which something is formed," from early French *molde* (same meaning), from Latin *modulus* "form, measure"]

³mold *vb* **1** : to work and press into shape ⟨*mold* loaves of bread⟩ **2** : to form in a mold **3** : to determine or influence the character of ⟨*mold* a child's mind⟩ — **mold·able** \'mōl-də-bəl\ *adj* — **mold·er** *n*

⁴mold *vb* : to become moldy [Middle English *moulen* "to become moldy"]

⁵mold *n* **1** : an often fuzzy surface growth of fungus especially on damp or decaying matter **2** : a fungus that produces mold

mold·er \'mōl-dər\ *vb* **mold·ered; mold·er·ing** \-d(ə-)riŋ\ : to crumble to bits by slow decay : DECAY

mold·ing \'mōl-diŋ\ *n* **1 a** : the act or work of a person who molds **b** : an object produced by molding **2** : a strip of material having a shaped surface and used as a decoration (as on a wall or the edge of a table)

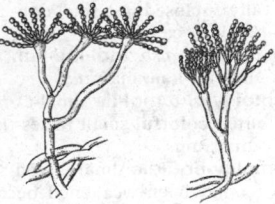

⁵mold 2

moldy \'mōl-dē\ *adj* **mold·i·er; -est** : resembling, containing, or covered with mold — **mold·i·ness** *n*

¹mole \'mōl\ *n* : a small usually brown and sometimes slightly raised permanent spot on the skin [Old English *māl* "spot on the skin"]

²mole *n* : any of numerous burrowing mammals with tiny eyes, concealed ears, and soft fur that eat insects [Middle English *mole* "burrowing animal"]

\ə\ abut	\au̇\ out	\i\ tip	\ȯ\ saw	\u̇\ foot
\ər\ further	\ch\ chin	\ī\ life	\ȯi\ coin	\y\ yet
\a\ mat	\e\ pet	\j\ job	\th\ thin	\yü\ few
\ā\ take	\ē\ easy	\ŋ\ sing	\t͟h\ this	\yu̇\ cure
\ä\ cot, cart	\g\ go	\ō\ bone	\ü\ food	\zh\ vision

[3]**mole** *n* : a pier made of heavy solid material (as concrete or stone) that protects a harbor from rough seas [from early French *mole* "stone pier," from early Italian *molo* (same meaning), derived from Latin *moles*, literally "a mass"]

mo·lec·u·lar \mə-'lek-yə-lər\ *adj* : of, relating to, or produced by molecules

molecular biology *n* : a branch of biology that investigates the structure and function of usually large molecules (as DNA and proteins) of living matter in order to understand their role in biological processes (as inheritance and cell function)

molecular formula *n* : a chemical formula that gives the total number of atoms of each element present in a molecule

molecular mass *n* : the mass of a molecule that is equal to the sum of the masses of all the atoms contained in the molecule's formula

molecular weight *n* : the weight of a molecule equal to the sum of the weights of the atoms contained in it

mol·e·cule \'mäl-i-ˌkyü(ə)l\ *n* **1** : the smallest particle of a substance having all the characteristics of the substance ⟨a *molecule* of water⟩ ⟨a *molecule* of oxygen⟩ **2** : a very small bit : PARTICLE

mole·hill \'mōl-ˌhil\ *n* **1** : a small mound or ridge of earth pushed up by a burrowing mole **2** : an unimportant obstacle or difficulty ⟨made a mountain out of a *molehill*⟩

mo·lest \mə-'lest\ *vb* **1** : to injure or disturb by interfering : ANNOY **2** : to make unwelcome sexual advances to; *esp* : to force physical sexual contact on — **mo·les·ta·tion** \ˌmōl-ˌes-'tā-shən, ˌmōl-əs-, ˌmäl-ˌes-\ *n* — **mo·lest·er** \mə-'les-tər\ *n*

mol·li·fy \'mäl-ə-ˌfī\ *vb* **-fied; -fy·ing 1** : to reduce the harshness or violence of **2** : to soothe in temper or disposition : CONCILIATE *synonyms* see PACIFY — **mol·li·fi·ca·tion** \ˌmäl-ə-fə-'kā-shən\ *n*

mol·lusk *or* **mol·lusc** \'mäl-əsk\ *n* : any of a large phylum of invertebrate animals (as snails, clams, and octopuses) with a soft body lacking segments and usually enclosed in a shell containing calcium — **mol·lus·can** *also* **mol·lus·kan** \mə-'ləs-kən, mä-\ *adj*

mollusk

mol·ly *also* **mol·lie** \'mäl-ē\ *n, pl* **mollies** : any of several often colorful small fishes that are often kept in tropical aquariums

[1]**mol·ly·cod·dle** \'mäl-ē-ˌkäd-ᵊl\ *n* : a person whose character has been weakened because of excessive pampering : SISSY

[2]**mollycoddle** *vb* **-cod·dled; -cod·dling** \-ˌkäd-liŋ, -ᵊl-iŋ\ : CODDLE 2, PAMPER

[1]**molt** \'mōlt\ *vb* : to shed hair, feathers, outer skin, shell, or horns with the cast-off parts being replaced by a new growth

[2]**molt** *n* : the act, process, or period of molting

mol·ten \'mōlt-ᵊn\ *adj* : melted especially by very great heat

mol·to \'mōl-tō, 'mol-\ *adv* : [2]MUCH 1, VERY — used in music directions

mo·lyb·de·num \mə-'lib-də-nəm\ *n* : a metallic element used in steel alloys to give greater strength and hardness — see ELEMENT table

mom \'mäm, 'məm\ *n* : [1]MOTHER 1a

mo·ment \'mō-mənt\ *n* **1** : a brief portion of time : INSTANT **2 a** : present time ⟨at the *moment* she is working on a novel⟩ **b** : a time of importance or success ⟨he has his *moments*⟩ **3** : IMPORTANCE, CONSEQUENCE ⟨an event of great *moment*⟩

mo·men·tari·ly \ˌmō-mən-'ter-ə-lē\ *adv* **1** : for a moment ⟨the pain eased *momentarily*⟩ **2** *archaic* : INSTANTLY **3** : at any moment ⟨we expect them *momentarily*⟩

mo·men·tary \'mō-mən-ˌter-ē\ *adj* : lasting only a moment *synonyms* see TRANSIENT

mo·ment·ly \'mō-mənt-lē\ *adv* : MOMENTARILY

mo·men·tous \mō-'ment-əs\ *adj* : very important ⟨a *momentous* decision⟩ — **mo·men·tous·ly** *adv*

mo·men·tum \mō-'ment-əm\ *n, pl* **-men·ta** \-'ment-ə\ *or* **-men·tums 1** : the characteristic of a moving body that is caused by its mass and its motion **2** : IMPETUS 1

momma *variant of* MAMA

mon- *or* **mono-** *combining form* **1** : one : single : alone ⟨*mono*tone⟩ **2** : one atom or group ⟨*mon*oxide⟩ [derived from Greek *monos* "alone, single"]

mon·arch \'män-ərk, -ˌärk\ *n* **1** : a person who reigns over a kingdom or empire: as **a** : a ruler who has total power ⟨absolute *monarch*⟩ **b** : someone who acts primarily as chief of state and who has only limited powers ⟨constitutional *monarch*⟩ **2** : someone or something like a monarch ⟨the oak is the *monarch* of the forest⟩ **3** : MONARCH BUTTERFLY — **mo·nar·chal** \mə-'när-kəl, mä-\ *or* **mo·nar·chi·al** \-kē-əl\ *adj*

monarch butterfly *n* : a large orange and black American butterfly that migrates in large numbers in the spring and fall and whose larva feeds on milkweed

mo·nar·chi·cal \mə-'när-ki-kəl, mä-\ *also* **mo·nar·chic** \-'när-kik\ *adj* : of or relating to a monarch or monarchy ⟨*monarchical* government⟩

mon·ar·chism \'män-ər-ˌkiz-əm\ *n* : the laws of monarchical government; *also* : belief in or support of these laws — **mon·ar·chist** \-kəst\ *n*

mon·ar·chy \'män-ər-kē\ *n, pl* **-chies 1** : total rule by one person **2** : a nation or country ruled by a monarch **3** : a form of government having a chief of state who inherits the position, rules for life, and holds powers varying from very limited to total

mon·as·tery \'män-ə-ˌster-ē\ *n, pl* **-ter·ies** : a place where a community of monks or nuns live and work — **mon·as·te·ri·al** \ˌmän-ə-'stir-ē-əl\ *adj*

mo·nas·tic \mə-'nas-tik\ *adj* **1** : of or relating to monks or monasteries **2** : resembling life in a monastery — **monastic** *n* — **mo·nas·ti·cal·ly** \-ti-k(ə-)lē\ *adv* — **mo·nas·ti·cism** \-tə-ˌsiz-əm\ *n*

Mon·day \'mən-dē\ *n* : the second day of the week

Word History In ancient times, it was believed that there were seven "planets," one of which was the moon. The seven days of the week were named after the seven "planets" in Latin. One of the days was named *dies Lunae*, which means "day of the moon." The Latin name was later translated into other languages. In Old English, *dies Lunae* became *mōnandæg*. The word *Monday* comes from the Old English *mōnandæg*. [Old English *mōnandæg* "Monday," literally "the moon's day," a translation of Latin *dies Lunae* "day of the moon"]

Mo·nel Metal \mō-ˌnel-\ *trademark* — used for an alloy primarily of nickel and copper

mo·ner·an \mō-'nir-ən, mə-\ *n* : PROKARYOTE — **moneran** *adj*

mon·e·tary \'män-ə-ˌter-ē *also* 'mən-\ *adj* : of or relating to money ⟨this administration's *monetary* policy⟩

mon·e·tize \'män-ə-ˌtīz *also* 'mən-\ *vb* **-tized; -tiz·ing** : to accept and set up (as gold) as money in its role of measuring the value of other kinds of money (as paper bills) — **mon·e·ti·za·tion** \ˌmän-ət-ə-'zā-shən *also* ˌmən-\ *n*

mon·ey \'mən-ē\ *n, pl* **moneys** *or* **mon·ies** \-ēz\ **1 a** : something (as coins or bills) generally accepted as a way of measuring value, as a way to trade value, and as a way to pay for goods and services **b** : an amount of money **2** : wealth calculated in terms of money **3** : the first, second, and third place winners in a horse or dog race —

usually used in the phrase *in the money* — **for one's money** : according to one's choice or opinion

Word History The wife of the Roman god Jupiter was Juno, but she was also known by several other names. One of them was *Moneta.* The Romans made coins at a temple that was dedicated to this goddess. For that reason the name *Moneta* came to mean "a place where coins are made," and later simply "coin" or "money." The Latin *Moneta* became *moneie* in early French. This early French word was borrowed into Middle English as *moneye.* From it we get the Modern English *money.* [Middle English *moneye* "money," from early French *moneie* (same meaning), from Latin *moneta* "coin, place where coins are made," from *Moneta* "a special name for the goddess Juno"; so called because the ancient Romans made coins at the temple of Juno Moneta — related to ²MINT]

mon·ey·bags \'mən-ē-ˌbagz\ *n sing or pl* : a wealthy person

money changer *n* : one whose business is the exchanging of one kind of money for the amount of other kinds of money that is equal in value

mon·eyed *or* **mon·ied** \'mən-ēd\ *adj* : having money : WEALTHY

mon·ey·lend·er \'mən-ē-ˌlen-dər\ *n* : one whose business is lending money; *esp* : PAWNBROKER

money market *n* : the trade in short-term negotiable instruments (as U.S. Treasury securities)

money order *n* : a written order purchased for a fee (as from a bank) to pay a particular amount of money to a specified person or company

Mon·gol \'mäŋ-gəl, 'män-ˌgōl\ *n* **1** : a member of one of the peoples of Mongolia who traditionally raise livestock **2** : MONGOLIAN 2

Mon·go·lian \män-'gōl-yən, mäŋ-, -'gō-lē-ən\ *n* **1** : a person born or living in Mongolia **2** : the language of the Mongol people — **Mongolian** *adj*

Mon·gol·oid \'mäŋ-gə-ˌlȯid\ *adj* : of or relating to a race of humankind that is native to Asia — **Mongoloid** *n*

mon·goose \'mäŋ-ˌgüs, 'mäŋ-\ *n, pl* **mon·goos·es** : any of various quick-moving mammals with a long slender body and long tail that are about the size of a ferret and feed chiefly on small animals and fruit

mongoose

¹mon·grel \'məŋ-grəl, 'mäŋ-\ *n* **1** : the offspring of parents of different breeds (as of dogs); *esp* : one whose ancestors are unknown **2** : a person or thing of mixed origin

²mongrel *adj* : of mixed or uncertain kind or origin

¹mon·i·tor \'män-ət-ər\ *n* **1 a** : a student appointed to assist a teacher **b** : a person that warns or instructs **c** : one that monitors or is used in monitoring; *esp* : a video screen used for display (as of television pictures or computer information) **2** : MONITOR LIZARD **3 a** : a heavily armored warship having low sides and revolving guns that was used against shipping in harbors and in river patrol **b** : a gunboat used to bombard coastal areas and riverbanks

²monitor *vb* **mon·i·tored; mon·i·tor·ing** \'män-ət-ə-riŋ, 'män-ə-triŋ\ : to watch, observe, or check for a special purpose ⟨*monitor* a broadcast for sound quality⟩

monitor lizard *n* : any of various large flesh-eating lizards of very warm areas in Africa, Australia, and Asia

monk \'məŋk\ *n* : a member of a religious community made up of men who agree to give up worldly life, remain poor and unmarried, and obey all laws of their community — **monk·ish** \'məŋ-kish\ *adj*

¹mon·key \'məŋ-kē\ *n, pl* **monkeys** **1** : any of a group of primate animals other than human beings that are furry and live in warm regions; *esp* : ones that are small and long-tailed as compared to the apes **2** : a ridiculous person : FOOL — **mon·key·ish** \-kē-ish\ *adj*

²monkey *vb* **mon·keyed; mon·key·ing** **1** : to act in a playful or mischievous manner **2** : MEDDLE, TAMPER ⟨don't *monkey* with the lawn mower⟩

mon·key·shine \'məŋ-kē-ˌshīn\ *n* : a mischievous trick : PRANK — usually used in plural

monkey wrench *n* : a wrench with one fixed and one adjustable jaw

monks·hood \'məŋ(k)s-ˌhůd\ *n* : any of a genus of poisonous plants related to the buttercups; *esp* : a tall Eurasian plant that is often grown for its white or purplish flowers

mono- — see MON-

mono·chro·mat·ic \ˌmän-ə-krō-'mat-ik\ *adj* **1** : having or consisting of one color **2** : consisting of radiation (as light) of a single wavelength

mono·chrome \'män-ə-ˌkrōm\ *n* : a painting, drawing, or photograph in a single color — **monochrome** *adj*

mon·o·cle \'män-i-kəl\ *n* : an eyeglass for one eye — **mon·o·cled** \-kəld\ *adj*

mono·cot \'män-ə-ˌkät\ *n* : MONOCOTYLEDON — **monocot** *adj*

mono·cot·y·le·don \ˌmän-ə-ˌkät-ᵊl-'ēd-ᵊn\ *n* : any of a group of flowering plants (as the palms and grasses) having an embryo with a single cotyledon and usually leaves with parallel veins and flower parts in groups of three — compare DICOTYLEDON — **mono·cot·y·le·don·ous** \-ᵊl-'ēd-ᵊn-əs\ *adj*

monocle

mono·cyte \'män-ə-ˌsīt\ *n* : a large white blood cell that is formed in the bone marrow and travels to the connective tissues where it develops into a macrophage

mon·oe·cious \mə-'nē-shəs, (')mä-\ *adj* : having on the same plant flowers with stamens only and flowers with pistils only

mo·nog·a·my \mə-'näg-ə-mē\ *n* : marriage with only one person at a time — **mo·nog·a·mous** \-məs\ *adj*

mono·gram \'män-ə-ˌgram\ *n* : an identifying or decorative symbol usually made up of a person's initials — **mono·grammed** \-ˌgramd\ *adj*

mono·lith \'män-ᵊl-ˌith\ *n* **1** : a single great stone often in the form of a monument or column **2** : something large and powerful (as a political organization) that is thought to function as a unified whole — **mono·lith·ic** \ˌmän-ᵊl-'ith-ik\ *adj*

mono·logue *also* **mono·log** \'män-ᵊl-ˌȯg, -ˌäg\ *n* **1** : a short dramatic work performed by one actor **2** : a long uninterrupted speech delivered by one person in the presence of others — **mono·logu·ist** \-ᵊl-ˌȯg-əst, -ˌäg-\ *or* **mo·no·lo·gist** \mə-'näl-ə-jəst; 'män-ᵊl-ˌȯg-əst, -ˌäg-\ *n*

mono·phon·ic \ˌmän-ə-'fän-ik\ *adj* : of or relating to sound recording or reproduction involving a single transmission path

mono·plane \'män-ə-ˌplān\ *n* : an airplane with only one set of wings

mo·nop·o·list \mə-'näp-ə-ləst\ *n* : one who monopolizes — **mo·nop·o·lis·tic** \-ˌnäp-ə-'lis-tik\ *adj*

mo·nop·o·lize \mə-'näp-ə-ˌlīz\ *vb* **-lized; -liz·ing** : to acquire or have complete control over ⟨always *monopolizing* the conversation⟩ — **mo·nop·o·li·za·tion** \-ˌnäp-ə-lə-'zā-shən\ *n* — **mo·nop·o·liz·er** \-'näp-ə-ˌlī-zər\ *n*

\ə\ **abut**	\aů\ **out**	\i\ **tip**	\ȯ\ **saw**	\ů\ **foot**
\ər\ **further**	\ch\ **chin**	\ī\ **life**	\ȯi\ **coin**	\y\ **yet**
\a\ **mat**	\e\ **pet**	\j\ **job**	\th\ **thin**	\yü\ **few**
\ā\ **take**	\ē\ **easy**	\ŋ\ **sing**	\th\ **this**	\yů\ **cure**
\ä\ **cot, cart**	\g\ **go**	\ō\ **bone**	\ü\ **food**	\zh\ **vision**

mo·nop·o·ly \mə-'näp-(ə-)lē\ *n, pl* **-lies 1 a** : complete control over the entire supply of goods or a service in a certain market **b** : complete possession **2** : a commercial product or service controlled by one person or company **3** : a company that has a monopoly

mono·rail \'män-ə-ˌrāl\ *n* : a single rail serving as a track for cars that balance on or hang from it; *also* : a car using such a track

monorail

mono·sac·cha·ride \ˌmän-ə-'sak-ə-ˌrīd\ *n* : a sugar that cannot be split into simpler sugars — called also *simple sugar*

mono·so·di·um glu·ta·mate \ˌmän-ə-ˌsōd-ē-əm-'glüt-ə-ˌmāt\ *n* : a sodium salt used for seasoning foods

mono·syl·la·ble \'män-ə-ˌsil-ə-bəl, ˌmän-ə-'sil-\ *n* : a word of one syllable — **mono·syl·lab·ic** \ˌmän-ə-sə-'lab-ik\ *adj*

mono·the·ism \'män-ə-(ˌ)thē-ˌiz-əm\ *n* : the belief that there is only one God — **mono·the·ist** \-ˌthē-əst\ *n* — **mono·the·is·tic** \ˌmän-ə-thē-'is-tik\ *adj*

mono·tone \'män-ə-ˌtōn\ *n* **1** : a series of syllables, words, or sentences on one unchanging key or pitch ⟨speak in a *monotone*⟩ **2** : a single unchanging musical tone **3** : a boring sameness or repetition ⟨a *monotone* of suburban houses⟩

mo·not·o·nous \mə-'nät-ᵊn-əs, -'nät-nəs\ *adj* **1** : uttered or sounded in one unchanging tone **2** : boring from being always the same ⟨a *monotonous* task⟩ — **mo·not·o·nous·ly** *adv* — **mo·not·o·nous·ness** *n*

mo·not·o·ny \mə-'nät-ᵊn-ē, -'nät-nē\ *n, pl* **-nies 1** : sameness of tone or sound **2** : lack of variety; *esp* : a lack of change that causes boredom

mono·treme \'män-ə-ˌtrēm\ *n* : any of an order of egg-laying mammals that include the platypuses and echidnas

mono·un·sat·u·rat·ed \ˌmän-ō-ˌən-'sach-ə-ˌrāt-ed\ *adj* : containing one double or triple bond per molecule — used especially of an oil, fat, or fatty acid

mon·ox·ide \mə-'näk-ˌsīd\ *n* : an oxide containing only one oxygen atom in the molecule

mon·sei·gneur \ˌmōn-ˌsän-'yər\ *n, pl* **mes·sei·gneurs** \ˌmā-ˌsān-'yər(z)\ : a high-ranking Frenchman (as a prince or archbishop) — used as a title before a title of office or rank

mon·sieur \məsh-(')yə(r), məs-, mə-'si(ə)r\ *n, pl* **mes·sieurs** \məsh-(')yə(r)(z), məs-, mäs-; mə-'si(ə)r(z)\ — used as a title equal to *Mister* for a Frenchman

mon·si·gnor \män-'sē-nyər, mən-\ *n, pl* **monsignors** *or* **mon·si·gno·ri** \ˌmän-'sēn-'yȯr-ē, -'yȯr-\ — used as a title for Roman Catholic priests

mon·soon \män-'sün\ *n* **1** : a periodic wind in the Indian Ocean and southern Asia **2** : the rainy season that accompanies the southwest monsoon **3** : rainfall that is associated with the monsoon season

¹mon·ster \'män(t)-stər\ *n* **1** : an animal or plant of abnormal form or structure **2** : a strange or horrible creature **3** : something unusually large **4** : an extremely wicked or cruel person

²monster *adj* : very large : ENORMOUS

mon·strance \'män(t)-strən(t)s\ *n* : a vessel in which the consecrated Host is exposed

mon·stros·i·ty \män-'sträs-ət-ē\ *n, pl* **-ties 1** : the condition of being monstrous **2** : something monstrous : MONSTER

mon·strous \'män(t)-strəs\ *adj* **1** : unusually large : GIGANTIC **2** : very ugly or vicious : HORRIBLE **3** : shockingly wrong or ridiculous **4** : very different from the usual form : ABNORMAL — **mon·strous·ly** *adv*

synonyms MONSTROUS, TREMENDOUS, STUPENDOUS, COLOSSAL mean of very great size. MONSTROUS suggests that something is unusually big when compared to others of its kind ⟨a *monstrous* cow⟩. TREMENDOUS suggests something so big that it causes wonder or fear ⟨the *tremendous* size of the blue whale⟩. STUPENDOUS suggests something that is amazing simply because of its size ⟨a *stupendous* wedding cake⟩. COLOSSAL suggests a size that is almost too great to imagine ⟨the *colossal* size of the largest planets⟩.

mon·tage \män-'täzh, mōn-\ *n* **1** : an artistic composition made up of several different kinds of items (as strips of newspaper, pictures, bits of wood) arranged together **2** : a rapid succession of distinct scenes or images in a motion picture to illustrate associated ideas

Mon·te·zu·ma's revenge \ˌmän-tə-'zü-məz-\ *n* : diarrhea contracted in Mexico especially by tourists [named after *Montezuma* II, 1466–1520, the last Aztec emperor of Mexico]

month \'mən(t)th\ *n, pl* **months** \'mən(t)s, 'mən(t)ths\ : one of the 12 parts into which the year is divided

¹month·ly \'mən(t)th-lē\ *adj* **1** : occurring, done, produced, or published every month **2** : due or calculated by the month ⟨*monthly* salary⟩ **3** : lasting a month — **monthly** *adv*

²monthly *n, pl* **monthlies 1** : a monthly magazine **2** *pl* : a menstrual period

mon·u·ment \'män-yə-mənt\ *n* **1** : something that serves as a memorial; *esp* : a building, pillar, stone, or statue honoring a person or event **2** : a work, saying, or deed that lasts or that is worth preserving ⟨the book is a *monument* of scholarship⟩ **3** : a boundary marker (as a stone) **4** : a place of historic interest or natural beauty set aside and maintained by the government as public property

mon·u·men·tal \ˌmän-yə-'ment-ᵊl\ *adj* **1** : of or relating to a monument **2** : serving as or resembling a monument : MASSIVE; *also* : highly significant : OUTSTANDING **3** : very great ⟨*monumental* stupidity⟩ — **mon·u·men·tal·ly** \-ᵊl-ē\ *adv*

¹moo \'mü\ *vb* : to make the low sound of a cow : LOW

²moo *n* : the sound a cow makes when it moos

mooch \'müch\ *vb* **1** : to wander about **2** : BEG 1, SPONGE — **mooch·er** *n*

¹mood \'müd\ *n* **1** : an emotional state of mind or feeling; *also* : the feeling expressed in a work of art or literature **2** : a dominant attitude or spirit ⟨the *mood* of the country was optimistic⟩ **3** : a distinctive atmosphere or context ⟨the dark *mood* of the movie⟩ [Old English *mōd* "a state of mind"]

²mood *n* : a set of forms of a verb that show whether the action or state expressed is to be thought of as a fact, a command, or a wish or possibility [an altered form of *mode*]

moody \'müd-ē\ *adj* **mood·i·er; -est 1** : frequently influenced by moods; *esp* : affected by changeable and gloomy moods or bad temper **2** : expressing a mood ⟨a *moody* face⟩ — **mood·i·ly** \'müd-ᵊl-ē\ *adv* — **mood·i·ness** \'müd-ē-nəs\ *n*

¹moon \'mün\ *n* **1 a** : the earth's natural satellite that shines by reflecting light from the sun and revolves about the earth in about 29½ days **b** : SATELLITE 2a **2** : an unspecified and usually long period of time ⟨took many *moons* to complete⟩ **3** : ¹MOONLIGHT — **moon·less** \-ləs\ *adj*

²moon *vb* : to spend time daydreaming

moon·beam \'mün-ˌbēm\ *n* : a ray of light from the moon

¹moon·light \-ˌlīt\ *n* : the light of the moon

²moonlight *vb* : to work at a second job in addition to a regular one — **moon·light·er** *n*

moon·lit \'mün-ˌlit\ *adj* : lighted by the moon

moon·roof \-ˌrüf, ˌrùf\ *n* : a glass sunroof

moon·scape \'mün-ˌskāp\ *n* : the surface of the moon as seen or as pictured

moon·shine \'mün-ˌshīn\ *n* **1** : ¹MOONLIGHT **2** : meaningless talk : NONSENSE **3** : alcoholic liquor; *esp* : illegally produced whiskey made from corn — **moon·shin·er** \-ˌshī-nər\ *n*

moon·stone \-ˌstōn\ *n* : a partly transparent shiny stone used as a gem

moon·struck \-ˌstrək\ *adj* **1** : mentally unbalanced **2** : romantically sentimental **3** : lost in daydreams or fantasy

moony \'mü-nē\ *adj* : DREAMY 2, MOONSTRUCK

¹**moor** \'mu̇(ə)r\ *n* : a boggy area; *esp* : one that is peaty and dominated by grasses and sedges [Old English *mōr* "an area of open and wet wasteland"]

²**moor** *vb* : to fasten in place with cables, lines, or anchors ⟨*moor* a boat⟩ [Middle English *moren* "to fasten (a boat) in place"] — **moor·age** \-ij\ *n*

Moor \'mu̇(ə)r\ *n* : one of a North African people that conquered Spain in the 8th century and ruled until 1492 [Middle English *More* "Moor," from early French *More* (same meaning), from Latin *Maurus* "a person from Mauretania (a country in Africa)"] — **Moor·ish** \-ish\ *adj*

moor·hen \'mu̇(ə)r-ˌhen\ *n* : a common gallinule found in the New World, Eurasia, and Africa

moor·ing \'mu̇(ə)r-iŋ\ *n* **1** : a place or object to which a boat or aircraft can be fastened **2** : a device or line by which a boat or aircraft is moored

moor·land \'mu̇(ə)r-lənd, -ˌland\ *n* : land consisting of moors

moose \'müs\ *n, pl* **moose** : a large cud-chewing mammal with broad flattened antlers and humped shoulders that is related to the deer and lives in forests of Canada, the northern U.S., Europe, and Asia

moose

¹**moot** \'müt\ *vb* **1** : to bring up for discussion **2** : ²DEBATE 1

²**moot** *adj* : open to question or discussion : DEBATABLE ⟨a *moot* question⟩

¹**mop** \'mäp\ *n* **1** : a tool for cleaning made of a bundle of cloth or yarn or a sponge fastened to a handle **2** : something resembling a mop ⟨a tangled *mop* of hair⟩

²**mop** *vb* **mopped; mop·ping** : to wipe or clean with or as if with a mop ⟨*mop* the floor⟩ ⟨*mopped* my brow with a handkerchief⟩

¹**mope** \'mōp\ *vb* **moped; mop·ing** **1** : to be in a dull and gloomy state **2** : to move slowly and aimlessly : DAWDLE — **mop·er** *n*

²**mope** *n* **1** : a person who lacks energy or enthusiasm **2** *pl* : low spirits : BLUES ⟨a fit of the *mopes*⟩

mo·ped \'mō-ˌped\ *n* : a lightweight low-powered motorbike that can be pedaled

mop·pet \'mäp-ət\ *n* : a young child

mo·raine \mə-'rān\ *n* : a pile of earth and stones carried and deposited by a glacier

¹**mor·al** \'mȯr-əl, 'mär-\ *adj* **1 a** : of or relating to the judgment of right and wrong in human behavior : ETHICAL **b** : expressing or teaching an idea of right behavior ⟨a *moral* poem⟩ **c** : agreeing with a standard of right behavior : GOOD ⟨*moral* conduct⟩ **d** : able to choose between right and wrong **2** : likely but not proved : VIRTUAL ⟨a *moral* certainty⟩ — **mor·al·ly** \-ə-lē\ *adv*

²**moral** *n* **1** : the lesson to be learned from a story or an experience **2** *pl* : moral conduct ⟨a high standard of *morals*⟩ **3** *pl* : moral teachings or rules

mo·rale \mə-'ral\ *n* : the mental and emotional condition (as of enthusiasm, spirit, or loyalty) of an individual or a group with regard to a task or goal to be accomplished

mor·al·ist \'mȯr-ə-ləst, 'mär-\ *n* **1** : a person who leads a moral life **2** : a person who teaches, studies, or points out morals **3** : a person who is concerned with regulating the morals of others

mor·al·is·tic \ˌmȯr-ə-'lis-tik, ˌmär-\ *adj* **1** : teaching or pointing out morals ⟨a *moralistic* story⟩ **2** : having or expressing a conservative moral attitude ⟨a *moralistic* attitude toward the problems of youth⟩

mo·ral·i·ty \mə-'ral-ət-ē\ *n, pl* **-ties** **1** : moral quality : VIRTUE ⟨judge the *morality* of an action⟩ **2** : a system of moral rules

morality play *n* : a type of play popular especially in the 15th and 16th centuries in which the characters stand for moral qualities (as virtue or vice) or conditions (as death)

mor·al·ize \'mȯr-ə-ˌlīz, 'mär-\ *vb* **-ized; -iz·ing** **1** : to explain in a moral sense : draw a moral from **2** : to make moral or morally better **3** : to make moral comments — **mor·al·i·za·tion** \ˌmȯr-ə-lə-'zā-shən, ˌmär-\ *n* — **mor·al·iz·er** \'mȯr-ə-ˌlī-zər, 'mär-\ *n*

mo·rass \mə-'ras\ *n* **1** : MARSH, SWAMP **2** : a situation that traps, confuses, or hinders

mor·a·to·ri·um \ˌmȯr-ə-'tōr-ē-əm, ˌmär-, -'tȯr-\ *n, pl* **-ri·ums** *or* **-ria** \-ē-ə\ **1** : a legally approved period of delay in the payment of a debt or the performance of a duty **2** : ²BAN 2, SUSPENSION ⟨a *moratorium* on atomic testing⟩

mo·ray eel \mə-'rā-, 'mȯr-ā-\ *n* : any of numerous often brightly colored eels that have sharp teeth capable of biting and live in warm seas — called also *moray*

mor·bid \'mȯr-bəd\ *adj* **1** : not healthful : DISEASED ⟨a *morbid* condition⟩ **2** : characterized by gloomy or sick ideas or feelings ⟨takes a *morbid* interest in funerals⟩ — **mor·bid·ly** *adv*

mor·bid·i·ty \mȯr-'bid-ət-ē\ *n, pl* **-ties** **1** : the quality or state of being morbid **2** : the rate at which a disease occurs in a group of individuals

mor·dant \'mȯrd-ᵊnt\ *adj* : SARCASTIC, BITING ⟨*mordant* criticism⟩

¹**more** \'mō(ə)r, 'mȯ(ə)r\ *adj* **1** : greater in amount, number, or size ⟨felt *more* pain⟩ **2** : ¹EXTRA, ADDITIONAL ⟨bought *more* apples⟩

²**more** *adv* **1** : in addition ⟨wait one day *more*⟩ **2** : to a greater or higher extent — often used with an adjective or adverb to form the comparative ⟨*more* active⟩ ⟨*more* actively⟩

³**more** *n* **1** : a greater amount or number ⟨got *more* than we expected⟩ ⟨the *more* I thought about it⟩ **2** : an additional amount or number ⟨the *more* the merrier⟩

mo·rel \mə-'rel, mȯ-\ *n* : any of several large edible fungi with a cap having indentations on the surface — called also *morel mushroom*

more or less *adv* **1** : to a varying or uncertain degree : SOMEWHAT ⟨they were *more or less* willing to help⟩ **2** : with small variations : APPROXIMATELY ⟨contains 16 acres *more or less*⟩

more·over \mōr-'ō-vər, mȯr-\ *adv* : in addition to what has been said : BESIDES

mo·res \'mō(ə)r-ˌāz, 'mȯ(ə)r- *also* -ēz\ *n pl* **1** : the unchanging customs of a particular group that are accepted by all group members as moral and necessary for the group's survival **2** : usual behavior : HABITS, MANNERS

Mor·gan \'mȯr-gən\ *n* : any of an American breed of light strong horses

mor·ga·nat·ic \ˌmȯr-gə-ˌnat-ik-\ *adj* : of, relating to, or being a legal and recognized marriage between a member

\ə\ abut	\au̇\ out	\i\ tip	\ȯ\ saw	\u̇\ foot
\ər\ further	\ch\ chin	\ī\ life	\ȯi\ coin	\y\ yet
\a\ mat	\e\ pet	\j\ job	\th\ thin	\yü\ few
\ā\ take	\ē\ easy	\ŋ\ sing	\th\ this	\yu̇\ cure
\ä\ cot, cart	\g\ go	\ō\ bone	\ü\ food	\zh\ vision

of a royal or noble family and a person of lower rank who does not take on the title of the higher ranked person and whose children do not acquire the title or inheritance of the parent of higher rank

morgue \\'mȯ(ə)rg\ *n* **1** : a place where the bodies of the dead are kept temporarily until they are identified or released for burial **2** : a department of a newspaper where reference material is filed

mor·i·bund \\'mȯr-ə-(‚)bənd, 'mär-\ *adj* : nearly dead

Mor·mon \\'mȯr-mən\ *n* : a member of the Church of Jesus Christ of Latter-day Saints founded by Joseph Smith in 1830 and accepting the Book of Mormon — **Mor·mon·ism** \\'mȯr-mə-‚niz-əm\ *n*

morn \\'mȯ(ə)rn\ *n* : MORNING

morn·ing \\'mȯr-niŋ\ *n* **1 a** : ²DAWN 1 **b** : the time from sunrise to noon **c** : the time from midnight to noon **2** : the first or early part : BEGINNING ⟨the *morning* of life⟩

morning glory *n* : any of various usually twining plants with showy trumpet-shaped flowers that usually close by the middle of the day; *also* : any of various related herbs, vines, shrubs, or trees

morning sickness *n* : nausea that occurs typically in the morning and that is usually associated with the early months of pregnancy

morning star *n* : a bright planet (as Venus) seen in the eastern sky before or at sunrise

mo·roc·co \mə-'räk-ō\ *n* : a fine leather made of goat skins tanned with sumac

mo·ron \\'mō(ə)r-‚än, 'mȯ(ə)r-\ *n* : a very stupid person — **mo·ron·ic** \mə-'rän-ik, mȯ-\ *adj*

mo·rose \mə-'rōs, mȯ-\ *adj* : SULLEN 1a, GLOOMY — **mo·rose·ly** *adv* — **mo·rose·ness** *n*

morph \\'mȯrf\ *vb* : to change in form or character [short for *metamorphose* "to change in form"]

mor·pheme \\'mȯr-‚fēm\ *n* : a word or a part of a word (as *re-* or *-call* in *recall*) that contains no smaller unit of meaning — **mor·phe·mic** \mȯr-'fē-mik\ *adj*

mor·phine \\'mȯr-‚fēn\ *n* : a bitter white habit-forming narcotic drug made from opium and used especially to deaden pain [derived from *Morpheus* "Greek god of dreams"]

mor·phol·o·gy \mȯr-'fäl-ə-jē\ *n* **1 a** : a branch of biology that deals with the form and structure of animals and plants **b** : the form and structure of a plant or animal or any of its parts **2** : the part of grammar dealing with word formation **3** : ¹STRUCTURE 3, FORM ⟨the *morphology* of rocks⟩ — **mor·pho·log·i·cal** \‚mȯr-fə-'läj-i-kəl\ *adj*

mor·ris \\'mȯr-əs, 'mär-\ *n* : a vigorous English dance traditionally performed by men wearing costumes and bells [Middle English *moreys* "Moorish"]

morris chair \‚mȯr-əs-, ‚mär-\ *n* : an easy chair with an adjustable back and removable cushions

mor·row \\'mär-ō, 'mȯr-\ *n* **1** *archaic* : MORNING **2** : the next day

Morse code \\'mȯrs-\ *n* : either of two codes consisting of dots and dashes or long and short sounds used for sending messages

---

INTERNATIONAL MORSE CODE

a · —	n — ·	á · — — · —	8 — — — · ·
b — · · ·	o — — —	ä · — · —	9 — — — — ·
c — · — ·	p · — — ·	é · · — · ·	0 — — — — —
d — · ·	q — — · —	ñ — — · — —	, — — · · — — (comma)
e ·	r · — ·	ö — — — ·	· — · — · — (period)
f · · — ·	s · · ·	ü · · — —	? · · — — · · (question mark)
g — — ·	t —	1 · — — — —	" · — · · — · (quotation marks)
h · · · ·	u · · —	2 · · — — —	: — — — · · · (colon)
i · ·	v · · · —	3 · · · — —	· — — — — · (apostrophe)
j · — — —	w · — —	4 · · · · —	- — · · · · — (hyphen)
k — · —	x — · · —	5 · · · · ·	/ — · · — · (slash)
l · — · ·	y — · — —	6 — · · · ·	(— · — — · (left parenthesis)
m — —	z — — · ·	7 — — · · ·	) — · — — · — (right parenthesis)

---

mor·sel \\'mȯr-səl\ *n* **1** : a small piece of food : BITE **2** : a small quantity or piece [Middle English *morsel* "a small piece of food," from early French *morsel* (same meaning), from *mors* "a bite," derived from Latin *morsus*, past participle of *mordēre* "to bite" — related to REMORSE; see *Word History* at REMORSE]

¹**mor·tal** \\'mȯrt-ᵊl\ *adj* **1** : capable of causing death ⟨a *mortal* wound⟩ **2** : certain to die ⟨animals are *mortal*⟩ **3** : extremely unfriendly ⟨a *mortal* enemy⟩ **4** : very great or severe ⟨in *mortal* fear⟩ **5** : ¹HUMAN 1 ⟨*mortal* limitations⟩ **6** : of, relating to, or connected with death ⟨*mortal* agony⟩ **synonyms** see DEADLY — **mor·tal·ly** \-ᵊl-ē\ *adv*

²**mortal** *n* : a human being

mor·tal·i·ty \mȯr-'tal-ət-ē\ *n*, *pl* **-ties** **1** : the quality or state of being mortal **2** : the death of large numbers (as of animals or people) **3 a** : the number of deaths in a given time or place **b** : the ratio of deaths occurring in a certain time in a given population to the number of individuals in the population

mortal sin *n* : a sin considered so serious or wicked as to deserve eternal punishment

¹**mor·tar** \\'mȯrt-ər\ *n* **1** : a strong deep bowl in which substances are pounded or crushed with a pestle **2** : a short muzzle-loading cannon used to fire shells at a low speed and at high angles

²**mortar** *n* : a building material made of lime and cement mixed with sand and water that is spread between bricks or stones so as to hold them together when it hardens — **mortar** *vb*

mor·tar·board \\'mȯrt-ər-‚bȯ(ə)rd, -‚bȯ(ə)rd\ *n* **1** : a board used to hold mortar while it is being applied **2** : an academic cap with a broad flat square top and tassel that is worn at graduation and other ceremonies

mortarboard 2

¹**mort·gage** \\'mȯr-gij\ *n* **1** : a transfer of rights to a piece of property (as a house) usually in return for a loan and that is canceled when the loan is paid **2** : the document recording such a transfer

²**mortgage** *vb* **mort·gaged; mort·gag·ing** **1** : to transfer rights to a piece of property by a mortgage **2** : to place under an obligation : pledge in advance

mort·gag·ee \‚mȯr-gi-'jē\ *n* : a person to whom property is mortgaged

mort·gag·or \‚mȯr-gi-'jȯ(ə)r\ *also* **mort·gag·er** \\'mȯr-gi-jər\ *n* : a person who mortgages his or her property

mor·ti·cian \mȯr-'tish-ən\ *n* : UNDERTAKER

mor·ti·fy \\'mȯrt-ə-‚fī\ *vb* **-fied; -fy·ing** **1** : to attempt to reduce or control bodily needs and desires through punishment and self-denial **2** : to embarrass greatly : HUMILIATE — **mor·ti·fi·ca·tion** \‚mȯrt-ə-fə-'kā-shən\ *n*

¹**mor·tise** \\'mȯrt-əs\ *n* : a hole or groove cut in a piece of wood or other material into which another piece fits so as to form a joint

²**mortise** *vb* **mor·tised; mor·tis·ing** **1** : to join or fasten securely especially by a tenon and mortise **2** : to cut a mortise in

¹**mor·tu·ary** \\'mȯr-chə-‚wer-ē\ *n*, *pl* **-ar·ies** : a place in which the bodies of the dead are kept until burial; *esp* : FUNERAL HOME

²**mortuary** *adj* : of or relating to death or burial of the dead

mo·sa·ic \mō-'zā-ik\ *n* **1** : a decoration on a surface made by setting small pieces of glass, tile, or stone of different colors into another material so as to make pictures or patterns **2** : the process of making mosaics **3** : something resembling a mosaic; *esp* : a virus disease of plants characterized by mottling of the foliage — **mosaic** *adj*

mo·sa·saur \'mō-zə-ˌsȯr\ *n* : any of various very large extinct fish-eating lizards of seas of the Cretaceous period with limbs resembling paddles [from Latin *Mosa* "the River Meuse" and Greek *sauros* "lizard"]

Mos·lem \'mäz-ləm *also* 'mäs-\ *variant of* MUSLIM

mosque \'mäsk\ *n* : a Muslim place of worship

mos·qui·to \mə-'skēt-ō\ *n, pl* **-toes** *also* **-tos** : any of numerous two-winged flies of which the females have a needle-like structure of the mouth region adapted to puncture the skin and suck the blood of animals [from Spanish *mosquito* "mosquito," literally "little fly," from *mosca* "fly"] — **mos·qui·to·ey** \-'skēt-ə-wē\ *adj*

mosquito

mosquito net *n* : a net for keeping out mosquitoes

moss \'mȯs\ *n* **1** : any of a class of plants that have no flowers and produce small leafy stems forming sex organs at their tips and that grow in patches like cushions clinging to rocks, bark, or damp ground **2** : any of various plants (as lichens) resembling mosses — compare REINDEER MOSS — **moss·like** \-ˌlīk\ *adj* — **mossy** \'mȯ-sē\ *adj*

mossy zinc *n* : a form of zinc made by pouring melted zinc into water

¹most \'mōst\ *adj* **1** : the majority of ⟨*most* people believe this⟩ **2** : greatest in amount or extent ⟨the *most* ability⟩

²most *adv* **1** : to the greatest or highest level or extent — often used with an adjective or adverb to form the superlative ⟨*most* active⟩ ⟨*most* actively⟩ **2** : to a very great extent ⟨a *most* careful driver⟩

³most *n* : the greatest amount, number, or part ⟨the *most* that can be accomplished⟩

⁴most *adv* : ALMOST ⟨the cost of *most* everything is higher⟩

-most \ˌmōst\ *adj suffix* : most ⟨inner*most*⟩ [Middle English *-most* "most"]

most·ly \'mōst-lē\ *adv* : for the greatest part : MAINLY

mote \'mōt\ *n* : a small particle : SPECK

mo·tel \mō-'tel\ *n* : a building or group of buildings which provide lodgings and in which the rooms are usually reached directly from an outdoor parking lot

mo·tet \mō-'tet\ *n* : a form of church music to be sung by several voices usually without accompanying instruments and with several melodies woven together

moth \'mȯth\ *n, pl* **moths** \'mȯthz, 'mȯths\ : any of a group of night-flying insects that are lepidopterans often with duller coloring, stouter bodies, and smaller wings than the related butterflies and with antennae which are often feathery

¹moth·ball \'mȯth-ˌbȯl\ *n* **1** : a ball (as of naphthalene) used to keep moths out of clothing **2** *pl* : protective storage ⟨a fleet put in *mothballs* after the war⟩

²mothball *vb* **1** : to remove a ship from use and protect from deterioration **2** : to withdraw from use or service and keep in reserve : put aside

moth–eat·en \'mȯ-ˌthēt-ᵊn\ *adj* **1** : eaten into by moths ⟨*moth-eaten* clothes⟩ **2** : so old as to be no longer acceptable or usable

¹moth·er \'məth-ər\ *n* **1 a** : a female parent **b** : a woman in authority; *esp* : a nun in charge of a convent **2** : an elderly woman **3** : ¹CAUSE 1, ORIGIN ⟨necessity is the *mother* of invention⟩ — **moth·er·hood** \-ˌhu̇d\ *n* — **moth·er·less** \-ləs\ *adj*

²mother *adj* **1 a** : of or relating to a mother ⟨*mother* love⟩ **b** : being in the relation of a mother to others ⟨a *mother* country⟩ **2** : gotten from or as if from one's mother

³mother *vb* **moth·ered; moth·er·ing** \'məth-(ə-)riŋ\ : to be or act as mother to

moth·er·board \'məth-ər-ˌbō(ə)rd, -ˌbȯ(ə)rd\ *n* : the main circuit board especially of a personal computer

Mother Car·ey's chicken \ˌməth-ər-ˌkar-ēz, -ˌker-\ *n* : STORM PETREL

Mother Hub·bard \ˌməth-ər-'həb-ərd\ *n* : a loose usually shapeless dress

moth·er–in–law \'məth-(ə)rən-ˌlȯ, 'məth-ərn-ˌlȯ\ *n, pl* **moth·ers–in–law** \'məth-ər-zən-\ : the mother of one's husband or wife

moth·er·land \'məth-ər-ˌland\ *n* : FATHERLAND

mother lode *n* : the main vein or deposit of an ore (as gold) in a region

moth·er·ly \'məth-ər-lē\ *adj* **1** : of, relating to, or characteristic of a mother ⟨*motherly* affection⟩ **2** : resembling a mother — **moth·er·li·ness** *n*

Mother Nature *n* : nature represented as a woman thought of as the source and guiding force of creation

moth·er–of–pearl \ˌməth-ə-rə(v)-'pər(-ə)l\ *n* : the hard pearly material that lines the shell of some mollusks (as mussels) and is often used for ornamental objects and buttons

mother of vinegar : a slimy mass of yeast cells and bacteria that forms on the surface of liquids in a process of alcoholic fermentation and is added to wine or cider to produce vinegar — called also *mother*

Mother's Day *n* : the second Sunday in May set aside for the honoring of mothers

mother tongue *n* **1** : one's native language **2** : a language from which another language develops

mo·tif \mō-'tēf\ *n* **1** : an important and usually repeating idea or theme in a work of art **2** : a feature in a decoration or design ⟨a flower *motif* in wallpaper⟩

mo·tile \'mōt-ᵊl, 'mō-ˌtīl\ *adj* : moving or able to move — **mo·til·i·ty** \mō-'til-ət-ē\ *n*

¹mo·tion \'mō-shən\ *n* **1** : a formal plan or suggestion for action offered according to the rules of a meeting ⟨a *motion* to adjourn⟩ **2 a** : an act or process of changing place or position : MOVEMENT **b** : an act or instance of moving the body or its parts : GESTURE — **mo·tion·less** \-ləs\ *adj* — **mo·tion·less·ly** *adv* — **mo·tion·less·ness** *n*

²motion *vb* **mo·tioned; mo·tion·ing** \'mō-sh(ə-)niŋ\ : to direct or signal by a movement or sign ⟨*motioned* me to come forward⟩

motion picture *n* **1** : a series of pictures projected on a screen rapidly one after another so as to give the appearance of a continuous picture in which the objects move **2** : MOVIE 2

motion sickness *n* : sickness caused by motion (as in travel by air, car, or ship) and characterized especially by nausea

mo·ti·vate \'mōt-ə-ˌvāt\ *vb* **-vat·ed; -vat·ing** : to provide with a reason for doing something : INDUCE

mo·ti·va·tion \ˌmōt-ə-'vā-shən\ *n* **1 a** : the act or process of motivating **b** : the condition of being motivated **2** : a motivating force or influence : INCENTIVE

¹mo·tive \'mōt-iv, *sense 2 is also* mō-'tēv\ *n* **1** : something (as a need or desire) that leads to or influences a person to do something ⟨their *motive* in running away was to avoid trouble⟩ **2** : MOTIF **synonyms** see CAUSE

²motive \'mōt-iv\ *adj* : of, relating to, or causing motion ⟨*motive* power⟩

¹mot·ley \'mät-lē\ *adj* **1** : having various colors **2** : composed of various often unlike kinds or parts ⟨a *motley* collection of junk⟩

²motley *n* **1 a** : a garment of mixed colors worn by a court jester **b** : ¹FOOL 2 **2** : a mixture of different elements

\ə\ abut	\au̇\ out	\i\ tip	\ȯ\ saw	\u̇\ foot
\ər\ further	\ch\ chin	\ī\ life	\ȯi\ coin	\y\ yet
\a\ mat	\e\ pet	\j\ job	\th\ thin	\yü\ few
\ā\ take	\ē\ easy	\ŋ\ sing	\th\ this	\yu̇\ cure
\ä\ cot, cart	\g\ go	\ō\ bone	\ü\ food	\zh\ vision

mo·to·cross \'mōt-ō-ˌkrȯs\ *n* : a motorcycle race over a course laid out on rough terrain; *also* : the sport of moto-cross racing

mo·to·neu·ron \ˌmōt-ə-'n(y)ü-ˌrän, -'n(y)u̇(ə)r-ˌän\ *n* : MOTOR NEURON

¹mo·tor \'mōt-ər\ *n* **1** : a machine that produces motion or power for doing work ⟨a gasoline *motor*⟩ ⟨electric *motors*⟩ **2** : MOTOR VEHICLE; *esp* : ²AUTOMOBILE — **mo·tor·less** \-ləs\ *adj*

²motor *adj* **1** : causing or giving motion ⟨*motor* power⟩ **2 a** : of, relating to, or being a nerve, neuron, or nerve fiber that carries a nerve impulse to a muscle causing movement ⟨*motor* nerves⟩ **b** : concerned with or involving muscular movement ⟨*motor* areas of the brain⟩ ⟨a *motor* reaction⟩ **3 a** : equipped with or driven by a motor **b** : of, relating to, or designed for use in an automobile ⟨a *motor* accident⟩ ⟨a *motor* mechanic⟩

³motor *vb* : to travel or transport by automobile : DRIVE

mo·tor·bike \'mōt-ər-ˌbīk\ *n* : a light motorcycle

mo·tor·boat \-ˌbōt\ *n* : a boat driven by a motor

mo·tor·cade \'mōt-ər-ˌkād\ *n* : a parade of motor vehicles

mo·tor·car \'mōt-ər-ˌkär\ *n* : ²AUTOMOBILE

motor court *n* : MOTEL

mo·tor·cy·cle \'mōt-ər-ˌsī-kəl\ *n* : a motorized vehicle for one or two passengers that has two wheels — **motorcy·cle** *vb* — **mo·tor·cy·clist** \-ˌsī-k(ə-)ləst\ *n*

motor home *n* : a large motor vehicle equipped as a complete traveling home

mo·tor·ist \'mōt-ə-rəst\ *n* : a person who travels by automobile

mo·tor·ize \'mōt-ə-ˌrīz\ *vb* **-ized; -iz·ing 1** : to equip with a motor **2** : to equip with motor-driven vehicles for transportation ⟨*motorized* troops⟩

mo·tor·man \'mōt-ər-mən\ *n* : an operator of a motor-driven vehicle (as a streetcar or a subway train)

motor neuron *n* : a neuron that passes from the central nervous system or a ganglion toward or to a muscle and carries a nerve impulse that causes movement — compare SENSORY NEURON

motor scooter *n* : a motorized vehicle with two or three wheels like a child's scooter but having a seat

mo·tor·truck \'mōt-ər-ˌtrək\ *n* : a self-propelled truck for transporting freight

motor vehicle *n* : a motorized vehicle (as an automobile or motorcycle) not operated on rails

¹mot·tle \'mät-³l\ *n* **1** : a colored spot **2** : a pattern of colored spots or blotches — **mot·tled** \-³ld\ *adj*

²mottle *vb* **mot·tled; mot·tling** \'mät-liŋ, -³l-iŋ\ : to mark with spots or blotches of different color or shades of color as if stained

mot·to \'mät-ō\ *n, pl* **mottoes** *also* **mottos 1** : a sentence, phrase, or word inscribed on something (as a coin or public building) to suggest its use or nature **2** : a short expression of a guiding rule of conduct

mould *chiefly British variant of* MOLD

moult *chiefly British variant of* MOLT

¹mound \'maund\ *n* **1** : a small hill or heap of dirt or stones (as one made to mark a grave) **2** : the slightly raised ground on which a baseball pitcher stands

²mound *vb* : to form into a mound

¹mount \'maunt\ *n* : MOUNTAIN — used especially before an identifying name ⟨*Mount* Everest⟩ [from Old English *munt* and early French *mont,* both meaning "mount" and both from Latin *mont-, mons* (same meaning)]

²mount *vb* **1 a** : ¹RISE 5a, ASCEND **b** : to go up : CLIMB ⟨*mount* a ladder⟩ **2** : to get up onto something ⟨*mount* a platform⟩ **3** : to furnish with riding animals or vehicles ⟨*mounted* infantry⟩ **4** : to increase rapidly in amount ⟨*mounting* debts⟩ **5** : to prepare for use, examination, or display especially by fastening in position on a support ⟨*mount* a picture on cardboard⟩ ⟨*mount* a specimen⟩ **6** : to furnish with scenery and costumes : STAGE **7** : to

place in position for the purpose of defense or observation ⟨*mounted* some guards⟩ [Middle English *mounten* "to increase, rise," from early French *monter* (same meaning), derived from Latin *mont-, mons* "hill, mount"]

³mount *n* **1** : FRAME, SUPPORT: as **a** : a jewelry setting **b** : a glass slide on which objects are placed for examination under a microscope **2** : SADDLE HORSE

moun·tain \'maunt-³n\ *n* **1** : an elevation higher than a hill **2** : a great mass or huge number ⟨a *mountain* of mail⟩

mountain ash *n* : any of various trees related to the roses and having leaves divided into numerous leaflets and red or orange-red fruits

mountain bike *n* : a bicycle with wide knobby tires and many gears for use on all kinds of terrain — **mountain bike** *vb*

moun·tain·eer \ˌmaunt-³n-'i(ə)r\ *n* **1** : a person who lives in the mountains **2** : a mountain climber

moun·tain·eer·ing \-'i(ə)r-iŋ\ *n* : the sport or technique of climbing mountains

mountain goat *n* : a cud-chewing mammal of the mountains of western North America that has a thick yellowish white hairy coat and slightly curved black horns and closely resembles a goat

mountain laurel *n* : a North American evergreen shrub of the heath family that has glossy leaves and pink or white cup-shaped flowers

mountain lion *n* : COUGAR

moun·tain·ous \'maunt-³n-əs, -nəs\ *adj* **1** : having many mountains **2** : resembling a mountain : HUGE

mountain goat

mountain sheep *n* : any of various wild sheep (as a bighorn sheep) that live in high mountains

moun·tain·side \'maunt-³n-ˌsīd\ *n* : the side of a mountain

mountain time *n, often cap M* : the time of the seventh time zone west of Greenwich that includes the Rocky Mountain states of the U.S.

moun·tain·top \'maunt-³n-ˌtäp\ *n* : the peak of a mountain

moun·te·bank \'maunt-i-ˌbaŋk\ *n* **1** : a person who peddles fake medicines (as at fairs and carnivals) by trickery **2** : a boastful dishonest pretender : CHARLATAN

Mount·ie \'maunt-ē\ *n* : a member of the Royal Canadian Mounted Police

mount·ing \'maunt-iŋ\ *n* : something that serves as a mount : SUPPORT ⟨a *mounting* for an engine⟩ ⟨a *mounting* for a diamond⟩

mourn \'mō(ə)rn, 'mȯ(ə)rn\ *vb* **1** : to feel or show grief or sorrow especially over someone's death **2** : to display the customary signs of grief for a death especially by wearing mourning — **mourn·er** *n*

mourn·ful \'mō(ə)rn-fəl, 'mȯ(ə)rn-\ *adj* **1** : expressing or full of sorrow : SORROWFUL ⟨a *mournful* face⟩ **2** : causing sorrow ⟨a *mournful* story⟩ — **mourn·ful·ly** \-fə-lē\ *adv* — **mourn·ful·ness** *n*

mourn·ing \'mōr-niŋ, 'mȯr-\ *n* **1** : the act of grieving **2** : an outward sign (as black clothes or a black arm band) of grief for a person's death ⟨to wear *mourning*⟩ **3** : a period of time during which signs of grief are shown

mourning cloak *n* : a blackish brown butterfly of Europe, Asia, and North America having a broad yellow border on the wings

mourning dove *n* : a dove of North America with a mournful call

¹mouse \'maůs\ *n, pl* **mice** \'mīs\ **1** : any of numerous small rodents with pointed snout, rather small ears, and a slender usually nearly hairless tail **2** : a person without spirit or courage **3** : a small hand-operated device used for computer input (as to control cursor movement on the display screen)

²mouse \'maůz\ *vb* **moused; mous·ing 1** : to hunt mice **2** : to search or move slyly and carefully (as a cat hunting mice) **3** : to search for carefully ⟨*mouse* out a scandal⟩

mouse pad *n* : a thin flat pad (as of rubber) on which a computer mouse is used

mous·er \'maů-zər\ *n* : a cat good at catching mice

mous·sa·ka \ˌmü-sə-'kä\ *n* : a Middle Eastern dish of ground meat (as lamb or beef) and sliced eggplant often topped with a seasoned sauce [from modern Greek *mousakas* "moussaka"]

¹mousse \'müs\ *n* **1** : a light whipped or molded food; *esp* : a cold dessert of sweetened and flavored whipped cream or egg whites and gelatin **2** : a foamy preparation used in styling hair

²mousse *vb* **moussed; mouss·ing** : to style (hair) with mousse

moustache *variant of* MUSTACHE

moustachio, moustachioed *variant of* MUSTACHIO, MUS-TACHIOED

mousy *or* **mous·ey** \'maů-sē, -zē\ *adj* **mous·i·er; -est** : of, relating to, or resembling a mouse: as **a** : ²QUIET 1a, STEALTHY **b** : ¹SHY 1a, TIMID **c** : dull in color : DRAB

¹mouth \'maůth\ *n, pl* **mouths** \'maůthz *also* 'maůths\ **1** : the opening through which food passes into the body of an animal and which in vertebrates is typically surrounded on the outside by the lips and encloses the tongue, gums, and teeth **2** : GRIMACE ⟨make a *mouth*⟩ **3** : an opening that is like a mouth ⟨the *mouth* of a cave⟩ ⟨the *mouth* of a container⟩ **4** : the place where a stream enters a larger body of water

²mouth \'maůth\ *vb* **1 a** : to speak or utter especially proudly or loudly : DECLAIM **b** : to repeat without belief or understanding ⟨*mouth* empty phrases⟩ **2 a** : to form with the lips without speaking ⟨the librarian *mouthed* "quiet"⟩ **b** : ¹MUMBLE 1 **3** : to take into the mouth — **mouth·er** *n*

mouthed \'maůthd, 'maůtht\ *adj* : having a mouth especially of a specified kind ⟨a large-*mouthed* jar⟩

mouth·ful \'maůth-ˌfůl\ *n* **1 a** : as much as a mouth will hold **b** : the amount put into the mouth at one time **2 a** : a small quantity **3 a** : a word or phrase that is very long or difficult to say **b** : a comment or remark that is rich in meaning ⟨you said a *mouthful*⟩

mouth organ *n* : HARMONICA

mouth·part \'maůth-ˌpärt\ *n* : a bodily structure that is near the mouth (as of an insect) especially when used to gather or eat food

mouth·piece \-ˌpēs\ *n* **1** : the part put to, between, or near the lips ⟨the *mouthpiece* of a trumpet⟩ ⟨the *mouthpiece* of a telephone⟩ **2** : someone who expresses another person's ideas : SPOKESPERSON

mouth–to–mouth \ˌmaůth-tə-ˌmaůth\ *adj* : of, relating to, or being a method of artificial respiration in which the rescuer's mouth is placed tightly over the victim's mouth in order to force air into the lungs by blowing hard enough every few seconds to inflate them ⟨*mouth-to-mouth* resuscitation⟩

mouth·wash \'maůth-ˌwȯsh, -ˌwäsh\ *n* : a liquid that usually kills germs and is used to clean the mouth and teeth and freshen the breath

mou·ton \'mü-ˌtän\ *n* : sheepskin that has been sheared, treated, and dyed to look like the pelt of a beaver or seal

¹mov·able *or* **move·able** \'mü-və-bəl\ *adj* **1** : capable of being moved : not fixed **2** : changing date from year to year ⟨Thanksgiving is a *movable* holiday⟩ — **mov·ably** \-blē\ *adv*

²movable *or* **moveable** *n* : a piece of property (as an article of furniture) that can be moved

¹move \'müv\ *vb* **moved; mov·ing 1** : to change the place or position of : SHIFT ⟨*move* the chair closer⟩ **2** : to go from one place to another ⟨*move* into the shade⟩ **3** : to set in motion ⟨*moved* their feet⟩ **4 a** : to cause a person to act or decide : PERSUADE ⟨the report *moved* me to change my mind⟩ **b** : to take action : ACT **5** : to affect the feelings of ⟨the sad story *moved* me to tears⟩ **6** : to suggest according to the rules of a meeting ⟨*move* to adjourn⟩ **7** : to change hands or cause to change hands through sale or rental ⟨the store's stock must be *moved*⟩ **8 a** : to change residence ⟨*moved* to Iowa⟩ **b** : to change place or position : STIR **9** : to cause to function : OPER-ATE ⟨this button *moves* the whole machine⟩ **10** : to proceed in a certain direction ⟨we're *moving* up in the world⟩ **11** : to carry on one's life in a particular environment ⟨*moves* in the best circles⟩ **12** : to go away : DEPART ⟨told them to *move* on⟩ **13** : to transfer a piece in a game (as chess) from one place to another **14** : to empty or cause to empty ⟨*move* the bowels⟩

²move *n* **1 a** : the act of moving a piece in a game **b** : the turn of a player to move **2 a** : a step taken to achieve a goal : MANEUVER **b** : the action of moving : MOVEMENT **c** : a change of residence or location — **on the move 1** : moving from place to place **2** : moving ahead or making progress

move·less \'müv-ləs\ *adj* : not moving : FIXED, MOTION-LESS

move·ment \'müv-mənt\ *n* **1 a** : the act or process of moving **b** : an instance or manner of moving ⟨observe the *movement* of a star⟩ **2** : a tendency or trend ⟨detected a *movement* toward fairer pricing⟩ **3 a** : a program or series of acts working toward a desired end ⟨a *movement* for political reform⟩ **b** : the group taking part in such a series of acts ⟨join the *movement*⟩ **4** : a mechanical arrangement (as of wheels) for causing a particular motion (as in a clock or watch) **5** : a section of a longer piece of music **6** : BOWEL MOVEMENT

mov·er \'mü-vər\ *n* : one that moves or sets something in motion; *esp* : a person or company that moves the belongings of others from one home to another

mov·ie \'mü-vē\ *n* **1** : MOTION PICTURE 1 **2 a** : a story represented in motion pictures **b** *pl* : a showing of a movie ⟨went to the *movies* yesterday⟩ **3** *pl* : the business of making movies : the motion-picture industry

mov·ie·go·er \-ˌgō-(ə)r\ *n* : a person who frequently attends the movies

mov·ing \'mü-viŋ\ *adj* **1** : changing place or position ⟨a *moving* target⟩ **2** : causing motion or action **3** : having the power to affect the feelings or sympathies ⟨a *moving* story⟩ **4 a** : of or relating to a change of residence ⟨*moving* expenses⟩ **b** : used for moving belongings from one place to another ⟨a *moving* van⟩ — **mov·ing·ly** *adv*

moving picture *n* : MOTION PICTURE

¹mow \'maů\ *n* **1** : a stack of hay or straw **2** : the part of a barn where hay or straw is stored [Old English *mūga* "heap, stack"]

²mow \'mō\ *vb* **mowed; mowed** *or* **mown** \'mōn\; **mow·ing 1** : to cut down with a scythe or machine ⟨*mow* hay⟩ **2** : to cut the standing leafy plant cover from ⟨*mow* a lawn⟩ **3** : to kill or destroy in great numbers **4** : to overcome completely ⟨*mow* down the other team⟩ [Old English *māwan* "to mow (as hay)"] — **mow·er** \'mō-(ə)r\ *n*

\ə\ **abut**	\aů\ **out**	\i\ **tip**	\ȯ\ **saw**	\ů\ **foot**
\ər\ **further**	\ch\ **chin**	\ī\ **life**	\ȯi\ **coin**	\y\ **yet**
\a\ **mat**	\e\ **pet**	\j\ **job**	\th\ **thin**	\yü\ **few**
\ā\ **take**	\ē\ **easy**	\ŋ\ **sing**	\th\ **this**	\yů\ **cure**
\ä\ **cot, cart**	\g\ **go**	\ō\ **bone**	\ü\ **food**	\zh\ **vision**

moz·za·rel·la \ˌmät-sə-ˈrel-ə\ *n* : a moist white rubbery mild-flavored cheese that is much used in Italian cooking

MP \ˈem-ˈpē\ *n* **1** : a member of the military police **2** : an elected member of a parliament [from *m*ilitary *p*olice]

MP3 \ˌem-(ˌ)pē-ˈthrē\ *n* **1** : a computer file format for the compression and storage of digital audio data **2** : a computer file (as a song) in MP3 format

Mr. \ˈmis-tər\ *n, pl* **Messrs.** \ˈmes-ərz\ **1** — used as a title before a man's last name or title of office ⟨*Mr.* Doe⟩ ⟨*Mr.* President⟩ **2** — used to form a title for a man who represents the thing indicated ⟨*Mr.* Punctuality⟩ ⟨*Mr.* Baseball⟩ [Middle English *Mr.*, an abbreviation of *master*]

MRI \ˌem-ˌär-ˈī\ *n* : MAGNETIC RESONANCE IMAGING

Mrs. \ˈmis-əz, -əs, *especially Southern* ˌmiz-əz, -əs, *or* (ˌ)miz\ *n, pl* **Mes·dames** \mā-ˈdäm, -ˈdam\ **1** — used as a title before a married woman's last name **2** — used to form a title for a woman who represents the thing indicated ⟨*Mrs.* Clever⟩ ⟨*Mrs.* Golf⟩ [an abbreviation of *mistress*]

MRSA \ˌem-ˌär-ˌes-ˈā, ˈmər-sə\ *n* : any of several strains of a bacterium that are resistant to many common antibiotics and may cause usually mild infections of the skin or sometimes more severe infections (as of the blood or lungs) [*m*ethicillin-*r*esistant *s*taphylococcus *a*ureus]

Ms. \(ˌ)miz\ *n, pl* **Mss.** *or* **Mses.** \ˈmiz-əz\ — used instead of *Miss* or *Mrs.* (as when it is unknown or unimportant whether the woman addressed is married or single) [probably a combination of *Miss* and *Mrs.*]

mu \ˈmyü, ˈmü\ *n* : the twelfth letter of the Greek alphabet — M or μ

¹much \ˈməch\ *adj* **more** \ˈmō(ə)r, ˈmȯ(ə)r\; **most** \ˈmōst\ **1** : great in quantity, amount, or extent ⟨has *much* money⟩ ⟨takes too *much* time⟩ **2** : great in importance or significance ⟨nothing *much* happened⟩

²much *adv* **more; most 1 a** : to a great or high level or extent ⟨*much* happier⟩ **b** : VERY ⟨*much* obliged⟩ **2** : just about : NEARLY ⟨looks *much* as it did years ago⟩ — **as much 1** : the same in quantity ⟨as *much* money⟩ **2** : to the same degree ⟨likes it just as *much*⟩

³much *n* **1** : a great quantity, amount, extent, or part ⟨*much* that was said is false⟩ **2** : something important or impressive ⟨not *much* to look at⟩

mu·ci·lage \ˈmyü-s(ə-)lij\ *n* **1** : a jellylike substance of various plants (as seaweeds or cacti) that is similar to plant gums **2** : a water solution of a gum or similar substance used especially as an adhesive

muck \ˈmək\ *n* **1** : soft moist barnyard manure **2** : DIRT 1, FILTH **3 a** : dark rich soil **b** : MUD, MIRE — **mucky** \ˈmək-ē\ *adj*

muck·rak·er \ˈmək-ˌrā-kər\ *n* : one of a group of writers noted for seeking out and exposing abuses and misconduct in American business, government, and society at the beginning of the 20th century — **muck·rake** \-ˌrāk\ *vb*

mu·cous \ˈmyü-kəs\ *adj* **1** : of, relating to, or resembling mucus ⟨*mucous* discharges⟩ **2** : producing or containing mucus ⟨a *mucous* gland⟩

mucous membrane *n* : a membrane rich in mucous glands; *esp* : one lining body passages and cavities (as of the nose or lungs) which connect directly or indirectly with the outside

mu·cus \ˈmyü-kəs\ *n* : a slippery sticky substance produced especially by mucous membranes which it moistens and protects

mud \ˈməd\ *n* : soft wet earth

mud dauber *n* : any of various wasps that construct mud cells in which the female places an egg with paralyzed insects or spiders as food for the larva

¹mud·dle \ˈməd-ᵊl\ *vb* **mud·dled; mud·dling** \ˈməd-liŋ, -ᵊl-iŋ\ **1** : to be or cause to be confused or bewildered : STU-

PEFY ⟨*muddled* by too much advice⟩ **2** : to mix up in a confused way ⟨*muddle* the household accounts⟩ **3** : to think or act in a confused way : BUNGLE ⟨*muddle* through a task⟩ — **mud·dler** \-lər, -ᵊl-ər\ *n*

²muddle *n* **1** : a state of confusion or bewilderment **2** : a confused mess : JUMBLE

¹mud·dy \ˈməd-ē\ *adj* **mud·di·er; -est 1** : filled or covered with mud ⟨a *muddy* pond⟩ ⟨*muddy* shoes⟩ **2** : resembling mud ⟨a *muddy* color⟩ ⟨*muddy* coffee⟩ **3** : not clear or bright ⟨a *muddy* complexion⟩ **4** : unclear in meaning : MUDDLED ⟨*muddy* thinking⟩ — **mud·di·ness** *n*

²muddy *vb* **mud·died; mud·dy·ing 1** : to soil or stain with or as if with mud **2** : to make cloudy or dull **3** : to become or cause to become confused

mud·flat \ˈməd-ˌflat\ *n* : a level area of land that lies just below the surface of water or that is repeatedly covered and left bare by the tide

mud·flow \ˈməd-ˌflō\ *n* : a moving mass of mud made up of soil and rainwater or melted snow

mud puppy *n* : a large North American salamander that has gills on the outside and is gray to rusty brown usually with bluish black spots

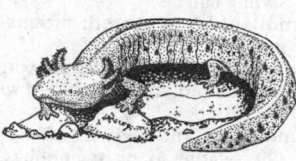
mud puppy

mud turtle *n* : any of various turtles that live on the bottom of bodies of fresh water and are related to the musk turtles

mu·ez·zin \m(y)ü-ˈez-ᵊn\ *n* : a crier who summons Muslims to prayer

¹muff \ˈməf\ *n* : a soft thick tubelike covering with open ends in which both hands may be inserted for protection from cold [from Dutch *mof* "a cover for the hands," from early French *moufle* "mitten"]

²muff *n* : a clumsy or bungled performance; *esp* : a failure to hold a ball in attempting a catch [probably from ¹*muff*] — **muff** *vb*

muf·fin \ˈməf-ən\ *n* : a bread made of batter containing egg that is baked in a small cup-shaped container

muf·fle \ˈməf-əl\ *vb* **muf·fled; muf·fling** \ˈməf-(ə-)liŋ\ **1** : to wrap up so as to conceal or protect **2** : to deaden the sound of ⟨*muffle* a cry⟩

muf·fler \ˈməf-lər\ *n* **1** : a scarf worn to protect the neck **2** : something that deadens noises; *esp* : a device attached to the exhaust system of an automobile

muf·ti \ˈməf-tē\ *n* : civilian clothes ⟨an off-duty soldier in *mufti*⟩

¹mug \ˈməg\ *n* **1** : a usually large drinking cup with a handle **2** : the face or mouth of a person **3** : ¹PUNK 1, THUG

²mug *vb* **mugged; mug·ging 1** : to make faces especially to attract attention : GRIMACE **2** : ²PHOTOGRAPH

³mug *vb* **mugged; mug·ging** : to assault especially with the intention of robbing — **mug·ger** *n*

mug·gy \ˈməg-ē\ *adj* **mug·gi·er; -est** : being warm and humid ⟨a *muggy* day in August⟩ — **mug·gi·ness** *n*

mug·hal \ˈmü-(ˌ)gəl\ *n* : ¹MOGUL 1

mug shot *n* : a photograph of a person's face; *esp* : a police photograph of a suspect's face or profile

Muhammadan *variant of* MOHAMMEDAN

mu·ja·hid·een *or* **mu·ja·hed·in** \mü-ˌja-hid-ˈēn, mù-, -ˌjä-\ *n pl* : Islamic guerrilla fighters especially in the Middle East [Arabic *mujāhidīn* "Islamic guerrilla fighters," plural form of *mujahīd* "a person who wages Islamic holy war"]

muk·luk \ˈmək-ˌlək\ *n* **1** : an Eskimo boot of sealskin or reindeer skin **2** : a boot with a soft leather sole worn over several pairs of socks

mu·lat·to \m(y)ù-ˈlat-ō\ *n, pl* **-toes** *or* **-tos 1** : a person with one black and one white parent **2** : a person of mixed white and black descent

mul·ber·ry \'məl-ˌber-ē\ *n* **1** : any of a genus of trees that have small edible usually purple fruits and leaves on which silkworms can be fed; *also* : the fruit of a mulberry **2** : a dark purple or purplish black

¹mulch \'məlch\ *n* : a covering (as of straw or sawdust) spread over the ground to protect the roots of plants from heat, cold, or evaporation, prevent soil loss, control weeds, enrich the soil, or keep fruit (as strawberries) clean

²mulch *vb* : to cover with mulch

¹mulct \'məlkt\ *n* : ¹FINE

²mulct *vb* **1** : to punish by a fine **2 a** : to defraud especially of money **b** : to obtain by dishonest means

mulberry 1

¹mule \'myü(ə)l\ *n* **1** : the hybrid offspring of a horse and a donkey; *esp* : the offspring of a male donkey and a female horse **2** : a very stubborn person **3** : a machine that draws and twists fiber into yarn or thread and winds it onto spindles [Middle English *mule* "the offspring of a donkey and a horse," from early French *mul* (same meaning), from Latin *multus* (same meaning)]

²mule *n* : a shoe or slipper that is open at the heel [from early French *mule* "slipper," from *mulleus* "a shoe worn by public officials"]

mule deer *n* : a long-eared deer of western North America that is larger and more heavily built than the white-tailed deer

mule skinner *n* : a driver of mules

mu·le·teer \ˌmyü-lə-'ti(ə)r\ *n* : a driver of mules

mul·ish \'myü-lish\ *adj* : STUBBORN 1a, INFLEXIBLE — **mul·ish·ly** *adv* — **mul·ish·ness** *n*

¹mull \'məl\ *vb* : to think about slowly and carefully : PONDER ⟨*mull* over an idea⟩ [Middle English *mullen* "to grind up or mix thoroughly," from *mul, mol* "dust"]

²mull *vb* : to sweeten, spice, and heat ⟨*mulled* wine⟩ [origin unknown]

mul·lein *also* **mul·len** \'məl-ən\ *n* : a tall herb related to the snapdragons and having coarse woolly leaves and spikes of usually yellow flowers

mul·let \'məl-ət\ *n, pl* **mullet** *or* **mullets** : any of a family of mostly gray food fishes chiefly of salt water — compare RED MULLET

mul·lion \'məl-yən\ *n* : a slender upright bar which separates sections of windows, doors, or screens — **mullion** *vb*

multi- *combining form* **1 a** : many : much ⟨multicolored⟩ **b** : more than two ⟨*multi*national⟩ ⟨*multi*racial⟩ **2** : many times over ⟨*multi*millionaire⟩ [derived from Latin *multus* "much, many"]

mul·ti·cel·lu·lar \ˌməl-ti-'sel-yə-lər, -ˌtī-\ *adj* : having or consisting of many cells — **mul·ti·cel·lu·lar·i·ty** \-ˌsel-yə-'lar-ət-ē\ *n*

mul·ti·col·ored \ˌməl-ti-'kəl-ərd\ *adj* : having, made up of, or including many colors

mul·ti·cul·tur·al \ˌməl-ti-'kəlch-rəl, -ˌtī-, -ə-rəl\ *adj* : of, relating to, reflecting, or adapted to diverse cultures ⟨a *multi*cultural society⟩ — **mul·ti·cul·tur·al·ism** \-rə-ˌliz-əm\ *n*

mul·ti·di·men·sion·al \ˌməl-ti-də-'mənch-nəl, -'menchən-ᵊl\ *adj* : made up of or involving two or more dimensions

mul·ti·fac·et·ed \-'fas-ət-əd\ *adj* : having many aspects or sides

mul·ti·far·i·ous \ˌməl-tə-'far-ē-əs, -'fer-\ *adj* : of many and various kinds ⟨the *multifarious* sounds of the city⟩

mul·ti·form \'məl-ti-ˌform\ *adj* : having many forms, shapes, or appearances

mul·ti·lat·er·al \ˌməl-ti-'lat-ə-rəl, -ˌtī-, -'la-trəl\ *adj* **1** : having many sides **2** : involving or taken part in by more than two nations or groups ⟨a *multilateral* treaty⟩ — **mul·ti·lat·er·al·ly** \-ē\ *adv*

mul·ti·lay·ered \ˌməl-ti-'lā-ərd, -'le(-ə)rd\ *or* **mul·ti·lay·er** \-'lā-ər, -'le(-ə)r\ *adj* : made up of or involving two or more layers or levels

¹mul·ti·me·dia \ˌməl-ti-'mēd-ē-ə\ *adj* : using or composed of more than one form of communication or expression ⟨*multimedia* software combining sound, video, and text⟩

²multimedia *n* : a technique (as the combining of sound, video, and text) for expressing ideas (as in communication, entertainment, or art) in which several media are employed; *also* : something (as software) using such a technique

mul·ti·mil·lion·aire \ˌməl-ti-ˌmil-yə-'na(ə)r, -ˌtī-, -'ne(ə)r, -'mil-yə-ˌna(ə)r, -ˌne(ə)r\ *n* : a person whose wealth is estimated at several millions (as of dollars)

¹mul·ti·na·tion·al \ˌməl-ti-'nash-nəl, -ən-ᵊl\ *adj* **1** : of, relating to, or involving more than two nations **2** : having divisions in more than two countries

²multinational *n* : a multinational corporation

¹mul·ti·ple \'məl-tə-pəl\ *adj* **1** : containing, involving, or consisting of more than one ⟨*multiple* copies⟩ **2** : ¹MANY 1 ⟨a person of *multiple* achievements⟩

²multiple *n* : the product of a quantity and a whole number ⟨35 is a *multiple* of 7⟩

mul·ti·ple–choice \ˌməl-tə-pəl-'chȯis\ *adj* **1** : having several answers from which one is to be chosen **2** : made up of multiple-choice questions ⟨a *multiple-choice* test⟩

multiple fruit *n* : a fruit (as a mulberry) formed from a cluster of flowers

multiple sclerosis *n* : a disease marked by patches of hardened tissue in the brain or spinal cord resulting in symptoms (as weakness or paralysis in the arms or legs or loss of balance and muscle coordination) that usually come and go

¹mul·ti·plex \'məl-tə-ˌpleks\ *adj* **1** : ¹MULTIPLE, MANY **2** : being or relating to a system of transmitting several messages simultaneously on the same circuit or channel

²multiplex *n* : a complex that houses several movie theaters

mul·ti·pli·cand \ˌməl-tə-pli-'kand\ *n* : the number that is to be multiplied by another

mul·ti·pli·ca·tion \ˌməl-tə-plə-'kā-shən\ *n* **1** : the act or process of multiplying **2** : a mathematical operation that takes two numbers and gives an answer equal to the sum of a column containing one of the numbers repeated the number of times of the other number ⟨the *multiplication* of 8 and 3 is the same as the sum of 8+8+8⟩

multiplication sign *n* : a symbol used to show multiplication: **a** : TIMES SIGN **b** : DOT 2b

mul·ti·pli·ca·tive \ˌməl-tə-'plik-ət-iv, 'məl-tə-plə-ˌkāt-\ *adj* : of, relating to, or associated with a mathematical operation of multiplication

multiplicative identity *n* : an element of a set that when multiplied by any other element of the set leaves the element unchanged ⟨the number 1 is a *multiplicative identity* in the set of real numbers⟩

multiplicative inverse *n* : an element (as a reciprocal) of a mathematical set that when multiplied by a given element gives the identity element ⟨in the set of all rational numbers the *multiplicative inverse* of 2 is $\frac{1}{2}$ since $2 \times \frac{1}{2} = 1$⟩

mul·ti·plic·i·ty \ˌməl-tə-'plis-ət-ē\ *n, pl* **-ties 1** : the quality or state of being multiple or various **2** : a great number

mul·ti·pli·er \'məl-tə-ˌplī(-ə)r\ *n* **1** : one that multiplies **2** : a number by which another number is multiplied

\ə\ **abut**	\au̇\ **out**	\i\ **tip**	\ȯ\ **saw**	\u̇\ **foot**
\ər\ **further**	\ch\ **chin**	\ī\ **life**	\ȯi\ **coin**	\y\ **yet**
\a\ **mat**	\e\ **pet**	\j\ **job**	\th\ **thin**	\yu̇\ **few**
\ā\ **take**	\ē\ **easy**	\ŋ\ **sing**	\tẖ\ **this**	\yu̇\ **cure**
\ä\ **cot, cart**	\g\ **go**	\ō\ **bone**	\ü\ **food**	\zh\ **vision**

mul·ti·ply \'məl-tə-ˌplī\ vb **-plied; -ply·ing 1 a** : to increase in number : make or become more numerous **b** : to produce offspring : BREED ⟨rabbits *multiply* rapidly⟩ **2 a** : to use in finding a product by multiplication ⟨*multiply* 7 and 8⟩ ⟨*multiply* 7 by 8⟩ **b** : to perform multiplication ⟨first divide and then *multiply*⟩

mul·ti·pur·pose \ˌməl-ti-'pər-pəs, -ˌtī-\ adj : having more than one use ⟨*multipurpose* furniture⟩

mul·ti·ra·cial \ˌməl-ti-'rā-shəl, -ˌtī-\ adj : composed of, relating to, or representing various races

mul·ti·stage \'məl-ti-ˌstāj\ adj : operating in or involving two or more stages ⟨a *multistage* rocket⟩

mul·ti·task·ing \-ˌtas-kiŋ\ n : the performance of multiple tasks at one time especially by a computer — **mul·ti·task** \-ˌtask\ vb

mul·ti·tude \'məl-tə-ˌt(y)üd\ n : a great number of things or people

synonyms MULTITUDE, CROWD, THRONG, MOB mean a large number of individuals. MULTITUDE usually suggests a truly great number ⟨*multitudes* made homeless by war⟩ ⟨a *multitude* of stars⟩. CROWD suggests a disorganized group that is closely packed together ⟨a *crowd* of onlookers at the scene of the accident⟩. THRONG suggests many people gathered together and wandering about ⟨*throngs* of people were at the fair⟩. MOB suggests disorderly behavior and disturbance and the possibility of violence ⟨an angry *mob* smashing windows⟩.

mul·ti·tu·di·nous \ˌməl-tə-'t(y)üd-nəs, -ᵊn-əs\ adj : consisting of a multitude ⟨*multitudinous* questions⟩

mul·ti·vi·ta·min \ˌməl-ti-'vīt-ə-mən\ adj : containing several vitamins and especially all known to be necessary to health ⟨a *multivitamin* pill⟩ — **multivitamin** n

¹mum \'məm\ adj : SILENT 1 ⟨keep *mum*⟩

²mum n : CHRYSANTHEMUM

³mum chiefly British variant of MOM

¹mum·ble \'məm-bəl\ vb **mum·bled; mum·bling** \-b(ə-)liŋ\ **1** : to speak softly and unclearly **2** : to eat with or as if with toothless gums ⟨a baby *mumbling* its food⟩ — **mum·bler** \-b(ə-)lər\ n — **mum·bly** \-b(ə-)lē\ adj

²mumble n : speech that is not clear enough to be understood

mum·bo jum·bo \ˌməm-bō-'jəm-bō\ n **1** : a complicated ceremony **2** : confusing or meaningless talk or activity

mum·mer \'məm-ər\ n **1** : a person who celebrates a holiday by making merry in disguise **2** : ACTOR

mum·mery \'məm-ə-rē\ n, pl **-mer·ies 1** : a performance by mummers **2** : a ridiculous ceremony

mum·mi·fy \'məm-i-ˌfī\ vb **-fied; -fy·ing 1** : to embalm and dry as or like a mummy **2** : to dry up like the skin of a mummy : SHRIVEL — **mum·mi·fi·ca·tion** \ˌməm-i-fə-'kā-shən\ n

mum·my \'məm-ē\ n, pl **mummies 1** : a body prepared for burial in the manner of the ancient Egyptians **2** : an unusually well-preserved body

mumps \'məm(p)s\ n sing or pl : a contagious disease caused by a virus and marked by fever and by swelling especially of salivary glands

munch \'mənch\ vb : to eat with a chewing action; also : to snack on ⟨*munched* popcorn and watched a movie⟩ — **munch·er** n

munch·ies \'mən-chēz\ n pl **1** : hunger pangs **2** : light snack foods

mun·dane \ˌmən-'dān, 'mən-ˌdān\ adj **1** : of or relating to the world : WORLDLY **2** : having to do with the practical details of everyday life — **mun·dane·ly** adv

mu·nic·i·pal \myu̇-'nis-(ə-)pəl\ adj : of or relating to a municipality ⟨*municipal* government⟩

mu·nic·i·pal·i·ty \myu̇-ˌnis-ə-'pal-ət-ē\ n, pl **-ties** : a self-governing city or town

mu·nif·i·cent \myu̇-'nif-ə-sənt\ adj **1** : very generous in giving ⟨a *munificent* host⟩ **2** : given generously or in plenty ⟨a *munificent* gift⟩ — **mu·nif·i·cent·ly** adv

mu·ni·tion \myu̇-'nish-ənz\ n : ARMAMENT 2, AMMUNITION

¹mu·ral \'myu̇r-əl\ adj **1** : of or relating to a wall **2** : applied to and made part of a wall surface ⟨a *mural* painting⟩

²mural n : a mural work of art

¹mur·der \'mərd-ər\ n **1** : the intentional and unlawful killing of a person **2** : something that is difficult or dangerous ⟨traffic was *murder* this morning⟩

²murder vb **mur·dered; mur·der·ing** \'mərd-(ə-)riŋ\ **1** : to commit murder **2** : to spoil by performing or using poorly ⟨*murder* a song⟩ ⟨*murder* the English language⟩ synonyms see KILL — **mur·der·er** \-ər-ər\ n

mur·der·ous \'mərd-(ə-)rəs\ adj **1** : intending or capable of causing murder or bloodshed : DEADLY ⟨*murderous* machine-gun fire⟩ **2** : very difficult to bear or withstand ⟨a *murderous* glance⟩ ⟨*murderous* heat⟩ — **mur·der·ous·ly** adv

murk \'mərk\ n : deep darkness or gloom; also : ¹FOG 1a

murky \'mər-kē\ adj **murk·i·er; -est 1** : very dark or gloomy **2** : FOGGY 1, MISTY **3** : difficult to understand ⟨a *murky* reply designed to confuse⟩ — **murk·i·ness** n

¹mur·mur \'mər-mər\ n **1** : a muttered complaint : GRUMBLE **2** : a low, faint, and continuous sound ⟨the *murmur* of bees⟩ **3** : an irregular heart sound typically indicating an abnormality in the heart's function or structure

²murmur vb **1** : to make a murmur ⟨the breeze *murmured* in the pines⟩ **2** : to say in a voice too low to be heard clearly — **mur·mur·er** n

mur·mur·ous \'mərm-(ə-)rəs\ adj : filled with or characterized by murmurs

Mur·phy's Law \'mər-fēz\ n : an observation that anything that can go wrong will go wrong

mur·rain \'mər-ən, 'mə-rən\ n : a disease that spreads among domestic animals or plants

murre \'mər\ n : a common black-and-white web-footed bird of northern seas; also : any of several related seabirds

mus·ca·tel \ˌməs-kə-'tel\ n : a sweet wine that is golden to dark amber in color

¹mus·cle \'məs-əl\ n **1 a** : a body tissue consisting of long cells that can contract and produce motion **b** : an organ that is a mass of muscle tissue attached at either end to a fixed point (as to bones) and that by contracting moves or stops the movement of a body part **2 a** : muscular strength : BRAWN **b** : ¹POWER 2 ⟨lacks the *muscle* to make good on campaign promises⟩

Word History People today are perhaps unlikely to think of their muscles as resembling mice. The ancient Romans, however, saw a likeness, especially in the major muscles of the arms and legs. For that reason the Latin word *musculus*, which originally meant "little mouse," came to be used to mean "muscle." [from Latin *musculus* "muscle, little mouse," from *mus* "mouse"]

²muscle vb **mus·cled; mus·cling** \'məs-(ə-)liŋ\ **1** : to force from a position ⟨was *muscled* out of office by political opponents⟩ **2** : to force one's way ⟨*muscled* through the crowd⟩

mus·cle–bound \'məs-əl-ˌbau̇nd\ adj : having abnormally large muscles that do not move and stretch easily

muscle shirt n : a close-fitting usually sleeveless T-shirt

muscle spindle n : a structure at the ending of a group of nerve fibers in a muscle that is sensitive to stretching of the muscle, consists of small striated muscle fibers richly supplied with nerve fibers, and is enclosed in a sheath of connective tissue — called also *stretch receptor*

Mus·co·vite \'məs-kə-ˌvīt\ n : a person born or living in Moscow — **Muscovite** adj

mus·cu·lar \'məs-kyə-lər\ adj **1 a** : of, relating to, or being muscle **b** : performed by the muscles **2** : having well-developed muscles : STRONG

muscular dys·tro·phy \-'dis-trə-fē\ n : an inherited disease characterized by increasing weakness of muscles

mus·cu·la·ture \'məs-kyə-lə-ˌchů(ə)r\ *n* : the muscles of the body or of one of its parts

¹**muse** \'myüz\ *vb* **mused; mus·ing** : PONDER [Middle English *musen* "to ponder," from early French *muser* "to gape, muse," Latin *musus* "mouth of an animal"]

²**muse** *n* **1** *cap* : any of the nine sister goddesses of song and poetry and the arts and sciences in Greek mythology **2** : a source of inspiration [Middle English *Muse* "one of the nine goddesses of the arts," from early French *Muse* (same meaning), from Latin *Musa* (same meaning), from Greek *Mousa* "Muse"]

mu·se·um \myů-'zē-əm\ *n* : a building in which interesting and valuable things (as works of art or historical or scientific objects) are collected and shown to the public

Word History The ancient Greeks worshipped nine sister goddesses, each of whom was called a *Mousa*. In English we now refer to them as the Muses. The Greeks believed that each Muse was the goddess of a particular art or science. A place that was dedicated to these goddesses — and to the arts and sciences for which they stood — was called a *Mouseion*. The Greek *Mouseion* became *Museum* in Latin, from which it was borrowed into English about 300 years ago. [from Latin *Museum* "a place devoted to the Muses, a place for the study of special arts and sciences," from Greek *Mouseion* (same meaning), from *Mouseios* "of the Muses," from *Mousa* "Muse, goddess of an art or science" — related to MUSIC]

¹**mush** \'məsh\ *n* **1** : cornmeal boiled in water or milk **2** : something soft and spongy or shapeless **3** : sickeningly sweet sentimentality [probably an altered form of *mash*] — **mush·i·ly** \-ə-lē\ *adv* — **mushy** \-ē\ *adj*

²**mush** *vb* : to travel over snow with a sled drawn by dogs — often used as a command to a dog team [probably from French *marchons* "let's move," from *marcher* "to move, march"] — **mush·er** *n*

³**mush** *n* : a trip across snow with a dog team

¹**mush·room** \'məsh-ˌrüm, -ˌrům\ *n* **1** : a fleshy part of a fungus that bears spores, grows above ground, and consists usually of a stem bearing a flattened cap; *esp* : one that is edible **2** : FUNGUS 1

²**mushroom** *vb* : to appear or develop suddenly or increase rapidly ⟨the population *mushroomed*⟩

mu·sic \'myü-zik\ *n* **1 a** : the art of producing pleasing or expressive combinations of tones especially with melody, rhythm, and usually harmony **b** : a musical composition set down on paper ⟨bring your *music*⟩ **2 a** : sounds that have rhythm, harmony, and melody **b** : an agreeable sound ⟨the *music* of a brook⟩ [Middle English *musik* "music," from early French *musike* (same meaning), from Latin *musica* (same meaning), from Greek *mousikē* "any art under the control or guidance of the Muses," derived from *Mousa* "Muse" — related to MUSEUM; see *Word History* at MUSEUM]

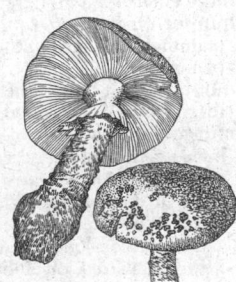

¹mushroom 1

¹**mu·si·cal** \'myü-zi-kəl\ *adj* **1 a** : of or relating to music or the writing or performance of music ⟨*musical* instruments⟩ **b** : having the pleasing harmonious qualities of music ⟨a *musical* voice⟩ **2** : fond of or gifted in music ⟨a *musical* family⟩ **3** : set to or accompanied by music — **mu·si·cal·ly** \-k(ə-)lē\ *adv*

²**musical** *n* : a film or play that tells a story and that includes both musical numbers and dialogue

musical comedy *n* : ²MUSICAL

mu·si·cale \ˌmyü-zi-'kal\ *n* : a usually private social gathering to hear music

mu·si·cal·i·ty \ˌmyü-zi-'kal-ət-ē\ *n* : the quality of being musical or melodious

music box *n* : a box containing a mechanical device that uses gears like those of a clock to play a tune

mu·si·cian \myů-'zish-ən\ *n* : a person who writes, sings, or plays music and especially as a profession — **mu·si·cian·ship** \-ˌship\ *n*

musk \'məsk\ *n* **1** : a strong-smelling substance obtained usually from the male musk deer and used in perfume; *also* : a substance of comparable odor that is from another animal (as a skunk) or is prepared artificially **2** : an odor of or resembling that of musk

musk deer *n* : any or several small hornless deers that live in the high regions of central Asia with the males producing musk

mus·keg \'məs-ˌkeg\ *n* : ¹BOG; *esp* : a bog of northern North America that is composed of many layers of half-decayed plants and especially sphagnum

mus·kel·lunge \'məs-kə-ˌlənj\ *n, pl* **muskellunge** : a large North American pike that may weigh over 60 pounds (27 kilograms) and is a valuable sport fish

mus·ket \'məs-kət\ *n* : a muzzle-loading firearm that was once used by soldiers

mus·ke·teer \ˌməs-kə-'ti(ə)r\ *n* : a soldier armed with a musket

mus·kie *or* **mus·ky** \'məs-kē\ *n, pl* **muskies** : MUSKELLUNGE

musk·mel·on \'məsk-ˌmel-ən\ *n* : any of various round to oval melons (as the cantaloupes or winter melons) of an Asian vine of the gourd family that have smooth or ridged skin and edible usually sweet flesh

musk ox *n* : a large shaggy-coated wild ox native to Greenland, Canada and Alaska with the males producing a strong odor similar to musk from glands below the eyes

musk·rat \'məs-ˌkrat\ *n, pl* **muskrat** *or* **muskrats** : a North American rodent that lives in or near the water, has a long scaly tail and webbed hind feet, and glossy usually dark brown fur; *also* : its fur or pelt

musk ox

musk turtle *n* : any of several small American freshwater turtles with a strong musky or bad-smelling odor

musky \'məs-kē\ *adj* **musk·i·er; -est** : having an odor of or resembling musk

Mus·lim \'məz-ləm, 'můs-, 'můz-\ *n* : a follower of Islam [from Arabic *muslim*, literally "one who surrenders (to God)"] — **Muslim** *adj*

mus·lin \'məz-lən\ *n* : a cotton fabric of plain weave [from French *mousseline* "muslin," derived from Arabic *mawşilī* "of Mosul (a city in Iraq)"]

¹**muss** \'məs\ *n* : a state of disorder : MESS — **mussy** \-ē\ *adj*

²**muss** *vb* : to make untidy : RUMPLE ⟨*mussed* my hair⟩

mus·sel \'məs-əl\ *n* **1** : any of various edible saltwater mollusks with a long dark hinged double shell **2** : any of numerous freshwater mollusks of rivers of the central U.S. whose hinged double shells are lined with mother-of-pearl

\ə\ **abut**	\aů\ **out**	\i\ **tip**	\ȯ\ **saw**	\ů\ **foot**
\ər\ **further**	\ch\ **chin**	\ī\ **life**	\ȯi\ **coin**	\y\ **yet**
\a\ **mat**	\e\ **pet**	\j\ **job**	\th\ **thin**	\yü\ **few**
\ā\ **take**	\ē\ **easy**	\ŋ\ **sing**	\th\ **this**	\yů\ **cure**
\ä\ **cot, cart**	\g\ **go**	\ō\ **bone**	\ü\ **food**	\zh\ **vision**

¹must \məs(t), 'məst\ *helping verb, present & past all persons*
must 1 : is commanded, requested, or urged to ⟨the train *must* stop⟩ ⟨you *must* read that book⟩ **2** : is forced, required, or obliged to ⟨leaves *must* fall⟩ ⟨one *must* eat to live⟩ ⟨we *must* be quiet⟩ **3** : is determined to ⟨if you *must* go⟩ **4** : is very likely to ⟨it *must* be time⟩ ⟨*must* have lost it⟩ **5** : is certain to ⟨the bus *must* be coming⟩

²must \'məst\ *n* : something required or absolutely necessary ⟨new shoes are a *must*⟩

mus·tache *also* **mous·tache** \'məs-,tash, (,)məs-'tash\ *n* **1** : the hair growing on the human upper lip **2** : hair or bristles about the mouth of a mammal (as a walrus)

mus·ta·chio *also* **mous·ta·chio** \(,)məs-'tash-(ē-)ō, -'täsh-\ *n, pl* **-chios** : MUSTACHE; *esp* : a large mustache — **mus·ta·chioed** *also* **mous·ta·chioed** \-(ē-)ōd\ *adj*

mus·tang \'məs-,taŋ\ *n* **1** : a small hardy wild horse of the western plains of the U.S. that is directly descended from horses brought in by the Spaniards **2** : BRONCO 1

Word History Many American cowboy practices can be traced back to those of northern Mexico. One such practice is a yearly roundup of unbranded or stray cattle. Centuries ago in Spain, cattle without owners were rounded up each year and sold. The Spanish word for this roundup was *mesta*, which came from a Latin phrase that meant "mixed animals." From *mesta*, the Spanish created the word *mestengo*, meaning "a wild or stray animal." In the form of Spanish spoken in Mexico, *mestengo* came to be used for wild or stray horses. As these horses became common in the western plains of the U.S., English borrowed the Mexican Spanish word *mestengo* as *mustang*. [from American Spanish *mestengo* "a wild or stray horse," from Spanish *mestengo* "a stray animal," derived from *mesta* "an annual roundup of stray cattle," from Latin *(animalia) mixta* "mixed animals"]

mus·tard \'məs-tərd\ *n* **1** : any of several yellow-flowered herbs related to the turnips and cabbages **2** : a yellow sharp-tasting powder of the seeds of a common mustard used in food seasonings or in medicine

mustard gas *n* : a poisonous gas used in war that has strongly irritating and especially blistering effects

mustard plaster *n* : a dressing made of a paste containing powdered mustard that is applied to the skin (as of the back or chest) to cause redness and irritation in the surface layers of the skin and reduce inflammation deeper down

¹mus·ter \'məs-tər\ *vb* **mus·tered; mus·ter·ing** \-t(ə-)riŋ\ **1 a** : to enroll formally ⟨was *mustered* into the army⟩ **b** : to assemble (as troops) for roll call or inspection **2** : to stir up or bring to action ⟨all the strength I could *muster*⟩

²muster *n* **1 a** : an act of assembling; *esp* : a formal military inspection or drill **b** : an assembled group : COLLECTION **2** : critical examination ⟨work that would never pass *muster*⟩

muster out *vb* : to discharge from service

mustn't \'məs-ᵊnt\ : must not

musty \'məs-tē\ *adj* **must·i·er; -est 1 a** : affected by dampness or mildew : MOLDY **b** : tasting or smelling of dampness and decay **2 a** : ¹STALE 2, TRITE ⟨*musty* proverbs⟩ **b** : OUTMODED, ANTIQUATED ⟨*musty* traditions⟩ — **must·i·ness** *n*

mu·ta·ble \'myüt-ə-bəl\ *adj* **1** : likely to change often : INCONSTANT **2 a** : capable of change **b** : able or likely to mutate — **mu·ta·bil·i·ty** \,myüt-ə-'bil-ət-ē\ *n*

¹mu·tant \'myüt-ᵊnt\ *adj* : of, relating to, or produced by mutation

²mutant *n* : a mutant individual

mu·tate \'myü-,tāt\ *vb* **mu·tat·ed; mu·tat·ing** : to undergo or cause to undergo mutation

mu·ta·tion \myü-'tā-shən\ *n* **1** : a basic and important change **2 a** : a permanent change in hereditary material involving either a change in the position of the genes on the chromosomes or a basic change in the chemical structure of a gene; *also* : the process of producing a mutation **b** : an individual, strain, or trait resulting from mutation

¹mute \'myüt\ *adj* **mut·er; mut·est 1** : unable to speak **2** : felt but not expressed in words ⟨*mute* sympathy⟩ **3** : not pronounced : SILENT ⟨the *mute* "b" in "thumb"⟩ — **mute·ly** *adv* — **mute·ness** *n*

²mute *n* **1** : a person who cannot or does not speak **2** : a device attached to or inserted into a musical instrument to reduce, soften, or muffle its tone **3** : ²STOP 9

³mute *vb* **mut·ed; mut·ing 1** : to muffle or reduce the sound of **2** : to tone down ⟨*muted* his criticism⟩

mu·ti·late \'myüt-ᵊl-,āt\ *vb* **-lat·ed; -lat·ing 1** : to make imperfect by cutting or altering severely : RUIN ⟨*mutilate* a play⟩ **2** : to cut off or destroy a necessary part (as a limb) : MAIM — **mu·ti·la·tion** \,myüt-ᵊl-'ā-shən\ *n* — **mu·ti·la·tor** \'myüt-ᵊl-,āt-ər\ *n*

M ²mute 2

mu·ti·neer \,myüt-ᵊn-'i(ə)r\ *n* : a person who is guilty of mutiny

mu·ti·nous \'myüt-ᵊn-əs, 'myüt-nəs\ *adj* **1** : inclined to or in a state of mutiny : REBELLIOUS ⟨a *mutinous* crew⟩ **2** : relating to or being mutiny ⟨*mutinous* acts⟩ — **mu·ti·nous·ly** *adv*

mu·ti·ny \'myüt-ᵊn-ē, 'myüt-nē\ *n, pl* **-nies** : refusal to obey authority; *esp* : a military outbreak against the officer in charge **synonyms** see REBELLION — **mutiny** *vb*

mutt \'mət\ *n* : a mongrel dog : CUR

mut·ter \'mət-ər\ *vb* **1** : ¹MUMBLE 1 **2** : to murmur complainingly or angrily : GRUMBLE — **mutter** *n* — **mut·ter·er** \-ər-ər\ *n*

mut·ton \'mət-ᵊn\ *n* : the flesh of a mature sheep used for food [from French *mouton* "sheep"]

mut·ton·chops \'mət-ᵊn-,chäps\ *n pl* : whiskers framing a man's face that are narrow at the temple and broad and round by the lower jaws

mu·tu·al \'myüch-(ə-)wəl, 'myü-chəl\ *adj* **1 a** : given and received in equal amount ⟨*mutual* favors⟩ **b** : having the same relation one to the other ⟨*mutual* enemies⟩ **2** : owned, shared, or enjoyed by two or more at the same time : JOINT ⟨our *mutual* friend⟩ ⟨*mutual* defense⟩ **3** : organized so that the customers share directly in the company's profits and losses ⟨a *mutual* savings bank⟩ ⟨a *mutual* insurance company⟩ — **mu·tu·al·ly** \-ē\ *adv*

mu·tu·al·ism \'myüch-(ə-)wə-,liz-əm, 'myü-chə-,liz-\ *n* : association between different kinds of organisms that benefits both

muu·muu \'mü-,mü\ *n* : a usually long, loose-fitting, and brightly-colored dress originally worn in Hawaii

¹muz·zle \'məz-əl\ *n* **1** : the nose and jaws of an animal : SNOUT **2** : a covering for the mouth and jaws of an animal used to keep it from eating or biting **3** : the open end of a weapon from which the missile is fired

²muzzle *vb* **muz·zled; muz·zling** \'məz-(ə-)liŋ\ **1** : to put a muzzle on **2** : to prevent free or normal expression by : GAG ⟨the dictator *muzzled* the press⟩

¹muzzle 1

muz·zle–load·er \ˌməz-əl-ˈ(l)ōd-ər\ *n* : a gun that is loaded through the muzzle — **muz·zle–load·ing** \-ˈ(l)ōd-iŋ\ *adj*

my \(ˈ)mī, mə\ *adj* : of or relating to me or myself ⟨*my* head⟩ ⟨kept *my* promise⟩ ⟨*my* injuries⟩

my·ce·li·um \mī-ˈsē-lē-əm\ *n, pl* **-lia** \-lē-ə\ : the part of the body of a fungus that does not reproduce and usually consists of a mass of hyphae that are often growing in something else (as soil, organic matter, or the tissues of a plant or animal host) — **my·ce·li·al** \-lē-əl\ *adj*

-my·cin \ˈmīs-ᵊn\ *combining form* : a substance made from a bacterium which resembles a fungus [strepto*mycin*]

my·col·o·gist \mī-ˈkäl-ə-jəst\ *n* : a person who is a specialist or expert in mycology

my·col·o·gy \mī-ˈkäl-ə-jē\ *n* **1** : a branch of biology dealing with fungi **2** : fungal life

my·cor·rhi·za \ˌmī-kə-ˈrī-zə\ *n, pl* **-zae** \-ˌzē\ *also* **-zas** : the joining of a fungus and the root of a plant in which the fungus grows around or through the root providing nutrients and water to it and receiving food from it

my·elin \ˈmī-ə-lən\ *n* : a soft white somewhat fatty material that forms a thick layer around the axons of some neurons

my·elin·at·ed \ˈmī-ə-lə-ˌnāt-əd\ *adj* : having a myelin covering ⟨*myelinated* nerve fibers⟩

myelin sheath *n* : a layer of myelin surrounding the axons of some neurons

my·nah *or* **my·na** \ˈmī-nə\ *n* : any of various Asian starlings; *esp* : one that is mostly black and is often tamed and trained to mimic words

myn·heer \mə-ˈne(ə)r\ *n* : a male Netherlander — used as a title equal to *Mr.*

myo·car·di·um \ˌmī-ə-ˈkärd-ē-əm\ *n* : the middle muscular layer of the wall of the heart

myo·fi·bril \ˌmī-ō-ˈfīb-rəl, -ˈfib-\ *n* : any of the long thin contracting protein subunits of a muscle cell that are composed of actin and myosin filaments

my·o·pia \mī-ˈō-pē-ə\ *n* **1** : the condition of being nearsighted **2** : a lack of foresight : a narrow view of something — **my·o·pic** \-ˈō-pik, -ˈäp-ik\ *adj*

my·o·sin \ˈmī-ə-sən\ *n* : a protein of muscle that with actin is active in muscular contraction

¹myr·i·ad \ˈmir-ē-əd\ *n* **1** : ten thousand **2** : a large but not specified or counted number ⟨*myriads* of stars⟩

²myriad *adj* : extremely numerous ⟨the *myriad* grains of sand on a beach⟩

myr·ia·pod *also* **myr·io·pod** \ˈmir-ē-ə-ˌpäd\ *n* : any of a group of arthropods including the millipedes and centipedes — **myriapod** *adj*

myrrh \ˈmər\ *n* : a brown slightly bitter gum obtained from African and Arabian trees and used especially in perfumes or formerly in incense

myr·tle \ˈmərt-ᵊl\ *n* **1** : a common evergreen shrub of southern Europe with leaves, fragrant white or rosy flowers, and black berries **2 a** : any of the family of chiefly tropical shrubs or trees (as eucalyptus or guava) to which the common myrtle belongs **b** : ¹PERIWINKLE

my·self \mī-ˈself, mə-\ *pron* **1** : the one that is I — used for emphasis or to show that the subject and object of the verb are the same ⟨I'll go my-

myrtle 1

self⟩ ⟨I'm going to get *myself* a new hobby⟩ **2** : my normal or healthy self ⟨didn't feel *myself* yesterday⟩

mys·te·ri·ous \mis-ˈtir-ē-əs\ *adj* : containing, suggesting, or presenting a mystery ⟨*mysterious* noises⟩; *also* : difficult and impossible to understand ⟨the *mysterious* ways of nature⟩ — **mys·te·ri·ous·ly** *adv*

mys·tery \ˈmis-t(ə-)rē\ *n, pl* **-ter·ies** **1 a** : a religious truth that cannot be fully understood **b** : any of the 15 events (as the Nativity, the Crucifixion, or the Assumption) which serve as subjects for meditation by Roman Catholics as they say the rosary **2 a** : something that has not been or cannot be explained ⟨where they went is a *mystery*⟩ **b** : a deep secret ⟨kept their plans a *mystery*⟩ **3** : a work of fiction dealing with the solution of a mysterious crime

> **synonyms** MYSTERY, ENIGMA, PUZZLE mean something which is hard to understand or explain. MYSTERY applies to what cannot be fully understood by human reason or easily explained ⟨the *mystery* surrounding the building of the pyramids⟩. ENIGMA applies to words or actions very difficult to interpret correctly ⟨what she meant by her last remark is an *enigma*⟩. PUZZLE applies to a tricky problem that challenges one to provide a solution ⟨the cause of the blast is a *puzzle*⟩.

mystery play *n* : a play in the Middle Ages based on stories from the Bible (as the creation of the world or the life and death of Jesus Christ)

¹mys·tic \ˈmis-tik\ *adj* **1** : MYSTICAL 1 **2** : of or relating to magic : OCCULT **3** : MYSTERIOUS, AWESOME

²mystic *n* : a person who seeks direct knowledge of God through meditation and prayer

mys·ti·cal \ˈmis-ti-kəl\ *adj* **1** : having a spiritual meaning or reality that is not immediately apparent to the senses or the mind **2** : of, relating to, or resulting from communication directly with God — **mys·ti·cal·ly** \-k(ə-)lē\ *adv*

mys·ti·cism \ˈmis-tə-ˌsiz-əm\ *n* **1** : the experience of mystical union or direct communication with God **2** : the belief that direct knowledge of God or of spiritual truth can be achieved through deep meditation

mys·ti·fy \ˈmis-tə-ˌfī\ *vb* **-fied; -fy·ing** : to confuse thoroughly the understanding of : PERPLEX ⟨*mystified* by his behavior⟩ **synonyms** see PUZZLE — **mys·ti·fi·ca·tion** \ˌmis-tə-fə-ˈkā-shən\ *n*

mys·tique \mis-ˈtēk\ *n* : an attitude of mystery and respect developing around something or someone ⟨the *mystique* of mountain climbing⟩

myth \ˈmith\ *n* **1** : a story often describing the adventures of superhuman beings that attempts to describe the origin of a people's customs or beliefs or to explain mysterious events (as the changing of the seasons) **2** : a person or thing that exists only in the imagination ⟨the dragon is a *myth*⟩ **3** : a popular belief that is false or unsupported

myth·i·cal \ˈmith-i-kəl\ *or* **myth·ic** \ˈmith-ik\ *adj* **1** : based on, described in, or being a myth ⟨Hercules is a *mythical* hero⟩ **2** : existing only in the imagination : IMAGINARY ⟨the author created a *mythical* town⟩ — **myth·i·cal·ly** \-i-k(ə-)lē\ *adv*

my·thol·o·gy \mith-ˈäl-ə-jē\ *n, pl* **-gies** **1** : a collection of myths; *esp* : the myths dealing with the gods and heroes of a particular people ⟨Greek *mythology*⟩ **2** : a branch of knowledge that deals with myths — **myth·o·log·i·cal** \ˌmith-ə-ˈläj-i-kəl\ *adj*

myxo·my·cete \ˌmik-sō-ˈmī-ˌsēt, -(ˌ)mī-ˈsēt\ *n* : SLIME MOLD

\ə\ abut	\au̇\ out	\i\ tip	\o̊\ saw	\u̇\ foot
\ər\ further	\ch\ chin	\ī\ life	\o̊i\ coin	\y\ yet
\a\ mat	\e\ pet	\j\ job	\th\ thin	\yü\ few
\ā\ take	\ē\ easy	\ŋ\ sing	\th\ this	\yu̇\ cure
\ä\ cot, cart	\g\ go	\ō\ bone	\ü\ food	\zh\ vision

N

n \\'en\ *n, often cap* **1** : the 14th letter of the English alphabet **2** : an unspecified quantity ⟨the numbers from 1 to *n*⟩

-n — see ¹-EN

nab \\'nab\ *vb* **nabbed; nab·bing** **1** : to seize and take into custody : ARREST **2** : to seize suddenly; *esp* : ¹STEAL 2a

na·bob \\'nā-ˌbäb\ *n* **1** : a governor of a province of the Mogul empire in India **2** : a person of great wealth or importance

na·celle \nə-'sel\ *n* : an enclosed shelter on an aircraft for an engine or sometimes for the crew

na·cho \\'nä-chō\ *n, pl* **nachos** : a tortilla chip topped with melted cheese and often additional toppings (as hot peppers or refried beans)

na·cre \\'nā-kər\ *n* : MOTHER-OF-PEARL

na·dir \\'nā-ˌdi(ə)r, 'nād-ər\ *n*
1 : the point of the celestial sphere that is directly opposite the zenith and directly under the observer **2** : the lowest point ⟨our hopes reached their *nadir*⟩

nadir 1: *1* nadir, *2* observer, *3* zenith

¹**nag** \\'nag\ *n* : ¹HORSE 1a; *esp* : a horse that is old and in poor condition [Middle English *nagge* "horse"]

²**nag** *vb* **nagged; nag·ging** **1** : to annoy by repeated faultfinding, scolding, or urging ⟨kept *nagging* me to let her come⟩ ⟨always *nags* him to clean his room⟩ **2** : to cause (someone) to feel annoyed or worried for a long period of time ⟨a problem that *nagged* at her⟩ [probably of Scandinavian origin] — **nag·ger** *n*

³**nag** *n* : a person who frequently nags

Na·hum \\'nā-(h)əm\ *n* — see BIBLE

na·iad \\'nā-əd, 'nī-, -ˌad\ *n, pl* **na·iads** *or* **na·ia·des** \-ə-ˌdēz\ **1** : one of the nymphs living in lakes, rivers, springs, and fountains **2** : a water-dwelling larva of some insects (as a mayfly, dragonfly, damselfly, or stone fly)

¹**nail** \\'nā(ə)l\ *n* **1** : a horny covering at the end of the fingers and toes of human beings, apes, and monkeys; *also* : a similar structure (as a claw) in other animals **2** : a slender usually pointed fastener with a head designed to be pounded in

²**nail** *vb* **1** : to fasten with or as if with a nail **2** : ¹CATCH 1, TRAP ⟨*nail* a thief⟩ **3** : to hit or strike in a forceful or accurate way ⟨*nailed* the ball⟩ **4** : to complete successfully ⟨*nailed* the dismount⟩ **5** : to settle, establish, or represent clearly and unmistakably ⟨*nail* down all the details⟩ — **nail·er** *n*

nail·brush \\'nāl-ˌbrəsh\ *n* : a small brush for cleaning the hands and fingernails

nail file *n* : a small flat file (as of metal or cardboard) that is used for shaping fingernails

na·ive *or* **na·ïve** \nä-'ēv\ *adj* **na·iv·er; na·iv·est** **1** : marked by honest simplicity : ARTLESS **2** : showing lack of experience or knowledge : CREDULOUS [from French *naïve* "having a natural simplicity and honesty," from early French *naïf* "being part of the nature of a person from birth, native, inborn," from Latin *nativus* "native," from *natus*, past participle of *nasci* "to be born" — related to NATIVE] — **na·ive·ly** *adv*

na·ïve·te *also* **na·ive·te** \(ˌ)nä-ˌēv(-ə)-'tā, nä-'ēv(-ə)-tä\ *n* **1** : the quality or state of being naive **2** : a naive remark or action

na·ked \\'nā-kəd, *especially Southern* 'nek-əd\ *adj* **1** : having no clothes on **2 a** : lacking a usual or natural covering (as of leaves, plants, or feathers) ⟨*naked* hills⟩ **b** : not enclosed in a case or covering ⟨a *naked* sword⟩ **c** : lacking protective covering parts (as membranes, scales, or shells) ⟨a *naked* seed⟩ **3** : ²PLAIN 2, UNADORNED ⟨the *naked* truth⟩ **4** : not aided by artificial means ⟨seen by the *naked* eye⟩ — **na·ked·ly** *adv* — **na·ked·ness** *n*

naked mole rat *n* : a burrowing rodent of Ethiopia, Somalia, and Kenya that resembles a mole, has nearly hairless wrinkled skin, and is practically blind

¹**name** \\'nām\ *n* **1** : a word or combination of words by which a person or thing is regularly known **2** : a descriptive often insulting word or phrase ⟨called him *names*⟩ **3** : REPUTATION 2 ⟨made a *name* for herself⟩ **4** : appearance as opposed to fact ⟨a friend in *name* only⟩

²**name** *vb* **named; nam·ing** **1** : to give a name to : CALL **2 a** : to mention or identify by name **b** : to accuse by name ⟨*name* the culprit⟩ **3** : to nominate for office : APPOINT ⟨*named* the diplomat Secretary of State⟩ **4** : to decide upon : CHOOSE ⟨*name* the date for a wedding⟩ **5** : to mention specifically ⟨*name* a price⟩ — **nam·er** *n*

³**name** *adj* **1** : bearing a name ⟨*name* tag⟩ **2** : having an established reputation ⟨*name* performers⟩ ⟨*name* brands⟩

name·less \\'nām-ləs\ *adj* **1** : having no name **2** : not marked with a name ⟨a *nameless* grave⟩ **3** : ¹UNKNOWN, ANONYMOUS ⟨a *nameless* hero⟩ **4 a** : impossible to describe ⟨*nameless* fears⟩ **b** : too disgusting or disturbing to be described ⟨*nameless* acts of cruelty⟩

name·ly \\'nām-lē\ *adv* : that is to say ⟨the cat family, *namely*, lions, tigers, and related animals⟩

name·sake \\'nām-ˌsāk\ *n* : one that has the same name as another; *esp* : one named after another

nan·keen \(')nan-'kēn\ *n* : a durable brownish yellow cotton fabric originally from China

nan·ny \\'nan-ē\ *n* : a woman who is paid to care for a young child usually in the child's home

nanny goat *n* : a female goat

nano— \\'nan-ō, -ə\ *combining form* **1** : very small ⟨*nano*technology⟩ **2** : one billionth part of ⟨*nano*gram⟩ [from Greek *nanos* "dwarf"]

nano·gram \\'nan-ə-ˌgram\ *n* : one billionth of a gram

nano·meter \\'nan-ə-ˌmēt-ər\ *n* : one billionth of a meter

nano·scale \\'nan-ə-ˌskā(ə)l\ *adj* : having dimensions usually measured in nanometers

nano·sec·ond \\'nan-ə-ˌsek-ənd, -ənt\ *n* : one billionth of a second

nano·tech \\'nan-ō-ˌtek\ *n* : NANOTECHNOLOGY

nano·tech·nol·o·gy \ˌnan-ō-tek-'näl-ə-jē\ *n* : the art of using and controlling materials on an atomic or molecular scale especially in order to create microscopic devices

¹**nap** \\'nap\ *vb* **napped; nap·ping** **1** : to sleep briefly especially during the day **2** : to be off guard ⟨was caught *napping*⟩ [Old English *hnappian* "to doze"]

²**nap** *n* : a short sleep especially during the day

³**nap** *n* : a hairy or downy surface on a woven fabric or leather [Middle English *noppe* "soft surface on a fabric," from early Dutch *noppe* "tuft of wool, nap"] — **nap·py** \\'nap-ē\ *adj*

⁴**nap** *vb* **napped; nap·ping** : to raise a nap on fabric or leather

na·palm \\'nā-ˌpäm, -ˌpälm\ *n* **1** : a thickener used to make gasoline jellylike (as for bombs) **2** : fuel made jellylike with napalm

nape \'nāp, 'nap\ *n* : the back of the neck

naph·tha \'naf-thə, 'nap-\ *n* : any of various often flammable liquids prepared from coal or petroleum and used especially to dissolve substances

naph·tha·lene \'naf-thə-ˌlēn, 'nap-\ *n* : a hydrocarbon in the form of crystals usually obtained from coal tar and used in chemical manufacture and as a moth repellent

nap·kin \'nap-kən\ *n*   **1** : a small square of cloth or paper used during a meal to wipe the lips or fingers and protect the clothes   **2** : a small cloth or towel [Middle English *nappekin* "napkin," from *nappe* "tablecloth," derived from Latin *mappa* "napkin" — related to APRON, MAP]

na·po·leon \nə-'pōl-yən, -'pō-lē-ən\ *n*   **1** : a former French 20-franc gold coin   **2** : an oblong pastry with a filling of cream, custard, or jelly

narc *also* **nark** \'närk\ *n, slang* : a person (as a government agent) who investigates narcotics violations

nar·cis·sism \'när-sə-ˌsiz-əm\ *n* : excessive love and admiration for oneself and especially one's own appearance — **nar·cis·sist** \-sist\ *n* — **nar·cis·sis·tic** \ˌnär-sə-'sis-tik\ *adj*

nar·cis·sus \när-'sis-əs\ *n, pl* **nar·cis·si** \-'sis-ˌī, -ē\ *or* **nar·cis·sus·es** *or* **nar·cissus** : DAFFODIL; *esp* : one whose flowers have a short tube and grow separately on the stalk

nar·co·sis \när-'kō-səs\ *n, pl* **nar·co·ses** \-'kō-ˌsēz\ : a dazed, unconscious, or inactive condition produced by chemicals (as narcotics)

¹nar·cot·ic \när-'kät-ik\ *n*   **1** : a drug (as opium or morphine) that in small doses dulls the senses, relieves pain, and causes sleep but in large doses has dangerous effects (as coma)   **2** : something that soothes, relieves, or lulls

²narcotic *adj*   **1** : acting as or being the source of a narcotic ⟨*narcotic* drugs⟩ ⟨the opium poppy is a *narcotic* plant⟩   **2** : of or relating to narcotics or their use or control ⟨*narcotic* laws⟩

na·res \'na(ə)r-(ˌ)ēz, 'ne(ə)r-\ *n pl* : the pair of openings of the nose or nasal cavity of a vertebrate

nar·rate \'na(ə)r-ˌāt, na-'rāt\ *vb* **nar·rat·ed; nar·rat·ing** : RELATE 1, TELL ⟨*narrate* a story⟩ — **nar·ra·tor** \'na(ə)r-ˌāt-ər, na-'rāt-, nə-; 'nar-ət-\ *n*

nar·ra·tion \na-'rā-shən, nə-\ *n*   **1** : the act or process or an instance of telling a story   **2** : ¹STORY 1a, NARRATIVE — **nar·ra·tion·al** \-shnəl, -shən-ᵊl\ *adj*

nar·ra·tive \'nar-ət-iv\ *n*   **1** : something (as a story) that is told or written   **2** : the art or practice of telling stories — **narrative** *adj*

   synonyms NARRATIVE, ACCOUNT, RECITAL mean a statement of facts or events. NARRATIVE suggests a series of connected events told like a story ⟨a *narrative* of the early pioneers⟩. ACCOUNT suggests a simple repeating of the facts or events ⟨give the police an *account* of what happened⟩. RECITAL may suggest either an account with many details or a list of memorized facts ⟨the speaker gave a *recital* of the scientist's many achievements⟩.

¹nar·row \'nar-ō\ *adj*   **1 a** : of slender width ⟨a *narrow* space⟩   **b** : of less than usual width ⟨*narrow* roads⟩   **2** : limited in size or scope ⟨a *narrow* selection of jeans⟩   **3** : not broad or open in views or opinions ⟨*narrow* in their thinking⟩   **4 a** : barely enough for the purpose : CLOSE ⟨won by a *narrow* margin⟩   **b** : barely successful ⟨a *narrow* escape⟩ — **nar·row·ly** *adv* — **nar·row·ness** *n*

²narrow *n* : a narrow part or passage; *esp* : a strait connecting two bodies of water — usually used in plural

³narrow *vb* : to lessen in width or extent : CONTRACT

nar·row–mind·ed \ˌnar-ō-'mīn-dəd\ *adj* : INTOLERANT 2, BIGOTED — **nar·row–mind·ed·ness** *n*

narwhal

nar·whal \'när-ˌwäl, -ˌhwäl, -wəl\ *n* : an arctic sea mammal that is about 20 feet (six meters) long, is related to the dolphins and whales and in the male has a long twisted ivory tusk

¹na·sal \'nā-zəl\ *n* : a nasal consonant

²nasal *adj*   **1** : of or relating to the nose   **2 a** : uttered with passage of air through the nose ⟨the *nasal* consonants \m\, \n\, and \ŋ\⟩ ⟨the *nasal* vowels in French⟩   **b** : marked by resonance produced through the nose ⟨speaking in a *nasal* tone⟩ — **na·sal·i·ty** \nā-'zal-ət-ē\ *n* — **na·sal·ly** \'nāz-(ə-)lē\ *adv*

nasal cavity *n* : an incompletely divided chamber that lies between the floor of the skull and the roof of the mouth and functions in the warming and filtering of inhaled air and in the sensing of odors

nas·tur·tium \nə-'stər-shəm, na-\ *n* : any of a genus of herbs with showy flowers and edible sharp-tasting seeds and leaves

nas·ty \'nas-tē\ *adj* **nas·ti·er; -est**   **1** : very dirty or foul : FILTHY   **2** : morally disgusting or degrading   **3** : DISAGREEABLE 1, UNPLEASANT ⟨*nasty* weather⟩   **4** : SPITEFUL, ILL-NATURED ⟨a *nasty* temper⟩ ⟨a *nasty* trick⟩   **5** : HARMFUL, DANGEROUS ⟨a *nasty* fall on the ice⟩ — **nas·ti·ly** \-tə-lē\ *adv* — **nas·ti·ness** \-tē-nəs\ *n*

na·tal \'nāt-ᵊl\ *adj* : of or relating to birth

na·tion \'nā-shən\ *n*   **1** : NATIONALITY 3   **2** : a community of people composed of one or more nationalities usually with its own territory and government   **3** : the territory of a nation

¹na·tion·al \'nash-nəl, -ən-ᵊl\ *adj*   **1** : of or relating to a nation ⟨*national* elections⟩   **2** : belonging to or maintained by the federal government ⟨*national* cemeteries⟩ — **na·tion·al·ly** \-ē\ *adv*

²national *n*   **1** : a person who owes allegiance to or is under the protection of a nation   **2** : a competition that is national in scope — usually used in plural ⟨qualified for the figure skating *nationals*⟩

national bank *n* : a commercial bank organized under laws passed by Congress and chartered by the federal government

national guard *n*   **1** *cap* : a militia force recruited by each state, equipped by the federal government, and subject to the call of either   **2** : a military force serving as a national police and defense force — **national guardsman** *n, often cap*

na·tion·al·ism \'nash-nəl-ˌiz-əm, -ən-ᵊl-\ *n* : loyalty and devotion to a nation especially as expressed in a glorifying of one nation above all others and a stressing of the promotion of its culture and interests

na·tion·al·ist \'nash-nəl-əst, -ən-ᵊl-əst\ *n*   **1** : a supporter of nationalism   **2** : a member of a group promoting national independence — **nationalist** *adj* — **na·tion·al·is·tic** \ˌnash-nəl-'is-tik, -ən-ᵊl-\ *adj*

na·tion·al·i·ty \ˌnash-(ə-)'nal-ət-ē\ *n, pl* **-ties**   **1** : the fact or state of belonging to a nation ⟨a person of French *nationality*⟩   **2** : political independence as a nation   **3** : a people having a common beginning, tradition, or language

na·tion·al·ize \'nash-nəl-ˌīz, -ən-ᵊl-\ *vb* **-ized; -iz·ing**   **1** : to make national   **2** : to remove from private ownership

\ə\ abut	\au̇\ out	\i\ tip	\ȯ\ saw	\u̇\ foot
\ər\ further	\ch\ chin	\ī\ life	\ȯi\ coin	\y\ yet
\a\ mat	\e\ pet	\j\ job	\th\ thin	\yü\ few
\ā\ take	\ē\ easy	\ŋ\ sing	\t͟h\ this	\yu̇\ cure
\ä\ cot, cart	\g\ go	\ō\ bone	\ü\ food	\zh\ vision

and place under government control ⟨*nationalize* railroads⟩ — **na·tion·al·i·za·tion** \-ə-ˈzā-shən\ *n*

national monument *n* : a place of historic, scenic, or scientific interest set aside for preservation usually by presidential proclamation

national park *n* : an area of special scenic, historical, or scientific importance set aside and maintained by a national government and in the U.S. by an act of Congress

na·tion·wide \ˌnā-shən-ˈwīd\ *adj* : extending throughout a nation ⟨*nationwide* phone service⟩

¹**na·tive** \ˈnāt-iv\ *adj* 1 : INBORN 1, NATURAL ⟨*native* ability⟩ 2 : born in a particular place or country ⟨*native* Hawaiians⟩ 3 : belonging to one because of the place or circumstances of one's birth ⟨my *native* language⟩ 4 a : grown, produced, or having its beginning in a particular region ⟨*native* art⟩ ⟨*native* stone⟩ b : living or growing naturally in a particular region ⟨*native* plants⟩ 5 : found in nature especially in a pure form : not artificially prepared ⟨*native* salt⟩ 6 *cap* : of, relating to, or being a member of an indigenous people of North or South America : NATIVE AMERICAN [Middle English *natif* "native," from early French *natif* (same meaning), from Latin *nativus* (same meaning), from *natus,* past participle of *nasci* "to be born" — related to INNATE, NAIVE, NATURE] — **na·tive·ly** *adv*

²**native** *n* 1 : one born or raised in a particular place ⟨a *native* of Milwaukee⟩ 2 : one of a people living in a place before the arrival of foreigners 3 : something native to or produced in a locality

Native American *n* : a member of any of the indigenous peoples of the western hemisphere; *esp* : a Native American of North America and especially the U.S. — compare AMERICAN INDIAN — **Native American** *adj*

na·tiv·i·ty \nə-ˈtiv-ət-ē, nā-\ *n, pl* **-ties** 1 *cap* : the birth of Jesus 2 : the time, place, or manner of being born : BIRTH

nat·ty \ˈnat-ē\ *adj* **nat·ti·er; -est** : trimly neat and tidy : SMART ⟨a *natty* suit⟩ — **nat·ti·ly** \ˈnat-ᵊl-ē\ *adv* — **nat·ti·ness** \ˈnat-ē-nəs\ *n*

¹**nat·u·ral** \ˈnach-(ə-)rəl\ *adj* 1 : born in or with one : INNATE ⟨*natural* ability⟩ 2 : being such by nature : BORN ⟨a *natural* musician⟩ 3 : BIOLOGICAL 2 ⟨her *natural* parents⟩ 4 a : growing without human care ⟨*natural* forests⟩ b : existing in or produced by nature ⟨*natural* scenery⟩ c : relating to or being natural food 5 : ¹HUMAN 1 ⟨it is not *natural* to howl at the moon⟩ 6 : of, relating to, or following the usual events and happenings of nature or the physical world : not miraculous ⟨*natural* causes⟩ 7 : not made or changed by humans ⟨*natural* silk⟩ ⟨a person's *natural* complexion⟩ 8 : being simple and sincere ⟨*natural* manners⟩ 9 : LIFELIKE ⟨the people in the picture look *natural*⟩ 10 a : having neither sharps nor flats in the key signature b : having a sharp or a flat changed in pitch by a natural sign — **nat·u·ral·ness** *n*

²**natural** *n* 1 a : a sign ♮ placed on a line or space of the musical staff to change a sharp or flat in the key signature back to the natural tone value b : a note or tone changed by the natural sign 2 : one naturally able to do or to learn easily how to do something ⟨a *natural* at golf⟩ 3 : AFRO

natural childbirth *n* : a system of managing childbirth in which the mother receives training in order to remain conscious and to help in the process of birth with little or no use of drugs (as anesthetics)

natural food *n* : food that has been processed as little as possible and contains no added artificial substances to keep it fresh or give it flavor

natural gas *n* : gas that comes from the earth's crust through natural openings or bored wells; *esp* : a flammable mixture of hydrocarbons and especially methane used chiefly as a fuel and raw material

natural history *n* : the study of natural objects and especially plants and animals as they live in nature from an amateur or popular point of view

nat·u·ral·ist \ˈnach-(ə-)rə-ləst\ *n* : a person who specializes in natural history — **naturalist** *adj*

nat·u·ral·i·za·tion \ˌnach-(ə-)rə-lə-ˈzā-shən\ *n* : the act or process of naturalizing : the state of being naturalized

nat·u·ral·ize \ˈnach-(ə-)rə-ˌlīz\ *vb* **-ized; -iz·ing** 1 : to introduce into common use ⟨*naturalize* a foreign word⟩ 2 : to become or cause to become established as if native ⟨*naturalized* weeds⟩ 3 : to give the rights and privileges of citizenship to ⟨*naturalize* a foreign-born person⟩

nat·u·ral·ly \ˈnach-(ə-)rə-lē, ˈnach-ər-lē\ *adv* 1 : by natural character or ability ⟨*naturally* affectionate⟩ 2 : according to the usual course of things ⟨we *naturally* wanted to go to the big game⟩ 3 a : without artificial aid ⟨hair that curls *naturally*⟩ b : in a simple and sincere manner ⟨speak *naturally*⟩ 4 : in a lifelike manner ⟨paints flowers *naturally*⟩

natural number *n* : the number 1 or any number (as 3, 12, or 432) obtained by adding 1 to it one or more times : a positive whole number

natural resource *n* : something (as a mineral, waterpower source, forest, or kind of animal) that is found in nature and is valuable to humans (as in providing a source of energy, recreation, or scenic beauty

natural science *n* : any of the sciences (as physics, chemistry, or biology) that deal with matter, energy, and their relationships and transformations or with measurable natural events

natural selection *n* : a natural process in which individuals or groups best adapted to the conditions under which they live survive and produce young and poorly adapted forms are eliminated

na·ture \ˈnā-chər\ *n* 1 : the basic quality, character, or way in which a thing or person exists or has been formed ⟨the *nature* of steel⟩ 2 : ¹KIND 1a, SORT ⟨and things of that *nature*⟩ 3 : DISPOSITION 3a, TEMPERAMENT ⟨a baby with a happy *nature*⟩ 4 : a power or set of forces thought of as controlling the universe 5 : natural feeling especially as shown in one's attitude toward others ⟨your generous *nature* is well-known⟩ 6 : humanity's original or natural condition : primitive life ⟨return to *nature*⟩ 7 : the physical universe ⟨the study of *nature*⟩ 8 : the workings of a living body ⟨leave a cure to *nature*⟩; *esp* : an excretory function — used in phrases like *the call of nature* 9 : natural scenery ⟨the beauties of *nature*⟩ [Middle English *nature* "normal or essential quality of something, nature," from early French *nature* (same meaning), from Latin *natura* (same meaning), from *natus,* past participle of *nasci* "to be born" — related to INNATE, NATIVE]

¹**naught** *also* **nought** \ˈnȯt, ˈnät\ *pron* : ¹NOTHING 2 ⟨their efforts came to *naught*⟩

²**naught** *also* **nought** *n* 1 : the quality or state of being nothing : NONEXISTENCE 2 : ¹ZERO 1 — see NUMBER table

naugh·ty \ˈnȯt-ē, ˈnät-\ *adj* **naugh·ti·er; -est** : behaving badly or improperly — **naugh·ti·ly** \ˈnȯt-ᵊl-ē, ˈnät-\ *adv* — **naugh·ti·ness** \ˈnȯt-ē-nəs, ˈnät-\ *n*

nau·sea \ˈnȯ-zē-ə, -sē-ə; ˈnȯ-zhə, -shə\ *n* 1 : a disturbed condition of the stomach in which one feels like vomiting 2 : extreme disgust

Word History The ancient Greeks were a seagoing people, so seasickness was not rare for them. Their word for seasickness, *nausia* or *nautia,* came from their word for ship, *naus.* But *nautia* or *nausia* also meant the worst symptom of seasickness, the stomach upset and urge to vomit. *Nausea,* as we call this feeling in English, can be caused by something other than the motion of a ship. The ancient Greeks and the ancient Romans, who spoke Latin, needed only one word for both seasickness and the upset in the stomach. The Romans borrowed the

Greek word, spelling it *nausea* in Latin. English took the word directly from Latin. [from Latin *nausea* "seasickness, the stomach upset that causes an urge to vomit," from Greek *nausia, nautia* (same meaning), literally "ship sickness," from *naus* "ship" — related to ASTRONAUT, NAUTICAL, NOISE; see *Word History* at NOISE]

nau·se·ate \'nȯ-zē-ˌāt, -sē-, -zhē-, -shē-\ *vb* **-at·ed; -at·ing** : to affect or become affected with nausea or disgust

nau·se·at·ing \'nȯ-zē-ˌāt-iŋ, -sē-, -zhē-, -shē-\ *adj* : causing nausea and especially disgust ⟨*nauseating* behavior⟩ — **nau·se·at·ing·ly** *adv*

nau·seous \'nȯ-shəs, 'nȯ-zē-əs\ *adj* : affected with or causing nausea or disgust ⟨feel *nauseous*⟩ ⟨a *nauseous* odor⟩ — **nau·seous·ly** *adv*

nau·ti·cal \'nȯt-i-kəl, 'nät-\ *adj* : of or relating to sailors, navigation, or ships [from Latin *nauticus* "nautical," from Greek *nautikos* (same meaning), from *nautēs* "sailor," from *naus* "ship" — related to ASTRONAUT, NAUSEA; see *Word History* at NAUSEA] — **nau·ti·cal·ly** \-k(ə-)lē\ *adv*

nautical mile *n* : any of various units of distance used for sea and air navigation equal to about 6076 feet (1852 meters)

nau·ti·lus \'nȯt-ᵊl-əs, 'nät-\ *n, pl* **nau·ti·lus·es** *or* **nau·ti·li** \-ᵊl-ˌī, -ˌē\ **1** : any of a genus of mollusks of the South Pacific and Indian oceans that are cephalopods and have a spiral chambered shell that is pearly on the inside — called also *chambered nautilus* **2** : PAPER NAUTILUS

nautilus 1

Na·va·jo *also* **Na·va·ho** \'nav-ə-ˌhō, 'näv-\ *n, pl* **Navajo** *or* **Navajos** *also* **Navaho** *or* **Navahos** : a member of an American Indian people of northern New Mexico and Arizona

na·val \'nā-vəl\ *adj* : of or relating to a navy or warships

naval stores *n pl* : products (as pitch, turpentine, or rosin) obtained from coniferous trees (as pines)

¹nave \'nāv\ *n* : the hub of a wheel

²nave *n* : the long central main part of a church

na·vel \'nā-vəl\ *n* : a hollowed out place on the outside wall of the middle of the abdomen marking the point of attachment of the umbilical cord

navel orange *n* : a usually seedless orange that contains a small or partial second fruit at one end resembling a navel

nav·i·ga·ble \'nav-i-gə-bəl\ *adj* **1 a** : deep and wide enough to permit passage to ships ⟨*navigable* rivers⟩ **b** : capable of being navigated ⟨*navigable* terrain⟩ **2** : capable of being steered ⟨a *navigable* balloon⟩ — **nav·i·ga·bil·i·ty** \ˌnav-i-gə-'bil-ət-ē\ *n*

nav·i·gate \'nav-ə-ˌgāt\ *vb* **-gat·ed; -gat·ing** **1 a** : to travel by water **b** : to sail over, on, or through ⟨*navigate* the Atlantic Ocean⟩ **2 a** : to direct one's course in a ship or aircraft **b** : to control the course of : STEER **3** : to make one's way about, over, or through ⟨*navigate* the new website⟩ ⟨*navigate* the school's halls⟩

nav·i·ga·tion \ˌnav-ə-'gā-shən\ *n* **1** : the act or practice of navigating **2** : the science of getting ships, aircraft, or spacecraft from place to place; *esp* : the method of figuring out position, course, and distance traveled — **nav·i·ga·tion·al** \-shnəl, -shən-ᵊl\ *adj*

nav·i·ga·tor \'nav-ə-ˌgāt-ər\ *n* : one that navigates or is qualified to navigate

nav·vy \'nav-ē\ *n, pl* **navvies** *chiefly British* : an unskilled laborer

na·vy \'nā-vē\ *n, pl* **navies** **1** : a fleet of ships **2** : a na-

tion's warships **3** *often cap* : a nation's complete equipment and organization for sea warfare **4** : a dark purplish blue

navy bean *n* : a kidney bean grown especially for its small white seeds that are valuable as food; *also* : its seed

navy yard *n* : a naval shore station where ships are built or repaired

na·wab \nə-'wäb\ *n* **1** : NABOB 1 **2** : NABOB 2

¹nay \'nā\ *adv* **1** : ¹NO 3 **2** : not merely this but also : not only so but ⟨the letter made him happy, *nay*, ecstatic⟩

²nay *n* **1** : DENIAL 1, REFUSAL **2 a** : a negative reply or vote **b** : one who votes no

Naz·a·rene \ˌnaz-ə-'rēn\ *n* : a person born or living in Nazareth — **Nazarene** *adj*

Na·zi \'nät-sē, 'nat-\ *n* : a member of a German fascist party controlling Germany from 1933 to 1945 — **Nazi** *adj* — **Na·zism** \'nät-ˌsiz-əm, 'nat-\ *n*

NCO \ˌen-(ˌ)sē-'ō\ *n* : NONCOMMISSIONED OFFICER

NC–17 \'en-ˌsē-ˌsev-ən-'tēn\ *certification mark* — used to certify that a motion picture is of such a nature that no one under the age of 17 can be admitted

-nd *symbol* — used after the figure 2 to indicate the ordinal number second ⟨2*nd*⟩ ⟨42*nd*⟩

Ne·an·der·thal \nē-'an-dər-ˌthȯl, -ˌtȯl; nā-'än-dər-ˌtäl\ *n* **1** *or* **Ne·an·der·tal** \-ˌtȯl, -ˌtäl\ : a primate mammal that belongs to the same family as human beings, lived from about 30,000 to 200,000 years ago, is known from skeletal remains in Europe, northern Africa, and western Asia, and is characterized especially by a stocky muscular build and prominent browridge — called also *Neanderthal man* **2** : one who suggests a caveman in appearance, behavior, or intelligence — **Neanderthal** *adj*

Ne·a·pol·i·tan ice cream \ˌnē-ə-ˌpäl-ət-ᵊn-\ *n* : a brick of ice cream with layers of different flavors (as vanilla, chocolate, and strawberry)

neap tide \'nēp-\ *n* : a tide of least range occurring at the first and third quarters of the moon

¹near \'ni(ə)r\ *adv* **1** : at, within, or to a short distance or time ⟨night was drawing *near*⟩ **2** : in a condition or state resembling or close to : ALMOST ⟨*near* dead⟩ **3** : NEARLY 1 ⟨*near* related⟩ [Old English *nēar* "nearer," comparative form of *nēah* "near, close" — related to NEIGHBOR, NIGH; see *Word History* at NEIGHBOR]

²near \(')ni(ə)r\ *prep* : close to ⟨standing *near* the door⟩

³near \'ni(ə)r\ *adj* **1** : closely related or associated ⟨her *nearest* and dearest friend⟩ **2 a** : not far away ⟨the *near* future⟩ **b** : barely avoided ⟨a *near* disaster⟩ **c** : almost not happening ⟨a *near* victory⟩ **3** : being the closer of two ⟨the *near* side of a hill⟩ **4** : ²DIRECT 1, SHORT ⟨the *nearest* route⟩ **5** : closely resembling a model or a genuine example ⟨*near* silk⟩ — **near·ness** *n*

⁴near \'ni(ə)r\ *vb* : to come near : APPROACH ⟨the ship was *nearing* the dock⟩

near·by \ni(ə)r-'bī, 'ni(ə)r-ˌbī\ *adv or adj* : close at hand

near·ly \'ni(ə)r-lē\ *adv* **1** : in a close manner or relationship ⟨*nearly* related⟩ **2** : almost but not quite ⟨*nearly* the same⟩ ⟨*nearly* missed the train⟩ **3** : to the least extent ⟨not *nearly* enough⟩

near·sight·ed \'ni(ə)r-'sīt-əd\ *adj* : able to see near things more clearly than distant ones : MYOPIC — **near·sight·ed·ness** *n*

neat \'nēt\ *adj* **1** : being orderly and clean : TIDY ⟨a *neat* roommate⟩ ⟨a *neat* closet⟩ **2** : not mixed or diluted : STRAIGHT 3d ⟨*neat* cement⟩ **3** : marked by tasteful simplicity ⟨*neat* furnishings⟩ **4** : marked by skill or ingenuity

\ə\ abut	\au̇\ out	\i\ tip	\ȯ\ saw	\u̇\ foot
\ər\ further	\ch\ chin	\ī\ life	\ȯi\ coin	\y\ yet
\a\ mat	\e\ pet	\j\ job	\th\ thin	\yü\ few
\ā\ take	\ē\ easy	\ŋ\ sing	\t͟h\ this	\yu̇\ cure
\ä\ cot, cart	\g\ go	\ō\ bone	\ü\ food	\zh\ vision

: ADROIT <a *neat* dive> **5** : ³FINE 4, SPLENDID <had a *neat* time> — **neat·ly** *adv* — **neat·ness** *n*

Word History Today a popular use of the word *neat* is to mean "fine, splendid." It is a use that does not appear to have much in common with earlier meanings of the word such as "tidy" or "undiluted." But in its newest sense of "splendid," something that is "neat" might be thought of as a brilliant or shining example of the best of its kind. And this idea is very close to the origin of the word. *Neat* first began to be used in English about 400 years ago. It was borrowed from the early French word *net,* which in turn was taken from Latin *nitidus,* meaning "bright, shining." At first *neat* was used in English with the same meaning, as in "a neat new metal pin." This original sense in time fell out of use. But the idea of something bright and clean and sparkling and new gave us other meanings. One of these is the sense of "tidy," as in "a neat room or desk." Perhaps the idea of something clean also gave rise to the sense of *neat* meaning "not mixed or diluted" with anything. The idea of "tidy" certainly must have been the basis of the sense of "marked by tasteful simplicity." And since all of these senses suggest something that is viewed as ideal, it is easy to understand that they should lead to the newest sense of *neat,* meaning "splendid." When first used in English, *splendid* also meant "shining," coming from a Latin verb meaning "to shine." [from earlier *neat* "bright, shining," from early French *net* (same meaning), from Latin *nitidus* (same meaning), from *nitēre* "to shine" — related to ³NET]

synonyms NEAT, TIDY, TRIM mean showing care and concern for order. NEAT stresses that something is clean in addition to being orderly <your clothes should always be *neat*>. TIDY suggests that something is continually kept orderly and neat <I work hard to keep my room *tidy*>. TRIM stresses that something is orderly and compact <*trim* comfortable houses>.

neb·u·la \'neb-yə-lə\ *n, pl* **-las** *or* **-lae** \-,lē, -,lī\ **1** : any of many huge clouds of gas or dust in deep space **2** : GALAXY — **neb·u·lar** \-lər\ *adj*

neb·u·lous \'neb-yə-ləs\ *adj* **1** : of, relating to, or resembling a nebula **2** : not clear or sharp : VAGUE — **neb·u·lous·ly** *adv* — **neb·u·lous·ness** *n*

¹**nec·es·sary** \'nes-ə-,ser-ē\ *adj* **1** : going to happen with no way of preventing it : INESCAPABLE <tests are a *necessary* part of school> **2** : being the only logically possible result <a *necessary* conclusion> **3** : being required : MANDATORY <it is *necessary* to attend all practices> **4** : absolutely needed : ESSENTIAL <food is *necessary* for life> [Middle English *necessarie* "necessary, required," derived from Latin *necesse* "necessary, unavoidable," from *ne-* "not" and *cedere* "to go, go away" — related to CONCEDE, SUCCEED] — **nec·es·sar·i·ly** \,nes-ə-'ser-ə-lē\ *adv*

²**necessary** *n, pl* **-sar·ies** : something necessary : REQUIREMENT <the *necessaries* of life>

ne·ces·si·tate \ni-'ses-ə-,tāt\ *vb* **-tat·ed; -tat·ing** : to make necessary <sick enough to *necessitate* staying home> — **ne·ces·si·ta·tion** \-,ses-ə-'tā-shən\ *n*

ne·ces·si·ty \ni-'ses-ət-ē, -'ses-tē\ *n, pl* **-ties** **1** : conditions that cannot be changed <forced by *necessity*> **2** : the quality or state of being in need : POVERTY **3 a** : something that is necessary : REQUIREMENT <the *necessities* for camping in comfort> **b** : an urgent need or desire <call in case of *necessity*>

neck \'nek\ *n* **1** : the part of the body connecting the head and the main part of the body **2** : the part of a garment covering or nearest to the neck **3 a** : something like a neck in shape or position <the *neck* of a bottle> <a *neck* of land> **b** : the part of a tooth between the crown and the root — **necked** \'nekt\ *adj*

neck and neck *adv or adj* : very close (as in a race)

neck·er·chief \'nek-ər-chəf, -,chif, -,chēf\ *n, pl* **-chiefs** *also* **neck·er·chieves** \-chəfs, -,chifs, -,chēvz, -,chēfs\ : a square of cloth worn folded about the neck like a scarf

neck·lace \'nek-ləs\ *n* : an ornament (as a string of beads) worn around the neck

neck·line \-,līn\ *n* : the outline of the neck opening of a garment

neck·tie \-,tī\ *n* : a narrow length of cloth worn about the neck and tied in front

neckerchief

neck·wear \-,wa(ə)r, -,we(ə)r\ *n* : articles (as scarves or neckties) for wear around the neck

nec·ro·man·cy \'nek-rə-,man(t)-sē\ *n* **1** : the art or practice of calling up the spirits of the dead for magical purposes **2** : MAGIC 1 — **nec·ro·man·cer** \-sər\ *n*

nec·rop·sy \'nek-,räp-sē\ *n, pl* **-sies** : AUTOPSY; *esp* : an autopsy performed on an animal

nec·tar \'nek-tər\ *n* **1** : the drink of the Greek and Roman gods **2** : a sweet liquid given off by plants and especially by the flowers and used by bees in making honey

nec·tar·ine \,nek-tə-'rēn\ *n* : a smooth-skinned peach; *also* : a tree producing this fruit

nec·tary \'nek-t(ə-)rē\ *n, pl* **-tar·ies** : a plant gland that secretes nectar

née *or* **nee** \'nā\ *adj* — used to identify a woman by her family name at birth <Mrs. Jane Doe, *née* Smith>

¹**need** \'nēd\ *n* **1** : necessary duty : OBLIGATION <no *need* to apologize> **2 a** : a lack of something necessary, desirable, or useful <the *need* for more doctors> **b** : something necessary or desired <a *need* for sympathy>; *also* : a mental or physical requirement for keeping a living thing in normal condition **3** : a situation requiring supply or relief <call whenever the *need* arises> <a friend in *need*> **4** : POVERTY 1, WANT <provide for those in *need*>

²**need** *vb* **1** : to be in want **2** : to be in need of : REQUIRE <they *need* advice> **3** : to be required or obliged <we *need* to look at the facts> <you *need* not answer> **4** : to be necessary <something *needs* to be done>

need·ful \'nēd-fəl\ *adj* : necessary for a purpose — **need·ful·ly** \-fə-lē\ *adv* — **need·ful·ness** *n*

¹**nee·dle** \'nēd-ᵊl\ *n* **1 a** : a small slender usually steel instrument that has an eye for thread or surgical sutures at one end and is used for sewing **b** : any of various devices for carrying thread and making stitches (as in crocheting or knitting) **c** : a slender hollow usually stainless steel instrument by which material is put into or taken from the body through the skin **d** : an extremely thin solid usually stainless steel instrument used in acupuncture and inserted through the skin **2 a** : a slender bar of magnetized steel that is free to turn (as in a compass) to show the direction of a magnetic field **b** : a slender pointer on a dial **3 a** : a slender pointed object (as a pointed crystal or an obelisk) **b** : a leaf (as of a pine) shaped like a needle **4** : a slender piece of jewel or steel with a rounded tip used in a phonograph to transmit vibrations from the record — **nee·dle·like** \'nēd-ᵊl-(,)līk\ *adj*

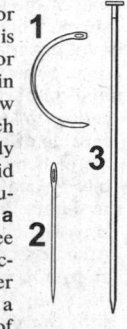

¹needle 1: *1* suture, *2* sewing, *3* knitting

²**needle** *vb* **nee·dled; nee·dling** \'nēd-liŋ, -ᵊl-iŋ\ **1** : ¹TEASE 2a, TAUNT **2** : to cause to take action by repeated stinging remarks — **nee·dler** \'nēd-lər, -ᵊl-ər\ *n*

nee·dle·fish \'nēd-ᵊl-,fish\ *n* **1** : any of various long flesh-eating fishes with long slender jaws and sharp teeth **2** : PIPEFISH

nee·dle·leaf \'nēd-ᵊl-ˌlēf\ adj : populated with trees having leaves that are needles ⟨*needleleaf* forests⟩; *also* : having leaves that are needles ⟨*needleleaf* trees⟩

nee·dle·point \'nēd-ᵊl-ˌpȯint\ n : embroidery done on canvas or plastic usually in simple even stitches across counted threads

need·less \'nēd-ləs\ adj : UNNECESSARY — **need·less·ly** adv

nee·dle·work \'nēd-ᵊl-ˌwərk\ n : work done with a needle; *esp* : work (as embroidery) other than plain sewing

needn't \'nēd-ᵊnt\ : need not

needs \'nēdz\ adv : because of necessity : NECESSARILY ⟨must *needs* be recognized⟩

needy \'nēd-ē\ adj **need·i·er; -est** **1** : being in want : very poor ⟨*needy* families⟩ **2** : marked by want of affection, attention, or emotional support ⟨a tendency to be emotionally *needy*⟩ — **need·i·ness** n

ne'er \(ˈ)ne(ə)r, (ˈ)na(ə)r\ adv : NEVER

ne'er–do–well \'ne(ə)r-dù-ˌwel, 'na(ə)r-\ n : an idle worthless person

ne·far·i·ous \ni-'far-ē-əs, -'fer-\ adj : very wicked : EVIL — **ne·far·i·ous·ly** adv — **ne·far·i·ous·ness** n

ne·gate \ni-'gāt\ vb **ne·gat·ed; ne·gat·ing 1** : to deny the existence or truth of **2** : to cause to be ineffective or invalid ⟨the discovery *negates* all previous theories⟩

ne·ga·tion \ni-'gā-shən\ n **1 a** : the action of negating : DENIAL **b** : a negative statement **2** : something that is the opposite of something positive ⟨death is the *negation* of life⟩

¹neg·a·tive \'neg-ət-iv\ adj **1** : marked by denial, prohibition, or refusal ⟨a *negative* reply⟩ **2** : not positive or helpful ⟨a *negative* attitude⟩ **3** : less than zero and opposite in sign to a positive number ⟨-2 is a *negative* number⟩ **b** : extending or measured in a direction opposite to one chosen as positive ⟨a *negative* angle⟩ **4 a** : of, being, or relating to electricity of a kind of which the electron is the elementary unit ⟨a *negative* charge⟩ **b** : having more electrons than protons ⟨a *negative* particle⟩ **c** : being the part toward which the electric current flows from the outside circuit ⟨the *negative* pole of a battery⟩ **5 a** : not indicating the presence of a particular germ or condition ⟨a *negative* TB test⟩ **b** : directed or moving away from a source of stimulation ⟨a *negative* tropism⟩ **6** : having the light and dark parts approximately opposite to those of the thing or person photographed — **neg·a·tive·ly** adv — **neg·a·tive·ness** n — **neg·a·tiv·i·ty** \ˌneg-ə-'tiv-ət-ē\ n

²negative n **1** : a reply that indicates denial or contradiction : REFUSAL **2** : something that is the opposite or negation of something else **3** : an expression (as the word *no*) of negation or denial **4** : a negative number **5** : the side that argues or votes against something in a debate **6** : a negative photographic image on transparent material used for printing positive pictures; *also* : the material that carries such an image

³negative vb **-tived; -tiv·ing 1** : to refuse to accept or approve **2** : to vote against **3** : DENY 1, CONTRADICT

negative sign n : MINUS SIGN

¹ne·glect \ni-'glekt\ vb **1** : to give little attention or respect to ⟨*neglected* their garden⟩ **2** : to leave undone or not attended to especially through carelessness ⟨don't *neglect* to feed the fish⟩ — **ne·glect·er** n

synonyms NEGLECT, DISREGARD, IGNORE mean to pass over something without giving it any or enough attention. NEGLECT suggests that one has not given enough attention to something that deserves or requires attention, but the lack of attention may not be deliberate ⟨you have been *neglecting* your homework⟩. DISREGARD suggests deliberately overlooking something usually because one feels that it is not worth noticing ⟨*disregarded* the "No Exit" sign and left through that door⟩. IGNORE suggests deliberately overlooking something

easily seen ⟨my grandmother politely *ignored* the messy room⟩.

²neglect n **1** : an act or instance of neglecting something ⟨his *neglect* of important responsibilities⟩ **2** : the condition of being neglected ⟨the stone wall was collapsing from years of *neglect*⟩

ne·glect·ful \ni-'glek(t)-fəl\ adj : given to neglecting : CARELESS — **ne·glect·ful·ly** \-fə-lē\ adv

neg·li·gee also **neg·li·gé** \ˌneg-lə-'zhā\ n **1** : a woman's long flowing dressing gown **2** : carelessly informal clothes [derived from French *négligé*, past participle of *négliger* "to neglect"]

neg·li·gence \'neg-li-jən(t)s\ n **1 a** : the quality or state of being negligent **b** : failure to take the care that a reasonably cautious person usually takes **2** : an act or instance of negligence

neg·li·gent \'neg-li-jənt\ adj **1** : marked by or likely to show neglect **2** : failing to take proper or normal care — **neg·li·gent·ly** adv

neg·li·gi·ble \'neg-li-jə-bəl\ adj : so small or unimportant as to deserve little or no attention ⟨a *negligible* error⟩ — **neg·li·gi·bly** \-blē\ adv

ne·go·tia·ble \ni-'gō-sh(ē-)ə-bəl\ adj : capable of being negotiated: as **a** : capable of being passed from one person to another without being signed in return for something of equal value ⟨*negotiable* bonds⟩ **b** : capable of being traveled over, dealt with, or accomplished ⟨*negotiable* roads⟩ ⟨some kind of agreement was *negotiable*⟩ **c** : open to discussion or change ⟨*negotiable* prices⟩ — **ne·go·tia·bil·i·ty** \-ˌgō-sh(ē-)ə-'bil-ət-ē\ n

ne·go·ti·ate \ni-'gō-shē-ˌāt\ vb **-at·ed; -at·ing 1 a** : to have a discussion with another so as to arrive at an agreement **b** : to arrange for or bring about by such discussion ⟨*negotiate* a treaty⟩ **2** : to transfer to another in return for something of equal value ⟨*negotiate* a check⟩ **3** : to get through, around, or over successfully ⟨*negotiate* a turn⟩ — **ne·go·ti·a·tion** \-ˌgō-shē-'ā-shən, -sē-\ n — **ne·go·ti·a·tor** \-'gō-shē-ˌāt-ər\ n

Ne·gri·to \nə-'grēt-ō\ n, pl **-tos** or **-toes** : a member of any of a group of dark-skinned peoples that are of small size and live in Oceania and southeastern Asia

ne·gri·tude \'neg-rə-ˌt(y)üd, 'nē-grə-\ n : awareness of and pride in the cultural aspects of the African heritage

Ne·gro \'nē-grō\ n, pl **Negroes** *sometimes offensive* : a member of a race of humankind native to Africa and classified according to physical features (as dark skin coloration) [from Spanish *Negro* or Portuguese *Negro* "a person of a black race," derived from Latin *nigr-, niger* "black"] — **Negro** adj, *sometimes offensive* — **Ne·groid** \'nē-ˌgrȯid\ adj or n, *often cap, sometimes offensive*

Ne·he·mi·ah \ˌnē-(h)ə-'mī-ə\ n — see BIBLE table

neigh \'nā\ vb : to make the loud drawn-out cry of a horse — **neigh** n

¹neigh·bor \'nā-bər\ n **1** : a person who lives near another **2** : a person or thing located near another ⟨Canada is a *neighbor* of the U.S.⟩ **3** : a fellow human being

Word History The words *near* and *nigh* are both related to—and have the same meaning as—the Old English word *nēah*. Another word which can be traced, at least in part, to *nēah* is *neighbor*. The combination of *nēah*, meaning "near," and *gebūr*, meaning "dweller," produced the Old English word *nēahgebūr*. This word was used for "a person living near another." The pronunciation and spelling of *nēahgebūr* has changed over the centuries to give us *neighbor*, but the word's basic meaning has remained the same. [Old English *nēahgebūr*

\ə\ **abut**	\au̇\ **out**	\i\ **tip**	\ȯ\ **saw**	\u̇\ **foot**
\ər\ **further**	\ch\ **chin**	\ī\ **life**	\ȯi\ **coin**	\y\ **yet**
\a\ **mat**	\e\ **pet**	\j\ **job**	\th\ **thin**	\yü\ **few**
\ā\ **take**	\ē\ **easy**	\ŋ\ **sing**	\th\ **this**	\yu̇\ **cure**
\ä\ **cot, cart**	\g\ **go**	\ō\ **bone**	\ü\ **food**	\zh\ **vision**

"neighbor," from *nēah* "near" + *gebūr* "dweller" — related to NEAR, NIGH]

²**neigh·bor** *vb* **neigh·bored; neigh·bor·ing** \-b(ə-)riŋ\ : to be next to or near to ⟨*neighboring* towns⟩

neigh·bor·hood \'nā-bər-ˌhud\ *n* **1** : the quality or state of being neighbors **2 a** : a place or region near : VICINITY **b** : a number or amount near ⟨cost in the *neighborhood* of $10⟩ **3 a** : the people living near one another **b** : a section lived in by people who consider themselves neighbors

neigh·bor·ly \'nā-bər-lē\ *adj* : of, relating to, or characteristic of neighbors; *esp* : FRIENDLY ⟨a *neighborly* welcome⟩ — **neigh·bor·li·ness** *n*

¹**nei·ther** \'nē-thər *also* 'nī-\ *pron* : not the one and not the other ⟨*neither* of the two⟩

²**neither** *conj* **1** : both not : equally not ⟨*neither* black nor white⟩ **2** : also not ⟨*neither* did I⟩

³**neither** *adj* : not either ⟨*neither* hand⟩

nek·ton \'nek-tən, -ˌtän\ *n* : strong-swimming water-dwelling animals (as whales, sharks, or squid) that are largely independent of the action of waves and currents

nem·a·to·cyst \'nem-ət-ə-ˌsist, ni-'mat-ə-\ *n* : one of the tiny stinging organs of various coelenterates (as jellyfishes and corals) used in catching prey

nem·a·tode \'nem-ə-ˌtōd\ *n* : any of a major group of long cylinder-shaped worms that are parasites in animals or plants or live in soil or water — called also *roundworm*

nem·e·sis \'nem-ə-səs\ *n, pl* **nem·e·ses** \-ə-ˌsēz\ **1 a** : one that punishes or avenges **b** : a formidable and usually victorious rival or opponent **2** : an act or instance of just punishment

neo- *combining form* : new : recent ⟨*neo*logism⟩ [from Greek *neos* "new"]

neo·clas·sic \ˌnē-ō-'klas-ik\ *adj* : of or relating to a renewal or a renewal with some changes of the classical style especially in literature, art, or music — **neo·clas·si·cal** \-'klas-i-kəl\ *adj* — **neo·clas·si·cism** \-'klas-ə-ˌsiz-əm\ *n*

neo·dym·i·um \ˌnē-ō-'dim-ē-əm\ *n* : a silver-white to yellow metallic chemical element — see ELEMENT table

Neo·lith·ic \ˌnē-ə-'lith-ik\ *adj* : of, relating to, or being the latest period of the Stone Age which is marked by the use of polished stone tools

ne·ol·o·gism \nē-'äl-ə-ˌjiz-əm\ *n* : a new word or expression — **ne·ol·o·gis·tic** \-ˌäl-ə-'jis-tik\ *adj*

¹**ne·on** \'nē-ˌän\ *n* **1** : a colorless odorless gaseous element found in very small amounts in air and used in electric lamps — see ELEMENT table **2 a** : a lamp in which the gas contains a large amount of neon that gives a reddish glow when a current is passed through it **b** : a sign composed of such lamps

²**neon** *adj* **1** : of, relating to, or using neon ⟨*neon* lights⟩ **2** : extremely bright : FLUORESCENT ⟨*neon* yellow⟩

neo·phyte \'nē-ə-ˌfīt\ *n* **1** : a person who has recently joined a religion **2** : BEGINNER, NOVICE

neo·plasm \'nē-ə-ˌplaz-əm\ *n* : TUMOR

neo·prene \'nē-ə-ˌprēn\ *n* : a synthetic rubber used in numerous products (as wet suits, mouse pads, and flexible pipes)

ne·pen·the \nə-'pen(t)-thē\ *n* : a potion used by the ancient peoples to dull pain and sorrow

neph·ew \'nef-yü\ *n* : a son of one's brother, sister, brother-in-law, or sister-in-law

ne·phri·tis \ni-'frīt-əs\ *n, pl* **ne·phrit·i·des** \-'frit-ə-ˌdēz\ : inflammation of the kidneys

neph·ron \'nef-ˌrän\ *n* : a single unit of the kidney that functions in filtering the blood and forming urine from waste products

nep·o·tism \'nep-ə-ˌtiz-əm\ *n* : favoritism shown to a relative (as in the distribution of political offices)

Nep·tune \'nep-ˌt(y)ün\ *n* : the planet eighth in order from the sun — see PLANET table — **Nep·tu·ni·an** \nep-'t(y)ü-nē-ən\ *adj*

nep·tu·ni·um \nep-'t(y)ü-nē-əm\ *n* : a radioactive metallic element similar to uranium and obtained in nuclear reactors in the production of plutonium — see ELEMENT table

nerd \'nərd\ *n* **1** : an unstylish, unattractive, or socially awkward person **2** : a person slavishly devoted to intellectual or academic pursuits — **nerdy** \'nər-dē\ *adj*

Ne·re·id \'nir-ē-əd\ *n* : any of the sea nymphs held in Greek mythology to be the daughters of the sea god Nereus

¹**nerve** \'nərv\ *n* **1** : TENDON ⟨strain every *nerve*⟩ **2** : one of the stringy bands of nervous tissue connecting the nervous system with other organs and carrying nerve impulses **3 a** : power of endurance or control ⟨a test of mind and *nerve*⟩ **b** : fearless boldness ⟨had the *nerve* to confront the mysterious stranger⟩ **c** : behavior marked by a rude or disrespectful boldness ⟨what *nerve* of her to say that⟩ **4 a** : a sore or sensitive point ⟨that remark hit a *nerve*⟩ **b** *pl* : a condition of being very nervous : JITTERS ⟨had a case of the *nerves* before her performance⟩ **5** : a vein in a leaf or in the wing of an insect **6** : the sensitive soft inner part of a tooth — **nerved** \'nərvd\ *adj*

²**nerve** *vb* **nerved; nerv·ing** : to give strength or courage to

nerve cell *n* : NEURON; *also* : CELL BODY

nerve center *n* : ¹CENTER 2c

nerve cord *n* **1** : a pair of closely united nerves that run along the inside of the body on the lower side of many long-bodied invertebrates (as earthworms and insects) **2** : a tube-shaped cord of nervous tissue in the back or upper side of a chordate above the notochord that makes up or develops into the central nervous system

nerve ending *n* : a structure forming an end of a nerve axon that is distant from the cell body

nerve fiber *n* : any of the long thin parts that lead to or away from the cell body of a neuron and include axons and dendrites

nerve gas *n* : a war gas damaging especially to the nervous and respiratory systems

nerve impulse *n* : the change in electrical charge that moves along the nerve fiber of a neuron in response to a stimulus (as pain) and serves to transmit a record of sensation from a receptor to the spinal cord or brain, relay a signal to another neuron, or carry an instruction to act to a muscle or gland

nerve·less \'nərv-ləs\ *adj* **1** : lacking strength or courage : FEEBLE **2** : showing or having control : not nervous — **nerve·less·ly** *adv*

nerve net *n* : a network of neurons that seem to be continuous one with another and carry impulses in all directions; *also* : a nervous system (as in a jellyfish) consisting of such a network

ner·vous \'nər-vəs\ *adj* **1 a** : of, relating to, or composed of neurons ⟨*nervous* tissue⟩ **b** : of or relating to the nerves **c** : having its source in or affected by the nerves ⟨*nervous* energy⟩ **2 a** : easily excited or irritated ⟨a *nervous* person⟩ **b** : TIMID, FEARFUL ⟨a *nervous* smile⟩ **3** : causing uncomfortable feelings ⟨a *nervous* situation⟩ — **ner·vous·ly** *adv* — **ner·vous·ness** *n*

nervous breakdown *n* : an attack of mental or emotional disorder that is severe enough to require hospitalization

nervous system *n* : the bodily system that receives stimuli, decides on their importance, and sends nerve impulses to the organs of action and that in vertebrates is made up of brain and spinal cord, nerves, ganglia, and parts of the receptor organs

nervy \'nər-vē\ *adj* **nerv·i·er; -est** **1 a** : showing calm courage : FEARLESS **b** : rudely bold ⟨a *nervy* salesperson⟩ **2** : EXCITABLE 1, NERVOUS — **nerv·i·ness** *n*

-ness \nəs\ *n suffix* : state : condition : quality ⟨good*ness*⟩ [Old English *-nes* (suffix) "state, condition, quality"]

¹nest \'nest\ *n* **1 a** : a place or structure where eggs are laid and hatched or young are raised ⟨a turtle's *nest*⟩ ⟨the *nest* of a bird⟩ ⟨a mouse's *nest*⟩ **b** : the home or shelter of an animal (as a squirrel or chimpanzee) **2 a** : a place of rest, retreat, or lodging : HOME ⟨grown children who have left the *nest*⟩ **b** : DEN 2, HANGOUT ⟨the robbers' *nest*⟩ **3** : the occupants of a nest ⟨a *nest* of baby birds⟩ **4** : a group of objects made to fit one within another ⟨a *nest* of measuring cups⟩

²nest *vb* **1** : to build or live in a nest ⟨robins *nested* in the tree⟩ **2** : to fit compactly together or within one another ⟨a set of tables that *nest* for storage⟩

nest egg *n* : a fund of money set aside as a reserve

nest·er \'nes-tər\ *n* **1** : one that nests **2** *West* : a person who settles on open range in order to farm

nes·tle \'nes-əl\ *vb* **nes·tled; nes·tling** \-(ə-)liŋ\ **1** : to lie close and snug : CUDDLE **2** : to settle as if in a nest — **nes·tler** \-(ə-)lər\ *n*

nest·ling \'nest-liŋ\ *n* : a young bird not yet able to leave the nest

¹net \'net\ *n* **1** : a fabric made of threads, cords, ropes, or wires that weave in and out with much open space **2** : something made of net: as **a** : a device for catching fish, birds, or insects **b** : a fabric barricade which divides a court in half (as in tennis or badminton) **c** : the fabric that encloses the sides and back of the goal (as in hockey or soccer) **3** : something that traps like a net ⟨a *net* of thorns⟩ **4** : a network of lines, fibers, or figures **5** *often cap* : INTERNET [Old English *nett* "net fabric"] — **net·like** \-,līk\ *adj* — **net·ted** \'net-əd\ *adj*

²net *vb* **net·ted; net·ting** **1** : to cover with or as if with a net **2** : to catch in or as if in a net ⟨*net* fish⟩ **3** : to hit the ball into the net in a racket game — **net·ter** *n*

³net *adj* : free from all charges or deductions ⟨*net* profit⟩ ⟨*net* weight⟩ [from earlier *net* "neat," from Middle English *net* "clean, bright," derived from Latin *nitidus* "bright, lustrous" — related to NEAT; see *Word History* at NEAT]

⁴net *vb* **net·ted; net·ting** : to gain or produce as profit ⟨*netted* five dollars on the sale⟩

⁵net *n* : a net amount, profit, weight, or price

net·book \'net-,bùk\ *n* : a small portable computer designed primarily for wireless Internet access

neth·er \'neth-ər\ *adj* : ³LOWER 1

neth·er·most \'neth-ər-,mōst\ *adj* : being the farthest down

neth·er·world \'neth-ər-,wərld\ *n* : the world of the dead

net·i·quette \'net-i-kət, -,ket\ *n* : etiquette governing communication on the Internet

net·i·zen \'net-ə-zən\ *n* : a user of the Internet

net·ting \'net-iŋ\ *n* **1** : NETWORK 1 **2** : the act or process of making a net

¹net·tle \'net-ᵊl\ *n* : any of several tall herbs with stinging hairs on the leaves and stems

²nettle *vb* **net·tled; net·tling** \'net-liŋ, -ᵊl-iŋ\ **1** : to sting with nettles **2** : ANNOY, VEX

net–veined \'net-'vānd\ *adj* : having veins that branch and come together again to form a network ⟨dicotyledons have *net-veined* leaves⟩ — compare PARALLEL-VEINED

¹net·work \'net-,wərk\ *n* **1** : a fabric or structure of cords or wires that cross with even spacings **2** : a system of lines or channels resembling a network **3** : a group or system of related or connected parts; *esp* : a group of connected radio or television stations **4** : a system of computers connected by communications lines

²network *vb* **1** : to cover with or join into a network **2** : to join together in a network ⟨*networked* the classroom's computers⟩

neu·ral \'n(y)ùr-əl\ *adj* : of, relating to, or affecting a nerve or the nervous system

neu·ral·gia \n(y)ù-'ral-jə\ *n* : pain that follows the course of a nerve; *also* : a condition marked by such pain

neu·ro·hor·mone \,n(y)ùr-ō-'hòr-,mōn\ *n* : a hormone produced by or acting on nervous tissue

neu·rol·o·gist \n(y)ù-'räl-ə-jəst\ *n* : a specialist in neurology; *esp* : a physician who specializes in identifying and treating diseases of the nervous system

neu·rol·o·gy \n(y)ù-'räl-ə-jē\ *n* : the scientific study of the nervous system — **neu·ro·log·i·cal** \,n(y)ùr-ə-'läj-i-kəl\ *or* **neu·ro·log·ic** \-'läj-ik\ *adj*

neu·ron \'n(y)ü-,rän, 'n(y)ù(ə)r-,än\ *n* : a grayish or reddish cell that is the basic working unit of the nervous system and has an axon and dendrites that carry nerve impulses

neu·ro·sis \n(y)ù-'rō-səs\ *n, pl* **neu·ro·ses** \-'rō-,sēz\ : any of various mental and emotional disorders that affect only part of a person's personality, are less serious than a psychosis, and involve unusual or extreme reactions (as abnormal fears, depression, or anxiety) to stress and conflict

neu·ros·po·ra \n(y)ù-'räs-pə-rə\ *n* : any of a genus of fungi that often have pink spores, are important in genetic research, and are severe pests in bakeries

neu·ro·sur·geon \,n(y)ùr-ō-'sər-jən\ *n* : a surgeon who specializes in performing surgery on the brain, spinal cord, or nerves — **neu·ro·sur·gery** \-'sərj-(ə-)rē\ *n*

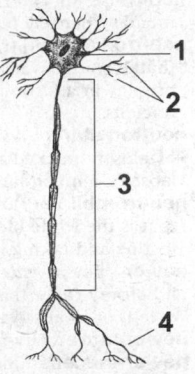

neuron: *1* cell body, *2* dendrite, *3* axon, *4* nerve ending

¹neu·rot·ic \n(y)ù-'rät-ik\ *adj* : of, relating to, being, or affected with neurosis — **neu·rot·i·cal·ly** \-i-k(ə-)lē\ *adv*

²neurotic *n* **1** : a person affected with a neurosis **2** : an emotionally unstable person

neu·ro·trans·mit·ter \,n(y)ùr-ō-tran(t)s-'mit-ər, -tranz-\ *n* : a substance (as acetylcholine) that carries a nerve impulse from one neuron to another across a synapse

¹neu·ter \'n(y)üt-ər\ *adj* **1** : relating to or being the class of words that ordinarily includes most of those referring to things that are neither male nor female ⟨a *neuter* noun⟩ ⟨the *neuter* gender⟩ **2** : lacking sex organs; *also* : having imperfectly developed sex organs

²neuter *n* **1 a** : a word or form of the neuter gender **b** : the neuter gender **2** : WORKER 2

³neuter *vb* : CASTRATE, ALTER 2

¹neu·tral \'n(y)ü-trəl\ *n* **1** : one that is neutral **2** : a neutral color **3** : a state in which transmission gears (as of a motor vehicle) are not in contact so that power from the engine is not passed to the drive shaft

²neutral *adj* **1 a** : not favoring either side in a quarrel, contest, or war **b** : of or relating to a neutral country ⟨*neutral* territory⟩ **2 a** : having no distinctive characteristics ⟨a *neutral* personality⟩ **b** : not feeling strongly one way or the other **3** : having no color that stands out **4** : neither acid nor basic **5** : not electrically charged — **neu·tral·ly** \-trə-lē\ *adv*

neu·tral·ism \'n(y)ü-trə-,liz-əm\ *n* : a policy of neutrality in international affairs

neu·tral·ist \'n(y)ü-trə-ləst\ *n* **1** : one that favors or practices neutrality **2** : one that favors keeping or making a state or region neutral

neu·tral·i·ty \n(y)ü-'tral-ət-ē\ *n* : the quality or state of being neutral especially in time of war

\ə\ **abut**	\aù\ **out**	\i\ **tip**	\ò\ **saw**	\ù\ **foot**
\ər\ **further**	\ch\ **chin**	\ī\ **life**	\òi\ **coin**	\y\ **yet**
\a\ **mat**	\e\ **pet**	\j\ **job**	\th\ **thin**	\yü\ **few**
\ā\ **take**	\ē\ **easy**	\ŋ\ **sing**	\th\ **this**	\yù\ **cure**
\ä\ **cot, cart**	\g\ **go**	\ō\ **bone**	\ü\ **food**	\zh\ **vision**

neu·tral·ize \'n(y)ü-trə-ˌlīz\ *vb* **-ized; -iz·ing 1** : to make chemically neutral ⟨*neutralize* an acid with a base⟩ **2** : to make ineffective : NULLIFY ⟨*neutralize* an opponent's move⟩ **3** : to make electrically neutral by combining equal positive and negative quantities **4** : to make politically neutral ⟨*neutralize* a country⟩ — **neu·tral·i·za·tion** \ˌn(y)ü-trə-lə-ˈzā-shən\ *n* — **neu·tral·iz·er** \'n(y)ü-trə-ˌlī-zər\ *n*

neu·tri·no \n(y)ü-ˈtrē-nō\ *n, pl* **-nos** : an uncharged elementary particle believed to have little or no mass

neu·tron \'n(y)ü-ˌträn\ *n* : an uncharged atomic particle that has a mass nearly equal to that of the proton and is present in all known atomic nuclei except the hydrogen nucleus

neutron star *n* : a very dense object in space that consists of closely packed neutrons and is produced by the collapse of a much larger star

neu·tro·phil \'n(y)ü-trə-ˌfil\ *n* : a cell with fine grains in it that is the white blood cell doing most of the work in collecting and taking in stray and foreign matter

nev·er \'nev-ər\ *adv* **1** : not ever : at no time ⟨I *never* saw it before⟩ ⟨*never* had a sick day in my life⟩ **2** : not to any extent or in any way ⟨*never* fear⟩

nev·er·more \ˌnev-ər-ˈmō(ə)r, -ˈmȯ(ə)r\ *adv* : never again

nev·er·the·less \ˌnev-ər-thə-ˈles\ *adv* : in spite of that : HOWEVER ⟨a tiring but *nevertheless* enjoyable day⟩

¹new \'n(y)ü\ *adj* **1** : not old : RECENT, MODERN ⟨*new* ways of thinking⟩ **2** : not the same as the former : taking the place of one that came before ⟨a *new* teacher⟩ **3** : recently discovered or learned about ⟨*new* lands⟩ ⟨*new* plants and animals⟩ **4** : not known or experienced before ⟨*new* feelings⟩ **5** : not accustomed ⟨*new* to this work⟩ **6** : beginning as a repeating of some previous act or thing ⟨the *new* year⟩ **7** : refreshed in spirits or vigor ⟨felt like a *new* person after my vacation⟩ **8** : being in a position or place for the first time ⟨a *new* member⟩ — **new·ness** *n*

synonyms NEW, NOVEL, ORIGINAL, FRESH mean having recently come into existence or use. NEW may apply to what is freshly made and unused ⟨*new* bricks⟩ or has not been known before ⟨*new* design⟩ or not experienced before ⟨starts a *new* job⟩. NOVEL applies to what is not only new but strange or untried ⟨a *novel* way of solving the problem⟩. ORIGINAL applies to what is the first of its kind to exist ⟨a person without one *original* idea⟩. FRESH applies to what has not lost its original qualities of newness such as liveliness, energy, or brightness ⟨*fresh* towels⟩ ⟨a *fresh* start in life⟩.

²new *adv* : just recently ⟨*new*-mown hay⟩

New Age *n* **1** : a way of thinking arising in late 20th century Western society and adapted from a variety of ancient and modern cultures that emphasizes beliefs (as reincarnation) outside the mainstream and that advances alternative approaches to spirituality, right living, and health **2** : a soft soothing form of instrumental music often used to promote relaxation — **new age** *adj, often cap* — **New Ag·er** \-ˈā-jər\ *n*

new·bie \'n(y)ü-bē\ *n* : a newcomer especially to cyberspace

¹new·born \'n(y)ü-ˈbȯ(ə)rn\ *adj* **1** : recently born **2** : born anew

²newborn *n, pl* **newborn** *or* **newborns** : a newborn individual

new·com·er \'n(y)ü-ˌkəm-ər\ *n* **1** : one recently arrived **2** : BEGINNER

new·el \'n(y)ü-əl\ *n* **1** : an upright post about which the steps of a circular staircase wind **2** : a post at the foot of a straight stairway or one at a landing

new·fan·gled \'n(y)ü-ˈfaŋ-gəld\ *adj* : of the newest style : NOVEL ⟨*newfangled* ideas⟩ ⟨a *newfangled* contraption⟩

new–fash·ioned \'n(y)ü-ˈfash-ənd\ *adj* : UP-TO-DATE 2, MODERN

New·found·land \'n(y)ü-fən-(d)lənd, -ˌ(d)land; n(y)ü-ˈfaùn-(d)lənd\ *n* : any of a breed of very large thick-coated dogs probably developed in Newfoundland

Newfoundland

new·ly \'n(y)ü-lē\ *adv* **1** : not long ago : RECENTLY ⟨a *newly* married couple⟩ **2** : from a totally fresh beginning : ANEW ⟨a *newly* furnished house⟩

new·ly·wed \'n(y)ü-lē-ˌwed\ *n* : a person recently married

new moon *n* : the moon's phase when its dark side is toward the earth; *also* : the thin curved outline of the moon seen shortly after sunset for a few days after the actual occurrence of the new moon phase

news \'n(y)üz\ *n* **1 a** : a report of recent events or of something unknown ⟨brought us the office *news*⟩ **b** : previously unknown information ⟨I've got *news* for you⟩ **c** : something having a specified influence or effect ⟨snow was good *news* for the ski resorts⟩ **2 a** : material reported in a newspaper or news periodical or on a newscast **b** : an event that is interesting enough to be reported **c** : NEWSCAST ⟨watched the *news* on television⟩

news agency *n* : an organization that supplies news to subscribing newspapers, magazines, and newscasters

news·boy \'n(y)üz-ˌbȯi\ *n* : a person who delivers or sells newspapers

news·cast \-ˌkast\ *n* : a radio or television broadcast of news — **news·cast·er** \-ˌkas-tər\ *n*

news·group \-ˌgrüp\ *n* : an electronic bulletin board on the Internet

news·let·ter \-ˌlet-ər\ *n* : a bulletin or small newspaper of interest chiefly to a special group

news·man \-mən, -ˌman\ *n* : one who gathers or reports the news : REPORTER, CORRESPONDENT

news·pa·per \'n(y)üz-ˌpā-pər, 'n(y)üs-\ *n* : a paper that is printed and distributed usually daily or weekly and contains news, articles of opinion, features, and advertising

news·pa·per·man \-ˌman\ *n* : one who owns or is employed by a newspaper; *esp* : one who writes or edits copy for a newspaper

news·print \'n(y)üz-ˌprint\ *n* : paper made chiefly from wood pulp and used mostly for newspapers

news·reel \-ˌrēl\ *n* : a short motion picture dealing with current events

news·stand \-ˌstand\ *n* : a place where newspapers and magazines are sold

news·wor·thy \-ˌwər-thē\ *adj* : sufficiently interesting to the average person to deserve reporting

newsy \'n(y)ü-zē\ *adj* **news·i·er; -est** : filled with news; *esp* : CHATTY 2 ⟨a *newsy* letter⟩

newt \'n(y)üt\ *n* : any of various small salamanders that live mostly in water

newt

New Testament *n* : the second of the two chief divisions of the Bible — see BIBLE table

new·ton \'n(y)üt-ᵊn\ *n* : the unit of force that is of such size that under its influence a body whose mass is one kilogram would experience an acceleration of one meter per second per second

New World *n* : the western hemisphere; *esp* : the continental landmass of North and South America

New Year *n* **1** : NEW YEAR'S DAY; *also* : the first days of the year **2** : ROSH HASHANAH

New Year's Day *n* : January 1 observed as a legal holiday in many countries

¹next \'nekst\ *adj* : coming immediately before or following ⟨the *next* page⟩ ⟨the house *next* to ours⟩

²next \(')nekst\ *prep* : ¹NEXT TO

³next \'nekst\ *adv* **1** : in the nearest time, place, or order following ⟨open this package *next*⟩ **2** : at the first time to come after this ⟨when *next* we meet⟩

next–door *adj* : located or living in the next building, house, apartment, or room ⟨*next-door* neighbors⟩

next door *adv* : in or to the next building, house, apartment, or room

¹next to *prep* : immediately following : being close to ⟨*next to* the head of her class⟩

²next to *adv* : very nearly : ALMOST

Nez Percé *or* **Nez Perce** \'nez-₁pərs, 'nes-'pe(ə)rs, *French* nā-per-sā\ *n, pl* **Nez Percé** *or* **Nez Percés** *or* **Nez Perce** *or* **Nez Perces** : a member of an American Indian people of central Idaho and neighboring parts of Washington and Oregon [French, literally "pierced nose"]

ni·a·cin \'nī-ə-sən\ *n* : an acid of the vitamin B complex that is found widely in plants and animals and is used especially against pellagra — called also *nicotinic acid*

ni·a·cin·amide \₁nī-ə-'sin-ə-₁mīd\ *n* : a compound of the vitamin B complex that is used like niacin

nib \'nib\ *n* **1** : ¹BILL 1, BEAK **2** : the point of a pen **3** : a part that is pointed or sticks out

nib·ble \'nib-əl\ *vb* **nib·bled; nib·bling** \-(ə-)liŋ\ : to bite or chew gently or bit by bit — **nibble** *n* — **nib·bler** \-(ə)lər\ *n*

ni·cad \'nī-₁kad\ *n* : a rechargeable battery made with nickel and cadmium electrodes

nice \'nīs\ *adj* **1** : finicky in tastes or habits **2** : not obvious : SUBTLE ⟨a *nice* distinction⟩ **3** : PLEASING, AGREEABLE ⟨a *nice* time⟩ ⟨a *nice* person⟩ **4** : well behaved : RESPECTABLE ⟨wasn't a *nice* thing to do⟩ **5** : done very well ⟨*nice* job!⟩ — **nice·ly** *adv* — **nice·ness** *n*

Word History Five hundred years ago, when *nice* was first used in English, it meant "foolish or stupid." This is not as surprising as it may seem, since it came through early French from the Latin *nescius,* meaning "ignorant." By the 16th century, the sense of being very particular or "finicky" had developed. In the 19th century, *nice* came to mean "pleasant or agreeable" and then "respectable," a sense quite unlike its original meaning. [Middle English *nice* "foolish, stupid," from early French *nice* (same meaning), from Latin *nescius* "ignorant," from *nescire* "not to know," from *ne-* "not" and *scire* "to know" — related to SCIENCE]

nice·ty \'nī-sət-ē, -stē\ *n, pl* **-ties** **1** : a dainty, delicate, or elegant thing ⟨enjoy the *niceties* of life⟩ **2** : a small point or detail ⟨*niceties* of table manners⟩ **3** : careful attention to details ⟨*nicety* is needed in making watches⟩ **4** : the point at which a thing is at its best ⟨roasted to a *nicety*⟩

niche \'nich\ *n* **1** : a hollowed-out place in a wall especially for a statue **2** : a place, use, or work for which a person is best fitted ⟨finally found her *niche*⟩ **3 a** : a habitat that contains the things necessary for a particular plant or animal to live **b** : the part that a particular living thing plays in an ecological community

¹nick \'nik\ *n* **1** : a small groove : NOTCH **2** : ¹CHIP 4 ⟨a *nick* in a cup⟩ **3** : the last moment at which the result of an event can be changed ⟨arrived in the *nick* of time⟩

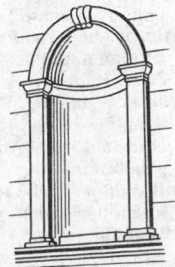

niche 1

²nick *vb* **1** : to make a nick in **2** : to wound or cut slightly ⟨*nicked* himself shaving⟩

¹nick·el \'nik-əl\ *n* **1** : a silver-white hard metallic element that can be hammered and shaped and is capable of a high polish, resistant to wearing away, and used chiefly in alloys — see ELEMENT table **2 a** *also* **nick·le** : the U.S. five-cent piece made of nickel and copper **b** : five cents

Word History When copper miners in the German state of Saxony first dug out chunks of what is now known to be nickel ore, they thought it was copper. But even though it was reddish-brown like copper, the ore broke easily and did not seem to have any use. Because they were at first fooled, the Germans called this ore *Kupfernickel,* meaning literally "copper demon" or "copper goblin." *Kupfer* is the German word for "copper" and *Nickel* in German means "demon" or "goblin." Even though the metal turned out to be quite valuable, it kept its old name. For a while the term was *copper nickel* in English, and then simply *nickel,* for both the metal and the American five-cent coin made out of a combination of nickel and copper. [derived from German *Kupfernickel* "a compound of nickel and arsenic," literally "copper demon," from *Kupfer* "copper" and *Nickel* "demon"]

²nick·el *vb* **-eled** *or* **-elled; -el·ing** *or* **-el·ling** \'nik-(ə-)liŋ\ : to plate with nickel

nick·el·ode·on \₁nik-ə-'lōd-ē-ən\ *n* **1** : an early movie theater charging five cents for admission **2** : JUKEBOX

nick·er \'nik-ər\ *vb* **nick·ered; nick·er·ing** \-(ə-)riŋ\ : NEIGH, WHINNY — **nicker** *n*

¹nick·name \'nik-₁nām\ *n* **1** : an often descriptive name (as "Shorty" or "Tex") given in addition to the one belonging to an individual **2** : a form of a proper name (as "Billy" for "William") used by family or friends

Word History The Middle English word *eke* meant "something added on." An *ekename* was therefore an added name given to a person or place. Many people who heard the phrase "an ekename," however, thought they were hearing "a nekename." Because of that confusion over the course of many years, the word *ekename* became *nekename.* Later changes in spelling have given us the modern word *nickname.* [Middle English *nekename* "an additional name," from the phrase *an ekename* (misunderstood as being *a nekename*), from *eke* "something added on" and *name* "name"]

²nickname *vb* : to give a nickname to

nic·o·tine \'nik-ə-₁tēn\ *n* : a poisonous substance found in tobacco and used as an insecticide

nic·o·tin·ic acid \₁nik-ə-'tē-nik-, -'tin-ik-\ *n* : NIACIN

nic·ti·tat·ing membrane \₁nik-tə-₁tāt-iŋ-\ *n* : a thin membrane found in many animals at the inner angle or beneath the lower lid of the eye and capable of extending across the eyeball

niece \'nēs\ *n* : a daughter of one's brother, sister, brother-in-law, or sister-in-law

nif·ty \'nif-tē\ *adj* **nif·ti·er; -est** : very good : very attractive — **nifty** *n*

nig·gard \'nig-ərd\ *n* : a mean stingy person : MISER — **niggard** *adj*

nig·gard·ly \'nig-ərd-lē\ *adj* **1** : STINGY 1, MISERLY **2** : characteristic of a niggard : SCANTY — **niggardly** *adv*

¹nigh \'nī\ *adv* **1** : near in place, time, or relationship **2** : ALMOST, NEARLY [Old English *nēah* "near, nigh" — related to NEAR, NEIGHBOR; see *Word History* at NEIGHBOR]

²nigh *adj* : not far : CLOSE, NEAR

\ə\ **abut**	\au̇\ **out**	\i\ **tip**	\ȯ\ **saw**	\u̇\ **foot**
\ər\ **further**	\ch\ **chin**	\ī\ **life**	\ȯi\ **coin**	\y\ **yet**
\a\ **mat**	\e\ **pet**	\j\ **job**	\th\ **thin**	\yü\ **few**
\ā\ **take**	\ē\ **easy**	\ŋ\ **sing**	\t͟h\ **this**	\yu̇\ **cure**
\ä\ **cot, cart**	\g\ **go**	\ō\ **bone**	\ü\ **food**	\zh\ **vision**

night \'nīt\ *n* **1** : the time between dusk and dawn when there is no sunlight **2** : NIGHTFALL **3** : the darkness of night — **night** *adj*

night blindness *n* : subnormal vision in faint light (as at night) — **night–blind** *adj*

night–bloom·ing ce·re·us \'nīt-ˌblüm-iŋ-'sir-ē-əs\ *n* : any of several cacti that bloom at night; *esp* : a slender spreading or climbing cactus often grown for its large showy fragrant white flowers

night·cap \'nīt-ˌkap\ **1** : a cap worn with nightclothes **2** : a drink taken at bedtime **3** : the final race or contest of a day's sports activities

night·clothes \-ˌklō(th)z\ *n pl* : garments worn in bed

night·club \-ˌkləb\ *n* : a place of entertainment open in the evening and usually serving food and liquor, having a floor show, and providing music for dancing

night crawler *n* : EARTHWORM; *esp* : a large earthworm found on the soil surface at night and often used as bait for fish

night·dress \'nīt-ˌdres\ *n* : NIGHTGOWN

night·fall \-ˌfȯl\ *n* : the coming of night : DUSK

night·gown \-ˌgau̇n\ *n* : a long loose garment worn in bed

night·hawk \-ˌhȯk\ *n* **1** : any of several insect-eating birds that resemble the related whip-poor-will **2** : NIGHT OWL

night·in·gale \'nīt-ᵊn-ˌgāl\ *n* **1** : an Old World thrush noted for the sweet song of the male **2** : any of several other birds noted for their sweet song or for singing at night

nightingale 1

night·ly \'nīt-lē\ *adj* **1** : of or relating to the night or every night **2** : happening, done, or produced by night or every night — **nightly** *adv*

night·mare \'nīt-ˌma(ə)r, -ˌme(ə)r\ *n* **1** : a frightening dream **2** : a frightening or horrible experience — **night·mar·ish** \-ish\ *adj*

   Word History In the Middle Ages many people believed in a type of evil spirit that was said to haunt people while they slept. Such a demon was known in Old English as a *mare*. Because it was believed to come in the night, it later became known in Middle English as a *nightmare*. It was not until the 16th century that the word *nightmare* came to mean "a frightening dream." This meaning probably came from the belief that such dreams were caused by evil spirits. [Middle English *nightmare* "evil spirit thought to haunt people during sleep," from *night* "night" and *mare* "spirit," from Old English *mare* "evil spirit haunting people in sleep"]

night owl *n* : a person who usually stays up late at night

night·shade \'nīt-ˌshād\ *n* : any of a family of herbs, shrubs, and trees having clusters of usually white, yellow, or purple flowers, and fruits that are berries and including many poisonous forms (as belladonna) and important food plants (as the potato, tomato, and eggplant)

night·shirt \-ˌshərt\ *n* : a nightgown resembling a shirt

night·stick \-ˌstik\ *n* : a police officer's club

night·time \'nīt-ˌtīm\ *n* : the time from dusk to dawn — **nighttime** *adj*

nil \'nil\ *n* : nothing at all : ZERO — **nil** *adj*

Ni·lot·ic \nī-'lät-ik\ *adj* : of or relating to the Nile or the peoples of the Nile basin

nim·ble \'nim-bəl\ *adj* **nim·bler** \-b(ə-)lər\; **nim·blest** \-b(ə-)ləst\ **1** : quick and light in motion : AGILE ⟨a *nimble* dancer⟩ **2** : quick in understanding and learning : CLEVER ⟨a *nimble* mind⟩ — **nim·ble·ness** \-bəl-nəs\ *n* — **nim·bly** \-blē\ *adv*

nim·bo·stra·tus \ˌnim-bō-'strāt-əs, -'strat-\ *n* : a low dark gray layer of cloud that usually produces rain or snow

nim·bus \'nim-bəs\ *n, pl* **nim·bi** \-ˌbī, -ˌbē\ *or* **nim·bus·es** **1** : a shining cloud about a god or goddess when on earth **2** : an indication (as a circle) of radiant light about the head of a drawn or sculptured god or saint **3** : a rain cloud

nimbus 2

nin·com·poop \'nin-kəm-ˌpüp, 'niŋ-\ *n* : a foolish or stupid person

nine \'nīn\ *n* **1** — see NUMBER table **2** : the ninth in a set or series **3** : a baseball team — **nine** *adj or pron*

nine·pin \-ˌpin\ *n* **1** *pl* : a bowling game resembling ten-pins played without the headpin **2** : a pin used in ninepins

nine·teen \(')nīn(t)-'tēn\ *n* — see NUMBER table — **nine·teen** *adj or pron* — **nine·teenth** \-'tēn(t)th\ *adj or n*

nine·ty \'nīnt-ē\ *n, pl* **nineties** **1** — see NUMBER table **2** *pl* : the numbers 90 to 99 and specifically the years 90 to 99 in a lifetime or century — **nine·ti·eth** \-ē-əth\ *adj or n* — **ninety** *adj or pron*

nin·ja \'nin-jə, -(ˌ)jä\ *n, pl* **ninja** *also* **ninjas** : a person trained in ancient Japanese arts of combat and self-defense and employed especially for espionage and assassinations

nin·ny \'nin-ē\ *n, pl* **ninnies** : a foolish or stupid person

ninth \'nīn(t)th\ *n, pl* **ninths** — see NUMBER table — **ninth** *adj or adv*

ni·o·bi·um \nī-'ō-bē-əm\ *n* : a shiny gray metallic element used in alloys — see ELEMENT table

¹nip \'nip\ *vb* **nipped; nip·ping** **1** : to catch hold of and squeeze tightly between two surfaces, edges, or points ⟨the dog *nipped* my ankle⟩ **2** : to cut off by pinching or clipping **3** : to destroy the growth or progress of ⟨*nipped* in the bud⟩ **4** : to make numb with cold : CHILL **5** : to seize suddenly and forcibly : SNATCH, STEAL **6** : to move quickly or nimbly [Middle English *nippen* "to nip"]

²nip *n* **1** : something (as a sharp stinging cold or a biting flavor) that nips ⟨cheese with a *nip*⟩ **2** : the act of nipping : PINCH, BITE **3** : a small portion : BIT

³nip *n* : a small quantity of liquor ⟨takes a *nip* now and then⟩ [probably a shortened form of *nipperkin* "a liquor container"; of unknown origin]

nip and tuck \ˌnip-ən-'tək\ *adj or adv* : so close that the advantage shifts rapidly from one contestant to another

nip·per \'nip-ər\ *n* **1** : a device (as pincers) for nipping — usually used in plural **2** : a small boy

nip·ple \'nip-əl\ *n* **1** : the small protruding part of the gland that in females produces milk and from which a baby or young mammal sucks milk **2** : something resembling a nipple; *esp* : the mouthpiece of a bottle from which an infant feeds

Nip·pon·ese \ˌnip-ə-'nēz, -'nēs\ *adj* : of or relating to Japan or Japanese : JAPANESE — **Nipponese** *n*

nip·py \'nip-ē\ *adj* **nip·pi·er; -est** **1** : quick in movement : NIMBLE, BRISK **2** : having a biting flavor **3** : CHILLY **1** ⟨a *nippy* day⟩

ni·sei \(')nē-'sā, ˌnē-'sā\ *n, pl* **nisei** *also* **niseis** : a son or daughter of immigrant Japanese parents who is born and educated in America [Japanese, literally "second generation"]

nit \'nit\ *n* **1** : the egg of a louse or similar insect; *also* : the insect itself when young **2** : a minor shortcoming

ni·ter \'nīt-ər\ *n* **1** : POTASSIUM NITRATE **2** : SODIUM NITRATE

nit·pick \'nit-ˌpik\ *vb* : to criticize for tiny faults that are usually of little importance — **nit·pick·er** *n*

ni·trate \'nī-ˌtrāt, -trət\ *n* **1** : a chemical compound formed by the reaction of nitric acid with another substance **2** : nitrate of sodium or potassium used as a fertilizer

nitric acid \'nī-trik-\ *n* : a strong liquid nitrogen-containing acid used in making fertilizers, explosives, and dyes

ni·tri·fi·ca·tion \ˌnī-trə-fə-'kā-shən\ *n* : the process of combining, mixing, or filling with nitrogen or one of its compounds; *esp* : the oxidation (as by bacteria) of ammonium salts to nitrites and then to nitrates

ni·tri·fi·er \'nī-trə-ˌfī(-ə)r\ *n* : any of various soil bacteria capable of nitrification

ni·tri·fy·ing \'nī-trə-ˌfī-iŋ\ *adj* : active in nitrification ⟨*nitrifying* bacteria⟩

ni·trite \'nī-ˌtrīt\ *n* : a salt of a certain unstable nitrogen-containing acid that is known only in solution or in the form of its salts

ni·tro·gen \'nī-trə-jən\ *n* : a colorless tasteless odorless element that occurs as a gas which makes up 78 percent of the atmosphere and that forms a part of all living tissues — see ELEMENT table — **ni·trog·e·nous** \nī-'träj-ə-nəs\ *adj*

nitrogen cycle *n* : a continuous series of natural processes by which nitrogen passes from air to soil to living things and back to the air by means of nitrogen fixation, nitrification, decay, and denitrification

nitrogen dioxide *n* : a reddish brown poisonous gas that is an air pollutant formed from automobile exhausts

nitrogen fixation *n* : the changing of free nitrogen in the air into a combined form (as ammonia) especially by bacteria in the soil and in roots

nitrogen–fixer *n* : any of various living things (as bacteria) in the soil that are capable of nitrogen fixation

nitrogen–fixing *adj* : capable of nitrogen fixation

nitrogen oxide *n* : any of various oxides of nitrogen: as **a** : NITROGEN DIOXIDE **b** : NITROUS OXIDE

ni·tro·glyc·er·in *or* **ni·tro·glyc·er·ine** \ˌnī-trə-'glis-(ə-)rən\ *n* : an oily explosive poisonous liquid used chiefly in making dynamite and in medicine to relax blood vessels

nitrous oxide *n* : a colorless gas that when inhaled causes loss of the ability to feel pain and sometimes produces laughter and is used especially in dentistry — called also *laughing gas*

nit·ty–grit·ty \'nit-ē-ˌgrit-ē, ˌnit-ē-'grit-ē\ *n* : what is essential and basic ⟨the *nitty-gritty* of the problem⟩

nit·wit \'nit-ˌwit\ *n* : a stupid or silly person

¹no \(')nō\ *adv* **1** — used to express the negative of an alternative ⟨shall we go to the game or *no*⟩ **2** : in no respect or degree — used in comparisons ⟨it is *no* better than I expected it to be⟩ **3** : not so — used to express disagreement or refusal ⟨*no*, I'm not hungry⟩ **4** — used with a following adjective to imply a meaning expressed by the opposite positive statement ⟨*no* uncertain terms⟩ **5** — used to emphasize a following negative or to introduce a statement that is clearer or has more emphasis ⟨has the right, *no*, the duty, to continue⟩ **6** — used to express surprise, doubt, or disbelief ⟨*no* — you don't say⟩

²no *adj* **1 a** : not any ⟨has *no* money⟩ **b** : hardly any : very little ⟨finished in *no* time⟩ **2** : not a ⟨I'm *no* expert⟩

³no \'nō\ *n, pl* **noes** *or* **nos** \'nōz\ **1** : an act or instance of refusing or denying by the use of the word *no* : DENIAL **2 a** : a negative vote or decision **b** *pl* : persons voting in the negative

no·bel·i·um \nō-'bel-ē-əm\ *n* : a radioactive metallic element produced artificially — see ELEMENT table

No·bel Prize \(ˌ)nō-ˌbel-\ *n* : an annual prize (as in literature, medicine, peace) established by the will of Alfred Nobel for the encouragement of people who work for the interests of humanity

no·bil·i·ty \nō-'bil-ət-ē\ *n, pl* **-ties 1** : the quality or state of being noble ⟨*nobility* of character⟩ **2** : the body of persons forming the noble class in a country or state ⟨a member of the *nobility*⟩

¹no·ble \'nō-bəl\ *adj* **no·bler** \-b(ə-)lər\; **no·blest** \-b(ə-)ləst\ **1** : FAMOUS, NOTABLE ⟨*noble* deed⟩ **2** : of high birth or rank : ARISTOCRATIC **3** : possessing very high qualities : EXCELLENT **4** : grand especially in appearance : IMPOSING ⟨a *noble* cathedral⟩ **5** : having or characterized by superiority of mind or character : MAGNANIMOUS ⟨a *noble* nature⟩ **6** : chemically inactive especially toward oxygen ⟨*noble* metal⟩ — **no·ble·ness** \-bəl-nəs\ *n* — **no·bly** \-blē\ *adv*

²noble *n* : a person of noble rank or birth

no·ble·man \'nō-bəl-mən\ *n* : a man of noble rank

no·ble·wom·an \-ˌwùm-ən\ *n* : a woman of noble rank

¹no·body \'nō-bəd-ē, -ˌbäd-ē\ *pron* : no person : not anybody ⟨*nobody* lives in that house⟩

²nobody *n, pl* **no·bod·ies** : a person of no importance

noc·tur·nal \näk-'tərn-ᵊl\ *adj* **1** : of, relating to, or occurring in the night ⟨a *nocturnal* journey⟩ **2** : active at night ⟨*nocturnal* insects⟩ [from early French *nocturnal, nocturnel* or Latin *nocturnalis*, both meaning "nocturnal," derived from earlier Latin *noct-, nox* "night" — related to EQUINOX] — **noc·tur·nal·ly** \-ᵊl-ē\ *adv*

noc·turne \'näk-ˌtərn\ *n* : a work of art dealing with evening or night; *esp* : a dreamy composition for the piano

¹nod \'näd\ *vb* **nod·ded; nod·ding 1** : to bend the head downward or forward (as in bowing or going to sleep or as a way of answering "yes") **2** : to move up and down ⟨the tulips *nodded* in the breeze⟩ **3** : to show by a nod of the head ⟨*nod* agreement⟩ **4** : to let one's attention roam for a moment and make an error — **nod·der** *n*

²nod *n* : the action of nodding

nod·al \'nōd-ᵊl\ *adj* : relating to, being, or located at or near a node

nod·ding \'näd-iŋ\ *adj* : bending downward or forward ⟨a plant with *nodding* flowers⟩

nod·dle \'näd-ᵊl\ *n* : ¹HEAD 1

nod·dy \'näd-ē\ *n, pl* **noddies** : any of several stout-bodied terns of warm seas

node \'nōd\ *n* **1 a** : a thickened or swollen enlargement (as of a joint with rheumatism) **b** : a mass of tissue in the body resembling a knot **2** : a point on a stem at which a leaf is inserted

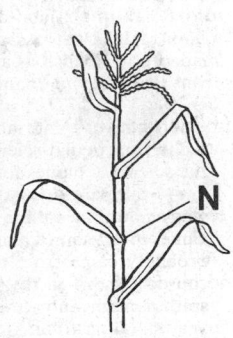

N node 2

nod·ule \'näj-(ˌ)ü(ə)l\ *n* **1** : a small rounded mass ⟨manganese *nodules* on the ocean floor⟩ **2** : a swelling on the root of a plant of the legume family that contains nitrogen-fixing bacteria — **nod·u·lar** \'näj-ə-lər\ *adj*

no·el \nō-'el\ *n* **1** : a Christmas carol **2** *cap* : the Christmas season [from French *noël* "Christmas, a carol," derived from Latin *natalis* "birthday"]

nog·gin \'näg-ən\ *n* **1** : a small mug **2** : a small quantity (as a gill) of drink **3** : a person's head

no–good \ˌnō-ˌgùd\ *adj* : having no worth, use, or chance of success — **no–good** \'nō-ˌgùd\ *n*

no–hit·ter \(')nō-'hit-ər\ *n* : a baseball game in which a pitcher allows the opposition no base hits

¹noise \'nòiz\ *n* **1** : a loud, confused, or senseless shouting or outcry **2 a** : ³SOUND 1b; *esp* : a loud, harsh, or unhar-

\ə\ **abut**	\aù\ **out**	\i\ **tip**	\ò\ **saw**	\ù\ **foot**
\ər\ **further**	\ch\ **chin**	\ī\ **life**	\òi\ **coin**	\y\ **yet**
\a\ **mat**	\e\ **pet**	\j\ **job**	\th\ **thin**	\yü\ **few**
\ā\ **take**	\ē\ **easy**	\ŋ\ **sing**	\th\ **this**	\yù\ **cure**
\ä\ **cot, cart**	\g\ **go**	\ō\ **bone**	\ü\ **food**	\zh\ **vision**

monious sound **b** : an unwanted signal in an electronic communication system

Word History Although loud noise may make us sick, we probably do not think of the words *noise* and *nausea* as having much in common. But the word *noise* came into English from early French, in which it meant "quarrel, loud noise." French had it from the Latin word *nausea* meaning "seasickness, nausea." Perhaps the original connection was with the unpleasant sounds or complaints made by seasick passengers or sailors. *Nausea,* after all, came from the Greek word for sailor, *nautēs.* [Middle English *noise* "noise," from early French *noise* "quarrel, loud noise," from Latin *nausea* "seasickness, nausea," derived from Greek *nautēs* "sailor" — related to NAUSEA; see *Word History* at NAUSEA]

²noise *vb* **noised; nois·ing** : to spread by rumor or report ⟨*noised* it about that we would be allowed to leave early⟩

noise·less \'nȯiz-ləs\ *adj* : making or causing no noise ⟨kittens on *noiseless* feet⟩ — **noise·less·ly** *adv*

noise·mak·er \'nȯiz-ˌmā-kər\ *n* : one that makes noise; *esp* : a device used to make noise at parties

noise pollution *n* : annoying or harmful noise (as of jet planes or automobiles) in an environment — called also *sound pollution*

noi·some \'nȯi-səm\ *adj* **1** : not wholesome ⟨a *noisome* slum⟩ **2** : disagreeable especially to the sense of smell : DISGUSTING ⟨*noisome* odors⟩

noisy \'nȯi-zē\ *adj* **nois·i·er; -est 1** : making noise **2** : full of or characterized by noise ⟨a *noisy* street⟩ — **nois·i·ly** \-zə-lē\ *adv* — **nois·i·ness** \-zē-nəs\ *n*

no·mad \'nō-ˌmad\ *n* **1** : a member of a people that has no fixed home but wanders from place to place **2** : an individual who roams about without a goal or purpose — **nomad** *or* **no·mad·ic** \nō-'mad-ik\ *adj* — **no·mad·ism** \'nō-ˌmad-ˌiz-əm\ *n*

no–man's–land \'nō-ˌmanz-ˌland\ *n* **1** : an unoccupied area between opposing armies **2** : an area of indefinite or uncertain character

nom de plume \ˌnäm-di-'plüm\ *n, pl* **noms de plume** \ˌnäm(z)-di-\ : PEN NAME [a phrase believed to have been made up in English as a French translation of *pen name;* from French *nom* "name" and *de* "of" and *plume* "(the) pen"]

no·men·cla·ture \'nō-mən-ˌklā-chər\ *n* : a system of terms used in a particular science, field of knowledge, or art; *esp* : the scientific names for plants and animals used in biology — compare BINOMIAL NOMENCLATURE [from Latin *nomenclatura* "a calling by name, list of names," derived from *nomen* "name" and *calatus,* past participle of *calare* "to call"]

nom·i·nal \'näm-ən-ᵊl, 'näm-nəl\ *adj* **1** : being such in name or form only ⟨the *nominal* head of the party⟩ **2** : very small : TRIFLING ⟨a *nominal* price⟩ — **nom·i·nal·ly** \-ē\ *adv*

nom·i·nate \'näm-ə-ˌnāt\ *vb* **-nat·ed; -nat·ing** : to choose as a candidate for election, appointment, or honor; *esp* : to propose for office ⟨*nominated* a senator for president⟩ — **nom·i·na·tor** \-ˌnāt-ər\ *n*

nom·i·na·tion \ˌnäm-ə-'nā-shən\ *n* **1** : the act, process, or an instance of nominating **2** : the state of being nominated

nom·i·na·tive \'näm-(ə-)nət-iv\ *adj* : being or belonging to the case of a noun or pronoun that is usually the subject of a verb — **nominative** *n*

nom·i·nee \ˌnäm-ə-'nē\ *n* : a person nominated for an office, duty, or position

no·mo·gram \'näm-ə-ˌgram, 'nō-mə-\ *n* : a set of several lines marked off to scale and arranged in such a way that by using a straightedge to connect known values on two lines an unknown value can be read at the point of intersection with another line

no·mo·graph \'näm-ə-ˌgraf, 'nō-mə-\ *n* : NOMOGRAM

non- \(')nän, ˌnän\ *prefix* : not : reverse of : absence of ⟨*non*resident⟩ ⟨*non*fiction⟩ [derived from Latin *non* "not"]

nonabsorbent	noncontradictory	nonhandicapped
nonacademic	noncontributory	nonhardy
nonacid	noncontrollable	nonhereditary
nonacidic	noncontrolled	nonhistorical
nonacting	noncontrolling	nonhuman
nonaction	noncontroversial	nonimmigrant
nonactivated	nonconventional	nonimmune
nonadhesive	nonconvertible	nonindustrial
nonadjacent	noncorporate	nonindustrialized
nonaggression	noncorrosive	noninfected
nonaggressive	noncreative	noninfectious
nonagricultural	noncriminal	noninfective
nonalcoholic	noncrisis	noninflammable
nonassertive	noncritical	noninstitutional
nonathlete	noncrystalline	noninstitutionalized
nonathletic	nondegenerate	noninstructional
nonattendance	nondelivery	nonintegrated
nonautomatic	nondemocratic	nonintellectual
nonbeliever	nondenominational	noninterchangeable
nonbelligerent	nonderivative	noninterference
nonbinding	nondescriptive	nonintersecting
nonbiodegradable	nondetachable	nonintoxicating
nonbiting	nondevelopment	nonionizing
nonbreakable	nondirected	nonirritating
noncaking	nondirectional	non–Jewish
non–Catholic	nondisabled	nonleaded
noncellular	nondisclosure	nonlegal
noncertified	nondiscrimination	nonlethal
non–Christian	nondiscriminatory	nonlexical
noncitizen	nondocumentary	nonliquid
nonclassical	nondollar	nonliteral
nonclerical	nondomestic	nonliterary
nonclinical	nondramatic	nonliving
noncoercive	nondurable	nonlocal
noncombat	nonedible	nonlogical
noncombative	noneducational	nonluminous
noncombustible	nonelastic	nonmagnetic
noncommercial	nonelected	nonmalleable
noncommitment	nonelection	nonmanagement
noncommitted	nonelective	nonmaterial
noncomparable	nonelectric	nonmaterialistic
noncompatible	nonelectrical	nonmeat
noncompetition	nonemergency	nonmechanical
noncompetitive	nonempirical	nonmedical
noncompetitor	nonending	nonmember
noncomplementary	nonexclusive	nonmembership
noncompliance	nonexempt	nonmetric
noncompliant	nonexplosive	nonmetrical
noncompressible	nonfarm	nonmigrant
nonconclusion	nonfarmer	nonmigratory
nonconducting	nonfatal	nonmilitant
nonconduction	nonfattening	nonmilitary
nonconductive	nonfatty	nonmolecular
nonconfidence	nonfederal	nonmotile
nonconfidential	nonfederated	nonmotorized
nonconflicting	nonfinancial	nonmoving
nonconfrontational	nonfissionable	nonmusical
nonconscious	nonflying	nonnational
nonconservative	nonfood	nonnative
nonconstitutional	nonfreezing	nonnatural
nonconstruction	nonfulfillment	nonnecessity
nonconstructive	nonfunctional	nonnegotiable
noncontact	nonfunctioning	nonnumerical
noncontagious	nongaseous	nonnutritious
noncontemporary	nongovernment	nonobservance
noncontinuous	nongovernmental	nonobservant
noncontradiction	nongrammatical	nonoccurrence

nonofficial
nonoily
nonoperating
nonoperational
nonoperative
nonorganic
nonorthodox
nonparallel
nonparalytic
nonparasitic
nonparticipant
nonparticipating
nonparticipation
nonparty
nonpaying
nonpayment
nonperformance
nonperformer
nonperishable
nonpersistent
nonpersonal
nonphysical
nonplastic
nonpoisonous
nonpolitical
nonpolitically
nonpolluting
nonporous
nonpossession
nonpractical
nonpracticing
nonpregnant
nonprint
nonproducing
nonprofessional
nonprofessionally
nonprogressive
nonpublic
nonracial
nonradioactive
nonrandom
nonrandomness
nonrated
nonrational
nonreactive
nonreactor
nonrealistic
nonreciprocal
nonrecurrent
nonrecyclable
nonreducing
nonreflecting
nonregulated
nonregulation
nonrelative
nonreligious
nonrenewable
nonrepresentative
nonresidential
nonrestricted
nonretractile
nonreusable
nonreversible
nonrotating
nonroutine
nonsalable
nonscientific
nonscientist
nonseasonal
nonsecure
nonsegregated
nonsegregation
nonselected
nonselective
nonsensational
nonsensitive
nonsensuous
nonserious
nonsexist
nonsexual
nonshrinkable
nonsinkable
nonsmoker
nonsmoking
nonsocial
nonsolar
nonspatial
nonspeaker
nonspeaking
nonspecialist
nonspecific
nonspectacular
nonspeculative
nonstationary
nonstatistical
nonstrategic
nonstructural
nonstructured
nonsubsidized
nonsuccess
nonsugar
nonsurgical
nonswimmer
nonsymbolic
nonsymmetric
nonsymmetrical
nontaxable
nontechnical
nontemporal
nontheatrical
nontoxic
nontraditional
nontransferable
nontropical
nontypical
nonuniform
nonuniformity
nonunionized
nonuniversal
nonurban
nonurgent
nonvalid
nonvegetarian
nonvenomous
nonviewer
nonviscous
nonvisual
nonvocal
nonvocational
nonvoter
nonvoting
nonwinning
nonwoody
nonwork
nonworker
nonworking

no·na·gon \ˈnō-nə-ˌgän\ *n* : a polygon of nine angles and nine sides

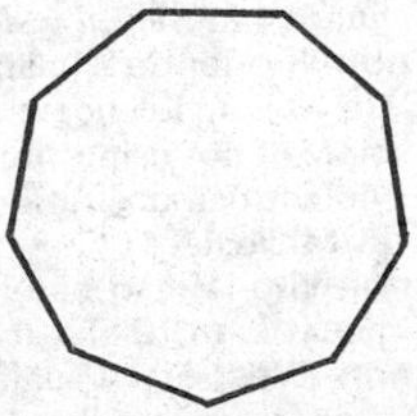
nonagon

non·busi·ness \ˈnän-ˈbiz-nəs, -nəz\ *adj* : not related to business; *esp* : not related to one's primary business

nonce \ˈnän(t)s\ *n* : the one, particular, or present occasion, purpose, or use ⟨for the *nonce*⟩

non·cha·lance \ˌnän-shə-ˈlän(t)s, ˈnän-shə-ˌlän(t)s\ *n* : the quality or state of being nonchalant

non·cha·lant \ˌnän-shə-ˈlänt, ˈnän-shə-ˌlänt\ *adj* : having a confident and easy manner ⟨face a crowd with *nonchalant* ease⟩ [from French *nonchalant* "not excited," derived from early French *nonchaloir* "to disregard, be unconcerned," from *non-* "not" and *chaloir* "to care," from Latin *calēre* "to be warm" — related to CAULDRON, CALORIE] — **non·cha·lant·ly** *adv*

non·com \ˈnän-ˌkäm\ *n* : NONCOMMISSIONED OFFICER

non·com·ba·tant \ˌnän-kəm-ˈbat-ᵊnt, (ˈ)nän-ˈkäm-bət-ənt\ *n* **1** : a member (as a chaplain) of the armed forces whose duties do not include fighting **2** : CIVILIAN — **noncombatant** *adj*

non·com·e·do·gen·ic \-ˌkäm-əd-ō-ˈjen-ik\ *adj* : not tending to clog pores ⟨a *noncomedogenic* moisturizing lotion⟩

non·com·mis·sioned officer \ˌnän-kə-ˌmish-ənd-\ *n* : an officer in the Army, Air Force, or Marine Corps appointed from among the enlisted personnel

non·com·mit·tal \ˌnän-kə-ˈmit-ᵊl\ *adj* : not telling or showing what a person thinks or has decided ⟨a *noncommittal* answer⟩ — **non·com·mit·tal·ly** \-ᵊl-ē\ *adv*

non·con·duc·tor \ˌnän-kən-ˈdək-tər\ *n* : a substance that conducts heat, electricity, or sound at a very low rate

non·con·form \-kən-ˈfȯ(ə)rm\ *vb* : to fail to conform — **non·con·form·er** *n*

non·con·form·ist \ˌnän-kən-ˈfȯr-məst\ *n* **1** *often cap* : a person who does not conform to an established church **2** : a person who does not conform to generally accepted standards or customs — **nonconformist** *adj, often cap*

non·con·for·mi·ty \ˌnän-kən-ˈfȯr-mət-ē\ *n* : failure or refusal to conform

noncooperation \ˌnän-kō-ˌäp-ə-ˈrā-shən\ *n* : failure or refusal to cooperate especially with the government

non·dairy \ˈnän-ˈde(ə)r-ē\ *adj* : containing no milk or milk products ⟨*nondairy* whipped topping⟩

non·de·duct·ible \-di-ˈdək-tə-bəl\ *adj* : not deductible; *esp* : not deductible for income tax purposes ⟨a *nondeductible* contribution⟩ — **non·de·duct·ibil·i·ty** \-ˌdək-tə-ˈbil-ət-ē\ *n*

non·de·script \ˌnän-di-ˈskript\ *adj* : belonging or appearing to belong to no particular class or kind : not easily described — **nondescript** *n*

non·de·struc·tive \-di-ˈstrək-tiv\ *adj* : not destructive; *esp* : not causing destruction of material being investigated or treated ⟨*nondestructive* testing of metal⟩ — **non·de·struc·tive·ly** *adv* — **non·de·struc·tive·ness** *n*

non·di·vid·ing \ˌnän-də-ˈvīd-iŋ\ *adj* : not undergoing cell division

¹none \ˈnən\ *pron* **1** : not any ⟨*none* of them went⟩ ⟨*none* of it is needed⟩ **2** : not one ⟨*none* of the family⟩ **3** : not any such thing or person ⟨half a loaf is better than *none*⟩

²none *adv* **1** : by no means : not at all ⟨*none* too soon to begin⟩ **2** : in no way : to no extent ⟨*none* the worse for wear⟩

non·ec·o·nom·ic \ˌnän-ˌek-ə-ˈnäm-ik, -ˌē-kə-\ *adj* : not economic; *esp* : having no economic importance or involvement

non·elec·tro·lyte \ˌnän-ə-ˈlek-trə-ˌlīt\ *n* : a substance (as sugar) that does not readily form ions when dissolved or melted and that is a poor conductor of electricity

non·en·ti·ty \nä-ˈnen(t)-ət-ē\ *n, pl* **-ti·ties** **1** : something that does not exist or exists only in the imagination **2** : a person of no importance

non·es·sen·tial \ˌnän-i-ˈsen-chəl\ *adj* : not necessary or essential — **nonessential** *n*

none·the·less \ˌnən-t͟hə-ˈles\ *adv* : NEVERTHELESS

non·ex·ist·ence \ˌnän-ig-ˈzis-təns\ *n* : absence of existence — **non·ex·ist·ent** \-tənt\ *adj*

non·fat \ˈnän-ˈfat\ *adj* : having no fat or fat solids : having the fat removed ⟨*nonfat* milk⟩

non·fer·rous \-ˈfer-əs\ *adj* **1** : not containing, including, or relating to iron **2** : of or relating to metals other than iron

non·fic·tion \ˈnän-ˈfik-shən\ *n* : literature or cinema that is not fictional — **non·fic·tion·al** \(ˈ)nän-ˈfik-shnəl, -shən-ᵊl\ *adj*

non·fig·u·ra·tive \-ˈfig-(y)ə-rət-iv\ *adj* : NONOBJECTIVE

non·flam·ma·ble \-ˈflam-ə-bəl\ *adj* : not flammable; *also*

\ə\ **abut**	\au̇\ **out**	\i\ **tip**	\ȯ\ **saw**	\u̇\ **foot**
\ər\ **further**	\ch\ **chin**	\ī\ **life**	\ȯi\ **coin**	\y\ **yet**
\a\ **mat**	\e\ **pet**	\j\ **job**	\th\ **thin**	\yü\ **few**
\ā\ **take**	\ē\ **easy**	\ŋ\ **sing**	\t͟h\ **this**	\yu̇\ **cure**
\ä\ **cot, cart**	\g\ **go**	\ō\ **bone**	\ü\ **food**	\zh\ **vision**

: not easily ignited and not burning rapidly if ignited — **non·flam·ma·bil·i·ty** \-ˌflam-ə-'bil-ət-ē\ n

non·flow·er·ing \(')nän-'flau̇-(ə-)riŋ\ adj : producing no flowers; esp : having no flowering stage in the life cycle

non·green \'nän-'grēn\ adj : having no chlorophyll ⟨nongreen plants⟩

no·nil·lion \nō-'nil-yən\ n — see NUMBER table

non·in·ter·ven·tion \ˌnän-ˌint-ər-'ven-chən\ n 1 : the state or habit of not intervening 2 : refusal or failure to intervene

non·in·volve·ment \-in-'välv-mənt, -'volv-\ n : absence of involvement or emotional attachment — **non·in·volved** \-'välvd, -'volvd\ adj

non·lit·er·ate \-'lit-ə-rət, -'lit-rət\ adj 1 : not literate 2 : having no written language — **nonliterate** n

non·met·al \(')nän-'met-ᵊl\ n : an element (as carbon or nitrogen) that lacks the characteristics of a metal

non·me·tal·lic \ˌnän-mə-'tal-ik\ adj 1 : not metallic 2 : of, relating to, or being a nonmetal

non·mor·al \-'mor-əl, -'mär-\ adj : not being moral or ethical

non·neg·a·tive \(')nän-'neg-ət-iv\ adj : not negative; esp : being either positive or zero ⟨a nonnegative number⟩

non·nu·cle·ar \(')nän-'n(y)ü-klē-ər\ adj 1 : not nuclear ⟨nonnuclear weapons⟩ 2 : not having nuclear weapons ⟨nonnuclear countries⟩

no-no \'nō-ˌnō\ n, pl **no-no's** or **no-nos** : something that is unacceptable or forbidden

non·ob·jec·tive \ˌnän-əb-'jek-tiv\ adj : intended to represent no natural or actual object or likeness ⟨nonobjective art⟩

no-nonsense adj : putting up with or including no nonsense : SERIOUS ⟨a no-nonsense manager⟩

¹**non·pa·reil** \ˌnän-pə-'rel\ adj : having no equal : PEERLESS

²**nonpareil** n 1 : an individual of unequaled excellence : PARAGON 2 : PAINTED BUNTING

non·par·ti·san \(')nän-'pärt-ə-zən, -sən\ adj : not partisan; esp : free from party ties, bias, or designation ⟨a nonpartisan ballot⟩ ⟨a nonpartisan committee⟩

non·patho·gen·ic \-ˌpath-ə-'jen-ik\ adj : not capable of causing disease

non·plus \(')nän-'pləs\ vb **non·plussed** also **non·plused**; **non·plus·sing** also **non·plus·ing** : to cause to be at a loss as to what to say, think, or do : PERPLEX

non·po·lar \-'pō-lər\ adj : not polar; esp : consisting of molecules not having a dipole ⟨a nonpolar solvent⟩

non·pre·scrip·tion \ˌnän-pri-'skrip-shən\ adj : capable of being bought without a doctor's prescription ⟨a nonprescription pain reliever⟩

non·pro·duc·tive \ˌnän-prə-'dək-tiv\ adj 1 : failing to produce : UNPRODUCTIVE ⟨a nonproductive oil well⟩ 2 : not directly productive ⟨nonproductive labor⟩

non·prof·it \'nän-'präf-ət\ adj : not existing or carried on for the purpose of making a profit ⟨a nonprofit organization⟩

non·pro·tein \-'prō-ˌtēn, -'prōt-ē-ən\ adj : not being or derived from protein ⟨the nonprotein part of an enzyme⟩ ⟨nonprotein nitrogen⟩

non·read·er \-'rēd-ər\ n 1 : one who does not or cannot read 2 : a child who is slow in learning to read — **non·read·ing** \-iŋ\ adj

non·res·i·dent \(')nän-'rez-əd-ənt, -'rez-dənt, -'rez-ə-ˌdent\ adj : not living in a particular place — **nonresident** n

non·re·sis·tance \ˌnän-ri-'zis-tən(t)s\ n : the policy or practice of yielding to authority even when unjust or cruel

non·re·sis·tant \-'tənt\ adj : not resistant; esp : unable to withstand the effects of a harmful substance (as an insecticide or antibiotic) ⟨nonresistant bacteria⟩

non·re·stric·tive \ˌnän-ri-'strik-tiv\ adj 1 : not serving or

tending to restrict 2 : not limiting the reference of the word or phrase modified ⟨a nonrestrictive clause⟩

non·re·turn·able \-ri-'tər-nə-bəl\ adj : not returnable; esp : not returnable to a dealer in exchange for a deposit ⟨nonreturnable bottles⟩ — **nonreturnable** n

non·sched·uled \(')nän-'skej-(ˌ)ü(ə)ld, -'skej-əld\ adj : licensed to carry passengers or freight by air without a regular schedule ⟨a nonscheduled airline⟩

non·sec·tar·i·an \ˌnän-(ˌ)sek-'ter-ē-ən\ adj : not having a sectarian character : not restricted to a particular religious group

non·sense \'nän-ˌsen(t)s, 'nän(t)-sən(t)s\ n 1 : foolish or meaningless words or actions 2 : things of no importance or value — **non·sen·si·cal** \nän-'sen(t)-si-kəl\ adj — **non·sen·si·cal·ly** \-k(ə-)lē\ adv — **non·sen·si·cal·ness** \-kəl-nəs\ n

non·skid \(')nän-'skid\ adj : designed to prevent skidding

non·stan·dard \(')nän-'stan-dərd\ adj 1 : not standard 2 : not agreeing in pronunciation, grammatical construction, idiom, or choice of word with the usage generally characteristic of educated native speakers of the language

non·stick \'nän-'stik\ adj : allowing easy removal of cooked food particles ⟨a nonstick coating in a pan⟩

non·stop \'nän-'stäp\ adj : done, made, or held without a stop ⟨a nonstop flight to Chicago⟩ — **nonstop** adv

non·sup·port \ˌnän(t)-sə-'pō(ə)rt, -'pó(ə)rt\ n : failure to support; esp : failure to provide legally required financial support

non·tast·er \(')nän-'tā-stər\ n : a person unable to taste the chemical phenylthiocarbamide

non·ther·mal \-'thər-məl\ adj : not produced by heat

non·threat·en·ing \-'thret-ᵊn-iŋ\ adj 1 : not constituting a threat ⟨a nonthreatening illness⟩ 2 : not likely to cause anxiety ⟨nonthreatening activities⟩; also : INNOCUOUS 2

non·union \(')nän-'yün-yən\ adj 1 : not belonging to a trade union ⟨nonunion carpenters⟩ 2 : not recognizing or favoring trade unions or their members ⟨nonunion employers⟩

non·use \-'yüs\ n 1 : failure to use ⟨nonuse of available material⟩ 2 : the fact or condition of not being used

non·us·er \-'yü-zər\ n : one who does not make use of something (as a harmful drug)

non·vas·cu·lar plant \-'vas-kyə-lər-\ n : a plant (as a moss or an alga) that has no specialized conducting system for carrying fluids

non·ver·bal \(')nän-'vər-bəl\ adj 1 : being other than verbal ⟨nonverbal symbols⟩ 2 : involving little use of language ⟨nonverbal tests⟩ — **non·ver·bal·ly** \-bə-lē\ adv

non·vi·o·lence \(')nän-'vī-ə-lən(t)s\ n 1 : the avoidance of the use of violence as a matter of principle; also : the principle of not using violence to achieve one's goals 2 : nonviolent demonstrations for the purpose of achieving political goals

non·vi·o·lent \(')nän-'vī-ə-lənt\ adj 1 : not using violence : PEACEFUL 2 : of, relating to, or marked by nonviolence

non-West·ern \(')nän-'wes-tərn\ adj 1 : not being part of the western tradition ⟨non-Western countries⟩ 2 : of or relating to non-Western societies ⟨non-Western values⟩

non·white \(')nän-'hwīt, -'wīt\ n : a person whose features and especially whose skin color are different from those of white people of northwestern Europe — **nonwhite** adj

non·wo·ven \(')nän-'wō-vən\ adj 1 : made of fibers held together by interlocking or bonding (as by chemical means) but not woven ⟨nonwoven fabric⟩ 2 : made of nonwoven fabric ⟨a nonwoven dress⟩ — **nonwoven** n

non·ze·ro \-'zē-rō, -'zi(ə)r-ō\ adj : being, having, or involving a value other than zero

noo·dle \'nüd-ᵊl\ n : a thin strip of dough made from flour, water, and usually eggs and cooked by boiling

nook \'nu̇k\ n 1 : an interior angle or corner formed usually by two walls ⟨a chimney nook⟩ 2 : a sheltered or hidden place ⟨a shady nook⟩

noon \'nün\ *n* : the middle of the day : 12 o'clock in the daytime — **noon** *adj*

Word History Noon has not always meant "12 o'clock in the daytime." In the ancient Roman way of keeping track of time, the hours of the day were counted from sunrise to sunset. The ninth hour of their day (about 3 p.m. nowadays) was called *nona,* Latin for "ninth." In the early period of English, the word was borrowed as *nōn,* also referring to the ninth hour after sunrise. By the 14th century, however, the word came to be used for midday, 12 o'clock, as we use it today. [Old English *nōn* "ninth hour from sunrise," derived from Latin *nona,* a feminine form of *nonus* "ninth," from *novem* "nine"]

noon·day \-,dā\ *n* : MIDDAY

no one *pron* : ¹NOBODY ⟨*no one* was home⟩

noon·tide \'nün-,tīd\ *n* : NOONTIME

noon·time \-,tīm\ *n* : the time of noon : MIDDAY

noose \'nüs\ *n* : a loop that passes through a knot at the end of a line so that it gets smaller when the other end of the line is pulled

nor \nər, (')nȯ(ə)r\ *conj* : and not ⟨not for you *nor* for me⟩ — used especially between two words or phrases preceded by *neither* ⟨neither here *nor* there⟩

nor·adren·a·line \,nȯr-ə-'dren-ᵊl-ən\ *n* : NOREPINEPHRINE

nor·epi·neph·rine \,nȯ(ə)r-,ep-ə-'nef-rən\ *n* : a hormone that causes blood vessels to contract and helps to transmit nerve impulses in the sympathetic nervous system and in some parts of the central nervous system

norm \'nȯ(ə)rm\ *n* **1** : ¹AVERAGE 2; *esp* : a set standard of development or achievement usually derived from the average or median achievement of a large group **2** : a common or typical practice or custom

¹**nor·mal** \'nȯr-məl\ *adj* **1** : ¹PERPENDICULAR 2 **2** : of the regular or usual kind **3 a** : relating to or marked by average intelligence or development **b** : free from sickness of body or mind : SANE, SOUND — **nor·mal·ly** \-mə-lē\ *adv*

²**normal** *n* **1** : a normal line **2** : a person or thing that is normal **3** : a form or state regarded as the usual : AVERAGE

normal curve *n* : a symmetrical bell-shaped curve that is often used as an approximation to the graph of scores or measurements consisting of many bunched values near the average in the middle and a few large and a few small values arranged toward the opposite ends

nor·mal·cy \'nȯr-məl-sē\ *n* : NORMALITY

nor·mal·i·ty \nȯr-'mal-ət-ē\ *n* : the quality or state of being normal

nor·mal·ize \'nȯr-mə-,līz\ *vb* **-ized; -iz·ing** : to make normal or average — **nor·mal·i·za·tion** \,nȯr-mə-lə-'zā-shən\ *n*

Nor·man \'nȯr-mən\ *n* **1** : one of the Scandinavians who conquered Normandy in the 10th century **2** : one of the people of mixed Norman and French blood who conquered England in 1066 **3** : a person born or living in Normandy — **Nor·man** *adj*

Norse \'nȯ(ə)rs\ *n* **1** *pl* **Norse a** : the Scandinavian people **b** : the Norwegian people **2 a** : NORWEGIAN 2 **b** : any of the Scandinavian languages — **Norse** *adj*

Norse·man \'nȯr-smən\ *n* : any of the ancient Scandinavians

¹**north** \'nȯ(ə)rth\ *adv* : to or toward the north

²**north** *adj* **1** : placed or lying toward or at the north ⟨the *north* entrance⟩ **2** : coming from the north ⟨a *north* wind⟩

³**north** *n* **1 a** : the direction to the left of one facing east **b** : the compass point opposite to south **2** *cap* : regions or countries north of a point that is mentioned or understood

north·bound \'nȯrth-,baùnd\ *adj* : headed north

¹**north·east** \nȯr-'thēst, *nautical* nȯ-'rēst\ *adv* : to or toward the northeast

²**northeast** *n* **1** : the direction between north and east **2** *cap* : regions or countries northeast of a point that is mentioned or understood

³**northeast** *adj* **1** : placed or lying toward or at the northeast ⟨the *northeast* corner⟩ **2** : coming from the northeast ⟨a *northeast* wind⟩

north·east·er \nȯr-'thē-stər, nȯ-'rē-\ *n* **1** : a strong northeast wind **2** : a storm with northeast winds

north·east·er·ly \nȯr-'thē-stər-lē\ *adv or adj* **1** : from the northeast **2** : toward the northeast

north·east·ern \nȯr-'thē-stərn\ *adj* **1** *often cap* : of, relating to, or characteristic of the Northeast **2** : lying toward or coming from the northeast

North·east·ern·er \nȯr-'thē-stə(r)-nər\ *n* : a person born or living in a northeastern region (as of the U.S.)

north·east·ward \nȯr-'thēs-twərd\ *adv or adj* : toward the northeast — **north·east·wards** \-twərdz\ *adv*

north·er \'nȯr-thər\ *n* **1** : a strong north wind **2** : a storm with north winds

¹**north·er·ly** \'nȯr-thər-lē\ *adj or adv* **1** : placed or lying toward the north ⟨the *northerly* border⟩ **2** : coming from the north ⟨a *northerly* wind⟩

²**northerly** *n, pl* **-lies** : a wind from the north

north·ern \'nȯr-thə(r)n\ *adj* **1** *cap* : of, relating to, or characteristic of the North **2** : lying toward or coming from the north ⟨a *northern* storm⟩ — **north·ern·most** \-,mōst\ *adj*

North·ern·er \'nȯr-thə(r)-nər\ *n* : a person born or living in the North (as of the U.S.)

northern harrier *n* : a common brown or grayish hawk especially of fields and marshes that has a white patch on the upper side near the base of the tail

northern hemisphere *n, often cap N&H* : the half of the earth that lies north of the equator

northern lights *n pl* : AURORA BOREALIS

north·land \'nȯrth-,land, -lənd\ *n, often cap* : land in the north : the north of a country or region

North·man \-mən\ *n* : NORSEMAN

north pole *n* **1 a** : *often cap N&P*: the northernmost point of the earth : the northern end of the earth's axis **b** : the point in the sky directly overhead at the north pole **2** : the pole of a magnet that points toward the north

north–seeking pole *n* : NORTH POLE 2

North Star *n* : the star toward which the northern end of the earth's axis very nearly points — called also *polestar*

north·ward \'nȯrth-wərd\ *adv or adj* : toward the north — **north·wards** \-wərdz\ *adv*

¹**north·west** \nȯrth-'west, *nautical* nȯr-'west\ *adv* : to or toward the northwest

²**northwest** *n* **1** : the direction between north and west **2** *cap* : the regions or countries northwest of a point that is mentioned or understood

³**northwest** *adj* **1** : coming from the northwest ⟨a *northwest* wind⟩ **2** : placed or lying toward or at the northwest ⟨the *northwest* corner⟩

north·west·er \nȯr(th)-'wes-tər\ *n* : a strong northwest wind

north·west·er·ly \nȯrth-'wes-tər-lē\ *adv or adj* **1** : from the northwest **2** : toward the northwest

north·west·ern \nȯrth-'wes-tərn\ *adj* **1** *often cap* : of, relating to, or characteristic of the Northwest **2** : lying toward or coming from the northwest

North·west·ern·er \nȯrth-'wes-tə(r)-nər\ *n* : a person born or living in a northwestern region (as of the U.S.)

north·west·ward \nȯrth-'wes-twərd\ *adv or adj* : toward the northwest — **north·west·wards** \-twərdz\ *adv*

\ə\ abut	\aù\ out	\i\ tip	\ȯ\ saw	\ù\ foot
\ər\ further	\ch\ chin	\ī\ life	\ȯi\ coin	\y\ yet
\a\ mat	\e\ pet	\j\ job	\th\ thin	\yü\ few
\ā\ take	\ē\ easy	\ŋ\ sing	\th\ this	\yù\ cure
\ä\ cot, cart	\g\ go	\ō\ bone	\ü\ food	\zh\ vision

Nor·way maple \ˌnȯ(ə)r-ˌwā-\ *n* : a Eurasian maple with dark green or often reddish or red-veined leaves that is often planted in the U.S. as a shade tree

Norway rat *n* : BROWN RAT

Nor·we·gian \nȯr-ˈwē-jən\ *n* **1** : a person born or living in Norway **2** : the Germanic language of the Norwegian people — **Norwegian** *adj*

nos *plural of* NO

¹nose \ˈnōz\ *n* **1 a** : the part of the face or head that contains the nostrils and covers the front or outer part of the nasal cavity; *also* : this part together with the nasal cavity **b** : the front part of the head above or sticking out beyond the jaws ⟨the length of a whale from the tip of the *nose* to the middle of the tail⟩ **2** : the sense of smell **3** : the organ of smell of a vertebrate **4** : something (as a point, edge, or projection) like a nose ⟨the *nose* of a plane⟩ **5** : an ability to discover ⟨a *nose* for news⟩ — **nosed** \ˈnōzd\ *adj*

²nose *vb* **nosed; nos·ing 1** : to detect by or as if by smell : SCENT **2** : to push or move with the nose **3** : to touch or rub with the nose : NUZZLE **4** : to search especially into other peoples' business : PRY **5** : to move ahead slowly or cautiously ⟨the boat *nosed* around the bend⟩

nose·bleed \ˈnōz-ˌblēd\ *n* : a bleeding from the nose

nose cone *n* : a protective cone forming the forward end of a rocket or missile

nose-dive \ˈnōz-ˌdīv\ *n* **1** : a downward nose-first plunge (as of an airplane) **2** : a sudden extreme drop (as in prices)

nose–dive *vb* **nose–dived; nose–div·ing** : to plunge suddenly or sharply

no—see—um \nō-ˈsē-əm\ *n* : any of various tiny two-winged flies that bite [from the words (as supposedly spoken by American Indians) *no see um* "you don't see them"]

nose·gay \-ˌgā\ *n* : a small bunch of flowers : POSY 1

nose out *vb* : to defeat by a narrow margin ⟨the home team barely *nosed out* the visitors⟩

nose·piece \-ˌpēs\ *n* : the end piece of a microscope body to which a lens or set of lenses is attached

nose·wheel \-ˌhwēl, -ˌwēl\ *n* : a landing-gear wheel under the nose of an aircraft

nos·tal·gia \nä-ˈstal-jə, nə-\ *n* : a longing for something past — **nos·tal·gic** \-jik\ *adj* — **nos·tal·gi·cal·ly** \-ji-k(ə-)lē\ *adv*

nos·tril \ˈnäs-trəl\ *n* : either of the outer openings of the nose through which one breathes; *also* : either fleshy wall forming a side of the nose [Old English *nosthyrl* "nostril," literally "nose hole," from *nosu* "nose" and *thyrel* "hole" — related to THRILL; see *Word History* at THRILL]

nosy *or* **nos·ey** \ˈnō-zē\ *adj* **nos·i·er; -est** : of a prying or inquisitive disposition or quality : INTRUSIVE — **nos·i·ly** \-zə-lē\ *adv* — **nos·i·ness** \-zē-nəs\ *n*

not \(ˈ)nät\ *adv* **1** — used to make a word or group of words negative ⟨the books are *not* here⟩ **2** — used to stand for the negative of a group of words that comes before ⟨is sometimes hard to see and sometimes *not*⟩

¹no·ta·ble \ˈnōt-ə-bəl\ *adj* **1** : deserving special notice : REMARKABLE ⟨a *notable* sight⟩ **2** : DISTINGUISHED, PROMINENT ⟨a *notable* writer⟩ — **no·ta·bly** \-blē\ *adv*

²notable *n* : a famous person

no·ta·rize \ˈnōt-ə-ˌrīz\ *vb* **-rized; -riz·ing** : to sign as a notary public to show that a document is authentic — **no·ta·ri·za·tion** \ˌnōt-ə-rə-ˈzā-shən\ *n*

no·ta·ry public \ˌnōt-ə-rē-\ *n, pl* **notaries public** *or* **no·tary publics** : a public officer who witnesses the making of a document (as a deed) and signs it to show that it is authentic — called also *notary*

no·ta·tion \nō-ˈtā-shən\ *n* **1** : ²NOTE 3a ⟨make *notations* on a paper⟩ **2** : the act of noting **3** : a system of marks, signs, figures, or characters used to give specified information ⟨musical *notation*⟩ ⟨scientific *notation*⟩ — **no·ta·tion·al** \-shnəl, -shən-ᵊl\ *adj*

¹notch \ˈnäch\ *n* **1** : a cut in the shape of a V in an edge or surface **2** : a narrow pass between mountains : GAP 3 : DEGREE 1, STEP ⟨turn the radio up a *notch*⟩

²notch *vb* **1** : to cut or make a notch in **2 a** : to mark or record by a notch **b** : ACHIEVE 2, SCORE

notched \ˈnächt\ *adj* : having a notch or notches

¹note \ˈnōt\ *vb* **not·ed; not·ing 1 a** : to notice or observe with care **b** : to record or preserve in writing **2** : to make special mention of : NOTICE — **not·er** *n*

²note *n* **1 a** : a musical sound : TONE **b** : an animal's cry, call, or sound ⟨a bird's *note*⟩ **c** : a symbol in music that by its shape and position on the staff shows the pitch of a tone and the length of time it is to be held **2** : a quality that shows a feeling ⟨a *note* of sadness in your voice⟩ **3 a** : something written down often to aid the memory ⟨I'll make a *note* of the appointment⟩ **b** : a brief and informal record **c** : a written or printed comment that helps explain part of the book ⟨*notes* in the back of the book⟩ **4 a** : a written promise to pay **b** : a piece of paper money **5 a** : a short informal letter **b** : a formal diplomatic or official communication **6 a** : REPUTATION 1, DISTINCTION ⟨a scientist of *note*⟩ **b** : careful notice ⟨take *note* of the exact time⟩ **synonyms** see ¹SIGN

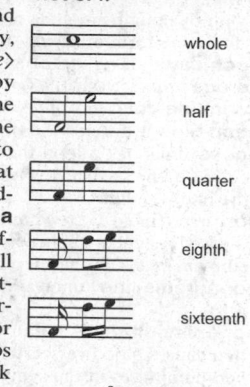

whole

half

quarter

eighth

sixteenth

²note 1c

note·book \ˈnōt-ˌbùk\ *n* **1** : a book for notes **2** : a portable computer that is similar to but usually smaller than a laptop

not·ed \ˈnōt-əd\ *adj* : well-known and highly regarded : FAMOUS — **not·ed·ly** *adv*

note·pad \ˈnōt-ˌpad\ *n* : ²PAD 4

note·wor·thy \ˈnōt-ˌwər-thē\ *adj* : worthy of note : REMARKABLE — **note·wor·thi·ness** *n*

¹noth·ing \ˈnəth-iŋ\ *pron* **1** : not anything ⟨there's *nothing* in the box⟩ **2** : one of no interest, value, or importance ⟨your opinion means *nothing* to me⟩ — **nothing doing** : by no means : definitely no

²nothing *adv* : not at all : in no way

³nothing *n* **1 a** : something that does not exist **b** : absence of quantity : ZERO **2** : something of little or no worth or importance — **noth·ing·ness** *n*

¹no·tice \ˈnōt-əs\ *n* **1** : warning or indication of something : ANNOUNCEMENT ⟨gave us *notice* of the change⟩ **2** : notification of the ending of an agreement at a specified time ⟨gave my employer *notice*⟩ **3** : ATTENTION 1, HEED ⟨take no *notice* of them⟩ **4** : a written or printed announcement **5** : a brief published criticism (as of a book)

²notice *vb* **no·ticed; no·tic·ing 1** : to make mention of : remark on **2** : to take notice of : OBSERVE, MARK ⟨*notice* details⟩

no·tice·able \ˈnōt-ə-sə-bəl\ *adj* **1** : worthy of notice ⟨*noticeable* for its fine coloring⟩ **2** : capable of being or likely to be noticed ⟨a *noticeable* improvement⟩ — **no·tice·ably** \-blē\ *adv*

synonyms NOTICEABLE, PROMINENT, OUTSTANDING, CONSPICUOUS mean attracting notice or attention. NOTICEABLE suggests that something is likely to be seen ⟨an essay with many *noticeable* mistakes⟩. PROMINENT suggests that something calls attention to itself by standing out from its surroundings ⟨a *prominent* bruise on the forehead⟩. OUTSTANDING applies to something that rises above and is better than others of the same kind ⟨an *outstanding* baseball player⟩. CONSPICUOUS applies to something that is easily observed and certain to attract attention ⟨his loud voice made him *conspicuous* at the party⟩.

no·ti·fi·ca·tion \ˌnōt-ə-fə-'kā-shən\ *n* **1** : the act or an instance of notifying **2** : written or printed matter that gives notice

no·ti·fy \'nōt-ə-ˌfī\ *vb* **-fied; -fy·ing** : to give notice to : INFORM ⟨*notify* the police⟩ — **no·ti·fi·er** \-ˌfī(-ə)r\ *n*

no·tion \'nō-shən\ *n* **1 a** : IDEA 2, CONCEPTION ⟨have a *notion* of a poem's meaning⟩ **b** : a belief held : OPINION **c** : a sudden wish or desire : WHIM ⟨just had a *notion* to go home⟩ **2** *pl* : small useful articles (as pins, needles, or thread)

no·to·chord \'nōt-ə-ˌkò(ə)rd\ *n* : a flexible supporting rod of cells that exists in the embryos of all chordates, remains in the adults of some primitive forms (as lancelets and lampreys), and is replaced by the backbone in most vertebrates

no·to·ri·ety \ˌnōt-ə-'rī-ət-ē\ *n, pl* **-eties** : the quality or state of being notorious

no·to·ri·ous \nō-'tōr-ē-əs, nə-, -'tòr-\ *adj* : generally known and talked of; *esp* : widely and unfavorably known   **synonyms** see FAMOUS — **no·to·ri·ous·ly** *adv*

¹not·with·stand·ing \ˌnät-with-'stan-diŋ, -with-\ *prep* : ²DESPITE ⟨we went ahead with our plan *notwithstanding* their objections⟩

²notwithstanding *adv* : NEVERTHELESS, HOWEVER

nou·gat \'nü-gət\ *n* : a candy of nuts or fruit pieces in a sugar paste

nought *variant of* NAUGHT

noun \'naùn\ *n* : a word that is the name of something (as a person, animal, place, thing, quality, idea, or action) and that is typically used in a sentence as subject or object of a verb or as object of a preposition

nour·ish \'nər-ish, 'nə-rish\ *vb* **1** : to promote the growth or development of **2 a** : to provide with food : FEED ⟨plants *nourished* by rain and soil⟩ **b** : to provide for : SUPPORT, MAINTAIN ⟨a friendship *nourished* by trust⟩

nour·ish·ing *adj* : giving nourishment : NUTRITIOUS

nour·ish·ment \'nər-ish-mənt, 'nə-rish-\ *n* **1** : something that nourishes : FOOD, NUTRIMENT **2** : the act of nourishing : the state of being nourished

no·va \'nō-və\ *n, pl* **novas** *or* **no·vae** \-vē, -ˌvī\ : a star that suddenly increases greatly in brightness and then within a few months or years grows dim again

¹nov·el \'näv-əl\ *adj* **1** : new and different from what has been known before **2** : original or striking in design or appearance ⟨a *novel* way to make money⟩   **synonyms** see NEW

²novel *n* : a long prose narrative that usually portrays imaginary characters and events

nov·el·ette \ˌnäv-ə-'let\ *n* : NOVELLA

nov·el·ist \'näv-(ə-)ləst\ *n* : a writer of novels

no·vel·la \nō-'vel-ə\ *n* : a work of fiction falling between a short story and a novel in length and complexity

nov·el·ty \'näv-əl-tē\ *n, pl* **-ties** **1** : something new or unusual **2** : the quality or state of being novel : NEWNESS **3** : a small article intended mainly as an unusual ornament or toy — usually used in plural

No·vem·ber \nō-'vem-bər\ *n* : the 11th month of the year
Word History The first calendar used in ancient Rome began the year with the month of March. The ninth month of the year was called *November,* from the Latin word *novem,* meaning "nine." When the name was first borrowed into Middle English from early French, it was spelled *Novembre.* But in time the original Latin spelling became the one used in English. [Middle English *Novembre* "November (the 11th month)," from early French *Novembre* (same meaning), from Latin *November* "November (ninth month)," from *novem* "nine"]

no·ve·na \nō-'vē-nə\ *n, pl* **no·ve·nas** *or* **no·ve·nae** \-nē\ : a Roman Catholic devotion in which prayers are said for the same intention on nine days in a row

nov·ice \'näv-əs\ *n* **1** : a new member of a religious order who is preparing to take the vows of religion **2** : a person who has no previous experience with something

no·vi·tiate \nō-'vish-ət\ *n* **1** : the period or state of being a novice **2** : NOVICE 1 **3** : a place where novices are trained

no·vo·caine \'nō-və-ˌkān\ *n* : a form of procaine; *also* : an anesthetic that is applied to and acts on only a small part of the body [*novo-,* from Latin *novus* "new" and *cocaine*]

¹now \(')naù\ *adv* **1 a** : at the present time ⟨they are busy *now*⟩ **b** : in the time immediately before the present ⟨thought of them just *now*⟩ **c** : in the time immediately to follow ⟨come in *now*⟩ **2** — used with the sense of present time weakened or lost (as to express command or introduce an important point) ⟨*now* hear this⟩ **3** : SOMETIMES ⟨*now* one and *now* another⟩ **4** : under the present circumstances ⟨*now* the trouble began⟩ **5** : by this time ⟨has been teaching *now* for twenty years⟩ — **now and then** : from time to time : OCCASIONALLY

²now *conj* : in view of the fact that : SINCE — often followed by *that* ⟨*now* that we are here⟩

³now \'naù\ *n* : the present time ⟨been ill up to *now*⟩

⁴now \'naù\ *adj* : of or relating to the present time : EXISTING ⟨the *now* president⟩

now·a·days \'naù-(ə-)ˌdāz\ *adv* : at the present time

no·way *adv* **1** \'nō-ˌwā\ *or* **no·ways** \-ˌwāz\ : NOWISE **2** usually **no way** \-'wā\ : certainly not

¹no·where \'nō-ˌhwe(ə)r, -ˌwe(ə)r, -ˌhwa(ə)r, -hwər, -wər\ *adv* **1** : not in or at any place **2** : to no place **3** : not at all : not to the least extent — usually used with *near* ⟨*nowhere* near enough⟩

²nowhere *n* : a place that does not exist ⟨sounds seeming to come from *nowhere*⟩

nowhere near *adv* : not nearly

no·wise \'nō-ˌwīz\ *adv* : not at all

nox·ious \'näk-shəs\ *adj* : harmful especially to health : UNWHOLESOME ⟨*noxious* fumes⟩

noz·zle \'näz-əl\ *n* : a short tube that narrows in the middle or toward one end and is often used (as on a hose or pipe) to direct or speed up a flow of fluid

-n't \(°)nt, ənt\ *vb combining form* : not ⟨is*n't*⟩

nth \'en(t)th\ *adj* **1** : numbered with an unspecified or indefinitely large ordinal number ⟨for the *nth* time⟩ **2** : UTMOST 2, EXTREME ⟨to the *nth* degree⟩

nu \'n(y)ü\ *n* : the 13th letter of the Greek alphabet — N or ν

nu·ance \'n(y)ü-ˌän(t)s, n(y)ü-'än(t)s\ *n* : a slight shade or degree of difference (as in color, tone, or meaning)

nub \'nəb\ *n* **1** : KNOB 1a, LUMP **2** : the main point of a matter ⟨the *nub* of the story⟩

nub·bin \'nəb-ən\ *n* **1** : a small or imperfect ear of corn; *also* : any small shriveled or undeveloped fruit **2** : a small part or bit

nub·ble \'nəb-əl\ *n* : a small knob or lump — **nub·bly** \-(ə-)lē\ *adj*

nub·by \'nəb-ē\ *adj* **nub·bi·er; -est** : having small knobs or lumps ⟨a *nubby* knit fabric⟩

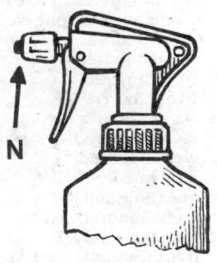

N nozzle

\ə\ abut	\aù\ out	\i\ tip	\ò\ saw	\ù\ foot
\ər\ further	\ch\ chin	\ī\ life	\òi\ coin	\y\ yet
\a\ mat	\e\ pet	\j\ job	\th\ thin	\yü\ few
\ā\ take	\ē\ easy	\ŋ\ sing	\th\ this	\yù\ cure
\ä\ cot, cart	\g\ go	\ō\ bone	\ü\ food	\zh\ vision

TABLE OF NUMBERS

CARDINAL NUMBERS[1]				ORDINAL NUMBERS[4]	
NAME[2]	SYMBOL			NAME[5]	SYMBOL[6]
	Arabic	Roman[3]			
zero or naught or cipher	0				
one	1	I		first	1st
two	2	II		second	2d or 2nd
three	3	III		third	3d or 3rd
four	4	IV		fourth	4th
five	5	V		fifth	5th
six	6	VI		sixth	6th
seven	7	VII		seventh	7th
eight	8	VIII		eighth	8th
nine	9	IX		ninth	9th
ten	10	X		tenth	10th
eleven	11	XI		eleventh	11th
twelve	12	XII		twelfth	12th
thirteen	13	XIII		thirteenth	13th
fourteen	14	XIV		fourteenth	14th
fifteen	15	XV		fifteenth	15th
sixteen	16	XVI		sixteenth	16th
seventeen	17	XVII		seventeenth	17th
eighteen	18	XVIII		eighteenth	18th
nineteen	19	XIX		nineteenth	19th
twenty	20	XX		twentieth	20th
twenty-one	21	XXI		twenty-first	21st
twenty-two	22	XXII		twenty-second	22d or 22nd
twenty-three	23	XXIII		twenty-third	23d or 23rd
twenty-four	24	XXIV		twenty-fourth	24th
twenty-five	25	XXV		twenty-fifth	25th
twenty-six	26	XXVI		twenty-sixth	26th
twenty-seven	27	XXVII		twenty-seventh	27th
twenty-eight	28	XXVIII		twenty-eighth	28th
twenty-nine	29	XXIX		twenty-ninth	29th
thirty	30	XXX		thirtieth	30th
thirty-one etc	31	XXXI		thirty-first etc	31st
forty	40	XL		fortieth	40th
fifty	50	L		fiftieth	50th
sixty	60	LX		sixtieth	60th
seventy	70	LXX		seventieth	70th
eighty	80	LXXX		eightieth	80th
ninety	90	XC		ninetieth	90th
one hundred	100	C		hundredth or one hundredth	100th
one hundred and one or one hundred one etc	101	CI		hundred and first or one hundred and first etc	101st
two hundred	200	CC		two hundredth	200th
three hundred	300	CCC		three hundredth	300th
four hundred	400	CD		four hundredth	400th
five hundred	500	D		five hundredth	500th
six hundred	600	DC		six hundredth	600th
seven hundred	700	DCC		seven hundredth	700th
eight hundred	800	DCCC		eight hundredth	800th
nine hundred	900	CM		nine hundredth	900th
one thousand or ten hundred etc	1,000	M		thousandth or one thousandth	1,000th
two thousand etc	2,000	MM		two thousandth etc	2,000th
five thousand	5,000	$\overline{\text{V}}$		five thousandth	5,000th
ten thousand	10,000	$\overline{\text{X}}$		ten thousandth	10,000th
one hundred thousand	100,000	$\overline{\text{C}}$		hundred thousandth or one hundred thousandth	100,000th
one million	1,000,000	$\overline{\text{M}}$		millionth or one millionth	1,000,000th

[1] The cardinal numbers are used in simple counting or in answer to "how many?" The words for these numbers may be used as nouns (he counted to *twelve*), as pronouns (*twelve* were found), or as adjectives (*twelve* girls).

[2] In formal writing the numbers one to one hundred and in less formal writing the numbers one to nine are commonly written out in words, while larger numbers are given in numerals. A number occurring at the beginning of a sentence is usually written out. Except in very formal writing numerals are used for dates. Arabic numbers from 1,000 to 9,999 are often written without commas (1000 to 9999). Year numbers are always written without commas (1783).

[3] The Roman numerals are written either in capitals or in lowercase letters.

[4] The ordinal numbers are used to show the order in which such items as names, objects, and periods of time are considered (the *twelfth* month; the *fourth* row of seats; the *18th* century).

[5] Each of the terms for the ordinal numbers except *first* and *second* is used for one of a number of parts into which a whole may be divided (a *fourth*; a *sixth*; a *tenth*) and as the denominator in fractions (*one fourth*; *three fifths*). When used as nouns the fractions are usually written as two words, although they are usually hyphenated as adjectives (a *two-thirds* majority). When fractions are written in numerals, the cardinal symbols are used (¼, ⅗, ⅚).

[6] The Arabic symbols for the cardinal numbers may sometimes be read as ordinals (January 1 = January first; 2 Samuel = Second Samuel). The Roman numerals are sometimes read as ordinals (Henry IV = Henry the Fourth); sometimes they are written with the ordinal suffixes (XIXth Dynasty).

DENOMINATIONS ABOVE ONE MILLION

American system[1]				British system[1]			
NAME	VALUE IN POWERS OF TEN	NUMBER OF ZEROS[2]	NUMBER OF GROUPS OF THREE 0'S AFTER 1,000	NAME	VALUE IN POWERS OF TEN	NUMBER OF ZEROS[2]	POWERS OF 1,000,000
billion	10^9	9	2	milliard	10^9	9	—
trillion	10^{12}	12	3	billion	10^{12}	12	2
quadrillion	10^{15}	15	4	trillion	10^{18}	18	3
quintillion	10^{18}	18	5	quadrillion	10^{24}	24	4
sextillion	10^{21}	21	6	quintillion	10^{30}	30	5
septillion	10^{24}	24	7	sextillion	10^{36}	36	6
octillion	10^{27}	27	8	septillion	10^{42}	42	7
nonillion	10^{30}	30	9	octillion	10^{48}	48	8
decillion	10^{33}	33	10	nonillion	10^{54}	54	9
				decillion	10^{60}	60	10

[1] The American system for numbers above one million was modeled on the French system but more recently the French system has been changed to correspond to the German and British systems. In the American system each of the denominations above 1,000 millions (the American *billion*) is 1,000 times greater than the one before (one trillion = 1,000 billions; one quadrillion = 1,000 trillions). In the British system the first denomination above 1,000 millions (the British *milliard*) is 1,000 times the preceding one, but each of the denominations above 1,000 milliards (the British *billion*) is 1,000,000 times the preceding one (one trillion = 1,000,000 billions; one quadrillion = 1,000,000 trillions). In recent years, however, British usage reflects increasing use of the American system in place of the British system.

[2] For ease in reading large numerals, the thousands, millions, and larger denominations are usually separated by commas (21,530; 1,155,465) or especially in technical writing by spaces (1 155 465). Serial numbers (as social security numbers) are often written with hyphens (042-24-4705).

---

nu·cle·ar \'n(y)ü-klē-ər\ *adj* **1** : of, relating to, or being a nucleus (as of a cell) **2** : of, relating to, or using the atomic nucleus ⟨*nuclear* reactions⟩ **3** : being or relating to energy or a weapon that involves a nuclear reaction ⟨*nuclear* energy⟩ ⟨a *nuclear* war⟩ ⟨*nuclear* power plants⟩

nuclear family *n* : a family group that consists only of father, mother, and children

nuclear membrane *n* : a double membrane enclosing a cell nucleus — called also *nuclear envelope*

nu·cle·ic acid \n(y)ü-ˌklā-ik-, -ˌklē-\ *n* : any of various acids (as DNA or RNA) composed of a chain of nucleotides and found especially in cell nuclei

nu·cle·o·lus \n(y)ü-'klē-ə-ləs\ *n, pl* **nu·cle·o·li** \-ˌlī\ : a sphere-shaped body in the cell nucleus that is associated with a particular part of a chromosome, and is rich in ribosomal RNA

nu·cleo·plasm \'n(y)ü-klē-ə-ˌplaz-əm\ *n* : the fluidlike substance in the nucleus of a cell in which the nucleolus and chromatin are suspended

nu·cle·o·tide \'n(y)ü-klē-ə-ˌtīd\ *n* : any of the basic units of structure of DNA or RNA that consist of a base (as adenine, cytosine, guanine, or thymine) joined to a sugar (as deoxyribose) with five carbon atoms in a molecule and to a phosphate group

nu·cle·us \'n(y)ü-klē-əs\ *n, pl* **nu·clei** \-klē-ˌī\ *also* **-cle·us·es** : a central point, group, or mass of something: as **a** : the small, brighter, and denser part of a galaxy or of the head of a comet **b** : a cell part that is characteristic of all living things with the exception of viruses, bacteria, and blue-green algae, that is necessary for heredity and for making proteins, that contains the chromosomes, and that is enclosed in a nuclear membrane **c** : a mass of gray matter or group of neurons in the central nervous system **d** : the central part of an atom that includes nearly all of the atomic mass and consists of protons and usually neutrons [from modern Latin *nucleus* "the central part of something," from Latin *nucleus* "kernel," derived from *nux* "nut"]

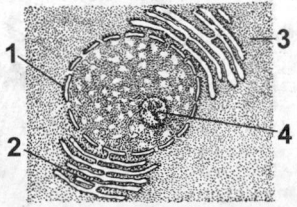

nucleus b: *1* nuclear membrane, *2* endoplasmic reticulum, *3* cytoplasm, *4* nucleolus

nu·clide \'n(y)ü-ˌklīd\ *n* : a kind of atom marked by the number of protons and neutrons and by the amount of energy contained in its nucleus

¹nude \'n(y)üd\ *adj* **nud·er; nud·est** : having no clothes on — **nude·ness** *n*

²nude *n* **1** : a nude human figure especially as shown in art **2** : the condition of being nude ⟨in the *nude*⟩

nudge \'nəj\ *vb* **nudged; nudg·ing** : to touch or push gently; *esp* : to attract the attention of by a push of the elbow — **nudge** *n*

nud·ism \'n(y)üd-ˌiz-əm\ *n* : the practice of going nude especially in private places (as beaches) that are separated from public areas — **nud·ist** \'n(y)üd-əst\ *n or adj*

nu·di·ty \'n(y)üd-ət-ē\ *n* : the quality or state of being nude

nug·get \'nəg-ət\ *n* : a solid lump especially of precious metal

nui·sance \'n(y)üs-ᵊn(t)s\ *n* : an annoying or troublesome person, thing, or way of doing something

null \'nəl\ *adj* **1** : having no legal or binding force : IN-VALID **2** : having no value : INSIGNIFICANT **3** : having no elements ⟨the *null* set⟩

null and void *adj* : having no force, binding power, or validity

nul·li·fi·ca·tion \ˌnəl-ə-fə-'kā-shən\ *n* **1** : the act of nullifying : the state of being nullified **2** : the action of a state blocking or attempting to prevent the enforcement within its territory of a federal law of the U.S. — **nul·li·fi·ca·tion·ist** \-sh(ə-)nəst\ *n*

nul·li·fy \'nəl-ə-ˌfī\ *vb* **-fied; -fy·ing** : to make null or valueless; *esp* : ANNUL

¹numb \'nəm\ *adj* **1** : lacking in sensation especially from cold or from an anesthetic **2** : lacking in emotion : INDIF-FERENT — **numb·ly** *adv* — **numb·ness** *n*

²numb *vb* : to make or become numb

¹num·ber \'nəm-bər\ *n* **1 a** : the total of persons, things, or units taken together : AMOUNT ⟨the *number* of people in the room⟩ **b** : the possibility of being counted ⟨mosquitoes in swarms beyond *number*⟩ **c** : a total that is not specified : MANY ⟨a *number* of accidents occur on wet roads⟩ **2 a** : a unit belonging to a mathematical system

\ə\ **abut**	\au̇\ **out**	\i\ **tip**	\ȯ\ **saw**	\u̇\ **foot**
\ər\ **further**	\ch\ **chin**	\ī\ **life**	\ȯi\ **coin**	\y\ **yet**
\a\ **mat**	\e\ **pet**	\j\ **job**	\th\ **thin**	\yü\ **few**
\ā\ **take**	\ē\ **easy**	\ŋ\ **sing**	\th\ **this**	\yu̇\ **cure**
\ä\ **cot, cart**	\g\ **go**	\ō\ **bone**	\ü\ **food**	\zh\ **vision**

and subject to its laws ⟨a *number* divisible by 2⟩ **b** *pl* : ARITHMETIC **3** : a quality of a word form that shows whether the word is singular or plural ⟨a verb agrees in *number* with its subject⟩ **4 a** : a word, symbol, or letter used to represent a mathematical number **b** : a certain numeral for telling one person or thing from another or from others ⟨a phone *number*⟩ **5** : one in a series ⟨the June *number* of a magazine⟩ **6** : a musical, theatrical, or literary selection — **by the numbers 1** : all together in time to a specific count or cadence **2** : in a manner lacking freshness and individuality

☞ The Table of Numbers is on page 540.

²number *vb* **num·bered; num·ber·ing** \-b(ə-)riŋ\ **1** : ¹COUNT 1a, ENUMERATE **2** : to claim as part of a total : INCLUDE ⟨was *numbered* among the guests⟩ **3** : to restrict to a definite number ⟨vacation days are *numbered* now⟩ **4** : to assign a number to ⟨*number* the pages of a scrapbook⟩ **5** : to add up to or have a total of ⟨our group *numbered* ten in all⟩ — **num·ber·er** \-bər-ər\ *n*

number crunch·er \-ˈkrən-chər\ *n* **1** : a computer that performs fast numerical calculations especially on large amounts of data **2** : a person concerned with complex numerical data — **number crunching** *n*

num·ber·less \ˈnəm-bər-ləs\ *adj* : too many to count : INNUMERABLE ⟨the *numberless* stars in the sky⟩

number line *n* : a line without ends whose points are matched to the real numbers by their distance from a given point labeled zero

Num·bers \ˈnəm-bərz\ *n* — see BIBLE table

numbskull *variant of* NUMSKULL

nu·mer·al \ˈn(y)üm-(ə-)rəl\ *n* **1** : a symbol or group of symbols representing a number **2** *pl* : numbers that designate by year a school or college class and that are awarded for distinction (as in sports)

nu·mer·ate \ˈn(y)ü-mə-ˌrāt\ *vb* **-at·ed; -at·ing** : ENUMERATE

nu·mer·a·tion \ˌn(y)ü-mə-ˈrā-shən\ *n* **1** : the act or process or a system or instance of counting or naming one by one ⟨a base 10 system of *numeration*⟩ **2** : the act of reading in words numbers expressed by numerals

nu·mer·a·tor \ˈn(y)ü-mə-ˌrāt-ər\ *n* **1** : the part of a fraction that is above the line and signifies the number to be divided by the denominator ⟨3 is the *numerator* of the fraction ³⁄₅⟩ **2** : one that counts something

nu·mer·ic \n(y)ù-ˈmer-ik\ *adj* : NUMERICAL; *esp* : indicating a number or a system of numbers ⟨a *numeric* code⟩

nu·mer·i·cal \n(y)ù-ˈmer-i-kəl\ *adj* **1** : of or relating to numbers **2** : shown in or involving numbers or a number system ⟨*numerical* order⟩ — **nu·mer·i·cal·ly** \-k(ə-)lē\ *adv*

nu·mer·ous \ˈn(y)üm-(ə-)rəs\ *adj* : consisting of great numbers ⟨*numerous* friends⟩ — **nu·mer·ous·ly** *adv*

nu·mis·mat·ics \ˌn(y)ü-məz-ˈmat-iks, -məs\ *n* : the study or collection of coins, paper money, and sometimes related objects (as medals) — **nu·mis·mat·ic** \-ik\ *adj* — **nu·mis·ma·tist** \n(y)ü-ˈmiz-mət-əst\ *n*

num·skull *or* **numb·skull** \ˈnəm-ˌskəl\ *n* : a stupid person

nun \ˈnən\ *n* : a woman belonging to a religious order; *esp* : one living under solemn vows of poverty, chastity, and obedience

nun·cio \ˈnən(t)-sē-ˌō, ˈnün(t)-\ *n, pl* **-ci·os** : a papal representative to a civil government

nun·nery \ˈnən-(ə-)rē\ *n, pl* **-ner·ies** : a convent of nuns

¹nup·tial \ˈnəp-shəl, -chəl\ *adj* **1** : of or relating to marriage or a wedding **2** : typical of the breeding season

²nuptial *n* : WEDDING — usually used in plural

¹nurse \ˈnərs\ *n* **1** : a woman who has the care of a young child **2** : a person skilled or trained in caring for the sick and in maintaining good health in those who are not sick and who works either independently or under the supervision of a physician **3** : a worker of a social insect (as an ant or bee) that cares for the young

²nurse *vb* **nursed; nurs·ing 1** : to feed at the breast : SUCKLE **2** : ¹REAR 3b, EDUCATE **3** : to manage with care or economy ⟨*nursed* the business through hard times⟩ **4** : to care for and wait on (as a young child or sick person) ⟨*nursed* me back to health⟩ **5** : to hold in one's memory ⟨*nurse* a grudge⟩ **6** : to treat with special care ⟨*nursed* the car over the rough road⟩ — **nurs·er** *n*

nurse·maid \ˈnər-ˌsmād\ *n* : a girl or woman employed to look after children

nurs·ery \ˈnərs-(ə-)rē\ *n, pl* **-er·ies 1 a** : a child's bedroom **b** : a place where children are temporarily cared for in their parents' absence **2** : a place where plants (as trees or shrubs) are grown for transplanting, for use as stocks in grafting, or for sale

nurs·ery·man \-mən\ *n* : a person who keeps or works in a plant nursery

nursery rhyme *n* : a short rhyme for children that often tells a story

nursery school *n* : a school for children usually under five years of age

nurse's aide *n* : a worker who assists trained nurses in a hospital by performing unspecialized services (as giving baths)

nurse shark *n* : a shark of warm waters that is active at night

nursing bottle *n* : ¹BOTTLE 3

nursing home *n* : a privately operated establishment where personal or nursing care is provided for persons (as the aged) who are unable to care for themselves properly

nurs·ling \ˈnər-sliŋ\ *n* **1** : one that is tended with special care **2** : a nursing child

nur·tur·ance \ˈnər-chə-rən(t)s\ *n* : affectionate care and attention — **nur·tur·ant** \-rənt\ *adj*

¹nur·ture \ˈnər-chər\ *n* **1** : TRAINING 1, UPBRINGING **2** : something that nourishes : FOOD

²nurture *vb* **nur·tured; nur·tur·ing** \ˈnərch-(ə-)riŋ\ **1** : to supply with nourishment **2** : EDUCATE 2 **3** : to further the development of : FOSTER

nut \ˈnət\ *n* **1 a** : a hard-shelled dry fruit (as a peanut in the shell) or seed (as a Brazil nut) with an inner kernel; *also* : this kernel **b** : a dry one-seeded fruit (as an acorn, hazelnut, or chestnut) that has a woody outer layer and does not break open when it is ripe **2** : a block of metal with a hole in it that is fastened to a bolt or screw by means of a screw thread within the hole **3** : the ridge on the upper end of the fingerboard of a stringed instrument over which the strings pass **4 a** : a foolish, odd, or crazy person **b** : ENTHUSIAST ⟨a movie *nut*⟩ [Old English *hnutu* "nut"]

nut·crack·er \ˈnət-ˌkrak-ər\ *n* : a device for cracking the shells of nuts

nut·hatch \ˈnət-ˌhach\ *n* : any of various small birds that climb trees and eat insects and are noted for their habit of going down tree trunks headfirst

nut·let \ˈnət-lət\ *n* : a small nut; *also* : a small fruit similar to a nut

nut·meg \ˈnət-ˌmeg\ *n* : a spice that consists of the ground seeds of a small tropical evergreen tree grown especially in Indonesia; *also* : the seed or tree

nuthatch

nu·tria \ˈn(y)ü-trē-ə\ *n* : a South American rodent that lives in or near water, has webbed feet and a nearly hairless tail, and has been introduced into the U.S. along the Gulf Coast and in the Pacific Northwest — called also *coypu*

¹nu·tri·ent \'n(y)ü-trē-ənt\ *adj* : furnishing nourishment

²nutrient *n* : a nutrient substance or ingredient

nu·tri·ment \'n(y)ü-trə-mənt\ *n* : something that nourishes

nu·tri·tion \n(y)ù-'trish-ən\ *n* 1 : the act or process of nourishing or being nourished; *esp* : the processes by which an animal or plant takes in and makes use of food substances 2 : NOURISHMENT 1

nu·tri·tion·al \n(y)ù-'trish-nəl, -ən-ᵊl\ *adj* : of or relating to nutrition — **nu·tri·tion·al·ly** \-ē\ *adv*

nu·tri·tion·ist \-'trish-(ə-)nist\ *n* : a specialist in the study of nutrition

nu·tri·tious \n(y)ù-'trish-əs\ *adj* : providing nutrients : NOURISHING

nu·tri·tive \'n(y)ü-trət-iv\ *adj* 1 : of or relating to nutrition 2 : NUTRITIOUS

nuts \'nəts\ *adj* 1 : ENTHUSIASTIC, KEEN ⟨was *nuts* about baseball⟩ 2 : CRAZY 1

nut·shell \'nət-ˌshel\ *n* : the shell of a nut — **in a nutshell** : in a very brief statement

nut·ty \'nət-ē\ *adj* **nut·ti·er; -est** 1 : containing or suggesting nuts (as in flavor) 2 : not showing good sense; *also* : mentally unbalanced — **nut·ti·ness** *n*

nuz·zle \'nəz-əl\ *vb* **nuz·zled; nuz·zling** \-(ə-)liŋ\ 1 : to push or rub with the nose 2 : to lie close : NESTLE

ny·lon \'nī-ˌlän\ *n* 1 : any of numerous strong tough elastic synthetic materials used especially in textiles and plastics 2 *pl* : stockings made of nylon [coined from meaningless word elements] — **nylon** *adj*

nymph \'nim(p)f\ *n* 1 : one of many goddesses in old legends represented as beautiful young girls living in mountains, forests, meadows, and waters 2 : any of various immature insects; *esp* : an immature insect (as a dragonfly or grasshopper) that differs from the adult chiefly in the size of the body and in its incompletely developed wings

O

o \'ō\ *n, often cap* 1 : the 15th letter of the English alphabet 2 : ¹ZERO 1

o' *also* \ə\ *prep* : OF ⟨one *o*'clock⟩

O *variant of* ¹OH

oaf \'ōf\ *n* : a stupid or awkward person [derived from *auf, alfe* "goblin's child," probably from Middle English *alven, elven* "elf, fairy," from Old English *elfen* "nymphs"] — **oaf·ish** \'ō-fish\ *adj* — **oaf·ish·ness** *n*

oak \'ōk\ *n, pl* **oaks** *or* **oak** 1 : any of various trees or shrubs closely related to the beeches and chestnuts and producing acorns 2 : the tough hard wood of the oak much used for furniture and flooring — **oak·en** \'ō-kən\ *adj*

oa·kum \'ō-kəm\ *n* : hemp or jute fiber soaked with tar or something like tar and used in caulking seams (as of wooden ships) and packing joints (as of pipes)

¹oar \'ō(ə)r, 'ȯ(ə)r\ *n* 1 : a long pole with a broad blade at one end used for rowing or steering a boat 2 : OARSMAN — **oared** \'ō(ə)rd, 'ȯ(ə)rd\ *adj*

²oar *vb* : ¹ROW 1

oar·lock \'ō(ə)r-ˌläk, 'ȯ(ə)r-\ *n* : a usually U-shaped device for holding an oar in place

oars·man \'ō(ə)rz-mən, 'ȯ(ə)rz-\ *n* : a person who rows especially in a racing crew

oa·sis \ō-'ā-səs\ *n, pl* **oa·ses** \-'ā-ˌsēz\ 1 : a fertile or green spot in a desert 2 : something or some place that provides refreshing relief

oat \'ōt\ *n* : a grain that is widely grown for its long loose clusters of seeds which are used for human food and for livestock feed — **oat·en** \'ōt-ᵊn\ *adj*

oath \'ōth\ *n, pl* **oaths** \'ōt͟hz, 'ōths\ 1 : a solemn appeal to God or to some deeply respected person or thing to witness to the truth of one's word or the sincerity of a promise ⟨under *oath* to tell the truth⟩ 2 : a careless or improper use of a sacred name; *also* : SWEARWORD

oat·meal \'ōt-ˌmēl, ōt-'mē(ə)l\ *n* 1 : oats husked and ground into meal or flattened into flakes 2 : a hot cereal made from oatmeal

Oba·di·ah \ˌō-bə-'dī-ə\ *n* — see BIBLE

¹ob·bli·ga·to \ˌäb-lə-'gät-ō\ *adj* : not to be left out — used as a direction in music

²obbligato *n, pl* **-tos** *also* **-ti** \-ē\ : an important melodic part usually played by a single instrument to accompany another instrument or a singer ⟨a violin *obbligato*⟩

ob·du·ra·cy \'äb-d(y)ə-rə-sē, äb-'d(y)ùr-ə-\ *n, pl* **-cies** : the quality or state of being obdurate

ob·du·rate \'äb-d(y)ə-rət, äb-'d(y)ùr-ət\ *adj* 1 a : stubbornly continuing to do wrong b : hardened in feelings 2 : hard to convince or persuade : UNYIELDING — **ob·du·rate·ly** *adv*

obe·di·ence \ō-'bēd-ē-ən(t)s, ə-\ *n* 1 : an act or instance of obeying 2 : the quality or state of being obedient

obe·di·ent \ō-'bēd-ē-ənt, ə-\ *adj* : willing to obey — **obe·di·ent·ly** *adv*

obei·sance \ō-'bēs-ᵊn(t)s, -'bās-\ *n* : a movement of the body (as a bow) made as a sign of respect

obe·lia \ō-'bēl-yə\ *n* : any of a genus of small marine hydroids that form colonies branched like trees

obe·lisk \'äb-ə-ˌlisk\ *n* : a four-sided pillar that becomes narrower toward the top and ends in a pyramid

obese \ō-'bēs\ *adj* : very fat — **obe·si·ty** \ō-'bē-sət-ē\ *n*

obey \ō-'bā, ə-\ *vb* **obeyed; obeying** 1 a : to follow the commands or guidance of ⟨*obeyed* her parents⟩ b : to be obedient ⟨trained the dog to *obey*⟩ 2 : to act in agreement with : CARRY OUT ⟨*obey* an order⟩ ⟨*obey* the rules⟩

obi \'ō-bē\ *n* : a broad sash worn with a Japanese kimono

obit·u·ary \ə-'bich-ə-ˌwer-ē\ *n, pl* **-ar·ies** : a notice of a person's death (as in a newspaper) — **obituary** *adj*

¹ob·ject \'äb-jikt\ *n* 1 : something that can be perceived by the senses ⟨I see an *object* in the distance⟩ 2 : something that is the target of thought or feeling ⟨an *object* of study⟩ ⟨the *ob-*

oat

obelisk

\ə\ abut	\aù\ out	\i\ tip	\ȯ\ saw	\ù\ foot
\ər\ further	\ch\ chin	\ī\ life	\ȯi\ coin	\y\ yet
\a\ mat	\e\ pet	\j\ job	\th\ thin	\yü\ few
\ā\ take	\ē\ easy	\ŋ\ sing	\t͟h\ this	\yù\ cure
\ä\ cot, cart	\g\ go	\ō\ bone	\ü\ food	\zh\ vision

ject of my affections⟩ **3** : the goal or purpose of some activity ⟨the *object* is to raise money⟩ **4** : a noun or term behaving like a noun that receives the action of a verb or completes the meaning of a preposition **5** : something (as an icon or window) on a computer screen that can be moved or used by itself — **ob·ject·less** \'äb-jik-tləs\ *adj*

²**ob·ject** \əb-'jekt\ *vb* **1** : to offer or mention as an objection ⟨*objected* that the price was too high⟩ **2** : to oppose something firmly usually with words ⟨*objected* to the plan⟩ — **ob·jec·tor** \-'jek-tər\ *n*

object ball \'äb-jik(t)-\ *n* : the ball first struck by the cue ball in pool or billiards

ob·jec·tion \əb-'jek-shən\ *n* **1** : an act of objecting **2** : a reason for or a feeling of disapproval ⟨my *objection* is this⟩ ⟨had *objections* to the plan⟩

ob·jec·tion·able \əb-'jek-sh(ə-)nə-bəl\ *adj* : arousing objection : OFFENSIVE ⟨uses *objectionable* language⟩ — **ob·jec·tion·ably** \-blē\ *adv*

¹**ob·jec·tive** \əb-'jek-tiv\ *adj* **1** : being outside of the mind and independent of it ⟨*objective* reality⟩ **2** : being or belonging to the case of a noun or pronoun that is an object of a transitive verb or a preposition **3** : dealing with facts without letting one's feelings interfere with them ⟨an *objective* judgment⟩ — **ob·jec·tive·ly** *adv* — **ob·jec·tiv·i·ty** \(,)äb-jek-'tiv-ət-ē, əb-\ *n*

²**objective** *n* **1** : a lens or system of lenses (as in a microscope) that forms an image of an object **2** : a goal or end of action *synonyms* see INTENTION

object lesson \'äb-jikt-\ *n* : a real example of how some general idea or role works

ob·jet d'art \,ȯb-,zhä-'där\ *n, pl* **ob·jets d'art** \,ȯb-,zhä-'där\ : an article of artistic value

ob·li·gate \'äb-lə-,gāt\ *vb* **-gat·ed; -gat·ing** : to make (someone) do something by law or because it is right

ob·li·ga·tion \,äb-lə-'gā-shən\ *n* **1** : an act of making oneself responsible for doing something **2 a** : something (as a promise or contract) that requires one to do something **b** : something one must do : DUTY **3** : a feeling of being indebted for an act of kindness

oblig·a·to·ry \ə-'blig-ə-,tȯr-ē, -,tȯr- *also* 'äb-li-gə-\ *adj* : not to be left out, forgotten, or ignored : being required

oblige \ə-'blīj\ *vb* **obliged; oblig·ing** **1** : to compel by pressure : ²FORCE 1 ⟨the soldiers were *obliged* to retreat⟩ **2 a** : to earn the gratitude of ⟨you will *oblige* me by coming early⟩ **b** : to do a favor for or do something as a favor ⟨glad to *oblige*⟩ — **oblig·er** *n*

oblig·ing \ə-'blī-jiŋ\ *adj* : willing to do favors — **oblig·ing·ly** *adv*

oblique \ō-'blēk, ə-, -'blīk\ *adj* **1** : having a slanting direction or position : neither perpendicular nor parallel **2** : having the axis not perpendicular to the base ⟨an *oblique* cone⟩ **3** : having no right angle ⟨an *oblique* triangle⟩ **4 a** : not straightforward or direct **b** : DEVIOUS — **oblique·ly** *adv* — **oblique·ness** *n*

oblique angle *n* : an acute or obtuse angle

oblit·er·ate \ə-'blit-ə-,rāt, ō-\ *vb* **-at·ed; -at·ing** : to remove or destroy completely : WIPE OUT — **oblit·er·a·tion** \-,blit-ə-'rā-shən\ *n*

obliv·i·on \ə-'bliv-ē-ən, ō-, ä-\ *n* **1** : the state of forgetting or having forgotten or of being unaware or unconscious **2** : the state of being forgotten

obliv·i·ous \ə-'bliv-ē-əs, ō-, ä-\ *adj* : not being conscious or aware ⟨*oblivious* to the danger⟩ ⟨*oblivious* of the crowd⟩ — **obliv·i·ous·ly** *adv* — **obliv·i·ous·ness** *n*

¹**ob·long** \'äb-,lȯŋ\ *adj* : longer in one direction than in the other ⟨an *oblong* shoe box⟩ ⟨an *oblong* watermelon⟩

²**oblong** *n* : an oblong figure or object

ob·nox·ious \äb-'näk-shəs, əb-\ *adj* : very disagreeable or offensive — **ob·nox·ious·ly** *adv* — **ob·nox·ious·ness** *n*

oboe \'ō-bō\ *n* : a musical instrument in the form of a slender tube that has a distinctive bright sound and that is played by blowing into a mouthpiece holding two reeds — **obo·ist** \'ō-,bō-əst\ *n*

oboe

Word History The musical instrument we now call an *oboe* was developed in France in the 17th century. The French called it a *hautbois*, a word pronounced something like English "o boy" and made up of *haut*, meaning "high," and *bois*, meaning "wood." The *hautbois* was the highest pitched member of a group of woodwind instruments played with a reed. For a time the English simply used the French word for the instrument. Sometimes they spelled it *hautbois*, sometimes *hautboy*, and sometimes they changed the spelling to *oboy* or *hoboy*. Meanwhile, the Italians took the French word as *oboe*, a spelling closer to the way they pronounced it. In the 18th century it became fashionable in England to prefer Italian musical terms. The English then started using the form *oboe* instead of *hautbois*, and so *oboe* is the form we use today. [from Italian *oboe* "oboe," from French *hautbois* (same meaning), from *haut* "high" and *bois* "wood"]

ob·scene \äb-'sēn, əb-\ *adj* **1** : REPULSIVE, DISGUSTING **2** : very shocking to one's sense of what is moral or decent — **ob·scene·ly** *adv*

ob·scen·i·ty \äb-'sen-ət-ē, əb-\ *n, pl* **-ties** **1** : the quality or state of being obscene **2** : something that is obscene

¹**ob·scure** \äb-'skyu̇(ə)r, əb-\ *adj* **1 a** : not having enough light : DARK, GLOOMY **b** : not clearly seen : FAINT ⟨*obscure* markings⟩ **2** : not easily understood or not clearly expressed ⟨an *obscure* passage⟩ **3 a** : hidden from view : REMOTE ⟨an *obscure* village⟩ **b** : not widely known ⟨an *obscure* poet⟩ — **ob·scure·ly** *adv*

²**obscure** *vb* **ob·scured; ob·scur·ing** : to make obscure

ob·scu·ri·ty \äb-'skyu̇r-ət-ē, əb-\ *n, pl* **-ties** **1** : something that is obscure **2** : the quality or state of being obscure

ob·se·qui·ous \əb-'sē-kwē-əs, äb-\ *adj* : ready or prompt to help or obey like a servant or slave at the wish or command of another person especially to gain favor

ob·serv·able \əb-'zər-və-bəl\ *adj* : able to be observed : NOTICEABLE — **ob·serv·ably** \-blē\ *adv*

ob·ser·vance \əb-'zər-vən(t)s\ *n* **1** : an established practice or ceremony ⟨religious *observances*⟩ **2** : an act of following a custom, rule, or law **3** : an act or instance of watching

ob·ser·vant \əb-'zər-vənt\ *adj* **1** : paying careful attention : WATCHFUL **2** : quick to observe : KEEN **3** : careful in observing : MINDFUL — **ob·ser·vant·ly** *adv*

ob·ser·va·tion \,äb-sər-'vā-shən, -zər-\ *n* **1** : an act or instance of observing a custom, rule, or law **2** : an act or the power of seeing or fixing the mind upon something **3** : an act of gathering information (as for scientific studies) by noting facts or occurrences ⟨weather *observations*⟩ **4** : an opinion formed or expressed after observing **5** : the state of being observed ⟨was in the hospital for *observation*⟩ *synonyms* see REMARK — **ob·ser·va·tion·al** \-shnəl, -shən-³l\ *adj*

ob·ser·va·to·ry \əb-'zər-və-,tȯr-ē, -,tȯr-\ *n, pl* **-ries** **1** : a place or institution equipped with instruments for observation of natural objects and events (as in astronomy) **2** : a place providing a wide view

ob·serve \əb-'zərv\ *vb* **ob·served; ob·serv·ing** **1** : to act in agreement with : OBEY ⟨*observe* the law⟩ **2** : to celebrate or honor (as a holiday) with special events or customs **3 a** : to watch carefully ⟨*observed* how the food was prepared⟩ **b** : to make a scientific observation of ⟨*observe* an eclipse⟩ **4** : to come to understand or know especially by thinking about facts that have been noted ⟨I have *observed* that it happens more often on Tuesdays⟩ **5** : to say as a remark ⟨*observed* that it was a fine day and we agreed⟩ **synonyms** see KEEP — **ob·serv·er** *n*

ob·sess \əb-'ses, äb-\ *vb* : to occupy the mind of completely or abnormally ⟨*obsessed* with this new scheme⟩

ob·ses·sion \äb-'sesh-ən, əb-\ *n* : a disturbing concern with an idea or feeling that cannot be put out of mind even when it is seen to be unreasonable; *also* : such a thought or feeling

ob·ses·sive \äb-'ses-iv, əb-\ *adj* : of, relating to, having, or being an obsession — **ob·ses·sive·ly** *adv*

ob·sid·i·an \əb-'sid-ē-ən\ *n* : a dark natural glass formed by the cooling of lava

ob·so·les·cence \,äb-sə-'les-ᵊn(t)s\ *n* : the process of becoming obsolete or the state of being nearly obsolete

ob·so·les·cent \,äb-sə-'les-ᵊnt\ *adj* : going out of use : becoming obsolete ⟨replacing *obsolescent* equipment⟩

ob·so·lete \,äb-sə-'lēt, 'äb-sə-,lēt\ *adj* **1** : no longer in use ⟨an *obsolete* word⟩ **2** : of a kind or style no longer current : OUTMODED ⟨*obsolete* machinery⟩ — **ob·so·lete·ly** *adv* — **ob·so·lete·ness** *n*

ob·sta·cle \'äb-sti-kəl\ *n* : something that stands in the way of progress or achievement : HINDRANCE ⟨drove around the *obstacles* in the road⟩ ⟨didn't let shortness be an *obstacle* to a basketball career⟩

ob·stet·ric \əb-'ste-trik, äb-\ *or* **ob·stet·ri·cal** \-tri-kəl\ *adj* : of or relating to childbirth or obstetrics

ob·ste·tri·cian \,äb-stə-'trish-ən\ *n* : a physician specializing in obstetrics

ob·stet·rics \əb-'ste-triks, äb-\ *n* : a branch of medical science that deals with childbirth and with the care of women before, during, and after childbirth

ob·sti·na·cy \'äb-stə-nə-sē\ *n* : the quality or state of being obstinate

ob·sti·nate \'äb-stə-nət\ *adj* **1** : sticking to an opinion, purpose, or course in spite of reason, arguments, or persuasion **2** : not easily overcome or removed ⟨an *obstinate* fever⟩ — **ob·sti·nate·ly** *adv*

synonyms OBSTINATE, DOGGED, STUBBORN mean unwilling to change course or give up one's intention. OBSTINATE suggests that one sticks to a course of action to the point of being unreasonable ⟨an *obstinate* player who would not pass the ball⟩. DOGGED suggests that one goes after something and never tires or quits ⟨a *dogged* reporter determined to get the real story⟩. STUBBORN suggests that one has a fixed mind and opposes all attempts to change it ⟨too *stubborn* to admit the mistake⟩.

ob·strep·er·ous \əb-'strep-(ə-)rəs, äb-\ *adj* : noisy and hard to control — **ob·strep·er·ous·ly** *adv* — **ob·strep·er·ous·ness** *n*

ob·struct \əb-'strəkt, äb-\ *vb* **1** : to close up by an obstacle ⟨a fallen tree *obstructed* the roadway⟩ **2** : to be or get in the way of : HINDER ⟨lying to the police *obstructs* justice⟩

ob·struc·tion \əb-'strək-shən, äb-\ *n* **1** : an act of obstructing : the state of being obstructed **2** : something that gets in the way : OBSTACLE

ob·struc·tion·ism \əb-'strək-shə-,niz-əm, äb-\ *n* : deliberate interference with business especially in a legislative body — **ob·struc·tion·ist** \-sh(ə-)nəst\ *n or adj*

ob·struc·tive \əb-'strək-tiv, äb-\ *adj* : tending or serving to obstruct

ob·tain \əb-'tān, äb-\ *vb* **1** : to gain or acquire usually by planning or effort **2** : to be generally recognized or established : PREVAIL **3b** ⟨good manners *obtained*⟩ **synonyms** see GET — **ob·tain·able** \-'tā-nə-bəl\ *adj*

ob·trude \əb-'trüd, äb-\ *vb* **ob·trud·ed; ob·trud·ing 1** : to stick out ⟨the tortoise *obtruded* its head⟩ **2** : to put forward without being asked ⟨*obtrude* one's views⟩

ob·tru·sive \əb-'trü-siv, äb-, -ziv\ *adj* : likely to obtrude — **ob·tru·sive·ly** *adv* — **ob·tru·sive·ness** *n*

ob·tuse \äb-'t(y)üs\ *adj* **ob·tus·er; -est 1** : not pointed or sharp : BLUNT **2 a** : being between 90° and 180° ⟨an *obtuse* angle⟩ **b** : having an obtuse angle ⟨an *obtuse* triangle⟩ **3** : not quick or keen of understanding or feeling — **ob·tuse·ness** *n*

ob·verse \'äb-,vərs, äb-'vərs\ *n* **1** : the side of something (as a coin) bearing the principal design or lettering **2** : a front or principal surface **3** : COUNTERPART 3

ob·vi·ate \'äb-vē-,āt\ *vb* **-at·ed; -at·ing** : to anticipate and take care of beforehand ⟨*obviate* an objection⟩

ob·vi·ous \'äb-vē-əs\ *adj* : easily found, seen, or understood : PLAIN ⟨an *obvious* mistake⟩ — **ob·vi·ous·ness** *n*

ob·vious·ly \'äb-vē-əs-lē\ *adv* **1** : in an obvious manner ⟨*obviously* enjoys her work⟩ ⟨dealing with an *obviously* difficult subject⟩ **2** : it is obvious ⟨*obviously*, this is only a beginning⟩

oc·a·ri·na \,äk-ə-'rē-nə\ *n* : a simple musical instrument usually having an oval body with finger holes and a projecting mouthpiece and producing soft flutelike tones

¹oc·ca·sion \ə-'kā-zhən\ *n* **1** : a favorable opportunity : a good chance ⟨sorry not to have had *occasion* to meet them⟩ **2** : a situation that provides a reason ⟨an *occasion* for rejoicing⟩ **3** : something that brings about an event ⟨the remark was the *occasion* of a bitter quarrel⟩ **4** : a time at which something happens ⟨on the *occasion* of the wedding⟩ **5** : a need that arises ⟨have *occasion* to travel⟩ **6** : a special event or ceremony : CELEBRATION ⟨a big *occasion*⟩

²occasion *vb* **-sioned; -sion·ing** \-'kāzh-(ə-)niŋ\ : to give occasion to : CAUSE

oc·ca·sion·al \ə-'kāzh-nəl, -ən-ᵊl\ *adj* **1** : of, relating to, or created for a particular occasion ⟨*occasional* verse⟩ **2** : happening, appearing, or met with now and then ⟨an *occasional* visitor⟩

oc·ca·sion·al·ly \-ē\ *adv* : from time to time ⟨*occasionally* goes to the movies⟩

Oc·ci·dent \'äk-səd-ənt, -sə-,dent\ *n* : ³WEST 2 [Middle English *occident* "the West," from early French *occident* (same meaning), from Latin *occident-, occidens* "the West, the part of the world lying in the direction in which the sun sets, the part of the world opposite the Orient," derived from *occidere* "to fall, set behind the horizon," from *oc-, ob-* "toward, over" and *cadere* "to fall"]

oc·ci·den·tal \,äk-sə-'dent-ᵊl\ *adj, often cap* **1** : of, relating to, or located in the Occident : WESTERN **2** : of or relating to Occidentals

Occidental *n* : a person of European ancestry

¹oc·cip·i·tal \äk-'sip-ət-ᵊl\ *adj* : of or relating to the back part of the head or skull or to the occipital bone

²occipital *n* : OCCIPITAL BONE

occipital bone *n* : a compound bone that forms the back part of the skull

Oc·ci·tan \'äk-sə-,tan\ *n* : a Romance language spoken in southern France

oc·clude \ə-'klüd, ä-\ *vb* **oc·clud·ed; oc·clud·ing 1** : to close up or block off **2** : to take up and hold by absorption or adsorption **3** : to come together with opposing surfaces in contact ⟨the teeth do not *occlude* properly⟩

oc·clud·ed front \ə-'klüd-əd-, ä-\ *n* : OCCLUSION 2

\ə\ abut	\aú\ out	\i\ tip	\ò\ saw	\ú\ foot
\ər\ further	\ch\ chin	\ī\ life	\öi\ coin	\y\ yet
\a\ mat	\e\ pet	\j\ job	\th\ thin	\yü\ few
\ā\ take	\ē\ easy	\ŋ\ sing	\th\ this	\yù\ cure
\ä\ cot, cart	\g\ go	\ō\ bone	\ü\ food	\zh\ vision

oc·clu·sion \ə-'klü-zhən\ *n* **1** : the coming together of the surfaces of the upper and lower teeth **2** : the front formed by a cold front overtaking a warm front and lifting the warm air over the cold air

¹oc·cult \ə-'kəlt, ä-\ *vb* : to shut off from view : COVER, ECLIPSE

²oc·cult \ə-'kəlt, ä-; 'äk-əlt\ *adj* **1** : beyond understanding : MYSTERIOUS **2** : of or relating to supernatural forces

³occult \ə-'kəlt, ä-; 'äk-əlt\ *n* : matters thought to involve the influence of supernatural forces

oc·cult·ism \ə-'kəl-‚tiz-əm, ä-; 'äk-‚əl-‚tiz-əm\ *n* : a belief in the action or influence of supernatural powers — **oc·cult·ist** \-'təst\ *n*

oc·cu·pan·cy \'äk-yə-pən-sē\ *n, pl* **-cies** **1** : the act or condition of occupying or taking possession ⟨takes *occupancy* on the first of the month⟩ **2** : the state of being occupied ⟨an *occupancy* limit of 5 persons⟩

oc·cu·pant \'äk-yə-pənt\ *n* : a person who occupies something; *esp* : ²RESIDENT 1

oc·cu·pa·tion \‚äk-yə-'pā-shən\ *n* **1** : one's business or profession **2** : the taking possession and control of an area ⟨*occupation* of a conquered country⟩

oc·cu·pa·tion·al \‚äk-yə-'pā-shnəl, -shən-ᵊl\ *adj* : of or relating to one's occupation ⟨a report on *occupational* health and safety⟩ — **oc·cu·pa·tion·al·ly** \-ē\ *adv*

oc·cu·py \'äk-yə-‚pī\ *vb* **-pied; -py·ing** **1 a** : to take up the attention or energies of ⟨reading *occupied* me most of the summer⟩ **b** : to fill up (space or time) ⟨sports *occupied* most of their spare time⟩ ⟨a liter of water *occupies* 1000 cubic centimeters of space⟩ **2 a** : to take or hold possession of ⟨enemy troops *occupied* the town⟩ **b** : to live in as owner or tenant ⟨*occupy* an apartment⟩ — **oc·cu·pi·er** \-‚pī(-ə)r\ *n*

oc·cur \ə-'kər\ *vb* **oc·curred; oc·cur·ring** \-'kər-iŋ\ **1** : to be found or met with : APPEAR ⟨plants that *occur* in meadows⟩ **2** : to come into existence : HAPPEN ⟨an accident *occurred* on the way to school⟩ ⟨success doesn't just *occur*, it is earned⟩ **3** : to come into the mind ⟨it just *occurred* to me⟩ [from Latin *occurrere* "to be found or met with, appear," literally, "to run up against," from *oc-, ob-* "in the way" and *currere* "to run" — related to CURRENT, INCUR]

oc·cur·rence \ə-'kər-ən(t)s, -'kə-rən(t)s\ *n* **1** : something that occurs **2** : the action or process of occurring **3** : the presence of a natural form or material in a particular place ⟨the *occurrence* of oil in Oklahoma⟩

ocean \'ō-shən\ *n* **1** : the whole body of salt water that covers nearly three fourths of the surface of the earth **2** : one of the large bodies of water into which the ocean is divided — **oce·an·ic** \‚ō-shē-'an-ik\ *adj*

ocean·go·ing \-‚gō-iŋ\ *adj* : made to travel on the ocean ⟨*oceangoing* ships⟩

ocean·og·ra·phy \‚ō-shə-'näg-rə-fē\ *n* : a science that deals with the ocean — **ocean·og·ra·pher** \‚ō-shə-'näg-rə-fər\ *n* — **ocean·o·graph·ic** \-nə-'graf-ik\ *adj* — **ocean·o·graph·i·cal·ly** \-i-k(ə-)lē\ *adv*

oce·lot \'äs-ə-‚lät, 'ō-sə-\ *n* : a medium-sized American wildcat that is found from Texas to northern Argentina and has a tawny yellow or grayish coat marked with black

ocher *or* **ochre** \'ō-kər\ *n* **1** : an earthy usually red or yellow and often impure iron ore used as coloring matter **2** : the color of yellow ocher

o'·clock \ə-'kläk\ *adv* **1** : according to the clock ⟨the time is three *o'clock*⟩ **2** — used for indicating position or direction as if on a clock dial ⟨an airplane approaching at eleven *o'clock*⟩

octa- *or* **octo-** *also* **oct-** *combining form* : eight [derived from Greek *oktō* and Latin *octo*, both meaning "eight"]

oc·ta·gon \'äk-tə-‚gän\ *n* : a polygon with eight angles and eight sides — **oc·tag·o·nal** \äk-'tag-ən-ᵊl\ *adj*

oc·ta·he·dron \‚äk-tə-'hē-drən\ *n, pl* **-drons** *or* **-dra** \-drə\ : a polyhedron that has eight faces

oc·tal \'äk-tᵊl\ *adj* : of, relating to, or being a number system with a base of eight

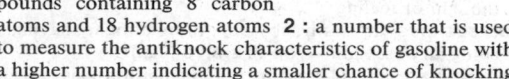
octagon

oc·tane \'äk-‚tān\ *n* **1** : any of several liquid chemical compounds containing 8 carbon atoms and 18 hydrogen atoms **2** : a number that is used to measure the antiknock characteristics of gasoline with a higher number indicating a smaller chance of knocking

oc·tave \'äk-tiv, -təv, -‚tāv\ *n* **1** : a group of eight lines of poetry (as the first eight lines of a sonnet) **2 a** : the difference in pitch between the first and eighth tone on the scale **b** : a tone or note that is eight steps above or below another note or tone **3** : a group of eight

octave 2

oc·ta·vo \äk-'tā-vō, -'tāv-ō\ *n, pl* **-vos** : a book made up of sheets of paper that have been folded to produce eight leaves

oc·tet \äk-'tet\ *n* **1 a** : a piece of music written for eight voices or eight instruments **b** : the performers of an octet **2** : a group or set of eight

oc·til·lion \äk-'til-yən\ *n* — see NUMBER table

Oc·to·ber \äk-'tō-bər\ *n* : the tenth month of the year

Word History According to its origin, the name *October*, which we know as the tenth month of the year, really means "eighth month." In the first calendar used in ancient Rome, the year had only ten months, starting in March and ending in December. The extra period between December and March was not considered part of the series of months. Later, when two extra months were added to the calendar, October became the tenth month but kept its old name. The Latin name came into Old English as *october* and into early French as *octobre*. It was spelled both ways in Middle English. But in time the influence of Latin fixed the spelling as *october*. [Middle English *October, Octobre* "the tenth month," from Old English *October* and early French *octobre* (both, same meaning), both from Latin *October* "the eighth month," from *octo* "eight"]

oc·to·ge·nar·i·an \‚äk-tə-jə-'ner-ē-ən\ *n* : a person whose age is between 80 and 89

oc·to·pus \'äk-tə-pəs\ *n, pl* **-pus·es** *or* **-pi** \-‚pī\ **1** : any of various sea mollusks that are cephalopods having eight muscular arms with two rows of suckers which hold objects (as its prey) **2** : something suggestive of an octopus; *esp* : a powerful grasping organization with many branches [from scientific Latin *Octopod-, Octopus* "octopus," from Greek *oktōpous*, literally, "eight-footed," from *oktō* "eight" and *pous* "foot"]

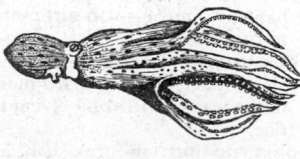
octopus 1

¹oc·u·lar \'äk-yə-lər\ *adj* : of or relating to the eye or to the eyesight

²ocular *n* : EYEPIECE

oc·u·list \'äk-yə-ləst\ *n* **1** : OPHTHALMOLOGIST **2** : OPTOMETRIST

¹OD \(ˈ)ō-ˈdē\ *n* : an overdose of a drug and especially a narcotic

²OD *vb* **OD'd** *or* **ODed** \(ˈ)ō-ˈdēd\; **OD'ing** \(ˈ)ō-ˈdē-iŋ\ : to become ill or die from an OD

odd \ˈäd\ *adj* **1** : being only one of a pair or set ⟨an *odd* shoe⟩ **2** : somewhat more than the number mentioned ⟨50-*odd* years ago⟩ **3 a** : being any number that cannot be divided evenly by 2 ⟨1, 3, 5, and 7 are *odd* numbers⟩ **b** : marked by an odd number ⟨an *odd* year⟩ **4** : additional to or apart from what is usual, expected, or planned on ⟨*odd* jobs⟩ **5** : not usual or traditional : STRANGE ⟨what an *odd* thing to do⟩ — **odd·ness** *n*

 Word History In the early Norse language, the word *oddi* was first used to mean "a point of land." Then, because one corner of a triangle looks something like a point of land sticking out into the sea, *oddi* came to mean "triangle." A triangle that has one long point, like a point of land, may be thought of as having two paired angles and one angle left over. In time, the Norse came to call something that was not matched or paired up "oddi." This was used for an odd number, one left over after all other numbers were paired up. It was also used for an odd man, one who in a voting situation could break a tie with his vote. When the word was taken into English in the Middle Ages, it had the meaning of an odd number like 3, 5, or 7 that cannot be divided evenly by 2. Later it came to mean something that stood out from others as being different or strange. [Middle English *odde* "odd," from an early Norse word *oddi* (noun) "a point of land, triangle, odd number"]

odd·ball \-ˌból\ *n* : a person who behaves strangely

odd·i·ty \ˈäd-ət-ē\ *n, pl* **-ties 1** : something odd **2** : the quality or state of being odd

odd·ly \ˈäd-lē\ *adv* **1** : in an odd manner ⟨was behaving *oddly*⟩ **2** : as is odd ⟨liked the work, *oddly* enough⟩

odd·ment \ˈäd-mənt\ *n* : something left over : REMNANT

odds \ˈädz\ *n pl* **1** : a difference by which one thing is favored over another ⟨the *odds* are in favor of our side⟩ **2 a** : the probability that one thing is so or will happen instead of another ⟨the *odds* are good it will rain today⟩ **b** : the ratio of the probability of one event to that of an event that can happen instead ⟨the *odds* of success to failure in throwing a six with two dice are 1 to 5⟩ **3** : a state of disagreement ⟨at *odds* with their neighbor⟩

odds and ends *n pl* : miscellaneous articles, leftovers, or things to do

ode \ˈōd\ *n* : a lyric poem that expresses a noble feeling with dignity

-ode \ˌōd\ *n combining form* **1** : way : path ⟨electro*de*⟩ **2** : electrode ⟨di*ode*⟩ [derived from Greek *hodos* "way, path"]

odif·er·ous \ō-ˈdif-(ə-)rəs\ *adj* : ODOROUS

odi·ous \ˈōd-ē-əs\ *adj* : causing hatred or strong dislike : worthy of hatred — **odi·ous·ly** *adv*

odi·um \ˈōd-ē-əm\ *n* **1** : the state of being generally hated **2** : the disgrace or shame attached to something considered hateful

odom·e·ter \ō-ˈdäm-ət-ər\ *n* : an instrument for measuring distance traveled (as by a vehicle)

odor \ˈōd-ər\ *n* : the quality of something that stimulates the sense of smell : SCENT; *also* : a sensation resulting from such stimulation — **odor·less** \-ləs\ *adj*

odor·if·er·ous \ˌōd-ə-ˈrif-(ə-)rəs\ *adj* : ODOROUS

odor·ous \ˈōd-ə-rəs\ *adj* : having or giving off an odor

od·ys·sey \ˈäd-ə-sē\ *n, pl* **-seys** : a long wandering or series of travels [named for the *Odyssey*, a long poem from ancient Greece telling the story of the 10-year wanderings of Odysseus, a Greek hero and king]

o'er \ˈō(ə)r, ˈȯ(ə)r\ *adv or prep* : OVER

of \əv, ˈəv, ˈäv\ *prep* **1** — used to indicate a point from which something is located ⟨north *of* the lake⟩ **2 a** — used to indicate origin ⟨*of* noble birth⟩ **b** — used to indi-

cate cause or reason ⟨afraid *of* the dark⟩ ⟨died *of* flu⟩ **c** : ¹BY 4 ⟨the plays *of* Shakespeare⟩ **d** : on the part of ⟨very kind *of* you⟩ **3 a** : made from ⟨a ring *of* gold⟩ **b** — used to indicate contents ⟨a cup *of* water⟩ **c** — used to indicate the number or amount in or making up something ⟨a class *of* 20 students⟩ ⟨interest *of* 5¼%⟩ **4 a** — used to indicate the whole that includes an amount or part mentioned first ⟨most *of* the team⟩ **b** — used to indicate the whole or quantity from which part is removed or used ⟨gave freely *of* their time⟩ **5 a** : relating to : ABOUT ⟨stories *of* her adventures⟩ **b** : in respect to ⟨slow *of* speech⟩ ⟨great *of* heart⟩ **6 a** — used to indicate belonging or possession ⟨queen *of* France⟩ ⟨courage *of* the pioneers⟩ **b** — used to indicate relationship between a result and something upon which an operation or procedure is performed to produce it ⟨the product *of* two numbers⟩ ⟨the solution *of* an equation⟩ **7** — used to indicate something that is removed ⟨cured *of* her disease⟩ ⟨relieved *of* his command⟩ ⟨rid the barn *of* rats⟩ **8** — used to indicate that an example belongs to a certain class ⟨the city *of* Rome⟩ **9** — used to indicate what a noun, verb, or adjective applies to ⟨love *of* nature⟩ ⟨cheated *of* a dollar⟩ ⟨fond *of* oranges⟩ **10** : having as a quality or possession ⟨a thing *of* no importance⟩ **11** : ²BEFORE 3 ⟨ten minutes *of* eight⟩

¹off \ˈȯf\ *adv* **1 a** : from a place or position ⟨march *off*⟩ ⟨stood 10 paces *off*⟩ ⟨drove the dogs *off*⟩ **b** : from a course : ASIDE ⟨turned *off* onto a side street⟩ **c** : into an unconscious state ⟨dozed *off*⟩ **2** : so as to be separated from support or close contact ⟨rolled to the edge of the table and *off*⟩ ⟨the handle came *off*⟩ **3** : so as to be divided ⟨surface marked *off* into squares⟩ **4** : so as to be stopped or finished ⟨shut *off* an engine⟩ ⟨a coat of paint to finish it *off*⟩ **5** : away from work ⟨took the day *off*⟩

²off \(ˈ)ȯf\ *prep* **1** : away from the surface, position, or place of ⟨take it *off* the table⟩ ⟨the ball bounced *off* the wall⟩ ⟨a path *off* the main road⟩ **2** — used to indicate the object of an action ⟨borrowed a dollar *off* him⟩ ⟨living *off* my parents⟩ **3 a** : released or freed from ⟨*off* duty⟩ **b** : below the usual level of ⟨*off* her game⟩ ⟨a dollar *off* the price⟩

³off \(ˈ)ȯf\ *adj* **1 a** : not left : RIGHT ⟨the *off* horse⟩ **b** : more distant ⟨the *off* side of the building⟩ **2** : started on the way ⟨*off* on a trip⟩ ⟨they're *off* and running⟩ **3 a** : not taking place ⟨the game is *off*⟩ **b** : not operating ⟨the radio is *off*⟩ **4 a** : not correct : WRONG ⟨these numbers are *off*⟩ ⟨your guess is way *off*⟩ **b** : not entirely sane **c** : small in degree : SLIGHT ⟨an *off* chance⟩ **5** : being not as busy as usual ⟨liked to vacation during the *off* season⟩ **6 a** : not very good : POOR ⟨an *off* grade of oil⟩ **b** : below or down from the normal ⟨stocks were *off*⟩ ⟨offered at 15% *off*⟩ **7** : provided for or taken care of ⟨we were better *off* before⟩

of·fal \ˈȯ-fəl, ˈäf-əl\ *n* : the waste or by-product of a process; *esp* : the inside organs of and parts trimmed from an animal killed and prepared for food ⟨fish *offal*⟩

¹off·beat \ˈȯf-ˌbēt\ *n* : a musical beat or part of a musical beat that is not accented

²offbeat *adj* : not ordinary : UNUSUAL

of·fend \ə-ˈfend\ *vb* **1** : to do wrong : SIN **2** : to cause to be angry or annoyed : DISPLEASE ⟨that language *offends* me⟩ — **of·fend·er** *n*

of·fense *or* **of·fence** \ə-ˈfen(t)s, *especially for sense 2* ˈäf-ˌen(t)s, ˈȯf-\ *n* **1** : something that offends **2 a** : an act of attacking : ASSAULT **b** : the method of attacking or attempting to score in a game or contest **c** : the side that is attempting to score **3 a** : the act of offending ⟨I meant no *offense*⟩ **b** : the state of being offended ⟨takes *offense* at

\ə\ abut	\au̇\ out	\i\ tip	\ȯ\ saw	\u̇\ foot
\ər\ further	\ch\ chin	\ī\ life	\ȯi\ coin	\y\ yet
\a\ mat	\e\ pet	\j\ job	\th\ thin	\yü\ few
\ā\ take	\ē\ easy	\ŋ\ sing	\ṯh\ this	\yu̇\ cure
\ä\ cot, cart	\g\ go	\ō\ bone	\ü\ food	\zh\ vision

any criticism⟩ **4 a** : a violation of a social or moral code **b** : a breaking of the law

synonyms OFFENSE, SIN, VICE, CRIME mean a violation of law. OFFENSE applies to the breaking of any law, rule, or code ⟨students will be expelled for major *offenses*⟩. SIN applies especially to a breaking of moral law ⟨the *sin* of greed⟩. VICE applies to a habit that degrades or ruins ⟨one of their worst *vices* was gambling⟩. CRIME applies to a serious offense punishable by the law of the state ⟨robbery is a *crime*⟩.

¹**of·fen·sive** \ə-'fen(t)-siv\ *adj* **1 a** : relating to or made or suited for attack ⟨*offensive* weapons⟩ **b** : of or relating to the attempt to score in a game or contest ⟨the *offensive* team⟩ **2** : causing painful or unpleasant sensations ⟨an *offensive* smell⟩ **3** : causing displeasure or resentment ⟨an *offensive* remark⟩ — **of·fen·sive·ly** *adv* — **of·fen·sive·ness** *n*

²**offensive** *n* **1** : the state or attitude of one who is making an attack ⟨on the *offensive*⟩ **2** : ²ATTACK 1 ⟨launch an *offensive*⟩

¹**of·fer** \'ȯf-ər, 'äf-\ *vb* **of·fered; of·fer·ing** \-(ə-)riŋ\ **1** : to present as an act of worship : SACRIFICE **2** : to present (something) to be accepted or rejected ⟨was *offered* the job⟩ ⟨*offer* $10 for the lamp⟩ ⟨*offer* fruit for sale⟩ **3 a** : to present for consideration : SUGGEST ⟨*offer* a suggestion⟩ **b** : to declare one's willingness ⟨*offered* to help⟩ **4** : to try to make or do : PUT UP ⟨*offered* stubborn resistance⟩ **5** : to make available ⟨the hut *offered* protection from the wind and rain⟩ **6** : to propose as payment ⟨I'll *offer* you $700 for that car⟩ [Old English *offrian* "to present as an act of worship," derived from Latin *offerre* "to present, offer," from *of-, ob-* "to, toward" and *ferre* "to bear, carry" — related to ¹DEFER, REFER]

²**offer** *n* **1** : an act or instance of offering ⟨an *offer* to help⟩ **2** : a price suggested by one prepared to buy : BID

of·fer·ing \'ȯf-(ə-)riŋ, 'äf-\ *n* **1** : the act of one who offers **2 a** : something offered **b** : a sacrifice offered as a part of worship **3** : a contribution to the support of a church

of·fer·to·ry \'ȯf-ə(r)-ˌtōr-ē, 'äf-, -ˌtȯr-\ *n, pl* **-ries** **1** *often cap* **a** : the offering of the sacramental bread and wine to God before they are consecrated **b** : a verse from a psalm said or sung at the beginning of the offertory **2 a** : the collection and presentation of the offerings of the congregation in church **b** : the music played or sung during an offertory

off·hand \'ȯf-'hand\ *adv or adj* : without previous thought or preparation ⟨can't say *offhand* how many there are⟩ ⟨made *offhand* excuses for his absence⟩

off·hand·ed \'ȯf-'han-dəd\ *adj* : OFFHAND ⟨*offhanded* remarks⟩ — **off·hand·ed·ly** *adv*

of·fice \'äf-əs, 'ȯf-\ *n* **1** : a special duty or post and especially one of authority in government ⟨hold public *office*⟩ **2** : a prescribed form or service of worship : RITE **3** : something done for another : SERVICE **4** : a place where a business is carried on ⟨ticket *office*⟩ ⟨a dentist's *office*⟩ **5** : a large government department ⟨Patent *Office*⟩

of·fice·hold·er \-ˌhōl-dər\ *n* : a person holding a public office

of·fi·cer \'äf-ə-sər, 'ȯf-\ *n* **1** : a person given the responsibility of enforcing the law ⟨a police *officer*⟩ **2** : a person who holds an office ⟨an *officer* of the company⟩ **3** : a person who holds a commission in the armed forces

¹**of·fi·cial** \ə-'fish-əl\ *n* **1** : a person who holds an office ⟨public *officials*⟩ **2** : a person who enforces the rules in a game or sport ⟨the *officials* of a football game⟩

²**official** *adj* **1** : of or relating to an office ⟨*official* duties⟩ **2** : having authority to perform a duty ⟨the *official* government of the 13 colonies⟩ **3** : prescribed or permitted by authority ⟨the *official* language⟩ ⟨an *official* American League baseball⟩ **4** : proper for a person in office ⟨an *official* greeting⟩ — **of·fi·cial·ly** \-'fish-(ə-)lē\ *adv*

of·fi·cial·dom \ə-'fish-əl-dəm\ *n* : officials as a class

of·fi·ci·ate \ə-'fish-ē-ˌāt\ *vb* **-at·ed; -at·ing** **1** : to perform a ceremony ⟨*officiate* at a wedding⟩ **2** : to act as an officer ⟨*officiated* at the annual meeting⟩ **3** : to enforce the rules of (a game or sport) ⟨*officiate* a soccer match⟩

of·fi·cious \ə-'fish-əs\ *adj* : volunteering one's services where they are not asked for or needed — **of·fi·cious·ly** *adv* — **of·fi·cious·ness** *n*

off·ing \'ȯf-iŋ, 'äf-\ *n* : the near future ⟨sees trouble in the *offing*⟩

off–key \'ȯf-'kē\ *adj or adv* : above or below the proper tone of a melody ⟨singing *off-key*⟩

off–limits \'ȯf-'flim-əts\ *adj* **1** : not to be entered or used by a certain group of people **2** : not to be discussed or considered ⟨questions about my salary are *off-limits*⟩

off–line \'ȯf-'flīn\ *adj* : not connected to or controlled by a computer ⟨an *off-line* printer⟩ — **off–line** *adv*

off of *prep* : ²OFF

off–ramp \'ȯf-ˌramp\ *n* : a ramp by which one leaves a limited-access highway

off–road \'ȯf-'rōd\ *adj* : of, relating to, done with, or being a vehicle designed especially to operate away from public roads

off–road·er \'ȯf-ˌrōd-ər\ *n* **1** : a driver of an off-road vehicle **2** : an off-road vehicle

off–season \'ȯf-ˌsēz-ᵊn\ *n* : a time when some activity is suspended or reduced

¹**off·set** \'ȯf-ˌset\ *n* **1** : a short shoot arising from the base of a plant and growing flat on the ground **2** : something that serves to make up for something else

²**off·set** \'ȯf-'set *also* ȯf-'set\ *vb* **-set; -set·ting** : to make up for ⟨gains in one state *offset* losses in another⟩

off–shoot \'ȯf-ˌshüt\ *n* **1** : something that branches out from something else **2** : a branch of a main stem of a plant

¹offset 1

¹**off–shore** \'ȯf-'shō(ə)r, -'shȯ(ə)r\ *adv* : from the shore : at a distance from the shore

²**off–shore** \'ȯf-ˌshō(ə)r, -ˌshȯ(ə)r\ *adj* **1** : coming or moving away from the shore ⟨an *offshore* breeze⟩ **2** : located off the shore ⟨*offshore* islands⟩ ⟨an *offshore* oil rig⟩

off·side \'ȯf-'sīd\ *adv or adj* : illegally in advance of the ball or puck

off·spring \'ȯf-ˌspriŋ\ *n, pl* **offspring** *also* **offsprings** : the young of a person, animal, or plant

off·stage \'ȯf-'stāj, -ˌstāj\ *adv or adj* : off or away from the stage

off–the–record *adj* : given or made privately and not meant for publication ⟨would only give the reporter *off=the-record* comments⟩

off–the–wall *adj* : very unusual : BIZARRE ⟨an *off-the-wall* sense of humor⟩

off–white \'ȯf-'hwīt, -'wīt\ *n* : a yellowish or grayish white

oft \'ȯft\ *adv* : OFTEN ⟨an *oft* neglected factor⟩

of·ten \'ȯ-fən, 'ȯf-tən\ *adv* : many times : FREQUENTLY

of·ten·times \-ˌtīmz\ *or* **oft·times** \'ȯf(t)-ˌtīmz\ *adv* : OFTEN

ogle \'ōg-əl *also* 'äg-\ *vb* **ogled; ogling** \-(ə-)liŋ\ : to look at in a flirting way or with unusual attention or desire — **ogle** *n* — **ogler** \-(ə-)lər\ *n*

ogre \'ō-gər\ *n* **1** : an ugly giant of fairy tales and folklore that eats people **2** : a dreaded person or object — **ogre·ish** \'ō-g(ə-)rish\ *adj*

¹**oh** *or* **O** \(')ō\ *interj* **1** — used to express an emotion (as astonishment or desire) or in response to a physical sensation (as pain) **2** — used in direct address ⟨*Oh* sir, you forgot your change⟩ **3** — used to express understanding

of a statement ⟨*oh,* that's what you mean⟩ **4** — used to introduce an example or a guess ⟨there are probably, *oh,* six or seven different ways to do that⟩

²oh \'ō\ *n* : ¹ZERO 1

ohm \'ōm\ *n* : a unit of electric resistance equal to the resistance of a circuit in which a potential difference of one volt produces a current of one ampere — **ohm·ic** \'ō-mik\ *adj*

ohm·me·ter \'ō(m)-ˌmēt-ər\ *n* : an instrument for indicating resistance in ohms directly

Ohm's law \'ōmz-\ *n* : a law in electricity that states that the current in a circuit is equal to the potential difference divided by the resistance of the circuit

¹-oid \ˌóid\ *n suffix* : something resembling a (specified) object or having a (specified) quality ⟨planet*oid*⟩

²-oid *adj suffix* : resembling : having the form or appearance of [derived from Greek *-oeidēs* "resembling, having a specified form"]

¹oil \'ói(ə)l\ *n* **1 a** : any of numerous greasy flammable usually liquid substances from plant, animal, or mineral sources that do not dissolve in water and are used especially as lubricants, fuels, and food **b** : PETROLEUM **2** : something (as a cosmetic) like oil or containing an oil ⟨bath *oil*⟩ ⟨suntan *oil*⟩ **3 a** : artist's paints made of pigments and oil **b** : a painting done in oils

²oil *vb* : to put oil in or on

oil·can \'ói(ə)l-ˌkan\ *n* : a can for oil; *esp* : a can with a spout that is designed to release oil drop by drop

oil·cloth \'ói(ə)l-ˌklóth\ *n* : cloth treated with oil or paint so as to be waterproof and used for table and shelf coverings

oil·er \'ói-lər\ *n* **1** : a person (as a worker) who oils something **2** : a device for applying oil

oil field *n* : a region rich in oil deposits

oil gland *n* : a gland (as of the skin) that gives off an oily substance

oil of wintergreen : a chemical compound made from salicylic acid and used in liniments and as a flavoring

oil paint *n* : paint made with a drying oil

oil painting *n* : a painting done with oil paints

oil palm *n* : a palm that is cultivated for its clusters of fruits from which a vegetable oil is obtained

oil·seed \'ói(ə)l-ˌsēd\ *n* : a seed or crop (as flaxseed) grown mainly for the oil obtained from it

oil shale *n* : a rock (as shale) from which oil can be recovered

oil·skin \'ói(ə)l-ˌskin\ *n* **1** : a waterproof cloth **2** : an oilskin raincoat **3** *pl* : an oilskin coat and trousers

oil slick *n* : a film of oil floating on water

oil well *n* : a well from which petroleum is obtained

oily \'ói-lē\ *adj* **oil·i·er; -est 1** : of, relating to, or consisting of oil **2 a** : covered or soaked with oil **b** : high in oils that are naturally produced ⟨*oily* skin⟩ — **oil·i·ness** *n*

oint·ment \'óint-mənt\ *n* : a semisolid greasy medicine for use on the skin

Ojib·wa *or* **Ojib·way** *or* **Ojib·we** \ō-'jib-wā\ *n, pl* **Ojibwa** *or* **Ojibwas** *or* **Ojibway** *or* **Ojibways** *or* **Ojibwe** *or* **Ojibwes** : a member of an American Indian people originally of Michigan

¹OK *or* **okay** \ō-'kā\ *adv or adj* : ALL RIGHT

Word History In the late 1830s Boston newspapers were filled with abbreviations. Abbreviation was apparently the fashion at that time. Any phrase might be shortened. The fad even went so far as to produce abbreviations for intentional misspellings. Such popular expressions as *N.G.* (no go) and *A.R.* (all right) gave way to *K.G.* (know go) and *O.W.* (oll wright). The abbreviation *O.K.* stood for *oll korrect,* a deliberate misspelling of *all correct.* Several of these abbreviated misspellings became popular for a time, but *O.K.* was the only one to gain a lasting place in the language. [an abbreviation of *oll korrect,* an altered form of *all correct*]

²OK *or* **okay** *n* : APPROVAL ⟨gave their *OK* to start the project⟩

³OK *or* **okay** *vb* **OK'd** *or* **okayed; OK'·ing** *or* **okay·ing** : APPROVE 2

oka·pi \ō-'käp-ē\ *n* : an African mammal closely related to the giraffe but lacking the long neck

okra \'ō-krə\ *n* : a tall herb related to the hollyhocks and grown for its edible green pods which are used especially in soups and stews; *also* : these pods

okapi

¹old \'ōld\ *adj* **1 a** : dating from the distant past ⟨an *old* custom⟩ **b** : having lasted or been such for a long time ⟨an *old* friend⟩ **2** *cap* : belonging to an early period in development ⟨*Old* Irish⟩ **3** : having existed for a specified length of time ⟨a child three years *old*⟩ **4** : having lived a long time ⟨*old* people⟩ **5** : FORMER 1 ⟨my *old* teachers⟩ **6** : showing the effects of time or use ⟨wore an *old* coat⟩ **7** : long familiar ⟨it's still the same *old* story⟩

synonyms OLD, ANCIENT, ANTIQUE, ARCHAIC mean having come into being or use in the distant past. OLD may apply to a period of time that is truly long or only longer than average ⟨*old* houses that were built two hundred years ago⟩ ⟨an *old* sweater of mine⟩. ANCIENT applies to things that happened or existed in the very distant past ⟨*ancient* custom⟩ or to things that still survive from early times ⟨the *ancient* pyramids of Egypt⟩. ANTIQUE applies to things that have been handed down from times gone by ⟨collected *antique* furniture⟩. ARCHAIC suggests something that has the characteristics of a much earlier time ⟨the play used *archaic* language so as to give the audience a feeling for those days⟩.

²old *n* : old or earlier time ⟨in days of *old*⟩

old country *n* : the country that a person has emigrated from

old·en \'ōl-dən\ *adj* : of or relating to earlier days

Old English *n* : the language of the English people before about 1100

old·fan·gled \'ōl(d)-'faŋ-gəld\ *adj* : OLD-FASHIONED

old–fash·ioned \'ōl(d)-'fash-ənd\ *adj* **1** : of, relating to, or like that of an earlier time ⟨*old-fashioned* clothes⟩ **2** : holding fast to old ways : CONSERVATIVE

Old French *n* : the French language from the 9th to the 16th century

Old Glory *n* : the flag of the U.S.

old–growth \'ōl(d)-'grōth\ *adj* : of, relating to, or being a forest characterized by the presence of large old trees, dead standing trees, and fallen rotting trees and that is usually in a late stage of development

old hand *n* : VETERAN 1

old·ish \'ōl-dish\ *adj* : somewhat old or elderly

old lady *n* **1** : one's wife or mother **2** : GIRLFRIEND; *esp* : a woman with whom a man lives

old maid *n* **1** : an elderly unmarried woman **2** : a very neat fussy person **3** : a card game in which all but one of the cards are matched in pairs and the player holding the

\ə\ abut	\au̇\ out	\i\ tip	\ȯ\ saw	\u̇\ foot
\ər\ further	\ch\ chin	\ī\ life	\ȯi\ coin	\y\ yet
\a\ mat	\e\ pet	\j\ job	\th\ thin	\yü\ few
\ā\ take	\ē\ easy	\ŋ\ sing	\th\ this	\yu̇\ cure
\ä\ cot, cart	\g\ go	\ō\ bone	\ü\ food	\zh\ vision

unmatched card at the end loses — **old–maid·ish** \ˈōl(d)-ˈmād-ish\ adj

old man n **1** : one's husband or father **2** cap O&M : a person (as one's boss or commanding officer) who is in charge **3** : BOYFRIEND; esp : a man with whom a woman lives

Old Norse n : the Germanic language of the Scandinavian peoples before about 1350

Old Prus·sian \-ˈprəsh-ən\ n : a language used until the 1600s in a region of northeastern Europe that borders the Baltic Sea

old·ster \ˈōl(d)-stər\ n : an old or elderly person

Old Style n : the way the calendar was calculated before the adoption of the Gregorian calendar

Old Testament n : the first of the two chief divisions of the Christian Bible — see BIBLE table

old–time \ˌōl(d)-ˈtīm\ adj **1** : of, relating to, or typical of an earlier period **2** : of long standing ⟨old-time residents⟩

old–tim·er \ˌōl(d)-ˈtī-mər\ n **1 a** : VETERAN 1 **b** : OLDSTER **2** : something old-fashioned

old wives' tale n : a belief that is not based on fact : SUPERSTITION

old–world \ˈōl-ˈ(d)wər(-ə)ld\ adj **1** : of or relating to the Old World **2** : having old-fashioned charm

Old World n : the eastern hemisphere except Australia; esp : the continent of Europe

ole·an·der \ˈō-lē-ˌan-dər\ n : a poisonous evergreen shrub with showy fragrant usually white, pink, or purple flowers

ole·fin \ˈō-lə-fən\ n : a chemical compound made up of carbon and hydrogen atoms that contains at least one double bond; esp : any of various long-chain synthetic polymers (as of ethylene) used especially as textile fibers

oleo \ˈō-lē-ˌō\ n, pl **ole·os** : MARGARINE

oleo·mar·ga·rine \ˌō-lē-ō-ˈmärj-(ə-)rən, -ˈmärj-ə-ˌrēn\ n : MARGARINE

O level n : the lowest of three levels of British examinations in a secondary school subject

ol·fac·tion \äl-ˈfak-shən, ōl-\ n : the sense of smell; also : the act or process of smelling

ol·fac·to·ry \äl-ˈfak-t(ə-)rē, ōl-\ adj : of, relating to, or concerned with the sense of smell

olfactory bulb n : either of two small round structures projecting from the lower surface of the brain above the nasal cavity that transmit stimuli from the olfactory nerves to other areas of the brain for processing

olfactory nerve n : either of a pair of sensory nerves that are the first cranial nerves, arise in the nose, and carry odor stimuli to the brain by way of the olfactory bulb

oli·gar·chy \ˈäl-ə-ˌgär-kē, ˈō-lə-\ n, pl **-chies 1** : government by the few **2** : a government in which a small group exercises control; also : a group exercising such control **3** : an organization controlled by a small group

Oli·go·cene \ˈäl-i-gō-ˌsēn, ˈō-li-; ə-ˈlig-ə-\ adj : of, relating to, or being an epoch of the Tertiary period of geological history or the corresponding series of rocks — see GEOLOGIC TIME table — **Oligocene** n

ol·ive \ˈäl-iv, -əv\ n **1** : a Mediterranean evergreen tree grown for its fruit; also : the edible fruit of the olive tree that is the source of an oil **2** : a yellowish green — **olive** adj

olive branch n **1** : a branch of the olive tree especially when used as a symbol of peace **2** : something meant to show intentions of peace or goodwill ⟨made a call to his former friend as an olive branch⟩

olive drab n **1** : a grayish olive color **2** : a wool or

olive 1

cotton fabric of an olive drab color; also : a uniform made out of this fabric

olive oil n : a pale yellow to yellowish green oil obtained from the pulp of olives and used especially as a salad oil, in cooking, and in soaps

ol·iv·ine \ˈäl-ə-ˌvēn\ n : a usually greenish mineral that is a silicate of magnesium and iron

olym·pi·ad \ə-ˈlim-pē-ˌad, ō-\ n, often cap **1** : one of the four-year periods between Olympic Games **2** : a celebration of the modern Olympic Games; also : a competition similar or compared to the Olympic Games ⟨the school's math olympiad⟩

¹**Olym·pi·an** \ə-ˈlim-pē-ən, ō-\ adj **1** : of or relating to Olympus **2** : relating to or proper for one of the Greek gods of Olympus : LOFTY

²**Olympian** adj **1** : of or relating to the ancient Greek region of Olympia **2** : OLYMPIC 2

³**Olympian** n : an athlete who competes in the Olympic Games

⁴**Olympian** n : one of the Greek gods living on Olympus

Olym·pic \ə-ˈlim-pik, ō-\ adj **1** : ¹OLYMPIAN **2** : of or relating to the Olympic Games ⟨the U.S. Olympic team⟩

Olympic Games n pl **1** : an ancient Greek festival held every fourth year and made up of contests in sports, music, and literature **2** : a series of international athletic contests held in a different country during the summer and the winter once every four years

Olym·pics \ə-ˈlim-piks, ō-\ n pl : OLYMPIC GAMES

om·buds·man \ˈäm-ˌbu̇dz-mən, ˈōm-, -bədz-, -ˌman; äm-ˈbu̇dz-, ōm-\ n, pl **om·buds·men** \-ˌmən\ : a government official who investigates complaints made by people about unfair acts of public officials

ome·ga \ō-ˈmeg-ə, -ˈmē-gə, -ˈmā-gə\ n : the 24th and last letter of the Greek alphabet — Ω or ω [from Greek ō mega, literally, "big o"]

om·elet also **om·elette** \ˈäm-(ə-)lət\ n : beaten eggs cooked without stirring and served folded in half

Word History Although the word omelet bears little resemblance to Latin lamina, the shape of an omelet does resemble a thin plate, which is what lamina, the ultimate source of omelet, means. The Latin noun lamella, a diminutive form of lamina, became lemelle "blade of a knife" in medieval French. La lemelle "the blade" was misinterpreted as l'alemelle, and so the word gained an initial vowel. In later French, alemelle or alumelle was altered (by substituting the suffix -ette for the suffix -elle) into allumette, which acquired the meaning "dish made with beaten eggs" (such a dish resembling a thin plate or blade). After a later alteration to omelette the word found its way into English. [from French omelette "omelet," derived from early French amelette, alemette, altered forms of alemelle "omelet," literally, "knife blade, thin plate," derived from la lemelle (same meaning), derived from Latin lamella "a small thin metal plate," from lamina "a thin plate"]

omen \ˈō-mən\ n : a happening believed to be a sign or warning of some future event

omi·cron \ˈäm-ə-ˌkrän, ˈōm-\ n : the 15th letter of the Greek alphabet — O or o [from Greek o mikron, literally, "small o"]

om·i·nous \ˈäm-ə-nəs\ adj : being or showing a sign of evil or misfortune to come ⟨ominous clouds⟩ — **om·i·nous·ly** adv

omis·sion \ō-ˈmish-ən, ə-\ n **1** : something omitted **2** : the act of omitting : the state of being omitted

omit \ō-ˈmit, ə-\ vb **omit·ted; omit·ting 1** : to leave out ⟨omitted your name from the list⟩ **2** : to fail to do : NEGLECT ⟨omitted to mention that it was my fault⟩

¹**om·ni·bus** \ˈäm-ni-(ˌ)bəs\ n : BUS

²**omnibus** adj **1** : of, relating to, or providing for many things at once **2** : containing or including many items ⟨an omnibus legislative bill⟩

om·nip·o·tence \äm-'nip-ət-ən(t)s\ *n* : the quality or state of being omnipotent

om·nip·o·tent \äm-'nip-ət-ənt\ *adj* : having power or authority without limit : ALMIGHTY — **om·nip·o·tent·ly** *adv*

om·ni·pres·ent \,äm-ni-'prez-°nt\ *adj* : present in all places at all times

om·ni·science \äm-'nish-ən(t)s\ *n* : the quality or state of being omniscient

om·ni·scient \äm-'nish-ənt\ *adj* : knowing everything [from modern Latin *omniscient-, omnisciens* "knowing all things, all-knowing," derived from *omni-* (from *omnis* "all") and *scient-, sciens* "knowing," from *scire* "to know" — related to SCIENCE] — **om·ni·scient·ly** *adv*

om·ni·vore \'äm-ni-ˌvō(ə)r, -ˌvȯ(ə)r\ *n* : one that is omnivorous

om·niv·o·rous \äm-'niv-(ə-)rəs\ *adj* : feeding on both animal and vegetable substances

¹on \(')ȯn, (')än\ *prep* **1 a** : in contact with and supported by ⟨the book *on* the table⟩ **b** : in a position in contact with or near ⟨a fly *on* the wall⟩ ⟨a town *on* the river⟩ **c** — used to indicate the location of something ⟨*on* the other side of the house⟩ ⟨*on* the right⟩ **2 a** — used to indicate means of being attached or supported ⟨*on* a string⟩ ⟨stood *on* one foot⟩ ⟨hang your coat *on* the peg⟩ ⟨you can rely *on* me⟩ ⟨lives *on* insects⟩ **b** — used to indicate means of being carried ⟨rode *on* a horse⟩ ⟨went *on* the bus⟩ ⟨have only five dollars *on* me⟩ **3** — used to indicate a time or an instance when something takes place ⟨*on* arriving home, I found your letter⟩ ⟨arrived *on* Monday⟩ ⟨news *on* the hour⟩ **4 a** — used to indicate the way something is done ⟨told her *on* the sly⟩ **b** — used to indicate what something is done with or done by ⟨cut *on* broken glass⟩ ⟨talk *on* the phone⟩ ⟨type *on* a keyboard⟩ ⟨displayed *on* a TV screen⟩ **5 a** : involved with or participating in : busy with ⟨*on* a committee⟩ ⟨*on* tour⟩ **b** : in a state or process of ⟨*on* fire⟩ ⟨*on* the increase⟩ **c** : in keeping with a goal or objective ⟨*on* schedule⟩ **6 a** — used to indicate a reason or basis ⟨*on* one condition⟩ ⟨interest of 10 cents *on* the dollar⟩ **b** — used to indicate who or what is responsible ⟨this treat is *on* me⟩ ⟨blamed it *on* the weather⟩ **7** — used to indicate someone or something an action or feeling is directed toward ⟨was creeping up *on* us⟩ ⟨have pity *on* me⟩ ⟨the joke's *on* you⟩ **8 a** : CONCERNING, ABOUT ⟨a book *on* cats⟩ ⟨agree *on* price⟩ **b** : with respect to ⟨go light *on* the salt⟩ ⟨short *on* cash⟩ **9** : following in series ⟨loss *on* loss⟩

²on \'ȯn, 'än\ *adv* **1** : in or into contact with a surface ⟨put the kettle *on*⟩ ⟨has new shoes *on*⟩ **2** : forward in space, time, or action ⟨went *on* home⟩ ⟨*on* came the storm⟩ ⟨getting *on* in years⟩ **3** : from one to another ⟨pass the word *on*⟩ ⟨and so *on*⟩ **4** : into operation or a position allowing operation ⟨turn the light *on*⟩

³on \'ȯn, 'än\ *adj* **1** : doing an activity (as a role in a play) ⟨you're *on* next⟩ **2 a** : being in operation ⟨the radio is *on*⟩ **b** : set so as to permit operation ⟨the switch is *on*⟩ **c** : taking place or being broadcast ⟨the game is *on*⟩ **3** : having been planned ⟨has nothing *on* for tonight⟩

¹once \'wən(t)s\ *adv* **1** : one time only ⟨will repeat the question *once*⟩ **2** : at any one time : EVER ⟨*once* you hesitate, it's too late⟩ **3** : at some time in the past : FORMERLY ⟨it was *once* done that way⟩ **4** : by one degree of relationship ⟨cousin *once* removed⟩ — **once and for all** **1** : in a final way or manner ⟨let's settle this *once and for all*⟩ **2** : for the last time ⟨I'm asking you *once and for all*⟩ — **once in a while** : from time to time

²once *n* : one single time ⟨just this *once*⟩ — **at once** **1** : at the same time : SIMULTANEOUSLY ⟨two people talking *at once*⟩ **2** : IMMEDIATELY 2 ⟨leave *at once*⟩

³once *conj* : AS SOON AS ⟨*once* that is done, all will be well⟩

once–over \'wən(t)-ˌsō-vər\ *n* : a quick glance or examination ⟨gave the menu the *once-over*⟩

on·cho·cer·ci·a·sis \ˌäŋ-kō-sər-'kī-ə-səs, \-ˌsēz\ *n, pl* **-a·ses** : RIVER BLINDNESS

on·co·gene \'äŋ-kō-jēn\ *n* : a gene having the potential to cause a normal cell to become cancerous

on·col·o·gist \än-'käl-ə-jist\ *n* : a physician specializing in oncology

on·col·o·gy \än-'käl-ə-jē\ *n* : a branch of medicine concerned with the study and treatment of tumors

on·com·ing \'ȯn-ˌkəm-iŋ, 'än-\ *adj* : coming nearer ⟨*oncoming* traffic⟩

¹one \'wən, ˌwən\ *adj* **1** : being a single unit or thing — see NUMBER table **2** : being a certain unit or thing ⟨early *one* morning⟩ **3 a** : being the same in kind or quality ⟨members of *one* class⟩ **b** : not divided **4** : not definitely fixed or placed ⟨will see you again *one* day⟩ **5** : ¹ONLY 2a ⟨the *one* person they wanted to see⟩

²one *n* **1** : the number indicating a single unit **2** : the first in a set or series **3** : a single person or thing ⟨has the *one*, but needs the other⟩ **4** : a one-dollar bill

³one *pron* **1** : a single member or individual ⟨saw *one* of your friends⟩ **2** : any person ⟨*one* never knows⟩

one another *pron* : EACH OTHER

one–dimensional *adj* **1** : having one dimension **2** : STEREOTYPED

one–horse *adj* : small and unimportant ⟨a *one-horse* town⟩

one·ness \'wən-nəs\ *n* : the quality, state, or fact of being one ⟨our *oneness* with the rest of humanity⟩

oner·ous \'än-ə-rəs, 'ō-nə-\ *adj* : being difficult and unpleasant to do or to deal with ⟨an *onerous* task⟩ — **oner·ous·ly** *adv*

one·self \(ˌ)wən-'self\ *pron* **1** : one's own self ⟨one can feel proud of *oneself*⟩ **2** : one's normal or healthy self

one–sid·ed \'wən-'sīd-əd\ *adj* **1 a** : having one side more developed **b** : having or happening on one side only **2** : favoring one side : PARTIAL ⟨a *one-sided* view of the case⟩ — **one–sid·ed·ly** *adv* — **one–sid·ed·ness** *n*

ones place *n* : UNITS PLACE

one·time \'wən-ˌtīm\ *adj* **1** : FORMER 1 ⟨a *onetime* boxing champion⟩ **2** : happening only once ⟨a *onetime* event⟩

one–to–one \ˌwən-tə-'wən\ *adj* : pairing each element of a set with one and only one element of another set ⟨a *one=to-one* correspondence between the real numbers and the points on a straight line⟩

one–way *adj* **1** : moving or allowing movement in one direction only **2** : ONE-SIDED 1b

on·go·ing \'ȯn-ˌgō-iŋ, 'än-\ *adj* : being in progress or movement

on·ion \'ən-yən\ *n* : a widely grown Asian herb related to the lilies and having edible bulbs that have a sharp odor and taste and are used as a vegetable and to season foods; *also* : its bulb

on·ion·skin \-ˌskin\ *n* : a thin strong nearly transparent paper of very light weight

online \'ȯn-'līn, 'än-\ *adj* : relating to or connected to a computer or telecommunications system (as the Internet) ⟨an *online* database⟩ — **online** *adv*

on·look·er \'ȯn-ˌlùk-ər, 'än-\ *n* : SPECTATOR

¹on·ly \'ōn-lē\ *adj* **1** : the best without doubt ⟨it's the *only* thing for me⟩ **2 a** : alone in or of a class or kind : SOLE ⟨the *only* survivor

onion

\ə\ abut	\aù\ out	\i\ tip	\ȯ\ saw	\ù\ foot
\ər\ further	\ch\ chin	\ī\ life	\ȯi\ coin	\y\ yet
\a\ mat	\e\ pet	\j\ job	\th\ thin	\yü\ few
\ā\ take	\ē\ easy	\ŋ\ sing	\th\ this	\yù\ cure
\ä\ cot, cart	\g\ go	\ō\ bone	\ü\ food	\zh\ vision

of the crash⟩ **b** : having no brother or sister ⟨an *only* child⟩ **3** : ²FEW 1 ⟨one of the *only* areas not yet explored⟩

²**only** *adv* **1 a** : as a single fact or instance and nothing more or different ⟨worked *only* in the mornings⟩ **b** : no one or nothing other than ⟨*only* you know⟩ **2** : at the very least ⟨it was *only* too true⟩ **3 a** : in the end ⟨it will *only* make you sick⟩ **b** : with the result ⟨found my pen, *only* to lose it again⟩ **4 a** : as recently as ⟨*only* last week⟩ **b** : in the immediate past ⟨*only* just saw her⟩

³**only** *conj* : except that ⟨I'd play, *only* I'm too tired⟩

on·o·mas·tics \ˌän-ə-ˈmas-tiks\ *n sing or pl* : the study of the proper names of people and places

on·o·mato·poe·ia \ˌän-ə-ˌmat-ə-ˈpē-(y)ə\ *n* **1** : the naming of a thing or action by imitation of natural sounds (as "buzz" or "hiss") **2** : the use of words whose sound suggests the sense (as for poetic effect) — **on·o·mato·poe·ic** \-ˈpē-ik\ *or* **on·o·mato·po·et·ic** \-pō-ˈet-ik\ *adj*

on–ramp \ˈȯn-ˌramp, ˈän-\ *n* : a ramp by which one enters a limited-access highway

on·rush \ˈȯn-ˌrəsh, ˈän-\ *n* : a rushing forward or onward — **on·rush·ing** \-iŋ\ *adj*

on·set \ˈȯn-ˌset, ˈän-\ *n* **1** : ²ATTACK 1 **2** : BEGINNING 1

on·shore \ˈȯn-ˌshō(ə)r, ˈän-, -ˌshȯ(ə)r\ *adj* **1** : moving toward the shore ⟨*onshore* winds⟩ **2** : situated on land ⟨*onshore* oil refinery⟩ — **on·shore** \ˈȯn-ˈshō(ə)r, ˈän-, -ˈshȯ(ə)r\ *adv*

on·slaught \ˈän-ˌslȯt, ˈȯn-\ *n* : a violent attack

on·stage \ˈȯn-ˈstāj, ˈän-\ *adv or adj* : on or onto a stage : on a part of the stage visible to the audience

on–tar·get \ˈȯn-ˈtär-gət, ˈän-\ *adj* : just right : ACCURATE ⟨gave him *on-target* advice⟩

on–the–job *adj* : received or learned while working at a job ⟨*on-the-job* training⟩

on·to \ˌȯn-tə, ˌän-; ˈȯn-tü, ˈän-\ *prep* **1** : to a position on or against ⟨leaped *onto* the horse⟩ ⟨climbed *onto* the roof⟩ **2** : in a state of knowing about or becoming aware of ⟨I'm *onto* their little game⟩

¹**on·ward** \ˈȯn-wərd, ˈän-\ *also* **on·wards** \-wərdz\ *adv* : toward or at a point lying ahead in space or time : FORWARD ⟨kept moving *onward*⟩

²**onward** *adj* : directed or moving onward ⟨the *onward* march of time⟩

on·yx \ˈän-iks\ *n* : chalcedony in parallel layers of different color

oo·dles \ˈüd-ᵊlz\ *n pl* : a great quantity

oo·gen·e·sis \ˌō-ə-ˈjen-ə-səs\ *n* : the process of female gamete formation including meiosis and formation of eggs

oo·lite \ˈō-ə-ˌlīt\ *n* : a rock consisting of small round grains usually of calcium carbonate firmly joined together

oo·long \ˈü-ˌlȯŋ\ *n* : tea made from leaves that have undergone partial fermentation before being dried

oops *or* **whoops** \ˈ(w)ù(ə)ps\ *interj* — used to express mild apology, surprise, or distress (as at spilling something or saying the wrong thing)

Oort cloud \ˈȯrt-\ *n* : a spherical shell of small icy bodies (as comets) that orbit the sun far beyond Pluto [named after Jan Oort, 1900–1992, Dutch astronomer]

oo·tid \ˈō-ə-ˌtid\ *n* : an egg cell after meiosis but before it is a fully mature egg

¹**ooze** \ˈüz\ *n* : soft mud or slime (as on the bottom of a lake)

²**ooze** *vb* **oozed**; **ooz·ing** **1** : to flow or leak slowly ⟨sap *oozed* from the tree⟩ **2** : EMIT 1a ⟨a manner that *oozed* confidence⟩

³**ooze** *n* : something that oozes

oozy \ˈü-zē\ *adj* **ooz·i·er**; **-est** : consisting of or resembling ooze

opac·i·ty \ō-ˈpas-ət-ē\ *n, pl* **-ties** : the quality or state of being opaque

opal \ˈō-pəl\ *n* : a mineral with changeable colors that is used as a gem

opaque \ō-ˈpāk\ *adj* **1** : not letting light through : not

transparent **2** : hard to understand **3** : dull of mind : STUPID — **opaque·ly** *adv* — **opaque·ness** *n*

ope \ˈōp\ *vb* **oped**; **op·ing** *archaic* : ²OPEN

¹**open** \ˈō-pən, ˈȯp-ᵊm\ *adj* **1** : allowing passage : not shut or blocked ⟨an *open* door⟩ ⟨*open* books⟩ ⟨*open* pores⟩ **2** : not enclosed or covered ⟨an *open* boat⟩ ⟨an *open* fire⟩ ⟨*open* wounds⟩ **3 a** : not secret : PUBLIC ⟨*open* dislike⟩ **b** : LIABLE 2 ⟨*open* to challenge⟩ **4 a** : free to be used, entered, or taken part in by all ⟨an *open* meeting⟩ ⟨an *open* golf tournament⟩ **b** : easy to enter, get through, or see ⟨*open* country⟩ **5** : not drawn together : spread out ⟨an *open* flower⟩ ⟨an *open* umbrella⟩ **6 a** : available for use : FREE ⟨keep an hour *open* tomorrow⟩ ⟨the only option *open* to us⟩ **b** : not decided or settled ⟨an *open* question⟩ **c** : waiting to be filled ⟨the job is still *open*⟩ **d** : available for purchase all or most of the time ⟨these items are in *open* stock⟩ **7** : ready to consider appeals or ideas ⟨an *open* mind⟩ ⟨*open* to suggestion⟩ **8** : not allowing the flow of electricity : being an incomplete electrical circuit ⟨an *open* switch⟩ — **open·ly** \ˈō-pən-lē\ *adv* — **open·ness** \ˈō-pən-nəs\ *n*

²**open** *vb* **opened** \ˈō-pənd, ˈȯp-ᵊmd\; **open·ing** \ˈōp-(ə-)niŋ\ **1 a** : to change or move from a shut or closed condition ⟨*open* a book⟩ ⟨the door *opened*⟩ **b** : to clear by or as if by removing something in the way ⟨*open* a road blocked with snow⟩ ⟨the clouds *opened*⟩ **c** : to make an opening in ⟨*open* a boil⟩ **2 a** : to make or become ready for use ⟨*open* a new store⟩ **b** : to make available for a certain purpose ⟨*open* land for settlement⟩ ⟨*opened* Japan to foreign trade⟩ ⟨the office *opens* at eight⟩ **c** : to access for use ⟨*open* the computer file⟩ **3** : to have an opening ⟨the rooms *open* onto a hall⟩ **4** : BEGIN 1, START ⟨*opened* fire⟩ ⟨*open* talks⟩

³**open** *n* **1** : open space; *esp* : ²OUTDOORS ⟨go out in the *open*⟩ **2** : a contest or tournament that is open **3** : a state or position that is public or is not concealed

open air *n* : ²OUTDOORS 1 — **open–air** *adj*

open–and–shut \ˌō-pən-ən-ˈshət\ *adj* **1** : perfectly plain : OBVIOUS **2** : easily settled ⟨an *open-and-shut* case⟩

open arms *n pl* : an eager or warm welcome ⟨greeted us with *open arms*⟩

open dating *n* : the placing of dates on goods (as dairy products) so that the consumer can tell how old they are

open door *n* : a policy of giving equal opportunity for trade to all nations — **open–door** *adj*

open·er \ˈōp-(ə-)nər\ *n* : something used for opening ⟨a bottle *opener*⟩ ⟨a conversation *opener*⟩ — **for openers** : to begin with

open–eyed \ˌō-pə-ˈnīd\ *adj* **1** : having the eyes open **2** : watching carefully : ALERT

open·hand·ed \ˌō-pən-ˈhan-dəd\ *adj* : GENEROUS 1 — **open·hand·ed·ly** *adv* — **open·hand·ed·ness** *n*

open–heart *adj* : of, relating to, or done on a heart temporarily stopped and surgically opened for repair of defects or damage ⟨*open-heart* surgery⟩

open·heart·ed \ˌō-pən-ˈhärt-əd\ *adj* **1** : FRANK **2** : GENEROUS 1 — **open·heart·ed·ly** *adv* — **open·heart·ed·ness** *n*

open–hearth *adj* : being or relating to a process of making steel from pig iron in a furnace that reflects heat from the roof onto the material

open house *n* : usually informal hospitality or entertainment for all comers

open·ing \ˈōp-(ə-)niŋ\ *n* **1** : an act or instance of making or becoming open ⟨the *opening* of a new store⟩ ⟨welcome to our grand *opening*⟩ **2** : something that is open: as **a** : ¹BREACH 2b **b** : an open place ⟨an *opening* in the woods⟩ **3** : BEGINNING 2 ⟨the *opening* of fishing season⟩ **4 a** : ¹OCCASION 1, CHANCE ⟨saw an *opening* to run with the ball⟩ **b** : a job opportunity ⟨*openings* for welders and machinists⟩

open letter *n* : a letter (as one addressed to an official) for the public to see and printed in a newspaper or magazine

open–mind·ed \ˌō-pən-'mīn-dəd\ *adj* : open to arguments or ideas : not prejudiced — **open–mind·ed·ly** *adv* — **open–mind·ed·ness** *n*

open·mouthed \ˌō-pən-'mau̇thd, -'mau̇tht\ *adj* **1** : having the mouth wide open **2** : struck with amazement or wonder

open season *n* : a time when it is legal to hunt game or catch fish that are legally protected at other times

open secret *n* : something supposed to be a secret but in fact generally known

open sentence *n* : a statement (as in mathematics) that contains at least one blank or unknown and that becomes true or false when the blank is filled or a quantity is substituted for the unknown ⟨"$n + 5 = 3$" and "It is divisible by 6" are *open sentences*⟩

open sesame *n* : something that always works to bring about a desired result ⟨believed education was the *open sesame* to the good life⟩ [from *open sesame*, the magical command used by Ali Baba to open the door of the robbers' den in the story *Ali Baba and the Forty Thieves*]

open up *vb* **1** : to make available **2** : to make visible or come into view ⟨the road *opens up* ahead⟩ **3** : to begin firing (as with a weapon or with questions)

open·work \'ō-pən-ˌwərk\ *n* : something made or work done so as to show openings through the fabric or material — **open–worked** \-ˌwərkt\ *adj*

¹opera *plural of* OPUS

²op·era \'äp-(ə-)rə\ *n* **1** : a play in which usually the entire text is sung with orchestral accompaniment **2** : the performance of an opera ⟨go to the *opera*⟩ — **op·er·at·ic** \ˌäp-ə-'rat-ik\ *adj*

op·er·a·ble \'äp-(ə-)rə-bəl\ *adj* **1** : fit, possible, or desirable to use **2** : likely to have a favorable result upon surgical treatment ⟨an *operable* cancer⟩

opera glasses *n pl* : small binoculars or field glasses of low power for use in a theater

op·er·ant \'äp-ə-rənt\ *adj* : of, relating to, or being operant conditioning or behavior reinforced by operant conditioning

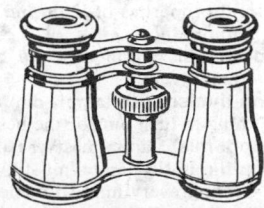

opera glasses

operant conditioning *n* : conditioning in which the desired behavior (as bar-pressing by a rat) or increasingly closer approximations to it are followed by a reinforcement (as delivery of food) that is needed, pleasant, or desired

op·er·ate \'äp-(ə-)ˌrāt\ *vb* **-at·ed; -at·ing** **1** : to work or cause to work in a proper way ⟨how to *operate* the new microwave oven⟩ **2** : to take effect ⟨a drug that *operates* quickly⟩ **3** : MANAGE 1 ⟨*operate* a business⟩ **4 a** : to perform an operation or a series of operations **b** : to perform surgery ⟨*operate* on a patient⟩ ⟨*operated* on an injured leg⟩ [from Latin *operatus*, past participle of *operari* "to work" — related to MANEUVER; see *Word History* at MANEUVER]

operating system *n* : software that controls the operation of a computer and directs the processing of the user's programs (as by controlling input and output functions)

op·er·a·tion \ˌäp-ə-'rā-shən\ *n* **1** : the act, process, method, or result of operating ⟨does the whole *operation* without stopping⟩ ⟨the *operation* of a drug⟩ **2** : the quality or state of being able to work or function ⟨put a factory into *operation*⟩ **3** : a procedure performed on a living body usually with medical instruments especially to restore health or repair damage or defect **4** : a mathematical or logical process (as addition or multiplication) for getting one mathematical expression from others according to a rule **5** : the process of putting military or naval forces into action ⟨naval *operations*⟩ **6** : a single step in a com-

puter program **7** : a usually small business or establishment ⟨ran a small *operation*⟩

op·er·a·tion·al \ˌäp-ə-'rā-shnəl, -shən-ᵊl\ *adj* **1** : of or relating to operation or an operation **2** : ready for operation

¹op·er·a·tive \'äp-(ə-)rət-iv, 'äp-ə-ˌrāt-\ *adj* **1** : producing a normal or desired effect **2** : being in operation

²operative *n* **1** : OPERATOR 1 **2 a** : a secret agent : SPY **b** : ²DETECTIVE

op·er·a·tor \'äp-(ə-)ˌrāt-ər\ *n* **1** : a person who operates something ⟨a computer *operator*⟩ ⟨the *operator* of an automobile⟩ **2** : a person in charge of a telephone switchboard

op·er·et·ta \ˌäp-ə-'ret-ə\ *n* : a light play set to music with speaking, singing, and dancing scenes

oph·thal·mol·o·gist \ˌäf-thə(l)-'mäl-ə-jəst, ˌäp-, -ˌthal-\ *n* : a physician specializing in ophthalmology — compare OPTICIAN 2, OPTOMETRIST

oph·thal·mol·o·gy \ˌäf-thə(l)-'mäl-ə-jē, ˌäp-, -ˌthal-\ *n* : a branch of medical science dealing with the structure, functions, and diseases of the eye

oph·thal·mo·scope \äf-'thal-mə-ˌskōp, äp-\ *n* : an optical instrument for viewing the inside of the eye

¹opi·ate \'ō-pē-ət, -ˌāt\ *n* **1** : a drug (as morphine or codeine) containing or made from opium and tending to cause sleep and relieve pain; *also* : ¹NARCOTIC 1 **2** : something restful or soothing ⟨the *opiate* of sleep⟩

²opiate *adj* **1 a** : containing or mixed with opium **b** : of, relating to, or being an opiate **2 a** : causing sleep **b** : causing dullness or idleness

opine \ō-'pīn\ *vb* **opined; opin·ing** : to have or express an opinion

opin·ion \ə-'pin-yən\ *n* **1** : a judgment about a person or thing ⟨a high *opinion* of themselves⟩ **2** : a belief based on experience and on seeing certain facts that falls short of positive knowledge **3 a** : a statement by an expert after careful study ⟨you better get a doctor's *opinion*⟩ **b** : a formal statement from a judge or court of the reasons for a legal decision ⟨read the court's *opinion* in that case⟩

synonyms OPINION, BELIEF, CONVICTION mean something that one thinks is true. OPINION suggests a judgment that may not be shared by all ⟨heard more than one *opinion* on that issue⟩. BELIEF suggests a view that one has come to accept fully in one's own mind ⟨a basic *belief* in a supreme being⟩. CONVICTION suggests a firm unchangeable belief ⟨a *conviction* that all life is valuable⟩.

opin·ion·at·ed \ə-'pin-yə-ˌnāt-əd\ *adj* : holding to one's own opinions and ideas too strongly

opi·um \'ō-pē-əm\ *n* **1** : a bitter brownish narcotic drug that causes addiction and is the dried juice of the unripe fruit capsule of the opium poppy **2** : something having an effect like that of opium

opium poppy *n* : an annual Eurasian poppy grown for opium, for its edible oily seeds, and for its showy flowers

opos·sum \(ə-)'päs-əm\ *n, pl* **opossums** *also* **opossum** : a common marsupial mammal mostly of the eastern U.S. that usually is active at night, has a tail that can wrap around and grasp objects (as tree branches), and is an expert climber [from *apossoun, opassom*, a word in

opossum

\ə\ abut	\au̇\ out	\i\ tip	\ȯ\ saw	\u̇\ foot
\ər\ further	\ch\ chin	\ī\ life	\ȯi\ coin	\y\ yet
\a\ mat	\e\ pet	\j\ job	\th\ thin	\yü\ few
\ā\ take	\ē\ easy	\ŋ\ sing	\th\ this	\yu̇\ cure
\ä\ cot, cart	\g\ go	\ō\ bone	\ü\ food	\zh\ vision

an Algonquian language of Virginia meaning, literally, "white dog"]

op·po·nent \ə-'pō-nənt\ *n* : a person or thing that opposes another

op·por·tune \ˌäp-ər-'t(y)ün\ *adj* : SUITABLE 1, TIMELY ⟨an *opportune* moment to act⟩ — **op·por·tune·ly** *adv*
Word History The Latin adjective *opportunus* was used to mean "fit, suitable, or convenient." It was formed from the prefix *op-, ob-,* meaning "at or toward" and *portus,* meaning "port or harbor." The Romans considered something "at the port" to be suitable and ready for use. The French took the word as *opportun* with the same basic meaning, and the word came into English as *opportune* in the 15th century. Nowadays it is often applied to a suitable or favorable time for something, or to something that occurs or is done at just the right time. [Middle English *opportune* "opportune, suitable, fit," from early French *opportun* (same meaning), from Latin *opportunus* "fit, suitable, convenient," from *op-, ob-* "toward, at" and *portus* "port, harbor"]

op·por·tun·ism \ˌäp-ər-'t(y)ü-ˌniz-əm\ *n* : the practice of taking advantage of opportunities or circumstances regardless of what one should do or what might happen

op·por·tun·ist \-'t(y)ü-nəst\ *n* : one that is opportunistic or that practices opportunism — **opportunist** *adj*

op·por·tu·nis·tic \-t(y)ü-'nis-tik\ *n* : taking advantage of opportunities as they arise: as **a** : exploiting opportunities with little regard to principle or consequences ⟨an *opportunistic* cheater⟩ **b** : feeding on whatever food is available ⟨*opportunistic* feeders⟩

op·por·tu·ni·ty \ˌäp-ər-'t(y)ü-nət-ē\ *n, pl* **-ties** 1 : a favorable combination of circumstances, time, and place 2 : a chance to better oneself

op·pos·able \ə-'pō-zə-bəl\ *adj* : capable of being placed against one or more of the remaining digits of a hand or foot ⟨the *opposable* human thumb⟩

op·pose \ə-'pōz\ *vb* **op·posed; op·pos·ing** 1 : to be or place opposite or against something 2 : to offer resistance to : stand against : RESIST

¹op·po·site \'äp-ə-zət, 'äp-sət\ *adj* **1 a** : being at the other end, side, or corner ⟨lived on *opposite* sides of the street⟩ ⟨the *opposite* sides of a rectangle⟩ **b** : being one of two angles of a four-sided figure (as a square or parallelogram) that are not next to each other **2 a** : being in a position to oppose or cancel out ⟨*opposite* sides of the question⟩ **b** : as different as possible : CONTRARY ⟨reached *opposite* conclusions⟩ ⟨went off in *opposite* directions⟩ **3** : being the other of a matching or contrasting pair ⟨the *opposite* sex⟩ — **op·po·site·ly** *adv* — **op·po·site·ness** *n*

²opposite *n* **1** : someone or something that is opposite **2** : ANTONYM **3** : ADDITIVE INVERSE; *esp* : the additive inverse of a real number ⟨+3 and –3 are *opposites*⟩

³opposite *adv* : on or to the opposite side

⁴opposite *prep* : across from and usually facing or on the same level with ⟨the house *opposite* ours⟩

op·po·si·tion \ˌäp-ə-'zish-ən\ *n* **1** : the state of being opposite **2** : the action of resisting ⟨offer *opposition* to a plan⟩ ⟨the *opposition* of two forces⟩ **3 a** : a group of persons (as a team or an enemy force) that oppose someone or something **b** *often cap* : a political party opposing the party in power

op·press \ə-'pres\ *vb* **1** : to control or rule in a harsh or cruel way ⟨a country *oppressed* by a dictator⟩ **2** : to cause to feel burdened in spirit ⟨*oppressed* by grief⟩ — **op·pres·sor** \-'pres-ər\ *n*

op·pres·sion \ə-'presh-ən\ *n* **1** : cruel or unjust use of authority or power **2** : a feeling of low spirits

op·pres·sive \ə-'pres-iv\ *adj* **1** : cruel or harsh without just cause ⟨*oppressive* taxes⟩ **2** : causing a feeling of op-

pression ⟨*oppressive* heat⟩ — **op·pres·sive·ly** *adv* — **op·pres·sive·ness** *n*

op·pro·bri·ous \ə-'prō-brē-əs\ *adj* : expressing very strong disapproval ⟨the *opprobrious* term "murderer"⟩

op·pro·bri·um \ə-'prō-brē-əm\ *n* : very strong disapproval

opt \'äpt\ *vb* : to make a choice

op·tic \'äp-tik\ *adj* : of or relating to vision or the eye [Middle English *optic* "relating to the eye," from Latin *opticus* (same meaning), from Greek *optikos* (same meaning), from *opsesthai* "to be going to see" — related to AUTOPSY]

op·ti·cal \'äp-ti-kəl\ *adj* **1** : relating to optics **2** : of or relating to vision **3 a** : of, relating to, or using light ⟨an *optical* telescope⟩ **b** : involving the use of a device that senses light to acquire information for a computer ⟨an *optical* scanner⟩ — **op·ti·cal·ly** \-k(ə-)lē\ *adv*

optical disk *n* : a disk with a plastic coating on which information (as music or computer data) is recorded in digital form and which is read by using a laser

optical fiber *n* : a single fiber-optic strand

optical illusion *n* : ILLUSION 1

op·ti·cian \äp-'tish-ən\ *n* **1** : a maker of or dealer in optical items and instruments **2** : a person who reads prescriptions for correction of vision, orders, prepares, and sometimes grinds lenses for eyeglasses, sells eyeglasses and contact lenses, and fits and adjusts eyeglasses — compare OPHTHALMOLOGIST, OPTOMETRIST

optic lobe *n* : either of a pair of lobes in the midbrain that are concerned with vision

optic nerve *n* : either of a pair of sensory nerves that are the second pair of cranial nerves and carry visual information from the retina of the eye to the brain

op·tics \'äp-tiks\ *n* : a science that deals with the nature and properties of light and the effects that it undergoes and produces

op·ti·mal \'äp-tə-məl\ *adj* : ²OPTIMUM — **op·ti·mal·ly** \-mə-lē\ *adv*

op·ti·mism \'äp-tə-ˌmiz-əm\ *n* : a habit of expecting everything to turn out for the best

op·ti·mist \'äp-tə-məst\ *n* : an optimistic person

op·ti·mis·tic \ˌäp-tə-'mis-tik\ *adj* : showing optimism : expecting everything to come out all right : HOPEFUL — **op·ti·mis·ti·cal·ly** \-ti-k(ə-)lē\ *adv*

¹op·ti·mum \'äp-tə-məm\ *n, pl* **-ma** \-mə\ *also* **-mums** : the best or most favorable amount or degree

²optimum *adj* : most desirable or satisfactory ⟨under *optimum* conditions⟩

op·tion \'äp-shən\ *n* **1** : the power or right to choose **2** : a right to buy or sell something at a specified price during a specified period ⟨took an *option* on the house⟩ **3** : something that may be chosen ⟨a CD player was one of the *options* on the car⟩

op·tion·al \'äp-shnəl, -shən-³l\ *adj* : left to one's choice : not required ⟨*optional* equipment on a new car⟩ — **op·tion·al·ly** \-ē\ *adv*

op·tom·e·trist \äp-'täm-ə-trəst\ *n* : a specialist licensed in optometry — compare OPHTHALMOLOGIST, OPTICIAN 2

op·tom·e·try \äp-'täm-ə-trē\ *n* : the profession of examining the eyesight and prescribing corrective lenses or eye exercises to improve vision and of diagnosing and sometimes treating diseases of the eye — **op·to·met·ric** \ˌäp-tə-'me-trik\ *adj*

op·u·lence \'äp-yə-lən(t)s\ *n* : great wealth

op·u·lent \'äp-yə-lənt\ *adj* : having or showing much wealth — **op·u·lent·ly** *adv*

opus \'ō-pəs\ *n, pl* **opera** \'ō-pə-rə, 'äp-ə-\ *also* **opus·es** \'ō-pə-səz\ : ¹WORK 7; *esp* : a musical composition or set of compositions

or \ər, (ˌ)ȯ(ə)r\ *conj* — used to indicate an alternative ⟨coffee *or* tea⟩ ⟨sink *or* swim⟩

¹-or \ər, ˌȯ(ə)r, ˈȯ(ə)r\ *n suffix* : one that does a specified thing ⟨elevat*or*⟩ [derived from Latin *-or* or *-ator,* both meaning "one that does something"]

²-or \ər\ *n suffix* : condition : activity ⟨demean*or*⟩ [derived from Latin *-or* "condition, activity"]

or·a·cle \ˈȯr-ə-kəl, ˈär-\ *n* **1** : a person (as a priestess of ancient Greece) through whom a god is believed to speak **2** : the place where a god speaks through an oracle **3** : an answer given by an oracle **4** : a person giving wise or final decisions or advice [Middle English *oracle* "a person through whom a god speaks," from early French *oracle* (same meaning), from Latin *oraculum* (same meaning), from *orare* "to speak, pray" — related to ADORE, ORATION]

orac·u·lar \ȯ-ˈrak-yə-lər, ə-\ *adj* **1** : of, relating to, or being an oracle **2** : resembling an oracle — **orac·u·lar·ly** *adv*

oral \ˈōr-əl, ˈȯr-, ˈär-\ *adj* **1** : uttered by the mouth : SPOKEN **2** : of, relating to, given by, or near the mouth ⟨*oral* hygiene⟩ — **oral·ly** \-ə-lē\ *adv*

synonyms ORAL, VERBAL mean expressed or communicated in words. ORAL applies only to the spoken word and not to what is written ⟨made an *oral* report before the class⟩. VERBAL applies to either speech or writing and may stress the use of words as opposed to other forms of expression or communication ⟨a test of your *verbal* and mathematical skills⟩.

¹or·ange \ˈär-inj, ˈȯr-, -ənj\ *n* **1 a** : a round usually sweet juicy fruit with a yellowish to reddish orange rind **b** : any of various small evergreen citrus trees having shiny leaves, fragrant white flowers, and fruits which are oranges **2** : a color between red and yellow

²orange *adj* **1** : of or relating to the orange **2** : of the color orange

or·ange·ade \ˌär-in-ˈjād, ˌȯr-, -ən-\ *n* : a drink made of orange juice, sugar, and water

orange hawkweed *n* : a European hawkweed that has bright orange-red flower heads and is a troublesome weed in northeastern North America

or·ange·wood \ˈär-inj-ˌwu̇d, ˈȯr-, -ənj-\ *n* : the wood of an orange tree

orang·utan \ə-ˈraŋ-ə-ˌtaŋ, -ˌtan\ *n* : a large anthropoid ape of Borneo and Sumatra that is about ⅔ as large as a gorilla, eats mostly plants, lives in trees, and has very long arms, long thin reddish brown hair, and a nearly hairless face

orate \ȯ-ˈrāt\ *vb* **orat·ed; orat·ing** : to speak as if giving an oration

ora·tion \ə-ˈrā-shən, ȯ-\ *n* : an important speech given on some special occasion [from Latin *oration-, oratio* "speech," from *oratus,* past participle of *orare* "to speak, pray" — related to ADORE, ORACLE]

orangutan

or·a·tor \ˈȯr-ət-ər, ˈär-\ *n* : a public speaker noted for skill and power in speaking

or·a·tor·i·cal \ˌȯr-ə-ˈtȯr-i-kəl, ˌär-ə-ˈtär-\ *adj* : of, relating to, or characteristic of an orator or oratory — **or·a·tor·i·cal·ly** \-k(ə-)lē\ *adv*

or·a·to·rio \ˌȯr-ə-ˈtȯr-ē-ˌō, ˌär-, -ˈtōr-\ *n, pl* **-ri·os** : a vocal and orchestral work usually dramatizing a religious subject without action or scenery

¹or·a·to·ry \ˈȯr-ə-ˌtōr-ē, ˈär-, -ˌtȯr-\ *n, pl* **-ries** : a place for prayer; *esp* : a private chapel

²oratory *n* **1** : the art of an orator **2** : oratorical language or speeches

orb \ˈȯ(ə)rb\ *n* **1** : something (as a planet) in the shape of a ball **2** : ¹EYE 1

¹or·bit \ˈȯr-bət\ *n* : one of the bone-lined cavities for the eyes in the vertebrate skull — called also *eye socket* [Middle English *orbit* "eye socket," from Latin *orbita* (same meaning), from earlier *orbita* "path, rut, track"]

²orbit *n* : the path taken by one body circling around another body ⟨the *orbit* of the earth around the sun⟩; *also* : one complete circle that makes up such a path [from Latin *orbita* "path, rut, track"] — **or·bit·al** \-ᵊl\ *adj*

³orbit *vb* **1** : to move in an orbit around : CIRCLE ⟨the moon *orbits* the earth⟩ **2** : to send up so as to move in an orbit ⟨*orbit* a satellite⟩

or·bit·er \ˈȯr-bət-ər\ *n* **1** : one that orbits **2** : SPACE SHUTTLE

or·chard \ˈȯr-chərd\ *n* **1** : a place where fruit or nut trees are grown **2** : the trees in an orchard

or·ches·tra \ˈȯr-kə-strə, -ˌkes-trə\ *n* **1** : the front part of the main floor of a theater **2** : a group of musicians who perform instrumental music using mostly stringed instruments

Word History In front of the ancient Greek stage was a semicircular space where a chorus danced, sang, and commented on the action of the play. The Greek word *orchēstra* referred to this space. It came from the verb *orcheisthai,* meaning "to dance." The word was borrowed into Latin, but the Roman orchestra was reserved for the seats of prominent persons, such as senators, instead of for a chorus. When English borrowed the word, it indicated the space occupied by a group of musicians, usually right in front of the stage. It also was used to refer to the group of musicians itself. Later, *orchestra* came to mean the forward part or all of the main floor of a theater. [from Latin *orchestra* "the place in front of the stage where prominent persons sit," from Greek *orchēstra* "a semicircular area in front of the stage of a theater where the chorus dances," from *orcheisthai* "to dance"]

or·ches·tral \ȯr-ˈkes-trəl\ *adj* : of, relating to, or written for an orchestra

or·ches·trate \ˈȯr-kə-ˌstrāt\ *vb* **-trat·ed; -trat·ing** **1** : to write or arrange music for an orchestra **2** : to arrange or combine so as to get the best effect — **or·ches·tra·tion** \ˌȯr-kə-ˈstrā-shən\ *n*

or·chid \ˈȯr-kəd\ *n* **1** : any plant or flower of a large family of plants that have usually showy flowers with three petals of which the middle petal is enlarged and differs from the others in shape and color **2** : a light purple

or·chis \ˈȯr-kəs\ *n* : ORCHID 1; *esp* : any of a genus of woodland plants having fleshy roots and a spur on the middle petal

or·dain \ȯr-ˈdān\ *vb* **1** : to make a person a Christian minister or priest by a special ceremony **2 a** : ²DECREE ⟨it was *ordained* by law⟩ **b** : DESTINE 1 ⟨we seem *ordained* to fail⟩

or·deal \ȯr-ˈdē(-ə)l\ *n* **1** : a method of deciding guilt or innocence by making the accused person take dangerous or painful tests ⟨*ordeal* by fire⟩ **2** : a severe test or experience

¹or·der \ˈȯrd-ər\ *vb* **or·dered; or·der·ing** \ˈȯrd-(ə-)riŋ\ **1** : to put in order : ARRANGE ⟨*ordered* the books alphabetically⟩ **2 a** : to give an order to or for ⟨*ordered* them to clean their rooms⟩ ⟨*order* groceries⟩ **b** : to command to go or come to a certain place ⟨*order* troops back to base⟩ **3** : to place an order ⟨have you *ordered* yet?⟩ — **or·der·er** \ˈȯrd-ər-ər\ *n*

\ə\ abut	\au̇\ out	\i\ tip	\ȯ\ saw	\u̇\ foot
\ər\ further	\ch\ chin	\ī\ life	\ȯi\ coin	\y\ yet
\a\ mat	\e\ pet	\j\ job	\th\ thin	\yü\ few
\ā\ take	\ē\ easy	\ŋ\ sing	\th\ this	\yu̇\ cure
\ä\ cot, cart	\g\ go	\ō\ bone	\ü\ food	\zh\ vision

²order *n* **1 a** : a group of people united in some way (as by living under the same religious rule or by loyalty to common interests and duties) ⟨an *order* of monks⟩ ⟨an *order* of knighthood⟩ **b** : the badge or emblem of such an order **c** : a military medal or award **2** *pl* : the Christian ministry ⟨in *orders*⟩ **3 a** : a rank or class in society ⟨the lower *orders*⟩ **b** : ¹CLASS 3a, KIND ⟨emergencies of this *order*⟩ **c** : a category of biological classification ranking above the family and below the class **4 a** : the way objects in space or events in time are arranged or follow one another ⟨the *order* of the seasons⟩ ⟨in alphabetical *order*⟩ **b** : the established way or arrangement ⟨the old *order*⟩ **c** : regular or harmonious arrangement or a condition having such an arrangement ⟨kept my room in *order*⟩ **5 a** : the state of things when law or authority is obeyed ⟨restored *order* after the riot⟩ **b** : a certain rule or direction : COMMAND ⟨that's an *order*⟩ **6 a** : a style of building **b** : a type of architectural column with its related parts **7** : good working condition ⟨out of *order*⟩ **8 a** : a direction to pay money, to buy or sell, or to supply goods or services **b** : goods or items bought or sold ⟨an *order* of eggs and toast⟩ — **in order** : APPROPRIATE ⟨an apology is *in order*⟩ — **in order to** *or* **in order that** : for the purpose of — **on the order of 1** : similar to : LIKE ⟨cloth *on the order of* tweed⟩ **2** : ABOUT ⟨spent *on the order of* $2000⟩ — **to order** : according to the instructions of an order ⟨a suit made *to order*⟩

²order 6b: *1* Corinthian, *2* Doric, *3* Ionic

or·dered \'ȯrd-ərd\ *adj* **1** : carefully regulated or managed ⟨led an *ordered* life⟩ ⟨an *ordered* landscape⟩ **2 a** : having the property that for any two different elements *a* and *b* either *a* is greater than *b* or *a* is less than *b* ⟨the set of real numbers is *ordered*⟩ **b** : having elements labeled by ordinal numbers ⟨an *ordered* pair has a first and a second element⟩

¹or·der·ly \'ȯrd-ər-lē\ *adj* **1 a** : arranged in some order or pattern ⟨*orderly* rows of houses⟩ **b** : ¹TIDY 1 ⟨kept my desk *orderly*⟩ **c** : regulated by law or system ⟨an *orderly* universe⟩ **d** : METHODICAL 2 ⟨an *orderly* thinker⟩ **2** : well behaved ⟨an *orderly* crowd⟩ — **or·der·li·ness** *n* — **orderly** *adv*

²orderly *n, pl* **-lies 1** : a soldier who carries messages and performs services for an officer **2** : a person who waits on others, cleans, and does general work in a hospital

or·di·nal \'ȯrd-nəl, -ᵊn-əl\ *n* : ORDINAL NUMBER

ordinal number *n* : a number indicating the place (as first, fifth, 22nd) of an item in an ordered sequence — compare CARDINAL NUMBER; see NUMBER table

or·di·nance \'ȯrd-nən(t)s, -ᵊn-ən(t)s\ *n* : a law or regulation especially of a city or town

¹or·di·nary \'ȯrd-ᵊn-ˌer-ē\ *n, pl* **-nar·ies 1** : regular or usual condition or course of things ⟨nothing out of the *ordinary*⟩ **2 a** *British* : a meal served to any person at a fixed price **b** *chiefly British* : a restaurant serving regular meals

²ordinary *adj* **1** : to be expected : NORMAL, USUAL ⟨*ordinary* problems⟩ **2** : neither good nor bad : AVERAGE ⟨an *ordinary* person⟩ — **or·di·nari·ly** \ˌȯrd-ᵊn-'er-ə-lē\ *adv* — **or·di·nari·ness** \'ȯrd-ᵊn-ˌer-ē-nəs\ *n*

or·di·nate \'ȯrd-nət, -ᵊn-ət, -ᵊn-ˌāt\ *n* : the number in an ordered pair of numbers (as *y* in (*x, y*)) that gives the location of a point along the y-axis — called also *y-coordinate;* compare ABSCISSA

or·di·na·tion \ˌȯrd-ᵊn-'ā-shən\ *n* : the act of ordaining : the state of being ordained

ord·nance \'ȯrd-nən(t)s\ *n* **1** : military supplies; *also* : the branch of the army that obtains and gives out military supplies **2** : ARTILLERY 1

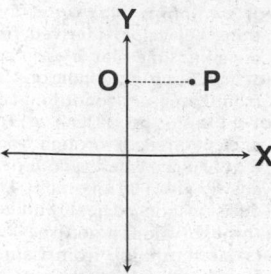

ordinate: *O* is the ordinate of point *P*

Or·do·vi·cian \ˌȯrd-ə-'vish-ən\ *adj* : of, relating to, or being a period of the Paleozoic era of geological history or the corresponding system of rocks — see GEOLOGIC TIME table — **Ordovician** *n*

¹ore \'ō(ə)r, 'ȯ(ə)r\ *n* : a mineral mined to obtain a substance that it contains ⟨iron *ore*⟩

²ore \'ər-ə\ *n, pl* **ore** : a unit of value equal to ¹/₁₀₀ krona or ¹/₁₀₀ krone [Swedish *öre* and Danish and Norwegian *øre*]

ore·ad \'ōr-ē-ˌad, 'ȯr-, -ē-əd\ *n* : a nymph of mountains and hills in Greek mythology

oreg·a·no \ə-'reg-ə-ˌnō\ *n, pl* **-nos** : a bushy mint with leaves used as a seasoning and a source of a fragrant oil

or·gan \'ȯr-gən\ *n* **1 a** : a keyboard musical instrument in which sets of pipes are sounded by compressed air **b** : an electronic keyboard musical instrument by which sounds like those of an organ are made **2** : a part (as a kidney or leaf) of a person, plant, or animal that consists of cells and tissues and is specialized to do a particular task — compare SYSTEM 1b **3** : a way of getting something done ⟨courts are *organs* of government⟩ **4** : a publication (as a newspaper or magazine) of a special group

or·gan·dy *also* **or·gan·die** \'ȯr-gən-dē\ *n, pl* **-dies** : a fine transparent cotton fabric with a stiff finish and a plain weave

or·gan·elle \ˌȯr-gə-'nel\ *n* : a structure (as a mitochondrion) in a cell that performs a special function

or·gan–grind·er \'ȯr-gən-ˌgrīn-dər\ *n* : a traveling street musician who plays a hand organ

or·gan·ic \ȯr-'gan-ik\ *adj* **1 a** : of, relating to, or arising in a bodily organ **b** : affecting the structure of the living thing ⟨an *organic* disease⟩ **2 a** : of, relating to, or obtained from living things ⟨*organic* matter⟩ **b** : of, relating to, or containing carbon compounds **c** : of, relating to, or dealt with by a branch of chemistry concerned with the carbon compounds of living things and most other carbon compounds **d** : relating to, producing, dealing in, or involving foods produced with the use of feed or fertilizer obtained from plants or animals and without the use of laboratory-made fertilizers, growth substances, antibiotics, or pesticides ⟨*organic* gardeners⟩ ⟨*organic* food stores⟩ **3 a** : forming an important part of a whole : FUNDAMENTAL **b** : having the parts related together ⟨an *organic* whole⟩ — **or·gan·i·cal·ly** \-i-k(ə-)lē\ *adv*

or·gan·ism \'ȯr-gə-ˌniz-əm\ *n* **1** : something having many related parts that function together as a whole **2** : an individual living thing that carries on the activities of life by means of organs which have separate functions but are dependent on each other : a living person, plant, or animal — **or·gan·is·mic** \ˌȯr-gə-'niz-mik\ *adj*

or·gan·ist \'ȯr-gə-nəst\ *n* : one who plays an organ

¹or·ga·ni·za·tion \ˌȯrg-(ə-)nə-'zā-shən\ *n* **1** : the act or process of organizing **2** : the condition or manner of being organized ⟨a high degree of *organization*⟩ **3** : a group of persons organized for some purpose ⟨a business *organization*⟩ — **or·ga·ni·za·tion·al** \-shnəl, -shən-ᵊl\ *adj*

²**organization** *adj* : behaving and thinking in a way that an organization would approve of

or·ga·nize \'òr-gə-ˌnīz\ *vb* **-nized; -niz·ing 1** : to make separate parts into one united whole : form or form into an organization **2** : to put into order : SYSTEMATIZE ⟨*organize* your work⟩ — **or·ga·niz·er** *n*

or·ga·nized *adj* : having an organization to plan and carry out activities ⟨*organized* baseball⟩

organ of Cor·ti \-'kòrt-ē\ : a complicated structure in the cochlea that is the chief part of the ear which receives sound and changes it into signals carrying information to the brain

or·gasm \'òr-ˌgaz-əm\ *n* : the climax of sexual excitement

or·gy \'òr-jē\ *n, pl* **orgies 1** : secret ceremonies in honor of an ancient Greek or Roman god usually celebrated by wild singing and dancing **2** : something (as a party) that resembles an orgy in lack of control

ori·el window \'ōr-ē-əl-, 'òr-\ *n* : a large window that sticks out from and is supported against a wall

ori·ent \'ōr-ē-ent, 'òr-\ *vb* **1 a** : to cause to face toward the east **b** : to set or arrange in a definite position especially in relation to the points of the compass **2** : to acquaint with a situation or environment ⟨*orient* new students⟩ **3** : to direct towards the interests of a particular group ⟨movies that are *oriented* toward teenagers⟩

Ori·ent \'ōr-ē-ənt, 'òr-, -ē-ˌent\ *n* : ³EAST 2; *esp* : the countries of eastern Asia

Word History The Romans had no magnetic compasses, so they depended on the position of the rising sun to determine directions in the daytime. The direction from which the sun

oriel window

rose (which we know as east) was called *oriens*. This word was formed from the verb *oriri*, meaning "to rise, come forth." The word *oriens* also came to be used for the part of the world in the direction from which the sun rose, that is, the area we call the East. The English word *Orient*, taken from the Latin *oriens*, was used for the same general area to the east of Europe, and especially eastern Asia. When the verb *orient* was first used in English, it meant "to set or face toward the east." To orient a church means to build it so that the aisles lead up to the main altar at the eastern end of the building. Other senses of the verb developed later. [Middle English *orient* "east," from Medieval French *orient* (same meaning), from Latin *orient-*, *oriens* "the direction in which the sun rises," from *oriri* "to rise" — related to ORIGIN]

ori·en·tal \ˌōr-ē-'ent-ᵊl, ˌòr-\ *adj, often cap* : of, relating to, or situated in Asia — **ori·en·tal·ly** \-ᵊl-ē\ *adv*

Oriental *n, sometimes offensive* : one who is a native of east Asia or is of east Asian descent

Oriental poppy *n* : an Asian perennial poppy commonly grown for its very large showy flowers

Oriental rug *n* : a handwoven or hand-knotted rug or carpet made in a country of central or southern Asia

ori·en·tate \'ōr-ē-ən-ˌtāt, 'òr-, -ˌen-\ *vb* **-tat·ed; -tat·ing** : ORIENT

ori·en·ta·tion \ˌōr-ē-ən-'tā-shən, ˌòr-ē-ˌen-\ *n* **1 a** : the act or process of orienting or of being oriented **b** : the state of being oriented **2** : a usually general or lasting direction of thought, inclination, or interest **3** : change of position by a cell or organism or by one of their parts in response to outside stimulus

ori·en·teer·ing \ˌōr-ē-ən-'tir-iŋ\ *n* : a competitive or noncompetitive recreational activity in which participants

find their way over an unfamiliar course (as in the woods) using a map and compass

-ories *plural of* -ORY

ori·fice \'òr-ə-fəs, 'är-\ *n* : an opening (as a mouth or hole) through which something may pass

ori·ga·mi \ˌòr-ə-'gäm-ē\ *n* : the Japanese art of folding paper into shapes

or·i·gin \'òr-ə-jən, 'är-\ *n* **1** : ANCESTRY 1, PARENTAGE ⟨of French *origin*⟩ **2 a** : a rising, beginning, or coming from a source **b** : basic source or cause **3** : the intersection of the x-axis and y-axis on a graph [Middle English *origine* "ancestry," from Latin *origin-*, *origo*, from *oriri* "to rise" — related to ABORIGINE, ORIENT; see *Word History* at ORIENT]

¹**orig·i·nal** \ə-'rij-ən-ᵊl, -nəl\ *n* : something from which a copy or translation is made

²**original** *adj* **1** : relating to or being the origin or beginning : FIRST, EARLIEST ⟨the *original* part of an old house⟩ ⟨*original* owners⟩ **2** : not copied or imitated from something else ⟨*original* paintings⟩ ⟨an *original* idea⟩ **3** : being an original **4** : able to think up new things : INVENTIVE ⟨an *original* artist⟩ **synonyms** see NEW

orig·i·nal·i·ty \ə-ˌrij-ə-'nal-ət-ē\ *n* **1** : the quality or state of being original : FRESHNESS ⟨the *originality* of an idea⟩ **2** : the power or ability to think, act, or do something in new ways : CREATIVITY ⟨an artist of great *originality*⟩

orig·i·nal·ly \ə-'rij-ən-ᵊl-ē, -nəl-ē\ *adv* **1** : in the beginning : in the first place ⟨it *originally* belonged to me⟩ **2** : in an original manner

original sin *n* **1** : the state of sin that according to Christian teaching all people are born in as a result of Adam's sin in Eden **2** : a very great and significant wrong ⟨the *original sin* of slavery⟩

orig·i·nate \ə-'rij-ə-ˌnāt\ *vb* **-nat·ed; -nat·ing 1** : to bring into existence : cause to be : INITIATE, INVENT **2** : to come into existence : ARISE — **orig·i·na·tion** \-ˌrij-ə-'nā-shən\ *n* — **orig·i·na·tor** \-'rij-ə-ˌnāt-ər\ *n*

ori·ole \'ōr-ē-ˌōl, 'òr-, -ē-əl\ *n* **1** : any of various usually brightly colored Old World birds related to the crows **2** : any of various New World birds that build hanging nests woven from various materials (as grass and leaves) and the males of which are usually black and yellow or orange and the females chiefly greenish or yellowish

Ori·on \ə-'rī-ən, ò-\ *n* : a group of stars on the equator east of Taurus represented on charts by the figure of a hunter with belt and sword

or·i·son \'òr-ə-sən, 'är-, -zən\ *n* **1** : PRAYER 1 **2** : PRAYER 2a

Or·lon \'ò(ə)r-ˌlän\ *trademark* — used for an acrylic fiber

¹**or·na·ment** \'òr-nə-mənt\ *n* **1** : something that adds beauty : DECORATION **2** : addition of something that beautifies ⟨a satin bow applied for *ornament*⟩

²**or·na·ment** \'òr-nə-ˌment\ *vb* : to provide with ornament : ADORN — **or·na·men·ta·tion** \ˌòr-nə-mən-'tā-shən, -ˌmen-\ *n*

¹**or·na·men·tal** \ˌòr-nə-'ment-ᵊl\ *adj* : of, relating to, or serving as ornament — **or·na·men·tal·ly** \-ᵊl-ē\ *adv*

²**ornamental** *n* : a decorative object; *esp* : a plant cultivated for its beauty rather than for use

or·nate \òr-'nāt\ *adj* : decorated in a fancy way — **or·nate·ly** *adv* — **or·nate·ness** *n*

or·nery \'òrn-(ə-)rē, 'ärn-\ *adj* **or·neri·er; -est** : having an irritable disposition — **or·neri·ness** *n*

or·ni·thol·o·gist \ˌòr-nə-'thäl-ə-jəst\ *n* : a person who specializes in ornithology

or·ni·thol·o·gy \ˌòr-nə-'thäl-ə-jē\ *n* : a branch of zoology dealing with birds

\ə\ **abut**	\aú\ **out**	\i\ **tip**	\ò\ **saw**	\ú\ **foot**
\ər\ **further**	\ch\ **chin**	\ī\ **life**	\òi\ **coin**	\y\ **yet**
\a\ **mat**	\e\ **pet**	\j\ **job**	\th\ **thin**	\yü\ **few**
\ā\ **take**	\ē\ **easy**	\ŋ\ **sing**	\th\ **this**	\yu̇\ **cure**
\ä\ **cot, cart**	\g\ **go**	\ō\ **bone**	\ü\ **food**	\zh\ **vision**

¹or·phan \ˈȯr-fən\ *n* **1** : a child whose parents are dead **2** : one who has had some protection or advantage taken away ⟨*orphans* of the storm⟩ — **orphan** *adj* — **or·phan·hood** \-ˌhůd\ *n*

²orphan *vb* **or·phaned; or·phan·ing** \ˈȯrf-(ə-)niŋ\ : to cause to become an orphan ⟨children *orphaned* by war⟩

or·phan·age \ˈȯrf-(ə-)nij\ *n* : an institution for the care of orphans

or·tho·clase \ˈȯr-thə-ˌklās, -ˌklāz\ *n* : a mineral consisting especially of potassium feldspar

orth·odon·tics \ˌȯr-thə-ˈdänt-iks\ *n* : a branch of dentistry dealing with faults in the arrangement and placing of teeth and with their correction (as by means of braces) — **orth·odon·tic** \-ˈdänt-ik\ *adj*

orth·odon·tist \ˌȯr-thə-ˈdänt-əst\ *n* : a dentist who specializes in orthodontics

or·tho·dox \ˈȯr-thə-ˌdäks\ *adj* **1** : holding established beliefs especially in religion ⟨an *orthodox* Christian⟩ **2** : approved as measuring up to some standard : USUAL, CONVENTIONAL ⟨take an *orthodox* approach to a problem⟩ **3** *cap* **a** : EASTERN ORTHODOX **b** : of or relating to Orthodox Judaism — **or·tho·dox·ly** *adv*

> **Word History** When someone has the same opinions and beliefs as those held by most other people, these opinions are usually considered the "right" opinions to have. In English such opinions might be called "orthodox." The English word *orthodox* comes originally from the Greek words *orthos,* meaning "right, true" and *doxa,* meaning "opinion." These two words were combined to form the Greek verb *orthodoxein,* meaning "to have the right opinion." From *orthodoxein* came the Greek adjective *orthodoxos,* which was borrowed into Latin as *orthodoxus.* The English adjective *orthodox* comes from this Latin adjective. [from early French *orthodoxe* or Latin *orthodoxus,* both meaning "orthodox," from Greek *orthodoxos* (same meaning), from *orthodoxein* "to have the right or true opinion," derived from *orthos* "right, true" and *doxa* "opinion"]

Orthodox Judaism *n* : Judaism that considers the Torah and Talmud sacred and that strictly follows Jewish laws and traditions in everyday life

or·tho·doxy \ˈȯr-thə-ˌdäk-sē\ *n, pl* **-dox·ies 1** : the quality or state of being orthodox **2** : an orthodox belief or practice

or·thog·ra·phy \ȯr-ˈthäg-rə-fē\ *n, pl* **-phies 1** : correct spelling **2** : a way or style of spelling — **or·tho·graph·ic** \ˌȯr-thə-ˈgraf-ik\ *also* **or·tho·graph·i·cal** \-i-kəl\ *adj* — **or·tho·graph·i·cal·ly** \-i-k(ə-)lē\ *adv*

or·tho·pe·dic \ˌȯr-thə-ˈpēd-ik\ *adj* **1** : of, relating to, or used in orthopedics **2** : marked by or affected with skeletal deformity, disorder, or injury

or·tho·pe·dics \ˌȯr-thə-ˈpēd-iks\ *n sing or pl* : a branch of medicine dealing with the correction or prevention of deformities, disorders, or injuries of the skeleton and structures (as tendons and ligaments) closely associated with it

or·tho·pe·dist \ˌȯr-thə-ˈpēd-əst\ *n* : a physician who specializes in orthopedics

¹-o·ry \ˌȯr-ē, ȯr-ē, (ə-)rē\ *n suffix, pl* **-ories** : place of or for ⟨observat*ory*⟩ [derived from Latin *-orius* (adjective suffix)]

²-ory *adj suffix* : of, relating to, serving for, or characterized by ⟨regulat*ory*⟩

oryx \ˈōr-iks, ˈȯr-, ˈär-\ *n, pl* **oryx** *or* **oryx·es** : any of several African antelopes having long horns that are straight or that curve backward

Osage \ō-ˈsāj, ˈō-ˌsāj\ *n, pl* **Osag·es** *or* **Osage** : a member of an American Indian people originally of Missouri

oryx

os·cil·late \ˈäs-ə-ˌlāt\ *vb* **-lat·ed; -lat·ing 1 a** : to swing backward and forward like a pendulum **b** : to move or travel back and forth between two points **2** : to have trouble deciding between opposing beliefs, feelings, or ideas — **os·cil·la·to·ry** \ˈäs-ə-lə-ˌtōr-ē, -ˌtȯr-\ *adj*

os·cil·la·tion \ˌäs-ə-ˈlā-shən\ *n* **1** : the action or state of oscillating : VIBRATION **2** : VARIATION 1, FLUCTUATION **3** : a single swing (as of an oscillating body) from one extreme limit to the other

os·cil·la·tor \ˈäs-ə-ˌlāt-ər\ *n* **1** : one that oscillates **2** : a device for producing alternating current; *esp* : a radio-frequency or audio-frequency generator

os·cil·lo·scope \ä-ˈsil-ə-ˌskōp, ə-\ *n* : an instrument in which the variations in a continually changing electrical quantity appear temporarily as a visible wave form on the screen of a cathode-ray tube

Osee \ˈō-ˌzē, ō-ˈzä-ə\ *n* : HOSEA

osier \ˈō-zhər\ *n* **1** : any of various willows with easily bent twigs used for making furniture and baskets **2** : a willow rod used for making baskets **3** : any of several American dogwoods

os·mi·um \ˈäz-mē-əm\ *n* : a hard brittle blue-gray or blue-black metallic element with a high melting point that is the heaviest metal known — see ELEMENT table

os·mo·sis \äz-ˈmō-səs, äs-\ *n* **1** : the passage of material (as a solvent) through a membrane (as of a plant or animal cell) that will not allow all kinds of molecules to pass **2** : a taking in (as of knowledge) as if by the process of osmosis — **os·mot·ic** \-ˈmät-ik\ *adj*

os·prey \ˈäs-prē, -ˌprā\ *n, pl* **ospreys** : a large hawk that is dark brown above and mostly white below and that feeds chiefly on fish — called also *fish hawk*

os·si·cle \ˈäs-i-kəl\ *n* : a small bone or bony structure (as one of the three small bones of the middle ear) [Latin, literally, "small bone"]

os·si·fi·ca·tion \ˌäs-ə-fə-ˈkā-shən\ *n* : the natural process of bone formation

os·si·fy \ˈäs-ə-ˌfī\ *vb* **-fied; -fy·ing 1** : to become or change into bone or bony tissue **2** : to become or make hardened or set in one's ways

os·ten·si·ble \ä-ˈsten(t)-sə-bəl, ə-\ *adj* : shown outwardly : APPARENT ⟨the *ostensible* purpose of his visit⟩

os·ten·si·bly \ä-ˈsten(t)-sə-blē, ə-\ *adv* : to all outward appearances : SEEMINGLY ⟨a statement *ostensibly* true⟩

os·ten·ta·tion \ˌäs-tən-ˈtā-shən\ *n* : unnecessary show to attract attention, admiration, or envy

os·ten·ta·tious \ˌäs-tən-ˈtā-shəs\ *adj* : fond of or showing ostentation — **os·ten·ta·tious·ly** *adv* — **os·ten·ta·tious·ness** *n*

os·teo·ar·thri·tis \ˌäs-tē-ō-är-ˈthrīt-əs\ *n* : arthritis marked by the breakdown of cartilage and bone of joints

os·te·o·blast \ˈäs-tē-ə-ˌblast\ *n* : a cell that forms bone

os·te·o·cyte \ˈäs-tē-ə-ˌsīt\ *n* : a bone cell that develops from an osteoblast trapped in one of the tiny spaces in bone

os·teo·path \ˈäs-tē-ə-ˌpath\ *n* : a person who practices osteopathy

os·te·op·a·thy \ˌäs-tē-ˈäp-ə-thē\ *n* : a system of treating diseases that uses procedures involving especially the manipulation of bones but does not exclude other treatment (as the use of drugs and surgery) — **os·teo·path·ic** \ˌäs-tē-ə-ˈpath-ik\ *adj*

os·te·o·po·ro·sis \ˌäs-tē-ō-pə-ˈrō-səs\ *n* : a condition affecting especially older women that is characterized by weak bones that are easily broken

ostler *variant of* HOSTLER

os·tra·cism \ˈäs-trə-ˌsiz-əm\ *n* **1** : a method of temporary banishment by popular vote without trial practiced in ancient Greece **2** : a general refusal to include someone as part of a social group

os·tra·cize \ˈäs-trə-ˌsīz\ *vb* **-cized; -ciz·ing** : to force to leave or refuse to include by ostracism

Word History The ancient Greek word *ostrakon* had several meanings, including "a shell" and "a fragment of pottery." Such pottery fragments were used in ancient Athens as ballots in a particular kind of popular vote. Once a year the citizens would gather in the marketplace to decide who, if anyone, should be forced to go away temporarily for the good of the city. Each voter wrote a name on an *ostrakon.* If enough votes were cast against one person, then that person was sent away from the city, or *ostracized.* [from Greek *ostrakizein* "to banish by voting with pottery fragments," from *ostrakon* "shell, pottery fragment"]

os·trich \'äs-trich, 'ôs-\ *n* **1** : a very large bird of Africa that often weighs as much as 300 pounds (140 kilograms) runs very quickly but cannot fly, and has large wing and tail feathers used especially formerly in dusters and fans and to adorn hats and clothing **2** : one who tries to avoid danger by refusing to face it

ostrich 1

¹oth·er \'əth-ər\ *adj* **1** : not being the one or ones first mentioned or included ⟨broke my *other* arm⟩ **2** : having one come before that is not included or counted : SECOND ⟨every *other* day⟩ **3** : not the same : DIFFERENT ⟨any *other* color would be better⟩ **4** : ADDITIONAL ⟨some *other* guests are coming⟩ **5** : recently past ⟨the *other* evening⟩

²other *n* **1** : a remaining one ⟨lift one foot and then the *other*⟩ **2** : a different or additional one ⟨the *others* came later⟩

³other *pron* : a different or additional one ⟨something or *other*⟩

⁴other *adv* : OTHERWISE 1 ⟨could not get there *other* than by helicopter⟩

¹other than *prep* : EXCEPT FOR, BESIDES ⟨*other than* that, nothing happened⟩

²other than *conj* : ³EXCEPT 2, BUT ⟨cannot enter *other than* by special permission⟩

oth·er·wise \'ə-thər-,wīz\ *adv* **1** : in a different way : DIFFERENTLY ⟨could not do *otherwise*⟩ **2** : in different circumstances ⟨*otherwise* we might have won⟩ **3** : in other respects ⟨the *otherwise* busy street⟩

oth·er·world \'əth-ər-,wərld\ *n* : a world beyond death

oto·lar·yn·gol·o·gy \'ōt-ō-,lar-ən-'gäl-ə-jē\ *n* : a medical specialty concerned with the ear, nose, and throat

ot·ter \'ät-ər\ *n, pl* **otter** *or* **otters** **1** : any of several water-dwelling mammals that are related to the weasels and minks, have webbed feet with claws and dark brown fur, and feed on other animals (as fish, clams, and crabs) that live in or near the water — compare SEA OTTER **2** : the fur or pelt of an otter

otter 1

ot·to·man \'ät-ə-mən\ *n, pl* **-mans** **1** *cap* : a citizen or government official of the Ottoman Empire **2** : an upholstered footstool

Ot·to·man \'ät-ə-mən\ *adj* : of or relating to the Ottoman Empire, its rulers, or its citizens or government officials

ouch \'auch\ *interj* — used to express sudden pain

ought \'ot\ *helping verb* **1** — used to express duty ⟨we *ought* to pay our debts⟩ **2** — used to express what it would be wise to do ⟨you *ought* to take care of yourself⟩

3 — used to express what is naturally expected ⟨they *ought* to be here by now⟩ **4** — used to express what is correct ⟨the result *ought* to be zero⟩

oughtn't \'ot-²nt\ : ought not

ounce \'aun(t)s\ *n* **1 a** : a unit of weight equal to ¹⁄₁₂ troy pound (about 31 grams) — see MEASURE table **b** : a unit of weight equal to ¹⁄₁₆ avoirdupois pound (about 28 grams) **c** : a small amount ⟨an *ounce* of common sense⟩ **2** : FLUID OUNCE

Word History The Latin word *uncia* was used to mean "a twelfth part of something." In reference to length, it meant one-twelfth of a *pes* "foot." In reference to weight, it meant one-twelfth of a *libra* "pound." *Uncia,* as a unit of length, came into Old English as *ince* or *ynce,* which became our *inch. Uncia,* as a unit of weight, came into Middle English from the early French word *unce* and became our *ounce.* In the present system of weights used in this country, the pound is divided into sixteen parts instead of twelve. The result is that the ounce, which originally meant one-twelfth, is now equal to one-sixteenth of a pound. [Middle English *unce, ounce* "ounce," from early French *unce* (same meaning), from Latin *uncia* "a twelfth part, ounce," from *unus* "one" — related to INCH, UNITE]

our \är, (')au̇(ə)r\ *adj* : of or relating to us or ourselves or ourself ⟨*our* house⟩ ⟨*our* actions⟩ ⟨*our* being chosen⟩

Our Father *n* : LORD'S PRAYER

ours \(')au̇(ə)rz, ärz\ *pron sing or pl* : that which belongs to us ⟨your yard is big and *ours* is small⟩

our·selves \är-'selvz, au̇(ə)r-\ *pron pl* **1** : our own selves — used for emphasis or to show that the subject and object of the verb are the same ⟨we amused *ourselves*⟩ ⟨we did it *ourselves*⟩ **2** : our normal or healthy selves ⟨just not *ourselves* today⟩

-ous \əs\ *adj suffix* **1** : full of : having plenty of ⟨clamor*ous*⟩ **2** : having : possessing the qualities of ⟨poison*ous*⟩ [derived from Latin *-osus* (adjective suffix)]

oust \'au̇st\ *vb* : to force or drive out (as from office or from possession of something)

oust·er \'au̇s-tər\ *n* : the act or an instance of ousting or being ousted

¹out \'au̇t\ *adv* **1 a** : in a direction away from the inside, center, or surface ⟨look *out* of a window⟩ **b** : ¹OUTDOORS ⟨it's raining *out*⟩ **c** : OUT-OF-BOUNDS **2** : from among others ⟨picked *out* a hat⟩ **3** : away from home, business, or the usual or proper place ⟨*out* to lunch⟩ ⟨left a word *out*⟩ **4** : into a state of loss or defeat ⟨was voted *out* of office⟩ **5** : into the possession or control of another ⟨lent *out* money⟩ **6** : into groups or shares ⟨sorted *out* her notes⟩ **7 a** : so as to be exhausted, completed, or discontinued ⟨the food ran *out*⟩ ⟨the light burned *out*⟩ **b** : at an end ⟨before the week is *out*⟩ **8 a** : in or into the open ⟨the sun came *out*⟩ **b** : ALOUD ⟨cried *out*⟩ **9 a** : to completion or satisfaction ⟨work the problem *out*⟩ **b** : to the full or a great extent or degree ⟨stretched *out* on the floor⟩ ⟨all decked *out*⟩ **10** : so as to put out or be put out in baseball ⟨the catcher threw the runner *out*⟩ ⟨grounded *out* to shortstop⟩

²out *vb* : to become known ⟨the truth will *out*⟩

³out \(,)au̇t\ *prep* — used to indicate an outward movement ⟨ran *out* the door⟩ ⟨looked *out* the window⟩

⁴out \'au̇t\ *adj* **1 a** : located outside or at a distance ⟨the *out* islands⟩ **b** : OUT-OF-BOUNDS **2** : not being in power ⟨the *out* party⟩ **3** : not allowed to continue batting, to occupy a base, or to score in baseball ⟨the runner was *out*⟩ **4** : directed outward or directing something outward ⟨put

\ə\ **abut**	\au̇\ **out**	\i\ **tip**	\ȯ\ **saw**	\u̇\ **foot**
\ər\ **further**	\ch\ **chin**	\ī\ **life**	\ȯi\ **coin**	\y\ **yet**
\a\ **mat**	\e\ **pet**	\j\ **job**	\th\ **thin**	\yü\ **few**
\ā\ **take**	\ē\ **easy**	\ŋ\ **sing**	\th\ **this**	\yu̇\ **cure**
\ä\ **cot, cart**	\g\ **go**	\ō\ **bone**	\ü\ **food**	\zh\ **vision**

the letter in the *out* basket⟩ **5** : ¹ABSENT 1, MISSING ⟨a basket with its bottom *out*⟩ **6** : no longer in fashion ⟨that style of pants is definitely *out*⟩ **7** : not to be considered ⟨that choice was *out* as far as we were concerned⟩ **8** : DETERMINED 1 ⟨was *out* to get revenge⟩ **9** : engaged in or attempting a particular activity ⟨won on his first time *out*⟩

⁵**out** \'aút\ *n* **1** : one who is out of power **2 a** : the putting out of a batter or base runner in baseball **b** : a player who has been put out **3** : a way of escaping from an embarrassing situation or a difficulty

out- *prefix* : in a manner that goes beyond ⟨*out*maneuver⟩ [derived from *out* (adverb)]

out–and–out \ˌaút-ᵊn-'(d)aút\ *adj* : being exactly what is stated : COMPLETE, THOROUGHGOING ⟨an *out-and-out* crook⟩

out·bid \(')aút-'bid\ *vb* **-bid; -bid·ding** : to make a higher bid than

¹**out·board** \'aút-ˌbō(ə)rd, -ˌbó(ə)rd\ *adj* **1** : located outboard **2** : having or using an outboard motor

²**outboard** *adv* **1** : outside a ship's hull : away from the long axis of a ship **2** : in a position closer to the wing tips of an airplane

³**outboard** *n* : OUTBOARD MOTOR

outboard motor *n* : a small internal-combustion engine with propeller attached for mounting at the stern of a small boat

out·bound \'aút-ˌbaúnd\ *adj* : outward bound ⟨*outbound* traffic⟩

out·brave \(')aút-'brāv\ *vb* **1** : to face or resist boldly **2** : to have more courage than

out·break \'aút-ˌbrāk\ *n* **1** : a sudden increase in activity use, or acceptance ⟨the *outbreak* of war⟩ **2** : something (as an epidemic or revolution) that breaks out ⟨an *outbreak* of measles⟩

out·breed·ing \-ˌbrēd-iŋ\ *n* : the interbreeding of individuals that are unrelated or only distantly related

out·build·ing \-ˌbil-diŋ\ *n* : a building separate from and smaller than the main one

out·burst \-ˌbərst\ *n* **1** : a sudden violent expression of strong feeling ⟨an *outburst* of anger⟩ **2** : a sudden increase in activity or growth

out·cast \-ˌkast\ *n* : a person who is cast out by society : PARIAH — **outcast** *adj*

out·caste \-ˌkast\ *n* **1** : a Hindu who has been forced out of a caste for violation of its rules **2** : one who has no caste

out·class \(')aút-'klas\ *vb* : to do or be so much better than as to appear of a higher class

out·come \'aút-ˌkəm\ *n* : ²RESULT 1

¹**out·crop** \'aút-ˌkräp\ *n* **1** : a coming out of bedrock to the surface of the ground **2** : the part of a rock formation that appears at the surface of the ground

²**out·crop** \'aút-ˌkräp, (')aút-'kräp\ *vb* **-cropped; -crop·ping** : to come to the surface : APPEAR ⟨granite *outcropping* through softer rocks⟩

out·crop·ping \'aút-ˌkrä-piŋ\ *n* : ¹OUTCROP

¹**out·cross** \'aút-ˌkrós\ *n* **1** : a cross made by outcrossing two individuals or strains **2** : the offspring resulting from an outcross

²**outcross** *vb* : to cross with an unrelated individual or strain or one that is only distantly related

out·cry \'aút-ˌkrī\ *n* **1** : a loud cry : CLAMOR **2** : a strong protest

out·dat·ed \(')aút-'dāt-əd\ *adj* : not up-to-date

out·dis·tance \-'dis-tən(t)s\ *vb* : to go far ahead of (as in a race) : OUTSTRIP

out·do \-'dü\ *vb* **-did** \-'did\; **-done** \-'dən\; **-do·ing** \-'dü-iŋ\ : to go beyond in achievement or performance **syn·onyms** see EXCEED

out·door \ˌaút-ˌdō(ə)r, -ˌdó(ə)r\ *also* **out·doors** \-ˌdō(ə)rz, -ˌdó(ə)rz\ *adj* **1** : of or relating to the outdoors ⟨an *out-*

door setting⟩ **2** : done outdoors ⟨*outdoor* games⟩ **3** : having no roof and walls ⟨an *outdoor* theater⟩

¹**out·doors** \(')aút-'dō(ə)rz, -'dó(ə)rz\ *adv* : outside a building : in or into the open air

²**outdoors** *n* **1** : a place away from or outside a building **2** : the world away from human dwellings

out·er \'aút-ər\ *adj* **1** : located on the outside or farther out ⟨the *outer* wall⟩ **2** : being away from a center ⟨the *outer* planets of the solar system⟩

outer ear *n* : the outer visible part of the ear that collects and directs sound waves toward the eardrum by way of a canal through the temporal bone

out·er·most \'aút-ər-ˌmōst\ *adj* : farthest out

outer space *n* : ¹SPACE 4; *esp* : the region beyond the solar system

out·er·wear \'aút-ər-ˌwa(ə)r, -ˌwe(ə)r\ *n* **1** : clothing for outdoor wear **2** : outer clothing as opposed to underwear

out·field \'aút-ˌfēld\ *n* **1** : the part of a baseball field beyond the infield and between the foul lines **2** : the players positioned in the outfield — **out·field·er** \-ˌfēl-dər\ *n*

out·fight \(')aút-'fīt\ *vb* **-fought** \-'fót\; **-fight·ing** : to fight better than : DEFEAT

¹**out·fit** \'aút-ˌfit\ *n* **1** : the equipment or clothing especially for some special purpose ⟨a camping *outfit*⟩ ⟨a sports *outfit*⟩ **2** : a group of persons working together or associated in the same activity ⟨soldiers in the same *outfit*⟩

²**outfit** *vb* **-fit·ted; -fit·ting** : to furnish with an outfit : EQUIP ⟨*outfit* an expedition⟩ — **out·fit·ter** *n*

out·flank \(')aút-'flaŋk\ *vb* : to get around the side of (a military formation) ⟨*outflank* the enemy⟩

out·flow \'aút-ˌflō\ *n* **1** : a flowing out ⟨an *outflow* of fans from the stadium⟩ **2** : something that flows out

out·fox \(')aút-'fäks\ *vb* : OUTWIT

out·go \'aút-ˌgō\ *n, pl* **outgoes** : money spent : OUTLAY

out·go·ing \'aút-ˌgō-iŋ\ *adj* **1 a** : going out : DEPARTING ⟨*outgoing* tide⟩ **b** : retiring from a position ⟨the *outgoing* governor⟩ **2** : being at ease and friendly when dealing with others ⟨an *outgoing* person⟩

out·grow \(')aút-'grō\ *vb* **-grew** \-'grü\; **-grown** \-'grōn\; **-grow·ing** **1** : to grow faster than **2** : to grow too large or too mature for ⟨*outgrew* their clothes⟩ ⟨*outgrow* playing with dolls⟩

out·growth \'aút-ˌgrōth\ *n* **1** : something that grows out of or develops from something else **2** : OFFSHOOT 1, BY-PRODUCT

out·guess \(')aút-'ges\ *vb* : to correctly foresee the plans, actions, or activities of

out·house \'aút-ˌhaús\ *n* : OUTBUILDING; *esp* : ²PRIVY 1

out·ing \'aút-iŋ\ *n* : a brief usually outdoor pleasure trip

out·land·er \'aút-ˌlan-dər\ *n* : a person from another country or region

out·land·ish \(')aút-'lan-dish\ *adj* : of strange appearance or manner : BIZARRE ⟨an *outlandish* costume⟩ — **out·land·ish·ly** *adv* — **out·land·ish·ness** *n*

out·last \(')aút-'last\ *vb* : to last longer than : SURVIVE

¹**out·law** \'aút-ˌló\ *n* **1** : a person who is not given the protection of the law **2** : a lawless person or one who is running away from the law **3** : an animal (as a horse) that is wild and hard to control — **outlaw** *adj*

²**outlaw** *vb* **1** : to deprive of the protection of law **2** : to make illegal ⟨dueling was *outlawed*⟩ — **out·law·ry** \'aút-ˌló(ə)r-ē\ *n*

out·lay \'aút-ˌlā\ *n* **1** : the act of spending **2** : an amount spent : PAYMENT

out·let \'aút-ˌlet, -lət\ *n* **1** : a place or opening through which something is let out : EXIT, VENT **2** : a means of release or satisfaction ⟨an *outlet* for her grief⟩ **3 a** : a market for a product **b** : an agency (as a store or dealer) through which a product is marketed **4** : an electrical device (as in a wall) into which an appliance may be plugged

¹**out·line** \'aút-ˌlīn\ *n* **1** : a line that traces or forms the

outer limits of an object or figure and shows its shape **2 a :** a drawing or picture giving only the outlines of something **b :** this method of drawing **3 a :** a brief summary or plan often in numbered divisions **b :** a brief treatment of a subject ⟨an *outline* of world history⟩

²out·line *vb* **1 :** to draw or trace the outline of **2 :** to indicate the main features or parts of ⟨*outlined* our responsibilities⟩

out·live \(')aút-'liv\ *vb* **:** to live longer than **:** OUTLAST

out·look \'aút-ˌlùk\ *n* **1 a :** a place offering a view **b :** a view from a particular place **2 :** POINT OF VIEW **3 :** conditions that seem to lie ahead ⟨the *outlook* for business⟩

out loud *adv* **:** loudly enough to be heard **:** ALOUD

out·ly·ing \'aút-ˌlī-iṇ\ *adj* **:** being far from a center or main body ⟨an *outlying* suburb⟩

out·ma·neu·ver \ˌaút-mə-'n(y)ü-vər\ *vb* **:** to be more skillful or successful than in maneuvering

out·mod·ed \(')aút-'mōd-əd\ *adj* **:** no longer acceptable, usable, or fashionable ⟨*outmoded* beliefs⟩

out·most \'aút-ˌmōst\ *adj* **:** OUTERMOST

out·num·ber \(')aút-'nəm-bər\ *vb* **:** to be more than in number ⟨girls *outnumber* boys in the class⟩

out of *prep* **1 a :** from within to the outside of ⟨walked *out of* the room⟩ **b** — used to indicate a change in quality, state, or form ⟨woke *out of* a deep sleep⟩ **c :** beyond the range or limits of ⟨moved *out of* sight⟩ **2 :** BECAUSE OF, FROM ⟨fled *out of* fear⟩ **3** — used to indicate source, material, or cause ⟨built *out of* old lumber⟩ **4** — used to indicate the state or condition of being without something especially that was there before ⟨the store is *out of* bread⟩ ⟨cheated us *out of* our savings⟩ **5 :** from among ⟨one *out of* four survived⟩ **6** — used to indicate the center of a business or activity ⟨runs her business *out of* her home⟩

out—of—bounds \ˌaút-ə(v)-'baún(d)z\ *adv or adj* **:** outside the limits of the playing area ⟨the pass went *out-of-bounds*⟩

out—of—date \-'dāt\ *adj* **:** OUTMODED, OBSOLETE

out—of—door \-'dō(ə)r, -'dò(ə)r\ *or* **out—of—doors** \-'dō(ə)rz, -'dò(ə)rz\ *adj* **1 :** OUTDOOR 1 **2 :** OUTDOOR 2

out—of—doors *n* **:** ²OUTDOORS

out of doors *adv* **:** ¹OUTDOORS

out—of—the—way \ˌaút-ə(v)-thə-'wā\ *adj* **1 :** being off the usual paths ⟨an *out-of-the-way* village⟩ **2 :** not commonly found or met **:** UNUSUAL ⟨the store specializes in *out-of-the-way* books⟩

out·pace \(')aút-'pās\ *vb* **:** OUTRUN

out·pa·tient \'aút-ˌpā-shənt\ *n* **:** a patient who visits a hospital for diagnosis or treatment without staying overnight — compare INPATIENT

out·play \(')aút-'plā\ *vb* **:** to play better than

out·post \'aút-ˌpōst\ *n* **1 :** a guard stationed at a distance from a military force or camp **2 :** the position occupied by an outpost **3 :** a settlement on a frontier or in a far-away place

out·pour·ing \-ˌpōr-iṇ, -ˌpòr-\ *n* **1 :** the act of pouring out **2 a :** something that pours out or is poured out **b :** OUTBURST 1

¹out·put \'aút-ˌpùt\ *n* **1 :** something produced: as **a :** agricultural or industrial production ⟨steel *output*⟩ **b :** mental or artistic production ⟨writing *output*⟩ **c :** the amount produced by a person in a given time **d :** power or energy delivered or produced by a machine or system ⟨light *output* of the sun⟩ **e :** the information produced by a computer **2 :** a point at which something (as power, an electronic signal, or data) comes out

²output *vb* **-put·ted** *or* **-put; -put·ting :** to produce as output

¹out·rage \'aút-ˌrāj\ *n* **1 :** a violent or brutal act **2 :** an act that hurts someone or shows disrespect for a person's feelings **3 :** the angry feelings caused by injury or insult [from early French *outrage* "an act of violence or brutality" from *outre* "beyond" (from Latin *ultra* "beyond") and *-age* "action"]

²outrage *vb* **-raged; -rag·ing 1 :** to cause to suffer violent injury or abuse **2 :** to cause to feel anger or resentment

out·ra·geous \aút-'rā-jəs\ *adj* **:** extremely annoying, insulting, or shameful **:** SHOCKING — **out·ra·geous·ly** *adv* — **out·ra·geous·ness** *n*

out·rank \(')aút-'raṇk\ *vb* **:** to rank higher or be more important than

ou·tré \ü-'trā\ *adj* **:** very strange or unusual **:** BIZARRE [French]

out·rid·er \'aút-ˌrīd-ər\ *n* **:** a mounted escort

out·rig·ger \'aút-ˌrig-ər\ *n* **1 :** a frame that extends from the side of a boat to prevent upsetting **2 :** a boat equipped with an outrigger

outrigger 2

¹out·right \(')aút-'rīt\ *adv* **1 a :** in entirety **:** COMPLETELY ⟨sold *outright*⟩ **b :** without holding back ⟨laughed *outright*⟩ **2 :** on the spot **:** INSTANTANEOUSLY ⟨killed *outright*⟩

²out·right \'aút-ˌrīt\ *adj* **1 :** being exactly what is stated ⟨an *outright* lie⟩ **2 :** given without restriction ⟨an *outright* gift⟩

out·run \(')aút-'rən\ *vb* **-ran** \-'ran\; **-run; -run·ning 1 :** to run or go faster than **2 :** EXCEED 1 ⟨our needs *outran* our funds⟩

out·sell \-'sel\ *vb* **-sold** \-'sōld\; **-sell·ing 1 :** to be sold more than ⟨corn *outsold* beets⟩ **2 :** to sell more than ⟨we *outsell* our competitors⟩

out·set \'aút-ˌset\ *n* **:** BEGINNING 1, START

out·shine \(')aút-'shīn\ *vb* **-shone** \-'shōn\; **-shin·ing 1 :** to shine brighter than **2 :** EXCEL, SURPASS

¹out·side \(')aút-'sīd, 'aút-ˌsīd\ *n* **1 :** a place or region beyond an enclosure or boundary **2 :** an outer side or surface **3 :** the extreme limit of a guess **:** MOST ⟨the crowd numbered 10,000 at the *outside*⟩

²outside *adj* **1 :** of, relating to, or being on the outside ⟨the *outside* edge⟩ **2 :** connected with or leading to the outside ⟨an *outside* door⟩ **3 :** coming from outside ⟨*outside* influences⟩ **4 :** barely possible **:** REMOTE ⟨an *outside* chance⟩

³outside *adv* **:** on or to the outside ⟨waited *outside* in the hall⟩; *esp* **:** ¹OUTDOORS ⟨took the dog *outside*⟩

⁴outside *prep* **1 :** on or to the outside of ⟨*outside* the house⟩ **2 :** beyond the limits of ⟨*outside* the law⟩ **3 :** ¹EXCEPT 2, BESIDES ⟨nobody *outside* a few close friends⟩

outside of *prep* **1 :** ⁴OUTSIDE 2 **2 :** EXCEPT FOR ⟨*outside of* her brother she is alone in the house⟩

out·sid·er \(')aút-'sīd-ər\ *n* **:** a person who does not belong to a particular group

¹out·size \'aút-ˌsīz\ *n* **:** a size different and especially larger than the standard

²outsize *also* **out·sized** \-ˌsīzd\ *adj* **:** unusually large or heavy

out·skirts \'aút-ˌskərts\ *n pl* **:** the parts far from the center of a place or town

out·smart \(')aút-'smärt\ *vb* **:** OUTWIT

out·spo·ken \aút-'spō-kən\ *adj* **:** direct and open in speech or expression **:** FRANK — **out·spo·ken·ness** \-kən-nəs\ *n*

out·spread \-'spred\ *vb* **-spread; -spread·ing :** to spread out **:** EXTEND — **out·spread** \'aút-ˌspred\ *adj*

out·stand·ing \-'stan-diṇ\ *adj* **1 :** sticking out **:** PROJECTING **2 a :** not yet paid **:** UNPAID ⟨*outstanding* bills⟩ **b :** continuing in being **:** UNRESOLVED ⟨problems *outstanding*⟩ **3 :** attracting notice especially because of excellence ⟨an *outstanding* scholar⟩ **synonyms** see NOTICEABLE — **out·stand·ing·ly** \-diṇ-lē\ *adv*

\ə\ abut	\aú\ out	\i\ tip	\ò\ saw	\ú\ foot
\ər\ further	\ch\ chin	\ī\ life	\òi\ coin	\y\ yet
\a\ mat	\e\ pet	\j\ job	\th\ thin	\yü\ few
\ā\ take	\ē\ easy	\ṇ\ sing	\th\ this	\yú\ cure
\ä\ cot, cart	\g\ go	\ō\ bone	\ü\ food	\zh\ vision

out·stay \\(')aut-'stā\\ *vb* **1** : to stay beyond or longer than ⟨*outstayed* their welcome⟩ **2** : to be able to hold out longer than

out·stretch \\aut-'strech\\ *vb* : to stretch out : EXTEND

out·strip \\-'strip\\ *vb* **-stripped; -strip·ping** **1** : to go faster or farther than ⟨*outstripped* the other runners⟩ **2 a** : EXCEL ⟨*outstripped* all rivals⟩ **b** : EXCEED 1 ⟨demand *outstrips* supply⟩

out–there \\aut-'tha(ə)r, -'th(ə)r\\ *adj* : UNCONVENTIONAL ⟨*out-there* styles⟩

¹out·ward \\'aut-wərd\\ *adj* **1** : moving or directed toward the outside or away from a center ⟨an *outward* flow⟩ **2** : showing on the outside ⟨*outward* signs of fear⟩

²outward *or* **out·wards** \\-wərdz\\ *adv* : toward the outside ⟨the city stretches *outward* for miles⟩ ⟨fold it *outward*⟩

out·ward·ly \\'aut-wərd-lē\\ *adv* : on the outside : in outward appearance ⟨*outwardly* calm⟩

out·wear \\(')aut-'wa(ə)r, -'we(ə)r\\ *vb* **-wore** \\-'wō(ə)r, -'wȯ(ə)r\\; **-worn** \\-'wō(ə)rn, -'wȯ(ə)rn\\; **-wear·ing** : to last longer than ⟨a fabric that *outwears* others⟩

out·weigh \\-'wā\\ *vb* : to be greater than in weight, value, or importance ⟨the benefits *outweigh* the disadvantages⟩

out·wit \\aut-'wit\\ *vb* **-wit·ted; -wit·ting** : to get the better of by cleverness **synonyms** see FRUSTRATE

¹out·work \\(')aut-'wərk\\ *vb* : to outdo in working

²out·work \\'aut-,wərk\\ *n* : a small protected position constructed outside a main defense (as a castle)

out·worn \\aut-'wō(ə)rn, -'wȯ(ə)rn\\ *adj* : WORN-OUT 1, OUT-OF-DATE ⟨an *outworn* system⟩

ou·zel \\'ü-zəl\\ *n* : DIPPER 2

ova *plural of* OVUM

¹oval \\'ō-vəl\\ *n* : an oval figure or object

²oval *adj* : having the shape or outline of an egg [from Latin *ovalis* (adjective) "having the shape of an egg," derived from earlier *ovum* "egg"]

oval window *n* : an oval opening between the middle ear and inner ear having the base of the stapes attached to its membrane

¹oval

ovar·i·an \\ō-'var-ē-ən, -'ver-\\ *adj* : of, relating to, or produced by an ovary ⟨*ovarian* hormones⟩

ova·ry \\'ōv-(ə-)rē\\ *n, pl* **-ries** **1** : one of the usually paired organs in the body of female animals that produces eggs and that in female vertebrates also produces sex hormones **2** : the enlarged rounded lower part of the pistil of a flower in which seeds are formed

ovate \\'ō-,vāt\\ *adj* : shaped like an egg in outline with the base wider than the end ⟨*ovate* leaves⟩

ova·tion \\ō-'vā-shən\\ *n* : a public expression of praise : enthusiastic applause

ov·en \\'əv-ən\\ *n* : a chamber (as in a stove) used for baking, heating, or drying

ov·en·bird \\-,bərd\\ *n* : an American warbler that builds a dome-shaped nest on the ground

¹over \\'ō-vər\\ *adv* **1 a** : across a barrier or space ⟨fly *over* to London⟩ **b** : in a direction down or forward and down ⟨fell *over*⟩ **c** : across the brim ⟨soup boiled *over*⟩ **d** : so as to bring the underside up ⟨turned his cards *over*⟩ **e** : from one person or side to another ⟨hand it *over*⟩ **f** : to one's home ⟨ask them *over*⟩ **g** : at a distance from a certain point ⟨two

ovenbird

streets *over*⟩ **h** : to agreement ⟨won them *over*⟩ **2** : ¹ACROSS **3** ⟨got their point *over*⟩ **3 a** : beyond a limit ⟨the show ran a minute *over*⟩ **b** : more than needed : too many or too much ⟨*over* fond of food⟩ **c** : till a later time (as the next day) : OVERNIGHT ⟨stay *over*⟩ ⟨sleep *over*⟩ **4** : so as to cover the whole surface ⟨windows boarded *over*⟩ **5** — used in a two-way radio transmission to indicate that a message is complete and a reply is expected **6 a** : ²THROUGH 2a ⟨read it *over*⟩ **b** : once more : AGAIN ⟨do it *over*⟩

²over \\,ō-vər, 'ō-\\ *prep* **1** : higher than : ABOVE ⟨towered *over* my mother⟩ ⟨flew *over* the lake⟩ **2 a** : above in authority, power, or worth ⟨respected those *over* us⟩ **b** : in front of : AHEAD OF, BEYOND ⟨a big lead *over* the others⟩ **3** : more than ⟨cost *over* $5⟩ **4 a** : down upon especially so as to cover ⟨laid a blanket *over* the child⟩ **b** : all through or throughout ⟨all *over* town⟩ ⟨went *over* her notes⟩ **c** : on or along the surface of ⟨*over* the road⟩ **5 a** : ²ACROSS ⟨jump *over* a stream⟩ **b** : to or on the other side of ⟨climb *over* the fence⟩ **c** : down from : OFF ⟨fell *over* the edge⟩ **6** : DURING ⟨*over* the past 25 years⟩ **7** — used to indicate an object of concern ⟨trouble *over* money⟩ **8** : by means of ⟨heard the news *over* the radio⟩

³over \\'ō-vər, ,ō-\\ *adj* **1** : having or being more than is needed or expected ⟨the balance was $3 *over*⟩ **2** : brought or having come to an end ⟨the day is *over*⟩

over- *prefix* **1** : so as to be greater, better, or stronger than **2** : so as to be too much or too great [from *over* (adverb or adjective)]

overabundance	overexaggerate	overprotect
overabundant	overexaggeration	overprotection
overambitious	overexcite	overprotective
overanxious	overexcited	overprotectiveness
overbake	overexert	overreact
overbold	overexertion	overreaction
overburden	overfamiliar	overrefined
overcareful	overfat	overrefinement
overcautious	overfertilization	oversensitive
overcomplicate	overgenerous	oversensitiveness
overcomplicated	overhasty	oversensitivity
overconfidence	overheat	overspecialization
overconfident	overindulge	overspecialize
overconfidently	overindulgence	overstuff
overconscientious	overindulgent	oversubtle
overcook	overlarge	oversuspicious
overcount	overload	overtax
overcritical	overlong	overtaxation
overdecorate	overmodest	overtip
overdependence	overnice	overtired
overdependent	overpay	overtrain
overdramatic	overpayment	overwater
overeager	overpopulate	overwind
overeagerness	overpopulation	overwithhold
overemphasis	overpraise	overzealous
overemphasize	overproduce	overzealousness
overenthusiastic	overproduction	

over·achiev·er \\,ōvər-ə-'chē-vər\\ *n* : one who achieves success over and above the standard or expected level especially at an early age — **over·achieve** \\-'chēv\\ *vb* — **over·achieve·ment** \\-mənt\\ *n*

over·act \\,ō-və-'rakt\\ *vb* **1** : to act more than is necessary **2** : to overact a part **3** : to exaggerate in acting

over·ac·tive \\,ō-və-'rak-tiv\\ *adj* : very active and especially abnormally so ⟨an *overactive* thyroid⟩ — **over·ac·tiv·i·ty** \\-rak-'tiv-ət-ē\\ *n*

¹over·age \\,ō-və-'rāj\\ *adj* : older than is normal for one's position ⟨*overage* students⟩

²over·age \\'ōv-(ə-)rij\\ *n* : ¹EXCESS 1, SURPLUS

¹over·all \\,ō-və-'ról\\ *adv* : as a whole : GENERALLY ⟨we find your work satisfactory, *overall*⟩

²**overall** \ˌō-və-ˈról, ˈō-və-ˌról\ *adj* **1** : including everything ⟨*overall* expenses⟩ **2** : viewed as a whole : GENERAL

over·alls \ˈō-və-ˌrólz\ *n pl* : loose trousers made of strong material usually with a bib and shoulder straps

over and above *prep* : ¹BESIDES

over and over *adv* : many times : OFTEN

over·arm \ˈō-və-ˌrärm\ *adj* **1** : ¹OVERHAND **2** : made with the arm lifted out of the water and stretched forward ⟨an *overarm* swimming stroke⟩

over·awe \ˌō-və-ˈró\ *vb* : to make quiet or peaceful with fear, respect, or wonder

over·bal·ance \ˌō-vər-ˈbal-ən(t)s\ *vb* **1** : to have greater weight or importance than ⟨your good qualities *overbalanced* your shortcomings⟩ **2** : to lose or cause to lose balance ⟨a boat *overbalanced* by shifting cargo⟩

over·bear \ˌō-vər-ˈba(ə)r, -ˈbe(ə)r\ *vb* **-bore** \-ˈbō(ə)r, -ˈbó(ə)r\; **-borne** \-ˈbō(ə)rn, -ˈbó(ə)rn *also* **-born** \-ˈbó(ə)rn\; **-bear·ing** **1** : to bring down by a stronger weight or force : OVERPOWER **2** : to exceed in importance or forcefulness : OUTWEIGH

overalls

over·bear·ing \-ˈba(ə)r-iŋ, -ˈbe(ə)r-\ *adj* : ARROGANT, DOMINEERING — **over·bear·ing·ly** *adv*

over·bid \ˌō-vər-ˈbid\ *vb* **-bid; -bid·ding** : to bid too high — **over·bid** \ˈō-vər-ˌbid\ *n*

over·bite \ˈō-vər-ˌbīt\ *n* : the projection of the upper front teeth over the lower front teeth when the biting surfaces of the teeth in the upper and lower jaws are in contact

over·board \ˈō-vər-ˌbō(ə)rd, -ˌbó(ə)rd\ *adv* **1** : over the side of a ship into the water **2** : to extremes of enthusiasm ⟨go *overboard* for a new fad⟩

over·buy \ˌō-vər-ˈbī\ *vb* **-bought** \-ˈbót\; **-buy·ing** : to buy more than is needed or can be afforded

¹**over·cast** *vb* **-cast; -cast·ing** **1** \ˌō-vər-ˈkast, ˈō-vər-ˌkast\ : DARKEN 1, OVERSHADOW **2** \ˈō-vər-ˌkast\ : to sew with stitches that prevent the material at the edge of a seam from coming apart

²**over·cast** \ˌō-vər-ˈkast, ˌō-vər-ˈkast\ *adj* : clouded over : GLOOMY ⟨an *overcast* night⟩

³**over·cast** \ˈō-vər-ˌkast\ *n* : COVERING; *esp* : a covering of clouds over the sky

over·charge \ˌō-vər-ˈchärj\ *vb* **1** : to charge too much **2** : to fill or load too full ⟨a cannon *overcharged* with powder⟩ — **over·charge** \ˈō-vər-ˌchärj\ *n*

over·cloud \-ˈklaúd\ *vb* : to overspread with clouds : DARKEN

over·coat \ˈō-vər-ˌkōt\ *n* : a warm coat worn over indoor clothing

over·come \ˌō-vər-ˈkəm\ *vb* **-came** \-ˈkām\; **-come; -com·ing** **1** : to gain an advantage or victory over ⟨*overcome* an enemy⟩ **2** : to make helpless or exhausted ⟨was *overcome* by gas⟩ **synonyms** see CONQUER

over·crowd \-ˈkraúd\ *vb* **1** : to cause to be too crowded **2** : to crowd together too much

over·do \-ˈdü\ *vb* **-did** \-ˈdid\; **-done** \-ˈdən\; **-do·ing** \-ˈdü-iŋ\ **1** : to do too much ⟨*overdoes* it getting ready for a party⟩ **2** : EXAGGERATE ⟨*overdo* praise⟩ **3** : to cook too long ⟨meat that is *overdone*⟩

¹**over·dose** \ˈō-vər-ˌdōs\ *n* : too great a dose — **over·dos·age** \ˌō-vər-ˈdō-sij\ *n*

²**over·dose** \ˌō-vər-ˈdōs\ *vb* **1** : to give an overdose or too many doses to **2** : to take or experience an overdose ⟨*overdosed* on heroin⟩

over·draft \ˈō-vər-ˌdraft\ *n* : an overdrawing of a bank account or the amount overdrawn

over·draw \ˌō-vər-ˈdró\ *vb* **-drew** \-ˈdrü\; **-drawn** \-ˈdrón\; **-draw·ing** **1** : to draw checks on (a bank account) for more than the balance in it **2** : EXAGGERATE, OVERSTATE

¹**over·dress** \ˌō-vər-ˈdres\ *vb* : to dress too formally or warmly for an occasion

²**over·dress** \ˈō-vər-ˌdres\ *n* : a dress worn over another

over·drive \ˈō-vər-ˌdrīv\ *n* : a transmission gear in an automobile that allows the drive shaft to operate at a speed greater than that of the engine crankshaft

over·due \ˌō-vər-ˈd(y)ü\ *adj* **1 a** : unpaid when due ⟨*overdue* bills⟩ **b** : not appearing or presented on time ⟨an *overdue* train⟩ ⟨an *overdue* book⟩ **2** : more than ready ⟨a country *overdue* for governmental reform⟩

over·eat \ˌō-vər-ˈēt\ *vb* **over·ate** \-ˈāt\; **-eat·en** \-ˈēt-ᵊn\; **-eat·ing** : to eat to excess — **over·eat·er** \-ˈēt-ər\ *n*

over·es·ti·mate \ˌō-və-ˈres-tə-ˌmāt\ *vb* **-mat·ed; -mat·ing** **1** : to estimate as being more than the actual size, quantity, or number ⟨*overestimated* how many would attend⟩ **2** : to place too high a value on : OVERRATE ⟨*overestimated* his abilities⟩ — **over·es·ti·mate** \-mət\ *n* — **over·es·ti·ma·tion** \-ˌres-tə-ˈmā-shən\ *n*

over·ex·pose \ˌō-və-rik-ˈspóz\ *vb* **-posed; -pos·ing** : to expose (as photographic material) for a longer time than is needed or desirable — **over·ex·po·sure** \-ˈspō-zhər\ *n*

over·ex·tend \ˌō-vər-ik-ˈstend\ *vb* : to extend or expand beyond a safe or reasonable point; *esp* : to commit (oneself) financially beyond what can be paid — **over·ex·ten·sion** \-ˈsten-shən\ *n*

over·feed \ˌō-vər-ˈfēd\ *vb* **-fed** \-ˈfed\; **-feed·ing** : to feed or eat to excess

over·fill \ˌō-vər-ˈfil\ *vb* : to fill to overflowing

over·fish \-ˈfish\ *vb* : to fish too much for (a kind of fish) or in (a certain area)

over·flight \ˈō-vər-ˌflīt\ *n* : a flight over an area

¹**over·flow** \ˌō-vər-ˈflō\ *vb* **1** : to cover with or as if with water : INUNDATE **2** : to flow over the brim or top of ⟨the river *overflowed* its banks⟩ **3** : to flow over bounds ⟨the creek *overflows* every spring⟩ **4** : to fill a space up and spread beyond its limits ⟨the paragraph *overflowed* the page⟩

²**over·flow** \ˈō-vər-ˌflō\ *n* **1** : a flowing over : FLOOD **2** : something that flows over : SURPLUS **3** : an outlet or container for liquid that overflows

over·fly \ˌō-vər-ˈflī\ *vb* **-flew** \-ˈflü\; **-flown** \-ˈflōn\; **-fly·ing** : to fly over; *esp* : to pass over in an aircraft or spacecraft

over·gar·ment \ˈō-vər-ˌgär-mənt\ *n* : an outer garment

over·graze \ˌō-vər-ˈgrāz\ *vb* **-grazed; -graz·ing** : to allow animals to graze (as a pasture) to the point of damaging the vegetation

over·grow \ˌō-vər-ˈgrō\ *vb* **-grew** \-ˈgrü\; **-grown** \-ˈgrōn\; **-grow·ing** **1** : to grow over so as to cover **2** : OUTGROW **3** : to grow too big ⟨an *overgrown* puppy⟩ **4** : to become grown over — **over·growth** \ˈō-vər-ˌgrōth\ *n*

overgrown *adj* : grown unusually or too big ⟨*overgrown* boys⟩ ⟨*overgrown* cities⟩

¹**over·hand** \ˈō-vər-ˌhand\ *adj* : made with the hand brought forward and down from above shoulder level ⟨an *overhand* pitch⟩ ⟨an *overhand* tennis stroke⟩ — **overhand** *adv* — **over·hand·ed** \-ˈhan-dəd\ *adv*

²**overhand** *n* : an overhand stroke (as in tennis)

overhand knot *n* : a small knot often used to prevent the end of a cord from pulling apart — see KNOT illustration

¹**over·hang** \ˈō-vər-ˌhaŋ, ˌō-vər-ˈhaŋ\ *vb* **-hung** \-ˌhəŋ, -ˈhəŋ\; **-hang·ing** **1** : to stick out or hang over **2** : THREATEN 3

²**over·hang** \ˈō-vər-ˌhaŋ\ *n* : a part that overhangs ⟨the *overhang* of a roof⟩

\ə\ abut	\aú\ out	\i\ tip	\ó\ saw	\ú\ foot
\ər\ further	\ch\ chin	\ī\ life	\ói\ coin	\y\ yet
\a\ mat	\e\ pet	\j\ job	\th\ thin	\yü\ few
\ā\ take	\ē\ easy	\ŋ\ sing	\th\ this	\yú\ cure
\ä\ cot, cart	\g\ go	\ō\ bone	\ü\ food	\zh\ vision

over·haul \ˌō-vər-ˈhȯl\ vb 1 : to make a thorough examination of and make necessary repairs and adjustments on ⟨*overhaul* an engine⟩ 2 : OVERTAKE 1a — **over·haul** \ˈō-vər-ˌhȯl\ n

¹**over·head** \ˌō-vər-ˈhed\ adv : above one's head : ALOFT ⟨geese flying *overhead*⟩

²**over·head** \ˈō-vər-ˌhed\ adj 1 : operating or lying above ⟨an *overhead* door⟩ 2 : of or relating to business expense

³**over·head** \ˈō-vər-ˌhed\ n 1 : general business expenses (as rent, heat, or insurance) 2 : a stroke in a racket game made above head height : SMASH

over·hear \ˌō-vər-ˈhi(ə)r\ vb **-heard** \-ˈhərd\; **-hear·ing** \-ˈhi(ə)r-iŋ\ : to hear without the speaker's knowledge or intention

over·joy \ˌō-vər-ˈjȯi\ vb : to fill with great joy

over·kill \-ˈkil\ n 1 : a much greater capacity for destruction than is needed for a particular target 2 : an excess beyond what is needed or suitable ⟨advertising *overkill*⟩

over·land \ˈō-vər-ˌland, -lənd\ adv or adj : by, on, or across land

over·lap \ˌō-vər-ˈlap\ vb 1 : to lay or lie over (something) so as to partly cover ⟨that piece *overlaps* the edge⟩ 2 : to have something in common ⟨political and social interests that often *overlap*⟩ 3 : to occupy the same area in part ⟨the photos *overlap*⟩ — **over·lap** \ˈō-vər-ˌlap\ n

¹**over·lay** \ˌō-vər-ˈlā\ vb **-laid** \-ˈlād\; **-lay·ing** 1 : to lay or spread over or across 2 : OVERLIE

²**over·lay** \ˈō-vər-ˌlā\ n : something (as a veneer on wood) that is overlaid

over·leap \ˌō-vər-ˈlēp\ vb **-leaped** or **-leapt** \-ˈlept also -ˈlept\; **-leap·ing** \-ˈlē-piŋ\ 1 : to leap over or across ⟨*overleap* a ditch⟩ 2 : to defeat (oneself) by going too far

over·learn \-ˈlərn\ vb : to continue to study or practice something after mastering it

over·lie \-ˈlī\ vb **-lay** \-ˈlā\; **-lain** \-ˈlān\; **-ly·ing** \-ˈlī-iŋ\ : to lie over or upon

over·look \ˌō-vər-ˈlu̇k\ vb 1 : to look over : INSPECT 2 **a** : to look down upon from above **b** : to provide a view of from above ⟨the mountain *overlooks* a lake⟩ 3 **a** : to fail to see : MISS **b** : to pay no attention to : IGNORE ⟨*overlook* a beginner's mistakes⟩

over·lord \ˈō-vər-ˌlȯ(ə)rd\ n 1 : a lord who rules over other lords 2 : an absolute or supreme ruler

over·ly \ˈō-vər-lē\ adv : to an excessive degree : TOO

over·mas·ter \ˌō-vər-ˈmas-tər\ vb : OVERPOWER, SUBDUE

over·match \-ˈmach\ vb 1 : to be more than a match for : DEFEAT 2 : to match with a stronger opponent ⟨a boxer who was badly *overmatched*⟩

¹**over·much** \ˌō-vər-ˈmach\ adj or adv : too much

²**over·much** \ˈō-vər-ˌmach, ˌō-vər-ˈmach\ n : too great an amount

¹**over·night** \ˌō-vər-ˈnīt\ adv 1 : on or during the evening or night ⟨stayed away *overnight*⟩ 2 : very quickly or suddenly ⟨became famous *overnight*⟩

²**overnight** adj 1 : of, lasting, or staying the night ⟨*overnight* trip⟩ ⟨an *overnight* guest⟩ 2 : SUDDEN 1 ⟨*overnight* stardom⟩ 3 : traveling during the night ⟨an *overnight* train⟩ 4 : delivered within one day's time ⟨*overnight* mail⟩

overnight bag n : a suitcase of a size to carry clothing and personal articles for an overnight trip — called also *overnight case*

over·night·er \ˌō-vər-ˈnīt-ər\ n 1 : OVERNIGHT BAG 2 : an overnight trip 3 : a person who stays overnight

¹**over·pass** \ˌō-vər-ˈpas\ vb 1 : to pass across, over, or beyond 2 : SURPASS 3 : ¹DISREGARD, IGNORE

²**over·pass** \ˈō-vər-ˌpas\ n 1 : a crossing (as of two highways or of a highway and railroad) at different levels usually by means of a bridge 2 : the upper level of an overpass

over·play \ˌō-vər-ˈplā\ vb 1 : EXAGGERATE, OVEREMPHASIZE ⟨newspapers *overplayed* the story⟩ 2 : to rely too much on the strength of ⟨*overplayed* my hand and lost⟩

over·pop·u·late \-ˈpäp-yə-ˌlāt\ vb : to populate too densely : cause to have too great a population ⟨the city was *overpopulated* and polluted⟩

over·pop·u·la·tion \-ˌpäp-yə-ˈlā-shən\ n : the condition of having too many people living in a certain area

over·pow·er \ˌō-vər-ˈpau̇(-ə)r\ vb 1 : to overcome by greater force : DEFEAT 2 : OVERWHELM 2 ⟨*overpowered* by hunger⟩ — **over·pow·er·ing·ly** \-ˈpau̇r-iŋ-lē\ adv

over·price \ˌō-vər-ˈprīs\ vb : to price too high

over·print \-ˈprint\ vb : to print over with something additional — **over·print** \ˈō-vər-ˌprint\ n

over·rate \ˌō-və(r)-ˈrāt\ vb : to rate, value, or estimate too highly ⟨a book that was *overrated*⟩

over·reach \-ˈrēch\ vb 1 : to reach above or beyond : OVERTOP 2 : to defeat (oneself) by trying to do or gain too much 3 : OUTWIT, TRICK 4 : to reach or go too far — **over·reach·er** n

over·ride \-ˈrīd\ vb **-rode** \-ˈrōd\; **-rid·den** \-ˈrid-ᵊn\; **-rid·ing** \-ˈrīd-iŋ\ 1 : to ride over or across : TRAMPLE 2 : to ride a horse too much or too hard 3 **a** : to take power away from : DOMINATE **b** : ANNUL 2 ⟨the congress *overrode* the president's veto⟩

over·ripe \-ˈrīp\ adj : passed beyond ripeness toward decay ⟨an *overripe* pear⟩

over·rule \-ˈrül\ vb 1 : to decide against ⟨the judge *overruled* the objection⟩ 2 : to reverse or set aside (a decision or ruling made by a lesser authority)

¹**over·run** \ˌō-və(r)-ˈrən\ vb **-ran** \-ˈran\; **-run**; **-run·ning** 1 **a** : to invade and occupy ⟨the island was *overrun* by the enemy⟩ **b** : to spread, swarm, or grow over ⟨a garden *overrun* with weeds⟩ ⟨rats *overran* the ship⟩ 2 : to run or go beyond or past ⟨*overran* third base⟩ ⟨the program *overran* the time allowed⟩ 3 : flow over ⟨the river *overran* its banks⟩

²**over·run** \ˈō-və(r)-ˌrən\ n 1 : an act or instance of overrunning 2 : the amount by which something overruns

over·sea \ˌō-vər-ˈsē, ˈō-vər-ˌsē\ adj or adv : OVERSEAS

over·seas \-ˈsēz, -ˌsēz\ adv or adj : beyond or across the sea

over·see \ˌō-vər-ˈsē\ vb **-saw** \-ˈsȯ\; **-seen** \-ˈsēn\; **-see·ing** 1 : to look down upon : SURVEY 2 **a** : to look over : EXAMINE **b** : SUPERINTEND, SUPERVISE

over·seer \ˈō-və(r)-ˌsi(ə)r, -ˌsē-ər; ˌō-və(r)-ˈsi(ə)r, -ˈsē-ər\ n : one that oversees : SUPERINTENDENT

over·sell \ˌō-vər-ˈsel\ vb **-sold** \-ˈsōld\; **-sell·ing** : to sell too much to or of

over·shad·ow \-ˈshad-ō\ vb 1 : to cast a shadow over : DARKEN 2 : to become more important than : OUTWEIGH ⟨the win *overshadowed* the player's injury⟩

over·shoe \ˈō-vər-ˌshü\ n : a shoe (as of rubber) worn over another for protection; esp : GALOSH

over·shoot \ˌō-vər-ˈshüt\ vb **-shot** \-ˈshät\; **-shoot·ing** 1 : to miss by going beyond ⟨the plane *overshot* the runway⟩ 2 : to shoot over or beyond ⟨*overshot* the target⟩

over·shot \ˈō-vər-ˌshät\ adj : moved by water shooting over from above ⟨an *overshot* waterwheel⟩

over·sight \-ˌsīt\ n 1 : the act or duty of overseeing : SUPERVISION ⟨have the *oversight* of a job⟩ 2 : an error or a leaving something out through carelessness or haste

over·sim·pli·fy \ˌō-vər-ˈsim-plə-ˌfī\ vb : to simplify something so much that the result is confusing, misleading, or wrong — **over·sim·pli·fi·ca·tion** \-ˌsim-plə-fə-ˈkā-shən\ n

over·size \-ˈsīz\ or **over·sized** \-ˈsīzd\ adj : being of more than normal or ordinary size ⟨*oversize* pillows⟩ ⟨an *oversize* shirt⟩

over·skirt \-ˌskərt\ n : a skirt worn over another skirt

over·sleep \ˌō-vər-ˈslēp\ vb **-slept** \-ˈslept\; **-sleep·ing** : to sleep beyond the usual time or beyond the time set for getting up

over·spread \-'spred\ *vb* **-spread; -spread·ing** : to spread over or above ⟨branches *overspreading* a garden path⟩

over·state \-'stāt\ *vb* : to state in too strong terms : EXAGGERATE — **over·state·ment** \-mənt\ *n*

over·stay \-'stā\ *vb* : to stay beyond the time or the limits of ⟨*overstayed* their welcome⟩

over·step \-'step\ *vb* : to step over or beyond : EXCEED ⟨*overstepped* their authority⟩

over·stock \-'stäk\ *vb* : to stock more than there is need or room for ⟨stores *overstocked* with toys⟩ — **over·stock** \'ō-vər-ˌstäk\ *n*

over·stuffed \ˌō-vər-'stəft\ *adj* **1** : stuffed too full **2** : covered completely and deeply with upholstery ⟨an *overstuffed* chair⟩

over·sub·scribe \-səb-'skrīb\ *vb* : to subscribe for more of than is available ⟨*oversubscribe* a stock issue⟩

over·sup·ply \-sə-'plī\ *n* : a supply that is too large : SURPLUS

overt \ō-'vərt, 'ō-(ˌ)vərt\ *adj* : open to view : not secret ⟨*overt* hostility⟩ — **overt·ly** *adv* — **overt·ness** *n*

over·take \ˌō-vər-'tāk\ *vb* **-took** \-'túk\; **-tak·en** \-'tā-kən\; **-tak·ing** **1 a** : to catch up with **b** : to catch up with and pass by **2** : to come upon suddenly ⟨a blizzard *overtook* the hunting party⟩

over–the–counter *adj* : sold legally without a prescription ⟨an *over-the-counter* pain reliever⟩

over·throw \-'thrō\ *vb* **-threw** \-'thrü\; **-thrown** \-'thrōn\; **-throw·ing** **1** : OVERTURN 1, UPSET ⟨lawn chairs *overthrown* by the gale⟩ **2** : ¹DEFEAT, DESTROY ⟨a government *overthrown* by rebels⟩ **3** : to throw a ball over or past ⟨*overthrew* second base⟩ **synonyms** see CONQUER — **over·throw** \'ō-vər-ˌthrō\ *n*

over·time \'ō-vər-ˌtīm\ *n* **1** : time beyond a set limit; *esp* : working time beyond a standard day or week **2** : the wage paid for overtime — **overtime** *adv or adj*

over·tone \-ˌtōn\ *n* **1** : any of a series of higher tones related to and produced along with a base tone that make up the whole sound of a musical tone **2** : an accompanying result, quality, or meaning : SUGGESTION ⟨the words carried an *overtone* of menace⟩

over·top \ˌō-vər-'täp\ *vb* **1** : to rise above the top of : go beyond in height ⟨*overtopped* my cousin by 3 inches⟩ **2** : SURPASS

over·ture \'ō-və(r)-ˌchù(ə)r, -chər\ *n* **1** : an opening offer : PROPOSAL ⟨the enemy made *overtures* for peace⟩ **2 a** : a musical composition played by the orchestra as the introduction to an opera or musical play **b** : a piece of music in the style of an overture for concert performance

over·turn \ˌō-vər-'tərn\ *vb* **1** : to turn over or upside down ⟨waves *overturned* the boat⟩ **2 a** : INVALIDATE, DESTROY ⟨*overturn* the group's unity⟩ **b** : ²REVERSE 2a ⟨*overturn* the court's ruling⟩ — **over·turn** \'ō-vər-ˌtərn\ *n*

¹over·use \-'yüz\ *vb* : to use too much ⟨an *overused* phrase⟩

²over·use \-'yüs\ *n* : too much use

over·val·ue \-'val-yü\ *vb* **1** : to give an excessive value to ⟨*overvalue* a stock⟩ **2** : to value too highly : place too much importance on ⟨*overvalued* the opinions of others⟩

over·view \'ō-vər-ˌvyü\ *n* : a general survey : SUMMARY

over·ween·ing \ˌō-vər-'wē-niŋ\ *adj* **1** : ARROGANT, CONCEITED **2** : IMMODERATE, EXAGGERATED ⟨*overweening* pride⟩ — **over·ween·ing·ly** *adv*

over·weigh \ˌō-vər-'wā\ *vb* : to weigh more than : OVERBALANCE ⟨it *overweighed* other considerations⟩

¹over·weight \'ō-vər-ˌwāt, *sense 2 is usually* ˌō-vər-'wāt\ *n* **1** : weight above what is required or allowed **2** : excessive or burdensome weight

²over·weight \ˌō-vər-'wāt\ *adj* : being more than the expected, normal, or proper weight; *esp* : having greater than normal bodily weight for one's age, height, and build

over·whelm \ˌō-vər-'hwelm, -'welm\ *vb* **1** : to cover over completely : SUBMERGE ⟨a boat *overwhelmed* by a wave⟩

2 : to overcome completely : CRUSH ⟨*overwhelmed* by grief⟩

over·whelm·ing \ˌō-vər-'hwel-miŋ, -wel-\ *adj* : GREAT 4, EXTREME ⟨an *overwhelming* response⟩ — **over·whelm·ing·ly** *adv*

over·win·ter \-'wint-ər\ *vb* : to spend or survive the winter ⟨the butterfly *overwinters* in Mexico⟩

over·work \-'wərk\ *vb* **1** : to work or cause to work too hard or long ⟨*overworked* the crew⟩ **2** : to use too much ⟨*overworked* phrases⟩ — **overwork** *n*

over·write \ˌō-və(r)-'rīt\ *vb* **-wrote** \-'rōt\; **-writ·ten** \-'rit-ᵊn\; **-writ·ing** \-'rīt-iŋ\ **1** : to write over the surface of : write on top of **2** : to write too much or in an overly elaborate style ⟨*overwritten* accounts of everyday events⟩

over·wrought \ˌō-və(r)-'rót\ *adj* **1** : extremely excited : AGITATED ⟨*overwrought* feelings⟩ **2** : decorated too much : OVERDONE

ovi·duct \'ō-və-ˌdəkt\ *n* : a tube for the passage of eggs from the ovary of an animal [from scientific Latin *oviductus* "oviduct," from Latin *ovi-* "egg" (from *ovum* "egg") and Latin *ductus* "tube, duct"]

ovip·a·rous \ō-'vip-(ə-)rəs\ *adj* : producing eggs that develop and hatch outside the body of the female

ovi·pos·i·tor \'ō-və-ˌpäz-ət-ər\ *n* : a specialized organ (as of an insect) for depositing eggs

ovoid \'ō-ˌvóid\ *adj* : OVATE

ovu·late \'äv-yə-ˌlāt, 'ōv-\ *vb* **-lat·ed; -lat·ing** : to produce eggs or release them from an ovary — **ovu·la·tion** \ˌäv-yə-'lā-shən, ˌōv-\ *n*

ovule \'äv-(ˌ)yü(ə)l, 'ōv-\ *n* **1** : an outgrowth of the ovary of a seed plant that after fertilization develops into a seed **2** : a small egg; *esp* : one in an early stage of growth

ovum \'ō-vəm\ *n, pl* **ova** \-və\ : ²EGG 1c

ow \'aú, 'ü\ *interj* — used especially to express sudden pain

owe \'ō\ *vb* **owed; ow·ing** **1 a** : to be obligated to pay or repay ⟨*owes* me $5⟩ **b** : to be indebted to ⟨*owes* the grocer for supplies⟩ **c** : to be in debt ⟨*owes* for her house⟩ **2** : to have or possess as something obtained from or given to ⟨*owes* much to good luck⟩ — **owe it** : to have a responsibility to do something ⟨*owes it* to us to apologize⟩

ow·ing \'ō-iŋ\ *adj* : due to be paid : OWED ⟨have bills *owing*⟩ ⟨claim no more than is *owing*⟩

owing to *prep* : BECAUSE OF ⟨absent *owing to* illness⟩

owl \'aú(ə)l\ *n* : any of an order of birds of prey that are active mainly at night and that have a broad head, very large eyes, and a powerful hooked beak and claws

owl·et \'aú-lət\ *n* : a young or small owl

owl·ish \'aú-lish\ *adj* : resembling or suggesting an owl — **owl·ish·ly** *adv* — **owl·ish·ness** *n*

¹own \'ōn\ *adj* : belonging to oneself or itself ⟨my *own* room⟩

²own *vb* **1 a** : to have or hold as property : POSSESS **b** : to have power or control over ⟨wanted to *own* her own life⟩ **2** : to admit that something is true : CONFESS ⟨*owned* to being scared⟩ ⟨if you broke the window, *own* up⟩ **synonyms** see ACKNOWLEDGE — **own·er** \'ō-nər\ *n* — **own·er·ship** \-ˌship\ *n*

³own *pron sing or pl* : one or ones belonging to oneself — used after a possessive ⟨dog of his *own*⟩ — **on one's own**

owl

\ə\ abut	\aú\ out	\i\ tip	\ó\ saw	\ú\ foot
\ər\ further	\ch\ chin	\ī\ life	\ói\ coin	\y\ yet
\a\ mat	\e\ pet	\j\ job	\th\ thin	\yü\ few
\ā\ take	\ē\ easy	\ŋ\ sing	\th\ this	\yú\ cure
\ä\ cot, cart	\g\ go	\ō\ bone	\ü\ food	\zh\ vision

: without outside help or control ⟨we're *on our own* now⟩ ⟨did the whole thing *on her own*⟩

ox \'äks\ *n, pl* **ox·en** \'äk-sən\ *also* **ox** **1** : a common large domesticated bovine mammal which is kept for milk, draft, and meat and of which the female is a cow and the male a bull; *esp* : an adult castrated male **2** : any various related bovine mammals (as the buffalo)

ox·blood \'äks-ˌbləd\ *n* : a medium reddish brown

ox·bow \-ˌbō\ *n* **1** : a U-shaped collar worn by a draft ox **2** : something (as a bend in a river) resembling an oxbow — **oxbow** *adj*

ox·cart \-ˌkärt\ *n* : a cart drawn by oxen

ox·eye \'äk-ˌsī\ *n* : any of several plants related to the daisies and having heads with both disk and ray flowers

oxeye daisy *n* : DAISY 1b

ox·ford \'äks-fərd\ *n* **1** : a low shoe laced over the middle of the foot **2** : OXFORD CLOTH

oxford cloth *n* : a soft strong cotton or synthetic fabric that has a weave that is plain or like that of a basket

ox·i·da·tion \ˌäk-sə-'dā-shən\ *n* **1** : the process of oxidizing **2** : the state or result of being oxidized — **ox·i·da·tive** \'äk-sə-ˌdāt-iv\ *adj*

oxford 1

oxidation state *n* : a positive or negative number that represents the effective charge of an atom or element and indicates the extent of or possibility for oxidation of the atom or element ⟨the usual *oxidation state* of sodium is +1 and of oxygen –2⟩ — called also *oxidation number*

ox·ide \'äk-ˌsīd\ *n* : a compound of oxygen with another element or a chemical group

ox·i·dize \'äk-sə-ˌdīz\ *vb* **-dized; -diz·ing** **1** : to combine with oxygen **2** : to remove hydrogen from especially by the action of oxygen **3** : to remove one or more electrons from (an atom, ion, or molecule) **4** : to become oxidized — **ox·i·diz·er** *n*

oxy·acet·y·lene \ˌäk-sē-ə-'set-əl-ən, -əl-ˌēn\ *adj* : of, relating to, or using a mixture of oxygen and acetylene ⟨*oxyacetylene* torch⟩

ox·y·gen \'äk-si-jən\ *n* : a reactive element that is found in water, rocks, and free as a colorless tasteless odorless gas which forms about 21 percent of the atmosphere, that is capable of combining with almost all elements, and that is necessary for life — see ELEMENT table

Word History Oxygen was discovered by two scientists working independently, Joseph Priestley of England and Carl Scheele of Sweden. However, it was the French chemist Antoine Lavoisier who later gave the gas its name. He said the most common characteristic of this element was its ability to combine with other substances to form acids. For this reason Lavoisier named it *oxygène,* literally meaning "acid producer." The origin of his word was two Greek elements, *oxys,* meaning "sharp, sour," and *-genēs,* meaning "born, generated." [from French *oxygène* "oxygen," literally, "acid producer," from *oxy-* "sharp, acid" (from Greek *oxys* "sharp, sour") and *-gène* "one that produces or generates" (from Greek *-genēs* "born, generated")]

ox·y·gen·ate \'äk-si-jə-ˌnāt, äk-'sij-ə-\ *vb* **-at·ed; -at·ing** : to combine or supply with oxygen — **ox·y·gen·ation** \ˌäk-si-jə-'nā-shən, äk-ˌsij-ə-\ *n*

oxygen debt *n* : a lack of oxygen that develops in the body during periods of intense activity and must be made good when the body returns to rest

oxygen mask *n* : a device worn over the nose and mouth through which oxygen is supplied from a storage tank

oxygen tent *n* : a flexible enclosure which can be placed over and around a person in bed and within which a flow of oxygen can be maintained

oxy·he·mo·glo·bin \ˌäk-si-'hē-mə-ˌglō-bən\ *n* : a compound of hemoglobin with oxygen that is the chief means of transportation of oxygen from the air (as in the lungs) by way of the blood to the tissues

ox·y·mo·ron \ˌäk-si-'mōr-ˌän, -'mor-\ *n, pl* **oxymorons** *also* **ox·y·mo·ra** \-'mōr-ə, -'mor-ə\ : a combination of contradictory words (as *cruel kindness*) [from Greek *oxymōros* "pointedly foolish," from Greek *oxys* "sharp, keen" and *mōros* "foolish"]

oy \'oi\ *interj* — used especially to express annoyance or dismay ⟨*oy,* what a mess⟩

oyez \ō-'yā, -'yes\ *imperative verb* — used as a call to gain attention before a public announcement

oys·ter \'oi-stər\ *n* : any of various marine mollusks that include important edible shellfish and have a rough uneven shell made up of two hinged parts and closed by a single muscle

oyster bed *n* : a place where oysters grow or are cultivated

oyster catcher *n* : any of several wading birds with stout legs, a heavy wedge-shaped bill, and often black and white plumage

oyster cracker *n* : a small salted usually round cracker

ozone \'ō-ˌzōn\ *n* **1** : a form of oxygen that is a bluish irritating sharp-smelling gas containing three atoms per molecule, and that is used especially in disinfecting, deodorizing, and bleaching **2** : pure and refreshing air

ozone hole *n* : an area of the ozone layer (as near the south pole) that is seasonally depleted of ozone

ozone layer *n* : a layer of the earth's atmosphere at heights of about 20 to 30 miles (32 to 48 kilometers) that is normally characterized by high ozone content which blocks most of the sun's ultraviolet radiation from entry into the lower atmosphere

P

p \'pē\ *n, often cap* : the 16th letter of the English alphabet

pa \'pä, 'po\ *n* : ¹FATHER 1a

¹pace \'pās\ *n* **1 a** : rate of moving especially on foot **b** : rate of progress ⟨the *pace* of the story was slow⟩ **2 a** : a manner of going on foot : GAIT **b** : a fast gait of a horse in which legs on the same side move together **3** : a single step or a measure based on the length of a human step

²pace *vb* **paced; pac·ing** **1** : to walk with slow steady steps ⟨*pacing* to and fro⟩ **2** : to cover at a walk ⟨*pace* the floor⟩ **3** : to measure by paces ⟨*pace* off twenty feet⟩ **4**

: to set or regulate the pace of ⟨tried to *pace* himself during the marathon⟩ — **pac·er** *n*

pace·mak·er \'pā-ˌsmā-kər\ *n* **1** : a group of cells or a bodily part (as of the heart) that serves to establish and maintain a rhythmic bodily activity **2** : an electrical device for steadying or establishing the heartbeat

pachy·derm \'pak-i-ˌdərm\ *n* : any of various usually thick-skinned mammals (as an elephant or a rhinoceros) that have hooves or nails resembling hooves; *esp* : ELEPHANT

pa·cif·ic \pə-'sif-ik\ *adj* **1** : tending to lessen or avoid fights or disagreements **2** : having a peaceful nature — **pa·cif·i·cal·ly** \-i-k(ə-)lē\ *adv*

Pacific salmon *n* : SALMON 1b

Pacific time *n* : the time of the 8th time zone west of Greenwich that includes the Pacific coastal region of the U.S. — see TIME ZONE illustration

pac·i·fi·er \'pas-ə-ˌfī(-ə)r\ *n* **1** : one that pacifies **2** : a usually nipple-shaped device for babies to suck or bite on

pac·i·fism \'pas-ə-ˌfiz-əm\ *n* : opposition to war or violence as a means of settling disputes — **pac·i·fist** \-fəst\ *n*

pac·i·fy \'pas-ə-ˌfī\ *vb* **-fied; -fy·ing** **1** : to make peaceful or quiet ⟨*pacify* a crying child⟩ **2** : to restore to a peaceful state : SETTLE, SUBDUE ⟨sent troops to *pacify* the country⟩ [Middle English *pacifien* "to soothe the anger or disturbance of, make peaceful," from Latin *pacificare* (same meaning), from *pac-, pax* "peace" — related to APPEASE, PEACE] — **pac·i·fi·ca·tion** \ˌpas-ə-fə-'kā-shən\ *n*

synonyms PACIFY, MOLLIFY, APPEASE, PLACATE mean to calm the feelings of. PACIFY suggests the quieting of persons who are upset or angry ⟨*pacify* a crying baby with a toy⟩. MOLLIFY suggests a comforting of hurt feelings ⟨an apology would probably *mollify* your friend⟩. APPEASE suggests dealing with another's anger or threats by giving in to demands ⟨some were willing to *appease* the dictator in order to keep peace⟩. PLACATE suggests changing anger or bitterness to goodwill ⟨the builders *placated* the people of the neighborhood by including a playground in their plans⟩.

¹pack \'pak\ *n* **1 a** : a bundle arranged for carrying especially on the back of a person or animal **b** : a group of items packaged as a unit ⟨a *pack* of cards⟩ **c** : PACKET 2, CONTAINER **d** : a stack of magnetic disks in a container for use as a storage device **2** : the contents of a pack **3 a** : a group of similar persons or animals ⟨a *pack* of thieves⟩ ⟨a wolf *pack*⟩ **b** : an organized troop (as of Cub Scouts) **4** : a tight mass or group; *esp* : a mass of ice chunks floating on the sea **5** : absorbent material (as gauze pads) used medically (as to apply medicine or moisture or to press upon a bodily part to stop bleeding) — compare ICE PACK 2 [Middle English *pack* "a bundle for carrying on the back"; of Germanic origin]

²pack *vb* **1 a** : to place articles in (as for transportation or storage) ⟨*pack* a suitcase⟩ **b** : to cover or fill so as to prevent passage (as of air or water) ⟨*pack* the joint of a pipe⟩ **c** : to place closely and securely in a container or bundle ⟨*pack* goods⟩ **2 a** : to crowd in ⟨people *packed* the hall⟩ **b** : to form into a pack ⟨ice is *packing* in the gorge⟩ **3** : to send or go away without delay ⟨*pack* a child off to school⟩ **4** : to transport on foot or on the back of an animal ⟨*pack* water from a spring⟩ **5** : ¹CARRY 6 ⟨*pack* a gun⟩ **6** : to be supplied with : POSSESS ⟨a storm *packing* hurricane winds⟩

synonyms PACK, CRAM, STUFF mean to fill something to its limit or beyond. PACK may suggest filling something up in a way that is tight but orderly ⟨*pack* a trunk⟩ or it may suggest filling something too much ⟨people were *packed* into the room like sardines⟩. CRAM usually suggests that something has been filled in a forceful, careless, or disorderly way ⟨*crammed* everything into one small box⟩. STUFF suggests filling something with as much as it will hold and often to the point that it bulges ⟨I *stuffed* my pockets with candy⟩.

³pack *vb* : to choose or bring together dishonestly so as to be assured of a favorable vote ⟨*pack* a jury⟩ [from obsolete *pack* "to make a secret agreement"]

¹pack·age \'pak-ij\ *n* **1** : a small or medium-sized pack : PARCEL **2** : a covering wrapper or container **3** : PACK-

AGE DEAL **4** : a collection of related items to be considered together ⟨presented his tax *package* to the nation⟩

²package *vb* **pack·aged; pack·ag·ing** : to make into or enclose in a package — **pack·ag·er** *n*

package deal *n* : an offer containing several items all or none of which must be accepted

package store *n* : a store that sells alcoholic beverages only in containers that may not be opened in the store

pack animal *n* : an animal (as a horse or donkey) used for carrying packs

packed \'pakt\ *adj* **1** : that is crowded or stuffed — often used in combination ⟨an action-*packed* story⟩ **2** : filled to capacity ⟨performed before a *packed* stadium⟩

pack·er \'pak-ər\ *n* : one that packs; *esp* : a dealer who prepares and packs foods for the market

pack·et \'pak-ət\ *n* **1** : a passenger boat carrying mail and cargo on a regular schedule **2** : a small bundle or parcel

pack ice *n* : sea ice formed into a mass by the crushing together of chunks and sheets of ice

pack·ing·house \'pak-iŋ-ˌhau̇s\ *n* : an establishment for preparing foods and especially meat

pack rat *n* **1** : WOOD RAT; *esp* : a bushy-tailed rodent of western North America that stores food and loose objects **2** : a person who collects or hoards especially unneeded items

pack·sad·dle \'pak-ˌsad-ᵊl\ *n* : a saddle that supports the load on the back of a pack animal

pack·thread \-ˌthred\ *n* : strong thread or twine used especially for sewing or tying packs or parcels

pact \'pakt\ *n* : AGREEMENT 2; *esp* : a treaty between countries [Middle English *pact* "agreement," from early French *pact* (same meaning), from Latin *pactum* (same meaning), derived from *pacisci* "to agree, contract"]

¹pad \'pad\ *vb* **pad·ded; pad·ding** **1** : to go on foot **2** : to move along with a muffled step [probably from early Dutch *paden* "to follow a path"]

²pad *n* **1 a** : a thin flat mat or cushion **b** : a guard worn to shield body parts against impact **c** : a piece of usually folded absorbent material (as gauze) **d** : a piece of material that holds ink for inking a rubber stamp **2 a** : the hairy foot of some mammals (as a fox or hare) **b** : the soft thickening of the underside of the foot or toes of some mammals (as dogs) **3** : a floating leaf of a water plant **4** : a number of sheets of writing paper glued together at one edge **5** : LAUNCHPAD **6 a** : living quarters : HOME **b** : ¹BED 1a [origin unknown]

³pad *vb* **pad·ded; pad·ding** **1** : to furnish with a pad or padding **2** : to expand with unnecessary or unimportant material ⟨*pad* a speech⟩

⁴pad *n* : a soft muffled or slapping sound

pad·ding \'pad-iŋ\ *n* : material used to pad something

¹pad·dle \'pad-ᵊl\ *vb* **pad·dled; pad·dling** \'pad-liŋ, -ᵊl-iŋ\ : to move the hands or feet about in shallow water [origin unknown]

²paddle *n* **1 a** : an instrument with a flat blade to move and steer a small boat (as a canoe) **b** : an instrument used for stirring, mixing, or hitting **c** : a short bat with a broad flat blade used to hit the ball in various games (as table tennis) **2** : one of the broad boards at the outer rim of a paddle wheel or waterwheel [Middle English *padell* "a device for cleaning a plow"]

³paddle *vb* **pad·dled; pad·dling** \'pad-liŋ, -ᵊl-iŋ\ **1** : to move or drive forward with or as if with a paddle **2** : to stir or mix with a paddle **3** : to beat with or as if with a paddle

\ə\ abut	\au̇\ out	\i\ tip	\ȯ\ saw	\u̇\ foot
\ər\ further	\ch\ chin	\ī\ life	\ȯi\ coin	\y\ yet
\a\ mat	\e\ pet	\j\ job	\th\ thin	\yü\ few
\ā\ take	\ē\ easy	\ŋ\ sing	\th\ this	\yu̇\ cure
\ä\ cot, cart	\g\ go	\ō\ bone	\ü\ food	\zh\ vision

paddle wheel *n* : a wheel with boards around its outer edge used to move a vessel

paddle wheel

pad·dock \'pad-ək, -ik\ *n* **1** : an enclosed area where animals are put to eat grass or to exercise **2** : an enclosed area where racehorses are saddled and paraded before moving to the racetrack

pad·dy \'pad-ē\ *n, pl* **paddies** : wet land in which rice is grown

pad·dy wagon \'pad-ē-\ *n* : PATROL WAGON

pad·lock \'pad-ˌläk\ *n* : a removable lock with a curved piece that snaps into a catch — **padlock** *vb*

pa·dre \'päd-rā, -rē\ *n* **1** : PRIEST **2** : a military chaplain [from Spanish or Italian or Portuguese *padre* "priest," literally, "father," all from Latin *pater* "father" — related to PATERNAL, PATRON, PATTERN]

pae·an \'pē-ən\ *n* : a song of joy, praise, or triumph

pa·el·la \pä-'el-ə, -'āl-yə, -'ā-yə\ *n* : a Spanish dish of rice, meat, seafood, vegetables, and spices

pa·gan \'pā-gən\ *n* **1** : HEATHEN 1 **2** : a person who is not religious — **pagan** *adj* — **pa·gan·ism** \-gə-ˌniz-əm\ *n*

Word History In ancient Rome a person living in a rural area or village was called *paganus,* a word derived from the Latin noun *pagus,* meaning "village, district." In time *paganus* came to refer to a civilian as opposed to a soldier. When Christianity became generally accepted in the towns and cities of the empire, *paganus* was used to refer to a villager who continued to worship the old gods. Christians used the term for anyone not of their faith or of the Jewish faith. The word in Old English for such a person was what is now *heathen.* In the 14th century, English borrowed the Latin *paganus* as *pagan,* and used it with the same meaning. In time both *heathen* and *pagan* also took on the meaning of "a person having no religion." [Middle English *pagan* "heathen," from Latin *paganus* (same meaning), from earlier *paganus* "person who lives in a rural area," from *pagus* "village, district"]

¹page \'pāj\ *n* **1** : a youth in the Middle Ages being trained for knighthood and in the service of a knight **2** : a youth serving a person of rank **3** : a person employed especially to deliver messages or perform personal services (as in a hotel) [Middle English *page* "a youth trained to serve a knight," from early French *page* (same meaning)]

²page *vb* **paged; pag·ing** **1** : to serve as a page **2** : to send for by calling out the name of **3** : to contact by means of a pager

³page *n* **1 a** : one side of a printed or written leaf **b** : the entire leaf **c** : the material printed or written on a page **2 a** : a written record ⟨the *pages* of history⟩ **b** : an event worth recording ⟨an exciting *page* in one's life⟩ **3 a** : a large section of computer memory **b** : the information found at a single World Wide Web address [from early French *page* "a leaf in a book," from Latin *pagina* (same meaning)]

⁴page *vb* **paged; pag·ing** **1** : to number or mark the pages of **2** : to turn the pages (as of a book or magazine) especially in a quick steady manner

pag·eant \'paj-ənt\ *n* **1** : an impressive exhibition or spectacle **2** : an entertainment consisting of scenes based on history or legend

pag·eant·ry \'paj-ən-trē\ *n, pl* **-tries** **1** : pageants and the presentation of pageants **2** : splendid display

pag·er \'pā-jər\ *n* : one that pages; *esp* : a small electronic device that beeps, vibrates, or flashes when it receives a special radio signal indicating an incoming message

pa·go·da \pə-'gōd-ə\ *n* : a tower in eastern Asia of several stories erected as a temple or memorial

pagoda

¹paid \'pād\ *past and past participle of* PAY

²paid *adj* : being or having been paid or paid for ⟨a *paid* political announcement⟩

pail \'pā(ə)l\ *n* **1** : a round container that is open at the top and has a handle : BUCKET **2** : the quantity held by a pail ⟨fetch a *pail* of water⟩

pail·ful \'pā(ə)l-ˌfúl\ *n* : PAIL 2

¹pain \'pān\ *n* **1** : PUNISHMENT **2** ⟨under *pain* of death⟩ **2 a** : physical suffering associated with disease, injury, or other bodily disorder ⟨a *pain* in the back⟩ **b** : a basic bodily sensation that is caused by something harmful, is accompanied by physical discomfort (as pricking, throbbing, or aching), and usually makes one try to escape its source **3** : mental distress : GRIEF **4** *pl* : the suffering experienced during childbirth **5** *pl* : great care or effort ⟨took *pains* with their work⟩ — **pain·less** \-ləs\ *adj* — **pain·less·ly** *adv*

²pain *vb* **1** : to cause pain in or to : HURT **2** : to give or feel pain

pain·ful \'pān-fəl\ *adj* : feeling or giving pain — **pain·ful·ly** \-f(ə-)lē\ *adv* — **pain·ful·ness** \-fəl-nəs\ *n*

pain·kill·er \'pān-ˌkil-ər\ *n* : something (as a drug) that relieves pain — **pain·kill·ing** \-iŋ\ *adj*

pains·tak·ing \'pān-ˌstā-kiŋ\ *adj* : taking or showing great care and effort ⟨a *painstaking* search⟩ — **pains·tak·ing·ly** \-kiŋ-lē\ *adv*

¹paint \'pānt\ *vb* **1** : to apply paint or a covering or coloring substance to ⟨*paint* a wall⟩ **2 a** : to make a picture or design by using paints ⟨*paint* a portrait⟩ **b** : to describe clearly ⟨*paint* a scene in words⟩ **3** : to practice the art of painting

²paint *n* **1** : MAKEUP 2 **2** : a mixture of coloring matter and a suitable liquid to form a thin coating when spread on a surface

paint·brush \'pānt-ˌbrəsh\ *n* **1** : a brush for applying paint **2 a** : INDIAN PAINTBRUSH 1 **b** : ORANGE HAWKWEED

painted bunting *n* : a brightly colored bunting found from the southern U.S. to Panama

painted lady *n* : a butterfly with brown, orange, black, and white wings that migrates long distances

painted turtle *n* : a common freshwater turtle of North America with a greenish black upper shell with yellow bands and red markings and a yellow lower shell

¹paint·er \'pānt-ər\ *n* : one that paints; *esp* : an artist who paints [from *paint* (verb) and *-er* (noun suffix)]

²pain·ter *n* : a line used for attaching or towing a boat [Middle English *paynter* "a line used for securing a boat," probably from early French *pentoir, penteur* "clothesline"]

³pain·ter *n* : COUGAR [an altered form of *panther*]

paint·ing *n* **1** : a painted work of art **2** : the art or occupation of painting

¹pair \'pa(ə)r, 'pe(ə)r\ *n, pl* **pairs** *also* **pair** **1** : two things that match or are meant to be used together ⟨a *pair* of hands⟩ ⟨a *pair* of gloves⟩ **2** : a thing having two connected matching parts ⟨a *pair* of scissors⟩ **3** : a set of two like or associated things [Middle English *paire* "two things that match or go together," from early French *paire* (same meaning), from Latin *paria* "equal things," from *par* "equal" — related to COMPARE, PAR, PEER, UMPIRE; see *Word History* at UMPIRE]

²pair *vb* **1** : to make a pair of or arrange in pairs ⟨*paired* off the animals⟩ **2** : to form a pair or pairs ⟨*paired* off for the next dance⟩

pais·ley \ˈpāz-lē\ *adj, often cap* : made with colorful curved figures ⟨a *paisley* shawl⟩ — **pais·ley** *n*

Pai·ute \ˈpī-ˌ(y)üt\ *n* : a member of an American Indian people originally of Utah, Arizona, Nevada, and California

pa·ja·mas \pə-ˈjäm-əz, -ˈjam-\ *n pl* : a loose lightweight usually two-piece garment worn for sleeping or lounging [from Hindi *pājāma* "loose lightweight trousers," from Persian *pā* "leg" and Persian *jāma* "garment"]

¹**pal** \ˈpal\ *n* : a close friend

²**pal** *vb* **palled; pal·ling** : to be or become pals

pal·ace \ˈpal-əs\ *n* **1** : the official residence of a ruler **2** : a large splendid house **3** : a large public building (as for a legislature, court, or governor) [Middle English *palais* "palace," from early French *palais* (same meaning), from Latin *palatium* (same meaning), from *Palatium,* name of one of the Seven Hills of Rome on which the Caesars had their residences]

pal·a·din \ˈpal-əd-ən\ *n* : a person who fights for a cause as a knight fought for a king in the Middle Ages

pa·lan·quin \ˌpal-ən-ˈkēn, -ˈk(w)in, pə-ˈlaŋ-kwən\ *n* : a boxlike structure in which a person is carried on the shoulders of servants using poles

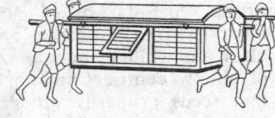

palanquin

pal·at·able \ˈpal-ət-ə-bəl\ *adj* **1** : agreeable to the taste **2** : AGREEABLE 1, ACCEPTABLE — **pal·at·abil·i·ty** \ˌpal-ət-ə-ˈbil-ət-ē\ *n* — **pal·at·ably** \ˈpal-ət-ə-blē\ *adv*

pal·ate \ˈpal-ət\ *n* **1** : the roof of the mouth that separates the mouth from the nasal cavity and is made up of a bony front part and a soft flexible back part **2** : the sense of taste

pa·la·tial \pə-ˈlā-shəl\ *adj* : of, resembling, or fit for a palace — **pa·la·tial·ly** \-shə-lē\ *adv*

¹**pa·la·ver** \pə-ˈlav-ər, -ˈläv-\ *n* **1** : a long discussion usually between persons of different levels of culture **2** : ²TALK 1; *esp* : idle or flattering talk

²**palaver** *vb* **pa·la·vered; pa·la·ver·ing** \-(ə-)riŋ\ : to talk especially at length or idly

¹**pale** \ˈpā(ə)l\ *adj* **pal·er; pal·est 1 a** : light in color or shade : not vivid ⟨a *pale* pink⟩ **b** : not having the warm skin color of a person in good health : PALLID ⟨became *pale*⟩ **2** : not bright or brilliant : DIM ⟨*pale* sunshine⟩ [Middle English *pale* "lacking in color," from early French *pale* (same meaning), from Latin *pallidus* (same meaning), from *pallēre* "to be pale"] — **pale·ly** *adv* — **pale·ness** *n*

²**pale** *vb* **paled; pal·ing** : to make or become pale

³**pale** *n* **1** : a stake or picket of a fence **2** : an enclosed place **3** : territory within clearly marked bounds or under a particular authority [Middle English *pale* "paling, picket," from early French *pal* "stake," from Latin *palus* (same meaning) — related to TRAVEL; see *Word History* at TRAVEL]

pale·face \ˈpā(ə)l-ˌfās\ *n* : a white person

Pa·leo·cene \ˈpā-lē-ə-ˌsēn\ *adj* : of, relating to, or being the earliest epoch of the Tertiary period of geological history or the corresponding series of rocks — see GEOLOGIC TIME table — **Paleocene** *n*

Pa·leo·lith·ic \ˌpā-lē-ə-ˈlith-ik\ *adj* : of, relating to, or being the earliest period of the Stone Age marked by rough or crudely chipped stone implements

pa·le·on·tol·o·gist \ˌpā-lē-ˌän-ˈtäl-ə-jəst\ *n* : a specialist in paleontology

pa·le·on·tol·o·gy \ˌpā-lē-ˌän-ˈtäl-ə-jē\ *n* : a science dealing with the life of past geological periods as known especially from fossil remains — **pa·le·on·to·log·i·cal** \-ˌänt-ᵊl-ˈäj-i-kəl\ *also* **pa·le·on·to·log·ic** \-ik\ *adj*

Pa·leo·zo·ic \ˌpā-lē-ə-ˈzō-ik\ *adj* : of, relating to, or being an era of geological history ending about 248,000,000 years ago in which vertebrates and land plants first appeared; *also* : relating to the corresponding system of rocks — see GEOLOGIC TIME table — **Paleozoic** *n*

pal·ette \ˈpal-ət\ *n* **1** : a thin usually oval board or tablet with a hole for the thumb at one end used by a painter to lay and mix pigments on **2** : the colors put on the palette

pal·frey \ˈpȯl-frē\ *n, pl* **palfreys** *archaic* : a saddle horse that is not a war-horse

pal·in·drome \ˈpal-ən-ˌdrōm\ *n* : a word, phrase, or sentence (as "Step on no pets") or a number (as 1881) that reads the same backward or forward

pal·ing \ˈpā-liŋ\ *n* **1** : ³PALE 1, PICKET **2** : pales or a fence of pales

¹**pal·i·sade** \ˌpal-ə-ˈsād\ *n* **1 a** : a stout high fence of stakes especially for defense **b** : a long strong pointed stake set close with others as a defense **2** : a line of steep cliffs

²**palisade** *vb* **-sad·ed; -sad·ing** : to surround or protect with palisades

palisade cell *n* : a cell of the palisade layer

palisade layer *n* : a layer of cylinder-shaped cells that are rich in chloroplasts and are found just beneath the upper epidermis of a leaf — compare SPONGY LAYER

¹**pall** \ˈpȯl\ *n* **1** : a heavy cloth covering for a coffin, hearse, or tomb **2** : a chalice cover made of a square piece of stiffened linen **3 a** : something that covers, darkens, or produces a gloomy effect ⟨a *pall* of black smoke⟩ **b** : a feeling of gloom ⟨his bad mood cast a *pall* over the celebration⟩

²**pall** *vb* : to become dull or uninteresting : lose the ability to give pleasure ⟨the excitement of the party quickly began to *pall*⟩

pal·la·di·um \pə-ˈlād-ē-əm\ *n* : a silver-white metallic element that is used especially in alloys — see ELEMENT table

pall·bear·er \ˈpȯl-ˌbar-ər, -ˌber-\ *n* : a person who helps to carry the coffin at a funeral

palled *past and past participle of* PAL

pal·let \ˈpal-ət\ *n* **1** : a straw-filled mattress **2** : a small, hard, or temporary bed

pal·li·ate \ˈpal-ē-ˌāt\ *vb* **-at·ed; -at·ing 1** : to make less harmful or harsh **2** : to find excuses for : EXCUSE

¹**pal·li·a·tive** \ˈpal-ē-ˌāt-iv, ˈpal-yət-\ *adj* : serving to palliate

²**palliative** *n* : something that palliates

pal·lid \ˈpal-əd\ *adj* : lacking healthy color : PALE — **pal·lid·ly** *adv*

palling *present participle of* PAL

pal·lor \ˈpal-ər\ *n* : paleness especially of the face

¹**palm** \ˈpäm, ˈpälm\ *n* **1** : any of a family of mostly tropical or subtropical woody trees, shrubs, or vines usually with a simple but often tall stem topped by a crown of very large feathery or fan-shaped leaves **2 a** : a palm leaf especially when carried as a symbol of victory or rejoicing **b** : an emblem of success or triumph [Old English *palm* "palm tree," from Latin *palma* "palm of the hand"; so called because the leaves resemble an outstretched hand] — **palm·like** \-ˌlīk\ *adj*

¹palm 1

²**palm** *n* **1** : the underside of the hand between the fingers and the wrist **2** : a measure of length

\ə\ **abut**	\au̇\ **out**	\i\ **tip**	\ȯ\ **saw**	\u̇\ **foot**
\ər\ **further**	\ch\ **chin**	\ī\ **life**	\ȯi\ **coin**	\y\ **yet**
\a\ **mat**	\e\ **pet**	\j\ **job**	\th\ **thin**	\yü\ **few**
\ā\ **take**	\ē\ **easy**	\ŋ\ **sing**	\th\ **this**	\yu̇\ **cure**
\ä\ **cot, cart**	\g\ **go**	\ō\ **bone**	\ü\ **food**	\zh\ **vision**

based on the width or length of the palm [Middle English *paume* "palm of the hand," from early French *paume* (same meaning), from Latin *palma* "palm of the hand"]

³palm *vb* : to conceal in or pick up secretly with the hand

pal·mate \'pal-ˌmāt, 'pälm-ˌāt, 'päm-\ *adj* : resembling a hand with the fingers spread ⟨*palmate* leaves⟩

palm·er \'päm-ər, 'päl-mər\ *n* : a person wearing two crossed palm leaves as a sign of having gone on a pilgrimage to the Holy Land

pal·met·to \pal-'met-ō\ *n, pl* **-tos** *or* **-toes** : any of several usually low-growing palms with fan-shaped leaves

palm·is·try \'päm-ə-strē, 'päl-mə-\ *n* : the art or practice of reading a person's character or future from markings on the palm of the hand — **palm·ist** \'päm-əst, 'päl-məst\ *n*

palm off *vb* : to get rid of or pass on (as something fake, useless, or of poor quality) in a dishonest way ⟨*palmed off* fake antiques on unsuspecting customers⟩

Palm Sunday *n* : the Sunday before Easter celebrated in memory of Jesus' entry into Jerusalem

palm·top \-ˌtäp\ *n* : a small portable computer that fits in the palm of the hand

palmy \'päm-ē, 'päl-mē\ *adj* **palm·i·er; -est** 1 : having palms ⟨a *palmy* beach⟩ 2 : marked by success : PROSPEROUS ⟨a *palmy* community⟩

pal·o·mi·no \ˌpal-ə-'mē-nō\ *n, pl* **-nos** : a horse with a light golden coat and cream or white mane and tail

pal·pa·ble \'pal-pə-bəl\ *adj* 1 : capable of being touched or felt : TANGIBLE 2 : easily sensed : NOTICEABLE 3 : easily understood or recognized : OBVIOUS ⟨a *palpable* error⟩ — **pal·pa·bil·i·ty** \ˌpal-pə-'bil-ət-ē\ *n* — **pal·pa·bly** \'pal-pə-blē\ *adv*

pal·pi·tate \'pal-pə-ˌtāt\ *vb* **-tat·ed; -tat·ing** : to beat rapidly and strongly : THROB, QUIVER

pal·pi·ta·tion \ˌpal-pə-'tā-shən\ *n* : an act or instance of palpitating; *esp* : an abnormally rapid beating of the heart

pal·pus \'pal-pəs\ *n, pl* **pal·pi** \-ˌpī, -ˌpē\ : a part that sticks out from a mouthpart of an arthropod and is used in sensing by touch or in feeding

pal·sied \'pól-zēd\ *adj* : affected with or as if with palsy

pal·sy \'pól-zē\ *n* 1 : PARALYSIS 2 : a condition marked by uncontrollable trembling or shaking of the body or a part (as the head or hands)

pal·ter \'pól-tər\ *vb* **pal·tered; pal·ter·ing** \-t(ə)riŋ\ 1 : to act or speak insincerely 2 : HAGGLE, BARGAIN — **pal·ter·er** \-tər-ər\ *n*

pal·try \'pól-trē\ *adj* **pal·tri·er; -est** 1 : PETTY 3, MEAN ⟨a *paltry* trick⟩ 2 : TRIVIAL 2, WORTHLESS ⟨a *paltry* sum⟩ — **pal·tri·ness** *n*

pam·pa \'pam-pə\ *n, pl* **pam·pas** \-pəz, -pəs\ : a wide generally grass-covered plain of South America

pam·per \'pam-pər\ *vb* **pam·pered; pam·per·ing** \-p(ə)riŋ\ : to treat with too much care and attention

pam·phlet \'pam(p)-flət\ *n* : a short printed publication with no cover or with a paper cover

pam·phle·teer \ˌpam(p)-flə-'ti(ə)r\ *n* : a writer of pamphlets usually attacking something or urging a cause — **pamphleteer** *vb*

¹pan \'pan\ *n* 1 **a** : a usually broad, shallow, and open container for cooking **b** : something resembling a pan 2 : a basin or depression in the earth ⟨a salt *pan*⟩ [Old English *panne* "pan for cooking," derived from Latin *patina* (same meaning)]

²pan *vb* **panned; pan·ning** 1 : to wash earthy material in a pan to concentrate bits of metal ⟨*pan* for gold⟩ 2 : to yield precious metal in panning 3 : to criticize severely

³pan *vb* **panned; pan·ning** : to move a motion-picture or television camera so as to keep a moving object in view or to scan a scene [from earlier *pan* "the process of panning," short for *panorama*]

pan·a·cea \ˌpan-ə-'sē-ə\ *n* : a remedy for all ills or difficulties : CURE-ALL

pan·a·ma \'pan-ə-ˌmä, -ˌmó\ *n, often cap* : a lightweight

hat made of narrow strips from the young leaves of a tropical American tree

Pan–Amer·i·can \ˌpan-ə-'mer-ə-kən\ *adj* : of, relating to, or involving the independent republics of North and South America

pan·broil \'pan-ˌbrói(ə)l\ *vb* : to cook uncovered on a hot metal surface (as a frying pan) with little or no fat

pan·cake \'pan-ˌkāk\ *n* : a flat cake usually made of thin batter and cooked on both sides on a griddle or in a frying pan

pan·chro·mat·ic \ˌpan-krō-'mat-ik\ *adj* : sensitive to light of all colors in the visible spectrum ⟨*panchromatic* film⟩

pan·cre·as \'paŋ-krē-əs, 'pan-\ *n* : a large gland of vertebrates that lies near the stomach and produces digestive enzymes and insulin — **pan·cre·at·ic** \ˌpaŋ-krē-'at-ik, ˌpan-\ *adj*

pancreatic duct *n* : a duct leading from the pancreas and opening into the duodenum

pancreatic juice *n* : a clear digestive fluid that contains enzymes produced by the pancreas and that flows into the duodenum

pan·da \'pan-də\ *n* 1 : RED PANDA 2 : a large black and white mammal of chiefly central China that feeds primarily on bamboo shoots and is now usually considered to be closely related to the bears — called also *giant panda*

panda 2

¹pan·dem·ic \pan-'dem-ik\ *adj* : occurring over a wide area and affecting many individuals ⟨*pandemic* malaria⟩

²pandemic *n* : a pandemic outbreak of a disease

pan·de·mo·ni·um \ˌpan-də-'mō-nē-əm\ *n* : a wild uproar : TUMULT [from *Pandemonium*, name of the place of demons in *Paradise Lost* by John Milton, from Greek *pan-* "all, every, completely" and Greek *daimon* "evil spirit, demon"]

pan·der \'pan-dər\ *or* **pan·der·er** \-dər-ər\ *n* : one who takes advantage of or profits from the weaknesses and mean desires of others — **pander** *vb*

pane \'pān\ *n* 1 : a piece, section, or side of something (as a sheet of glass in a window) 2 : one of the sections (as of 50 or 100 stamps) into which a sheet of postage stamps is divided

pan·e·gy·ric \ˌpan-ə-'jir-ik, -'jī-rik\ *n* : formal or elaborate praise

¹pan·el \'pan-ᵊl\ *n* 1 **a** : a list or a group of persons selected as jurors **b** : a group of persons who discuss a topic before an audience **c** : a group of entertainers or guests who are players in a quiz or guessing game on a radio or television program 2 : a separate or different part of a surface: as **a** : a usually rectangular and sunken or raised section of a door, wall, or ceiling **b** : a flat usually rectangular piece of construction material (as plywood) made to form part of a surface **c** : a lengthwise section of cloth (as in a skirt or dress) 3 **a** : a thin flat piece of wood on which a picture is painted **b** : a painting on such a surface 4 : a usually vertical mount for controls or dials (as of instruments of measurement)

²panel *vb* **-eled** *or* **-elled; -el·ing** *or* **-el·ling** : to furnish or decorate with panels

pan·el·ing \'pan-ᵊl-iŋ\ *n* : panels joined in a continuous surface

pan·el·ist \'pan-ᵊl-əst\ *n* : a member of a panel

pan·fish \'pan-ˌfish\ *n* : a small food fish (as a sunfish) usually caught with a hook and line and not sold in stores

pan·fry \'pan-ˌfrī, pan-'frī\ *vb* **pan·fried; pan·fry·ing** : to cook in a frying pan with a small amount of fat

pang \'paŋ\ *n* : a sudden sharp attack of pain or distress

pan·go·lin \'paŋ-gə-lən, 'pan-\ *n* : any of several Asian and African toothless mammals having the body covered with large overlapping horny scales

¹pan·han·dle \'pan-,han-dᵊl\ *n* : a narrow strip of territory that extends from a larger territory (as a state) ⟨the Texas *Panhandle*⟩

²panhandle *vb* **-dled; -dling** : to beg for money on the street — **pan·han·dler** \-(d)lər, -dᵊl-ər\ *n*

¹pan·ic \'pan-ik\ *n* **1** : a sudden overpowering fright especially without reasonable cause; *also* : extreme anxiousness **2** : a sudden widespread fright concerning financial affairs causing hurried selling and a sharp fall in prices — **panic** *adj* — **pan·icky** \'pan-i-kē\ *adj*

Word History The ancient Greeks worshiped a god of pastures, flocks, and shepherds whom they named *Pan*. Pan was believed to be able to cause great fear at times. The people of Athens believed that it was Pan who had caused the Persians to flee in terror from the battle of Marathon. The Greek adjective *panikos,* literally meaning "of Pan," was used to describe the kind of sudden fear that Pan was thought to cause. The English word *panic* comes from Greek *panikos.* [Greek *panikon* "fear caused by Pan, panic," from *panikos* "relating to the fear caused by Pan," literally, "of Pan," from *Pan,* name of a god of woods and shepherds]

²panic *vb* **pan·icked** \-ikt\; **pan·ick·ing** : to affect or be affected with panic

pan·i·cle \'pan-i-kəl\ *n* : a branched flower cluster (as of a lilac or some grasses) in which each branch from the main stem has one or more flowers

pan·ic–strick·en \'pan-ik-,strik-ən\ *adj* : overcome with panic

pa·ni·no \pə-'nē-nō\ *n, pl* **pa·ni·ni** \-nē\ : a usually grilled sandwich made with Italian bread

panned *past and past participle of* PAN

pan·nier \'pan-yər, 'pan-ē-ər\ *n* : a large basket; *esp* : one carried on the back of an animal or the shoulder of a person

panning *present participle of* PAN

panicle

pan·o·ply \'pan-ə-plē\ *n, pl* **-plies** **1** : a full suit of armor **2** : a protective covering **3** : a magnificent arrangement or display — **pan·o·plied** \-plēd\ *adj*

pan·ora·ma \,pan-ə-'ram-ə, -'räm-\ *n* **1** : a picture shown a part at a time by being unrolled before the spectator **2** : a full and clear view in every direction **3** : a complete presentation of a subject — **pan·oram·ic** \-'ram-ik\ *adj*

pan out *vb* : TURN OUT 5; *esp* : SUCCEED

pan·pipe \'pan-,pīp\ *n* : a musical instrument made up of several short pipes of different lengths fixed together and played by blowing air across the top — usually used in plural

pan·sy \'pan-zē\ *n, pl* **pansies** : a garden plant that is related to the violets and has large velvety flowers with five petals usually in shades of yellow, purple, or brownish red; *also* : its flower

pant \'pant\ *vb* **1 a** : to breathe hard or quickly : GASP **b** : to make a puffing sound **c** : to move forward with panting ⟨the car *panted* up the hill⟩ **2** : to wish for eagerly : YEARN **3** : to utter with panting ⟨ran up and *panted* out the message⟩ — **pant** *n*

pan·ta·loon \,pant-ᵊl-'ün\ *n* **1** *pl* : close-fitting trousers usually with straps passing under the insteps **2** : loose-fitting usually shorter than ankle-length trousers — see *Word History* at PANTS

pan·ther \'pan(t)-thər\ *n, pl* **panthers** *also* **panther** **1** : LEOPARD; *esp* : one that is black **2** : COUGAR **3** : JAGUAR

pant·ie *or* **panty** \'pant-ē\ *n, pl* **pant·ies** : a woman's or child's undergarment covering the lower trunk — usually used in plural

pan·to·graph \'pant-ə-,graf\ *n* : an instrument for copying something (as a map or plan) by hand using a previously chosen scale

pan·to·mime \'pant-ə-,mīm\ *n* **1** : PANTOMIMIST **2** : a performance in which a story is told by expressive movements of the body or face **3** : expression of information by movements of the body or face — **pantomime** *vb*

pan·to·mim·ist \'pant-ə-,mim-əst, -,mīm-\ *n* : an actor or dancer in pantomimes

pan·to·then·ic acid \,pant-ə-,then-ik-\ *n* : an oily acid of the vitamin B complex found in all living tissues and necessary for growth

pan·try \'pan-trē\ *n, pl* **pantries** : a small room in which food and dishes are kept [Middle English *panetrie* "pantry," derived from early French *panetier* "servant in charge of food storage," from *pan* "bread," from Latin *panis* "bread, food" — related to COMPANION]

pants \'pan(t)s\ *n pl* **1** : an outer garment extending from the waist to the ankle and covering each leg separately : TROUSERS **2** : UNDERPANTS; *esp* : PANTIE

Word History A form of comic entertainment that had its start in Italy became popular throughout Europe several hundred years ago. A small group of actors would put on a play with a standard set of humorous characters. One of the standard characters was a bad-tempered old man called *Pantalone* or *Pantaloon.* Pantaloon always wore a tight-fitting combination of trousers and stockings. Because he did, such clothing became known as *pantaloons.* The word *pantaloons,* which was later used for various types of trousers, is still sometimes heard today. The usual term now, however, is *pants,* which is a short way of saying *pantaloons.* [a shortened form of *pantaloons* "trousers," from *Pantaloon, Pantalone,* name of a clown in stage entertainment]

pant·suit \'pant-,süt\ *n* : a woman's outfit consisting usually of a long jacket and pants made of the same material

panty hose *n pl* : a one-piece undergarment for women consisting of hosiery combined with panties

pap \'pap\ *n* : soft or bland food for infants or invalids

pa·pa \'päp-ə\ *n* : ¹FATHER 1a

pa·pa·cy \'pā-pə-sē\ *n, pl* **-cies** **1** : the office of pope **2** : the term of a pope's reign **3** *cap* : the government of the Roman Catholic Church of which the pope is the head

pa·pa·in \pə-'pā-ən, -'pī-ən\ *n* : an enzyme in papaya juice used especially to make meat tender and in medicine

pa·pal \'pā-pəl\ *adj* : of or relating to the pope or the papacy — **pa·pal·ly** \-pə-lē\ *adv*

papaw *variant of* PAWPAW

pa·pa·ya \pə-'pī-ə\ *n* : an oblong edible yellow fruit with many black seeds that grows on a tropical American tree with large leaves; *also* : the tree

¹pa·per \'pā-pər\ *n* **1 a** : a thin sheet made usually from rags, wood, straw, or bark and used to write or print on, to wrap things in, or to cover walls **b** : a sheet or piece of paper **2 a** : a piece of paper having something written or printed on it **b** : a written composition **3** : NEWSPAPER **4** : WALLPAPER [Middle English *papir* "paper," from early French *papier* (same meaning), from Latin *papyrus* "paper, papyrus" — related to PAPYRUS]

pansy

\ə\ abut	\au̇\ out	\i\ tip	\ȯ\ saw	\u̇\ foot
\ər\ further	\ch\ chin	\ī\ life	\ȯi\ coin	\y\ yet
\a\ mat	\e\ pet	\j\ job	\th\ thin	\yu̇\ few
\ā\ take	\ē\ easy	\ŋ\ sing	\th\ this	\yu̇\ cure
\ä\ cot, cart	\g\ go	\ō\ bone	\ü\ food	\zh\ vision

²**paper** *vb* **pa·pered; pa·per·ing** \'pā-p(ə-)riŋ\ : to cover or line with paper and especially wallpaper ⟨*paper* a room⟩ — **pa·per·er** \-pər-ər\ *n*

³**paper** *adj* **1 a** : of, relating to, or made of paper or cardboard ⟨*paper* carton⟩ ⟨*paper* mills⟩ **b** : PAPERY ⟨nuts with *paper* shells⟩ **2** : NOMINAL 1

pa·per·back \'pā-pər-,bak\ *n* : a book with a flexible paper binding — **paperback** *adj*

paper birch *n* : a North American birch with white bark that peels off the tree easily

pa·per·board \-,bō(ə)rd, -,bȯ(ə)rd\ *n* : CARDBOARD

paper clip *n* : a length of wire bent into flat loops that is used to hold papers together

pa·per·hang·er \'pā-pər-,haŋ-ər\ *n* : a person who applies wallpaper to walls especially as an occupation — **pa·per·hang·ing** \-,haŋ-iŋ\ *n*

paper money *n* : money consisting of government notes and bank notes

paper mulberry *n* : an Asian tree related to the mulberries and widely grown as a shade tree

paper nautilus *n* : a mollusk with eight arms that is related to the octopuses and of which the female has a thin fragile shell — called also *argonaut*

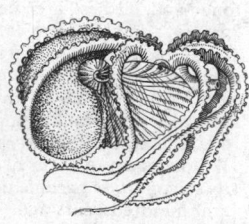

paper nautilus

paper trail *n* : documents (as financial records or published materials) from which a person's actions may be traced or opinions learned

paper wasp *n* : a wasp that builds a nest out of papery material

pa·per·weight \'pā-pər-,wāt\ *n* : an object used to hold down loose papers by its weight

pa·per·work \-,wərk\ *n* : routine office or record-keeping work

pa·pery \'pā-p(ə-)rē\ *adj* : resembling paper in thinness or firmness — **pa·per·i·ness** *n*

pa·pier–mâ·ché \,pā-pər-mə-'shā, ,pap-,yā-mə-; -(,)ma-\ *n* : a light strong molding material made of paper pulp mixed with glue and other substances [French, literally, "chewed paper"] — **papier–mâché** *adj*

pa·pil·la \pə-'pil-ə\ *n, pl* **-pil·lae** \-'pil-ē, -,ī\ : a small bodily structure (as one on the surface of the tongue) that often contains taste buds) that resembles a tiny nipple in form

pa·poose \pa-'püs, pə-\ *n* : a North American Indian infant

pa·pri·ka \pə-'prē-kə, pa-\ *n* : a mild red spice consisting of the dried finely ground fruit of various cultivated sweet peppers

Pap smear \'pap-\ *n* : a test for the early detection of cancer especially of the cervix of the uterus using cells that are shed or scraped off and stained in a special way — called also *Pap test*

pa·py·rus \pə-'pī-rəs\ *n, pl* **pa·py·ri** \-'pī(ə)r-ē, -,ī\ *also* **pa·py·rus·es 1** : a tall sedge of the Nile valley **2** : the soft central part of papyrus stems especially when made into strips and pressed into a writing material **3** : a writing on or written scroll of papyrus [Middle English *papyrus* "papyrus," from Latin *papyrus* "papyrus, paper," from Greek *papyros* "papyrus" — related to PAPER]

papyrus 1

par \'pär\ *n* **1 a** : the fixed value of the unit of money of one country expressed in terms of the unit of money of another country **b** : the face value or issuing price of a stock or bond **2** : common level : EQUALITY **3** : an accepted standard (as of health) ⟨not feeling up to *par*⟩ **4** : the standard score for a golf hole or course [from Latin *par* (noun) "one that is equal," from *par* (adjective) "equal" — related to COMPARE, PAIR, PEER, UMPIRE; see *Word History* at UMPIRE] — **par** *adj*

par·a·ble \'par-ə-bəl\ *n* : a short simple story illustrating a moral or spiritual truth

pa·rab·o·la \pə-'rab-ə-lə\ *n* **1** : a curve formed by the intersection of a cone with a plane parallel to a straight line in its surface : a curve formed by a point moving so that its distance from a fixed point is equal to its distance from a fixed line **2** : something that is bowl-shaped — **par·a·bol·ic** \,par-ə-'bäl-ik\ *adj*

¹**para·chute** \'par-ə-,shüt\ *n* **1** : a folding umbrella-shaped device of light fabric used especially for making a safe jump from an aircraft **2** : something (as the bunch of hairs on a dandelion seed) that is like a parachute in form, use, or operation

²**parachute** *vb* **-chut·ed; -chut·ing** : to transport or come down by means of a parachute — **para·chut·ist** \-,shüt-əst\ *n*

¹**pa·rade** \pə-'rād\ *n* **1** : great show or display **2** : a formation of a body of troops before a superior officer **3** : a public procession **4** : a crowd of strolling people ⟨the Easter *parade*⟩

²**parade** *vb* **pa·rad·ed; pa·rad·ing 1 a** : to cause to march **b** : to march in a parade **2** : ²PROMENADE **3** : SHOW OFF 1 ⟨*parade* one's knowledge⟩ **synonyms** see SHOW — **pa·rad·er** *n*

para·di·chlo·ro·ben·zene \,par-ə-,dī-,klōr-ə-'ben-,zēn, -,klȯr-, -,ben-'zēn\ *n* : a white compound that contains chlorine and benzene and is used chiefly in moth balls

par·a·digm \'par-ə-,dīm, -,dim\ *n* **1** : an example showing how something is to be done : MODEL **2** : an example of a conjugation or declension showing a word in all its inflectional forms — **par·a·dig·mat·ic** \,par-ə-dig-'mat-ik\ *adj*

par·a·dise \'par-ə-,dīs, -,dīz\ *n* **1** : EDEN 2 **2** : HEAVEN 2 **3** : a place or state of great happiness [Middle English *paradis* "the Garden of Eden," from early French *paradis* (same meaning), from Latin *paradisus* (same meaning), from Greek *paradeisos* "Garden of Eden," literally, "enclosed park"]

par·a·dox \'par-ə-,däks\ *n* **1 a** : a statement that seems to go against common sense but may still be true **b** : a false statement that at first seems true **2** : a person or thing having qualities that seem to be opposites — **par·a·dox·i·cal** \,par-ə-'däk-si-kəl\ *adj* — **par·a·dox·i·cal·ly** \-k(ə-)lē\ *adv*

par·af·fin \'par-ə-fən\ *n* : a flammable waxy substance obtained from wood, coal, or petroleum and used chiefly in coating and sealing, in candles, and in drugs and cosmetics

par·a·gon \'par-ə-,gän, -gən\ *n* : a model of excellence or perfection

¹**para·graph** \'par-ə-,graf\ *n* **1** : a part of a writing or speech that develops in an organized manner one point of a subject or gives the words of one speaker **2** : a short written article (as in a newspaper) complete in one section

²**paragraph** *vb* : to divide into or write paragraphs

par·a·keet \'par-ə-,kēt\ *n* : any of numerous usually small slender parrots with a long tail

Par·a·li·pom·e·non \,par-ə-lə-'päm-ə-,nän, -lī-\ *n* : CHRONICLES

par·al·lax \'par-ə-,laks\ *n* : the apparent shift in position of an object as seen from two different points not on a straight line with the object

¹**par·al·lel** \'par-ə-,lel\ *adj* **1** : lying or moving in the same direction but always the same distance apart ⟨*parallel* lines⟩ ⟨the train tracks are *parallel*⟩ **2 a** : being or relating to an electrical circuit having a number of conductors

in parallel **b** : being or relating to a connection in a computer system in which the bits of a byte are transmitted over separate wires at the same time **3** : ³LIKE, SIMILAR ⟨*parallel* situations⟩

²**parallel** *n* **1** : a parallel line, curve, or surface **2 a** : one of the imaginary circles on the surface of the earth parallel to the equator that mark latitude **b** : a corresponding line on a globe or map **3 a** : COUNTERPART 1, EQUAL ⟨a victory without *parallel*⟩ **b** : SIMILARITY 1, LIKENESS **c** : a tracing of similarity ⟨draw a *parallel* between two periods of history⟩ **4** : an arrangement of electrical devices in a circuit in which the same potential difference is applied to two or more resistances with each resistance on a parallel branch

³**parallel** *vb* **1** : to be like or equal to **2** : to lie, run, or move in a direction parallel to ⟨the highway *parallels* the river⟩

⁴**parallel** *adv* : in a parallel manner — often used with *with* or *to*

parallel bars *n pl* : a pair of horizontal bars that are used for swinging and balancing exercises in gymnastics

par·al·lel·ism \ˈpar-ə-ˌlel-ˌiz-əm\ *n* : the quality or state of being parallel; *esp* : similarity of construction of word groups especially for effect or rhythm

par·al·lel·o·gram \ˌpar-ə-ˈlel-ə-ˌgram\ *n* : a four-sided figure whose opposite sides are parallel and of equal length

par·al·lel–veined \ˌpar-ə-ˌlel-ˈvānd\ *adj* : having veins that are arranged nearly parallel to one another and do not branch and come together again ⟨monocotyledons such as grasses and lilies have *parallel-veined* leaves⟩ — compare NET-VEINED

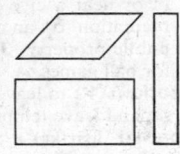

parallelogram

pa·ral·y·sis \pə-ˈral-ə-səs\ *n, pl* **-y·ses** \-ə-ˌsēz\ : complete or partial loss of function especially when involving motion or sensation in a part of the body

¹**par·a·lyt·ic** \ˌpar-ə-ˈlit-ik\ *adj* **1** : affected with, marked by, or causing paralysis **2** : of, relating to, or resembling paralysis

²**paralytic** *n* : one affected with paralysis

par·a·lyze \ˈpar-ə-ˌlīz\ *vb* **-lyzed; -lyz·ing** **1** : to affect with paralysis **2** : to make powerless or unable to act, function, or move

par·a·me·cium \ˌpar-ə-ˈmē-sh(ē-)əm, -sē-əm\ *n, pl* **-cia** \-sh(ē-)ə, -sē-ə\ *also* **-ciums** : any of a genus of one-celled somewhat slipper-shaped mostly freshwater protozoans that move by cilia

para·med·ic \ˌpar-ə-ˈmed-ik\ *n* **1** : a person who works in a health field by helping a physician (as by taking X-rays or giving injections) **2** : a specially trained person with a license to provide a wide range of emergency services (as the giving of intravenous drugs) before or during transport to a hospital [from *para-* "alongside of, associated with in a secondary or assisting role" and *medic* "a person trained in or studying medical work"; *para-* derived from Greek *para* "beside, alongside of" and *medic* from Latin *medicus* "physician"]

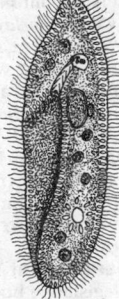

paramecium

para·med·i·cal \ˌpar-ə-ˈmed-i-kəl\ *adj* : concerned with helping with the work of highly trained medical professionals ⟨a *paramedical* aide⟩

pa·ram·e·ter \pə-ˈram-ət-ər\ *n* **1** : an independent variable used to express the coordinates of a point ⟨if the coordinates (*x, y*) of a point are given by the functions $x = f(t)$ and $y = g(t)$ then the *parameter* is the variable *t*⟩ **2** : any of a set of properties whose values determine the characteristics or behavior of something ⟨*parameters* of

the atmosphere such as temperature, pressure, and density⟩ — **para·met·ric** \ˌpar-ə-ˈme-trik\ *adj*

par·a·mount \ˈpar-ə-ˌmaunt\ *adj* : superior to all others : SUPREME ⟨of *paramount* importance⟩

par·a·mour \ˈpar-ə-ˌmur\ *n* : a partner in a sexual relationship other than that of husband and wife

para·noia \ˌpar-ə-ˈnȯi-ə\ *n* **1** : a serious mental disorder marked especially by feelings of persecution or an exaggerated sense of one's own importance usually without hallucinations **2** : a tendency toward being overly suspicious and distrustful

¹**para·noid** \ˈpar-ə-ˌnȯid\ *adj* **1** : resembling paranoia **2** : marked especially by suspiciousness, distrust, and feelings of persecution **3** : extremely fearful ⟨grew *paranoid* about losing her job⟩

²**paranoid** *n* : one who is paranoid

par·a·pet \ˈpar-ə-pət, -ˌpet\ *n* **1** : a wall of earth or stone to protect soldiers **2** : a low wall or railing at the edge of a platform, roof, or bridge

par·a·pher·na·lia \ˌpar-ə-fə(r)-ˈnāl-yə\ *n sing or pl* **1** : personal belongings **2** : FURNISHINGS, APPARATUS ⟨purchased all the necessary *paraphernalia* of the sport⟩

¹**para·phrase** \ˈpar-ə-ˌfrāz\ *n* : a way of stating something (as a written work) again by giving the meaning in different words

²**paraphrase** *vb* **-phrased; -phras·ing** : to give the meaning in different words ⟨*paraphrased* the author's account⟩ — **para·phras·er** *n*

para·pro·fes·sion·al \ˌpar-ə-prə-ˈfesh-nəl, -ən-ºl\ *n* : a person trained to assist a professional person (as a teacher or doctor) — **paraprofessional** *adj*

par·a·site \ˈpar-ə-ˌsīt\ *n* **1** : a person who lives at the expense of another **2** : a living thing which lives in or on another living thing in parasitism **3** : a person dependent on something else for life or support without making proper return

par·a·sit·ic \ˌpar-ə-ˈsit-ik\ *adj* : of or relating to parasites or their way of life : being a parasite — **par·a·sit·i·cal·ly** \-i-k(ə-)lē\ *adv*

par·a·sit·ism \ˈpar-ə-sə-ˌtiz-əm, -ˌsīt-ˌiz-\ *n* : a close association between living things of two or more kinds of which one is a parasite obtaining benefits from the other which is a host and is usually harmed in some way

par·a·sit·ize \ˈpar-ə-sə-ˌtīz, -ˌsīt-ˌīz\ *vb* **-ized; -iz·ing** : to infest or live on or with as a parasite ⟨an insect that *parasitizes* many mammals⟩

para·sol \ˈpar-ə-ˌsȯl\ *n* : a light umbrella for protection against the sun

para·sym·pa·thet·ic \ˌpar-ə-ˌsim-pə-ˈthet-ik\ *adj* : of, relating to, being, or acting on the parasympathetic nervous system

parasol

parasympathetic nervous system *n* : the part of the autonomic nervous system that is concerned with controlling the body during normal routine situations and that tends to cause secretion of the digestive and salivary glands and slow the heart rate and that acts on bodily organs by releasing acetylcholine at the ends of nerve fibers supplying them — compare SYMPATHETIC NERVOUS SYSTEM

\ə\ **abut**	\au̇\ **out**	\i\ **tip**	\ȯ\ **saw**	\u̇\ **foot**
\ər\ **further**	\ch\ **chin**	\ī\ **life**	\ȯi\ **coin**	\y\ **yet**
\a\ **mat**	\e\ **pet**	\j\ **job**	\th\ **thin**	\yü\ **few**
\ā\ **take**	\ē\ **easy**	\ŋ\ **sing**	\th\ **this**	\yu̇\ **cure**
\ä\ **cot, cart**	\g\ **go**	\ō\ **bone**	\ü\ **food**	\zh\ **vision**

par·a·thor·mone \ˌpar-ə-'thȯr-ˌmōn\ *n* : PARATHYROID HORMONE

para·thy·roid \ˌpar-ə-'thī-ˌrȯid\ *adj* : of, relating to, or produced by the parathyroid glands

parathyroid gland *n* : any of usually four small endocrine glands next to or located in the thyroid gland that produce parathyroid hormone

parathyroid hormone *n* : a hormone that is produced by the parathyroid glands and controls the amount of calcium and phosphorus in the blood

para·troops \'par-ə-ˌtrüps\ *n pl* : troops trained and equipped to parachute from an airplane — **para·troop** \-ˌtrüp\ *adj* — **para·troop·er** \-ˌtrü-pər\ *n*

¹**para·ty·phoid** \ˌpar-ə-'tī-ˌfȯid, -(ˌ)tī-'fȯid\ *adj* 1 : resembling typhoid fever 2 : of or relating to paratyphoid or the bacteria that cause it

²**paratyphoid** *n* : a disease caused by bacteria, resembling typhoid fever, and usually occurring from eating contaminated food

par·boil \'pär-ˌbȯil\ *vb* : to boil briefly usually before cooking in another manner

¹**par·cel** \'pär-səl\ *n* 1 : a part of a whole : PORTION 2 : a plot of land 3 : a group or collections of persons or things ⟨told a *parcel* of lies⟩ 4 : a wrapped bundle

²**parcel** *vb* **par·celed** *or* **par·celled; par·cel·ing** *or* **par·cel·ling** \'pär-s(ə-)liŋ\ 1 : to divide into parts : DISTRIBUTE 2 : to wrap up into a parcel

parcel post *n* 1 : a mail service handling parcels 2 : packages handled by parcel post

parch \'pärch\ *vb* 1 : to toast by dry heat 2 : to wilt with heat

parched \'pärcht\ *adj* : deprived of natural moisture ⟨*parched* hillsides⟩; *also* : THIRSTY ⟨*parched* hikers⟩

parch·ment \'pärch-mənt\ *n* 1 : the skin of a sheep or goat prepared as a writing material 2 : a paper like parchment 3 : something written on parchment

¹**par·don** \'pärd-ᵊn\ *n* : the excusing of an offense without a penalty — **par·don·able** \'pärd-nə-bəl, -ᵊn-ə-bəl\ *adj* — **par·don·ably** \-blē\ *adv*

²**pardon** *vb* **par·doned; par·don·ing** \'pärd-niŋ, -ᵊn-iŋ\ 1 : to free from penalty 2 : to forgive an offense

pare \'pa(ə)r, 'pe(ə)r\ *vb* **pared; par·ing** 1 : to cut or shave off the outside or the ends of ⟨*pare* an apple⟩ 2 : to reduce as if by paring ⟨*pare* expenses⟩

par·e·gor·ic \ˌpar-ə-'gȯr-ik, -'gōr-, -'gär-\ *n* : a liquid mixture of opium and camphor in alcohol used especially to relieve pain

pa·ren·chy·ma \pə-'reŋ-kə-mə\ *n* 1 : the tissue of an animal organ (as a gland) that performs the work of the organ as compared to tissue which only gives support or serves as a framework 2 : a tissue of higher plants consisting of thin-walled living cells that remain capable of cell division even when mature, are the location where photosynthesis takes place and materials and food are stored, and make up much of the substance of leaves and roots and the pulp of fruits as well as parts of stems and supporting structures

par·ent \'par-ənt, 'per-\ *n* 1 a : one that is a father or mother b : an animal or plant that produces offspring 2 : the original source of something — **parent** *adj* — **par·ent·hood** \-ˌhu̇d\ *n*

par·ent·age \'par-ənt-ij, 'per-\ *n* : descent from parents or ancestors : LINEAGE

pa·ren·tal \pə-'rent-ᵊl\ *adj* : of, typical of, or being parents

pa·ren·the·sis \pə-'ren(t)-thə-səs\ *n, pl* **-the·ses** \-thə-ˌsēz\ 1 : a word, phrase, or sentence inserted in a passage to explain or comment on it 2 : one of a pair of marks ( ) used to enclose a parenthesis or to group units in a mathematical expression — **par·en·thet·ic** \ˌpar-ən-'thet-ik\ *or* **par·en·thet·i·cal** \-'thet-i-kəl\ *adj* — **par·en·thet·i·cal·ly** \-i-k(ə-)lē\ *adv*

par·ent·ing \'par-ənt-iŋ, 'per-\ *n* : the raising of a child by its parents

par ex·cel·lence \ˌpär-ˌek-sə-'läns\ *adv or adj* : in the highest degree : above all others

par·fait \pär-'fā\ *n* 1 : a custard containing whipped cream and syrup frozen without stirring 2 : a dessert of layers of fruit, syrup, ice cream, and whipped cream

pa·ri·ah \pə-'rī-ə\ *n* : a person despised or rejected by society : OUTCAST

pa·ri·etal \pə-'rī-ət-ᵊl\ *adj* : of, relating to, or forming the upper back wall of the head

par·ing \'pa(ə)r-iŋ, 'pe(ə)r-\ *n* 1 : the act of cutting away an edge or surface 2 : something pared off

par·ish \'par-ish\ *n* 1 a : a section of a church district in the care of a priest or minister b : the persons who live in and attend the church of such a section 2 : the members of a church 3 : a division of the state of Louisiana that is similar to a county in other states

pa·rish·io·ner \pə-'rish-(ə-)nər\ *n* : a member or resident of a parish

par·i·ty \'par-ət-ē\ *n, pl* **-ties** : the quality or state of being equal or equivalent : EQUALITY

¹**park** \'pärk\ *n* 1 : an area around a country house used for recreation (as hunting or riding) 2 a : a piece of ground in or near a city or town kept as a place of beauty or recreation b : an area maintained in its natural state as a public property 3 : PARKING LOT 4 : an enclosed field for ball games

²**park** *vb* 1 : to leave a vehicle standing temporarily 2 : to set and leave temporarily ⟨*park* yourself in that chair⟩

par·ka \'pär-kə\ *n* : a very warm jacket with a hood

parking lot *n* : an outdoor area for parking motor vehicles

Par·kin·son's disease \'pär-kən-sənz-\ *n* : a disease chiefly of later life that tends to get steadily worse and is marked especially by stiff and trembling muscles, slowness of movement, and a shuffling way of walking

parka

park·way \'pär-ˌkwā\ *n* : a broad landscaped highway

par·lance \'pär-lən(t)s\ *n* : manner of speech

par·lay \'pär-ˌlā, -lē\ *vb* : to increase or change into something of much greater value ⟨*parlayed* a drawback into an asset⟩ [from *parlay* "to make a series of bets so that winnings from earlier bets are all wagered on later contests," from French *paroli* (noun) "a parlayed bet," from an Italian dialect word *paroli*, plural of *parolo* "a parlayed bet," perhaps from *para* "equal"]

par·ley \'pär-lē\ *vb* **par·leyed; par·ley·ing** : to speak with another : CONFER; *esp* : to discuss terms with an enemy [derived from early French *parler* "to speak" — related to PARLIAMENT, PARLOR; see *Word History* at PARLOR] — **parley** *n*

par·lia·ment \'pär-lə-mənt *also* 'pärl-yə-\ *n* : the supreme legislative body of various political units ⟨the British *parliament*⟩ [Middle English *parliament* "a council for discussing government business," from early French *parlement* (same meaning), from *parler* "to speak" — related to PARLEY, PARLOR; see *Word History* at PARLOR]

par·lia·men·tar·i·an \ˌpär-lə-ˌmen-'ter-ē-ən, -mən- *also* ˌpärl-yə-\ *n* : an expert in parliamentary procedure

par·lia·men·ta·ry \ˌpär-lə-'ment-ə-rē, -'men-trē *also* ˌpärl-yə-\ *adj* 1 : of, relating to, or enacted by a parliament 2 : of or relating to government by a cabinet whose members belong to and are responsible to the legislature 3 : of or according to the rules governing the way in which official meetings (as of a parliament or congress) are conducted ⟨*parliamentary* procedure⟩

par·lor \'pär-lər\ *n* **1** : a room in a home, hotel, or club used for conversation or the reception of guests **2** : any of various business places ⟨funeral *parlor*⟩ ⟨beauty *parlor*⟩

> **Word History** In some monasteries during the Middle Ages, monks were not allowed to speak except when they were in a special room. Such a room was known in early French as a *parlour*. The word *parlour* comes from the French verb *parler*, which means "to speak." In the 13th century, *parlour* was borrowed into English as *parlor*. Eventually it acquired the meaning that it has today. Other English words that can be traced to the verb *parler* include *parley* and *parliament*. [Middle English *parlour* "a room for receiving and talking with guests," from early French *parlour* (same meaning), from *parler* "to speak" — related to PARLEY, PARLIAMENT]

par·lous \'pär-ləs\ *adj* : DANGEROUS 1, RISKY — **par·lous·ly** *adv*

Par·me·san \'pär-mə-ˌzän, -ˌzhän, -zən, -ˌzan\ *n* : a very hard dry sharply flavored cheese that is sold grated or in wedges

pa·ro·chi·al \pə-'rō-kē-əl\ *adj* **1** : of or relating to a parish **2** : restricted or limited in range or scope : NARROW, PROVINCIAL ⟨a *parochial* point of view⟩ — **pa·ro·chi·al·ism** \-kē-ə-ˌliz-əm\ *n* — **pa·ro·chi·al·ly** \-kē-ə-lē\ *adv*

parochial school *n* : a school maintained by a religious body

par·o·dy \'par-əd-ē\ *n, pl* **-dies** **1** : a written or musical work in which the style of an author or work is imitated for comic effect **2** : a poor imitation — **par·o·dist** \-əd-əst\ *n* — **parody** *vb*

¹pa·role \pə-'rōl\ *n* : an early release of a prisoner who meets specified requirements

²parole *vb* **pa·roled; pa·rol·ing** : to release on parole — **pa·rol·ee** \pə-ˌrō-'lē\ *n*

pa·rot·id \pə-'rät-əd\ *adj* : of or relating to the parotid gland

parotid gland *n* : either of a pair of large salivary glands located below and in front of the ear

par·ox·ysm \'par-ək-ˌsiz-əm\ *n* **1** : a fit, attack, or sudden increase of symptoms (as of a disease) that occurs, quiets down, and occurs again and again ⟨a *paroxysm* of coughing⟩ **2** : a sudden violent emotion or action ⟨*paroxysms* of rage⟩

par·quet \'pär-ˌkā, pär-'kā\ *n* : a flooring of parquetry

par·que·try \'pär-kə-trē\ *n, pl* **-tries** : a patterned wood inlay used especially for floors

¹par·rot \'par-ət\ *n* **1** : any of numerous usually brightly colored tropical birds marked by a strong hooked bill, by toes arranged in pairs with two in front and two behind, and often by the ability to mimic speech **2** : a person who repeats the words of others without understanding what they mean

parquetry

²parrot *vb* : to repeat words like a parrot

parrot fever *n* : PSITTACOSIS

parrot fish *n* : any of various sea fishes that are related to the perches and have the teeth united into a cutting plate resembling a beak

par·ry \'par-ē\ *vb* **par·ried; par·ry·ing** **1** : to turn aside skillfully : DEFLECT ⟨*parry* a blow⟩ **2** : EVADE 1 ⟨*parry* an embarrassing question⟩ — **parry** *n*

parse \'pärs, 'pärz\ *vb* **parsed; pars·ing** **1** : to analyze a sentence by naming its parts and their relations to each other **2** : to give the part of speech of a word and explain its relation to others in a sentence

Par·si *also* **Par·see** \'pär-ˌsē\ *n* : a Zoroastrian descended from Persian refugees settled principally at Bombay

par·si·mo·ny \'pär-sə-ˌmō-nē\ *n* : the quality of being overly sparing with money : MISERLINESS — **par·si·mo·ni·ous** \ˌpär-sə-'mō-nē-əs\ *adj* — **par·si·mo·ni·ous·ly** *adv* — **par·si·mo·ni·ous·ness** *n*

pars·ley \'pär-slē\ *n, pl* **parsleys** : a European herb related to the carrot and widely grown for its finely divided leaves which are used to season or decorate foods; *also* : the leaves

pars·nip \'pär-snəp\ *n* : a Eurasian herb related to the carrot and grown for its long white root which is cooked as a vegetable; *also* : this root

parsnip

par·son \'pärs-ᵊn\ *n* **1** : a minister in charge of a parish **2** : a member of the clergy; *esp* : a Protestant pastor [Middle English *persone* "parson," from early French *persone* (same meaning), from Latin *persona*, literally, "person"; so called because the parson was the legal "person" representing the church]

par·son·age \'pär-snij, 'pärs-ᵊn-ij\ *n* : the house provided by a church for its pastor

¹part \'pärt\ *n* **1 a** : one of the pieces into which something can be divided **b** : one of the equal units of which something is composed ⟨a fifth *part* for each⟩ **c** : a portion of a plant or animal body : MEMBER, ORGAN ⟨wash the injured *part*⟩ **d** : a particular melody or line of music for one voice or instrument or a certain group of voices or instruments in harmony with others **e** : a piece of a machine or equipment **2** : a person's share, duty, or function ⟨did my *part*⟩ **3** : one of the sides in a conflict ⟨take another's *part* in a quarrel⟩ **4** : a general area : REGION — usually used in plural ⟨you're not from around these *parts*⟩ **5** : a role in a play **6** : the line where the hair is divided in combing — **for the most part** : in general ⟨*for the most part* the class was well behaved⟩ — **in part** : PARTLY ⟨the program was sponsored *in part* by public donations⟩ — **on the part of** : relating to the one specified ⟨an enthusiastic response *on the part of* students⟩

> **synonyms** PART, PORTION, SECTION, FRAGMENT mean something less than the whole. PART is a general word and can be used when it is not necessary to be exact ⟨they ran only *part* of the way⟩. PORTION suggests a part that is assigned or given as one's share ⟨divided the food into six *portions*⟩. SECTION applies to a part that is fairly small or is clearly seen as a unit ⟨the sports *section* of the newspaper⟩. FRAGMENT applies to a part made by or as if by breaking something ⟨while digging they found *fragments* of old pottery⟩ ⟨some ancient literature is now known only in *fragments*⟩.

²part *vb* **1** : to separate from or leave someone : go away : DEPART **2** : to become separated, detached, or broken ⟨the ice *parted*⟩ **3** : to give up possession or control ⟨wouldn't *part* with their old car⟩ **4 a** : to divide into parts **b** : to separate by combing on each side of a line **synonyms** see SEPARATE

³part *adv* : PARTLY ⟨was only *part* right⟩

par·take \pär-'tāk, pər-\ *vb* **par·took** \-'tůk\; **par·tak·en** \-'tā-kən\; **par·tak·ing** **1 a** : to take a share or part ⟨*partake* of a meal⟩ **b** : to take part in something ⟨all may *partake* in the ceremony⟩ **2** : to have some of the qualities of something ⟨the story *partook* of the nature of drama⟩ — **par·tak·er** *n*

\ə\ **abut**	\aů\ **out**	\i\ **tip**	\ȯ\ **saw**	\ů\ **foot**
\ər\ **further**	\ch\ **chin**	\ī\ **life**	\ȯi\ **coin**	\y\ **yet**
\a\ **mat**	\e\ **pet**	\j\ **job**	\th\ **thin**	\yů\ **few**
\ā\ **take**	\ē\ **easy**	\ŋ\ **sing**	\th\ **this**	\yü\ **cure**
\ä\ **cot, cart**	\g\ **go**	\ō\ **bone**	\ü\ **food**	\zh\ **vision**

synonyms PARTAKE, PARTICIPATE, SHARE mean to take part together. PARTAKE applies especially to the common enjoyment of food and drink ⟨shall we *partake* of the feast prepared for us?⟩. PARTICIPATE suggests an undertaking or activity in which persons work or act as a group ⟨the whole class *participated* in singing the songs⟩. SHARE can apply either to situations in which one person allows another the use or enjoyment of some possession ⟨she was nice enough to *share* her lunch with me⟩ or to situations involving the use of something by two or more people ⟨my brother and I *share* a bedroom⟩.

par·the·no·gen·e·sis \ˌpär-thə-nō-ʹje-nə-səs\ *n* : reproduction especially among lower plants and invertebrates in which a germ cell that has not undergone fertilization develops into a new individual

par·tial \ʹpär-shəl\ *adj* 1 : inclined to favor one side over another : BIASED 2 : fond of someone or something ⟨*partial* to pizza⟩ 3 : relating to or being a part rather than the whole : not total or complete ⟨a *partial* eclipse⟩ ⟨a *partial* rhyme⟩ — **par·tial·ly** \ʹpärsh-(ə-)lē\ *adv*

par·tial·i·ty \ˌpär-shē-ʹal-ət-ē, pär-ʹshal-\ *n, pl* **-ties** 1 : the quality or state of being partial 2 : a special taste or liking

partial product *n* : a product of the multiplicand and one digit of a two or more digit multiplier

par·tic·i·pant \pər-ʹtis-ə-pənt, pär-\ *n* : one that participates

par·tic·i·pate \pər-ʹtis-ə-ˌpāt, pär-\ *vb* **-pat·ed; -pat·ing** : to take part or have a share in something in common with others ⟨*participate* in sports⟩ synonyms see PARTAKE — **par·tic·i·pa·tion** \-ˌtis-ə-ʹpā-shən\ *n* — **par·tic·i·pa·tor** \-ʹtis-ə-ˌpāt-ər\ *n*

par·ti·cip·i·al \ˌpärt-ə-ʹsip-ē-əl\ *adj* : of, relating to, or formed with a participle ⟨*participial* phrase⟩ — **par·ti·cip·i·al·ly** \-ē-ə-le\ *adv*

par·ti·ci·ple \ʹpärt-ə-ˌsip-əl\ *n* : a word that functions like an adjective and also shows such features of a verb as tense and voice and the ability to take an object

par·ti·cle \ʹpärt-i-kəl\ *n* 1 : one of the very small parts of matter (as a molecule, atom, or electron) 2 : a very small quantity or piece 3 : the smallest possible portion

par·ti·cle·board \-ˌbō(ə)rd, -ˌbȯ(ə)rd\ *n* : a board made of very small pieces of wood stuck together

¹**par·tic·u·lar** \pə(r)-ʹtik-(y)ə-lər, -ʹtik-lər\ *adj* 1 : of or relating to the separate parts of a whole ⟨each *particular* item on the list⟩ 2 : of or relating to a single person or thing ⟨my *particular* skills⟩ 3 : very unusual : SPECIAL ⟨a storm of *particular* violence⟩ 4 : hard to please : FASTIDIOUS ⟨*particular* about their clothes⟩

²**particular** *n* : an individual fact, detail, or item — **in particular** : PARTICULARLY 2

par·tic·u·lar·i·ty \pə(r)-ˌtik-yə-ʹlar-ət-ē\ *n, pl* **-ties** 1 : a very small detail 2 : careful attention to detail : EXACTNESS, CARE

par·tic·u·lar·ize \pə(r)-ʹtik-(yə-)lə-ˌrīz\ *vb* **-ized; -iz·ing** : to state in detail : SPECIFY — **par·tic·u·lar·i·za·tion** \-ˌtik-(yə-)lə-rə-ʹzā-shən\ *n*

par·tic·u·lar·ly \pə(r)-ʹtik-yə-(lər-)lē, -yə-lə-lē; pə(r)-ʹtik-(ə-)lē\ *adv* 1 : in a particular manner 2 : to an unusual degree : ESPECIALLY

par·tic·u·late \pər-ʹtik-yə-lət, pär-, -ˌlāt\ *n* : a substance made up of very small separate particles

¹**part·ing** \ʹpärt-iŋ\ *n* 1 : SEPARATION 1, DIVISION 2 : a place where a division or separation occurs ⟨a *parting* of the ways⟩ 3 : LEAVE-TAKING ⟨shake hands at *parting*⟩

²**parting** *adj* 1 : being in the process of departing 2 : serving to divide : SEPARATING 3 : given, taken, or performed at parting ⟨a *parting* kiss⟩

par·ti·san \ʹpärt-ə-zən\ *n* 1 : a person who is strongly devoted to a particular cause or group 2 : GUERRILLA — **partisan** *adj* — **par·ti·san·ship** \-ˌship\ *n*

par·ti·tion \pər-ʹtish-ən, pär-\ *n* 1 : DIVISION 1a, SEPARATION 2 : an interior dividing wall 3 : ¹PART 1a, SECTION — **partition** *vb* — **par·ti·tion·er** \-ʹtish-(ə-)nər\ *n*

part·ly \ʹpärt-lē\ *adv* : in some measure or degree : not completely ⟨a statement that is only *partly* true⟩

part·ner \ʹpärt-nər\ *n* 1 : one associated in action with another : COLLEAGUE 2 : either of a couple who dance together 3 : one of two or more persons who play together in a game against an opposing side 4 : a person with whom one shares an intimate relationship : one member of a couple 5 : a member of a partnership

part·ner·ship \ʹpärt-nər-ˌship\ *n* 1 : the state of being a partner 2 : a business organization owned by two or more persons who agree to share the profits and losses

part of speech : a class of words (as adjectives, adverbs, conjunctions, interjections, nouns, prepositions, pronouns, or verbs) identified according to the kinds of ideas they express and the way they work in a sentence

partook *past of* PARTAKE

par·tridge \ʹpär-trij\ *n, pl* **partridge** *or* **par·tridg·es** : any of several plump Old World birds related to the common chicken and often hunted as game; *also* : any of various North American birds (as a bobwhite or ruffed grouse) that are related to and resemble partridges of the Old World

partridge

par·tridge·ber·ry \-ˌber-ē\ *n* : an evergreen plant of the eastern U.S. and Canada that grows along the ground and produces somewhat tart scarlet berries; *also* : its berry

part–song \ʹpärt-ˌsȯn\ *n* : a song consisting of two or more voice parts

part–time \ʹpärt-ˌtīm\ *adj or adv* : involving or working less than a full or regular schedule

par·tu·ri·tion \ˌpärt-ə-ʹrish-ən, ˌpär-chə-\ *n* : CHILDBIRTH

part·way \ʹpärt-ˌwā\ *adv* : to a part of a distance ⟨followed us *partway* home⟩

¹**par·ty** \ʹpärt-ē\ *n, pl* **parties** 1 : one side in a dispute or contest ⟨the *parties* to a lawsuit⟩ 2 : a group of persons organized to influence or direct the policies of a government 3 : a person or group that takes part with others in an action or affair ⟨a mountain-climbing *party*⟩ 4 : a particular individual : PERSON ⟨get the right *party* on the telephone⟩ 5 : a detail of soldiers 6 : a social gathering; *also* : entertainment for such a gathering — **party** *adj*

²**party** *vb* **par·tied; par·ty·ing** : to give or attend parties

party poop·er \-ʹpü-pər\ *n* : one who spoils the pleasure of others especially at a party : KILLJOY

pas·cal \pas-ʹkal\ *n* 1 : a unit of pressure in the metric system equal to one newton per square meter 2 *usu cap* P *or all cap* : a computer programming language developed from ALGOL [named for Blaise *Pascal* 1623–1662 French mathematician]

Pas·cal's triangle \pas-ʹkalz-\ *n* : a set of numbers which are arranged in rows in the shape of a triangle with the top row containing only 1, the next row 1 1, the following row 1 2 1, and in general the nth row containing the coefficients in the expansion of $(a + b)^n$ as n equals 0, 1, 2, 3, etc.

pas·chal \ʹpas-kəl\ *adj* : of or relating to Passover or Easter [from earlier *Pasch* "Passover, Easter," derived from Greek *pascha* "Passover," from Hebrew *pesaḥ* "Passover"]

pa·sha \ʹpäsh-ə, ʹpash-ə, pə-ʹshä\ *n* : an official (as in Turkey or northern Africa) of high rank

¹**pass** \ʹpas\ *vb* 1 : ¹MOVE 2, PROCEED 2 a : to go away ⟨the pain will soon *pass*⟩ b : ¹DIE 1 — often used with *on* 3 : to go by or beyond or move past 4 : to go or allow to

go across, over, or through ⟨let no one *pass*⟩ **5 :** to change or transfer ownership or possession ⟨recipes *passed* down through the family⟩ **6 :** HAPPEN 2, OCCUR **7 a :** to gain the approval of a legislative body ⟨the bill *passed* both houses⟩ **b :** to approve officially ⟨*pass* a new law⟩ **8 :** to go or allow to go through an examination or course of study successfully ⟨*passed* my French course⟩ **9 :** to cause to be considered ⟨*passed* for an expert⟩ **10 :** to transfer or become transferred from one person to another ⟨*pass* the butter⟩ ⟨*pass* a football⟩ **11 :** to decide not to bid, bet, or draw in a card game **12 :** to cause or permit to elapse : SPEND ⟨*pass* time⟩ **13 :** to state judicially ⟨*pass* sentence⟩ — **pass·er** *n* — **pass muster :** to gain approval or acceptance — **pass the buck :** to shift a responsibility to someone else — **pass the hat :** to take up a collection of money

²**pass** *n* **1 :** PASSAGE 2a, WAY **2 :** a gap in a mountain range

³**pass** *n* **1 :** the act or an instance of passing : PASSAGE **2 :** ACCOMPLISHMENT 1, REALIZATION — used in the phrases *come to pass* and *bring to pass* **3 :** SITUATION 3, CONDITION ⟨have come to a strange *pass*⟩ **4 :** a written permission to enter or leave or to move about freely ⟨a soldier's three-day *pass*⟩ **5 :** a moving of the hands over or along something **6 :** a transfer of a ball or puck from one player to another; *esp* : FORWARD PASS **7 :** BASE ON BALLS **8 :** an act of passing in a card game **9 :** EFFORT 2, TRY ⟨make a *pass* at it⟩

pass·able \ˈpas-ə-bəl\ *adj* **1 :** capable of being passed, crossed, or traveled on ⟨*passable* roads⟩ **2 :** barely good enough : TOLERABLE ⟨a *passable* imitation⟩ — **pass·ably** \-blē\ *adv*

pas·sage \ˈpas-ij\ *n* **1 :** the action or process of passing from one place or condition to another **2 a :** a road, path, channel, or course by which something can pass **b :** CORRIDOR 1 **3 a :** ¹VOYAGE, JOURNEY **b :** a right to travel as a passenger ⟨book *passage* on an airplane⟩ **4 :** the passing of a law **5 :** a usually brief portion of a written work or speech or of a musical composition

pas·sage·way \-ˌwā\ *n* **:** a road or way by which a person or thing may pass

pass away *vb* **:** ¹DIE 1

pass·book \ˈpas-ˌbuk\ *n* **:** BANKBOOK

pas·sé \pa-ˈsā\ *adj* **:** OUTMODED, OUT-OF-DATE [French, literally, "past, gone by"]

pas·sel \ˈpas-əl\ *n* **:** a large number : GROUP

pas·sen·ger \ˈpas-ⁿn-jər\ *n* **:** a person riding in or on a vehicle

passenger pigeon *n* **:** an extinct but formerly very common North American pigeon that migrated long distances

pass·er·by \ˌpas-ər-ˈbī\ *n, pl* **pass·ers·by** \ˌpas-ərz-\ **:** one who passes by

¹**pass·ing** \ˈpas-iŋ\ *n* **1 :** the act of one that passes or causes to pass **2 :** DEATH 1 — **in passing :** by the way : INCIDENTALLY

²**passing** *adj* **1 :** going by or past ⟨the *passing* crowd⟩ **2 :** lasting only for a short time; *esp* : showing haste or lack of attention : HASTY, SUPERFICIAL ⟨a *passing* glance⟩ **3 :** used for the act or process of passing ⟨the *passing* lane⟩ **4 :** given on satisfactory completion of an examination or course of study ⟨a *passing* grade⟩

pas·sion \ˈpash-ən\ *n* *often cap* **1 :** the sufferings of Jesus between the night of the Last Supper and his death **2 a** *pl* **:** the emotions in general **b :** strong feeling or emotion **3 a :** great affection : LOVE **b :** a strong liking **c :** an object of desire or deep interest

pas·sion·ate \ˈpash-(ə-)nət\ *adj* **1 :** excited or easily excited to strong feeling **2 :** showing or expressing strong feeling **3 :** strongly affected with sexual desire — **pas·sion·ate·ly** *adv*

passion play *n, often cap 1st P* **:** a play representing scenes connected with Jesus' suffering and crucifixion

Passion Sunday *n* **:** the 5th Sunday in Lent

Pas·sion·tide \ˈpash-ən-ˌtīd\ *n* **:** the last two weeks of Lent

Passion Week *n* **1 :** HOLY WEEK **2 :** the 2nd week before Easter

¹**pas·sive** \ˈpas-iv\ *adj* **1 a :** not active but acted upon ⟨*passive* spectators⟩ **b :** indicating that the person or thing represented by the subject is acted on by the verb ⟨"was hit" in "he was hit by the ball" is *passive*⟩ **2 a :** not operating **b :** of, relating to, or making use of the sun's heat usually without the aid of mechanical devices **3 :** offering no resistance — **pas·sive·ly** *adv* — **pas·sive·ness** *n* — **pas·siv·i·ty** \pa-ˈsiv-ət-ē\ *n*

²**passive** *n* **1 :** a passive verb form **2 :** the passive voice

passive immunity *n* **:** temporary immunity acquired by transfer (as by injection) of antibodies especially from an individual with active immunity

passive resistance *n* **:** resistance especially to a government or an occupying power characterized mainly by noncooperation

pass·key \ˈpas-ˌkē\ *n* **1 :** a key for opening two or more locks **2 :** SKELETON KEY

pass off *vb* **:** to give a false identity to : describe untruthfully

pass out *vb* **:** to lose consciousness

Pass·over \ˈpas-ˌō-vər\ *n* **:** a Jewish holiday celebrated in March or April in honor of the freeing of the Hebrews from slavery in Egypt [so called because in Exodus 12:23–27 the Lord passes over the homes of the Israelites in killing the firstborn in Egypt]

pass over \(ˈ)pas-ˈō-vər\ *vb* **1 :** to ignore in passing **2 :** to pay no attention to

pass·port \ˈpas-ˌpō(ə)rt, -ˌpȯ(ə)rt\ *n* **1 :** a government-issued document that serves to identify a citizen and allows him or her to travel to foreign countries **2 :** something that allows a person to reach a desired goal ⟨education can be a *passport* to a successful future⟩

pass·word \-ˌwərd\ *n* **1 :** a word or phrase that must be spoken by a person in order to pass a guard **2 :** a secret series of numbers or letters required for access to a computer

¹**past** \ˈpast\ *adj* **1 a :** AGO ⟨10 years *past*⟩ **b :** just gone by ⟨for the *past* few months⟩ **2 :** having existed or taken place in a period before the present ⟨*past* customs⟩ **3 :** of, relating to, or being a verb tense that in English is usually formed by internal vowel change (as in *sang*) or by the addition of a suffix (as in *laughed*) and that expresses time gone by **4 :** no longer serving ⟨a *past* president⟩

²**past** *prep* **1 :** ²BEYOND 1 ⟨*past* 50 years old⟩ ⟨half *past* ten⟩ **2 :** in a course by and then beyond ⟨the road goes *past* the house⟩

³**past** *n* **1 :** a former time or event **2 a :** PAST TENSE **b :** a verb form in the past tense **3 :** a past life or history; *esp* : a past life that is secret or questionable

⁴**past** *adv* **:** so as to pass by ⟨a deer ran *past*⟩

pas·ta \ˈpäs-tə\ *n* **1 :** a dough of flour, eggs, and water made in different shapes and dried (as spaghetti or macaroni) or used fresh (as ravioli) **2 :** a dish of cooked pasta

¹**paste** \ˈpāst\ *n* **1 a :** a dough rich in fat used for pastry **b :** a candy made by evaporating fruit with sugar or by flavoring a gelatin, starch, or gum arabic preparation **c :** a smooth food product made by evaporation or grinding ⟨almond *paste*⟩ **2 :** a preparation of flour or starch and water used for sticking things together **3 :** a soft plastic substance or mixture **4 :** a very brilliant glass used for artificial gems [Middle English *paste* "pastry dough,"

\ə\ **abut**	\aù\ **out**	\i\ **tip**	\ò\ **saw**	\ù\ **foot**
\ər\ **further**	\ch\ **chin**	\ī\ **life**	\òi\ **coin**	\y\ **yet**
\a\ **mat**	\e\ **pet**	\j\ **job**	\th\ **thin**	\yü\ **few**
\ā\ **take**	\ē\ **easy**	\ŋ\ **sing**	\th\ **this**	\yù\ **cure**
\ä\ **cot, cart**	\g\ **go**	\ō\ **bone**	\ü\ **food**	\zh\ **vision**

from early French *paste* (same meaning), from Latin *pasta* "paste, dough"]

²**paste** *vb* **past·ed; past·ing** **1** : to stick on or together by paste **2** : to cover with something pasted on **3** : to put (something cut or copied from a computer document) into another part of the document or into another document

³**paste** *vb* **past·ed; past·ing** : to hit hard [an altered form of earlier *baste* "to hit, beat"]

paste·board \'pās(t)-ˌbō̇(ə)rd, -ˌbȯ(ə)rd\ *n* : CARDBOARD

¹**pas·tel** \pas-'tel\ *n* **1 a** : a paste made of ground color and used for making crayons **b** : a crayon of such paste **2** : a drawing in pastel **3** : any of various pale or light colors

²**pastel** *adj* **1** : of, relating to, or made with pastels **2** : pale and light in color

pas·tern \'pas-ˌtərn\ *n* : the part of the foot of a horse between the fetlock and the top of the hoof; *also* : the corresponding part of some other four-footed animals

pas·teur·i·za·tion \ˌpas-chə-rə-'zā-shən, ˌpas-tə-\ *n* : the process of heating a liquid (as milk) to a temperature high enough and keeping it at that temperature long enough to kill many objectionable germs and then cooling it rapidly without causing a major change in its chemical composition

pas·teur·ize \'pas-chə-ˌrīz, 'pas-tə-\ *vb* **-ized; -iz·ing** : to expose to pasteurization [named for Louis *Pasteur* 1822–1895 French chemist] — **pas·teur·iz·er** *n*

pas·time \'pas-ˌtīm\ *n* : something that helps to make time pass agreeably

past master *n* **1** : one who has held the office of master (as in a club or lodge) **2** : one who is expert

pas·tor \'pas-tər\ *n* : a minister or priest in charge of a church or parish — **pas·tor·ship** \-ˌship\ *n*

¹**pas·to·ral** \'pas-t(ə-)rəl\ *adj* **1 a** : of or relating to shepherds or rural life **b** : devoted to or based on livestock raising **2** : of or relating to the pastor of a church

²**pas·to·ral** \'pas-t(ə-)rəl, *sense 3 is often* ˌpas-tə-'räl, -'ral\ *n* **1** : a literary work dealing with shepherds or rural life **2** : a rural picture or scene **3** : PASTORALE

pas·to·rale \ˌpas-tə-'räl, -'ral\ *n* : a piece of music for instruments or voices that suggests rural scenes

pas·tor·ate \'pas-t(ə-)rət\ *n* **1** : the office, duties, or term of service of a pastor **2** : a body of pastors

past participle *n* : a participle that expresses completed action and that is one of the principal parts of the verb ⟨"raised" in "Many hands were raised" and "thrown" in "The ball has been thrown" are *past participles*⟩

past perfect tense *n* : a verb tense formed in English with *had* and expressing an action or state completed at or before a past time spoken of

pas·tra·mi \pə-'sträm-ē\ *n* : a highly seasoned smoked beef

past·ry \'pā-strē\ *n, pl* **pastries** **1** : sweet baked goods (as cakes or tarts) made of dough or having a crust made of enriched dough **2** : a piece of pastry

past tense *n* : a verb tense expressing action or state in the past

pas·tur·age \'pas-chə-rij\ *n* : ¹PASTURE

¹**pas·ture** \'pas-chər\ *n* **1** : plants (as grass) for feeding especially grazing animals **2** : land or a plot of land used for grazing

²**pasture** *vb* **pas·tured; pas·tur·ing** **1** : ¹GRAZE 1 **2** : to feed (as cattle) on pasture

pas·ture·land \'pas-chər-ˌland\ *n* : ¹PASTURE 2

¹**pas·ty** \'pas-tē\ *n, pl* **pas·ties** : ¹PIE; *esp* : a meat pie

²**pasty** \'pā-stē\ *adj* **past·i·er; -est** : resembling paste; *esp* : pale and unhealthy in appearance — **past·i·ness** *n*

P pastern

PA system \pē-'ā-\ *n* : PUBLIC-ADDRESS SYSTEM

¹**pat** \'pat\ *n* **1** : a light blow especially with the hand or a flat instrument **2** : a light tapping sound **3** : something (as butter) shaped into a small flat portion

²**pat** *vb* **pat·ted; pat·ting** **1** : to strike lightly with the hand or a flat instrument : strike or beat gently **2** : to flatten, smooth, or shape with pats **3** : to tap or stroke gently with the hand to soothe or to show affection or approval

³**pat** *adj* **pat·ter; pat·test** **1** : exactly suited : APT, TIMELY ⟨a *pat* answer⟩ **2** : learned exactly ⟨have a lesson down *pat*⟩ **3** : ¹FIRM 2b, UNYIELDING ⟨stand *pat*⟩

¹**patch** \'pach\ *n* **1** : a piece of material used to mend or cover a hole, a torn place, or a weak spot **2** : a shield (as of cloth) worn over an injured eye **3** : a small piece : SCRAP **4 a** : a small area or plot different from its surroundings ⟨a *patch* of oats⟩ ⟨a *patch* of blistered skin⟩ **b** : a spot of color : BLOTCH **5** : a piece of cloth worn (as on the shoulder of a uniform) as an ornament or insignia

²**patch** *vb* **1** : to mend, cover, or fill up a hole or weak spot in **2** : to provide with a patch **3 a** : to make out of patches **b** : to mend or put together especially hastily or clumsily **c** : to deal with successfully : SETTLE — usually used with *up* ⟨*patched* up their differences⟩ **synonyms** see MEND

patch pocket *n* : a pocket that is sewn on the outside of a garment

patch test *n* : a test for finding out if a person is sensitive to an allergy-producing substance that is made by putting small pads soaked with the substance to be tested on the unbroken skin

patch·work \'pach-ˌwərk\ *n* **1** : something made up of various parts **2** : pieces of cloth of various colors and shapes sewn together usually in a pattern — **patch·work** *adj*

patchy \'pach-ē\ *adj* **patch·i·er; -est** : consisting of or marked by patches : resembling patchwork

pate \'pāt\ *n* : ¹HEAD 1; *esp* : the top of the head — **pat·ed** \'pāt-əd\ *adj*

patchwork 2

pa·tel·la \pə-'tel-ə\ *n, pl* **pa·tel·lae** \-'tel-ē, -ˌī\ *or* **-tellas** : KNEECAP

pat·en \'pat-°n\ *n* **1** : a plate of precious metal for the eucharistic bread **2** : a metal plate **3** : a thin disk (as of metal)

¹**pat·ent** *sense 1 is* 'pat-°nt, *sense 2 is* 'pāt-, 'pat-\ *adj* **1 a** : protected by a patent **b** : of, relating to, or concerned with patents ⟨a *patent* lawyer⟩ **c** : ²PROPRIETARY 2 ⟨a *patent* can opener⟩ **2** : ²PLAIN 4a, OBVIOUS ⟨a *patent* lie⟩ — **pat·ent·ly** *adv*

²**pat·ent** \'pat-°nt\ *n* **1** : an official document granting a right or privilege; *esp* : a writing granting to an inventor for a term of years the only right to make, use, or sell his or her invention **2** : the right granted by a patent

³**pat·ent** \'pat-°nt\ *vb* : to protect by patent — **pat·ent·able** \'pat-°n-tə-bəl\

pat·en·tee \ˌpat-°n-'tē\ *n* : one to whom a patent is granted

pat·ent leather \ˌpat-°n(t)-\ *n* : a leather with a hard smooth glossy surface

patent medicine *n* : a medicine (as cough syrup) available for sale to the public without a doctor's prescription, that is protected by a trademark, has contents which may not be fully disclosed, and especially in the past was often of unproven effectiveness

pa·ter·nal \pə-'tərn-°l\ *adj* **1** : FATHERLY ⟨*paternal* advice⟩ **2** : received or inherited from one's father **3** : related through the father ⟨a *paternal* grandfather⟩ [from Latin *paternalis* "fatherly," from earlier *paternus* (same meaning), from *pater* "father" — related to PADRE, PA-TRON, PATTERN] — **pa·ter·nal·ly** \-ᵊl-ē\ *adv*

pa·ter·ni·ty \pə-'tər-nət-ē\ *n* **1** : the state of being a father **2** : origin from a father

path \'path, 'pȧth\ *n, pl* **paths** \'pathz, 'paths, 'pȧthz, 'pȧths\ **1 a** : a track made by foot travel **b** : a track constructed for a particular use (as horseback riding) **2 a** : the way along which something moves : COURSE **b** : a way of life, conduct, or thought — **path·less** \-ləs\ *adj*

pa·thet·ic \pə-'thet-ik\ *adj* : causing one to feel tenderness, pity, or sorrow — **pa·thet·i·cal·ly** \-i-k(ə-)lē\ *adv*

path·find·er \'path-,fīn-dər, 'pȧth-\ *n* : one that discovers a way and especially a new route in unexplored regions

patho·gen \'path-ə-jən\ *n* : a germ (as a bacterium or virus) that causes disease

patho·gen·ic \,path-ə-'jen-ik\ *adj* : causing or capable of causing disease

patho·log·i·cal \,path-ə-'läj-i-kəl\ *also* **patho·log·ic** \-ik\ *adj* **1** : of or relating to pathology **2** : changed or caused by disease **3** : being such to a degree that is extreme, excessive, or abnormal ⟨a *pathological* liar⟩ — **patho·log·i·cal·ly** \-i-k(ə-)lē\ *adv*

pa·thol·o·gist \pə-'thäl-ə-jəst, pa-\ *n* : a specialist in pathology

pa·thol·o·gy \pə-'thäl-ə-jē\ *n, pl* **-gies** **1** : the study of diseases and especially of the changes in the body produced by them **2** : something abnormal; *esp* : the disorders in structure and function that occur in a particular disease

pa·thos \'pā-,thäs, -,thȯs\ *n* : an element in life or in artistic representation of it that moves one to pity

path·way \'path-,wā, 'pȧth-\ *n* : PATH

pa·tience \'pā-shən(t)s\ *n* : the quality or state of being patient

¹pa·tient \'pā-shənt\ *adj* **1** : putting up with pains or hardships calmly or without complaint **2** : showing calm self-control **3** : not hasty or reckless **4** : STEADFAST 2, PERSEVERING ⟨years of *patient* labor⟩ — **pa·tient·ly** *adv*

²patient *n* : an individual awaiting or under medical care and treatment

pa·tio \'pat-ē-,ō *also* 'pät-\ *n, pl* **pa·ti·os** **1** : COURTYARD; *esp* : an inner court open to the sky **2** : an often paved recreation area next to a dwelling

pa·tois \'pa-,twä, 'pä-\ *n, pl* **patois** \-,twäz\ : DIALECT

pa·tri·arch \'pā-trē-,ärk\ *n* **1 a** : one of the Old Testament fathers of the human race or of the Hebrew people **b** : the father and ruler of a family or tribe **c** : an old man deserving respect **2** : any of various bishops of highest rank and dignity — **pa·tri·ar·chal** \,pā-trē-'är-kəl\ *adj*

pa·tri·ar·chy \'pā-trē-,är-kē\ *n, pl* **-chies** **1** : social organization in which the father is head of the family and ancestry and inheritance are traced in the male line **2** : a society organized according to the principles of patriarchy

pa·tri·cian \pə-'trish-ən\ *n* **1** : a member of one of the original citizen families of ancient Rome **2** : a person of high birth or position : ARISTOCRAT — **patrician** *adj*

pat·ri·mo·ny \'pa-trə-,mō-nē\ *n, pl* **-nies** **1** : an estate inherited from one's father or ancestors **2** : something passed down from one's father or ancestors : HERITAGE — **pat·ri·mo·ni·al** \,pa-trə-'mō-nē-əl\ *adj*

pa·tri·ot \'pā-trē-ət, -trē-,ät\ *n* : a person who loves his or her country and supports its authority and interests

pa·tri·ot·ic \,pā-trē-'ät-ik\ *adj* **1** : having or showing patriotism — **pa·tri·ot·i·cal·ly** \-i-k(ə-)lē\ *adv* **2** : suitable or proper for a patriot

pa·tri·ot·ism \'pā-trē-ə-,tiz-əm\ *n* : love of one's own country

¹pa·trol \pə-'trōl\ *n* **1 a** : the action of going the rounds of an area for observation or guard **b** : the person or group doing the patrolling **2** : a part of a Boy Scout or Girl Scout troop

²patrol *vb* **pa·trolled; pa·trol·ling** : to carry out a patrol or a patrol of — **pa·trol·ler** *n*

pa·trol·man \pə-'trōl-mən\ *n* : a police officer who has a regular beat

patrol wagon *n* : an enclosed police truck used to carry prisoners

pa·tron \'pā-trən\ *n* **1** : a person chosen as a special guardian or supporter ⟨a *patron* of poets⟩ **2** : one who gives generous support or approval ⟨a *patron* of the arts⟩ **3** : a person who buys the goods or uses the services offered (as by a business) [Middle English *patroun* "a special guardian or protector," from early French *patrun, patron* (same meaning), from Latin *patronus* "patron, patron saint," from earlier *patronus* "defender," from *patr-, pater* "father" — related to PADRE, PATERNAL, PATTERN]

pa·tron·age \'pa-trə-nij, 'pā-\ *n* **1** : the support or influence of a patron **2** : business or activity provided by patrons **3** : the power to give out government jobs, contracts, or favors

pa·tron·ess \'pā-trə-nəs\ *n* : a woman who is a patron: as **a** : a woman chosen as a special guardian or supporter **b** : a woman who gives generous support or approval

pa·tron·ize \'pā-trə-,nīz, 'pa-\ *vb* **-ized; -iz·ing** **1** : to act as a patron to or of : give aid or support to ⟨*patronize* the arts⟩ **2** : to act as if one were better than **3** : to be a patron of ⟨*patronize* a store⟩ ⟨*patronize* the library⟩ — **pa·tron·iz·ing·ly** \-,nī-ziŋ-lē\ *adv*

patron saint *n* : a saint to whom a person, society, church, or place is dedicated

pa·troon \pə-'trün\ *n* : a landowner of a large estate in New York or New Jersey granted by the Dutch

patted *past and past participle of* ²PAT

¹pat·ter \'pat-ər\ *vb* : to talk quickly and smoothly or mechanically [Middle English *patren* "to patter, chant prayers mechanically," from *paternoster* "Lord's Prayer, Our Father," derived from Latin *pater noster* "our father" (first words of the prayer)]

²patter *n* **1** : JARGON 2, CANT **2** : fast talk used especially to attract attention or to entertain

³patter *vb* **1** : to strike or pat rapidly and repeatedly ⟨rain *pattering* on a roof⟩ **2** : to run with quick light-sounding steps [from *pat* "to tap or strike"]

⁴patter *n* : a series of quick light sounds ⟨the *patter* of little feet⟩

¹pat·tern \'pat-ərn\ *n* **1** : something worth imitating or using as a guide **2** : a model or guide for making something ⟨a dress *pattern*⟩ **3** : an artistic form, figure, or design ⟨chintz with a small *pattern*⟩ **4** : a set of characteristics that are displayed repeatedly ⟨behavior *patterns*⟩ [Middle English *patron* "pattern," from early French *patron* (same meaning), from Latin *patronus* "patron, patron saint," from earlier *patronus* "defender, protector," from *patr-, pater* "father" — related to PADRE, PATERNAL, PATRON] — **patterned** \-ərnd\ *adj*

synonyms PATTERN, EXAMPLE, MODEL, IDEAL mean someone or something that one should follow or imitate. PATTERN suggests a carefully worked out design that should be followed closely ⟨other countries have used our laws as a *pattern*⟩. EXAMPLE applies to something that should be followed or sometimes to something certainly not to be followed ⟨set a good *example* for others⟩ ⟨they were punished for bad behavior and let that be an *example* for you⟩. MODEL suggests that the person or thing imitated is very worthy of imitation ⟨a leader who can be a *model* for all children⟩. IDEAL suggests some-

\ə\ abut	\aů\ out	\i\ tip	\ȯ\ saw	\ů\ foot
\ər\ further	\ch\ chin	\ī\ life	\ȯi\ coin	\y\ yet
\a\ mat	\e\ pet	\j\ job	\th\ thin	\yü\ few
\ā\ take	\ē\ easy	\ŋ\ sing	\th\ this	\yů\ cure
\ä\ cot, cart	\g\ go	\ō\ bone	\ü\ food	\zh\ vision

thing real or imagined that is thought to be the best of its kind that can exist ⟨the *ideal* of beauty⟩.

²**pattern** *vb* : to make or design by following a pattern

patting *present participle of* ²PAT

pat·ty *also* **pat·tie** \'pat-ē\ *n, pl* **patties** **1** : a little pie **2** : a small flat cake of chopped food **b** : a small flat candy

pau·ci·ty \'pȯ-sət-ē\ *n* : smallness of number or quantity : SCARCITY ⟨a *paucity* of experience⟩

paunch \'pȯnch, 'pänch\ *n* **1** : the belly together with its contents **2** : POTBELLY 1

paunchy \'pȯn-chē, 'pän-\ *adj* **paunch·i·er; -est** : having a potbelly — **paunch·i·ness** *n*

pau·per \'pȯ-pər\ *n* : a very poor person; *esp* : one supported by charity — **pau·per·ism** \-pə-ˌriz-əm\ *n* — **pau·per·ize** \-ˌrīz\ *vb*

¹**pause** \'pȯz\ *n* **1** : a temporary stop or rest **2** : the sign ⌢ placed over or under a musical note, chord, or rest to show that it is to be held longer than usual **3** : a reason for pausing ⟨a thought that should give *pause*⟩ [Middle English *pause* "a temporary stop, pause," from Latin *pausa* "a pause" — related to ¹REPOSE]

²**pause** *vb* **paused; paus·ing** **1** : to stop temporarily **2** : to linger for a time ⟨*pause* on a high note⟩

pave \'pāv\ *vb* **paved; pav·ing** : to lay or cover with material (as stone or concrete) that forms a firm level surface for travel — **pave the way** : to prepare a smooth easy way

pave·ment \'pāv-mənt\ *n* **1** : a paved surface (as of a street) **2** : the material with which something is paved

pa·vil·ion \pə-'vil-yən\ *n* **1** : a usually large tent with a peaked or rounded top **2** : a lightly constructed building serving as a shelter in a park, garden, or athletic field **3** : a part of a building that extends from the main part **4** : a building partly or completely detached from the main building or group of buildings

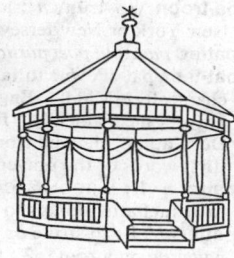
pavilion 2

Word History The Latin word *papilio* meant "butterfly." In a later stage of Latin, *papilio* also came to be used to mean "a tent." Probably this happened because the top of a colorful tent looked like the spread wings of a butterfly. This meaning of the word was borrowed into early French as *pavillioun*. Later still, the French word came into English and is now spelled *pavilion*. Over the years *pavilion* has acquired additional meanings in English, all having to do with a building of some kind. But a tent that is large and richly decorated—as colorful as a butterfly—is still sometimes called a *pavilion*. [Middle English *pavillioun* "a large decorated tent," from early French *pavillioun* "tent," from Latin *papilion-, papilio* "butterfly"]

pav·ing \'pā-viŋ\ *n* : PAVEMENT

¹**paw** \'pȯ\ *n* **1** : the foot of a four-footed animal (as a lion or dog) having claws; *also* : the foot of an animal **2** : a human hand especially when large or clumsy

²**paw** *vb* **1** : to touch or strike with a paw **2** : to touch or handle clumsily or rudely ⟨*pawed* the merchandise⟩ **3** : to scrape or beat with or as if with a hoof **4** : to grab at wildly **5** : to search especially carelessly or roughly ⟨*pawed* through the box of letters⟩

pawl \'pȯl\ *n* : a tongue or sliding bolt on a machine part that is made to fall into notches on another part (as a ratchet wheel) so as to permit motion in only one direction

¹**pawn** \'pȯn, 'pän\ *n* **1** : the piece of least value in the game of chess **2** : one that can be used to further the purposes of another [Middle English *pown* "chess piece represent-

ing an ordinary soldier," from early French *peoun, paun* (same meaning), from Latin *pedon-, pedo* "foot soldier," derived from earlier *ped-, pes* "foot" — related to PEDESTRIAN]

²**pawn** *n* **1** : something given as a guarantee of repayment of a loan **2** : the state of being pledged ⟨the watch was in *pawn*⟩ [Middle English *paun* "something given as a guarantee of repayment of a loan"]

³**pawn** *vb* : to leave as a guarantee of repayment of a loan ⟨*pawn* a watch⟩ — **pawn·er** *n*

pawn·bro·ker \'pȯn-ˌbrō-kər, 'pän-\ *n* : a person who makes a business of lending money and keeping personal property as a guarantee — **pawn·bro·king** \-kiŋ\ *n*

Paw·nee \pȯ-'nē, pä-\ *n* : a member of an American Indian people originally of Nebraska and Kansas

pawn·shop \'pȯn-ˌshäp, 'pän-\ *n* : a pawnbroker's shop

paw·paw *also* **pa·paw** *n* **1** \pə-'pȯ\ : PAPAYA **2** \'päp-(ˌ)ȯ, 'pȯp-\ : a North American tree having purple flowers and an edible fruit with green skin; *also* : its fruit

¹**pay** \'pā\ *vb* **paid** \'pād\ *also in sense 6* **payed; pay·ing** **1** : to give (as money) in return for services received or for something bought ⟨*pay* the taxi driver⟩ ⟨*pay* for a ticket⟩ **2** : to give what is owed ⟨*pay* a tax⟩ **3** : to get even with ⟨*pay* someone back for an insult⟩ **4** : to give or offer freely ⟨*pay* a compliment⟩ ⟨*pay* attention⟩ **5 a** : to return value or profit to ⟨it *pays* to drive carefully⟩ **b** : to give as a return ⟨a bank account *paying* eight percent⟩ **6** : to make slack and allow to run out ⟨*pay* out a rope⟩ — **pay·er** \'pā-ər\ *also* **pay·or** \'pā-ər, pā-'ó(ə)r\ *n*

²**pay** *n* **1 a** : the act of paying **b** : the state of being paid or employed for money **2** : something paid; *esp* : ²WAGE, SALARY

³**pay** *adj* **1** : containing or leading to something valuable **2** : having a coin slot for receiving money for use ⟨a *pay* phone⟩

pay·able \'pā-ə-bəl\ *adj* : that may, can, or must be paid ⟨accounts *payable*⟩

pay·check \'pā-ˌchek\ *n* : a check in payment of wages or salary

pay·day \'pā-ˌdā\ *n* : a regular day on which wages are paid

pay dirt *n* **1** : earth or ore that produces a profit for a miner **2** : a useful or profitable discovery or object

pay·ee \pā-'ē\ *n* : one to whom money is paid or is to be paid

pay·load \'pā-ˌlōd\ *n* : something (as cargo, passengers, instruments, or explosives) carried by a vehicle in addition to what is necessary for its operation

pay·mas·ter \-ˌmas-tər\ *n* : an officer or agent of an employer whose duty it is to pay salaries or wages

pay·ment \'pā-mənt\ *n* **1** : the act of paying **2** : money given to pay a debt **3** : ²PAY 2

pay·off \'pā-ˌȯf\ *n* **1** : ¹PROFIT 2 **2** : the last and most interesting part of an incident ⟨the *payoff* of a story⟩

pay off \(')pā-'ȯf\ *vb* **1** : to pay in full ⟨*pay off* a mortgage⟩ **2** : to produce a profit ⟨investments that *pay off*⟩

pay–per–view *n* : a cable television service by which customers can order access to a particular broadcast for a fee

pay·roll \'pā-ˌrōl\ *n* **1** : a list of persons entitled to receive pay with the amounts due to each **2** : the amount of money necessary to pay those on a payroll

pay up *vb* : to pay in full

PC \ˌpē-'sē\ *n, pl* **PCs** *or* **PC's** : PERSONAL COMPUTER

PDA \ˌpē-ˌdē-'ā\ *n* : an electronic device that is small enough to be held in the hand and is used especially to store and organize personal information (as addresses and schedules) [*personal digital assistant*]

pea \'pē\ *n, pl* **peas** *also* **pease** \'pēz\ **1 a** : a plant of the legume family that is widely grown for its pods of protein-rich edible rounded seeds **b** : the seed of a pea **2** : a plant (as the sweet pea) related to the pea

peace \'pēs\ *n* **1** : a state of quiet; *esp* : freedom from public disturbance or war **2** : freedom from upsetting thoughts or feelings **3** : harmony in personal relations **4 a** : a state or period of peace between governments **b** : an agreement to end a war [Middle English *pees* "peace," from early French *pes, pees* (same meaning), from Latin *pac-, pax* "peace" — related to APPEASE, PACIFY]

peace·able \'pē-sə-bəl\ *adj* **1** : PEACEFUL 1 **2** : PEACEFUL 3 — **peace·ably** \-blē\ *adv*

peace·ful \'pēs-fəl\ *adj* **1** : enjoying peace and quiet ⟨a *peaceful* people⟩ **2** : ²QUIET 1c, TRANQUIL ⟨a *peaceful* countryside⟩; *esp* : not at war **3** : not involving violence or force ⟨settled the conflict by *peaceful* means⟩ **synonyms** see CALM — **peace·ful·ly** \-fə-lē\ *adv* — **peace·ful·ness** *n*

peace·keep·ing \'pē-ˌskē-piŋ\ *n* : the enforcing of a truce between countries or groups by an international military force

peace·mak·er \'pē-ˌsmā-kər\ *n* : a person who settles an argument or stops a fight — **peace·mak·ing** \-kiŋ\ *n or adj*

peace·time \'pē-ˌstīm\ *n* : a time when a nation is not at war

peach \'pēch\ *n* **1** : a sweet juicy fruit with white or yellow flesh, a thin fuzzy skin, and a single seed enclosed in a rough stony covering that is produced by a low spreading Chinese tree related to the plums and cherries and grown in most temperate areas; *also* : this tree **2** : a moderate yellowish pink

pea·cock \'pē-ˌkäk\ *n* : the male of a very large Asian pheasant having a very long brightly colored tail that can be spread or raised, a small crest of upright feathers on the top of the head, and in most forms brilliant blue or green feathers on the neck and shoulders

peacock

pea jacket \'pē-\ *n* : a heavy woolen double-breasted jacket originally worn by sailors

¹peak \'pēk\ *n* **1** : a part of a piece of clothing that is pointed or sticks out; *esp* : the front part of a cap or hat **2 a** : the top of a hill or mountain **b** : a mountain all by itself **3** : the highest point of development ⟨the *peak* of perfection⟩ — **peak** *adj*

²peak *vb* : to reach or cause to come to a peak, point, or maximum

¹peaked \'pēkt *also* 'pē-kəd\ *adj* : having a peak : POINTED ⟨a *peaked* roof⟩

²peak·ed \'pē-kəd\ *adj* : looking pale and sick

peal \'pē(ə)l\ *n* **1** : the loud ringing of bells **2** : a loud sound or series of sounds ⟨a *peal* of laughter⟩ ⟨a *peal* of thunder⟩ — **peal** *vb*

pea·nut \'pē-(ˌ)nət\ *n* **1** : a plant of the legume family that has yellow flowers and is grown for its underground pods of oily nutlike edible seeds which yield peanut oil or are crushed to make peanut butter; *also* : this pod or one of the oily edible seeds it contains **2** *pl* : a very small amount

peanut butter *n* : a paste made chiefly of ground roasted peanuts

peanut oil *n* : a colorless to yellow fatty oil that is obtained from peanuts

pear \'pa(ə)r, 'pe(ə)r\ *n* : a fruit that is commonly larger at the end opposite the stem and typi-

peanut 1

cally has a pale green or brownish skin and juicy flesh; *also* : a tree that bears pears and is related to the apple

¹pearl \'pər(-ə)l\ *n* **1 a** : a dense smooth shiny body that is considered a gem and is formed in layers as an abnormal growth in the body of some mollusks usually around something irritating (as a grain of sand) which has gotten into the shell **b** : MOTHER-OF-PEARL **2** : something like a pearl (as in shape, color, or value) **3** : a light bluish gray

²pearl *adj* **1** : of, relating to, or resembling pearl **2** : made of pearls

pearl onion *n* : a very small onion that is usually pickled

pearly \'pər-lē\ *adj* **pearl·i·er**; **-est** : resembling pearls or mother-of-pearl

peas·ant \'pez-ᵊnt\ *n* **1** : a European small farmer or farm laborer **2** : a member of a similar agricultural class elsewhere

peas·ant·ry \-ᵊn-trē\ *n* : peasants as a group

pease *plural of* PEA

peat \'pēt\ *n* : a dark brown or blackish material that is the remains of plants partly decayed in water and is sometimes dug up and dried for use as fuel

peat moss *n* : SPHAGNUM

¹peb·ble \'peb-əl\ *n* **1** : a small rounded stone **2** : an uneven, wrinkled, or grainy surface — **peb·ble·like** \-əl-ˌ(l)īk\ *adj* — **peb·bly** \-(ə-)lē\ *adj*

²pebble *vb* **peb·bled**; **peb·bling** \'peb-(ə-)liŋ\ : to produce an uneven, wrinkled, or grainy surface on

pe·can \pi-'kän, -'kan\ *n* : an oblong edible nut that usually has a thin shell and is the fruit of a tall tree of the central and southern U.S.; *also* : this tree which is one of the hickories

pec·ca·dil·lo \ˌpek-ə-'dil-ō\ *n, pl* **-loes** *or* **-los** : a slight offense or fault

pec·ca·ry \'pek-ə-rē\ *n, pl* **-ries** : either of two American mammals of warm regions that gather in herds, are active usually at night, and look like but are much smaller than the related pigs

peccary

¹peck \'pek\ *n* **1** : see MEASURE table **2** : a large quantity ⟨a *peck* of trouble⟩ [Middle English *pek* "unit of measure," from early French *pek* (same meaning)]

²peck *vb* **1 a** : to strike with the bill : thrust the beak into **b** : to make by pecking ⟨*peck* holes⟩ **2** : to strike with a sharp instrument (as a pick) **3** : to pick up with the bill ⟨a chicken *pecking* corn⟩ **4** : to bite daintily : NIBBLE ⟨*peck* at one's food⟩ [Middle English *pecken* "to strike or pierce repeatedly," perhaps from early German *pekken* (same meaning)]

³peck *n* **1** : a mark or hole made by pecking **2** : a quick sharp stroke

pecking order *also* **peck order** *n* **1** : a basic pattern of social organization within a flock of poultry in which each bird pecks another lower in the scale without being pecked in return and allows pecking by one of higher rank **2** : a social order with ranks or classes

pec·tin \'pek-tən\ *n* : any of various substances in plant tissues that dissolve in water and produce a gel which is the basis of fruit jellies; *also* : a commercial product rich in pectins

\ə\ **abut**	\au̇\ **out**	\i\ **tip**	\ȯ\ **saw**	\u̇\ **foot**
\ər\ **further**	\ch\ **chin**	\ī\ **life**	\ȯi\ **coin**	\y\ **yet**
\a\ **mat**	\e\ **pet**	\j\ **job**	\th\ **thin**	\yü\ **few**
\ā\ **take**	\ē\ **easy**	\ŋ\ **sing**	\t͟h\ **this**	\yu̇\ **cure**
\ä\ **cot, cart**	\g\ **go**	\ō\ **bone**	\ü\ **food**	\zh\ **vision**

pec·to·ral \'pek-t(ə-)rəl\ *adj* : of, relating to, or situated in, near, or on the chest

pectoral fin *n* : either of a pair of fins of a fish that correspond to the front limbs of a four-footed animal — compare PELVIC FIN

pectoral muscle *n* : any of the muscles which connect the front walls of the chest with the bones of the upper arm and shoulder and of which there are two on each side in the human body

pe·cu·liar \pi-'kyül-yər\ *adj* 1 : characteristic of only one person, thing, or place ⟨a custom *peculiar* to England⟩ 2 : different from the usual or normal ⟨*peculiar* behavior⟩ *synonyms* see CHARACTERISTIC — **pe·cu·liar·ly** *adv*

pe·cu·liar·i·ty \pi-ˌkyül-'yar-ət-ē, -ˌkyü-lē-'ar-\ *n, pl* **-ties** 1 : the quality or state of being peculiar 2 : something different or individual 3 : something odd or abnormal

pe·cu·ni·ary \pi-'kyü-nē-ˌer-ē\ *adj* : of, relating to, or consisting of money

ped·a·gog·ics \ˌped-ə-'gäj-iks\ *n* : PEDAGOGY

ped·a·gogue \'ped-ə-ˌgäg\ *n* : TEACHER, SCHOOLMASTER

Word History In ancient Greece a rich family had many servants. One of the servants was in charge of caring for the children. This servant's duties included escorting the children to and from school. As a name for this servant, the Greek prefix *paid-*, meaning "child," and the noun *agōgos*, meaning "leader," were combined to form *paid-agōgos*. This word might be translated literally as "child-leader." The English word *pedagogue* can be traced to the Greek *paidagōgos*. It is now a name for a person who leads children by teaching them, rather than just by escorting them. [Middle English *pedagoge* "teacher," from early French *pedagoge* (same meaning), from Latin *paedagogus* (same meaning), from Greek *paidagōgos* "a servant who escorted children to school," from *paid-* "child" and *agōgos* "leader"]

ped·a·go·gy \'ped-ə-ˌgōj-ē *also* -ˌgäj-ē\ *n* : the art, science, or profession of teaching : EDUCATION — **ped·a·gog·i·cal** \-i-kəl\ *adj* — **ped·a·gog·i·cal·ly** \-i-k(ə-)lē\ *adv*

¹**ped·al** \'ped-ᵊl\ *n* : a lever (as on a piano, bicycle, or sewing machine) worked by the foot [from early French *pedale* "a foot lever on an organ," from Italian *pedale* (same meaning), from Latin *pedalis* "of the foot," from *ped-, pes* "foot" — related to PEDESTRIAN]

²**pedal** *vb* **ped·aled** *also* **ped·alled; ped·al·ing** *also* **ped·al·ling** \'ped-ᵊl-iŋ, -liŋ\ 1 : to use or work the pedals of something 2 : to ride a bicycle

pedal pushers *n pl* : women's and girls' calf-length trousers

ped·ant \'ped-ᵊnt\ *n* 1 : a person who shows off his or her learning 2 : a dull and overly exact teacher — **pe·dan·tic** \pi-'dant-ik\ *adj* — **pe·dan·ti·cal·ly** \-i-k(ə-)lē\ *adv*

ped·ant·ry \'ped-ᵊn-trē\ *n, pl* **-ries** : dull and overly exact presentation of knowledge or learning

ped·dle \'ped-ᵊl\ *vb* **ped·dled; ped·dling** \-liŋ, -ᵊl-iŋ\ 1 : to travel about especially from house to house with goods for sale 2 : to sell from place to place usually in small quantities 3 : to present (something) in a manner that is intended to convince others of its value ⟨*peddled* her opinion to her friends⟩ — **ped·dler** *also* **ped·lar** \'ped-lər\ *n*

ped·es·tal \'ped-əs-tᵊl\ *n* 1 : the support or foot of a column 2 : the base of something upright (as a vase, lamp, or statue) 3 : a position of high regard

¹**pe·des·tri·an** \pə-'des-trē-ən\ *adj* 1 : not interesting : ORDINARY 2 a : going on foot b : of, relating to, or designed for walking ⟨*pedestrian* traffic⟩ ⟨a *pedestrian* mall⟩ [from Latin *pedestr-, pedestris* "going on foot," from *ped-, pes* "foot" — related to CENTIPEDE, IMPEDE, ¹PAWN, PEDAL] — **pe·des·tri·an·ism** \-trē-ə-ˌniz-əm\ *n*

²**pedestrian** *n* : a person who is walking

pe·di·a·tri·cian \ˌpēd-ē-ə-'trish-ən\ *n* : a doctor who specializes in pediatrics

pe·di·at·rics \ˌpēd-ē-'a-triks\ *n* : a branch of medicine concerned with the development, care, and diseases of babies and children — **pe·di·at·ric** \-trik\ *adj*

pe·dic·u·lo·sis \pi-ˌdik-yə-'lō-səs\ *n* : the condition of having lice (as in the hair or on the body)

ped·i·cure \'ped-i-ˌkyu̇(ə)r\ *n* : care of the feet, toes, and toenails; *also* : a single treatment of these parts

ped·i·gree \'ped-ə-ˌgrē\ *n* 1 : a table or list showing the line of ancestors of a person or animal 2 : an ancestral line : LINEAGE 3 : purity of breed recorded by a pedigree — **ped·i·greed** \-ˌgrēd\ *adj*

ped·i·ment \'ped-ə-mənt\ *n* : a triangular space forming the gable of a roof in classic architecture

P pediment

pe·dom·e·ter \pi-'däm-ət-ər\ *n* : an instrument that measures the distance one covers in walking

pe·dun·cle \'pē-ˌdəŋ-kəl, pi-'dəŋ-\ *n* : a narrow part by which some larger part or the body of a living thing is attached; *esp* : a stalk that supports a flower cluster

peek \'pēk\ *vb* 1 : to look cautiously or briefly 2 : to look through a crack or hole or from a hiding place — **peek** *n*

¹**peel** \'pē(ə)l\ *vb* 1 : to strip off an outer layer of ⟨*peel* an apple⟩ 2 : to strip or tear off ⟨*peeled* off their coats⟩ 3 a : to come off in strips or patches ⟨the paint is *peeling*⟩ b : to lose an outer layer (as of skin) ⟨your face is *peeling*⟩ — **peel·er** *n*

²**peel** *n* : an outer covering and especially the skin or rind of a fruit

peel·ing \'pē-liŋ\ *n* : a peeled-off piece or strip (as of skin or rind)

¹**peep** \'pēp\ *vb* 1 : to make a feeble shrill sound as of a bird newly hatched 2 : to speak with a small weak voice [Middle English *pepen* "to peep, make the sound of a young bird"; the word began as an imitation of the sound made by a young bird]

²**peep** *n* : a quick high-pitched sound

³**peep** *vb* 1 : PEEK 2, PEER 2 : to show slightly ⟨crocuses *peeping* through the snow⟩ [Middle English *pepen* "to peek," an altered form of earlier *piken* "to peek"]

⁴**peep** *n* 1 : the first appearance ⟨the *peep* of dawn⟩ 2 : a brief or sly look

¹**peep·er** \'pē-pər\ *n* : any of various tree frogs that peep; *esp* : SPRING PEEPER

²**peeper** *n* 1 : one that peeps; *esp* : PEEPING TOM 2 : ¹EYE 1

peep·hole \'pēp-ˌhōl\ *n* : a hole or crack to peep through

peep·ing Tom \ˌpē-piŋ-'täm\ *n* : a person who spies into the windows of private dwellings

Word History According to an ancient English legend, the lord of the town of Coventry had burdened the citizens with heavy taxes. His wife, Lady Godiva, was constantly urging the lord to lower the taxes. Finally he promised to do away with the taxes, but only if Lady Godiva would ride naked on a horse through the town. Wanting to help the townspeople, Godiva agreed and made the ride, covered only by her very long hair. For their part, the people decided to stay in their homes and not look at her nakedness. However, a tailor named Tom could not resist the temptation to peep at her. For this, it is said, he was struck blind. He is remembered as "Peeping Tom," and his name is used for a person who sneakily peeps at the private activities of others.

¹**peer** \'pi(ə)r\ *n* 1 : a person of the same rank or class as another 2 a : a member of one of the five ranks of the British nobility b : ²NOBLE [Middle English *peer* "one on equal standing with another," derived from early French *per* (adjective) "equal," from Latin *par* "equal" — related to COMPARE, PAIR, PAR, UMPIRE; see *Word History* at UMPIRE]

²**peer** \'pi(ə)r\ *vb* **1** : to look closely or curiously ⟨*peered* into the dark closet⟩ **2** : ³PEEP 2 [perhaps an altered and shortened form of *appear*]

peer·age \'pi(ə)r-ij\ *n* **1** : NOBILITY 2 **2** : a list or register of peers

peer·less \'pi(ə)r-ləs\ *adj* : having no equal ⟨*peerless* beauty⟩ — **peer·less·ly** *adv* — **peer·less·ness** *n*

¹**peeve** \'pēv\ *vb* **peeved; peev·ing** : to make irritable or resentful : ANNOY, IRRITATE

²**peeve** *n* **1** : a feeling or mood of resentment **2** : something one finds annoying ⟨a pet *peeve*⟩

pee·vish \'pē-vish\ *adj* **1** : IRRITABLE **2** : STUBBORN 1a — **pee·vish·ly** *adv* — **pee·vish·ness** *n*

pee·wee \'pē-wē\ *n* **1** : PEWEE **2** : a tiny person or thing

¹**peg** \'peg\ *n* **1 a** : a small usually cylindrical pointed piece (as of wood) used to pin down or fasten things or to fit into or close holes ⟨a tent *peg*⟩ **b** : a tapered wooden piece in a musical instrument (as a violin) that is turned to tighten or loosen a string to adjust pitch **2** : a piece that sticks out and is used as a support or boundary marker **3** : ¹STEP 5, DEGREE ⟨take someone down a *peg*⟩ **4** : ²THROW 1 ⟨a quick *peg* to first base⟩

²**peg** *vb* **pegged; peg·ging** **1 a** : to fasten or mark with pegs **b** : to fix or hold (as prices) at a level or rate of increase **2** : to place in a class or group **3** : ¹THROW 1a **4** : to work steadily and diligently

Peg·a·sus \'peg-ə-səs\ *n* : a group of stars that is located just north of Aquarius and Pisces and that is recognized by four bright stars in the form of a large square

Peg–Board \'peg-,bō(ə)rd, -,bȯ(ə)rd\ *trademark* — used for material (as fiberboard) with evenly spaced holes into which hooks may be inserted for the storage or display of articles

peg·ma·tite \'peg-mə-,tīt\ *n* : a grainy variety of granite that occurs in layers in rock

Pe·king·ese *or* **Pe·kin·ese** \,pē-kən-'ēz, -kiŋ-, -'ēs\ *n, pl* **Pekingese** *or* **Pekinese** **1 a** : the Chinese dialect of Peking **b** : a person born or living in Peking **2** : any of a Chinese breed of small short-legged dogs with a broad flat face and a long soft coat

Pekingese 2

Pe·king man \,pē-,kiŋ-\ *n* : an extinct prehistoric human being known from skeletal and cultural remains in cave deposits found in northeastern China and now classified with the direct ancestor of modern human beings

pe·koe \'pē-kō\ *n* : a black tea made from small-sized tea leaves especially in India and Ceylon

pel·age \'pel-ij\ *n* : the hairy covering of an animal

pe·lag·ic \pə-'laj-ik\ *adj* : of, relating to, or living or occurring in the open sea : OCEANIC ⟨*pelagic* fish⟩

pel·ar·go·ni·um \,pe-lär-'gō-nē-əm\ *n* : GERANIUM 2

pelf \'pelf\ *n* : MONEY 1a, RICHES

pel·i·can \'pel-i-kən\ *n* : any of a genus of large web-footed birds with a very large bill having a pouch on the lower part used to scoop in fish for food

pel·la·gra \pə-'lag-rə, -'lāg-, -'läg-\ *n* : a disease caused by a diet with too little niacin and protein and marked by a skin rash, digestive disorders, and mental symptoms (as irritability and confusion)

pelican

pel·let \'pel-ət\ *n* **1 a** : a little ball (as of food or medicine) **b** : a wad of material (as of bones and fur) that could not be digested and was regurgitated by a bird of prey (as an owl) **2 a** : BULLET 1 **b** : a piece of small shot

pel·li·cle \'pel-i-kəl\ *n* : a thin skin, film, or membrane (as of a paramecium)

pell–mell \'pel-'mel\ *adv* **1** : in confusion or disorder **2** : in great haste — **pell–mell** *adj*

pel·lu·cid \pə-'lü-səd\ *adj* : extremely clear or transparent

¹**pelt** \'pelt\ *n* : a usually unfinished skin with its hair, wool, or fur [Middle English *pelt* "skin and attached fur of an animal"]

²**pelt** *vb* **1** : to strike with a series of blows, missiles, or words **2** : HURL 1, THROW **3** : to beat against again and again **4** : to move quickly [Middle English *pelten* "to hit with a series of blows, pelt"]

pel·vic \'pel-vik\ *adj* : of, relating to, or located in or near the pelvis ⟨*pelvic* bones⟩

pelvic fin *n* : either of a pair of fins of a fish that correspond to the hind limbs of a four-footed animal — compare PECTORAL FIN

pelvic girdle *n* : an arch of bone or cartilage that supports the hind limbs of a vertebrate

pel·vis \'pel-vəs\ *n, pl* **pel·vis·es** *or* **pel·ves** \'pel-,vēz\ : a basin-shaped structure in the skeleton of many vertebrates formed by the pelvic girdle and the nearby bones of the spine; *also* : its cavity

Pem·broke Welsh corgi \'pem-,brōk-, -,brùk-\ *n* : any of a breed of Welsh corgis with pointed ears, straight forelegs, and a short tail — called also *Pembroke*

pem·mi·can \'pem-i-kən\ *n* : dried lean meat pounded fine and mixed with melted fat

¹**pen** \'pen\ *n* **1** : a small enclosure for animals **2** : a small place of confinement or storage [Middle English]

²**pen** *vb* **penned; pen·ning** : to shut in a pen

³**pen** *n* : an instrument for writing or drawing with ink

Word History The words *pen* and *pencil* look very much alike, and the writing instruments themselves have much in common. But these two words are not at all related. *Pen* can be traced back to the Latin word *penna* or *pinna*, meaning "feather." The early pens were made of long feathers trimmed to a point to hold ink. In time, pens came to be made with metal points and later with rolling balls instead of points. For this reason we no longer associate the word *pen* with feathers. *Pencil* can be traced to the Latin word *penicillus*, which meant "little tail" or "brush." (It also gave us our word *penicillin*.) The first pencils were artists' brushes that had fine hairs drawn to a point, like the tail of a tiny animal. From these first pencils, used for painting fine lines, the word came to be used for other instruments used to draw marks. Some pencils were sticks of charcoal. Others were sticks of slate or lead. Still others were sticks of colored material like crayons. In time, we began using our modern wood and graphite pencils, which are not at all like the original "little tails." [Middle English *penne* "a writing instrument made from a bird's feather," from early French *penne* "a bird's feather, pen," from Latin *penna, pinna* "feather"]

⁴**pen** *vb* **penned; pen·ning** : to write especially with a pen

⁵**pen** *n, slang* : PENITENTIARY [a shortened form of *penitentiary*]

pe·nal \'pēn-²l\ *adj* : of or relating to punishment ⟨*penal* laws⟩ ⟨a *penal* colony⟩

pe·nal·ize \'pēn-²l-,īz, 'pen-\ *vb* **-ized; -iz·ing** **1** : to give a penalty to **2** : to place at a disadvantage

\ə\ **abut**	\au̇\ **out**	\i\ **tip**	\ȯ\ **saw**	\u̇\ **foot**
\ər\ **further**	\ch\ **chin**	\ī\ **life**	\ȯi\ **coin**	\y\ **yet**
\a\ **mat**	\e\ **pet**	\j\ **job**	\th\ **thin**	\yü\ **few**
\ā\ **take**	\ē\ **easy**	\ŋ\ **sing**	\th\ **this**	\yu̇\ **cure**
\ä\ **cot, cart**	\g\ **go**	\ō\ **bone**	\ü\ **food**	\zh\ **vision**

pen·al·ty \'pen-ᵊl-tē\ *n, pl* **-ties 1** : punishment for a crime or offense **2** : something forfeited when one fails to do what one has agreed to do **3** : disadvantage, loss, or hardship due to some action or condition **4** : a punishment or handicap given for breaking a rule in a sport or game

pen·ance \'pen-ən(t)s\ *n* **1** : an act showing sorrow or regret for sin **2** : a sacrament consisting of regret for sin, confession to a priest, an act showing sorrow or regret ordered by the confessor, and forgiveness

pence *plural of* PENNY

pen·chant \'pen-chənt\ *n* : a strong liking

¹**pen·cil** \'pen(t)-səl\ *n* **1** : an instrument for writing, drawing, or marking consisting of or containing a slender cylinder or strip of a solid marking substance **2** : something like a pencil in form or use ⟨an eyebrow *pencil*⟩ [Middle English *pensel* "an artist's brush, pencil," from early French *pincel* (same meaning), derived from Latin *penicillus*, literally, "little tail" — related to PENICILLIN; see *Word History* at ³PEN]

²**pencil** *vb* **-ciled** *or* **-cilled; -cil·ing** *or* **-cil·ling** \'pen(t)-s(ə)liŋ\ : to mark, draw, or write with or as if with a pencil

pen·dant *also* **pen·dent** \'pen-dənt\ *n* : something that hangs down especially as an ornament

pen·dent *or* **pen·dant** \'pen-dənt\ *adj* **1** : sticking out or hanging over **2** : supported from above **3** : ²PENDING 1

¹**pend·ing** \'pen-diŋ\ *prep* : while waiting for ⟨held in jail *pending* a trial⟩

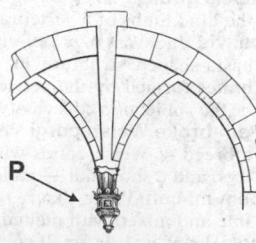

P pendant

²**pending** *adj* **1** : not yet decided or acted on ⟨bills *pending* in Congress⟩ **2** : being about to take place ⟨signs of a *pending* victory⟩

pen·du·lous \'pen-jə-ləs\ *adj* **1** : hanging so as to swing freely **2** : hanging downward — **pen·du·lous·ly** *adv*

pen·du·lum \'pen-jə-ləm\ *n* : a body hung from a fixed point so as to swing freely back and forth under the action of gravity [from scientific Latin *pendulum* "something suspended so as to swing freely," from Latin *pendulus* "suspended," from *pendēre* "to hang" — related to DEPEND, PERPENDICULAR]

pe·ne·plain *also* **pe·ne·plane** \'pēn-i-ˌplān, 'pen-\ *n* : a large almost flat land surface shaped by erosion

pen·e·tra·ble \'pen-ə-trə-bəl\ *adj* : capable of being penetrated — **pen·e·tra·bil·i·ty** \ˌpen-ə-trə-'bil-ət-ē\ *n*

pen·e·trate \'pen-ə-ˌtrāt\ *vb* **-trat·ed; -trat·ing 1 a** : to pass into or through **b** : to enter by piercing **2** : to come to understand **3** : to move deeply

pen·e·trat·ing *adj* **1** : having the power of entering or piercing ⟨*penetrating* cold⟩ **2** : ACUTE 3, DISCERNING ⟨a *penetrating* mind⟩ — **pen·e·trat·ing·ly** \-ˌtrāt-iŋ-lē\ *adv*

pen·e·tra·tion \ˌpen-ə-'trā-shən\ *n* **1** : the act or process of penetrating **2 a** : the depth to which something penetrates **b** : keen understanding

pen·guin \'peŋ-gwən, 'pen-\ *n* : any of various short-legged seabirds of the southern hemisphere that cannot fly and have wings functioning as flippers and used in swimming

pen·i·cil·lin \ˌpen-ə-'sil-ən\ *n* : any of several antibiotics or a mixture of these produced by penicillia or in the laboratory and used especially against round disease-producing bacteria [from scientific Latin *Penicillium* "a genus of molds producing antibiotics," from Latin *penicillus,* literally, "little tail" — related to PENCIL]

penguin

pen·i·cil·li·um \ˌpen-ə-'sil-ē-əm\ *n, pl* **-lia** \-ē-ə\ : any of a genus of fungi of which most are blue molds found chiefly on moist nonliving organic matter (as decaying fruit)

pen·in·su·la \pə-'nin(t)-s(ə-)lə, -'nin-chə-lə\ *n* : a piece of land nearly surrounded by water or sticking out into the water [from Latin *paeninsula* "peninsula," from *paene-* "almost" and *insula* "island" — related to INSULATE, ISLE, ISOLATE] — **pen·in·su·lar** \-s(ə-)lər, -chə-lər\ *adj*

pe·nis \'pē-nəs\ *n, pl* **pe·nis·es** *also* **pe·nes** \'pē-ˌnēz\ : a male organ of copulation containing a channel through which sperm leaves the body that in mammals including human beings also serves to discharge urine from the body — **pe·nile** \-ˌnīl\ *adj*

pen·i·tence \'pen-ə-tən(t)s\ *n* : sorrow for one's sins or faults : REPENTANCE — **pen·i·tent** \-tənt\ *adj* — **pen·i·tent·ly** *adv*

penitent *n* : a person who repents or is doing penance

pen·i·ten·tial \ˌpen-ə-'ten-chəl\ *adj* : of or relating to penitence or penance — **pen·i·ten·tial·ly** \-'tench-(ə-)lē\ *adv*

pen·i·ten·tia·ry \ˌpen-ə-'tench-(ə-)rē\ *n, pl* **-ries** : a usually state or federal prison in which criminals are kept

pen·knife \'pen-ˌnīf\ *n* : a small pocketknife usually with only one blade [so called from the fact that it was originally used for sharpening the points of quill (feather) pens]

pen·light \-ˌlīt\ *n* : a small flashlight resembling a fountain pen in size or shape

pen·man \-mən\ *n* : AUTHOR 1

pen·man·ship \-mən-ˌship\ *n* **1** : the art or practice of writing with the pen **2** : quality or style of handwriting

pen name *n* : a false name used by an author

pen·nant \'pen-ənt\ *n* **1** : a flag with a usually tapering or forked tail that is used especially for signaling **2** : a flag that serves as the emblem of championship

pen·ni·less \'pen-i-ləs, 'pen-ᵊl-əs\ *adj* : having no money : very poor

pen·non \'pen-ən\ *n* **1** : a long triangular or forked streamer attached to the head of a lance as a flag **2** : ²FLAG 1, PENNANT

Penn·syl·va·nia Dutch \ˌpen(t)-səl-ˌvā-nyə-, -nē-ə-\ *n* **1** : a people living mostly in eastern Pennsylvania whose culture goes back to the German migrations of the 18th century **2** : the German dialect of the Pennsylvania Dutch — **Pennsylvania Dutchman** *n*

Penn·syl·va·nian \ˌpen(t)-səl-'vā-nyən, -nē-ən\ *adj* **1** : of or relating to Pennsylvania or its people **2** : of, relating to, or being the later part of the Carboniferous period in the Paleozoic era of geological history in North America marked by the first appearance of reptiles; *also* : relating to the corresponding system of rocks — see GEOLOGIC TIME table — **Pennsylvanian** *n*

pen·ny \'pen-ē\ *n, pl* **pen·nies** \-ēz\ *or* **pence** \'pen(t)s\ **1 a** : a British unit of money formerly equal to ¹/₂₄₀ pound but now equal to ¹/₁₀₀ pound **b** : a coin representing this unit **2** *pl* **pennies** : CENT **3** : a sum of money ⟨earn an honest *penny*⟩

penny arcade *n* : an amusement center where each device for entertainment may be operated for a small sum

pen·ny·weight \'pen-ē-ˌwāt\ *n* — see MEASURE table

pen·ny–wise \-ˌwīz\ *adj* : wise only in small or unimportant matters

pen pal *n* : a friend made and kept through letter-writing

¹**pen·sion** \'pen-chən\ *n* : a sum paid regularly to a person especially following retirement or to surviving dependents

²**pension** *vb* **pen·sioned; pen·sion·ing** \'pench-(ə-)niŋ\ : to pay a pension to

pen·sion·er \'pench-(ə-)nər\ *n* : a person who receives or lives on a pension

pen·sive \'pen(t)-siv\ *adj* **1** : dreamily thoughtful **2** : suggestive of sad thoughtfulness — **pen·sive·ly** *adv* — **pen·sive·ness** *n*

pen·stock \'pen-ˌstäk\ *n* **1** : a gate or valve for regulating a flow (as of water) **2** : a pipe for carrying water

pent \'pent\ *adj* : shut up : CONFINED ⟨*pent*-up feelings⟩

pen·ta·gon \'pent-ə-ˌgän\ *n* : a polygon of five angles and five sides

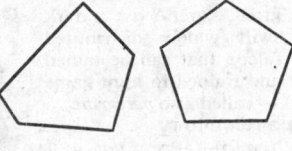

pentagon

pen·tag·o·nal \pen-'tag-ən-ᵊl\ *adj* **1** : having five sides and five angles **2** : having a pentagon as a cross section or as a base ⟨a *pentagonal* pyramid⟩

pen·tam·e·ter \pen-'tam-ət-ər\ *n* : a line of verse consisting of five metrical feet

pen·tath·lon \pen-'tath-lən, -ˌlän\ *n* : an athletic contest made up of five different track-and-field events

Pen·te·cost \'pent-i-ˌkȯst, -ˌkäst\ *n* **1** : SHABUOTH **2** : the seventh Sunday after Easter observed as a Christian church festival in memory of the appearance of the Holy Spirit to the apostles — **Pen·te·cos·tal** \ˌpent-i-'käs-tᵊl, -'kȯs-\ *adj or n*

pent·house \'pent-ˌhaus\ *n* **1** : a sloping roof or a shed attached to a wall or building **2** : a structure (as an apartment) built on the roof of a building

pen·tose \'pen-ˌtōs\ *n* : any of various sugars containing five carbon atoms in a molecule

pe·nult \'pē-ˌnəlt, pi-'nəlt\ *n* : the next to the last syllable of a word

pen·ul·ti·mate \pi-'nəl-tə-mət\ *adj* : next to the last — **penultimate** *n*

pen·um·bra \pə-'nəm-brə\ *n, pl* **-brae** \-brē, -ˌbrī\ *or* **-bras** : the partial shadow surrounding a perfect shadow (as in an eclipse) — **pen·um·bral** \-brəl\ *adj*

pe·nu·ri·ous \pə-'n(y)ùr-ē-əs\ *adj* **1** : marked by or suffering from penury **2** : extremely stingy : MISERLY — **pe·nu·ri·ous·ly** *adv* — **pe·nu·ri·ous·ness** *n*

pen·u·ry \'pen-yə-rē\ *n* : extreme poverty

pe·on \'pē-ˌän, -ən\ *n* **1** : a poor farm laborer especially in Latin America **2** : a person who does hard or dull work — **pe·on·age** \'pē-ə-nij\ *n*

pe·o·ny \'pē-ə-nē\ *n, pl* **-nies** : any of a genus of plants that are widely grown for their large red, pink, or white flowers

¹peo·ple \'pē-pəl\ *n, pl* **people** **1** *pl* : HUMAN BEINGS, PERSONS — often used in compounds instead of *persons* ⟨sales*people*⟩ **2** *pl* : the members of a family : KINDRED **3** *pl* : the mass of a community as distinguished from a special class **4** *pl* **peoples** : a body of persons united by a common culture, tradition, or sense of kinship, and usually language **5** : the body of voters of a state

²people *vb* **peo·pled; peo·pling** \'pē-p(ə-)liŋ\ **1** : to supply or fill with people **2** : INHABIT

¹pep \'pep\ *n* : brisk energy : LIVELINESS — **pep·pi·ness** \-ē-nəs\ *n* — **pep·py** \-ē\ *adj*

²pep *vb* **pepped; pep·ping** : to put pep into : STIMULATE ⟨let's try to *pep* things up⟩

pe·po \'pē-pō\ *n* : a fleshy many-seeded fruit (as a pumpkin, squash, melon, or cucumber) of the gourd family that has a hard rind and is technically classified as a berry [Latin "a melon"]

¹pep·per \'pep-ər\ *n* **1** : either of two sharp-tasting products from the fruit of an Indian plant used especially as a seasoning **a** : BLACK PEPPER **b** : WHITE PEPPER **2** : a woody vine with rounded leaves and flowers arranged in a spike that is widely cultivated in the tropics for its red berries from which pepper is prepared **3** : any of several products similar to pepper that are obtained from close relatives of the pepper **4 a** : any of a genus of tropical American herbs and shrubs of the nightshade family widely cultivated for their many-seeded fruits that usual-

ly have fleshy walls; *esp* : one whose fruits are hot peppers or sweet peppers **b** : the fruit of a pepper that is usually green when unripe and yellow or red when ripe — **pepper** *adj*

²pepper *vb* **pep·pered; pep·per·ing** \'pep-(ə-)riŋ\ **1** : to sprinkle, cover, or season with or as if with pepper ⟨*pepper* the stew⟩ ⟨a face *peppered* with freckles⟩ **2** : to hit with a shower of blows or objects

pep·per·corn \'pep-ər-ˌkȯ(ə)rn\ *n* : a dried berry of the black pepper

peppered moth *n* : a European moth that normally has white wings with small black specks but often has black wings in areas with heavy air pollution

pep·per·mint \'pep-ər-ˌmint, -mənt\ *n* **1** : a mint with stalks of small usually pink flowers that is the source of an oil which is sharp in flavor and is used especially to flavor candies **2** : candy flavored with peppermint

peppermint 1

pep·per·o·ni \ˌpep-ə-'rō-nē\ *n* : a highly seasoned beef and pork sausage

pep·pery \'pep-(ə-)rē\ *adj* **1** : of, relating to, or having the qualities of pepper : HOT **2** : having a hot temper **3** : FIERY 3a

pep·sin \'pep-sən\ *n* **1** : an enzyme given off by glands in the wall of the stomach that begins the digestion of most proteins **2** : a preparation of pepsin obtained especially from the stomach of the hog and used in medicine

pep·tic \'pep-tik\ *adj* **1** : relating to or promoting digestion **2** : resulting from the action of digestive juices ⟨a *peptic* ulcer of the stomach⟩

pep·ti·dase \'pep-tə-ˌdās, -ˌdāz\ *n* : an enzyme that breaks down simple peptides

pep·tide \'pep-ˌtīd\ *n* : any of various substances that are usually obtained by the partial breakdown of proteins

pep·tone \'pep-ˌtōn\ *n* : any of various products that result from the partial breakdown of proteins and that dissolve in water

per \(')pər\ *prep* **1** : by means of **2** : to or for each ⟨$10 *per* day⟩ **3** : as indicated by : ACCORDING TO ⟨*per* list price⟩

¹per·ad·ven·ture \'pər-əd-ˌven-chər, 'per-; ˌpər-əd-'ven-, ˌper-\ *adv, archaic* : PERHAPS, POSSIBLY

²peradventure *n* : a possibility of error or uncertainty

per·am·bu·late \pə-'ram-byə-ˌlāt\ *vb* **-lat·ed; -lat·ing** **1** : to walk over or through **2** : STROLL, RAMBLE — **per·am·bu·la·tion** \-ˌram-byə-'lā-shən\ *n*

per·am·bu·la·tor \pə-'ram-byə-ˌlāt-ər\ *n* **1** : one that perambulates **2** *chiefly British* : a baby carriage

per an·num \(ˌ)pər-'an-əm\ *adv* : in or for each year : ANNUALLY

per·cale \(ˌ)pər-'kā(ə)l, 'pər-ˌkā(ə)l, (ˌ)pər-'kal\ *n* : a fine closely woven cotton cloth used especially to make sheets and pillowcases

per cap·i·ta \(ˌ)pər-'kap-ət-ə\ *adv or adj* : by or for each person ⟨*per capita* income⟩

per·ceive \pər-'sēv\ *vb* **perceived; per·ceiv·ing** **1** : UNDERSTAND 1a, COMPREHEND **2** : to become aware of through the senses and especially through sight — **per·ceiv·er** *n*

¹per·cent \pər-'sent\ *adv* : in the hundred : of each hundred

²percent *adj* : measured or counted on the basis of a whole divided into one hundred parts ⟨a five *percent* increase⟩

\ə\ abut	\au\ out	\i\ tip	\ȯ\ saw	\u\ foot
\ər\ further	\ch\ chin	\ī\ life	\ȯi\ coin	\y\ yet
\a\ mat	\e\ pet	\j\ job	\th\ thin	\yu\ few
\ā\ take	\ē\ easy	\ŋ\ sing	\th\ this	\yu\ cure
\ä\ cot, cart	\g\ go	\ō\ bone	\ü\ food	\zh\ vision

[3]**percent** *n, pl* **percent** *or* **percents** **1** : one part in a hundred : HUNDREDTH ⟨50 *percent* of the students⟩ **2** : PERCENTAGE 1 ⟨a large *percent* of her allowance⟩

per·cent·age \pər-'sent-ij\ *n* **1 a** : a part of a whole expressed in hundredths ⟨a high *percentage* of students attended⟩ **b** : the result obtained by multiplying a number by a percent ⟨the *percentage* equals the rate times the base⟩ **2 a** : PROBABILITY 3a ⟨play the *percentages*⟩ **b** : favorable odds

per·cep·ti·ble \pər-'sep-tə-bəl\ *adj* : capable of being noticed or observed ⟨a *perceptible* change⟩ — **per·cep·ti·bly** \-blē\ *adv*

per·cep·tion \pər-'sep-shən\ *n* **1** : a result of perceiving : OBSERVATION **2** : awareness of surrounding objects, conditions, or forces through sensation ⟨color *perception*⟩ **3** : capacity for understanding

per·cep·tive \pər-'sep-tiv\ *adj* : capable of or showing a keen ability to observe and understand

[1]**perch** \'pərch\ *n* **1** : a roost for a bird **2** : a raised seat or position [Middle English *perche* "a peg on which something is hung," from early French *perche* (same meaning), from Latin *pertica* "pole"]

[2]**perch** *vb* **1** : to place on a perch **2** : to land, settle, or rest on or as if on a perch

[3]**perch** *n, pl* **perch** *or* **perch·es** **1** : a common North American freshwater fish that is yellowish with dark green vertical stripes and is a popular food and sport fish — called also *yellow perch* **2** : any of various fishes related to or resembling the

[3]*perch* 1

perch [Middle English *perche* "a kind of fish," from early French *perche* (same meaning), from Latin *perca* (same meaning), from Greek *perkē* "perch (fish)"]

per·chance \pər-'chan(t)s\ *adv* : PERHAPS, POSSIBLY

Per·che·ron \'pər-chə-,rän, -shə-\ *n* : any of a breed of powerful draft horses that originated in France

per·chlo·rate \(')pər-'klō(ə)r-,āt, -'klō(ə)r-\ *n* : a chemical compound formed by the reaction of perchloric acid with another substance

per·chlo·ric acid \(,)pər-,klōr-ik-, -,klȯr-\ *n* : a fuming strong acid that is a powerful oxidizing agent when heated

per·co·late \'pər-kə-,lāt\ *vb* **-lat·ed; -lat·ing** **1** : to trickle or cause to trickle through something porous : FILTER, SEEP ⟨water *percolating* through sand⟩ **2** : to prepare coffee in a percolator **3** : to be or become spread through : PENETRATE

per·co·la·tion \,pər-kə-'lā-shən\ *n* : the act or process of percolating

per·co·la·tor \'pər-kə-,lāt-ər\ *n* : a coffeepot in which boiling water rising through a tube is repeatedly turned downward through a basket with holes that contains ground coffee beans to make coffee

per·cus·sion \pər-'kəsh-ən\ *n* **1** : the act of tapping sharply; *esp* : the striking of a percussion cap so as to set off the charge in a firearm **2** : the striking of sound sharply on the ear

percussion cap *n* : [1]CAP 4

percussion instrument *n* : a musical instrument (as a drum, cymbal, or maraca) sounded by striking or shaking — compare BRASS INSTRUMENT, STRINGED INSTRUMENT, WOODWIND

per·cus·sion·ist \pər-'kəsh-(ə-)nəst\ *n* : a person who plays percussion instruments

per di·em \(,)pər-dē-əm, -'dī-\ *adv* : by the day : for each day — **per diem** *adj*

per·di·tion \pər-'dish-ən\ *n* **1** : eternal damnation **2** : HELL 2

per·e·gri·nate \'per-ə-grə-,nāt\ *vb* **-nat·ed; -nat·ing** : to travel especially on foot — **per·e·gri·na·tion** \,per-ə-grə-'nā-shən\ *n*

per·e·grine falcon \'per-ə-grən-, -,grēn-\ *n* : a dark swift widely distributed falcon that can be tamed and trained to hunt game — called also *peregrine*

peregrine falcon

pe·remp·to·ry \pə-'rem(p)-t(ə-)rē\ *adj* **1** : not to be refused ⟨a *peremptory* summons from the boss⟩ **2** : expressing command ⟨called for silence with a *peremptory* gesture⟩ **3** : showing the attitude of one accustomed to command : ARROGANT ⟨the *peremptory* tone caused resentment⟩ — **pe·remp·to·ri·ly** \-t(ə-)rə-lē\ *adv* — **pe·remp·to·ri·ness** \-t(ə-)rē-nəs\ *n*

[1]**pe·ren·ni·al** \pə-'ren-ē-əl\ *adj* **1** : present at all seasons of the year ⟨*perennial* springs⟩ **2** : living for several years usually with new leafy growth produced from the base each year ⟨*perennial* daisies⟩ **3 a** : PERSISTENT 1, CONSTANT **b** : RECURRENT ⟨flooding is a *perennial* problem⟩ — **pe·ren·ni·al·ly** \-ē-ə-lē\ *adv*

[2]**perennial** *n* : a perennial plant

[1]**per·fect** \'pər-fikt\ *adj* **1 a** : being entirely without fault or defect : FLAWLESS **b** : meeting all requirements : ACCURATE, EXACT ⟨a *perfect* circle⟩ ⟨a *perfect* copy⟩ **c** : PURE 3, TOTAL ⟨*perfect* stillness⟩ **d** : [1]COMPLETE 1, WHOLE **2** : of an extreme kind ⟨a *perfect* fool⟩ **3** : of, relating to, or being a verb form in the perfect tense **4** : having both stamens and pistil ⟨a *perfect* flower⟩ [Middle English *perfit* "complete, thoroughly or accurately done," from early French *parfit* (same meaning), from Latin *perfectus* "complete, perfect," derived from *perficere* "to carry out, complete," from *per-* "completely" and *-ficere*, from *facere* "to make, do" — related to ARTIFICIAL, FASHION, SATISFY] — **per·fect·ness** \-fik(t)-nəs\ *n*

[2]**per·fect** \pər-'fekt *also* 'pər-fikt\ *vb* **1** : to make perfect **2** : to bring to final form — **per·fect·er** *n*

[3]**per·fect** \'pər-fikt\ *n* **1** : PERFECT TENSE **2** : a verb form in the perfect tense

per·fect·ible \pər-'fek-tə-bəl *also* 'pər-fik-\ *adj* : capable of improvement or perfection — **per·fect·ibil·i·ty** \pər-,fek-tə-'bil-ət-ē *also* ,pər-fik-\ *n*

per·fec·tion \pər-'fek-shən\ *n* **1** : the quality or state of being perfect **2** : a perfect quality or thing **3** : a degree of accuracy or excellence that cannot be bettered ⟨cooked to *perfection*⟩ **4** : the act or process of perfecting

per·fec·tion·ist \pər-'fek-sh(ə-)nəst\ *n* : a person who is not content with anything less than perfection — **perfectionist** *adj*

per·fect·ly \'pər-fik-(t)lē\ *adv* **1** : in a perfect manner ⟨understand *perfectly*⟩ **2** : QUITE 1, ALTOGETHER ⟨I was *perfectly* willing⟩

perfect number *n* : a whole number that is equal to the sum of all its divisors except itself ⟨28 is a *perfect number* because it is the sum of $1 + 2 + 4 + 7 + 14$⟩

perfect square *n* : a whole number whose square root is a whole number ⟨9 is a *perfect square*⟩

perfect tense *n* : a verb tense that expresses an action or state completed at the time of speaking or at a time spoken of

per·fid·i·ous \(,)pər-'fid-ē-əs\ *adj* : of, relating to, or characterized by perfidy : TREACHEROUS — **per·fid·i·ous·ly** *adv* — **per·fid·i·ous·ness** *n*

per·fi·dy \'pər-fəd-ē\ *n, pl* **-dies** : the quality or state of being faithless or disloyal : TREACHERY

per·fo·rate \'pər-fə-,rāt\ *vb* **-rat·ed; -rat·ing** : to make a hole or series of holes through; *esp* : to make a line of holes to make tearing easy and neat ⟨sheets of stamps are *perforated*⟩ — **per·fo·rate** \ˈpər-f(ə-)rət, -fə-ˌrāt\ *adj* — **per·fo·ra·tor** \-fə-ˌrāt-ər\ *n*

per·fo·ra·tion \ˌpər-fə-ˈrā-shən\ *n* **1** : the act or process of perforating **2** : a hole, pattern, or series of holes made by perforating

per·force \pər-ˈfō(ə)rs, -ˈfȯ(ə)rs\ *adv* : by force of circumstances or of necessity

per·form \pə(r)-ˈfȯ(ə)rm\ *vb* **1 a** : CARRY OUT, DO **b** : ²ACT 4, FUNCTION **2** : to do something requiring special skill **3 a** : to do according to rules or in an established way ⟨*perform* a wedding⟩ **b** : to give a performance of ⟨*perform* a play⟩ — **per·form·able** \-ˈfȯr-mə-bəl\ *adj* — **per·form·er** \-ˈfȯr-mər\ *n*

per·for·mance \pə(r)-ˈfȯr-mən(t)s\ *n* **1 a** : the doing of an action **b** : something accomplished : DEED, FEAT **2 a** : the action of representing a character in a play **b** : a public presentation **3** : the manner in which something performs ⟨an engine's *performance*⟩

¹per·fume \ˈpər-ˌfyüm, (ˌ)pər-ˈfyüm\ *n* **1** : the scent of something usually sweet-smelling **2** : a substance that gives off a pleasant odor; *esp* : a liquid containing fragrant oils (as from flowers) mixed with alcohol and applied to the body to give it a pleasant odor

²per·fume \(ˌ)pər-ˈfyüm, ˈpər-ˌfyüm\ *vb* **-fumed; -fum·ing** : to fill with a pleasing odor (as of flowers)

per·fum·ery \pə(r)-ˈfyüm-(ə-)rē\ *n, pl* **-er·ies 1** : the art or process of making perfume **2** : a place where perfumes are made

per·func·to·ry \pər-ˈfəŋ(k)-t(ə-)rē\ *adj* **1** : done mechanically or carelessly ⟨a *perfunctory* inspection⟩ **2** : lacking in interest or enthusiasm : INDIFFERENT — **per·func·to·ri·ly** \-t(ə-)rə-lē\ *adv* — **per·func·to·ri·ness** \-t(ə-)rē-nəs\ *n*

per·haps \pər-ˈ(h)aps, ˈpraps\ *adv* : possibly but not certainly [from *per* (preposition) "by, according to" and *haps,* plural of *hap* "chance, chance occurrence" — related to HAPPEN, HAPPY, MISHAP]

peri·anth \ˈper-ē-ˌanth\ *n* : the outer part of a flower made up of the calyx and corolla especially when united into one part

peri·car·di·um \ˌper-ə-ˈkärd-ē-əm\ *n, pl* **-dia** \-ē-ə\ : the cone-shaped structure of membrane that encloses the vertebrate heart and the nearby parts of the large arteries and veins leading to or away from it — **peri·car·di·al** \-ē-əl\ *adj*

peri·gee \ˈper-ə-jē\ *n* : the point nearest a planet (as the earth) or other body (as a moon) reached by an object orbiting it — compare APOGEE

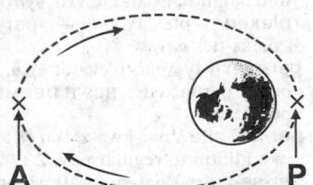

perigee: *P* perigee, *A* apogee

peri·he·lion \ˌper-ə-ˈhēl-yən\ *n* : the point in the path of a heavenly body (as a planet) that is nearest to the sun

per·il \ˈper-əl\ *n* **1** : the state of being in danger of injury, loss, or destruction **2** : something that presents immediate danger ⟨*perils* of the highway⟩ **synonyms** see DANGER

per·il·ous \ˈper-ə-ləs\ *adj* : full of or involving peril — **per·il·ous·ly** *adv* — **per·il·ous·ness** *n*

pe·rim·e·ter \pə-ˈrim-ət-ər\ *n* : the boundary of a shape or area; *also* : the length of such a boundary

pe·ri·od \ˈpir-ē-əd\ *n* **1** : the completion of a cycle, a series of events, or an action **2** : a point . used to mark the end (as of a declarative sentence or an abbreviation) **3 a** : a portion of time marked by some repeating event **b** : the

length of time required for a motion or event to complete a cycle and begin to repeat itself ⟨the *period* of a pendulum⟩ **c** : a single occurrence of menstruation **4 a** : ¹STAGE 4e **b** : a division of geologic time longer than an epoch and included in an era **c** : a stage or portion of time in the history of something ⟨the colonial *period*⟩ **5 a** : one of the divisions of the school day **b** : one of the divisions of the playing time of a game **6** : a series of elements of increasing atomic number as listed in horizontal rows in the periodic table

synonyms PERIOD, ERA, AGE mean a portion of time. PERIOD can be used of any portion of time, no matter how long or short ⟨talked for a *period* of five minutes⟩ ⟨was a farmer for a *period* of twenty years⟩. ERA suggests a period of history noted for new or remarkable events ⟨an *era* of space exploration⟩. AGE suggests a long period of time that is associated with an important person ⟨the *age* of Thomas Jefferson⟩ or an outstanding thing ⟨the atomic *age*⟩.

pe·ri·od·ic \ˌpir-ē-ˈäd-ik\ *adj* **1** : occurring at regular intervals **2** : consisting of or containing a series of repeated stages ⟨*periodic* vibrations⟩

¹pe·ri·od·i·cal \ˌpir-ē-ˈäd-i-kəl\ *adj* **1** : PERIODIC 1 **2** : published at regular intervals — **pe·ri·od·i·cal·ly** \-k(ə-)lē\ *adv*

²periodical *n* : a periodical publication

periodic table *n* : an arrangement of chemical elements in order of atomic number that groups elements with common characteristics in the same area of the table

peri·odon·tal \ˌper-ē-ō-ˈdänt-ᵊl\ *adj* **1** : surrounding or occurring about the teeth **2** : affecting tissues that surround or occur about the teeth ⟨*periodontal* disease⟩

peri·os·te·um \ˌper-ē-ˈäs-tē-əm\ *n, pl* **-tea** \-tē-ə\ : the membrane of connective tissue that covers all bones except at the surfaces in a joint

peri·pa·tet·ic \ˌper-ə-pə-ˈtet-ik\ *adj* : going about from place to place : ITINERANT

¹pe·riph·er·al \pə-ˈrif-(ə-)rəl\ *adj* **1** : of, relating to, located in, or forming a periphery **2** : ¹AUXILIARY, SUPPLEMENTARY ⟨*peripheral* equipment⟩ — **pe·riph·er·al·ly** \-ē\ *adv*

²peripheral *n* : a device connected to a computer to provide communication (as input and output) or extra storage capacity

peripheral nervous system *n* : the part of the nervous system that is outside the central nervous system and is made up of the autonomic nervous system, the spinal nerves, and the cranial nerves except the optic nerve

pe·riph·ery \pə-ˈrif-(ə-)rē\ *n, pl* **-er·ies 1** : the boundary or surface of a body or figure **2** : the outer or outermost part

peri·scope \ˈper-ə-ˌskōp\ *n* : an instrument containing lenses and mirrors by which an observer (as on a submerged submarine) can get a view that would otherwise be blocked — **peri·scop·ic** \ˌper-ə-ˈskäp-ik\ *adj*

per·ish \ˈper-ish\ *vb* : to pass away completely : become destroyed

per·ish·able \ˈper-ish-ə-bəl\ *adj* : likely to spoil or decay ⟨*perishable* fruit⟩ — **perishable** *n*

peri·stal·sis \ˌper-ə-ˈstȯl-səs, -ˈstäl-, -ˈstal-\ *n, pl* **-stal·ses** \-ˌsēz\ : the contracting and expanding movements by which food and waste products of digestion are forced through parts (as the esophagus and intestine) of the digestive system — **peri·stal·tic** \-tik\ *adj*

periscope

\ə\ abut	\au̇\ out	\i\ tip	\ȯ\ saw	\u̇\ foot
\ər\ further	\ch\ chin	\ī\ life	\ȯi\ coin	\y\ yet
\a\ mat	\e\ pet	\j\ job	\th\ thin	\yü\ few
\ā\ take	\ē\ easy	\ŋ\ sing	\th\ this	\yu̇\ cure
\ä\ cot, cart	\g\ go	\ō\ bone	\ü\ food	\zh\ vision

peri·to·ne·um \ˌper-ət-ᵊn-'ē-əm\ *n, pl* **-ne·ums** *or* **-nea** \-'nē-ə\ : the smooth transparent membrane that lines the cavity of the abdomen and encloses the abdominal and pelvic organs

peri·to·ni·tis \ˌper-ət-ᵊn-'īt-əs\ *n* : inflammation of the peritoneum

peri·wig \'per-i-ˌwig\ *n* : WIG

¹per·i·win·kle \'per-i-ˌwiŋ-kəl\ *n* : an evergreen herb that spreads along the ground and has shiny leaves and blue or white flowers [Old English *perwince* "periwinkle vine," from Latin *pervinca* (same meaning)]

²periwinkle *n* **1** : any of various small edible marine snails of coastal regions **2** : the shell of a periwinkle [Old English *pinewincle* "an edible sea snail"]

per·jure \'pər-jər\ *vb* **per·jured; per·jur·ing** \'pərj-(ə-)riŋ\ : to make (oneself) guilty of perjury — **per·jur·er** \'pər-jər-ər\ *n*

per·ju·ry \'pərj-(ə-)rē\ *n, pl* **-ries** : the act or crime of swearing to what one knows is untrue

perk \'pərk\ *vb* **1** : to lift quickly or alertly ⟨the dog *perked* up its ears⟩ **2** : to make fresher in appearance ⟨new paint *perked* up the room⟩ **3** : to become more lively or cheerful — usually used with *up* ⟨we *perked* up at the good news⟩

perky \'pər-kē\ *adj* **perk·i·er; -est** : being lively and cheerful — **perk·i·ness** *n*

per·lite \'pər-ˌlīt\ *n* : a glassy mineral of volcanic origin that when expanded by heat foms a lightweight material capable of absorbing liquids (as water)

¹perm \'pərm\ *n* : ²PERMANENT

²perm *vb* : to give (hair) a permanent

per·ma·frost \'pər-mə-ˌfròst\ *n* : a permanently frozen layer at variable depth below the surface in frigid regions of a planet (as earth)

¹per·ma·nent \'pərm(-ə)-nənt\ *adj* : lasting or intended to last for a very long time : not temporary or changing *synonyms* see LASTING — **per·ma·nence** \-nən(t)s\ *n* — **per·ma·nen·cy** \-nən-sē\ *n* — **per·ma·nent·ly** *adv* — **per·ma·nent·ness** *n*

²permanent *n* : a long-lasting hair wave produced by mechanical and chemical means

permanent magnet *n* : a magnet that retains its magnetism after removal of the magnetizing force

permanent press *n* : the process of treating a fabric chemically to resist wrinkling — **permanent–press** *adj*

permanent tooth *n* : one of the second set of teeth of a mammal that follow the milk teeth, usually last into old age, and in human beings are 32 in number

per·me·abil·i·ty \ˌpər-mē-ə-'bil-ət-ē\ *n* : the quality or state of being permeable

per·me·able \'pər-mē-ə-bəl\ *adj* : having pores or openings that permit liquids or gases to pass through ⟨a *permeable* membrane⟩ ⟨*permeable* limestone⟩

per·me·ate \'pər-mē-ˌāt\ *vb* **-at·ed; -at·ing** **1** : to spread throughout ⟨a room *permeated* with the scent of flowers⟩ **2** : to pass through something which has pores or small openings or is of loose texture : seep through ⟨water *permeates* sand⟩ — **per·me·ation** \ˌpər-mē-'ā-shən\ *n*

Perm·ian \'pər-mē-ən\ *adj* : of, relating to, or being the latest period of the Paleozoic era of geological history or the corresponding system of rocks — see GEOLOGIC TIME table — **Permian** *n*

per·mis·si·ble \pər-'mis-ə-bəl\ *adj* : that may be permitted : ALLOWABLE — **per·mis·si·bil·i·ty** \-ˌmis-ə-'bil-ət-ē\ *n* — **per·mis·si·ble·ness** \-'mis-ə-bəl-nəs\ *n* — **per·mis·si·bly** \-blē\ *adv*

per·mis·sion \pər-'mish-ən\ *n* **1** : the act of permitting **2** : the consent of a person in authority ⟨has *permission* to leave⟩

per·mis·sive \pər-'mis-iv\ *adj* **1** : granting or tending to grant permission : ALLOWING **2** : not forbidden : ALLOWABLE — **per·mis·sive·ly** *adv* — **per·mis·sive·ness** *n*

¹per·mit \pər-'mit\ *vb* **per·mit·ted; per·mit·ting** **1** : to consent to : give permission : ALLOW **2** : to make possible : give an opportunity ⟨if time *permits*⟩ — **per·mit·ter** *n*

²per·mit \'pər-ˌmit, pər-'mit\ *n* : a written statement of permission given by one having authority : LICENSE

per·mu·ta·tion \ˌpər-myù-'tā-shən\ *n* : an ordered arrangement of a set of objects

per·ni·cious \pər-'nish-əs\ *adj* : very destructive or harmful ⟨a *pernicious* disease⟩ — **per·ni·cious·ly** *adv*

pernicious anemia *n* : a severe anemia in which the red blood cells decrease in number and increase in size and which is caused by a reduced ability to absorb vitamin B_{12}

per·o·ra·tion \'per-ər-ˌā-shən, 'pər-\ *n* : the last part of a speech

per·ox·ide \pə-'räk-ˌsīd\ *n* : an oxide containing a high proportion of oxygen; *esp* : HYDROGEN PEROXIDE

¹per·pen·dic·u·lar \ˌpər-pən-'dik-yə-lər\ *adj* **1** : exactly vertical or upright **2** : forming a right angle with each other or with a given line or plane [Middle English *perpendiculer* "exactly upright," from early French *perpendiculer* (same meaning), from Latin *perpendicularis* (same meaning), derived from *per-* "thoroughly" and *pendēre* "to hang" — related to DEPEND, PENDULUM] — **per·pen·dic·u·lar·ly** *adv*

²perpendicular *n* : a perpendicular line

per·pe·trate \'pər-pə-ˌtrāt\ *vb* **-trat·ed; -trat·ing** : to be guilty of doing : COMMIT — **per·pe·tra·tion** \ˌpər-pə-'trā-shən\ *n* — **per·pe·tra·tor** \'pər-pə-ˌtrāt-ər\ *n*

per·pet·u·al \pər-'pech-(ə-)wəl, -'pech-əl\ *adj* **1** : continuing forever : EVERLASTING **2** : occurring continually : CONSTANT — **per·pet·u·al·ly** \-ē-\ *adv*

per·pet·u·ate \pər-'pech-ə-ˌwāt\ *vb* **-at·ed; -at·ing** : to make perpetual or cause to last indefinitely — **per·pet·u·a·tion** \-ˌpech-ə-'wā-shən\ *n* — **per·pet·u·a·tor** \-'pech-ə-ˌwāt-ər\ *n*

per·pe·tu·ity \ˌpər-pə-'t(y)ü-ət-ē\ *n, pl* **-ities** **1** : perpetual existence **2** : endless time : ETERNITY

per·plex \pər-'pleks\ *vb* **1** : to block the understanding of; *esp* : CONFUSE 1a, BEWILDER **2** : to make difficult to understand : COMPLICATE *synonyms* see PUZZLE — **per·plexed** \-'plekst\ *adj* — **per·plexed·ly** \-'plek-səd-lē, -'pleks-tlē\ *adv*

per·plex·i·ty \pər-'plek-sət-ē\ *n, pl* **-ties** **1** : the state of being perplexed : BEWILDERMENT **2** : something that perplexes

per·qui·site \'pər-kwə-zət\ *n* **1** : a privilege or profit made in addition to regular pay **2** : ¹⁰TIP

per·se·cute \'pər-si-ˌkyüt\ *vb* **-cut·ed; -cut·ing** **1** : to treat continually in a way meant to be cruel or harmful; *esp* : to cause to suffer because of belief **2** : ANNOY, PESTER — **per·se·cu·tor** \-ˌkyüt-ər\ *n* — **per·se·cu·to·ry** \-kyü-ˌtōr-ē, -ˌtòr-\ *adj*

per·se·cu·tion \ˌpər-si-'kyü-shən\ *n* **1** : the act or practice of persecuting **2** : the condition of being persecuted

Per·seus \'pər-ˌsüs, -sē-əs\ *n* : a northern group of stars between Taurus and Cassiopeia

per·se·ver·ance \ˌpər-sə-'vir-ən(t)s\ *n* : the action, state, or an instance of persevering

per·se·vere \ˌpər-sə-'vi(ə)r\ *vb* **-vered; -ver·ing** : to keep at something in spite of difficulties, opposition, or discouragement

per·se·ver·ing \ˌpər-sə-'vi(ə)r-iŋ\ *adj* : showing perseverance — **per·se·ver·ing·ly** *adv*

Per·sian \'pər-zhən\ *n* **1** : a native or inhabitant of an-

perpendicular

²perpendicular

cient Persia or modern Iran **2** : the language of the Persians — **Persian** *adj*

Persian cat *n* : any of a breed of domestic cats with a round head, stocky body, and long silky fur

Persian lamb *n* : a pelt that is obtained from a karakul lamb and has very silky tightly curled fur

per·si·flage \'pər-si-ˌfläzh, 'per-\ *n* : silly or lightly joking talk

per·sim·mon \pər-'sim-ən\ *n* **1** : any of a genus of trees with hard fine wood, oblong leaves, and small bell-shaped white flowers **2** : the usually orange fruit of a persimmon that resembles a plum and is edible when fully ripe but usually very bitter when unripe

Persian cat

per·sist \pər-'sist, -'zist\ *vb* **1** : to continue to do something in spite of opposition, warnings, or pleas : PERSEVERE **2** : to last on and on : continue to exist — **per·sist·er** *n*

per·sis·tence \pər-'sis-tən(t)s, -'zis-\ *n* **1** : the act or fact of persisting **2** : the quality of being persistent

per·sis·tent \pər-'sis-tənt, -'zis-\ *adj* **1** : continuing, existing, or acting for a long or longer than usual time ⟨a *persistent* cold⟩ ⟨*persistent* gills⟩ **2** : stubbornly determined — **per·sis·tent·ly** *adv*

per·son \'pər-sᵊn\ *n* **1** : HUMAN BEING, INDIVIDUAL — used in combination especially by those who prefer to avoid *man* in compounds that apply to both sexes ⟨chair*person*⟩ **2** : a character or part in or as if in a play **3** : the body of a human being **4** : reference to the speaker, to one spoken to, or to one spoken of as indicated especially by means of certain pronouns [Middle English *person* "human being," from early French *persone* (same meaning), from Latin *persona* "person, character in a play," originally "an actor's mask"] — **in person** : as one who is or was actually present ⟨the president appeared *in person*⟩ ⟨spoke to her *in person*⟩

per·son·able \'pər-snə-bəl\ *adj* : pleasing in appearance or manner — **per·son·able·ness** *n*

per·son·age \'pər-snij, -ᵊn-ij\ *n* **1** : an important or famous person **2** : a character in a book or play

¹**per·son·al** \'pər-snəl, -ᵊn-əl\ *adj* **1** : of, relating to, or belonging to a person : PRIVATE ⟨*personal* property⟩ **2 a** : done in person **b** : proceeding from or directed to a single person **c** : carried on between individuals directly **3** : relating to the person or body ⟨your *personal* appearance⟩ **4** : closely related to an individual : INTIMATE **5** : indicating grammatical person

²**personal** *n* : a short paragraph or ad in a newspaper relating to personal matters

personal computer *n* : a small general-purpose computer with a microprocessor

personal effects *n pl* : privately owned items (as clothing or jewelry) normally worn or carried on the person

per·son·al·i·ty \ˌpərs-ᵊn-'al-ət-ē, ˌpər-'snal-\ *n, pl* **-ties** **1** : the state of being a person **2** : the whole collection of individual emotions and behavior that make one person different from others : INDIVIDUALITY **3** : an insulting mention of a person ⟨use *personalities* in an argument⟩ **4** : pleasing qualities of character ⟨has lots of *personality*⟩ **5** : a person who is well-known ⟨a television *personality*⟩

per·son·al·ize \'pərs-nə-ˌlīz, -ᵊn-ə-\ *vb* **-ized; -iz·ing** **1** : PERSONIFY 1 **2** : to make personal; *esp* : to mark as belonging to a particular person ⟨*personalized* stationery⟩

per·son·al·ly \'pərs-nə-lē, -ᵊn-ə-\ *adv* **1** : in person ⟨attend to the matter *personally*⟩ **2** : as a person : in personality ⟨*personally* attractive⟩ **3** : for oneself : as far as oneself is concerned ⟨*personally*, I am against it⟩

personal pronoun *n* : a pronoun (as *I, you,* or *they*) used as a substitute for a noun that names a definite person or thing

per·son·al·ty \'pərs-nəl-tē, -ᵊn-əl-\ *n, pl* **-ties** : personal property as distinguished from real estate

per·son·i·fi·ca·tion \pər-ˌsän-ə-fə-'kā-shən\ *n* **1** : the representation of a thing or idea as a person or by the human form **2** : an imaginary being thought of as representing a thing or an idea ⟨Uncle Sam is the *personification* of the U.S.⟩ **3** : a perfect example : EMBODIMENT ⟨you are the very *personification* of generosity⟩

per·son·i·fy \pər-'sän-ə-ˌfī\ *vb* **-fied; -fy·ing** **1** : to think of or represent as a person ⟨*personify* the forces of nature⟩ **2** : to be the perfect example of ⟨she *personified* kindness⟩

per·son·nel \ˌpərs-ᵊn-'el\ *n* : a group of persons employed (as in a public service, a factory, or an office)

¹**per·spec·tive** \pər-'spek-tiv\ *n* **1** : the art or technique of painting or drawing a scene so that objects in it seem to have depth and distance **2** : the relationship in which a subject or its parts are viewed mentally ⟨places the issues in *perspective*⟩ **b** : POINT OF VIEW ⟨from a conservative *perspective*⟩ **3** : the power to understand things in their true relationship to each other ⟨try to keep your *perspective* and not get flustered⟩ **4** : the appearance to the eye of objects in space with respect to their distance and positions in relation to each other

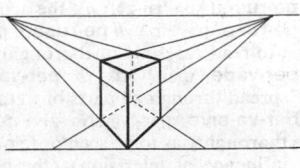

¹perspective 1

²**perspective** *adj* : of, relating to, or seen in perspective

per·spi·ca·cious \ˌpər-spə-'kā-shəs\ *adj* : having or showing keen understanding — **per·spi·ca·cious·ly** *adv* — **per·spi·cac·i·ty** \-'kas-ət-ē\ *n*

per·spic·u·ous \pər-'spik-yə-wəs\ *adj* **1** : plain to the understanding : CLEAR **2** : expressing oneself clearly — **per·spi·cu·ity** \ˌpər-spə-'kyü-ət-ē\ *n* — **per·spic·u·ous·ly** \pər-'spik-yə-wə-slē\ *adv* — **per·spic·u·ous·ness** *n*

per·spi·ra·tion \ˌpər-spə-'rā-shən\ *n* **1** : the act or process of perspiring **2** : a salty fluid given off by the sweat glands : SWEAT

per·spire \pər-'spī(ə)r\ *vb* **per·spired; per·spir·ing** : to give off perspiration : SWEAT

per·suade \pər-'swād\ *vb* **per·suad·ed; per·suad·ing** : to win over to a belief or to a course of action by argument or earnest request — **per·suad·able** \-'swād-ə-bəl\ *adj* — **per·suad·er** *n*

per·sua·si·ble \pər-'swā-zə-bəl, -'swā-sə-\ *adj* : capable of being persuaded

per·sua·sion \pər-'swā-zhən\ *n* **1** : the act of persuading **2** : the power or ability to persuade **3** : the state of being persuaded **4 a** : a way of believing; *esp* : a system of religious beliefs **b** : a group having the same religious beliefs

per·sua·sive \pər-'swā-siv, -ziv\ *adj* : tending to persuade ⟨a *persuasive* argument⟩ — **per·sua·sive·ly** *adv* — **per·sua·sive·ness** *n*

pert \'pərt\ *adj* **1** : IMPUDENT **2** : being trim and chic **3** : VIVACIOUS, LIVELY — **pert·ly** *adv* — **pert·ness** *n*

per·tain \pər-'tān\ *vb* **1** : to belong to a person or thing as a part, quality, or function ⟨duties that *pertain* to an office⟩ **2** : to have reference ⟨books *pertaining* to birds⟩

per·ti·na·cious \ˌpərt-ᵊn-'ā-shəs\ *adj* **1** : holding strongly to an opinion, purpose, or course of action **2** : stubborn-

\ə\ **abut**	\aů\ **out**	\i\ **tip**	\ò\ **saw**	\ů\ **foot**
\ər\ **further**	\ch\ **chin**	\ī\ **life**	\òi\ **coin**	\y\ **yet**
\a\ **mat**	\e\ **pet**	\j\ **job**	\th\ **thin**	\yü\ **few**
\ā\ **take**	\ē\ **easy**	\ŋ\ **sing**	\th\ **this**	\yů\ **cure**
\ä\ **cot, cart**	\g\ **go**	\ō\ **bone**	\ü\ **food**	\zh\ **vision**

ly or annoyingly persistent — **per·ti·na·cious·ly** *adv* — **per·ti·na·cious·ness** *n* — **per·ti·nac·i·ty** \-'as-ət-ē\ *n*

per·ti·nence \'pərt-ᵊn-ən(t)s, 'pərt-nən(t)s\ *n* : the quality or state of being pertinent : RELEVANCE

per·ti·nen·cy \'pərt-ᵊn-ən-sē, 'pərt-nən-sē\ *n* : PERTINENCE

per·ti·nent \'pərt-ᵊn-ənt, 'pərt-nənt\ *adj* : having to do with the matter being thought about or discussed : RELEVANT ⟨a *pertinent* question⟩ — **per·ti·nent·ly** *adv*

per·turb \pər-'tərb\ *vb* : to disturb greatly especially in mind — **per·turb·able** \-'tər-bə-bəl\ *adj*

per·tur·ba·tion \ˌpərt-ər-'bā-shən, ˌpər-ˌtər-\ *n* **1** : the action of perturbing **2** : the state of being perturbed — **per·tur·ba·tion·al** \-shnəl, -shən-ᵊl\ *adj*

per·tus·sis \pər-'təs-əs\ *n* : WHOOPING COUGH

pe·ruke \pə-'rük\ *n* : a kind of wig popular in the 17th and 18th centuries

pe·rus·al \pə-'rü-zəl\ *n* : the action of perusing

pe·ruse \pə-'rüz\ *vb* **pe·rused; pe·rus·ing** : ¹READ 1a; *esp* : to read carefully or thoroughly — **pe·rus·er** *n*

per·vade \pər-'vād\ *vb* **per·vad·ed; per·vad·ing** : to spread through all parts of : PERMEATE

per·va·sive \pər-'vā-siv, -ziv\ *adj* : spread throughout so thoroughly as to be seen or felt everywhere ⟨the *pervasive* influence of television⟩ ⟨the *pervasive* dampness of the mines⟩ — **per·va·sive·ly** *adv* — **per·va·sive·ness** *n*

per·verse \(ˌ)pər-'vərs, 'pər-ˌvərs\ *adj* **1** : morally bad : CORRUPT **2** : stubborn in opposing what is right, reasonable, or accepted : WRONGHEADED **3** : IRRITABLE, CRANKY **4** : marked by perversion : PERVERTED — **per·verse·ly** *adv* — **per·verse·ness** *n*

per·ver·sion \pər-'vər-zhən\ *n* **1 a** : the action of perverting **b** : the state of being perverted **2** : abnormal sexual behavior

per·ver·si·ty \pər-'vər-sət-ē, -stē\ *n, pl* **-ties** : the quality, state, or an instance of being perverse

¹per·vert \pər-'vərt\ *vb* **1** : to cause to turn away from what is good or true or right : CORRUPT **2** : to put to a wrong use **3** : to give a wrong meaning to : MISINTERPRET

²per·vert \'pər-ˌvərt\ *n* : one that is perverted; *esp* : one given to some form of sexual perversion

per·vert·ed \pər-'vərt-əd\ *adj* : marked by perversion

Pe·sach \'pä-ˌsäk\ *n* : PASSOVER

pe·se·ta \pə-'sāt-ə\ *n* **1** : the former basic unit of money of Spain **2** : a coin or bill representing one peseta

pes·ky \'pes-kē\ *adj* **pes·ki·er; -est** : TROUBLESOME 2 — **pes·ki·ly** \-kə-lē\ *adv* — **pes·ki·ness** \-kē-nəs\ *n*

pe·so \'pā-sō\ *n, pl* **pesos** **1** : an old silver coin of Spain or Spanish America **2 a** : the basic unit of money of Argentina, Chile, Colombia, Cuba, Dominican Republic, Mexico, Philippines, and Uruguay **b** : a coin or bill representing one peso

pes·si·mism \'pes-ə-ˌmiz-əm\ *n* **1** : a tending to expect the worst possible outcome **2** : a belief that evil is more common than good in life — **pes·si·mist** \-məst\ *n*

pes·si·mis·tic \ˌpes-ə-'mis-tik\ *adj* : of, relating to, or marked by pessimism : GLOOMY — **pes·si·mis·ti·cal·ly** \-ti-k(ə-)lē\ *adv*

pest \'pest\ *n* **1** : an epidemic disease which causes a large number of deaths; *esp* : ¹PLAGUE 2 **2** : something resembling a pest in destructiveness; *esp* : a plant or animal harmful to human beings or human concerns (as agriculture) **3** : one that pesters or annoys : NUISANCE — **pesty** \'pes-tē\ *adj*

pes·ter \'pes-tər\ *vb* **pes·tered; pes·ter·ing** \-t(ə-)riŋ\ : ANNOY, BOTHER

pest·hole \'pest-ˌhōl\ *n* : a place in which diseases are common

pes·ti·cide \'pes-tə-ˌsīd\ *n* : a substance used to destroy pests — **pes·ti·cid·al** \ˌpes-tə-'sīd-ᵊl\ *adj*

pes·tif·er·ous \pes-'tif-(ə-)rəs\ *adj* **1** : dangerous to society : PERNICIOUS **2** : TROUBLESOME 2

pes·ti·lence \'pes-tə-lən(t)s\ *n* : a contagious or infectious epidemic disease that spreads quickly and is often fatal; *esp* : BUBONIC PLAGUE

pes·ti·lent \'pes-tə-lənt\ *adj* **1** : dangerous or destructive to life : DEADLY ⟨a *pestilent* drug⟩ **2** : harmful or dangerous to society : PERNICIOUS **3** : causing displeasure or annoyance ⟨a *pestilent* child⟩ **4** : INFECTIOUS 1, CONTAGIOUS ⟨a *pestilent* disease⟩

pes·ti·len·tial \ˌpes-tə-'len-chəl\ *adj* : causing or likely to cause pestilence

pes·tle \'pes-əl, 'pes-tᵊl\ *n* : a usually club-shaped tool for pounding or grinding substances in a mortar

pes·to \'pes-tō\ *n* : a sauce made especially of fresh basil, garlic, oil, pine nuts, and grated cheese

pestle with mortar

¹pet \'pet\ *n* **1** : someone given special treatment or consideration ⟨teacher's *pet*⟩ **2** : a tame animal kept for pleasure rather than for use

²pet *adj* **1** : kept or treated as a pet ⟨a *pet* rabbit⟩ **2** : showing fondness ⟨a *pet* name⟩ **3** : ²FAVORITE ⟨my *pet* project⟩

³pet *vb* **pet·ted; pet·ting** **1** : FONDLE, CARESS **2** : to treat as a pet : PAMPER **3** : to engage in embracing, caressing, and kissing

⁴pet *n* : a spell of sulkiness or anger

pet·al \'pet-ᵊl\ *n* : one of the often brightly colored modified leaves that make up the corolla of a flower — **pet·aled** *or* **pet·alled** \-ᵊld\ *adj* — **pet·al·like** \-ᵊl-ˌ(l)īk\ *adj*

pe·ter \'pēt-ər\ *vb* **1** : to slowly come to an end — usually used with *out* ⟨her popularity *petered* out⟩ **2** : to become exhausted — usually used with *out* ⟨raked half the lawn before he *petered* out⟩

Pe·ter \'pēt-ər\ *n* — see BIBLE table

pet·i·ole \'pet-ē-ˌōl\ *n* : the thin stem of a leaf

pe·tite \pə-'tēt\ *adj* : having a small trim figure

pe·tit four \ˌpet-ē-'fō(ə)r, -'fò(ə)r\ *n, pl* **petits fours** *or* **petit fours** \-ē-'fō(ə)rz, -'fò(ə)rz\ : a small frosted cake

¹pe·ti·tion \pə-'tish-ən\ *n* **1** : an earnest request : ENTREATY **2** : a formal written request made to a superior or authority

²petition *vb* **pe·ti·tioned; pe·ti·tion·ing** \-'tish-(ə-)niŋ\ : to make a request to or for; *esp* : to make a formal written request — **pe·ti·tion·er** \-(ə-)nər\ *n*

pet·it jury \ˌpet-ē-\ *n* : a jury of 12 persons for a trial in court

petr- *or* **petri-** *or* **petro-** *combining form* **1** : stone : rock **2** : petroleum ⟨*petro*chemical⟩ [Greek *petros* "stone" and *petra* "rock"]

pe·trel \'pe-trəl, 'pē-\ *n* : any of various seabirds with long wings that fly far from land

Pe·tri dish \ˌpē-trē-\ *n* : a small shallow dish of thin glass or plastic with a loose cover used especially for cultures of bacteria

pet·ri·fac·tion \ˌpe-trə-'fak-shən\ *n* **1** : the process of petrifying or state of being petrified **2** : something that is petrified

Petri dish

pet·ri·fi·ca·tion \ˌpe-trə-fə-'kā-shən\ *n* : PETRIFACTION

pet·ri·fy \'pe-trə-ˌfī\ *vb* **-fied; -fy·ing** **1** : to convert into stone or a stony substance by the penetration of water and the depositing of minerals which were dissolved in the water ⟨*petrified* wood⟩ **2** : to make lifeless or inactive : DEADEN **3** : to paralyze with fear, amazement, or awe : STUN

pet·ro·chem·i·cal \,pe-trō-'kem-i-kəl\ n : a chemical obtained from petroleum or natural gas

pet·rol \'pe-trəl, -,träl\ n, chiefly British : GASOLINE

pe·tro·leum \pə-'trō-lē-əm, -'trōl-yəm\ n : an oily flammable liquid that may vary from almost colorless to black, is obtained from wells drilled in the ground, and is the source of gasoline, kerosene, fuel oils, and other products

petroleum jelly n : a tasteless, odorless, and oily or greasy substance from petroleum that is used especially in ointments and dressings

¹**pet·ti·coat** \'pet-ē-,kōt\ n : a skirt or slip worn under a dress or outer skirt

²**petticoat** adj : of, relating to, or controlled by women : FEMALE ⟨petticoat government⟩

pet·ti·fog \'pet-ē-,fòg, -,fäg\ vb **-fogged; -fog·ging 1** : to engage in legal trickery **2** : to argue about unimportant details : BICKER — **pet·ti·fog·ger** n — **pet·ti·fog·gery** \-,fòg-(ə-)rē, -,fäg-\ n

petting zoo n : a collection of farm animals or gentle exotic animals for children to pet and feed

pet·tish \'pet-ish\ adj : IRRITABLE, PEEVISH — **pet·tish·ly** adv — **pet·tish·ness** n

pet·ty \'pet-ē\ adj **pet·ti·er; -est 1** : lesser in rank or importance : MINOR ⟨a petty prince⟩ **2** : having little or no importance or meaning ⟨petty details⟩ **3** : having or displaying a mean narrow-minded attitude : SMALL-MINDED [Middle English pety "small, minor," an altered form of petit (same meaning), from early French petit "small"] — **pet·ti·ly** \'pet-ᵊl-ē\ adv — **pet·ti·ness** \'pet-ē-nəs\ n

petty cash n : a small amount of money kept on hand in an office to pay for minor items

petty officer n : an officer in the Navy or Coast Guard appointed from among enlisted personnel

petty officer first class n : a naval petty officer with a rank just below that of chief petty officer

petty officer second class n : a naval petty officer with a rank just below that of petty officer first class

petty officer third class n : a naval petty officer with a rank just below that of petty officer second class

pet·u·lance \'pech-ə-lən(t)s\ n : the quality or state of being petulant

pet·u·lant \'pech-ə-lənt\ adj : marked by displays of rudeness or ill temper — **pet·u·lant·ly** adv

pe·tu·nia \pi-'t(y)ün-yə\ n : any of a genus of tropical South American herbs of the nightshade family widely grown for their showy funnel-shaped flowers

pew \'pyü\ n : one of the benches with backs and sometimes doors set in rows in a church

pe·wee \'pē-wē\ n : any of various small grayish or greenish brown birds that eat flying insects

pew·ter \'pyüt-ər\ n **1** : any of various metallic substances made mostly of tin; esp : a dull metallic substance containing lead formerly used for utensils **2** : utensils made of pewter — **pewter** adj

pew

pey·o·te \pā-'ōt-ē\ n **1** : a drug containing mescaline that causes hallucinations and is obtained from the dried round and flattened tops of a small spineless cactus of the southwestern U.S. and Mexico **2** : the cactus from which peyote is obtained — called also mescal

PG \'pē-'jē\ trademark — used to certify that a motion picture is of such a nature that persons of all ages may be admitted but parental guidance is suggested

PG–13 \,pē-,jē-,thər(t)-'tēn\ trademark — used to certify that a motion picture is of such a nature that persons of all ages may be admitted but parental guidance is suggested especially for children under 13 years of age

pH \(')pē-'āch\ n : a number used in expressing acidity or alkalinity on a scale whose values run from 0 to 14 with 7 representing neutrality, numbers less than 7 increasing acidity, and numbers greater than 7 increasing alkalinity; also : the condition represented by such a number

phage \'fāj also 'fäzh\ n : BACTERIOPHAGE

phago·cyte \'fag-ə-,sīt\ n : a cell (as a white blood cell) that takes in and breaks down foreign material (as bacteria) and waste

pha·lanx \'fā-,laŋ(k)s\ n, pl **pha·lanx·es** or **pha·lan·ges** \fə-'lan-(,)jēz, fā-\ **1** : a body of heavily armed infantry of ancient Greece **2** pl phalanges : one of the bones of a finger or toe of a vertebrate

phal·a·rope \'fal-ə-,rōp\ n : any of various small shorebirds that resemble sandpipers but have thicker toes and are good swimmers

phal·lus \'fal-əs\ n, pl **phal·li** \'fal-,ī, -,ē\ or **phal·lus·es 1** : a symbol or likeness of the male sex organ **2** : PENIS — **phal·lic** \'fal-ik\ adj

Phan·er·o·zo·ic \,fan-ə-rə-'zō-ik\ adj : of, relating to, or being an eon of geological history that is made up of the Paleozoic, Mesozoic, and Cenozoic eras or the corresponding systems of rocks — see GEOLOGIC TIME table — **Phanerozoic** n

phan·tasm \'fan-,taz-əm\ n **1** : a misleading image or appearance (as a mirage) : ILLUSION **2** : GHOST, SPECTER **3** : a product of the imagination : FANTASY — **phan·tas·mal** \fan-'taz-məl\ adj

phantasy variant of FANTASY

¹**phan·tom** \'fant-əm\ n : something (as a ghost) that seems to be there but is not real : APPARITION

²**phantom** adj **1** : suggesting or being a phantom **2** : existing in name only : not real : FICTITIOUS ⟨phantom voters⟩

pha·raoh \'fe(ə)r-ō, 'fa(ə)r-; 'fā-rō\ n, often cap : a ruler of ancient Egypt [Old English pharao "pharaoh," from Latin pharaon-, pharao (same meaning), from Greek pharaō (same meaning), from Hebrew par'ōh "pharaoh," of Egyptian origin]

¹**phar·ma·ceu·ti·cal** \,fär-mə-'süt-i-kəl\ adj : of, relating to, or involved in pharmacy or the manufacture and sale of medicinal drugs ⟨a pharmaceutical company⟩ — **phar·ma·ceu·ti·cal·ly** \-i-k(ə-)lē\ adv

²**pharmaceutical** n : a drug or preparation used in medicine

phar·ma·cist \'fär-mə-səst\ n : one trained in pharmacy

phar·ma·col·o·gist \,fär-mə-'käl-ə-jəst\ n : a person who specializes in pharmacology

phar·ma·col·o·gy \,fär-mə-'käl-ə-jē\ n **1** : the study of drugs, their composition, effects, and use in medicine **2** : the properties and reactions of drugs especially with relation to their medical value — **phar·ma·co·log·i·cal** \-kə-'läj-i-kəl\ also **phar·ma·co·log·ic** \-'läj-ik\ adj — **phar·ma·co·log·i·cal·ly** \-i-k(ə-)lē\ adv

phar·ma·co·poe·ia also **phar·ma·co·pe·ia** \,fär-mə-kə-'pē-(y)ə\ n **1** : a book describing drugs, chemicals, and preparations used in medicine **2** : a collection or stock of medicinal drugs

phar·ma·cy \'fär-mə-sē\ n, pl **-cies 1** : the art, practice, or profession of preparing drugs according to a doctor's prescription **2 a** : a place where medicines are made or distributed **b** : DRUGSTORE

\ə\ abut	\aú\ out	\i\ tip	\ò\ saw	\ù\ foot
\ər\ further	\ch\ chin	\ī\ life	\òi\ coin	\y\ yet
\a\ mat	\e\ pet	\j\ job	\th\ thin	\yü\ few
\ā\ take	\ē\ easy	\ŋ\ sing	\th\ this	\yù\ cure
\ä\ cot, cart	\g\ go	\ō\ bone	\ü\ food	\zh\ vision

pha·ryn·geal \ˌfar-ən-ˈjē-əl, fə-ˈrin-j(ē-)əl\ *adj* : relating to, located in, or produced in the region of the pharynx

phar·ynx \ˈfar-iŋ(k)s\ *n, pl* **pha·ryn·ges** \fə-ˈrin-(ˌ)jēz\ *also* **phar·ynx·es** : a tube extending from the back of the nasal cavity and mouth to the esophagus in vertebrate animals that is the passage through which air passes to the larynx and food to the esophagus

¹**phase** \ˈfāz\ *n* **1** : a particular appearance or state in a repeating series of changes ⟨*phases* of the moon⟩ **2** : a step or part in a series of events or actions : STAGE **3** : a particular part or feature (as of an activity, situation, or a subject being considered) : ASPECT **4** : a physically different portion or kind of matter present in a mixed system ⟨the three *phases* ice, water, and steam⟩

²**phase** *vb* **phased; phas·ing 1** : to do in steps according to a plan **2** : to introduce in stages — usually used with *in* ⟨*phase* in new models⟩

phase out *vb* : to discontinue doing, producing, or using ⟨*phasing out* old machinery⟩

pheas·ant \ˈfez-ᵊnt\ *n, pl* **pheasant** *or* **pheasants** : any of numerous large long-tailed brightly colored birds that are related to the domestic chicken and many of which are raised as ornamental or game birds

phe·no·bar·bi·tal \ˌfē-nō-ˈbär-bə-ˌtȯl\ *n* : a drug that is a barbiturate used to calm one down and cause sleep

phe·nol \ˈfē-ˌnȯl, -ˌnȯl; fi-ˈnȯl, -ˈnȯl\ *n* : a white poisonous acidic compound present in tars from coal and wood that when dissolved to make a weak liquid mixture is used as a disinfectant — **phe·no·lic** \fi-ˈnō-lik, -ˈnäl-ik\ *adj*

phe·nol·phtha·lein \ˌfēn-ᵊl-ˈthal-ē-ən, -ˈthal-ˌēn, -ˈthāl-\ *n* : a white or yellowish white compound used as a laxative and as an acid-base indicator because its solution is brilliant red in alkalies and clear in acids

phe·nom·e·nal \fi-ˈnäm-ən-ᵊl\ *adj* **1** : of, relating to, or being a phenomenon **2** : very remarkable : EXTRAORDINARY ⟨a *phenomenal* memory⟩ — **phe·nom·e·nal·ly** \-ᵊl-ē\ *adv*

phe·nom·e·non \fi-ˈnäm-ə-ˌnän, -nən\ *n, pl* **-na** \-nə, -ˌnä\ *or* **-nons 1** *pl* **phenomena** : an observable fact or event **2** : a fact, feature, or event of scientific interest **3 a** : a rare or important fact or event **b** *pl* **phenomenons** : an exceptional, unusual, or abnormal person or thing

phe·no·type \ˈfē-nə-ˌtīp\ *n* : the visible characteristics of a plant or animal that result from the combined effects of the genes and the environment — **phe·no·typ·ic** \ˌfē-nə-ˈtip-ik\ *adj*

phe·nyl·ke·ton·uria \ˌfen-ᵊl-ˌkēt-ᵊn-ˈ(y)ùr-ē-ə, ˌfēn-\ *n* : an inherited disease of human beings that is marked by the inability to break down and process a certain chemical in the body and may cause severe brain damage if not treated properly

phen·yl·thio·car·ba·mide \ˌfen-ᵊl-ˌthī-ō-ˈkär-bə-ˌmīd\ *n* : a compound that is extremely bitter or tasteless depending on the presence or absence of a single dominant gene in the taster — called also *PTC*

pher·o·mone \ˈfer-ə-ˌmōn\ *n* : a chemical substance (as a scent) that is produced by an animal and serves as a signal to other individuals of the same species to engage in some kind of behavior (as mating)

phi \ˈfī\ *n* : the 21st letter of the Greek alphabet — Φ or φ

phi·al \ˈfī(-ə)l\ *n* : VIAL

phi·lan·der \fə-ˈlan-dər\ *vb* **phi·lan·dered; phi·lan·der·ing** \-d(ə-)riŋ\ : to be sexually unfaithful to one's wife — **phi·lan·der·er** \-dər-ər\ *n*

phil·an·throp·ic \ˌfil-ən-ˈthräp-ik\ *adj* : of, relating to, or devoted to philanthropy : CHARITABLE, BENEVOLENT — **phil·an·throp·i·cal** \-ˈthräp-i-kəl\ *adj*

phi·lan·thro·py \fə-ˈlan(t)-thrə-pē\ *n, pl* **-pies 1** : a spirit of goodwill toward all people especially when expressed in active efforts to help others **2** : a charitable act or gift **3** : an organization which distributes or is supported by

charitable contributions — **phi·lan·thro·pist** \-pəst\ *n*

phi·lat·e·list \fə-ˈlat-ᵊl-əst\ *n* : someone who collects or studies postage stamps

phi·lat·e·ly \fə-ˈlat-ᵊl-ē\ *n* : the collection and study of postage stamps — **phil·a·tel·ic** \ˌfil-ə-ˈtel-ik\ *adj*

¹**-phile** \ˌfīl\ *n combining form* : one that loves or is strongly attracted to ⟨audio*phile*⟩ [from Greek *-philos* "loving"]

²**-phile** *adj combining form* : being strongly attracted to

Phi·le·mon \fə-ˈlē-mən, fī-\ *n* — see BIBLE table

phil·har·mon·ic \ˌfil-ər-ˈmän-ik, ˌfil-(ˌ)(h)är-\ *n* : SYMPHONY ORCHESTRA

Phi·lip·pi·ans \fə-ˈlip-ē-ənz\ *n* — see BIBLE table

Phi·lis·tine \ˈfil-ə-ˌstēn; fə-ˈlis-tən, -ˌtēn\ *n* **1** : a member of an ancient race that lived in the coastal regions of Palestine **2** *often not cap* **a** : a person who dislikes or is indifferent to art and cultural activities and whose only interest is in making money **b** : a person who lacks taste or knowledge — **philistine** *adj, often cap*

philo·den·dron \ˌfil-ə-ˈden-drən\ *n, pl* **-drons** *also* **-dra** \-drə\ : any of several plants of the arum family that are often grown for their showy usually shiny leaves

phi·lol·o·gy \fə-ˈläl-ə-jē\ *n* : the study of language and especially of historical development in languages — **phil·o·log·i·cal** \ˌfil-ə-ˈläj-i-kəl\ *adj* — **phi·lol·o·gist** \fə-ˈläl-ə-jəst\ *n*

phi·los·o·pher \fə-ˈläs-(ə-)fər\ *n* **1 a** : a person who seeks wisdom or enlightenment : SCHOLAR, THINKER **b** : a student of philosophy **2** : a person who is calm and patient when faced with trouble

philosopher's stone *n* **1** : an imaginary stone, substance, or mixture believed by alchemists to have the power to change other metals into gold **2** : an elusive or imaginary key to success

philo·soph·i·cal \ˌfil-ə-ˈsäf-i-kəl\ *also* **philo·soph·ic** \-ik\ *adj* **1** : of, relating to, or based on philosophy **2** : characterized by the attitude of a philosopher; *esp* : calm and patient when faced with trouble — **philo·soph·i·cal·ly** \-i-k(ə-)lē\ *adv*

phi·los·o·phize \fə-ˈläs-ə-ˌfīz\ *vb* **-phized; -phiz·ing 1** : to think like a philosopher **2** : to talk about life as if one were a philosopher — **phi·los·o·phiz·er** *n*

phi·los·o·phy \fə-ˈläs-(ə-)fē\ *n, pl* **-phies 1** : the study of the basic ideas about knowledge, truth, right and wrong, religion, and the nature and meaning of life **2** : the philosophical teachings or principles of a person or group ⟨Greek *philosophy*⟩ **3** : the general principles of a field of study or activity ⟨the *philosophy* of history⟩ **4** : someone's basic beliefs about the way people should live

phish·ing \ˈfish-iŋ\ *n* : a scam by which an e-mail user is fooled into revealing personal information — **phish·er** \-ər\ *n*

phle·bot·o·my \fli-ˈbät-ə-mē\ *n* : the removal of blood from a vein chiefly for transfusion or diagnosis and widely used in the past to treat many types of disease but now limited to the treatment of only a few specific conditions

phlegm \ˈflem\ *n* **1** : thick mucus produced in abnormal quantity in the respiratory passages **2 a** : cold indifference **b** : calm fortitude — **phlegmy** \ˈflem-ē\ *adj*

phleg·mat·ic \fleg-ˈmat-ik\ *adj* : not easily excited : slow to respond [from earlier *phlegm* "one of the four body fluids once believed to affect a person's health," from Middle English *fleume* (same meaning), from early French *fleume* (same meaning), from Latin *phlegma* (same meaning), from Greek *phlegma* "flame, phlegm" — see *Word History* at HUMOR] — **phleg·mat·i·cal·ly** \-i-k(ə-)lē\ *adv*

phlo·em \ˈflō-ˌem\ *n* : a tissue of higher plants that contains sieve tubes serving to carry dissolved food material and that lies mostly outside the cambium — compare XYLEM

phlox \'fläks\ *n, pl* **phlox** *or* **phlox-es** : any of a genus of American herbs widely grown for their showy clusters of usually white, pink, or purplish flowers

phlox

-phobe \,fōb\ *n combining form* : one fearing or disliking [from Greek *-phobos* "fearing"] — **-pho-bic** \'fō-bik\ *adj combining form*

pho·bia \'fō-bē-ə\ *n* : an unreasonable, abnormal, and lasting fear of something

phoe·be \'fē-bē\ *n* : any of several American flycatchers; *esp* : one of the eastern U.S. that has a slight crest and is plain grayish brown above and yellowish white below

Phoe·ni·cian \fi-'nish-ən, -'nē-shən\ *n* **1** : a person born or living in ancient Phoenicia **2** : the Semitic language of ancient Phoenicia — **Phoenician** *adj*

phoe·nix \'fē-niks\ *n* : a legendary bird which was thought to live for 500 years, burn itself to death, and then rise newborn from the ashes

phon- *or* **phono-** *combining form* : sound : voice : speech ⟨*phonic*⟩ ⟨*phonograph*⟩ [from Greek *phōnē* "voice, sound"]

pho·na·tion \fō-'nā-shən\ *n* : the act or process of producing speech sounds — **pho·nate** \'fō-,nāt\ *vb*

1phone \'fōn\ *n* **1** : HEADPHONE **2** : **1**TELEPHONE **3** : SMARTPHONE

2phone *vb* **phoned; phon·ing** : **2**TELEPHONE

-phone \,fōn\ *n combining form* : sound ⟨homo*phone*⟩ — often in names of musical instruments and sound-sending devices ⟨radio*phone*⟩ ⟨xylo*phone*⟩ [from Greek *phōnē* "voice, sound"]

pho·neme \'fō-,nēm\ *n* : one of the smallest units of speech that distinguishes one utterance from another ⟨\n\ and \t\ in "pin" and "pit" are different *phonemes*⟩

pho·ne·mic \fə-'nē-mik\ *adj* **1** : of, relating to, or having the characteristics of a phoneme **2** : being different phonemes — **pho·ne·mi·cal·ly** \-mi-k(ə-)lē\ *adv*

pho·net·ic \fə-'net-ik\ *adj* **1 a** : of or relating to spoken language or speech sounds ⟨*phonetic* differences between Old English and Modern English⟩ **b** : of or relating to phonetics **2** : representing speech sounds ⟨*phonetic* spelling⟩ [from modern Latin *phoneticus* "relating to speech sounds," from Greek *phōnētikos* (same meaning), derived from *phōnē* "voice, sound" — related to EUPHONY, SYMPHONY] — **pho·net·i·cal·ly** \-i-k(ə-)lē\ *adv*

pho·net·ics \fə-'net-iks\ *n* : the study and classification of speech sounds — **pho·ne·ti·cian** \,fō-nə-'tish-ən\ *n*

pho·nic \'fän-ik *also* 'fō-nik\ *adj* **1** : of, relating to, or producing sound **2** : of or relating to speech sounds or to phonics — **pho·ni·cal·ly** \-(ə-)lē\ *adv*

phon·ics \'fän-iks\ *n* : a method of teaching beginners to read and pronounce words by learning the characteristic sounds of letters, letter groups, and especially syllables

pho·no·graph \'fō-nə-,graf\ *n* : an instrument that reproduces sound recorded on a grooved disk — **pho·no·graph·ic** \,fō-nə-'graf-ik\ *adj* — **pho·no·graph·i·cal·ly** \-i-k(ə-)lē\ *adv*

1pho·ny *also* **pho·ney** \'fō-nē\ *adj* **pho·ni·er; -est** : not genuine or real: as **a** (1) : intended to deceive or mislead (2) : **2**COUNTERFEIT 1 ⟨a *phony* $10 bill⟩ **b** : causing suspicion : probably dishonest ⟨sounds like a *phony* excuse to me⟩ **c** : FICTITIOUS, FALSE ⟨gave a *phony* name to the police⟩ — **pho·ni·ness** *n*

2phony *also* **phoney** *n, pl* **phonies** *also* **phoneys** : a phony person or thing

phoo·ey \'fü-ē\ *interj* — used to express disapproval or disgust

phos·phate \'fäs-,fāt\ *n* **1** : a salt of a phosphoric acid **2** : a drink made of carbonated water and fruit syrup with a little phosphoric acid added for tang

phos·pho·lip·id \,fäs-fō-'lip-əd\ *n* : a phosphorus-containing fatty substance that forms the main structural part of a cell membrane

phos·phor \'fäs-fər, -,fò(ə)r\ *n* : a substance exhibiting phosphorescence

phos·pho·res·cence \,fäs-fə-'res-ᵊn(t)s\ *n* **1** : a light given off at low temperatures that is caused by the absorption of radiations (as X-rays or ultraviolet light) and continuing for a noticeable time after these radiations have stopped **2** : an enduring light given off with little heat

phos·pho·res·cent \,fäs-fə-'res-ᵊnt\ *adj* : exhibiting phosphorescence

phos·phor·ic acid \fäs-,fòr-ik-, -,fär-\ *n* : any of several oxygen-containing acids of phosphorus

phos·pho·rus \'fäs-f(ə)rəs\ *n* **1** : a phosphorescent substance; *esp* : one that glows in the dark **2** : a nonmetallic element that occurs widely especially as phosphates — see ELEMENT table — **phos·phor·ic** \fäs-'fòr-ik, -'fär-\ *adj* — **phos·pho·rous** \'fäs-f(ə-)rəs; fäs-'fōr-əs, -'fòr-\ *adj*

phot- *or* **photo-** *combining form* **1** : light ⟨*photon*⟩ ⟨*photography*⟩ **2** : photograph : photographic ⟨*photocopy*⟩ **3** : photoelectric ⟨*photocell*⟩ [from Greek *phot-, phos* "light"]

1pho·to \'fōt-ō\ *n, pl* **photos** : **1**PHOTOGRAPH

2photo *vb* : **2**PHOTOGRAPH

3photo *adj* : PHOTOGRAPHIC 1

pho·to·cell \'fōt-ō-,sel\ *n* : PHOTOELECTRIC CELL

pho·to·copy \'fōt-ə-,käp-ē\ *n* : a copy of usually printed material made using a process in which an image is formed by the action of light on an electrically charged surface — **photocopy** *vb*

pho·to·elec·tric \,fōt-ō-i-'lek-trik\ *adj* : involving, relating to, or using any of various electrical effects due to the action of radiation (as light) on matter

photoelectric cell *n* : a device in which variations of light are converted into corresponding variations in an electric current

photoelectric effect *n* : the giving off of free electrons from a metal surface when light strikes it

photo finish *n* **1** : a finish of a race in which contestants are so close that a photograph of them crossing the finish line has to be examined to decide the winner **2** : a close contest (as in an election)

pho·to·gen·ic \,fōt-ə-'jen-ik, -'jēn-\ *adj* : suitable for being photographed : likely to photograph well ⟨a *photogenic* child⟩ — **pho·to·ge·ni·cal·ly** \-i-k(ə-)lē\ *adv*

1pho·to·graph \'fōt-ə-,graf\ *n* : a picture obtained by photography

2photograph *vb* **1** : to take a photograph of **2** : to take photographs **3** : to be photographed — **pho·tog·ra·pher** \fə-'täg-rə-fər\ *n*

pho·to·graph·ic \,fōt-ə-'graf-ik\ *adj* **1** : relating to, obtained by, or used in photography ⟨*photographic* supplies⟩ **2** : capable of remembering details exactly ⟨a *photographic* memory⟩ — **pho·to·graph·i·cal·ly** \-i-k(ə-)lē\ *adv*

pho·tog·ra·phy \fə-'täg-rə-fē\ *n* : the art or process of making pictures by means of a camera that directs the image of an object onto a surface (as film) that is sensitive to light

pho·to·mi·cro·graph \,fōt-ə-'mī-krə-,graf\ *n* : a photograph of a microscope image

\ə\ **abut**		\au̇\ **out**	\i\ **tip**	\ò\ **saw**	\u̇\ **foot**
\ər\ **further**		\ch\ **chin**	\ī\ **life**	\òi\ **coin**	\y\ **yet**
\a\ **mat**		\e\ **pet**	\j\ **job**	\th\ **thin**	\yü\ **few**
\ā\ **take**		\ē\ **easy**	\ŋ\ **sing**	\t͟h\ **this**	\yu̇\ **cure**
\ä\ **cot, cart**		\g\ **go**	\ō\ **bone**	\ü\ **food**	\zh\ **vision**

pho·ton \'fō-ˌtän\ *n* : a tiny particle or bundle of electro-magnetic radiation

pho·to·pe·ri·od \ˌfōt-ō-'pir-ē-əd\ *n* : a recurring cycle of light and dark periods as it affects the growth and functioning of a plant or animal

pho·to·play \'fōt-ō-ˌplā\ *n* : MOVIE 2a

pho·to·shop \'fōt-(ˌ)ō-ˌshäp\ *vb* **-shopped; -shop·ping** *often cap* : to alter an image with computer software

pho·to·sphere \'fōt-ə-ˌsfi(ə)r\ *n* : the shining surface of the sun or a star — **pho·to·spher·ic** \ˌfōt-ə-'sfir-ik, -'sfer-\ *adj*

pho·to·syn·the·sis \ˌfōt-ə-'sin(t)-thə-səs\ *n* : the process by which plants and some bacteria and protists that contain chlorophyll make carbohydrates from water and from carbon dioxide in the air in the presence of light — **pho·to·syn·thet·ic** \-sin-'thet-ik\ *adj*

pho·to·tax·is \ˌfōt-ə-'tak-səs\ *n* : a movement of a living thing that is made in response to light

pho·tot·ro·pism \fō-'tä-trə-ˌpiz-əm\ *n* : a movement or growing in a particular direction that is made by a living thing in response to light — **pho·to·tro·pic** \ˌfōt-ə-'träp-ik\ *adj*

phrag·mi·tes \frag-'mī-ˌtēz\ *n* : any of various tall reeds with large feathery clusters of flowers

¹phrase \'frāz\ *n* **1** : a brief expression; *esp* : one commonly used **2** : a small unit of a musical passage usually several measures long **3** : a group of two or more words that express a single idea but do not form a complete sentence ⟨"out the door" in "they ran out the door" is a *phrase*⟩ — **phras·al** \'frā-zəl\ *adj* — **phras·al·ly** \-zə-lē\ *adv*

²phrase *vb* **phrased; phras·ing 1** : to express in words **2** : to divide into musical phrases

phrase·ol·o·gy \ˌfrā-zē-'äl-ə-jē, frā-'zäl-\ *n* **1** : manner of speaking and writing : STYLE **2** : choice of words

phras·ing \'frā-ziŋ\ *n* **1** : PHRASEOLOGY 1 **2** : the act, method, or result of grouping notes into musical phrases

phy·lac·tery \fə-'lak-t(ə-)rē\ *n, pl* **-ter·ies 1** : either of two small square leather boxes containing scripture passages on slips of paper that are traditionally worn on the left arm and the head by Jewish men during morning prayers **2** : AMULET

phy·log·e·ny \fī-'läj-ə-nē\ *n, pl* **-nies** : the development of a group of related living things by evolution over a long period of time in contrast to the development of a particular individual from its first immature stage to an adult

phylactery 1

phy·lum \'fī-ləm\ *n, pl* **phy·la** \-lə\ : a group of animals or in some classifications plants sharing one or more major characteristics that set them apart from all other animals or plants and forming one of the main categories in biological classification that ranks above the class and below the kingdom — compare DIVISION 8

phys ed \'fiz-'ed\ *n* : PHYSICAL EDUCATION

phys·ic \'fiz-ik\ *n* : a remedy for disease; *esp* : a strong laxative

phys·i·cal \'fiz-i-kəl\ *adj* **1 a** : having material existence **b** : of or relating to material things **2 a** : of or relating to natural science **b** : of or relating to physics **3** : of or relating to the body : BODILY — **phys·i·cal·ly** \-k(ə-)lē\ *adv*

physical education *n* : instruction in the care and development of the body

physical examination *n* : an examination of the bodily functions and condition of a person

physical geography *n* : a branch of geography that deals with the physical features and changes of the earth

physical science *n* : any of the natural sciences (as physics, geology, and astronomy) that deal primarily with nonliving materials

physical therapist *n* : a person who is a specialist in physical therapy

physical therapy *n* : the treatment of disease, injury, or disability especially by massage, exercise, water, or heat

phy·si·cian \fə-'zish-ən\ *n* : a specialist in healing human diseases; *esp* : one educated and licensed to practice medicine

phys·i·cist \'fiz-(ə-)səst\ *n* : a specialist in physics

phys·ics \'fiz-iks\ *n* **1** : a science that deals with matter and energy and their actions upon each other in the fields of mechanics, heat, light, electricity, sound, and the atomic nucleus **2** : physical composition, characteristics, or processes ⟨the *physics* of sound⟩

phys·iog·no·my \ˌfiz-ē-'ä(g)-nə-mē\ *n, pl* **-mies** : facial features or expression thought to reveal qualities of mind or character

phys·iog·ra·phy \ˌfiz-ē-'äg-rə-fē\ *n* : a branch of geography that deals with the exterior features and changes of the earth — **phys·iog·ra·pher** \-fər\ *n* — **phys·io·graph·ic** \ˌfiz-ē-ō-'graf-ik\ *adj*

phys·i·o·log·i·cal \ˌfiz-ē-ə-'läj-i-kəl\ *or* **phys·i·o·log·ic** \-'läj-ik\ *adj* **1** : of or relating to physiology **2** : characteristic of healthy or normal functioning of the body — **phys·i·o·log·i·cal·ly** \-i-k(ə-)lē\ *adv*

phys·i·ol·o·gist \ˌfiz-ē-'äl-ə-jəst\ *n* : a specialist in physiology

phys·i·ol·o·gy \ˌfiz-ē-'äl-ə-jē\ *n* **1** : a branch of biology dealing with the processes and activities by which life is carried on and which are special features of the functioning of living things, tissues, and cells **2** : the life processes and activities of a living thing or any of its parts or of a particular bodily process

phys·io·ther·a·py \ˌfiz-ē-ō-'ther-ə-pē\ *n* : PHYSICAL THERAPY

phy·sique \fə-'zēk\ *n* : the build of a person's body

-phyte \ˌfīt\ *n combining form* : plant having a (specified) characteristic or habitat ⟨sporo*phyte*⟩ [from Greek *phyton* "plant"]

phy·to·plank·ton \ˌfī-tō-'plaŋ(k)-tən, -ˌtän\ *n* : plankton that is composed of plants

pi \'pī\ *n, pl* **pis** \'pīz\ **1** : the 16th letter of the Greek alphabet — Π or π **2 a** : the symbol π representing the ratio of the circumference of a circle to its diameter **b** : the ratio itself having a value of approximately 3.1416

pi·a·nis·si·mo \ˌpē-ə-'nis-ə-ˌmō\ *adv or adj* : very softly — used as a direction in music

¹pi·a·no \pē-'än-ō\ *adv or adj* : in a soft or quiet manner — used as a direction in music

²pi·ano \pē-'an-ō\ *n, pl* **pianos** : a musical instrument consisting of a large frame holding steel wire strings that sound when struck by felt-covered hammers which are operated from a keyboard [from Italian *piano* "a keyboard musical instrument," a shortened form of *pianoforte*, from *piano* "soft" and *forte* "loud"; so called because, unlike earlier keyboard instruments, it could be played with varying degrees of loudness] — **pi·a·nist** \pē-'an-əst, 'pē-ə-nəst\ *n*

²piano

pi·ano·forte \pē-'an-ə-ˌfō(ə)rt, -ˌfó(ə)rt, -ˌfört-ē\ *n* : ²PIANO

pi·as·tre \pē-'as-tər, -'äs-\ *n* : a basic unit of money equal to ¹⁄₁₀₀ Egyptian, Lebanese, or Syrian pound

pi·az·za \pē-'az-ə, *sense 1 is usually* -'at-sə, -'ät-\ *n, pl* **piaz-**

zas *or* **pi·az·ze** \-'at-sā, -'ät-\ **1** *pl piazze* : an open square especially in an Italian town : PLAZA **2 a** : a long hall with an arched roof **b** *dialect* : VERANDA, PORCH

pi·broch \'pē-,bräk, -,bräk\ *n* : a set of variations for the Scottish bagpipe

pi·ca \'pī-kə\ *n* : a typewriter type providing 10 characters to the inch

pic·a·dor \'pik-ə-,dò(ə)r\ *n, pl* **picadors** \-,dò(ə)rz\ *or* **pic·a·do·res** \,pik-ə-'dòr-ēz, -'dòr-\ : a rider on horseback in a bullfight who jabs the bull with a lance

pic·a·resque \,pik-ə-'resk, ,pē-kə-\ *adj* : of, relating to, or being a type of fiction which presents the adventures of a usually rascally character ⟨a *picaresque* novel⟩

pic·a·yune \,pik-ē-'(y)ün\ *adj* : of little value : PALTRY; *also* : PETTY 3

pic·ca·lil·li \,pik-ə-'lil-ē\ *n* : a spicy relish of chopped vegetables

pic·co·lo \'pik-ə-,lō\ *n, pl* **-los** : a small shrill flute [from Italian *piccolo* "piccolo," a shortened form of *piccolo flauto* "little flute"] — **pic·co·lo·ist** \-əst\ *n*

¹**pick** \'pik\ *vb* **1** : to strike, pierce, or break up with a pointed tool **2 a** : to remove matter from bit by bit by or as if by plucking ⟨*picked* the bone clean⟩ **b** : to gather by plucking ⟨*pick* berries⟩ **c** : to pluck with a pick or with the fingers ⟨*pick* a guitar⟩ **3 a** : ¹SELECT, CHOOSE ⟨*pick* out a dress⟩ **b** : to make (one's way) slowly and carefully ⟨*picked* their way through the rubble⟩ **4** : to steal or pilfer from ⟨*pick* pockets⟩ **5** : to start (a fight) with someone else deliberately **6** : to dig at or into : PROBE ⟨*picking* his teeth⟩ **7** : to eat sparingly or in a finicky manner ⟨*picked* at her dinner⟩ **8** : to unlock without a key ⟨*pick* a lock⟩ [Middle English *piken* "to pierce, pick," from Old English *pīcian* (same meaning) and from early French *piquer* "to prick" — related to ³PIKE] — **pick·er** *n* — **pick on** : to single out especially for criticism, teasing, or bullying ⟨always *picking on* smaller children⟩

²**pick** *n* **1** : a blow or stroke with a pointed instrument **2 a** : the act or opportunity of choosing : CHOICE ⟨take your *pick*⟩ **b** : the best or choicest one or portion ⟨took only the *pick* of the crop⟩ **c** : one that is picked ⟨his *pick* for vice president⟩

³**pick** *n* **1** : a heavy tool with a wooden handle and a blade pointed at one or both ends used especially to loosen or break up soil or rock **2** : a slender pointed instrument ⟨ice *pick*⟩ **3** : a small thin piece of metal or plastic used to pluck a stringed instrument **4** : a comb with long widely spaced teeth used in grooming hair [Middle English *pik* "a pick for digging"]

pickaback *variant of* PIGGYBACK

pick·ax \'pik-,aks\ *n* : ³PICK 1

picked \'pikt\ *adj* : selected as being the best available ⟨a *picked* crew⟩

pick·er·el \'pik-(ə-)rəl\ *n, pl* **pickerel** *or* **pickerels** **1** : either of two fishes resembling but smaller than the related pike **2** : WALLEYE

pickerel 1

pick·er·el·weed \-,wēd\ *n* : a plant mostly of the eastern U.S. and Canada that grows in shallow water and has large arrow-shaped leaves and blue flowers

¹**pick·et** \'pik-ət\ *n* **1** : a pointed stake or post (as for a fence) **2** : a soldier or a group of soldiers assigned to stand guard **3** : a person (as a striking worker or a demonstrator) on a picket line

²**picket** *vb* **1** : to enclose, fence, or strengthen with pickets **2 a** : to guard with a picket **b** : to station as a picket **3** : ²TETHER ⟨*picket* a horse⟩ **4 a** : to station pickets or act as a picket at ⟨*picket* a factory⟩ **b** : to serve as a picket — **pick·et·er** *n*

picket line *n* **1** : a position held by a line of military pickets **2** : a line of individuals (as striking workers or protestors) who are demonstrating against a business, organization, or institution

pick·ings \'pik-iŋz\ *n pl* **1** : something available or left over; *esp* : eatable remains **2** : yield or return for the effort put forth ⟨easy *pickings*⟩ ⟨slim *pickings*⟩

¹**pick·le** \'pik-əl\ *n* **1** : a liquid used for preserving or cleaning; *esp* : a saltwater or vinegar solution in which foods are preserved : BRINE **2** : an unpleasant or difficult situation : PLIGHT **3** : an article of food (as a cucumber) preserved in a saltwater or vinegar solution

²**pickle** *vb* **pick·led; pick·ling** \'pik-(ə-)liŋ\ : to treat, preserve, or clean in or with a pickle

pick·led *adj* : preserved with pickle

pick—me—up \'pik-mē-,əp\ *n* : something that stimulates or refreshes

pick off *vb* **1** : to shoot or bring down one by one or with a single shot **2** : to put out (a base runner who is off base) with a quick throw

pick out *vb* **1** : to see or detect with some difficulty ⟨*picked out* the trail in the snow⟩ **2** : to play the notes of by ear or one by one ⟨*pick out* a tune⟩

pick over *vb* : to examine in order to select the best or remove the unwanted

pick·pock·et \'pik-,päk-ət\ *n* : a thief who steals from pockets and purses

pick·up \'pik-,əp\ *n* **1 a** : an increase in activity ⟨a *pickup* in business⟩ **b** : ACCELERATION 1 **2** : one (as a hitchhiker or chance acquaintance) that is picked up **3 a** : the changing of mechanical movements into electrical energy in the reproduction of sound **b** : a device (as on a phonograph) for making such a change **4 a** : the receiving of sound or an image into a radio or television transmitting device **b** : a device (as a microphone or a television camera) for converting sound or an image into electrical signals **5** : a light truck with an open body and low sides — called also *pickup truck*

pick up \(')pik-'əp\ *vb* **1 a** : to take hold of and lift ⟨*picked* the book *up*⟩ **b** : to gather together : COLLECT ⟨*picked up* every piece⟩ **c** : to clean up : TIDY ⟨*pick up* your room⟩ **2** : to take (passengers or freight) into a vehicle **3 a** : to acquire without great effort or by chance ⟨*pick up* a habit⟩ ⟨*picked up* a nasty cold⟩ **b** : to gain by study or experience ⟨*picked up* a new language while traveling⟩ **c** : to obtain especially by buying or as a bargain ⟨*picked up* the shirts on sale⟩ **d** : to form a brief or chance acquaintance with a stranger **e** : to take into custody ⟨was *picked up* by the police⟩ **4** : to find and follow ⟨*picked up* the outlaw's trail⟩ **5** : to bring within range of sight or hearing ⟨a radio that *picks up* foreign broadcasts⟩ **6** : to gather or regain speed or strength

picky \'pik-ē\ *adj* **pick·i·er; -est** : FUSSY 2b, FINICKY

¹**pic·nic** \'pik-(,)nik\ *n* **1** : a meal eaten outdoors often during a trip away from home **2 a** : a pleasant or carefree experience ⟨breaking a leg is no *picnic*⟩ **b** : an easy task **3** : a shoulder of pork that is often smoked and boned — **pic·nic·ky** *adj*

²**picnic** *vb* **pic·nicked; pic·nick·ing** : to go on a picnic : eat as if on a picnic — **pic·nick·er** *n*

pi·co- \'pē-kō, -kə\ *combining form* : one trillionth part of [probably from Spanish *pico* "small amount," literally, "peak, beak"]

pi·cot \'pē-kō, pē-'kō\ *n* : one of a series of small loops forming an ornamental edging on ribbon or lace

pic·to·gram \'pik-tə-,gram\ *n* : PICTOGRAPH

\ə\ abut	\aú\ out	\i\ tip	\ò\ saw	\ú\ foot
\ər\ further	\ch\ chin	\ī\ life	\òi\ coin	\y\ yet
\a\ mat	\e\ pet	\j\ job	\th\ thin	\yü\ few
\ā\ take	\ē\ easy	\ŋ\ sing	\th\ this	\yú\ cure
\ä\ cot, cart	\g\ go	\ō\ bone	\ü\ food	\zh\ vision

pic·to·graph \'pik-tə-ˌgraf\ *n* **1** : an ancient or prehistoric drawing or painting on a rock wall **2** : one of the symbols of a system of picture writing **3** : a diagram representing statistical information by pictures which can be varied in color, size, or number to indicate change — **pic·to·graph·ic** \ˌpik-tə-'graf-ik\ *adj*

pictograph 1

pic·to·ri·al \pik-'tōr-ē-əl, -'tȯr-\ *adj* **1** : of or relating to painting or drawing ⟨*pictorial* art⟩ **2** : consisting of or illustrated by pictures ⟨*pictorial* magazines⟩ **3** : suggesting or communicating vivid mental images ⟨*pictorial* poetry⟩ — **pic·to·ri·al·ly** \-ē-ə-lē\ *adv*

¹pic·ture \'pik-chər\ *n* **1** : a design or image made on a surface (as by painting, drawing, or photography) **2 a** : a clear description in words ⟨the book gives us a *picture* of another way of life⟩ **b** : a mental image : IDEA ⟨do you get the *picture*?⟩ **3** : a particular combination of circumstances : SITUATION ⟨an improvement of the economic *picture*⟩ **4 a** : an exact likeness : COPY **b** : a perfect symbol of something : EMBODIMENT ⟨the *picture* of health⟩ **5 a** : an image on a screen **b** : MOTION PICTURE — **picture** *adj*

²picture *vb* **pic·tured; pic·tur·ing** \'pik-chə-riŋ, 'pik-shriŋ\ **1** : to draw or paint a picture of : DEPICT **2** : to describe vividly **3** : to form a mental image of : IMAGINE

picture book *n* : a book that consists entirely or chiefly of pictures

picture graph *n* : PICTOGRAPH 3

picture–perfect *adj* : completely flawless : PERFECT ⟨made a *picture-perfect* landing⟩

pic·tur·esque \ˌpik-chə-'resk\ *adj* **1 a** : resembling or suitable for a painted picture ⟨a *picturesque* landscape⟩ **b** : CHARMING, QUAINT ⟨*picturesque* customs⟩ **2** : calling forth a striking mental picture ⟨a *picturesque* story⟩ **synonyms** see GRAPHIC — **pic·tur·esque·ly** *adv* — **pic·tur·esque·ness** *n*

picture tube *n* : a cathode-ray tube on which the picture in a television set appears

picture window *n* : a large window designed to frame a view

picture writing *n* : pictures that stand for actions or facts

pid·dling \'pid-liŋ, -liŋ, -ᵊl-ən, -ᵊl-iŋ\ *adj* : lacking size or importance : TRIVIAL

pid·gin \'pij-ən\ *n* : a simplified speech used for communication by people who speak different languages

pie \'pī\ *n* : a dish consisting of a pastry crust and a filling (as of fruit or meat)

¹pie·bald \'pī-ˌbȯld\ *adj* : spotted or blotched with two different colors and especially with black and white ⟨a *piebald* horse⟩

²piebald *n* : a piebald animal (as a horse)

¹piece \'pēs\ *n* **1** : a part cut, torn, or broken from a thing : FRAGMENT ⟨a *piece* of string⟩ **2** : one of a class, group, or set of things ⟨a *piece* of mail⟩ ⟨a three-*piece* suit⟩ ⟨a chess *piece*⟩ **3** : a usually unspecified distance ⟨down the road a *piece*⟩ **4** : a portion marked off ⟨a *piece* of land⟩ **5** : a single item or example ⟨a *piece* of news⟩ **6** : a standard quantity or size in which an article is made or sold ⟨buy lumber by the *piece*⟩ **7** : something made, composed, or written ⟨a *piece* written for the piano⟩ **8** : ¹COIN 1 ⟨a 50-cent *piece*⟩ **9** : FIREARM **10** : EXAMPLE 1 ⟨a nice *piece* of acting⟩ — **of a piece** : of the same kind or character throughout : CONSISTENT — **piece of one's mind** : a severe scolding — **to pieces** **1** : without reserve or restraint : COMPLETELY ⟨love him *to pieces*⟩ **2** : out of

control : CRAZY ⟨went *to pieces* from the news⟩ **3** : into parts ⟨an old book falling *to pieces*⟩

²piece *vb* **pieced; piec·ing** **1** : to repair, form, or complete by adding pieces ⟨helped to *piece* a quilt⟩ ⟨*pieced* a jigsaw puzzle⟩ **2** : to join into a whole ⟨*pieced* their stories together⟩ — **piec·er** *n*

piece by piece *adv* : a little at a time

pièce de ré·sis·tance \pē-ˌes-də-rə-ˌzē-'stän(t)s\ *n, pl* **pièces de ré·sis·tance** *same*\ **1** : the main dish of a meal **2** : an outstanding item or event : SHOWPIECE [French, literally, "piece of resistance"]

¹piece·meal \'pē-ˌsmēl\ *adv* **1** : one piece at a time : GRADUALLY **2** : in pieces : APART

²piecemeal *adj* : done, made, or accomplished piece by piece or in an incomplete way ⟨*piecemeal* reforms⟩

piece of cake : something easy to do ⟨the quiz was a *piece of cake*⟩

piece of eight : an old Spanish peso of eight reals

piece·work \'pē-ˌswərk\ *n* : work paid for at a rate based on the number of articles produced rather than the time spent working — **piece·work·er** \-ˌswər-kər\ *n*

pie chart *n* : a circular chart that is divided into parts shaped like pieces of pie in such a way that the size of each piece represents the relative quantity or frequency of something — called also *circle graph, pie graph*

pied \'pīd\ *adj* : having blotches of two or more colors

pied·mont \'pēd-ˌmänt\ *adj* : lying or formed at the base of mountains — **piedmont** *n*

pie plant *n* : garden rhubarb

pier \'pi(ə)r\ *n* **1** : a support for a bridge **2** : a structure built out into the water for use as a landing place or walk or to protect or form a harbor **3** : an upright supporting part (as a pillar or buttress) of a building or structure

pierce \'pi(ə)rs\ *vb* **pierced; pierc·ing** **1 a** : to run into or through as a pointed weapon does : STAB **b** : to enter or thrust into sharply or painfully **2** : to make a hole in or through ⟨have one's ears *pierced*⟩ **3** : to force or make a way into or through ⟨*pierce* the enemy's line⟩ **4** : to penetrate with the eye or mind : see through **5** : to stir the emotions of : MOVE — **pierc·er** *n*

pierced *adj* **1** : having holes **2** : having a hole for the attachment of a piece of jewelry ⟨*pierced* ears⟩ ⟨a *pierced* tongue⟩ **3** : designed for pierced ears ⟨*pierced* earrings⟩

¹pierc·ing *adj* : having the ability to enter, pierce, or penetrate: as **a** : loud and shrill ⟨*piercing* screams⟩ **b** : PERCEPTIVE, KEEN ⟨a *piercing* glance⟩ **c** : very cold ⟨a *piercing* wind⟩ — **pierc·ing·ly** \'pir-siŋ-lē\ *adv*

²piercing *n* : a piece of jewelry (as a ring or stud) that is attached to pierced flesh

pier glass *n* : a tall narrow mirror

pie·ro·gi *also* **pi·ro·gi** \pə-'rō-gē\ *n, pl* **-gi** *also* **-gies** : a case of dough filled with meat, cheese, or vegetables and cooked by boiling and then panfrying

pi·ety \'pī-ət-ē\ *n, pl* **pi·eties** **1** : the quality or state of being pious : dutifulness in religion **2** : a pious act

pif·fle \'pif-əl\ *n* : NONSENSE 1

pig \'pig\ *n* **1 a** : a young domesticated swine usually weighing less than 120 pounds (54 kilograms) — compare HOG 1a **b** : a wild or domesticated swine of any age or weight **2 a** : PORK **b** : PIGSKIN 1 **3** : a dirty, gluttonous, or repulsive person **4** : a metal cast (as of iron) poured directly from the smelting furnace into a mold

pi·geon \'pij-ən\ *n* **1** : any of numerous birds with a stout body, usually short legs, and smooth feathers; *esp* : any of many varieties of the rock dove that are domesticated or have escaped from domestication and live in cities and towns throughout most of the world **2** : someone who is easily fooled or cheated

¹pi·geon·hole \-ˌhōl\ *n* : a small open compartment (as in a desk) for keeping letters or papers

²pigeonhole *vb* : to place in or as if in the pigeonhole of a desk

pi·geon–toed \ˌpij-ən-'tōd\ *adj* : having the toes and front of the foot turned inward

pig·gish \'pig-ish\ *adj* : resembling or suggesting a pig (as in greed or dirtiness) — **pig·gish·ly** *adv*

[1]**pig·gy·back** \'pig-ē-ˌbak\ *also* **pick·a·back** \'pig-ē-ˌbak, 'pik-ə-\ *adv or adj* **1** : on the back or shoulders **2** : on a railroad flatcar

[2]**piggyback** *n* : the act of carrying piggyback

piggy bank *n* : a bank for coins often shaped like a pig

pig·head·ed \'pig-'hed-əd\ *adj* : STUBBORN 1a, OBSTINATE

pig iron *n* : crude iron that is the direct product of the blast furnace and when refined yields steel, wrought iron, or high-purity iron

pig latin *n, often cap L* : a play language usually formed by placing the first consonants and "-ay" at the end of each word (as "utshay the oorday" for "shut the door")

pig·let \'pig-lət\ *n* : a baby pig

pig·ment \'pig-mənt\ *n* **1** : a substance that gives color to other materials; *esp* : a powder mixed with a liquid to give color **2** : a natural coloring matter in animals and plants — **pig·ment·ed** \-mənt-əd, -ˌment-\ *adj*

pig·men·ta·tion \ˌpig-mən-'tā-shən, -ˌmen-\ *n* : a coloring with pigment; *esp* : an amount of bodily pigment that is greater than normal

pigmy *variant of* PYGMY

pig out *vb* **pigged out; pig·ging out** : to eat greedily

pig·pen \'pig-ˌpen\ *n* **1** : a pen for pigs **2** : a dirty or messy place

pig·skin \-ˌskin\ *n* **1** : the skin of a swine or leather made of it **2** : FOOTBALL 2

pig·sty \'pig-ˌstī\ *n* : PIGPEN

pig·tail \-ˌtāl\ *n* : a tight braid of hair — **pig·tailed** \-ˌtāld\ *adj*

pig·weed \-ˌwēd\ *n* : any of various weedy plants especially of the two families to which the goosefoots and amaranths belong

pi·ka \'pē-kə\ *n* : any of various small short-eared mammals of rocky uplands of Asia and western North America that are related to the rabbits

pigtail

[1]**pike** \'pīk\ *n* **1** : PIKESTAFF 1 **2** : a sharp point or spike (as the tip of a spear) [Old English *pic* "pick used for digging"] — **piked** \'pīkt\ *adj*

[2]**pike** *n, pl* **pike** *or* **pikes** **1** : a large freshwater fish with a long body and long snout that is valued for food and sport and is widely distributed in cool northern waters **2** : any of various fishes related to or like the pike [Middle English *pike* "a fish," from *pic* "a pick used for digging"]

[3]**pike** *n* : a long wooden pole with a steel point once used as a weapon [from early French *pique* "a long weapon of war," from *piquer* "to prick," probably derived from a Latin word *picus* "woodpecker" — related to [1]PICK]

[4]**pike** *n* : TURNPIKE [a shortened form of *turnpike*]

pik·er \'pī-kər\ *n* **1** : one who does things on a small scale; *esp* : one who gambles with a small amount of money **2** : CHEAPSKATE, CHISELER

pike·staff \'pīk-ˌstaf\ *n* **1** : a sharply pointed walking stick **2** : the shaft of a soldier's pike

pi·laf *also* **pi·laff** \pi-'läf, 'pē-ˌläf\ *or* **pi·lau** \pi-'lō, -'lo, 'pē-; *Southern often* 'pər-lü, -lō\ *n* : a dish made of seasoned rice and often meat

pi·las·ter \'pī-ˌlas-tər\ *n* : an upright rectangular column that ornaments or helps to support a wall from which it sticks out slightly

[1]**pile** \'pī(ə)l\ *n* : a long slender post usually of timber, steel, or concrete driven into the ground to support a load [Old English *pīl* "dart, stake," from Latin *pilum* "spear, javelin"]

[2]**pile** *vb* **piled; pil·ing** : to drive piles into

[3]**pile** *n* **1 a** : a quantity of things heaped together **b** : a heap of wood for burning a corpse or a sacrifice **2** : a great amount **3** : REACTOR 2 [Middle English *pile* "pier of a bridge, heap, stack," from early French *pille* "pier of a bridge," from Latin *pila* "pillar"]

[4]**pile** *vb* **piled; pil·ing** **1** : to lay or place something in a pile : STACK **2** : to heap in abundance : LOAD **3** : to move or push forward hastily or in a disorganized way : CROWD ⟨*piled* into the car⟩

[5]**pile** *n* **1** : a coat or surface of usually short close fine furry hairs **2** : raised loops on the surface of a fabric which may be cut or uncut and which produce a velvety or fuzzy texture [Middle English *pile* "furry surface," from early French *peil, pil* "hair, coat with thick nap," from Latin *pilus* "hair" — related to CATERPILLAR; see *Word History* at CATERPILLAR] — **piled** *adj*

[6]**pile** *n* **1** : HEMORRHOID 1 **2** *pl* : HEMORRHOID 2 [Middle English *pile* "hemorrhoid," perhaps derived from Latin *pila* "ball"]

pi·le·at·ed woodpecker \ˌpī-lē-ˌāt-əd-, ˌpil-ē-\ *n* : a North American woodpecker that is black with a red crest and white on the wings and sides of the neck

pile driver *n* : a machine for hammering piles into place

pil·fer \'pil-fər\ *vb* **pil·fered; pil·fer·ing** \-f(ə-)riŋ\ : to steal articles of small value or in small amounts — **pil·fer·age** \-f(ə-)rij\ *n* — **pil·fer·er** \-fər-ər\ *n*

pil·grim \'pil-grəm\ *n* **1** : one who journeys in foreign lands : TRAVELER **2** : a person who travels to a shrine or holy place to worship **3** *cap* : one of the English colonists who founded the first permanent settlement in New England at Plymouth in 1620

pil·grim·age \'pil-grə-mij\ *n* : a journey of a pilgrim — **pilgrimage** *vb*

pil·ing \'pī-liŋ\ *n* : a structure of piles (as one built in or near water)

[1]**pill** \'pil\ *n* **1 a** : medicine or a food supplement in a small rounded mass to be swallowed whole **b** *often cap* : an oral contraceptive — usually used with *the* **2** : something resembling a pill in shape or size **3** : something unpleasant that must be accepted or endured **4** : an unpleasant or tiresome person

[2]**pill** *vb, of a garment* : to develop small balls of fiber on the surface because of wear

[1]**pil·lage** \'pil-ij\ *n* : the act of robbing by force especially in war

[2]**pillage** *vb* **pil·laged; pil·lag·ing** : to strip of goods and possessions with ruthless violence : PLUNDER, LOOT — **pil·lag·er** *n*

[1]**pil·lar** \'pil-ər\ *n* **1** : a firm upright support (as for a roof) **2** : a column or shaft standing alone (as for a monument) **3** : a supporting or important member or part ⟨a *pillar* of society⟩

[2]**pillar** *vb* : to provide or support with or as if with pillars ⟨a long *pillared* hall⟩

pill·box \'pil-ˌbäks\ *n* **1** : a small usually shallow box for pills **2** : a small low fortification for machine guns and antitank weapons **3** : a small round hat without a brim

pill bug *n* : WOOD LOUSE; *esp* : a wood louse able to curl itself into a ball

pil·lion \'pil-yən\ *n* **1** : a cushion or pad placed behind a saddle for an ex-

[1]pillar 1

\ə\ abut	\au̇\ out	\i\ tip	\o̊\ saw	\u̇\ foot
\ər\ further	\ch\ chin	\ī\ life	\oi\ coin	\y\ yet
\a\ mat	\e\ pet	\j\ job	\th\ thin	\yü\ few
\ā\ take	\ē\ easy	\ŋ\ sing	\th\ this	\yu̇\ cure
\ä\ cot, cart	\g\ go	\ō\ bone	\ü\ food	\zh\ vision

tra rider **2** : a saddle for a passenger on a motorcycle or bicycle

pil·lo·ry \\'pil-(ə-)rē\\ *n, pl* **-ries** **1** : a device formerly used for the public punishment of wrongdoers that consists of a wooden frame with holes in which the head and hands can be locked **2** : exposure to public scorn or ridicule — **pillory** *vb*

¹pil·low \\'pil-ō\\ *n* : a bag filled with soft or springy material used as a cushion usually for the head of a person lying down

²pillow *vb* **1** : to place on or as if on a pillow **2** : to serve as a pillow for

pil·low·case \\'pil-ō-‚kās\\ *n* : a removable covering for a pillow

¹pi·lot \\'pī-lət\\ *n* **1 a** : a person who steers a ship **b** : a person qualified to guide a ship into and out of a port or in specified waters **2** : someone who provides guidance and direction : LEADER **3** : one who flies or is qualified to fly an aircraft or spacecraft **4** : PILOT LIGHT — **pi·lot·less** \\-ləs\\ *adj*

²pilot *vb* : to act as pilot of : GUIDE

³pilot *adj* : serving as a guiding or tracing device, as an activating or auxiliary unit, or to test a new invention or idea ⟨a *pilot* study⟩

pilot balloon *n* : a small unmanned balloon sent up to show the direction and speed of the wind

pilot fish *n* : a fish with a narrow body and a widely forked tail that often swims near a shark

pi·lot·house \\'pī-lət-‚haús\\ *n* : an enclosed place for the helmsman of a ship that contains the steering and navigating equipment

pilot light *n* : a small permanent flame used to ignite gas at a burner

pilot whale *n* : either of two mostly black medium-sized toothed whales related to the dolphins

pi·men·to \\pə-'ment-ō\\ *n, pl* **-tos** *or* **-to** : PIMIENTO

pi·mien·to \\pə-'ment-ō, pəm-'yent-\\ *n, pl* **-tos** : any of various sweet peppers that have thick flesh and a mild flavor and are used especially as a stuffing for olives and as a source of paprika

pim·ple \\'pim-pəl\\ *n* : a small swelling of the skin often containing pus : PUSTULE — **pim·pled** \\-pəld\\ *adj* — **pim·ply** \\-p(ə-)lē\\ *adj*

¹pin \\'pin\\ *n* **1 a** : a piece of wood, metal, or plastic used especially for fastening things together or for hanging one thing from another **b** : something that resembles a pin especially in long slender form ⟨a *pin* that makes an electrical connection⟩ **c** : one of the pieces that make up the target in various games (as bowling) **d** : the staff of the flag marking a hole on a golf course **e** : a peg for regulating the tension of the strings of a musical instrument **2 a** : a very thin small pointed metal pin with a head used especially for fastening cloth **b** : ³LITTLE 1, TRIFLE ⟨doesn't care a *pin* what they think⟩ **c** : an ornament or emblem fastened to clothing with a pin **d** : a device (as a hairpin or safety pin) for fastening **3** : ¹LEG 1

²pin *vb* **pinned; pin·ning** **1 a** : to fasten, join, or secure with or as if with a pin **b** : to prevent or be prevented from moving ⟨*pinned* under the wreckage⟩ **2** : to assign the blame or responsibility for

pin·afore \\'pin-ə-‚fō(ə)r, -‚fó(ə)r\\ *n* : a low-necked sleeveless garment worn especially by children

pi·ña·ta \\pēn-'yät-ə\\ *n* : a decorated container filled with candies, fruits, and gifts which is hung up to be broken open with sticks by blindfolded persons during festivities [Spanish, literally, "pot"]

pin·ball machine \\'pin-‚ból-\\ *n* : a game in which a ball shot by a plunger scores points as it rolls around a slanting surface among pins and targets

pince–nez \\pan(t)-'snā\\ *n, pl* **pince–nez** \\-'snā(z)\\ : eyeglasses clipped to the nose by a spring

pince-nez

pin·cer \\'pin-chər, 'pin(t)-sər\\ *n* **1** *pl* : an instrument having two handles and two jaws that is used to grip things **2** : a claw (as of a lobster) resembling a pair of pincers — **pin·cer·like** \\-‚līk\\ *adj*

¹pinch \\'pinch\\ *vb* **1 a** : to squeeze between the finger and thumb or between the jaws of an instrument **b** : to nip off (a bud) to control flowering or prune the tip of (a young shoot) to cause branching **c** : to squeeze painfully **2** : to cause to appear thin, haggard, or shrunken ⟨a face *pinched* with cold⟩ **3 a** : to be thrifty or stingy **b** : to restrain or limit narrowly **4 a** : ¹STEAL 2a **b** : ¹ARREST 2 **5 a** : ³NARROW, TAPER **b** : to sharply reduce the length or quantity of

²pinch *n* **1 a** : a critical time or point : EMERGENCY ⟨help out in a *pinch*⟩ **b** : painful pressure or stress ⟨the *pinch* of hunger⟩ **2 a** : an act of pinching **b** : as much as may be taken between the finger and thumb ⟨a *pinch* of salt⟩ **c** : a small amount **3 a** : THEFT **b** : a police raid; *also* : ²ARREST 2

pinch·er \\'pin-chər\\ *n* **1** : one that pinches **2** *pl* : PINCER 1

pinch hitter *n* **1** : a baseball player sent in to bat for another especially when a hit is needed **2** : a person called upon to do another's work in an emergency — **pinch–hit** \\(')pinch-'hit\\ *vb*

pin·cush·ion \\'pin-‚kúsh-ən\\ *n* : a small cushion in which pins may be stuck

¹pine \\'pīn\\ *vb* **pined; pin·ing** **1** : to lose energy, health, or weight through grief, worry, or distress ⟨*pine* away⟩ **2** : to long for very much **synonyms** see YEARN

²pine *n* **1** : any of a genus of evergreen trees that have narrow needles for leaves, cones, and wood ranging from very soft to hard and that include valuable timber trees as well as many ornamentals **2** : the white or yellow wood of a pine — **pin·ey** *also* **piny** \\'pī-nē\\ *adj*

pi·ne·al gland \\'pī-nē-əl, pī-'nē-\\ *n* : a small usually cone-shaped part of the brain of most vertebrates that has an eyelike structure in reptiles and produces melatonin especially in response to darkness — called also *pineal body*

²pine 1

pine·ap·ple \\'pī-‚nap-əl\\ *n* : a tropical plant with stiff spiny sword-shaped leaves and a short flowering stalk that develops into an edible fruit with usually pale yellow sweet juicy flesh and very thick skin; *also* : this fruit [Middle English *pinappel* "the cone of a pine"; so called because the fruit looks like the cone from a pine tree]

pine cone *n* : the cone of a pine tree

pine tar *n* : tar obtained from pinewood and used especially in roofing and soaps and in the treatment of skin diseases

pine·wood \\'pīn-‚wúd\\ *n* **1** : the wood of a pine tree **2** : a wood or growth of pines

pin·feath·er \\'pin-‚feth-ər\\ *n* : an incompletely developed feather just breaking through the skin

ping \\'piŋ\\ *n* **1** : a sharp sound like that of a bullet striking **2** : ²KNOCK 3b — **ping** *vb*

Ping–Pong \'piŋ-ˌpäŋ, -ˌpȯŋ\ *trademark* — used for table tennis

pin·head \'pin-ˌhed\ *n* **1** : the head of a pin **2** : a very dull or stupid person : FOOL

pin·head·ed \-ˌhed-əd\ *adj* : lacking intelligence or understanding : STUPID — **pin·head·ed·ness** *n*

pin·hole \-ˌhōl\ *n* : a very small hole made by or as if by a pin

¹pin·ion \'pin-yən\ *n* **1** : the end part of a bird's wing; *also* : a bird's wing **2** : a feather of a bird's pinion

²pinion *vb* **1** : to restrain especially by binding the arms **2** : to prevent a bird from flying especially by cutting off the pinion of one wing

³pinion *n* **1** : a gear with a small number of teeth designed to fit together with a larger wheel or rack **2** : the smallest of a set of gearwheels

¹pink \'piŋk\ *n* **1** : any of a genus of herbs that have narrow leaves and are often grown for their showy usually pink flowers produced singly or in clusters **2** : the highest degree ⟨athletes in the *pink* of condition⟩ [origin unknown]

²pink *n* : a pale red — **pink** *adj* — **pink·ish** \'piŋ-kish\ *adj* — **pink·ness** *n*

³pink *vb* : to cut cloth, leather, or paper in an ornamental pattern or with a saw-toothed edge [from earlier *pink* "stab, pierce," from Middle English *pinken* "to thrust"]

pink·eye \'piŋ-ˌkī\ *n* : a contagious disease in which the inner surface of the eyelid and part of the eyeball become pinkish and sore

pin·kie *or* **pin·ky** \'piŋ-kē\ *n, pl* **pinkies** : LITTLE FINGER [probably from Dutch *pinkje* "little finger"]

pinking shears *n pl* : dressmaking shears that make a zig-zag cut

pin money *n* : money for small expenses

pin·na \'pin-ə\ *n, pl* **pin·nae** \'pin-ē, -ˌī\ *or* **pin·nas** **1** : a feather, wing, or fin or a part like one **2** : the part of the ear that is outside the head and is made of cartilage

pin·nace \'pin-əs\ *n* **1** : a light sailing ship **2** : a ship's boat

pin·na·cle \'pin-i-kəl\ *n* **1** : a slender tower generally coming to a point at the top **2** : a high pointed peak **3** : the highest point of achievement or development

pin·nate \'pin-ˌāt\ *adj* : resembling a feather especially in having similar parts arranged on opposite sides of a long thin central part like a stem ⟨a *pinnate* leaf⟩ — **pin·nate·ly** *adv*

pinned *past and past participle of* PIN

pinning *present participle of* PIN

pin·ni·ped \'pin-ə-ˌped\ *n* : any of a group of mammals (as seals, sea lions, and walruses) that typically live in oceans but bear their young on land or on floating sheets of ice, have front and hind flippers, and eat other animals (as fish)

pi·noch·le \'pē-ˌnək-əl\ *n* : a card game played with two cards of each suit with 9 the lowest card

pi·ñon *or* **pin·yon** \'pin-ˌyōn, -ˌyän, -yən; pin-'yōn\ *n, pl* **piñons** *or* **pinyons** *or* **pi·ño·nes** \pin-'yō-nēz\ : any of various small pines of western North America with edible seeds; *also* : the edible seed of a piñon

¹pin·point \'pin-ˌpȯint\ *n* **1** : the point of a pin **2** : an extremely small or sharp point ⟨a *pinpoint* of light in the darkness⟩

²pinpoint *vb* : to locate or identify exactly ⟨*pinpoint* your career interests⟩

³pinpoint *adj* **1** : extremely fine or exact ⟨*pinpoint* accuracy⟩ **2** : located, fixed, or directed with great exactness

pin·prick \'pin-ˌprik\ *n* : a small puncture made by or as if

¹pink 1

by a pin; *also* : a small but unpleasant sensation ⟨the steady *pinprick* of a guilty conscience⟩

pins and needles *n pl* : a pricking tingling feeling in an arm or leg that is recovering from numbness — **on pins and needles** : in a nervous or jumpy state of expectation

pin·stripe \'pin-ˌstrīp\ *n* : a very thin stripe on a fabric; *also* : a suit with such stripes — **pin–striped** \-ˌstrīpt\ *adj*

pint \'pīnt\ *n* **1** — see MEASURE table **2** : a pint container

pin·tail \'pin-ˌtāl\ *n, pl* **pintail** *or* **pintails** : a bird (as a duck or grouse) with long central tail feathers

¹pin·to \'pin-tō\ *n, pl* **pintos** *also* **pintoes** : a horse or pony marked with patches of white and another color

²pinto *adj* : PIED, MOTTLED

pinto bean *n* : a spotted kidney bean used for food; *also* : a plant producing pinto beans that is often used to feed livestock

pint–size \'pīnt-ˌsīz\ *or* **pint–sized** \-ˌsīzd\ *adj* : TINY, SMALL

pin tuck *n* : a very narrow tuck

pin·wale \'pin-ˌwāl\ *adj* : made with narrow wales ⟨*pinwale* corduroy⟩

pin·wheel \-ˌhwēl\ *n* **1** : a fireworks device in the form of a spinning wheel of colored fire **2** : a toy made of fanlike blades that spin in the wind at the end of a stick

pin·worm \-ˌwərm\ *n* : any of numerous small roundworms that infest the intestines of various vertebrates; *esp* : one that infests human beings

pin·yin \'pin-'yin\ *n, often cap* : a system for writing Chinese words by using Roman letters to represent the sounds

pinyon *variant of* PIÑON

¹pi·o·neer \ˌpī-ə-'ni(ə)r\ *n* **1** : a person or group that explores new areas of thought or activity ⟨*pioneers* of American medicine⟩ **2** : one of the first to settle in an area : COLONIST — **pioneer** *adj*

²pioneer *vb* **1** : to act as a pioneer **2** : to open or prepare for others to follow; *esp* : ²SETTLE 2a **3** : to begin or take part in the development of something new

pi·ous \'pī-əs\ *adj* **1** : having or showing love for deity : DEVOUT **2** : displaying great loyalty to a person or thing (as a family, custom, or philosophy) **3** : marked by a false show of goodness ⟨a *pious* fraud⟩ **4** : deserving praise : WORTHY ⟨a *pious* effort⟩ — **pi·ous·ly** *adv* — **pi·ous·ness** *n*

¹pip \'pip\ *vb* **pipped; pip·ping** **1** : to break through the shell of the egg in hatching **2** : to be broken by a pipping bird ⟨eggs starting to *pip*⟩ [imitative word]

²pip *n* **1** : a dot or spot (as on dice or playing cards) that indicates numerical value **2** : BLIP [origin unknown]

³pip *n* **1** : a small fruit seed ⟨apple *pips*⟩ **2** : something very good of its kind [a shortened form of *pippin* "a kind of apple"]

¹pipe \'pīp\ *n* **1 a** : a musical instrument consisting of a tube of reed, wood, or metal that is played by blowing **b** : one of the tubes of a pipe organ **c** : BAGPIPE — usually used in plural **d** : the whistle, call, or note especially of a bird or an insect **2** : a long tube or hollow body for carrying a substance (as water, steam, or gas) **3** : a tube with a small bowl at one end used for smoking tobacco **4** : a large barrel used especially to hold oil or wine

²pipe *vb* **piped; pip·ing** **1 a** : to play on a pipe **b** : to receive on board or signal the departure of by the sounding of a boatswain's pipe **2** : to speak, call, or play with a high shrill tone **3** : to furnish or trim with piping **4** : to carry by or as if by pipes ⟨*pipe* water⟩ — **pip·er** *n*

\ə\ abut	\au̇\ out	\i\ tip	\ȯ\ saw	\u̇\ foot
\ər\ further	\ch\ chin	\ī\ life	\ȯi\ coin	\y\ yet
\a\ mat	\e\ pet	\j\ job	\th\ thin	\yü\ few
\ā\ take	\ē\ easy	\ŋ\ sing	\th\ this	\yu̇\ cure
\ä\ cot, cart	\g\ go	\ō\ bone	\ü\ food	\zh\ vision

pipe cleaner *n* : a piece of flexible wire in which tufted fabric is twisted and which is used to clean the stem of a tobacco pipe

pipe down *vb* : to stop talking or making noise

pipe dream *n* : an unreal and fantastic idea, wish, or story

pipe·fish \'pīp-ˌfish\ *n* : any of various long slender fishes that are related to the sea horses and have a tube-shaped snout and a body covered with bony plates

pipe fitter *n* : a person who installs and repairs piping

pipe·line \'pī-ˌplīn\ *n* **1** : a line of pipe with pumps, valves, and control devices for carrying liquids, gases, or finely divided solids **2** : a direct channel for information or supplies

pipe organ *n* : ORGAN 1a

pi·pette \pī-'pet\ *n* : a device for measuring and transferring small volumes of liquid that typically consists of a narrow glass tube into which the liquid is drawn by suction and kept by blocking the upper end — **pipette** *vb*

pipe up *vb* : SPEAK OUT

pip·ing \'pī-piŋ\ *n* **1 a** : the music of a pipe **b** : a shrill sound or call ⟨the *piping* of frogs⟩ **2** : a quantity or system of pipes **3** : a narrow fold of fabric used to decorate seams or edges

piping hot *adj* : very hot

pip–squeak \'pip-ˌskwēk\ *n* : one that is small or insignificant

pi·quan·cy \'pē-kən-sē\ *n* : the quality or state of being piquant

pipette

pi·quant \'pē-kənt, -ˌkänt\ *adj* **1** : agreeably stimulating to the taste; *esp* : SPICY 1 **2** : pleasingly exciting ⟨a *piquant* bit of gossip⟩ — **pi·quant·ly** *adv*

¹pique \'pēk\ *n* **1** : offense taken by one treated with disrespect or looked down upon **2** : a sudden feeling of resentment

²pique *vb* **piqued; piqu·ing** **1** : to arouse anger or resentment in : IRRITATE; *esp* : to offend by treating with disrespect **2** : EXCITE 1, AROUSE ⟨the package *piqued* my curiosity⟩

pi·qué *or* **pi·que** \pi-'kā, 'pē-ˌkā\ *n* : a ribbed fabric of cotton, rayon, or silk

pi·ra·cy \'pī-rə-sē\ *n, pl* **-cies** **1** : robbery on the high seas **2** : the use of another's production or invention without permission

pi·ra·nha \pə-'ran-yə, -'rän-(y)ə\ *n* : any of various usually small flesh-eating South American freshwater fishes that have very sharp teeth, often occur in groups, and include some that may attack human beings and animals in the water

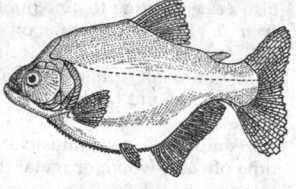

piranha

¹pi·rate \'pī-rət\ *n* : a person who commits piracy — **pi·rat·i·cal** \pə-'rat-i-kəl, pī-\ *adj* — **pi·rat·i·cal·ly** \-i-k(ə-)lē\ *adv*

²pirate *vb* **pi·rat·ed; pi·rat·ing** : to take by piracy ⟨*pirate* an invention⟩

pirogi *variant of* PIEROGI

pi·rogue \'pē-ˌrōg\ *n* **1** : DUGOUT 1 **2** : a boat like a canoe

pir·ou·ette \ˌpir-ə-'wet\ *n* : a rapid whirling of the body; *esp* : a full turn on the toe or ball of one foot in ballet — **pirouette** *vb*

pis *plural of* PI

Pi·sces \'pī-ˌsēz\ *n* **1** : a group of stars between Aquarius and Aries usually pictured as a pair of fish **2 a** : the 12th sign of the zodiac — see ZODIAC table **b** : a person whose sign of the zodiac is Pisces

pis·ta·chio \pə-'stash-(ē-ˌ)ō, -'stäsh-\ *n, pl* **-chios** : a small Asian tree that is related to the sumacs and has a fruit containing a greenish edible seed; *also* : its seed

pis·til \'pis-t³l\ *n* : the seed-producing part of a flower consisting usually of stigma, style, and ovary [from scientific Latin *pistillum* "pistil," from Latin *pistillum* "pestle for grinding material in a mortar"]

pis·til·late \'pis-tə-ˌlāt\ *adj* : having pistils; *esp* : having pistils but no stamens

pis·tol \'pis-t³l\ *n* : a short firearm made to be aimed and fired with one hand [from early French *pistole* "pistol," from German *pistole* (same meaning), derived from Czech *píšt'ala*, literally, "pipe, fife"]

pis·to·le·ro \ˌpis-tə-'ler-ō\ *n, pl* **-ros** : GUNMAN

pistol–whip *vb* : to beat with a pistol

pis·ton \'pis-tən\ *n* : a sliding piece moved by or moving against the pressure of a fluid (as steam or hot gases) that usually consists of a short solid cylinder moving within a larger hollow cylinder

¹pit \'pit\ *n* **1** : a hole, shaft, or cavity in the ground ⟨a gravel *pit*⟩ **2** : an area set off from and often sunken below neighboring areas: as **a** : an enclosure where animals (as cocks) are set to fight **b** : the space occupied by an orchestra in a theater **3 a** : a hollowed or indented area especially in the surface of the body ⟨the *pit* of the stomach⟩ **b** : an indented scar (as from a boil) **4** *pl* : ³WORST 1 ⟨it's the *pits*⟩ **5** : any of the areas alongside an auto racetrack used for servicing cars during a race — often used in plural with *the* [Old English *pytt* "pit, hole in the ground"]

²pit *vb* **pit·ted; pit·ting** **1 a** : to put into or store in a pit **b** : to make pits in; *esp* : to scar with pits **2** : to set against another in a fight or contest ⟨*pitted* the courageous fighter against the champion⟩ **3** : to become marked with pits

³pit *n* : the stone of a fruit (as the cherry or peach) that is a drupe [from Dutch *pit* "the seed-containing stone of a fruit"]

⁴pit *vb* **pit·ted; pit·ting** : to remove the pit from ⟨*pitted* dates⟩

pi·ta \'pēt-ə\ *n* : a thin flat bread

pit–a–pat \ˌpit-i-'pat\ *n* : PITTER-PATTER — **pit–a–pat** *adv or adj* — **pit–a–pat** *vb*

pit bull *n* : a dog of any of several breeds originally developed for fighting and noted for strength and stamina

pit bull terrier *n* **1** : PIT BULL **2** : AMERICAN PIT BULL TERRIER

¹pitch \'pich\ *n* **1** : a dark sticky substance left over from distilling tar and used in making roofing paper, in waterproofing seams, and in paving **2** : resin from various cone-bearing trees [Old English *pic* "a tarlike substance," from Latin *pic-, pix* (same meaning)]

²pitch *vb* : to cover, smear, or treat with pitch

³pitch *vb* **1** : to erect and fix firmly in place ⟨*pitch* a tent⟩ **2** : to throw usually toward a certain point ⟨*pitch* hay into a wagon⟩ **3** : to present or advertise especially in a high-pressure way **4 a** : to fix or set at a particular pitch or level ⟨*pitch* a tune too high⟩ ⟨a test *pitched* at a 5th-grade reading level⟩ **b** : to cause to be set at a certain angle : SLOPE **5 a** : to fall or plunge forward ⟨*pitch* from a cliff⟩ **b** : to move in such a way that one end falls while the other end rises ⟨a ship *pitching* in a rough sea⟩ **c** : ²BUCK 1a ⟨a *pitching* horse⟩ **6 a** : to throw a ball to a batter **b** : to play ball as a pitcher [Middle English *pichen* "to thrust, drive, fix firmly"]

⁴pitch *n* **1** : the action or a manner of pitching; *esp* : an up-and-down movement **2** : slope or degree of slope **3** : the forward distance advanced by a propeller as it makes one revolution **4** : the amount or level of something (as a feeling) ⟨excitement reached a high *pitch*⟩ **5 a** : highness or lowness of sound **b** : a standard frequency for tuning instruments ⟨the oboe sounded the *pitch*⟩ **6 a** : a high-pressure sales talk **b** : RECOMMENDATION 1 ⟨made a *pitch* for tax cuts⟩ **7** : the delivery of a baseball by a pitcher to a batter — **pitched** \'picht\ *adj*

pitch–black \'pich-'blak\ *adj* : extremely dark or black

pitch·blende \'pich-,blend\ *n* : a brown to black mineral that is a source of uranium and radium

pitch–dark \'pich-'därk\ *adj* : extremely dark

pitched battle \'pich(t)-\ *n* : a fiercely fought battle in which the opposing forces are locked in close combat

¹**pitch·er** \'pich-ər\ *n* : a container for holding and pouring liquids that usually has a lip or spout and a handle [Middle English *picher* "container for pouring liquids," from early French (same meaning), from Latin *bicarius* "drinking vessel, goblet"]

²**pitcher** *n* : one that pitches; *esp* : a baseball player who pitches [from *pitch* "to erect in place, throw a ball" and *-er*, noun suffix]

pitcher plant *n* : any of various plants with modified leaves which form a tube resembling a pitcher for catching and digesting insects

pitch·fork \'pich-,fȯ(ə)rk\ *n* : a tool with a long handle and usually two to five metal prongs that is used especially in pitching hay — **pitchfork** *vb*

pitch in *vb* **1** : to begin to work **2** : to contribute to a common task ⟨all the students *pitched in* to make the dance a success⟩

pitch·out \'pich-,aút\ *n* **1** : a pitch in baseball deliberately out of reach of the batter to let the catcher check or put out a base runner **2** : a lateral pass in football between two backs behind the line of scrimmage

pitch pipe *n* : a small pipe blown to establish the pitch in singing or in tuning an instrument

pitchfork

pitchy \'pich-ē\ *adj* **1 a** : full of pitch : TARRY **b** : of, relating to, or having the qualities of pitch **2** : PITCH-BLACK

pit·e·ous \'pit-ē-əs\ *adj* : of a kind to move to pity ⟨*piteous* cries for help⟩ — **pit·e·ous·ly** *adv*

pit·fall \'pit-,fȯl\ *n* **1** : ¹TRAP 1, SNARE; *esp* : a covered or camouflaged pit used to capture animals or people **2** : a danger or difficulty that is hidden or is not easily recognized

pith \'pith\ *n* **1 a** : the loose spongy tissue that forms the center of the stem in most plants and probably functions chiefly in storage **b** : the spongy inside of a bone or feather **2** : the essential part : CORE ⟨the *pith* of the problem⟩

pithy \'pith-ē\ *adj* **pith·i·er**; **-est** **1** : consisting of or filled with pith **2** : being short and to the point ⟨a *pithy* saying⟩ — **pith·i·ly** \'pith-ə-lē\ *adv* — **pith·i·ness** \'pith-ē-nəs\ *n*

piti·able \'pit-ē-ə-bəl\ *adj* : PITIFUL — **piti·ably** \-blē\ *adv*

piti·ful \'pit-i-fəl\ *adj* **1** : deserving or arousing pity or sympathy ⟨a *pitiful* mongrel⟩ **2** : deserving pitying scorn (as by not being adequate) ⟨a *pitiful* excuse⟩ — **piti·ful·ly** \-f(ə-)lē\ *adv*

piti·less \'pit-i-ləs, 'pit-ªl-əs\ *adj* : having no pity : HARSH, CRUEL — **piti·less·ly** *adv*

pi·ton \'pē-,tän\ *n* : a spike or peg that is driven into a rock or ice surface for support (as for a mountain climber)

pit stop *n* **1** : a stop at the pits during an automobile race **2 a** : a stop (as during a trip) for fuel, food, or rest or for use of a restroom **b** : a place where a pit stop is or can be made

pit·tance \'pit-ªn(t)s\ *n* : a small portion, amount, or allowance especially of money

pitted *past and past participle of* PIT

pit·ter–pat·ter \'pit-ər-,pat-ər, 'pit-ē-,pat-\ *n* : a rapid series of light sounds or beats — **pit·ter–pat·ter** \,pit-ər-'pat-, ,pit-ē-'pat-\ *adv or adj* — **pitter–patter** *like adv*\ *vb*

pitting *present participle of* PIT

¹**pi·tu·i·tary** \pə-'t(y)ü-ə-,ter-ē\ *adj* : of, relating to, or being the pituitary gland

²**pituitary** *n, pl* **-tar·ies** : PITUITARY GLAND

pituitary gland *n* : a small oval endocrine organ located at the base of the brain that produces various hormones that regulate especially growth and reproduction — called also *pituitary body*

pit viper *n* : any of various mostly New World poisonous snakes that have a small pit on each side of the head and hollow fangs with holes in them

¹**pity** \'pit-ē\ *n, pl* **pit·ies** **1** : sympathetic sorrow for one suffering, distressed, or unhappy : COMPASSION **2** : something to be regretted ⟨it's a *pity* you can't go⟩

²**pity** *vb* **pit·ied**; **pity·ing** : to feel pity for

¹**piv·ot** \'piv-ət\ *n* **1** : a shaft or pin on which something turns **2** : something on which something else turns or depends : a central member, part, or point

²**pivot** *vb* **1** : to turn on or as if on a pivot ⟨the guns are mounted in such a way as to *pivot* easily⟩ ⟨the future *pivots* on what is done today⟩ **2** : to provide with, mount on, or attach by a pivot

piv·ot·al \'piv-ət-ªl\ *adj* **1** : of, relating to, or functioning as a pivot **2** : extremely important : CRITICAL ⟨a *pivotal* discovery⟩ — **piv·ot·al·ly** \-ªl-ē\ *adv*

pix·el \'pik-səl, -,sel\ *n* : any of the small elements that together make up an image (as on a television screen) or sensor (as in a camera) [from *pix*, an altered form of *pictures*, and *element*]

pix·ie *also* **pixy** \'pik-sē\ *n, pl* **pix·ies** : a mischievous elf or fairy — **pix·ie·ish** \-sē-ish\ *adj*

piz·za \'pēt-sə\ *n* : a dish made typically of thinly rolled bread dough spread with a spiced mixture usually including tomatoes and cheese and often other toppings and baked — called also *pizza pie* [from Italian *pizza* "pizza"]

piz·ze·ria \,pēt-sə-'rē-ə\ *n* : an establishment where pizzas are made or sold

piz·zi·ca·to \,pit-si-'kät-ō\ *adv or adj* : by means of plucking by the fingers instead of bowing — used as a direction in music

pj's \(')pē-'jāz\ *n pl* : PAJAMAS

¹**plac·ard** \'plak-ərd, -,ärd\ *n* : a notice posted in a public place : POSTER

²**plac·ard** \'plak-,ärd, -ərd\ *vb* **1** : to post in a public place **2** : to announce by or as if by posting

pla·cate \'plāk-,āt, 'plak-\ *vb* **pla·cat·ed**; **pla·cat·ing** : to calm the anger or bitterness of **synonyms** see PACIFY

¹**place** \'plās\ *n* **1** : an available space : ROOM ⟨make a *place* for the newcomer⟩ **2 a** : a region not made clear in description ⟨all over the *place*⟩ **b** : a building or spot set apart for a special purpose ⟨a *place* of learning⟩ **3 a** : a certain region or center of population ⟨a nice *place* to visit⟩ **b** : ¹HOUSE 1, DWELLING ⟨nice *place* you have here⟩ ⟨our summer *place*⟩ **4** : a certain part of a surface or body : SPOT ⟨a sore *place* on my shoulder⟩ ⟨lost my *place* in the book⟩ **5** : relative position in a scale or series ⟨kept them in their *place*⟩ ⟨in the first *place*, you're wrong⟩ ⟨finished in last *place*⟩ **6 a** : a proper position ⟨the *place* of education in society⟩ **b** : a suitable moment or point ⟨this is not the *place* to discuss that problem⟩ **7 a** : an available seat or accommodation ⟨needs a *place* to stay⟩ **b** : usual space or use ⟨paper towels take the *place* of linen⟩ **8** : the position of a digit in a numeral ⟨the number 316 has three *places*⟩ ⟨in 2.718 the digit 1 is two *places* after the decimal point⟩ **9** : JOB 3, POSITION **10** : a

\ə\ abut	\aú\ out	\i\ tip	\ȯ\ saw	\ú\ foot
\ər\ further	\ch\ chin	\ī\ life	\ȯi\ coin	\y\ yet
\a\ mat	\e\ pet	\j\ job	\th\ thin	\yü\ few
\ā\ take	\ē\ easy	\ŋ\ sing	\th\ this	\yú\ cure
\ä\ cot, cart	\g\ go	\ō\ bone	\ü\ food	\zh\ vision

public square **11** : a short street **12** : second position at the finish (as of a horse race)

²place *vb* **placed; plac·ing 1** : to put or arrange in a certain place or position **2 a** : to appoint to a position ⟨was *placed* in command⟩ **b** : to find a job or home for ⟨*place* a child for adoption⟩ **3 a** : to assign to a position in a series or category : RANK **b** : ¹ESTIMATE 1 ⟨*placed* the value of the ring too high⟩ **c** : to identify by association ⟨couldn't quite *place* her face⟩ **4** : to give an order for ⟨*place* a bet⟩ **5** : to come in second (as in a horse race)

pla·ce·bo \plə-'sē-bō\ *n, pl* **-bos** : a medicine that usually has no effect on a disease and is prescribed by a doctor for the mental relief it offers a patient [from Latin *placebo* "I shall please"]

place·hold·er \'plās-ˌhōl-dər\ *n* : a symbol used in mathematics in the place of a numeral not yet known

place·kick \'plā-ˌskik\ *n* : a kick in football made with the ball held in place on the ground — **place·kick** *vb*

place mat *n* : a small table mat on which a place setting is laid

place·ment \'plā-smənt\ *n* **1** : an act or instance of placing; *esp* : the assignment of a person to a suitable place (as a class in school or a job) **2** : PLACEKICK

pla·cen·ta \plə-'sent-ə\ *n, pl* **-cen·tas** *or* **-cen·tae** \-'sent-ē\ : the organ in most mammals by which the fetus is joined to the uterus of the mother and is nourished — **pla·cen·tal** \-'sent-ᵊl\ *adj*

plac·er \'plas-ər\ *n* : a deposit of sand or gravel containing particles of valuable mineral (as gold)

place setting *n* : a set of dishes and silverware for one person

place value *n* : the value of the location of a digit in a number ⟨in 425 the location of the digit 2 has a *place value* of ten while the digit itself indicates that there are two tens⟩

plac·id \'plas-əd\ *adj* : peacefully free of interruption or disturbance : PEACEFUL, CALM ⟨a *placid* disposition⟩ — **pla·cid·i·ty** \pla-'sid-ət-ē, plə-\ *n* — **plac·id·ly** \'plas-əd-lē\ *adv*

plack·et \'plak-ət\ *n* : a slit in a garment (as a skirt) which closes after the garment has been put on

pla·gia·rism \'plā-jə-ˌriz-əm\ *n* **1** : an act of plagiarizing **2** : something plagiarized — **pla·gia·rist** \-rəst\ *n* — **pla·gia·ris·tic** \ˌplā-jə-'ris-tik\ *adj*

pla·gia·rize \'plā-jə-ˌrīz\ *vb* **-rized; -riz·ing** : to steal and pass off (as the ideas or words of another) as one's own ⟨*plagiarized* a classmate's homework⟩ — **pla·gia·riz·er** *n*

¹plague \'plāg\ *n* **1 a** : a disastrous evil **b** : a large number of destructive pests ⟨a *plague* of locusts⟩ **2** : an epidemic disease causing a high rate of death : PESTILENCE; *esp* : a serious disease that is caused by a bacterium, occurs or has occurred in several forms including bubonic plague, and is usually passed to human beings from infected rodents and especially rats by the bite of a flea or is passed directly from person to person **3** : a cause or occasion of annoyance : NUISANCE

²plague *vb* **plagued; plagu·ing 1** : to strike or afflict with or as if with disease or evil **2** : to cause worry or distress to ⟨*plagued* by a sense of guilt⟩

plaid \'plad\ *n* **1** : a rectangular length of tartan worn over the shoulder as part of the Scottish national costume **2** : a fabric with a tartan pattern **3 a** : TARTAN 1 **b** : a pattern of unevenly spaced repeated stripes crossing at right angles — **plaid** *adj*

¹plain \'plān\ *n* : a broad area of level or rolling treeless country [Middle English *plain* "a stretch of nearly level treeless country," from early French *plain* (same meaning), derived from Latin *planus* "flat" — related to ¹PLANE]

²plain *adj* **1** : having no pattern or decoration ⟨her dress

was *plain*⟩ **2** : free of added or extra matter : PURE ⟨a glass of *plain* water⟩ **3** : open and clear to the sight ⟨in *plain* view⟩ **4 a** : clear to the mind ⟨your meaning was *plain*⟩ **b** : FRANK, BLUNT ⟨*plain* speaking⟩ **5 a** : of common or average accomplishments or position : ORDINARY ⟨*plain* people⟩ **b** : not complicated or hard to do ⟨*plain* sewing⟩ **6** : neither ugly nor beautiful — **plain·ly** *adv* — **plain·ness** \'plān-nəs\ *n*

³plain *adv* : in a plain or simple manner

⁴plain *adv* : to a complete degree : TOTALLY ⟨were *plain* overcome by all the problems⟩ [partly from Middle English *plein* (adjective) "entire, complete" (derived from Latin *plenus* "full") and partly from *plain* (adverb) "in a plain manner" (derived from Latin *planus* "flat, level")]

plain·clothes·man \'plān-'klō(th)z-mən, -ˌman\ *n* : a police officer who does not wear a uniform on duty

Plains \'plānz\ *adj* : of or relating to North American Indians of the Great Plains or to their culture

plains·man \'plānz-mən\ *n* : a person who lives on the plains

plain·song \'plān-ˌsȯŋ\ *n* : a chant of worship sung in various Christian ceremonies

plain·spo·ken \-'spō-kən\ *adj* : speaking or spoken frankly

plaint \'plānt\ *n* **1** : a crying out : WAIL **2** : ¹PROTEST, COMPLAINT

plain·tiff \'plānt-əf\ *n* : the complaining party in a lawsuit

plain·tive \'plānt-iv\ *adj* : showing or expressing sorrow : MOURNFUL, SAD ⟨a *plaintive* sigh⟩ — **plain·tive·ly** *adv* — **plain·tive·ness** *n*

plain weave *n* : a weave in which the threads cross by lacing together alternately — **plain-woven** *adj*

¹plait \'plāt, 'plat\ *vb* **1** : PLEAT 1 **2 a** : ¹BRAID 1 **b** : to make by braiding ⟨*plaiting* a basket⟩ — **plait·er** *n*

²plait *n* **1** : a flat fold : PLEAT **2** : a flat braid (as of hair)

¹plan \'plan\ *n* **1** : a drawing or diagram showing the parts or outline of something **2** : a method or scheme of acting, doing, or arranging ⟨a civil defense *plan*⟩ ⟨vacation *plans*⟩ **3** : GOAL 2, AIM ⟨our *plan* was to stop them at the bridge⟩ — **plan·less** \-ləs\ *adj*

synonyms PLAN, PLOT, SCHEME mean a method of making or doing something or achieving a goal. PLAN suggests that some thinking was done beforehand and often that the thinking resulted in something written down or pictured ⟨a *plan* for a new school⟩. PLOT suggests a complicated carefully shaped plan of several parts. PLOT can be used of the plan of a story ⟨a novel with a good *plot*⟩ or it can be used of a secret and usually evil plan ⟨a *plot* to take over the government⟩. SCHEME suggests a sly plan often motivated by self-interest ⟨a *scheme* to cheat simple people⟩.

²plan *vb* **planned; plan·ning 1** : to form a plan of or for : to arrange the parts or details of ahead of time ⟨*plan* a church⟩ ⟨*plan* a party⟩ **2** : to have in mind : INTEND **3** : to make plans — **plan·ner** *n*

pla·nar·ia \plə-'nar-ē-ə, -'ner-\ *n* : PLANARIAN; *esp* : any of a common freshwater genus

pla·nar·i·an \plə-'nar-ē-ən, -'ner-\ *n* : any of an order of small soft-bodied mostly water-dwelling flatworms having cilia; *esp* : one living in fresh water and having two eyespots and a triangular head

¹plane \'plān\ *vb* **planed; plan·ing 1** : to make smooth or level especially with a plane **2** : to remove by planing — often used with *away* or *off* [Middle English *planen* "to make smooth or level," from early French *planer* (same meaning), derived from Latin *planus* "level" — related to ¹PLAIN] — **plan·er** *n*

²plane *n* : a tool for smoothing or shaping wood

³plane *n* **1 a** : a surface in which a straight line

planarian

PLANETS *

| NAME | SYMBOL | MEAN DISTANCE FROM THE SUN | | | PERIOD OF REVOLUTION | PERIOD OF ROTATION | EQUATORIAL DIAMETER | | MASS |
		astronomical units	million miles	million kilometers	days or years	hours or days	miles	kilometers	relative to Earth
Mercury	☿	0.39	35.99	57.91	87.97 d.	58.65 d.	3,033	4,879	0.06
Venus	♀	0.72	67.25	108.21	224.70 d.	243.02 d.	7,522	12,104	0.82
Earth	⊕	1.00	92.98	149.60	365.26 d.	23.93 h.	7,928	12,756	1.00
Mars	♂	1.52	141.67	227.94	686.99 d.	24.62 h.	4,222	6,794	0.11
Jupiter	♃	5.20	483.78	778.41	11.86 y.	9.92 h.	88,865	142,984	317.82
Saturn	♄	9.54	886.72	1,426.73	29.47 y.	10.66 h.	74,914	120,536	95.16
Uranus	♅	19.19	1,784.32	2,870.97	84.02 y.	17.24 h.	31,770	51,118	14.54
Neptune	♆	30.07	2,795.68	4,498.25	164.79 y.	16.11 h.	30,782	49,528	17.15

*In 2006 the International Astronomical Union defined *planet* in a way that excluded Pluto, classifying it instead as a *dwarf planet*. A number of astronomers dislike the change, and discussion continues. However, most of the general public has accepted the change.

joining any two points on the surface also lies completely on the surface **b** : a flat or level surface **2** : a level of existence or development ⟨on the intellectual *plane*⟩ **3 a** : one of the main supporting surfaces of an airplane **b** : AIRPLANE

⁴plane *adj* **1** : having no elevations or depressions : FLAT **2 a** : of, relating to, or dealing with planes ⟨*plane* geometry⟩ **b** : lying within a plane ⟨a *plane* curve⟩ [from Latin *planus* "level"]

⁵plane *vb* **planed; plan·ing** **1** : to fly while keeping the wings still **2** : to travel by airplane [from French *planer* "to fly while keeping the wings motionless," from *plain* "level, plain"; so called from the fact that the wings of a soaring bird form a level surface]

plan·et \'plan-ət\ *n* : a heavenly body other than a comet, asteroid, or satellite that travels in orbit around the sun; *also* : such a body orbiting another star

Word History Most of the stars seem to have fixed positions when they are compared to other stars. There are some heavenly bodies, however, that clearly change their positions in relation to the stars and to each other. They seem to wander about among the fixed stars. The ancient Greek name for such a heavenly body was *planēs*, which means "wanderer." The English word *planet* comes from the Greek *planēs*. Unlike the ancient Greeks, we now know that the planets "wander" across the sky because they are revolving around the sun. [Middle English *planete* "planet," from early French *planet* (same meaning), from Latin *planeta* (same meaning), from Greek *planēt-*, *planēs* "planet," literally, "wanderer"]

plan·e·tar·i·um \,plan-ə-'ter-ē-əm\ *n, pl* **-i·ums** *or* **-ia** \-ē-ə\ **1** : a device that projects images of heavenly bodies on a ceiling shaped like a dome **2** : a building or room housing a planetarium

plan·e·tary \'plan-ə-,ter-ē\ *adj* **1 a** : of or relating to a planet **b** : having a motion like that of a planet ⟨*planetary* electrons of the atomic nucleus⟩ **2** : WORLDWIDE, GLOBAL ⟨a matter of *planetary* concern⟩

plan·e·tes·i·mal \,plan-ə-'tes-ə-məl, -tez-\ *n* : one of numerous small solid heavenly bodies which may have existed at an early stage of the development of the solar system and from which the planets may have been formed

plan·e·toid \'plan-ə-,toid\ *n* **1** : a body resembling a planet **2** : ASTEROID

¹plank \'plaŋk\ *n* **1** : a wide heavy thick board **2** : an item in the list of beliefs and goals of a political party

²plank *vb* **1** : to cover or floor with planks **2** : to set down forcefully ⟨*planked* the book on the table⟩ **3** : to cook and serve on a board ⟨*planked* steak⟩

plank·ton \'plaŋ(k)-tən, -,tän\ *n* : the floating or weakly swimming animal and plant life of a body of water — **plank·ton·ic** \plaŋ(k)-'tän-ik\ *adj*

pla·no–con·cave \,plā-nō–kän-'kāv, -'kän-,kāv\ *adj* : flat on one side and concave on the other

pla·no–con·vex \,plā-nō–kän-'veks, -'kän-,veks, -kən-'veks\ *adj* : flat on one side and convex on the other

¹plant \'plant\ *vb* **1 a** : to put or set in the ground to grow ⟨*plant* seeds⟩ **b** : to set permanently in the consciousness of : IMPLANT ⟨*plant* good habits⟩ **2 a** : to cause to become established ⟨*plant* colonies⟩ **b** : to stock or provide with something usually to grow or increase ⟨*plant* fields to corn⟩ ⟨*plant* a stream with trout⟩ **3 a** : to place or fix in the ground ⟨*planted* stakes to hold the vines⟩ **b** : to place firmly or forcibly ⟨*planted* themselves right in our way⟩ **4** : to place or introduce so as to mislead ⟨*plant* a spy⟩

²plant *n* **1** : any of a kingdom of mostly photosynthetic living things usually lacking the ability to move from place to place under their own power, having no obvious nervous or sensory organs, possessing cellulose cell walls, and often having a body that is able to keep growing without taking on a fixed size and shape **2 a** : the land, buildings, and equipment of an organization ⟨the college *plant*⟩ **b** : a building or workshop for the manufacture of a product : FACTORY **c** : POWER PLANT **3** : something or someone planted ⟨left muddy footprints as a *plant* to confuse the police⟩ — **plant·like** \-,līk\ *adj*

¹plan·tain \'plant-ᵊn\ *n* : any of several common weeds having a short stem or none at all, leaves with parallel veins, and a long stalk of tiny greenish flowers

²plantain *n* : the large greenish starchy fruit of a kind of banana plant that is eaten cooked and is an important food in the tropics; *also* : this plant

plan·ta·tion \plan-'tā-shən\ *n* **1** : a group of plants and especially trees planted and cared for **2** : a settlement in a new country or region : COLONY **3** : a planted area; *esp* : an agricultural estate worked by laborers

plant·er \'plant-ər\ *n* **1** : one that plants or cultivates ⟨a mechanical corn *planter*⟩; *esp* : a person who owns or operates a plantation **2** : a container in which ornamental plants are grown

plant food *n* **1** : FOOD 2b **2** : FERTILIZER

plant hormone *n* : a substance other than food that in small amounts changes one of the life processes of a plant; *esp* : one made by the plant itself and acting somewhere other than at the site where it is produced

plan·ti·grade \'plant-ə-,grād\ *adj* : walking on the sole with the heel touching the ground ⟨human beings are *plantigrade*⟩

plant kingdom *n* : a basic group of natural objects that includes all living and extinct plants — compare ANIMAL KINGDOM, MINERAL KINGDOM

¹plantain

\ə\ abut	\au̇\ out	\i\ tip	\ȯ\ saw	\u̇\ foot
\ər\ further	\ch\ chin	\ī\ life	\ȯi\ coin	\y\ yet
\a\ mat	\e\ pet	\j\ job	\th\ thin	\yü\ few
\ā\ take	\ē\ easy	\ŋ\ sing	\t̲h̲\ this	\yu̇\ cure
\ä\ cot, cart	\g\ go	\ō\ bone	\ü\ food	\zh\ vision

plant louse *n* : APHID; *also* : any of various small insects that are like aphids

plaque \'plak\ *n* **1** : an ornamental pin; *esp* : an honorary badge **2** : a flat thin piece (as of metal) used for decoration or inscribed as a memorial or marker **3** : a sticky usually colorless film on teeth that is formed by and contains bacteria

plash \'plash\ *n* : ²SPLASH — **plash** *vb*

plas·ma \'plaz-mə\ *n* **1** : the watery part of blood, lymph, or milk **2** : a collection of charged particles that shows some characteristics of a gas but that differs from a gas in being a good conductor of electricity and in being affected by a magnetic field

plasma membrane *n* : CELL MEMBRANE

plas·mo·di·um \plaz-'mōd-ē-əm\ *n, pl* **-dia** \-ē-ə\ : a parasite that causes malaria

¹plas·ter \'plas-tər\ *n* **1** : a medicated or protective dressing consisting of a film (as of cloth or plastic) spread with a substance that clings to the skin ⟨adhesive *plaster*⟩ **2** : a paste (as of lime, water, and sand) that hardens on drying and is used for coating walls and ceilings — **plas·tery** \-t(ə-)rē\ *adj*

²plaster *vb* **plas·tered; plas·ter·ing** \-t(ə-)riŋ\ **1** : to apply a plaster to **2** : to cover over as if with a coat of plaster **3** : to smooth down with a sticky or shiny substance ⟨*plastered* my hair down⟩ **4** : to fasten or apply tightly to another surface ⟨wet clothes *plastered* to his body⟩ **5** : to affix to or place on especially in large numbers ⟨*plaster* posters to a wall⟩ **6** : to apply plaster — **plas·ter·er** \-tər-ər\ *n*

plas·ter·board \'plas-tər-,bō(ə)rd, -,bȯ(ə)rd\ *n* : DRYWALL

plaster cast *n* : a rigid dressing of gauze filled with plaster of paris

plaster of par·is \-'par-əs\ *often cap 2nd P* : a white powder made from gypsum that mixes with water to form a paste that hardens quickly and is used chiefly for casts and molds

¹plas·tic \'plas-tik\ *adj* **1** : capable of being molded or modeled ⟨*plastic* clay⟩ **2** : marked by or using modeling ⟨sculpture is a *plastic* art⟩ **3** : made or consisting of a plastic ⟨*plastic* dishes⟩ — **plas·ti·cal·ly** \-ti-k(ə-)lē\ *adv*

²plastic *n* : a plastic substance; *esp* : any of numerous synthetic or processed materials that can be formed into objects, films, or fibers

plas·tic·i·ty \pla-'stis-ət-ē\ *n* : the quality or state of being plastic; *esp* : capacity for being molded or changed in form or shape

plastic surgeon *n* : a surgeon skilled in plastic surgery

plastic surgery *n* : surgery concerned with the repair or improvement of lost, injured, defective, or misshapen parts of the body

plas·tid \'plas-təd\ *n* : any of various small bodies (as chloroplasts) that occur in the cytoplasm of cells of photosynthetic organisms (as plants) and that often serve as centers for special activities (as storage of starch)

plat \'plat\ *n* **1** : a small plot of ground **2** : a plan or map of an area with lots marked out

¹plate \'plāt\ *n* **1 a** : a flat thin piece of material **b** : metal in sheets ⟨steel *plate*⟩ **c** : a thin layer of one metal deposited on another **2 a** : one of the broad metal pieces used in armor **b** : armor made of plates **3** : a usually flat bony or horny bodily part forming part of a covering of an animal (as some fishes or reptiles) **4** : HOME PLATE **5** : any of the huge movable segments into which the earth's lithosphere is divided and which are held to float on and travel over the mantle **6 a** : precious metal; *esp* : silver bullion **b** : vessels (as bowls or cups) used in the home and made of or plated with precious metal (as silver) **7 a** : a shallow usually circular dish from which food is eaten or served **b** : a main food course served on a plate ⟨a *plate* of spaghetti⟩ **c** : food and service for one person ⟨a dinner at $10 a *plate*⟩ **d** : a dish or pouch used in taking

a collection (as in a church) **8 a** : a prepared surface from which printing is done **b** : a sheet of material (as plastic or glass) coated with a chemical sensitive to light for use in a camera **9** : LICENSE PLATE **10** : the part of a denture that holds the false teeth and fits to the mouth; *also* : a set of false teeth **11** : a full-page illustration ⟨an art book with color *plates*⟩ — **plate·like** \-,līk\ *adj*

²plate *vb* **plat·ed; plat·ing** : to cover or equip with plate ⟨*plate* the teapot with silver⟩

pla·teau \pla-'tō, 'pla-,tō\ *n, pl* **plateaus** *or* **pla·teaux** \-'tōz, -,tōz\ **1** : a broad flat area of high land **2** : a stable level, period, or condition [from French *plateau* "flat land raised above the surrounding land," from early French *plateau* "platter, plate"]

plate·ful \'plāt-,fu̇l\ *n* : a quantity to fill a plate

plate glass *n* : fine glass in large sheets that has been ground and polished

plate·let \'plāt-lət\ *n* : one of the tiny colorless disk-shaped bodies of the blood of mammals that assist in blood clotting

plate tectonics *n* **1** : a theory in geology: the lithosphere of the earth is divided into a small number of moving plates whose movements cause seismic activity (as earthquakes) **2** : the process of plate movement — **plate–tectonic** *adj*

plat·form \'plat-,fȯrm\ *n* **1** : a declaration of the beliefs and goals of a political party or candidate **2 a** : a level usually raised surface ⟨a railroad station *platform*⟩ **b** : a raised floor or stage for performers or speakers **3** : a thick sole for a shoe or a shoe with such a sole

plat·ing \'plāt-iŋ\ *n* **1** : the act or process of covering especially with metal plate **2** : a coating of metal plates or plate ⟨armor *plating*⟩ ⟨the *plating* wore off the spoons⟩

¹plat·i·num \'plat-nəm, -ᵊn-əm\ *n* : a heavy precious grayish white metallic element that is used especially as a catalyst and in jewelry — see ELEMENT table

²platinum *adj* : qualifying for a platinum record — **go platinum** : to have enough sales to qualify for a platinum record

platinum record *n* : a platinum phonograph record awarded to a singer or group whose album has sold at least one million copies

plat·i·tude \'plat-ə-,t(y)üd\ *n* **1** : the quality or state of being dull or not stimulating **2** : an obvious, stale, or shallow remark

pla·toon \plə-'tün, pla-\ *n* **1** : a part of a military company consisting of two or more squads **2** : a group of football players sent into or withdrawn from the game as a body

platoon sergeant *n* : a noncommissioned officer in the army with a rank just below that of first sergeant

plat·ter \'plat-ər\ *n* **1** : a large plate used especially for serving meat **2** : a phonograph record

platy \'plat-ē\ *n, pl* **platy** *or* **plat·ys** *or* **plat·ies** : either of two small freshwater fish that are often kept in tropical aquariums and are noted for their varied and brilliant colors

platy·pus \'plat-i-pəs, -,pu̇s\ *n, pl* **platy·pus·es** *also* **platy·pi** \-,pī, -,pē\ : a small water-dwelling egg-laying mammal of eastern Australia and Tasmania with a fleshy bill resembling that of a duck, webbed feet, and a broad flattened tail

platypus

plau·dit \'plȯd-ət\ *n* **1** : APPLAUSE **2** : enthusiastic approval — usually used in plural ⟨received the *plaudits* of the critics⟩ [from Latin *plaudite*, a form of *plaudere* "to clap" — related to

APPLAUD, EXPLODE, PLAUSIBLE; see *Word History* at EX-
PLODE, PLAUSIBLE]

plau·si·ble \'plȯ-zə-bəl\ *adj* **1** : seemingly fair, reasonable,
or valuable but often not so ⟨a *plausible* excuse⟩ **2** : appearing worthy of belief ⟨the argument was both *plausible* and powerful⟩ — **plau·si·bil·i·ty** \ˌplȯ-zə-'bil-ət-ē\ *n*
— **plau·si·bly** \'plȯ-zə-blē\ *adv*

Word History A plausible explanation is one that sounds
as if it could be true. Such an explanation is not usually
greeted with applause, but the origin of *plausible* suggests that it might be. *Plausible* comes from the Latin
word *plausibilis,* meaning "worthy of applause." The
first use of *plausible* in English was to describe a person
or thing that deserved special praise. That use is now
obsolete. To call something *plausible* now is to praise it
only slightly, if at all. [from Latin *plausibilis* "deserving
applause, pleasing," from *plausus,* past participle of
plaudere "to clap" — related to APPLAUD, EXPLODE,
PLAUDIT; see *Word History* at EXPLODE]

¹play \'plā\ *n* **1 a** : a brisk handling or using ⟨the *play* of a
sword⟩ **b** : the conduct, course, or action of a game ⟨rain
held up *play*⟩ **c** : a particular act or maneuver in a game
⟨a great *play* by the shortstop⟩ **d** : one's turn in a game
⟨it's your *play*⟩ **2 a** : exercise or activity for amusement
⟨children at *play*⟩ **b** : absence of any bad intention ⟨said
it in *play*⟩ **c** : the act or an instance of playing on words
: PUN **d** : the act of playing a game and risking something
on an uncertain event : GAMBLING, GAMING **3 a** : a way
or manner of acting or proceeding : ACTION, CONDUCT
⟨fair *play*⟩ **b** : OPERATION 1, ACTIVITY **c** : brisk or light
movement ⟨the light *play* of a breeze⟩ **d** : freedom of
motion ⟨too much *play* in the steering wheel⟩ **e** : opportunity for action ⟨the new job gave *play* to my talents⟩ **4
a** : the stage representation of an action or story **b** : a
dramatic composition : DRAMA — **in play** : in condition
or position to be legitimately played ⟨the ball was *in play*⟩
— **out of play** : not in play

²play *vb* **1 a** : to engage in sport or recreation and especially in activity for amusement ⟨children *playing*⟩ **b** : to
treat or behave lightly or without respect that is due ⟨*play*
with a new idea⟩ **c** : to make use of double meaning or
the similarity of sound of two words for humorous effect
: PUN **d** : to handle something in an absentminded way
: TOY ⟨*played* with the pencil⟩ **2 a** : to take advantage
⟨*played* upon the people's fears⟩ **b** : to move swiftly or
lightly ⟨shadows *playing* on the wall⟩ **c** : to move freely
d : to let go in a stream ⟨hoses *playing* on the fire⟩ **3 a**
: to sound in performance ⟨listen to an organ *playing*⟩ **b**
: to be staged or presented ⟨what's *playing* at the movies⟩
4 : to behave in a particular way ⟨*play* safe⟩ **5 a** : to take
part in ⟨*play* cards⟩ ⟨*play* ball⟩ **b** : to pretend to take part
in the activities of ⟨children *playing* house⟩ **c** : to do for
amusement or from mischief ⟨*play* a trick on someone⟩
6 a : to perform on or as if on the stage ⟨*play* a part⟩ **b**
: to act the part of ⟨*play* the fool⟩ **7 a** : to contend against
in a game ⟨*playing* the Dodgers today⟩ **b** : to put or keep
in action ⟨*play* a card in a game⟩ ⟨*play* a fish on a line⟩ **8**
: to cause something to produce music or sound ⟨*play* the
piano⟩ ⟨*play* a record⟩ — **play·able** \'plā-ə-bəl\ *adj* —
play ball : COOPERATE

play·act·ing \'plā-ˌak-tiŋ\ *n* **1** : performance in theatrical
productions **2** : behavior that is not sincere or natural

play·back \'plā-ˌbak\ *n* : the action of reproducing recorded sound or pictures often immediately after recording

play back \(')plā-'bak\ *vb* : to perform a playback of (a
disc or tape)

play·bill \'plā-ˌbil\ *n* : a poster advertising a play

play·boy \-ˌbȯi\ *n* : a man whose chief interest is the pursuit of pleasure

play down *vb* : to attach little importance to : MINIMIZE

play·er \'plā-ər\ *n* **1 a** : a person who plays a game **b**

: MUSICIAN **c** : ACTOR **2** : a device for playing recorded
material (as music) ⟨an MP3 *player*⟩

player piano *n* : a piano containing an automatic playing
mechanism

play·fel·low \'plā-ˌfel-ō\ *n* : PLAYMATE

play·ful \'plā-fəl\ *adj* **1** : full of play ⟨fond of playing ⟨a
playful kitten⟩ **2** : HUMOROUS ⟨a *playful* tone of voice⟩
— **play·ful·ly** \-fə-lē\ *adv* — **play·ful·ness** *n*

play·ground \'plā-ˌgraünd\ *n* : a piece of land used for
games and recreation especially by children

play·house \-ˌhaüs\ *n* **1** : THEATER 1 **2** : a small house for
children to play in

playing card *n* : any of a set of cards marked to show rank
and suit (as spades, hearts, diamonds, or clubs) and used
in playing games

playing field *n* : a field for various games; *esp* : the part of
a field marked off for play

play·let \'plā-lət\ *n* : a short play

play·mate \'plā-ˌmāt\ *n* : a companion in play

play–off \'plā-ˌȯf\ *n* **1** : a final contest or series of contests
to break a tie **2** : a series of contests played after the end
of the regular season to determine a championship — often used in plural

play off \(')plā-'ȯf\ *vb* : to break a tie by a play-off

play out *vb* **1** : to perform to the end **2 a** : to use up or
finish **b** : to become exhausted : TIRE **3** : UNREEL, UN-
FOLD

play·pen \'plā-ˌpen\ *n* : a portable enclosure in which a
baby or young child is placed to play

play·thing \-ˌthiŋ\ *n* : ¹TOY 2

play up *vb* : EMPHASIZE

play·wright \'plā-ˌrīt\ *n* : a person who writes plays

pla·za \'plaz-ə, 'pläz-\ *n* : a public square in a city or town

plea \'plē\ *n* **1** : a defendant's answer to a lawsuit or to a
criminal charge ⟨a *plea* of guilty⟩ **2** : something offered
as an excuse ⟨left early with the *plea* of a headache⟩ **3**
: an earnest appeal ⟨a *plea* for mercy⟩

plead \'plēd\ *vb* **plead·ed** \'plēd-əd\ *or* **pled** \'pled\;
plead·ing 1 : to argue a case in a court of law **2** : to
answer to a claim or charge in a court of law ⟨*plead* not
guilty⟩ **3 a** : to argue for or against a claim ⟨*plead* a case
before a jury⟩ **b** : to appeal earnestly : BEG **4** : to offer
as a defense, apology, or excuse ⟨*plead* sickness⟩ —
plead·er *n*

pleas·ant \'plez-ᵊnt\ *adj* **1** : giving pleasure : AGREEABLE
⟨a *pleasant* day⟩ **2** : having or marked by pleasing manners, behavior, or appearance ⟨the new teacher is very
pleasant⟩ — **pleas·ant·ly** *adv* — **pleas·ant·ness** *n*

pleas·ant·ry \'plez-ᵊn-trē\ *n, pl* **-ries 1** : agreeable playfulness in conversation **2 a** : a humorous act or speech **b**
: a light or casual polite remark

¹please \'plēz\ *vb* **pleased; pleas·ing 1** : to give pleasure
or satisfaction ⟨the new show will really *please* you⟩ **2**
: to feel the desire : LIKE ⟨do what you *please*⟩

²please *adv* — used to express politeness in a request
⟨*please* come in⟩

pleas·ing \'plē-ziŋ\ *adj* : giving pleasure : AGREEABLE —
pleas·ing·ly *adv*

plea·sur·able \'plezh-(ə-)rə-bəl, 'plāzh-\ *adj* : PLEASANT 1
— **plea·sur·ably** \-blē\ *adv*

plea·sure \'plezh-ər, 'plāzh-\ *n* **1** : a particular desire or
purpose : INCLINATION ⟨what's your *pleasure*⟩ **2** : the
feeling that comes when one's wishes are met **3** : a source
of delight or joy

synonyms PLEASURE, JOY, ENJOYMENT mean the agreeable feeling that accompanies getting something good or

\ə\ abut	\au̇\ out	\i\ tip	\ȯ\ saw	\u̇\ foot
\ər\ further	\ch\ chin	\ī\ life	\ȯi\ coin	\y\ yet
\a\ mat	\e\ pet	\j\ job	\th\ thin	\yü\ few
\ā\ take	\ē\ easy	\ŋ\ sing	\th\ this	\yu̇\ cure
\ä\ cot, cart	\g\ go	\ō\ bone	\ü\ food	\zh\ vision

much wanted. PLEASURE suggests an inner satisfaction rather than an open display of feeling ⟨the *pleasure* felt after helping others⟩. JOY suggests a very strong feeling that is shown openly ⟨you could see the winner's *joy*⟩. ENJOYMENT suggests a conscious reaction to something intended to make one happy ⟨the songs added to our *enjoyment* of the movie⟩.

¹**pleat** \'plēt\ *vb* **1** : to fold or arrange in pleats ⟨*pleat* a skirt⟩ **2** : ¹BRAID 1 — **pleat·er** *n*

²**pleat** *n* : a fold (as in cloth) made by doubling material over on itself

ple·be·ian \pli-'bē-(y)ən\ *n* **1** : a member of the common people in ancient Rome **2** : one of the common people — **plebeian** *adj*

pleb·i·scite \'pleb-ə-ˌsīt, -sət\ *n* : a vote by which the people of an entire country or district express an opinion for or against a proposal especially on a choice of government or ruler

plec·trum \'plek-trəm\ *n, pl* **plec·tra** \-trə\ *or* **plectrums** : ³PICK 3

¹**pledge** \'plej\ *n* **1** : the handing over of something to another to assure that the giver will keep his or her promise; *also* : the thing handed over **2** : the state of being held as a security ⟨given in *pledge*⟩ **3** : something that is a token or sign of something else ⟨the ring is a *pledge* of love⟩ **4** : ²TOAST 3 **5** : a promise or agreement that must be kept

²**pledge** *vb* **pledged; pledg·ing 1** : to give as a pledge **2** : to drink to the health of : ³TOAST **3** : to obligate by a pledge ⟨*pledged* myself to give $50⟩ **4** : to promise by a pledge ⟨*pledge* money to charity⟩

Ple·ia·des \'plē-ə-ˌdēz\ *n pl* : a loose cluster of stars in Taurus that is easily seen by a person with average sight

Pleis·to·cene \'plīs-tə-ˌsēn\ *adj* : of, relating to, or being the earlier epoch of the Quaternary period of geological history or the corresponding series of rocks — see GEOLOGIC TIME table — **Pleistocene** *n*

ple·na·ry \'plē-nə-rē, 'plen-ə-\ *adj* **1** : complete in all ways : FULL ⟨*plenary* powers⟩ **2** : including all who have a right to attend ⟨a *plenary* session of an assembly⟩

pleni·po·ten·tia·ry \ˌplen-ə-pə-'tench-(ə-)rē, -'ten-chē-ˌer-ē\ *n, pl* **-ries** : a person and especially a diplomatic agent having full power to carry on business — **plenipotentiary** *adj*

plen·i·tude \'plen-ə-ˌt(y)üd\ *n* : the quality or state of being full or plentiful : ABUNDANCE

plen·te·ous \'plent-ē-əs\ *adj* : PLENTIFUL 2 — **plen·te·ous·ly** *adv*

plen·ti·ful \'plent-i-fəl\ *adj* **1** : giving or containing plenty ⟨a *plentiful* land⟩ **2** : present in large numbers or amount ⟨*plentiful* rain⟩ — **plen·ti·ful·ly** \-fə-lē\ *adv*

synonyms PLENTIFUL, AMPLE, ABUNDANT, COPIOUS mean more than enough yet not too much. PLENTIFUL suggests a great or rich supply ⟨vegetables are cheap when *plentiful*⟩. AMPLE suggests an amount more than enough to meet a particular need ⟨an income *ample* for the way that I live⟩. ABUNDANT suggests a supply far greater than needed ⟨an unexpectedly *abundant* corn harvest⟩. COPIOUS suggests more often a large quantity or number than a rich supply ⟨took *copious* notes during the lecture⟩.

plen·ti·tude \'plen(t)-ə-ˌt(y)üd\ *n* : PLENITUDE

¹**plen·ty** \'plent-ē\ *n* **1 a** : a full supply ⟨had *plenty* of time to finish⟩ **b** : a large number or amount ⟨is in *plenty* of trouble⟩ **2** : the state of being plentiful ⟨times of *plenty*⟩

²**plenty** *adv* : QUITE 2 ⟨the game was *plenty* exciting⟩

ple·sio·saur \'plē-sē-ə-ˌsȯ(ə)r, -zē-\ *n* : any of a group of large Mesozoic marine reptiles with flattened bodies and limbs changed into paddles

pleu·ra \'plu̇r-ə\ *n, pl* **pleu·rae** \'plu̇(ə)r-ˌē, -ˌī\ *or* **pleuras** : the delicate membrane lining each half of the chest of mammals and folded back over the surface of the lung of the same side — **pleu·ral** \'plu̇r-əl\ *adj*

pleu·ri·sy \'plu̇r-ə-sē\ *n* : inflammation of the pleura usually with fever, painful breathing, and coughing

plex·i·glass \'plek-si-ˌglas\ *n* : a transparent acrylic plastic often used in place of glass

plex·us \'plek-səs\ *n, pl* **plex·us·es** : a network especially of blood vessels or nerves

pli·able \'plī-ə-bəl\ *adj* **1** : possible to bend without breaking **2** : easily influenced — **pli·abil·i·ty** \ˌplī-ə-'bil-ət-ē\ *n*

pli·ant \'plī-ənt\ *adj* **1** : PLIABLE 1, FLEXIBLE ⟨*pliant* willow twigs⟩ **2** : PLIABLE 2, YIELDING **3** : adjusting to changing conditions : ADAPTABLE — **pli·ant·ly** *adv*

plied *past and past participle of* PLY

pli·ers \'plī-(ə)rz\ *n pl* : a small pincers for holding small objects or for bending and cutting wire

plies *plural of* PLY

¹**plight** \'plīt\ *vb* : to put or give in pledge — **plight·er** *n*

²**plight** *n* : a usually bad condition or state : PREDICAMENT ⟨in a sorry *plight*⟩

pliers

plinth \'plin(t)th\ *n* **1** : the lowest part of the base of an architectural column **2** : a block used as a base (as for a vase)

Plio·cene \'plī-ə-ˌsēn\ *adj* : of, relating to, or being the latest epoch of the Tertiary period of geological history or the corresponding series of rocks — see GEOLOGIC TIME table — **Pliocene** *n*

plod \'pläd\ *vb* **plod·ded; plod·ding 1** : to walk heavily or slowly : TRUDGE **2** : to work or study with effort **3** : to progress or develop slowly — **plod** *n* — **plod·der** *n* — **plod·ding·ly** \-iŋ-lē\ *adv*

plonk *variant of* PLUNK

plop \'pläp\ *vb* **plopped; plop·ping 1** : to make or move with a sound like that of something dropping into water **2** : to set, drop, or throw heavily ⟨*plopped* myself in a chair⟩ — **plop** *n*

¹**plot** \'plät\ *n* **1** : a small area of ground : LOT ⟨a cemetery *plot*⟩ **2** : a plan of a floor of a building **3** : the main story (as of a literary work or movie) **4** : an evil or unlawful scheme **5** : ¹DIAGRAM, CHART **synonyms** see PLAN

²**plot** *vb* **plot·ted; plot·ting 1 a** : to make a plot, map, or plan of **b** : to mark, note, or locate on a map or chart ⟨*plot* a ship's position⟩ **2** : to plan especially secretly : SCHEME **3 a** : to locate and mark (a point) by means of coordinates **b** : to make (a curve) by marking out a number of plotted points — **plot·ter** *n*

plough *chiefly British variant of* PLOW

plo·ver \'pləv-ər, 'plō-vər\ *n, pl* **plover** *or* **plovers** : any of numerous shorebirds differing from the related sandpipers in having shorter bills

¹**plow** \'plau̇\ *n* **1** : a farm machine used to cut, lift, and turn over soil **2** : a device (as a snowplow) used to spread or clear away material on the ground

²**plow** *vb* **1** : to open, break up, or work with a plow ⟨*plow* a furrow⟩ **2** : to move forcefully into or through ⟨a ship *plowing* the waves⟩ **3** : to go steadily and with great effort ⟨*plow* through a report⟩ **4** : to clear away snow from with a plow ⟨*plow* the road⟩

plow·boy \'plau̇-ˌbȯi\ *n* **1** : a boy who guides a plow or leads the horse drawing it **2** : a country youth

plow·man \-mən\ *n* **1** : one that plows **2** : a farm laborer

plow·share \-ˌshe(ə)r, -ˌsha(ə)r\ *n* : the part of a plow that cuts the earth

ploy \'plȯi\ *n* : a trick designed to embarrass or upset an opponent

¹**pluck** \'plək\ *vb* **1 a** : to pull or pick off or out ⟨*pluck* a flower⟩ **b** : to remove something (as feathers) from by or as if by plucking ⟨*pluck* a chicken⟩ **2** : to move or separate forcibly : SNATCH ⟨*plucked* the child from danger⟩ **3**

: to play by pulling the strings ⟨*pluck* a guitar⟩ — **pluck-er** *n*

²pluck *n* **1** : a sharp pull : TUG **2** : COURAGE, SPIRIT

plucky \'plǝk-ē\ *adj* **pluck·i·er; -est** : COURAGEOUS, BRAVE

¹plug \'plǝg\ *n* **1** : a piece used to close or fill a hole **2** : a flat cake of tightly pressed tobacco leaves **3** : something of lesser quality; *esp* : a worn-out horse **4** : SPARK PLUG 1 **5** : a lure with several hooks used in casting for fish **6** : a device usually on a cord used to make an electrical connection by putting it into another part (as a socket) **7** : a piece of favorable publicity

¹plug 5

²plug *vb* **plugged; plug·ging 1** : to stop, make tight, or secure with or as if with a plug ⟨*plug* the leak with tar⟩ **2** : to hit with a bullet : SHOOT **3** : to advertise or publicize over and over **4** : to become plugged — usually used with *up* ⟨the drain was *plugged* up⟩ **5** : to keep steadily at work or in action ⟨*plugged* away at my homework⟩ — **plug·ger** *n* — **plug into** : to connect or become connected to by or as if by means of a plug ⟨the generator *plugs into* the power grid⟩

plug-in \'plǝg-ˌin\ *n* : software that adds to the capabilities of a larger program (as a browser)

plug in *vb* : to establish an electric circuit by inserting a plug

plum \'plǝm\ *n* **1 a** : any of numerous trees and shrubs related to the peach and cherries and having globe-shaped to oval edible fruits with an oblong stone **b** : the smooth-skinned fruit of a plum **2** : a raisin when used in desserts (as puddings or cake) **3** : something very desirable **4** : a dark reddish purple — **plum·like** \-ˌlīk\ *adj*

plum·age \'plü-mij\ *n* : the feathers of a bird

¹plumb \'plǝm\ *n* : a weight attached to a line especially to show a vertical direction or distance — **out of plumb** *or* **off plumb** : not vertical or true

²plumb *adv* **1** : straight down or up : VERTICALLY **2** *chiefly dialect* : to a complete degree : ABSOLUTELY **3** : in a direct manner : EXACTLY

³plumb *vb* **1** : to measure, adjust, or test with a plumb ⟨*plumb* a wall⟩ ⟨plumb the depth of the well⟩ **2** : to see into and come to understand ⟨*plumbed* their motives⟩

⁴plumb *adj* : exactly vertical or true ⟨the wall is *plumb*⟩

plumb bob *n* : the metal bob of a plumb line

plumb·er \'plǝm-ǝr\ *n* : a person who puts in or repairs the pipes and fixtures involved in the distribution and use of water in a building

plumber's helper *n* : PLUNGER b

plumb·ing \'plǝm-iŋ\ *n* **1** : a plumber's work **2** : a system of pipes for supplying and carrying off water in a building

plumb line *n* : a line that has a weight (as a plumb bob) at one end and is used to find out whether something is vertical or to measure depth

¹plume \'plüm\ *n* **1** : a feather of a bird; *esp* : one that is large and showy **2 a** : a feather or tuft of feathers worn as an ornament (as on a hat) **b** : a deserved prize or reward **3** : something that resembles a feather (as in shape or lightness) ⟨a *plume* of smoke⟩ — **plumy** \'plü-mē\ *adj*

²plume *vb* **plumed; plum·ing 1** : to provide or adorn with feathers **2** : to act with too much pride in oneself ⟨*plumed* himself on his swimming skill⟩ **3** : to arrange the feathers of : PREEN ⟨a bird *pluming* itself⟩

¹plum·met \'plǝm-ǝt\ *n* **1** : ¹PLUMB **2** : PLUMB LINE

²plummet *vb* : to fall straight down : PLUNGE

¹plump \'plǝmp\ *vb* **1** : to drop, sink, or come in contact suddenly or heavily ⟨*plumped* down in the chair⟩ **2** : to support someone or something strongly — used with *for*

⟨*plump* for a candidate⟩ [Middle English *plumpen* "to drop or sink heavily"]

²plump *n* : a sudden plunge, fall, or blow

³plump *adv* **1** : with a sudden or heavy drop **2** : ¹DIRECTLY 1 ⟨ran *plump* into the wall⟩

⁴plump *vb* : to make or become plump ⟨*plump* up a pillow⟩ [*plump* (adjective) "rounded, chubby," from Middle English *plump* "dull, blunt"]

⁵plump *adj* : having a full rounded form : CHUBBY — **plump·ness** *n*

plum pudding *n* : a rich boiled or steamed pudding containing fruits (as raisins) and spices

plum tomato *n* : a small oblong tomato

plu·mule \'plü-myü(ǝ)l\ *n* : the shoot or bud of a plant embryo or seedling that is located between the cotyledons and grows into the stem and leaves

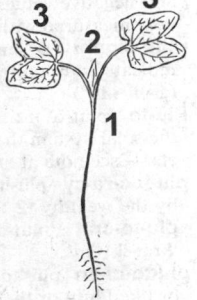

plumule:
1 hypocotyl,
2 plumule,
3 cotyledons

¹plun·der \'plǝn-dǝr\ *vb* **plun·dered; plun·der·ing** \-d(ǝ-)riŋ\ : to rob especially openly and by force (as in a raid) — **plun·der·er** \-dǝr-ǝr\ *n*

²plunder *n* **1** : an act of plundering **2** : something taken by force or theft : LOOT

¹plunge \'plǝnj\ *vb* **plunged; plung·ing 1** : to push or drive into something with force ⟨*plunged* a knife into the pie⟩ **2** : to leap or dive into water **3 a** : to rush with reckless haste ⟨*plunged* into debt⟩ **b** : to bring into an unpleasant state ⟨*plunged* the family into gloom⟩ **4** : to dip or move suddenly downward or forward and downward ⟨the road *plunges* along the slope⟩

²plunge *n* : a sudden dive, leap, or rush

plung·er \'plǝn-jǝr\ *n* : one that plunges: as **a** : a device (as a piston in a pump) that acts with a plunging motion **b** : a rubber suction cup on a handle used to free plumbing traps and waste outlets of something blocking them

plunk \'plǝŋk\ *or* **plonk** \'pläŋk, 'plòŋk\ *vb* **1** : to make or cause to make a hollow, metallic, or harsh sound ⟨*plunk* the strings of a banjo⟩ **2** : to drop or set down suddenly ⟨*plunk* a suitcase on the bench⟩ — **plunk** *n*

¹plu·ral \'plùr-ǝl\ *adj* : of, relating to, or being a word form used to indicate more than one ⟨*plural* nouns⟩ — **plu·ral·ly** \-ǝ-lē\ *adv*

²plural *n* : a form of a word used to show that more than one person or thing is meant

plu·ral·i·ty \plù-'ral-ǝt-ē\ *n, pl* **-ties 1** : the state of being plural or numerous **2 a** : the greater number or part ⟨a *plurality* of the nations want peace⟩ **b** : the number of votes by which one candidate wins over another **c** : a number of votes cast for a candidate in a contest of more than two candidates that is greater than the number cast for any other candidate but is not more than half the total votes cast

plu·ral·ize \'plùr-ǝ-ˌlīz\ *vb* **-ized; -iz·ing** : to make plural or express in the plural form — **plu·ral·i·za·tion** \ˌplùr-ǝ-lǝ-'zā-shǝn\ *n*

¹plus \'plǝs\ *adj* **1** : mathematically positive ⟨a *plus* quantity⟩ **2** : having, receiving, or being in addition to what is expected ⟨now she is *plus* a kitten⟩ **3** : falling high in a certain range ⟨a grade of C *plus*⟩ **4** : electrically positive

\ǝ\ **abut**	\au̇\ **out**	\i\ **tip**	\ò\ **saw**	\u̇\ **foot**
\ǝr\ **further**	\ch\ **chin**	\ī\ **life**	\ȯi\ **coin**	\y\ **yet**
\a\ **mat**	\e\ **pet**	\j\ **job**	\th\ **thin**	\yü\ **few**
\ā\ **take**	\ē\ **easy**	\ŋ\ **sing**	\th\ **this**	\yu̇\ **cure**
\ä\ **cot, cart**	\g\ **go**	\ō\ **bone**	\ü\ **food**	\zh\ **vision**

²**plus** *n, pl* **plus·es** \'pləs-əz\ *also* **plus·ses 1** : an added quantity **2** : something that is an advantage ⟨that the machine operated quietly was a *plus*⟩

³**plus** *prep* : increased by : with the addition of ⟨4 *plus* 5 is 9⟩

¹**plush** \'pləsh\ *n* : a fabric like a very thick soft velvet

²**plush** *adj* **1** : made of or like plush **2** : very luxurious ⟨a *plush* home⟩

plus/minus sign *n* : the sign ± used to mean that a quantity (as 2 in "the square root of 4 is ± 2") takes on both a positive and a negative value or to indicate a plus or minus quantity (as 5 in "the scale was accurate to ± 5 grams") — called also *plus/minus symbol*

plus or minus *adj* : indicating a quantity whose positive and negative values establish the limits of a range of values ⟨measured with an accuracy of *plus or minus* 1 gram⟩

plus sign *n* : a sign + used especially in mathematics to indicate addition (as in 8 + 6 = 14) or a positive quantity (as in +10°)

Plu·to \'plüt-ō\ *n* : a large object in the outermost part of the solar system that is often considered one of the planets — see note at PLANET table

plu·toc·ra·cy \plü-'täk-rə-sē\ *n, pl* **-cies 1** : government by the wealthy **2** : a controlling class of the wealthy — **plu·to·crat** \'plüt-ə-ˌkrat\ *n* — **plu·to·crat·ic** \ˌplüt-ə-'krat-ik\ *adj*

plu·to·ni·an \plü-'tō-nē-ən\ *adj, often cap* : of, relating to, or like Pluto or the lower world : INFERNAL

plu·to·ni·um \plü-'tō-nē-əm\ *n* : a radioactive metallic element that is formed by decay of neptunium and found in minute quantities in pitchblende and that produces atomic energy by fission — see ELEMENT table

¹**ply** \'plī\ *vb* **plied; ply·ing 1 a** : to use steadily or forcefully ⟨*ply* an ax⟩ **b** : to work at ⟨*ply* one's trade⟩ **2** : to keep furnishing or supplying something to ⟨*ply* a guest with food⟩ **3** : to go or travel regularly [Middle English *plien*, a shortened form of *applien* "to apply"]

²**ply** *n, pl* **plies** : one of the folds, layers, or strands of which something (as yarn or plywood) is made up [Middle English *plien* "to fold," from early French *plier* (same meaning), from Latin *plicare* (same meaning)]

Plym·outh Rock \ˌplim-əth-\ *n* : any of an American breed of medium-sized domestic chickens having a single comb

ply·wood \'plī-ˌwùd\ *n* : a strong board made by gluing thin sheets of wood together under heat and pressure

PMS \ˌpē-ˌem-'es\ *n* : PREMENSTRUAL SYNDROME

pneu·mat·ic \n(y)ù-'mat-ik\ *adj* **1** : of, relating to, or using air, wind, or other gas **2** : moved or worked by air pressure ⟨a *pneumatic* drill⟩ **3** : made to hold or be inflated with compressed air ⟨*pneumatic* tires⟩ [from Latin *pneumaticus* "relating to or using air," from Greek *pneumatikos* (same meaning), from *pneumat-, pneuma* "air, breath"] — **pneu·mat·i·cal·ly** \-i-k(ə-)lē\ *adv*

pneu·mo·coc·cus \ˌn(y)ü-mə-'käk-əs\ *n, pl* **-coc·ci** \-'käk-(s)ī, -'käk-(ˌ)(s)ē\ : a bacterium that causes pneumonia — **pneu·mo·coc·cal** \-'käk-əl\ *adj*

pneu·mo·nia \n(y)ù-'mō-nyə\ *n* : a disease of the lungs marked by inflammation, congestion, fever, cough, and difficulty in breathing and caused especially by infection

¹**poach** \'pōch\ *vb* : to cook in simmering liquid ⟨*poached* eggs⟩ [Middle English *pochen* "to boil an egg without its shell so that the white covers the yolk like a bag," from early French *pocher* (same meaning), from earlier *pochier*, literally, "to put into a bag," from *poche* "bag, pocket"]

²**poach** *vb* : to hunt or fish unlawfully [from early French *pocher* "to hunt or fish unlawfully"] — **poach·er** *n*

po'·boy \'pō-ˌbòi\ *also* **poor boy** *n* : ²SUBMARINE 2

pock \'päk\ *n* : a small swelling on the skin like a pimple (as in chicken pox or smallpox); *also* : the scar it leaves

¹**pock·et** \'päk-ət\ *n* **1 a** : a small bag carried by a person

: PURSE **b** : a small bag open at the top or side inserted in a garment ⟨coat *pocket*⟩ **2** : supply of money : MEANS **3** : CONTAINER; *esp* : a bag at the corner or side of a billiard table **4** : something like a pocket ⟨a *pocket* of gold in a mine⟩ **5** : AIR POCKET

²**pocket** *vb* **1 a** : to put or enclose in a pocket ⟨*pocketed* the change⟩ **b** : to take for one's own use especially dishonestly ⟨*pocket* the profits⟩ **2** : to set aside : SUPPRESS ⟨*pocketed* my anger⟩ **3** : to supply with pockets

³**pocket** *adj* **1 a** : small enough to fit in the pocket **b** : smaller than the usual size ⟨a *pocket* park⟩ **2** : carried in or paid from one's pocket ⟨*pocket* expenses⟩

pock·et·book \'päk-ət-ˌbùk\ *n* **1** *often* **pocket book** : a small especially paperback book **2** : a container for money and personal papers : WALLET **3 a** : ¹PURSE 1 **b** : HANDBAG 2 **4** : financial resources : INCOME ⟨a price suited to your *pocketbook*⟩

pock·et·ful \'päk-ət-ˌfùl\ *n, pl* **pocketfuls** \-ˌfùlz\ *or* **pock·ets·ful** \-əts-ˌfùl\ : as much or as many as the pocket will contain

pocket gopher *n* : GOPHER 2a

pock·et·knife \'päk-ət-ˌnīf\ *n* : a knife that has one or more blades that fold into the handle and that can be carried in the pocket

pocket money *n* : money for small personal expenses

pock·et·size \'päk-ət-ˌsīz\ *also* **pock·et–sized** \-ˌsīzd\ *adj* : of a size convenient for carrying in the pocket

pocket veto *n* : a veto of a legislative bill by an executive (as the president) accomplished through holding the bill unsigned until after the session of the legislature is over

¹**pock·mark** \'päk-ˌmärk\ *n* : the scar caused by smallpox or acne; *also* : an imperfection suggesting a pockmark

²**pockmark** *vb* : to cover with or as if with pockmarks

¹**pod** \'päd\ *n* **1** : a fruit that is dry when ripe and then splits open to free its seeds; *esp* : LEGUME 2 **2** : any of various natural protective coverings (as a cocoon) or cases (as for grasshopper eggs) **3** : a streamlined compartment under the wings or body of an airplane used as a container (as for fuel or a jet engine)

²**pod** *n* : a number of animals (as whales) clustered together

pod·cast \'päd-ˌkast\ *n* : a program made available digitally for automatic download over the Internet — **podcast** *vb* — **pod·cast·er** *n*

po·di·a·trist \pə-'dī-ə-trəst\ *n* : a specialist in podiatry — called also *chiropodist*

po·di·a·try \pə-'dī-ə-trē\ *n* : medical care and treatment of the human foot — called also *chiropody*

po·di·um \'pōd-ē-əm\ *n, pl* **podiums** *or* **po·dia** \-ē-ə\ : a raised platform especially for an orchestral conductor

po·em \'pō-əm, -im, 'pōm, *also* 'pō-ˌem\ *n* : a composition in verse

po·esy \'pō-ə-zē, -sē\ *n, pl* **po·esies** : poetic form or composition : POETRY

po·et \'pō-ət, -it\ *n* : a person who writes poetry

po·et·ess \'pō-ət-əs, -it-\ *n* : a girl or woman who writes poetry

po·et·ic \pō-'et-ik\ *adj* **1** : of, relating to, or characteristic of poets or poetry ⟨*poetic* words⟩ **2** : written in verse — **po·et·i·cal** \-i-kəl\ *adj* — **po·et·i·cal·ly** \-k(ə-)lē\ *adv*

poet laureate *n, pl* **poets laureate** *or* **poet laureates 1** : a poet appointed by an English ruler as a member of the royal household and formerly expected to write poems for court and national occasions **2** : a poet regarded by a country or region as its most outstanding

po·et·ry \'pō-ə-trē, -i-trē\ *n* **1 a** : writing usually with a rhythm that repeats : VERSE **b** : the productions of a poet : POEMS **2** : writing chosen and arranged to create a certain emotional response through meaning, sound, and rhythm

po·go stick \'pō-gō-\ *n* : a pole with a strong spring at the bottom and two footrests on which a person stands and moves along by jumping [from *Pogo*, a trademark]

poi \'pȯi\ *n, pl* **poi** *or* **pois** : a Hawaiian food made of cooked taro root pounded to a paste and often fermented

poi·gnan·cy \'pȯi-nyən-sē\ *n* : the quality or state of being poignant

poi·gnant \'pȯi-nyənt\ *adj* **1** : painfully affecting the feelings : SHARP, PIERCING ⟨*poignant* grief⟩ **2** : deeply affecting : TOUCHING — **poi·gnant·ly** *adv*

poi·ki·lo·therm \pȯi-'kē-lə-,thərm, -'kil-ə-\ *n* : an animal (as a frog) with a temperature that tends to change with and is similar to or slightly higher than the environment : a cold-blooded organism

poin·set·tia \pȯin-'set-ē-ə, -'set-ə\ *n* : a showy Mexican and Central American plant with large scarlet bracts that grow like petals about its small yellow flowers

poinsettia

¹point \'pȯint\ *n* **1 a** : an individual detail : ITEM ⟨two *points* that were important to remember⟩ **b** : a distinguishing detail : CHARACTERISTIC ⟨politeness was a strong *point*⟩ **c** : the chief part or meaning ⟨the *point* of the joke⟩ **2** : a goal to be achieved : PURPOSE ⟨there's no *point* in continuing⟩ **3 a** : a geometric element that has position but no dimensions and is pictured as a small dot **b** : a usually small or precise place : LOCALITY ⟨a starting *point*⟩ **c** : an exact moment ⟨at this *point* they were interrupted⟩ **d** : a step, stage, or degree in development or rank ⟨the melting *point* of ice⟩ ⟨up to a *point* it was a good performance⟩ **4 a** : the usually sharp or tapering end of something (as a sword or pencil) : TIP **b** : either of two metal pieces in a distributor through which the circuit is made or broken **5** : a piece of land that sticks out **6 a** : a very small mark : DOT **b** : PUNCTUATION MARK; *esp* : PERIOD 2 **c** : DECIMAL POINT **7 a** : one of the 32 marks indicating direction on a compass used by seamen **b** : the difference of 11¼ degrees between two such adjacent points **8** : a unit used in giving a value or score ⟨scored fifteen *points*⟩ **9** : the action of pointing — **beside the point** : IRRELEVANT — **in point of** : in the matter of ⟨*in point of* fact⟩ — **to the point** : PERTINENT ⟨a remark that was quite *to the point*⟩

²point *vb* **1 a** : to furnish with a point ⟨*point* a pencil with a knife⟩ **b** : to give force to ⟨*point* up a remark with actual examples⟩ **2 a** : PUNCTUATE 1 **b** : to separate a fraction from a whole number by a decimal point ⟨*point* off three decimal places⟩ **3 a** : to show the position or direction of especially by extending a finger ⟨*point* out a house⟩ **b** : to direct someone's attention to ⟨*point* out a mistake⟩ **c** : to indicate game by freezing into a fixed position with head and gaze directed toward the object hunted ⟨a dog that *points* well⟩ **4** : to turn, face, or cause to be turned in a particular direction : AIM ⟨*point* the boat upstream⟩ **5** : to indicate the fact or probability of something ⟨everything *points* to a bright future⟩

point–blank \'pȯint-'blaŋk\ *adj* **1** : aimed at a target from a very short distance away ⟨fired from *point-blank* range⟩ **2** : ¹BLUNT 3, DIRECT ⟨a *point-blank* refusal⟩ — **point–blank** *adv*

point·ed \'pȯint-əd\ *adj* **1** : having a point **2 a** : being to the point : PERTINENT **b** : aimed at a particular person or group ⟨*pointed* remarks⟩ — **point·ed·ly** *adv* — **point·ed·ness** *n*

point·er \'pȯint-ər\ *n* **1** : one that points; *esp* : a rod used to direct attention **2** : a large short-haired dog with long ears and short

hair that hunts by scent, and points game **3** : a useful hint : TIP ⟨*pointers* on how to study⟩

point·less \'pȯint-ləs\ *adj* **1** : lacking meaning : SENSELESS ⟨a *pointless* remark⟩ **2** : INEFFECTIVE 1 ⟨*pointless* attempts to be funny⟩ — **point·less·ly** *adv* — **point·less·ness** *n*

point of view : a way of looking at or thinking about something : STANDPOINT

pointy \'pȯin-tē\ *adj* **point·i·er; -est** **1** : coming to a rather sharp point **2** : having parts that stick out sharply here and there

¹poise \'pȯiz\ *vb* **poised; pois·ing** **1 a** : ²BALANCE 5; *esp* : to hold or make firm or steady by balancing **b** : to hold without motion in a steady position : HOVER ⟨a bird *poised* in the air⟩ **2** : to put into readiness : BRACE ⟨*poised* for action⟩

²poise *n* **1** : ¹BALANCE 4, EQUILIBRIUM **2 a** : a dignified self-confident manner ⟨a speaker of great *poise*⟩ **b** : a way of carrying oneself : BEARING

¹poi·son \'pȯiz-ən\ *n* **1** : a substance that by its chemical action can kill or injure a living thing **2** : something destructive or harmful [Middle English *poison* "poison, a poisonous drink," from early French *poison* "drink, potion, poison," from Latin *potion-, potio* "a drink, potion" — related to POTION]

²poison *vb* **poi·soned; poi·son·ing** \'pȯiz-niŋ, -ᵊn-iŋ\ **1 a** : to injure or kill with poison **b** : to put poison in or on ⟨*poisoned* the air with its fumes⟩ **2** : to exert a harmful influence on : CORRUPT ⟨*poisoned* their minds⟩ — **poi·son·er** \'pȯiz-nər, -ᵊn-ər\ *n*

³poison *adj* : POISONOUS ⟨a *poison* plant⟩

poison gas *n* : a poisonous gas or a liquid or a solid giving off poisonous vapors designed (as in chemical warfare) to kill or injure

poison ivy *n* **1** : a usually climbing plant that is related to the sumacs, has leaves usually with three leaflets, greenish flowers, white berries, and leaves and stems that when bruised and touched may cause an itching rash on the skin **2** : a skin rash caused by poison ivy

poison oak *n* : any of several shrubby plants related to poison ivy and causing a similar rash

poi·son·ous \'pȯiz-nəs, -ᵊn-əs\ *adj* : containing poison : having or causing an effect of poison — **poi·son·ous·ly** *adv*

poison sumac *n* : a swamp shrub related to poison ivy and causing a similar rash but having leaves with 7 to 13 leaflets

¹poke \'pōk\ *n, chiefly Southern & Midland* : ¹BAG 1a, SACK [Middle English *poke* "bag, sack," from an early French dialect word *poke* (same meaning)]

²poke *vb* **poked; pok·ing** **1 a** : JAB, PROD ⟨*poke* a stick at a snake⟩ ⟨*poked* me in the ribs⟩ **b** : ¹THRUST 2, STAB **c** : to produce by piercing, stabbing, or jabbing ⟨*poke* a hole⟩ **2** : to stick out or cause to stick out ⟨*poked* her head out the window⟩ **3** : to be nosy especially about things that do not concern one **4** : to search over or through usually without purpose : RUMMAGE ⟨*poking* around in the attic⟩ **5** : to move slowly or lazily ⟨they were just *poking* along home⟩ [Middle English *poken* "to jab, prod"] — **poke fun at** : DERIDE, MOCK

³poke *n* : a quick thrust : JAB

¹pok·er \'pō-kər\ *n* : one that pokes; *esp* : a metal rod for stirring a fire

²po·ker \'pō-kər\ *n* : a card game in which a player bets on the value of his or her hand

\ə\ **abut**	\au̇\ **out**	\i\ **tip**	\ȯ\ **saw**	\u̇\ **foot**
\ər\ **further**	\ch\ **chin**	\ī\ **life**	\ȯi\ **coin**	\y\ **yet**
\a\ **mat**	\e\ **pet**	\j\ **job**	\th\ **thin**	\yü\ **few**
\ā\ **take**	\ē\ **easy**	\ŋ\ **sing**	\t̲h̲\ **this**	\yu̇\ **cure**
\ä\ **cot, cart**	\g\ **go**	\ō\ **bone**	\ü\ **food**	\zh\ **vision**

poke·weed \'pō-ˌkwēd\ *n* : an American herb with spikes of white flowers, dark purple juicy berries, a poisonous root, and young shoots sometimes used as greens

poky *or* **pok·ey** \'pō-kē\ *adj* **pok·i·er; -est 1** : being small and cramped ⟨a *poky* room⟩ **2** : so slow as to be annoying — **pok·i·ness** *n*

po·lar \'pō-lər\ *adj* **1 a** : of or relating to a geographical pole or the region around it **b** : coming from or having the characteristics of a polar region ⟨*polar* cold⟩ **2** : of or relating to one or more poles (as of a magnet) **3** : diametrically opposite **4** : showing polarity ⟨water molecules are *polar*⟩

pokeweed

polar bear *n* : a large creamy-white fish-eating bear that lives in arctic regions

polar body *n* : a cell that separates from the immature ovum during meiosis and that contains a nucleus produced in the first or second division of meiosis but very little cytoplasm

Po·lar·is \pə-'lar-əs, -'lär-\ *n* : NORTH STAR

po·lari·scope \pō-'lar-ə-ˌskōp\ *n* : an instrument for studying the characteristics of substances in polarized light

po·lar·i·ty \pō-'lar-ət-ē, pə-\ *n, pl* **-ties 1** : the condition of having poles and especially magnetic or electrical poles **2** : attraction toward a particular object or in a specific direction

po·lar·ize \'pō-lə-ˌrīz\ *vb* **-ized; -iz·ing 1** : to cause to vibrate (as light waves) in a definite pattern **2** : to give physical polarity to **3** : to break up into opposing groups **4** : to become polarized — **po·lar·i·za·tion** *n*

Po·lar·oid \'pō-lə-ˌroid\ *trademark* — used for a material that polarizes light or for a camera

¹**pole** \'pōl\ *n* **1** : a long slender piece of material (as wood or metal) ⟨telephone *poles*⟩ **2** : ROD 2a [Old English *pāl* "stake, pole"]

²**pole** *vb* **poled; pol·ing** : to push or move with a pole ⟨*pole* a boat⟩ — **pol·er** *n*

³**pole** *n* **1** : either end of an axis of a globe and especially of the earth's axis **2 a** : one of the two terminals of an electric cell or battery **b** : one of two or more regions in a magnetized body at which the magnetism seems to be concentrated **3** : either of two specialized areas at opposite ends of an axis in an organism or cell ⟨chromosomes moving toward the *poles* of a dividing cell⟩ [Middle English *pool* "axis of the earth," from Latin *polus* (same meaning), from Greek *polos* "pivot, pole"]

Pole \'pōl\ *n* : a person born or living in Poland

pole bean *n* : a cultivated bean with long coiling stems that is usually trained to grow upright on supports

pole·cat \'pōl-ˌkat\ *n, pl* **polecats** *or* **polecat 1** : a brown to black European flesh-eating mammal related to the weasels **2** : ¹SKUNK 1

polecat 1

Word History A polecat is not a cat at all, and its name has nothing to do with poles. The European polecat looks like a large weasel with a bandit's mask of darker fur around its eyes. The polecat has long been known as a killer of poultry, and its name reflects its reputation. *Polecat* was spelled *polcat* in Middle English. This word was probably formed from *pol* or *poul*, the early French word for "cock," and the Middle English word *cat*. During the Middle English period people often gave the name *cat* to small animals, like the polecat, that looked something like the ordinary house cat. [Middle English *polcat* "polecat," probably from early French *pol, poul* "cock" and Middle English *cat* "cat, a small animal"]

po·lem·ic \pə-'lem-ik\ *n* : an aggressive attack on the opinions or beliefs of another — **po·lem·i·cal** \-'lem-i-kəl\ *also* **polemic** *adj* — **po·lem·i·cal·ly** \-i-k(ə-)lē\ *adv*

po·len·ta \pō-'len-tə\ *n* : mush made of chestnut meal, cornmeal, or grain

pole·star \'pōl-ˌstär\ *n* : NORTH STAR

pole vault *n* : a track-and-field event in which contestants use a pole to jump for height over a crossbar — **pole–vault** *vb* — **pole–vault·er** *n*

¹**po·lice** \pə-'lēs\ *vb* **po·liced; po·lic·ing 1** : to control, regulate, or keep in order by use of police ⟨*police* a city⟩ **2** : to make clean and put in order ⟨*police* the area⟩

²**police** *n, pl* **police 1** : the department of government that keeps order and enforces law, investigates crimes, and makes arrests **2** *pl* : members of a police force **3** : a private or military force like a police force ⟨campus *police*⟩

police dog *n* **1** : a dog trained to help police (as in drug detection) **2** : GERMAN SHEPHERD

police force *n* : a body of officers trained and entrusted by a government to keep public peace, enforce laws, and prevent and detect crime

po·lice·man \pə-'lē-smən\ *n* : POLICE OFFICER

police officer *n* : a member of a police force

police state *n* : a state in which the activities of the people are under the power of the government often acting through a secret police force

po·lice·wom·an \pə-'lē-ˌswùm-ən\ *n* : a woman who is a police officer

¹**pol·i·cy** \'päl-ə-sē\ *n, pl* **-cies** : a course of action chosen in order to guide people in making decisions ⟨a country's foreign *policy*⟩

²**policy** *n, pl* **-cies** : a document that contains the agreement made by an insurance company with a person whose life or property is insured

pol·i·cy·hold·er \'päl-ə-sē-ˌhōl-dər\ *n* : the owner of an insurance policy

po·lio \'pō-lē-ˌō\ *n* : POLIOMYELITIS

po·lio·my·eli·tis \ˌpō-lē-ˌō-ˌmī-ə-'līt-əs\ *n* : an infectious virus disease marked by inflammation of nerve cells in the spinal cord accompanied by fever and often paralysis and wasting of muscles — called also *infantile paralysis*

¹**pol·ish** \'päl-ish\ *vb* **1** : to make smooth and glossy usually by rubbing **2** : to smooth or improve in manners, condition, or style **3** : to bring to a highly developed or finished state ⟨*polish* a technique⟩ — **pol·ish·er** *n*

²**polish** *n* **1 a** : a smooth glossy surface : LUSTER **b** : good manners : REFINEMENT **2** : the action or process of polishing **3** : a substance prepared for use in polishing ⟨shoe *polish*⟩ ⟨nail *polish*⟩

¹**Pol·ish** \'pō-lish\ *adj* : of, relating to, or characteristic of Poland, the Poles, or Polish

²**Polish** *n* : the Slavic language of the Poles

polish off *vb* : to finish off or dispose of rapidly or completely ⟨*polished off* the whole meal⟩

po·lite \pə-'līt\ *adj* **po·lit·er; -est 1** : showing good taste or training : REFINED ⟨*polite* society⟩ ⟨*polite* forms of address⟩ **2** : showing consideration and courtesy : COURTEOUS — **po·lite·ly** *adv* — **po·lite·ness** *n*

pol·i·tic \'päl-ə-ˌtik\ *adj* : wise especially in dealing with others or in carrying out a policy

po·lit·i·cal \pə-'lit-i-kəl\ *adj* **1** : of or relating to a government or the conduct of government **2** : of or relating to politics **3** : organized in governmental terms ⟨*political* units⟩ **4** : involving, concerned with, or accused of acts against a government or political system ⟨*political* prisoners⟩ — **po·lit·i·cal·ly** \-k(ə-)lē\ *adv*

politically correct *adj* : following the belief that language and practices which could offend political sensibilities (as in matters of sex or race) should be eliminated — **political correctness** *n*

political science *n* : the study of government and politics — **political scientist** *n*

pol·i·ti·cian \ˌpäl-ə-ˈtish-ən\ *n* : a person who takes an active part in party politics or in government business

pol·i·tics \ˈpäl-ə-ˌtiks\ *n sing or pl* **1 a** : POLITICAL SCIENCE **b** : the art of guiding or influencing governmental policy **c** : the art of winning and holding control over a government **2** : political affairs or business; *esp* : competition between groups or individuals for power and leadership **3** : political opinions

pol·ka \ˈpōl-kə\ *n* : a lively dance that originated in Bohemia — **polka** *vb*

pol·ka dot \ˈpō-kə-\ *n* : a dot in a textile pattern of evenly spaced dots

¹poll \ˈpōl\ *n* **1 a** : ¹HEAD 1 **b** : the top or back of the head **2 a** : the casting or recording of votes **b** : the place where votes are cast or recorded — usually used in plural ⟨at the *polls*⟩ **3** : a questioning of persons to obtain information or opinions

²poll *vb* **1 a** : to take and record the votes of **b** : to request each member of to declare his or her vote individually ⟨*poll* a jury⟩ **2** : to receive votes in an election ⟨the candidate *polled* 10,000 votes⟩ **3** : to question (people) or cover (an area) in a poll **4** : to cast one's vote at a poll — **poll·er** \ˈpō-lər\ *n*

pol·lack *or* **pol·lock** \ˈpäl-ək\ *n, pl* **pollack** *or* **pollock** **1** : an important food fish of the northern Atlantic that resembles the related cods but is darker **2** : an important food fish of the northern Pacific that is related to and resembles the pollack of the northern Atlantic

polled \ˈpōld\ *adj* : having no horns ⟨*polled* cattle⟩

pol·len \ˈpäl-ən\ *n* : a mass of tiny particles in the anthers of a flower that fertilize the seeds and usually appear as fine yellow dust

pollen basket *n* : a flat or hollow area bordered with stiff hairs on the hind leg of a bee in which it carries pollen to the hive or nest

pollen grain *n* : one of the microscopic grains of which pollen is made up

pollen sac *n* : one of the pouches of a seed plant anther in which pollen is formed

pollen tube *n* : a tube that is formed by a pollen grain as it grows down the style and that carries the sperm nuclei to the embryo sac of a flower

pol·li·nate \ˈpäl-ə-ˌnāt\ *vb* **-nat·ed; -nat·ing** : to place pollen on the stigma of

pol·li·na·tion \ˌpäl-ə-ˈnā-shən\ *n* : the act or process of pollinating

pol·li·na·tor \ˈpäl-ə-ˌnāt-ər\ *n* : something (as an insect) that pollinates flowers

poll·ster \ˈpōl-stər\ *n* : one that conducts a poll or collects data obtained by a poll

poll tax *n* : a tax of a fixed amount per adult person that is often linked to the right to vote

pol·lut·ant \pə-ˈlüt-ənt\ *n* : something that pollutes

pol·lute \pə-ˈlüt\ *vb* **pol·lut·ed; pol·lut·ing** : to make impure; *esp* : to spoil (as a natural resource) with waste made by humans ⟨industrial wastes *polluted* the river⟩

pol·lu·tion \pə-ˈlü-shən\ *n* **1** : the action of polluting : the state of being polluted ⟨air *pollution*⟩ — compare NOISE POLLUTION, THERMAL POLLUTION **2** : POLLUTANT

Pol·lux \ˈpäl-əks\ *n* : a bright star in Gemini [derived from Latin *Pollux* "Pollux, one of the twin heroes of Greek mythology," from Greek *Polydeukēs* "Pollux" — see *Word History* at GEMINI]

pol·ly·wog *or* **pol·li·wog** \ˈpäl-ē-ˌwäg, -ˌwȯg\ *n* : TADPOLE

po·lo \ˈpō-lō\ *n* : a game played by teams of players on horseback using long-handled mallets to drive a wooden ball — **po·lo·ist** \ˈpō-lō-əst\ *n*

po·lo·naise \ˌpäl-ə-ˈnāz, ˌpō-lə-\ *n* : a dignified 19th century Polish dance [from French *polonaise* "a fancy woman's dress or gown," literally, "a Polish gown," from *polonaise* (adjective), feminine form of *polonais* "Polish"]

po·lo·ni·um \pə-ˈlō-nē-əm\ *n* : a radioactive metallic element that is found in pitchblende and decays to form lead — see ELEMENT table

polo shirt *n* : a close-fitting pullover shirt of knitted fabric

pol·ter·geist \ˈpōl-tər-ˌgīst\ *n* : a mischievous ghost thought to be the cause of mysterious noises (as rappings)

pol·troon \päl-ˈtrün\ *n* : COWARD

poly- *combining form* : many : several [Middle English *poly-* "many," from Latin *poly-* (same meaning), derived from Greek *polys* "many, several, much"]

poly·an·thus \ˌpäl-ē-ˈan(t)-thəs\ *n* **1** : any of various hybrid primroses **2** : a narcissus having small white or yellow flowers

poly·chro·mat·ic \ˌpäl-i-krō-ˈmat-ik\ *adj* : showing a variety or change of colors : MULTICOLORED

poly·chrome \ˈpäl-i-ˌkrōm\ *adj* : relating to, made with, or decorated in several colors ⟨*polychrome* pottery⟩

poly·dac·ty·ly \ˌpäl-i-ˈdak-tə-lē\ *n* : the condition of having extra fingers or toes

poly·es·ter \ˈpäl-ē-ˌes-tər\ *n* : any of a group of polymers that consist basically of repeated units of an ester and are used chiefly in making fibers or plastics

poly·eth·yl·ene \ˌpäl-ē-ˈeth-ə-ˌlēn\ *n* : a lightweight plastic resistant to chemicals and moisture and used chiefly in packaging

po·lyg·a·mous \pə-ˈlig-ə-məs\ *adj* **1** : of or relating to marriage in which a spouse has more than one mate at one time **2** : having more than one mate at one time — **po·lyg·a·mist** \-məst\ *n* — **po·lyg·a·my** \-mē\ *n*

poly·glot \ˈpäl-i-ˌglät\ *adj* **1** : speaking or writing several languages **2** : containing or composed of several languages — **polyglot** *n*

poly·gon \ˈpäl-i-ˌgän\ *n* : a geometric figure that is closed, that lies in a plane, and whose edges are all straight lines ⟨triangles, squares, and pentagons are all *polygons*⟩ — **po·lyg·o·nal** \pə-ˈlig-ən-ᵊl\ *adj*

poly·graph \ˈpäl-i-ˌgraf\ *n* : an instrument for recording changes in several bodily functions (as blood pressure and rate of breathing) at the same time — compare LIE DETECTOR

poly·he·dron \ˌpäl-i-ˈhē-drən\ *n, pl* **-drons** *or* **-dra** \-drə\ : a geometric solid whose faces are each flat polygons — **poly·he·dral** \-drəl\ *adj*

poly·mer \ˈpäl-ə-mər\ *n* : a chemical compound or mixture of compounds that is formed by combination of smaller molecules and consists basically of repeating structural units — **poly·mer·ic** \ˌpäl-ə-ˈmer-ik\ *adj*

polyhedron

po·ly·mer·i·za·tion \pə-ˌlim-ə-rə-ˈzā-shən, ˌpäl-ə-mə-rə-\ *n* : a chemical reaction in which two or more small molecules combine to form larger molecules — **po·ly·mer·ize** \pə-ˈlim-ə-ˌrīz, ˈpäl-ə-mə-\ *vb*

\ə\ **abut**	\aú\ **out**	\i\ **tip**	\ó\ **saw**	\ú\ **foot**
\ər\ **further**	\ch\ **chin**	\ī\ **life**	\ói\ **coin**	\y\ **yet**
\a\ **mat**	\e\ **pet**	\j\ **job**	\th\ **thin**	\yü\ **few**
\ā\ **take**	\ē\ **easy**	\ŋ\ **sing**	\th\ **this**	\yú\ **cure**
\ä\ **cot, cart**	\g\ **go**	\ō\ **bone**	\ü\ **food**	\zh\ **vision**

Poly·ne·sian \ˌpäl-ə-'nē-zhən, -shən\ *n* **1** : a member of any of the native peoples of Polynesia **2** : a group of languages spoken in Polynesia — **Polynesian** *adj*

¹poly·no·mi·al \ˌpäl-i-'nō-mē-əl\ *n* : an algebraic expression having two or more terms ⟨the *polynomial* a² + 2ab – b²⟩

²polynomial *adj* : relating to, composed of, or expressed as one or more polynomials ⟨7023 written as 7(10³) + 0(10²) + 2(10¹) + 3(10⁰) is in *polynomial* form⟩

pol·yp \'päl-əp\ *n* : an invertebrate animal (as a sea anemone or a coral) that is a coelenterate having a hollow cylinder-shaped body closed and attached at one end and opening at the other by a central mouth surrounded by tentacles armed with minute stinging organs

po·lyph·o·ny \pə-'lif-ə-nē\ *n* : music consisting of two or more independent but harmonious melodies — **poly·phon·ic** \ˌpäl-i-'fän-ik\ *adj*

poly·sac·cha·ride \ˌpäl-i-'sak-ə-ˌrīd\ *n* : a carbohydrate that can be broken down into two or more small sugar molecules

poly·sty·rene \ˌpäl-i-'stī(ə)r-ˌēn\ *n* : a stiff transparent plastic used chiefly in molded products, foams, and sheet materials

poly·syl·lab·ic \ˌpäl-i-sə-'lab-ik\ *adj* : having many syllables; *esp* : having more than three syllables — **poly·syl·lab·i·cal·ly** \-'lab-i-k(ə)lē\ *adv* — **poly·syl·la·ble** \'päl-i-ˌsil-ə-bəl, ˌpäl-i-'sil-\ *n*

poly·tech·nic \ˌpäl-i-'tek-nik\ *adj* : relating to or devoted to instruction in many technical arts or applied sciences ⟨a *polytechnic* school⟩

poly·the·ism \'päl-i-(ˌ)thē-ˌiz-əm\ *n* : belief in or worship of more than one god — **poly·the·ist** \-ˌthē-əst\ *adj or n* — **poly·the·is·tic** \ˌpäl-i-thē-'is-tik\ *adj*

poly·un·sat·u·rat·ed \ˌpäl-ē-ˌən-'sach-ə-ˌrāt-əd\ *adj, of an oil or fatty acid* : having many double or triple bonds in a molecule

pome \'pōm\ *n* : a fleshy fruit (as an apple or pear) consisting of a central core that has usually five seeds and is surrounded by a thick fleshy outer layer

pome·gran·ate \'päm-(ə-)ˌgran-ət, 'pəm-ˌgran-\ *n* : a reddish fruit about the size of an orange that has a thick leathery skin and many seeds in a pulp of tart flavor; *also* : a tropical Asian tree that produces pomegranates [Middle English *poumgrenet* "pomegranate," from early French *pomme garnette* "pomegranate," literally, "seedy fruit"; *pomme* from earlier *pome* "apple" and *grenate* derived from Latin *granum* "grain, seed" — related to GARNET, GRAIN, GRENADE; see *Word History* at GARNET]

Pom·er·a·nian \ˌpäm-ə-'rā-nē-ən, -nyən\ *n* : any of a breed of very small compact dogs having long hair

¹pom·mel \'pəm-əl, 'päm-\ *n* : the knob on the hilt of a sword or at the front of a saddle

²pom·mel \'pəm-əl\ *vb* **-meled** *or* **-melled**; **-mel·ing** *or* **-mel·ling** \-(ə-)liŋ\ : ³POUND 2a, PUMMEL

pomp \'pämp\ *n* **1** : a show of magnificence : SPLENDOR ⟨the *pomp* of a royal ceremony⟩ **2** : showy display

pom·pa·dour \'päm-pə-ˌdō(ə)r, -ˌdȯ(ə)r\ *n* : a hairdo in which the hair is combed high over the forehead; *also* : hair dressed in this style

pom·pa·no \'päm-pə-ˌnō, 'pəm-\ *n, pl* **-no** *or* **-nos** : a food fish that occurs along the coasts of the western Atlantic and the Gulf of Mexico having a narrow body and forked tail; *also* : any of several related fishes

pom–pom \'päm-ˌpäm\ *n* **1** : a fluffy ball used as trimming on clothing **2** : a handheld usually brightly colored fluffy ball waved by cheerleaders

P ¹pommel

pomp·ous \'päm-pəs\ *adj* **1** : making a show of importance or dignity ⟨a *pompous* manner⟩ **2** : having an overly high opinion of one's importance ⟨a *pompous* politician⟩ — **pomp·ous·ly** *adv* — **pomp·ous·ness** *n*

pon·cho \'pän-chō\ *n, pl* **ponchos 1** : a cloak like a blanket with a slit in the middle for the head **2** : a waterproof garment like a poncho

pond \'pänd\ *n* : a body of water usually smaller than a lake

pon·der \'pän-dər\ *vb* **pon·dered; pon·der·ing** \-d(ə-)riŋ\ : to consider carefully — **pon·der·er** \-dər-ər\ *n*

synonyms PONDER, MEDITATE, RUMINATE mean to consider or examine closely or deliberately. PONDER implies prolonged thinking about a matter often with a careful consideration and weighing of different aspects or alternatives ⟨*pondered* her next chess move⟩. MEDITATE implies a definite focusing of one's thoughts on something so as to understand it deeply ⟨*meditated* on the meaning of life⟩. RUMINATE implies going over the same matter in one's thoughts again and again but suggests a more casual and less focused approach ⟨*ruminating* on the possibilities the future might hold⟩.

pon·der·o·sa pine \ˌpän-də-ˌrō-sə-, -zə-\ *n* : a tall timber pine of western North America with long needles in groups of 2 or 3; *also* : its strong reddish straight-grained wood

pon·der·ous \'pän-d(ə-)rəs\ *adj* **1** : very heavy **2** : unpleasantly dull ⟨fell asleep during the *ponderous* speech⟩ — **pon·der·ous·ly** *adv* — **pon·der·ous·ness** *n*

pond lily *n* : WATER LILY

pond scum *n* **1** : SPIROGYRA; *also* : any of various related algae **2** : a mass of tangled threads of algae in still water

pond·weed \'pän-ˌdwēd\ *n* : any of several water plants with leaves that float or are under the water and spikes of greenish flowers

pone \'pōn\ *n, Southern & Midland* : CORN PONE

pon·gee \(ˈ)pän-'jē, 'pän-ˌjē\ *n* **1** : a thin soft silk fabric of Chinese origin **2** : an imitation of pongee in cotton or synthetic fiber

pon·iard \'pän-yərd\ *n* : a slender dagger

pon·tiff \'pänt-əf\ *n* : BISHOP 1; *esp, often cap* : POPE — **pon·tif·i·cal** \pän-'tif-i-kəl\ *adj*

¹pon·tif·i·cate \pän-'tif-i-kət, -'tif-ə-ˌkāt\ *n* : the office or term of office of a pontiff

²pon·tif·i·cate \pän-'tif-ə-ˌkāt\ *vb* **-cat·ed; -cat·ing** : to speak pompously

pon·toon \pän-'tün\ *n* **1** : a flat-bottomed boat **2** : a float used in building a floating bridge **3** : a float of an airplane [from French *ponton* "a floating bridge, punt," from Latin *ponton-, ponto* (same meaning), from *pont-, pons* "bridge" — related to ¹PUNT]

P pontoon 3

po·ny \'pō-nē\ *n, pl* **ponies 1** : a small horse; *esp* : a horse of any of several breeds of very small compact animals **2** : a word-for-word translation of a foreign language text

pony express *n, often cap P&E* : a rapid postal system across the western U.S. in 1860–61 that operated by changing horses and riders along the way

po·ny·tail \'pō-nē-ˌtāl\ *n* : a hairstyle in which the hair is pulled together and banded usually at the back of the head so as to resemble the tail of a pony

pooch \'püch\ *n* : ¹DOG 1a

poo·dle \'püd-°l\ *n* : any of a breed of active intelligent dogs that have thick curly coats of solid color and that occur in three sizes

Word History Poodles often have their coats cut in different patterns. Both their haircuts and their name go back to a time when poodles were kept not as house pets but as retrievers. Poodles were especially good at retrieving game in the water. The dogs were good swimmers, and they had heavy coats that kept them warm even in icy water. Hunters cut their dogs' hair shorter in a pattern that would make swimming easier. Cutting poodles' hair in a pattern soon became a tradition. The German name for this skillful swimmer was *Pudelhund.* This word combined *pudeln,* meaning "to splash," and *hund,* meaning "dog." It was then shortened to *Pudel,* which English borrowed as *poodle.* [from German *Pudel,* a shortened form of *Pudelhund* "poodle," from *pudeln* "to splash" and *Hund* "dog"]

pooh \ˈpü, ˈpu̇\ *interj* — used to express disapproval

pooh–pooh \ˈpü-ˌpü, pü-ˈpü\ *also* **pooh** \ˈpü\ *vb* **1** : to express scorn or impatience **2** : to treat with scorn : DERIDE ⟨*pooh-pooh* the idea of ghosts⟩

¹pool \ˈpül\ *n* **1** : a small deep body of water **2** : a small body of standing liquid : PUDDLE **3** : SWIMMING POOL [Old English *pōl* "a small body of water"]

²pool *vb* : to form a pool

³pool *n* **1** : the money bet by a number of persons on an event or in a game **2** : a game played on a billiard table having six pockets with usually 15 object balls **3** : a common fund for making investments **4 a** : a readily available supply ⟨a *pool* of talent⟩ ⟨a typing *pool*⟩ **b** : a group sharing in some activity ⟨a car *pool*⟩ [from French *poule* "the amount of money bet in a card game," literally, "hen," derived from early French *poul* "a male chicken, cock" — related to PULLET]

⁴pool *vb* : to contribute to a common fund or effort ⟨*pooled* their resources⟩

poop \ˈpüp\ *n* : an enclosed raised structure at the stern of a ship

¹poor \ˈpu̇(ə)r, ˈpō(ə)r\ *adj* **1** : lacking riches or possessions **2** : less than enough ⟨a *poor* crop⟩ **3** : not good in quality or character of work **4** : lacking fertility ⟨*poor* land⟩ **5** : not satisfactory ⟨the patient had a *poor* day⟩ **6** : lacking in signs of wealth or good taste ⟨*poor* furnishings⟩ **7** : worthy of pity or sympathy ⟨the *poor* kitten hurt its paw⟩ — **poor·ly** *adv* — **poor·ness** *n*

²poor *n pl* : poor people ⟨charity for the *poor*⟩

poor boy *variant of* PO'BOY

poor farm *n* : a farm kept by the government for the support and employment of poor people

poor·house \ˈpu̇(ə)r-ˌhau̇s, ˈpō(ə)r-\ *n* : a place maintained at public expense to house poor people

poor·ly \ˈpu̇(ə)r-lē, ˈpō(ə)r-\ *adj* : somewhat ill

¹pop \ˈpäp\ *vb* **popped**; **pop·ping** **1** : to burst or cause to burst with a pop ⟨the balloon *popped*⟩ ⟨we *popped* corn⟩ **2** : to go, come, push, or enter quickly or suddenly ⟨*pop* into bed⟩ ⟨*popped* a grape into my mouth⟩ **3** : to shoot with a gun **4** : to bulge from the sockets ⟨eyes *popping* with surprise⟩ **5** : to hit a pop fly [Middle English *poppen* "to hit, burst open"; a word created to imitate the sound made when something bursts open]

²pop *n* **1** : a sharp explosive sound **2** : a shot from a gun **3** : a flavored carbonated beverage

³pop *adv* : like or with a pop : SUDDENLY

⁴pop *n* : ¹FATHER 1a [a shortened form of *poppa,* an altered form of *papa*]

⁵pop *adj* **1 a** : POPULAR 2 ⟨*pop* music⟩ **b** : of or relating to pop music ⟨a *pop* singer⟩ **2** : of, relating to, or being the behavior and interests of average people and especially young people [a shortened form of *popular*]

⁶pop *n* : popular music ⟨listens to *pop*⟩

pop·corn \ˈpäp-ˌkȯ(ə)rn\ *n* : corn with kernels that burst open to form a white starchy mass when heated; *also* : the popped kernels

pope \ˈpōp\ *n, often cap* : the head of the Roman Catholic Church

pop·eyed \ˈpäp-ˌīd\ *adj* : having eyes that bulge

pop fly *n* : a short high fly in baseball

pop·gun \ˈpäp-ˌgən\ *n* : a toy gun that usually shoots corks and makes a popping sound

pop·in·jay \ˈpäp-ən-ˌjā\ *n* : a proud talkative thoughtless person

pop·lar \ˈpäp-lər\ *n* **1** : any of a genus of slender quick= growing trees (as an aspen or cottonwood) that have catkins for flowers and are related to the willows **2** : the wood of a poplar

pop·lin \ˈpäp-lən\ *n* : a strong ribbed fabric in plain weave

pop·over \ˈpäp-ˌō-vər\ *n* : a quick bread shaped like a hollow muffin and made from eggs, milk, and flour

pop·per \ˈpäp-ər\ *n* : one that pops; *esp* : a utensil for popping corn

pop·py \ˈpäp-ē\ *n, pl* **poppies** : any of a genus of herbs that have milky juice, showy flowers, and a fruit that is a capsule and include one that is the source of opium and several that are grown as ornamental plants

Pop·si·cle \ˈpäp-ˌsik-əl\ *trademark* — used for flavored and colored water frozen on a stick

pop·u·lace \ˈpäp-yə-ləs\ *n* **1** : the common people : MASSES **2** : POPULATION 1

pop·u·lar \ˈpäp-yə-lər\ *adj* **1** : of, relating to, or coming from the whole body of people ⟨*popular* government⟩ **2** : suitable for the average person (as in low price or ease of understanding) ⟨*popular* prices⟩ ⟨*popular* science⟩ **3** : generally current : PREVALENT ⟨*popular* opinion⟩ **4** : commonly liked or approved ⟨a *popular* teacher⟩ [from Latin *popularis* "of the people," from *populus* "the people" — related to PUBLIC] — **pop·u·lar·i·ty** \ˌpäp-yə-ˈlar-ət-ē\ *n* — **pop·u·lar·ly** *adv*

pop·u·lar·ize \ˈpäp-yə-lə-ˌrīz\ *vb* **-ized**; **-iz·ing** : to make popular — **pop·u·lar·i·za·tion** \ˌpäp-yə-lə-rə-ˈzā-shən\ *n* — **pop·u·lar·iz·er** \ˈpäp-yə-lə-ˌrī-zər\ *n*

pop·u·late \ˈpäp-yə-ˌlāt\ *vb* **-lat·ed**; **-lat·ing** **1** : to have a place in : OCCUPY, INHABIT **2** : to provide with inhabitants : PEOPLE

pop·u·la·tion \ˌpäp-yə-ˈlā-shən\ *n* **1** : the whole number of people living in a country or region **2** : the act or process of populating **3** : a group of one or more species of organisms living in a particular area or habitat

pop·u·lous \ˈpäp-yə-ləs\ *adj* : having a large population

¹pop-up \ˈpäp-ˌəp\ *n* **1** : POP FLY **2** : a pop-up window on a computer screen

²pop-up *adj* **1** : of, relating to, or having a part or device that pops up ⟨a *pop-up* book⟩ **2** : appearing suddenly on a computer screen ⟨a *pop-up* window⟩

por·ce·lain \ˈpōr-s(ə-)lən, ˈpȯr-\ *n* : a hard white ceramic ware used especially for dishes and chemical utensils

porch \ˈpōrch, ˈpȯrch\ *n* : a covered entrance to a building usually with a separate roof

por·cu·pine \ˈpȯr-kyə-ˌpīn\ *n* : any of various rather large slow= moving mostly plant-eating rodents with stiff sharp quills among the hairs on the body [Middle English *porke despyne* "porcupine," from early French *porc espin,* literally, "thorny pig," derived from Latin *porcus* "pig" and *spina* "spine, prickle" — related to PORK, PORPOISE, SPINE; see *Word History* at PORPOISE]

porcupine fish *n* : any of several fish chiefly of tropical seas that have the body covered with spines

porcupine

and that can puff themselves up with air or water like a balloon when threatened

¹pore \'pō(ə)r, 'pȯ(ə)r\ *vb* **pored; por·ing** : to read with great attention : STUDY ⟨*pore* over a book⟩

²pore *n* : a tiny opening or space (as in the skin or the soil) — **pored** \'pō(ə)rd, 'pȯ(ə)rd\ *adj*

por·gy \'pȯr-gē\ *n, pl* **porgies** *also* **porgy** : a blue-spotted silvery red food fish of the coasts of Europe and America; *also* : any of various other related or similar fishes

pork \'pō(ə)rk, 'pȯ(ə)rk\ *n* : the flesh of a pig used for food [Middle English *pork* "meat from a pig," from early French *porc* "pig," from Latin *porcus* "pig" — related to PORCUPINE, PORPOISE; see *Word History* at PORPOISE]

pork·er \'pōr-kər, 'pȯr-\ *n* : HOG 1a; *esp* : a young pig fattened for use as fresh pork

por·nog·ra·phy \pȯr-'näg-rə-fē\ *n* : pictures or writings describing sexual behavior and intended to cause sexual excitement — **por·no·graph·ic** \ˌpȯr-nə-'graf-ik\ *adj*

po·ros·i·ty \pə-'räs-ət-ē, pōr-'äs-, pȯ-'räs-\ *n, pl* **-ties** : the quality or state of being porous

po·rous \'pōr-əs, 'pȯr-\ *adj* **1** : full of pores **2** : capable of absorbing liquids

por·phy·ry \'pȯr-f(ə-)rē\ *n, pl* **-ries** : a rock consisting of feldspar crystals set firmly in a compact dark red or purple base of glassy or fine-grained texture — **por·phy·rit·ic** \ˌpȯr-fə-'rit-ik\ *adj*

por·poise \'pȯr-pəs\ *n*
1 : any of several small toothed whales with blunt rounded snouts that live and travel in groups : DOLPHIN 1a
Word History The small whale we call a porpoise is a swift and graceful swimmer.

porpoise 1

However, both its name and *pork,* the English word for the meat of hogs, can be traced back to Latin *porcus,* meaning "pig." The porpoise's rounded face must have reminded the ancient Romans of a pig's snout. They named the animal *porcus marinus,* meaning "pig of the sea." In the Middle Ages this became *porcopiscus,* from Latin *porcus* "pig" and *piscis* "fish." In early French the word was borrowed as *porpeis.* It is from the French that we derived our English word *porpoise.* [Middle English *porpoys* "porpoise," from early French *porpeis* (same meaning), from Latin *porcopiscis,* literally, "pig fish," from *porcus* "pig" and *piscis* "fish"; originally in Latin called *porcus marinus,* literally, "pig of the sea" — related to PORCUPINE, PORK]

por·ridge \'pȯr-ij, 'pär-\ *n* : a soft food made by boiling meal or a vegetable in milk or water until it thickens ⟨oatmeal *porridge*⟩

por·rin·ger \'pȯr-ən-jər, 'pär-\ *n* : a low metal bowl or cup with a handle

¹port \'pōrt, 'pȯrt\ *n* **1** : a place where ships may take shelter from storms **2** : a harbor town or city where ships load or unload cargo **3** : AIRPORT [Middle English *port* "a place for ships to be secured," from Old English *port* and early French *port* (both, same meaning), from Latin *portus* (same meaning)]

²port *n* **1 a** : an opening (as in machinery) for gas, steam, or water to go in or out **b** : a place of entry into a system **2** : PORTHOLE 1 **3** : ¹JACK 7 [Middle English *porte* "gate, an opening in the side of a ship for light or moving cargo in or out," from early French *porte* "door, gate," from Latin *porta* "passage, gate" — related to PORTAL]

³port *vb* : to turn (the helm of a ship) to the left — used chiefly as a command

⁴port *n* : the left side of a ship or aircraft looking forward [probably from ¹*port* "a place for ships to be secured" or ²*port* "an opening in the side of a ship"; so called from the

fact that very early sailing vessels would keep the left side toward the port because the steering mechanism was always on the right side — see *Word History* at STARBOARD] — **port** *adj*

⁵port *n* : a rich sweet wine [named for *Oporto,* a city in Portugal from which the wine was exported]

por·ta·ble \'pōrt-ə-bəl, 'pȯrt-\ *adj* : possible to carry or move about ⟨a *portable* computer⟩ [Middle English *portable* "capable of being carried or moved about," from early French *portable* (same meaning), from Latin *portabilis* (same meaning), from earlier *portare* "to carry" — related to PORTFOLIO, TRANSPORT]

¹por·tage \'pōrt-ij, 'pȯrt-; pōr-'täzh\ *n* **1** : the carrying of boats or goods overland from one body of water to another **2** : a route for such carrying

²portage *vb* **por·taged; por·tag·ing** : to go or carry over a portage

por·tal \'pōrt-ᵊl, 'pȯrt-\ *n* : a large or magnificent door or gate [Middle English *portal* "door, the structure around a door," from early French *portal* (same meaning), derived from Latin *portalis* (adjective) "of a gate," from *porta* "gate, passage" — related to ²PORT]

portal vein *n* : a vein that carries blood from the digestive organs and spleen to the liver

port·cul·lis \pōrt-'kəl-əs, pȯrt-\ *n* : a heavy iron gate that can be lowered to prevent entrance (as to a castle)

por·tend \pȯr-'tend, pōr-\ *vb* : to give a sign or warning of beforehand ⟨the distant thunder *portended* a storm⟩

por·tent \'pȯ(ə)r-ˌtent, 'pō(ə)r-\ *n* : a sign or warning of a coming event : OMEN

por·ten·tous \pȯr-'tent-əs, pōr-\ *adj* **1** : being a portent : THREATENING **2** : causing wonder — **por·ten·tous·ly** *adv* — **por·ten·tous·ness** *n*

portcullis

¹por·ter \'pōrt-ər, 'pȯrt-\ *n, chiefly British* : DOORKEEPER

²porter *n* **1** : a person who carries baggage (as at a hotel) **2** : a railroad employee who waits on passengers **3** : a dark heavy ale

por·ter·house \'pōrt-ər-ˌhau̇s, 'pȯrt-\ *n* : a beefsteak with a large piece of tenderloin on a T-shaped bone

port·fo·lio \pōrt-'fō-lē-ˌō, pȯrt-\ *n, pl* **-lios** **1** : a case for carrying papers or drawings **2** : the office and functions of a minister of state or member of a cabinet **3** : the stocks and bonds held by an investor or investment firm [an altered form of earlier *porto folio* "portfolio," from Italian *portafoglio* (same meaning), from *portare* "to carry" and *foglio* "leaf, sheet"; *portare* from Latin *portare* "to carry" and *foglio* from Latin *folium* "leaf" — related to FOLIAGE, PORTABLE]

port·hole \'pōrt-ˌhōl, 'pȯrt-\ *n* **1** : an opening in the side of a ship or aircraft **2** : an opening (as in a wall) to shoot through

por·ti·co \'pōrt-i-ˌkō, 'pȯrt-\ *n, pl* **-coes** *or* **-cos** : a row of columns supporting a roof around or at the entrance of a building

¹por·tion \'pōr-shən, 'pȯr-\ *n* **1 a** : one's share of a whole ⟨a *portion* of food⟩ **b** : DOWRY **2** : one's lot or fate **3** : a part of a whole **synonyms** see PART

²portion *vb* **por·tioned; por·tion·ing** \-sh(ə-)niŋ\ : APPORTION

port·land cement \ˌpōrt-lən(d)-, ˌpȯrt-\ *n* : a cement made by burning and grinding a mixture usually of clay and limestone

port·ly \'pōrt-lē, 'pȯrt-\ *adj* **port·li·er; -est** : heavy of body : STOUT — **port·li·ness** *n*

port·man·teau \pȯrt-'man-tō, pȯrt-\ *n, pl* **-teaus** *or* **-teaux** \-tōz\ : TRAVELING BAG

por·trait \'pōr-trət, 'pȯr-, -ˌtrāt\ *n* **1** : a picture of a person usually showing the face **2** : a portrayal in words

por·tray \pōr-'trā, pȯr-\ *vb* **1** : to make a portrait of **2 a** : to describe in words **b** : to play the role of — **por·tray·er** *n*

por·tray·al \pōr-'trā(-ə)l, pȯr-\ *n* **1** : the act or process of portraying : REPRESENTATION **2** : PORTRAIT 1

Por·tu·guese \'pōr-chə-ˌgēz, 'pȯr-, -ˌgēs; ˌpȯr-chə-'gēz, ˌpȯr-, -'gēs\ *n, pl* **Portuguese** **1** : a person born or living in Portugal **2** : the language of Portugal and Brazil — **Portuguese** *adj*

Portuguese man–of–war *n, pl* **Portuguese man–of–wars** *also* **Portuguese men–of–war** : any of several large colonial invertebrate animals that are hydrozoans and float on the surface of the sea by means of a large gas-filled structure like a bag and have long tentacles capable of delivering a painful sting

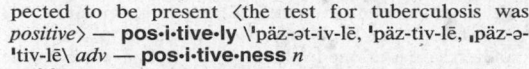

Portuguese man-of-war

¹pose \'pōz\ *vb* **posed; pos·ing** **1 a** : to hold or cause to hold a special position of the body ⟨*posed* for fashion photographers⟩ **b** : to pretend to be what one is not ⟨*pose* as a soldier⟩ **2** : to offer for consideration ⟨*posed* a question⟩

²pose *n* **1** : a position of the body held for a special purpose **2** : a pretended attitude ⟨my cheerfulness was a *pose*⟩

¹pos·er \'pō-zər\ *n* : a puzzling or baffling question

²poser *n* : a person who poses

po·seur \pō-'zər\ *n* : a person who pretends to be what he or she is not

posh \'päsh\ *adj* : ELEGANT 1, FASHIONABLE

posies *plural of* POSY

¹po·si·tion \pə-'zish-ən\ *n* **1 a** : the manner in which something is placed or arranged **b** : a certain arrangement of the body ⟨exercise while in a sitting *position*⟩ **2** : a stand taken on a question **3** : the point or area occupied by something **4 a** : one's rank in an organization or in society **b** : JOB 3 [Middle English *posycion* "position," from early French *posicioun* (same meaning), from Latin *positio* "position," from *ponere* "to put, place" — related to ¹COMPOUND] — **po·si·tion·al** \-'zish-(ə-)nəl\ *adj*

²position *vb* **po·si·tioned; po·si·tion·ing** \-'zish-(ə-)niŋ\ : to put in a certain position

¹pos·i·tive \'päz-ət-iv, 'päz-tiv\ *adj* **1 a** : clearly or definitely stated ⟨*positive* orders⟩ **b** : filled with confidence : CERTAIN ⟨were *positive* we would win⟩ **2** : of, relating to, or having the form of an adjective or adverb that shows no degree of comparison **3 a** : having or showing real existence or activity ⟨*positive* change in temperature⟩ **b** : having the light and dark areas the same as in the original subject ⟨a *positive* photographic image⟩ **c** : being numerically greater than zero ⟨+2 is a *positive* number⟩ **d** : reckoned or proceeding in a direction taken as that of increase or progress **e** : directed or moving toward the source of a stimulus ⟨a *positive* tropism⟩ **4 a** : of, being, or relating to electricity of which the proton is the smallest unit and which is produced in a glass rod rubbed with silk ⟨a *positive* charge⟩ **b** : charged with positive electricity : having a deficiency of electrons ⟨a *positive* particle⟩ **c** : being the part from which the current flows to the external circuit ⟨the *positive* pole of a storage battery⟩ **d** : electron-collecting — used of an electrode in an electron tube **5 a** : showing acceptance or approval ⟨a *positive* answer to the question⟩ **b** : showing the presence especially of a condition, substance, or living thing sus-

pected to be present ⟨the test for tuberculosis was *positive*⟩ — **pos·i·tive·ly** \'päz-ət-iv-lē, 'päz-tiv-lē, ˌpäz-ə-'tiv-lē\ *adv* — **pos·i·tive·ness** *n*

²positive *n* : something positive: as **a** : the positive degree or a positive form in a language **b** : a positive photograph or a print from a negative

pos·i·tron \'päz-ə-ˌträn\ *n* : a positively charged particle having the same mass and size of charge as the electron

pos·se \'päs-ē\ *n* **1** : a group of people called upon by a sheriff for help (as in pursuit of a criminal) **2** : a number of people organized to make a search (as for a lost child)

pos·sess \pə-'zes\ *vb* **1 a** : to have and hold as property : OWN **b** : to have as a characteristic, knowledge, or skill ⟨*possesses* a keen wit⟩ **2** : to enter into and control firmly : DOMINATE ⟨*possessed* by a demon⟩ ⟨whatever *possessed* you to do that⟩ — **pos·sess·or** \-'zes-ər\ *n*

pos·ses·sion \pə-'zesh-ən\ *n* **1 a** : the act of possessing or holding as one's own : OWNERSHIP **b** : control of property without regard to ownership **2 a** : something held as one's own **b** : an area under the control of but not actually part of a nation ⟨island *possessions* of the U.S.⟩ **3** : control by an idea or influence from outside oneself

¹pos·ses·sive \pə-'zes-iv\ *adj* **1** : of, relating to, or being a grammatical case that shows ownership or a similar relation **2** : showing the desire to possess or control ⟨a *possessive* attitude⟩ — **pos·ses·sive·ly** *adv* — **pos·ses·sive·ness** *n*

²possessive *n* **1** : the possessive case **2** : a noun or pronoun in the possessive case

pos·si·bil·i·ty \ˌpäs-ə-'bil-ət-ē\ *n, pl* **-ties** **1** : the state or fact of being possible **2** : something possible

pos·si·ble \'päs-ə-bəl\ *adj* **1** : being something that can be done or brought about ⟨a task *possible* only to skilled workers⟩ **2** : being something that may or may not occur ⟨plan against *possible* dangers⟩ **3** : able or fitted to be or to become ⟨a *possible* site for a camp⟩

pos·si·bly \'päs-ə-blē\ *adv* **1** : by possible means : by any possibility ⟨that cannot *possibly* be true⟩ **2** : PERHAPS ⟨may *possibly* recover⟩

pos·sum \'päs-əm\ *n* : OPOSSUM

¹post \'pōst\ *n* **1** : a piece of timber or metal fixed upright especially as a support : PILLAR **2** : a pole or stake set up as a marker ⟨the starting *post*⟩ **3** : a metallic fixture attached to an electrical device (as a battery) for making connections [Old English *post* "an upright timber for support, pillar," from Latin *postis* (same meaning)]

²post *vb* **1 a** : to fix notices to or on a suitable place (as a bulletin board) **b** : to publish or announce by or as if by a notice ⟨*posted* the students' grades⟩ **2** : to forbid persons from entering or using by putting up warning notices ⟨*post* a trout stream⟩ **3** : ²SCORE 1a ⟨*posted* a 72 for the round⟩ **4** : to publish (as a message) in an online forum

³post *n* **1** *chiefly British* : POSTAL SERVICE **2** *chiefly British* : the mail handled by the post **3** *chiefly British* : a single shipment of mail **4** : something (as a message) that is posted online [from early French *poste* "a relay station, one who carries messages," from early Italian *posta* "relay station," derived from *porre* (verb) "to place," from Latin *ponere* "to place" — related to ⁵POST]

⁴post *vb* **1** : to ride or travel with haste : HURRY **2** : ²MAIL **3** : to transfer a bookkeeping item from a book of original entry to an account book **4** : to make familiar with a subject : INFORM

⁵post *n* **1 a** : the place at which a soldier or guard is stationed **b** : a station or task to which a person is assigned **c** : a place to which troops are assigned : CAMP **2** : an office or position to which a person is appointed   **3** : TRADING POST [from early French *poste* "place where soldiers are stationed," from early Italian *posto* (same meaning), derived from *porre* (verb) "to place," from Latin *ponere* "to place" — related to ³POST]

⁶**post** *vb* **1** : to station in a given place ⟨*post* a guard⟩   **2** : to give as a guarantee of payment ⟨*post* a bond⟩

post- *prefix*   **1 a** : after : later ⟨*post*date⟩   **b** : behind   **2** : following : later than ⟨*post*script⟩ [derived from Latin *post* "after, later"]

post·age \'pō-stij\ *n* : the charge fixed by law for carrying an article by mail

postage stamp *n* : a government stamp used on mail to show that postage has been paid

post·al \'pōs-tᵊl\ *adj* : of or relating to mail or to the post office

postal card *n*   **1** : a blank card with a postage stamp printed on it   **2** : POSTCARD 1

postal service *n* : a government department in charge of handling the mail

post·card \'pōs(t)-ˌkärd\ *n*   **1** : a card on which a message may be sent by mail without an envelope   **2** : POSTAL CARD 1

post·con·sum·er \ˌpōs(t)-kən-'sü-mər\ *adj*   **1** : discarded by a consumer ⟨*postconsumer* waste⟩   **2** : having been used and recycled for reuse in another consumer product ⟨*postconsumer* plastics⟩

post·date \(')pōs(t)-'dāt\ *vb*   **1** : to assign a date to that is later than the actual or current date ⟨*postdate* a check⟩   **2** : to follow in time

post·er \'pō-stər\ *n* : a notice or advertisement for posting in a public place or for decorative or pictorial display

¹**pos·te·ri·or** \pō-'stir-ē-ər, pä-\ *adj*   **1** : later in time : SUBSEQUENT   **2** : located behind or toward the back — **pos·te·ri·or·ly** *adv*

²**pos·te·ri·or** \pä-'stir-ē-ər, pō-\ *n* : the hind end of the body; *esp* : BUTTOCK 2a

pos·ter·i·ty \pä-'ster-ət-ē\ *n*   **1** : the line of individuals descended from one ancestor   **2** : all future generations

pos·tern \'pōs-tərn, 'päs-\ *n*   **1** : a back door or gate   **2** : a private or side entrance or way — **postern** *adj*

post exchange *n* : a store at a military post that sells to people in or associated with the armed forces

¹**post·grad·u·ate** \(')pōst-'graj-(ə-)wət, -ə-ˌwāt\ *adj* : of, relating to, or engaged in formal studies after graduation : ²GRADUATE 2

²**postgraduate** *n* : a student continuing his or her education after graduation

post·haste \'pōst-'hāst\ *adv* : with great speed ⟨sent *posthaste* for the doctor⟩

post·hole \'pōst-ˌhōl\ *n* : a hole sunk in the ground to hold a fence post

post·hu·mous \'päs-chə-məs\ *adj*   **1** : born after the death of the father ⟨a *posthumous* son⟩   **2** : published after the death of the author   **3** : following or occurring after one's death ⟨*posthumous* fame⟩ ⟨a *posthumous* award⟩ — **post·hu·mous·ly** *adv*

pos·til·ion *or* **pos·til·lion** \pō-'stil-yən, pə-\ *n* : a person who rides as a guide on the left-hand horse of a pair drawing a coach

post·lude \'pōst-ˌlüd\ *n* : a closing piece of music; *esp* : an organ piece at the end of a church service

post·man \'pōs(t)-mən, -ˌman\ *n* : LETTER CARRIER

post·mark \-ˌmärk\ *n* : a mark canceling the postage stamp on a piece of mail and giving the date and place of sending — **postmark** *vb*

post·mas·ter \-ˌmas-tər\ *n* : a person in charge of a post office

postmaster general *n, pl* **postmasters general** : an official in charge of a national post office department or postal service

post me·ri·di·em \ˌpōs(t)-mə-'rid-ē-əm, -ē-ˌem\ *adj* : being after noon — abbreviation *p.m.*

post·mis·tress \'pōs(t)-ˌmis-trəs\ *n* : a woman in charge of a post office

¹**post·mor·tem** \(')pōs(t)-'mort-əm\ *adj* : done or occurring after death

²**postmortem** *n*   **1** : AUTOPSY   **2** : an analysis or discussion of an event after it is over

postmortem examination *n* : AUTOPSY

post·na·sal drip \'pōst-ˌnā-zəl\ *n* : a flow of mucus from the passages of the nose onto the back of the throat that occurs especially as a result of allergies

post·na·tal \(')pōst-'nāt-ᵊl\ *adj* : following birth; *also* : of or relating to a newborn child ⟨*postnatal* care⟩

post office *n*   **1** : POSTAL SERVICE   **2** : a local branch of the postal service handling the mail for a particular place

post·paid \'pōs(t)-'pād\ *adv* : with postage paid by the sender

post·pone \pōs(t)-'pōn\ *vb* **-poned; -pon·ing** : to put off (as an action or event) until a later time ⟨rain forced us to *postpone* the picnic⟩ — **post·pone·ment** \-mənt\ *n*

post road *n* : a road over which mail is carried

post·script \'pōs(t)-ˌskript\ *n* : a note or series of notes added at the end of a letter, article, or book

¹**pos·tu·late** \'päs-chə-ˌlāt\ *vb* **-lat·ed; -lat·ing** : to claim as true : assume as a postulate ⟨*postulates* that all people are created equal⟩

²**pos·tu·late** \'päs-chə-lət, -ˌlāt\ *n* : a statement or claim assumed to be true especially as the basis of a process of reasoning

¹**pos·ture** \'päs-chər\ *n*   **1** : the position of one part of the body with relation to other parts : the general way of holding the body   **2** : a particular condition or state ⟨a country's defense *posture*⟩ — **pos·tur·al** \-chə-rəl\ *adj*

²**posture** *vb* **pos·tured; pos·tur·ing** : to take a particular posture : POSE

post·war \'pōst-'wó(ə)r\ *adj* : of, relating to, or being a period after a war ⟨*postwar* Europe⟩

po·sy \'pō-zē\ *n, pl* **posies**   **1** : a bunch of flowers : BOUQUET   **2** : ¹FLOWER 1c

¹**pot** \'pät\ *n*   **1 a** : a deep rounded container for household purposes ⟨cooking *pot*⟩   **b** : the quantity held by a pot ⟨a *pot* of tea⟩   **2** : an enclosed trap for catching fish or lobsters   **3 a** : a large quantity or sum   **b** : the total of the bets at stake at one time   **4** : ¹RUIN 1 ⟨business went to *pot*⟩

¹pot 1a

²**pot** *vb* **pot·ted; pot·ting**   **1** : to preserve in a sealed pot, jar, or can   **2** : to plant or grow in a pot

³**pot** *n* : MARIJUANA [perhaps from Mexican Spanish *potiguaya* "marijuana"]

po·ta·ble \'pōt-ə-bəl\ *adj* : suitable for drinking — **po·ta·bil·i·ty** \ˌpōt-ə-ə-'bil-ət-ē\ *n*

pot·ash \'pät-ˌash\ *n* : potassium or a potassium compound

po·tas·si·um \pə-'tas-ē-əm\ *n* : a silver-white soft light metallic element that has a low melting point and occurs abundantly in nature especially combined in minerals — see ELEMENT table

potassium chlorate \-'klō(ə)r-ˌāt, -'kló(ə)r-\ *n* : a salt used to supply oxygen for matches, fireworks, and explosives

potassium chloride *n* : a salt used as a fertilizer

potassium cyanide *n* : a very poisonous salt used especially to obtain gold and silver from ore

potassium dichromate \-(')dī-'krō-ˌmāt, -'dī-krō-\ *n* : a salt that can be dissolved in water, forms large orange-red crystals, and is used especially in dyeing and photography

potassium hydroxide n : a white solid that dissolves in water to form a very alkaline liquid and is used especially in making soap

potassium nitrate n : a salt used in making gunpowder, as a fertilizer, and in medicine

potassium permanganate \-(ˌ)pər-ˈmaŋ-gə-ˌnāt\ n : a dark purple salt used especially as a disinfectant

potassium sulfate n : a white salt used especially as a fertilizer

po·ta·to \pə-ˈtāt-ō, pət-ˈāt-\ n, pl **-toes** 1 : SWEET POTATO 1 2 a : an erect South American herb widely cultivated for its thick starchy edible underground tubers **b** : one of these edible tubers — called also *Irish potato, spud, white potato*

potato beetle n : COLORADO POTATO BEETLE

potato bug n : COLORADO POTATO BEETLE

potato chip n : a thin slice of potato fried in deep fat

potbellied pig n : any of an Asian breed of small pigs having a straight tail, potbelly, and black, white, or black and white coat

potbellied stove n : a stove with a rounded or bulging body — called also *potbelly stove*

pot·bel·ly \ˈpät-ˌbel-ē\ n 1 : an enlarged abdomen or one that bulges outward 2 : POTBELLIED STOVE — **pot·bel·lied** \-ˈbel-ēd\ adj

po·ten·cy \ˈpōt-ᵊn-sē\ n, pl **-cies** : the quality or state of being potent ⟨vitamins of high *potency*⟩; *esp* : power to bring about a certain result

po·tent \ˈpōt-ᵊnt\ adj 1 : having or wielding force, authority, or influence : POWERFUL ⟨*potent* arguments for a strong defense⟩ 2 a : very effective ⟨*potent* medicine⟩ **b** : rich in a particular quality : STRONG ⟨*potent* tea⟩ — **po·tent·ly** adv

po·ten·tate \ˈpōt-ᵊn-ˌtāt\ n : a person who has controlling power : SOVEREIGN

¹**po·ten·tial** \pə-ˈten-chəl\ adj : capable of becoming real : POSSIBLE ⟨aware of the *potential* dangers in a scheme⟩ — **po·ten·tial·ly** \-ˈtench-(ə-)lē\ adv

²**potential** n 1 a : something that can develop or become actual : POSSIBILITY ⟨a *potential* for injury⟩ **b** : ¹PROMISE 3 ⟨an invention with great *potential*⟩ 2 a : the work required to move a single positive charge from a reference point (as at infinity) to a point in question **b** : POTENTIAL DIFFERENCE

potential difference n : the difference in potential between two points that represents the work involved or the energy released in the transfer of a unit quantity of electricity from one point to the other

potential energy n : the amount of energy a thing (as a weight raised to a height or a coiled spring) has because of its position or because of the arrangement of its parts

po·ten·ti·al·i·ty \pə-ˌten-chē-ˈal-ət-ē\ n, pl **-ties** 1 : the ability to develop or to come into existence 2 : ²POTENTIAL 1a

pot·ful \ˈpät-ˌful\ n : the quantity held by a pot

pot·head \ˈpät-ˌhed\ n : a person who frequently smokes marijuana

poth·er \ˈpäth-ər\ n : ¹FUSS 1

pot·herb \ˈpät-ˌ(h)ərb\ n : an herb whose leaves or stems are boiled for use as greens; *also* : one (as mint) used to season food

pot holder n : a small cloth pad used for handling hot cooking utensils

pot·hole \ˈpät-ˌhōl\ n : a deep round hole (as in a road)

pot·hook \-ˌhuk\ n : an S-shaped hook for hanging pots over an open fire

po·tion \ˈpō-shən\ n : a mixture of liquids (as a medicine or poison) [Middle English *pocioun* "a mixture of liquids," from early French *poisun, pocioun* (same meaning), from Latin *potion-, potio* "a drink, potion," from *potare* "to drink" — related to POISON]

pot·luck \ˈpät-ˈlək\ n 1 a : a regular meal for which no special preparations have been made **b** : a meal to which people bring food to share 2 : whatever is offered or available in given circumstances or at a given time

pot·pie \-ˈpī\ n : pastry-covered meat and vegetables cooked in a deep dish

pot·pour·ri \ˌpō-pu-ˈrē\ n 1 : a jar of flower petals and spices used for scent 2 : a miscellaneous collection : MEDLEY

pot roast n : a piece of meat (as beef) cooked by braising usually on top of the stove

pot·shot \ˈpät-ˌshät\ n 1 : a shot taken in a casual manner or at an easy target 2 : a critical remark made in a random manner

pot·tage \ˈpät-ij\ n : a thick soup of vegetables or vegetables and meat

potted past and past participle of POT

¹**pot·ter** \ˈpät-ər\ n : one that makes pottery

²**potter** vb : ³PUTTER — **pot·ter·er** n

potter's field n : a public burial place for the poor, unknown persons, and criminals

potter's wheel n : a horizontal disk revolving on a spindle and carrying the clay being shaped by a potter

pot·tery \ˈpät-ə-rē\ n, pl **-ter·ies** 1 : a place where clay articles (as pots and vases) are made 2 : the art of the potter : CERAMICS 3 : articles made from clay that is shaped while moist and hardened by heat

potting present participle of POT

pot·ty \ˈpät-ē\ n : TOILET 2b, BATHROOM

¹**pouch** \ˈpauch\ n 1 : a small bag that can be closed (as with a string) ⟨tobacco *pouch*⟩ 2 : a structure in the form of a bag; *esp* : one for carrying the young on the abdomen of a female marsupial (as a kangaroo or opossum) — **pouched** \ˈpaucht\ adj

potter's wheel

²**pouch** vb : to put or form into or as if into a pouch

poul·tice \ˈpōl-təs\ n : a soft usually heated mass that often contains medicine, is spread on cloth, and is applied especially to sores

poul·try \ˈpōl-trē\ n : domesticated birds kept for eggs or meat [Middle English *pultrie* "fowl raised for food," from early French *pulletrie* (same meaning), from *pulleter* "one who raises poultry," from *pullet* "chicken" — related to PULLET]

poul·try·man \-mən\ n : one who raises or deals in poultry

pounce \ˈpaun(t)s\ vb **pounced; pounc·ing** 1 : to swoop down on and seize something ⟨a cat waiting to *pounce*⟩ 2 : to make a sudden assault or approach ⟨a clerk *pounced* on me immediately⟩ — **pounce** n

¹**pound** \ˈpaund\ n, pl **pounds** also **pound** 1 : any of various units of mass and weight; *esp* : a unit in general use among English-speaking peoples equal to 16 ounces (about 0.454 kilograms) — see MEASURE table 2 a : the basic unit of money of the United Kingdom — called also *pound sterling* **b** : any of several basic units of money (as of Egypt, Lebanon, or Syria) **c** : a coin or bill representing one pound [Old English *pund* "pound weight," from Latin *pondo* (same meaning)]

²**pound** n 1 : a public enclosure for stray animals ⟨the dog *pound*⟩ 2 : an enclosure within which fish or shellfish are

\ə\ abut	\au̇\ out	\i\ tip	\ȯ\ saw	\u̇\ foot
\ər\ further	\ch\ chin	\ī\ life	\ȯi\ coin	\y\ yet
\a\ mat	\e\ pet	\j\ job	\th\ thin	\yü\ few
\ā\ take	\ē\ easy	\ŋ\ sing	\th\ this	\yu̇\ cure
\ä\ cot, cart	\g\ go	\ō\ bone	\ü\ food	\zh\ vision

caught or stored [Old English *pund-* "an enclosure for animals"]

³**pound** *vb* **1** : to crush to powder or pulp by beating **2 a** : to strike heavily or again and again ⟨*pound* the piano⟩ **b** : to produce by pounding ⟨*pound* out a tune on the piano⟩ **c** : ¹DRIVE 1b ⟨*pound* a nail⟩ **3** : to move heavily ⟨the horses *pounded* along the lane⟩ [Old English *pūnian* "to beat into a powder"] — **pound·er** *n*

⁴**pound** *n* : an act or sound of pounding

pound cake *n* : a cake made with a large amount of butter and eggs

pour \'pō(ə)r, 'pȯ(ə)r\ *vb* **1** : to flow or to cause to flow in a stream ⟨*pour* the tea⟩ ⟨tears *pouring* down their cheeks⟩ **2** : to let loose something without restraint ⟨*poured* out my troubles to anyone who would listen⟩ **3** : to rain very hard — **pour·er** *n*

¹**pout** \'pau̇t\ *vb* **1** : to show displeasure by pushing out the lips **2** : ¹SULK

²**pout** *n* **1** : an act of pouting **2** *pl* : a state of bad humor

pov·er·ty \'päv-ərt-ē\ *n* **1** : the state of being poor : lack of money or possessions : WANT **2** : a small supply : DEARTH ⟨a *poverty* of information about the new disease⟩ **3** : lack of fertility ⟨*poverty* of the soil⟩

pov·er·ty–strick·en \-ˌstrik-ən\ *adj* : very poor : DESTITUTE

POW \ˌpē-ˌō-'dəb-əl-(ˌ)yü\ *n* : PRISONER OF WAR

¹**pow·der** \'pau̇d-ər\ *n* **1 a** : dry material made up of fine particles **b** : something (as a food, medicine, or cosmetic) made in or changed to the form of a powder **2** : a solid explosive used in shooting or blasting

²**powder** *vb* **1** : to sprinkle or cover with or as if with powder **2** : to crush to or become powder — **pow·der·er** \-ər-ər\ *n*

powder blue *n* : a pale blue

powder horn *n* : a flask for carrying gunpowder; *esp* : one made of the horn of an ox or cow

pow·dery \'pau̇d-ə-rē\ *adj* **1 a** : resembling or consisting of powder **b** : easily made into a powder : CRUMBLY **2** : covered with or as if with powder : DUSTY

powdery mildew *n* : a fungus that is a parasite and produces a large number of powdery spores on the host; *also* : a plant disease caused by such a fungus

¹**pow·er** \'pau̇(-ə)r\ *n* **1 a** : possession of control, authority, or influence over others ⟨a politician hungry for *power*⟩ **b** : one having such power; *esp* : an independent state ⟨China is a major *power* in Asia⟩ **2** : ability to act or do something ⟨lose the *power* of speech⟩ **3 a** : physical might **b** : mental strength **4** : the number of times as indicated by an exponent a number occurs as a factor in a product; *also* : the product obtained by raising a number to a power ⟨10^3, or $10\cdot10\cdot10$, is the 3rd *power* of 10⟩ **5 a** : force or energy that is or can be applied to work ⟨electric *power*⟩ **b** : the time rate at which work is done or energy given off or transferred **6** : MAGNIFICATION 2b

synonyms POWER, ENERGY, STRENGTH mean the ability to put out effort or force. POWER applies to the ability to act, whether only possible or actually used ⟨the king had the *power* to coin money⟩. ENERGY applies to stored-up power that can be used to do work ⟨the sun could be a great source of new *energy* for us⟩. STRENGTH applies to that quality which gives a person or thing the ability to put out force or to oppose another's force or attack ⟨test the *strength* of this rope⟩.

²**power** *adj* : relating to, supplying, or using power ⟨a *power* drill⟩ ⟨*power* failure⟩

³**power** *vb* : to supply with power

pow·er·boat \'pau̇(-ə)r-ˌbōt\ *n* : MOTORBOAT

power dive *n* : a dive of an airplane accelerated by the power of the engine — **power–dive** *vb*

pow·er·ful \'pau̇(-ə)r-fəl\ *adj* : full of or having power or influence : STRONG, EFFECTIVE — **pow·er·ful·ly** \-f(ə-)lē\ *adv*

pow·er·house \'pau̇(-ə)r-ˌhau̇s\ *n* **1** : POWER PLANT **2** : a person or thing having unusual strength or energy

pow·er·less \'pau̇(-ə)r-ləs\ *adj* **1** : lacking power, force, or energy **2** : lacking authority to act — **pow·er·less·ly** *adv* — **pow·er·less·ness** *n*

power plant *n* : a building in which electric power is generated

power station *n* : POWER PLANT

power strip *n* : an electrical device that converts a single power outlet into several outlets

power up *vb* : to cause to operate ⟨*power up* the computer⟩

pow·wow \'pau̇-ˌwau̇\ *n* **1** : an American Indian ceremony or social gathering **2** : a meeting for discussion — **powwow** *vb*

pox \'päks\ *n* : a disease (as chicken pox) that is caused by a virus and produces a rash on the skin

PR \ˌpē-'är\ *n* : PUBLIC RELATIONS

prac·ti·ca·ble \'prak-ti-kə-bəl\ *adj* **1** : capable of being done, put into practice, or accomplished : FEASIBLE ⟨a *practicable* plan⟩ **2** : USABLE ⟨a *practicable* weapon⟩ — **prac·ti·ca·bil·i·ty** \ˌprak-ti-kə-'bil-ət-ē\ *n*

prac·ti·cal \'prak-ti-kəl\ *adj* **1** : of or relating to action and practice rather than ideas or thought ⟨for *practical* purposes⟩ **2** : being such in practice or effect : VIRTUAL ⟨a *practical* failure⟩ **3** : capable of being put to use or account : USEFUL ⟨a *practical* knowledge of farming⟩ **4** : good at putting ideas or plans into action ⟨a *practical* mind⟩ — **prac·ti·cal·i·ty** \ˌprak-ti-'kal-ət-ē\ *n*

practical joke *n* : a joke involving something that is done rather than said; *esp* : a trick played on a person — **practical joker** *n*

prac·ti·cal·ly \'prak-ti-k(ə-)lē\ *adv* **1** : in a practical manner ⟨talked *practically* about the problem⟩ **2** : ALMOST, NEARLY ⟨*practically* everyone went to the game⟩

practical nurse *n* : a nurse who cares for the sick professionally without having the training or experience required of a registered nurse; *esp* : LICENSED PRACTICAL NURSE

¹**prac·tice** *also* **prac·tise** \'prak-təs\ *vb* **prac·ticed** *or* **prac·tised**; **prac·tic·ing** *or* **prac·tis·ing** **1** : to perform or work at over and over so as to become skilled ⟨*practice* juggling⟩ **2** : CARRY OUT, APPLY ⟨*practice* what you preach⟩ **3** : to do or perform often or usually ⟨*practice* politeness⟩ **4** : to engage in or work at as a profession ⟨*practice* medicine⟩ — **prac·tic·er** *n*

²**practice** *also* **practise** *n* **1 a** : actual performance or application **b** : a repeated or usual action ⟨it was our *practice* to rise early⟩ **c** : the usual way of doing something ⟨local *practice*⟩ **2 a** : action done over and over in order to acquire skill ⟨*practice* makes perfect⟩ **b** : the condition of being skilled through practice ⟨get in *practice*⟩ **3 a** : continuous work in a profession ⟨the *practice* of law⟩ **b** : a professional business ⟨the doctor has expanded her *practice*⟩ *synonyms* see HABIT

prac·ticed *or* **prac·tised** \'prak-təst\ *adj* **1** : EXPERIENCED, SKILLED ⟨a *practiced* chef⟩ **2** : learned by practice

prac·ti·tio·ner \prak-'tish-(ə-)nər\ *n* : a person who practices a profession and especially law or medicine

prae·tor \'prēt-ər\ *n* : an ancient Roman official ranking below a consul and acting as a judge

¹**prae·to·ri·an** \prē-'tōr-ē-ən, -'tȯr-\ *adj* **1** : of or relating to a Roman praetor **2** *often cap* : of, relating to, or being the bodyguard of a Roman emperor ⟨the *praetorian* guard⟩

²**praetorian** *n, often cap* : a member of the praetorian guard

prag·mat·ic \prag-'mat-ik\ *also* **prag·mat·i·cal** \-i-kəl\ *adj* : concerned with practical matters rather than intellectual or artistic matters — **prag·mat·i·cal·ly** \-i-k(ə-)lē\ *adv*

prag·ma·tism \'prag-mə-ˌtiz-əm\ *n* **1** : a practical approach to problems and affairs **2** : a doctrine that truth is to be tested by the practical effects of belief — **prag-ma·tist** \-mət-əst\ *adj or n*

prai·rie \'pre(ə)r-ē\ *n* : a large area of level or rolling grass-land

prairie chicken *n* : a grouse of the prairies of the central U.S. with the males having a patch of bare skin on either side of the neck which is inflated with air during court-ship displays

prairie dog *n* : a black-tailed buff or grayish rodent of central and west-ern U.S. prairies that is related to the squirrels and usually lives in colonies with many burrows

prairie dog

prairie schooner *n* : a long covered wagon used by pioneers to cross the prairies

praise \'prāz\ *vb* **praised; prais·ing** **1** : to express approval of : COM-MEND **2** : to glorify (a god or a saint) especially in song [Middle English *preisen* "to praise," from early French *preisier, priser* "to praise, prize," from Latin *pretiare* "to prize," from earlier *pretium* (noun) "price, money" — related to PRICE] — **praise** *n*

praise·wor·thy \-,wər-thē\ *adj* : worthy of praise

pra·line \'prä-,lēn, 'prā-\ *n* : a candy of nuts in boiled brown sugar or maple sugar

prance \'pran(t)s\ *vb* **pranced; pranc·ing** **1** : to rise up or move about on the hind legs **2** : to ride on a prancing horse **3** : to walk or move about in a lively and proud manner : STRUT — **prance** *n* — **pranc·er** \'pran(t)-sər\ *n*

prank \'praŋk\ *n* : a playful or mischievous act : TRICK — **prank·ish** \'praŋ-kish\ *adj* — **prank·ish·ness** *n*

prank·ster \'praŋ(k)-stər\ *n* : a player of pranks

pra·seo·dym·i·um \,prā-zē-ō-'dim-ē-əm\ *n* : a yellowish white metallic element used especially in alloys and in coloring glass greenish yellow — see ELEMENT table

prate \'prāt\ *vb* **prat·ed; prat·ing** : to talk at great length but with little meaning : CHATTER — **prate** *n*

prat·fall \'prat-,fȯl\ *n* : a fall on the backside

prat·tle \'prat-ᵊl\ *vb* **prat·tled; prat·tling** \-liŋ, -ᵊl-iŋ\ **1** : PRATE **2** : ¹BABBLE 1a — **prattle** *n* — **prat·tler** \-lər, -ᵊl-ər\ *n*

prawn \'prȯn, 'prän\ *n* **1** : any of numerous wide-spread edible crustaceans that resemble shrimps **2** : ¹SHRIMP 1; *esp* : a large shrimp

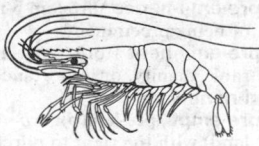

prawn 1

pray \'prā\ *vb* **1** : to ask earnestly : BEG 〈I *pray* you, tell me where they went〉 **2** : to address God with adoration, confession, pleading, or thanksgiving

prayer \'pra(ə)r, 'pre(ə)r\ *n* **1** : the act or practice of pray-ing to God 〈a moment of silent *prayer*〉 **2 a** : a set of words addressed to God 〈a *prayer* of thanksgiving〉 **b** : an earnest request or wish : PLEA **3** : a religious practice consisting chiefly of prayers 〈had regular family *prayers*〉

prayer·ful \'pra(ə)r-fəl, 'pre(ə)r-\ *adj* **1** : given to or marked by prayer : DEVOUT **2** : ²EARNEST 1 — **prayer-ful·ly** \-fə-lē\ *adv*

praying mantis *n* : MANTIS; *esp* : a European mantis that is now found in the U.S.

pre- *prefix* **1 a** : earlier than : before 〈*pre*historic〉 **b** : in preparation for : required for 〈*pre*medical〉 **2** : in ad-vance : beforehand 〈*pre*pay〉 **3** : in front of : front 〈*pre*-molar〉 [Latin *prae-* "before," from Latin *prae* "in front of, before"]

preach \'prēch\ *vb* **1 a** : to deliver a sermon : utter pub-licly **b** : to set forth in a sermon 〈*preach* the gospel〉 **2** : to urge publicly : ADVOCATE 〈*preach* brotherhood〉

preach·er \'prē-chər\ *n* : one that preaches; *esp* : ¹MINIS-TER 1b

pre·am·ble \'prē-,am-bəl, prē-'am-\ *n* **1** : an introduction (as to a law) that often gives the reasons for the parts that follow **2** : something that comes before and leads to something else

pre·ar·range \,prē-ə-'rānj\ *vb* : to arrange beforehand — **pre·ar·range·ment** \-mənt\ *n*

Pre·cam·bri·an \(')prē-'kam-brē-ən\ *adj* : of, relating to, or being the earliest era of geological history extending to the beginning of the Phanerozoic eon about 544,000,000 years ago; *also* : relating to the rocks formed during this time — see GEOLOGIC TIME table — **Precambrian** *n*

pre·car·i·ous \pri-'kar-ē-əs, -'ker-\ *adj* **1** : depending on unknown conditions or chance events **2** : dangerously lacking in security or steadiness 〈*precarious* health〉 — **pre·car·i·ous·ly** *adv* — **pre·car·i·ous·ness** *n*

pre·cau·tion \pri-'kȯ-shən\ *n* **1** : care taken in advance : FORESIGHT **2** : a measure taken beforehand to prevent harm or to bring about a good result 〈take *precautions* against fire〉 — **pre·cau·tion·ary** \-shə-,ner-ē\ *adj*

pre·cede \pri-'sēd\ *vb* **pre·ced·ed; pre·ced·ing** : to be, go, or come before (as in rank, position, or time)

pre·ce·dence \'pres-əd-ən(t)s, pri-'sēd-ᵊn(t)s\ *n* **1** : the act or fact of preceding (as in time) **2** : consideration based on order of importance : PRIORITY 〈your safety takes *pre-cedence*〉

¹pre·ce·dent \pri-'sēd-ᵊnt, 'pres-əd-ənt\ *adj* : going before in time, order, arrangement, or importance

²prec·e·dent \'pres-əd-ənt\ *n* **1** : an earlier occurrence of something similar **2** : something that may serve as an example or rule to be followed in the future

pre·ced·ing \pri-'sēd-iŋ\ *adj* : going before : PREVIOUS

pre·cept \'prē-,sept\ *n* : a command or principle intended as a general rule of action

pre·cep·tor \pri-'sep-tər, 'prē-,sep-\ *n* **1** : TEACHER, TU-TOR **2** : the principal of a school

pre·ces·sion \prē-'sesh-ən\ *n* : a comparatively slow cir-cling of the rotation axis of a spinning body about an-other line intersecting it — **pre·cess** \prē-'ses, 'prē-,ses\ *vb*

pre·cinct \'prē-,siŋ(k)t\ *n* **1** : an administrative district especially of a town or city 〈a police *precinct*〉 〈an elec-toral *precinct*〉 **2** : a surrounding or enclosed area 〈within the *precincts* of the college〉

pre·cious \'presh-əs\ *adj* **1** : of great value or high price 〈diamonds and other *precious* stones〉 **2** : greatly loved : DEAR 〈*precious* memories〉 [Middle English *precious* "of great value," from early French *precios* (same meaning), from Latin *pretiosus* (same meaning), from *pretium* "price, money" — related to PRICE] — **pre·cious·ly** *adv* — **pre·cious·ness** *n*

prec·i·pice \'pres-(ə-)pəs\ *n* : a very steep and high face of a rock or mountain

¹pre·cip·i·tate \pri-'sip-ə-,tāt\ *vb* **-tat·ed; -tat·ing** **1 a** : to throw violently : HURL **b** : to fall headlong **2** : to bring about suddenly 〈an event that *precipitated* war〉 **3 a** : to separate or cause to separate from solution or suspension **b** : to change from a vapor to a liquid or solid and fall as rain or snow — **pre·cip·i·ta·tor** \-,tāt-ər\ *n*

²pre·cip·i·tate \pri-'sip-ət-ət, -ə-,tāt\ *n* : a usually solid sub-stance separated from a solution or suspension by chemi-cal or physical change

\ə\ abut	\au̇\ out	\i\ tip	\ȯ\ saw	\u̇\ foot
\ər\ further	\ch\ chin	\ī\ life	\ȯi\ coin	\y\ yet
\a\ mat	\e\ pet	\j\ job	\th\ thin	\yü\ few
\ā\ take	\ē\ easy	\ŋ\ sing	\th\ this	\yu̇\ cure
\ä\ cot, cart	\g\ go	\ō\ bone	\ü\ food	\zh\ vision

³pre·cip·i·tate \pri-'sip-ət-ət\ *adj* : HASTY 2 ⟨a *precipitate* attack⟩ — **pre·cip·i·tate·ly** *adv*

pre·cip·i·ta·tion \pri-,sip-ə-'tā-shən\ *n* **1** : unwise haste **2** : the process of precipitating or of forming a precipitate **3** : water or the amount of water that falls to the earth as hail, rain, sleet, or snow

pre·cip·i·tous \pri-'sip-ət-əs\ *adj* **1** : showing unwise and unnecessary haste : RASH ⟨a *precipitous* act⟩ **2** : steep like a precipice ⟨a *precipitous* slope⟩ **synonyms** see STEEP — **pre·cip·i·tous·ly** *adv* — **pre·cip·i·tous·ness** *n*

pré·cis \prā-'sē, 'prā-sē\ *n, pl* **pré·cis** \-'sēz, -sēz\ : a brief summary of the essential points of something

pre·cise \pri-'sīs\ *adj* **1** : exactly or sharply explained or stated **2** : very exact ⟨*precise* scales⟩ ⟨the *precise* time⟩ **3** : agreeing exactly with a rule or standard **synonyms** see CORRECT — **pre·cise·ly** *adv* — **pre·cise·ness** *n*

¹pre·ci·sion \pri-'sizh-ən\ *n* : the quality or state of being precise : EXACTNESS, ACCURACY

²precision *adj* **1** : designed for very accurate measurement or operation ⟨a *precision* gauge⟩ **2** : marked by precision ⟨*precision* drilling⟩

pre·clude \pri-'klüd\ *vb* **pre·clud·ed; pre·clud·ing** : to make impossible beforehand : PREVENT ⟨the injury *precluded* the possibility of a career in sports⟩

pre·co·cious \pri-'kō-shəs\ *adj* : showing the qualities or abilities of an adult at an unusually early age ⟨a *precocious* child⟩ — **pre·co·cious·ly** *adv* — **pre·co·cious·ness** *n* — **pre·coc·i·ty** \pri-'käs-ət-ē\ *n*

Word History The process of growing from a child to an adult is sometimes thought of as being like the slow ripening of fruit. That was the image which gave us the word *precocious.* Like many English words, *precocious* comes from Latin. The Latin prefix *prae-,* meaning "ahead of, before," and the verb *coquere,* meaning "to ripen, cook," were combined to form the adjective *praecoc-, praecox,* which meant "ripening early or before its time." The Latin word was first used to describe certain plants and fruits. In time it also came to refer to other things that mature before their usual time. [from Latin *praecoc-, praecox* "ripening early, ripening before its time," from *prae-* "ahead of, before" and *coquere* "to ripen, cook"]

pre·con·ceive \,prē-kən-'sēv\ *vb* : to form (an opinion or idea) beforehand ⟨*preconceived* notions about foreign lands⟩ — **pre·con·cep·tion** \-'sep-shən\ *n*

pre·cook \(')prē-'kůk\ *vb* : to cook partially or entirely before final cooking or reheating

pre·cur·sor \pri-'kər-sər, 'prē-,kər-\ *n* **1** : PREDECESSOR **2** : a substance or cell from which another substance or cell is formed

pre·da·ceous *or* **pre·da·cious** \pri-'dā-shəs\ *adj* : living by preying on others : PREDATORY 2

pre·date \(')prē-'dāt\ *vb* : ANTEDATE 1

pre·da·tion \pri-'dā-shən\ *n* : a way of life in which food is obtained mostly by killing and eating animals

pred·a·tor \'pred-ət-ər, -ə-,tò(ə)r\ *n* : an animal that obtains food mostly by killing and eating other animals

pred·a·to·ry \'pred-ə-,tōr-ē, -,tòr-\ *adj* **1** : of, relating to, or marked by robbing or using others for personal gain ⟨*predatory* raids⟩ **2** : living by predation ⟨*predatory* animals⟩

pre·de·ces·sor \'pred-ə-,ses-ər, 'prēd-\ *n* : one that precedes; *esp* : a person who has held a position or office before another [Middle English *predecessour* "predecessor," from early French *predecesseur* (same meaning), from Latin *praedecessor* "one that goes before," from *prae-* "before, pre-," and *decessor* "retiring governor," from *decedere* "to depart," from *de-* "from" and *cedere* "to go, go away" — related to ANCESTOR, CONCEDE]

pre·des·ti·na·tion \(,)prē-,des-tə-'nā-shən\ *n* **1 a** : the act of predestining **b** : the state of being predestined **2** : the

doctrine that God has predestined some persons to eternal happiness and others to eternal punishment

pre·des·tine \(')prē-'des-tən\ *vb* : to decide beforehand especially by divine command

pre·de·ter·mine \,prēd-i-'tər-mən\ *vb* **1** : PREDESTINE **2** : to decide or settle beforehand ⟨meet at a *predetermined* place⟩ — **pre·de·ter·mi·na·tion** \-,tər-mə-'nā-shən\ *n*

pre·dic·a·ment \pri-'dik-ə-mənt\ *n* : a difficult, puzzling, or trying situation : FIX

¹pred·i·cate \'pred-i-kət\ *n* : the part of a sentence or clause that expresses what is said about the subject ⟨"threw the ball" in "the child threw the ball" is the *predicate*⟩ — **pred·i·ca·tive** \'pred-i-kət-iv, 'pred-ə-,kāt-\ *adj*

²pred·i·cate \'pred-ə-,kāt\ *vb* **-cat·ed; -cat·ing** : ²BASE 2 ⟨your theory is *predicated* on the belief that ghosts exist⟩ — **pred·i·ca·tion** \,pred-ə-'kā-shən\ *n*

³pred·i·cate \'pred-i-kət\ *adj* : belonging to the predicate; *esp* : completing the meaning of a linking verb ⟨*hot* in "the sun is hot" is a *predicate* adjective⟩ — compare ATTRIBUTIVE

pre·dict \pri-'dikt\ *vb* : to declare in advance : foretell on the basis of observation, experience, or reasoning [from Latin *praedictus,* past participle of *praedicere* "to predict, tell ahead of time," from *prae-* "pre-, earlier than, before" and *dicere* "to say" — related to DICTATE] **synonyms** see FORETELL — **pre·dict·able** \-'dik-tə-bəl\ *adj* — **pre·dict·ably** \-blē\ *adv*

pre·dic·tion \pri-'dik-shən\ *n* **1** : an act of predicting **2** : something predicted : FORECAST ⟨a *prediction* that there would be an earthquake⟩ — **pre·dic·tive** \-'dik-tiv\ *adj*

pre·di·lec·tion \,pred-ᵊl-'ek-shən, ,prēd-\ *n* : a natural liking for something ⟨a *predilection* for adventure stories⟩

pre·dis·pose \,prēd-is-'pōz\ *vb* : to dispose in advance : make susceptible : INCLINE — **pre·dis·po·si·tion** \,prē-,dis-pə-'zish-ən\ *n*

pre·dom·i·nance \pri-'däm-ə-nən(t)s\ *n* : the quality or state of being predominant

pre·dom·i·nant \pri-'däm-ə-nənt\ *adj* : greater in importance, strength, influence, or authority : PREVAILING ⟨the *predominant* color in a painting⟩ — **pre·dom·i·nant·ly** *adv*

pre·dom·i·nate \pri-'däm-ə-,nāt\ *vb* **1** : to be predominant : PREVAIL **2** : to go beyond others in number or quantity ⟨cottages *predominated*⟩ — **pre·dom·i·na·tion** \-,däm-ə-'nā-shən\ *n*

pre·em·i·nence \prē-'em-ə-nən(t)s\ *n* : the quality or state of being preeminent

pre·em·i·nent \prē-'em-ə-nənt\ *adj* : having supreme rank, dignity, or importance : OUTSTANDING — **pre·em·i·nent·ly** *adv*

pre·empt \prē-'em(p)t\ *vb* **1 a** : to settle upon (as public land) with the right to purchase before others **b** : to take by such a right **2** : to take before someone else can : APPROPRIATE ⟨*preempt* a seat at the stadium⟩ **3** : to take the place of ⟨the president's speech *preempted* the regular program⟩ — **pre·emp·tion** \-'em(p)-shən\ *n* — **pre·emp·tive** \-'em(p)-tiv\ *adj* — **pre·emp·tor** \-tər\ *n*

preen \'prēn\ *vb* **1** : to groom with the bill ⟨a bird *preening* its feathers⟩ **2** : to make one's appearance neat and tidy ⟨*preened* in front of the mirror⟩

pre·ex·ist \,prē-ig-'zist\ *vb* : to exist before something else

pre·ex·is·tence \,prē-ig-'zis-tən(t)s\ *n* : existence in a former state or before something else; *esp* : existence of the soul before its union with the body — **pre·ex·is·tent** \-tənt\ *adj*

pre·fab \(')prē-'fab, 'prē-,fab\ *n* : a prefabricated structure

pre·fab·ri·cate \(')prē-'fab-ri-,kāt\ *vb* : to manufacture the parts of something beforehand so that it can be built by putting the parts together — **pre·fab·ri·ca·tion** \,prē-,fab-ri-'kā-shən\ *n*

¹pref·ace \'pref-əs\ *n* : a section that introduces a book or a speech

²**preface** *vb* **pref·aced; pref·ac·ing** : to introduce by or begin with a preface ⟨*prefaced* the talk with a funny story⟩

pre·fect \'prē-ˌfekt\ *n* **1** : a high official or judge (as of ancient Rome or France) **2** : a student assistant in some schools

pre·fec·ture \'prē-ˌfek-chər\ *n* **1** : the office or term of office of a prefect **2** : the district governed by a prefect — **pre·fec·tur·al** \prē-'fek-chə-rəl\ *adj*

pre·fer \pri-'fər\ *vb* **pre·ferred; pre·fer·ring 1** : to choose or like better than another ⟨*prefer* dark clothes⟩ **2** : to present for action or consideration ⟨*prefer* charges against a thief⟩

pref·er·a·ble \'pref-(ə-)rə-bəl, 'pref-ər-bəl\ *adj* : worthy to be preferred : more desirable — **pref·er·a·bil·i·ty** \ˌpref-(ə-)rə-'bil-ət-ē\ *n* — **pref·er·a·bly** \'pref-(ə-)rə-blē, 'pref-ər-\ *adv*

pref·er·ence \'pref-ərn(t)s, 'pref-(ə-)rən(t)s\ *n* **1 a** : the act of preferring **b** : the state of being preferred **2** : the power or opportunity of choosing ⟨gave him his *preference*⟩ **3** : one that is preferred : FAVORITE ⟨my *preference* is soul music⟩ **4** : the act of giving advantages to some over others ⟨show *preference* in giving out jobs⟩

pref·er·en·tial \ˌpref-ə-'ren-chəl\ *adj* **1** : of or relating to preference **2** : showing preference ⟨*preferential* treatment⟩ **3** : creating or using preference in trading **4** : permitting the showing of order of preference (as of candidates in an election) ⟨a *preferential* ballot⟩ — **pref·er·en·tial·ly** \-'rench-(ə-)lē\ *adv*

pre·fer·ment \pri-'fər-mənt\ *n* **1** : advancement or promotion in dignity, office, or rank **2** : a position or office of honor or importance

pre·fig·ure \(')prē-'fig-yər, *especially British* -'fig-ər\ *vb* **1** : to show, suggest, or announce by an earlier type, image, or likeness ⟨the first crocus *prefigures* the arrival of spring⟩ **2** : to picture or imagine beforehand ⟨*prefigure* the outcome of the game⟩ — **pre·fig·u·ra·tion** \(ˌ)prē-ˌfig-(y)ə-'rā-shən\ *n* — **pre·fig·ure·ment** \(')prē-'fig-yər-mənt, *especially British* -'fig-ər-\ *n*

¹**pre·fix** \'prē-ˌfiks, prē-'fiks\ *vb* : to place in front; *esp* : to add as a prefix ⟨*prefix* a syllable to a word⟩

²**pre·fix** \'prē-ˌfiks\ *n* : a letter or group of letters that comes at the beginning of a word and has a meaning of its own

preg·nan·cy \'preg-nən(t)-sē\ *n, pl* **-cies** : the condition of being pregnant : GESTATION

preg·nant \'preg-nənt\ *adj* **1** : containing a developing embryo, fetus, or unborn offspring within the body **2** : full of meaning ⟨a *pregnant* pause⟩ — **preg·nant·ly** *adv*

pre·heat \(')prē-'hēt\ *vb* : to heat beforehand ⟨*preheat* the oven to 400 degrees⟩

pre·hen·sile \prē-'hen(t)-səl\ *adj* : capable of grasping especially by wrapping around ⟨a *prehensile* tail⟩

pre·His·pan·ic \ˌprē-(h)i-'span-ik\ *adj* : of, relating to, or being the time prior to Spanish conquests in the western hemisphere

pre·his·tor·ic \ˌprē-(h)is-'tor-ik, -'tär-\ *adj* : of, relating to, or existing in times before written history ⟨*prehistoric* animals⟩ — **pre·his·tor·i·cal·ly** \-i-k(ə-)lē\ *adv*

pre·his·to·ry \(')prē-'his-t(ə-)rē\ *n* : the study of prehistoric man — **pre·his·to·ri·an** \ˌprē-(h)is-'tōr-ē-ən, -'tòr-\ *n*

pre·judge \(')prē-'jəj\ *vb* : to judge before receiving all or enough of the facts — **pre·judg·ment** \-'jəj-mənt\ *n*

¹**prej·u·dice** \'prej-əd-əs\ *n* **1** : injury or damage to a case at law or to one's rights **2 a** : a favoring or dislike of something without good reason **b** : unfriendly feelings directed against an individual, a group, or a race [Middle English *prejudice* "injury from a judgment, an opinion formed before knowing the facts," from early French *prejudice* (same meaning), from Latin *praejudicium* "previous judgment," from *prae-* "pre-, before" and *judi-*

cium "judgment," from *judic-*, *judex* "judge," from *jus* "right, law" and *dicere* "to say" — related to JUDGE, JUST]

²**prejudice** *vb* **-diced; -dic·ing 1** : to cause damage to (as a case at law) ⟨newspaper stories *prejudiced* the murder case⟩ **2** : to cause to have prejudice : BIAS ⟨the incident *prejudiced* them against that company⟩

prej·u·di·cial \ˌprej-ə-'dish-əl\ *adj* : tending to cause damage : DETRIMENTAL

prel·ate \'prel-ət\ *n* : a high-ranking member of the clergy (as a bishop)

¹**pre·lim·i·nary** \pri-'lim-ə-ˌner-ē\ *n, pl* **-nar·ies** : something preliminary

²**preliminary** *adj* : coming before the main part or item : INTRODUCTORY — **pre·lim·i·nar·i·ly** \-ˌlim-ə-'ner-ə-lē\ *adv*

pre·lit·er·ate \(')prē-'lit-ə-rət, -'li-trət\ *adj* : existing before or lacking the use of writing ⟨*preliterate* societies⟩

¹**pre·lude** \'prel-ˌ(y)üd, 'prā-ˌl(y)üd\ *n* **1** : something that comes before and prepares for the main or more important parts ⟨the wind was a *prelude* to the storm⟩ **2 a** : a short musical introduction (as to an opera) **b** : a musical piece (as an organ solo) played at the beginning of a church service

²**prelude** *vb* **pre·lud·ed; pre·lud·ing** : to give, play, or serve as a prelude

pre·ma·ture \ˌprē-mə-'t(y)ú(ə)r, -'chú(ə)r\ *adj* : happening, coming, existing, or done before the proper or usual time; *esp* : born after a period of pregnancy of less than 37 weeks ⟨*premature* babies⟩ — **pre·ma·ture·ly** *adv* — **pre·ma·tu·ri·ty** \-'t(y)ùr-ət-ē, -'chùr-\ *n*

pre·med·i·cal \(')prē-'med-i-kəl\ *adj* : coming before and preparing for the study of medicine

pre·med·i·tate \pri-'med-ə-ˌtāt, 'prē-\ *vb* : to think about and plan beforehand ⟨*premeditated* murder⟩ — **pre·med·i·ta·tion** \pri-ˌmed-ə-'tā-shən, ˌprē-\ *n*

pre·men·stru·al \(')prē-'men(t)-strə-wəl\ *adj* : of, relating to, occurring in, or being the time period just preceding menstruation ⟨*premenstrual* symptoms⟩

premenstrual syndrome *n* : a varying group of symptoms experienced by some women prior to menstruation that may include irritability, insomnia, fatigue, anxiety, depression, headache, and abdominal pain — called also *PMS*

¹**pre·mier** \pri-'m(y)i(ə)r, 'prē-mē-ər, 'prem-ē-\ *adj* **1** : first in position, rank, or importance : PRINCIPAL **2** : first in time : EARLIEST

²**premier** *n* : the chief minister of government : PRIME MINISTER — **pre·mier·ship** \-ˌship\ *n*

¹**pre·miere** \pri-'mye(ə)r, -'mi(ə)r\ *n* : a first performance or showing ⟨*premiere* of a play⟩

²**premiere** *adj* : PREMIER

¹**prem·ise** \'prem-əs\ *n* **1** : a statement taken to be true and used as a basis for argument or reasoning **2** *pl* **a** : a piece of land with the buildings on it **b** : a building or part of a building usually with its grounds

²**pre·mise** \'prem-əs, pri-'mīz\ *vb* **pre·mised; pre·mis·ing** : to base on certain assumptions ⟨a conclusion *premised* on stereotypes⟩

¹**pre·mi·um** \'prē-mē-əm\ *n* **1 a** : a reward for an act **b** : a sum above and above a regular or stated price **c** : something given free or at a lower price with the purchase of a product or service **2** : the amount paid for a contract of insurance **3** : a high or extra value ⟨put a *premium* on accuracy⟩ [Latin *praemium* "booty, profit, reward," from *prae-* "before" + *emere* "to take, buy"]

²**premium** *adj* : of high quality, value, or price

\ə\ **abut**	\aú\ **out**	\i\ **tip**	\ò\ **saw**	\ú\ **foot**
\ər\ **further**	\ch\ **chin**	\ī\ **life**	\òi\ **coin**	\y\ **yet**
\a\ **mat**	\e\ **pet**	\j\ **job**	\th\ **thin**	\yü\ **few**
\ā\ **take**	\ē\ **easy**	\ŋ\ **sing**	\th\ **this**	\yú\ **cure**
\ä\ **cot, cart**	\g\ **go**	\ō\ **bone**	\ü\ **food**	\zh\ **vision**

pre·mix \prē-'miks, 'prē-\ *vb* : to mix before use

¹**pre·mo·lar** \(')prē-'mō-lər\ *adj* : located in front of the molar teeth; *also* : being or relating to the premolars

²**premolar** *n* : any of the double-pointed grinding teeth which are located between the canines and the true molars and of which there are two on each side of each jaw

pre·mo·ni·tion \ˌprē-mə-'nish-ən, ˌprem-ə-\ *n* : a feeling that something is going to happen ⟨a *premonition* of disaster⟩ — **pre·mon·i·to·ry** \pri-'män-ə-ˌtōr-ē, -ˌtor-\ *adj*

pre·na·tal \(')prē-'nāt-°l\ *adj* : occurring or existing before birth ⟨*prenatal* care⟩ ⟨*prenatal* development⟩

pre·oc·cu·pied \(')prē-'äk-yə-ˌpīd\ *adj* 1 : lost in thought : ENGROSSED 2 : already occupied

pre·oc·cu·py \(')prē-'äk-yə-ˌpī\ *vb* 1 : to hold the attention of beforehand 2 : to take possession of before another — **pre·oc·cu·pa·tion** \(ˌ)prē-ˌäk-yə-'pā-shən\ *n*

pre·or·dain \ˌprē-or-'dān\ *vb* : FOREORDAIN — **pre·or·di·na·tion** \(ˌ)prē-ˌord-°n-'ā-shən\ *n*

pre·pack·age \(')prē-'pak-ij\ *vb* : to package (as food) before offering for sale

prep·a·ra·tion \ˌprep-ə-'rā-shən\ *n* 1 : the action or process of making ready in advance 2 : a state of being prepared : READINESS 3 : an act or measure that prepares ⟨busy with *preparations* for the picnic⟩ 4 : something prepared ⟨a medicinal *preparation*⟩

pre·pa·ra·to·ry \pri-'par-ə-ˌtōr-ē, -ˌtor-\ *adj* : preparing or serving to prepare for something : INTRODUCTORY

preparatory school *n* 1 : a usually private school preparing students primarily for college 2 *British* : a private elementary school preparing students primarily for public schools

pre·pare \pri-'pa(ə)r, -'pe(ə)r\ *vb* **pre·pared; pre·par·ing** 1 : to make ready beforehand ⟨*prepared* us for the news⟩ ⟨*prepare* for a test⟩ 2 : to put together the elements of : COMPOUND ⟨*prepare* a prescription⟩ — **pre·par·er** *n*

pre·pared \pri-'pa(ə)rd, -'pe(ə)rd\ *adj* : treated with a special process : given a special treatment

pre·pared·ness \pri-'par-əd-nəs, -'per- *also* -'pa(ə)rd-nəs *or* -'pe(ə)rd-\ *n* : the quality or state of being prepared; *esp* : a state of readiness for war

pre·pay \(')prē-'pā\ *vb* **pre·paid** \-'pād\; **pre·pay·ing** : to pay or pay for in advance — **pre·pay·ment** \-'pā-mənt\ *n*

pre·pon·der·ance \pri-'pän-d(ə-)rən(t)s\ *n* : a greater quantity, number, weight, or importance ⟨the *preponderance* of evidence suggests that the accused is guilty⟩

pre·pon·der·ant \pri-'pän-d(ə-)rənt\ *adj* 1 : having greater weight, force, or influence : PREDOMINANT 2 : having greater frequency — **pre·pon·der·ant·ly** *adv*

prep·o·si·tion \ˌprep-ə-'zish-ən\ *n* : a word or group of words that combines with a noun or pronoun to form a phrase that usually acts as an adverb, adjective, or noun ⟨"with" in "the house with the red door" is a *preposition*⟩ — **prep·o·si·tion·al** \-'zish-nəl, -ən-°l\ *adj*

pre·pos·sess \ˌprē-pə-'zes\ *vb* 1 : PREOCCUPY 1 2 : to influence beforehand especially so as to win approval

pre·pos·sess·ing *adj* : creating a good impression : ATTRACTIVE ⟨a *prepossessing* appearance⟩

pre·pos·ses·sion \ˌprē-pə-'zesh-ən\ *n* 1 : an attitude, belief, or impression formed beforehand : PREJUDICE 2 : great concern with just one idea or object

pre·pos·ter·ous \pri-'päs-t(ə-)rəs\ *adj* : making little or no sense : ABSURD — **pre·pos·ter·ous·ly** *adv* — **pre·pos·ter·ous·ness** *n*

Word History The familiar expression "putting the cart before the horse" comes very close to the literal sense of the word *preposterous*. The Romans formed their Latin adjective *praeposterus* from *prae-*, meaning "before," and *posterus*, meaning "following." They at first used it to mean "having that first which ought to be last," like having a cart ahead of the horse that is pulling it. *Praeposterus* was used to describe something that was out of the normal or logical order or position. From this devel-

oped the more general sense of "ridiculous, absurd." These meanings were borrowed into English in the 16th century. Although *preposterous* is seldom used in its literal sense nowadays, we still use it to describe something that seems so unreasonable as to be ridiculous. [from Latin *praeposterus*, literally, "having the rear part in front," from *prae-* "in front, before" and *posterus* "coming behind, following"]

prep school *n* : PREPARATORY SCHOOL

pre·puce \'prē-ˌpyüs\ *n* : FORESKIN

pre·re·cord·ed \ˌprē-ri-'kȯ(ə)rd-əd\ *adj* : recorded in advance of presentation or use ⟨a *prerecorded* television program⟩

pre·reg·is·tra·tion \ˌprē-ˌrej-ə-'strā-shən\ *n* : a special registration prior to an official registration period ⟨*preregistration* for spring semester courses⟩; *also* : a registration prior to an event, activity, or program ⟨*preregistration* for basketball was held last month⟩

pre·req·ui·site \(')prē-'rek-wə-zət\ *n* : something required beforehand or necessary as preparation for something else ⟨the course is a *prerequisite* for advanced study⟩ — **prerequisite** *adj*

pre·rog·a·tive \pri-'räg-ət-iv\ *n* : a special right or privilege given because of one's rank or position

¹**pres·age** \'pres-ij\ *n* 1 : OMEN 2 : a warning or suggestion of future events

²**pre·sage** \'pres-ij, pri-'sāj\ *vb* **pre·saged; pre·sag·ing** 1 : to give a sign or warning of : PORTEND 2 : FORETELL, PREDICT

pres·by·ter \'prez-bət-ər, 'pres-\ *n* : a member of the governing body of an early Christian church

Pres·by·te·ri·an \ˌprez-bə-'tir-ē-ən, ˌpres-\ *adj* 1 *often not cap* : having a system of representative governing councils of ministers and elders 2 : of, relating to, or being a Protestant Christian church that is presbyterian in government — **Presbyterian** *n* — **Pres·by·te·ri·an·ism** \-ē-ə-ˌniz-əm\ *n*

¹**pre·school** \'prē-ˌskül\ *adj* : of, relating to, or being the period in a child's life to the age of five or six that ordinarily precedes attendance at school

²**preschool** *n* : a school for children usually younger than those attending elementary school or kindergarten : NURSERY SCHOOL

pre·school·er \'prē-ˌskü-lər\ *n* : a child of preschool age

pre·science \'prēsh-(ē-)ən(t)s, 'presh-\ *n* : FORESIGHT 1

pre·scient \'prēsh-(ē-)ənt, 'presh-\ *adj* : having foresight — **pre·scient·ly** *adv*

pre·scribe \pri-'skrīb\ *vb* **pre·scribed; pre·scrib·ing** 1 : to lay down as a rule of action ⟨the route that was *prescribed*⟩ 2 : to order or direct the use of something as a remedy ⟨the doctor *prescribed* an antibiotic⟩ — **pre·scrib·er** *n*

pre·scrip·tion \pri-'skrip-shən\ *n* 1 : the action of prescribing rules or directions 2 a : a written direction or order for the preparation and use of a medicine b : a medicine that is prescribed — **pre·scrip·tive** \-'skrip-tiv\ *adj*

pres·ence \'prez-°n(t)s\ *n* 1 : the fact or state of being present ⟨no one noticed the stranger's *presence*⟩ 2 : position close to a person ⟨in the *presence* of a guest⟩ 3 : a person's appearance ⟨a stately *presence*⟩ 4 : something felt or believed to be present ⟨a ghostly *presence*⟩

presence of mind : ability to think clearly and act quickly in an emergency

¹**pres·ent** \'prez-°nt\ *n* : something presented

²**pre·sent** \pri-'zent\ *vb* 1 a : to introduce one person to another b : to bring before the public ⟨*present* a play⟩ 2 : to make a gift to ⟨*presented* me with a watch⟩ 3 : to give or hand over with ceremony ⟨*present* a medal⟩ 4 : to make an accusation against someone ⟨*present* a charge⟩ 5 : to offer to view : DISPLAY, SHOW ⟨*presents* a fine appearance⟩ **synonyms** see GIVE — **pre·sent·er** *n*

³**pres·ent** \'prez-³nt\ *adj* **1** : being or going on now : not past or future ⟨the *present* situation⟩ **2** : being before or near a person or in sight : being at a certain place and not elsewhere ⟨all the pupils were *present*⟩ ⟨was *present* at the ceremony⟩ **3** : of, relating to, or being a verb tense that expresses present time or the time of speaking

⁴**pres·ent** \'prez-³nt\ *n* **1 a** : PRESENT TENSE **b** : a verb form in the present tense **2** : the present time

pre·sent·able \pri-'zent-ə-bəl\ *adj* : having a satisfactory or pleasing appearance — **pre·sent·ably** \-blē\ *adv*

pre·sen·ta·tion \ˌprē-ˌzen-'tā-shən, ˌprez-³n-, ˌprēz-³n-\ *n* **1** : the act of presenting **2 a** : something (as a gift or an award) presented **b** : something set forth for attention (as a play or a sales demonstration) **3** : the position in which the fetus lies in the uterus in labor with respect to the opening through which it passes in birth — **pre·sen·ta·tion·al** \-shnəl, -shən-³l\ *adj*

pres·ent–day \'prez-³nt-ˌdā\ *adj* : being or happening now

pre·sen·ti·ment \pri-'zent-ə-mənt\ *n* : a feeling that something will or is about to happen

pres·ent·ly \'prez-³nt-lē\ *adv* **1** *archaic* : at once **2** : before long : after a while ⟨*presently* they arrived⟩ **3** : at the present time : NOW ⟨she is *presently* working⟩

pre·sent·ment \pri-'zent-mənt\ *n* : the act of presenting to an authority a statement of the matter to be dealt with ⟨a *presentment* returned by a grand jury⟩

present participle \'prez-³nt-\ *n* : a participle that expresses present action, that in English is formed with the suffix *-ing,* and that indicates action going on

present perfect tense *n* : a tense formed in English with *have* and expressing action or state completed at the time of speaking

present tense *n* : a tense that expresses action or state in the present time and is used of what is true at the time of speaking or is always true

pres·er·va·tion \ˌprez-ər-'vā-shən\ *n* : a keeping from injury, loss, or decay

¹**pre·ser·va·tive** \pri-'zər-vət-iv\ *adj* : having the power of preserving

²**preservative** *n* : something that preserves or has the power of preserving; *esp* : a substance added to food to prevent spoiling or discoloring

¹**pre·serve** \pri-'zərv\ *vb* **pre·served; pre·serv·ing 1** : to keep or save from injury, loss, or ruin : PROTECT ⟨*preserve* the republic⟩ **2** : MAINTAIN 1, CONTINUE ⟨*preserve* silence⟩ **3** : to prepare (as vegetables, fruits, or meats) to be kept for future use — **pre·serv·er** *n*

²**preserve** *n* **1** : fruit cooked in sugar or made into jams or jellies ⟨strawberry *preserves*⟩ **2** : an area where natural resources (as fish, game, or trees) are protected

pre·set \(')prē-'set\ *vb* **pre·set; pre·set·ting** : to set ahead of time ⟨*preset* the oven to 350 degrees⟩

pre·shrink \(')prē-'shriŋk\ *vb* **pre·shrank** \-'shraŋk\; **pre·shrunk** \-'shrəŋk\ : to shrink (as a fabric) before making into a garment so that the garment will not shrink much when washed

pre·side \pri-'zīd\ *vb* **pre·sid·ed; pre·sid·ing 1** : to be in the place of authority : act as president, chairperson, or moderator ⟨*preside* over a meeting⟩ **2** : to be in charge

pres·i·den·cy \'prez-əd-ən-sē, 'prez-dən-; 'prez-ə-ˌden(t)-sē\ *n, pl* **-cies 1** : the office of president **2** : the term during which a president holds office

pres·i·dent \'prez-əd-ənt, 'prez-dənt, 'prez-ə-ˌdent\ *n* **1** : a person who presides over a meeting **2** : the chief officer of an organization ⟨a bank *president*⟩ ⟨college *president*⟩ ⟨*president* of our club⟩ **3** : the chief executive officer or the chief of state in a republic — **pres·i·den·tial** \ˌprez(ə)-'den-chəl\ *adj*

Presidents' Day *n* : WASHINGTON'S BIRTHDAY 2

¹**pre·soak** \(')prē-'sōk\ *vb* : to soak before washing

²**pre·soak** \'prē-ˌsōk\ *n* **1** : an instance of presoaking **2** : a product used for presoaking clothes

pre·sort \(ˌ)prē-'sȯ(ə)rt\ *vb* : to sort (outgoing mail) by zip code usually before delivery to a post office

¹**press** \'pres\ *n* **1** : ²CROWD 1, THRONG **2** : a machine or device that uses pressure to shape, flatten, squeeze, or stamp ⟨a cookie *press*⟩ ⟨a cider *press*⟩ **3** : ¹CLOSET 2 **4 a** : an act of pressing : PRESSURE **b** : an aggressive defense in basketball **5** : the smoothed and creased condition of a freshly pressed garment **6 a** : PRINTING PRESS **b** : a printing or publishing business **7 a** : the gathering and publishing or broadcasting of news **b** : the newspapers and magazines of a country **c** : news reporters and broadcasters

¹press 2

²**press** *vb* **1** : to bear down upon : push steadily against **2** : to squeeze so as to force out the juice or contents of ⟨*press* apples to make cider⟩ **3** : to flatten out or smooth by bearing down upon (as with an iron) ⟨*press* clothes⟩ **4 a** : to put pressure on : FORCE, COMPEL ⟨*pressed* by business to return⟩ **b** : to ask or urge strongly ⟨*pressed* us to go with them⟩ **5 a** : to insist on ⟨didn't *press* the issue⟩ **b** : to make a demand ⟨*pressing* for higher wages⟩ **6 a** : to crowd closely ⟨reporters *pressed* around the celebrity⟩ **b** : to force or push one's way ⟨*pressed* deeper into the jungle⟩ — **press·er** *n*

³**press** *vb* : to force into emergency service

press agent *n* : a person employed to establish and keep up good public relations by publicity

press conference *n* : an interview given by a public figure to the press

presser foot *n* : a piece on a sewing machine that holds the fabric down while stitching

press·ing \'pres-iŋ\ *adj* : needing one's immediate attention ⟨a *pressing* issue⟩ — **press·ing·ly** \-iŋ-lē\ *adv*

press secretary *n* : a person in charge of relations with the press for a public figure

¹**pres·sure** \'presh-ər\ *n* **1** : a force or influence that cannot be avoided ⟨social *pressure*⟩ **2** : the application of force to something by something else in direct contact with it ⟨keep steady *pressure* on the gas pedal⟩ **3 a** : the action of a force against an opposing force **b** : the force applied over a surface divided by its area **c** : the force exerted as a result of the weight of the atmosphere **4** : the stress or burden of matters demanding attention ⟨works well under *pressure*⟩

²**pressure** *vb* **pres·sured; pres·sur·ing** \'presh-(ə-)riŋ\ **1** : to apply pressure to **2** : PRESSURIZE

pressure cooker *n* : a utensil for cooking or preserving foods by means of steam under pressure — **pressure–cook** \ˌpresh-ər-'kùk\ *vb*

pressure point *n* : a point where a blood vessel runs near a bone and can be compressed (as to stop bleeding) by applying pressure against the bone

pres·sur·ize \'presh-ə-ˌrīz\ *vb* **-ized; -iz·ing 1** : to maintain near-normal atmospheric pressure in ⟨*pressurize* an airplane cabin⟩ **2** : to apply pressure to — **pres·sur·iza·tion** \ˌpresh-(ə-)rə-'zā-shən\ *n*

pres·ti·dig·i·ta·tion \ˌpres-tə-ˌdij-ə-'tā-shən\ *n* : SLEIGHT OF HAND 1 — **pres·ti·dig·i·ta·tor** \-'dij-ə-ˌtāt-ər\ *n*

\ə\ abut	\aú\ out	\i\ tip	\ó\ saw	\ú\ foot
\ər\ further	\ch\ chin	\ī\ life	\ói\ coin	\y\ yet
\a\ mat	\e\ pet	\j\ job	\th\ thin	\yü\ few
\ā\ take	\ē\ easy	\ŋ\ sing	\th\ this	\yú\ cure
\ä\ cot, cart	\g\ go	\ō\ bone	\ü\ food	\zh\ vision

pres·tige \pre-'stēzh, -'stēj\ *n* : importance in the eyes of other people — **pres·ti·gious** \-'stij-əs\ *adj* — **pres·ti·gious·ly** *adv* — **pres·ti·gious·ness** *n*

pres·to \'pres-tō\ *adv or adj* **1** : suddenly as if by magic ⟨a wave of the hand and, *presto*, it's gone⟩ **2** : at a rapid tempo — used as a direction in music

pre·sum·ably \pri-'zü-mə-blē\ *adv* : one would presume : it seems likely : PROBABLY ⟨*presumably* he'll come later⟩

pre·sume \pri-'züm\ *vb* **pre·sumed; pre·sum·ing 1** : to undertake without permission or good reason : DARE ⟨*presume* to question the authority of a superior⟩ **2** : to expect or assume with confidence : feel sure ⟨I *presume* you'll fly if you do go⟩ **3** : to suppose to be true without proof ⟨*presume* a person innocent until proved guilty⟩ — **pre·sum·able** \-'zü-mə-bəl\ *adj*

pre·sump·tion \pri-'zəm(p)-shən\ *n* **1** : presumptuous attitude or behavior **2 a** : strong reason for believing something to be so in spite of lack of proof **b** : something believed but not proved

pre·sump·tu·ous \pri-'zəm(p)-ch(ə-w)əs\ *adj* : going beyond what is proper — **pre·sump·tu·ous·ly** *adv* — **pre·sump·tu·ous·ness** *n*

pre·sup·pose \ˌprē-sə-'pōz\ *vb* : to take something to be true : suppose ahead of time ⟨the book *presupposes* its readers will know something about the subject⟩ — **pre·sup·po·si·tion** \(ˌ)prē-ˌsəp-ə-'zish-ən\ *n*

pre·sweet·ened \'prē-'swēt-ᵊnd\ *adj* : sweetened by the manufacturer ⟨*presweetened* cereal⟩

¹**pre·teen** \'prē-'tēn\ *n* : a boy or girl not yet 13 years old

²**preteen** *adj* **1** : relating to or produced for children especially in the 9 to 12 year-old age group ⟨*preteen* fashions⟩ **2** : being younger than 13 years old

¹**pre·tend** \pri-'tend\ *vb* **1** : to give the appearance of being, having, or doing ⟨I don't *pretend* to be a doctor, but you should do something about that cough⟩ **2** : to make believe : act a part or role ⟨*pretend* to be a bear⟩ ⟨*pretend* I'm your boss. What would you say?⟩

²**pretend** *adj* : IMAGINARY, MAKE-BELIEVE

pre·tend·er \pri-'ten-dər\ *n* **1** : a person who pretends **2** : a person who claims a throne without right

pre·tense *or* **pre·tence** \'prē-'ten(t)s, pri-'ten(t)s\ *n* **1** : a claim usually not supported by facts **2** : the quality or state of being pretentious ⟨free from *pretense*⟩ **3** : an effort to reach a certain condition or quality ⟨let's have some *pretense* of order around here⟩ ⟨the book makes no *pretense* at completeness⟩ **4** : a pretended purpose ⟨was there under false *pretenses*⟩ **5** : a false show : SIMULATION ⟨a *pretense* of indifference⟩

pre·ten·sion \pri-'ten-chən\ *n* **1** : PRETENSE 1 **2** : something one hopes to reach : ASPIRATION, AMBITION ⟨has serious *pretensions* as a writer⟩ **3** : PRETENSE 2

pre·ten·tious \pri-'ten-chəs\ *adj* : appearing or trying to appear more important or more valuable than is the case — **pre·ten·tious·ly** *adv* — **pre·ten·tious·ness** *n*

pret·er·it *or* **pret·er·ite** \'pret-ə-rət\ *n* : PAST TENSE

pre·ter·nat·u·ral \ˌprēt-ər-'nach-(ə-)rəl\ *adj* : beyond what is natural : unable to be explained by ordinary means — **pre·ter·nat·u·ral·ly** \-'nach-(ə-)rə-lē, -'nach-ər-lē\ *adv*

pre·test \'prē-'test\ *n* : a test to find out if students are prepared for further studies

pre·text \'prē-ˌtekst\ *n* : a reason put forward in order to hide the real reason

pre·treat \(')prē-'trēt\ *vb* : to treat (as soiled clothes) before laundering — **pre·treat·ment** \-mənt\ *n*

¹**pret·ty** \'prit-ē, 'purt-\ *adj* **pret·ti·er; -est** : delicately or gracefully attractive to the eye or ear ⟨a *pretty* face⟩ ⟨*pretty* tunes⟩ **synonyms** see BEAUTIFUL — **pret·ti·ly** \'prit-ᵊl-ē, 'purt-ᵊl-ē\ *adv* — **pret·ti·ness** \'prit-ē-nəs, 'purt-\ *n*

²**pret·ty** \'prit-ē, pərt-ē\ *adv* : in some degree : FAIRLY, MODERATELY ⟨*pretty* big⟩ ⟨was *pretty* much ignored⟩

³**pretty** \like ¹\ *n, pl* **pretties** : a pretty person or thing

pret·zel \'pret-səl\ *n* : a brown cracker that is salted and usually hard and shaped like a loose knot

Word History Pretzels were probably first made in the U.S. during the 19th century by immigrants from Germany. The English word *pretzel* comes from the German *Brezel*. The familiar knot-shaped pretzel has been known in Germanic countries for centuries. Its German name comes from the Latin *brachiatus*, which means "having branches like arms." The pretzel likely got its name because its knot shape looks something like a pair of folded arms. [from German *Brezel* "pretzel," derived from Latin *brachiatus* (adjective) "having branches like arms," from *brachium*, "arm" — related to ²BRACE]

pre·vail \pri-'vā(ə)l\ *vb* **1** : to win against opposition : be successful ⟨our team *prevailed*⟩ ⟨truth will *prevail* over error⟩ ⟨believed injustice should not *prevail*⟩ **2** : to urge successfully ⟨*prevailed* upon me to play a few tunes⟩ **3 a** : to be frequent ⟨the storms that *prevail* there in winter⟩ **b** : to be or continue to be in use or fashion ⟨lower rates *prevail* in the evening⟩ ⟨customs that still *prevail*⟩

pre·vail·ing \pri-'vā-lin\ *adj* **1** : having greater force or influence **2 a** : most frequent ⟨*prevailing* winds⟩ **b** : generally current : COMMON — **pre·vail·ing·ly** *adv*

prev·a·lence \'prev-(ə-)lən(t)s\ *n* **1** : the state of being prevalent **2** : the degree to which something is prevalent; *esp* : the part of a population that is affected with a particular disease at a given time

prev·a·lent \'prev-(ə-)lənt\ *adj* : accepted, practiced, or happening often or over a wide area — **prev·a·lent·ly** *adv*

pre·var·i·cate \pri-'var-ə-ˌkāt\ *vb* **-cat·ed; -cat·ing** : ³LIE 1 — **pre·var·i·ca·tion** \-ˌvar-ə-'kā-shən\ *n* — **pre·var·i·ca·tor** \-'var-ə-ˌkāt-ər\ *n*

pre·vent \pri-'vent\ *vb* **1** : to keep from happening ⟨*prevent* accidents⟩ **2** : to hold or keep back : HINDER, STOP ⟨bad weather *prevented* us from leaving⟩ — **pre·vent·able** *also* **pre·vent·ible** \-ə-bəl\ *adj*

pre·ven·ta·tive \pri-'vent-ət-iv\ *adj or n* : PREVENTIVE

pre·ven·tion \pri-'ven-chən\ *n* : the act or practice of preventing something ⟨the *prevention* of fires⟩

¹**pre·ven·tive** \pri-'vent-iv\ *n* : something that prevents; *esp* : something used to prevent disease

²**preventive** *adj* : concerned with or used for prevention ⟨*preventive* measures⟩ ⟨*preventive* medicine⟩

¹**pre·view** \'prē-ˌvyü\ *vb* : to view or show in advance

²**preview** *n* **1** : a showing of something (as a movie) before regular showings **2** *also* **pre·vue** \-ˌvyü\ : a showing of bits from a movie that is to be shown in the near future

pre·vi·ous \'prē-vē-əs\ *adj* : going before in time or order : PRECEDING, PRIOR — **pre·vi·ous·ly** *adv*

previous to *prep* : PRIOR TO, BEFORE

pre·war \'prē-'wȯ(ə)r\ *adj* : occurring or existing before a war

pre·wash \(')prē-'wȯsh, -'wäsh\ *vb* : to wash beforehand

pre·writ·ing \'prē-ˌrīt-in\ *n* : planning and getting ideas in order before writing

¹**prey** \'prā\ *n* **1** : an animal hunted or killed by another animal for food **2** : a person who is helpless or unable to escape attack : VICTIM **3** : the act or habit of seizing and pouncing upon

²**prey** *vb* **preyed; prey·ing 1 a** : to seize and eat something as prey **b** : to do violent or dishonest acts ⟨robbers who *preyed* on travelers⟩ **2** : to have a harmful effect ⟨fears that *prey* on the mind⟩

¹**price** \'prīs\ *n* **1** : the quantity of one thing and especially money that is exchanged or demanded in exchange for another **2** : ²REWARD 1 ⟨a *price* on an outlaw's head⟩ **3** : the cost at which something is gotten or done ⟨victory at any *price*⟩ [Middle English *pris* "prize, price," from early French *pris* (same meaning), from Latin *pretium* "price, money" — related to APPRECIATE, PRAISE, PRECIOUS, ¹PRIZE]

synonyms PRICE, CHARGE, FEE mean payment in exchange for something. PRICE usually refers to the payment asked for goods ⟨the *price* of a pair of shoes⟩. CHARGE usually refers to the payment asked for services ⟨the *charge* for dry-cleaning a pair of pants⟩. FEE refers to a charge fixed (as by law or a business) for a service or permit ⟨the *fee* for a driver's license⟩.

²**price** *vb* **priced; pric·ing** 1 : to set a price on 2 : to ask the price of — **pric·er** *n*

price·less \'prī-sləs\ *adj* 1 : too valuable to have a price : not to be bought at any price 2 : very funny or strange ⟨a *priceless* remark⟩

¹**prick** \'prik\ *n* 1 : a mark or small wound made by a pointed instrument 2 : something sharp or pointed 3 : an instance of pricking 4 : the sensation of being pricked

²**prick** *vb* 1 : to pierce slightly with a sharp point 2 : to have or cause a feeling of or as if of being pricked 3 : to point forward or upward ⟨the dog's ears *pricked* up at the sound⟩ — **prick up one's ears** : to listen with close attention

prick·er \'prik-ər\ *n* 1 : one that pricks 2 : ¹PRICKLE 1

¹**prick·le** \'prik-əl\ *n* 1 : a small sharp point or a sharp pointed part (as a thorn on a plant) that sticks out 2 : a slight stinging or tingling sensation

²**prickle** *vb* **prick·led; prick·ling** \'prik-(ə-)liŋ\ 1 : to prick slightly 2 : to cause or feel a slight stinging or tingling sensation

prick·ly \'prik-lē, -ə-lē\ *adj* **prick·li·er; -est** 1 : full of or covered with prickles ⟨*prickly* plants⟩ 2 : marked by slight stinging or tingling ⟨a *prickly* sensation⟩ — **prick·li·ness** *n*

prickly heat *n* : a rash around the openings of the sweat glands with pimples, itching, and tingling that is caused by inflammation

prickly pear *n* 1 : any of numerous cacti with spines and usually flat stem segments 2 : the pear-shaped sweet edible pulpy fruit of a prickly pear

¹**pride** \'prīd\ *n* 1 : too high an opinion of one's own ability or worth : a feeling of being better than others 2 : a reasonable and justifiable sense of one's own worth : SELF-RESPECT 3 : a sense of pleasure that comes from some act or possession 4 : something of which one is proud ⟨our *pride* and joy⟩ 5 : a group of lions

²**pride** *vb* **prid·ed; prid·ing** : to think highly of (oneself)

pride·ful \'prīd-fəl\ *adj* : full of pride — **pride·ful·ly** \-fə-lē\ *adv* — **pride·ful·ness** *n*

prickly pear 1

pried *past and past participle of* PRY

priest \'prēst\ *n* : a person who has the authority to lead or perform religious ceremonies [Old English *prēost* "priest," derived from Latin *presbyter* "priest, elder," from Greek *presbyteros*, comparative form of *presbys* "old man, elder"]

priest·ess \'prē-stəs\ *n* : a woman who is a priest

priest·hood \'prēst-ˌhu̇d, 'prē-ˌstu̇d\ *n* 1 : the office or dignity of a priest 2 : the whole group of priests

priest·ly \'prēst-lē\ *adj* **priest·li·er; -est** 1 : of or relating to a priest or the priesthood 2 : characteristic of or suitable for a priest — **priest·li·ness** *n*

prig \'prig\ *n* : a person who annoys others by being too careful about conforming to what is socially acceptable (as in speech and manners) — **prig·gish** \'prig-ish\ *adj* — **prig·gish·ly** *adv* — **prig·gish·ness** *n*

prim \'prim\ *adj* **prim·mer; prim·mest** : very fussy about one's appearance and behavior — **prim·ly** *adv* — **prim·ness** *n*

pri·ma·cy \'prī-mə-sē\ *n, pl* **-cies** 1 : the state of being first (as in time, place, or rank) 2 : the office or dignity of a bishop of the highest rank

pri·ma don·na \ˌprim-ə-'dän-ə, ˌprē-mə-\ *n, pl* **prima donnas** 1 : a principal female singer in an opera or concert organization 2 : a person who is easily hurt or upset or is stuck-up [Italian, literally, "first lady"; *prima* from Latin *prima*, a feminine form of *primus* "first," *donna* from Latin *domina* "lady, mistress," a feminine form of *dominus* "master" — related to DAME, PRIME]

pri·mal \'prī-məl\ *adj* 1 : of or relating to the first period or state : PRIMITIVE 2 : first in importance : BASIC

pri·mar·i·ly \prī-'mer-ə-lē\ *adv* 1 : for the most part : CHIEFLY 2 : in the first place : ORIGINALLY

¹**pri·ma·ry** \'prī-ˌmer-ē, 'prim-(ə-)rē\ *adj* 1 : first in time or development : INITIAL, PRIMITIVE ⟨the *primary* stage of a civilization⟩ 2 a : of first rank, importance, or value ⟨our *primary* duties⟩ b : ¹BASIC 1, FUNDAMENTAL ⟨the family is the *primary* unit of human association⟩ c : of, relating to, or being one of the principal flight feathers of a bird's wing located on the outer joint d : of, relating to, or being the strongest of three levels of stress in pronunciation 3 a : not made or coming from something else : FIRST-HAND ⟨a *primary* source of information⟩ b : of, relating to, or being the current or circuit that is connected to the source of electricity in an induction coil or transformer

²**primary** *n, pl* **-ma·ries** 1 : one of the usually nine or ten strong flight feathers on the outer joint of a bird's wing 2 : PRIMARY COLOR 3 : an election in which members of a political party nominate candidates for office 4 : the coil that is connected to the source of electricity in an induction coil or transformer — called also *primary coil*

primary color *n* : any of a set of colors from which all other colors may be made with the colors for light being red, green, and blue and for pigments or paint being red, yellow, and blue

pri·mate \'prī-ˌmāt *or especially for 1* -mət\ *n* 1 : a bishop or archbishop of the highest rank in a district, nation, or church 2 : any of an order of mammals that are characterized by hands and feet that grasp, a relatively large complex brain, and vision in which objects are seen in three dimensions and that includes human beings, apes, monkeys, and related forms (as lemurs and tarsiers)

pri·ma·tol·o·gy \ˌprī-mə-'täl-ə-jē\ *n* : the study of primates and especially primates other than human beings — **pri·ma·tol·o·gist** \-jist\ *n*

¹**prime** \'prīm\ *n* 1 : the first part : the earliest stage 2 : the most vigorous, prosperous, or satisfying stage or period ⟨in the *prime* of one's life⟩ 3 : the best individual or part 4 : PRIME NUMBER 5 : the symbol ′ [Old English *prīm* "a religious service for the first hour of the day," from Latin *prima (hora)* "first (hour)," from *primus* "first" — related to PREMIER, PRIMA DONNA, PRIMEVAL, PRINCE]

²**prime** *adj* 1 : first in time : ORIGINAL 2 a : of, relating to, or being a prime number b : expressed as a product of prime factors ⟨the *prime* factorization of 12 is 2 · 2 · 3⟩ 3 a : first in rank or importance ⟨our *prime* responsibility⟩ b : being highest in quality or value ⟨*prime* farmland⟩ c : of the highest grade of meat ⟨*prime* beef⟩

³**prime** *vb* **primed; prim·ing** 1 : to get ready for firing by putting in priming ⟨*prime* a rifle⟩ 2 : to put a first color or coating on (an unpainted surface) 3 : to put into working order by filling ⟨*prime* a pump⟩ 4 : to make (someone) ready to do something ⟨teams *primed* to win⟩

prime meridian *n* : the meridian of 0° longitude from which other longitudes are calculated

\ə\ **abut**	\au̇\ **out**	\i\ **tip**	\ȯ\ **saw**	\u̇\ **foot**
\ər\ **further**	\ch\ **chin**	\ī\ **life**	\ȯi\ **coin**	\y\ **yet**
\a\ **mat**	\e\ **pet**	\j\ **job**	\th\ **thin**	\yü\ **few**
\ā\ **take**	\ē\ **easy**	\ŋ\ **sing**	\t͟h\ **this**	\yu̇\ **cure**
\ä\ **cot, cart**	\g\ **go**	\ō\ **bone**	\ü\ **food**	\zh\ **vision**

prime minister *n* : the chief officer of the government in some countries

prime number *n* : a whole number other than 0 or ±1 that is not divisible without a remainder by any other whole numbers except ±1 and ± itself

¹**prim·er** \'prim-ər, *especially British* 'prī-mər\ *n* **1** : a small book for teaching children to read **2** : a book that introduces a subject ⟨a *primer* of chemistry⟩ **3** : a short informative piece of writing ⟨a *primer* on healthy eating⟩

²**prim·er** \'prī-mər\ *n* **1** : a device (as a cap or tube) containing a small explosive charge that is used for setting off a larger explosive charge (as in a cartridge) **2** : material used in priming a surface

prime time *n* : the time in the evening when television has its largest number of viewers

pri·me·val \prī-'mē-vəl\ *adj* : belonging to the earliest time : PRIMITIVE [from Latin *primaevus* "relating to the very earliest ages," from *primus* "first" and *aevum* "age" — related to PRIME] — **pri·me·val·ly** \-və-lē\ *adv*

prim·ing \'prī-min\ *n* **1** : the explosive used in priming a charge **2** : ²PRIMER 2

¹**prim·i·tive** \'prim-ət-iv\ *adj* **1 a** : of or relating to the earliest age or period ⟨*primitive* forests⟩ ⟨the *primitive* church⟩ **b** : closely resembling an ancient ancestor ⟨a *primitive* fish⟩ **2** : belonging to or characteristic of an early stage of development ⟨*primitive* tools⟩ **3** : of or relating to a people or culture that lacks a written language and advanced technologies ⟨*primitive* societies⟩ **4** : being or made by a self-taught artist — **prim·i·tive·ly** *adv* — **prim·i·tive·ness** *n*

²**primitive** *n* **1** : something primitive : something basic or original **2** : a member of a primitive people

pri·mor·di·al \prī-'mord-ē-əl\ *adj* : first created or developed : PRIMEVAL — **pri·mor·di·al·ly** \-ē-ə-lē\ *adv*

primp \'primp\ *vb* : to dress or arrange in a careful or fussy manner

prim·rose \'prim-,rōz\ *n* : any of a genus of herbs with large leaves arranged at the base of the stem and showy variously colored flowers in clusters on leafless stalks

primrose

prince \'prin(t)s\ *n* **1** : MONARCH 1 **2** : a son or grandson of a monarch : a male member of a royal family **3** : a nobleman of very high rank **4** : a person of high standing in his class or profession [Middle English *prince* "ruler, king," from early French *prince* (same meaning), from Latin *princip-, princeps* "leader, initiator," literally, "one who takes the first part," from *primus* "first" and *capere* "to take" — related to PRIME]

Prince Al·bert \prin-'sal-bərt\ *n* : a long double-breasted coat

prince consort *n, pl* **princes consort** : the husband of a reigning queen

prince·ly \'prin(t)-slē\ *adj* **prince·li·er; -est 1** : of or relating to a prince **2** : suitable for a prince ⟨a *princely* sum⟩

prin·cess \'prin(t)-səs, 'prin-,ses, prin-'ses\ *n* **1** : a daughter or granddaughter of a monarch : a female member of a royal family **2** : the wife of a prince

¹**prin·ci·pal** \'prin(t)-s(ə-)pəl, -sə-bəl\ *adj* : most important : CHIEF ⟨the *principal* ingredient of the stew⟩ — **prin·ci·pal·ly** \-ē, prin(t)-splē\ *adv*

²**principal** *n* **1 a** : a leading or most important person **b** : the head of a school **2** : a sum of money that is placed to earn interest, is owed as a debt, or is used as a fund

prin·ci·pal·i·ty \,prin(t)-sə-'pal-ət-ē\ *n, pl* **-ties** : a small territory that is ruled by a prince

principal parts *n pl* : the infinitive, the past tense, and the past and present participles of an English verb

prin·ci·ple \'prin(t)-s(ə-)pəl, -sə-bəl\ *n* **1** : a general or basic truth on which other truths or theories can be based ⟨scientific *principles*⟩ **2** : a rule of conduct ⟨a person of high *principles*⟩ **3** : a law or fact of nature which makes possible the working of a machine or device ⟨the *principle* of magnetism⟩ ⟨the *principle* of the lever⟩

prin·ci·pled \'prin(t)-s(ə-)pəld, -sə-bəld\ *adj* : based on or marked by principle ⟨high-*principled*⟩

prink \'prink\ *vb* : PRIMP

¹**print** \'print\ *n* **1 a** : a mark made by pressure **b** : something that has been stamped with an impression or formed in a mold ⟨a *print* of butter⟩ **2 a** : printed state or form ⟨put a manuscript into *print*⟩ **b** : printed matter **c** : printed letters **3** : a picture, copy, or design made by printing (as from an engraving or a photographic negative) **4 a** : cloth with a printed pattern **b** : an article of such cloth

²**print** *vb* **1** : to put or stamp something in or on **2 a** : to make a copy of by pressing paper against an inked surface (as type or an engraving) **b** : to stamp with a design by pressure ⟨*print* wallpaper⟩ **c** : to publish in printed form ⟨*print* a newspaper⟩ **d** : to write or cause to be written on a surface (as a computer display screen) for viewing ⟨the computer will *print* the message at the top of the screen⟩ **e** : PRINT OUT **3** : to write in separate letters like those made by a typewriter **4** : to make a picture from a photographic negative

print·able \'print-ə-bəl\ *adj* : considered suitable to be published

print·er \'print-ər\ *n* **1** : a person whose business is printing **2** : a device used for printing or for making printouts

printer's devil *n* : an apprentice in a printing office

print·ing \'print-in\ *n* **1** : the process of putting something in printed form **2** : the art or business of a printer

printing press *n* : a machine that produces printed copies

print·mak·er \'print-,mā-kər\ *n* : an artist who makes prints

print·out \'print-,aut\ *n* : a printed record produced by a computer

print out \(')print-'aut\ *vb* : to produce a printed record of

¹**pri·or** \'prī-(ə)r\ *n* : a monk who is head of a priory

²**prior** *adj* **1** : earlier in time or order : PREVIOUS ⟨better than in *prior* years⟩ ⟨without *prior* warning⟩ **2** : being more important than something else : having priority ⟨has a *prior* claim to our attention⟩

pri·or·ess \'prī-ə-rəs\ *n* : a nun who is head of a priory

pri·or·i·ty \prī-'or-ət-ē, -'är-\ *n, pl* **-ties 1** : the quality or state of coming before another in time or importance **2** : a condition of being given attention before others ⟨this project has top *priority*⟩

prior to *prep* : in advance of : BEFORE

pri·o·ry \'prī-(ə-)rē\ *n, pl* **-ries** : a religious house under a prior or prioress

prise *chiefly British variant of* ⁵PRIZE

prism \'priz-əm\ *n* **1** : a polyhedron with two opposite ends that are parallel polygons and faces that are each parallelograms **2** : a transparent object that usually has three sides and bends light so that it breaks up into rainbow colors

pris·on \'priz-ⁿn\ *n* **1** : a state of confinement or captivity **2** : a place where criminals or prisoners are locked up

prison camp *n* : a camp where prisoners are held

pris·on·er \'priz-nər, -ⁿn-ər\ *n* : a person who has been captured or locked up

prisoner of war : a member of the armed forces of a nation who has been captured by the enemy

pris·tine \'pris-,tēn\ *adj* **1** : not spoiled, polluted, or corrupted (as by civilization) ⟨a *pristine* forest⟩ **2** : being fresh and clean ⟨*pristine* new math books⟩

prith·ee \'prith-ē, 'prith-\ *interj, archaic* — used to express a wish or request

pri·va·cy \'prī-və-sē\ *n, pl* **-cies 1 a** : the quality or state of being out of the sight and hearing of other people : SE-CLUSION ⟨the *privacy* of the home⟩ **b** : freedom from being intruded upon ⟨one's right to *privacy*⟩ **2** : SECRECY 2 ⟨talk in *privacy*⟩

¹pri·vate \'prī-vət\ *adj* **1** : having to do with or for the use of a single person or group : not public ⟨*private* property⟩ ⟨a *private* beach⟩ **2 a** : not holding any public office ⟨a *private* citizen⟩ **b** : not relating to one's official position : PERSONAL ⟨*private* letters⟩ ⟨your own *private* opinion⟩ **3** : not known or meant to be known publicly ⟨*private* meetings⟩ ⟨keep personal information *private*⟩ **4** : not under public control ⟨a *private* school⟩ — **pri·vate·ly** *adv* — **pri·vate·ness** *n*

²private *n* **1** *pl* : PRIVATE PARTS **2** : a person of low or lowest rank in an organized group (as a police or fire department); *esp* : an enlisted person of the lowest ranks in the army or marine corps — **in private** : where no one else can hear ⟨would like to speak to you *in private*⟩

private detective *n* : PRIVATE INVESTIGATOR

¹pri·va·teer \ˌprī-və-'ti(ə)r\ *n* **1** : an armed private ship permitted by its government to make war on ships of an enemy country **2** : a sailor on a privateer

²privateer *vb* : to cruise in or as a privateer

private first class *n* : an enlisted person with a rank just below corporal in the army or just below lance corporal in the marines

private investigator *n* : a person who does detective work and is not a member of a police force

private parts *n pl* : the genital organs on the outside of the body

pri·va·tion \prī-'vā-shən\ *n* : the state of being deprived

priv·et \'priv-ət\ *n* : a shrub that is related to the olive, has small white flowers, and is widely used for hedges

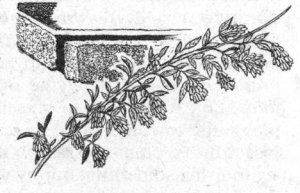

privet

¹priv·i·lege \'priv(-ə)-lij\ *n* : a right or liberty granted as a favor or benefit especially to some and not others

²privilege *vb* **-leged; -leg·ing** : to grant a privilege to

priv·i·leged \'priv(-ə)-lijd\ *adj* : having more things and a better chance in life than most people ⟨*privileged* classes of society⟩

priv·i·ly \'priv-ə-lē\ *adv* : in secret : PRIVATELY

¹privy \'priv-ē\ *adj* **1** : ¹PRIVATE 3, SECRET **2** : ¹PRIVATE 2b, PERSONAL **3** : sharing in a secret ⟨*privy* to the conspiracy⟩

²privy *n, pl* **priv·ies 1** : a small building without plumbing used as a toilet **2** : TOILET 2b

¹prize \'prīz\ *n* **1** : something won or to be won in a contest **2** : something unusually valuable or eagerly sought [Middle English *pris* "prize, price, value," from early French *pris* (same meaning), from Latin *pretium* "price, money" — related to PRICE]

²prize *adj* **1 a** : awarded a prize ⟨a *prize* essay⟩ **b** : awarded as a prize ⟨*prize* money⟩ **2** : outstanding of its kind ⟨a *prize* fool⟩ ⟨a *prize* student⟩

³prize *vb* **prized; priz·ing 1** : to estimate the value of **2** : to value highly : TREASURE [Middle English *prisen* "to appraise, esteem," from early French *prisier* (same meaning), from Latin *pretiare* (same meaning), from earlier *pretium* (noun) "price, value"]

⁴prize *n* : something taken (as in war) especially at sea [Middle English *prise* "something taken by force or

threat," from early French *prise* "taking, seizure," from *prendre* "to take," from Latin *prehendere* "to take"]

⁵prize *vb* **prized; priz·ing** : to force or move with or as if with a lever : PRY

prize·fight \'prīz-ˌfīt\ *n* : a contest between professional boxers for pay — **prize·fight·er** \-ər\ *n* — **prize·fight·ing** \-iŋ\ *n*

prize·win·ner \-ˌwin-ər\ *n* : a winner of a prize — **prize·win·ning** \-ˌwin-iŋ\ *adj*

¹pro \'prō\ *n, pl* **pros** \'prōz\ : an argument or evidence in favor of something ⟨discuss the *pros* and cons⟩ [Middle English *pro* "an argument in favor of something," from Latin *pro* (preposition) "in favor of, for"]

²pro *adv* : in favor of something

³pro *n or adj* : PROFESSIONAL [a shortened form of *professional*]

¹pro- *prefix* : located in front of or at the front of ⟨*protho*rax⟩ [derived from Greek *pro* "before, forward"]

²pro- *prefix* **1** : taking the place of : substituting for ⟨*pro*noun⟩ **2** : favoring : supporting ⟨*pro*-American⟩ [derived from Latin *pro* "in front of, for"]

pro·ac·tive \prō-'ak-tiv\ *adj* : acting in anticipation of future problems, needs, or changes — **pro·ac·tive·ly** *adv*

prob·a·bil·i·ty \ˌpräb-ə-'bil-ət-ē\ *n, pl* **-ties 1** : the quality or state of being probable **2** : something probable **3 a** : a measure of how often a particular event will happen if something which results in any of a number of possible events is done repeatedly ⟨the *probability* of a coin coming up heads is ½⟩ **b** : a branch of mathematics concerned with the study of probabilities

prob·a·ble \'präb-ə-bəl\ *adj* : reasonably sure but not certain of happening or being true : LIKELY

prob·a·bly \'präb-(ə-)blē, 'präb-lē\ *adv* : without much doubt : very likely

¹pro·bate \'prō-ˌbāt\ *n* **1** : proof before a probate court that the will of a deceased person is genuine **2** : judicial determination of the legal force of a will

²probate *vb* **pro·bat·ed; pro·bat·ing** : to establish by probate as genuine and as having legal force

probate court *n* : a court that probates wills and administers estates of deceased persons

pro·ba·tion \prō-'bā-shən\ *n* **1** : a period of trial for finding out or testing a person's fitness (as for a job or school) **2** : the suspending of a convicted offender's sentence during good behavior under the supervision of a probation officer — **pro·ba·tion·al** \-shnəl, -shən-ᵊl\ *adj* — **pro·ba·tion·ary** \-shə-ˌner-ē\ *adj*

pro·ba·tion·er \prō-'bā-sh(ə-)nər\ *n* : a person who is on probation

probation officer *n* : an officer appointed to supervise convicted offenders on probation

¹probe \'prōb\ *n* **1** : a slender medical instrument especially for examining a cavity (as a deep wound) **2** : a device used to penetrate or send back information especially from outer space **3** : a careful investigation **4** : an attempt to explore or learn about some unknown place ⟨a space *probe*⟩

²probe *vb* **probed; prob·ing 1** : to examine with or as if with a probe **2** : to investigate thoroughly — **prob·er** *n*

pro·bi·ty \'prō-bət-ē\ *n* : HONESTY, UPRIGHTNESS

¹prob·lem \'präb-ləm\ *n* **1** : something to be worked out or solved ⟨a *problem* in arithmetic⟩ **2 a** : something that is hard to understand, deal with, or correct ⟨social *problems*⟩ ⟨have a *problem* with the car⟩ **b** : something that causes one trouble or irritation ⟨of course the mosquitoes

\ə\ **abut**	\au̇\ **out**	\i\ **tip**	\ȯ\ **saw**	\u̇\ **foot**
\ər\ **further**	\ch\ **chin**	\ī\ **life**	\ȯi\ **coin**	\y\ **yet**
\a\ **mat**	\e\ **pet**	\j\ **job**	\th\ **thin**	\yü\ **few**
\ā\ **take**	\ē\ **easy**	\ŋ\ **sing**	\th\ **this**	\yu̇\ **cure**
\ä\ **cot, cart**	\g\ **go**	\ō\ **bone**	\ü\ **food**	\zh\ **vision**

are a *problem*⟩ **c** : difficulty in understanding or accepting ⟨I have a *problem* with your attitude⟩

²problem *adj* **1** : dealing with a problem of human conduct or social justice ⟨a *problem* play⟩ **2** : difficult to deal with ⟨a *problem* child⟩

prob·lem·at·ic \ˌpräb-lə-ˈmat-ik\ *also* **prob·lem·at·i·cal** \-ˈmat-i-kəl\ *adj* **1** : difficult to solve or decide : PUZZLING ⟨a *problematic* situation⟩ **2** : not settled : UNCERTAIN ⟨their future is still *problematic*⟩ **3** : open to question ⟨the evidence is *problematic*⟩

pro·bos·cis \prə-ˈbäs-əs, -kəs\ *n*, *pl* **-bos·cis·es** *also* **-bos·ci·des** \-ˈbäs-ə-ˌdēz\ **1** : a long flexible snout; *esp* : the trunk of an elephant **2** : a long tube-shaped bodily part (as the sucking organ of a butterfly) in the mouth region of an invertebrate

pro·caine \ˈprō-ˌkān\ *n* : a drug that is used as a local anesthetic in dentistry and medicine

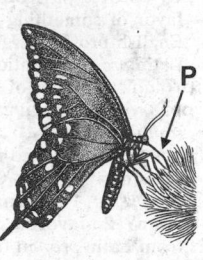

P proboscis 2

pro·ce·dure \prə-ˈsē-jər\ *n* **1** : a manner or method in which a business or action is carried on **2 a** : a series of steps followed in a regular definite order ⟨the *procedure* for acquiring a passport⟩ **b** : a set of instructions for a computer that has a name by which it can be called into action — **pro·ce·dur·al** \-ˈsēj-(ə-)rəl\ *adj*

pro·ceed \prō-ˈsēd, prə-\ *vb* **1** : to come from a source **2 a** : to continue after a pause or interruption **b** : to go or act by an orderly method **3 a** : to carry on an action, process, or movement **b** : to be in the process of being done ⟨the work is *proceeding* well⟩ **4** : to go forward or onward : ADVANCE

pro·ceed·ing *n* **1** : PROCEDURE 2a **2** *pl* : things that happen ⟨kept an eye on the *proceedings*⟩ **3** : a legal action

pro·ceeds \ˈprō-ˌsēdz\ *n pl* : the money or profit that comes from a business deal

¹pro·cess \ˈpräs-ˌes, ˈprōs-, -əs\ *n*, *pl* **pro·cess·es** \-ˌes-əz, -ə-səz, -ə-ˌsēz\ **1 a** : ²ADVANCE 1 ⟨the *process* of time⟩ **b** : something going on **2 a** : a natural continuing action or series of actions or changes ⟨the *process* of growth⟩ ⟨life *processes*⟩ ⟨mental *processes*⟩ **b** : a series of actions or operations leading to a result ⟨a manufacturing *process*⟩ **3** : the carrying on of a legal action ⟨due *process* of law⟩ **4** : a bodily part that sticks out or is conspicuous : OUTGROWTH ⟨a bony *process*⟩

²process *vb* **1** : to change or prepare by special treatment ⟨*process* foods⟩ **2 a** : to take care of according to a routine ⟨*process* people looking for a job⟩ ⟨*process* insurance claims⟩ **b** : to take in and organize for use in a variety of ways ⟨computers *process* data⟩ ⟨*process* information⟩

process cheese *n* : cheese made by blending several lots of cheese

pro·ces·sion \prə-ˈsesh-ən\ *n* **1** : continuous forward movement : PROGRESSION **2** : a group of individuals moving along in an orderly often ceremonial way ⟨a funeral *procession*⟩

¹pro·ces·sion·al \prə-ˈsesh-nəl, -ən-ᵊl\ *n* : a musical composition (as a hymn) written for a procession

²processional *adj* : of, relating to, or moving in a procession

pro·ces·sor \ˈpräs-ˌes-ər, ˈprōs-\ *n* **1** : a person or machine that processes **2** : a part of a computer that processes data; *esp* : CPU

pro–choice \prō-ˈchȯis\ *adj* : favoring the legalization of abortion

pro·claim \prō-ˈklām\ *vb* **1** : to announce publicly ⟨*proclaimed* his innocence⟩ **2** : to declare formally ⟨*proclaim* a holiday⟩ — **pro·claim·er** *n*

proc·la·ma·tion \ˌpräk-lə-ˈmā-shən\ *n* **1** : the act of proclaiming **2** : something proclaimed

pro·cliv·i·ty \prō-ˈkliv-ət-ē\ *n*, *pl* **-ties** : a natural tendency of the mind or personality ⟨showed artistic *proclivities* at an early age⟩; *esp* : such a tendency toward something bad ⟨a *proclivity* for violence⟩

pro·con·sul \(ˈ)prō-ˈkän(t)-səl\ *n* : an administrator in a modern colony, dependency, or occupied area

pro·cras·ti·nate \p(r)ə-ˈkras-tə-ˌnāt, prō-\ *vb* **-nat·ed; -nat·ing** : to keep putting off something that should be done — **pro·cras·ti·na·tion** \-ˌkras-tə-ˈnā-shən\ *n* — **pro·cras·ti·na·tor** \-ˈkras-tə-ˌnāt-ər\ *n*

pro·cre·ate \ˈprō-krē-ˌāt\ *vb* **-at·ed; -at·ing** : to bring forth offspring : REPRODUCE

proc·tor \ˈpräk-tər\ *n* : a person who supervises students during an examination — **proctor** *vb*

proc·u·ra·tor \ˈpräk-yə-ˌrāt-ər\ *n* : a person who handles the business affairs of another : AGENT

pro·cure \prə-ˈkyu̇(ə)r\ *vb* **pro·cured; pro·cur·ing** **1** : to get possession of ⟨managed to *procure* tickets to the big game⟩ **2** : BRING ABOUT, ACHIEVE ⟨*procured* an audience with the pope⟩ **synonyms** see GET — **pro·cur·able** \-ˈkyu̇r-ə-bəl\ *adj* — **pro·cure·ment** \-ˈkyu̇(ə)r-mənt\ *n*

¹prod \ˈpräd\ *vb* **prod·ded; prod·ding** **1** : to poke with something **2** : to stir a person or animal to action ⟨kept *prodding* me to reveal the secret⟩ — **prod·der** *n*

²prod *n* **1** : something used for prodding **2** : an act of prodding : a sharp urging or reminder

¹prod·i·gal \ˈpräd-i-gəl\ *adj* : carelessly wasteful ⟨a *prodigal* spender⟩ — **prod·i·gal·i·ty** \ˌpräd-ə-ˈgal-ət-ē\ *n* — **prod·i·gal·ly** \ˈpräd-i-g(ə)lē\ *adv*

²prodigal *n* : somebody who wastes money carelessly

pro·di·gious \prə-ˈdij-əs\ *adj* **1** : exciting amazement or wonder ⟨performs *prodigious* feats⟩ **2** : very big : HUGE ⟨a *prodigious* amount of food⟩ — **pro·di·gious·ly** *adv*

prod·i·gy \ˈpräd-ə-jē\ *n*, *pl* **-gies** **1** : an amazing event or action : WONDER **2** : an unusually talented child

¹pro·duce \prə-ˈd(y)üs\ *vb* **pro·duced; pro·duc·ing** **1** : to bring to view : EXHIBIT ⟨*produce* evidence⟩ ⟨*produced* a permit when asked⟩ **2** : to give birth or rise to ⟨a tree *producing* good fruit⟩ ⟨the offspring an insect can *produce*⟩ **3** : to prepare to present to the public ⟨*produce* a play⟩ **4** : to cause to be or happen : BRING ABOUT ⟨the insect bite *produced* a rash⟩ ⟨this will *produce* results⟩ **5 a** : to bring something out by work ⟨*produced* a magazine article⟩ **b** : ²MANUFACTURE 2 ⟨a factory *producing* steel⟩ — **pro·duc·ible** \-ˈd(y)ü-sə-bəl\ *adj*

²pro·duce \ˈpräd-(ˌ)üs, ˈprōd- *also* -(ˌ)yüs\ *n* **1** : something produced **2** : fresh fruits and vegetables

pro·duc·er \prə-ˈd(y)ü-sər\ *n* **1** : one that produces; *esp* : a person who grows agricultural products or manufactures articles **2** : a person who supervises or finances a play, a movie, or a radio or television program **3** : a living thing (as a green plant) that makes its food from simple inorganic substances (as carbon dioxide and nitrogen) and many of which are food sources for other organisms — compare CONSUMER 2

prod·uct \ˈpräd-(ˌ)əkt\ *n* **1** : the number or expression resulting from the multiplication of two or more numbers or expressions ⟨15 is the *product* of 3 and 5⟩ **2** : something produced

pro·duc·tion \prə-ˈdək-shən\ *n* **1** : something produced **2** : the act or process of producing **3** : the amount produced : total output ⟨annual *production* of coal⟩ **4** : something exaggerated out of proportion to its importance ⟨made a big *production* out of ordering lunch⟩

pro·duc·tive \prə-ˈdək-tiv\ *adj* **1** : having the power to produce plentifully ⟨*productive* soil⟩ ⟨*productive* fishing waters⟩ **2** : producing something ⟨efforts *productive* of much good⟩ **3** : giving results ⟨a *productive* meeting⟩ — **pro·duc·tive·ly** *adv* — **pro·duc·tive·ness** *n*

pro·duc·tiv·i·ty \(ˌ)prō-ˌdək-ˈtiv-ət-ē, ˌpräd-(ˌ)ək-, prə-ˌdək-\ *n* **1** : the quality or state of being productive **2**

: the rate of production at which food for other living things is made by living things that are producers

prof \'präf\ *n* : PROFESSOR

¹pro·fane \prō-'fān, prə-\ *vb* **pro·faned; pro·fan·ing 1** : to treat (something sacred) with great disrespect **2** : to put to a wrong or vulgar use : DEBASE — **prof·a·na·tion** \ˌpräf-ə-'nā-shən, ˌprō-fə-\ *n* — **pro·fa·na·to·ry** \prō-'fan-ə-ˌtōr-ē, -ˌtȯr-\ *adj*

²profane *adj* **1** : not concerned with religion or religious purposes : SECULAR, WORLDLY **2** : showing no respect for holy things ⟨*profane* language⟩ — **pro·fane·ly** *adv*

pro·fan·i·ty \prō-'fan-ət-ē, prə-\ *n, pl* **-ties 1** : the quality or state of being profane **2** : profane language

pro·fess \prə-'fes\ *vb* **1** : to declare openly or freely ⟨*profess* confidence in a friend⟩ **2** : ¹PRETEND 1, CLAIM ⟨*professed* to be our friends⟩

pro·fessed \prə-'fest\ *adj* **1** : openly declared ⟨failed in its *professed* task⟩ **2** : claiming to be qualified ⟨a *professed* expert⟩

pro·fess·ed·ly \prə-'fes-əd-lē, -'fest-lē\ *adv* **1** : by one's own declaration ⟨a *professedly* serious novelist⟩ **2** : supposedly but not really ⟨was *professedly* open to all, but actually was not⟩

pro·fes·sion \prə-'fesh-ən\ *n* **1** : the act of taking the vows of a religious community **2** : a public declaring or claiming (as of a belief, faith, or opinion) **3 a** : an occupation (as medicine, law, or teaching) that requires specialized knowledge and often advanced education **b** : a principal occupation or employment **c** : the people working in a profession ⟨the legal *profession*⟩

¹pro·fes·sion·al \prə-'fesh-nəl, -ən-ᵊl\ *adj* **1 a** : of, relating to, or resembling that of a profession **b** : having a particular profession as a permanent career ⟨a *professional* soldier⟩ **2 a** : taking part for money in an activity (as sport) that others do for pleasure ⟨*professional* golfers⟩ **b** : engaged in by persons who are paid ⟨*professional* football⟩ — **pro·fes·sion·al·ly** \-ē\ *adv*

²professional *n* : a person who engages in an activity professionally

pro·fes·sion·al·ize \prə-'fesh-nəl-ˌīz, -ən-ᵊl-\ *vb* **-ized; -iz·ing** : to give a professional nature to

pro·fes·sor \prə-'fes-ər\ *n* : a teacher especially of the highest rank at a college or university — **pro·fes·so·ri·al** \ˌprō-fə-'sōr-ē-əl, ˌpräf-ə-, -'sȯr-\ *adj* — **pro·fes·so·ri·al·ly** \-ē-ə-lē\ *adv*

pro·fes·sor·ship \prə-'fes-ər-ˌship\ *n* : the office, duties or position of a professor

prof·fer \'präf-ər\ *vb* **prof·fered; prof·fer·ing** \'präf-(ə-)riŋ\ : ¹OFFER 2 — **proffer** *n*

pro·fi·cien·cy \prə-'fish-ən-sē\ *n, pl* **-cies** : the quality or state of being proficient

pro·fi·cient \prə-'fish-ənt\ *adj* : very good at doing something especially through practice **synonyms** see SKILLFUL — **pro·fi·cient·ly** *adv*

¹pro·file \'prō-ˌfīl\ *n* **1** : a head or face seen or drawn from the side **2** : something seen in outline **3** : a vertical section of soil that shows the various layers **4** : a set of data often in the form of a graph that shows the important characteristics of something ⟨read her psychological *profile*⟩ **5** : level of activity that attracts attention ⟨tried to keep a low *profile*⟩

¹profile 1

²profile *vb* **pro·filed; pro·fil·ing 1** : to represent in profile **2** : to produce a profile of

¹prof·it \'präf-ət\ *n* **1** : the gain or benefit from something **2** : the gain after all the expenses are subtracted from the amount received — **prof·it·less** \-ləs\ *adj*

²profit *vb* **1** : to get some good out of something : GAIN ⟨*profit* by experience⟩ **2** : to be of use to (someone) : BENEFIT ⟨an agreement that *profited* us all⟩

prof·it·able \'präf-ət-ə-bəl, 'präf-tə-bəl\ *adj* : producing profit — **prof·it·ably** \-blē\ *adv*

prof·i·teer \ˌpräf-ə-'ti(ə)r\ *n* : a person who makes an unfair profit especially on essential goods during an emergency — **profiteer** *vb*

prof·li·ga·cy \'präf-li-gə-sē\ *n* : the quality or state of being profligate

prof·li·gate \'präf-li-gət\ *adj* **1** : wicked in character or morals : DISSIPATED **2** : very wasteful — **profligate** *n*

pro·found \prə-'faùnd\ *adj* **1** : having or showing great knowledge or understanding ⟨a *profound* thinker⟩ **2** : very deeply felt ⟨*profound* sorrow⟩ **3** : ABSOLUTE 1a, COMPLETE ⟨a *profound* silence⟩ — **pro·found·ly** \-'faùn-(d)lē\ *adv* — **pro·found·ness** \-'faùn(d)-nəs\ *n*

pro·fun·di·ty \prə-'fən-dət-ē\ *n, pl* **-ties 1** : great knowledge or understanding **2** : something profound

pro·fuse \prə-'fyüs\ *adj* **1** : pouring forth in great amounts ⟨*profuse* apologies⟩ ⟨*profuse* in their thanks⟩ **2** : very plentiful ⟨a *profuse* harvest⟩ ⟨a *profuse* variety of minerals⟩ — **pro·fuse·ly** *adv*

pro·fu·sion \prə-'fyü-zhən\ *n* : a plentiful supply : great quantity ⟨lilacs blooming in *profusion*⟩

prog·e·ny \'präj-(ə-)nē\ *n, pl* **-nies 1** : human descendants : CHILDREN **2** : offspring of animals or plants

pro·ges·ter·one \prō-'jes-tə-ˌrōn\ *n* : a hormone that is produced by the corpus luteum and causes the uterus to change so that it provides a suitable environment for a fertilized egg

prog·no·sis \präg-'nō-səs\ *n, pl* **prog·no·ses** \-'nō-ˌsēz\ **1** : the prospect of recovery of an individual who has a disease based on the usual course of the disease and the characteristics of the individual who is sick **2** : ²FORECAST

prog·nos·ti·cate \präg-'näs-tə-ˌkāt\ *vb* **-cat·ed; -cat·ing** : PREDICT, PROPHESY — **prog·nos·ti·ca·tor** \-ˌkāt-ər\ *n*

prog·nos·ti·ca·tion \(ˌ)präg-ˌnäs-tə-'kā-shən\ *n* : ²FORECAST

¹pro·gram \'prō-ˌgram, -grəm\ *n* **1** : a brief usually written outline describing a presentation (as of a concert or play) **2** : the performance of a program ⟨received a trophy at the awards *program*⟩; *esp* : a performance that is broadcast **3** : a plan of action ⟨a *program* of regular dental checkups⟩ ⟨a political *program*⟩ **4** : a set of step-by-step instructions that tell a computer to do something with data

²program *vb* **pro·grammed** *or* **pro·gramed** \-ˌgramd, -grəmd\; **pro·gram·ming** *or* **pro·gram·ing 1** : to provide with a program ⟨*program* a computer⟩ **2** : to direct the thinking or behavior of (someone) as if by a computer program ⟨he's been *programmed* to believe he can succeed if he tries⟩ — **pro·gram·ma·ble** \'prō-ˌgram-ə-bəl\ *adj*

pro·gramme *chiefly British variant of* PROGRAM

pro·gram·mer *also* **pro·gram·er** \'prō-ˌgram-ər, -grə-mər\ *n* : a person who writes computer programs

pro·gram·ming *also* **pro·gram·ing** \'prō-ˌgram-iŋ, -grə-miŋ\ *n* **1** : the planning, scheduling, or performing of a program ⟨advocates less violence in television *programming*⟩ **2** : the design and production of computer programs

program music *n* : music that is inspired by or that describes a story or a sequence of images

\ə\ abut	\aù\ out	\i\ tip	\ȯ\ saw	\ù\ foot
\ər\ further	\ch\ chin	\ī\ life	\ȯi\ coin	\y\ yet
\a\ mat	\e\ pet	\j\ job	\th\ thin	\yü\ few
\ā\ take	\ē\ easy	\ŋ\ sing	\th\ this	\yù\ cure
\ä\ cot, cart	\g\ go	\ō\ bone	\ü\ food	\zh\ vision

¹**prog·ress** \'präg-rəs, -ˌres, *chiefly British* 'prō-ˌgres\ *n* **1** : a moving toward a goal ⟨the *progress* of a ship⟩ **2** : gradual improvement or advancement ⟨the *progress* of science⟩

²**pro·gress** \prə-'gres\ *vb* **1** : to move forward : ADVANCE, PROCEED ⟨the story *progressed*⟩ ⟨how is the experiment *progressing*?⟩ **2** : to move toward a higher, better, or more advanced stage

pro·gres·sion \prə-'gresh-ən\ *n* **1** : the action of progressing or moving forward **2** : a continuous and connected series (as of acts, events, or steps) **3** : a changing from one chord to another by means of several notes or chords coming one after the other

¹**pro·gres·sive** \prə-'gres-iv\ *adj* **1 a** : of, relating to, or showing progress or progression **b** : making use of or interested in new ideas ⟨a *progressive* city⟩ **c** : of or relating to an educational theory emphasizing informal classrooms and encouraging self-expression ⟨a *progressive* school⟩ **2 a** : moving forward or onward : ADVANCING ⟨the *progressive* movements of the hands of a clock⟩ **b** : spreading and becoming worse ⟨a *progressive* disease⟩ **c** : increasing in rate as the base amount increases ⟨a *progressive* tax⟩ **3** : of, relating to, or being a verb form that expresses action or state in progress at the time of speaking or a time spoken of ⟨*am seeing* and *is being seen* are *progressive* forms⟩ — **pro·gres·sive·ly** *adv* — **pro·gres·sive·ness** *n*

²**progressive** *n* : a person believing in gradual political change and social improvement by government action

pro·hib·it \prō-'hib-ət\ *vb* **1** : to forbid by authority ⟨*prohibit* parking⟩ **2** : to make impossible ⟨the high walls *prohibit* escape⟩

pro·hi·bi·tion \ˌprō-ə-'bish-ən\ *n* **1** : the act of prohibiting **2** : an order forbidding something **3** *often cap* : the forbidding by law of the sale and manufacture of alcoholic beverages

pro·hi·bi·tion·ist \'prō-ə-'bish-(ə-)nəst\ *n* : a person who is in favor of prohibiting the manufacture and sale of alcoholic beverages

pro·hib·i·tive \prō-'hib-ət-iv\ *adj* : likely to discourage use or purchase ⟨*prohibitive* prices⟩ — **pro·hib·i·tive·ly** *adv*

¹**proj·ect** \'präj-ˌekt, -ikt\ *n* **1** : a plan or scheme to do something **2** : a task or problem in school ⟨my science *project*⟩ **3** : a group of houses or apartment buildings built according to a single plan; *esp* : one built with government help to provide low-cost housing

²**pro·ject** \prə-'jekt\ *vb* **1 a** : to work out in the mind **b** : to plan, figure, or estimate for the future ⟨*project* next year's costs⟩ **2** : to throw forward **3** : STICK OUT 1a **4** : to cause to fall upon a surface ⟨*project* motion pictures on a screen⟩

pro·jec·tile \prə-'jek-t³l\ *n* : something (as a bullet or rocket) thrown or driven forward especially from or for use as a weapon

pro·jec·tion \prə-'jek-shən\ *n* **1** : a method of showing a curved surface (as the earth) on a flat one (as a map) **2** : the act of throwing or shooting forward **3** : something that sticks out **4** : the act or process of projecting something on a surface (as by motion pictures or slides) **5** : an estimate of what might happen in the future based on what is happening now

pro·jec·tion·ist \prə-'jek-sh(ə-)nəst\ *n* : a person who operates a motion-picture projector or television equipment

pro·jec·tor \prə-'jek-tər\ *n* : a machine for projecting an image or pictures upon a surface ⟨a motion-picture *projector*⟩ ⟨a slide *projector*⟩

pro·kary·ote \prō-'kar-ē-ˌōt\ *n* : an organism (as a bacterium) that is typically single-celled and does not have a nucleus or most of the cell structures (as mitochondria) characteristic of eukaryotes

pro·leg \'prō-ˌleg\ *n* : a fleshy leg on the abdomen of some insect larvae

pro·le·tar·i·an \ˌprō-lə-'ter-ē-ən\ *n* : a member of the proletariat — **proletarian** *adj*

pro·le·tar·i·at \ˌprō-lə-'ter-ē-ət, -'tar-, -ē-ˌat\ *n* **1** : the lowest social or economic class of a community **2** : industrial workers who sell their labor to live

pro—life \prō-'līf\ *adj* : opposed to abortion

pro·lif·er·ate \prə-'lif-ə-ˌrāt\ *vb* **-at·ed; -at·ing** : to grow or increase rapidly — **pro·lif·er·a·tion** \-ˌlif-ə-'rā-shən\ *n*

pro·lif·ic \prə-'lif-ik\ *adj* **1** : producing young or fruit in large numbers ⟨a *prolific* orchard⟩ **2** : highly inventive : PRODUCTIVE ⟨a *prolific* writer⟩ **synonyms** see FERTILE — **pro·lif·i·cal·ly** \-'lif-i-k(ə-)lē\ *adv*

pro·lix \prō-'liks, 'prō-(ˌ)liks\ *adj* : too long-winded or wordy — **pro·lix·i·ty** \prō-'lik-sət-ē\ *n*

pro·logue \'prō-ˌlòg\ *n* **1** : an introduction to a book or play **2** : an act or event that comes before or introduces something

pro·long \prə-'lòn\ *vb* : to make longer in time ⟨*prolonged* the visit⟩

pro·lon·ga·tion \(ˌ)prō-ˌlòn-'gā-shən\ *n* **1** : a making longer **2** : something that prolongs or is prolonged

prom \'präm\ *n* : a formal dance given by a high school or college class [a shortened form of *promenade* "a march by couples at the beginning of a formal ball"]

¹**prom·e·nade** \ˌpräm-ə-'nād, -'näd\ *n* **1** : a walk or ride for pleasure or to be seen **2** : a place for strolling **3** : a part of a square dance in which couples move counterclockwise in a circle

²**promenade** *vb* **-nad·ed; -nad·ing 1** : to take a stroll in public **2** : to perform a promenade in a dance

pro·me·thi·um \prə-'mē-thē-əm\ *n* : a radioactive metallic element obtained from the splitting of uranium atoms — see ELEMENT table

prom·i·nence \'präm(-ə)-nən(t)s\ *n* **1** : the quality, state, or fact of being prominent : DISTINCTION ⟨a person of *prominence*⟩ **2** : something (as a mountain) that is prominent **3** : a mass of gas resembling a cloud that arises from the chromosphere of the sun

prom·i·nent \'präm(-ə)-nənt\ *adj* **1** : sticking out beyond a surface or line **2** : easily noticeable ⟨the *prominent* sound was the drumbeat⟩ **3** : DISTINGUISHED, EMINENT ⟨our most *prominent* citizens⟩ **synonyms** see NOTICEABLE — **prom·i·nent·ly** *adv*

prom·is·cu·ity \ˌpräm-əs-'kyü-ət-ē\ *n, pl* **-ities** : the quality or state of being promiscuous

pro·mis·cu·ous \prə-'mis-kyə-wəs\ *adj* **1** : composed of all sorts of persons and things : MISCELLANEOUS **2** : not restricted to one person or class; *esp* : not restricted to one sexual partner — **pro·mis·cu·ous·ly** *adv*

¹**prom·ise** \'präm-əs\ *n* **1** : a statement by a person that he or she will or will not do something ⟨a *promise* to pay within a month⟩ **2** : something promised **3** : a cause or ground for hope ⟨give *promise* of success⟩ ⟨shows *promise*⟩ [Middle English *promisse, promis* "promise," derived from Latin *promissus,* past participle of *promittere* "to send forth, promise," from *pro-* "forward, forth" and *mittere* "to send, throw" — related to MESSAGE]

²**promise** *vb* **prom·ised; prom·is·ing 1** : to give a promise about one's own actions ⟨I *promise* to clean my room this afternoon⟩ **2** : to give reason to expect ⟨dark clouds *promising* rain⟩ — **prom·i·sor** \ˌpräm-ə-'sò(ə)r\ *n*

promised land *n* : a better place or state that one hopes to reach [so called from the biblical promise God made in Genesis 17:8 and Exodus 3:8 to give the land of Canaan to Abraham and his descendants]

prom·is·ing \'präm-ə-siŋ\ *adj* : likely to turn out well ⟨a *promising* student⟩ — **prom·is·ing·ly** \-siŋ-lē\ *adv*

prom·is·so·ry \'präm-ə-ˌsōr-ē, -ˌsòr-\ *adj* : containing a promise to pay ⟨a *promissory* note⟩

prom·on·to·ry \'präm-ən-ˌtōr-ē, -ˌtòr-\ *n, pl* **-ries** : a high point of land sticking out into the sea

pro·mote \prə-'mōt\ *vb* **pro·mot·ed; pro·mot·ing** **1 :** to move up in position or rank ⟨was *promoted* to the next grade⟩ **2 :** to help (something) grow or develop ⟨good soil *promotes* plant growth⟩ **3 :** to help increase the sales of ⟨a sports star *promoting* a new product⟩

pro·mot·er \prə-'mōt-ər\ *n* **:** a person who promotes; *esp* **:** one who finances a sporting event ⟨a *promoter* of prize-fights⟩

pro·mo·tion \prə-'mō-shən\ *n* **1 :** a moving up in position or rank **2 :** the promoting of something — **pro·mo·tion·al** \-shnəl, -shən-ᵊl\ *adj*

¹prompt \'präm(p)t\ *vb* **1 :** to lead to do something ⟨curiosity *prompted* her to ask the question⟩ **2 :** to remind of something forgotten or poorly learned ⟨*prompt* an actor⟩ **3 :** to be the cause of : INSPIRE ⟨pride *prompted* the act⟩

²prompt *adj* **1 a :** being ready and quick to act ⟨*prompt* to answer⟩ **b :** being on time : PUNCTUAL ⟨*prompt* in arriving⟩ **2 :** done at once : given without delay ⟨*prompt* assistance⟩ **synonyms** see QUICK — **prompt·ly** *adv* — **prompt·ness** *n*

³prompt *n* **:** something that prompts : REMINDER

prompt·er \'präm(p)-tər\ *n* **:** a person who reminds another of the words to be spoken next (as in a play)

promp·ti·tude \'präm(p)-tə-ˌt(y)üd\ *n* **:** the quality or habit of being prompt : PROMPTNESS

pro·mul·gate \'präm-əl-ˌgāt; prō-'məl-\ *vb* **-gat·ed; -gat·ing** **:** to make known or make public ⟨*promulgate* a new law⟩ — **pro·mul·ga·tion** \ˌpräm-əl-'gā-shən, ˌprō-(ˌ)məl-\ *n*

prone \'prōn\ *adj* **1 :** likely to be or act a certain way ⟨was *prone* to laziness⟩ ⟨accident-*prone*⟩ **2 :** lying flat; *esp* **:** lying face down ⟨he was *prone* on the floor⟩ — **prone** *adv* — **prone·ness** \'prōn-nəs\ *n*

prong \'prȯŋ, 'präŋ\ *n* **1 :** ¹FORK 1 **2 :** one of the sharp points of a fork : TINE **3 :** a slender pointed part that sticks out (as on an antler) **4 :** something resembling a prong ⟨there are two *prongs* to the argument⟩ — **pronged** \'prȯŋd, 'präŋd\ *adj*

prong·horn \'prȯŋ-ˌhȯ(ə)rn, 'präŋ-\ *n, pl* **pronghorn** *or* **pronghorns** **:** a cud-chewing horned mammal of treeless parts of western North America resembling an antelope — called also *pronghorn antelope*

pronghorn

pro·nom·i·nal \prō-'näm-ən-ᵊl\ *adj* **:** of, relating to, or being a pronoun

pro·noun \'prō-ˌnaùn\ *n* **:** a word that is used as a substitute for a noun

pro·nounce \prə-'naùn(t)s\ *vb* **pro·nounced; pro·nounc·ing** **1 :** to state in an official or solemn way ⟨I *pronounce* you husband and wife⟩ ⟨the judge *pronounced* sentence⟩ **2 :** to give as an opinion ⟨*pronounced* the party a success⟩ **3 a :** to use the voice to make the sounds of ⟨practice *pronouncing* foreign words⟩ **b :** to say or speak correctly ⟨I can't *pronounce* your name⟩ — **pro·nounc·er** *n*

pro·nounced \prə-'naùn(t)st\ *adj* **:** very noticeable ⟨walk with a *pronounced* limp⟩ — **pro·nounc·ed·ly** \-'naùn(t)-səd-lē\ *adv*

pro·nounce·ment \prə-'naùn(t)-smənt\ *n* **:** an official or solemn statement or announcement

pron·to \'prän-ˌtō\ *adv* **:** without delay : right away

pro·nun·ci·a·tion \prə-ˌnən(t)-sē-'ā-shən\ *n* **:** the act or way of pronouncing a word or words

¹proof \'prüf\ *n* **1 a :** evidence of truth or correctness ⟨gave *proof* of her statement⟩ **b :** an act or process of showing or finding out that something is true especially by reasoning or by experiment ⟨a *proof* that the theorem is true⟩ ⟨put a theory to the *proof*⟩ **2 a :** a copy (as of something set in type) taken for study and correction **b** **:** a test print made from a photographic negative

²proof *adj* **:** designed or made to prevent or keep out something that could be harmful ⟨this lock is *proof* against tampering⟩ — often used in compounds ⟨water*proof*⟩

³proof *vb* **:** to activate (yeast) by mixing with water

proof·read \'prü-ˌfrēd\ *vb* **-read** \-ˌfred\; **-read·ing** **:** to read over and fix mistakes in — **proof·read·er** *n*

¹prop \'präp\ *n* **:** something that props or supports

²prop *vb* **propped; prop·ping** **1 a :** to hold up or keep from falling or slipping by placing a support under or against ⟨*prop* up a broken chair⟩ **b :** to support by placing against something ⟨*propped* the rake against a tree⟩ **2** **:** to give help, encouragement, or support to ⟨*propped* up by his faith in times of crisis⟩

³prop *n* **:** PROPERTY 4

⁴prop *n* **:** PROPELLER

pro·pa·gan·da \ˌpräp-ə-'gan-də, ˌprō-pə-\ *n* **:** an organized spreading of certain ideas; *also* **:** the ideas spread in this way — **pro·pa·gan·dist** \-dəst\ *n or adj* — **pro·pa·gan·dis·tic** \-ˌgan-'dis-tik\ *adj*

pro·pa·gan·dize \ˌpräp-ə-'gan-ˌdīz, ˌprō-pə-\ *vb* **-dized; -diz·ing** **1 :** to spread propaganda **2 :** to try to influence by propaganda

prop·a·gate \'präp-ə-ˌgāt\ *vb* **-gat·ed; -gat·ing** **1 :** to have or cause to have offspring : MULTIPLY 1 ⟨ways to *propagate* plants without seeds⟩ ⟨*propagate* an apple by grafting⟩ **2 :** to cause (as an idea or belief) to spread out and affect a greater number or wider area ⟨*propagate* a faith⟩

prop·a·ga·tion \ˌpräp-ə-'gā-shən\ *n* **:** the act or process of propagating: as **a :** multiplication (as of a kind of living thing) in number of individuals **b :** the spreading of something (as a belief) abroad or into new regions

pro·pane \'prō-ˌpān\ *n* **:** a heavy flammable gas found in crude petroleum and natural gas and used especially as fuel and in the chemical industry

pro·pel \prə-'pel\ *vb* **pro·pelled; pro·pel·ling** **:** to push or drive usually forward or onward ⟨a bicycle is *propelled* by pedals⟩ ⟨*propelled* by the crowd⟩

pro·pel·lant *also* **pro·pel·lent** \prə-'pel-ənt\ *n* **:** something that propels: as **a :** fuel plus a chemical to supply oxygen used by a rocket engine **b :** a gas under pressure in a can for expelling the contents when the pressure is released

pro·pel·ler \prə-'pel-ər\ *n* **:** a device consisting of a hub fitted with blades that is made to turn rapidly by an engine and is used especially for propelling airplanes and ships

P

P propeller

pro·pen·si·ty \prə-'pen(t)-sət-ē\ *n, pl* **-ties :** a natural inclination or liking **:** BENT ⟨a *propensity* for bright colors⟩ ⟨a *propensity* to daydream⟩

prop·er \'präp-ər\ *adj* **1 :** belonging naturally to something : SPECIAL ⟨diseases *proper* to the tropics⟩ **2 :** considered without surrounding places, things, or events ⟨lived outside the city *proper*⟩ **3 a :** strictly accurate : CORRECT ⟨the *proper* way to pronounce the word⟩ **b** **:** obeying social rules : APPROPRIATE ⟨the *proper* way to address the mayor⟩ **4 :** suitable because of an essential

\ə\ abut		\au̇\ out	\i\ tip	\ȯ\ saw	\u̇\ foot
\ər\ further		\ch\ chin	\ī\ life	\ȯi\ coin	\y\ yet
\a\ mat		\e\ pet	\j\ job	\th\ thin	\yü\ few
\ā\ take		\ē\ easy	\ŋ\ sing	\th̲\ this	\yu̇\ cure
\ä\ cot, cart		\g\ go	\ō\ bone	\ü\ food	\zh\ vision

nature or condition ⟨*proper* lighting to work by⟩ **syn-onyms** see FIT — **pro·per·ness** *n*

proper adjective *n* : an adjective formed from a proper noun ⟨"Italian" in "Italian paintings" is a *proper adjective*⟩

proper fraction *n* : a fraction in which the numerator is less than the denominator

prop·er·ly \'präp-ər-lē\ *adv* **1** : in a fit or suitable way ⟨behave *properly* in church⟩ **2** : according to fact : COR-RECTLY ⟨*properly* labeled goods⟩ ⟨*properly* speaking, whales are not fish⟩

proper name *n* : PROPER NOUN

proper noun *n* : a noun that names a particular person, place, or thing

prop·er·tied \'präp-ərt-ēd\ *adj* : owning property

prop·er·ty \'präp-ərt-ē\ *n, pl* **-ties 1** : a special quality of something ⟨the commutative *property* of addition⟩ ⟨sweetness is a *property* of sugar⟩ **2** : something (as land, goods, or money) that is owned ⟨that lamp is my aunt's *property*⟩; *esp* : a piece of real estate ⟨a business *property*⟩ **3** : something other than scenery or costumes that is used in a play or movie — **prop·er·ty·less** \-ē-ləs\ *adj*

pro·phase \'prō-ˌfāz\ *n* **1** : the first stage of mitosis or the second division of meiosis in which chromosomes be-come visible as tightly coiled threadlike structures **2** : the first stage of the first division of meiosis in which chro-mosomes become visible and pair with homologous chro-mosomes to undergo synapsis

proph·e·cy \'präf-ə-sē\ *n, pl* **-cies 1** : the sayings of a prophet **2** : the foretelling of the future ⟨the gift of *prophecy*⟩ **3** : something foretold : PREDICTION

proph·e·sy \'präf-ə-ˌsī\ *vb* **-sied; -sy·ing 1** : to speak or write like a prophet **2** : FORETELL, PREDICT — **proph·e·si·er** \-ˌsī(-ə)r\ *n*

proph·et \'präf-ət\ *n* **1** : one who declares publicly a mes-sage that one believes has come from God or a god **2** : one who foretells future events

proph·et·ess \'präf-ət-əs\ *n* : a woman who is a prophet

pro·phet·ic \prə-'fet-ik\ *or* **pro·phet·i·cal** \-'fet-i-kəl\ *adj* : of or relating to a prophet or prophecy — **pro·phet·i·cal·ly** \-i-k(ə-)lē\ *adv*

Proph·ets \'präf-əts\ *n pl* : the second part of the Hebrew Bible — see BIBLE table

¹pro·phy·lac·tic \ˌprō-fə-'lak-tik\ *adj* **1** : guarding from or preventing the spread or occurrence of disease or infec-tion **2** : tending to prevent or ward off

²prophylactic *n* : something prophylactic; *esp* : a device and especially a condom for preventing infection or preg-nancy

pro·pi·ti·ate \prō-'pish-ē-ˌāt\ *vb* **-at·ed; -at·ing** : to gain or regain the favor or goodwill of — **pro·pi·ti·a·tion** \-ˌpish-ē-'ā-shən\ *n* — **pro·pi·tia·to·ry** \-'pish-(ē-)ə-ˌtōr-ē, -ˌtȯr-\ *adj*

pro·pi·tious \prə-'pish-əs\ *adj* **1** : giving favorable signs of the success of something to come : PROMISING ⟨a *propi-tious* first interview⟩ **2** : likely to produce good results ⟨a *propitious* undertaking⟩

pro·po·nent \prə-'pō-nənt, 'prō-ˌpō-nənt\ *n* : one who ar-gues in favor of something ⟨a *proponent* of recycling⟩

¹pro·por·tion \p(r)ə-'pōr-shən, -'pȯr-\ *n* **1** : the size, num-ber, or amount of one thing or group as compared to the size, number, or amount of another ⟨the *proportion* of boys to girls in our class is three to one⟩ **2** : a balanced or pleasing arrangement ⟨out of *proportion*⟩ **3** : a state-ment of the equality of two ratios (as ⁴⁄₈ = ¹⁰⁄₅) — com-pare ²EXTREME 2 ⁴MEAN 2b **4** : a fair or just share ⟨did our *proportion* of the work⟩ **5** : DIMENSION 1b ⟨a crisis of large *proportions*⟩ ⟨the *proportions* of a room⟩ — **in proportion** : PROPORTIONAL 1

²proportion *vb* **-tioned; -tion·ing** \-sh(ə-)niŋ\ **1** : to adjust something to fit with something else **2** : to make the parts of go well with each other

pro·por·tion·al \p(r)ə-'pōr-shnəl, -'pȯr-, -shən-ᵊl\ *adj* **1 a** : being equivalent in size, amount, or strength **b** : having the same or a constant ratio **2** : set with reference to proportions — **pro·por·tion·al·i·ty** \-ˌpōr-shə-'nal-ət-ē, -ˌpȯr-\ *n* — **pro·por·tion·al·ly** \-'pōr-shnə-lē, -'pȯr-, -shən-ᵊl-ē\ *adv*

pro·por·tion·ate \p(r)ə-'pōr-sh(ə-)nət, -'pȯr-\ *adj* : PRO-PORTIONAL 1 — **pro·por·tion·ate·ly** *adv*

pro·pos·al \prə-'pō-zəl\ *n* **1** : a stating or putting forward something for consideration **2 a** : something proposed : SUGGESTION **b** : an offer of marriage

pro·pose \prə-'pōz\ *vb* **pro·posed; pro·pos·ing 1** : to make a suggestion to be thought over and talked about : SUGGEST ⟨*propose* a new theory⟩ **2** : to make plans : INTEND ⟨*propose* to buy a new house⟩ **3** : to suggest for filling a place or office ⟨*propose* someone for member-ship⟩ **4** : to make an offer of marriage — **pro·pos·er** *n*

prop·o·si·tion \ˌpräp-ə-'zish-ən\ *n* **1** : something offered to be thought about or accepted : PROPOSAL ⟨a business *proposition*⟩ **2** : an expression (as in logic) to be proved or explained **3** : something of a certain kind which one must deal with ⟨the mine will never be a paying *proposi-tion*⟩ ⟨fixing that roof will be a tough *proposition*⟩

pro·pound \prə-'paůnd\ *vb* : PROPOSE 1 — **pro·pound·er** *n*

¹pro·pri·etary \p(r)ə-'prī-ə-ˌter-ē\ *n, pl* **-etar·ies** : PROPRI-ETOR 1

²proprietary *adj* **1 a** : of or relating to a proprietor ⟨*pro-prietary* rights⟩ **b** : resembling that of a proprietor ⟨a *proprietary* pride in their hometown⟩ **2** : made and sold by one having the exclusive right to manufacture and sell ⟨a *proprietary* drug⟩ **3** : privately owned and managed ⟨a *proprietary* nursing home⟩

pro·pri·etor \prə-'prī-ət-ər\ *n* **1** : a person to whom own-ership of a colony is granted **2** : a person who is owner ⟨the *proprietor* of the store⟩ — **pro·pri·etor·ship** \-ˌship\ *n*

pro·pri·ety \p(r)ə-'prī-ət-ē\ *n, pl* **-eties 1** : the quality or state of being proper ⟨questioned the *propriety* of expel-ling him for such a minor offense⟩ **2** : correctness in manners or behavior : POLITENESS **3** *pl* : the rules and customs of behavior followed by polite people

prop root *n* : a root that braces or supports a plant

pro·pul·sion \prə-'pəl-shən\ *n* **1** : the action or process of propelling **2** : something that propels — **pro·pul·sive** \-'pəl-siv\ *adj*

pro ra·ta \(ˈ)prō-'rät-ə, -'rät-ə\ *adv* : in proportion to the share of each : PROPORTIONATELY — **pro rata** *adj*

pro·rate \(ˈ)prō-'rāt\ *vb* **pro·rat·ed; pro·rat·ing** : to divide or spread proportionately ⟨*prorate* a weekly wage for three days of work⟩ — **pro·ra·tion** \prō-'rā-shən\ *n*

pros *plural of* ¹PRO ³PRO

pro·sa·ic \prō-'zā-ik\ *adj* : being dull, ordinary, or unin-teresting — **pro·sa·i·cal·ly** \-'zā-ə-k(ə-)lē\ *adv*

pro·sce·ni·um \prō-'sē-nē-əm\ *n* **1** : the part of a stage in front of the curtain **2** : the wall containing the arch that frames the stage

pro·scribe \prō-'skrīb\ *vb* **pro·scribed; pro·scrib·ing** : PROHIBIT 1

pro·scrip·tion \prō-'skrip-shən\ *n* **1** : the act of proscribing : the state of being pro-scribed **2** : PROHIBI-TION 2

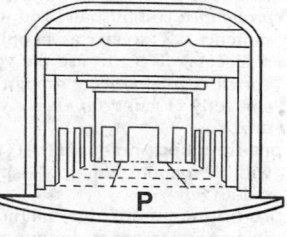

P proscenium 1

prose \'prōz\ *n* **1** : the ordinary language that people use when they speak or write **2** : writing that does not have the repeating rhythm used in poetry — **prose** *adj*

pros·e·cute \'präs-i-ˌkyüt\ vb **-cut·ed; -cut·ing** **1** : to follow up to the end : keep at ⟨*prosecute* a war⟩ **2** : to carry on a legal action against an accused person to prove his or her guilt — **pros·e·cut·able** \-ˌkyüt-ə-bəl\ adj

prosecuting attorney n : DISTRICT ATTORNEY

pros·e·cu·tion \ˌpräs-i-ˈkyü-shən\ n **1** : the act or process of prosecuting; *esp* : the bringing and continuance of a criminal case **2** : the one bringing charges of crime against a person being tried; *esp* : the state's lawyers in a criminal case

pros·e·cu·tor \'präs-i-ˌkyüt-ər\ n : a person (as a district attorney) who prosecutes especially a criminal case as lawyer for the state

pros·e·lyte \'präs-ə-ˌlīt\ n : a new convert especially to a religion

pros·e·ly·tize \'präs-(ə)lə-ˌtīz\ vb **-tized; -tiz·ing** **1** : to talk someone into changing religious faith **2** : to try to get new people to join one's cause or group

prose poem n : a composition in prose that has some of the qualities of a poem

pro·sim·i·an \(ˈ)prō-ˈsim-ē-ən\ n : a mammal (as a lemur) that is one of the lower primates — **prosimian** adj

pros·o·dy \'präs-əd-ē\ n, pl **-dies** : the study of the structure of poetry

¹**pros·pect** \'präs-ˌpekt\ n **1** : a wide view **2** : looking forward to something : ANTICIPATION ⟨the *prospect* of a good time⟩ **3** : something that is waited for or expected : POSSIBILITY ⟨what is the *prospect* of our seeing you again soon?⟩ **4 a** : a possible buyer or customer **b** : a likely candidate ⟨a presidential *prospect*⟩

²**prospect** vb : to explore especially for mineral deposits ⟨*prospecting* for gold⟩

pro·spec·tive \prə-ˈspek-tiv also ˈprä-ˌspek-, prō-ˈspek-, prä-ˈspek-\ adj **1** : likely to come about ⟨*prospective* benefits⟩ **2** : likely to become ⟨a *prospective* buyer⟩

pros·pec·tor \'präs-ˌpek-tər\ n : a person who explores a region in search of valuable minerals (as metals or oil)

pro·spec·tus \prə-ˈspek-təs, prä-\ n, pl **-tus·es** : a printed statement that describes something (as a new business) and is sent out to people who may want to take part (as by investing)

pros·per \'präs-pər\ vb **pros·pered; pros·per·ing** \-p(ə-)riŋ\ **1** : to succeed or make money in something one is doing **2** : THRIVE 1, FLOURISH **3** : to cause to become prosperous

pros·per·i·ty \prä-ˈsper-ət-ē\ n : the state of being prosperous or successful

pros·per·ous \'präs-p(ə-)rəs\ adj **1** : having or showing success or financial good fortune **2** : strong and healthy in growth — **pros·per·ous·ly** adv

pros·tate \'präs-ˌtāt\ n : PROSTATE GLAND — **pros·tat·ic** \prä-ˈstat-ik\ adj

prostate gland n : a body around the base of the male urethra in mammals that is part muscle and part gland and produces a whitish fluid that is a major part of semen

pros·the·sis \präs-ˈthē-səs, 'präs-thə-\ n, pl **-the·ses** \-ˌsēz\ : an artificial device that replaces a missing part of the body

¹**pros·ti·tute** \'präs-tə-ˌt(y)üt\ vb **-tut·ed; -tut·ing** : to put (as one's talents) to unworthy uses : DEBASE

²**prostitute** n : a person who engages in sexual activities for money

pros·ti·tu·tion \ˌpräs-tə-ˈt(y)ü-shən\ n **1** : the acts or practices of a prostitute **2** : the state of being prostituted

¹**pros·trate** \'präs-ˌtrāt\ adj **1** : stretched out with the face on the ground **2** : completely overcome or exhausted ⟨*prostrate* with grief⟩ **3** : trailing on the ground ⟨a *prostrate* shrub⟩

²**prostrate** vb **pros·trat·ed; pros·trat·ing** **1** : to throw or put into a prostrate position **2** : to bring to a weak or powerless condition ⟨*prostrated* with grief⟩

pros·tra·tion \prä-ˈstrā-shən\ n **1 a** : the act of assuming a prostrate position **b** : the state of being prostrate **2** : complete physical or mental exhaustion : COLLAPSE

prosy \'prō-zē\ adj **pros·i·er; -est** : PROSAIC

prot·ac·tin·i·um \ˌprōt-ˌak-ˈtin-ē-əm\ n : a shiny metallic radioactive element of short life — see ELEMENT table

pro·tag·o·nist \prō-ˈtag-ə-nəst\ n : the chief character in a play, novel, or story

pro·te·an \'prōt-ē-ən\ adj : easily taking different shapes or roles [from *Proteus*, a god of the sea in Greek mythology who could change his form at will]

pro·tect \prə-ˈtekt\ vb : to cover or shield from something that would destroy or injure : GUARD

pro·tec·tion \prə-ˈtek-shən\ n **1 a** : the act of protecting ⟨under our *protection*⟩ **b** : the state of being protected ⟨the open boat offered no *protection* from the weather⟩ **2** : a person or thing that protects

pro·tec·tive \prə-ˈtek-tiv\ adj : giving or meant to give protection — **pro·tec·tive·ly** adv — **pro·tec·tive·ness** n

protective coloration n : coloration by which a living thing appears less visible or less attractive to predators

pro·tec·tor \prə-ˈtek-tər\ n **1** : a person or thing that protects or is intended to protect **2** : a person who takes charge of a kingdom while the king or queen is too young to rule : REGENT

pro·tec·tor·ate \prə-ˈtek-t(ə-)rət\ n **1 a** : government by a protector **b** : the office or period of rule of a protector **2** : a small country ruled by a larger one

pro·té·gé \'prōt-ə-ˌzhā\ n : a person under the care or training of someone influential especially for the furthering of his or her career [French, from *protéger* "to protect"]

pro·tein \'prō-ˌtēn, 'prōt-ē-ən\ n : any of numerous substances that consist of chains of amino acids, contain the elements carbon, hydrogen, nitrogen, oxygen, and often sulfur, include many compounds (as enzymes and hormones) essential for life, and are supplied by various foods (as meat, milk, eggs, nuts, and beans) — **pro·tein·aceous** \ˌprōt-ᵊn-ˈā-shəs, ˌprō-ˌtēn-, ˌprōt-ē-ən-\ adj

pro tem·po·re \prō-ˈtem-pə-rē\ adv : for the present ⟨president *pro tempore*⟩

Pro·tero·zo·ic \ˌprät-ə-rə-ˈzō-ik, ˌprōt-\ adj : of, relating to, or being an eon of geologic time between the Archean and the Phanerozoic eons that exceeds in length all of following geologic time and is marked by rocks which contain fossils indicating the existence of algae and small soft-bodied animals resembling worms and jellyfish; *also* : relating to the corresponding system of rocks — see GEOLOGIC TIME table — **Proterozoic** n

¹**pro·test** \'prō-ˌtest\ n : a complaint, objection, or display of unwillingness or disapproval

²**pro·test** \prə-ˈtest, 'prō-ˌtest, prō-ˈtest\ vb **1** : to declare positively : ASSERT ⟨*protested* their innocence⟩ **2 a** : to make a protest against ⟨*protested* the higher tax rate⟩ **b** : to object strongly ⟨*protest* against a new highway⟩ — **pro·test·er** or **pro·tes·tor** \-ˈtes-tər, -tes-\ n

prot·es·tant \'prät-əs-tənt, sense 2 is also prə-ˈtes-\ n **1** cap : a member of one of several Christian churches that separated from the Roman Catholic church in the 16th century or of a church founded by members of these churches **2** : one who protests — **protestant** adj, often cap — **Prot·es·tant·ism** \'prät-əs-tənt-ˌiz-əm\ n

pro·tes·ta·tion \ˌprät-əs-ˈtā-shən, ˌprō-ˌtes-\ n **1** : the act of protesting **2** : a positive declaration

pro·tho·rax \(ˈ)prō-ˈthō(ə)r-ˌaks, -ˈthó(ə)r-\ n : the first segment of the thorax of an insect

pro·tist \'prōt-əst\ n : any of a kingdom of organisms that resemble plants or animals or both, are one-celled and

\ə\ abut	\aú\ out	\i\ tip	\ò\ saw	\ú\ foot
\ər\ further	\ch\ chin	\ī\ life	\òi\ coin	\y\ yet
\a\ mat	\e\ pet	\j\ job	\th\ thin	\yü\ few
\ā\ take	\ē\ easy	\ŋ\ sing	\th\ this	\yú\ cure
\ä\ cot, cart	\g\ go	\ō\ bone	\ü\ food	\zh\ vision

sometimes colonial or less often many-celled, and that typically include the protozoans, most algae, and often some fungi (as slime molds) — **pro·tis·tan** \prō-'tis-tən\ *adj or n*

pro·to·col \'prōt-ə-ˌkȯl\ *n* **1** : an original copy or record of a document **2** : a code of diplomatic or military rules of behavior **3** : a set of rules for the formatting of data in an electronic communications system ⟨network *protocols*⟩

pro·ton \'prō-ˌtän\ *n* : an atomic particle that occurs in the nucleus of every atom and carries a positive charge equal in size to the negative charge of an electron — **pro·ton·ic** \prō-'tän-ik\ *adj*

pro·to·plan·et \'prōt-ō-ˌplan-ət\ *n* : a whirling mass of gas that rotates around a star and is believed to become a planet — **pro·to·plan·e·tary** \ˌprōt-ō-'plan-ə-ˌter-ē\ *adj*

pro·to·plasm \'prōt-ə-ˌplaz-əm\ *n* : a mixture of various organic and inorganic substances (as proteins and water) that makes up the living nucleus, cytoplasm, plastids, and mitochondria of the cell and is considered the physical basis of life — **pro·to·plas·mic** \ˌprōt-ə-'plaz-mik\ *adj*

pro·to·type \'prōt-ə-ˌtīp\ *n* : an original model on which something is patterned

pro·to·zoa \ˌprōt-ə-'zō-ə\ *n pl* : microorganisms that are protozoans

pro·to·zo·an \ˌprōt-ə-'zō-ən\ *n* : any of a phylum or group of microorganisms (as amoebas and paramecia) that are single-celled protists and have varied structure and physiology and often complicated life cycles — **protozoan** *adj*

pro·to·zo·ol·o·gist \ˌprōt-ə-zō-'äl-ə-jəst, -zə-'wäl-\ *n* : a specialist in protozoology

pro·to·zo·ol·o·gy \ˌprōt-ə-zō-'äl-ə-jē, -zə-'wäl-\ *n* : a branch of zoology dealing with protozoans

pro·tract \prō-'trakt\ *vb* : PROLONG

pro·trac·tor \prō-'trak-tər\ *n* : an instrument for drawing and measuring angles

pro·trude \prō-'trüd\ *vb* **pro·trud·ed; pro·trud·ing** : to stick out or cause to stick out

pro·tru·sion \prō-'trü-zhən\ *n* **1** : the act of protruding : the state of being protruded **2** : something that protrudes

protractor

pro·tu·ber·ance \prō-'t(y)ü-b(ə-)rən(t)s\ *n* **1** : the quality or state of bulging beyond a surrounding surface **2** : ²BULGE

pro·tu·ber·ant \prō-'t(y)ü-b(ə-)rənt\ *adj* : bulging beyond the surrounding surface

proud \'praúd\ *adj* **1 a** : having or displaying excessive self-esteem ⟨a *proud* manner⟩ **b** : much pleased ⟨*proud* parents of a hero⟩ **c** : having proper self-respect ⟨too *proud* to beg⟩ **2** : MAGNIFICENT 1, GLORIOUS ⟨a *proud* record⟩ **3** : VIGOROUS 1, SPIRITED ⟨a *proud* horse⟩ — **proud·ly** *adv*

prove \'prüv\ *vb* **proved; proved** *or* **prov·en** \'prü-vən\; **prov·ing** **1** : to test by an experiment or a standard ⟨*prove* gold⟩ **2 a** : to show the truth of by evidence ⟨*prove* the charges⟩ ⟨*proved* she could handle the job⟩ **b** : to check the correctness of (as an arithmetic solution) **3** : to show the genuineness of ⟨*prove* a will⟩ **4** : to turn out especially after trial or test ⟨the new automobile engine *proved* to be impractical⟩ — **prov·able** \'prü-və-bəl\ *adj*

Pro·ven·çal \ˌpräv-ən-'säl, ˌprōv-\ *n* **1** : a person born or living in Provence **2** : OCCITAN — **Provençal** *adj*

prov·en·der \'präv-ən-dər\ *n* **1** : dry food for domestic animals : FEED **2** : FOOD 1

prov·erb \'präv-ˌərb\ *n* : a brief popular saying expressing a wise thought

pro·ver·bi·al \prə-'vər-bē-əl\ *adj* **1** : of, relating to, or re-

sembling a proverb ⟨*proverbial* wisdom⟩ **2** : commonly spoken of ⟨the *proverbial* beginner's luck⟩ — **pro·ver·bi·al·ly** \-bē-ə-lē\ *adv*

Prov·erbs \'präv-ˌərbz\ *n* — see BIBLE table

pro·vide \prə-'vīd\ *vb* **pro·vid·ed; pro·vid·ing** **1** : to take care of beforehand ⟨*provide* against a possible scarcity⟩ **2** : to state a condition or stipulation ⟨the contract *provided* for 10 paid holidays⟩ **3** : to supply what is needed for support ⟨*provides* for a large family⟩ **4** : to supply or furnish for use ⟨cows *provide* milk⟩ [Middle English *providen* "to provide," from Latin *providēre*, literally, "to see ahead," from *pro-* "ahead, forward" and *vidēre* "to see" — related to VISION] — **pro·vid·er** *n*

pro·vid·ed \prə-'vīd-əd\ *conj* : IF 1

prov·i·dence \'präv-əd-ən(t)s, -ə-ˌden(t)s\ *n* **1 a** *often cap* : divine guidance or care **b** *cap* : God as the guide and protector of all human beings **2** : the quality or state of being provident : PRUDENCE

prov·i·dent \'präv-əd-ənt, -ə-ˌdent\ *adj* **1** : providing for future needs **2** : FRUGAL — **prov·i·dent·ly** *adv*

prov·i·den·tial \ˌpräv-ə-'den-chəl\ *adj* **1** : of, relating to, or determined by Providence ⟨*providential* guidance⟩ **2** : FORTUNATE, TIMELY ⟨a *providential* escape⟩ — **prov·i·den·tial·ly** \-'dench-(ə-)lē\ *adv*

prov·ince \'präv-ən(t)s\ *n* **1 a** : a country or region brought under the control of the ancient Roman government **b** : a usually large division of a country having its own government ⟨Canadian *provinces*⟩ **c** *pl* : all of a country except the chief cities **2** : the jurisdiction of an archbishop or metropolitan **3** : proper or appropriate business or area of skill, knowledge, or interest ⟨a legal question outside the physician's *province*⟩

¹pro·vin·cial \prə-'vin-chəl\ *n* **1** : a person living in or coming from a province **2** : a provincial person

²provincial *adj* **1** : of, relating to, or coming from a province **2 a** : limited in outlook : NARROW **b** : lacking the ways and manners of city people **3** : of or relating to a style (as in furniture) marked by simple design and plain decoration ⟨a French *provincial* table⟩ — **pro·vin·ci·al·i·ty** \-ˌvin-chē-'al-ət-ē\ *n* — **pro·vin·cial·ly** \-'vinch-(ə-)lē\ *adv*

pro·vin·cial·ism \prə-'vin-chə-ˌliz-əm\ *n* **1** : a local word, phrase, or idiom **2** : the quality or state of being provincial

proving ground *n* : a place for scientific testing

¹pro·vi·sion \prə-'vizh-ən\ *n* **1 a** : the act or process of providing ⟨*provision* of transportation for the trip⟩ **b** : something done beforehand : PREPARATION ⟨make *provision* for emergencies⟩ **2** : a stock of materials or supplies; *esp* : a stock of food — usually used in plural **3** : ¹CONDITION 1 ⟨a constitutional *provision*⟩

²provision *vb* **pro·vi·sioned; pro·vi·sion·ing** \-'vizh-(ə-)niŋ\ : to supply with provisions

pro·vi·sion·al \prə-'vizh-nəl, -ən-ᵊl\ *adj* : serving for the time being ⟨a *provisional* government⟩ ⟨*provisional* arrangements⟩ — **pro·vi·sion·al·ly** \-ē\ *adv*

pro·vi·so \prə-'vī-zō\ *n, pl* **-sos** *or* **-soes** **1** : a sentence or clause in a legal document in which a condition is stated **2** : a limiting statement ⟨released them with the *proviso* that they behave⟩

prov·o·ca·tion \ˌpräv-ə-'kā-shən\ *n* **1** : the act of provoking **2** : something that provokes

pro·voc·a·tive \prə-'väk-ət-iv\ *adj* : serving or tending to provoke ⟨*provocative* comments⟩ — **pro·voc·a·tive·ly** *adv* — **pro·voc·a·tive·ness** *n*

pro·voke \prə-'vōk\ *vb* **pro·voked; pro·vok·ing** **1** : to excite to anger **2** : to stir up : BRING ABOUT ⟨*provoke* an argument⟩ [Middle English *provoken* "to arouse to strong feeling or action," from early French *provoquer* (same meaning), from Latin *provocare* "to call forth, stir up," from *pro-* "forth, forward" and *vocare* "to call" — related to ADVOCATE, REVOKE, VOCATION]

synonyms PROVOKE, EXCITE, STIMULATE mean to arouse into doing or feeling something. PROVOKE stresses the feeling or action called forth ⟨my stories usually *provoke* laughter⟩. EXCITE suggests the stirring up of great feeling ⟨news of the victory *excited* joy and relief⟩. STIMULATE suggests a rousing out of laziness, inactivity, or unconcern ⟨a speech that *stimulated* the crowd to shout slogans⟩.

pro·vok·ing \prə-'vō-kiŋ\ *adj* : causing mild anger : ANNOYING ⟨a *provoking* delay⟩ — **pro·vok·ing·ly** \-kiŋ-lē\ *adv*

pro·vost \'prō-ˌvōst, 'präv-əst, *before* "marshal" *often* ˌprō-vō\ *n* : a high managing officer (as in a university)

provost marshal *n* : a military police chief

prow \'praú\ *n* : the bow of a ship

prow·ess \'praú-əs\ *n* **1** : great bravery especially in battle **2** : very great ability ⟨athletic *prowess*⟩

prowl \'praú(ə)l\ *vb* **1** : to move about or wander in a secretive manner in or as if in search of prey **2** : to roam over like a wild beast ⟨*prowl* the streets⟩ — **prowl** *n* — **prowl·er** *n*

prowl car *n* : SQUAD CAR

prox·im·i·ty \präk-'sim-ət-ē\ *n* : the state or condition of being near : NEARNESS

proxy \'präk-sē\ *n, pl* **prox·ies** **1** : authority held by one person to act for another (as in voting) **2 a** : a person holding authority to act for another **b** : a written paper giving a person such authority — **proxy** *adj*

prude \'prüd\ *n* : a person who is easily shocked or offended by things that do not shock or offend others — **prud·ish** \'prüd-ish\ *adj* — **prud·ish·ly** *adv* — **prud·ish·ness** *n*

pru·dence \'prüd-ᵊn(t)s\ *n* **1** : the ability to govern and discipline oneself by the use of reason **2** : skill and good judgment in the management of affairs

pru·dent \'prüd-ᵊnt\ *adj* **1** : clever and careful in action and judgment ⟨it's *prudent* to save some of your money⟩ **2** : DISCREET **3** : FRUGAL — **pru·dent·ly** *adv*

pru·den·tial \prü-'den-chəl\ *adj* **1** : of, relating to, or resulting from prudence **2** : using prudence

prud·ery \'prüd-(ə-)rē\ *n, pl* **-er·ies** **1** : the quality or state of being prudish **2** : a prudish remark or act

¹prune \'prün\ *n* : a dried plum

²prune *vb* **pruned; prun·ing** **1 a** : to reduce by getting rid of matter that is not necessary or wanted ⟨*prune* an essay⟩ ⟨*prune* a budget⟩ **b** : to remove as unnecessary **2** : to cut off the parts of a woody plant that are dead or not wanted ⟨*prune* the hedge⟩ — **prun·er** *n*

pru·ri·ent \'prúr-ē-ənt\ *adj* : having or revealing indecent desires or thoughts — **pru·ri·ent·ly** *adv*

¹pry \'prī\ *vb* **pried; pry·ing** : to look closely : PEER; *esp* : to search curiously into other people's affairs [Middle English *prien* "to look at closely"]

²pry *vb* **pried; pry·ing** **1** : to raise, move, or pull apart with or as if with a lever ⟨*pry* off a tight lid⟩ **2** : to force out, detach, or open with difficulty ⟨could not *pry* a secret out of her⟩ [an altered form of *prize* "to move with or as if with a lever"]

³pry *n* : a tool for prying

pry·ing *adj* : given to asking about other people's affairs especially in an annoying or meddlesome way **synonyms** see CURIOUS — **pry·ing·ly** \-iŋ-lē\ *adv*

psalm \'säm, 'sälm\ *n* **1** : a sacred song or poem **2** *cap* : one of the hymns that make up the Old Testament Book of Psalms

Word History The Greek word *psallein* originally meant "to pull" or "to pluck." It then came to be used with the meaning "to play a stringed musical instrument." From this verb came the noun *psalmos,* which literally meant "the twanging of a harp." Since harp music often accompanied singing, *psalmos* took on the meaning of "a song sung to harp music" and later simply "a song or poem."

It was borrowed into Latin as *psalmus* and came into English as *psalm.* [Old English *psealm* "psalm," from Latin *psalmus* (same meaning), from Greek *psalmos* "psalm," literally, "twanging of a harp," from *psallein* "to pluck, play a stringed musical instrument"]

psalm·ist \'säm-əst, 'säl-məst\ *n* : a writer or composer of psalms

psalm·o·dy \'säm-əd-ē, 'säl-məd-\ *n, pl* **-dies** **1** : the art or practice of singing psalms in worship **2** : a collection of psalms

Psalms \'sämz, 'sälmz\ *n* — see BIBLE table

Psal·ter \'sòl-tər\ *n* **1** : the Book of Psalms in the Bible **2** : a collection of Psalms

psal·tery *also* **psal·try** \'sòl-t(ə-)rē\ *n, pl* **-ter·ies** *also* **-tries** : an ancient stringed musical instrument resembling the zither

p's and q's \ˌpēz-ᵊn-'kyüz\ *n* : something (as manners) that one should be careful about ⟨always minded my *p's and q's* around my aunts and uncles⟩

pseud- *or* **pseudo-** *combining form* : not genuine : fake [derived from Greek *pseudēs* "false"]

pseu·do \'süd-ō\ *adj* : not genuine : FAKE

pseud·onym \'süd-ᵊn-ˌim\ *n* : a fictitious name; *esp* : PEN NAME

pseu·do·pod \'süd-ə-ˌpäd\ *n* : PSEUDOPODIUM

pseu·do·po·di·um \ˌsüd-ə-'pōd-ē-əm\ *n, pl* **-po·dia** \-ē-ə\ : an outward extension of part of a cell that is produced by the pressure of moving cytoplasm (as in an amoeba) and that helps to move the cell and to take in its food

pshaw \'shò\ *interj* — used to express irritation, contempt, or disbelief

psi \'sī\ *n* : the 23rd letter of the Greek alphabet — Ψ *or* ψ

psi·lo·cy·bin \ˌsī-lə-'sī-bən\ *n* : a chemical that is obtained from a fungus and causes hallucinations

psit·ta·co·sis \ˌsit-ə-'kō-səs\ *n* : an infectious disease of birds caused by a bacterium, marked by diarrhea and loss of weight and strength, and capable of being passed on to human beings — called also *parrot fever*

pso·ri·a·sis \sə-'rī-ə-səs\ *n* : a skin disease characterized by red patches often covered with white scales

psych *or* **psyche** \'sīk\ *vb* **psyched; psych·ing** **1** : to make oneself psychologically ready — usually used with *up* ⟨*psyched* themselves up for the race⟩ **2** : to make uneasy — often used with *out* ⟨*psych* out an opponent⟩

psy·che \'sī-kē\ *n* **1** : ¹SOUL 2, SELF **2** : ¹MIND 2

¹psy·che·del·ic \ˌsī-kə-'del-ik\ *adj* **1** : of, relating to, or being a drug (as LSD) that produces abnormal often extreme mental effects (as hallucinations) **2 a** : imitating the effects of psychedelic drugs **b** : glowing brightly

²psychedelic *n* : a psychedelic drug

psy·chi·a·trist \sə-'kī-ə-trəst, sī-\ *n* : a specialist in psychiatry

psy·chi·a·try \sə-'kī-ə-trē, sī-\ *n* : a branch of medicine that deals with disorders of the mind, emotions, or behavior — **psy·chi·at·ric** \ˌsī-kē-'a-trik\ *adj*

¹psy·chic \'sī-kik\ *also* **psy·chi·cal** \-ki-kəl\ *adj* **1** : of or relating to the psyche **2** : not physical; *esp* : not to be explained by knowledge of natural laws **3** : sensitive to influences or forces believed to come from beyond the natural world — **psy·chi·cal·ly** \-ki-k(ə-)lē\ *adv*

²psychic *n* : a psychic person (as a medium)

psy·cho \'sī-kō\ *n* : a person of unsound mind — not used technically [short for *psychopath*]

psycho- *combining form* : mind : mental processes and activities ⟨*psycho*therapy⟩ [derived from Greek *psychē* "soul, mind, principle of life"]

\ə\ abut	\aú\ out	\i\ tip	\ò\ saw	\ú\ foot
\ər\ further	\ch\ chin	\ī\ life	\òi\ coin	\y\ yet
\a\ mat	\e\ pet	\j\ job	\th\ thin	\yü\ few
\ā\ take	\ē\ easy	\ŋ\ sing	\t̲h̲\ this	\yú\ cure
\ä\ cot, cart	\g\ go	\ō\ bone	\ü\ food	\zh\ vision

psy·cho·ac·tive \ˌsī-kō-ˈak-tiv\ *adj* : affecting the mind or behavior ⟨*psychoactive* drugs⟩

psy·cho·anal·y·sis \ˌsī-kō-ə-ˈnal-ə-səs\ *n, pl* **-y·ses** \-ˌsēz\ : a method of explaining and treating mental and emotional disorders by having the patient talk freely about himself or herself and especially about dreams, problems, and early childhood memories and experiences

psy·cho·an·a·lyst \ˌsī-kō-ˈan-ᵊl-əst\ *n* : a medical specialist who uses psychoanalysis to treat patients with mental or emotional disorders

psy·cho·an·a·lyt·ic \ˌsī-kō-ˌan-ᵊl-ˈit-ik\ *also* **psy·cho·an·a·lyt·i·cal** \-i-kəl\ *adj* : of, relating to, or using psychoanalysis or its principles and techniques

psy·cho·an·a·lyze \ˌsi-kō-ˈan-ᵊl-ˌīz\ *vb* : to treat by means of psychoanalysis

psy·cho·log·i·cal \ˌsī-kə-ˈläj-i-kəl\ *also* **psy·cho·log·ic** \-ˈläj-ik\ *adj* **1 a** : of or relating to psychology **b** : MENTAL 1 **2** : meant to influence the will or mind — **psy·cho·log·i·cal·ly** \-i-k(ə)lē\ *adv*

psy·chol·o·gist \sī-ˈkäl-ə-jəst\ *n* : a specialist in psychology

psy·chol·o·gy \sī-ˈkäl-ə-jē\ *n, pl* **-gies** **1** : the science or study of mind and behavior **2** : the particular ways in which an individual or group thinks or behaves [from scientific Latin *psychologia* "the study of the mind and behavior," derived from Greek *psychē* "soul, mind" and Greek *-logia* "science, study"]

psy·cho·path \ˈsī-kə-ˌpath\ *n* : a mentally ill or unstable person; *esp* : one who does not feel guilty about not living up to normal social and moral responsibilities and exhibits a disregard for the feelings and safety of others

psy·cho·sis \sī-ˈkō-səs\ *n, pl* **-cho·ses** \-ˈkō-ˌsēz\ : a serious mental illness marked by loss of or greatly lessened ability to test whether what one is thinking and feeling about the real world is really true

psy·cho·so·mat·ic \ˌsī-kō-sə-ˈmat-ik\ *adj* : of, relating to, or being symptoms of the body that are caused by disturbances (as stress) originating in the mind

psy·cho·ther·a·pist \ˌsī-kō-ˈther-ə-pəst\ *n* : a person (as a doctor or psychologist) who treats patients by psychotherapy

psy·cho·ther·a·py \ˌsī-kō-ˈther-ə-pē\ *n* : treatment of mental or emotional disorder or of related bodily illnesses by psychological means

¹psy·chot·ic \sī-ˈkät-ik\ *adj* : of, relating to, or marked by psychosis

²psychotic *n* : a psychotic person

psy·chrom·e·ter \sī-ˈkräm-ət-ər\ *n* : an instrument for measuring the water vapor in the atmosphere by means of the difference in the readings of two thermometers when one of them is kept wet so that it is cooled by evaporation

ptar·mi·gan \ˈtär-mi-gən\ *n, pl* **ptarmigan** *or* **ptarmigans** : any of various grouses of northern regions with completely feathered feet

PT boat \(ˈ)pē-ˈtē-\ *n* : a high-speed motorboat usually equipped with torpedoes, machine guns, and depth charges

PTC \ˌpē-ˌtē-ˈsē\ *n* : PHENYLTHIOCARBAMIDE

ptarmigan

pte·ri·do·phyte \tə-ˈrid-ə-ˌfīt\ *n* : any of a group of vascular plants that have roots, stems, and leaves, reproduce by spores instead of by flowers and seeds, and include the ferns, club mosses, horsetails, and their extinct relatives

ptero·dac·tyl \ˌter-ə-ˈdak-tᵊl\ *n* : any of various extinct flying reptiles having a featherless membrane extending from the body along the arms and forming the supporting surface of the wings [from scientific Latin *Pterodactylus* "pterodactyl," from Greek *pteron* "wing" and Greek *daktylos* "finger"]

ptero·saur \ˈter-ə-ˌsȯ(ə)r\ *n* : PTERODACTYL

pto·maine \ˈtō-ˌmān, tō-ˈmān\ *n* : any of various often poisonous compounds formed by the action of decay-producing bacteria on nitrogen-containing matter (as proteins)

ptomaine poisoning *n* : food poisoning caused by bacteria or their products

pty·a·lin \ˈtī-ə-lən\ *n* : an enzyme found in the saliva of many animals that helps change starch into sugar

pub \ˈpəb\ *n, chiefly British* : PUBLIC HOUSE 2

pu·ber·ty \ˈpyü-bərt-ē\ *n* **1** : the condition of being or the period of becoming first capable of reproducing sexually that is brought on by the production of sex hormones and the maturing of the sex organs (as the testes and ovaries) and is marked by the development of secondary sex characteristics (as male facial hair growth and female breast development) and by the occurrence of the first menstruation in the female **2** : the age at which puberty occurs often defined legally as 14 in boys and 12 in girls

pu·bic \ˈpyü-bik\ *adj* : of, relating to, or located near the pubis

pu·bis \ˈpyü-bəs\ *n, pl* **pu·bes** \-ˌbēz\ : the front and lower of the three principal bones composing each half of the pelvis

¹pub·lic \ˈpəb-lik\ *adj* **1 a** : of, relating to, belonging to, or affecting all the people ⟨*public* law⟩ **b** : provided by the government ⟨*public* education⟩ **c** : relating to or engaged in the service of the community or nation ⟨*public* life⟩ **2** : of or relating to community interests as opposed to private affairs ⟨a radio program in the *public* interest⟩ **3** : devoted to the general welfare ⟨needed leaders with *public* spirit⟩ **4** : open to or shared by all ⟨a *public* meeting⟩ ⟨the *public* library⟩ **5 a** : generally known ⟨the story became *public*⟩ **b** : WELL-KNOWN ⟨a *public* figure⟩ **6** : supported by income from public funds and private contributions rather than by commercials ⟨*public* television⟩ [Middle English *publique* "relating to the people as a whole, public," from early French *publique* (same meaning), from Latin *publicus* "belonging to the people as a whole," from *populus* "the people" — related to POPULAR, REPUBLIC] — **pub·lic·ly** *adv*

²public *n* **1** : a place open or visible to people ⟨seen in *public*⟩ **2** : the people as a whole ⟨a lecture open to the *public*⟩ **3** : a particular group of people ⟨a writer's *public*⟩

public–address system *n* : a set of equipment including microphone and loudspeakers used for broadcasting to a large audience in an auditorium or out of doors

pub·li·can \ˈpəb-li-kən\ *n* : a tax collector for the ancient Romans

pub·li·ca·tion \ˌpəb-lə-ˈkā-shən\ *n* **1** : the act or process of publishing **2** : a published work

public house *n* **1** : INN, HOTEL **2** *chiefly British* : a licensed saloon or bar

pub·li·cist \ˈpəb-lə-səst\ *n* **1 a** : an expert in international law **b** : an expert on public affairs **2** : PRESS AGENT

pub·lic·i·ty \(ˌ)pə-ˈblis-ət-ē\ *n* **1** : the condition of being public or publicly known **2** : an act or device designed to attract public interest; *esp* : information with a news value designed to further the interests of a place, person, or cause **3 a** : an action that gains public attention **b** : the attention so gained

pub·li·cize \ˈpəb-lə-ˌsīz\ *vb* **-cized; -ciz·ing** : to give publicity to

public relations *n* **1** : the business of creating public goodwill for a person, firm, or institution **2** : the degree of understanding and goodwill achieved

public school *n* **1** : a British private school that gives a liberal education and prepares students for the universities **2** : an elementary or secondary school supported by taxes and operated by a local government

public servant *n* : a governmental official or employee

public service *n* **1** : the business of supplying a commodity (as electricity or gas) or service (as transportation) to any or all members of a community **2** : governmental employment; *esp* CIVIL SERVICE

public utility *n* : a business organization performing a public service and subject to special governmental regulation

public works *n pl* : works (as schools, highways, or docks) constructed with public funds for public use

pub·lish \ˈpəb-lish\ *vb* **1** : to make generally known : make public announcement of **2 a** : to produce or release for publication; *esp* : ²PRINT 2c **b** : to print the work of ⟨*publish* a poet⟩ — **pub·lish·able** \-ə-bəl\ *adj*

pub·lish·er \ˈpəb-lish-ər\ *n* : one that publishes; *esp* : one that sends out and offers for sale printed matter (as books, magazines, or newspapers)

¹**puck** \ˈpək\ *n* : a fairy or spirit who plays tricks on human beings [Old English *pūca* "evil spirit"]

²**puck** *n* : a rubber disk used in ice hockey [from a dialect word *puck* "to hit, poke," probably from Irish *poc* "butt, stroke in hurling," literally, "buck (male deer)"]

¹**puck·er** \ˈpək-ər\ *vb* **puck·ered**; **puck·er·ing** \-(ə-)riŋ\ : to contract into folds or wrinkles ⟨*pucker* one's lips⟩

²**pucker** *n* : a fold or wrinkle caused by puckering — **puck·ery** \ˈpək-(ə-)rē\ *adj*

pud·ding \ˈpu̇d-iŋ\ *n* **1** : a boiled or baked soft food usually with a cereal base ⟨corn *pudding*⟩ **2** : a soft, spongy, or thick creamy dessert ⟨bread *pudding*⟩

pudding stone *n* : ³CONGLOMERATE 1

¹**pud·dle** \ˈpəd-ᵊl\ *n* : a very small pool (as of dirty or muddy water)

²**puddle** *vb* **pud·dled**; **pud·dling** \ˈpəd-liŋ, -ᵊl-iŋ\ **1** : to make muddy **2** : to cover with puddles — **pud·dler** \-lər, -ᵊl-ər\ *n*

pudgy \ˈpəj-ē\ *adj* **pudg·i·er**; **-est** : short and plump — **pudg·i·ness** *n*

pueb·lo \pü-ˈeb-lō, ˈpweb-, pyü-ˈeb-\ *n, pl* **pueblos** **1** : an American Indian village of Arizona or New Mexico consisting of flat-roofed stone or adobe houses joined in groups sometimes several stories high **2** *cap* : a member of any of several American Indian peoples of Arizona and New Mexico [from Spanish *pueblo* "village," literally, "people," from Latin *populus* "people"]

pu·er·ile \ˈpyu̇(-ə)r-əl, -ˌīl\ *adj* : showing a lack of maturity, seriousness, or good judgment ⟨*puerile* remarks⟩ — **pu·er·il·i·ty** \ˌpyu̇(-ə)r-ˈil-ət-ē\ *n*

¹**puff** \ˈpəf\ *vb* **1 a** : to blow in short gusts **b** : to breathe hard : PANT ⟨*puffed* as we climbed the hill⟩ **c** : to blow by or as if by puffs ⟨the locomotive *puffed* smoke⟩ **2** : to swell or become swollen with or as if with air ⟨the sprained ankle *puffed* up⟩ ⟨*puffed* up with pride⟩

²**puff** *n* **1 a** : an act or instance of puffing : WHIFF, GUST **b** : a cloud (as of smoke or steam) given off in a puff **2** : a light pastry that rises high in baking **3 a** : a slight swelling **b** : a small fluffy pad for applying cosmetic powder **c** : a quilted bed covering — **puff·i·ness** \ˈpəf-ē-nəs\ *n* — **puffy** \ˈpəf-ē\ *adj*

³**puff** *adj* : of, relating to, or designed for promotion or flattery ⟨a *puff* piece⟩

puff adder *n* : HOGNOSE SNAKE

puff·ball \ˈpəf-ˌbȯl\ *n* : any of various often edible globe-shaped fungi that release ripe spores in a cloud resembling smoke when they are touched

puff·er \ˈpəf-ər\ *n* **1** : one that puffs **2** : PUFFER FISH

puffer fish *n* : any of various scaleless fishes chiefly of tropical seas which can puff themselves up with air or water when threatened and most of which are highly poisonous — called also *blowfish, puffer*

puf·fin \ˈpəf-ən\ *n* : any of several seabirds that are related

to the auks and have a short thick neck and a deep grooved bill marked with different colors

pug \ˈpəg\ *n* : any of a breed of small sturdy compact dogs having a short coat, tightly curled tail, and broad wrinkled face

pug

pu·gi·list \ˈpyü-jə-ləst\ *n* : ¹BOXER — **pu·gi·lis·tic** \ˌpyü-jə-ˈlis-tik\ *adj*

pug·na·cious \ˌpəg-ˈnā-shəs\ *adj* : showing a readiness to fight *synonyms* see BELLIGERENT — **pug·na·cious·ly** *adv* — **pug·nac·i·ty** \-ˈnas-ət-ē\ *n*

pug nose *n* : a usually short nose turning up at the end — **pug–nosed** \ˈpəg-ˈnōzd\ *adj*

puis·sance \ˈpwis-ᵊn(t)s, ˈpyü-ə-sən(t)s\ *n* : STRENGTH 1, POWER — **puis·sant** \-ᵊnt, -sənt\ *adj*

puke \ˈpyük\ *vb* **puked**; **puk·ing** : ²VOMIT — **puke** *n*

pule \ˈpyü(ə)l\ *vb* **puled**; **pul·ing** : ¹WHINE, WHIMPER

¹**pull** \ˈpu̇l\ *vb* **1** : to separate forcibly from a natural or firm attachment ⟨*pull* a tooth⟩ ⟨*pull* up carrots⟩ **2 a** : to use force on so as to cause or tend to cause motion toward the force ⟨*pull* a wagon⟩ ⟨*pull* at a rope⟩ **b** : to stretch repeatedly ⟨*pull* taffy⟩ **c** : to strain by stretching ⟨*pull* a tendon⟩ **d** : ¹MOVE 1 ⟨the car *pulled* out of the driveway⟩ **3** : to draw apart : TEAR **4** : ¹REMOVE 2 ⟨*pulled* the pitcher in the third inning⟩ **5** : to bring into the open ⟨*pulled* a knife⟩ **6** : to carry out with skill or daring : COMMIT ⟨*pull* a robbery⟩ **7** : ATTRACT 2 ⟨*pull* customers⟩ — **pull·er** *n* — **pull oneself together** : to regain one's calmness — **pull one's leg** : to deceive someone playfully — **pull together** : to work in harmony : COOPERATE

²**pull** *n* **1 a** : the act or an instance of pulling **b** : the effort put forth in pulling ⟨a long *pull* uphill⟩ **2** : special influence ⟨got his job through *pull*⟩ **3** : a device for pulling ⟨a drawer *pull*⟩ **4** : a force that attracts or influences ⟨the *pull* of gravity⟩ **5** : an injury resulting from abnormal straining or stretching ⟨a muscle *pull*⟩

pull–down \ˈpu̇l-ˌdȧu̇n\ *adj* : appearing on a computer screen below a selected item ⟨a *pull-down* menu⟩

pul·let \ˈpu̇l-ət\ *n* : a young hen; *esp* : a hen of the domestic chicken that is less than a year old [Middle English *polet* "a young chicken or fowl," from early French *pullet* (same meaning), derived from earlier *pulle, poule* "young animal," from Latin *pullus* "young animal, chicken" — related to ³POOL, POULTRY]

pul·ley \ˈpu̇l-ē\ *n, pl* **pulleys** : a small wheel with a grooved rim used with a rope or chain to change the direction of a pulling force and in combination to increase the force applied for lifting

Pull·man \ˈpu̇l-mən\ *n* : a railroad passenger car with comfortable furnishings especially for night travel

¹**pull·over** \ˌpu̇l-ˌō-vər\ *adj* : put on by being pulled over the head ⟨*pullover* sweater⟩

²**pull·over** \ˈpu̇l-ˌō-vər\ *n* : a pullover garment

pull through *vb* : to help through or to survive a dangerous or difficult period or situation ⟨had pneumonia but she *pulled through*⟩

pul·mo·nary \ˈpu̇l-mə-ˌner-ē, ˈpəl-\ *adj* **1** : relating to, affecting, or occurring in the lungs **2** : carried on by the lungs ⟨*pulmonary* respiration⟩

\ə\ abut	\au̇\ out	\i\ tip	\ȯ\ saw	\u̇\ foot
\ər\ further	\ch\ chin	\ī\ life	\ȯi\ coin	\y\ yet
\a\ mat	\e\ pet	\j\ job	\th\ thin	\yü\ few
\ā\ take	\ē\ easy	\ŋ\ sing	\th\ this	\yu̇\ cure
\ä\ cot, cart	\g\ go	\ō\ bone	\ü\ food	\zh\ vision

pulmonary artery *n* : an artery that carries oxygen-poor blood containing carbon dioxide from the right side of the heart to the lungs

pulmonary circulation *n* : the passage of oxygen-poor blood from the right side of the heart through arteries to the lungs where it picks up oxygen and is returned to the left side of the heart by veins

pulmonary vein *n* : a vein that returns oxygen-rich blood from the lungs to the left side of the heart

¹pulp \'pəlp\ *n* **1 a** : the soft juicy or fleshy part of a fruit or vegetable ⟨the *pulp* of an apple⟩ **b** : a mass of vegetable matter from which the juice or moisture has been squeezed ⟨*pulp* left in orange juice⟩ **2** : the soft sensitive tissue that fills the central cavity of a tooth **3** : a material prepared chiefly from wood but also from other materials (as rags) and used in making paper products **4** : pulpy state ⟨beaten to a *pulp*⟩ **5** : a magazine or book on cheap paper and often dealing with sensational material

²pulp *vb* : to make into a pulp — **pulp·er** *n*

pul·pit \'pul-ˌpit *also* 'pəl-, -pət\ *n* **1** : a raised platform or high desk used in preaching or leading a worship service **2** : the preaching profession **3** : a job as a preacher

pulp·wood \'pəlp-ˌwud\ *n* : wood (as of aspen, hemlock, pine, or spruce) used in making pulp for paper

pulpy \'pəl-pē\ *adj* **pulp·i·er; -est** : resembling or consisting of pulp — **pulp·i·ness** *n*

pul·sate \'pəl-ˌsāt\ *vb* **pul·sat·ed; pul·sat·ing 1** : to throb or move rhythmically **2** : to exhibit a pulse or pulsation : BEAT ⟨a heart *pulsating*⟩

pul·sa·tion \ˌpəl-'sā-shən\ *n* : a rhythmic vibrating or expanding and contracting movement or action (as of an artery); *also* : a single throb of such movement

¹pulse \'pəls\ *n* : the edible seeds of several crops (as peas, beans, or lentils) of the legume family; *also* : a plant yielding pulse

²pulse *n* **1** : a regular throbbing caused in the arteries by the contractions of the heart **2 a** : rhythmical beating or throbbing **b** : PULSATION, BEAT, THROB **3 a** : a brief variation of a quantity (as electrical current) whose value is normally constant **b** : an electromagnetic wave or a sound wave lasting only a short length of time

³pulse *vb* **pulsed; puls·ing** : to display a pulse or pulsation ⟨the veins in his forehead *pulsed*⟩

pul·ver·ize \'pəl-və-ˌrīz\ *vb* **-ized; -iz·ing 1** : to beat or grind into a powder or dust **2** : to destroy as if by pulverizing

pu·ma \'p(y)ü-mə\ *n, pl* **pumas** *also* **puma** : COUGAR

pum·ice \'pəm-əs\ *n* : a very light glass that is formed by the rapid cooling of lava from volcanoes, is full of small holes, and is used especially in powder form for smoothing and polishing

pum·mel \'pəm-əl\ *vb* **-meled** *or* **-melled; -mel·ing** *or* **-mel·ling** \-(ə-)liŋ\ **1** : ³POUND 2a, BEAT ⟨knead and *pummel* the dough⟩ **2** : to defeat decisively ⟨*pummeled* the competition⟩

¹pump \'pəmp\ *n* : a device that raises, transfers, delivers, or compresses fluids especially by suction or pressure or both

²pump *vb* **1** : to raise, transfer, or compress by means of a pump ⟨*pump* up water⟩ **2** : to free (as from water or air) by the use of a pump ⟨*pump* a boat dry⟩ **3** : to fill by using a pump ⟨*pump* up a tire⟩ **4** : to draw, force, or drive onward in the manner of a pump ⟨the heart *pumps* blood into the arteries⟩ **5** : to move up and down like a pump handle ⟨*pump* the hand of a friend⟩ **6 a** : to question again and again to find out something **b** : to draw out by such questioning — **pump·er** *n*

³pump *n* : a low shoe gripping the foot chiefly at the toe and heel

pum·per·nick·el \'pəm-pər-ˌnik-əl\ *n* : a dark coarse somewhat sour rye bread

pump·kin \'pəm(p)-kən\ *n* **1** : the usually round orange fruit of a vine of the gourd family widely used as food;

also : a fruit (as a crookneck squash) of a closely related vine **2** : a usually hairy prickly vine that produces pumpkins **3** : a strong orange color

pump·kin·seed \-ˌsēd\ *n* **1** : a small brightly colored North American freshwater sunfish **2** : BLUEGILL

pun \'pən\ *n* : the humorous use of a word in such a way as to suggest different meanings or of words having the same sound but different meanings — **pun** *vb*

¹punch \'pənch\ *vb* **1 a** : ¹PROD 1, POKE **b** : ¹DRIVE 1a, HERD ⟨*punch* cattle⟩ **2 a** : to strike with the fist **b** : to press, strike, or cause to work by or as if by punching ⟨*punch* a typewriter⟩ **3** : to pierce or stamp with a punch **4** : to enter (as data) by punching keys [Middle English *pouncen, punchen* "emboss, pierce," probably from *pounce* "punching tool, dagger, talon"] — **punch·er** *n*

²punch *n* **1** : a quick blow with or as if with the fist **2** : effective force ⟨the team was well trained but lacked *punch*⟩

³punch *n* **1 a** : a tool for piercing, cutting, or stamping or for driving a nail **b** : a device or machine for cutting holes or notches (as in paper or cardboard) **2** : a hole or notch made by a punch

⁴punch *n* : a drink made of various and usually many ingredients and often flavored with wine or liquor [perhaps from a word in Hindi & Urdu (the official language of Pakistan) *pāc* "five"; so called from the fact that it originally had five ingredients]

pun·cheon \'pən-chən\ *n* : a large barrel of varying size

punc·til·io \ˌpəŋ(k)-'til-ē-ˌō\ *n, pl* **-ios 1** : a small but important detail of conduct in a ceremony or in following a set of rules **2** : careful following of set ways of doing things (as in social conduct)

punc·til·i·ous \ˌpəŋ(k)-'til-ē-əs\ *adj* : following exactly the details of proper ways of behaving — **punc·til·i·ous·ly** *adv* — **punc·til·i·ous·ness** *n*

punc·tu·al \'pəŋ(k)-chə-(-wə)l\ *adj* : acting or usually acting at an appointed time or at a regularly scheduled time ⟨the trains were *punctual*⟩ — **punc·tu·al·i·ty** \ˌpəŋ(k)-chə-'wal-ət-ē\ *n* — **punc·tu·al·ly** \'pəŋ(k)-chə-(-wə)-lē\ *adv*

punc·tu·ate \'pəŋ(k)-chə-ˌwāt\ *vb* **-at·ed; -at·ing 1** : to mark or divide with punctuation marks **2** : to interrupt at intervals ⟨a speech *punctuated* by a harsh cough⟩

punc·tu·a·tion \ˌpəŋ(k)-chə-'wā-shən\ *n* : the act, prac-

PUNCTUATION MARKS

.	period (*or chiefly Brit* full stop)
,	comma
;	semicolon
:	colon
'	apostrophe
' '	quotation marks, single (*or chiefly Brit* inverted commas)
" "	quotation marks, double (*or chiefly Brit* inverted commas)
« »	guillemets
?	question mark
¿ ?	question marks, Spanish
!	exclamation point
¡ !	exclamation points, Spanish
‽	interrobang
@	at sign
/	slash (*or diagonal or slant or solidus or virgule*)
\	backslash
. . .	ellipsis
-	hyphen
⹀	double hyphen
–	dash (*or en dash*)
—	dash (*or em dash*)
~	swung dash
( )	parentheses
[ ]	brackets, square (*or brackets*)
⟨ ⟩	brackets, angle
{ }	braces (*or curly brackets*)

tice, or system of inserting punctuation marks in written matter to make the meaning clear and separate parts (as clauses or sentences)

punctuation mark *n* : any of various marks or signs used in punctuation

¹**punc·ture** \'pəŋ(k)-chər\ *n* **1** : the act of puncturing **2** : a hole or wound made by puncturing ⟨a slight *puncture* of the skin⟩ ⟨a tire *puncture*⟩

²**puncture** *vb* **punc·tured; punc·tur·ing** \'pəŋ(k)-chə-riŋ, 'pəŋ(k)-shriŋ\ **1** : to make a hole with a point ⟨a nail *punctured* the tire⟩ **2** : to suffer a puncture of ⟨*punctured* the tire on a nail⟩ **3** : to become punctured ⟨worn tires *puncture* easily⟩ **4** : to make useless or ridiculous as if by a puncture ⟨*puncture* an argument⟩

pun·gen·cy \'pən-jən-sē\ *n* : the quality or state of being pungent

pun·gent \'pən-jənt\ *adj* **1** : sharply exciting to the mind ⟨*pungent* criticism⟩ ⟨*pungent* wit⟩ **2** : causing a sharp or irritating sensation; *esp* : sharp or harsh to the sense of taste or smell — **pun·gent·ly** *adv*

pun·ish \'pən-ish\ *vb* **1** : to cause to experience pain or suffering for having done wrong ⟨*punish* criminals with imprisonment⟩ **2** : to inflict punishment for ⟨*punish* misbehavior⟩ **3** : to deal with or handle severely or roughly ⟨badly *punished* by an opponent⟩ — **pun·ish·able** \-ə-bəl\ *adj* — **pun·ish·er** *n*

> **synonyms** PUNISH, DISCIPLINE mean to put a penalty on someone for doing wrong. PUNISH stresses giving some kind of pain or suffering to the wrongdoer rather than trying to reform the person ⟨*punished* the burglars by sending them to prison⟩. DISCIPLINE suggests penalizing the wrongdoer but stresses the effort to bring the person under control ⟨parents must *discipline* their children⟩.

pun·ish·ment \'pən-ish-mənt\ *n* **1 a** : the act of punishing **b** : the state or fact of being punished ⟨persons undergoing *punishment*⟩ **2** : the penalty for a fault or crime ⟨the *punishment* for robbery⟩ **3** : severe, rough, or disastrous treatment

pu·ni·tive \'pyü-nət-iv\ *adj* **1** : of or relating to punishment or penalties ⟨*punitive* law⟩ **2** : intended to inflict punishment ⟨a *punitive* expedition against outlaws⟩ — **pu·ni·tive·ly** *adv*

¹**punk** \'pəŋk\ *n* **1** : a petty gangster or hoodlum **2 a** : PUNK ROCK **b** : a punk rock musician **c** : a person who wears punk styles [origin unknown]

²**punk** *adj* **1** : very poor in quality ⟨played a *punk* game⟩ **2** : being in poor health ⟨feeling *punk* today⟩ **3 a** : of or relating to punk rock **b** : relating to or being a style (as of clothing or hair) first inspired by punk rock

punk rock *n* : rock music marked by extreme expressions of anger and social discontent

¹**punt** \'pənt\ *n* : a long narrow flat-bottomed boat with square ends usually pushed along with a pole [Old English *punt* "a flat-bottomed boat pushed along with a pole," from Latin *ponton-, ponto* "punt, floating bridge, pontoon" — related to PONTOON]

²**punt** *vb* : to propel (as a punt) with a pole

¹**punt**

³**punt** *vb* : to kick a football before it touches the ground when dropped from the hands [origin unknown] — **punt·er** *n*

⁴**punt** *n* : the act or an instance of punting a ball

pu·ny \'pyü-nē\ *adj* **pu·ni·er; -est** : slight or lesser in power, size, or importance : WEAK [from early French *puisné* "younger," literally, "born afterward," from *puis* "afterward" and *né* "born"] — **pu·ni·ness** *n*

pup \'pəp\ *n* : PUPPY; *also* : one of the young of various animals (as a seal or rat)

pu·pa \'pyü-pə\ *n, pl* **pu·pae** \-pē, -ˌpī\ *or* **pupas** : a stage of an insect (as a bee, moth, or beetle) having complete metamorphosis that occurs between the larva and the adult, is usually enclosed in a cocoon or case, and goes through changes inside by which structures of the larva are replaced by those of the adult — **pu·pal** \'pyü-pəl\ *adj*

pu·pate \'pyü-ˌpāt\ *vb* **pu·pat·ed; pu·pat·ing** : to become a pupa : pass through the stage of the pupa — **pu·pa·tion** \pyü-'pā-shən\ *n*

¹**pu·pil** \'pyü-pəl\ *n* **1** : a child or young person in school or in the care of a tutor or teacher **2** : one who has been taught or influenced by a person of fame : DISCIPLE [Middle English *pupille* "a child under the care of a guardian," from early French *pupille* (same meaning), from Latin *pupillus* "a boy under the care of a guardian" and *pupilla* "a girl under the care of a guardian"; *pupillus* derived from *pupus* "boy"; *pupilla* derived from *pupa* "girl, doll" — related to ²PUPIL]

²**pupil** *n* : the usually round opening in the iris that contracts and expands to control the amount of light entering the eye

> **Word History** If you look into another person's eye, you can see a small reflection of yourself. That small image made the ancient Romans think of a doll. Thus, they called the part of the eye in which it appears the *pupilla*. This word literally meant "little doll." The English word for that part of the eye, *pupil,* can be traced to the Latin *pupilla. Pupilla* also had another meaning. A little girl who was an orphan and was in the care of a guardian was called a *pupilla.* A little boy in the same situation was called a *pupillus.* From these two Latin words we get the other English *pupil,* meaning "a young student in the care of a tutor or in school." [derived from Latin *pupilla* "pupil of the eye, girl under care of a guardian," literally, "little doll," derived from *pupa* "doll, girl"; so called because the tiny image of oneself seen in another's eye is like a tiny doll]

pup·pet \'pəp-ət\ *n* **1** : a doll moved by hand or by strings or wires **2** : DOLL 1 **3** : a person or a government whose acts are controlled by an outside force or influence

pup·pe·teer \ˌpəp-ə-'ti(ə)r\ *n* : one who works puppets

pup·py \'pəp-ē\ *n, pl* **puppies** : a young domestic dog; *esp* : one less than a year old

pur·blind \'pər-ˌblīnd\ *adj* **1** : partly blind **2** : lacking in understanding

¹**pur·chase** \'pər-chəs\ *vb* **pur·chased; pur·chas·ing** : to get by paying money for : BUY ⟨*purchase* a house⟩ — **pur·chas·able** \-chə-sə-bəl\ *adj* — **pur·chas·er** *n*

²**purchase** *n* **1** : an act or instance of purchasing **2** : something purchased **3** : a secure hold, grasp, or place to stand ⟨could not get a *purchase* on the ledge⟩

pure \'pyu̇(ə)r\ *adj* **1** : not mixed with anything else : free from everything that might make dirty, change, or lower the quality ⟨*pure* water⟩ **2** : free from sin or guilt; *esp* : CHASTE 1 **3** : nothing other than ⟨*pure* nonsense⟩ **4** : not applied to everyday problems : THEORETICAL ⟨*pure* science⟩ ⟨*pure* mathematics⟩ **5 a** : of unmixed ancestry **b** : producing offspring which do not vary from the type of the parents or among themselves with respect to one or more characters

pure·bred \-'bred\ *adj* : bred from members of a recognized breed, strain, or kind without cross-breeding over many generations — **pure·bred** \-ˌbred\ *n*

¹**pu·ree** \pyu̇-'rā, -'rē\ *n* **1** : a paste or thick liquid usually

\ə\ abut	\au̇\ out	\i\ tip	\ȯ\ saw	\u̇\ foot
\ər\ further	\ch\ chin	\ī\ life	\ȯi\ coin	\y\ yet
\a\ mat	\e\ pet	\j\ job	\th\ thin	\yü\ few
\ā\ take	\ē\ easy	\ŋ\ sing	\t̲h̲\ this	\yu̇\ cure
\ä\ cot, cart	\g\ go	\ō\ bone	\ü\ food	\zh\ vision

made by rubbing cooked food through a sieve **2** : a thick soup having pureed vegetables as a base

²**puree** *vb* **pu·reed; pu·ree·ing** : to boil soft and then rub through a sieve

pure·ly \'pyů(ə)r-lē\ *adv* **1** : to the full or entire extent **2** : without the addition of anything harmful or different **3** : for no other reason than : ONLY ⟨done *purely* for fun⟩ **4** : in an innocent manner

¹**pur·ga·tive** \'pər-gət-iv\ *adj* : tending to act as a strong laxative

²**purgative** *n* : a strong laxative

pur·ga·to·ry \'pər-gə-ˌtōr-ē, -ˌtór-\ *n, pl* **-ries** : a state after death in which according to Roman Catholic belief the souls of those who die in God's grace are purified of their sins by suffering

¹**purge** \'pərj\ *vb* **purged; purg·ing** **1** : to make clean **2** : to have or cause strong and usually repeated emptying of the bowels

²**purge** *n* **1** : an act or instance of purging **2** : something that purges

pu·ri·fy \'pyůr-ə-ˌfī\ *vb* **-fied; -fy·ing** : to make or become pure — **pu·ri·fi·ca·tion** \ˌpyůr-ə-fə-'kā-shən\ *n* — **pu·ri·fi·er** \'pyůr-ə-ˌfī(-ə)r\ *n*

Pu·rim \'půr-(ˌ)im, půr-'im\ *n* : a Jewish holiday observed in February or March that celebrates the rescue of the Jews from a plot to massacre them [from Hebrew *pūrīm* (plural), literally, "lots cast in determining something by chance"; so called because Haman in the biblical story in Esther 9:24–26 cast lots to decide a day on which he planned to destroy the Jews]

pu·rine \'pyů(ə)r-ˌēn\ *n* : any of a group of bases including several (as adenine or guanine) that are important parts of DNA and RNA

pur·ism \'pyů(ə)r-ˌiz-əm\ *n* : a strict following of what is considered absolutely correct especially in the use of words — **pur·ist** \-əst\ *n*

pu·ri·tan \'pyůr-ət-ᵊn\ *n* **1** *cap* : a member of a 16th and 17th century Protestant group in England and New England opposing many customs of the Church of England **2** : one who practices or preaches a stricter moral code than is generally followed — **puritan** *adj, often cap* — **pu·ri·tan·i·cal** \ˌpyůr-ə-'tan-i-kəl\ *adj* — **pu·ri·tan·ism** \'pyůr-ət-ᵊn-ˌiz-əm\ *n, often cap*

pu·ri·ty \'pyůr-ət-ē\ *n* **1** : the quality or state of being pure : freedom from impurities **2** : freedom from guilt or sin

¹**purl** \'pərl\ *vb* : to invert the stitches in knitting [from obsolete *pirl* "to twist"]

²**purl** *n* **1** : a swirling stream **2** : a gentle murmur [perhaps of Scandinavian origin]

³**purl** *vb* **1** : ²EDDY, SWIRL **2** : to make a murmuring sound

pur·lieu \'pərl-ˌyü\ *n* **1** : an outlying or neighboring district **2** *pl* : SURROUNDINGS

pur·loin \(ˌ)pər-'lóin, 'pər-ˌlóin\ *vb* : ¹STEAL 2a — **pur·loin·er** *n*

¹**pur·ple** \'pər-pəl\ *adj* **pur·pler** \-p(ə-)lər\; **pur·plest** \-p(ə-)ləst\ : of the color purple

²**purple** *n* : a color midway between red and blue

³**purple** *vb* **pur·pled; pur·pling** \'pər-p(ə-)liŋ\ : to turn purple

Purple Heart *n* : a U.S. military decoration awarded to any member of the armed forces wounded or killed in action

pur·plish \'pər-p(ə-)lish\ *adj* : somewhat purple

¹**pur·port** \'pər-ˌpō(ə)rt, -ˌpô(ə)rt\ *n* **1** : meaning stated, suggested, or hinted **2** : the main point of a talk or subject

²**pur·port** \(ˌ)pər-'pō(ə)rt, -'pô(ə)rt\ *vb* : to give the impression of being ⟨*purports* to be a physician⟩

pur·pose \'pər-pəs\ *n* **1** : something set up as an end to be attained **2** : an object or result achieved ⟨worked to little *purpose*⟩ **synonyms** see INTENTION — **pur·pose·ful** \-fəl\ *adj* — **pur·pose·ful·ly** \-fə-lē\ *adv* — **pur·pose·ful·**

ness \-fəl-nəs\ *n* — **pur·pose·less** \-pəs-ləs\ *adj* — **on purpose** : by intention

pur·pose·ly \'pər-pəs-lē\ *adv* : with a clear or known purpose

purr \'pər\ *n* : a low murmuring sound of a contented cat — **purr** *vb*

¹**purse** \'pərs\ *n* **1** : a small container (as a wallet) for money; *esp* : a woman's pocketbook **2** : a source of supply or support **3** : a sum of money offered as a prize or present [Old English *purs* "a small bag for money, purse," from Latin *bursa* "purse," from earlier *bursa* "oxhide," from Greek *byrsa* (same meaning) — related to DISBURSE, REIMBURSE]

²**purse** *vb* **pursed; purs·ing** **1** : to put into a purse **2** : ¹PUCKER ⟨*pursed* lips⟩

purs·er \'pər-sər\ *n* : an official on a ship who keeps accounts and attends to passengers

pur·su·ance \pər-'sü-ən(t)s\ *n* : the act of pursuing or carrying out ⟨in *pursuance* of their plans⟩

pur·su·ant to \pər-'sü-ənt-\ *prep* : in carrying out : ACCORDING TO

pur·sue \pər-'sü\ *vb* **pur·sued; pur·su·ing** **1** : to follow in order to catch up with and seize **2** : to try to obtain or accomplish : SEEK ⟨*pursue* pleasure⟩ **3** : to proceed along ⟨*pursue* a northerly course⟩ **4** : to engage in : PRACTICE ⟨*pursue* a hobby⟩ **5** : to continue to distress severely : HAUNT ⟨*pursued* by fear⟩ [Middle English *pursuen* "to follow in order to capture or kill," derived from early French *pursure, pursiure* (same meaning), derived from Latin *prosequi* "to follow after, pursue," from *pro-* "forward" and *sequi* "to follow" — related to SEQUEL] **synonyms** see CHASE — **pur·su·er** *n*

pur·suit \pər-'süt\ *n* **1** : the act of pursuing **2** : an activity done especially for pleasure

pur·vey \(ˌ)pər-'vā, 'pər-ˌvā\ *vb* **pur·veyed; pur·vey·ing** : to supply usually as a business — **pur·vey·ance** \-ən(t)s\ *n* — **pur·vey·or** \-ər\ *n*

pus \'pəs\ *n* : thick cloudy usually yellowish white fluid matter formed at a place of inflammation and infection (as an abscess) and containing white blood cells, tissue debris, and germs

¹**push** \'půsh\ *vb* **1** : to press against with force in order to drive **2** : to force forward, downward, or outward **3** : to go or make go ahead ⟨*push* the job to completion⟩ **4** : to press hard against so as to involve in difficulty ⟨was *pushed* for time⟩ **5** : to engage in the sale of (illegal drugs)

²**push** *n* **1** : a strong advance against obstacles **2** : a sudden thrust : SHOVE **3** : a steady applying of force in a direction away from the body from which it comes

push–button *adj* **1** : operated or done by means of push buttons ⟨a *push-button* phone⟩ **2** : using or dependent on complicated automatic machines ⟨*push-button* warfare⟩ ⟨a *push-button* civilization⟩

push button *n* : a small button or knob that when pushed operates something especially by closing an electric circuit

push·cart \'půsh-ˌkärt\ *n* : a cart pushed by hand

push·er \'půsh-ər\ *n* **1** : one that pushes **2** : a seller of illegal drugs

push·over \'půsh-ˌō-vər\ *n* **1** : an opponent easy to defeat or incapable of resistance **2** : someone unable to resist an attraction or appeal **3** : something easily done : SNAP

push–up \'půsh-ˌəp\ *n* : an exercise performed while lying facedown by raising and lowering the body with the straightening and bending of the arms

pu·sil·lan·i·mous \ˌpyü-sə-'lan-ə-məs\ *adj* : COWARDLY

¹**puss** \'půs\ *n* **1** : CAT 1a **2** : GIRL 1 [origin unknown]

²**puss** *n, slang* : ¹FACE 1 [from Irish *pus* "mouth"]

pussy \'půs-ē\ *n, pl* **puss·ies** **1** : CAT 1a **2** : a catkin of the pussy willow

pussy·foot \-ˌfůt\ *vb* **1** : to walk or move in a careful or sneaky manner **2** : to avoid taking a firm stand (as in a dispute)

pussy willow *n* : a willow having large silky catkins

pus·tule \'pəs-chü(ə)l\ *n* **1** : a small elevation of the skin having an inflamed base and containing pus **2** : a small elevation resembling a pimple or blister

¹put \'pu̇t\ *vb* **put; put·ting 1 a** : to place in or move into a position or relationship ⟨*put* the book down⟩ **b** : to throw with an overhand pushing motion ⟨*put* the shot⟩ **c** : to bring into a state or condition ⟨*put* it to use⟩ ⟨*put* the matter right⟩ ⟨*put* us at risk⟩ **2 a** : to cause to undergo something ⟨was *put* to death⟩ **b** : IMPOSE 1a ⟨*put* a special tax on luxuries⟩ **3** : to set before one for judgment or decision (as by a formal vote) ⟨*put* the motion⟩ **4** : ⁴EXPRESS 1a ⟨*put* your feelings into words⟩ **5 a** : to devote or urge to an activity or end ⟨*put* them to work⟩ **b** : ²INVEST 1 ⟨*put* our money in the company⟩ **6 a** : ¹ESTIMATE 1 ⟨*put* the time at about eleven⟩ **b** : ATTACH 5 ⟨*puts* a high value on friendship⟩ **7** : ¹GO 1, PROCEED ⟨the ship *put* to sea⟩ — **put forth 1** : DISCLOSE, ISSUE **2** : to bring into action **3** : to produce or send out by growth ⟨*put forth* leaves⟩ — **put forward** : PROPOSE 1 ⟨*put forward* a theory⟩ — **put in mind** : REMIND — **put together 1** : to create as a whole : CONSTRUCT **2** : ADD 1b, COMBINE — **put to it** : to give difficulty to ⟨was *put to it* to keep up⟩

²put *n* : a throw made with an overhand pushing motion

³put *adj* : FIXED 1a, SET ⟨stay *put* until I come back⟩

put about *vb* : to change course or direction ⟨after sailing north, they *put about* and headed east⟩

put across *vb* : to gain or communicate successfully ⟨*put across* a plan⟩

put by *vb* : to lay aside : SAVE ⟨have money *put by* for an emergency⟩

put down *vb* **1** : to bring to an end by force ⟨*put down* a riot⟩ **2** : to write down (as in a list) **3** : BELITTLE, CRITICIZE — **put–down** \'pu̇t-ˌdau̇n\ *n*

put in *vb* **1** : to make or make as a request, offer, or declaration ⟨*put in* a plea of guilty⟩ ⟨*put in* for a job at the store⟩ **2** : to spend at some activity or place ⟨*put in* six hours at the office⟩ **3** : ¹PLANT 1a ⟨*put in* a crop⟩ **4** : to enter a harbor or port ⟨the freighter *put in* for overnight⟩

put off *vb* **1** : to cause negative feelings in ⟨your sloppy appearance *put* them *off*⟩ **2** : to hold back to a later time : DEFER ⟨*put off* my visit to the dentist⟩ **3** : to rid oneself of ⟨*put off* your coat⟩

put–on \'pu̇t-ˌȯn, -ˌän\ *n* **1** : a false appearance or presentation ⟨my bravery was all a *put-on*⟩ **2** : a joke in which someone is fooled

put on \(')pu̇t-'ȯn, -'än\ *vb* **1 a** : to dress oneself in **b** : to make part of one's appearance or behavior **c** : ¹PRETEND 1 ⟨*put on* a show of anger⟩ **2** : EXAGGERATE, OVERSTATE ⟨they're *putting* it *on* when they make such claims⟩ **3** : PERFORM 3b, PRODUCE ⟨*put on* an entertaining act⟩ **4** : ²KID 1, FOOL ⟨you're *putting* me *on*⟩ — **put–on** *adj*

put–out \'pu̇t-ˌau̇t\ *n* : the act of causing a base runner or batter to be out in baseball

put out \ˌpu̇t-'au̇t, 'pu̇t-\ *vb* **1** : EXTINGUISH 1 ⟨*put* the fire *out*⟩ **2** : EXERT 1, USE ⟨*put out* all my strength to move the piano⟩ **3** : ¹PRODUCE 4 **4** : IRRITATE 1, PROVOKE ⟨my father was *put out* by my failure⟩ **5** : to cause to be out (as in baseball) **6** : to set out from shore ⟨Columbus *put out* for the New World⟩

put over *vb* : PUT ACROSS ⟨*put over* a song⟩

pu·tre·fac·tion \ˌpyü-trə-'fak-shən\ *n* **1** : the rotting of organic matter **2** : the state of being putrefied : CORRUPTION

pu·tre·fy \'pyü-trə-ˌfī\ *vb* **-fied; -fy·ing** : to make or become putrid : ROT 1a

pu·trid \'pyü-trəd\ *adj* **1 a** : being in a state of putrefac-

tion : ROTTEN ⟨*putrid* meat⟩ **b** : characteristic of putrefaction : FOUL ⟨a *putrid* odor⟩ **2** : morally objectionable

putt \'pət\ *n* : a golf stroke made to cause the ball to roll into or near the hole — **putt** *vb*

¹put·ter \'pu̇t-ər\ *n* : one that puts [from *put* and *-er* (noun suffix)]

²putt·er \'pət-ər\ *n* **1** : a golf club used in putting **2** : a person who putts [from *putt* and *-er* (noun suffix)]

³put·ter \'pət-ər\ *vb* **1** : to move or act without obvious purpose **2** : to work by chance or without skill [an altered form of earlier *potter* "to move about idly without aim or purpose"] — **put·ter·er** \-ər-ər\ *n*

put through *vb* : to carry to a conclusion ⟨*put through* a number of reforms⟩

putting *present participle of* PUT

¹put·ty \'pət-ē\ *n, pl* **putties** : a soft cement (as for holding glass in a window frame)

²putty *vb* **put·tied; put·ty·ing** : to cement or seal up with putty

putty knife *n* : a tool with a broad flat metal blade used especially for applying putty and for scraping

put up *vb* **1 a** : to prepare for later use ⟨*put up* a lunch⟩; *esp* : ³CAN 1 ⟨*put up* peaches⟩ **b** : to put away out of use ⟨*put up* your sword⟩ **2 a** : to nominate for election **b** : to offer for public sale ⟨*put* their possessions *up* for auction⟩ **3** : to give or obtain food and shelter : LODGE ⟨*put* us *up* overnight⟩ **4** : ¹BUILD 1, ERECT **5** : CARRY ON 2 ⟨*put up* a struggle⟩ **6** : to make available ⟨*put up* a prize for the best essay⟩ — **put up to** : to urge or cause to do ⟨*put* them *up to* doing the stunts⟩ — **put up with** : to endure or tolerate without complaint or attempt at retaliation ⟨*put up with* their insults⟩

¹puz·zle \'pəz-əl\ *vb* **puz·zled; puz·zling** \-(ə-)liŋ\ **1** : to confuse the understanding of **2** : to solve with difficulty or cleverness — **puz·zler** \-(ə-)lər\ *n*

synonyms PUZZLE, PERPLEX, MYSTIFY mean to baffle (someone) by preventing the understanding of something. PUZZLE suggests that a particular part of something is hard to understand or explain ⟨it is the cause of the disease that *puzzles* doctors⟩. PERPLEX adds a suggestion of worry or distress ⟨*perplexed* by the sudden departure of their friend⟩. MYSTIFY stresses the completeness of one's failure to understand ⟨the magic trick *mystified* the audience⟩.

²puzzle *n* **1** : PUZZLEMENT 1 **2 a** : something that puzzles **b** : a question, problem, or device designed for testing skill or cleverness **synonyms** see MYSTERY

puz·zle·ment \'pəz-əl-mənt\ *n* **1** : the state of being puzzled **2** : ²PUZZLE 2a

pyg·my \'pig-mē\ *n, pl* **pygmies 1** *cap* : one of a small people of equatorial Africa ranging under five feet (1.5 meters) in height **2** : a person or thing very small for its kind : DWARF — **pygmy** *adj*

Word History In ancient Greek the word *pygmē* was used to mean "a measure of length from the elbow to the knuckles." It also came to refer to the fist. From this word Greek writers formed the word *pygmaios* for "a tiny person no longer than the forearm." They were assumed to be writing about imaginary figures, not real people. Later, this Greek word was taken into Latin as *pygmaeus*, meaning "dwarf." From Latin *pygmaeus* English formed the word *pygmy*. In the 19th century this word was applied to a member of a race of small people found living in Africa. [Middle English *pigmei* "pygmy, dwarf," from Latin *pygmaeus* (noun and adjective) "pygmy, dwarfish," from Greek *pygmaios* (same meaning), liter-

\ə\ **abut**	\au̇\ **out**	\i\ **tip**	\ȯ\ **saw**	\u̇\ **foot**
\ər\ **further**	\ch\ **chin**	\ī\ **life**	\ȯi\ **coin**	\y\ **yet**
\a\ **mat**	\e\ **pet**	\j\ **job**	\th\ **thin**	\yü\ **few**
\ā\ **take**	\ē\ **easy**	\ŋ\ **sing**	\th\ **this**	\yu̇\ **cure**
\ä\ **cot, cart**	\g\ **go**	\ō\ **bone**	\ü\ **food**	\zh\ **vision**

ally, "one no longer than the forearm," from *pygmē* "fist, measure of length from the elbow to the knuckles"]

py·ja·mas \pə-'jä-məz\ *chiefly British variant of* PAJAMAS

py·lon \'pī-ˌlän, -lən\ *n* **1** : a tower for supporting a long span of wire; *also* : any of various structures like a tower **2** : a post or tower marking a prescribed course of flight for an airplane

py·lo·rus \pī-'lōr-əs, -'lȯr-\ *n, pl* **-lo·ri** \-'lō(ə)r-ˌī, -ˌē\ : the opening in a vertebrate animal from the stomach into the intestine — **py·lo·ric** \pī-'lȯr-ik, pə-, -'lȯr-\ *adj*

py·or·rhea \ˌpī-ə-'rē-ə\ *n* : an inflammation with pus of the sockets of the teeth leading usually to loosening of the teeth

¹pyr·a·mid \'pir-ə-ˌmid\ *n*
1 : a massive structure built especially in ancient Egypt that usually has a square base and four triangular sides meeting at a point **2** : something that resembles a pyramid in shape or organization ⟨the social *pyramid*⟩ **3** : a polyhedron that has a polygon for its base and triangles that meet at a point at the top for its sides — **py·ra·mi·dal** \pə-'ram-əd-ᵊl, ˌpir-ə-'mid-\ *adj*

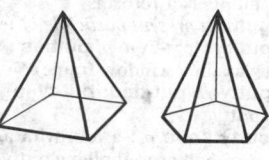

¹pyramid 3

²pyramid *vb* : to build up in the form of a pyramid

pyre \'pī(ə)r\ *n* : a heap of wood for burning a dead body; *also* : a pile of material to be burned

py·re·thrum \pī-'rē-thrəm, -'reth-rəm\ *n* **1** : any of several chrysanthemums that have finely divided leaves and include ornamental plants as well as important sources of insecticides **2** : an insecticide consisting of the dried heads of some Old World pyrethrums

Py·rex \'pī(ə)r-ˌeks\ *trademark* — used for glass and glassware that is resistant to heat, chemicals, and electricity

pyr·i·dox·ine \ˌpir-ə-'däk-ˌsēn, -sən\ *n* : an alcohol of the vitamin B₆ group found especially in cereals

py·rim·i·dine \pī-'rim-ə-ˌdēn, pə-\ *n* : any of a group of bases including several (as cytosine and thymine) that are important parts of DNA or RNA

py·rite \'pī-ˌrīt\ *n* : a common mineral that consists of iron combined with sulfur, has a pale brass-yellow color and metallic luster, and is used especially in making sulfuric acid

pyro- *combining form* : fire : heat [derived from Greek *pyr-* "fire"]

py·ro·lu·site \ˌpī-rō-'lü-ˌsīt\ *n* : a mineral consisting of manganese dioxide that is of an iron-black or dark steel-gray color and metallic luster, is usually soft, and is the most important ore of manganese

py·ro·ma·nia \ˌpī-rō-'mā-nē-ə\ *n* : an abnormal continuous desire to start fires

py·ro·ma·ni·ac \-ˌak\ *n* : a person who exhibits pyromania

py·rox·ene \pī-'räk-ˌsēn\ *n* : any of various silicate minerals that usually contain aluminum, calcium, sodium, magnesium, or iron

py·ru·vic acid \pī-ˌrü-vik-\ *n* : an acid that can be formed from either glucose or glycogen and is an important chemical in the production of energy from food in animals

Pythagorean theorem *n* : a theorem in geometry: the square of the length of the hypotenuse of a right triangle equals the sum of the squares of the lengths of the other two sides

py·thon \'pī-ˌthän, -thən\ *n* : any of various large nonpoisonous snakes especially of Africa, Asia, and Australia that squeeze and suffocate their prey and include some of the largest snakes living at the present time

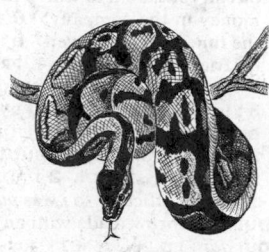

python

Word History *Python* in Greek legend, was the name of a monstrous serpent that lived in the caves of Mt. Parnassus near the town of Delphi. This serpent attacked the mother of the god Apollo. Zeus, fortunately, came to her aid and removed her to a place of safety. Later, Apollo sought revenge for the attack. With bow and arrow he hunted the dreaded Python. After struggling with and finally slaying the serpent, Apollo buried it in the temple at Delphi. To celebrate this victory a festival of games was held, including athletic and musical contests and a dramatic performance of Apollo's slaying of Python. These games continued to be held every four years until the 4th century A.D. They were called the Pythian games and ranked second to the Olympic games in popularity. Its was not until the 19th century that the word *python* was used for a large snake that crushes its prey. [named for *Python,* a monstrous serpent in Greek Legend]

Q

q \'kyü\ *n, often cap* : the 17th letter of the English alphabet

Q-tip \'kyü-ˌtip\ *trademark* — used for a cotton-tipped swab

¹quack \'kwak\ *n* : the cry of a duck; *also* : a sound resembling this cry [a word created to imitate the sound made by a duck]

²quack *vb* : to make a quack

³quack *n* : a person who makes false claims to special knowledge or ability; *esp* : one who pretends to have medical skill [a shortened form of earlier *quacksalver* "a person who pretends to have medical skill"; of Dutch origin]

⁴quack *adj* : of, relating to, or used by a person who is a quack ⟨*quack* medicines⟩

quack·ery \'kwak-(ə-)rē\ *n* : the practices or claims of a quack

quack grass *n* : a European grass that is found throughout North America as a weed and that spreads by creeping underground stems

quad \'kwäd\ *n* : QUADRUPLET

quad·ran·gle \'kwäd-ˌraŋ-gəl\ *n* **1** : ²QUADRILATERAL **2 a** : a four-sided enclosure especially when surrounded by buildings **b** : the buildings enclosing a quadrangle — **qua·dran·gu·lar** \kwä-'draŋ-gyə-lər\ *adj*

quad·rant \'kwäd-rənt\ *n* **1** : an arc of 90° : one quarter of a circle **2** : any of the four quarters into which something is divided by two real or imaginary lines that intersect each other at right angles

quad·ra·phon·ic \ˌkwäd-rə-'fän-ik\ *adj* : of or relating to the transmission, recording, or reproduction of sound using four transmission channels

¹qua·drat·ic \kwä-'drat-ik\ *adj* : involving or consisting of terms in which no variable is

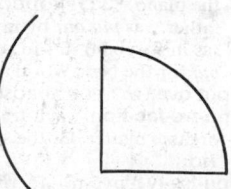

quadrant 1

raised to a power higher than 2 ⟨a *quadratic* expression⟩ ⟨a *quadratic* function⟩

²**quadratic** *n* : a quadratic polynomial or equation

quadratic equation *n* : an equation containing one term in which the unknown is squared and no term in which it is raised to a power higher than 2 ⟨solve for *x* in the *quadratic equation* $x^2 - 4x + 4 = 0$⟩

quadratic formula *n* : a formula that gives the solutions of the general quadratic equation $ax^2 + bx + c = 0$ and that is usually written in the form

$$x = \frac{-b \pm \sqrt{b^2 - 4ac}}{2a}$$

quadri- *or* **quadr-** *or* **quadru-** *combining form* : four [derived from Latin *quattuor* "four"]

¹**quad·ri·lat·er·al** \ˌkwäd-rə-ˈlat-ə-rəl, -ˈla-trəl\ *adj* : having four sides

²**quadrilateral** *n* : a polygon with four sides and four angles

qua·drille \kwä-ˈdril, k(w)ə-\ *n* : a square dance for four couples or music for this dance

qua·dril·lion \kwä-ˈdril-yən\ *n* — see NUMBER table

quad·ri·ple·gic \ˌkwäd-rə-ˈplē-jik\ *n* : a person who is paralyzed in both arms and both legs

quad·ru·ped \ˈkwäd-rə-ˌped\ *n* : an animal having four feet

¹**qua·dru·ple** \kwä-ˈdrüp-əl, -ˈdrəp-; ˈkwäd-rəp-\ *vb* **qua·dru·pled; qua·dru·pling** \-(ə-)liŋ\ : to make or become four times as great or as many

²**quadruple** *adj* **1** : having four units or members **2** : being four times as great or as many **3** : marked by four beats per measure ⟨*quadruple* time⟩ — **quadruple** *n*

qua·dru·plet \kwä-ˈdrü-plət, -ˈdrəp-lət; ˈkwäd-rə-plət\ *n* **1** : a combination of four of a kind **2** : one of four offspring born at one birth

qua·dru·pli·cate \kwä-ˈdrü-pli-kət\ *n* **1** : four copies all alike — used with *in* ⟨papers typed in *quadruplicate*⟩ **2** : one of four things exactly alike; *esp* : one of four identical copies

quaff \ˈkwäf, ˈkwaf\ *vb* : to drink freely — **quaff** *n*

quag·mire \ˈkwag-ˌmī(ə)r, ˈkwäg-\ *n* **1** : soft spongy wet ground that shakes or gives way under the foot **2** : a difficult situation from which it is hard to escape

¹**quail** \ˈkwā(ə)l\ *n, pl* **quail** *or* **quails** : any of various mostly small plump game birds (as the bobwhite) that are related to the common domestic chicken [Middle English *quaile* "quail (bird)," from early French *quaile* (same meaning), from Latin *quaccula* (same meaning), of imitative origin]

¹quail

²**quail** *vb* : to lose courage : shrink in fear [Middle English *quailen* "to wither, decline," from early Dutch *quelen* (same meaning)]

quaint \ˈkwānt\ *adj* : unusual or different in quality or appearance; *esp* : pleasingly old-fashioned or unfamiliar ⟨a *quaint* fishing village⟩ — **quaint·ly** *adv* — **quaint·ness** *n*

¹**quake** \ˈkwāk\ *vb* **quaked; quak·ing** **1** : to shake or vibrate usually from shock or lack of stability **2** : to tremble or shudder usually from cold or fear

²**quake** *n* : a shaking or trembling; *esp* : EARTHQUAKE

quak·er \ˈkwā-kər\ *n* **1** : one that quakes **2** *cap* : FRIEND 4 — **Quak·er·ism** \-kə-ˌriz-əm\ *n*

qual·i·fi·ca·tion \ˌkwäl-ə-fə-ˈkā-shən\ *n* **1** : the act or an instance of qualifying **2** : the state of being qualified **3 a** : a special skill, knowledge, or ability that fits a person for

a particular work or position **b** : a condition that must be met (as to gain a privilege)

qual·i·fied \ˈkwäl-ə-ˌfīd\ *adj* **1** : having the necessary qualifications : FITTED **2** : limited in some way ⟨a *qualified* yes to the question⟩

qual·i·fi·er \ˈkwäl-ə-ˌfī-(ə)r\ *n* **1** : a person or thing that meets requirements **2** : a word or word group that limits the meaning of another word or word group : MODIFIER

qual·i·fy \ˈkwäl-ə-ˌfī\ *vb* **-fied; -fy·ing** **1 a** : to make less general or more limited : MODIFY ⟨*qualify* a statement⟩ **b** : to make less harsh or strict : MODERATE ⟨*qualify* a punishment⟩ **c** : to limit the meaning of (as a noun) **2** : to describe in a particular way ⟨would you *qualify* her as smart⟩ **3 a** : to fit or be fit (as by training, skill, or ability) for a special purpose ⟨*qualify* for a race⟩ **b** : ²LICENSE ⟨*qualified* to practice law⟩

qual·i·ta·tive \ˈkwäl-ə-ˌtāt-iv\ *adj* : of, relating to, or involving quality or kind — **qual·i·ta·tive·ly** *adv*

qual·i·ty \ˈkwäl-ət-ē\ *n, pl* **-ties** **1 a** : basic and individual nature ⟨a person with a kindly *quality*⟩ **b** : a basic characteristic ⟨hardness is a *quality* of steel⟩ **2** : grade of excellence ⟨food of high *quality*⟩ **3** : high social rank ⟨marry a person of *quality*⟩ **4** : something that sets a person or thing apart **5** : TIMBRE

quality point *n* : GRADE POINT

quality point average *n* : GRADE POINT AVERAGE

qualm \ˈkwäm, ˈkwälm *also* ˈkwȯm\ *n* **1** : a sudden attack of illness, faintness, or nausea **2** : a sudden fear **3** : a feeling of doubt or indecision in matters of right and wrong ⟨had *qualms* about coming home late⟩ — **qualmy** \-ē\ *adj*

> **synonyms** QUALM, SCRUPLE, COMPUNCTION mean an uneasy feeling about what one is doing or going to do. QUALM suggests an uneasy fear that one is not following one's conscience or better judgment ⟨started having *qualms* about going along with the crowd⟩. SCRUPLE suggests doubt about the rightness of an act based upon one's moral code ⟨citizens with *scruples* won't cheat on their taxes⟩. COMPUNCTION suggests an inner feeling that one is doing wrong to another person ⟨don't you have any *compunctions* about spreading gossip?⟩.

qualm·ish \ˈkwäm-ish, ˈkwälm- *also* ˈkwȯm-ish\ *adj* **1** : feeling qualms : NAUSEATED **2** : of, relating to, or producing qualms — **qualm·ish·ness** *n*

quan·da·ry \ˈkwän-d(ə-)rē\ *n, pl* **-ries** : a state of confusion or doubt : DILEMMA ⟨in a *quandary* about which to choose⟩

quan·ti·ta·tive \ˈkwän(t)-ə-ˌtāt-iv\ *adj* : of, relating to, or involving the measurement of quantity — **quan·ti·ta·tive·ly** *adv* — **quan·ti·ta·tive·ness** *n*

quan·ti·ty \ˈkwän(t)-ət-ē\ *n, pl* **-ties** **1 a** : an amount or number that is not fixed **b** : a great amount or number ⟨buys food in *quantity*⟩ **2 a** : the character of something that makes it possible to measure or number it **b** : something on which a mathematical operation can be performed ⟨multiply the *quantity* x by y⟩ [Middle English *quantite* "amount," from early French *quantité* (same meaning), derived from Latin *quantus* "how much?, how large?"]

¹**quan·tum** \ˈkwänt-əm\ *n, pl* **quan·ta** \ˈkwänt-ə\ : the smallest amount of many forms of energy (as light)

²**quantum** *adj* : of or relating to the principles of quantum theory ⟨*quantum* physics⟩

quantum theory *n* : a theory in physics based on the idea that radiant energy (as light) is composed of small separate packets of energy

¹**quar·an·tine** \'kwȯr-ən-ˌtēn, 'kwär-\ *n* **1** : a period during which a ship arriving in port and suspected of carrying contagious disease is forbidden contact with the shore **2** : a limiting or forbidding of movements of persons or goods that is designed to prevent the spread of disease or pests **3** : the period during which a person with a contagious disease is under quarantine **4** : a place where persons are kept in quarantine

Word History As bad as contagious diseases are today, they were much more frightening in the Middle Ages. No effective treatment or cure was known then. When it was found out that ships could carry diseases from port to port, authorities acted to protect their citizens. Any ship suspected of carrying a disease was forced to remain offshore for a time. Usually about forty days had to pass before it was allowed to dock. Then if no signs of disease were found on the ship, it was allowed to unload its passengers and cargo. The Italians called this restriction period *quarantena*. They based the word on a French word *quarantaine*, meaning "a period of forty days." This French word was derived from the Latin *quadraginta*, meaning "forty." It was the Italian word that was taken into English as *quarantine* in the 17th century. [from Italian *quarantena* "quarantine, period of forty days," probably from early French *quarantaine* "period of forty days," from earlier *quarante* "forty," from Latin *quadraginta* "forty," from *quadra-* "four"]

²**quarantine** *vb* **-tined; -tin·ing** : to put or hold in quarantine : ISOLATE

quark \'kwȯrk, 'kwärk\ *n* : any of several particles that are believed to be components of heavier particles (as protons or neutrons)

¹**quar·rel** \'kwȯr-(-ə)l, 'kwär-(-ə)l\ *n* **1** : a cause of dispute or complaint **2** : an angry difference of opinion : DISPUTE

²**quarrel** *vb* **-reled** *or* **-relled; -rel·ing** *or* **-rel·ling** **1** : to find fault ⟨I *quarrel* with your version of what happened⟩ **2** : to argue forcefully or loudly : SQUABBLE — **quar·rel·er** *or* **quar·rel·ler** *n*

quar·rel·some \'kwȯr-(-ə)l-səm, 'kwär-(-ə)l-\ *adj* : usually ready to quarrel **synonyms** see BELLIGERENT

¹**quar·ry** \'kwȯr-ē, 'kwär-\ *n, pl* **quarries** **1** : an animal hunted as game or prey **2** : something sought or chased after

Word History The quarry a hunter chases is not related to the quarry that supplies building stones. The word for a hunter's quarry can be traced back to a ceremony that was once part of every successful hunt. The hounds used for chasing the game were rewarded after the kill by being allowed to eat part of the dead animal, which was given to them on a piece of hide. The French word for this hounds' share was *cureie* or *quereie*, which was borrowed into Middle English as *querre*. The word later came to be used for the live game animal itself. Now a quarry is anything that is pursued. [Middle English *querre* "the part of a game animal given to the hounds," from early French *cureie, quereie* (same meaning), from *cuir* "skin, hide" (on which the animal parts were placed), from Latin *corium* (same meaning)]

²**quarry** *n, pl* **quarries** : an open pit usually for obtaining building stone, slate, or limestone [Middle English *quarey*, an altered form of *quarrere* "a place for digging stones for use in building," from Latin *quadrus* "hewn stone," literally, "squared stone," from Latin *quadrum* "a square"]

³**quarry** *vb* **quar·ried; quar·ry·ing** **1** : to dig or take from or as if from a quarry **2** : to make a quarry in — **quar·ri·er** *n*

quart \'kwȯ(ə)rt\ *n* **1** — see MEASURE table **2** : a container or measure having a capacity of one quart

¹**quar·ter** \'kwȯ(r)t-ər\ *n* **1** : one of four equal parts **2** : a unit (as of weight or length) that equals one fourth of some larger unit **3 a** : any of four 3-month divisions of a year **b** : a school term of about 12 weeks **c** : a coin worth

a fourth of a dollar **d** : the sum of 25 cents **e** : one fourth part of a slaughtered animal including a leg ⟨a *quarter* of beef⟩ **f** : a fourth part of the moon's period ⟨a moon in its first *quarter*⟩ **g** : one of the four equal parts into which the playing time of some games is divided **4** : someone or something (as a place, direction, or group) not named ⟨complaints came from all *quarters*⟩ **5 a** : a particular division or district of a city **b** : an assigned station especially of a member of a crew ⟨call to *quarters*⟩ **c** *pl* : the place where one lives : LODGING **6** : MERCY 1a ⟨show no *quarter* to the enemy⟩ [Middle English *quarter* "a fourth part," from early French *quarter* (same meaning), derived from Latin *quartus* "a fourth"] — **at close quarters** : at close range or in immediate contact

²**quarter** *vb* **1 a** : to divide into four equal parts **b** : to separate into parts ⟨peel and *quarter* an orange⟩ **2** : to provide with lodging or shelter

³**quarter** *adj* : consisting of or equal to a quarter

quar·ter·back \'kwȯ(r)t-ər-ˌbak\ *n* : an offensive football back who calls the signals and directs the offensive play of the team — **quarterback** *vb*

quar·ter·deck \-ˌdek\ *n* : the part of the upper deck that is located toward the rear of a ship

quarter horse *n* : any of a breed of stocky muscular horses capable of high speed for short distances

quarter horse

Word History *Quarter horse* might seem like a strange name for an animal that is not only full-sized but quite sturdy and muscular. However, the breed gets its name not because it is a fraction of a horse but because it can run very fast for short distances. Unlike the slender, long-legged Thoroughbred horse, the compact quarter horse is built for quick bursts of speed. For about a quarter-mile the quarter horse probably can run faster than any other breed of horse. After that distance the quarter horse begins to slow down and can be beaten in a race with other horses.

quarter hour *n* **1** : any of the quarter points of an hour **2** : 15 minutes

quar·ter·ing \'kwȯ(r)t-ə-riŋ\ *adj* : coming from a direction behind and to the side (as of a ship) ⟨a *quartering* wind⟩

¹**quar·ter·ly** \'kwȯ(r)t-ər-lē\ *adv* : four times a year ⟨interest compounded *quarterly*⟩

²**quarterly** *adj* : coming or happening every three months ⟨*quarterly* premium⟩ ⟨*quarterly* meeting⟩

³**quarterly** *n, pl* **-lies** : a magazine published four times a year

quar·ter·mas·ter \'kwȯ(r)t-ər-ˌmas-tər\ *n* : an army officer who provides clothing and supplies for troops

quarter note *n* : a musical note equal in time to ¼ of a whole note

quarter rest *n* : a musical rest equal in time to a quarter note

quar·ter·staff \'kwȯ(r)t-ər-ˌstaf\ *n, pl* **-staves** \-ˌstavz, -ˌstāvz\ : a long strong staff used long ago as a weapon

quar·tet *also* **quar·tette** \kwȯr-'tet\ *n* **1 a** : a musical composition for four instruments or voices **b** : the performers of a quartet **2** : a group or set of four

quar·to \'kwȯrt-ō\ *n, pl* **quartos** : a book made up of sheets of paper that have been folded into four leaves

quartz \'kwȯ(ə)rts\ *n* : a common mineral consisting of silicon dioxide that is often found in the form of colorless transparent crystals but is sometimes (as in amethysts, agates, and jaspers) brightly colored

quartz·ite \'kwȯrt-ˌsīt\ *n* : a compact grainy rock composed of quartz and made from sandstone by the earth's heat and pressure

qua·sar \'kwā-ˌzär *also* -ˌsär\ *n* : any of the very distant starlike heavenly objects that give off very strong blue and ultraviolet light and powerful radio waves

¹quash \'kwäsh, 'kwȯsh\ *vb* : to put down completely : QUELL ⟨*quash* a rebellion⟩ [Middle English *quashen* "to smash," from early French *quasser, casser* (same meaning), from Latin *quassare* "to shake violently, shatter," from *quatere* "to shake"]

²quash *vb* : to cancel by court action ⟨*quash* a criminal charge⟩ [Middle English *quashen* "to nullify," from early French *casser, quasser* "to annul," from Latin *cassare* (same meaning), from earlier Latin *cassus* "void"]

qua·si \'kwā-ˌzī, -ˌsī; 'kwäz-ē, 'kwäs-\ *combining form* : in some sense or degree ⟨*quasi*-historical⟩ ⟨*quasi*-officially⟩ [from Latin *quasi* "as if"]

Qua·ter·na·ry \'kwät-ə(r)-ˌner-ē, kwə-'tər-nə-rē\ *adj* : of, relating to, or being the period of geological history from the end of the Tertiary period to the present time or the corresponding system of rocks — see GEOLOGIC TIME table — **Quaternary** *n*

qua·train \'kwä-ˌtrān\ *n* : a unit or group of four lines of verse

¹qua·ver \'kwā-vər\ *vb* **qua·vered; qua·ver·ing** \'kwāv-(ə-)riŋ\ **1** : ¹TREMBLE 1 **2** : to utter sound in trembling unsteady tones ⟨a voice that *quavered*⟩ **3** : to say or sing with a quavering voice — **qua·ver·ing·ly** \'kwāv-(ə-)riŋ-lē\ *adv* — **qua·very** \'kwāv-(ə-)rē\ *adj*

²quaver *n* **1** : EIGHTH NOTE **2** : a trembling sound

quay \'kē, 'k(w)ā\ *n* : a structure built along the bank of a waterway for use as a landing place

quea·sy *also* **quea·zy** \'kwē-zē\ *adj* **quea·si·er; -est 1** : somewhat nauseated ⟨the boat ride made me *queasy*⟩ **2** : full of doubt ⟨*queasy* about taking the test⟩ — **quea·si·ly** \-zə-lē\ *adv* — **quea·si·ness** \-zē-nəs\ *n*

Que·chua \'kech-(ə-)wə, kā-'chü-ə\ *n, pl* **Quechua** *or* **Quechuas** : a family of closely related languages spoken by American Indian peoples of Peru, Bolivia, Ecuador, Colombia, Chile, and Argentina

¹queen \'kwēn\ *n* **1** : the wife or widow of a king **2** : a woman who rules a kingdom in her own right **3 a** : a woman of supreme rank, power, or attractiveness ⟨a society *queen*⟩ **b** : something thought of as female and being at the top in a particular field ⟨*queen* of the ocean liners⟩ **4** : the most powerful piece in the game of chess **5** : a playing card bearing the figure of a queen **6** : the fertile fully developed female of social bees, ants, and termites whose purpose is to lay eggs [Old English *cwēn* "woman, wife, queen"]

²queen *vb* **1** : to act like a queen; *esp* : put on airs **2** : to become or promote to a queen in chess

Queen Anne's lace \-'anz-\ *n* : an herb native to Eurasia but found growing throughout North America that has a whitish root and flat lacelike clusters of tiny white flowers and from which the cultivated carrot originated — called also *wild carrot*

queen·ly \'kwēn-lē\ *adj* : resembling a queen

queen mother *n* : the widowed mother of the king or queen who is currently reigning

queen–size \'kwēn-ˌsīz\ *adj* : having a size of about 60 inches by 80 inches (about 1.5 by 1.9 meters) ⟨a *queen=size* bed⟩

¹queer \'kwi(ə)r\ *adj* **1** : oddly unlike the usual or normal ⟨a *queer* smell⟩ **2** : not quite well : QUEASY ⟨feeling a little *queer* today⟩ — **queer·ish** \-ish\ *adj* — **queer·ly** *adv* — **queer·ness** *n*

²queer *vb* : to spoil the effect or success of : DISRUPT ⟨a sudden storm *queered* our plans⟩

quell \'kwel\ *vb* **1** : to put down by force ⟨*quell* a riot⟩ **2** : ³QUIET ⟨*quell* fears⟩ — **quell·er** *n*

quench \'kwench\ *vb* **1** : EXTINGUISH 1 ⟨*quench* a fire⟩ **2** : to bring to an end **3** : SATISFY 2b ⟨*quench* your thirst⟩ — **quench·able** \'kwen-chə-bəl\ *adj* — **quench·er** *n*

quer·u·lous \'kwer-(y)ə-ləs\ *adj* **1** : always eager to complain **2** : showing a complaining attitude ⟨a *querulous* voice⟩ — **quer·u·lous·ly** *adv* — **quer·u·lous·ness** *n*

¹que·ry \'kwi(ə)r-ē, 'kwe(ə)r-\ *n, pl* **queries** : ¹QUESTION 1a

²query *vb* **que·ried; que·ry·ing 1** : to ask questions about especially in order to clear up doubts **2** : to put as a question ⟨*queried* the matter to their teacher⟩ **3** : to ask questions of ⟨*queried* the professor⟩

¹quest \'kwest\ *n* **1** : an act or instance of seeking **2 a** : ²SEARCH ⟨in *quest* of game⟩ **b** : an adventurous journey by a knight in a tale of olden days

²quest *vb* **1** : to go on a quest : SEEK **2** : to search for : PURSUE **3** : to ask for : DEMAND

¹ques·tion \'kwes-chən, 'kwesh-\ *n* **1 a** : something asked ⟨try to make your *questions* brief⟩ **b** : a topic to be talked or argued about ⟨arms control and other *questions* of the day⟩ **c** : a suggestion to be voted on ⟨put the *question* to the members⟩ **2 a** : an act or instance of asking : INQUIRY **b** : OBJECTION 1 ⟨obey without *question*⟩ **c** : POSSIBILITY 1 ⟨no *question* of escape⟩

²question *vb* **1** : to ask questions of or about **2** : to doubt the correctness of ⟨*question* the decision of the judges⟩ **3** : to look at or consider carefully : EXAMINE — **ques·tion·er** *n* — **ques·tion·ing·ly** \-chə-niŋ-lē\ *adv*

ques·tion·able \'kwes-chə-nə-bəl, 'kwesh-\ *adj* **1** : open to doubt, question, or challenge : not certain or exact ⟨milk of *questionable* purity⟩ ⟨a *questionable* decision⟩ **2** : believed to be bad, false, or unsound : DUBIOUS ⟨*questionable* motives⟩ — **ques·tion·ably** \-blē\ *adv*

question mark *n* : a punctuation mark ? used chiefly at the end of a sentence to indicate a direct question

ques·tion·naire \ˌkwes-chə-'na(ə)r, -'ne(ə)r\ *n* : a set of questions to be asked of a number of persons usually in order to gather information (as on opinions)

quet·zal \ket-'säl, -'sal\ *n, pl* **quetzals** *or* **quet·za·les** \-'säl-ās\ : a brightly colored Central American bird with green feathers, a red breast, and in the male tail feathers often over two feet (60 centimeters) in length

¹queue \'kyü\ *n* **1** : a pigtail usually worn hanging at the back of the head **2** : a waiting line ⟨a *queue* at a ticket window⟩ **3** : a sequence of messages or jobs held in temporary storage in a computer awaiting transmission or processing

Word History The Latin word *cauda* or *coda*, meaning "tail," passed into French and in time ended up being spelled *queue*. English borrowed this word, giving it the meaning "a long braid of hair," one that hangs from a person's head like a tail. This sense is still in use, but we more commonly refer to such a braid as a *pigtail* today. In the 19th century, *queue* came to be used for something else that looked like a tail—a number of people waiting in line. [from French *queue*, literally, "tail," from Latin *coda, cauda* "tail" — related to CODA, COWARD, ³CUE; see *Word History* at COWARD]

²queue *vb* **queued; queu·ing** *or* **queue·ing 1** : to arrange or form in a queue **2** : to line up or wait in a queue ⟨the crowd *queued* up for tickets⟩ — **queu·er** *n*

¹quib·ble \'kwib-əl\ *vb* **quib·bled; quib·bling** \-(ə-)liŋ\ **1** : to talk about unimportant things rather than the real point ⟨stop *quibbling* about words and tell what happened⟩ **2** : to find fault or argue over unimportant points ⟨people ignored the main point of the speech and *quibbled* about its length⟩ — **quib·bler** \-(ə-)lər\ *n*

\ə\ **abut**		\au̇\ **out**	\i\ **tip**	\ȯ\ **saw**	\u̇\ **foot**
\ər\ **further**		\ch\ **chin**	\ī\ **life**	\ȯi\ **coin**	\y\ **yet**
\a\ **mat**		\e\ **pet**	\j\ **job**	\th\ **thin**	\yü\ **few**
\ā\ **take**		\ē\ **easy**	\ŋ\ **sing**	\th̲\ **this**	\yu̇\ **cure**
\ä\ **cot, cart**		\g\ **go**	\ō\ **bone**	\ü\ **food**	\zh\ **vision**

²quibble *n* **1** : a statement that deals with a minor matter and not the real point under discussion **2** : a minor objection or criticism

¹quick \ˈkwik\ *adj* **1** *archaic* : not dead : LIVING, ALIVE **2 a** : fast in understanding, thinking, or learning : mentally keen **b** : reacting with speed and alertness **c** : aroused immediately and easily ⟨*quick* temper⟩ **d** : fast in development or occurrence ⟨gave a *quick* look⟩ **e** : marked by speed, readiness, or promptness of action or movement — **quick** *adv* — **quick·ly** *adv* — **quick·ness** *n*
  synonyms QUICK, PROMPT, READY, APT mean able to respond right away. QUICK stresses that the response is immediate and often suggests that the ability is part of one's nature ⟨she always had a *quick* mind⟩. PROMPT suggests that the ability to respond quickly is the product of training and discipline ⟨the store gives *prompt* service⟩. READY suggests ease or smoothness in response ⟨he always had a *ready* answer to any question⟩. APT stresses the person's intelligence or talent that allows the giving of a quick response ⟨an *apt* student who learned computer programming in no time⟩.

²quick *n* **1** : living persons ⟨the *quick* and the dead⟩ **2** : a very tender area of flesh (as under a fingernail) **3** : one's innermost feelings ⟨hurt to the *quick* by the remark⟩ **4** : the very center of something : HEART ⟨the *quick* of the matter⟩

quick bread *n* : a bread made with baking powder or baking soda that does not have to be allowed to rise before baking

quick·en \ˈkwik-ən\ *vb* **quick·ened; quick·en·ing** \-(ə-)niŋ\ **1 a** : to make or become alive : REVIVE ⟨warm spring days that *quickened* the earth⟩ **b** : AROUSE 2, STIMULATE ⟨curiosity *quickened* her interest⟩ **2** : to make or become quicker : HASTEN ⟨*quickened* her steps⟩ **3 a** : to begin growth and development ⟨seeds *quickening* in the soil⟩ **b** : to reach the stage of fetal growth at which motion is begun

quick–freeze \ˈkwik-ˈfrēz\ *vb* **-froze** \-ˈfrōz\; **-fro·zen** \-ˈfrōz-ən\; **-freez·ing** : to freeze food so rapidly that the natural juices and flavor are not lost

quick·ie \ˈkwik-ē\ *n* : something done or made in a hurry

quick·sand \ˈkwik-ˌsand\ *n* : a deep mass of loose sand mixed with water into which heavy objects sink

quick·sil·ver \-ˌsil-vər\ *n* : MERCURY 1a
  Word History The metal mercury resembles silver in color. Unlike silver and most other metals, though, mercury is liquid at ordinary temperatures. For that reason it is able to flow and to move almost as if it were alive. The Old English word for mercury was *cwicseolfor,* a combination of *cwic,* meaning "alive" or "moving," and *seolfor,* meaning "silver." The Modern English *quicksilver* comes from the Old English *cwicseolfor.* [Old English *cwicseolfor,* from *cwic* "alive" and *seolfor* "silver"]

quick–tem·pered \ˈkwik-ˈtem-pərd\ *adj* : easily angered : IRASCIBLE

quick–wit·ted \ˈkwik-ˈwit-əd\ *adj* : quick in thinking and understanding : mentally alert **synonyms** see INTELLIGENT — **quick–wit·ted·ness** *n*

quid \ˈkwid\ *n* : a lump of something chewable

qui·es·cent \kwī-ˈes-ᵊnt, kwē-\ *adj* : marked by a lack of action or movement — **qui·es·cence** \-ᵊn(t)s\ *n* — **qui·es·cent·ly** *adv*

¹qui·et \ˈkwī-ət\ *n* : the quality or state of being quiet — **on the quiet** : in a secretive manner

²quiet *adj* **1 a** : marked by little or no motion, activity, or noise : CALM **b** : ¹GENTLE 2b, EASYGOING ⟨a *quiet* disposition⟩ **c** : not disturbed : PEACEFUL ⟨enjoyed a *quiet* dinner for two⟩ **2** : not colorful or showy : CONSERVATIVE ⟨*quiet* clothes⟩ **3** : hidden from public view ⟨a *quiet* corner⟩ — **quiet** *adv* — **qui·et·ly** *adv* — **qui·et·ness** *n*

³quiet *vb* : to make or become quiet — **qui·et·er** *n*

qui·etude \ˈkwī-ə-ˌt(y)üd\ *n* : the state of being quiet : TRANQUILLITY

qui·etus \kwī-ˈēt-əs\ *n* **1** : a final freeing from something (as a debt or duty) **2** : something that quiets or brings under control ⟨put the *quietus* on their celebration⟩

quill \ˈkwil\ *n* **1 a** : the hollow tubelike part of a feather **b** : one of the large stiff feathers of the wing or tail **2** : one of the hollow sharp spines of a porcupine or hedgehog **3** : a pen made from a feather

¹quilt \ˈkwilt\ *n* : a bed cover made of two layers of cloth with a filling of wool, cotton, or down held together by patterned stitching

²quilt *vb* : to construct (as by padding, covering with patterns, or sewing layers together) like a quilt — **quilt·er** *n*

quilt·ing *n* **1** : material that is quilted or used for making quilts **2** : the process of quilting

quince \ˈkwin(t)s\ *n* : the fruit of an Asian tree that resembles a yellow apple with hard flesh and is used especially for marmalade, jelly, and preserves; *also* : a tree that bears quinces

qui·nine \ˈkwī-ˌnīn *also* ˈkwin-ˌīn\ *n* : a bitter white drug obtained from cinchona bark and used especially to treat malaria

qui·noa \ki-ˈnō-ə\ *n* : a goosefoot that occurs in the Andes and has starchy seeds that are used as food and ground into flour; *also* : its seeds

quince

Quin·qua·ge·si·ma \ˌkwiŋ-kə-ˈjes-ə-mə, -ˈjā-zə-\ *n* : the Sunday before Lent

quint \ˈkwint\ *n* : QUINTUPLET

quin·tal \ˈkwint-ᵊl\ *n* : HUNDREDWEIGHT

quin·tes·sence \kwin-ˈtes-ᵊn(t)s\ *n* **1** : the purest form of something **2** : the most perfect type or example [Middle English *quintessence* "the substance from which heavenly bodies are formed (according to medieval belief)," from early French *quinte essence* (same meaning), from Latin *quinta essentia,* literally, "fifth essence," from earlier *quinta,* feminine form of *quintus* "fifth," and earlier *essentia* "essence"] — **quint·es·sen·tial** \ˌkwint-ə-ˈsen-chəl\ *adj*

quin·tet \kwin-ˈtet\ *n* **1 a** : a musical composition for five instruments or voices **b** : the performers of a quintet **2** : a group or set of five

quin·til·lion \kwin-ˈtil-yən\ *n* — see NUMBER table

¹quin·tu·ple \kwin-ˈt(y)üp-əl, -ˈtəp-; ˈkwint-əp-\ *adj* **1** : having five units or members **2** : being five times as great or as many — **quintuple** *n*

²quintuple *vb* **quin·tu·pled; quin·tu·pling** \-(ə-)liŋ\ : to make or become five times as great or as many

quin·tu·plet \kwin-ˈtəp-lət, -ˈt(y)üp-; ˈkwint-əp-\ *n* **1** : a group of five **2** : one of five offspring born at one birth

¹quip \ˈkwip\ *n* **1** : a clever remark **2** : a witty or funny saying

²quip *vb* **quipped; quip·ping** : to make quips

quirk \ˈkwərk\ *n* **1** : a sudden turn, twist, or curve **2** : an odd personal habit : IDIOSYNCRASY — **quirky** \ˈkwər-kē\ *adj*

quirt \ˈkwərt\ *n* : a riding whip with a short handle and a rawhide tip

quis·ling \ˈkwiz-liŋ\ *n* : one who helps the invaders of one's own country [named for Vidkun *Quisling* 1887–1945, a Norwegian politician who helped the German invaders in World War II]

¹quit \ˈkwit\ *adj* : released from duty, responsibility, or penalty : FREE ⟨*quit* of debt⟩

²quit *vb* quit *also* **quit·ted; quit·ting 1** : to make full payment to or for : REPAY ⟨*quit* a debt⟩ **2** : ²CONDUCT 4 ⟨the children *quit* themselves well in the woods⟩ **3 a** : to depart from : LEAVE ⟨*quit* the scene of the accident⟩ **b** : to bring to an end : ABANDON **c** : to give up (as an action or activity) for good ⟨*quit* bragging⟩ ⟨*quit* a job⟩ **4** : to admit defeat : SURRENDER

quite \'kwīt\ *adv* **1** : beyond question or doubt : COMPLETELY ⟨*quite* alone⟩ ⟨*quite* sure⟩ **2** : MORE OR LESS 1, RATHER ⟨we live *quite* near the school⟩

quits \'kwits\ *adj* : even or equal with another (as by repaying a debt, returning a favor, or paying back an enemy)

quit·tance \'kwit-ᵊn(t)s\ *n* **1 a** : a freeing from a debt or responsibility **b** : a document certifying quittance **2** : something given in return : RECOMPENSE

quit·ter \'kwit-ər\ *n* : a person who gives up too easily

¹quiv·er \'kwiv-ər\ *n* **1** : a case for carrying arrows **2** : the arrows in a quiver [Middle English *quiver* "a case for carrying arrows," from early French *quivre* (same meaning); of Germanic origin]

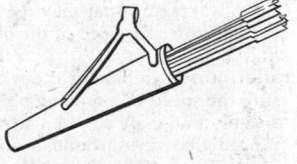

¹quiver

²quiver *vb* **quiv·ered; quiv·er·ing** \'kwiv-(ə-)riŋ\ : to move with a slight shaking motion [Middle English *quiveren* "to quiver," probably from *quiver* "agile, quick"]

³quiver *n* : the act or action of quivering : TREMOR

quix·ot·ic \kwik-'sät-ik\ *adj* : impractical especially in the foolish pursuit of ideals [from Don *Quixote*, hero of the novel *Don Quixote de la Mancha* by Cervantes] — **quix·ot·i·cal·ly** \-'sät-i-k(ə-)lē\ *adv*

¹quiz \'kwiz\ *n, pl* **quiz·zes 1** : a person who mocks **2** : the act or action of quizzing; *esp* : a short oral or written test

²quiz *vb* **quizzed; quiz·zing 1** : to make fun of : MOCK **2** : to ask many questions — **quiz·zer** *n*

quiz·zi·cal \'kwiz-i-kəl\ *adj* **1** : teasing in a good-natured way **2 a** : showing doubt in a good-natured way **b** : showing puzzlement or curiosity — **quiz·zi·cal·ly** \-k(ə-)lē\ *adv*

quoit \'kwāt, 'k(w)òit\ *n* **1** : a ring of iron or circle of rope to be thrown over a peg in a game **2** *pl* : a game played with quoits

quo·rum \'kwōr-əm, 'kwòr-\ *n* : the number of members of an organization required to be present in order for business to be carried on

quo·ta \'kwōt-ə\ *n* **1** : a share or part assigned to each member of a group **2** : the number or amount making up a quota

quot·able \'kwōt-ə-bəl\ *adj* : fit for or worth quoting

quo·ta·tion \kwō-'tā-shən\ *n* **1** : the act or process of quoting **2** : the prices currently bid or offered for stocks, bonds, or goods **3** : something that is quoted

quotation mark *n* : one of a pair of punctuation marks " " or ' ' used chiefly to indicate the beginning and the end of a direct quotation

¹quote \'kwōt\ *vb* **quot·ed; quot·ing 1** : to repeat (someone else's words) exactly ⟨*quote* Shakespeare⟩ **2** : to give as an example **3** : to set off written material by quotation marks

²quote *n* **1** : QUOTATION 3 **2** : QUOTATION MARK

quoth \(')kwōth\ *vb past, archaic* : SAID — used chiefly in the first and third persons and placed before the subject

quo·tient \'kwō-shənt\ *n* : the number resulting from the division of one number by another ⟨dividing 10 by 5 gives a *quotient* of 2⟩ [Middle English *quocient*, an altered form of Latin *quotiens* "how many times?"]

R

r \'är\ *n, often cap* : the 18th letter of the English alphabet

R *certification mark* — used to certify that a motion picture is of such a nature that admission is restricted to persons over a specified age (as 17) unless accompanied by a parent or guardian

rab·bi \'rab-ī\ *n* **1** : ¹MASTER 1a, TEACHER — used as a term of address for Jewish religious leaders **2** : a professionally trained leader of a Jewish congregation [Old English *rabbi* "term of address used for Jewish religious leaders," from Latin *rabbi* (same meaning), from Greek *rhabbi* (same meaning), from Hebrew *rabbī* "my master," from *rabh* "master" and the suffix *-ī* "my"] — **rab·bin·ic** \rə-'bin-ik, ra-\ *or* **rab·bin·i·cal** \-i-kəl\ *adj*

rab·bin·ate \'rab-ə-nət, -ˌnāt\ *n* **1** : the office of a rabbi **2** : a group of rabbis

rab·bit \'rab-ət\ *n, pl* **rabbit** *or* **rabbits** : any of various small burrowing mammals with long ears and short tails that differ from the related hares especially in being born with the eyes closed and without fur; *also* : the pelt of a rabbit

rabbit

rabbit punch *n* : a short chopping blow to the back of the neck — **rabbit–punch** *vb*

rab·ble \'rab-əl\ *n* **1** : a crowd that is noisy and hard to control : MOB **2** : a group of people looked down upon as ignorant and hard to control

rab·ble–rous·er \'rab-əl-ˌraü-zər\ *n* : a person who stirs up the people especially to hatred or violence

ra·bid \'rab-əd *also* 'rā-bəd\ *adj* **1** : extremely violent : FURIOUS **2** : going to extreme lengths (as in interest or opinion) ⟨*rabid* supporters⟩ **3** : affected with rabies ⟨a *rabid* dog⟩ — **ra·bid·ly** *adv*

ra·bies \'rā-bēz\ *n* : a disease of the nervous system of mammals that is caused by a virus usually passed on by the bite of an animal already infected with it and is always deadly if untreated

rac·coon *also* **ra·coon** \ra-'kün\ *n, pl* **raccoon** *or* **raccoons** *also* **racoon** *or* **racoons** : a small North American mammal that is mostly gray with a black mask, has a bushy ringed tail, lives chiefly in trees and is active at night, and eats a varied diet

raccoon

\ə\ **abut**	\au̇\ **out**	\i\ **tip**	\ȯ\ **saw**	\u̇\ **foot**
\ər\ **further**	\ch\ **chin**	\ī\ **life**	\ȯi\ **coin**	\y\ **yet**
\a\ **mat**	\e\ **pet**	\j\ **job**	\th\ **thin**	\yü\ **few**
\ā\ **take**	\ē\ **easy**	\ŋ\ **sing**	\th\ **this**	\yu̇\ **cure**
\ä\ **cot, cart**	\g\ **go**	\ō\ **bone**	\ü\ **food**	\zh\ **vision**

including small animals, fruits, eggs, and insects; *also* : the pelt of a raccoon [Virginia Algonquian *raugroughcoon, arocoun* "racoon"]

¹race \'rās\ *n* **1** : a strong or rapid current of water or its channel **2 a** : a contest of speed **b** : a contest involving progress toward a goal ⟨the *race* for governor⟩ [Middle English *ras* "the act of running, a rapid current of water," of Norse origin]

²race *vb* **raced; rac·ing** **1** : to take part in a race **2** : to go, move, or function at top speed ⟨people *racing* for safety⟩ ⟨a heart *racing* from excitement⟩ **3** : to take part in a race against ⟨I'll *race* you home⟩ **4** : to cause the engine of a motor vehicle to go fast especially when in neutral

³race *n* **1 a** : a group of people of common ancestry or stock ⟨the English *race*⟩ ⟨scion of a noble *race*⟩ **b** : a class or kind of people unified by common interests, habits, or characteristics ⟨a new *race* of scientists⟩ **2 a** : a variety or breed of animals or plants **b** : a category of humankind that shares certain distinctive physical traits **3** : a major group of living things ⟨the human *race*⟩ [from early French *race* "generation," from early Italian *razza* (same meaning)]

race·course \'rā-,skō(ə)rs, -,skȯ(ə)rs\ *n* : a place for racing

race·horse \'rās-,hȯ(ə)rs\ *n* : a horse bred or kept for racing

rac·er \'rā-sər\ *n* **1** : one that races or is used for racing **2** : any of various long swift usually black or bluish American snakes

race·run·ner \'rās-,rən-ər\ *n* : a North American lizard that has a long tail and moves quickly

race·track \'rā-,strak\ *n* : a usually oval course on which races are run

race·way \'rā-,swā\ *n* **1** : a channel for a current of water **2** : RACETRACK; *esp* : one for harness racing

ra·cial \'rā-shəl\ *adj* : of, relating to, or based on race — **ra·cial·ly** \-shə-lē\ *adv*

ra·cial·ism \'rā-shə-,liz-əm\ *n* : RACISM — **ra·cial·ist** \-ləst\ *n or adj* — **ra·cial·is·tic** \rā-shə-'lis-tik\ *adj*

rac·ism \'rā-,siz-əm\ *n* **1** : belief that certain races of people are by birth and nature superior to others **2** : discrimination or hatred based on race — **rac·ist** \'rā-səst\ *n or adj*

¹rack \'rak\ *n* **1** : a framework for holding fodder for livestock **2** : an instrument of torture on which a body is stretched **3** : a framework or stand on or in which articles are placed ⟨hat *rack*⟩ ⟨bicycle *rack*⟩ **4** : a bar with teeth on one side for fitting together with those of a pinion **5** : a pair of antlers

¹rack 4: *R* rack, *P* pinion

²rack *vb* **1** : to cause to suffer torture, pain, sorrow, or ruin ⟨*racked* by a cough⟩ **2** : to stretch or strain violently ⟨*racked* his brains for the answer⟩ **3** : to place (as pool balls) in a rack

³rack *n* : either of two gaits of a horse: **a** : PACE 2b **b** : a fast showy gait similar to the pace but in which the feet of the same side do not touch down at the same time

⁴rack *n* : a cut of meat from a lamb or pig that includes some of the rib section

¹rack·et *or* **rac·quet** \'rak-ət\ *n* **1** : a light implement consisting of a handle attached to an open frame with a network of strings stretched across it that is used to hit the object in play (as in tennis, badminton, or racquetball) **2** : ²PADDLE 1c [from early French *raquette* "racket" derived from Latin *rasceta* "wrist," from Arabic *rusgh* (same meaning)]

²racket *n* **1** : a loud confused noise **2 a** : a dishonest scheme for obtaining money (as by cheating or threats) **b**

: an easy way to make money or earn a living ⟨is that all you do? What a *racket*⟩ [origin unknown]

³racket *vb* : to make a racket

rack·e·teer \,rak-ə-'ti(ə)r\ *n* : one who gets money or advantages by using force or threats — **racketeer** *vb*

rack up *vb* : ²SCORE 4a ⟨*racked* 30 points *up* in the first half⟩

racoon *variant of* RACCOON

rac·quet·ball \'rak-ət-,bȯl\ *n* : a game for two or four played on a four-walled court with short-handled rackets and a rubber ball; *also* : the ball used in this game

¹racy \'rā-sē\ *adj* **rac·i·er; -est** **1** : full of energy or keen enjoyment **2** : slightly indecent or improper ⟨*racy* jokes⟩ — **rac·i·ly** \-sə-lē\ *adv* — **rac·i·ness** \-sē-nəs\ *n*

²racy *adj* **racier; -est** : being long-bodied and lean

ra·dar \'rā-,där\ *n* : a device that sends out radio waves for detecting and locating an object by the reflection of the radio waves and that may use this reflection to find out the position and speed of the object [from *radio detecting and ranging*]

radar gun *n* : a handheld device that uses radar to measure the speed of a moving object

¹ra·di·al \'rād-ē-əl\ *adj* **1** : arranged or having parts arranged like rays around a common center ⟨the *radial* form of a starfish⟩ **2** : relating to, placed like, or moving along a bodily radius (as the bone of the forearm) — **ra·di·al·ly** \-ē-ə-lē\ *adv*

²radial *n* **1** : a radial part **2** : a tire in which the ply cords are at right angles to the centerline of the tread — called also *radial tire*

radial symmetry *n* : plant and animal symmetry in which similar parts are arranged in a balanced way around the center of the body — compare BILATERAL SYMMETRY

ra·di·ance \'rād-ē-ən(t)s\ *n* : the quality or state of being radiant

radial symmetry

ra·di·ant \'rād-ē-ənt\ *adj* **1 a** : giving out or reflecting light ⟨a *radiant* jewel⟩ **b** : vividly bright and gleaming **2** : glowing with love, confidence, or happiness ⟨a *radiant* smile⟩ **3** : transmitted by radiation ⟨*radiant* heat⟩ **synonyms** see BRIGHT — **ra·di·ant·ly** *adv*

radiant energy *n* : energy transmitted in the form of electromagnetic waves (as heat waves, light waves, radio waves, X-rays)

ra·di·ate \'rād-ē-,āt\ *vb* **-at·ed; -at·ing** **1** : to proceed in a direct line from or toward a center **2 a** : to send out rays : SHINE **b** : to come forth in the form or as if in the form of rays **3** : to spread around from or as if from a center [Latin *radiare* "to proceed from or toward a center," from *radius* "ray, beam, spoke" — related to RADIO, RADIUS, ²RAY]

ra·di·a·tion \,rād-ē-'ā-shən\ *n* **1** : the action or process of radiating; *esp* : the process of giving off radiant energy in the form of waves or particles **2** : something that is radiated; *esp* : energy radiated in the form of waves or particles — **ra·di·a·tion·al** \-shnəl, -shən-ᵊl\ *adj*

ra·di·a·tor \'rād-ē-,āt-ər\ *n* : one that radiates; *esp* : any of various devices (as a set of pipes or tubes) for transferring heat from a fluid within to an area or object outside

¹rad·i·cal \'rad-i-kəl\ *adj* **1** : of, relating to, or proceeding from a root **2 a** : departing sharply from the usual or ordinary : EXTREME **b** : of or relating to radicals in politics — **rad·i·cal·ly** \-k(ə-)lē\ *adv* — **rad·i·cal·ness** *n*

Word History Our word *radical* was formed from the Latin adjective *radicalis*, which simply meant "of or relating to a root." The Latin word *radix* meant "root." This meaning was kept when the word *radicalis* came into English as *radical,* but new senses developed too. Since a root is at the bottom of something, *radical* came to describe what is at the base or beginning, in other words, what is "basic, fundamental." Later, *radical* was used to describe something that was extremely different from the usual. Then, as a noun *radical* came to be applied to a person who wants to make extreme or "radical" changes in the government or in society. In mathematics, a radical sign indicates a root of a number. The words *radish* and *eradicate* also come from the Latin *radix.* [Middle English *radical* "relating to a root," from Latin *radicalis* (same meaning), from earlier *radic-,* *radix* "root" — related to ERADICATE, RADISH]

²radical *n* **1** : ¹ROOT 5 **2** : a person who favors rapid and sweeping changes especially in laws and methods of government **3** : a group of atoms bonded together that is considered as a unit in various kinds of reactions **4 a** : a mathematical expression (as $\sqrt{x}$) involving a radical sign **b** : RADICAL SIGN

rad·i·cal·ism \'rad-i-kə-ˌliz-əm\ *n* : the quality or state of being radical

rad·i·cal·ize \'rad-i-kə-ˌlīz\ *vb* **-ized; -iz·ing** : to make radical

radical sign *n* : the sign √ placed before an expression in mathematics to indicate that its root is to be found

rad·i·cand \ˌrad-ə-'kand\ *n* : the expression under a radical sign

radii *plural of* RADIUS

¹ra·dio \'rād-ē-ˌō\ *n, pl* **ra·di·os 1** : the sending or receiving of signals using electromagnetic waves without a connecting wire ⟨*radio* includes television and radar⟩; *esp* : the use of these waves to carry sound that has been changed into electrical energy **2** : a radio receiving set ⟨a transistor *radio*⟩ **3** : the radio broadcasting industry [a shortened form of *radiotelegraphy,* literally, "telegraphy by rays"; *radio-* from French *radio-* "radial, radiating," from Latin *radius* "ray, beam, spoke" — related to RADIATE, RADIUS, ²RAY]

²radio *adj* **1** : of, relating to, or operated by radiant energy especially at radio frequencies **2** : of, relating to, or used in radio or a radio ⟨*radio* commercials⟩

³radio *vb* : to communicate or send a message to by radio

radio- *combining form* **1** : radiant energy : radiation ⟨*radio*active⟩ **2** : radioactive ⟨*radio*carbon⟩ [derived from Latin *radius* "ray, beam, spoke"]

ra·dio·ac·tive \ˌrād-ē-ō-'ak-tiv\ *adj* : of, caused by, or exhibiting radioactivity — **ra·dio·ac·tive·ly** *adv*

ra·dio·ac·tiv·i·ty \-ˌak-'tiv-ət-ē\ *n* : the giving off of rays of energy or particles by the breaking apart of atoms of certain elements (as uranium)

radio astronomy *n* : astronomy dealing with electromagnetic waves of radio frequency received from outside the earth's atmosphere — **radio astronomer** *n*

ra·dio·car·bon \ˌrād-ē-ō-'kär-bən\ *n* : radioactive carbon; *esp* : CARBON 14

radiocarbon dating *n* : CARBON DATING

radio frequency *n* : any of the electromagnetic wave frequencies between about 3 kilohertz and 300 gigahertz that are used especially in radio and television transmission and in radar

ra·dio·gram \'rād-ē-ō-ˌgram\ *n* : a message transmitted by radio

ra·dio·iso·tope \ˌrād-ē-ō-'ī-sə-ˌtōp\ *n* : a radioactive isotope

ra·di·o·lar·i·an \ˌrād-ē-ō-'lar-ē-ən, -'ler-\ *n* : any of various usually ball-shaped marine protozoans that have small spines radiating from the shell and have a skeleton containing silica

ra·di·ol·o·gy \ˌrād-ē-'äl-ə-jē\ *n* : a branch of medicine concerned with the use of radiant energy (as X-rays) or radioactive material in the diagnosis and treatment of disease

— **ra·dio·log·i·cal** \-ə-'läj-i-kəl\ *or* **ra·dio·log·ic** \-ik\ *adj* — **ra·di·ol·o·gist** \-'äl-ə-jist\ *n*

ra·dio·man \'rād-ē-ō-ˌman\ *n* : a radio operator (as on a ship)

ra·di·om·e·ter \ˌrād-ē-'äm-ət-ər\ *n* : an instrument for measuring the strength of radiant energy — **ra·dio·met·ric** \ˌrād-ē-ō-'me-trik\ *adj* — **ra·di·om·e·try** \-'äm-ə-trē\ *n*

ra·dio·phone \'rād-ē-ə-ˌfōn\ *n* : RADIOTELEPHONE

ra·dio·sonde \'rād-ē-ō-ˌsänd\ *n* : a miniature radio transmitter that is carried aloft (as by a balloon) with instruments for sensing and broadcasting atmospheric conditions

ra·dio·tele·phone \ˌrād-ē-ō-'tel-ə-ˌfōn\ *n* : a telephone that uses radio waves without the use of connecting wires — **ra·dio·te·le·pho·ny** \-tə-'lef-ə-nē, -'tel-ə-ˌfō-nē\ *n*

radio telescope *n* : a radio receiver-antenna combination used for observation in radio astronomy

radio wave *n* : an electromagnetic wave with radio frequency

rad·ish \'rad-ish, 'red-\ *n* : the crisp edible root of a plant related to the mustards that is usually eaten raw as a vegetable; *also* : a plant that produces radishes [Old English *rædic* "radish," from Latin *radic-, radix* "root" — related to ERADICATE, RADICAL; see *Word History* at RADICAL]

ra·di·um \'rād-ē-əm\ *n* : a strongly radioactive shining white metallic element that is chemically similar to barium, occurs in combination in very small quantities in minerals (as pitchblende), and is used in the treatment of cancer — see ELEMENT table

ra·di·us \'rād-ē-əs\ *n, pl* **ra·dii** \-ē-ˌī\ *also* **ra·di·us·es 1** : the bone on the thumb side of the human forearm; *also* : a corresponding bone of other vertebrates **2** : a line extending from the center of a circle or sphere to the circumference or surface **3 a** : the length of a radius **b** : a circular area defined by a given radius ⟨deer may wander within a *radius* of several miles⟩ **4** : a radial part or plane [from Latin *radius* "ray, beam, spoke" — related to RADIATE, RADIO, ²RAY]

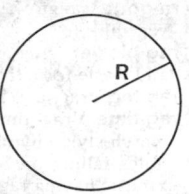

R radius 2

ra·don \'rā-ˌdän\ *n* : a heavy radioactive gaseous element formed by the breaking apart of radium atoms — see ELEMENT table

rad·u·la \'raj-ə-lə\ *n* : a tough band bearing teeth that occurs in some mollusks (as snails and slugs) and is used to scrape or tear off food and bring it into the mouth

raf·fia \'raf-ē-ə\ *n* : fiber from a palm of Madagascar and Africa used as a cord for weaving various articles (as baskets or hats) and for tying

raff·ish \'raf-ish\ *adj* **1** : vulgarly crude or flashy ⟨*raffish* language⟩ **2** : careless about moral behavior : DISREPUTABLE — **raff·ish·ly** *adv* — **raff·ish·ness** *n*

¹raf·fle \'raf-əl\ *vb* **raf·fled; raf·fling** \'raf-(ə-)liŋ\ : to dispose of by a raffle ⟨*raffle* off a turkey⟩

²raffle *n* : the sale of chances for a prize whose winner is the one whose ticket is picked at a drawing

¹raft \'raft\ *n* : a flat structure (as a group of logs fastened together) for support or transportation on water [Middle English *rafte* "rafter, raft"; of Norse origin]

²raft *vb* : to transport or move on or by means of a raft

³raft *n* : a large amount or number [probably an altered form of earlier *raff* "jumble"]

\ə\ abut	\au̇\ out	\i\ tip	\ȯ\ saw	\u̇\ foot
\ər\ further	\ch\ chin	\ī\ life	\ȯi\ coin	\y\ yet
\a\ mat	\e\ pet	\j\ job	\th\ thin	\yü\ few
\ā\ take	\ē\ easy	\ŋ\ sing	\t̲h̲\ this	\yu̇\ cure
\ä\ cot, cart	\g\ go	\ō\ bone	\ü\ food	\zh\ vision

raf·ter \\'raf-tər\\ *n* : one of the usually sloping timbers that support a roof — **raf·tered** \\-tərd\\ *adj*

¹rag \\'rag\\ *n* **1** : a waste or worn piece of cloth **2** *pl* : shabby or very worn clothing ⟨dressed in *rags*⟩ **3** : NEWSPAPER; *esp* : a low quality newspaper

²rag *vb* **ragged; rag·ging 1** : to rail at : SCOLD **2** : TORMENT 2, TEASE [origin unknown] — **rag on** : to make fun of

³rag *n* : a composition in ragtime

rag·a·muf·fin \\'rag-ə-,məf-ən\\ *n* : a poorly clothed often dirty child

rag·bag \\'rag-,bag\\ *n* **1** : a bag for scraps of cloth **2** : a collection of various things

rag doll *n* : a cloth doll that is stuffed and usually painted

¹rage \\'rāj\\ *n* **1 a** : very strong and uncontrolled anger **b** : a fit of violent anger **2** : violent action (as of wind or sea) **3** : FAD ⟨the current *rage*⟩ **synonyms** see ANGER

²rage *vb* **raged; rag·ing 1** : to be in a rage **2** : to continue out of control ⟨the fire *raged* for hours⟩

rag·ged \\'rag-əd\\ *adj* **1** : having a rough or uneven edge or outline ⟨*ragged* cliffs⟩ **2 a** : torn or worn to or as if to tatters ⟨a *ragged* dress⟩ **b** : wearing tattered clothes ⟨a *ragged* child⟩ **3** : done in an uneven way ⟨a *ragged* performance⟩ — **rag·ged·ly** *adv* — **rag·ged·ness** *n*

rag·gedy \\'rag-əd-ē\\ *adj* **-ged·i·er; -est** : RAGGED 2

raging *adj* **1** : causing great pain or distress **2** : VIOLENT 1, WILD ⟨a *raging* fire⟩ **3** : EXTRAORDINARY ⟨a *raging* success⟩

rag·lan sleeve \\'rag-lən-\\ *n* : a sleeve sewn in by seams slanted from the underarm to the neck

rag·man \\'rag-,man\\ *n* : a collector of or dealer in rags

ra·gout \\ra-'gü\\ *n* : a highly seasoned stew of meat and vegetables

rag·pick·er \\'rag-,pik-ər\\ *n* : a person who collects rags and waste for a living

rag·tag \\'rag-,tag\\ *adj* : RAGGED 2b

rag·time \\'rag-,tīm\\ *n* **1** : music played with a strong march-style rhythm and a lively melody with accented notes falling on beats that are not usually accented **2** : music having ragtime rhythm

rag·weed \\'rag-,wēd\\ *n* : any of various chiefly North American weedy herbs related to the daisies and producing pollen irritating to the eyes and noses of some persons

rah \\'rä, 'rȯ\\ *interj* : HOORAY — used to cheer a team on

¹raid \\'rād\\ *n* : a sudden attack or invasion

²raid *vb* : to make a raid on — **raid·er** *n*

¹rail \\'rā(ə)l\\ *n* **1 a** : a bar extending from one support to another and serving as a guard or barrier **b** : RAILING 1 **2 a** : a bar of steel forming a track for wheeled vehicles **b** : RAILROAD [Middle English *raile* "bar, rail," from early French *raille, reille* "bar, ruler," from Latin *regula* "straightedge, ruler," from *regere* "to lead straight, govern, rule" — related to REGENT, REGULATE, RULE]

²rail *vb* : to provide with a railing

³rail *n, pl* **rails** *or* **rail** : any of various small wading birds related to the cranes [Middle English *raile* "rail (the bird)," from early French *raalie* (same meaning)]

ragweed

³rail

⁴rail *vb* : to scold or complain in harsh or bitter language [Middle English *railen* "to scold, be abusive to," from early French *railler* "to mock," probably derived from Latin *ragere* "to neigh"] — **rail·er** *n*

rail·car \\-,kär\\ *n* : a railroad car

rail·ing \\'rā-liŋ\\ *n* **1** : a barrier (as a fence) consisting of rails and their supports **2** : material for rails

rail·lery \\'rā-lə-rē\\ *n, pl* **-ler·ies** : an act or an instance of making fun of somebody in a good-natured way

¹rail·road \\'rā(ə)l-,rōd\\ *n* **1** : a permanent road that has parallel steel rails which make a track for cars **2** : a railroad together with the lands, buildings, locomotives, cars, and other equipment that belong to it

²railroad *vb* **1 a** : to send by railroad **b** : to work on a railroad **2 a** : to push (as a bill) through a legislature in a rush **b** : to convict and send to prison without very much evidence or by means of false charges — **rail·road·er** *n*

rail·road·ing *n* : the building or operation of a railroad

rail·way \\'rā(ə)l-,wā\\ *n* : ¹RAILROAD

rai·ment \\'rā-mənt\\ *n* : CLOTHING 1

¹rain \\'rān\\ *n* **1 a** : water falling in drops from clouds **b** : the falling of such water **2 a** : RAINSTORM **b** *pl* : the rainy season **3** : rainy weather ⟨a week of *rain*⟩ **4** : a heavy fall ⟨a *rain* of arrows⟩ — **rain·less** \\-ləs\\ *adj*

²rain *vb* **1** : to fall as water in drops from the clouds **2** : to send down rain **3** : to fall like rain ⟨ashes *rained* from the volcano⟩ **4** : to give in large amounts ⟨*rained* blows on each other⟩ — **rain cats and dogs** : to rain very hard

rain·bow \\'rān-,bō\\ *n* : an arc or circle of colors that appears in the sky opposite the sun and is caused by the sun shining through raindrops, spray, or mist

rainbow trout *n* : a large trout native to western North America that usually has red or pink stripes with black dots on its sides — compare STEELHEAD

rain·coat \\'rān-,kōt\\ *n* : a coat of waterproof or water-resistant material

rain date *n* : an alternative date set aside for use if a scheduled event must be postponed due to rain

rain·drop \\-,dräp\\ *n* : a drop of rain

rain·fall \\-,fȯl\\ *n* **1** : a fall of rain **2** : amount of precipitation ⟨an annual *rainfall* of 20 inches⟩

rain forest *n* **1** : an often tropical woodland with a high annual rainfall and very tall evergreen trees with tops forming a continuous layer — called also *tropical rain forest* **2** : TEMPERATE RAIN FOREST

rain gauge *n* : an instrument for measuring rainfall

raincoat

rain·mak·ing \\'rān-,mā-kiŋ\\ *n* : the action or process of attempting to produce rain by artificial means — **rain·mak·er** \\-kər\\ *n*

rain out *vb* : to interrupt or prevent (as a sports event) by rain — **rain·out** \\'rān-,aut\\ *n*

rain·proof \\-'prüf\\ *adj* : keeping rain out

rain·storm \\-,stȯ(ə)rm\\ *n* : a storm of or with rain

rain·wa·ter \\-,wȯt-ər, -,wät-\\ *n* : water falling or fallen as rain

rain·wear \\-,wa(ə)r, -,we(ə)r\\ *n* : waterproof or water-resistant clothing — called also *rain gear*

rainy \\'rā-nē\\ *adj* **rain·i·er; -est** : having much rain

rainy day *n* : a period of need or want ⟨set a little money aside for a *rainy day*⟩ — **rainy–day** *adj*

¹raise \\'rāz\\ *vb* **raised; rais·ing 1** : to cause to rise ⟨*raise* a window⟩ ⟨*raise* dust⟩ **2 a** : ¹AWAKE, AROUSE ⟨enough noise to *raise* the dead⟩ **b** : to recall from or as if from death **c** : to stir up : INCITE ⟨*raise* a rebellion⟩ **3 a** : to set upright by lifting or building ⟨*raise* a monument⟩ **b** : to lift up ⟨*raise* your hand⟩ **c** : to place higher especially in rank : PROMOTE ⟨was *raised* to captain⟩ **d** : HEIGHTEN 1, INVIGORATE ⟨*raise* the spirits⟩ **4** : ²COL-LECT 1b ⟨*raise* funds⟩ **5 a** : to look after the growth and development of : GROW ⟨*raise* hogs⟩ ⟨*raise* corn⟩ **b** : BRING UP 1, REAR 3b ⟨*raise* a child⟩ ⟨was *raised* in the city⟩ **6** : BRING ABOUT ⟨*raised* a laugh⟩ **7** : to bring to notice ⟨*raise* an issue⟩ **8 a** : to increase the strength of ⟨don't *raise* your voice⟩ **b** : to increase the amount of ⟨*raise* the rent⟩ **c** : to increase a bid or bet **9** : to make light and airy ⟨*raise* dough⟩ **10** : to multiply a quantity by itself a specified number of times ⟨*raise* two to the fourth power⟩ **11** : to bring into sight on the horizon by approaching ⟨*raised* land at last⟩ **12** : to cause to form on the skin ⟨*raise* a blister⟩ — **rais·er** *n* — **raise eyebrows** : to cause surprise or mild disapproval ⟨a comment that *raised eyebrows*⟩ — **raise the bar** : to set a higher stan-dard ⟨new software that *raises the bar* for competitors⟩

synonyms RAISE, LIFT, HEAVE, HOIST mean to move from a lower to a higher place or position. RAISE often suggests a suitable or intended higher position to which something is brought ⟨*raise* the flag to the top of the pole⟩. LIFT suggests a bringing up especially from the ground and may also suggest the need for exertion in order to pick up something heavy ⟨*lift* some boxes onto the table⟩. HEAVE suggests lifting with great effort or strain ⟨*heave* those bales of hay onto the truck⟩. HOIST often suggests the use of mechanical means to increase the force applied in raising something very heavy ⟨*hoist* the crates onto the ship⟩.

²**raise** *n* **1** : an increase in the amount of a bet or bid **2** : an increase in pay

raised *adj* **1** : done in relief ⟨*raised* needlework⟩ **2** : hav-ing a nap ⟨*raised* fabric⟩

rai·sin \ˈrāz-ᵊn\ *n* : a grape usually rich in sugar that has been dried

ra·ja *or* **ra·jah** \ˈräj-ə, ˈräzh-\ *n* : an Indian or Malay prince or chief [from Hindi and Urdu (the official language of Pakistan) *rājā* "prince, chief"]

¹**rake** \ˈrāk\ *n* **1** : a garden tool with a long handle and prongs at the end **2** : a machine for gathering hay [Old English *racu* "a tool for gathering up grass or straw"]

²**rake** *vb* **raked; rak·ing 1** : to gather, loosen, or smooth with or as if with a rake ⟨*rake* leaves⟩ ⟨*raking* in money⟩ **2 a** : to touch in passing over lightly **b** : ¹SCRATCH 1, SCRAPE **3** : to search through : RANSACK ⟨*rake* the rec-ords for evidence⟩ **4** : to sweep the length of with or as if with gunfire — **rak·er** *n*

³**rake** *n* : LIBERTINE [a shortened form of earlier *rakehell* (same meaning)]

¹**rak·ish** \ˈrā-kish\ *adj* : of or resembling that of a rake : DISSOLUTE [from *rake* "libertine"] — **rak·ish·ly** *adv* — **rak·ish·ness** *n*

²**rakish** *adj* **1** : having a trim or streamlined look that sug-gests speed ⟨a *rakish* ship⟩ ⟨a *rakish* sports car⟩ **2** : JAUN-TY, DASHING ⟨*rakish* clothes⟩ [from earlier *rake* "the amount of slope or lean of a ship's mast or the amount of overhang of a ship's bow"] — **rak·ish·ly** *adv* — **rak·ish·ness** *n*

rale \ˈral, ˈräl\ *n* : an abnormal sound that accompanies the sounds of normal breathing (as in bronchitis)

¹**ral·ly** \ˈral-ē\ *vb* **ral·lied; ral·ly·ing 1 a** : to bring or come together for a common purpose ⟨*rallied* to the cause⟩ **b** : to bring back to order ⟨*rallied* the retreating troops⟩ **2** : to rouse from low spirits or weakness ⟨the patient *ral-lied*⟩ **3** : to make a comeback ⟨the team *rallied* in the fourth quarter⟩ ⟨stock prices *rallied* at the close of trad-ing⟩ [from French *rallier* "to call or come together for a common purpose," from early French *ralier* (same mean-ing), from *re-* "again, back" and *alier* "to unite"]

²**rally** *n*, *pl* **rallies 1** : the action of rallying **2** : a big meet-ing intended to arouse enthusiasm **3** : a series of shots hit back and forth between players (as in tennis) before a point is won

³**rally** *vb* **ral·lied; ral·ly·ing** : to tease in a good-natured way [from French *railler* "to mock, tease," from early French *railler* (same meaning) — related to ⁴RAIL]

¹**ram** \ˈram\ *n* **1** : a male sheep **2** : BATTERING RAM

²**ram** *vb* **rammed; ram·ming 1** : to strike or strike against with violence : CRASH **2** : to force in, down, or through by or as if by driving or pressing — **ram·mer** *n*

RAM \ˈram\ *n* : a computer memory that acts as the main storage available to the user for programs and data — compare ROM

Ram·a·dan \ˈrä-mə-ˌdän, ˌrä-mə-ˈdän\ *n* : the ninth month of the Islamic year observed as sacred with daily fasting from dawn to sunset [from Arabic *Ramaḍān*]

¹**ram·ble** \ˈram-bəl\ *vb* **ram·bled; ram·bling** \-b(ə-)liŋ\ **1** : to move from place to place for no special reason **2** : to talk or write without a clear purpose or point **3** : to grow or extend irregularly **synonyms** see WANDER

²**ramble** *n* **1** : a long stroll with no particular destination **2** : a rambling story or discussion

ram·bler \ˈram-blər\ *n* **1** : a person who rambles **2** : a climbing rose with flexible stems and rather small flowers in large clusters

ram·bunc·tious \ram-ˈbəŋ(k)-shəs\ *adj* : not under con-trol : UNRULY, EXUBERANT — **ram·bunc·tious·ly** *adv* — **ram·bunc·tious·ness** *n*

ram·i·fi·ca·tion \ˌram-ə-fə-ˈkā-shən\ *n* **1** : the act or pro-cess of branching **2** : OUTGROWTH 1 ⟨the *ramifications* of the decision⟩

ram·i·fy \ˈram-ə-ˌfī\ *vb* **-fied; -fy·ing** : to spread out or split up into branches or divisions

ram·jet \ˈram-ˌjet\ *n* : a jet engine that depends on the speed of flight for the compression of the air it takes in rather than using a mechanical compressor

ramp \ˈramp\ *n* : a sloping way or plane: as **a** : a sloping passage or roadway connecting different levels **b** : a slope for launching boats

¹**ram·page** \ˈram-ˌpāj, (ˈ)ram-ˈpāj\ *vb* **ram·paged; ram-pag·ing** : to rush wildly about

²**ram·page** \ˈram-ˌpāj\ *n* : a course of violent or reckless action or behavior — **ram·pa·geous** \ram-ˈpā-jəs\ *adj* — **ram·pa·geous·ly** *adv*

ram·pant \ˈram-pənt *also* -ˌpant\ *adj* **1** : standing on the hind legs like a horse rearing **2** : not checked in growth or spread ⟨rumor ran *rampant*⟩ — **ram·pant·ly** *adv*

ram·part \ˈram-ˌpärt, -pərt\ *n* : a broad bank or wall raised as a protective barrier; *also* : any barrier that provides protection

¹**ram·rod** \ˈram-ˌräd\ *n* : a rod for ramming the charge down the barrel in a muzzle-loading firearm

²**ramrod** *adj* : not flexible : very strict

³**ramrod** *adv* : in a fully upright position : RIGIDLY ⟨sat *ramrod* straight⟩

ram·shack·le \ˈram-ˌshak-əl\ *adj* : looking ready to fall down ⟨a *ramshackle* old barn⟩

ran *past of* RUN

¹**ranch** \ˈranch\ *n* **1** : a place for the raising of livestock (as cattle, horses, or sheep) on range **2** : a farm devoted to a specific crop or kind of animal ⟨a fruit *ranch*⟩ ⟨a mink *ranch*⟩ **3** : RANCH HOUSE 2

²**ranch** *vb* : to live or work on a ranch

ranch·er \ˈran-chər\ *n* : a person who owns or works on a ranch

ran·che·ro \ran-ˈche(ə)r-ō, rän-\ *n*, *pl* **-ros** : RANCHER

ranch house *n* **1** : the main house on a ranch **2** : a one-story house usually with a low=pitched roof

ranch house 2

ranch·man \'ranch-mən\ *n* : RANCHER

ran·cid \'ran(t)-səd\ *adj* : having a strong disagreeable smell or taste ⟨*rancid* butter⟩ — **ran·cid·i·ty** \ran-'sid-ət-ē\ *n*

ran·cor \'raŋ-kər\ *n* : deep hatred — **ran·cor·ous** \-k(ə-)rəs\ *adj* — **ran·cor·ous·ly** *adv*

rand \'rand, 'ränd, 'ränt\ *n, pl* **rand** **1** : the basic unit of money of South Africa **2** : a coin or bill representing one rand

ran·dom \'ran-dəm\ *adj* **1** : showing no clear plan, purpose, or pattern ⟨a *random* arrangement⟩ **2** : having a definite and especially an equal probability of occurring ⟨a *random* number⟩ — **ran·dom·ly** *adv* — **ran·dom·ness** *n* — **at random** : without definite aim, direction, rule, or method ⟨subjects chosen *at random*⟩

ran·dom–ac·cess \ˌran-dəm-'ak-ˌses\ *adj* : permitting access to stored data in any order the user desires

random–access memory *n* : RAM

ran·dom·ize \'ran-də-ˌmīz\ *vb* **-ized; -iz·ing** : to make random ⟨shuffling *randomizes* playing cards⟩

rang *past of* RING

¹range \'rānj\ *n* **1** : a series of things in a line ⟨a *range* of mountains⟩ **2** : a cooking stove **3** **a** : open land over which livestock may roam and feed **b** : the place where a certain kind of animal or plant naturally lives **4** : the act of ranging about **5** **a** : the maximum distance a weapon can shoot, a missile can travel, or a vehicle can go without refueling **b** : the distance between a weapon and its target **c** : a place where shooting is practiced ⟨a rifle *range*⟩ **6** **a** : the distance or amount included or gone over : SCOPE ⟨the *range* of one's knowledge⟩ **b** : the extent of pitch covered by a voice or instrument or a melody **7** **a** : a sequence, series, or scale between limits ⟨out of our price *range*⟩ ⟨a wide *range* of colors⟩ **b** : the difference between the least and greatest of a set of values

²range *vb* **ranged; rang·ing** **1** **a** : to set in a row or in proper order **b** : to set in place among others of the same kind **2** : to roam freely **3** : to vary within limits ⟨the temperature *ranged* from 50° to 90°⟩

range finder *n* : a device used to find out the distance of an object (as a target)

range·land \'rānj-ˌland\ *n* : land used or suitable for livestock range

rang·er \'rān-jər\ *n* **1** : FOREST RANGER **2** **a** : a member of a body of troops who range over a region **b** : a soldier in an army unit with special training (as parachute jumping and scuba diving) for making surprise attacks and raids

rangy \'rān-jē\ *adj* **rang·i·er; -est** **1** : having long limbs and a long body ⟨*rangy* cattle⟩ **2** : tall and slender in body build ⟨a *rangy* athlete⟩ — **rang·i·ness** *n*

ra·ni *or* **ra·nee** \rä-'nē, 'rän-ˌē\ *n* : a Hindu queen : a raja's wife

¹rank \'raŋk\ *adj* **1** : strong and active in growth ⟨*rank* weeds⟩ **2** : offensively gross or vulgar : FOUL ⟨*rank* language⟩ **3** **a** : very noticeable ⟨*rank* dishonesty⟩ **b** : ²OUT-RIGHT 1 ⟨*rank* beginners⟩ **4** : offensive in odor or flavor — **rank·ly** *adv* — **rank·ness** *n*

²rank *n* **1** : ³ROW 1, SERIES **2** **a** : a line of soldiers standing side by side **b** : the body of enlisted persons in an army ⟨rose from the *ranks*⟩ **3** : a group of individuals classed together — usually used in plural ⟨in the *ranks* of the unemployed⟩ **4** : position within a group ⟨a poet of high *rank*⟩ **5** : official grade or position ⟨the *rank* of general⟩ **6** : high social position ⟨a person of *rank*⟩

³rank *vb* **1** : to arrange in lines or in a formation **2** : to determine the position of in relation to others : RATE ⟨a highly *ranked* player⟩ **3** : to come before in rank ⟨a captain *ranks* a lieutenant⟩ **4** : to take or have a certain position in a group ⟨*ranks* third in the class⟩

rank and file *n* **1** : the enlisted persons of one of the armed forces **2** : the ordinary members that make up the body of a group when considered apart from the leaders

ran·kle \'raŋ-kəl\ *vb* **ran·kled; ran·kling** \-k(ə-)liŋ\ : to cause anger, irritation, or deep bitterness

Word History The Greek word *drakōn,* meaning "serpent, dragon," was borrowed into Latin as *draco.* Later, the noun *dracunculus,* meaning "little serpent," was formed from *draco.* The French borrowed this noun as *draoncle* or *raoncle* but used it for "a festering sore or ulcer." It seems that the form of such a sore looked something like the form of a small serpent. From the noun the French formed the verb *rancler,* "to fester." In the 14th century, the verb was taken into English as *rankle,* with the same meaning. Our word *dragon* also comes from the Greek *drakōn* by way of the Latin *draco.* [Middle English *ranclen* "to fester," from early French *rancler* (same meaning), derived from earlier *draoncle, raoncle* "a festering sore," from Latin *dracunculus* "little serpent, little dragon," from earlier *draco* "serpent, dragon," from Greek *drakon* "serpent, dragon" — related to DRAGON]

ran·sack \'ran-ˌsak, (')ran-'sak\ *vb* **1** : to search thoroughly **2** : to search through in order to rob — **ran·sack·er** *n*

¹ran·som \'ran(t)-səm\ *n* **1** : something paid or demanded for the freedom of a captured person **2** : the act of ransoming

²ransom *vb* : to free from captivity or punishment by paying a price — **ran·som·er** *n*

¹rant \'rant\ *vb* : to talk loudly and wildly — **rant·er** *n*

²rant *n* : loud and wild speech

¹rap \'rap\ *n* **1** : a sharp blow or knock **2** **a** : a sharp criticism **b** : a bad reputation that is often not deserved ⟨given a bad *rap*⟩ **3** **a** : the blame for or unfavorable consequences of an action ⟨took the *rap*⟩ **b** : a criminal charge ⟨a murder *rap*⟩ [Middle English *rappe* "a hard blow"]

²rap *vb* **rapped; rap·ping** **1** : to give a quick sharp blow : KNOCK **2** : to utter suddenly with force

³rap *n* : the least bit ⟨doesn't care a *rap*⟩

⁴rap *vb* **rapped; rap·ping** **1** : to talk freely and frankly **2** : to perform rap

⁵rap *n* **1** : an informal talk : CHAT, CONVERSATION; *also* : a line of talk : PATTER **2** **a** : a rhythmic chanting often in unison of usually rhymed couplets to a musical accompaniment **b** : a musical piece so performed

ra·pa·cious \rə-'pā-shəs\ *adj* **1** : very greedy **2** : PREDATORY 2 — **ra·pa·cious·ly** *adv* — **ra·pa·cious·ness** *n*

ra·pac·i·ty \rə-'pas-ət-ē\ *n* : the quality of being rapacious

¹rape \'rāp\ *n* : an herb related to the mustards that is grown for animals to graze on and for its seeds which are used as birdseed and as a source of oil — compare *canola* [Middle English *rape* "the herb rape," from Latin *rapa, rapum* "turnip, rape"]

²rape *vb* **raped; rap·ing** **1** *archaic* : to take away by force **2** : to have sexual relations with by force [Middle English *rapen* "to take away by force," from Latin *rapere* "to seize"] — **rap·er** *n* — **rap·ist** \'rā-pəst\ *n*

³rape *n* : an act or instance of raping

¹rap·id \'rap-əd\ *adj* : very fast **synonyms** see FAST — **ra·pid·i·ty** \rə-'pid-ət-ē, ra-\ *n* — **rap·id·ly** *adv* — **rap·id·ness** *n*

²rapid *n* : a part of a river where the current flows fast usually over rocks — usually used in plural

rapid eye movement *n* : rapid movement of the eyes which occurs during the dreaming period of sleep

rap·id–fire \ˌrap-əd-'fī(ə)r\ *adj* **1** : able to fire shots rapidly ⟨a *rapid-fire* weapon⟩ **2** : marked by a rapid rate or pace ⟨spoke *rapid-fire* Spanish⟩

rapid transit *n* : fast public passenger transportation (as by subway) in cities

ra·pi·er \ˈrā-pē-ər\ *n* : a straight sword with a narrow blade having both edges sharp

rap·ine \ˈrap-ən, -ˌīn\ *n* : the seizing and carrying away of something by force

rap·pel \ra-ˈpel, ra-\ *vb* **-pelled** *also* **-peled**; **-pel·ling** *also* **-pel·ing** : to descend (as from a cliff) by sliding down a rope

rap·per \ˈrap-ər\ *n* : one that raps or is used for rapping: as **a** : a door knocker **b** : a performer of rap music

rap·port \ra-ˈpō(ə)r, -ˈpȯ(ə)r\ *n* : a friendly relationship

rap·proche·ment \ˌrap-ˌrōsh-ˈmän\ *n* : establishment of or state of having friendly relations

rap·scal·lion \rap-ˈskal-yən\ *n* : RASCAL

rapt \ˈrapt\ *adj* : showing complete delight or interest ⟨listened with *rapt* attention⟩ — **rapt·ly** \ˈrap-(t)lē\ *adv* — **rapt·ness** \ˈrap(t)-nəs\ *n*

rap·tor \ˈrap-tər\ *n* : BIRD OF PREY [Latin *raptor* "plunderer," from *rapere* "to seize"]

rap·ture \ˈrap-chər\ *n* : a strong feeling of joy, delight, or love — **rap·tur·ous** \-chə-rəs, -shrəs\ *adj* — **rap·tur·ous·ly** *adv* — **rap·tur·ous·ness** *n*

¹**rare** \ˈra(ə)r, ˈre(ə)r\ *adj* **rar·er**; **rar·est** **1** : not thick or dense : THIN ⟨the atmosphere is *rare* at high altitudes⟩ **2** : very fine : EXCELLENT, SPLENDID ⟨a *rare* June day⟩ **3** : very uncommon ⟨rain is *rare* in the desert⟩ ⟨a collection of *rare* books⟩ [Middle English *rare* "thin," from Latin *rarus* "rare"] — **rare·ness** *n*

> **synonyms** RARE, SCARCE mean being in short supply. RARE usually applies to an object or quality of which only a few examples are to be found and which is thus greatly prized and cherished ⟨a *rare* gem⟩. SCARCE applies to something that for the present is in too short supply to meet the demand for it ⟨food was *scarce* that winter⟩.

²**rare** *adj* **rar·er**; **rar·est** : cooked so that the inside is still red ⟨*rare* roast beef⟩ [Old English *hrēre* "boiled lightly"]

rare·bit \ˈra(ə)r-bət, ˈre(ə)r-\ *n* : WELSH RABBIT

rar·efac·tion \ˌrar-ə-ˈfak-shən, ˌrer-\ *n* **1** : the action or process of rarefying **2** : the state of being rarefied **3** : a state or region of minimum pressure in a substance (as air) being traveled through by a wave formed by compression (as sound)

rar·efy *also* **rar·i·fy** \ˈrar-ə-ˌfī, ˈrer-\ *vb* **-efied**; **-efy·ing** : to make or become rare, thin, or less dense

rare·ly \ˈra(ə)r-lē, ˈre(ə)r-\ *adv* : not often : SELDOM

rar·ing \ˈra(ə)r-ən, ˈre(ə)r-, -iŋ\ *adj* : full of enthusiasm or eagerness ⟨*raring* to go⟩

rar·i·ty \ˈrar-ət-ē, ˈrer-\ *n, pl* **-ties** **1** : the quality, state, or fact of being rare **2** : someone or something rare

ras·cal \ˈras-kəl\ *n* **1** : a mean or dishonest person **2** : a mischievous person

ras·cal·i·ty \ra-ˈskal-ət-ē\ *n, pl* **-ties** : the actions or character of a rascal

ras·cal·ly \ˈras-kə-lē\ *adj* : of or resembling that of a rascal ⟨a *rascally* trick⟩ — **rascally** *adv*

¹**rash** \ˈrash\ *adj* : marked by or coming from being too hasty in speech or action or in making decisions ⟨a *rash* promise⟩ — **rash·ly** *adv* — **rash·ness** *n*

²**rash** *n* **1** : a breaking out of the skin with red spots **2** : many instances in a short time ⟨a *rash* of fires⟩

¹**rasp** \ˈrasp\ *vb* **1** : to rub with or as if with a rough file ⟨*rasp* off a rough edge⟩ **2** : IRRITATE 1 **3** : to speak or say in an irritated tone **4** : to make a harsh grating sound

²**rasp** *n* **1** : a coarse file with cutting points instead of lines **2** : a rasping sound or sensation

rasp·ber·ry \ˈraz-ˌber-ē, -b(ə-)rē\ *n* **1 a** : any of various black or red edible berries that are rounder and smaller than the related blackberries **b** : a usually prickly plant that produces raspberries **2** : a sound of scorn made by sticking out the tongue and blowing hard so as to make it vibrate

raspy \ˈras-pē\ *adj* **rasp·i·er**; **-est** : making a harsh grating sound ⟨a *raspy* voice⟩

¹**rat** \ˈrat\ *n* **1** : any of various rodents that have brown, black, white, or grayish fur and a long usually nearly hairless tail and that look like but are larger than the related mice **2** : a person who betrays friends **3** : a person who spends much time in a specified place ⟨a mall *rat*⟩ — **rat·like** \-ˌlīk\ *adj*

²**rat** *vb* **rat·ted**; **rat·ting** **1** : to betray, desert, or inform on one's friends ⟨didn't *rat* on us⟩ ⟨*ratted* them out⟩ **2** : to catch or hunt rats

rat·able *or* **rate·able** \ˈrāt-ə-bəl\ *adj* : able to be rated or estimated

ratch·et \ˈrach-ət\ *n* **1** : a mechanical device that consists of a bar or wheel having slanted teeth into which a pawl drops so as to allow motion in one direction only **2** : PAWL

R ratchet 1

¹**rate** \ˈrāt\ *vb* **rat·ed**; **rat·ing** : to scold violently : BERATE [Middle English *raten* "to scold violently"]

²**rate** *n* **1 a** : a constant ratio between two things ⟨a *rate* of exchange⟩ **b** : a price or charge set according to a scale or standard ⟨hotel *rates*⟩ ⟨tax *rate*⟩ **2** : a quantity, amount, or degree of something measured in units of something else ⟨the unemployment *rate*⟩ **3** : a level of quality : CLASS [Middle English *rate* "an estimated or determined value," from early French *rate* (same meaning), derived from Latin *rata*, literally, "fixed, determined," from *(pro) rata (parte)* "according to the fixed proportion"] — **at any rate** : without regard to or in spite of other considerations

³**rate** *vb* **rat·ed**; **rat·ing** **1** : CONSIDER 3, REGARD ⟨was *rated* a good pianist⟩ **2** : to set an estimate on : EVALUATE **3** : to determine the rank, class, or position of : GRADE ⟨*rate* a movie⟩ **4** : to have a rating : be classed ⟨*rates* high in math⟩ **5** : to have a right to : DESERVE ⟨*rate* a promotion⟩

rath·er \ˈrath-ər, ˈräth-, ˈrəth-\ *adv* **1** : more willingly ⟨would *rather* stay home⟩ **2** : more exactly : more properly ⟨my father, or, *rather*, my stepfather⟩ **3** : INSTEAD ⟨was no better but *rather* grew worse⟩ **4** : ²SOMEWHAT ⟨*rather* cold today⟩

¹**rather than** *conj* **1** — used to indicate negation or a contrary choice or wish ⟨*rather than* continue the argument, he walked away⟩ ⟨chose to sing *rather than* play violin⟩ **2** : and not ⟨happy *rather than* sad⟩ ⟨why one thing *rather than* another?⟩

²**rather than** *prep* : INSTEAD OF ⟨*rather than* being pleased, she was angry⟩

rat·i·fi·ca·tion \ˌrat-ə-fə-ˈkā-shən\ *n* : the action of ratifying

rat·i·fy \ˈrat-ə-ˌfī\ *vb* **-fied**; **-fy·ing** : to give legal or official approval to ⟨*ratify* a treaty⟩

rat·ing \ˈrāt-iŋ\ *n* : a position within a grading system ⟨credit *rating*⟩

\ə\ abut	\au̇\ out	\i\ tip	\ȯ\ saw	\u̇\ foot
\ər\ further	\ch\ chin	\ī\ life	\ȯi\ coin	\y\ yet
\a\ mat	\e\ pet	\j\ job	\th\ thin	\yü\ few
\ā\ take	\ē\ easy	\ŋ\ sing	\th\ this	\yu̇\ cure
\ä\ cot, cart	\g\ go	\ō\ bone	\ü\ food	\zh\ vision

rapier (caption beside sword illustration)

ra·tio \'rā-shō, -shē-,ō\ *n, pl* **ra·tios** **1** : the quotient of two numbers or mathematical expressions ⟨the *ratio* of 6 to 3 may be expressed as 6:3, 6/3, and 2⟩ **2** : the relationship in quantity, amount, or size between two or more things ⟨women outnumbered men in the *ratio* of three to one⟩

¹ra·tion \'rash-ən, 'rā-shən\ *n* **1 a** : a food allowance for one day **b** *pl* : ¹PROVISION 2 **2** : the amount one is allowed by authority

²ration *vb* **ra·tioned; ra·tion·ing** \'rash-(ə-)niŋ, 'rāsh-\ **1** : to control the amount one can use ⟨during the war the government *rationed* gasoline⟩ **2** : to use sparingly ⟨*ration* your water on the hike⟩

¹ra·tio·nal \'rash-nəl, -ən-ºl\ *adj* **1 a** : having the ability to reason ⟨*rational* beings⟩ **b** : relating to, based on, or showing reason : REASONABLE 2 ⟨*rational* behavior⟩ **2** : relating to or involving rational numbers ⟨a *rational* fraction⟩ — **ra·tio·nal·ly** \-ē\ *adv*

²rational *n* : something rational; *esp* : RATIONAL NUMBER

ra·tio·nale \,rash-ə-'nal\ *n* : a basic reason or explanation for something

ra·tio·nal·i·ty \,rash-ə-'nal-ət-ē\ *n* : the quality or state of being rational

ra·tio·nal·ize \'rash-nə-,līz, -ən-ºl-,īz\ *vb* **-ized; -iz·ing** **1** : to bring into agreement with reason or cause something to seem believable **2** : to remove irrational expressions from ⟨*rationalize* a denominator⟩ — **ra·tio·nal·i·za·tion** \,rash-nə-lə-'zā-shən, -ən-ºl-ə-\ *n*

rational number *n* : a number that can be expressed as a whole number or the quotient of two whole numbers

rat·line \'rat-lən\ *n* : any of the small cross ropes attached to the shrouds of a ship so as to form the steps of a rope ladder

rat snake *n* : any of various large nonpoisonous snakes that eat rodents and birds and that kill their prey by squeezing and suffocating it

rat·tan \ra-'tan, rə-\ *n* **1** : a climbing palm with very long tough stems **2** : a part of a rattan stem used especially for furniture and wickerwork

rat·ter \'rat-ər\ *n* : a rat-catching dog or cat

ratline

¹rat·tle \'rat-ºl\ *vb* **rat·tled; rat·tling** \'rat-liŋ, -ºl-iŋ\ **1** : to make or cause to make a rattle ⟨windows *rattling* in the wind⟩ **2** : CHATTER 2 ⟨*rattled* on and on about the party⟩ **3** : to move with a rattle ⟨the old truck *rattled* down the street⟩ **4** : to say or do in a brisk lively way ⟨*rattled* off the answers⟩ **5** : to disturb the calmness of : UPSET ⟨the question *rattled* the speaker⟩

²rattle *n* **1** : a series of short sharp sounds : CLATTER **2** : a device (as a toy) for making a rattling sound **3** : a rattling organ at the end of a rattlesnake's tail made up of horny joints

rat·tler \'rat-lər, -ºl-ər\ *n* : RATTLESNAKE

rat·tle·snake \'rat-ºl-,snāk\ *n* : any of various poisonous American snakes with a rattle at the end of the tail

rat·tle·trap \-,trap\ *n* : something (as an old car) that is rickety and makes rattling noises

¹rat·tling \'rat-liŋ\ *adj* : very brisk : LIVELY ⟨going at a *rattling* pace⟩

²rattling *adv* : ²VERY 1 ⟨a *rattling* good tale⟩

rat·tly \'rat-lē, -ºl-ē\ *adj* : likely to rattle : making a rattle ⟨a *rattly* old car⟩

rat·ty \'rat-ē\ *adj* **rat·ti·er; -est** **1 a** : full of rats ⟨*ratty* dockside warehouses⟩ **b** : of or relating to rats **2** : SHABBY 2a ⟨a *ratty* old sweater⟩

rau·cous \'ró-kəs\ *adj* **1** : being harsh and unpleasant ⟨a *raucous* voice⟩ **2** : behaving in a rough and noisy way ⟨a *raucous* crowd⟩ — **rau·cous·ly** *adv* — **rau·cous·ness** *n*

¹rav·age \'rav-ij\ *n* : violently destructive action or effect

²ravage *vb* **rav·aged; rav·ag·ing** : to attack or act upon with great violence ⟨a forest *ravaged* by fire⟩ — **rav·age·ment** \-mənt\ *n* — **rav·ag·er** *n*

¹rave \'rāv\ *vb* **raved; rav·ing** **1** : to talk wildly as if crazy **2** : to talk with great enthusiasm ⟨*raved* about the new play⟩ — **rav·er** *n*

²rave *n* : a statement of enthusiastic praise

¹rav·el \'rav-əl\ *vb* **-eled** *or* **-elled; -el·ing** *or* **-el·ling** \-(ə-)liŋ\ : UNRAVEL 1 — **rav·el·er** *or* **rav·el·ler** \-(ə-)lər\ *n*

²ravel *n* : something that is raveled

rav·el·ing *or* **rav·el·ling** \'rav(-ə-)liŋ, -lən\ *n* : something raveled or frayed; *esp* : a thread raveled out of a fabric

¹ra·ven \'rā-vən\ *n* : a bird of Europe, Asia, northern Africa, and America that has glossy black feathers and is larger than the related crow

²raven *adj* : shiny and black like a raven's feathers ⟨*raven* hair⟩

rav·en·ous \'rav-(ə-)nəs\ *adj* : very eager for food or satisfaction — **rav·en·ous·ly** *adv* — **rav·en·ous·ness** *n*

ra·vine \rə-'vēn\ *n* : a small narrow valley with steep sides that is larger than a gully and smaller than a canyon

rav·i·o·li \,rav-ē-'ō-lē, ,räv-\ *n, pl* **ravioli** *also* **raviolis** \-lēz\ : little pockets of pasta with a filling (as of meat or cheese) [Italian, from a plural of a dialect word *raviolo*, literally, "little turnip"]

rav·ish \'rav-ish\ *vb* **1** : to seize and take away by violence **2** : RAPE 2 **3** : to overcome with a feeling and especially a feeling of joy or delight — **rav·ish·er** *n*

rav·ish·ing \'rav-ish-iŋ\ *adj* : very attractive or pleasing — **rav·ish·ing·ly** \-iŋ-lē\ *adv*

¹raw \'ró\ *adj* **raw·er** \'ró-(ə)r\; **raw·est** \'ró-əst\ **1** : not cooked ⟨a *raw* carrot⟩ **2 a** : being in or nearly in the natural state : not processed or purified ⟨*raw* milk⟩ ⟨*raw* sewage⟩ **b** : not in a finished, organized, or polished form ⟨the *raw* edge of a seam⟩ ⟨*raw* data⟩ **3 a** : having the surface scraped or roughened ⟨*raw* red hands⟩ **b** : very sore or irritated ⟨a *raw* throat⟩ **4** : not trained or experienced ⟨a *raw* recruit⟩ **5** : unpleasantly damp or cold ⟨a *raw* wind⟩ — **raw·ly** *adv* — **raw·ness** *n*

²raw *n* : a raw place or state

raw-boned \'ró-'bōnd\ *adj* : extremely thin : GAUNT

raw deal *n* : an instance of unfair treatment

¹raw·hide \'ró-,hīd\ *n* **1** : a whip of untanned hide **2** : untanned cattle skin

²rawhide *vb* **raw·hid·ed; raw·hid·ing** : to whip or drive with or as if with a rawhide

raw material *n* : something from which a useful or desirable product can be manufactured or produced ⟨wheat and rye are the *raw materials* for a flour mill⟩ ⟨collect *raw material* for writing a story⟩

¹ray \'rā\ *n* : any of numerous flat broad fishes (as stingrays and skates) usually living on the sea bottom and having eyes on the upper surface of their bodies, a long narrow tail, and a skeleton made of cartilage [Middle English *raye* "the ray (fish)," from early French *raie* (same meaning), from Latin *raia* (same meaning)]

²ray *n* **1 a** : one of the lines of light that appear to be given off by a bright object **b** : a thin beam of radiant energy (as light) **c** : a stream of particles (as electrons) traveling in the same line **2 a** : any of a group of lines coming from a common center **b** : HALF LINE **3** : a plant or animal structure that resembles a ray: as **a** : VASCULAR RAY **b** : one of the bony rods in the fin of a fish **4** : a tiny bit ⟨a *ray* of

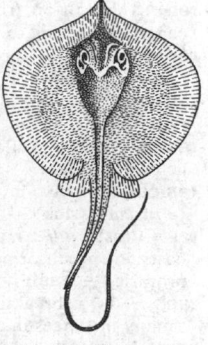

¹ray

hope⟩ [Middle English *ray* "a beam of light," from early French *rai* (same meaning), from Latin *radius* "ray, beam, spoke" — related to RADIATE, RADIO, RADIUS]

rayed \'rād\ *adj* : having rays

ray flower *n* : one of the flowers with long flat petals that grow on the outer edge of the head of a plant (as a daisy) of the composite family — compare *disk flower*

ray·on \'rā-ˌän\ *n* : a yarn, thread, or fabric made from fibers produced chemically from cellulose

raze \'rāz\ *vb* **razed; raz·ing** : to destroy completely by knocking down or breaking to pieces : DEMOLISH ⟨*razed* the building⟩

ra·zor \'rā-zər\ *n* : a sharp cutting instrument used to shave off hair

ra·zor·back \-ˌbak\ *n* : a thin-bodied long-legged half-wild hog chiefly of the southeastern U.S. with long stiff hairs down the center of its back

razor clam *n* : any of various marine mollusks having a shell made of two long narrow hinged parts

razz \'raz\ *vb* : ¹TEASE 2a

RBI \ˌär-ˌbē-'ī, 'rib-ē\ *n, pl* **RBIs** *or* **RBI** : a run in baseball that is driven in by a batter [*r*un *b*atted *in*]

-rd *symbol* — used after the figure 3 to indicate the ordinal number *third* ⟨3rd⟩ ⟨63rd⟩

re \'rā\ *n* : the second note of the musical scale

re- \(')rē *before* '-*stressed syllable,* (ˌ)rē *before* ˌ-*stressed syllable,* ˌrē *before unstressed syllable*\ *prefix* **1** : again ⟨refill⟩ **2** : back : backward ⟨recall⟩ [derived from Latin *re-, red-* "again, back, against"]

reacquire	rebury	redivision
reactivate	rebuy	redraft
reactivation	recalculate	redraw
readdress	recalculation	reeligibility
readjust	rechannel	reeligible
readjustment	recharter	reemerge
readmission	recheck	reemergence
readmit	recolor	reemission
readopt	recommission	reemit
reaffirm	recompile	reemphasis
reanalysis	recomputation	reemphasize
reanalyze	recompute	reenergize
reanimate	reconceive	reenlist
reanimation	reconcentrate	reenlistment
reappear	reconcentration	reenroll
reappearance	reconception	reequip
reapplication	recondense	reestablish
reapply	reconnect	reestablishment
reappoint	reconnection	reevaluate
reappointment	reconquer	reevaluation
reappraisal	reconquest	reexamination
reappraise	reconsecrate	reexamine
reapprove	reconsecration	reexplore
reargue	recontact	reface
rearrest	recontaminate	refinance
reassemble	recontamination	refind
reassembly	reconvene	refix
reassess	recopy	refloat
reassessment	recross	refold
reassign	recut	reformat
reassignment	rededicate	refreeze
reattach	rededication	refurnish
reattachment	redeliver	regather
reawaken	redelivery	regild
rebalance	redeposit	regive
rebaptism	redigestion	regrade
rebaptize	rediscover	regrind
rebid	rediscovery	rehandle
reboil	redispose	rehear
reboot	redissolve	reheat
rebroadcast	redistill	reimpose
reburial	redivide	reimposition

reincorporate	reorientation	restudy
reincorporation	repack	restyle
reinjure	repaint	resubmission
reinsert	repeople	resubmit
reinsertion	rephotograph	resummon
reinstall	rephrase	resupply
reintroduce	replay	resurvey
reintroduction	repopulate	resynthesis
reinvade	reprice	resynthesize
reinvasion	repurchase	retag
rekindle	reread	retaste
relaunch	rerecord	reteach
relearn	reroll	retest
relight	resaw	retie
reload	reschedule	retrace
remeasure	rescore	retransmission
remeasurement	reseal	retransmit
remelt	resealable	retry
remix	reseat	retype
remold	resell	reunification
rename	resettle	reunify
renumber	resew	rewash
reoccupy	reshow	reweave
reoccur	resow	reweigh
reoccurrence	restage	rewire
reorient	restock	
reorientate	restrengthen	

're \(ə)r\ *vb* : ¹ARE ⟨sorry, we'*re* sold out⟩

¹reach \'rēch\ *vb* **1** : to stretch out : EXTEND ⟨*reached* out her arm⟩ **2 a** : to touch or move to touch or take by sticking out a part of the body (as the hand) or something held in the hand ⟨couldn't *reach* the apple, even standing on tiptoes⟩ ⟨*reached* for the catsup⟩ **b** : to extend or stretch to ⟨their land *reaches* the river⟩ **c** : to get up to or as far as : come to ⟨your letter *reached* me yesterday⟩ ⟨tried to *reach* an agreement⟩ **d** : to communicate with ⟨tried to *reach* you by phone⟩ **3** : ²HAND 2, PASS ⟨please *reach* me the salt⟩ — **reach·able** \'rē-chə-bəl\ *adj* — **reach·er** *n*

²reach *n* **1** : an unbroken stretch (as of a river) **2 a** : the action or an act of reaching **b** : the distance one can reach ⟨kept it in easy *reach*⟩ **c** : ability to stretch so as to touch something ⟨you have a long *reach*⟩ **d** : the ability to reach something as if by using the hands ⟨a new car is beyond our *reach* right now⟩

re·act \rē-'akt\ *vb* **1** : to act or behave in response (as to stimulation or an influence) ⟨the colonists *reacted* to the tax by boycotting tea⟩ **2** : to oppose a force or influence — usually used with *against* ⟨*reacted* against their unfair treatment⟩ **3** : to go through or cause to go through a chemical reaction

re·ac·tant \rē-'ak-tənt\ *n* : a substance that enters into and is changed by a chemical reaction

re·ac·tion \rē-'ak-shən\ *n* **1 a** : the act or process or an instance of reacting ⟨our *reaction* to the news⟩ **b** : an action or attitude opposing current political or social forces or ideas **2** : a bodily response to a stimulus; *esp* : the response of the body to a foreign substance (as a drug) **3** : the force that opposes the action of a force applied to one body by another body **4 a** : chemical transformation or change : the action between atoms or molecules to form one or more new substances **b** : a process involving change in atomic nuclei

¹re·ac·tion·ary \rē-'ak-shə-ˌner-ē\ *adj* : of, relating to, or favoring old-fashioned political or social ideas

\ə\ abut	\aù\ out	\i\ tip	\ȯ\ saw	\ù\ foot
\ər\ further	\ch\ chin	\ī\ life	\ȯi\ coin	\y\ yet
\a\ mat	\e\ pet	\j\ job	\th\ thin	\yü\ few
\ā\ take	\ē\ easy	\ŋ\ sing	\th\ this	\yù\ cure
\ä\ cot, cart	\g\ go	\ō\ bone	\ü\ food	\zh\ vision

²reactionary *n, pl* **-ar·ies** : a reactionary person

re·ac·tive \rē-'ak-tiv\ *adj* **1** : of or relating to reaction **2** : reacting or tending to react — **re·ac·tive·ly** *adv* — **re·ac·tive·ness** *n* — **re·ac·tiv·i·ty** \(ˌ)rē-ˌak-'tiv-ət-ē\ *n*

re·ac·tor \rē-'ak-tər\ *n* **1** : one that reacts **2** : a device for the controlled release of nuclear energy (as for producing heat)

¹read \'rēd\ *vb* **read** \'red\; **read·ing** \'rēd-iŋ\ **1 a** : to go over and take in and understand the meaning of letters or symbols ⟨learn to *read*⟩ ⟨*read* braille⟩ ⟨can you *read* decimals⟩ ⟨I can't *read* your writing⟩ **b** : to study the movements of (a speaker's lips) and so understand what is being said **c** : to speak aloud written or printed words ⟨*read* us a story⟩ **d** : to go over and take in the contents of ⟨*reading* a book⟩ **e** : to understand the written form of ⟨*reads* Spanish⟩ **f** : to be able to be read **2** : to learn from what one has seen in writing or printing ⟨*read* about the fire⟩ **3 a** : to discover or figure out the meaning of ⟨*read* palms⟩ **b** : FORETELL, PREDICT ⟨able to *read* his fortune⟩ **c** : to watch carefully in order to tell what will happen ⟨*reading* the rapids while canoeing⟩ **4** : to show by numbers or letters ⟨the thermometer *reads* zero⟩ **5 a** : to acquire data or information ⟨a scanner *reads* the bar code⟩ **b** : to send to or get from storage ⟨*read* your program back in⟩ — **read between the lines** : to understand more than is directly stated

²read \'red\ *adj* : taught or informed by reading ⟨a well=*read* person⟩

read·able \'rēd-ə-bəl\ *adj* : able to be read easily — **read·abil·i·ty** \ˌrēd-ə-'bil-ət-ē\ *n* — **read·ably** \-blē\ *adv*

read·er \'rēd-ər\ *n* **1** : a person who reads **2 a** : a device that makes a readable image ⟨a microfilm *reader*⟩ **b** : a machine for acquiring data (as for a computer) ⟨a card *reader*⟩ **3** : a book for learning or practicing reading

read·er·ship \'rēd-ər-ˌship\ *n* : a group of readers

read·ing \'rēd-iŋ\ *n* **1** : something to be read or for reading **2** : a particular version **3** : the number or fact shown on an instrument ⟨the thermometer *reading* was 20 degrees⟩ **4** : an individual explanation of something

read–on·ly memory \'rēd-'ōn-lē-\ *n* : ROM

read·out \'rēd-ˌaȯt\ *n* : an electronic device that displays information (as data from a calculator); *also* : the information displayed

¹ready \'red-ē\ *adj* **readi·er; -est 1** : prepared for use or action ⟨dinner is *ready*⟩ **2** : likely to do something ⟨*ready* to cry⟩ **3** : WILLING 1 ⟨*ready* to give aid⟩ **4** : showing ease and promptness ⟨a *ready* answer⟩ **5** : available right away : HANDY ⟨*ready* money⟩ **synonyms** see QUICK — **readi·ly** \'red-ᵊl-ē\ *adv* — **readi·ness** \'red-ē-nəs\ *n*

²ready *vb* **read·ied; ready·ing** : to make ready : PREPARE

¹ready–made \ˌred-ē-'mād\ *adj* : made beforehand for immediate use ⟨*ready-made* clothes⟩

²ready–made *n* : something that is ready-made

ready room *n* : a room in which a pilot or an astronaut waits before a mission

ready–to–wear \ˌred-ēt-ə-'wa(ə)r, -'we(ə)r\ *adj* : made in a standard size and not for any particular person

¹re·al \'rē(-ə)l, 'ri(-ə)l\ *adj* **1** : of, relating to, or made up of land and buildings ⟨*real* property⟩ **2 a** : not artificial or fake : GENUINE ⟨*real* leather⟩; *also* : being exactly what the name implies ⟨a *real* professional⟩ **b** : not imaginary : ACTUAL ⟨*real* life⟩ **c** : belonging to or containing elements that belong to the set of real numbers ⟨an equation with two *real* solutions⟩ **3** : ABSOLUTE 1a, COMPLETE ⟨there's a *real* surprise at the end⟩ [Middle English *real* "real, relating to things," from early French *real* (same meaning), derived from Latin *res* "thing, matter" — related to REBUS, REPUBLIC] — **re·al·ness** *n* — **for real 1** : in earnest : SERIOUSLY ⟨arguing *for real*⟩ **2** : GENUINE 2 ⟨couldn't believe the offers were *for real*⟩ **3** : truly good or capable of success ⟨not yet sure if this team is *for real*⟩

synonyms REAL, ACTUAL, TRUE mean agreeing with known facts. REAL may suggest that a thing is what it appears to be ⟨*real* gold⟩. ACTUAL stresses that someone or something does or did occur or exist ⟨was Robin Hood an *actual* person?⟩. TRUE may apply to something that is real or actual ⟨a *true* story⟩ or to something that agrees with a standard ⟨seaweeds are not *true* plants⟩.

²real *adv* : ²VERY 1 ⟨we had a *real* good time⟩

³re·al \rä-'äl\ *n, pl* **re·als** *or* **re·ales** \-'äl-ās\ : an old silver coin of Spain

⁴re·al \rā-'äl\ *n, pl* **re·als** *or* **reis** \'räsh, 'räs, 'räzh, 'räz\ **1** : the basic unit of money of Brazil **2** : a coin or bill representing one real

real estate *n* : property consisting of buildings and land

re·align \ˌre-ə-'līn\ *vb* : to align again; *esp* : to reorganize or make new groupings of — **re·align·ment** \-mənt\ *n*

real image *n* : an image of an object formed by rays of light coming to a focus (as after passing through a lens)

re·al·ism \'rē-ə-ˌliz-əm, 'ri-ə-\ *n* **1** : willingness to face facts and to give in to what is necessary **2** : the showing of things as they really are in art, literature, and theater — **re·al·ist** \-ləst\ *adj or n*

re·al·is·tic \ˌrē-ə-'lis-tik, ˌri-ə-\ *adj* **1** : true to life or nature ⟨a *realistic* painting⟩ **2** : ready to see things as they really are and deal with them sensibly ⟨a *realistic* approach⟩ — **re·al·is·ti·cal·ly** \-ti-k(ə-)lē\ *adv*

re·al·i·ty \rē-'al-ət-ē\ *n, pl* **-ties 1** : the quality or state of being real **2** : someone or something real or actual ⟨our dream became a *reality*⟩ **3** : television programming that shows videos of actual occurrences (as police chases, stunts, or natural disasters) — **in reality** : in actual fact

re·al·ize \'rē-ə-ˌlīz, 'ri-ə-\ *vb* **-ized; -iz·ing 1** : to bring into being : ACCOMPLISH ⟨*realize* a lifelong ambition⟩ **2** : to get by sale or effort : GAIN ⟨*realize* a profit⟩ **3** : to be aware of ⟨*realized* their danger⟩ — **re·al·iz·able** \-ˌlī-zə-bəl\ *adj* — **re·al·i·za·tion** \ˌrē-ə-lə-'zā-shən, ˌri-ə-\ *n*

real—life *adj* : happening in reality : being like real life

re·al·ly \'rē-(ə-)lē, 'ri(-ə)l-ē\ *adv* **1** : in actual fact : ACTUALLY ⟨didn't *really* mean it⟩ **2** : without question : TRULY ⟨a *really* beautiful day⟩ **3** : ²VERY 2 ⟨look *really* close⟩ ⟨he runs *really* fast⟩ **4** : to be honest : FRANKLY

realm \'relm\ *n* **1** : KINGDOM 1 **2** : field of influence or activity ⟨the *realm* of art⟩

real number *n* : a number (as −2, 3, ⅞, .25, 12, π) that is rational or irrational

Re·al·tor \'rē(-ə)l-tər, -ˌtȯ(ə)r\ *collective mark* — used for a real estate agent who is a member of the National Association of Realtors

re·al·ty \'rē(-ə)l-tē\ *n, pl* **-ties** : REAL ESTATE

¹ream \'rēm\ *n* **1** : a quantity of paper that may equal 480, 500, or 516 sheets **2** : a great amount — usually used in plural ⟨*reams* of notes⟩ [Middle English *reme* "a quantity of paper," from early French *reme* (same meaning), from Arabic *rizma*, literally, "bundle"]

²ream *vb* : to shape, make larger, or smooth out with a reamer [probably from Old English *rēman* "to open up"]

ream·er \'rē-mər\ *n* : a tool with cutting edges for enlarging or shaping a hole

reap \'rēp\ *vb* **1 a** : to cut (as grain) or clear (as a field) with a sickle, scythe, or machine **b** : ²HARVEST 1 ⟨*reap* a crop⟩ **2** : to get as a result ⟨*reap* the benefit of hard work⟩

reamer

reap·er \'rē-pər\ *n* **1** : a worker who reaps crops **2** : a machine for reaping grain

re·ap·por·tion \ˌrē-ə-'pōr-shən, -'pȯr-\ *vb* **1** : to apportion (as a house of representatives) again **2** : to make a new apportionment — **re·ap·por·tion·ment** \-shən-mənt\ *n*

¹rear \'ri(ə)r\ *vb* **1 :** to put up by building : CONSTRUCT **2** : to raise or set on end **3 a :** to take care of the breeding and raising of ⟨*rear* cattle⟩ **b :** to bring by continuous care to a stage at which one is fully grown or self-sufficient ⟨*rear* children⟩ **4 :** to rise high **5 :** to rise up on the hind legs ⟨the horse *reared* in fright⟩

²rear *n* **1 :** the part (as of an army) or area farthest from the enemy **2 :** BUTTOCK 2a **3 :** the space or position at the back

³rear *adj* : being at the back

rear admiral *n* : a naval commissioned officer with a rank just below that of vice admiral

rear guard *n* : soldiers who protect the rear of an army

re·arm \(')rē-'ärm\ *vb* : to arm again with new or better weapons — **re·ar·ma·ment** \-'är-mə-mənt\ *n*

rear·most \'ri(ə)r-,mōst\ *adj* : farthest in the rear : LAST

re·ar·range \,rē-ə-'rānj\ *vb* : to arrange again usually in a different way ⟨*rearranged* the furniture⟩ — **rearrangement** *n*

rear·view mirror \,ri(ə)r-,vyü-\ *n* : a mirror (as in a car) that gives a view to the rear

¹rear·ward \'ri(ə)r-wərd\ *adj* **1 :** located at, near, or toward the rear **2 :** directed toward the rear : BACKWARD — **rear·ward·ly** *adv*

²rearward *also* **rear·wards** \-wərdz\ *adv* : at, near, or toward the rear : BACKWARD

¹rea·son \'rēz-ᵊn\ *n* **1 a :** a statement given to explain a belief or act ⟨gave a *reason* for my absence⟩ **b :** a good basis ⟨*reasons* for thinking life may exist on other planets⟩ **c :** the thing that makes some fact understandable : CAUSE ⟨wanted to know the *reason* for earthquakes⟩ **2 a :** the power to think : INTELLIGENCE **b :** a sound mind **synonyms** see CAUSE — **within reason** : within reasonable limits — **with reason** : with good cause

²reason *vb* **rea·soned; rea·son·ing** \'rēz-niŋ, -ᵊn-iŋ\ **1 :** to talk with another in order to cause a change of mind ⟨*reason* with someone⟩ **2 a :** to use the power of reason **b :** to state or conclude by use of reason ⟨*reasoned* that both statements couldn't be true⟩

rea·son·able \'rēz-nə-bəl, -ᵊn-ə-bəl\ *adj* **1 a :** not beyond what is usual or expected : MODERATE ⟨a *reasonable* request⟩ ⟨a *reasonable* chance of success⟩ **b :** not expensive ⟨*reasonable* prices⟩ **2 :** able to reason : RATIONAL ⟨a *reasonable* person⟩ — **rea·son·abil·i·ty** \,rēz-nə-'bil-ət-ē, -ᵊn-ə-\ *n* — **rea·son·able·ness** \'rēz-nə-bəl-nəs, -ᵊn-ə-\ *n* — **rea·son·ably** \-blē\ *adv*

rea·son·ing *n* **1 :** the use of reason **2 :** the reasons used in and the proofs that result from thought : ARGUMENT

re·as·sur·ance \,rē-ə-'shúr-ən(t)s\ *n* : the action of reassuring : the state of being reassured

re·as·sure \,rē-ə-'shü(ə)r\ *vb* **1 :** to assure again **2 :** to give fresh confidence to : free from fear

re·ata \rē-'at-ə, -'ät-\ *n* : LARIAT

¹re·bate \'rē-,bāt, ri-'bāt\ *vb* **re·bat·ed; re·bat·ing :** to make a rebate of : give as a rebate

²re·bate \'rē-,bāt\ *n* : a return of part of a payment or an amount owed

¹reb·el \'reb-əl\ *adj* **1 :** being or fighting against one's government or ruler **2 :** not obeying

²rebel *n* : a person who refuses to give in to authority

³re·bel \ri-'bel\ *vb* **re·belled; re·bel·ling 1 :** to be against or fight against authority and especially the authority of one's government **2 :** to feel or show anger or strong dislike

re·bel·lion \ri-'bel-yən\ *n* **1 :** open opposition to authority **2 :** open fighting against authority (as one's government) **synonyms** REBELLION, REVOLUTION, UPRISING, MUTINY mean an outbreak against authority. REBELLION suggests an outbreak that is serious and widespread but often does not succeed ⟨the *rebellion* lasted a year before the government put it down⟩. REVOLUTION applies to a successful rebellion that ends in a major change (as of government) ⟨the American *revolution* brought about the creation of a new country⟩. UPRISING suggests a rebellion that quickly fails ⟨*uprisings* on the frontier⟩. MUTINY applies to an outbreak against authority at sea ⟨the sailors planned a *mutiny*⟩.

re·bel·lious \ri-'bel-yəs\ *adj* **1 :** taking part in rebellion **2 :** tending to fight against or disobey authority — **re·bel·lious·ly** *adv* — **re·bel·lious·ness** *n*

re·birth \(')rē-'bərth\ *n* **1 :** a new or second birth **2 :** a return to importance

re·born \(')rē-'bȯ(ə)rn\ *adj* : born again

¹re·bound \ri-'baúnd\ *vb* **1 :** to spring back on hitting something **2 :** to recover from a loss or disappointment **3 :** to gain possession of a rebound in basketball

²re·bound \'rē-,baúnd, ri-'baúnd\ *n* **1 :** the action of rebounding : a springing back **2 a :** a basketball or hockey puck that rebounds **b :** the act of gaining possession of a basketball rebound ⟨led the league in *rebounds*⟩ **3 :** an immediate reaction especially to a loss or disappointment

re·bo·zo \ri-'bō-zō, -sō\ *n, pl* **-zos :** a long scarf worn chiefly by Mexican women

re·branch \(')rē-'branch\ *vb* : to branch again ⟨the stream branched and *rebranched*⟩

¹re·buff \ri-'bəf\ *vb* : to refuse or check sharply ⟨the suggestion was *rebuffed*⟩

²rebuff *n* : a refusal to meet an advance or offer

re·build \(')rē-'bild\ *vb* **-built** \-'bilt\; **-build·ing 1 :** to make important repairs to or changes in ⟨*rebuild* an old house⟩ **2 :** to build again ⟨planned to *rebuild* after the fire⟩

¹re·buke \ri-'byük\ *vb* **re·buked; re·buk·ing :** to criticize sharply
    synonyms REBUKE, REPRIMAND, ADMONISH, CHIDE mean to express criticism of. REBUKE suggests a severe or stern criticism ⟨*rebuked* the students for bad conduct at the concert⟩. REPRIMAND suggests a formal and often public or official rebuke ⟨the general was *reprimanded* by the President for an unwise speech⟩. ADMONISH suggests an earnest or friendly warning or piece of advice ⟨we were *admonished* for not trying hard enough⟩. CHIDE suggests a mild scolding that expresses displeasure or disappointment ⟨my parents *chided* me for my table manners⟩.

²rebuke *n* : an expression of strong disapproval

re·bus \'rē-bəs\ *n* : a riddle or puzzle made up of letters, pictures, and symbols whose names sound like the syllables and words of a phrase or sentence [from Latin *rebus* "by things," from *res* "thing, matter" — related to REAL, REPUBLIC]

rebus

re·but \ri-'bət\ *vb* **re·but·ted; re·but·ting 1 :** to oppose by argument **2 :** to prove to be wrong especially by argument or by proof that the opposite is true

re·but·tal \ri-'bət-ᵊl\ *n* : the act of rebutting; *also* : argument or proof that rebuts

re·cal·ci·trance \ri-'kal-sə-trən(t)s\ *n* : the state of being recalcitrant

re·cal·ci·trant \ri-'kal-sə-trənt\ *adj* : stubbornly refusing to give in to authority

¹re·call \ri-'kȯl\ *vb* **1 :** CANCEL 2a, REVOKE ⟨*recalled* the order⟩ **2 a :** to call back ⟨soldiers *recalled* to active duty⟩ ⟨*recalled* cars with brake problems⟩ **b :** to bring back to

\ə\ **abut**	\aú\ **out**	\i\ **tip**	\ȯ\ **saw**	\ú\ **foot**
\ər\ **further**	\ch\ **chin**	\ī\ **life**	\ȯi\ **coin**	\y\ **yet**
\a\ **mat**	\e\ **pet**	\j\ **job**	\th\ **thin**	\yü\ **few**
\ā\ **take**	\ē\ **easy**	\ŋ\ **sing**	\t̲h̲\ **this**	\yú\ **cure**
\ä\ **cot, cart**	\g\ **go**	\ō\ **bone**	\ü\ **food**	\zh\ **vision**

mind : REMEMBER ⟨*recalled* seeing her somewhere before⟩ — **re·call·able** \-ˈkȯ-lə-bəl\ *adj*

²**re·call** \ri-ˈkȯl, ˈrē-ˌkȯl\ *n* **1** : a command to return **2** : a way in which a public official may be removed from office by vote of the people **3** : remembrance of what has been learned or experienced **4** : the act of canceling (as an order) **5** : a call by a manufacturer for the return of a product that may be defective or contaminated

re·cant \ri-ˈkant\ *vb* : to take back publicly an opinion or belief — **re·can·ta·tion** \ˌrē-ˌkan-ˈtā-shən\ *n*

¹**re·cap** \ˈrē-ˌkap, ri-ˈkap\ *vb* **re·capped; re·cap·ping** : RECAPITULATE ⟨now, to *recap* the news⟩

²**re·cap** \ˈrē-ˌkap\ *n* : a brief summary : RECAPITULATION

³**re·cap** \(ˈ)rē-ˈkap\ *vb* **re·capped; re·cap·ping** : ¹RETREAD 1

⁴**re·cap** \ˈrē-ˌkap\ *n* : ²RETREAD 2

re·ca·pit·u·late \ˌrē-kə-ˈpich-ə-ˌlāt\ *vb* **-lat·ed; -lat·ing** : to give a brief summary : SUMMARIZE — **re·ca·pit·u·la·tion** \-ˌpich-ə-ˈlā-shən\ *n*

re·cap·ture \(ˈ)rē-ˈkap-chər\ *vb* **1** : to capture again ⟨*recaptured* the escaped prisoner⟩ **2** : to experience again ⟨trying to *recapture* those happy times⟩

re·cast \(ˈ)rē-ˈkast\ *vb* **-cast; -cast·ing** **1** : to cast again ⟨*recast* a cannon⟩ ⟨*recast* a play⟩ **2** : to change around : REVISE, REMODEL ⟨*recast* a sentence to make it clearer⟩

re·cede \ri-ˈsēd\ *vb* **re·ced·ed; re·ced·ing** **1 a** : to move back or away ⟨the flood waters *receded*⟩ **b** : to slant backward ⟨a *receding* forehead⟩ **2** : to grow less or smaller ⟨a *receding* debt⟩

¹**re·ceipt** \ri-ˈsēt\ *n* **1** : RECIPE 2 **2** : the act or process of receiving **3** : something received — usually used in plural **4** : a written statement saying that money or goods have been received

²**receipt** *vb* **1** : to give a receipt for **2** : to mark as paid ⟨*receipt* a bill⟩

re·ceiv·able \ri-ˈsē-və-bəl\ *adj* **1** : capable of being received **2** : not yet paid : DUE ⟨accounts *receivable*⟩

re·ceiv·ables \ri-ˈsē-və-bəlz\ *n pl* : amounts of money receivable

re·ceive \ri-ˈsēv\ *vb* **re·ceived; re·ceiv·ing** **1** : to take or get something that is given, paid, or sent ⟨*receive* the money⟩ ⟨*receive* a letter⟩ **2** : to welcome on arrival : GREET ⟨*receive* friends⟩ **3** : to hold a reception ⟨*receive* from four to six o'clock⟩ **4** : ²EXPERIENCE ⟨*receive* a shock⟩ **5** : to change incoming radio waves into sounds or pictures [Middle English *receiven* "to gain possession of," from early French *receivre* (same meaning), from Latin *recipere* "receive, take back," from *re-* "back, again" and *capere* "to take" — related to ACCEPT, CAPTURE]

re·ceiv·er \ri-ˈsē-vər\ *n* : one that receives: as **a** : a person appointed to take control of property that is involved in a lawsuit or of a business that is bankrupt or is being reorganized **b** : equipment for receiving radio or television broadcasts **c** : a device for changing electricity or radio waves into light or sound **d** : an offensive football player who may catch a forward pass

re·ceiv·er·ship \ri-ˈsē-vər-ˌship\ *n* **1** : the office or role of a receiver **2** : the state of being in the control of a receiver

re·cen·cy \ˈrēs-ᵊn-sē\ *n* : the state of being recent

re·cent \ˈrēs-ᵊnt\ *adj* **1 a** : of or relating to a time not long past ⟨*recent* history⟩ **b** : having lately appeared or come into existence : NEW, FRESH ⟨*recent* events⟩ **2** *cap* : HOLOCENE — **re·cent·ly** *adv* — **re·cent·ness** *n*

re·cep·ta·cle \ri-ˈsep-ti-kəl\ *n* **1** : something used to receive and contain smaller objects : CONTAINER **2** : the enlarged end of a flower stalk upon which the parts of the flower grow

re·cep·tion \ri-ˈsep-shən\ *n* **1** : the act or process of receiving, welcoming, or accepting ⟨a warm *reception*⟩ **2** : the receiving of a radio or television broadcast **3** : a social gathering ⟨a wedding *reception*⟩

re·cep·tion·ist \ri-ˈsep-sh(ə-)nəst\ *n* : an office employee who greets callers, answers questions, and arranges appointments

re·cep·tive \ri-ˈsep-tiv\ *adj* **1** : able or willing to receive especially ideas **2** : able to receive and pass on stimuli ⟨the *receptive* part of the retina⟩ — **re·cep·tive·ly** *adv* — **re·cep·tive·ness** *n* — **re·cep·tiv·i·ty** \ˌrē-ˌsep-ˈtiv-ət-ē, ri-\ *n*

re·cep·tor \ri-ˈsep-tər\ *n* **1** : a cell or group of cells that receives stimuli : SENSE ORGAN **2** : a molecule (as protein) on the surface or in the inside of a cell that recognizes and joins to specific molecules causing a certain activity within the cell to begin

¹**re·cess** \ˈrē-ˌses, ri-ˈses\ *n* **1** : a hidden or secret place **2 a** : a space or little hollow set back (as from the main line of a coast or mountain range) **b** : ALCOVE 1 **3** : a brief period for relaxation between periods of work

²**recess** *vb* **1** : to put into a recess ⟨*recessed* lighting⟩ **2** : to make a recess in **3** : to interrupt for or take a recess

re·ces·sion \ri-ˈsesh-ən\ *n* **1** : the act or fact of receding or withdrawing **2** : a group of individuals departing in an orderly often ceremonial way **3** : a downward turn in business activity; *also* : the period of such a downward turn

re·ces·sion·al \ri-ˈsesh-nəl, -ən-ᵊl\ *n* : a hymn or musical piece at the conclusion of a service or program; *also* : RECESSION 2

¹**re·ces·sive** \ri-ˈses-iv\ *adj* **1** : tending to go back **2** : producing a bodily characteristic (as eye color) when homozygous and not masked by a copy of the gene that is dominant ⟨*recessive* genes⟩; *also* : exhibited by the body only when the determining gene is homozygous ⟨blue eye color is a *recessive* trait⟩ — **re·ces·sive·ly** *adv* — **re·ces·sive·ness** *n*

²**recessive** *n* **1** : a recessive characteristic or gene **2** : an individual that has one or more recessive characteristics

re·charge \rē-ˈchärj\ *vb* **1** : to make a new attack **2** : to charge again; *esp* : to restore the chemical energy of (a storage battery) so it may be used again **3** : to make or become restored in energy or spirit : RENEW ⟨needed some time to relax and *recharge*⟩ — **re·charge·able** \-ˈchär-jə-bəl\ *adj* — **re·charg·er** \-jər\ *n*

rec·i·pe \ˈres-ə-(ˌ)pē\ *n* **1** : PRESCRIPTION 2a **2** : a set of instructions for making something (as a food dish) from various things ⟨a *recipe* for beef stew⟩ **3** : method of proceeding ⟨a *recipe* for success⟩

re·cip·i·ent \ri-ˈsip-ē-ənt\ *n* : one that receives ⟨the *recipient* of many honors⟩ — **recipient** *adj*

¹**re·cip·ro·cal** \ri-ˈsip-rə-kəl\ *adj* **1** : done, given, or felt equally by both sides ⟨*reciprocal* affection⟩ **2** : related to each other in such a way that one completes the other or is the equal of the other ⟨*reciprocal* agreements⟩ — **re·cip·ro·cal·ly** \-k(ə-)lē\ *adv*

²**reciprocal** *n* **1** : something in a reciprocal relationship to another **2** : either of a pair of numbers (as 9 and ⅑ or ⅔ and ³⁄₂) whose product is one

re·cip·ro·cate \ri-ˈsip-rə-ˌkāt\ *vb* **-cat·ed; -cat·ing** **1** : to give and take mutually : EXCHANGE **2** : to make a return for something ⟨*reciprocate* a favor⟩ — **re·cip·ro·ca·tion** \ri-ˌsip-rə-ˈkā-shən\ *n*

rec·i·proc·i·ty \ˌres-ə-ˈpräs-ət-ē\ *n, pl* **-ties** **1** : shared dependence, cooperation, or exchange between persons, groups, or states **2** : an exchange of commercial benefits between countries

re·cit·al \ri-ˈsīt-ᵊl\ *n* **1** : a reciting of something; *esp* : a story told in detail **2** : a program of music usually given by a single performer ⟨a piano *recital*⟩ **3** : a public performance by music or dance pupils **synonyms** see NARRATIVE — **re·cit·al·ist** \-ᵊl-əst\ *n*

rec·i·ta·tion \ˌres-ə-ˈtā-shən\ *n* **1** : a complete telling or listing of something **2** : the act or an instance of reading or repeating aloud especially before an audience **3** : a student's oral reply to questions

rec·i·ta·tive \ˌres-(ə-)tə-ˈtēv\ *n* : a style of singing without a fixed rhythm that imitates speech and is used sometimes in operas and oratorios; *also* : a passage in this style — **recitative** *adj*

re·cite \ri-ˈsīt\ *vb* **re·cit·ed; re·cit·ing 1** : to repeat from memory or read aloud before an audience ⟨*recite* a poem⟩. **2** : to tell all the details of **3** : to answer questions about a lesson — **re·cit·er** *n*

reck·less \ˈrek-ləs\ *adj* : showing lack of caution : IRRESPONSIBLE, WILD — **reck·less·ly** *adv* — **reck·less·ness** *n*

reck·on \ˈrek-ən\ *vb* **reck·oned; reck·on·ing** \-(ə-)niŋ\ **1 a** : ¹COUNT 1a, COMPUTE ⟨*reckon* the days till her birthday⟩ **b** : to estimate by calculating ⟨*reckon* the height of a building⟩ **2** : CONSIDER 3, REGARD ⟨was *reckoned* among the leaders⟩ **3** *chiefly dialect* : THINK 2, SUPPOSE **4** : to look forward to as certain : DEPEND ⟨*reckon* on support⟩ — **reck·on·er** \-(ə-)nər\ *n*

reck·on·ing *n* **1** : the act or an instance of calculating **2** : a settling of accounts ⟨day of *reckoning*⟩

re·claim \ri-ˈklām\ *vb* **1** : to make someone better in behavior or character : REFORM ⟨*reclaim* criminals⟩ **2** : to change to a desirable condition or state ⟨*reclaim* the desert for agriculture⟩; *also* : to restore to a previous natural state ⟨*reclaim* mining sites⟩ **3** : to obtain from a waste product or by-product : RECOVER ⟨*reclaimed* wool⟩ — **re·claim·able** \-ˈklā-mə-bəl\ *adj*

rec·la·ma·tion \ˌrek-lə-ˈmā-shən\ *n* : the act or process of reclaiming : the state of being reclaimed

re·cline \ri-ˈklīn\ *vb* **re·clined; re·clin·ing 1** : to lean or cause to lean backwards **2** : ¹REPOSE 2, LIE ⟨*reclining* on the sofa⟩

re·cluse \ˈrek-ˌlüs, ri-ˈklüs\ *n* : a person who lives away from others — **re·clu·sive** \ri-ˈklü-siv, -ziv\ *adj*

rec·og·ni·tion \ˌrek-ig-ˈnish-ən, ˌrek-əg-\ *n* **1** : the act of recognizing **2** : acknowledgment of something done or given ⟨got a medal in *recognition* of bravery⟩ **3** : formal acknowledgment of the political existence of a government or nation **4** : special attention or notice

re·cog·ni·zance \ri-ˈkäg-nə-zən(t)s, -ˈkän-ə-\ *n* : a recorded legal promise to do something (as to appear in court)

rec·og·nize \ˈrek-ig-ˌnīz, ˈrek-əg-\ *vb* **-nized; -niz·ing 1** : to be willing to admit : ACKNOWLEDGE ⟨*recognized* my own faults⟩ **2** : to admit as qualified to be heard at a meeting ⟨*recognizes* the delegate from Arkansas⟩ **3** : to grant diplomatic recognition to ⟨*recognized* the new government⟩ **4** : to take approving notice of ⟨*recognize* an act of bravery with a medal⟩ **5** : to show one is acquainted with ⟨*recognize* someone with a nod⟩ **6** : to know and remember upon seeing ⟨I didn't *recognize* you in that new hairdo⟩ [derived from early French *reconoistre* "to recognize," from Latin *recognoscere* (same meaning), from *re-* "again" and *cognoscere* "to know" — related to CONNOISSEUR, INCOGNITO] — **rec·og·niz·abil·i·ty** \ˌrek-ig-ˌnī-zə-ˈbil-ət-ē, ˌrek-əg-\ *n* — **rec·og·niz·able** \ˈrek-əg-ˌnī-ze-bəl, ˈrek-ig-\ *adj* — **rec·og·niz·ably** \-ˌnī-zə-blē\ *adv*

¹re·coil \ri-ˈkȯi(ə)l\ *vb* **1 a** : to fall back under pressure : RETREAT **b** : to shrink back ⟨*recoil* in horror⟩ **2** : to spring back to or as if to a starting point ⟨the compressed spring *recoiled* upon release⟩ ⟨the big gun *recoiled* upon firing⟩

²re·coil \ˈrē-ˌkȯil, ri-ˈkȯi(ə)l\ *n* **1** : the act or action of recoiling **2** : the distance through which something (as a spring) recoils

rec·ol·lect \ˌrek-ə-ˈlekt\ *vb* **1** : to recall to mind : REMEMBER **2** : to remind oneself of something temporarily forgotten

re—col·lect \ˌrē-kə-ˈlekt\ *vb* : to collect again; *esp* : ¹RALLY 2, RECOVER

rec·ol·lec·tion \ˌrek-ə-ˈlek-shən\ *n* **1** : the action or power of recalling to mind **2** : something recalled to the mind *synonyms* see MEMORY

re·com·bi·na·tion \ˌrē-ˌkäm-bə-ˈnā-shən\ *n* : the formation of new combinations of genes

re·com·bine \ˌrē-kəm-ˈbīn\ *vb* **1** : to combine again or anew **2** : to undergo or cause to undergo recombination

rec·om·mend \ˌrek-ə-ˈmend\ *vb* **1** : to make a statement in praise of ⟨*recommend* a person for a promotion⟩ **2** : to cause to receive favorable attention ⟨children *recommended* by their good manners⟩ **3** : to put forward or suggest as one's advice, as one's choice, or as having one's support — **rec·om·mend·able** \-ˈmen-də-bəl\ *adj* — **rec·om·mend·er** *n*

rec·om·men·da·tion \ˌrek-ə-mən-ˈdā-shən, -ˌmen-\ *n* **1** : the act of recommending **2** : a thing or course of action recommended **3** : something that recommends ⟨a written *recommendation*⟩

re·com·mit \ˌrē-kə-ˈmit\ *vb* **1** : to refer (as a bill) again to a committee **2** : to commit again — **re·com·mit·ment** \-mənt\ *n* — **re·com·mit·tal** \-ˈmit-ᵊl\ *n*

rec·om·pense \ˈrek-əm-ˌpen(t)s\ *vb* **-pensed; -pens·ing** : to pay for or pay back — **recompense** *n*

rec·on·cile \ˈrek-ən-ˌsīl\ *vb* **-ciled; -cil·ing 1** : to make friendly again ⟨*reconcile* friends who have quarreled⟩ **2** : to settle by agreement : ADJUST ⟨*reconcile* differences⟩ **3** : to make agree ⟨a story that cannot be *reconciled* with the facts⟩ **4** : to cause to give in or to accept : make content ⟨*reconciled* myself to the loss⟩ — **rec·on·cil·able** \ˌrek-ən-ˈsī-lə-bəl, ˈrek-ən-ˌsīl-\ *adj* — **rec·on·cile·ment** \ˈrek-ən-ˌsīl-mənt\ *n* — **rec·on·cil·er** *n* — **rec·on·cil·i·a·tion** \ˌrek-ən-ˌsil-ē-ˈā-shən\ *n*

re·con·dite \ˈrek-ən-ˌdīt, ri-ˈkän-\ *adj* **1** : hidden from sight **2** : difficult to understand : DEEP ⟨a *recondite* subject⟩

re·con·di·tion \ˌrē-kən-ˈdish-ən\ *vb* : to return to good condition ⟨*reconditioned* a used car⟩

re·con·firm \ˌrē-kən-ˈfərm\ *vb* **1** : to confirm again **2** : to establish more strongly — **re·con·fir·ma·tion** \(ˌ)rē-ˌkän-fər-ˈmā-shən\ *n*

re·con·nais·sance \ri-ˈkän-ə-zən(t)s\ *n* : a survey (as of enemy territory) to gain information

re·con·noi·ter *or* **re·con·noi·tre** \ˌrē-kə-ˈnȯit-ər *also* ˌrekə-\ *vb* **-noi·tered** *or* **-noi·tred; -noi·ter·ing** *or* **-noi·tring** : to make a reconnaissance (as in preparation for military action)

re·con·sid·er \ˌrē-kən-ˈsid-ər\ *vb* : to consider again especially with the possibility of change or reversal — **re·con·sid·er·a·tion** \-ˌsid-ə-ˈrā-shən\ *n*

re·con·sti·tute \(ˈ)rē-ˈkän(t)-stə-ˌt(y)üt\ *vb* : to return to a former condition by adding water

re·con·struct \ˌrē-kən-ˈstrəkt\ *vb* : to construct again : REBUILD, REMODEL

re·con·struc·tion \ˌrē-kən-ˈstrək-shən\ *n* **1 a** : the action of reconstructing : the state of being reconstructed **b** *often cap* : the reorganization and reestablishment of the Confederate states in the Union after the American Civil War **2** : something reconstructed

re·con·ver·sion \ˌrē-kən-ˈvər-zhən\ *n* : conversion back to a previous state

re·con·vert \ˌrē-kən-ˈvərt\ *vb* : to convert back

¹re·cord \ri-ˈkȯ(ə)rd\ *vb* **1 a** : to set down in writing **b** : to deposit an authentic official copy of ⟨*record* a deed⟩ **c** : to register permanently ⟨events *recorded* in history⟩ **d** : INDICATE 1a, READ ⟨the thermometer *recorded* 40°⟩ **2** : to give evidence of **3** : to change sound or visual images

\ə\ **abut**	\au̇\ **out**	\i\ **tip**	\ȯ\ **saw**	\u̇\ **foot**
\ər\ **further**	\ch\ **chin**	\ī\ **life**	\ȯi\ **coin**	\y\ **yet**
\a\ **mat**	\e\ **pet**	\j\ **job**	\th\ **thin**	\yü\ **few**
\ā\ **take**	\ē\ **easy**	\ŋ\ **sing**	\th̲\ **this**	\yu̇\ **cure**
\ä\ **cot, cart**	\g\ **go**	\ō\ **bone**	\ü\ **food**	\zh\ **vision**

into a form (as on magnetic tape) that can be listened to or watched at a later time

²**rec·ord** \'rek-ərd *also* -,ȯrd\ *n* **1** : the state or fact of being recorded ⟨on *record*⟩ **2 a** : something that recalls or tells about past events **b** : an official writing that records what has been said or done by a group, organization, or official **c** : an authentic official copy of a document **3 a** : the known or recorded facts about something or someone ⟨my school *record*⟩ **b** : a recorded top performance or achievement ⟨broke the high jump *record*⟩ **4** : something on which sound or visual images have been recorded

³**rec·ord** \'rek-ərd\ *adj* : setting a record : outstanding among other like things ⟨a *record* crop⟩ ⟨*record* prices⟩

re·cord·er \ri-'kȯrd-ər\ *n* **1** : a person or device that records **2** : a musical instrument consisting of a usually wooden tube with finger holes and a whistle mouthpiece

re·cord·ing \ri-'kȯrd-iŋ\ *n* : ²RECORD 4

rec·ord player \'rek-ərd-\ *n* : an electronic instrument for playing phonograph records

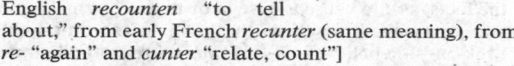

recorder 2

¹**re·count** \ri-'kaůnt\ *vb* : to tell about in detail : NARRATE ⟨*recount* an adventure⟩ [Middle English *recounten* "to tell about," from early French *recunter* (same meaning), from *re-* "again" and *cunter* "relate, count"]

²**re·count** \(')rē-'kaůnt\ *vb* : to count again [from English *re-* (prefix) and *count*]

³**re·count** \'rē-,kaůnt, (')rē-'kaůnt\ *n* : a second or fresh count (as of election votes)

re·coup \ri-'küp\ *vb* **1** : to make up for : RECOVER ⟨*recoup* a loss⟩ **2** : REIMBURSE, COMPENSATE ⟨*recoup* a person for losses⟩ — **re·coup·ment** \-'küp-mənt\ *n*

re·course \'rē-,kō(ə)rs, -,kȯ(ə)rs; ri-'kō(ə)rs, -'kȯ(ə)rs\ *n* **1** : a turning for assistance or protection ⟨have *recourse* to the law⟩ **2** : a source of help or strength : RESORT

re·cov·er \ri-'kəv-ər\ *vb* **re·cov·ered; re·cov·er·ing** \-'kəv-(ə-)riŋ\ **1** : REGAIN 1 ⟨*recover* a lost wallet⟩ ⟨*recovered* my breath⟩ **2** : to regain or bring back to normal health, self-confidence, or position ⟨stumbled, then *recovered* myself⟩ ⟨*recovered* from the flu⟩ **3** : to make up for ⟨*recover* lost time⟩ **4** : to obtain something useful by separating it from a source (as ore or waste) : RECLAIM ⟨*recover* gold from gravel⟩ — **re·cov·er·able** \-'kəv-(ə-)rə-bəl\ *adj*

re–cov·er \(')rē-'kəv-ər\ *vb* : to cover again

re·cov·ery \ri-'kəv-(ə-)rē\ *n, pl* **-er·ies** : the act or process or an instance of recovering

recovery room *n* : a hospital room where patients are temporarily placed for special care and observation after an operation

¹**rec·re·ant** \'rek-rē-ənt\ *adj* **1** : crying for mercy : COWARDLY **2** : unfaithful to duty or allegiance

²**recreant** *n* **1** : COWARD **2** : one that is unfaithful : BETRAYER, DESERTER

rec·re·ate \'rek-rē-,āt\ *vb* **-at·ed; -at·ing** **1** : to give new life or freshness to **2** : to take recreation — **rec·re·ative** \-,āt-iv\ *adj*

re–cre·ate \,rē-krē-'āt\ *vb* : to create again especially in the imagination — **re–cre·ation** \-'ā-shən\ *n* — **re–cre·ative** \-'āt-iv\ *adj*

rec·re·ation \,rek-rē-'ā-shən\ *n* **1** : refreshment of mind or body after work or worry : DIVERSION **2** : a way of refreshing mind or body ⟨hiking and gardening are our favorite *recreations*⟩ — **rec·re·ation·al** \-shnəl, -shən-°l\ *adj*

recreational vehicle *n* : a vehicle designed for recreational use (as in camping); *esp* : MOTOR HOME

re·crim·i·nate \ri-'krim-ə-,nāt\ *vb* **-nat·ed; -nat·ing** **1** : to make a return charge against an accuser **2** : to respond bitterly — **re·crim·i·na·tion** \-,krim-ə-'nā-shən\ *n*

re·cru·des·cence \,rē-krü-'des-°n(t)s\ *n* : a renewal or breaking out again especially of something unhealthy or dangerous ⟨a *recrudescence* of conflict⟩

¹**re·cruit** \ri-'krüt\ *vb* **1 a** : to increase the number of by enlisting new members **b** : to get the services of : ENGAGE ⟨*recruited* new teachers⟩ **2** : REPLENISH ⟨*recruited* their finances⟩ **3** : to return or increase the health, energy, or strength of — **re·cruit·er** *n* — **re·cruit·ment** \-'krüt-mənt\ *n*

²**recruit** *n* : a newcomer to a field or activity; *esp* : a newly enlisted or drafted member of the armed forces

Word History The French formed the noun *recrute,* meaning "fresh growth," from their verb *recroistre* "to grow up again." This verb was taken from the Latin verb *recrescere,* which had the same meaning. Later, someone saw a likeness between "a fresh growth of plants" and "a fresh supply of soldiers." Thus they began using the word *recrute* for the new soldiers. In the 17th century this sense of *recrute* came to the attention of the English. They borrowed the word as *recruit* and began using it as a verb and noun. In time it acquired broader senses not related to the military. [from French *recrute, recrue* (noun) "new growth, a batch of new soldiers," derived from early French *recroistre* "to grow up again," from Latin *recrescere* (same meaning), from *re-* "again" and *crescere* "to grow"]

re·crys·tal·lize \(')rē-'kris-tə-,līz\ *vb* : to form or cause to form crystals after being dissolved or melted — **re·crys·tal·li·za·tion** \(,)rē-,kris-tə-lə-'zā-shən\ *n*

rect·an·gle \'rek-,taŋ-gəl\ *n* : a four-sided polygon that has four right angles and each pair of opposite sides parallel and of the same length [from Latin *rectangulus* "having a right angle," from earlier Latin *rectus* "right" and *angulus* "angle"]

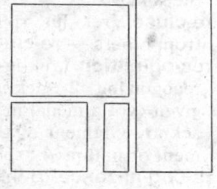

rectangle

rect·an·gu·lar \rek-'taŋ-gyə-lər\ *adj* **1** : shaped like a rectangle ⟨a *rectangular* building⟩ **2** : having edges, faces, or surfaces that meet at right angles : having faces or surfaces shaped like rectangles ⟨a *rectangular* solid⟩ ⟨*rectangular* blocks⟩

rec·ti·fy \'rek-tə-,fī\ *vb* **-fied; -fy·ing** : to set or make right **synonyms** see CORRECT — **rec·ti·fi·able** \-,fī-ə-bəl\ *adj* — **rec·ti·fi·ca·tion** \,rek-tə-fə-'kā-shən\ *n*

rec·ti·tude \'rek-tə-,t(y)üd\ *n* **1** : the quality or state of being straight **2** : moral honesty : RIGHTEOUSNESS

rec·tor \'rek-tər\ *n* **1** : a member of the clergy who has charge of a church or parish **2** : the priest in charge of certain Roman Catholic religious houses **3** : the head of a university or school

rec·to·ry \'rek-t(ə-)rē\ *n, pl* **-ries** : a residence of a rector or a parish priest

rec·tum \'rek-təm\ *n, pl* **rectums** *or* **rec·ta** \-tə\ : the end of the large intestine that links the colon to the anus — **rec·tal** \-t°l\ *adj*

rec·tus \'rek-təs\ *n, pl* **rec·ti** \-,tī, -,tē\ : any of several straight muscles (as of the abdomen)

re·cum·bent \ri-'kəm-bənt\ *adj* **1** : being in a state of rest **2** : lying down

re·cu·per·ate \ri-'k(y)ü-pə-,rāt\ *vb* **-at·ed; -at·ing** : RECOVER 2; *esp* : to regain health or strength — **re·cu·per·a·tion** \-,k(y)ü-pə-'rā-shən\ *n*

re·cu·per·a·tive \-,rāt-iv, -rət-iv\ *adj* : of, relating to, or aiding in recuperation ⟨the body's *recuperative* powers⟩

re·cur \ri-'kər\ *vb* **re·curred; re·cur·ring** **1** : to go or come back in thought or discussion **2** : to come again into the mind **3** : to occur or appear again — **re·cur·rence** \-'kər-ən(t)s, -'kə-rən(t)s\ *n*

re·cur·rent \ri-'kər-ənt, -'kə-rənt\ *adj* : returning from time to time ⟨a *recurrent* fever⟩ — **re·cur·rent·ly** *adv*

re·curved \(')rē-'kərvd\ *adj* : curved backward or inward ⟨*recurved* claws⟩

re·cy·cla·ble \(')rē-'sī-klə-bəl\ *adj* : fit for or capable of being recycled ⟨*recyclable* plastic bottles⟩

re·cy·cle \(')rē-'sī-kəl\ *vb* : to process (as liquid body waste, glass, or cans) in order to regain materials for human use

¹red \'red\ *adj* **red·der; red·dest** **1** : of the color red **2 a** : flushed especially with anger or embarrassment **b** : BLOODSHOT ⟨eyes *red* from weeping⟩ **3 a** : openly supporting sweeping social or political change especially by force **b** : encouraging, aiding, or furthering Communism : COMMUNIST **c** : of or relating to the U.S.S.R. or a Communist country — **red·ly** *adv* — **red·ness** *n*

²red *n* **1** : a color like that of blood or a ruby **2** : one that is of a red color **3** : a dye that colors red **4 a** : a person who seeks the overthrow of a social or political order : REVOLUTIONARY **b** *often cap* : a member or follower of a Communist party : COMMUNIST **5** : the condition of showing a loss ⟨in the *red*⟩

red alga *n* : any of various algae that usually grow in the ocean and are of reddish color

re·date \rē-'dāt\ *vb* **1** : to date again or anew **2** : to change the date of : give a different date to

red·bird \'red-,bərd\ *n* : any of several birds (as a cardinal) with mostly red feathers

red blood cell *n* : a reddish cell of the blood that contains hemoglobin and carries oxygen from the lungs to the tissues — called also *erythrocyte, red blood corpuscle, red cell, red corpuscle*

red–blood·ed \'red-'bləd-əd\ *adj* : ENERGETIC, VIGOROUS

red·breast \-,brest\ *n* : a bird (as a robin) with a reddish breast

red·cap \-,kap\ *n* : ²PORTER 1

red–car·pet \-'kär-pət\ *adj* : marked by ceremonial courtesy ⟨*red-carpet* treatment⟩

red cedar *n* **1** : any of several U.S. evergreen trees that are conifers with scalelike leaves and fragrant red or reddish brown wood **2** : the wood of a red cedar

red cell *n* : RED BLOOD CELL

red clover *n* : a European clover that has globe-shaped reddish purple flowers and is grown for animals to graze on and as a cover crop

red·coat \'red-,kōt\ *n* : a British soldier especially during the American Revolution

red corpuscle *n* : RED BLOOD CELL

red cross *n* : a red-colored cross on a white background used as a badge for hospitals and for members of a worldwide organization that helps the suffering especially in areas of war or disaster

red deer *n* : ELK 2 — used for one of Europe, Africa, and Asia

Red Delicious *n* : a usually large apple with sweet crisp juicy flesh and dark red skin

red·den \'red-ᵊn\ *vb* **red·dened; red·den·ing** \'red-niŋ, -ᵊn-iŋ\ : to make or become red; *esp* : ¹BLUSH 1

red·dish \'red-ish\ *adj* : somewhat red — **red·dish·ness** *n*

red dwarf *n* : a star having much lower surface temperature, brightness, mass, and size than the sun

re·dec·o·rate \(')rē-'dek-ə-,rāt\ *vb* : to freshen or change a decorative scheme — **re·dec·o·ra·tion** \(,)rē-,dek-ə-'rā-shən\ *n*

re·deem \ri-'dēm\ *vb* **1** : to buy or win back **2 a** : to free from captivity especially by paying a ransom **b** : to free from the penalties of sin **3** : to change for the better : REFORM ⟨sinners not easily *redeemed*⟩ **4** : to remove the obligation of by payment ⟨the government redeems

savings bonds⟩ **5** : to make good : FULFILL ⟨*redeem* a promise⟩ — **re·deem·able** \-'dē-mə-bəl\ *adj* — **re·deem·er** \-'dē-mər\ *n*

re·de·fine \,rē-di-'fīn\ *vb* **1** : to define (as a concept) again ⟨*redefined* their terms⟩ **2** : to reexamine or reevaluate especially with a view to change ⟨*redefine* our goals⟩

re·demp·tion \ri-'dem(p)-shən\ *n* : the act or process or an instance of redeeming — **re·demp·tive** \-'dem(p)-tiv\ *adj*

re·de·sign \,rēd-i-'zīn\ *vb* : to change what something looks like, is used for, or contains — **redesign** *n*

re·de·vel·op \,rē-di-'vel-əp\ *vb* : to develop again; *esp* : REDESIGN, REBUILD — **re·de·vel·op·er** *n* — **re·de·vel·op·ment** \-mənt\ *n*

red fox *n* : a usually orange-red to reddish brown fox with a white-tipped tail — compare SILVER FOX

red giant *n* : a very large star with a relatively low surface temperature

red fox

red–hand·ed \'red-'han-dəd\ *adv or adj* : in the act of doing something wrong

red·head \-,hed\ *n* : a person having red hair

red·head·ed \-'hed-əd\ *adj* : having red hair or a red head

redheaded woodpecker *n* : a North American woodpecker that has a red head, a black back, and white patches on the wings

red herring *n* : something intended to distract attention from the real problem

red–hot \'red-'hät\ *adj* **1** : glowing red with heat **2** : marked by much feeling, enthusiasm, or energy ⟨a *red=hot* political campaign⟩ **3** : of or relating to the immediate present : including the very latest information ⟨*red=hot* news⟩

re·di·rect \,rēd-ə-'rekt, ,rē-(,)dī-\ *vb* : to change the course or direction of — **re·di·rec·tion** \-'rek-shən\ *n*

re·dis·trib·ute \,rē-də-'strib-yət\ *vb* **1** : to change the distribution of **2** : to spread to other areas — **re·dis·tri·bu·tion** \-,dis-trə-'byü-shən\ *n*

re·dis·trict \(')rē-'dis-(,)trikt\ *vb* : to divide into new districts; *esp* : to reorganize the legislative districts of

red lead *n* : an orange-red to brick-red oxide of lead used in storage-battery plates, in glass, and in paint

red–let·ter \'red-,let-ər\ *adj* : worth remembering especially in a happy or joyful way ⟨a *red-letter* day⟩ [from the practice of marking holy days in red letters in church calendars]

red maple *n* : a North American maple that has reddish twigs and rather soft wood and grows mainly in moist soils

red marrow *n* : BONE MARROW b

red meat *n* : meat (as beef) that is reddish in color when raw

red mullet *n* : either of two red or reddish goatfishes of warm seas that are used as food

re·do \(')rē-'dü\ *vb* **-did** \-'did\; **-done** \-'dən\; **-do·ing** \-'dü-iŋ\ : to do over or again; *esp* : REDECORATE

red oak *n* **1** : any of various North American oaks with acorns that take two years to mature and leaves with bristles on the edge **2** : the wood of a red oak

red·o·lence \'red-ᵊl-ən(t)s\ *n* **1** : the quality or state of being redolent **2** : ¹SCENT 1b, AROMA

\ə\ **abut**	\au̇\ **out**	\i\ **tip**	\ȯ\ **saw**	\u̇\ **foot**
\ər\ **further**	\ch\ **chin**	\ī\ **life**	\ȯi\ **coin**	\y\ **yet**
\a\ **mat**	\e\ **pet**	\j\ **job**	\th\ **thin**	\yü\ **few**
\ā\ **take**	\ē\ **easy**	\ŋ\ **sing**	\th\ **this**	\yu̇\ **cure**
\ä\ **cot, cart**	\g\ **go**	\ō\ **bone**	\ü\ **food**	\zh\ **vision**

red·o·lent \'red-ᵊl-ənt\ *adj* **1** : AROMATIC **2** : full of a fragrance or odor : SCENTED ⟨a room *redolent* of cooked cabbage⟩

re·dou·ble \(')rē-'dəb-əl\ *vb* : to make or become doubled (as in size or amount) ⟨*redoubled* their efforts⟩

re·doubt·able \ri-'daut-ə-bəl\ *adj* : causing fear or dread : FORMIDABLE ⟨a *redoubtable* warrior⟩ — **re·doubt·ably** \-blē\ *adv*

re·dound \ri-'daund\ *vb* : to have a result for good or bad

red panda *n* : a long-tailed mammal that is related to and resembles the raccoon, has long reddish brown fur, feeds especially on bamboo leaves, and is found from the Himalayas to China — called also *lesser panda*

red pepper *n* **1** : a mature red sweet pepper or hot pepper **2** : CAYENNE

¹**re·dress** \ri-'dres\ *vb* : to set (as a wrong) right : REMEDY, RELIEVE — **re·dress·er** *n*

²**re·dress** \ri-'dres, 'rē-,dres\ *n* **1 a** : relief from distress **b** : the way or possibility of seeking a remedy **2** : something that makes up for wrong or loss **3** : an act or instance of redressing

red panda

red–shaft·ed flicker \'red-'shaf-təd-\ *n* : a flicker of western North America with light red on the underside of the tail and wings and in the male a red streak on each side of the base of the bill

red·shift \'red-'shift\ *n* : displacement of a spectrum especially of a heavenly body toward longer wavelengths

red snapper *n* : any of several reddish sea fishes including some used for food or sport

red spider *n* : SPIDER MITE

red spruce *n* : a spruce of the eastern U.S. and Canada that is an important source of lumber and pulpwood

red squirrel *n* : a common North American squirrel that has reddish upper parts and is smaller than the gray squirrel

red·start \'red-,stärt\ *n* : an American warbler with a black and orange male

red–tailed hawk \,red-,tāld-\ *n* : an American hawk that has a rather short usually reddish tail and feeds mostly on small rodents (as mice) — called also *redtail*

red tape *n* : rules and regulations that waste people's time

red tide *n* : seawater discolored and made poisonous by the presence of large numbers of dinoflagellates

re·duce \ri-'d(y)üs\ *vb* **re·duced; re·duc·ing** **1** : to make smaller in size, amount, or number ⟨*reduce* the number of accidents⟩; *esp* : to lose weight by dieting **2** : to bring to a specified state or condition **3 a** : to lower in grade or rank : DEMOTE **b** : to be driven by poverty or need ⟨was *reduced* to begging⟩ **c** : to lessen the strength of **4** : to change an arithmetic expression to a simpler form without changing its value ⟨*reduce* a fraction to lowest terms⟩ **5** : to break down (as by crushing or grinding) ⟨*reduce* stone to powder⟩ **6 a** : DEOXIDIZE **b** : to combine with or subject to the action of hydrogen **c** : to add one or more electrons to (an atom or ion or molecule) — **re·duc·er** *n* — **re·duc·ibil·i·ty** \-,d(y)ü-sə-'bil-ət-ē\ *n* — **re·duc·ible** \-'d(y)ü-sə-bəl\ *adj*

re·duc·tion \ri-'dək-shən\ *n* **1** : the act or process of reducing : the state of being reduced **2 a** : something made by reducing **b** : the amount by which something is reduced in price **3** : MEIOSIS; *esp* : halving of the chromosome number in the reduction division — **re·duc·tive** \-'dək-tiv\ *adj*

reduction division *n* : the first meiotic cell division in the formation of sex cells in which the number of chromosomes in each cell is halved; *also* : MEIOSIS

re·dun·dan·cy \ri-'dən-dən-sē\ *n, pl* **-cies** **1** : the quality or state of being redundant **2 a** : the use of unnecessary words **b** : an act or instance of needless repetition

re·dun·dant \ri-'dən-dənt\ *adj* **1** : more than what is necessary or normal **2** : using or having more words than necessary : REPETITIOUS — **re·dun·dant·ly** *adv*

re·du·pli·cate \ri-'d(y)ü-pli-,kāt, 'rē-\ *vb* : to make or perform again : COPY — **re·du·pli·cate** \-kət\ *adj*

re·du·pli·ca·tion \ri-,d(y)ü-pli-'kā-shən, ,rē-\ *n* : an act or instance of doubling or repeating : DUPLICATION — **re·du·pli·ca·tive** \ri-'d(y)ü-pli-,kāt-iv, 'rē-\ *adj*

red–winged blackbird \,red-,wiŋd-\ *n* : an American blackbird of which the adult male is black with a patch of bright red on the wing — called also *redwing blackbird*

red-winged blackbird

red·wood \'red-,wud\ *n* : a tall cone-producing evergreen tree mostly of coastal California that is related to the bald cypresses and sometimes grows to be 360 feet (110 meters) tall; *also* : its light long-lasting brownish red wood

re·echo \(')rē-'ek-ō\ *vb* : to echo back : REVERBERATE

reed \'rēd\ *n* **1 a** : any of various tall slender grasses of wet areas that have stems with large joints **b** : a stem of such a grass **c** : a growth or mass of reeds **2** : a musical instrument made of the hollow joint of a plant **3** : a thin flexible strip (as of cane, wood, metal, or plastic) fastened at one end to the mouthpiece of a musical instrument (as a clarinet) or over an air opening (as in an accordion) and set in vibration by an air current (as the breath)

re·ed·u·cate \(')rē-'ej-ə-,kāt\ *vb* : to train again; *esp* : to cause to develop new attitudes or habits through education — **re·ed·u·ca·tion** \(,)rē-,ej-ə-'kā-shən\ *n*

reedy \'rēd-ē\ *adj* **reed·i·er; -est** **1** : full of or covered with reeds ⟨a *reedy* marsh⟩ **2** : made of or resembling reeds; *esp* : long and slender like a reed ⟨*reedy* arms⟩

¹**reef** \'rēf\ *n* **1** : a part of a sail taken in or let out in regulating size **2** : the reduction in sail area made by reefing [Middle English *riff* "reef of a sail"; of Norse origin]

²**reef** *vb* : to reduce the area of (a sail) by rolling or folding a portion

³**reef** *n* : a chain of rocks or coral or a ridge of sand at or near the surface of water [from Dutch *rif* "reef of rocks or sand"; of Scandinavian origin]

¹**reef·er** \'rē-fər\ *n* **1** : one that reefs **2** : a close-fitting jacket of thick cloth

²**reefer** *n* : a marijuana cigarette

¹**reek** \'rēk\ *n* **1** : VAPOR 1, FOG **2** : a strong or disagreeable fume or odor

²**reek** *vb* **1** : to give off smoke or vapor **2 a** : to have a strong or unpleasant smell ⟨the kitchen *reeks* of garlic⟩ ⟨clothes *reeking* of tobacco smoke⟩ **b** : to give a strong impression of some feature or quality ⟨she *reeks* of snobbery⟩ — **reeky** \'rē-kē\ *adj*

¹**reel** \'rē(ə)l\ *n* **1 a** : a device that can be turned round and round and on which something flexible is wound **b** : a device which is set on the handle of a fishing pole and used for winding up or letting out the line **c** : a narrow spool with a rim used to guide photographic film or magnetic tape **2** : a quantity of something wound on a reel **3** : a frame for drying clothes

²**reel** *vb* **1** : to wind on or as if on a reel **2** : to pull (as a fish) by reeling a line **3** : to wind or turn a reel — **reel·able** \'rē-lə-bəl\ *adj* — **reel·er** *n*

³**reel** *vb* **1 a** : to whirl around ⟨*reeling* in a dance⟩ **b** : to be in a whirl ⟨heads *reeling* with excitement⟩ **2** : to fall back (as from a blow) **3** : to walk or move unsteadily

⁴**reel** *n* : a reeling motion

⁵reel *n* : a lively dance originally of the Scottish Highlands; *also* : the music for this dance

re·elect \ˌrē-ə-ˈlekt\ *vb* : to elect for another term in office — **re·elec·tion** \-ˈlek-shən\ *n*

reel off *vb* : to tell or recite rapidly and easily ⟨*reeled off* the right answers⟩

re·en·act \ˌrē-ə-ˈnakt\ *vb* **1** : to enact again **2** : to perform again — **re·en·act·ment** \-ˈnak(t)-mənt\ *n*

re·en·ter \(ˈ)rē-ˈent-ər\ *vb* : to enter again ⟨*reentered* the building⟩

re·en·trance \(ˈ)rē-ˈen-trən(t)s\ *n* : REENTRY

re·en·try \(ˈ)rē-ˈen-trē\ *n* **1** : a second or new entry **2** : the action of reentering the earth's atmosphere after travel in space

reeve \ˈrēv\ *n* : an English manor officer of the Middle Ages

ref \ˈref\ *n* : ¹REFEREE 2

re·fash·ion \(ˈ)rē-ˈfash-ən\ *vb* : to make again : MAKE OVER, ALTER

re·fec·to·ry \ri-ˈfek-t(ə-)rē\ *n, pl* **-ries** : a dining hall

refectory table *n* : a long narrow table with heavy legs

refectory table

re·fer \ri-ˈfər\ *vb* **re·ferred**; **re·fer·ring** **1** : to explain in terms of a general cause ⟨*referred* the defeat to poor training⟩ **2** : to go, send, or guide to some person or place for treatment, help, advice, or information ⟨*refer* them to a dictionary⟩ ⟨*refer* a patient to a specialist⟩ ⟨*refer* to the dictionary for the meaning of a word⟩ **3** : to have relationship : RELATE ⟨the asterisk *refers* to a footnote⟩ **4** : to call attention : make reference ⟨no one *referred* to yesterday's quarrel⟩ [Middle English *referren, referen* "to think of or place in a certain relationship, make a connection with in the mind," derived from Latin *referre*, literally, "to carry back," from *re-* "back, again" and *ferre* "to bear, carry, yield" — related to ¹DEFER, OFFER] — **re·fer·able** \ˈref-(ə-)rə-bəl, ri-ˈfər-ə-\ *adj* — **re·fer·rer** \ri-ˈfər-ər\ *n*

¹ref·er·ee \ˌref-ə-ˈrē\ *n* **1** : a person to whom something that is to be investigated or decided is referred **2** : a sports official usually having final authority in conducting a game

²referee *vb* **-eed**; **-ee·ing** : to conduct as a referee

¹ref·er·ence \ˈref-ərn(t)s, ˈref-(ə-)rən(t)s\ *n* **1** : the act of referring **2** : a relation to or concern with something : RESPECT ⟨with *reference* to what was said⟩ **3 a** : a remark referring to something : ALLUSION ⟨made *reference* to our agreement⟩ **b** : a sign or indication referring a reader to another book or portion of a written work **c** : use as sources of information ⟨volumes for ready *reference*⟩ **4 a** : a person to whom questions as to another person's honesty or ability can be addressed **b** : a statement of the qualifications of a person seeking employment or appointment given by someone familiar with them **c** : a book, document, or portion of a written work to which a reader is referred

²reference *adj* : used or usable for reference ⟨a *reference* point⟩

reference mark *n* : a conventional mark (as *, †, or ‡) placed in written or printed text to call the reader's attention especially to a footnote

ref·er·en·dum \ˌref-ə-ˈren-dəm\ *n, pl* **-da** \-də\ *or* **-dums** : the idea or practice of letting voters approve or disapprove laws or suggested laws; *also* : such a vote

ref·er·ent \ˈref-(ə-)rənt\ *n* : something that refers or is referred to; *esp* : the thing a word represents — **referent** *adj*

re·fer·ral \ri-ˈfər-əl\ *n* : the act or an instance of referring

re·fig·ure \rē-ˈfig-yər\ *vb* **1** : to figure again or anew ⟨*refigure* the shipping charges⟩ **2** : to give new meaning or use to ⟨*refigure* old-fashioned styles⟩

¹re·fill \(ˈ)rē-ˈfil\ *vb* : to fill or become filled again — **re·fill·able** \-ˈfil-ə-bəl\ *adj*

²re·fill \ˈrē-ˌfil\ *n* : a new or fresh supply of something ⟨a *refill* for a ball-point pen⟩

re·fine \ri-ˈfīn\ *vb* **re·fined**; **re·fin·ing** **1** : to come or bring to a pure state ⟨*refine* sugar⟩ **2** : to make or become improved **3** : to free from what is vulgar **4** : to improve by introducing something that makes a small difference ⟨*refined* upon the older methods⟩ — **re·fin·er** *n*

re·fined \ri-ˈfīnd\ *adj* **1** : socially well-trained : WELL‑BRED, CULTIVATED ⟨very *refined* manners⟩ **2** : freed from impurities : PURE ⟨*refined* sugar⟩ **3** : carried to a fine point : SUBTLE ⟨*refined* measurements⟩

re·fine·ment \ri-ˈfīn-mənt\ *n* **1** : the action or process of refining **2** : the state of being refined : CULTIVATION **3 a** : something that has been refined ⟨*refinements* in dress and behavior⟩ **b** : something intended to improve or refine

re·fin·ery \ri-ˈfīn-(ə-)rē\ *n, pl* **-er·ies** : a building and equipment for refining metals, oil, or sugar

re·fin·ish \(ˈ)rē-ˈfin-ish\ *vb* : to give (as furniture) a new surface — **re·fin·ish·er** *n*

re·fit \(ˈ)rē-ˈfit\ *vb* : to get ready for use again ⟨*refit* a ship for service⟩ — **re·fit** \ˈrē-ˌfit, (ˈ)rē-ˈfit\ *n*

re·flect \ri-ˈflekt\ *vb* **1** : to bend or throw back waves of light, sound, or heat ⟨a polished surface *reflects* light⟩ **2** : to give back an image or likeness of as if by a mirror **3** : to bring as a result **4** : to cast disapproval or blame ⟨our bad conduct *reflects* upon our training⟩ **5** : to think seriously and carefully : MEDITATE

reflecting telescope *n* : REFLECTOR 2

re·flec·tion \ri-ˈflek-shən\ *n* **1** : an instance of reflecting; *esp* : the return of light or sound waves from a surface **2** : the production of an image by or as if by a mirror **3** : an image produced by or as if by a mirror **4** : something that brings blame or disgrace ⟨a *reflection* on my honesty⟩ **5** : an opinion formed or a remark made after careful thought **6** : careful thought ⟨much *reflection* on the problem⟩ — **re·flec·tion·al** \-shnəl, -shən-ᵊl\ *adj*

re·flec·tive \ri-ˈflek-tiv\ *adj* **1** : capable of reflecting light, images, or sound waves **2** : marked by reflection : THOUGHTFUL **3** : of, relating to, or caused by reflection — **re·flec·tive·ly** *adv* — **re·flec·tive·ness** *n* — **re·flec·tiv·i·ty** \ˌrē-ˌflek-ˈtiv-ət-ē, ri-\ *n*

re·flec·tor \ri-ˈflek-tər\ *n* **1** : one that reflects; *esp* : a polished surface for reflecting light or heat **2** : a telescope in which the principal light-gathering element is a mirror

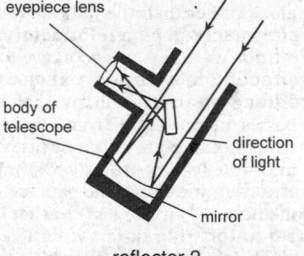

reflector 2

¹re·flex \ˈrē-ˌfleks\ *n* **1** : an automatic response to a stimulus in which a nerve message passes from a sense organ to the spinal cord and then to a point of action (as a muscle or gland) often without 2nd Passing to the brain ⟨the knee-jerk *reflex*⟩ — compare HABIT 3 **2** *pl* : the power of acting or responding with enough speed ⟨an athlete with great *reflexes*⟩

²reflex *adj* **1** : produced in reaction, resistance, or return

\ə\ **abut**	\au̇\ **out**	\i\ **tip**	\o̅\ **saw**	\u̇\ **foot**
\ər\ **further**	\ch\ **chin**	\ī\ **life**	\o̅i\ **coin**	\y\ **yet**
\a\ **mat**	\e\ **pet**	\j\ **job**	\th\ **thin**	\yü\ **few**
\ā\ **take**	\ē\ **easy**	\ŋ\ **sing**	\t̲h̲\ **this**	\yu̇\ **cure**
\ä\ **cot, cart**	\g\ **go**	\o̅\ **bone**	\ü\ **food**	\zh\ **vision**

2 : of, relating to, or produced by a reflex of the nervous system ⟨*reflex* action⟩ — **re·flex·ly** *adv*

reflex arc *n* : the complete nervous path involved in a reflex

re·flex·ion \ri-ˈflek-shən\ *chiefly British variant of* REFLECTION

¹**re·flex·ive** \ri-ˈflek-siv\ *adj* **1** : turned back upon itself **2** : of, relating to, or being an action directed back upon the doer or the grammatical subject **3** : of, relating to, or being a relation which exists between a thing and itself ⟨the relation of equality or "is equal to" is *reflexive* but the relation "is the parent of" is not⟩ **4** : characterized by behavior that occurs automatically without thinking ⟨a *reflexive* response⟩ — **re·flex·ive·ly** *adv*

²**reflexive** *n* : a pronoun that refers to the grammatical subject and is the object of the verb ⟨in the sentence "We forced ourselves to finish the assignment," the word "ourselves" is a *reflexive*⟩

re·flux \ˈrē-ˌfləks\ *n* : a flowing back : EBB

re·for·es·ta·tion \(ˌ)rē-ˌfȯr-ə-ˈstā-shən, -ˌfär-\ *n* : the action of renewing a forest by planting seeds or young trees — **re·for·est** \(ˈ)rē-ˈfȯr-əst, -ˈfär-\ *vb*

¹**re·form** \ri-ˈfȯ(ə)rm\ *vb* **1** : to make better by removal of faults ⟨*reform* a prisoner⟩ **2** : to correct or improve one's own behavior or habits — **re·form·able** \-ˈfȯr-mə-bəl\ *adj*

²**reform** *n* **1** : improvement in what is bad **2** : a removal or correction of an abuse, a wrong, or errors

re–form \(ˈ)rē-ˈfȯ(ə)rm\ *vb* : to form again ⟨the ice re=formed on the lake⟩

ref·or·ma·tion \ˌref-ər-ˈmā-shən\ *n* **1** : the act of reforming : the state of being reformed **2** *cap* : a 16th century series of religious actions which led to establishment of the Protestant churches — **ref·or·ma·tion·al** \-shnəl, -shən-ᵊl\ *adj*

re·for·ma·tive \ri-ˈfȯr-mət-iv\ *adj* : tending or likely to reform

¹**re·for·ma·to·ry** \ri-ˈfȯr-mə-ˌtōr-ē, -ˌtȯr-\ *adj* : REFORMATIVE

²**reformatory** *n, pl* **-ries** : an institution for reforming usually young or female criminals or those in jail for the first time

re·form·er \ri-ˈfȯr-mər\ *n* : one that works for reform

Reform Judaism *n* : a 19th and 20th century development of Judaism marked by the nonobservance of much legal tradition no longer considered appropriate, by simplified traditional ceremonies, and by stress on the religious rather than the national quality of Judaism

reform school *n* : a reformatory for boys or girls

re·fract \ri-ˈfrakt\ *vb* : to cause to go through refraction

refracting telescope *n* : REFRACTOR

re·frac·tion \ri-ˈfrak-shən\ *n* : the bending of a ray when it passes at an angle from one medium into another in which its speed is different (as when light passes from air into water) — **re·frac·tive** \-ˈfrak-tiv\ *adj*

refractive index *n* : the ratio of the speed of light in one medium (as air or glass) to that in another medium

re·frac·tor \ri-ˈfrak-tər\ *n* : a telescope in which the principal light-gathering element is a lens

re·frac·to·ry \ri-ˈfrakt(ə-)rē\ *adj* **1** : resisting control or authority : STUBBORN ⟨a *refractory* child⟩ **2** : resistant to treatment : UNRESPONSIVE **3** : capable of enduring high temperatures — **re·frac·to·ri·ness** \-t(ə-)rē-nəs\ *n*

¹**re·frain** \ri-ˈfrān\ *vb* : to hold oneself back ⟨*refrain* from laughing⟩

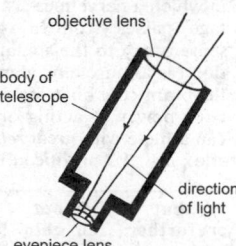

objective lens

body of telescope

direction of light

eyepiece lens

refractor

²**refrain** *n* : a regularly repeated phrase or verse of a poem or song : CHORUS

re·fresh \ri-ˈfresh\ *vb* **1** : to make fresh or fresher : REVIVE ⟨sleep *refreshes* the body⟩ ⟨*refreshed* my memory by looking at my notes⟩ **2** : to restore or maintain by renewing supply

re·fresh·en \ri-ˈfresh-ən\ *vb* : REFRESH

re·fresh·er \ri-ˈfresh-ər\ *n* **1** : something that refreshes **2** : review or instruction designed especially to keep one familiar with professional progress

re·fresh·ing \ri-ˈfresh-iŋ\ *adj* : serving to refresh; *esp* : pleasing because of freshness or newness

re·fresh·ment \ri-ˈfresh-mənt\ *n* **1** : the act of refreshing : the state of being refreshed **2 a** : something that refreshes **b** *pl* : a light meal ⟨*refreshments* will be served after the meeting⟩

re·fried beans \(ˌ)rē-ˌfrīd-\ *n pl* : beans cooked with seasonings, fried, then mashed and fried again

re·frig·er·ant \ri-ˈfrij-(ə-)rənt\ *n* : a substance used in refrigeration

re·frig·er·ate \ri-ˈfrij-ə-ˌrāt\ *vb* **-at·ed; -at·ing** : to make or keep cold or cool; *esp* : to freeze or chill food to preserve it — **re·frig·er·a·tion** \-ˌfrij-ə-ˈrā-shən\ *n*

re·frig·er·a·tor \ri-ˈfrij-ə-ˌrāt-ər\ *n* : a device or room for keeping articles (as food) cool

re·fu·el \(ˈ)rē-ˈfyü-əl\ *vb* : to provide with or take on more fuel

ref·uge \ˈref-ˌyüj\ *n* **1** : shelter or protection from danger or distress **2** : a place that provides shelter or protection ⟨wildlife *refuges*⟩

ref·u·gee \ˌref-yu̇-ˈjē, ˈref-yu̇-ˌjē\ *n* : a person who flees for safety especially to a foreign country [from French *réfugié*, past participle of *réfugier* "to put in a place of safety," from Latin *refugium* "a refuge," from *refugere* "to run away from, escape," from *re-* "again, against" and *fugere* "to run away, flee" — related to CENTRIFUGAL, FUGITIVE]

re·ful·gence \ri-ˈfu̇l-jən(t)s, -ˈfəl-\ *n* : a radiant or shining quality or state : BRILLIANCE — **re·ful·gent** \-jənt\ *adj*

¹**re·fund** \ri-ˈfənd, ˈrē-ˌfənd\ *vb* : to return money in repayment — **re·fund·able** \-ə-bəl\ *adj*

²**re·fund** \ˈrē-ˌfənd\ *n* **1** : the act of refunding **2** : an amount of money refunded

³**re·fund** \(ˈ)rē-ˈfənd\ *vb* : to fund a debt again

re·fur·bish \ri-ˈfər-bish\ *vb* : to brighten or freshen up : RENOVATE ⟨*refurbish* an old house⟩ — **re·fur·bish·ment** \-mənt\ *n*

re·fus·al \ri-ˈfyü-zəl\ *n* **1** : the act of refusing or denying **2** : the opportunity or right of refusing or taking (as a purchase) before others

¹**re·fuse** \ri-ˈfyüz\ *vb* **re·fused; re·fus·ing** **1** : to say one will not accept : REJECT ⟨*refused* the money⟩ **2 a** : to show or express positive unwillingness ⟨*refused* to act⟩ **b** : to say one will not grant : DENY ⟨was *refused* entrance⟩ **3** : to withhold the accepting, following, or permitting of something *synonyms* see DECLINE — **re·fus·er** *n*

²**ref·use** \ˈref-ˌyüs, -ˌyüz\ *n* : worthless things : TRASH

ref·u·ta·tion \ˌref-yu̇-ˈtā-shən\ *n* : the act or process of refuting : DISPROOF

re·fute \ri-ˈfyüt\ *vb* **re·fut·ed; re·fut·ing** : to prove wrong by argument or evidence : show to be false ⟨*refute* the testimony of a witness⟩ — **re·fut·able** \-ˈfyüt-ə-bəl\ *adj* — **re·fut·er** *n*

re·gain \ri-ˈgān\ *vb* **1** : to gain or get again ⟨*regained* my health⟩ **2** : to get back to : reach again ⟨*regain* the shore⟩

re·gal \ˈrē-gəl\ *adj* **1** : of, relating to, or suitable for a king **2** : of remarkable excellence or magnificence : SPLENDID — **re·gal·ly** \ˈrē-gə-lē\ *adv*

re·gale \ri-ˈgā(ə)l\ *vb* **re·galed; re·gal·ing** **1** : to entertain richly **2** : to give pleasure or amusement to **3** : to feast oneself : FEED

re·ga·lia \ri-'gāl-yə\ *n sing or pl* **1** : the emblems and symbols (as the crown) of royalty **2** : the emblem of an office or association **3** : special dress : FINERY

¹re·gard \ri-'gärd\ *n* **1 a** : CONSIDERATION 2, CONCERN ⟨little *regard* for others' feelings⟩ **b** : the act or an instance of looking : GAZE **2 a** : the worth or estimation in which something is held **b** : a feeling of respect and affection : ESTEEM ⟨a high *regard* for my teacher⟩ **c** *pl* : friendly greetings ⟨give them my *regards*⟩ **3** : ¹REFERENCE 2, RESPECT ⟨this is in *regard* to your unpaid balance⟩ **4** : a point to be taken into consideration ⟨nothing to worry about in that *regard*⟩

²regard *vb* **1** : to pay attention to : take into consideration **2 a** : to show respect or consideration for **b** : to have a high opinion of **3** : to look at **4** *archaic* : to relate to **5** : to think of : look upon ⟨*regarded* you as a friend⟩ — **as regards** : with respect to : REGARDING

re·gard·ful \ri-'gärd-fəl\ *adj* **1** : HEEDFUL, OBSERVANT **2** : full or expressive of regard or respect : RESPECTFUL

re·gard·ing *prep* : CONCERNING

¹re·gard·less \ri-'gärd-ləs\ *adj* : having or taking no regard : HEEDLESS, CARELESS ⟨*regardless* of what might happen⟩

²regardless *adv* : in spite of everything

re·gat·ta \ri-'gät-ə, -'gat-\ *n* : a boat race or a series of boat races

re·gen·cy \'rē-jən-sē\ *n, pl* **-cies** **1** : the office, authority, or government of a regent or body of regents **2** : the period of rule of a regent or body of regents

¹re·gen·er·ate \ri-'jen-(ə-)rət\ *adj* : spiritually reborn or renewed

²re·gen·er·ate \ri-'jen-ə-,rāt\ *vb* **1** : to cause to be reborn spiritually **2** : to reform completely in ways of thinking and behaving **3** : to generate or produce again; *esp* : to replace (a lost or damaged body part) by a new growth of tissue **4** : to give new life to : REVIVE ⟨land *regenerated* by rotation of crops⟩

re·gen·er·a·tion \ri-jen-ə-'rā-shən, ,rē-\ *n* : an act or the process of regenerating : the state of being regenerated

re·gen·er·a·tive \ri-'jen-ə-,rāt-iv\ *adj* **1** : of, relating to, or marked by regeneration **2** : tending to regenerate

re·gent \'rē-jənt\ *n* **1** : a person who governs a kingdom when a monarch is not able to **2** : a member of a governing group (as of a state university) [Middle English *regent* "one who governs," from early French *regent* or Latin *regent-, regens* (both, same meaning), from earlier Latin *regens,* a form of the verb *regere* "to lead straight, govern, rule" — related to ¹RAIL, REGULATE, RULE] — **regent** *adj*

reg·gae \'reg-(,)ā, 'rāg-\ *n* : popular music of Jamaican origin that combines native styles with elements of U.S. black popular music and is performed at moderate tempos with the accent on the offbeat

reg·i·cide \'rej-ə-,sīd\ *n* **1** : a person who kills or helps to kill a king **2** : the killing of a king — **reg·i·cid·al** \,rej-ə-'sīd-əl\ *adj*

re·gime *also* **ré·gime** \rā-'zhēm, ri-\ *n* **1 a** : REGIMEN 1 **b** : a regular pattern of doing something **2 a** : a method of rule or management **b** : a form of government or administration; *esp* : a governmental or social system **c** : a period of rule of a regime

reg·i·men \'rej-ə-mən, -,men\ *n* **1** : a regular course of treatment **2** : a form of government : RULE

¹reg·i·ment \'rej-(ə-)mənt\ *n* : a military unit consisting usually of a number of battalions — **reg·i·men·tal** \,rej-ə-'ment-əl\ *adj*

²reg·i·ment \'rej-ə-,ment\ *vb* **1** : to organize for the sake of regulation or control **2** : to make orderly or the same as others — **reg·i·men·ta·tion** \,rej-ə-mən-'tā-shən, -,men-\ *n*

reg·i·men·tals \,rej-ə-'ment-əlz\ *n pl* **1** : a regimental uniform **2** : military dress

re·gion \'rē-jən\ *n* **1** : an area, division, or district of administration **2 a** : a part, portion, or area having no fixed boundaries ⟨darker *regions* of the night sky⟩ **b** : a broad geographic area ⟨never visited the southwestern *region* of the U.S.⟩ **3** : an indefinite area surrounding a specified body part ⟨a pain in the *region* of the heart⟩ **4** : a set of points any two of which can be connected by a line lying wholly within the set together with none, some, or all of the points on its boundary ⟨a rectangular *region*⟩

re·gion·al \'rēj-nəl, -ən-əl\ *adj* **1** : of, relating to, or characteristic of a region **2** : affecting a particular region : LOCALIZED ⟨*regional* pain⟩ — **re·gion·al·ly** \-ē\ *adv*

re·gion·al·ism \'rēj-nəl-,iz-əm, -ən-əl-\ *n* **1** : the quality of being conscious of and loyal to a particular region **2** : the practice of using a particular region as the setting in art or literature **3** : an individual quality (as of speech) of a geographic area — **re·gion·al·ist** \-əst\ *n or adj* — **re·gion·al·is·tic** \,rēj-nəl-'is-tik, -ən-əl-\ *adj*

¹reg·is·ter \'rej-ə-stər\ *n* **1 a** : a written record or list of items **b** : a book for such a record ⟨a *register* of deeds⟩ **2** : a part of the range of a human voice or a musical instrument made up of tones similarly produced or of the same quality **3** : a device (as in a floor or wall) that regulates the flow of heated air from a furnace **4 a** : an automatic device registering a number or a quantity **b** : a number or quantity registered by such a device

¹register 3

²register *vb* **reg·is·tered; reg·is·ter·ing** \-st(ə-)riŋ\ **1 a** : to record exactly and legally in a register ⟨*register* a will⟩ **b** : to enroll especially as a voter or student **c** : to record automatically : INDICATE ⟨the thermometer *registered* zero⟩ **2** : to get special protection for (a piece of mail) by prepayment of a fee **3** : to show by expression and bodily movements alone ⟨your face *registered* surprise⟩ **4** : to write one's name in a register ⟨*register* at a hotel⟩ ⟨*register* for the draft⟩ **5** : to make an impression ⟨your name didn't *register* with me⟩

³register *n* : REGISTRAR

registered nurse *n* : a graduate trained nurse who has been licensed to practice by a state authority — called also *RN*

reg·is·trant \'rej-ə-strənt\ *n* : one that registers or is registered

reg·is·trar \'rej-ə-,strär\ *n* : an official who records or keeps records

reg·is·tra·tion \,rej-ə-'strā-shən\ *n* **1** : an act or the fact of registering **2** : something recorded in a register **3** : the number of individuals registered : ENROLLMENT **4** : a document certifying an act of registering ⟨automobile *registration*⟩

reg·is·try \'rej-ə-strē\ *n, pl* **-tries** **1** : REGISTRATION 3 **2** : a place of registration **3 a** : a book in which things are recorded exactly and legally **b** : something recorded in a registry

re·gress \ri-'gres\ *vb* : to go or cause to go back especially to a previous level or condition

re·gres·sion \ri-'gresh-ən\ *n* : an act or the fact of regressing

re·gres·sive \ri-'gres-iv\ *adj* **1** : of, relating to, or tending toward regression **2** : gradually decreasing ⟨a *regressive* tax⟩

\ə\ abut	\au̇\ out	\i\ tip	\ȯ\ saw	\u̇\ foot
\ər\ further	\ch\ chin	\ī\ life	\ȯi\ coin	\y\ yet
\a\ mat	\e\ pet	\j\ job	\th\ thin	\yü\ few
\ā\ take	\ē\ easy	\ŋ\ sing	\th\ this	\yu̇\ cure
\ä\ cot, cart	\g\ go	\ō\ bone	\ü\ food	\zh\ vision

¹re·gret \ri-ˈgret\ *vb* **re·gret·ted; re·gret·ting** **1 a** : to mourn the loss or death of **b** : to miss very much **2** : to be keenly sorry for **3** : to experience regret

²regret *n* **1** : sorrow aroused by events beyond one's control **2 a** : an expression of sorrow or disappointment **b** *pl* : a note politely turning down an invitation — **re·gret·ful** \-ˈgret-fəl\ *adj*

re·gret·ful·ly \ri-ˈgret-fə-lē\ *adv* **1** : in a way that is full of regret ⟨I must *regretfully* decline your invitation⟩ **2** : I regret : we regret ⟨*regretfully*, we can't go⟩

re·gret·ta·ble \ri-ˈgret-ə-bəl\ *adj* : deserving regret

re·gret·ta·bly \ri-ˈgret-ə-blē\ *adv* **1** : to an extent deserving regret ⟨a *regrettably* big decline in wages⟩ **2** : it is regrettable : UNFORTUNATELY ⟨*regrettably*, I could not agree⟩

re·group \(ˈ)rē-ˈgrüp\ *vb* : to form into a new group ⟨in order to subtract 129 from 531 *regroup* 531 into 5 hundreds, 2 tens, and 11 ones⟩

re·grow \(ˈ)rē-ˈgrō\ *vb* **-grew** \-ˈgrü\; **-grown** \-ˈgrōn\; **-grow·ing** : to grow (as a missing part) again

re·growth \(ˈ)rē-ˈgrōth\ *n* : the process of regrowing ⟨conditions affecting forest *regrowth*⟩; *also* : a result or product of regrowing ⟨cattle grazing on pasture *regrowth*⟩

¹reg·u·lar \ˈreg-yə-lər\ *adj* **1** : belonging to a religious community and living by its rules **2 a** : formed, built, arranged, or ordered according to an established rule, law, or type **b** : having all sides or faces equal and all angles equal ⟨a square is a *regular* polygon⟩ **c** : even or balanced in form or structure; *esp* : having radial symmetry ⟨*regular* flowers⟩ **3 a** : being in the habit of following a method : ORDERLY, METHODICAL **b** : returning or acting at fixed times **4 a** : following established or prescribed uses or rules **b** : being such without any doubt : COMPLETE, UNMITIGATED ⟨a *regular* scoundrel⟩ **c** : following the normal or usual manner of changing tense ⟨*regular* verbs⟩ **5** : of, relating to, or being a permanent army of a country — **reg·u·lar·ly** \ˈreg-yə-lər-lē\ *adv*

²regular *n* **1** : a member of the clergy who belongs to a religious community **2** : a soldier in a regular army **3** : a player on an athletic team who usually starts every game

reg·u·lar·i·ty \ˌreg-yə-ˈlar-ət-ē\ *n, pl* **-ties** **1** : the quality or state of being regular **2** : something that is regular

reg·u·lar·ize \ˈreg-yə-lə-ˌrīz\ *vb* **-ized; -iz·ing** : to make regular

reg·u·late \ˈreg-yə-ˌlāt\ *vb* **-lat·ed; -lat·ing** **1 a** : to govern or direct according to rule **b** : to bring under the control of authority ⟨*regulate* prices⟩ **2** : to bring order or method to ⟨*regulate* one's habits⟩ **3** : to fix or adjust the time, amount, degree, or rate of ⟨*regulate* the pressure of a tire⟩ ⟨the brain *regulates* the heartbeat⟩ [from Latin *regulatus*, past participle of *regulare* "to regulate, direct," from *regula* "a rule, straightedge" — related to ¹RAIL, REGENT, RULE] — **reg·u·la·tor** \-ˌlāt-ər\ *n* — **reg·u·la·to·ry** \-lə-ˌtōr-ē, -ˌtȯr-\ *adj*

¹reg·u·la·tion \ˌreg-yə-ˈlā-shən\ *n* **1** : the act of regulating : the state of being regulated **2 a** : a rule or order telling how something is to be done ⟨safety *regulations* in a factory⟩ **b** : a rule or order having the force of law

²regulation *adj* : being in agreement with regulations ⟨a *regulation* baseball⟩

re·gur·gi·tate \(ˈ)rē-ˈgər-jə-ˌtāt\ *vb* **-tat·ed; -tat·ing** : to throw or be thrown back or out again ⟨*regurgitate* undigested food⟩ — **re·gur·gi·ta·tion** \(ˌ)rē-ˌgər-jə-ˈtā-shən\ *n*

re·ha·bil·i·tate \ˌrē-(h)ə-ˈbil-ə-ˌtāt\ *vb* **-tat·ed; -tat·ing** **1** : to restore to a former status or reputation **2 a** : to restore to a state of efficiency, good management, or repair ⟨*rehabilitate* slum areas⟩ **b** : to restore to a condition of health or useful and constructive activity ⟨*rehabilitate* criminals⟩ — **re·ha·bil·i·ta·tion** \-ˌbil-ə-ˈtā-shən\ *n*

re·hash \(ˈ)rē-ˈhash\ *vb* : to present or use (as an argu-

ment) again in another form without much change or improvement — **re·hash** \ˈrē-ˌhash\ *n*

re·hears·al \ri-ˈhər-səl\ *n* **1** : a private performance or practice session in preparation for a public appearance **2** : a practice exercise : TRIAL

re·hearse \ri-ˈhərs\ *vb* **re·hearsed; re·hears·ing** **1 a** : to say again : REPEAT **b** : to recount in order : ENUMERATE ⟨they *rehearsed* their complaints in a letter⟩ **2 a** : to practice (a play or scene) for public performance **b** : to train or instruct (as actors) by rehearsal **3** : to engage in a rehearsal — **re·hears·er** *n*

Word History In the Middle Ages, French farmers used a tool they called a *herce*. This was a triangular wooden frame with sturdy pegs or teeth on one side. It was pulled over plowed farmland to break up the soil in order to make it smooth for planting. The early French verb used to describe this action was *hercier*, which meant "to harrow." In most cases the process had to be repeated over and over, so the word *rehercier* was formed, meaning "to harrow again" or "reharrow." In time, *rehercier* came to be used with more general meanings like "to go over something again (and again)," as in repeating a school lesson or a story. The word came into Middle English as *rehersen*, meaning "to say again, repeat." Through the years the English word, now spelled *rehearse*, has picked up new meanings. Perhaps the most familiar one now is "to go through (a scene or play) over and over for practice until it is ready for performance." [Middle English *rehersen* "to say again, repeat," from early French *rehercier* "to go over again and again," literally, "to harrow again," from *re-* "again" and *hercier* "to harrow," from *herce* "a harrow"]

re·hy·drate \(ˈ)rē-ˈhī-ˌdrāt\ *vb* : to restore fluid to (something dehydrated) — **re·hy·dra·tion** \ˌrē-ˌhī-ˈdrā-shən\ *n*

reichs·mark \ˈrīk-ˌsmärk\ *n, pl* **reichsmarks** *also* **reichsmark** : the German unit of money from 1925 to 1948

¹reign \ˈrān\ *n* **1** : the authority or rule of a monarch **2** : the time during which a monarch reigns

²reign *vb* **1** : to govern as a monarch **2** : to exercise authority in the manner of a monarch **3** : to be usual or widespread ⟨silence *reigned*⟩

reign of terror : a period marked by violence that is often carried out by those in power and produces terror among the people involved

re·im·burse \ˌrē-əm-ˈbərs\ *vb* **-bursed; -burs·ing** : to pay back : REPAY ⟨*reimburse* travel expenses⟩ [from *re-* "again, back" and obsolete *imburse* "pay, put in the pocket," from Latin *imbursare* (same meaning), from earlier *in-* "in" and *bursa* "purse, small leather bag" — related to DISBURSE, PURSE] — **re·im·burs·able** \-ˈbər-sə-bəl\ *adj* — **re·im·burse·ment** \-ˈbər-smənt\ *n*

¹rein \ˈrān\ *n* **1** : a line or strap fastened to a bit on each side for controlling an animal (as a horse) — usually used in plural **2 a** : an influence that slows, limits, or holds back ⟨kept the child under a tight *rein*⟩ **b** : controlling or guiding power — usually used in plural ⟨seized the *reins* of government⟩ **3** : complete freedom : SCOPE ⟨gave full *rein* to her imagination⟩

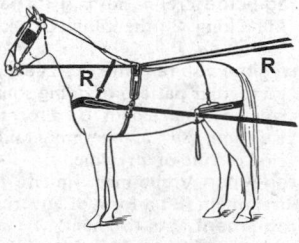

R **¹rein 1**

²rein *vb* : to check, control, or stop by or as if by reins ⟨*reined* in the horse⟩ ⟨couldn't *rein* his impatience⟩

re·in·car·nate \ˌrē-ən-ˈkär-ˌnāt\ *vb* **-nat·ed; -nat·ing** : to give a new or different body or form to

re·in·car·na·tion \(ˌ)rē-ˌin-ˌkär-ˈnā-shən\ *n* **1** : the action of reincarnating : the state of being reincarnated **2** : rebirth in new bodies or forms of life; *esp* : a rebirth of a soul in a new human body

rein·deer \ˈrān-ˌdi(ə)r\ *n, pl* **reindeer** *also* **rein·deers** : CARIBOU — used especially for one of the Old World

reindeer moss *n* : a gray lichen of northern regions that has many branches and is an important food for caribou

re·in·fec·tion \ˌrē-ən-ˈfek-shən\ *n* : infection following recovery from another infection of the same kind — **re·in·fect** \ˌre-ən-ˈfekt\ *vb*

re·in·force \ˌrē-ən-ˈfō(ə)rs, -ˈfȯ(ə)rs\ *vb* **1** : to strengthen by additional assistance, material, or support ⟨*reinforce* the elbows of a jacket⟩ ⟨*reinforce* the argument with facts⟩ **2** : to strengthen or increase by fresh additions ⟨were *reinforcing* their pitching staff⟩ ⟨*reinforce* our troops⟩ **3** : to stimulate (a person or animal) with a reinforcer; *also* : to increase the frequency of (a response) with a reinforcer

re·in·force·ment \ˌrē-ən-ˈfōr-smənt, -ˈfȯr-\ *n* **1** : the action of reinforcing : the state of being reinforced **2** : something that reinforces

re·in·forc·er \ˌrē-ən-ˈfōr-sər, -ˈfȯr-\ *n* **1** : one that reinforces **2** : a stimulus (as a reward or the removal of something unpleasant) given after a desired action or reply that helps to make the individual act or reply in the same way when the conditions are repeated

re·in·state \ˌrē-ən-ˈstāt\ *vb* **-stat·ed; -stat·ing** : to place again in a former position or condition ⟨*reinstate* an official⟩ — **re·in·state·ment** \-mənt\ *n*

re·in·ter·pret \ˌrē-ən-ˈtər-prət\ *vb* : to interpret again; *esp* : to give a new or different interpretation to — **re·in·ter·pre·ta·tion** \-ˌtər-prə-ˈtā-shən\ *n*

re·in·vent \ˌrē-ən-ˈvent\ *vb* **1** : to make as if for the first time something already invented ⟨*reinvent* the wheel⟩ **2** : to remake or redo completely ⟨*reinvented* his musical style⟩ — **re·in·ven·tion** \-ˈven-chən\ *n*

re·in·vest \ˌrē-ən-ˈvest\ *vb* : to invest again or anew — **re·in·vest·ment** \-ˈves(t)-mənt\ *n*

re·is·sue \ˈish-ü\ *vb* : to issue again; *esp* : to cause to become available again ⟨*reissue* a stamp⟩ — **reissue** *n*

re·it·er·ate \rē-ˈit-ə-ˌrāt\ *vb* **-at·ed; -at·ing** : to say or do over again or repeatedly — **re·it·er·a·tion** \(ˌ)rē-ˌit-ə-ˈrā-shən\ *n* — **re·it·er·a·tive** \rē-ˈit-ə-ˌrāt-iv, -rət-\ *adj* — **re·it·er·a·tive·ly** *adv* — **re·it·er·a·tive·ness** *n*

¹re·ject \ri-ˈjekt\ *vb* **1** : to refuse to admit, believe, or receive **2** : to throw away as useless or unsatisfactory **3** : to refuse to grant or consider **4** : to cause the rejection of by the immune system ⟨the body of the patient started to *reject* the transplanted heart⟩ **synonyms** see DECLINE

²re·ject \ˈrē-ˌjekt\ *n* : a rejected person or thing

re·jec·tion \ri-ˈjek-shən\ *n* **1** : the action of rejecting : the state of being rejected **2** : something rejected **3** : the process by which the immune system causes foreign tissue (as of a skin graft or transplanted organ) to separate from and stop functioning with the tissues of the animal or human being that has received it

re·joice \ri-ˈjȯis\ *vb* **re·joiced; re·joic·ing** **1** : to give joy to : GLADDEN ⟨news that *rejoices* the heart⟩ **2** : to feel joy or great delight ⟨*rejoice* over a friend's good luck⟩ — **re·joic·er** *n* — **re·joic·ing·ly** \-ˈjȯi-siŋ-lē\ *adv*

re·joic·ing \ri-ˈjȯi-siŋ\ *n* **1** : the action of one that rejoices **2** : a time or an expression of joy

re·join *vb* **1** \(ˈ)rē-ˈjȯin\ : to join again : return to ⟨*rejoined* my family after a week in camp⟩ **2** \ri-\ : to say in reply

re·join·der \ri-ˈjȯin-dər\ *n* : ²REPLY; *esp* : an answer to a reply

re·ju·ve·nate \ri-ˈjü-və-ˌnāt\ *vb* **-nat·ed; -nat·ing** : to make young or youthful again : give new vigor to — **re·ju·ve·na·tion** \-ˌjü-və-ˈnā-shən\ *n* — **re·ju·ve·na·tor** \-ˈjü-və-ˌnāt-ər\ *n*

relaid *past and past participle of* RELAY

¹re·lapse \ri-ˈlaps, ˈrē-ˌlaps\ *n* : a relapsing; *esp* : a recurrence of illness after a period of improvement

²re·lapse \ri-ˈlaps\ *vb* **re·lapsed; re·laps·ing** : to slip or fall back into a former worse state — **re·laps·er** *n*

re·late \ri-ˈlāt\ *vb* **re·lat·ed; re·lat·ing** **1** : to give an account of : TELL ⟨*relate* a story⟩ **2** : to show or establish a relationship between ⟨*relate* cause and effect⟩ **3** : to have relationship or connection : REFER ⟨the readings *relate* to the class discussions⟩ **4** : to have or establish a social relationship ⟨the way a child *relates* to a teacher⟩ **5** : to respond especially in a favorable way ⟨can't *relate* to that kind of music⟩ — **re·lat·able** \-ˈlāt-ə-bəl\ *adj*

re·lat·ed *adj* **1** : connected through a relation that is known or can be discovered ⟨painting and the *related* arts⟩ **2** : connected by common ancestry or by marriage

re·lat·er *or* **re·la·tor** \ri-ˈlāt-ər\ *n* : one that relates : NARRATOR

re·la·tion \ri-ˈlā-shən\ *n* **1** : the act of telling or describing **2** : CONNECTION 2, RELATIONSHIP ⟨the *relation* of employer to employee⟩ **3** : a related person : RELATIVE **4** : ¹REFERENCE 2, RESPECT ⟨in *relation* to this matter⟩ **5 a** : the state of sharing an interest (as in social or business matters) **b** *pl* : business or public affairs ⟨good trade *relations*⟩ ⟨foreign *relations*⟩ **c** *pl* : dealings between persons or groups ⟨improved his *relations* with his family⟩ — **re·la·tion·al** \-shnəl, -shən-ᵊl\ *adj*

re·la·tion·ship \ri-ˈlā-shən-ˌship\ *n* **1** : the state of being related ⟨study language *relationships*⟩ **2** : KINSHIP ⟨claimed *relationship* with the mayor⟩; *also* : a specific instance or type of this ⟨family *relationships*⟩ **3** : a state of affairs existing between those having shared dealings ⟨good doctor-patient *relationships*⟩

¹rel·a·tive \ˈrel-ət-iv\ *n* **1** : a word referring grammatically to one that comes before it **2** : a person connected with another by blood or marriage

²relative *adj* **1 a** : introducing a subordinate clause that qualifies an expressed or implied antecedent ⟨*relative* pronoun⟩ **b** : introduced by a word having such an antecedent ⟨*relative* clause⟩ **2** : RELEVANT, PERTINENT ⟨questions *relative* to the topic⟩ **3** : existing in comparison to something else ⟨the *relative* value of two houses⟩ **4** : having the same key signature — used of major and minor keys and scales — **rel·a·tive·ness** *n*

relative humidity *n* : the amount of water vapor actually present in the air compared to the greatest amount possible at the same temperature

rel·a·tive·ly \ˈrel-ət-iv-lē\ *adv* : ²SOMEWHAT

relative to *prep* : in relation to ⟨the angle of the pole *relative to* the ground⟩

rel·a·tiv·is·tic \ˌrel-ət-iv-ˈis-tik\ *adj* : of, relating to, or characterized by relativity — **rel·a·tiv·is·ti·cal·ly** \-ti-k(ə-)lē\ *adv*

rel·a·tiv·i·ty \ˌrel-ə-ˈtiv-ət-ē\ *n, pl* **-ties** **1** : the quality or state of being relative; *esp* : dependence on something else **2 a** : a theory in physics that considers mass and energy to be equal and that states that a moving object will experience changes in mass, size, and time which are related to its speed and are not noticeable except at speeds approaching that of light **b** : an extension of relativity theory to include gravity and its related acceleration effects

re·lax \ri-ˈlaks\ *vb* **1** : to make or become loose or less tense ⟨*relaxed* my attention⟩ **2** : to make or become less severe or strict ⟨*relax* discipline⟩ **3** : to get rid of nervous tension or anxiety ⟨couldn't *relax* in crowds⟩ **4** : to rest or enjoy oneself away from one's usual duties ⟨*relaxed* at the beach⟩ — **re·lax·er** *n*

¹re·lax·ant \ri-'lak-sənt\ *adj* : producing relaxation

²relaxant *n* : a relaxing agent; *esp* : a drug that causes muscular relaxation

re·lax·ation \ˌrē-ˌlak-'sā-shən, ri-\ *n* **1** : the act of relaxing : the state of being relaxed **2** : a relaxing activity or pastime ⟨play the guitar as a *relaxation*⟩ **3** : the lengthening that characterizes inactive muscle

re·laxed \ri-'lakst\ *adj* **1** : lacking in precision or strictness ⟨was very *relaxed* for a new parent⟩ **2** : not worried or tense ⟨found her in a *relaxed* moment⟩ **3** : easy of manner : INFORMAL ⟨a *relaxed* style of comedy⟩ **4** : somewhat loose-fitting and usually casual in style ⟨*relaxed* jeans⟩ — **re·laxed·ly** \-'lak-səd-lē, -'laks-tlē\ *adv* — **re·laxed·ness** \-'lak-səd-nəs, -'laks(t)-nəs\ *n*

¹re·lay \'rē-ˌlā\ *n* **1** : a fresh supply (as of horses or people) arranged to relieve others **2 a** : a race between teams in which each team member covers an assigned part of the course **b** : one of the divisions of a relay **3** : an electromagnetic device in which the opening or closing of one circuit operates another device (as a switch in another circuit) **4** : the act of passing along (as a message or a ball) by stages; *also* : one of such stages ⟨the shortstop's *relay* from center field was too late to catch the runner⟩

²re·lay \'rē-ˌlā, ri-'lā\ *vb* **re·layed; re·lay·ing 1 a** : to place or arrange in relays **b** : to provide with relays **2** : to pass along by stages ⟨news was *relayed* by satellites⟩

³re·lay \(')rē-'lā\ *vb* **-laid** \-'lād\; **-lay·ing** : to lay again

¹re·lease \ri-'lēs\ *vb* **re·leased; re·leas·ing 1** : to set free (as from confinement) ⟨*release* a prisoner⟩ ⟨*release* a bird from a cage⟩ **2** : to relieve from something that holds or burdens ⟨*released* from our promise⟩ **3** : to give up in favor of another : RELINQUISH ⟨*release* a claim to property⟩ **4** : to give permission for publication, performance, exhibition, or sale of (as a movie or news story) — **re·leas·able** \-'lē-sə-bəl\ *adj*

²release *n* **1** : relief or rescue from sorrow, suffering, or trouble **2 a** : a discharge from an obligation (as a debt) **b** : a giving up of a right or claim **3** : the act or an instance of setting free or letting go **4** : a document that contains a release **5** : the state of being freed **6** : a device adapted to hold or release a mechanism as required **7 a** : the act of permitting performance or publication **b** : the matter released; *esp* : a statement prepared for the press

re·leas·er \ri-'lē-sər\ *n* : one that releases; *esp* : a stimulus that serves to start complicated reflex behavior

rel·e·gate \'rel-ə-ˌgāt\ *vb* **-gat·ed; -gat·ing 1** : to remove or dismiss to a less important place ⟨*relegate* some old books to the attic⟩ **2** : to refer or hand over for decision or carrying out ⟨*relegate* that matter to a special committee⟩ — **rel·e·ga·tion** \ˌrel-ə-'gā-shən\ *n*

re·lent \ri-'lent\ *vb* **1** : to become less severe, harsh, or strict **2** : SLACKEN

re·lent·less \ri-'lent-ləs\ *adj* : not lessening in severity, intensity, strength, or pace : UNRELENTING ⟨*relentless* criticism⟩ — **re·lent·less·ly** *adv* — **re·lent·less·ness** *n*

rel·e·vance \'rel-ə-vən(t)s\ *n* : relation to the matter at hand : PERTINENCE

rel·e·van·cy \'rel-ə-vən-sē\ *n, pl* **-cies** : RELEVANCE

rel·e·vant \'rel-ə-vənt\ *adj* : having something to do with the matter being considered : PERTINENT ⟨a *relevant* question⟩ — **rel·e·vant·ly** *adv*

re·li·abil·i·ty \ri-ˌlī-ə-'bil-ət-ē\ *n, pl* **-ties** : the quality or state of being reliable

re·li·able \ri-'lī-ə-bəl\ *adj* : fit to be trusted : DEPENDABLE — **re·li·able·ness** *n* — **re·li·ably** \-blē\ *adv*

re·li·ance \ri-'lī-ən(t)s\ *n* **1** : the act of relying **2** : the condition or attitude of one who relies : DEPENDENCE **3** : something or someone relied on

re·li·ant \ri-'lī-ənt\ *adj* : having reliance on something or

someone : TRUSTING ⟨*reliant* on the family for news⟩ — **re·li·ant·ly** *adv*

rel·ic \'rel-ik\ *n* **1** : an object treated with great respect because of its connection with a saint or martyr **2** : something left behind after decay or disappearance ⟨*relics* of ancient cities⟩

rel·ict \'rel-ikt\ *n* **1** : WIDOW **2** : a small surviving group of a formerly widespread plant or animal species that continues to exist in an isolated area

relied *past and past participle of* RELY

re·lief \ri-'lēf\ *n* **1 a** : removal or lightening of something painful, troubling, burdensome, or dangerous **b** : WELFARE 2a **c** : military assistance to a post or force in extreme danger **d** : a means of breaking boredom : DIVERSION ⟨a quick swim was a welcome *relief* from the job⟩ **2** : release from duty **3** : one that takes the place of another on duty **4**

relief 5b

: the legal correction of a wrong **5 a** : elevation of figures or designs from the background (as in sculpture) **b** : a work of art with such raised figures **c** : projecting detail or figures in sculpture **6** : sharpness of outline ⟨a roof in bold *relief* against the sky⟩ **7** : the elevations of a land surface ⟨a map showing *relief*⟩

relief map *n* : a map or model in which unevenness of surface is shown in relief

relief pitcher *n* : a baseball pitcher who takes over for another during a game

re·lieve \ri-'lēv\ *vb* **re·lieved; re·liev·ing 1** : to free partly or wholly from a burden or from distress ⟨*relieve* parents of worry⟩ **2** : to bring about the removal or reduction of ⟨efforts to *relieve* world hunger⟩ **3** : to release from a post or duty ⟨*relieve* a sentry⟩ **4** : to break the sameness of ⟨a black dress *relieved* by a white collar⟩ **5** : to put or stand out in relief : set off by contrast (as in sculpture or painting) **6** : to discharge the bladder or bowels of (oneself) — **re·liev·er** *n*

re·li·gion \ri-'lij-ən\ *n* **1 a** : the service and worship of God or the supernatural **b** : belief in or devotion to religious faith or observance **c** : the state of a person in the religious life ⟨a nun in her 20th year of *religion*⟩ **2** : a set or system of religious attitudes, beliefs, and ways of doing things **3** : a cause, principle, or system of beliefs held with faith and strong feeling

¹re·li·gious \ri-'lij-əs\ *adj* **1** : devoted to God or to the powers or forces believed to govern life ⟨a very *religious* person⟩ **2** : of or relating to religion ⟨*religious* beliefs⟩ **3** : very devoted and faithful ⟨performed his duties with *religious* regularity⟩ — **re·li·gious·ly** *adv* — **re·li·gious·ness** *n*

²religious *n, pl* **religious** : a member of a religious order

re·line \(')rē-'līn\ *vb* : to put new lines on or a new lining in ⟨*reline* a coat⟩

re·lin·quish \ri-'liŋ-kwish\ *vb* **1** : to withdraw or retreat from : leave behind ⟨*relinquished* their homes and sailed to the New World⟩ **2** : to give over to the control or possession of another ⟨*relinquish* a title⟩ **3** : to let go of : RELEASE ⟨*relinquish* your grip on the bar⟩ ⟨few leaders willingly *relinquish* power⟩ — **re·lin·quish·ment** \-mənt\ *n*

rel·i·quary \'rel-ə-ˌkwer-ē\ *n, pl* **-quar·ies** : a small box or shrine in which sacred relics are kept

¹rel·ish \'rel-ish\ *n* **1** : a pleasing appetizing taste **2** : a small bit added for flavor : DASH **3 a** : enjoyment or delight in something ⟨eat with great *relish*⟩ **b** : a strong liking **4** : a highly seasoned food (as of pickles or mustard) eaten with other food to add flavor

²**relish** *vb* **1** : to add relish to **2** : to be pleased by : ENJOY **3** : to eat or drink with pleasure — **rel·ish·able** \-ə-bəl\ *adj*

re·live \(')rē-'liv\ *vb* : to live over again; *esp* : to experience again in the imagination

re·lo·cate \(')rē-'lō-ˌkāt, ˌrē-lō-'kāt\ *vb* **1** : to locate again **2** : to move to a new location ⟨*relocate* a factory⟩ — **re·lo·ca·tion** \ˌrē-lō-'kā-shən\ *n*

re·luc·tance \ri-'lək-tən(t)s\ *n* : the quality or state of being reluctant

re·luc·tant \ri-'lək-tənt\ *adj* : showing doubt or unwillingness ⟨*reluctant* to answer⟩ — **re·luc·tant·ly** *adv*

re·ly \ri-'lī\ *vb* **re·lied; re·ly·ing 1** : to have confidence based on experience ⟨someone you can *rely* on⟩ **2** : to be dependent ⟨the system on which we *rely* for water⟩

REM \'rem\ *n* : RAPID EYE MOVEMENT

¹**re·main** \ri-'mān\ *vb* **1 a** : to be a part not destroyed, taken, or used up ⟨little *remained* after the fire⟩ **b** : to be something yet to be shown, done, or treated ⟨that *remains* to be seen⟩ **2** : to stay in the same place or with the same person or group; *esp* : to stay behind **3** : to continue unchanged ⟨the weather *remained* cold⟩

²**remain** *n* **1** : whatever is left over or behind — usually used in plural ⟨the *remains* of a meal⟩ **2** *pl* : a dead body

re·main·der \ri-'mān-dər\ *n* **1** : a remaining group or part **2** : the number left after a subtraction **3** : the final undivided part that is left over after division and is smaller than the divisor ⟨dividing 7 by 3 gives you 2 with a *remainder* of 1⟩

¹**re·make** \(')rē-'māk\ *vb* **-made** \-'mād\; **-mak·ing** : to make anew or in a different form

²**re·make** \'rē-ˌmāk\ *n* : one that has been remade; *esp* : a new version of a motion picture

¹**re·mand** \ri-'mand\ *vb* **1** : to send back a case to another court for further action **2** : to return to custody or be held longer or to await trial

²**remand** *n* : the act of remanding : the state of being remanded ⟨sent back on *remand*⟩

¹**re·mark** \ri-'märk\ *n* **1** : the act of remarking : NOTICE **2** : mention of that which deserves attention or notice **3** : a briefly expressed opinion

   synonyms REMARK, OBSERVATION, COMMENT mean something said or written that gives an opinion. REMARK suggests a quick thought or offhand judgment ⟨made a brief *remark* about the weather⟩. OBSERVATION suggests a careful opinion expressed after looking closely at something ⟨she published her *observations* on whales after ten years of study⟩. COMMENT suggests a remark that is meant to explain or criticize ⟨after the play was over, he made his *comments* on it⟩.

²**remark** *vb* **1** : to take note of ⟨*remarked* his strange manner⟩ **2** : to express as a comment ⟨"Nice day," she *remarked*⟩ **3** : to make a comment ⟨*remarked* on how well the team was doing⟩

re·mark·able \ri-'mär-kə-bəl\ *adj* : worthy of being or likely to be noticed especially as being uncommon or extraordinary — **re·mark·able·ness** *n* — **re·mark·ably** \-blē\ *adv*

re·mar·ry \rē-'mar-ē\ *vb* : to marry again : to marry after an earlier marriage — **re·mar·riage** \-ij\ *n*

re·match \(')rē-'mach, 'rē-ˌmach\ *n* : a second meeting between the same contestants

re·me·di·a·ble \ri-'mēd-ē-ə-bəl\ *adj* : capable of being made better

re·me·di·al \ri-'mēd-ē-əl\ *adj* : intended to make something better ⟨*remedial* measures⟩ ⟨*remedial* classes⟩

re·me·di·a·tion \ri-ˌmēd-ē-'ā-shən\ *n* : the act or process of remedying ⟨*remediation* of reading problems⟩

¹**rem·e·dy** \'rem-əd-ē\ *n, pl* **-dies 1** : a medicine or treatment that cures or relieves **2** : something that corrects an evil, rights a wrong, or makes up for a loss

²**remedy** *vb* **-died; -dy·ing** : to provide or serve as a remedy for : RELIEVE

re·mem·ber \ri-'mem-bər\ *vb* **-bered; -ber·ing** \-b(ə-)riŋ\ **1** : to bring to mind or think of again ⟨*remembers* the old days⟩ **2 a** : to keep in mind for attention ⟨*remember* friends at Christmas⟩ **b** : ¹REWARD 1 ⟨was *remembered* in the will⟩ **3** : to keep in the memory ⟨*remember* the facts for the test⟩ **4** : to pass along greetings from ⟨*remember* us to your family⟩ — **re·mem·ber·able** \-b(ə-)rə-bəl\ *adj* — **re·mem·ber·er** \-bər-ər\ *n*

re·mem·brance \ri-'mem-brən(t)s\ *n* **1** : the act of remembering **2** : something remembered **3 a** : something (as a souvenir) that serves to keep in or bring to mind : REMINDER **b** : something (as a greeting or gift) recalling or expressing friendship **synonyms** see MEMORY

re·mind \ri-'mīnd\ *vb* : to put in mind of something : cause to remember ⟨*remind* a child that it is bedtime⟩ — **re·mind·er** *n*

rem·i·nisce \ˌrem-ə-'nis\ *vb* **-nisced; -nisc·ing** : to talk or think about things that happened in the past ⟨*reminisced* about old times⟩

rem·i·nis·cence \ˌrem-ə-'nis-°n(t)s\ *n* **1 a** : a recalling to mind of a past experience ⟨had a pleasant *reminiscence* of a favorite childhood toy⟩ **b** : the process of thinking or telling about past experiences ⟨spent a pleasant hour in *reminiscence*⟩ **2** : an account of a memorable experience — often used in plural **synonyms** see MEMORY

rem·i·nis·cent \ˌrem-ə-'nis-°nt\ *adj* **1** : of, relating to, or engaging in reminiscence **2** : reminding one of someone or something else

re·miss \ri-'mis\ *adj* **1** : careless in the performance of work or duty ⟨*remiss* in paying one's bills⟩ **2** : showing neglect or lack of attention ⟨service at the restaurant was *remiss*⟩ — **re·miss·ly** *adv* — **re·miss·ness** *n*

re·mis·si·ble \ri-'mis-ə-bəl\ *adj* : capable of being forgiven ⟨*remissible* sins⟩ — **re·mis·si·bly** \-blē\ *adv*

re·mis·sion \ri-'mish-ən\ *n* **1** : the act or process of remitting **2** : a state or period during which something is remitted

¹**re·mit** \ri-'mit\ *vb* **re·mit·ted; re·mit·ting 1 a** : to release from the guilt or penalty of : PARDON ⟨*remit* sins⟩ **b** : to keep from demanding or calling for ⟨*remit* a penalty⟩ **2** : to give over for consideration, judgment, decision, or action ⟨*remit* the proposal to a special committee⟩ **3** : to send money especially in payment **4** : to lessen in intensity or severity often temporarily : MODERATE ⟨the fever had *remitted*⟩ — **re·mit·ment** \-'mit-mənt\ *n* — **re·mit·ta·ble** \-'mit-ə-bəl\ *adj* — **re·mit·ter** *n*

²**remit** *n* **1** : an act of remitting **2** : something remitted to another person or authority

re·mit·tal \ri-'mit-°l\ *n* : REMISSION

re·mit·tance \ri-'mit-°n(t)s\ *n* **1** : money sent especially in payment **2** : a sending of money (as to a distant place)

rem·nant \'rem-nənt\ *n* **1** : a surviving usually small part ⟨*remnants* of a great civilization⟩ **2** : something that remains or is left over ⟨a *remnant* of cloth⟩

re·mod·el \(')rē-'mäd-°l\ *vb* : to change the structure of

re·mon·strance \ri-'män(t)-strən(t)s\ *n* : an act or instance of protest

re·mon·strant \ri-'män(t)-strənt\ *adj* : strongly objecting or opposing — **re·mon·strant·ly** *adv*

\ə\ abut	\au̇\ **out**	\i\ **tip**	\ȯ\ **saw**	\u̇\ **foot**
\ər\ **further**	\ch\ **chin**	\ī\ **life**	\ȯi\ **coin**	\y\ **yet**
\a\ **mat**	\e\ **pet**	\j\ **job**	\th\ **thin**	\yü\ **few**
\ā\ **take**	\ē\ **easy**	\ŋ\ **sing**	\t̲h̲\ **this**	\yu̇\ **cure**
\ä\ **cot, cart**	\g\ **go**	\ō\ **bone**	\ü\ **food**	\zh\ **vision**

re·mon·strate \ri-'män-ˌstrāt\ *vb* **-strat·ed; -strat·ing** : to present and urge reasons in opposition ⟨*remonstrate* with a student for being late⟩

rem·o·ra \'rem-ə-rə\ *n* : any of various marine fishes that have a suction disk on the top of the head by means of which they cling especially to other fishes

re·morse \ri-'mȯ(ə)rs\ *n* : a deep regret coming from a sense of guilt for past wrongs : SELF-REPROACH

remora: remoras on a tiger shark

Word History The Latin verb *remordēre* literally meant "to bite again." The Romans, however, usually used it with the meaning "to torment," because being tormented was like getting bitten again and again. A noun derivative of this verb is *remorsus,* which in early French was used to form the noun *remors.* This noun was used to refer to the deep regret that torments one for having done something wrong. In the 15th century, this French word was taken into English as *remorse* with the same meaning. [Middle English *remorse* "a deep regret for having done wrong," from early French *remors* (same meaning), from Latin *remorsus,* noun derivative of *remordēre* "to bite again," from *mordēre* "to bite" — related to MORSEL]

re·morse·ful \ri-'mȯrs-fəl\ *adj* : moved or marked by remorse — **re·morse·ful·ly** \-fə-lē\ *adv* — **re·morse·ful·ness** *n*

re·morse·less \ri-'mȯr-sləs\ *adj* : having no remorse : MERCILESS ⟨*remorseless* cruelty⟩ — **re·morse·less·ly** *adv* — **re·morse·less·ness** *n*

¹**re·mote** \ri-'mōt\ *adj* **re·mot·er; -est** **1** : far removed in place, time, or relation ⟨*remote* countries⟩ ⟨*remote* ages⟩ ⟨*remote* cousins⟩ **2** : SECLUDED 1 ⟨a *remote* valley⟩ **3** : acting, acted on, or controlled indirectly or from a distance ⟨*remote* computer operation⟩ **4** : small in degree : SLIGHT ⟨a *remote* possibility⟩ **5** : distant in manner : ALOOF — **re·mote·ly** *adv* — **re·mote·ness** *n*

²**remote** *n* : REMOTE CONTROL 2

remote control *n* **1** : control (as by a radio signal) of operation from a point some distance away ⟨operated by *remote control*⟩ **2** : a device for controlling something from a distance ⟨a *remote control* for a VCR⟩

¹**re·mount** \(')rē-'maůnt\ *vb* **1** : to mount something again ⟨*remount* the picture on better cardboard⟩ **2** : to mount again ⟨*remount* at once and ride back⟩

²**re·mount** \'rē-ˌmaůnt, (')rē-'maůnt\ *n* : a fresh horse to take the place of one no longer available

re·mov·able *also* **re·move·able** \ri-'mü-və-bəl\ *adj* : possible to remove — **re·mov·abil·i·ty** \-ˌmü-və-'bil-ət-ē\ *n* — **re·mov·able·ness** \-'mü-və-bəl-nəs\ *n* — **re·mov·ably** \-blē\ *adv*

re·mov·al \ri-'mü-vəl\ *n* : the act of removing : the fact of being removed

¹**re·move** \ri-'müv\ *vb* **re·moved; re·mov·ing** **1** : to change or cause to change to another location, position, station, or residence ⟨*remove* soldiers to the front⟩ **2** : to move by lifting, pushing aside, or taking away or off ⟨*remove* your hat⟩ **3** : to dismiss from office ⟨the treasurer was *removed* after a year⟩ **4** : to get rid of : ELIMINATE 1 ⟨*remove* a tumor⟩ **5** : to go away **6** : to be capable of being removed ⟨a bottle cap that *removes* easily⟩

²**remove** *n* **1** : REMOVAL; *esp* : ²MOVE 2c **2 a** : a distance separating one thing from another **b** : a degree or stage of separation ⟨at one *remove*⟩

re·moved \ri-'müvd\ *adj* **1** : being a generation older or younger ⟨the children of your first cousin are your first

cousins once *removed*⟩ **2** : far away or separate in space, time, or character ⟨a town far *removed* from cities⟩

re·mov·er \ri-'müv-ər\ *n* : something (as a chemical) used in removing a substance ⟨paint *remover*⟩

re·mu·ner·ate \ri-'myü-nə-ˌrāt\ *vb* **-at·ed; -at·ing** : to pay an equivalent to for a service, loss, or expense : RECOMPENSE — **re·mu·ner·a·tor** \-ˌrāt-ər\ *n*

re·mu·ner·a·tion \ri-ˌmyü-nə-'rā-shən\ *n* **1** : something that pays back an equivalent **2** : an act or fact of paying back an equivalent

re·mu·ner·a·tive \ri-'myü-nə-rət-iv, -ˌrāt-\ *adj* **1** : serving to remunerate **2** : PROFITABLE ⟨made a highly *remunerative* investment⟩ — **re·mu·ner·a·tive·ly** *adv* — **re·mu·ner·a·tive·ness** *n*

re·nais·sance \ˌren-ə-'sän(t)s, -'zän(t)s\ *n* **1** *cap* : the period of European history between the 14th and 17th centuries marked by a flourishing of art and literature inspired by ancient times and by the beginnings of modern science **2** *often cap* : a movement or period of great activity (as in literature, science, and the arts)

re·nal \'rēn-ᵊl\ *adj* : relating to, involving, or located in the region of the kidneys

re·name \(')rē-'nām\ *vb* : to give a new name to

re·na·scence \ri-'nas-ᵊn(t)s, -'nās-\ *n, often cap* : RENAISSANCE 2

re·na·scent \-ᵊnt\ *adj* : rising again into being or more intense activity or effect

rend \'rend\ *vb* **rent** \'rent\ *also* **rend·ed; rend·ing** **1** : to remove from place by force : WREST **2** : to split or tear apart or in pieces by force **3** : to tear (the hair or clothing) as a sign of anger, grief, or despair **4** : to affect as if splitting or tearing ⟨silence *rent* by a scream⟩

ren·der \'ren-dər\ *vb* **ren·dered; ren·der·ing** \-d(ə-)riŋ\ **1** : to obtain by heating ⟨*render* lard from fat⟩ **2 a** : to furnish or give to another : DELIVER ⟨*render* a report⟩ ⟨*render* aid⟩ **b** : ¹SURRENDER 1, GIVE UP ⟨*rendered* their lives to save others⟩ **3** : to give in return ⟨*render* thanks⟩ **4 a** : to cause to be or become ⟨*render* a person helpless⟩ **b** : PERFORM 3a ⟨*render* a salute⟩ **c** : PERFORM 3b ⟨*render* a song⟩ **d** : TRANSLATE 3a, b ⟨*render* Latin into English⟩ — **ren·der·able** \-d(ə-)rə-bəl\ *adj* — **ren·der·er** \-dər-ər\ *n*

¹**ren·dez·vous** \'rän-di-ˌvü, -dā-\ *n, pl* **ren·dez·vous** \-ˌvüz\ **1 a** : a place agreed on for assembling or meeting **b** : a place that many people visit **2** : a planned meeting [early French *rendezvous* "a place to meet," from the phrase *rendez vous* "present yourself"]

²**rendezvous** *vb* **-voused** \-ˌvüd\; **-vous·ing** \-ˌvü-iŋ\; **-vouses** \-ˌvüz\ : to come or bring together at a rendezvous

ren·di·tion \ren-'dish-ən\ *n* : an act or result of rendering ⟨sang their *rendition* of the old song⟩

¹**ren·e·gade** \'ren-i-ˌgād\ *n* **1** : a person who deserts a faith, cause, or party **2** : a person who rejects lawful or acceptable behavior

²**renegade** *adj* **1** : having deserted a faith, cause, or party **2** : having rejected tradition : UNCONVENTIONAL

re·nege \ri-'nig, -'neg, -'nēg, -'nāg\ *vb* **re·neged; re·neg·ing** **1** : DENY **2** : to go back on a promise or agreement ⟨*reneged* on paying the debt⟩ — **re·neg·er** *n*

re·new \ri-'n(y)ü\ *vb* **1** : to make or become new, fresh, or strong again ⟨strength *renewed* by a night's rest⟩ **2** : to restore to existence ⟨*renew* the splendor of a palace⟩ **3** : to do or make again ⟨*renew* a complaint⟩ **4** : to begin again : RESUME ⟨*renewed* efforts to make peace⟩ **5** : to put in a fresh supply of : REPLACE ⟨*renew* the water in a tank⟩ **6** : to grant or obtain an extension of : continue in force for another period ⟨*renew* a lease⟩ ⟨*renew* a subscription⟩ — **re·new·er** *n*

re·new·able \ri-'n(y)ü-ə-bəl\ *adj* **1** : capable of being renewed **2** : capable of being replaced by natural ecological cycles or sound management procedures ⟨*renewable* resources like water, wildlife, forests, and grasslands⟩

re·new·al \ri-'n(y)ü-əl\ *n* **1** : the act of renewing : the state of being renewed **2** : something renewed **3** : the rebuilding of a large area by a public authority ⟨urban *renewal*⟩

ren·net \'ren-ət\ *n* **1 a** : the contents of the stomach of a young animal and especially a calf **b** : a part of the lining of the stomach that is used to curdle milk **2** : something used to curdle milk; *esp* : RENNIN

ren·nin \'ren-ən\ *n* : a stomach enzyme that curdles milk

re·nom·i·nate \(')rē-'näm-ə-,nāt\ *vb* : to nominate again especially for a term right after one just served — **re·nom·i·na·tion** \(,)rē-,näm-ə-'nā-shən\ *n*

re·nounce \ri-'naun(t)s\ *vb* **re·nounced; re·nounc·ing 1** : to give up, refuse, or resign usually by public declaration ⟨*renounced* the throne⟩ **2** : to refuse to follow, obey, or recognize any further : REPUDIATE ⟨*renounced* the authority of her political party⟩ — **re·nounce·ment** \-'naun(t)-smənt\ *n* — **re·nounc·er** *n*

ren·o·vate \'ren-ə-,vāt\ *vb* **-vat·ed; -vat·ing** : to make like new again : put in good condition — **ren·o·va·tion** \,ren-ə-'vā-shən\ *n* — **ren·o·va·tor** \'ren-ə-,vāt-ər\ *n*

re·nown \ri-'naun\ *n* : a state of being widely known and highly honored : FAME

re·nowned \ri-'naund\ *adj* : having renown : CELEBRATED **synonyms** see FAMOUS

¹rent \'rent\ *n* : money paid for the use of property : a periodic payment made by a tenant to the owner for the use of the owner's property [Middle English *rente* "income from property," from early French *rente* "payment, income," derived from Latin *rendere* "to yield"] — **for rent** : available for use or service at a price

²rent *vb* **1** : to take and hold property under an agreement to pay rent **2** : to give the possession and use of in return for rent ⟨*rented* a cottage to friends⟩ **3** : to be for rent ⟨the room *rents* for $40 a week⟩ — **rent·able** \-ə-bəl\ *adj*

³rent *past and past participle of* REND

⁴rent *n* **1** : an opening (as in cloth) made by or as if by tearing **2** : an act or instance of tearing [from a dialect word *rent* "to tear," from Middle English *renten,* an altered form of *renden* "to tear, rend"]

¹rent·al \'rent-ᵊl\ *n* **1** : an amount paid or collected as rent **2** : something for rent **3** : an act of renting

²rental *adj* **1** : of, relating to, or available for rent ⟨a *rental* car⟩ **2** : dealing in rental property ⟨a *rental* agency⟩

rent·er \'rent-ər\ *n* : one that rents; *esp* : TENANT

re·nun·ci·a·tion \ri-,nən(t)-sē-'ā-shən\ *n* : the act or practice of renouncing

re·open \(')rē-'ō-pən, -'ōp-ᵊn\ *vb* **1** : to open again **2** : to take up again : RESUME ⟨*reopen* the discussion⟩

¹re·or·der \(')rē-'órd-ər\ *vb* **1** : to arrange in a different way **2** : to place a reorder

²reorder *n* : an order like a previous order placed with the same supplier

re·or·ga·ni·za·tion \(,)rē-,órg-(ə-)nə-'zā-shən\ *n* : the act of reorganizing : the state of being reorganized; *esp* : the changing of the financial structure of a business

re·or·ga·nize \(')rē-'ór-gə-,nīz\ *vb* : to organize again or anew; *esp* : to bring about a reorganization (as of a business) — **re·or·ga·niz·er** *n*

¹rep \'rep\ *n* : ²REPRESENTATIVE ⟨sales *rep*⟩

²rep *n* : REPETITION 1b

re·pack·age \(')rē-'pak-ij\ *vb* : to package again or anew; *esp* : to put into a more attractive form

¹re·pair \ri-'pa(ə)r, -'pe(ə)r\ *vb* : to make one's way : GO ⟨*repair* to an inner office⟩

²repair *vb* **1** : to put back in good condition ⟨*repair* a broken toy⟩ **2** : to make up for : REMEDY ⟨*repair* an injustice⟩ **synonyms** see MEND — **re·pair·able** \-'par-ə-bəl, -'per-\ *adj* — **re·pair·er** \-ər\ *n*

³repair *n* **1 a** : the act or process of repairing ⟨make *repairs*⟩ **b** : the result of repairing ⟨a tire with three re-

pairs⟩ **2 a** : condition with respect to soundness or need of fixing ⟨the car is in poor *repair*⟩ **b** : good condition ⟨a house in *repair*⟩

re·pair·man \ri-'pa(ə)r-,man, -'pe(ə)r-, -mən\ *n* : a person whose occupation is making repairs ⟨TV *repairman*⟩

rep·a·ra·ble \'rep-(ə-)rə-bəl\ *adj* : capable of being repaired

rep·a·ra·tion \,rep-ə-'rā-shən\ *n* **1** : a repairing or keeping in repair ⟨a building in need of constant *reparation*⟩ **2** : the act of making up for a wrong **3** : money or materials paid or to be paid by a country losing a war to the winner to make up for damages done in the war — usually used in plural

re·par·a·tive \ri-'par-ət-iv\ *adj* : of, relating to, or serving to repair

rep·ar·tee \,rep-ər-'tē, -,är-, -'tā\ *n* **1** : a clever witty reply **2** : skill in making clever replies

re·past \ri-'past\ *n* **1** : something taken as food : MEAL **2** : the act of taking food

¹re·pa·tri·ate \(')rē-'pā-trē-,āt, -'pa-\ *vb* **-at·ed; -at·ing** : to return to the country of origin, allegiance, or citizenship ⟨*repatriate* prisoners of war⟩ — **re·pa·tri·a·tion** \(,)rē-,pā-trē-'ā-shən, -,pa-\ *n*

²re·pa·tri·ate \(')rē-'pā-trē-ət, -tre-,āt\ *n* : one that is repatriated

re·pay \(')rē-'pā\ *vb* **-paid** \-'pād\; **-pay·ing 1** : to pay back ⟨*repay* a loan⟩ **2** : to make a return payment to ⟨*repay* a creditor⟩ — **re·pay·able** \-'pā-ə-bəl\ *adj* — **re·pay·ment** \-'pā-mənt\ *n*

re·peal \ri-'pē(ə)l\ *vb* : to do away with especially by legislative action ⟨*repeal* a law⟩ — **repeal** *n* — **re·peal·able** \-'pē-lə-bəl\ *adj*

re·peal·er \-'pē-lər\ *n* : one that repeals; *esp* : a legislative act that cancels or does away with an earlier act

¹re·peat \ri-'pēt\ *vb* **1 a** : to say or state again ⟨*repeated* the question⟩ **b** : to say from memory : RECITE ⟨*repeat* a poem⟩ **c** : to say after another ⟨*repeat* the following words after me⟩ **2** : to make, do, or perform again ⟨*repeat* a mistake⟩ **3** : to present (oneself) again in the same words or way ⟨hate *repeating* myself⟩ — **re·peat·able** \-ə-bəl\ *adj*

²re·peat \ri-'pēt, 'rē-,pēt\ *n* **1** : the act of repeating **2** : something repeated **3 a** : a musical passage to be repeated in performance **b** : a sign that consists of two dots one above the other and that is placed before and after a musical passage to be repeated **4** : a repetition of a radio or television program

re·peat·ed \ri-'pēt-əd\ *adj* : done or happening again and again : FREQUENT

re·peat·ed·ly \-lē\ *adv* : at frequent intervals : OFTEN

re·peat·er \ri-'pēt-ər\ *n* **1** : a firearm that fires several times without reloading **2** : a person who violates the laws again and again **3** : a student who is taking a class or course again

repeating decimal *n* : a decimal in which after a certain point a particular digit or sequence of digits repeats itself indefinitely — compare TERMINATING DECIMAL

re·pel \ri-'pel\ *vb* **re·pelled; re·pel·ling 1 a** : to drive back ⟨*repel* the enemy⟩ **b** : to fight against : RESIST **2** : to refuse to accept : REJECT ⟨*repel* a suggestion⟩ **3 a** : to be incapable of sticking to, mixing with, taking up, or holding ⟨a fabric that *repels* water⟩ **b** : to force away or apart or tend to do so by mutual action at a distance ⟨two like electrical charges *repel* each other⟩ **4** : DISGUST ⟨a sight that *repelled* everyone⟩ — **re·pel·ler** *n*

\ə\ abut	\au\ out	\i\ tip	\ò\ saw	\ù\ foot
\ər\ further	\ch\ chin	\ī\ life	\òi\ coin	\y\ yet
\a\ mat	\e\ pet	\j\ job	\th\ thin	\yü\ few
\ā\ take	\ē\ easy	\ŋ\ sing	\th\ this	\yù\ cure
\ä\ cot, cart	\g\ go	\ō\ bone	\ü\ food	\zh\ vision

re·pel·len·cy \ri-ˈpel-ən-sē\ *n* : the quality of repelling : the ability to repel

¹re·pel·lent *also* **re·pel·lant** \ri-ˈpel-ənt\ *adj* **1** : serving or tending to drive away — often used in combination ⟨a water-*repellent* jacket⟩ **2** : causing disgust — **re·pel·lent·ly** *adv*

²repellent *also* **repellant** *n* : something that repels; *esp* : a substance used to keep off pests (as insects)

re·pent \ri-ˈpent\ *vb* **1** : to feel sorrow for one's sin and make up one's mind to do what is right **2** : to feel sorry for or dissatisfied with something one has done : REGRET — **re·pent·er** *n*

re·pen·tance \ri-ˈpent-ᵊn(t)s\ *n* : the action or process of repenting especially for one's sins

re·pen·tant \ri-ˈpent-ᵊnt\ *adj* : feeling or showing repentance — **re·pen·tant·ly** *adv*

re·per·cus·sion \ˌrē-pər-ˈkəsh-ən, ˌrep-ər-\ **1** : a return action or effect **2** : a widespread, indirect, or unexpected effect of something said or done ⟨the new policy had *repercussions* for everyone⟩

re·per·cus·sive \ˌrē-pər-ˈkəs-iv, ˌrep-ər-\ *adj* : of, marked by, or creating repercussion

rep·er·toire \ˈrep-ə(r)-ˌtwär\ *n* **1** : a list or supply of dramas, operas, pieces, or parts that a company or person is prepared to perform **2** : a supply of skills or devices possessed by a person ⟨passing is part of the *repertoire* of a quarterback⟩

rep·er·to·ry \ˈrep-ə(r)-ˌtōr-ē, -ˌtor-\ *n, pl* **-ries** **1** : a place where something may be found **2 a** : REPERTOIRE **b** : a company that performs different plays or pieces in the course of a season **c** : a theater in which such a company performs

rep·e·ti·tion \ˌrep-ə-ˈtish-ən\ *n* **1 a** : the act or an instance of repeating **b** : a motion or exercise (as a push-up) that is repeated and usually counted **2** : something repeated

rep·e·ti·tious \ˌrep-ə-ˈtish-əs\ *adj* : marked by repetition; *esp* : tiresomely repeating — **rep·e·ti·tious·ly** *adv* — **rep·e·ti·tious·ness** *n*

re·pet·i·tive \ri-ˈpet-ət-iv\ *adj* : REPETITIOUS — **re·pet·i·tive·ly** *adv* — **re·pet·i·tive·ness** *n*

re·pine \ri-ˈpīn\ *vb* **1** : to feel or express sadness or discontent : COMPLAIN **2** : to long restlessly for something — **re·pin·er** *n*

re·place \ri-ˈplās\ *vb* **1** : to put back in a proper or former place ⟨*replace* a card in a file⟩ **2** : to take the place of ⟨paper money has *replaced* gold coins⟩ **3** : to put something new in the place of ⟨*replace* a broken dish⟩ — **re·place·able** \-ˈplā-sə-bəl\ *adj*

re·place·ment \ri-ˈplā-smənt\ *n* **1** : the act of replacing : the state of being replaced **2** : one that replaces another : SUBSTITUTE

replacement set *n* : a set of elements any one of which may be used to replace a given variable or placeholder in a mathematical sentence or expression (as an equation)

re·plant \(ˈ)rē-ˈplant\ *vb* **1** : to plant again or anew ⟨*replanted* the tree farther from the house⟩ **2** : to provide with new plants ⟨*replanted* the park⟩

re·plen·ish \ri-ˈplen-ish\ *vb* : to make full or complete once more ⟨*replenish* a supply of fuel⟩ — **re·plen·ish·er** *n* — **re·plen·ish·ment** \-mənt\ *n*

re·plete \ri-ˈplēt\ *adj* **1** : fully or well provided or filled ⟨a book *replete* with illustrations⟩ **2** : well fed — **re·plete·ness** *n*

re·ple·tion \ri-ˈplē-shən\ *n* **1** : the act of eating too much : the state of being fed too much ⟨made sick by *repletion*⟩ **2** : fulfillment of a need or desire : SATISFACTION

rep·li·ca \ˈrep-li-kə\ *n* **1** : a close reproduction especially by the maker of the original **2** : a copy exact in all details : DUPLICATE

¹rep·li·cate \ˈrep-lə-ˌkāt\ *vb* **-cat·ed; -cat·ing** **1** : ²DUPLI-

CATE 1, REPEAT **2** : to produce one or more exact copies of itself ⟨DNA *replicates* in the cell nucleus⟩

²rep·li·cate \ˈrep-li-kət\ *n* : one of several identical experiments, processes, or samples

rep·li·ca·tion \ˌrep-lə-ˈkā-shən\ *n* **1** : very exact copying or duplication **2** : an act or process of copying or duplication

¹re·ply \ri-ˈplī\ *vb* **re·plied; re·ply·ing** **1** : to respond in words or writing ⟨*reply* to a letter⟩ **2** : to do something in response; *esp* : to return gunfire or an attack **3** : to give as an answer ⟨*replied* not a word⟩ — **re·pli·er** \-ˈplī(-ə)r\ *n*

²reply *n, pl* **replies** : something said, written, or done in answer or response

¹re·port \ri-ˈpō(ə)rt, -ˈpȯ(ə)rt\ *n* **1 a** : common talk : RUMOR **b** : REPUTATION 1 ⟨people of evil *report*⟩ **2** : a usually detailed account or statement ⟨a news *report*⟩ ⟨wrote a *report* of the meeting⟩ **3** : an explosive noise ⟨the *report* of a gun⟩

²report *vb* **1** : to make a statement about or description of : RELATE **2 a** : to describe and discuss in a newspaper article or broadcast ⟨*report* a baseball game⟩ **b** : to act as a reporter ⟨*report* on the latest developments⟩ **3 a** : to return or present (a matter officially given over to a committee) with conclusions and suggestions **b** : to make known to the proper authorities ⟨*report* a fire⟩ **c** : to make a charge of misconduct against ⟨*report* a student for lateness⟩ **4 a** : to present oneself ⟨*report* for duty⟩ **b** : to work as a subordinate ⟨*reports* to the vice president⟩

re·port·able \-ˈpōrt-ə-bəl, -ˈpȯrt-\ *adj* **1** : worth reporting ⟨a *reportable* development⟩ **2** : required by law to be reported ⟨*reportable* income⟩

report card *n* : a report containing a student's grades that is regularly sent by a school to the student's parents or guardian

re·port·ed·ly \ri-ˈpōrt-əd-lē, -ˈpȯrt-\ *adv* : according to report

re·port·er \ri-ˈpōrt-ər, -ˈpȯrt-\ *n* : a person who reports; *esp* : one employed by a newspaper, magazine, or radio or television station to gather, write, or report news

re·por·to·ri·al \ˌrep-ə(r)-ˈtōr-ē-əl, ˌrēp-, -ˈtȯr-\ *adj* : of, relating to, or characteristic of a reporter or report — **re·por·to·ri·al·ly** \-ē-ə-lē\ *adv*

¹re·pose \ri-ˈpōz\ *vb* **re·posed; re·pos·ing** **1** : to lay at rest ⟨*reposed* her head on a cushion⟩ **2** : to lie at rest ⟨*reposing* on the couch⟩ [Middle English *reposen* "to lay at rest," from early French *reposer* (same meaning), from Latin *repausare* (same meaning), from earlier *re-* "back, again" and *pausare* "to stop," from Latin *pausa* "a pause" — related to PAUSE]

²repose *n* **1** : a state of resting after effort or strain; *esp* : rest in sleep **2** : freedom from disturbance or excitement : CALM ⟨the *repose* of the forest⟩ **3** : absence or stopping of activity or movement ⟨a face in *repose*⟩

³re·pose *vb* **re·posed; re·pos·ing** **1** : to place (as trust or confidence) in someone or something **2** : to place for control, management, or use [Middle English *reposen* "to replace," from Latin *reponere* "replace"]

re·pose·ful \ri-ˈpōz-fəl\ *adj* : likely to bring on relaxation — **re·pose·ful·ly** \-fə-lē\ *adv* — **re·pose·ful·ness** *n*

re·po·si·tion \ˌrē-pə-ˈzish-ən\ *vb* : to change the position of

re·pos·i·to·ry \ri-ˈpäz-ə-ˌtōr-ē, -ˌtȯr-\ *n, pl* **-ries** **1** : a place or container where something is deposited or stored **2** : one that contains or stores something immaterial ⟨a *repository* of knowledge⟩

re·pos·sess \ˌrē-pə-ˈzes\ *vb* : to regain or retake possession of — **re·pos·ses·sion** \-ˈzesh-ən\ *n*

rep·re·hend \ˌrep-ri-ˈhend\ *vb* : to find fault with usually with sternness

rep·re·hen·si·ble \ˌrep-ri-ˈhen(t)-sə-bəl\ *adj* : worthy of or deserving blame or condemnation ⟨*reprehensible* acts⟩ — **rep·re·hen·si·ble·ness** *n* — **rep·re·hen·si·bly** \-blē\ *adv*

rep·re·hen·sion \ˌrep-ri-ˈhen-chən\ *n* : the act of reprehending : CONDEMNATION

rep·re·sent \ˌrep-ri-ˈzent\ *vb* 1 : to serve as a sign or symbol of ⟨the flag *represents* our country⟩ 2 : to present a picture, image, or likeness of : PORTRAY ⟨this picture *represents* a scene at Queen Elizabeth's court⟩ 3 a : to take the place of in some respect b : to act for or in the place of (as in a legislative body) c : to manage the legal and business affairs of ⟨he *represented* one of the sport's top athletes⟩ 4 : to describe as having a certain character or quality ⟨*represented* himself as being poor⟩ 5 : to serve as an example or instance of — **rep·re·sent·able** \-ə-bəl\ *adj* — **rep·re·sent·er** *n*

rep·re·sen·ta·tion \ˌrep-ri-ˌzen-ˈtā-shən\ *n* 1 : one (as a picture or symbol) that represents something else 2 : the act or action of representing : the state of being represented (as in a legislative body) — **rep·re·sen·ta·tion·al** \ˌrep-ri-ˌzen-ˈtā-shnəl, -shən- ²l\ *adj*

¹**rep·re·sen·ta·tive** \ˌrep-ri-ˈzent-ət-iv\ *adj* 1 : serving to represent ⟨a painting *representative* of a battle⟩ 2 : standing or acting for another especially through delegated authority 3 : of, based upon, or being a government in which the people are represented by persons chosen from among them usually by election 4 : serving as a typical example of the thing mentioned ⟨a *representative* athlete⟩ — **rep·re·sen·ta·tive·ly** *adv* — **rep·re·sen·ta·tive·ness** *n*

²**representative** *n* 1 : a typical example of a group, class, or quality 2 : one that represents another or others : DELEGATE; *esp* : a member of the house of representatives of the U.S. Congress or a state legislature

re·press \ri-ˈpres\ *vb* 1 a : to check by or as if by pressure ⟨injustice was *repressed*⟩ b : to put down by force : SUBDUE 2 a : to hold in by self-control ⟨*repressed* a laugh⟩ b : to prevent the natural or normal expression, activity, or development of ⟨*repress* one's anger⟩ 3 : to shut out of consciousness ⟨*repressed* a painful past⟩ — **re·press·ible** \-ˈpres-ə-bəl\ *adj* — **re·pres·sive** \-ˈpres-iv\ *adj*

re·pressed \ri-ˈprest\ *adj* 1 : subjected to or marked by repression ⟨a *repressed* child⟩ 2 : characterized by a keeping in check

re·pres·sion \ri-ˈpresh-ən\ *n* 1 : the act of repressing : the state of being repressed 2 : a process of the mind by which painful or disturbing thoughts or desires are kept from conscious awareness

re·pres·sor \ri-ˈpres-ər\ *n* : one that represses; *esp* : a protein that keeps a special region of a chromosome from acting to start the manufacture of messenger RNA

¹**re·prieve** \ri-ˈprēv\ *vb* **re·prieved; re·priev·ing** 1 : to delay the punishment of (as a condemned prisoner) 2 : to give relief or deliverance to for a time

²**reprieve** *n* 1 a : the act of reprieving : the state of being reprieved b : a postponing of a prison or death sentence 2 : a temporary escape (as from pain or trouble)

¹**rep·ri·mand** \ˈrep-rə-ˌmand\ *n* : a severe or formal criticism

²**reprimand** *vb* : to criticize (a person) severely especially from a position of authority **synonyms** see REBUKE

¹**re·print** \(ˈ)rē-ˈprint\ *vb* : to print again or make a reprint of — **re·print·er** *n*

²**re·print** \ˈrē-ˌprint\ *n* 1 : a new or additional printing without change in the text 2 : a separately printed piece of writing

re·pri·sal \ri-ˈprī-zəl\ *n* 1 : the use of force short of war by one nation against another in return for damage or loss suffered ⟨economic *reprisals*⟩ 2 : an act of getting back at especially in war

¹**re·proach** \ri-ˈprōch\ *n* 1 a : something that deserves blame or disgrace ⟨their dirty yard is a *reproach* to the whole street⟩ b : loss of reputation : DISGRACE 2 : the act or action of disapproving ⟨was beyond *reproach*⟩ 3 : an expression of disapproval — **re·proach·ful** \-fəl\ *adj* — **re·proach·ful·ly** \-fə-lē\ *adv* — **re·proach·ful·ness** *n*

²**reproach** *vb* : to find fault with : BLAME ⟨*reproached* him for his cowardice⟩ — **re·proach·able** \-ˈprō-chə-bəl\ *adj* — **re·proach·er** *n* — **re·proach·ing·ly** \-ˈprō-chiŋ-lē\ *adv*

¹**rep·ro·bate** \ˈrep-rə-ˌbāt\ *vb* **-bat·ed; -bat·ing** : to condemn strongly as unworthy or evil — **rep·ro·ba·tion** \ˌrep-rə-ˈbā-shən\ *n*

²**reprobate** *adj* 1 : doomed to hell : CONDEMNED 2 : being without any morals : CORRUPT 3 : of, relating to, or characteristic of a wicked person

³**reprobate** *n* : a wicked person

re·pro·cess \rē-ˈpräs-es, -ˈprōs-, -es\ *vb* : to subject to a special process or treatment in preparation for reuse

re·pro·duce \ˌrē-prə-ˈd(y)üs\ *vb* 1 a : to produce new individuals of the same kind b : to cause to exist again ⟨*reproduce* water from steam⟩ c : to imitate closely ⟨sound effects can *reproduce* the sound of thunder⟩ d : to present again e : to make an image or copy of ⟨*reproduce* a face on canvas⟩ f : to translate a recording into sound 2 : to go through reproduction ⟨her voice *reproduces* well⟩ 3 : to produce offspring — **re·pro·duc·er** *n*

re·pro·duc·tion \ˌrē-prə-ˈdək-shən\ *n* 1 : the act or process of reproducing; *esp* : the process by which plants and animals produce offspring 2 : something reproduced : COPY

re·pro·duc·tive \ˌrē-prə-ˈdək-tiv\ *adj* : of, relating to, or capable of reproduction

re·proof \ri-ˈprüf\ *n* : criticism for a fault : REBUKE

re·prove \ri-ˈprüv\ *vb* **re·proved; re·prov·ing** 1 : to scold or correct usually in a gentle way ⟨*reprove* a tardy student⟩ 2 : to express disapproval of ⟨*reprove* a fault⟩

¹**rep·tile** \ˈrep-t²l, -ˌtīl\ *n* : any of a group of cold-blooded air-breathing vertebrates (as snakes, lizards, turtles, and alligators) that usually lay eggs and have skin covered with scales or bony plates

²**reptile** *adj* : characteristic of a reptile : REPTILIAN

rep·til·ian \rep-ˈtil-ē-ən\ *adj* : of, relating to, or resembling reptiles

re·pub·lic \ri-ˈpəb-lik\ *n* 1 : a government having a chief of state who is not a monarch and who is usually a president 2 : a government in which supreme power belongs to the citizens through their right to vote 3 : a political unit having a republican form of government 4 : a political and territorial unit of the former nations of the U.S.S.R., Czechoslovakia, or Yugoslavia [from French *république* "republic," derived from Latin *respublica* "republic, public matters, commonweal," literally "public things," from *res* "thing, matter" and *publica,* a feminine form of *publicus* "relating to the people as a whole, public" — related to PUBLIC, REAL, REBUS]

¹**re·pub·li·can** \ri-ˈpəb-li-kən\ *adj* 1 a : of, relating to, or resembling a republic b : favoring or supporting a republic 2 *cap* a : DEMOCRATIC-REPUBLICAN b : of, relating to, or being one of the two major political parties in the U.S.

²**republican** *n* 1 : one that favors or supports a republican form of government 2 *cap* a : a member of a political party favoring republicanism b : a member of the Democratic-Republican party or of the Republican party of the U.S.

\ə\ abut	\au̇\ out	\i\ tip	\ȯ\ saw	\u̇\ foot
\ər\ further	\ch\ chin	\ī\ life	\ȯi\ coin	\y\ yet
\a\ mat	\e\ pet	\j\ job	\th\ thin	\yü\ few
\ā\ take	\ē\ easy	\ŋ\ sing	\t̲h̲\ this	\yu̇\ cure
\ä\ cot, cart	\g\ go	\ō\ bone	\ü\ food	\zh\ vision

re·pub·li·can·ism \ri-'pəb-li-kə-,niz-əm\ *n* **1** : support or desire for a republican form of government **2** : the principles or ideas of republican government **3** *cap* : the principles, policy, or practices of the Republican party of the U.S.

re·pu·di·ate \ri-'pyüd-ē-,āt\ *vb* **-at·ed; -at·ing** **1** : to refuse to have anything to do with **2** : to refuse to accept or pay *⟨repudiate* a debt⟩ — **re·pu·di·a·tion** \-,pyüd-ē-'ā-shən\ *n* — **re·pu·di·a·tor** \-'pyüd-ē-,āt-ər\ *n*

re·pug·nance \ri-'pəg-nən(t)s\ *n* : a strong feeling of dislike

re·pug·nant \ri-'pəg-nənt\ *adj* **1** : INCOMPATIBLE 1 **2** : causing a feeling of dislike or disgust : REPULSIVE — **re·pug·nant·ly** *adv*

¹re·pulse \ri-'pəls\ *vb* **re·pulsed; re·puls·ing** **1** : to drive or beat back : REPEL *⟨repulse* an attack⟩ **2** : to cause dislike or disgust in

²repulse *n* **1** : a cold unfriendly rejection **2** : the action of driving back an attacker

re·pul·sion \ri-'pəl-shən\ *n* **1** : the action of repulsing : the state of being repulsed **2** : the force with which bodies, particles, or like forces repel one another **3** : a feeling of great dislike : REPUGNANCE

re·pul·sive \ri-'pəl-siv\ *adj* : causing disgust — **re·pul·sive·ly** *adv* — **re·pul·sive·ness** *n*

rep·u·ta·ble \'rep-yət-ə-bəl\ *adj* : having a good reputation : RESPECTABLE — **rep·u·ta·bil·i·ty** \,rep-yət-ə-'bil-ət-ē\ *n* — **rep·u·ta·bly** \'rep-yət-ə-blē\ *adv*

rep·u·ta·tion \,rep-yə-'tā-shən\ *n* **1** : overall quality or character as seen or judged by people in general ⟨a car with a good *reputation*⟩ **2** : notice by other people of some quality or ability ⟨has the *reputation* of being a good tennis player⟩ **3** : a place in public regard : good name ⟨trying to protect his *reputation*⟩

¹re·pute \ri-'pyüt\ *vb* **re·put·ed; re·put·ing** : to have the opinion that : CONSIDER *⟨reputed* to be a millionaire⟩

²repute *n* **1** : REPUTATION 1 **2** : good reputation ⟨a scientist of *repute*⟩

re·put·ed \ri-'pyüt-əd\ *adj* **1** : having a good reputation ⟨a highly *reputed* lawyer⟩ **2** : believed by most people to be such ⟨the movie was a *reputed* success⟩

re·put·ed·ly *adv* : according to reputation or general belief

¹re·quest \ri-'kwest\ *n* **1** : an asking for something **2** : something asked for ⟨granted me three *requests*⟩ **3** : the condition of being requested ⟨tickets are available upon *request*⟩

²request *vb* **1** : to make a request to or of **2** : to ask for — **re·quest·er** *or* **re·quest·or** \ri-'kwest-ər\ *n*

re·qui·em \'rek-wē-əm *also* 'rāk- *or* 'rēk-\ *n* **1** : a mass for a dead person **2** : a musical service or composition in honor of the dead [Middle English *requiem* "a mass for the dead," from Latin *requiem* "rest," the first word of the phrase *Requiem aeternam dona eis* "Eternal rest grant to them," said or sung at the begining of the mass]

requiem shark *n* : any of several large sharks (as the tiger shark) usually found in warm seas that sometimes attack human beings

re·quire \ri-'kwī(ə)r\ *vb* **re·quired; re·quir·ing** **1** : to have a need for ⟨a game that *requires* skill⟩ **2** : ¹ORDER 2a ⟨the law *requires* that everyone pay the tax⟩

re·quire·ment \ri-'kwī(ə)r-mənt\ *n* : something that is required or necessary ⟨*requirements* for graduation⟩

req·ui·site \'rek-wə-zət\ *adj* : needed for reaching a goal or achieving a purpose — **requisite** *n* — **req·ui·site·ness** *n*

¹req·ui·si·tion \,rek-wə-'zish-ən\ *n* **1** : the act of requiring or demanding **2** : a demand or request made by proper authority ⟨a *requisition* for supplies⟩ **3** : the state of being in demand or use ⟨the cars were in *requisition*⟩

²requisition *vb* **-si·tioned; -si·tion·ing** \-'zish-niŋ, -ən-iŋ\ : to make a requisition for

re·quit·al \ri-'kwīt-ᵊl\ *n* **1** : something given in payment or in return **2** : the act or action of requiting : the state of being requited

re·quite \ri-'kwīt\ *vb* **re·quit·ed; re·quit·ing** **1** : to make return for : REPAY **2** : to make suitable return to for a service or an injury ⟨*requited* her for her help⟩ — **re·quit·er** *n*

re·ra·di·ate \(')rē-'rād-ē-,āt\ *vb* : to radiate anew ⟨the ground *reradiates* the heat obtained from the sun⟩ — **re·ra·di·a·tion** \(,)rē-,rād-ē-'ā-shən\ *n*

¹re·run \(')rē-'rən\ *vb* **-ran; -run; -run·ning** : to run again or anew

²re·run \'rē-,rən, (')rē-'rən\ *n* **1** : the act or action or an instance of rerunning **2** : a television program or movie that is rerun

re·sale \'rē-,sāl, (')rē-'sā(ə)l\ *n* : the act or an instance of selling again

re·scind \ri-'sind\ *vb* **1** : CANCEL 2a ⟨*rescind* a contract⟩ **2** : to do away with by legislative action ⟨*rescind* a law⟩ — **re·scind·er** *n* — **re·scind·ment** \-mənt\ *n*

re·scis·sion \ri-'sizh-ən\ *n* : an act of rescinding

res·cue \'res-kyü\ *vb* **res·cued; res·cu·ing** : to free from danger or evil : SAVE — **res·cue** *n* — **res·cu·er** *n*

¹re·search \ri-'sərch, 'rē-,sərch\ *n* **1** : careful study and investigation for the purpose of discovering and explaining new knowledge **2** : the collecting of information about a subject

²research *vb* **1** : to search or investigate thoroughly ⟨*research* her options⟩ **2** : to do research for ⟨*research* a book⟩ — **re·search·er** *n*

re·seed \(')rē-'sēd\ *vb* : to sow seed on again

re·sem·blance \ri-'zem-blən(t)s\ *n* **1 a** : the quality or state of resembling : SIMILARITY **b** : a point of likeness **2** : REPRESENTATION 1

re·sem·ble \ri-'zem-bəl\ *vb* **-bled; -bling** \-b(ə-)liŋ\ : to be like or similar to ⟨he *resembles* his father⟩

re·send \rē-'send\ *vb* **-sent** \-'sent\; **-send·ing** : to send again or back ⟨*resent* a returned letter⟩

re·sent \ri-'zent\ *vb* : to feel or state annoyance or anger at

re·sent·ful \ri-'zent-fəl\ *adj* **1** : full of resentment ⟨felt *resentful* of her success⟩ **2** : caused or marked by resentment ⟨a *resentful* reply to a letter⟩ — **re·sent·ful·ly** \-fə-lē\ *adv* — **re·sent·ful·ness** *n*

re·sent·ment \ri-'zent-mənt\ *n* : a feeling of angry displeasure at something regarded as a wrong, insult, or injury

res·er·va·tion \,rez-ər-'vā-shən\ *n* **1** : the act of reserving **2** : an arrangement to have something (as a motel room or a seat on a plane) held for one's use **3** : something reserved for a special use; *esp* : an area of public lands so reserved (as for use by American Indians) **4 a** : a limiting condition : EXCEPTION ⟨agree without *reservations*⟩ **b** : ²DOUBT 1 ⟨had *reservations* about joining the team⟩

¹re·serve \ri-'zərv\ *vb* **re·served; re·serv·ing** **1** : to keep in store for future or special use ⟨*reserve* that shirt for special occasions⟩ **2** : to hold over to a future time or place : DEFER ⟨*reserve* judgment on that matter⟩ **3** : to arrange to have set aside and held for one's use ⟨*reserve* a hotel room⟩

²reserve *n* **1** : something stored or available for future use : STOCK ⟨oil *reserves*⟩ **2 a** : military forces held back or available for later use — usually used in plural **b** : the military forces of a country not part of the regular services **3** : an area of land set apart ⟨a wild game *reserve*⟩ **4** : restraint, closeness, or caution in one's words and behavior **5** : ¹SUBSTITUTE ⟨the *reserves* of the football team⟩ — **in reserve** : set aside for future or special use

re·served \ri-'zərvd\ *adj* **1** : cautious in words and actions ⟨a *reserved* young man⟩ **2** : kept or set apart or aside for future or special use ⟨a *reserved* table⟩ **synonyms** see SILENT — **re·serv·ed·ly** \-'zər-vəd-lē\ *adv* — **re·ser·ved·ness** \-'zər-vəd-nəs\ *n*

re·serv·ist \ri-'zər-vəst\ *n* : a member of a military reserve

res·er·voir \'rez-ə(r)v-ˌwär, -ə(r)v-ˌ(w)ȯr\ *n* **1** : a place where something is kept in store; *esp* : an artificial or natural lake where water is collected as a water supply **2** : an extra supply : RESERVE **3** : a living thing (as a fly or mouse) in which a parasite (as a bacterium) that is harmful to some other living thing lives and multiplies [from French *réservoir* "place where something is kept in reserve," from *reserver* "to reserve, keep for future use"]

reservoir 1

re·set \rē-'set\ *vb* **-set; -set·ting** **1** : to set again or anew ⟨*reset* a diamond in a new setting⟩ **2** : to change the reading of often to zero ⟨*reset* a stopwatch⟩ — **reset** \'rē-ˌset\ *n* — **re·set·table** \-'set-ə-bəl\ *adj*

re·shape \(')rē-'shāp\ *vb* : to give a new form to — **re·shap·er** *n*

re·shuf·fle \(')rē-'shəf-əl\ *vb* **1** : to shuffle again **2** : to reorganize usually by switching around existing parts ⟨the president *reshuffled* the cabinet⟩ — **reshuffle** *n*

re·side \ri-'zīd\ *vb* **re·sid·ed; re·sid·ing** **1** : to live permanently or continuously ⟨*reside* in St. Louis⟩ **2** : to be present as a part or quality ⟨the power of veto *resides* in the president⟩ — **re·sid·er** *n*

res·i·dence \'rez-əd-ən(t)s, -ə-ˌden(t)s\ *n* **1** : the act or state of living or working continuously in a place ⟨physicians in *residence* in a hospital⟩ ⟨*residence* abroad⟩ **2 a** : the place where one lives **b** : the status of a legal resident **3 a** : the period during which a person resides in a place **b** : a period of actual study, research, or teaching at a college or university

res·i·den·cy \'rez-əd-ən-sē, -ə-ˌden(t)-\ *n, pl* **-cies** **1 a** : a usually official place of residence **b** : a state or period of residence ⟨a four-year *residency* in the country⟩ **c** : RESIDENCE 2b ⟨applied for *residency*⟩ **2 a** : a period of advanced training especially in a medical specialty that typically follows graduation from medical school **b** : RESIDENCE 3b

¹res·i·dent \'rez-əd-ənt, -ə-ˌdent\ *adj* **1** : living in a place for some length of time **2** : working on a regular or full-time basis ⟨a *resident* physician⟩ **3** : not migrating to other areas ⟨*resident* birds⟩

²resident *n* **1** : one who resides in a place **2** : a person (as a physician) serving a residency

res·i·den·tial \ˌrez-(ə)-'den-chəl\ *adj* **1** : used as a residence or by residents ⟨a *residential* hotel⟩ **2** : suitable for or containing residences ⟨a *residential* neighborhood⟩ **3** : of or relating to residence or residences **4** : provided to patients staying in a facility ⟨*residential* treatment⟩ — **res·i·den·tial·ly** \-'dench-(ə-)lē\ *adv*

¹re·sid·u·al \ri-'zij-(ə-)wəl, -'zij-əl\ *adj* **1** : of, relating to, or being a residue **2** : leaving a residue that is effective for some time afterward — **re·sid·u·al·ly** \-ē\ *adv*

²residual *n* : a residual product, substance, or result

res·i·due \'rez-ə-ˌd(y)ü\ *n* : whatever remains after a part is taken, set apart, or lost or after the completion of a process

re·sign \ri-'zīn\ *vb* **1** : to give up by a formal or official act ⟨*resign* an office⟩ **2** : to give up an office or position : QUIT **3** : to yield to without resistance ⟨*resign* oneself to disappointment⟩

res·ig·na·tion \ˌrez-ig-'nā-shən\ *n* **1 a** : an act of resigning **b** : a formal notice of this act **2** : the quality or the feeling of a person who is resigned

re·signed \ri-'zīnd\ *adj* : giving in patiently (as to loss, sorrow, or misfortune) — **re·sign·ed·ly** \-'zī-nəd-lē\ *adv* — **re·sign·ed·ness** \-'zī-nəd-nəs\ *n*

re·sil·ience \ri-'zil-yən(t)s\ *n* **1** : the ability of a body to regain its original size and shape after being compressed, bent, or stretched : ELASTICITY **2** : the ability to recover from or adjust to misfortune or change

re·sil·ien·cy \ri-'zil-yən-sē\ *n* : RESILIENCE

re·sil·ient \ri-'zil-yənt\ *adj* : characterized or marked by resilience [from Latin *resilient-, resiliens,* present participle of *resilire* "to jump back, rebound," from *re-* "back, again" and *salire* "to leap, spring" — related to ASSAULT, INSULT, SOMERSAULT] — **re·sil·ient·ly** *adv*

res·in \'rez-°n\ *n* **1** : any of various yellowish or brownish substances (as rosin) that are obtained from the gum or sap of some trees (as the pine) and are used in varnishes and plastics and in medicine **2** : any of various manufactured products that are similar to natural resins in properties and are used chiefly in plastics — **res·in·ous** \'rez-nəs, -°n-əs\ *adj*

re·sist \ri-'zist\ *vb* **1** : to fight against : OPPOSE ⟨*resist* temptation⟩ **2** : to withstand the force or effect of ⟨material that *resists* water⟩

re·sis·tance \ri-'zis-tən(t)s\ *n* **1 a** : an act or instance of resisting : OPPOSITION **b** : a method of resisting **2** : the ability to resist ⟨the body's *resistance* to disease⟩ **3** : an opposing or slowing force **4** : the opposition offered by a body or substance to the passage through it of a steady electric current **5** : a source of resistance **6** *often cap* : a secret organization in a conquered or nearly conquered country fighting against enemy forces

re·sis·tant \ri-'zis-tənt\ *adj* : giving, capable of, or showing resistance — often used in combination ⟨wrinkle-*resistant* clothes⟩

re·sist·er \-'zis-tər\ *n* : one that resists; *esp* : one who actively opposes the policies of a government

re·sist·i·bil·i·ty \ri-ˌzis-tə-'bil-ət-ē\ *n* **1** : the quality or state of being resistible **2** : the ability to resist

re·sist·ible \ri-'zis-tə-bəl\ *adj* : capable of being resisted

re·sist·less \ri-'zist-ləs\ *adj* **1** : too strong to be resisted **2** : giving no resistance — **re·sist·less·ly** *adv* — **re·sist·less·ness** *n*

re·sis·tor \ri-'zis-tər\ *n* : a device offering electrical resistance

res·o·lute \'rez-ə-ˌlüt\ *adj* **1** : marked by firm determination ⟨a *resolute* character⟩ **2** : ¹STEADY ⟨a *resolute* gaze⟩ — **res·o·lute·ly** *adv* — **res·o·lute·ness** *n*

res·o·lu·tion \ˌrez-ə-'lü-shən\ *n* **1 a** : the act or process of changing to simpler form **b** : the act of answering ⟨the *resolution* of a problem⟩ **c** : the act of determining **2 a** : the process or capability of distinguishing (as parts of an object or sources of light) **b** : a measure of the sharpness of an image or of the sharpness with which a device can produce or record an image ⟨a printer with a *resolution* of 1200 dots per inch⟩ **3 a** : something that is resolved ⟨New Year *resolutions*⟩ **b** : DETERMINATION 4 **4** : a formal statement of the feelings, wishes, or decision of a group **5** : the point in a work of literature at which the main conflict is worked out

¹re·solve \ri-'zälv, -'zȯlv\ *vb* **re·solved; re·solv·ing** **1** : to break up or separate into individual parts **2 a** : to clear up : DISPEL ⟨*resolve* doubts⟩ **b** : to find an answer or solution to **3** : to reach a decision about : DECIDE ⟨*resolve* to study harder⟩ **4** : to declare or decide by a formal resolution and vote — **re·solv·able** \-'zäl-və-bəl, -'zȯl-\ *adj* — **re·solv·er** *n*

²resolve *n* **1** : something resolved : RESOLUTION **2** : firmness of purpose

re·solved \ri-'zälvd, -'zȯlvd\ *adj* : RESOLUTE 1

\ə\ **abut**	\aů\ **out**	\i\ **tip**	\ȯ\ **saw**	\ů\ **foot**
\ər\ **further**	\ch\ **chin**	\ī\ **life**	\ȯi\ **coin**	\y\ **yet**
\a\ **mat**	\e\ **pet**	\j\ **job**	\th\ **thin**	\yü\ **few**
\ā\ **take**	\ē\ **easy**	\ŋ\ **sing**	\th\ **this**	\yů\ **cure**
\ä\ **cot, cart**	\g\ **go**	\ō\ **bone**	\ü\ **food**	\zh\ **vision**

res·o·nance \'rez-ᵊn-ən(t)s, -nən(t)s\ *n* **1** : the quality or state of being resonant **2** : a reinforcement of sound (as a musical tone) in a vibrating body or system caused by waves from another body vibrating at nearly the same rate **3** : a vibrating quality of a voice sound

res·o·nant \'rez-ᵊn-ənt, 'rez-nənt\ *adj* **1** : continuing to sound **2** : of, relating to, or showing resonance **3** : strengthened and enriched by resonance — **res·o·nant·ly** *adv*

res·o·nate \'rez-ᵊn-ₐāt\ *vb* **-nat·ed; -nat·ing 1** : to produce or exhibit resonance **2 a** : to respond as if by resonance ⟨*resonate* to the music⟩ **b** : to strike a chord ⟨a message that *resonates* with voters⟩

res·o·na·tor \'rez-ᵊn-ₐāt-ər\ *n* : something (as a device for increasing the resonance of a musical instrument) that resounds or resonates

¹**re·sort** \ri-'zȯ(ə)rt\ *n* **1 a** : someone or something that is looked to for help ⟨a last *resort*⟩ **b** : RECOURSE 1 ⟨have *resort* to force⟩ **2 a** : frequent, habitual, or general visiting ⟨a place of popular *resort*⟩ **b** : a frequently visited place : HANGOUT **c** : a place providing recreation and entertainment especially to vacationers ⟨a ski *resort*⟩

²**resort** *vb* **1** : to go especially frequently or habitually **2** : to turn to for aid, relief, or advantage ⟨*resort* to violence⟩

re·sound \ri-'zaund\ *vb* **1** : to become filled with sound : REVERBERATE ⟨the hall *resounded* with cheers⟩ **2** : to sound loudly ⟨the organ *resounds* throughout the hall⟩ **3** : to become renowned

re·sound·ing *adj* **1** : producing or marked by resonant sound **2** : leaving no doubt : CLEAR ⟨a *resounding* success⟩ — **re·sound·ing·ly** \-'zaun-diŋ-lē\ *adv*

re·source \'rē-ₛsō(ə)rs, -ₜzō(ə)rs, -ₛsȯ(ə)rs, -ₜzȯ(ə)rs; ri-'sō(ə)rs, -'zō(ə)rs, -'sȯ(ə)rs, -'zȯ(ə)rs\ *n* **1 a** : a new or a reserve source of supply or support **b** *pl* : a usable stock or supply (as of money, products, or energy) ⟨mineral *resources*⟩ **c** : NATURAL RESOURCE **2** : the possibility of relief or recovery ⟨left helpless without *resource*⟩ **3** : the ability to meet and deal with difficult situations

re·source·ful \ri-'sōrs-fəl, -'sȯrs-, -'zōrs-, -'zȯrs-\ *adj* : able to deal well with new or difficult situations — **re·source·ful·ly** \-fə-lē\ *adv* — **re·source·ful·ness** *n*

¹**re·spect** \ri-'spekt\ *n* **1** : relation to or concern with something specified : REFERENCE ⟨with *respect* to your last letter⟩ **2 a** : high or special regard : ESTEEM **b** *pl* : expressions of regard or courtesy ⟨pay my *respects* to your family⟩ **3** : ¹DETAIL 1b ⟨perfect in all *respects*⟩

²**respect** *vb* **1** : to consider worthy of high regard : ESTEEM **2** : to avoid interfering with ⟨*respected* their wishes⟩ — **re·spect·er** *n*

re·spect·able \ri-'spek-tə-bəl\ *adj* **1** : worthy of respect : REPUTABLE **2** : decent or correct in character or behavior : PROPER ⟨*respectable* people⟩ **3** : fair in size, quality, or quantity ⟨a *respectable* amount of money⟩ **4** : fit to be seen : PRESENTABLE ⟨*respectable* clothes⟩ — **re·spect·abil·i·ty** \-ₛspek-tə-'bil-ət-ē\ *n* — **re·spect·able·ness** \-'spek-tə-bəl-nəs\ *n* — **re·spect·ably** \-blē\ *adv*

re·spect·ful \ri-'spekt-fəl\ *adj* : marked by or showing respect ⟨a *respectful* manner⟩ ⟨*respectful* of others⟩ — **re·spect·ful·ly** \-fə-lē\ *adv* — **re·spect·ful·ness** *n*

re·spect·ing *prep* : CONCERNING

re·spec·tive \ri-'spek-tiv\ *adj* : not the same or shared : SEPARATE ⟨they hurried to their *respective* homes⟩

re·spec·tive·ly \ri-'spek-tiv-lē\ *adv* : each in the order given ⟨John and Mary were 12 and 13 years old *respectively*⟩

re·spell \(')rē-'spel\ *vb* : to spell again or in another way; *esp* : to spell out according to a phonetic system — **re·spell·ing** *n*

res·pi·ra·tion \ₛres-pə-'rā-shən\ *n* **1** : the act or process of breathing **2** : the physical processes (as breathing and diffusion) by which a living thing obtains the oxygen it needs to produce energy and eliminate waste gases (as carbon dioxide) **3** : any of various chemical reactions (as oxidation) in cells that release energy from food molecules (as glucose)

res·pi·ra·tor \'res-pə-ₛrāt-ər\ *n* **1** : a device covering the mouth and nose especially to prevent the breathing in of harmful substances (as dust or fumes) **2** : a device used to maintain artificial respiration

re·spi·ra·to·ry \'res-p(ə-)rə-ₛtōr-ē, ri-'spī-rə-, -ₛtȯr-\ *adj* : of or relating to respiration or the organs of respiration ⟨*respiratory* diseases⟩

respiratory system *n* : a system of organs used in breathing that in human beings consists of the nose, nasal passages, pharynx, larynx, trachea, bronchi and lungs

re·spire \ri-'spī(ə)r\ *vb* **re·spired; re·spir·ing** : to engage in respiration; *esp* : BREATHE 1

re·spite \'res-pət *also* ri-'spīt\ *n* **1** : a short delay : POSTPONEMENT **2** : a period of rest or relief

re·splen·dence \ri-'splen-dən(t)s\ *n* : the quality or state of being resplendent : SPLENDOR

re·splen·den·cy \-dən-sē\ *n* : RESPLENDENCE

re·splen·dent \ri-'splen-dənt\ *adj* : so bright as to seem to glow ⟨fields *resplendent* with flowers⟩ ⟨*resplendent* in a new red coat⟩ — **re·splen·dent·ly** *adv*

re·spond \ri-'spänd\ *vb* **1** : to say something in return : make an answer **2 a** : to react in response ⟨note how the animal's eyes *respond* to light⟩ **b** : to have a favorable reaction ⟨the patient is *responding* to treatment⟩

re·sponse \ri-'spän(t)s\ *n* **1** : an act or instance of replying : ANSWER **2** : words said or sung by the people or choir in a religious service **3** : a reaction of a living thing to a stimulus

re·spon·si·bil·i·ty \ri-ₛspän(t)-sə-'bil-ət-ē\ *n, pl* **-ties 1** : the quality or state of being responsible **2** : the quality of being dependable **3** : something for which one is responsible ⟨neglected his *responsibilities*⟩

re·spon·si·ble \ri-'spän(t)-sə-bəl\ *adj* **1 a** : being the one who must answer or account for something ⟨the committee *responsible* for the job⟩ **b** : being the cause or explanation ⟨the germ *responsible* for the disease⟩ **2 a** : able to meet one's obligations : RELIABLE ⟨a *responsible* citizen⟩ **b** : able to choose for oneself between right and wrong **3** : requiring a person to take charge of or to be trusted with important matters ⟨a *responsible* job⟩ — **re·spon·si·ble·ness** *n* — **re·spon·si·bly** \-blē\ *adv*

re·spon·sive \ri-'spän(t)-siv\ *adj* **1** : giving response : being an answer ⟨a *responsive* smile⟩ **2** : quick to respond or react sympathetically : SENSITIVE ⟨*responsive* to the needs of the poor⟩ — **re·spon·sive·ly** *adv* — **re·spon·sive·ness** *n*

¹**rest** \'rest\ *n* **1** : ¹SLEEP 1 **2 a** : freedom from activity **b** : a state marked by lack of motion or activity **3** : a place for resting or lodging **4 a** : a silence in music equal in time to a note of the same name **b** : a character standing for such a silence **5** : something used for support ⟨a head *rest*⟩ — **at rest** : resting especially in sleep or death

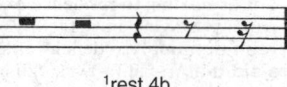

¹rest 4b

²**rest** *vb* **1 a** : to get rest by lying down : SLEEP **b** : to give rest to **c** : to lie dead **2** : to not take part in work or activity **3** : to be free from anxiety or disturbance **4** : to place or be placed for or as if for support **5 a** : to be based or founded **b** : to fix or be fixed in hope or confidence ⟨*rested* their hopes on their children⟩ **6** : to stop presenting evidence in a law case ⟨the defense *rests*⟩

³**rest** *n* : something that is left over or behind : REMAINDER ⟨ate the *rest* of the soup⟩

re·start \rē-'stärt\ *vb* **1** : to start anew ⟨*restarted* the car⟩

2 a : to resume (as an activity) after an interruption ⟨will *restart* the game⟩ **b** : to resume operation ⟨the rides will *restart* after one hour⟩ — **restart** \'rē-ˌstärt\ *n*

re·state \(ˈ)rē-ˈstāt\ *vb* : to state again or in another way

re·state·ment \-mənt\ *n* **1** : something that is restated **2** : the act of restating

res·tau·rant \'res-t(ə-)rənt, -tə-ˌränt\ *n* : a business place where meals or refreshments may be bought [from French *restaurant* "food that restores, restaurant," from *restaurer* "to restore, renew"]

res·tau·ra·teur \ˌres-tə-rə-ˈtər\ *also* **res·tau·ran·teur** \-ˌrän-\ *n* : a person who owns or runs a restaurant

rest·ed \'res-təd\ *adj* : having had enough rest or sleep

rest·ful \'rest-fəl\ *adj* : giving or suggesting rest : QUIET ⟨a *restful* scene⟩ — **rest·ful·ly** \-fə-lē\ *adv* — **rest·ful·ness** *n*

rest home *n* : a place that provides housing and general care for the aged or sick

rest house *n* : a building used for shelter by travelers

rest·ing *adj* : not growing or active : DORMANT 2b ⟨a *resting* spore⟩

res·ti·tu·tion \ˌres-tə-ˈt(y)ü-shən\ *n* : the giving of something back to its rightful owner or the giving of something of equal value (as for loss or damage)

res·tive \'res-tiv\ *adj* **1** : stubbornly fighting control : BALKY ⟨a *restive* horse⟩ **2** : showing impatience or uneasiness : FIDGETY ⟨the crowd grew *restive*⟩ — **res·tive·ly** *adv* — **res·tive·ness** *n*

rest·less \'rest-ləs\ *adj* **1** : being without rest : giving no rest ⟨a *restless* night⟩ **2** : always moving ⟨the *restless* sea⟩ **3** : showing one to be uneasy ⟨*restless* pacing back and forth⟩ — **rest·less·ly** *adv* — **rest·less·ness** *n*

res·to·ra·tion \ˌres-tə-ˈrā-shən\ *n* **1** : an act of restoring or the condition of being restored **2** : something (as a building) that has been restored

¹re·stor·a·tive \ri-ˈstōr-ət-iv, -ˈstȯr-\ *adj* : of or relating to restoration; *esp* : having power to restore ⟨the *restorative* value of food and rest⟩

²restorative *n* : something that serves to restore to consciousness or health

re·store \ri-ˈstō(ə)r, -ˈstȯ(ə)r\ *vb* **re·stored; re·stor·ing 1** : ¹RETURN 5 ⟨*restored* the purse to its owner⟩ **2** : to put or bring back into existence or use ⟨*restore* harmony after an argument⟩ **3** : to bring back to or put back into an earlier or original state ⟨*restore* an old house⟩ **4** : to put again in possession of something ⟨*restore* the king to the throne⟩ — **re·stor·able** \-ˈstōr-ə-bəl, -ˈstȯr-\ *adj* — **re·stor·er** *n*

re·strain \ri-ˈstrān\ *vb* **1 a** : to prevent from doing something **b** : to keep back : CURB ⟨*restrain* one's anger⟩ **c** : to limit or keep under control ⟨*restrain* trade⟩ **2** : to take away liberty; *esp* : to place under arrest or restraint — **re·strain·able** \-ˈstrā-nə-bəl\ *adj* — **re·strain·er** *n*

re·strained \ri-ˈstrānd\ *adj* : marked by restraint : showing careful control — **re·strain·ed·ly** \-ˈstrā-nəd-lē\ *adv*

re·straint \ri-ˈstrānt\ *n* **1** : the act of restraining : the state of being restrained ⟨held in *restraint*⟩ **2** : a restraining force or influence **3** : control over one's behavior ⟨act with *restraint*⟩

re·strict \ri-ˈstrikt\ *vb* **1** : to keep within bounds **2** : to place under limits as to use **synonyms** see LIMIT

re·strict·ed *adj* : being or placed under limits or restrictions ⟨a *restricted* outlook⟩ ⟨a *restricted* area⟩

re·stric·tion \ri-ˈstrik-shən\ *n* **1** : something (as a law or rule) that restricts **2** : an act of restricting : the condition of being restricted

re·stric·tive \ri-ˈstrik-tiv\ *adj* **1** : serving or likely to restrict **2** : limiting the reference of a modified word or phrase — **restrictive** *n* — **re·stric·tive·ly** *adv* — **re·stric·tive·ness** *n*

rest·room \'rest-ˌrüm, -ˌrum\ *n* : a room or set of rooms that includes sinks and toilets

re·struc·ture \rē-ˈstrək-chər\ *vb* : to change the makeup, organization, or pattern of

¹re·sult \ri-ˈzəlt\ *vb* **1** : to come about as an effect, consequence, or conclusion ⟨disease *results* from infection⟩ **2** : to have as an effect ⟨the disease *results* in death⟩

²result *n* **1** : something that comes about as an effect or end **2** : a good or clear effect ⟨this method gets *results*⟩ **3** : something obtained by calculation or investigation — **re·sult·ful** \-fəl\ *adj* — **re·sult·less** \-ləs\ *adj*

¹re·sul·tant \ri-ˈzəlt-ᵊnt\ *adj* : coming from or resulting from something else — **re·sul·tant·ly** *adv*

²resultant *n* : something that results : OUTCOME; *esp* : the single vector that is the sum of a given set of vectors

re·sume \ri-ˈzüm\ *vb* **re·sumed; re·sum·ing 1** : to take again : occupy again ⟨*resume* your seats⟩ **2** : to begin again or go back to ⟨*resumed* the game the next day⟩

ré·su·mé *or* **re·su·me** *also* **re·su·mé** \'rez-ə-ˌmā\ *n* **1** : a brief statement : SUMMARY ⟨a *résumé* of the news⟩ **2** : a short account of one's career and qualifications for a job

re·sump·tion \ri-ˈzəm(p)-shən\ *n* : the action of resuming

re·sur·face \rē-ˈsər-fəs\ *vb* **1** : to provide with a new or fresh surface ⟨*resurface* the table⟩ **2** : to come again to the surface (as of water) — **re·sur·fac·er** \-fə-sər\ *n*

re·sur·gence \ri-ˈsər-jən(t)s\ *n* : a rising again into life, activity, or notice

re·sur·gent \-jənt\ *adj* : undergoing or tending to produce resurgence

res·ur·rect \ˌrez-ə-ˈrekt\ *vb* **1** : to raise from the dead : bring back to life **2** : to bring to attention or into use again

res·ur·rec·tion \ˌrez-ə-ˈrek-shən\ *n* **1 a** *cap* : the rising of Jesus from the dead **b** *often cap* : the rising again to life of all the human dead before the final judgment **2** : RESURGENCE, REVIVAL — **res·ur·rec·tion·al** \-shnəl, -shən-ᵊl\ *adj*

re·sus·ci·tate \ri-ˈsəs-ə-ˌtāt\ *vb* **-tat·ed; -tat·ing 1** : to bring back from apparent death or from unconsciousness **2** : REVIVE 1

re·sus·ci·ta·tion \ri-ˌsəs-ə-ˈtā-shən\ *n* : an act or procedure that attempts to resuscitate; *also* : the state of being resuscitated — compare CARDIOPULMONARY RESUSCITATION

re·sus·ci·ta·tor \ri-ˈsəs-ə-ˌtāt-ər\ *n* : one that resuscitates; *esp* : a device used to restore or assist the respiration of a person who is not breathing normally

ret \'ret\ *vb* **ret·ted; ret·ting** : to soak a plant (as flax) to loosen the fiber from the woody tissue

¹re·tail \'rē-ˌtāl\ *vb* : to sell in small amounts to people for their own use — **re·tail·er** *n*

²retail *n* : the sale of products or goods in small quantities to people for their own use

³retail *adj* : of, relating to, or engaged in selling by retail ⟨*retail* stores⟩

⁴retail *adv* : in small quantities : from a retailer

re·tain \ri-ˈtān\ *vb* **1 a** : to keep in possession or use ⟨you will *retain* your rights as a citizen⟩ **b** : to keep in pay or in one's service; *esp* : to employ by paying a retainer ⟨*retain* an attorney⟩ **c** : REMEMBER 3 ⟨I can't *retain* phone numbers⟩ **2** : to hold secure or unchanged ⟨land *retains* heat longer than water⟩

¹re·tain·er \ri-ˈtā-nər\ *n* : a fee paid (as to a lawyer) for advice or services or for a claim upon services in case of need

\ə\ **abut**	\au̇\ **out**	\i\ **tip**	\o̅\ **saw**	\u̇\ **foot**
\ər\ **further**	\ch\ **chin**	\ī\ **life**	\o̅i\ **coin**	\y\ **yet**
\a\ **mat**	\e\ **pet**	\j\ **job**	\th\ **thin**	\yü\ **few**
\ā\ **take**	\ē\ **easy**	\ŋ\ **sing**	\th̲\ **this**	\yu̇\ **cure**
\ä\ **cot, cart**	\g\ **go**	\ō\ **bone**	\ü\ **food**	\zh\ **vision**

²**re·tain·er** *n* **1** : a servant or follower in a wealthy household **2** : one that retains **3** : a usually removable dental device used to hold teeth in correct position especially following orthodontic treatment (as with braces) — called also *bite plate*

¹**re·take** \(')rē-'tāk\ *vb* **-took** \-'tŭk\; **-tak·en** \-'tā-kən\; **-tak·ing** : to take again; *esp* : to photograph again

²**re·take** \'rē-ˌtāk\ *n* : a second photographing or photograph

re·tal·i·ate \ri-'tal-ē-ˌāt\ *vb* **-at·ed; -at·ing** : to return (as an injury) in kind : get revenge — **re·tal·i·a·tion** \-ˌtal-ē-'ā-shən\ *n* — **re·tal·ia·to·ry** \-'tal-yə-ˌtōr-ē, -ˌtòr-\ *adj*

re·tard \ri-'tärd\ *vb* : to slow up especially by preventing or checking progress — HINDER — **re·tard·er** *n*

re·tar·dant \ri-'tärd-ᵊnt\ *adj* : serving or tending to retard ⟨flame-*retardant* fabrics⟩

re·tar·da·tion \ˌrē-ˌtär-'dā-shən\ *n* **1** : an act or instance of retarding **2** : the extent to which something is retarded **3** : an unusual slowness especially of intellectual or physical development; *esp* : MENTAL RETARDATION

re·tard·ed \ri-'tärd-əd\ *adj, sometimes offensive* : slow or limited in intellectual or emotional development

retch \'rech, *British* rēch\ *vb* **1** : ²VOMIT 1 **2** : to try to vomit

re·tell \rē-'tel\ *vb* **-told** \-'tōld\; **-tel·ling** **1** : to tell again or in another form **2** : to count again

re·ten·tion \ri-'ten-chən\ *n* **1** : the act of retaining : the state of being retained **2** : power of retaining **3** : something retained

re·ten·tive \ri-'tent-iv\ *adj* : having ability to retain ⟨a *retentive* memory⟩ — **re·ten·tive·ly** *adv* — **re·ten·tive·ness** *n*

re·think \rē-'thiŋk\ *vb* **-thought** \-'thòt\; **-think·ing** : to think about again : RECONSIDER

ret·i·cence \'ret-ə-sən(t)s\ *n* **1** : the quality or state of being reticent **2** : an instance of being reticent **3** : RELUCTANCE

ret·i·cent \'ret-ə-sənt\ *adj* **1** : tending not to talk or give out information **2** : quiet in tone or appearance **3** : RELUCTANT **synonyms** see SILENT — **ret·i·cent·ly** *adv*

re·tic·u·lar \ri-'tik-yə-lər\ *adj* : RETICULATE

re·tic·u·late \ri-'tik-yə-lət\ *adj* : resembling a net

ret·i·cule \'ret-i-ˌkyü(ə)l\ *n* : a handbag that is closed by pulling a string

ret·i·na \'ret-ᵊn-ə, 'ret-nə\ *n, pl* **retinas** *also* **ret·i·nae** \-ᵊn-ˌē, -ˌī\ : the light-sensitive inner layer lining the back of the eye that contains the rods and cones and converts the images formed by the lens into signals which reach the brain by way of the optic nerve — **ret·i·nal** \-ᵊn-əl, -nəl\ *adj*

ret·i·nol \'ret-ᵊn-ˌòl, -ˌōl\ *n* : the most common form of vitamin A

ret·i·nue \'ret-ᵊn-ˌ(y)ü\ *n* : a group of helpers, servants, or followers

re·tire \ri-'tī(ə)r\ *vb* **re·tired; re·tir·ing** **1** : to get away from action or danger : RETREAT **2** : to go away especially to be alone **3** : to give up or cause to give up one's job **4** : to go to bed **5** : to put out (a batter or side) in baseball **6** : to win permanent possession of (as a trophy)

re·tired *adj* **1** : SECLUDED 1 ⟨a *retired* village⟩ **2** : not working at active duties or business

re·tir·ee \ri-ˌtī-'rē\ *n* : a person who has retired from a job or profession

¹**re·tire·ment** \ri-'tī(ə)r-mənt\ *n* : an act of retiring : the state of being retired; *esp* : the leaving of one's job permanently

²**retirement** *adj* : of, relating to, or made for retired persons ⟨a *retirement* community⟩

re·tir·ing \ri-'tī(ə)r-iŋ\ *adj* : RESERVED 1, SHY — **re·tir·ing·ly** \-iŋ-lē\ *adv* — **re·tir·ing·ness** *n*

re·tool \(')rē-'tül\ *vb* **1** : to equip again with new or different tools ⟨*retool* a factory⟩ **2** : to make changes or improvements to ⟨*retool* that idea⟩

¹**re·tort** \ri-'tò(ə)rt\ *vb* **1** : to answer back : reply angrily or sharply **2** : to reply to an argument with an opposing argument [from Latin *retortus,* past participle of *retorquēre,* literally "to twist back, hurl back," from *re-* "back, again" and *torquēre* "to twist" — related to DISTORT, EXTORT, TORTURE]

²**retort** *n* : a quick, witty, or angry reply

³**re·tort** \ri-'tò(ə)rt, 'rē-ˌtò(ə)rt\ *n* : a container in which substances are distilled or broken down by heat [from early French *retorte* "a vessel in which substances are distilled," derived from Latin *retortus,* past participle of *retorquēre* "to twist"; probably so called from its shape]

re·touch \(')rē-'təch\ *vb* : TOUCH UP; *esp* : to change (as a photographic negative) in order to produce a more desirable appearance — **re·touch** \'rē-ˌtəch, (')rē-'təch\ *n* — **re·touch·er** \(')rē-'təch-ər\ *n*

³retort

re·tract \ri-'trakt\ *vb* **1** : to draw or pull back or in ⟨a cat can *retract* its claws⟩ **2** : to withdraw (as an offer, a statement, or a claim) ⟨the newspaper *retracted* the story⟩ — **re·tract·able** \-'trak-tə-bəl\ *adj*

re·trac·tile \ri-'trak-tᵊl, -ˌtīl\ *adj* : capable of being drawn back or in ⟨the *retractile* claws of a cat⟩

re·trac·tion \ri-'trak-shən\ *n* **1** : a statement taking back something previously said **2** : an act of retracting : the state of being retracted **3** : the ability to retract

re·trac·tor \ri-'trak-tər\ *n* : one that retracts; *esp* : a muscle that draws an organ or part in or back

re·train \rē-'trān\ *vb* **1** : to train again or anew **2** : to become retrained — **re·train·able** \-'trā-nə-bəl\ *adj*

re·trans·late \ˌrē-tran(t)s-'lāt, -tranz-\ *vb* : to translate into another language ⟨*retranslated* the German translation into English⟩ — **re·trans·la·tion** \-'lā-shən\ *n*

¹**re·tread** \(')rē-'tred\ *vb* **re·tread·ed; re·tread·ing** **1** : to put a new tread on (a worn tire) **2** : to make over as if new ⟨*retread* an old plot⟩

²**re·tread** \'rē-ˌtred\ *n* **1** : a retreaded tire **2** : something made or done again especially in a slightly altered form

¹**re·treat** \ri-'trēt\ *n* **1 a** : an act of going away especially from something difficult, dangerous, or disagreeable **b** : a military retreat from the enemy **c** : a signal for retreating **2** : a place of privacy or safety : REFUGE **3** : a period of withdrawal for prayer, meditation, study, or instruction under a director ⟨went on a spiritual *retreat*⟩

²**retreat** *vb* **1** : to make a retreat **2** : to slope backward — **re·treat·er** *n*

re·trench \ri-'trench\ *vb* **1** : LESSEN, REDUCE **2** : to reduce expenses : ECONOMIZE — **re·trench·ment** \-mənt\ *n*

re·tri·al \(')rē-'trī(-ə)l\ *n* : a second trial, experiment, or test

ret·ri·bu·tion \ˌre-trə-'byü-shən\ *n* : something given in payment for a wrong : PUNISHMENT

re·trib·u·tive \ri-'trib-yət-iv\ *adj* : of, relating to, or marked by retribution ⟨*retributive* justice⟩ — **re·trib·u·tive·ly** *adv*

re·trib·u·to·ry \ri-'trib-yə-ˌtōr-ē, -ˌtòr-\ *adj* : RETRIBUTIVE

re·triev·al \ri-'trē-vəl\ *n* : an act or process of retrieving

re·trieve \ri-'trēv\ *vb* **re·trieved; re·triev·ing** **1** : to find and bring in killed or wounded game ⟨teach a dog how to *retrieve*⟩ **2** : to recover or make good a loss or damage ⟨*retrieved* artifacts from the shipwreck⟩ **3** : to get and bring back; *esp* : to recover (as information) from storage — **re·triev·able** \-'trē-və-bəl\ *adj*

re·triev·er \ri-'trē-vər\ *n* : one that retrieves; *esp* : a dog (as a golden retriever) of any of several breeds having a heavy water-resistant coat and used especially for retrieving game

retriever

ret·ro \'ret-rō\ *adj* : relating to, reviving, or being the styles and especially the fashions of the past

retro- *prefix* : backward : back ⟨*retro*-rocket⟩ [derived from Latin *re-* "back, again" and Latin *-tro* (the final part of *intro* "within")]

ret·ro·ac·tive \‚re-trō-'ak-tiv\ *adj* : intended to apply or take effect at a date in the past ⟨a *retroactive* pay raise⟩ — **ret·ro·ac·tive·ly** *adv*

ret·ro·fire \'re-trō-‚fī(-ə)r\ *vb* : to ignite a retro-rocket — **retrofire** *n*

ret·ro·fit \'re-trō-‚fit\ *vb* : to install (new or modified parts or equipment) in something previously manufactured or constructed

ret·ro·grade \'re-trə-‚grād\ *adj* **1** : having a backward direction or motion **2** : tending toward or resulting in a worse or previous state

ret·ro·gress \‚re-trə-'gres\ *vb* : to move backward

ret·ro·gres·sion \-'gresh-ən\ *n* **1** : movement backwards **2** : return to a previous and less complicated level of development or organization

ret·ro·rock·et \'re-trō-‚räk-ət\ *n* : a rocket (as on a space vehicle) used to slow forward motion

ret·ro·spect \'re-trə-‚spekt\ *n* : a looking back on or a thinking about past events

ret·ro·spec·tion \‚re-trə-'spek-shən\ *n* **1** : the act or power of recalling the past **2** : RETROSPECT

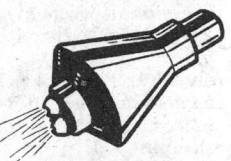

retro-rocket

¹ret·ro·spec·tive \‚re-trə-'spek-tiv\ *adj* : of, relating to, or given to retrospection — **ret·ro·spec·tive·ly** *adv*

²retrospective *n* : an exhibition, compilation, or performance of work that an artist has done in the past

ret·ro·vi·rus \'re-trō-‚vī-rəs\ *n* : any of a group of RNA-containing viruses (as HIV) that replicate by becoming incorporated into the chromosomes of infected cells in the form of DNA which is produced from the viral RNA

retted *past and past participle of* RET

retting *present participle of* RET

¹re·turn \ri-'tərn\ *vb* **1 a** : to come or go back **b** : to go back in thought or practice ⟨*returned* to his old ways⟩ **2** : ¹REPLY 3, ANSWER **3** : to make an official report of ⟨the jury *returned* a verdict⟩ **4** *British* : to elect to office **5** : to bring, carry, send, or put back ⟨*return* a book to the library⟩ ⟨*return* borrowed money⟩ **6** : to bring in (as profit) : YIELD **7 a** : to give or perform in return ⟨*return* a compliment⟩ **b** : to respond to in a similar way ⟨*return* kindness with kindness⟩ **c** : to give back to the owner ⟨*return* that lawnmower⟩ **8 a** : to hit back (as a tennis ball) **b** : to run with (a football) after the possession of the ball changes from one team to the other (as by a fumble or a punt) — **re·turn·er** *n*

²return *n* **1 a** : the act of coming back to or from a place or condition **b** : a regular or frequent occurrence : RECURRENCE ⟨the *return* of spring⟩ **2 a** : a report of the results of voting — usually used in plural ⟨election *returns*⟩ **b** : a statement of income to be taxed ⟨a tax re-

turn⟩ **3** : a means for bringing something (as water) back to its starting point **4** : the profit from labor, investment, or business : YIELD **5 a** : the act of returning something to an earlier place, condition, or ownership **b** : something returned **6** : something given in payment or exchange ⟨ask nothing in *return* for a favor⟩ **7** : the action or an instance of returning a ball (as in tennis or football)

³return *adj* **1** : played or given in return ⟨a *return* call⟩ ⟨a *return* game⟩ **2** : used for returning ⟨a *return* ticket⟩ **3** : of, relating to, or causing a return to a place or condition ⟨a *return* envelope⟩

re·turn·able \ri-'tər-nə-bəl\ *adj* : that may or must be returned ⟨*returnable* bottles⟩

re·turn·ee \ri-‚tər-'nē\ *n* : one who returns

re·union \(')rē-'yün-yən\ *n* **1** : the act of reuniting : the state of being reunited **2** : a reuniting of persons after separation ⟨a class *reunion*⟩

re·unite \‚rē-yü-'nīt\ *vb* : to come or bring together again after a separation

re·us·able \(')rē-'yü-zə-bəl\ *adj* : capable of being used again or repeatedly

re·use \(')rē-'yüz\ *vb* : to use again especially in a different way — **re·use** \-'yüs\ *n*

¹rev \'rev\ *n* : a revolution of a motor

²rev *vb* **revved; rev·ving 1** : to increase the revolutions per minute of (a motor) **2** : to make more active or effective — used with *up* ⟨needed to *rev* up the campaign⟩ **3** : EXCITE 1 — usually used with *up* ⟨the concert *revved* us up⟩

re·val·u·ate \(')rē-'val-yə-‚wāt\ *vb* **-at·ed; -at·ing** : REVALUE — **re·val·u·a·tion** \(‚)rē-‚val-yə-'wā-shən\ *n*

re·val·ue \(')rē-'val-yü\ *vb* : to make a new valuation of : REAPPRAISE

re·vamp \(')rē-'vamp\ *vb* **1** : to make like new again : RENOVATE **2** : ¹REVISE

re·veal \ri-'vē(ə)l\ *vb* **1** : to make known : DIVULGE **2** : to show plainly : DISPLAY — **re·veal·er** *n*

synonyms REVEAL, DISCLOSE, TELL, BETRAY mean to make known what has been or should be concealed. REVEAL may apply to making known ordinary information or to making known truths that are usually beyond the range of human vision or reason ⟨*revealed* his age to the interviewer⟩ ⟨their mission was *revealed* to them in a dream⟩. DISCLOSE most often involves the giving out of information previously kept secret ⟨*disclosed* to the media that the leaders of the two countries had met privately⟩. TELL stresses that the information made known is necessary or useful ⟨why didn't you *tell* her that the concert was canceled?⟩. BETRAY implies either that disclosing the information involves wrongdoing or that the disclosure is against one's will ⟨*betrayed* plans for a new computer to the firm's chief rival⟩ ⟨though I said nothing, my face *betrayed* my concern⟩.

rev·eil·le \'rev-ə-lē\ *n* **1** : a signal to get up in the morning **2** : a bugle call at about sunrise signaling the first military formation of the day [from French *réveillez* "wake up!"]

¹rev·el \'rev-əl\ *vb* **-eled** *or* **-elled; -el·ing** *or* **-el·ling** \-(ə-)liŋ\ **1** : to take part in a revel : be noisy in a festive manner **2** : to take great delight in something — **rev·el·er** *or* **rev·el·ler** \-(ə-)lər\ *n*

²revel *n* : a noisy or merry celebration

rev·e·la·tion \‚rev-ə-'lā-shən\ *n* **1** : an act of revealing or making known divine truth **2 a** : an act of revealing to view **b** : something that is revealed; *esp* : a surprising or astonishing disclosure

Rev·e·la·tion \‚rev-ə-'lā-shən\ *n* — see BIBLE table

\ə\ **abut**	\au̇\ **out**	\i\ **tip**	\ȯ\ **saw**	\u̇\ **foot**
\ər\ **further**	\ch\ **chin**	\ī\ **life**	\ȯi\ **coin**	\y\ **yet**
\a\ **mat**	\e\ **pet**	\j\ **job**	\th\ **thin**	\yü\ **few**
\ā\ **take**	\ē\ **easy**	\ŋ\ **sing**	\t̲h̲\ **this**	\yu̇\ **cure**
\ä\ **cot, cart**	\g\ **go**	\ō\ **bone**	\ü\ **food**	\zh\ **vision**

re·ve·la·to·ry \\'rev-ə-lə-ˌtōr-ē, -ˌtȯr-, ri-'vel-ə-\\ *adj* : of or relating to revelation

rev·el·ry \\'rev-əl-rē\\ *n, pl* **-ries** : rough and noisy merry-making

¹re·venge \\ri-'venj\\ *vb* **re·venged; re·veng·ing** **1** : to get even for a wrong done ⟨*revenge* myself on my enemies⟩ **2** : to give injury in return for ⟨*revenge* an insult⟩ — **re·veng·er** *n*

²revenge *n* **1** : a desire to pay back injury for injury **2** : an act or instance of revenging **3** : a chance for getting satisfaction — **re·venge·ful** \\-fəl\\ *adj* — **re·venge·ful·ly** \\-fə-lē\\ *adv* — **re·venge·ful·ness** *n*

rev·e·nue \\'rev-ə-ˌn(y)ü\\ *n* **1** : the income produced by a given source **2** : the income that a government collects for public use

rev·e·nu·er \\'rev-ə-ˌn(y)ü-ər\\ *n* : a revenue department officer

re·ver·ber·ant \\ri-'vər-b(ə-)rənt\\ *adj* : tending to reverberate — **re·ver·ber·ant·ly** *adv*

re·ver·ber·ate \\ri-'vər-bə-ˌrāt\\ *vb* **-at·ed; -at·ing** : to continue in or as if in a series of echoes — **re·ver·ber·a·tion** \\-ˌvər-bə-'rā-shən\\ *n*

re·vere \\ri-'vi(ə)r\\ *vb* **re·vered; re·ver·ing** : to show devotion and honor to : think of with reverence

¹rev·er·ence \\'rev-(ə-)rən(t)s, 'rev-ərn(t)s\\ *n* **1** : honor or respect felt or shown : DEFERENCE **2** : the state of being revered or honored

²reverence *vb* **-enced; -enc·ing** : to think of or treat with reverence

¹rev·er·end \\'rev-(ə-)rənd, 'rev-ərnd\\ *adj* **1** : worthy of reverence : REVERED ⟨these *reverend* halls⟩ **2** — used as a title for a member of the clergy ⟨the *Reverend* Ms. Doe⟩ ⟨the *Reverend* John Doe⟩ ⟨the *Reverend* Mother Superior⟩

²reverend *n* : a member of the clergy

rev·er·ent \\'rev-(ə-)rənt, 'rev-ərnt\\ *adj* : very respectful : showing reverence — **rev·er·ent·ly** *adv*

rev·er·en·tial \\ˌrev-ə-'ren-chəl\\ *adj* **1** : showing or having a quality of reverence **2** : inspiring reverence — **rev·er·en·tial·ly** \\-'rench-(ə-)lē\\ *adv*

rev·er·ie *also* **rev·ery** \\'rev-(ə-)rē\\ *n, pl* **-er·ies** **1** : ¹DAYDREAM **2** : the condition of being lost in thought

re·ver·sal \\ri-'vər-səl\\ *n* : an act or the process of reversing

¹re·verse \\ri-'vərs\\ *adj* **1** : opposite or contrary to a previous or normal condition ⟨*reverse* order⟩ **2** : acting or working in a manner opposite to the usual **3** : bringing about backward movement ⟨*reverse* gear⟩ [Middle English *revers* "opposite or contrary to a previous or normal condition," from early French *revers* (same meaning), from Latin *reversus* "turned back," from *revertere* "to turn back," from *re-* "again" + *vertere* "to turn" — related to CONVERSE, VERSATILE, VERTICAL, VICE VERSA] — **re·verse·ly** *adv*

²reverse *vb* **re·versed; re·vers·ing** **1** : to turn completely about or upside down or inside out **2 a** : to overthrow or set aside a legal decision by an opposite decision **b** : to change to the contrary ⟨*reverse* a policy⟩ **3 a** : to go or cause to go in the opposite direction **b** : to put (as a car) into reverse **4** : to undo the effect of (as a condition) ⟨face creams that promise to *reverse* the signs of aging⟩ — **re·vers·er** *n*

³reverse *n* **1** : something directly opposite to something else **2** : an act or instance of reversing; *esp* : a change for the worse **3** : the back part of something **4** : a gear that reverses something

¹re·vers·ible \\ri-'vər-sə-bəl\\ *adj* **1** : capable of being reversed or of reversing ⟨a *reversible* chemical reaction⟩ **2 a** : having two finished usable sides ⟨*reversible* fabrics⟩ **b** : wearable with either side out ⟨a *reversible* coat⟩ — **re·vers·ibil·i·ty** \\-ˌvər-sə-'bil-ət-ē\\ *n* — **re·vers·ibly** \\-'vər-sə-blē\\ *adv*

²reversible *n* : a reversible cloth or garment

re·ver·sion \\ri-'vər-zhən\\ *n* **1** : a right of future possession (as of property or a title) **2 a** : an act or the process of returning (as to an earlier condition) **b** : a product of reversion **3** : an act or instance of turning the opposite way : the state of being so turned

re·vert \\ri-'vərt\\ *vb* **1** : to come or go back ⟨*reverted* to the customs of their ancestors⟩ **2** : to experience reversion

¹re·view \\ri-'vyü\\ *n* **1** : a formal inspection of troops by officers **2** : a general survey **3** : an act of looking something over especially for flaws **4 a** : a discussion by a critic of the quality of something (as a book or play) **b** : a magazine filled mostly with reviews and essays **5 a** : a look at past events **b** : a fresh study of material studied before **6** : REVUE

²review *vb* **1** : to look at a thing again **2** : to study or examine again ⟨*review* a lesson⟩ **3** : to make a formal inspection of (as troops) **4** : to discuss the quality of (as a book or play) **5** : to look back on ⟨*review* one's accomplishments⟩ — **re·view·er** *n*

re·vile \\ri-'vī(ə)l\\ *vb* **re·viled; re·vil·ing** : to speak to or about in an insulting way — **re·vile·ment** \\-mənt\\ *n* — **re·vil·er** *n*

¹re·vise \\ri-'vīz\\ *vb* **re·vised; re·vis·ing** **1** : to look over again in order to correct or improve ⟨*revise* a book report⟩ **2** : to make a new, corrected, improved, or up-to-date version or arrangement of ⟨*revise* a dictionary⟩ — **re·vis·er** *or* **re·vi·sor** \\-'vī-zər\\ *n*

²re·vise \\'rē-ˌvīz, ri-'vīz\\ *n* : an act of revising : REVISION

Revised Standard Version *n* : a revision of the American Standard Version of the Bible published in 1946 and 1952

Revised Version *n* : a British revision of the Authorized Version of the Bible published in 1881 and 1885

re·vi·sion \\ri-'vizh-ən\\ *n* **1** : an act of revising (as an essay) **2** : a revised version — **re·vi·sion·ary** \\-'vizh-ə-ˌner-ē\\ *adj*

re·vis·it \\rē-'viz-ət\\ *vb* : to visit again : return to

re·vi·tal·ize \\(')rē-'vīt-ᵊl-ˌīz\\ *vb* **-ized; -iz·ing** : to give new life or vigor to — **re·vi·tal·i·za·tion** \\(ˌ)rē-ˌvīt-ᵊl-ə-'zā-shən\\ *n*

re·viv·al \\ri-'vī-vəl\\ *n* **1** : a reviving of interest (as in art, literature, or religion) **2** : a new presentation or publication (as of a book, play, or movie) **3** : a new growth or increase ⟨a *revival* of business⟩ **4** : a meeting or series of meetings conducted by a preacher to arouse religious emotions or to make converts

re·viv·al·ism \\ri-'vī-və-ˌliz-əm\\ *n* : the spirit or methods found at religious revivals

re·viv·al·ist \\ri-'vīv-(ə-)ləst\\ *n* : one who conducts revivals

re·vive \\ri-'vīv\\ *vb* **re·vived; re·viv·ing** **1** : to make (someone or something) strong, active, or healthy again **2** : to bring back into use or popularity ⟨trying to *revive* an old custom⟩ — **re·viv·er** *n*

re·vo·ca·ble \\'rev-ə-kə-bəl\\ *adj* : capable of being revoked ⟨a *revocable* privilege⟩

re·vo·ca·tion \\ˌrev-ə-'kā-shən\\ *n* : an act or instance of revoking

re·voke \\ri-'vōk\\ *vb* **re·voked; re·vok·ing** : to put an end to (as a law, order, or privilege) by taking away or canceling [Middle English *revoken* "to take back, withdraw," from early French *revoquer* (same meaning), from Latin *revocare* "to call back," from *re-* "back, again" and *vocare* "to call" — related to ADVOCATE, PROVOKE, VOCATION] — **re·vok·er** *n*

¹re·volt \\ri-'vōlt\\ *vb* **1** : to rise up against the authority of a ruler or government **2** : to feel or cause to feel disgust or shock — **re·volt·er** *n*

²revolt *n* **1** : an act or instance of revolting **2** : an open and often violent rising up against authority

re·volt·ing *adj* : very offensive : DISGUSTING — **re·volt·ing·ly** *adv*

rev·o·lu·tion \ˌrev-ə-'lü-shən\ *n* **1 a** : the action by a heavenly body of going round in an orbit **b** : the time taken to complete one orbit **2** : completion of a course (as of years) : CYCLE **3 a** : the action or motion of revolving : a turning round a center or axis : ROTATION **b** : a single complete turn (as of a wheel or a phonograph record) **4 a** : a sudden, extreme, or complete change **b** : a basic change in government; *esp* : the overthrow of one government and the substitution of another by the governed *synonyms* see REBELLION

rev·o·lu·tion·ary \ˌrev-ə-'lü-shə-ˌner-ē\ *adj* **1 a** : of, relating to, or involving a revolution ⟨*revolutionary* war⟩ **b** : favoring revolution **c** : being or bringing about a big or important change ⟨a *revolutionary* new product⟩ **2** *cap* : of or relating to the American Revolution — **revolutionary** *n*

rev·o·lu·tion·ist \ˌrev-ə-'lü-sh(ə-)nəst\ *n* **1** : a person who takes part in a revolution **2** : a person who believes in revolution as a means of bringing about change — **revolutionist** *adj*

rev·o·lu·tion·ize \ˌrev-ə-'lü-shə-ˌnīz\ *vb* **-ized; -iz·ing** **1** : to overthrow the established government of **2** : to cause a person to become a revolutionist **3** : to change greatly or completely ⟨an invention that *revolutionized* the industry⟩ — **rev·o·lu·tion·iz·er** *n*

re·volve \ri-'välv, -'vȯlv\ *vb* **re·volved; re·volv·ing** **1** : to think over carefully **2 a** : to move in an orbit **b** : to turn on or as if on an axis : ROTATE **3** : RECUR **3** **4** : to have as a main point ⟨the argument *revolved* around wages⟩ [Middle English *revolven* "to turn over in the mind, cause to go around (on an axis)," from Latin *revolvere* "to roll back, cause to return," from *re-* "back, again" and *volvere* "to roll" — related to VOLUME; see *Word History* at VOLUME] — **re·volv·able** \-'väl-və-bəl, -'vȯl-\ *adj*

re·volv·er \ri-'väl-vər, -'vȯl-\ *n* : a handgun having a revolving cylinder holding several bullets all of which may be shot without loading again

re·volv·ing *adj* : likely to revolve or recur

re·vue \ri-'vyü\ *n* : a theatrical entertainment consisting usually of brief and often funny sketches and songs

re·vul·sion \ri-'vəl-shən\ *n* **1** : a strong pulling or drawing away : WITHDRAWAL **2 a** : a sudden or strong reaction or change **b** : a sense of complete dislike — **re·vul·sive** \-'vəl-siv\ *adj*

revved *past and past participle of* REV

revving *present participle of* REV

re·wake \(')rē-'wāk\ *vb* **-waked** *or* **-woke** \-'wōk\; **-waked** *or* **-wo·ken** \-'wō-kən\ *or* **-woke; -wak·ing** : to waken again

¹re·ward \ri-'wȯrd\ *vb* : to give a reward to or for — **re·ward·er** *n*

²reward *n* **1** : something (as money) given or offered in return for a service (as the return of something lost) **2** : a stimulus (as food) that is given to an organism after a correct or desired way of behaving and that makes the behavior more probable in the future

re·ward·ing *adj* : giving satisfaction ⟨a *rewarding* experience⟩

¹re·wind \rē-'wīnd\ *vb* **-wound** \-'wau̇nd\; **-wind·ing** : to wind again; *esp* : to reverse the winding of (as a video tape)

²re·wind \'rē-ˌwīnd\ *n* : a function of an electronic device that reverses a recording to a previous portion

re·word \(')rē-'wərd\ *vb* : to state in different words

re·work \(')rē-'wərk\ *vb* : to work again or anew: as **a** : ¹REVISE **2**, REWRITE **b** : to reprocess (as used material) for further use

¹re·write \(')rē-'rīt\ *vb* **-wrote** \-'rōt\; **-writ·ten** \-'rit-ən\; **-writ·ing** \-'rīt-ing\ : to write over again : REVISE — **re·writ·er** \-'rīt-ər\ *n*

²re·write \'rē-ˌrīt\ *n* : something rewritten

rey·nard \'rān-ərd, 'ren-\ *n, often cap* : ¹FOX **1a** [derived from *Renart, Renard,* the name of a fox who was the hero of an early French epic poem *Roman de Renart*]

re·zone \(')rē-'zōn\ *vb* : to alter the zoning of ⟨*rezoned* the neighborhood for business⟩

rhap·so·dize \'rap-sə-ˌdīz\ *vb* **-dized; -diz·ing** : to speak or write with great praise

rhap·so·dy \'rap-səd-ē\ *n, pl* **-dies** **1** : a written or spoken expression of great emotion **2** : a musical composition of irregular form — **rhap·sod·ic** \rap-'säd-ik\ *also* **rhap·sod·i·cal** \-i-kəl\ *adj* — **rhap·sod·i·cal·ly** \-i-k(ə-)lē\ *adv*

rhea \'rē-ə\ *n* : either of two large three-toed South American birds that cannot fly and resemble but are smaller than the African ostrich

rhe·ni·um \'rē-nē-əm\ *n* : a rare heavy metallic element that is obtained either as a gray powder or as a hard silver-white metal and is used especially in catalysts and alloys — see ELEMENT table

rheo·stat \'rē-ə-ˌstat\ *n* : a resistor for regulating an electric current by the use of variable resistances — **rheo·stat·ic** \ˌrē-ə-'stat-ik\ *adj*

rhe·sus monkey \ˌrē-səs-\ *n* : a pale brown Asian monkey often used in medical research

rhea

rhet·o·ric \'ret-ə-rik\ *n* **1** : the art of speaking or writing effectively **2** : the study or use of the principles and rules of composition **3 a** : skill in the effective use of speech **b** : language that is not honest, sincere, or meaningful — **rhet·o·ri·cian** \ˌret-ə-'rish-ən\ *n*

rhe·tor·i·cal \ri-'tȯr-i-kəl, -'tär-\ *adj* **1** : of, relating to, or dealing with rhetoric ⟨*rhetorical* studies⟩ **2** : used only for a colorful effect and not expected to be answered ⟨a *rhetorical* question⟩ — **rhe·tor·i·cal·ly** \-k(ə-)lē\ *adv*

rheum \'rüm\ *n* : a watery discharge from the mucous membranes especially of the eyes or nose — **rheumy** \'rü-mē\ *adj*

rheu·mat·ic \ru̇-'mat-ik\ *adj* : of, relating to, characteristic of, or suffering from rheumatism — **rheu·mat·i·cal·ly** \-'mat-i-k(ə-)lē\ *adv*

rheumatic fever *n* : a disease especially of young people that is characterized by fever, by inflammation and pain in and around the joints, and by inflammation of the membranes surrounding the heart and the heart valves

rheu·ma·tism \'rü-mə-ˌtiz-əm\ *n* : any of various conditions marked by stiffness, pain, or swelling in muscles or joints

Rh factor \är-'āch-\ *n* : a protein on the red blood cells of some people that is one of the substances used to classify human blood as to compatibility for transfusion and that when present in a fetus but not the mother causes a serious condition in which the mother produces antibodies that cross the placenta and attack the red blood cells of the fetus [from *rh*esus monkey, the animal in which the Rh factor was found]

rhine·stone \'rīn-ˌstōn\ *n* : a colorless imitation diamond of high luster made usually of glass or paste [named after the *Rhine* river in Europe, near where were found the rock crystals that were originally used as substitutes for diamonds]

\ə\ **abut**	\au̇\ **out**	\i\ **tip**	\ȯ\ **saw**	\u̇\ **foot**
\ər\ **further**	\ch\ **chin**	\ī\ **life**	\ȯi\ **coin**	\y\ **yet**
\a\ **mat**	\e\ **pet**	\j\ **job**	\th\ **thin**	\yü\ **few**
\ā\ **take**	\ē\ **easy**	\ng\ **sing**	\th\ **this**	\yu̇\ **cure**
\ä\ **cot, cart**	\g\ **go**	\ō\ **bone**	\ü\ **food**	\zh\ **vision**

rhi·no \'rī-nō\ *n, pl* rhinos *also* **rhino** : RHINOCEROS

rhi·noc·er·os \rī-'näs-(ə-)rəs\ *n, pl* -noc·er·os·es *also* -noc·er·os : any of various large plant-eating mammals of Africa and Asia that are related to the horse and have a thick skin with little hair, three toes on each foot, and one or two heavy upright horns on the snout

rhinoceros

Word History One of the largest animals found on land today is the thick-skinned rhinoceros. Another of the animal's characteristics, besides large size, is found on its snout. All rhinoceroses have at least one horn, and some have two horns. The English name for this animal with a horn or horns on its snout was borrowed from Latin *rhinoceros.* The Latin name, in turn, came from the Greek word *rhinokerōs,* which literally means "nose-horned." This word is made up of the Greek word *rhin-, rhis,* meaning "nose" and the word *keras,* meaning "horn." [Middle English *rinoceros* "rhinoceros," from Latin *rhinocerot-, rhinoceros* (same meaning), from Greek *rhinokerōt-, rhinokerōs,* literally "nose-horned," from *rhin-, rhis* "nose" and *keras* "horn"]

rhi·zoid \'rī-,zoid\ *n* : a structure (as a hypha of a fungus) that functions like a root in support or absorption

rhi·zome \'rī-,zōm\ *n* : a rootlike, often thickened, and usually horizontal underground plant stem that produces shoots above and roots below

Rh–negative \,är-,āch-\ *adj* : lacking Rh factor on the red blood cells

rho \'rō\ *n* : the 17th letter of the Greek alphabet — P or ρ

Rhode Is·land Red \rō-,dī-lən(d)-\ *n* : any of a U.S. breed of domestic chickens with rich brownish red feathers

rho·di·um \'rōd-ē-əm\ *n* : a rare silvery white hard metallic element that is resistant to attack by acids, occurs in nickel ores, and is used in platinum alloys — see ELEMENT table

rho·do·den·dron \,rōd-ə-'den-drən\ *n* : any of a genus of trees and shrubs of the heath family that often have leathery evergreen leaves and showy clusters of yellow, white, pink, red, or purple flowers [from scientific Latin *rhododendron* "rhododendron," derived from Greek *rhodon* "rose" and Greek *dendron* "tree"]

rhododendron

rhom·bic \'räm-bik\ *adj* **1** : having the form of a rhombus **2** : of, relating to, or being a form of crystal having three unequal axes at right angles to each other

rhom·boid \'räm-,bòid\ *n* : a parallelogram with no right angles and with each side differing in length from the two other sides it comes in contact with — **rhomboid** *adj* — **rhom·boi·dal** \räm-'bòid-ᵊl\ *adj*

rhom·bus \'räm-bəs\ *n, pl* **rhom·bus·es** *or* **rhom·bi** \-,bī, -,bē\ : a parallelogram with all four sides of equal length and usually with no right angles

Rh–pos·i·tive \,är-,āch-'päz-ət-iv, -'päz-tiv\ *adj* : having Rh factor on the red blood cells

rhu·barb \'rü-,bärb\ *n* **1** : a plant related to buckwheat and having large green leaves with thick juicy pink or red

stems that are used for food **2** : a heated dispute or argument

¹rhyme *also* **rime** \'rīm\ *n* **1 a** : close similarity in the final sounds of two or more words or lines of verse **b** : one of two or more words having this similarity in sound **2 a** : rhyming verse **b** : a composition in verse that rhymes

²rhyme *also* **rime** *vb* **rhymed** *also* **rimed; rhym·ing** *also* **rim·ing 1 a** : to make rhymes : put into rhyme **b** : to compose rhyming verse **2** : to end in syllables that rhyme **3** : to cause to rhyme : use as rhyme ⟨*rhymed* "moon" with "June"⟩ — **rhym·er** *n*

rhyme scheme *n* : the arrangement of rhymes in a stanza or a poem

rhy·o·lite \'rī-ə-,līt\ *n* : a very acid volcanic rock that is the lava form of granite — **rhy·o·lit·ic** \,rī-ə-'lit-ik\ *adj*

rhythm \'rith-əm\ *n* **1** : a flow of rising and falling sounds in language that is produced in verse by a regular repeating of stressed and unstressed syllables **2** : a flow of sound in music having regular accented beats **3** : a particular or typical pattern of rhythm **4** : a movement or activity in which some action repeats regularly ⟨the *rhythm* of breathing⟩

rhythm and blues *n* : popular music with elements of blues and African-American folk music

rhyth·mic \'rith-mik\ *or* **rhyth·mi·cal** \-mi-kəl\ *adj* : of, relating to, or having rhythm — **rhyth·mi·cal·ly** \-mi-k(ə-)lē\ *adv*

rhythm method *n* : a method of birth control in which a couple does not have sexual intercourse during the time when ovulation is most likely to occur

ri·a·ta \rē-'at-ə, -'ät-\ *n* : LARIAT

¹rib \'rib\ *n* **1 a** : one of the series of curved bones of the chest of most vertebrates that are joined to the spinal column in pairs and help to support the body wall and protect the organs inside **b** : a cut of meat including a rib **2** : something (as a piece of wire supporting the fabric of an umbrella) resembling a rib **3 a** : a major vein of an insect's wing or of a leaf **b** : one of the parallel ridges in a knitted or woven fabric

¹rib 1a

²rib *vb* **ribbed; rib·bing 1** : to furnish or enclose with ribs **2** : to form ribs in a fabric in knitting or weaving — **rib·ber** *n*

³rib *vb* **ribbed; rib·bing** : to make jokes about : KID — **rib·ber** *n*

rib·ald \'rib-əld\ *adj* : marked by or using coarse or indecent language or humor ⟨*ribald* jokes⟩ — **rib·ald·ry** \-əl-drē\ *n*

rib·bon \'rib-ən\ *n* **1 a** : a narrow usually closely woven strip of colorful fabric (as silk) used especially for decoration **b** : a ribbon worn as a military decoration or as a symbol of a medal **c** : a ribbon given as an award in a competition **2** : a strip of inked fabric (as in a typewriter) **3** : TATTER 1, SHRED — usually used in plural ⟨torn to *ribbons*⟩ — **rib·bon·like** \-,līk\ *adj*

rib cage *n* : the bony enclosing wall of the chest consisting chiefly of the ribs and their connecting parts

ri·bo·fla·vin \,rī-bə-'flā-vən\ *n* : a vitamin of the vitamin B complex that helps growth and is found both free (as in milk) and combined with other substances (as in liver) — called also *vitamin B₂*

ri·bo·nu·cle·ic acid \,rī-bō-n(y)ù-,klē-ik-, -,klā-\ *n* : RNA

ri·bose \'rī-,bōs\ *n* : a sugar that has five carbon atoms and five oxygen atoms in each molecule and is part of RNA — compare DEOXYRIBOSE

ri·bo·som·al RNA \,rī-bə-'sō-məl-\ *n* : an RNA that is one of the structural elements of ribosomes — called also *rRNA*

ri·bo·some \'rī-bə-ˌsōm\ *n* : one of numerous small RNA-containing particles in a cell that are sites of protein synthesis

rice \'rīs\ *n* **1** : a southeast Asian grass widely grown in warm wet areas especially for its seeds which are used for food **2** : the seeds of rice

rice paper *n* : a thin papery material made from the spongy inner part of the stem of an Asian shrub or small tree related to the ginseng

ric·er \'rī-sər\ *n* : a kitchen utensil in which soft foods (as boiled potatoes) are pressed through a strainer

rich \'rich\ *adj* **1** : having great wealth : WEALTHY **2 a** : having high value ⟨a *rich* harvest⟩ **b** : COSTLY 1, VALUABLE ⟨*rich* robes⟩ **3 a** : having a large supply of some usually desirable quality or thing ⟨a land *rich* in resources⟩ **b** : of pleasingly strong odor ⟨*rich* perfumes⟩ **c** : very productive : FRUITFUL, FERTILE ⟨a *rich* mine⟩ ⟨*rich* soils⟩ **d** : containing much seasoning, fat, or sugar ⟨*rich* food⟩ **e** : high in fuel content ⟨*rich* mixture⟩ **4 a** : vivid and deep in color ⟨*rich* red⟩ **b** : full and mellow in tone and quality ⟨*rich* voice⟩ **5** : very amusing ⟨a play with many *rich* lines⟩ — **rich·ness** *n*

Rich·ard Roe \ˌrich-ər-'drō\ *n* : a party to legal proceedings whose true name is unknown

rich·en \'rich-ən\ *vb* **rich·ened; rich·en·ing** \-(ə-)niŋ\ : to make rich or richer

rich·es \'rich-əz\ *n pl* : things that make one rich : WEALTH [Middle English *richesse*, originally not a plural but a singular noun meaning "richness"]

rich·ly \'rich-lē\ *adv* **1** : in a rich manner ⟨*richly* dressed⟩ **2** : in full measure : AMPLY ⟨*richly* deserved⟩

Rich·ter scale \'rik-tər-\ *n* : a scale for expressing the strength of an earthquake

rick \'rik\ *n* : a stack or pile (as of hay or grain) in the open air

rick·ets \'rik-əts\ *n* : a disease of young people and animals in which the bones are soft and deformed due to an inability of the body to use calcium and phosphorus because of a lack of vitamin D

rick·ett·sia \rik-'et-sē-ə\ *n, pl* **-si·as** *or* **-si·ae** \-sē-ˌē, -sē-ˌī\ : any of various bacteria including several that cause diseases (as Rocky Mountain spotted fever and typhus) in human beings — **rick·ett·si·al** \-sē-əl\ *adj*

rick·ety \'rik-ət-ē\ *adj* **1** : in weak physical condition ⟨a *rickety* old man⟩ **2** : UNSOUND 3, SHAKY ⟨a *rickety* wagon⟩

rick·ey \'rik-ē\ *n, pl* **rickeys** : a drink flavored with lime

rick·rack *or* **ric·rac** \'rik-ˌrak\ *n* : a flat braid woven to form zigzags and used especially as trimming on clothing

rick·shaw *also* **rick·sha** \'rik-ˌshȯ\ *n* : a small hooded carriage with two wheels that is pulled by one person and was used originally in Japan

rickshaw

¹ric·o·chet \'rik-ə-ˌshā, *British also* -ˌshet\ *n* **1** : a bouncing off at an angle (as of a bullet off a flat surface) **2** : an object that ricochets

²ricochet *vb* **-cheted** \-ˌshād\ *also* **-chet·ted** \-ˌshet-əd\; **-chet·ing** \-ˌshā-iŋ\ *also* **-chet·ting** \-ˌshet-iŋ\ : to bounce off at an angle

ri·cot·ta \ri-'kät-ə\ *n* : a soft, white Italian cheese

rid \'rid\ *vb* **rid** *also* **rid·ded; rid·ding** : to make free : RELIEVE ⟨*rid* yourself of worries⟩ ⟨get *rid* of that junk⟩

rid·dance \'rid-ᵊn(t)s\ *n* : the act of ridding : the state of being rid of

rid·den \'rid-ᵊn\ *adj* : extremely concerned with or burdened by ⟨guilt-*ridden*⟩ ⟨slum-*ridden*⟩

¹rid·dle \'rid-ᵊl\ *n* **1** : a baffling, misleading, or puzzling question presented as a problem to be solved or guessed : CONUNDRUM **2** : something or someone difficult to understand [Old English *rǣdelse* "opinion, riddle"]

²riddle *vb* **rid·dled; rid·dling** \'rid-liŋ, -ᵊl-iŋ\ **1** : to find the answer for a riddle or mystery **2** : to create a riddle for : MYSTIFY **3** : to speak in riddles — **rid·dler** \-lər, -ᵊl-ər\ *n*

³riddle *n* : a coarse sieve [Old English *hriddel* "a coarse sieve"]

⁴riddle *vb* **rid·dled; rid·dling** \'rid-liŋ, -ᵊl-iŋ\ **1** : to sift or separate with or as if with a riddle **2 a** : to pierce with many holes ⟨*riddled* the car with bullets⟩ **b** : to spread through ⟨a book *riddled* with mistakes⟩

¹ride \'rīd\ *vb* **rode** \'rōd\; **rid·den** \'rid-ᵊn\; **rid·ing** \'rīd-iŋ\ **1 a** : to go or be carried along on an animal's back or on or in a vehicle (as a boat, automobile, or airplane) **b** : to sit on and control so as to be carried along ⟨*ride* a bicycle⟩ **2 a** : to be supported and usually carried along by ⟨a surfboard *rides* the waves⟩ **b** : to float at anchor **c** : to remain afloat through : SURVIVE ⟨*ride* out a storm⟩ **3 a** : ¹CARRY 1 ⟨*rode* the child on my back⟩ **b** : to travel over a surface ⟨the car *rides* well⟩ **4 a** : ¹TEASE 2a **b** : OPPRESS 2 ⟨*ridden* by fears⟩ **5** : to depend on something

²ride *n* **1** : an act of riding; *esp* : a trip on horseback or by vehicle ⟨a *ride* in the country⟩ **2** : a mechanical device (as at an amusement park) for riding on **3** : a means of transportation ⟨needs a *ride* to work⟩

ride·able *also* **rid·able** \'rīd-ə-bəl\ *adj* : fit for riding on or over ⟨a *rideable* horse⟩ ⟨a *rideable* road⟩

rid·er \'rīd-ər\ *n* **1** : one that rides **2 a** : an addition to a document **b** : an additional clause to a legislative bill **3** : something that lies over or moves along on another piece ⟨the scale had *riders* to measure weight⟩ — **rid·er·less** \-ləs\ *adj*

¹ridge \'rij\ *n* : a raised or elevated part or·area: as **a** : a range of hills or mountains **b** : the line made where two sloping surfaces come together ⟨the *ridge* of a roof⟩ — **ridged** \'rijd\ *adj*

²ridge *vb* **ridged; ridg·ing** : to form into or extend in ridges

ridge·pole \'rij-ˌpōl\ *n* **1** : the highest horizontal timber in a sloping roof to which the upper ends of the rafters are fastened **2** : the horizontal pole at the top of a tent

ridgy \'rij-ē\ *adj* : having or rising in ridges

¹rid·i·cule \'rid-ə-ˌkyü(ə)l\ *n* : the act of making fun of someone or something : DERISION

²ridicule *vb* **-culed; -cul·ing** : to make fun of : DERIDE — **rid·i·cul·er** *n*

ri·dic·u·lous \rə-'dik-yə-ləs\ *adj* : causing or deserving ridicule : ABSURD, PREPOSTEROUS — **ri·dic·u·lous·ly** *adv* — **ri·dic·u·lous·ness** *n*

rid·ing \'rīd-iŋ\ *adj* **1** : used for or when riding ⟨*riding* boots⟩ **2** : operated by a rider ⟨a *riding* mower⟩

rife \'rīf\ *adj* **1** : WIDESPREAD 1, PREVALENT ⟨lands where famine is *rife*⟩ **2** : supplied in large amounts ⟨the town was *rife* with rumors⟩ — **rife·ly** *adv*

¹rif·fle \'rif-əl\ *vb* **rif·fled; rif·fling** \'rif-(ə-)liŋ\ **1** : to form, flow over, or move in riffles **2** : to ruffle slightly : RIPPLE **3 a** : to flip or leaf through in a hurry **b** : to shuffle playing cards by separating the deck into two parts and sliding the thumbs along the edges so that the cards are mixed

²riffle *n* **1 a** : a shallow extending across a stream bed and causing broken water **b** : a stretch of water flowing over a riffle **2** : a small wave or succession of small waves : RIPPLE **3** : the act or process of shuffling (as cards)

riff·raff \'rif-ˌraf\ *n* **1** : a class of people who are looked down upon : RABBLE **2** : RUBBISH — **riffraff** *adj*

¹ri·fle \'rī-fəl\ *vb* **ri·fled; ri·fling** \-f(ə-)liŋ\ **1** : to search through fast and roughly especially in order to steal ⟨*rifled* the coat pockets for loose change⟩ **2** : ¹STEAL 2a [Middle English *riflen* "to steal or carry away by force," from early French *rifler* "to scrape off, plunder"; of Germanic origin] — **ri·fler** \-f(ə-)lər\ *n*

²rifle *vb* **ri·fled; ri·fling** \-f(ə-)liŋ\ : to cut spiral grooves on the inside of a barrel of ⟨*rifled* arms⟩ [perhaps from French *rifler* "to scratch, file," from early French, "to scrape off, plunder"]

³rifle *n* **1 a** : a weapon with a long rifled barrel that is designed to be fired from the shoulder **b** : a rifled artillery piece **2** *pl* : a body of soldiers armed with rifles

⁴rifle *vb* **ri·fled; ri·fling** \-f(ə-)liŋ\ : to hit or throw a ball with great force

ri·fle·man \'rī-fəl-mən\ *n* **1** : a soldier armed with a rifle **2** : a person skilled in shooting with a rifle

ri·fle·ry \'rī-fəl-rē\ *n* : the practice of shooting at targets with a rifle

ri·fling \'rī-f(ə)liŋ\ *n* **1** : the act or process of making spiral grooves **2** : a system of spiral grooves inside the barrel of a gun causing a bullet when fired to spin about its longer axis

¹rift \'rift\ *n* **1 a** : an opening made by splitting or separation : CLEFT **b** : a normal geological fault **2** : a break in friendly relations : BREACH

²rift *vb* : ²CLEAVE, SPLIT

rift valley *n* : a long valley formed by the sinking of the earth's crust between two parallel or nearly parallel faults or groups of faults

¹rig \'rig\ *vb* **rigged; rig·ging** **1** : to fit out (as a ship) with rigging **2** : CLOTHE 1a, DRESS — usually used with *out* **3 a** : to furnish with gear : EQUIP **b** : to set up usually for temporary use : CONSTRUCT ⟨*rig* up a temporary shelter⟩ [Middle English *riggen* "to fit out a ship with rigging"] — **rig·ger** *n*

²rig *n* **1** : the shape, number, and arrangement of sails and masts of a ship that sets it apart from ships of other types ⟨the *rig* of a schooner⟩ **2** : EQUIPAGE 2 ; *esp* : a carriage with its horse : CLOTHING 1 **4** : tackle, equipment, or machinery fitted for a certain purpose ⟨an oil-drilling *rig*⟩

³rig *vb* **rigged; rig·ging** : to fix in advance so that the outcome will be known ⟨*rig* an election⟩ [from earlier *rig* (noun) "a cheating trick," of unknown origin]

Ri·gel \'rī-jəl, -gəl\ *n* : a bright star in the left foot of the Orion star group

rig·ging \'rig-iŋ, -ən\ *n* **1** : the ropes and chains used aboard a ship especially in working sail and supporting masts and spars **2** : equipment for supporting and working something (as theater scenery)

¹right \'rīt\ *adj* **1** : RIGHTEOUS 1, UPRIGHT **2** : following what is just, good, or proper ⟨*right* conduct⟩ **3** : agreeing with facts or truth : CORRECT ⟨the *right* answer⟩ **4** : ²APPROPRIATE, SUITABLE ⟨the *right* person for the job⟩ ⟨the *right* tool⟩ **5** : STRAIGHT 1 ⟨a *right* line⟩ **6** : GENUINE 1, REAL **7 a** : of, relating to, situated on, or being the side of the body which is away from the side on which the heart is mostly located ⟨the *right* leg⟩ **b** : located nearer to the right side of the body ⟨the *right* arm of the chair⟩ **8** : being shaped in such a way that a line drawn from the middle of the top to the middle of the base is perpendicular to the base ⟨a *right* cone⟩ **9** : being or meant to be the side on top, in front, or on the outside ⟨landed *right* side up⟩ ⟨*right* side out⟩ **10** : acting or judging in a way that agrees with truth or fact ⟨time proved us *right*⟩ **11** : healthy in mind or body ⟨did not feel *right*⟩ **12** : most worth having or seeking ⟨the *right* neighborhoods⟩ ⟨the *right* people⟩ — **right·ness** *n*

²right *n* **1** : the ideal of what is just and good **2** : something to which one has a just claim — often used in plural ⟨the *right* to freedom of religion⟩ ⟨the movie *rights* to a story⟩ **3** : something that one may properly claim as due ⟨knowing the truth is her *right*⟩ **4** : the cause of truth or justice ⟨fighting for *right*⟩ **5 a** : the right side or the part on the right side **b** : a turn to the right ⟨take a *right* at the stop sign⟩ **6** : the quality or state of being factually correct ⟨there's both *right* and wrong in that argument⟩ **7** *often cap* : the members of a European legislative body sitting to the right of the officer in charge and holding more conservative political views than other members **8** *often cap* : political conservatives — **by rights** : with reason or justice : PROPERLY — **to rights** : into proper order ⟨put your room *to rights*⟩

³right *adv* **1** : according to right ⟨live *right*⟩ **2** : in the exact location or position : PRECISELY ⟨*right* where you left it⟩ **3** : in a suitable, proper, or desired manner ⟨hold your pen *right*⟩ **4** : in a direct line or course ⟨go *right* home⟩ **5** : according to fact or truth : TRULY ⟨guess *right*⟩ ⟨heard *right*⟩ **6** : all the way ⟨windows *right* to the floor⟩ **7** : without delay : IMMEDIATELY ⟨*right* at 2 o'clock⟩ **8** : to a great degree : VERY ⟨a *right* pleasant day⟩

⁴right *vb* **1** : to make right (something wrong or unjust) **2 a** : to adjust or restore to the proper state or condition **b** : to bring or restore to an upright position **3** : to become upright — **right·er** *n*

right angle *n* : an angle whose measure is 90° : an angle whose sides are perpendicular to each other — **right–an·gled** \'rīt-'aŋ-gəld\ *or* **right–an·gle** \-gəl\ *adj*

right away *adv* : without delay : IMMEDIATELY

right circular cone *n* : CONE 2a

right circular cylinder *n* : a cylinder with bases that are circles and with the line joining the centers of the two bases perpendicular to both bases

right angle

righ·teous \'rī-chəs\ *adj* **1** : acting rightly : UPRIGHT **2 a** : according to what is right ⟨*righteous* actions⟩ **b** : caused by an insult to one's sense of what is right ⟨*righteous* anger⟩ — **righ·teous·ly** *adv* — **righ·teous·ness** *n*

right field *n* **1** : the part of the baseball outfield to the right looking out from the home plate **2** : the position of the player defending right field — **right fielder** *n*

right·ful \'rīt-fəl\ *adj* **1** : ¹JUST 2a **2** : having a just or legal claim : LEGITIMATE ⟨the *rightful* owner⟩ — **right·ful·ly** \-fə-lē\ *adv* — **right·ful·ness** *n*

right–hand \'rīt-ˌhand\ *adj* **1** : located on the right **2** : RIGHT-HANDED 1 **3** : relied on most of all ⟨*right-hand* man⟩

right–hand·ed \'rīt-'han-dəd\ *adj* **1** : using the right hand more easily than the left **2** : done or made with or for the right hand **3** : having or moving with a clockwise turn or twist — **right–hand·ed·ly** *or* **right–hand·ed** *adv* — **right–hand·ed·ness** *n* — **right–hand·er** \-'han-dər\ *n*

right·ist \'rīt-əst\ *n, often cap* : a person with conservative political views — **rightist** *adj, often cap*

right·ly \'rīt-lē\ *adv* **1** : in agreement with right conduct **2** : in the right or proper manner **3** : in agreement with truth or fact

right–mind·ed \'rīt-'mīn-dəd\ *adj* : likely to do what is right

right now *adv* **1** : RIGHT AWAY **2** : at the present time

right–of–way \ˌrīt-ə(v)-'wā\ *n, pl* **rights–of–way** **1** : a legal right to pass over another person's land **2** : the area over which a right-of-way exists **3** : the right of certain traffic to go ahead of other traffic **4** : PRIORITY 1 ⟨gave the bill the *right-of-way* in the Senate⟩

right on *interj* — used to show agreement or to give encouragement

right prism *n* : a prism that has exactly two bases and whose other sides are all rectangles that are perpendicular to these bases

right triangle *n* : a triangle having a right angle

right·ward \ˈrīt-wərd\ *adj or adv* : toward, at, or to the right

rig·id \ˈrij-əd\ *adj* **1** : not flexible : STIFF, HARD **2 a** : very fixed in one's opinion or habits : UNYIELDING **b** : carefully observed : SCRUPULOUS ⟨follows a *rigid* exercise program⟩ **3** : exact and accurate in procedure [from Latin *rigidus*, "rigid," from *rigēre* "to be stiff" — related to RIGOR MORTIS] — **ri·gid·i·ty** \rə-ˈjid-ət-ē\ *n* — **rig·id·ly** \ˈrij-əd-lē\ *adv* — **rig·id·ness** *n*

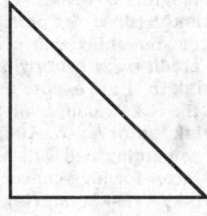

right triangle

rig·ma·role *also* **rig·a·ma·role** \ˈrig-(ə-)mə-ˌrōl\ *n* **1** : confused or meaningless talk : NONSENSE **2** : a complicated and often unnecessary procedure

rig·or \ˈrig-ər\ *n* **1 a** : the quality of not being flexible or yielding **b** : an act or instance of being strict or harsh **2** : a shuddering caused by a chill **3** : a condition that makes life difficult or uncomfortable; *esp* : extreme cold **4** : strict precision : EXACTNESS ⟨logical *rigor*⟩

rig·or mor·tis \ˌrig-ər-ˈmȯrt-əs\ *n* : temporary stiffness of muscles occurring after death [from scientific Latin, literally "stiffness of death," from Latin *rigēre* "to be stiff" — related to RIGID]

rig·or·ous \ˈrig-(ə-)rəs\ *adj* **1** : very strict **2** : marked by great differences of temperature or climate **3** : very accurate — **rig·or·ous·ly** *adv* — **rig·or·ous·ness** *n*

rile \ˈrī(ə)l\ *vb* **riled**; **ril·ing** **1** : to make angry **2** : ROIL 1

rill \ˈril\ *n* : a very small brook

¹rim \ˈrim\ *n* **1 a** : an outer edge especially of something curved **b** : BRINK 1 **2** : the outer part of a wheel joined to the hub usually by spokes — **rim·less** \-ləs\ *adj*

²rim *vb* **rimmed**; **rim·ming** **1** : to provide with a rim : serve as a rim for : BORDER **2** : to run around the rim of ⟨the putt *rimmed* the cup⟩

¹rime \ˈrīm\ *n* **1** : ¹FROST 2 **2** : CRUST 3a, INCRUSTATION

²rime *vb* **rimed**; **rim·ing** : to cover with or as if with rime

³rime *variant of* RHYME

rim·rock \ˈrim-ˌräk\ *n* **1** : the top layer or layers of rock on a plateau that remains as a vertical surface after the land near it is worn away **2** : the edge or surface of a layer of rimrock

rimy \ˈrī-mē\ *adj* **rim·i·er**; **-est** : covered with rime : FROSTY

rind \ˈrīnd\ *n* : the bark of a tree; *also* : a usually hard or tough outer layer (as the skin of a fruit)

¹ring \ˈriŋ\ *n* **1** : a circular band for holding, connecting, hanging, or pulling or for packing or sealing ⟨a key *ring*⟩ ⟨a towel *ring*⟩ **2** : a circular band usually of precious metal worn on the finger **3** : something circular in shape ⟨smoke *rings*⟩ **4** : an often circular space for shows and contests ⟨a circus *ring*⟩ ⟨a boxing *ring*⟩ **5** : ANNUAL RING **6** : a group of persons involved in selfish or dishonest activities ⟨a *ring* of thieves⟩ **7** *pl* : a pair of rings suspended from above and used for hanging, swinging, and balancing tricks in gymnastics [Old English *hring* "a circular band"] — **ringed** \ˈriŋd\ *adj* — **ring·like** \ˈriŋ-ˌlīk\ *adj*

²ring *vb* **ringed**; **ring·ing** \ˈriŋ-iŋ\ **1** : to place or form a ring around : ENCIRCLE **2** : to provide with a ring **3** : to throw a ring over (the mark) in a game where curved objects (as horseshoes) are tossed at a mark **4** : to form or take the shape of a ring

³ring *vb* **rang** \ˈraŋ\; **rung** \ˈrəŋ\; **ring·ing** \ˈriŋ-iŋ\ **1** : to make a clear and vibrating sound when struck ⟨church bells *ringing*⟩ **2** : to cause to sound especially by striking ⟨*rang* the bell⟩ **3** : to announce by or as if by ringing

⟨*ring* an alarm⟩ ⟨*ring* in the new year⟩ **4** : to sound loudly ⟨cheers *rang* out⟩ **5 a** : to be filled with echoing sound : RESOUND ⟨the whole hall *rang* with their cheers⟩ **b** : to have the feeling of being filled with a humming sound ⟨his ears were *ringing*⟩ **6** : to be filled with talk or news ⟨the whole town *rang* with news of the victory⟩ **7** : to seem to have some particular quality ⟨her story *rings* true⟩ **8 a** : to call for especially by bell ⟨*ring* for the servants⟩ **b** *chiefly British* : to call on the telephone ⟨will *ring* you up tomorrow⟩ [Old English *hringan* "to ring"] — **ring a bell** : to sound familiar ⟨yes, that name *rings a bell*⟩

⁴ring *n* **1** : a set of bells **2** : a clear sound made by or as if by vibrating metal **3** : a tone like that of a bell **4** : a continuous or repeating loud noise **5** : something that suggests a certain quality ⟨a story with the *ring* of truth⟩ **6 a** : the act or an instance of ringing **b** : a telephone call

ring·bolt \ˈriŋ-ˌbōlt\ *n* : a bolt with a ring through a loop at one end

¹ring·er \ˈriŋ-ər\ *n* **1** : one that sounds especially by ringing **2 a** : one that enters a competition with a false identity **b** : one that strongly resembles another — often used with *dead* ⟨a dead *ringer* for the senator⟩

²ringer *n* : a quoit or horseshoe that falls right over a peg

ring finger *n* : the third finger of the left hand counting the index finger as the first

ring·git \ˈriŋ-git\ *n, pl* **ringgit** *or* **ringgits** **1** : the basic unit of money of Malaysia **2** : a coin or bill representing one ringgit

ring·lead·er \ˈriŋ-ˌlēd-ər\ *n* : a leader especially of a group of persons who cause trouble

ring·let \ˈriŋ-lət\ *n* **1** : a small ring or circle **2** : a long curl (as of hair)

ring·mas·ter \ˈriŋ-ˌmas-tər\ *n* : one in charge of performances in a ring (as of a circus)

ring–necked \ˈriŋ-ˈnekt\ *or* **ring–neck** \-ˈnek\ *adj* : having a ring of color around the neck

ring–necked pheasant *n* : a Eurasian pheasant that has a white neck ring in the male and that has been widely introduced in North America as a game bird

ring·side \ˈriŋ-ˌsīd\ *n* : the area just outside a ring (as at a prizefight) — **ringside** *adj*

ring-necked pheasant

ring stand *n* : a metal stand consisting of a long upright rod attached to a heavy rectangular base used with rings and clamps for supporting laboratory equipment

ring–tailed \ˈriŋ-ˈtā(ə)ld\ *adj* : having a tail marked with rings of different colors

ring·tone \ˈriŋ-ˌtōn\ *n* : the sound made by a cell phone to signal an incoming call

ring up *vb* : to add up and record on a cash register

ring·worm \ˈriŋ-ˌwərm\ *n* : a contagious skin disease caused by fungi and marked by ring-shaped discolored patches

rink \ˈriŋk\ *n* **1** : a sheet of ice laid out for curling, ice hockey, or ice-skating **2** : an enclosed place for rollerskating

¹rinse \ˈrin(t)s\ *vb* **rinsed**; **rins·ing** **1 a** : to wash lightly with water ⟨*rinse* out your mouth⟩ ⟨*rinse* the apple before

\ə\ **abut**	\au̇\ **out**	\i\ **tip**	\ȯ\ **saw**	\u̇\ **foot**
\ər\ **further**	\ch\ **chin**	\ī\ **life**	\ȯi\ **coin**	\y\ **yet**
\a\ **mat**	\e\ **pet**	\j\ **job**	\th\ **thin**	\yü\ **few**
\ā\ **take**	\ē\ **easy**	\ŋ\ **sing**	\th\ **this**	\yu̇\ **cure**
\ä\ **cot, cart**	\g\ **go**	\ō\ **bone**	\ü\ **food**	\zh\ **vision**

you eat it⟩ **b** : to clean off with clear water the soap left over from washing ⟨*rinse* the dishes⟩ **2** : to treat (hair) with a rinse — **rins·er** *n*

²rinse *n* **1** : an act of rinsing **2 a** : liquid used for rinsing **b** : a solution that temporarily tints hair

¹ri·ot \ˈrī-ət\ *n* **1** : public violence, disturbance, or disorder **2** : a varied display of color **3** : something or someone very funny

²riot *vb* : to create or take part in a riot — **ri·ot·er** *n*

riot act *n* : a strong scolding or warning — used in the phrase *read the riot act*

ri·ot·ous \ˈrī-ət-əs\ *adj* **1 a** : of the nature of a riot **b** : taking part in rioting **2** : ABUNDANT ⟨a garden *riotous* with flowers⟩ — **ri·ot·ous·ly** *adv*

¹rip \ˈrip\ *vb* **ripped; rip·ping 1** : to tear, cut apart, or open **2** : to slash or slit with or as if with a sharp blade **3** : to go with a rush — **rip·per** *n*

²rip *n* : a torn place : TEAR

³rip *n* : a body of water made rough by the meeting of opposing currents or by passing over a rough bottom

⁴rip *n* : a person who acts wild or gets into trouble [probably a shortened and altered form of *reprobate* (noun)]

rip cord *n* : a cord or wire pulled by a parachute jumper to release a parachute out of its container

ripe \ˈrīp\ *adj* **rip·er; rip·est 1** : fully grown and developed ⟨a *ripe* tomato⟩ **2** : having mature knowledge, understanding, or judgment **3** : ¹READY 1 ⟨*ripe* for action⟩ **4** : brought to just the right state — **ripe·ly** *adv* — **ripe·ness** *n*

rip·en \ˈrī-pən\ *vb* **rip·ened; rip·en·ing** \ˈrīp-(ə-)niŋ\ : to make or become ripe

rip—off \ˈrip-ˌȯf\ *n* : an act or an instance of ripping off

rip off \ˈrip-ˈȯf\ *vb* **1** : ROB 1a; *also* : to cheat someone : DEFRAUD **2** : ¹STEAL 2a

ri·poste \ri-ˈpōst\ *n* **1** : a fencer's quick return thrust **2** : a quick reply or action in return

rip·ping \ˈrip-iŋ\ *adj, chiefly British* : very good ⟨had a *ripping* time⟩

¹rip·ple \ˈrip-əl\ *vb* **rip·pled; rip·pling** \-(ə-)liŋ\ **1 a** : to become or cause to become covered with small waves **b** : to flow in small waves **2** : to make a sound like that of water flowing in small waves ⟨laughter *rippled* through the crowd⟩ **3** : to move with a wavy motion

²ripple *n* **1 a** : the disturbing of the surface of water **b** : a small wave or a mark like a small wave **2** : a sound like that of rippling water

rip·ply \ˈrip-lē\ *adj* : having ripples

rip—roar·ing \ˈrip-ˈrōr-iŋ, -ˈrȯr-\ *adj* : noisily excited or exciting

rip·saw \ˈrip-ˌsȯ\ *n* : a saw for cutting wood in the direction of the grain

¹rise \ˈrīz\ *vb* **rose** \ˈrōz\; **ris·en** \ˈriz-ᵊn\; **ris·ing** \ˈrī-ziŋ\ **1 a** : to get up from lying, kneeling, or sitting **b** : to get up from sleep or from one's bed **2** : to return from death **3** : to take up arms ⟨the people *rose* in rebellion⟩ **4** : to appear above the horizon ⟨sun *rises* at six⟩ **5 a** : to move upward : ASCEND ⟨smoke *rises*⟩ **b** : to extend upward ⟨hill *rises* to a great height⟩ **6** : to swell in size or volume ⟨the river was *rising*⟩ ⟨bread dough *rises*⟩ **7 a** : to become encouraged ⟨their spirits *rose*⟩ **b** : to grow stronger ⟨felt her anger *rising*⟩ **8 a** : to gain a higher rank or position ⟨*rose* to colonel⟩ **b** : to increase in quantity or number ⟨prices were *rising*⟩ **9 a** : ARISE 2b ⟨an ugly rumor had *risen*⟩ **b** : to come into being : ORIGINATE ⟨river *rises* in the hills⟩ **10** : to show oneself equal to a demand or test ⟨*rise* to the occasion⟩

²rise \ˈrīz\ *n* **1** : an act of rising : a state of being risen **2** : BEGINNING 1, ORIGIN **3** : the distance of one point above another **4** : an increase in amount, number, or volume **5 a** : an upward slope **b** : a spot higher than surrounding ground **6** : an angry reaction

ris·er \ˈrī-zər\ *n* **1** : one that rises (as from sleep) ⟨an early *riser*⟩ **2** : the upright board between two stair treads

ris·i·ble \ˈriz-ə-bəl\ *adj* **1** : able to laugh **2** : arousing laughter : FUNNY

¹risk \ˈrisk\ *n* **1** : possibility of loss or injury **2** : someone or something that presents a risk ⟨a bad *risk*⟩ ⟨a good credit *risk*⟩ **synonyms** see DANGER

²risk *vb* **1** : to expose to danger ⟨*risked* her life⟩ **2** : to take the risk or danger of ⟨*risked* breaking his neck⟩

risk factor *n* : something that increases the possibility that something bad will happen ⟨cigarette smoking is a *risk factor* for lung cancer⟩

risky \ˈris-kē\ *adj* **risk·i·er; -est** : having or bringing risk : DANGEROUS

ri·tar·dan·do \ri-ˌtär-ˈdän-dō, ˌrē-\ *adv or adj* : with a gradual slowing of tempo — used as a direction in music — **ritardando** *n*

rite \ˈrīt\ *n* **1 a** : a fixed form for a ceremony **b** : the ceremonial practices of a church or group of churches **2** : a ceremonial act or action

¹rit·u·al \ˈrich-(ə-)wəl, ˈrich-əl\ *adj* **1** : of or relating to rites or a ritual ⟨a *ritual* dance⟩ **2** : according to religious law or social custom — **rit·u·al·ly** \-ē\ *adv*

²ritual *n* **1** : an established form for a ceremony **2 a** : a system of rites **b** : a ceremonial act or action **c** : a formal and customarily repeated act or series of acts

rit·u·al·ism \ˈrich-(ə-)wəl-ˌiz-əm, ˈrich-əl-\ *n* : the use of ritual — **rit·u·al·is·tic** \ˌrich-(ə-)wəl-ˈis-tik, ˌrich-əl-\ *adj*

ritzy \ˈrit-sē\ *adj* **ritz·i·er; -est 1** : very fashionable **2** : STUCK-UP, SNOBBISH [from *Ritz*, name of a group of elegant hotels]

¹ri·val \ˈrī-vəl\ *n* **1 a** : one of two or more trying to get what only one can have **b** : COMPETITOR **2** : one that equals another : PEER

Word History The English word *rival* can be traced to the Latin word *rivus*, meaning "a stream." From *rivus* came the Latin *rivalis*, which meant "one who uses the same stream as another." Those who must share a stream may argue about who has the right to use the water. Such disputes are common when two people want the same thing. The Latin word *rivalis* in time came to be used for other people who are also likely to fight with each other. It meant "a man in love with the same woman as another man." This sense of *rivalis* came into English as *rival*. [from early French *rival* "rival," from Latin *rivalis* "one using the same stream as another, a rival in love," from *rivalis* (adjective) "of a stream," from *rivus* "stream"]

²rival *adj* : of, relating to, or being a rival

³rival *vb* **ri·valed** *or* **ri·valled; ri·val·ing** *or* **ri·val·ling** \ˈrīv-(ə-)liŋ\ **1** : to be in competition with **2** : to be as good as or almost as good as ⟨manufacture linens that *rival* the world's best⟩

ri·val·ry \ˈrī-vəl-rē\ *n, pl* **-ries** : the act of rivaling : the state of being a rival : COMPETITION

rive \ˈrīv\ *vb* **rived** \ˈrīvd\; **riv·en** \ˈriv-ən\ *also* **rived; riv·ing** \ˈrī-viŋ\ **1** : to tear apart **2** : to become split or cause to split

riv·er \ˈriv-ər\ *n* **1** : a natural stream of water larger than a brook or creek **2** : a large stream or flow ⟨the jet stream is a *river* of air⟩ [Middle English *rivere* "river," from early French *rivere* (same meaning), derived from Latin *riparius* "related to or located on the bank of a river," from *ripa* "shore"]

riv·er·bank \ˈriv-ər-ˌbaŋk\ *n* : the bank of a river

riv·er·bed \-ˌbed\ *n* : the channel occupied or once occupied by a river

river blindness *n* : a human disease of Africa and tropical America that is caused by a parasitic nematode worm passed on by the bite of a blackfly and that usually results in blindness if untreated — called also *onchocerciasis*

riv·er·boat \-ˌbōt\ *n* : a boat used (as for carrying passengers or freight) on a river

riv·er·side \-ˌsīd\ *n* : the side or bank of a river

¹riv·et \'riv-ət\ *n* : a metal bolt with a head at one end used for uniting two or more pieces by passing the shank through a hole in each piece and then beating or pressing down the plain end so as to make a second head

²rivet *vb* **1** : to fasten with or as if with rivets **2** : to attract and hold (as one's eyes or attention) completely — **riv·et·er** *n*

riv·u·let \'riv-(y)ə-lət\ *n* : a small stream

ri·yal \rē-'yäl\ *n* **1** : the basic unit of money of Qatar and Saudi Arabia **2** : a bill representing one riyal

RN \ˌär-'en\ *n* : REGISTERED NURSE

RNA \ˌär-en-'ā\ *n* : any of various nucleic acids that are typically found in the cytoplasm of cells, are usually composed of a single chain of nucleotides, differ from DNA in containing ribose as the five-carbon sugar instead of deoxyribose, and that function mostly in protein synthesis — called also *ribonucleic acid;* compare MESSENGER RNA, RIBOSOMAL RNA, TRANSFER RNA

¹roach \'rōch\ *n, pl* **roach** *also* **roach·es** : any of various fishes including some sunfishes and shiners

²roach *n* : COCKROACH

road \'rōd\ *n* **1** : ROADSTEAD — often used in plural **2 a** : an open way for vehicles, persons, and animals **b**

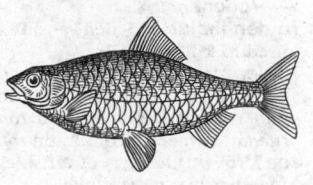

¹roach

: ROADBED **2 3** : PATH 2b ⟨the *road* to success⟩ **4** : ¹RAILROAD **5** : a series of visits to several places or the travel necessary to get there ⟨the team plays five games on the *road*⟩ ⟨traveled with the *road* company of the play⟩

road·bed \-ˌbed\ *n* **1** : the foundation of a road or railroad **2** : the part of the surface of a road that vehicles travel on

road·block \-ˌbläk\ *n* : a blocking of a road (as by police officers)

road·house \-ˌhaus\ *n* : a bar or inn usually outside city limits

road·run·ner \'rō-ˌdrən-ər\ *n* : a long-tailed ground-dwelling bird of the southwestern U.S. that usually travels by running — called also *chaparral bird, chaparral cock*

¹road·side \'rōd-ˌsīd\ *n* : the strip of land along a road : the side of a road

roadrunner

²roadside *adj* : located by the side of a road ⟨*roadside* hamburger stand⟩

road·stead \'rōd-ˌsted\ *n* : a place less enclosed than a harbor where ships may ride at anchor

road·ster \'rōd-stər\ *n* : an automobile with an open body and a folding fabric top that seats two

road test *n* : a test (as of a vehicle or of a person's ability to drive) made on the road

road·way \'rōd-ˌwā\ *n* **1 a** : the strip of land over which a road passes **b** : ROAD 2a **2** : the part of a bridge used by vehicles

roam \'rōm\ *vb* : to go or go over from place to place without a plan ⟨*roam* the hills⟩ ⟨cattle *roaming* in search of water⟩ **synonyms** see WANDER — **roam·er** *n*

¹roan \'rōn\ *adj* : of a dark color (as black, red, or brown) sprinkled with white ⟨a *roan* horse⟩

²roan *n* : an animal (as a horse) with a roan coat

¹roar \'rō(ə)r, 'ro(ə)r\ *vb* **1** : to utter a long full loud sound ⟨the lion *roared*⟩ **2** : to laugh loudly **3** : to say with a roar — **roar·er** \'rōr-ər, 'ror-\ *n*

²roar *n* **1 a** : the deep loud cry of a wild animal (as a lion) **b** : a loud deep cry or shout **2** : a loud confused sound ⟨the *roar* of the crowd⟩

roar·ing \'rōr-iŋ, 'ror-\ *adj* : very active or strong ⟨a *roaring* fire⟩ ⟨does a *roaring* business⟩ ⟨a *roaring* headache⟩

¹roast \'rōst\ *vb* **1** : to cook with dry heat (as in an oven) **2** : to be or make very hot **3** : to criticize severely in either a serious or joking way

²roast *n* **1** : a piece of meat roasted or suitable for roasting **2** : an outing at which food is roasted **3** : severe criticism or kidding

³roast *adj* : cooked by roasting ⟨*roast* beef⟩ ⟨*roast* pork⟩

roast·er \'rō-stər\ *n* **1** : a device for roasting meat **2** : something (as a young chicken) suitable for roasting

rob \'räb\ *vb* **robbed; rob·bing 1 a** : to take something away from a person or place in secrecy or by force, threat, or trickery **b** : to take away as loot : STEAL **2** : to keep from getting something due, expected, or desired — **rob·ber** *n*

robber fly *n* : any of various two-winged flies that eat insects and are covered with coarse bristly hairs

rob·bery \'räb-(ə-)rē\ *n, pl* **-ber·ies** : the act, practice, or an instance of robbing

¹robe \'rōb\ *n* **1** : a long loose or flowing garment **2** : a covering or wrap for the lower body

²robe *vb* **robed; rob·ing 1** : to clothe or cover with or as if with a robe **2** : ¹DRESS 2a

rob·in \'räb-ən\ *n* **1** : a small European thrush with an orange red face, throat, and breast **2** : a large North American thrush with a grayish back and head and a brick red breast

ro·bot \'rō-ˌbät\ *n* **1 a** : a machine that looks and acts like a human being **b** : a capable but unfeeling person **2** : a device that automatically performs tasks that are complicated and often continuously repeated — **ro·bot·ic** \rō-'bät-ik\ *adj* — **ro·bot·i·cal·ly** \-i-k(ə-)lē\ *adv*

Word History In 1923 a play by the Czech author Karel Čapek introduced the word *robot* to English. The title of the play, *R.U.R.,* stood for "Rossum's Universal Robots," a fictional company that manufactured robots. These humanlike machines were supposed to perform all the hard, dull, and dangerous work for people, but they finally became resentful and rebelled, killing all humans. Čapek formed the word *robot* for his machines from the Czech *robota,* meaning "forced labor." The play was very popular and its ideas made a strong impression. As a result, the word *robot* came to have several meanings, including "a human being who has become brutal and insensitive or machinelike because of overwork and mistreatment." It is used today for machines that may not look human but do perform the kind of dangerous or dull work that Rossum's Universal Robots were supposed to have done. [from Czech *robot* "a machine that looks like a human being and performs dull or dangerous work," from *robota* "forced labor, work"]

ro·bust \rō-'bəst, 'rō-(ˌ)bəst\ *adj* : being strong and vigorously healthy — **ro·bust·ly** *adv* — **ro·bust·ness** \-'bəs(t)-nəs, -(ˌ)bəs(t)-\ *n*

roc \'räk\ *n* : a bird of fable so big it was supposed to be able to carry off an elephant

Ro·chelle salt \rō-ˌshel-\ *n* : a salt of potassium and sodium that is used as a laxative

¹rock \ˈräk\ *vb* **1** : to move back and forth in or as if in a cradle **2 a** : to sway or cause to sway back and forth **b** : to cause to be upset ⟨*rocked* by the news⟩ [Old English *roccian* "to move back and forth as in a cradle"]

²rock *n* **1** : a rocking movement **2** : popular music usually having a fast tempo, strong beat, and much repetition

³rock *n* **1** : a large mass of stone **2 a** : solid mineral deposits **b** : a lump or piece of rock **3** : something like a rock in firmness : SUPPORT [Middle English *rokke* "stone, rock," from an early French dialect word *roke* (same meaning)] — **rock·like** *adj*

rock–and–roll *n* : ²ROCK 2

rock bass *n* : a sunfish spotted with brown that is found especially in the upper Mississippi valley and Great Lakes region

rock bottom *n* : the lowest point or level

rock·bound \ˈräk-ˌbau̇nd\ *adj* : surrounded or covered with rocks

rock candy *n* : boiled sugar crystallized on a string

rock crystal *n* : transparent quartz

rock dove *n* : a bluish gray dove of Europe and Asia that is found throughout most of North America — compare PIGEON

rock·er \ˈräk-ər\ *n* **1 a** : a curving piece of wood or metal on which an object (as a cradle) rocks **b** : a structure or device (as a chair) that rocks on rockers **2** : a device that works with a rocking motion **3** : a rock singer, musician, fan, or song — **off one's rocker** CRAZY 1

¹rock·et \ˈräk-ət\ *n* **1** : a firework that is driven through the air by the gases produced by a burning substance **2** : a jet engine that operates like a firework rocket but carries its own oxygen for burning the fuel and is therefore able to run without the oxygen of the air **3** : an object (as a missile) that is driven by a rocket [from Italian *rocchetta*, literally "a small stick or rod on which wool is held for spinning," from *rocca* "distaff"; probably so called because of its shape]

²rocket *vb* **1** : to transport by a rocket ⟨*rocket* a satellite into orbit⟩ **2** : to rise swiftly ⟨a singer who *rocketed* to stardom⟩ **3** : to travel rapidly in or as if in a rocket

rock·et·ry \ˈräk-ə-trē\ *n* : the study of, experimenting with, or use of rockets

rocket ship *n* : a spaceship driven by rockets

rocket sled *n* : a rocket-propelled vehicle that runs usually on a single rail and is used mainly in aviation research

rock garden *n* : a garden laid out among rocks or decorated with rocks

rock hound *n* : a person who collects rocks and minerals as a hobby

rocking chair *n* : a chair mounted on rockers

rocking horse *n* : a toy horse mounted on rockers

rock lobster *n* : SPINY LOBSTER

rock 'n' roll \ˌräk-ən-ˈrōl\ *n* : ²ROCK 2

rock salt *n* : common salt in large crystals or masses

rock·weed \ˈräk-ˌwēd\ *n* : any of various brown algae commonly growing attached to rocks along shores

rocking horse

rock wool *n* : a material resembling wool made by blowing a jet of steam through melted rock and used chiefly for heat and sound insulation

¹rocky \ˈräk-ē\ *adj* **rock·i·er; -est** : full of or consisting of rocks — **rock·i·ness** *n*

²rocky *adj* **rock·i·er; -est** **1** : weak and confused and unsteady on one's feet **2** : marked by obstacles or problems : DIFFICULT ⟨a *rocky* start⟩ — **rock·i·ness** \-ē-nəs\ *n*

Rocky Mountain sheep *n* : BIGHORN SHEEP

Rocky Mountain spotted fever *n* : a disease that is caused by a bacterium passed on by the bite of a tick and that is characterized by chills, fever, headache, pains in the muscles and joints, and a red to purple rash

ro·co·co \rə-ˈkō-kō, rō-kə-ˈkō\ *adj* : of or relating to a style of artistic expression common in the 18th century marked by fancy curved forms and much ornament — **rococo** *n*

rod \ˈräd\ *n* **1 a** : a straight slender stick or bar **b** : a stick or bundle of twigs used in whipping a person **c** : a pole with a line and usually a reel attached for fishing **2 a** : a unit of length — see MEASURE table **b** : a square rod **3** : any of the cells in the retina that are shaped like rods and respond to dim light **4** *slang* : HANDGUN — **rod·less** \-ləs\ *adj* — **rod·like** \-ˌlīk\ *adj*

rode *past of* RIDE

ro·dent \ˈrōd-³nt\ *n* : any of an order of fairly small mammals (as mice, squirrels, or beavers) that have sharp front teeth used for gnawing [derived from Latin *rodent-, rodens*, a form of *rodere* "to gnaw" — related to ERODE] — **rodent** *adj*

ro·den·ti·cide \rō-ˈdent-ə-ˌsīd\ *n* : a chemical substance used to kill rodents

ro·deo \ˈrōd-ē-ˌō, rə-ˈdā-ō\ *n, pl* **-de·os** **1** : a roundup of cattle **2** : an exhibition featuring cowboy skills (as riding and roping) [from Spanish *rodear* "to surround," from *rueda* "a wheel," from Latin *rota* (same meaning)]

roe \ˈrō\ *n* : the eggs of a fish especially while still bound together in a membrane

roent·gen \ˈrent-gən, ˈrənt-, -jən\ *n* : the international unit of measurement for X-rays and gamma rays that is based on their ability to produce charged particles in the air

roent·gen·i·um \rent-ˈgən-ē-əm, rənt-, -ˈjen-\ *n* : a short-lived radioactive element produced artificially — see ELEMENT table

roentgen ray *n, often cap 1st R* : X-RAY

Ro·ga·tion Day \rō-ˈgā-shən-\ *n* : one of the Christian days of prayer especially for the harvest observed on the three days before Ascension Day and by Roman Catholics also on April 25

rog·er \ˈräj-ər\ *interj* — used especially in radio and signaling to say that a message has been received and understood

rogue \ˈrōg\ *n* **1** : a dishonest or wicked person **2** : a mischievous individual

rogue elephant *n* : a vicious elephant that separates from the herd and roams alone

rogues' gallery *n* : a collection of pictures of persons arrested as criminals

rogu·ish \ˈrō-gish\ *adj* **1** : of, relating to, or being a rogue **2** : playfully mischievous — **rogu·ish·ly** *adv* — **rogu·ish·ness** *n*

roil \ˈrȯi(ə)l, *sense 2 is also* ˈrī(ə)l\ *vb* **1** : to make cloudy or muddy by stirring up ⟨*roil* the water of a brook⟩ **2** : to rouse the anger of

rois·ter \ˈrȯi-stər\ *vb* **rois·tered; rois·ter·ing** \-st(ə-)riŋ\ : to have a noisy good time — **rois·ter·er** \-stər-ər\ *n*

role *also* **rôle** \ˈrōl\ *n* **1 a** : a character assigned or taken on **b** : a socially expected behavior pattern usually determined by an individual's status in a particular society **c** : a part played by an actor or singer ⟨a starring *role*⟩ **2** : ¹FUNCTION 2a ⟨the *role* of enzymes in digestion⟩ [from French *rôle* "part played by an actor," literally "scroll"; so called because before the use of books, the actor's parts were written on scrolls]

role model *n* : a person whose behavior in a certain role is imitated by others

role–play \ˈrōl-ˌplā, -ˈplā\ *vb* : to act out the role of ⟨*role-play* an interviewer⟩

¹roll \ˈrōl\ *n* **1 a** : a written document that may be rolled up : SCROLL **b** : an official list of names ⟨the voter *rolls*⟩ **2**

a : something or a quantity of something that is rolled up or rounded as if rolled ⟨*rolls* of fat⟩ **b** : a small piece of baked bread dough **c** : paper money folded or rolled

²**roll** *vb* **1** : to move or cause to move by turning over and over on a surface without sliding **2 a** : to put a wrapping around **b** : to form into a ball or roll **3** : to make smooth, even, or firm with or as if with a roller **4 a** : to move on rollers or wheels **b** : to begin or cause to begin operating or moving ⟨*roll* the cameras⟩ ⟨let's get *rolling*⟩ **5** : to sound with a full echoing tone or with a continuous beating sound ⟨*roll* a drum⟩ ⟨thunder *rolled*⟩ **6** : to have an abundant supply ⟨*rolling* in money⟩ **7 a** : to move onward or around as if on a wheel or scroll ⟨the days *roll* by⟩ ⟨lines *rolling* off the screen of a computer⟩ **b** : to rotate on an axis **8** : to flow in a continuous stream ⟨money was *rolling* in⟩ **9** : to move with a side-to-side sway : ROCK

³**roll** *n* **1 a** : a sound produced by rapid strokes on a drum **b** : a heavy echoing sound ⟨the *roll* of thunder⟩ **2** : a rolling movement or an action involving such movement

roll bar *n* : an overhead metal bar in an automobile that is designed to protect riders in case the automobile overturns

roll call *n* : the action of calling off a list of names (as for checking attendance); *also* : a time for a roll call

roll·er \ˈrō-lər\ *n* **1 a** : a turning cylinder over or on which something is moved or which is used to press, shape, spread, or smooth something **b** : a rod on which something (as a map or a shade) is rolled up **c** : a small wheel (as of a roller skate) **2** : a long heavy wave on the sea **3** : one that rolls or rolls over

roller bearing *n* : a bearing in which a rotating part turns on rollers held in a circular frame or cage

roll·er coast·er \ˈrō-lər-ˌkō-stər, ˈrō-lē-ˌkō-\ *n* : an elevated railway (as in an amusement park) with sharp curves and steep slopes on which cars roll

roller rink *n* : RINK 2

roller skate *n* : a skate that goes on wheels instead of a runner — **roller-skate** *vb*

rol·lick \ˈräl-ik\ *vb* : ¹FROLIC — **rollick** *n*

rol·lick·ing \ˈräl-ik-iŋ\ *adj* : full of fun and good spirits

rolling pin *n* : a cylinder (as of wood) used to roll out dough

rolling stock *n* : wheeled vehicles owned or used by a railroad or trucking company

rolling pin

roll·top desk \ˌrōl-ˌtäp-\ *n* : a desk with a cover that can be slid up or down

roll up *vb* : to build up by many additions one after the other ⟨the winning candidate *rolled up* a large majority⟩

¹**ro·ly-po·ly** \ˌrō-lē-ˈpō-lē\ *adj* : being short and fat

²**roly-poly** *n, pl* **-lies** : a roly-poly person or thing

ROM \ˈräm\ *n* : a usually small computer memory that contains special-purpose information (as a program) which cannot be altered — compare RAM

ro·maine \rō-ˈmān\ *n* : a lettuce with a tall loose head of long crisp leaves — called also *romaine lettuce*

¹**Ro·man** \ˈrō-mən\ *n* **1 a** : a person born or living in Rome **b** : a citizen of the Roman Empire **2** *not cap* : roman letters or type

²**Roman** *adj* **1** : of or relating to Rome or the Romans or the empire of which Rome was the original capital **2 a** : ¹LATIN 2 **b** : of or relating to the Latin language **3** *not cap* : of or relating to a type style with upright characters (as in "these definitions") **4** : of or relating to the Roman Catholic Church

Roman candle *n* : a firework that is a long tube that shoots out balls or stars of fire one at a time

Roman Catholic *adj* : of or relating to the body of Christians having levels of authority under the pope, a liturgy centered in the Mass, and a body of beliefs laid down by the church as the only interpreter of revealed truth — **Roman Catholic** *n* — **Roman Catholicism** *n*

¹**ro·mance** \rō-ˈman(t)s, ˈrō-ˌman(t)s\ *n* **1 a** : an old tale of knights and noble ladies **b** : an adventure story **c** : a love story **2** : LOVE AFFAIR **3** : an attraction or appeal to one's feelings ⟨the *romance* of the old West⟩

Word History As the Roman Empire spread throughout Europe, the Latin language developed many dialects. In these dialects, the original Latin was changed by the native languages spoken before the conquest. These dialects were called *romanz* in early French and became the bases of what we call Romance languages today. Even after the fall of Rome, serious writing was done in Latin. But in what is now France, popular verse stories about knights, dragons, ghosts, and battles were written in the local dialect. Soon *romanz* came to mean one of these stories, and the word was borrowed into Middle English. Since many of the stories were about love affairs, *romance* came to mean "a love story," and then "a love affair." In the late 18th and early 19th centuries, a group of poets, including Shelley, Byron, Keats, and Wordsworth, were labeled *Romantic* because they wrote poetry about the same kinds of things as were found in the old romances—noble love, courage, and ghostly beings. [Middle English *romauns* "a story of adventure or legend," from early French *romanz* "French language, something written in French," from Latin *romanice* "in a vernacular (as opposed to Latin)," from Latin *Romanus* "Gallic Romance speaker (as opposed to a Frank)," from *Romanus* "Roman"]

²**romance** *vb* **ro·manced; ro·manc·ing** **1** : to have romantic thoughts or ideas **2** : to carry on a love affair with

Ro·mance \rō-ˈman(t)s, ˈrō-ˌman(t)s\ *adj* : of, relating to, or being the languages (as French, Italian, or Spanish) developed from Latin

Ro·man·esque \ˌrō-mə-ˈnesk\ *adj* : relating to or being an old style of architecture (as for churches) coming before Gothic architecture and having round arches, thick heavy walls, and few small windows

Ro·ma·ni·an \rù-ˈmā-nē-ən, rō-\ *also* **Ru·ma·ni·an** \rù-\ *n* **1** : a person born or living in Romania **2** : the Romance language of the Romanians — **Romanian** *also* **Rumanian** *adj*

Roman numeral *n* : a numeral in a system of numbers based on the ancient Roman system — see NUMBER table

Ro·ma·no \rə-ˈmän-ō, rō-\ *n* : a hard sharp cheese used grated

Ro·mans \ˈrō-mənz\ *n* — see BIBLE table

Ro·mansch *or* **Ro·mansh** \rō-ˈmänch\ *n* : a Romance language spoken in parts of Switzerland

¹**ro·man·tic** \rō-ˈmant-ik\ *n* : a romantic person; *esp* : a romantic writer, composer, or artist

²**romantic** *adj* **1** : of, relating to, or resembling a romance ⟨*romantic* writing⟩ **2** : IMAGINARY **3** : IMPRACTICAL ⟨a *romantic* scheme⟩ **4 a** : stressing or appealing to the emotions or imagination ⟨a *romantic* spot⟩ **b** *often cap* : of or relating to romanticism **5** : of, relating to, or associated with love — **ro·man·ti·cal·ly** \-i-k(ə-)lē\ *adv*

ro·man·ti·cism \rō-ˈmant-ə-ˌsiz-əm\ *n* **1** *often cap* : a literary and artistic movement marked chiefly by an emphasis on the imagination and emotions **2** : the quality or state of being romantic — **ro·man·ti·cist** \-səst\ *n, often cap*

\ə\ abut	\aù\ out	\i\ tip	\ò\ saw	\ù\ foot
\ər\ further	\ch\ chin	\ī\ life	\òi\ coin	\y\ yet
\a\ mat	\e\ pet	\j\ job	\th\ thin	\yü\ few
\ā\ take	\ē\ easy	\ŋ\ sing	\th\ this	\yù\ cure
\ä\ cot, cart	\g\ go	\ō\ bone	\ü\ food	\zh\ vision

ro·man·ti·cize \rō-'mant-ə-ˌsīz\ *vb* **-cized; -ciz·ing** **1** : to make romantic : show in a romantic way **2** : to have romantic ideas — **ro·man·ti·ci·za·tion** \-ˌmant-ə-sə-'zā-shən\ *n*

Rom·a·ny \'räm-ə-nē, 'rō-mə-\ *n, pl* **-nies** **1** : GYPSY 1 **2** : the Indic language of the Gypsies — **Romany** *adj*

¹romp \'rämp\ *n* : rough and noisy play : FROLIC

²romp *vb* : to play in a rough and noisy way

romp·er \'räm-pər\ *n* : a child's one-piece garment with the lower part shaped like bloomers — usually used in plural

rood \'rüd\ *n* : ¹CROSS 1b, CRUCIFIX

¹roof \'rüf, 'ruf\ *n, pl* **roofs** \'rüfs, 'rufs, 'rüvz, 'ruvz\ **1 a** : the upper covering part of a building **b** : a place to live : HOME ⟨a *roof* over one's head⟩ **2** : the upper boundary of the mouth **3** : something resembling a roof in form, position, or purpose — **roofed** \'rüft, 'ruft\ *adj* — **roof·less** \'rüf-ləs, 'ruf-\ *adj* — **roof·like** \-ˌlīk\ *adj*

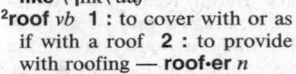

¹roof 1: *1* gambrel, *2* mansard

²roof *vb* **1** : to cover with or as if with a roof **2** : to provide with roofing — **roof·er** *n*

roof·ing *n* : material for a roof

roof·top \'rüf-ˌtäp, 'ruf-\ *n* : ¹ROOF 1a; *esp* : the outer surface of a flat roof

roof·tree \-ˌtrē\ *n* : RIDGEPOLE 1

¹rook \'ruk\ *n* : a common Old World crow that nests and sleeps in groups usually in treetops [Old English *hrōc* "crowlike bird"]

²rook *vb* : ¹CHEAT 1, SWINDLE

³rook *n* : a chessman that can move parallel to the sides of the board across any number of unoccupied squares [Middle English *rok* "chess piece," from early French *roc* (same meaning), from Arabic *rukhkh* (same meaning); of Persian origin]

rook·ery \'ruk-ə-rē\ *n, pl* **-er·ies** : the place where a group of birds or social mammals (as penguins or seals) breed, nest, or raise their young

rook·ie \'ruk-ē\ *n* : BEGINNER, RECRUIT; *esp* : a first-year player in a professional sport

¹room \'rüm, 'rum\ *n* **1** : space used or available for something ⟨houseplants that take up little *room*⟩ ⟨enough *room* to run and play⟩ **2 a** : a part of the inside of a building that is divided off **b** : such a part used as a lodging **3** : the people in a room **4** : a suitable opportunity : CHANCE ⟨*room* for improvement⟩

²room *vb* : to live in or share a room as a lodger

room·er \'rü-mər, 'rum-ər\ *n* : LODGER

room·ful \'rüm-ˌful, 'rum-\ *n, pl* **roomfuls** \-ˌfulz\ *or* **rooms·ful** \'rümz-ˌful, 'rumz-\ **1** : as much or as many as a room will hold **2** : the persons or objects in a room

rooming house *n* : a house where rooms are rented to lodgers

room·mate \'rüm-ˌmāt, 'rum-\ *n* : one of two or more persons sharing a room or dwelling

roomy \'rü-mē, 'rum-ē\ *adj* **room·i·er; -est** : having plenty of room — **room·i·ness** *n*

¹roost \'rüst\ *n* **1** : a support on which birds rest **2** : a place where birds often roost

²roost *vb* : to settle down for rest or sleep : PERCH

roost·er \'rü-stər\ *n* **1** : an adult male domestic chicken **2** : an adult male bird

¹root \'rüt, 'rut\ *n* **1 a** : the leafless usually underground part of a plant that absorbs water and minerals, stores food, and holds the plant in place **b** : an underground plant part especially when fleshy and edible **2 a** : the part of a tooth within the socket **b** : the base or end of a

bodily part (as a hair or a fingernail) or the part by which it is attached to the body **3 a** : an original cause : SOURCE ⟨the *roots* of evil⟩ **b** : the ancestors of a person or a group of persons ⟨people tracing their *roots*⟩ **c** : something that lies under and supports ⟨the *roots* of a mountain chain⟩ **d** : ¹CORE 1, HEART ⟨the *root* of the problem⟩ **e** : a close relationship with a social environment ⟨has *roots* in the South⟩ **4 a** : a number that when multiplied by itself a given number of times equals a specified number ⟨2 is a 4th *root* of 16 because 2 x 2 x 2 x 2 = 16⟩ **b** : a solution of a polynomial equation with one unknown ⟨$(x + 1)(x - 1) = 0$ has the *roots* $x = -1$ and $x = 1$⟩ **5** : a word or part of a word from which other words are formed ⟨"butler" and "bottle" come from the same Latin *root*⟩ [Old English *rōt* "root of a plant"; of Norse origin] — **root·ed** \-əd\ *adj* — **root·less** \-ləs\ *adj* — **root·like** \-ˌlīk\ *adj*

²root *vb* **1 a** : to form or enable to form roots **b** : to fix or become fixed by or as if by roots : take root **2** : to remove by or as if by pulling out the roots ⟨*root* out spies⟩

³root *vb* : to turn up or dig in the soil with the snout ⟨pigs *rooting* for fungi⟩

⁴root \'rüt, 'rut\ *vb* **1** : ²CHEER 2 **2** : to wish for the success of someone or something ⟨*rooting* for the underdog⟩ [perhaps an altered form of *rout*, a rare word meaning "to low or bellow like cattle"] — **root·er** *n*

root beer *n* : a sweet carbonated drink flavored with extracts of roots and herbs

root canal *n* : the space in the root of a tooth that contains soft sensitive tissue; *also* : a dental procedure to save a tooth by removing this tissue when diseased or injured and filling the space with a protective material

root cap *n* : a layer of dead cells that forms a protective cover over the growing tip of a root

root cellar *n* : an underground storage area for vegetables and especially those (as carrots) with enlarged roots

root hair *n* : one of the threadlike outgrowths near the tip of a rootlet that function in absorption of water and minerals

root·let \'rüt-lət, 'rut-\ *n* : a small root

root pressure *n* : the pressure that is caused by the absorption of soil water and that helps to push water up the plant stem from the roots

root·stock \'rüt-ˌstäk, 'rut-\ *n* **1** : RHIZOME **2** : a root or part of a root to which an aboveground plant part is grafted

¹rope \'rōp\ *n* **1 a** : a large stout cord of strands (as of fiber or wire) twisted or braided together **b** : LARIAT **c** : a noose used for hanging **2** : a row or string (as of beads) made by or as if by braiding, twining, or threading **3** *pl* : the special way things are done (as on a job) ⟨learn the *ropes*⟩

²rope *vb* **roped; rop·ing** **1 a** : to bind, fasten, or tie with a rope **b** : to set off or divide by a rope ⟨*rope* off a street for a neighborhood carnival⟩ **c** : to catch with a lasso **2** : to draw as if with a rope ⟨*roped* her friends into helping with the project⟩ — **rop·er** *n*

rope·walk \-ˌwok\ *n* : a place where rope is made

rope·walk·er \-ˌwo-kər\ *n* : an acrobat who performs on a tightrope

ropy \'rō-pē\ *adj* **rop·i·er; -est** **1** : capable of being drawn into a sticky thread : VISCOUS **2** : resembling rope — **rop·i·ness** *n*

Roque·fort \'rōk-fərt\ *trademark* — used for a blue cheese made in France of sheep's milk

Ror·schach test \'rō(ə)r-ˌshäk-\ *n* : a psychological test in which a person is asked to tell what he or she sees in and thinks about ink blots of varying designs and colors and which is used to measure certain traits of personality

ro·sa·ry \'rōz-(ə-)rē\ *n, pl* **-ries** **1** *often cap* : a Roman Catholic devotion consisting of meditation on usually five sacred mysteries during recitation of five decades of Hail Marys of which each begins with an Our Father and ends with a Gloria Patri **2** : a string of beads used in counting prayers especially of the Roman Catholic rosary

Word History *Rosary* is ultimately borrowed from Latin *rosarium*, a derivative of *rosa*, "rose." In classical Latin *rosarium* referred to a bed or garden of roses. In the Middle Ages rose gardens became particularly associated with Mary, and artists would give a rose-garden setting to the Annunciation, the announcement made to Mary by an angel that she would be the Messiah's mother. *Rosarium* could also refer to a rose garland or wreath for the head that Mary made or wore in various legends. When sequences of prayers to the Virgin became a popular devotion in the 1400s, it is not surprising that Latin *rosarium* was applied to them. Later the word was also applied to the strings of beads used in reciting the rosary prayers. [from Latin *rosarium* "rosary prayers, rosary beads," from earlier *rosarium* "rose garden," derived from *rosa* "rose"]

¹rose *past of* RISE

²rose \'rōz\ *n* **1 a** : any of a genus of usually prickly sometimes climbing shrubs that have compound leaves and showy often fragrant white, yellow, red, pink, or orange flowers **b** : the flower of a rose **2** : a medium purplish red — **rose·like** \-,līk\ *adj*

³rose *adj* **1** : of, relating to, resembling, or used for the rose or roses **2** : of the color rose

rose–breast·ed grosbeak \,rōz-'bres-təd-\ *n* : a grosbeak of eastern North America of which the male is chiefly black and white with a rose-red breast and the female is a grayish brown with a streaked breast

rose·bud \'rōz-,bəd\ *n* : the bud of a rose

rose·bush \-,bush\ *n* : a shrub that produces roses

rose–col·ored \-,kəl-ərd\ *adj* **1** : having a rose color ⟨a lamp with a *rose-colored* shade⟩ **2** : OPTIMISTIC ⟨a *rose-colored* view of the problem⟩

rose hip *n* : the ripened usually red or orange fruit of a rose

rose·mary \'rōz-,mer-ē\ *n* : a fragrant shrubby mint with grayish green needlelike leaves used as a seasoning; *also* : the leaves of rosemary [an altered form of Middle English *rosmarine* "rosemary," from Latin *rosmarinus*, literally, "dew of the sea," from *ros* "dew" and *marinus* "of the sea"]

Ro·set·ta stone \rō-,zet-ə-\ *n* : a black stone with inscriptions in Egyptian hieroglyphics and Greek that gave the first clue to understanding hieroglyphics

ro·sette \rō-'zet\ *n* **1** : a badge or ornament of ribbon gathered in the shape of a rose **2** : a design of leaves or flowers used as a decoration **3** : a circular cluster of leaves developed on a plant (as at the base of a dandelion)

rose·wood \'rōz-,wud\ *n* **1** : any of various tropical trees with hard dark red to purplish wood that is streaked with black and is used especially for making

rosette 2

furniture and musical instruments **2** : the wood of a rosewood

Rosh Ha·sha·nah \,rōsh-hə-'shō-nə, ,rōsh-ə-, ,räsh-, -'shän-ə\ *n* : the Jewish New Year observed as a religious holiday in September or October [from Hebrew *rōsh hashshānāh*, literally, "beginning of the year"]

¹ros·in \'räz-ºn, 'rȯz-\ *n* : an amber-colored to almost black brittle resin obtained especially from pine trees and used especially in making varnish and on violin bows

²rosin *vb* : to rub (as the bow of a violin) with rosin

ros·ter \'räs-tər\ *n* : a list usually of people belonging to some group

ros·trum \'räs-trəm\ *n, pl* **rostra** \-trə\ *or* **rostrums 1** : a stage or platform from which to give a speech **2** : a bodily part (as a snout) that resembles a bird's beak

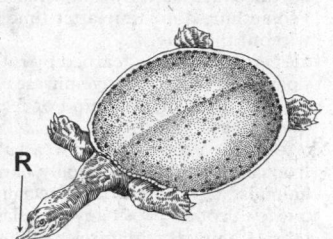

R rostrum 2

Word History *Rostrum,* a "raised platform for speakers," goes back to the collecting of war souvenirs by the ancient Romans. Warships in those days had pointed beams, called "beaks," sticking out from the bows. They were used to ram and sink enemy ships. To celebrate a great naval victory, the Romans gathered the beaks of the losers' ships. They hung them in back of the speaker's platform in the Forum in Rome. The Latin word for the ship's beak was *rostrum*. The plural, *rostra*, soon came to be used for the speaker's platform. In time *rostra* came to be used for any speaker's platform, not just one decorated with the beaks of ships. In the 18th century English began using the Latin singular form *rostrum* to mean "a speaker's platform." [from Latin *Rostra* "the speaker's platform in the Forum," from *rostra*, plural of *rostrum* "ship's beak"]

rosy \'rō-zē\ *adj* **ros·i·er; -est 1** : of the color rose **2** : PROMISING, HOPEFUL ⟨the outlook was *rosy*⟩ ⟨*rosy* prospects⟩ — **ros·i·ly** \-zə-lē\ *adv* — **ros·i·ness** \-zē-nəs\ *n*

¹rot \'rät\ *vb* **rot·ted; rot·ting 1 a** : to decay due to the action of fungi or bacteria **b** : to become unsafe or weak (as from use or chemical action) **2** : to go to ruin **3** : to cause to rot

²rot *n* **1 a** : the process of rotting : the state of being rotten **b** : something rotten or rotting **2 a** : a disease of plants or animals marked by the decay of tissue **b** : an area of decayed tissue ⟨pruned the *rot* from the tree trunk⟩ **3** : NONSENSE 1 ⟨don't talk *rot*⟩

¹ro·ta·ry \'rōt-ə-rē\ *adj* **1 a** : turning on an axis like a wheel ⟨a *rotary* blade⟩ **b** : taking place about an axis ⟨*rotary* motion⟩ **2** : having a rotating part ⟨a *rotary* lawn mower⟩

²rotary *n, pl* **-ries 1** : a rotary machine **2** : a road junction formed around a central circle about which traffic moves in one direction only

ro·tate \'rō-,tāt\ *vb* **ro·tat·ed; ro·tat·ing 1** : to turn or cause to turn about an axis or a center ⟨the earth *rotates*⟩ **2 a** : to do or cause to do something in turn **b** : to pass in a series ⟨the seasons *rotate*⟩ **3** : to cause to grow one after the other on the same land ⟨*rotate* alfalfa and corn⟩ — **ro·tat·able** \-,tāt-ə-bəl\ *adj* — **ro·ta·tor** \-,tāt-ər\ *n*

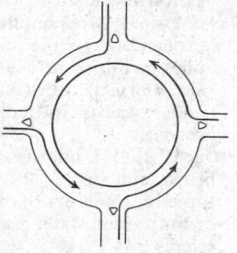

²rotary 2

ro·ta·tion \rō-'tā-shən\ *n* **1 a** : the act of rotating especially on an axis **b** : one complete turn **2** : CROP ROTATION — **ro·ta·tion·al** \-shnəl, -shən-ºl\ *adj*

¹rote \\'rōt\ *n* **1** : the use of memory usually without thinking about it ⟨learn by *rote*⟩ ⟨repeat something by *rote*⟩ **2** : something done time after time in an automatic way or without thinking

²rote *adj* **1** : done or learned by rote ⟨*rote* learning of multiplication tables⟩ ⟨a *rote* phrase⟩ **2** : done or carried out without engaging the mind or feelings ⟨*rote* duties⟩ ⟨ask a *rote* question⟩

ro·te·none \\'rōt-ⁿn-ˌōn\ *n* : a substance obtained from tropical plants that is usually harmless to warm-blooded animals but is poisonous especially to insects

ro·ti·fer \\'rōt-ə-fər\ *n* : any of a class of tiny aquatic invertebrate animals with circles of cilia on one end that look like moving wheels when moving

ro·tis·ser·ie \rō-'tis-(ə-)rē\ *n* : an appliance fitted with a spit on which food is rotated before or over a source of heat

ro·tor \\'rōt-ər\ *n* **1** : a part that rotates in a stationary part (as in an electrical machine) **2** : a complete system of rotating blades that support a helicopter in flight

ro·to·till·er \\'rōt-ə-ˌtil-ər\ *n* : a landscaping machine with rotating blades that lift and turn over soil [from *Rototiller*, a trademark]

rot·ten \\'rät-ⁿn\ *adj* **1** : having rotted **2** : morally bad **3** : very unpleasant or worthless ⟨did a *rotten* job⟩ — **rot·ten·ly** *adv* — **rot·ten·ness** \-ⁿn-(n)əs\ *n*

ro·tund \rō-'tənd, 'rō-ˌtənd\ *adj* **1** : somewhat round **2** : ⁵PLUMP — **ro·tun·di·ty** \rō-'tən-dət-ē\ *n*

ro·tun·da \rō-'tən-də\ *n* **1** : a round building; *esp* : one covered by a dome **2 a** : a large round room **b** : a large central area (as in a hotel)

rouble *variant of* RUBLE

¹rouge \\'rüzh, *especially Southern* 'rüj\ *n* **1** : a cosmetic used to give a red color to the cheeks or lips **2** : a red powder consisting essentially of ferric oxide used for polishing (as glass or metal)

²rouge *vb* **rouged; roug·ing** : to put rouge on

¹rough \\'rəf\ *adj* **1 a** : having an uneven surface : not smooth **b** : covered with or made up of coarse and often shaggy hair or bristles ⟨a *rough*-coated terrier⟩ **2 a** : not calm ⟨*rough* seas⟩ **b** : being harsh or violent ⟨*rough* treatment⟩ **c** : difficult to take or deal with ⟨we've had some *rough* times⟩ **3 a** : harsh to the ear **b** : coarse or rugged in nature or look **4** : not complete or exact ⟨a *rough* draft⟩ ⟨*rough* estimate⟩; *also* : ¹APPROXIMATE ⟨this will give you a *rough* idea of the house⟩ — **rough·ish** \\'rəf-ish\ *adj* — **rough·ly** *adv* — **rough·ness** *n*

synonyms ROUGH, HARSH, RUGGED mean not smooth or even. ROUGH implies having points, bristles, ridges, or projections on the surface ⟨*rough* wood⟩. HARSH implies having a surface that is unpleasant to the touch ⟨a *harsh* brush⟩. RUGGED implies an uneven land surface and suggests difficulty of travel ⟨*rugged* mountain roads⟩.

²rough *n* **1** : uneven ground covered with high grass, brush, and stones **2** : the rugged or unpleasant part of something ⟨nature in the *rough*⟩ **3** : something in a crude or unfinished state; *also* : such a state ⟨a diamond in the *rough*⟩

³rough *adv* : in a rough way : not smoothly ⟨the engine idled *rough*, but ran smoothly at high speed⟩

⁴rough *vb* **1** : ROUGHEN **2** : to handle roughly : BEAT ⟨*roughed* up by hoodlums⟩ **3** : to shape or make in a rough way ⟨*rough* out a plan⟩ — **rough it** : to live without ordinary comforts

rough·age \\'rəf-ij\ *n* : FIBER 1f

rough·en \\'rəf-ən\ *vb* **rough·ened; rough·en·ing** \-(ə-)niŋ\ : to make or become rough

rough–hewn \\'rəf-'hyün\ *adj* **1** : being rough or unfinished ⟨*rough-hewn* beams⟩ **2** : lacking smooth manners or social grace

¹rough·house \\'rəf-ˌhaüs\ *n* : violence or rough noisy play

²rough·house \-ˌhaüs, -ˌhaüz\ *vb* **rough·housed; rough·hous·ing** : to take part in roughhouse

rough·neck \\'rəf-ˌnek\ *n* **1** : a rough person : ROWDY **2** : a worker on a crew drilling oil wells

Rough Rider *n* : a member of the cavalry led by Theodore Roosevelt in the Spanish-American War

rough·shod \\'rəf-'shäd\ *adv* : with no consideration for the wishes or feelings of others — usually used in the phrase *ride roughshod over* or *run roughshod over*

rou·lette \rü-'let\ *n* **1** : a gambling game in which players bet on which compartment of a revolving wheel a small ball will come to rest in **2** : a wheel or disk with teeth around the outside [from French *roulette*, literally, "small wheel"]

¹round \\'raünd\ *adj* **1 a** : having every part of the surface or circumference the same distance from the center **b** : shaped like a cylinder ⟨a *round* peg⟩ **c** : nearly round ⟨a *round* face⟩ **2** : ⁵PLUMP **3 a** : ¹COMPLETE 1 ⟨a *round* dozen⟩ **b** : nearly correct or exact to a certain decimal place ⟨use the *round* number 1400 for the exact figure 1411⟩ **c** : LARGE ⟨a good *round* sum⟩ **4** : moving in or forming a circle **5** : having lifelike fullness ⟨a *round* character in a story⟩ **6** : having fullness of tone **7** : having curves rather than angles — **round·ish** \\'raün-dish\ *adj* — **round·ness** \\'raün(d)-nəs\ *n*

²round *adv* : ¹AROUND

³round *n* **1** : something (as a circle, globe, or ring) that is round **2** : a song in which three or four singers sing the same melody and words one after another at intervals **3** : ²RUNG **4** : an indirect or circling path **5 a** : a regularly covered route ⟨a watchman's *rounds*⟩ **b** : a series of calls or stops regularly made ⟨a doctor on her *rounds* in the hospital⟩ **6** : a drink apiece served at one time to each person in a group **7** : a series or cycle of repeated actions or events ⟨opened a new *round* of disarmament talks⟩ **8 a** : one shot fired by a soldier or weapon **b** : ammunition for one shot **9** : a unit of play in a contest or game ⟨a *round* of golf⟩ **10** : a cut of beef especially between the rump and the lower leg — **in the round 1** : in full sculptured form unattached to a background **2** : with a center stage surrounded by an audience on all sides ⟨theater *in the round*⟩

⁴round *vb* **1 a** : to make or become round **b** : to pronounce a sound with rounding of the lips **2** : to go or pass around ⟨*rounded* the curve⟩ **3** : to bring to completion — often used with *off* or *out* **4** : to express as a round number; *esp* : to drop any digits to the right of a given decimal place and increase the last remaining digit by 1 if the first dropped digit is 5 or greater ⟨4.57268 *rounded* off to three decimal places is 4.573⟩ **5** : to follow a winding course

⁵round \(')raünd\ *prep* : ²AROUND

round·about \\'raün-də-ˌbaüt\ *adj* : not direct ⟨went a *roundabout* way⟩

round dance *n* **1** : a folk dance in which participants form a ring and move in a certain direction **2** : a series of movements performed by a bee to indicate that a source of food is nearby

round·ed \\'raün-dəd\ *adj* : curving or round in shape

roun·de·lay \\'raün-də-ˌlā\ *n* : a simple song with refrain

round·house \\'raünd-ˌhaüs\ *n* **1** : a circular building where locomotives are kept or repaired **2** : a blow with the hand made with a wide swing

round·ly \\'raün-(d)lē\ *adv* **1** : in a thorough way : COMPLETELY ⟨was *roundly* ignored⟩ **2** : in plain or strong language ⟨*roundly* criticized the plan⟩

round–robin \\'raün-ˌdräb-ən\ *n* **1** : a letter (as of protest) whose signers put their signatures in a circle so the receiver cannot tell who signed first **2** : a tournament in which every contestant plays once against every other contestant

round–shoul·dered \'rauṅ(d)-'shōl-dərd\ *adj* : having the shoulders stooping or rounded

round steak *n* : a steak cut from the round of beef

round table \'rauṅ(d)-,tā-bəl\ *n* **1** *cap R&T* : the large round table of King Arthur and his knights **2** *usually* **round·ta·ble** : a meeting of several persons for discussion

round·up \'rauṅ-,dəp\ *n* **1** : the gathering together of animals (as cows) on the range by riding around them and driving them in **2** : a gathering together of scattered persons or things **3** : ²SUMMARY ⟨a *roundup* of the news⟩

round up \'rauṅ-'dəp\ *vb* **1** : to collect (as cattle) by circling and driving **2** : to gather in or bring together

round·worm \'rauṅ-,dwərm\ *n* : a nematode worm (as a hookworm); *also* : a related round-bodied worm without segments as compared to a flatworm

rouse \'rauz\ *vb* **roused; rous·ing** **1** : ¹AWAKE 1 **2** : to make or become active : stir up

rous·ing \'rau̇-ziŋ\ *adj* **1** : having the power to rouse one ⟨sang a *rousing* hymn⟩ ⟨a *rousing* speech⟩ **2** : very good : EXCEPTIONAL ⟨a *rousing* business⟩

roust·about \'rau̇-stə-,bau̇t\ *n* : a person (as a deckhand, dock worker, or oil field worker) who does heavy labor

¹rout \'rau̇t\ *vb* **1** : to poke around with the snout : ³ROOT **2** : to dig or cut a groove in (as wood or metal) **3 a** : to drive by force ⟨*routed* out of their homes⟩ **b** : to cause to come out especially from bed

²rout *n* **1** : a state of wild confusion and disorderly retreat **2** : a disastrous defeat

³rout *vb* **rout·ed; rout·ing** **1** : to put to flight **2** : to defeat completely

¹route \'rüt, 'rau̇t\ *n* **1** : ROAD 2a, HIGHWAY ⟨U.S. *Route* 66⟩ **2** : a course of action toward a goal ⟨the best *route* to peace⟩ **3 a** : an established, selected, or assigned course of travel ⟨explorers looking for a new *route* to the Indies⟩ ⟨air *routes* to Europe⟩ **b** : a territory to be gone over regularly ⟨a newspaper *route*⟩

²route *vb* **rout·ed; rout·ing** : to send or transport by a certain route ⟨*route* heavy traffic around the city⟩

¹rout·er \'rau̇t-ər\ *n* : a machine for cutting out the surface of wood or metal

²rout·er \'rüt-ər, 'rau̇t-\ *n* : one that routes; *esp* : a device that sends data from one place to another within a computer network or between computer networks

¹rou·tine \rü-'tēn\ *n* **1** : a standard or regular way of doing something **2** : an often repeated speech or formula **3** : a part (as of an act or a sports performance) that is carefully worked out so it can be repeated often ⟨a comedy *routine*⟩ ⟨a dance *routine*⟩ ⟨a gymnastic *routine*⟩ **4** : a set of computer instructions that will perform a certain job

²routine *adj* **1** : ²COMMONPLACE, ORDINARY **2** : done or happening in a usual or standard way — **rou·tine·ly** *adv*

rove \'rōv\ *vb* **roved; rov·ing** : ROAM

¹ro·ver \'rō-vər\ *n* : ¹PIRATE

²rov·er \'rō-vər\ *n* : a person who roves around : ROAMER

rov·ing \'rō-viŋ\ *n* : a slightly twisted roll or strand of textile fibers

¹row \'rō\ *vb* **1** : to move a boat by means of oars **2** : to travel or carry in a rowboat **3** : to pull an oar in a crew [Old English *rōwan* "to propel a boat with oars"] — **row·er** \'rō(-ə)r\ *n*

²row *n* : an act or instance of rowing

³row *n* **1 a** : a series of persons or things arranged in a usually straight line; *esp* : a horizontal arrangement of items **b** : the line along which such objects are arranged ⟨planted the corn in parallel *rows*⟩ **2** : ¹WAY 1a, STREET [Middle English *rawe* "a number of objects arranged in a line"]

⁴row \'rau̇\ *n* : a noisy disturbance or quarrel [origin unknown]

⁵row \'rau̇\ *vb* : to have a row : FIGHT, QUARREL

row·boat \'rō-,bōt\ *n* : a boat made to be rowed

¹row·dy \'rau̇d-ē\ *adj* **row·di·er; -est** : rough or loud in behavior — **row·di·ness** *n*

²rowdy *n, pl* **rowdies** : a rowdy person

row·el \'rau̇(-ə)l\ *n* : a disk on the end of a spur that has sharp points around its edge

row house \'rō-\ *n* : any of a row of houses connected by common sidewalls

row·ing \'rō-iŋ\ *n* : the sport of racing long narrow boats rowed by oars

row·lock \'räl-ək, 'rəl-; 'rō-,läk\ *n, chiefly British* : OARLOCK

roy·al \'rȯi(-ə)l\ *adj* **1** : of or relating to a sovereign : REGAL **2** : fit for a king or queen ⟨a *royal* welcome⟩ — **roy·al·ly** \'rȯi-ə-lē\ *adv*

royal blue *n* : a purplish blue

roy·al·ist \'rȯi-ə-ləst\ *n* : a person who supports a sovereign — **royalist** *adj*

royal jelly *n* : a substance rich in vitamins and proteins that is secreted from glands in the head of honeybees and is fed to all very young larvae and to all maturing queen bees

roy·al·ty \'rȯi(-ə)l-tē\ *n, pl* **-ties** **1** : royal status or power **2** : royal character or conduct **3** : members of a royal family **4 a** : a share of a product or profit (as of a mine) claimed by the owner for allowing another to use the property **b** : a payment made to the owner of a patent or copyright for the use of it

rRNA \,är-,är-,en-'ā\ *n* : RIBOSOMAL RNA

RSS \,är-,es-'es\ *n* : a computer document format that enables updates to websites to be easily distributed

¹rub \'rəb\ *vb* **rubbed; rub·bing** **1 a** : to move along the surface of a body with pressure **b** : to wear away or chafe with friction **2** : to scour, polish, erase, spread, or smear by pressure and friction — **rub elbows** *or* **rub shoulders** : to associate in a friendly way : MINGLE — **rub the wrong way** : to cause to be angry : IRRITATE

²rub *n* **1 a** : something that gets in the way : DIFFICULTY **b** : something that is annoying **2** : the act of rubbing

¹rub·ber \'rəb-ər\ *n* **1** : something used in rubbing, polishing, scraping, or cleaning **2 a** : an elastic substance obtained from the milky juice of various tropical plants **b** : any of various synthetic substances like rubber **3** : something made of or resembling rubber: as **a** : a rubber overshoe **b** : a rectangular slab of white rubber in the middle of a baseball infield on which a pitcher stands while pitching **4** : CONDOM — **rub·ber·like** \-,līk\ *adj* — **rub·bery** \'rəb-(ə-)rē\ *adj*

²rubber *n* **1** : a contest that consists of an odd number of games (as card games) and is won by the side that takes a majority (as two out of three) **2** : an extra game played to decide the winner of a tie

rubber band *n* : a continuous band made of rubber for holding things together : ELASTIC

rub·ber·ized \'rəb-ə-,rīzd\ *adj* : coated or soaked with rubber

rub·ber·neck \'rəb-ər-,nek\ *vb* : to look around or stare with great curiosity

rubber plant *n* : a plant that produces rubber; *esp* : an Asian tree related to the mulberries that is widely raised as a houseplant

rubber–stamp *vb* : to approve, endorse, or dispose of as a matter of routine or at the command of another

rubber stamp *n* : a stamp with a printing face made of rubber

rubber tree *n* : a tree that produces rubber; *esp* : a South American tree that is often grown on plantations as a commercial source of rubber

rub·bing \'rəb-iŋ\ *n* : an image of a raised or indented surface made by placing paper over it and rubbing the paper with something colored

rubbing alcohol *n* : a cooling and soothing solution for use on the outside of the body that contains an alcohol and water

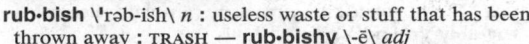

rubber stamp

rub·bish \'rəb-ish\ *n* : useless waste or stuff that has been thrown away : TRASH — **rub·bishy** \-ē\ *adj*

rub·ble \'rəb-əl\ *n* **1** : rough broken stones or bricks used in building **2** : a confused mass of rough or broken things

rub·down \'rəb-ˌdaùn\ *n* : a brisk rubbing of the body (as to relax tired muscles)

ru·bel·la \rü-'bel-ə\ *n* : GERMAN MEASLES

ru·bi·cund \'rü-bi-(ˌ)kənd\ *adj* : RUDDY 1

ru·bid·i·um \rü-'bid-ē-əm\ *n* : a soft silvery metallic element that reacts violently with water — see ELEMENT table

rub in *vb* : to keep reminding someone of something unpleasant ⟨you don't have to *rub* it *in*⟩

ru·ble *also* **rou·ble** \'rü-bəl\ *n* **1** : the basic unit of money of Russia and formerly of the U.S.S.R. **2** : a coin representing one ruble

rub off *vb* : to become transferred ⟨the ink *rubbed off* on my fingers⟩ ⟨a positive attitude can *rub off* on others⟩

rub out *vb* : to remove by or as if by erasing

ru·bric \'rü-brik\ *n* **1** : a name or heading under which something is classified : CLASSIFICATION ⟨different problems under the general *rubric* of ecology⟩ **2** : an explanation or set of instructions at the beginning of a text (as a book) **3** : a guide listing criteria for grading or scoring tests, projects, or papers

¹ru·by \'rü-bē\ *n, pl* **rubies** **1** : a precious stone of a deep red color **2** : the dark red color of the ruby

²ruby *adj* : dark red in color

ru·by–throat·ed hummingbird \ˌrü-bē-ˌthrōt-əd-\ *n* : a hummingbird of eastern North America that has a bright shiny green back, whitish underparts, and in the adult male a shiny red throat

ruck·sack \'rək-ˌsak, 'rùk-\ *n* : KNAPSACK

ruck·us \'rək-əs, 'rùk-, 'rùk-\ *n* : ⁴ROW

ruc·tion \'rək-shən\ *n* : a noisy disturbance : UPROAR

rud·der \'rəd-ər\ *n* : a flat movable piece (as of wood or metal) attached to the rear of a ship or aircraft for steering

rud·dy \'rəd-ē\ *adj* **rud·di·er; -est 1** : having a healthy reddish color **2** : ¹RED 1, REDDISH — **rud·di·ly** \'rəd-əl-ē\ *adv* — **rud·di·ness** \'rəd-ē-nəs\ *n*

rude \'rüd\ *adj* **rud·er; rud·est 1** : IMPOLITE **2** : not refined or cultured **3** : being sudden and forceful ⟨a *rude* awakening⟩ **4** : being in a rough or unfinished state : roughly made — **rude·ly** *adv* — **rude·ness** *n*

ru·di·ment \'rüd-ə-mənt\ *n* **1** : a basic principle or skill — usually used in plural ⟨the *rudiments* of grammar⟩ **2 a** : something unformed or undeveloped : BEGINNING — usually used in plural **b** : a body part so underdeveloped

R rudder

in size or structure that it is unable to perform its normal function

ru·di·men·ta·ry \ˌrüd-ə-'ment-ə-rē, -'men-trē\ *adj* **1** : ELEMENTARY 1, FUNDAMENTAL **2** : very imperfectly developed or represented only by a small part compared to the fully developed form ⟨a *rudimentary* tail⟩

¹rue \'rü\ *vb* **rued; ru·ing** : to feel sorrow or regret for

²rue *n* : ²REGRET 1, SORROW

rue·ful \'rü-fəl\ *adj* **1** : exciting pity or sympathy **2** : MOURNFUL 1, REGRETFUL — **rue·ful·ly** \-fə-lē\ *adv*

ruff \'rəf\ *n* **1** : a large round collar of pleated muslin or linen worn by men and women in the 16th and 17th centuries **2** : a fringe of long hairs or feathers growing around or on the neck of an animal — **ruffed** \'rəft\ *adj*

ruffed grouse *n* : a grouse of the U.S. and Canada with the male having tufts of shiny black feathers around the neck

ruf·fi·an \'rəf-ē-ən\ *n* : a brutal person : BULLY — **ruffian** *adj* — **ruf·fi·an·ly** *adj*

ruff 1

¹ruf·fle \'rəf-əl\ *vb* **ruf·fled; ruf·fling** \'rəf-(ə-)liŋ\ **1 a** : to disturb the smoothness of **b** : ¹TROUBLE 1a, VEX **2** : to erect (as feathers) in or like a ruff **3** : to make into a ruffle

²ruffle *n* **1** : a state or cause of irritation **2 a** : a strip of fabric gathered or pleated on one edge **b** : RUFF 2 — **ruf·fly** \'rəf-(ə-)lē\ *adj*

³ruffle *n* : a low vibrating drumbeat that is less loud than a roll

rug \'rəg\ *n* : a piece of thick heavy fabric usually with a nap or pile used as a floor covering

rug·by \'rəg-bē\ *n, often cap* : a football game between two teams in which play is continuous and the team that has the ball may run with it, kick it, or pass it sideways or backward but is not allowed to block or make forward passes [named for *Rugby* School in England where the game was first played]

rug·ged \'rəg-əd\ *adj* **1** : having a rough uneven surface ⟨hiking on *rugged* trails⟩ ⟨the *rugged* surface of the moon⟩ **2** : having wrinkles or uneven features ⟨their *rugged* faces⟩ ⟨*rugged* good looks⟩ **3** : having a rough but strong or sturdy character ⟨*rugged* pioneers⟩ **4** : involving hardship : presenting a severe test of physical, mental, or moral strength ⟨a *rugged* winter⟩ ⟨*rugged* training⟩ ⟨the *rugged* life of a sailor⟩ **5** : being strong and tough ⟨*rugged* enough to stand hard use⟩ **synonyms** see ROUGH — **rug·ged·ly** *adv* — **rug·ged·ness** *n*

¹ru·in \'rü-ən, -in\ *n* **1** : complete collapse or destruction **2** : the remains of something destroyed — usually used in plural ⟨the *ruins* of a city⟩

²ruin *vb* **1** : to reduce to ruins **2 a** : to damage beyond repair **b** : ³BANKRUPT — **ru·in·er** *n*

ru·in·a·tion \ˌrü-ə-'nā-shən\ *n* : ¹RUIN 1

ru·in·ous \'rü-ə-nəs\ *adj* : causing or tending to cause ruin : DESTRUCTIVE — **ru·in·ous·ly** *adv*

¹rule \'rül\ *n* **1 a** : a guide or principle for conduct or action **b** : an accepted method, custom, or habit **c** : REGULATION 2, BYLAW **2** : a broad statement generally found to be true ⟨as a *rule* we don't have much snow here⟩ **3** : the exercise of authority or control : GOVERNMENT **4** : RULER 2 [Middle English *reule* "a guide for proper actions," from early French *reule* (same meaning), from Latin *regula* "straightedge, ruler," from *regere* "to lead straight, govern, rule" — related to ¹RAIL, REGENT, REGULATE]

²rule *vb* **ruled; rul·ing 1** : to have power over : CONTROL, DIRECT **2 a** : to exercise authority or power over **b** : to be supreme or outstanding in **3** : to give or state as a considered decision **4** : to mark with lines drawn along or as if along the straight edge of a ruler   *synonyms* see GOVERN

rule of thumb 1 : a method based on experience and common sense **2** : a general principle that is roughly correct

rule out *vb* : to eliminate the possibility of

rul·er \'rü-lər\ *n* **1** : ¹SOVEREIGN 1 **2** : a straight strip of material (as wood or metal) marked off in units and used as a guide in drawing lines or for measuring

rul·ing \'rü-liŋ\ *n* : an official decision (as by a judge)

rum \'rəm\ *n* : an alcoholic liquor made from molasses or sugarcane

Rumanian *variant of* ROMANIAN

rum·ba \'rəm-bə, 'rùm-\ *n* : a dance of Cuban origin

¹**rum·ble** \'rəm-bəl\ *vb* **rum·bled; rum·bling** \-b(ə-)liŋ\ : to make or move with a low heavy rolling sound ⟨thunder *rumbled* in the distance⟩

²**rumble** *n* : a low heavy rolling sound

rumble seat *n* : a folding seat in the back of an old-fashioned automobile that is not covered by the top over the front seat

ru·men \'rü-mən\ *n, pl* **ru·mi·na** \-mə-nə\ *or* **ru·mens** : the large first compartment of the stomach of a cud= chewing mammal (as a cow) in which cellulose is broken down by the action of microorganisms and in which food is stored prior to chewing

¹**ru·mi·nant** \'rü-mə-nənt\ *n* : a cud-chewing mammal

²**ruminant** *adj* **1 a** : chewing the cud **b** : of or relating to a group of hoofed mammals (as sheep, oxen, deer, and camels) that chew the cud and have a complex 3- or 4-chambered stomach **2** : given to or engaged in contemplation : MEDITATIVE

ru·mi·nate \'rü-mə-,nāt\ *vb* **-nat·ed; -nat·ing 1** : to spend time thinking : MEDITATE **2** : to chew the cud : bring up and chew again what has been chewed slightly and swallowed   *synonyms* see PONDER — **ru·mi·na·tion** \,rü-mə-'nā-shən\ *n*

¹**rum·mage** \'rəm-ij\ *vb* **rum·maged; rum·mag·ing** : to make an active search especially by moving, turning, or looking through the contents of a place or container ⟨*rummaging* through the attic⟩

²**rummage** *n* : a confused miscellaneous collection of articles

rummage sale *n* : a sale of miscellaneous articles especially to raise money (as for a church or charity)

rum·my \'rəm-ē\ *n* : a card game in which each player tries to lay down cards in groups of three or more

¹**ru·mor** \'rü-mər\ *n* **1** : a widely held opinion having no known source : HEARSAY **2** : a statement or story that is in circulation but has not been proved to be true

²**rumor** *vb* **ru·mored; ru·mor·ing** \'rüm-(ə-)riŋ\ : to tell by rumor : spread a rumor

rump \'rəmp\ *n* **1 a** : upper rounded part of the hindquarters of a 4-legged animal **b** : BUTTOCK 2a **2** : a cut of beef between the loin and round

rum·ple \'rəm-pəl\ *vb* **rum·pled; rum·pling** \-p(ə-)liŋ\ : ²WRINKLE, MUSS

rum·pus \'rəm-pəs\ *n* : a noisy commotion

¹**run** \'rən\ *vb* **ran** \'ran\; **run; run·ning 1 a** : to go at a pace faster than a walk **b** : to take to flight : FLEE ⟨made the enemy *run*⟩ **2** : to move or allow to move freely about ⟨chickens *running* loose⟩ ⟨*running* around without a coat⟩ **3 a** : to go or cause to go rapidly or hurriedly ⟨*run* and get the doctor⟩ **b** : to go in pursuit of : CHASE ⟨had *run* the woodchuck into its hole⟩ **4** : to do something by or as if by running ⟨*run* errands⟩ **5 a** : to take part in a race **b** : to be or cause to be a candidate in an election ⟨*ran* for mayor⟩ **6 a** : to move on or as if on wheels **b** : to ravel lengthwise ⟨stockings guaranteed not to *run*⟩ **7 a** : to go back and forth ⟨the bus *runs* every hour⟩ **b** : to migrate or move in schools; *esp* : to go up a river to spawn

⟨shad are *running* in the river⟩ **8 a** : OPERATE 1 ⟨I can *run* that machine⟩ ⟨left the engine *running*⟩ **b** : to cause to be treated or operated on : PROCESS ⟨*ran* my program on the computer⟩ **9** : to continue in force or operation ⟨the contract has two years to *run*⟩ ⟨the play *ran* for six months⟩ **10** : to pass into a specified condition ⟨*run* into debt⟩ **11 a** : to move as a liquid : FLOW **b** : to dissolve and spread out ⟨colors guaranteed not to *run*⟩ **c** : to give off liquid ⟨my nose is *running*⟩ **12** : to tend to develop a specified quality or feature ⟨one of those people who *run* to fat⟩ **13 a** : EXTEND 4 ⟨the boundary line *runs* east⟩ **b** : to be in a certain form or order **14 a** : to occur again and again ⟨a song *running* through my head⟩ ⟨a condition that *runs* in their family⟩ **b** : to exist or occur in a continuous range of variation **15** : to be in circulation ⟨speculation *ran* wild⟩ **16** : ²TRACE 2a ⟨*ran* the rumor to its source⟩ **17** : to slip through or past ⟨*run* a blockade⟩ **18** : to pass over, across, or through **19 a** : to cause or allow to go ⟨*ran* the rascals out of town⟩ ⟨*ran* the car off the road⟩ **b** : to be in charge of : MANAGE ⟨*run* a factory⟩ **20** : to make oneself liable to : INCUR ⟨*ran* the risk of discovery⟩ — **run across** : to meet or find by chance — **run a fever** *or* **run a temperature** : to have a fever — **run into** : to meet by chance — **run riot 1** : to behave wildly **2** : to occur in great quantity — **run short** *or* **run low** : to be running out ⟨supplies were *running short*⟩ ⟨*run low* on fuel⟩

²**run** *n* **1 a** : an act or the action of running **b** : a fast gallop **c** : an annual migration of fish up a river especially to spawn; *also* : a group of fish migrating especially to spawn **d** : a running race ⟨the 1500-meter *run*⟩ **e** : a score made in baseball by a base runner reaching home plate **2 a** *chiefly Midland* : CREEK 2 **b** : something that flows especially during a certain time ⟨the first *run* of maple sap⟩ **3 a** : the horizontal distance from one point to another **b** : general tendency or direction **4** : a continuous series especially of similar things ⟨a long *run* of cloudy days⟩ **5** : sudden heavy demands from depositors, creditors, or customers ⟨a *run* on a bank⟩ **6** : the quantity of work turned out in a continuous operation; *also* : a period of continuous operation **7** : the usual or normal kind ⟨average *run* of students⟩ **8 a** : the distance covered in a period of continuous traveling **b** : regular course or trip ⟨the bus makes four *runs* daily⟩ **c** : freedom of movement ⟨has the *run* of the house⟩ **9 a** : a way, track, or path often traveled by animals **b** : an enclosure for animals where they may feed or exercise **10 a** : an inclined course (as for skiing) **b** : a track or guide on which something runs **11** : a ravel in a knitted fabric **12** *pl* : DIARRHEA ⟨had a bad case of the *runs*⟩ — **on the run 1** : while running : without stopping **2** : running away

run·about \'rən-ə-,baùt\ *n* : a small motorboat used especially for pleasure

run·a·gate \'rən-ə-,gāt\ *n* **1** : ²VAGABOND **2** : ¹RUNAWAY 1

run·around \'rən-ə-,raùnd\ *n* : deceptive or delaying action especially in response to a request

¹**run·away** \'rən-ə-,wā\ *n* **1** : a person who runs away : FUGITIVE **2** : the act of running away out of control; *also* : something (as a horse) that is running out of control

²**runaway** *adj* **1** : running away : FUGITIVE **2** : being out of control

run away \,rən-ə-'wā\ *vb* **1** : to leave in a hurry especially to escape from danger or confinement **2** : to leave home

run·back \'rən-,bak\ *n* : ²RETURN 7

\ə\ abut	\aù\ out	\i\ tip	\o̊\ saw	\ù\ foot
\ər\ further	\ch\ chin	\ī\ life	\o̊i\ coin	\y\ yet
\a\ mat	\e\ pet	\j\ job	\th\ thin	\yü\ few
\ā\ take	\ē\ easy	\ŋ\ sing	\t̲h̲\ this	\yù\ cure
\ä\ cot, cart	\g\ go	\ō\ bone	\ü\ food	\zh\ vision

run·down \\'rən-ˌdau̇n\ *n* : an item by item report : SUM-MARY

run–down \\'rən-'dau̇n\ *adj* **1** : being in poor condition ⟨a *run-down* farm⟩ **2** : being in or indicating poor health ⟨that *run-down* feeling⟩

run down \\'rən-'dau̇n\ *vb* **1** : to collide with and knock down **2 a** : to chase until exhausted or captured **b** : to find by search : trace the source of **3** : to stop operating because of the exhaustion of an energy source ⟨the battery *ran down*⟩

rune \\'rün\ *n* : any of the characters of an alphabet used by the Germanic peoples from about the 3rd to the 13th centuries — **ru·nic** \\'rü-nik\ *adj*

ᚲᚢᛈᚠᚱᚤ

rune

¹rung *past participle of* ³RING

²rung \\'rəŋ\ *n* : a rounded part placed as a crosspiece between the legs of a chair; *also* : one of the crosspieces of a ladder

run–in \\'rən-ˌin\ *n* : an angry dispute : QUARREL

run·ner \\'rən-ər\ *n* **1 a** : one that runs **b** : BASE RUNNER **2** : MESSENGER **3** : a thin piece or part on which something slides **4 a** : a slender creeping stem that arises from the base of a plant; *esp* : STOLON **b** : a plant (as a strawberry) that forms or spreads by runners **5 a** : a long narrow carpet (as for a hall) **b** : a narrow decorative cloth cover for a table or dresser top

run·ner–up \\'rən-ə-ˌrəp\ *n, pl* **runners–up** : the competitor in a contest who finishes next to the winner

¹run·ning \\'rən-iŋ\ *n* : the action of running — **in the running** : having a chance to win a contest — **out of the running** : having no chance to win a contest

²running *adj* **1** : going on steadily : CONTINUOUS ⟨a *running* battle⟩ **2** : measured in a straight line **3** : done while running or with a running start ⟨a *running* jump⟩ **4** : made or trained for running ⟨a *running* track⟩ ⟨*running* shoes⟩ ⟨a *running* horse⟩

³running *adv* : one after another : in a row : CONSECUTIVELY ⟨for three days *running*⟩

running board *n* : a narrow step at the side of an automobile

running knot *n* : a knot (as a slipknot) that slides along the line around which it is tied

running light *n* : any of the lights on a vehicle (as a ship) that show size, position, or direction

running mate *n* : a candidate running for a lesser office (as vice president) who is on the same ticket with the candidate for the top office

running stitch *n* : a small even stitch run in and out in cloth

run·ny \\'rən-ē\ *adj* **run·ni·er; -est** **1** : too soft and liquid ⟨the scrambled eggs are *runny*⟩ **2** : giving off a liquid ⟨a *runny* nose⟩

run·off \\'rən-ˌȯf\ *n* **1** : a final contest or election to decide an earlier one that has not given the victory to one competitor **2** : water from rain or snow that flows over the surface of the ground and finally into streams

run off \\'rən-'ȯf, ˌrən-\ *vb* **1** : to produce rapidly **2** : to decide by a runoff **3** : to drive away **4** : RUN AWAY 1 — **run off with** : to carry off : STEAL

run–of–the–mill \ˌrən-ə-(v)-thə-'mil\ *adj* : ²AVERAGE 2, ORDINARY

¹run–on \\'rən-ˌȯn, -ˌän\ *adj* : continuing without pause from one line of verse to another

²run–on \\'rən-ˌȯn, -ˌän\ *n* **1** : a dictionary entry that is run on **2** : RUN-ON SENTENCE

run on \\'rən-'ȯn, ˌrən-, -'än\ *vb* **1** : to keep going : CONTINUE **2** : to talk or tell at length **3** : to place or add (as an entry in a dictionary) at the end of an entry

run–on sentence *n* : a sentence formed from two or more sentences improperly joined (as "I didn't see the red light, officer, I was looking the other way")

run out *vb* **1** : to come to an end : EXPIRE ⟨time *ran out* before we could tie the game⟩ **2** : to become exhausted or used up ⟨our supplies were *running out*⟩ — **run out of** : to use up the available supply of ⟨better stop before we *run out of* gas⟩

run over *vb* **1 a** : ¹OVERFLOW 2 **b** : ¹OVERFLOW 3 **2** : to go beyond a limit ⟨the show may *run over* a minute or two⟩ **3** : to go over or rehearse quickly ⟨let's *run over* those lines again⟩ **4** : to collide with, knock down, and often drive over

runt \\'rənt\ *n* : an unusually small person or animal — **runty** \-ē\ *adj*

run through *vb* **1** : to pierce with or as if with a sword **2** : to spend or use up wastefully ⟨*ran through* the money in no time⟩ **3** : to read or rehearse without pausing

run up *vb* : to cause to pile up : ACCUMULATE ⟨*ran up* a big telephone bill⟩

run·way \\'rən-ˌwā\ *n* **1** : ²RUN 9a **2** : a paved strip of ground (as at an airport) for the landing and takeoff of aircraft **3** : a support (as a track, pipe, or trough) on which something runs

ru·pee \rü-'pē, 'rü-ˌpē\ *n* **1** : the basic unit of money of any of several countries (as of India and Pakistan) **2** : a coin representing one rupee [from a word in Hindi and Urdu (the main language of Pakistan) *rūpaiyā* "a unit of money"]

ru·pi·ah \rü-'pē-ə\ *n, pl* **rupiah** *or* **rupiahs** **1** : the basic unit of money of Indonesia **2** : a coin or bill representing one rupiah

¹rup·ture \\'rəp-chər\ *n* **1** : a break in peaceful or friendly relations **2** : a breaking or tearing apart (as of body tissue) ⟨a *rupture* in an artery⟩ **3** : HERNIA [Middle English *ruptur* "a breach of the peace," from early French *rupture* "a breach of the peace" or Latin *ruptura* "fracture, break," from Latin *ruptus,* past participle of *rumpere* "to break" — related to CORRUPT, INTERRUPT]

²rupture *vb* **rup·tured; rup·tur·ing** **1** : to part by violence : BREAK **2** : to produce a rupture in **3** : to have a rupture

ru·ral \\'ru̇r-əl\ *adj* : of or relating to the country, country people or life, or agriculture

rural free delivery *n* : the free delivery of mail on routes in country districts

rural route *n* : a postal route in a rural free delivery area

ruse \\'rüs, 'rüz\ *n* : a clever way to fool someone : TRICK **synonyms** see TRICK

¹rush \\'rəsh\ *n* : any of various marsh plants that are monocotyledons often having hollow stems sometimes used to weave chair seats and mats [Old English *rysc* "the rush plant"]

²rush *vb* **1** : to move forward or act with haste or eagerness **2** : to perform in a short time or at high speed ⟨*rushed* the job through⟩ **3** : to urge on to greater speed ⟨don't *rush* me⟩ **4** : to run toward or against in attack : CHARGE [Middle English *russhen* "to rush," from early French *ruser* "to drive off, repulse," from Latin *recusare* "to oppose"] — **rush·er** *n*

³rush *n* **1** : a violent forward motion ⟨a *rush* of wind⟩ **2** : a burst of activity or speed **3** : an eager migration of people usually to a new place in search of wealth ⟨the gold *rush*⟩

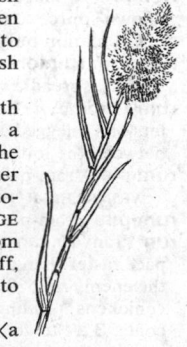

¹rush

⁴rush *adj* : demanding special speed or hurry ⟨*rush* orders⟩ ⟨the *rush* season⟩

rush hour *n* : a period of the day when traffic is very heavy or business is very brisk

rusk \\'rəsk\ *n* : a sweet or plain bread baked, sliced, and baked again until dry and crisp

¹rus·set \\'rəs-ət\ *n* **1** : coarse homespun usually reddish brown cloth **2** : a reddish brown **3** : any of various usually late-ripening apples that have rough mostly russet-colored skins

²russet *adj* : of the color russet

Rus·sian \\'rəsh-ən\ *n* **1** : a person born or living in Russia **2** : a Slavic language of the Russian people — **Russian** *adj*

Russian dressing *n* : a salad dressing usually containing mayonnaise and chili sauce

Russian wolfhound *n* : BORZOI

Rus·so- \\'rəs-ō, 'rəsh-; ˌrəs-ə\ *combining form* : Russian and ⟨*Russo*-Japanese⟩ [from the English words *Russia*, *Russian*]

¹rust \\'rəst\ *n* **1** : a reddish brittle coating formed on iron especially when chemically attacked by moist air and composed chiefly of ferric oxide **2 a** : any of numerous destructive diseases of plants caused by fungi and characterized by reddish brown spots **b** : any of an order of fungi that cause plant rusts **3** : a reddish brown

²rust *vb* : to form or cause to form rust ⟨iron *rusts*⟩

¹rus·tic \\'rəs-tik\ *adj* : of, relating to, or suitable for the country or country people : RURAL — **rus·ti·cal·ly** \-ti-k(ə-)lē\ *adv* — **rus·tic·i·ty** \ˌrəs-'tis-ət-ē\ *n*

²rustic *n* : a person living or raised in the country

¹rus·tle \\'rəs-əl\ *vb* **rus·tled; rus·tling** \\'rəs-(ə-)liŋ\ **1** : to make or cause to make a rustle **2** : to act or move with energy **3** : to steal (as cattle) from the range — **rus·tler** \\'rəs-(ə-)lər\ *n*

²rustle *n* : a quick series of small sounds ⟨the *rustle* of leaves⟩

rust·proof \\'rəst-'prüf\ *adj* : protected against rusting

rusty \\'rəs-tē\ *adj* **rust·i·er; -est** **1** : affected by or as if by rust **2** : less skilled and slow through lack of practice or old age **3** : of the color rust — **rust·i·ly** \-tə-lē\ *adv* — **rust·i·ness** \-tē-nəs\ *n*

¹rut \\'rət\ *n* **1** : a track worn by a wheel or by frequent passage **2** : a usual or fixed routine ⟨I need a change — I'm getting in a *rut*⟩ [probably derived from early French *route* "route, way"] — **rut·ty** \\'rət-ē\ *adj*

²rut *vb* **rut·ted; rut·ting** : to make a rut in

³rut *n* : the period during which male animals (as elk or deer) display behavior associated with the urge to breed [Middle English *rutte* "state of sexual excitement," from early French *ruit* "rut, disturbance," from Latin *rugitus* "roar," from earlier *rugire* "to roar"]

⁴rut *vb* **rut·ted; rut·ting** : to exhibit behavior associated with the rut — used of a male animal

ru·ta·ba·ga \ˌrüt-ə-'bā-gə, ˌrüt-, -'beg-ə\ *n* : a turnip with a large yellowish root that is eaten as a vegetable; *also* : the root

Ruth \\'rüth\ *n* — see BIBLE table

ru·the·ni·um \rü-'thē-nē-əm\ *n* : a hard brittle grayish rare metallic element used especially in alloys and catalysts — see ELEMENT table

ruth·er·ford·ium \ˌrəth-ər-'förd-ē-əm\ *n* : a radioactive element that is produced artificially — see ELEMENT table [scientific Latin, from Ernest Rutherford, 1871–1937, British physicist]

ruth·less \\'rüth-ləs\ *adj* : having no pity : MERCILESS, CRUEL — **ruth·less·ly** *adv* — **ruth·less·ness** *n*

RV \ˌär-'vē\ *n* : RECREATIONAL VEHICLE

Rx \ˌär-'eks\ *n* : PRESCRIPTION 2a [derived from abbreviation for Latin *recipe* "prescription," literally, "take"]

-ry \rē\ *n suffix, pl* **-ries** : -ERY ⟨wizard*ry*⟩ ⟨citizen*ry*⟩ [derived from early French *-erie* (a noun suffix)]

rye \\'rī\ *n* **1** : a hardy annual cereal grass widely grown for grain and as a cover crop; *also* : its seeds **2** : RYE BREAD **3** : whiskey distilled from rye or from rye and malt

rye bread *n* : bread made entirely or partly from rye flour

rye 1

S

s \\'es\ *n, often cap* **1** : the 19th letter of the English alphabet **2** : a grade rating a student's work as satisfactory

¹-s \s *after a voiceless consonant sound, z after a voiced consonant sound or a vowel sound*\ *n pl suffix* — used to form the plural of most nouns that do not end in *s, z, sh,* or *ch* or in *y* following a consonant ⟨head*s*⟩ ⟨book*s*⟩ ⟨boy*s*⟩ ⟨belief*s*⟩, to form the plural of proper nouns that end in *y* following a consonant ⟨Mary*s*⟩, and with or without a preceding apostrophe to form the plural of abbreviations, numbers, letters, and symbols used as nouns ⟨MC*s*⟩ ⟨4*s*⟩ ⟨#*s*⟩ ⟨B*'s*⟩ [derived from Old English *-as*, an ending on plural nouns]

²-s *adv suffix* — used to form adverbs indicating usual or repeated action or state ⟨at home Sunday*s*⟩ ⟨shops morning*s*⟩

³-s *vb suffix* — used to form the third person singular present of most verbs that do not end in *s, z, sh,* or *ch* or in *y* following a consonant ⟨fall*s*⟩ ⟨take*s*⟩ ⟨play*s*⟩

¹'s \like -'s\ *vb* **1 a** : IS ⟨she*'s* here⟩ **b** : WAS ⟨when*'s* the last time you ate?⟩ **2** : HAS ⟨he*'s* seen them⟩ **3** : DOES ⟨what*'s* he want?⟩

²'s \s\ *pron* : US — used with *let* ⟨let*'s*⟩

-'s \s *after voiceless consonant sounds other than* s, sh, ch; z *after vowel sounds and voiced consonant sounds other than* z, zh, j; əz *after* s, sh, ch, z, zh, j\ *n suffix or pron suffix* — used to form the possessive of singular nouns ⟨boy*'s*⟩, of plural nouns not ending in *s* ⟨children*'s*⟩, of some pronouns ⟨anyone*'s*⟩, and of word groups functioning as nouns ⟨the man in the corner*'s* hat⟩ or pronouns ⟨someone else*'s*⟩

Sab·bath \\'sab-əth\ *n* **1** : the 7th day of the week observed from Friday evening to Saturday evening as a day of rest and worship by Jews and some Christians **2** : the day of the week (as among Christians) set aside in a religion for rest and worship [Middle English *sabat* "the seventh day of the week for rest and worship," from early French *sabat* and Old English *sabat* (both, same meaning), both from Latin *sabbatum* "Sabbath," from Greek *sabbaton* (same meaning), from Hebrew *shabbāth*, literally, "rest"]

sab·bat·i·cal \sə-'bat-i-kəl\ *or* **sab·bat·ic** \-'bat-ik\ *adj* **1** : of or relating to the Sabbath ⟨*sabbatical* laws⟩ **2** : of or relating to a leave granted usually every seventh year (as to a professor) for rest, travel, or research

\ə\ **abut**	\au̇\ **out**	\i\ **tip**	\ȯ\ **saw**	\u̇\ **foot**
\ər\ **further**	\ch\ **chin**	\ī\ **life**	\ȯi\ **coin**	\y\ **yet**
\a\ **mat**	\e\ **pet**	\j\ **job**	\th\ **thin**	\yü\ **few**
\ā\ **take**	\ē\ **easy**	\ŋ\ **sing**	\th\ **this**	\yu̇\ **cure**
\ä\ **cot, cart**	\g\ **go**	\ō\ **bone**	\ü\ **food**	\zh\ **vision**

sa·ber or **sa·bre** \'sā-bər\ n : a cavalry sword with a curved blade

sa·ber–toothed tiger \,sā-bər-,tüth(t)-\ n : any of various large prehistoric extinct cats with very long curved upper canine teeth

Sa·bine \'sā-,bīn\ n : a member of an ancient Italic people conquered by Rome in 290 B.C. — **Sabine** adj

sa·ble \'sā-bəl\ n, pl **sables** **1** : the color black **2 a** or pl **sable** : a meat-eating mammal of northern Europe and Asia related to the martens and valued for its soft rich brown fur **b** : the fur or pelt of a sable — **sable** adj

sable 2a

¹**sab·o·tage** \'sab-ə-,täzh\ n **1** : destruction of an employer's property or the action of making it difficult to work by discontented workers **2** : destructive or blocking action carried on by enemy agents or sympathizers to make a nation's war effort more difficult

Word History Because the word *sabotage* appears related to French *sabot*, "wooden shoe," some people have thought that in the first cases of *sabotage* in France, industrial workers must have thrown their *sabots* into machinery in order to damage it. In fact, there is no evidence for such an etymology. The French verb *saboter* is known in the sense "to damage an employer's property" in the early 1900s but this meaning is perhaps based on an earlier sense "to carry out clumsily, botch, bungle," first attested in 1808. This meaning is in turn usually explained as proceeding from a yet older sense, "to make a clattering noise with sabots," on the premise that walking with wooden shoes suggests clumsy performance. It is hard to know if these diverse meanings are a single line of development, or if the associations evoked in Frenchmen by this piece of peasant footwear brought about episodes of verb creation from the same noun. [from French *sabotage* "destruction of property to hinder a manufacturing or war effort," from *saboter* "to clatter around wearing sabots, botch," from *sabot* "a wooden shoe"]

²**sabotage** vb **-taged; -tag·ing** : to practice sabotage on : WRECK

sab·o·teur \,sab-ə-'tər, -'t(y)ù(ə)r\ n : a person who performs sabotage

sac \'sak\ n : a pouch in an animal or plant often containing a fluid ⟨a food-storage *sac*⟩ — **sac·like** \-,līk\ adj

sac·cha·rin \'sak-(ə-)rən\ n : a very sweet white substance that is used as a calorie-free sweetener [derived from Latin *saccharum* "sugar," from Greek *sakcharon* "sugar"; of Sanskrit origin]

sac·cha·rine \'sak-(ə-)rən, -ə-,rēn\ -ə-,rīn\ adj **1 a** : of, relating to, or resembling sugar or its characteristics ⟨*saccharine* taste⟩ **b** : producing or containing sugar ⟨*saccharine* fluids⟩ **2** : overly sweet ⟨a *saccharine* smile⟩

sac·er·do·tal \,sas-ər-'dōt-ᵊl, ,sak-\ adj : of or relating to priests or a priesthood : PRIESTLY — **sac·er·do·tal·ly** \-ᵊl-ē\ adv

sac fungus n : ASCOMYCETE

sa·chem \'sā-chəm\ n : a North American Indian chief

sa·chet \sa-'shā\ n : a small bag containing a perfumed powder for scenting clothes and linens

¹**sack** \'sak\ n **1** : a flexible container (as of paper) : BAG **2** : SACKFUL **3** : discharge from employment — usually used with *get* or *give* **4** : ¹BUNK 3, BED [Middle English

sak "bag, sackcloth," from early French *sacc* (same meaning), from Latin *saccus* "bag" and later Latin *saccus* "sackcloth," both from Greek *sakkos* "bag, sackcloth" — related to ⁴SACK] — **sack·like** \-,līk\ adj

²**sack** vb **1** : to put in a sack **2** : DISMISS 2, FIRE

³**sack** n : any of several white wines imported to England from Spain and the Canary Islands in the 16th and 17th centuries [from early French *sec* "dry to the taste, not sweet," from Latin *siccus* (same meaning)]

⁴**sack** vb **1** : to loot after capture **2** : ²PILLAGE, LOOT [from English *sack* "the action of looting," from early French *sac* (same meaning), from early Italian *sacco*, literally, "a bag," from Latin *saccus* "bag" — related to ¹SACK]

⁵**sack** n : the looting of a captured town

sack·cloth \'sak-,(k)lòth\ n **1** : rough cloth for sacks **2** : a garment of sackcloth worn as a sign of sorrow

sack coat n : a man's jacket with a straight back

sack·ful \'sak-,fúl\ n, pl **sackfuls** \-,fúlz\ : the quantity that fills a sack

sack·ing \'sak-iŋ\ n : strong rough cloth from which sacks are made

sac·ra·ment \'sak-rə-mənt\ n **1** : a religious act that is a sign or symbol of a spiritual existence **2** cap : BLESSED SACRAMENT — **sac·ra·men·tal** \,sak-rə-'ment-ᵊl\ adj — **sac·ra·men·tal·ly** \-ᵊl-ē\ adv

sa·cred \'sā-krəd\ adj **1** : set apart in honor of someone (as a god) ⟨a mountain *sacred* to Jupiter⟩ **2** : HOLY **3** ⟨the *sacred* name of Jesus⟩ **3** : ¹RELIGIOUS 2 ⟨*sacred* songs⟩ **4** : deserving respect or honor ⟨a *sacred* right⟩ [Middle English *sacred* "sacred," derived from early French *sacrer* "to make holy, dedicate to God," from Latin *sacrare* (same meaning), from *sacr-, sacer* "sacred, holy" — related to CONSECRATE, SACRIFICE] — **sa·cred·ly** adv — **sa·cred·ness** n

¹**sac·ri·fice** \'sak-rə-,fīs, -fəs\ n **1** : an act of offering something precious to God or a god; *esp* : the killing of a victim on an altar **2** : something offered in sacrifice **3** : a giving up of something especially for the sake of someone else; *also* : something so given up **4** : loss of profit ⟨sell goods at a *sacrifice*⟩ [Middle English *sacrifice* "the act of offering something to God or a god," from early French *sacrifice* (same meaning), from Latin *sacrificium* "sacrifice," from *sacr-, sacer* "sacred" and *-ficium*, from *facere* "to do, make" — related to SACRED]

²**sac·ri·fice** \'sak-rə-,fīs, -,fīz\ vb **-ficed; -fic·ing** **1** : to offer or perform as a sacrifice **2** : to give up for the sake of something else **3** : to sell at a loss **4** : to make a sacrifice hit — **sac·ri·fic·er** n

sacrifice fly n : an outfield fly in baseball caught by a fielder after which a base runner scores

sacrifice hit n : a bunt in baseball that allows a runner to advance one base while the batter is put out

sac·ri·fi·cial \,sak-rə-'fish-əl\ adj : of or relating to sacrifice — **sac·ri·fi·cial·ly** \-ə-lē\ adv

sac·ri·lege \'sak-rə-lij\ n : theft or violation of something sacred — **sac·ri·le·gious** \,sak-rə-'lij-əs, -'lē-jəs\ adj — **sac·ri·le·gious·ly** adv — **sac·ri·le·gious·ness** n

sac·ris·tan \'sak-rə-stən\ n **1** : a church officer in charge of the sacristy **2** : SEXTON

sac·ris·ty \'sak-rə-stē\ n, pl **-ties** : VESTRY

sac·ro·sanct \'sak-rō-,saŋ(k)t\ adj : most sacred, holy, or respected : INVIOLABLE — **sac·ro·sanc·ti·ty** \,sak-rō-'saŋ(k)-tət-ē\ n

sa·crum \'sak-rəm, 'sā-krəm\ n, pl **sa·cra** \'sak-rə, 'sā-krə\ : a triangular bone at the base of the spinal column that connects with or forms a part of the pelvis and in human beings consists of five united vertebrae

sad \'sad\ adj **sad·der; sad·dest** **1** : filled with or expressing grief or unhappiness ⟨*sad* songs⟩ **2** : causing grief or unhappiness : DEPRESSING ⟨*sad* news⟩ — **sad·ly** adv

sad·den \'sad-ᵊn\ *vb* **sad·dened; sad·den·ing** \-niŋ, -ᵊn-iŋ\ : to make or become sad

¹sad·dle \'sad-ᵊl\ *n* **1 a** : a padded and leather-covered seat for a horseback rider **b** : a padded part of a harness **c** : a bicycle or motorcycle seat **2** : something like a saddle in shape, position, or use; *esp* : a support for an object — **in the saddle** : in control or command

¹saddle 1a

²saddle *vb* **sad·dled; sad·dling** \'sad-liŋ, -ᵊl-iŋ\ **1** : to put a saddle on **2** : ENCUMBER 1, BURDEN

sad·dle·bag \'sad-ᵊl-,bag\ *n* : one of a pair of covered pouches laid across the back of a horse behind the saddle or hanging over the rear wheel of a bicycle or motorcycle

sad·dle·bow \-,bō\ *n* : the raised front part of a saddle

saddle horse *n* : a horse suited for or trained for riding

sad·dler \'sad-lər\ *n* : one that makes, repairs, or sells horse equipment (as saddles)

sad·dlery \'sad-lə-rē, 'sad-ᵊl-rē\ *n, pl* **-dler·ies** : the work, articles of trade, or shop of a saddler

saddle shoe *n* : a shoe having a piece of different color or leather across the instep

saddle sore *n* **1** : a sore on the back of a horse caused by an ill-fitting or improperly adjusted saddle **2** : an irritation or sore on parts of the rider's body caused by rubbing against the saddle

sad·dle·tree \'sad-ᵊl-,trē\ *n* : the frame of a saddle

sa·dism \'sā-,diz-əm, 'sad-,iz-\ *n* **1** : abnormal behavior in which sexual pleasure is obtained by hurting another **2 a** : pleasure taken in cruelty **b** : very great cruelty — **sa·dis·tic** \sə-'dis-tik *also* sā-\ *adj*

sa·dist \'sād-əst, 'sad-\ *n* : an individual who practices sadism

sad·ness \'sad-nəs\ *n* : the quality, state, or fact of being sad

sa·fa·ri \sə-'fär-ē, -'far-\ *n* : a hunting expedition especially in eastern Africa

¹safe \'sāf\ *adj* **saf·er; saf·est** **1** : freed or secure from danger, harm, or loss **2** : successful at getting to a base in baseball without being put out ⟨the runner was *safe*⟩ **3** : providing safety **4** : not threatening danger ⟨*safe* medicine⟩ **5 a** : CAUTIOUS ⟨a *safe* driver⟩ **b** : TRUSTWORTHY [Middle English *sauf* "safe, unhurt," from early French *sauf* (same meaning), from Latin *salvus* "safe, healthy" — related to ³SAGE, SAVE] — **safe·ly** *adv* — **safe·ness** *n*

²safe *n* : a container to keep articles (as valuables) safe

safe–deposit box *n* : a box (as in the vault of a bank) for the safe storage of valuables

¹safe·guard \'sāf-,gärd\ *n* : something that protects and gives safety : DEFENSE

²safeguard *vb* : to make safe or secure : PROTECT

safe·keep·ing \'sāf-'kē-piŋ\ *n* : PROTECTION 1, CUSTODY

safe·light \'sā-,flīt\ *n* : a darkroom lamp with a filter to screen out light that is harmful to film or paper

safe sex *n* : sexual activity and especially sexual intercourse in which various measures (as the use of latex condoms) are taken to avoid disease (as AIDS) transmitted by sexual contact — called also *safer sex*

safe·ty \'sāf-tē\ *n, pl* **safeties** **1** : the state or condition of being safe : freedom from hurt, injury, or loss **2** : a protective device (as on a pistol) to prevent accidental operation **3 a** : a score of two points for the defensive team in football when an offensive ballcarrier is tackled behind the offensive team's goal line **b** : a defensive football player whose position is far back from the line of scrimmage

safety belt *n* : a belt for fastening a person to an object to prevent falling or injury

safety match *n* : a match that can be struck only on a specially prepared surface

safety pin *n* : a pin in the form of a clasp with a guard covering its point

safety razor *n* : a razor with a guard for the blade to prevent deep cuts

safety valve *n* **1** : a valve that opens automatically (as when steam pressure becomes too great) **2** : OUTLET 2

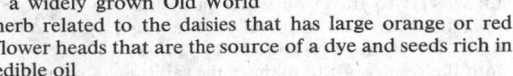

safety pin

saf·flow·er \'saf-,laú(-ə)r\ *n* : a widely grown Old World herb related to the daisies that has large orange or red flower heads that are the source of a dye and seeds rich in edible oil

safflower oil *n* : a polyunsaturated edible oil obtained from the seeds of the safflower

saf·fron \'saf-rən\ *n* **1** : the orange usually powdered dried stigmas of a purple-flowered crocus that are used especially to color or flavor foods **2** : an orange to orange yellow color

¹sag \'sag\ *vb* **sagged; sag·ging** **1** : to droop or sink below the normal or right level **2** : to become less firm or strong — **sag·gy** \'sag-ē\ *adj*

²sag *n* **1** : a sagging part or area ⟨the *sag* in a rope⟩ **2** : an instance or amount of sagging

sa·ga \'säg-ə\ *n* **1** : a tale of figures and events of Norway and Iceland from history or legend **2** : a story of heroic deeds

sa·ga·cious \sə-'gā-shəs\ *adj* : quick and wise in understanding and judgment — **sa·ga·cious·ness** *n* — **sa·gac·i·ty** \-'gas-ət-ē\ *n*

sag·a·more \'sag-ə-,mō(ə)r, -,mó(ə)r\ *n* **1** : an Algonquian Indian chief **2** : SACHEM

¹sage \'sāj\ *adj* **sag·er; sag·est** : ²WISE 1, PRUDENT ⟨*sage* advice⟩ [Middle English *sage* "wise," from early French *sage* (same meaning), derived from Latin *sapere* "to be wise, taste, have good taste" — related to INSIPID, SAVANT] — **sage·ly** *adv* — **sage·ness** *n*

²sage *n* : a very wise person

³sage *n* **1** : a European mint with fragrant leaves that is used especially to flavor meat **2** : SAGEBRUSH [Middle English *sage* "sage plant," from early French *sage, salge* (same meaning), from Latin *salvia* "sage plant used for health," from *salvus* "safe, healthy" — related to SAFE, SAVE]

sage·brush \'sāj-,brəsh\ *n* : any of several low shrubby North American plants related to the daisies; *esp* : a common plant with a bitter juice that smells like sage and is widespread on the plains of the western U.S.

Sag·it·tar·i·us \,saj-ə-'ter-ē-əs\ *n* **1** : a group of stars between Scorpio and Capricorn usually pictured as a creature that is half man half horse with a bow and arrow **2 a** : the ninth sign of the zodiac — see ZODIAC table **b** : a person whose sign of the zodiac is Sagittarius [from Latin *Sagittarius,* literally, "archer"]

sa·go \'sā-gō\ *n, pl* **sagos** : a dry granulated or powdered starch prepared from spongy tissue inside the stem of a sago palm

sago palm *n* : a palm or cycad that yields sago; *esp* : any of various tall tropical palms that have leaves with numerous leaflets

\ə\ abut	\aú\ out	\i\ tip	\ó\ saw	\ú\ foot
\ər\ further	\ch\ chin	\ī\ life	\ói\ coin	\y\ yet
\a\ mat	\e\ pet	\j\ job	\th\ thin	\yü\ few
\ā\ take	\ē\ easy	\ŋ\ sing	\th\ this	\yú\ cure
\ä\ cot, cart	\g\ go	\ō\ bone	\ü\ food	\zh\ vision

sa·gua·ro \sə-'wär-ə, -'wär-ō, -'gwär-ō\ *n, pl* **-ros** : a cactus of desert regions of the southwestern U.S. and Mexico that has a spiny branched trunk, bears white flowers and edible reddish fruit, and may reach a height of up to 50 feet (16 meters)

said *past and past participle of* SAY

saguaro

¹**sail** \'sā(ə)l, *as last element in compounds often* səl\ *n* **1 a** : a sheet of fabric (as canvas) used to catch wind to move a craft through water or over ice **b** : the sails of a ship ⟨under full *sail*⟩ **c** *pl usually* **sail** : a ship with sails **2** : something like a sail **3** : a journey by ship

²**sail** *vb* **1** : to travel on water in a ship ⟨*sail* the seas⟩ **2** : to travel by a sailing craft **3** : to move or glide along ⟨*sailed* into the room⟩ **4** : to manage the sailing of — **sail into** : to go at something eagerly ⟨*sailed into* their dinner⟩

sail·boat \'sā(ə)l-ˌbōt\ *n* : a boat equipped with sails

sail·cloth \-ˌklȯth\ *n* : a heavy canvas

sail·fish \-ˌfish\ *n* : any of a genus of large sea fishes that are related to the swordfish and marlins and have long slender jaws and a very large fin like a sail on the back

sail·or \'sā-lər\ *n* : a person who sails : SEAMAN

sail·plane \'sā(ə)l-ˌplān\ *n* : a glider designed to rise in an upward current of air

¹**saint** \'sānt; *when a name follows* (ˌ)sānt *or* sənt\ *n* **1** : a holy and godly person; *esp* : one who is declared to be worthy of special honor **2** : a person who is very good especially about helping others

²**saint** \'sānt\ *vb* : CANONIZE

Saint Ag·nes' Eve \sānt-ˌag-nə-səz-, -ˌag-nəs-\ *n* : the night of January 20 when a woman is traditionally thought to dream of her future husband

Saint An·drew's cross \-ˌan-ˌdrüz-\ *n* : a cross shaped like the letter X

Saint Ber·nard \ˌsānt-bər-'närd\ *n* : any of a breed of large powerful dogs developed in the Swiss Alps and formerly used in aiding lost travelers

Saint Bernard

saint·ed \'sānt-əd\ *adj* : SAINTLY

saint·hood \'sānt-ˌhu̇d\ *n* **1** : the quality or state of being a saint **2** : saints as a group

saint·ly \'sānt-lē\ *adj* **saint·li·er; -est** : relating to, resembling, or proper for a saint : HOLY — **saint·li·ness** *n*

Saint Pat·rick's Day \-'pa-triks-\ *n* : March 17 celebrated in honor of St. Patrick

saint·ship \'sānt-ˌship\ *n* : SAINTHOOD 1

Saint Valentine's Day *n* : VALENTINE'S DAY

saith \(')seth, 'sā-əth\ *archaic present third singular of* SAY

¹**sake** \'sāk\ *n* **1** : GOAL 2, PURPOSE ⟨for the *sake* of argument⟩ **2** : the good of something : ADVANTAGE ⟨the *sake* of our country⟩ [Old English *sacu* "guilt, legal action"]

²**sa·ke** *or* **sa·ki** \'säk-ē\ *n* : a Japanese alcoholic drink made from rice [Japanese]

sa·laam \sə-'läm\ *n* : a greeting performed by bowing very low with the palm on the forehead [from Arabic *salām* "a greeting," literally, "peace"] — **salaam** *vb*

sal·able *or* **sale·able** \'sā-lə-bəl\ *adj* : capable of being or good enough to be sold — **sal·abil·i·ty** \ˌsā-lə-'bil-ət-ē\ *n*

sal·ad \'sal-əd\ *n* **1** : green vegetables (as lettuce) often with tomato, cucumber, or radish served with dressing **2** : a cold dish (as of meat, shellfish, fruit, or vegetables) usually prepared with a dressing

salad bar *n* : a self-service counter in a restaurant featuring a selection of salad makings and dressings

salad dressing *n* : a sauce for a salad

salad oil *n* : a vegetable oil fit for use in salad dressings

sal·a·man·der \'sal-ə-ˌman-dər\ *n* **1** : an imaginary creature not harmed by fire **2** : any of an order of amphibians that are covered with scaleless usually smooth moist skin and look like lizards

sa·la·mi \sə-'läm-ē\ *n* : highly seasoned sausage of pork and beef

sal am·mo·ni·ac \ˌsal-ə-'mō-nē-ˌak\ *n* : AMMONIUM CHLORIDE

sal·a·ried \'sal-(ə-)rēd\ *adj* : receiving or paying a salary ⟨a *salaried* position⟩

sal·a·ry \'sal-(ə-)rē\ *n, pl* **-ries** : money paid at regular times for work or services : STIPEND

Word History The word *salary* is a loanword from Latin *salarium*, a derivative of *sal*, "salt," and perhaps originally short for *salarium argentum*, "salt money." According to a customary explanation, it was at one time money paid to Roman soldiers with which they were supposed to buy salt, but nothing in the known history of the word supports this. From the evidence of documents and inscriptions, the *salarium* was a fixed payment, introduced under the rule of Caesar Augustus, that was made to officials of a certain rank. The word was also applied to various other fees and payments to individuals by the Roman state or a community. Presumably *salarium* was a kind of euphemism, since the sums involved were much greater than would have been needed just to buy salt. [Middle English *salarie* "money paid to a worker," from Latin *salarium* "salt money, pension, salary," derived from *sal* "salt"]

sale \'sā(ə)l\ *n* **1** : the act of selling; *esp* : the exchange of property for a price **2** : ¹AUCTION **3** : a selling of goods at lower than usual prices **4** *pl* **a** : the business of selling **b** : total amounts of money received — **for sale** : available for purchase — **on sale 1** : available for purchase **2** : selling at a lower than usual price

sales·clerk \'sā(ə)lz-ˌklərk\ *n* : a person employed to sell goods in a store

sales·man \-mən\ *n* : one who sells in a specific territory or in a store — **sales·man·ship** \-ˌship\ *n*

sales·peo·ple \-ˌpē-pəl\ *n pl* : people employed to sell goods or services

sales·per·son \-ˌpərs-ᵊn\ *n* : a person employed to sell goods or services

sales tax *n* : a tax paid on the purchase of goods and services and collected by the seller

sales·wom·an \'sā(ə)lz-ˌwu̇m-ən\ *n* : a woman employed to sell goods especially in a store

sal·i·cyl·ic acid \ˌsal-ə-ˌsil-ik-\ *n* : a weak acid used especially in the form of salts to relieve pain and fever

sa·lient \'sā-lyənt, 'sā-lē-ənt\ *adj* **1** : sticking outward ⟨a *salient* angle⟩ **2** : very important or noticeable — **sa·lient·ly** *adv*

sa·line \'sā-ˌlēn, -ˌlīn\ *adj* **1** : consisting of or containing salt ⟨a *saline* solution⟩ **2** : of, relating to, or resembling salt — **sa·lin·i·ty** \sā-'lin-ət-ē, sə-\ *n*

sa·li·va \sə-'lī-və\ *n* : a fluid containing water, protein, salts, and often a starch-splitting enzyme that is secreted into the mouth by salivary glands

sal·i·vary \'sal-ə-ˌver-ē\ *adj* : of or relating to saliva or the salivary glands

salivary gland *n* : any of various glands that secrete saliva into the mouth

sal·i·vate \'sal-ə-ˌvāt\ *vb* **-vat·ed; -vat·ing** : to produce or secrete saliva especially in large amounts — **sal·i·va·tion** \ˌsal-ə-ˈvā-shən\ n

Salk vaccine \ˈsȯ(l)k-\ n : a polio vaccine that contains inactivated virus [named for Jonas *Salk* died 1985 an American doctor who developed the vaccine]

sal·low \ˈsal-ō\ adj : of an unhealthy yellowish color ⟨*sallow* complexion⟩

¹**sal·ly** \ˈsal-ē\ n, pl **sallies** **1** : an action of rushing or bursting out; *esp* : a sudden attack of surrounded troops upon the attackers **2** : a witty remark : QUIP **3** : EXCURSION 1a, JAUNT

²**sally** vb **sal·lied; sal·ly·ing** **1** : to leap or burst out suddenly **2** : SET OUT 2, DEPART ⟨*sallied* out to see the town⟩

salm·on \ˈsam-ən\ n, pl **salmon** also **salmons** **1** : any of various large food and game fishes that are related to the trouts, have reddish or pinkish flesh, live in oceans or large lakes, and swim up rivers or streams to deposit or fertilize eggs: as **a** : one of the northern Atlantic that does not die after breeding — called also *Atlantic salmon* **b** : any of several fishes (as the Chinook salmon) of the northern Pacific that usually die after breeding — called also *Pacific salmon* **2** : SALMON PINK

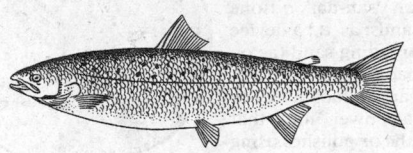

salmon 1b

salm·on·ber·ry \-ˌber-ē\ n : a showy red-flowered raspberry of the Pacific coast of North America; *also* : its edible salmon-colored fruit

sal·mo·nel·la \ˌsal-mə-ˈnel-ə\ n, pl **-nel·lae** \-ˈnel-ē, -ˌī\ or **-nellas** or **-nella** : any of a genus of rod-shaped bacteria that cause various illnesses (as food poisoning) in human beings and other warm-blooded animals

salmon pink n : a strong yellowish pink

sa·lon \sə-ˈlän, ˈsal-ˌän\ n **1** : an apartment or living room of stylish design **2** : a social gathering held in a salon **3 a** : an art gallery **b** : an annual exhibition of art **4** : a stylish business establishment

sa·loon \sə-ˈlün\ n **1** : a public room for socializing especially on a ship **2** : BARROOM

sal·sa \ˈsȯl-sə, ˈsäl-\ n **1** : a spicy sauce of tomatoes, onions, and hot peppers **2** : popular Latin American music with elements of rhythm and blues, jazz, and rock

¹**salt** \ˈsȯlt\ n **1 a** : a compound in the form of crystals that consists of sodium chloride and is used especially for seasoning or preserving food and in industry — called also *common salt* **b** : any of numerous compounds formed by replacement of part or all of the hydrogen of an acid by a metal or by a group acting like a metal **2** : an element that gives an appealing or enlivening quality to (as one's life) **3** : SKEPTICISM — usually used in the phrases *with a grain of salt* and *with a pinch of salt* **4** : SAILOR

²**salt** vb : to treat, preserve, flavor, or supply with salt

³**salt** adj **1 a** : containing salt : SALINE, SALTY ⟨*salt* water⟩ **b** : having or being one of the four basic taste sensations — compare BITTER 1, ¹SOUR 1, ¹SWEET 1b **2** : prepared for use or seasoned with salt ⟨*salt* pork⟩ — **salt·ness** n

salt–and–pepper adj : having dark and light color intermingled in small flecks ⟨a *salt-and-pepper* beard⟩

salt away vb : to lay away safely : SAVE

salt·bush \ˈsȯlt-ˌbu̇sh\ n : any of various shrubby plants of dry regions that are related to the goosefoots

salt·cel·lar \ˈsȯlt-ˌsel-ər\ n : a small container for holding salt at table

salt flat n : an area of land covered with a crust of salt left by evaporation of water

sal·tine \sȯl-ˈtēn\ n : a square crisp cracker usually sprinkled with salt

salt lake n : a lake that has become salty through evaporation

salt lick n : ²LICK 3

salt marsh n : flat land that is overflowed by salt water

salt pan n : an undrained natural depression in which water gathers and leaves a deposit of salt on evaporation

salt·shak·er \ˈsȯlt-ˌshā-kər\ n : a container having a top with holes in it for sprinkling salt

salt·wa·ter \ˈsȯlt-ˌwȯt-ər, -ˌwät-\ adj : relating to, living in, or consisting of salt water

salty \ˈsȯl-tē\ adj **salt·i·er; -est** **1** : seasoned with or containing salt : tasting of or like salt **2** : having the flavor of or suggesting the sea or things related to the sea **3** : ¹RACY 2 ⟨a *salty* remark⟩ — **salt·i·ness** n

sa·lu·bri·ous \sə-ˈlü-brē-əs\ adj : favorable to health — **sa·lu·bri·ous·ly** adv — **sa·lu·bri·ous·ness** n

sal·u·tary \ˈsal-yə-ˌter-ē\ adj **1** : producing a good result **2** : furthering good health — **sal·u·tari·ness** n

sal·u·ta·tion \ˌsal-yə-ˈtā-shən\ n **1** : an expression of greeting, goodwill, or courtesy **2** : the word or phrase of greeting that begins a letter — **sal·u·ta·tion·al** \-shnəl, -shən-əl\ adj

sa·lu·ta·to·ri·an \sə-ˌlüt-ə-ˈtōr-ē-ən, -ˈtȯr-\ n : the graduating student usually second highest in rank

¹**sa·lu·ta·to·ry** \sə-ˈlüt-ə-ˌtōr-ē, -ˌtȯr-\ adj : expressing salutations or welcome

²**salutatory** n, pl **-ries** : a salutatory address

¹**sa·lute** \sə-ˈlüt\ vb **sa·lut·ed; sa·lut·ing** **1** : to greet with courteous words or a bow **2 a** : to honor by a standard military ceremony **b** : to show respect to by taking the proper position ⟨*salute* an officer⟩ — **sa·lut·er** n

²**salute** n **1** : SALUTATION 1, GREETING **2 a** : a sign or ceremony of goodwill, compliment, or respect **b** : the position taken by a person saluting a military officer

¹**sal·vage** \ˈsal-vij\ n **1** : money paid for saving a wrecked or endangered ship or its cargo or passengers **2** : the act of saving a ship or possessions in danger of being lost **3** : something saved or recovered (as from a wreck or fire)

²**salvage** vb **sal·vaged; sal·vag·ing** : to rescue or save especially from wreckage or ruin — **sal·vage·able** \-ə-bəl\ adj — **sal·vag·er** n

sal·va·tion \sal-ˈvā-shən\ n **1** : the saving of a person from sin **2** : something that saves **3** : the saving from danger or evil

¹**salve** \ˈsav, ˈsàv\ n : a healing ointment

²**salve** vb **salved; salv·ing** : to ease or soothe with or as if with a salve

sal·ver \ˈsal-vər\ n : a serving tray

sal·vo \ˈsal-vō\ n, pl **salvos** or **salvoes** **1 a** : the firing of two or more guns at the same time at one target or in a salute **b** : the release all at once of a rack of bombs or rockets **2** : the firing of one gun after another in a group of artillery pieces **3** : a sudden burst (as of cheers)

sa·ma·ra \ˈsam-ə-rə; sə-ˈmar-ə, -ˈmär-\ n : a dry usually one-seeded winged fruit (as of an elm tree) that does not split open when ripe

sa·mar·i·um \sə-ˈmer-ē-əm, -ˈmar-\ n : a pale gray shiny metallic element — see ELEMENT table

¹**same** \ˈsām\ adj **1** : resembling in every respect ⟨the *same* answer as before⟩ **2** : not another ⟨the *same* school⟩ **3** : very much alike ⟨on the *same* day last year⟩

synonyms SAME, IDENTICAL, EQUAL mean not different or not differing from one another. SAME suggests that the things being compared are really one thing and not two or more ⟨saw the *same* truck twice⟩. IDENTICAL usually suggests that two or more things are like each other in every way ⟨these plates are *identical*⟩. EQUAL suggests that the things being compared are like each other in some specific way ⟨singers of *equal* talent⟩.

²same *pron* : the same one or ones

same·ness \'sām-nəs\ *n* **1** : the quality or state of being the same : IDENTITY **2** : MONOTONY 2, UNIFORMITY

Samoa time *n* : the time of the 11th time zone west of Greenwich that includes American Samoa

sam·o·var \'sam-ə-ˌvär\ *n* : a container with a faucet used especially in Russia for tea

Sam·o·yed \'sam-ə-ˌyed, 'sam-ˌȯi-ˌed\ *n* : any of a breed of medium-sized white or cream-colored sled dogs developed in Siberia

sam·pan \'sam-ˌpan\ *n* : a flat-bottomed Chinese boat usually moved by oars

sampan

¹sam·ple \'sam-pəl\ *n* **1** : a part or thing that shows the quality of the whole or group **2** : a part (as a set of individuals chosen from a whole population) used for investigating the whole

²sample *vb* **sam·pled; sam·pling** \-p(ə-)liŋ\ : to judge the quality of by a sample

¹sam·pler \'sam-plər\ *n* : a piece of needlework typically having letters or verses on it done in various stitches as an example of skill

²sam·pler \'sam-p(ə-)lər\ *n* **1** : one that collects or examines samples **2** : a collection of samples

sample space *n* : the set of all the possible results of a statistical experiment ⟨if you flip a coin once, the *sample space* is {heads, tails}⟩

Sam·u·el \'sam-yə(-wə)l\ *n* — see BIBLE table

sam·u·rai \'sam-(y)ə-ˌrī\ *n, pl* **samurai** : a warrior serving a Japanese feudal lord and practicing a code of conduct which valued honor over life

san·a·to·ri·um \ˌsan-ə-'tōr-ē-əm, -'tȯr-\ *n, pl* **-ri·ums** *or* **-ria** \-ē-ə\ : an establishment for the care and treatment especially of people recovering from illness or having a disease likely to last a long time — called also *sanitarium*

sanc·ti·fy \'saŋ(k)-tə-ˌfī\ *vb* **-fied; -fy·ing** **1** : to set apart as sacred **2** : to make free from sin — **sanc·ti·fi·ca·tion** \ˌsaŋ(k)-tə-fə-'kā-shən\ *n*

sanc·ti·mo·ni·ous \ˌsaŋ(k)-tə-'mō-nē-əs\ *adj* : pretending to be devoted — **sanc·ti·mo·ni·ous·ly** *adv* — **sanc·ti·mo·ni·ous·ness** *n*

¹sanc·tion \'saŋ(k)-shən\ *n* **1** : an action taken to enforce a law or rule **2** : official permission or approval **3** : a measure used to punish or prevent an action

²sanction *vb* **-tioned; -tion·ing** \-sh(ə-)niŋ\ **1** : to officially accept or allow **2** : to impose a penalty upon

sanc·ti·ty \'saŋ(k)-tət-ē\ *n, pl* **-ties** **1** : HOLINESS 1, SAINTLINESS **2** : the quality or state of being holy or sacred

sanc·tu·ary \'saŋ(k)-chə-ˌwer-ē\ *n, pl* **-ar·ies** **1** : a holy or sacred place **2** : the most sacred part of a place of worship **3** : a building or room for religious worship **4** : a place that provides shelter or protection ⟨a wildlife *sanctuary*⟩ **5** : protection provided by a sanctuary

sanc·tum \'saŋ(k)-təm\ *n, pl* **sanctums** *also* **sanc·ta** \-tə\ **1** : a sacred place **2** : a place where one is free from being bothered

¹sand \'sand\ *n* **1** : loose material in grains produced by the natural breaking up of rocks **2** : a soil made up mostly of sand

²sand *vb* **1** : to sprinkle with sand **2** : to smooth by rubbing with sandpaper

san·dal \'san-d³l\ *n* : a shoe consisting of a sole strapped to the foot

san·dal·wood \-ˌwu̇d\ *n* : the close-grained fragrant yellowish wood of an Asian tree often used in carving and cabinetwork; *also* : the tree that yields this wood

sand·bag \'san(d)-ˌbag\ *n* : a bag filled with sand

sand·bank \-ˌbaŋk\ *n* : a large deposit of sand

sand·bar \-ˌbär\ *n* : a ridge of sand formed in water by tides or currents

sand·blast \-ˌblast\ *vb* : to cut or clean with sand driven at high speed by or as if by compressed air — **sand·blast·er** *n*

sand·box \-ˌbäks\ *n* : a box for holding sand especially for children to play in

sand·bur \'san(d)-ˌbər\ *n* : any of a genus of grasses mostly of warm sandy areas that produce small prickly dry fruits; *also* : one of these fruits

sand dollar *n* : any of various round flat sea urchins that usually live in shallow water and on sandy bottoms

sand·er \'san-dər\ *n* : one that sands: as **a** : a device for spreading sand (as on icy roads); *also* : a truck that carries such a device **b** : a power tool that smooths or polishes using a rough material (as sandpaper)

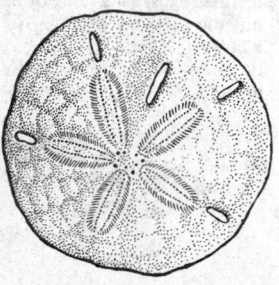
sand dollar

sand flea *n* **1** : a flea found in sandy places **2** : any of numerous tiny leaping crustaceans common on ocean beaches

sand fly *n* : any of various small two-winged flies that bite

sand·glass \'san(d)-ˌglas\ *n* : an instrument (as an hourglass) for measuring time by the running of sand

sand·hill crane \ˌsand-ˌhil-\ *n* : a crane of North America and Siberia that is chiefly bluish gray with red on the top of the head

sand·lot \'san-(d)lät\ *n* : a vacant lot especially when used by youngsters for unorganized sports — **sandlot** *adj* — **sand·lot·ter** \-ˌ(d)lät-ər\ *n*

sand·man \'san(d)-ˌman\ *n* : the magical being of folklore who is said to make children sleepy by sprinkling sand in their eyes

¹sand·pa·per \-ˌpā-pər\ *n* : paper with rough material (as sand) glued on one side and used for smoothing and polishing

²sandpaper *vb* : to rub with or as if with sandpaper

sand·pip·er \-ˌpī-pər\ *n* : any of numerous small shorebirds with usually long bills and legs

sand·stone \-ˌstōn\ *n* : a rock made of sand held together by a natural cement

sand·storm \-ˌstȯ(ə)rm\ *n* : a storm of wind (as in a desert) that drives clouds of sand

sand trap *n* : a hazard on a golf course consisting of a hollow containing sand

¹sand·wich \'san-(ˌ)(d)wich\ *n* **1** : one or more slices of bread or a roll with a filling or spread **2** : something resembling a sandwich

Word History John Montagu, 4th Earl of Sandwich, was famous in 18th century England as a powerful political figure. He was also known to be fond of playing cards. The story was told that he once spent an entire night at the card table. Instead of leaving the game to have dinner, he ordered that slices of meat be brought to him between two pieces of bread. In that way he could continue playing while he ate. This convenient type of food soon became popular throughout England. Because of the story about the Earl, it became known as the *sand-*

wich. [named for John Montagu, 4th Earl of *Sandwich,* died 1792, English diplomat]

²**sandwich** *vb* **1** : to insert between two or more things **2** : to make a place for : CROWD

sandwich man *n* : one who advertises or pickets a place of business by wearing an advertising board in front and behind

sandy \'san-dē\ *adj* **sand·i·er; -est** **1** : consisting of, containing, or sprinkled with sand **2** : of a yellowish gray color

sane \'sān\ *adj* **san·er; san·est** **1** : mentally sound and healthy **2** : proceeding from a sound mind : RATIONAL, SENSIBLE — **sane·ly** *adv* — **sane·ness** \'sān-nəs\ *n*

sang *past of* SING

san·gui·nary \'saŋ-gwə-ˌner-ē\ *adj* **1** : willing or eager to cause bloodshed : BLOODTHIRSTY **2** : BLOODY 2

san·guine \'saŋ-gwən\ *adj* **1** : having the color of blood **2 a** : SANGUINARY 1 **b** : RUDDY 1 **3** : CHEERFUL 1a, HOPEFUL ⟨a *sanguine* disposition⟩ **4** : CONFIDENT, OPTIMISTIC ⟨*sanguine* of success⟩ [Middle English *sanguin* "having the color of blood," from early French *sanguin* (same meaning), from Latin *sanguineus* (same meaning), from *sanguin-, sanguis* "blood" — see *Word History* at HUMOR] — **san·guine·ly** *adv* — **san·guin·i·ty** \saŋ-ˈgwin-ət-ē, san-\ *n*

san·i·tar·i·an \ˌsan-ə-ˈter-ē-ən\ *n* : a person who specializes in public health and matters of sanitation

san·i·tar·i·um \ˌsan-ə-ˈter-ē-əm\ *n, pl* **-i·ums** *or* **-ia** \-ē-ə\ : SANATORIUM

san·i·tary \'san-ə-ˌter-ē\ *adj* **1** : of or relating to health : HYGIENIC ⟨*sanitary* laws⟩ **2** : free from filth, infection, or dangers to health

sanitary landfill *n* : LANDFILL

sanitary napkin *n* : a disposable absorbent pad that is used to absorb uterine flow (as during menstruation)

san·i·ta·tion \ˌsan-ə-ˈtā-shən\ *n* **1** : the act or process of making sanitary **2** : the promotion of community hygiene and disease prevention especially by keeping up sewage systems, by collecting and disposing of trash and garbage, and by cleaning streets

san·i·tize \'san-ə-ˌtīz\ *vb* **-tized; -tiz·ing** : to make sanitary (as by cleaning or sterilizing)

san·i·ty \'san-ət-ē\ *n* : the quality or state of being sane

San Jo·se scale \ˌsan-ə-ˌzā-\ *n* : a scale insect introduced into North America from Asia that is very destructive to fruit trees

sank *past of* SINK

sans \(ˌ)sanz\ *prep* : ¹WITHOUT 2a

san·se·vie·ria \ˌsan(t)-sə-ˈvir-ē-ə\ *n* : any of a genus of tropical herbs that are related to the agaves and have spotted or striped sword-shaped leaves — called also *snake plant*

San·skrit \'san-ˌskrit\ *n* : an ancient Indic language of India and of Hinduism — **Sanskrit** *adj*

San·ta Claus \'sant-ē-ˌklôz, 'sant-ə-\ *n* : the spirit of Christmas represented by a fat jolly old man in a red suit who gives toys to children [from Dutch *Sinterklaas,* an altered form of Dutch *Sint Nikolaas* "Saint Nicholas"]

San·ta Ger·tru·dis \ˌsant-ə-(ˌ)gər-ˈtrüd-əs\ *n* : any of a breed of red beef cattle that were developed from a cross between Brahmans and shorthorns and that are tolerant of hot climates

Santa Gertrudis

¹**sap** \'sap\ *n* **1** : the fluid part of a plant; *esp* : a watery solution that circulates through a

higher plant and carries food and nutrients **2** : bodily health and vigor : VITALITY 3b **3** : a foolish person who is easily tricked or cheated

²**sap** *vb* **sapped; sap·ping** **1** : UNDERMINE **2** ⟨heavy waves *sapped* the seawall⟩ **2** : to weaken gradually ⟨illness *sapped* my strength⟩

sa·pi·ence \'sā-pē-ən(t)s, 'sap-ē-\ *n* : WISDOM 1a, SAGENESS

sa·pi·ent \'sā-pē-ənt, 'sap-ē-\ *adj* : ²WISE 1, DISCERNING — **sa·pi·ent·ly** *adv*

sap·ling \'sap-liŋ\ *n* : a young tree

sap·o·dil·la \ˌsap-ə-ˈdil-ə\ *n* : a tropical American evergreen tree with hard reddish wood, a rough-skinned brownish fruit with sweet flesh, and a milky sap that is the source of chicle

sap·phire \'saf-ˌī(ə)r\ *n* **1** : a clear bright blue precious stone **2** : a deep purplish blue [Middle English *safir* "sapphire," from early French *safir* (same meaning), from Latin *sapphirus* "sapphire," from Greek *sappheiros* (same meaning), perhaps of Semitic origin] — **sapphire** *adj*

sap·py \'sap-ē\ *adj* **sap·pi·er; -est** **1** : full of sap **2 a** : foolishly sentimental **b** : FOOLISH, SILLY — **sap·pi·ness** *n*

sap·ro·phyte \'sap-rə-ˌfīt\ *n* : a living thing (as a fungus) that lives on the dead or decaying material of plants and animals — **sap·ro·phyt·ic** \ˌsap-rə-ˈfit-ik\ *adj*

sap·suck·er \'sap-ˌsək-ər\ *n* : any of various North American woodpeckers that drill holes in trees in order to obtain sap and insects for food

sap·wood \-ˌwu̇d\ *n* : the young sap-containing and usually lighter-colored wood found just beneath the bark of a tree — compare HEARTWOOD

sa·ran \sə-ˈran\ *n* : a tough flexible plastic resin

sarape *variant of* SERAPE

sar·casm \'sär-ˌkaz-əm\ *n* : the use of words that mean the opposite of what the speaker really thinks in order to insult, show irritation, or be funny

Word History Anyone who has suffered from the sarcastic remarks of others will not be too surprised to learn that *sarcasm,* "a cutting remark," comes from a Greek verb, *sarkazein,* that literally means "to tear flesh like a dog." Very early, though, this Greek verb came to mean "to bite one's lip in rage," and "to gnash one's teeth," and finally "to sneer." The Greek noun *sarkasmos,* from which the English *sarcasm* comes, meant "a sneering or hurtful remark." But even today sarcasm is often described as sharp, cutting, or wounding, recalling in a faint way the original meaning of the Greek verb. [from French *sarcasme* or Latin *sarcasmos,* both meaning "sarcasm," from Greek *sarkasmos* "sarcasm," from *sarkazein* "to tear flesh, bite the lips in rage, sneer," from *sark-, sarx* "flesh"]

sar·cas·tic \sär-ˈkas-tik\ *adj* **1** : containing sarcasm ⟨a *sarcastic* remark⟩ **2** : being in the habit of using sarcasm ⟨a *sarcastic* person⟩ — **sar·cas·ti·cal·ly** \-ti-k(ə-)lē\ *adv*

sar·coph·a·gus \sär-ˈkäf-ə-gəs\ *n, pl* **-gi** \-ˌgī, -ˌjī, -ˌgē\ *also* **-gus·es** : a stone coffin

sar·dine \sär-ˈdēn\ *n, pl* **sardines** *also* **sardine** : any of various young or very small fish often preserved in oil for food

sar·don·ic \sär-ˈdän-ik\ *adj* : SCORNFUL, MOCKING — **sar·don·i·cal·ly** \-ˈdän-i-k(ə-)lē\ *adv*

sar·gas·so \sär-ˈgas-ō\ *n, pl* **-sos** **1** : SARGASSUM **2** : a mass of floating plants and especially sargassums

\ə\ **abut**	\au̇\ **out**	\i\ **tip**	\ȯ\ **saw**	\u̇\ **foot**
\ər\ **further**	\ch\ **chin**	\ī\ **life**	\ȯi\ **coin**	\y\ **yet**
\a\ **mat**	\e\ **pet**	\j\ **job**	\th\ **thin**	\yü\ **few**
\ā\ **take**	\ē\ **easy**	\ŋ\ **sing**	\th\ **this**	\yu̇\ **cure**
\ä\ **cot, cart**	\g\ **go**	\ō\ **bone**	\ü\ **food**	\zh\ **vision**

sar·gas·sum \sär-'gas-əm\ *n* : any of a genus of brown algae that have a leafy branching body and air bladders and that often grow in free-floating masses in the ocean

sa·ri *also* **sa·ree** \'sär-ē\ *n* : a garment worn by women in southern Asia that consists of a long cloth draped around the body and head or shoulder

sa·rong \sə-'ròŋ, -'räŋ\ *n* : a loose skirt made of a long strip of cloth wrapped loosely around the body and worn by men and women of the Malay island group and many Pacific islands

sar·sa·pa·ril·la \sas-(ə)pə-'ril-ə, särs-\ *n* **1** : the dried roots of any of several tropical American woody plants used especially as a flavoring; *also* : a plant that produces sarsaparilla **2** : a sweetened carbonated beverage flavored with sassafras and an oil from a birch

sar·to·ri·al \sär-'tōr-ē-əl, -'tòr-\ *adj* : of or relating to a tailor or tailored clothes — **sar·to·ri·al·ly** \-ē-ə-lē\ *adv*

¹**sash** \'sash\ *n* : a broad band (as of silk) worn around the waist or over the shoulder

²**sash** *n, pl* **sash** *also* **sash·es** **1** : the frame in which panes of glass are set in a window or door **2** : the movable part of a window

Sas·quatch \'sas-ˌkwach, -ˌkwäch\ *n* : BIGFOOT

sass \'sas\ *vb* : to reply to in a rude disrespectful way — **sass** *n*

sas·sa·fras \'sas-(ə)ˌfras\ *n* : a tall eastern North American tree that is related to the laurels and has fragrant yellow flowers and bluish black berries; *also* : its dried root bark used formerly in medicine or as a flavoring

sari

sassafras

sassy \'sas-ē\ *adj* **sass·i·er; -est** : given to back talk : IMPUDENT

sat *past and past participle of* SIT

Sa·tan \'sāt-ᵊn\ *n* : ¹DEVIL 1 [Middle English *Satan* "Satan," from early French *Satan* (same meaning), from Latin *Satan* (same meaning), from Greek *Satan* "Satan," from Hebrew *śāṭān* "adversary"] — **sa·tan·ic** \sə-'tan-ik, sā-\ *adj* — **sa·tan·i·cal·ly** \-'tan-i-k(ə)lē\ *adv*

satch·el \'sach-əl\ *n* : a small bag often with a shoulder strap

sate \'sāt\ *vb* **sat·ed; sat·ing** **1** : to fill especially with food beyond desire : GLUT **2** : to satisfy fully : SATIATE

sa·teen \sa-'tēn\ *n* : a glossy cotton fabric resembling satin

sat·el·lite \'sat-ᵊl-ˌīt\ *n* **1** : a follower resembling a slave **2 a** : a heavenly body orbiting another of larger size **b** : a man-made object or vehicle intended to orbit the earth, the moon, or another heavenly body **3** : a country controlled by a more powerful country — **satellite** *adj*

Word History Although it is now closely connected with the modern world of space exploration, *satellite* is actually a very old word. Its origin can be traced to the Latin word *satelles,* meaning "one who escorts or follows after an important person." This is also the original meaning of *satellite* in English. Because such heavenly bodies as the moon can be thought of as "escorts" of the planets they orbit, they also became known as *satellites.* The satellites of modern times made by humans got their name because they, like the moon, orbit the earth. [from early French *satellite* "a person who follows or escorts someone of importance," from Latin *satellit-, satelles* "escort, attendant"]

satellite dish *n* : a microwave dish for receiving usually television transmissions from an orbiting satellite

¹**sa·ti·ate** \'sā-sh(ē-)ət\ *adj* : filled to excess

²**sa·ti·ate** \'sā-shē-ˌāt\ *vb* **-at·ed; -at·ing** : to satisfy (as a need or desire) fully or to excess — **sa·ti·a·tion** \ˌsā-shē-'ā-shən, -sē-\ *n*

sa·ti·ety \sə-'tī-ət-ē\ *n* : the quality or state of being fed or gratified to or beyond fullness

sat·in \'sat-ᵊn\ *n* : a fabric (as of silk) with smooth shiny face and dull back — **satin** *adj* — **sat·iny** \'sat-nē, 'sat-ᵊn-ē\ *adj*

satin weave *n* : a weave that produces a fabric with a smooth face

sat·ire \'sa-ˌtī(ə)r\ *n* : something meant to make fun of and show the weaknesses of human nature or a particular person — **sa·tir·ic** \sə-'tir-ik\ *or* **sa·tir·i·cal** \-'tir-i-kəl\ *adj* — **sa·tir·i·cal·ly** \-i-k(ə)lē\ *adv*

sat·i·rist \'sat-ə-rəst\ *n* : a person who satirizes

sat·i·rize \'sat-ə-ˌrīz\ *vb* **-rized; -riz·ing** : to make fun of or show the weaknesses of by using satire

sat·is·fac·tion \ˌsat-əs-'fak-shən\ *n* **1 a** : the quality or state of being satisfied **b** : a cause of satisfaction **2** : something that makes up for a loss or injury **3** : ASSURANCE 2

sat·is·fac·to·ry \ˌsat-əs-'fak-t(ə-)rē\ *adj* : giving satisfaction — **sat·is·fac·to·ri·ly** \-t(ə-)rə-lē\ *adv* — **sat·is·fac·to·ri·ness** \-t(ə-)rə-nəs\ *n*

sat·is·fy \'sat-əs-ˌfī\ *vb* **-fied; -fy·ing** **1** : to do what has been agreed upon ⟨*satisfy* a contract⟩ **2 a** : to make happy : PLEASE ⟨the movie's ending *satisfied* everyone⟩ **b** : to meet the needs of : APPEASE ⟨*satisfied* their hunger⟩ **3** : CONVINCE ⟨*satisfied* that they are innocent⟩ **4** : FULFILL 2, MEET ⟨*satisfy* requirements⟩ **5** : to make true by fulfilling a condition ⟨values that *satisfy* an equation⟩ [Middle English *satisfien* "fulfill an obligation," from early French *satisfier* (same meaning), from Latin *satisfacere* (same meaning), from *satis* "enough" and *facere* "to do, make" — related to FASHION, PERFECT] — **sat·is·fi·able** \-ˌfī-ə-bəl\ *adj* — **sat·is·fy·ing·ly** \-ˌfī-iŋ-lē\ *adv*

sa·trap \'sā-ˌtrap, 'sa-\ *n* **1** : the governor of a division of ancient Persia **2** : a ruler who is controlled by a higher authority

sat·u·rate \'sach-ə-ˌrāt\ *vb* **-rat·ed; -rat·ing** **1** : to soak or fill with something to the point where no more can be absorbed or dissolved ⟨*saturate* water with salt⟩ **2** : to fill completely with something that penetrates : STEEP **synonyms** see SOAK

sat·u·rat·ed \'sach-ə-ˌrāt-əd\ *adj* **1** : full of moisture **2 a** : being a mixture that is unable to absorb or dissolve any more of a substance at a given temperature and pressure **b** : being a carbon compound having no double or triple bonds between carbon atoms ⟨*saturated* fats⟩

sat·u·ra·tion \ˌsach-ə-'rā-shən\ *n* **1** : the act or process of saturating **2** : the state of being saturated

Sat·ur·day \'sat-ərd-ē\ *n* : the seventh day of the week

Word History Several of the days of the week, such as Tuesday and Wednesday, get their English names from Germanic gods, but Saturday gets its name from a Roman one. *Saturnus* was the name of an important Roman god of agriculture, known in English as *Saturn.* The Old English word *sæterndæg,* "Saturn's day," came originally from the god's Latin name. The modern English *Saturday* comes from the Old English *sæterndæg.* [Old English *sæterndæg,* literally, "Saturn's day," derived from Latin *Saturnus* "Saturn"]

Sat·urn \'sat-ərn\ *n* : the planet sixth in order from the sun — see PLANET table

sat·ur·na·lia \ˌsat-ər-'nāl-yə\ *n sing or pl* **1** *cap* : the festival of the god Saturn celebrated in ancient Rome with feasting and wild revelry **2** : a celebration involving wild behavior : ORGY — **sat·ur·na·lian** \-yən\ *adj*

sat·ur·nine \'sat-ər-ˌnīn\ *adj* : SULLEN 1a

sa·tyr \'sāt-ər, 'sat-\ *n* **1** *often cap* : a forest god believed by the ancient Greeks to have the ears and tail of a horse or goat and to enjoy rowdy pleasures **2** : a man having strong sexual desire

1sauce \'sòs\ *n* **1** : a thick liquid that is eaten with or on food to add flavor ⟨a tangy pasta *sauce*⟩ ⟨ice cream with chocolate *sauce*⟩ **2** : boiled or canned fruit ⟨cranberry *sauce*⟩ **3** : rude or impolite language or actions

2sauce *vb* **sauced; sauc·ing 1** : to add sauce to : SEASON **2** : to be rude or impudent to

sauce·pan \'sò-ˌspan\ *n* : a small cooking pan with a handle

sau·cer \'sò-sər\ *n* **1** : a small round shallow dish in which a cup is set **2** : something like a saucer especially in shape

saucy \'sòs-ē\ *adj* **sauc·i·er; -est 1** : marked by bold rudeness or disrespect : IMPUDENT ⟨a *saucy* child⟩ ⟨a *saucy* answer⟩ **2** : 2SMART 6a, TRIM ⟨a *saucy* little hat⟩ — **sauc·i·ly** \-ə-lē\ *adv* — **sauc·i·ness** \-ē-nəs\ *n*

sau·er·bra·ten \'saù(-ə)r-ˌbrät-ᵊn\ *n* : beef soaked in vinegar and seasonings before being roasted

sau·er·kraut \'saù(-ə)r-ˌkraut\ *n* : finely cut cabbage fermented in brine [German, from *sauer* "sour" + *Kraut* "greens"]

sau·na \'saù-nə, 'sò-nə\ *n* : a Finnish steam bath

saun·ter \'sònt-ər, 'sänt-\ *vb* : to walk along in an idle or leisurely manner : STROLL — **saunter** *n* — **saun·ter·er** \-ər-ər\ *n*

sau·ri·an \'sòr-ē-ən\ *n* : any of a group of reptiles including the lizards and in older classifications the crocodiles and various extinct forms (as the dinosaurs) that look like lizards — **saurian** *adj*

sau·sage \'sò-sij\ *n* **1** : highly seasoned ground meat (as pork) usually stuffed in casings **2** : a roll of sausage meat in a casing

sau·té \sò-'tā, sō-\ *vb* **sau·téed** *or* **sau·téd; sau·té·ing** : to fry in a small amount of fat

sau·terne \sō-'tərn, sò-, -'te(ə)rn\ *n* : a semisweet golden table wine

1sav·age \'sav-ij\ *adj* **1** : not tamed ⟨*savage* beasts⟩ **2** : very cruel and unrestrained ⟨a *savage* beating⟩ **3** : not cultivated : WILD ⟨the *savage* wilderness⟩ **4** : not civilized ⟨*savage* customs⟩ **5** : very critical or harsh — **sav·age·ly** *adv* — **sav·age·ness** *n*

Word History In Latin the adjective *silvaticus*, a derivative of *silva*, "forest," meant "growing or living in the forest." Because forest life is wild, the adjective easily acquired the meaning "wild, uncultivated" in later Latin as well as in the spoken Latin of the declining Roman Empire. Medieval French inherited *silvaticus*, altered to *salvaticus*, as *salvage* or *sauvage*, which was borrowed into Middle English. Medieval French *sauvage* retained the source meanings "wild, uncultivated (of fruit)" and "untamed (of animals)." But it could also be applied to humans, in which case its meanings could range from "lacking civilization, barbarous" to "fierce, cruel." English *savage* has had all these senses at some point in its history. [Middle English *savage* "untamed, wild," from early French *salvage, savage,* (same meaning), from Latin *salvaticus,* an altered form of earlier *silvaticus* "of the woods, wild," from *silva* "woods, forest"]

2savage *n* **1** : a person belonging to a group with a low level of civilization **2** : a brutal person

sav·age·ry \'sav-ij-(ə-)rē\ *n, pl* **-ries 1** : savage disposition or action : CRUELTY **2** : the state of being savage

sa·van·na *also* **sa·van·nah** \sə-'van-ə\ *n* : a grassland (as of eastern Africa or northern South America) containing scattered trees

sa·vant \sa-'vänt, -'vän; sə-'vant, 'sav-ənt\ *n* **1** : SCHOLAR 2b **2** : a person who does not have normal intelligence but who has very unusual mental abilities that other people do not have [from French *savant,* a form of the verb

savoir "to know," from Latin *sapere* "to be wise, taste, have good taste" — related to INSIPID, 1SAGE]

1save \'sāv\ *vb* **saved; sav·ing 1 a** : to deliver from sin **b** : to rescue or deliver from danger or harm ⟨*saved* his friend from drowning⟩ **c** : to keep from injury, destruction, waste, or loss ⟨*save* the coat from damage by moths⟩ **d** : to store (data) in a computer or on a storage device (as a flash drive) **2 a** : to put aside for future use ⟨*save* a little for later⟩ **b** : to put aside money ⟨*saved* up for a new bike⟩ **3 a** : to make unnecessary : AVOID ⟨it will *save* your having to go back again⟩ **b** : to keep from being lost to an opponent ⟨*saved* the game⟩ **4 a** : to avoid unnecessary waste or expense : ECONOMIZE ⟨*save* on heat⟩ **b** : to spend less money ⟨buy now and *save*⟩ **c** : to spend less by ⟨*save* 25 percent⟩ [Middle English *saven* "to deliver from sin," from early French *salver* (same meaning), from Latin *salvare* "to save," from earlier *salvus* "safe, healthy" — related to SAFE, 3SAGE] — **sav·er** *n* — **save the day** : to solve or avert a problem ⟨her quick thinking *saved the day*⟩

2save *n* **1** : a play that prevents an opponent from scoring or winning **2** : the action of a relief pitcher in baseball in successfully protecting a team's lead; *also* : official credit for a save

3save *prep* : 1EXCEPT 2 ⟨no hope *save* one⟩

1sav·ing \'sā-viŋ\ *n* **1** : the act of rescuing **2 a** : something saved **b** *pl* : money saved over a period of time

2saving *prep* **1** : 2EXCEPT 2, SAVE **2** : without disrespect to

3saving *conj* : 3EXCEPT

savings account *n* : an account (as in a bank) on which interest is usually paid and from which withdrawals can be made

savings and loan association *n* : an association organized to hold savings of members and to invest chiefly in mortgage loans

savings bank *n* : a bank that receives and invests savings and pays interest to depositors

savings bond *n* : a registered U.S. bond that comes in values of $50 to $10,000

sav·ior *or* **sav·iour** \'sāv-yər\ *n* : one that saves from danger or destruction; *esp, cap* : MESSIAH 1b

1sa·vor \'sā-vər\ *n* **1** : the taste and odor of something **2** : something clearly marking one as different from others — **sa·vor·less** \-ləs\ *adj*

2savor *vb* **sa·vored; sa·vor·ing** \'sāv-(ə-)riŋ\ **1** : to have a specified smell or quality **2** : to give flavor to **3** : to taste or smell with pleasure : RELISH — **sa·vor·er** \'sā-vər-ər\ *n*

1sa·vory \'sāv-(ə-)rē\ *adj* : pleasing to the taste or smell — **sa·vor·i·ness** *n*

2sa·vo·ry \'sāv-(ə-)rē\ *n, pl* **-ries** : either of two European mints with leaves used in cooking as seasonings

1sav·vy \'sav-ē\ *vb* **sav·vied; sav·vy·ing** : COMPREHEND 1, UNDERSTAND

2savvy *n* : useful understanding : SHREWDNESS

3savvy *adj* **sav·vi·er; -est** : having a practical understanding or knowledge of something ⟨a *savvy* stock market investor⟩

1saw *past of* SEE

2saw \'sò\ *n* : a hand or power tool or a machine used to cut

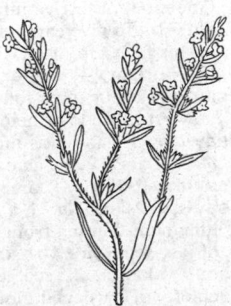

2savory

\ə\ abut	\aù\ out	\i\ tip	\ò\ saw	\ù\ foot
\ər\ further	\ch\ chin	\ī\ life	\òi\ coin	\y\ yet
\a\ mat	\e\ pet	\j\ job	\th\ thin	\yü\ few
\ā\ take	\ē\ easy	\ŋ\ sing	\th\ this	\yù\ cure
\ä\ cot, cart	\g\ go	\ō\ bone	\ü\ food	\zh\ vision

hard material and equipped usually with a tooth-edged blade

³saw *vb* **sawed** \'sȯd\; **sawed** *or* **sawn** \'sȯn\; **saw·ing** \'sȯ(-)iŋ\ : to cut or shape with a saw

⁴saw *n* : a common saying : PROVERB

saw·buck \'sȯ-ˌbək\ *n* **1** : SAWHORSE **2** *slang* : a 10-dollar bill

saw·dust \'sȯd-(ˌ)əst\ *n* : tiny particles (as of wood) made by a saw in cutting

sawed–off \'sȯ-ˌdȯf\ *adj* : having an end sawed off ⟨a *sawed-off* shotgun⟩

saw·fish \'sȯ-ˌfish\ *n* : any of several mostly tropical rays that resemble sharks but have a long flat snout with sharp toothlike structures along both edges

saw·fly \-ˌflī\ *n* : any of numerous insects related to the wasps and bees in which the female has a serrated organ used to cut holes in plants where she lays eggs

saw grass *n* : a sedge with leaves that have sharp jagged edges

saw·horse \'sȯ-ˌhȯ(ə)rs\ *n* : a frame on which wood is laid for sawing by hand

saw·mill \-ˌmil\ *n* : a mill or machine for sawing logs

saw–toothed \-ˈtütht\ *adj* : having an edge or outline like the teeth of a saw

saw·yer \'sȯ-yər, 'sȯi-ər\ *n* : a person who saws timber

sax \'saks\ *n* : SAXOPHONE

Sax·on \'sak-sən\ *n* : a member of a Germanic people conquering England with the Angles and Jutes in the 5th century A.D. and joining with them to form the Anglo-Saxon people

sax·o·phone \'sak-sə-ˌfōn\ *n* : a musical instrument of the woodwind class consisting of a usually curved metal tube with finger keys and a reed mouthpiece [named for Antoine "Adolph" *Sax* 1814–1894 a Belgian maker of musical instruments] — **sax·o·phon·ist** \-ˌfō-nəst\ *n*

saxophone

¹say \'sā\ *vb* **said** \'sed\; **say·ing** \'sā-iŋ\; **says** \'sez\ **1 a** : to express in words : STATE ⟨*say* what you mean using as few words as possible⟩ **b** : to state as opinion or belief : DECLARE ⟨*said* to be the best you can get⟩ **2 a** : ²UTTER 2, PRONOUNCE ⟨can't *say* more than three words without laughing⟩ **b** : RECITE 1, REPEAT ⟨*said* my prayers⟩ **3 a** : INDICATE 2, SHOW ⟨the clock *says* five minutes after ten⟩ **b** : to give expression to : COMMUNICATE ⟨the look on his face *said* it all⟩ **4** : SUPPOSE 1, ASSUME ⟨let's *say* you're right⟩ — **say·er** \'sā-ər\ *n*

²say *n* **1** : an expression of opinion ⟨had my *say*⟩ **2** : the power to decide or help decide ⟨had no *say* in the plans⟩

³say *adv* **1** : about as much or as many as ⟨is worth, *say*, ten dollars⟩ **2** : as an example ⟨pick any state, *say* Iowa⟩

say·ing \'sā-iŋ\ *n* : something frequently said : PROVERB

say–so \'sā-ˌsō\ *n* **1 a** : one's unsupported word **b** : a judgment coming from a person of authority **2** : a right of last decision : AUTHORITY

¹scab \'skab\ *n* **1** : scabies of domestic animals **2** : a crust chiefly of hardened blood that forms over and protects a wound **3** : a worker who takes the place of a striking worker **4** : a plant disease in which crusted spots form on stems or leaves

²scab *vb* **scabbed; scab·bing 1** : to become covered with a scab **2** : to act as a scab

scab·bard \'skab-ərd\ *n* : a protective case for a sword, dagger, or bayonet

scab·by \'skab-ē\ *adj* **scab·bi·er; -est 1 a** : covered with or full of scabs ⟨*scabby* skin⟩ **b** : diseased with scab ⟨a *scabby* plant⟩ **2** : CONTEMPTIBLE ⟨a *scabby* trick⟩

sca·bies \'skā-bēz\ *n, pl* **scabies** : an itch or mange caused by mites living as parasites under the skin

scads \'skadz\ *n pl* : a great quantity

scaf·fold \'skaf-əld *also* -ˌōld\ *n* **1 a** : an elevated platform built as a support for workers **b** : a platform on which a criminal is executed **2** : a supporting framework

scaf·fold·ing \'skaf-əl-diŋ, -ˌōl-\ *n* **1** : a system of scaffolds **2** : materials for scaffolds

scal·able \'skā-lə-bəl\ *adj* **1** : capable of being scaled **2** : capable of being easily expanded or improved on demand ⟨a *scalable* computer network⟩ — **scal·abil·i·ty** \ˌskā-lə-ˈbil-ət-ē\ *n*

¹sca·lar \'skā-lər, -ˌlär\ *adj* **1** : arranged like a ladder : GRADUATED ⟨*scalar* chain of authority⟩ **2 a** : able to be represented by a point on a scale ⟨a *scalar* quantity⟩ **b** : of or relating to a scalar ⟨*scalar* multiplication⟩

²scalar *n* **1** : a real number rather than a vector **2** : a quantity (as mass or time) that has a magnitude which can be described by a real number but no direction

sca·la·re \skə-ˈla(ə)r-ē, -ˈle(ə)r-, -ˈlär-\ *n* : ANGELFISH 2

scal·a·wag *or* **scal·ly·wag** \'skal-i-ˌwag\ *n* **1** : RASCAL 2 **2** : a white Southerner acting as a Republican in the time of reconstruction after the American Civil War

¹scald \'skȯld\ *vb* **1** : to burn with or as if with hot liquid or steam **2 a** : to cover with boiling water or steam **b** : to bring to a temperature just below the boiling point ⟨*scald* milk⟩ **3** : ¹SCORCH 1

²scald *n* : an injury to the body caused by scalding

scald·ing \'skȯl-diŋ\ *adj* **1** : causing the sensation of scalding or burning **2** : as hot as if boiling ⟨*scalding* water⟩ **3** : very hot **4** : BITING, SCATHING

¹scale \'skā(ə)l\ *n* **1 a** : either pan of a balance **b** : ¹BALANCE 1 — usually used in plural **2** : a device for weighing ⟨a bathroom *scale*⟩ [Middle English *scale* "bowl, pan or tray of a balance," of Norse origin]

²scale *vb* **scaled; scal·ing 1** : to weigh in scales **2** : to have a specified weight

³scale *n* **1 a** : any of the small stiff flat plates that form an outer covering on the body of some animals and especially fishes and reptiles **b** : a small thin plate that resembles an animal scale ⟨*scales* of mica⟩ ⟨the *scales* on a moth's wing⟩ **2** : a small thin flake (as of dandruff) shed from the skin **3** : a thin layer or coating formed especially on metal (as iron) ⟨boiler *scale*⟩ **4** : a special leaf that covers a bud of a seed plant **5 a** : SCALE INSECT **b** : a disease of plants caused by a scale insect [Middle English *scale* "a plate on the skin of a fish," from early French *escale* (same meaning); of Germanic origin] — **scale·less** \'skā(ə)l-ləs\ *adj* — **scale·like** \'skā(ə)l-ˌlīk\ *adj*

⁴scale *vb* **scaled; scal·ing 1** : to remove scale or the scales from ⟨*scale* a boiler⟩ ⟨*scale* fish⟩ **2** : to take off in scales or thin layers ⟨*scale* the bark off a tree⟩ **3** : to come off in scales or shed scales : FLAKE **4** : to throw a flat object so as to sail in air or skip on water

⁵scale *n* **1** : a series of tones going up or down in pitch with each tone having a fixed relationship to those above and below it **2 a** : a series of spaces marked by lines and used to measure distances or to register something (as the height of the mercury in a thermometer) **b** : a divided line on a map or chart indicating the length (as an inch) used to represent a larger unit of measure (as a mile) **c** : an instrument consisting of a strip (as of wood, plastic, or metal) with spaces on its surface that are evenly divided and numbered for measuring distances or amounts **3** : a series divided into classes **4** : the size of a picture, plan, or model of a thing compared to the size of the thing itself **5** : size in comparison ⟨do things on a large *scale*⟩ **6** : a rule by which something can be measured or judged [Middle English *scale* "ladder," from Latin *scala* "ladder, staircase," from earlier *scalae* (plural) "stairs, rungs, ladder"]

⁶scale *vb* **scaled; scal·ing 1** : to climb by or as if by a ladder ⟨*scale* a wall⟩ ⟨*scale* a cliff⟩ **2 a** : to arrange in order with the highest assigned one value (as a grade of A) and the lowest another value (as a grade of D) with the rest placed in groups between the two ⟨*scale* a test⟩ **b** : to measure by or as if by a scale **c** : to make, regulate, or estimate by a rule ⟨*scale* down the budget⟩ — **scal·er** *n*

scaled \ˈskā(ə)ld\ *adj* : furnished with or adjusted to a scale ⟨a *scaled* line⟩

scale insect *n* : any of numerous small insects related to aphids and including many destructive plant pests in which the males have wings, the females are scale-covered and are often permanently attached to a host plant, and the young suck the juices of plants

sca·lene \ˈskā-ˌlēn, skā-ˈlēn\ *adj* : having sides that are each a different length ⟨a *scalene* triangle⟩

scal·lion \ˈskal-yən\ *n* : GREEN ONION

¹scal·lop \ˈskäl-əp, ˈskal-\ *n* **1 a** : any of a family of marine mollusks with a two-part ribbed shell **b** : a muscle of the scallop used for food **2** : one of the two parts of a scallop shell **3** : one of a continuous series of rounded half-circles forming a border (as on lace)

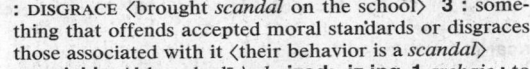
¹scallop 2

²scallop *vb* **1** : to bake in a sauce usually covered with seasoned bread or cracker crumbs ⟨*scalloped* potatoes⟩ **2** : to shape, cut, or make an edge in scallops

scallywag *variant of* SCALAWAG

¹scalp \ˈskalp\ *n* **1** : the part of the skin and flesh of the head usually covered with hair **2** : a part of the human scalp cut or torn from an enemy especially as a sign of victory

²scalp *vb* **1** : to remove the scalp from **2** : to buy and resell at much higher prices ⟨*scalp* theater tickets⟩ — **scalp·er** *n*

scal·pel \ˈskal-pəl *also* skal-ˈpel\ *n* : a small straight thin-bladed knife used especially in surgery

scaly \ˈskā-lē\ *adj* **scal·i·er; -est 1 a** : covered with, composed of, or resembling scale or scales **b** : FLAKY 2 ⟨*scaly* skin⟩ **2** : infested with scale insects ⟨*scaly* fruit⟩

scam \ˈskam\ *n* : a fraudulent or deceptive act or operation ⟨lost $500 in a business *scam*⟩ [origin unknown] — **scam** *vb*

scamp \ˈskamp\ *n* : RASCAL 2

scam·per \ˈskam-pər\ *vb* **scam·pered; scam·per·ing** \-p(ə-)riŋ\ : to run lightly and usually playfully about — **scamper** *n*

¹scan \ˈskan\ *vb* **scanned; scan·ning 1** : to read or mark verses so as to show stress and rhythm ⟨*scan* poetry⟩ **2 a** : to examine thoroughly ⟨*scanned* their faces for signs of anger⟩ **b** : to make a wide sweeping search of ⟨*scanning* the field with binoculars⟩ **c** : to look through or over hastily ⟨*scanned* the headlines⟩ **d** : to examine systematically (as by passing a beam of radiation over or through) in order to obtain data especially for display or storage ⟨*scanned* the patient's heart⟩ ⟨*scan* the photos into the computer⟩ **3** : to move across in successive lines to form an image on a cathode-ray tube ⟨the electron beam *scans* the face of the picture tube⟩

²scan *n* **1** : the act or process of scanning **2** : an image formed by scanning something: as **a** : a picture of the distribution of radioactive material in something (as a bodily organ) **b** : a picture of part of the body made (as by a computer) by combining separate pictures taken from different angles or of different sections

scan·dal \ˈskan-dᵊl\ *n* **1** : a crime against faith that causes another to sin **2** : loss of or damage to one's reputation

: DISGRACE ⟨brought *scandal* on the school⟩ **3** : something that offends accepted moral standards or disgraces those associated with it ⟨their behavior is a *scandal*⟩

scan·dal·ize \ˈskan-də-ˌlīz\ *vb* **-ized; -iz·ing 1** *archaic* : to speak of in a false or vicious way **2** : to shock the moral sense of ⟨their actions *scandalized* the neighbors⟩

scan·dal·ous \ˈskan-d(ə-)ləs\ *adj* **1** : harmful to one's reputation : DEFAMATORY ⟨denied the truth of the *scandalous* rumors⟩ **2** : SHOCKING ⟨*scandalous* behavior⟩ — **scan·dal·ous·ly** *adv*

scan·di·um \ˈskan-dē-əm\ *n* : a silvery white metallic element found together with other rare elements — see ELEMENT table

scan·ner \ˈskan-ər\ *n* : one that scans: as **a** : a device that senses recorded information **b** : a radio receiver that scans a range of frequencies for a signal **c** : a device that scans an image or document especially for use or storage on a computer ∼ **d** : a device for scanning a living body to collect medical information

scan·sion \ˈskan-chən\ *n* : the analysis of verse to show its meter

¹scant \ˈskant\ *adj* **1 a** : barely or scarcely enough; *esp* : not quite coming up to a certain measure ⟨a *scant* cup of milk⟩ **b** : lacking in size or quantity : MEAGER, SCANTY ⟨*scant* growth⟩ **2** : having a small or short supply ⟨*scant* of breath⟩ — **scant·ly** *adv* — **scant·ness** *n*

²scant *vb* : SKIMP 1, STINT

scant·ling \ˈskant-liŋ, -lən\ *n* : a small piece of lumber; *esp* : one of the upright pieces in the frame of a house

scanty \ˈskant-ē\ *adj* **scant·i·er; -est** : very small in size or amount ⟨*scanty* nourishment⟩ ⟨*scanty* bikinis⟩ **synonyms** see MEAGER — **scant·i·ly** \ˈskant-ᵊl-ē\ *adv* — **scant·i·ness** \ˈskant-ē-nəs\ *n*

scape·goat \ˈskāp-ˌgōt\ *n* : a person or thing taking the blame for others

scap·u·la \ˈskap-yə-lə\ *n, pl* **-lae** \-ˌlē, -ˌlī\ *or* **-las** : SHOULDER BLADE

scap·u·lar \ˈskap-yə-lər\ *n* **1** : a long wide band of cloth with an opening for the head worn front and back over the shoulders by monks **2** : a pair of small cloth squares joined by shoulder tapes and worn under the clothing on the breast and back especially for religious purposes

¹scar \ˈskär\ *n* **1** : a mark left (as on the skin) after injured tissue has healed **2** : a mark on a stem or branch where a leaf or fruit has separated **3** : a mark (as on furniture) resembling a scar **4** : a lasting injury from a bad experience

²scar *vb* **scarred; scar·ring 1** : to mark with or form a scar **2** : to do lasting injury to **3** : to become scarred

scar·ab \ˈskar-əb\ *n* **1** : any of a family of large stout beetles (as a dung beetle) **2** : an ornament or a gem made to represent a scarab; *esp* : one used in ancient Egypt as a symbol of eternal life

scarce \ˈske(ə)rs, ˈska(ə)rs\ *adj* **scarc·er; scarc·est** : lacking in quantity or number : not plentiful ⟨food is *scarce*⟩ **synonyms** see RARE — **scarce·ness** *n*

scarce·ly \ˈske(ə)rs-lē, ˈska(ə)rs-\ *adv* **1** : by a narrow margin : only just ⟨had *scarcely* made the train in time⟩ **2 a** : certainly not ⟨could *scarcely* tell them

scarab 1

\ə\ **abut**	\au̇\ **out**	\i\ **tip**	\ȯ\ **saw**	\u̇\ **foot**
\ər\ **further**	\ch\ **chin**	\ī\ **life**	\ȯi\ **coin**	\y\ **yet**
\a\ **mat**	\e\ **pet**	\j\ **job**	\th\ **thin**	\yü\ **few**
\ā\ **take**	\ē\ **easy**	\ŋ\ **sing**	\th̲\ **this**	\yu̇\ **cure**
\ä\ **cot, cart**	\g\ **go**	\ō\ **bone**	\ü\ **food**	\zh\ **vision**

they were wrong⟩ **b** : probably not ⟨could *scarcely* have chosen a better leader⟩

scar·ci·ty \'sker-sət-ē, 'skar-\ *n, pl* **-ties** : the quality or state of being scarce : a very small supply

¹**scare** \'ske(ə)r, 'ska(ə)r\ *vb* **scared; scar·ing** **1** : to frighten suddenly : ALARM **2** : to become scared

²**scare** *n* **1** : a sudden fright **2** : a widespread state of alarm : PANIC

scare·crow \'ske(ə)r-ˌkrō, 'ska(ə)r-\ *n* : an object usually suggesting a human figure that is set up to scare birds away from crops

scare up *vb* : to find or get together with much labor or difficulty ⟨managed to *scare up* the money⟩

¹**scarf** \'skärf\ *n, pl* **scarves** \'skärvz\ *or* **scarfs** **1** : a broad band of cloth worn about the shoulders, around the neck, over the head, or about the waist **2** : RUNNER 5b

²**scarf** *vb* : ³SCOFF 1 ⟨*scarfed* down my sandwich⟩

scar·i·fy \'skar-ə-ˌfī, 'sker-\ *vb* **-fied; -fy·ing** : to make scratches or small cuts in

scar·let \'skär-lət\ *n* **1** : scarlet cloth or clothes **2** : a bright red — **scarlet** *adj*

scarlet fever *n* : a contagious disease caused by a bacterium and characterized by fever, swelling, pain in the nose, throat, and mouth, and a red rash

scarlet runner bean *n* : a tropical American high-climbing bean with large bright red flowers and red and black seeds

scarlet tanager *n* : an American tanager of which the male is scarlet with black wings during the breeding season and the female is olive

scarp \'skärp\ *n* **1** : a line of cliffs produced by faulting or erosion **2** : a low steep slope along a beach caused by wave erosion — **scarped** *adj*

scar tissue *n* : connective tissue forming a scar

scary \'ske(ə)r-ē, 'ska(ə)r-\ *adj* **scar·i·er; -est** **1** : causing fright : ALARMING ⟨a *scary* movie⟩ **2** : easily scared : TIMID **3** : feeling alarm or fright : SCARED, FRIGHTENED ⟨*scary* feeling⟩ — **scar·i·ly** \-ə-lē\ *adv*

¹**scat** \'skat\ *vb* **scat·ted; scat·ting** **1** : to go away quickly — often used to drive away an animal (as a cat) **2** : to move fast : SCOOT

²**scat** *n* : the feces deposited by an animal ⟨bear *scat*⟩

³**scat** *n* : jazz singing with meaningless syllables

⁴**scat** *vb* **scat·ted; scat·ting** : to sing by making up meaningless syllables to go with the music

¹**scathe** \'skāth\ *n* : HARM 1, INJURY — **scathe·less** \-ləs\ *adj*

²**scathe** *vb* **scathed; scath·ing** **1** : to do harm to : INJURE; *esp* : to injure by fire : SCORCH, SEAR **2** : to attack with very harsh accusations

scath·ing \'skā-thiŋ\ *adj* : painfully harsh ⟨a *scathing* look⟩ — **scath·ing·ly** \-thiŋ-lē\ *adv*

scat·ter \'skat-ər\ *vb* **1** : to cause to separate widely ⟨wind *scattered* the dry leaves⟩ **2** : to place or leave here and there ⟨*scattered* their toys all over the house⟩ **3** : to sow widely and without pattern **4** : to separate and go in different directions ⟨the crowd *scattered*⟩ **5** : to occur or fall without pattern ⟨lakes *scattered* everywhere in the hills⟩

scat·ter·brain \'skat-ər-ˌbrān\ *n* : a silly careless person incapable of concentration — **scat·ter·brained** \-ˌbrānd\ *adj*

¹**scat·ter·ing** \'skat-ə-riŋ\ *n* **1** : an act or process in which something scatters or is scattered **2** : something scattered; *esp* : a small number or amount placed or found here and there ⟨a *scattering* of visitors⟩

²**scattering** *adj* **1** : going in various directions **2** : found or placed far apart and in no pattern

scatter rug *n* : THROW RUG

scav·enge \'skav-ənj, -inj\ *vb* **scav·enged; scav·eng·ing** : to collect usable things from what has been discarded

scav·en·ger \'skav-ən-jər\ *n* **1** : someone or something that scavenges **2** : an organism (as a vulture or hyena) that usually feeds on dead or decaying matter

Word History In the U.S., *scavenger* is not the title of a particular occupation, but it is in Great Britain. There it means "street cleaner," which is a use close to the original meaning. In English towns in the Middle Ages, a tax was placed on goods offered for sale by merchants who came from another town for market day. This tax was called a *skawage*, from an early French dialect word *escauwage*, meaning "a showing or inspection (of goods)." The *skawage* gave the local merchants an advantage and discouraged outsiders from selling in the town. In this way it was like our modern-day *tariff*, or "tax on imports." The official whose duty it was to collect this tax was called the *skawager*. This word was later spelled *scavager* and then *scavenger*. When the towns came to need someone to keep the streets clean, this duty also became the job of the scavenger. The word *scavenger* is now used in the British Isles for all street cleaners. By the time British colonists started towns in America, the skawage tax was no longer collected, and the word *scavenger* came to be used here in its more general sense of "someone who collects usable things from what has been discarded." [from earlier *scavager*, from early French *skawageour* "one who collects a tax on goods sold by merchants from another town," from an early French dialect word *escauver* "to inspect"]

scavenger hunt *n* : a party contest in which players are sent out usually in pairs to obtain without buying unusual objects within a fixed length of time

sce·nar·io \sə-'nar-ē-ˌō, -'ner-, -'när-\ *n, pl* **-i·os** **1 a** : an outline of a play **b** : the text of an opera **2** : SCREENPLAY **3** : a sequence of events especially when imagined

sce·nar·ist \sə-'nar-əst, -'ner-, -'när-\ *n* : a writer of scenarios

scene \'sēn\ *n* **1 a** : a division of an act during which there is no change of scene or break in time **b** : a single situation or conversation in a play ⟨the love *scene*⟩ **c** : a small part of a motion picture or a television program **2 a** : a stage setting ⟨change *scenes*⟩ **b** : a view or sight that looks like a picture ⟨a winter *scene*⟩ **3** : the place of an event or action : LOCALE ⟨the *scene* of the crime⟩ **4** : a display of anger or misconduct ⟨made a *scene* when accused of the crime⟩ **5 a** : area of activity ⟨the music *scene*⟩ **b** : SITUATION 3 ⟨the *scene* got serious when the police arrived⟩ — **behind the scenes** **1** : out of public view; *also* : in secret ⟨decisions reached *behind the scenes*⟩ **2** : in a position to see or control the hidden workings ⟨the lawyer *behind the scenes*⟩

scen·ery \'sēn-(ə-)rē\ *n* **1** : the painted scenes or hangings and accessories used on a theater stage **2** : a view or landscape resembling a beautiful painting ⟨mountain *scenery*⟩ **3** : one's usual surroundings ⟨needed a change of *scenery*⟩

scene–steal·er \'sēn-ˌstē-lər\ *n* : an actor who draws attention though he or she is not intended to be the center of attraction

sce·nic \'sē-nik\ *adj* **1** : of or relating to stage scenery **2** : of or relating to natural scenery ⟨a *scenic* route⟩ **3** : representing an action or event in pictured form ⟨*scenic* wallpaper⟩

¹**scent** \'sent\ *n* **1 a** : an odor left by an animal **b** : a particular and usually agreeable odor **2 a** : sense of smell ⟨a keen *scent*⟩ **b** : power of detection : NOSE 5 **3** : a course of pursuit or discovery ⟨thrown off the *scent*⟩ **4** : ¹HINT 1, INKLING ⟨a *scent* of trouble⟩ **5** : ¹PERFUME 2 **6** : a mixture prepared for use as a lure in hunting or fishing

²**scent** *vb* **1 a** : to become aware of or follow through the sense of smell ⟨the dog *scented* a rabbit⟩ **b** : to get a hint of ⟨*scent* trouble⟩ **2** : to fill with an odor : PERFUME ⟨*scent* a handkerchief⟩

scent·ed *adj* : having scent; *esp* : filled with perfume

scep·ter \'sep-tər\ *n* **1** : a baton carried by a ruler as an emblem of authority **2** : authority of an empire or a ruler : SOVEREIGNTY — **scep·tered** \-tərd\ *adj*

scep·tic, scep·ti·cal, scep·ti·cism *chiefly British variant of* SKEPTIC, SKEPTICAL, SKEPTICISM

¹**sched·ule** \'skej-ü(ə)l, -əl, *Canadian also* 'shej-, *British usually* 'shed-yü(ə)l\ *n* **1 a** : a written or printed list or catalog ⟨a *schedule* of social events⟩ **b** : TIMETABLE ⟨a plane *schedule*⟩ **c** : a *schedule* for completion of the school⟩ **2** : ¹PROGRAM 3, AGENDA ⟨my *schedule* for tomorrow⟩

²**schedule** *vb* **sched·uled; sched·ul·ing 1** : to place in a schedule ⟨*schedule* a meeting⟩ **2** : to make a schedule of ⟨*scheduled* my income and debts⟩

sche·mat·ic \ski-'mat-ik\ *adj* : of, relating to, or forming a scheme, plan, or diagram : DIAGRAMMATIC — **sche·mat·i·cal·ly** \-'mat-i-k(ə-)lē\ *adv*

sche·ma·tize \'skē-mə-ˌtīz\ *vb* **-tized; -tiz·ing** : to form or form into a scheme or regular arrangement

¹**scheme** \'skēm\ *n* **1** : a pictorial sketch or outline **2** : a brief statement in an outline, table, or list **3** : a plan or program of action ⟨a new *scheme* for better insurance coverage⟩; *esp* : a sly or secret one ⟨a *scheme* to seize control of the territory⟩ **4** : a regular or organized design, arrangement, or pattern ⟨the color *scheme* of a room⟩ ⟨your whole *scheme* of life⟩ **synonyms** see PLAN

²**scheme** *vb* **schemed; schem·ing 1** : to form a scheme for **2** : to form plans; *esp* : to engage in a plot — **schem·er** *n*

schem·ing \'skē-miŋ\ *adj* : being in the habit of forming schemes; *esp* : SNEAKY, DECEPTIVE

schil·ling \'shil-iŋ\ *n* **1** : the former basic unit of money of Austria until 2002 **2** : a coin representing one schilling

schism \'siz-əm, 'skiz-\ *n* **1 a** : DIVISION 6, SEPARATION **b** : lack of harmony : DISCORD **2 a** : division in or separation from a church or religious body **b** : the offense of promoting schism

¹**schis·mat·ic** \siz-'mat-ik, skiz-\ *n* : one who creates or takes part in schism

²**schismatic** *adj* : of, relating to, or guilty of schism

schist \'shist\ *n* : a metamorphic rock that can be split along nearly parallel planes

schizo·phre·nia \ˌskit-sə-'frē-nē-ə\ *n* : a serious mental illness that is a psychosis and is characterized by a distorted view and understanding of the real world, by greatly reduced ability to carry out one's daily tasks, and by abnormal ways of thinking, feeling, and behaving

¹**schizo·phren·ic** \ˌskit-sə-'fren-ik\ *adj* : of, relating to, or affected with schizophrenia

²**schizophrenic** *n* : a person affected with schizophrenia

schle·miel *also* **shle·miel** \shlə-'mē(ə)l\ *n* : an unlucky clumsy person : CHUMP

schmaltz *also* **schmalz** \'shmȯlts\ *n* : sentimental music or art — **schmaltzy** \'shmȯlt-sē\ *adj*

schmooze *or* **shmooze** \'shmüz\ *vb* **schmoozed** *or* **shmoozed; schmooz·ing** *or* **shmooz·ing** : to converse informally : CHAT; *also* : to chat in a friendly and persuasive manner especially so as to gain favor, business, or connections [Yiddish *shmuesn* "to chat," from Hebrew *shĕmū'ôth* "news, rumor"] — **schmooz·er** \'shmü-zər\ *n*

schmoozy \'shmü-zē\ *adj* : of, relating to, characterized by, or given to schmoozing ⟨a *schmoozy* salesclerk⟩

schmuck \'shmək\ *n, slang* : a stupid or foolish person

schnau·zer \'shnaủt-sər, 'shnaủ-zər, snaủ-\ *n* : any of a German breed of dogs with a long head, pointed ears, and wiry coat

scepter 1

schol·ar \'skäl-ər\ *n* **1** : a person who attends a school or studies under a teacher : PUPIL **2 a** : a person who has done advanced study in a special area **b** : a learned person **3** : a holder of a scholarship — **schol·ar·ly** *adj*

schol·ar·ship \'skäl-ər-ˌship\ *n* **1** : money given (as by a college) to a student to help pay for further education **2** : the character, qualities, or achievements of a scholar **synonyms** see KNOWLEDGE

scho·las·tic \skə-'las-tik\ *adj* : of or relating to schools or scholars — **scho·las·ti·cal·ly** \-ti-k(ə-)lē\ *adv*

¹**school** \'skül\ *n* **1 a** : a place or establishment for teaching and learning ⟨public *schools*⟩ ⟨a music *school*⟩ **b** : a faculty or division within an institution for higher education devoted to teaching, study, and research in a particular area of knowledge : COLLEGE ⟨*school* of law⟩ ⟨graduate *school*⟩ **2 a** : a session of school ⟨missed *school* yesterday⟩ **b** : SCHOOLHOUSE **c** : the students or students and teachers of a school ⟨the whole *school* was at the assembly⟩ **3** : a group of persons having the same opinions and beliefs or accepting the same methods or leaders; *also* : the shared opinions, beliefs, or methods of such a group

Word History The English word *school* comes from the Greek *scholē*. The original meaning of *scholē* was "leisure." To the Greeks it seemed natural that one's leisure should be spent learning and thinking. *Scholē* therefore came to mean not only "leisure" but also "a place for learning." Many Greeks were later employed by the Romans as teachers, and the Romans borrowed the Greek word as *schola*. The Latin word *schola* in time came into Old English as *scōl*. [Old English *scōl* "a place for learning," from Latin *schola* (same meaning), from Greek *scholē* "leisure, discussion, lecture, school"]

²**school** *vb* **1** : to teach or drill in a specific skill or area of knowledge ⟨well *schooled* in languages⟩ **2** : to discipline or make used to something ⟨*school* oneself in patience⟩

³**school** *n* : a large number of water-dwelling animals of one kind (as fish) swimming together

school·bag \'skül-ˌbag\ *n* : a bag for carrying schoolbooks and school supplies

school board *n* : a board in charge of local public schools

school·book \'skül-ˌbůk\ *n* : a school textbook

school·boy \-ˌbȯi\ *n* : a boy attending school

school bus *n* : a vehicle for transporting children to and from school

school·child \'skül-ˌchīld\ *n* : a child attending school

school·fel·low \-ˌfel-ō\ *n* : SCHOOLMATE

school·girl \-ˌgər(-ə)l\ *n* : a girl attending school

school·house \-ˌhaủs\ *n* : a building used as a school

school·ing \'skül-iŋ\ *n* **1** : instruction in school : EDUCATION **2** : the cost of going to school

school·marm \'skül-ˌmä(r)m\ *or* **school·ma'am** \-ˌmäm, -ˌmam\ *n* : a woman who is a schoolteacher especially in a rural or small-town school

school·mas·ter \-ˌmas-tər\ *n* : a man who teaches school

school·mate \-ˌmāt\ *n* : a companion at school

school·mis·tress \-ˌmis-trəs\ *n* : a woman who teaches school

school·room \-ˌrüm, -ˌrüm\ *n* : CLASSROOM

school·teach·er \-ˌtē-chər\ *n* : a person who teaches school

school·time \-ˌtīm\ *n* : the time for beginning a session of school or during which school is held

school·work \-ˌwərk\ *n* : lessons done in classes at school or assigned to be done at home

\ə\ **abut**		\aủ\ **out**	\i\ **tip**	\ȯ\ **saw**	\ủ\ **foot**
\ər\ **further**		\ch\ **chin**	\ī\ **life**	\ȯi\ **coin**	\y\ **yet**
\a\ **mat**		\e\ **pet**	\j\ **job**	\th\ **thin**	\yü\ **few**
\ā\ **take**		\ē\ **easy**	\ŋ\ **sing**	\th\ **this**	\yủ\ **cure**
\ä\ **cot, cart**		\g\ **go**	\ō\ **bone**	\ü\ **food**	\zh\ **vision**

school·yard \-ˌyärd\ *n* : the playground of a school

schoo·ner \ˈskü-nər\ *n* **1** : a ship with a fore-and-aft rig and two or more masts **2** : a large tall glass (as for beer) **3** : PRAIRIE SCHOONER

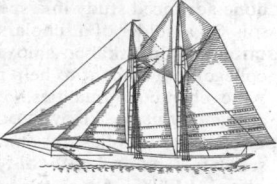

schooner 1

schot·tische \ˈshät-ish, shä-ˈtēsh\ *n* : a slow dance with steps similar to those of a polka; *also* : music for this dance

schuss \ˈshus, ˈshüs\ *vb* : to ski directly down a slope at high speed — **schuss** *n*

schwa \ˈshwä\ *n* **1** : a vowel that is not stressed and is the usual sound of the first and last vowels of the English word *America* **2** : the symbol ə commonly used for a schwa and sometimes also for a similarly pronounced stressed vowel (as in *cut*)

sci·at·i·ca \sī-ˈat-i-kə\ *n* : pain along the course of a sciatic nerve especially in the back of the thigh; *also* : pain in or near the hips

sciatic nerve \sī-ˌat-ik-\ *n* : a nerve that runs down the back of the thigh and is the largest nerve in the body

sci·ence \ˈsī-ən(t)s\ *n* **1 a** : an area of knowledge that is an object of study **b** : something (as a sport or technique) that may be studied or learned like a science ⟨have it down to a *science*⟩ **c** : any of the natural sciences (as biology, physics, or chemistry) **2** : knowledge covering general truths or the operation of general laws especially as obtained and tested through the scientific method [Middle English *science* "the state of knowing, knowledge," from early French *science* (same meaning), from Latin *scientia* (same meaning), from *scient-, sciens* "knowing," from *scire* "to know" — related to CONSCIOUS, NICE, OMNISCIENT; see *Word History* at NICE]

science fair *n* : an exhibition of science projects typically prepared and presented by schoolchildren

science fiction *n* : fiction that deals with the influence of real or imagined science on society or individuals — **sci·ence–fic·tion·al** \ˈsī-ən(t)s-ˈfik-shnəl, -shən-ᵊl\ *adj*

sci·en·tif·ic \ˌsī-ən-ˈtif-ik\ *adj* : of, relating to, or exhibiting the methods or rules of science — **sci·en·tif·i·cal·ly** \-ˈtif-i-k(ə-)lē\ *adv*

scientific method *n* : the rules and procedures for the pursuit of knowledge involving the finding and stating of a problem, the collection of facts through observation and experiment, and the making and testing of ideas that need to be proven right or wrong

scientific notation *n* : a system of writing numbers as the product of a number between 1 and 10 and a power of 10 ⟨999.9 is expressed in *scientific notation* as 9.999×10^2⟩

sci·en·tist \ˈsī-ənt-əst\ *n* : a person skilled in science and especially natural science : a scientific investigator

sci–fi \ˈsī-ˈfī\ *n* : SCIENCE FICTION — **sci–fi** *adj*

scim·i·tar \ˈsim-ət-ər, -ə-ˌtär\ *n* : a sword with a curved blade used in the past especially in the Middle East and western Asia

scin·til·late \ˈsint-ᵊl-ˌāt\ *vb* **-lat·ed; -lat·ing 1** : to give off sparks **2** : to flash or gleam as if throwing off sparks ⟨eyes *scintillating* with anger⟩ — **scin·til·lant** \-ᵊl-ənt\ *adj* — **scin·til·la·tion** \ˌsint-ᵊl-ˈā-shən\ *n*

sci·on \ˈsī-ən\ *n* **1** : a living part (as a bud or stem) that is cut from a plant and joined to another plant in grafting **2 a** : ²DESCENDANT 1, CHILD **b** : HEIR 1

¹scis·sor \ˈsiz-ər\ *n* : SCISSORS

²scissor *vb* **scis·sored; scis·sor·ing** \-(ə-)riŋ\ : to cut with scissors or shears ⟨*scissored* the paper into strips⟩

scis·sors \ˈsiz-ərz\ *n sing or pl* **1** : a cutting instrument having two blades whose cutting edges slide past each other **2** : a gymnastic feat in which the leg movements suggest the opening and closing of scissors

scissors kick *n* : a swimming kick in which the legs move like scissors

scle·ra \ˈskler-ə\ *n* : the dense fibrous white or bluish white tissue that forms the outer covering of the back five-sixths of the eye and is replaced in front by the transparent cornea with which it is continuous

scle·ro·sis \sklə-ˈrō-səs\ *n* : an abnormal hardening of a tissue or body part (as arteries or muscles) that occurs in several serious diseases — compare MULTIPLE SCLEROSIS

¹scle·rot·ic \sklə-ˈrät-ik\ *adj* **1** : being or relating to the sclera **2** : of, relating to, or affected with sclerosis

²sclerotic *n* : SCLERA

sclerotic coat *n* : SCLERA

¹scoff \ˈskäf, ˈskȯf\ *n* : an expression of scorn or mockery

²scoff *vb* : JEER, RIDICULE — **scoff·er** *n*

³scoff *vb* **1** : to eat greedily ⟨*scoffed* dinner⟩ **2** : ¹SNATCH 2 ⟨*scoffed* up the free gifts⟩

¹scold \ˈskōld\ *n* : a person who scolds constantly

²scold *vb* **1** : to find fault noisily or angrily **2** : to criticize severely or angrily

sco·lex \ˈskō-ˌleks\ *n, pl* **sco·li·ces** *also* **sco·le·ces** \-lə-ˌsēz\ : the head of a tapeworm

sco·li·o·sis \ˌskō-lē-ˈō-səs\ *n, pl* **-o·ses** \-ˌsēz\ : an abnormal sideways curving of the spine

sconce \ˈskän(t)s\ *n* : a lamp or candlestick or group of candlesticks fastened to a wall

scone \ˈskōn, ˈskän\ *n* : a quick bread baked on a griddle or in an oven

¹scoop \ˈsküp\ *n* **1 a** : a large shovel (as for shoveling coal) **b** : a tool or utensil shaped like a shovel for digging into a soft substance and lifting out a portion **c** : a round utensil with a handle for dipping out soft food (as ice cream) **d** : a small tool for cutting or gouging **2** : an act or the action of scooping : a motion made with or as if with a scoop **3 a** : the amount held by a scoop ⟨a *scoop* of ice cream⟩ **b** : a hole made by scooping **4 a** : information of immediate interest ⟨what's the *scoop*⟩ **b** : the reporting of a news story ahead of competitors — **scoop·ful** \-ˌfu̇l\ *n*

sconce

²scoop *vb* **1** : to take out or up with or as if with a scoop **2** : to make hollow **3** : to report a news story ahead of — **scoop·er** *n*

scoot \ˈsküt\ *vb* **1** : to go suddenly and swiftly : DART **2** : to slide especially while seated ⟨*scoot* over⟩ — **scoot** *n*

scoot·er \ˈsküt-ər\ *n* **1** : a child's vehicle consisting of a narrow base between a front and a back wheel and guided by a handle attached to the front wheel **2** : MOTOR SCOOTER

¹scope \ˈskōp\ *n* **1** : space or opportunity for action or thought ⟨full *scope* for expression⟩ **2** : area or amount included, reached, or viewed : RANGE ⟨a subject broad in *scope*⟩ [from Italian *scopo* "aim, purpose, goal," from Greek *skopos* "watcher, goal, aim" — related to BISHOP, EPISCOPAL, HOROSCOPE; see *Word History* at BISHOP]

²scope *n* : any of various instruments for viewing: as **a** : MICROSCOPE **b** : ¹TELESCOPE **c** : OSCILLOSCOPE [by shortening]

-scope *combining form* : means for viewing : instrument for viewing ⟨kaleido*scope*⟩ [derived from Greek *skopos* "watcher, goal, aim"]

sco·pol·amine \skō-ˈpäl-ə-ˌmēn\ *n* : a poisonous substance that is found in some plants of the nightshade family and that is used in medicine (as to prevent nausea or dilate the pupil of the eye)

¹scorch \'skȯrch\ *vb* **1** : to burn on the surface **2** : to burn so as to dry, wilt, or turn brown

²scorch *n* **1** : a result of scorching **2** : a browning of plant tissues usually caused by disease or heat

scorched earth *n* : land stripped of anything that could be of use to an invading enemy force

scorch·er \'skȯr-chər\ *n* : someone or something that scorches; *esp* : a very hot day

¹score \'skō(ə)r, 'skȯ(ə)r\ *n, pl* **scores 1** *or pl* **score a** : TWENTY **b** : a group of 20 things — often used in combination with a cardinal number ⟨five*score*⟩ **2** : a line made with or as if with a sharp instrument **3** : a duty or injury kept in mind for later action ⟨had some old *scores* to settle⟩ **4** : ¹REASON 1b, GROUND ⟨you have nothing to worry about on that *score*⟩ **5** : the complete written music showing all of the individual parts of a large piece (as a symphony) **6 a** : a number expressing accomplishment (as in a game or a test) or worth (as of a product) ⟨had a *score* of 80 out of a possible 100⟩ **b** : a record of points made by competing teams or players ⟨the final *score* was 4–3⟩ **c** : an act (as a goal, run, or touchdown) that gains points in any of various games or contests **7** : the facts of a situation ⟨we won't know what the *score* is until the laboratory results are in⟩ — **score·less** \-ləs\ *adj*

²score *vb* **scored; scor·ing 1 a** : to set down in an account : RECORD **b** : to keep score in a game or contest **2** : to mark with lines, grooves, scratches, or notches **3** : BERATE, SCOLD **4 a** : to make or cause to make a score in or as if in a game : TALLY ⟨*score* a run⟩ **b** : ACHIEVE 2, WIN ⟨*scored* a big success⟩ **5** : ¹GRADE 3, MARK **6** : to arrange (a musical composition) for performance — **scor·er** *n* — **score points** : to gain favor, status, or advantage

score·board \'skō(ə)r-,bō(ə)rd, 'skȯ(ə)r-,bȯ(ə)rd\ *n* : a large board for displaying the score of a game or match

score·card \-,kärd\ *n* : a card for recording the score (as of a game)

score·keep·er \-,kē-pər\ *n* : a person appointed to record the score during the progress of a game or contest

sco·ria \'skōr-ē-ə, 'skȯr-\ *n, pl* **-ri·ae** \-ē-,ē, -ē-,ī\ : rough cindery lava

¹scorn \'skȯ(ə)rn\ *n* **1** : a feeling of anger and disgust **2** : someone or something very much disliked

²scorn *vb* **1** : to show scorn for **2** : to reject or dismiss because of scorn : DISDAIN ⟨*scorned* local traditions⟩ — **scorn·er** *n*

scorn·ful \'skȯrn-fəl\ *adj* : feeling or showing scorn **synonyms** see CONTEMPTUOUS — **scorn·ful·ly** \-fə-lē\ *adv*

Scor·pio \'skȯr-pē-,ō\ *n* **1** : a group of stars between Libra and Sagittarius usually pictured as a scorpion **2 a** : the eighth sign of the zodiac — see ZODIAC table **b** : a person whose sign of the zodiac is Scorpio

scor·pi·on \'skȯr-pē-ən\ *n* : any of an order of invertebrates that are arachnids and that have a long jointed body and a slender tail with a poisonous stinger at the end

Scot \'skät\ *n* : a person born or living in Scotland

scotch \'skäch\ *vb* **1** *archaic* : to injure so as to make temporarily harmless **2** : to stamp out : CRUSH; *esp* : to put an end to by showing the untruth of ⟨*scotch* a rumor⟩

¹Scotch \'skäch\ *adj* : ¹SCOTTISH

²Scotch *n* **1** : SCOTS **2 Scotch** *pl* : the people of Scotland **3** *often not cap* : whiskey made in Scotland especially from barley

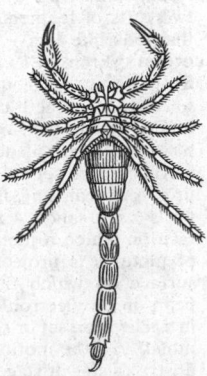
scorpion

Scotch·man \'skäch-mən\ *n* : SCOTSMAN

Scotch terrier *n* : SCOTTISH TERRIER

Scotch·wom·an \'skäch-,wùm-ən\ *n* : SCOTSWOMAN

sco·ter \'skōt-ər\ *n, pl* **scoters** *or* **scoter** : any of several ducks of coasts of Eurasia, Canada, and the U.S.

scot–free \'skät-'frē\ *adj* : completely free from duty, harm, or penalty ⟨get off *scot-free*⟩ [from earlier *scot* "money owed"]

scoter

Scot·land Yard \,skät-lən(d)-'yärd\ *n* : the detective division of the London area police

¹Scots \'skäts\ *adj* : ¹SCOTTISH

²Scots *n* : the English language of Scotland

Scots·man \'skät-smən\ *n* : a person born or living in Scotland

Scots·wom·an \-,swùm-ən\ *n* : a woman born or living in Scotland

scot·tie \'skät-ē\ *n* **1** *cap* : SCOTCHMAN **2** : SCOTTISH TERRIER

¹Scot·tish \'skät-ish\ *adj* : of, relating to, or characteristic of Scotland, the people of Scotland, or the Scots language

²Scottish *n* : ²SCOTS

Scottish terrier *n* : any of an old Scottish breed of terrier with short legs, a long head with small ears that stand straight up, a broad deep chest, and a thick rough coat

scoun·drel \'skaùn-drəl\ *n* : a mean or wicked person : VILLAIN — **scoun·drel·ly** \-drə-lē\ *adj*

¹scour \'skaù(ə)r\ *vb* **1** : to move about or through quickly especially in search ⟨*scoured* the woods for the missing child⟩ **2** : to examine thoroughly and rapidly ⟨*scoured* the legal documents⟩

²scour *vb* **1 a** : to rub hard with something rough in order to clean **b** : to remove by rubbing hard and washing ⟨*scour* spots from the stove⟩ **2** : to free from foreign substances or impurities by or as if by washing **3** : to wear away (as by water) : ERODE ⟨a stream *scouring* its banks⟩ — **scour·er** *n*

³scour *n* : an action or result of scouring

¹scourge \'skərj\ *n* **1** : ²WHIP 1, LASH **2** : someone or something that is an instrument of punishment or criticism **3** : AFFLICTION 2

²scourge *vb* **scourged; scourg·ing 1** : to whip severely : FLOG **2** : to cause severe suffering to : DEVASTATE

scouring rush *n* : HORSETAIL

¹scout \'skaùt\ *vb* **1** : to go about and observe in search of information : RECONNOITER **2 a** : to make a search ⟨*scout* about for firewood⟩ **b** : to find by searching ⟨*scouted* up the necessary supplies⟩ [Middle English *scouten* "to explore an area for information," from early French *escouter* "to listen," from Latin *auscultare* "to listen"]

²scout *n* **1 a** : one sent to obtain information and especially to survey in preparation for military action in war **b** : a person who searches for talented newcomers ⟨a baseball *scout*⟩ **2** : the act or an instance of scouting : RECONNAISSANCE **3** *often cap* **a** : BOY SCOUT **b** : GIRL SCOUT **4** : ²INDIVIDUAL 2, PERSON ⟨you're a good *scout*⟩

³scout *vb* **1** : DERIDE, MOCK **2** : to reject as foolish [of Scandinavian origin]

scout·ing \'skaùt-iŋ\ *n* **1** : the action of one that scouts **2**

\ə\ **abut**	\aù\ **out**	\i\ **tip**	\ȯ\ **saw**	\ù\ **foot**
\ər\ **further**	\ch\ **chin**	\ī\ **life**	\ȯi\ **coin**	\y\ **yet**
\a\ **mat**	\e\ **pet**	\j\ **job**	\th\ **thin**	\yü\ **few**
\ā\ **take**	\ē\ **easy**	\ŋ\ **sing**	\th\ **this**	\yù\ **cure**
\ä\ **cot, cart**	\g\ **go**	\ō\ **bone**	\ü\ **food**	\zh\ **vision**

often cap : the activities of the various Boy Scout and Girl Scout groups

scout·mas·ter \'skaut-ˌmas-tər\ *n* : the leader of a band of scouts and especially of a troop of Boy Scouts

scow \'skau\ *n* : a large flat-bottomed boat with broad square ends used chiefly for transporting sand, gravel, or refuse

¹**scowl** \'skau(ə)l\ *vb* **1** : to make a frowning expression of displeasure **2** : to exhibit or express with a scowl — **scowl·er** *n* — **scowl·ing·ly** \'skau-liŋ-lē\ *adv*

²**scowl** *n* : an expression of displeasure on the face : FROWN

¹**scrab·ble** \'skrab-əl\ *vb* **scrab·bled; scrab·bling** \-(ə-)liŋ\ **1** : to scratch or scrape about frantically with hands or paws **2** : ¹SCRAMBLE 2 **3** : to struggle by or as if by scraping or scratching ⟨*scrabble* for a living⟩ — **scrab·bler** \-(ə-)lər\ *n*

²**scrabble** *n* : an act or instance of scrabbling

scrag \'skrag\ *n* : a lean person or animal

scrag·gly \'skrag-(ə-)lē\ *adj* **scrag·gli·er; -est** : of rough or uneven outline : RAGGED, UNKEMPT ⟨a *scraggly* beard⟩

scrag·gy \'skrag-ē\ *adj* **scrag·gi·er; -est** **1** : ¹ROUGH 3b, JAGGED ⟨*scraggy* cliffs⟩ **2** : being lean and long : SCRAWNY

scram \'skram\ *vb* **scrammed; scram·ming** : to go away at once ⟨*scram,* you're not wanted⟩

¹**scram·ble** \'skram-bəl\ *vb* **scram·bled; scram·bling** \-b(ə-)liŋ\ **1 a** : to move with urgency or panic **b** : to move or climb hastily on all fours **2** : to strive or struggle for something ⟨*scramble* for front seats⟩ **3 a** : to toss or mix together : JUMBLE **b** : to cook the mixed whites and yolks of eggs by stirring them while frying — **scram·bler** \-b(ə-)lər\ *n*

²**scramble** *n* **1** : a scrambling movement **2** : a disordered mess

¹**scrap** \'skrap\ *n* **1** *pl* : pieces of discarded or leftover food **2** : a small bit : FRAGMENT **3** : things discarded as worthless [Middle English *scrap* "discarded bits of food"; of Norse origin]

²**scrap** *vb* **scrapped; scrap·ping** **1** : to break up into scrap **2** : to discard as worthless

³**scrap** *n* : ¹QUARREL 2, FIGHT [origin unknown]

⁴**scrap** *vb* **scrapped; scrap·ping** : ²QUARREL 2, FIGHT — **scrap·per** *n*

scrap·book \'skrap-ˌbuk\ *n* : a book of blank pages for miscellaneous items (as clippings and pictures)

¹**scrape** \'skrāp\ *vb* **scraped; scrap·ing** **1 a** : to remove by repeated strokes of an edged tool ⟨*scrape* off rust⟩ **b** : to clean or smooth by rubbing **2 a** : to rub or cause to rub so as to make a harsh noise **b** : to damage or injure by dragging or rubbing against a rough surface ⟨*scraped* his knee on the pavement⟩ **3 a** : to gather with difficulty and little by little ⟨*scrape* together a few dollars⟩ **b** : to barely get by ⟨*scraped* through with low grades⟩ — **scrap·er** *n*

²**scrape** *n* **1 a** : the act or process of scraping **b** : a sound, mark, or injury made by scraping **2** : a bow made with a pulling back of the foot **3 a** : a disagreeable situation **b** : ALTERCATION, FIGHT

scrap·ing \'skrā-piŋ\ *n* : something scraped off or together — usually used in plural

scrap·ple \'skrap-əl\ *n* : a seasoned mush of meat scraps and cornmeal set in a mold and served in fried slices

scrap·py \'skrap-ē\ *adj* **scrap·pi·er; -est** **1** : QUARRELSOME **2** : having an aggressive and determined spirit — **scrap·pi·ness** *n*

¹**scratch** \'skrach\ *vb* **1** : to scrape, rub, or injure with or as if with the claws or nails **2** : to act on (a desire) — used with *itch* ⟨*scratch* the itch to travel⟩ **3** : to make a living by hard work and saving **4 a** : to cancel or erase by or as if by drawing a line through **b** : to withdraw (an entry) from competition **5** : to write or draw especially hastily

or carelessly : SCRAWL **6** : to scrape or rub oneself lightly especially to relieve itching **7** : to make a thin harsh sound ⟨this pen *scratches*⟩ — **scratch·er** *n* — **scratch one's back** : to do a favor for with the expectation of like return — **scratch one's head** : to be or become confused — **scratch the surface** : to make a modest effort or start

²**scratch** *n* **1** : a mark (as a line) or injury made by scratching; *also* : a slight wound **2** : the sound of scratching **3** : the line from which competitors start in a race **4** : satisfactory state or performance ⟨not up to *scratch*⟩ — **from scratch** **1** : from a point at which nothing has been done ahead of time ⟨made a new plan *from scratch*⟩ **2** : without using a prepared mixture of ingredients ⟨bake a cake *from scratch*⟩

scratch hit *n* : a batted ball that is not hit hard but that results in a base hit

scratch test *n* : a test that is used to determine if a person is allergic to a substance and is made by rubbing some of that substance into small scratches on the skin

scratchy \'skrach-ē\ *adj* **scratch·i·er; -est** **1** : likely to scratch or make sore or raw : PRICKLY ⟨*scratchy* woolens⟩ **2** : making a scratching noise **3** : marked or made with scratches ⟨a *scratchy* surface⟩ ⟨*scratchy* handwriting⟩ **4** : uneven in quality : RAGGED ⟨played a *scratchy* game of golf⟩ **5** : somewhat sore ⟨a *scratchy* throat⟩ — **scratch·i·ness** *n*

scrawl \'skrol\ *vb* : to write or draw awkwardly, hastily, or carelessly : SCRIBBLE — **scrawl** *n* — **scrawly** \'skro-lē\ *adj*

scraw·ny \'skro-nē\ *adj* **scraw·ni·er; -est** : poorly nourished : SKINNY — **scraw·ni·ness** *n*

¹**scream** \'skrēm\ *vb* **1** : to cry out, sound, or utter loudly and shrilly **2** : to move with great speed **3 a** : to produce or give a vivid, startling, or alarming effect or expression **b** : to protest, demand, or complain forcefully — **scream·er** *n*

²**scream** *n* **1** : a loud shrill long cry or noise ⟨*screams* of terror⟩ **2** : a very funny person or thing

scream·ing \'skrē-miŋ\ *adj* **1** : noticeable as if by screaming ⟨*screaming* headlines⟩ ⟨a *screaming* red⟩ **2** : very funny **3** : extremely fast or powerful ⟨the speedboat was a *screaming* machine⟩ — **scream·ing·ly** *adv*

¹**screech** \'skrēch\ *n* **1** : a shrill harsh cry usually expressing pain or terror **2** : a sound like a screech ⟨the *screech* of brakes⟩

²**screech** *vb* **1** : to cry out usually in terror or pain **2** : to make a sound like a screech ⟨the car *screeched* to a halt⟩ **synonyms** see SHOUT — **screech·er** *n*

screech·ing \'skrē-chiŋ\ *adj* : SUDDEN 1a ⟨her career came to a *screeching* halt⟩

screech owl *n* : either of two small North American owls that have two tufts of feathers on the head that look like ears

¹**screen** \'skrēn\ *n* **1** : a device used to hide or protect ⟨a window *screen*⟩ **2** : something that serves to shelter, protect, or conceal ⟨a *screen* of fighter planes⟩ **3** : a network of wire set in a frame and used for separating different-sized parts (as of sand) **4 a** : a flat surface on which a picture or series of pictures is projected **b** : the surface on which the image appears in an electronic display (as in a television set or computer terminal) **5** : the motion-picture industry ⟨a star of stage and *screen*⟩

²**screen** *vb* **1** : to guard from injury or danger **2 a** : to shelter, protect, or separate with or as

screech owl

if with a screen **b** : to pass through a screen to separate the parts of different sizes ⟨*screen* gravel⟩ **c** : to remove by or as if by a screen ⟨*screens* out much harmful radiation⟩ **d** : to examine in order to separate into groups or to select or eliminate ⟨carefully *screened* everyone applying for the job⟩ **3** : to provide with a screen ⟨*screen* a porch⟩ **4** : to project on a screen ⟨*screen* a movie⟩

screen·ing \'skrē-niŋ\ *n* : a net (as of metal or plastic) used especially for screens

screen·play \'skrēn-ˌplā\ *n* : the written form of a story prepared for film production

screen saver *n* : a computer program that usually displays various images on the screen of a computer that is on but not in use

screen·writ·er \-ˌrīt-ər\ *n* : a writer of screenplays

¹**screw** \'skrü\ *n* **1 a** : a simple machine consisting of a solid cylinder with a winding groove around it and a correspondingly grooved hollow cylinder into which it fits **b** : a nail-shaped or rod-shaped metal piece with a winding groove used for fastening solid pieces together **2 a** : something having the shape of a screw : SPIRAL **b** : the act of screwing tight : TWIST **c** : a screw-shaped device (as a corkscrew) **3** : PROPELLER — **screw·like** \-ˌlīk\ *adj* — **have a screw loose** : to be mentally unbalanced ⟨I must *have a screw looose* for agreeing to do this⟩

²**screw** *vb* **1 a** : to attach, fasten, or close with a screw **b** : to operate, tighten, or adjust with a screw **c** : to turn or twist on a screwlike thread **2** : to twist out of shape ⟨a face *screwed* up in pain⟩ **3** : to increase in amount ⟨trying to *screw* up enough nerve to ask⟩ — **screw·er** *n*

screw around *vb* **1** : to waste time with unproductive activity : DALLY **2** : to have sexual relations with someone outside of a marriage

¹**screw·ball** \'skrü-ˌbȯl\ *n* **1** : a baseball pitch that moves away from a straight path in a direction opposite to a curve **2** : a crazy person : NUT

²**screwball** *adj* : ²ZANY, NUTTY

screw·driv·er \'skrü-ˌdrī-vər\ *n* : a tool for turning screws

screw eye *n* : a screw having a head in the form of a loop

screw propeller *n* : PROPELLER

screw-up \'skrü-ˌəp\ *n* **1** : one who screws up **2** : ²BOTCH, BLUNDER

screw up *vb* **1** : to tighten, fasten, or lock by or as if by a screw ~ **2 a** : ¹BOTCH **b** : to cause to act in a crazy or confused way

screw·worm \'skrü-ˌwərm\ *n* : the larva of a blowfly of the warm parts of America that develops in the wounds or sores of mammals and may cause disease or death; *also* : the blowfly itself

screwy \'skrü-ē\ *adj* **screw·i·er; -est 1** : oddly different and unfamiliar ⟨knew something was *screwy*⟩ **2** : CRAZY 1, INSANE ⟨completely *screwy* people⟩ — **screw·i·ness** *n*

scrib·ble \'skrib-əl\ *vb* **scrib·bled; scrib·bling** \-(ə-)liŋ\ : to write or draw hastily or carelessly [Middle English *scriblen* "to write hurriedly or carelessly," from Latin *scribillare* (same meaning), from earlier *scribere* "to write" — related to SCRIBE] — **scribble** *n* — **scrib·bler** \'skrib-(ə-)lər\ *n*

¹**scribe** \'skrīb\ *n* **1** : a scholar of the Jewish law in New Testament times **2 a** : a public secretary or clerk **b** : a person who copies manuscripts [Middle English *scribe* "one of a class of scholars and copiers of the Scriptures in ancient Israel," from Latin *scriba* "official writer," from *scribere* "to write" — related to CIRCUMSCRIBE, DESCRIPTION, SCRIBBLE, SCRIPTURE, SHROVE TUESDAY]

²**scribe** *vb* **scribed; scrib·ing** : to mark or make by cutting or scratching with a pointed instrument

¹**scrim·mage** \'skrim-ij\ *n* **1** : a minor battle : SKIRMISH **2** : the play between two football teams that begins with the snap of the ball **3** : practice play between a team's squads or a practice game between two teams

²**scrimmage** *vb* **scrim·maged; scrim·mag·ing** : to take part in a scrimmage — **scrim·mag·er** *n*

scrimp \'skrimp\ *vb* **1** : to make too small or short : SKIMP **2** : ECONOMIZE 1

scrim·shaw \'skrim-ˌshȯ\ *n* : carved or engraved articles made originally by American whalers usually from baleen or whale teeth [origin unknown]

scrip \'skrip\ *n* **1** : a document showing that the holder has the right to something (as stock or land) **2** : paper money made by the government for temporary use in an emergency

script \'skript\ *n* **1 a** : something written : TEXT **b** : the written text of a stage play, screenplay, or broadcast **2** : letters and figures written by hand : HANDWRITING

scrip·to·ri·um \skrip-'tōr-ē-əm, -'tȯr-\ *n, pl* **-ria** \-ē-ə\ : a copying room in a monastery for use by scribes in the Middle Ages

scrip·tur·al \'skrip-chə-rəl, 'skrip-shrəl\ *adj* : of, relating to, or agreeing with a sacred writing; *esp* : BIBLICAL — **scrip·tur·al·ly** \-ē\ *adv*

scrip·ture \'skrip-chər\ *n* **1 a** *cap* : the books of the Old and New Testaments or of either of them : BIBLE — often used in plural **b** *often cap* : a portion of writing from the Bible **2** : the sacred writings of a religion [Middle English *scripture, Scripture* "the books of the Bible," from Latin *scriptura* (same meaning), from earlier *scriptura* "the act or product of writing," from *scriptus,* past participle of *scribere* "to write" — related to SCRIBE]

script·writ·er \'skrip-ˌtrīt-ər\ *n* : a person who writes scripts (as screenplays for television or movies)

scriv·en·er \'skriv-(ə-)nər\ *n* : a professional copyist or writer : SCRIBE

scrod \'skräd\ *n* : a young fish (as a cod or haddock); *esp* : one split and boned for cooking

¹**scroll** \'skrōl\ *n* **1** : a roll of paper or animal skin that has been prepared as a writing surface; *esp* : one on which something is written or engraved **2** : an ornament resembling a loosely or partly rolled scroll

²**scroll** *vb* : to move (as text or graphics) up or down or across a display screen as if by unrolling a scroll

scroll·work \-ˌwərk\ *n* : ornamental work (as in metal or wood) having a scroll or scrolls

scrooge \'skrüj\ *n, often cap* : a miserly person

scro·tum \'skrōt-əm\ *n, pl* **scro·ta** \'skrōt-ə\ *or* **scro·tums** : the pouch on the outside of the body that in most male mammals contains the testes

scrounge \'skraunj\ *vb* **scrounged; scroung·ing 1** : to collect by or as if by rummaging ⟨*scrounge* around for firewood⟩ **2** : to get by coaxing or persuading ⟨*scrounge* a dollar from a friend⟩ — **scroung·er** *n*

¹**scrub** \'skrəb\ *n* **1 a** : a thick growth of small or stunted shrubs or trees **b** : an area of land covered with scrub **2** : a domestic animal of mixed or unknown parentage and usually inferior build **3** : a person of small size or low social rank **4** : a player not belonging to the first string — **scrub** *adj*

²**scrub** *vb* **scrubbed; scrub·bing** : to rub hard in cleaning or washing ⟨*scrub* clothes⟩ — **scrub·ber** *n*

³**scrub** *n* : an act or instance of scrubbing

scrub·by \'skrəb-ē\ *adj* **scrub·bi·er; -est 1** : of small size

¹scroll 1

or poor quality : STUNTED ⟨*scrubby* cattle⟩ **2** : covered with or consisting of scrub ⟨a *scrubby* hill⟩

scrub·land \'skrəb-ˌland\ *n* : land covered with scrub

scruff \'skrəf\ *n* : the skin of the back of the neck : NAPE

scruffy \'skrəf-ē\ *adj* **scruff·i·er; -est** : dirty or shabby in appearance ⟨a *scruffy* beard⟩

scrump·tious \'skrəm(p)-shəs\ *adj* : DELIGHTFUL, EXCELLENT; *esp* : DELICIOUS — **scrump·tious·ly** *adv*

scrunch \'skrənch\ *vb* **1 a** : ¹CRUNCH 1, CRUSH ⟨*scrunch* a paper cup⟩ **b** : to make or move with a crunching sound ⟨cinders *scrunching* underfoot⟩ **2 a** : to draw or squeeze together tightly **b** : CRUMPLE 1 ⟨*scrunch* up a piece of paper⟩ **c** : to cause (as one's facial features) to draw together ⟨*scrunched* up his nose⟩ **3** : CROUCH, HUNCH

scrunch·ie *or* **scrunchy** \'skrən-chē\ *n, pl* **scrunchies** : a fabric-covered elastic used for holding back hair (as in a ponytail)

¹**scru·ple** \'skrü-pəl\ *n* **1** — see MEASURE table **2** : a tiny part or quantity [Middle English *scriple* "a unit of weight," from Latin *scrupulus* "small sharp stone"]

²**scruple** *n* **1** : a moral consideration or rule of conduct that makes one uneasy or makes action difficult **2** : a sense of guilt felt when one does wrong ⟨acted without *scruple*⟩ **synonyms** see QUALM

Word History Having a sharp pebble in your shoe can be painful enough to keep you from walking until you remove it. That fact was well known by the ancient Romans, who regularly wore sandals. *Scruple* comes from the Latin word *scrupulus,* which originally meant "a small sharp stone." The ancient Romans also used *scrupulus* to refer to a feeling or thought that might keep a person from doing something that was not quite right. It seemed to them to affect the conscience in the same way that a tiny stone in the shoe would keep a person from being able to walk. This second meaning of *scrupulus* is the one that still survives in our English word *scruple.* [from early French *scruple* "scruple," from Latin *scrupulus* "scruple, a small sharp stone"]

³**scruple** *vb* **scru·pled; scru·pling** \-p(ə-)liŋ\ : to have scruples

scru·pu·lous \'skrü-pyə-ləs\ *adj* **1** : full of or having scruples : STRICT **2** : being very exact : PAINSTAKING ⟨working with *scrupulous* care⟩ — **scru·pu·lous·ly** *adv* — **scru·pu·lous·ness** *n*

scru·ti·nize \'skrüt-ᵊn-ˌīz\ *vb* **-nized; -niz·ing** : to examine very closely : INSPECT

scru·ti·ny \'skrüt-ᵊn-ē, 'skrüt-nē\ *n, pl* **-nies** : a close inspection : EXAMINATION

scu·ba \'sk(y)ü-bə\ *n* : equipment used for breathing while swimming underwater [*self-contained underwater breathing apparatus*]

scuba diver *n* : one who swims underwater with scuba gear — **scuba dive** *vb*

¹**scud** \'skəd\ *vb* **scud·ded; scud·ding** : to move or run swiftly ⟨clouds *scudding* across the sky⟩

²**scud** *n* **1** : the act of scudding **2** : light clouds driven by the wind

¹**scuff** \'skəf\ *vb* **1** : to scrape the feet in walking : SHUFFLE **2** : to become rough or scratched through wear

²**scuff** *n* : a noise or act of scuffing

scuf·fle \'skəf-əl\ *vb* **scuf·fled; scuf·fling** \-(ə-)liŋ\ **1** : to struggle roughly at close quarters **2 a** : to move with a scuff : SCURRY **b** : to scuff one's feet — **scuffle** *n*

¹**scull** \'skəl\ *n* **1 a** : an oar used at the stern of a boat to drive it forward with a side-to-side motion **b** : one of a pair of short oars for use by one person **2** : a boat driven by one or more pairs of sculls

²**scull** *vb* : to move a boat by a scull or sculls — **scull·er** *n*

scul·lery \'skəl-(ə-)rē\ *n, pl* **-ler·ies** : a room for cleaning and storing dishes and utensils, washing vegetables, and similar work

scul·lion \'skəl-yən\ *n* : a kitchen helper

scul·pin \'skəl-pən\ *n, pl* **sculpins** *also* **sculpin** **1** : any of numerous spiny large-headed usually scaleless fishes with fanlike fins **2** : a fish of the southern California coast that has poisonous spines on the fin on the back and is caught for food and sport

sculpin

sculpt \'skəlpt\ *vb* : ²SCULPTURE, CARVE

sculp·tor \'skəlp-tər\ *n* : a person who makes sculptures

sculp·tress \'skəlp-trəs\ *n* : a woman who is a sculptor

¹**sculp·ture** \'skəlp-chər\ *n* **1** : the act, process, or art of carving or cutting hard substances, modeling plastic substances, or casting melted metals into works of art **2 a** : work produced by sculpture **b** : a piece of such work — **sculp·tur·al** \-chə-rəl, -shrəl\ *adj*

²**sculpture** *vb* **sculp·tured; sculp·tur·ing** \'skəlp-chə-riŋ, 'skəlp-shriŋ\ **1** : to make sculptures **2** : to shape by or as if by carving or molding

scum \'skəm\ *n* **1 a** : matter that has risen to or formed on the surface of a liquid often as a slimy covering — compare POND SCUM 2 **b** : a film formed on a solid or gelatinous object ⟨soap *scum*⟩ **2** : a loathsome or worthless person or group of people — **scum·my** \'skəm-ē\ *adj*

scup·per \'skəp-ər\ *n* : an opening above the upper deck in the side of a boat through which water drains overboard

scup·per·nong \'skəp-ər-ˌnóŋ, -ˌnän\ *n* : a large yellowish green plum-flavored grape

scur·ri·lous \'skər-ə-ləs, 'skə-rə-\ *adj* **1** : vulgar and evil ⟨*scurrilous* crooks⟩ **2** : containing indecent words or harsh abuse ⟨*scurrilous* attacks on the senator⟩ — **scur·ri·lous·ly** \'skər-ə-ləs-lē, 'skə-rə-\ *adv*

scur·ry \'skər-ē, 'skə-rē\ *vb* **scur·ried; scur·ry·ing** : to move briskly : SCAMPER — **scurry** *n*

¹**scur·vy** \'skər-vē\ *n* : a disease caused by lack of vitamin C and characterized by loosening of the teeth, softening of the gums, and bleeding under the skin

²**scurvy** *adj* **scur·vi·er; -est** : CONTEMPTIBLE, MEAN ⟨a *scurvy* practice⟩

scutch·eon \'skəch-ən\ *n* : ESCUTCHEON

¹**scut·tle** \'skət-ᵊl\ *n* : a metal pail for carrying coal [Middle English *scutel* "a shallow basket for carrying things," from Latin *scutella* "drinking bowl"]

²**scuttle** *n* : a small opening (as in the deck of a ship or the roof of a house) with a lid or cover; *also* : its lid [Middle English *skotell* "lid of a scuttle"]

³**scuttle** *vb* **scut·tled; scut·tling** **1** : to sink by cutting holes through the bottom or sides ⟨*scuttle* a ship⟩ **2** : to put an end to by a deliberate act ⟨*scuttle* a conference⟩

⁴**scuttle** *vb* **scut·tled; scut·tling** \'skət-liŋ, -ᵊl-iŋ\ : SCURRY [probably a combination of ¹*scud* and ²*shuttle*]

⁵**scuttle** *n* **1** : a quick scuffing pace **2** : a short swift run

scut·tle·butt \'skət-ᵊl-ˌbət\ *n* : ¹RUMOR 1, GOSSIP

scythe \'sīth, sī\ *n* : a tool that has a curved blade on a long curved handle and is used for mowing grass or grain by hand

sea \'sē\ *n* **1 a** : a great body of salty water that covers much of the earth; *also* : the waters of the earth **b** : a body of salt water not

scythe

as large as an ocean ⟨the Mediterranean *Sea*⟩ **c** : OCEAN 1 **d** : an inland body of water either salt or fresh ⟨the *Sea* of Galilee⟩ **2** : rough water ⟨a high *sea* swept the deck⟩ **3** : something suggesting the sea (as in great size or depth) ⟨a golden *sea* of wheat⟩ **4** : a life involving marine travel ⟨hoped to make a career of the *sea*⟩ **5** : ²MARE — **sea** *adj* — **at sea 1** : on the sea; *esp* : on a sea voyage **2** : without landmarks for guidance : LOST, BEWILDERED — **to sea** : to or on the open sea

sea anemone *n* : any of several invertebrate sea animals that are coelenterates, look like flowers, and have clusters of brightly colored tentacles around the mouth

sea·bag \'sē-ˌbag\ *n* : a canvas bag used especially by a sailor for gear (as clothes)

sea bass *n* : any of numerous marine fishes that are usually smaller and more active than the related groupers; *esp* : a food and sport fish of the Atlantic coast of the U.S.

sea·bed \'sē-ˌbed\ *n* : the floor of a sea or ocean

sea·bird \'sē-ˌbərd\ *n* : a bird (as a gull or an albatross) that lives on or near the open ocean

sea·board \'sē-ˌbō(ə)rd, -ˌbò(ə)rd\ *n* : SEACOAST; *also* : the country bordering a seacoast — **seaboard** *adj*

sea·borg·i·um \sē-'bòr-gē-əm\ *n* : a short-lived radioactive element that is produced artificially — see ELEMENT table [from G.T. *Seaborg*, 1912–1999, American chemist]

sea breeze *n* : a cooling daytime breeze blowing inland from the sea

sea·coast \'sē-ˌkōst\ *n* : the shore of the sea

sea cow *n* : MANATEE, DUGONG

sea cucumber *n* : any of a class of invertebrate sea animals that are echinoderms with a long tough flexible muscular body resembling a cucumber and having tentacles surrounding the mouth at one end

sea devil *n* : MANTA RAY

sea dog *n* : an experienced sailor

sea fan *n* : any of various invertebrate sea animals that form fan-shaped colonies and are coelenterates related to the corals and sea anemones

sea·far·er \'sē-ˌfar-ər, -ˌfer-\ *n* : a person who travels over the ocean : MARINER

sea·far·ing \'sē-ˌfar-iŋ, -ˌfer-\ *n* : a traveling over the sea as work or recreation — **seafaring** *adj*

sea·floor \-ˌflō(ə)r, -ˌflò(ə)r\ *n* : SEABED

sea·food \-ˌfüd\ *n* : edible marine fish and shellfish

sea·go·ing \-ˌgō-iŋ\ *adj* : designed or used for sea travel

sea green *n* **1** : a medium green or bluish green **2** : a medium yellow green

sea gull *n* : a gull that lives near the sea

sea horse *n* **1** : a mythical animal half horse and half fish **2** : a small fish with bony plates covering its body and a head that looks like a horse's head

¹seal \'sē(ə)l\ *n, pl* **seals** *also* **seal 1** : any of numerous marine mammals that live mostly in cold regions, feed especially on fish, mate and give birth to young on land, and use short webbed flippers to swim and dive **2 a** : the soft dense fur of a seal **b** : leather made from the skin of a seal [Old English *seolh* "seal (marine animal)"]

²seal *vb* : to hunt seals

³seal *n* **1 a** : something (as a pledge) that makes safe or secure ⟨under *seal* of secrecy⟩ **b** : a device with a cut or raised design or figure that can be pressed or stamped into paper or wax to form a mark (as for certifying a signature) **c** : a usually ornamental adhesive stamp that may be used to close a letter or package ⟨Christmas *seals*⟩ **2 a** : something that is at-

sea horse 2

tached to a closed container and has to be broken in order to open the container **b** : a tight and perfect closing ⟨test the *seal* of the jars⟩ [Middle English *sele, seel* "pledge, guarantee," from early French *seal, sel* (same meaning), from Latin *sigillum* "seal," literally, "small sign, small image," from *signum* "mark, sign, image" — related to ¹SIGN]

⁴seal *vb* **1** : to mark with a seal ⟨*seal* a deed⟩ **2** : to close with or as if with a seal ⟨the sheriff *sealed* the area⟩ ⟨ice *sealed* the ships into the harbor⟩ **3** : to decide finally

sea lamprey *n* : a lamprey of the Atlantic coast that is also found in the Great Lakes and that attaches to and feeds on other fishes with its round sucking mouth

sea·lane \'sē-ˌlān\ *n* : an established sea route

sea lavender *n* : any of a genus of mostly coastal plants that produce clusters of tiny pink to purplish flowers

sea legs *n pl* : bodily adjustment to the motion of a ship at sea indicated especially by ability to walk steadily and by freedom from seasickness

¹seal·er \'sē-lər\ *n* **1** : an official who certifies weights and measures **2** : a substance used on a surface to be painted that prevents the paint from sinking in

²sealer *n* : a person or a ship engaged in hunting seals

sea lettuce *n* : any of several marine green algae that are thin and edible — called also *ulva*

sea level *n* : the height of the surface of the sea midway between the average high and low tides

sea lily *n* : CRINOID; *esp* : a crinoid that has a stalk

sealing wax *n* : a composition that is plastic when warm and is used for sealing (as letters)

sea lion *n* : any of several large Pacific seals that have small ears on the outside of the body

sea lettuce

seal off *vb* : to close tightly

seal·skin \'sē(ə)l-ˌskin\ *n* **1** : the fur or pelt of a fur seal **2** : a garment (as a coat) of sealskin — **sealskin** *adj*

¹seam \'sēm\ *n* **1** : the fold, line, or groove made by sewing together or joining two edges or two pieces ⟨the *seams* of a dress⟩ ⟨the *seams* of a boat⟩ **2 a** : a raised or sunken line : GROOVE, FURROW, WRINKLE **b** : a layer (as of rock) between clearly different layers ⟨coal *seams*⟩ — **seamless** \-ləs\ *adj* — **at the seams** : to the full or entire extent : COMPLETELY ⟨falling apart *at the seams*⟩

²seam *vb* **1** : to join with a seam **2** : to mark with a line, scar, or wrinkle ⟨creeks *seam* the valley⟩ ⟨a face *seamed* with age⟩

sea·man \'sē-mən\ *n* **1** : SAILOR, MARINER **2** : a naval enlisted person with a rank below those of petty officers; *esp* : an enlisted person with a rank just below that of petty officer third class

seaman apprentice *n* : a naval enlisted person with a rank just below that of seaman

seaman recruit *n* : a naval enlisted person of the lowest rank

sea·man·ship \'sē-mən-ˌship\ *n* : the art or skill of handling, working, and navigating a ship

sea mile *n* : NAUTICAL MILE

sea monkey *n* : a brine shrimp that hatches from a dormant egg and is sometimes raised in aquariums

\ə\ **abut**	\au̇\ **out**	\i\ **tip**	\ȯ\ **saw**	\u̇\ **foot**
\ər\ **further**	\ch\ **chin**	\ī\ **life**	\ȯi\ **coin**	\y\ **yet**
\a\ **mat**	\e\ **pet**	\j\ **job**	\th\ **thin**	\yü\ **few**
\ā\ **take**	\ē\ **easy**	\ŋ\ **sing**	\th\ **this**	\yu̇\ **cure**
\ä\ **cot, cart**	\g\ **go**	\ō\ **bone**	\ü\ **food**	\zh\ **vision**

sea·mount \'sē-,maunt\ *n* : a submarine mountain

seam·stress \'sēm(p)-strəs\ *n* : a woman who sews especially for a living

seamy \'sē-mē\ *adj* **seam·i·er; -est** : not pleasing or presentable : SORDID ⟨the *seamy* side of the city⟩ — **seam·i·ness** *n*

sé·ance \'sā-,än(t)s\ *n* **1** : a meeting for discussion : SESSION **2** : a meeting to receive the communications of spirits

sea otter *n* : a large marine otter of northern Pacific coasts that feeds mostly on shellfish (as clams, crabs, and sea urchins) and can grow to nearly six feet (two meters) in length

sea·plane \'sē-,plān\ *n* : an airplane designed to take off from and land on the water

sea·port \-,pō(ə)rt, -,pȯ(ə)rt\ *n* : a port, harbor, or town within reach of seagoing ships

sea·quake \'sē-,kwāk\ *n* : a submarine earthquake

¹sear \'si(ə)r\ *vb* **1** : to cause withering or drying : PARCH, SHRIVEL ⟨harsh winds that *sear* and burn⟩ **2 a** : to burn, scorch, mark, or injure with or as if with sudden heat **b** : to cook the surface of quickly with intense heat ⟨*sear* a steak⟩

²sear *n* : a mark or scar left by searing

¹search \'sərch\ *vb* **1 a** : to go through or look carefully and thoroughly in an effort to find or discover something ⟨*search* a room⟩ ⟨*search* for a lost child⟩ **b** : to look in the pockets or the clothing of for something hidden ⟨*search* an arrested person⟩ **2** : to find or come to know by or as if by careful investigation or examination — usually used with *out* **3** : to use a computer to find information in (as a database, network, or website) **synonyms** see SEEK — **search·er** *n* — **search·ing·ly** \'sər-chiŋ-lē\ *adv*

²search *n* : an act of searching : an attempt to get, find, or seek out

search engine *n* : computer software used to search data (as text or a database) for specified information; *also* : a website that uses such software

search·light \'sərch-,līt\ *n* : a device for casting a beam of light; *also* : a beam of light cast by it

search warrant *n* : a warrant making legal a search of a specified place (as a house) for stolen goods or unlawful possessions (as illegal drugs)

sea·scape \'sē-,skāp\ *n* **1** : a view of the sea **2** : a picture representing a scene at sea

Sea Scout *n* : one enrolled in the Boy Scouts of America program that provides training in seamanship

sea serpent *n* : a large marine animal resembling a snake often reported to have been seen but never proved to be real

sea·shell \'sē-,shel\ *n* : the shell of a marine animal and especially a mollusk

sea·shore \-,shō(ə)r, -,shȯ(ə)r\ *n* : the shore of a sea : SEACOAST

sea·sick \-,sik\ *adj* : sick or as if sick in the stomach from the pitching or rolling of a ship — **sea·sick·ness** *n*

sea·side \-,sīd\ *n* : the land bordering the sea : SEACOAST

sea slug *n* **1** : SEA CUCUMBER **2** : any of several marine mollusks that have no shell

¹sea·son \'sēz-ᵊn\ *n* **1 a** : a suitable or natural time or occasion ⟨a *season* for all things⟩ **b** : an indefinite period of time : WHILE ⟨willing to wait a *season*⟩ **2 a** : a period of the year associated with something in particular that happens every year ⟨the baseball *season*⟩ **b** : a period marked by special activity especially in some field ⟨tourist *season*⟩ **c** : a period in which a place is most often visited **d** : one of the four quarters into which the year is commonly divided — compare AUTUMN 1, SPRING, ¹SUMMER 1, WINTER 1 **e** : the time of a major holiday **3** : SEASONING **4** : the schedule of official games played or to be played by a sports team during a playing season ⟨got

through the *season* undefeated⟩ — **in season 1** : at the right or fitting time **2** : in a state or at the stage of greatest fitness (as for eating) ⟨peaches are *in season*⟩ **3** : at the legally established time for being hunted or caught — **out of season** : not in season ⟨fined for hunting *out of season*⟩

²season *vb* **sea·soned; sea·son·ing** \'sēz-niŋ, -ᵊn-iŋ\ **1** : to make pleasant to the taste by adding seasoning ⟨a *seasoned* stew⟩ **2 a** : to make or become suitable for use (as by drying) ⟨*season* lumber⟩ **b** : to make fit by experience ⟨a *seasoned* sailor⟩ — **sea·son·er** \'sēz-nər, -ᵊn-ər\ *n*

sea·son·able \'sēz-nə-bəl, -ᵊn-ə-bəl\ *adj* : suitable to the season or situation : TIMELY ⟨a *seasonable* frost⟩ ⟨*seasonable* advice⟩ — **sea·son·ably** \-blē\ *adv*

sea·son·al \'sēz-nəl, -ᵊn-əl\ *adj* : of, relating to, or restricted to a particular season ⟨*seasonal* industries⟩ — **sea·son·al·ly** \-nə-lē, -ᵊn-ə-lē\ *adv*

sea·son·ing \'sēz-niŋ, -ᵊn-iŋ\ *n* : something (as a spice or herb) that seasons

season ticket *n* : a ticket (as to all of a team's games) good for a specified season

sea star *n* : STARFISH

¹seat \'sēt\ *n* **1 a** : something (as a chair) intended to be sat in or on **b** : the part of something on which one rests in sitting ⟨*seat* of the trousers⟩ ⟨a chair *seat*⟩ **c** : the part of the body on which a person sits : BUTTOCK 2a **2 a** : the place on or at which a person sits ⟨had three *seats* for the game⟩ **b** : a right of sitting usually as a member ⟨a *seat* in the senate⟩ **c** : MEMBERSHIP 1 **3** : a place or area where something is located ⟨the *seat* of the pain⟩ ⟨*seats* of learning⟩; *esp* : a place (as a city) from which authority is exercised ⟨the new *seat* of the government⟩ **4** : posture in or way of sitting especially on horseback **5** : a part or surface on which another part or surface rests — **seat·ed** \-əd\ *adj*

²seat *vb* **1 a** : to place in or on a seat ⟨*seat* a guest⟩ **b** : to provide seats for ⟨a theater *seating* 1000 persons⟩ **2** : to repair the seat of or provide a new seat for ⟨*seat* a chair⟩ — **seat·er** *n*

seat belt *n* : a strap designed to hold a person in a seat (as in an automobile or airplane)

sea trout *n* **1** : a trout or char that lives mostly in the ocean but goes up rivers to breed and lay eggs **2** : any of various sea fishes (as the weakfish) that look like trout

sea turtle *n* : any of various large marine turtles (as the green turtle or the loggerhead) that have paddle-shaped feet to aid in swimming

sea urchin *n* : any of a class of small marine invertebrate animals that are echinoderms, usually live on or burrow in the sea bottom, and are enclosed in roundish shells covered with spines that can move

sea urchin

sea·wall \'sē-,wȯl\ *n* : a wall or bank to prevent sea waves from wearing away the shore

¹sea·ward \'sē-wərd\ *n* : the direction or side away from land and toward the open sea

²seaward *adj* **1** : going or located toward the sea **2** : coming from the sea ⟨a *seaward* wind⟩

³seaward *also* **sea·wards** \-wərdz\ *adv* : toward the sea

sea·wa·ter \'sē-,wȯt-ər, -,wät-\ *n* : water in or from the sea

sea·way \-,wā\ *n* **1 a** : a route for travel on the sea **b** : an ocean traffic lane **2** : a rough sea **3** : a deep inland waterway that admits ocean shipping

sea·weed \-,wēd\ *n* : a plant growing in the sea; *esp* : a marine alga (as a kelp)

sea·wor·thy \-ˌwər-thē\ *adj* : fit or safe for a sea voyage ⟨a *seaworthy* ship⟩ — **sea·wor·thi·ness** *n*

se·ba·ceous gland \si-'bā-shəs-\ *n* : any of the skin glands that secrete an oily lubricating substance at the base of hairs or onto the skin

se·cant \'sē-ˌkant, -kənt\ *n* **1** : a straight line that intersects a curve at two or more points **2** : a trigonometric function that is the ratio between the hypotenuse in a right triangle and the side next to an acute angle

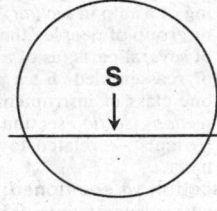

S secant 1

se·cede \si-'sēd\ *vb* **se·ced·ed; se·ced·ing** : to withdraw from an organization (as a nation, church, or political party)

se·ces·sion \si-'sesh-ən\ *n* : the act of seceding

se·ces·sion·ist \-'sesh-(ə-)nəst\ *n* : one who joins in or supports a secession — **se·ces·sion·ism** \-ˌniz-əm\ *n* — **secessionist** *adj*

se·clude \si-'klüd\ *vb* **se·clud·ed; se·clud·ing** **1** : to keep away from others : SECRETE, HIDE ⟨*secluded* themselves⟩ **2** : to shut away : SCREEN, ISOLATE ⟨a cottage *secluded* by forests⟩

se·clud·ed *adj* **1** : hidden from view ⟨a *secluded* valley⟩ **2** : living in seclusion : SOLITARY ⟨*secluded* monks⟩ — **se·clud·ed·ness** *n*

se·clu·sion \si-'klü-zhən\ *n* **1** : the act of secluding : the state of being secluded **2** : a secluded place — **se·clu·sive** \-siv, -ziv\ *adj* — **se·clu·sive·ly** *adv* — **se·clu·sive·ness** *n*

¹sec·ond \'sek-ənd *also* -ənt\ *adj* **1** — see NUMBER table **2 a** : next to the first in time, order, importance, or rank ⟨*second* violin⟩ ⟨*second* place⟩ **b** : ¹OTHER 2 ⟨elects a mayor every *second* year⟩ **c** : resembling or suggesting an original : ANOTHER ⟨a *second* Shakespeare⟩ [Middle English *second* "next to the first in position, order, or time," from early French *secund* (same meaning), from Latin *secundus* "second, following, favorable," from *sequi* "to follow" — related to SEQUEL] — **second** *adv* — **sec·ond·ly** *adv*

²second *n* **1 a** — see NUMBER table **b** : one next after the first in time, order, importance, or rank **2** : one who assists another (as in a duel or prizefight) **3** : the difference in pitch between the first tone and the second tone of a scale **4** : a damaged or imperfect article (as of merchandise) **5** : the act of seconding a motion **6** : SECOND BASE **7** : the second gear or speed in an automobile **8** *pl* : a second helping of food

³second *n* **1 a** : the 60th part of a minute of angular measure **b** : the 60th part of a minute of time; *esp* : the international unit of time related to the period of the radiation corresponding to a change between the two levels of the ground state of a particular isotope of the cesium atom **2** : ¹INSTANT, MOMENT ⟨I'll be back in a *second*⟩ [Middle English *secounde* "the 60th part of a minute," from Latin *secunda* (same meaning), derived from earlier *secundus* (adjective) "second (in order), following, favorable"; so called from the fact that the minute is the first level of division of a degree or hour and this is the second level]

⁴second *vb* **1** : to give support or encouragement to : ASSIST **2** : to encourage that something be debated or voted on ⟨*second* a motion⟩ [from Latin *secundare* "to give support to, assist," from *secundus* (adjective) "second, following, favorable"] — **sec·ond·er** *n*

¹sec·ond·ary \'sek-ən-ˌder-ē\ *adj* **1 a** : of second rank, importance, or value ⟨*secondary* considerations⟩ **b** : of, relating to, or being the second strongest of the three or four levels of stress ⟨the last syllable of "refrigerate" has *secondary* stress⟩ **2 a** : coming from something original or basic **b** : of, relating to, or being the current created by a change in the primary current or the circuit of the created current in an induction coil or transformer ⟨a *secondary* coil⟩ ⟨*secondary* voltage⟩ **3 a** : of, relating to, or being a second rank or grade in a series **b** : of or relating to a secondary school — **sec·ond·ari·ly** \ˌsek-ən-'der-ə-lē\ *adv*

²secondary *n, pl* **-ar·ies** **1** : the defensive football players who line up behind the line of scrimmage **2** : any of the quill feathers attached to the ulna of the wing of a bird **3** : the coil through which the secondary current passes in an induction coil or transformer — called also *secondary coil*

secondary color *n* : a color formed by mixing equal amounts of two primary colors

secondary school *n* : a school for students above elementary or grammar school level and below college level

secondary sex characteristic *n* : a physical characteristic (as the growth of breasts in the human female or the showy feathers of a male bird) that appears in members of one sex at puberty or in seasonal breeders at breeding season and is not directly concerned with reproduction

second base *n* : the base that must be touched second by a base runner in baseball or the position of the player defending the area around it

second baseman *n* : the player defending the area to the right of second base

second–best *adj* : next to the best

second–class *adj* **1** : of or relating to a class next below the first or highest class **2 a** : ¹INFERIOR 3, MEDIOCRE **b** : deprived of wealth or social rank

second cousin *n* : the child of one's parent's first cousin

second–degree burn *n* : a burn characterized by pain, blistering, and destruction of the top layers of the skin that is accompanied by the accumulation of blood and fluid in the tissues beneath the burned area

second fiddle *n* : a person who fills a secondary role

second growth *n* : forest trees that come up naturally after removal of the first growth by cutting or by fire

sec·ond–guess \ˌsek-ᵊŋ-'ges, -ən-\ *vb* **1** : to question or criticize actions or decisions of (someone) often after the results of those actions or decisions are known **2** : PREDICT — **sec·ond–guess·er** *n*

sec·ond·hand \ˌsek-ən-'hand\ *adj* **1** : not original : taken from someone else ⟨*secondhand* reports⟩ **2 a** : having had a previous owner ⟨a *secondhand* car⟩ **b** : selling used goods ⟨a *secondhand* store⟩ — **secondhand** *adv*

second hand *n* : the hand marking seconds on a timepiece

secondhand smoke *n* : tobacco smoke that is exhaled by smokers or is given off by burning tobacco and is inhaled by persons nearby

second lieutenant *n* : a military commissioned officer of the lowest rank

second person *n* : a set of words or forms (as pronouns or verb forms) referring to the one to whom the utterance in which they occur is addressed

sec·ond–rate \ˌsek-ən-'(d)rāt\ *adj* : of second or ordinary quality or value : MEDIOCRE

second–string *adj* : being a substitute player as distinguished from a regular [from the reserve bowstring carried by an archer in case the first breaks]

second wind *n* : new energy or ability to continue

se·cre·cy \'sē-krə-sē\ *n, pl* **-cies** **1** : the habit of keeping secrets : SECRETIVENESS **2** : the quality or state of being hidden or concealed

\ə\ **abut**	\au̇\ **out**	\i\ **tip**	\ȯ\ **saw**	\u̇\ **foot**
\ər\ **further**	\ch\ **chin**	\ī\ **life**	\ȯi\ **coin**	\y\ **yet**
\a\ **mat**	\e\ **pet**	\j\ **job**	\th\ **thin**	\yü\ **few**
\ā\ **take**	\ē\ **easy**	\ŋ\ **sing**	\t͟h\ **this**	\yu̇\ **cure**
\ä\ **cot, cart**	\g\ **go**	\ō\ **bone**	\ü\ **food**	\zh\ **vision**

¹se·cret \'sē-krət\ *adj* **1 a** : hidden or kept from knowledge or view **b** : working in secret as a spy or detective : UNDERCOVER ⟨a *secret* agent⟩ **2** : SECLUDED 1 ⟨a *secret* valley⟩ — **se·cret·ly** *adv*

synonyms SECRET, COVERT, CLANDESTINE, SURREPTITIOUS mean done without attracting observation. SECRET implies concealment on any grounds for any reason ⟨met at a *secret* location⟩. COVERT stresses the fact of not being open or declared ⟨*covert* intelligence operations⟩. CLANDESTINE implies secrecy usually for an evil, illicit, or unauthorized purpose and often emphasizes the fear of being discovered ⟨a *clandestine* meeting of conspirators⟩. SURREPTITIOUS applies to action or behavior done secretly often with skillful avoidance of detection and in violation of custom, law, or authority ⟨the *surreptitious* stockpiling of weapons⟩.

²secret *n* **1 a** : something that cannot be explained : MYSTERY **b** : something kept from the knowledge of others or shared only privately with a few **2** : something taken to be necessary to gain a desired end ⟨the *secret* of a long life⟩ — **in secret** : in a private place or manner

sec·re·tar·i·at \,sek-rə-'ter-ē-ət, -ē-,at\ *n* **1** : the secretaries of an organization **2** : the division of administration of a governmental organization ⟨the United Nations *secretariat*⟩

sec·re·tary \'sek-rə-,ter-ē\ *n, pl* **-tar·ies** **1** : a person employed to handle records, letters, and routine work for another person **2** : an officer of a business corporation or society who has charge of the letters and records **3** : a government official in charge of a division ⟨*Secretary* of State⟩ **4** : a desk with a top section for books — **sec·re·tar·i·al** \,sek-rə-'ter-ē-əl\ *adj*

secretary–general *n, pl* **secretaries—general** : a principal officer of administration ⟨*secretary-general* of the United Nations⟩

secretary 4

¹se·crete \si-'krēt\ *vb* **se·cret·ed; se·cret·ing** : to produce and give off a secretion ⟨glands that *secrete* saliva⟩

²se·crete \si-'krēt, 'sē-krət\ *vb* **se·cret·ed; se·cret·ing** : to deposit or conceal in a hiding place

se·cre·tion \si-'krē-shən\ *n* **1 a** : the process of giving off a substance (as saliva) **b** : a substance produced and given off by a gland; *esp* : one (as an enzyme) that performs a specific useful function in the body **2** : CONCEALMENT 1

se·cre·tive \'sē-krət-iv, si-'krēt-\ *adj* : having a tendency toward secrecy and concealment : not frank or open — **se·cre·tive·ly** *adv* — **se·cre·tive·ness** *n*

secret police *n* : a police organization operating mostly in secrecy and especially for the political purposes of its government and often using methods of terrorists

Secret Service *n* : a division of the U.S. Department of Homeland Security chiefly in charge of stopping crimes against the nation's financial system and protecting the president and other national and visiting world leaders

sect \'sekt\ *n* **1 a** : a religious group having beliefs that differ greatly from those of the main body **b** : a religious body consisting of members having similar beliefs **2 a** : a group of people having the same beliefs or following the same leader **b** : PARTY 1 **c** : FACTION

¹sec·tar·i·an \sek-'ter-ē-ən\ *adj* **1** : of, relating to, or characteristic of a sect or sectarian **2** : not willing to consider other points of view ⟨a *sectarian* mind⟩ — **sec·tar·i·an·ism** \-ē-ə-,niz-əm\ *n*

²sectarian *n* **1** : a member of a sect **2** : a person who won't consider the ideas or opinions of others

¹sec·tion \'sek-shən\ *n* **1** : a part cut off or separated ⟨a *section* of an orange⟩ **2** : a part of a written work ⟨the sports *section* of the newspaper⟩ **3** : the appearance that a thing has or would have if cut straight through ⟨a drawing of a ship in *section*⟩ **4** : a part of an area, community, or group of people ⟨the business *section* of town⟩ **5** : one of several parts (as of a bookcase) that may be assembled or reassembled **6** : a part of an orchestra composed of one class of instruments ⟨the brass *section*⟩ [from Latin *section-, sectio* "section, the act of cutting," from *secare* "to cut" — related to DISSECT, INSECT] **synonyms** see PART

²section *vb* **sec·tioned; sec·tion·ing** \-sh(ə-)niŋ\ **1** : to cut or separate into or become cut or separated into parts or sections **2** : to represent in sections (as by a drawing)

sec·tion·al \'sek-shnəl, -shən-ᵊl\ *adj* **1 a** : of or relating to a section **b** : local or regional in type ⟨*sectional* interests⟩ **2** : consisting of or divided into sections ⟨*sectional* furniture⟩ — **sec·tion·al·ly** \-ē\ *adv*

sec·tion·al·ism \'sek-shnə-,liz-əm, -shən-ᵊl-,iz-\ *n* : too much devotion to the interests of a region

sec·tor \'sek-tər, -,tȯ(ə)r\ *n* **1 a** : the part of a circle included between two radii **b** : an area assigned to a military commander to defend **2** : a part of society ⟨the public *sector*⟩ ⟨the industrial *sector*⟩

sec·u·lar \'sek-yə-lər\ *adj* **1 a** : not spiritual : WORLDLY ⟨*secular* concerns⟩ **b** : not religious ⟨*secular* music⟩ **c** : of, relating to, or regulated by the state rather than the church ⟨*secular* courts⟩ **2** : of or relating to members of the clergy who do not belong to a religious community ⟨a *secular* priest⟩ — **sec·u·lar·ly** *adv*

sec·u·lar·ism \'sek-yə-lə-,riz-əm\ *n* : the belief that religion and religious considerations should be ignored — **sec·u·lar·ist** \-rəst\ *n* — **secularist** *also* **sec·u·lar·is·tic** \,sek-yə-lə-'ris-tik\ *adj*

sec·u·lar·ize \'sek-yə-lə-,rīz\ *vb* **-ized; -iz·ing** **1** : to make secular **2** : to transfer to civil use, possession, or control from that of the church — **sec·u·lar·i·za·tion** \,sek-yə-lə-rə-'zā-shən\ *n*

¹se·cure \si-'kyu̇(ə)r\ *adj* **se·cur·er; se·cur·est** **1** : easy in mind : CONFIDENT ⟨*secure* in the knowledge that help was near⟩ **2 a** : providing safety : SAFE ⟨a *secure* hideaway⟩ ⟨is *secure* against attack⟩ **b** : TRUSTWORTHY, DEPENDABLE ⟨*secure* foundation⟩ **3** : ¹SURE 5a, CERTAIN ⟨victory is *secure*⟩ [from Latin *securus* "safe, secure," literally, "without care," from *se* "without" and *cura* "care" — related to CURE, SURE; see *Word History* at CURE] — **se·cure·ly** *adv*

²secure *vb* **se·cured; se·cur·ing** **1 a** : to make safe : GUARD, SHIELD ⟨*secure* a supply line from enemy raids⟩ **b** : to assure payment of **2 a** : to take into custody ⟨*secure* a prisoner⟩ **b** : to fasten tightly ⟨*secure* a door⟩ **3** : to acquire as the result of effort ⟨*secure* employment⟩ **synonyms** see GET

se·cure·ment \si-'kyu̇(ə)r-mənt\ *n* : the act or process of making secure

se·cu·ri·ty \si-'kyu̇r-ət-ē\ *n, pl* **-ties** **1** : the state of being secure : SAFETY **2** : something given as a pledge ⟨*security* for a loan⟩ **3** : a document (as a stock certificate or bond) providing evidence of ownership ⟨government *securities*⟩ **4** : something that secures : PROTECTION; *esp* : measures taken to guard against spying or destructive actions ⟨concerns over national *security*⟩

se·dan \si-'dan\ *n* **1** : a portable often covered chair that is designed to hold one person and to be carried on poles by two people **2** : an enclosed automobile that seats four to seven persons including the driver in a single compartment and has a permanent top

se·date \si-'dāt\ *adj* : quiet in manner or conduct : STAID, SOBER — **se·date·ly** *adv* — **se·date·ness** *n*

¹**sed·a·tive** \'sed-ət-iv\ *adj* : tending to calm or to ease tension

²**sedative** *n* : a sedative medicine

sed·en·tary \'sed-ᵊn-₁ter-ē\ *adj* **1** : not migratory : SETTLED ⟨*sedentary* birds⟩ **2** : doing or requiring much sitting ⟨a *sedentary* job⟩

sedge \'sej\ *n* : any of a family of plants of marshy areas that are related to the grasses and have solid often three-sided stems

sed·i·ment \'sed-ə-mənt\ *n* **1** : the material from a liquid that settles to the bottom **2** : material (as stones and sand) deposited by water, wind, or glaciers — **sed·i·ment** \-₁ment\ *vb*

sed·i·men·ta·ry \₁sed-ə-'ment-ə-rē, -'men-trē\ *adj* **1** : of, relating to, or containing sediment **2** : formed by or from sediment ⟨*sedimentary* rock⟩ — compare IGNEOUS, METAMORPHIC

sed·i·men·ta·tion \₁sed-ə-mən-'tā-shən, -₁men-\ *n* : the action or process of depositing sediment

se·di·tion \si-'dish-ən\ *n* : the stirring up of feelings against lawful authority

se·di·tious \si-'dish-əs\ *adj* : of, relating to, or causing sedition ⟨*seditious* statements⟩

se·duce \si-'d(y)üs\ *vb* **se·duced; se·duc·ing** **1** : to persuade to be disobedient or disloyal **2** : to persuade to do wrong ⟨*seduced* into crime⟩ **3** : to persuade to have sexual intercourse especially for the first time — **se·duc·er** *n* — **se·duc·tion** \-'dək-shən\ *n*

se·duc·tive \si-'dək-tiv\ *adj* : tending to seduce : ALLURING, TEMPTING — **se·duc·tive·ly** *adv* — **se·duc·tive·ness** *n*

se·duc·tress \si-'dək-trəs\ *n* : a woman who seduces

sed·u·lous \'sej-ə-ləs\ *adj* : steadily industrious : DILIGENT — **sed·u·lous·ly** *adv*

se·dum \'sēd-əm\ *n* : any of a genus of herbs that have fleshy leaves and clusters of yellow, white, or pink flowers

¹**see** \'sē\ *vb* **saw** \'sȯ\; **seen** \'sēn\; **see·ing** \'sē-iŋ\ **1 a** : to become aware of by means of the eyes or have the power of sight ⟨*see* a bird⟩ ⟨a person who cannot *see*⟩ **b** : to give or pay attention ⟨*see*, the bus is coming⟩ **2 a** : to have experience of : UNDERGO ⟨had *seen* life on a farm⟩ **b** : to know or find out by investigation ⟨*see* what's wrong with the car⟩ **c** : to acknowledge or consider something being pointed out ⟨*see*, I told you it would rain⟩ **3 a** : to form a mental picture of : VISUALIZE ⟨I can *see* it now in my mind⟩ **b** : to understand the meaning or importance of ⟨I *see* what you mean⟩ **c** : to be aware of : RECOGNIZE ⟨*sees* only our faults⟩ **d** : to imagine as a possibility ⟨couldn't *see* him as a crook⟩ **4 a** : to provide for ⟨had enough money to *see* them through⟩ **b** : to make sure ⟨*see* that the job gets done⟩ **5 a** : to call on : VISIT ⟨*see* a sick friend⟩ **b** **(1)** : to keep company with especially in courtship or dating ⟨had been *seeing* each other for a year⟩ **(2)** : to grant an interview to ⟨the president will *see* you⟩ **6** : ACCOMPANY 1, ESCORT ⟨I'll *see* you home⟩ — **see after** : to attend to : care for ⟨*saw after* my mother⟩ — **see eye to eye** : to have a common point of view : AGREE — **see red** : to become very angry — **see the light** : to discover or realize a truth — **see things** : HALLUCINATE — **see through** : to learn the true nature of ⟨*saw through* the scheme⟩ — **see to** : to provide for the needs of ⟨*saw to* the children's education⟩

²**see** *n* **1** : the city in which a bishop's church is located **2** : the area in which a bishop has authority : DIOCESE

see·able \'sē-ə-bəl\ *adj* : capable of being seen

¹**seed** \'sēd\ *n, pl* **seed** *or* **seeds** **1 a** : the grains of plants used for sowing **b** : a fertilized ripened ovule of a flowering plant that contains an embryo and is capable of producing a new plant; *also* : a plant structure (as a spore or small dry fruit) capable of producing a new plant **c** : SEMEN; *also* : MILT **2** : the children of one individual ⟨the *seed* of David⟩ **3** : something from which growth takes place : GERM **4** : a competitor who has been seeded in a tournament ⟨the top *seed*⟩ — **seed** *adj* — **seed·ed** \-əd\ *adj* — **seed·like** \-₁līk\ *adj* — **go to seed** *or* **run to seed** : to lose effectiveness : DECAY, DETERIORATE

²**seed** *vb* **1** : to produce or shed seeds ⟨weeds that *seed* freely⟩ **2** : to plant seeds in : SOW ⟨*seed* a lawn with grass⟩ **3** : to treat (a cloud) with solid particles to convert water droplets into ice crystals in an attempt to produce rain **4** : to remove seeds from **5** : to rank (a player or team) in a tournament on the basis of previous record ⟨was *seeded* second in the state tournament⟩

seed·bed \'sēd-₁bed\ *n* : soil or a bed of soil prepared for planting seed

seed·case \-₁kās\ *n* : a dry hollow fruit (as a pod) that contains seeds

seed coat *n* : the hard protective outer covering of a seed

seed·eat·er \'sēd-₁ēt-ər\ *n* : a bird (as a finch) that eats mostly seeds

seed·er \'sēd-ər\ *n* : a machine for planting or sowing seeds

seed leaf *n* : COTYLEDON

seed·less \'sēd-ləs\ *adj* : having no seeds ⟨*seedless* grapes⟩

seed·ling \'sēd-liŋ\ *n* **1** : a young plant grown from seed **2** : a tree before it becomes a sapling — **seedling** *adj*

seed plant *n* : a plant that bears seeds : SPERMATOPHYTE

seed·pod \'sēd-₁päd\ *n* : ¹POD 1

seedy \'sēd-ē\ *adj* **seed·i·er; -est** **1** : containing or full of seeds ⟨a *seedy* fruit⟩ **2** : not being in good shape : SHABBY ⟨*seedy* clothes⟩ — **seed·i·ness** *n*

see·ing \'sē-iŋ\ *conj* : in consideration of the fact that

Seeing Eye *trademark* — used for a dog trained to guide the blind

seek \'sēk\ *vb* **sought** \'sȯt\; **seek·ing** **1** : to go to ⟨*seek* the shade on a sunny day⟩ **2 a** : to go in search of : look for ⟨*seek* out the guilty person⟩ **b** : to try to discover ⟨*seek* the truth⟩ **3** : to ask for : REQUEST ⟨*seeks* advice⟩ **4** : to try to acquire or gain : aim at ⟨*seeking* public office⟩ **5** : to make an attempt : TRY ⟨*seek* to find a way⟩ ⟨*sought* to improve my work⟩ — **seek·er** *n*

synonyms SEEK, SEARCH, HUNT mean to look for something. SEEK may imply looking for either material or mental things ⟨*seeking* new friends⟩ ⟨*seeks* the truth⟩. SEARCH suggests looking for something in a careful, thorough way ⟨we *searched* all over the house for the letter⟩. HUNT suggests a long pursuit, as if one were going after game ⟨I *hunted* all day for the right gift⟩.

seem \'sēm\ *vb* **1** : to give the impression of being : APPEAR ⟨the request *seems* reasonable⟩ **2 a** : to appear to a person's own mind or opinion ⟨can't *seem* to solve the problem⟩ **b** : to appear to be ⟨there *seems* no reason for worry⟩

seem·ing \'sē-miŋ\ *adj* : appearing to be real or true : APPARENT ⟨suspicious of their *seeming* enthusiasm⟩ — **seem·ing·ly** *adv*

seem·ly \'sēm-lē\ *adj* **seem·li·er; -est** **1** : ATTRACTIVE, HANDSOME **2** : being in good taste : PROPER ⟨*seemly* behavior⟩ **3** : suitable for the occasion, purpose, or person : FIT ⟨a *seemly* reply⟩ — **seem·li·ness** *n* — **seemly** *adv*

seen *past participle of* SEE

see out *vb* : to continue with until the end : FINISH

seep \'sēp\ *vb* : to flow or pass slowly through small openings : OOZE

sedge

\ə\ **abut**	\aú\ **out**	\i\ **tip**	\ȯ\ **saw**	\ú\ **foot**
\ər\ **further**	\ch\ **chin**	\ī\ **life**	\ȯi\ **coin**	\y\ **yet**
\a\ **mat**	\e\ **pet**	\j\ **job**	\th\ **thin**	\yü\ **few**
\ā\ **take**	\ē\ **easy**	\ŋ\ **sing**	\t̲h̲\ **this**	\yú\ **cure**
\ä\ **cot, cart**	\g\ **go**	\ō\ **bone**	\ü\ **food**	\zh\ **vision**

seep·age \'sē-pij\ *n* **1** : the process of seeping **2** : a quantity of fluid that has seeped through something

seer \'si(ə)r, *especially for sense 1 also* 'sē-ər\ *n* **1** : someone or something that sees **2** : a person who foresees or foretells events

seer·suck·er \'si(ə)r-,sək-ər\ *n* : a light fabric usually striped and having parallel wrinkles

¹**see·saw** \'sē-,sò\ *n* **1 a** : an up-and-down or backward-and-forward motion or movement **b** : a contest or struggle in which now one side now the other has the lead **2 a** : a game in which two children or groups of children ride on opposite ends of a plank balanced in the middle so that one end goes up as the other goes down **b** : the plank used in the game of seesaw — **seesaw** *adj*

²**seesaw** *vb* **see·sawed; see·saw·ing 1** : to move like a seesaw **2** : to play on a seesaw

seethe \'sēth\ *vb* **seethed; seeth·ing 1** : to churn or foam as if boiling ⟨the river rapids *seethed*⟩ **2** : to be upset or in a state of great excitement ⟨was *seething* with rage⟩

¹**seg·ment** \'seg-mənt\ *n* **1** : any of the parts into which a thing is divided or naturally separates : SECTION, DIVISION **2 a** : a part cut off from a geometric figure by a line; *esp* : the part of a circle enclosed by a chord and an arc **b** : a part of a straight line included between two points — called also *line segment* — **seg·ment·ed** \'seg-,ment-əd, seg-'ment-\ *adj*

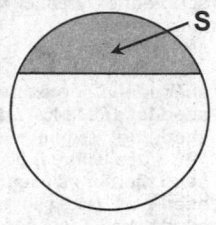

S ¹segment 2a

²**seg·ment** \'seg-,ment\ *vb* : to separate into segments

seg·men·ta·tion \,seg-mən-'tā-shən, -,men-\ *n* : the process of dividing into segments; *esp* : the formation of many cells from a single cell (as in a developing egg)

sego lily \,sē-gō-\ *n* : a western North American herb related to the lilies and having usually white flowers with purplish or yellow markings

seg·re·gate \'seg-ri-,gāt\ *vb* **-gat·ed; -gat·ing** : to separate from others or from the general mass : ISOLATE; *esp* : to separate by races [from Latin *segregatus* "set apart," from *segregare* "to set apart," from *se-* "apart, without" and *gregare* "gather together into a flock or herd," from *greg-, grex* "flock, herd" — related to AGGREGATE, CONGREGATE]

segregated *adj* **1 a** : set apart from others of the same kind or group **b** : divided in facilities or administered separately for members of different groups or races **c** : restricted to one group or race by a policy of segregation ⟨*segregated* schools⟩ **2** : practicing or maintaining segregation especially of races

seg·re·ga·tion \,seg-ri-'gā-shən\ *n* **1** : the act or process of segregating : the state of being segregated **2** : the separation or isolation of a race, class, or group (as by restriction to an area or by separate schools)

seg·re·ga·tion·ist \,seg-ri-'gā-sh(ə-)nəst\ *n* : a person who believes in, practices, or encourages segregation especially of races

sei·gneur \sān-'yər\ *n, often cap* : ¹LORD 1, SEIGNIOR

sei·gnior \sān-'yò(ə)r, 'sān-,yò(ə)r\ *n* : a man of rank or authority

sei·gniory *or* **sei·gnory** \'sān-yə-rē\ *n, pl* **-gnior·ies** *or* **-gnor·ies** : the territory of a lord : DOMAIN

¹**seine** \'sān\ *n* : a large fishing net kept hanging in the water by weights and floats

²**seine** *vb* **seined; sein·ing** : to fish with or catch with a seine

seism- *or* **seismo-** *combining form*

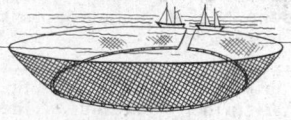

¹seine

: earthquake : vibration ⟨*seismo*graph⟩ [Greek *seismos* "earthquake," from *seiein* "to shake"]

seis·mic \'sīz-mik, 'sīs-\ *adj* : of, subject to, or caused by an earthquake or an earth vibration caused by something else (as an explosion)

seis·mic·i·ty \sīz-'mis-ət-ē, sīs-\ *n* : the relative frequency and distribution of earthquakes

seis·mo·gram \'sīz-mə-,gram, 'sīs-\ *n* : the record of an earth tremor as made by a seismograph

seis·mo·graph \'sīz-mə-,graf, 'sīs-\ *n* : a device to measure and record vibrations of the earth — **seis·mo·graph·ic** \,sīz-mə-'graf-ik, ,sīs-\ *adj* — **seis·mog·ra·phy** \sīz-'mäg-rə-fē, sīs-\ *n*

seis·mol·o·gy \sīz-'mäl-ə-jē, sīs-\ *n* : a science that deals with earthquakes and with artificially produced vibrations of the earth — **seis·mo·log·i·cal** \,sīz-mə-'läj-i-kəl, ,sīs-\ *adj* — **seis·mol·o·gist** \sīz-'mäl-ə-jəst, sīs-\ *n*

seis·mom·e·ter \sīz-'mäm-ət-ər, sīs-\ *n* : a seismograph that measures the actual movements of the ground

seize \'sēz\ *vb* **seized; seiz·ing 1** : to take possession of by force ⟨the wind *seized* the hat off my head⟩ **2** : to take prisoner : ARREST **3 a** : to take hold of suddenly or with force : CLUTCH **b** : to understand fully and clearly : COMPREHEND ⟨*seize* an idea quickly⟩ **4** : to attack or overwhelm suddenly (as with fever) — **seiz·er** *n*

sei·zure \'sē-zhər\ *n* **1** : the act of seizing : the state of being seized **2** : a sudden attack (as of disease); *esp* : the physical signs (as extreme twitching of muscles) of an episode of abnormal brain activity (as in epilepsy)

se·lag·i·nel·la \sə-,laj-ə-'nel-ə\ *n* : any of a genus of plants that are related to the club mosses and have branching stems and scalelike leaves

sel·dom \'sel-dəm\ *adv* : not often : RARELY

¹**se·lect** \sə-'lekt\ *vb* **1** : to pick out from a number or group : CHOOSE **2** : to choose (a particular action or a section of text on a computer screen) especially using a mouse

²**select** *adj* **1** : chosen from a number or group to include the best or most suitable individuals ⟨invited only a few *select* employees⟩ **2** : of special value or excellence : SUPERIOR, CHOICE ⟨a *select* hotel⟩

se·lec·tion \sə-'lek-shən\ *n* **1** : the act of selecting : the state of being selected ⟨*selection* of the best poem was difficult⟩ ⟨cheered my *selection* as athlete of the year⟩ **2 a** : one that is selected : CHOICE **b** : a collection of selected things **3** : any natural or artificial process that tends to favor the survival and reproduction of some individuals but not of others with the result that only the inherited characteristics of the favored individuals continue to be passed on

se·lec·tive \sə-'lek-tiv\ *adj* : of or relating to selection : selecting or tending to select ⟨*selective* shoppers⟩

se·lect·man \si-'lek(t)-,man, -mən; -,lek(t)-'man\ *n* : one of a group of town officials elected annually in some of the New England states

se·lec·tor \sə-'lek-tər\ *n* : someone or something that selects

se·le·ni·um \sə-'lē-nē-əm\ *n* : an element that is sensitive to light and is used especially in glass, alloys, and electronic devices — see ELEMENT table

¹**self** \'self, *Southern also* 'sef\ *pron* : MYSELF 1, HIMSELF, HERSELF ⟨check that can be paid to *self*⟩ ⟨a room for *self*, son, and daughter⟩

²**self** \'self\ *n, pl* **selves** \'selvz, *Southern also* 'sevz\ **1** : a person thought of as an individual apart from everyone else **2** : a particular side of a person's disposition ⟨your better *self*⟩ **3** : personal interest ⟨without thought of *self*⟩

self- *combining form* **1 a** : oneself or itself ⟨*self*-pitying⟩ **b** : of oneself or itself ⟨*self*-destructive⟩ ⟨*self*-sacrifice⟩ **c** : by oneself or itself ⟨*self*-made⟩ ⟨*self*-propelled⟩ **2 a** : to, with, for, or toward oneself or itself ⟨*self*-addressed⟩ **b**

: of or in oneself or itself ⟨*self*-evident⟩ **c** : from or by means of oneself or itself ⟨*self*-fertile⟩

self–act·ing \'sel-'fak-tiŋ\ *adj* : acting or capable of acting of or by itself : AUTOMATIC

self–ac·tu·al·ize \sel-'fak-ch(ə-w)əl-ˌīz, -sh(ə-w)əl-\ *vb* : to realize fully one's potential — **self–ac·tu·al·i·za·tion** \-ˌfak-ch(ə-w)ə-lə-'zā-shən, -ˌfaksh-wə-\ *n*

self–ad·dressed \ˌsel-fə-'drest, 'sel-'fad-ˌrest\ *adj* : addressed for return to the sender ⟨*self-addressed* envelope⟩

self–ad·mi·ra·tion \ˌsel-ˌfad-mə-'rā-shən\ *n* : SELF= CONCEIT

self–ap·point·ed \ˌsel-fə-'pȯint-əd\ *adj* : appointed by oneself usually without qualifications ⟨a *self-appointed* guardian⟩

self–as·ser·tion \ˌsel-fə-'sər-shən\ *n* **1** : the act of asserting oneself or one's own rights or claims **2** : the act of asserting that one is better than others — **self–as·ser·tive** \-'sərt-iv\ *adj*

self–as·sur·ance \ˌsel-fə-'shur-ən(t)s\ *n* : SELF= CONFIDENCE

self–as·sured \ˌsel-fə-'shu̇(ə)rd\ *adj* : sure of oneself : having self-confidence

self–aware·ness \ˌsel-fə-'wa(ə)r-nəs, -'we(ə)r-\ *n* : an awareness of one's own personality or individuality

self–cen·tered \'self-'sent-ərd\ *adj* : interested chiefly in one's own self : SELFISH — **self–cen·tered·ness** *n*

self–con·ceit \ˌself-kən-'sēt\ *n* : an exaggerated opinion of oneself : VANITY — **self–con·ceit·ed** \-əd\ *adj*

self–con·cept \'self-'kän-ˌsept\ *n* : the mental image one has of oneself

self–con·fessed \ˌself-kən-'fest\ *adj* : openly admitted by oneself ⟨a *self-confessed* forger⟩

self–con·fi·dence \'self-'kän-fəd-ən(t)s, -fə-ˌden(t)s\ *n* : confidence in oneself and in one's powers and abilities — **self–con·fi·dent** \-fəd-ənt, -fə-ˌdent\ *adj* — **self–con·fi·dent·ly** *adv*

self–con·scious \'self-'kän-chəs\ *adj* : uncomfortably conscious of oneself as an object of the observation of others — **self–con·scious·ly** *adv* — **self–con·scious·ness** *n*

self–con·tained \ˌself-kən-'tānd\ *adj* **1** : enough or complete in itself **2 a** : showing self-control **b** : keeping one's thoughts and feelings to oneself — **self–con·tain·ment** \-'tān-mənt\ *n*

self–con·trol \ˌself-kən-'trōl\ *n* : control over one's own impulses, emotions, or acts — **self–con·trolled** \-'trōld\ *adj*

self–de·cep·tion \ˌself-di-'sep-shən\ *n* : the act of deceiving oneself : the state of being deceived by oneself

self–de·feat·ing \ˌself-di-'fēt-iŋ\ *adj* : acting to defeat its own purpose

self–de·fense \ˌself-di-'fen(t)s\ *n* : the act of defending oneself, one's property, or a close relative

self–de·ni·al \ˌself-di-'nī(-ə)l\ *n* : the refusal to satisfy one's own desires

self–de·struc·tion \ˌself-di-'strək-shən\ *n* : destruction of oneself; *esp* : SUICIDE 1 — **self–de·struc·tive** \-'strək-tiv\ *adj*

self–de·ter·mi·na·tion \ˌself-di-ˌtər-mə-'nā-shən\ *n* **1** : free choice of one's own acts without outside pressure **2** : the deciding by the people of a place of the form of government they will have

self–di·rect·ed \ˌself-də-'rek-təd, -dī-\ *adj* : directed by oneself and not by an outside force or agency ⟨a *self= directed* personality⟩

self–dis·ci·pline \'self-'dis-ə-plən\ *n* : correction or regulation of oneself for the sake of improvement

self–doubt \'self-'daut\ *n* : a lack of faith in oneself — **self–doubt·ing** \-iŋ\ *adj*

self–ed·u·cat·ed \'self-'ej-ə-ˌkāt-əd\ *adj* : educated by one's own efforts without formal instruction

self–em·ployed \ˌsel-fim-'plȯid\ *adj* : earning income from one's own business or profession rather than salary or wages from an employer

self–es·teem \ˌsel-fə-'stēm\ *n* **1** : a confidence and satisfaction in oneself : SELF-RESPECT **2** : an exaggerated opinion of one's own abilities : SELF-CONCEIT

self–ev·i·dent \'sel-'fev-əd-ənt, -ə-ˌdent\ *adj* : having no need of proof ⟨*self-evident* truths⟩

self–ex·plan·a·to·ry \ˌsel-fik-'splan-ə-ˌtōr-ē, -ˌtȯr-\ *adj* : understandable without explanation

self–ex·pres·sion \ˌsel-fik-'spresh-ən\ *n* : the expression of one's own personality

self–fer·til·i·za·tion \ˌself-ˌfərt-ᵊl-ə-'zā-shən\ *n* : fertilization of a plant or animal by its own pollen or sperm — **self–fer·til·ize** \'self-'fərt-ᵊl-ˌīz\ *vb*

self–gov·ern·ment \'self-'gəv-ər(n)-mənt, -'gəv-ᵊm-ənt\ *n* **1** : control over one's own actions : SELF-CONTROL **2** : government by action of the people making up a community; *esp* : democratic government — **self–gov·erned** \-'gəv-ərnd\ *adj* — **self–gov·ern·ing** \-ər-niŋ\ *adj*

self–help \'self-'help\ *n* : the act of bettering oneself or overcoming one's problems without dependence on others

self–hood \'self-ˌhud\ *n* : INDIVIDUALITY 1

self–iden·ti·ty \ˌsel-ˌfī-'den(t)-ət-ē\ *n* : INDIVIDUALITY 1

self·ie \'sel-fē\ *n, pl* **self·ies** : an image of oneself taken by oneself using a digital camera especially for posting on social networks

self–im·age \'sel-'fim-ij\ *n* : one's ideas about oneself or one's role

self–im·por·tance \ˌsel-fim-'pȯrt-ᵊn(t)s, -ən(t)s\ *n* : an exaggerated opinion of one's own importance — **self–im·por·tant** \-ᵊnt, -ənt\ *adj* — **self–im·por·tant·ly** *adv*

self–im·posed \ˌsel-fim-'pōzd\ *adj* : imposed on one by oneself : voluntarily assumed

self–im·prove·ment \ˌsel-ˌfim-'prüv-mənt\ *n* : improvement of oneself by one's own actions

self–in·crim·i·na·tion \ˌsel-fin-ˌkrim-ə-'nā-shən\ *n* : incrimination of oneself; *esp* : the giving of evidence or answering of questions which would leave one liable to be tried for a crime

self–in·dul·gence \ˌsel-fin-'dəl-jən(t)s\ *n* : the quality or state of being self-indulgent

self–in·dul·gent \ˌsel-fin-'dəl-jənt\ *adj* : pleasing one's own desires too easily

self–in·flict·ed \ˌsel-fin-'flik-təd\ *adj* : inflicted by oneself ⟨a *self-inflicted* wound⟩

self–in·ter·est \'sel-'fin-trəst, -'fint-ə-rəst\ *n* **1** : a concern for one's own advantage ⟨acted out of *self-interest* and fear⟩ **2** : one's own interest or advantage ⟨our *self-interest* demands that we help others⟩

self·ish \'sel-fish\ *adj* : taking care of oneself without thought for others — **self·ish·ly** *adv* — **self·ish·ness** *n*

self·less \'sel-fləs\ *adj* : having no concern for self : UN-SELFISH — **self·less·ly** *adv* — **self·less·ness** *n*

self–made \'self-'mād\ *adj* **1** : made by one's own actions **2** : raised from poverty by one's own efforts ⟨a *self-made* person⟩

self–pity \'self-'pit-ē\ *n* : pity for oneself; *esp* : too much attention to one's misfortunes — **self–pity·ing** \-ē-iŋ\ *adj*

self–pol·li·na·tion \ˌself-ˌpäl-ə-'nā-shən\ *n* : pollination of a flower by its own pollen or sometimes by pollen from another flower on the same plant — **self–pol·li·nate** \'self-'päl-ə-ˌnāt\ *vb*

self–por·trait \'self-'pȯr-trət, -'pȯr-, -ˌtrāt\ *n* : a portrait of oneself made by oneself

\ə\ **abut**	\au̇\ **out**	\i\ **tip**	\ȯ\ **saw**	\u̇\ **foot**
\ər\ **further**	\ch\ **chin**	\ī\ **life**	\ȯi\ **coin**	\y\ **yet**
\a\ **mat**	\e\ **pet**	\j\ **job**	\th\ **thin**	\yü\ **few**
\ā\ **take**	\ē\ **easy**	\ŋ\ **sing**	\th\ **this**	\yu̇\ **cure**
\ä\ **cot, cart**	\g\ **go**	\ō\ **bone**	\ü\ **food**	\zh\ **vision**

self–pos·sessed \ˌself-pə-ˈzest\ *adj* : having or showing self-possession : CALM

self–pos·ses·sion \ˌself-pə-ˈzesh-ən\ *n* : control of one's emotions or reactions : COMPOSURE

self–pres·er·va·tion \ˌself-ˌprez-ər-ˈvā-shən\ *n* : the keeping of oneself from destruction or harm

self–pro·claimed \ˌself-prō-ˈklāmd\ *adj* : SELF-STYLED

self–pro·duced \ˌself-prə-ˈd(y)üst\ *adj* : produced by oneself or itself

self–pro·pelled \ˌself-prə-ˈpeld\ *adj* : having within itself the means for its own movement

self–pro·pel·ling \ˌself-prə-ˈpel-iŋ\ *adj* : SELF-PROPELLED

self–pro·tec·tive \ˌself-prə-ˈtek-tiv\ *adj* : serving or tending to protect oneself

self–re·gard \ˌsel-fri-ˈgärd\ *n* : regard for or consideration of oneself or one's own interests

self–re·li·ance \ˌsel-fri-ˈlī-ənts\ *n* : trust in one's own efforts and abilities — **self–re·li·ant** \-ənt\ *adj*

self–re·proach \ˌsel-fri-ˈprōch\ *n* : the act of blaming or accusing oneself

self–re·spect \ˌsel-fri-ˈspekt\ *n* **1** : a proper respect for oneself as a human being **2** : regard for one's own standing or position — **self–re·spect·ing** \-ˈspek-tiŋ\ *adj*

self–re·straint \ˌsel-fri-ˈstrānt\ *n* : proper control over one's actions or emotions

self–righ·teous \ˈsel-ˈfrī-chəs\ *adj* : strongly convinced of the rightness of one's actions or beliefs — **self–righ·teous·ly** *adv* — **self–righ·teous·ness** *n*

self–ris·ing flour \ˌsel-ˌfrī-ziŋ-\ *n* : a mixture of flour, salt, and a leavening agent — called also *self-raising flour*

self–rule \ˈsel-ˈfrül\ *n* : SELF-GOVERNMENT 2

self–sac·ri·fice \ˈself-ˈsak-rə-ˌfis, -fəs\ *n* : an unselfish giving over of oneself or one's own interest for others — **self–sac·ri·fic·ing** \-ˌfī-siŋ\ *adj*

self·same \ˈself-ˌsām\ *adj* : exactly the same : IDENTICAL

self–sat·is·fac·tion \ˌself-ˌsat-əs-ˈfak-shən\ *n* : a usually overly satisfied feeling about oneself or one's achievements

self–sat·is·fied \ˈself-ˈsat-əs-ˌfīd\ *adj* : feeling or showing self-satisfaction

self–seal·ing \ˈself-ˈsē-liŋ\ *adj* : capable of sealing itself (as after puncture) ⟨a *self-sealing* tire⟩

self–seek·er \ˈself-ˈsē-kər\ *n* : one who selfishly advances one's own ends — **self–seek·ing** \-kiŋ\ *n or adj*

self–serve \ˈself-ˈsərv\ *adj* : permitting self-service

self–ser·vice \ˈself-ˈsər-vəs\ *n* : the serving of oneself (as in a restaurant or gas station) with things to be paid for at a cashier's desk or by means of a mechanism that is operated by coins — **self–service** *adj*

self–start·er \ˈself-ˈstärt-ər\ *n* : a person who is ambitious

self–styled \ˈself-ˈstī(ə)ld\ *adj* : called by oneself ⟨*self-styled* experts⟩

self–suf·fi·cien·cy \ˌself-sə-ˈfish-ən-sē\ *n* : the quality or state of being self-sufficient

self–suf·fi·cient \ˌself-sə-ˈfish-ənt\ *adj* : able to take care of oneself without outside help : INDEPENDENT

self–sup·port \ˌself-sə-ˈpō(ə)rt, -ˈpȯ(ə)rt\ *n* : independent support of oneself or itself

self–sup·port·ing \-iŋ\ *adj* : characterized by self-support: as **a** : meeting one's needs by one's own efforts or output **b** : supporting itself or its own weight ⟨a *self-supporting* wall⟩

self–taught \ˈself-ˈtȯt\ *adj* **1** : having knowledge or skills acquired by one's own efforts without formal instruction ⟨a *self-taught* musician⟩ **2** : learned by oneself ⟨*self-taught* knowledge⟩

self–will \ˈself-ˈwil\ *n* : a stubborn sticking to one's own desires or ideas — **self–willed** \-ˈwild\ *adj*

self–wind·ing \ˈself-ˈwīn-diŋ\ *adj* : not needing to be wound by hand ⟨a *self-winding* watch⟩

self–worth \-ˈwərth\ *n* : SELF-ESTEEM

sell \ˈsel\ *vb* **sold** \ˈsōld\; **sell·ing** **1** : to betray a person or duty — often used with *out* **2** : to exchange in return for money or something else of value ⟨*sell* groceries⟩ **3 a** : to develop a belief in the truth, value, or desirability of ⟨trying to *sell* a program to Congress⟩ **b** : to bring around to a favorable way of thinking ⟨tried to *sell* the children on reading⟩ **4** : to achieve a sale; *also* : to achieve satisfactory sales ⟨hoped that the new car would *sell*⟩ **5** : to be sold or priced ⟨these *sell* for a dollar apiece⟩ — **sell·er** *n* — **sell short** : to put too low a value on the ability, strength, or importance of

sell·out \ˈsel-ˌaut\ *n* **1** : the act or an instance of selling out **2** : a show, contest, or exhibition for which all seats are sold

sell out \(ˈ)sel-ˈaut\ *vb* : to dispose of all of one's goods by sale

sel·vage *or* **sel·vedge** \ˈsel-vij\ *n* : an edge of cloth so woven that it will not ravel

selves *plural of* ²SELF

se·man·tic \si-ˈmant-ik\ *adj* **1** : of or relating to meaning in language **2** : of or relating to semantics — **se·man·ti·cal·ly** \-ˈmant-i-k(ə-)lē\ *adv*

se·man·tics \si-ˈmant-iks\ *n sing or pl* : the study of meanings and changes of meaning — **se·man·ti·cist** \si-ˈmant-ə-səst\ *n*

sem·a·phore \ˈsem-ə-ˌfō(ə)r, -ˌfȯ(ə)r\ *n* **1** : a device for sending signals that can be seen by the receiver **2** : a system of sending signals with two flags held one in each hand

sem·blance \ˈsem-blən(t)s\ *n* **1** : outward and often misleading appearance or show **2** : one that resembles another : LIKENESS, IMAGE

semaphore 2: alphabet; 3 positions following Z: error, end of word, numerals follow; numerals 1, 2, 3, 4, 5, 6, 7, 8, 9, 0 same as A through J

se·men \ˈsē-mən\ *n* : a sticky whitish fluid of the male reproductive tract that contains the sperm

se·mes·ter \sə-ˈmes-tər\ *n* : either of two terms of about 18 weeks each that make up a school year

semi- \ˈsem-i, ˈsem-, -ˌī\ *prefix* **1** : half in amount or value ⟨*semi*tone⟩ **2** : occurring halfway through a certain time period ⟨*semi*annual⟩ **3** : to some extent : partly : incompletely ⟨*semi*tropical⟩ **4** : partial : incomplete ⟨*semi*darkness⟩ [Latin *semi-* "half"]

semi·an·nu·al \ˌsem-ē-ˈan-yə(-wə)l, ˌsem-ˌī-\ *adj* : occurring every six months or twice a year — **semi·an·nu·al·ly** \-ē\ *adv*

semi·aquat·ic \ˌsem-ē-ə-ˈkwät-ik, ˌsem-ˌī-, -ˈkwat-\ *adj* : growing well in or very near water; *also* : living near and often entering water but not living in it

semi·ar·id \ˌsem-ē-ˈar-əd, ˌsem-ˌī-\ *adj* : marked by light rainfall; *esp* : having from about 10 to 20 inches (25 to 51 centimeters) of annual precipitation

semi·cir·cle \ˈsem-i-ˌsər-kəl\ *n* **1** : half of a circle **2** : an object or arrangement of objects in the form of a half circle — **semi·cir·cu·lar** \ˌsem-i-ˈsər-kyə-lər\ *adj*

semicircular canal *n* : any of the loop-shaped tubes in the ear that contain fluid and tiny hairs and help to maintain the body's sense of balance

semi·clas·si·cal \ˌsem-i-ˈklas-i-kəl, ˌsem-ˌī-\ *adj* **1** : having some of the characteristics of the classical **2** : of or relating to a classical musical composition that has become generally popular

semi·co·lon \'sem-i-ˌkō-lən\ *n* : a punctuation mark that can be used to separate parts of a sentence which need clearer separation than would be shown by a comma, to separate main clauses which have no conjunction between, and to separate phrases and clauses containing commas

semi·con·duc·tor \ˌsem-i-kən-'dək-tər, ˌsem-ˌī-\ *n* : any of a class of solids (as germanium) that have an ability to conduct electricity between that of a conductor and that of an insulator — **semi·con·duct·ing** \-tiŋ\ *adj*

semi·con·scious \ˌsem-i-'kän-chəs, ˌsem-ˌī-\ *adj* : partially conscious — **semi·con·scious·ness** *n*

semi·dark·ness \ˌsem-i-'därk-nəs, ˌsem-ˌī-\ *n* : partial darkness

¹**semi·fi·nal** \ˌsem-i-'fīn-ᵊl\ *adj* **1** : coming before the final round in a tournament **2** : of or taking part in a semifinal

²**semi·fi·nal** \'sem-i-ˌfīn-ᵊl\ *n* : a semifinal match or game — **semi·fi·nal·ist** \ˌsem-i-'fīn-ᵊl-əst\ *n*

semi·for·mal \ˌsem-i-'fȯr-məl, ˌsem-ˌī-\ *adj* : being or suitable for an event that is not too formal

¹**semi·month·ly** \ˌsem-i-'mən(t)th-lē, ˌsem-ˌī-\ *n* : a semimonthly publication

²**semimonthly** *adj* : occurring twice a month

³**semimonthly** *adv* : twice a month

sem·i·nar \'sem-ə-ˌnär\ *n* **1** : a course of study followed by a group of advanced students **2** : a meeting of a seminar or a room for such meetings **3** : a meeting for giving and discussing information ⟨a sales *seminar*⟩

sem·i·nar·i·an \ˌsem-ə-'ner-ē-ən\ *n* : a student in a seminary

sem·i·nary \'sem-ə-ˌner-ē\ *n, pl* **-nar·ies** **1** : a private school at or above the high school level **2** : a school for the training of priests, ministers, or rabbis

Word History The English word *seminary* and its Latin source *seminarium*, a derivative of *semen*, "seed," both originally denoted a nursery for young plants. Roman authors sometimes used the Latin word figuratively, but English has gone much further in extending the meaning of the word, while the use of the old sense "nursery for plants" is now obsolete. The use of *seminary* in reference to training schools for Roman Catholic clergy dates from the 16th century. Today the word refers equally to Catholic, Protestant, or Jewish colleges for training priests, ministers, or rabbis. *Seminary* has also been applied to other kinds of schools. When they were first formed in the 19th century, colleges for women were called "female seminaries" or "seminaries for young ladies." [Middle English *seminary* "seedbed, nursery, from Latin *seminarium* (same meaning), from *semen* "seed"]

sem·i·nif·er·ous tubule \ˌsem-ə-'nif-(ə-)rəs-\ *n* : any of the coiled threadlike tubes that make up most of the testis and produce sperm cells

Sem·i·nole \'sem-ə-ˌnōl\ *n* : a member of an American Indian people of Florida

semi·of·fi·cial \ˌsem-ē-ə-'fish-əl, ˌsem-ˌī-\ *adj* : having some official authority or standing

semi·per·me·able \ˌsem-i-'pər-mē-ə-bəl, ˌsem-ˌī-\ *adj* : partially but not freely or entirely permeable; *esp* : permeable to some usually small molecules but not to other usually larger particles — **semi·per·me·abil·i·ty** \-ˌpər-mē-ə-'bil-ət-ē\ *n*

semi·pre·cious \ˌsem-i-'presh-əs, ˌsem-ˌī-\ *adj* : of less value than a precious stone

semi·pri·vate \ˌsem-i-'prī-vət, ˌsem-ˌī-\ *adj* : shared with one other or a few others ⟨a *semiprivate* hospital room⟩

semi·pro \'sem-i-ˌprō, 'sem-ˌī-\ *adj or n* : SEMIPROFESSIONAL

semi·pro·fes·sion·al \ˌsem-i-prə-'fesh-nəl, -ən-ᵊl, ˌsem-ˌī-\ *adj* **1** : engaging in an activity for pay but not as a full-time occupation **2** : engaged in by semiprofessional players ⟨*semiprofessional* football⟩ — **semiprofessional** *n*

semi·re·li·gious \ˌsem-i-ri-'lij-əs, ˌsem-ˌī-\ *adj* : somewhat religious in character

semi·skilled \ˌsem-i-'skild, ˌsem-ˌī-\ *adj* : having or requiring less training than skilled labor and more than unskilled labor

semi·soft \ˌsem-i-'sȯft, ˌsem-ˌī-\ *adj* : moderately soft; *esp* : firm but easily cut ⟨*semisoft* cheese⟩

semi·sol·id \ˌsem-i-'säl-əd, ˌsem-ˌī-\ *adj* : having the qualities of both a solid and a liquid — **semisolid** *n*

semi·sweet \ˌsem-i-'swēt, ˌsem-ˌī-\ *adj* : slightly sweetened ⟨*semisweet* chocolate⟩

Sem·ite \'sem-ˌīt\ *n* : a member of any of a group of peoples of southwestern Asia chiefly represented by the Jews and Arabs

Se·mit·ic \sə-'mit-ik\ *adj* : of or relating to the Semites; *esp* : of, relating to, or characteristic of the Jews

semi·tone \'sem-i-ˌtōn, 'sem-ˌī-\ *n* : the smallest difference in pitch between any two tones of a scale

semi·trail·er \'sem-i-ˌtrā-lər, 'sem-ˌī-\ *n* **1** : a freight trailer that when attached is supported at its forward end by the truck tractor **2** : a trucking rig made up of a tractor and a semitrailer

semi·trop·i·cal \ˌsem-i-'träp-i-kəl, ˌsem-ˌī-\ *also* **semi·trop·ic** \-ik\ *adj* : SUBTROPICAL

¹**semi·week·ly** \ˌsem-i-'wē-klē, ˌsem-ˌī-\ *adj* : occurring twice a week — **semiweekly** *adv*

²**semiweekly** *n* : a publication that comes out twice a week

sem·o·li·na \ˌsem-ə-'lē-nə\ *n* : a grainy powder that is milled from hard wheat (as durum wheat) and is often used to make pasta (as spaghetti)

sen·ate \'sen-ət\ *n* : an official law-making group or council: as **a** : the supreme council of the ancient Roman republic and empire **b** : the higher branch of a legislature of a nation, state, or province [Middle English *senat* "lawmaking council of ancient Rome," from early French *senat* (same meaning), from Latin *senatus*, literally, "council of elders," from *sen-, senex* "old" — related to SENIOR]

sen·a·tor \'sen-ət-ər\ *n* : a member of a senate — **sen·a·tor·ship** \-ˌship\ *n*

sen·a·to·ri·al \ˌsen-ə-'tōr-ē-əl, -'tȯr-\ *adj* : of or relating to a senator or a senate ⟨*senatorial* office⟩

send \'send\ *vb* **sent** \'sent\; **send·ing** **1** : to cause to go ⟨*sent* the pupil home⟩ ⟨*sent* a message⟩; *esp* : to set in motion by physical force ⟨*sent* the ball into right field⟩ ⟨*send* a rocket to the moon⟩ **2** : to cause to happen ⟨whatever fate may *send*⟩ **3** : to put or bring into a certain condition ⟨*sent* them into a rage⟩ **4 a** : to cause someone to pass a message on or do an errand — often used with *out* ⟨*send* out for lunch⟩ **b** : to dispatch a request or order — often used with *away* ⟨*sent* away for skates⟩ — **send·er** *n* — **send for** : to request by message to come ⟨the principal *sent for* the child⟩ — **send packing** : to send off roughly or in disgrace

send–off \'sen-ˌdȯf\ *n* : a demonstration of goodwill and enthusiasm for the beginning of something new (as a trip)

Sen·e·ca \'sen-i-kə\ *n* : a member of an American Indian people of western New York

sen·e·schal \'sen-ə-shəl\ *n* : an agent or bailiff who managed a lord's estate in feudal times

se·nile \'sēn-ˌīl *also* 'sen-\ *adj* : of, relating to, or characteristic of old age ⟨*senile* weakness⟩; *esp* : showing a loss of mental ability usually associated with old age [from Latin *senilis* "showing the features of old age," from *sen-, senex* "old" — related to SENIOR]

\ə\ **abut**	\au̇\ **out**	\i\ **tip**	\ȯ\ **saw**	\u̇\ **foot**
\ər\ **further**	\ch\ **chin**	\ī\ **life**	\ȯi\ **coin**	\y\ **yet**
\a\ **mat**	\e\ **pet**	\j\ **job**	\th\ **thin**	\yü\ **few**
\ā\ **take**	\ē\ **easy**	\ŋ\ **sing**	\th\ **this**	\yu̇\ **cure**
\ä\ **cot, cart**	\g\ **go**	\ō\ **bone**	\ü\ **food**	\zh\ **vision**

se·nil·i·ty \si-'nil-ət-ē\ *n* : the quality or state of being senile; *esp* : the physical and mental weakness of old age

¹se·nior \'sē-nyər\ *n* **1** : a person who is older than another ⟨five years my *senior*⟩ **2 a** : a person with higher standing or rank **b** : a student in the final year of high school or college [Middle English *senior* "a person older than another specific person," from Latin *senior* (same meaning), from *senior* (adjective) "older, elder," from *sen-*, *senex* "old" — related to SENATE, SENILE, SENOR, SIR]

²senior *adj* **1** : being older — used to distinguish a father from a son with the same name ⟨John Doe, *Senior*⟩ **2** : higher ranking ⟨*senior* officers⟩ ⟨the *senior* partner of the law firm⟩ **3** : of or relating to seniors in an educational institution ⟨the *senior* class⟩

senior airman *n* : a temporary rank in the air force just below that of a sergeant

senior chief petty officer *n* : a naval petty officer with a rank just below that of a master chief petty officer

senior citizen *n* : an elderly person; *esp* : one who has retired

se·nior·i·ty \sēn-'yòr-ət-ē, -'yär-\ *n* **1** : the quality or state of being senior **2** : a privileged position arrived at by length of service

senior master sergeant *n* : a noncommissioned officer in the air force with a rank just below that of chief master sergeant

sen·na \'sen-ə\ *n* **1** : CASSIA 2; *esp* : one used as a medicine **2** : the dried leaves or pods of various cassias used as a strong laxative

se·nor *or* **se·ñor** \sān-'yò(ə)r\ *n, pl* **senors** *or* **se·ño·res** \-'yō(ə)r-ās, -'yò(ə)r-\ : a Spanish or Spanish-speaking man — used as a title equivalent to *Mr.* [from Spanish *señor* "man, gentleman," from Latin *senior* "superior, lord," from earlier *senior* (adjective) "elder, older," from *sen-*, *senex* "old" — related to SENIOR]

se·no·ra *or* **se·ño·ra** \sān-'yōr-ə, -'yòr-\ *n* : a married Spanish or Spanish-speaking girl or woman — used as a title equivalent to *Mrs.*

se·no·ri·ta *or* **se·ño·ri·ta** \sān-yə-'rēt-ə\ *n* : an unmarried Spanish or Spanish-speaking girl or woman — used as a title equivalent to *Miss*

sen·sa·tion \sen-'sā-shən, sən-\ *n* **1 a** : a mental process (as seeing, hearing, or smelling) that results from stimulation of a sense organ **b** : awareness (as of heat or pain) due to stimulation of a sense organ **c** : an indefinite bodily feeling **2 a** : a state of excited interest or feeling **b** : a cause of such excitement

sen·sa·tion·al \sen-'sā-shnəl, -shən-ᵊl, sən-\ *adj* **1** : of or relating to sensation or the senses **2** : arousing a strong and usually shallow interest or emotional reaction ⟨*sensational* news⟩ **3** : exceedingly or unexpectedly excellent or great ⟨a *sensational* diving catch⟩ — **sen·sa·tion·al·ly** \-ē\ *adv*

¹sense \'sen(t)s\ *n* **1** : a meaning or one of a set of meanings a word, phrase, or story may have **2 a** : the power to become aware of by means of sense organs **b** : a specialized function or mechanism (as sight, hearing, smell, taste, or touch) of the body that involves the action and effect of a stimulus on a sense organ ⟨the pain *sense*⟩ **3 a** : a particular sensation or kind of sensation ⟨a good *sense* of balance⟩ **b** : awareness arrived at through or as if through the senses ⟨a vague *sense* of danger⟩ **c** : an awareness and appreciation of something ⟨a fine *sense* of humor⟩ **4 a** : INTELLIGENCE 1 **b** : good reason or excuse ⟨no *sense* in waiting⟩

²sense *vb* **sensed; sens·ing** **1** : to become aware of through the senses **2** : to be or become conscious of ⟨*sense* danger⟩ **3** : to detect automatically especially in response to a physical quantity (as light or movement)

sense·less \'sen(t)-sləs\ *adj* **1** : ¹UNCONSCIOUS **2** ⟨knocked *senseless*⟩ **2** : FOOLISH, STUPID **3** : POINTLESS **1**, MEANINGLESS ⟨a *senseless* act⟩ — **sense·less·ly** *adv* — **sense·less·ness** *n*

sense organ *n* : a body part (as an eye or ear) that receives stimuli (as light or sound) in such a way as to excite nerve cells to send information to the brain

sen·si·bil·i·ty \ˌsen(t)-sə-'bil-ət-ē\ *n, pl* **-ties** **1** : ability to receive sensations : SENSITIVENESS **2** : response to a pleasurable or painful impression (as praise or criticism) **3** : the emotion or feeling of which a person is capable

sen·si·ble \'sen(t)-sə-bəl\ *adj* **1** : possible to take in by the senses or by reason or understanding ⟨felt a *sensible* chill⟩ ⟨her distress was *sensible* from the way she acted⟩ **2** : capable of being made aware of or of feeling ⟨*sensible* to pain⟩ **3** : AWARE ⟨*sensible* of the increasing heat⟩ **4** : showing or containing good sense or reason : REASONABLE ⟨a *sensible* arrangement⟩ — **sen·si·ble·ness** *n* — **sen·si·bly** \-blē\ *adv*

sen·si·tive \'sen(t)-sət-iv, 'sen(t)-stiv\ *adj* **1** : capable of responding to stimulation **2 a** : easily or strongly affected or hurt ⟨a *sensitive* child⟩ **b** : capable of showing very small differences : DELICATE ⟨*sensitive* scales⟩ **c** : readily affected or changed by the action of a certain thing ⟨plants *sensitive* to light⟩ — **sen·si·tive·ly** *adv* — **sen·si·tive·ness** *n*

sensitive plant *n* : any of several mimosas with leaves that fold or droop when touched

sen·si·tiv·i·ty \ˌsen(t)-sə-'tiv-ət-ē\ *n, pl* **-ties** : the quality or state of being sensitive

sen·si·tize \'sen(t)-sə-ˌtīz\ *vb* **-tized; -tiz·ing** : to make or become sensitive

sen·sor \'sen-ˌsò(ə)r, 'sen(t)-sər\ *n* : a device that detects a physical quantity (as a movement or a beam of light) and responds by transmitting a signal

sen·so·ry \'sen(t)s-(ə-)rē\ *adj* **1** : of or relating to sensation or to the senses ⟨*sensory* stimulation⟩ **2** : carrying nerve impulses from the sense organs toward or to the brain : AFFERENT ⟨a *sensory* nerve⟩

sensory neuron *n* : a neuron that transmits nerve impulses from a sense organ (as an eye or nose) toward the central nervous system — compare MOTOR NEURON

sen·su·al \'sench-(ə-)wəl, 'sen-shəl\ *adj* **1** : relating to or consisting in the pleasing of the senses **2** : devoted to the pleasures of the senses — **sen·su·al·i·ty** \ˌsen-chə-'wal-ət-ē\ *n* — **sen·su·al·ly** \'sench-(ə-)wə-lē, 'sen-shə-lē\ *adv*

sen·su·ous \'sench-(ə-)wəs\ *adj* **1 a** : having to do with the senses or with things perceived by the senses **b** : producing an agreeable effect on the senses ⟨mild *sensuous* breezes⟩ **2** : able to be easily influenced through the senses — **sen·su·ous·ly** *adv* — **sen·su·ous·ness** *n*

sent *past and past participle of* SEND

¹sen·tence \'sent-ᵊn(t)s, -ᵊnz\ *n* **1 a** : JUDGMENT 2; *esp* : one pronounced by a court in a criminal proceeding and specifying the punishment **b** : the punishment set by a court **2 a** : a grammatically self-contained group of words that expresses a statement, a question, a command, a wish, or an exclamation **b** : a mathematical or logical statement (as an equation) in words or symbols — **sen·ten·tial** \sen-'ten-chəl\ *adj*

²sentence *vb* **sen·tenced; sen·tenc·ing** **1** : to impose a judgment on ⟨*sentenced* them to prison⟩ **2** : to cause to suffer something

sentence fragment *n* : a word, phrase, or clause that lacks the self-contained structure of a sentence but is written and punctuated like a complete sentence

sen·ten·tious \sen-'ten-chəs\ *adj* : containing or using phrases which sound more important than they are

sen·tient \'sen-ch(ē-)ənt\ *adj* **1** : capable of sensing or feeling ⟨*sentient* beings⟩ **2** : AWARE ⟨*sentient* of one's surroundings⟩

sen·ti·ment \'sent-ə-mənt\ *n* **1 a** : a thought or attitude influenced by feeling **b** : a certain notion : OPINION **2** : tender feelings of affection or yearning

sen·ti·men·tal \ˌsent-ə-'ment-ᵊl\ *adj* **1 a** : marked by feeling or sentiment **b** : resulting from feeling rather than reason or thought **2** : having an excess of sentiment or sensibility — **sen·ti·men·tal·ly** \-ᵊl-ē\ *adv*

sen·ti·men·tal·ism \ˌsent-ə-'ment-ᵊl-ˌiz-əm\ *n* **1** : a tendency to be sentimental **2** : an overly sentimental idea or statement — **sen·ti·men·tal·ist** \-ᵊl-əst\ *n*

sen·ti·men·tal·i·ty \ˌsent-ə-ˌmen-'tal-ət-ē, -mən-\ *n, pl* **-ties** **1** : the quality or state of being sentimental and especially overly sentimental **2** : a sentimental idea or its expression

sen·ti·nel \'sent-(ə-)nəl\ *n* : SENTRY

sen·try \'sen-trē\ *n, pl* **sen·tries** : ¹GUARD 3a; *esp* : a soldier standing guard at a point of passage

se·pal \'sēp-əl, 'sep-\ *n* : one of the specialized leaves that form the calyx of a flower

sep·a·ra·ble \'sep-(ə-)rə-bəl\ *adj* : capable of being separated or distinguished — **sep·a·ra·bil·i·ty** \ˌsep-(ə-)rə-'bil-ət-ē\ *n*

¹sep·a·rate \'sep-ə-ˌrāt\ *vb* **-rat·ed; -rat·ing** **1 a** : to set or keep apart ⟨*separate* the pages with a slip of paper⟩ **b** : to make a distinction between : DISTINGUISH ⟨*separate* fact from fiction⟩ **c** : ²SORT 1 ⟨*separate* mail⟩ **d** : to spread widely in space or time : SCATTER ⟨widely *separated* homesteads⟩ **2** : to end a relationship with that is bound by a contract ⟨*separated* from the army⟩ **3** : to isolate or become isolated from a mixture ⟨*separate* cream from milk⟩ **4** : to become divided or detached : come apart **5** : to cease to live together as man and wife **6** : to go in different directions

   synonyms SEPARATE, PART, DIVIDE mean to break into parts or to keep apart. SEPARATE may suggest that things have been put into different groups, or that a thing has been removed from a group, or that something has been put between like things ⟨*separate* the good eggs from the bad eggs⟩ ⟨a fence *separates* the yards⟩. PART suggests that the things to be separated are closely joined in some way ⟨nothing could *part* the two friends⟩. DIVIDE suggests separating by cutting or breaking into pieces or sections ⟨*divide* the pie into six equal servings⟩.

²sep·a·rate \'sep-(ə-)rət\ *adj* **1** : set or kept apart ⟨the motel contains fifty *separate* units⟩ **2** : not shared with another : INDIVIDUAL ⟨*separate* rooms⟩ **3** : having independent existence ⟨the *separate* pieces of a puzzle⟩ — **sep·a·rate·ly** *adv* — **sep·a·rate·ness** *n*

³sep·a·rate \'sep-(ə-)rət\ *n* : an article of dress designed to be worn interchangeably with others to form different outfits — usually used in plural

sep·a·ra·tion \ˌsep-ə-'rā-shən\ *n* **1** : the act or process of separating : the state of being separated **2 a** : a point or line of division **b** : a space that comes between things : GAP **3 a** : a formal separating of husband and wife by agreement but without divorce **b** : the ending of a relationship that is bound by a contract (as employment or military service)

sep·a·rat·ist \'sep-(ə-)rət-əst\ *n* : a person who favors separation (as from a church or party) — **sep·a·rat·ism** \-rə-ˌtiz-əm\ *n* — **separatist** *adj*

sep·a·ra·tor \'sep-ə-ˌrāt-ər\ *n* : one that separates; *esp* : a device for separating liquids (as cream from milk) of different densities or liquids from solids

¹se·pia \'sē-pē-ə\ *n* **1** : a brown pigment made from the ink of cuttlefishes **2** : a brownish gray

²sepia *adj* : of the color sepia

se·poy \'sē-ˌpȯi\ *n* : a native of India employed as a soldier in the service of a European power

Sep·tem·ber \sep-'tem-bər, səp-\ *n* : the ninth month of the year

   Word History The ancient Romans originally used a calendar which began the year with the month of March. The seventh month of the year was called *September*, from *septem*, a Latin word meaning "seven." The name

was spelled *Septembre* when it was borrowed from early French into Middle English, but eventually the English spelling was changed to that of the original Latin. [Middle English *Septembre* "the month of September," from Old English *September* and early French *Septembre* (both, same meaning), both from Latin *September* "the seventh month," from *septem* "seven"]

sep·tet *also* **sep·tette** \sep-'tet\ *n* **1** : a musical composition for seven instruments or voices **2** : a group or set of seven; *esp* : the musicians that perform a septet

sep·tic sore throat \'sep-tik-\ *n* : STREP THROAT

septic tank *n* : a tank in which solid sewage is broken down by bacteria

sep·til·lion \sep-'til-yən\ *n* — see NUMBER table

sep·tu·a·ge·nar·i·an \(ˌ)sep-ˌt(y)ü-ə-jə-'ner-ē-ən, ˌsep-tə-ˌwäj-ə-\ *n* : a person who is 70 or more but less than 80 years old — **septuagenarian** *adj*

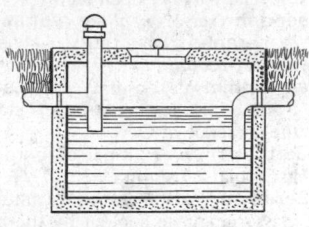
septic tank

Sep·tu·a·ges·i·ma \ˌsep-tə-wə-'jes-ə-mə, -'jā-zə-\ *n* : the third Sunday before Lent

sep·tum \'sep-təm\ *n, pl* **sep·ta** \-tə\ : a dividing wall or membrane especially between bodily spaces or masses of soft tissue

sep·ul·cher *or* **sep·ul·chre** \'sep-əl-kər\ *n* **1** : a place of burial : TOMB **2** : a container for religious relics especially in an altar

se·pul·chral \sə-'pəl-krəl\ *adj* **1** : of or relating to the burial of the dead **2** : DISMAL, GLOOMY

sep·ul·ture \'sep-əl-chù(ə)r\ *n* **1** : BURIAL **2** : SEPULCHER

se·quel \'sē-kwəl\ *n* **1** : an event that follows or comes afterward : RESULT **2** : a book, motion picture, or television program that continues a story begun in a preceding one [Middle English *sequel, sequele* "follower, series," from early French *sequelle* (same meaning), from Latin *sequella, sequela* "follower," from *sequi* "to follow" — related to CONSECUTIVE, PURSUE, ¹SECOND, SEQUENCE]

se·quence \'sē-kwən(t)s, -ˌkwen(t)s\ *n* **1 a** : a continuous or connected series **b** : a set of several shots or scenes developing a single subject (as in a movie) ⟨a chase *sequence* in a spy movie⟩ **2** : the order in which things are or should be connected, related, or dated ⟨the *sequence* of events⟩ **3 a** : ²RESULT 1, CONSEQUENCE **b** : a development that follows something else [Middle English *sequence* "a hymn, a connected series," derived from Latin *sequentia* "state or fact of following, succession," from *sequent-, sequens*, a form of the verb *sequi* "to follow" — related to SEQUEL]

se·quen·tial \si-'kwen-chəl\ *adj* **1** : of, relating to, or arranged in a sequence ⟨*sequential* file systems⟩ **2** : following in sequence — **se·quen·tial·ly** \-'kwench-(ə-)lē\ *adv*

se·ques·ter \si-'kwes-tər\ *vb* **-tered; -ter·ing** \-t(ə-)riŋ\ **1** : to set apart : SEGREGATE ⟨the jury was *sequestered* until a verdict was reached⟩ **2** : to take custody of (as personal property) until a demand is satisfied

se·ques·tra·tion \ˌsēk-wəs-'trā-shən, ˌsek-\ *n* : the act of sequestering : the state of being sequestered

se·quin \'sē-kwən\ *n* : a small piece of shiny metal or plastic used as an ornament especially on clothes

\ə\ abut	\aù\ out	\i\ tip	\ȯ\ saw	\ù\ foot
\ər\ further	\ch\ chin	\ī\ life	\ȯi\ coin	\y\ yet
\a\ mat	\e\ pet	\j\ job	\th\ thin	\yü\ few
\ā\ take	\ē\ easy	\ŋ\ sing	\th\ this	\yù\ cure
\ä\ cot, cart	\g\ go	\ō\ bone	\ü\ food	\zh\ vision

se·quined *or* **se·quinned** \'sē-kwənd\ *adj* : ornamented with or as if with sequins

se·quoia \si-'kwói-(y)ə\ *n* : either of two huge cone-bearing California trees that are related to the bald cypresses and may grow to a height of over 300 feet (90 meters): **a** : GIANT SEQUOIA **b** : REDWOOD

sera *plural of* SERUM

se·ra·glio \sə-'ral-yō\ *n, pl* **-glios** : the rooms assigned to women in a Muslim household

se·ra·pe *or* **sa·ra·pe** \sə-'räp-ē\ *n* : a colorful woolen shawl worn over the shoulders especially by Mexican men

ser·aph \'ser-əf\ *n, pl* **ser·a·phim** \-ə-,fim\ *or* **seraphs** : SERAPHIM — **se·raph·ic** \sə-'raf-ik\ *adj*

ser·a·phim \'ser-ə-,fim\ *n, pl* **seraphim** : one of the 6-winged angels standing in the presence of God

Serb \'sərb\ *n* **1** : a person born or living in Serbia **2** : SERBIAN 2

Ser·bi·an \'sər-bē-ən\ *n* **1** : SERB 1 **2** : a Slavic language spoken by the people of Serbia — **Serbian** *adj*

Ser·bo–Cro·a·tian \,sər-(,)bō-krō-'ā-shən\ *n* : the Serbian and Croatian languages together with the Slavic speech of Bosnia, Herzegovina, and Montenegro considered as a single language with regional variants

sere \'si(ə)r\ *adj* : being dry and withered ⟨*sere* leaves⟩

serape

¹**ser·e·nade** \,ser-ə-'nād\ *n* : music as sung or played outdoors at night for a woman

²**serenade** *vb* **-nad·ed; -nad·ing** : to entertain with or perform a serenade — **ser·e·nad·er** *n*

ser·en·dip·i·ty \,ser-ən-'dip-ət-ē\ *n* : the gift of finding valuable or agreeable things not looked for

se·rene \sə-'rēn\ *adj* **1** : showing complete calm **2 a** : clear and free of storms ⟨*serene* skies⟩ **b** : shining bright and steady **synonyms** see CALM — **se·rene·ly** *adv* — **se·rene·ness** \-'rēn-nəs\ *n*

se·ren·i·ty \sə-'ren-ət-ē\ *n* : the quality or state of being serene : PEACEFULNESS

serf \'sərf\ *n* : a servant or laborer of olden times who was treated as part of the land worked on and went along with the land if it was sold [from French *serf* "a slave bound to a certain piece of land," from early French, from Latin *servus* "slave, servant" — related to SERVANT; see *Word History* at SLAVE] — **serf·dom** \-dəm\ *n*

serge \'sərj\ *n* : a durable cloth woven with diagonal ridges

ser·geant \'sär-jənt\ *n* **1** : a military noncommissioned officer with any of the ranks above corporal in the army or the marines or above airman first class in the air force; *esp* : an enlisted person with the rank just below that of staff sergeant **2** : a police officer ranking in the U.S. just below captain or sometimes lieutenant [Middle English *sergeant* "sergeant, attendant, servant," from early French *sergent, serjant* (same meaning), from Latin *servient-, serviens,* a form of the verb *servire* "to serve"]

sergeant at arms : an officer of a court of law or a lawmaking body appointed to keep order

sergeant first class *n* : an enlisted person in the army with a rank just below that of master sergeant

sergeant major *n, pl* **sergeants major** *or* **sergeant majors** **1** : a noncommissioned officer (as in the army) serving as chief enlisted assistant in a headquarters **2** : an enlisted person of the highest rank in the army or marines

sergeant major of the army : a sergeant major who advises the senior commanding officer of the army

sergeant major of the marine corps : a sergeant major who advises the senior commanding officer of the marines

¹**se·ri·al** \'sir-ē-əl\ *adj* **1** : consisting of or arranged in a series, rank, or row ⟨*serial* order⟩ **2** : appearing in parts or numbers that follow regularly ⟨a *serial* story⟩ **3** : being or relating to a connection in a computer system in which the bits of a byte are transmitted one at a time over a single wire — **se·ri·al·ly** \-ē-ə-lē\ *adv*

²**serial** *n* **1** : a work appearing (as in a magazine or on television) in parts at regular intervals **2** : one part of a serial work — **se·ri·al·ist** \'sir-ē-ə-ləst\ *n*

se·ri·al·ize \'sir-ē-ə-,līz\ *vb* **-ized; -iz·ing** : to arrange or publish in serial form

serial number *n* : a number showing place in a series and used as a means of identification

seri·cul·ture \'ser-ə-,kəl-chər\ *n* : the production of raw silk by raising silkworms

se·ries \'si(ə)r-ēz\ *n, pl* **series** **1** : a number of things or events arranged in order and connected by being alike in some way ⟨a concert *series*⟩ ⟨a *series* of talks⟩ **2** : a division of rock formations smaller than a system comprising rocks deposited during an epoch **3** : an arrangement of the parts of or elements in an electric circuit whereby the whole current passes through each part or element without branching **4** : a group of sentence elements of the same rank that follow one after another and are joined together ⟨the phrase "a bowl of oranges, apples, and bananas" has a *series* of three nouns⟩ — **in series** : in a serial arrangement

ser·if \'ser-əf\ *n* : any of the short lines crossing the upper and lower ends of the strokes of a printed letter

se·ri·ous \'sir-ē-əs\ *adj* **1** : thoughtful or quiet in appearance or manner **2 a** : requiring much thought or work ⟨*serious* study⟩ **b** : of or relating to a matter of importance ⟨a *serious* novel⟩ **3** : not joking or funny **4** : having important or dangerous possible consequences ⟨a *serious* injury⟩ — **se·ri·ous·ly** *adv* — **se·ri·ous·ness** *n*

synonyms SERIOUS, SOLEMN, EARNEST mean not funny or not playful. SERIOUS suggests being concerned about really important things ⟨doctors are *serious* about finding a cure⟩. SOLEMN stresses dignity along with full seriousness ⟨a sad and *solemn* occasion⟩. EARNEST stresses that one is sincere and has serious intentions ⟨an *earnest* student working hard for good grades⟩.

se·ri·ous–mind·ed \,sir-ē-ə-'smīn-dəd\ *adj* : having a serious disposition or trend of thought

ser·mon \'sər-mən\ *n* **1** : a public speech usually by a priest, minister, or rabbi for the purpose of giving religious instruction **2** : a speech on conduct or duty

se·rous membrane \'sir-əs-\ *n* : a thin membrane (as the peritoneum) with cells that secrete a watery fluid

ser·pent \'sər-pənt\ *n* : a usually large snake

ser·pen·tine \'sər-pən-,tēn, -,tīn\ *adj* **1** : of or resembling a serpent **2** : winding or turning one way and another ⟨a *serpentine* path through the woods⟩

ser·rate \'se(ə)r-,āt, sə-'rāt\ *adj* : having a saw-toothed edge ⟨a *serrate* leaf⟩

ser·rat·ed \'ser-,āt-əd, sə-'rāt-\ *adj* : notched or toothed on the edge ⟨a knife with a *serrated* blade⟩ [derived from Latin *serratus,* past participle of *serrare* "to saw," from *serra* "a saw" — related to SIERRA]

ser·ried \'ser-ēd\ *adj* : crowded or pressed together

A B C

S serif

se·rum \'sir-əm\ *n, pl* **serums** *or* **se·ra** \'sir-ə\ **1** : BLOOD SERUM **2** : ANTISERUM

ser·vant \'sər-vənt\ *n* : one that serves others; *esp* : a person hired to perform household or personal services [Middle English *servant* "servant," from early French *servant* (same meaning), from a form of *servir* "to serve," from Latin *servire* "to be a slave, serve," from *servus* "slave, servant" — related to SERF; see *Word History* at SLAVE]

¹serve \'sərv\ *vb* **served; serv·ing 1 a** : to be a servant **b** : to give the service and respect due **c** : to work through or perform a term of service ⟨*served* five years in the marines⟩ **d** : to be in prison for or during ⟨*served* a 10-year sentence⟩ **2 a** : to act officially as a clergyman or priest ⟨*serve* at mass⟩ **b** : to assist as server at mass **3 a** : to be of use : answer a purpose ⟨the tree *serves* as shelter⟩ **b** : to be favorable or convenient ⟨when the time *serves*⟩ **c** : to hold an office : perform a duty ⟨*serve* on a jury⟩ **4** : to be enough for ⟨a pie that will *serve* eight people⟩ **5 a** : to help persons to food ⟨as at a table or counter⟩ **b** : to set out portions of food or drink **6 a** : to furnish or supply with something needed or desired **b** : to wait on customers **7** : to treat or act toward in a certain way ⟨they *served* me ill⟩ **8** : to bring to notice, deliver, or carry out as required by law ⟨*serve* a summons⟩ **9** : to make a serve (as in tennis) — **serve one right** : to be deserved

²serve *n* : the act of putting the ball or shuttlecock in play (as in tennis or badminton)

serv·er \'sər-vər\ *n* **1** : a person who serves food or drink **2** : the player who puts a ball in play **3** : something (as a tray) used in serving food or drink **4** : a computer in a network that is used to provide services (as access to files or the delivery of e-mail) to other computers

¹ser·vice \'sər-vəs\ *n* **1 a** : the occupation or function of serving ⟨in active *service*⟩ **b** : employment as a servant ⟨entered the queen's *service*⟩ **2 a** : the work or action performed by one that serves ⟨gives good *service*⟩ **b** : ²HELP 1, USE, BENEFIT ⟨be of *service* to them⟩ **c** : availability for use ⟨I'll place a car at your *service*⟩ **3** : a religious ceremony or rite ⟨the burial *service*⟩ **4 a** : the act of serving **b** : a helpful act : good turn ⟨did us a *service*⟩ **c** : useful labor that does not produce goods — usually used in plural ⟨charge for professional *services*⟩ **d** : ²SERVE **5** : a set of articles for a particular use ⟨a tea *service*⟩ **6 a** : a branch of public employment or the people working in it ⟨the consular *service*⟩ **b** : a nation's armed forces ⟨called into the *service*⟩ **7** : an organization for supplying some public demand or keeping up and repairing something ⟨television sales and *service*⟩ — **ser·vice** *adj*

¹service 5

²service *vb* **ser·viced; ser·vic·ing** : to work at taking care of and repairing ⟨*service* cars⟩

ser·vice·able \'sər-və-sə-bəl\ *adj* **1** : prepared for or capable of service : USEFUL **2** : lasting or wearing well in use — **ser·vice·abil·i·ty** \ˌsər-və-sə-'bil-ət-ē\ *n* — **ser·vice·able·ness** \'sər-və-sə-bəl-nəs\ *n*

ser·vice·ber·ry \'sər-vəs-ˌber-ē *also* 'sär-\ *n* **1** : any of various North American trees or shrubs related to the roses that are sometimes grown for their showy white flowers and edible purplish to red fruit — called also *Juneberry, shadbush* **2** : the fruit of a serviceberry

service charge *n* : a fee charged for a particular service often in addition to a basic fee

service club *n* **1** : a club of business or professional men or women organized for their common benefit and active in community service **2** : a recreation center for enlisted persons provided by one of the armed services

ser·vice·man \'sər-və-ˌsman, -smən\ *n* : a member of the armed forces

service mark *n* : a mark used to identify a service offered to customers

service module *n* : a part of a space vehicle containing oxygen, water, fuel cells, fuel tanks, and the main rocket engine

service station *n* : GAS STATION

ser·vice·wom·an \'sər-və-ˌswum-ən\ *n* : a woman who is a member of the armed forces

ser·vile \'sər-vəl, -ˌvīl\ *adj* **1** : of or appropriate to a slave **2** : lacking spirit or independence : SUBMISSIVE — **ser·vile·ly** \-və(l)-lē, -ˌvīl-lē\ *adv* — **ser·vil·i·ty** \(ˌ)sər-'vil-ət-ē\ *n*

serv·ing \'sər-viŋ\ *n* : a helping of food or drink ⟨another *serving* of vegetables⟩

ser·vi·tor \'sər-vət-ər, -və-ˌtò(ə)r\ *n* : a male servant

ser·vi·tude \'sər-və-ˌt(y)üd\ *n* : a condition in which one does not have the freedom to determine one's own life

ses·a·me \'ses-ə-mē\ *n* **1** : a hairy herb of warm regions that is grown for its seeds; *also* : its small somewhat flat seeds that are used as a source of oil and to flavor food **2** : OPEN SESAME

sesqui- *combining form* : one and a half times ⟨*sesquicentennial*⟩ [from Latin *sesqui-* "one and a half," literally, "and a half," derived from *semi-* "half"]

ses·qui·cen·ten·ni·al \ˌses-kwi-sen-'ten-ē-əl\ *n* : a 150th anniversary or its celebration — **sesquicentennial** *adj*

ses·sile \'ses-ˌīl, -əl\ *adj* **1** : attached directly by the base and not raised upon a stalk ⟨a *sessile* leaf⟩ **2** : permanently attached and not free to move about : SEDENTARY ⟨*sessile* coral polyps⟩

sesame 1

ses·sion \'sesh-ən\ *n* **1** : a meeting or series of meetings of a body (as a court or legislature) for the carrying on of business **2** : the period between the first meeting of a legislative or judicial body and the last meeting **3** : the period during the year or day in which a school has classes

ses·tet \se-'stet\ *n* : a group of six lines of poetry (as the last six lines of a sonnet)

¹set \'set\ *vb* **set; set·ting 1** : to cause to sit **2** : to give (a fowl) eggs to hatch or provide (eggs) with suitable conditions for hatching **3 a** : to put or fix in a place, condition, or position ⟨*set* a dish on the table⟩ ⟨*set* a trap⟩ ⟨*set* a watch⟩ **b** : to place (a story or performance) in a specified setting ⟨a book *set* in a small town⟩ **4** : to direct with fixed attention ⟨had *set* my heart on a new bike⟩ **5** : to cause to be, become, or do ⟨slaves were *set* free⟩ **6** : to

\ə\ **abut**	\au̇\ **out**	\i\ **tip**	\ȯ\ **saw**	\u̇\ **foot**
\ər\ **further**	\ch\ **chin**	\ī\ **life**	\ȯi\ **coin**	\y\ **yet**
\a\ **mat**	\e\ **pet**	\j\ **job**	\th\ **thin**	\yü\ **few**
\ā\ **take**	\ē\ **easy**	\ŋ\ **sing**	\th\ **this**	\yu̇\ **cure**
\ä\ **cot, cart**	\g\ **go**	\ō\ **bone**	\ü\ **food**	\zh\ **vision**

start on purpose ⟨*set* a fire⟩ **7** : to fix or decide on as a time, limit, or regulation ⟨*set* a price⟩ ⟨*set* a wedding day⟩ **8 a** : to establish as the best performance ⟨*set* a record⟩ **b** : to furnish as a pattern or model ⟨*set* an example⟩ **9** : to restore to normal position or connection ⟨*set* a broken bone⟩ **10 a** : to put in order for immediate use ⟨*set* the table⟩ **b** : to put in order for printing ⟨*set* type by hand⟩ **c** : to put into type or something like type (as on photographic film) ⟨*set* the first word in italic⟩ **11** : to wave, curl, or arrange hair by wetting and drying **12** : to fix in a setting or frame ⟨*set* diamonds in a ring⟩ **13** : ²VALUE 1, RATE ⟨*set* the loss at $2000⟩ **14** : to put and fix in a direction ⟨*set* our faces toward home once more⟩ **15** : to fix firmly : give rigid form to ⟨*set* his jaw in determination⟩ **16** : to become or cause to become firm or solid ⟨the gelatin is *setting*⟩ **17** : to form and bring to maturity ⟨the old tree still *sets* a good crop of apples⟩ **18** *chiefly dialect* : SIT 1a, b **19** : to cover and warm eggs to hatch them ⟨the hen has been *setting* for several days⟩ **20** : to pass below the horizon ⟨the sun *sets*⟩ **21** : to apply oneself to some activity ⟨*set* to work⟩ **22** : to have a certain direction in motion : FLOW **23** : to become permanent ⟨if you don't wash that fast the stain will *set*⟩ — **set about** : to begin to do — **set apart 1** : to reserve for a certain use **2** : to make noticeable — **set aside 1** : ¹DISCARD 2 **2** : to set apart for some purpose : RESERVE, SAVE **3** : ANNUL 2, OVERRULE ⟨the verdict was *set aside* by the court⟩ — **set eyes on** : to catch sight of : SEE ⟨loved her from the minute he *set eyes on* her⟩ — **set foot in** : ENTER 1 — **set foot on** : to step onto — **set forth 1** : to make known ⟨*set forth* an idea⟩ **2** : to start out on a journey : SET OUT — **set in motion** : to give movement to : BEGIN ⟨*set* the plan *in motion*⟩ — **set one's hand to** : to become engaged in : UNDERTAKE — **set one's sights on** : to determine to get or accomplish ⟨*set their sights on* winning the game⟩ — **set store** : to consider valuable or trustworthy — used with *by* or *on* — **set to music** : to provide music for — **set upon** : to attack usually with violence : ASSAULT

²**set** *n* **1 a** : the act or action of setting **b** : the condition of being set **2** : a number of persons or things of the same kind that belong or are used together ⟨the social *set*⟩ ⟨a *set* of dishes⟩ **3** : direction of flow ⟨the *set* of the wind⟩ **4** : the form or movement of the body or of its parts ⟨the *set* of the shoulders⟩ **5** : an artificial setting for a scene of a play or movie **6** : a group of tennis games that make up a match **7** : a group of mathematical elements (as numbers or points) **8** : an electronic device ⟨a television *set*⟩

³**set** *adj* **1** : showing great determination ⟨*set* against going⟩ **2** : fixed by authority ⟨a *set* rule⟩ **3** : not very willing to change ⟨*set* in their ways⟩ **4 a** : FIXED 1a, RIGID ⟨a *set* smile⟩ **b** : BUILT-IN ⟨a *set* tub for washing⟩ **5** : prepared for use or action : READY ⟨are you all *set*?⟩

se·ta \'sēt-ə\ *n, pl* **se·tae** \'sē-,tē\ : a slender usually rigid or bristly and springy organ or part of an animal or plant

set·back \'set-,bak\ *n* : a slowing of progress : a temporary defeat

set down *vb* **1** : to cause to sit down : SEAT **2** : to place at rest on a surface or on the ground **3** : to land (an airplane) on the ground or water **4** : ESTABLISH 2 ⟨the government *set down* laws⟩ **5** : to put in writing

set–in \,set-,in\ *adj* : cut separately and stitched in ⟨*set-in* sleeves⟩

set in *vb* **1** : ¹INSERT 2 **2** : to make its appearance : BEGIN ⟨winter *set in* early⟩

set·line \'set-,līn\ *n* : a long heavy fishing line to which several hooks are attached in a row

set off *vb* **1 a** : to cause to show up clearly ⟨bright flowers *set off* by dark shadows⟩ **b** : to separate from others : make noticeable ⟨a direct quotation *set off* by quotation marks⟩ **2 a** : to cause to go off or explode ⟨*set off* an alarm⟩ ⟨*set off* a firecracker⟩ **b** : to cause to start : BEGIN

⟨*set* an argument *off* by your remarks⟩ **3** : to start out on a course or a trip ⟨*set off* for home⟩ ⟨*set off* in a boat⟩

set out *vb* **1** : to begin with a definite purpose : UNDERTAKE ⟨deliberately *set out* to win⟩ **2** : to start out on a course, a journey, or a career ⟨*set out* to be a doctor⟩ ⟨*set out* for Spain⟩

set·tee \se-'tē\ *n* **1** : a long seat with a back **2** : a medium-sized sofa with arms and a back

set·ter \'set-ər\ *n* **1** : someone or something that sets **2** : a large long-coated dog (as an Irish setter) used in hunting birds that is trained to point on finding game

set theory *n* : a branch of mathematics that deals with sets and with relations between sets — **set–the·o·ret·ic** \-,thē-ə-'ret-ik\ *adj*

set·ting \'set-iŋ\ *n* **1** : the manner, position, or direction in which something is set ⟨change a thermostat *setting*⟩ **2** : a frame or holder in which something is mounted ⟨a *setting* for a diamond⟩ **3** : the background (as time and place) of the action of a story or performance **4** : the articles of tableware required for setting a place at table ⟨two *settings* of silver⟩ **5** : a batch of eggs for hatching

¹**set·tle** \'set-²l\ *n* : a long wooden bench with arms and a high solid back

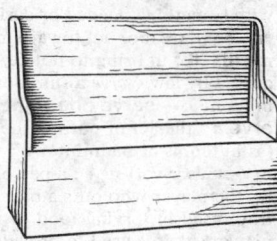

¹settle

²**settle** *vb* **set·tled; set·tling** \'set-liŋ, -²l-iŋ\ **1** : to place so as to stay ⟨*settled* into a chair⟩ **2 a** : to establish in a place to live : COLONIZE ⟨*settled* the West⟩ **b** : to make one's home ⟨*settle* in the country⟩ **3** : to make or become quiet : CALM ⟨rocking *settled* the baby⟩ **4** : DECIDE 1 ⟨*settle* the question⟩ **5** : to put in order : make final arrangements ⟨*settle* an estate⟩ ⟨*settle* a bill⟩ **6** : to adjust differences ⟨*settle* a quarrel⟩ **7 a** : to come to rest ⟨birds *settling* on a branch⟩ **b** : to descend usually slowly and stay down ⟨mist *settling* in the valley⟩ **8 a** : to sink gradually or to the bottom ⟨the foundations of the house *settled*⟩ — often used with *out* ⟨dust particles *settling* out⟩ **b** : to sink in a liquid ⟨sediment *settles* to the bottom⟩ **9** : to apply oneself — usually used with *down* ⟨*settle* down to study⟩ **10** : to take up an ordered life — often used with *down* ⟨marry and *settle* down⟩ — **settle for** : to be content with ⟨would not *settle for* a tie score⟩

set·tle·ment \'set-²l-mənt\ *n* **1** : the act of settling : the condition of being settled **2** : final payment (as of a bill) **3 a** : a place or region newly settled **b** : a small village **4** : SETTLEMENT HOUSE

settlement house *n* : an institution providing various community services to people in a crowded part of a city

set·tler \'set-lər, -²l-ər\ *n* : a person who settles in a new region : COLONIST

set·up \'set-,əp\ *n* : the way in which something is set up : ORGANIZATION, ARRANGEMENT

set up \(')set-'əp\ *vb* **1** : to place in position ⟨*set up* a target⟩ **2 a** : ²ERECT 1 ⟨*set up* a building⟩ **b** : to assemble the parts of ⟨*set up* a machine⟩ **3** : to cause to happen ⟨the wind *sets up* a humming in the wires⟩ **4** : to put in operation : FOUND, INAUGURATE ⟨*set up* a school⟩ **5** : to put in operation as a way of living ⟨*set up* housekeeping⟩ — **set up shop** : to establish one's business

sev·en \'sev-ən\ *n* **1** — see NUMBER table **2** : the seventh in a set or series ⟨the *seven* of hearts⟩ — **seven** *adj or pron*

sev·en–league \'sev-ən-,lēg\ *adj* : crossing seven leagues at a stride ⟨*seven-league* boots⟩

seven seas *n pl* : all the waters or oceans of the world ⟨had sailed the *seven seas*⟩

sev·en·teen \ˌsev-ən-ˈtēn\ *n* — see NUMBER table — **sev·enteen** *adj or pron* — **sev·en·teenth** \-ˈtēn(t)th\ *adj or n*

seventeen–year locust *n* : a cicada of the U.S. with a life span of seventeen years in the North and of thirteen years in the South that spends only a few weeks as a winged adult and lives most of its life as a wingless underground nymph which feeds on roots

sev·enth \ˈsev-ən(t)th\ *n* **1** — see NUMBER table **2** : the difference in pitch between the first tone and the seventh tone of a scale — **seventh** *adj or adv*

sev·en·ty \ˈsev-ən-tē\ *n, pl* **-ties** — see NUMBER table — **sev·en·ti·eth** \-tē-əth\ *adj or n* — **seventy** *adj or pron*

sev·er \ˈsev-ər\ *vb* **sev·ered; sev·er·ing** \-(ə-)riŋ\ **1** : to put or keep apart : DIVIDE; *esp* : to cut off or through **2** : to come or break apart

¹**sev·er·al** \ˈsev-(ə-)rəl\ *adj* **1** : separate or distinct from one another : DIFFERENT 〈federal union of the *several* states〉 **2** : being more than two but not very many 〈*several* persons〉 — **sev·er·al·ly** \-ē\ *adv*

²**several** *pron* : a small number : more than two but not very many 〈*several* of the guests〉

sev·er·ance \ˈsev-(ə-)rən(t)s\ *n* : the act or process of severing : the state of being severed

se·vere \sə-ˈvi(ə)r\ *adj* **se·ver·er; -est 1 a** : strict in judgment, discipline, or government 〈a *severe* ruler〉 **b** : serious in feeling or manner : GRAVE **2** : not using unnecessary ornament : PLAIN 〈a *severe* style〉 **3** : inflicting pain, distress, or hardship 〈*severe* wounds〉 〈a *severe* winter〉 **4** : requiring great effort 〈a *severe* test〉 — **se·vere·ly** *adv*

se·ver·i·ty \sə-ˈver-ət-ē\ *n, pl* **-ties** : the quality or state of being severe

sew \ˈsō\ *vb* **sewed; sewn** \ˈsōn\ *or* **sewed; sew·ing 1** : to join or fasten by stitches 〈*sew* on a button〉 **2** : to work with needle and thread

sew·age \ˈsü-ij\ *n* : waste materials carried off by sewers

¹**sew·er** \ˈsō(-ə)r\ *n* : one that sews

²**sew·er** \ˈsü-ər, ˈsù(-ə)r\ *n* : a usually covered drain to carry off water and sewage

sew·er·age \ˈsü-ə-rij, ˈsù(-ə)r-ij\ *n* **1** : SEWAGE **2** : the removal and disposal of sewage and surface water by sewers **3** : a system of sewers

sew·ing \ˈsō-iŋ\ *n* **1** : the act, method, or occupation of one that sews **2** : material that has been or is to be sewed

sewing machine *n* : a machine for sewing

sew up *vb* **1** : to get exclusive use or control of **2** : to make certain of

sex \ˈseks\ *n* **1** : either of two groups into which many living things are divided according to their roles in reproduction and which consist of males or females **2** : the physical and behavioral characteristics that make males and females different from each other **3** : sexual activity; *esp* : SEXUAL INTERCOURSE [Middle English *sex* "category of living things according to reproductive roles," from Latin *sexus* (same meaning)]

sex- *or* **sexi-** *combining form* : six 〈*sex*tet〉 [from Latin *sex* "six"]

sex·a·ge·nar·i·an \ˌsek-sə-jə-ˈner-ē-ən, (ˌ)sek-ˌsaj-ə-\ *n* : a person who is 60 or more but less than 70 years old — **sexagenarian** *adj*

sex cell *n* : an egg cell or a sperm cell

sex chromosome *n* : either of a pair of chromosomes (as the human X chromosome or the human Y chromosome) in a sexually reproducing organism that are inherited differently in the two sexes and are concerned with the determination of sex

sex gland *n* : GONAD

sex hormone *n* : a hormone (as estrogen or testosterone) that affects the growth or function of the reproductive organs or the development of secondary sex characteristics

sex·ism \ˈsek-ˌsiz-əm\ *n* : distinction and especially unjust distinction based on sex and made against one person or group in favor of another; *esp* : distinctions made against women — **sex·ist** \ˈsek-səst\ *adj or n*

sex–linked \ˈsek-ˌsliŋ(k)t\ *adj* **1** : located on one type of sex chromosome but not on the other 〈a *sex-linked* gene〉 **2** : controlled by a sex-linked gene 〈a *sex-linked* characteristic〉 — **sex–link·age** \-ˌsliŋ-kij\ *n*

sex·tant \ˈsek-stənt\ *n* : a navigational instrument for measuring the angle between the horizon and the sun or a star in order to find out the latitude (as of a ship)

sex·tet \sek-ˈstet\ *n* **1** : a musical composition for six instruments or voices **2** : a group or set of six

sex·til·lion \sek-ˈstil-yən\ *n* — see NUMBER table

sex·ton \ˈsek-stən\ *n* : an official of a church who takes care of church buildings and property

sextant

¹**sex·tu·ple** \sek-ˈst(y)üp-əl, -ˈstəp-; ˈsek-stəp-\ *adj* **1** : having six units or members **2** : being six times as great or as many — **sextuple** *n*

²**sextuple** *vb* **sex·tu·pled; sex·tu·pling** \-(ə-)liŋ\ : to make or become six times as much or as many

sex·tu·plet \sek-ˈstəp-lət, -ˈst(y)üp-; ˈsek-st(y)əp-\ *n* **1** : a combination of six of a kind **2** : one of six offspring born at one birth

sex·u·al \ˈseksh-(ə-)wəl, ˈsek-shəl\ *adj* **1** : of or relating to sex or the sexes 〈*sexual* differences〉 **2** : having or involving sex 〈*sexual* reproduction〉 — **sex·u·al·ly** \ˈseksh-(ə-)wə-lē, ˈseksh-(ə-)lē\ *adv*

sexual harassment *n* : uninvited and unwelcome verbal or physical behavior of a sexual nature especially by a person in authority toward a subordinate (as an employee or student)

sexual intercourse *n* : sexual union especially involving penetration of the vagina by the penis

sex·u·al·i·ty \ˌsek-shə-ˈwal-ət-ē\ *n* : the quality or state of being sexual

sexually transmitted disease *n* : STD

sexual relations *n pl* : SEXUAL INTERCOURSE

sexy \ˈsek-sē\ *adj* **sex·i·er; -est** : sexually exciting : EROTIC — **sex·i·ness** *n*

sfor·zan·do \sfȯrt-ˈsän-dō, -ˈsan-\ *adj* : played with special stress or accent — used as a direction in music

shab·by \ˈshab-ē\ *adj* **shab·bi·er; -est 1** : dressed in worn clothes **2 a** : worn and faded from wear 〈a *shabby* sofa〉 **b** : ill kept : DILAPIDATED 〈*shabby* houses〉 **3** : not fair or generous 〈*shabby* treatment〉 — **shab·bi·ly** \ˈshab-ə-lē\ *adv* — **shab·bi·ness** \ˈshab-ē-nəs\ *n*

Sha·bu·oth \shə-ˈvü-ˌōt(h), -ˌōs, -əs\ *n* : a Jewish holiday celebrated in May or June to commemorate the revelation of the Ten Commandments at Mount Sinai

shack \ˈshak\ *n* **1** : HUT, SHANTY **2** : a room or similar enclosed structure for a particular person or use 〈a radio *shack*〉

¹**shack·le** \ˈshak-əl\ *n* **1** : a ring or band that prevents free use of the legs or arms **2** : something that prevents free action — usually used in plural **3** : a U-shaped metal device for joining or fastening something

²**shackle** *vb* **shack·led; shack·ling** \ˈshak-(ə-)liŋ\ **1 a** : to bind with shackles 〈the guard *shackled* the prisoner〉 **b** : to make fast with a shackle **2** : to deprive of freedom of

\ə\ abut	\aù\ out	\i\ tip	\ȯ\ saw	\ù\ foot
\ər\ further	\ch\ chin	\ī\ life	\ȯi\ coin	\y\ yet
\a\ mat	\e\ pet	\j\ job	\th\ thin	\yü\ few
\ā\ take	\ē\ easy	\ŋ\ sing	\th\ this	\yù\ cure
\ä\ cot, cart	\g\ go	\ō\ bone	\ü\ food	\zh\ vision

action : HINDER ⟨*shackled* by poverty⟩ — **shack·ler** \-(ə-)lər\ *n*

shad \'shad\ *n, pl* **shad** : any of several sea fishes that are related to the her- rings, swim up rivers to lay or fertilize eggs, and include important food fishes

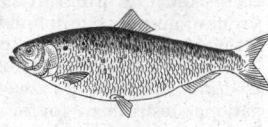

shad

shad·bush \'shad-ˌbush\ *n* : SERVICEBERRY 1

¹**shade** \'shād\ *n* 1 : partial darkness ⟨the trees cast *shade*⟩ 2 : space sheltered from the heat and bright light of the sun ⟨sit in the *shade* of a tree⟩ 3 *pl* : the shadows that gather as darkness falls ⟨the *shades* of night⟩ 4 : ¹SPIRIT 2b, GHOST 5 : something that blocks off or cuts down light, sun, or heat ⟨a lamp *shade*⟩ ⟨a window *shade*⟩ 6 : the darkening of some objects in a painting or drawing to suggest that they are in shade 7 : the darkness or light- ness of a color ⟨four *shades* of brown⟩ 8 : a very small difference or amount ⟨just a *shade* taller⟩ ⟨*shades* of meaning⟩ — **shade·less** \-ləs\ *adj*

²**shade** *vb* **shad·ed; shad·ing** 1 : to shelter from light or heat 2 : to mark with changes of light or color ⟨*shade* a drawing⟩ 3 : to show or begin to have slight differences of color, value, or meaning — **shad·er** *n*

shade tree *n* : a tree grown chiefly to make shade

¹**shad·ow** \'shad-ō\ *n* 1 : shade within certain bounds ⟨the valley was in *shadow*⟩ 2 : a reflected image (as in a mir- ror) 3 : shelter from danger or view 4 **a** : an imperfect and faint representation **b** : an imitation of something 5 : the dark figure cast on a surface by a body that is be- tween the surface and the light ⟨my *shadow* stays with me⟩ 6 : ¹PHANTOM 7 *pl* : darkness caused by the setting of the sun ⟨twilight *shadows*⟩ 8 : a shaded part of a pic- ture 9 : a form from which the substance has departed : REMNANT, VESTIGE 10 **a** : an inseparable companion or follower **b** : a person who shadows as a spy or detective 11 : a very little bit : TRACE ⟨not a *shadow* of a doubt⟩ 12 : a source of gloom or unhappiness — **shad·ow·less** \-ləs\ *adj* — **shad·ow·like** \-ˌlīk\ *adj*

²**shadow** *vb* 1 : to cast a shadow on 2 : to follow espe- cially secretly : TRAIL — **shad·ow·er** \'shad-ə-wər\ *n*

shad·ow·box \'shad-ō-ˌbäks\ *vb* : to box with an imagi- nary opponent as a form of training

shad·owy \'shad-ə-wē\ *adj* 1 **a** : not realistic ⟨*shadowy* dreams of glory⟩ **b** : dim as a shadow ⟨the *shadowy* area between good and bad⟩ 2 : full of shade ⟨a *shadowy* lane⟩

shady \'shād-ē\ *adj* **shad·i·er; -est** 1 : casting a shadow : giving shade 2 : sheltered from the sun's rays ⟨a *shady* grove⟩ 3 : not right or honest ⟨a *shady* business deal⟩ — **shad·i·ly** \'shād-ᵊl-ē\ *adv* — **shad·i·ness** \'shād-ē-nəs\ *n*

shaft \'shaft\ *n, pl* **shafts** \'shaf(t)s, *in sense 1c also* 'shavz\ 1 **a** : the long handle of a weapon (as a spear) **b** : ¹SPEAR 1, LANCE **c** *or pl* **shaves** \'shavz\ : ¹POLE 1; *esp* : one of two poles between which a horse is hitched to pull a ve- hicle **d** : an arrow especially for a longbow 2 : a narrow beam of light 3 : something suggestive of the shaft of an arrow or spear ⟨the *shaft* or trunk of a tree⟩ 4 : the han- dle of a tool or instrument (as a hammer or golf club) 5 : a tall monument (as a column) 6 : an opening or pas- sage straight down through the floors of a building ⟨an air *shaft*⟩ 7 : a commonly cylindrical bar used to support rotating pieces or to transmit power or motion by rota- tion 8 : a mine opening for finding or mining ore 9 : the midrib of a feather 10 : the part of a hair that is visible above the surface of the skin

¹**shag** \'shag\ *n* 1 **a** : a shaggy tangled mass or covering **b** : a rug or carpeting with long yarns that do not stand up 2 : a strong coarse tobacco cut into fine shreds

²**shag** *vb* **shagged; shag·ging** 1 : to chase after and re- turn a ball 2 : to catch a ball

shag·bark hickory \'shag-ˌbärk-\ *n* : a hickory of the east- ern U.S. and Canada with a gray shaggy outer bark that peels off in long strips — called also *shagbark*

shag·gy \'shag-ē\ *adj* **shag·gi·er; -est** 1 : covered with or made up of long, coarse, or tangled growth 2 : having a rough or hairy surface — **shag·gi·ly** \'shag-ə-lē\ *adv* — **shag·gi·ness** \'shag-ē-nəs\ *n*

shah \'shä, 'shò\ *n* : a ruler of Iran until the 1979 revolu- tion

¹**shake** \'shāk\ *vb* **shook** \'shuk\; **shak·en** \'shā-kən\; **shak·ing** 1 : to move irregularly to and fro : QUIVER, TREMBLE ⟨*shaking* with cold⟩ 2 : to become unsteady : TOTTER 3 : to cause to move in a usually quick jerky manner 4 : to free oneself from ⟨*shake* off a cold⟩ 5 : to cause to become weaker ⟨*shake* one's faith⟩ 6 : to force out of a place by quick jerky movements ⟨*shake* dust from a blanket⟩ 7 : to clasp (hands) in greeting or as a sign of goodwill or agreement — **shak·able** \'shā-kə-bəl\ *adj* — **shake a leg** : to hurry up

²**shake** *n* 1 : an act of shaking 2 *pl* : a condition of trem- bling (as from chill) 3 : something produced by shaking; *esp* : MILK SHAKE 4 : a very brief period of time ⟨ready in two *shakes*⟩ 5 *pl* : one that stands out especially in importance, ability, or merit — usually used in the phrase *no great shakes* 6 : a long shingle 7 : ³DEAL 2 ⟨a fair *shake*⟩

shake·down \'shāk-ˌdaun\ *n* : a testing under operating conditions of something new (as a ship) for possible faults or for the operators to become more familiar with it ⟨a *shakedown* cruise⟩

shak·er \'shā-kər\ *n* 1 : a utensil or machine used in shak- ing 2 *cap* : a member of a religious group originating in England and practicing a communal life

Shake·spear·ean *or* **Shake·spear·ian** \shāk-'spir-ē-ən\ *adj* : of, relating to, or having the characteristics of Shakespeare or his writings

shake–up \'shā-ˌkəp\ *n* : an act or instance of shaking up; *esp* : a reorganization that has extreme effects ⟨lost their jobs in an office *shake-up*⟩

shake up \(')shā-'kəp\ *vb* 1 : to jar by or as if by a physi- cal shock ⟨the accident *shook up* both drivers⟩ ⟨the news *shook* us *up*⟩ 2 : to bring about an extensive reorganiza- tion of

sha·ko \'shak-ō, 'shāk-\ *n, pl* **sha·kos** *or* **sha·koes** : a stiff military cap with a high crown and plume

shako

shaky \'shā-kē\ *adj* **shak·i·er; -est** 1 **a** : lacking firmness **b** : lacking in au- thority or reliability : QUESTIONABLE ⟨*shaky* data⟩ 2 : marked by shaking : TREMBLING 3 : likely to give way or break down — **shak·i·ly** \-kə-lē\ *adv* — **shak·i·ness** \-kē-nəs\ *n*

shale \'shā(ə)l\ *n* : a rock with a fine grain formed from clay, mud, or silt — **shal·ey** \'shā-lē\ *adj*

shall \shəl, (')shal\ *helping verb, past* **should** \shəd, (')shud\; *present sing & pl* **shall** 1 : am or are going to or expect- ing to : WILL ⟨I *shall* write today⟩ 2 : is or are compelled to : MUST ⟨they *shall* not pass⟩

shal·lop \'shal-əp\ *n* : a small open boat moved by oars or sails

¹**shal·low** \'shal-ō\ *adj* 1 : having little depth ⟨*shallow* wa- ter⟩ 2 : showing little knowledge, thought, or feeling — **shal·low·ly** *adv* — **shal·low·ness** *n*

²**shallow** *n* : a shallow place or area in a body of water — usually used in plural

shalt \shəlt, (')shalt\ *archaic present 2nd singular of* SHALL

¹**sham** \'sham\ *n* 1 : a trick that deceives : HOAX 2 : some- thing resembling an article of personal or household linen

and used in place of or over it **3** : an imitation or counterfeit giving the impression of being real

²sham *vb* **shammed; sham·ming** : to act in a deceiving way

³sham *adj* : not real : FALSE ⟨*sham* pearls⟩

sham·ble \'sham-bəl\ *vb* **sham·bled; sham·bling** \-b(ə-)liŋ\ : to walk awkwardly with dragging feet : SHUFFLE — **shamble** *n*

sham·bles \'sham-bəlz\ *n sing or pl* **1** : a place or state of destruction ⟨the hurricane left the city in a *shambles*⟩ **2** : a scene or state of disorder or confusion : MESS ⟨this room is a *shambles*⟩ ⟨an economy in *shambles*⟩

¹shame \'shām\ *n* **1 a** : a painful emotion caused by having done something wrong or improper **b** : ability to feel shame ⟨have you no *shame*?⟩ **2** : ¹DISHONOR 1, DISGRACE **3** : something that brings disgrace or causes shame or strong regret **4** : something to be regretted : PITY ⟨it's a *shame* you'll miss the show⟩

²shame *vb* **shamed; sham·ing** **1** : to bring shame to : DISGRACE **2** : to cause to feel shame **3** : to force by causing to feel guilty ⟨they were *shamed* into confessing⟩

shame·faced \'shām-'fāst\ *adj* **1** : showing modesty : BASHFUL **2** : showing shame : ASHAMED — **shame·faced·ly** \-'fā-səd-lē, -'fāst-lē\ *adv* — **shame·faced·ness** \-'fā-səd-nəs, -'fās(t)-nəs\ *n*

Word History The Old English word *scamfæst* was formed by a combination of the noun *scamu,* meaning "shame," and the adjective *fæst,* meaning "firmly fixed or bound, fast." The meaning of *scamfæst* was "bound by shame" or, more simply, "bashful." Over the course of many years, Old English *scamfæst* was changed to modern English *shamefaced*. The change from *-fæst* to *-faced* occurred because many people misunderstood *-fæst*. They substituted a more familiar word for one they did not know. The belief that bashfulness shows in a person's face probably also influenced the change. [an altered form of earlier *shamefast*, from Old English *scamfæst* "bound by shame, bashful," from *scamu* "shame" and *fæst* "fixed, fast"]

shame·ful \'shām-fəl\ *adj* **1** : bringing shame ⟨*shameful* behavior⟩ **2** : arousing the feeling of shame ⟨a *shameful* sight⟩ — **shame·ful·ly** \-fə-lē\ *adv* — **shame·ful·ness** \-fəl-nəs\ *n*

shame·less \'shām-ləs\ *adj* **1** : having no shame **2** : showing lack of shame — **shame·less·ly** *adv* — **shame·less·ness** *n*

¹sham·poo \sham-'pü\ *vb* : to wash (as the hair) with soap and water or with a special preparation — **sham·poo·er** *n*

²shampoo *n* **1** : an act or instance of shampooing **2** : a cleaner used in shampooing

sham·rock \'sham-,räk\ *n* : a plant of folk legend with leaves composed of three leaflets that is associated with St. Patrick and Ireland; *also* : any of several plants (as a clover or a wood sorrel) or their leaves that resemble, are worn to represent, or are held to be the shamrock of legend [from Irish *seamróg,* literally, "little clover"]

shang·hai \shaŋ-'hī\ *vb* **shang·haied; shang·hai·ing** **1** : to put aboard a ship by force often with the help of liquor or a drug **2** : to put by threat or force into or as if into a place of detention **3** : to put by trickery into an undesirable position [from *Shanghai,* a major seaport in China; so called because this method was formerly sometimes used to get sailors for ships sailing to eastern Asia]

shank \'shaŋk\ *n* **1 a** : the part of the leg between the knee and the ankle in human beings or a similar part in various other vertebrates **b** : a cut of meat (as beef or lamb) from usually the upper part of a leg **2 a** : the straight shaft (as of a nail, pin, or fishhook) **b** : the narrow part of the sole of a shoe beneath the instep **3** : a part of a tool that connects the acting part with a part by which it is held or moved ⟨the *shank* of a drill bit⟩ ⟨the

shank of a key⟩ **4** : a part of something by which it can be attached: as **a** : a part that sticks out on the back of a solid button **b** : a short stem of thread that holds a sewn button away from the cloth — **shanked** \'shan(k)t\ *adj*

shan't \(')shant, (')shänt\ : shall not

¹shanty *variant of* CHANTEY

²shan·ty \'shant-ē\ *n, pl* **shanties** : SHACK, HUT

shan·ty·town \-,taùn\ *n* : a usually poor town or section of a town made up mostly of shanties

¹shape \'shāp\ *vb* **shaped; shap·ing** **1** : to give a certain form or shape to ⟨*shape* the dough into loaves⟩ **2** : to change in shape so as to fit neatly and closely ⟨a hat *shaped* close to the head⟩ **3** : DEVISE 1, PLAN **4** : to make fit especially for some purpose ⟨*shaping* the minds of future leaders⟩ **5** : to take on or approach a definite form — often used with *up* — **shap·er** *n*

²shape *n* **1** : outward appearance : FORM ⟨the *shape* of a pearl⟩ **2** : the outline of a body : FIGURE ⟨a square *shape*⟩ **3** : definite form and arrangement ⟨a plan now taking *shape*⟩ **4** : something having a certain form **5** : the condition in which something or someone is at a certain time ⟨the car was in poor *shape*⟩ — **shaped** \,shāpt\ *adj*

shape·less \'shā-pləs\ *adj* **1** : having no fixed or regular shape **2 a** : deprived of usual or normal shape **b** : not shapely — **shape·less·ly** *adv* — **shape·less·ness** *n*

shape·ly \'shā-plē\ *adj* **shape·li·er; -est** : having a regular or pleasing shape ⟨a *shapely* figure⟩ — **shape·li·ness** *n*

shape up \(')shāp\ *vb* : to improve to a good condition or standard ⟨*shape up* and start studying⟩

shard \'shärd\ *n* : a piece or fragment of something brittle (as pottery)

¹share \'she(ə)r, 'sha(ə)r\ *n* **1** : a portion belonging to, due to, or contributed by an individual **2** : the part given or belonging to one of a number owning something together ⟨sold my *share* of the business⟩ **3** : any of the equal portions or interests into which the property of a corporation is divided ⟨100 *shares* of stock⟩

²share *vb* **shared; shar·ing** **1** : to divide and distribute in portions ⟨*shared* the lunch⟩ **2** : to use, experience, or enjoy with others **3** : to give or be given a share : take a part ⟨*share* in planning the program⟩ *synonyms* see PARTAKE — **shar·er** *n*

share·crop \'she(ə)r-,kräp, 'sha(ə)r-\ *vb* **share·cropped; share·crop·ping** : to farm or produce as a sharecropper

share·crop·per \'she(ə)r-,kräp-ər, 'sha(ə)r-\ *n* : a farmer who works land for the owner in return for a share of the value of the crop

share·hold·er \-,hōl-dər\ *n* : one that owns or holds a share in property; *esp* : STOCKHOLDER

share·ware \-,wa(ə)r, -,we(ə)r\ *n* : software with usually only basic capability which is available for trial use at little or no cost but which can be upgraded for a fee

¹shark \'shärk\ *n* : any of numerous marine fishes that have rough grayish skin and a skeleton made of cartilage, that usually prey on other animals and are sometimes dangerous to people, and that include some caught for the oil in their livers or for their hide from which a leather is made — **shark·like** \'shär-,klīk\ *adj*

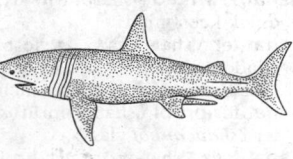

¹shark

²**shark** *n* **1** : a sly greedy person who takes advantage of others ⟨a loan *shark*⟩ **2** : a person who outdoes others especially in a certain area ⟨a *shark* at arithmetic⟩

shark·skin \'shärk-ˌskin\ *n* **1** : the hide of a shark or leather made from it **2** : a smooth durable material with small woven designs that looks like the hide of a shark

¹**sharp** \'shärp\ *adj* **1 a** : having a thin keen edge or fine point ⟨a *sharp* knife⟩ **b** : briskly cold : NIPPING ⟨*sharp* biting wind⟩ **2 a** : alert in understanding : QUICK-WITTED ⟨a *sharp* student⟩ **b** : having very good ability to see or hear ⟨you have *sharp* eyes⟩ **c** : keen in attention to one's own interest sometimes to the point of being dishonest ⟨a *sharp* customer⟩ **3 a** : full of activity or energy : BRISK ⟨keep up a *sharp* pace⟩ **b** : EAGER ⟨a *sharp* appetite⟩ **4 a** : CURT, ANGRY ⟨a *sharp* reply⟩ **b** : causing intense mental or physical distress ⟨a *sharp* pain⟩ ⟨*sharp* criticism⟩ **5** : having a strong odor or flavor ⟨*sharp* cheese⟩ **6 a** : ending in a point or edge ⟨*sharp* features⟩ ⟨*sharp* mountain peaks⟩ **b** : involving an abrupt change ⟨a *sharp* turn⟩ ⟨a *sharp* drop in the temperature⟩ **c** : clear in outline or detail : DISTINCT ⟨a *sharp* image⟩ **d** : set forth with clarity and distinctness ⟨*sharp* contrast⟩ **7 a** : higher by a half step than the pitch of the note indicated by the letter name **b** : higher than the true pitch **8** : STYLISH, DRESSY — **sharp·ly** *adv* — **sharp·ness** *n*

synonyms SHARP, KEEN, ACUTE mean having or showing alertness and clear understanding. SHARP suggests quick understanding, cleverness, and sometimes trickery ⟨*sharp* traders⟩. KEEN suggests quickness, enthusiasm, and a mind of deep understanding ⟨a *keen* observer of human behavior⟩. ACUTE suggests the power to think clearly and to see small differences ⟨*acute* powers of reasoning⟩.

²**sharp** *adv* **1** : in a sharp manner : SHARPLY ⟨sang *sharp*⟩ **2** : at an exact time ⟨arrive by four o'clock *sharp*⟩

³**sharp** *n* **1** : a musical note or tone one half step higher than the note or tone indicated by the letter name; *also* : a character ♯ on a line or space of the staff indicating such a note or tone **2** : a needle with a small eye for sewing by hand

⁴**sharp** *vb* **1** : to raise in pitch especially by a half step **2** : to sing or play above the true pitch

sharp·en \'shär-pən\ *vb* **sharp·ened; sharp·en·ing** \'shärp-(ə-)niŋ\ **1** : to make or become sharp or sharper ⟨*sharpen* a pencil⟩ ⟨a better lens *sharpened* the image⟩ ⟨pain that suddenly *sharpened*⟩ **2** : IMPROVE ⟨*sharpen* one's skills⟩ — **sharp·en·er** \'shärp-(ə-)nər\ *n*

sharp·er \'shär-pər\ *n* : ²CHEAT 2, SWINDLER

sharp·eyed \'shär-'pīd\ *adj* : having keen sight; *also* : keen in observing or seeing through ⟨a *sharp-eyed* hiker spotted the rare bird⟩

sharp·shoot·er \'shärp-ˌshüt-ər\ *n* : one skilled in shooting : a good marksman — **sharp·shoot·ing** \-ˌshüt-iŋ\ *n*

sharp·wit·ted \'shärp-'wit-əd\ *adj* : having or showing a quick keen mind

shat·ter \'shat-ər\ *vb* **1** : to break or fall to pieces ⟨the window *shattered*⟩ **2** : to damage badly : RUIN, WRECK ⟨the bad news will *shatter* their morale⟩

shat·ter·proof \ˌshat-ər-'prüf\ *adj* : made so as not to shatter ⟨*shatterproof* glass⟩

shat·ters \'shat-ərz\ *n pl* : broken pieces ⟨the vase lay in *shatters*⟩

¹**shave** \'shāv\ *vb* **shaved; shaved** *or* **shav·en** \'shā-vən\; **shav·ing 1 a** : to cut off in thin layers or shreds **b** : to cut off closely **2 a** : to cut the hair from (as the head) close to the roots **b** : to cut off hair or beard close to the skin **3** : to come close to or touch lightly in passing ⟨the tire *shaved* the curb⟩

²**shave** *n* **1** : a tool for shaving or cutting thin slices **2** : an act or process of shaving especially the beard **3** : a narrow escape ⟨a close *shave*⟩

shav·er \'shā-vər\ *n* **1** : a person who shaves **2** : a tool or machine for shaving; *esp* : an electric-powered razor **3** : BOY 1, YOUNGSTER

shaves *plural of* SHAFT

shav·ing \'shā-viŋ\ *n* **1** : the act of one that shaves **2** : something shaved off ⟨wood *shavings*⟩

¹**shawl** \'shȯl\ *n* : a square or oblong piece of woven or knitted fabric used especially as a covering for the head or shoulders

²**shawl** *vb* : to wrap in or as if in a shawl

Shaw·nee \shȯ-'nē, shä-\ *n* : a member of an American Indian people originally of the central Ohio valley

shay \'shā\ *n, chiefly dialect* : a two-wheeled carriage; *esp* : CHAISE

¹**she** \(')shē\ *pron* : that female one ⟨*she* is my wife⟩

²**she** \'shē\ *n* : a female person or animal — often used in combination ⟨*she*-cat⟩

sheaf \'shēf\ *n, pl* **sheaves** \'shēvz\ **1** : a bundle of stalks and ears of grain **2** : a group of things often fastened together and resembling a sheaf of grain ⟨a *sheaf* of arrows⟩ ⟨a *sheaf* of papers⟩ — **sheaf·like** \'shē-ˌflīk\ *adj*

¹**shear** \'shi(ə)r\ *vb* **sheared; sheared** *or* **shorn** \'shō(ə)rn, 'shȯ(ə)rn\; **shear·ing 1** : to cut the hair or wool from ⟨*shearing* sheep⟩ **2** : to deprive of by or as if by cutting off ⟨*shorn* of power⟩ **3** : to become divided under the action of a shear ⟨the bolt may *shear* off⟩ — **shear·er** *n*

²**shear** *n* **1 a** : a cutting tool similar or identical to a pair of scissors but typically larger — usually used in plural **b** : any of various cutting tools or machines operating by the action of opposed cutting edges of metal — usually used in plural **2** : an action or force that causes or tends to cause two parts of a body to slide on each other in a direction parallel to their plane of contact

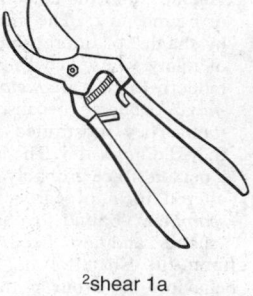

²shear 1a

shear·wa·ter \'shi(ə)r-ˌwȯt-ər, -ˌwät-\ *n* : any of numerous marine birds related to the petrels and albatrosses that often skim close to the water during flight

sheath \'shēth\ *n, pl* **sheaths** \'shēthz, 'shēths\ **1** : a case for a blade (as of a knife) **2** : a covering especially of a body part that is like a sheath in form or use

sheathe \'shēth\ *vb* **sheathed; sheath·ing 1** : to put into a sheath ⟨*sheathe* your sword⟩ **2** : to cover with something that protects ⟨*sheathe* a ship's bottom with copper⟩ — **sheath·er** *n*

sheath·ing \'shē-thiŋ, -thiŋ\ *n* : material used to sheathe something; *esp* : the first covering of boards or of waterproof material on the outside wall of a frame house or on a timber roof

sheath knife *n* : a knife having a fixed blade and designed to be carried in a sheath

¹**sheave** \'shiv, 'shēv\ *n* : a grooved wheel : PULLEY

²**sheave** \'shēv\ *vb* **sheaved; sheav·ing** : to gather and bind into a sheaf

she·bang \shi-'baŋ\ *n* : everything involved that is under consideration — usually used in the phrase *the whole shebang*

¹**shed** \'shed\ *vb* **shed; shed·ding 1** : to keep out : REPEL ⟨raincoats *shed* water⟩ **2 a** : to cause (blood) to flow from a cut or wound **b** : to pour forth in drops ⟨*shed* tears⟩ **c** : to give off or out ⟨the sun *sheds* light and heat⟩ **3 a** : to cast (as a natural covering) aside ⟨a snake *sheds* its skin⟩ **b** : to let fall (as leaves) **4** : to rid oneself of : DISCARD ⟨*shed* extra pounds⟩ — **shed·der** *n*

²**shed** *n* : a structure built for shelter or storage

she'd \\(ˌ)shēd\ : she had : she would

sheen \'shēn\ *n* : a bright or shining condition ⟨the *sheen* of satin⟩

sheep \'shēp\ *n, pl* **sheep** 1 : any of various cud-chewing mammals that are stockier than the related goats and lack a beard in the male; *esp* : one raised for its wool, skin, or flesh 2 : a weak helpless person who is easily led

sheep·dog \'shēp-ˌdȯg\ *n* : a dog used to tend, drive, or guard sheep

sheep·fold \'shēp-ˌfōld\ *n* : a pen or shelter for sheep

sheep·herd·er \'shēp-ˌhərd-ər\ *n* : a worker in charge of a flock of sheep — **sheep·herd·ing** \-ˌhərd-iŋ\ *n*

sheep·ish \'shē-pish\ *adj* 1 : resembling a sheep (as in being meek or shy) 2 : embarrassed especially over being found out in a fault ⟨a *sheepish* look⟩ — **sheep·ish·ly** *adv* — **sheep·ish·ness** *n*

sheeps·head \'shēps-ˌhed\ *n* : any of several fishes; *esp* : a food fish of the Atlantic and Gulf coasts of the U.S. with broad front teeth

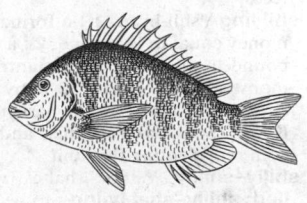

sheepshead

sheep·skin \'shēp-ˌskin\ *n* 1 : the skin of a sheep or leather made from it 2 : DI-PLOMA

¹sheer \'shi(ə)r\ *adj* 1 : very thin or transparent ⟨*sheer* stockings⟩ 2 a : being such to the fullest degree : UTTER ⟨*sheer* nonsense⟩ b : taken or acting apart from everything else ⟨by *sheer* force⟩ 3 : very steep : being almost straight up and down ⟨a *sheer* drop to the sea⟩ [from earlier *sheer* "shining," from Middle English *sheer* "freed from guilt," probably from an early Norse word *skærr* "pure"] *synonyms* see STEEP — **sheer·ly** *adv* — **sheer·ness** *n*

²sheer *adv* 1 : in a complete manner : ALTOGETHER 2 : straight up or down with no break : PERPENDICULARLY

³sheer *vb* : to swerve from a course [perhaps an altered form of *shear* "to cut, cut off"]

⁴sheer *n* : a turn or change in the course of a ship

¹sheet \'shēt\ *n* 1 : a broad piece of cloth (as an article of bedding used next to the body) 2 a : a usually rectangular piece of paper b : an unbound page of a book — usually used in plural c : a newspaper, magazine, or occasional publication ⟨a gossip *sheet*⟩ d : the unseparated postage stamps printed by one impression of a plate on a single piece of paper; *also* : PANE 2 3 : a broad surface of something ⟨a *sheet* of ice⟩ 4 : a portion of something that is thin in comparison to its length and width ⟨a *sheet* of iron⟩ [Old English *scēte, scīete* "broad piece of cloth, sheet"] — **sheet·like** *adj*

²sheet *vb* : to cover with a sheet : SHROUD

³sheet *n* : a rope or chain that regulates the angle at which a sail is set in relation to the wind [Old English *scēata* "lower corner of a sail"]

sheet·ing \'shēt-iŋ\ *n* : material in the form of sheets or suitable for forming into sheets

sheet metal *n* : metal in the form of a sheet

sheet music *n* : music printed on unbound sheets of paper

Sheet·rock \'shēt-ˌräk\ *trademark* — used for drywall

sheikh *or* **sheik** \'shēk, *for sense 1 also* 'shāk\ *n* 1 a : an Arab leader, ruler, or prince b : a leader of a Muslim organization or group 2 *usually* **sheik** : a man supposed to be irresistibly attractive to romantic young women — **sheik·dom** \-dəm\ *n*

shek·el \'shek-əl\ *n* 1 : an ancient unit of weight or value; *esp* : a Hebrew unit equal to about 252 grains troy (about 16.3 grams) 2 : a coin weighing one shekel 3 : the basic unit of money of Israel

shelf \'shelf\ *n, pl* **shelves** \'shelvz\ 1 : a flat piece (as of wood or metal) set parallel to and above a floor (as on a wall or in a bookcase) to hold objects 2 : something (as a sandbar or ledge of rock) that suggests a shelf — **shelf-like** \'shel-ˌflīk\ *adj* — **on the shelf** : in a state of idleness or uselessness

shelf fungus *n* : BRACKET FUNGUS

shelf life *n* : the period of time something may be stored and still be good enough to use

¹shell \'shel\ *n* 1 a : a hard stiff covering of an animal (as a turtle or beetle) b : the outer covering of an egg (as of a bird or reptile) 2 : the outer covering of a nut, fruit, or seed especially when hard or tough 3 : shell material or shells especially of mollusks 4 : something like a shell: as a : a framework or outside structure b : a bottom crust for a pie ⟨a *pastry* shell⟩ c : a concrete arched roof (as over an outdoor stage) ⟨a band *shell*⟩ 5 : a way of behaving that hides one's feelings ⟨coming out of one's *shell*⟩ 6 : a shell-bearing mollusk 7 : a narrow light racing boat rowed by one or more persons using long oars 8 a : an object filled with an explosive to be shot from cannon b : a metal or paper case holding the explosive charge and shot or bullet used in small arms — **shell** *adj*

²shell *vb* 1 a : to remove from a natural enclosing cover (as a shell or husk) : SHUCK ⟨*shell* peas⟩ b : to remove the grains from (as an ear of corn) 2 : to shoot shells at or upon 3 : to fall out of the pod or husk 4 : to collect shells (as from a beach)

she'll \\(ˌ)shē(ə)l, shil\ : she shall : she will

¹shel·lac \shə-'lak\ *n* 1 : purified lac 2 : a preparation of lac dissolved in alcohol and used as a wood filler or finish

²shellac *vb* **shel·lacked; shel·lack·ing** : to coat or treat with shellac

shel·lack·ing \shə-'lak-iŋ\ *n* : a lopsided defeat

shell bean *n* 1 : a bean grown primarily for its edible seeds — compare SNAP BEAN 2 : the edible seed of a bean

shelled \'sheld\ *adj* 1 : having a shell especially of a specified kind ⟨pink-*shelled*⟩ ⟨hard-*shelled*⟩ 2 a : having the shell removed ⟨*shelled* nuts⟩ ⟨*shelled* oysters⟩ b : removed from the cob ⟨*shelled* corn⟩

shell·fish \'shel-ˌfish\ *n* : an invertebrate animal that lives in water and has a shell; *esp* : an edible mollusk (as an oyster) or crustacean (as a crab)

shell shock *n* : any of numerous nervous conditions appearing in soldiers exposed to modern warfare

shell–shocked \'shel-ˌshäkt\ *adj* 1 : affected with shell shock 2 : mentally confused, upset, or exhausted as the result of being under too much stress

shelly \'shel-ē\ *adj* **shell·i·er; -est** 1 : full of or covered with shells and especially seashells ⟨a *shelly* beach⟩ 2 : consisting of a shell or shells ⟨a crab's *shelly* home⟩

¹shel·ter \'shel-tər\ *n* 1 a : something that covers or protects ⟨an air raid *shelter*⟩ ⟨a fallout *shelter*⟩ b : a place that provides food and lodging (as to the homeless) c : a place that houses and feeds stray or unwanted animals 2 : the state of being protected ⟨take *shelter* from a storm⟩

²shelter *vb* **shel·tered; shel·ter·ing** \-t(ə-)riŋ\ 1 : to be a shelter for : provide with shelter 2 : to find and use a shelter

shelve \'shelv\ *vb* **shelved; shelv·ing** 1 : to place on a shelf ⟨*shelve* books⟩ 2 : to put off or aside : DEFER ⟨*shelve* a project⟩ — **shelv·er** *n*

shelv·ing \'shel-viŋ\ *n* : material to make shelves from; *also* : the shelves themselves

\ə\ abut	\au̇\ out	\i\ tip	\ȯ\ saw	\u̇\ foot
\ər\ further	\ch\ chin	\ī\ life	\ȯi\ coin	\y\ yet
\a\ mat	\e\ pet	\j\ job	\th\ thin	\yü\ few
\ā\ take	\ē\ easy	\ŋ\ sing	\t͟h\ this	\yu̇\ cure
\ä\ cot, cart	\g\ go	\ō\ bone	\ü\ food	\zh\ vision

she·nan·i·gans \shə-'nan-i-gənz\ *n pl* : funny or mischievous activity

¹shep·herd \'shep-ərd\ *n* **1** : a person who takes care of sheep **2** : GERMAN SHEPHERD

²shepherd *vb* : to care for as or as if a shepherd

shep·herd·ess \'shep-ərd-əs\ *n* : a woman who takes care of sheep

shepherd's check *n* : a pattern of small black-and-white checks especially in a fabric

sher·bet \'shər-bət\ *n* : a frozen dessert of fruit juice to which milk, egg white, or gelatin is added before freezing

sher·iff \'sher-əf\ *n* : an official of a county who is in charge of enforcing the law [Middle English *shirreve* "sheriff," from Old English *scīrgerēfa* "sheriff," from *scīr* "shire, county" and *gerēfa* "a government agent"]

sher·pa \'she(ə)r-pə, 'shər-\ *n* : a member of a people living on the high southern slopes of the Himalayas who are known for providing support for foreign trekkers and mountain climbers

sher·ry \'sher-ē\ *n, pl* **sherries** : a wine with a nutty flavor
Word History It is common to name wines after the part of a country where they are made. The wine called *sherry* today was first made in a town originally called, in Spanish, *Xeres*. The English approximation of the Spanish pronunciation was \'sher-ēz\, spelled *sherris*. After a time, people thought that *sherris* was a plural and so made a singular form, *sherry*, by cutting off the supposed plural ending. The \sh\ sound symbolized by *x* in Spanish (later by *j*) changed to a \k\ or \h\, so that the modern Spanish pronunciation of *Jerez* is even less like English *sherry*. [named for *Xeres* (now spelled *Jerez*), a city in Spain where the wine was originally made]

she's \(ˌ)shēz\ : she is : she has

Shet·land pony \ˌshet-lən(d)-\ *n* : any of a breed of small strong short-legged ponies developed in the Shetland Islands and having a thick coat and long mane and tail

Shetland sheepdog *n* : any of a breed of small dogs that have a long thick coat and look like miniature collies

Shia *or* **Shi·'a** \'shē-(ˌ)ä\ *n, pl* **Shia** *or* **Shi·'a** *also* **Shi·as** *or* **Shi·'as** **1** : one of the two main branches of Islam **2** : a Muslim who is a member of the Shia branch of Islam : SHIITE

shib·bo·leth \'shib-ə-ləth *also* -ˌleth\ *n* **1 a** : a slogan especially of a party or group **b** : an idea or saying that is commonly believed **2** : some behavior or use of language that identifies a person as belonging to a group

shied *past and past participle of* SHY

¹shield \'shē(ə)ld\ *n* **1** : a broad piece of armor carried on the arm to protect oneself in battle **2** : something that serves as a defense or protection **3** : the ancient mass of hard rock that forms the core of a continent

²shield *vb* : to cover or screen with or as if with a shield

shield volcano *n* : a broad rounded volcano that is built up from many layers of lava

shier *comparative of* SHY

shies *plural of* SHY

shiest *superlative of* SHY

¹shift \'shift\ *vb* **1** : to exchange for another of the same kind **2 a** : to change the place, position, or direction of **b** : to make a change in place, position, or direction ⟨the wind *shifted*⟩ **c** : to change the gear rotating the transmission shaft of an automobile **3** : to get along without help : FEND ⟨left the others to *shift* for themselves⟩

²shift *n* **1** : a means or device for getting something done **2 a** : ²SLIP 5a **b** : CHEMISE 2 **3** : the act of shifting **4** : a

¹shield 1

group of workers who work together during a scheduled period of time; *also* : the period of time during which they work **5** : GEARSHIFT

shift·er \'shif-tər\ *n* : one that shifts; *esp* : GEARSHIFT

shift key *n* : a key on a keyboard that when pressed allows a different set of characters to be produced by the other keys

shift·less \'shif(t)-ləs\ *adj* : lacking in ambition : LAZY — **shift·less·ly** *adv* — **shift·less·ness** *n*

shifty \'shif-tē\ *adj* **shift·i·er; -est** **1** : not worthy of trust : TRICKY **2** : indicating a tricky character ⟨*shifty* eyes⟩ — **shift·i·ly** \-tə-lē\ *adv* — **shift·i·ness** \-tē-nəs\ *n*

Shi·ite *or* **Shi·'ite** \'shē-ˌīt\ *n, pl* -ites *or* -ites : a Muslim who is a member of the Shia branch of Islam

shil·le·lagh \shə-'lā-lē\ *n* : ¹CUDGEL [named for *Shillelagh*, a town in Ireland noted for its oak trees]

shil·ling \'shil-iŋ\ *n* **1** : a former unit of British money equal to ¹⁄₂₀ pound **2** : a coin equal to ¹⁄₂₀ pound in any of several countries of the Commonwealth of Nations **3** : any of several early American coins **4 a** : the basic unit of money of Kenya, Somalia, Tanzania, and Uganda **b** : a coin representing this unit

shilly–shally \'shil-ē-ˌshal-ē\ *vb* **shilly–shal·lied; shilly–shal·ly·ing** : to be unable to make up one's mind : show hesitation

shim·mer \'shim-ər\ *vb* **shim·mered; shim·mer·ing** \-(ə-)riŋ\ : to shine with a wavering light : GLIMMER — **shimmer** *n*

¹shin \'shin\ *n* : the front part of the leg below the knee

shille-lagh

²shin *vb* **shinned; shin·ning** : SHINNY

shin·bone \'shin-ˌbōn, -ˌbōn\ *n* : TIBIA 1

shin·dig \'shin-ˌdig\ *n* : a big fancy party

shin·dy \'shin-dē\ *n, pl* **shindies** : ⁴ROW

¹shine \'shīn\ *vb* **shone** \'shōn\ *or* **shined; shin·ing** **1** : to give light ⟨the stars *shone* brightly⟩ **2** : to be glossy : GLEAM ⟨polished the buttons until they *shone* like gold⟩ **3** : to be outstanding : show talent ⟨on stage where I could really *shine*⟩ **4** : to cause to give light ⟨*shine* a flashlight⟩ **5** : to make bright by polishing ⟨*shined* my shoes⟩

²shine *n* **1** : brightness from light given off or reflected **2** : fair weather : SUNSHINE ⟨rain or *shine*⟩ **3** : LIKING, FANCY ⟨took a *shine* to them⟩ **4** : a polish given to shoes

shin·er \'shī-nər\ *n* **1** : one that shines **2** : a silvery fish; *esp* : any of numerous small freshwater American fishes related to the carp **3** : BLACK EYE

¹shin·gle \'shiŋ-gəl\ *n* **1** : a small thin piece of building material for laying in overlapping rows as a covering for the roof or sides of a building **2** : a small sign **3** : a woman's short haircut — **shin·gle·like** \-ˌlīk\ *adj*

shiner 2

²shingle *vb* **shin·gled; shin·gling** \-g(ə-)liŋ\ **1** : to cover with or as if with shingles **2** : to cut and shape the hair in a shingle

shin·ing \'shī-niŋ\ *adj* **1** : giving forth or reflecting a steady light : GLOWING **2** : OUTSTANDING 2 ⟨a *shining* example⟩ **synonyms** see BRIGHT — **shin·ing·ly** *adv*

shin·ny \'shin-ē\ *vb* **shin·nied; shin·ny·ing** : to climb up or down something vertical by grasping it with the arms and legs and moving oneself by repeated jerks ⟨*shinnied* up the pole⟩

Shin·to \'shin-ˌtō\ *n* : a religion native to Japan

shiny \'shī-nē\ *adj* **shin·i·er; -est** : having a smooth glossy surface ⟨a *shiny* new car⟩

¹ship \'ship\ *n* **1** : a large seagoing boat **2** : a ship's crew **3** : AIRSHIP, AIRPLANE, SPACECRAFT

²ship *vb* **shipped; ship·ping** **1 a** : to place or receive on board a ship for transportation by water **b** : to cause to be transported 〈had her boxes *shipped* home〉 **2** : to take into a ship or boat 〈*ship* oars〉 **3** : to sign on as a crew member of a ship **4** : to take in (as water) over the side

-ship \,ship\ *n suffix* **1** : state : condition : quality 〈friend*ship*〉 〈apprentice*ship*〉 **2** : position : office : duties 〈profesor*ship*〉 **3** : art : skill : activity 〈horseman*ship*〉 〈penman*ship*〉 **4** : one having or entitled to be called by a (specified) title 〈his Lord*ship*〉 〈her Lady*ship*〉 **5** : the whole body of persons included in a class 〈a large reader*ship*〉 [Old English *-scipe* "condition, something having a certain quality"]

¹ship·board \'ship-,bō(ə)rd, -,bȯ(ə)rd\ *n* **1** : the side of a ship **2** : ¹SHIP 1 〈met on *shipboard*〉

²shipboard *adj* : existing or taken place on board a ship 〈a *shipboard* romance〉

ship·build·er \-,bil-dər\ *n* : one who designs or builds ships — **ship·build·ing** \-diŋ\ *n*

ship·load \-'lōd, -,lōd\ *n* : as much or as many as a ship will hold 〈a *shipload* of corn〉 〈*shiploads* of immigrants〉

ship·mate \-,māt\ *n* : a fellow sailor

ship·ment \'ship-mənt\ *n* **1** : the act of shipping **2** : the goods shipped

ship·pa·ble \'ship-ə-bəl\ *adj* : suitable for shipping

ship·per \'ship-ər\ *n* : one who ships goods

ship·ping \'ship-iŋ\ *n* **1** : the body of ships in one place or belonging to one port or country **2** : the act or business of one that ships goods

ship·shape \'ship-'shāp\ *adj* : being neat and orderly : TIDY

ship·worm \-,wərm\ *n* : any of various marine clams that have a wormlike body and a shell used for burrowing in underwater wood and that cause damage to ships and wharves

¹ship·wreck \-,rek\ *n* **1** : a wrecked ship **2** : the destruction or loss of a ship

²shipwreck *vb* **1** : to cause to experience shipwreck 〈a storm that *shipwrecked* the sailors〉 **2** : to destroy (a ship) by driving ashore or sinking

ship·yard \'ship-,yärd\ *n* : a place where ships are built or repaired

shire \'shī(ə)r, *in place-name compounds* ,shi(ə)r, shər\ *n* **1** : a county in England **2** : any of a British breed of tall draft horses

shirk \'shərk\ *vb* : to get out of doing especially what one ought to do : AVOID 3, EVADE 〈*shirked* their duty〉 — **shirk·er** *n*

shirr \'shər\ *vb* **1** : to draw cloth together in a shirring **2** : to cook eggs removed from the shell by baking

shirr·ing \'shər-iŋ\ *n* : a decorative gathering (as of cloth) made by drawing up the material along two or more parallel lines of stitching

shirt \'shərt\ *n* **1** : a garment for the upper part of the body usually with a collar, sleeves, a front opening, and a tail long enough to be tucked inside pants or a skirt **2** : UNDERSHIRT

shirt·sleeve \-,slēv\ *n* : the sleeve of a shirt — **in shirt-sleeves** : wearing a shirt but no coat

shirt·tail \-,tāl\ *n* : the part of a shirt that reaches below the waist especially in the back

shirt·waist \-,wāst\ *n* : a woman's tailored garment (as a dress or blouse) with details copied from men's shirts

shirty \'shərt-ē\ *adj, chiefly British* : being annoyed : ANGRY

shish ke·bab \'shish-kə-,bäb\ *n* : cubes of meat marinated and cooked on skewers

¹shiv·er \'shiv-ər\ *n* : one of the small pieces into which a brittle thing is broken by great force [Middle English *shiver* "a small piece of something that is broken"]

²shiver *vb* **shiv·ered; shiv·er·ing** \'shiv-(ə-)riŋ\ : to break into many small pieces : SHATTER

³shiver *vb* **shiv·ered; shiv·er·ing** \'shiv-(ə-)riŋ\ : to shake involuntarily (as from cold or fear) [Middle English *shiveren*, an altered form of *chiveren* "to tremble, shiver"]

⁴shiver *n* **1** : an instance of shivering **2** : a thrill of emotion and especially of fear — usually used in plural with *the* 〈a ghost story that would give you the *shivers*〉

shiv·ery \'shiv-(ə-)rē\ *adj* **1** : marked by shivers **2** : causing shivers

shlemiel *variant of* SCHLEMIEL

shmooze *variant of* SCHMOOZE

¹shoal \'shōl\ *adj* : ¹SHALLOW 1 〈*shoal* water〉 [Old English *sceald* "shallow"]

²shoal *n* **1** : a place where a sea, lake, or river is shallow **2** : a sandbank or sandbar just below the surface of the water

³shoal *n* : ³SCHOOL 〈a *shoal* of pilot fish〉 [Old English *scolu* "great number"]

shoat \'shōt\ *n* : a young hog and especially one that has been weaned

¹shock \'shäk\ *n* : a bunch of sheaves of grain or stalks of corn set on end (as in a field) [Middle English *shock* "bunch of stalks"]

²shock *n* **1** : the sudden violent collision of bodies in a fight 〈the *shock* of combat〉 **2** : a violent shake or jerk 〈an earthquake *shock*〉 **3 a** : a sudden or violent disturbance of the mind or feelings 〈the *shock* of defeat〉 **b** : something that causes such a disturbance 〈the news came as a *shock*〉 **c** : a state of being so disturbed 〈were in *shock* when they heard the true story〉 **4** : a state of bodily collapse that is often marked by a drop in blood pressure and volume and that is usually caused by a severe injury, burn, or hemorrhage **5** : the effect of a strong charge of electricity passing through the body of a person or animal [from early French *choc* "a violent collision, shock," from *choquer* (verb) "to strike against," from earlier *choquier* (same meaning); probably of Germanic origin]

³shock *vb* **1** : to strike with surprise, horror, or disgust 〈were *shocked* by her behavior〉 **2** : to affect by electrical shock **3** : to drive into or out of by or as if by a shock 〈*shocked* the public into action〉 — **shock·er** *n*

⁴shock *n* : a thick bushy mass 〈a *shock* of hair〉 [from earlier *shock* (adjective) "bushy," probably derived from *shock* (noun) "a bunch of stalks" because of the similarity of the appearance of bushy hair to a bunch of stalks of grain]

shock absorber *n* : a device for absorbing the energy of sudden shocks in machinery or structures

shock·ing *adj* : causing horror or disgust 〈a *shocking* crime〉 〈*shocking* behavior〉 — **shock·ing·ly** \-iŋ-lē\ *adv*

shock·proof \'shäk-,prüf\ *adj* **1** : incapable of being shocked **2 a** : resistant to damage by shock **b** : unlikely to cause shock 〈a *shockproof* switch〉

shock wave *n* : a wave formed by the sudden compression (as by an earthquake or supersonic aircraft) of the substance through which the wave travels

shod·dy \'shäd-ē\ *adj* **shod·di·er; -est** : poorly done or made 〈*shoddy* construction〉 〈*shoddy* furniture〉 — **shod·di·ly** \'shäd-ᵊl-ē\ *adv* — **shod·di·ness** \'shäd-ē-nəs\ *n*

¹shoe \'shü\ *n* **1 a** : an outer covering for the human foot usually having a thick and somewhat stiff sole and heel and a lighter upper part **b** : HORSESHOE 1 **2** *pl* : another's place or point of view 〈suppose you were in your

\ə\ **abut**	\au̇\ **out**	\i\ **tip**	\ȯ\ **saw**	\u̇\ **foot**
\ər\ **further**	\ch\ **chin**	\ī\ **life**	\ȯi\ **coin**	\y\ **yet**
\a\ **mat**	\e\ **pet**	\j\ **job**	\th\ **thin**	\yü\ **few**
\ā\ **take**	\ē\ **easy**	\ŋ\ **sing**	\t̲h̲\ **this**	\yu̇\ **cure**
\ä\ **cot, cart**	\g\ **go**	\ō\ **bone**	\ü\ **food**	\zh\ **vision**

friend's *shoes*⟩ **3** : the part of a brake that presses on the wheel of a vehicle

²**shoe** *vb* **shod** \'shäd\ *also* **shoed** \'shüd\; **shoe·ing** \'shü-iŋ\ : to put a shoe on : furnish with shoes; *esp* : to put a shoe or shoes on a horse

shoe·horn \-ˌhȯrn\ *n* : a curved piece (as of metal) to help in putting on a shoe

shoe·lace \-ˌlās\ *n* : a lace or string for fastening a shoe

shoe·mak·er \-ˌmā-kər\ *n* : a person who makes or repairs shoes

shoe·string \-ˌstriŋ\ *n* **1** : SHOELACE **2** : a small sum of money ⟨start a business on a *shoestring*⟩

shoe tree *n* : a foot-shaped device that can be put into a shoe to preserve its shape

sho·gun \'shō-gən\ *n* : any of a line of military governors ruling Japan until the revolution of 1867–68

shone *past and past participle of* SHINE

shoo \'shü\ *vb* : to scare, drive, or send away by or as if by crying *shoo* ⟨*shooed* everyone out of the kitchen⟩

shoo-fly pie \'shü-ˌflī-\ *n* : a pie made of molasses or brown sugar with a crumbly topping

shoo–in \'shü-ˌin\ *n* : one that is a certain and easy winner

shook *past of* SHAKE

shook–up \ˌshu̇k-'əp\ *adj* : nervously upset : AGITATED

¹**shoot** \'shüt\ *vb* **shot** \'shät\; **shoot·ing** **1 a** : to let fly or cause to be driven forward with force ⟨*shoot* an arrow⟩ **b** : to cause a missile to be driven out of ⟨*shoot* a gun⟩ **c** : to cause a weapon to discharge a missile ⟨*shoot* at a target⟩ **2 a** : to send (a marble) forward by snapping the thumb **b** : to hit or throw (as a ball or puck) toward a goal **c** : to score by shooting ⟨*shoot* a basket⟩ **d** : ²PLAY 5a ⟨*shoot* pool⟩ **3** : to strike with a missile from a bow or gun; *esp* : to kill by so doing ⟨*shot* a deer⟩ **4** : to push or slide into or out of a fastening ⟨*shot* the door bolt⟩ **5 a** : to push or thrust forward swiftly ⟨lizards *shooting* out their tongues⟩ **b** : to grow rapidly ⟨the corn is *shooting* up⟩ **6 a** : to go, move, or pass rapidly ⟨they *shot* past on skis⟩ **b** : to pass swiftly along ⟨*shoot* the rapids in a canoe⟩ **c** : to stream out suddenly : SPURT **d** : to dart with a piercing sensation ⟨*shooting* pains⟩ **7** : to take the altitude of ⟨*shoot* the sun with a sextant⟩ **8** : to take a picture or series of pictures or television images of — **shoot·er** *n* — **shoot at** *or* **shoot for** : to try to accomplish : strive for — **shoot the breeze** : ¹TALK 5a, CHAT — **shoot the works** : to put forth all one's efforts

²**shoot** *n* **1 a** : a plant stem with its leaves and branches especially when not yet mature **b** : OFFSHOOT 1 **2 a** : an act of shooting **b** : a hunting trip or party **c** : a shooting match

shooting star *n* : a meteor appearing as a temporary streak of light in the night sky

shoot–out \'shüt-ˌau̇t\ *n* : a battle fought with handguns or rifles

¹**shop** \'shäp\ *n* **1** : a place of business : OFFICE **2 a** : a building or room where goods are sold retail **b** *also* **shoppe** \'shäp\ : a small store offering a specialized line of goods ⟨a gift *shop*⟩ **3** : a place where workers are doing a particular kind of work especially with machinery ⟨a *print* shop⟩ **4 a** : a school laboratory equipped for industrial arts education **b** : INDUSTRIAL ARTS ⟨take *shop* as a freshman⟩ ⟨metal *shop*⟩ **5** : SHOPTALK ⟨talk *shop*⟩

²**shop** *vb* **shopped; shop·ping** **1** : to visit shops for the purpose of looking over and buying goods **2** : to look for the best buy ⟨*shop* around for a new car⟩ — **shop·per** *n*

shop·keep·er \'shäp-ˌkē-pər\ *n* : STOREKEEPER 2

shop·lift \-ˌlift\ *vb* : to steal merchandise on display in stores

shop·lift·er \-ˌlif-tər\ *n* : a person who shoplifts

shopping center *n* : a group of retail stores and service establishments usually located in a suburban area and having a large parking lot

shopping mall *n* : MALL 3

shop·talk \'shäp-ˌtȯk\ *n* : talk about or related to one's work or special interests

shop·worn \-ˌwȯ(ə)rn, -ˌwȯ(ə)rn\ *adj* **1** : faded or soiled from being too long in a store **2** : stale from too much use of familiarity ⟨*shopworn* suggestions⟩

¹**shore** \'shō(ə)r, 'shȯ(ə)r\ *n* : the land along the edge of a body of water (as the sea) [Middle English *shore* "the land on the edge of a body of water"]

²**shore** *vb* **shored; shor·ing** : to support with one or more bracing timbers ⟨*shore* up a house foundation⟩ [Middle English *shoren* "to support, brace"]

³**shore** *n* : a prop or support placed under or against something to support it

shore·bird \'shō(ə)r-ˌbərd, 'shȯ(ə)r-\ *n* : any of a group of birds (as a plover or sandpiper) that frequent the seashore

S ³shore

shore·line \-ˌlīn\ *n* : the line where a body of water touches the shore

shore patrol *n* : a branch of a navy with guard and police functions

shore·ward \'shō(ə)r-wərd, 'shȯ(ə)r-\ *or* **shore·wards** \-wərdz\ *adv* : toward the shore

shor·ing \'shȯr-iŋ, 'shȯr-\ *n* : a group of things that shore something up

shorn *past participle of* SHEAR

¹**short** \'shȯ(ə)rt\ *adj* **1** : having little length or height : not long or tall **2 a** : not long in time : BRIEF ⟨a *short* delay⟩ **b** : not great in distance ⟨a *short* walk⟩ **3** : not remembering for long ⟨a *short* memory⟩ **4** : of, relating to, or being one of the vowel sounds \ə, a, e, i, u̇\ and sometimes \ä\ and \ȯ\ **5 a** : not coming up to the regular standard or to what is needed ⟨gave *short* measure⟩ ⟨in *short* supply⟩ **b** : not reaching far enough ⟨the throw was *short*⟩ **c** : not having enough ⟨*short* of cash⟩ **6** : easily upset ⟨has a *short* temper⟩ **7** : FLAKY 2, CRUMBLY **8** : cut down to a brief length ⟨a *short* tax form⟩ ⟨"doc" is *short* for "doctor"⟩ — **short·ish** \-ish\ *adj* — **in short order** : with speed and promptness

²**short** *adv* **1** : with suddenness ⟨stopped *short*⟩ **2** : so as not to reach as far as expected ⟨fell *short* of the mark⟩

³**short** *n* **1** : a short signal or sound (as in Morse Code) **2** *pl* **a** : pants that reach to the knees or not as far as the knees **b** : short underpants **3** : SHORT CIRCUIT — **for short** : as an abbreviation ⟨named Katherine or Kate *for short*⟩ — **in short** : as a brief summary

⁴**short** *vb* : SHORT-CIRCUIT

short·age \'shȯrt-ij\ *n* : a lack in the amount needed : DEFICIT ⟨a *shortage* of cash⟩ ⟨a gasoline *shortage*⟩

short·bread \'shȯrt-ˌbred\ *n* : a cookie made of flour, sugar, and lots of shortening

short·cake \-ˌkāk\ *n* : a dessert made of rich biscuit dough baked and served with sweetened fruit ⟨strawberry *shortcake*⟩

short·change \-'chānj\ *vb* **1** : to give less than the correct amount of change to **2** : to give less than due : CHEAT

short–cir·cuit \-'sər-kət\ *vb* : to make a short circuit in or have a short circuit

short circuit *n* : an electrical connection made between points in an electric circuit between which current does not normally flow

short·com·ing \'shȯrt-ˌkəm-iŋ, (')shȯrt-'kəm-\ *n* : ¹FAULT 1b

¹**short·cut** \'shȯrt-ˌkət, -'kət\ *n* : a shorter, quicker, or easier way ⟨a *shortcut* through the woods⟩ ⟨a *shortcut* to fame⟩

²**shortcut** *vb* **-cut; -cut·ting** : to take or use a shortcut

short division *n* : mathematical division in which the steps are performed one after another without writing out the remainders

short·en \'shȯrt-ᵊn\ *vb* **short·ened; short·en·ing** \'shȯrt-niŋ, -ᵊn-iŋ\ **1** : to make or become short or shorter **2** : to add shortening to (as pastry dough) — **short·en·er** \-nər, -ᵊn-ər\ *n*

short·en·ing \'shȯrt-niŋ, -ᵊn-iŋ\ *n* **1** : a making or becoming short or shorter **2** : a fat (as butter or lard) used in baking especially to make pastry flaky or crumbly

short fuse *n* : a tendency to get angry easily

short–haired \'shȯrt-ˌha(ə)rd, -ˌhe(ə)rd\ *adj* : having short hair or fur ⟨a *short-haired* cat⟩

short·hand \'shȯrt-ˌhand\ *n* **1** : a method of rapid writing by using symbols for sounds, words, or phrases **2** : a short or quick way of showing or saying something — **shorthand** *adj*

short–hand·ed \-'han-dəd\ *adj* : having or working with fewer than the usual number of people

short–haul \-ˌhȯl\ *adj* : traveling or involving a short distance ⟨*short-haul* flights⟩

short·horn \-ˌhȯ(ə)rn\ *n* : any of a breed of roan, red, white, or red and white beef and dairy cattle that have short horns and were originally developed in England

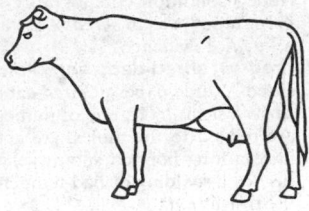

shorthorn

short–horned grasshopper \ˌshȯrt-ˌhȯrn(d)-\ *n* : any of a family of grasshoppers with short antennae

short hundredweight *n* : HUNDREDWEIGHT 1

short–lived \'shȯrt-'līvd, -ˌlivd\ *adj* : living or lasting only a short time ⟨*short-lived* blooms⟩ ⟨*short-lived* joy⟩

short·ly \'shȯrt-lē\ *adv* **1** : in a few words : BRIEFLY **2** : in or within a short time : SOON ⟨will arrive *shortly*⟩ ⟨*shortly* after sunset⟩

short·ness \'shȯrt-nəs\ *n* : the quality or state of being short ⟨*shortness* of breath⟩

short–order \ˌshȯrt-ˌȯrd-ər\ *adj* : preparing or serving food that can be cooked quickly when a customer orders it ⟨a *short-order* cook⟩

short–range \-'rānj\ *adj* **1** : involving or taking into account only a short period of time ⟨*short-range* plans⟩ **2** : relating to or fit for short distances ⟨*short-range* radar⟩

short shrift *n* : little or no attention or consideration ⟨gave the problem *short shrift*⟩

short·sight·ed \'shȯrt-'sīt-əd\ *adj* **1** : NEARSIGHTED **2** : showing a failure to think ahead : lacking foresight ⟨a *shortsighted* policy⟩ — **short·sight·ed·ly** *adv* — **short·sight·ed·ness** *n*

short·stop \'shȯrt-ˌstäp\ *n* : the baseball infielder whose position is between second and third base

short story *n* : a short work of fiction usually dealing with a few characters and a single event

short–tem·pered \'shȯrt-'tem-pərd\ *adj* : easily angered

short–term \-'tərm\ *adj* : SHORT-RANGE ⟨*short-term* goals⟩

short ton *n* — see MEASURE table

short·wave \'shȯrt-'wāv\ *n* : a radio wave with a wavelength between 10 and 100 meters

Sho·shone \shə-'shōn(-ē), 'shō-ˌshōn\ *or* **Sho·sho·ni** \shə-'shō-nē\ *n, pl* **Shoshones** *or* **Shoshoni** *also* **Shoshone** *or* **Shoshonis** : a member of a group of American Indian peoples of California, Idaho, Nevada, Utah, and Wyoming

¹**shot** \'shät\ *n* **1 a** : an action of shooting **b** : an aimed discharge of a weapon (as a gun or cannon) **c** : a stroke or throw in a game; *esp* : an attempt at scoring **d** : an injection of something (as a medicine or vaccine) into the body ⟨penicillin *shots*⟩ **2 a** *pl* **shot** : something sent by shooting; *esp* : small lead or steel pellets forming a charge for a shotgun **b** : a heavy metal ball thrown for distance in the shot put **3** : the flight of a missile or the distance it travels : RANGE ⟨within rifle *shot*⟩ **4** : a person who shoots ⟨a good *shot*⟩ **5 a** : ²ATTEMPT 1, TRY ⟨take another *shot* at the puzzle⟩ **b** : CHANCE ⟨has a good *shot* at winning⟩ **6 a** : ¹PHOTOGRAPH **b** : a single portion of a movie or a television program shot by one camera without stopping **7 a** : a small measure or amount of alcoholic liquor **b** : a small amount applied at one time : DOSE

²**shot** *past and past participle of* SHOOT

³**shot** *adj* **1** : marked or streaked with a different color ⟨blue *shot* with silver⟩ ⟨hair *shot* with gray⟩ **2** : brought to a state of ruin or uselessness ⟨my nerves were *shot*⟩ ⟨the tires are *shot*⟩

shot·gun \'shät-ˌgən\ *n* : a firearm used to fire small shot at short range

shot put *n* : a field event in which a heavy metal ball is heaved for distance — **shot–put·ter** \-ˌpu̇t-ər\ *n*

should \shəd, (')shu̇d\ *past of* SHALL **1** : ought to ⟨you *should* study harder⟩ ⟨they *should* be here soon⟩ **2** : happen to ⟨if you *should* see them, say hello for me⟩ **3** — used to express what is probable or expected ⟨they *should* be here by now⟩ **4** — used as a more polite or less assured form of shall ⟨*should* I turn out the lights?⟩

¹**shoul·der** \'shōl-dər\ *n* **1** : the part of the body of a person or animal where the arm or foreleg joins the body **2** : a cut of meat including the upper joint of the foreleg and attached parts **3** : the part of a garment at the wearer's shoulder **4** : a part that resembles a person's shoulder ⟨*shoulder* of a hill⟩ **5** : the edge of a road

²**shoulder** *vb* **shoul·dered; shoul·der·ing** \-d(ə-)riŋ\ **1** : to push with one's shoulder ⟨*shouldered* him aside⟩ **2** : to accept as one's burden or responsibility ⟨*shoulder* the blame⟩

shoulder blade *n* : the flat triangular bone of the back of the shoulder that forms a joint with the humerus of the upper arm — called also *scapula*

shoulder strap *n* : a strap worn over the shoulder to hold up an article or a garment

should·est \'shu̇d-əst\ *archaic past 2nd singular of* SHALL

shouldn't \'shu̇d-ᵊnt\ : should not

shouldst \shədst, (')shu̇dst\ *archaic past 2nd singular of* SHALL

¹**shout** \'shau̇t\ *vb* **1** : to utter a sudden loud cry ⟨*shouted* for joy⟩ **2** : to utter in a loud voice ⟨*shouted* out the answers⟩ — **shout·er** *n*

synonyms SHOUT, SHRIEK, SCREECH mean to utter a loud cry. SHOUT suggests any kind of loud cry that is meant to be heard either far away or above other noise ⟨we *shouted* to them across the street⟩. SHRIEK suggests a high-pitched cry that is a sign of strong feeling ⟨the children *shrieked* with joy⟩. SCREECH suggests a drawn-out shriek that is usually without words and is very harsh and unpleasant ⟨the cats fought and *screeched*⟩.

²**shout** *n* : a loud cry or call

¹**shove** \'shəv\ *vb* **shoved; shov·ing** **1** : to push with steady force **2** : to push along or away carelessly or rudely ⟨*shoved* her out of the way⟩ **3** : DEPART 1 — usually used with *off* ⟨time to *shove* off for home⟩ — **shov·er** *n*

²**shove** *n* : an act or instance of shoving

\ə\ abut	\au̇\ out	\i\ tip	\ȯ\ saw	\u̇\ foot
\ər\ further	\ch\ chin	\ī\ life	\ȯi\ coin	\y\ yet
\a\ mat	\e\ pet	\j\ job	\th\ thin	\yü\ few
\ā\ take	\ē\ easy	\ŋ\ sing	\t͟h\ this	\yu̇\ cure
\ä\ cot, cart	\g\ go	\ō\ bone	\ü\ food	\zh\ vision

¹shov·el \ˈshəv-əl\ *n* **1** : a broad scoop with a handle used for lifting and throwing loose material (as dirt or snow) **2** : SHOVELFUL

²shovel *vb* **-eled** *or* **-elled; -el·ing** *or* **-el·ling** \ˈshəv-(ə-)liŋ\ **1** : to lift and throw with a shovel ⟨*shovel* snow⟩ **2** : to dig or clean out with a shovel ⟨*shovel* out the sheep pens⟩ **3** : to throw or carry roughly or in a mass as if with a shovel ⟨stop *shoveling* the food into your mouth⟩

shov·el·er *or* **shov·el·ler** \ˈshəv-(ə-)lər\ *n* **1** : one that shovels **2** : any of several freshwater ducks having a large and very broad bill

shov·el·ful \ˈshəv-əl-ˌful\ *n, pl* **shovelfuls** \-ˌfulz\ *also* **shov·els·ful** \-əlz-ˌful\ : as much as a shovel will hold

¹show \ˈshō\ *vb* **showed; shown** \ˈshōn\ *or* **showed; show·ing** **1** : to place in sight : present so as to be seen **2** : REVEAL 2 ⟨*showed* strong feeling⟩ **3** : to give from or as if from a position of authority ⟨we'll *show* them no mercy⟩ **4** : TEACH 1, INSTRUCT ⟨*showed* me a few chords on the guitar⟩ **5** : PROVE 2a ⟨that *shows* we're right⟩ **6** : to give indication or record of ⟨his grades *show* some improvement⟩ **7** : ²USHER 1, GUIDE ⟨*showed* them to a seat⟩ **8** : to be noticeable ⟨the patch hardly *shows*⟩ ⟨the determination *showed* in her face⟩ **9** : to present (an animal) for judging in a show **10** : to be third or at least third (as in a horse race)

    synonyms SHOW, EXHIBIT, DISPLAY, PARADE mean to present something in a way that will draw attention. SHOW suggests letting another see or examine ⟨*show* me a picture of your family⟩. EXHIBIT suggests putting something out in public ⟨the children *exhibited* their drawings at the fair⟩. DISPLAY stresses putting something out in the open where others may see it clearly ⟨*display* sale items in front of the store⟩. PARADE suggests making a great show of something ⟨look at them *parading* their new bikes⟩.

²show *n* **1** : a display made for effect ⟨a *show* of strength⟩ **2 a** : a false outward appearance ⟨made a *show* of friendship⟩ **b** : a true indication : SIGN ⟨a *show* of reason⟩ **3** : a ridiculous spectacle **4** : an entertainment or exhibition especially by performers (as on TV or the stage) **5** : a competitive exhibition (as of animals) to demonstrate quality **6** : third place at the finish (as of a horse race)

show·biz \-ˌbiz\ *n* : SHOW BUSINESS

show·boat \ˈshō-ˌbōt\ *n* : a river steamboat used as a traveling theater

show business *n* : the arts, occupations, and companies that make up the entertainment industry

¹show·case \-ˌkās\ *n* : a protective glass case in which things are displayed

²showcase *vb* : to exhibit especially in an attractive or favorable way ⟨*showcase* new talent⟩

show·down \-ˌdaun\ *n* : the test of strength that finally settles a dispute

¹show·er \ˈshau(-ə)r\ *n* **1 a** : a short fall of rain over a small area **b** : a similar fall of sleet, hail, or snow **2** : something resembling a shower ⟨a *shower* of sparks⟩ **3** : a party where gifts are given especially to a bride or pregnant woman **4** : a bath in which water is sprayed on a person; *also* : a device for providing such a bath

²shower *vb* **1** : to rain or fall in or as if in a shower **2** : to bathe in a shower **3** : to wet with fine spray or drops **4** : to provide in great quantity ⟨*showered* them with attention⟩

show·man \ˈshō-mən\ *n* **1** : the producer of a theatrical show **2** : a person having a special skill for presenting something in a dramatic way — **show·man·ship** \-ˌship\ *n*

show–off \ˈshō-ˌof\ *n* **1** : the act of showing off **2** : a person who shows off

show off \(ˈ)shō-ˈof\ *vb* **1** : to display proudly **2** : to try to attract attention by conspicuous behavior

show·piece \ˈshō-ˌpēs\ *n* : a very fine example used for exhibition

show·place \-ˌplās\ *n* : a place (as an estate or building) that is regarded as a very fine example

show·room \-ˌrüm, -ˌrum\ *n* : a room where merchandise (as new cars) is displayed for sale or where samples are displayed ⟨a carpet *showroom*⟩

show·time \ˈshō-ˌtīm\ *n* : the scheduled or actual time at which a show or something likened to a show begins

show up *vb* **1** : to reveal the true nature of by uncovering faults : EXPOSE ⟨were *shown up* for the fools they really are⟩ **2** : to be where one is expected to be : ARRIVE ⟨*showed up* on time⟩

showy \ˈshō-ē\ *adj* **show·i·er; -est** **1** : attracting attention : STRIKING ⟨*showy* blossoms⟩ **2** : given to or marked by much outward display : GAUDY ⟨*showy* jewelry⟩ — **show·i·ly** \ˈshō-ə-lē\ *adv* — **show·i·ness** \ˈshō-ē-nəs\ *n*

shrap·nel \ˈshrap-nᵊl\ *n, pl* **shrapnel** **1** : a shell designed to burst and scatter metal balls with which it is filled along with jagged fragments of the case **2** : metal pieces from an exploded bomb, shell, or mine

¹shred \ˈshred\ *n* **1 a** : a long narrow piece cut or torn off : SCRAP ⟨*shreds* of cloth⟩ **b** *pl* : a shredded, damaged, or ruined condition ⟨the loss tore his confidence to *shreds*⟩ ⟨reputation was in *shreds*⟩ **2** : a small amount : BIT ⟨not a *shred* of evidence⟩

²shred *vb* **shred·ded; shred·ding** : to cut or tear into shreds ⟨*shred* paper⟩ ⟨*shred* cabbage⟩ — **shred·der** *n*

shrew \ˈshrü\ *n* **1** : any of numerous small mammals that are related to the moles, are active mostly at night, and have a long pointed snout, very small eyes, and velvety fur **2** : a scolding or bad-tempered woman — **shrew·ish** \ˈshrü-ish\ *adj*

shrewd \ˈshrüd\ *adj* : showing quick practical cleverness : ASTUTE ⟨a *shrewd* observer⟩; *also* : marked by clever dealing that takes advantage ⟨a *shrewd* negotiator⟩ — **shrewd·ly** *adv* — **shrewd·ness** *n*

¹shriek \ˈshrēk\ *vb* **1** : to utter a sharp shrill cry **2** : to cry out in a high-pitched voice **synonyms** see SHOUT

²shriek *n* : a sharp shrill cry

shrift \ˈshrift\ *n, archaic* : the confession of sins to a priest or the hearing of a confession by a priest

¹shrill \ˈshril\ *vb* : to make a high sharp piercing sound : SCREAM

²shrill *adj* : having a sharp high sound ⟨a *shrill* whistle⟩ — **shrill** *adv* — **shrill·ness** *n* — **shril·ly** \ˈshril-lē\ *adv*

³shrill *n* : a shrill sound

¹shrimp \ˈshrimp\ *n, pl* **shrimps** *or* **shrimp** **1** : any of numerous small mostly marine shellfish that are crustaceans related to the lobsters, that have a long slender body, an abdomen that is very thin from side to side, and long legs, and that include some important as food **2** : a very small or unimportant person or thing — **shrimp·like** \-ˌlīk\ *adj*

²shrimp *vb* : to fish for or catch shrimps

shrimp·er \ˈshrimp-ər\ *n* **1** : a shrimp fisherman **2** : a boat used in fishing for shrimps

shrine \ˈshrīn\ *n* **1** : a case or box for sacred relics (as the bones of a saint) **2** : a place in which devotion is paid to a saint or deity ⟨a Buddhist *shrine*⟩ **3** : a place that is considered sacred ⟨visited the *shrines* of American independence⟩

¹shrimp 1

¹shrink \ˈshriŋk\ *vb* **shrank** \ˈshraŋk\ *or* **shrunk** \ˈshrəŋk\; **shrunk** *or* **shrunk·en** \ˈshrəŋ-kən\; **shrink·ing** **1** : to curl up or withdraw in or as if in fear or pain ⟨*shrink* in horror⟩ **2** : to make or become smaller ⟨*shrink* cloth by washing⟩ ⟨meat *shrinks* in cooking⟩ — **shrink·er** *n*

²shrink *n, slang* : PSYCHIATRIST

shrink·age \'shriŋ-kij\ *n* : the amount by which something shrinks or becomes less

shrive \'shrīv\ *vb* **shrived** *or* **shrove** \'shrōv\; **shriv·en** \'shriv-ən\ *or* **shrived**; **shriv·ing** \'shrī-viŋ\ **1** : to hear the confession of and administer the Roman Catholic sacrament of penance to : PARDON **2** *archaic* : to confess one's sins especially to a priest

shriv·el \'shriv-əl\ *vb* **-eled** *or* **-elled**; **-el·ing** *or* **-el·ling** \-(ə-)liŋ\ : to shrink and become dry and wrinkled

¹shroud \'shraùd\ *n* **1** : the cloth placed over or around a dead body **2** : something that covers or shelters like a shroud ⟨a *shroud* of secrecy⟩ **3** : one of the ropes that go from the masthead of a ship to the sides to provide support to the mast

²shroud *vb* : to cover with or as if with a shroud ⟨*shrouded* in fog⟩

Shrove·tide \'shrōv-,tīd\ *n* : the three days just before Ash Wednesday

Shrove Tuesday \'shrōv-\ *n* : the Tuesday before Ash Wednesday [Middle English *schroftewesday* "Shrove Tuesday," from *schrof*, from *shriven* "to shrive, give a penance or pardon to," and *tewesday* "Tuesday"; *shriven*, from Old English *scrifan* "to shrive, prescribe," from Latin *scribere* "to write" — related to SCRIBE, TUESDAY; see *Word History* at TUESDAY]

shrub \'shrəb\ *n* : a woody plant that has several stems and is smaller than most trees

shrub·bery \'shrəb-(ə-)rē\ *n, pl* **-ber·ies** : a group of shrubs or an area where shrubs are growing

shrub·by \'shrəb-ē\ *adj* **shrub·bi·er; -est 1** : consisting of or covered with shrubs ⟨a *shrubby* hillside⟩ **2** : resembling a shrub ⟨a *shrubby* palm⟩

shrug \'shrəg\ *vb* **shrugged; shrug·ging** : to draw or hunch up the shoulders usually to express doubt, uncertainty, or lack of interest — **shrug** *n*

shrug off *vb* **1** : to brush aside as not important **2** : to take off (a garment) by wriggling out

¹shuck \'shək\ *n* **1** : the outer covering of a nut or of an ear of corn **2** : the shell of an oyster or clam

²shuck *vb* **1** : to remove the shucks of **2** : to throw aside — often used with *off*

¹shud·der \'shəd-ər\ *vb* **shud·dered; shud·der·ing** \-(ə-)riŋ\ **1** : to tremble with fear or horror or from cold ⟨*shuddered* just thinking about it⟩ **2** : ¹SHAKE 1, QUIVER ⟨the train slowed and *shuddered* to a halt⟩

²shudder *n* : an act of shuddering : SHIVER — **shud·dery** \-(ə-)rē\ *adj*

¹shuf·fle \'shəf-əl\ *vb* **shuf·fled; shuf·fling** \-(ə-)liŋ\ **1** : to mix in a disorderly mass **2** : to push out of sight **3 a** : to mix cards to change their order in the pack **b** : to move from place to place **4 a** : to walk or move by sliding or dragging the feet ⟨*shuffling* along⟩ **b** : to move by sliding along or back and forth without lifting ⟨*shuffled* her feet⟩ — **shuf·fler** \-(ə-)lər\ *n*

²shuffle *n* **1 a** : an act of shuffling **b** : a disorderly mass or pile **2** : a sliding or dragging walk

shuf·fle·board \'shəf-əl-,bō(ə)rd, -,bò(ə)rd\ *n* : a game in which players try to push disks into scoring areas of a diagram marked on a smooth surface

shul \'shùl\ *n* : SYNAGOGUE

shun \'shən\ *vb* **shunned; shun·ning** : to avoid purposely or by habit ⟨*shunned* her former friends⟩ — **shun·ner** *n*

¹shunt \'shənt\ *vb* **1** : to turn off to one side or out of the way : SHIFT **2** : to switch (as a train) from one track to another — **shunt·er** *n*

²shunt *n* : a method or device for turning or pushing aside; *esp* : a conductor joining two points in an electrical circuit so as to form a path through which a portion of the current may pass

shush \'shəsh, 'shùsh\ *vb* : to urge to be quiet — **shush** *n*

shut \'shət\ *vb* **shut; shut·ting 1** : to move into position so as to close an opening ⟨*shut* the door⟩ **2** : to close so

as to forbid entrance or leaving ⟨*shut* the cottage for the winter⟩ **3** : to keep in a place by enclosing or by blocking the way out : IMPRISON ⟨*shut* them in jail⟩ **4** : to close by bringing parts together ⟨*shut* your eyes⟩ **5** : to stop or cause to stop operation ⟨*shut* both stores for a week⟩ ⟨the plant *shut* down⟩

shut·down \'shət-,daùn\ *n* : an ending of an activity

shute *variant of* CHUTE

shut–in \'shət-,in\ *n* : a sick person unable to go outdoors

shut–off \'shət-,òf\ *n* **1** : something that shuts off **2** : an instance of shutting off : INTERRUPTION, STOPPAGE

shut off \,shət-'òf\ *vb* **1** : to stop the flow of ⟨*shut off* the water⟩ **2 a** : to stop the operation of ⟨*shut* the motor *off*⟩ **b** : to cease operating ⟨the light *shuts off* automatically⟩ **3** : to make or keep separate ⟨*shut off* from the rest of the world⟩

shut·out \'shət-,aùt\ *n* : a game in which one side fails to score

shut out \,shət-'aùt\ *vb* **1** : to keep something out : EXCLUDE **2** : to keep an opponent from scoring in a game

¹shut·ter \'shət-ər\ *n* **1** : a movable cover for a window that swings on hinges like a door **2** : a device in a camera that opens to allow light to enter when a picture is taken

²shutter *vb* : to close with or by shutters ⟨kept the house *shuttered*⟩

shut·ter·bug \'shət-ər-,bəg\ *n* : a photography enthusiast

¹shut·tle \'shət-ᵊl\ *n* **1** : an instrument used in weaving to carry the thread back and forth from side to side through the threads that run lengthwise **2 a** : a vehicle that goes back and forth regularly over an often short route ⟨the airport *shuttle*⟩ ⟨space *shuttle*⟩ **b** : an established route used by a shuttle

²shuttle *vb* **shut·tled; shut·tling** \'shət-liŋ, -ᵊl-iŋ\ **1** : to move or travel back and forth often **2** : to transport in, by, or as if by a shuttle ⟨*shuttled* the children to school⟩

shut·tle·cock \'shət-ᵊl-,käk\ *n* : a small and very light cone-shaped object that is used in playing badminton

shut up *vb* **1** : to cause a person to stop talking **2** : to stop writing or speaking

¹shy \'shī\ *adj* **shi·er** *or* **shy·er** \'shī(-ə)r\; **shi·est** *or* **shy·est** \'shī-əst\ **1 a** : easily frightened : TIMID **b** : not feeling comfortable around people : not wanting or able to call attention to oneself **2** : having less than a full or an expected amount or number ⟨we were about ten dollars *shy* of our goal⟩ — **shy·ly** *adv* — **shy·ness** *n*

synonyms SHY, BASHFUL, DIFFIDENT mean feeling awkward around others. SHY suggests not wanting to meet or talk with people either by habit or for special reasons ⟨at the new school I was *shy* at first⟩. BASHFUL suggests being shy and afraid like a very young child ⟨they were *bashful* and would hide when company came⟩. DIFFIDENT suggests not putting oneself forward because of a lack of self-confidence ⟨in art class he was *diffident* about his work⟩.

²shy *vb* **shied; shy·ing 1** : to draw back in sudden dislike or distaste ⟨*shied* from publicity⟩ **2** : to move quickly to one side in fright ⟨the horse *shied*⟩

³shy *n, pl* **shies** : a sudden move to one side

shy·ster \'shī-stər\ *n* : a crooked lawyer or politician

S ¹shutter 1

\ə\ **abut**	\aù\ **out**	\i\ **tip**	\ò\ **saw**	\ù\ **foot**
\ər\ **further**	\ch\ **chin**	\ī\ **life**	\òi\ **coin**	\y\ **yet**
\a\ **mat**	\e\ **pet**	\j\ **job**	\th\ **thin**	\yü\ **few**
\ā\ **take**	\ē\ **easy**	\ŋ\ **sing**	\th\ **this**	\yù\ **cure**
\ä\ **cot, cart**	\g\ **go**	\ō\ **bone**	\ü\ **food**	\zh\ **vision**

si \'sē\ *n* : the seventh note of a scale : TI

¹Si·a·mese \ˌsī-ə-'mēz, -'mēs\ *adj* : of or relating to Thailand, the Thais, or their language

²Siamese *n, pl* **Siamese** **1** : THAI 1 **2** : THAI 2

Siamese cat *n* : any of a breed of slender blue-eyed domestic cats with short hair and a light-colored body and darker ears, paws, tail, and face

Siamese twin *n* : either of a pair of human or animal twins born joined together

Si·be·ri·an husky \sī-ˌbir-ē-ən-\ *n* : any of a breed of medium-sized dogs that were developed to pull sleds and that have a thick coat and a bushy tail

¹sib·i·lant \'sib-ə-lənt\ *adj* : having or producing the sound of or a sound like the *s* or the *sh* in *sash*

²sibilant *n* : a sibilant speech sound (as English \s\, \z\, \sh\, \zh\, \ch (=tsh)\, or \j (=dzh)\)

sib·ling \'sib-liŋ\ *n* : one of two or more individuals having the same parents or sometimes only one parent in common

sick \'sik\ *adj* **1 a** : affected with disease or ill health **b** : of, relating to, or intended for use in sickness ⟨*sick* pay⟩ ⟨a *sick* ward⟩ **c** : affected with or accompanied by nausea : QUEASY 1 ⟨felt *sick* to her stomach⟩ **2 a** : badly upset by strong emotion ⟨*sick* with shame⟩ ⟨worried *sick*⟩ **b** : tired of something from having too much of it ⟨*sick* of their whining⟩ **c** : filled with disgust ⟨such gossip makes me *sick*⟩ **3** : mentally or emotionally unsound or disturbed ⟨*sick* thoughts⟩

sick bay *n* : a place on a ship used as a hospital

sick·bed \'sik-ˌbed\ *n* : the bed on which a sick person lies

sick·en \'sik-ən\ *vb* **sick·ened; sick·en·ing** \-(ə-)niŋ\ : to make or become sick

sick·en·ing \'sik-(ə-)niŋ\ *adj* : causing sickness or disgust ⟨a *sickening* sight⟩ — **sick·en·ing·ly** *adv*

sick·ish \'sik-ish\ *adj* **1** : somewhat nauseated **2** : somewhat sickening ⟨a *sickish* odor⟩

¹sick·le \'sik-əl\ *n* : a tool with a sharp curved metal blade and a short handle used to cut grass

²sickle *vb* **sick·led; sick·ling** \'sik-(ə-)liŋ\ : to change into a sickle cell ⟨the ability of red blood cells to *sickle*⟩

sickle cell *n* : an abnormal red blood cell that is crescent-shaped

sickle–cell anemia *n* : a serious inherited disease in which small blood vessels become blocked with sickle cells and which occurs mostly in people of African, Mediterranean, or southwest Asian ancestry

sick·ly \'sik-lē\ *adj* **sick·li·er; -est** **1** : somewhat sick : often ailing ⟨was *sickly* as a child⟩ **2** : caused by or associated with ill health ⟨a *sickly* complexion⟩ **3 a** : tending to produce disease ⟨a *sickly* climate⟩ **b** : appearing as if sick ⟨a *sickly* flame⟩ **c** : not growing well : ⟨a *sickly* plant⟩ **d** : SICKENING ⟨a *sickly* odor⟩

sick·ness \'sik-nəs\ *n* **1** : ill health : ILLNESS **2** : a specific disease : MALADY **3** : NAUSEA 1

sick·room \'sik-ˌrüm, -ˌrùm\ *n* : a room in which a sick person stays

¹side \'sīd\ *n* **1 a** : the right or left part of the trunk of the body ⟨a pain in the *side*⟩ ⟨stood at her *side*⟩ **b** : the entire right or left half of the animal body ⟨a *side* of beef⟩ **2** : a place, space, or direction away from or beyond a central point or line ⟨set it to one *side*⟩ **3** : a surface or line forming a border or face of an object ⟨a cube has six *sides*⟩ **4** : an outer part of a thing considered as facing in a certain direction ⟨the back *side* of the moon⟩ **5 a** : a straight-line segment forming part of the boundary of a geometric figure ⟨*side* of a square⟩ **b** : one of the longer surfaces that form the boundary of a solid ⟨lay the book on its *side*⟩ **c** : either surface of a thin object ⟨one *side* of a record⟩ **6** : a position or part of something viewed as opposite or different from another ⟨my *side* of the story⟩ ⟨try to look on the good *side*⟩ ⟨never saw this *side* of his personality⟩ **7** : a body of contestants ⟨our *side* won⟩ **8** : a line of ancestors traced back from either parent ⟨a grandfather

on his mother's *side*⟩ **9** : a side dish ordered separately ⟨a *side* of fries⟩ — **on the side** **1** : in addition to but not included in the main portion ⟨a salad with dressing *on the side*⟩ **2** : in addition to one's main occupation ⟨selling insurance *on the side*⟩ — **this side of** : short of : ALMOST ⟨behavior just *this side of* reckless⟩

²side *adj* **1** : of, relating to, or located on the side ⟨*side* window⟩ **2** : going toward or coming from the side ⟨*side* wind⟩ **3** : being in addition to something more important : INCIDENTAL ⟨a *side* issue⟩

³side *vb* **sid·ed; sid·ing** **1** : to take the same side ⟨*sided* with our friend in the argument⟩ **2** : to put siding on ⟨*side* a house⟩

side·arm \'sīd-ˌärm\ *adj* : done with the arm extending out to the side ⟨a *sidearm* pitch in baseball⟩ — **sidearm** *adv*

side·arm \'sīd-ˌärm\ *n* : a weapon (as a sword or revolver) worn at the side or in the belt

side·board \'sīd-ˌbō(ə)rd, -ˌbò(ə)rd\ *n* : a piece of furniture for holding dishes, silverware, and table linen

side·burns \'sīd-ˌbərnz\ *n pl* : hair growing on the side of the face in front of the ears

Word History During the American Civil War, the Union general Ambrose Everett Burnside became known for the long bushy whiskers he wore on the sides of his face. Burnside was a popular figure in the city of Washington during the early days of the war. His unusual appearance caught the public eye, and other men soon began growing long whiskers like his. Such whiskers, which became the fashion throughout America, were originally called *burnsides* after the general. By the 1880s the order of the two words comprising *burnsides* was reversed to give *sideburns*, probably by analogy with "side-whiskers." [an altered form of *burnsides* "long whiskers at the side of the face," named for Ambrose Everett *Burnside* 1824–1881 American general]

side by side *adv* : beside one another

side·car \'sīd-ˌkär\ *n* : a car attached to the side of a motorcycle for a passenger

sid·ed \'sīd-əd\ *adj* : having sides often of a stated number or kind ⟨steep-*sided* mountains⟩ ⟨four-*sided* figures⟩

side dish *n* : food served separately along with the main course

side effect *n* : an often harmful and unwanted effect (as of a drug) that occurs along with the basic desired effect ⟨the environmental *side effects* of using chemicals to kill pests⟩

side·kick \'sīd-ˌkik\ *n* : one who is another's pal, partner, or helper

side·light \-ˌlīt\ *n* **1** : light from the side **2** : incidental or extra information

side·line \-ˌlīn\ *n* **1** : a line marking the side of a playing field or court **2** : a business or job done in addition to one's regular occupation

¹side·long \'sīd-ˌlòŋ\ *adv* : out of the corner of one's eye ⟨glanced *sidelong* at the food on the table⟩

²sidelong \ˌsīd-ˌlòŋ\ *adj* **1** : made to one side or out of the corner of one's eye ⟨a *sidelong* glance⟩ **2** : INDIRECT 2

side·sad·dle \-ˌsad-ᵊl\ *n* : a saddle for women in which the rider sits with both legs on one side of the horse — **sidesaddle** *adv*

side·show \-ˌshō\ *n* : a small show off to the side offered in addition to a main show (as of a circus)

side·slip \-ˌslip\ *vb* : to slide sideways — **sideslip** *n*

side·spin \-ˌspin\ *n* : motion that causes a ball to spin sideways

side–split·ting \-ˌsplit-iŋ\ *adj* : very funny ⟨a *side-splitting* joke⟩

side·step \-ˌstep\ *vb* **1** : to take a step to the side **2** : to avoid by a

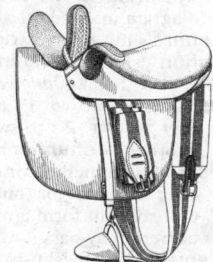
sidesaddle

step to the side ⟨*sidestep* a blow⟩ **3** : to avoid answering or dealing with ⟨*sidestep* a question⟩

side street *n* : a street joining and often ending at a main road

side·stroke \-ˌstrōk\ *n* : a swimming stroke made while lying on the side by sweeping the arms downward and backward underwater while the legs do a scissors kick

¹**side-swipe** \-ˌswīp\ *vb* : to hit along the side with a blow that bounces off at an angle ⟨*sideswiped* a parked car⟩

²**sideswipe** *n* **1** : an instance of sideswiping : a blow from an angle that bounces off **2** : an indirectly related disapproving remark, allusion, or reference ⟨a *sideswipe* at the senator's voting record⟩

¹**side·track** \ˈsīd-ˌtrak\ *n* : SIDING 1

²**sidetrack** *vb* **1** : to transfer from a main railroad line to a siding **2** : to turn aside from a main purpose or use ⟨got *sidetracked* by all the phone calls⟩

side·walk \ˈsīd-ˌwȯk\ *n* : a usually paved walk at the side of a street or road

side·wall \-ˌwȯl\ *n* **1** : a wall forming the side of something **2** : the side of an automotive tire between the tread shoulder and the rim

side·ward \ˈsīd-wərd\ *or* **side·wards** \-wərdz\ *adv or adj* : toward the side

side·ways \ˈsīd-ˌwāz\ *adv or adj* **1** : from one side ⟨viewed the stage *sideways*⟩ **2** : with one side forward ⟨turn *sideways*⟩ **3** : to one side ⟨fell *sideways*⟩

side–whis·kers \-ˌhwis-kərz, -ˌwis-\ *n pl* : whiskers on the side of the face usually worn long

side·wind·er \-ˌwīn-dər\ *n* : a small rattlesnake of the southwestern U.S. that moves by thrusting its body diagonally forward in a series of flat S-shaped loops

sidewinder

side·wise \ˈsīd-ˌwīz\ *adv or adj* : SIDEWAYS

sid·ing \ˈsīd-iŋ\ *n* **1** : a short railroad track connected with the main track **2** : material used to cover the outside walls of frame buildings ⟨vinyl *siding*⟩

si·dle \ˈsīd-ᵊl\ *vb* **si·dled; si·dling** \ˈsīd-liŋ, -ᵊl-iŋ\ : to go or move with one side forward ⟨the waiter *sidled* around the end of the counter⟩

siege \ˈsēj\ *n* **1** : the placing of an army around a fortified place or city to force it to surrender **2** : a lasting attack (as of illness) — **lay siege to 1** : to attack militarily **2** : to pursue diligently or persistently ⟨*laid siege to* his work⟩

si·en·na \sē-ˈen-ə\ *n* : an artist's pigment that is either brownish yellow or reddish brown

si·er·ra \sē-ˈer-ə\ *n* : a range of mountains especially with jagged peaks [from Spanish *sierra* "a range of jagged mountains," literally, "a saw," from Latin *serra* "a saw" — related to SERRATED]

si·es·ta \sē-ˈes-tə\ *n* : a nap or rest especially in the afternoon

Word History In the ancient Roman way of keeping track of time, the hours of the day were counted from sunrise to sunset. The hour when the sun was most nearly directly overhead was their sixth hour, or *sexta hora* in Latin. As Latin developed into Spanish on the Iberian Peninsula, *sexta* became *siesta*. In some countries, like Spain, it may be too hot to work in the middle of the day. There it is the custom to take a short nap until the heat begins to lessen. This rest period is called *siesta* in Spanish, and this word has come directly into English

with the same meaning. [from Spanish *siesta* "an afternoon nap or rest period," from Latin *sexta (hora)* "sixth (hour), noon"; so called because the Romans counted the hours from sunrise]

¹**sieve** \ˈsiv\ *n* : a device with meshes or holes to separate finer particles from coarser ones or solids from liquids

²**sieve** *vb* **sieved; siev·ing** : to put through a sieve : SIFT ⟨*sieve* the tomatoes to remove the seeds⟩

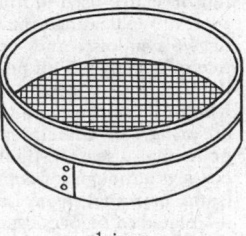

¹sieve

sieve tube *n* : a tube that is composed of an end-to-end series of thin-walled living cells, transports food substances in plants, and is found in the phloem

sift \ˈsift\ *vb* **1 a** : to put through a sieve ⟨*sift* flour⟩ **b** : to separate or separate out by or as if by putting through a sieve **2** : to go through especially to sort out what is useful or valuable ⟨*sift* evidence⟩ ⟨*sift* through a pile of papers⟩ — **sift·er** *n*

¹**sigh** \ˈsī\ *vb* **1** : to take or let out a long loud breath (as in weariness or relief) **2** : to make a sound like sighing ⟨wind *sighing* in the branches⟩ **3** : YEARN 1 ⟨*sighing* for the good old days⟩

²**sigh** *n* **1** : an often involuntary act of sighing especially when expressing a feeling **2** : the sound of gently moving or escaping air ⟨the *sighs* of a summer breeze⟩

¹**sight** \ˈsīt\ *n* **1** : something that is seen : SPECTACLE **2 a** : something that is worth seeing ⟨showed us the *sights* of the city⟩ **b** : something that is peculiar, funny, or messy ⟨you're a *sight*⟩ **3** : the process, power, or function of seeing; *esp* : the animal sense of which the sense organ is the eye and by which the position, shape, and color of objects are perceived **4** : the act of seeing ⟨knows him by *sight*⟩ ⟨faints at the *sight* of blood⟩ **5** : the perception of an object within the visual field ⟨lost *sight* of the plane⟩ **6** : the space over which a person can see ⟨a ship came into *sight*⟩ **7** : a device that aids the eye in aiming or in finding the direction of an object **8** *pl* : ASPIRATION 3a, GOAL 2 ⟨set her *sights* on a career in law⟩ — **out of sight** : very good — **sight for sore eyes** : someone or something one is very glad to see

²**sight** *vb* **1** : to get or catch sight of ⟨several bears were *sighted*⟩ **2** : to look at through or as if through a sight

sight·ed \ˈsīt-əd\ *adj* : having sight ⟨clear-*sighted*⟩

sight·less \ˈsīt-ləs\ *adj* : lacking sight : BLIND — **sight·less·ness** *n*

sight·ly \ˈsīt-lē\ *adj* : pleasant to look at — **sight·li·ness** *n*

sight–read \ˈsīt-ˌrēd\ *vb* **-read** \-ˌred\; **-read·ing** \-ˌrēd-iŋ\ : to read something written in a foreign language or play music without first practicing or studying it

sight·see \ˈsīt-ˌsē\ *vb* **-saw; -see·ing** : to go about seeing sights of interest — **sight·se·er** \-ˌsē-ər, -ˌsi(ə)r\ *n*

sight·see·ing \-ˌsē-iŋ\ *adj* : engaged in, devoted to, or used for seeing things and places of interest ⟨a *sightseeing* bus⟩ — **sight·seeing** *n*

sight unseen *adv* : without inspection or estimate of worth ⟨bought it *sight unseen*⟩

sig·ma \ˈsig-mə\ *n* : the 18th letter of the Greek alphabet — Σ or σ or ς

¹**sign** \ˈsīn\ *n* **1 a** : a motion, action, or movement of the hand by which a thought is expressed or a command or

\ə\ **abut**	\au̇\ **out**	\i\ **tip**	\ȯ\ **saw**	\u̇\ **foot**
\ər\ **further**	\ch\ **chin**	\ī\ **life**	\ȯi\ **coin**	\y\ **yet**
\a\ **mat**	\e\ **pet**	\j\ **job**	\th\ **thin**	\yü\ **few**
\ā\ **take**	\ē\ **easy**	\ŋ\ **sing**	\th\ **this**	\yu̇\ **cure**
\ä\ **cot, cart**	\g\ **go**	\ō\ **bone**	\ü\ **food**	\zh\ **vision**

wish made known ⟨made a *sign* for them to be quiet⟩ **b** : ¹SIGNAL 1 **c** : SIGN LANGUAGE **2** : a mark having a generally understood meaning and used in place of words **3** : one of the 12 parts of the zodiac **4 a** : a symbol (as a flat or sharp) used in musical notation **b** : a symbol (as ÷ or √) indicating a mathematical operation; *also* : one of two symbols + and – characterizing a number as positive or negative **5** : a public notice that advertises something or gives information **6 a** : something that indicates what is present or is to come ⟨no *sign* of life⟩ ⟨first *signs* of spring⟩ **b** : something that provides evidence of plant or animal disease [Middle English *signe* "a gesture that conveys a thought or command," from early French *signe* (same meaning), from Latin *signum* "mark, sign, image" — related to DESIGNATE, ³SEAL, ¹SIGNAL, SIGNIFICANT]
synonyms SIGN, MARK, TOKEN, NOTE, SYMPTOM mean an indication of something that is not readily perceived. SIGN applies to any indication that can be perceived by the senses or by reason ⟨encouraging *signs* for business⟩. MARK suggests something characteristic of a thing in contrast to general outward appearance ⟨a *mark* of good upbringing⟩. TOKEN applies to something serving as proof of a thing that is without physical form ⟨a *token* of my affection⟩. NOTE suggests a distinguishing mark or characteristic ⟨a *note* of sarcasm in her voice⟩. SYMPTOM suggests an outward indication of an inward change or condition ⟨frequent arguments were a *symptom* of their growing dislike for one another⟩.

²**sign** *vb* **1 a** : to make or place a sign on **b** : to represent or indicate by a sign **2** : to write one's name on to show that one accepts, agrees with, or is responsible for ⟨*sign* a check⟩ ⟨*sign* a letter⟩ ⟨*sign* a contract⟩ **3** : to hire by getting to sign something (as a contract) ⟨*sign* a new ball player⟩ **4** : to use sign language — **sign·ee** \ˌsī-'nē\ *n* — **sign·er** *n*

¹**sig·nal** \'sig-nᵊl\ *n* **1** : an act, event, or word that serves to start some action **2** : a sound or motion of a part of the body made to give warning or command **3** : an object placed to give notice or warning ⟨a traffic *signal*⟩ **4 a** : the message, sound, or effect transmitted in electronic communication (as radio or television) **b** : a radio wave or electric current that transmits a message or effect (as in radio or television) [Middle English *signal* "signal, sign," derived from Latin *signalis* "of a sign," from earlier *signum* "mark, sign, image" — related to SIGN]

²**signal** *vb* **sig·naled** *or* **sig·nalled**; **sig·nal·ing** *or* **sig·nal·ling** \-nə-liŋ\ **1** : to notify by a signal **2** : to communicate by or as if by signals — **sig·nal·er** *n*

³**signal** *adj* **1** : unusually great ⟨a *signal* honor⟩ ⟨a *signal* achievement⟩ **2** : used in signaling ⟨a *signal* light⟩ — **sig·nal·ly** \-nə-lē\ *adv*

sig·nal·ize \'sig-nə-ˌlīz\ *vb* **-ized**; **-iz·ing** : to make well-known : point out clearly

sig·nal·man \'sig-nᵊl-mən, -ˌman\ *n* : a person who sends signals or works with signals

sig·na·ture \'sig-nə-ˌchủ(ə)r, -chər\ *n* **1** : the name of a person written by that person **2** : a notation used in music to indicate the key or the rhythm

sign·board \'sīn-ˌbō(ə)rd, -ˌbȯ(ə)rd\ *n* : a board with a notice or sign on it

sig·nif·i·cance \sig-'nif-i-kən(t)s\ *n* **1** : ¹MEANING 1 **2** : the quality of being of notable worth or influence **synonyms** see IMPORTANCE

sig·nif·i·cant \sig-'nif-i-kənt\ *adj* **1** : having much importance **2** : probably caused by something other than chance ⟨a statistically *significant* relationship between vitamin deficiency and disease⟩ **3** : having meaning and especially a hidden or special meaning ⟨gave us a *significant* wink⟩ [from Latin *significant-, significans,* present participle of *significare* "to signify, indicate," from *signum* "mark, sign, image" — related to SIGN] — **sig·nif·i·cant·ly** *adv*

significant digit *n* : any of the digits of a number beginning with the first digit on the left that is not zero and ending with the last on the right that is either not zero or that is a zero but is considered to be exact — called also *significant figure*

sig·ni·fi·ca·tion \ˌsig-nə-fə-'kā-shən\ *n* : the meaning that a term or symbol has or is meant to have

sig·ni·fy \'sig-nə-ˌfī\ *vb* **-fied**; **-fy·ing** **1** : ²MEAN 2, DENOTE **2** : to show especially by a sign : make known ⟨*signified* their agreement by nodding⟩ **3** : to have importance : MATTER ⟨doesn't *signify* much what you wear⟩

sign in *vb* : to make a record of one's arrival or presence ⟨use a password to *sign in* on the computer⟩

sign language *n* **1** : a formal language using a system of hand movements for communication (as by the deaf) **2** : a way of communicating mainly by hand and arm movements as often used by people speaking different languages

sign off \(')sī-'nȯf\ *vb* : to announce the end (as of a program or broadcast)

sign of the cross : a movement of the hand forming a cross especially on forehead, shoulders, and breast to profess Christian faith or ask divine protection or blessing

sign on \(')sī-'nȯn, -'nän\ *vb* **1** : to hire oneself by or as if by a signature ⟨*signed on* as a member of the crew⟩ **2** : to announce the beginning of broadcasting

sign out *vb* **1** : to make a record of one's departure ⟨have to *sign out* before getting off-line⟩ **2** : to record or approve the release or departure of ⟨*signed out* the library books⟩

sign·post \'sīn-ˌpōst\ *n* **1** : a post with signs on it to direct travelers **2** : something that points the way

sign up \(')sī-'nəp\ *vb* : to sign one's name in order to get, do, or take something ⟨*signed up* for Spanish⟩ — **sign-up** *n or adj*

Sikh \'sēk\ *n* : a believer in a religion of India that was founded about 1500 and that believes in one God and rejects idols and caste — **Sikh·ism** \-ˌiz-əm\ *n*

si·lage \'sī-lij\ *n* : fodder (as hay or corn) fermented (as in a silo) to produce a rich moist feed for livestock

¹**si·lence** \'sī-lən(t)s\ *n* **1** : the state of keeping or being silent — often used as an interjection ⟨*"Silence!"* demanded the maestro⟩ **2** : the state of there being no sound or noise : STILLNESS ⟨in the *silence* of the night⟩ **3 a** : a state of not mentioning **b** : SECRECY 2 ⟨research done in *silence*⟩

²**silence** *vb* **si·lenced**; **si·lenc·ing** **1** : to stop the noise or speech of : cause to be silent ⟨*silenced* the class⟩ **2** : SUPPRESS 1 ⟨*silencing* opposing views⟩

si·lenc·er \'sī-lən-sər\ *n* : a device used on small arms to reduce the sound of firing

si·lent \'sī-lənt\ *adj* **1** : not speaking ⟨stood *silent* before the court⟩ **2** : tending not to say much ⟨a very *silent* person⟩ **3** : free from sound or noise : STILL **4** : done or felt without speaking ⟨*silent* reading⟩ ⟨*silent* grief⟩ **5 a** : making no mention ⟨history is *silent* about this incident⟩ **b** : not active in running a business ⟨a *silent* partner⟩ **6** : not pronounced ⟨*silent* "e" in "came"⟩ ⟨the "b" in "doubt" is *silent*⟩ **7** : made without recorded sound ⟨*silent* movies⟩ — **si·lent·ly** *adv*
synonyms SILENT, TACITURN, RETICENT, RESERVED mean tending not to talk. SILENT suggests a habit of never saying more than one must ⟨a *silent* person who leads by example rather than words⟩. TACITURN suggests that by nature one dislikes talking and may also prefer being alone ⟨a *taciturn* farmer who did not welcome visitors⟩. RETICENT suggests a dislike of talking about one's own business ⟨the new neighbor was *reticent* about her job⟩. RESERVED suggests that one is rigid and quiet during conversation ⟨the *reserved* couple did not join in the lively talk at dinner⟩.

silent treatment *n* : an act of completely ignoring a person or thing by being silent especially as a means of expressing contempt or disapproval ⟨gave him the *silent treatment* after their breakup⟩

¹**sil·hou·ette** \ˌsil-ə-ˈwet\ *n* **1 a** : a picture (as a drawing or cutout) of the outline of an object filled in with a solid usually black color **b** : a profile portrait done in silhouette **2** : the outline of an object seen or as if seen against the light

²**silhouette** *vb* **-ett·ed; -ett·ing** : to represent by a silhouette; *also* : to show against a light background ⟨ducks *silhouetted* against the evening sky⟩ — **sil·hou·et·tist** \-ˈwet-ist\ *n*

¹silhouette 1b

sil·i·ca \ˈsil-i-kə\ *n* : a compound that consists of the dioxide of silicon and occurs in various forms (as in quartz, opal, and sand)

sil·i·cate \ˈsil-i-ˌkāt, ˈsil-ə-kət\ *n* : a chemical salt that consists of a metal combined with silicon and oxygen and is used especially in building materials (as bricks)

sil·i·con \ˈsil-i-kən, ˈsil-ə-ˌkän\ *n* : a nonmetallic element that occurs combined as the most abundant element after oxygen in the earth's crust and is used especially in alloys and electronic devices — see ELEMENT table

silicon dioxide *n* : SILICA

sil·i·cone \ˈsil-ə-ˌkōn\ *n* : any of various silicon compounds that contain carbon and hydrogen, are obtained as oily or greasy substances or plastics, and are used especially for water-resistant and heat-resistant lubricants and varnishes

sil·i·co·sis \ˌsil-ə-ˈkō-səs\ *n* : a serious lung disease that is characterized by scar tissue in the lungs and shortness of breath and is caused by inhaling silica dusts for a long time

silk \ˈsilk\ *n* **1** : a fine continuous protein fiber produced by various insect larvae usually to form their cocoons; *esp* : a strong glossy elastic fiber produced by silkworms and used to weave cloth **2** : thread, yarn, or fabric made from silk **3** : something resembling silk: as **a** : the thread produced by a spider **b** : the cluster of thin threadlike parts at the end of an ear of corn that are styles of the ovaries

silk·en \ˈsil-kən\ *adj* **1** : made of or with silk **2** : resembling silk especially in soft smooth feel **3** : pleasantly smooth ⟨a *silken* voice⟩

silk moth *n* : the silkworm moth

silk screen *n* : a method of printing in which a design is produced by forcing colored ink through a piece of fabric that has been treated so that the ink cannot pass through some parts

silk·worm \ˈsil-ˌkwərm\ *n* : any of various moth larvae that spin a large amount of silk to make a cocoon; *esp* : a wrinkled hairless yellowish caterpillar that is the larva of an Asian moth, is raised in captivity on mulberry leaves, and produces a strong silk that is the silk most often used for thread or cloth

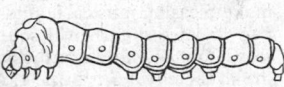

silkworm

silky \ˈsil-kē\ *adj* **silk·i·er; -est** **1** : soft and smooth as silk **2** : having or covered with fine soft hairs, plumes, or scales — **silk·i·ly** \-kə-lē\ *adv* — **silk·i·ness** \-kē-nəs\ *n*

sill \ˈsil\ *n* **1** : a horizontal piece (as a timber) that forms the lowest part of a supporting structure: as **a** : the horizontal piece at the base of a window **b** : the timber or stone at the foot of a door : THRESHOLD **2** : a flat mass of igneous rock injected while melted between other rocks

sil·ly \ˈsil-ē\ *adj* **sil·li·er; -est** **1** : weak in mind : FOOLISH **2** : not showing common sense or good judgment : ABSURD ⟨a *silly* plan⟩ **3** : lacking in seriousness or importance ⟨playing *silly* games⟩ **4** : being stunned or dazed ⟨scared *silly*⟩ — **sil·li·ness** \ˈsil-ē-nəs\ *n*

si·lo \ˈsī-lō\ *n, pl* **silos** **1** : a trench, pit, or especially a tall cylinder (as of wood or concrete) used for making and storing silage **2** : an underground structure for housing a missile

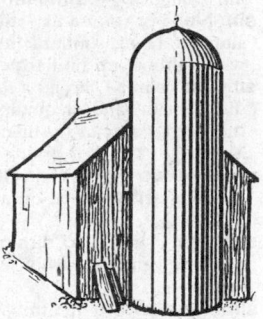

silo 1

¹**silt** \ˈsilt\ *n* **1** : very small particles left as sediment from water; *also* : a soil made up mostly of silt with little clay **2** : a deposit of sediment (as by a river) — **silty** \ˈsil-tē\ *adj*

²**silt** *vb* : to make or become choked, blocked, filled, or covered with silt ⟨the river channel *silted* up⟩

Si·lu·ri·an \sī-ˈlu̇r-ē-ən, sə-\ *adj* : of, relating to, or being a period of the Paleozoic era of geological history marked by the first appearance of land plants; *also* : relating to the corresponding system of rocks — see GEOLOGIC TIME table — **Silurian** *n*

silvan *variant of* SYLVAN

¹**sil·ver** \ˈsil-vər\ *n* **1** : a soft white metallic element that takes a high polish and is a better conductor of heat and electricity than any other substance — see ELEMENT table **2 a** : coin made of silver **b** : articles (as tableware) made of or plated with silver **c** : tableware made of other metals (as stainless steel) **3** : a medium gray **4** : a silver medal awarded as the second prize in a competition

²**silver** *adj* **1** : relating to, made of, or yielding silver ⟨*silver* jewelry⟩ ⟨*silver* ore⟩ **2** : SILVERY 1

³**silver** *vb* **sil·vered; sil·ver·ing** \ˈsilv-(ə-)riŋ\ : to coat with or as if with silver — **sil·ver·er** \ˈsil-vər-ər\ *n*

silver bromide *n* : a compound that is easily affected by light and is much used in photography

sil·ver·fish \ˈsil-vər-ˌfish\ *n* : any of various small wingless insects; *esp* : one that is found in houses and feeds on paper products, clothing, and other starchy materials

silver fox *n* : a color form of the common red fox in which the pelt is black tipped with white

silver iodide *n* : a compound that darkens when exposed to light and is used in photography, rainmaking, and medicine

silver lining *n* : a consoling or hopeful prospect ⟨looked for the *silver lining* in a bad situation⟩

silver nitrate *n* : a compound used especially in photography and as an antiseptic in medicine

silver plate *n* **1** : a plating of silver **2** : tableware plated with silver

sil·ver·smith \ˈsil-vər-ˌsmith\ *n* : a person who makes articles of silver

sil·ver·ware \-ˌwa(ə)r, -ˌwe(ə)r\ *n* **1** : tableware made of or plated with silver **2** : ¹SILVER 2c

sil·very \ˈsilv-(ə-)rē\ *adj* **1** : having a shine like silver **2** : containing or consisting of silver

Sim·chas To·rah \ˌsim-kə-ˈstȯr-ə, -ˈstȯr-\ *n* : a Jewish holiday observed in October or November in celebration of the completion of the annual reading of the Torah [from Hebrew *śimḥath tōrāh* "rejoicing of the Torah"]

\ə\ **abut**	\au̇\ **out**	\i\ **tip**	\ȯ\ **saw**	\u̇\ **foot**
\ər\ **further**	\ch\ **chin**	\ī\ **life**	\ȯi\ **coin**	\y\ **yet**
\a\ **mat**	\e\ **pet**	\j\ **job**	\th\ **thin**	\yü\ **few**
\ā\ **take**	\ē\ **easy**	\ŋ\ **sing**	\th\ **this**	\yu̇\ **cure**
\ä\ **cot, cart**	\g\ **go**	\ō\ **bone**	\ü\ **food**	\zh\ **vision**

¹**sim·i·an** \'sim-ē-ən\ *adj* : of, relating to, or resembling monkeys or apes

²**simian** *n* : ¹MONKEY 1, ¹APE 1

sim·i·lar \'sim-(ə-)lər\ *adj* **1** : having qualities in common **2** : not differing in shape but only in size or position ⟨*similar* triangles⟩ — **sim·i·lar·ly** *adv*

sim·i·lar·i·ty \,sim-ə-'lar-ət-ē\ *n, pl* **-ties 1** : the quality or state of being similar : RESEMBLANCE **2** : a point in which things are similar : CORRESPONDENCE

sim·i·le \'sim-ə-(,)lē\ *n* : a figure of speech in which things different in kind or quality are compared by the use of the word *like* or *as* (as in *eyes like stars*) — compare METAPHOR

si·mil·i·tude \sə-'mil-ə-,t(y)üd\ *n* **1** : a visible likeness **2** : a comparison based on an imagined likeness **3** : SIMILARITY 2

sim·mer \'sim-ər\ *vb* **sim·mered; sim·mer·ing** \-(ə-)riŋ\ : to stew gently below or just at the boiling point — **simmer** *n*

simmer down *vb* **1** : to become calm or peaceful **2** : to become reduced by or as if by simmering ⟨a broth *simmered down* to half⟩

¹**sim·per** \'sim-pər\ *vb* **sim·pered; sim·per·ing** \-p(ə-)riŋ\ **1** : to smile in a foolish manner ⟨fans *simpering* at the star⟩ **2** : to say with a simper ⟨*simpered* an apology⟩ — **sim·per·er** \-pər-ər\ *n*

²**simper** *n* : a silly smile

sim·ple \'sim-pəl\ *adj* **sim·pler** \-p(ə-)lər\; **sim·plest** \-p(ə-)ləst\ **1** : free from dishonesty or vanity : INNOCENT **2** : not wealthy ⟨*simple* folks⟩ **3** : lacking in education, experience, or intelligence **4 a** : free from complications ⟨a *simple* melody⟩ ⟨neat *simple* clothing⟩ **b** : consisting of only one main clause and no subordinate clauses ⟨a *simple* sentence⟩ **c** : consisting of only the verb ⟨a *simple* predicate⟩ **5** : not compound ⟨a *simple* eye⟩ **6 a** : not divided into branches or leaflets ⟨a *simple* leaf⟩ **b** : developing from a single ovary ⟨*simple* fruits⟩ **7** : ¹UTTER, ABSOLUTE ⟨the *simple* truth⟩ **8** : easy to understand or perform ⟨*simple* instructions⟩ ⟨a *simple* explanation⟩ — **sim·ple·ness** \-pəl-nəs\ *n*

simple fraction *n* : a fraction with whole numbers for the numerator and denominator — compare COMPLEX FRACTION

simple fracture *n* : a breaking of a bone in such a way that the skin is not broken and bone fragments do not stick out — compare COMPOUND FRACTURE

simple interest *n* : interest paid or figured on the original amount only of a loan or on the amount of an account

simple machine *n* : any of various elementary devices formerly considered as the elements of which all machines are composed and including the lever, the wheel and axle, the pulley, the inclined plane, the wedge, and the screw

sim·ple-mind·ed \,sim-pəl-'mīn-dəd\ *adj* **1** : UNSOPHISTICATED 1 **2** : FOOLISH

simple sugar *n* : MONOSACCHARIDE

sim·ple·ton \'sim-pəl-tən\ *n* : a person lacking in common sense

sim·plic·i·ty \sim-'plis-ət-ē\ *n, pl* **-ties 1** : the quality or state of being simple **2** : HONESTY, STRAIGHTFORWARDNESS **3 a** : clearness of expression **b** : the quality or state of being plain **4** : FOLLY 1, SILLINESS

sim·pli·fy \'sim-plə-,fī\ *vb* **-fied; -fy·ing** : to make simple or simpler — **sim·pli·fi·ca·tion** \,sim-plə-fə-'kā-shən\ *n* — **sim·pli·fi·er** \'sim-plə-,fī-(ə-)r\ *n*

sim·plis·tic \sim-'plis-tik\ *adj* **1** : SIMPLE 8 **2** : characterized by too much simplicity : not involving or dealing with related complexities ⟨a *simplistic* explanation of the situation⟩ — **sim·plis·ti·cal·ly** \-ti-k(ə-)lē\ *adv*

sim·ply \'sim-plē\ *adv* **1 a** : in a clear manner ⟨stated the directions *simply*⟩ **b** : in a plain manner ⟨*simply* dressed⟩ **c** : in a direct manner : CANDIDLY ⟨told the story as *sim-*

ply as a child would⟩ **2 a** : for nothing more than ⟨eats *simply* to keep alive⟩ **b** : without any question : TRULY ⟨*simply* marvelous⟩

sim·u·late \'sim-yə-,lāt\ *vb* **-lat·ed; -lat·ing** : to give the appearance or effect of : IMITATE

simulated *adj* : made to look genuine : FAKE ⟨*simulated* pearls⟩

sim·u·la·tion \,sim-yə-'lā-shən\ *n* **1** : the act or process of simulating **2** : an object that is not genuine **3** : the imitation by one system or process of the way in which another system or process works ⟨a computer *simulation* of spaceflight⟩

sim·u·la·tor \'sim-yə-,lāt-ər\ *n* : one that simulates; *esp* : a device that enables the operator to experience under test conditions events similar to those likely to occur in a real situation

si·mul·ta·neous \,sī-məl-'tā-nē-əs, -nyəs\ *adj* **1** : existing or occurring at the same time **2** : satisfied by the same values of the variables ⟨*simultaneous* equations⟩ [from Latin *simul* "at the same time, together" and English *-taneous* (as in *instantaneous*) — related to ASSEMBLE, ENSEMBLE] — **si·mul·ta·neous·ly** *adv*

¹**sin** \'sin\ *n* **1** : a breaking of a moral law **2** : an action that is or is felt to be bad **synonyms** see OFFENSE

²**sin** *vb* **sinned; sin·ning** : to commit a sin

¹**since** \(')sin(t)s\ *adv* **1** : from a definite past time until now ⟨has stayed there ever *since*⟩ **2** : before the present time : AGO ⟨long *since* dead⟩ **3** : after a time in the past ⟨has *since* become rich⟩

²**since** *prep* : from or after a specified time in the past ⟨*since* summer, the team has improved⟩

³**since** *conj* **1** : at a time or times in the past after or later than ⟨has held a job *since* he graduated⟩ : from the time in the past when ⟨ever *since* I was a child⟩ **2** : for the reason that : BECAUSE ⟨*since* you're ready, we'll go now⟩

sin·cere \sin-'si(ə)r\ *adj* **sin·cer·er; sin·cer·est 1** : TRUSTWORTHY, STRAIGHTFORWARD ⟨a *sincere* friend⟩ **2** : GENUINE 1, REAL ⟨a *sincere* interest in painting⟩ — **sin·cere·ly** *adv* — **sin·cer·i·ty** \-'ser-ət-ē, -'sir-\ *n*

sine \'sīn\ *n* : a trigonometric function that for an acute angle in a right triangle is the ratio of the side opposite the angle to the hypotenuse

sin·ew \'sin-yü *also* 'sin-ü\ *n* **1** : TENDON; *esp* : one prepared for use as a cord or thread **2** : solid strength : POWER

sin·ewy \'sin-yə-wē *also* 'sin-ə-\ *adj* **1** : full of sinews : STRINGY ⟨*sinewy* meat⟩ **2** : STRONG 1 ⟨*sinewy* arms⟩

sin·ful \'sin-fəl\ *adj* : marked by or full of sin : WICKED — **sin·ful·ly** \-fə-lē\ *adv* — **sin·ful·ness** *n*

¹**sing** \'siŋ\ *vb* **sang** \'saŋ\ *or* **sung** \'səŋ\; **sung; sing·ing** \'siŋ-iŋ\ **1 a** : to produce musical sounds by means of the voice **b** : to utter with musical sounds ⟨*sing* a song⟩ **c** : ¹CHANT 2, INTONE ⟨parts of the mass were *sung*⟩ **2** : to make pleasing musical sounds ⟨birds *singing* at dawn⟩ **3** : to make a slight shrill sound ⟨a kettle *singing* on the stove⟩ **4** : to express enthusiastically ⟨*sing* the praises of life in the city⟩ **5** : ¹BUZZ 1, RING ⟨ears *singing* from the sudden descent⟩ **6** : to affect or bring to a place or state by singing ⟨*sing* a baby to sleep⟩ ⟨*sing* the blues away⟩ **7** : to call aloud : cry out ⟨*sing* out when you find them⟩ — **sing·able** \'siŋ-ə-bəl\ *adj*

²**sing** *n* : a session of group singing

¹**singe** \'sinj\ *vb* **singed** \'sinjd\; **singe·ing** \'sin-jiŋ\ : to burn slightly; *esp* : to remove hair, down, or fuzz from usually by passing briefly over a flame

²**singe** *n* : a slight burn : SCORCH

¹**sing·er** \'siŋ-ər\ *n* : one that sings

²**sing·er** \'sin-jər\ *n* : one that singes

¹**sin·gle** \'siŋ-gəl\ *adj* **1** : not married; *esp* : never having been married **2** : being alone : being the only one ⟨the *single* survivor of the disaster⟩ **3** : consisting of one ⟨a *single* standard⟩ **4** : having only one row of petals or ray

flowers around the center of a blossom ⟨a *single* rose⟩ **5 a** : consisting of a separate whole : INDIVIDUAL ⟨each *single* citizen⟩ **b** : of, relating to, or involving only one person **6** : being a whole ⟨a *single* world⟩ **7** : designed for the use of one person only ⟨a *single* room⟩ ⟨a *single* bed⟩ — **sin·gle·ness** *n*

²**single** *n* **1 a** : a separate individual person or thing **b** : an unmarried adult **c** (1) : a recording having one short tune on each side (2) : a music recording having two or more tracks that is shorter than a full-length album **2** : a hit in baseball that enables a batter to reach first base safely **3** *pl* : a game (as of tennis) between two players

³**single** *vb* **sin·gled; sin·gling** \'siŋ-g(ə-)liŋ\ **1** : to select (a person or thing) from a number or group — usually used with *out* **2** : to make a single in baseball

single bond *n* : a chemical bond in which one pair of electrons is shared by two atoms in a molecule especially when the atoms can share more than one pair of electrons — compare DOUBLE BOND, TRIPLE BOND

sin·gle–breast·ed \ˌsiŋ-gəl-'bres-təd\ *adj* : having a center closing with one row of buttons and no overlapping lapel ⟨*single-breasted* coat⟩

single file *n* : a line of persons or things arranged one behind another — **single file** *adv*

sin·gle–hand·ed \ˌsiŋ-gəl-'han-dəd\ *adj* **1** : managed or done by one person **2** : working alone : lacking help — **sin·gle–hand·ed·ly** *adv*

sin·gle–mind·ed \-'mīn-dəd\ *adj* : having only one purpose : DETERMINED ⟨a *single-minded* devotion to stopping crime⟩ — **sin·gle–mind·ed·ly** *adv*

sin·glet \'siŋ-glət\ *n, chiefly British* : UNDERSHIRT

sin·gle–tree \'siŋ-gəl-(ˌ)trē\ *n* : WHIFFLETREE

sin·gly \'siŋ-g(ə-)lē\ *adv* **1** : by or with oneself : INDIVIDUALLY **2** : in a single-handed manner

¹**sing·song** \'siŋ-ˌsȯŋ\ *n* : a monotonous rhythm or a monotonous rise and fall of pitch

²**singsong** *adj* : having a monotonous rhythm

¹**sin·gu·lar** \'siŋ-gyə-lər\ *adj* **1 a** : of or relating to a separate person or thing : INDIVIDUAL **b** : of, relating to, or constituting a word form denoting one person, thing, or instance ⟨a *singular* noun⟩ **c** : of or relating to a single instance or to something considered by itself **2** : EXCEPTIONAL 1 **3** : different from general expectations : PECULIAR — **sin·gu·lar·ly** *adv*

²**singular** *n* : something that is singular; *esp* : the singular number, the inflectional form denoting it, or a word in that form

sin·gu·lar·i·ty \ˌsiŋ-gyə-'lar-ət-ē\ *n, pl* **-ties** **1** : the quality or state of being singular **2** : something that is singular : PECULIARITY **3** : a point or region of infinite density which is held to be the final state of matter falling into a black hole

sin·is·ter \'sin-əs-tər\ *adj* **1** : especially evil or leading to evil : BAD **2** : threatening evil, harm, or danger : OMINOUS [Middle English *sinistre* "unlucky, unfavorable," from Latin *sinistr-, sinister* "left, on the left side, awkward, unfavorable"; so called because the ancient Romans believed that omens seen on the left side told of bad things to come] — **sin·is·ter·ly** *adv*

¹**sink** \'siŋk\ *vb* **sank** \'saŋk\ *or* **sunk** \'səŋk\; **sunk; sink·ing** **1 a** : to move or cause to move downward usually so as to be below the surface or swallowed up ⟨feet *sinking* into deep mud⟩ ⟨*sink* a ship⟩ **b** : to descend gradually lower and lower ⟨the sun *sank* behind the hills⟩ **2** : to lessen in amount or strength **3** : to fall to or into a lower status (as of quality, worth, or number) : DECLINE ⟨*sink* into decay⟩ **4 a** : to penetrate or cause to penetrate ⟨*sank* my ax into the tree⟩ **b** : to become absorbed ⟨the water *sank* into the dry ground⟩ **5** : to form by digging or boring ⟨*sink* a well⟩ **6** : ²INVEST 1 ⟨*sank* a million dollars in the new company⟩ **7** : to fail in strength, spirits, or health ⟨my heart *sank*⟩ — **sink·able** \'siŋ-kə-bəl\ *adj*

²**sink** *n* **1 a** : CESSPOOL **b** : ²SEWER **2** : a stationary basin for washing (as in a kitchen) connected with a drain and usually a water supply

sink·er \'siŋ-kər\ *n* **1** : one that sinks; *esp* : a weight for sinking a line or net **2** : DOUGHNUT 1

sink·hole \'siŋk-ˌhōl\ *n* : a hollow place in which drainage collects

sinking fund *n* : a fund set up for paying off the original amount of a debt when it falls due

sinned *past and past participle of* SIN

sin·ner \'sin-ər\ *n* : one that sins

sinning *present participle of* SIN

Si·no- \ˌsī-nō, 'sī-\ *combining form* **1** : Chinese **2** : Chinese and ⟨*Sino*-American⟩ [derived from Greek *Sinai* "Chinese"]

sin·u·os·i·ty \ˌsin-yə-'wäs-ət-ē\ *n, pl* **-ties** **1** : the quality or state of being sinuous **2** : something that is sinuous : winding turn

sin·u·ous \'sin-yə-wəs\ *adj* : of a snakelike or wavy form : WINDING — **sin·u·ous·ly** *adv*

si·nus \'sī-nəs\ *n* : a hollow place : CAVITY; *esp* : any of several cavities in the skull that usually connect with the nostrils

si·nus·itis \ˌsī-n(y)ə-'sīt-əs\ *n* : inflammation of a sinus

Siou·an \'sü-ən\ *n* **1** : an American Indian language stock of central and southeastern North America **2** : a member of any of the American Indian peoples speaking Siouan languages

Sioux \'sü\ *n, pl* **Sioux** \'sü(z)\ **1** : DAKOTA **2** : SIOUAN

¹**sip** \'sip\ *vb* **sipped; sip·ping** **1** : to drink in small quantities or little by little **2** : to take sips from : TASTE — **sip·per** *n*

²**sip** *n* **1** : the act of sipping **2** : a small amount taken by sipping

¹**si·phon** *also* **sy·phon** \'sī-fən\ *n* **1** : a bent tube through which a liquid can be drawn by means of air pressure up and over the edge of one container and into another container at a lower level **2** : any of various tube-shaped organs in animals and especially mollusks that are used to draw in or pass off fluids

²**siphon** *also* **syphon** *vb* **si·phoned** *also* **sy·phoned; si·phon·ing** *also* **sy·phon·ing** \'sīf-(ə-)niŋ\ : to draw off or pass off by or as if by a siphon ⟨*siphoned* off money for a vacation⟩

¹siphon 1

sir \(')sər\ *n* **1** : a man having the right to be addressed as *sir* — used as a title before the given name of a knight or baronet **2** : a title of respect used in addressing a man without using his name [Middle English *sir* "a man of rank or position," from *sire* "a father," from early French *sire* "lord, superior," from Latin *senior* (adjective) "older, elder" — related to SENIOR]

Sirach \'sī-rak\ *n* — see BIBLE table

¹**sire** \'sī(ə)r\ *n* **1** : ¹FATHER 1a **2** *archaic* : a male ancestor : FOREFATHER **3** : the male parent of an animal and especially of a domestic animal

²**sire** *vb* **sired; sir·ing** : BEGET 1 — used especially of domestic animals

\ə\ abut	\au̇\ out	\i\ tip	\ȯ\ saw	\u̇\ foot
\ər\ further	\ch\ chin	\ī\ life	\ȯi\ coin	\y\ yet
\a\ mat	\e\ pet	\j\ job	\th\ thin	\yü\ few
\ā\ take	\ē\ easy	\ŋ\ sing	\t͟h\ this	\yu̇\ cure
\ä\ cot, cart	\g\ go	\ō\ bone	\ü\ food	\zh\ vision

si·ren \\'sī-rən *for sense 3 also* sī-'rēn\ *n* **1** *often cap* : one of a group of womanlike creatures in Greek mythology that lured mariners to destruction by their singing **2** : a tempting woman **3** : a device often electrically operated for producing a loud shrill warning sound ⟨ambulance *siren*⟩

Word History In the Greek epic poem *The Odyssey*, Homer tells of the adventures of Odysseus on his voyage home after the Trojan War. One of these adventures involves a couple of sea nymphs, called Sirens, who are half woman and half bird. They attract sailors by the beauty of their singing, which causes the ships to crash on the rocks. To avoid such a fate, Odysseus has his sailors' ears filled with wax so that they cannot hear the Sirens' song. He has himself tied to a mast so that he cannot steer the ship toward the rocks. It works. The ship succeeds in getting past the Sirens, who are then so upset that they drown themselves. The word *siren* lives on, however. It was taken into Latin, French, and English. It has been used for "a tempting woman," but its chief use is for "a loud-sounding warning device." Its sound is far from beautiful, but it does signal danger. [Middle English *siren* "a partly female creature in Greek legend whose beautiful singing lured sailors to their deaths," from early French *siren* and Latin *siren* (both, same meaning), from Greek *seirēn* (same meaning)]

Sir·i·us \\'sir-ē-əs\ *n* : the brightest star in the night sky — called also *Dog Star* [Middle English *Sirius* "the brightest star," from Latin *Sirius* (same meaning), from Greek *Seirios* "the brightest star," literally, "burning, scorching" — see *Word History* at DOG DAYS]

sir·loin \\'sər-,loin\ *n* : a cut of meat and especially of beef from the part just in front of the rump

sirup *variant of* SYRUP

si·sal \\'sī-səl, -zəl\ *n* **1** : a strong durable white fiber used to make ropes and twine **2** : a widely grown tropical Mexican agave with leaves that produce sisal

sis·sy \\'sis-ē\ *n, pl* **sissies** **1** : a man or boy who appears feminine or behaves in a feminine manner **2** : a fearful or cowardly person — **sissy** *adj*

sis·ter \\'sis-tər\ *n* **1** : a female who has one or both parents in common with another individual **2** *often cap* : a member of a religious community of women : NUN **3 a** : a fellow female member of a group **b** : a girl or woman who shares a common national or racial origin with another ⟨*sister* schools⟩ ⟨*sister* ships⟩ **5** *chiefly British* : ¹NURSE 2 — **sis·ter·ly** *adj or adv*

sis·ter·hood \\'sis-tər-,hùd\ *n* **1** : the state of being a sister **2** : a community or society of sisters

sis·ter–in–law \\'sis-t(ə-)rən-,lò, -tərn-,lò\ *n, pl* **sis·ters–in–law** \-tər-zən-\ **1** : the sister of one's spouse **2 a** : the wife of one's brother **b** : the wife of one's spouse's brother

sit \\'sit\ *vb* **sat** \\'sat\; **sit·ting** **1 a** : to rest on the buttocks or haunches ⟨*sit* in a chair⟩ **b** : to cause to be seated ⟨*sit* yourself down⟩ **c** : ²PERCH 2, ROOST 2 **2** : to provide seats or seating room for ⟨the car *sits* five people⟩ **3** : to occupy a place as a member of an official body ⟨*sit* in Congress⟩ **4** : to hold a session ⟨the court is now *sitting*⟩ **5** : to cover eggs for hatching : ²BROOD 1 **6** : to pose for a portrait or photograph : serve as a model **7** : to lie or rest in a condition or location ⟨the vase *sits* on the table⟩ **8** : to remain inactive ⟨the car *sits* in the garage⟩ **9** : BABYSIT — **sit on one's hands** : to fail to take action — **sit pretty** : to be in a highly favorable situation — **sit tight** : to keep one's position without change

sit·com \\'sit-,käm\ *n* : SITUATION COMEDY

sit–down \\'sit-,daun\ *n* : a strike in which the workers stop work and refuse to leave their places of employment — called also *sit-down strike*

site \\'sīt\ *n* **1** : local position (as of a building, town, or monument) **2** : the place or scene of an occurrence or event ⟨a picnic *site*⟩ **3** : WEBSITE

sit–in \\'sit-,in\ *n* : an act of sitting in seats or on the floor (as in a restaurant or office) as a means of organized protest

Sit·ka spruce \,sit-kə-\ *n* : a tall spruce of the northern Pacific coast of North America with thin reddish brown bark and flat needles; *also* : its wood

sit·ter \\'sit-ər\ *n* : one that sits; *esp* : a person who babysits

¹sit·ting \\'sit-iŋ\ *n* **1** : an act of one that sits; *esp* : a single occasion of continuous sitting ⟨finished the portrait in one *sitting*⟩ **2 a** : a brooding over eggs for hatching **b** : SETTING 5 **3** : SESSION 1 ⟨*sitting* of the legislature⟩

²sitting *adj* : used in or for sitting ⟨a *sitting* position⟩

sitting duck *n* : an easy or defenseless target

sitting room *n* : LIVING ROOM

sit·u·ate \\'sich-ə-,wāt\ *vb* **-at·ed; -at·ing** : to place in a site or situation : LOCATE

sit·u·at·ed \\'sich-ə-,wāt-əd\ *adj* **1** : placed in a site or situation **2** : provided with money or possessions ⟨not rich but comfortably *situated*⟩

sit·u·a·tion \,sich-ə-'wā-shən\ *n* **1 a** : the way in which something is placed in relation to its surroundings **b** : SITE 1 **2 a** : a position or place of employment : POST, JOB **b** : position in life : STATUS **3** : position with respect to conditions and circumstances ⟨the military *situation*⟩ **4** : relative position or combination of events and conditions at a particular moment

situation comedy *n* : a radio or television comedy series that involves a continuing cast of characters in different stories not related to each other

sit–up \\'sit-,əp\ *n* : an exercise done by lying on the back and rising up to a sitting position by bending forward at the waist without lifting the feet and returning to the original position

six \\'siks\ *n* **1** — see NUMBER table **2** : the sixth in a set or series — **six** *adj or pron* — **at sixes and sevens** : in disorder : CONFUSED

six–gun \\'siks-,gən\ *n* : a revolver with six chambers

six·pence \\'sik-spən(t)s, *U.S. also* -,spen(t)s\ *n* **1** : the sum of six pence **2** *pl* **sixpence** *or* **six·penc·es** : a coin representing six pence

six–shoot·er \\'sik(s)-'shüt-ər\ *n* : SIX-GUN

six·teen \(')sik-'stēn\ *n* — see NUMBER table — **six·teen** *adj or pron* — **six·teenth** \-'tēn(t)th\ *adj or n*

sixteenth note *n* : a musical note with a time value one sixteenth that of a whole note

sixteenth rest *n* : a musical rest equal in time to a sixteenth note

sixth \\'siks(t)th, 'siks(t)\ *n, pl* **sixths** **1** — see NUMBER table **2** : the difference in pitch between the first tone and the sixth tone of a scale — **sixth** *adj or adv* — **sixth·ly** \\'siksth-lē, 'sikst-\ *adv*

sixth sense *n* : a special ability to sense something that does not involve the five senses

six·ty \\'sik-stē\ *n, pl* **sixties** — see NUMBER table — **six·ti·eth** \-stē-əth\ *adj or n* — **sixty** *adj or pron*

siz·able *or* **size·able** \\'sī-zə-bəl\ *adj* : fairly large : CONSIDERABLE — **siz·ably** \-blē\ *adv*

¹size \\'sīz\ *n* **1** : physical extent or bulk **2 a** : the measurements of a thing **b** : relative amount or number **3** : one of a series of measures especially of manufactured articles (as of clothing) usually identified by numbers or letters [Middle English *sise* "a law, a law controlling weights and measures used in the marketplace, a fixed portion of food and drink," from early French *sise* (same meaning), from earlier *assise* "a lawmaking session, legal action," from *asseoir* "to seat," derived from Latin *assidere* "to sit beside, assist (a judge)," from *ad-* "toward, near" and *sedēre* "to sit"]

²size *vb* **sized; siz·ing** **1** : to make a particular size **2** : to arrange, grade, or classify according to size **3** : to form a judgment of — used with *up* ⟨*sizing* up the candidates⟩
³size \'sīz, ˌsīz\ *adj* : SIZED 1 ⟨medium-*size*⟩
⁴size \'sīz\ *n* : a gluey material (as a preparation of glue, flour, or varnish) used for filling the pores in a surface (as of plaster), as a stiffener (as of fabric), or as an adhesive [Middle English *sise* "something gluey used as a filler, stiffener, or adhesive"]
⁵size *vb* **sized; siz·ing** : to apply size to
sized \'sīzd, ˌsīzd\ *adj* **1** : having a specified size ⟨small=*sized*⟩ **2** : arranged or adjusted according to size
siz·ing \'sī-ziŋ\ *n* : ⁴SIZE
siz·zle \'siz-əl\ *vb* **siz·zled; siz·zling** \-(ə-)liŋ\ : to make a hissing sound in or as if in burning or frying — **sizzle** *n* — **siz·zler** \-(ə-)lər\ *n*
ska \'skä\ *n* : popular music of Jamaican origin that combines elements of traditional Caribbean rhythms and jazz [perhaps an alteration of *scat* "jazz singing with meaningless syllables"]
¹skate \'skāt\ *n* : any of numerous rays that have broad wing-like fins
²skate *n* **1** : a metallic runner fitting the sole of a shoe or a shoe with a permanently attached runner used for gliding on ice **2** : ROLLER SKATE
³skate *vb* **skat·ed; skat·ing** **1** : to glide along on skates **2** : to slide or move as if on skates — **skat·er** *n*
¹skate·board \'skāt-ˌbō(ə)rd, -ˌbȯ(ə)rd\ *n* : a short board mounted on small wheels that is used for coasting and for performing athletic stunts
²skateboard *vb* : to ride or perform stunts on a skateboard — **skate·board·er** \-ˌbȯrd-ər, -ˌbȯrd-\ *n*
skate park *n* : an outdoor area having structures and surfaces for roller-skating and skateboarding
skat·ing \'skāt-iŋ\ *n* : the act, art, or sport of gliding on skates
skeet \'skēt\ *n* : trapshooting in which clay targets are thrown in such a way as to simulate the angle of flight of a bird
skein \'skān\ *n* : a looped length of yarn or thread put up in a loose twist after it is taken from the reel
skel·e·tal \'skel-ət-ᵊl\ *adj* : of, relating or attached to, forming, or resembling a skeleton ⟨*skeletal* muscles⟩ ⟨the *skeletal* system⟩
¹skel·e·ton \'skel-ət-ᵊn\ *n* **1** : a firm supporting or protecting structure or framework of a living thing; *esp* : a framework made of bone or sometimes cartilage that supports the soft tissues and protects the internal organs of a vertebrate (as a fish or human being) — compare ENDOSKELETON, EXOSKELETON **2** : a very thin person or animal **3** : something forming a structural framework
²skeleton *adj* **1** : of, consisting of, or resembling a skeleton ⟨a *skeleton* hand⟩ **2** : consisting of the smallest possible number of persons who can get a job done ⟨a *skeleton* crew⟩
skeleton key *n* : a key made to open many locks
skep·tic \'skep-tik\ *n* : a person slow to believe or ready to question : DOUBTER
skep·ti·cal \'skep-ti-kəl\ *adj* : relating to or marked by doubt — **skep·ti·cal·ly** \-k(ə-)lē\ *adv*
skep·ti·cism \'skep-tə-ˌsiz-əm\ *n* : an attitude of doubt
¹sketch \'skech\ *n* **1 a** : a rough drawing representing the chief features of an object or scene **b** : a rough draft (as

of a story) **2** : a brief description or outline **3** : a short comedy piece
²sketch *vb* **1** : to make a sketch, rough draft, or outline of **2** : to draw or paint a sketch — **sketch·er** *n*
sketch·book \'skech-ˌbùk\ *n* : a book of or for sketches
sketchy \'skech-ē\ *adj* **sketch·i·er; -est** **1** : of the nature of a sketch : roughly outlined **2** : lacking completeness, clearness, or substance : SLIGHT, VAGUE
skew \'skyü\ *vb* **1** : to take a slanting course : move or turn aside : SWERVE **2** : to distort from a true value or symmetrical form ⟨*skewed* the facts to fit their theory⟩
¹skew·er \'skyü-ər, 'skyü(-ə)r\ *n* **1** : a long pin for keeping meat in form while roasting or for holding small pieces of meat and vegetables for broiling **2** : something shaped or used like a meat skewer
²skewer *vb* : to fasten or pierce with or as if with a skewer
skew lines *n pl* : straight lines that do not intersect and are not in the same plane
skew·ness \'skyü-nəs\ *n* : lack of straightness or of agreement in size, shape, or position of parts on opposite sides of a dividing line or center
¹ski \'skē\ *n, pl* **skis** : one of a pair of narrow strips of wood, metal, or plastic curving upward in front that are used for gliding over snow or water [from Norwegian *ski* "a ski," from an early Norse word *skīth* "a stick of wood"]
²ski *vb* **skied; ski·ing** : to glide on skis — **ski·er** *n*
ski boot *n* : a boot or shoe used for skiing; *esp* : a heavy rigid boot that extends above the ankle
¹skid \'skid\ *n* **1** : a log or plank for supporting something (as above the ground) **2** : one of the logs, planks, or rails along or on which something heavy is rolled or slid **3** : a device placed under a carriage wheel to prevent its turning **4** : a runner used as part of the landing gear of an airplane or helicopter **5** : the act of skidding : SLIDE
²skid *vb* **skid·ded; skid·ding** **1** : to haul along, slide, hoist, or store on skids **2** : to slide without rotating ⟨the wheels *skidded*⟩ **3** : to fail to grip the roadway; *esp* : to slip sideways on the road ⟨the car *skidded* on an icy road⟩
skid row \-ˈrō\ *n* : a district of cheap saloons and cheap rooming houses in which vagrants and alcoholics live
skies *plural of* SKY
skiff \'skif\ *n* : any of various small boats; *esp* : a flat-bottomed rowboat
ski·ing \'skē-iŋ\ *n* : the art or sport of gliding and jumping on skis
ski jump *n* **1** : a jump made by a person wearing skis **2** : a specially prepared course or track from which a skier makes a jump — **ski jump** *vb* — **ski jump·er** *n*

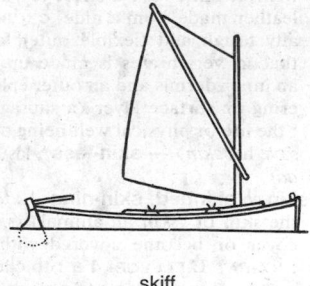

skiff

ski lift *n* : a machine that consists usually of a series of bars or seats hanging from a moving cable and that is used to carry skiers or sightseers up a long slope
skill \'skil\ *n* **1** : ability that comes from training or practice **2** : a developed or acquired ability : ACCOMPLISHMENT ⟨reading *skills*⟩
skilled \'skild\ *adj* **1** : having skill : EXPERT ⟨*skilled* workers⟩ **2** : requiring skill and training ⟨a *skilled* trade⟩
skil·let \'skil-ət\ *n* : FRYING PAN

¹skate

\ə\ abut	\aù\ out	\i\ tip	\ȯ\ saw	\ù\ foot
\ər\ further	\ch\ chin	\ī\ life	\ȯi\ coin	\y\ yet
\a\ mat	\e\ pet	\j\ job	\th\ thin	\yü\ few
\ā\ take	\ē\ easy	\ŋ\ sing	\th̲\ this	\yù\ cure
\ä\ cot, cart	\g\ go	\ō\ bone	\ü\ food	\zh\ vision

skill·ful \'skil-fəl\ *adj* **1** : having or showing skill **2** : accomplished with skill ⟨a *skillful* defense⟩ — **skill·ful·ly** \-fə-lē\ *adv* — **skill·ful·ness** *n*

synonyms SKILLFUL, PROFICIENT, ADEPT, EXPERT mean having the knowledge and experience needed to succeed at what one does. SKILLFUL suggests being very able at doing a particular job ⟨a *skillful* truck driver⟩. PROFICIENT suggests a sure ability that comes from training and practice ⟨a *proficient* waiter who can handle several tables at once⟩. ADEPT suggests having a native ability as well as a learned skill at something ⟨she is *adept* at getting people to work together⟩. EXPERT suggests having a thorough knowledge of a subject as well as being very skillful at working in it ⟨*expert* guides led us through the cave⟩.

¹skim \'skim\ *vb* **skimmed; skim·ming 1 a** : to clear a liquid of scum or floating substance : remove (as film or scum) from the surface of a liquid **b** : to remove cream from by skimming **2** : to glance through (as a book) for the chief ideas or the plot **3** : to throw so as to bounce along the surface of water **4** : to pass swiftly or lightly over : glide or skip along, above, or near a surface

²skim *n* **1** : a thin layer, coating, or film **2** : the act of skimming **3** : something skimmed; *esp* : SKIM MILK

³skim *adj* : having the cream removed by skimming

skim·mer \'skim-ər\ *n* : one that skims; *esp* : a flat scoop or spoon with holes that is used for skimming

skimmer

skim milk *n* : milk from which the cream has been removed — called also *skimmed milk*

skimp \'skimp\ *vb* **1** : to give not enough or barely enough attention or effort to or funds for **2** : to save by or as if by skimping : SCRIMP

skimpy \'skim-pē\ *adj* **skimp·i·er; -est** : barely enough : SCANTY — **skimp·i·ly** \-pə-lē\ *adv* — **skimp·i·ness** \-pē-nəs\ *n*

¹skin \'skin\ *n* **1 a** : the outer layer of an animal when separated from the body usually with its hair or feathers : HIDE, PELT **b** : a sheet of parchment or fine-grained leather made from a hide **c** : ¹BOTTLE 1b **2 a** : the usually tough and flexible outer layer of an animal body that in vertebrates is made up of two layers including an inner dermis and an outer epidermis **b** : an outer covering or surface layer ⟨a sausage *skin*⟩ ⟨apple *skins*⟩ **3** : the life or physical well-being of a person ⟨made sure to save his *skin*⟩ — **skin·less** \-ləs\ *adj* — **skinned** \'skind\ *adj*

²skin *vb* **skinned; skin·ning 1** : to strip, scrape, or rub off the skin of ⟨*skin* an animal⟩ ⟨*skinned* my knee⟩ **2** : to cover or become covered with or as if with skin **3** : ¹CHEAT 1, FLEECE **4 a** : to climb up or down ⟨*skin* up and down a rope⟩ **b** : to pass or get by with little room to spare

skin–deep \'skin-'dēp\ *adj* **1** : as deep as the skin **2** : not thorough or lasting in impression : SUPERFICIAL

skin–dive \'skin-,dīv\ *vb* : to swim underwater with a face mask and flippers and sometimes with a portable breathing device — **skin diver** *n* — **skin–div·ing** \-,dī-viŋ\ *n*

skin–flint \'skin-,flint\ *n* : a person who is very stingy in money matters : MISER

skin graft *n* : skin transferred from a donor area to grow new skin at a place where the skin has been destroyed or stripped away (as by burning); *also* : the procedure by which such a piece of skin is removed and transferred to a new area

skink \'skiŋk\ *n* : any of a family of mostly small lizards with smooth scales

skin·ner \'skin-ər\ *n* **1** : one that removes and processes or deals in skins, pelts, or hides **2** : a driver of draft animals; *esp* : MULE SKINNER

skin·ny \'skin-ē\ *adj* **skin·ni·er; -est 1** : resembling skin : MEMBRANOUS ⟨a *skinny* layer⟩ **2** : very thin **synonyms** see LEAN — **skin·ni·ness** *n*

skin·ny–dip \'skin-ē-,dip\ *vb* : to swim in the nude — **skin·ny–dip·per** *n*

skin·tight \'skin-'tīt\ *adj* : closely fitted to the figure

¹skip \'skip\ *vb* **skipped; skip·ping 1 a** : to move or proceed with leaps and bounds **b** : to bounce or cause to bounce off one point after another ⟨*skipping* stones⟩ **c** : to leap over lightly **2** : to leave hurriedly or secretly ⟨*skip* town⟩ **3 a** : to pass over or leave out (as a section, item, or step) ⟨*skipped* the dull parts of the book⟩ **b** : to promote or cause to be promoted to a grade higher than the next grade in school **c** : to fail to attend ⟨*skipped* the meeting⟩

²skip *n* **1 a** : a light bouncing step **b** : a manner of moving by alternating hops and steps **2** : a failure to do something; *also* : something not done

ski pole *n* : a pole that has an encircling disk set a little above the point and a strap for the hand at the top and is used as an aid in skiing

¹skip·per \'skip-ər\ *n* **1** : one that skips **2** : any of various insects that differ from the related butterflies especially in having stout bodies, smaller wings, and usually antennae with curved ends [*skip* (verb) and *-er* (noun suffix)]

²skipper *n* : the master of a ship; *esp* : the master of a fishing, small trading, or pleasure boat [Middle English *skipper* "the master of a ship," from early Dutch *schipper* (same meaning), from *schip* "ship"]

¹skir·mish \'skər-mish\ *n* **1** : a minor fight between small bodies of troops **2** : a minor dispute or contest

²skirmish *vb* **1** : to engage in a skirmish **2** : to search about (as for supplies) — **skir·mish·er** *n*

¹skirt \'skərt\ *n* **1 a** : a free-hanging part of a garment extending from the waist down **b** : a separate free-hanging garment usually worn by women and girls covering the body from the waist down **c** : either of two flaps on a saddle covering the bars on which the stirrups are hung **2** *pl* : OUTSKIRTS **3** : a part or attachment serving as a rim, border, or edging

²skirt *vb* **1 a** : to go or pass around or about; *esp* : to go around or keep away from in order to avoid danger or discovery **b** : to escape or miss by a narrow margin **2** : to be, lie, or move along an edge, border, or margin

skit \'skit\ *n* : a humorous story or sketch; *esp* : a sketch included in a dramatic performance

ski tow *n* **1** : a machine that consists usually of a moving rope which a skier grasps to be pulled to the top of a slope **2** : SKI LIFT

skit·ter \'skit-ər\ *vb* : to glide or skip lightly or quickly : skim along a surface

skit·tish \'skit-ish\ *adj* **1** : lively or frisky in action **2** : easily frightened : RESTIVE ⟨a *skittish* horse⟩ **3** : BASHFUL — **skit·tish·ly** *adv* — **skit·tish·ness** *n*

skoal \'skōl\ *n* : ²TOAST 3, HEALTH — often used as an interjection

skul·dug·gery *or* **skull·dug·gery** \,skəl-'dəg-(ə-)rē\ *n, pl* **-ger·ies** : sneaky or dishonest behavior : TRICKERY

skulk \'skəlk\ *vb* **1** : to move in a sly or secret manner : SNEAK **2** : to hide or conceal oneself from cowardice or fear or with treacherous intention **synonyms** see LURK — **skulk·er** *n*

skull \'skəl\ *n* **1** : the case of bone or cartilage that forms the skeleton of the head and face, encloses the brain, and supports the jaws of vertebrates **2** : the location of understanding or intelligence : MIND — **skulled** \'skəld\ *adj*

skull and cross·bones \-'krós-,bōnz\ *n, pl* **skulls and crossbones** : a representation of a human skull over crossbones used as a warning of danger to life

skull·cap \'skəl-,kap\ *n* : a close-fitting cap; *esp* : a light cap without brim for indoor wear

¹**skunk** \'skəŋk\ *n, pl* **skunks** *also* **skunk 1** : any of various black-and-white North American mammals related to the weasels that give off a fluid with a sharp and unpleasant smell when threatened **2** : a mean hateful person [from a word in Massachusett (an extinct Algonquian language spoken in Massachusetts)]

¹skunk 1

²**skunk** *vb* : to defeat completely; *esp* : to prevent entirely from scoring or succeeding : SHUT OUT

skunk cabbage *n* : either of two North American herbs that grow in wet areas, bloom in late winter or early spring, and have an odor like that of a skunk

sky \'skī\ *n, pl* **skies 1** : the upper atmosphere : the vast arch or dome that seems to spread over the earth **2** : HEAVEN 2 **3** : ¹WEATHER, CLIMATE ⟨the forecast is for sunny *skies* tomorrow⟩

sky blue *n* : a pale to light blue

sky·cap \'skī-,kap\ *n* : one employed to carry hand luggage at an airport

sky·div·ing \-,dī-viŋ\ *n* : the sport of jumping from an airplane and carrying out various body maneuvers before opening a parachute — **sky·dive** \-,dīv\ *vb* — **sky·div·er** *n*

¹**sky–high** \-'hī\ *adv* **1 a** : high into the air **b** : to a high level or degree **2** : in an enthusiastic manner **3** : to bits : APART

²**sky–high** *adj* : extremely expensive ⟨prices are *sky-high*⟩

sky·jack·er \-,jak-ər\ *n* : a person who takes control of a flying airplane by threat of violence — **sky·jack** \-,jak\ *vb*

¹**sky·lark** \'skī-,lärk\ *n* : a common Old World lark noted for its continuous song uttered mostly while flying

²**skylark** *vb* : to play wild pranks : FROLIC — **sky·lark·er** *n*

sky·light \'skī-,līt\ *n* : a window or group of windows in a roof or ceiling

sky·line \-,līn\ *n* **1** : the line where earth and sky or water and sky seem to meet : HORIZON **2** : an outline (as of buildings or mountains) against the sky

¹**sky·rock·et** \'skī-,räk-ət\ *n* : ¹ROCKET 1

²**skyrocket** *vb* **1** : to shoot up suddenly ⟨costs have *sky-rocketed*⟩ **2** : to cause to rise or increase rapidly

sky·scrap·er \'skī-,skrā-pər\ *n* : a very tall building

sky·ward \'skī-wərd\ *adv* **1** : toward the sky ⟨gaze *sky-ward*⟩ **2** : to a higher level

sky·writ·ing \'skī-,rīt-iŋ\ *n* : writing formed in the sky by means of smoke or vapor released from an airplane — **sky·writ·er** \-,rīt-ər\ *n*

slab \'slab\ *n* : a thick flat piece or slice (as of stone, wood, or bread)

¹**slack** \'slak\ *adj* **1** : CARELESS 2 **2** : not energetic ⟨a *slack* pace⟩ **3 a** : not tight : not tense or taut ⟨a *slack* rope⟩ **b** : lacking in firmness : WEAK, SOFT ⟨*slack* control⟩ **4** : not busy ⟨a *slack* season⟩ — **slack·ly** *adv* — **slack·ness** *n*

²**slack** *vb* **1 a** : to be or become slack or careless in performing or doing **b** : LESSEN ⟨the wind *slacked* off⟩ **2** : to avoid work or duty **3** : LOOSEN 2 **4 a** : to cause to lessen **b** : SLAKE 4

³**slack** *n* **1** : a stopping of movement or flow **2** : a part of something that hangs loose without strain ⟨take up the *slack* of a rope⟩ **3** *pl* : trousers especially for casual wear **4** : a dull season or period : LULL **5** : additional tolerance or relief from pressure ⟨cut me some *slack*⟩

slack·en \'slak-ən\ *vb* **slack·ened; slack·en·ing** \-(ə-)niŋ\ **1** : to make or become slower or less energetic ⟨*slacken* speed⟩ **2** : to make less taut : LOOSEN ⟨*slacken* sail⟩ **3** : to become careless

slack·er \'slak-ər\ *n* : one who avoids work or a duty

slag \'slag\ *n* : waste left after the melting of ores and the separation of the metal from them

slain *past participle of* SLAY

slake \'slāk, *senses* 3 & 4 *are also* 'slak\ *vb* **slaked; slak·ing 1** *archaic* : ABATE, MODERATE **2** : to relieve or satisfy with water or liquid : QUENCH ⟨*slaked* our thirst⟩ **3** : to become slaked **4** : to cause (lime) to heat and crumble by treatment with water

sla·lom \'släl-əm\ *n* **1** : skiing in a zigzag or wavy course between upright poles **2** : a timed skiing race over such a course

¹**slam** *vb* **slammed; slam·ming 1** : to strike or beat hard **2** : to shut with force and noise : BANG ⟨*slammed* the door⟩ **3** : to set or slap down violently or noisily ⟨*slammed* the books down on the table⟩ **4** : to make a banging noise **5** : to criticize harshly

²**slam** *n* **1** : a heavy blow **2 a** : a noisy violent closing **b** : a banging noise especially from the slamming of a door **3** : a cutting or violent criticism

slam–bang \'slam-'baŋ\ *adj* **1** : very noisy or violent **2** : having fast-paced often nonstop action

slam dunk *n* : DUNK SHOT — **slam–dunk** \'slam-'dəŋk\ *vb*

¹**slan·der** \'slan-dər\ *n* **1** : the making of false statements that damage another's reputation **2** : a false and harmful oral statement about a person — **slan·der·ous** \-d(ə-)rəs\ *adj* — **slan·der·ous·ly** *adv*

²**slander** *vb* **slan·dered; slan·der·ing** \-d(ə-)riŋ\ : to utter slander against : DEFAME — **slan·der·er** \-dər-ər\ *n*

slang \'slaŋ\ *n* **1** : special language used by a particular group **2** : an informal nonstandard vocabulary composed of invented words, changed words, and exaggerated or humorous figures of speech — **slang** *adj*

slangy \'slaŋ-ē\ *adj* **slang·i·er; -est 1** : of, relating to, or being slang : containing slang **2** : being in the habit of using slang — **slang·i·ness** *n*

¹**slant** \'slant\ *vb* **1** : to turn or incline from a straight line or a level : SLOPE **2** : to interpret or present according to a special viewpoint

²**slant** *n* **1** : a slanting direction, line, or plane : SLOPE **2** : something that slants **3** : a way of looking at something ⟨get a new *slant* on the problem⟩ — **slant** *adj* — **slanty** \'slant-ē\ *adj*

slant height *n* **1** : the distance along the surface of a right circular cone from the edge of the base to the vertex **2** : the altitude of a side of a regular pyramid

slant·ways \'slant-,wāz\ *adv* : SLANTWISE

slant·wise \'slant-,wīz\ *adv or adj* : so as to slant : in a slanting direction or position

¹**slap** \'slap\ *n* **1** : a quick sharp blow especially with the open hand **2** : a noise like that of a slap

²**slap** *vb* **slapped; slap·ping 1 a** : to strike with or as if with the open hand **b** : to make a sound like that of slapping **2** : to put, place, or throw with careless haste or force ⟨*slapped* the book down on the desk⟩

³**slap** *adv* : ¹DIRECTLY 2, SMACK

slap·dash \'slap-,dash, -'dash\ *adj* : HAPHAZARD, SLIP-SHOD

slap·jack \'slap-,jak\ *n* **1** : PANCAKE **2** : a card game in which each player tries to be the first to slap his or her hand on any jack that appears faceup

slap shot *n* : a hard shot in ice hockey that is made with a swinging stroke

\ə\ **abut**	\au̇\ **out**	\i\ **tip**	\ȯ\ **saw**	\u̇\ **foot**
\ər\ **further**	\ch\ **chin**	\ī\ **life**	\ȯi\ **coin**	\y\ **yet**
\a\ **mat**	\e\ **pet**	\j\ **job**	\th\ **thin**	\yü\ **few**
\ā\ **take**	\ē\ **easy**	\ŋ\ **sing**	\th\ **this**	\yu̇\ **cure**
\ä\ **cot, cart**	\g\ **go**	\ō\ **bone**	\ü\ **food**	\zh\ **vision**

slap·stick \'slap-ˌstik\ *n* : comedy stressing horseplay — **slapstick** *adj*

¹**slash** \'slash\ *vb* **1** : to cut by sweeping and pointless blows **2** : to whip or strike with or as if with a cane **3** : to criticize without mercy **4** : to cut slits in (as a skirt) to reveal a different color or material **5** : to reduce sharply : CUT ⟨*slash* prices⟩ — **slash·er** *n*

²**slash** *n* **1** : the act of slashing; *also* : a long cut or stroke made by slashing **2** : an ornamental slit in a garment **3** : a mark / used to mean "or" (as in *and/or*), "and or" (as in *bottles/cans*), or "per" (as in *kilometers/hour*)

slash pine *n* : a pine of the southeastern U.S. that is an important source of turpentine, lumber, and pulpwood

slat \'slat\ *n* : a thin narrow flat strip of wood, plastic, or metal ⟨the *slats* of a venetian blind⟩ — **slat·ted** \'slat-əd\ *adj*

¹**slate** \'slāt\ *n* **1** : a piece of construction material (as layered rock) prepared as a shingle for roofing and siding **2** : a dense fine-grained rock formed by compression of shales or other rocks that splits readily into thin layers or plates **3** : a tablet of material (as slate) used for writing on **4 a** : a written or unwritten record (as of deeds) ⟨started with a clean *slate*⟩ **b** : a list of candidates for nomination or election **5 a** : a dark purplish gray **b** : a gray similar in color to common roofing slate — **slate** *adj* — **slate·like** \-ˌlīk\ *adj*

²**slate** *vb* **slat·ed; slat·ing 1** : to cover with slate or a slate-like substance ⟨*slate* a roof⟩ **2** : to register or schedule for a special purpose or action ⟨*slate* a meeting⟩ — **slat·er** *n*

slat·tern \'slat-ərn\ *n* : an untidy sloppy woman

slat·tern·ly \-lē\ *adj* : untidy and dirty through carelessness — **slat·tern·li·ness** *n*

slaty \'slāt-ē\ *adj* **1** : of, containing, or characteristic of slate **2** : of a purplish gray color

¹**slaugh·ter** \'slȯt-ər\ *n* **1** : the act of killing; *esp* : the butchering of livestock for market **2** : destruction of human lives in large numbers (as in war or a massacre)

²**slaughter** *vb* **1** : to kill an animal for food : BUTCHER **2** : to kill without mercy or in large numbers : MASSACRE — **slaugh·ter·er** \'slȯt-ər-ər\ *n*

slaugh·ter·house \'slȯt-ər-ˌhaus\ *n* : an establishment where animals are butchered

Slav \'släv, 'slav\ *n* : a native speaker of a Slavic language

¹**slave** \'slāv\ *n* **1** : a person who is owned by another person and can be sold at the owner's will **2** : a person who has lost self-control and is controlled by something or someone else ⟨a *slave* to bad habits⟩ **3** : a person who performs difficult or boring work : DRUDGE — **slave** *adj*
Word History In the Middle Ages, Germanic people fought and raided other peoples, especially the Slavic peoples to the east. They took a great many captives there and sold them as slaves throughout Europe. The Slavic people were so common as slaves that writers of the time used the Latin word for "Slav," *Sclavus,* to mean "a personal slave." The Latin word became *sclave* in Middle English and then *slave* in Modern English. Of course slavery and slaves had existed long before the Middle Ages. The ancient Romans used the Latin word *servus* for "slave." This Latin word is the ancestor of our word *servant*. In French, *servus* became *serf* and was used for a slave who belonged to a piece of land rather than to an individual. *Serf* has continued to mean this in both French and English, although serfs themselves no longer exist. [Middle English *sclave* "slave," from early French *esclave* (same meaning), derived from Latin *Sclavus* "Slav"]

²**slave** *vb* **slaved; slav·ing** : to work like a slave : DRUDGE

slave driver *n* **1** : a supervisor of slaves at work **2** : a harsh boss

slave·hold·er \'slāv-ˌhōl-dər\ *n* : an owner of slaves — **slave·hold·ing** \-diŋ\ *adj or n*

¹**sla·ver** \'slav-ər, 'släv-\ *vb* **sla·vered; sla·ver·ing** \-(ə-)riŋ\ : DROOL 2, SLOBBER

²**slav·er** \'slā-vər\ *n* : a person or ship engaged in the slave trade

slav·ery \'slāv-(ə-)rē\ *n* **1** : DRUDGERY, TOIL **2 a** : the state of being a slave **b** : the practice of slaveholding

¹**Slav·ic** \'slav-ik, 'släv-\ *adj* : of, relating to, or characteristic of the Slavs or their languages

²**Slavic** *n* : a branch of the Indo-European language family including Belarusian, Bulgarian, Czech, Polish, Serbian and Croatian, Slovene, Russian, and Ukrainian

slav·ish \'slā-vish\ *adj* **1** : of or characteristic of a slave **2** : lacking in independence or originality ⟨*slavish* imitators⟩ — **slav·ish·ly** *adv* — **slav·ish·ness** *n*

¹**Sla·von·ic** \slə-'vän-ik\ *adj* : ¹SLAVIC

²**Slavonic** *n* : ²SLAVIC

slaw \'slȯ\ *n* : COLESLAW

slay \'slā\ *vb* **slew** \'slü\; **slain** \'slān\; **slay·ing** : to put to death violently and in great numbers — **slay·er** *n*

slea·zy \'slē-zē *also* 'slā-\ *adj* **slea·zi·er; -est 1** : not firm in texture : FLIMSY **2** : made carelessly of poor material : SHODDY — **slea·zi·ly** \-zə-lē\ *adv* — **slea·zi·ness** \-zē-nəs\ *n*

¹**sled** \'sled\ *n* **1** : a vehicle usually on runners for transportation especially over snow or ice **2** : a small sled used especially by children for coasting on snow-covered slopes

²**sled** *vb* **sled·ded; sled·ding** : to ride or carry on a sled or sleigh — **sled·der** *n*

sled dog *n* : a dog trained to draw a usually large sled especially in the Arctic regions

¹**sledge** \'slej\ *n* : ¹SLEDGEHAMMER

²**sledge** *n* : a strong heavy sled

³**sledge** *vb* **sledged; sledg·ing** : to travel with or transport on a sledge

sled dog

¹**sledge·ham·mer** \'slej-ˌham-ər\ *n* : a large heavy hammer usually used with both hands — **sledgehammer** *vb*

²**sledgehammer** *adj* : marked by directness or strong force ⟨a *sledgehammer* approach to the problem⟩

¹**sleek** \'slēk\ *vb* : to make or become sleek

²**sleek** *adj* **1 a** : smooth and glossy as if polished ⟨*sleek* dark hair⟩ **b** : having a smooth healthy well-groomed look ⟨*sleek* cattle grazing⟩ **2** : having a prosperous look or manner — **sleek·ly** *adv* — **sleek·ness** *n*

¹**sleep** \'slēp\ *n* **1** : the natural periodic loss of consciousness during which the powers of the body are restored **2** : a state resembling sleep: as **a** : a state of inactivity (as hibernation) like sleep **b** : DEATH 4 ⟨put my pet cat to *sleep*⟩; *also* : ¹COMA, TRANCE **c** : a state marked by loss of feeling followed by tingling ⟨my foot's gone to *sleep*⟩ — **sleep·like** \'slē-ˌplīk\ *adj*

²**sleep** *vb* **slept** \'slept\; **sleep·ing 1** : to rest or be in a state of sleep **2** : to get rid of or spend in or by sleep ⟨*slept* off his headache⟩ **3** : to provide sleeping space for ⟨the boat *sleeps* six⟩ **4** : to have sexual intercourse

sleep·er \'slē-pər\ *n* **1** : one that sleeps **2** : a horizontal beam to support something on or near ground level **3** : SLEEPING CAR **4** : someone or something considered unlikely to succeed that suddenly becomes successful

sleeping bag *n* : a long fabric bag that is warmly lined for sleeping outdoors or in a camp or tent

sleeping car *n* : a railroad passenger car having berths for sleeping

sleeping pill *n* : a drug that is taken as a tablet or capsule to bring on sleep

sleeping sickness *n* **1** : a serious disease found in tropical Africa that is characterized by fever, headache, sleepiness, and confusion and is passed on by tsetse flies **2** : any of various virus diseases in which sleepiness is a major symptom

sleep·less \'slē-pləs\ *adj* **1** : not able to sleep **2** : marked by the absence of sleep ⟨a *sleepless* night⟩ **3** : unceasingly alert or active — **sleep·less·ly** *adv* — **sleep·less·ness** *n*

sleep·over \'slēp-ō-vər\ *n* : an overnight stay at another's home or an instance of having others stay at one's own home

sleep·walk \'slēp-ˌwȯk\ *vb* : to walk while or as if while asleep — **sleep·walk·er** \-ˌwȯ-kər\ *n*

sleepy \'slē-pē\ *adj* **sleep·i·er; -est 1** : ready to fall asleep **2** : quietly inactive ⟨a *sleepy* village⟩ — **sleep·i·ly** \-pə-lē\ *adv* — **sleep·i·ness** \-pē-nəs\ *n*

    synonyms SLEEPY, SOMNOLENT, DROWSY mean having the urge or tendency to sleep. SLEEPY may suggest that one is merely aware of a desire to go to sleep ⟨felt *sleepy* after a long day⟩. SOMNOLENT is more likely to suggest the slowness or laziness of one who is sleepy by nature ⟨a *somnolent* child who did not take part in games⟩. DROWSY suggests strong feelings of numbness and sleepiness that can be hard to get rid of ⟨felt *drowsy* after a big meal⟩.

sleepy·head \-ˌhed\ *n* : a sleepy person

¹sleet \'slēt\ *n* : frozen or partly frozen rain — **sleety** \'slēt-ē\ *adj*

²sleet *vb* : to shower sleet

sleeve \'slēv\ *n* **1** : the part of a garment covering the arm **2** : a part that fits over or around something like a sleeve — **sleeved** \'slēvd\ *adj* — **sleeve·less** \'slēv-ləs\ *adj*

¹sleigh \'slā\ *n* : an open usually horse-drawn vehicle with runners for use on snow or ice

²sleigh *vb* : to drive or travel in a sleigh

sleight \'slīt\ *n* **1 a** : sly trickery **b** : ¹TRICK 1d, STRATAGEM **2** : DEXTERITY, SKILL

¹sleigh

sleight of hand : skill especially in juggling or magic tricks **2** : a magic or juggling trick requiring skill with the hands

slen·der \'slen-dər\ *adj* **1** : ¹THIN 1, SLIM **2** : limited or not enough in amount : MEAGER ⟨a *slender* income⟩ — **slen·der·ly** *adv* — **slen·der·ness** *n*

¹sleuth \'slüth\ *n* : ²DETECTIVE

    Word History In Middle English the word *sleuth* meant "the track or trail left by an animal or person." After the 15th century *sleuth* was seldom used except in such words as *sleuth-dog* and *sleuthhound*. These were terms for a dog trained to follow a track or trail. The sleuthhound became well known for its eager and thorough pursuit of an object. Later the word *sleuthhound* came to be used for a "detective." The modern word *sleuth* first came into use as a shortened form of *sleuthhound*. [a shortened form of *sleuthhound* "a dog that follows a track or trail by scent," from Middle English *sleuth* "a track or trail"; of Norse origin]

²sleuth *vb* : to act as a detective

¹slew \'slü\ *past of* SLAY

²slew *variant of* ¹SLOUGH 1

³slew *also* **slue** *vb* : to turn, twist, or swing about especially out of a course : VEER

⁴slew *n* : a large number

¹slice \'slīs\ *n* **1 a** : a thin flat piece cut from something ⟨*slice* of bread⟩ **b** : a wedge-shaped piece (as of pie or cake) **2** : the flight of a ball curving to the right when hit by someone right-handed or to the left when hit by someone left-handed

²slice *vb* **sliced; slic·ing 1 a** : to cut with or as if with a knife **b** : to cut something into slices **2** : to hit a ball so that a slice results — **slic·er** *n*

¹slick \'slik\ *vb* : to make sleek or smooth

²slick *adj* **1 a** : having a smooth surface : SLIPPERY ⟨a *slick* road⟩ **b** : having or showing skill and style but no depth ⟨*slick* writing⟩ **2 a** : CLEVER 3; *esp* : TRICKY 1 **b** : quick and neat in action : SKILLFUL — **slick·ly** *adv* — **slick·ness** *n*

³slick *n* : something that is smooth or slippery; *esp* : a smooth patch of water covered with a film of oil

slick·er \'slik-ər\ *n* **1** : a long loose raincoat often of rubberized cloth or plastic **2** : a sly clever crook

¹slide \'slīd\ *vb* **slid** \'slid\; **slid·ing** \'slīd-iŋ\ **1 a** : to move or cause to move smoothly along a surface **b** : to coast on snow or ice **c** : to fall or dive feetfirst or headfirst when approaching a base in baseball **2** : to slip and fall by a loss of footing, balance, or support **3 a** : to move or pass smoothly and easily **b** : to move, pass, or put so as not to be noticed **4** : to become worse gradually

²slide *n* **1** : the act or motion of sliding **2** : a loosened mass that slides ⟨a rock *slide*⟩ **3 a** : a sloping surface down which a person or thing slides **b** : something (as a cover for an opening) that operates or adjusts by sliding **4 a** : a small transparent picture or image that can be projected on a screen **b** : a small usually rectangular glass or plastic plate used to hold an object to be examined under a microscope

slid·er \'slīd-ər\ *n* **1** : one that slides **2** : a baseball pitch thrown like a fastball but breaking similarly to a curve **3** : a small meat sandwich typically served on a bun; *esp* : a small hamburger

slide rule *n* : an instrument used for calculation that in its simple form consists of a ruler with a movable middle piece

slide·way \'slīd-ˌwā\ *n* : a way along which something slides

slier *comparative of* SLY

sliest *superlative of* SLY

¹slight \'slīt\ *adj* **1 a** : having a slim or delicate build : not stout **b** : lacking in strength or substance : FLIMSY, FRAIL **c** : lacking weight, solidity, or importance : TRIVIAL **2** : small of its kind or in amount — **slight·ly** *adv* — **slight·ness** *n*

²slight *vb* **1** : to treat with disrespect **2** : to perform or attend to carelessly and without proper attention to detail

³slight *n* **1** : an act or an instance of slighting **2** : a humiliating discourtesy

slight·ing \'slīt-iŋ\ *adj* : characterized by disregard or disrespect — **slight·ing·ly** *adv*

¹slim \'slim\ *adj* **slim·mer; slim·mest 1** : of small diameter or thickness in comparison with the height or length **2 a** : low in quality or quantity : SLIGHT **b** : SCANTY, SMALL ⟨has a *slim* chance of winning⟩ — **slim·ly** *adv* — **slim·ness** *n*

²slim *vb* **slimmed; slim·ming** : to make or become slender

slime \'slīm\ *n* **1** : soft moist earth or clay; *esp* : sticky slippery or sticky mud **2** : a slippery or sticky substance; *esp* : one that various animals (as slugs or catfishes) secrete onto their skin

slime mold *n* : either of two groups of organisms that reproduce by spores and form slimy masses composed of amoeboid cells that fuse to form a giant cell with many nuclei or that gather tightly together without fusing

\ə\ **abut**	\aů\ **out**	\i\ **tip**	\ȯ\ **saw**	\ů\ **foot**
\ər\ **further**	\ch\ **chin**	\ī\ **life**	\ȯi\ **coin**	\y\ **yet**
\a\ **mat**	\e\ **pet**	\j\ **job**	\th\ **thin**	\yü\ **few**
\ā\ **take**	\ē\ **easy**	\ŋ\ **sing**	\th\ **this**	\yů\ **cure**
\ä\ **cot, cart**	\g\ **go**	\ō\ **bone**	\ü\ **food**	\zh\ **vision**

slimy \'slī-mē\ *adj* **slim·i·er; -est 1 a** : of, relating to, or resembling slime : VISCOUS **b** : covered with or producing slime **2** : VILE 1a, OFFENSIVE — **slim·i·ness** *n*

¹sling \'sliŋ\ *vb* **slung** \'sləŋ\; **sling·ing** \'sliŋ-iŋ\ **1** : to throw with a sudden sweeping motion ⟨*slung* the sweater over her shoulder⟩ **2** : to throw with a sling — **sling·er** \'sliŋ-ər\ *n*

²sling *n* **1 a** : a short strap with strings fastened to its ends that is whirled round to throw something (as a stone) **b** : SLINGSHOT **2** : something (as a rope or chain) used to hoist, lower, support, or carry something; *esp* : a bandage hanging from the neck to support an arm or hand **3** : a slinging or hurling of or as if of a missile

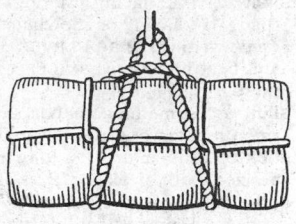

²sling 2

³sling *vb* **slung** \'sləŋ\; **sling·ing** \'sliŋ-iŋ\ **1** : to put in or move or support with a sling **2** : to hang from two points ⟨*sling* a hammock⟩

sling·shot \'sliŋ-ˌshät\ *n* : a forked stick with an elastic band attached for shooting small stones

slink \'sliŋk\ *vb* **slunk** \'sləŋk\; **slink·ing** : to move or go sneakily : creep along (as in fear or shame)

slinky \'sliŋ-kē\ *adj* **slink·i·er; -est 1** : sneakily quiet ⟨*slinky* movements⟩ **2** : following the lines of the figure in a gracefully flowing manner ⟨*slinky* dresses⟩

¹slip \'slip\ *vb* **slipped; slip·ping 1 a** : to move easily and smoothly : SLIDE ⟨*slip* the knife into its sheath⟩ **b** : to move or place quietly or sneakily ⟨*slipped* from the room⟩ **c** : to pass without being noticed or used ⟨let the opportunity *slip*⟩ **2 a** : to get away from ⟨*slipped* his pursuers⟩ **b** : to free from : SHED ⟨the dog *slipped* its collar⟩ **c** : to escape the attention or memory of ⟨it *slipped* my mind⟩ **d** : to express or become expressed unintentionally ⟨the secret *slipped* out⟩ **e** : to cause to slide open : RELEASE ⟨*slip* a bolt⟩ **3** : to let a knitting stitch pass from one needle to another without working a new stitch **4 a** : to slide out of place, away from a support, or from one's grasp **b** : to slide so as to fall or lose balance ⟨*slipped* on the ice⟩ **5** : to cause to slide especially in putting, passing, or inserting easily or quickly ⟨*slip* into a coat⟩ **6** : to fall from some level or standard usually gradually or by degrees [Middle English *slippen* "to move by sliding, to move quietly or unnoticed"; of Germanic origin]

²slip *n* **1 a** : a sloping ramp that extends out into the water and serves for landing or repairing ships **b** : a place for a ship between two piers **2** : the act or an instance of departing secretly or hurriedly **3** : a mistake in judgment, selected course of action, or way of doing things : BLUNDER, MISSTEP **4** : the act or an instance of slipping down or out of place ⟨a *slip* on the ice⟩; *also* : a sudden mishap **5 a** : an undergarment made in dress length with shoulder straps **b** : PILLOWCASE

³slip *n* **1** : a small shoot or twig cut for planting or grafting : CUTTING **2 a** : a long narrow strip of material **b** : a small piece of paper ⟨a sales *slip*⟩ [Middle English *slippe* "a small shoot or twig for planting or grafting"; probably of Germanic origin]

⁴slip *n* : thin wet clay used in pottery for casting, for decoration, or as a cement [Old English *slypa* "slime, paste"]

slip·cov·er \'slip-ˌkəv-ər\ *n* : a removable covering for a piece of furniture

slip·knot \-ˌnät\ *n* : a knot that slips along a line around which it is made — see KNOT illustration

slip·page \'slip-ij\ *n* **1** : an act, instance, or process of slipping **2** : a loss in transmission of power

slipped disk *n* : an injury in which one of the disks of cartilage between the vertebrae slips out of place, puts pressure on spinal nerves, and causes back and leg pain

slip·per \'slip-ər\ *n* : a light low shoe without laces that is easily slipped on or off — **slip·pered** \-ərd\ *adj*

slip·pery \'slip-(ə-)rē\ *adj* **slip·peri·er; -est 1** : having a surface smooth enough to cause one to slide or lose one's hold **2** : not worthy of trust : TRICKY, CRAFTY — **slip·peri·ness** *n*

slip·shod \'slip-ˈshäd\ *adj* : very careless : SLOVENLY

slip-up \'slip-ˌəp\ *n* **1** : ²MISTAKE 2 **2** : MISCHANCE 2

slip up \slip-ˈəp\ *vb* : to make a mistake : BLUNDER

¹slit \'slit\ *vb* **slit; slit·ting 1 a** : to make a slit in : SLASH **b** : to cut off or away : SEVER **2** : to cut into long narrow strips — **slit·ter** *n*

²slit *n* : a long narrow cut or opening — **slit** *adj* — **slit·less** \-ləs\ *adj*

slith·er \'slith-ər\ *vb* **1** : to slide or cause to slide on or as if on a loose gravelly surface **2** : to slip or slide like a snake

slith·ery \'slith-ə-rē\ *adj* : having a slippery surface, texture, or quality

¹sliv·er \'sliv-ər\ *n* **1** : a long slender piece cut or torn off : SPLINTER **2** : a small and narrow portion ⟨a *sliver* of pie⟩

²sliver *vb* **sliv·ered; sliv·er·ing** \'sliv-(ə-)riŋ\ : to cut or form into slivers : SPLINTER

slob \'släb\ *n* : a dirty, nasty, or rude person — **slob·by** \'slä-bē\ *adj*

¹slob·ber \'släb-ər\ *vb* **slob·bered; slob·ber·ing** \-(ə-)riŋ\ **1** : to let saliva or liquid dribble from the mouth : DROOL **2** : to show feeling in an exaggerated way : GUSH

²slobber *n* **1** : dripping saliva **2** : silly exaggerated show of feeling

sloe \'slō\ *n* : the tart bluish black globe-shaped fruit of the blackthorn; *also* : BLACKTHORN

sloe—eyed \'slō-ˈīd\ *adj* **1** : having soft dark bluish or purplish black eyes **2** : having slanted eyes

sloe gin *n* : a sweet reddish liqueur flavored chiefly with sloes

slog \'släg\ *vb* **slogged; slog·ging 1** : to hit hard : BEAT **2** : to work in a steady determined manner — **slog·ger** *n*

slo·gan \'slō-gən\ *n* **1** : a word or phrase that calls to battle **2** : a word or phrase used by a party, a group, or a business to attract attention

Word History The clans of Scotland were groups of related families that joined together, especially to defend against outsiders. In the old days these outsiders might be other clans, but usually they were the English to the south. When it was time to gather members of the clan for a battle, the Scots would shout the *sluagh-gairm,* which meant "army cry." It is made up of the Scottish Gaelic word *sluagh,* meaning "army," and *ghairm,* meaning "call, cry." This came into English as *slogorn* and later became *slogan.* At first *slogan* meant a "battle cry" or "rallying cry." Later it came to be used for "a motto or phrase used by a group to attract attention." [from earlier *slogorn* "war cry, rallying cry," from Scottish Gaelic, the ancient language of Scotland, *sluagh-gairm* "army cry," from *sluagh* "army" and *ghairm* "call, cry"]

slo—mo \'slō-ˌmō\ *n* : SLOW MOTION — **slo—mo** *adj*

sloop \'slüp\ *n* : a sailboat with one mast and a fore-and-aft mainsail and jib

¹slop \'släp\ *n* **1** : soft mud : SLUSH **2** : thin

sloop

tasteless drink or liquid food — usually used in plural **3** : liquid spilled or splashed **4 a** : food waste (as garbage) fed to animals : SWILL **b** : waste given off by the body — usually used in plural

²slop *vb* **slopped; slop·ping 1** : to spill on or over **2** : to feed slop to ⟨*slop* the pigs⟩

¹slope \'slōp\ *adj* : that slants : SLOPING

²slope *vb* **sloped; slop·ing** : to take a slanting direction : give a slant to : INCLINE — **slop·er** *n*

³slope *n* **1** : ground that forms a natural or artificial incline **2** : upward or downward slant or degree of slant **3** : the ratio of the change in a vertical direction to the change in a horizontal direction between any two points on the graph of a straight line

slope—intercept form *n* : the equation of a straight line in the form $y = mx + b$ where m is the slope of the line and b is its y-intercept

slop·py \'släp-ē\ *adj* **slop·pi·er; -est 1 a** : wet so as to spatter easily : SLUSHY **b** : wet with or as if with something slopped over **2** : SLOVENLY, CARELESS ⟨a *sloppy* dresser⟩ **3** : overly sentimental — **slop·pi·ly** \'släp-ə-lē\ *adv* — **slop·pi·ness** \'släp-ē-nəs\ *n*

¹slosh \'släsh\ *n* **1** : SLUSH 1 **2** : the slap or splash of liquid

²slosh *vb* **1** : to struggle through or splash about in or with water, mud, or slush **2** : to move with a splashing motion

¹slot \'slät\ *n* : a long narrow opening, groove, or passage : SLIT, NOTCH

²slot *vb* **slot·ted; slot·ting** : to cut a slot in

slot car *n* : a toy racing car that fits into a groove and is guided electrically by remote control

sloth \'slóth, 'slōth\ *n* **1** : the quality or state of being lazy **2** : any of several slow-moving mammals of the tropical forests of Central and South America that are related to the armadillos, live in trees, and feed on leaves, shoots, and fruits

sloth·ful \'slóth-fəl, 'slōth-\ *adj* : LAZY 1, SLUGGISH, INDOLENT — **sloth·ful·ly** \-fə-lē\ *adv*

slot machine *n* **1** : a machine whose operation is begun when a coin is dropped into a slot **2** : a coin-operated gambling machine that pays off for the matching of symbols on wheels spun by a handle

sloth 2

¹slouch \'slaúch\ *n* **1** : an awkward, lazy, or unqualified person **2** : a manner of walking, sitting, or standing characterized by an awkward stooping of head and shoulders

²slouch *vb* : to walk, sit, or stand with a slouch — **slouch·er** *n*

slouchy \'slaú-chē\ *adj* **slouch·i·er; -est** : slouching or untidy especially in appearance

¹slough \'slü, 'slaú; *in the U.S.* (except New England) 'slü *is usual for sense 1;* 'slaú *is more frequent for sense 2*\ *n* **1** *also* **slew** *or* **slue** \'slü\ : a wet and marshy or muddy place (as a swamp or backwater) **2** : a discouraged, degraded, or hopeless state [Old English *slōh* "swamp"]

²slough \'sləf\ *also* **sluff** *n* **1** : the cast-off skin of a snake **2** : a mass of dead tissue separating from living tissue **3** : something that may be shed or cast off [Middle English *slughe* "the cast-off skin of a snake"]

³slough \'sləf\ *also* **sluff** *vb* **1 a** : to cast off or become cast off **b** : to cast off one's skin **c** : to separate dead tissue from living tissue **d** : to get rid of or discard as bothersome, objectionable, or not to one's advantage **2** : to crumble slowly and fall away

Slo·vak \'slō-ˌväk, -ˌvak\ *n* **1** : a member of a Slavic people of Slovakia **2** : the Slavic language of the Slovak

people — **Slovak** *adj* — **Slo·va·ki·an** \slō-'väk-ē-ən, -'vak-\ *adj or n*

slov·en \'sləv-ən\ *n* : a slovenly person : SLOB

Slo·vene \'slō-ˌvēn\ *n* **1** : a member of a Slavic people living largely in Slovenia **2** : the language of the Slovenes — **Slovene** *adj* — **Slo·ve·ni·an** \slō-'vē-nē-ən\ *adj or n*

slov·en·ly \'sləv-ən-lē\ *adj* **1 a** : untidy especially in dress or person **b** : lazily careless **2** : characteristic of a sloven — **slov·en·li·ness** *n* — **slovenly** *adv*

¹slow \'slō\ *adj* **1 a** : not quick to understand ⟨a *slow* learner⟩ **b** : STUPID **c** : naturally slow-moving **2 a** : unwilling to take prompt action **b** : not easily aroused or excited ⟨was *slow* to anger⟩ **3 a** : moving, flowing, or proceeding without speed or at less than usual speed ⟨traffic was *slow*⟩ **b** : not vigorous or active ⟨a *slow* fire⟩ **c** : taking place at a low rate or over a considerable period of time ⟨*slow* progress in negotiations⟩ **4** : having qualities that hinder or stop rapid progress or action ⟨a *slow* racetrack⟩ **5 a** : registering behind or below what is correct ⟨the clock is *slow*⟩ **b** : that is behind the time at a specified time or place **6** : lacking in activity or liveliness ⟨a *slow* market⟩ — **slow·ish** \'slō-ish\ *adj* — **slow·ly** *adv* — **slow·ness** *n*

²slow *adv* : in a slow manner

³slow *vb* : to make or go slow or slower — often used with *down* or *up*

slow·down \'slō-ˌdaún\ *n* : a slowing down

slow motion *n* : action in a film or television picture apparently taking place more slowly than it actually occurred — **slow—motion** *adj*

slow·poke \'slō-ˌpōk\ *n* : a very slow person

sludge \'sləj\ *n* **1** : MUD, MIRE **2** : a muddy or slushy mass; *esp* : solid matter produced by water and sewage treatment processes — **sludgy** \'sləj-ē\ *adj*

¹slue *variant of* ¹SLOUGH 1

²slue *variant of* ³SLEW

¹slug \'sləg\ *n* **1** : SLUGGARD **2 a** : a small piece of shaped metal (as a bullet) **b** : a metal disk used in place of a coin in a coin-operated machine **3** : any of numerous long wormlike land mollusks that are related to the snails but have only an underdeveloped shell or none at all **4** : a single drink of liquor : SHOT [Middle English *slugge* "a lazy person"; of Scandinavian origin]

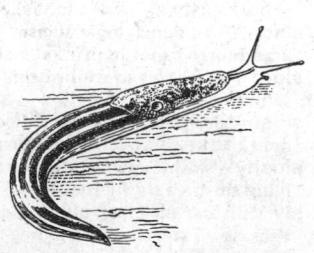

¹slug 3

²slug *n* : a heavy blow especially with the fist [perhaps from earlier *slug* (verb) "to load (a weapon) with slugs"]

³slug *vb* **slugged; slug·ging** : to strike heavily with or as if with the fist or a bat

slug·gard \'sləg-ərd\ *n* : a lazy person — **sluggard** *adj*

slugger *n* : one (as a batter or boxer) that strikes hard or with heavy blows

slug·gish \'sləg-ish\ *adj* : slow in movement or reaction by habit or condition — **slug·gish·ly** *adv* — **slug·gish·ness** *n*

¹sluice \'slüs\ *n* **1** : an artificial passage for water with a gate for controlling its flow or changing its direction **2** : a body of water held back by a gate or a stream flowing through a gate **3** : a device (as a floodgate) for controlling the flow of water **4** : a channel that carries off surplus

\ə\ **abut**	\aú\ **out**	\i\ **tip**	\ó\ **saw**	\ú\ **foot**
\ər\ **further**	\ch\ **chin**	\ī\ **life**	\ói\ **coin**	\y\ **yet**
\a\ **mat**	\e\ **pet**	\j\ **job**	\th\ **thin**	\yü\ **few**
\ā\ **take**	\ē\ **easy**	\ŋ\ **sing**	\th\ **this**	\yú\ **cure**
\ä\ **cot, cart**	\g\ **go**	\ō\ **bone**	\ü\ **food**	\zh\ **vision**

water **5** : a long sloping trough (as for floating logs to a sawmill)

²**sluice** *vb* **sluiced; sluic·ing 1** : to draw off by or through a sluice **2 a** : to wash with or in water running through or from a sluice **b** : DRENCH, FLUSH

¹**slum** \'sləm\ *n* : a thickly populated section especially of a city marked by crowding, dirty run-down housing, and generally poor living conditions

²**slum** *vb* **slummed; slum·ming** : to visit slums especially out of curiosity — **slum·mer** *n*

¹**slum·ber** \'sləm-bər\ *vb* **slum·bered; slum·ber·ing** \-b(ə-)riŋ\ **1** : to sleep usually lightly **2** : to exist without being active ⟨a *slumbering* volcano⟩ — **slum·ber·er** \-bər-ər\ *n*

²**slumber** *n* : ¹SLEEP

slum·ber·ous *or* **slum·brous** \'sləm-b(ə-)rəs\ *adj* **1** : very sleepy **2** : causing or tending to cause sleep : SOPORIFIC

slum·lord \'sləm-lo(ə)rd\ *n* : a landlord who receives high profits from renting substandard housing

¹**slump** \'sləmp\ *vb* **1** : to drop or slide down suddenly : COLLAPSE **2** : to assume a stooped posture : SLOUCH **3** : to fall off sharply

²**slump** *n* : a marked or continued reduction especially in economic activity or prices

slung *past and past participle of* SLING

slunk *past and past participle of* SLINK

¹**slur** \'slər\ *vb* **slurred; slur·ring 1 a** : to slide or slip over without proper mention, consideration, or emphasis **b** : to perform hurriedly : SKIMP **2** : to sing or play successive musical notes of different pitch in a smooth or connected manner **3** : to speak unclearly

²**slur** *n* **1 a** : a curved line connecting notes to be sung or played without a break **b** : the combination of two or more slurred tones **2** : a slurring manner of speech

³**slur** *vb* **slurred; slur·ring 1** : to make an insulting remark about : DISPARAGE **2** : to make unclear : OBSCURE

⁴**slur** *n* **1 a** : damaging criticism **b** : ¹DISHONOR 1, SHAME **2** : a blurred spot in printed matter : SMUDGE

slurp \'slərp\ *vb* : to eat or drink noisily or with a sucking sound — **slurp** *n*

slush \'sləsh\ *n* **1** : partly melted or watery snow **2** : soft mud : MIRE **3** : overly sentimental material

slushy \'sləsh-ē\ *adj* **slush·i·er; -est** : full of or resembling slush ⟨a *slushy* road⟩

sly \'slī\ *adj* **sli·er** *or* **sly·er** \'slī(-ə)r\; **sli·est** *or* **sly·est** \'slī-əst\ **1 a** : clever at hiding one's goals or purpose **b** : tending to secrecy or concealment **2** : lightly mischievous ⟨a *sly* smile⟩ *synonyms* see CUNNING — **sly·ly** *adv* — **sly·ness** *n* — **on the sly** : in a secret manner

¹**smack** \'smak\ *n* **1** : characteristic or slight taste or flavor **2** : a small quantity [Old English *smæc* "a characteristic taste or flavor"]

²**smack** *vb* : to have a flavor, trace, or suggestion

³**smack** *vb* **1** : to close and open the lips noisily especially in eating **2** : to kiss usually loudly **3** : to make or give a sharp slap or blow

⁴**smack** *n* **1** : a quick sharp noise made by rapidly opening and closing the lips **2** : a loud kiss **3** : a sharp slap or blow

⁵**smack** *adv* : in a square and sharp manner : DIRECTLY ⟨hit me *smack* in the face⟩

smack–dab \'smak-'dab\ *adv* : EXACTLY 1b ⟨*smack-dab* in the middle⟩

¹**small** \'smol\ *adj* **1** : little in size **2** : little in amount ⟨a *small* supply⟩ **3** : not very much : MINOR ⟨*small* success⟩ **4** : not important ⟨a *small* matter⟩ **5** : operating on a limited scale ⟨*small* dealers⟩ **6** : ¹SOFT 1c ⟨a *small* voice⟩ **7** : not generous : MEAN, PETTY ⟨a *small* nature⟩ **8** : made up of few or little units ⟨a *small* crowd⟩ **9** : ¹HUM-BLE 1, MODEST ⟨a *small* beginning⟩ **10** : having been humiliated or humbled ⟨felt very *small* to be caught

cheating⟩ — **small·ish** \'smo-lish\ *adj* — **small·ness** \'smol-nəs\ *n*

²**small** *adv* **1** : in or into small pieces ⟨cut the meat *small*⟩ **2** : in a small manner ⟨most businesses begin *small*⟩

³**small** *n* : a part smaller and especially narrower than the rest ⟨the *small* of the back⟩

small arm *n* : a firearm fired while held in the hands — usually used in plural

small calorie *n* : CALORIE 1a

small capital *n* : a letter having the form of but smaller than a capital letter (as in THESE WORDS) — called also **small cap**

small–claims court *n* : a court intended to simplify the settling of disputes over small debts

small–fry \'smol-ˌfrī\ *adj* **1** : ¹MINOR 1, UNIMPORTANT **2** : of or relating to children : CHILDISH

small intestine *n* : the long narrow part of the intestine between the stomach and the colon in which food is mostly digested, from which digested food is absorbed into the body, and which consists of the duodenum, jejunum, and ileum

small–mind·ed \'smol-'mīn-dəd\ *adj* **1** : having narrow interests, sympathies, or outlook **2** : typical of a small-minded person : PETTY — **small–mind·ed·ness** *n*

small·mouth bass \ˌsmol-ˌmauth-\ *n* : a black bass that lives in clear rivers and lakes and is bronze green above and lighter below — called also *smallmouth black bass*

small potatoes *n* : someone or something of trivial importance or worth

small·pox \'smol-ˌpäks\ *n* : a sometimes deadly disease that is caused by a virus, is characterized by fever and a skin rash, and is believed to have been wiped out worldwide as a result of vaccination

small talk *n* : light or informal conversation

¹**smart** \'smärt\ *vb* **1** : to cause or feel a sharp stinging pain **2** : to feel mental distress (as regret, resentment, or embarrassment)

²**smart** *adj* **1** : causing a sharp stinging sensation **2** : marked by forceful activity or vigorous strength **3** : BRISK 1, SPIRITED ⟨a *smart* pace⟩ **4 a** : mentally alert : BRIGHT ⟨a *smart* teacher⟩ **b** : sharp in scheming : SHREWD **5 a** : WITTY, CLEVER **b** : IMPUDENT, FLIPPANT **6 a** : stylish or elegant in dress or appearance **b** : WORLD-LY-WISE, KNOWING **c** : FASHIONABLE **7 a** : being a guided missile ⟨a *smart* bomb⟩ **b** : operating by automation ⟨a *smart* machine tool⟩ — **smart·ly** *adv* — **smart·ness** *n*

³**smart** *adv* : in a smart manner

⁴**smart** *n* : a smarting pain; *esp* : a stinging pain in one small part of the body

smart al·eck \'smärt-ˌal-ik, -ˌel-\ *n* : a person who likes to show off in a clever or witty but annoying way — **smart–al·ecky** \-ˌal-ə-kē, -ˌel-\ *or* **smart–aleck** *adj*

smart card *n* : a small plastic card that has a tiny built-in computer chip to store and process data

smart·en \'smärt-ᵊn\ *vb* **smart·ened; smart·en·ing** \'smärt-niŋ, -ᵊn-iŋ\ **1** : to make smart or smarter; *esp* : SPRUCE, FRESHEN ⟨*smartened* themselves for the party⟩ **2** : to make or become more alert or informed ⟨*smarten* up, before it's too late⟩

smart·phone \'smärt-ˌfōn\ *n* : a cell phone that includes additional functions (as e-mail or an Internet browser)

smarty *or* **smart·ie** \'smärt-ē\ *n, pl* **smart·ies** : SMART AL-ECK

¹**smash** \'smash\ *vb* **1** : to break into pieces by violence : SHATTER **2** : to drive, throw, or move violently especially with a destructive effect **3** : to destroy completely : WRECK **4** : to go to pieces suddenly : COLLAPSE — **smash·er** *n*

²**smash** *n* **1 a** : a heavy blow or attack **b** : a hard overhand stroke (as in tennis) **2** : the condition of being smashed **3 a** : the action or sound of smashing; *esp* : a wreck due to collision : CRASH **b** : complete collapse : RUIN; *esp*

: BANKRUPTCY **4** : a striking success : HIT ⟨the new play is a *smash*⟩

smash·up \'smash-ˌəp\ *n* **1** : a complete collapse **2** : a destructive collision of motor vehicles

smat·ter·ing \'smat-ə-riŋ\ *n* **1** : a small amount of knowledge ⟨a *smattering* of French⟩ **2** : a small scattered number

¹smear \'smi(ə)r\ *n* **1** : a spot made by or as if by an oily or sticky substance : SMUDGE **2** : material smeared on a surface; *esp* : material prepared for microscopic examination by smearing on a slide — compare PAP SMEAR **3** : a usually unproven charge or accusation

²smear *vb* **1 a** : to spread with something oily or sticky **b** : to spread over a surface **2 a** : to stain, smudge, or dirty by or as if by smearing **b** : to harm the reputation of **3** : to blot out or blur by or as if by smearing — **smear·er** *n*

smeary \'smi(ə)r-ē\ *adj* **1** : marked by smears **2** : likely to cause smears

¹smell \'smel\ *vb* **smelled** \'smeld\ *or* **smelt** \'smelt\; **smell·ing** **1** : to become aware of an odor by means of the sense organs located in the nose ⟨*smell* dinner cooking⟩ **2** : to detect or become aware of as if by the sense of smell ⟨*smell* trouble⟩ **3** : to use the sense of smell **4 a** : to have or give off an odor ⟨the candles *smell* like roses⟩ **b** : to have a disagreeable odor : STINK **c** : to give a hint or trace of something ⟨the plan *smells* of trickery⟩ — **smell·er** *n* — **smell a rat** : to have a suspicion of something wrong — **smell blood** : to sense an opponent's weakness — **smell the roses** : to enjoy life

²smell *n* **1** : ODOR, SCENT **2** : the process or power of becoming aware of an odor; *also* : the sense by which one detects odor **3** : a special quality associated with a given source : AURA ⟨the *smell* of adventure⟩ **4** : an act of smelling

smelling salts *n pl* : a strong-smelling preparation of ammonia in water used to wake someone who has fainted

smelly \'smel-ē\ *adj* **smell·i·er; -est** : having a smell and especially a bad smell ⟨*smelly* socks⟩

¹smelt \'smelt\ *n, pl* **smelts** *or* **smelt** : any of several very small food fishes that look like the related trouts and live in fresh water or in coastal sea waters

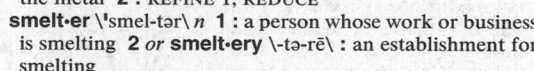
¹smelt

²smelt *vb* **1** : to melt (as ore) usually in order to separate the metal **2** : REFINE 1, REDUCE

smelt·er \'smel-tər\ *n* **1** : a person whose work or business is smelting **2** *or* **smelt·ery** \-tə-rē\ : an establishment for smelting

smid·gen *also* **smid·geon** *or* **smid·gin** \'smij-ən\ *or* **smidge** \'smij\ *n* : a small amount : BIT

¹smile \'smī(ə)l\ *vb* **smiled; smil·ing** **1** : to have, produce, or exhibit a smile **2 a** : to look with amusement or ridicule **b** : to be fortunate or agreeable ⟨the weather *smiled* on our plans⟩ **3** : to express by a smile ⟨both parents *smiled* their approval⟩ — **smil·er** *n* — **smil·ing·ly** \'smī-liŋ-lē\ *adv*

²smile *n* : a change of facial expression in which the eyes brighten and the corners of the mouth curve slightly upward especially in expression of amusement, pleasure, approval, or sometimes scorn

¹smil·ey \'smī-lē\ *adj* : exhibiting a smile : frequently smiling

²smiley *n* : EMOTICON

smirch \'smərch\ *vb* **1** : to make dirty, stained, or discolored especially by smearing with something that soils **2** : to bring discredit or disgrace on — **smirch** *n*

smirk \'smərk\ *vb* : to smile in an insincere or smug manner — **smirk** *n*

smirky \'smər-kē\ *adj* **smirk·i·er; -est** : suggesting or being a smirk

smite \'smīt\ *vb* **smote** \'smōt\; **smit·ten** \'smit-ᵊn\ *or* **smote; smit·ing** \'smīt-iŋ\ **1** : to strike sharply or heavily especially with the hand or a hand weapon **2 a** : to kill or injure by smiting **b** : to attack or afflict suddenly and harmfully ⟨*smitten* by disease⟩ **3** : to affect like a sudden hard blow ⟨*smitten* with terror⟩ **4** : CAPTIVATE, TAKE 6 ⟨*smitten* with the kitten⟩ — **smit·er** \'smīt-ər\ *n*

smith \'smith\ *n* **1** : a worker in metals : BLACKSMITH **2** : one who constructs, builds, or produces something : MAKER — often used in combination ⟨gun*smith*⟩

smith·er·eens \ˌsmith-ə-'rēnz\ *n pl* : small broken pieces : BITS

smithy \'smith-ē *also* 'smith-\ *n, pl* **smith·ies** **1** : the workshop of a smith **2** : BLACKSMITH

¹smock \'smäk\ *n* **1** *archaic* : a woman's undergarment; *esp* : CHEMISE 1 **2** : a light loose garment worn usually over regular clothing for protection from dirt

¹smock 2

²smock *vb* : to embroider or shirr with smocking

smock·ing \'smäk-iŋ\ *n* : a decorative embroidery or shirring made by gathering cloth in regularly spaced round tucks

smog \'smäg *also* 'smóg\ *n* : a thick haze caused by the action of sunlight on air polluted especially by smoke and automobile exhaust fumes [from *smoke* and *fog*]

smog·gy \'smäg-ē *also* 'smóg-ē\ *adj* **smog·gi·er; -est** : having a lot of smog

¹smoke \'smōk\ *n* **1** : the gas of burning materials (as coal, wood, or tobacco) made visible by small particles of carbon floating in it **2** : a mass or column of smoke **3** : something that has little substance or value or that doesn't last very long **4** : something that hides **5 a** : something to smoke (as a cigarette) **b** : an act of smoking tobacco — **smoke·like** \'smō-ˌklīk\ *adj*

²smoke *vb* **smoked; smok·ing** **1 a** : to give off or exhale smoke **b** : to give off too much smoke **2 a** : to inhale and exhale the fumes of burning plant material and especially tobacco **b** : to use in smoking ⟨*smoke* a pipe⟩ **3 a** : to drive away by smoke **b** : to blacken or discolor with smoke **c** : to use smoke to give (as meat or cheese) flavor and keep from spoiling — **smok·er** *n*

smoke and mirrors *n* : something intended to disguise or draw attention away especially from an unpleasant issue

smoke detector *n* : an alarm that activates automatically when it detects smoke — called also *smoke alarm*

smoke·house \'smōk-ˌhaus\ *n* : a building where meat or fish is given flavor and kept from spoiling by the use of smoke

smoke jumper *n* : a forest firefighter who parachutes to locations otherwise difficult to reach

smoke·less \'smō-kləs\ *adj* : producing or containing little or no smoke ⟨*smokeless* fuel⟩

smoke screen *n* : a screen of or as if of smoke to make observation or detection difficult

smoke·stack \'smōk-ˌstak\ *n* : a large chimney or pipe for carrying away smoke (as on a factory or ship)

smoke tree *n* : either of two shrubs or small trees that are related to the cashew and have large clusters of tiny flowers that look like clouds of smoke

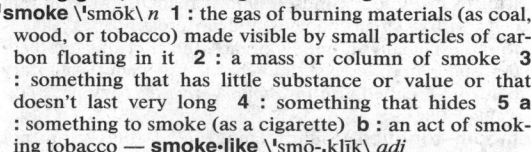
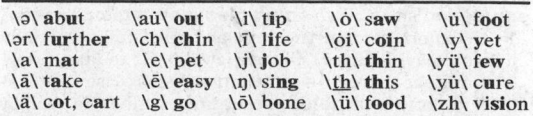

\ə\ **abut**	\au̇\ **out**	\i\ **tip**	\ȯ\ **saw**	\u̇\ **foot**
\ər\ **further**	\ch\ **chin**	\ī\ **life**	\ȯi\ **coin**	\y\ **yet**
\a\ **mat**	\e\ **pet**	\j\ **job**	\th\ **thin**	\yü\ **few**
\ā\ **take**	\ē\ **easy**	\ŋ\ **sing**	\t͟h\ **this**	\yu̇\ **cure**
\ä\ **cot, cart**	\g\ **go**	\ō\ **bone**	\ü\ **food**	\zh\ **vision**

smoky *also* **smok·ey** \'smō-kē\ *adj* **smok·i·er; -est 1** : giving off smoke especially in large quantities ⟨*smoky* stoves⟩ **2** : resembling or suggestive of smoke ⟨a *smoky* flavor⟩ **3** : filled with or darkened by smoke ⟨a *smoky* room⟩ — **smok·i·ly** \-kə-lē\ *adv* — **smok·i·ness** \-kē-nəs\ *n*

¹**smol·der** *or* **smoul·der** \'smōl-dər\ *n* : a slow smoky fire

²**smolder** *or* **smoulder** *vb* **smol·dered** *or* **smoul·dered; smol·der·ing** *or* **smoul·der·ing** \-d(ə-)riŋ\ **1** : to burn slowly with smoke and usually without flame ⟨fire was *smoldering* in the pit⟩ **2** : to exist or continue in a hidden or controlled state ⟨discontent *smoldered* for years before the revolt⟩ **3** : to burn inwardly ⟨anger *smoldered* in my heart⟩

smooch \'smüch\ *vb* : ¹KISS 1, PET — **smooch** *n*

¹**smooth** \'smüth\ *adj* **1 a** : having a continuous even surface : not rough ⟨a *smooth* skin⟩ **b** : not hairy **2** : free from obstacles or difficulties ⟨a *smooth* path⟩ **3** : even and uninterrupted in flow or flight **4** : flattering but not truthfully so ⟨a *smooth* talker⟩ **5 a** : calm in manner or behavior ⟨a *smooth* disposition⟩ **b** : AMIABLE, COURTEOUS **6** : not sharp or harsh ⟨a *smooth* sherry⟩ — **smooth·ly** *adv* — **smooth·ness** *n*

²**smooth** *vb* **1** : to make smooth ⟨*smooth* the edge of a board⟩ **2 a** : to free from what is harsh or disagreeable : POLISH ⟨*smoothed* out my style⟩ **b** : to make calm : SOOTHE **3** : to make (as a fault) seem of little importance in order to avoid bad feelings ⟨*smoothed* things over with apologies⟩ **4** : to free from trouble or difficulty ⟨*smoothed* the way for a quick end to the dispute⟩ **5** : to press flat ⟨*smoothed* down the folds of the tablecloth⟩ **6** : to cause to lie evenly and in order : PREEN ⟨*smooths* down its feathers⟩ — **smooth·er** *n*

smooth muscle *n* : muscle that is made up of long thin cells with a single nucleus and no cross stripes, that is found especially in hollow organs and parts (as the bladder and blood vessels), and that is not under voluntary control — called also *involuntary muscle;* compare STRIATED MUSCLE

smooth–tongued \'smüth-'təŋd\ *adj* : flattering but not truthfully so

smoothy *or* **smooth·ie** \'smü-thē\ *n, pl* **smooth·ies 1** : a smooth-tongued person **2** : a person with well-bred manners

smor·gas·bord \'smȯr-gəs-ˌbō(ə)rd, -ˌbȯ(ə)rd\ *n* : a self-service luncheon or supper offering a large variety of foods and dishes [from Swedish *smörgåsbord* "a buffet meal," from *smörgås* "open sandwich" and *bord* "table"]

smote *past of* SMITE

smoth·er \'sməth-ər\ *vb* **smoth·ered; smoth·er·ing** \-(ə-)riŋ\ **1** : to be overcome or killed through lack of air **2** : to overcome or kill by depriving of air or exposing to smoke or fumes **3 a** : to prevent the development or actions of ⟨*smother* a child with too much care⟩ **b** : to cover up : SUPPRESS ⟨*smother* a yawn⟩ **c** : to cover thickly ⟨steak *smothered* with mushrooms⟩

¹**smudge** \'sməj\ *vb* **smudged; smudg·ing 1 a** : to make a smudge on **b** : to soil as if by smudging **2** : to make a smudge ⟨a chalk that does not *smudge*⟩ **3** : to become smudged ⟨charcoal drawings *smudge* easily⟩

²**smudge** *n* **1 a** : a blurry spot or streak : SMEAR **b** : ²STAIN 2 **2** : a fire made to smoke (as for protecting fruit from frost) — **smudgy** \'sməj-ē\ *adj*

smug \'sməg\ *adj* **smug·ger; smug·gest** : highly satisfied with oneself : COMPLACENT — **smug·ly** *adv* — **smug·ness** *n*

smug·gle \'sməg-əl\ *vb* **smug·gled; smug·gling** \-(ə-)liŋ\ **1** : to export or import secretly and unlawfully especially to avoid paying taxes ⟨*smuggle* jewels⟩ **2** : to take, bring, or introduce secretly — **smug·gler** \'sməg-lər\ *n*

¹**smut** \'smət\ *vb* **smut·ted; smut·ting 1** : to stain, soil, or affect (a crop or plant) with smut **2** : to become affected by smut

²**smut** *n* **1** : matter that soils or blackens; *esp* : a particle of soot **2** : any of various destructive diseases of plants caused by fungi that transform plant organs (as seeds) into dark masses of spores; *also* : a fungus that causes a smut **3** : indecent language, pictures, or writing

smut·ty \'smət-ē\ *adj* **smut·ti·er; -est 1** : soiled or tainted with smut ⟨a *smutty* face⟩ **2** : affected with smut fungus ⟨*smutty* plants⟩ **3** : OBSCENE 2, INDECENT ⟨*smutty* jokes⟩ — **smut·ti·ly** \'smət-ᵊl-ē\ *adv* — **smut·ti·ness** \'smət-ē-nəs\ *n*

snack \'snak\ *n* : a light meal : LUNCH

snack bar *n* : a public eating place where snacks are served usually at a counter

¹**snag** \'snag\ *n* **1 a** : a tree or branch when stuck underwater and not visible from the surface **b** : a standing dead tree **2** : an uneven or broken part sticking out from a smooth surface ⟨caught my sweater on a *snag*⟩ **3** : a concealed or unexpected difficulty ⟨our plans hit a *snag*⟩

²**snag** *vb* **snagged; snag·ging** : to catch on or as if on a snag

snag·gle·tooth \'snag-əl-ˌtüth\ *n* : a tooth that sticks out, is uneven, or is broken — **snag·gle·toothed** \ˌsnag-əl-'tütht\ *adj*

snail \'snā(ə)l\ *n* **1** : any of numerous small mollusks that are gastropods usually with a spiral shell and that include some living on land and others living in water **2** : a slow-moving person or thing

snail mail *n* **1** : mail delivered by a postal system **2** : ¹MAIL 4

¹**snake** \'snāk\ *n* **1** : any of numerous limbless reptiles that have a long body and salivary glands often capable of producing venom which is injected through fangs **2** : a mean or treacherous person — **snake·like** \'snā-ˌklīk\ *adj*

²**snake** *vb* **snaked; snak·ing** : to crawl, wind, or move like a snake

snake·bird \'snāk-ˌbərd\ *n* : ANHINGA

snake·bite \-ˌbīt\ *n* : the bite of a snake and especially a poisonous snake

snake in the grass : a secretly unfaithful friend

snake plant *n* : SANSEVIERIA

snake·root \'snā-ˌkrüt, -ˌkrut\ *n* : any of various plants sometimes believed to be a cure for snake-bites or illness; *also* : the root of a snakeroot

snake·skin \'snāk-ˌskin\ *n* : the skin of a snake or leather made from it

snaky *also* **snak·ey** \'snā-kē\ *adj* **1** : of or resembling a snake **2** : full of snakes — **snak·i·ly** \-kə-lē\ *adv*

snakeroot

¹**snap** \'snap\ *vb* **snapped; snap·ping 1 a** : to make a sudden closing of the jaws : seize something sharply with the mouth ⟨fish *snapping* at the bait⟩ **b** : to grasp at something eagerly ⟨*snapped* at the chance to travel⟩ **c** : to take possession of at once — usually used with *up* ⟨*snap* up a bargain⟩ **2** : to speak sharply or irritably ⟨*snap* at a questioner⟩ **3 a** : to break or break apart suddenly especially with a sharp sound ⟨the twig *snapped*⟩ ⟨*snapped* the bone in two⟩ **b** : to give way or cause to give way suddenly under stress ⟨the rope *snapped*⟩ **c** : to bring to a sudden end ⟨*snapped* the opposing team's winning streak⟩ **4** : to make or cause to make a sharp or crackling sound ⟨*snap* a whip⟩ **5 a** : to close or fit in place with a quick movement ⟨the lid *snapped* shut⟩ **b** : to put into or remove

from a position by a sudden movement or with a snapping sound ⟨*snap* off a switch⟩ **c** : to close by snaps or fasteners ⟨*snapped* up the snowsuit⟩ **6 a** : to move briskly or sharply ⟨*snapped* to attention⟩ **b** : to undergo a sudden and rapid change (as from one condition to another) ⟨*snapped* out of his bad mood⟩ **c** : to put a (football) in play especially by passing or handing backward between the legs **d** : to take a snapshot of

²**snap** *n* **1** : a quick closing (as of the mouth in biting or of scissors in cutting); *esp* : a biting or snatching with the teeth or jaws **2** : something that is easy and presents no problems : CINCH **3** : a small amount : BIT ⟨don't care a *snap*⟩ **4 a** : a sudden snatching at something **b** : a quick short movement **c** : a sudden sharp breaking **5** : a sound made by snapping something ⟨shut the book with a *snap*⟩ **6** : a sudden spell of harsh weather ⟨a cold *snap*⟩ **7** : a catch or fastening that closes or locks with a click ⟨*snap* of a bracelet⟩ **8** : a thin brittle cookie **9** : SNAPSHOT **10** : smartness of movement or speech : ENERGY **11** : an act or instance of snapping a football

³**snap** *adj* **1** : made suddenly or without careful thought ⟨a *snap* judgment⟩ **2** : shutting or fastening with a click or by means of a device that snaps ⟨a *snap* lock⟩ **3** : unusually easy ⟨a *snap* course⟩

snap·back \'snap-ˌbak\ *n* : a sudden rebound or recovery

snap back \(')snap-'bak\ *vb* : to make a quick recovery ⟨*snap back* after an illness⟩

snap bean *n* : a bean grown primarily for its long pods that are cooked as a vegetable while they are still young and tender and before their seeds have become enlarged — compare SHELL BEAN

snap·drag·on \'snap-ˌdrag-ən\ *n* : a widely grown herb having showy usually pink, red, white, or yellow two-lipped flowers

snap·per \'snap-ər\ *n, pl* **snappers 1 a** : something that snaps **b** : SNAPPING TURTLE **2** *pl also* **snapper a** : any of a large family of active flesh-eating fishes of warm seas that are important as food and sport fishes **b** : any of several immature fishes (as the young of the bluefish) that resemble a snapper

snapping turtle *n* : either of two large American freshwater turtles that have a large head, powerful jaws, and a long tail

snapping turtle

snap·pish \'snap-ish\ *adj* **1** : marked by snapping irritable speech : IRASCIBLE ⟨a *snappish* disposition⟩ **2** : apt to bite ⟨a *snappish* dog⟩ — **snap·pish·ly** *adv*

snap·py \'snap-ē\ *adj* **snap·pi·er; -est 1** : SNAPPISH 1 **2 a** : quickly made or done **b** : full of life : LIVELY **c** : briskly cold **d** : STYLISH, SMART ⟨a *snappy* dresser⟩ — **snap·pi·ly** \'snap-ə-lē\ *adv*

snap·shot \'snap-ˌshät\ *n* : a photograph taken usually with a small hand-held camera

¹**snare** \'sna(ə)r, 'sne(ə)r\ *n* **1 a** : a trap often consisting of a noose for catching small animals or birds **b** : something by which one is entangled, trapped, or deceived **2** : one of the catgut strings or metal spirals stretched across the bottom of a snare drum

²**snare** *vb* **snared; snar·ing 1** : to capture or entangle by or as if by use of a snare **2** : to win by skillful or deceptive measures **synonyms** see CATCH — **snar·er** *n*

snare drum *n* : a small two-headed drum that can be worn at the side while marching and that has a band of snares stretched across the lower head to rattle when the head vibrates to give the drum its special sound

¹**snarl** \'snär(-ə)l\ *n* **1** : a tangle especially of hairs or thread : KNOT **2** : a tangled situation ⟨a traffic *snarl*⟩ [Middle

English *snarle* "snare, noose," probably from snarlen "to trap, entangle"]

²**snarl** *vb* : to get into a tangle

³**snarl** *vb* **1** : to growl with a snapping or showing of teeth **2** : to speak in an angry way **3** : to utter with a snarl [from obsolete *snar* "to growl"] — **snarl·er** *n*

⁴**snarl** *n* : an angry growl

¹**snatch** \'snach\ *vb* **1** : to seize or try to seize something quickly or suddenly **2** : to grasp or take suddenly or hastily : GRAB — **snatch·er** *n*

²**snatch** *n* **1 a** : a brief period ⟨slept in *snatches*⟩ **b** : something brief, hurried, or in small bits **2** : a snatching at or of something

snaz·zy \'snaz-ē\ *adj* **snaz·zi·er; -est** : attractive in a flashy way ⟨a *snazzy* tie⟩

¹**sneak** \'snēk\ *vb* **sneaked** \'snēkt\ *or* **snuck** \'snək\; **sneak·ing 1** : to go about in a sly or secret manner **2** : to put, bring, or take in a sly manner **synonyms** see LURK

²**sneak** *n* **1** : a person who acts in a secret or sly manner **2** : the act or an instance of sneaking

³**sneak** *adj* **1** : carried on secretly : CLANDESTINE **2** : occurring without warning ⟨a *sneak* attack⟩

sneak·er \'snē-kər\ *n* **1** : one that sneaks **2** : a sports shoe (as of canvas) with a rubber sole

sneak·ing \'snē-kiŋ\ *adj* **1** : FURTIVE, UNDERHAND **2 a** : not openly expressed ⟨a *sneaking* admiration for an opponent⟩ **b** : being a thought, feeling, or suspicion that makes one uneasy ⟨a *sneaking* feeling we would fail⟩

sneaky \'snē-kē\ *adj* **sneak·i·er; -est 1** : behaving in a sly or secret manner **2** : marked by secrecy or slyness ⟨a *sneaky* trick⟩ — **sneak·i·ly** \-kə-lē\ *adv* — **sneak·i·ness** \-kē-nəs\ *n*

¹**sneer** \'sni(ə)r\ *vb* **1** : to smile or laugh with expressions of scorn **2** : to speak or write in a scorning manner — **sneer·er** *n*

²**sneer** *n* : a sneering expression or remark

sneeze \'snēz\ *vb* **sneezed; sneez·ing** : to force the breath out through the nose or mouth in a sudden violent noisy action — **sneeze** *n* — **sneez·er** *n* — **sneeze at** : to treat lightly : DISDAIN

¹**snick** \'snik\ *vb* : to make or cause to make a snick

²**snick** *n* : a slight often metallic sound : CLICK

¹**snick·er** \'snik-ər\ *vb* **snick·ered; snick·er·ing** \-(ə-)riŋ\ : to give a small and often mean or sly laugh

²**snicker** *n* : an act or sound of snickering

snide \'snīd\ *adj* **1** : ²LOW 9b, MEAN ⟨a *snide* trick⟩ **2** : slyly uncomplimentary or insulting ⟨*snide* remarks⟩

¹**sniff** \'snif\ *vb* **1** : to draw air into the nose in short breaths loud enough to be heard ⟨*sniffed* at the cheese⟩ **2** : to show or express scorn ⟨*sniffed* at simple jobs⟩ **3** : to smell or inhale by taking short breaths ⟨*sniff* perfume⟩ **4** : to detect by or as if by smelling ⟨*sniff* out trouble⟩ — **sniff·er** *n*

²**sniff** *n* **1** : the act or sound of sniffing **2** : an odor or amount sniffed

sniff·ish \'snif-ish\ *adj* : SCORNFUL, DISDAINFUL ⟨a *sniffish* boss⟩ — **sniff·ish·ly** *adv*

¹**snif·fle** \'snif-əl\ *vb* **snif·fled; snif·fling** \-(ə-)liŋ\ **1** : to sniff repeatedly **2** : to speak with or as if with sniffling

²**sniffle** *n* **1** *pl* : a common cold in which the main symptom is a runny nose **2** : an act or sound of sniffling

snig·ger \'snig-ər\ *vb* **snig·gered; snig·ger·ing** \-(ə-)riŋ\ : ¹SNICKER — **snigger** *n*

¹**snip** \'snip\ *n* **1** : a small piece that is snipped off : FRAGMENT **2** : an act or sound of snipping **3** : a rude person

²**snip** *vb* **snipped; snip·ping** : to cut or cut off with or as if with shears or scissors; *esp* : to clip suddenly or by bits

¹**snipe** \'snīp\ *n, pl* **snipes** *or* **snipe** : any of several birds that have a long slender bill, live mostly in marshy areas, and are related to the sandpipers

²**snipe** *vb* **sniped; snip·ing 1** : to shoot at exposed individuals of an enemy's forces from a usually concealed point **2** : to attack with unfair or cutting remarks — **snip·er** *n*

¹snipe

snip·pet \'snip-ət\ *n* : a small part, piece, or thing

snip·py \'snip-ē\ *adj* **snip·pi·er; -est 1** : SHORT-TEMPERED, SNAPPISH **2** : rudely brief : CURT

snips \'snips\ *n pl* : hand shears used especially for cutting sheet metal ⟨tin *snips*⟩

¹**snitch** \'snich\ *n* : a person who snitches : TATTLETALE, INFORMER [origin unknown]

²**snitch** *vb* : INFORM 2, TATTLE — **snitch·er** *n*

³**snitch** *vb* : to take by sly or secret action; *esp* : PILFER ⟨*snitched* more candy⟩ [probably alteration of *snatch*]

sniv·el \'sniv-əl\ *vb* **-eled** *or* **-elled; -el·ing** *or* **-el·ling** \-(ə-)liŋ\ **1** : to draw mucus up the nose loud enough to be heard **2** : to cry or whine with sniffling **3** : to speak or act in a whining manner — **sniv·el·er** \-(ə-)lər\ *n*

snob \'snäb\ *n* **1** : one who imitates, admires, or seeks association with those of higher social position **2** : one who looks down upon those felt to be less important

Word History *Snob* is an old word in English for "a cobbler, a person who makes or repairs shoes." Cobblers came to be thought of as representative of all of the working-class or lower-class people. In time the name *snob* came to be applied to the lower classes as distinguished from the nobility, the landowners, and the rich merchants. From its being used for any member of the lower class, *snob* soon came to mean "a person who pretends to be a member of a higher class, one who imitates the clothing, speech, and manners of the nobility." Nowadays the word means "anyone who acts as if he or she were better than others." [from obsolete *snob* "a member of the lower classes," from a dialect word *snob* "cobbler, shoemaker"]

snob appeal *n* : the appeal (as from high price) that a product has for a snobbish person

snob·bery \'snäb-(ə-)rē\ *n* : snobbish conduct

snob·bish \'snäb-ish\ *adj* : of, relating to, or being a snob ⟨a *snobbish* attitude⟩ — **snob·bish·ly** *adv* — **snob·bish·ness** *n*

snob·bism \'snäb-,iz-əm\ *n* : SNOBBERY

snob·by \'snäb-ē\ *adj* **snob·bi·er; -est** : SNOBBISH

snood \'snüd\ *n* : a net or fabric bag for holding hair pinned or tied on at the back of the head

¹**snoop** \'snüp\ *vb* : to look or search especially in a sneaking or meddlesome manner — **snoop·er** *n*

²**snoop** *n* : one that snoops

snoopy \'snü-pē\ *adj* : being in the habit of snooping especially for personal information about others

snoot \'snüt\ *n* **1** : SNOUT 1 **2** : ¹NOSE 1a **3** : a snooty person : SNOB

snooty \'snüt-ē\ *adj* **snoot·i·er; -est** : SNOBBISH — **snoot·i·ly** \'snüt-ᵊl-ē\ *adv* — **snoot·i·ness** \'snüt-ē-nəs\ *n*

snooze \'snüz\ *vb* **snoozed; snooz·ing** : to take a nap : DOZE — **snooze** *n*

snooze button *n* : a button on an alarm clock that stops and resets the alarm for a short time later to allow for more rest

snore \'snō(ə)r, 'snó(ə)r\ *vb* : to breathe with a rough hoarse noise while sleeping — **snore** *n* — **snor·er** *n*

¹**snor·kel** \'snór-kəl\ *n* **1** : a tube or tubes that can be extended above the surface of the water to supply air to and remove exhaust from a submerged submarine **2** : a tube used by swimmers for breathing with the head under water

²**snorkel** *vb* **snor·keled; snor·kel·ing** \-k(ə-)liŋ\ : to swim underwater using a snorkel

¹snorkel 2

¹**snort** \'snó(ə)rt\ *vb* **1 a** : to force air violently through the nose with a rough harsh sound **b** : to express scorn, anger, or surprise by a snort **2** : to take in (a drug) by inhaling through the nose — **snort·er** *n*

²**snort** *n* **1** : an act or sound of snorting **2** : a drink of liquor usually taken by itself in one swallow

snot \'snät\ *n* **1** : nasal mucus **2** : a snotty person

snot·ty \'snät-ē\ *adj* **snot·ti·er; -est 1** : soiled with nasal mucus ⟨a *snotty* nose⟩ **2** : annoyingly or spitefully unpleasant ⟨a *snotty* reply⟩

snout \'snaút\ *n* **1 a** : a long nose or muzzle (as of a pig) that sticks out **b** : a front part of the head of an animal that sticks out like the snout of a pig **c** : the human nose especially when large or ugly **2** : something resembling a snout — **snout·ed** \-əd\ *adj*

snout beetle *n* : WEEVIL

¹**snow** \'snō\ *n* **1 a** : small white ice crystals formed directly from the water vapor of the air **b** : a fall of snow crystals : a mass of snow crystals that have fallen to earth **2** : something resembling snow: as **a** : a dessert made of stiffly beaten egg whites, sugar, and fruit ⟨pineapple *snow*⟩ **b** *slang* : COCAINE

²**snow** *vb* **1** : to fall or cause to fall in or as snow ⟨it had been *snowing* all day⟩ **2** : to cover, shut in, or imprison with or as if with snow ⟨we were *snowed* in for two days⟩ ⟨the desk was *snowed* under by papers⟩ **3** : to deceive, persuade, or charm with insincere or flattering talk ⟨couldn't *snow* her with his compliments⟩

¹**snow·ball** \'snō-,ból\ *n* **1** : a round mass of snow pressed or rolled together **2** : a viburnum widely grown for its ball-shaped clusters of white flowers — called also *snowball bush*

²**snowball** *vb* **1** : to throw snowballs at **2** : to increase or expand at a rapidly accelerating rate ⟨problems *snowball* when early trouble signs are ignored⟩

snow·bank \'snō-,baŋk\ *n* : a mound or slope of snow

snow·bird \-,bərd\ *n* : any of several small birds (as a junco) seen chiefly in winter

snow–blind \-,blīnd\ *or* **snow–blind·ed** \-,blīn-dəd\ *adj* : affected with snow blindness

snow blindness *n* : inflammation and inability to stand light caused by glare reflected from snow or ice

snow·blow·er \'snō-,blō-(ə)r\ *n* : a machine in which a rotating device picks up and throws snow aside

snow·board \-,bō(ə)rd, -,bó(ə)rd\ *n* : a board like a wide ski ridden in a surfing position over snow — **snowboard** *vb* — **snow·boarder** *n* — **snow·board·ing** *n*

snow·bound \-'baúnd\ *adj* : shut in or blockaded by snow

snow·cap \-,kap\ *n* : a covering cap of snow (as on a mountain peak) — **snow·capped** \-,kapt\ *adj*

snow·drift \-,drift\ *n* : a bank of drifted snow

snow·drop \-,dräp\ *n* : a European plant that is related to the amaryllises and produces nodding white flowers that often appear while snow is still on the ground

snow·fall \-,ból\ *n* **1** : a fall of snow **2** : the amount of snow that falls in a single storm or in a certain period

snow fence *n* : a fence placed across the usual path of the wind to protect something (as a road) from snowdrifts

snow·flake \'snō-ˌflāk\ *n* : a flake or crystal of snow

snowflake

snow leopard *n* : a large cat of central Asia with long heavy grayish white fur marked with brownish black spots and rings

snow line *n* : the lower edge of an area of permanent snow (as a mountain peak)

snow·man \'snō-ˌman, -'man\ *n* : snow shaped to resemble a person

snow·mo·bile \'snō-mō-ˌbēl\ *n* : any of various motor vehicles for travel on snow — **snow·mo·bil·er** \-ˌbē-lər\ *n* — **snow·mo·bil·ing** \-ˌbē-liŋ\ *n*

snow pea *n* : a cultivated pea that has flat edible pods; *also* : the pods

snow·plow \-ˌplau̇\ *n* : any of various devices used for clearing away snow

¹snow·shoe \-ˌshü\ *n* : a light frame (as of wood or aluminum) strung with a net that is attached to the foot to prevent sinking in soft snow

²snowshoe *vb* **snow·shoed; snow·shoe·ing** : to travel on snowshoes

snowshoe hare *n* : a rather large hare of northern North America with heavily furred hind feet and a coat that is brown in summer but usually white in winter — called also *snowshoe rabbit*

snow·slide \'snō-ˌslīd\ *n* : an avalanche of snow

snow·storm \-ˌstȯrm\ *n* : a storm of falling snow

snow·suit \-ˌsüt\ *n* : a one-piece or two-piece lined garment worn by children

snow thrower *n* : SNOWBLOWER

snow tire *n* : an automobile tire with a tread designed to give added traction on snow

snow tube *n* : a large inflatable ring-shaped tube used for sliding down a snow-covered slope

snow under *vb* **1** : to overwhelm especially beyond the ability to absorb or deal with something **2** : to defeat by a large amount

snow–white \'snō-'hwīt, -'wīt\ *adj* : white as snow

snowy \'snō-ē\ *adj* **snow·i·er; -est** **1** : marked by or covered with snow ⟨a *snowy* day⟩ ⟨*snowy* mountaintops⟩ **2 a** : whitened by or as if by snow ⟨an orchard *snowy* with apple blossoms⟩ **b** : SNOW-WHITE

snowy owl *n* : a large chiefly arctic owl that nests on the ground and is white or white spotted with brown

snowy owl

¹snub \'snəb\ *vb* **snubbed; snub·bing** **1** : to check or stop with a reply that hurts : REBUKE **2 a** : to check (as a line) suddenly while running out especially by turning around a fixed object (as a post) **b** : to check the motion of by snubbing a line **3** : to deliberately ignore or treat rudely **4** : to put out by crushing — **snub·ber** *n*

²snub *n* : an act or an instance of snubbing; *esp* : ²REBUFF

³snub *or* **snubbed** \'snəbd\ *adj* : STUBBY, BLUNT

snub–nosed \'snəb-'nōzd\ *adj* : having a stubby and usually slightly turned-up nose

¹snuff \'snəf\ *vb* **1** : to cut off the burned end of the wick of a candle so as to brighten the light **2** : to put an end to

: EXTINGUISH ⟨*snuff* out a candle⟩ ⟨*snuff* out a life⟩ [Middle English *snoffe* "the burned end of a candle wick"]

²snuff *vb* **1** : to draw forcibly through or into the nostrils **2** : to sniff so as to smell [perhaps derived from Dutch *snuffen* "to sniff"]

³snuff *n* : powdered tobacco especially for inhaling through the nostrils [from Dutch *snuf*, a shortened form of *snuftabak* "powdered tobacco," from *snuffen* "to snuff, sniff" and *tabak* "tobacco"] — **up to snuff** : in good shape

snuff·box \'snəf-ˌbäks\ *n* : a small box for snuff

¹snuf·fle \'snəf-əl\ *vb* **snuf·fled; snuf·fling** \-(ə-)liŋ\ **1** : to snuff or sniff usually loudly and over and over again **2** : to breathe through a partly blocked nose with a sniffing sound **3** : ¹WHINE 1

²snuffle *n* : the sound made in snuffling

¹snug \'snəg\ *vb* **snugged; snug·ging** **1** : to settle or lie down : SNUGGLE **2** : to make snug

²snug *adj* **snug·ger; snug·gest** **1 a** : SEAWORTHY **b** : ²TRIM, NEAT **c** : fitting closely and comfortably ⟨a *snug* coat⟩ **2** : enjoying or providing warm secure shelter and comfort : COZY ⟨a *snug* cottage⟩ **3** : fairly large ⟨a *snug* fortune⟩ **4** : offering safe concealment ⟨a *snug* harbor⟩ — **snug** *adv* — **snug·ly** *adv* — **snug·ness** *n*

snug·gery \'snəg-(ə-)rē\ *n, pl* **-ger·ies** *chiefly British* : a snug cozy place; *esp* : a small comfortable room

snug·gle \'snəg-əl\ *vb* **snug·gled; snug·gling** \-(ə-)liŋ\ **1** : to curl up comfortably or cozily : CUDDLE **2** : to pull in close especially for comfort or in affection : NESTLE

¹so \(')sō, *especially before adj or adv followed by "that"* sə\ *adv* **1 a** : in a manner or way that is indicated or suggested ⟨do you really think *so*⟩ ⟨it *so* happened that all were wrong⟩ — often used as a substitute for a preceding clause ⟨I didn't like it and told her *so*⟩ **b** : in the same manner or way : ALSO ⟨worked hard and *so* did we⟩ **c** : ¹THEN 2 ⟨and *so* home and to bed⟩ **2 a** : to an indicated or suggested amount or way ⟨had never been *so* happy⟩ **b** : very much ⟨I loved them *so*⟩ **c** : to a definite but not specified amount ⟨can only do *so* much in a day⟩ **d** : most certainly : INDEED ⟨you did *so* do it⟩ **e** : most decidedly : SURELY ⟨I *so* don't believe you⟩ **3** : for a reason that has just been stated : THEREFORE ⟨is honest and *so* returned the wallet⟩

²so \(')sō\ *conj* **1 a** : with the result that ⟨the way you speak is good, *so* every word is clear⟩ **b** : in order that ⟨be quiet *so* that I can sleep⟩ **2** *archaic* : provided that **3** : for that reason ⟨don't want to go, *so* I won't⟩ **4 a** — used to introduce a statement or question ⟨*so* here we are⟩ often to belittle a point under discussion ⟨*so* what?⟩ **b** — used interjectionally to indicate awareness of a discovery ⟨*so*, that's who did it⟩ — **so as to** : in order to ⟨keep quiet *so as to* not attract attention⟩

³so \'sō\ *adj* **1** : agreeing with actual facts : TRUE ⟨said things that were not *so*⟩ **2** : marked by a definite order ⟨my books are always just *so*⟩

⁴so \ˌsō, 'sō\ *pron* **1** : such as has been specified : the same ⟨if you have to sign up for the trip, do *so* as soon as possible⟩ **2** : approximately that ⟨20 years or *so*⟩

⁵so \'sō\ *n* : ¹SOL

¹soak \'sōk\ *vb* **1 a** : to lie covered with a liquid **b** : to place in a liquid to wet or as if to wet thoroughly **2 a** : to enter or pass through something by or as if by pores : PERMEATE **b** : to penetrate or affect the mind or feelings **3** : to draw out by or as if by steeping ⟨*soak* the dirt out⟩ **4** : to draw in by or as if by suction or absorption ⟨*soaked* up the sunshine⟩ **5** : to cause to pay too much — **soak·er** *n*

\ə\ **abut**	\au̇\ **out**	\i\ **tip**	\ȯ\ **saw**	\u̇\ **foot**
\ər\ **further**	\ch\ **chin**	\ī\ **life**	\ȯi\ **coin**	\y\ **yet**
\a\ **mat**	\e\ **pet**	\j\ **job**	\th\ **thin**	\yü\ **few**
\ā\ **take**	\ē\ **easy**	\ŋ\ **sing**	\th\ **this**	\yu̇\ **cure**
\ä\ **cot, cart**	\g\ **go**	\ō\ **bone**	\ü\ **food**	\zh\ **vision**

synonyms SOAK, SATURATE, STEEP, DRENCH mean to pass or to be passed through a liquid. SOAK suggests dunking something in a liquid for a long time in order to soften or clean it ⟨let the dirty rags *soak* for several hours⟩. SATURATE stresses soaking something to the point where no more liquid can be absorbed ⟨the sponge is *saturated* with water⟩. STEEP applies to the soaking of something so that some part of the thing passes into the liquid ⟨allow the tea to *steep* for five minutes⟩. DRENCH suggests a thorough wetting from something that pours down ⟨the rain *drenched* our clothes⟩.

²**soak** *n* **1** : the act or process of soaking : the state of being soaked **2** : DRUNKARD

so–and–so \'sō-ən-ˌsō\ *n, pl* **so–and–sos** *or* **so–and–so's** \-ən-ˌsōz\ : an unnamed or unspecified person or thing

¹**soap** \'sōp\ *n* **1** : a substance that is usually made by the action of alkali on fat, dissolves in water, and is used for washing **2** : a salt of a fatty acid **3** : SOAP OPERA

²**soap** *vb* : to rub soap over or into

soap·ber·ry \'sōp-ˌber-ē\ *n* : any of a genus of mostly tropical woody plants; *also* : the fruit of a soapberry that is sometimes used as a substitute for soap

soap·box \-ˌbäks\ *n* : something used as a platform (as on a street) by someone giving a speech to passersby — **soapbox** *adj*

soap opera *n* : a radio or television drama presented in a series of continuing stories and characters and intended to appeal to the emotions [so called because the advertisers on these programs were usually soap manufacturers — see *Word History* at HORSE OPERA]

soap·stone \'sōp-ˌstōn\ *n* : a soft stone having a soapy feel and composed essentially of talc, chlorite, and often some magnetite

soap·suds \-ˌsədz\ *n pl* : ¹SUDS 1

soapy \'sō-pē\ *adj* **soap·i·er; -est 1** : smeared with or full of soap ⟨a *soapy* face⟩ **2** : containing or combined with soap **3** : resembling or having the qualities of soap — **soap·i·ness** \-pē-nəs\ *n*

¹**soar** \'sō(ə)r, 'sȯ(ə)r\ *vb* **1 a** : to fly aloft or about ⟨the plane *soared* into the sky⟩ **b** : to sail or hover in the air often at a great height : GLIDE ⟨an eagle *soaring* in lazy circles⟩ **2** : to rise or increase very noticeably (as in position, value, or price) ⟨admission fees *soared*⟩

²**soar** *n* : the act of soaring : upward flight

¹**sob** \'säb\ *vb* **sobbed; sob·bing 1** : to weep especially with short gasping sounds **2** : to bring to a specified state by sobbing ⟨*sobbed* myself to sleep⟩ **3 a** : to make a sound like that of sobbing ⟨the wind *sobbed* through the trees⟩ **b** : to utter with sobs ⟨*sobbed* out their story⟩

²**sob** *n* **1** : an act of sobbing **2** : a sound of or like that of sobbing

¹**so·ber** \'sō-bər\ *adj* **so·ber·er** \-bər-ər\; **so·ber·est** \-b(ə-)rəst\ **1 a** : sparing especially in the use of food and drink **b** : not drunk **2** : having a serious attitude : SOLEMN **3** : having a quiet tone or color **4** : well reasoned and balanced ⟨a *sober* decision⟩ — **so·ber·ly** \-bər-lē\ *adv* — **so·ber·ness** *n*

²**sober** *vb* **so·bered; so·ber·ing** \-b(ə-)riŋ\ : to make or become sober

so·bri·ety \sə-'brī-ət-ē\ *n* : the quality or state of being sober

so·bri·quet *also* **sou·bri·quet** \'sō-bri-ˌkā, -ˌket; ˌsō-bri-'kā, -'ket\ *n* : a descriptive name or phrase : NICKNAME

so–called \'sō-'kȯld\ *adj* : commonly or popularly but often inaccurately so named ⟨your *so-called* friend⟩

soc·cer \'säk-ər\ *n* : a football game with 11 players on a side in which a round ball is advanced by kicking it or by hitting it with any part of the body except the hands and arms

Word History Soccer is the world's most popular sport. In most countries, however, its name is not *soccer* but *football*. In England, where the modern game started, it is usually called either *football* or *association football*. The latter name comes from the fact that the rules of the game were standardized when the *Football Association* was founded in England in 1863. The word *soccer* comes from the last three letters of the abbreviation *assoc.*, which stands for "association." Although the word *soccer* was first used in England, the only countries where it is now the usual name for the sport are the U.S. and Canada. [by shortening and alteration of *association football*]

so·cia·bil·i·ty \ˌsō-shə-'bil-ət-ē\ *n, pl* **-ties 1** : the quality or state of being sociable : AFFABILITY **2** : the act or an instance of being sociable

¹**so·cia·ble** \'sō-shə-bəl\ *adj* **1** : likely to seek or enjoy companionship : AFFABLE, FRIENDLY ⟨*sociable* people⟩ **2** : leading to friendliness or pleasant social relations [from early French *sociable* "social, sociable," from Latin *sociabilis* (same meaning), from *sociare* "to join, associate," from *socius* "ally, companion" — related to ASSOCIATE] — **so·cia·bly** \-blē\ *adv*

²**sociable** *n* : ²SOCIAL

¹**so·cial** \'sō-shəl\ *adj* **1 a** : devoted to or engaged in for sociability ⟨*social* events⟩ ⟨my *social* life⟩ **b** : ¹SOCIABLE 1 **2** : of or relating to human society ⟨*social* institutions⟩ **3 a** : tending to form cooperative relationships with others ⟨we are *social* beings⟩ **b** : living or growing by nature in groups or communities ⟨bees are *social* insects⟩ **4 a** : of, relating to, or based on rank in a particular society ⟨not accepted as their *social* equal⟩ **b** : of or relating to fashionable society ⟨a *social* leader⟩

²**social** *n* : a friendly gathering usually for a special reason ⟨an ice cream *social*⟩

social climber *n* : one who attempts to gain a higher social position or be accepted in fashionable society

so·cial·ism \'sō-shə-ˌliz-əm\ *n* : any of various social systems based on shared or governmental ownership and administration of the means of production and distribution of goods — **so·cial·ist** \'sōsh-(ə-)ləst\ *n* — **socialist** *or* **so·cial·is·tic** \ˌsō-shə-'lis-tik\ *adj* — **so·cial·is·ti·cal·ly** \-ti-k(ə-)lē\ *adv*

so·cial·ite \'sō-shə-ˌlīt\ *n* : a person well-known in fashionable society

so·cial·ize \'sō-shə-ˌlīz\ *vb* **-ized; -iz·ing 1** : to make social; *esp* : to make fit for a social environment **2** : to take part in social activities ⟨*socializing* with friends after work⟩ — **so·cial·i·za·tion** \ˌsōsh-(ə-)lə-'zā-shən\ *n* — **so·cial·iz·er** \'sō-shə-ˌlī-zər\ *n*

so·cial·ly \'sōsh-(ə-)lē\ *adv* **1** : in a social manner ⟨birds living *socially* together⟩ **2** : with respect to society ⟨*socially* disadvantaged⟩

social media *n sing or pl* : forms of electronic communication (as websites for social networking and microblogging) through which users create online communities to share information, ideas, personal messages, and other content (as videos)

social networking *n* : the creation and maintenance of personal and business relationships especially online

social science *n* **1** : a science that deals with human society or its elements (as family, state, or race) and with institutions and relationships in an organized community **2** : a science (as economics) dealing with a particular side of human society

social scientist *n* : a person who specializes in social science

social security *n* **1** : the idea or system by which the public provides for the security of individuals and their families **2** *cap both Ss* : a U.S. government program established in 1935 to include old-age and survivors insurance, contributions to state unemployment insurance, and old-age assistance

social studies *n pl* : the studies dealing with human relationships and the way society works (as history, civics, economics, and geography)

social work *n* : any of various professional activities or methods concerned especially with providing services (as counseling, job training, or financial assistance) designed to promote social well-being (as of the economically disadvantaged) — **social worker** *n*

¹**so·ci·e·ty** \sə-'sī-ət-ē\ *n, pl* **-et·ies** 1 : the community life thought of as a system within which the individual lives ⟨rural *society*⟩ 2 : people for the most part ⟨the benefit of *society*⟩ 3 : an association of persons for some purpose ⟨the school French *society*⟩ 4 : a part of a community thought of as a unit set apart by common interests or values; *esp* : the group or set of fashionable persons 5 : a system or group of living things that depend on each other and usually form a social unit (as a hive of bees) 6 : the state of being with other people — **so·ci·e·tal** \-ət-ºl\ *adj*

²**society** *adj* : of, relating to, or characteristic of fashionable society

so·cio·log·i·cal \ˌsō-sē-ə-'läj-i-kəl, ˌsō-sh(ē-)ə-\ *also* **so·cio·log·ic** \-ik\ *adj* 1 : of or relating to sociology or its methods 2 : concerned with or relating to social needs and problems — **so·cio·log·i·cal·ly** \-i-k(ə-)lē\ *adv*

so·ci·ol·o·gist \ˌsō-sē-'äl-ə-jəst, ˌsō-shē-\ *n* : a person who specializes in sociology

so·ci·ol·o·gy \ˌsō-sē-'äl-ə-jē, ˌsō-shē-\ *n* : the science of society, social institutions, and social relationships

¹**sock** \'säk\ *n, pl* **socks** *also* **sox** \'säks\ : a knitted or woven covering for the foot usually extending above the ankle and sometimes to the knee [Old English *socc* "a low shoe or slipper," from Latin *soccus* (same meaning)]

²**sock** *vb* : to hit, strike, or apply forcefully : deliver a blow [origin unknown]

³**sock** *n* : a violent blow : PUNCH

sock·et \'säk-ət\ *n* : an opening or hollow that forms a holder for something ⟨the eye *socket*⟩ ⟨screwed the light bulb into the *socket*⟩

¹**sod** \'säd\ *n* 1 **a** : TURF 1 **b** : the grass-covered and herb-covered surface of the ground 2 : one's native land

²**sod** *vb* **sod·ded; sod·ding** : to cover with sod or turfs

so·da \'sōd-ə\ *n* 1 **a** : SODIUM CARBONATE **b** : SODIUM BICARBONATE 2 **a** : SODA WATER **b** : SODA POP **c** : a sweet drink consisting of soda water, flavoring, and often ice cream

soda cracker *n* : a cracker leavened with bicarbonate of soda and cream of tartar

soda fountain *n* 1 : a device for drawing soda water 2 : the equipment and counter for the preparation and serving of carbonated drinks, sodas, sundaes, and ice cream

soda jerk *n* : one who prepares and serves soft drinks and ice cream at a soda fountain

so·dal·i·ty \sō-'dal-ət-ē\ *n, pl* **-ties** : an organized society or fellowship; *esp* : a Roman Catholic association for the purposes of devotion or charity

soda pop *n* : a soft drink consisting of soda water with added flavoring and a sweet syrup

soda water *n* : a beverage consisting of carbonated water

sod·den \'säd-ºn\ *adj* 1 : heavy with moisture : SOAKED 2 **a** : dull or lacking in expression **b** : SLUGGISH, DULL ⟨*sodden* minds⟩ — **sod·den·ly** *adv*

so·di·um \'sōd-ē-əm\ *n* : a soft waxy silver-white metallic element that is chemically very active and is common in nature in combined form — see ELEMENT table

sodium bicarbonate *n* : a white weakly alkaline salt used especially in baking powders and fire extinguishers and in medicine as an antacid — called also *baking soda, bicarbonate of soda*

sodium carbonate *n* : a sodium salt used especially in making soaps and chemicals, in water softening, in cleaning and bleaching, and in photography

sodium chloride *n* : a chemical compound that consists of crystals having equal numbers of sodium and chlorine atoms : SALT 1a

sodium citrate *n* : a salt used especially to prevent stored blood from clotting

sodium fluoride *n* : a salt that is added in tiny amounts to drinking water and toothpastes to prevent tooth decay

sodium hydroxide *n* : a white brittle solid that is strongly alkaline and is used especially in making soap, rayon, and paper

sodium nitrate *n* : a salt used as a fertilizer and to preserve meat

sodium nitrite *n* : a salt used especially in the manufacture of dyes and as a meat preservative

sodium sulfate *n* : a bitter salt used especially in detergents, in the manufacture of rayon, and in dyeing and finishing textiles

sodium thio·sul·fate \-ˌthī-ə-'səl-ˌfāt\ *n* : a chemical compound used especially in photography to make images permanent and in bleaching

so·fa \'sō-fə\ *n* : a long upholstered seat usually with arms and a back and often convertible into a bed

sofa bed *n* : a sofa that can be made to serve as a bed

¹**soft** \'sȯft\ *adj* 1 **a** : having a pleasing, comfortable, or soothing effect : GENTLE, MILD ⟨*soft* breezes⟩ **b** : not bright or glaring ⟨*soft* lighting⟩ **c** : pleasing to the ear : quiet in pitch or volume ⟨*soft* voices⟩ **d** : smooth or delicate in appearance or feel ⟨a *soft* silk⟩ 2 : demanding little effort : EASY ⟨a *soft* job⟩ 3 : sounding as in *ace* and *gem* — used of *c* and *g* 4 : gently or gradually curved or rounded : not harsh or jagged ⟨*soft* hills⟩ 5 **a** : having a mild gentle disposition : DOCILE **b** : showing sympathetic understanding ⟨took a *soft* stand toward the rebels⟩ 6 : lacking in strength : FEEBLE ⟨*soft* from easy living⟩ 7 : mentally weak 8 **a** : yielding to physical pressure ⟨a *soft* mattress⟩ ⟨*soft* metals such as lead⟩ **b** : not as hard as others of its kind 9 : free from substances (as calcium and magnesium salts) that prevent lathering of soap ⟨*soft* water⟩ 10 : occurring at such a speed and in such a way that a destructive crash is avoided ⟨a *soft* landing on the moon⟩ — **soft·ly** *adv* — **soft·ness** \'sȯf(t)-nəs\ *n*

²**soft** *adv* : in a soft manner

soft·ball \'sȯf(t)-ˌbȯl\ *n* : baseball played on a small diamond with a ball that is larger than a baseball and that is pitched underhand; *also* : the ball used in this game

soft–boiled \-'bȯi(ə)ld\ *adj* : lightly boiled so that the contents are soft ⟨*soft-boiled* eggs⟩

soft coal *n* : BITUMINOUS COAL

soft drink *n* : a sweet flavored beverage containing no alcohol; *esp* : SODA POP

soft·en \'sȯ-fən\ *vb* **soft·ened; soft·en·ing** \'sȯf-(ə-)niŋ\ 1 : to make or become soft or softer 2 : to lessen the strength of — **soft·en·er** \'sȯf-(ə-)nər\ *n*

soft·heart·ed \'sȯft-'härt-əd\ *adj* : MERCIFUL, SYMPATHETIC — **soft·heart·ed·ly** *adv* — **soft·heart·ed·ness** *n*

soft–serve \'sȯf(t)-ˌsərv\ *n* : smooth soft ice cream made in and dispensed from a freezer in which it is continuously churned

soft–shell \'sȯf(t)-ˌshel\ *or* **soft–shelled** \-'sheld\ *adj* : having a soft or fragile shell especially as a result of recent shedding ⟨*soft-shell* crabs⟩

soft–shoe \'sȯf(t)-'shü\ *n* : a form of stage dancing developed from tap dancing but done with soft-soled shoes and at a slower tempo and more relaxed rhythm

soft soap *n* 1 : a partly liquid soap 2 : FLATTERY 2

\ə\ **abut**	\aú\ **out**	\i\ **tip**	\ȯ\ **saw**	\ú\ **foot**
\ər\ **further**	\ch\ **chin**	\ī\ **life**	\ȯi\ **coin**	\y\ **yet**
\a\ **mat**	\e\ **pet**	\j\ **job**	\th\ **thin**	\yü\ **few**
\ā\ **take**	\ē\ **easy**	\ŋ\ **sing**	\th\ **this**	\yu̇\ **cure**
\ä\ **cot, cart**	\g\ **go**	\ō\ **bone**	\ü\ **food**	\zh\ **vision**

soft–soap \'sȯf(t)-'sōp\ *vb* : to soothe or coax with flattery — **soft–soap·er** *n*

soft·ware \'sȯf-ˌtwa(ə)r, -ˌtwe(ə)r\ *n* : the programs and related information used by a computer

soft wheat *n* : a wheat with soft kernels high in starch but usually low in protein

soft·wood \'sȯf-ˌtwu̇d\ *n* **1** : the wood of a tree (as a pine or fir) that produces cones as compared to that of a tree (as a maple) that is a broad-leaved flowering plant — compare HARDWOOD 1 **2** : a tree that produces softwood

softy *or* **soft·ie** \'sȯf-tē\ *n, pl* **soft·ies 1** : WEAKLING **2** : a silly or sentimental person

sog·gy \'säg-ē, 'sȯg-\ *adj* **sog·gi·er; -est** : heavy with water or moisture : SOAKED, SODDEN — **sog·gi·ly** \'säg-ə-lē, 'sȯg-\ *adv* — **sog·gi·ness** \'säg-ē-nəs, 'sȯg-\ *n*

¹soil \'sȯi(ə)l\ *vb* : to make or become dirty [Middle English *soilen* "to corrupt, make dirty," from early French *soiller* "to wallow," from *soil* "pigsty"]

²soil *n* **1 a** : SOILAGE, STAIN **b** : moral soilage : CORRUPTION **2** : something that soils or pollutes

³soil *n* **1** : firm land : EARTH **2** : the loose surface material of the earth in which plants grow **3** : ¹COUNTRY 2b, LAND **4** : an environment in which something may take root and grow ⟨slums are fertile *soil* for crime⟩ [Middle English *soil* "earth," from early French *soil* (same meaning), derived from Latin *solea* "sole, sandal, foundation timber"]

soil·age \'sȯi-lij\ *n* : the act of soiling : the state of being soiled

soil·less \'sȯi(ə)l-ləs\ *adj* : carried on without soil ⟨*soilless* agriculture⟩

soil science *n* : the science of soils

soil scientist *n* : a person who specializes in soil science

soi·ree *or* **soi·rée** \swä-'rā\ *n* : an evening party or social gathering

¹so·journ \'sō-jərn, sō-'jərn\ *n* : a temporary stay

²sojourn *vb* : to stay as a temporary resident : STOP ⟨*sojourned* for a month at a resort⟩ — **so·journ·er** *n*

¹sol \'sōl\ *n* : the fifth note of the musical scale [from Latin *sol* "the fifth note of the scale"]

²sol \'säl, 'sȯl\ *n, pl* **so·les** \'sō-ˌlās\ **1** : the basic unit of money of Peru **2** : a coin representing one sol [American Spanish, from Spanish, "sun," from Latin]

³sol \'säl, 'sȯl\ *n* : a colloid in which tiny solid particles are scattered throughout a liquid [derived from *sol*ution]

¹so·lace \'säl-əs *also* 'sōl-\ *n* **1** : comfort in times of grief or worry **2** : something that gives comfort

²solace *vb* **so·laced; so·lac·ing 1** : to give solace to : CONSOLE **2** : to make cheerful

so·lar \'sō-lər, -ˌlär\ *adj* **1** : of, derived from, relating to, or caused by the sun **2** : measured by the earth's course in relation to the sun ⟨*solar* time⟩ ⟨*solar* year⟩ **3 a** : produced or operated by the action of the sun's light or heat ⟨*solar* energy⟩ **b** : using the sun's rays especially to produce heat or electricity ⟨a *solar* house⟩ [Middle English *solar* "derived from or related to the sun," from Latin *solaris* (same meaning), from *sol* "sun" — related to SUNDAY; see *Word History* at SUNDAY]

solar cell *n* : a photoelectric cell that converts sunlight into electrical energy and is used as a power source

solar collector *n* : any of various devices for the absorption of solar radiation for the heating of water or buildings or the production of electricity

solar eclipse *n* : an eclipse of the sun by the moon

solar flare *n* : a sudden temporary outburst of energy from a small area of the sun's surface

so·lar·i·um \sō-'lar-ē-əm, sə-, -'ler-\ *n, pl* **-ia** \-ē-ə\ *also* **-i·ums** : a room exposed to the sun

solar panel *n* : a group of solar cells forming a flat surface (as on a spacecraft)

so·lar plexus \'sō-lər-\ *n* **1** : a network of nerves in the abdomen behind the stomach that contains ganglia sending nerve fibers to the internal organs of the abdomen **2** : the general area of the stomach below the sternum

solar system *n* : a star with the group of heavenly bodies that revolve around it; *esp* : the sun with the planets, moons, asteroids, and comets that orbit it

solar wind *n* : the continuous radiation of charged particles from the sun's surface

sold *past and past participle of* SELL

¹sol·der \'säd-ər, 'sȯd-\ *n* : a metal or a mixture of metals (as of lead and tin) used when melted to join metallic surfaces

²solder *vb* **sol·dered; sol·der·ing** \-(ə-)riŋ\ **1** : to unite or repair with solder **2** : to become joined or renewed by or as if by the use of solder — **sol·der·er** \-ər-ər\ *n*

soldering iron *n* : a usually electrical device used for soldering

¹sol·dier \'sōl-jər\ *n* **1 a** : a person in military service and especially in the army **b** : an enlisted person **2** : a worker in something strongly believed in **3** : a termite or ant with a large head and jaws that is a member of a caste that protects the colony — **sol·dier·ly** *adj*

²soldier *vb* **sol·diered; sol·dier·ing** \ˌsōlj-(ə-)riŋ\ : to serve as or act like a soldier

soldier of fortune : one who follows a military career wherever there is promise of profit, adventure, or pleasure

sol·diery \'sōlj-(ə-)rē\ *n* : a body of soldiers

¹sole \'sōl\ *n* **1** : the underside of a foot **2** : the part of footwear on which the sole of the foot rests [Middle English *sole* "the underside of the foot or shoe," from early French *sole* (same meaning), from Latin *solea* "sandal"] — **soled** \'sōld\ *adj*

²sole *vb* **soled; sol·ing** : to furnish with a sole ⟨*sole* shoes⟩

³sole *n* : any of various flatfishes that have a small mouth, small fins, and small closely set eyes and that include some fishes used for food [Middle English *sole* "a type of flatfish," from early French *sole* (same meaning), from Latin *solea* "sandal, a flatfish"]

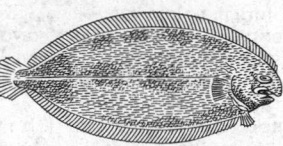

³sole

⁴sole *adj* **1** *archaic* : having no companion : ALONE **2 a** : having no sharer ⟨*sole* owner⟩ **b** : being the only one **3** : acting independently and without assistance or interference ⟨the *sole* judge⟩ **4** : belonging only to the one person, unit, or group named ⟨given *sole* authority⟩ [Middle English *sole* "alone," from early French *seul* (same meaning), from Latin *solus* "alone" — related to DESOLATE, SOLITUDE, SOLO] — **sole·ness** *n*

so·le·cism \'säl-ə-ˌsiz-əm, 'sō-lə-\ *n* **1** : an ungrammatical combination of words in a sentence **2** : a social blunder

sole·ly \'sō(l)-lē\ *adv* **1** : without another : SINGLY, ALONE **2** : ²ONLY 1a ⟨done *solely* for money⟩

sol·emn \'säl-əm\ *adj* : being serious and dignified in appearance or behavior *synonyms* see SERIOUS — **so·lem·ni·ty** \sə-'lem-nət-ē\ *n* — **sol·emn·ly** \'säl-əm-lē\ *adv*

sol·em·nize \'säl-əm-ˌnīz\ *vb* **-nized; -niz·ing 1** : to observe or honor with solemnity **2** : to perform with ceremony; *esp* : to unite in marriage with religious ceremony **3** : to make solemn : DIGNIFY — **sol·em·ni·za·tion** \ˌsäl-əm-nə-'zā-shən\ *n*

so·le·noid \'sō-lə-ˌnȯid, 'säl-ə-\ *n* : a coil of wire commonly in the form of a long cylinder that when carrying a current acts as a magnet so that a movable core is drawn into the coil when a current flows

soli *plural of* SOLO

so·lic·it \sə-'lis-ət\ *vb* **1** : ENTREAT, BEG; *esp* : to approach with a request or appeal **2** : to appeal for ⟨*solicited* the help of neighbors⟩ **3 a** : to lead especially into evil **b** : to approach for sinful purposes — **so·lic·i·ta·tion** \-ˌlis-ə-ˈtā-shən\ *n*

so·lic·i·tor \sə-ˈlis-ət-ər\ *n* **1** : one that solicits **2** : a British lawyer **3** : the chief law officer of a city, town, county, or government division

so·lic·i·tous \sə-ˈlis-ət-əs\ *adj* **1** : full of concern or fears : APPREHENSIVE **2** : very careful **3** : anxiously willing : EAGER — **so·lic·i·tous·ly** *adv*

so·lic·i·tude \sə-ˈlis-ə-ˌt(y)üd\ *n* **1** : the state of being solicitous : ANXIETY **2** : too much care or attention

¹sol·id \ˈsäl-əd\ *adj* **1 a** : not hollow **b** : written as one word ⟨a *solid* compound⟩ **2** : having, involving, or dealing with solids : CUBIC **2** ⟨a *solid* geometric shape⟩ **3 a** : not loose or spongy : COMPACT ⟨a *solid* mass of rock⟩ **b** : neither gaseous nor liquid ⟨*solid* ice⟩ ⟨*solid* waste⟩ **4** : of good sturdy quality or kind ⟨*solid* comfort⟩ ⟨*solid* reasons⟩ **5 a** : not interrupted ⟨for three *solid* hours⟩ **b** : being in complete agreement : UNANIMOUS, UNITED ⟨*solid* for pay increases⟩ **6 a** : thoroughly dependable : RELIABLE ⟨a *solid* citizen⟩ **b** : earnest or important in purpose ⟨*solid* reading⟩ **7** : of one material, kind, or color ⟨*solid* gold⟩ **synonyms** see HARD — **solid** *adv* — **sol·id·ly** *adv* — **sol·id·ness** *n*

²solid *n* **1** : a geometric figure or element (as a cube or a sphere) having three dimensions **2** : a solid substance : a substance that keeps its size and shape

sol·i·dar·i·ty \ˌsäl-ə-ˈdar-ət-ē\ *n* : unity (as of a group) that produces or is based on shared interests and goals

so·lid·i·fy \sə-ˈlid-ə-ˌfī\ *vb* **-fied; -fy·ing** : to make or become solid, compact, or hard

so·lid·i·ty \sə-ˈlid-ət-ē\ *n, pl* **-ties** **1** : the quality or state of being solid **2** : something solid

solid–state *adj* **1** : relating to the characteristics and structure of solid material **2** : using semiconductor devices rather than electron tubes ⟨a *solid-state* radio⟩

so·lil·o·quize \sə-ˈlil-ə-ˌkwīz\ *vb* **-quized; -quiz·ing** : to give a soliloquy : talk to oneself

so·lil·o·quy \sə-ˈlil-ə-kwē\ *n, pl* **-quies** **1** : the act of talking to oneself **2** : a dramatic speech that represents a series of unspoken thoughts

sol·i·taire \ˈsäl-ə-ˌta(ə)r, -ˌte(ə)r\ *n* **1** : a single gem (as a diamond) set alone **2** : a card game played by one person alone

¹sol·i·tary \ˈsäl-ə-ˌter-ē\ *adj* **1** : all alone ⟨a *solitary* traveler⟩ **2** : seldom visited : LONELY **3** : being the only one : SOLE ⟨*solitary* example⟩ **4** : growing or living alone : not forming part of a group or cluster ⟨flowers at the end of the stalk and *solitary*⟩ ⟨the *solitary* wasps⟩ — **sol·i·tari·ly** \ˌsäl-ə-ˈter-ə-lē\ *adv* — **sol·i·tari·ness** \ˈsäl-ə-ˌter-ē-nəs\ *n*

²solitary *n, pl* **-tar·ies** : one who lives or seeks to live a solitary life : RECLUSE, HERMIT

sol·i·tude \ˈsäl-ə-ˌt(y)üd\ *n* **1** : the quality or state of being alone or far-off from society : SECLUSION, LONELINESS **2** : a lonely place (as a desert) [Middle English *solitude* "the state of being alone," from early French *solitude* (same meaning), from Latin *solitudin-, solitudo* (same meaning), from *solus* "alone" — related to DESOLATE, ⁴SOLE, SOLO]

¹so·lo \ˈsō-lō\ *n, pl* **solos** **1** *or pl* **so·li** \ˈsō-lē\ : a piece of music written to be performed by one voice or one instrument **2** : an action in which there is only one performer [from Italian *solo* "a part in music performed without accompaniment," from *solo* (adjective) "alone," from Latin *solus* "alone" — related to DESOLATE, ⁴SOLE, SOLITUDE]

²solo *adv or adj* : without a companion : ALONE

³solo *vb* **so·loed; so·lo·ing** \-(ˌ)lō-iŋ, -lə-wiŋ\ : to perform by oneself; *esp* : to fly an airplane without one's instructor

so·lo·ist \ˈsō-lə-wəst, -(ˌ)lō-əst\ *n* : one who performs a solo

so·lon \ˈsō-lən, -ˌlän\ *n* **1** : a wise and skillful giver of a collection of laws **2** : a member of a legislative body

so long \sō-ˈlȯn\ *interj* — used to express good-bye or farewell

so long as *conj* **1** : during and up to the end of the time that : WHILE ⟨*so long as* you are here, I feel safe⟩ **2** : provided that ⟨you may go, *so long as* you behave yourself⟩

sol·stice \ˈsäl-stəs, ˈsōl-, -ˌstis\ *n* **1** : the point in the apparent path of the sun at which the sun is farthest north or south of the equator **2** : the time of the sun's passing a solstice which occurs on June 22nd and on December 22nd

sol·u·bil·i·ty \ˌsäl-yə-ˈbil-ət-ē\ *n* **1** : the quality or state of being soluble **2** : the amount of a substance that will dissolve in a given amount of another substance

sol·u·ble \ˈsäl-yə-bəl\ *adj* **1** : capable of being dissolved in a liquid ⟨sugar is *soluble* in water⟩ **2** : capable of being solved or explained : SOLVABLE ⟨a *soluble* problem⟩

so·lu·tion \sə-ˈlü-shən\ *n* **1 a** : an act or process of solving **b** : an answer to a problem : EXPLANATION **c** : SOLUTION SET **2 a** : an act or the process by which a solid, liquid, or gaseous substance is dissolved in a liquid **b** : a liquid in which something has been dissolved **c** : the condition of being dissolved

solution set *n* : a set of values that are solutions for an equation; *also* : TRUTH SET

solv·able \ˈsäl-və-bəl, ˈsȯl-\ *adj* : capable of being solved ⟨a *solvable* problem⟩

Sol·vay process \ˈsäl-ˌvā-\ *n* : a process for making sodium carbonate from common salt using carbon dioxide and ammonia

solve \ˈsälv, ˈsȯlv\ *vb* **solved; solv·ing** : to find a solution for ⟨*solve* a puzzle⟩

sol·ven·cy \ˈsäl-vən-sē, ˈsȯl-\ *n* : the quality or state of being solvent

¹sol·vent \ˈsäl-vənt, ˈsȯl-\ *adj* : able to pay all legal debts

²solvent *n* : a usually liquid substance capable of dissolving one or more other substances

so·mat·ic \sō-ˈmat-ik, sə-\ *adj* : of, relating to, or affecting the body especially as compared to the mind or the tissue producing the germ cells

somatic cell *n* : any cell of an animal or plant other than a germ cell

som·ber *or* **som·bre** \ˈsäm-bər\ *adj* **1** : so shaded as to be dark and gloomy **2** : ²MELANCHOLY 1, GRAVE ⟨a *somber* mood⟩ **3** : dull or dark colored — **som·ber·ly** *adv* — **som·ber·ness** *n*

som·bre·ro \səm-ˈbre(ə)r-ō, säm-\ *n, pl* **-ros** : a tall hat with a very wide brim worn especially in the Southwest and Mexico [from Spanish *sombrero* "a wide-brimmed hat," from *sombra* "shade"]

sombrero

¹some \ˈsəm, *for sense 2b* səm *without stress*\ *adj* **1** : being one unknown, unnamed, or unspecified unit or thing ⟨*some* person knocked⟩ **2 a** : being one, a part, or an unspecified number of something (as a class or group) named ⟨*some* birds can't fly⟩ **b** : being of an unspecified amount or number ⟨give me *some* water⟩ ⟨have *some* apples⟩ **3** : worthy of notice or consideration ⟨that was *some* party⟩

\ə\ **abut**	\au̇\ **out**	\i\ **tip**	\ȯ\ **saw**	\u̇\ **foot**
\ər\ **further**	\ch\ **chin**	\ī\ **life**	\ȯi\ **coin**	\y\ **yet**
\a\ **mat**	\e\ **pet**	\j\ **job**	\th\ **thin**	\yü\ **few**
\ā\ **take**	\ē\ **easy**	\ŋ\ **sing**	\t̲h̲\ **this**	\yu̇\ **cure**
\ä\ **cot, cart**	\g\ **go**	\ō\ **bone**	\ü\ **food**	\zh\ **vision**

²some \'səm\ *pron* **1** : a part or quantity of something ⟨*some* of the milk⟩ ⟨*some* of the apples⟩ **2** : an indefinite additional amount ⟨ran a mile and then *some*⟩

³some \'səm, ,səm\ *adv* **1** : reasonably close to : ABOUT ⟨*some* eighty houses⟩ **2 a** : ²SOMEWHAT ⟨felt *some* better⟩ **b** : to some degree ⟨the cut bled *some*⟩

-some \səm\ *adj suffix* **1** : having the quality or nature of the thing specified ⟨burden*some*⟩ **2** : causing a (specified) feeling or condition ⟨fear*some*⟩ [Old English *-sum* "having a particular quality, action, or effect"]

¹some·body \'səm-,bäd-ē, -bəd-\ *pron* : one or some person of no certain or known identity ⟨did *somebody* knock?⟩

²somebody *n* : a person of position or importance ⟨wanted to be *somebody*⟩

some·day \'səm-,dā\ *adv* : at some future time ⟨may *someday* travel the world⟩

some·how \-,haù\ *adv* : in one way or another ⟨we'll manage *somehow*⟩

some·one \-(,)wən\ *pron* : ¹SOMEBODY ⟨*someone* took my money⟩

some·place \-,plās\ *adv* : ¹SOMEWHERE 1 ⟨fell *someplace* over there⟩

¹som·er·sault \'səm-ər-,sólt\ *n* : a leap or roll in which a person turns heels over head [from early French *sombresaut* "somersault," derived from Latin *super* "over" and *saltus* "leap," from *salire* "to jump" — related to RESILIENT]

²somersault *vb* : to perform a somersault

¹som·er·set \'səm-ər-,set\ *n* : ¹SOMERSAULT

²somerset *vb* **-set·ed; -set·ing** : ²SOMERSAULT

¹some·thing \'səm(p)-thiŋ, *especially in rapid speech or for sense 2* 'səmp-ᵊm\ *pron* **1** : some unnamed or unspecified thing ⟨*something* must be done about it⟩ **2** : an important person or thing ⟨decided to make *something* of myself⟩ — **something else** : something or someone special or extraordinary

²something *adv* **1** : ²SOMEWHAT ⟨was *something* less than perfect⟩ **2** : ²VERY 1 ⟨snores *something* awful⟩

¹some·time \'səm-,tīm\ *adv* **1** : at some time in the future ⟨I'll do it *sometime*⟩ **2** : at some unspecified or uncertain point of time ⟨*sometime* last night⟩

²sometime *adj* : having been at an earlier time : FORMER, LATE ⟨*sometime* mayor⟩

some·times \'səm-,tīmz, (,)səm-'tīmz\ *adv* : at times : now and then : OCCASIONALLY ⟨speaks *sometimes* very fast⟩

some·way \'səm-,wā\ *also* **some·ways** \-,wāz\ *adv* : in some way : SOMEHOW ⟨tried to make him *someway* understand⟩

¹some·what \'səm-,(h)wät, -,(h)wət, (,)səm-'(h)wät, -'(h)wət\ *pron* : some unspecified part or amount : SOMETHING ⟨*somewhat* of what you say is true⟩

²somewhat *adv* : in some measure : SLIGHTLY ⟨*somewhat* comfortable⟩

¹some·where \'səm-,(h)we(ə)r, -,(h)wa(ə)r, -(,)(h)wər\ *adv* **1** : in, at, or to a place unknown or unspecified ⟨mentions it *somewhere*⟩ **2** : reasonably close to ⟨*somewhere* around nine o'clock⟩

²somewhere *n* : an unnamed place ⟨went to *somewhere* in France⟩

some·wheres \'səm-,(h)we(ə)rz, -,(h)wa(ə)rz, -(,)(h)wərz\ *adv, chiefly dialect* : ¹SOMEWHERE

som·no·lence \'säm-nə-lən(t)s\ *n* : the state of being sleepy or ready to fall asleep : DROWSINESS

som·no·lent \'säm-nə-lənt\ *adj* : showing signs of not being fully awake **synonyms** see SLEEPY

so much as *adv* : ³EVEN 5 ⟨nobody would *so much as* look at you⟩

son \'sən\ *n* **1 a** : a male offspring especially of human parents **b** : a human male descendant **2** *cap* : the second person of the Trinity **3** : a man or boy closely associated with or thought of as a child of something (as a country, race, or religion)

so·nar \'sō-,när\ *n* : a device for detecting the presence and location of submerged objects (as submarines) by sound waves

so·na·ta \sə-'nät-ə\ *n* : a piece of music written for instruments and usually having three or four main parts in different styles and different keys

song \'sóŋ\ *n* **1** : the act or art of singing **2** : poetical composition : POETRY **3** : a short piece of music with words intended to be sung **4** : a characteristic sound or series of sounds (as of a bird) **5 a** : a melody for a lyric poem or ballad **b** : a poem easily set to music **6** : a small amount ⟨can be bought for a *song*⟩

song·bird \-,bərd\ *n* : a bird that utters a series of musical tones

song·fest \'sóŋ-,fest\ *n* : an informal session of group singing of popular or folk songs

Song of Sol·o·mon \-'säl-ə-mən\ — see BIBLE table

Song of Songs — see BIBLE table

song sparrow *n* : a common sparrow of North America that is brownish above and mostly white below and is noted for its sweet cheerful song

song·ster \'sóŋ(k)-stər\ *n* **1** : a person that sings **2** : a book of songs

song·stress \'sóŋ(k)-strəs\ *n* : a woman who is a singer

song·writ·er \'sóŋ-,rīt-ər\ *n* : a person who composes words or music or both especially for popular songs

son·ic \'sän-ik\ *adj* : using, produced by, or relating to sound waves

sonic boom *n* : a sound like that of an explosion produced when a shock wave formed at the nose of an aircraft traveling at supersonic speed reaches the ground

son–in–law \'sən-ən-,lò\ *n, pl* **sons–in–law** \'sən-zən-\ : the husband of one's daughter

son·net \'sän-ət\ *n* : a poem of 14 lines usually rhyming by a fixed scheme

son·ne·teer \,sän-ə-'ti(ə)r\ *n* : a writer of sonnets

son·ny \'sən-ē\ *n* : a young boy — used chiefly as a term of address

so·nor·i·ty \sə-'nór-ət-ē, -'när-\ *n, pl* **-ties** : the quality or state of being sonorous : RESONANCE

so·no·rous \sə-'nór-əs, -'nór-; 'sän-ə-rəs\ *adj* **1** : producing sound (as when struck) **2** : full or loud in sound : RESONANT — **so·no·rous·ly** *adv*

soon \'sün, *especially New England* 'sùn\ *adv* **1** : before long : without delay ⟨*soon* after sunrise⟩ **2** : in a speedy way ⟨as *soon* as possible⟩ **3** *archaic* : before the usual time **4** : by choice ⟨would as *soon* do it now⟩

soot \'sùt, 'sət, 'süt\ *n* : a black powder formed when something is burned; *esp* : the fine powder consisting chiefly of carbon that colors smoke

sooth \'süth\ *n, archaic* : the quality or state of being true : TRUTH, REALITY

soothe \'süth\ *vb* **soothed; sooth·ing 1** : to please by or as if by attention or concern : PLACATE **2** : ALLEVIATE, RELIEVE ⟨the lotion *soothed* his sunburn⟩ **3** : to bring comfort : calm down ⟨music *soothes* the soul⟩

sooth·ing \'sü-thiŋ\ *adj* : tending to soothe ⟨*soothing* sounds⟩

sooth·say·er \'süth-,sā-ər\ *n* : a person who claims to foretell events — **sooth·say·ing** \-,sā-iŋ\ *n*

sooty \'sùt-ē, 'sət-, 'süt-\ *adj* **soot·i·er; -est 1 a** : of, relating to, or producing soot ⟨*sooty* fires⟩ **b** : soiled with soot ⟨*sooty* buildings⟩ **2** : of the color of soot ⟨*sooty* birds⟩ — **soot·i·ness** \-ē-nəs\ *n*

¹sop \'säp\ *n* **1** *chiefly dialect* : a piece of food dipped or soaked in a liquid (as bread dipped in milk or gravy) **2** : a bribe or gift for soothing or winning approval

²sop *vb* **sopped; sop·ping 1 a** : to soak or dip in or as if in liquid **b** : to wet thoroughly **2** : to mop or soak up ⟨*sopping* up gravy with bread⟩

soph·ism \'säf-,iz-əm\ *n* : a misleading argument that seems reasonable

soph·ist \'säf-əst\ *n* : one who argues by the use of sophisms

¹**so·phis·ti·cate** \sə-'fis-tə-ˌkāt\ *vb* **-cat·ed; -cat·ing** : to cause to become sophisticated — **so·phis·ti·ca·tion** \-ˌfis-tə-'kā-shən\ *n*

²**so·phis·ti·cate** \sə-'fis-ti-kət, -tə-ˌkāt\ *n* : a sophisticated person

so·phis·ti·cat·ed \sə-'fis-tə-ˌkāt-əd\ *adj* **1 a** : deprived of native or original plainness **b** : very complicated : COMPLEX ⟨*sophisticated* instruments⟩ **c** : WORLDLY-WISE, KNOWING ⟨a *sophisticated* young graduate⟩ **2 a** : finely experienced and aware ⟨a *sophisticated* observer⟩ **b** : appealing to one's intelligence ⟨a *sophisticated* novel⟩ — **so·phis·ti·cat·ed·ly** *adv*

soph·ist·ry \'säf-ə-strē\ *n* : reasoning or arguments typical of a sophist

soph·o·more \'säf-ˌmō(ə)r, -ˌmö(ə)r; 'säf-°m-ˌō(ə)r, -ˌȯ(ə)r\ *n* : a student in his or her second year at a 4-year high school or college

soph·o·mor·ic \ˌsäf-ə-'mōr-ik, -'mȯr-, -'mär-\ *adj* **1** : conceited and overconfident of knowledge but poorly informed and immature ⟨a *sophomoric* argument⟩ **2** : lacking in maturity, taste, or judgment ⟨*sophomoric* humor⟩

So·pho·ni·as \ˌsäf-ə-'nī-əs, ˌsō-fə-\ *n* : ZEPHANIAH

sop·ping \'säp-iŋ\ *adj* : thoroughly wet

sop·py \'säp-ē\ *adj* **sop·pi·er; -est 1** : soaked through **2** : very wet

¹**so·pra·no** \sə-'pran-ō, -'prän-\ *adj* **1** : relating to the soprano voice or part **2** : having a high range ⟨*soprano* sax⟩ [from Italian *soprano* "relating to a soprano or soprano part," from *sopra* "above," from Latin *supra* "above"]

²**soprano** *n, pl* **-nos 1** : the highest voice part in harmony for four parts with men's and women's voices — compare ALTO 1b, ²BASS 1a, TENOR 2a **2** : the highest singing voice of women or boys; *also* : a person with this voice

sor·bet \sȯr-'bā\ *n* : a fruit-flavored ice served especially as a dessert

sor·cer·er \'sȯrs-(ə-)rər\ *n* : a person who practices sorcery : WIZARD

sor·cer·ess \'sȯrs-(ə-)rəs\ *n* : a woman who practices sorcery : WITCH

sor·cery \'sȯrs-(ə-)rē\ *n* : the use of powers gotten with the help of or by the control of evil spirits : WITCHCRAFT

sor·did \'sȯrd-əd\ *adj* **1** : very dirty : FILTHY ⟨*sordid* surroundings⟩ **2** : VILE 1a ⟨a *sordid* life⟩ **3** : meanly greedy : COVETOUS — **sor·did·ly** *adv* — **sor·did·ness** *n*

¹**sore** \'sō(ə)r, 'sȯ(ə)r\ *adj* **sor·er; sor·est 1 a** : causing pain or distress ⟨a *sore* subject⟩ **b** : full of pain : TENDER ⟨*sore* muscles⟩ **c** : hurt or red and swollen so as to be or seem painful ⟨*sore* runny eyes⟩ **2** : accompanied by difficulties, hardship, or exertion ⟨in a *sore* situation⟩ **3** : ANGRY 1a ⟨my friend is *sore* at me⟩ — **sore·ness** *n*

²**sore** *n* **1** : a sore spot on the body; *esp* : one (as an ulcer) with the tissues broken and usually infected **2** : a cause of pain : AFFLICTION

³**sore** *adv* : SORELY

sore·head \'sō(ə)r-ˌhed, 'sȯ(ə)r-\ *n* : a person easily angered or discontented — **sorehead** *or* **sore·head·ed** \-'hed-əd\ *adj*

sore·ly \'sō(ə)r-lē, 'sȯ(ə)r-\ *adv* : in a sore manner

sore throat *n* : a throat that is painful because of inflammation

sor·ghum \'sȯr-gəm\ *n* **1** : any of a genus of Old World tropical grasses that look like corn; *esp* : one cultivated for grain, forage, or syrup **2** : syrup made from a sorghum

so·ror·i·ty \sə-'rȯr-ət-ē, -'rär-\ *n, pl* **-ties** : a club of women especially at a college

sorghum 1

[from Latin *sororitas* "sisterhood," from earlier *soror* "sister"]

¹**sor·rel** \'sȯr-əl, 'sär-\ *n* **1** : a brownish orange to light brown **2** : a sorrel-colored animal; *esp* : a light reddish brown horse often with cream mane and tail

²**sorrel** *n* : any of various plants (as dock or wood sorrel) with sour juice

¹**sor·row** \'sär-ō, 'sȯr-\ *n* **1 a** : sadness felt after a loss (as of something loved) **b** : a cause of grief or sadness **2** : a display of grief or sadness

    synonyms SORROW, GRIEF, WOE mean distress of mind. SORROW suggests a feeling that something has been lost and often feelings of guilt and regret ⟨expressed *sorrow* for having caused the accident⟩. GRIEF stresses feeling great sorrow usually for a special reason ⟨their *grief* when their pet died⟩. WOE suggests feeling hopeless and miserable ⟨all my troubles left me in a state of *woe*⟩.

²**sorrow** *vb* : to feel or express sorrow : GRIEVE

sor·row·ful \'sär-ō-fəl, 'sȯr-, -ə-fəl\ *adj* **1** : full of or showing sorrow ⟨a *sorrowful* good-bye⟩ **2** : expressive of or causing sorrow ⟨*sorrowful* eyes⟩ — **sor·row·ful·ly** \-f(ə-)lē\ *adv*

sor·ry \'sär-ē, 'sȯr-\ *adj* **sor·ri·er; -est 1** : feeling sorrow or regret **2** : MOURNFUL 2, SAD **3** : causing sorrow, pity, or scorn : WRETCHED — **sor·ri·ness** \-ē-nəs\ *n*

¹**sort** \'sȯ(ə)rt\ *n* **1 a** : a group of persons or things that have something in common : CLASS **b** : PERSON 1, INDIVIDUAL ⟨not a bad *sort*⟩ **2 a** *archaic* : method or manner of acting : WAY, MANNER **b** : general disposition : NATURE ⟨people of an evil *sort*⟩ — **all sorts of** : many different : all kinds of ⟨knows *all sorts of* people⟩ — **of sorts** *or* **of a sort** : of an unimportant or just average kind ⟨a poet *of sorts*⟩ — **out of sorts 1** : somewhat ill **2** : easily angered : IRRITABLE

²**sort** *vb* **1** : to separate and arrange by kind or class : CLASSIFY ⟨*sort* mail⟩ ⟨*sort* out socks by color⟩ **2** : AGREE 6, SUIT ⟨our views *sort* poorly with theirs⟩ **3** : SEARCH ⟨*sort* through some old papers⟩ — **sort·er** *n*

sor·tie \'sȯrt-ē, sȯr-'tē\ *n* : a sudden rushing out of troops from a position of defense against the enemy : SALLY — **sortie** *vb*

sort of \ˌsȯrt-ə(v), -ər\ *adv* : to a moderate degree : SOMEWHAT ⟨acted *sort of* wild⟩

so·rus \'sōr-əs, 'sȯr-\ *n, pl* **so·ri** \'sō(ə)r-ˌī, 'sȯ(ə)r-, -ˌē\ : any of the dots on the underside of a fertile fern frond consisting of a cluster of spores

SOS \ˌes-(ˌ)ō-'es, ˌes-ə-'wes\ *n* **1** : an international radio code distress signal used by ships and aircraft calling for help **2** : a call for help

¹**so-so** \'sō-'sō\ *adv* : fairly well : TOLERABLY, PASSABLY ⟨played the violin only *so-so*⟩

²**so-so** *adj* : neither very good nor very bad ⟨a *so-so* performance⟩

sot \'sät\ *n* : DRUNKARD

sot·to vo·ce \ˌsät-ō-'vō-chē\ *adv or adj* **1** : in a whisper; *also* : in private **2** : very softly ⟨play the last part *sotto voce*⟩ [from Italian *sottovoce*, literally, "under the voice"]

sou \'sü\ *n* : a French bronze coin of the period before 1914 worth 5 centimes

soubriquet *variant of* SOBRIQUET

¹**souf·flé** \sü-'flā, 'sü-ˌflā\ *n* : a delicate spongy hot dish lightened in baking by stiffly beaten egg whites ⟨cheese *soufflé*⟩ [derived from French *soufflé*, past participle of *souffler* "to blow up, inflate"]

\ə\ **abut**	\au̇\ **out**	\i\ **tip**	\ȯ\ **saw**	\u̇\ **foot**
\ər\ **further**	\ch\ **chin**	\ī\ **life**	\ȯi\ **coin**	\y\ **yet**
\a\ **mat**	\e\ **pet**	\j\ **job**	\th\ **thin**	\yü\ **few**
\ā\ **take**	\ē\ **easy**	\ŋ\ **sing**	\<u>th</u>\ **this**	\yu̇\ **cure**
\ä\ **cot, cart**	\g\ **go**	\ō\ **bone**	\ü\ **food**	\zh\ **vision**

²**soufflé** or **souf·fléed** \-'flād, -₁flād\ adj : puffed by or in cooking ⟨*soufflé* omelet⟩

sough \'saů, 'səf\ vb : to make a moaning or sighing sound — **sough** n

sought past and past participle of SEEK

¹**soul** \'sōl\ n **1** : the spiritual part of a person believed to give life to the body and in many religions thought to live forever **2 a** : the necessary part of something **b** : a person who leads or stirs others to action : LEADER ⟨the *soul* of the campaign⟩ **3 a** : the part of one's personality having to do with feelings and the sense of what is right and wrong ⟨felt my *soul* rebel against injustice⟩ **b** : spiritual force : FERVOR **4** : PERSON ⟨a kind *soul*⟩ **5 a** : a strong positive feeling conveyed especially by black American performers **b** : SOUL MUSIC — **souled** \'sōld\ adj

²**soul** adj **1** : of or relating to black Americans or their culture ⟨*soul* food⟩ **2** : designed for or controlled by blacks ⟨*soul* radio stations⟩

soul·ful \'sōl-fəl\ adj : full of or expressing feeling ⟨*soulful* music⟩ — **soul·ful·ly** \-fə-lē\ adv — **soul·ful·ness** n

soul·less \'sōl-ləs\ adv : having no soul or no greatness or nobleness of mind or feeling — **soul·less·ly** adv

soul music n : music that originated in black American gospel singing, is closely related to rhythm and blues, and is characterized by intensity of feeling and earthiness

soul–search·ing \'sōl-₁sər-chiŋ\ n : examination of one's conscience and especially one's reasons and values

¹**sound** \'saůnd\ adj **1 a** : not diseased or weak : HEALTHY ⟨a *sound* mind in a *sound* body⟩ **b** : free from imperfection or rot **2** : ¹SOLID 4, FIRM ⟨a building of *sound* construction⟩ **3** : not faulty : VALID, RIGHT ⟨a *sound* argument⟩ **4 a** : THOROUGH 1 ⟨a *sound* revenge⟩ **b** : not disturbed ⟨a *sound* sleep⟩ **c** : SEVERE 3 ⟨a *sound* beating⟩ **5** : showing good judgment or sense ⟨*sound* advice⟩ [Old English *gesund* "free from injury or disease"] — **sound·ly** \'saůn-(d)lē\ adv — **sound·ness** \'saůn(d)-nəs\ n

²**sound** adv : to the full extent : THOROUGHLY ⟨*sound* asleep⟩

³**sound** n **1 a** : the sensation of hearing **b** : a particular impression obtained by hearing : NOISE, TONE **c** : the energy of vibration that causes the sensation of hearing **2 a** : one of the noises that together make up human speech ⟨the *sound* of "th" in "this"⟩ **b** : a series of spoken noises **3 a** : meaningless noise **b** : the suggestion carried or given by something heard or said ⟨the excuse has a suspicious *sound*⟩ **4** : hearing distance : EARSHOT ⟨within *sound* of my voice⟩ [Middle English *soun* "a sound, something that can be heard," from early French *son* (same meaning), from Latin *sonus* "a sound" — related to UNISON]

⁴**sound** vb **1 a** : to make or cause to make a sound **b** : RESOUND ⟨the auditorium *sounded* with applause⟩ **c** : RESOUND 2 ⟨cheers are *sounding* throughout the gymnasium⟩ **d** : to give a signal by sound ⟨the bugle *sounds* to battle⟩ **2** : PRONOUNCE 3a ⟨*sound* each word clearly⟩ **3** : to put into words : VOICE **4 a** : to make known : PROCLAIM **b** : to order, signal, or indicate by a sound ⟨*sound* the alarm⟩ **5** : to make or give an impression especially when heard ⟨*sounds* incredible⟩

⁵**sound** n : a long passage of water that is wider than a strait and often connects two larger bodies of water or forms a channel between the mainland and an island [Old English *sund* "a sea, swimming"]

⁶**sound** vb **1 a** : to measure the depth of (as with a sounding line) : FATHOM **b** : to look into or investigate the possibility **2** : to try to find out the views or intentions of : PROBE ⟨*sounded* me out on the idea⟩ **3** : to dive down suddenly ⟨a *sounding* whale⟩ [Middle English *sounden* "to measure the depth of," from early French *sonder* (same meaning), from *sonde* "a line used for measuring depths"; probably of Germanic origin]

sound barrier n : the sudden large increase in resistance that the air offers to an aircraft nearing the speed of sound

sound·board \'saůn(d)-₁bō(ə)rd, -₁bó(ə)rd\ n **1** : a thin board under the strings of a musical instrument (as a piano) that vibrates slightly from the sound made by the strings and serves to strengthen the sound given off by the instrument **2** : SOUNDING BOARD 1

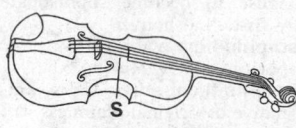

S soundboard 1

sound effects n pl : effects that imitate sounds called for in the script of a play, radio or television program, or motion picture

sound·er \'saůn-dər\ n : one that sounds; esp : a device for making soundings

sound·ing \'saůn-diŋ\ n **1 a** : measurement of depth especially with a sounding line **b** : the depth found by sounding **2** : an investigation, test, or sampling of opinion or intention

sounding board n **1** : a structure behind or over a speaker's platform to make sound uttered from it clear **2** : a means for helping to spread opinions **3** : a person or group on whom new ideas or opinions are tested

sounding line n : a line, wire, or cord weighted at one end for sounding

sound·less \'saůn-(d)ləs\ adj : making no sound : SILENT — **sound·less·ly** adv

sound off vb **1** : to count while marching **2** : to voice one's opinions freely with force

sound pollution n : NOISE POLLUTION

sound·proof \'saůn(d)-'prüf\ adj : designed to prevent sound from entering or leaving — **soundproof** vb

sound track n : the area on a motion-picture film that carries the sound record

sound truck n : a truck equipped with a loudspeaker

sound waves n pl : waves formed by compression of the material (as air) through which they travel regardless of whether they can be heard

soup \'süp\ n **1** : a liquid food with a meat, fish, or vegetable stock as a base and often containing pieces of solid food **2** : something like or suggesting soup (as a heavy fog) [from early French *supe* "soup"; of Germanic origin]

souped–up \'süpt-'əp\ adj : improved or increased in power, performance, or appeal ⟨a *souped-up* car⟩ — **soup up** vb

soupy \'sü-pē\ adj **soup·i·er; -est 1** : resembling soup **2** : thickly foggy or cloudy

¹**sour** \'saů(ə)r\ adj **1** : having or being an acid or tart taste that is one of the four taste sensations — compare BITTER 1 ³SALT 1b ¹SWEET 1b **2 a** : having become acid through spoiling ⟨*sour* milk⟩ **b** : indicating decay : PUTRID ⟨a *sour* odor⟩ **3** : UNPLEASANT, DISAGREEABLE ⟨a *sour* look⟩ ⟨played a *sour* note⟩ **4** : acid in reaction ⟨*sour* soil⟩ — **sour·ly** adv — **sour·ness** n

²**sour** n **1 a** : something sour **b** : the basic taste sensation produced by acid stimuli **2** : a cocktail made with liquor, lemon or lime juice, sugar, and sometimes soda water

³**sour** vb : to become or make sour

sour ball n : a round piece of hard candy having a sour flavor

source \'sō(ə)rs, 'só(ə)rs\ n **1 a** : a force that gives rise to something : CAUSE ⟨a *source* of strength⟩ **b** : a point where something begins **c** : a person or a publication that supplies information **2** : the beginning of a stream of water ⟨the *source* of the Nile⟩ **3** : a firsthand document or main reference work

sour cherry *n* : a small cherry tree widely grown for its soft tart bright red to nearly black fruits; *also* : its fruit

sour cream *n* : a thick cream soured by the addition of a special kind of bacterium and used especially in cooking

sour·dough \'saů(ə)r-ˌdō\ *n* **1** : a dough in which fermentation is active and which is used to start fermentation in other dough (as in making bread) **2** : an old-time prospector in Alaska or northwestern Canada

sour grapes *n pl* : the act of making something seem unimportant after it becomes impossible to gain

sou·sa·phone \'sü-zə-ˌfōn\ *n* : a large circular tuba that goes over the player's shoulder and has a wide bell that faces forward [named for John Philip *Sousa* 1854–1932 American band leader and composer]

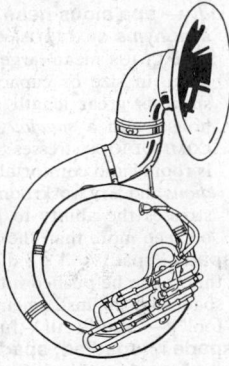
sousaphone

¹souse \'saůs\ *vb* **soused;** **sous·ing 1** : ²PICKLE **2 a** : to plunge in liquid : IMMERSE **b** : to wet thoroughly : DRENCH **3** : to make or become drunk

²souse *n* **1** : something pickled; *esp* : seasoned and chopped meat trimmed from pork, fish, or shellfish **2** : an act of sousing : WETTING **3** : DRUNKARD

¹south \'saůth\ *adv* : to or toward the south

²south *adj* **1** : situated toward or at the south (the *south* entrance) **2** : coming from the south (a *south* wind)

³south *n* **1 a** : the direction to the right of one facing east **b** : the compass point opposite to north **2** *cap* : regions or countries south of a point that is mentioned or understood; *esp* : the southeastern part of the U.S.

south·bound \'saůth-ˌbaůnd\ *adj* : headed south (a *southbound* train)

¹south·east \saů-'thēst, *nautical* saů-'ēst\ *adv* : to or toward the southeast

²southeast *n* **1** : the direction between south and east **2** *cap* : regions or countries southeast of a point that is mentioned or understood

³southeast *adj* **1** : situated toward or at the southeast (the *southeast* corner) **2** : coming from the southeast (a *southeast* wind)

south·east·er \saů-'thē-stər, saů-'ē-\ *n* : a storm, strong wind, or gale coming from the southeast

south·east·er·ly \saů-'thē-stər-lē, saů-'ē-\ *adv or adj* **1** : from the southeast **2** : toward the southeast

south·east·ern \saů-'thē-stərn, saů-'ē-\ *adj* **1** *often cap* : of, relating to, or characteristic of the Southeast **2** : lying toward or coming from the southeast

South·east·ern·er \saů-'thē-stə(r)-nər, saů-'ē-\ *n* : a person born or living in a southeastern region (as of the U.S.)

south·east·ward \saů-'thēs-twərd, saů-'ēs-\ *adv or adj* : toward the southeast — **south·east·wards** \-twərdz\ *adv*

south·er·ly \'səth-ər-lē\ *adv or adj* **1** : toward the south **2** : coming from the south

south·ern \'səth-ərn\ *adj* **1** *cap* : of, relating to, or characteristic of the South **2** : lying toward or coming from the south — **south·ern·most** \-ˌmōst\ *adj*

Southern Cross *n* : four bright stars in the southern hemisphere that are placed as if at the ends of a cross; *also* : the group of stars of which these four are the brightest

South·ern·er \'səth-ə(r)-nər\ *n* : a person born or living in the South (as of the U.S.)

southern hemisphere *n, often cap S&H* : the half of the earth that lies south of the equator

southern lights *n pl* : AURORA AUSTRALIS

south·land \'saůth-ˌland, -lənd\ *n, often cap* : land in the south : the south of a country or region

south·paw \'saůth-ˌpȯ\ *n* : a left-handed person; *esp* : a left-handed baseball pitcher — **southpaw** *adj*

south pole *n* **1** *often cap S&P* : the southernmost point of the earth : the southern end of the earth's axis **2** : the pole of a magnet that points toward the south

south–seeking pole *n* : SOUTH POLE 2

south·ward \'saůth-wərd\ *adv or adj* : toward the south — **south·wards** \-wərdz\ *adv*

¹south·west \saůth-'west, *nautical* saů-'west\ *adv* : to or toward the southwest

²southwest *n* **1** : the direction between south and west **2** *cap* : regions or countries southwest of a point that is mentioned or understood

³southwest *adj* **1** : coming from the southwest (a *southwest* wind) **2** : situated toward or at the southwest (the *southwest* corner)

south·west·er \saů(th)-'wes-tər\ *n* : a storm or wind from the southwest

south·west·er·ly \saů(th)-'wes-tər-lē\ *adv or adj* **1** : from the southwest **2** : toward the southwest

south·west·ern \saů(th)-'wes-tərn\ *adj* **1** : lying toward or coming from the southwest **2** *often cap* : of, relating to, or characteristic of the Southwest

South·west·ern·er \saů(th)-'wes-tə(r)-nər\ *n* : a person born or living in a southwestern region (as of the U.S.)

south·west·ward \saů(th)-'wes-twərd\ *adv or adj* : toward the southwest — **south·west·wards** \-twərdz\ *adv*

sou·ve·nir \'sü-və-ˌni(ə)r, ˌsü-və-'ni(ə)r\ *n* : something that serves as a reminder : MEMENTO

sou'·west·er \saů-'wes-tər\ *n* **1** : a long waterproof coat worn especially at sea during stormy weather **2** : a waterproof hat with a wide slanting brim longer in back than in front

sou'wester 2

¹sov·er·eign \'säv-(ə-)rən, 'säv-ərn, 'səv-\ *n* **1** : a person, body of persons, or a state possessing sovereignty; *esp* : a monarch exercising supreme authority in a state **2** : an old British gold coin

²sovereign *adj* **1** : ¹CHIEF 2, HIGHEST (a citizen's *sovereign* duty) **2** : supreme in power or authority (a *sovereign* ruler) **3** : politically independent : AUTONOMOUS (a *sovereign* state)

sov·er·eign·ty \'säv-(ə-)rən-tē, 'säv-ərn-, 'səv-\ *n, pl* **-ties** **1 a** : supreme power especially over a politically organized unit : DOMINION **b** : freedom from outside control : AUTONOMY **c** : the condition of being sovereign or a sovereign **2** : one (as a country) that is sovereign

so·vi·et \'sōv-ē-ˌet, 'säv-, -ē-ət\ *n* **1 a** : an elected governing council in the Union of Soviet Socialist Republics **2** *pl, cap* : the people and especially the political and military leaders of the Union of Soviet Socialist Republics [from Russian *sovet* "council"] — **soviet** *adj, often cap*

\ə\ abut	\aů\ out	\i\ tip	\ȯ\ saw	\ů\ foot
\ər\ further	\ch\ chin	\ī\ life	\ȯi\ coin	\y\ yet
\a\ mat	\e\ pet	\j\ job	\th\ thin	\yü\ few
\ā\ take	\ē\ easy	\ŋ\ sing	\th\ this	\yů\ cure
\ä\ cot, cart	\g\ go	\ō\ bone	\ü\ food	\zh\ vision

so·vi·et·ize \'sōv-ē-ˌet-ˌīz, 'säv-, -ē-ət-\ *vb* **-ized; -iz·ing** *often cap* **1** : to bring under Soviet control **2** : to force to be like the Soviets — **so·vi·et·iza·tion** \ˌsōv-ē-ˌet-ə-'zā-shən, ˌsäv-ē-, -ət-\ *n, often cap*

¹sow \'saú\ *n* : an adult female hog; *also* : the adult female of various other animals (as a bear)

²sow \'sō\ *vb* **sowed; sown** \'sōn\ *or* **sowed; sow·ing 1 a** : to plant seed for growth especially by scattering **b** : ¹PLANT 1a **c** : to scatter with or as if with seed **d** : to put into a selected environment : DISTRIBUTE **2** : to set in motion : FOMENT ⟨*sowing* the seeds of suspicion⟩ **3** : to spread over a wide area : DISPERSE, DISSEMINATE — **sow·er** \'sō(-ə)r\ *n*

sow·bel·ly \'saú-ˌbel-ē\ *n* : fat salt pork or bacon

sow bug \'saú-\ *n* : WOOD LOUSE; *esp* : a wood louse capable of curling itself into a ball

sox *plural of* SOCK

soy \'sói\ *n* **1** : SOY SAUCE **2** : SOYBEAN

soya \'sói-(y)ə\ *n* : SOYBEAN

soy·bean \'sói-'bēn, -ˌbēn\ *n* : a hairy annual Asian plant of the legume family widely grown for its edible seeds rich in oil and proteins, as food for livestock, and for soil improvement; *also* : its seed

soy sauce *n* : a brown sauce made from soybeans and used especially in Chinese and Japanese cooking

spa \'spä, 'spó\ *n* **1 a** : a mineral spring **b** : a resort area with mineral springs **2** : a commercial establishment (as a resort) offering programs and equipment devoted especially to health, fitness, weight loss, beauty, or relaxation [named for *Spa*, a place in Belgium that has a natural mineral spring and health resort]

¹space \'spās\ *n* **1** : a period of time **2 a** : a limited extent in one, two, or three dimensions : DISTANCE, AREA, VOLUME **b** : an area set apart or available ⟨parking *space*⟩ ⟨floor *space*⟩ **3** : the limitless three-dimensional extent in which all things exist and move **4** : the region beyond the earth's atmosphere **5** : a blank area separating words or lines **6** : an available seat on a public vehicle

²space *vb* **spaced; spac·ing** : to place with space between ⟨*space* out the chairs one foot apart⟩

space–age \'spā-ˌsāj\ *adj* : of or relating to the age of space exploration; *esp* : ¹MODERN 1 ⟨*space-age* technology⟩

space cadet *n* : a person who is confused, forgetful, or very inattentive

space·craft \'spā-ˌskraft\ *n, pl* **spacecraft** : a vehicle for travel beyond the earth's atmosphere

space·flight \'spās-ˌflīt\ *n* : flight beyond the earth's atmosphere

space heater *n* : an usually portable device for heating a small area

space·man \'spā-ˌsman, -smən\ *n* **1** : one who travels outside the earth's atmosphere **2** : a visitor to earth from outer space

space medicine *n* : a branch of medicine concerned with the effects of spaceflight on the human body

space opera *n* : science fiction that deals with fantastic situations involving space travelers and beings from other worlds [from *space* and *opera*, following the pattern of *soap opera, horse opera* — see *Word History* at HORSE OPERA]

space out *vb* : to become inattentive or distracted ⟨*spaced out* halfway through the lecture⟩

space·port \'spā-ˌspō(ə)rt, -ˌspó(ə)rt\ *n* : a place for testing and launching spacecraft

space·ship \'spās-ˌship, 'spāsh-\ *n* : SPACECRAFT

space shuttle *n* : a spacecraft designed to transport people and cargo between earth and space that can be used repeatedly

space station *n* : an artificial satellite designed to stay in orbit permanently and to be occupied by humans for long periods

space suit *n* : a suit equipped to make life in space possible for its wearer

space walk *n* : a period of movement in space outside a spacecraft by an astronaut

space suit

spac·ing \'spā-siŋ\ *n* **1** : an arrangement in space **2** : the distance between any two objects in an arranged series

spa·cious \'spā-shəs\ *adj* : large or vast in size or capacity — **spa·cious·ly** *adv* — **spa·cious·ness** *n*

synonyms SPACIOUS, COMMODIOUS, CAPACIOUS mean larger than the average in size or capacity. SPACIOUS suggests great length and width ⟨a house with a *spacious* front lawn⟩. COMMODIOUS stresses that something is roomy and comfortable ⟨a *commodious* and airy workroom⟩. CAPACIOUS stresses the ability to hold, contain, or keep more than the average ⟨a *capacious* closet⟩.

¹spade \'spād\ *n* **1** : a digging tool like a shovel made so that it can be pushed into the ground with the foot **2** : a spade-shaped instrument [Old English *spadu* "a digging tool"] — **spade·ful** \-ˌfúl\ *n*

²spade *vb* **spad·ed; spad·ing** : to dig with or use a spade

³spade *n* **1** : a black figure resembling an inverted heart with a short stem at the bottom used to indicate a suit of playing cards **2** : a card of the suit of spades [from Italian *spada* or Spanish *espada*, both meaning "broad sword" and both from Latin *spatha* "blade"]

spade·work \'spād-ˌwərk\ *n* **1** : work done with the spade **2** : the hard plain work that must be done at the beginning of a project

spa·ghet·ti \spə-'get-ē\ *n* : a food made chiefly of a mixture of flour and water dried in the form of thin solid strings

Word History The Italian word *spago* means "cord, string." The suffix *-etto* in Italian, like the suffix *-ette* in English, means "little one." Added together, *spago* and *-etto* become *spaghetto*, which means "little string." "Little string" describes very well the shape of a strand of spaghetti. The word *spaghetti* is actually the plural form of *spaghetto*. [from Italian *spaghetti* "pasta made in long strings," from *spaghetti*, plural of *spaghetto* "little string," from *spago* "string"]

spaghetti strap *n* : very thin fabric shoulder strap

spake \'spāk\ *archaic past of* SPEAK

¹spam \'spam\ *n* : unsolicited usually commercial e-mail sent to a large number of addresses

²spam *vb* : to send spam to — **spam·mer** *n*

¹span \'span\ *n* **1** : the distance from the end of the thumb to the end of the little finger of a spread hand; *also* : an English unit of length equal to 9 inches (about 22.9 centimeters) **2 a** : a limited portion of time ⟨*span* of life⟩ **b** : the spread (as of an arch) from one support to another **c** : the portion supported to form a span [Old English *spann* "distance measured by the outstretched hand"]

²span *vb* **spanned; span·ning 1 a** : to measure by or as if by the hand with fingers and thumb extended **b** : ²MEASURE 2 **2 a** : to reach or extend across ⟨a bridge *spans* the river⟩ ⟨a career that *spans* four decades⟩ **b** : to place or construct a span over

³span *n* : a pair of animals (as mules) driven together [from Dutch *span* "a pair of animals driven together," derived from earlier *spannen* "to hitch up"]

span·dex \'span-ˌdeks\ *n* : any of various synthetic elastic textile fibers

¹span·gle \'spaŋ-gəl\ *n* **1** : a small piece of shining metal or plastic used for ornamentation on clothing **2** : a small glittering object

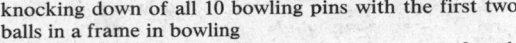

²spangle *vb* **span·gled; span·gling** \'spaŋ-g(ə-)liŋ\ : to set or sprinkle with or as if with spangles

Span·glish \'spaŋ-glish, -lish\ *n* : Spanish marked by many borrowings from English; *also* : any of various combinations of Spanish and English

Span·iard \'span-yərd\ *n* : a person born or living in Spain

span·iel \'span-yəl\ *n* : a member of any of several breeds of small or medium-sized mostly short-legged dogs that usually have long wavy hair and large drooping ears

spaniel

Span·ish \'span-ish\ *n* **1** : the Romance language of Spain and of the countries colonized by Spaniards **2 Spanish** *pl* : the people of Spain — **Spanish** *adj*

Spanish American *n* **1** : a person born or living in one of the countries of America in which Spanish is the national language **2** : a person living in the U.S. whose native language is Spanish and whose culture is of Spanish origin — **Spanish–American** *adj*

Spanish moss *n* : a plant related to the pineapple that forms hanging tufts of grayish green threadlike strands on trees from the southern U.S. to Argentina

Spanish moss

Spanish omelet *n* : an omelet made usually with chopped green pepper, onion, and tomato

Spanish rice *n* : rice cooked with onions, green peppers, and tomatoes

spank \'spaŋk\ *vb* : to strike on the buttocks with the open hand — **spank** *n*

¹spank·ing \'spaŋ-kiŋ\ *adj* : BRISK 1, LIVELY ⟨a *spanking* breeze⟩

²spanking *adv* : ²VERY 2 ⟨a *spanking* clean floor⟩ ⟨*spanking* new⟩

span·ner \'span-ər\ *n, chiefly British* : ²WRENCH 2

¹spar \'spär\ *n* **1** : a stout pole **2** : a long rounded usually wood or metal piece (as a mast, boom, or yard) to which a sail is fastened [Middle English *sparre* "a stout pole, a pole used to support a sail on a ship"]

²spar *vb* **sparred; spar·ring** **1** : to box or make boxing movements with the fists for practice or in fun **2** : ²SKIRMISH 1 [Middle English *sparren* "to dart, spring"]

¹spare \'spa(ə)r, 'spe(ə)r\ *vb* **spared; spar·ing** **1** : to keep from being punished or harmed : show mercy ⟨*spared* the prisoners⟩ **2** : to free of the need to do something ⟨*spare* yourself the trouble⟩ **3** : to hold off from doing or spending ⟨*spare* no cost⟩ **4** : to use or give out in small amounts ⟨more pancakes, please, and don't *spare* the syrup⟩ **5 a** : to give up as not really needed ⟨can you *spare* me a few minutes⟩ ⟨couldn't *spare* a dime⟩ **b** : to have left over ⟨got there with time to *spare*⟩ [Old English *sparian* "to refrain from harming"]

²spare *adj* **spar·er; spar·est** **1** : held in reserve ⟨a *spare* tire⟩ **2** : being over what is needed ⟨*spare* time⟩ **3** : not generous or wasteful : SPARING **4** : somewhat thin **5** : not abundant or plentiful : SCANTY [Middle English *spare* "being extra or more than is needed"] — **spare·ly** *adv* — **spare·ness** *n*

³spare *n* **1** : a spare or duplicate piece or part **2** : the

knocking down of all 10 bowling pins with the first two balls in a frame in bowling

spare·ribs \'spa(ə)r-ˌ(r)ibz, 'spe(ə)r-\ *n pl* : a cut of pork ribs separated from the bacon strips [derived from a German dialect word *ribbesper* "pickled pork ribs roasted on a spit," derived from *ribbe* "rib" and *sper* "spear, spit"; probably spelled *spareribs* in English because of the misunderstanding of the meaning of the German word *sper*]

spar·ing \'spa(ə)r-iŋ, 'spe(ə)r-\ *adj* : careful in the use of money or supplies — **spar·ing·ly** \-iŋ-lē\ *adv*

¹spark \'spärk\ *n* **1 a** : a small bit of a burning material **b** : a hot glowing bit struck from a mass **2** : a short bright flash of electricity between two points **3** : ²SPARKLE 1 **4** : a small amount that could grow into something larger ⟨still has a *spark* of decency⟩ [Old English *spearca* "spark"]

²spark *vb* **1** : to give off or cause to give off sparks **2** : to cause to get going ⟨the question *sparked* quite an argument⟩ ⟨*sparked* the team to victory⟩

³spark *vb* : WOO 1, COURT [from earlier *spark* (noun) "a foolish young man, boyfriend"] — **spark·er** *n*

sparking plug *n, British* : SPARK PLUG 1

¹spar·kle \'spär-kəl\ *vb* **spar·kled; spar·kling** \-k(ə-)liŋ\ **1 a** : to throw out sparks **b** : to give off small flashes of light ⟨the diamond *sparkled*⟩ **2** : to do or play very well ⟨*sparkled* at shortstop⟩ **3** : EFFERVESCE 1 ⟨*sparkling* wine⟩ **4** : to become lively or active ⟨the conversation *sparkled*⟩

²sparkle *n* **1** : a little flash of light **2** : the quality of sparkling **3** : the quality or state of being effervescent

spar·kler \'spär-klər\ *n* **1** : DIAMOND 1b **2** : a firework that throws off very bright sparks as it burns

spark plug *n* **1** : a device used in an engine to produce a spark that ignites a fuel mixture **2** : one that begins something or drives something forward

sparky \'spär-kē\ *adj* **spark·i·er; -est** : being lively and active ⟨*sparky* children⟩ — **spark·i·ly** \-kə-lē\ *adv*

sparred *past and past participle of* SPAR

sparring *present participle of* SPAR

sparring partner *n* : a person with whom a boxer spars for practice during training

spar·row \'spar-ō\ *n* **1** : any of several small songbirds that have usually brownish or grayish feathers and are related to the finches; *esp* : HOUSE SPARROW **2** : any of numerous finches (as the song sparrow) that resemble the true sparrows

spark plug 1

sparrow hawk *n* : any of various small hawks

sparse \'spärs\ *adj* **spars·er; spars·est** : of few and scattered elements; *esp* : not thickly grown or settled **synonyms** see MEAGER — **sparse·ly** *adv* — **sparse·ness** *n* — **spar·si·ty** \'spär-sət-ē\ *n*

¹Spar·tan \'spärt-ᵊn\ *n* **1** : a person born or living in ancient Sparta **2** : a person of great courage and self-discipline

²Spartan *adj* **1** : of or relating to Sparta in ancient Greece **2** *often not cap* **a** : marked by strict self-discipline or self-denial ⟨a *Spartan* athlete⟩ **b**

sparrow hawk

\ə\ abut	\au̇\ out	\i\ tip	\o̊\ saw	\u̇\ foot
\ər\ further	\ch\ chin	\ī\ life	\o̊i\ coin	\y\ yet
\a\ mat	\e\ pet	\j\ job	\th\ thin	\yu̇\ few
\ā\ take	\ē\ easy	\ŋ\ sing	\th\ this	\yu̇\ cure
\ä\ cot, cart	\g\ go	\ō\ bone	\ü\ food	\zh\ vision

: marked by absence of comfort and luxury ⟨a *Spartan* room⟩ — **spar·tan·ly** *adv*

spasm \'spaz-əm\ *n* **1** : a sudden uncontrolled contracting of muscles ⟨back *spasms*⟩ **2** : a sudden violent and temporary effort, emotion, or outburst ⟨a *spasm* of creativity⟩ — **spasm** *vb*

spas·mod·ic \spaz-'mäd-ik\ *adj* **1 a** : relating to or affected or characterized by spasm ⟨*spasmodic* movements⟩ **b** : resembling a spasm especially in sudden violence **2** : acting or going now and then : INTERMITTENT ⟨*spasmodic* activity⟩ **3** : subject to outburst of emotional excitement : EXCITABLE — **spas·mod·i·cal·ly** \-'mäd-ik(ə-)lē\ *adv*

spas·tic \'spas-tik\ *adj* : of, relating to, characterized by, or affected with or as if with spasms ⟨*spastic* colon⟩

¹spat \'spat\ *past and past participle of* SPIT

²spat *n, pl* **spat** *or* **spats** : a young oyster [origin unknown]

³spat *n* : a cloth or leather covering for the instep and ankle [a shortened form of *spatterdash* "a protective covering for the ankle or leg"]

⁴spat *n* **1** : a brief unimportant quarrel : DISPUTE **2** : a sound like that of rain falling in large drops

⁵spat *vb* **spat·ted; spat·ting 1** : to have a spat : QUARREL **2** : to strike with a sound like that of rain falling in large drops

spate \'spāt\ *n* : a sudden flood or rush

spa·tial \'spā-shəl\ *adj* : of or relating to space — **spa·tial·ly** \'spāsh-(ə-)lē\ *adv*

¹spat·ter \'spat-ər\ *vb* **1** : to splash with drops or small bits of something wet ⟨*spatter* the paper with paint⟩ **2** : to scatter by splashing ⟨*spattered* mud all over my coat⟩

²spatter *n* **1** : the act or sound of spattering **2** : a drop or splash spattered on something : a spot or stain due to spattering

spat·u·la \'spach-ə-lə\ *n* : an instrument with a thin flexible blade used especially for spreading or mixing soft substances or lifting

spav·in \'spav-ən\ *n* : a swelling of the hock of a horse associated with strain

spav·ined \'spav-ənd\ *adj* **1** : affected with spavin **2** : old and decrepit

¹spawn \'spón, 'spän\ *vb* **1** : to deposit or fertilize eggs ⟨fish swimming upstream to *spawn*⟩ **2** : to produce young especially in large numbers **3** : GENERATE, BRING FORTH — **spawn·er** *n*

²spawn *n* **1** : the eggs of aquatic animals (as fishes or oysters) that lay many small eggs **2** : PRODUCT 2, OFFSPRING; *also* : something produced in large quantities

spay \'spā\ *vb* : to remove the ovaries and uterus of (a female animal)

speak \'spēk\ *vb* **spoke** \'spōk\; **spo·ken** \'spō-kən\; **speak·ing 1** : to utter words : TALK **2** : to utter in words ⟨*speak* the truth⟩ **3** : to mention in speech or writing ⟨*spoke* of being ill⟩ **4** : to serve as spokesperson ⟨*spoke* for the group⟩ **5** : to express feelings in ways other than by words ⟨actions *speak* louder than words⟩ **6** : to use or be able to use in talking ⟨*speaks* Spanish⟩ — **speak·able** \'spē-kə-bəl\ *adj* — **to speak of** : worth mentioning or noticing ⟨no improvement *to speak of*⟩

speak·easy \'spē-,kē-zē\ *n, pl* **-eas·ies** : a place where alcoholic drinks are illegally sold

speak·er \'spē-kər\ *n* **1** : a person who speaks **2** : a person who conducts a meeting (as of a legislature) **3** : LOUDSPEAKER

speak·er·ship \'spē-kər-,ship\ *n* : the position of speaker of a legislature

speak out *vb* **1** : to speak loudly and clearly **2** : to speak freely and confidently ⟨was never afraid to *speak out* on the issues⟩

speak up *vb* : SPEAK OUT

¹spear \'spi(ə)r\ *n* **1** : a weapon with a long straight handle and sharp head or blade used for throwing or jabbing **2** : an instrument with a sharp point and curved hooks used in spearing fish **3** : SPEARMAN

²spear *vb* : to pierce or strike with or as if with a spear — **spear·er** *n*

³spear *n* : a usually young blade, shoot, or sprout (as of grass)

spear·fish \'spi(ə)r-,fish\ *vb* : to fish with a spear

spear·gun \-,gən\ *n* : a gun that shoots a spear and is used for spearfishing

¹spear·head \-,hed\ *n* **1** : the head or point of a spear **2** : a person, thing, or group that is the leading force (as in a development or attack)

²spearhead *vb* : to serve as leader of ⟨*spearhead* a campaign for better schools⟩

spear·man \'spi(ə)r-mən\ *n* : a soldier armed with a spear

spear·mint \-,mint, -mənt\ *n* : a common mint grown for flavoring and especially for its fragrant oil

spec \'spek\ *n* : SPECIFICATION 2a — usually used in plural

¹spe·cial \'spesh-əl\ *adj* **1 a** : being unusual and especially better in some way ⟨a *special* occasion⟩ **b** : being very dear or liked very well ⟨a *special* friend⟩ **2** : different from others of the same kind : UNIQUE ⟨a *special* case⟩ **3** : being or having more than the usual : ADDITIONAL, EXTRA ⟨a *special* edition⟩ **4** : designed for a certain purpose or occasion ⟨a *special* diet⟩ — **spe·cial·ly** \'spesh-(ə-)lē\ *adv*

²special *n* **1** : one that is used for a special service or occasion ⟨caught the commuter *special* to work⟩ **2** : something (as a television program) that is not part of a regular series **3** : a featured dish at a restaurant ⟨the *specials* of the day⟩

spearmint

special delivery *n* : delivery of mail by messenger for an extra fee

special education *n* : classes or instruction designed for students with special educational needs

spe·cial·ist \'spesh-(ə-)ləst\ *n* **1** : a person who studies or works at a special occupation or branch of learning ⟨an eye *specialist*⟩ **2** : an enlisted person in the army with a rank similar to that of corporal — **specialist** *or* **spe·cial·is·tic** \,spesh-ə-'lis-tik\ *adj*

spe·ci·al·i·ty \,spesh-ē-'al-ət-ē\ *n, pl* **-ties** : SPECIALTY

spe·cial·i·za·tion \,spesh-(ə-)lə-'zā-shən\ *n* **1** : a making or becoming specialized **2 a** : a change in the structure of a body part so that it becomes suited for performing a particular function or of a whole plant or animal so that it is suited for life in a particular environment **b** : a body part or an organism changed by specialization

spe·cial·ize \'spesh-ə-,līz\ *vb* **-ized; -iz·ing 1** : to limit one's attention or energy to one business, subject, or study **2** : to undergo specialization

specialized *adj* **1** : characterized by or exhibiting biological specialization **2** : designed, trained, or fitted for one particular purpose or occupation

special relativity *n* : RELATIVITY 2a

spe·cial·ty \'spesh-əl-tē\ *n, pl* **-ties 1** : a product of a special kind or of special excellence ⟨eggs were the cook's *specialty*⟩ **2** : something a person specializes in or has special knowledge of

spe·ci·a·tion \,spē-shē-'ā-shən, -sē-\ *n* : the formation of a new species (as that occurring as a result of isolation in a geographic area)

spe·cie \'spē-shē, -sē\ *n* : money in coin

spe·cies \'spē-shēz, -sēz\ *n, pl* **species 1** : a class of things of the same kind and with the same name : KIND **2** : a category of living things that ranks below a genus, is made up of related individuals able to produce fertile offspring, and is identified by a two-part scientific name

¹**spe·cif·ic** \spi-'sif-ik\ *adj* **1** : relating to or being an example of a certain kind of thing ⟨a *specific* case⟩ ⟨was the question *specific* or general?⟩ **2 a** : restricted to a particular individual, situation, effect, or reaction ⟨a disease *specific* to humans⟩ ⟨a *specific* enzyme⟩ **b** : having one particular effect or influence (as on a body part or a disease) ⟨quinine is *specific* for malaria⟩ **3** : clearly and exactly presented or stated ⟨gave them *specific* directions⟩ **4** : of, relating to, or being a species — **spe·cif·i·cal·ly** \-'sif-i-k(ə-)lē\ *adv*

²**specific** *n* **1** : something specially adapted to a purpose or use; *esp* : a drug or remedy specific for a particular disease **2** *pl* : things that are specific : DETAILS, PARTICULARS ⟨get down to *specifics*⟩

spec·i·fi·ca·tion \,spes-(ə-)fə-'kā-shən\ *n* **1** : the act or process of specifying **2 a** : a description of work to be done or materials to be used — usually used in plural ⟨the architect's *specifications* for a new building⟩ **b** : a single specified item

specific gravity *n* : the ratio of the density of a substance to the density of some other substance (as water) taken as a standard when both densities are obtained by weighing in air

specific heat *n* : the heat in calories required to raise the temperature of one gram of a substance one degree Celsius

spec·i·fic·i·ty \,spes-ə-'fis-ət-ē\ *n* : the quality or condition of being specific; *esp* : the condition of taking part in or of acting as a catalyst in only one or a few chemical reactions ⟨the *specificity* of an enzyme⟩

spec·i·fy \'spes-ə-,fī\ *vb* **-fied; -fy·ing 1** : to name or mention exactly and clearly ⟨*specify* the cause⟩ **2** : to include in a specification ⟨*specify* oak flooring⟩

spec·i·men \'spes-(ə-)mən\ *n* **1** : a part or a single thing that shows what the whole thing or group is like : SAMPLE **2** : a portion of material for use in testing or examination ⟨a blood *specimen*⟩ **3** : PERSON 1, INDIVIDUAL ⟨he's a tough *specimen*⟩

spe·cious \'spē-shəs\ *adj* : having a false look of being fair, just, or right ⟨a *specious* argument⟩ — **spe·cious·ly** *adv* — **spe·cious·ness** *n*

¹**speck** \'spek\ *n* **1** : a small spot or blemish **2** : a very small amount : BIT ⟨just a *speck* more milk⟩

²**speck** *vb* : to make specks on or in

¹**speck·le** \'spek-əl\ *n* : a small mark (as of color)

²**speckle** *vb* **speck·led; speck·ling** \'spek-(ə-)liŋ\ : to mark with speckles

specs \'speks\ *n pl* : ¹GLASS 2b

spec·ta·cle \'spek-ti-kəl\ *n* **1 a** : an unusual or impressive public display **b** : an object of curious or annoyed attention ⟨made a *spectacle* of yourself at the party⟩ **2** *pl* : ¹GLASS 2b [Middle English *spectacle* "spectacle," from early French *spectacle* (same meaning), from Latin *spectaculum* (same meaning), from *spectare* "to watch," from *specere* "to look, look at" — related to AUSPICE, EXPECT]

spec·ta·cled \'spek-ti-kəld\ *adj* **1** : having or wearing glasses **2** : having markings that look like a pair of glasses ⟨a *spectacled* bear⟩

spec·tac·u·lar \spek-'tak-yə-lər, spək-\ *adj* : of, relating to, or being a spectacle : exciting to see : SENSATIONAL ⟨a *spectacular* sunset⟩ — **spec·tac·u·lar·ly** *adv*

spec·ta·tor \'spek-,tāt-ər, spek-'tāt-\ *n* : a person who looks on (as at a sports event) — **spectator** *adj*

spec·ter *or* **spec·tre** \'spek-tər\ *n* **1** : GHOST **2** : something that bothers the mind

spec·tral \'spek-trəl\ *adj* **1** : of, relating to, or suggesting a specter : GHOSTLY **2** : of, relating to, or made by a spectrum

spec·tro·graph \'spek-t(r)ə-,graf\ *n* : an instrument for spreading radiation (as of light or sound) into a spectrum and photographing or mapping the spectrum

spec·trom·e·ter \spek-'träm-ət-ər\ *n* **1** : an instrument for producing a spectrum **2** : an instrument that spreads particles or radiation into an ordered sequence (as by mass or energy)

spec·tro·pho·tom·e·ter \,spek-trō-fə-'täm-ət-ər\ *n* : an instrument for measuring the strengths of the light in different parts of a spectrum

spec·tro·scope \'spek-trə-,skōp\ *n* : an instrument that produces spectra from or by the use of electromagnetic waves (as of light) — **spec·tros·co·py** \spek-'träs-kə-pē\ *n*

spec·trum \'spek-trəm\ *n, pl* **spec·tra** \-trə\ *or* **spec·trums 1 a** : the group of different colors including red, orange, yellow, green, blue, indigo, and violet arranged in the order of their wavelengths and seen when white light passes through a prism and falls on a surface or when sunlight is scattered by water droplets to form a rainbow **b** : ELECTROMAGNETIC SPECTRUM **2** : a continuous range or series ⟨a wide *spectrum* of interests⟩

spec·u·late \'spek-yə-,lāt\ *vb* **-lat·ed; -lat·ing 1** : to think or wonder about a subject ⟨*speculating* about the future⟩ **2** : to engage in a business deal in which much profit may be made although at a big risk — **spec·u·la·tor** \-,lāt-ər\ *n*

spec·u·la·tion \,spek-yə-'lā-shən\ *n* **1** : thoughts or guesses about something ⟨much *speculation* about who the new teacher would be⟩ **2** : the taking of a big risk in business in hopes of making a big profit

spec·u·la·tive \'spek-yə-lət-iv, -,lāt-\ *adj* **1 a** : of or relating to mental speculation ⟨*speculative* knowledge⟩ **b** : CURIOUS 1 ⟨a *speculative* glance⟩ **2** : of or relating to financial speculation — **spec·u·la·tive·ly** *adv*

spec·u·lum \'spek-yə-ləm\ *n, pl* **-la** \-lə\ *also* **-lums** : an instrument that is inserted into a bodily passage in order to help in inspection or the giving of medicine

speech \'spēch\ *n* **1** : the communication or expression of thoughts in spoken words **2 a** : something that is spoken **b** : a public talk **3** : a form of communication (as a language or dialect) used by a particular group **4** : the power of expressing or communicating thoughts by speaking

speech·less \'spēch-ləs\ *adj* **1** : unable to speak **2** : not speaking for a time : SILENT ⟨*speechless* with surprise⟩ — **speech·less·ly** *adv* — **speech·less·ness** *n*

¹**speed** \'spēd\ *n* **1 a** : the act or state of moving swiftly : SWIFTNESS **b** : rate of motion : VELOCITY **2** : quickness in movement or action **3** : a transmission gear in motor vehicles or bicycles ⟨a 10-*speed* bicycle⟩ **4** : METHAMPHETAMINE; *also* : a related drug — **up to speed** : operating at full effectiveness or capability

²**speed** *vb* **sped** \'sped\ *or* **speed·ed; speed·ing 1 a** : to move or cause to move fast **b** : to go or drive at too high a speed **2** : to increase the speed of : ACCELERATE — often used with *up*

speed·boat \'spēd-,bōt\ *n* : a fast motorboat

speed bump *n* : a low raised ridge across a roadway (as in a parking lot) to limit vehicle speed

speed dial *n* : a telephone function by which a stored number can be dialed by pressing only one key — **speed–dial** *vb*

speed·er \'spēd-ər\ *n* : a person who drives faster than the legal speed limit

speed limit *n* : the highest or lowest speed allowed by law in a certain area

speed of light *n* : a fundamental physical constant that is the speed at which electromagnetic radiation travels in a

\ə\ **abut**	\au̇\ **out**	\i\ **tip**	\ȯ\ **saw**	\u̇\ **foot**
\ər\ **further**	\ch\ **chin**	\ī\ **life**	\ȯi\ **coin**	\y\ **yet**
\a\ **mat**	\e\ **pet**	\j\ **job**	\th\ **thin**	\yu̇\ **few**
\ā\ **take**	\ē\ **easy**	\ŋ\ **sing**	\th\ **this**	\yu̇\ **cure**
\ä\ **cot, cart**	\g\ **go**	\ō\ **bone**	\ü\ **food**	\zh\ **vision**

vacuum and that has a value of 299,792,458 meters per second

speed·om·e·ter \spi-'däm-ət-ər\ *n* **1** : an instrument that measures speed **2** : an instrument that both measures speed and records distance traveled

speed–read·ing \'spēd-ˌrēd-iŋ\ *n* : a method of reading rapidly by skimming

speed·ster \'spēd-stər\ *n* : one that goes or can go very fast

speed·way \'spēd-ˌwā\ *n* : a racetrack for racing cars or motorcycles

speedy \'spēd-ē\ *adj* **speed·i·er; -est** : moving or taking place fast — **speed·i·ly** \'spēd-ᵊl-ē\ *adv* — **speed·i·ness** \'spēd-ē-nəs\ *n*

spe·le·ol·o·gy \ˌspē-lē-'äl-ə-jē, ˌspel-ē-\ *n* : the scientific study or exploration of caves — **spe·le·o·log·i·cal** \-ə-'läj-i-kəl\ *adj* — **spe·le·ol·o·gist** \-'äl-ə-jist\ *n*

¹**spell** \'spel\ *n* **1 a** : a spoken word or form of words believed to have magic power **b** : a state of enchantment **2** : a very strong influence or attraction [Old English *spell* "talk, tale"]

²**spell** *vb* : to put under a spell : BEWITCH

³**spell** *vb* **spelled** \'speld\; **spell·ing** : to take the place of for a time : RELIEVE ⟨if we *spell* each other we won't get tired⟩ [Old English *spelian* "to take the place of, relieve"]

⁴**spell** *vb* **spelled** \'speld, 'spelt\; **spell·ing 1 a** : to name, write, or print the letters of in order **b** : to be the letters of ⟨"c-a-t" *spells* "cat"⟩ **2** : to amount to : MEAN ⟨what you do could *spell* the difference between life and death⟩ ⟨that usually *spells* trouble⟩ [Middle English *spellen* "to mean, signify, read by spelling out letters," from early French *espeleir* (same meaning); of Germanic origin]

⁵**spell** *n* **1** : one's turn at work or duty **2** : a period spent in a job or occupation **3 a** : a short period of time **b** : a stretch of a specified type of weather ⟨a hot *spell*⟩ **4** : a period of bodily or mental distress or disorder : ATTACK, FIT ⟨a *spell* of coughing⟩ ⟨fainting *spells*⟩ [probably an altered form of Old English *spale* "a substitute"; the spelling probably influenced in Middle English by the similar word *spelen* "to substitute for, relieve"]

spell·bind \'spel-ˌbīnd\ *vb* **-bound** \-ˌbaund\; **-bind·ing** : to hold by or as if by a spell : FASCINATE

spell·bind·er \'spel-ˌbīn-dər\ *n* **1** : a very powerful speaker **2** : one that compels attention

spell·bound \'spel-'baund\ *adj* : held by or as if by a spell

spell–checker *n* : a computer program that identifies possible misspellings in a block of text by comparing the text with a database of accepted spellings — **spell–check** \'spel-ˌchek\ *vb*

spell·er \'spel-ər\ *n* **1** : a person who spells words especially in a certain way ⟨a poor *speller*⟩ **2** : a book with exercises for teaching spelling

spell·ing \'spel-iŋ\ *n* : the forming of words from letters; *also* : the letters composing a word

spelling bee *n* : a spelling contest in which each contestant who spells a word wrong is eliminated

spell out *vb* **1** : to make very plain ⟨each one's duties were *spelled out* in detail⟩ **2** : to write or print in letters and in full ⟨numbers are to be *spelled out*⟩

spelt \'spelt\ *chiefly British past and past participle of* SPELL

spe·lunk·er \spi-'ləŋ-kər, 'spē-ˌləŋ-\ *n* : a person who makes a hobby of exploring or studying caves — **spe·lunk·ing** \-kiŋ\ *n*

spend \'spend\ *vb* **spent** \'spent\; **spend·ing 1** : to pay out : EXPEND **2** : to cause or allow (as time) to pass ⟨*spent* the day with friends⟩ **3 a** : ¹EXHAUST 1, WEAR OUT **b** : to use wastefully : SQUANDER — **spend·er** *n*

spend·able \'spen-də-bəl\ *adj* : available for spending

spending money *n* : money for small personal expenses

spend·thrift \'spen(d)-ˌthrift\ *n* : one who spends wastefully — **spendthrift** *adj*

spent \'spent\ *adj* **1** : used up **2** : drained of energy

sperm \'spərm\ *n, pl* **sperm** *or* **sperms 1** : SEMEN **2** : a mobile male gamete that has a long and thin or rounded head and a long thin tail that acts as a flagellum — called also *spermatozoon, sperm cell*

sper·ma·ce·ti \ˌspər-mə-'sēt-ē, -'set-\ *n* : a waxy solid obtained from the oil of some sea-dwelling mammals and especially the sperm whale and used mostly in the past in ointments, cosmetics, and candles

sper·ma·tid \'spər-mət-əd\ *n* : any of the cells produced in meiosis that form sperm cells

sper·ma·to·gen·e·sis \(ˌ)spər-ˌmat-ə-'jen-ə-səs\ *n, pl* **-e·ses** \-ə-ˌsēz\ : the process of male gamete formation including meiosis and formation of sperm cells

sper·ma·to·phyte \(ˌ)spər-'mat-ə-ˌfīt\ *n* : any of a group of plants that produce seeds and include the gymnosperms and flowering plants

sper·ma·to·zo·on \(ˌ)spər-ˌmat-ə-'zō-ən, ˌspər-mət-\ *n, pl* **-zoa** \-'zō-ə\ : SPERM 2

sperm cell *n* : SPERM 2

sper·mi·cide \'spər-mə-ˌsīd\ *n* : a preparation or substance (as in a contraceptive) used to kill sperm

sperm whale *n* : a large toothed whale with a large chamber in the skull that contains a fluid mixture of spermaceti and oil

sperm whale

¹**spew** \'spyü\ *vb* : to send or come out in a flood or gush

²**spew** *n* : matter that is spewed out

sphag·num \'sfag-nəm\ *n* **1** : any of a large genus of mosses that usually grow in wet areas (as bogs) and become compacted with other plant matter to form peat **2** : a mass of sphagnum plants

sphere \'sfi(ə)r\ *n* **1 a** : a globe-shaped body : BALL, GLOBE **b** : a solid geometric shape whose surface is made up of all the points that are an equal distance from the point that is the shape's center **c** : the surface of a sphere **2** : a field of influence or activity ⟨the public *sphere*⟩ — **sphe·ric·i·ty** \sfir-'is-ət-ē\ *n*

spher·i·cal \'sfir-i-kəl, 'sfer-\ *adj* : relating to or having the form of a sphere or part of a sphere — **spher·i·cal·ly** \-k(ə-)lē\ *adv*

spher·oid \'sfi(ə)r-ˌoid, 'sfe(ə)r-\ *n* : a figure resembling a flattened sphere

sphinc·ter \'sfiŋ(k)-tər\ *n* : a ringlike muscle surrounding a body opening that is able to make the opening smaller or close it

sphinx \'sfiŋ(k)s\ *n, pl* **sphinx·es** *or* **sphin·ges** \'sfin-ˌjēz\ : an ancient Egyptian image having the body of a lion and the head of a man, ram, or hawk

sphinx moth *n* : HAWK MOTH

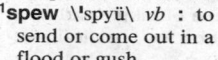

sphinx

sphyg·mo·ma·nom·e·ter \ˌsfig-mō-mə-'näm-ət-ər\ *n* : an instrument for measuring blood pressure

¹**spice** \'spīs\ *n* **1** : a plant product (as pepper or nutmeg) that has a strong pleasant smell and is used to season or flavor food **2** : something that adds interest ⟨variety is the *spice* of life⟩ **3** : a fragrant odor : PERFUME

²**spice** *vb* **spiced; spic·ing** : to season with or as if with spices

spice–bush \'spīs-ˌbush\ *n* : a fragrant shrub of the eastern U.S. and Canada that is related to the laurels and has clusters of small greenish yellow flowers and usually red berries

spick–and–span or **spic–and–span** \‚spik-ən-'span\ *adj*
1 : quite new and unused **2** : very clean and neat ⟨kept
the cabin *spick-and-span*⟩

spic·ule \'spik-yü(ə)l\ *n* : a small hard needlelike structure; *esp* : one of the tiny calcium- or silica-containing
bodies that support the tissues of various invertebrates
and especially sponges

spicy \'spī-sē\ *adj* **spic·i·er; -est 1** : flavored with or containing spice **2** : somewhat shocking or indecent ⟨a *spicy*
story⟩ — **spic·i·ly** \-sə-lē\ *adv* — **spic·i·ness** \-sē-nəs\ *n*

spi·der \'spīd-ər\ *n* **1** : any of an order of arachnids that
have two or more pairs of abdominal organs for spinning
threads of silk used in making cocoons for their eggs,
nests for themselves, or webs for catching their prey **2** : a
cast-iron frying pan

spider crab *n* : any of numerous crabs with very long legs
and nearly triangular bodies

spider mite *n* : any of various mites that spin webs and
include some that attack plants — called also *red spider*

spider plant *n* : any of several plants that are related to
the lilies, have long narrow leaves and hanging stems often producing small plants at the end, and are often
grown as houseplants

spi·der·web \'spīd-ər-‚web\ *n* : the silken web spun by
most spiders and used as a resting place and a trap for
small prey

spi·dery \'spīd-ə-rē\ *adj* **1** : resembling a spider; *also*
: long and thin like the legs of a spider **2** : resembling a
spiderweb ⟨*spidery* handwriting⟩ ⟨*spidery* lace⟩ **3** : full of
spiders

spied *past and past participle of* ¹SPY

¹spiel \'spē(ə)l\ *vb* : to talk in a fast, smooth, and usually
colorful manner — **spiel·er** \'spē-lər\ *n*

²spiel *n* : fast smooth usually colorful talk often intended
to sell something

spies *plural of* ²SPY

spiffy \'spif-ē\ *adj* **spiff·i·er; -est** : fine looking : SMART ⟨a
spiffy sports jacket⟩

spig·ot \'spig-ət, 'spik-ət\ *n* **1** : a plug used to stop the
vent in a barrel **2** : FAUCET

¹spike \'spīk\ *n* **1** : a very
large nail **2 a** : one of the
metal objects set in the sole
and heel of a shoe (as a
baseball shoe) to prevent
slipping **b** *pl* : a pair of
shoes having spikes **3** : an
unbranched antler of a
young deer **4** : the act or
an instance of spiking (as in volleyball) **5** : a pointed element (as in a graph) [Middle English *spike* "a large nail";
probably of Scandinavian origin]

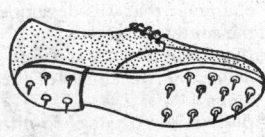

¹spike 2a

²spike *vb* **spiked; spik·ing 1** : to fasten or furnish with
spikes **2** : to pierce or cut with or on a spike **3** : to add
alcoholic liquor to a drink **4** : to drive (as a volleyball)
sharply downward **5** : to increase sharply ⟨battery sales
spiked after the storm⟩

³spike *n* **1** : an ear of grain **2** : a long usually rather narrow cluster in which the blossoms grow close
to the central stem [Middle English *spik* "a head of a stalk
of grain, ear," from Latin *spica* (same meaning)]

spiked \'spīkt\ *adj* **1** : having sharp points **2** : arranged in
stiff clumps ⟨*spiked* hair⟩

spike·let \'spī-klət\ *n* : one of the small few-flowered
spikes that occur in grasses and sedges

spike·nard \'spīk-‚närd\ *n* : a North American herb with a
fragrant root and clusters of small whitish flowers

spiky *also* **spikey** \'spī-kē\ *adj* **spik·i·er; -est** : of, relating
to, or characterized by spikes ⟨*spiky* barbed wire⟩ —
spik·i·ness \-kē-nəs\ *n*

spile \'spī(ə)l\ *n* : a spout inserted in a tree to draw off sap

¹spill \'spil\ *vb* **spilled** \'spild, 'spilt\ *also* **spilt** \'spilt\;
spill·ing 1 : to cause (blood) to flow by wounding or
killing **2 a** : to cause or allow to fall, flow, or run out by
accident ⟨*spilled* some flour on the floor⟩ **b** : to fall or
run out so as to be lost or wasted ⟨the milk *spilled*⟩ **c** : to
spread beyond limits ⟨crowds *spilled* into the streets⟩ **3**
: to throw off or out ⟨a horse *spilled* its rider⟩ **4** : to let
out : GIVE AWAY ⟨*spilled* the secret⟩ — **spill·able** \'spil-
ə-bəl\ *adj* — **spill·er** *n* — **spill one's guts** : to make
known especially personal information — **spill the
beans** : to give a secret away by talking without thinking

²spill *n* **1 a** : an act or instance of spilling **b** : a fall from a
horse or vehicle **2** : something spilled ⟨cleaning up an oil
spill⟩

spill·age \'spil-ij\ *n* **1** : the act or process of spilling **2**
: the quantity that spills

spill·way \'spil-‚wā\ *n* : a passage for extra water to run
over or around a dam

¹spin \'spin\ *vb* **spun** \'spən\; **spin·ning 1** : to draw out
and twist into yarn or thread ⟨*spun* the fleece into thread⟩
2 a : to produce by drawing out and twisting fibers ⟨*spin*
thread⟩ **b** : to form threads or a web or cocoon by giving
off a sticky fluid that quickly hardens into silk **3** : to turn
or cause to turn round and round rapidly **4** : to feel as if
in a whirl ⟨my head was *spinning*⟩ **5** : to tell using the
imagination ⟨*spin* a yarn⟩ **6** : to move swiftly on wheels
or in a vehicle **7** : to make, shape, or produce by or as if
by spinning ⟨*spun* sugar⟩

²spin *n* **1 a** : the act of spinning something **b** : a rapid
whirling motion **2** : a short trip in a vehicle ⟨go for a
spin⟩ **3 a** : a plunging descent or downward spiral **b** : a
state of mental confusion **4** : a special point of view,
emphasis, or interpretation

spin·ach \'spin-ich\ *n* : a widely grown plant with dark
green leaves that are used as food; *also* : the leaves

spi·nal \'spīn-ᵊl\ *adj* **1** : of, relating to, or located near the
backbone **2** : of, relating to, or affecting the spinal cord

spinal column *n* : BACKBONE 1

spinal cord *n* : the cord of nervous tissue that extends
from the brain along the back in the cavity of the backbone, branches to form the spinal nerves, carries nerve
impulses to and from the brain, and helps to control reflex actions

spinal nerve *n* : any of the paired nerves which arise from
the spinal cord and pass to various parts of the body and
of which there are normally 31 pairs in human beings

spin·dle \'spin-dᵊl\ *n* **1 a** : a slender round
rod or stick with tapered ends by which
thread or yarn is twisted in spinning by hand
and on which it is wound **b** : a device consisting of a long spike fixed so that papers
can be stuck on it for filing **2** : something
shaped like a spindle: as **a** : a network of fibers along which the chromosomes are distributed during cell division **b** : MUSCLE
SPINDLE **3** : something (as an axle or shaft)
shaped or turned like a spindle or on which
something turns

spin·dly \'spin-(d)lē, -dᵊl-ē\ *adj* **spin·dli·er;
-est** : of a tall or long and thin appearance
that often suggests physical weakness ⟨*spindly* legs⟩

spin·drift \'spin-‚drift\ *n* : spray blown from
waves

spindle 1a

spine \'spīn\ *n* **1 a** : BACKBONE 1 **b** : something resembling a backbone **c** : the part of a book to

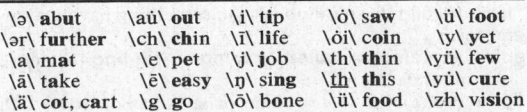

\ə\ **abut**	\aú\ **out**	\i\ **tip**	\ó\ **saw**	\ú\ **foot**
\ər\ **further**	\ch\ **chin**	\ī\ **life**	\ói\ **coin**	\y\ **yet**
\a\ **mat**	\e\ **pet**	\j\ **job**	\th\ **thin**	\yü\ **few**
\ā\ **take**	\ē\ **easy**	\ŋ\ **sing**	\th\ **this**	\yú\ **cure**
\ä\ **cot, cart**	\g\ **go**	\ō\ **bone**	\ü\ **food**	\zh\ **vision**

which the pages are attached **2** : a stiff pointed usually sharp projecting part of a plant or animal ⟨protective *spines* cover the body of a porcupine fish⟩ ⟨cactus *spines* are formed from leaves⟩ [Middle English *spine* "thorn, spinal column," from Latin *spina* (same meaning) — related to PORCUPINE]

spine·less \'spīn-ləs\ *adj* **1** : having no spines, thorns, or prickles **2 a** : having no backbone : INVERTEBRATE **b** : lacking spirit, courage, or determination — **spine·less·ly** *adv* — **spine·less·ness** *n*

spin·et \'spin-ət\ *n* : a low piano built with the strings running up and down

spin·na·ker \'spin-i-kər\ *n* : a large triangular sail set on a long light pole and used when sailing with the wind pushing from behind or nearly so

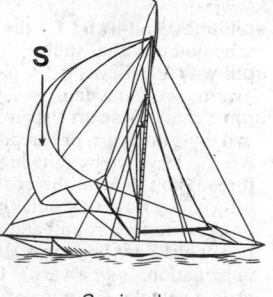

S spinnaker

spin·ner \'spin-ər\ *n* **1** : one that spins **2** : a fishing lure that spins when drawn through the water

spin·ner·et \,spin-ə-'ret\ *n* : an organ especially of a spider or caterpillar that has a small hole through which the sticky fluid produced by the silk glands is forced and hardens to form a silk thread

spinning *present participle of* SPIN

spinning jen·ny \'spin-iŋ-,jen-ē\ *n* : an early machine for spinning wool or cotton by means of many spindles

spinning reel *n* : a fishing reel that has a moving arm which winds the line around the spool and which locks out of the way during casting so the line can wind off freely

spinning wheel *n* : a small machine driven by the hand or foot for spinning yarn or thread

spin—off \'spin-,óf\ *n* **1** : something that results from work done to produce a different product : BY-PRODUCT ⟨household products that are *spin-offs* of space research⟩ **2** : something that imitates or comes from an earlier work or product ⟨a *spin-off* of a hit TV show⟩

spin·ster \'spin(t)-stər\ *n* **1** : a woman whose occupation is to spin **2** : an unmarried woman past the usual age for marrying — **spin·ster·hood** \-,hùd\ *n* — **spin·ster·ish** \-st(ə-)rish\ *adj* — **spin·ster·ly** *adv*

spiny \'spī-nē\ *adj* **spin·i·er; -est** **1** : full of difficulties, obstacles, or problems : THORNY **2** : having or covered with spines, thorns, or prickles — **spin·i·ness** *n*

spiny anteater *n* : ECHIDNA

spiny lobster *n* : any of several edible crustaceans that differ from the related true lobsters in having a simple unenlarged first pair of legs and a spiny carapace

spi·ra·cle \'spir-i-kəl, 'spī-ri-\ *n* : any of the openings in the body of an arthropod and especially of an insect through which air enters a trachea

¹**spi·ral** \'spī-rəl\ *adj* **1** : winding or circling around a center and gradually getting closer to or farther away from it ⟨the *spiral* curve of a watch spring⟩ **2** : winding around an axis like the thread of a screw ⟨a *spiral* staircase⟩ — **spi·ral·ly** \-rə-lē\ *adv*

²**spiral** *n* **1 a** : a curve in a plane that winds around a point while getting closer to or farther away from it **b** : a curve (as a helix) in space that winds around an axis **2** : a single turn or coil in a spiral object **3** : something having a spiral form

³**spiral** *vb* **-raled** *or* **-ralled; -ral·ing** *or* **-ral·ling** : to move in a spiral path

spire \'spī(ə)r\ *n* **1** : a blade or stalk (as of grass) that

gradually becomes thinner and narrower near the top **2** : a sharp pointed tip (as of a tree or antler) **3 a** : a pointed roof especially of a tower **b** : STEEPLE — **spired** \'spī(ə)rd\ *adj*

spi·rea *or* **spi·raea** \spī-'rē-ə\ *n* : any of a genus of shrubs related to the roses and having small usually white or pink flowers in dense clusters

spirea

spi·ril·lum \spī-'ril-əm\ *n, pl* **-ril·la** \-'ril-ə\ : any of a genus of long curved bacteria with a bunch of flagella at both ends; *also* : any spiral thread-shaped bacterium (as a spirochete)

¹**spir·it** \'spir-ət\ *n* **1** : a force within a human being thought to give the body life, energy, and power : SOUL **2 a** *cap* : HOLY SPIRIT **b** : a being (as a ghost) whose existence cannot be explained by the known laws of nature **3** : ¹MOOD ⟨in good *spirits*⟩ **4** : a lively or brisk quality ⟨answered with *spirit*⟩ **5** : real meaning or intention ⟨the *spirit* of the law⟩ **6** : an attitude governing one's actions ⟨said in a *spirit* of fun⟩ **7 a** : a distilled alcoholic liquor — usually used in plural **b** : a solution in alcohol — often used in plural ⟨*spirits* of camphor⟩ [Middle English *spirit* "a life-giving force," derived from Latin *spiritus*, literally, "breath"]

²**spirit** *vb* : to carry off secretly or mysteriously

spir·it·ed \'spir-ət-əd\ *adj* : full of courage or energy ⟨a *spirited* discussion⟩ — **spir·it·ed·ly** *adv*

spir·it·less \'spir-ət-ləs\ *adj* : lacking courage or energy — **spir·it·less·ly** *adv* — **spir·it·less·ness** *n*

¹**spir·i·tu·al** \'spir-ich-(ə-)wəl, -ich-əl\ *adj* **1** : of, relating to, or consisting of spirit : not bodily or material **2** : of or relating to sacred or religious matters **3** : related or joined in spirit ⟨our *spiritual* home⟩ — **spir·i·tu·al·i·ty** \,spir-ich-ə-'wal-ət-ē\ *n* — **spir·i·tu·al·ly** \'spir-ich-(ə-)wəl-ē, -ich-əl-ē\ *adv* — **spir·i·tu·al·ness** *n*

²**spiritual** *n* : a religious song usually of a very emotional character that was developed especially among blacks in the southern U.S.

spir·i·tu·al·ism \'spir-ich-(ə-)wə-,liz-əm, -ich-ə-,liz-\ *n* : a belief that the spirits of the dead communicate with the living

spi·ro·chete *also* **spi·ro·chaete** \'spī-rə-,kēt\ *n* : any of a group of slender coiled bacteria including one that causes syphilis

spi·ro·gy·ra \,spī-rə-'jī-rə\ *n* : any of a genus of freshwater green algae with spiral chloroplasts

¹**spit** \'spit\ *n* **1** : a thin pointed rod for holding meat over a fire **2** : a small point of land that runs out into a body of water [Old English *spitu* "a long rod for holding meat over a fire to cook"]

²**spit** *vb* **spit** *or* **spat** \'spat\; **spit·ting** **1 a** : to cause (as saliva) to spurt from the mouth : EXPECTORATE **b** : to express by or as if by spitting : make a spitting sound **2 a** : to give off briskly : EMIT **b** : to rain lightly or snow in flurries [Old English *spittan* "to spit (saliva) from the mouth"] — **spit·ter** *n*

³**spit** *n* **1 a** : SALIVA **b** : the act of spitting **2** : a foamy secretion produced by spittlebugs **3** : perfect likeness ⟨the *spit* and image of her father⟩

spit·ball \'spit-,ból\ *n* **1** : paper chewed and rolled into a ball to be thrown or shot at someone or something **2** : a baseball pitch thrown after the ball has been moistened with spit or sweat

¹**spite** \'spīt\ *n* : dislike or hatred for another person with a wish to torment, anger, or defeat — **in spite of** : without being prevented by ⟨failed *in spite of* all our work⟩ ⟨went ahead *in spite of* the difficulties⟩

²**spite** *vb* **spit·ed; spit·ing** : ANNOY, OFFEND ⟨did it to *spite* me⟩

spite·ful \'spīt-fəl\ *adj* : filled with or showing spite : MALICIOUS — **spite·ful·ly** \-fə-lē\ *adv* — **spite·ful·ness** *n*

spit·fire \'spit-ˌfī(ə)r\ *n* : an easily angered or highly emotional person

spitting image *n* : perfect likeness

spit·tle \'spit-ᵊl\ *n* **1** : SALIVA **2** : ³SPIT 2

spit·tle·bug \-ˌbəg\ *n* : any of numerous leaping insects that produce and cover themselves with foam in the young stages

spittle insect *n* : SPITTLEBUG

spit·toon \spi-'tün\ *n* : a container to spit into

spit up *vb* : REGURGITATE, VOMIT ⟨the baby *spit up* twice⟩ — **spit–up** *n*

spitz \'spits\ *n* : a member of any of several breeds of heavy-coated dogs with ears standing straight up and a tail curled over the back

¹**splash** \'splash\ *vb* **1 a** : to cause (something liquid or sloppy) to move and scatter roughly ⟨*splash* water⟩ **b** : to wet, soil, or stain by spattering with something liquid or sloppy ⟨*splashed* by a passing car⟩ **2** : to move or strike with a splashing sound ⟨*splash* through a puddle⟩ ⟨a brook *splashing* over rocks⟩ **3** : to spread or scatter like a splashed liquid ⟨the sunset *splashed* the sky with red⟩ — **splash·er** *n*

²**splash** *n* **1 a** : splashed material **b** : a spot or smear from or as if from splashed liquid **2** : the sound or action of splashing

splash·down \'splash-ˌdaůn\ *n* : the landing of a spacecraft in the ocean

splashy \'splash-ē\ *adj* **splash·i·er; -est 1** : attracting attention or meant to attract attention ⟨would have preferred a less *splashy* debut⟩ **2** : being bright, bold, and colorful ⟨a *splashy* shirt⟩ ⟨*splashy* posters⟩

splat \'splat\ *n* : a splattering or slapping sound

splat·ter \'splat-ər\ *vb* **1** : ¹SPATTER 1 **2** : to scatter or fall in or as if in drops — **splatter** *n*

splay \'splā\ *vb* : to spread out or apart ⟨a colt with legs *splayed* out⟩

spleen \'splēn\ *n* **1** : an organ containing many blood vessels that is located near the stomach or intestine of most vertebrates, destroys worn-out red blood cells, filters the blood, and produces some white blood cells **2** : feelings of anger or ill will that are often not expressed

splen·did \'splen-dəd\ *adj* **1** : having or showing splendor : BRILLIANT **2** : impressive in beauty, grandeur, or excellence ⟨a *splendid* job⟩ ⟨a *splendid* palace⟩ **3** : EXCELLENT ⟨had a *splendid* time at the beach⟩ [from Latin *splendidus* "splendid, brilliant," from *splendēre* "to shine"] — **splen·did·ly** *adv* — **splen·did·ness** *n*

synonyms SPLENDID, GORGEOUS, GLORIOUS, SUBLIME mean very impressive. SPLENDID suggests that something is far above the ordinary in excellence, beauty, or grandeur ⟨a *splendid* jewel⟩. GORGEOUS suggests a rich splendor especially in a display of color ⟨a *gorgeous* red dress⟩. GLORIOUS suggests that something is radiant with light or beauty ⟨a *glorious* sunset⟩. SUBLIME suggests a noble grandeur almost beyond human understanding ⟨the Grand Canyon is a *sublime* sight⟩.

splen·dif·er·ous \splen-'dif-(ə-)rəs\ *adj* : SPLENDID 1

splen·dor \'splen-dər\ *n* **1** : great brightness : BRILLIANCE ⟨the *splendor* of the sun⟩ **2** : POMP 1, GLORY ⟨the *splendor* of ancient Rome⟩ **3** : something splendid ⟨the *splendors* of the past⟩ — **splen·dor·ous** *also* **splen·drous** \'splen-d(ə-)rəs\ *adj*

sple·net·ic \spli-'net-ik\ *adj* : marked by bad temper : TESTY, GRUMPY

¹**splice** \'splīs\ *vb* **spliced; splic·ing 1** : to unite (as two ropes) by weaving the strands together **2** : to unite (as

pieces of film) by connecting the ends together **3** : to unite, link, or insert as if by splicing — **splic·er** *n*

²**splice** *n* : a joining or joint made by splicing

²splice

¹**splint** \'splint\ *n* **1** : a thin flexible strip of wood woven together with others in making a chair seat or basket **2** : ¹SPLINTER **3** : material or a device used to protect a body part (as a broken arm) and keep it in place

²**splint** *vb* : to support and hold in place with or as if with a splint or splints

splint bone *n* : one of the small slender bones in the leg of a horse

¹**splin·ter** \'splint-ər\ *n* : a thin piece split or torn off lengthwise : SLIVER — **splinter** *adj*

²**splinter** *vb* **splin·tered; splin·ter·ing** \'splint-ə-riŋ, 'splin-triŋ\ : to divide or break into splinters

¹**split** \'split\ *vb* **split; split·ting 1 a** : to divide lengthwise or by layers ⟨*split* a log⟩ **b** : to divide or separate as if by forcing apart ⟨*split* the town⟩ ⟨families were often *split up*⟩ **c** : to mark (a ballot) or cast (a vote) for candidates of different parties **2 a** : to burst or break apart or in pieces **b** : to affect as if by breaking up or tearing apart ⟨a roar that *split* the air⟩ **3 a** : to divide into shares ⟨we *split* the profit⟩ **b** : to divide into groups or parts ⟨we'll *split up*; you take the left fork⟩ ⟨they *split* into two teams⟩ **c** : to become separated off ⟨*split* from the group⟩ **4** : DEPART 1 ⟨*split* for the party⟩ **5** *British* : INFORM 2, TELL — usually used with *on* — **split·ter** *n* — **split hairs** : to make small and unimportant distinctions — **split one's sides** : to laugh heartily

²**split** *n* **1** : a narrow break made by or as if by splitting : CRACK **2** : the act or process of splitting : DIVISION **3** : the act of lowering oneself to the floor or leaping into the air with the legs extended in a straight line and in opposite directions

³**split** *adj* : divided by or as if by splitting ⟨a *split* lip⟩

split infinitive *n* : an infinitive with *to* having a modifier between the *to* and the verbal (as in "to really start")

split–lev·el \'split-ˌlev-əl\ *n* : a house divided so that the floor in one part is about halfway between two floors in the other

split pea *n* : a dried pea that has had the outer skin removed and that is split into two parts

split personality *n* **1** : a mental and emotional disorder in which the personality becomes separated into two or more parts each of which controls behavior part of the time **2** : a double character or nature ⟨a city with a *split personality*⟩

split second *n* : a small fraction of a second : FLASH

split–second *adj* **1** : occurring in a split second ⟨a *split-second* decision⟩ **2** : extremely precise ⟨*split-second* timing⟩

split·ting \'split-iŋ\ *adj* : very severe ⟨a *splitting* headache⟩

splotch \'spläch\ *n* : BLOTCH 2, SPOT — **splotch** *vb* — **splotchy** \'spläch-ē\ *adj*

¹**splurge** \'splərj\ *n* : an instance of spending more than usual

²**splurge** *vb* **splurged; splurg·ing** : indulge oneself or spend lavishly

¹**splut·ter** \'splət-ər\ *n* **1** : a confused noise (as of trying to talk too fast) **2** : a splashing or sputtering sound

²**splutter** *vb* **1** : to make a noise as if spitting **2** : to speak or say in haste or confusion

\ə\ abut	\aů\ out	\i\ tip	\ȯ\ saw	\ů\ foot
\ər\ further	\ch\ chin	\ī\ life	\ȯi\ coin	\y\ yet
\a\ mat	\e\ pet	\j\ job	\th\ thin	\yü\ few
\ā\ take	\ē\ easy	\ŋ\ sing	\th\ this	\yů\ cure
\ä\ cot, cart	\g\ go	\ō\ bone	\ü\ food	\zh\ vision

¹spoil \'spȯi(ə)l\ *n* : stolen goods : PLUNDER

²spoil *vb* **spoiled** \'spȯi(ə)ld, 'spȯi(ə)lt\ *also* **spoilt** \'spȯi(ə)lt\; **spoil·ing** 1 : ²PLUNDER, ROB 2 a : to damage badly : RUIN ⟨*spoiled* my new sweater⟩ b : to damage the quality or effect of ⟨a quarrel *spoiled* the party⟩ c : to decay or lose freshness, value, or usefulness by being kept too long ⟨the milk *spoiled*⟩ 3 : to damage the disposition of by letting get away with too much ⟨*spoil* a child⟩ 4 : to have an eager desire ⟨*spoiling* for a fight⟩

spoil·age \'spȯi-lij\ *n* : the action of spoiling or the condition of being spoiled

spoil·er \'spȯi-lər\ *n* 1 a : one that spoils b : one (as a political candidate) having little or no chance of winning but capable of depriving a rival of success 2 : a device (as on an airplane or automobile) used to disrupt airflow and decrease lift 3 : information about the plot of a book, motion picture, or television program that can spoil a reader's or a viewer's sense of surprise or suspense

spoil·sport \'spȯi(ə)l-ˌspō(ə)rt, -ˌspȯ(ə)rt\ *n* : a person who spoils the fun of others

¹spoke \'spōk\ *past and archaic past participle of* SPEAK

²spoke *n* 1 : one of the small bars extending from the hub of a wheel to support the rim 2 : something resembling the spoke of a wheel

spo·ken \'spō-kən\ *adj* 1 : given by or using speech ⟨a *spoken* message⟩ ⟨the *spoken* language⟩ 2 : speaking in a specified manner ⟨soft-*spoken*⟩ ⟨plain*spoken*⟩

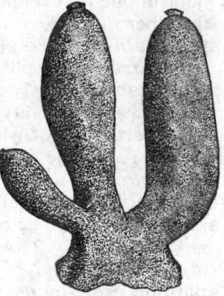

S ²spoke 1

spokes·man \'spōk-smən\ *n* : a person who speaks for another or for a group

spokes·mod·el \-ˌsmäd-ᵊl\ *n* : a model who is a spokesman or spokeswoman

spokes·per·son \'spōk-ˌspərs-ᵊn\ *n* : SPOKESMAN

spokes·wom·an \'spōk-ˌswu̇m-ən\ *n* : a woman who speaks for another or for a group

spon·dee \'spän-ˌdē\ *n* : a metrical foot consisting of two accented syllables (as in *tom-tom*) — **spon·da·ic** \spän-'dā-ik\ *adj*

¹sponge \'spənj\ *n* 1 a : a springy mass of fibers and spicules that forms the skeleton of a group of aquatic animals and is able to absorb water freely; *also* : a piece of this material or of a natural or synthetic product with similar properties used especially for cleaning b : any of the phylum of primitive mostly marine animals that are the source of natural sponges, have a body of loosely connected cells with a skeleton supported by spicules or flexible fibers, and are filter feeders that live permanently attached to a solid surface as adults 2 : a pad (as of folded gauze) used in surgery and medicine (as to soak up fluids or apply medicine) 3 : one who lives on others : SPONGER 4 a : raised dough (as for yeast bread) b : a whipped dessert usually containing egg whites

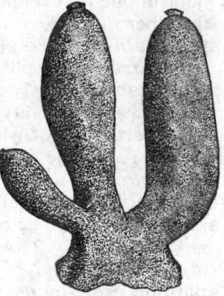

¹sponge 1b

²sponge *vb* **sponged; spong·ing** 1 : to clean or wipe with or as if with a sponge 2 : to absorb with or like a sponge 3 : to get something or live at the expense of another — **spong·er** *n*

sponge cake *n* : a light cake made without shortening

spon·gin \'spən-jən\ *n* : a protein that is the main element making up the flexible fibers in sponge skeletons

spongy \'spən-jē\ *adj* **spong·i·er; -est** : resembling a

sponge in appearance or in ability to absorb : soft and full of holes or moisture — **spong·i·ness** *n*

spongy cell *n* : one of the chlorophyll-containing cells of the spongy layer of a plant leaf

spongy layer *n* : a layer of loosely packed and irregularly shaped chlorophyll-bearing cells that fills the part of a leaf between the palisade layer and the lower epidermis — called also *spongy parenchyma, spongy tissue*

¹spon·sor \'spän(t)-sər\ *n* 1 : a person who takes the responsibility for some other person or thing 2 : GODPARENT 3 a : a person or an organization that pays for or plans and carries out a project or activity b : a person or an organization that pays the cost of a radio or television program — **spon·sor·ship** \-ˌship\ *n*

²sponsor *vb* **spon·sored; spon·sor·ing** \'spän(t)s-(ə-)riŋ\ : to act as sponsor for

spon·ta·ne·ity \ˌspänt-ən-'ē-ət-ē, ˌspänt-ᵊn-, -'ā-ət-\ *n* : the quality or state of being spontaneous

spon·ta·ne·ous \spän-'tā-nē-əs\ *adj* 1 : done, said, or produced freely and naturally ⟨*spontaneous* laughter⟩ 2 : acting or taking place without any outside force or cause — **spon·ta·ne·ous·ly** *adv* — **spon·ta·ne·ous·ness** *n*

spontaneous combustion *n* : a bursting of material into flame from the heat produced within itself by chemical action (as oxidation)

spontaneous generation *n* : the coming into existence of living things directly from lifeless matter instead of from other living things

spoof \'spüf\ *vb* : to make good-natured fun of — **spoof** *n*

¹spook \'spük\ *n* 1 : GHOST, SPECTER 2 : ²SPY 2

²spook *vb* : to make or become frightened : SCARE

spooky \'spü-kē\ *adj* **spook·i·er; -est** 1 : relating to, resembling, or suggesting ghosts ⟨*spooky* houses⟩ 2 : SKITTISH 2 ⟨a *spooky* horse⟩ — **spook·i·ness** *n*

spool \'spül\ *n* 1 : a cylinder which has a rim at each end and on which something (as thread, wire, or tape) is wound 2 : material wound on a spool

¹spoon \'spün\ *n* 1 : a utensil with a small shallow bowl and a handle that is used especially in eating and cooking 2 : something (as a fishing lure) that resembles a spoon in shape [Old English *spōn* "a chip of wood"]

²spoon *vb* : to take up in or as if in a spoon

spoon·bill \'spün-ˌbil\ *n* : any of several wading birds related to the ibises that have a bill with a broad, flat, and rounded tip

spoon bread *n* : soft bread made of cornmeal mixed with milk, eggs, and shortening and served with a spoon

spoo·ner·ism \'spü-nə-ˌriz-əm\ *n* : a mixing up of usually the initial sounds of two or more words (as in "tons of soil" for "sons of toil")

spoonbill

spoon–feed \'spün-ˌfēd\ *vb* **-fed** \-ˌfed\; **-feed·ing** : to feed by means of a spoon

spoon·ful \'spün-ˌfu̇l\ *n, pl* **spoonfuls** \-ˌfu̇lz\ *also* **spoons·ful** \'spünz-ˌfu̇l\ : as much as a spoon can hold

spoor \'spu̇(ə)r, 'spō(ə)r, 'spȯ(ə)r\ *n* : a track, a trail, a scent, or droppings especially of a wild animal

spo·rad·ic \spə-'rad-ik\ *adj* : occurring or done now and then — **spo·rad·i·cal·ly** \-'rad-i-k(ə-)lē\ *adv*

spo·ran·gi·um \spə-'ran-jē-əm\ *n, pl* **-gia** \-jē-ə\ : a sac or case within which spores are produced and stored

¹**spore** \'spō(ə)r, 'spȯ(ə)r\ *n* : a reproductive body that is produced by fungi and by some plants and microorganisms (as ferns and bacteria) and that usually consists of a single cell and is able to produce a new individual either by developing by itself or after fusion with another spore — **spored** \'spō(ə)rd, 'spȯ(ə)rd\ *adj*

²**spore** *vb* **spored; spor·ing** : to produce or reproduce by spores

spore case *n* : SPORANGIUM

spo·ro·phyte \'spōr-ə-ˌfīt, 'spȯr-\ *n* : the individual or generation of a plant having alternating sexual and asexual generations that produces asexual spores — compare GAMETOPHYTE

spo·ro·zo·an \ˌspōr-ə-'zō-ən, ˌspȯr-\ *n* : any of a large group of parasitic one-celled animals (as the parasites that cause malaria) that have a complicated life cycle usually involving both asexual and sexual generations often in different hosts — **sporozoan** *adj*

spor·ran \'spȯr-ən, 'spär-\ *n* : a pouch usually of skin with the fur on that is worn in front of the kilt by Highlanders in full dress

¹**sport** \'spō(ə)rt, 'spȯ(ə)rt\ *vb* **1** : to amuse oneself : FROLIC **2** : to speak or act in fun **3** : SHOW OFF 1

²**sport** *n* **1 a** : PASTIME, RECREATION **b** : physical activity (as hunting, running, or an athletic game) engaged in for pleasure **2 a** : JEST 2 **b** : ¹FUN **3** ⟨make *sport* of someone⟩ **3** : a person who shows good sportsmanship **4** : an individual that shows a sudden major change from the normal type usually as a result of a mutation ⟨a yellow *sport* among the red apples⟩

³**sport** *or* **sports** *adj* : of, relating to, or suitable for sports ⟨*sports* equipment⟩; *also* : made in a style suitable for casual or informal wear ⟨a *sport* coat⟩

sport·ing \'spōrt-iŋ, 'spȯrt-\ *adj* **1** : of, relating to, or suitable for sport ⟨*sporting* events⟩ ⟨*sporting* dogs⟩ **2** : involving about as much risk as a sports competitor would expect to take ⟨a *sporting* chance⟩

sport·ive \'spōrt-iv, 'spȯrt-\ *adj* : FROLICSOME, PLAYFUL — **sport·ive·ly** *adv* — **sport·ive·ness** *n*

sports car *n* : a low usually two-passenger automobile designed for high-speed driving

sports·cast \'spō(ə)rt-ˌskast, 'spȯ(ə)rt-\ *n* : a broadcast of a sports event — **sports·cast·er** *n*

sports·man \'spō(ə)rt-smən, 'spȯ(ə)rt-\ *n* **1** : a person who engages in or is interested in sports and especially outdoor sports **2** : ²SPORT 3 — **sports·man·like** \-ˌlīk\ *adj* — **sports·man·ly** \-lē\ *adj*

sports·man·ship \'spō(ə)rt-smən-ˌship, 'spȯ(ə)rt-\ *n* : fair play, respect for opponents, and gracious behavior in winning or losing

sports medicine *n* : a field of medicine concerned with the prevention and treatment of injuries and disorders that are related to participation in sports

sports·wear \'spō(ə)rt-ˌswa(ə)r, 'spȯ(ə)rt-, -ˌswe(ə)r\ *n* : clothes suitable for sports or for casual or informal wear

sports·wom·an \-ˌswum-ən\ *n* : a woman who engages in or is interested in sports and especially outdoor sports

sports·writ·er \'spō(ə)rts-ˌrīt-ər, 'spȯ(ə)rts-\ *n* : a person who writes about sports (as for a newspaper)

sport–util·i·ty vehicle \'spȯrt-yü-'til-ət-ē-\ *n* : a rugged automotive vehicle similar to a station wagon but built on a light truck chassis

sporty \'spōrt-ē, 'spȯrt-\ *adj* **sport·i·er; -est** : of or relating to sports; *also* : being or having the look of being suitable for sports ⟨*sporty* clothes⟩ — **sport·i·ly** \'spȯrt-ᵊl-ē, 'spȯrt-\ *adv* — **sport·i·ness** \'spȯrt-ē-nəs, 'spȯrt-\ *n*

spor·u·la·tion \ˌspȯr-(y)ə-'lā-shən, ˌspȯr-\ *n* : formation of or division into spores

¹**spot** \'spät\ *n* **1** : something bad that others know about one : FAULT **2 a** : a small area that is different (as in color) from the main part **b** : an area marred or marked (as by dirt) **c** : a small diseased or decayed area on the body surface of a plant or animal ⟨*spots* of rot on a leaf⟩ ⟨*spots* of chicken pox⟩ **3 a** : a small quantity or amount **b** : a particular place ⟨a good *spot* for a picnic⟩ ⟨a sore *spot*⟩ **4** : a particular position (as in an organization or on a program) **5** : ¹SPOTLIGHT 2 **6** : a position usually of difficulty or embarrassment ⟨put someone in a *spot*⟩ **7** : a short broadcast announcement or advertisement — **on the spot 1** : at once : IMMEDIATELY **2** : at the place of action **3** : in a difficult situation

²**spot** *vb* **spot·ted; spot·ting 1** : to mark or become marked with or as if with spots **2** : to single out : IDENTIFY ⟨*spot* a friend in a crowd⟩

³**spot** *adj* **1 a** : done on the spot ⟨*spot* coverage of the news⟩ **b** : paid upon delivery ⟨*spot* cash⟩ **c** : involving immediate cash payment ⟨the *spot* market for oil⟩ **d** : broadcast between scheduled programs ⟨*spot* announcements⟩ **2** : made from time to time or in a few places or instances ⟨a *spot* check⟩

spot–check \'spät-ˌchek\ *vb* : to make a spot check

spot·less \'spät-ləs\ *adj* : free from spots or blemishes : perfectly clean or pure ⟨a *spotless* kitchen⟩ ⟨a *spotless* reputation⟩ — **spot·less·ly** *adv* — **spot·less·ness** *n*

¹**spot·light** \'spät-ˌlīt\ *n* **1 a** : a spot of light used to light up a particular area, person, or thing (as on a stage) **b** : public notice **2** : a light designed to direct a narrow strong beam of light on a small area

²**spotlight** *vb* **-light·ed** *or* **-lit; -light·ing 1** : to light up with a spotlight **2** : to bring to public attention

spot·ted \'spät-əd\ *adj* : marked with spots ⟨a *spotted* cat⟩

spotted fever *n* : any of various diseases (as Rocky Mountain spotted fever and typhus) that are characterized by fever and spots on the skin

spotted owl *n* : a rare dark brown owl with white spots above and dark stripes below that is found from British Columbia to southern California and central Mexico

spotted turtle *n* : a small freshwater turtle of the eastern U.S. with a blackish shell covered with round yellow spots

spot·ter \'spät-ər\ *n* **1** : a person who removes spots **2** : a person who keeps watch : OBSERVER **3** : a person who helps another during exercise (as to prevent injury)

spot·ty \'spät-ē\ *adj* **spot·ti·er; -est 1** : having spots **2** : not always the same especially in quality ⟨your work has been *spotty*⟩ — **spot·ti·ly** \'spät-ᵊl-ē\ *adv* — **spot·ti·ness** \'spät-ē-nəs\ *n*

spouse \'spaus *also* 'spauz\ *n* : a married person : HUSBAND, WIFE — **spou·sal** \'spau-zəl, -səl\ *adj*

¹**spout** \'spaut\ *vb* **1** : to shoot (as liquid) out with force ⟨wells *spouting* oil⟩ **2** : to speak with a long and quick flow of words so as to sound important **3** : to flow out with force : SPURT ⟨blood *spouted* from the wound⟩ — **spout·er** *n*

²**spout** *n* **1** : a tube, pipe, or hole through which something (as rainwater) spouts **2** : a sudden strong stream of fluid

¹**sprain** \'sprān\ *n* **1** : a sudden or severe twisting of a joint with stretching or tearing of ligaments **2** : a condition that results from a sprain and is usually marked by pain and swelling

S sporran

\ə\ **abut**	\au̇\ **out**	\i\ **tip**	\ȯ\ **saw**	\u̇\ **foot**
\ər\ **further**	\ch\ **chin**	\ī\ **life**	\ȯi\ **coin**	\y\ **yet**
\a\ **mat**	\e\ **pet**	\j\ **job**	\th\ **thin**	\yü\ **few**
\ā\ **take**	\ē\ **easy**	\ŋ\ **sing**	\th\ **this**	\yu̇\ **cure**
\ä\ **cot, cart**	\g\ **go**	\ō\ **bone**	\ü\ **food**	\zh\ **vision**

²**sprain** *vb* : to injure by a sudden or severe twist

sprawl \'spról\ *vb* **1** : to lie or sit with arms and legs spread out ⟨*sprawled* on the couch watching TV⟩ **2** : to spread out in an uneven or awkward way ⟨a *sprawling* city⟩ — **sprawl** *n*

¹**spray** \'sprā\ *n* : a usually flowering branch or shoot

²**spray** *n* **1** : liquid flying in fine drops like water blown from a wave **2 a** : a burst of fine mist (as from an atomizer) **b** : a device (as an atomizer) for scattering a spray

³**spray** *vb* **1** : to scatter or apply as a spray **2** : to scatter spray on or into — **spray·er** *n*

spray gun *n* : a device for spraying liquids (as paints and insecticides)

¹**spread** \'spred\ *vb* **spread; spread·ing 1 a** : to open over a larger area ⟨*spread* out a map⟩ **b** : to stretch out : EXTEND ⟨*spread* her arms wide⟩ **2 a** : to scatter over an area ⟨*spread* fertilizer⟩ **b** : to give out over a period or among a group ⟨*spread* the work over several weeks⟩ **c** : to put a layer of on a surface ⟨*spread* butter on bread⟩ **d** : to cover something with ⟨*spread* the cloth on the table⟩ **e** : to prepare for a meal : SET ⟨*spread* a table⟩ **3 a** : to become or cause to become widely known ⟨*spread* the news⟩ ⟨the panic *spread* rapidly⟩ **b** : to extend the range or occurrence of ⟨*spread* a disease⟩ **4** : to stretch or move apart ⟨*spread* one's fingers⟩ — **spread·able** \'spred-ə-bəl\ *adj*

²**spread** *n* **1 a** : the act or process of spreading ⟨the *spread* of education⟩ **b** : the extent of spreading ⟨the *spread* of a bird's wings⟩ **2** : a very noticeable display in a newspaper or magazine ⟨a two-page *spread*⟩ **3 a** : a food to be spread on bread or crackers ⟨a cheese *spread*⟩ **b** : a very fine meal : FEAST **c** : a cloth cover for a table or bed **4** : distance between two points

spread–ea·gle \'spred-,ē-gəl\ *vb* **-ea·gled; -ea·gling** \-,ē-g(ə-)liŋ\ : to stand or move with arms and legs spread wide

spread·er \'spred-ər\ *n* : one that spreads: as **a** : an implement for scattering material **b** : a small knife used especially for spreading butter

spread·sheet \'spred-,shēt\ *n* : an accounting program for a computer; *also* : the ledger layout simulated by such a program

spree \'sprē\ *n* : an outburst of activity ⟨a buying *spree*⟩

sprier *comparative of* SPRY

spriest *superlative of* SPRY

sprig \'sprig\ *n* : a small shoot or twig especially with leaves or flowers

spright·ly \'sprīt-lē\ *adj* **spright·li·er; -est** : full of spirit : LIVELY — **spright·li·ness** *n* — **sprightly** *adv*

¹**spring** \'spriŋ\ *vb* **sprang** \'spraŋ\ *or* **sprung** \'sprəŋ\; **sprung; spring·ing** \'spriŋ-iŋ\ **1 a** : to appear or grow quickly ⟨the weeds *sprang* up overnight⟩ **b** : to come from by birth or descent ⟨*sprang* from an immigrant family⟩ **c** : to come into being : ARISE ⟨towns *sprang* up across the plains⟩ **2** : to move suddenly forward or upward : LEAP ⟨a lion crouched and waiting to *spring*⟩ ⟨*sprang* up the path⟩ ⟨*sprang* to my feet⟩ **3** : to have (a leak) appear **4 a** : to move by elastic force ⟨the lid *sprang* shut⟩ **b** : to become warped or bent ⟨the door has *sprung*⟩ **5 a** : to cause to operate suddenly ⟨*spring* a trap⟩ **b** : to produce suddenly ⟨*sprung* a surprise on us⟩ **6** : ¹PAY 1 — usually used with *for* ⟨*spring* for a new pair of shoes⟩ **7** : to release or cause to be released from confinement (as jail)

²**spring** *n* **1** : a source of supply; *esp* : a source of water coming up from the ground **2 a** : the season between winter and summer including in the northern hemisphere usually the months of March, April, and May **b** : a time or season of growth or development **3** : an elastic body or device that recovers its original shape when released after being squeezed or stretched **4 a** : the act or an instance of leaping up or forward **b** : elastic power or force ⟨the *spring* in your step⟩

spring beauty *n* : a spring herb that sends up a two-leaved stem and has delicate pink flowers

spring·board \'spriŋ-,bō(ə)rd, -,bó(ə)rd\ *n* **1** : a flexible board usually fastened at one end and used for jumping high in gymnastics or diving **2** : a point of departure ⟨a *springboard* to success in business⟩

spring·bok \'spriŋ-,bäk\ *n, pl* **springbok** *or* **springboks** : a swift and graceful gazelle of southern African noted for its habit of leaping suddenly into the air

spring·er spaniel \,spriŋ-ər-\ *n* : a medium-sized sporting dog of either of two breeds used chiefly for finding small game and driving it from cover: **a** : ENGLISH SPRINGER SPANIEL **b** : WELSH SPRINGER SPANIEL

spring fever *n* : a lazy or restless feeling often associated with the coming of spring

spring peeper *n* : a small brown tree frog of the eastern U.S. and Canada with a shrill piping call

spring roll *n* : EGG ROLL; *also* : any of various similar appetizers

spring tide *n* : a greater than usual tide that occurs at each new moon and full moon

spring·time \'spriŋ-,tīm\ *n* : the season of spring

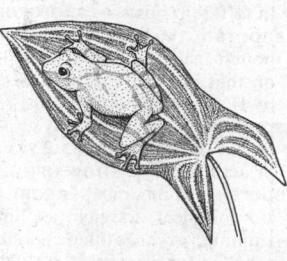
spring peeper

spring·wood \-,wùd\ *n* : the soft light-colored inner part of an annual ring of wood that is made up of large thin-walled cells and develops early in the growing season — compare SUMMERWOOD

springy \'spriŋ-ē\ *adj* **spring·i·er; -est 1** : having an elastic quality ⟨green *springy* wood⟩ **2** : having or showing a lively and energetic movement ⟨walks with a *springy* step⟩ — **spring·i·ly** \'spriŋ-ə-lē\ *adv* — **spring·i·ness** \'spriŋ-ē-nəs\ *n*

¹**sprin·kle** \'spriŋ-kəl\ *vb* **sprin·kled; sprin·kling** \-k(ə-)liŋ\ **1** : to scatter in drops or particles ⟨*sprinkle* water⟩ ⟨*sprinkle* grass seed over the soil⟩ **2 a** : to scatter over or in or among ⟨*sprinkle* the spaghetti with grated cheese⟩ **b** : to wet lightly ⟨*sprinkle* clothes before ironing⟩ **3** : to rain lightly in scattered drops — **sprin·kler** \-k(ə-)lər\ *n*

²**sprinkle** *n* **1** : the act or an instance of sprinkling; *esp* : a light rain **2** : SPRINKLING

sprin·kling \'spriŋ-kliŋ\ *n* : a very small number or amount

¹**sprint** \'sprint\ *vb* : to run at top speed especially for a short distance — **sprint·er** *n*

²**sprint** *n* **1** : a short run at top speed **2** : a race over a short distance

sprite \'sprīt\ *n* : ELF, FAIRY

sprock·et \'spräk-ət\ *n* **1** : one of many points that stick up on the rim of a wheel shaped so as to fit into the links of a chain **2** : a wheel having sprockets

¹**sprout** \'spraùt\ *vb* **1** : to grow or spring up as or as if a sprout **2** : to send out new growth ⟨potatoes kept too warm will *sprout* in the bag⟩ **3** : to send forth or up : cause to develop : GROW

sprocket

²**sprout** *n* **1 a** : ²SHOOT 1a; *esp* : a young shoot (as from a

seed or root) **2** *pl* : edible young shoots especially from recently germinated seeds (as of alfalfa)

¹spruce \'sprüs\ *vb* **spruced; spruc·ing** : to make or make oneself spruce ⟨*spruce* up a room⟩ ⟨*spruce* up a bit before going out to dinner⟩

²spruce *adj* **spruc·er; spruc·est** : neat or stylish in appearance — **spruce·ly** *adv* — **spruce·ness** *n*

³spruce *n* **1** : any of a genus of usually pyramid-shaped evergreen trees that are related to the pines and have soft light wood **2** : the wood of a spruce

sprung *past and past participle of* SPRING

spry \'sprī\ *adj* **spri·er** *or* **spry·er** \'sprī(-ə)r\; **spri·est** *or* **spry·est** \'sprī-əst\ : light and easy in motion : NIMBLE, SPRIGHTLY ⟨a *spry* 75-year-old⟩ — **spry·ly** *adv* — **spry·ness** *n*

spud \'spəd\ *n* : POTATO 2b

spume \'spyüm\ *n* : ¹FOAM 1

spu·mo·ni *also* **spu·mo·ne** \spù-'mō-nē\ *n* : ice cream in layers of different colors and flavors often with candied fruits and nuts [from Italian *spumone,* a form of *spuma* "foam"]

spun *past and past participle of* SPIN

spun glass *n* : FIBERGLASS

spunk \'spəŋk\ *n* **1** : COURAGE, PLUCK **2** : ¹SPIRIT 4

Word History Spunk now means "spirit, readiness to fight against odds, courage." It is somewhat surprising to learn that it comes from a Latin word for something that seems quite the opposite: "sponge." The Latin word for "sponge," *spongia,* came into Scottish Gaelic, the Celtic language of the Scottish Highlands, as *spong* and meant "sponge." But it also came to mean "tinder," the light, dry material used to start a fire. Tinder was often dry, spongy wood that would ignite easily and looked like sponge. A person who fought courageously and without complaining, especially against strong opponents, was thought of as catching fire. This flaring up of the human spirit was compared to the bursting into flame of tinder. Thus, a person who had this quality was said to have spunk. [from earlier *spunk* "tinder," from Scottish Gaelic *spong* "sponge, tinder," from Latin *spongia* "sponge"]

spunky \'spəŋ-kē\ *adj* **spunk·i·er; -est** : full of spunk : SPIRITED — **spunk·i·ly** \-kə-lē\ *adv* — **spunk·i·ness** \-kē-nəs\ *n*

spun sugar *n* : sugar that has been boiled and spun into fine threads usually for cotton candy

¹spur \'spər\ *n* **1 a** : a pointed device fastened to the back of a rider's boot and used to urge a horse on **b** *pl* : recognition for achievement **2** : something that makes one want to do something : INCENTIVE **3 a** : a stiff sharp pointed part (as a horny spine on the leg of a rooster) **b** : a hollow flower part that sticks out especially on a petal (as of a columbine) or on a sepal (as of a larkspur) **4** : a mass of jagged rock coming out from the side of a mountain **5** : a short section of railway track coming away from the main line — **on the spur of the moment** : by a sudden decision : without thinking about it long

²spur *vb* **spurred; spur·ring** **1** : to urge a horse on with spurs **2** : to move to action : INCITE, STIMULATE

spu·ri·ous \'spyùr-ē-əs\ *adj* : not genuine or authentic : FALSE — **spu·ri·ous·ly** *adv* — **spu·ri·ous·ness** *n*

spurn \'spərn\ *vb* : to reject or thrust aside with scorn — **spurn·er** *n*

spur–of–the–moment *adj* : made or done by the sudden making up of one's mind ⟨a *spur-of-the moment* decision⟩

spurred \'spərd\ *adj* **1** : wearing spurs **2** : having one or more spurs ⟨a *spurred* violet⟩

¹spurt \'spərt\ *vb* **1** : to pour out suddenly : SPOUT **2** : ¹SQUIRT 1

²spurt *n* : a sudden pouring out : JET

³spurt *n* **1** : a short period of time : MOMENT **2** : a brief burst of effort, activity, or development ⟨a *spurt* of work⟩ ⟨a growth *spurt*⟩

⁴spurt *vb* : to make a spurt

Sput·nik \'spùt-nik, 'spət-\ *n* : any of a series of satellites launched by the Soviet Union beginning in 1957

¹sput·ter \'spət-ər\ *vb* **1** : to spit or squirt pieces of food or saliva noisily from the mouth **2** : to speak or utter hastily or explosively in confusion or excitement ⟨*sputtered* out protests⟩ **3** : to make explosive popping sounds ⟨the motor *sputtered* and died⟩ — **sput·ter·er** \-ər-ər\ *n*

²sputter *n* : the act or sound of sputtering

spu·tum \'sp(y)üt-əm\ *n, pl* **spu·ta** \-ə\ : material that is spit or coughed up from the lungs and bronchi and is made up mostly of mucus

¹spy \'spī\ *vb* **spied; spy·ing** **1** : to watch, inspect, or examine secretly : act as a spy **2** : to catch sight of : SEE ⟨*spied* a friend in the crowd⟩

²spy *n, pl* **spies** **1** : one that watches the movement or actions of others especially in secret **2** : a person who tries secretly to obtain information for one country in the territory of another usually unfriendly country

spy·glass \'spī-ˌglas\ *n* : a small telescope

squab \'skwäb\ *n, pl* **squabs** *or* **squab** : a young bird; *esp* : a young pigeon about four weeks old and ready for use as food

spyglass

¹squab·ble \'skwäb-əl\ *n* : a noisy quarrel usually over unimportant things

²squabble *vb* **squab·bled; squab·bling** \'skwäb-(ə-)liŋ\ : to quarrel noisily for little or no reason : WRANGLE — **squab·bler** \-(ə-)lər\ *n*

squad \'skwäd\ *n* **1** : a small organized group of soldiers; *esp* : a small unit that can be easily directed in the field **2** : a small group engaged in a common effort or occupation ⟨a football *squad*⟩ ⟨a rescue *squad*⟩

squad car *n* : a police car connected by radio with headquarters

squad·ron \'skwäd-rən\ *n* : any of several units of military organization

squal·id \'skwäl-əd\ *adj* **1** : filthy or degraded as a result of neglect or the lack of money **2** : VILE 1a **synonyms** see DIRTY — **squal·id·ly** *adv* — **squal·id·ness** *n*

¹squall \'skwòl\ *vb* : to cry out with a harsh sound : SCREAM — **squall·er** *n*

²squall *n* : a harsh cry or scream

³squall *n* **1** : a sudden violent wind often with rain or snow **2** : a short-lived commotion

⁴squall *vb* : to blow as a squall

squal·ly \'skwò-lē\ *adj* **squall·i·er; -est** : marked by squalls : GUSTY, STORMY

squa·lor \'skwäl-ər\ *n* : filthy or degraded conditions resulting from negelct or lack of money

squa·mous \'skwā-məs, 'skwä-\ *adj* : of, relating to, or being an epithelium that consists at least in its outer layers of small flattened scalelike cells

squan·der \'skwän-dər\ *vb* **squan·dered; squan·der·ing** \-d(ə-)riŋ\ : to spend foolishly or wastefully ⟨*squandered* all her money on video games⟩ — **squan·der·er** \-dər-ər\ *n*

¹square \'skwa(ə)r, 'skwe(ə)r\ *n* **1** : an instrument having at least one right angle and two straight edges used to draw or test right angles **2** : a rectangle with all four sides

\ə\ **abut**	\aù\ **out**	\i\ **tip**	\ò\ **saw**	\ù\ **foot**
\ər\ **further**	\ch\ **chin**	\ī\ **life**	\òi\ **coin**	\y\ **yet**
\a\ **mat**	\e\ **pet**	\j\ **job**	\th\ **thin**	\yü\ **few**
\ā\ **take**	\ē\ **easy**	\ŋ\ **sing**	\th\ **this**	\yù\ **cure**
\ä\ **cot, cart**	\g\ **go**	\ō\ **bone**	\ü\ **food**	\zh\ **vision**

equal **3** : any of the four-sided spaces marked out on a board for playing games **4** : the product of a number multiplied by itself ⟨4 is the *square* of 2⟩ **5 a** : an open place or area formed at the meeting of two or more streets **b** : ¹BLOCK 7a — **on the square 1** : at right angles **2** : in a fair open manner : HONESTLY — **out of square** : not at an exact right angle

²square *adj* **squar·er; squar·est 1 a** : having four equal sides and four right angles ⟨a *square* piece of paper⟩ **b** : forming a right angle ⟨a *square* corner⟩ **c** : having a square base ⟨a *square* pyramid⟩ **2 a** : being approximately a cube ⟨a *square* cabinet⟩ **b** : of a shape suggesting strength and toughness ⟨a *square* jaw⟩ ⟨*square* shoulders⟩ **c** : having the shape of a square as its cross section ⟨a *square* tower⟩ **3 a** : being a unit of area that has the shape of a square and sides of a specified unit length ⟨a *square* foot⟩ **b** : being of a specified length in each of two equal dimensions ⟨10 feet *square*⟩ **4 a** : exactly adjusted : well made **b** : ¹JUST 2a, FAIR ⟨a *square* deal⟩ **c** : leaving no balance : SETTLED **d** : being tied in score ⟨the golfers were all *square* after five holes⟩ **e** : large enough to satisfy ⟨three *square* meals a day⟩ **5** : not knowing or following the latest styles — **square·ness** *n*

³square *vb* **squared; squar·ing 1** : to form with right angles, straight edges, and flat surfaces : make square or rectangular ⟨*square* a timber⟩ **2** : to bring to a right angle ⟨*squared* his shoulders⟩ **3 a** : to multiply (a number) by itself : to raise (a number) to the second power **b** : to find a square equal in area to ⟨*square* a circle⟩ **4** : to agree or make agree ⟨his story does not *square* with the facts⟩ **5** : ²BALANCE 1, SETTLE ⟨*square* an account⟩ **6** : to mark off into squares **7** : ²BRIBE, FIX **8** : to take a fighting stance ⟨the two *squared* off⟩

⁴square *adv* : in a direct, firm, or honest manner ⟨looked her *square* in the eye⟩

square away *vb* : to put in order or readiness

square bracket *n* : ¹BRACKET 3a

square dance *n* : a lively dance for sets of four couples who form the sides of a square — **square–dance** *vb* — **square dancer** *n* — **square dancing** *n*

square knot *n* : a knot made of two reverse half-knots and typically used to join the ends of two cords — see KNOT illustration

square·ly *adv* **1** : in a plain or honest manner ⟨we must *squarely* face the problem⟩ **2 a** : EXACTLY 1a, PRECISELY ⟨*squarely* in the middle⟩ **b** : so as to make solid contact ⟨hit the ball *squarely*⟩ **3** : in a square form or manner : so as to be square ⟨a *squarely* cut dress⟩

square measure *n* : a unit or system of units for measuring area — see MEASURE table, METRIC SYSTEM table

square number *n* : a whole number (as 1, 4, or 9) that is the square of another whole number

square one *n* : the first stage or starting point ⟨back to *square one*⟩

square–rigged \'skwa(ə)r-ˌrigd, 'skwe(ə)r-\ *adj* : having the principal sails extended on yards fastened in a horizontal position to the masts at their center

square–rig·ger \-ˈrig-ər\ *n* : a square-rigged ship

square root *n* : a number that when squared equals a specified number ⟨+3 and -3 are both a *square root* of 9⟩

square shooter *n* : a just or honest person

squar·ish \'skwa(ə)r-ish, 'skwe(ə)r-\ *adj* : somewhat square in form or appearance

¹squash \'skwäsh, 'skwȯsh\ *vb* **1** : to press or beat into a pulp or a flat mass : CRUSH ⟨*squash* a beetle⟩ **2** : to put an end to by force : SUPPRESS, SQUELCH ⟨*squash* a revolt⟩ **3** : ¹SQUEEZE 1c, PRESS ⟨*squashed* into the seat⟩ [from Middle English *squachen* "to crush, annul," from early French *esquacher* (same meaning)]

²squash *n* **1** : the sudden fall of a heavy soft body or the sound of such a fall **2** : a crushing sound **3** : a crushed

mass **4** : a game played in a four-walled court with a racket and a rubber ball

³squash *n, pl* **squash·es** *or* **squash** : any of various fruits of plants of the gourd family that are used especially as vegetables; *also* : a plant and typically a vine that produces squashes [a shortened and altered form of earlier *isquoutersquash* "the squash plant or fruit"; of American Indian origin]

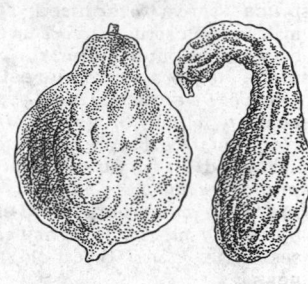
³squash

squash bug *n* : a large black American bug that is destructive to squash vines

squash racquets *n* : ²SQUASH 4

squashy \'skwäsh-ē, 'skwȯsh-\ *adj* **squash·i·er; -est** : easily squashed : SOFT

¹squat \'skwät\ *vb* **squat·ted; squat·ting 1** : to sit or cause (oneself) to sit on one's heels **2** : to occupy land as a squatter **3** : to crouch close to the ground ⟨a hare *squatting* in the grass⟩

²squat *n* **1** : the act of squatting **2** : a squatting posture

³squat *adj* **squat·ter; squat·test 1** : being in a squatting posture **2** : low to the ground **3** : being short and thick — **squat·ly** *adv* — **squat·ness** *n*

squat·ter \'skwät-ər\ *n* **1** : one that squats **2 a** : one that settles on land without right or title or payment of rent **b** : one that settles on public land under government regulation with the purpose of acquiring title

squat·ty \'skwät-ē\ *adj* **squat·ti·er; -est** : ³SQUAT 3, THICKSET

¹squawk \'skwȯk\ *vb* **1** : to utter a harsh short scream **2** : to complain or protest loudly or forcefully ⟨students *squawked* about the new dress code⟩ — **squawk·er** *n*

²squawk *n* **1** : a harsh short scream **2** : a noisy complaint

¹squeak \'skwēk\ *vb* **1** : to make a short shrill cry or noise **2** : to pass, succeed, or win by a narrow margin ⟨barely *squeaked* by⟩ **3** : to utter in a shrill tone

²squeak *n* **1** : a sharp shrill cry or sound **2** : ²ESCAPE 1 ⟨a close *squeak*⟩

squeaky \'skwē-kē\ *adj* **squeak·i·er; -est** : making or likely to make a shrill sound ⟨a *squeaky* door⟩

¹squeal \'skwē(ə)l\ *vb* **1** : to make a long shrill cry or noise **2 a** : INFORM 2 ⟨*squealed* to the teacher⟩ **b** : COMPLAIN 1, PROTEST **3** : to utter with or as if with a squeal — **squeal·er** *n*

²squeal *n* : a long shrill cry or noise

squea·mish \'skwē-mish\ *adj* **1 a** : easily made sick : QUEASY **b** : affected with nausea : NAUSEATED **2** : easily shocked or disgusted — **squea·mish·ly** *adv* — **squea·mish·ness** *n*

squee·gee \'skwē-ˌjē\ *n* : a blade of leather or rubber set on a handle and used for spreading or wiping liquid material on, across, or off a surface (as a window) — **squee·gee** *vb*

¹squeeze \'skwēz\ *vb* **squeezed; squeez·ing 1 a** : to press together from the opposite sides of : COMPRESS ⟨*squeeze* wet clay into a ball⟩ **b** : to get by squeezing ⟨*squeeze* juice from a lemon⟩ **c** : to force or thrust by compression : CROWD ⟨*squeezed* into the car⟩ **2 a** : to force (as by threats) money, goods, or services from ⟨*squeezed* their tenants mercilessly⟩ **b** : to reduce the amount of ⟨rising costs *squeezed* profits⟩ **3** : to gain or win by a narrow margin — **squeez·er** *n*

²squeeze *n* **1** : an act or instance of squeezing **2** : financial pressure ⟨put the *squeeze* on someone⟩ **3** *slang* : a romantic partner ⟨she's my main *squeeze*⟩

¹squelch \'skwelch\ *n* **1 :** a sound of or as if of a squishy substance under suction ⟨the *squelch* of mud⟩ **2 :** a remark that silences an opponent

²squelch *vb* **1 a :** to fall or stamp on so as to crush **b :** to put an end to by force : QUELL, SILENCE **2 :** to make or cause to make a sucking sound **3 :** to splash through water, slush, or mire — **squelch·er** *n*

squib \'skwib\ *n* **:** a short humorous or witty writing or speech

squid \'skwid\ *n, pl* **squid** *or* **squids :** any of numerous sea mollusks that are cephalopods and have eight short arms and two usually longer tentacles, a long thin body with a fin on each side, and a slender internal shell

squig·gle \'skwig-əl\ *n* **:** a short wavy twist or line : CURLICUE

squinch \'skwinch\ *vb* **1 :** to screw up (the face or eyes) : SQUINT ⟨*squinched* in the bright light⟩ **2 :** to make more compact **3 :** to crouch down or draw together

¹squint \'skwint\ *vb* **1 a :** to look with a side glance (as in jealousy or disdain) **b :** to be cross-eyed **2 :** to look or peer with eyes partly closed — **squint·er** *n*

²squint *n* **1 :** inability to direct both eyes to the same object due to a fault of the muscles of the eyeball **2 :** the act or an instance of squinting — **squinty** \'skwint-ē\ *adj*

squint–eyed \'skwint-'īd\ *adj* **1 :** having eyes that are partly closed **2 :** looking with a side glance (as in envy or ill will)

¹squire \'skwī(ə)r\ *n* **1 :** one who carries the shield or armor of a knight **2 a :** a male servant **b :** a lady's escort **3 a :** an owner of a country estate **b :** JUSTICE OF THE PEACE

²squire *vb* **squired; squir·ing :** to attend as a squire or escort

squirm \'skwərm\ *vb* **1 :** to twist about like an eel or a worm ⟨*squirmed* in their seats⟩ **2 :** to feel very embarrassed ⟨undeserved praise made us *squirm*⟩ — **squirmy** \'skwər-mē\ *adj*

¹squir·rel \'skwər-(ə)l, 'skwə-rəl\ *n, pl* **squirrels** *also* **squirrel 1 :** any of various small or medium-sized rodents; *esp* **:** one with a long bushy tail and strong hind legs used especially for leaping from tree branch to tree branch **2 :** the fur of a squirrel

Word History When a squirrel sits up to eat or to look around, it often raises its bushy tail up against its back and over its head as if to shade itself. The ancient Greeks noticed this habit, and they called the animal *skiouros*. This word was made up of *skia*, meaning "shadow," and *oura*, "tail." The Romans turned this into the Latin word *sciurus*, which made its way into early French as *esquirel*. English *squirrel* was borrowed from the French. [Middle English *squirel* "squirrel," from early French *esquirel* (same meaning), derived from Latin *sciurus* (same meaning), from Greek *skiouros* "squirrel," from *skia* "shadow" and *oura* "tail"]

¹squirrel 1

²squirrel *vb* **-reled** *or* **-relled; -rel·ing** *or* **-rel·ling :** to store up for future use — often used with *away* ⟨*squirreled* away all his spare change⟩

¹squirt \'skwərt\ *vb* **1 :** to come forth or shoot out in a sudden rapid stream : SPURT **2 :** to wet with a sudden rapid stream

²squirt *n* **1 a :** a small quick stream : JET **b :** the action of squirting **2 :** a disrespectful youngster

squirt gun *n* **:** WATER PISTOL

squishy \'skwish-ē\ *adj* **squish·i·er; -est :** being soft, yielding, and damp

SRO *n* **:** a house, apartment building, or residential hotel in which low-income or welfare tenants live in single rooms

S–shaped \'es-ˌshāpt, 'esh-\ *adj* **:** having the shape of a capital S

SST \ˌes-(ˌ)es-'tē\ *n* **:** an airplane used to transport people and goods at supersonic speeds

¹-st — see ²-EST

²-st *symbol* — used after the figure 1 to indicate the ordinal number first ⟨1*st*⟩ ⟨81*st*⟩

¹stab \'stab\ *n* **1 :** a wound produced by a pointed object or weapon **2 :** a thrust of a pointed weapon **3 :** EFFORT 2, TRY ⟨I'll take a *stab* at it⟩

²stab *vb* **stabbed; stab·bing 1 :** to wound or pierce by the thrust of a pointed object or weapon **2 :** ¹THRUST 1, DRIVE — **stab·ber** *n*

sta·bil·i·ty \stə-'bil-ət-ē\ *n, pl* **-ties :** the condition of being stable

sta·bi·lize \'stā-bə-ˌlīz\ *vb* **-lized; -liz·ing 1 :** to make or become stable, fixed, or firm **2 :** to hold steady (as by means of a stabilizer) — **sta·bi·li·za·tion** \ˌstā-bə-lə-'zā-shən\ *n*

sta·bi·liz·er \'stā-bə-ˌlī-zər\ *n* **:** one (as a chemical or a device) that stabilizes something; *esp* **:** a fixed surface for stabilizing the motion of an airplane

¹sta·ble \'stā-bəl\ *n* **1 :** a building in which domestic animals are sheltered and fed; *esp* **:** such a building having stalls or compartments ⟨a horse *stable*⟩ **2 a :** the racehorses of one owner **b :** a group of athletes (as boxers) under one management [Middle English *stable* "a place where animals are sheltered," from early French *estable* (same meaning), from Latin *stabulum* (same meaning), from *stare* "to stand"]

²stable *vb* **sta·bled; sta·bling** \-b(ə-)liŋ\ **:** to put, keep, or live in or as if in a stable

³stable *adj* **sta·bler** \-b(ə-)lər\; **sta·blest** \-b(ə-)ləst\ **1 a :** firmly established : FIXED, STEADFAST ⟨a *stable* community⟩ **b :** not easily changed or affected ⟨a *stable* government⟩ **c :** not likely to change suddenly or greatly ⟨a *stable* income⟩ **2 a :** steady in purpose : CONSTANT **b :** not subject to insecurity or emotional illness : SANE ⟨*stable* personalities⟩ **3 :** not readily changing in chemical composition or physical state ⟨a *stable* compound⟩ [Middle English *stable* "fixed, not moving or changing," from early French *estable* (same meaning), from Latin *stabilis* (same meaning), from *stare* "to stand"] — **sta·ble·ness** \-bəl-nəs\ *n* — **sta·bly** \-b(ə-)lē\ *adv*

sta·bler \'stā-b(ə-)lər\ *n* **:** one that keeps a stable

stac·ca·to \stə-'kät-ō\ *adj* **1 :** cut short so as not to sound connected ⟨*staccato* notes⟩ **2 :** made up of rapid disconnected elements or sounds ⟨*staccato* blasts of a horn⟩ — **staccato** *adv* — **staccato** *n*

¹stack \'stak\ *n* **1 :** a large pile (as of hay, straw, or grain) usually shaped like a cone **2 a :** an orderly pile of objects usually one on top of the other ⟨a *stack* of dishes⟩ **b :** a large number or amount **3 :** CHIMNEY 1, SMOKESTACK **4 :** a structure with shelves for storing books — usually used in plural

²stack *vb* **:** to arrange in or form a stack : PILE ⟨*stacked* the dishes on the table⟩ — **stack·er** *n*

stack·able \'stak-ə-bəl\ *adj* **:** easily stacked

stack up *vb* **:** MEASURE UP 2, COMPARE ⟨see how you *stack up* against the champion⟩

\ə\ **abut**	\au̇\ **out**	\i\ **tip**	\ȯ\ **saw**	\u̇\ **foot**
\ər\ **further**	\ch\ **chin**	\ī\ **life**	\ȯi\ **coin**	\y\ **yet**
\a\ **mat**	\e\ **pet**	\j\ **job**	\th\ **thin**	\yü\ **few**
\ā\ **take**	\ē\ **easy**	\ŋ\ **sing**	\th\ **this**	\yu̇\ **cure**
\ä\ **cot, cart**	\g\ **go**	\ō\ **bone**	\ü\ **food**	\zh\ **vision**

sta·di·um \'stād-ē-əm\ *n, pl* **-dia** \-ē-ə\ *or* **-di·ums** **1** : a course for footraces in ancient Greece with rows of seats for spectators **2** *pl usually* **stadiums** : a large usually roofless building with rows of seats for spectators at modern sports events

Word History A *stadion* in ancient Greece was a unit of measurement equal to about 180 meters. One of the most important events in the ancient Olympic Games was a footrace exactly one stadion long. The course on which the race was run, including the raised seats from which spectators watched, was also known as a *stadion*. This word was later borrowed into Latin as *stadium*. In time, it also came to be used to refer to larger structures in which different kinds of athletic contests were held. That is how the English word *stadium* is usually used. [Middle English *stadium* "a course for races in ancient Greece, a large structure for sports events," from Latin *stadium* (same meaning), from Greek *stadion* "a course for footraces, a unit of measurement"]

¹**staff** \'staf\ *n, pl* **staffs** \'stafs, 'stavz\ *or* **staves** \'stavz, 'stāvz\ **1 a** : a pole, stick, rod, or bar used as a support or as a sign of authority ⟨a flag hanging limp on its *staff*⟩ **b** : the long handle of a weapon (as a lance or pike) **c** : ¹CLUB 1a, CUDGEL **2** : something that

¹staff 3

is a source of strength ⟨bread is the *staff* of life⟩ **3** : the five horizontal lines and the spaces between them on which music is written **4** *pl* **staffs a** : a group of persons serving as assistants to or employees under a chief ⟨a hospital *staff*⟩ **b** : military officers who assist a commanding officer in planning and management but who do not take part in actual combat — **staff** *adj*

²**staff** *vb* : to supply with a staff or with workers

staff·er \'staf-ər\ *n* : a member of a staff and especially a newspaper staff

staff sergeant *n* : a military enlisted person with a rank just below that of platoon sergeant in the army, below that of gunnery sergeant in the marines, and below that of technical sergeant in the air force

¹**stag** \'stag\ *n, pl* **stags 1** *or pl* **stag** : an adult male deer especially of one of the larger kinds **2 a** : a social gathering of men only **b** : a man who attends a dance or party unaccompanied by a woman

²**stag** *adj* **1** : intended for men only ⟨a *stag* party⟩ **2** : unaccompanied by someone of the opposite sex — **stag** *adv*

¹**stage** \'stāj\ *n* **1 a** : one of the levels into which a structure can be divided **b** : a floor of a building **c** : a shelf or layer especially as one of a series **2 a** : a raised platform **b** : a part of a theater including the acting area **c** : the small platform of a microscope on which an object is placed for examination **3 a** : a center of attention : scene of action **b** : the theatrical profession or art **4 a** : a place of rest formerly provided for those traveling by stagecoach **b** : the distance between stopping places in a journey **c** : STAGE COACH ⟨traveling by *stage*⟩ **5 a** : a period or step in a process, activity, or development ⟨an early *stage* of a disease⟩ **b** : one of the periods of the growth and development of a plant or animal ⟨the larval *stage* of a beetle⟩; *also* : an individual in such a stage **6** : one of two or more sections of a rocket each having its own fuel and engine ⟨a three-*stage* missile⟩ — **on the stage** : in or into the acting profession

²**stage** *vb* **staged; stag·ing** : to produce or show publicly on or as if on the stage ⟨*stages* two plays each year⟩ ⟨*stage* a track meet⟩

stage·coach \'stāj-ˌkōch\ *n* : a coach pulled by horses

that carries passengers and mail and runs on a schedule between established stops

stage direction *n* : a playwright's instruction to a director and actors

stage fright *n* : nervousness felt at appearing before an audience

stage·hand \'stāj-ˌhand\ *n* : a stage worker who handles scenery, properties, or lights

stage manager *n* : a person who is in charge of the stage and the related details of a theatrical production

stage·struck \'stāj-ˌstrək\ *adj* : fascinated by the stage; *esp* : having an eager desire to become an actor

stage whisper *n* : a loud whisper by an actor intended to be heard by the spectators but supposed not to be heard by persons on the stage

¹**stag·ger** \'stag-ər\ *vb* **stag·gered; stag·ger·ing** \-(ə-)riŋ\ **1** : to move or cause to move unsteadily from side to side as if about to fall **2 a** : to begin to doubt and waver : become less confident **b** : to cause to doubt, waver, or hesitate : OVERWHELM ⟨were *staggered* by the problems they had to face⟩ **3** : to place or arrange in a zigzag or alternate but regular way — **stag·ger·er** \-ər-ər\ *n*

²**stagger** *n* **1** *pl* : an abnormal condition of domestic animals associated with damage to the central nervous system and marked by unsteady movements and falling **2** : a reeling or unsteady gait or stance

stag·ger·ing *adj* : so great as to cause one to stagger : ASTONISHING, OVERWHELMING ⟨a *staggering* achievement⟩ ⟨*staggering* medical bills⟩ — **stag·ger·ing·ly** \'stag-(ə-)riŋ-lē\ *adv*

stag·hound \'stag-ˌhaund\ *n* : a large heavy hound once used in hunting deer and other large animals

stag·ing \'stā-jiŋ\ *n* **1** : SCAFFOLDING 1 **2** : the putting of a play on the stage

stag·nant \'stag-nənt\ *adj* **1** : not flowing in a current or stream : MOTIONLESS **2** : not active or brisk ⟨*stagnant* business⟩

stag·nate \'stag-ˌnāt\ *vb* **stag·nat·ed; stag·nat·ing** : to be or become stagnant — **stag·na·tion** \stag-'nā-shən\ *n*

¹**staid** \'stād\ *adj* **1** : not easily changed : SETTLED, FIXED ⟨a *staid* opinion⟩ **2 a** : calm and serious in manner, attitude, or style **b** : not bold, bright, or showy ⟨*staid* colors⟩ — **staid·ly** *adv* — **staid·ness** *n*

²**staid** *past and past participle of* STAY

¹**stain** \'stān\ *vb* **1** : to soil or discolor especially in spots **2** : to give color to (as by dyeing) : TINGE **3 a** : ¹CORRUPT 1 ⟨a fine mind *stained* by jealousy⟩ **b** : ¹DISGRACE ⟨the scandal *stained* his reputation⟩ — **stain·er** *n*

²**stain** *n* **1** : a soiled or discolored spot **2** : a mark of guilt or disgrace ⟨bore the *stain* of their father's crime⟩ **3** : something (as a dye) used in staining: as **a** : a dye or pigment capable of penetrating the pores of wood **b** : a dye or mixture of dyes used in microscopy to make very small and transparent structures visible, to color tissue elements so that they can be told apart, and to produce specific chemical reactions — **stain·less** \'stān-ləs\ *adj*

stained glass *n* : glass colored or stained for use in windows

stainless steel *n* : an alloy of steel and chromium that is highly resistant to stain, rust, and corrosion

stair \'sta(ə)r, 'ste(ə)r\ *n* **1** : a series of steps or flights of steps for passing from one level to another — often used in plural ⟨ran down the *stairs*⟩ **2** : one step of a stairway

stair·case \-ˌkās\ *n* : a flight of stairs with the supporting structures

stair·way \-ˌwā\ *n* : one or more flights of stairs usually with landings to pass from one level to another

stair·well \-ˌwel\ *n* : a vertical shaft in which stairs are located

¹**stake** \'stāk\ *n* **1** : a pointed piece (as of wood or metal) driven or to be driven into the ground especially as a marker or support **2** : a post to which a person is bound

for execution by burning **3 a** : something that is staked for gain or loss **b** : the prize in a contest **c** : an interest or share in a business **4** : GRUBSTAKE — **at stake** : in a position to be lost or won ⟨lots of money *at stake*⟩

²stake *vb* **staked; stak·ing 1 a** : to mark the limits of by stakes ⟨*stake* out a mining claim⟩ **b** : to tie to a stake **c** : to fasten up or support (as plants) with stakes **2 a** : ²BET **1 b** : to back financially

sta·lac·tite \stə-'lak-ˌtīt\ *n* : a deposit of calcium carbonate resembling an icicle hanging from the roof or sides of a cavern [from scientific Latin *stalactites* "stalactite," from Greek *stalaktos* (adjective) "dripping"]

sta·lag·mite \stə-'lag-ˌmīt\ *n* : a deposit of calcium carbonate like an inverted stalactite formed on the floor of a cave by the drip of water [from scientific Latin *stalagmites* "stalagmite," from Greek *stalagma* "a drop" or Greek *stalagmos* "the act or result of dripping"]

1 stalactite, 2 stalagmite

¹stale \'stā(ə)l\ *adj* **stal·er; stal·est 1** : having lost a good taste or quality from age ⟨*stale* food⟩ **2** : used or heard so often as to be dull ⟨*stale* news⟩ **3** : not so strong, effective, or energetic as before ⟨felt *stale* from lack of exercise⟩ — **stale·ly** \'stā(ə)l-lē\ *adv* — **stale·ness** *n*

²stale *vb* **staled; stal·ing** : to make or become stale

¹stale·mate \'stā(ə)l-ˌmāt\ *n* **1** : a position in chess that results in a draw when the only piece to be moved is the king which cannot be moved without being exposed to attack by the other player's piece **2** : a drawn or undecided contest : DEADLOCK ⟨the two sides reached a *stalemate* in their negotiations⟩

²stalemate *vb* **stale·mat·ed; stale·mat·ing** : to bring into a stalemate ⟨the talks were *stalemated* over the issue of payment⟩

¹stalk \'stok\ *n* **1** : a slender upright object or supporting or connecting structure ⟨the *stalk* of a goblet⟩ **2** : a plant stem especially of a plant that is not woody ⟨*stalks* of asparagus⟩ — **stalked** \'stokt\ *adj* — **stalky** \'sto-kē\ *adj*

²stalk *vb* **1 a** : to hunt slowly and quietly ⟨*stalk* deer⟩ **b** : to go through (an area) in search of prey ⟨*stalk* the woods for deer⟩ **2** : to walk in a stiff or proud manner ⟨*stalked* out of the room⟩ **3** : to pursue obsessively and to the point of harassment — **stalk·er** *n*

³stalk *n* **1** : the act of stalking **2** : a stalking manner of walking

¹stall \'stol\ *n* **1** : a compartment for a domestic animal in a stable or barn **2 a** : a seat in the choir of a church with back and sides wholly or partly enclosed **b** *chiefly British* : a front orchestra seat in a theater — usually used in plural **3** : a booth, stand, or counter at which articles are displayed for sale **4** : a small compartment ⟨a shower *stall*⟩; *esp* : one with a toilet or urinal [Old English *steall* "stall for an animal"]

²stall *vb* **1** : to put into or keep in a stall **2** : to stop or cause to stop usually by accident ⟨*stall* an engine⟩ **3** : to experience or cause (an aircraft) to experience a stall in flying

³stall *n* : the condition of an aircraft or a wing of an aircraft in which lift is lost and the aircraft or wing tends to drop

⁴stall *n* : a trick to deceive or delay [an altered form of earlier *stale* "lure"]

⁵stall *vb* : to distract attention or make excuses to gain time ⟨try to *stall* them until I get the place cleaned up⟩

stal·lion \'stal-yən\ *n* : a male horse; *esp* : one kept especially for breeding

¹stal·wart \'stol-wərt\ *adj* : marked by outstanding strength

and vigor of mind, body, or spirit ⟨has *stalwart* common sense⟩ ⟨a *stalwart* team of rescuers⟩ — **stal·wart·ly** *adv*

²stalwart *n* **1** : a stalwart person **2** : a loyal supporter (as in politics)

sta·men \'stā-mən\ *n, pl* **stamens** *also* **sta·mi·na** \'stā-mə-nə, 'stam-ə-\ : an organ of a flower that consists of an anther and a filament and produces the pollen

stam·i·na \'stam-ə-nə\ *n* : VIGOR 1, ENDURANCE

sta·mi·nate \'stā-mə-nət, 'stam-ə-, -ˌnāt\ *adj* : having stamens; *esp* : having stamens but no pistils ⟨*staminate* flowers⟩

¹stam·mer \'stam-ər\ *vb* **stam·mered; stam·mer·ing** \-(ə-)riŋ\ : to speak or utter with involuntary stops and much repeating — **stam·mer·er** \-ər-ər\ *n*

²stammer *n* : an act or instance of stammering

¹stamp \'stamp; *senses 1b & 2 are also* 'stämp *or* 'stomp\ *vb* **1 a** : to pound or crush with a heavy instrument **b** : to strike or beat forcibly with the bottom of the foot **c** : to put an end to or destroy by or as if by stamping with the foot **2** : to walk heavily or noisily **3 a** : ¹IMPRINT 1, IMPRINT ⟨*stamp* the bill "paid"⟩ **b** : to attach a stamp to ⟨*stamp* a letter⟩ **4** : to form with a stamp or die **5** : CHARACTERIZE 1 ⟨*stamped* as reliable workers⟩ — **stamp·er** *n*

²stamp *n* **1** : a device or instrument for stamping **2** : the mark made by stamping **3** : a sign of a special quality ⟨a *stamp* of genius⟩ **4** : the act of stamping **5 a** : a stamped or printed paper attached to something to show that a tax or fee has been paid **b** : POSTAGE STAMP

¹stam·pede \stam-'pēd\ *n* **1** : a wild rush or flight of frightened animals **2** : a sudden movement of a crowd of people [from a word in the Spanish of Mexico and the American Southwest, *estampida* "stampede," from Spanish *estampida* "a crash, loud noise," from *estamper* "to pound, stamp"]

²stampede *vb* **stam·ped·ed; stam·ped·ing 1** : to run away or cause (as cattle) to run away in panic **2** : to act together or cause to act together suddenly and without thought

stance \'stan(t)s\ *n* **1** : a way of standing or being placed : POSTURE ⟨a soldier with an erect *stance*⟩ **2** : a way of thinking or feeling ⟨took an opposing *stance* on the issue⟩

¹stanch *also* **staunch** \'stonch, 'stänch\ *vb* **1** : to stop the flow of ⟨*stanch* tears⟩; *also* : to stop the flow of blood from (a wound) **2** : to stop in its course ⟨trying to *stanch* the crime wave⟩

²stanch *variant of* ²STAUNCH

stan·chion \'stan-chən\ *n* **1** : an upright bar, post, or support **2** : a device that fits loosely around an animal's neck and limits forward and backward motion (as in a stall)

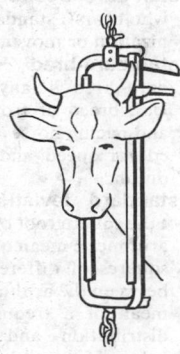

stanchion 2

¹stand \'stand\ *vb* **stood** \'stud\; **stand·ing 1 a** : to support oneself on the feet in an erect position **b** : to be a specified height when fully erect ⟨*stands* six feet two⟩ **c** : to rise to one's feet **2** : to take up and keep a usually specified position or attitude ⟨*stand* aside⟩ ⟨can you *stand* on your head⟩ ⟨where do we *stand* on this question⟩ **3** : to be in a particular state or situation ⟨*stands* accused⟩ **4** *chiefly British* : to be a candidate : RUN **5 a** : to have a relative position in or as if in a scale ⟨*stands* first in the class⟩ **b** : to be in a position to gain or lose ⟨*stands* to make a profit⟩ **6 a** : to rest, remain, or set upright on a base or lower end ⟨a ladder *standing* against a wall⟩ **b** : to occupy a place or location ⟨a house *standing* on a hill⟩ **7 a** : to remain without moving ⟨rainwater *standing* in stagnant pools⟩ **b** : to remain in effect ⟨the order *stands*⟩ **8** : to exist in a certain form ⟨you must take or leave our offer as it *stands*⟩ **9 a** : to put up with or resist successfully : BEAR ⟨*stand* pain⟩ ⟨the building *stood* the pressure of the storm⟩ ⟨this book will *stand* the test of time⟩ **b** : to derive benefit or enjoyment from ⟨you look like you could *stand* some sleep⟩ **c** : to go through the experience of ⟨*stand* trial⟩ **10** : to perform the duty of ⟨*stand* guard⟩ **11** : to pay for ⟨I'll *stand* dinner⟩ **12** : to cause to stand : set upright — **stand·er** *n* — **stand for 1** : to be a symbol for : REPRESENT **2** : to put up with : PERMIT ⟨would not *stand for* bad manners⟩ — **stand one's ground** : to maintain one's position

²**stand** *n* **1** : an act or instance of stopping or staying in one place **2 a** : a halt for defense or resistance **b** : a stop made to give a performance ⟨was booked for a three-night *stand*⟩ **3 a** : a place or post where one stands **b** : a position especially with respect to an issue ⟨took a *stand* against higher taxes⟩ **4 a** : the place occupied by a witness testifying in court **b** : a row of seats for spectators of an outdoor sport or spectacle **c** : a raised platform (as for a speaker) **5** : a small often open-air structure for a small retail business ⟨a hot-dog *stand*⟩ **6** : a support (as a rack or table) on or in which something may be placed ⟨umbrella *stands*⟩ ⟨a bicycle *stand*⟩ **7** : a group of plants growing in a continuous area ⟨a good *stand* of wheat⟩

¹**stan·dard** \'stan-dərd\ *n* **1 a** : a figure used as an emblem by an organized body of people ⟨the eagle was the Roman legion's *standard*⟩ **b** : the personal flag of the ruler of a state **2 a** : something set up by authority or by general consent as a rule for measuring or as a model ⟨a *standard* of weight⟩ ⟨*standards* of good manners⟩ **b** : the basis of value in a monetary system ⟨the gold *standard*⟩ **3** : a structure that serves as a support ⟨a lamp *standard*⟩

²**standard** *adj* **1** : used as or meeting a standard established by law or custom ⟨*standard* weight⟩ **2** : regularly and widely used ⟨*standard* practice in the trade⟩ **3** : having recognized and permanent value ⟨*standard* reference works⟩ **4** : well established by usage in the speech or writing of the educated and widely recognized as acceptable ⟨*standard* spelling⟩

stan·dard–bear·er \'stan-dərd-₁bar-ər, -₁ber-\ *n* **1** : one who bears a standard or banner **2** : the leader of an organization or movement

stan·dard·bred \'stan-dərd-₁bred\ *n* : any of a U.S. breed of trotting and pacing horses noted for speed and endurance

standard deviation *n* : the square root of the arithmetic mean of the squares of differences between the arithmetic mean of a frequency distribution and the values of the variable

standardbred

stan·dard·ize \'stan-dərd-₁īz\ *vb* **-ized; -iz·ing** : to compare with or make agree with a standard — **stan·dard·i·za·tion** \₁stan-dərd-ə-'zā-shən\ *n*

standard of living : the necessities, comforts, and luxuries that a person or group is accustomed to

standard time *n* : the time established by law or by general usage over a region or country

¹**stand·by** \'stan(d)-₁bī\ *n, pl* **stand·bys** \-₁bīz\ : one available or to be relied on especially in emergencies

²**standby** *adj* **1** : held near at hand and ready for use ⟨*standby* equipment⟩ **2** : relating to the act of standing by ⟨a *standby* period⟩ **3** : of or relating to a mode of transportation (as airline service) in which the passengers must wait for an available unreserved spot ⟨a *standby* ticket⟩

³**standby** *adv* : as a standby passenger ⟨flying *standby*⟩

stand by \(')stan(d)-'bī\ *vb* **1** : to be present ⟨*stood by*, watching the game⟩ **2** : to be or to get ready to act ⟨ambulances are *standing by*⟩ **3** : to remain loyal or faithful ⟨*stood by* us to the end⟩ ⟨*stood by* his decision⟩

stand·ee \stan-'dē\ *n* : one who occupies standing room

stand–in \'stan-₁din\ *n* **1** : someone employed to occupy an actor's place while lights and camera are readied **2** : ¹SUBSTITUTE

stand in \(')stan-'din\ *vb* : to act as a stand-in

¹**stand·ing** \'stan-diŋ\ *adj* **1 a** : not yet cut or harvested ⟨*standing* timber⟩ **b** : upright on the feet or base : ERECT ⟨a *standing* pose⟩ **2 a** : not flowing : STAGNANT ⟨*standing* water⟩ **b** : remaining at the same level, degree, or amount until canceled ⟨a *standing* offer⟩ **c** : continuing in existence or use for an unlimited length of time : PERMANENT ⟨a *standing* army⟩ ⟨*standing* committees⟩ **3** : done from a standing position ⟨*standing* jump⟩ ⟨a *standing* ovation⟩

²**standing** *n* **1** : the action or position of one that stands **2** : length of existence or service : DURATION ⟨a quarrel of long *standing*⟩ **3 a** : position or rank as compared with others ⟨had the highest *standing* in the class⟩ **b** : good reputation ⟨people of *standing* in the community⟩

standing room *n* : space available for spectators or passengers to stand in after all seats are filled

standing wave *n* : a vibration of a body or physical system in which the amplitude varies from place to place, is constantly zero at fixed points, and does not appear to move

stand·off \'stan-₁dof\ *n* : a contest or game in which there is no winner : DRAW

stand·off·ish \stan-'do-fish\ *adj* : not friendly : ALOOF

stand·out \'stan-₁daut\ *n* : one that is well-known or outstanding especially because of excellence

stand out \(')stan-'daut\ *vb* **1** : to stick out from a surface : PROJECT **2** : to be easily seen or recognized

stand pat *vb* **1** : to play one's hand as dealt in draw poker without drawing **2** : to oppose or resist change — **stand·pat·ter** \'stan(d)-₁pat-ər\ *n* — **stand·pat·ism** \-₁pat-₁iz-əm\ *n*

stand·point \'stan(d)-₁point\ *n* : a position from which things are viewed and according to which they are compared and judged

stand·still \-₁stil\ *n* : a state marked by absence of motion or activity : STOP ⟨traffic was at a *standstill*⟩

stand up *vb* **1** : to rise to a standing position **2** : to remain in good condition ⟨*stands up* to repeated washings⟩ **3** : to fail to keep an appointment with — **stand up for** : to defend against attack or criticism — **stand up to 1** : to meet fairly and fully **2** : to face boldly

stank *past of* STINK

stan·za \'stan-zə\ *n* : a division of a poem consisting of a series of lines arranged together in a usually repeating pattern of rhythm and rhyme — **stan·za·ic** \stan-'zā-ik\ *adj*

sta·pes \'stā-pēz\ *n, pl* **stapes** *or* **sta·pe·des** \'stā-pə-₁dēz\ : STIRRUP 2

staph \'staf\ *n* : STAPHYLOCOCCUS; *also* : an infection with staphylococci

staph·y·lo·coc·cus \₁staf-(ə-)lō-'käk-əs\ *n, pl* **-coc·ci** \-'käk-₁(s)ī, -₁(₁)(s)ē\ : any of a group of round bacteria that cause various diseases (as food poisoning and skin infections) and that occur especially in irregular clusters

— **staph·y·lo·coc·cal** \-'käk-əl\ *also* **staph·y·lo·coc·cic** \-'käk-(s)ik\ *adj*

¹**sta·ple** \'stā-pəl\ *n* : a usually U-shaped fastener: as **a** : a piece of metal with sharp points to be driven into a surface to hold something (as a hook, rope, or wire) **b** : a piece of thin wire that is driven through papers and bent over at the ends to fasten them together or driven through thin material to fasten it to something else **c** : a usually metal surgical fastener used to hold layers of tissue together (as in the closing of a wound) [Old English *stapol* "post"]

²**staple** *vb* **sta·pled; sta·pling** \-p(ə-)liŋ\ : to fasten with staples

³**staple** *n* **1** : a chief product of business or farming of a place **2 a** : something in widespread and constant use or demand **b** : the chief part of something ⟨potatoes are the *staple* of their diet⟩ **3** : RAW MATERIAL **4** : textile fiber (as wool or rayon) suitable for spinning into yarn [Middle English *staple* "a major market town, place for exporting"; of Dutch origin]

⁴**staple** *adj* **1** : used, needed, or enjoyed constantly usually by many individuals **2** : produced regularly or in large quantities ⟨*staple* crops such as wheat and rice⟩ **3** : ¹PRINCIPAL, CHIEF ⟨bamboo is the *staple* diet of the panda⟩

sta·pler \'stā-p(ə-)lər\ *n* : a device that staples

¹**star** \'stär\ *n* **1 a** : a natural body visible in the sky especially at night that gives off light or shines by reflection **b** : a ball-shaped gaseous celestial body (as the sun) of great mass that shines by its own light **2** : a planet or an arrangement of the planets that is believed in astrology to influence one's life — usually used in plural **3** : a figure or thing (as an asterisk or badge) with five or more points that represents or resembles a star **4 a** : the principal member of a theater or opera company **b** : a very talented or popular performer ⟨football *stars*⟩ ⟨TV *stars*⟩ — **star·like** \-ˌlīk\ *adj*

²**star** *vb* **starred; star·ring 1** : to sprinkle or adorn with stars **2 a** : to mark with a star as being superior **b** : to mark with an asterisk **3** : to present in the role of a star **4** : to play the most important role ⟨will produce and *star* in a new play⟩ **5** : to perform outstandingly ⟨*starred* at shortstop in the series⟩

³**star** *adj* **1** : of, relating to, or being a star **2** : being of outstanding excellence : PREEMINENT ⟨*star* athlete⟩ ⟨our *star* trumpeter⟩

¹**star·board** \'stär-bərd\ *n* : the right side of a ship or aircraft looking forward

Word History The word *starboard* has nothing whatever to do with stars. The *star-* part of the word used to be spelled *stēor-* in Old English and referred to the steering oar or rudder of a ship. In those days the rudder was located on the side of the ship to the right of a person facing toward the bow. Nowadays, of course, the rudder is at the stern. The *-board* part of the word refers not to a plank but to a whole side of a ship. This meaning survives today in the verb to *board* a ship or airplane. The side opposite the starboard is usually called the *port.* The name probably comes from the fact that this side faced the port or dock when the ship was steered into a harbor. The port side is sometimes also called the *larboard.* The *lar-* part of this word was spelled *lade-* in Old English. It probably came from the verb *laden,* meaning "to load." So the *larboard* was the side from which the cargo was loaded and unloaded. [Old English *stēorbord* "starboard, side of a ship from which it is steered," from *stēor* "steering oar" and *bord* "the side of a ship"]

²**starboard** *adj* : of, relating to, or situated to starboard

¹**starch** \'stärch\ *vb* : to stiffen with or as if with starch

²**starch** *n* **1** : a white odorless tasteless carbohydrate that is the chief form in which carbohydrate is stored in plants, is an important food, and is used also in adhesives, in laundering, and in pharmacy and medicine **2** : a stiff formal manner : FORMALITY **3** : VITALITY 2, SPUNK

starchy \'stär-chē\ *adj* **starch·i·er; -est 1** : containing, consisting of, or resembling starch ⟨*starchy* foods⟩ **2** : consisting of or marked by formality or stiffness — **starch·i·ness** *n*

star–crossed \'stär-ˌkrȯst\ *adj* : UNLUCKY 1, UNFORTUNATE [so called from the idea that stars control the lives and actions of people]

star·dom \'stärd-əm\ *n* : the status or position of a star

¹**stare** \'sta(ə)r, 'ste(ə)r\ *vb* **stared; star·ing** : to look hard and long often with wide-open eyes ⟨*stare* at a stranger⟩ **synonyms** see GAZE — **star·er** *n*

²**stare** *n* : the act or an instance of staring

star·fish \'stär-ˌfish\ *n* : any of a class of echinoderms that have five arms arranged evenly around a central disk and feed largely on mollusks (as oysters)

star fruit *n* : a green to yellow tropical Asian fruit that has the shape of a 5-pointed star when cut across the middle — called also *carambola*

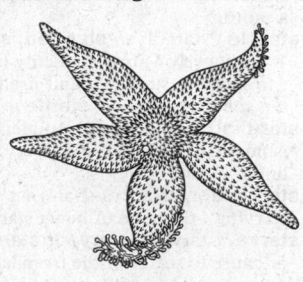

starfish

star·gaze \-ˌgāz\ *vb* **-gazed; -gaz·ing 1** : to gaze at stars **2** : to stare absentmindedly : DAYDREAM — **star·gaz·er** *n*

¹**stark** \'stärk\ *adj* **1** : STRONG 1, ROBUST **2 a** : STIFF 1, MOTIONLESS ⟨*stark* in death⟩ **b** : INFLEXIBLE 3, STRICT ⟨*stark* discipline⟩ **3** : ¹SHEER 2a, UTTER ⟨*stark* nonsense⟩ **4 a** : ¹BARREN 2a, DESOLATE ⟨a *stark* landscape⟩ **b** : having few or no ornaments : BARE **5** : UNADORNED, HARSH ⟨*stark* realism⟩ — **stark·ly** *adv*

²**stark** *adv* : WHOLLY, ABSOLUTELY ⟨*stark* mad⟩

star·let \'stär-lət\ *n* : a young movie actress

star·light \'stär-ˌlīt\ *n* : the light given by the stars

star·ling \'stär-liŋ\ *n* : any of a family of usually dark-colored birds that tend to flock together; *esp* : a dark brown or in summer glossy greenish black European bird that has been brought to the U.S. and is often considered a pest

star·lit \'stär-ˌlit\ *adj* : lighted by the stars

star–nosed mole \'stär-nōzd-\ *n* : a black long-tailed mole of the northeastern U.S. and southeastern Canada that is found near or in water and has a bunch of pink fleshy projections surrounding the nostrils which are used as feelers in searching for food

Star of Da·vid \-'dā-vəd\ : a 6-pointed star used as a symbol of Judaism

star·ry \'stär-ē\ *adj* **star·ri·er; -est 1** : full of stars ⟨*starry* heavens⟩ **2** : of, relating to, or consisting of stars : STELLAR ⟨*starry* light⟩ **3** : shining like stars : SPARKLING ⟨*starry* eyes⟩

Stars and Bars *n sing or pl* : the first flag of the Confederate States of America

Stars and Stripes *n sing or pl* : the flag of the U.S.

star·shine \'stär-ˌshīn\ *n* : STARLIGHT

star·ship \'stär-ˌship\ *n* : a vehicle designed for travel between stars

star–span·gled \'stär-ˌspaŋ-gəld\ *adj* : adorned with stars

¹**start** \'stärt\ *vb* **1** : to move suddenly and sharply : give a sudden twitch or jerk (as in surprise) **2** : to come or bring

\ə\ **abut**	\au̇\ **out**	\i\ **tip**	\ȯ\ **saw**	\u̇\ **foot**
\ər\ **further**	\ch\ **chin**	\ī\ **life**	\ȯi\ **coin**	\y\ **yet**
\a\ **mat**	\e\ **pet**	\j\ **job**	\th\ **thin**	\yu̇\ **few**
\ā\ **take**	\ē\ **easy**	\ŋ\ **sing**	\th\ **this**	\yu̇\ **cure**
\ä\ **cot, cart**	\g\ **go**	\ō\ **bone**	\ü\ **food**	\zh\ **vision**

into being, activity, or operation ⟨who *started* the rumor⟩ ⟨*started* a camp for youngsters⟩ ⟨fire *started* in the cellar⟩ ⟨the game *started* late⟩ **3** : to stick out or seem to stick out : PROTRUDE ⟨eyes that *started* from their sockets⟩ **4** : SET OUT 2, BEGIN ⟨*start* to school⟩ **5** : to take part or cause to take part in a game or contest **6** : to cause to move, act, or operate ⟨*start* the motor⟩

²start *n* **1 a** : a quick unwilled bodily reaction **b** : a brief and sudden action or movement **2** : a beginning of movement, activity, or development ⟨get an early *start*⟩ **3** : a lead or advantage at the beginning of a race or competition : HEAD START **4** : a place of beginning

start·er \'stärt-ər\ *n* : someone or something that starts something or causes something else to start ⟨the *starter* of a motor⟩

star·tle \'stärt-ᵊl\ *vb* **star·tled; star·tling** \'stärt-liŋ, -ᵊl-iŋ\ **1** : to move or jump suddenly (as in surprise or fright) **2** : to frighten suddenly and usually not seriously ⟨the kitten *startles* easily⟩ — **startle** *n*

star·tling *adj* : causing a sudden fright, surprise, or astonishment ⟨a *startling* discovery⟩ — **star·tling·ly** \'stärt-liŋ-lē, -ᵊl-iŋ-\ *adv*

star·va·tion \stär-'vā-shən\ *n* : the act or an instance of starving : the state of being starved

starve \'stärv\ *vb* **starved; starv·ing** **1** : to suffer or die or cause to suffer or die from lack of food **2** : to suffer or die or cause to suffer or die from a lack of something other than food ⟨a child *starving* for affection⟩ [Old English *steorfan* "to die (from any cause)"]

starve·ling \'stärv-liŋ\ *n* : one thin and weakened by or as if by lack of food

¹stash \'stash\ *vb* : to store in a usually secret place for future use

²stash *n* **1** : a hiding place ⟨used the cupboard as a secret *stash*⟩ **2** : something stored or hidden away ⟨had a *stash* of money in the closet⟩

¹state \'stāt\ *n* **1 a** : manner or condition of being ⟨a *state* of readiness⟩ **b** : condition of mind or disposition ⟨in a highly nervous *state*⟩ **2 a** : a condition or stage of the physical makeup of something ⟨water in the gaseous *state*⟩ **b** : a stage in the growth or development of a plant or animal ⟨the larval *state*⟩ **3 a** : a politically organized body of people usually occupying a definite territory **b** : the political organization of such a body of people **4** : one of the units of a nation having a federal government ⟨the United *States* of America⟩ **5** : the territory of a state — **state·less** \-ləs\ *adj*

²state *adj* **1** : suitable or used for ceremonies or official occasions ⟨*state* robes⟩ **2** : of or relating to a national state or to one state of a federal government ⟨a *state* church⟩ ⟨a *state* legislature⟩ **3** : of or relating to the government : GOVERNMENTAL ⟨*state* secrets⟩

³state *vb* **stated; stat·ing** **1** : to set by regulation or authority ⟨the law *stated* times for inspection⟩ **2** : to express in words ⟨*state* an opinion⟩

state bird *n* : a bird selected (as by the legislature) as an emblem of a state of the U.S.

state·craft \'stāt-ˌkraft\ *n* : the art of conducting government affairs

stat·ed \'stāt-əd\ *adj* **1** : being set or fixed ⟨a *stated* procedure for elections⟩ **2** : set down clearly ⟨*stated* goals⟩

state flower *n* : a flowering plant selected (as by the legislature) as an emblem of a state of the U.S.

state·hood \'stāt-ˌhu̇d\ *n* : the condition of being a state; *esp* : the condition or status of one of the states of the U.S.

state·house \'stāt-ˌhau̇s\ *n* : the building in which a state legislature meets

state·ly \'stāt-lē\ *adj* **state·li·er; -est** : impressively grand in appearance, manner, or size — **state·li·ness** *n*

state·ment \'stāt-mənt\ *n* **1** : the act or process of stating **2 a** : something stated : REPORT, ASSERTION **b** : PROPOSI-

TION 2 **3** : a brief summarized record of activity in a financial account over a particular period of time ⟨a monthly bank *statement*⟩ **4** : an instruction in a computer program

state·room \'stāt-ˌrüm, -ˌru̇m\ *n* : a private room on a ship or on a railroad car

state·side \'stāt-ˌsīd\ *adj* : of or relating to the U.S. as considered from outside its continental limits

states·man \'stāt-smən\ *n* : a person engaged in fixing the policies and conducting the affairs of a government; *esp* : one having unusual wisdom and skill in such matters — **states·man·like** \-ˌlīk\ *adj* — **states·man·ly** \-lē\ *adj* — **states·man·ship** \-ˌship\ *n*

states' rights *n pl* : all rights not given to the federal government by the U.S. Constitution nor forbidden by it to the separate states

state·wide \'stāt-'wīd\ *adj* : including all parts of a state

¹stat·ic \'stat-ik\ *adj* **1** : of or relating to bodies at rest or forces that are balanced ⟨*static* friction⟩ **2** : showing little change ⟨a *static* population⟩ **3** : marked by a lack of movement, liveliness, or progress **4** : of, relating to, or producing stationary charges of electricity (as those produced by friction)

²static *n* : noise produced in a radio or television receiver by atmospheric or electrical disturbances

static electricity *n* : electricity that consists of isolated stationary charges

static line *n* : a cord attached to a parachute pack and to an airplane to open the parachute after a jumper clears the plane

¹sta·tion \'stā-shən\ *n* **1** : the place or position in which something or someone stands or is assigned to stand or remain **2** : a regular stopping place : DEPOT ⟨drove him to the bus *station*⟩ **3 a** : a post or area of duty or occupation **b** : a stock farm or ranch of Australia or New Zealand **4** : social or official position : RANK ⟨a person of high *station*⟩ **5** : a place for specialized scientific observation and study especially in or near the field or in natural surroundings ⟨a biological *station*⟩ ⟨a weather *station*⟩ **6** : a place established to provide a public service ⟨police *station*⟩ ⟨fire *station*⟩ ⟨power *station*⟩ **7 a** : a complete collection of radio or television equipment for transmitting or receiving **b** : the place in which such a station is located

²station *vb* **sta·tioned; sta·tion·ing** \'stā-sh(ə-)niŋ\ : to assign to or set in a station or position : POST ⟨*station* a guard at the door⟩

sta·tion·ary \'stā-shə-ˌner-ē\ *adj* **1** : fixed in a station, course, or position : IMMOBILE ⟨a *stationary* loudspeaker⟩ **2** : unchanging in condition ⟨a *stationary* population⟩

station break *n* : a pause in a radio or television broadcast for announcement of the identity of the network or station

sta·tio·ner \'stā-sh(ə-)nər\ *n* : one that sells stationery

sta·tio·nery \'stā-shə-ˌner-ē\ *n* **1** : materials (as paper, pens, and ink) for writing or typing **2** : letter paper usually accompanied with matching envelopes

sta·tion·mas·ter \'stā-shən-ˌmas-tər\ *n* : an official in charge of the operation of a railroad station

station wagon *n* : an automobile that has a large open area behind the back seat instead of a trunk and that has a door at the back for loading and unloading things

sta·tis·tic \stə-'tis-tik\ *n* : a single item of information in a statistical collection

stat·is·ti·cian \ˌstat-ə-'stish-ən\ *n* : a person who specializes in statistics

sta·tis·tics \stə-'tis-tiks\ *n sing or pl* : a branch of mathematics dealing with the collection and study of numerical data; *also* : a collection of such numerical data — **sta·tis·ti·cal** \-'tis-ti-kəl\ *adj* — **sta·tis·ti·cal·ly** \-ti-k(ə-)lē\ *adv*

stat·u·ary \'stach-ə-ˌwer-ē\ *n, pl* **-ar·ies** **1** : ¹SCULPTURE 1 **2** : a collection of statues — **statuary** *adj*

stat·ue \'stach-ü\ *n* : a likeness (as of a person) sculptured, modeled, or cast in a solid substance (as marble)

stat·u·esque \,stach-ə-'wesk\ *adj* : resembling a statue especially in size, gracefulness, or beauty; *esp* : tall and attractive ⟨a *statuesque* actress⟩

stat·u·ette \,stach-ə-'wet\ *n* : a small statue

stat·ure \'stach-ər\ *n* **1** : natural height (as of a person) in an upright position **2** : quality or status gained by growth, development, or achievement ⟨artists of *stature*⟩

sta·tus \'stāt-əs, 'stat-\ *n* **1** : position or rank in relation to others : STANDING **2** : state or condition with respect to circumstances : SITUATION

sta·tus quo \,stāt-ə-'skwō, ,stat-\ *n* : the way things are now ⟨chose to keep the *status quo* rather than make changes⟩

stat·ute \'stach-üt, -ət\ *n* : a law put into effect by the legislative branch of a government

statute mile *n* : MILE 1

stat·u·to·ry \'stach-ə-,tōr-ē, -,tȯr-\ *adj* **1** : of or relating to statutes **2** : regulated by statute **3** : punishable by statute

¹staunch *variant of* ¹STANCH

²staunch *or* **stanch** \'stȯnch, 'stänch\ *adj* **1 a** : WATERTIGHT 1, SOUND ⟨a *staunch* ship⟩ **b** : strongly built : SUBSTANTIAL ⟨*staunch* foundations⟩ **2** : steadfast in loyalty or principle ⟨a *staunch* friend⟩ **synonyms** see FAITHFUL — **staunch·ly** *adv*

¹stave \'stāv\ *n* **1** : a wooden stick **2** : one of the narrow strips of wood or iron plates placed edge to edge to form the sides, covering, or lining of a vessel (as a barrel or cask) or structure **3** : STANZA **4** : ¹STAFF 3

²stave *vb* **staved** *or* **stove** \'stōv\; **stav·ing 1** : to break in the staves of (a cask) **2** : to smash a hole in ⟨*stave* in a boat⟩

stave off *vb* : to force or keep away : fend off ⟨*stave off* trouble⟩

staves *plural of* STAFF

S ¹stave 2

¹stay \'stā\ *n* : a strong rope or wire used to steady or brace something (as a mast) [Old English *stæg* "a strong rope used to steady or support something"]

²stay *vb* : to fasten (as a smokestack) with stays

³stay *vb* **1** : to stop going forward : PAUSE **2** : to continue in a place or condition : REMAIN ⟨*stayed* at home⟩ **3** : to stand firm **4** : to take up residence : LODGE ⟨*stayed* in a hotel⟩ **5** : ¹WAIT 1a **6** : to last out (as a race) **7** : ²CHECK 2, HALT ⟨*stay* an execution⟩ [Middle English *stayen* "to stop going forward," from early French *ester* "to stand, stay," from Latin *stare* "to stand"]

⁴stay *n* **1** : the action of halting : the state of being stopped **2** : a stopping of a procedure by court or executive order **3** : a residence or visit in a place

⁵stay *n* **1** : something that serves as a prop : SUPPORT **2** : a thin firm strip (as of plastic) used for stiffening a garment (as a corset) or part (as a shirt collar) [from early French *estaie* "a support, prop"; of Germanic origin]

⁶stay *vb* : to provide support for

staying power *n* : ability, influence, or strength enough to keep going through a difficult task ⟨a candidate with the *staying power* to make it to the election⟩

STD \,es-,tē-'dē\ *n* : any of various diseases (as syphilis and gonorrhea) that are usually transmitted by direct sexual contact and that include some (as hepatitis and AIDS) that may be contracted by other than sexual means

stead \'sted\ *n* **1** : ADVANTAGE 3, SERVICE ⟨their knowledge of French stood them in good *stead*⟩ **2** : the place usually taken or duty carried out by the one mentioned ⟨acted in the mayor's *stead*⟩

stead·fast \'sted-,fast\ *adj* **1 a** : firmly fixed in place **b** : not subject to change ⟨a *steadfast* purpose⟩ **2** : firm in

belief, determination, or allegiance ⟨*steadfast* friends⟩ **synonyms** see FAITHFUL — **stead·fast·ly** *adv* — **stead·fast·ness** \-,fas(t)-nəs\ *n*

¹steady \'sted-ē\ *adj* **stead·i·er; -est 1 a** : firm in position : FIXED **b** : direct or sure in movement ⟨took *steady* aim⟩ **2 a** : ¹REGULAR 3, UNIFORM ⟨a *steady* pace⟩ **b** : not changing much : STABLE ⟨*steady* prices⟩ **3 a** : not easily moved or upset : RESOLUTE **b** : constant in feeling, principle, purpose, or attachment : DEPENDABLE — **steadi·ly** \'sted-ᵊl-ē\ *adv* — **steadi·ness** \'sted-ē-nəs\ *n*

²steady *vb* **stead·ied; steady·ing** : to make, keep, or become steady

³steady *adv* : in a steady manner : STEADILY

⁴steady *n, pl* **stead·ies** : one that is steady; *esp* : a boyfriend or girlfriend with whom one goes steady

steady state *n* : a state or condition of a system or process that does not change or changes only slightly over time ⟨on the average a living cell maintains a *steady state*⟩

steady state theory *n* : a theory in astronomy that states that the universe has always existed and has always been expanding

steak \'stāk\ *n* **1** : a slice of meat and especially beef **2** : a slice of a large fish (as swordfish)

¹steal \'stē(ə)l\ *vb* **stole** \'stōl\; **sto·len** \'stō-lən\; **steal·ing 1** : to come or go secretly or quietly ⟨*stole* out of the room⟩ **2 a** : to take and carry away without right and with the intention of keeping the property of another : ROB **b** : to take in a sneaky way and without permission ⟨*steal* a kiss⟩ **c** : to take entirely to oneself or beyond one's proper share ⟨*steal* the show⟩ **3 a** : SMUGGLE 2 **b** : to accomplish or get in a concealed or unobserved manner ⟨*steal* a nap⟩ **4 a** : to seize, gain, or win by trickery, skill, or daring ⟨the basketball player *stole* the ball⟩ **b** : to gain a base in baseball by running without the aid of a hit or an error — **steal·er** *n* — **steal one's thunder** : to grab attention from another especially by presenting an idea or plan first; *also* : to claim credit for another's idea

²steal *n* **1** : the act or an instance of stealing **2** : something offered or purchased at a low price : BARGAIN

¹stealth \'stelth\ *n* **1** : sly or secret action **2** : a design style intended to make an aircraft difficult to detect by radar

²stealth *adj* : intended not to attract attention : STEALTHY 2 ⟨a *stealth* campaign⟩

stealthy \'stel-thē\ *adj* **stealth·i·er; -est 1** : slow, deliberate, and secret in action or character **2** : intended to escape observation : FURTIVE — **stealth·i·ly** \-thə-lē\ *adv*

¹steam \'stēm\ *n* **1 a** : the invisible vapor into which water is changed when heated to the boiling point **b** : the mist formed when water vapor cools **2** : water vapor kept under pressure so as to supply energy for heating, cooking, or mechanical work; *also* : the power so generated **3 a** : driving force : POWER ⟨arrived under their own *steam*⟩ **b** : built-up tension ⟨let off a little *steam*⟩

²steam *vb* **1** : to rise or pass off as vapor **2** : to give off steam or vapor **3** : to move or travel by or as if by the power of steam ⟨*steamed* up the river⟩ **4** : to be angry : BOIL ⟨was *steaming* over the insult⟩ **5** : to expose to the action of steam (as for softening or cooking) ⟨*steamed* clams⟩

steam·boat \'stēm-,bōt\ *n* : a boat driven by steam

steam engine *n* : an engine driven by steam

steam·er \'stē-mər\ *n* **1** : a container in which something is steamed **2 a** : a ship driven by steam **b** : an engine, machine, or vehicle run by steam

steam iron *n* : a pressing iron with a compartment holding water that is converted to steam by the iron's heat and

\ə\ **abut**	\au̇\ **out**	\i\ **tip**	\ȯ\ **saw**	\u̇\ **foot**
\ər\ **further**	\ch\ **chin**	\ī\ **life**	\ȯi\ **coin**	\y\ **yet**
\a\ **mat**	\e\ **pet**	\j\ **job**	\th\ **thin**	\yü\ **few**
\ā\ **take**	\ē\ **easy**	\ŋ\ **sing**	\th\ **this**	\yu̇\ **cure**
\ä\ **cot, cart**	\g\ **go**	\ō\ **bone**	\ü\ **food**	\zh\ **vision**

given off through holes in the bottom onto the fabric being pressed

steam·roll·er \'stēm-ˌrō-lər\ *n* : a machine formerly driven by steam that has wide heavy rollers for pressing down and smoothing roads

steam·ship \'stēm-ˌship\ *n* : STEAMER 2a

steam shovel *n* : a power machine for digging that was formerly operated by steam

steam turbine *n* : a turbine that is driven by the pressure of steam discharged at high speed against the turbine blades

steamy \'stē-mē\ *adj* **steam·i·er; -est** **1** : consisting of, characterized by, or full of steam **2** : hot and humid ⟨*steamy* weather⟩ **3** : EROTIC — **steam·i·ly** \-mə-lē\ *adv*

stea·ric acid \stē-ˌar-ik-, ˌsti(ə)r-ik-\ *n* : acid obtained by the hydrolysis of a hard fat (as tallow) with alkali

stea·rin \'stē-ə-rən, 'sti(ə)r-ən\ *n* : a chemical compound that is the chief substance in beef fat

steed \'stēd\ *n* : ¹HORSE 1a; *esp* : a lively horse

¹steel \'stē(ə)l\ *n* **1** : commercial iron that contains carbon in any amount up to about 1.7 percent as a necessary part **2** : an article (as a sword) made of steel **3** : a hard cold quality ⟨answered with *steel* in her voice⟩

²steel *vb* : to fill with courage or determination

³steel *adj* **1** : made of or like steel **2** : of or relating to the production of steel

steel·head \'stē(ə)l-ˌhed\ *n, pl* **steelhead** *also* **steelheads** : a rainbow trout that migrates to the sea to mature and returns to rivers to breed — called also *steelhead trout*

steel wool *n* : a rough material composed of long fine steel shavings and used especially for cleaning and polishing

steely \'stē-lē\ *adj* **steel·i·er; -est** **1** : made of steel **2** : resembling steel (as in hardness or color) ⟨a *steely* gaze⟩ — **steel·i·ness** *n*

steel·yard \'stē(ə)l-ˌyärd\ *n* : a balance on which something to be weighed is hung from the shorter arm of a lever and is balanced by a weight that slides along the longer arm which is marked with a scale

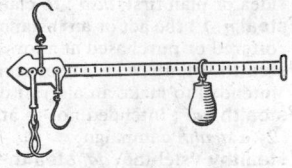

steelyard

¹steep \'stēp\ *adj* **1** : having a very sharp slope : almost straight up-and-down **2** : being or characterized by a very rapid decline or increase **3** : too great or high ⟨*steep* prices⟩ — **steep·ly** *adv*

synonyms STEEP, PRECIPITOUS, SHEER mean having a slope that is close to exactly upright. STEEP implies such sharpness of pitch that going up or down is very difficult ⟨a *steep* hill⟩. PRECIPITOUS applies to a slope so sharp that it is almost straight up-and-down ⟨the river winds through a *precipitous* gorge⟩. SHEER suggests an unbroken precipitous expanse ⟨*sheer* cliffs that made the climbers hesitate⟩.

²steep *n* : a sharply sloping place

³steep *vb* **1 a** : to soak in liquid (as for drawing out a flavor) at a temperature under the boiling point ⟨*steep* tea⟩ **b** : to undergo the process of soaking in a liquid **2** : to fill with or involve deeply ⟨*steeped* in learning⟩ **synonyms** see SOAK

steep·en \'stē-pən\ *vb* **steep·ened; steep·en·ing** \'stēp-(ə-)niŋ\ : to make or become steeper

stee·ple \'stē-pəl\ *n* **1** : a tall structure usually having a small spire at the top and built on top of a church tower **2** : a church tower — **stee·pled** \-pəld\ *adj*

stee·ple·chase \'stē-pəl-ˌchās\ *n* **1 a** : a race over the countryside on horses **b** : a horse race on a special course with obstacles (as hedges and walls) **2** : a footrace of usu-

ally 3,000 meters over hurdles and a water jump [so called from the fact that originally the races were across the countryside in a direct line toward a distant church steeple sighted rising above the other buildings] — **stee·ple·chas·er** \-ˌchā-sər\ *n*

¹steer \'sti(ə)r\ *n* **1** : a male domestic ox castrated before sexual maturity and especially one raised for beef **2** : an ox less than four years old

²steer *vb* **1** : to direct the course or the course of : GUIDE ⟨*steer* by the stars⟩ ⟨*steer* a boat⟩ ⟨*steer* a conversation⟩ **2** : to follow a course of action **3** : to be guided ⟨an automobile that *steers* well⟩ — **steer·able** \'stir-ə-bəl\ *adj* — **steer·er** \'stir-ər\ *n* — **steer clear** : to keep entirely away ⟨*steer clear* of arguments⟩

steer·age \'sti(ə)r-ij\ *n* **1** : the act or practice of steering; *also* : DIRECTION 1 **2** : a section in a passenger ship for passengers paying the lowest fares

steering wheel *n* : a wheel for steering something by hand

stego·sau·rus \ˌsteg-ə-'sȯr-əs\ *n* : any of a genus of 4-footed planteating dinosaurs having bony plates and spikes on the back and tail and whose fossil remains are found in the Upper Jurassic rocks of Colorado and Wyoming

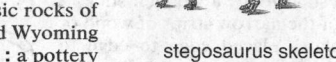

stegosaurus skeleton

stein \'stīn\ *n* : a pottery mug for beer

stel·lar \'stel-ər\ *adj* **1** : of or relating to the stars ⟨*stellar* light⟩ **2 a** : ¹PRINCIPAL, LEADING ⟨a *stellar* role⟩ **b** : OUTSTANDING **3** ⟨a *stellar* performance⟩

¹stem \'stem\ *n* **1 a** : the main stalk of a plant that develops buds and shoots and usually grows above the ground **b** : a plant part (as the stalk of a leaf or flower) that supports some other part **2** : the bow of a ship **3** : the basic part of a word to which prefixes or suffixes may be added **4** : something held to resemble a plant stem: as **a** : the short upright line from the head of a musical note **b** : the part of a tobacco pipe from the bowl outward **c** : a main or heavy stroke of a letter **d** : the cylindrical support of a piece of stemware (as a wine glass) **e** : a shaft of a watch used for winding [Old English *stefn, stemn* "stem of a plant, stem of a ship"] — **stem·less** \-ləs\ *adj* — **from stem to stern** : ¹THROUGHOUT 1, THOROUGHLY

²stem *vb* **stemmed; stem·ming** **1** : to remove the stem from **2** : to have or trace a beginning or growth : DERIVE ⟨illness that *stemmed* from unsanitary conditions⟩

³stem *vb* **stemmed; stem·ming** : to make progress against

⁴stem *vb* **stemmed; stem·ming** **1** : to stop or check by or as if by damming ⟨*stem* the flow of blood from the wound⟩ **2** : to become checked or stopped [Middle English *stemmen* "to dam up"; of Norse origin]

stem cell *n* : a simple cell that can become a cell (as a blood cell or skin cell) with a special function

stemmed \'stemd\ *adj* : having a stem

stem·ware \'stem-ˌwa(ə)r, -ˌwe(ə)r\ *n* : glass vessels (as goblets) mounted on a stem

stem–wind·er \'stem-ˌwīn-dər\ *n* **1** : a watch wound by an inside mechanism turned by a knob on the stem **2** : something that is first-rate of its kind; *esp* : a stirring speech

stench \'stench\ *n* : a very disagreeable smell : STINK 1

¹sten·cil \'sten(t)-səl\ *n* **1** : a piece of material (as a sheet of paper) with lettering or a design that is cut out and through which ink or paint is forced onto a surface to be printed **2** : a design or print produced with a stencil

²stencil *vb* **-ciled** *or* **-cilled; -cil·ing** *or* **-cil·ling** \-s(ə-)liŋ\ **1** : to paint with a stencil **2** : to produce by a stencil

steno \'sten-ō\ *n, pl* **sten·os** : STENOGRAPHER

ste·nog·ra·pher \stə-'näg-rə-fər\ *n* **1** : a writer of short-hand **2** : one employed chiefly to take and make a copy of dictation

ste·nog·ra·phy \stə-'näg-rə-fē\ *n* : the art or process of writing in shorthand — **steno·graph·ic** \,sten-ə-'graf-ik\ *adj* — **steno·graph·i·cal·ly** \-'graf-i-k(ə-)lē\ *adv*

sten·tor \'sten-,tô(ə)r, 'stent-ər\ *n* : any of a genus of trumpet-shaped one-celled animals that are protozoans living in fresh water and moving by means of cilia

sten·to·ri·an \sten-'tôr-ē-ən, -'tor-\ *adj* : very loud ⟨a *stentorian* voice⟩ [from *Stentōr*, a Greek messenger at the time of the Trojan War noted for having a very loud voice]

¹step \'step\ *n* **1** : a rest for the foot in going up or down : STAIR, RUNG **2 a** : a movement made by raising the foot and bringing it down elsewhere **b** : a combination of foot or foot and body movements in a repeated pattern **c** : manner of walking : STRIDE ⟨knows me by my *step*⟩ **d** : FOOTPRINT **e** : the sound of a footstep **3 a** : the space passed over in one step **b** : a short distance ⟨only a *step* away⟩ **c** : the height of one stair **4** *pl* : ¹COURSE 2, WAY ⟨guided their *steps* down the path⟩ **5 a** : a level or rank in a scale ⟨one *step* nearer graduation⟩ **b** : a stage in a process **6** : an action, proceeding, or measure often occurring as one in a series ⟨took *steps* to correct the situation⟩ **7** : a musical scale degree — **step·like** \-,līk\ *adj* — **stepped** \'stept\ *adj*

²step *vb* **stepped; step·ping 1 a** : to move or take by raising the foot and bringing it down elsewhere or by moving each foot in order ⟨*step* three paces⟩ ⟨*stepped* ashore⟩ **b** : ¹DANCE 1 **2 a** : to go on foot : WALK ⟨*step* outside⟩ **b** : to move briskly ⟨really *stepped* along⟩ **3** : to press down with the foot ⟨*step* on a nail⟩ **4** : to come as if at a single step ⟨*step* into a good job⟩ **5** : to measure by steps — **step·per** *n*

step·broth·er \'step-,brəth-ər\ *n* : a son of one's stepparent by a former partner

step–by–step \,step-bī-'step\ *adj* : GRADUAL

step·child \'step-,chīld\ *n* : a child of one's wife or husband by a former partner

step·daugh·ter \-,dot-ər\ *n* : a daughter of one's wife or husband by a former partner

step down \(')step-'daún\ *vb* **1** : to lower the voltage of (a current) using a transformer **2** : to decrease or reduce especially by one or more steps ⟨*stepped down* the volume⟩ **3** : RESIGN 2, RETIRE ⟨will *step down* as chairman at the end of this year⟩ — **step–down** \-,daún\ *adj*

step·fa·ther \'step-,fäth-ər\ *n* : the husband of one's mother when distinct from one's natural or legal father

step–in \-,in\ *n* : an article of clothing (as a dress or shoes) that can be put on by being stepped into

step·lad·der \-,lad-ər\ *n* : a short ladder that has broad flat steps and two pairs of legs connected by a hinge at the top and that opens at the bottom to become freestanding

step·moth·er \-,məth-ər\ *n* : the wife of one's father when distinct from one's natural or legal mother

step out *vb* : to go away from a place usually for a short distance and for a short time

step·par·ent \'step-,par-ənt, -,per-\ *n* : a person who is a stepmother or stepfather

steppe \'step\ *n* : land in regions of wide temperature range (as in southeastern Europe and parts of Asia) that is dry, usually rather level, and covered with grass

step·ping–stone \'step-iŋ-,stōn\ *n* **1** : a stone on which to step (as in crossing a stream) **2** : something aiding in progress or advancement ⟨a *stepping-stone* to success⟩

step·sis·ter \'step-,sis-tər\ *n* : a daughter of one's stepparent by a former partner

step·son \-,sən\ *n* : a son of one's husband or wife by a former partner

step stool *n* : a stool with one or two steps beneath the seat

step up *vb* **1** : to increase the voltage of (a current) using a transformer **2** : to increase or advance ⟨*step up* production⟩ **3 a** : to come forward ⟨*stepped up* to accept responsibility⟩ **b** : to succeed in meeting a challenge (as by greater effort or better performance) — **step–up** \'step-,əp\ *adj*

-ster \stər\ *n combining form* **1** : one that does or handles or operates ⟨team*ster*⟩ **2** : one that makes or uses ⟨song*ster*⟩ **3** : one that is associated with or participates in ⟨gang*ster*⟩ **4** : one that is ⟨young*ster*⟩ [Old English *-estre* "female agent"]

¹ste·reo \'ster-ē-,ō, 'stir-\ *n* **1** : stereophonic reproduction **2** : a stereophonic sound system

²stereo *adj* **1** : of or relating to the seeing of objects in three dimensions **2** : STEREOPHONIC

ste·reo·phon·ic \,ster-ē-ə-'fän-ik, ,stir-\ *adj* : of or relating to sound reproduction designed to create the effect of listening to the original

ste·re·op·ti·con \,ster-ē-ə-'äp-ti-kən, ,stir-\ *n* : a projector for transparent slides

ste·reo·scope \'ster-ē-ə-,skōp, 'stir-\ *n* : an optical instrument that blends two slightly different pictures of the same subject to give the effect of depth

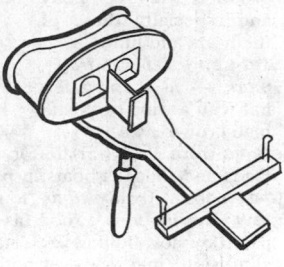
stereoscope

ste·reo·scop·ic \,ster-ē-ə-'skäp-ik\ *adj* **1** : of or relating to the stereoscope **2** : characterized by the seeing of objects in three dimensions ⟨*stereoscopic* vision⟩

¹ste·reo·type \'ster-ē-ə-,tīp, 'stir-\ *n* **1** : a printing plate made by casting melted metal in a mold **2** : something agreeing with a pattern; *esp* : an idea that many people have about a thing or a group and that may often be untrue or only partly true

²stereotype *vb* **1** : to make a stereotype from **2** : to develop a mental stereotype about ⟨unfairly *stereotyped* salesmen as dishonest⟩

ste·reo·typed \'ster-ē-ə-,tīpt, 'stir-\ *adj* : following a pattern : lacking originality ⟨*stereotyped* characters in the book⟩

ster·ile \'ster-əl\ *adj* **1** : not able to produce fruit, crops, or offspring : not fertile ⟨*sterile* soil⟩ **2** : free from microscopic living things and especially germs (as bacteria and viruses) ⟨a *sterile* dressing for a wound⟩ — **ste·ril·i·ty** \stə-'ril-ət-ē\ *n*

ster·il·ize \'ster-ə-,līz\ *vb* **-ized; -iz·ing** : to make sterile: as **a** : to deprive of the power of reproduction ⟨had their cat *sterilized*⟩ **b** : to free of microscopic living things and especially germs (as bacteria) ⟨*sterilize* the dental instruments⟩ — **ster·il·i·za·tion** \,ster-ə-lə-'zā-shən\ *n*

ster·il·iz·er \'ster-ə-,lī-zər\ *n* : one that sterilizes something; *esp* : a device used for sterilizing by steam, boiling water, or dry heat

¹ster·ling \'stər-liŋ\ *n* **1** : British money **2** : sterling silver or articles of it [so called from the phrase "a pound sterling," meaning the British pound as a monetary unit, but originally "a pound (by weight) of sterlings," from Middle English *sterling* "silver penny"]

²sterling *adj* **1** : of or relating to British sterling **2** : being or made of an alloy of 925 parts of silver with 75 parts of copper ⟨*sterling* silver⟩ **3** : EXCELLENT

\ə\ **abut**	\au̇\ **out**	\i\ **tip**	\ȯ\ **saw**	\u̇\ **foot**
\ər\ **further**	\ch\ **chin**	\ī\ **life**	\ȯi\ **coin**	\y\ **yet**
\a\ **mat**	\e\ **pet**	\j\ **job**	\th\ **thin**	\yü\ **few**
\ā\ **take**	\ē\ **easy**	\ŋ\ **sing**	\th\ **this**	\yu̇\ **cure**
\ä\ **cot, cart**	\g\ **go**	\ō\ **bone**	\ü\ **food**	\zh\ **vision**

¹**stern** \'stərn\ *adj* **1 a** : hard and severe in nature or manner ⟨a *stern* judge⟩ **b** : expressing severe displeasure : HARSH ⟨a *stern* look⟩ **2** : not inviting or attractive : FORBIDDING, GRIM **3** : firm and not changeable : STOUT, RESOLUTE ⟨*stern* determination⟩ — **stern·ly** *adv* — **stern·ness** \'stərn-nəs\ *n*

²**stern** *n* **1** : the rear end of a boat **2** : a rear part

ster·num \'stər-nəm\ *n, pl* **sternums** *or* **ster·na** \-nə\ : a flat narrow piece of bone or cartilage in the chest that connects the ribs in most vertebrates other than fishes — called also *breastbone*

stern–wheel·er \'stərn-'hwē-lər\ *n* : a paddle-wheel steamer having a stern wheel instead of side wheels

ste·roid \'stir-ˌȯid, 'ster-\ *n* : any of various chemical compounds that include numerous hormones (as estrogen and testosterone) — compare ANABOLIC STEROID

stetho·scope \'steth-ə-ˌskōp *also* 'steth-\ *n* : a medical instrument used for listening to sounds produced in the body and especially those of the heart and lungs

Stet·son \'stet-sən\ *trademark* — used for a felt hat with a wide brim and high crown

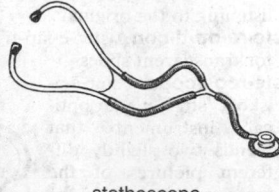

stethoscope

ste·ve·dore \'stēv-(ə-)ˌdō(ə)r, -ˌdȯ(ə)r\ *n* : a person who loads and unloads boats in port [from Spanish *estibador* "stevedore," from *estibar* "to pack"]

¹**stew** \'st(y)ü\ *n* **1** : food (as meat with vegetables) prepared by slow boiling **2** : a state of excitement, worry, or confusion ⟨in a *stew* over nothing⟩

²**stew** *vb* **1** : to boil slowly : SIMMER **2** : to become excited or worried : FRET

stew·ard \'st(y)ü-ərd, 'st(y)ù(-ə)rd\ *n* **1** : a manager of a large home, estate, or organization **2** : a person employed to manage the supply and distribution of food and attend the needs of passengers (as on a train, airplane, or ship) [Old English *stīweard,* literally, "keeper of the hall, keeper of the sty," from *stī* "hall, sty" and *weard* "ward, guard, keeper"]

stew·ard·ess \'st(y)ü-ərd-əs, 'st(y)ù(-ə)rd-\ *n* : a woman who does the job of a steward; *esp* : one who attends the needs of passengers (as on an airplane)

stew·ard·ship \'st(y)ü-ərd-ˌship, 'st(y)ù(-ə)rd-\ *n* **1** : the office and duties of a steward **2** : the careful and responsible management of something entrusted to one's care ⟨*stewardship* of our natural resources⟩

¹**stick** \'stik\ *n* **1** : a cut or broken branch of twig especially when dry and dead **2** : a long slender piece of wood or metal: as **a** : a club or staff used as a weapon **b** : WALKING STICK **1 3** : something used for striking or moving an object in a game **4** : something like a stick in shape or use ⟨a *stick* of dynamite⟩ **5** : something prepared in a long and slender form ⟨carrot *sticks*⟩ ⟨a *stick* of butter⟩ **6** : a person who is dull or lifeless **7** *pl* : remote usually rural districts ⟨way out in the *sticks*⟩ [Old English *sticca*]

²**stick** *vb* **stuck** \'stək\; **stick·ing** **1 a** : to stab with something pointed : PIERCE **b** : to kill by piercing **2** : to cause to penetrate ⟨*stuck* a needle in my finger⟩ **3 a** : to fasten by pushing in : ATTACH ⟨*stuck* a flower in my buttonhole⟩ **b** : to push out, up, or under ⟨*stuck* out my hand⟩ **4** : to put or set in a specified place or position ⟨*stuck* the cap on my head⟩ **5** : to cling to a surface ⟨snowflakes *stuck* on the windowpane⟩ **6 a** : to bring to a halt : prevent the movement or action of ⟨the car got *stuck* in traffic⟩ **b** : ¹BAFFLE 1, STUMP ⟨got *stuck* on the first problem⟩ **7 a** : ¹CHEAT 1, DEFRAUD **b** : to burden with something disagreeable ⟨*stuck* with the job of cleaning up⟩ **8** : to become fixed in place by or as if by gluing ⟨his foot *stuck* in

the mud⟩ **9 a** : to remain in a place, situation, or environment ⟨decided to *stick* where he was⟩ **b** : to hold to something tightly : CLING ⟨she *stuck* to her story⟩ **10** : to become blocked or jammed ⟨the desk drawer always *sticks*⟩ **11** : to be unable to proceed (as through fear or conscience) [Old English *stician*] — **stick one's neck out** : to make oneself vulnerable (as to criticism or punishment) by taking a risk — **stick to one's guns** : to maintain one's position especially in the face of opposition — **stuck on** : infatuated with

stick around *vb* : to stay or wait about : LINGER

stick·ball \'stik-ˌbȯl\ *n* : baseball played on the street or in a small area with a broomstick and a lightweight ball

stick·er \'stik-ər\ *n* **1** : something that pierces with a point **2 a** : something that clings (as a bur) or causes clinging (as glue) **b** : a slip of paper with gummed back that clings to a surface

stick figure *n* : a drawing showing the head of a human being or animal as a circle and all other parts as straight lines

stick insect *n* : any of various usually wingless insects that have a long body resembling a stick — called also *walking stick*

stick–in–the–mud \'stik-ən-thə-ˌməd\ *n* : one who is slow, old-fashioned, or unprogressive

stick·le·back \'stik-əl-ˌbak\ *n* : any of numerous small scaleless fishes that have two or more sharp spines on the back

stick·ler \'stik-(ə-)lər\ *n* **1** : a person who insists on exactness or completeness in the observance of something ⟨a *stickler* for the rules⟩ **2** : something that baffles or puzzles

stickleback

stick out *vb* **1 a** : to extend out : PROJECT **b** : to be noticeable ⟨you will certainly *stick out* with that red hat and coat⟩ **2** : to put up with : ENDURE ⟨*stuck* it *out* to the bitter end⟩

stick·pin \'stik-ˌpin\ *n* : an ornamental pin worn in a necktie

stick·tight \-ˌtīt\ *n* : BUR MARIGOLD

stick·up \'stik-ˌəp\ *n* : a robbery at gunpoint : HOLDUP

stick up \'stik-'əp\ *vb* **1** : to stand upright or on end : PROTRUDE **2** : to rob at gunpoint — **stick up for** : to speak or act in defense of : SUPPORT

sticky \'stik-ē\ *adj* **stick·i·er; -est 1 a** : ¹ADHESIVE, GLUEY ⟨*sticky* syrup⟩ **b** : coated with a sticky substance ⟨the tabletop was *sticky*⟩ **2** : MUGGY, HUMID ⟨a hot *sticky* day⟩ **3** : tending to stick ⟨*sticky* windows⟩ — **stick·i·ly** \'stik-ə-lē\ *adv* — **stick·i·ness** \'stik-ē-nəs\ *n*

¹**stiff** \'stif\ *adj* **1 a** : not easily bent : RIGID **b** : not easily moved ⟨*stiff* muscles⟩ ⟨*stiff* valves⟩ **2 a** : marked by moral courage **b** : not easy or graceful in manner **3** : hard fought ⟨a *stiff* fight⟩ **4 a** : exerting great force : STRONG ⟨a *stiff* wind⟩ **b** : POTENT 2b ⟨a *stiff* dose⟩ **5** : not flowing easily : THICK ⟨beat egg whites until *stiff*⟩ **6 a** : HARSH 3, SEVERE ⟨a *stiff* penalty⟩ **b** : RUGGED ⟨*stiff* terrain⟩ **7** : EXPENSIVE 2, STEEP ⟨a *stiff* price⟩ — **stiff·ly** *adv* — **stiff·ness** *n*

²**stiff** *adv* **1** : in a stiff manner **2** : to a stiff state or condition ⟨frozen *stiff*⟩ **3** : to an extreme degree ⟨bored *stiff*⟩

³**stiff** *n* **1** : CORPSE **2** : PERSON ⟨you lucky *stiff*⟩

stiff·en \'stif-ən\ *vb* **stiff·ened; stiff·en·ing** \-(ə-)niŋ\ : to make or become stiff or stiffer — **stiff·en·er** \-(ə-)nər\ *n*

sti·fle \'stī-fəl\ *vb* **sti·fled; sti·fling** \-f(ə-)liŋ\ **1** : to kill by depriving of or die from lack of oxygen or air : SMOTHER **2** : to keep in check by deliberate effort : REPRESS ⟨trying to *stifle* a sneeze⟩ — **sti·fling·ly** \-f(ə-)liŋ-lē\ *adv*

stig·ma \'stig-mə\ *n, pl* **stig·ma·ta** \stig-'mät-ə, 'stig-mət-ə\ *or* **stigmas** **1 a** : a mark of shame : STAIN **b** : an identifying mark or characteristic; *esp* : a specific sign

that indicates the presence of a disease **2** *stigmata pl*
: bodily marks or pains resembling the wounds of Jesus
when nailed on the cross **3 a** : a small spot, scar, or opening on a plant or animal **b** : the upper part of the pistil of
a flower which receives the pollen grains and on which
they start to grow — **stig·mat·ic** \stig-'mat-ik\ *adj*

stig·ma·tize \'stig-mə-ˌtīz\ *vb* **-tized; -tiz·ing** : to mark
with a stigma; *esp* : to describe or identify as disgraceful

stile \'stī(ə)l\ *n* **1** : a step or set of steps for passing over a
fence or wall **2** : TURNSTILE

sti·let·to \stə-'let-ō\ *n, pl* **-tos** *or* **-toes** : a slender dagger

¹still \'stil\ *adj* **1 a** : not moving ⟨lying quiet and *still*⟩ **b**
: of, relating to, or being an ordinary photograph rather
than a motion picture **2** : uttering no sound : QUIET **3 a**
: TRANQUIL, CALM **b** : free from noise or commotion
: PEACEFUL [Old English *stille* "not moving"] — **stillness** *n*

²still *vb* **1 a** : to make quiet : CALM ⟨*still* their fears⟩ **b** : to
put to an end : SETTLE **2** : to make or become motionless
or silent : QUIET

³still *adv* **1** : without motion ⟨sit *still*⟩ **2** : up to this or that
time ⟨*still* lives there⟩ ⟨while it's *still* hot⟩ **3** : in spite of
that : NEVERTHELESS ⟨those who take care can *still* make
mistakes⟩ **4 a** : ³EVEN 4 ⟨a *still* more difficult problem⟩
b : beyond this : IN ADDITION, YET ⟨won *still* another
tournament⟩

⁴still *n* **1** : ¹QUIET, SILENCE **2** : a still photograph

⁵still *n* **1** : DISTILLERY **2** : a device used in distillation
[from earlier *still* (verb) "to distill," from Middle English
stillen, a shortened form of *distillen* "to distill"]

still·birth \'stil-ˌbərth, -'bərth\ *n* : the birth of a dead baby

still·born \-'bò(ə)rn\ *adj* : dead at birth

still life *n, pl* **still lifes** : a picture of an arrangement of
objects

stilly \'stil-ē\ *adj* : showing stillness : CALM, QUIET

stilt \'stilt\ *n* **1** : one of two poles each
with a rest or strap for the foot used to
elevate the wearer above the ground in
walking **2** : a stake or post used to support a structure above ground or water
level

stilt·ed \'stil-təd\ *adj* : not easy and natural ⟨*stilted* speech⟩

stim·u·lant \'stim-yə-lənt\ *n* **1** : something (as a drug) that temporarily increases the activity or efficiency of the
body or one of its parts ⟨a heart *stimulant*⟩ **2** : STIMULUS 1 — **stimulant** *adj*

stim·u·late \'stim-yə-ˌlāt\ *vb* **-lat·ed;
-lat·ing** **1** : to make active or more active : ANIMATE, AROUSE ⟨*stimulate* in-
dustry⟩ **2** : to act on as a bodily stimulus or stimulant   **synonyms** see
PROVOKE

stim·u·la·tion \ˌstim-yə-'lā-shən\ *n* : the
act or result of stimulating

stilt 1

stim·u·lus \'stim-yə-ləs\ *n, pl* **-li** \-ˌlī, -ˌlē\ **1** : something
that rouses or stirs to action : INCENTIVE **2** : something
(as an environmental change) that acts to partly change
bodily activity (as by exciting a sensory organ) ⟨heat,
light, and sound are common physical *stimuli*⟩

¹sting \'stiŋ\ *vb* **stung** \'stəŋ\; **sting·ing** \'stiŋ-iŋ\ **1 a** : to
prick painfully especially with a sharp or poisonous sting-
er ⟨*stung* by a bee⟩ **b** : to affect with or feel quick piercing pain or smart ⟨hail *stung* their faces⟩ **2** : to cause to
suffer mentally ⟨*stung* with regret⟩ **3** : OVERCHARGE 1,
CHEAT ⟨got *stung* on the deal⟩ **4** : to use a stinger ⟨bees
sting⟩

²sting *n* **1 a** : the act of stinging **b** : a wound or pain
caused by or as if by stinging **2** : STINGER 2 — **sting·less**
\'stiŋ-ləs\ *adj*

sting·er \'stiŋ-ər\ *n* **1** : one that stings; *esp* : a piercing
blow or remark **2** : a sharp organ of some animals (as
bees or scorpions) that is used to wound, paralyze, or kill
prey or an enemy by piercing and injecting a poisonous
fluid

sting·ray \'stiŋ-ˌrā\ *n* : any of numerous rays that have one or
more large sharp stinging spines
near the base of the whiplike tail

stin·gy \'stin-jē\ *adj* **stin·gi·er;
-est** **1** : not generous : giving, using, or spending as little as possible **2** : SCANTY, MEAGER ⟨a *stingy*
portion⟩ — **stin·gi·ly** \-jə-lē\ *adv*
— **stin·gi·ness** \-jē-nəs\ *n*

¹stink \'stiŋk\ *vb* **stank** \'staŋk\ *or*
stunk \'stəŋk\; **stunk; stink·ing**
1 : to give off or cause to have an
unpleasant smell ⟨the garbage pail
stinks⟩ **2** : to be very bad or unpleasant ⟨that news really *stinks*⟩
— **stink·er** *n*

²stink *n* **1** : a strong unpleasant
odor : STENCH **2** : a public outcry
against something : FUSS ⟨made a big *stink* when asked to
leave⟩ — **stinky** \'stiŋ-kē\ *adj*

stink·bug \'stiŋk-ˌbəg\ *n* : any of various true bugs that
give off a bad smell

¹stint \'stint\ *vb* **1** : to be sparing or stingy ⟨not *stinting*
with their praise⟩ **2** : to limit in share or portion : cut
short in amount ⟨*stint* the children's allowance⟩ — **stint-
er** *n*

²stint *n* **1** : RESTRICTION 1, LIMITATION ⟨gave without
stint⟩ **2 a** : a quantity of work assigned **b** : a period of
time spent at a particular activity ⟨served a brief *stint* as a
waiter⟩

stipe \'stīp\ *n* : a short stalk
supporting the cap of a
mushroom

sti·pend \'stī-ˌpend, -pənd\
n : a sum of money paid at
regular times for services
or expenses

stip·ple \'stip-əl\ *vb* **stip-
pled; stip·pling** \-(ə-)liŋ\
: to apply (as paint or ink)
by repeated small touches
— **stipple** *n* — **stip·pler**
\-(ə-)lər\ *n*

stip·u·late \'stip-yə-ˌlāt\ *vb*
-lat·ed; -lat·ing : to demand or insist on as part
of an agreement

stingray

S stipe

stip·u·la·tion \ˌstip-yə-'lā-shən\ *n* : something required as
part of an agreement

stip·ule \'stip-yü(ə)l\ *n* : either of a pair of small leaflike
parts at the base of the petiole of a leaf in many plants —
see LEAF illustration

¹stir \'stər\ *vb* **stirred; stir·ring** **1 a** : to make or cause to
make an especially small movement or change of position
⟨the leaves were barely *stirring*⟩ **b** : to disturb the quiet
of : AGITATE ⟨the bear *stirred* up the bees⟩ **2** : to mix,
dissolve, or make especially by a continued circular
movement ⟨*stir* the pudding⟩ **3 a** : to rouse to action or
strong feeling : INCITE ⟨his pleas *stirred* the crowd⟩ **b** : to
call forth (as a memory) : EVOKE ⟨*stirred* thoughts of

home⟩ **c :** to cause to take place : PROVOKE ⟨*stir* up trouble⟩ **4 :** to be active or busy ⟨not a creature was *stirring*⟩ — **stir·rer** *n*

²stir *n* **1 a :** a state of disturbance, upset, or action **b** : widespread notice and discussion : IMPRESSION **2 :** a small movement **3 :** a stirring movement

¹stir–fry \'stər-ˌfrī\ *vb* : to fry quickly over high heat while stirring continuously

²stir–fry \-ˌfrī\ *n* : a dish of something stir-fried

stir·ring \'stər-iŋ\ *adj* : MOVING 3, INSPIRING ⟨a *stirring* speech⟩

stir·rup \'stər-əp *also* 'stir-əp *or* 'stə-rəp\ *n* **1 :** either of a pair of small light frames often of metal hung by straps from a saddle and used as a support for the foot of a horseback rider **2 :** the innermost bone of the chain of three small bones in the middle ear of a mammal — called also *stapes*

¹stitch \'stich\ *n* **1 :** a sudden sharp pain especially in the side **2 a :** one in-and-out movement of a threaded needle in sewing or embroidering **b :** a portion of thread left in the material after one stitch **3 :** a single loop of thread or yarn around a tool (as a knitting needle) **4 :** a series of stitches formed in a particular way — **in stitches :** in a state of uncontrollable laughter

²stitch *vb* **1 a :** to join with or as if with stitches ⟨*stitched* a seam⟩ **b :** to make, mend, or decorate with or as if with stitches **2 :** to do needlework : SEW — **stitch·er** *n*

stoat \'stōt\ *n* : a common ermine of northern regions especially in its brown summer coat

¹stock \'stäk\ *n* **1 a** *archaic* : ¹STUMP **2 b** *archaic* : a log or block of wood **c** *archaic* : something without life or consciousness **d :** a dull, stupid, or lifeless person **2 a** *pl* : a timber frame with holes to contain the feet or feet and hands of a wrongdoer as public punishment **b :** the part of a crossbow or long gun that is held against the shoulder or in the hand when in use **3 a :** the main stem of a plant : TRUNK **b :** a plant or plant part that is joined to a living branch or stem and makes up the lower or underground parts in a graft **4 a :** the original (as a human being, race, or language) from which others descend : SOURCE **b** : ANCESTRY 2, LINEAGE **5 a :** the equipment or goods of an establishment **b :** farm animals : LIVESTOCK **6 a :** the ownership element of a corporation divided to give the owners an interest and usually voting power **b :** a portion of such stock **7 :** a wide band or scarf worn about the neck especially by some members of the clergy **8 a :** liquid in which meat, fish, or vegetables have been simmered and which is used to make soup, gravy, or sauce **b** : RAW MATERIAL **9 :** confidence placed in someone or something **10 :** the production and presentation of plays by a stock company — **in stock :** in the store and ready for delivery

²stock *vb* **1 :** to fit to or with a stock **2 :** to provide with or acquire stock or a stock ⟨*stock* up on food⟩ **3 :** to get or keep a stock of ⟨a store that *stocks* only the finest goods⟩

³stock *adj* **1 :** kept regularly in stock ⟨a *stock* model⟩ **2** : commonly used or brought forward : STANDARD ⟨the *stock* answer⟩

¹stock·ade \stä-'kād\ *n* **1 :** a line of stout posts set firmly to form a defense **2 a :** an enclosure or pen made with posts and stakes **b :** an enclosure in which prisoners are kept

²stockade *vb* **stock·ad·ed; stock·ad·ing :** to protect or surround with a stockade

stock·bro·ker \'stäk-ˌbrō-kər\ *n* : one that handles orders to buy and sell stocks

stock car *n* : a racing car that is similar to regular cars

stock certificate *n* : a formal legal document showing evidence of ownership of one or more shares of the stock of a corporation

stock company *n* **1 :** a corporation whose resources are represented by stock **2 :** a theatrical company without outstanding stars

stock exchange *n* **1 :** a place where the buying and selling of stocks is conducted **2 :** an association of stockbrokers

stock·fish \'stäk-ˌfish\ *n* : fish (as cod, haddock, or hake) dried hard in the open air without salt

stock·hold·er \'stäk-ˌhōl-dər\ *n* : an owner of stocks

stock·ing \'stäk-iŋ\ *n* **1 :** a close-fitting usually knit covering for the foot and leg **2 :** ¹SOCK

stocking cap *n* : a long knitted cone-shaped cap usually with an ornament at the pointed end

stock market *n* : STOCK EXCHANGE 1

stock·pile \'stäk-ˌpīl\ *n* : an extra supply especially of something necessary accumulated within a country for use during a shortage — **stockpile** *vb*

stock·room \-ˌrüm, -ˌrùm\ *n* : a storage place for supplies or goods used in a business

stock–still \-'stil\ *adj* : very still : MOTIONLESS ⟨stood *stock-still*⟩

stocky \'stäk-ē\ *adj* **stock·i·er; -est :** compact, sturdy, and quite thick in build : THICKSET — **stock·i·ly** \'stäk-ə-lē\ *adv* — **stock·i·ness** \-ē-nəs\ *n*

stock·yard \'stäk-ˌyärd\ *n* : a yard in which livestock are kept temporarily for slaughter, market, or shipping

stodgy \'stäj-ē\ *adj* **stodg·i·er; -est 1 :** moving in a slow struggling way especially as a result of physical bulkiness **2 :** having no excitement or interest : DULL, BORING ⟨a *stodgy* day⟩ **3 :** very old-fashioned in attitude or point of view — **stodg·i·ly** \'stäj-ə-lē\ *adv*

¹sto·ic \'stō-ik\ *n* : one not easily excited or upset

²stoic *or* **sto·i·cal** \'stō-i-kəl\ *adj* : unconcerned about pleasure or pain — **sto·ical·ly** \-i-k(ə-)lē\ *adv*

stoke \'stōk\ *vb* **stoked; stok·ing 1 :** to stir up or tend (as a fire) **2 :** to supply (as a furnace) with fuel **3 :** to feed plentifully — **stok·er** *n*

¹stole \'stōl\ *past of* STEAL

²stole *n* **1 :** a long narrow band worn around the neck by bishops and priests in ceremonies **2 :** a long wide scarf or similar covering worn by women usually across the shoulders

stolen *past participle of* STEAL

stol·id \'stäl-əd\ *adj* : having or expressing little or no feeling : not easily stirred or excited ⟨a *stolid* person⟩ — **stol·id·ly** *adv*

sto·lon \'stō-lən, -ˌlän\ *n* : a horizontal branch from the base of a plant that produces new plants from buds at its tip or nodes (as in the strawberry) — called also *runner*

S stolon

sto·ma \'stō-mə\ *n, pl* **sto·ma·ta** \-mət-ə\ : a small opening which is surrounded by two guard cells and through which moisture and gases pass in and out of the epidermis of a leaf

¹stom·ach \'stəm-ək, -ik\ *n* **1 a :** a pouch of the vertebrate digestive system into which food passes from the esophagus for mixing and digestion before passing to the duodenum of the small intestine **b :** a cavity with a similar function in an invertebrate animal **c :** the part of the body that contains the stomach : BELLY, ABDOMEN **2 a** : desire for food caused by hunger : APPETITE **b :** ²DESIRE 1, INCLINATION ⟨had no *stomach* for an argument⟩

²stomach *vb* : TOLERATE 1 ⟨could not *stomach* the smell⟩

stom·ach·ache \'stəm-ək-ˌāk, -ik-\ *n* : pain in or near the stomach

stom·ach·er \'stəm-i-kər\ *n* : the center front section of an upper part of a woman's dress appearing between the laces of an outer garment (as in 16th century costume)

sto·mate \'stō-ˌmāt\ *n* : STOMA

stomp \'stämp, 'stȯmp\ *vb* : ¹STAMP 2 〈*stomped* angrily out of the room〉 — **stomp** *n* — **stomp·er** *n*

stomping ground *n* : a favorite or frequently sought-out place 〈the museum became my new *stomping ground*〉; *also* : familiar territory 〈returned to the *stomping grounds* of my youth〉

¹stone \'stōn\ *n* **1 a** : earth or mineral matter hardened in a mass **b** : a piece of rock not as fine as gravel 〈throw *stones*〉 **c** : a piece of rock used for some special purpose (as for a monument or in construction) **d** : GEM 1b **2 a** : CALCULUS 2a **b** : a stony seed or one (as of a plum) enclosed in a stony cover **3** *pl usually* **stone** : any of various units of weight; *esp* : a British unit equal to 14 pounds (6.3 kilograms)

²stone *adj* : of, relating to, or made of stone

³stone *vb* **stoned; ston·ing 1** : to throw stones at; *esp* : to kill by hitting with stones **2** : to remove the stones or seeds of (a fruit) — **ston·er** *n*

⁴stone *adv* : in a complete manner : ENTIRELY 〈the soup is *stone* cold〉 — often used in combination 〈they are *stone=* broke〉

Stone Age *n* : the oldest period in which human beings are known to have existed that is marked by the use of stone tools

stone–blind \'stōn-'blīnd\ *adj* : totally blind

stone·cut·ter \-ˌkət-ər\ *n* **1** : a person who cuts, carves, or puts a finish on stone **2** : a machine for putting a finish on stone — **stone·cut·ting** \-ˌkət-iŋ\ *n*

stone–deaf \-'def\ *adj* : totally deaf

stone fly *n* : any of an order of 4-winged insects of which the immature stages have gills and live in water and that are used by fishermen for bait when immature or fully developed

stone–ground \'stōn-'graund\ *adj* : ground by the use of millstones 〈*stone-ground* flour〉

stone·ma·son \'stōn-ˌmās-ᵊn\ *n* : a mason who builds with stone

stone's throw *n* : a short distance 〈lives within a *stone's throw* of the school〉

stone·ware \-ˌwa(ə)r, -ˌwe(ə)r\ *n* : a clay pottery used for storage utensils, tile, and ornamental wares

stone·washed \-ˌwȯsht, -ˌwäsht\ *adj* : subjected to a washing process during manufacture that includes using stones especially to create a softer fabric 〈*stonewashed* jeans〉

stone·work \-ˌwərk\ *n* **1** : a structure or part built of stone : MASONRY **2** : the shaping, preparation, or setting of stone

stony *also* **ston·ey** \'stō-nē\ *adj* **ston·i·er; -est 1 a** : full of stones 〈*stony* soil〉 **b** : hard as stone 〈a *stony* seed〉 **2** : PITILESS, UNFEELING 〈a *stony* stare〉 — **ston·i·ly** \'stōn-ᵊl-ē\ *adv*

stood *past and past participle of* STAND

stooge \'stüj\ *n* **1** : one who follows or serves another without thinking **2** : an actor who usually by asking questions prepares the way for a principal comedian's jokes — **stooge** *vb*

stool \'stül\ *n* **1 a** : a seat without back or arms supported by three or four legs or by a central post **b** : FOOTSTOOL **2 a** : a seat used while urinating or having a bowel movement **b** : a mass of bodily waste discharged from the intestine in a bowel movement

stool pigeon *n* : a person acting as a spy or informer for the police [from *stool pigeon* "a pigeon tied to a stool and used as a decoy to draw other birds into a net"]

¹stoop \'stüp\ *vb* **1 a** : to bend down or over **b** : to stand or walk with the head and shoulders or the upper part of the body bent forward **2** : to degrade oneself 〈*stoop* to lying〉 [Old English *stūpian* "to stoop, bend over"]

²stoop *n* **1** : an act of bending the body forward **2** : a forward bend of the back and shoulders that is temporary or by habit

³stoop *n* : a porch, platform, or entrance stairway at a house door [from Dutch *stoep* "porch, stoop"]

¹stop \'stäp\ *vb* **stopped; stop·ping 1** : to close an opening by filling or blocking it : PLUG 〈nose *stopped* up by a cold〉 **2** : RESTRAIN 1a, PREVENT 〈*stopped* me from going〉 **3** : to interrupt or prevent from continuing or occurring : CHECK 〈couldn't *stop* the noise〉 **4** : to instruct one's bank not to pay 〈*stop* payment on a check〉 **5** : to halt the movement or progress of 〈*stop* the car〉 **6** : to change the pitch of (as a violin string) by pressing with the finger **7 a** : to bring action or operation to an end 〈the motor *stopped*〉 **b** : to come to an end 〈sit down when the music *stops*〉 **8** : to make a visit 〈*stopping* with friends for a week〉

²stop *n* **1** : CESSATION, END 〈his father put a *stop* to the arguing〉 **2 a** : a series of similar organ pipes that vary by pitch but have the same tone quality **b** : STOP KNOB — often used in phrases like *pull out all the stops* to suggest holding nothing back **3** : something that delays, blocks, or brings to a halt : IMPEDIMENT, OBSTACLE **4** : a device for halting or limiting motion 〈the door was held open by a *stop*〉 **5** : the act of stopping : the state of being stopped 〈the train was brought to a sudden *stop*〉 **6** : a halt in a journey : STAY 〈made a quick *stop* to refuel〉 **7** : a stopping place 〈a bus *stop*〉 **8** *chiefly British* : any of several punctuation marks **9** : a consonant in the uttering of which there is a step (as in the "p" of "apt" or the "g" of "tiger") when the breath passage is completely closed **10** : a function of an electronic device that stops a recording

³stop *adj* : serving to stop : designed to stop 〈*stop* line〉 〈*stop* signal〉

stop bath *n* : an acid bath used to stop the development of a photographic negative or print

stop·cock \'stäp-ˌkäk\ *n* : a faucet for stopping or regulating flow (as through a pipe)

stop·gap \'stäp-ˌgap\ *n* : something that fills a gap : a temporary substitute

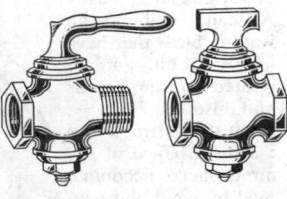

stopcock

stop knob *n* : one of the handles by which an organist draws or shuts off a particular stop

stop·light \'stäp-ˌlīt\ *n* : TRAFFIC SIGNAL

stop·over \-ˌō-vər\ *n* **1** : a stop in the course of one's journey **2** : a stopping place on a journey

stop·page \'stäp-ij\ *n* : the act of stopping : the state of being stopped

¹stop·per \'stäp-ər\ *n* **1** : one that brings to a halt : CHECK **2** : one that closes, shuts, or fills up; *esp* : something used to plug an opening

²stopper *vb* : to close or fasten with or as if with a stopper

stop·watch \'stäp-ˌwäch\ *n* : a watch having a hand or a digital display that can be started and stopped for exact timing (as of a race)

stor·able \'stōr-ə-bəl, 'stȯr-\ *adj* : suitable for storage : capable of being stored 〈*storable* fruits〉

stor·age \'stōr-ij, 'stȯr-\ *n* **1 a** : space or a place for storing **b** : an amount stored **c** : MEMORY 5 **2 a** : the act of storing : the state of being stored **b** : the price charged for storing something

\ə\ abut	\au̇\ out	\i\ tip	\ȯ\ saw	\u̇\ foot
\ər\ further	\ch\ chin	\ī\ life	\ȯi\ coin	\y\ yet
\a\ mat	\e\ pet	\j\ job	\th\ thin	\yü\ few
\ā\ take	\ē\ easy	\ŋ\ sing	\th\ this	\yu̇\ cure
\ä\ cot, cart	\g\ go	\ō\ bone	\ü\ food	\zh\ vision

storage battery *n* : a cell or connected group of cells that converts chemical energy into electrical energy by reversible chemical reactions and that may be recharged by passing a current through it in the direction opposite to that of its discharge — called also *storage cell*

¹**store** \'stō(ə)r, 'stȯ(ə)r\ *vb* **stored; stor·ing** **1** : LAY AWAY, ACCUMULATE ⟨*store* vegetables for winter use⟩ **2** : to provide with what is needed : FURNISH, SUPPLY ⟨*store* a ship with provisions⟩ **3 a** : to deposit in a place (as a warehouse) for safekeeping or disposal ⟨*stored* my furniture until I found a new apartment⟩ **b** : to record information in a device (as a computer) **4** : to provide storage room for : HOLD ⟨racks for *storing* basketballs⟩

²**store** *n* **1 a** : something stored ⟨a *store* of good jokes⟩ **b** *pl* : accumulated supplies (as of food) : STOCK ⟨a ship's *stores*⟩ **2** : ¹VALUE 3, IMPORTANCE ⟨a family that set great *store* by tradition⟩ **3** : a place where goods are sold : SHOP — **in store** : ready for use or action : in preparation ⟨there's a surprise *in store* for you⟩

³**store** *adj* : purchased from a store : READY-MADE ⟨*store* clothes⟩ ⟨*store* bread⟩

store·house \'stō(ə)r-ˌhaus, 'stȯ(ə)r-\ *n* **1** : a building for storing goods **2** : a large supply : REPOSITORY ⟨a *storehouse* of information⟩

store·keep·er \-ˌkē-pər\ *n* **1** : one who is in charge of stores **2** : one who manages a store or shop

store·room \-ˌrüm, -ˌrum\ *n* : a room for the storing of goods or supplies

store·wide \-'wīd\ *adj* : including all or most merchandise in a store ⟨a *storewide* sale⟩

¹**sto·ried** \'stōr-ēd, 'stȯr-\ *adj* **1** : decorated with designs representing scenes from story or history ⟨a *storied* tapestry⟩ **2** : having an interesting history ⟨a *storied* castle⟩

²**storied** *or* **sto·reyed** \'stōr-ēd, 'stȯr-\ *adj* : having stories ⟨a two-*storied* house⟩

stork \'stȯ(ə)rk\ *n* : any of various large mostly African and Asian wading birds that have long stout bills and are related to the herons and ibises

stork

¹**storm** \'stȯ(ə)rm\ *n* **1 a** : a disturbance of the atmosphere accompanied by wind and usually by rain, snow, hail, sleet, or thunder and lightning **b** : a heavy fall of rain, snow, or hail **c** : a serious disturbance of any element of nature **2** : a disturbed state : a sudden or violent commotion **3** : a heavy discharge of objects ⟨fired a *storm* of arrows at the castle⟩ **4** : a violent outburst ⟨a *storm* of protest⟩ **5** : a violent attack on a defended position — **by storm** : by or as if by using a bold swift direct movement especially with the intent of defeating or winning over quickly ⟨took the fashion world *by storm*⟩ — **up a storm** : in a remarkable or energetic fashion ⟨dancing *up a storm*⟩

²**storm** *vb* **1 a** : to blow with violence **b** : to rain, hail, snow, or sleet heavily **2** : to attack by storm ⟨*stormed* ashore⟩ ⟨*storm* the fort⟩ **3** : to show violent feeling : RAGE ⟨*storming* at the unusual delay⟩ **4** : to rush about violently ⟨the mob *stormed* through the streets⟩

storm petrel *n* : any of various small dark petrels that usually return to land only to nest typically in burrows — called also *Mother Carey's chicken*

storm window *n* : a glass window that is placed outside an ordinary window as a protection against severe weather

stormy \'stȯr-mē\ *adj* **storm·i·er; -est** **1** : relating to, marked by, or being a sign of a storm ⟨a *stormy* day⟩ ⟨*stormy* skies⟩ **2** : characterized by or subject to angry or intense disagreements or strong emotional outbursts ⟨a *stormy* conference⟩ — **storm·i·ly** \-mə-lē\ *adv* — **storm·i·ness** \-mē-nəs\ *n*

stormy petrel *n* **1** : STORM PETREL **2** : a person who is fond of conflict or disagreement

¹**sto·ry** \'stōr-ē, 'stȯr-\ *n, pl* **stories** **1 a** : an account of incidents or events **b** : ANECDOTE **2 a** : a fictional tale shorter than a novel; *esp* : SHORT STORY **b** : the main tale of a written work **3** : a widely told rumor **4** : FIB, LIE, FALSEHOOD **5** : a news article or broadcast [Middle English *storie* "tale," from early French *estoire, estorie* (same meaning), from Latin *historia* "tale, history"]

²**story** *also* **sto·rey** \'stōr-ē, 'stȯr-\ *n, pl* **stories** *also* **storeys** : a set of rooms or an area making up one floor level of a building [Middle English *storie*, from Latin *historia* "tale, illustration, story of a building," from earlier Latin, "tale, history"; probably so called from the use of narrative paintings on the window levels of medieval buildings]

sto·ry·tell·er \'stōr-ē-ˌtel-ər, 'stȯr-\ *n* : a teller of stories

stoup \'stüp\ *n* **1** : a container (as a large glass) for beverages **2** : a basin for holy water at the entrance of a church

¹**stout** \'staut\ *adj* **1** : strong of character : BRAVE, BOLD **2** : physically or materially strong : STURDY, VIGOROUS **3** : FORCEFUL ⟨a *stout* attack⟩ **4** : bulky in body : OVERWEIGHT — **stout·ly** *adv* — **stout·ness** *n*

²**stout** *n* : a dark heavy beer

stout·heart·ed \'staut-'härt-əd\ *adj* : COURAGEOUS, BOLD — **stout·heart·ed·ly** *adv*

¹**stove** \'stōv\ *n* **1** : an appliance that burns fuel or uses electricity to provide heat (as for cooking or heating) **2** : KILN

²**stove** *past and past participle of* ²STAVE

stove·pipe \'stōv-ˌpīp\ *n* **1** : a metal pipe for carrying off smoke from a stove **2** : a tall silk hat

stow \'stō\ *vb* **1** : to put away : STORE ⟨*stowed* their belongings in the closet⟩ **2 a** : ARRANGE 1, PACK ⟨quickly *stowed* the cargo⟩ **b** : ²LOAD 1a ⟨*stowed* the ships to capacity⟩ **3** : to eat or drink up ⟨*stow* away a meal⟩

stow·age \'stō-ij\ *n* **1 a** : an act or process of stowing **b** : goods stowed or to be stowed **2 a** : ability to store **b** : a place for storage

stow·away \'stō-ə-ˌwā\ *n* : one who stows away : an unregistered passenger

stow away \ˌstō-ə-'wā\ *vb* : to hide aboard a vehicle to obtain transportation

¹**strad·dle** \'strad-ᵊl\ *vb* **strad·dled; strad·dling** \'strad-liŋ, -ᵊl-iŋ\ **1** : to stand, sit, or walk with the legs wide apart **2** : to approve or seem to approve two apparently opposite sides ⟨*straddle* a question⟩ — **strad·dler** \-lər, -ᵊl-ər\ *n*

²**straddle** *n* : the act or position of one that straddles

strafe \'strāf\ *vb* **strafed; straf·ing** : to fire on at close range and especially with machine guns from low-flying airplanes ⟨*strafed* the village⟩ — **straf·er** *n*

strag·gle \'strag-əl\ *vb* **strag·gled; strag·gling** \-(ə-)liŋ\ **1** : to wander from a course or way : ROVE, STRAY **2** : to trail off from others of its kind ⟨little cabins *straggling* off into the woods⟩ — **strag·gler** \-(ə-)lər\ *n*

¹**straight** \'strāt\ *adj* **1 a** : free from curves, bends, angles, or unevenness ⟨*straight* hair⟩ ⟨*straight* timber⟩ **b** : formed by a point moving continuously in the same direction ⟨a *straight* line⟩ **2 a** : holding to a proper course or method ⟨a *straight* thinker⟩ **b** : FRANK, CANDID ⟨a *straight* answer⟩ **3** : VERTICAL 2, UPRIGHT ⟨the picture isn't quite *straight*⟩ **4 a** : exhibiting truth, fairness, and honesty : JUST ⟨*straight* dealings⟩ **b** : correctly ordered or arranged ⟨set the kitchen *straight*⟩; *also* : CORRECT ⟨get the facts *straight*⟩ **c** : CONSECUTIVE ⟨five *straight* hours⟩ **d** : having nothing added ⟨*straight* liquor⟩ **e** : making no

exceptions in one's voting for a political party ⟨voted a *straight* ticket⟩ **f** : not varying from a pattern ⟨writes *straight* humor⟩ **g** : CONVENTIONAL **h** : not using or under the influence of drugs **i** : ¹HETEROSEXUAL **5** : being the only form of payment ⟨on *straight* commission⟩ — **straight·ness** *n*

²**straight** *adv* : in a straight manner, course, or line ⟨came *straight* home from school⟩

¹**straight·away** \'strāt-ə-,wā\ *adj* **1** : proceeding in a straight line : continuous in direction : STRAIGHTFORWARD **2** : IMMEDIATE 4 ⟨made a *straightaway* reply⟩

²**straightaway** *n* : the straight part of a racetrack : STRETCH

³**straight·away** \,strāt-ə-'wā\ *adv* : without delay : IMMEDIATELY ⟨found an answer *straightaway*⟩

straight·edge \'strāt-,ej\ *n* : a bar or piece of wood, metal, or plastic with a straight edge for testing straight lines and surfaces or for cutting along or drawing straight lines

straight·en \'strāt-ᵊn\ *vb* **straight·ened; straight·en·ing** \'strāt-niŋ, -ᵊn-iŋ\ : to make or become straight — usually used with *up* or *out* ⟨*straighten* up a room⟩ ⟨*straightened* out the problem⟩ — **straight·en·er** \'strāt-nər, -ᵊn-ər\ *n*

straight face *n* : a face giving no evidence of feeling and especially of amusement — **straight–faced** \'strāt-'fāst\ *adj*

¹**straight·for·ward** \(')strāt-'fȯr-wərd\ *adj* **1** : OUTSPOKEN, CANDID ⟨a *straightforward* reply⟩ **2** : proceeding in a straight course or manner : DIRECT — **straight·for·ward·ly** *adv* — **straight·for·ward·ness** *n*

²**straightforward** *also* **straight·for·wards** \-wərdz\ *adv* : in a straightforward manner

straight·way \'strāt-'wā, -,wā\ *adv* : RIGHT AWAY, IMMEDIATELY

¹**strain** \'strān\ *n* **1 a** : LINEAGE, ANCESTRY **b** : a group of plants or animals that look alike but have characteristics (as the ability to resist disease) that make them slightly different : VARIETY 3b ⟨a strong *strain* of winter wheat⟩ **2 a** : a quality or disposition that is natural or runs through a family ⟨a *strain* of genius in the family⟩ **b** : a small amount : TRACE, STREAK ⟨a *strain* of sadness⟩ **3** : MELODY 2, TUNE **4** : the manner or style of something said or of a course of action or conduct

²**strain** *vb* **1 a** : to draw tight : cause to clasp firmly **b** : to stretch to maximum extension and tightness **2 a** : to try one's hardest : STRIVE **b** : to injure or be injured by overuse, misuse, or pressure ⟨*strained* the heart by overwork⟩ ⟨*strain* one's back by lifting⟩ **3 a** : to pass or cause to pass through or as if through a strainer : FILTER **b** : to remove by straining ⟨*strain* lumps out of the gravy⟩ **4** : to stretch beyond a proper limit ⟨*strain* the truth⟩

³**strain** *n* **1** : an act of straining or the state of being strained **2** : bodily injury caused by too much tension, effort, or use ⟨heart *strain*⟩; *esp* : one resulting from a wrench or twist and involving severe stretching of muscles or ligaments ⟨back *strain*⟩

strained \'strānd\ *adj* **1** : not easy or natural : FORCED ⟨a *strained* smile⟩ **2** : brought close to war ⟨*strained* relations between countries⟩

strain·er \'strā-nər\ *n* : one that strains; *esp* : a device (as a screen or filter) to hold solid pieces while a liquid passes through

strait \'strāt\ *n* **1 a** : a narrow channel connecting two large bodies of water — often used in plural **b** : ISTHMUS **2** : a situation of confusion or distress — often used in plural ⟨in difficult *straits*⟩

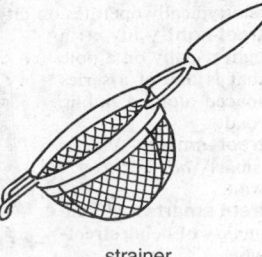

strainer

strait·en \'strāt-ᵊn\ *vb* **strait·ened; strait·en·ing** \'strāt-niŋ, -ᵊn-iŋ\ : to limit or restrict especially in resources ⟨*straitened* by misfortune⟩

strait·jack·et *also* **straight·jack·et** \'strāt-,jak-ət\ *n* : a cover or outer garment of strong material (as canvas) used to restrict the movement of the arms as a means of controlling a violent prisoner or patient

strait·laced *or* **straight·laced** \'strāt-'lāst\ *adj* : very strict or proper in actions, beliefs, or point of view

¹**strand** \'strand\ *n* : the land bordering a body of water : SHORE, BEACH [Old English *strand* "shore"]

²**strand** *vb* **1** : to run aground : BEACH ⟨boats *stranded* by the storm⟩ **2** : to leave in a strange or an unfavorable place especially without a way of departing ⟨*stranded* in a strange city⟩

³**strand** *n* **1** : one of the fibers, threads, strings, or wires twisted or braided to make a cord, rope, or cable **2** : something resembling a strand ⟨a *strand* of pearls⟩ ⟨a *strand* of DNA⟩ **3** : one of the elements of a complicated whole ⟨the *strands* of a legal argument⟩ [Middle English *strond* "strand, fiber"]

strand·ed \'stran-dəd\ *adj* : having a strand or strands especially of a specified kind or number — usually used in combination ⟨double-*stranded* DNA⟩

strange \'strānj\ *adj* **strang·er; strang·est** **1** : not native to or naturally belonging in a place **2 a** : not known, heard, or seen before ⟨*strange* surroundings⟩ **b** : causing surprise or wonder because not usual : noticeably unusual ⟨*strange* clothes⟩ **3** : UNEASY 1 ⟨feels *strange* on the first day of school⟩ [Middle English *strange* "foreign," from early French *estrange* (same meaning), from Latin *extraneus*, literally, "external, coming from the outside," from *extra* "outside" — related to EXTRA-] — **strange·ly** *adv* — **strange·ness** *n*

strang·er \'strān-jər\ *n* **1** : one who is strange **2 a** : FOREIGNER **b** : GUEST 1, VISITOR **c** : a person with whom or a thing with which one is unacquainted

stran·gle \'straŋ-gəl\ *vb* **stran·gled; stran·gling** \-g(ə-)liŋ\ **1** : to choke to death by squeezing the throat **2** : to cause (someone or something) to choke or suffocate **3** : to suppress or hinder the rise, growth, or expression of ⟨these rules are *strangling* my creativity⟩ **4** : to become strangled **5** : to die by or as if by interference with breathing — **stran·gler** \-g(ə-)lər\ *n*

stran·gle·hold \'straŋ-gəl-,hōld\ *n* **1** : an illegal wrestling hold by which one's opponent is choked **2** : a force or influence that chokes or blocks freedom of development or expression

stran·gu·late \'straŋ-gyə-,lāt\ *vb* **-lat·ed; -lat·ing** : STRANGLE 1

stran·gu·la·tion \,straŋ-gyə-'lā-shən\ *n* **1** : an act or process of strangling **2** : the state of being strangled

¹**strap** \'strap\ *n* **1** : a band, plate, or loop of metal for tying objects together or for clamping an object in position **2 a** : a narrow usually flat strip of a flexible material and especially leather used for fastening, holding together, or wrapping **b** : something made of a strap forming a loop ⟨boot *strap*⟩ **c** : a strip of leather used for whipping **d** : ¹STROP

²**strap** *vb* **strapped; strap·ping** **1** : to fasten with or attach by a strap **2** : to beat or punish with a strap **3** : ²STROP **4** : to cause to suffer from an extreme scarcity ⟨I'm *strapped* for cash⟩

strap·less \'strap-ləs\ *adj* : having no strap; *esp* : made or worn without shoulder straps ⟨*strapless* evening gown⟩

strap·ping \'strap-iŋ\ *adj* : ROBUST ⟨a *strapping* young man⟩

\ə\ abut	\au̇\ out	\i\ tip	\ȯ\ saw	\u̇\ foot
\ər\ further	\ch\ chin	\ī\ life	\ȯi\ coin	\y\ yet
\a\ mat	\e\ pet	\j\ job	\th\ thin	\yü\ few
\ā\ take	\ē\ easy	\ŋ\ sing	\th\ this	\yu̇\ cure
\ä\ cot, cart	\g\ go	\ō\ bone	\ü\ food	\zh\ vision

strat·a·gem \'strat-ə-jəm\ *n* **1** : a trick in war for deceiving and outwitting the enemy **2** : a clever trick or scheme **synonyms** see TRICK

stra·te·gic \strə-'tē-jik\ *adj* **1** : of, relating to, or showing strategy ⟨*strategic* value of the position⟩ ⟨a *strategic* retreat⟩ **2 a** : required for the conduct of war ⟨*strategic* supplies⟩ **b** : of great importance within a whole or for a planned purpose ⟨mentioned *strategic* points⟩ **3** : designed or trained to strike at what makes an enemy powerful ⟨*strategic* bomber⟩ — **stra·te·gi·cal** \-ji-kəl\ *adj* — **stra·te·gi·cal·ly** \-ji-k(ə-)lē\ *adv*

strat·e·gist \'strat-ə-jəst\ *n* : one skilled in strategy

strat·e·gize \-ˌjīz\ *vb* **-gized; -giz·ing** : to devise a strategy or course of action ⟨*strategized* with her teammates⟩

strat·e·gy \'strat-ə-jē\ *n, pl* **-gies** **1** : the science and art of employing the forces of a country in peace or war; *esp* : the science and art of military command exercised to meet the enemy in combat under favorable conditions **2 a** : a careful plan or method **b** : the art of making or employing plans or tricks to achieve a goal

strat·i·fi·ca·tion \ˌstrat-ə-fə-'kā-shən\ *n* **1** : the act or process of arranging or becoming arranged in layers or strata **2** : the state of being arranged in layers or strata

strat·i·fy \'strat-ə-ˌfī\ *vb* **-fied; -fy·ing** : to form, deposit, or arrange in layers ⟨*stratified* rock⟩

stra·tig·ra·phy \strə-'tig-rə-fē\ *n* : geology that deals with the beginnings, composition, distribution, and succession of the layers of rock in the earth's crust

stra·to·cu·mu·lus \ˌstrat-ō-'kyü-myə-ləs, ˌstrat-\ *n* : layered cumulus consisting of large balls or rolls of dark cloud which often cover the whole sky especially in winter

strato·sphere \'strat-ə-ˌsfi(ə)r\ *n* : an upper portion of the atmosphere above the troposphere where temperature changes little and clouds rarely form

stra·tum \'strāt-əm, 'strat-\ *n, pl* **stra·ta** \-ə\ **1** : a layer of a substance; *esp* : one of a series of layers ⟨a rock *stratum*⟩ ⟨a *stratum* of earth⟩ ⟨the deep *stratum* of the skin⟩ **2** : a level of society consisting of persons of the same or similar rank or position

stra·tus \'strāt-əs, 'strat-\ *n, pl* **stra·ti** \'strāt-ˌī, 'strat-\ : a cloud form extending over a large area at altitudes of usually 2000 to 7000 feet (600 to 2100 meters)

¹**straw** \'strȯ\ *n* **1 a** : stalks of grain after threshing; *also* : any dry stalky plant part used like grain straw (as for bedding or in packing) ⟨pine *straw*⟩ **b** : a natural or artificial fiber used for weaving or braiding **2** : a dry coarse stem especially of a cereal grass **3 a** : something of small worth or importance ⟨not worth a *straw*⟩ **b** : something too weak to provide help in a desperate situation ⟨clutch at any *straw* in a crisis⟩ **4** : a tube usually of plastic for sucking up a beverage — **strawy** \'strȯ(-)ē\ *adj*

²**straw** *adj* **1** : made of straw ⟨a *straw* hat⟩ **2** : of the pale yellow color of straw

straw·ber·ry \'strȯ-ˌber-ē, -b(ə-)rē\ *n* : an edible juicy red fruit of a low-growing herb with white flowers and long slender runners; *also* : a plant that bears strawberries

straw boss *n* : a person in charge of a small group of workers

straw vote *n* : an unofficial vote — called also *straw poll*

¹**stray** \'strā\ *n* **1** : a domestic animal that is wandering loose or is lost **2** : a person or thing that strays

²**stray** *vb* **1** : to wander from a group or from the proper place : ROAM ⟨the dog *strayed* from the yard⟩ **2** : to wander from a fixed or chosen route or at random ⟨accidentally *strayed* off the path⟩ **3** : to become distracted from an argument or chain of thought ⟨*strayed* from the point⟩ — **stray·er** *n*

³**stray** *adj* **1** : having strayed or been lost ⟨a *stray* dog⟩ **2** : occurring in one place and another or at random ⟨a few *stray* hairs⟩

¹**streak** \'strēk\ *n* **1** : a line or mark of a different color or

texture from its background : STRIPE **2** : the color of the fine powder of a mineral obtained by scratching or rubbing against a hard white surface **3 a** : a narrow band of light **b** : a lightning bolt **4 a** : a small amount : TRACE, STRAIN ⟨*streak* of stubbornness⟩ **b** : a brief period or series ⟨a *streak* of luck⟩ ⟨was on a winning *streak*⟩ **5** : a narrow layer ⟨a *streak* of fat in bacon⟩

²**streak** *vb* **1** : to make or have streaks on or in **2** : to move swiftly : RUSH ⟨a jet *streaking* across the sky⟩

streak camera *n* : a camera for recording very fast or short-lived things (as shock waves)

streaked \'strēkt, 'strē-kəd\ *adj* : marked with streaks or lines of color

streaky \'strē-kē\ *adj* **streak·i·er; -est** **1** : having or showing streaks **2** : likely to vary : CHANGEABLE ⟨a *streaky* hitter in baseball⟩ — **streak·i·ness** *n*

¹**stream** \'strēm\ *n* **1** : a body of running water (as a river or brook) flowing on the earth; *also* : any body of flowing fluid (as water or gas) **2** : a steady flow ⟨a *stream* of words⟩ **3** : a ray of light

²**stream** *vb* **1** : to flow or cause to flow in or as if in a stream **2 a** : to give off a bodily fluid in large amounts ⟨her eyes were *streaming*⟩ **b** : to become wet with a discharge of bodily fluid ⟨*streaming* with perspiration⟩ **3** : to trail out at full length ⟨hair *streaming* in the wind⟩ **4** : to pour in large numbers ⟨complaints came *streaming* in⟩ **5** : to transfer (digital data, such as audio or video material) in a continuous stream especially for immediate processing or playback

stream·er \'strē-mər\ *n* **1 a** : a flag that streams in the wind; *esp* : PENNANT 1 **b** : a long narrow wavy strip suggesting a banner floating in the wind **2** *pl* : AURORA BOREALIS

stream·ing \'strē-miŋ\ *adj* : playing continuously as data is sent to a computer over the Internet ⟨*streaming* video⟩

stream·let \'strēm-lət\ *n* : a small stream

stream·line \'strēm-ˌlīn\ *vb* **1** : to design or construct with an outline which makes motion through water or air easier **2** : to bring up to date : MODERNIZE **3** : to make simpler, more effective, or more productive

stream·lined \-ˌlīnd\ *adj* **1 a** : designed or constructed to make or as if to make motion through water or air easier **b** : stripped of everything unnecessary : SIMPLIFIED **2** : made more modern

¹**street** \'strēt\ *n* **1 a** : a public way especially in a city, town, or village usually including sidewalks and being wider than an alley or lane **b** : the part of a street reserved for vehicles **c** : a public way with the property along it ⟨lived on Maple *Street*⟩ **2** : the people occupying property on a street ⟨the whole *street* was excited⟩ [Old English *strǣt* "street," from Latin *strata* "paved road," derived from earlier *stratus*, past participle of *sternere* "to spread out"]

²**street** *adj* **1** : of or relating to the street or streets ⟨a *street* door⟩ ⟨a *street* map⟩ ⟨*street* clothes⟩ **2** : of or relating to the environment of the street ⟨*street* people⟩

street·car \-ˌkär\ *n* : a passenger vehicle that runs on rails and typically operates on city streets

street·light \-ˌlīt\ *n* : a light usually on a pole that is one of a series spaced along a public road

street–smart \'strēt-ˌsmärt\ *adj* : STREETWISE

street smarts *n pl* : the quality of being streetwise

street·wise \'strēt-ˌwīz\ *adj* : having the

streetcar

knowledge needed to survive in difficult or dangerous places or situations in a city

strength \'stren(k)th\ *n* **1** : the quality or state of being strong **2** : power to resist force **3** : power to resist attack **4 a** : the power to have an effect **b** : degree of concentration ⟨the *strength* of a liquid cleaner⟩ **c** : intensity of light, color, sound, or odor **5** : a strong quality ⟨list the *strengths* and weaknesses of the book⟩ **6** : force as measured in numbers ⟨army at full *strength*⟩ **7** : something or someone providing force or firmness : [2]SUPPORT ⟨her family was her *strength*⟩ **synonyms** see POWER

strength·en \'stren(k)-thən\ *vb* **strength·ened; strength·en·ing** \'stren(k)th-(ə-)niŋ\ : to make or become stronger — **strength·en·er** \-(ə-)nər\ *n*

stren·u·ous \'stren-yə-wəs\ *adj* **1 a** : very active : ENERGETIC ⟨leads a *strenuous* life⟩ **b** : FERVENT, ZEALOUS ⟨*strenuous* protest⟩ **2** : showing or requiring great energy ⟨*strenuous* tasks⟩ **synonyms** see VIGOROUS — **stren·u·ous·ly** *adv*

strep \'strep\ *n* : STREPTOCOCCUS

strep throat *n* : a sore throat that is marked by inflammation of the throat and pharynx and by fever and weakness and is caused by infection with streptococci

strep·to·coc·cus \,strep-tə-'käk-əs\ *n, pl* **-coc·ci** \-'käk-ˌ(s)ī, -ˌ(ˌ)(s)ē\ : any of various mostly parasitic round bacteria that occur in pairs or chains and include some that cause diseases in human beings and animals

strep·to·my·ces \,strep-tə-'mī-ˌsēz\ *n, pl* **streptomyces** : any of various mostly soil bacteria including some that form antibiotics as by-products of their metabolism

strep·to·my·cin \,strep-tə-'mīs-ᵊn\ *n* : an antibiotic produced by a soil streptomyces and used especially in the treatment of some infections (as tuberculosis) caused by bacteria

[1]**stress** \'stres\ *n* **1 a** : a force that acts when one body or part of a body presses on, pulls on, pushes against, or tends to squeeze or twist another body or part of a body **b** : the change in shape caused in a body by such a force **c** : a physical, chemical, or emotional factor that causes bodily or mental tension and may be involved in causing some diseases; *also* : a state of tension resulting from a stress **2** : special importance given to something : EMPHASIS, WEIGHT ⟨lay *stress* on a point⟩ **3** : relative force or loudness of sound ⟨"finally" has the *stress* on the first syllable⟩ **4** : [1]ACCENT 4 — **stress·less** \-ləs\ *adj*

[2]**stress** *vb* **1** : to subject to physical or emotional stress ⟨*stressing* the equipment⟩ ⟨this traffic is *stressing* me out⟩ **2** : to pronounce with stress ⟨*stress* the last syllable⟩ **3** : EMPHASIZE ⟨*stressed* the importance of teamwork⟩ **4** : to feel stress ⟨*stressing* about the big test⟩

stressed–out \'strest-'aút\ *adj* : suffering from high levels of physical or especially psychological stress

stress·ful \'stres-fəl\ *adj* : full of or tending to cause stress — **stress·ful·ly** \-fə-lē\ *adv*

stress mark *n* : a mark used with (as before, after, or over) a written syllable in the respelling of a word to show that this syllable is to be stressed when spoken : ACCENT MARK

[1]**stretch** \'strech\ *vb* **1** : to extend (as one's body) in a flat position ⟨*stretched* out on the bed⟩ **2** : to reach out ⟨*stretched* my arm⟩ **3 a** : to extend or become extended in length or width or both : SPREAD ⟨*stretched* his neck to see what was going on⟩ **b** : to extend over a continuous period ⟨the dynasty *stretches* back several centuries⟩ **4** : to draw up (one's body) from a cramped, stooping, or relaxed position ⟨awoke and *stretched* myself⟩ **5** : to pull tight ⟨*stretch* the canvas on the frame⟩ **6 a** : to enlarge or expand especially by force **b** : to make excessive demands on : STRAIN ⟨*stretched* her already thin patience⟩ **7** : to cause to reach or continue ⟨*stretch* a wire between two posts⟩ **8** : EXAGGERATE ⟨*stretch* the truth⟩ **9** : to become extended without breaking **10** : to extend one's

body or limbs ⟨*stretched* before jogging⟩ — **stretch·abil·i·ty** \,strech-ə-'bil-ət-ē\ *n* — **stretch·able** \'strech-ə-bəl\ *adj* — **stretch one's legs** : to take a walk in order to relieve stiffness caused by prolonged sitting

[2]**stretch** *n* **1** : an exercise of something beyond ordinary or normal limits ⟨*stretch* of the imagination⟩ **2** : the extent to which something may be stretched **3** : the act of stretching (as of the body) : the state of being stretched **4 a** : an extent in length or area ⟨a *stretch* of woods⟩ **b** : a continuous period of time ⟨silent for a *stretch*⟩ **5** : a term of imprisonment **6** : either of the straight sides of a racecourse; *esp* : HOMESTRETCH 1 **7** : the ability to be stretched

[3]**stretch** *adj* **1** : easily stretched : ELASTIC ⟨*stretch* socks⟩ **2** : longer than the standard size ⟨a *stretch* limousine⟩

stretch·er \'strech-ər\ *n* **1** : one that stretches; *esp* : a device or machine for stretching or expanding something **2** : a device that resembles a cot and is used for carrying a sick, injured, or dead person

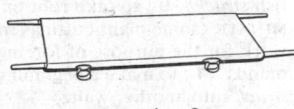

stretcher 2

stretch receptor *n* : MUSCLE SPINDLE

strew \'strü\ *vb* **strewed; strewed** *or* **strewn** \'strün\; **strew·ing** **1** : to spread (as seeds) by scattering **2** : to cover by or as if by scattering something over or on ⟨*strewing* the highways with litter⟩ **3** : to spread around as if sowing seeds : DISSEMINATE

stri·at·ed \'strī-ˌāt-əd\ *adj* : having or showing lines, bands, or grooves

striated muscle *n* : muscle tissue that is made up of long thin cells with many nuclei and with alternate light and dark stripes, that usually connects to and moves the vertebrate skeleton, and that is mostly under voluntary control — compare SMOOTH MUSCLE, VOLUNTARY MUSCLE

stri·a·tion \strī-'ā-shən\ *n* **1** : the fact or state of being striated **2** : a tiny groove, scratch, or channel especially when one of a parallel series **3** : any of the alternate dark and light cross bands of a myofibril of striated muscle

strick·en \'strik-ən\ *adj* **1** : troubled with disease, misfortune, or sorrow **2** : hit or wounded by or as if by an object that was thrown

strict \'strikt\ *adj* **1** : permitting no avoidance or escape ⟨under *strict* orders⟩ **2 a** : kept with great care : ABSOLUTE ⟨*strict* secrecy⟩ **b** : carefully obeying rules or a code of conduct **3** : completely correct : EXACT, PRECISE ⟨in the *strict* meaning of the word⟩ — **strict·ly** \'strik-(t)lē\ *adv* — **strict·ness** \'strik(t)-nəs\ *n*

stric·ture \'strik-chər\ *n* **1** : an abnormal narrowing of a bodily passage; *also* : the narrowed part **2** : a negative criticism : CENSURE

[1]**stride** \'strīd\ *vb* **strode** \'strōd\; **strid·den** \'strid-ᵊn\; **strid·ing** \'strīd-iŋ\ **1** : to move with or as if with long even steps ⟨*strode* across the room⟩ **2** : to take a very long step — **strid·er** \'strīd-ər\ *n*

[2]**stride** *n* **1** : a step or the distance covered by a step **2** : a way of striding **3** : the most effective natural pace — often used in the phrase *hit one's stride* **4** : a step forward : ADVANCE ⟨made great *strides* toward their goal⟩ — **in stride** : with little or no emotional reaction ⟨took the news *in stride*⟩

stri·dent \'strīd-ᵊnt\ *adj* : harsh sounding : GRATING, SHRILL ⟨a *strident* voice⟩ — **stri·dent·ly** *adv*

\ə\ abut	\aú\ out	\i\ tip	\ó\ saw	\ú\ foot
\ər\ further	\ch\ chin	\ī\ life	\ói\ coin	\y\ yet
\a\ mat	\e\ pet	\j\ job	\th\ thin	\yü\ few
\ā\ take	\ē\ easy	\ŋ\ sing	\th\ this	\yú\ cure
\ä\ cot, cart	\g\ go	\ō\ bone	\ü\ food	\zh\ vision

strife \'strīf\ *n* **1** : bitter sometimes violent disagreement ⟨political *strife*⟩ **2** : ²STRUGGLE 2, FIGHT

¹**strike** \'strīk\ *vb* **struck** \'strək\; **struck** *also* **strick·en** \'strik-ən\; **strik·ing** \'strī-kiŋ\ **1** : to take a course : GO ⟨*strike* across the field⟩ **2 a** : to deliver a stroke or blow : HIT **b** : to attack or seize especially with fangs or claws ⟨*struck* by a snake⟩ **3** : to remove or cancel with or as if with a stroke of the pen ⟨*struck* out a word in the text⟩ **4** : to lower, take down, or take apart ⟨*strike* a flag⟩ ⟨*strike* camp⟩ **5 a** : to indicate or become indicated by a clock, bell, or chime ⟨the hour had just *struck*⟩ **b** : to indicate by sounding ⟨the clock *struck* one⟩ **6** : to pierce or penetrate or to cause to pierce or penetrate ⟨the wind seemed to *strike* through our clothes⟩ **7** : to make a military attack : FIGHT ⟨*strike* for freedom⟩ **8** : to seize the bait ⟨a fish *struck*⟩ **9** : to take root or cause to take root : GERMINATE ⟨some plant cuttings *strike* quickly⟩ **10** : to stop work for the purpose of forcing an employer to meet demands **11** : to make a beginning : LAUNCH ⟨the orchestra *struck* into another waltz⟩ **12** : to cause to suffer pain or distress suddenly ⟨*struck* down at the height of her career⟩ **13 a** : to bring into forceful contact ⟨*struck* my knee against the seat⟩ **b** : to come into contact or collision with ⟨the car *struck* the tree⟩ **c** : to fall on ⟨sunlight *strikes* your face⟩ **14** : to affect with a strong feeling ⟨*struck* by its beauty⟩ **15 a** : to produce by stamping ⟨*strike* a coin⟩ **b** : to cause to ignite by friction ⟨*strike* a match⟩ **16** : to produce on a musical instrument by hitting or plucking strings ⟨*strike* a chord on the piano⟩ **17 a** : to come to mind ⟨the answer *struck* me suddenly⟩ **b** : to appear remarkable or make a strong impression on : IMPRESS ⟨I was *struck* by its beauty⟩ **18 a** : to come to ⟨*strike* the main road⟩ **b** : to come upon : DISCOVER ⟨*strike* gold⟩ **19** : to take on : ASSUME ⟨*strike* a pose⟩

²**strike** *n* **1** : an act or instance of striking **2 a** : a stopping of work by a body of workers to force an employer to meet demands **b** : a temporary stopping of normal activities in protest against an act or condition ⟨a hunger *strike*⟩ **3** : a pull on a line by a fish in striking **4** : a stroke of good luck; *esp* : a discovery of a valuable mineral deposit **5** : a baseball pitch that passes through the strike zone or that is swung at without being hit fair **6** : ¹DISADVANTAGE 2a, HANDICAP ⟨their poor attendance was a *strike* against them⟩ **7** : the knocking down of all the pins with the first ball in bowling **8** : a military attack

strike·bound \'strīk-ˌbau̇nd\ *adj* : experiencing a strike ⟨a *strikebound* factory⟩

strike·break·er \-ˌbrā-kər\ *n* : a person hired to replace a striking worker

strike·break·ing \-ˌbrā-kiŋ\ *n* : action designed to break up a strike

strike down *vb* : to make null and void : ANNUL ⟨*struck down* the proposal⟩; *esp* : to declare (a law) illegal and unenforceable ⟨the court *struck down* the law⟩

strike off *vb* : to produce in an effortless manner ⟨*strike off* a poem for the occasion⟩

strike·out \'strī-ˌkau̇t\ *n* : an out in baseball resulting from a batter's being charged with three strikes

strike out \(ˈ)strī-ˈkau̇t\ *vb* **1** : to enter upon a course of action ⟨*struck out* on my own after graduation⟩ **2** : to make an out or cause to make an out in baseball by a strikeout ⟨the shortstop *struck out*⟩ ⟨the pitcher *struck* him *out* with a curve⟩

strike·over \'strī-ˌkō-vər\ *n* : an act or instance of striking a typewriter letter, number, or symbol on a spot already occupied by another

strik·er \'strī-kər\ *n* : a worker on strike

strike up *vb* **1** : to begin or cause to begin to sing or play ⟨*strike up* the band⟩ **2** : to cause to begin ⟨*strike up* a conversation⟩

strike zone *n* : the area (as from the armpits to the tops of the knees of a batter) over home plate through which a baseball pitch must pass to be called a strike

strik·ing \'strī-kiŋ\ *adj* : attracting attention : REMARKABLE, IMPRESSIVE ⟨a *striking* costume⟩ ⟨a *striking* resemblance⟩ — **strik·ing·ly** *adv*

¹**string** \'striŋ\ *n* **1** : a cord usually used to fasten or tie **2** : a thin tough plant structure (as the fiber connecting the halves of a bean pod) **3 a** : the gut, wire, or nylon cord of a musical instrument that is plucked, bowed, or struck to produce a sound **b** *pl* : the stringed instruments of an orchestra **4** : the gut, wire, or cord of a racket or shooting bow **5 a** : a group of objects threaded on a string ⟨a *string* of pearls⟩ **b** : a series of things arranged in or as if in a line ⟨a *string* of automobiles⟩ **c** : a series of like items (as units of information, marks, or words) **d** : the animals and especially horses belonging to or used by one individual **6** : any of several squads of players on a team that are grouped together according to skill ⟨the second *string* of a football team⟩ **7** : a series in time : SUCCESSION, SEQUENCE **8** *pl* : requirements or obligations connected with something ⟨an agreement with no *strings* attached⟩

²**string** *vb* **strung** \'strəŋ\; **string·ing** \'striŋ-iŋ\ **1** : to equip (as a tennis racket) with strings **2 a** : to thread on or as if on a string ⟨*string* beads⟩ **b** : to tie, hang, or fasten with string **3** : to hang by the neck ⟨*strung* up from a high tree⟩ **4** : to remove the strings of ⟨*string* beans⟩ **5 a** : to extend or stretch like a string ⟨*string* wires from tree to tree⟩ **b** : to set out in a line or series

³**string** *adj* : of or relating to stringed musical instruments ⟨the *string* section of an orchestra⟩

string along *vb* **1** : to go along : AGREE ⟨*string* along with the majority⟩ **2** : DECEIVE 1, FOOL ⟨would *string* us *along* with false promises⟩

string bass *n* : DOUBLE BASS

string bean *n* **1** : a bean of one of the older varieties of kidney bean that have stringy fibers on the lines of separation of the pods; *also* : SNAP BEAN **2** : a very tall thin person

stringed instrument \'striŋd-\ *n* : any of a group of musical instruments (as the violin, harp, or piano) that is played by plucking or striking or by drawing a bow across tense strings — compare BRASS INSTRUMENT, PERCUSSION INSTRUMENT, WOODWIND 1

strin·gent \'strin-jənt\ *adj* **1** : tying, drawing, or pressing tight **2** : strict in setting standards or following rules ⟨*stringent* training⟩ — **strin·gent·ly** *adv*

string·er \'striŋ-ər\ *n* **1** : one that strings **2** : a long piece of wood or metal used for support or strengthening in a building (as under a floor)

string·ing \'striŋ-iŋ\ *n* : the material with which a racket is strung

stringy \'striŋ-ē\ *adj* **string·i·er; -est** : containing, consisting of, or resembling string ⟨*stringy* cheese⟩ ⟨*stringy* hair⟩ — **string·i·ness** *n*

¹**strip** \'strip\ *vb* **stripped** \'stript\ *also* **stript; strip·ping 1 a** : to remove clothing, covering, or surface substance from **b** : UNDRESS ⟨*stripped* and showered⟩ **c** : ¹PLUNDER, SPOIL ⟨troops *stripped* the town after capturing it⟩ **d** : to take away all duties, honors, or special rights **2 a** : to remove a layer that covers : SKIN, PEEL ⟨*strip* bark from a tree⟩ **b** : to remove unimportant material from **c** : to remove furniture, equipment, or accessories from **3** : to make bare or clear (as by cutting or grazing) **4** : to tear or damage the screw thread of (as a bolt or nut) — **strip·per** *n*

²**strip** *n* **1** : a long narrow piece or area ⟨*strips* of bacon⟩ ⟨a *strip* of land⟩ **2** : AIRSTRIP

strip cropping *n* : the growing of a food crop (as corn) in alternate strips with a crop (as hay) that forms sod and helps keep the soil from being worn away — **strip–crop** \-ˌkräp\ *vb*

¹stripe \'strīp\ *n* : a stroke or blow with a rod or part of a whip

²stripe *vb* **striped** \'strīpt\; **strip·ing** : to make stripes on

³stripe *n* **1** : a line or long narrow section differing in color or appearance from the background **2** : a piece of braid (as on the sleeve) to indicate military rank or length of service — **stripe·less** \'strī-pləs\ *adj*

striped \'strīpt, 'strī-pəd\ *adj* : having stripes or streaks

striped bass *n* : a large silvery marine food and sport fish that has black horizontal stripes on the sides, occurs along the Atlantic coast of the U.S., and has been introduced into inland waters (as lakes) along the Pacific coast

strip·ling \'strip-liŋ\ *n* : a youth just passing from boyhood to manhood

strip mine *n* : a mine that is worked from the earth's surface by the stripping away of covering material — **strip–mine** *vb*

strive \'strīv\ *vb* **strove** \'strōv\ *also* **strived** \'strīvd\; **striv·en** \'striv-ən\ *or* **strived; striv·ing** \'strī-viŋ\ **1** : to try hard : ENDEAVOR ⟨*strive* to win⟩ **2** : to struggle against : CONTEND — **striv·er** \'strī-vər\ *n*

strobe \'strōb\ *n* : a device that produces a very brief strong flash of light (as for photography) and that can be used repeatedly

strode *past of* STRIDE

¹stroke \'strōk\ *vb* **stroked; strok·ing** **1** : to rub gently in one direction **2** : to pass the hand over gently in kindness or tenderness [Old English *strācian* "stroke, caress"] — **strok·er** *n*

²stroke *n* **1** : the act of striking; *esp* : a blow with a weapon or instrument **2** : a single unbroken movement; *esp* : one of a series of repeated or to-and-fro movements **3** : a striking of the ball in a game; *esp* : a striking or attempt to strike the ball that counts as the scoring unit in golf **4 a** : a sudden action or process that results in something being struck ⟨*stroke* of lightning⟩ **b** : an unexpected result ⟨*stroke* of luck⟩ **5** : sudden weakening or loss of consciousness or the power to feel or move caused by the breaking or blocking (as by a clot) of a blood vessel in the brain — called also *apoplexy* **6** : one of a series of movements that pushes against something ⟨*stroke* of an oar⟩ **7** : a vigorous or energetic effort by which something is done, produced, or accomplished ⟨a *stroke* of genius⟩ **8** : the movement or the distance of the movement in either direction of a mechanical part (as a piston) having a forward and backward motion **9** : the sound of a bell being struck ⟨at the *stroke* of twelve⟩ **10 a** : a mark made by a single movement of a tool ⟨a *stroke* of the pen⟩ **b** : one of the lines of a letter of the alphabet [Middle English *stroke* "act of striking"]

³stroke *vb* **stroked; strok·ing** **1** : to show or cancel with a line ⟨*stroked* out my name⟩ **2** : ¹HIT 1a ⟨gently *stroked* the ball toward the hole⟩

stroll \'strōl\ *vb* : to walk in a leisurely or idle manner : RAMBLE — **stroll** *n*

stroll·er \'strō-lər\ *n* **1** : one that strolls **2** : a small carriage in which a baby sits and can be pushed around

strong \'stroŋ\ *adj* **strong·er** \'stroŋ-gər\; **strong·est** \'stroŋ-gəst\ **1** : having or marked by great physical power : ROBUST **2** : having moral or mental power **3** : having great resources (as of wealth) **4** : of a specified number ⟨an army ten thousand *strong*⟩ **5** : being great or striking ⟨a *strong* resemblance⟩ **6** : FORCEFUL, COGENT ⟨*strong* arguments⟩ **7** : not mild or weak : having much of some quality ⟨*strong* coffee⟩ ⟨*strong* acid⟩ ⟨*strong* glasses⟩ **8** : moving with rapidity or force ⟨*strong* wind⟩ **9** : ENTHUSIASTIC, ZEALOUS ⟨a *strong* believer in peace⟩ **10** : not easily captured or overcome ⟨a *strong* fort⟩ **11** : well established : FIRM ⟨*strong* traditions⟩ **12** : having a disgusting or powerful odor or flavor : RANK **13** : of, relating to, or being a verb that forms the past tense by a change in the root vowel and the past participle usually by the addition of *-en* with or without change of the root vowel (as *strive, strove, striven* or *drink, drank, drunk*) — **strong** *adv* — **strong·ly** \'stroŋ-lē\ *adv*

synonyms STRONG, STURDY, TOUGH mean showing the power to hold out against opposing force. STRONG suggests great power of body or material ⟨a *strong* person is needed to lift that⟩ ⟨a *strong* rope for pulling heavy loads⟩. STURDY suggests the ability to endure pressure or hard use ⟨a *sturdy* table⟩. TOUGH suggests firmness and elasticity in a thing ⟨a *tough* fabric that will last many years⟩ or energetic hardiness or determination in a person ⟨a *tough* opponent⟩.

strong·box \'stroŋ-ˌbäks\ *n* : a strongly made container for money or valuables

strong force *n* : the force between the particles of an atomic nucleus that acts to hold the nucleus together and is the strongest known force

strong·hold \'stroŋ-ˌhōld\ *n* : FORTRESS

strong–mind·ed \'stroŋ-'mīn-dəd\ *adj* : very independent in thought and judgment — **strong–mind·ed·ness** *n*

stron·ti·um \'strän-ch(ē-)əm, 'stränt-ē-əm\ *n* : a soft metallic element that can be hammered and shaped, occurs only in combination, and is used in color TV picture tubes and red fireworks — see ELEMENT table

strontium 90 *n* : a heavy radioactive form of strontium having the mass number 90 that is present in nuclear waste and fallout

¹strop \'sträp\ *n* : a usually leather band for sharpening a razor

²strop *vb* **stropped; strop·ping** : to sharpen on a strop ⟨*strop* a razor⟩

stro·phe \'strō-fē\ *n* : a division of a poem : STANZA — **stro·phic** \'strō-fik, 'sträf-ik\ *adj*

strove *past and chiefly dialect past participle of* STRIVE

struck *past and past participle of* STRIKE

struc·tur·al \'strək-chə-rəl, 'strək-shrəl\ *adj* **1** : of, relating to, or affecting structure ⟨*structural* weaknesses⟩ **2** : used or formed for use in construction ⟨*structural* steel⟩ — **struc·tur·al·ly** \-ē\ *adv*

structural formula *n* : an expanded molecular formula showing the arrangement within the molecule of atoms and of bonds

¹strop

¹struc·ture \'strək-chər\ *n* **1** : the action of building : CONSTRUCTION **2** : something constructed or arranged in a definite pattern of organization **3** : manner of construction : the arrangement or relationship of elements (as particles, parts, or organs) in a substance, body, or system ⟨soil *structure*⟩ ⟨the *structure* of a plant⟩ ⟨molecular *structure*⟩ ⟨social *structure*⟩ ⟨the *structure* of a language⟩ — **struc·ture·less** \-ləs\ *adj*

²structure *vb* **struc·tured; struc·tur·ing** \'strək-chə-riŋ, 'strək-shriŋ\ : to form into a structure : ORGANIZE

stru·del \'strüd-ᵊl, 'shtrüd-\ *n* : a pastry made of thin dough rolled up with filling and baked

¹strug·gle \'strəg-əl\ *vb* **strug·gled; strug·gling** \-(ə-)liŋ\ **1** : to make a great effort to overcome someone or something : STRIVE ⟨*struggling* with the problem⟩ **2** : to proceed with difficulty or with great effort ⟨*struggled* through the snow⟩ — **strug·gler** \-(ə-)lər\ *n*

²struggle *n* **1** : ²FIGHT 1a, CONTEST ⟨a power *struggle*⟩ **2** : a violent or strenuous effort or exertion ⟨a *struggle* to make ends meet⟩

struggle for existence : competition (as for food, space, or light) of members of a natural population that tends to

\ə\ abut	\au̇\ out	\i\ tip	\ȯ\ saw	\u̇\ foot
\ər\ further	\ch\ chin	\ī\ life	\ȯi\ coin	\y\ yet
\a\ mat	\e\ pet	\j\ job	\th\ thin	\yü\ few
\ā\ take	\ē\ easy	\ŋ\ sing	\th\ this	\yu̇\ cure
\ä\ cot, cart	\g\ go	\ō\ bone	\ü\ food	\zh\ vision

eliminate weaker or less efficient individuals and thereby to increase the chance of the stronger or more efficient individuals to pass on their traits

strum \'strəm\ *vb* **strummed; strum·ming** : to play a stringed instrument by brushing the strings with the fingers — **strum·mer** *n*

strung *past and past participle of* STRING

¹**strut** \'strət\ *vb* **strut·ted; strut·ting 1** : to walk in a stiff proud way **2** : to parade (as clothes) with a show of pride — **strut·ter** *n*

²**strut** *n* **1** : a bar or brace to resist pressure in the direction of its length **2** : a strutting step or walk

strych·nine \'strik-,nīn, -nən, -,nēn\ *n* : a bitter poison that is obtained from certain plants, acts as a stimulant to the central nervous system, and is used especially as a rat poison

¹**stub** \'stəb\ *n* **1** : ¹STUMP 2 **2** : a pen with a short blunt point **3** : a short part left after a larger part has been broken off or used up ⟨a pencil *stub*⟩ **4 a** : a small part of a check kept as a record of the contents of the check **b** : the part of a ticket returned to the user

²**stub** *vb* **stubbed; stub·bing 1** : to put out (as a cigarette) by crushing **2** : to strike (as one's toe) against an object

stub·ble \'stəb-əl\ *n* **1** : the stem ends of herbs and especially cereal grasses remaining attached to the ground after harvest **2** : a rough surface or growth resembling stubble — **stub·bly** \-(ə-)lē\ *adj*

stub·born \'stəb-ərn\ *adj* **1 a** : hard to convince, persuade, or move ⟨*stubborn* as a mule⟩ **b** : having or characterized by a firm idea or purpose : DETERMINED ⟨*stubborn* courage⟩ **2** : done or continued in a firm and determined manner ⟨*stubborn* refusal⟩ **3** : difficult to handle, manage, or treat ⟨*stubborn* hair⟩ **synonyms** see OBSTINATE — **stub·born·ly** *adv* — **stub·born·ness** \-ərn-(n)əs\ *n*

stub·by \'stəb-ē\ *adj* : resembling a stub especially in shortness and broadness ⟨*stubby* fingers⟩

stuc·co \'stək-ō\ *n, pl* **stuccos** *or* **stuccoes** : a plaster used to cover exterior walls or decorate interior walls — **stuc·coed** \-ōd\ *adj*

stuck *past and past participle of* STICK

stuck-up \'stək-'əp\ *adj* : having too high an opinion of one's own worth or ability : CONCEITED

¹**stud** \'stəd\ *n* **1** : a group of animals and especially horses kept primarily for breeding **2** : a male animal (as a stallion) kept for breeding [Old English *stōd*]

²**stud** *n* **1** : one of the smaller upright supports in the framing of the walls of a building to which the wall materials are fastened **2 a** : a knob, pin, bolt, or nail with a large head used for ornament or protection **b** : a solid button used on a garment as a fastener or ornament **3** : one of the metal or rubber cleats used on a snow tire to provide a better grip [Old English *studu*]

³**stud** *vb* **stud·ded; stud·ding 1** : to furnish (as a wall) with studs **2** : to decorate, cover, or protect with studs **3** : to set or be set thickly together ⟨water *studded* with islands⟩

stu·dent \'st(y)üd-ᵊnt, *chiefly Southern* -ənt\ *n* **1** : SCHOLAR 1; *esp* : one who attends a school or college **2** : one who studies ⟨a *student* of life⟩

student council *n* : a group elected from a body of students to serve as representatives in student government

student government *n* : the organization and management of student life, recreation, or discipline by various student organizations in a school or college

stud·ied \'stəd-ēd\ *adj* **1** : carefully thought out or prepared : THOUGHTFUL ⟨your judgments are always *studied* and fair⟩ **2** : KNOWLEDGEABLE, LEARNED ⟨*studied* in the craft of blacksmithing⟩ **3** : INTENTIONAL, DELIBERATE ⟨a *studied* insult⟩ — **stud·ied·ly** *adv*

stu·dio \'st(y)üd-ē-,ō\ *n, pl* **-dios 1 a** : the working place of an artist **b** : a place for the study of an art **2** : a place

where motion pictures are made **3** : a place for the transmission of radio or television programs

studio couch *n* : an upholstered usually backless couch that can be made to serve as a double bed by sliding from underneath it the frame of a single cot

stu·di·ous \'st(y)üd-ē-əs\ *adj* **1** : devoted to, fond of, or concerned with study ⟨a *studious* child⟩ ⟨*studious* habits⟩ **2** : of determined purpose : EARNEST ⟨made a *studious* effort to obey the rules⟩ — **stu·di·ous·ly** *adv* — **stu·di·ous·ness** *n*

¹**study** \'stəd-ē\ *n, pl* **stud·ies 1** : a state of thinking about something steadily : REVERIE **2 a** : use of the mind to acquire knowledge ⟨years of *study*⟩ **b** : careful or prolonged consideration ⟨the proposed change is under *study*⟩ **c** : a careful examination or investigation of something; *also* : a report or publication based on such a study **3** : a building or room devoted to study, reading, or writing **4 a** : a division or area of learning : SUBJECT ⟨American *studies*⟩ **b** : the actions or work of a student ⟨returned to her *studies* after vacation⟩ **5 a** : a person who learns or memorizes something (as a part in a play) — usually used with an adjective ⟨he's a quick *study*⟩

²**study** *vb* **stud·ied; study·ing 1** : to engage in study or the study of ⟨*studied* hard⟩ ⟨liked to *study* geography⟩ **2** : to give close attention to ⟨*study* a part in a play⟩ ⟨*studied* the request carefully⟩

study hall *n* **1** : a room in a school where students can study **2** : a period in a student's day set aside for study and homework

¹**stuff** \'stəf\ *n* **1** : supplies or equipment that people need or use **2** : writing, conversation, or ideas often of little or temporary worth **3** : something mentioned or understood but not named ⟨sold tons of the *stuff*⟩ **4 a** : basic part of something : SUBSTANCE ⟨the *stuff* of greatness⟩ **b** : body of knowledge ⟨teachers who know their *stuff*⟩ **5 a** : actions or talk of a particular kind ⟨how do they get away with such *stuff*⟩ **b** : special knowledge or ability ⟨a person who has the right *stuff* will do well here⟩

²**stuff** *vb* **1 a** : to fill by or as if by packing things in ⟨was *stuffing* her pockets with candy⟩ **b** : to eat too much ⟨don't *stuff* yourself with pizza⟩ **c** : to fill with a stuffing ⟨*stuffed* the pillow⟩ **2** : to fill with ideas or information ⟨*stuffed* their heads with facts⟩ **3** : to fill or block up ⟨a sore throat and *stuffed* nose⟩ **4** : to put or push into something especially carelessly or with little concern ⟨*stuffed* the clothes into the drawer⟩ **synonyms** see PACK — **stuff·er** *n*

stuff·ing \'stəf-iŋ\ *n* : material used to stuff something; *esp* : a seasoned mixture used to stuff meat or poultry

stuffy \'stəf-ē\ *adj* **stuff·i·er; -est 1** : SULLEN 1, ILL-HUMORED **2 a** : lacking fresh air ⟨a *stuffy* room⟩ **b** : stuffed or choked up ⟨had a *stuffy* feeling in my head⟩ **3** : lacking in pep or interest : DULL, STODGY **4** : SELF-RIGHTEOUS — **stuff·i·ly** \'stəf-ə-lē\ *adv* — **stuff·i·ness** \'stəf-ē-nəs\ *n*

stul·ti·fy \'stəl-tə-,fī\ *vb* **-fied; -fy·ing 1** : to cause to appear or be stupid, foolish, or very unreasonable **2** : to make worthless or useless ⟨*stultify* creativity⟩

stum·ble \'stəm-bəl\ *vb* **stum·bled; stum·bling** \-b(ə-)liŋ\ **1** : to trip in walking or running **2 a** : to walk unsteadily **b** : to speak or act in a hesitant or clumsy manner **3** : to come or happen unexpectedly or by chance ⟨*stumbled* onto the ruins of an old fort⟩ — **stum·ble** *n* — **stum·bler** \-b(ə-)lər\ *n* — **stum·bling·ly** \-b(ə-)liŋ-lē\ *adv*

stumbling block \'stəm-bliŋ-\ *n* **1** : an obstacle to belief or understanding **2** : an obstacle to progress

¹**stump** \'stəmp\ *n* **1** : the base of a bodily part (as an arm or leg) remaining after the rest is removed **2** : the part of a plant and especially a tree remaining attached to the root after the top is cut off **3** : a part (as of a pencil) re-

maining after the rest is worn away or lost : STUB **4** : a place or occasion for political public speaking

²**stump** *vb* **1 a** : ¹CHALLENGE 3 **b** : PERPLEX 1, CONFOUND **2 a** : to walk or walk over heavily or clumsily **b** : ²STUB **2 3** : to go about making political speeches ⟨*stump* the state for a candidate⟩ [probably an altered form of earlier *stump* (noun) "a challenge"] — **stumper** *n*

stumpy \'stəm-pē\ *adj* **stump·i·er; -est 1** : short and thick : SQUAT **2** : full of stumps

stun \'stən\ *vb* **stunned; stun·ning 1** : to make senseless or dizzy by or as if by a blow **2** : to overcome with astonishment or disbelief ⟨*stunned* by the news⟩ — **stun** *n*

stung *past and past participle of* STING

stun gun *n* : a weapon designed to stun or immobilize (as by electric shock) rather than kill or injure

stunk *past and past participle of* STINK

stun·ner \'stən-ər\ *n* : one that stuns or is stunning

stun·ning \'stən-iŋ\ *adj* **1** : causing astonishment or disbelief ⟨*stunning* news⟩ **2** : unusually impressive especially in beauty or excellence ⟨a *stunning* view⟩ ⟨a *stunning* effort⟩ — **stun·ning·ly** *adv*

¹**stunt** \'stənt\ *vb* : to hold back the normal growth, development, or progress of [from a dialect word *stunt* "stubborn, abrupt, stunted," probably of Scandinavian origin]

²**stunt** *n* : an unusual or difficult feat performed or attempted usually to gain attention or publicity [origin unknown]

³**stunt** *vb* : to perform stunts

stu·pe·fy \'st(y)ü-pə-ˌfī\ *vb* **-fied; -fy·ing 1** : ASTONISH, BEWILDER ⟨the strange sight *stupefied* the crowd⟩ **2** : to make stupid, groggy, or numb ⟨*stupefied* by the huge meal⟩

stu·pen·dous \st(y)ü-'pen-dəs\ *adj* : amazing especially because of great size or height ⟨*stupendous* gorges⟩ **syn·onyms** see MONSTROUS — **stu·pen·dous·ly** *adv* — **stu·pen·dous·ness** *n*

stu·pid \'st(y)ü-pəd\ *adj* **1 a** : dull of mind : DENSE **b** : given to unwise decisions or actions : UNTHINKING **2** : dulled in feeling or sensation **3** : showing or resulting from foolish thinking or acting : SENSELESS ⟨a *stupid* mistake⟩ **4** : not interesting or worthwhile : BORING ⟨a *stupid* movie⟩ — **stu·pid·ly** *adv* — **stu·pid·ness** *n*

stu·pid·i·ty \st(y)ü-'pid-ət-ē\ *n, pl* **-ties 1** : the quality or state of being stupid **2** : something (as an idea or act) that is stupid

stu·por \'st(y)ü-pər\ *n* **1** : a condition of greatly dulled or completely suspended sense or feeling ⟨drifted into a pleasant, dreamy *stupor*⟩ **2** : a state of dullness or lack of interest resulting often from stress or shock

stur·dy \'stərd-ē\ *adj* **stur·di·er; -est 1 a** : firmly built or made ⟨a *sturdy* ship⟩ **b** : strong and healthy in body : HARDY, ROBUST **2** : ¹FIRM 3, RESOLUTE ⟨*sturdy* self-reliance⟩ — **stur·di·ly** \'stərd-ᵊl-ē\ *adj* — **stur·di·ness** \'stərd-ē-nəs\ *n*

stur·geon \'stər-jən\ *n* : any of various usually large long-bodied fishes having a thick skin covered with rows of bony plates that are valued especially for their eggs which are made into caviar

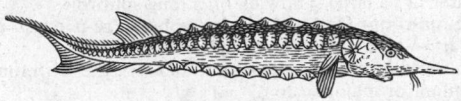

sturgeon

¹**stut·ter** \'stət-ər\ *vb* : to speak in an uneven way with involuntary repeating or interruption of sounds — **stut·ter·er** \-ər-ər\ *n*

²**stutter** *n* **1** : an act or instance of stuttering **2** : a speech disorder involving stuttering

¹**sty** \'stī\ *n, pl* **sties** *also* **styes** : PIGPEN [Old English *stig* "a pen for swine"]

²**sty** *or* **stye** \'stī\ *n, pl* **sties** *or* **styes** : a painful red swelling of a skin gland on the edge of an eyelid [a shortened form of obsolete *styan* "a painful swelling of a gland on the edge of the eyelid," from Old English *stīgend* (same meaning), from *stīgan* "to rise up"]

¹**style** \'stī(ə)l\ *n* **1 a** : a way of expressing oneself (as in speaking or writing) **b** : a particular way by which something is done, created, or performed ⟨a unique *style* of horseback riding⟩ ⟨the classical *style* of dance⟩ **2 a** : STYLUS 1 **b** : a column built so that its shadow indicates the time of day **c** : the narrow long middle part of the pistil of a flower which bears the stigma at its tip **3 a** : the state of being popular : FASHION ⟨clothes that are always in *style*⟩ **b** : fashionable elegance **c** : beauty, grace, or ease of doing something ⟨handled the awkward moment with *style*⟩ **4** : the custom or plan followed in spelling, capitalization, punctuation, and arrangement and display of type — **style·less** \-ləs\ *adj*

²**style** *vb* **styled; styl·ing 1** : to call by an identifying term : NAME ⟨*style* themselves scientists⟩ **2 a** : to give a particular style to ⟨cuts and *styles* hair⟩ **b** : to design or make in agreement with an accepted way of doing something — **styl·er** *n*

styl·ish \'stī-lish\ *adj* : having style; *esp* : FASHIONABLE — **styl·ish·ly** *adv* — **styl·ish·ness** *n*

styl·ist \'stī-ləst\ *n* **1** : a person known for an outstanding style ⟨a song *stylist*⟩ ⟨a prose *stylist*⟩ **2** : one who develops, designs, or advises on styles ⟨a hair *stylist*⟩ — **sty·lis·tic** \stī-'lis-tik\ *adj* — **sty·lis·ti·cal·ly** \-ti-k(ə-)lē\ *adv*

styl·ize \'stī(ə)l-ˌīz\ *vb* **styl·ized; styl·iz·ing** : to represent or design according to a style or pattern rather than according to nature or tradition

sty·lus \'stī-ləs\ *n, pl* **sty·li** \'stī(ə)l-ˌī\ *also* **sty·lus·es** \'stī-lə-səz\ **1** : an instrument used by the ancients for writing on wax tablets **2** : ¹NEEDLE 4

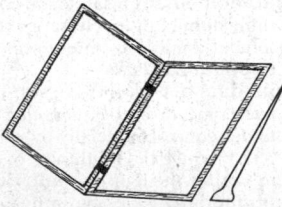

stylus 1 with Roman wax tablet

sty·mie \'stī-mē\ *vb* **sty·mied; sty·mie·ing** : to present an obstacle to : stand in the way of ⟨an unexpected snowstorm *stymied* travelers' plans⟩

Sty·ro·foam \'stī-rə-ˌfōm\ *trademark* — used for an expanded stiff plastic

sua·sion \'swā-zhən\ *n* : the act of influencing or persuading ⟨moral *suasion*⟩

suave \'swäv\ *adj* **suav·er; -est** : smoothly polite and agreeable ⟨a *suave* young man⟩ — **suave·ly** *adv* — **suave·ness** *n* — **sua·vi·ty** \'swäv-ət-ē\ *n*

¹**sub** \'səb\ *n* : ¹SUBSTITUTE

²**sub** *vb* **subbed; sub·bing** : to act as a substitute

³**sub** *n* : ²SUBMARINE

sub- *prefix* **1** : under : beneath : below ⟨*sub*soil⟩ ⟨*sub*freezing⟩ **2 a** : being at a lower rank or secondary level ⟨*sub*station⟩ **b** : division or lesser part of ⟨*sub*committee⟩ ⟨*sub*topic⟩ **c** : involving a secondary stage or process ⟨*sub*let⟩ ⟨*sub*contract⟩ **3** : less than completely, perfectly, or typically : somewhat ⟨*sub*dominant⟩ **4** : bordering upon ⟨*sub*arctic⟩ [from Latin *sub-* "under, below"]

\ə\ abut	\aú\ out	\i\ tip	\ò\ saw	\ú\ foot
\ər\ further	\ch\ chin	\ī\ life	\òi\ coin	\y\ yet
\a\ mat	\e\ pet	\j\ job	\th\ thin	\yü\ few
\ā\ take	\ē\ easy	\ŋ\ sing	\th\ this	\yu̇\ cure
\ä\ cot, cart	\g\ go	\ō\ bone	\ü\ food	\zh\ vision

sub·ant·arc·tic \ˌsəb-ant-'ärk-tik, -'ärt-ik\ *adj* : of, relating to, or being a region just outside the antarctic circle ⟨*subantarctic* islands⟩ ⟨*subantarctic* seals⟩

sub·arc·tic \ˌsəb-'ärk-tik, -səb-'ärt-ik\ *adj* : of, relating to, or being regions immediately outside of the arctic circle or regions similar to these in climate or conditions of life ⟨*subarctic* waters⟩ ⟨*subarctic* plants⟩

sub·com·mit·tee \'səb-kə-ˌmit-ē, ˌsəb-kə-'mit-ē\ *n* : a part of a committee usually organized for a certain purpose

sub·com·pact \'səb-'käm-ˌpakt\ *n* : an automobile smaller than a compact

¹**sub·con·scious** \ˌsəb-'kän-chəs, 'səb-\ *adj* : existing in the mind but not immediately available to consciousness ⟨a *subconscious* motive⟩ — **sub·con·scious·ly** *adv*

²**subconscious** *n* : the mental activities just below the limit of consciousness

sub·con·ti·nent \'səb-'känt-ᵊn-ənt, -'känt-nənt, -ˌkänt-\ *n* : a large area of land smaller than a continent; *esp* : a major subdivision of a continent ⟨the Indian *subcontinent*⟩ — **sub·con·ti·nen·tal** \ˌsəb-ˌkänt-ᵊn-'ent-ᵊl\ *adj*

sub·con·tract \'səb-'kän-ˌtrakt, -ˌkän-\ *n* : a contract between a party to an original contract and a third party who usually agrees to supply work or materials required in the original contract — **sub·con·tract** \ˌsəb-'kän-ˌtrakt, 'səb-; ˌsəb-kən-'trakt\ *vb* — **sub·con·trac·tor** \ˌsəb-'kän-ˌtrak-tər, 'səb-; ˌsəb-kən-'trak-tər\ *n*

sub·cu·ta·ne·ous \ˌsəb-kyù-'tā-nē-əs\ *adj* : being, living, occurring, or given under the skin ⟨*subcutaneous* parasites⟩

sub·di·vide \ˌsəb-də-'vīd\ *vb* **1** : to divide the parts of something into more parts **2** : to divide into several parts; *esp* : to divide a piece of land into building lots

sub·di·vi·sion \ˌsəb-də-'vizh-ən\ *n* **1** : the act or process of subdividing **2** : one of the parts into which something is subdivided

sub·dom·i·nant \ˌsəb-'däm(-ə)-nənt, 'səb-\ *n* **1** : something dominant to a lesser or partial degree **2** : the fourth tone of a major or minor scale (as F in the scale of C) — **subdominant** *adj*

sub·due \səb-'d(y)ü\ *vb* **sub·dued; sub·du·ing** **1** : to overcome in battle ⟨*subdued* the enemy⟩ **2** : to bring under control especially by willpower ⟨*subdued* his fears⟩ **3** : to reduce the brightness or strength of : SOFTEN ⟨tried to *subdue* the light⟩ — **sub·du·er** *n*

subdued *adj* : lacking in liveliness, intensity, or strength ⟨*subdued* colors⟩

sub·en·try \'səb-ˌen-trē\ *n* : an entry (as in a catalog) made under a more general entry

sub·freez·ing \'səb-'frē-ziŋ\ *adj* : being or marked by temperature below the freezing point (as of water) ⟨*subfreezing* weather⟩

sub·group \'səb-ˌgrüp\ *n* : a group whose members usually share some common quality that makes them different from the other members of a larger group to which they belong

sub·head \'səb-ˌhed\ *n* **1** : a heading under which one of the divisions of a subject is listed **2** : a title or headline coming after the main title or headline

sub·head·ing \'səb-ˌhed-iŋ\ *n* : SUBHEAD

¹**sub·ject** \'səb-jikt\ *n* **1 a** : a person under the authority or control of another **b** : a person who owes loyalty to a monarch or state **2 a** : a department of knowledge or learning **b** : an individual (as a person or a mouse) that is studied or experimented on **c** : the person or thing discussed : TOPIC ⟨the *subject* of an essay⟩ **3** : a noun or term functioning as a noun about which something is stated in the predicate of a sentence ⟨"child" in "the child threw the ball" is the *subject*⟩

²**subject** *adj* **1** : owing obedience or loyalty to another **2 a** : likely to be affected by ⟨*subject* to temptation⟩ **b** : having a tendency ⟨*subject* to catching colds⟩ **3** : depending on ⟨*subject* to your approval⟩

³**sub·ject** \səb-'jekt\ *vb* **1 a** : to bring under control or rule **b** : to make responsive to the discipline and control of a superior **2** : to make likely ⟨his poor conduct *subjected* him to criticism⟩ **3** : to cause or force to put up with something difficult, unpleasant, or inconvenient ⟨unwilling to *subject* us to embarrassment⟩ — **sub·jec·tion** \səb-'jek-shən\ *n*

sub·jec·tive \(ˌ)səb-'jek-tiv\ *adj* **1** : of, relating to, or being a subject **2** : of, relating to, or arising within one's self or mind : PERSONAL ⟨a *subjective* point of view⟩ — **sub·jec·tive·ly** *adv* — **sub·jec·tiv·i·ty** \(ˌ)səb-ˌjek-'tiv-ət-ē\ *n*

subject matter *n* : matter presented for consideration in discussion, thought, or study ⟨the poem's *subject matter*⟩

sub·ju·gate \'səb-ji-ˌgāt\ *vb* **-gat·ed; -gat·ing** **1** : to bring under control and rule as a subject : CONQUER **2** : to make willing to submit to others : SUBDUE — **sub·ju·ga·tion** \ˌsəb-ji-'gā-shən\ *n* — **sub·ju·ga·tor** \'səb-ji-ˌgāt-ər\ *n*

¹**sub·junc·tive** \səb-'jəŋ(k)-tiv\ *adj* : of, relating to, or being a verb form that represents an act or state not as fact but as conditional or possible or viewed emotionally (as with doubt or desire) ⟨the verb "were" is in the *subjunctive* mood in "if I were you, I wouldn't go"⟩

²**subjunctive** *n* : the subjunctive mood of a verb or a verb in this mood

sub·lease \'səb-ˌlēs, -'lēs\ *n* : a lease by a tenant of part or all of leased property to another person — **sublease** *vb*

sub·let \'səb-'let\ *vb* **-let; -let·ting** **1** : to lease or rent all or part of a leased or rented property **2** : to hire a third party to perform under a subcontract the work included in an original contract : SUBCONTRACT

sub·li·mate \'səb-lə-ˌmāt\ *vb* **-mat·ed; -mat·ing** **1** : ¹SUBLIME **2** : to direct the expression of (a desire or emotion) from an unacceptable form to one that is considered proper by one's culture or society — **sub·li·ma·tion** \ˌsəb-lə-'mā-shən\ *n*

¹**sub·lime** \sə-'blīm\ *vb* **sub·limed; sub·lim·ing** : to change or cause to change from a solid to a gaseous form and sometimes back to solid form without passing through a liquid form

²**sublime** *adj* **sub·lim·er; -est** **1** : grand or noble in thought, expression, or manner ⟨*sublime* truths⟩ **2** : having an impressive quality that inspires awe ⟨*sublime* beauty⟩ **synonyms** see SPLENDID — **sub·lime·ly** *adv* — **sub·lime·ness** *n*

sub·lim·i·nal \(ˌ)səb-'lim-ən-ᵊl, 'səb-\ *adj* **1** : not strong enough to produce a sensation or a mental awareness ⟨*subliminal* stimuli⟩ **2** : existing or functioning below the level of conscious awareness ⟨the *subliminal* mind⟩ ⟨*subliminal* advertising⟩ — **sub·lim·i·nal·ly** \-ē\ *adv*

sub·ma·chine gun \ˌsəb-mə-'shēn-ˌgən\ *n* : a lightweight automatic portable firearm

sub·mar·gin·al \ˌsəb-'märj-nəl, 'səb-, -ən-ᵊl\ *adj* **1** : located near or beneath a margin or a marginal part **2** : inadequate for some end or use ⟨farming *submarginal* land⟩

¹**sub·ma·rine** \'səb-mə-ˌrēn, ˌsəb-mə-'rēn\ *adj* : UNDERWATER; *esp* : UNDERSEA ⟨*submarine* plants⟩

²**submarine** *n* **1** : a naval vessel designed to operate underwater **2** : a large sandwich on a long split roll

sub·ma·ri·ner \'səb-mə-ˌrē-nər, ˌsəb-mə-'rē-nər *also* ˌsəb-'mar-ə-\ *n* : a member of a submarine crew

sub·me·di·ant \ˌsəb-'mēd-ē-ənt, 'səb-\ *n* : the sixth tone of a minor or major scale

sub·merge \səb-'mərj\ *vb* **sub·merged; sub·merg·ing** **1** : to put or go underwater ⟨the whale *submerged*⟩ **2** : to cover or become covered with or as if with water ⟨floods *submerged* the town⟩

sub·merse \səb-'mərs\ *vb* **sub·mersed; sub·mers·ing** : SUBMERGE

¹**sub·mers·ible** \səb-'mər-sə-bəl\ *adj* : capable of being submerged ⟨*submersible* pumps⟩

²submersible *n* : something that is submersible; *esp* : ²SUBMARINE 1

sub·mer·sion \-'mər-zhən, -shən\ *n* : the action of submerging : the state of being submerged

sub·min·ia·ture \ˌsəb-'min-ē-ə-ˌchů(ə)r, 'səb-, -'min-i-ˌchů(ə)r, -'min-yə-, -chər\ *adj* : very small ⟨*subminiature* electronic equipment⟩

sub·mis·sion \səb-'mish-ən\ *n* **1** : an act of submitting something (as for consideration or comment); *also* : something submitted (as a musical composition) **2** : the condition of being humble or obedient **3** : an act of submitting to the authority or control of another

sub·mis·sive \səb-'mis-iv\ *adj* : inclined or willing to submit to others : YIELDING [from Latin *submissus*, past participle of *submittere* "to let down," from *sub-* "under, below" and *mittere* "to send, throw" — related to MESSAGE] — **sub·mis·sive·ly** *adv* — **sub·mis·sive·ness** *n*

sub·mit \səb-'mit\ *vb* **sub·mit·ted; sub·mit·ting 1** : to subject to a process or treatment ⟨the metal was *submitted* to analysis⟩ **2** : to present to another for review or decision ⟨*submit* a question to the court⟩ ⟨*submit* a report⟩ **3** : to put forward as an opinion, reason, or idea ⟨we *submit* that the facts have not been established⟩ **4** : to give in to the authority, control, or choice of another **synonyms** see YIELD

sub·nor·mal \ˌsəb-'nor-məl, 'səb-\ *adj* : being lower, smaller, or less than what is considered normal ⟨*subnormal* temperatures⟩ — **sub·nor·mal·i·ty** \ˌsəb-nor-'mal-ət-ē\ *n* — **sub·nor·mal·ly** \ˌsəb-'nor-mə-lē, 'səb-\ *adv*

sub·note·book \'səb-ˌnōt-ˌbůk\ *n* : a portable computer similar to but smaller and lighter than a notebook computer

¹sub·or·di·nate \sə-'bord-ᵊn-ət, -'bord-nət\ *adj* **1** : placed in or occupying a lower class or rank ⟨a *subordinate* officer⟩ **2** : yielding to or controlled by authority **3 a** : of, relating to, or being a clause that functions as a noun, adjective, or adverb **b** : SUBORDINATING — **sub·or·di·nate·ly** *adv* — **sub·or·di·nate·ness** *n*

²subordinate *n* : one that is subordinate

³sub·or·di·nate \sə-'bord-ᵊn-ˌāt\ *vb* **-nat·ed; -nat·ing** : to make subordinate — **sub·or·di·na·tion** \-ˌbord-ᵊn-'ā-shən\ *n* — **sub·or·di·na·tive** \-'bord-ᵊn-ˌāt-iv\ *adj*

sub·or·di·nat·ing \sə-'bord-ᵊn-ˌāt-iŋ\ *adj* : introducing and linking a subordinate clause to a main clause ⟨a *subordinating* conjunction⟩

sub·plot \'səb-ˌplät\ *n* : a subordinate plot in fiction or drama

¹sub·poe·na \sə-'pē-nə\ *n* : an order in writing commanding a person named in it to appear in court under a penalty for failure to appear [from the Latin phrase *sub poena* "under penalty"; used as the beginning words of the order]

²subpoena *vb* **-naed; -na·ing** : to serve or summon with a subpoena

sub·po·lar \ˌsəb-'pō-lər, 'səb-\ *adj* **1** : SUBARCTIC **2** : SUBANTARCTIC

sub·rou·tine \ˌsəb-(ˌ)rü-'tēn\ *n* : a sequence of computer instructions for performing a specified task that can be used repeatedly

sub-Sa·ha·ran \ˌsəb-sə-'har-ən, 'səb-, -'her-, -'här-\ *adj* : of, relating to, or being the part of Africa south of the Sahara

sub·scribe \səb-'skrīb\ *vb* **sub·scribed; sub·scrib·ing 1** : to make known one's approval by or as if by signing ⟨we *subscribe* to your plan⟩ **2** : to agree to give or contribute by signing one's name with the amount promised ⟨*subscribe* fifty dollars to the fund⟩ **3 a** : to enter one's name for a publication or service **b** : to receive a periodical or service regularly on order **4** : to feel favorably inclined ⟨I *subscribe* to your sentiments⟩ — **sub·scrib·er** *n*

sub·script \'səb-ˌskript\ *n* : a distinguishing symbol (as a letter or number) immediately below or below and to the right or left of another written character — **sub·script** *adj*

sub·scrip·tion \səb-'skrip-shən\ *n* **1** : an act or instance of subscribing **2** : something (as a document containing a signature) that is subscribed **3** : an arrangement for providing, receiving, or making use of something of a continuing or periodic nature on a prepayment plan; *esp* : a purchase of a certain number of future issues (as of a magazine)

sub·sense \'səb-ˌsen(t)s\ *n* : a subordinate division of a sense (as in a dictionary)

sub·se·quent \'səb-si-kwənt, -sə-ˌkwent\ *adj* : following in time, order, or place ⟨*subsequent* events⟩ — **subsequent** *n* — **sub·se·quent·ly** \-ˌkwent-lē, -kwənt-\ *adv*

sub·ser·vi·ence \səb-'sər-vē-ən(t)s\ *n* **1** : a subordinate place or function **2** : obedience befitting one of a menial position

sub·ser·vi·en·cy \səb-'sər-vē-ən-sē\ *n* : SUBSERVIENCE

sub·ser·vi·ent \səb-'sər-vē-ənt\ *adj* **1** : useful in an inferior capacity : SUBORDINATE **2** : inclined or willing to submit to others : SUBMISSIVE — **sub·ser·vi·ent·ly** *adv*

sub·set \'səb-ˌset\ *n* : a mathematical set that is a part of another mathematical set ⟨the set of even numbers is a *subset* of the set of all numbers⟩

sub·side \səb-'sīd\ *vb* **sub·sid·ed; sub·sid·ing 1** : to sink or fall to the bottom : SETTLE **2** : to become quiet or less : ABATE ⟨as the fever *subsides*⟩ ⟨my anger *subsided*⟩ — **sub·si·dence** \səb-'sīd-ᵊn(t)s, 'səb-səd-ən(t)s\ *n*

¹sub·sid·iary \səb-'sid-ē-ˌer-ē, -'sid-ə-rē\ *adj* : of secondary importance ⟨*subsidiary* streams⟩

²subsidiary *n, pl* **-iar·ies** : one that is subsidiary; *esp* : a company wholly controlled by another

sub·si·dize \'səb-sə-ˌdīz, -zə-\ *vb* **-dized; -diz·ing** : to aid or furnish with a subsidy — **sub·si·di·za·tion** \ˌsəb-səd-ə-'zā-shən, ˌsəb-zəd-\ *n* — **sub·si·diz·er** *n*

sub·si·dy \'səb-səd-ē, -zəd-\ *n, pl* **-dies** : a grant or gift especially of money; *esp* : a grant by a government to a private person or company or to another government to assist an undertaking thought helpful to the public

sub·sist \səb-'sist\ *vb* **1** : to have or continue to have existence : BE, PERSIST **2** : to have or get the necessities of life (as food and clothing); *esp* : to nourish oneself ⟨*subsisting* on roots and berries⟩

sub·sis·tence \səb-'sis-tən(t)s\ *n* **1 a** : real being : EXISTENCE **b** : the condition of remaining in existence : CONTINUATION, PERSISTENCE **2 a** : means of subsisting **b** : the minimum (as of food and shelter) necessary to support life — **sub·sis·tent** \-tənt\ *adj*

sub·soil \'səb-ˌsoil\ *n* : a layer of weathered material that lies just under the surface soil

sub·son·ic \ˌsəb-'sän-ik, 'səb-\ *adj* **1** : of, relating to, or being a speed less than that of sound in air **2** : moving, capable of moving, or using air currents moving at a subsonic speed

sub·spe·cies \'səb-ˌspē-shēz, -sēz\ *n* : a category in biological classification that ranks just below a species and includes a physically recognizable and geographically separate group of individuals whose members can breed successfully with members of other subspecies of the same species where their ranges overlap — **sub·spe·cif·ic** \ˌsəb-spi-'sif-ik\ *adj*

sub·stance \'səb-stən(t)s\ *n* **1 a** : essential nature : ESSENCE ⟨divine *substance*⟩ **b** : the fundamental or essential part, quality, or meaning ⟨the *substance* of the speech⟩ **2 a** : physical material from which something is made **b** : material of particular or definite chemical con-

\ə\ abut	\aů\ out	\i\ tip	\ȯ\ saw	\ů\ foot
\ər\ further	\ch\ chin	\ī\ life	\ȯi\ coin	\y\ yet
\a\ mat	\e\ pet	\j\ job	\th\ thin	\yü\ few
\ā\ take	\ē\ easy	\ŋ\ sing	\th\ this	\yů\ cure
\ä\ cot, cart	\g\ go	\ō\ bone	\ü\ food	\zh\ vision

stitution 〈an oily *substance*〉 **c** : something (as drugs or alcoholic beverages) considered harmful and usually subject to legal restriction 〈*substance* abuse〉 **3** : material possessions : PROPERTY 〈a person of *substance*〉

sub·stan·dard \ˌsəb-ˈstan-dərd, ˈsəb-\ *adj* **1** : varying from or falling short of a standard or norm 〈*substandard* housing〉 **2** : following a pattern of linguistic usage that is not considered standard 〈*substandard* English〉

sub·stan·tial \səb-ˈstan-chəl\ *adj* **1 a** : consisting of or relating to substance : MATERIAL **b** : not imaginary : REAL 〈the *substantial* world〉 **c** : IMPORTANT 1, ESSENTIAL 〈*substantial* differences〉 **2** : enough to satisfy and nourish 〈a *substantial* meal〉 **3 a** : PROSPEROUS 〈a *substantial* farmer〉 **b** : considerable in quantity : significantly large 〈a *substantial* increase〉 **4** : firmly constructed 〈a *substantial* building〉 — **sub·stan·ti·al·i·ty** \-ˌstan-chē-ˈal-ət-ē\ *n* — **sub·stan·tial·ly** \-ˈstanch-(ə-)lē\ *adv*

sub·stan·ti·ate \səb-ˈstan-chē-ˌāt\ *vb* **-at·ed; -at·ing** **1** : to give substance or form to : EMBODY **2** : to establish by proof or evidence 〈*substantiate* a claim〉 — **sub·stan·ti·a·tion** \-ˌstan-chē-ˈā-shən\ *n*

¹sub·stan·tive \ˈsəb-stən-tiv\ *n* : a word or word group that functions in a sentence as a noun — **sub·stan·ti·val** \ˌsəb-stən-ˈtī-vəl\ *adj*

²substantive *adj* **1** : of, relating to, or being completely independent **2** : real rather than apparent 〈*substantive* evidence〉 **3** : having the function of a grammatical substantive 〈a *substantive* phrase〉 **4** : considerable in amount or numbers : SUBSTANTIAL 〈made *substantive* progress〉 **5** : creating and defining rights and duties 〈*substantive* law〉 **6** : involving matters of major or practical importance to all concerned 〈*substantive* discussions among world leaders〉 — **sub·stan·tive·ly** *adv*

sub·sta·tion \ˈsəb-ˌstā-shən\ *n* **1** : a branch post office **2** : a subsidiary station in which electric current is transformed

¹sub·sti·tute \ˈsəb-stə-ˌt(y)üt\ *n* : a person or thing that takes the place of another — **substitute** *adj*

²substitute *vb* **-tut·ed; -tut·ing** **1** : to put in the place of another : REPLACE **2** : to serve as a substitute — **sub·sti·tu·tion** \ˌsəb-stə-ˈt(y)ü-shən\ *n*

sub·strate \ˈsəb-ˌstrāt\ *n* **1** : an underlying layer: as **a** : SUBSTRATUM a **b** : the base on which an organism lives or over which it moves 〈the soil is the *substrate* of most plants〉 **2** : a substance acted upon (as by an enzyme)

sub·stra·tum \ˈsəb-ˌstrāt-əm, -ˌstrat-\ *n* : an underlying support or layer: as **a** : the material of which something is made **b** : a layer beneath the surface layer of soil : SUBSOIL **c** : SUBSTRATE b

sub·struc·ture \ˈsəb-ˌstrək-chər\ *n* : an underlying or supporting part of a structure

sub·sume \səb-ˈsüm\ *vb* **sub·sumed; sub·sum·ing** : to include or place within something larger or more general 〈red, yellow, and green are *subsumed* under the term "color"〉

sub·teen \ˈsəb-ˈtēn\ *n* : a child nearing adolescence

sub·ter·fuge \ˈsəb-tər-ˌfyüj\ *n* **1** : the action of deceiving usually by slyness in order to avoid some unpleasant circumstance (as to escape blame) **2** : a plan or trick that employs sly deception

sub·ter·ra·nean \ˌsəb-tə-ˈrā-nē-ən, -nyən\ *adj* **1** : being, lying, or operating under the surface of the earth **2** : existing or working in secret : HIDDEN

sub·ti·tle \ˈsəb-ˌtīt-ᵊl\ *n* **1** : a secondary or explanatory title **2** : a printed statement or bit of dialogue appearing on the screen between the scenes of a silent movie or appearing as a translation at the bottom of the screen during the scenes of a movie in a foreign language — **subtitle** *vb*

sub·tle \ˈsət-ᵊl\ *adj* **sub·tler** \ˈsət-lər, -ᵊl-ər\; **sub·tlest** \ˈsət-ləst, -ᵊl-əst\ **1 a** : DELICATE 1, ELUSIVE 〈a *subtle* fragrance〉 **b** : difficult to understand or distinguish 〈*subtle* differences in vowel sounds〉 **2** : marked by a keen

ability to understand 〈a *subtle* mind〉 **3** : SLY 1a, CRAFTY 〈*subtle* flattery〉 **4** : working slowly but effectively : INSIDIOUS 〈a *subtle* poison〉 [Middle English *sotil, subtile* "delicate," from early French *sotil* (same meaning), from Latin *subtilis* "delicate," literally, "finely woven," from *sub* "under, close to" and *tela* "fabric woven on a loom"] — **sub·tle·ness** \ˈsət-ᵊl-nəs\ *n* — **sub·tly** \ˈsət-lē, ˈsət-ᵊl-(l)ē\ *adv*

sub·tle·ty \ˈsət-ᵊl-tē\ *n, pl* **-ties** **1** : the quality or state of being subtle **2** : something subtle

sub·ton·ic \ˌsəb-ˈtän-ik, ˈsəb-\ *n* : LEADING TONE

sub·top·ic \ˈsəb-ˌtäp-ik\ *n* : a topic (as in a composition) that is a division of a main topic

sub·to·tal \ˈsəb-ˌtōt-ᵊl\ *n* : the sum of part of a series of figures

sub·tract \səb-ˈtrakt\ *vb* **1** : to take away (as one part or number) from another : DEDUCT 〈*subtract* 5 from 9〉 **2** : to perform a subtraction

sub·trac·tion \səb-ˈtrak-shən\ *n* **1** : an act or instance of subtracting **2** : the operation of deducting one number from another

sub·trac·tive \səb-ˈtrak-tiv\ *adj* : being or involving subtraction

sub·tra·hend \ˈsəb-trə-ˌhend\ *n* : a number that is to be subtracted from another number

sub·trop·i·cal \ˌsəb-ˈträp-i-kəl, ˈsəb-\ *also* **sub·trop·ic** \-ˈträp-ik\ *adj* : of, relating to, or being the regions bordering on the tropical zone 〈*subtropical* forests〉

sub·trop·ics \ˌsəb-ˈträp-iks, ˈsəb-\ *n pl* : subtropical regions

sub·unit \ˈsəb-ˌyü-nət\ *n* : a unit that forms an individually distinct part of a more comprehensive unit

sub·urb \ˈsəb-ˌərb\ *n* **1 a** : a part of a city or town near its outer edge **b** : a smaller community close to a city **2 pl** : the area of homes close to or surrounding a city [Middle English *suburb* "part around the outer edge of a city," from early French (same meaning), from Latin *suburbium* (same meaning), from *sub* "under, close to" and *urbs* "city"] — **sub·ur·ban** \sə-ˈbər-bən\ *adj or n*

sub·ur·ban·ite \sə-ˈbər-bə-ˌnīt\ *n* : a person who lives in the suburbs

sub·ur·bia \sə-ˈbər-bē-ə\ *n* : the suburbs of a city

sub·ver·sion \səb-ˈvər-zhən\ *n* : the act of overthrowing : the state of being overthrown; *esp* : an attempt to overthrow or undermine a government or political system by persons working secretly within the country involved — **sub·ver·sive** \-ˈvər-siv, -ziv\ *adj or n* — **sub·ver·sive·ly** *adv*

sub·vert \səb-ˈvərt\ *vb* **1** : to overturn or overthrow from the foundation **2** : to undermine the morals, allegiance, or faith of : CORRUPT — **sub·vert·er** *n*

sub·way \ˈsəb-ˌwā\ *n* **1** : an underground passage **2** : a usually electric underground railway

sub·woof·er \-ˈwuf-ər\ *n* : a loudspeaker producing only the lowest frequencies

sub·ze·ro \ˌsəb-ˈzē-rō\ *adj* : being or marked by temperature below zero

suc·ceed \sək-ˈsēd\ *vb* **1 a** : to come next after another in office or position or in possession of an estate; *esp* : to inherit sovereignty **b** : to follow after another in order **2 a** : to turn out well **b** : to reach a desired end or object : be successful 〈students who *succeed* in school〉 [Middle English *succeden* "to come after," from Latin *succedere* "to go up, follow after," from *sub-* "under, near" and *cedere* "to go, yield" — related to CONCEDE, NECESSARY] — **suc·ceed·er** *n*

suc·cess \sək-ˈses\ *n* **1 a** : degree or measure of succeeding **b** : satisfactory completion of something **c** : the gaining of wealth, respect, or fame **2** : a person or thing that succeeds

suc·cess·ful \sək-ˈses-fəl\ *adj* **1** : resulting or ending in success **2** : gaining or having gained success — **suc·cess·ful·ly** \-fə-lē\ *adv* — **suc·cess·ful·ness** *n*

suc·ces·sion \sək-'sesh-ən\ *n* **1** : the order, action, or right of succeeding to a throne, title, or property **2 a** : a repeated following of one person or thing after another **b** : a series of one-way changes in the composition of a biological community in which one group of plants or animals is replaced by a different group — **suc·ces·sion·al** \-'sesh-nəl, -ən-ᵊl\ *adj*

suc·ces·sive \sək-'ses-iv\ *adj* : following in order : following each other without interruption ⟨failed in three *successive* tries⟩ — **suc·ces·sive·ly** *adv* — **suc·ces·sive·ness** *n*

suc·ces·sor \sək-'ses-ər\ *n* : one that follows; *esp* : a person who succeeds to a throne, title, estate, or office

suc·cinct \(ˌ)sək-'siŋ(k)t, sə-'siŋ(k)t\ *adj* : marked by short concise expression without wasted words — **suc·cinct·ly** *adv* — **suc·cinct·ness** *n*

¹suc·cor \'sək-ər\ *n* : RELIEF 1a

²succor *vb* **suc·cored; suc·cor·ing** \'sək-(ə-)riŋ\ : to go to the aid of (one in need or distress) : RELIEVE — **suc·cor·er** \'sək-ər-ər\ *n*

suc·co·tash \'sək-ə-ˌtash\ *n* : lima or shell beans and green corn cooked together

suc·cu·lence \'sək-yə-lən(t)s\ *n* : the state of being succulent

¹suc·cu·lent \'sək-yə-lənt\ *adj* **1 a** : full of juice : JUICY ⟨*succulent* cherries⟩ **b** : moist and tasty ⟨a *succulent* meal⟩ **c** : having fleshy tissues that conserve moisture ⟨*succulent* plants⟩ **2** : rich in interest ⟨a *succulent* book⟩ — **suc·cu·lent·ly** *adv*

²succulent *n* : a succulent plant (as a cactus or an aloe)

suc·cumb \sə-'kəm\ *vb* **1** : to yield to force or pressure ⟨*succumb* to temptation⟩ **2** : ¹DIE 1 ⟨many of the early settlers *succumbed* during the winter⟩

¹such \(ˈ)səch, (ˌ)sich\ *adj* **1** : of a kind or character to be indicated or suggested ⟨a coat *such* as a doctor wears⟩ **2** : having a quality already specified ⟨deeply moved by *such* acts of kindness⟩ **3** : so great : so remarkable ⟨*such* a storm⟩ ⟨*such* courage⟩ **4** : of the same class, type, or sort : SIMILAR ⟨opened three *such* stores⟩

²such *pron* **1** : such a person or thing ⟨has a plan if it may be called *such*⟩ **2** : someone or something stated, implied, or exemplified ⟨*such* was the result⟩ ⟨*such* were the Romans⟩ **3** : someone or something of the same kind ⟨ships and planes and *such*⟩

³such *adv* **1** : to such a degree : SO ⟨*such* tall buildings⟩ **2** : ²VERY 1 ⟨hasn't been in *such* good spirits lately⟩

¹such·like \'səch-ˌlīk\ *adj* : of like kind : SIMILAR ⟨the third *suchlike* event⟩

²suchlike *pron* : someone or something of the same sort : a similar person or thing ⟨pencils, pens, and *suchlike*⟩

¹suck \'sək\ *vb* **1 a** : to draw in liquid and especially mother's milk with the mouth **b** : to draw liquid from by action of the mouth ⟨*suck* an orange⟩; *also* : to draw something from or consume by such action ⟨*suck* a candy⟩ **c** : to apply the mouth to in order to or as if to suck out a liquid ⟨*sucked* my thumb⟩ **2** : to take something in or up or remove something from by or as if by suction ⟨plants *sucking* moisture from the soil⟩ **3** : to act in an overly flattering or attentive manner ⟨*suck* up to the boss⟩

²suck *n* **1** : a sucking movement or force **2** : the act of sucking

suck·er \'sək-ər\ *n* **1 a** : one that sucks **b** : a part of an animal's body used for sucking or for clinging by suction **2** : a shoot from the roots or lower part of the

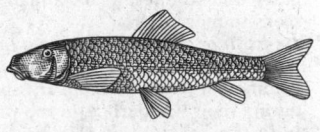

sucker 3

stem of a plant **3** : any of numerous freshwater fishes related to the carps that usually have thick soft lips for sucking in food **4** : LOLLIPOP **5** : a person easily fooled or cheated **6** : a person irresistibly attracted to something ⟨a *sucker* for historical novels⟩

sucker punch *vb* : to punch (a person) suddenly and usually without any obvious reason — **sucker punch** *n*

suck·ing louse *n* : any of an order of wingless insects that include the true lice and have mouthparts used for sucking body fluids

suck·le \'sək-əl\ *vb* **suck·led; suck·ling** \-(ə-)liŋ\ : to give or draw milk from the breast or udder

suck·ling \'sək-liŋ\ *n* : a young mammal still sucking milk from its mother

su·crase \'sü-ˌkrās\ *n* : an enzyme that splits sucrose into glucose and fructose

su·crose \'sü-ˌkrōs\ *n* : a sweet sugar obtained especially from sugarcane or sugar beets

suc·tion \'sək-shən\ *n* **1** : the act or process of sucking **2 a** : the action or process of drawing something (as liquid or dust) into a space (as a vacuum cleaner or a pump) by removing air from the space **b** : the force caused by suction

suction cup *n* : a cup of glass or of a flexible material (as rubber) in which a partial vacuum is produced when applied to a surface

sud·den \'səd-ᵊn\ *adj* **1 a** : happening or coming unexpectedly ⟨a *sudden* shower⟩ **b** : changing angle or character all at once ⟨a *sudden* turn in the road⟩ **2** : marked by or showing haste ⟨a *sudden* decision⟩ **3** : made or brought about in a short time ⟨a *sudden* cure⟩ — **sud·den·ly** *adv* — **sud·den·ness** \'səd-ᵊn-(n)əs\ *n* — **all of a sudden** : sooner than was expected : SUDDENLY

sudden death *n* : extra play to break a tie in a sports contest in which the first to score or gain the lead wins

su·do·ku \sü-'dō-kü\ *n* : a puzzle in which several numbers are to be filled into a 9x9 grid of squares so that every row, every column, and every 3x3 box contains the numbers 1 through 9 [from Japanese *sūdoku*, short for *sūji wa dokushin ni kagiru* "the numbers must remain single" (i.e., the digits can occur only once)]

¹suds \'sədz\ *n pl* **1** : soapy water especially when frothy **2** : the froth on soapy water

²suds *vb* : to form suds

sudsy \'səd-zē\ *adj* **suds·i·er; -est** : full of suds

sue \'sü\ *vb* **sued; su·ing** **1** : to seek justice from a person by bringing a legal action **2** : to make a request or application : PLEAD — usually used with *for* or *to* ⟨the weaker nation *sued* for peace⟩ — **su·er** *n*

suede *also* **suède** \'swād\ *n* **1** : leather rubbed on one side to produce a velvety surface **2** : a cloth fabric that looks and feels like suede [from French *gants de Suède* "Swedish gloves," from *Suède* "Sweden"]

su·et \'sü-ət\ *n* : the hard fat around the kidneys in beef and mutton from which tallow is made

suf·fer \'səf-ər\ *vb* **suf·fered; suf·fer·ing** \-(ə-)riŋ\ **1** : to feel or endure pain **2** : to experience something unpleasant ⟨*suffer* a defeat⟩ **3** : to bear loss or damage ⟨the business *suffered* during the storm⟩ **4** : ¹PERMIT 1, ALLOW — **suf·fer·able** \'səf-(ə-)rə-bəl\ *adj* — **suf·fer·able·ness** *n* — **suf·fer·ably** \-blē\ *adv* — **suf·fer·er** \'səf-ər-ər\ *n*

suf·fer·ance \'səf-(ə-)rən(t)s\ *n* **1** : consent or approval implied by a lack of interference or failure to enforce a prohibition **2** : power or ability to put up with

suf·fer·ing *n* **1** : the state or experience of one that suffers **2** : a pain or injury endured

suf·fice \sə-'fīs\ *vb* **suf·ficed; suf·fic·ing** **1** : to meet or satisfy a need : be sufficient ⟨a brief note will *suffice*⟩ **2** : to be competent or capable **3** : to be enough for

suf·fi·cien·cy \sə-'fish-ən-sē\ *n, pl* **-cies** **1** : sufficient means to meet one's needs **2** : the quality or state of being sufficient : ADEQUACY

suf·fi·cient \sə-'fish-ənt\ *adj* : enough to achieve a goal or fill a need — **suf·fi·cient·ly** *adv*

¹suf·fix \'səf-,iks\ *n* : a letter or group of letters that comes at the end of a word and has a meaning of its own — **suf·fix·al** \-,ik-səl\ *adj* — **suf·fix·less** \-,iks-ləs\ *adj*

²suf·fix \'səf-,iks, (,)sə-'fiks\ *vb* : to attach as a suffix — **suf·fix·ation** \,səf-,ik-'sā-shən\ *n*

suf·fo·cate \'səf-ə-,kāt\ *vb* **-cat·ed; -cat·ing** **1 a** : to stop the breathing of (as by strangling) **b** : to deprive of oxygen **c** : to make uncomfortable by want of fresh air **2** : to become suffocated; *esp* : to die or suffer from being unable to breathe or from lack of oxygen — **suf·fo·ca·tion** \,səf-ə-'kā-shən\ *n*

suf·frage \'səf-rij\ *n* : the right of voting; *also* : the exercise of such right

suf·frag·ette \,səf-ri-'jet\ *n* : a woman who supported voting rights for women when women were not allowed to vote

suf·frag·ist \'səf-ri-jəst\ *n* : a person who supports extending voting rights especially to women

suf·fuse \sə-'fyüz\ *vb* **suf·fused; suf·fus·ing** : to spread over or through in the manner of fluid or light — **suf·fu·sion** \-'fyü-zhən\ *n* — **suf·fu·sive** \-'fyü-siv, -ziv\ *adj*

¹sug·ar \'shùg-ər\ *n* **1** : a sweet substance that is made up wholly or mostly of sucrose, is colorless or white when pure, is obtained from plants (as sugarcane or sugar beets), is a source of dietary carbohydrate, and is used as a sweetener and preservative of other foods **2** : any of various water-soluble compounds that vary widely in sweetness and make up the simpler carbohydrates

²sugar *vb* **sug·ared; sug·ar·ing** \'shùg-(ə-)riŋ\ **1** : to make something less hard to take or put up with ⟨*sugar* advice with praise⟩ **2** : to sprinkle or mix with sugar **3** : to change to crystals of sugar ⟨candy *sugars* when cooked too long⟩ **4** : to make maple syrup or maple sugar

sugar beet *n* : a white-rooted beet grown for the sugar in its roots

sugar bush *n* : woods in which sugar maples are more numerous than other kinds of trees

sug·ar·cane \'shùg-ər-,kān\ *n* : a tall tropical grass that has a thick jointed stem and is widely grown in warm regions as a source of sugar

sug·ar·coat \,shùg-ər-'kōt\ *vb* : to coat with or as if with sugar

sug·ar·house \'shùg-ər-,haùs\ *n* : a building where maple sap is boiled to make maple syrup and maple sugar

sug·ar·less \'shùg-ər-ləs\ *adj* : containing no sugar ⟨*sugarless* gum⟩

sug·ar·loaf \-,lōf\ *n* **1** : refined sugar molded into a cone **2** : a hill or mountain shaped like a sugarloaf — **sugarloaf** *adj*

sugar maple *n* : a maple tree of eastern North America with hard wood that is much used for cabinetwork and sap that is the chief source of maple syrup and maple sugar

sugarcane

sug·ar·plum \'shùg-ər-,pləm\ *n* : a round piece of candy

sug·ary \'shùg-(ə-)rē\ *adj* **1** : too sweetly sentimental **2** : containing, resembling, or tasting of sugar

sug·gest \sə(g)-'jest\ *vb* **1 a** : to put (as a thought) into a person's mind **b** : to propose as an idea or possibility ⟨*suggest* going for a walk⟩ **2** : to call to mind through close connection or association ⟨the fire *suggests* arson⟩ — **sug·gest·er** *n*

sug·gest·ible \sə(g)-'jes-tə-bəl\ *adj* : easily influenced by suggestion — **sug·gest·ibil·i·ty** \-,jes-tə-'bil-ət-ē\ *n*

sug·ges·tion \sə(g)-'jes-chən, -'jesh-\ *n* **1 a** : the act or process of suggesting **b** : something (as a thought or plan) that is suggested **2 a** : the process by which a physical or mental state is influenced by a thought or idea ⟨the power of *suggestion*⟩ **b** : the process by which one thought leads to another especially through association of ideas **c** : a way of influencing attitudes and behavior hypnotically **3** : a slight indication ⟨a *suggestion* of a smile⟩

sug·ges·tive \sə(g)-'jes-tiv\ *adj* **1 a** : giving a suggestion : INDICATIVE ⟨*suggestive* of a past era⟩ **b** : full of suggestions : stimulating thought **c** : stirring mental associations **2** : suggesting something improper or indecent — **sug·ges·tive·ly** *adv* — **sug·ges·tive·ness** *n*

sui·cide \'sü-ə-,sīd\ *n* **1 a** : the act of killing oneself purposely **b** : ruin of one's own interests ⟨risking political *suicide*⟩ **2** : a person who commits or attempts suicide — **sui·cid·al** \,sü-ə-'sīd-ºl\ *adj* — **suicide** *adj*

suing *present participle of* SUE

¹suit \'süt\ *n* **1** : an action or process in a court for enforcing a right or claim **2** : an act or instance of requesting earnestly; *esp* : COURTSHIP **3** : a number of things used together : SET **4 a** : an outer costume of two or more pieces **b** : a costume to be worn for a special purpose or under particular conditions ⟨gym *suit*⟩ **5 a** : all the cards of one kind (as spades or hearts) in a pack of playing cards **b** : all the dominoes bearing the same number

²suit *vb* **1** : to outfit with clothes : DRESS **2** : to make suitable : ADAPT ⟨*suit* the action to the word⟩ **3 a** : to be proper for ⟨a mood that *suits* the occasion⟩ **b** : to be becoming to ⟨that dress *suits* you⟩ **4** : to meet the needs or desires of : PLEASE ⟨*suits* me fine⟩ **5** : to be in accordance : AGREE ⟨the job *suits* with your abilities⟩ **6** : to be appropriate or satisfactory ⟨these prices do not *suit*⟩

suit·able \'süt-ə-bəl\ *adj* **1** : adapted to a use or purpose ⟨food *suitable* for human consumption⟩ **2** : being fit or right for a use or group ⟨clothes *suitable* to the occasion⟩ ⟨a movie *suitable* for children⟩ **3** : QUALIFIED 1, CAPABLE ⟨looking for a *suitable* replacement⟩ **synonyms** see FIT — **suit·abil·i·ty** \,süt-ə-'bil-ət-ē\ *n* — **suit·able·ness** \'süt-ə-bəl-nəs\ *n* — **suit·ably** \-blē\ *adv*

suit·case \'süt-,kās\ *n* : a portable case designed to hold a traveler's clothing and personal articles

suite \'swēt, *sense 2c is also* 'süt\ *n* **1** : the personal staff accompanying a ruler, diplomat, or dignitary on official business **2** : a group of things forming a unit or making up a collection: as **a** : a group of rooms occupied as a unit **b** : a piece of music for an orchestra usually consisting of several independent pieces written in the form of special dances or taken as selections from a larger work (as a ballet) **c** : a set of matched furniture for a room ⟨a bedroom *suite*⟩

suit·or \'süt-ər\ *n* **1** : one that petitions or pleads **2** : a party to a suit at law **3** : a man who courts a woman or seeks to marry her

Suk·koth *or* **Suk·kot** \'sùk-əs, -,ōt, -,ōth, -,ōs\ *n* : a Jewish harvest festival celebrated in September or October to commemorate the temporary shelters used by the Jews during their wanderings in the wilderness

sul·fa \'səl-fə\ *adj* : of, relating to, or containing sulfanilamide or the sulfa drugs

sulfa drug *n* : any of various synthetic drugs that stop or slow the growth of bacteria and are derived especially from sulfanilamide

sul·fa·nil·amide \ˌsəl-fə-'nil-ə-ˌmīd, -məd\ *n* : a compound in the form of crystals that is the parent compound of most of the sulfa drugs

sul·fate \'səl-ˌfāt\ *n* : a compound and especially a salt formed by the reaction of sulfuric acid with another substance

sul·fide \'səl-ˌfīd\ *n* : a compound of sulfur with one or more other elements : a salt of hydrogen sulfide

sul·fur *also* **sul·phur** \'səl-fər\ *n* : a nonmetallic element that occurs either free or combined especially in sulfides and sulfates, is found in proteins, exists in several forms including yellow crystals, and is used especially in the chemical and paper industries, in strengthening rubber, and in medicine for treating skin diseases — see ELE-MENT table

sulfur dioxide *n* : a heavy strong-smelling gas that is used especially in making sulfuric acid, in bleaching, in preserving things, and as a refrigerant and that is a major substance in air pollution especially in industrial areas

sul·fu·ric \ˌsəl-'fyu̇(ə)r-ik\ *adj* : of, relating to, or containing sulfur

sulfuric acid *n* : a heavy oily strong acid that is colorless when pure and eats away at many solid substances

sul·fu·rous *also* **sul·phu·rous** \'səl-f(y)ə-rəs *also for sense 1* ˌsəl-'fyu̇r-əs\ *adj* **1** : of, relating to, or containing sulfur **2 a** : of, relating to, or dealing with the fire of hell : IN-FERNAL **b** : FIERY 3a, INFLAMED ⟨a *sulfurous* sermon⟩ **c** : PROFANE 2, BLASPHEMOUS ⟨*sulfurous* language⟩

sulfurous acid *n* : a weak acid known especially in mixtures of sulfur dioxide with water and through its salts and used in bleaching

¹sulk \'səlk\ *vb* : to be silently angry, upset, or irritable

²sulk *n* **1** : the state of one sulking — often used in plural ⟨had a case of the *sulks*⟩ **2** : a sulky mood ⟨was in a *sulk*⟩

¹sulky \'səl-kē\ *adj* **sulk·i·er; -est** : acting or tending to act silently angry, upset, or irritable — **sulk·i·ly** \-kə-lē\ *adv* — **sulk·i·ness** \-kē-nəs\ *n*

²sulky *n, pl* **sulk·ies** : a light two-wheeled vehicle that is pulled by a horse and has a seat for the driver only and usually no body

sul·len \'səl-ən\ *adj* **1 a** : gloomily or resentfully silent : not sociable **b** : suggesting a sullen state ⟨*sullen* refusal⟩ **2** : dull in sound or color **3** : DISMAL, GLOOMY ⟨a *sullen* sky⟩ — **sul·len·ly** *adv* — **sul·len·ness** \'səl-ən-(n)əs\ *n*

sul·ly \'səl-ē\ *vb* **sul·lied; sul·ly·ing** : to make soiled or tarnished

sul·tan \'səlt-ᵊn\ *n* : a king or ruler especially of a Muslim state

sul·ta·na \ˌ(ˌ)səl-'tan-ə\ *n* **1** : a woman who is a member of a sultan's family; *esp* : a sultan's wife **2** : a pale yellow seedless grape grown for raisins and wine; *also* : a raisin prepared by drying this grape

sul·tan·ate \'səlt-ᵊn-ˌāt\ *n* **1** : a state or country governed by a sultan **2** : the power or position of a sultan

sul·try \'səl-trē\ *adj* **sul·tri·er; -est** **1** : very hot and humid ⟨a *sultry* day⟩ **2** : burning hot ⟨*sultry* sun⟩ **3** : exciting or capable of exciting romantic passion ⟨*sultry* glances⟩ — **sul·tri·ly** \-trə-lē\ *adv* — **sul·tri·ness** \-trē-nəs\ *n*

¹sum \'səm\ *n* **1** : an indefinite or specified amount of money **2** : the whole amount ⟨the *sum* of your experience⟩ **3 a** : a summary of the chief points or thoughts **b** : the main point ⟨the *sum* and substance of an argument⟩ **4 a** : the result of adding numbers ⟨the *sum* of 5 and 7 is 12⟩ **b** : a problem in arithmetic — **in sum** : in short : BRIEFLY

²sum *vb* **summed; sum·ming** **1** : to calculate the sum of

: TOTAL **2** : to reach a sum : AMOUNT — usually used with *to*

su·mac *also* **su·mach** \'sü-ˌmak, 'shü-\ *n* **1** : a material used in tanning and dyeing made of the leaves and other parts of sumac **2** : any of a genus of trees, shrubs, and woody vines related to the cashew and having leaves turning to brilliant colors in autumn, spikes or loose clusters of red or whitish berries, and in some cases leaves or berries that are irritating to the skin — compare POI-SON IVY, POISON OAK, POISON SUMAC

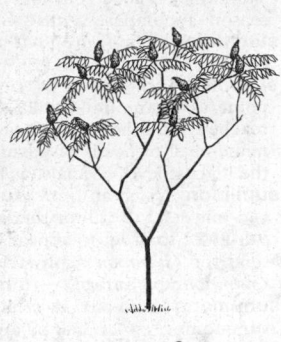

sumac 2

Su·me·ri·an \sü-'mer-ē-ən, -'mir-\ *n* **1** : a native of Sumer **2** : the language of the Sumerians that has no known relationships to other languages — **Sumerian** *adj*

sum·ma cum lau·de \ˌsum-ə-ˌkum-'laud-ə, -'laud-ē; ˌsəm-ə-ˌkəm-'lȯd-ē\ *adv or adj* : with highest distinction ⟨graduated *summa cum laude*⟩ [Latin]

sum·ma·ri·za·tion \ˌsəm-(ə-)rə-'zā-shən\ *n* **1** : the act of summarizing **2** : ²SUMMARY

sum·ma·rize \'səm-ə-ˌrīz\ *vb* **-rized; -riz·ing** **1** : to tell in or reduce to a summary **2** : to make a summary — **sum·ma·riz·able** \ˌsəm-ə-'rī-zə-bəl\ *adj* — **sum·ma·riz·er** *n*

¹sum·ma·ry \'səm-ə-rē\ *adj* **1** : expressing or covering the main points briefly : CONCISE ⟨a *summary* account⟩ **2** : done without delay or formality : quickly carried out ⟨a *summary* dismissal⟩ — **sum·mari·ly** \(ˌ)sə-'mer-ə-lē\ *adv*

²summary *n, pl* **-ries** : a short statement of the main points (as in a book or report)

sum·ma·tion \(ˌ)sə-'mā-shən\ *n* **1** : the act or process of forming a sum : ADDITION **2** : ¹SUM 2, TOTAL **3** : a final part of an argument reviewing points made and expressing conclusions

¹sum·mer \'səm-ər\ *n* **1** : the season between spring and autumn that usually includes the months of June, July, and August in the northern hemisphere **2** : the warmer half of the year **3** : one of the years of one's life ⟨a child of eight *summers*⟩ **4** : a time of fulfillment

²summer *adj* : of or for the summer ⟨*summer* flowers⟩ ⟨a *summer* job⟩

³summer *vb* **sum·mered; sum·mer·ing** \'səm-(ə-)riŋ\ **1** : to pass the summer **2** : to keep or carry through the summer; *esp* : to provide (as cattle or sheep) with pasture during the summer

sum·mer·house \'səm-ər-ˌhaus\ *n* **1** : a house for summer residence **2** : a covered structure in a garden or park designed to provide a shady resting place in summer

summer school *n* : a school or school session conducted in summer especially to help students make faster progress toward a diploma or degree, to make up credits lost through absence or failure, or to round out professional education

summer squash *n* : any of various garden squashes closely related to the pumpkins and used as a vegetable while immature and before hardening of the seeds and rind

sum·mer·time \'səm-ər-ˌtīm\ *n* : the summer season or a period like summer

sum·mer·wood \-ˌwud\ *n* : the harder and heavier outer

\ə\ **abut**	\au̇\ **out**	\i\ **tip**	\ȯ\ **saw**	\u̇\ **foot**
\ər\ **further**	\ch\ **chin**	\ī\ **life**	\ȯi\ **coin**	\y\ **yet**
\a\ **mat**	\e\ **pet**	\j\ **job**	\th\ **thin**	\yü\ **few**
\ā\ **take**	\ē\ **easy**	\ŋ\ **sing**	\th\ **this**	\yu̇\ **cure**
\ä\ **cot, cart**	\g\ **go**	\ō\ **bone**	\ü\ **food**	\zh\ **vision**

portion of an annual ring of wood that is made up of small thick-walled cells and develops late in the growing season — compare SPRINGWOOD

sum·mery \'səm-(ə-)rē\ *adj* : of, resembling, or fit for summer

sum·mit \'səm-ət\ *n* **1** : ¹TOP 1a, APEX; *esp* : the highest point (as of a mountain) **2** : the topmost level that can be reached **3 a** : the highest level of officials; *esp* : the diplomatic level of heads of government **b** : a conference of the highest-level officials (as heads of government)

sum·mon \'səm-ən\ *vb* **sum·moned; sum·mon·ing** \-(ə-)niŋ\ **1** : to call or send for in order to meet : CONVENE **2** : to order to appear before a court of law **3** : to send for ⟨*summon* a physician⟩ **4** : to call into being ⟨*summon* up courage⟩ — **sum·mon·er** \-(ə-)nər\ *n*

¹sum·mons \'səm-ənz\ *n, pl* **sum·mons·es** **1** : the act of summoning; *esp* : a call by authority to appear at a place named or to attend to some duty **2** : a warning or notice to appear in court **3** : a call, signal, or knock that summons

²summons *vb* : SUMMON 2

su·mo \'sü-mō\ *n* : a Japanese form of wrestling in which a contestant loses if forced out of the ring or if any part of the body except the soles of the feet touches the ground [Japanese]

sump \'səmp\ *n* : a pit or reservoir serving as a container or as a drain for liquids

sump·tu·ous \'səm(p)-ch(ə-w)əs\ *adj* : involving large expense : LAVISH, LUXURIOUS ⟨a *sumptuous* feast⟩ — **sump·tu·ous·ly** *adv* — **sump·tu·ous·ness** *n*

sum total *n* : total result : TOTALITY

sum up *vb* **1** : to state concisely ⟨a sentence that *sums up* the important ideas⟩ **2** : to present a summary

¹sun \'sən\ *n* **1 a** : the star around which the planets revolve, from which they receive heat and light, and which has an average distance from the earth of about 93,000,000 miles (150,000,000 kilometers), a diameter of 864,000 miles (1,390,000 kilometers), and a mass 332,000 times greater than earth **b** : a star like the sun **2** : the heat or light given off by the sun : SUNSHINE **3** : one resembling the sun usually in brilliance **4** : the rising or setting of the sun ⟨from *sun to sun*⟩ — **in the sun** : in the public eye — **under the sun** : in the world : on earth

²sun *vb* **sunned; sun·ning** **1** : to expose to or as if to the rays of the sun **2** : to sun oneself

sun·baked \'sən-bākt\ *adj* **1** : heated, parched, or compressed especially by too much sunlight **2** : baked by exposing to sunshine ⟨*sunbaked* bricks⟩

sun·bath \'sən-ˌbath, -ˌbath\ *n* : the action of sunbathing

sun·bathe \-ˌbāth\ *vb* : to expose oneself to sunlight or a sunlamp especially to get a tan — **sun·bath·er** \-ˌbā-thər\ *n*

sun·beam \-ˌbēm\ *n* : a ray of sunlight

sun·block \-ˌbläk\ *n* : a preparation (as a lotion) applied to the skin to prevent sunburn (as by physically blocking out the sun's rays)

sun·bon·net \-ˌbän-ət\ *n* : a woman's bonnet with a wide brim framing the face and usually having a ruffle at the back to protect the neck from the sun

¹sun·burn \-ˌbərn\ *vb* **-burned** \-ˌbərnd\ *or* **-burnt** \-ˌbərnt\; **-burn·ing** **1** : to burn or discolor by the sun **2** : to become sunburned

²sunburn *n* : a sore red state of the skin caused by too much sunlight

sunbonnet

sun·burst \'sən-ˌbərst\ *n* **1** : a flash of sunlight especially through a break in the clouds **2 a** : a jeweled pin representing a sun surrounded by rays **b** : a design in the form of rays extending from a central point

sun·dae \'sən-dē\ *n* : a serving of ice cream topped with fruit, syrup, or nuts

¹Sun·day \'sən-dē\ *n* : the first day of the week : the Christian Sabbath

> **Word History** It was believed in ancient times that there were seven "planets," including the sun and the moon. The days of the week were named in Latin for these "planets." One of the days was named *dies solis,* meaning "day of the sun." The Latin name was later translated into other languages. *Dies solis* became *sunnandæg* in Old English. The modern English *Sunday* comes from the Old English *sunnandæg.* [Old English *sunnandæg* "Sunday," from *sunne* "sun" + *dæg* "day"]

²Sunday *adj* **1** : of, relating to, or associated with Sunday **2** : ¹BEST 1 ⟨*Sunday* suit⟩

Sunday school *n* : a school held on Sunday for religious education

sun·der \'sən-dər\ *vb* **sun·dered; sun·der·ing** \-d(ə-)riŋ\ : to break or force apart or in two

sun·dew \'sən-d(y)ü\ *n* : any of a genus of wetland herbs that trap and digest insects with the sticky hairlike glands on their leaves

sun·di·al \-ˌdī(-ə)l\ *n* : a device to show the time of day by the position of the shadow cast on a marked plate or disk usually by an object with a straight edge

sun·down \-ˌdaun\ *n* : SUNSET 2

sun·down·er \-ˌdau-nər\ *n, Australian* : ²TRAMP 1, HOBO

sundial

sun·dries \'sən-drēz\ *n pl* : miscellaneous small articles (as pins or needles)

sun·dry \'sən-drē\ *adj* : MISCELLANEOUS, SEVERAL, VARIOUS ⟨for *sundry* reasons⟩

sun·fish \'sən-ˌfish\ *n* **1** : a very large sea fish that is flattened from side to side and has long fins and a small mouth **2** : any of a family of North American freshwater fishes that are related to the perches, are often brightly colored, and usually have a body that is flattened from side to side

sun·flow·er \-ˌflau(-ə)r\ *n* : any of a genus of tall herbs that are often grown for their large showy flower heads with yellow ray flowers and for their oil-rich seeds

sung *past and past participle of* SING

sun·glass·es \'sən-ˌglas-əz\ *n pl* : glasses to protect the eyes from the sun

sun god *n, often cap S&G* : a god that represents the sun in various religions

sun goddess *n, often cap S&G* : a goddess that represents the sun in various religions

sunflower

sunk *past and past participle of* SINK

sunk·en \'sən-kən\ *adj* **1** : being submerged; *esp* : lying at the bottom of a body of water ⟨*sunken* ships⟩ **2** : fallen in : HOLLOW ⟨*sunken* cheeks⟩ **3 a** : lying in a depression

⟨a *sunken* garden⟩ **b** : constructed below the normal floor level ⟨a *sunken* living room⟩

sun·lamp \'sən-ˌlamp\ *n* : an electric lamp that is made to give off radiation of wavelengths from ultraviolet to infrared

sun·less \'sən-ləs\ *adj* : lacking sunshine : DARK

sun·light \'sən-ˌlīt\ *n* : the light of the sun : SUNSHINE

sun·lit \-ˌlit\ *adj* : lighted by or as if by the sun

Sun·ni \'su̇n-(n)ē\ *n, pl* **-nis** *or* **-ni** **1** : one of the two main branches of Islam **2** : a Muslim who is a member of the Sunni branch of Islam

sun·ny \'sən-ē\ *adj* **sun·ni·er; -est** **1** : bright with sunshine **2** : MERRY 1 ⟨a *sunny* smile⟩ — **sun·ni·ly** \'sən-ᵊl-ē\ *adv* — **sun·ni·ness** \'sən-ē-nəs\ *n*

sun·rise \'sən-ˌrīz\ *n* **1** : the apparent rising of the sun above the horizon; *also* : the accompanying atmospheric effects (as color) **2** : the time at which the sun rises

sun·roof \-ˌrüf, -ˌru̇f\ *n* : a panel in the roof of an automobile that can be opened

sun·screen \-ˌskrēn\ *n* : a preparation (as a lotion) applied to the skin to prevent sunburn (as by chemically absorbing the sun's rays)

sun·set \-ˌset\ *n* **1** : the apparent sinking of the sun below the horizon; *also* : the accompanying atmospheric effects **2** : the time at which the sun sets

sun·shade \-ˌshād\ *n* : something (as a parasol) used to protect from the sun's rays

sun·shine \-ˌshīn\ *n* **1 a** : the sun's light or direct rays **b** : the warmth and light given by the sun's rays **2** : one (as a person or a condition) that spreads warmth, cheer, or happiness — **sun·shiny** \-ˌshī-nē\ *adj*

sun·spot \-ˌspät\ *n* : one of the dark spots that appear from time to time on the sun's surface and are usually visible only through a telescope

sun·stroke \-ˌstrōk\ *n* : a heatstroke caused by staying in the sun for too long

sun·tan \-ˌtan\ *n* : a browning of the skin from being exposed to the rays of the sun — **sun·tanned** \-ˌtand\ *adj*

sun·up \-ˌəp\ *n* : SUNRISE 2

¹sun·ward \'sən-wərd\ *adv* : toward the sun ⟨the planet tilted *sunward*⟩

²sunward *adj* : facing the sun

¹sup \'səp\ *vb* **supped; sup·ping** : to eat dinner : DINE [Old English *sūpan, suppan* "to eat or drink in gulps"]

²sup *n* : a mouthful especially of liquid : SIP

³sup *vb* **supped; sup·ping** **1** : to eat the evening meal **2** : to make one's supper — used with *on* or *off* ⟨*supped* on roast beef⟩ [Middle English *suppen, soupen* "to eat the evening meal," from early French *super* (same meaning), from *supe* "soup, sop"]

¹su·per \'sü-pər\ *adj* **1** : used as an overall term of approval ⟨a *super* cook⟩ **2** : very large or powerful ⟨a *super* atomic bomb⟩ **3** : showing the characteristics of its type to an extreme degree ⟨*super* secrecy⟩

²super *n* **1** : an actor not listed with the regular cast **2** : SUPERINTENDENT, SUPERVISOR

³super *adv* **1** : ²VERY 1, EXTREMELY ⟨a *super* fast car⟩ **2** : to a degree exceeding the usual or normal ⟨*super* critical⟩

super- *prefix* **1 a** : over and above : higher in quantity, quality, or degree than : more than ⟨*super*fine⟩ ⟨*super*human⟩ **b** : exceeding or so as to exceed what is usual or normal ⟨*super*cool⟩ **c** : bigger, better, or more important than others of the same kind ⟨*super*highway⟩ ⟨*super*star⟩ **2 a** : situated or placed above, on, or at the top of ⟨*super*impose⟩ **b** : next above or higher ⟨*super*tonic⟩ [derived from Latin *super* "over, above"]

su·per·abun·dant \ˌsü-pə-rə-'bən-dənt\ *adj* : more than ample : EXCESSIVE ⟨*superabundant* zeal⟩ ⟨a *superabundant* harvest⟩ — **su·per·abun·dance** \-dən(t)s\ *n* — **su·per·abun·dant·ly** *adv*

su·per·an·nu·ate \ˌsü-pə-'ran-yə-ˌwāt\ *vb* **-at·ed; -at·ing** **1** : to retire and pension because of age or infirmity **2** : to become retired **3** : to become outdated — **su·per·an·nu·a·tion** \-ˌran-yə-'wā-shən\ *n*

su·per·an·nu·at·ed *adj* : too old for work or use

su·perb \su̇-'pərb\ *adj* : outstandingly excellent, impressive, or beautiful ⟨*superb* quality⟩ ⟨was a *superb* pianist⟩ — **su·perb·ly** *adv* — **su·perb·ness** *n*

su·per·cil·ious \ˌsü-pər-'sil-ē-əs, -'sil-yəs\ *adj* : coolly and disdainfully proud : SNOBBISH — **su·per·cil·ious·ly** *adv* — **su·per·cil·ious·ness** *n*

su·per·com·put·er \'sü-pər-kəm-ˌpyüt-ər\ *n* : a large very fast mainframe used especially for scientific computations

su·per·con·ti·nent \'sü-pər-ˌkänt-ᵊn-ənt, -ˌkänt-nənt\ *n* : a former large continent which is assumed to have existed and from which other continents broke off and drifted away

¹su·per·cool \ˌsü-pər-'kül\ *vb* : to cool below the freezing point while remaining liquid

²supercool *adj* : extremely cool: as **a** : showing extraordinary reserve and self-control **b** : being the latest style or fashion ⟨*supercool* sunglasses⟩

su·per·fi·cial \ˌsü-pər-'fish-əl\ *adj* **1 a** : of or relating to a surface **b** : lying on, not going below, or affecting only the surface ⟨*superficial* wounds⟩ **2** : not thorough : SHALLOW ⟨a *superficial* inspection⟩ — **su·per·fi·ci·al·i·ty** \-ˌfish-ē-'al-ət-ē\ *n* — **su·per·fi·cial·ly** \-'fish-(ə-)lē\ *adv*

su·per·fine \ˌsü-pər-'fīn\ *adj* **1** : overly refined or nice **2** : extremely fine ⟨*superfine* toothbrush bristles⟩ **3** : of high quality or grade — used especially of merchandise

su·per·flu·ity \ˌsü-pər-'flü-ət-ē\ *n, pl* **-ties** **1** : an amount in excess **2** : something unnecessary or superfluous

su·per·flu·ous \su̇-'pər-flə-wəs\ *adj* : going beyond what is enough or necessary : EXTRA [Middle English *superfluous* "more than is needed," from Latin *superfluus*, literally, "running over," from *superfluere* "to overflow," from *super-* "over, in addition," and *fluere* "to flow" — related to FLUID] — **su·per·flu·ous·ly** \su̇-'pər-flə-wəs-lē\ *adv*

su·per·glue \'sü-pər-ˌglü\ *n* : a very strong glue — **superglue** *vb*

su·per·heat \ˌsü-pər-'hēt\ *vb* **1 a** : to heat (steam) to a higher temperature than the normal boiling point of water **b** : to heat a liquid above the boiling point without converting into vapor **2** : to heat very much or excessively

su·per·he·ro \'sü-per-ˌhē-rō, -ˌhi(ə)r-ō\ *n* : a fictional hero having extraordinary or superhuman powers; *also* : a very successful person

su·per·high·way \ˌsü-pər-'hī-ˌwā\ *n* **1** : a highway designed for high-speed traffic **2** : INTERNET

su·per·hu·man \ˌsü-pər-'hyü-mən, -'yü-\ *adj* **1** : being above the human : DIVINE ⟨*superhuman* beings⟩ **2** : going beyond normal human power, size, or capability ⟨a *superhuman* effort⟩ — **su·per·hu·man·ly** *adv* — **su·per·hu·man·ness** *n*

su·per·im·pose \ˌsü-pə-rim-'pōz\ *vb* : to place or lay over or above something — **su·per·im·po·si·tion** \-ˌrim-pə-'zish-ən\ *n*

su·per·in·tend \ˌsü-p(ə-)rin-'tend, ˌsü-pərn-\ *vb* : to be in charge of : DIRECT

su·per·in·ten·dence \ˌsü-p(ə-)rin-'ten-dən(t)s, ˌsü-pərn-\ *n* : the act or function of superintending or directing

su·per·in·ten·den·cy \ˌsü-p(ə-)rin-'ten-dən-sē\ *n, pl* **-cies** : the office or post of a superintendent

\ə\ **abut**	\au̇\ **out**	\i\ **tip**	\o̅\ **saw**	\u̇\ **foot**
\ər\ **further**	\ch\ **chin**	\ī\ **life**	\ȯi\ **coin**	\y\ **yet**
\a\ **mat**	\e\ **pet**	\j\ **job**	\th\ **thin**	\yü\ **few**
\ā\ **take**	\ē\ **easy**	\ŋ\ **sing**	\t̲h̲\ **this**	\yu̇\ **cure**
\ä\ **cot, cart**	\g\ **go**	\ō\ **bone**	\ü\ **food**	\zh\ **vision**

su·per·in·ten·dent \ˌsü-p(ə-)rin-ˈten-dənt, ˌsü-pərn-\ *n* : a person who directs, manages, or maintains something

¹su·pe·ri·or \sù-ˈpir-ē-ər\ *adj* **1** : situated higher up : UPPER **2** : of higher rank, quality, or importance **3** : courageously or calmly indifferent (as to something painful) **4 a** : greater in quantity or numbers ⟨escaped by *superior* speed⟩ **b** : excellent of its kind : BETTER ⟨a *superior* memory⟩ **5** : covering or including more things ⟨a genus is *superior* to a species⟩ **6** : feeling that one is better or more important than others — **su·pe·ri·or·ly** *adv*

²superior *n* **1** : one who is above another in rank, station, or office; *esp* : the head of a religious house or order **2** : one that goes beyond another in quality or merit

su·pe·ri·or·i·ty \sù-ˌpir-ē-ˈòr-ət-ē, -ˈär-\ *n, pl* **-ties** : the state or fact of being superior

superior vena cava *n* : the branch of the vena cava that returns blood to the heart from the upper or front part of the body including the head and front limbs

¹su·per·la·tive \sù-ˈpər-lət-iv\ *adj* **1** : of, relating to, or being the form of an adjective or adverb that shows the highest or lowest degree of comparison **2** : better than all others : SUPREME — **su·per·la·tive·ly** *adv*

²superlative *n* **1** : the superlative degree or a superlative form in a language **2** : the superlative or utmost degree of something **3** : a superlative person or thing

su·per·man \ˈsü-pər-ˌman\ *n* : a person with extraordinary or superhuman power

su·per·mar·ket \ˈsü-pər-ˌmär-kət\ *n* : a self-service market selling foods and household merchandise

su·per·mi·cro \-ˌmī-krō\ *n* : a very fast and powerful microcomputer

su·per·mini \-ˌmin-ē\ *n* : SUPERMINICOMPUTER

su·per·mini·com·put·er \-ˈmin-ē-kəm-ˌpyüt-ər\ *n* : a very fast and powerful minicomputer

su·per·nal \sù-ˈpərn-ᵊl\ *adj* **1 a** : being or coming from on high **b** : HEAVENLY **3** ⟨*supernal* music⟩ **2** : located in or belonging to the sky — **su·per·nal·ly** \-ᵊl-ē\ *adv*

su·per·nat·u·ral \ˌsü-pər-ˈnach-(ə-)rəl\ *adj* **1** : of or relating to an order of existence beyond the visible observable universe; *esp* : of or relating to God or a god, demigod, spirit, or devil **2 a** : departing from what is usual or normal especially so as to appear to go beyond the laws of nature **b** : attributed to an invisible agent (as a ghost or spirit) — **supernatural** *n* — **su·per·nat·u·ral·ly** \-ˈnach-(ə-)rə-lē, -ˈnach-ər-lē\ *adv*

su·per·no·va \ˌsü-pər-ˈnō-və\ *n* : the explosion of a very large star in which the star temporarily gives off up to one billion times more energy than the sun

¹su·per·nu·mer·ary \ˌsü-pər-ˈn(y)ü-mə-ˌrer-ē\ *adj* : exceeding the usual or needed number : EXTRA

²supernumerary *n, pl* **-ar·ies** **1** : a supernumerary person or thing **2** : an actor employed to play a small usually nonspeaking part

su·per·phos·phate \ˌsü-pər-ˈfäs-ˌfāt\ *n* : a soluble mixture of phosphates used as fertilizer

su·per·pose \ˌsü-pər-ˈpōz\ *vb* **-posed; -pos·ing** : to place or lay over or above another especially so as to make all like parts coincide ⟨congruent triangles can be *superposed*⟩ — **su·per·po·si·tion** \-pə-ˈzish-ən\ *n*

su·per·pow·er \ˈsü-pər-ˌpaù(-ə)r\ *n* : an extremely powerful nation

su·per·sat·u·rat·ed \ˌsü-pər-ˈsach-ə-ˌrāt-əd\ *adj* : containing an amount of something greater than the amount required for saturation by having been cooled from a higher temperature to a temperature below that at which saturation occurs ⟨a *supersaturated* solution⟩ ⟨air *supersaturated* with water vapor⟩

su·per·scribe \ˈsü-pər-ˌskrīb\ *vb* **-scribed; -scrib·ing** **1** : to write (as a name or address) on the outside or cover of **2** : to write or engrave on the top or outside

su·per·script \ˈsü-pər-ˌskript\ *n* : a distinguishing symbol (as a numeral or letter) written immediately above or above and to the side of another character — **super-script** *adj*

su·per·scrip·tion \ˌsü-pər-ˈskrip-shən\ *n* **1** : something superscribed **2** : the act of superscribing

su·per·sede \ˌsü-pər-ˈsēd\ *vb* **-sed·ed; -sed·ing** **1** : to force out of use as inferior **2** : to take the place, room, or position of : REPLACE **3** : to remove in favor of another [Middle English *superceden* "to defer," from early French *superceder*, from Latin *supersedēre* "to sit on top of, refrain from," from *super* "over, above," and *sedēre* "to sit"] — **su·per·sed·er** *n* — **su·per·se·dure** \-ˈsē-jər\ *n*

su·per·sen·si·tive \ˌsü-pər-ˈsen(t)-sət-iv, -ˈsen(t)-stiv\ *adj* : HYPERSENSITIVE — **su·per·sen·si·tiv·i·ty** \-ˌsen(t)-sə-ˈtiv-ət-ē\ *n*

su·per·ses·sion \ˌsü-pər-ˈsesh-ən\ *n* : the act of superseding : the state of being superseded

su·per·son·ic \ˌsü-pər-ˈsän-ik\ *adj* **1** : ULTRASONIC **2** : of, being, or relating to speeds from one to five times the speed of sound in air **3** : moving, capable of moving, or using air currents moving at supersonic speed ⟨a *supersonic* airplane⟩ — **su·per·son·i·cal·ly** \-i-k(ə-)lē\ *adv*

su·per·star \ˈsü-pər-ˌstär\ *n* : a star (as in sports or the movies) who is considered extremely talented, has great public appeal, and can usually command a high salary — **su·per·star·dom** \-dəm\ *n*

su·per·sti·tion \ˌsü-pər-ˈstish-ən\ *n* **1** : a belief or practice resulting from ignorance, fear of the unknown, or trust in magic **2** : an unreasoning fear of nature, the unknown, or God resulting from superstition

su·per·sti·tious \ˌsü-pər-ˈstish-əs\ *adj* : of, relating to, or influenced by superstition — **su·per·sti·tious·ly** *adv*

su·per·store \-ˌstō(ə)r, -ˌstó(ə)r\ *n* : a very large store often offering a wide variety of goods for sale

su·per·tank·er \ˈsü-pər-ˌtaŋ-kər\ *n* : a very large cargo ship fitted with tanks for carrying large amounts of liquid

su·per·ton·ic \ˌsü-pər-ˈtän-ik\ *n* : the second tone of a major or minor scale

su·per·vene \ˌsü-pər-ˈvēn\ *vb* **-vened; -ven·ing** : to take place as an additional or unlooked-for development — **su·per·ven·tion** \-ˈven-chən\ *n*

su·per·ve·nient \ˌsü-pər-ˈvē-nyənt\ *adj* : coming or occurring as something additional or unexpected

su·per·vise \ˈsü-pər-ˌvīz\ *vb* **-vised; -vis·ing** : SUPERINTEND, OVERSEE [from Latin *supervisus*, past participle of *supervidēre* "to oversee," from *super-* "over, above" and *vidēre* "to see" — related to VISION]

su·per·vi·sion \ˌsü-pər-ˈvizh-ən\ *n* : the act of supervising; *esp* : a critical watching and directing (as of activities)

su·per·vi·sor \ˈsü-pər-ˌvī-zər\ *n* : a person who supervises; *esp* : an officer in charge of a unit or an operation of a business, government, or school — **su·per·vi·so·ry** \ˌsü-pər-ˈvīz-(ə-)rē\ *adj*

su·per·wom·an \ˈsü-pər-ˌwùm-ən\ *n* : an exceptional woman; *esp* : a woman who succeeds in having a career and raising a family

su·pine \sù-ˈpīn\ *adj* **1** : lying on the back or with the face upward **2** : showing mental or moral indifference : LAZY — **su·pine·ly** *adv* — **su·pine·ness** \-ˈpīn-nəs\ *n*

supped *past and past participle of* SUP

sup·per \ˈsəp-ər\ *n* **1 a** : the evening meal especially when dinner is eaten at midday **b** : a social affair having a supper **2** : a light meal served late in the evening

supping *present participle of* SUP

sup·plant \sə-ˈplant\ *vb* **1** : to take the place of (another) especially by force or treachery **2 a** : to root out and supply a substitute for **b** : to gain the place of and serve as a substitute for especially by reason of superior excellence or power — **sup·plan·ta·tion** \ˌ(ˌ)sə-ˌplan-ˈtā-shən\ *n* — **sup·plant·er** \sə-ˈplant-ər\ *n*

¹sup·ple \ˈsəp-əl\ *adj* **sup·pler** \ˈsəp-(ə-)lər\; **sup·plest** \ˈsəp-(ə-)ləst\ **1** : readily adaptable to new situations ⟨a *supple* mind⟩ **2 a** : capable of being bent without creases or breaks : PLIANT ⟨*supple* leather⟩ **b** : able to bend or twist with ease : LIMBER ⟨the *supple* legs of a dancer⟩ — **sup·ple·ness** \-əl-nəs\ *n*

²**supple** *vb* **sup·pled; sup·pling** \'səp-(ə-)liŋ\ : to make soft and easy to bend

¹**sup·ple·ment** \'səp-lə-mənt\ *n* **1** : something that supplies what is needed or makes an addition ⟨vitamin pills used as dietary *supplements*⟩ **2** : an arc or angle that when added to a given arc or angle equals 180 degrees — **sup·ple·men·tal** \,səp-lə-'ment-ᵊl\ *adj*

²**sup·ple·ment** \'səp-lə-,ment\ *vb* : to add to ⟨*supplement* their incomes by doing odd jobs⟩ — **sup·ple·men·ta·tion** \,səp-lə-,men-'tā-shən, -mən-\ *n*

sup·ple·men·ta·ry \,səp-lə-'ment-ə-rē, -'men-trē\ *adj* **1** : added as a supplement : ADDITIONAL **2** : being or relating to a supplement or a supplementary angle

supplementary angle *n* : one of two angles or arcs whose sum is 180 degrees — usually used in plural

¹**sup·pli·ant** \'səp-lē-ənt\ *n* : one who asks earnestly

²**suppliant** *adj* : humbly asking — **sup·pli·ant·ly** *adv*

sup·pli·cant \'səp-li-kənt\ *n* : one who asks earnestly — **supplicant** *adj* — **sup·pli·cant·ly** *adv*

sup·pli·cate \'səp-lə-,kāt\ *vb* **-cat·ed; -cat·ing** **1** : to make a humble appeal; *esp* : to pray to God **2** : to ask earnestly and humbly — **sup·pli·ca·tion** \,səp-lə-'kā-shən\ *n*

¹**sup·ply** \sə-'plī\ *vb* **sup·plied; sup·ply·ing** **1** : to add as a supplement **2 a** : to provide for : SATISFY ⟨enough to *supply* the demand⟩ **b** : to make available for use ⟨*supplied* the necessary money⟩ **c** : to satisfy the needs or wishes of — **sup·pli·er** \-'plī-(ə-)r\ *n*

²**supply** *n, pl* **supplies** **1 a** : the quantity or amount of something that is needed or available ⟨the nation's oil *supply*⟩ **b** : ²STORE 1b — usually used in plural **2** : the act or process of filling a want or need **3** : the quantities of goods or services offered for sale at a particular time or at one price

¹**sup·port** \sə-'pō(ə)rt, -'pó(ə)rt\ *vb* **1** : to endure bravely or quietly : BEAR **2 a** : to promote the interests or cause of **b** : to uphold or defend as true or right : ADVOCATE ⟨*supports* fair play⟩ **c** : to argue or vote for ⟨*support* a candidate⟩ **d** : ¹ASSIST, HELP ⟨bombers *supported* the ground troops⟩ **e** : to provide evidence for : VERIFY ⟨they cannot *support* the claim⟩ **3** : to pay the costs of : MAINTAIN ⟨*supports* a large family⟩ **4 a** : to hold up or in position or serve as a foundation or prop for ⟨posts *support* the porch roof⟩ **b** : to keep up the price of (as milk or wheat) by buying large amounts to store at a certain price **5** : to keep something going : SUSTAIN ⟨not enough air to *support* life⟩ — **sup·port·able** \-ə-bəl\ *adj* — **sup·port·ive** \-'pōrt-iv, -'pórt-\ *adj*

²**support** *n* **1 a** : the act or process of supporting : the condition of being supported **b** : assistance provided by a company to users of its products ⟨customer *support*⟩ **2** : someone or something that supports

sup·port·er \sə-'pōrt-ər, -'pórt-\ *n* : one that supports; *esp* : one who argues or votes for someone or something

support hose *n* : elastic stockings

support system *n* : a network of people who provide someone with practical or emotional support

sup·pose \sə-'pōz\ *vb* **sup·posed; sup·pos·ing** **1** : to take as true or as a fact for the sake of argument ⟨*suppose* a fire should break out⟩ **2** : to hold as an opinion : BELIEVE ⟨they *supposed* they were on the right bus⟩ **3** : to come to a conclusion arrived at by guessing ⟨who do you *suppose* will win⟩

sup·posed \sə-'pōzd\ *sense 1 usually* -'pō-zəd, *senses 2 & 3 often* -'pōst\ *adj* **1** : believed to be true or real ⟨a *supposed* cure⟩ **2** : considered probable or certain : EXPECTED ⟨they are *supposed* to be here tomorrow⟩ **3** : required by or as if by authority ⟨you are *supposed* to listen to your parents⟩ — **sup·pos·ed·ly** \-'pō-zəd-lē *also* -'pōz-dlē\ *adv*

sup·po·si·tion \,səp-ə-'zish-ən\ *n* **1** : something that is supposed **2** : the act of supposing — **sup·po·si·tion·al** \-'zish-nəl, -ən-ᵊl\ *adj*

sup·press \sə-'pres\ *vb* **1** : to put down by authority or force ⟨*suppress* a rebellion⟩ **2 a** : to keep from being known ⟨tried to *suppress* the news⟩ **b** : to stop the publication or distribution of ⟨*suppressed* the test results⟩ **3** : to hold back : REPRESS ⟨*suppress* feelings of jealousy⟩ ⟨*suppressed* a cough⟩ **4** : to slow or stop the growth or development of : STUNT — **sup·press·ible** \-ə-bəl\ *adj* — **sup·pres·sion** \-'presh-ən\ *n* — **sup·pres·sive** \-'pres-iv\ *adj* — **sup·pres·sor** \-'pres-ər\ *n*

sup·pres·sant \sə-'pres-ᵊnt\ *n* : an agent (as a drug) that tends to suppress or reduce in intensity rather than eliminate something ⟨a cough *suppressant*⟩

sup·pu·rate \'səp-yə-,rāt\ *vb* **-rat·ed; -rat·ing** : to form or give off pus — **sup·pu·ra·tion** \,səp-yə-'rā-shən\ *n*

supra- *prefix* **1** : SUPER- 2a ⟨*supra*renal⟩ **2** : going beyond ⟨*supra*national⟩ [derived from Latin *supra* "above, beyond"]

su·pra·na·tion·al \,sü-prə-'nash-nəl, -ən-ᵊl\ *adj* : going beyond national boundaries or authority

su·prem·a·cist \sə-'prem-ə-səst\ *n* : a person who believes that one group (as the white race) should control all others

su·prem·a·cy \sə-'prem-ə-sē\ *n, pl* **-cies** **1** : the quality or state of being supreme **2** : supreme authority or power

su·preme \sə-'prēm, sü-\ *adj* **1** : highest in rank or authority **2** : highest in degree or quality **3** : greatest in degree ⟨giving one's life is the *supreme* sacrifice⟩ [from Latin *supremus,* a form of *superus* "upper," from *super* "over, above"] — **su·preme·ly** *adv* — **su·preme·ness** *n*

Supreme Being *n* : GOD 1

supreme court *n* : the highest court in a political unit (as the U.S. or one of its states)

sur- *prefix* : over ⟨*sur*print⟩ ⟨*sur*tax⟩ [derived from Latin *super* "over, above"]

sur·cease \'sər-,sēs, (,)sər-'sēs\ *n* : a stopping of action; *esp* : a temporary halt

¹**sur·charge** \'sər-,chärj\ *vb* **1 a** : OVERCHARGE 1 **b** : to charge an extra fee **2** : ¹OVERLOAD **3** : to mark a new value or a surcharge on a stamp

²**surcharge** *n* **1** : an additional tax or charge **2** : a burden that is too great **3 a** : a mark on top of a stamp that changes the value **b** : a stamp bearing such a mark

sur·cin·gle \'sər-,siŋ-gəl\ *n* : a belt or band passing around the body of a horse to bind a saddle or pack fast to the horse's back

sur·coat \'sər-,kōt\ *n* : an outer coat or cloak; *esp* : one worn over armor

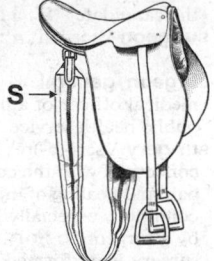

S surcingle

¹**sure** \'shu̇(ə)r, *especially Southern* 'shō(ə)r\ *adj* **1** : firmly established : STEADFAST ⟨a *sure* hold⟩ **2** : RELIABLE, TRUSTWORTHY ⟨a *sure* friend⟩ **3** : having no doubt : CONFIDENT ⟨I'm *sure* I'm right⟩ **4** : not to be doubted : CERTAIN ⟨*sure* evidence⟩ **5 a** : bound to happen : INEVITABLE ⟨*sure* disaster⟩ **b** : bound as if by fate ⟨we are *sure* to win⟩ [Middle English *seur, sure* "safe from danger or harm," from early French *seur* (same meaning), from *securus* "secure" — related to SECURE] — **sure·ness** *n* — **for sure** : without doubt : with certainty — **to be sure** : it must be admitted

\ə\ **abut**	\au̇\ **out**	\i\ **tip**	\ȯ\ **saw**	\u̇\ **foot**
\ər\ **further**	\ch\ **chin**	\ī\ **life**	\ȯi\ **coin**	\y\ **yet**
\a\ **mat**	\e\ **pet**	\j\ **job**	\th\ **thin**	\yü\ **few**
\ā\ **take**	\ē\ **easy**	\ŋ\ **sing**	\th\ **this**	\yu̇\ **cure**
\ä\ **cot, cart**	\g\ **go**	\ō\ **bone**	\ü\ **food**	\zh\ **vision**

²**sure** *adv* **1** : SURELY 1b **2** : SURELY 2

sure–fire \ˌshu̇r-ˈfī(ə)r\ *adj* : certain to get results

sure–foot·ed \ˈshu̇(ə)r-ˈfu̇t-əd\ *adj* : not likely to stumble or fall — **sure–foot·ed·ly** *adv* — **sure–foot·ed·ness** *n*

sure·ly \ˈshu̇(ə)r-lē\ *adv* **1 a** : with confidence ⟨answered quickly and *surely*⟩ **b** : without doubt : CERTAINLY ⟨they will *surely* be heard from again⟩ **2** : beyond question : TRULY ⟨I *surely* am tired this afternoon⟩

sure·ty \ˈshu̇r-ət-ē, ˈshu̇(ə)rt-ē\ *n, pl* **-ties** **1** : sure knowledge : CERTAINTY **2** : a formal agreement to do something : GUARANTEE **3** : one who takes legal responsibility for another's debt or failure in duty

¹**surf** \ˈsərf\ *n* **1** : waves that break upon the shore **2** : the foam, splash, and sound of breaking waves

²**surf** *vb* **1** : to ride the surf (as on a surfboard) **2** : to scan the offerings of (as television or the Internet) for something of interest

¹**sur·face** \ˈsər-fəs\ *n* **1** : the outside of an object or body ⟨on the *surface* of the water⟩ ⟨the earth's *surface*⟩ **2** : any flat or curved two-dimensional area in space ⟨the *surface* of a cube⟩ **3** : the outside appearance ⟨on the *surface* the plan seems good⟩ — **surface** *adj*

²**surface** *vb* **sur·faced; sur·fac·ing** **1 a** : to make smooth **b** : to apply the surface layer to ⟨*surface* a road⟩ **2** : to bring or come to the surface **3** : to come into public view ⟨letters that recently *surfaced*⟩

surface tension *n* : the attractive force felt by surface molecules of a liquid from the molecules beneath that tends to draw the surface molecules into the mass of the liquid and makes the liquid take the shape having the least surface area

sur·fac·ing *n* : material forming or used to form a surface

surf·board \ˈsərf-ˌbō(ə)rd, -ˌbȯ(ə)rd\ *n* : a lightweight board used in the sport of surfing — **surf·board·er** *n* — **surf·board·ing** \-iŋ\ *n*

¹**sur·feit** \ˈsər-fət\ *n* **1** : a supply that is more than enough : EXCESS **2** : an enjoyment of something (as food or drink) beyond what is good or necessary **3** : disgust caused by excess

²**surfeit** *vb* : to feed, supply, or enjoy to the point of excess

surf·ing \ˈsər-fiŋ\ *n* : the sport of riding the surf especially on a surfboard

¹**surge** \ˈsərj\ *vb* **surged; surg·ing** **1** : to rise and fall actively **2** : to move in or as if in waves

²**surge** *n* **1** : a swelling, rolling, or sweeping forward like that of a wave : an onward rush ⟨a *surge* of support for the candidate⟩ **2** : a large wave or billow : SWELL

sur·geon \ˈsər-jən\ *n* : a physician who specializes in surgery

surgeon general *n, pl* **surgeons general** : the chief medical officer of a branch of the armed services or of a public health service

sur·gery \ˈsərj-(ə-)rē\ *n, pl* **-ger·ies** **1** : medical science concerned with the correction of physical defects, the repair and healing of injuries, and the treatment of diseased conditions especially by operations **2 a** : the work done by a surgeon : OPERATION **3 3** : a room or area where surgery is performed [Middle English *surgerie* "surgery," from early French *cirurgerie, surgerie* (same meaning), from Latin *chirurgia* (same meaning), derived from Greek *cheirourgos* "surgeon," from *cheirourgos* "doing by hand," from *cheir* "hand" and *ergon* "work"]

sur·gi·cal \ˈsər-ji-kəl\ *adj* : of, relating to, or associated with surgeons or surgery ⟨*surgical* skills⟩ ⟨*surgical* equipment⟩ ⟨a *surgical* fever⟩ — **sur·gi·cal·ly** \-k(ə-)lē\ *adv*

sur·ly \ˈsər-lē\ *adj* **sur·li·er; -est** : having a rude unfriendly disposition — **sur·li·ness** *n*

Word History The word *surly,* which describes someone with a very bad temper, was at one time spelled *sirly.* It comes from the familiar word *sir,* which has been used for centuries as a title of respect for a gentleman or nobleman. *Sirly* was originally used to describe a person

who behaves in a very proud way—the kind of person who might insist on being called "sir." It was similar in meaning to the word *lordly.* Many years of use brought about the changes in spelling and in meaning that have given us the modern word *surly.* [Middle English *serreli* "lordly, imperious," from *sir* "a man of rank"]

¹**sur·mise** \sər-ˈmīz\ *vb* **sur·mised; sur·mis·ing** : to form an idea of based on very little evidence : GUESS

²**sur·mise** \sər-ˈmīz, ˈsər-ˌmīz\ *n* : a thought or idea based on little evidence : CONJECTURE

sur·mount \sər-ˈmau̇nt\ *vb* **1** : OVERCOME 1 ⟨*surmount* an obstacle⟩ **2** : to get to the top of : CLIMB **3** : to stand or lie at the top of : CROWN ⟨a weather vane *surmounts* the roof⟩ — **sur·mount·able** \-ə-bəl\ *adj*

sur·name \ˈsər-ˌnām\ *n* **1** : an added name : NICKNAME **2** : the name held in common by members of a family — **surname** *vb*

sur·pass \sər-ˈpas\ *vb* **1** : to be greater, better, or stronger than **2** : to go beyond the reach, powers, or capacity of *synonyms* see EXCEED — **sur·pass·able** \-ə-bəl\ *adj*

sur·plice \ˈsər-pləs\ *n* : a loose white outer garment worn at church services

sur·plus \ˈsər-(ˌ)pləs\ *n* **1** : the amount more than what is required or necessary : EXCESS **2** : an excess of income over spending — **surplus** *adj*

¹**sur·prise** \sə(r)-ˈprīz\ *n* **1 a** : an attack made without warning **b** : an act or an instance of coming upon someone suddenly **2** : something that surprises **3** : the state of being surprised : ASTONISHMENT

²**surprise** *also* **sur·prize** *vb* **sur·prised** *also* **sur·prized; sur·pris·ing** *also* **sur·priz·ing** **1 a** : to attack without warning **b** : to capture by an unexpected attack **2** : to come upon unexpectedly **3** : to fill with wonder or amazement because unexpected — **sur·pris·er** *n*

sur·pris·ing \sə(r)-ˈprī-ziŋ\ *adj* : causing surprise : AMAZING

sur·pris·ing·ly \-lē\ *adv* **1** : in a surprising manner : to a surprising degree ⟨a *surprisingly* fast runner⟩ **2** : it is surprising that ⟨*surprisingly,* no one disagreed⟩

¹**sur·ren·der** \sə-ˈren-dər\ *vb* **-dered; -der·ing** \-d(ə-)riŋ\ **1** : to give over to the power, control, or possession of another especially by force **2** : to give oneself over to something *synonyms* see YIELD

²**surrender** *n* : the giving of oneself or something into the power of another person or thing

sur·rep·ti·tious \ˌsər-əp-ˈtish-əs, ˌsə-rəp-\ *adj* : done, made, or acquired in secret *synonyms* see SECRET — **sur·rep·ti·tious·ly** *adv* — **sur·rep·ti·tious·ness** *n*

sur·rey \ˈsər-ē, ˈsə-rē\ *n, pl* **surreys** : a horse-drawn carriage that has two wide seats and four wheels [from earlier *Surrey cart,* named for *Surrey,* a county in England where it was first made]

surrey

sur·ro·gate \ˈsər-ə-ˌgāt, ˈsə-rə-, -gət\ *n* **1** : one appointed to act in place of another : DEPUTY **2** : a court officer in some states who handles the settling of wills

¹**sur·round** \sə-ˈrau̇nd\ *vb* : to enclose on all sides : ENCIRCLE

²**surround** *n* : something (as a border) that surrounds

sur·round·ings \sə-ˈrau̇n-diŋz\ *n pl* : the circumstances, conditions, or objects by which one is surrounded

sur·tax \ˈsər-ˌtaks\ *n* : an additional tax over and above a general tax

sur·veil·lance \sər-ˈvā-lən(t)s *also* -ˈvāl-yən(t)s *or* -ˈvā-ən(t)s\ *n* : close watch ⟨under *surveillance*⟩

¹**sur·vey** \sər-ˈvā, ˈsər-ˌvā\ *vb* **sur·veyed; sur·vey·ing** **1** : to look over and examine closely **2** : to find out the size,

shape, and position of (as an area of land) **3** : to gather information from or about **4** : to make a survey

²sur·vey \'sər-ˌvā, sər-'vā\ *n, pl* **surveys** : the act or an instance of surveying or of applying the principles and methods of surveying; *also* : something that is surveyed

sur·vey·ing \sər-'vā-iŋ\ *n* : a branch of mathematics concerned with finding the area of any part of the earth's surface, the lengths and directions of the boundary lines, and the shape of the surface and with accurately showing the results on paper

sur·vey·or \sər-'vā-ər\ *n* : one that surveys; *esp* : one whose occupation is surveying land

sur·viv·al \sər-'vī-vəl\ *n* **1** : the act or fact of living or continuing longer than another person or thing ⟨*survival* of half the population after the epidemic⟩ **2** : a continuation of life despite difficult conditions ⟨skills for *survival* in the desert⟩ **3** : one that survives

survival of the fittest : NATURAL SELECTION

sur·vive \sər-'vīv\ *vb* **sur·vived; sur·viv·ing 1** : to remain alive : continue to exist **2** : to remain alive after the death of ⟨*survived* by three children⟩ **3** : to continue to exist or live after ⟨*survived* the flood⟩ — **sur·vi·vor** \-'vī-vər\ *n*

sus·cep·ti·bil·i·ty \sə-ˌsep-tə-'bil-ət-ē\ *n, pl* **-ties 1** : the quality or state of being susceptible; *esp* : lack of ability to resist some outside agent (as a disease-causing germ or drug) **2 a** : a susceptible disposition or nature **b** *pl* : one's emotional state : FEELINGS

sus·cep·ti·ble \sə-'sep-tə-bəl\ *adj* **1** : being of such a nature as to permit some action or operation ⟨a theory *susceptible* to proof⟩ **2** : having little resistance ⟨persons *susceptible* to colds⟩ **3** : easily affected or impressed ⟨*susceptible* to flattery⟩ — **sus·cep·ti·bly** \-blē\ *adv*

su·shi \'sü-shē, 'sùsh-ē\ *n* : cold rice formed into any of various shapes and topped or wrapped with pieces of often raw seafood or vegetables

¹sus·pect \'səs-ˌpekt\ *adj* : regarded with suspicion

²sus·pect \'səs-ˌpekt\ *n* : one that is suspected; *esp* : a person suspected of a crime

³sus·pect \sə-'spekt\ *vb* **1** : to have doubts about **2** : to believe to be guilty without proof ⟨*suspect* someone of theft⟩ **3** : to suppose to be true or likely ⟨I *suspect* that it will rain⟩

sus·pend \sə-'spend\ *vb* **1** : to force to give up some right or position for a time ⟨*suspend* a student from school⟩ **2 a** : to stop or do away with for a time ⟨*suspend* bus service⟩ **b** : to put off on certain conditions ⟨*suspend* a lawbreaker's sentence⟩ **3 a** : to hang so as to be free on all sides except at the point of support **b** : to keep from falling or sinking by some invisible support ⟨dust *suspended* in the air⟩ **c** : to put or hold in suspension ⟨*suspended* sediment⟩

suspended animation *n* : temporary suspension of the bodily functions necessary to maintain life

sus·pend·er \sə-'spen-dər\ *n* **1** : one that suspends **2** : one of two bands worn across the shoulders to hold up one's pants or skirt — usually used in plural ⟨a pair of *suspenders*⟩

sus·pense \sə-'spen(t)s\ *n* **1** : the state of being suspended : SUSPENSION **2 a** : mental uncertainty : ANXIETY **b** : pleasant excitement caused by wondering what will happen ⟨a novel of *suspense*⟩ **3** : the state of being undecided — **sus·pense·ful** \-fəl\ *adj*

sus·pen·sion \sə-'spen-chən\ *n* **1 a** : the act or an instance of suspending **b** : the state of being suspended **c** : the period during which someone or something is suspended **2** : the act of hanging : the state of being hung **3** : the state of a substance when its particles are mixed with but not dissolved in a fluid or solid; *also* : a substance in this state **4** : something suspended **5** : the system of devices (as springs) supporting the upper part of a vehicle on the axles

suspension bridge *n* : a bridge that has its roadway suspended from two or more cables usually passing over towers and strongly anchored at the ends

¹sus·pi·cion \sə-'spish-ən\ *n* **1** : the act or an instance of suspecting or being suspected **2** : a feeling that something is wrong without definite evidence **3** : a small amount **synonyms** see DOUBT

²suspicion *vb* **sus·pi·cioned; sus·pi·cion·ing** \-'spish-(ə-)niŋ\ *chiefly substandard* : ³SUSPECT

sus·pi·cious \sə-'spish-əs\ *adj* **1** : likely to arouse suspicion : QUESTIONABLE ⟨*suspicious* behavior⟩ **2** : likely to suspect or distrust ⟨*suspicious* of strangers⟩ **3** : showing suspicion ⟨a *suspicious* glance⟩ — **sus·pi·cious·ly** *adv* — **sus·pi·cious·ness** *n*

sus·tain \sə-'stān\ *vb* **1** : to give support or relief to **2** : to supply with nourishment ⟨food *sustains* our bodies⟩ **3** : to keep up : PROLONG ⟨a book that will *sustain* your interest⟩ **4** : to support the weight of : CARRY **5** : to keep up the spirits of ⟨hope *sustained* the people⟩ **6 a** : to bear up under : ENDURE **b** : ²EXPERIENCE, UNDERGO ⟨*sustained* a serious wound⟩ **7 a** : to support as true, legal, or just **b** : to allow or admit as right ⟨the court *sustained* the motion⟩ **8** : PROVE 2a, CONFIRM — **sus·tain·able** \-'stā-nə-bəl\ *adj* — **sus·tain·er** *n*

sus·te·nance \'səs-tə-nən(t)s\ *n* **1 a** : means of support, maintenance, or existence **b** : NOURISHMENT 1 **2** : the act of sustaining : the state of being sustained; *esp* : a supplying with the necessities of life **3** : something that gives support, help, or strength

¹su·ture \'sü-chər\ *n* **1 a** : a stitch made with a suture **b** : a strand or fiber used to sew parts of the living body **c** : the act or process of sewing with sutures **2** : the line of connection in an immovable joint (as between the bones of the skull); *also* : such a joint

²suture *vb* **su·tured; su·tur·ing** \'süch-(ə-)riŋ\ : to unite, close, or secure with sutures ⟨*suture* a wound⟩

SUV \ˌes-ˌyü-'vē\ *n* : SPORT-UTILITY VEHICLE

svelte \'sfelt\ *adj* : slender and graceful in form [from French *svelte* "slender, sleek," from Italian *svelto* (same meaning), derived from *svellere* "to pluck out," derived from Latin *evellere* "to pluck"] — **svelte·ly** *adv* — **svelte·ness** *n*

¹swab \'swäb\ *n* **1 a** : ¹MOP 1 **b** : a wad of absorbent material usually wound around one end of a small stick and used especially for applying medicine or for removing material (as from a wound); *also* : a sample taken with a swab **2** : SAILOR

²swab *vb* **swabbed; swab·bing** : to use a swab on

swad·dle \'swäd-ᵊl\ *vb* **swad·dled; swad·dling** \'swäd-liŋ, -ᵊl-iŋ\ : to wrap an infant with swaddling clothes

swaddling clothes *n pl* : narrow strips of cloth wrapped around an infant to restrict movement

swag \'swag\ *n* : goods acquired by unlawful means

¹swag·ger \'swag-ər\ *vb* **swag·gered; swag·ger·ing** \-(ə-)riŋ\ **1** : to behave in a very proud manner; *esp* : to walk with a proud strut **2** : ²BOAST 1 — **swag·ger·er** \-ər-ər\ *n* — **swag·ger·ing·ly** \-(ə-)riŋ-lē\ *adv*

²swagger *n* : an act or instance of swaggering

swag·man \'swag-mən\ *n, chiefly Australian* : ²TRAMP 1, HOBO

Swa·hi·li \swä-'hē-lē\ *n, pl* **Swahili** *or* **Swahilis 1** : a member of a Bantu-speaking people of Zanzibar and the adjacent coast of Africa **2** : a Bantu language that is a trade and governmental language over much of East Africa and in the Congo region

\ə\ **abut**	\aú\ **out**	\i\ **tip**	\ò\ **saw**	\ú\ **foot**
\ər\ **further**	\ch\ **chin**	\ī\ **life**	\òi\ **coin**	\y\ **yet**
\a\ **mat**	\e\ **pet**	\j\ **job**	\th\ **thin**	\yü\ **few**
\ā\ **take**	\ē\ **easy**	\ŋ\ **sing**	\th\ **this**	\yù\ **cure**
\ä\ **cot, cart**	\g\ **go**	\ō\ **bone**	\ü\ **food**	\zh\ **vision**

swain \'swān\ *n* **1** : ²RUSTIC; *esp* : ¹SHEPHERD 1 **2** : a male admirer or lover

¹**swal·low** \'swäl-ō\ *n* **1** : any of a family of small birds that have long pointed wings and usually a deeply forked tail and that feed on insects caught while in flight **2** : any of several birds that look like true swallows [Old English *swealwe* "the swallow"]

¹swallow 1

²**swallow** *vb* **1 a** : to take into the stomach through the mouth and throat **b** : to perform the actions used in swallowing something ⟨clear your throat and *swallow* before answering⟩ **2** : to take in as if by swallowing : ENGULF **3** : to accept or believe without question, protest, or anger ⟨a hard story to *swallow*⟩ **4** : to keep from expressing or showing : REPRESS ⟨*swallowed* my anger⟩ [Old English *swelgan* "to swallow"] — **swal·low·er** \'swäl-ə-wər\ *n*

³**swallow** *n* **1** : an act of swallowing **2** : an amount that can be swallowed at one time

swal·low·tail \'swäl-ō-ˌtāl\ *n* **1** : a deeply forked and tapering tail (as of a swallow) **2** : any of various usually large butterflies in which the hind wing is elongated into a process that resembles a tail — **swal·low–tailed** \ˌswäl-ō-ˈtāld\ *adj*

swam *past of* SWIM

swa·mi \'swäm-ē\ *n* **1** : a Hindu priest or religious teacher — used as a title **2** : SEER 2

¹**swamp** \'swämp, 'swȯmp\ *n* : wet spongy land often partly covered with water

²**swamp** *vb* **1** : to fill or become filled with or as if with water **2** : OVERWHELM **2** ⟨was *swamped* with work⟩

swamp·land \'swäm-ˌpland, 'swȯm-\ *n* : ¹SWAMP

swampy \'swäm-pē, 'swȯm-\ *adj* **swamp·i·er; -est** : consisting of, relating to, or resembling swamp — **swamp·i·ness** *n*

swan \'swän\ *n, pl* **swans** *also* **swan** : any of various large heavy-bodied long-necked usually pure white water birds with webbed feet that are related to but larger than the geese

swan

¹**swank** \'swaŋk\ *vb* : SHOW OFF 2, SWAGGER

²**swank** *n* **1** : showy display or pride in dress or manners **2** : ELEGANCE 2

³**swank** *or* **swanky** \'swaŋ-kē\ *adj* **swank·er** *or* **swank·i·er; -est** **1** : marked by showy display : OSTENTATIOUS ⟨a *swank* limousine⟩ **2** : fashionably elegant ⟨a *swank* restaurant⟩ — **swank·i·ly** \'swaŋ-kə-lē\ *adv* — **swank·i·ness** \-kē-nəs\ *n*

swan song *n* : a farewell appearance or final act or public statement [from the legend that a dying swan sings a beautiful song]

swap \'swäp\ *vb* **swapped; swap·ping** : to give in exchange : make an exchange : TRADE — **swap** *n*

sward \'swȯ(ə)rd\ *n* : the grassy surface of land : TURF

¹**swarm** \'swȯ(ə)rm\ *n* **1** : a great number of honeybees leaving together from a hive with a queen to start a new colony elsewhere; *also* : a colony of honeybees settled in a hive **2** : a large number grouped together and usually in motion ⟨*swarms* of sightseers⟩ ⟨a *swarm* of meteors⟩

²**swarm** *vb* **1** : to form and leave a hive in a swarm **2** : to move or gather in a swarm : THRONG ⟨spectators *swarmed* into the stadium⟩ **3** : to contain or fill with a swarm

swar·thy \'swȯr-thē, -thē\ *adj* **swar·thi·er; -est** : having a dark complexion — **swar·thi·ness** *n*

¹**swash** \'swäsh, 'swȯsh\ *vb* **1** : ¹BLUSTER **2 2** : to make violent noisy movements **3** : to move with a splashing sound

²**swash** *n* **1** : ²SWAGGER **2** : a dashing of water against or upon something

swash·buck·ler \'swäsh-ˌbək-lər, 'swȯsh-\ *n* : a swaggering or daring soldier or adventurer; *also* : a story or movie about such a man

swash·buck·ling \'swäsh-ˌbək-(ə-)liŋ, 'swȯsh-\ *adj* **1** : acting in the manner of a swashbuckler **2** : characteristic of, marked by, or done by swashbucklers ⟨*swashbuckling* adventure⟩ ⟨a *swashbuckling* tale⟩

swas·ti·ka \'swäs-ti-kə *also* swä-ˈstē-kə\ *n* : a symbol in the form of a cross with the ends of the arms bent at right angles all in the same direction [from a word in Sanskrit (the ancient language of India) *svastika* "a symbol in the form of a cross with bent arms," from *svasti* "well-being"]

swat \'swät\ *vb* **swat·ted; swat·ting** : to hit with a quick hard blow — **swat** *n* — **swat·ter** *n*

swatch \'swäch\ *n* **1** : a sample piece (as of fabric) or a collection of samples **2** : ¹PATCH 3 ⟨*swatches* of hair⟩

swath \'swäth, 'swȯth\ *or* **swathe** \'swäth, 'swȯth, 'swäth\ *n* **1 a** : the sweep of a scythe or machine in mowing or the path cut in one course **b** : a row of cut grain or grass **2** : a long broad strip or belt **3** : a space destroyed as if by a mowing machine

¹**swathe** \'swäth, 'swȯth, 'swäth\ *vb* **swathed; swath·ing** **1** : to bind, wrap, or swaddle with or as if with a bandage **2** : ENVELOP

²**swathe** \'swäth, 'swȯth, 'swäth\ *or* **swath** \'swäth, 'swäth, 'swȯth, 'swȯth\ *n* : a band used in swathing

¹**sway** \'swā\ *n* **1** : the action or an instance of swaying or of being swayed **2** : a bending or twisting caused by or as if by swaying **3** : controlling force or influence : RULE

²**sway** *vb* **1 a** : to swing or cause to swing slowly back and forth **b** : to move gently from an upright to a leaning position **2** : to change often between one point, position, or opinion and another **3** : to have a strong influence upon — **sway·er** *n*

sway·backed \'swā-ˈbakt\ *also* **sway·back** \-ˈbak, -ˌbak\ *adj* : having an unusually sagging back ⟨a *swaybacked* mare⟩ — **sway·back** *n*

swear \'swa(ə)r, 'swe(ə)r\ *vb* **swore** \'swō(ə)r, 'swȯ(ə)r\; **sworn** \'swō(ə)rn, 'swȯ(ə)rn\; **swear·ing** **1** : to make a statement or promise under oath **2 a** : to state as true under oath ⟨a *sworn* statement⟩ **b** : to state or promise strongly or sincerely ⟨I *swear* that I was there⟩ **3 a** : to give an oath to ⟨the witness was *sworn*⟩ **b** : to bind by an oath ⟨*swore* us to secrecy⟩ **4** : to take an oath **5** : to use bad or vulgar language — **swear·er** *n* — **swear by** : to place great confidence in — **swear off** : to promise to give up ⟨*swear off* desserts⟩

swear in *vb* : to place into office by the giving of an oath

swear·word \'swa(ə)r-ˌwərd, 'swe(ə)r-\ *n* : a bad or vulgar word

¹**sweat** \'swet\ *vb* **sweat** *or* **sweat·ed; sweat·ing** **1** : to give off salty moisture through the pores of the skin : PERSPIRE **2** : to give off or cause to give off moisture **3** : to collect drops of moisture on the surface ⟨a pitcher of ice water *sweats* on a hot day⟩ **4 a** : to undergo anxiety or stress ⟨*sweated* through the test⟩ **b** *slang* : to worry about **5** : to get rid of or lose by perspiring ⟨*sweat* off weight⟩ **6** : to work very hard

²**sweat** *n* **1** : hard work **2** : moisture coming from the sweat glands of the skin : PERSPIRATION **3** : moisture gathering in drops on a surface

sweat·band \'swet-ˌband\ *n* **1** : a band lining the edge of a hat or cap to prevent sweat damage **2** : a band of material worn around the head or wrist to absorb sweat

sweat·er \'swet-ər\ *n* **1** : one that sweats or causes sweating **2** : a knitted or crocheted jacket or pullover

sweat gland *n* : a gland of the skin that gives off perspiration and opens by a tiny pore in the skin

sweat lodge *n* : a hut, lodge, or cavern heated by steam from water poured on hot stones and used especially by American Indians for ritual or therapeutic sweating

sweat out *vb* : to suffer or wait through the course of ⟨*sweated out* the afternoon waiting for the results⟩

sweat·pants \'swet-ˌpan(t)s\ *n pl* : pants of soft absorbent material worn especially for exercise

sweat·shirt \-ˌshərt\ *n* : a loose collarless usually long-sleeved pullover or jacket of soft absorbent material

sweat·shop \-ˌshäp\ *n* : a shop or factory in which employees work long hours at low wages under unhealthy conditions

sweaty \'swet-ē\ *adj* **sweat·i·er; -est** **1** : causing sweat ⟨*sweaty* work⟩ **2** : wet or stained with or smelling of sweat ⟨*sweaty* socks⟩ — **sweat·i·ly** \'swet-ᵊl-ē\ *adv* — **sweat·i·ness** \'swet-ē-nəs\ *n*

swede \'swēd\ *n* **1** *cap* **a** : a person born or living in Sweden **b** : a person of Swedish ancestry **2** *chiefly British* : RUTABAGA

Swed·ish \'swēd-ish\ *n* **1** : the Germanic language spoken in Sweden **2 Swedish** *pl* : the people of Sweden — **Swedish** *adj*

¹**sweep** \'swēp\ *vb* **swept** \'swept\; **sweep·ing 1 a** : to remove from a surface with or as if with a broom or brush ⟨*sweep* the dirt off the rug⟩ **b** : to remove or take with a single continuous forceful action ⟨*swept* the books off the desk⟩ **c** : to drive or carry along with great force **2 a** : to clean with or as if with a broom or brush ⟨*sweep* the floor⟩ **b** : to move across or along swiftly, violently, or overwhelmingly ⟨a storm *swept* across the plains⟩ **c** : to win all of ⟨the presidential candidate *swept* the western states⟩ **3** : to move with stately or sweeping movements ⟨*swept* into the room⟩ **4** : to move or extend in a wide curve or range — **sweep·er** *n*

²**sweep** *n* **1** : a long movable pole on a post that is used to raise and lower a bucket (as in a well) **2 a** : an act or instance of sweeping **b** : a decisive victory **c** : a winning of all the contests **3 a** : a movement of great range and force **b** : a curving or circular course or line **c** : ¹RANGE 6a, SCOPE ⟨outside the *sweep* of our vision⟩ **4** : CHIMNEY SWEEP **5** : SWEEPSTAKES

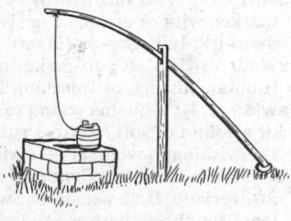

²sweep 1

¹**sweep·ing** *n* **1** : the act or action of one that sweeps **2** *pl* : things collected by sweeping

²**sweeping** *adj* **1 a** : moving or extending in a wide curve or over a wide area **b** : having a curving line or form **2** : BROAD 5 ⟨*sweeping* reforms⟩ ⟨*sweeping* generalizations⟩ — **sweep·ing·ly** \'swē-piŋ-lē\ *adv*

sweep–second hand \'swēp-ˌsek-ənd-, -ᵊnt-\ *n* : a hand marking seconds on a timepiece that is read from the same dial as the minute hand

sweep·stakes \'swēp-ˌstāks\ *also* **sweep–stake** \-ˌstāk\ *n, pl* **sweepstakes** *also* **sweep–stakes 1 a** : a race or contest in which the entire prize may be awarded to the winner **b** : ²CONTEST, COMPETITION **2** : any of various lotteries

¹**sweet** \'swēt\ *adj* **1 a** : pleasing to the taste **b** : being or causing the one of the four basic taste sensations that is caused especially by table sugar and is identified especially by the taste buds at the front of the tongue — compare BITTER 1, ³SALT 1b, ¹SOUR 1 **c** : having a relatively large sugar content ⟨*sweet* wine⟩ **2 a** : pleasing to the mind or feelings : AGREEABLE ⟨victory is *sweet*⟩ **b**

: marked by gentle good humor or kindliness ⟨a *sweet* elderly couple⟩ **c** : FRAGRANT ⟨a *sweet* smell⟩ **d** : delicately pleasing to the ear or eye ⟨a *sweet* melody⟩ **e** : very good or appealing ⟨a *sweet* sports car⟩ ⟨a *sweet* deal⟩ **3** : much loved : DEAR **4 a** : not sour, stale, or spoiled ⟨*sweet* milk⟩ **b** : not salt or salted : FRESH ⟨*sweet* butter⟩ **c** : not having too much acid ⟨*sweet* soil⟩ **d** : free from foul gases and odors **5** — used as an intensive ⟨take your own *sweet* time⟩ — **sweet·ish** \-ish\ *adj* — **sweet·ly** *adv* — **sweet·ness** *n* — **sweet on** : in love with

²**sweet** *adv* : in a sweet way

³**sweet** *n* **1 a** : a food (as a candy) having a high sugar content **b** *British* : DESSERT **2** : a sweet taste sensation **3** : a pleasant or agreeable experience, possession, or state **4** : ¹DARLING 1

sweet basil *n* : a mint that has clusters of whitish or purple flowers and leaves often used as a seasoning in cooking

sweet·bread \'swēt-ˌbred\ *n* : the thymus or pancreas of a young animal (as a calf) used as food

sweet·bri·ar *also* **sweet·bri·er** \-ˌbrī(-ə)r\ *n* : a rose with stout curved prickles and white to deep rosy pink flowers — called also *eglantine*

sweet clover *n* : any of a genus of herbs of the legume family widely grown for soil improvement or hay

sweet corn *n* : corn with soft kernels containing a large amount of sugar

sweet·en \'swēt-ᵊn\ *vb* **sweet·ened; sweet·en·ing** \'swēt-niŋ, -ᵊn-iŋ\ : to make or become sweet — **sweet·en·er** \'swēt-nər, -ᵊn-ər\ *n*

sweet·en·ing *n* **1** : the act or process of making sweet **2** : something that sweetens

sweet gum *n* : a North American tree that has lobed leaves, hard wood, and a long-stemmed woody round fruit; *also* : its wood

sweet·heart \'swēt-ˌhärt\ *n* : a person whom one loves

sweet·meat \-ˌmēt\ *n* : a food (as a candied fruit or piece of candy) rich in sugar

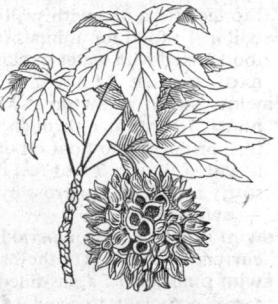

sweet gum

sweet pea *n* **1** : a widely grown Italian herb of the legume family with slender climbing stems and large fragrant flowers **2** : the flower of a sweet pea

sweet pepper *n* : a large mild-flavored thick-walled pepper; *also* : a pepper plant that bears sweet peppers

sweet potato *n* **1** : a tropical vine related to the morning glories and having variously shaped leaves and purplish flowers; *also* : its large sweet starchy root that is cooked and eaten as a vegetable **2** : OCARINA

sweet tooth *n* : a craving or fondness for sweets

sweet wil·liam \swēt-'wil-yəm\ *n, often cap W* : a widely grown Eurasian pink with small white to deep red or purple flowers that are often spotted or banded and grow in flat clusters on upright stems

¹**swell** \'swel\ *vb* **swelled; swelled** *or* **swol·len** \'swō-lən\; **swell·ing 1 a** : to expand (as in size, volume, or numbers) gradually beyond a normal or original limit ⟨rivers *swollen* by rain⟩ ⟨the population *swelled*⟩ **b** : to become abnormally enlarged or puffed up ⟨the sprained ankle

\ə\ **abut**	\au̇\ **out**	\i\ **tip**	\ȯ\ **saw**	\u̇\ **foot**
\ər\ **further**	\ch\ **chin**	\ī\ **life**	\ȯi\ **coin**	\y\ **yet**
\a\ **mat**	\e\ **pet**	\j\ **job**	\th\ **thin**	\yü\ **few**
\ā\ **take**	\ē\ **easy**	\ŋ\ **sing**	\th\ **this**	\yu̇\ **cure**
\ä\ **cot, cart**	\g\ **go**	\ō\ **bone**	\ü\ **food**	\zh\ **vision**

swelled badly〉 **c** : to form a bulge or lump **2** : to fill or become filled with pride **3** : to fill or become filled with emotion 〈his heart was *swollen* with jealousy〉 **synonyms** see EXPAND

²**swell** *n* **1 a** : a rounded lump **b** : the condition of bulging **2** : a long rolling wave or series of waves in the open sea **3** : a gradual increase and decrease of the loudness of a musical sound; *also* : a sign marking a swell **4** : a fashionably dressed person

³**swell** *adj* : very good : EXCELLENT

swell·ing \'swel-iŋ\ *n* **1** : something that is swollen; *esp* : a swollen part of the body **2** : the condition of being swollen

¹**swel·ter** \'swel-tər\ *vb* **swel·tered; swel·ter·ing** \-t(ə-)riŋ\ **1** : to suffer, sweat, or be faint from heat **2** : to overcome with heat

²**swelter** *n* : a state of great heat

swel·ter·ing *adj* : very hot — **swel·ter·ing·ly** *adv*

swept *past and past participle of* SWEEP

swept–back \'swep(t)-'bak\ *adj* : slanting toward the tail of an airplane to form an acute angle with the body 〈*swept-back* wings〉

swerve \'swərv\ *vb* **swerved; swerv·ing** : to turn aside suddenly from a straight line or course — **swerve** *n*

¹**swift** \'swift\ *adj* **1** : moving or capable of moving with great speed 〈a *swift* runner〉 **2** : occurring suddenly or within a very short time 〈a *swift* change in weather〉 **synonyms** see FAST — **swift·ly** *adv* — **swift·ness** \'swif(t)-nəs\ *n*

²**swift** *adv* : in a swift manner

³**swift** *n* : any of numerous small mostly dark birds that are related to the hummingbirds but resemble swallows

¹**swig** \'swig\ *n* : a quantity drunk at one time

²**swig** *vb* **swigged; swig·ging** : to drink in long gulps

¹**swill** \'swil\ *vb* **1** : DRENCH **2** : to drink or eat greedily **3** : to feed (as a pig) with swill — **swill·er** *n*

²**swill** *n* **1** : food for animals (as pigs) made from scraps of food mixed with water or skimmed or sour milk **2** : GARBAGE, REFUSE **3** : ¹SWIG

¹**swim** \'swim\ *vb* **swam** \'swam\; **swum** \'swəm\; **swim·ming 1** : to move through water by moving arms, legs, fins, or tail **2** : to float on or in or be covered with or as if with a liquid **3** : to feel dizzy 〈my head *swam* in the stuffy room〉 **4** : to cross by swimming 〈*swim* a stream〉 — **swim·mer** *n*

²**swim** *n* **1** : an act or period of swimming **2** : the main current of activity 〈in the *swim* of things〉

swim bladder *n* : a gas-filled expandable sac in fish that serves especially to regulate buoyancy which allows fish to remain at different depths without sinking

swimmer's ear *n* : redness, swelling, and pain of the ear canal that typically occurs when water trapped in the ear canal during swimming becomes infected usually with bacteria

swim·ming \'swim-iŋ\ *adj* : marked by, capable of, or used in or for swimming

swim·ming·ly \'swim-iŋ-lē\ *adv* : very well : SPLENDIDLY

swimming pool *n* : a large tank built for swimming

swim·suit \'swim-ˌsüt\ *n* : a suit for swimming or bathing

swim·wear \-ˌwa(ə)r, -ˌwe(ə)r\ *n* : clothing suitable for swimming

¹**swin·dle** \'swin-dᵊl\ *vb* **swin·dled; swin·dling** \-(d)liŋ, -dᵊl-iŋ\ : to get money or property from by dishonest means : CHEAT — **swin·dler** \-(d)lər, -dᵊl-ər\ *n*

²**swindle** *n* : an act or instance of swindling : FRAUD

swine \'swīn\ *n, pl* **swine 1** : any of a family of stout-bodied short-legged hoofed mammals with a thick bristly skin and a long

swine 1

snout; *esp* : a domestic animal developed from the European wild boar and raised for meat **2** : a nasty person

swine·herd \'swīn-ˌhərd\ *n* : a person who tends swine

¹**swing** \'swiŋ\ *vb* **swung** \'swəŋ\; **swing·ing** \'swiŋ-iŋ\ **1 a** : to move quickly in a sweeping curve 〈*swing* an ax〉 **b** : to sway or cause to sway to and fro or turn on an axis or hinge 〈*swung* the door open〉 **c** : to face or move in another direction 〈go forward, then *swing* to the right〉 **2 a** : to hang or be hung so as to permit swaying or turning **b** : to die by hanging **c** : to hang freely from support **d** : to change quickly between extremes 〈sales *swung* up sharply〉 **3** : to handle successfully : MANAGE 〈can you *swing* the purchase of a car〉 **4 a** : to move along with free swaying movements **b** : to start up in a smooth vigorous manner 〈ready to *swing* into action〉 **c** : to hit at something with a sweeping movement **5** : to be lively, exciting, and up-to-date 〈a town that really *swings*〉 — **swing·er** \'swiŋ-ər\ *n*

²**swing** *n* **1** : an act of swinging **2** : a swinging movement, blow, or rhythm **3** : the distance that something swings 〈a pendulum with a 5-foot *swing*〉 **4** : a swinging seat usually hung by ropes or chains **5 a** : a curving course or outline **b** : a course beginning and ending at the same point 〈a *swing* through town〉 **c** : a sudden change in state or condition 〈mood *swings*〉 — **swing** *adj*

swin·ish \'swī-nish\ *adj* : of, suggesting, or characteristic of swine : BEASTLY — **swin·ish·ly** *adv*

¹**swipe** \'swīp\ *vb* **swiped; swip·ing 1** : to strike or wipe with a sweeping motion **2** : PILFER **3** : to slide (a card with a magnetic strip or bar code) through a slot in a reading device so that information stored on the strip can be processed (as in making a purchase)

²**swipe** *n* : a strong sweeping blow

¹**swirl** \'swər(-ə)l\ *n* **1** : a whirling mass or motion : EDDY **2** : whirling confusion 〈lost in the *swirl* of events〉 **3** : a twisting shape, mark, or pattern

²**swirl** *vb* **1** : to move with or pass in a swirl **2** : to be marked with or arranged in swirls **3** : to cause to swirl — **swirl·ing·ly** \'swər-liŋ-lē\ *adv*

¹**swish** \'swish\ *vb* : to make, move, or strike with a soft rubbing, hissing, or splashing sound

²**swish** *n* **1** : a hissing sound (as of a whip cutting the air) or a sound of soft surfaces rubbing against each other **2** : a swishing movement — **swishy** \-ē\ *adj*

Swiss \'swis\ *n* **1** *pl* **Swiss a** : a person born or living in Switzerland **b** : a person of Swiss ancestry **2** : a pale yellow firm cheese with many large holes — **Swiss** *adj*

Swiss chard *n* : a beet of a variety lacking an enlarged root and having large leaves and juicy stalks often cooked as a vegetable; *also* : the stalks

Swiss steak *n* : a steak pounded with flour and cooked usually with vegetables and seasonings

¹**switch** \'swich\ *n* **1** : a slender flexible whip, rod, or twig **2** : an act or an instance of switching **3** : a bunch of long hairs at the end of the tail of an animal (as a cow) **4** : a device made usually of two movable rails and necessary connections and designed to turn a train or streetcar from one track to another **5** : a device for making, breaking, or changing the connections in an electrical circuit

²**switch** *vb* **1** : to strike or whip with or as if with a switch **2** : to lash from side to side **3** : to turn, shift, or change by or as if by operating a switch 〈*switch* off the light〉 〈*switched* to a different channel〉 **4** : to change one for another : EXCHANGE 〈*switch* seats〉 — **switch·er** *n*

switch·back \'swich-ˌbak\ *n* : a zigzag road, trail, or section of railroad tracks for climbing a steep hill

switch·blade \-ˌblād\ *n* : a pocketknife with a spring-operated blade

switch·board \-ˌbō(ə)rd, -ˌbȯ(ə)rd\ *n* : a device (as in a telephone exchange) consisting of a panel on which are mounted electric switches so arranged that a number of circuits may be connected, combined, and controlled

switch–hit·ter \-ˌhit-ər\ *n* : a baseball player who can bat either left-handed or right-handed

switch·man \-mən\ *n* : one who attends a railroad switch

switch·yard \-ˌyärd\ *n* : a place where railroad cars are switched from one track to another and trains are made up

¹swiv·el \'swiv-əl\ *n* : a device joining two parts so that one or both can turn freely

²swivel *vb* **-eled** *or* **-elled; -el·ing** *or* **-el·ling** \'swiv-(ə-)liŋ\ : to turn on or as if on a swivel

swivel chair *n* : a chair that swivels on its base

swollen *past participle of* SWELL

¹swoon \'swün\ *vb* **1** : ²FAINT **2** : to drift or fade gradually — **swoon·er** *n* — **swoon·ing·ly** \'swü-niŋ-lē\ *adv*

²swoon *n* **1** : a partial or total loss of consciousness **2** : a dreamlike state

¹swoop \'swüp\ *vb* : to dive or pounce suddenly like a hawk on its prey

²swoop *n* **1** : an act or instance of swooping **2** : a single quickly effective effort — often used with *fell* ⟨solved everything at one fell *swoop*⟩

swoosh \'swüsh, 'swu̇sh\ *vb* : to make or move with a rushing sound — **swoosh** *n*

swop *chiefly British variant of* SWAP

sword \'sō(ə)rd, 'sȯ(ə)rd\ *n* **1** : a weapon having a long blade usually with a sharp point and edge **2** : the use of force — **sword·like** \-ˌlīk\ *adj*

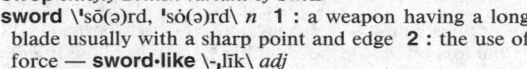

^1swivel

sword·fish \-ˌfish\ *n* : a very large ocean fish that has a long swordlike beak formed by the bones of the upper jaw and is an important food and game fish

swordfish

sword·play \-ˌplā\ *n* : the art or skill of using a sword especially in fencing

swords·man \'sō(ə)rdz-mən, 'sȯ(ə)rdz-\ *n* **1** : one who fights with a sword **2** : one skilled in the use of the sword

swords·man·ship \'sō(ə)rdz-mən-ˌship, 'sȯ(ə)rdz-\ *n* : SWORDPLAY

sword·tail \'sō(ə)rd-ˌtāl, 'sȯ(ə)rd-\ *n* : a small brightly marked Central American fish often kept in tropical aquariums and bred in many colors

swore *past of* SWEAR

sworn *past participle of* SWEAR

swum *past participle of* SWIM

swung *past and past participle of* SWING

syc·a·more \'sik-ə-ˌmō(ə)r, -ˌmȯ(ə)r\ *n* **1** : a Eurasian maple with yellowish green flowers that is widely planted as a shade tree **2** : a large spreading tree of the eastern and central U.S. that has light-brown bark peeling off in thin flakes and small round brown fruits hanging on long stalks

sy·co·phant \'sik-ə-fənt *also* -ˌfant\ *n* : a person who flatters another in order to get ahead — **sy·co·phan·tic** \ˌsik-ə-'fant-ik\ *adj* — **sy·co·phan·ti·cal·ly** \-'fant-i-k(ə-)lē\ *adv*

sy·enite \'sī-ə-ˌnīt\ *n* : an igneous rock composed chiefly of feldspar

syl·la·bary \'sil-ə-ˌber-ē\ *n, pl* **-bar·ies** : a set of written characters each of which stands for a syllable

syl·lab·ic \sə-'lab-ik\ *adj* : of, relating to, or being syllables — **syl·lab·i·cal·ly** \-i-k(ə-)lē\ *adv*

syl·lab·i·ca·tion \sə-ˌlab-ə-'kā-shən\ *n* : the forming of syllables : the division of words into syllables — **syl·lab·i·cate** \-'lab-ə-ˌkāt\ *vb*

syl·lab·i·fi·ca·tion \sə-ˌlab-ə-fə-'kā-shən\ *n* : SYLLABICA-TION

syl·lab·i·fy \sə-'lab-ə-ˌfī\ *vb* **-fied; -fy·ing** : to form or divide into syllables

syl·la·ble \'sil-ə-bəl\ *n* **1** : a unit of spoken language that consists of one or more vowel sounds alone or with one or more consonant sounds preceding or following **2** : one or more letters (as *syl, la,* and *ble*) in a word (as *syl·la·ble*) usually set off from the rest of the word by a centered dot or a hyphen and treated as guides to division at the end of a line

syl·la·bus \'sil-ə-bəs\ *n, pl* **-bi** \-ˌbī, -ˌbē\ *or* **-bus·es** : a brief outline (as of a course of study)

syl·lo·gism \'sil-ə-ˌjiz-əm\ *n* : a brief form for stating an argument that consists of two statements and a conclusion that must be true if these two statements are true — **syl·lo·gis·tic** \ˌsil-ə-'jis-tik\ *adj*

sylph \'silf\ *n* : a slender graceful woman or girl — **sylph·like** \'sil-ˌflīk\ *adj*

syl·van *also* **sil·van** \'sil-vən\ *adj* **1 a** : living or located in the woods or forest **b** : of, relating to, or characteristic of the woods or forest **2** : having lots of woods or trees : WOODED

sym·bi·ont \'sim-ˌbī-ˌänt, -bē-\ *n* : an individual living in symbiosis; *esp* : the smaller member of a symbiotic pair

sym·bi·o·sis \ˌsim-ˌbī-'ō-səs, -bē-\ *n, pl* **-o·ses** \-'ō-ˌsēz\ **1** : the living together in close association of two different kinds of organisms (as a fungus and an alga making up a lichen) especially when such an association is of benefit to both **2** : a cooperative relationship (as between two persons or groups) — **sym·bi·ot·ic** \-'ät-ik\ *adj* — **sym·bi·ot·i·cal·ly** \-i-k(ə-)lē\ *adv*

sym·bol \'sim-bəl\ *n* **1** : something that stands for something else; *esp* : something real that stands for or suggests another thing that cannot in itself be pictured or shown ⟨the lion is a *symbol* of courage⟩ **2** : a letter, character, or sign used instead of a word or group of words ⟨the sign + is the *symbol* for addition⟩ **synonyms** see EMBLEM

sym·bol·ic \sim-'bäl-ik\ *also* **sym·bol·i·cal** \-i-kəl\ *adj* **1** : of, relating to, or using symbols or symbolism ⟨a *symbolic* meaning⟩ ⟨*symbolic* art⟩ **2** : having the function or meaning of a symbol — **sym·bol·i·cal·ly** \-i-k(ə-)lē\ *adv*

sym·bol·ism \'sim-bə-ˌliz-əm\ *n* **1** : the art or practice of using symbols **2** : a system of symbols or representations

sym·bol·ist \'sim-bə-ləst\ *n* **1** : a user of symbols or symbolism (as in poetry) **2** : an expert in the explaining of symbols — **symbolist** *adj*

sym·bol·is·tic \ˌsim-bə-'lis-tik\ *adj* : SYMBOLIC

sym·bol·ize \'sim-bə-ˌlīz\ *vb* **-ized; -iz·ing** : to serve as a symbol of — **sym·bol·i·za·tion** \ˌsim-bə-lə-'zā-shən\ *n*

sym·met·ri·cal \sə-'me-tri-kəl\ *or* **sym·met·ric** \-trik\ *adj* : having, involving, or showing symmetry — **sym·met·ri·cal·ly** \-tri-k(ə-)lē\ *adv*

sym·me·try \'sim-ə-trē\ *n, pl* **-tries** **1** : balanced proportions **2** : close agreement in size, shape, and relative position of parts on opposite sides of a dividing line or plane or around a central point — compare BILATERAL SYM-METRY, RADIAL SYMMETRY

sym·pa·thet·ic \ˌsim-pə-'thet-ik\ *adj* **1** : fitting one's mood or disposition ⟨a *sympathetic* atmosphere for quiet study⟩ **2 a** : feeling favorable ⟨*sympathetic* with their aims⟩ **b** : marked by kindly or pleased appreciation ⟨a *sympathetic* study of modern music⟩ **3** : given to or arising from sympathy and sensitivity to others ⟨a *sympathetic* personality⟩ **4 a** : of or relating to the sympathetic nervous system **b** : controlled by or acting on the sympathetic nerves — **sym·pa·thet·i·cal·ly** \-i-k(ə-)lē\ *adv*

sympathetic nervous system *n* : the part of the autonomic nervous system that is concerned especially with preparing the body to react to situations of stress or

\ə\ **abut**	\au̇\ **out**	\i\ **tip**	\ȯ\ **saw**	\u̇\ **foot**
\ər\ **further**	\ch\ **chin**	\ī\ **life**	\ȯi\ **coin**	\y\ **yet**
\a\ **mat**	\e\ **pet**	\j\ **job**	\th\ **thin**	\yü\ **few**
\ā\ **take**	\ē\ **easy**	\ŋ\ **sing**	\th\ **this**	\yu̇\ **cure**
\ä\ **cot, cart**	\g\ **go**	\ō\ **bone**	\ü\ **food**	\zh\ **vision**

emergency, that controls expansion of the pupil of the eye and air passages, increases the heart rate, slows digestion, and narrows most blood vessels, and that is made up of nerve fibers that trigger the release of norepinephrine — compare PARASYMPATHETIC NERVOUS SYSTEM

sympathetic vibration *n* : a vibration produced in one body by vibrations of exactly the same period in a neighboring body

sym·pa·thize \'sim-pə-ˌthīz\ *vb* **-thized; -thiz·ing 1** : to share in suffering or grief : to feel or show sympathy **2** : to be in favor of something — **sym·pa·thiz·er** *n*

sym·pa·thy \'sim-pə-thē\ *n, pl* **-thies 1** : a relationship between persons or things in which whatever affects one also affects the other **2 a** : the readiness to think or feel alike that makes for a common bond **b** : readiness to favor or support **3** : the act of or capacity for entering into or sharing the feelings or interests of another **4** : a showing of sorrow for another's loss, grief, or misfortune

sym·phon·ic \sim-'fän-ik\ *adj* **1** : HARMONIOUS 1 **2** : of, relating to, or having the form of a symphony or symphony orchestra — **sym·phon·i·cal·ly** \-i-k(ə-)lē\ *adv*

sym·pho·ny \'sim(p)-fə-nē\ *n, pl* **-nies 1** : harmonious arrangement (as of sound or color) ⟨a *symphony* of sounds in the forest⟩ **2** : a usually long musical composition for a full orchestra **3** : SYMPHONY ORCHESTRA [Middle English *symphonie* "pleasing arrangement of sounds," from early French *symphonie* (same meaning), derived from Greek *syn-* "together" and *phōnē* "voice, sound" — related to EUPHONY, PHONETIC]

symphony orchestra *n* : a large orchestra of wind, string, and percussion instruments that plays symphonic works

sym·po·sium \sim-'pō-zē-əm *also* -zh(ē-)əm\ *n, pl* **-sia** \-zē-ə, -zh(ē-)ə\ *or* **-siums 1** : a group meeting at which there are several speeches and often a group discussion **2** : a collection of opinions on a subject [from earlier *symposium* "a social gathering at which there is a free exchange of ideas," from Latin *symposium* "a party with much drinking and conversation," derived from Greek *sympinein* "to drink together," from *syn-* "together with" and *pinein* "to drink" — related to SYNONYMOUS]

symp·tom \'sim(p)-təm\ *n* **1** : a change in a living thing that indicates the presence of a disease or other physical disorder; *esp* : one (as a headache) that can be felt or sensed only by the individual affected **2** : something that shows that something else exists : INDICATION *synonyms* see ¹SIGN — **symp·tom·less** \-ləs\ *adj*

symp·tom·at·ic \ˌsim(p)-tə-'mat-ik\ *adj* **1 a** : being a symptom (as of disease) ⟨an itchy skin rash is *symptomatic* of poison ivy⟩ **b** : concerned with, affecting, or having symptoms ⟨a *symptomatic* patient⟩ **2** : showing a quality or identity : CHARACTERISTIC — **symp·tom·at·i·cal·ly** \-i-k(ə-)lē\ *adv*

syn·a·gogue *also* **syn·a·gog** \'sin-ə-ˌgäg\ *n* **1** : a Jewish congregation **2** : the house of worship of a Jewish congregation [Middle English *synagoge* "a Jewish congregation," from early French *synagoge* (same meaning), from Latin *synagoga* (same meaning), from Greek *synagōgē* "synagogue, assembly," from *synagein* "to bring together," from *syn-* "together with" and *agein* "to lead" — related to SYNONYMOUS]

syn·apse \'sin-ˌaps, sə-'naps\ *n* : the point at which a nerve impulse passes from one neuron to another

syn·ap·sis \sə-'nap-səs\ *n, pl* **-ap·ses** \-ˌsēz\ : the pairing of homologous chromosomes that occurs in prophase of the first meiotic division and during which crossing-over may occur

syn·chro·nize \'siŋ-krə-ˌnīz, 'sin-\ *vb* **-nized; -niz·ing** : to cause to agree in time ⟨*synchronize* your watches⟩

syn·chro·nous \'siŋ-krə-nəs, 'sin-\ *adj* : happening or existing at the same time : SIMULTANEOUS [from Latin *synchronos* "synchronous," from Greek *synchronos* (same

meaning), from *syn-* "together, along with" and *chronos* "time" — related to CHRONICLE, SYNONYMOUS]

syn·cline \'sin-ˌklīn\ *n* : a place in the earth's crust where the rock layers curve downward — compare ANTICLINE

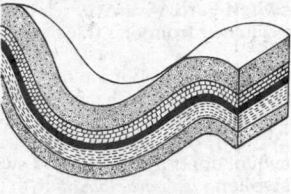
syncline

syn·co·pate \'siŋ-kə-ˌpāt, 'sin-\ *vb* **-pat·ed; -pat·ing 1** : to cut short : CLIP, ABBREVIATE **2** : to change or affect (musical rhythm) by syncopation — **syn·co·pa·tor** \-ˌpāt-ər\ *n*

syn·co·pa·tion \ˌsiŋ-kə-'pā-shən, ˌsin-\ *n* **1** : a temporary accenting of a normally weak beat in music to vary the rhythm **2** : a syncopated rhythm, passage, or dance step

syncopation 2

syn·co·pe \'siŋ-kə-(ˌ)pē, 'sin-\ *n* **1** : ³FAINT, ²SWOON 1 **2** : the loss of one or more sounds or letters in the middle of a word (as in *fo'c'sle* for *forecastle*)

¹syn·di·cate \'sin-di-kət\ *n* **1** : an association of persons involved in some official duty or business **2** : an association of people involved in organized crime **3** : a business concern that sells materials for publication at the same time in a number of newspapers or magazines

²syn·di·cate \'sin-də-ˌkāt\ *vb* **-cat·ed; -cat·ing 1** : to operate as a syndicate **2** : to sell (as a cartoon) for publication in several newspapers or magazines at once; *also* : to sell the work of (as a writer) in this way ⟨a *syndicated* columnist⟩ **3** : to join to form a syndicate — **syn·di·ca·tion** \ˌsin-də-'kā-shən\ *n* — **syn·di·ca·tor** \'sin-də-ˌkāt-ər\ *n*

syn·drome \'sin-ˌdrōm\ *n* : a group of signs and symptoms that occur together and characterize a particular abnormality or condition

syn·er·gism \'sin-ər-ˌjiz-əm\ *n* : action between individual parts or forces that produces a total result that is greater than the sum of the individual results — **syn·er·gist** \-jəst\ *n*

syn·er·gis·tic \ˌsin-ər-'jis-tik\ *adj* : of, relating to, or able to act in synergism ⟨*synergistic* drugs⟩

syn·od \'sin-əd\ *n* **1** : a meeting of church leaders **2** : the governing or advisory council of a church — **syn·od·al** \'sin-əd-ᵊl\ *adj* — **syn·od·i·cal** \sə-'näd-i-kəl\ *adj*

syn·onym \'sin-ə-ˌnim\ *n* : a word having the same or almost the same meaning as another word in the same language — **syn·onym·i·ty** \ˌsin-ə-'nim-ət-ē\ *n*

syn·on·y·mize \sə-'nän-ə-ˌmīz\ *vb* **-mized; -miz·ing** : to list or discuss the synonyms of a word

syn·on·y·mous \sə-'nän-ə-məs\ *adj* **1** : alike in meaning **2** : suggesting the same thing ⟨a brand name that is *synonymous* with quality⟩ [from Latin *synonymus* "synonymous," from Greek *synōnymos*, literally, "having the same name," from *syn-* "together, along with" and *onyma, onoma* "name" — related to ANONYMOUS, SYMPOSIUM, SYNAGOGUE, SYNCHRONOUS] — **syn·on·y·mous·ly** *adv*

syn·on·y·my \sə-'nän-ə-mē\ *n, pl* **-mies 1 a** : the study or discussion of synonyms **b** : a list or collection of synonyms often defined and discussed **2** : the quality or state of being synonymous

syn·op·sis \sə-'näp-səs\ *n, pl* **-op·ses** \-'näp-ˌsēz\ : a brief statement or outline (as of a story)

syn·tac·tic \sin-'tak-tik\ *or* **syn·tac·ti·cal** \-ti-kəl\ *adj* : of, relating to, or according to the rules of syntax — **syn-tac-ti-cal-ly** \-ti-k(ə-)lē\ *adv*

syn-tax \'sin-ˌtaks\ *n* : the way in which words are put together to form phrases, clauses, or sentences

syn-the-sis \'sin(t)-thə-səs\ *n, pl* **-the-ses** \-thə-ˌsēz\ **1** : the combination of parts or elements so as to form a whole; *esp* : the production of a substance by union of chemically simpler substances **2 a** : the combining of often very different ideas into an ordered whole **b** : the product so formed

syn-the-size \'sin(t)-thə-ˌsīz\ *vb* **-sized; -siz-ing** : to combine or produce by synthesis

syn-the-siz-er \-ˌsī-zər\ *n* **1** : one that synthesizes **2** : a computer-controlled device that creates and modifies sound (as for producing music)

¹syn-thet-ic \sin-'thet-ik\ *adj* **1** : relating to or involving synthesis **2** : of, relating to, or produced by chemical synthesis; *esp* : produced artificially ⟨*synthetic* drugs⟩ ⟨*synthetic* fibers⟩ — **syn-thet-i-cal-ly** \-'thet-i-k(ə-)lē\ *adv*

²synthetic *n* : a product of chemical synthesis

syph-i-lis \'sif-(ə-)ləs\ *n* : a venereal disease that is caused by a spirochete and if left untreated is marked by a series of three stages extending over many years — **syph-i-lit-ic** \ˌsif-ə-'lit-ik\ *adj or n*

sy-phon *variant of* SIPHON

Syr-i-ac \'sir-ē-ˌak\ *n* **1** : a literary language based on an eastern Aramaic dialect and used as the literary and liturgical language by several eastern Christian churches **2** : Aramaic spoken by Christian communities — **Syriac** *adj*

sy-rin-ga \sə-'riŋ-gə\ *n* : MOCK ORANGE

¹sy-ringe \sə-'rinj *also* 'sir-inj\ *n* : a device used to inject fluids into or withdraw them from the body or its cavities

²syringe *vb* **sy-ringed; sy-ring-ing** : to flush or cleanse with or as if with a syringe

syr-inx \'sir-iŋks\ *n* : the sound-producing organ of birds

syr-up *or* **sir-up** \'sər-əp, 'sir-əp, 'sə-rəp\ *n* **1** : a thick solution of sugar and water often containing a flavoring or a medicine **2** : the juice of a fruit or plant with some of the water removed — **syr-upy** \-ē\ *adj*

sys-op \'sis-ˌäp\ *n* : the administrator of a computer bulletin board [*sys*tem *op*erator]

sys-tem \'sis-təm\ *n* **1 a** : a group of objects or units combined to form a whole and to move or work together ⟨the railroad *system*⟩ ⟨a park *system*⟩ **b** : a group of bodily organs that together carry on one or more vital functions ⟨the digestive *system*⟩ **c** : the body considered as a functional unit ⟨a *system* weakened by disease⟩ **d** : an orderly plan or method of governing or arranging ⟨a democratic *system* of government⟩ **e** : a major division of rocks usually larger than a series and including all formed during a period or era **2 a** : a set of ideas or statements that explains the order or functioning of a whole **b** : a method of classifying, representing, or arranging ⟨a decimal *system* of numbers⟩ — **sys-tem-less** \-ləs\ *adj*

sys-tem-at-ic \ˌsis-tə-'mat-ik\ *adj* **1** : relating to or forming a system ⟨*systematic* thought⟩ **2** : presented or worked out as a system **3** : carried out or acting with thoroughness or regularity ⟨*systematic* efforts⟩ — **sys-tem-at-i-cal-ly** \-i-k(ə-)lē\ *adv*

sys-tem-atize \'sis-tə-mə-ˌtīz\ *vb* **-atized; -atiz-ing** : to make into or arrange according to a system

sys-tem-ic \sis-'tem-ik\ *adj* : of, relating to, or common to a system: as **a** : of or relating to the body as a whole ⟨a *systemic* disease⟩ **b** : concerned with the circulation that supplies blood to the bodily tissues through the aorta rather than the circulation involved in carrying blood through the pulmonary artery

systemic circulation *n* : the passage of oxygen-rich blood from the left side of the heart through arteries to all organs and tissues of the body and the return of oxygen-poor blood through veins to the right side of the heart

systems analyst *n* : a person who studies a procedure or business to find out its goals and purposes and to discover the best ways to accomplish them

sys-to-le \'sis-tə-lē\ *n* : the contraction of the heart by which the blood is forced onward and the circulation kept up — compare DIASTOLE

sys-tol-ic \sis-'täl-ik\ *adj* : of, relating to, caused by, or occurring during systole ⟨*systolic* blood pressure⟩

T

t \tē\ *n, pl* **t's** *or* **ts** \'tēz\ *often cap* : the 20th letter of the English alphabet — **to a T** : in a perfect manner

't \t\ *pron* : ¹IT ⟨'twill do⟩

¹tab \'tab\ *n* **1 a** : a short flap or tag used as an aid in filing, pulling, or hanging **b** : something inserted **2 a** : close watch ⟨keep *tabs* on fashion trends⟩ **b** : ³BILL 2, CHECK **3** : a key on a keyboard especially for arranging information in columns

²tab *vb* **tabbed; tab-bing** **1** : to furnish or ornament with tabs **2** : to select or name for a special purpose : DESIGNATE ⟨*tabbed* as the team's next captain⟩ **3** : to hit the tab key on a keyboard

tab-ard \'tab-ərd\ *n* **1** : a cloak worn by a knight over his armor and ornamented with his arms **2** : a herald's cape or coat ornamented with the lord's arms

tab-by \'tab-ē\ *n, pl* **tab-bies** **1** : a domestic cat with a striped and spotted coat **2** : a female cat

tabby 1

Word History A silk cloth with a striped or wavy pattern was once made in a section of the ancient city of Baghdad in what is now Iraq. The Arabic name for the cloth was *'attābī*, from *Al-'Attābīya*, the name of the part of the city where it was made. Through Latin, the French borrowed this word for the cloth, calling it *tabis*. This word in turn became *tabby* in English. People saw a resemblance between the striped or wavy pattern of the silk and cats that had striped or spotted markings on their fur. Thus these cats came to be called *tabby* cats after the cloth. [from French *tabis* "a silk fabric with a lustrous wavy finish," from Latin *attabi* (same meaning), from Arabic *'attābī* (same meaning), from *Al-'Attābīya*, name of a part of Baghdad where the cloth was made]

tab-er-na-cle \'tab-ər-ˌnak-əl\ *n* **1 a** *often cap* : a tent used as a place of worship by the Israelites during their wanderings in the wilderness with Moses **b** *archaic* : a

\ə\ **abut**	\au̇\ **out**	\i\ **tip**	\ȯ\ **saw**	\u̇\ **foot**
\ər\ **further**	\ch\ **chin**	\ī\ **life**	\ȯi\ **coin**	\y\ **yet**
\a\ **mat**	\e\ **pet**	\j\ **job**	\th\ **thin**	\yü\ **few**
\ā\ **take**	\ē\ **easy**	\ŋ\ **sing**	\th\ **this**	\yu̇\ **cure**
\ä\ **cot, cart**	\g\ **go**	\ō\ **bone**	\ü\ **food**	\zh\ **vision**

dwelling place **2** : a locked box used to hold Communion breads **3** : a house of worship

¹**ta·ble** \ˈtā-bəl\ *n* **1** : TABLET 1a **2 a** : a piece of furniture with a smooth flat top fixed on legs **b** : food served at a meal **c** : a group of people assembled at a table **3 a** : an orderly arrangement of facts or figures in rows or columns for quick reference ⟨a *table* of weights⟩ ⟨the multiplication *table*⟩ **b** : a short list ⟨the *table* of contents⟩ **4** : PLATEAU 1

²**table** *vb* **ta·bled; ta·bling** \-b(ə-)liŋ\ **1** : TABULATE **2** : to remove a parliamentary motion from consideration for an unspecified period of time **3** : to put on a table

tab·leau \ˈtab-ˌlō, ta-ˈblō\ *n, pl* **tab·leaux** \-ˌlōz, -blōz\ *also* **tableaus** : a scene or event shown by a group of persons in costume who remain silent and motionless

ta·ble·cloth \ˈtā-bəl-ˌklȯth\ *n* : a covering spread over a dining table before the places are set

ta·ble·land \ˈtā-bəl-ˌ(l)and\ *n* : PLATEAU 1

table salt *n* : salt for use on food and in cooking

ta·ble·spoon \ˈtā-bəl-ˌspün\ *n* **1** : a large spoon used especially for serving food **2** : a unit of measure used in cooking equal to ½ fluid ounce (about 15 milliliters)

ta·ble·spoon·ful \ˌtā-bəl-ˈspün-ˌfül, ˈtā-bəl-ˌspün-\ *n, pl* **ta·ble·spoon·fuls** \-ˌfülz\ *also* **ta·ble·spoons·ful** \-ˈspünz-ˌfül, -ˌspünz-\ **1** : as much as a tablespoon can hold **2** : TABLESPOON 2

table sugar *n* : ¹SUGAR 1; *esp* : white sugar granules

tab·let \ˈtab-lət\ *n* **1 a** : a flat slab suited for an inscription **b** : ²PAD 4 **2 a** : a compressed or molded block of a solid material **b** : a small usually round mass of material containing medicine ⟨aspirin *tablet*⟩ **3 a** : GRAPHICS TABLET **b** *or* **tablet computer** : a mobile computing device that has a flat rectangular form, is usually controlled by means of a touch screen, and is typically used for accessing the Internet, watching videos, and reading e-books

table talk *n* : informal conversation at or as if at a dining table

table tennis *n* : a game resembling tennis that is played on a table with wooden paddles and a small hollow plastic ball

ta·ble·top \ˈtā-bəl-ˌtäp\ *n* : the top of a table

ta·ble·ware \ˈtā-bəl-ˌwa(ə)r, -ˌwe(ə)r\ *n* : utensils (as of china, glass, or silver) for table use

table wine *n* : a wine suitable for serving with food

tab·loid \ˈtab-ˌlȯid\ *n* : a newspaper about half the page size of an ordinary newspaper containing short often sensational news stories and many photographs

¹**ta·boo** *also* **ta·bu** \tə-ˈbü, ta-\ *adj* : prohibited by a taboo [from *tabu*, a word in a language of the people of a South Sea island, meaning "taboo"]

²**taboo** *also* **tabu** *n, pl* **taboos** *also* **tabus** **1** : a prohibition against touching, saying, or doing something for fear of immediate harm by a superhuman force **2** : a prohibition established by social custom

ta·bor \ˈtā-bər\ *n* : a small drum with one head used to accompany a pipe played by the same person

tab·u·lar \ˈtab-yə-lər\ *adj* **1** : having a flat surface **2 a** : arranged or entered in a table **b** : computed by means of a table

tab·u·late \ˈtab-yə-ˌlāt\ *vb* **-lat·ed; -lat·ing** : to count and record in an orderly way ⟨*tabulate* votes⟩ — **tab·u·la·tion** \ˌtab-yə-ˈlā-shən\ *n* — **tab·u·la·tor** \ˈtab-yə-ˌlāt-ər\ *n*

ta·chom·e·ter \ta-ˈkäm-ət-ər, tə-\ *n* : a device for indicating speed of rotation [from Greek *tachos* "speed" and English *meter* "an instrument for measuring"]

tabor

tac·it \ˈtas-ət\ *adj* **1** : expressed without words or speech **2** : understood or made known (as by an act or by silence) though not actually expressed ⟨*tacit* approval⟩ — **tac·it·ly** *adv* — **tac·it·ness** *n*

tac·i·turn \ˈtas-ə-ˌtərn\ *adj* : tending to not speak **synonyms** see SILENT — **tac·i·tur·ni·ty** \ˌtas-ə-ˈtər-nət-ē\ *n* — **tac·i·turn·ly** \ˈtas-ə-ˌtərn-lē\ *adv*

¹**tack** \ˈtak\ *vb* **1** : to fasten or attach especially with tacks **2** : to join in a slight or hasty manner **3** : to add on in order to complete **4 a** : to change the direction of a sailing ship by shifting the sails **b** : to change from one tack to another **5** : to follow a zigzag course — **tack·er** *n*

²**tack** *n* **1** : a small short sharp-pointed nail usually with a broad flat head **2 a** : the direction a ship is sailing as shown by the position the sails are set in ⟨on the port *tack*⟩ **b** : a change of course from one tack to another **3** : a zigzag movement on land **4** : a course or method of action ⟨try a new *tack*⟩ **5** : a slight or temporary sewing or fastening

³**tack** *n* : stable gear; *esp* : equipment (as a saddle and bridle) for use on a saddle horse

tack·i·ness \ˈtak-ē-nəs\ *n* : the quality or state of being tacky

¹**tack·le** \ˈtak-əl, *nautical often* ˈtāk-\ *n* **1** : a set of special equipment : GEAR ⟨fishing *tackle*⟩ **2** : an arrangement of ropes and wheels for hoisting or pulling something heavy **3 a** : the act or an instance of tackling **b** : a football player who is positioned on the line of scrimmage and inside the ends

²**tackle** *vb* **tack·led; tack·ling** \ˈtak-(ə-)liŋ\ **1** : to seize or take hold of especially in order to stop or throw down **2** : to set about dealing with ⟨*tackle* a problem⟩ — **tack·ler** \-(ə-)lər\ *n*

¹**tacky** \ˈtak-ē\ *adj* **tack·i·er; -est** : somewhat sticky to the touch ⟨*tacky* varnish⟩

²**tacky** *adj* **tack·i·er; -est** **1** : SHABBY 2b, SEEDY **2** : marked by lack of style or good taste ⟨a *tacky* outfit⟩

ta·co \ˈtäk-ō\ *n, pl* **tacos** \-ōz\ : a usually fried tortilla that is folded or rolled and stuffed with a mixture (as of seasoned meat, cheese, and lettuce) [from the Spanish spoken in Mexico *taco* "taco"]

tac·o·nite \ˈtak-ə-ˌnīt\ *n* : a flinty rock high enough in iron content to be used as a low-grade iron ore

tact \ˈtakt\ *n* : the ability to deal with others without offending them — **tact·less** \ˈtak-tləs\ *adj* — **tact·less·ly** *adv* — **tact·less·ness** *n*

tact·ful \ˈtakt-fəl\ *adj* : having or showing tact — **tact·ful·ly** \-fə-lē\ *adv* — **tact·ful·ness** *n*

tac·tic \ˈtak-tik\ *n* **1** : a method of arranging and moving forces in combat **2** : a planned action for a particular purpose

tac·ti·cal \ˈtak-ti-kəl\ *adj* : of or relating to tactics — **tac·ti·cal·ly** \-k(ə-)lē\ *adv*

tac·ti·cian \tak-ˈtish-ən\ *n* : one skilled in tactics

tac·tics \ˈtak-tiks\ *n sing or pl* **1 a** : the science and art of arranging and moving forces in combat **b** : the art or skill of using available means to accomplish an end **2** : a system or method of proceeding

tac·tile \ˈtak-tᵊl, -ˌtīl\ *adj* : of, relating to, or used in the sense of touch [from French *tactile* or Latin *tactilis*, both meaning "capable of being touched or felt," from Latin *tangere* "to touch" — related to TANGENT, TANGIBLE]

tad \ˈtad\ *n* **1** : BOY 1 **2** : ²BIT 1 — **a tad** : SOMEWHAT ⟨was *a tad* rude to us⟩

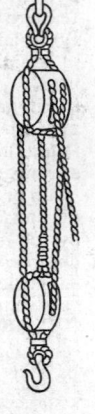

¹tackle 2

tad·pole \'tad-ˌpōl\ *n*
: the larva of a frog or
toad that has a round-
ed body and a long
tail, breathes with
gills, and lives in wa-
ter — called also *pol-
lywog*

tadpole in stages

Word History A
young tadpole looks
like a large head
with a tail. In time it
will develop back
legs and then front
legs. Finally it will
lose its tail and be-
come a toad or a frog. Our word for this immature form
of a toad or frog comes from Middle English *taddepol*.
This word was a combination of two others, *tode*, meaning "toad," and *polle*, meaning "head." [Middle English
taddepol "tadpole," from *tode* "toad" and *polle* "head"]

tae kwon do \'tī-'kwän-'dō\ *n, often cap T&K&D* : a Korean art of self-defense resembling karate

taf·fe·ta \'taf-ət-ə\ *n* : a crisp shiny fabric used especially
for women's clothing

taff·rail \'taf-ˌrāl, -rəl\ *n* : the rail around the stern of a ship

taf·fy \'taf-ē\ *n, pl* **taffies** : a candy usually of molasses or
brown sugar boiled and pulled until soft and chewy

¹**tag** \'tag\ *n* **1** : a loose hanging piece of cloth : TATTER **2**
: a metal or plastic binding on an end of a shoelace **3**
: TAG LINE **4 a** : something (as a marker) used for identification; *specif* : HANGTAG **b** : a part of a computer file
that controls the format or layout of a document or that
indicates a hyperlink (as "<it>" to indicate italic type)
[Middle English *tagge* "a hanging piece of loose cloth"; of
Germanic origin]

²**tag** *vb* **tagged; tag·ging 1** : to provide or mark with or as
if with a tag **2** : to follow closely and continuously **3**
: ²LABEL 3

³**tag** *n* **1** : a game in which one player who is it chases the
others and tries to touch one of them to make that person
it **2** : an act or instance of tagging a runner in baseball
[origin unknown]

⁴**tag** *vb* **tagged; tag·ging 1** : to touch in a game of tag **2**
: to put out (a runner) in baseball by touching with the
ball or with the gloved hand holding the ball

Ta·ga·log \tə-'gäl-əg, -ˌòg\ *n, pl* **Tagalog** *or* **Tagalogs 1**
: a member of the native people of the Philippine island
of Luzon **2** : the language of the Tagalog people

tag·along \'tag-ə-ˌlòŋ\ *n* : one that tags along

tag along \ˌtag-ə-'lòŋ\ *vb* : to follow another's lead especially in going from one place to another

tag end *n* : TAIL END

tag line *n* : a final line (as in a joke)

tag up *vb* : to touch a base before running in baseball after
a fly ball is caught

tai chi \'tī-'jē, -'chē\ *n, often cap T&C* : an ancient Chinese
system of movements performed for meditation or exercise

tai·ga \'tī-gə\ *n* : a moist northern forest that consists
mostly of cone-producing trees (as pines, spruces, and
firs) and begins where the tundra ends

¹**tail** \'tā(ə)l\ *n* **1** : the rear end or a lengthened growth from
the rear end of the body of an animal **2** : something resembling an animal's tail ⟨the *tail* of a kite⟩ ⟨the *tail* of a
comet⟩ **3** *pl* : full evening dress for men **4** : the back,
last, lower, or rear part of something ⟨the *tail* of an air-
plane⟩ **5** : the reverse of a coin **6** : one (as a detective)
who follows or keeps watch on someone **7** : a location
not far behind ⟨a posse on the outlaw's *tail*⟩ — **tailed**
\'tā(ə)ld\ *adj* — **tail·less** \'tā(ə)l-ləs\ *adj* — **tail·like**
\-ˌlīk\ *adj*

²**tail** *adj* : being at or coming from the rear

³**tail** *vb* **1** : to make or furnish with a tail **2 a** : to follow or
be drawn behind like a tail **b** : to follow closely to observe : SHADOW — **tail·er** *n*

tail·bone \'tā(ə)l-ˌbōn\ *n* : COCCYX

tail end *n* : the last part ⟨the *tail end* of summer⟩

¹**tail·gate** \'tā(ə)l-ˌgāt\ *n* : a panel at the back end of a vehicle (as a station wagon) that can be let down for loading
and unloading

²**tailgate** *vb* **tail·gat·ed; tail·gat·ing** : to drive dangerously
close behind another vehicle

tail·light \'tā(ə)l-ˌlīt\ *n* : a red warning light mounted at the
rear of a vehicle

¹**tai·lor** \'tā-lər\ *n* : a person whose occupation is making or
making adjustments in outer garments

²**tailor** *vb* **1** : to make or fashion as the work of a tailor **2**
: to make or make suitable for a special need or purpose

tai·lor·bird \'tā-lər-ˌbərd\ *n* : any of a genus of warblers
mostly of Asia that stitch leaves together to support and
hide their nests

tai·lored \'tā-lərd\ *adj* **1** : fashioned or fitted like a tailor's
work **2** : CUSTOM-MADE

tai·lor·ing \'tā-lə-riŋ\ *n* **1 a** : the business or occupation of
a tailor **b** : the work or quality of work of a tailor **2** : the
making or adapting of something to suit a particular purpose

tai·lor-made \ˌtā-lər-'mād\ *adj* **1** : made by or as if by a
tailor; *esp* : marked by exact fit and simple style **2** : made
or as if made to take care of a particular need

tailor's ham \'tā-lərz-\ *n* : a cushion used especially by
tailors for pressing curved areas of garments

tailor's tack *n* : a long loose stitch with a double thread to
fasten seams before thorough sewing

tail·piece \'tā(ə)l-ˌpēs\ *n* **1** : a piece added at the end **2** : a
device to which the strings of a stringed instrument are
fastened

tail pipe *n* : an outlet by which engine exhaust gases are
expelled from a vehicle (as an automobile or jet aircraft)

tail·spin \'tā(ə)l-ˌspin\ *n* : ²SPIN 3

tail wind *n* : a wind having the same general direction as
the course of a moving object (as an aircraft)

¹**taint** \'tānt\ *vb* **1** : to touch or affect slightly with something bad **2** : ²SPOIL 2c, DECAY

²**taint** *n* **1** : a trace of decay : STAIN **2** : a spoiling influence
— **taint·less** \-ləs\ *adj*

¹**take** \'tāk\ *vb* **took** \'tùk\; **tak·en** \'tā-kən\; **tak·ing 1** : to
lay hold of : GRASP ⟨*take* my hand⟩ **2** : ²CAPTURE 1 ⟨*take*
a fort⟩ **3** : ¹WIN 3a ⟨*take* first prize⟩ **4** : to get possession
of (as by buying, capturing, or killing) ⟨*took* several trout
with hook and line⟩ **5** : to seize and affect suddenly ⟨*tak-
en* with a fever⟩ **6** : CAPTIVATE, DELIGHT ⟨was much
taken with the new neighbors⟩ **7** : ¹EXTRACT 4 ⟨*take* material from an encyclopedia⟩ **8** : SUBTRACT 1 ⟨*take* 78
from 112⟩ **9** : to put an end to (as life) **10** : to find out
by testing or examining ⟨*take* a patient's temperature⟩ **11**
: ¹SELECT, CHOOSE ⟨I *took* the red one⟩ **12** : ASSUME 1
⟨*take* office⟩ ⟨*take* charge⟩ **13 a** : to let in and hold : AD-
MIT, ACCOMMODATE ⟨the boat was *taking* water fast⟩
⟨the suitcase won't *take* another thing⟩ **b** : to be affected
harmfully by (as a disease) : CONTRACT ⟨*take* a cold⟩ **c**
: to become soaked with or make part of itself : ABSORB
⟨this cloth *takes* dye very well⟩ ⟨plants *take* up water⟩ **14**
: to be guided by : FOLLOW ⟨*take* my advice⟩ **15** : to introduce into the body ⟨*take* your medicine⟩ **16 a** : to
submit to ⟨*took* the punishment without complaining⟩ **b**
: WITHSTAND ⟨can *take* a lot of punishment⟩ **17 a** : to
subscribe to ⟨*takes* two newspapers⟩ **b** : to enroll in for

\ə\ **abut**	\au̇\ **out**	\i\ **tip**	\o̅\ **saw**	\u̇\ **foot**	
\ər\ **further**	\ch\ **chin**	\ī\ **life**	\o̅i\ **coin**	\y\ **yet**	
\a\ **mat**	\e\ **pet**	\j\ **job**	\th\ **thin**	\yü\ **few**	
\ā\ **take**	\ē\ **easy**	\ŋ\ **sing**	\th\ **this**	\yu̇\ **cure**	
\ä\ **cot, cart**	\g\ **go**	\o̅\ **bone**	\ü\ **food**	\zh\ **vision**	

study ⟨*take* a course in history⟩ ⟨*take* piano lessons⟩ **c** : to keep from swinging at (a baseball pitch) ⟨*take* a strike⟩ **18 a** : UNDERSTAND 3, INTERPRET ⟨I *took* it to mean something different⟩ **b** : CONSIDER 3 ⟨wanted to be *taken* for a genius⟩ **19** : to react in a certain way ⟨*take* pride in one's work⟩ ⟨*take* offense⟩ **20** : to be formed or used with ⟨this verb *takes* an object⟩ **21** : to lead, carry, or cause to go along to another place ⟨*take* a package home⟩ ⟨*take* me to your leader⟩ **22 a** : to make use of ⟨*take* a vacation⟩ **b** : to proceed to occupy ⟨*take* a chair⟩ **23** : ²NEED 2, REQUIRE ⟨this job *takes* a lot of time⟩ ⟨I *take* a larger size⟩ **24** : to obtain an image or copy of ⟨*take* a photograph⟩ ⟨*take* fingerprints⟩ **25** : to set out to make, do, or perform ⟨*take* a walk⟩ ⟨*took* a new job⟩ **26** : to set out or go ⟨*take* after the escaped prisoner⟩ **27** : to have effect (as by absorption) ⟨a dye that *takes* well⟩ — **tak·er** *n* — **take a back seat** : to have or put in a lower position ⟨entertainment *takes a back seat* to food and shelter⟩ — **take advantage of 1** : to use to advantage : profit by **2** : to treat (someone) unfairly : EXPLOIT — **take after 1** : to take as an example : FOLLOW **2** : to look like : RESEMBLE ⟨*take after* their parents⟩ — **take a hike** *also* **take a walk** : to go away : LEAVE — **take care** : to be careful — **take care of** : to attend to or provide for the needs, operation, or treatment of — **take charge** : to assume care or control — **take effect 1** : to go into effect **2** : to have an expected or intended effect : be effective — **take five** *or* **take ten** : to take a break especially from work — **take for** : to suppose to be; *esp* : to suppose mistakenly to be — **take for granted** : to assume as true, real, or expected — **take hold** : to become attached or established — **take into account** : to make allowance for : CONSIDER — **take in vain** : to use a name without proper respect — **take no prisoners** : to be merciless or relentless — **take one's time** : to be slow or unhurried about doing something — **take part** : PARTICIPATE, SHARE — **take place** : to come about or occur : HAPPEN — **take the floor** : to rise (as in a meeting) to speak — **take to 1** : to go to or into ⟨*take* to the streets in protest⟩ **2** : to be drawn or attracted to — **take to court** : to bring before a judicial body; *esp* : SUE 1 — **take to task** : to scold for a fault — **take turns** : ¹ALTERNATE 1

²**take** *n* **1** : an act or the action of taking **2** : something taken : PROCEEDS, CATCH **3 a** : a scene filmed or televised at one time without stopping the camera **b** : a sound recording made during a single recording period **4** : mental response or reaction

take·away \ˈtā-kə-ˌwā\ *n* **1** *chiefly British* : TAKEOUT 3 **2** : an act or instance of taking possession of the ball or puck from an opposing team

take back *vb* : RETRACT 2, WITHDRAW ⟨*take back* an insulting remark⟩

take·down \ˈtāk-ˌdau̇n\ *n* : the action or an act of taking down — **take·down** \ˌtāk-ˈdau̇n\ *adj*

take down \(ˈ)tāk-ˈdau̇n\ *vb* **1 a** : to pull to pieces **b** : DISASSEMBLE **2** : to lower the spirit or pride of : HUMBLE **3** : to write down or record by mechanical means

take–home pay \ˌtāk-ˌhōm-\ *n* : the part of one's salary or wages remaining after deductions (as of income tax payments or union dues)

take in *vb* **1 a** : to reduce the length of ⟨*take in* a slack line⟩ **b** : to make smaller by enlarging seams or tucks ⟨*take in* a coat⟩ **2 a** : to receive as a guest or resident **b** : to give shelter to **3** : to receive and do at home for pay ⟨*take in* washing⟩ **4** : to include within fixed limits ⟨the camp *took in* several acres⟩ **5** : ATTEND 4 ⟨*take in* a movie⟩ **6** : to observe and think about so as to understand ⟨paused to *take* the situation *in*⟩ **7** : to deceive so as to take advantage of ⟨*taken in* by a hard luck story⟩

taken *past participle of* TAKE

take–no–prisoners *adj* : having a fierce, relentless, or merciless character ⟨*take-no-prisoners* politics⟩

take·off \ˈtā-ˌkȯf\ *n* **1** : ¹IMITATION 2; *esp* : PARODY 1 **2 a** : a rise or leap from a surface in making a jump or flight in an aircraft or spacecraft **b** : an action of starting out **3** : a spot at which one takes off

take off \(ˈ)tā-ˈkȯf\ *vb* **1 a** : ¹REMOVE 2 ⟨*take* your hat *off*⟩ **b** : to take away : DEDUCT ⟨*take off* 10 percent⟩ **2** : ¹RELEASE 1 ⟨*take* the brake *off*⟩ **3** : to spend (some time) away from an activity or occupation ⟨*took* two weeks *off* in August⟩ **4 a** : to start off or away often suddenly ⟨*took off* without saying goodbye⟩ **b** : to begin flight ⟨planes *taking off*⟩ **c** : to develop or grow rapidly

take on *vb* **1** : to struggle with as an opponent **2** : ¹EMPLOY 2 ⟨*took on* more workers⟩ **3** : to acquire (as an appearance or quality) as one's own ⟨*take on* weight⟩ **4** : to make an unusual show of one's feelings especially of grief or anger ⟨don't *take on* so⟩

take·out \ˈtā-ˌkau̇t\ *n* **1** : the action or an act of taking out **2** : something taken out or made to be taken out **3** : prepared food packaged to be eaten away from its place of sale

take out \(ˈ)tā-ˈkau̇t\ *vb* **1 a** : to take away : DEDUCT **b** : ¹REMOVE 4 **2** : to find release for : VENT ⟨*took out* their anger on me⟩ **3** : to conduct or escort into the open or to a public entertainment **4** : to take as payment in another form ⟨*took* the debt *out* in goods⟩ **5** : to obtain from the proper authority ⟨*take out* a charter⟩ **6** : to start on a course : SET OUT

take over \(ˈ)tā-ˈkō-vər\ *vb* : to get control or possession of or responsibility for something — **take·over** \ˈtā-ˌkō-vər\ *n*

take–up \ˈtā-ˌkəp\ *n* **1** : a device in a sewing machine for drawing up the slack thread as the needle rises in completing a stitch **2** : a device for winding photographic film on a reel, core, or spool

take up \(ˈ)tā-ˈkəp\ *vb* **1** : to begin to occupy ⟨*took up* their positions⟩ **2** : to begin to engage in : UNDERTAKE ⟨*took up* swimming⟩ **3** : to absorb or incorporate into itself ⟨plants *taking up* water and minerals⟩ **4** : to pull up or in so as to tighten or to shorten ⟨*take up* the slack⟩ — **take up for** : to take the part or side of — **take up with** : to begin to associate with

tak·ings \ˈtā-kiŋz\ *n pl, chiefly British* : receipts especially of money

talc \ˈtalk\ *n* : a very soft mineral that consists of a silicate of magnesium, has a soapy feel, and is used especially in making talcum powder

tal·cum powder \ˈtal-kəm-\ *n* : a powder composed of perfumed talc or talc and a mild antiseptic for sprinkling or rubbing over the skin

tale \ˈtā(ə)l\ *n* **1** : something told ⟨a *tale* of woe⟩ **2** : a story about an imaginary event ⟨a fairy *tale*⟩ **3** : a false story : LIE **4** : a piece of harmful gossip ⟨spread *tales* about us⟩

tale·bear·er \-ˌbar-ər, -ˌber-\ *n* : a person who spreads gossip, scandal, or rumors — **tale·bear·ing** \-iŋ\ *adj or n*

tal·ent \ˈtal-ənt\ *n* **1** : an ancient unit of weight and money **2** : the natural abilities of a person **3** : a special often athletic, creative, or artistic ability **4** : persons of talent in a field or activity [Middle English *talent* "an ancient unit of weight and money"; in sense 1 from Old English *talente* (same meaning), from Latin *talenta*, plural of *talentum* "unit of weight or money," from Greek *talanton* "pan of a scale, weight"; in senses 2–4 so called from the parable of the talents told by Jesus (Matthew 25:14–30)] **synonyms** see ABILITY — **tal·ent·ed** \-ən-təd\ *adj*

talent scout *n* : a person engaged in discovering and recruiting people with special talents

talent show *n* : a show consisting of a series of performances by amateurs who may be selected for special recognition as performers

tal·is·man \ˈtal-ə-smən, -əz-mən\ *n, pl* **talismans** : a ring or stone carved with symbols and believed to have magical powers : CHARM

¹talk \'tȯk\ *vb* **1** : to express in speech ⟨*talk* sense⟩ **2** : to speak about : DISCUSS ⟨*talk* business⟩ **3** : to influence, affect, or cause by talking ⟨*talked* us into agreeing⟩ **4** : to use for communicating ⟨*talk* sign language⟩ **5 a** : to express or exchange ideas by means of spoken words **b** : to communicate in any way ⟨the computer *talks* to the printer⟩ **6 a** : to spread gossip **b** : to reveal secret information ⟨tried to make the suspect *talk*⟩ — **talk·er** *n* — **talk back** : to answer disrespectfully

²talk *n* **1** : the act or an instance of talking **2** : a way of speaking **3** : pointless or useless discussion ⟨all *talk* and no action⟩ **4** : a formal discussion or exchange of views : CONFERENCE **5** : ¹RUMOR 1, GOSSIP **6** : the topic of comment or gossip ⟨it's the *talk* of the town⟩

talk·a·tive \'tȯ-kət-iv\ *adj* : fond of talking — **talk·a·tive·ness** *n*

synonyms TALKATIVE, LOQUACIOUS, GARRULOUS, VOLUBLE mean fond of talking. TALKATIVE suggests a regular willingness to talk or join in a conversation ⟨a *talkative* neighbor⟩. LOQUACIOUS suggests the ability of a person who speaks easily and smoothly ⟨the *loquacious* host of a television show⟩. GARRULOUS suggests a wish to talk that often continues to the point of being foolish and boring ⟨a *garrulous* person running on about the good old days⟩. VOLUBLE suggests a ready, rapid, and seemingly endless flow of speech ⟨a *voluble* salesclerk who told customers more than they cared to know⟩.

talk down *vb* : to speak in an overly simple manner as if to a person who does not know much

talking book *n* : AUDIOBOOK

talk·ing–to \'tȯ-kiŋ-ˌtü\ *n* : an often wordy scolding

talk over *vb* : DISCUSS 1

talk show *n* : a radio or television program in which persons engage in discussions or are interviewed

talky \'tȯ-kē\ *adj* : TALKATIVE

tall \'tȯl\ *adj* **1 a** : having unusually great height **b** : of a specified height ⟨five feet *tall*⟩ **2 a** : large in amount, extent, or degree ⟨a *tall* order to fill⟩ **b** : greatly exaggerated : IMPROBABLE ⟨a *tall* tale⟩ **synonyms** see HIGH — **tall** *adv* — **tall·ness** *n*

tal·lith \'täl-əs, -ət, -əth\ *or* **tal·lis** \-əs\ *n* : a shawl with fringed corners traditionally worn over the head or shoulders by Jewish men especially during morning prayers

tal·low \'tal-ō\ *n* : the solid fat of cattle and sheep used chiefly in soap, candles, and lubricants

tall ship *n* : a sailing vessel with at least two masts; *esp* : SQUARE-RIGGER

¹tal·ly \'tal-ē\ *n, pl* **tallies** **1** : a device for keeping a count **2 a** : a recorded account **b** : a total recorded **3** : a score or point made (as in a game)

²tally *vb* **tal·lied; tal·ly·ing** **1** : to keep a count of **2** : to make a tally : SCORE **3** : CORRESPOND 1, AGREE

tal·ly·ho \ˌtal-ē-'hō\ *n, pl* **tallyhos** : a call of a huntsman at sight of the fox

Tal·mud \'täl-ˌmu̇d, 'tal-məd\ *n* : the writings that declare Jewish law and tradition — **Tal·mu·dic** \tal-'mu̇d-ik, -'myüd-, -'məd-, täl-'mu̇d-\ *adj*

tal·on \'tal-ən\ *n* : the claw of an animal and especially of a bird of prey

ta·lus \'tā-ləs\ *n* : a pile of rocks broken off from and found at the base of a cliff or steep slope

ta·ma·le \tə-'mäl-ē\ *n* : cornmeal dough rolled with ground meat or beans seasoned usually with chili, wrapped in corn husks, and steamed

tam·a·rack \'tam-(ə-)ˌrak\ *n* **1** : any of several American larches; *esp* : one of the northern U.S. and Canada **2** : the wood of a tamarack

tam·a·rind \'tam-ə-rənd, -rind\ *n* : a tropical tree of the legume family that has hard yellowish wood, feathery leaves, and red-striped yellow flowers; *also* : its fruit which has a sour pulp used especially for preserves or as a seasoning in cooking

tam·a·risk \'tam-ə-ˌrisk\ *n* : any of a genus of chiefly desert shrubs of Eurasia and Africa that have small narrow leaves and clusters of tiny flowers

tam·bou·rine \ˌtam-bə-'rēn\ *n* : a shallow drum with one head and loose metal disks at the sides that is played by shaking or striking with the hand

¹tame \'tām\ *adj* **tam·er; tam·est** **1** : changed from the wild state so as to become useful and obedient to human beings : DOMESTICATED ⟨a *tame* elephant⟩ **2** : made gentle and obedient **3** : lacking spirit or interest : DULL — **tame·ly** *adv* — **tame·ness** *n*

²tame *vb* **tamed; tam·ing** **1 a** : to make or become tame ⟨*tame* a lion⟩ **b** : to subject to cultivation ⟨wilderness *tamed* by farmers⟩ **2** : to bring under control : SUBDUE ⟨*tame* your temper⟩ — **tam·er** *n*

tam–o'–shan·ter \'tam-ə-ˌshant-ər\ *n* : a Scottish cap with a tight headband, wide flat circular crown, and usually a pompom [named for *Tam o' Shanter*, hero of a poem by Robert Burns 1759–1796 Scottish poet]

tam-o'-shanter

tamp \'tamp\ *vb* **1** : to drive in or down by a series of blows **2** : to put a check on : LESSEN ⟨*tamp* down rumors⟩ — **tamp·er** *n*

tam·per \'tam-pər\ *vb* **tam·pered; tam·per·ing** \-p(ə-)riŋ\ **1** : to interfere in a secret or wrongful way **2 a** : to interfere so as to cause a weakening or change for the worse **b** : to try foolish or dangerous experiments **synonyms** see MEDDLE

tam·pon \'tam-ˌpän\ *n* : a wad of absorbent material (as cotton) placed in a body cavity or canal usually to absorb secretions (as from menstruation) or to stop heavy or uncontrolled bleeding

¹tan \'tan\ *vb* **tanned; tan·ning** **1** : to change hide into leather especially by soaking in a tannin solution **2** : to make or become tan or brown especially by exposing to the sun **3** : THRASH 2a, WHIP

²tan *adj* **tan·ner; tan·nest** : of the color tan

³tan *n* **1** : a brown color given to the skin especially by exposure to the sun **2** : a light yellowish brown — **tan·nish** \'tan-ish\ *adj*

tan·a·ger \'tan-i-jər\ *n* : any of numerous small mostly tropical American birds that are often brightly colored — compare SCARLET TANAGER

tanager

¹tan·dem \'tan-dəm\ *n* **1 a** : a two-seated carriage drawn by horses hitched one behind the other **b** : TANDEM BICYCLE **2** : a group of two or more arranged one behind the other

Word History *Tandem* is used to describe many

\ə\ **abut**	\au̇\ **out**	\i\ **tip**	\ȯ\ **saw**	\u̇\ **foot**
\ər\ **further**	\ch\ **chin**	\ī\ **life**	\ȯi\ **coin**	\y\ **yet**
\a\ **mat**	\e\ **pet**	\j\ **job**	\th\ **thin**	\yü\ **few**
\ā\ **take**	\ē\ **easy**	\ŋ\ **sing**	\t͟h\ **this**	\yu̇\ **cure**
\ä\ **cot, cart**	\g\ **go**	\ō\ **bone**	\ü\ **food**	\zh\ **vision**

things that involve the connecting of one object to another similar object behind it. A tandem tractor-trailer truck has one trailer hitched behind another, which is attached to the truck body, or tractor. A bicycle built for two is called a tandem bicycle because it has one seat and set of pedals behind another. The first use of the word *tandem* in English was for a carriage pulled by one horse hitched behind, rather than beside, another. Whoever first used the term in English apparently was making a play on words. The Latin word *tandem* meant "at length" referring to time, but in English *tandem* came to mean "at length" or "lengthwise," referring to position. [from Latin *tandem* "at length, at last"]

²tandem *adv or adj* : one behind another

tandem bicycle *n* : a bicycle for two or more persons sitting tandem

tang \'taŋ\ *n* **1** : a sharp often lingering flavor **2** : a sharp odor

tandem bicycle

tan·ge·lo \'tan-jə-ˌlō\ *n, pl* **-los** : the fruit of a tree that is a hybrid between a tangerine and a grapefruit; *also* : the tree

¹tan·gent \'tan-jənt\ *adj* : touching a curve or surface at only one point ⟨a straight line *tangent* to a circle⟩ [from Latin *tangent-, tangens* "touching," from *tangere* "to touch" — related to CONTACT, TACTILE, TANGIBLE]

²tangent *n* **1** : a trigonometric function that for an acute angle in a right triangle is the ratio of the side opposite the angle to the side next to it **2** : a line that is tangent **3** : a sudden change of course ⟨the speaker went off on a *tangent*⟩ — **tan·gen·tial** \tan-ˈjen-chəl\ *adj* — **tan·gen·tial·ly** \-ˈjench-(ə-)lē\ *adv*

tan·ger·ine \'tan-jə-ˌrēn, ˌtan-jə-ˈrēn\ *n* : any of various mandarin oranges having a usually deep orange skin and pulp; *also* : a tree producing tangerines

¹tan·gi·ble \'tan-jə-bəl\ *adj* **1** : capable of being touched **2** : capable of being understood and appreciated [from Latin *tangibilis* "tangible," from *tangere* "to touch" — related to CONTACT, TACTILE, TANGENT] — **tan·gi·bil·i·ty** \ˌtan-jə-ˈbil-ət-ē\ *n* — **tan·gi·bly** \'tan-jə-blē\ *adv*

²tangible *n* : something tangible

¹tan·gle \'taŋ-gəl\ *vb* **tan·gled; tan·gling** \-g(ə-)liŋ\ **1** : to make or become involved so as to complicate or confuse : be or become entangled **2** : to twist or become twisted together into a mass hard to straighten out again

²tangle *n* **1** : a tangled twisted mass (as of vines or hairs) confusedly woven together : SNARL **2** : a complicated or confused state or condition

tan·go \'taŋ-gō\ *n, pl* **tangos** : a ballroom dance of Latin American origin to music in ²/₄ time and marked by pauses between steps and a variety of body postures; *also* : the music for a tango — **tango** *vb*

tan·gram \'taŋ-grəm, 'tan-\ *n* : a Chinese puzzle made by cutting a square of thin material into a number of pieces which can be recombined into many different figures

tangy \'taŋ-ē\ *adj* **tang·i·er; -est** : having or suggestive of a tang

¹tank \'taŋk\ *n* **1** : a usually large container for holding, transporting, or storing liquids **2** : an enclosed heavily armed and armored combat vehicle that moves on beltlike tracks

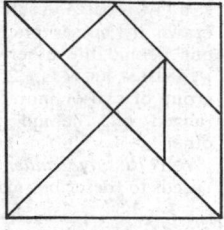

tangram

²tank *vb* : to place, store, or treat in a tank

tan·kard \'taŋ-kərd\ *n* : a tall one-handled drinking vessel; *esp* : a silver or pewter mug with a lid

tank·er \'taŋ-kər\ *n* : a vehicle (as a ship, truck, or aircraft) designed for the transportation of liquids

tank top *n* : a sleeveless collarless shirt with a low neckline

tanned *past and past participle of* TAN

tan·ner \'tan-ər\ *n* : a person who tans hides

tan·nery \'tan-(ə-)rē\ *n, pl* **tan·ner·ies** : a place where hides are tanned

tannest *superlative of* TAN

tan·nic acid \ˌtan-ik-\ *n* : TANNIN

tan·nin \'tan-ən\ *n* : any of various substances from plants (as the oak or sumac) used in tanning leather, dyeing fabric and yarn, the making of ink, and in medicine

tan·ning \'tan-iŋ\ *n* **1** : the art or process by which an animal skin is tanned **2** : a browning of the skin especially by exposure to the sun **3** : a usually severe whipping

tan·ta·lite \'tant-ᵊl-ˌīt\ *n* : a mineral consisting of a heavy dark shiny oxide of tantalum and other metals

tan·ta·lize \'tant-ᵊl-ˌīz\ *vb* **-lized; -liz·ing** : to tease or torment by or as if by presenting something desirable to the view but continually keeping it out of reach — **tan·ta·liz·ing·ly** \-ˌī-ziŋ-lē\ *adv*

Word History In Greek mythology, King Tantalus offended the gods, so they punished him in a truly terrible way. He was forced to stand in a lake whose water came up to his neck. But every time Tantalus became thirsty and bent over to drink, the water level dropped so that he could never reach it. Above his head were branches loaded with delicious fruits. Yet every time Tantalus reached up to take a fruit, the branches moved up out of reach, leaving him hungry. Thus, Tantalus was always in torment, and from his name comes the English word for tormenting or teasing someone in a similar way. [from Greek *Tantalus,* name of a king in mythology]

tan·ta·lum \'tant-ᵊl-əm\ *n* : a gray-white metallic element found in rare minerals and used especially in electronic devices — see ELEMENT table

tan·ta·mount \'tant-ə-ˌmaúnt\ *adj* : equal in value, meaning, or effect

tan·trum \'tan-trəm\ *n* : a fit of bad temper

¹tap \'tap\ *n* **1** : FAUCET, SPIGOT **2** : the procedure of removing fluid from a container or cavity by tapping [Old English *tæppa* "a plug for a hole (as in a wine cask)"] — **on tap 1** : ready to be drawn ⟨root beer *on tap*⟩ **2** : on hand : AVAILABLE

²tap *vb* **tapped; tap·ping** **1** : to release or cause to flow by making a hole or by drawing a plug from a container or cavity ⟨*tap* wine from a cask⟩ **2 a** : to make a hole in so as to let out or draw off a fluid ⟨*tap* maple trees⟩ **b** : to draw from or upon ⟨*tap* the nation's resources⟩ — **tap·per** *n*

³tap *vb* **tapped; tap·ping** : to strike or cause to strike lightly especially with a slight sound ⟨*tap* on a window⟩ ⟨*tap* one's foot⟩ [Middle English *tappen* "to strike lightly, tap," from early French *taper* "to strike with the side of the hand"; of Germanic origin] — **tap·per** *n*

⁴tap *n* **1** : a light blow or its sound **2** : a small metal plate for the sole and heel of a shoe (as for tap dancing)

tap dance *n* : a dance tapped out loudly by means of shoes to which taps have been added — **tap–dance** *vb* — **tap dancer** *n* — **tap dancing** *n*

¹tape \'tāp\ *n* **1** : a narrow band of woven fabric **2** : a string stretched breast-high above the finishing line of a race **3** : a narrow flexible strip or band; *esp* : MAGNETIC TAPE **4** : a recording made on magnetic tape

²tape *vb* **taped; tap·ing** **1** : to fasten, tie, bind, cover, or support with tape **2** : to measure with a tape measure **3** : TAPE-RECORD

tape deck *n* : a device used to play back and often to record on magnetic tapes that usually has to be connected to an audio system

tape measure *n* : a tape marked off in units (as inches or centimeters) and used for measuring

¹**ta·per** \'tā-pər\ *n* **1 a** : a long waxed wick used especially for lighting lamps, pipes, or fires **b** : a slender candle **2 a** : a tapering form or figure **b** : gradual lessening of thickness, diameter, or width in a long object **c** : a gradual decrease

²**taper** *vb* **ta·pered; ta·per·ing** \'tā-p(ə-)riŋ\ **1** : to make or become gradually smaller toward one end **2** : to become gradually less and less

tape–re·cord \ˌtā-pri-'kȯ(ə)rd\ *vb* : to make a recording of on magnetic tape ⟨*tape-record* a concert⟩

tape recorder *n* : a device for recording on and playing back magnetic tapes

taper off *vb* : to stop or lessen gradually

tap·es·try \'tap-ə-strē\ *n, pl* **-tries** : a heavy cloth that has designs or pictures woven into it and is used especially as a wall hanging — **tap·es·tried** \-strēd\ *adj*

tape·worm \'tāp-ˌwərm\ *n* : any of a group of flatworms that are parasites of the intestines of vertebrate animals including human beings

tap·i·o·ca \ˌtap-ē-'ō-kə\ *n* : grains or flakes of starch from the cassava root that are used especially in puddings and as a thickening in liquid foods; *also* : a food (as pudding) that contains tapioca

ta·pir \'tā-pər\ *n, pl* **tapir** *or* **tapirs** : any of several al plant-eating hoofed mammals of tropical America and southeastern Asia that are related to the horse and rhinoceros and have a long flexible snout, a very short tail, and short thick legs

tapir

tap·root \'tap-ˌrüt, -ˌrut\ *n* : a large main root that grows straight down and gives off many smaller side roots — compare FIBROUS ROOT

taps \'taps\ *n sing or pl* **1** : the last bugle call at night blown as a signal to put out the lights **2** : a similar call blown at military funerals and memorial services

tap water *n* : water as it comes from a tap (as in a home)

¹**tar** \'tär\ *n* **1 a** : a dark usually thick sticky liquid obtained by distilling wood, coal, or peat **b** : a substance that resembles tar; *esp* : a sticky substance that is formed by burning tobacco **2** : SAILOR — **tar·like** \-ˌlīk\ *adj*

²**tar** *vb* **tarred; tar·ring** : to smear with or as if with tar

ta·ran·tu·la \tə-'ranch-(ə-)lə, -'rant-ᵊl-ə\ *n* : any of a family of large hairy American spiders that usually move slowly and have a sharp bite but are not very poisonous to human beings

tar·dy \'tärd-ē\ *adj* **tar·di·er; -est** **1** : moving slowly : SLUGGISH **2** : not on time : LATE — **tar·di·ly** \'tärd-ə-lē\ *adv* — **tar·di·ness** \'tärd-ē-nəs\ *n*

tare \'ta(ə)r, 'te(ə)r\ *n* : a weed of grain fields especially of biblical times

tar·get \'tär-gət\ *n* **1** : a mark to shoot at **2** : a person or thing that is talked about, criticized, or laughed at **3** : a goal to be achieved : OBJECTIVE

tar·iff \'tar-əf\ *n* **1 a** : a list of taxes placed by a government on imported or in some countries exported goods **b** : a tax or rate of tax set up in a tariff list **2** : a list of rates or charges of a business or public service company

tar·mac \'tär-ˌmak\ *n* : a road, apron, or runway paved with layers of crushed stone covered with tar

¹**tar·nish** \'tär-nish\ *vb* **1** : to make or become dull, dim, or discolored ⟨silver *tarnishes*⟩ **2** : to bring disgrace or cast doubt on ⟨*tarnished* the family's good name⟩

²**tarnish** *n* : something that tarnishes; *esp* : a film of chemically changed material on the surface of a metal (as silver)

ta·ro \'tär-ō, 'tar-, 'ter-\ *n, pl* **taros** : a large-leaved tropical Asian plant grown throughout the tropics for its edible starchy rounded underground stem; *also* : the stem typically cooked as a vegetable or ground into flour

tarp \'tärp\ *n* : TARPAULIN

tar paper *n* : a heavy paper coated with or soaked in tar for use especially in building

tar·pau·lin \tär-'pȯ-lən, 'tär-pə-\ *n* : a piece of material (as waterproof canvas) used for protecting exposed objects

tar·pon \'tär-pən\ *n, pl* **tarpon** *or* **tarpons** : a large silvery sport fish found in the Gulf of Mexico and warm coastal waters of the Atlantic Ocean

¹**tar·ry** \'tar-ē\ *vb* **tar·ried; tar·ry·ing** **1** : to be slow in coming or going **2** : to stay in or at a place

²**tar·ry** \'tär-ē\ *adj* : of, resembling, or covered with tar

¹**tar·sal** \'tär-səl\ *adj* : of or relating to the tarsus

²**tarsal** *n* : a tarsal part (as a bone or cartilage)

tar sand *n* : sand or sandstone that is naturally soaked with heavy sticky portions of petroleum

tar·si·er \'tär-sē-ər, -sē-ˌā\ *n* : any of several small tree-dwelling primate mammals of a group of islands of southeastern Asia that are related to the lemurs, are active at night, and have large eyes and a long tail

tar·sus \'tär-səs\ *n, pl* **tar·si** \-ˌsī, -ˌsē\ **1** : the part of the foot of a vertebrate between the metatarsus and the leg; *also* : the small bones that support this part of the foot and include bones of the ankle, heel, and arch **2** : the lower and longest part of a bird's leg **3** : the part of the limb of an arthropod (as an insect) most distant from the body

¹**tart** \'tärt\ *adj* **1** : pleasantly sharp or sour to the taste **2** : having a sharp or biting quality ⟨a *tart* voice⟩ — **tart·ly** *adv* — **tart·ness** *n*

²**tart** *n* : a small pie or pastry shell containing jelly, custard, or fruit

tar·tan \'tärt-ᵊn\ *n* **1** : a plaid textile design of Scottish origin **2** : a fabric or garment with tartan design

¹**tar·tar** \'tärt-ər\ *n* **1** : a substance consisting mostly of cream of tartar that is found in the juice of grapes and is deposited in wine casks as a reddish crust or sediment **2** : a hard crust that forms on the teeth and consists of plaque that has become hardened with mineral salts (as of calcium)

²**tartar** *n* **1** *cap* : a member of any of the chiefly Mongolian peoples who invaded parts of Asia and eastern Europe during the Middle Ages **2** : a person who is often angry or violent

tartan 1

tar·tar sauce *or* **tar·tare sauce** \ˌtärt-ər-\ *n* : a sauce made chiefly of mayonnaise and chopped pickles

tase \'tāz\ *vb* : to attack with a stun gun

Ta·ser \'tā-zər\ *trademark* — used for a gun that fires electrified darts to stun and immobilize a person

task \'task\ *n* : a piece of assigned work

synonyms TASK, DUTY, JOB, CHORE mean a piece of work to be done. TASK suggests work given by a person in a position of authority ⟨the boss used to give me every hard *task*⟩. DUTY stresses that one is responsible for doing the work ⟨the *duty* of the police is to protect the people⟩. JOB may suggest that the work is necessary, hard, or important ⟨was given the *job* of choosing photos for the yearbook⟩. CHORE suggests a small routine piece of work that is necessary for keeping a house or farm ⟨taking out the garbage is a daily *chore*⟩.

\ə\ **abut**	\au̇\ **out**	\i\ **tip**	\ȯ\ **saw**	\u̇\ **foot**
\ər\ **further**	\ch\ **chin**	\ī\ **life**	\ȯi\ **coin**	\y\ **yet**
\a\ **mat**	\e\ **pet**	\j\ **job**	\th\ **thin**	\yü\ **few**
\ā\ **take**	\ē\ **easy**	\ŋ\ **sing**	\t͟h\ **this**	\yu̇\ **cure**
\ä\ **cot, cart**	\g\ **go**	\ō\ **bone**	\ü\ **food**	\zh\ **vision**

task·mas·ter \-ˌmas-tər\ *n* : one that assigns a task or burdens another with labor

Tas·ma·ni·an devil \(ˌ)taz-ˌmā-nē-ən-\ *n* : a burrowing marsupial of Tasmania that eats other animals, is about the size of a small dog, and has powerful jaws and a mostly black coat

¹**tas·sel** \'tas-əl *also especially of corn* 'tȧs-, 'tȯs-\ *n* **1** : a hanging ornament made of a bunch of cords fastened at one end **2** : something resembling a tassel; *esp* : the male flower cluster on the top of some plants and especially corn

²**tassel** *vb* -**seled** *or* -**selled**; -**sel·ing** *or* -**sel·ling** \-(ə-)liŋ\ : to adorn with or put forth tassels

¹**taste** \'tāst\ *vb* **tast·ed**; **tast·ing** **1** : ²EXPERIENCE, UNDERGO ⟨*taste* the joy of flying⟩ **2** : to test the flavor of something by taking a little into the mouth **3** : to eat or drink especially in small quantities **4** : to recognize by or as if by the sense of taste ⟨can *taste* the onion in it⟩ **5** : to have a specific flavor ⟨this milk *tastes* sour⟩

²**taste** *n* **1 a** : a small amount tasted **b** : a small sample of experience ⟨her first *taste* of success⟩ **2** : the sense that recognizes and tells apart the sweet, sour, bitter, or salty quality of a dissolved substance and is controlled by taste buds on the tongue **3 a** : the quality of a dissolved substance that can be identified by the sense of taste **b** : a sensation obtained from a substance in the mouth that is usually produced by the sense of taste in combination with those of touch and smell : FLAVOR **4** : a personal liking ⟨had expensive *tastes*⟩ **5 a** : the ability to choose and enjoy what is good and beautiful ⟨a person of *taste*⟩ **b** : aesthetic quality : STYLE ⟨in bad *taste*⟩

taste bud *n* : any of the sense organs by means of which taste is recognized and which are usually on the surface of the tongue

taste·ful \'tāst-fəl\ *adj* : having or showing good taste — **taste·ful·ly** \-fə-lē\ *adv* — **taste·ful·ness** *n*

taste·less \'tāst-ləs\ *adj* **1** : lacking flavor : FLAT ⟨*tasteless* soup⟩ **2** : not having or showing good taste ⟨a *tasteless* joke⟩ — **taste·less·ly** *adv* — **taste·less·ness** *n*

tast·er \'tā-stər\ *n* : one that tastes: as **a** : a person who has the duty of tasting food or drink prepared for another person especially to test for poison **b** : a person who is able to taste the chemical phenylthiocarbamide

tasty \'tā-stē\ *adj* **tast·i·er**; -**est** **1** : pleasing to the taste : SAVORY **2** : very attractive or interesting — **tast·i·ly** \-stə-lē\ *adv* — **tast·i·ness** \-stē-nəs\ *n*

tat \'tat\ *vb* **tat·ted**; **tat·ting** : to work at or make by tatting

tat·ter \'tat-ər\ *n* **1** : a part torn and left hanging : SHRED **2** *pl* : tattered clothing : RAGS — **tatter** *vb*

tat·tered \'tat-ərd\ *adj* **1** : wearing ragged clothes ⟨a *tattered* barefoot child⟩ **2** : torn in shreds : RAGGED ⟨a *tattered* flag⟩

tat·ting \'tat-iŋ\ *n* **1** : a delicate handmade lace formed usually by looping and knotting with a single thread and a small shuttle **2** : the act or process of making tatting

tatting 1

¹**tat·tle** \'tat-ᵊl\ *vb* **tat·tled**;
tat·tling \'tat-liŋ, -ᵊl-iŋ\ : to tell secrets : BLAB

²**tattle** *n* **1** : idle talk : CHATTER **2** : GOSSIP 2a

tat·tler \'tat-lər, -ᵊl-ər\ *n* : TATTLETALE

tat·tle·tale \'tat-ᵊl-ˌtāl\ *n* : a person who tattles

¹**tat·too** \ta-'tü\ *n* **1** : a call sounded shortly before taps as notice to go to quarters **2** : a rapid rhythmic rapping [from earlier *taptoo* "a call to go to quarters for the night," from Dutch *taptoe* (same meaning), from the phrase *tap toe!* "taps shut!," used as a signal that the taps, or faucets, on the wine casks in a barroom were closed for the night]

²**tattoo** *vb* : to mark or color the skin with a tattoo [from a

word in the native language of Tahiti *tatau* (noun) "the act of marking or coloring the skin"]

³**tattoo** *n* : a mark or figure fixed upon the body by using a needle to put color under the skin

tau \'taù, 'tȯ\ *n* : the 19th letter of the Greek alphabet — T or τ

taught *past and past participle of* TEACH

taunt \'tȯnt, 'tänt\ *vb* : to provoke or challenge in a mocking or insulting manner : jeer at — **taunt** *n* — **taunt·er** *n* — **taunt·ing·ly** \-iŋ-lē\ *adv*

taupe \'tōp\ *n* : a brownish gray

Tau·rus \'tȯr-əs\ *n* **1** : a group of stars between Aries and Gemini usually pictured as a bull **2 a** : the second sign of the zodiac — see ZODIAC table **b** : a person born under the sign of Taurus

taut \'tȯt\ *adj* **1 a** : drawn to the limit : not slack ⟨*taut* rope⟩ **b** : HIGH-STRUNG, TENSE ⟨*taut* nerves⟩ **2** : kept in proper order or condition ⟨a *taut* ship⟩ **synonyms** see TIGHT — **taut·ly** *adv* — **taut·ness** *n*

tau·tol·o·gy \tȯ-'täl-ə-jē\ *n, pl* -**gies** : needless repetition of an idea, statement, or word; *also* : an instance of such repetition ⟨"a beginner who has just started" is a *tautology*⟩ — **tau·to·log·i·cal** \ˌtȯt-ᵊl-'äj-i-kəl\ *adj*

tav·ern \'tav-ərn\ *n* **1** : an establishment where alcoholic liquors are sold to be drunk on the premises **2** : INN

taw \'tȯ\ *n* **1** : a marble used as a shooter **2** : the line from which players shoot at marbles

taw·dry \'tȯd-rē, 'täd-\ *adj* **taw·dri·er**; -**est** : cheap and showy — **taw·dri·ly** \-rə-lē\ *adv* — **taw·dri·ness** \-rē-nəs\ *n*

¹**taw·ny** \'tȯ-nē, 'tän-ē\ *adj* **taw·ni·er**; -**est** : of the color tawny — **taw·ni·ness** *n*

²**tawny** *n, pl* **tawnies** : a brownish orange to light brown color

¹**tax** \'taks\ *vb* **1** : to require to pay a tax **2** : to accuse of something ⟨*taxed* them with carelessness⟩ **3** : to make heavy demands on : STRAIN ⟨*taxed* our strength⟩ — **tax·er** *n*

²**tax** *n* **1** : a charge usually of money set by authority on persons or property for public purposes **2** : something (as an effort or duty) that makes heavy demands : STRAIN

tax·able \'tak-sə-bəl\ *adj* : subject to tax ⟨*taxable* goods⟩

tax·a·tion \tak-'sā-shən\ *n* : the action of taxing; *esp* : the establishing of taxes

¹**taxi** \'tak-sē\ *n, pl* **tax·is** \-sēz\ *also* **tax·ies** : TAXICAB; *also* : a similarly operated boat or airplane

²**taxi** *vb* **tax·ied**; **taxi·ing**; **tax·is** *or* **tax·ies** **1** : to operate an airplane slowly on the ground under its own power **2** : to ride in or transport by taxi

taxi·cab \'tak-sē-ˌkab\ *n* : an automobile that carries passengers for a fare usually based on the distance traveled

Word History In the days of horse-drawn vehicles, one type of carriage was called a *cabriolet*, from a French word meaning "leap." This name was fitting since the carriage was so light it bounced or "leaped" about on the rough roads of the time. In time the name *cabriolet* was shortened to *cab*. These cabs were popular as vehicles carrying passengers for a fee. They were equipped with a taximeter, a device that automatically recorded the distance traveled and showed what fee or "tax" the passenger owed. In time this carriage or "cab" with its taximeter came to be called a *taximeter cab*. When the automobile took over from carriages the job of carrying passengers for a fee, it took over the name *taximeter cab* as well. This name was soon shortened to *taxicab*, and that was later shortened to *taxi* and sometimes just *cab*. [from earlier *taximeter cab*, from French *taximètre*, literally "tax meter," and English *cab*, a shortened form of *cabriolet* "a one-horse carriage"]

taxi·der·mist \'tak-sə-ˌdər-məst\ *n* : a person who practices taxidermy

taxi·der·my \'tak-sə-ˌdər-mē\ *n* : the skill or occupation of preparing, stuffing, and mounting skins of animals [derived from Greek *taxis* "arrangement" and Greek *derma* "skin" and English *-y*, noun suffix] — **taxi·der·mic** \,tak-sə-'dər-mik\ *adj*

tax·is \'tak-səs\ *n, pl* **tax·es** \'tak-,sēz\ : a reflex movement by a freely moving organism in relation to a stimulus (as a light or a change in temperature); *also* : a reflex reaction involving such movement — compare TROPISM

tax·on·o·mist \tak-'sän-ə-məst\ *n* : a person who specializes in taxonomy and especially the taxonomy of plants and animals

tax·on·o·my \tak-'sän-ə-mē\ *n* **1** : the study of scientific classification **2** : CLASSIFICATION 2a; *esp* : orderly classification of living things according to their presumed natural relationships — **tax·o·nom·ic** \,tak-sə-'näm-ik\ *adj*

tax·pay·er \'tak-,spā-ər\ *n* : one that pays or is responsible for paying a tax

Tay–Sachs disease \'tā-'saks-\ *n* : a hereditary disease that is caused by the absence of an enzyme, is characterized by a buildup of lipids in the nervous tissue, and causes death in early childhood — called also *Tay-Sachs*

TB \(')tē-'bē\ *n* : TUBERCULOSIS

T–ball \'tē-,bòl\ *n* : baseball for youngsters in which the ball is batted from a tee rather than being pitched

T cell *n* : any of the lymphocytes (as a helper T cell) that usually mature in the thymus and take an active part in immune responses — compare B CELL

tea \'tē\ *n* **1 a** : a shrub related to the camellias that has fragrant white flowers and is grown mainly in China, Japan, India, and Sri Lanka **b** : the leaves and leaf buds of the tea prepared for use in beverages **c** : a beverage prepared from tea by soaking the prepared leaves and buds in boiling water **2** : a drink or medicine made by soaking parts (as leaves or dried roots) of plants other than the tea shrub ⟨ginger *tea*⟩ **3 a** : a late afternoon serving of tea and a light meal **b** : a party, snack, or meal at which tea is served

tea 1a

tea bag *n* : a bag usually of filter paper holding enough tea for an individual serving

teach \'tēch\ *vb* **taught** \'tòt\; **teach·ing** **1** : to assist in learning how to do something : show how ⟨*teach* a child to read⟩ **2** : to guide the studies of : INSTRUCT ⟨*teach* a class⟩ **3** : to give lessons in : instruct pupils in ⟨*teach* music⟩ **4** : to be a teacher **5** : to cause to learn : cause to know the effects of an action ⟨the experience *taught* him to be more careful⟩

teach·able \'tē-chə-bəl\ *adj* : capable of being taught; *esp* : able and willing to learn — **teach·abil·i·ty** \,tē-chə-'bil-ət-ē\ *n*

teach·er \'tē-chər\ *n* : one that teaches; *esp* : a person whose occupation is to instruct

teach·ing *n* **1** : the act, practice, or profession of a teacher **2** : something taught; *esp* : DOCTRINE

tea·cup \'tē-,kəp\ *n* : a small cup used with a saucer for hot beverages

teak \'tēk\ *n* **1** : a tall timber tree of southeastern Asia **2** : the hard durable yellowish brown wood of a teak — called also *teak·wood* \'tē-,kwůd\

tea·ket·tle \'tē-,ket-ʔl\ *n* : a covered kettle that is used for boiling water and has a handle and a spout

teal \'tē(ə)l\ *n, pl* **teal** *or* **teals** : any of various small short-necked ducks

¹team \'tēm\ *n* **1** : two or more animals used to pull the same vehicle or piece of machinery; *also* : these animals

with their harness and attached vehicle **2** : a number of persons associated together in work or activity

²team *vb* **1** : to join in a team **2** : to haul with or drive a team **3** : to form a team

team·mate \'tēm-,māt\ *n* : a fellow member of a team

team·ster \'tēm(p)-stər\ *n* : a person who drives a team or truck

team·work \'tēm-,wərk\ *n* : the work or activity of a number of persons acting together as a team

tea·pot \'tē-,pät\ *n* : a pot that is used for brewing and serving tea and that has a spout

¹tear \'ti(ə)r\ *n* **1** : a drop of the salty liquid that keeps the eye and the inner eyelids moist **2** *pl* : an act of crying or grieving ⟨burst into *tears*⟩ [Old English *tēar* "a drop of liquid from the eye"] — **teary** \'ti(ə)r-ē\ *adj*

²tear *vb* : to fill with tears : shed tears ⟨eyes *tearing* in the wind⟩

³tear \'ta(ə)r, 'te(ə)r\ *vb* **tore** \'tō(ə)r, 'tò(ə)r\; **torn** \'tō(ə)rn, 'tò(ə)rn\; **tear·ing** **1 a** : to separate or pull apart by force ⟨*tore* a page from the pad⟩ **b** : to injure by or as if by tearing : LACERATE ⟨*tear* the skin⟩ **2** : to divide or throw into disorder by the pull of contrary forces ⟨a mind *torn* by doubts⟩ **3** : to remove by force ⟨children *torn* from their parents⟩ **4** : to cause by force or violent means ⟨*tore* a hole in the wall⟩ **5** : to move or act with violence, haste, or force ⟨*tearing* down the street⟩ [Old English *teran* "to pull apart"] — **tear·er** *n*

⁴tear \'ta(ə)r, 'te(ə)r\ *n* **1** : the act of tearing **2** : damage from being torn; *esp* : a torn place ⟨mending a *tear* in my sleeve⟩

tear down *vb* : to knock down and break into pieces ⟨*tear down* an old building⟩

tear·drop \'ti(ə)r-,dräp\ *n* **1** : ¹TEAR 1 **2** : something (as a pendent gem) shaped like a dropping tear

tear·ful \'ti(ə)r-fəl\ *adj* : flowing with, accompanied by, or causing tears — **tear·ful·ly** \-fə-lē\ *adv*

tear·gas \'ti(ə)r-,gas\ *vb* : to use tear gas on

tear gas *n* : any of various substances that cause eye irritation and blind the eyes with tears when released into the air and that are used mostly to scatter mobs

tea·room \'tē-,rüm, -,rům\ *n* : a restaurant serving light meals

¹tease \'tēz\ *vb* **teased; teas·ing** **1** : to untangle and lay parallel by combing or carding ⟨*tease* wool⟩ **2 a** : to annoy continually : PESTER, TORMENT **b** : TANTALIZE **c** : to make fun of — **teas·er** *n* — **teas·ing·ly** \'tē-ziŋ-lē\ *adv*

²tease *n* **1 a** : the act of teasing **b** : the state of being teased **2** : one that teases

tea·sel \'tē-zəl\ *n* : an Old World prickly herb with flower heads covered with stiff hooked bracts

tea·spoon \'tē-,spün, -'spün\ *n* **1** : a small spoon used especially for eating soft foods and stirring beverages **2** : a unit of measure used especially in cooking equal to ⅙ fluid ounce or ⅓ tablespoon (about 5 milliliters)

tea·spoon·ful \'tē-,spün-,fúl, -'spün-\ *n, pl* **tea·spoon·fuls** \-,fúlz\ *also* **tea·spoons·ful** \-,spünz-,fúl, -'spünz-\ : as much as a teaspoon can hold **2** : TEASPOON 2

teat \'tit, 'tēt\ *n* : the part of a breast or udder through which milk is drawn : NIPPLE

teasel

¹tech \'tek\ *n* : TECHNICIAN ⟨lab *techs*⟩ ⟨a computer *tech*⟩

\ə\ **abut**	\aú\ **out**	\i\ **tip**	\ò\ **saw**	\ů\ **foot**	
\ər\ **further**	\ch\ **chin**	\ī\ **life**	\òi\ **coin**	\y\ **yet**	
\a\ **mat**	\e\ **pet**	\j\ **job**	\th\ **thin**	\yü\ **few**	
\ā\ **take**	\ē\ **easy**	\ŋ\ **sing**	\th\ **this**	\yů\ **cure**	
\ä\ **cot, cart**	\g\ **go**	\ō\ **bone**	\ü\ **food**	\zh\ **vision**	

²tech *n* : TECHNOLOGY

tech·ne·tium \tek-'nē-sh(ē-)əm\ *n* : a radioactive metallic element obtained especially from nuclear fuel as a product of uranium fission — see ELEMENT table

tech·ni·cal \'tek-ni-kəl\ *adj* **1 a** : having special knowledge especially of a mechanical or scientific subject ⟨*technical* experts⟩ **b** : used in special fields of knowledge ⟨*technical* language⟩ **2** : of or relating to a particular subject; *esp* : of or relating to a practical subject organized on scientific principles ⟨*technical* training⟩ **3** : existing by laws or rules ⟨a *technical* knockout⟩ **4** : of or relating to technique ⟨*technical* skill⟩ — **tech·ni·cal·ly** \-k(ə-)lē\ *adv*

tech·ni·cal·i·ty \tek-nə-'kal-ət-ē\ *n, pl* **-ties** **1** : something technical; *esp* : a detail that means something only to a specialist ⟨a legal *technicality*⟩ **2** : the quality or state of being technical

technical sergeant *n* : an enlisted person in the air force with a rank just below a master sergeant

tech·ni·cian \tek-'nish-ən\ *n* **1** : a specialist in the technical details of a subject or occupation ⟨a medical *technician*⟩ **2** : a person skilled in the techniques especially of an art

tech·nique \tek-'nēk\ *n* **1 a** : the manner in which details are treated (as by a writer) or basic physical movements are used (as by a dancer) **b** : ability to treat such details or use such movements ⟨perfect piano *technique*⟩ **2 a** : technical methods especially in scientific research ⟨laboratory *technique*⟩ **b** : a method of accomplishing a desired aim ⟨a *technique* for handling complaints⟩

tech·nol·o·gist \tek-'näl-ə-jəst\ *n* : a person who specializes in technology

tech·nol·o·gy \tek-'näl-ə-jē\ *n, pl* **-gies** **1** : the use of science in solving problems (as in industry or engineering) **2** : a technical method of doing something — **tech·no·log·i·cal** \tek-nə-'läj-i-kəl\ *adj*

tech·no—pop \'tek-nō-päp\ *n* : popular music featuring chiefly the use of synthesizers

tec·ton·ic \tek-'tän-ik\ *adj* : of or relating to tectonics

tec·ton·ics \tek-'tän-iks\ *n* **1** : a branch of geology concerned with the structure of the crust of a planet (as earth) or moon and especially with the formation of folds and faults in it **2** : TECTONISM

tec·to·nism \'tek-tə-niz-əm\ *n* : the process of deformation that produces the earth's continents, ocean basins, mountains, folds, and faults

ted·dy bear \'ted-ē-\ *n* : a stuffed toy bear

te·dious \'tēd-ē-əs, 'tē-jəs\ *adj* : tiring because of length or dullness : BORING — **te·dious·ly** *adv* — **te·dious·ness** *n*

te·di·um \'tēd-ē-əm\ *n* : the quality or state of being tedious : BOREDOM

¹tee \'tē\ *n* **1** : the letter *t* **2** : something shaped like a capital T — **to a tee** : in a perfect manner : EXACTLY ⟨the new shirt fits me *to a tee*⟩

²tee *n* **1 a** : a small peg on which a golf ball is set to be struck **b** : an adjustable post on which a ball is placed for batting (as in T-ball) **2** : the area from which a golf ball is struck in starting play on a hole

³tee *vb* **teed; tee·ing** : to place on a tee ⟨*teed* up the ball⟩

teem \'tēm\ *vb* : to become filled : ABOUND ⟨a stream *teeming* with fish⟩

teen \'tēn\ *n* : TEENAGER — **teen** *adj*

teen·age \'tē-nāj\ *or* **teen·aged** \-nājd\ *adj* : of, being, or relating to people in their teens

teen·ag·er \'tē-nā-jər\ *n* : a person in his or her teens

teens \'tēnz\ *n pl* **1** : the numbers 13 through 19; *esp* : the years 13 through 19 in a lifetime or century **2** : teenage persons : TEENAGERS

tee·ny \'tē-nē\ *adj* **tee·ni·er; -est** : TINY

teeny-bop·per \'tē-nē-bäp-ər\ *n* : a young teenager who is

enthusiastically devoted to popular music and to current fads

tee·ny—wee·ny \tē-nē-'wē-nē\ *adj* : TINY

tee off *vb* **1** : to hit a golf ball from a tee in starting play on a hole **2** : BEGIN 1, START

teepee *variant of* TEPEE

tee shirt *variant of* T-SHIRT

tee·ter \'tēt-ər\ *vb* **1 a** : to move unsteadily ⟨*teetered* on the edge and fell over the side⟩ **b** : WAVER 1 **2** : ²SEESAW 2 — **teeter** *n*

tee·ter·board \-bō(ə)rd, -bò(ə)rd\ *n* **1** : ¹SEESAW 2b **2** : a board placed on a raised support so that a person standing on one end of the board is thrown into the air if another person jumps on the opposite end

tee·ter—tot·ter \'tēt-ər-tät-ər\ *n* : ¹SEESAW 2b

teeth *plural of* TOOTH

teethe \'tēth\ *vb* **teethed; teeth·ing** : to experience the emergence of one's teeth through the gums : grow teeth

Tef·lon \'tef-län\ *trademark* — used for synthetic fluorine-containing resins used especially for nonstick coatings

tele- *combining form* **1** : at or over a distance ⟨*tele*gram⟩ **2** : television ⟨*tele*cast⟩

tele·cast \'tel-i-kast\ *vb* **-cast** *also* **-cast·ed; -cast·ing** : to broadcast by television — **telecast** *n* — **tele·cast·er** *n*

tele·com·mute \'tel-i-kə-myüt\ *vb* : to work at home using an electronic link (as the Internet) with a cental office — **tele·com·mut·er** *n*

tele·gram \'tel-ə-gram, *Southern also* -grəm\ *n* : a message sent by telegraph

¹tele·graph \'tel-ə-graf\ *n* : an electric device or system for sending messages by a code over wires — **tele·graph·ic** \tel-ə-'graf-ik\ *adj* — **tele·graph·i·cal·ly** \-'graf-i-k(ə-)lē\ *adv*

²telegraph *vb* **1** : to send by or as if by telegraph ⟨*telegraphed* a message⟩ **2** : to send a telegram to ⟨*telegraphed* home for money⟩ — **te·leg·ra·pher** \tə-'leg-rə-fər\ *n*

te·leg·ra·phy \tə-'leg-rə-fē\ *n* : the use or operation of a telegraph system or equipment

tele·mar·ket·ing \tel-ə-'mär-kət-iŋ\ *n* : the marketing of goods or services by telephone — **tele·mar·ket·er** \-ər\ *n*

tele·me·ter \'tel-ə-mēt-ər\ *n* : an electrical apparatus used to transmit measurements taken by automatic instruments especially by radio to a distant station — **teleme·ter** *vb*

te·lem·e·try \tə-'lem-ə-trē\ *n* **1** : the process of transmitting data by telemeter **2** : data transmitted by telemetry

te·lep·a·thy \tə-'lep-ə-thē\ *n* : apparent communication from one mind to another without speech or signs — **tele·path·ic** \tel-ə-'path-ik\ *adj* — **tele·path·i·cal·ly** \-'path-i-k(ə-)lē\ *adv*

¹tele·phone \'tel-ə-fōn\ *n* : an instrument for transmitting and receiving sounds over long distances by electricity

²telephone *vb* **-phoned; -phon·ing** **1** : to communicate by telephone **2** : to send by telephone **3** : to speak to by telephone

telephone booth *n* : an enclosure within which one may stand or sit while making a telephone call

tele·pho·to \tel-ə-'fōt-ō\ *adj* : being a camera lens designed to give a large image of a distant object

tele·print·er \'tel-ə-print-ər\ *n* : a device that produces hard copy from signals received over a communications circuit; *esp* : TELETYPEWRITER

¹tele·scope \'tel-ə-skōp\ *n* : a tubular instrument for viewing dis-

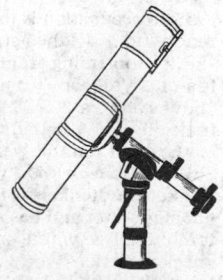

¹telescope

tant objects (as objects in outer space) by focusing light rays with mirrors or lenses

²tele·scope *vb* **-scoped; -scop·ing 1** : to slide or cause to slide one within another like the cylindrical sections of a hand telescope **2** : to run together like the sections of a telescope

tele·scop·ic \ˌtel-ə-ˈskäp-ik\ *adj* **1** : of, relating to, or performed with a telescope **2** : seen or discoverable only by a telescope 〈*telescopic* stars〉 **3** : able to discern objects at a distance 〈*telescopic* vision〉 **4** : having parts that telescope — **tele·scop·i·cal·ly** \-i-k(ə-)lē\ *adv*

tele·thon \ˈtel-ə-ˌthän\ *n* : a long television program usually to raise funds for a charity

Tele·type \ˈtel-ə-ˌtīp\ *trademark* — used for a teletypewriter

tele·type·writ·er \ˌtel-ə-ˈtīp-ˌrīt-ər\ *n* : a printing device resembling a typewriter that is used to send and receive signals over telephone lines

tel·evan·ge·list \ˌtel-i-ˈvan-jə-ləst\ *n* : an evangelist who conducts regularly televised religious programs — **tel·evan·ge·lism** \-ˌliz-əm\ *n*

tele·vise \ˈtel-ə-ˌvīz\ *vb* **-vised; -vis·ing** : to broadcast by television 〈*televised* the ball game〉

tele·vi·sion \ˈtel-ə-ˌvizh-ən\ *n* **1** : an electronic system of transmitting images with sound over a wire or through space by devices that change light and sound into electrical waves and then change these back into light and sound **2** : a television receiving set **3** : the television broadcasting industry

¹tel·ex \ˈtel-ˌeks\ *n* **1** : a communication service involving teletypewriters connected by wire through automatic exchanges **2** : a message sent by telex

²telex *vb* **1** : to send (as a message) by telex **2** : to communicate with by telex

tell \ˈtel\ *vb* **told** \ˈtōld\; **tell·ing 1** : ¹COUNT 1a, ENUMERATE **2 a** : to describe in detail : NARRATE 〈*tell* a story〉 **b** : to give an account 〈an article *telling* of her experience〉 **c** : ¹SAY 1a, UTTER 〈*tell* a lie〉 **3 a** : to make known : REVEAL 〈*tell* a secret〉 **b** : to express in words 〈can't *tell* you how pleased we are〉 **4** : to give information to : INFORM 〈*tell* me as soon as the package gets here〉 **5** : ¹ORDER 2a, DIRECT 〈*told* us to wait〉 **6** : to find out by observing 〈can *tell* the child is honest〉 **7** : to act as a tattletale 〈*tell* on a cheater〉 **8** : to have a noticeable effect 〈the pressure began to *tell* on them〉 **9** : to be evidence of : INDICATE 〈smiles *telling* of success〉 **synonyms** see REVEAL

tell·er \ˈtel-ər\ *n* **1** : one that tells 〈a *teller* of tales〉 **2** : a person who counts votes (as in a legislative body) **3** : a bank employee who receives and pays out money

tell·ing \ˈtel-iŋ\ *adj* : producing a noticeable effect : EFFECTIVE 〈the most *telling* evidence〉 — **tell·ing·ly** \-iŋ-lē\ *adv*

tell off *vb* : ²SCOLD 2, REPRIMAND 〈*told* him *off* for spreading rumors〉

¹tell·tale \ˈtel-ˌtāl\ *n* **1** : TALEBEARER, INFORMER **2** : an outward sign : INDICATION

²telltale *adj* : indicating or giving evidence of something 〈*telltale* fingerprints〉

tel·lu·ri·um \tə-ˈlur-ē-əm, te-\ *n* : an element that occurs in a silvery white brittle form having a metallic shine or in combination with metals and is used especially in alloys and catalysts — see ELEMENT table

telo·phase \ˈtel-ə-ˌfāz, ˈtēl-\ *n* **1** : the final stage of mitosis and of the second division of meiosis in which two new nuclei form each with a set of chromosomes **2** : the final stage in the first division of meiosis in which half the original number of chromosomes gather at opposite ends of the cell

te·mer·i·ty \tə-ˈmer-ət-ē\ *n* : the quality or state of being recklessly or foolishly bold

temp \ˈtemp\ *n* : TEMPERATURE

¹tem·per \ˈtem-pər\ *vb* **tem·pered; tem·per·ing** \-p(ə-)riŋ\ **1** : ²MODERATE 1, SOFTEN 〈*temper* justice with mercy〉 **2** : to control by reducing : SUBDUE 〈*temper* one's anger〉 **3** : to bring (as steel or glass) to the desired hardness or strength by heating and cooling **4** : to be or become tempered

²temper *n* **1** : characteristic manner of feeling 〈the *temper* of the times〉 **2** : the hardness or toughness of a substance 〈the *temper* of a knife blade〉 **3 a** : a characteristic state of mind or state of feeling : DISPOSITION **b** : calmness of mind : COMPOSURE 〈lost my *temper*〉 **c** : state of feeling or state of mind at a particular time **d** : a state of anger 〈left in a *temper*〉 **e** : the quality of being easily angered 〈has a hot *temper*〉

tem·pera \ˈtem-pə-rə\ *n* : a process of painting in which the colors are mixed with substances (as egg, glue, or gum) other than oil

tem·per·a·ment \ˈtem-p(ə-)rə-mənt\ *n* **1** : a person's attitude as it affects what he or she says or does 〈nervous *temperament*〉 **2** : the quality of being very excitable or irritable

tem·per·a·men·tal \ˌtem-p(ə-)rə-ˈment-ᵊl\ *adj* **1** : of or relating to temperament 〈*temperamental* peculiarities〉 **2 a** : likely to be easily upset 〈a *temperamental* movie star〉 **b** : unpredictable in performance 〈a *temperamental* motor〉 — **tem·per·a·men·tal·ly** \-ᵊl-ē\ *adv*

tem·per·ance \ˈtem-p(ə-)rən(t)s, -pərn(t)s\ *n* **1** : control over one's acts, thoughts, or feelings : MODERATION, RESTRAINT **2** : the use of little or no alcoholic drink

tem·per·ate \ˈtem-p(ə-)rət\ *adj* **1** : being or kept within limits **2** : not going too far in satisfying one's needs or desires **3** : not drinking much liquor **4** : marked by self-control : RESTRAINED 〈*temperate* speech〉 **5** : having or associated with a climate that is usually mild without extremely cold or extremely hot temperatures — **tem·per·ate·ly** *adv* — **tem·per·ate·ness** *n*

temperate rain forest *n* : woodland that has a temperate climate with heavy rainfall and that usually includes numerous kinds of trees but differs from a tropical rain forest in having one or two very common major trees

temperate zone *n, often cap T&Z* : the area or region between the Tropic of Cancer and the arctic circle or the Tropic of Capricorn and the antarctic circle — compare FRIGID ZONE, TORRID ZONE

tem·per·a·ture \ˈtem-pə(r)-ˌchùr, ˈtem-p(ə-)rə-ˌchùr, -chər\ *n* **1** : the degree of hotness or coldness of something (as air, water, or the body) as shown by a thermometer **2** : FEVER 1a 〈have a *temperature*〉

temperature inversion *n* : INVERSION 3

tem·pered \ˈtem-pərd\ *adj* **1** : made moderate 〈strictness *tempered* by compassion〉 **2** : having a particular kind of temper — used in combination 〈a bad-*tempered* dog〉 **3** : brought to the desired state (as of hardness, toughness, or flexibility) 〈*tempered* steel〉 〈*tempered* glass〉

tem·pest \ˈtem-pəst\ *n* **1** : a violent wind; *esp* : one accompanied by rain, hail, or snow **2** : a violent commotion : UPROAR

tem·pes·tu·ous \tem-ˈpes-chə-wəs, -ˈpesh-\ *adj* : VIOLENT 1, STORMY 〈a *tempestuous* sea〉 〈a *tempestuous* relationship〉 — **tem·pes·tu·ous·ly** *adv* — **tem·pes·tu·ous·ness** *n*

tem·plate \ˈtem-plət\ *n* **1** : a gauge, pattern, or mold (as a thin plate or board) used as a guide to the form of a piece being made **2** : something that establishes or serves as a pattern

¹tem·ple \ˈtem-pəl\ *n* : a building for worship

\ə\ abut	\aú\ out	\i\ tip	\ó\ saw	\ú\ foot
\ər\ further	\ch\ chin	\ī\ life	\ói\ coin	\y\ yet
\a\ mat	\e\ pet	\j\ job	\th\ thin	\yü\ few
\ā\ take	\ē\ easy	\ŋ\ sing	\th\ this	\yù\ cure
\ä\ cot, cart	\g\ go	\ō\ bone	\ü\ food	\zh\ vision

²temple *n* : the flattened space on each side of the forehead of some mammals including human beings

tem·po \'tem-pō\ *n, pl* **tem·pi** \-pē\ *or* **tempos** **1** : the rate of speed at which a musical piece or passage is to be played or sung **2** : rate of motion or activity

tem·po·ral \'tem-p(ə-)rəl\ *adj* **1** : of or relating to time as opposed to eternity **2 a** : of or relating to earthly life **b** : of or relating to material as opposed to spiritual concerns — **tem·po·ral·ly** \-ē\ *adv*

temporal bone *n* : a compound bone that is located on the side of the skull of some mammals including human beings and is composed of four major parts

tem·po·rary \'tem-pə-ˌrer-ē\ *adj* : not permanent : lasting for a limited time ⟨a *temporary* shortage⟩ [from Latin *temporarius* "lasting for only a short time," from *tempus* "time" — related to ¹TENSE] — **tem·po·rari·ly** \ˌtem-pə-'rer-ə-lē\ *adv*

tem·po·rize \'tem-pə-ˌrīz\ *vb* **-rized; -riz·ing** **1** : to act to suit the time or occasion : COMPROMISE **2** : to draw out discussions so as to gain time : DELAY — **tem·po·riz·er** \'tem-pə-ˌrī-zər\ *n*

tempt \'tem(p)t\ *vb* **1** : to persuade or try to persuade to do wrong by promise of pleasure or gain **2** : to risk the dangers of ⟨*tempt* fate⟩ **3 a** : to get to do something ⟨*tempted* her to taste the cake⟩ **b** : to cause to have a certain feeling ⟨was *tempted* to quit⟩ — **tempt·able** \'tem(p)-tə-bəl\ *adj* — **tempt·er** *n*

temp·ta·tion \tem(p)-'tā-shən\ *n* **1** : the act of tempting : the state of being tempted especially to evil **2** : something tempting

tempt·ing \'tem(p)-tiŋ\ *adj* : having a strong attraction ⟨the food all looked *tempting*⟩ — **tempt·ing·ly** *adv*

tempt·ress \'tem(p)-trəs\ *n* : a woman who tempts

ten \'ten\ *n* **1** — see NUMBER table **2** : the tenth in a set or series ⟨the *ten* of hearts⟩ **3** : something having ten units or members **4** : a 10-dollar bill — **ten** *adj or pron*

ten·a·ble \'ten-ə-bəl\ *adj* : capable of being held, maintained, or defended ⟨a *tenable* argument⟩

te·na·cious \tə-'nā-shəs\ *adj* **1 a** : not easily pulled apart **b** : tending to stick **2 a** : holding fast or tending to hold fast : PERSISTENT ⟨people *tenacious* of their opinions⟩ ⟨old ideas are *tenacious*⟩ **b** : RETENTIVE ⟨a *tenacious* memory⟩ — **te·na·cious·ly** *adv* — **te·na·cious·ness** *n*

te·nac·i·ty \tə-'nas-ət-ē\ *n* : the quality or state of being tenacious

ten·an·cy \'ten-ən-sē\ *n, pl* **-cies** **1 a** : the temporary possession or use of another's property **b** : the period of such use or possession **2** : the ownership of property

¹ten·ant \'ten-ənt\ *n* **1** : one who occupies property of another especially for rent **2** : OCCUPANT

²tenant *vb* : to hold or occupy as a tenant : INHABIT

tenant farmer *n* : a farmer who works land owned by another and pays rent either in cash or in shares of produce

Ten Commandments *n pl* : the commandments of God given to Moses on Mount Sinai

¹tend \'tend\ *vb* **1** : to pay attention ⟨*tend* to business⟩ **2 a** : to take care of ⟨*tended* her sick father⟩ **b** : to help the growth or development of ⟨*tend* the garden⟩ **3** : to have responsibility for as caretaker ⟨*tended* sheep⟩ **4** : to manage the operation of or do the necessary work connected with ⟨*tend* the fire⟩

²tend *vb* **1** : to move or turn in a certain direction ⟨the road *tends* to the right⟩ **2** : to be likely ⟨a person who *tends* to slouch⟩

ten·den·cy \'ten-dən-sē\ *n, pl* **-cies** **1** : a direction or approach toward a place, object, result, or limit **2** : a leaning toward a particular kind of thought or action : INCLINATION

¹ten·der \'ten-dər\ *adj* **1** : having a soft or yielding quality ⟨*tender* steak⟩ **2 a** : physically weak : DELICATE ⟨a *tender* plant⟩ **b** : IMMATURE, YOUNG ⟨children of *tender* years⟩ **3** : LOVING, AFFECTIONATE ⟨a *tender* look⟩ **4** : showing care : CONSIDERATE **5** : not harsh or stern : GENTLE, MILD ⟨*tender* irony⟩ **6** : sensitive to touch : very easily hurt ⟨a *tender* bruise⟩ **7** : demanding careful and sensitive handling ⟨a *tender* subject⟩ [Middle English *tender* "tender, fragile," from early French *tendre* (same meaning), from Latin *tener* "having a soft yielding texture, tender, young"] — **ten·der·ly** *adv* — **ten·der·ness** *n*

²tender *vb* **ten·dered; ten·der·ing** \-d(ə-)riŋ\ **1** : to offer in payment **2** : to present for acceptance ⟨*tendered* my resignation⟩ [Middle English *tendren* "to offer in payment," from early French *tendre* "to stretch out, offer," from Latin *tendere* "to stretch" — related to ²TENSE]

³tender *n* **1** : an offer of money in payment of a debt **2** : an offer made for acceptance; *esp* : a bid for a contract **3** : something that may by law be offered in payment; *esp* : MONEY

⁴tend·er \'ten-dər\ *n* : one that tends or takes care: as **a** : a ship used to attend other ships (as to supply food) **b** : a boat that carries passengers or freight between shore and a larger ship **c** : a car attached to a locomotive for carrying fuel and water [from *tend* "to look after" and *-er*, noun suffix]

⁵tender *n* : an often breaded strip of usually breast meat ⟨chicken *tenders*⟩ [probably short for *tenderloin*]

ten·der·foot \'ten-dər-ˌfüt\ *n, pl* **ten·der·feet** \-ˌfēt\ *also* **ten·der·foots** \-ˌfüts\ **1** : a person who is not hardened to a rough outdoor life **2** : BEGINNER

ten·der·heart·ed \ˌten-dər-'härt-əd\ *adj* : easily moved to love, pity, or sorrow : COMPASSIONATE

ten·der·ize \'ten-də-ˌrīz\ *vb* **-ized; -iz·ing** : to make (meat or meat products) tender by using a process or substance that breaks down connective tissue — **ten·der·i·za·tion** \ˌten-d(ə-)rə-'zā-shən\ *n* — **ten·der·iz·er** \'ten-də-ˌrī-zər\ *n*

ten·der·loin \'ten-dər-ˌloin\ *n* : a strip of tender meat (as beef or pork) on each side of the backbone

ten·don \'ten-dən\ *n* : a tough cord or band of dense white connective tissue that links a muscle to some other part (as a bone)

ten·dril \'ten-drəl\ *n* **1** : a slender leafless winding stem by which some climbing plants fasten themselves to a support **2** : something that curls like a tendril ⟨*tendrils* of hair⟩

T tendril 1

ten·e·ment \'ten-ə-mənt\ *n* **1 a** : a house used as a dwelling **b** : APARTMENT 1, FLAT **c** : TENEMENT HOUSE **2** : DWELLING

tenement house *n* : APARTMENT BUILDING; *esp* : one housing poorer families in a city

te·net \'ten-ət\ *n* : a widely held belief; *esp* : one held in common by members of a group or profession

ten·fold \'ten-ˌfōld, -'fōld\ *adj* **1** : having 10 units or members **2** : being 10 times as much or as many — **ten·fold** *adv*

ten·nis \'ten-əs\ *n* : a game played with rackets and a light elastic ball by two players or two pairs of players on a level court divided by a low net

tennis shoe *n* : a lightweight sneaker suitable for wear when playing tennis

ten·on \'ten-ən\ *n* : a projecting part in a piece of material (as wood) for insertion into a mortise to make a joint

¹ten·or \'ten-ər\ *n* **1** : the general meaning of something spoken or written ⟨the *tenor* of the book⟩ **2 a** : the next to lowest musical part in harmony for four parts — compare ALTO 1b, ²BASS 1a, ²SOPRANO 1 **b** : the highest natural adult male singing voice or a person who has such a voice **c** : a person or instrument performing a part next above a bass part **3** : a continuing in a course, movement, or activity ⟨the *tenor* of my life⟩

²tenor *adj* : relating to or having the range or part of a tenor

ten·pen·ny nail \ten-ˌpen-ē-\ *n* : a nail three inches (about 7.6 centimeters) long

ten·pin \'ten-ˌpin\ *n* **1** : a large bottle-shaped bowling pin **2** *pl* : a bowling game using 10 tenpins and a large ball

tens digit \'tenz-\ *n* : the numeral (as 5 in 456) in the tens place

¹tense \'ten(t)s\ *n* : a form of a verb used to show the past, present, or future time of the action or state it denotes [Middle English *tens* "time, tense," from early French *tens* (same meaning), from Latin *tempus* "time" — related to TEMPORARY]

²tense *adj* **tens·er; tens·est** **1** : stretched tight : made taut : RIGID ⟨*tense* muscles⟩ **2** : feeling or showing nervous tension ⟨a *tense* smile⟩ **3** : marked by strain or uncertainty ⟨a *tense* moment⟩ [from Latin *tensus* "stretched tight," from *tendere* "to stretch" — related to ²TENDER] **synonyms** see TIGHT — **tense·ly** *adv* — **tense·ness** *n*

³tense *vb* **tensed; tens·ing** : to make or become tense

ten·sion \'ten-chən\ *n* **1 a** : the act or action of stretching or the condition or degree of being stretched to stiffness ⟨*tension* of a muscle⟩ **b** : ¹STRESS 1c **2 a** : a state of mental unrest that is often accompanied by physical signs (as perspiring) of emotion **b** : a state of unfriendliness between individuals or groups

ten·sor \'ten(t)-sər, 'ten-ˌsó(ə)r\ *n* : a muscle that stretches a part

ten–speed \'ten-ˌspēd\ *n* : a bicycle with ten possible combinations of gears

tens place *n* : the place two to the left of the decimal point in a number expressed in the Arabic system of writing numbers ⟨2 is in the *tens place* in the number 124.6⟩

¹tent \'tent\ *n* **1** : a portable shelter (as of nylon) stretched and supported by poles **2 a** : something that resembles a tent or that serves as a shelter; *esp* : an enclosure placed over the head and shoulders to hold in oxygen or vapors given for medical reasons ⟨an oxygen *tent*⟩ **b** : the web of a tent caterpillar

²tent *vb* **1** : to live in a tent **2** : to cover with or as if with a tent

ten·ta·cle \'tent-i-kəl\ *n* **1** : any of various long flexible structures that stick out usually around the head or mouth of an animal (as a jellyfish or sea anemone) and are used especially for feeling or grasping **2** : something that resembles a tentacle especially in or as if in grasping or feeling out **b** : a sensitive hair on a plant — **ten·ta·cled** \-kəld\ *adj*

ten·ta·tive \'tent-ət-iv\ *adj* **1** : not fully worked out or developed ⟨*tentative* plans⟩ **2** : HESITANT, UNCERTAIN ⟨a *tentative* smile⟩ — **ten·ta·tive·ly** *adv*

tent caterpillar *n* : any of several destructive caterpillars that live in groups and construct large silken webs on trees

tenth \'ten(t)th\ *n, pl* **tenths** \'ten(t)s, 'ten(t)ths\ **1** — see NUMBER table **2** : one of 10 equal parts of something **3** : the one numbered 10 in a countable series — **tenth** *adj or adv*

tenths digit *n* : the numeral (as 5 in 4.56) in the tenths place in a number expressed in the Arabic system of writing numbers

tenths place *n* : the first place to the right of the decimal point in a number expressed in the Arabic system of writing numbers ⟨4 is in the *tenths place* in the number 12.46⟩

ten·u·ous \'ten-yə-wəs\ *adj* : having little substance or strength : FLIMSY, WEAK ⟨a *tenuous* hold on reality⟩ — **ten·u·ous·ly** *adv*

ten·ure \'ten-yər\ *n* : the act, right, manner, or term of holding something (as property, a position, or an office); *esp* : a status granted after a trial period to a teacher that gives protection from dismissal except for serious cause determined by formal proceedings — **ten·ur·ial** \te-'nyùr-ē-əl\ *adj*

ten·ured \-yərd\ *adj* : having tenure ⟨*tenured* teachers⟩

te·pee *or* **tee·pee** *also* **ti·pi** \'tē-pē\ *n* : a cone-shaped tent usually of skins used as a home especially by American Indians of the Great Plains [from *tʰípi*, a word in the language of the Dakota Indians meaning "a dwelling tent," from *tʰí-* "to dwell"]

tep·id \'tep-əd\ *adj* **1** : LUKEWARM ⟨a *tepid* bath⟩ **2** : lacking enthusiasm or conviction : HALFHEARTED ⟨a *tepid* response⟩

te·qui·la \tə-'kē-lə, tā-\ *n* : a Mexican liquor made from the fermented juice of an agave

tepee

tera- \'ter-ə\ *combining form* : trillion ⟨*tera*watt⟩ [from Greek *teras* "monster"]

tera·byte \'ter-ə-ˌbīt\ *n* : 1024 gigabytes; *also* : one trillion bytes

tera·watt \'ter-ə-ˌwät\ *n* : a unit of power equal to one trillion watts

ter·bi·um \'tər-bē-əm\ *n* : a rare metallic element — see ELEMENT table

ter·cet \'tər-sət\ *n* : a unit or group of three lines of verse

te·re·do \tə-'rēd-ō, -'rād-ō\ *n, pl* **-dos** : SHIPWORM

¹term \'tərm\ *n* **1** : ¹END 1b **2** : a fixed period of time; *esp* : the time for which something lasts : DURATION ⟨served two *terms*⟩ ⟨the new school *term*⟩ **3** *pl* : conditions that limit the nature and scope of something (as an agreement) ⟨could not accept their *terms*⟩ **4 a** : a word or expression that has an exact meaning in some uses or is limited to a particular field ⟨legal *terms*⟩ **b** *pl* : words of a particular kind ⟨spoke in glowing *terms*⟩ **5 a** : a mathematical expression (as $3x$ in $x^2 + 3x - y$) connected to another by a plus or a minus sign **b** : an element (as a numerator) of a fraction or proportion **6** *pl* **a** : personal relationship ⟨on good *terms* with the neighbors⟩ **b** : AGREEMENT 1b ⟨come to *terms* after much compromise⟩ **c** : a state of acceptance or understanding ⟨came to *terms* with not making the team⟩ — **in terms of** : with respect to or in relation to ⟨thinks of everything *in terms of* money⟩ — **on one's own terms** : in accordance with one's wishes : in one's own way ⟨prefers to live *on his own terms*⟩

²term *vb* : to apply a term to : CALL, NAME

¹ter·ma·gant \'tər-mə-gənt\ *n* : a nagging woman

²termagant *adj* : noisily nagging

¹ter·mi·nal \'tərm-nəl, -ən-ᵊl\ *adj* **1 a** : of, relating to, or forming an end ⟨a *terminal* pillar of a temple⟩ **b** : growing at the end of a branch or stem ⟨a *terminal* bud⟩ **2 a** : of, relating to, or occurring in a term or each term ⟨make *terminal* payments on a car⟩ **b** : leading finally to death ⟨a *terminal* illness⟩ **3** : occurring at or being the end of a period or series — **ter·mi·nal·ly** \-ē\ *adv*

²terminal *n* **1** : a part that forms the end **2** : a device attached to the end of a wire or cable or to electrical equipment for making connections **3 a** : either end of a trans-

\ə\ abut	\aù\ out	\i\ tip	\ò\ saw	\ù\ foot
\ər\ further	\ch\ chin	\ī\ life	\òi\ coin	\y\ yet
\a\ mat	\e\ pet	\j\ job	\th\ thin	\yü\ few
\ā\ take	\ē\ easy	\ŋ\ sing	\th\ this	\yù\ cure
\ä\ cot, cart	\g\ go	\ō\ bone	\ü\ food	\zh\ vision

portation line (as a railroad or shipping line) with its offices and freight and passenger stations **b** : a freight or passenger station that serves a large area or acts as a junction between lines ⟨a bus *terminal*⟩ **c** : a town at the end of a transportation line **4** : a device (as in a computer system) used for data entry and display

ter·mi·nate \'tər-mə-₁nāt\ *vb* **-nat·ed; -nat·ing 1 a** : to bring or come to an end : CLOSE ⟨*terminate* a meeting⟩ **b** : to form the conclusion of ⟨review questions *terminate* each chapter⟩ **2** : to serve as a limit or boundary of : BOUND ⟨a fence *terminated* the yard⟩ **3** : to reach an end point or line ⟨the racecourse *terminates* at the park entrance⟩ — **ter·mi·na·ble** \'tərm-(ə-)nə-bəl\ *adj* — **ter·mi·na·tion** \₁tər-mə-'nā-shən\ *n* — **ter·mi·na·tor** \'tər-mə-₁nāt-ər\ *n*

ter·mi·nat·ing decimal *n* : a decimal which can be written as a sequence of digits (as 3.25) or for which all the digits to the right of some place are zero (as 1.40000. . .) — compare REPEATING DECIMAL

ter·mi·nol·o·gy \₁tər-mə-'näl-ə-jē\ *n, pl* **-gies** : the special terms or expressions used in a field ⟨the *terminology* of law⟩

term insurance *n* : insurance that covers a limited period of time and pays only for losses that occur during that period

ter·mi·nus \'tər-mə-nəs\ *n, pl* **ter·mi·ni** \-₁nī, -₁nē\ *or* **-nus·es 1** : final goal : finishing point **2** : a post or stone marking a boundary **3 a** : either end of a transportation line or travel route **b** : the station or town at such a place

ter·mite \'tər-₁mīt\ *n* : any of a group of pale-colored soft-bodied social insects that feed on wood, live in colonies consisting of winged sexual forms, wingless sterile workers, and often soldiers, and that include some very destructive to wooden structures and trees — called also *white ant*

term paper *n* : a major written assignment in a school or college course involving a student's individual research and study in a subject area

tern \'tərn\ *n* : any of numerous sea birds that often have a forked tail, black cap, and white or gray body and that in comparison to the related gulls have a smaller and slenderer body and bill and narrower wings

tern

¹**ter·race** \'ter-əs\ *n* **1 a** : a flat roof or open platform **b** : a level area next to a building **2 a** : a raised piece of land with the top leveled off **b** : one of a group of horizontal ridges made in a hillside to conserve moisture and prevent loss of soil for agriculture **3** : a row of houses on raised ground or a sloping site

²**terrace** *vb* **ter·raced; ter·rac·ing** : to make into a terrace or supply with terraces

ter·ra–cot·ta \₁ter-ə-'kät-ə\ *n, pl* **terra–cottas 1** : a glazed or unglazed baked clay used for pottery, statues, and building materials; *also* : something made of this material **2** : a brownish orange [from Italian *terra cotta,* literally "baked earth," derived from Latin *terra* "earth" and Latin *coquere* "to cook"]

ter·ra fir·ma \-'fər-mə\ *n* : dry land : SOLID GROUND

ter·rain \tə-'rān *also* te-\ *n* : the surface features of an area of land ⟨rough *terrain*⟩

ter·ra·pin \'ter-ə-pən, 'tar-\ *n* : any of various North American turtles living in fresh or somewhat salty water

ter·rar·i·um \tə-'rar-ē-əm, -'rer-\ *n, pl* **-ia** \-ē-ə\ *or* **-i·ums** : a transparent enclo-

terrapin

sure used for keeping and observing small animals and plants indoors

ter·res·tri·al \tə-'res-trē-əl, -'res-chəl, -'resh-chəl\ *adj* **1** : of or relating to the earth or its living things **2 a** : of or relating to land as distinct from air or water ⟨*terrestrial* transportation⟩ **b** : living on or in or growing from land ⟨*terrestrial* plants⟩ ⟨*terrestrial* birds⟩

ter·ri·ble \'ter-ə-bəl\ *adj* **1** : causing terror or awe : FEARFUL, DREADFUL ⟨a *terrible* disaster⟩ **2 a** : very great in degree ⟨made a *terrible* mess of things⟩ ⟨a *terrible* cold⟩ **b** : very bad in quality ⟨*terrible* music⟩ — **ter·ri·bly** \-blē\ *adv*

ter·ri·er \'ter-ē-ər\ *n* : any of various usually small energetic dogs originally used by hunters to drive game animals from their holes

Word History Today most terriers are kept as pets. However, there was a time when the dogs were widely used for hunting. Terriers are usually small dogs with short legs, and they were used to dig game animals such as foxes, badgers, and weasels out of their holes. The dogs were also trained to go into a hole after a game animal and drive it out. The French name for these dogs was *chen terrer,* meaning "earth dog." English borrowed only the word *terrier,* which can be traced back to Latin *terra,* meaning "earth." [Middle English *terryer* "a small dog used for hunting burrowing animals," from early French *(chen) terrer,* literally "earth dog," from *terre* "earth," derived from Latin *terra* (same meaning)]

ter·rif·ic \tə-'rif-ik\ *adj* **1** : causing terror : TERRIBLE ⟨*terrific* destruction⟩ **2** : very great in degree : EXTRAORDINARY ⟨a car going at *terrific* speed⟩ **3** : unusually good ⟨makes *terrific* chili⟩ — **ter·rif·i·cal·ly** \-i-k(ə-)lē\ *adv*

ter·ri·fy \'ter-ə-₁fī\ *vb* **-fied; -fy·ing** : to fill with terror — **ter·ri·fy·ing·ly** \-₁fī-iŋ-lē\ *adv*

ter·ri·to·ri·al \₁ter-ə-'tōr-ē-əl, -'tòr-\ *adj* **1** : of or relating to a territory ⟨*territorial* claims⟩ **2** : organized chiefly for territorial defense ⟨a *territorial* army⟩ **3** : showing or involving territoriality ⟨*territorial* birds⟩ — **territorial** *n* — **ter·ri·to·ri·al·ly** \-ē-ə-lē\ *adv*

ter·ri·to·ri·al·i·ty \₁ter-ə-₁tōr-ē-'al-ət-ē, -₁tòr-\ *n* : the pattern of behavior associated with the defense of an animal's territory

ter·ri·to·ry \'ter-ə-₁tōr-ē, -₁tòr-\ *n, pl* **-ries 1 a** : a geographic area belonging to or under the control of a government **b** : a part of the U.S. not included within any state but having a separate governing body **2 a** : an assigned area ⟨a sales representative's *territory*⟩ **b** : an area that is occupied and defended by an animal or group of animals

ter·ror \'ter-ər\ *n* **1** : a state of great fear **2** : a cause of great fear **3** : a dreadful person or thing; *esp* : an unruly child **4** : violent or destructive acts (as bombing) committed by a group as a way of achieving its goals

ter·ror·ism \'ter-ər-₁iz-əm\ *n* : the use of terror as a means of achieving a goal — **ter·ror·ist** \-ər-əst\ *adj or n*

ter·ror·ize \'ter-ər-₁īz\ *vb* **-ized; -iz·ing 1** : to fill with terror **2** : to force by threat or violence — **ter·ror·i·za·tion** \₁ter-ər-ə-'zā-shən\ *n*

ter·ry \'ter-ē\ *n, pl* **terries** : an absorbent fabric with an even surface of uncut loops — called also *terry cloth*

terse \'tərs\ *adj* **ters·er; ters·est** : being brief and to the point : CONCISE ⟨a *terse* summary⟩; *also* : CURT, BRUSQUE ⟨dismissed me with a *terse* "no"⟩ — **terse·ly** *adv* — **terse·ness** *n*

ter·ti·ary \'tər-shē-₁er-ē\ *adj* **1** : of third rank, importance, or value **2** *cap* : of, relating to, or being the earliest period of the Cenozoic era of geological history marked by the formation of high mountains (as the Alps and Himalayas) and the rise in importance of mammals on land; *also* : relating to the corresponding system of rocks — see GEOLOGIC TIME table

Tertiary *n* : the Tertiary period or system of rocks

¹test \'test\ *n* **1** : a means of finding out the nature, quality, or value of something ⟨put the new car to the *test*⟩ **2** : a procedure or method for identifying something ⟨a *test* for starch⟩ ⟨allergy *tests*⟩ **3** : a set of questions or problems designed to find out a person's knowledge, skills, or intelligence **4** : a result of or rating based on a test ⟨uses 80-pound *test* fishing line⟩

²test *vb* **1** : to put to test or proof : TRY ⟨*test* out your strength⟩ **2 a** : to take part in a test ⟨actors *testing* for roles in the play⟩ **b** : to achieve or be assigned a rating on the basis of tests ⟨the class *tested* high in math⟩ **3** : to use tests as a way to analyze or identify ⟨*test* for copper⟩ — **test·able** \'tes-tə-bəl\ *adj*

³test *n* : a firm or rigid covering (as a shell) of many invertebrates

tes·ta \'tes-tə\ *n, pl* **tes·tae** \-,tē, -,tī\ : the hard outer coat of a seed

tes·ta·ment \'tes-tə-mənt\ *n* **1** *cap* : either of the two chief parts of the Bible **2 a** : actual proof : EVIDENCE ⟨the result is *testament* to her determination and hard work⟩ **b** : an expression of belief : CREED **3** : the legal instructions for the distribution of a person's belongings after death : WILL — **tes·ta·men·ta·ry** \,tes-tə-'ment-ə-rē, -'men-trē\ *adj*

tes·ta·tor \'tes-,tāt-ər, tes-'tāt-\ *n* : a person who leaves a will in force at the time of death

test bed *n* : a vehicle (as an airplane) used for testing new equipment; *also* : any device, facility, or means for testing something in development

test·cross \'test-,kròs, 'tes-\ *n* : a cross between an individual displaying a recessive trait and one displaying a dominant trait to determine whether or not the dominant trait is heterozygous

test·ed \'tes-təd\ *adj* : examined or qualified through testing ⟨time-*tested* principles⟩

¹tes·ter \'tēs-tər, 'tes-\ *n* : a canopy or a frame for a canopy over a bed, pulpit, or altar

²test·er \'tes-tər\ *n* : one that tests

testes *plural of* TESTIS

tes·ti·cle \'tes-ti-kəl\ *n* : TESTIS

tes·ti·fy \'tes-tə-,fī\ *vb* **-fied;** **-fy·ing** **1 a** : to make a statement based on personal knowledge or belief ⟨could *testify* to the student's devotion to her studies⟩ **b** : to make a formal statement of what one swears is true ⟨*testified* in court⟩ **2** : to give outward proof : serve as a sign of ⟨yawns *testifying* to fatigue⟩ — **tes·ti·fi·er** \-,fī-(-ə)r\ *n*

¹tester

¹tes·ti·mo·ni·al \,tes-tə-'mō-nē-əl\ *adj* : being a testimonial

²testimonial *n* **1 a** : a recommendation of a product or service **b** : a letter of recommendation **2** : something given or said to show affection or respect : TRIBUTE

tes·ti·mo·ny \'tes-tə-,mō-nē\ *n, pl* **-nies** **1** : firsthand evidence ⟨according to the *testimony* of eyewitnesses⟩ **2** : a statement made by a witness under oath especially in a court **3** : a public declaration of religious experience

tes·tis \'tes-təs\ *n, pl* **tes·tes** \'tes-,tēz\ : an oval-shaped male reproductive gland that produces sperm and secretes testosterone and that in most mammals is contained within the scrotum

tes·tos·ter·one \te-'stäs-tə-,rōn\ *n* : a male hormone produced by the testes that causes the development of the male reproductive system and secondary sex characteristics

test pilot *n* : a pilot who puts new aircraft through tests

test tube *n* : a tube of thin glass closed at one end and used especially in chemistry and biology

tes·ty \'tes-tē\ *adj* **tes·ti·er;** **-est** : easily annoyed : IRRITABLE — **tes·ti·ly** \-tə-lē\ *adv* — **tes·ti·ness** \-tē-nəs\ *n*

tet·a·nus \'tet-ə-nəs\ *n* **1** : a dangerous infectious disease marked by contraction of the muscles especially of the jaws and caused by a poison made by a bacterium that usually enters the body through a wound — compare LOCKJAW **2** : contraction of a muscle for a much longer time than normal that results from rapidly repeated motor nerve impulses

¹tête-à-tête \,tāt-ə-,tāt\ *n* : a private conversation between two persons [French, literally "head-to-head"]

²tête-à-tête \,tāt-ə-'tāt\ *adv* : in private

³tête-à-tête \,tāt-ə-,tāt\ *adj* : being face-to-face : PRIVATE

¹teth·er \'teth-ər\ *n* : a line by which something (as an animal or a balloon) is fastened so as to limit its range

²tether *vb* **teth·ered;** **teth·er·ing** \'teth-(ə-)riŋ\ : to fasten or hold with or as if with a tether ⟨felt *tethered* to my desk⟩

teth·er·ball \'teth-ər-,bòl\ *n* : a game played with a ball suspended by a string from an upright pole in which the object is to wrap the string around the pole by striking the ball in a direction opposite to that of one's opponent

tet·ra \'te-trə\ *n* : any of various small brightly colored South American fishes often kept in tropical aquariums

tetra- *combining form* : four : having four : having four parts [derived from Greek *tetra-* "four"]

tet·ra·chord \'te-trə-,kò(ə)rd\ *n* : a series of four tones : half an octave

tet·ra·cy·cline \,te-trə-'sī-,klēn\ *n* : a yellow crystalline antibiotic produced by a soil bacterium or made synthetically

tet·ra·eth·yl lead \,te-trə-,eth-əl-'led\ *n* : a heavy oily poisonous liquid added to gasoline to prevent engines from knocking

tet·ra·he·dron \,te-trə-'hē-drən\ *n, pl* **-drons** *or* **tetrahedra** \-drə\ : a polyhedron that has four faces — **tet·ra·he·dral** \-drəl\ *adj*

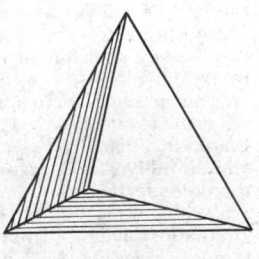

tetrahedron

te·tram·e·ter \te-'tram-ət-ər\ *n* : a line of verse consisting of four metrical feet

Teu·ton \'t(y)üt-ᵊn\ *n* **1** : a member of an ancient probably Germanic or Celtic people **2** : a member of a people speaking a Germanic language; *esp* : GERMAN 1 — **Teu·ton·ic** \t(y)ü-'tän-ik\ *adj*

Teutonic *n* : the Germanic languages

Tex–Mex \'tek-'smeks\ *adj* : of, relating to, or being the Mexican-American culture or food found especially in southern Texas [from *Tex*as and *Mex*ico]

¹text \'tekst\ *n* **1** : the original words of a work of literature **2 a** : the main body of printed or written matter on a page **b** : the main part of a book **3 a** : a passage from the Bible chosen for the subject of a sermon **b** : a subject on which one writes or speaks **4** : matter handled with a computer that is chiefly in the form of words **5** : TEXTBOOK **6** : TEXT MESSAGE

²text *vb* **1** : to send a text message from one cell phone to another **2** : to communicate by text messaging

text·book \'teks(t)-,bùk\ *n* : a book used in the study of a subject

\ə\ **abut**	\aù\ **out**	\i\ **tip**	\ò\ **saw**	\ù\ **foot**
\ər\ **further**	\ch\ **chin**	\ī\ **life**	\òi\ **coin**	\y\ **yet**
\a\ **mat**	\e\ **pet**	\j\ **job**	\th\ **thin**	\yü\ **few**
\ā\ **take**	\ē\ **easy**	\ŋ\ **sing**	\th\ **this**	\yù\ **cure**
\ä\ **cot, cart**	\g\ **go**	\ō\ **bone**	\ü\ **food**	\zh\ **vision**

tex·tile \'tek-ˌstīl, 'teks-t°l\ *n* : CLOTH 1; *esp* : a woven or knit cloth

text message *n* : a short message sent electronically usually from one cell phone to another

text mes·sag·ing \-'mes-i-jiŋ\ *n* : the sending of text messages electronically especially from one cell phone to another

tex·tu·al \'teks-chə(-wə)l\ *adj* : of, relating to, or based on a text — **tex·tu·al·i·ty** \ˌteks-chə-'wal-ət-ē\ *n* — **tex·tu·al·ly** \'tek-chə-(wə)l-ē\ *adv*

¹tex·ture \'teks-chər\ *n* **1** : the structure, feel, and appearance of something (as a fabric) ⟨the smooth *texture* of silk⟩ ⟨wood with a rough *texture*⟩ **2** : a quality that identifies something — **tex·tured** \-chərd\ *adj*

²texture *vb* **tex·tured; tex·tur·ing** : to give a particular texture to ⟨*texture* a ceiling⟩

tex·tur·ize \'teks-chə-ˌrīz\ *vb* **-ized; -iz·ing** : ²TEXTURE

¹-th — see ¹-ETH

²-th *or* **-eth** *adj suffix* — used to form ordinal numbers ⟨hundred*th*⟩ ⟨forti*eth*⟩ [Old English *-tha, -ta* (a suffix used in forming ordinal numbers)]

Thai \'tī\ *n* **1** : a person born or living in Thailand **2** : the official language of Thailand

thal·a·mus \'thal-ə-məs\ *n, pl* **thal·a·mi** \-ˌmī, -ˌmē\ : a subdivision of the forebrain that receives nerve impulses and sends them on to the appropriate parts of the brain cortex

thal·li·um \'thal-ē-əm\ *n* : a soft poisonous metallic element that has characteristics similar to lead — see ELEMENT table

¹than \thən, (')than\ *conj* **1** : when compared to the way, extent, or degree in or to which ⟨10 is less *than* 20⟩ ⟨older *than* I am⟩ ⟨easier said *than* done⟩ **2** : different from in kind, manner, or identity ⟨adults other *than* parents⟩

²than *prep* : in comparison with ⟨you are taller *than* me⟩

thane \'thān\ *n* **1** : a man in England during the Middle Ages who received lands from the king in return for military service **2** : a lord in Scotland during the Middle Ages

thank \'thaŋk\ *vb* **1** : to express gratitude to ⟨*thanked* her for the present⟩ **2** : to hold responsible ⟨had only myself to *thank* for my loss⟩

thank·ful \'thaŋk-fəl\ *adj* : feeling or showing thanks — **thank·ful·ly** \-fə-lē\ *adv* — **thank·ful·ness** *n*

thank·less \'thaŋ-kləs\ *adj* **1** : not appreciated by others ⟨a *thankless* job⟩ **2** : not showing or feeling gratitude — **thank·less·ly** *adv* — **thank·less·ness** *n*

thanks \'thaŋ(k)s\ *n pl* **1** : kindly or grateful thoughts : GRATITUDE ⟨express my *thanks* for their kindness⟩ **2** : an expression of gratitude ⟨give *thanks* before the meal⟩ ⟨many *thanks*⟩

thanks·giv·ing \thaŋ(k)s-'giv-iŋ\ *n* **1** : the act of giving thanks **2** : a prayer expressing gratitude **3** *cap* : THANKSGIVING DAY

Thanksgiving Day *n* : a day for giving thanks for divine goodness: as **a** : the fourth Thursday in November observed as a legal holiday in the U.S. **b** : the second Monday in October observed as a legal holiday in Canada

thanks to *prep* : with the help of : BECAUSE OF ⟨arrived early, *thanks to* good weather⟩ — **no thanks to** : not as a result of any help from ⟨we finished, *no thanks to* you⟩

thank–you \'thaŋ-ˌkyü\ *n* : a polite expression of one's gratitude

¹that \(')that\ *pron, pl* **those** \(')thōz\ **1 a** : the person, thing, or idea shown, mentioned, or understood from the situation ⟨*that* is my father⟩ **b** : the time, action, or event specified ⟨after *that* I went to bed⟩ **c** : the kind or thing specified as follows ⟨the purest water is *that* produced by distillation⟩ **2** : the one farther away ⟨*those* are elms and these are maples⟩ **3** : the one : the thing : the kind ⟨the richest ore is *that* found higher up⟩

²that *conj* **1 a** — used to introduce a noun clause serving especially as the subject or object of a verb ⟨*that* she has succeeded is certain⟩ ⟨said *that* I was afraid⟩ ⟨the reason for his absence is *that* he is ill⟩ **b** — used to introduce a clause that modifies a noun or adjective ⟨certain *that* this is true⟩ ⟨the fact *that* you are here⟩ **c** — used to introduce a clause that modifies an adverb or adverbial expression ⟨will go anywhere *that* he is invited⟩ **2** — used alone or after *so* or *in order* to introduce a clause expressing purpose ⟨saved money so *that* I could buy a bicycle⟩ **3** — used to introduce a clause giving a reason ⟨delighted *that* you could visit⟩ **4** — used especially after an expression including the word *so* or *such* to introduce a clause naming a result ⟨worked so hard *that* they became exhausted⟩

³that \thət, (ˌ)that\ *adj, pl* **those 1** : being the one named or understood ⟨*that* boy did it⟩ **2** : being the one farther away ⟨this chair or *that* one⟩

⁴that \thət, (ˌ)that\ *pron* **1** : WHO, WHOM, ²WHICH ⟨the girl *that* smiled⟩ ⟨the person *that* you spoke to⟩ ⟨the house *that* Jack built⟩ **2** : at, in, or on which : by, to, or with which ⟨each year *that* the awards are given⟩

⁵that \'that\ *adv* **1** : to such an extent ⟨need a nail about *that* long⟩ **2** : ²VERY 1, EXTREMELY ⟨it's not *that* important⟩

¹thatch \'thach\ *vb* : to cover with or as if with thatch

²thatch *n* **1** : a plant material (as straw) used to cover the roof of a building **2** : a mat of plant matter (as grass clippings) that has accumulated on the soil surface of a grassy area (as a lawn)

¹thaw \'thȯ\ *vb* **1** : to melt or cause to melt ⟨ice on the pond is *thawing*⟩ **2** : to become free of the effects of cold temperatures by being exposed to warmth ⟨frozen foods *thawed* before cooking⟩

²thaw *n* **1** : the action, fact, or process of thawing **2** : a period of time warm enough to thaw ice and snow

¹the \thə *(especially before consonant sounds and sometimes vowel sounds in Southern speech),* thē *(before vowel sounds);* 1e *is often* 'thē\ *definite article* **1 a** — used to indicate that a following noun or term functioning as a noun has been already made known by context or by circumstance ⟨put *the* cat out⟩ **b** — used to indicate that a following noun or term functioning as a noun is a unique or a particular member of its class ⟨*the* President⟩ ⟨*the* sun⟩ **c** — used before nouns that designate natural phenomena or points of the compass ⟨*the* night is cold⟩ ⟨wind came from *the* east⟩ **d** — used before a noun denoting time to indicate reference to what is present or immediate or is under consideration ⟨in *the* future⟩ **e** — used before names of some parts of the body or of the clothing as an equivalent of a possessive adjective ⟨how's *the* arm today⟩ ⟨grabbed me by *the* collar⟩ **f** — used before the name of a branch of human activity ⟨*the* law⟩ **g** — used in prepositional phrases to indicate that the noun in the phrase serves as a basis for calculation ⟨sold by *the* dozen⟩ **h** — used before a proper name (as of a ship or a well-known building) ⟨*the* Mayflower⟩ **i** — used before a proper name to indicate the distinctive characteristics of a person or thing ⟨*the* John Doe that we know wouldn't lie⟩ **j** — used before the plural form of a surname to indicate all the members of a family ⟨*the* Johnsons⟩ **k** — used before the plural form of a numeral that is a multiple of ten to denote a particular decade of a century or of a person's life ⟨life in *the* twenties⟩ **l** — used before the name of something used in daily life to indicate reference to the individual thing, part, or supply thought of as at hand ⟨talked on *the* telephone⟩ **m** — used to designate one of a class as the best, most typical, best known, or most worth singling out ⟨this is *the* life⟩ ⟨was *the* player in today's game⟩ **2 a** — used with a modified noun to limit the application of the noun to that specified by the modifier ⟨*the* right answer⟩ ⟨Peter *the* Great⟩ **b** — used before an absolute adjective or an ordinal number ⟨nothing but *the* best⟩ ⟨payment is due on *the* first⟩ **c** — used before a noun to limit its application to that specified by a following element in the sentence ⟨*the* poet Wordsworth⟩ ⟨didn't have *the* time to write⟩ **d** — used after a person's name to indicate a characteristic trait or notorious activity specified by the following noun ⟨Jack *the* Ripper⟩ **3 a** — used before a singular noun to indicate that the noun is to be understood as representative of a whole class ⟨good advice for *the* beginner⟩ **b** — used before an adjective functioning as a noun to indicate an abstract idea ⟨an essay on *the* sublime⟩ **4** — used before a noun or an adjective functioning as a noun to indicate reference to a group as a whole ⟨*the* rich⟩ ⟨*the* homeless⟩

²the *adv* **1** : than before : than otherwise ⟨none *the* wiser for attending⟩ **2 a** : to what extent ⟨*the* sooner the better⟩ **b** : to that extent ⟨the sooner *the* better⟩

the·ater *or* **the·atre** \'thē-ət-ər, 'thi-ət-\ *n* **1** : a building or area for dramatic performances or for showing movies **2** : a place like a theater; *esp* : a room often with rising rows of seats (as for a lecture) **3** : a place of significant events or action ⟨a *theater* of war⟩ **4** : plays or the performance of plays ⟨a course in American *theater*⟩ [Middle English *theatre* "outdoor structure for watching public performances (in ancient Greece and Rome)," from early French *theatre* (same meaning), from Latin *theatrum* (same meaning), from Greek *theatron*, literally "a place for viewing," from *theasthai* "to view," from *thea* "action of seeing, sight, view" — related to THEORY]

the·ater·go·er \-ˌgō-(ə-)r\ *n* : a person who frequently goes to the theater

the·at·ri·cal \thē-'a-tri-kəl\ *adj* **1** : of or relating to the theater ⟨a *theatrical* costume⟩ **2** : marked by pretended or excessive emotion ⟨a *theatrical* speech⟩ — **the·at·ri·cal·ly** \-k(ə-)lē\ *adv*

the·at·ri·cals \thē-'a-tri-kəlz\ *n pl* : the performance of plays

thee \(')thē\ *pron, objective case of* THOU

theft \'theft\ *n* : the act of stealing

their \thər, (ˌ)the(ə)r, (ˌ)tha(ə)r\ *adj* : of or relating to them or themselves ⟨*their* clothes⟩ ⟨they all have *their* theories⟩ ⟨*their* being seen⟩

theirs \'the(ə)rz, 'tha(ə)rz\ *pron* : their one : their ones ⟨the house is *theirs*⟩ ⟨these books are *theirs*⟩ ⟨*theirs* are on the table⟩

the·ism \'thē-ˌiz-əm\ *n* : belief in the existence of God as creator and ruler of the universe — **the·ist** \'thē-əst\ *n* — **the·is·tic** \thē-'is-tik\ *adj*

them \(th)əm, (')them, *after p, b, v, f, also* ᵊm\ *pron, objective case of* THEY

theme \'thēm\ *n* **1 a** : a subject for a work of literature, art, or music ⟨guilt and punishment is the *theme* of the story⟩ **b** : a specific and distinctive quality, characteristic, or concern ⟨the house was decorated in a country *theme*⟩ **2** : a written exercise : COMPOSITION — **the·mat·ic** \thi-'mat-ik\ *adj*

theme park *n* : an amusement park in which the structures and settings are based on a central theme

them·selves \thəm-'selvz, them-\ *pron* **1** : their own selves ⟨nations that govern *themselves*⟩ ⟨they *themselves* were present⟩ **2** : their normal or healthy condition ⟨were *themselves* again after a nights rest⟩

¹then \(')then\ *adv* **1** : at that time ⟨it was *then* believed the world was flat⟩ **2** : soon after that ⟨walked to the door, *then* turned⟩ **3 a** : following next after in order ⟨first came the clowns, *then* came the elephants⟩ **b** : in addition : BESIDES ⟨*then* there are the pots and pans to wash⟩ **4 a** : in that case ⟨take it, *then,* if you want it so much⟩ **b** : according to that ⟨your mind is made up, *then*⟩ **c** : as it appears ⟨the case, *then,* is closed⟩ **d** : as a necessary result ⟨if you were there, *then* you saw me⟩

²then \'then\ *n* : that time ⟨wait until *then*⟩

³then \'then\ *adj* : existing or acting at or belonging to the time mentioned ⟨the *then* governor⟩

thence \'then(t)s *also* 'then(t)s\ *adv* **1** : from that place ⟨proceeding *thence* directly to class⟩ **2** : from that fact or circumstance ⟨a natural conclusion follows *thence*⟩

thence·forth \'then(t)s-ˌfō(ə)rth, -ˌfȯ(ə)rth *also* 'then(t)s-\ *adv* : from that time forward : THEREAFTER ⟨the park was *thenceforth* open to residents only⟩

thence·for·ward \then(t)s-'fȯr-wərd *also* then(t)s-\ *also* **thence·for·wards** \-wərdz\ *adv* : onward from that place or time : THENCEFORTH

the·oc·ra·cy \thē-'äk-rə-sē\ *n, pl* **-cies** **1** : government of a country by officials believed to have divine guidance **2** : a country governed by a theocracy

the·od·o·lite \thē-'äd-ᵊl-ˌīt\ *n* : a very precise surveyor's transit

the·ol·o·gy \thē-'äl-ə-jē\ *n, pl* **-gies** **1** : the study of religion **2** : a set of religious beliefs — **theo·lo·gian** \ˌthē-ə-'lō-jən\ *n* — **theo·log·i·cal** \-'läj-i-kəl\ *adj*

the·o·rem \'thē-ə-rəm, 'thi(-ə)r-əm\ *n* **1** : a formula, proposition, or statement in mathematics or logic that has been or is to be proved from other formulas or propositions **2** : an idea accepted or proposed as a demonstrable truth

the·o·ret·i·cal \ˌthē-ə-'ret-i-kəl, ˌthi(-ə)r-'et-\ *also* **the·o·ret·ic** \-ik\ *adj* **1 a** : relating to or having the character of theory : ABSTRACT **b** : limited to theory or speculation : SPECULATIVE ⟨*theoretical* physics⟩ **2** : existing only in theory : HYPOTHETICAL ⟨a *theoretical* situation⟩ — **the·o·ret·i·cal·ly** \-i-k(ə-)lē\ *adv*

the·o·rist \'thē-ə-rəst, 'thi(-ə)r-əst\ *n* : a person who theorizes

the·o·rize \'thē-ə-ˌrīz\ *vb* **-rized; -riz·ing** : to form a theory : SPECULATE — **the·o·riz·er** *n*

the·o·ry \'thē-ə-rē, 'thi(-ə)r-ē\ *n, pl* **-ries** **1** : the general ideas or principles of an art or science ⟨music *theory*⟩ **2** : a general principle or set of principles that explains facts or events of the natural world ⟨wave *theory* of light⟩ **3** : a belief, policy, or procedure proposed or followed as the basis of action ⟨her method is based on the *theory* that all dogs can be trained⟩ **b** : an ideal set of facts, principles, or circumstances — often used in the phrase *in theory* ⟨in *theory,* everyone can receive a score of 100 on the test⟩ **4** : an idea that is the starting point for argument or investigation ⟨the *theory* of relativity⟩ [from Latin *theoria* "a looking at or considering of facts, theory," from Greek *theōria* "theory, action of viewing, consideration," from *theōrein* "to look at, consider," — related to THEATER]

ther·a·peu·tic \ˌther-ə-'pyüt-ik\ *adj* : of or relating to the treatment of diseases or disorders by using healing agents or methods ⟨*therapeutic* studies⟩; *also* : CURATIVE, MEDICINAL ⟨*therapeutic* diets⟩

ther·a·peu·tics \ˌther-ə-'pyüt-iks\ *n* : a branch of medical science dealing with the use of remedies

ther·a·pist \'ther-ə-pəst\ *n* : a person who specializes in therapy; *esp* : a person trained in methods of treatment other than the use of drugs or surgery ⟨a speech *therapist*⟩

ther·a·py \'ther-ə-pē\ *n, pl* **-pies** : treatment of an abnormal state of the mind or body

¹there \'tha(ə)r, 'the(ə)r\ *adv* **1** : in or at that place ⟨stand over *there*⟩ **2** : to or into that place ⟨went *there* every year⟩ **3** : at that point or stage ⟨stop right *there* before you say something you'll regret⟩ **4** : in that matter, re-

\ə\ **abut**	\au̇\ **out**	\i\ **tip**	\ȯ\ **saw**	\u̇\ **foot**
\ər\ **further**	\ch\ **chin**	\ī\ **life**	\ȯi\ **coin**	\y\ **yet**
\a\ **mat**	\e\ **pet**	\j\ **job**	\th\ **thin**	\yü\ **few**
\ā\ **take**	\ē\ **easy**	\ŋ\ **sing**	\th\ **this**	\yu̇\ **cure**
\ä\ **cot, cart**	\g\ **go**	\ō\ **bone**	\ü\ **food**	\zh\ **vision**

spect, or relation ⟨*there* is where I disagree with you⟩ **5** — used as an interjection to show satisfaction, approval, soothing, or defiance ⟨*there*, it's finished at last⟩ ⟨so *there*⟩

²**there** \(ˌ)tha(ə)r, (ˌ)the(ə)r *also* thər\ *pron* — used to introduce a sentence or clause ⟨*there* will come a time⟩

³**there** *like* ¹\ *n* **1** : that place or position ⟨get away from *there*⟩ **2** : that point ⟨you take it from *there*⟩

there·abouts *also* **there·about** \ˌthar-ə-ˈbaut(s), ˌther-; ˈthar-ə-ˌbaut(s), ˈther-\ *adv* **1** : near that place or time ⟨came from that town or *thereabouts*⟩ **2** : near that number, degree, or quantity ⟨fifty people or *thereabouts*⟩

there·af·ter \tha-ˈraf-tər, the-\ *adv* : after that ⟨it was returned shortly *thereafter*⟩

there·at \tha-ˈrat, the-\ *adv* **1** : at that place **2** : at that occurrence : on that account

there·by \ˈtha(ə)r-ˈbī, the(ə)r-; ˈtha(ə)r-ˌbī, ˈthe(ə)r-\ *adv* **1** : by that : by that means ⟨*thereby* lost her chance to win⟩ **2** : connected with or with reference to that ⟨*thereby* hangs a tale⟩

there'd \ˈtherd, ˈther-əd\ : there had : there would

there·for \tha(ə)r-ˈfō(ə)r, the(ə)r-\ *adv* : for or in return for that ⟨ordered a change and gave his reasons *therefor*⟩

there·fore \ˈtha(ə)r-ˌfō(ə)r, ˈthe(ə)r-, -ˌfȯ(ə)r\ *adv* : for that reason : CONSEQUENTLY ⟨he lost the bet, *therefore* he must pay⟩

there·from \tha(ə)r-ˈfrəm, the(ə)r-, -ˈfräm\ *adv* : from that or it ⟨learned much *therefrom*⟩

there·in \tha-ˈrin, the-\ *adv* **1** : in or into that place, time, or thing ⟨the world and all *therein*⟩ **2** : in that particular or respect ⟨*therein* they disagreed⟩

there'll \ˈther(-ə)l\ : there will : there shall

there·of \tha-ˈrəv, -ˈräv, the-\ *adv* **1** : of that or it ⟨the problem and solution *thereof*⟩ **2** : from that cause or particular : THEREFROM

there·on \tha-ˈrȯn, -ˈrän, the-\ *adv* : on that ⟨the highway and structures *thereon*⟩

there's \ˈtherz, thərz\ : there is : there has

there·to \tha(ə)r-ˈtü, the(ə)r-\ *adv* : to that ⟨voiced no complaints *thereto*⟩

there·to·fore \ˈthart-ə-ˌfō(ə)r, ˈthert-, -ˌfȯ(ə)r\ *adv* : up to that time ⟨noticed the *theretofore* undetected mistake⟩

there·un·to \tha-ˈrən-tü, the-; ˌthar-ən-ˈtü, ˌther-\ *adv, archaic* : THERETO

there·upon \ˈthar-ə-ˌpȯn, ˈther-, -ˌpän\ *adv* **1** : on that matter ⟨they disagreed *thereupon*⟩ **2** : THEREFORE **3** : immediately after that ⟨saw his bad grades and *thereupon* cut off his allowance⟩

there've \ˈtherv, thərv\ : there have

there·with \tha(ə)r-ˈwith, the(ə)r-, -ˈwith\ *adv* : with that ⟨led a simple life and was happy *therewith*⟩

there·with·al \ˈtha(ə)r-with-ˈȯl, ˈthe(ə)r-, -with-\ *adv* : THEREWITH

¹**ther·mal** \ˈthər-məl\ *adj* **1** : of or relating to a hot spring ⟨*thermal* springs⟩ **2** : of, relating to, caused by, or saving heat ⟨*thermal* energy⟩ ⟨*thermal* underwear⟩ — **ther·mal·ly** \-mə-lē\ *adv*

²**thermal** *n* : a rising body of warm air

thermal pollution *n* : the release of heated liquid (as water used by a factory) into a natural body of water at a temperature harmful to the environment

ther·mo·cou·ple \ˈthər-mə-ˌkəp-əl\ *n* : a device for measuring temperature in which a pair of wires of different metals (as copper and iron) are joined and the free ends of the wires are connected to an instrument (as a voltmeter) that measures the difference in potential created at the junction of the two metals

ther·mo·gram \ˈthər-mə-ˌgram\ *n* : a photograph that shows differences in temperature between different parts of an object (as the body or a building)

ther·mo·graph \ˈthər-mə-ˌgraf\ *n* : a recording thermometer

ther·mom·e·ter \thə(r)-ˈmäm-ət-ər\ *n* : an instrument for measuring temperature; *esp* : one consisting of a glass bulb attached to a fine glass tube with a numbered scale and containing a liquid (as mercury or colored alcohol) that is sealed in and rises and falls with changes of temperature — **ther·mo·met·ric** \ˌthər-mə-ˈme-trik\ *adj*

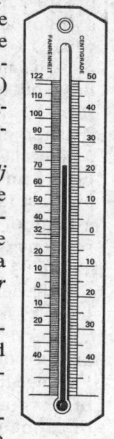

ther-mometer

ther·mo·nu·cle·ar \ˌthər-mō-ˈn(y)ü-klē-ər\ *adj* : of or relating to the transformations in the nucleus of atoms of low atomic weight (as hydrogen) that require a very high temperature (as in the hydrogen bomb or in the sun) ⟨a *thermonuclear* reaction⟩ ⟨a *thermonuclear* weapon⟩

ther·mo·plas·tic \ˌthər-mə-ˈplas-tik\ *adj* : capable of softening or melting when heated and of hardening again when cooled ⟨*thermoplastic* synthetic fibers⟩

ther·mos \ˈthər-məs\ *n* : a container (as a bottle) with a vacuum between an inner and an outer wall used to keep material (as liquids) hot or cold

ther·mo·stat \ˈthər-mə-ˌstat\ *n* : a device that automatically controls temperature — **ther·mo·stat·ic** \ˌthər-mə-ˈstat-ik\ *adj* — **ther·mo·stat·i·cal·ly** \-i-k(ə-)lē\ *adv*

ther·mo·tax·is \ˌthər-mə-ˈtak-səs\ *n* : a taxis in which temperature is the stimulus directing the movement of an organism

the·sau·rus \thi-ˈsȯr-əs\ *n, pl* **the·sau·ri** \-ˈsȯ(ə)r-ˌī, -ˌē\ *or* **the·sau·rus·es** \-ˈsȯr-ə-səz\ : a book of words and their synonyms [from scientific Latin *thesaurus* "treasury, storehouse, book of words," from Latin *thesaurus* "treasure, collection," from Greek *thēsauros* (same meaning) — related to TREASURE]

these *plural of* THIS

the·sis \ˈthē-səs\ *n, pl* **the·ses** \ˈthē-ˌsēz\ **1** : a statement put forth for discussion or proof : HYPOTHESIS **2** : a long essay presenting the results of original research

Thes·sa·lo·nians \ˌthes-ə-ˈlō-nyənz, -nē-ənz\ *n* — see BIBLE table

the·ta \ˈthāt-ə, ˈthēt-\ *n* : the eighth letter of the Greek alphabet — Θ or θ

they \(ˈ)thā\ *pron* **1** : those ones ⟨*they* won the game⟩ **2** : some people ⟨*they* say it will be a hard winter⟩

they'd \(ˌ)thād\ : they had : they would

they'll \(ˌ)thā(ə)l, thel\ : they shall : they will

they're \thər, (ˌ)the(ə)r\ : they are

they've \(ˌ)thāv\ : they have

thi·a·mine \ˈthī-ə-ˌmən, -ˌmēn\ *also* **thi·a·min** \-mən\ *n* : a vitamin of the B complex that is necessary for normal metabolism and nerve function and is found in many plants and animals — called also *vitamin B₁*

¹**thick** \ˈthik\ *adj* **1** : having or being of great depth or extent from one surface to its opposite ⟨a *thick* plank⟩ **2** : heavily built : THICKSET **3 a** : having units closely packed together : DENSE ⟨a *thick* forest⟩ **b** : occurring in large numbers : NUMEROUS ⟨flies were *thick* in the barn⟩ **c** : VISCOUS **2** ⟨*thick* syrup⟩ **4** : marked by haze, fog, or mist ⟨*thick* weather⟩ **5** : measuring in thickness ⟨12 inches *thick*⟩ **6 a** : not clearly spoken ⟨*thick* speech⟩ **b** : plainly obvious ⟨a *thick* French accent⟩ **7** : STUPID **1a** ⟨too *thick* to understand⟩ **8** : associated on close terms : INTIMATE ⟨those two are really *thick*⟩ **9** : going beyond what is proper or enough ⟨the flattery was a bit *thick*⟩ — **thick·ish** \-ish\ *adj* — **thick·ly** *adv*

²**thick** *n* **1** : the most crowded or active part ⟨in the *thick* of things⟩ **2** : the part of greatest thickness ⟨the *thick* of the thumb⟩

³**thick** *adv* : in a thick manner : so as to be thick : THICKLY ⟨*misfortunes came thick and fast*⟩

thick and thin *n* : every difficulty and problem ⟨was loyal through *thick and thin*⟩

thick·en \ˈthik-ən\ *vb* **thick·ened; thick·en·ing** \-(ə-)niŋ\ **1** : to make or become thick, dense, or viscous ⟨*thicken* gravy with flour⟩ **2** : to become complicated ⟨the plot *thickens*⟩ — **thick·en·er** \-(ə-)nər\ *n*

thick·en·ing *n* **1** : the act of making or becoming thick ⟨underwent a gradual *thickening*⟩ **2** : a thickened part or place **3** : something used to thicken

thick·et \ˈthik-ət\ *n* **1** : a thick usually small patch of shrubbery, small trees, or underbrush **2** : something resembling a thicket in being crowded together or impenetrable ⟨a *thicket* of fans⟩

thick·head·ed \ˈthik-ˈhed-əd\ *adj* : STUPID 1a

thick·ness \ˈthik-nəs\ *n* **1** : the quality or state of being thick **2** : the smallest of three dimensions ⟨length, width, and *thickness*⟩ **3** : the thick part of something **4** : ¹LAYER 2 ⟨a single *thickness* of canvas⟩

thick·set \ˈthik-ˈset\ *adj* **1** : closely placed or planted **2** : of short stout build : STOCKY

thick–skinned \-ˈskind\ *adj* **1** : having a thick skin **2** : not easily bothered by criticism or insult

thief \ˈthēf\ *n, pl* **thieves** \ˈthēvz\ : one that steals

thieve \ˈthēv\ *vb* **thieved; thiev·ing** : ¹STEAL 2a, ROB

thiev·ery \ˈthēv-(ə-)rē\ *n, pl* **-er·ies** : the action of stealing : THEFT

thiev·ish \ˈthē-vish\ *adj* **1** : of, relating to, or characteristic of a thief **2** : given to stealing — **thiev·ish·ly** *adv* — **thiev·ish·ness** *n*

thigh \ˈthī\ *n* : the part of the leg that extends from the hip to the knee

thigh·bone \-ˈbōn, -ˌbōn\ *n* : FEMUR 1

thig·mo·tax·is \ˌthig-mə-ˈtak-səs\ *n* : a taxis in which contact especially with a solid or rigid surface is the stimulus directing the movement of an organism

thig·mot·ro·pism \thig-ˈmä-trə-ˌpiz-əm\ *n* : a tropism in which contact especially with a solid or rigid surface is the stimulus directing the movement of an organism

thim·ble \ˈthim-bəl\ *n* : a cap or cover used in sewing to protect the finger that pushes the needle

¹**thin** \ˈthin\ *adj* **thin·ner; thin·nest** **1** : having little extent from one surface to its opposite ⟨*thin* paper⟩ **2** : having widely scattered units ⟨*thin* hair⟩ **3** : having too little flesh ⟨a tall *thin* boy⟩ **4** : less dense than normal ⟨*thin* air⟩ **5** : lacking substance or strength ⟨*thin* broth⟩ ⟨*thin* excuses⟩ **6** : somewhat weak or shrill ⟨a *thin* voice⟩ **synonyms** see LEAN — **thin·ly** *adv* — **thin·ness** \ˈthin-nəs\ *n* — **on thin ice** : in a dangerous situation

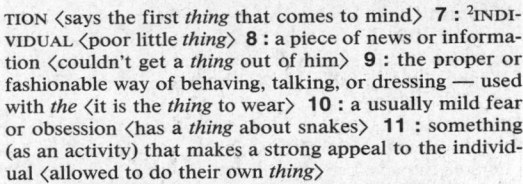

thimble

²**thin** *vb* **thinned; thin·ning** **1** : to make or become thin **2** : to reduce in number especially to prevent crowding ⟨*thin* young carrots in the garden⟩

thine \ˈthīn\ *pron, archaic* : thy one : thy ones

thing \ˈthiŋ\ *n* **1 a** : a matter of concern : AFFAIR ⟨many *things* to do⟩ **b** *pl* : state of affairs ⟨*things* are improving⟩ **c** : SITUATION **3** ⟨look at this *thing* another way⟩ **d** : EVENT 1a, CIRCUMSTANCE ⟨the flood was a terrible *thing*⟩ **e** : something one does well or likes to do ⟨do your *thing*⟩ **2 a** : ¹DEED 1, ACT ⟨do great *things*⟩ **b** : a product of work or activity ⟨likes to build *things*⟩ **c** : the aim of effort or activity ⟨the *thing* is to get well⟩ **3** : a particular object; *esp* : a lifeless object ⟨how do you work this *thing*?⟩ **4** *pl* : BELONGINGS ⟨pack your *things*⟩ **b** : an article of clothing ⟨not a *thing* to wear⟩ **5 a** : ¹DETAIL 1b ⟨checks every little *thing*⟩ **b** : a material or substance of a particular kind ⟨avoid starchy *things*⟩ **6** : IDEA 2, NO-

TION ⟨says the first *thing* that comes to mind⟩ **7** : ²INDIVIDUAL ⟨poor little *thing*⟩ **8** : a piece of news or information ⟨couldn't get a *thing* out of him⟩ **9** : the proper or fashionable way of behaving, talking, or dressing — used with *the* ⟨it is the *thing* to wear⟩ **10** : a usually mild fear or obsession ⟨has a *thing* about snakes⟩ **11** : something (as an activity) that makes a strong appeal to the individual ⟨allowed to do their own *thing*⟩

thing·am·a·bob \ˈthiŋ-ə-mə-ˌbäb\ *n* : THINGAMAJIG

thing·am·a·jig *or* **thing·um·a·jig** \ˈthiŋ-ə-mə-ˌjig\ *n* : something that is hard to classify or whose name is unknown or forgotten

think \ˈthiŋk\ *vb* **thought** \ˈthȯt\; **think·ing** **1** : to form or have in the mind ⟨afraid to *think* what might happen⟩ **2** : to have as an opinion : BELIEVE ⟨*think* it's so⟩ **3** : to hold in the mind for some time : PONDER ⟨*think* the matter over⟩ ⟨*think* about it⟩ **4** : to call to mind : REMEMBER ⟨never *thought* to ask⟩ ⟨he never *thinks* to call home⟩ **5** : to use the power of reason ⟨*think* before you write your answer⟩ **6** : to have an opinion ⟨they *think* highly of you⟩ **7** : to have concern ⟨I must *think* of my family first⟩ **8** : to invent by thinking — usually used with *up* ⟨always *thinking* up new schemes⟩ — **think·able** \ˈthiŋ-kə-bəl\ *adj* — **think·er** *n* — **think better of** : to reconsider and make a wiser decision — **think much of** : to view with satisfaction — usually used in negative constructions ⟨didn't *think much of* the idea⟩

¹**thinking** *n* **1** : the action of using one's mind to produce thoughts **2 a** : OPINION 1, JUDGMENT ⟨it is, to my *thinking*, utter nonsense⟩ **b** : ²THOUGHT 2 ⟨the current *thinking* on the subject⟩

²**thinking** *adj* : marked by use of the power of thinking ⟨*thinking* citizens⟩

thinking cap *n* : a state or mood in which one thinks ⟨put on your *thinking cap*⟩

think tank *n* : an organization formed to think up new solutions especially for social and scientific problems

thin·ner \ˈthin-ər\ *n* : one that thins; *esp* : a liquid (as turpentine) used to thin paint

thin–skinned \ˈthin-ˈskind\ *adj* **1** : having a thin skin ⟨*thin-skinned* oranges⟩ **2** : easily bothered by criticism or insult

¹**third** \ˈthərd\ *adj* **1 a** — see NUMBER table **b** : being next after the second in time, order, or importance ⟨the *third* taxi in line⟩ **2** : being one of three equal parts of something ⟨a *third* share of the money⟩ — **third** *adv* — **third·ly** *adv*

²**third** *n* **1 a** — see NUMBER table **b** : one next after a second in time, order, or importance ⟨the *third* in line⟩ **2** : one of three equal parts of something ⟨a *third* of the pie⟩ **3** : the difference in pitch between the first tone and the third tone of a scale **4** : the third forward gear or speed of a motor vehicle **5** : THIRD BASE

third base *n* : the base that must be touched third by a base runner in baseball or the position of the player defending the area around it

third baseman *n* : the player defending the area around third base

third class *n* : the class next below second class in a classification — **third–class** *adj*

third degree *n* : brutal treatment of a prisoner by the police in order to get a confession

third–degree burn *n* : a burn in which the whole thickness of the skin and sometimes underlying tissues are destroyed with loss of fluid and often shock

\ə\ abut	\au̇\ out	\i\ tip	\ȯ\ saw	\u̇\ foot
\ər\ further	\ch\ chin	\ī\ life	\ȯi\ coin	\y\ yet
\a\ mat	\e\ pet	\j\ job	\th\ thin	\yü\ few
\ā\ take	\ē\ easy	\ŋ\ sing	\th\ this	\yu̇\ cure
\ä\ cot, cart	\g\ go	\ō\ bone	\ü\ food	\zh\ vision

third party *n* **1** : a person other than the main participants ⟨a *third party* to the legal proceedings⟩ **2 a** : a political party operating usually for a limited time in addition to the two major parties in a 2-party system **b** : MINOR PARTY

third person *n* **1** : a set of words or forms (as verb forms or pronouns) referring to someone or something that is neither the speaker or writer of the utterance in which they occur nor the one to whom that utterance is addressed; *also* : a word or form belonging to such a set **2** : a writing style using verbs and pronouns of the third person

third–rate \'thər-'drāt\ *adj* : of third quality or value; *esp* : worse than second-rate

third world *n, often cap T&W* : the poor and underdeveloped nations of the world

¹thirst \'thərst\ *n* **1 a** : a feeling of dryness in the mouth and throat that accompanies a desire for liquids; *also* : the bodily condition (as of dehydration) that causes thirst **b** : a strong desire to drink **2** : a strong desire : CRAVING ⟨a *thirst* for fame⟩

²thirst *vb* **1** : to feel thirsty **2** : to have a strong desire : CRAVE

thirsty \'thər-stē\ *adj* **thirst·i·er; -est 1 a** : feeling thirst **b** : needing moisture ⟨*thirsty* land⟩ **2** : having a strong desire ⟨*thirsty* for knowledge⟩ — **thirst·i·ly** \-stə-lē\ *adv*

thir·teen \,thər(t)-'tēn, 'thər(t)-\ *n* — see NUMBER table — **thirteen** *adj or pron* — **thir·teenth** \-'tēn(t)th\ *adj or n*

thir·ty \'thərt-ē\ *n, pl* **thirties 1** — see NUMBER table **2** *pl* : the numbers 30 to 39; *esp* : the years 30 to 39 in a lifetime or century — **thir·ti·eth** \-ē-əth\ *n or adj* — **thirty** *adj or pron*

¹this \(')this, thəs\ *pron, pl* **these** \(')thēz\ **1** : the person, thing, or idea that is present or near in place, time, or thought or that has just been mentioned ⟨*these* are my friends⟩ **2** : the one nearer ⟨*this* is iron and that is tin⟩

²this *adj, pl* **these 1** : being the one that is present or near in place, time, or thought or that has just been mentioned ⟨*this* book is mine⟩ ⟨early *this* morning⟩ ⟨friends all *these* years⟩ **2** : the nearer at hand ⟨*this* car or that one⟩ ⟨I like *these* colors better than those⟩

³this \'this\ *adv* : to the degree suggested by something in the present situation ⟨didn't expect to wait *this* long⟩

this·tle \'this-əl\ *n* : any of various prickly plants related to the daisies and having often showy heads of mostly tubular flowers — **this·tly** \'this-(ə-)lē\ *adj*

this·tle·down \'this-əl-,daùn\ *n* : the mass of seed-carrying fluffy bristles from the ripe flower head of a thistle

thistle tube *n* : a usually glass funnel tube with a mouth that spreads out and a bulging top

¹thith·er \'thith-ər *also* 'thith-\ *adv* : to that place : THERE ⟨I shall go *thither*⟩

²thither *adj* : being on the other and farther side ⟨the *thither* bank of a river⟩

tho *variant of* THOUGH

thole \'thōl\ *also* **thole·pin** \-,pin\ *n* : a peg or pin on the rim of a boat that holds an oar in place

thong \'thòn\ *n* **1** : a strip of leather used especially for fastening something **2** : a sandal held on the foot by a thong fitting between the toes and connected by a strap across the top or around the sides of the foot

tho·rac·ic \thə-'ras-ik\ *adj* : of, relating to, located in, or involving the thorax ⟨the *thoracic* cavity⟩

tho·rax \'thōr-,aks, 'thòr-\ *n, pl* **tho·rax·es** *or* **tho·ra·ces** \'thōr-ə-,sēz, 'thòr-\ **1** : the part of the body of a

thistle

mammal between the neck and the abdomen; *also* : its cavity in which the heart and lungs lie **2** : the middle of the three main divisions of the body of an insect

tho·ri·um \'thōr-ē-əm, 'thòr-\ *n* : a radioactive metallic element — see ELEMENT table

thorn \'thò(ə)rn\ *n* **1** : a woody plant bearing sharp processes (as prickles or spines); *esp* : HAWTHORN **2** : a sharp stiff process on a plant; *esp* : a stem modified into a short, stiff, and leafless sharp point **3** : something or someone that causes distress or irritation — often used in the phrase *thorn in one's side* — **thorned** \'thò(ə)rnd\ *adj* — **thorn·less** \'thò(ə)rn-ləs\ *adj*

thorny \'thòr-nē\ *adj* **thorn·i·er; -est 1** : full of or covered with thorns ⟨*thorny* rose bushes⟩ **2** : full of difficulties ⟨a *thorny* problem⟩ — **thorn·i·ness** *n*

thor·ough \'thər-ō, 'thə-rō\ *adj* **1** : marked by or carried out to completion : EXHAUSTIVE ⟨a *thorough* search⟩ **2** : careful about detail ⟨a *thorough* worker⟩ [Middle English *thorow* "thorough," from Old English *thuruh, thurh* "through" — related to THRILL, THROUGH; see *Word History* at THRILL] — **thor·ough·ly** *adv* — **thor·ough·ness** *n*

¹thor·ough·bred \'thər-ə-,bred, 'thə-rə-\ *adj* **1** : bred from the best stock through a long line : PUREBRED ⟨*thoroughbred* dogs⟩ **2** *cap* : of, relating to, or being a Thoroughbred horse

²thoroughbred *n* **1** : a purebred or pedigreed animal **2** *cap* : any of an English breed of light speedy horses kept chiefly for racing

thor·ough·fare \'thər-ə-,fa(ə)r, 'thə-rə-, -,fe(ə)r\ *n* **1** : a street or road open at both ends **2** : a main road

thor·ough·go·ing \,thər-ə-'gō-iŋ, ,thə-rə-\ *adj* : THOROUGH 1, COMPLETE ⟨*thoroughgoing* cooperation⟩

²Thoroughbred 2

those *plural of* THAT

¹thou \(')thaù\ *pron, archaic* : the person addressed

²thou \'thaù\ *n, pl* **thou** : a thousand of something (as dollars) ⟨paid 15 *thou* for the car⟩

¹though \(')thō\ *conj* : in spite of the fact or possibility that ⟨*though* it was raining, we went hiking⟩

²though *adv* : ²HOWEVER 2, NEVERTHELESS ⟨not for long, *though*⟩

¹thought *past and past participle of* THINK

²thought \'thòt\ *n* **1** : the act or process of thinking **2** : serious consideration : careful attention ⟨give *thought* to the future⟩ **3** : power of thinking and especially of reasoning and judging **4** : power of imagining ⟨beauty beyond *thought*⟩ **5** : a product of thinking (as an idea, fancy, or invention) ⟨share your *thoughts* with us⟩

thought·ful \'thòt-fəl\ *adj* **1 a** : lost in thought **b** : marked by careful thinking ⟨a *thoughtful* essay⟩ **2** : considerate of the needs of others ⟨a kind and *thoughtful* friend⟩ — **thought·ful·ly** \-fə-lē\ *adv* — **thought·ful·ness** *n*

thought·less \'thòt-ləs\ *adj* **1 a** : not careful and alert **b** : done without thinking beforehand ⟨*thoughtless* actions⟩ **2** : lacking concern for others : INCONSIDERATE ⟨a *thoughtless* remark⟩ — **thought·less·ly** *adv* — **thought·less·ness** *n*

thought–out \'thòt-'aùt\ *adj* : produced or arrived at through careful and thorough consideration ⟨a well *thought-out* plan⟩

thou·sand \'thaùz-ᵊn(d)\ *n, pl* **thousands** *or* **thousand 1**

— see NUMBER table **2 :** a very large number ⟨*thousands* of ants⟩ — **thousand** *adj*

thou·sand–leg·ger \ˌthaủz-ᵊn-ˈ(d)leg-ər, -ˈ(d)lāg-\ *n* : MILLIPEDE

thousands digit \ˈthaủz-ᵊn(d)z-\ *n* : the numeral (as 1 in 1456) in the thousands place

thousands place *n* : the place four to the left of the decimal point in a number expressed in the Arabic system of writing numbers

thou·sandth \ˈthaủz-ᵊn(t)th\ *n* **1 :** one of 1000 equal parts of something **2 :** the one numbered 1000 in a countable series — see NUMBER table — **thousandth** *adj*

thrall \ˈthrȯl\ *n* **1 :** ¹SLAVE 1 **2 a :** a state of servitude or submission ⟨in *thrall* to his emotions⟩ **b :** a state of complete attention ⟨the play held me in *thrall*⟩ — **thrall·dom** *or* **thral·dom** \ˈthrȯl-dəm\ *n*

thrash \ˈthrash\ *vb* **1 :** THRESH 1 **2 a :** to strike forcefully especially with a long instrument (as a whip) : FLOG **b :** to defeat decisively or severely ⟨*thrashed* the visiting team⟩ **3 :** to move or stir about violently ⟨something was *thrashing* wildly in the water⟩ **4 :** to go over again and again ⟨*thrash* the matter over⟩ ⟨*thrash* out a plan⟩

¹**thrash·er** \ˈthrash-ər\ *n* : one that thrashes or threshes

²**thrasher** *n* : any of various long-tailed American songbirds that have a usually long curved bill and are related to the mockingbird

¹**thread** \ˈthred\ *n* **1 :** a thin fine cord formed by spinning and twisting short fibers into a continuous strand **2 :** something that resembles a thread ⟨*threads* of a spiderweb⟩ **3 :** the ridge or groove that winds around a screw **4 :** a train of thought that connects the parts in a sequence (as of ideas or events) ⟨lost the *thread* of the story⟩ — **thread·like** \-ˌlīk\ *adj*

²**thread** *vb* **1 :** to put a thread in working position in ⟨*thread* a needle⟩ **2 :** to pass through in the manner of a thread ⟨*thread* film through a camera⟩ **3 :** to make a way through or between ⟨a river *threading* narrow valleys⟩; *also* : to make (one's way) carefully ⟨had to *thread* their way between the mountains⟩ **4 :** to put together on a thread : STRING ⟨*thread* beads⟩ **5 :** to weave together with or as if with threads : INTERSPERSE ⟨dark hair *threaded* with gray⟩ — **thread·er** *n*

thread·bare \ˈthred-ˌba(ə)r, -ˌbe(ə)r\ *adj* **1 :** worn so much that the thread shows : SHABBY ⟨*threadbare* clothes⟩ **2 :** barely adequate ⟨a *threadbare* store with few items⟩ ⟨a *threadbare* event lacking excitement⟩ **3 :** having lost freshness and interest from overuse ⟨*threadbare* jokes⟩

thready \ˈthred-ē\ *adj* **1 :** consisting of or bearing fine threads or fibers ⟨a *thready* bark⟩ **2 :** lacking in fullness or vigor : THIN ⟨a *thready* voice⟩

threat \ˈthret\ *n* **1 :** an expression of an intent to do harm ⟨stop making *threats*⟩ **2 :** something that threatens ⟨the crumbling cliff was a *threat* to the village below⟩ **3 :** an indication of something impending ⟨the sky held a *threat* of rain⟩

threat·en \ˈthret-ᵊn\ *vb* **threat·ened; threat·en·ing** \ˈthret-niŋ, -ᵊn-iŋ\ **1 :** to utter threats : make threats against ⟨*threaten* tresspassers with arrest⟩ **2 :** to give signs or warning of ⟨clouds *threatening* rain⟩ **3 :** to be an imminent danger to : MENACE ⟨*hunger threatens* the town⟩ **4 :** to announce as intended or possible ⟨the workers *threatened* a strike⟩ ⟨*threatened* to buy a car⟩ **5 :** to cause to feel insecure or anxious ⟨felt *threatened* by his friend's success⟩ — **threat·en·ing·ly** \ˈthret-niŋ-lē, -ᵊn-iŋ-\ *adv*

three \ˈthrē\ *n* **1** — see NUMBER table **2 :** the third in a set or series ⟨the *three* of hearts⟩ **3 a :** something having three units or members **b :** THREE-POINTER — **three** *adj or pron*

3–D \ˈthrē-ˈdē\ *n* : the three-dimensional form or a picture produced in it

three–deck·er \ˈthrē-ˈdek-ər\ *n* : something made with three floors or layers

three–dimensional *adj* **1 :** of, relating to, or having three dimensions (as length, width, and height) **2 :** giving the appearance of depth or varying distances

three–fold \ˈthrē-ˌfōld, -ˈfōld\ *adj* **1 :** having three parts or members **2 :** being three times as great or as many — **threefold** *adv*

three–legged race \ˈthrē-ˈleg-əd-, -ˈlegd-\ *n* : a race between pairs of competitors with each partner having one leg tied to the adjoining leg of the other partner

three–pence \ˈthrep-ən(t)s, ˈthrip-, ˈthrəp-, *U.S. also* ˈthrē-ˌpen(t)s\ *n* **1** *pl* **threepence** *or* **three·penc·es** : a coin worth three pennies **2 :** the sum of three British pennies

three–pen·ny \ˈthrep-(ə-)nē, ˈthrip-, ˈthrəp-, *U.S. also* ˈthrē-ˌpen-ē\ *adj* : costing or worth threepence

three–pointer *n* : a basketball shot or field goal from beyond the three-point line

three–point line *n* : a line on a basketball court forming an arc at a set distance (as 22 feet) from the basket beyond which a field goal counts for three points

three–ring circus *n* **1 :** a circus with performances occuring in three different rings at the same time **2 a** : something wild, confusing, or chaotic ⟨five activities at one time turned the classroom into a *three-ring circus*⟩ **b** : something made into a spectacle ⟨the actor's court appearance became a *three-ring circus*⟩

three R's *n pl* : the basic subjects (as reading, writing, arithmetic) taught in elementary school

three·score \ˈthrē-ˈskō(ə)r, -ˈskȯ(ə)r\ *adj* : SIXTY

three·some \ˈthrē-səm\ *n* : a group of three

three–toed sloth \ˌthrē-ˌtōd-\ *n* : any of a genus of sloths having three claws on each foot — compare TWO-TOED SLOTH

three–wheel·er \ˈthrē-ˌhwē-lər, -ˌwē-\ *n* : any of various vehicles having three wheels

thren·o·dy \ˈthren-əd-ē\ *n, pl* **-dies** : a song of mourning or sorrow

thresh \ˈthrash, ˈthresh\ *vb* **1 :** to separate seed from a harvested plant especially by using a machine or tool ⟨*thresh* wheat⟩ **2 :** THRASH 4 ⟨*thresh* over a problem⟩ **3** : THRASH 3 ⟨*threshed* about in bed⟩

thresh·er \ˈthrash-ər, ˈthresh-\ *n* **1 a :** a person who threshes **b :** THRESHING MACHINE **2 :** THRESHER SHARK

thresher shark *n* : a large shark that has a very long curved upper lobe on its tail which it often uses in rounding up and stunning fish to feed on

thresher shark

threshing machine *n* : a machine used for separating grain or seeds from straw

thresh·old \ˈthresh-ˌ(h)ōld\ *n* **1 :** the section of wood or stone that lies under a door **2 a :** ¹ENTRANCE 2a **b :** the place or point of beginning ⟨at the *threshold* of an adventure⟩ **3 :** the point or level at which a physical or mental effect begins to be produced ⟨the *threshold* of hearing⟩

threw *past of* THROW

thrice \ˈthrīs\ *adv* **1 :** three times **2 :** to a high degree

thrift \ˈthrift\ *n* : careful management especially of money

thrift·less \ˈthrift-ləs\ *adj* : careless in the handling of money or resources

\ə\ **abut**		\aủ\ **out**	\i\ **tip**	\ȯ\ **saw**	\ủ\ **foot**
\ər\ **further**		\ch\ **chin**	\ī\ **life**	\ȯi\ **coin**	\y\ **yet**
\a\ **mat**		\e\ **pet**	\j\ **job**	\th\ **thin**	\yü\ **few**
\ā\ **take**		\ē\ **easy**	\ŋ\ **sing**	\t͟h\ **this**	\yủ\ **cure**
\ä\ **cot, cart**		\g\ **go**	\ō\ **bone**	\ü\ **food**	\zh\ **vision**

thrift shop *n* : a shop that sells secondhand articles and is often run by a charity

thrifty \\'thrif-tē\\ *adj* **thrift·i·er; -est** **1** : doing well because of hard work and thrift : PROSPEROUS **2** : growing strongly ⟨*thrifty* cattle⟩ **3** : tending to save money *synonyms* see FRUGAL — **thrift·i·ly** \\-tə-lē\\ *adv*

¹**thrill** \\'thril\\ *vb* **1** : to experience or cause to experience a sudden strong feeling of excitement ⟨the news *thrilled* him⟩ **2** : VIBRATE 2, TREMBLE ⟨a voice *thrilling* with emotion⟩

Word History Today when we speak of being thrilled, we are referring to a very pleasing experience. But it was not always so. The Old English word *thyrlian*, which gave us *thrill*, meant "to pierce" as with an arrow or spear. The Old English word came from an earlier word *thyrel*, meaning "hole." *Thyrel* has also given us two other Modern English words, *through* and *thorough*. It has also given us the last half of the word *nostril*, which literally means "nose hole." During the Middle English period the verb *thyrlian* became *thirlen* and continued to mean "to pierce." It also was the basis of the new verb *thrillen*, meaning "to penetrate." Then a connection was made between the physical sensation of being pierced and the emotional feeling of being suddenly and sharply excited. A new sense was born, which became the chief meaning of our *thrill*. [Middle English *thirlen, thrillen* "to pierce," from Old English *thyrlian* (same meaning) from *thyrel* "a hole," from *thurh* "through" — related to NOSTRIL, THOROUGH, THROUGH]

²**thrill** *n* **1 a** : a sudden strong emotion often accompanied by a tingling sensation ⟨gets a *thrill* of excitement from riding the roller coaster⟩ ⟨felt a *thrill* of fear⟩ **b** : something that thrills ⟨seeing my picture in the newspaper was a *thrill*⟩ **2** : VIBRATION 1b

thril·ler \\'thril-ər\\ *n* : one that thrills; *esp* : a work of fiction or drama with a great deal of action, mystery, adventure, or suspense

thrive \\'thrīv\\ *vb* **thrived** *or* **throve** \\'thrōv\\; **thrived** *also* **thriv·en** \\'thriv-ən\\; **thriv·ing** \\'thrī-viŋ\\ **1** : to grow vigorously : do well : FLOURISH **2** : to gain in wealth or possessions : PROSPER

throat \\'thrōt\\ *n* **1** : the part of the neck in front of the spinal column; *also* : the passage through the neck to the stomach and lungs **2** : something (as an end part) that resembles the throat — **throat·ed** \\-əd\\ *adj*

throaty \\'thrōt-ē\\ *adj* **throat·i·er; -est** : uttered or produced in deep low tones from or as if from low in the throat ⟨a *throaty* voice⟩ — **throat·i·ly** \\'thrōt-ᵊl-ē\\ *adv*

throb \\'thräb\\ *vb* **throbbed; throb·bing** **1** : to beat hard or fast (as from fright or pain) ⟨her injured ankle was *throbbing*⟩ **2** : to beat or vibrate with a steady rhythm — **throb** *n*

throe \\'thrō\\ *n* **1** : PANG ⟨death *throes*⟩ ⟨*throes* of childbirth⟩ **2** *pl* : a hard or painful struggle ⟨a state in the *throes* of revolution⟩

throm·bo·sis \\thräm-'bō-səs\\ *n, pl* **throm·bo·ses** \\-'bō-ˌsēz\\ : the formation or presence of a blood clot within a blood vessel

throm·bus \\'thräm-bəs\\ *n, pl* **throm·bi** \\-ˌbī, -ˌbē\\ : a clot of blood formed within a blood vessel and remaining attached to its place of origin — compare EMBOLUS

¹**throne** \\'thrōn\\ *n* **1** : the chair of state of a monarch or bishop **2** : royal power and dignity

²**throne** *vb* **throned; thron·ing** : to seat on a throne : ENTHRONE

¹**throng** \\'throŋ\\ *n* **1** : a large number of people gathered together ⟨a *throng* of over 3000⟩ **2** : a large number : CROWD ⟨a *throng* of fans⟩ ⟨a *throng* of cars⟩ *synonyms* see MULTITUDE

²**throng** *vb* **thronged; throng·ing** \\'throŋ-iŋ\\ **1** : to crowd upon or into ⟨a celebrity *thronged* by fans⟩ ⟨shoppers

thronged the mall⟩ **2** : to move, pass, or crowd together in great numbers ⟨the commuters *thronged* towards the station⟩

¹**throt·tle** \\'thrät-ᵊl\\ *vb* **throt·tled; throt·tling** \\'thrät-liŋ, -ᵊl-iŋ\\ **1** : to slow or stop the breathing of : CHOKE, STRANGLE **2** : to reduce the speed of (an engine) by closing the throttle — **throt·tler** \\-lər, -ᵊl-ər\\ *n*

²**throttle** *n* **1** : a valve controlling the flow of steam or fuel to an engine **2** : a lever controlling a throttle — **at full throttle** : at maximum speed or capacity ⟨jet engines operating *at full throttle*⟩ ⟨the project is proceeding *at full throttle*⟩

¹**through** \\(')thrü\\ *prep* **1 a** : in at one side and out at the opposite side of ⟨drove *through* the town⟩ **b** : by way of ⟨left *through* the window⟩ **c** : in the midst of : AMONG ⟨a path *through* the trees⟩ **d** : without stopping for ⟨drove *through* a red light⟩ **2 a** : by means of ⟨succeeded *through* hard work⟩ **b** : because of ⟨failed *through* lack of planning⟩ **3** : over the whole of ⟨all *through* the country⟩ **4 a** : from the beginning to the end of : DURING ⟨worked *through* the summer⟩ **b** : to and including ⟨Monday *through* Friday⟩ **5 a** : to a point of completion or exhaustion in ⟨got *through* the book⟩ **b** : to a state of official acceptance or approval ⟨got the bill *through* the legislature⟩ [Old English *thurh* "through" — related to THOROUGH, THRILL; see *Word History* at THRILL]

²**through** \\'thrü\\ *adv* **1 a** : from one end or side to the other ⟨let these people go *through*, please⟩ **b** : over the whole distance ⟨shipped *through* to Des Moines⟩ **2 a** : from beginning to end ⟨read the book *through* at one sitting⟩ **b** : to completion, conclusion, or accomplishment ⟨see the job *through*⟩ **3** : in or to every part : COMPLETELY ⟨wet *through*⟩ **4** : into the open : OUT ⟨break *through*⟩

³**through** \\'thrü\\ *adj* **1** : allowing free or continuous passage ⟨a *through* road⟩ **2** : going from point of origin to destination without changes or transfers ⟨a *through* train⟩ **3** : coming from and going to points outside a local area ⟨a lane for *through* traffic only⟩ **4** : having reached the end ⟨is *through* with the job⟩

¹**through·out** \\thrü-'aut\\ *adv* **1** : in or to every part : EVERYWHERE ⟨of one color *throughout*⟩ **2** : during the whole time or action : from beginning to end ⟨remained loyal *throughout*⟩

²**throughout** *prep* **1** : in or to every part of ⟨*throughout* the house⟩ **2** : during the whole time of ⟨*throughout* the evening⟩

throve *past of* THRIVE

¹**throw** \\'thrō\\ *vb* **threw** \\'thrü\\; **thrown** \\'thrōn\\; **throw·ing** **1 a** : to send through the air especially with a quick forward motion of the arm ⟨*threw* the ball over the fence⟩ **b** : ³PITCH 5b ⟨*threw* a no-hitter⟩ **2 a** : to cause to fall ⟨a horse jumped and *threw* its rider⟩ **b** : to cast (oneself) heavily or forcefully ⟨*threw* herself on the sofa⟩ **c** : to get the better of : OVERCOME ⟨the problem didn't *throw* her⟩ **3 a** : to put suddenly in a certain condition or position ⟨*threw* her arms around him⟩ ⟨*threw* him into prison⟩ **b** : to bring to bear : EXERT ⟨*threw* all their efforts into repairing the house⟩ **4** : to put on or take off quickly ⟨*throw* on a coat⟩ **5** : to form or shape on a potter's wheel **6** : to move to an open or closed position ⟨*throw* a switch⟩ **7** : to lose (a game or contest) on purpose **8** : to commit oneself for help, support, or protection ⟨*threw* himself on the mercy of the court⟩ **9** : to indulge in ⟨*threw* a temper tantrum⟩ **10** : to give for entertainment ⟨*throw* a party⟩ — **throw·er** \\'thrō(-ə)r\\ *n* — **throw one's weight around** *or* **throw one's weight about** : to exercise influence or authority especially to an excessive degree or in an objectionable manner

synonyms THROW, TOSS, FLING, HURL mean to drive something swiftly through space often by a movement of the arm. THROW is the broadest word and can be used of almost any motion and driving force <*throw* a ball> <the sudden stop *threw* the groceries to the floor of the car>. TOSS suggests a light or careless throwing <*toss* a coin to see which side comes up> <*tossed* the paper away>. FLING suggests a quick tossing often at no particular target <*flung* the coat on the chair and ran out of the room>. HURL suggests a throwing with strong force <*hurled* rocks at the old cans they were using as targets>.

²**throw** *n* **1** : an act of throwing **2** : a method of throwing an opponent in wrestling or judo **3** : the distance something is or may be thrown **4** : a loose covering (as for a sofa) **5** : a woman's light wrap

¹**throw·a·way** \'thrō-ə-ˌwā\ *n* : something that is or is designed to be thrown away especially after one use

²**throw·a·way** \ˌthrō-ə-ˌwā\ *adj* : designed to be thrown away : DISPOSABLE <*throwaway* cans and bottles>

throw away \ˌthrō-ə-'wā\ *vb* **1** : to get rid of : DISCARD <*threw* the old ones *away*> **2** : SQUANDER, WASTE <careful not to *throw* money *away*>

throw·back \'thrō-ˌbak\ *n* : something that has changed back to an earlier type or phase

throw off *vb* : to send out : EMIT <a sparkler *throws off* sparks>

throw out *vb* **1** : to reject or get rid of as worthless or unnecessary : THROW AWAY **2** : to remove from a place, position, or participation

throw rug *n* : a rug of such a size that several can be used (as to fill vacant places) in a room

throw up *vb* **1** : to build or raise hurriedly or quickly <*threw up* the window> **2** : to give up : QUIT <just wanted to *throw* the whole thing *up*> **3** : ²VOMIT 1

thru *variant of* THROUGH

thrum \'thrəm\ *vb* **thrummed; thrum·ming** : to sound or speak with a steady or boring rhythm — **thrum** *n*

thrush \'thrəsh\ *n* : any of a large family of small or medium-sized songbirds that are mostly of a plain color often with spotted underparts

¹**thrust** \'thrəst\ *vb* **thrust; thrust·ing** **1** : to push or drive with force : SHOVE **2** : to cause to enter or pierce something by pushing <*thrust* a knife into the bread> **3** : to press or force the acceptance of upon someone <*thrust* new responsibilities upon her>

²**thrust** *n* **1 a** : a push or lunge with a pointed weapon **b** : a military attack **2** : the force produced by a propeller or jet

thrush

or rocket engine that drives an aircraft or rocket forward **3 a** : a forward or upward push **b** : a movement (as by a group of people) in a particular direction

thrust·er \'thrəs-tər\ *n* : one that thrusts; *esp* : an engine that produces thrust by discharging a jet of fluid or a stream of particles

thru·way \'thrü-ˌwā\ *n* : EXPRESSWAY

¹**thud** \'thəd\ *vb* **thud·ded; thud·ding** : to move or strike so as to make a dull sound

²**thud** *n* **1** : ⁴BLOW 1 **2** : a dull sound : THUMP 1

thug \'thəg\ *n* : RUFFIAN

Word History *Thug* was the name given by the British in India in the 19th century to a member of a band of thieves and murderers. A thug would pretend to be friendly with a traveler and offer to share a journey. Then as soon as it was safe to do so, the thug would strangle and rob his companion. The word *thug* comes from *ṅhag*, a word in the Indian language Hindi meaning one of these robbers. Since thugs made travel danger-

ous, the British government rounded up most of them, and in a few years they were no longer a threat. The word *thug*, however, has lasted till today and even taken on the broader meaning of "ruffian." [from Hindi and Urdu *ṅhag*, literally "thief"]

thu·li·um \'th(y)ü-lē-əm\ *n* : a soft rare metallic element — see ELEMENT table

¹**thumb** \'thəm\ *n* **1 a** : the short thick first finger of the human hand next to the index finger **b** : the similar structure in lower animals **2** : the part of a glove or mitten that covers the thumb

²**thumb** *vb* **1** : to turn pages with the thumb <*thumb* through a book> **2** : to seek or get a ride in a passing automobile by sticking out one's thumb

thumb drive *n* : FLASH DRIVE

¹**thumb·nail** \'thəm-ˌnāl, -'nā(ə)l\ *n* **1** : the nail of the thumb **2** : a miniature computer graphic sometimes connected by a hyperlink to a larger version

²**thumb·nail** \ˌthəm-ˌnāl\ *adj* : ¹BRIEF <wrote a *thumbnail* sketch of the poet>

thumb·print \'thəm-ˌprint\ *n* : an impression made by the thumb

thumb·tack \'thəm-ˌtak\ *n* : a tack with a broad flat head for pressing into a board or wall with the thumb

thump \'thəmp\ *vb* **1** : to strike or beat with something thick or heavy so as to cause a dull sound **2** : to beat heavily : POUND — **thump** *n*

¹**thun·der** \'thən-dər\ *n* **1** : the loud sound that follows a flash of lightning **2** : a noise like thunder

²**thunder** *vb* **thun·dered; thun·der·ing** \-d(ə-)riŋ\ **1 a** : to produce thunder **b** : to produce a sound like thunder <horses *thundered* down the road> **2** : to utter loudly <the people *thundered* their approval> — **thun·der·er** \-dər-ər\ *n*

thun·der·bolt \'thən-dər-ˌbōlt\ *n* : a flash of lightning and the thunder that follows it

thun·der·clap \-ˌklap\ *n* **1** : a clap of thunder **2** : something sharp, loud, or sudden like a clap of thunder

thun·der·cloud \-ˌklaud\ *n* : a dark storm cloud that produces lightning and thunder

thun·der·head \-ˌhed\ *n* : a large cumulus cloud often appearing before a thunderstorm

thunder lizard *n* : BRONTOSAURUS

thun·der·ous \'thən-d(ə-)rəs\ *adj* **1** : producing thunder **2** : making a noise like thunder <*thunderous* applause> — **thun·der·ous·ly** *adv*

thun·der·show·er \'thən-dər-ˌshau̇(-ə)r\ *n* : a shower accompanied by lightning and thunder

thun·der·storm \-ˌstȯ(ə)rm\ *n* : a storm accompanied by lightning and thunder

thun·der·struck \-ˌstrək\ *adj* : stunned as if struck by a thunderbolt : ASTONISHED <*thunderstruck* at the news>

thunk \'thəŋk\ *vb* : to make a flat hollow sound — **thunk** *n*

Thurs·day \'thərz-dē\ *n* : the fifth day of the week

Word History Among the many gods worshiped by the Germanic people who lived in northern Europe in ancient times was one whose name was *Thor*. Thor was the god of thunder, weather, and crops. In the early Norse language, the fifth day of the week was known as *thōrsdagr*, literally "day of Thor," in his honor. The Norse name came into Old English as *thursdæg*, which in time became the Modern English *Thursday*. [Old English *thursdæg*, from early Norse *thōrsdagr*, literally "day of Thor"]

\ə\ **abut**	\au̇\ **out**	\i\ **tip**	\ȯ\ **saw**	\u̇\ **foot**
\ər\ **further**	\ch\ **chin**	\ī\ **life**	\ȯi\ **coin**	\y\ **yet**
\a\ **mat**	\e\ **pet**	\j\ **job**	\th\ **thin**	\yü\ **few**
\ā\ **take**	\ē\ **easy**	\ŋ\ **sing**	\th\ **this**	\yu̇\ **cure**
\ä\ **cot, cart**	\g\ **go**	\ō\ **bone**	\ü\ **food**	\zh\ **vision**

thus \\'thəs\ *adv* **1** : in this or that manner or way ⟨described it *thus*⟩ **2** : to this degree or extent : so ⟨a mild winter *thus* far⟩ **3** : because of this or that : HENCE ⟨attendence was poor, *thus* the meeting was canceled⟩ **4** : as an example

thwack \\'thwak\ *vb* : to strike with or as if with something flat or heavy : WHACK — **thwack** *n*

¹**thwart** \\'thwȯ(ə)rt\ *vb* **1** : to stand in the way of : hinder by opposing ⟨she *thwarted* me at every opportunity⟩ **2** : to defeat the hopes, desires, or plans of ⟨the goalie *thwarted* their attempts to score⟩ [Middle English *thwerten* (verb) "oppose, hinder," from *thwert* (adverb) "across"] **synonyms** see FRUSTRATE — **thwart•er** *n*

²**thwart** \\'thwȯ(ə)rt, *nautical often* 'thȯ(ə)rt\ *adv* : ¹ACROSS 1 [Middle English *thwert* "across"; of Norse origin]

³**thwart** *adj* : situated or placed across something else

⁴**thwart** *n* : a rower's seat extending across a boat

thy \(,)thī\ *adj, archaic* : of, relating to, or done by or to thee or thyself

thyme \\'tīm *also* 'thīm\ *n* **1** : any of a genus of Eurasian mints with small fragrant leaves; *esp* : one grown for use in seasoning food **2** : thyme leaves used as a seasoning

thy•mine \\'thī-,mēn\ *n* : a pyrimidine base that is one of the bases coding hereditary information in DNA — compare ADENINE, CYTOSINE, GUANINE, URACIL

thy•mus \\'thī-məs\ *n, pl* **thy•mus•es** *also* **thy•mi** \-,mī\ : a gland that is found in the young of most vertebrates usually in the chest near the heart, that before and for a time after birth has very important effects on the production and development of T cells, and that becomes less active and gradually shrinks or disappears with age

¹**thy•roid** \\'thī-,rȯid\ *adj* : of, relating to, or being the thyroid gland

²**thyroid** *n* : a large endocrine gland at the base of the neck of most vertebrates that produces iodine-containing hormones (as thyroxine) that affect growth, development, and metabolism — called also *thyroid gland*

thyroid–stimulating hormone *n* : a hormone secreted by the pituitary gland that controls the formation and release of the thyroid hormones

thy•ro•tro•pin \,thī-rə-'trō-pən\ *n* : THYROID-STIMULATING HORMONE

thy•rox•ine *or* **thy•rox•in** \thī-'räk-sən, -,sēn\ *n* : an iodine-containing hormone that is produced by the thyroid gland and is used to treat thyroid disorders

thy•self \thī-'self\ *pron, archaic* : YOURSELF

ti \\'tē\ *n* : the seventh note of the musical scale

ti•ara \tē-'ar-ə, -'er-, -'är-\ *n* **1** : a crown worn by the pope **2** : a decorative headband worn by women on special occasions

Ti•bet•an \tə-'bet-ᵊn\ *n* **1** : a member of the native race of Tibet **2** : the language of the Tibetan people — **Tibetan** *adj*

tib•ia \\'tib-ē-ə\ *n, pl* **-i•ae** \-ē-,ē, -ē-,ī\ *also* **-i•as** **1** : the inner and usually larger of the two bones of the vertebrate leg that is located between the knee and the ankle — called also *shinbone* **2** : the fourth joint of the

thyme 1

tiara 2

leg of an insect between the femur and the tarsus — **tib•i•al** \-ē-əl\ *adj*

tib•io•fib•u•la \,tib-ē-ō-'fib-yə-lə\ *n* : a single bone that replaces the tibia and fibula in a frog or toad

tic \\'tik\ *n* **1** : a regularly repeated twitching movement of a particular muscle and especially one of the face **2** : a particular form of behavior or speech that is often repeated ⟨"you know" is a verbal *tic*⟩

¹**tick** \\'tik\ *n* **1** : any of numerous bloodsucking invertebrates that are arachnids larger than the related mites, attach themselves to warm-blooded animals to feed, and include important carriers of infectious diseases [Middle English *tyke, teke* "tick"]

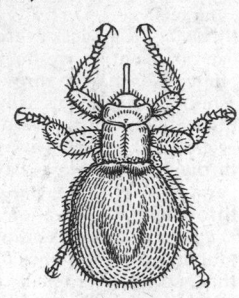

¹tick

²**tick** *n* **1** : the fabric case of a mattress, pillow, or cushion **2** : TICKING [Middle English *tike* "a fabric case for a mattress"; probably of Dutch origin]

³**tick** *n* **1** : a light rhythmic tap or beat ⟨the *tick* of a clock⟩ **2** : a small mark used to direct attention to something or to check an item on a list [Middle English *tek* "a rhythmic tap or beat"]

⁴**tick** *vb* **1 a** : to make the sound of a tick or a series of ticks **b** : to mark, count, or announce by or as if by ticking beats **2** : to work at a regular or proper pace : RUN **3** : to mark with a written tick : CHECK

⁵**tick** *n* : ¹CREDIT 3a, TRUST ⟨bought on *tick*⟩ [a shortened form of *ticket* "a slip recording a business deal"]

tick•er \\'tik-ər\ *n* **1** : ²WATCH 4 **2 a** : a telegraphic machine that receives stock prices and news and prints them out on a paper ribbon **b** : a strip of information that moves across the top or bottom of a television or computer screen **3** *slang* : HEART 1a

ticker tape *n* : the paper ribbon on which a telegraphic ticker prints

¹**tick•et** \\'tik-ət\ *n* **1** : ¹TAG 4, LABEL ⟨price *ticket*⟩ **2** : a summons or warning issued to a traffic offender ⟨got a *ticket* for speeding⟩ **3** : a paper or token showing that a fare or admission fee has been paid **4** : a list of candidates **5** : a slip or card recording a business deal [from obsolete French *etiquet* "a notice attached to something," derived from early French *estiquier* "to attach"; of Dutch origin — related to ETIQUETTE]

²**ticket** *vb* **1** : to attach a ticket to : LABEL **2** : to give a traffic ticket to

tick•ing \\'tik-iŋ\ *n* : a strong fabric used especially as a covering for mattresses and pillows

¹**tick•le** \\'tik-əl\ *vb* **tick•led; tick•ling** \-(ə-)liŋ\ **1** : to touch a body part lightly so as to cause uneasiness, laughter, or jerky movements **2** : to have a tingling or prickling sensation **3 a** : to excite or stir up agreeably : PLEASE ⟨food that *tickles* your taste buds⟩ **b** : to stir to laughter or merriment ⟨were *tickled* by the clown's antics⟩ — **tick•ler** \\'tik-(ə-)lər\ *n*

²**tickle** *n* **1** : the act of tickling **2** : a tickling sensation **3** : something that tickles

tick•lish \\'tik-(ə-)lish\ *adj* **1** : sensitive to tickling **2** : TOUCHY 1 ⟨*ticklish* about his baldness⟩ **3** : requiring delicate handling ⟨a *ticklish* subject⟩ — **tick•lish•ly** *adv* — **tick•lish•ness** *n*

tick–tack–toe *or* **tic–tac–toe** \,tik-,tak-'tō\ *n* : a game in which two players by turns put crosses and zeros in compartments of a figure formed by two vertical lines crossing two horizontal lines and each tries to get a row of three crosses or three zeros before the opponent does

tick·tock \'tik-ˌtäk, -ˌtäk\ *n* : the ticking sound of a clock [imitative]

tid·al \'tīd-ᵊl\ *adj* : of or relating to tides : rising and falling or flowing and ebbing at regular times

tidal wave *n* **1** : an unusually high sea wave that is triggered especially by an earthquake **2** : an unusual rise of water alongshore due to strong winds

tid·bit \'tid-ˌbit\ *also* **tit·bit** \'tit-ˌbit\ *n* **1** : a small tasty piece of food **2** : a pleasing bit (as of news)

tid·dle·dy·winks *or* **tid·dly·winks** \'tid-ᵊl-(d)ē-ˌwiŋ(k)s, 'tid-lē-ˌwiŋ(k)s\ *n* : a game in which players snap small disks from a flat surface into a small container

¹tide \'tīd\ *n* **1** : the alternate rising and falling of the surface of the ocean that occurs twice a day and is caused by the gravitational attraction of the sun and moon occurring unequally on different parts of the earth **2** : the flow of the incoming or outgoing tide **3** : something that rises and falls like the tides of the sea

²tide *vb* **tid·ed; tid·ing** : to enable to overcome or put up with a difficulty ⟨money to *tide* us over⟩

tide·land \'tīd-ˌland, -lənd\ *n* : land overflowed during high tide

tide pool *n* : a pool of salt water left (as in a rock basin) when the tide recedes

tide·wa·ter \-ˌwȯt-ər, -ˌwät-\ *n* **1** : water overflowing land at high tide **2** : low-lying coastal land

tid·ings \'tīd-iŋz\ *n pl* : NEWS 2b ⟨good *tidings*⟩

¹ti·dy \'tīd-ē\ *adj* **ti·di·er; -est** **1** : well ordered and cared for **2** : LARGE, SUBSTANTIAL ⟨a *tidy* price⟩ **synonyms** see NEAT

²tidy *vb* **ti·died; ti·dy·ing** **1** : to put in order ⟨*tidy* up the room⟩ **2** : to make things tidy

³tidy *n, pl* **tidies** : a fancy covering used to protect the back, arms, or headrest of a chair or sofa from wear or soiling

¹tie \'tī\ *n* **1** : a line, ribbon, or cord used for fastening, uniting, or drawing something closed **2 a** : a structural part (as a beam) holding two pieces together **b** : one of the cross supports to which railroad rails are fastened **3** : a bond of kinship or affection ⟨family *ties*⟩ **4** : a curved line joining two musical notes of the same pitch and used to indicate a single tone sustained through the time value of the two notes **5 a** : an equality in number : DEADLOCK ⟨the game ended in a *tie*⟩ **b** : a contest that ends with an equal score **6** : NECKTIE

²tie *vb* **tied; ty·ing** \'tī-iŋ\ *or* **tie·ing** **1 a** : to fasten, attach, or close by means of a tie **b** : to form a knot or bow in ⟨*tie* your scarf⟩ **2** : to limit the freedom or actions of ⟨responsibilities *tied* us down⟩ **3 a** : to make or have an equal score with in a contest ⟨the two teams *tied*⟩ **b** : to come up with something equal to ⟨*tied* the score⟩

tie–dye·ing \'tī-ˌdī-iŋ\ *n* : a hand method of producing patterns in textiles by tying portions of the fabric so that they will not absorb the dye — **tie–dye** \-ˌdī\ *n* — **tie–dyed** *adj*

tie in \(')tī-'in\ *vb* **1** : to bring into connection with something **2** : to become connected ⟨illustrations that *tie in* with the text⟩ — **tie–in** \'tī-ˌin\ *n*

¹tier \'ti(ə)r\ *n* : a row, rank, or layer usually arranged in a series one above the other — **tiered** \'ti(ə)rd\ *adj*

²tier *vb* **1** : to place or arrange in tiers **2** : to rise in tiers

³ti·er *or* **ty·er** \'tī(-ə)r\ *n* : a person or thing that ties

tie–up \'tī-ˌəp\ *n* **1** : a slowing or stopping especially of traffic or business **2** : CONNECTION 2, ASSOCIATION

tie up \(')tī-'əp\ *vb* **1** : to fasten securely **2 a** : to use in such a manner as not to be available for other purposes ⟨money *tied up* in stocks⟩ **b** : to keep from working or going ⟨traffic was *tied up* for hours⟩ **3** : to have a relationship with something else ⟨this *ties up* with what you said before⟩

tiff \'tif\ *n* : a minor quarrel

ti·ger \'tī-gər\ *n, pl* **ti·gers** *also* **tiger** **1** : a large Asian flesh‐eating mammal of the same family as the domestic cat with a coat that is typically light brown to orange with mostly vertical black stripes **2** : any of several large wildcats (as the jaguar or cougar) **3** : a domestic cat with a striped coat

tiger 1

tiger beetle *n* : any of numerous active beetles with strong jaws that eat other insects, have larvae which build tunnels in the soil, and include some capable of giving a painful bite

tiger cat *n* **1** : any of various medium-sized wildcats (as the ocelot) with a striped or spotted coat **2** : a striped or sometimes spotted tabby cat

ti·ger·ish \'tī-g(ə-)rish\ *adj* : of or resembling a tiger

tiger lily *n* : an Asian garden lily that has nodding usually orange-colored flowers spotted with black

tiger moth *n* : any of a family of stout-bodied moths usually with broad striped or spotted wings

tiger shark *n* : a large brown or gray shark of warm seas that sometimes attacks human beings

tiger swallowtail *n* : a large swallowtail of eastern North America that is mostly yellow with black borders and black stripes on the wings

¹tight \'tīt\ *adj* **1** : so close in structure as not to allow something (as liquid, gas, or light) to pass through ⟨a *tight* roof⟩ **2 a** : fixed very firmly in place ⟨loosen a *tight* jar cover⟩ **b** : not slack or loose ⟨kept the rope *tight*⟩ ⟨a *tight* knot⟩ **c** : fitting too closely ⟨*tight* shoes⟩ **3** : difficult to get through or out of ⟨in a *tight* spot⟩ ⟨on a *tight* schedule⟩ **4 a** : firm in control ⟨kept a *tight* hand on affairs⟩ **b** : STINGY 1 **5** : very closely packed or compressed ⟨a *tight* bale of hay⟩ **6** : low in supply : SCARCE ⟨money is *tight* just now⟩ — **tight·ly** *adv* — **tight·ness** *n*

synonyms TIGHT, TAUT, TENSE mean drawn or stretched to the limit. TIGHT may suggest that one thing is drawn around another as closely as possible ⟨the collar fit snugly around the dog's neck but was not too *tight*⟩. TAUT suggests pulling (as of a rope) until there is no give or slack ⟨a *taut* line between two poles⟩. TENSE suggests that something is so strained that it cannot function correctly ⟨if your muscles are too *tense*, you won't be able to run well⟩.

²tight *adv* **1 a** : in a tight manner ⟨hold on *tight*⟩ **b** : so as to be tight ⟨shut the door *tight*⟩ ⟨wound the spring *tight*⟩ **2** : in a deep and uninterrupted manner : SOUNDLY ⟨sleep *tight*⟩

tight·en \'tīt-ᵊn\ *vb* **tight·ened; tight·en·ing** \'tīt-niŋ, -ᵊn-iŋ\ : to make or become tight or tighter — **tight·en·er** \-nər, -ᵊn-ər\ *n*

tight·fist·ed \'tīt-'fis-təd\ *adj* : STINGY 1

tight–lipped \-'lipt\ *adj* **1** : having the lips closed tight (as in determination) **2** : not liking to speak : TACITURN

tight·rope \-ˌrōp\ *n* : a rope or wire stretched tight for acrobats to perform on

tights \'tīts\ *n pl* : a garment closely fitted to the body and covering it from the neck down or from the waist down

tight·wad \'tīt-ˌwäd\ *n* : a stingy person

ti·gress \'tī-grəs\ *n* : a female tiger

\ə\ abut	\au̇\ out	\i\ tip	\ȯ\ saw	\u̇\ foot
\ər\ further	\ch\ chin	\ī\ life	\ȯi\ coin	\y\ yet
\a\ mat	\e\ pet	\j\ job	\th\ thin	\yü\ few
\ā\ take	\ē\ easy	\ŋ\ sing	\th\ this	\yu̇\ cure
\ä\ cot, cart	\g\ go	\ō\ bone	\ü\ food	\zh\ vision

tike *variant of* TYKE

til·de \'til-də\ *n* : a mark ˜ placed especially over the letter *n* (as in Spanish *señor*) to indicate a sound that is approximately \ny\

¹**tile** \'tī(ə)l\ *n* **1** *pl* **tiles** *or* **tile a** : a flat or curved piece (as of fired clay, stone, or concrete) used especially for roofs or floors **b** : a pipe of earthenware used for a drain **2** : a thin piece of material (as linoleum or rubber) for covering floors or walls

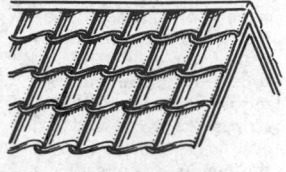

¹tile 1a

²**tile** *vb* **tiled; til·ing** : to cover with tiles

¹**till** *or* '**til** *also* **til** \t°l, təl, (,)til\ *prep or conj* : UNTIL ⟨won't finish *till* next week⟩ [Old English *til* "until"]

²**till** \'til\ *vb* : to work by plowing, sowing, and raising crops on or in ⟨*tilled* the land⟩ ⟨help *till* the soil⟩ [Old English *tilian* "to work (land) by plowing and raising crops"] — **till·able** \-ə-bəl\ *adj*

³**till** \'til\ *n* : a drawer for money

⁴**till** \'til\ *n* : a mixture of clay, sand, gravel, and boulders deposited by a glacier [origin unknown]

till·age \'til-ij\ *n* **1** : the process of tilling land **2** : cultivated land

¹**till·er** \'til-ər\ *n* : a person who tills; *also* : CULTIVATOR

²**til·ler** \'til-ər\ *n* : a lever used to turn the rudder of a boat from side to side

¹**tilt** \'tilt\ *vb* **1** : to move or shift so as to slant or tip **2** : to take part in a contest with lances : JOUST — **tilt·er** *n*

²**tilt** *n* **1** : a contest on horseback in which two opponents charging with lances try to unhorse each other : JOUST **2** : a contest with words between opponents **3** : ¹SPEED 1b ⟨at full *tilt*⟩ **4** : the act of tilting : the state or position of being tilted

tilth \'tilth\ *n* **1** : TILLAGE 2 **2** : the state of a soil with respect to the suitability of its particle size and structure for growing crops

tilt·me·ter \'tilt-,mēt-ər\ *n* : an instrument that measures the tilt of the earth's surface

tim·ber \'tim-bər\ *n* **1 a** : growing trees or their wood **b** — used interjectionally to warn of a falling tree **2** : wood for use in making something **3** : a usually large piece of wood squared or finished for use — **timber** *adj*

tim·ber·land \-,land\ *n* : wooded land especially with timber fit for sale

tim·ber·line \-,līn\ *n* : the upper limit beyond which trees do not grow (as on mountains) — called also *tree line*

timber wolf *n* : GRAY WOLF

tim·bre \'tam-bər, 'tim-\ *n* : the quality of a sound or musical tone determined by its overtones and different for each voice or instrument

tim·brel \'tim-brəl\ *n* : a small hand drum or tambourine

¹**time** \'tīm\ *n* **1 a** : the period during which an action, process, or condition exists or continues : DURATION ⟨was gone a long *time*⟩ ⟨it rained all the *time* during our vacation⟩ **b** : part of the day when one is free to do as one pleases ⟨find *time* for reading⟩ **2** : a point or period when something occurs : OCCASION ⟨remember the *time* you entered the pie-eating contest⟩ **3** : a set or usual moment or hour for something to happen, begin, or end ⟨arrived ahead of *time*⟩ **4 a** : a historical period : AGE ⟨in your grandparents' *time*⟩ **b** : conditions of a specified period ⟨*times* are hard⟩ ⟨move with the *times*⟩ **5** : a prison sentence ⟨doing *time* for robbery⟩ **6** : the rhythmic grouping of beats in music shown in the time signature **7 a** : a moment, hour, day, or year as indicated by a clock or calendar ⟨what *time* is it⟩ **b** : a system of determining time **8 a** : one of a series of repeated instances or actions ⟨told you many *times*⟩ **b** *pl* : added or accumulated

quantities or examples ⟨five *times* greater⟩ **c** *pl* : equal parts of which an indicated number make up a greater quantity ⟨five *times* smaller⟩ **d** : ²TURN 5b ⟨three *times* at bat⟩ **9** : a person's experience during a certain period ⟨had the *time* of their lives⟩ ⟨had quite a *time* staying in the saddle⟩ **10** : TIME-OUT ⟨called *time*⟩ — **at times** : now and then — **from time to time** : once in a while : OCCASIONALLY — **in no time** : in the shortest possible time — **in time 1** : early enough **2** : in the course of time : EVENTUALLY **3** : at the correct speed in music — **on time 1** : at the time set **2** : on an installment payment plan — **time after time** : over and over again — **time and again** : over and over again

²**time** *vb* **timed; tim·ing 1** : to arrange or set the time or rate at which something happens **2** : to measure or record the time, duration, or rate of ⟨*timed* the race⟩

time and a half *n* : payment of a worker (as for working overtime) at one and one half times the regular wage rate

time capsule *n* : a container holding historical records or objects representative of current culture that is placed (as in a cornerstone) for preservation until discovery by some future age

time card *n* : a card used with a time clock to record an employee's starting and quitting times each day

time clock *n* : a clock that stamps an employee's starting and quitting times on his or her time card

time deposit *n* : a deposit in a bank that is to be paid after a specified time has gone by

time exposure *n* : a photograph taken by the exposure of film for a definite time usually of more than one half second

time–hon·ored \'tī-,män-ərd\ *adj* : being in use for a long time ⟨*time-honored* traditions⟩

time·keep·er \'tīm-,kē-pər\ *n* **1** : a clerk who keeps records of the time worked by employees **2** : an official who keeps track of the playing time in a sports contest

time lag *n* : the period of time between two related happenings (as a cause and its effect)

time·less \'tīm-ləs\ *adj* : not restricted to a certain time or date — **time·less·ly** *adv* — **time·less·ness** *n*

time·ly \'tīm-lē\ *adj* **time·li·er; -est 1** : coming early or at the right time **2** : especially suitable for the time ⟨a *timely* book⟩ — **time·li·ness** *n*

time machine *n* : a fictional machine that allows one to travel backward or forward in time

time–out \'tī-'maut\ *n* **1** : a stopping of play (as in a game) usually for a short time **2** : a quiet period used especially as a way to discipline children

time·piece \'tīm-,pēs\ *n* : a device (as a clock or watch) to measure time

tim·er \'tī-mər\ *n* **1 a** : TIMEPIECE **b** : TIMEKEEPER 2 **2** : a clocklike device that turns something on or off at a set time or gives a signal at the end of a period of time

times \,tīmz\ *prep* : multiplied by ⟨two *times* seven is fourteen⟩

time–sav·ing \'tīm-,sā-viŋ\ *adj* : designed to get something done quicker — **time–sav·er** \-,sā-vər\ *n*

time·scale \'tīm-,skāl\ *n* : an arrangement of events used as a measure of the duration or age of a period of history or geologic or cosmic time

time–shar·ing \'tīm-,she(ə)r-iŋ, -,sha(ə)r-\ *n* : use of a computer system by many users at the same time

time signature *n* : a sign used to indicate musical meter and usually written with one number above another with the bottom number indicating the kind of note used as a unit of time and the top number indicating the number of these units in each measure

times sign \'tīm(z-)\ *n* : the symbol × used to indicate multiplication

time·ta·ble \'tīm-,tā-bəl\ *n* **1** : a table telling when a plane, bus, or train leaves or arrives **2** : a list showing the order in which something is planned to be done

time–test·ed \-ˌtes-təd\ *adj* : proven effective over a long period of time ⟨*time-tested* methods⟩

time zone *n* : a geographic region within which the same standard time is used

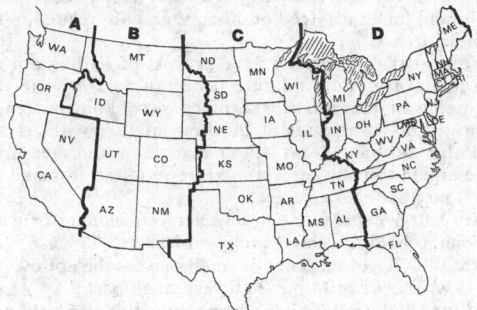

time zone: *A* Pacific time, *B* mountain time, *C* central time, *D* eastern time

tim·id \'tim-əd\ *adj* : feeling or showing a lack of courage or self-confidence : SHY — **ti·mid·i·ty** \tə-'mid-ət-ē\ *n* — **tim·id·ly** \'tim-əd-lē\ *adv* — **tim·id·ness** *n*

tim·ing \'tī-miŋ\ *n* **1** : selection for best effect of the exact moment for beginning or doing something **2** : observation and recording (as by a stopwatch) of the time taken by something

tim·o·rous \'tim-(ə-)rəs\ *adj* : easily frightened : FEARFUL — **tim·o·rous·ly** *adv* — **tim·o·rous·ness** *n*

tim·o·thy \'tim-ə-thē\ *n* : a European grass that has long cylinder-shaped spikes and is widely grown in the U.S. for hay

Tim·o·thy \'tim-ə-thē\ *n* — see BIBLE table

tim·pa·ni *also* **tym·pa·ni** \'tim-pə-nē\ *n pl* : a set of two or three kettledrums played by one performer — **tim·pa·nist** \-nəst\ *n*

¹tin \'tin\ *n* **1** : a soft shiny bluish white metallic element that is used in combination with other metals, as a protective coating, and in tinfoil — see ELEMENT table **2 a** : a container made of metal (as tinplate) ⟨a pie *tin*⟩ **b** : a sealed can holding food — **tin** *adj*

²tin *vb* **tinned; tin·ning 1** : to cover or plate with tin or a mixture of tin with another metal **2** : to put up or pack in tins : CAN

tin can *n* : a container for food made of metal (as tinplate or aluminum)

tinc·ture \'tiŋ(k)-chər\ *n* **1** : a substance that colors, dyes, or stains **2** : a solution that contains a medical substance (as a drug) mixed with alcohol ⟨*tincture* of iodine⟩

tin·der \'tin-dər\ *n* : a material that burns easily and can be used as kindling

tin·der·box \-ˌbäks\ *n* **1** : a metal box for holding tinder and usually a flint and steel for striking a spark **2** : something that can easily catch fire

tine \'tīn\ *n* : a slender pointed part : PRONG ⟨the *tines* of a fork⟩

tin·foil \'tin-ˌfȯil\ *n* : a thin metal sheeting usually of aluminum or an alloy of tin and lead

¹tinge \'tinj\ *vb* **tinged; tinge·ing** *or* **ting·ing** \'tin-jiŋ\ : to color or flavor slightly

²tinge *n* : a slight coloring, flavor, or quality ⟨a reddish *tinge*⟩ ⟨a *tinge* of mystery⟩

tin·gle \'tiŋ-gəl\ *vb* **tin·gled; tin·gling** \'tiŋ-g(ə-)liŋ\ : to feel or cause a prickling or thrilling sensation — **tingle** *n* — **tin·gly** \-g(ə-)lē\ *adj*

¹tin·ker \'tiŋ-kər\ *n* : a person who travels around and earns a living by repairing household utensils (as pots and pans)

²tinker *vb* **tin·kered; tin·ker·ing** \'tiŋ-k(ə-)riŋ\ : to repair or adjust something in an unskilled or experimental manner ⟨*tinkering* with his car⟩ — **tin·ker·er** \-kər-ər\ *n*

tin·kle \'tiŋ-kəl\ *vb* **tin·kled; tin·kling** \-k(ə-)liŋ\ : to make or cause to make a series of short high ringing or clinking sounds — **tinkle** *n*

tin liz·zie \-'liz-ē\ *n* : a small cheap early automobile

tin·ny \'tin-ē\ *adj* **tin·ni·er; -est** : resembling or suggesting tin

tin·plate \'tin-'plāt\ *n* : thin sheet iron or steel coated with tin — **tin–plate** *vb*

tin·sel \'tin(t)-səl\ *n* **1** : a thread, strip, or sheet of metal, paper, or plastic used to produce a glittering effect **2** : something that seems attractive but is of little worth

tin·smith \'tin-ˌsmith\ *n* : a worker in tin or sometimes other metals

¹tint \'tint\ *n* **1 a** : a slight or pale coloring **b** : any of various shades of a color **2** : a variation of a color made by adding white to it

²tint *vb* : to give or apply a tint or color to ⟨*tinted* glasses⟩

tin·tin·nab·u·la·tion \ˌtin-tə-ˌnab-yə-'lā-shən\ *n* : the ringing of bells or a similar sound

tin·type \-ˌtīp\ *n* : an early photograph consisting of a positive image taken directly on a thin iron plate having a darkened surface

tin·ware \'tin-ˌwa(ə)r, -ˌwe(ə)r\ *n* : objects made of tinplate

ti·ny \'tī-nē\ *adj* **ti·ni·er; -est** : very small : MINUTE — **ti·ni·ness** *n*

¹tip \'tip\ *vb* **tipped; tip·ping 1** : TURN OVER 1a ⟨*tipped* over a glass⟩ **2** : to bend from a straight position : SLANT ⟨the bench *tips* on the uneven floor⟩ **3** : to raise and tilt forward ⟨*tipped* his hat⟩ [Middle English *tipen* "to upset, overturn"]

²tip *n* : the act or an instance of tipping ⟨a *tip* of the hat⟩

³tip *vb* **tipped; tip·ping 1** : to attach a tip to **2** : to cover or decorate the tip of

⁴tip *n* **1** : the pointed or rounded end of something **2** : a small piece or part serving as an end, cap, or point [Middle English *tip* "a pointed end"] — **tipped** \'tipt\ *adj* — **on the tip of one's tongue 1** : about to be uttered **2** : just escaping memory

⁵tip *n* : a light touch or blow : TAP [Middle English *tippe* "a light touch or blow"]

⁶tip *vb* **tipped; tip·ping** : to hit a baseball so that it glances off the bat

⁷tip *n* : a piece of useful or secret information given ⟨got a *tip* on how to prepare for the test⟩ [origin unknown]

⁸tip *vb* **tipped; tip·ping** : to give useful or secret information to ⟨someone must have *tipped* them off⟩

⁹tip *vb* **tipped; tip·ping** : to give a tip to ⟨*tip* the waiter⟩ [probably derived from earlier *tip* (verb) "to strike lightly"]

¹⁰tip *n* : a small sum of money given for a service

tipi *variant of* TEPEE

¹tip–off \'tip-ˌȯf\ *n* **1** : a warning that something is going to happen **2** : a telltale sign

²tip–off *n* : the start of a basketball game when the ball is thrown in the air and a player from each team jumps up and tries to get the ball

tip·per \'tip-ər\ *n* : one that tips

tip·pet \'tip-ət\ *n* **1** : a long hanging part of a garment (as on a sleeve or cape) **2** : a shoulder cape usually with hanging ends

tip·ple \'tip-əl\ *vb* **tip·pled; tip·pling** \-(ə-)liŋ\ : to drink liquor especially by habit — **tip·pler** \-(ə-)lər\ *n*

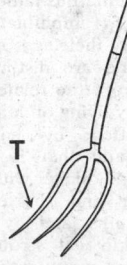

T tine

\ə\ **abut**	\au̇\ **out**	\i\ **tip**	\ȯ\ **saw**	\u̇\ **foot**
\ər\ **further**	\ch\ **chin**	\ī\ **life**	\ȯi\ **coin**	\y\ **yet**
\a\ **mat**	\e\ **pet**	\j\ **job**	\th\ **thin**	\yü\ **few**
\ā\ **take**	\ē\ **easy**	\ŋ\ **sing**	\th\ **this**	\yu̇\ **cure**
\ä\ **cot, cart**	\g\ **go**	\ō\ **bone**	\ü\ **food**	\zh\ **vision**

tip·sy \\'tip-sē\ *adj* **tip·si·er; -est** : unsteady or foolish from drinking

¹**tip·toe** \\'tip-ˌtō, -'tō\ *n* **1** : the tip of a toe **2** : the ends of the toes

²**tiptoe** *adv or adj* : on or as if on tiptoe

³**tiptoe** *vb* **tip·toed; tip·toe·ing** : to walk on tiptoe

¹**tip–top** \\'tip-'täp, -ˌtäp\ *n* : the highest point

²**tip–top** *adj* : very good : EXCELLENT ⟨in *tip-top* shape⟩ — **tip–top** *adv*

ti·rade \\'tī-ˌrād, 'tī-ˌrād\ *n* : a long violent angry speech : HARANGUE

¹**tire** \\'tī(ə)r\ *vb* **tired; tir·ing 1** : to become weary **2** : to decrease greatly or completely the physical strength of **3** : to wear out the patience or attention of : BORE
  synonyms TIRE, WEARY, FATIGUE, EXHAUST mean to make someone unwilling or unable to continue doing something. TIRE suggests a loss of strength or patience ⟨all that lifting really *tired* me⟩. WEARY suggests that one has reached a point where one cannot put up with something anymore ⟨I'm *wearied* by these endless complaints⟩. FATIGUE suggests very great tiredness brought about by much effort or strain ⟨the long climb up the mountain greatly *fatigued* her⟩. EXHAUST suggests that one's energy of mind or body has been all used up ⟨the race had *exhausted* him and he fell asleep at once⟩.

²**tire** *n* **1** : a metal hoop that forms the tread of a wheel **2** : a rubber cushion that usually contains compressed air and fits around a wheel ⟨automobile *tires*⟩

¹**tired** \\'tī(ə)rd\ *adj* **1** : ¹WEARY 1 **2** : used over and over again ⟨the same *tired* old excuse⟩ — **tired·ly** *adv* — **tired·ness** *n*

²**tired** *adj* : having tires

tire·less \\'tī(ə)r-ləs\ *adj* : seeming never to get tired ⟨a *tireless* worker⟩ — **tire·less·ly** *adv*

tire·some \\'tī(ə)r-səm\ *adj* : likely to tire one because of length or dullness : BORING ⟨a *tiresome* lecture⟩ — **tire·some·ly** *adv*

'tis \\'tiz, (ˌ)tiz\ : it is

tis·sue \\'tish-ü\ *n* **1** : a fine lightweight fabric **2** : a piece of soft absorbent paper **3** : a mass or layer of cells usually of one kind together with the uniting or enclosing substance around and between them that form the basic structural materials of a plant or an animal — compare CONNECTIVE TISSUE

tissue paper *n* : a thin paper used especially to wrap delicate articles

¹**tit** \\'tit\ *n* : TEAT

²**tit** *n* : any of various small plump often long-tailed birds of Eurasia and Africa that are related to the chickadees and titmice

ti·tan \\'tīt-³n\ *n* **1** *cap* : one of a family of giants overthrown by the gods of ancient Greece **2** : one of gigantic size, power, or achievement

ti·tan·ic \tī-'tan-ik\ *adj* : enormous in size, force, or power

ti·ta·ni·um \tī-'tān-ē-əm, tə-\ *n* : a silvery gray light strong metallic element found combined in various minerals and used especially in alloys (as in steel) — see ELEMENT table

titbit *variant of* TIDBIT

¹**tithe** \\'tīth\ *vb* **tithed; tith·ing** : to pay or give a tithe [Old English *teogothian* "to give a tenth part," from *teogotha* "tenth"] — **tith·er** *n*

²**tithe** *n* : a tenth part (as of one's income) given especially as a contribution to a church

tit·il·late \\'tit-³l-ˌāt\ *vb* **-lat·ed; -lat·ing 1** : ¹TICKLE 1 **2** : to excite pleasurably — **tit·il·la·tion** \ˌtit-³l-'ā-shən\ *n*

¹**ti·tle** \\'tīt-³l\ *n* **1 a** : a legal right to the ownership of property **b** : the document that is evidence of a right **2** : the name given to something (as a book, song, or job) to identify or describe it **3** : a word or group of words attached to a person's name to show honor, rank, or office **4** : CHAMPIONSHIP 2 ⟨won the batting *title*⟩

²**title** *vb* **ti·tled; ti·tling** \\'tīt-liŋ, -³l-iŋ\ : to call by a title

ti·tled \\'tīt-³ld\ *adj* : having a title especially of nobility

title page *n* : a page of a book bearing the title

tit·mouse \\'tit-ˌmaus\ *n, pl* **tit·mice** \-ˌmīs\ : any of several small North American songbirds that usually have small bills and long tails, feed on insects, and are related to the chickadees

ti·tra·tion \tī-'trā-shən\ *n* : the process of finding out the strength of a liquid mixture (as of an acid in water) by dripping another mixture (as of a base) of known strength into a known amount of the first mixture with usually another substance that will change color and measuring the amount of the second mixture required to make the first mixture change color

tit·ter \\'tit-ər\ *vb* : to laugh in a nervous manner or while trying to hold the laugh back — **titter** *n*

tit·tle \\'tit-³l\ *n* **1** : a point or small sign (as the dot over an *i*) in writing or printing **2** : a very small part

tit·u·lar \\'tich-(ə-)lər\ *adj* : being something in title only : NOMINAL ⟨the *titular* head of state⟩ — **tit·u·lar·ly** *adv*

Ti·tus \\'tīt-əs\ *n* — see BIBLE table

Ti·Vo \\'tē-(ˌ)vō\ *vb* **Ti·Voed; Ti·Vo·ing** : to record a television program with a DVR

tiz·zy \\'tiz-ē\ *n, pl* **tizzies** : a very excited and mixed-up state of mind

T lymphocyte *n* : T CELL

TNT \ˌtē-ˌen-'tē\ *n* : a flammable poisonous compound used as a high explosive

¹**to** \tə, tü, (')tü\ *prep* **1 a** — used to indicate movement or something suggesting movement toward a place, person, or thing reached ⟨walked *to* school⟩ ⟨send data *to* disk storage⟩ ⟨went back *to* my first idea⟩ **b** — used to indicate direction ⟨a mile *to* the south⟩ ⟨your back *to* the window⟩ **c** — used to indicate contact ⟨apply polish *to* the table⟩ **d** — used to indicate a limit ⟨the water was up *to* my waist⟩ **2** — used to indicate purpose, result, or end ⟨came *to* our aid⟩ ⟨broke *to* pieces⟩ ⟨sentenced *to* death⟩ **3 a** : ²BEFORE 3 ⟨at quarter *to* five⟩ **b** : ¹UNTIL ⟨from nine *to* five⟩ **4** — used to indicate belonging, accompanying, or responding ⟨the key *to* the lock⟩ ⟨dance *to* live music⟩ ⟨not much you could say *to* that⟩ **5 a** — used to indicate a relation of likeness or unlikeness ⟨similar *to* mine⟩ **b** — used to indicate agreement ⟨salt *to* taste⟩ **c** — used to indicate a proportion in terms of number or amount ⟨packed 10 *to* the box⟩ **6 a** — used to indicate the relation of adjective to noun ⟨agreeable *to* all of us⟩ or verb to complement ⟨sticks *to* business⟩ **b** — used to indicate one that receives an action ⟨spoke *to* the teacher⟩ ⟨give it *to* me⟩ **7** : for no one but ⟨had the house *to* ourselves⟩ **8** — used to mark an infinitive ⟨likes *to* swim⟩ and often used by itself in place of an infinitive ⟨I didn't mean *to*⟩

²**to** \\'tü\ *adv* **1** : in the direction toward ⟨run *to* and fro⟩ **2** : into contact especially with a frame ⟨snapped her purse *to*⟩ ⟨wind blew the door *to*⟩ **3** : to a state of consciousness or awareness ⟨brings him *to* with smelling salts⟩

toad \\'tōd\ *n* : any of numerous tailless leaping amphibians that lay their eggs in water and are distinguished from the related frogs by living on land more often, by having a build that is shorter and thicker with weaker and shorter hind limbs, and by having skin that is rough, dry and warty rather than smooth and moist

toad

toad·stool \-ˌstül\ *n* : a fungus that has an umbrella-shaped cap : MUSHROOM; *esp* : one that is poisonous or unfit for food

¹**toady** \'tōd-ē\ *n, pl* **toad·ies** : a person who flatters another in the hope of receiving favors

²**toady** *vb* **toad·ied; toady·ing** : to behave like a toady — **toady·ism** \-ē-ˌiz-əm\ *n*

to–and–fro \ˌtü-ən-'frō\ *adj* : forward and backward

¹**toast** \'tōst\ *vb* **1** : to make crisp, hot, and brown by heat ⟨*toast* bread⟩ **2** : to warm completely

²**toast** *n* **1** : sliced toasted bread **2 a** : a person in whose honor other people drink **b** : a highly admired person ⟨the *toast* of the town⟩ **3** : an act of drinking in honor of a person

³**toast** *vb* : to suggest or drink to as a toast

toast·er \'tō-stər\ *n* : an electrical appliance for toasting

toaster oven *n* : an electrical kitchen appliance that bakes, broils, and toasts and that fits on a countertop

toasty \'tō-stē\ *adj* **toast·i·er; -est** : comfortably warm

to·bac·co \tə-'bak-ō\ *n, pl* **-cos** **1** : any of a genus of chiefly American plants of the nightshade family that have sticky leaves and tube-shaped flowers; *esp* : a tall upright tropical American herb with pink or white flowers that is grown for its leaves **2** : the leaves of cultivated tobacco prepared for use in smoking or chewing or as snuff

tobacco mosaic *n* : any of a group of virus diseases of tobacco and related plants

to–be \tə-'bē\ *adj* : that is to be : FUTURE — often used in combination ⟨a bride-*to-be*⟩

To·bi·as \tə-'bī-əs\ *n* : TOBIT

To·bit \'tō-bət\ *n* — see BIBLE table

¹**to·bog·gan** \tə-'bäg-ən\ *n* : a long light sled made without runners and curved up at the front

²**toboggan** *vb* : to slide on a toboggan

to·coph·er·ol \tō-'käf-ə-ˌról, -ˌról\ *n* : VITAMIN E

toc·sin \'täk-sən\ *n* **1** : an alarm bell or the ringing of it **2** : a warning signal

¹**to·day** \tə-'dā\ *adv* **1** : on or for this day **2** : at the present time : NOWADAYS

²**today** *n* : the present day, time, or age

tod·dle \'täd-ºl\ *vb* **tod·dled; tod·dling** \'täd-liŋ, -ºl-iŋ\ : to walk with short unsteady steps like a young child — **toddle** *n*

tod·dler \'täd-lər, -ºl-ər\ *n* : a young child — **tod·dler·hood** \-ˌhüd\ *n*

to–do \tə-'dü\ *n, pl* **to–dos** \-'düz\ : ¹FUSS, STIR, COMMOTION

¹**toe** \'tō\ *n* **1 a** : one of the jointed parts of the front end of a vertebrate foot **b** : the front end or part of a foot or hoof **c** : the front end or part of something worn on the foot **2** : something that resembles a toe

²**toe** *vb* **toed; toe·ing** : to touch, reach, or kick with the toes

toed \'tōd\ *adj* : having a toe or toes especially of a specified kind or number ⟨five-*toed*⟩ ⟨round-*toed* shoes⟩

toe·hold \'tō-ˌhōld\ *n* : a hold or support for the toes (as in climbing)

toe·nail \-ˌnāl, -'nā(ə)l\ *n* : a nail of a toe

tof·fee *also* **tof·fy** \'tó-fē, 'täf-ē\ *n, pl* **toffees** *also* **toffies** : candy made by boiling sugar and butter together

to·fu \'tō-fü\ *n* : a soft food product prepared by coagulating soybean milk — called also *bean curd*

tobacco 1

to·ga \'tō-gə\ *n* : the loose outer garment worn in public by citizens of ancient Rome

to·geth·er \tə-'geth-ər\ *adv* **1** : in or into one group, body, or place ⟨gathered *together*⟩ **2** : in touch or in partnership with each other ⟨in business *together*⟩ ⟨the doors banged *together*⟩ **3 a** : at one time ⟨they all cheered *together*⟩ **b** : one after the other : in order ⟨work for hours *together*⟩ **4 a** : in or by combined effort ⟨worked *together* to clear the road⟩ **b** : in or into agreement ⟨get *together* on a plan⟩ **c** : in or into an organized or orderly arrangement ⟨pull yourself *together*⟩ **5 a** : to each other ⟨add the numbers *together*⟩ **b** : considered as a whole ⟨all *together* there were 15 of us⟩ — **to·geth·er·ness** *n*

toga

¹**tog·gle** \'täg-əl\ *n* : a crosspiece attached to the end of or to a loop in a rope, chain, or belt to prevent slipping or to serve as a fastening or as a grip for tightening ⟨used a stick as a *toggle* in tightening a rope⟩

²**toggle** *vb* **1** : to fasten with or as if with a toggle **2** : to furnish with a toggle **3** : to switch between two options especially of an electronic device usually by pressing a single button or a simple key combination

toggle bolt *n* : a bolt that has a nut with wings that close for passage through a small hole and spring open after passing through the hole to keep the bolt from slipping back through

toggle switch *n* : an electric switch operated by pushing a lever through a small angle

togs \'tägz, 'tógz\ *n pl* : CLOTHING 1; *esp* : a set of clothes and accessories for a specified use ⟨riding *togs*⟩ ⟨skiing *togs*⟩

¹**toil** \'tói(ə)l\ *n* : long hard labor

Word History Even though we have machines to do much of our hard work today, much long, hard toil must still be done by hand. Our Modern English word *toil*, however, comes from a Latin word for a laborsaving machine. The ancient Romans built a machine for crushing olives to produce olive oil. This machine was called a *tudicula*. This Latin word was formed from the word *tudes*, meaning "hammer," because the machine had little hammers to crush the olives. From this came the Latin verb *tudiculare*, meaning "to crush or grind." Early French used this Latin verb as the basis for its verb, spelled *toiller*, which meant "to make dirty, fight, wrangle." From this came the noun *toyl*, meaning "battle, disturbance, confusion." This early French noun in time was taken into Middle English as *toile*, meaning "argument, battle." The earliest sense of our Modern English *toil* was "a long, hard struggle in battle." It is natural enough that in time this came to be used to refer to any long hard effort. [Middle English *toile* "battle, argument," derived from early French *toyl* "battle, disturbance, confusion," from *toiller* (verb) "make dirty, fight, wrangle," from Latin *tudiculare* "crush, grind," from *tudicula* "machine with hammers for beating olives," from *tudes* "hammer"]

²**toil** *vb* **1** : to work hard and long **2** : to go on with effort ⟨*toiling* up a steep hill⟩ *synonyms* see WORK — **toil·er** *n*

toi·let \'tói-lət\ *n* **1** : the act or process of dressing and making oneself neat **2 a** : BATHROOM **b** : a fixture that consists usually of a bowl that is flushed with water and a seat and is used for defecation and urination

toilet paper *n* : a thin soft sanitary absorbent paper usually in a roll for bathroom use

toi·let·ry \'tȯi-lə-trē\ *n, pl* **-ries** : something (as a soap, lotion, toothpaste, or cologne) used in grooming oneself

toilet water *n* : a scented liquid (as cologne) for use especially after bathing

toil·some \'tȯi(ə)l-səm\ *adj* : requiring much effort

to·ken \'tō-kən\ *n* **1** : an outward sign **2** : something (as an act, gesture, or object) that serves as a sign or symbol ⟨a white flag is a *token* of surrender⟩ **3 a** : SOUVENIR **b** : INDICATION **2** ⟨this is only a *token* of what we hope to accomplish⟩ **4** : a piece resembling a coin that has a special use ⟨a bus *token*⟩ **synonyms** see EMBLEM, ¹sign — **by the same token** : for the same reason

told *past and past participle of* TELL

tol·er·able \'täl-(ə-)rə-bəl, 'täl-ər-bəl\ *adj* **1** : capable of being put up with ⟨*tolerable* pain⟩ **2** : fairly good ⟨a *tolerable* singing voice⟩ — **tol·er·ably** \-blē\ *adv*

tol·er·ance \'täl-(ə-)rən(t)s\ *n* **1 a** : ability to put up with something harmful or unpleasant **b** : the ability to adjust to a food or drug so that its effects are experienced less strongly **2** : sympathy for or acceptance of feelings, habits, or beliefs that are different from one's own

tol·er·ant \'täl-(ə-)rənt\ *adj* : showing tolerance — **tol·er·ant·ly** *adv*

tol·er·ate \'täl-ə-ˌrāt\ *vb* **-at·ed; -at·ing** **1** : to allow something to be or be done without making a move to stop it : put up with ⟨refused to *tolerate* such treatment⟩ **2** : to withstand the action of ⟨plants that *tolerate* drought⟩ ⟨*tolerate* a drug⟩ — **tol·er·a·tion** \ˌtäl-ə-'rā-shən\ *n*

¹toll \'tōl\ *n* **1** : a tax paid for a privilege (as the use of a highway or bridge) **2** : a charge paid for a service **3** : the cost in life or health ⟨the death *toll* from the hurricane⟩ [Middle English *toll* "a tax or fee paid to be allowed to do something," from early French *toll* (same meaning), derived from Latin *telonium* "a house where duties on imports are paid and ships' cargoes are checked," derived from Greek *telos* "tax, toll"]

²toll *vb* **1** : to announce or call by the sounding of a bell **2** : to sound with slow strokes ⟨the bell *tolls* solemnly⟩ [Middle English *tollen* "to pull, drag, or toll (a bell)," perhaps from Middle English *toilen* "to struggle"]

³toll *n* : the sound of a tolling bell

toll·booth \'tōl-ˌbüth\ *n* : a booth where tolls are paid

toll call *n* : a long-distance telephone call

toll·gate \'tōl-ˌgāt\ *n* : a point where vehicles stop to pay a toll

toll·house \-ˌhau̇s\ *n* : a house or booth where tolls are collected

tom \'täm\ *n* : the male of various animals: as **a** : TOM CAT **b** : a male turkey

tom·a·hawk \'täm-i-ˌhȯk\ *n* : a light ax used as a weapon especially by North American Indians — **tomahawk** *vb*

to·ma·to \tə-'māt-ō *also* -'mät-\ *n, pl* **-toes** **1** : a usually large

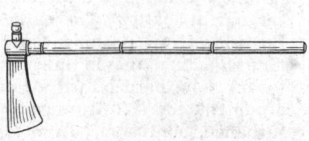

tomahawk

rounded red or sometimes yellow pulpy berry that is eaten as a vegetable **2** : a widely grown South American plant of the nightshade family that produces tomatoes [derived from Spanish *tomate* "tomato," from the name for this plant in the ancient language of the Aztecs]

tomb \'tüm\ *n* **1** : ²GRAVE 1 **2** : a house or burial chamber for dead people

tom·boy \'täm-ˌbȯi\ *n* : a girl who enjoys things some people think are more suited to boys — **tom·boy·ish** \-ish\ *adj* — **tom·boy·ish·ness** *n*

tomb·stone \'tüm-ˌstōn\ *n* : GRAVESTONE

tom·cat \'täm-ˌkat\ *n* : a male domestic cat

tome \'tōm\ *n* : a big thick book

tom·fool·ery \täm-'fül-(ə-)rē\ *n* : playful or foolish behavior

tom·my gun \'täm-ē-ˌgən\ *n* : SUBMACHINE GUN

¹to·mor·row \tə-'mär-ō, -'mȯr-\ *adv* : on or for the day after today

²tomorrow *n* : the day after today

tom–tom \'täm-ˌtäm, 'təm-ˌtäm\ *n* : a usually long and narrow drum commonly beaten with the hands

ton \'tən\ *n, pl* **tons** *also* **ton** **1** — see MEASURE table **2** : METRIC TON

ton·al \'tōn-ᵊl\ *adj* : of or relating to a musical tone — **ton·al·ly** \-ᵊl-ē\ *adv*

to·nal·i·ty \tō-'nal-ət-ē\ *n, pl* **-ties** : the character of a piece of music based on its key or on the relation of its tones and chords to a particular keynote

¹tone \'tōn\ *n* **1 a** : a musical sound having a definite pitch : the sound of a note **b** : WHOLE STEP **2** : accent or pitch of the voice especially when used to express an emotion or a change in meaning ⟨spoke in a sharp *tone*⟩ **3** : style or manner of expression ⟨reply in a friendly *tone*⟩ ⟨the author's *tone* shows his or her attitude toward the subject⟩ **4 a** : a shade of color ⟨decorated in soft *tones*⟩ **b** : a color that changes another ⟨gray with a blue *tone*⟩ **5 a** : a healthy state of the body or any of its parts **b** : normal tension or ability to respond to stimuli; *esp* : the state of normal tension of a muscle in which it is partly contracted **6** : general character or quality ⟨the city's upbeat *tone*⟩ [Middle English *tone* "a musical sound, a sound from the voice," from Latin *tonus* "tension, tone, pitch," from Greek *tonos* "act of stretching, tension, tone, pitch"; so called because the pitch of the tone of a stringed musical instrument is related to how tightly the strings are stretched]

²tone *vb* **toned; ton·ing** **1** : to give tone to : STRENGTHEN ⟨vitamins to *tone* up the system⟩ **2** : to soften in color, appearance, or sound — often used with *down*

tone-deaf \'tōn-ˌdef\ *adj* : not noticing small differences in musical pitch

tone language *n* : a language (as Chinese) in which changes in tone of words that otherwise sound alike indicate different meanings

tongs \'täŋz, 'tȯŋz\ *n pl* : a device for taking hold of something that consists usually of two movable pieces joined at one end

¹tongue \'təŋ\ *n* **1** : a fleshy movable muscular part of the floor of the mouth of most vertebrates that has sensory organs (as taste buds) and small glands and functions especially in taking and swallowing food and in human beings as a speech organ **2** : the flesh of a tongue (as of beef) used as food **3** : the power of communication : SPEECH **4** : LANGUAGE 1a **5** : something resembling a tongue (as in being long and fastened at one end) — **tongue·less** \-ləs\ *adj* — **tongue·like** \-ˌlīk\ *adj*

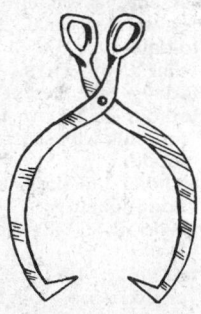

tongs

²tongue *vb* **tongued; tongu·ing** \'təŋ-iŋ\ **1** : to touch or lick with or as if with the tongue **2** : to separate individual notes when playing a wind instrument by interrupting the stream of wind with the tongue

tongue–in–cheek *adj* : not meant to be taken seriously

tongue in cheek *adv* : in a tongue-in-cheek manner

tongue–lash·ing \'təŋ-ˌlash-iŋ\ *n* : a severe scolding

tongue–tied \-ˌtīd\ *adj* : unable to speak clearly or freely (as from shyness)

tongue twister *n* : a word, phrase, or sentence that is hard to say because of a series of similar consonant sounds (as in "twin-screw steel cruiser" or "rubber baby-buggy bumpers")

¹**ton·ic** \'tän-ik\ *adj* **1** : making (as the mind or body) stronger or healthier **2** : relating to or based on the first tone of a scale ⟨*tonic* chord⟩ ⟨*tonic* harmony⟩

²**tonic** **1 a** : a medicine that increases body tone **b** : a liquid to be used on the hair or scalp **c** *chiefly New England* : SODA POP **d** : TONIC WATER **2** : the first tone of a scale

tonic water *n* : a carbonated beverage flavored with a small amount of quinine, lemon, and lime

¹**to·night** \tə-'nīt\ *adv* : on this present night or the night following this present day

²**tonight** *n* : the present or the coming night

ton·nage \'tən-ij\ *n* **1** : a tax on ships based on tons carried **2** : ships in terms of the total number of tons that are or can be carried **3** : total weight in tons shipped, carried, or mined

ton·sil \'tän(t)-səl\ *n* : either of a pair of oval-shaped masses of spongy tissue that lie one on each side of the throat at the back of the mouth

ton·sil·lec·to·my \,tän(t)-sə-'lek-tə-mē\ *n, pl* **-mies** : the surgical removal of the tonsils

ton·sil·li·tis \,tän(t)-sə-'līt-əs\ *n* : inflammation of the tonsils

ton·sure \'tän-chər\ *n* : a haircut with the top of the head shaved worn especially by monks [Middle English *tonsure* "the act of shaving a part of the top of the head," derived from Latin *tonsura* "the act of shearing," from *tonsus*, past participle of *tondēre* "to shear"] — **ton·sured** \-chərd\ *adj*

too \(')tü\ *adv* **1** : in addition : ALSO ⟨sell the house and the furniture *too*⟩ **2** : to a degree greater than wanted or needed ⟨the soup is *too* hot⟩ ⟨this has gone on *too* long⟩ **3** : ²VERY 1 ⟨the climb was not *too* hard⟩

took *past of* TAKE

¹**tool** \'tül\ *n* **1** : a device (as a hammer, saw, knife, or wrench) used or worked by hand or by a machine **2 a** : something used in doing one's job as if it were a tool ⟨a scholar's books are his *tools*⟩ **b** : something that helps to gain an end ⟨hard work is a *tool* for success⟩ **3** : a person used by another : DUPE **synonyms** *see* IMPLEMENT

²**tool** *vb* **1** : to shape, form, or finish with a tool **2** : to equip a plant or industry with machines and tools for production

tool·box \'tül-,bäks\ *n* : a chest to store tools in

tool·mak·er \-,mā-kər\ *n* : one (as an animal or a human being) that makes tools — **tool·mak·ing** \-kiŋ\ *n*

tool·shed \-,shed\ *n* : a small building to store tools in

¹**toot** \'tüt\ *vb* **1** : to sound a short blast ⟨a horn *tooted*⟩ **2** : to blow or sound an instrument (as a horn) especially in short blasts ⟨*toot* a whistle⟩ — **toot·er** *n*

²**toot** *n* : a short blast (as on a horn)

tooth \'tüth\ *n, pl* **teeth** \'tēth\ **1 a** : one of the hard bony structures that are usually located on the jaws of vertebrates and are used for seizing and chewing food and as weapons **b** : any of various usually hard and sharp structures especially around the mouth of an invertebrate **2 a** : something like or suggesting the tooth of an animal in shape, arrangement, or action ⟨the *tooth* of a saw⟩ **b** : one of the projections on the rim of a cogwheel that fit between the projections on another part especially to transmit force : COG — **tooth·less** \'tüth-ləs\ *adj* — **tooth·like** \-,līk\ *adj*

tooth·ache \'tü-,thāk\ *n* : pain in or near a tooth

tooth and nail *adv* : as hard as one can ⟨fighting *tooth and nail*⟩

tooth·brush \'tüth-,brəsh\ *n* : a brush for cleaning the teeth

toothed \'tütht\ *adj* **1** : having teeth especially of a specified kind or number **2** : JAGGED, NOTCHED

toothed whale *n* : any of a group of whales, dolphins, and porpoises with numerous sharp cone-shaped teeth — compare BALEEN WHALE

tooth·paste \'tüth-,pāst\ *n* : a paste for cleaning the teeth

tooth·pick \-,pik\ *n* : a pointed instrument (as a thin piece of wood) for removing substances caught between the teeth

tooth powder *n* : a powder for cleaning the teeth

tooth·some \'tüth-səm\ *adj* : pleasing to the taste : DELICIOUS ⟨*toothsome* pies⟩

toothy \'tü-thē\ *adj* **tooth·i·er; -est** : having or showing many usually large teeth ⟨a *toothy* grin⟩ — **tooth·i·ly** \-thə-lē\ *adv*

¹**top** \'täp\ *n* **1 a** : the highest point, level, or part of something ⟨the *top* of the hill⟩ ⟨sang at the *top* of her voice⟩ **b** : the upper end, edge, or surface ⟨the *top* of the page⟩ ⟨filled the glass to the *top*⟩ **c** : the stalk and leaves of a plant and especially one with edible roots ⟨beet *tops*⟩ **2** : an upper piece, lid, or covering ⟨blouses, shirts, and *tops*⟩ ⟨put the *top* on the jar⟩ **3** : the highest position ⟨reached the *top* of the profession⟩ [Old English *top* "highest point"] — **topped** \'täpt\ *adj* — **on top of** : in addition to

²**top** *vb* **topped; top·ping** **1** : to remove or cut the top of ⟨*top* a tree⟩ **2** : to cover with a top or on the top ⟨*topped* the sundae with nuts⟩ **3** : to be better than **4** : to go over the top of **5** : to hit the top part of ⟨*top* a golf ball⟩

³**top** *adj* : of, relating to, or being at the top

⁴**top** *n* : a child's toy that has a point on which it can be made to spin [Old English *top* "a spinning toy"]

to·paz \'tō-,paz\ *n* : a mineral in the form of usually yellow to brownish yellow crystals that is valued as a gem

top·coat \'täp-,kōt\ *n* : a lightweight overcoat

top dollar *n* : the highest amount being paid for an article, product, or service ⟨paid *top dollar* for the tickets⟩

top–dress \-,dres\ *vb* : to apply material to (as land or a road) without working it in; *esp* : to scatter fertilizer over (land)

top·dress·ing \-,dres-iŋ\ *n* : a material used to top-dress soil

top·gal·lant \(')täp-'gal-ənt, tə-'gal-\ *n* : a mast or sail next above the topmast or topsail

top hat *n* : a man's hat with a tall crown

top–heavy \'täp-,hev-ē\ *adj* : having the top part too heavy for the lower part

¹**to·pi·ary** \'tō-pē-,er-ē\ *adj* **1 a** : relating to or being the art or practice of topiary **b** : shaped or created by topiary ⟨a *topiary* elephant⟩ **2** : characterized by or containing topiary ⟨a *topiary* garden⟩

²**topiary** *n, pl* **-ar·ies** **1** : the art or practice of training and trimming trees or shrubs into odd or ornamental shapes **2** : a garden or park containing plants shaped by topiary; *also* : a plant or plants shaped by topiary

top·ic \'täp-ik\ *n* **1** : a heading in an outline of a subject or explanation **2** : the subject or a section of a subject (as of a speech or a report)

top hat

\ə\ **abut**	\au̇\ **out**	\i\ **tip**	\ȯ\ **saw**	\u̇\ **foot**
\ər\ **further**	\ch\ **chin**	\ī\ **life**	\ȯi\ **coin**	\y\ **yet**
\a\ **mat**	\e\ **pet**	\j\ **job**	\th\ **thin**	\yü\ **few**
\ā\ **take**	\ē\ **easy**	\ŋ\ **sing**	\th\ **this**	\yu̇\ **cure**
\ä\ **cot, cart**	\g\ **go**	\ō\ **bone**	\ü\ **food**	\zh\ **vision**

top·i·cal \'täp-i-kəl\ *adj* **1** : designed to be applied to or to work on a specific place or part (as of the body) ⟨a *topical* medicine⟩ **2 a** : of or relating to topics ⟨*topical* outline⟩ **b** : referring to the topics of the day or place ⟨*topical* jokes⟩ — **top·i·cal·ly** \-k(ə-)lē\ *adv*

topic sentence *n* : a sentence that states the main thought of a paragraph

top·knot \'täp-ˌnät\ *n* : a tuft of feathers or hair on the top of the head

top·mast \-ˌmast, -məst\ *n* : the mast next above the lower mast

top·min·now \-ˌmin-ō\ *n* : any of several small surface-feeding fishes

top·most \-ˌmōst\ *adj* : highest of all

top–notch \-'näch\ *adj* : of the highest quality : FIRST-RATE ⟨a *top-notch* performance⟩

top–of–the–line *adj* : TOP-NOTCH ⟨*top-of-the-line* camera equipment⟩

to·po·graph·ic \ˌtäp-ə-'graf-ik, ˌtōp-ə-\ *or* **to·po·graph·i·cal** \-'graf-i-kəl\ *adj* : of, relating to, or showing topography ⟨a *topographic* map⟩ — **to·po·graph·i·cal·ly** \-k(ə-)lē\ *adv*

to·pog·ra·phy \tə-'päg-rə-fē\ *n* **1** : the art or practice of showing on maps or charts the heights and depths of the features of a place **2** : the shape and height and depth of the features of a place

to·pol·o·gy \tə-'päl-ə-jē\ *n* : a branch of mathematics concerned with the properties of geometric figures that do not change when the figure is twisted or stretched in certain ways — **to·po·log·i·cal** \ˌtäp-ə-'läj-i-kəl, ˌtōp-\ *adj* — **to·pol·o·gist** \tə-'päl-ə-jist\ *n*

top·per \'täp-ər\ *n* **1** : one that tops **2** : TOP HAT

top·ping \'täp-iŋ\ *n* : a food served on top of another to make it look or taste better

top·ple \'täp-əl\ *vb* **top·pled; top·pling** \-(ə-)liŋ\ **1** : to fall over from being too heavy at the top **2** : to push over

top·sail \'täp-ˌsāl, -səl\ *also* **top·s'l** \-səl\ *n* **1** : the sail next above the lowermost sail on a mast in a square-rigged ship **2** : the sail set above and sometimes on the gaff in a fore-and-aft rigged ship

T topsail 2

top secret *adj* **1** : protected by a high degree of secrecy ⟨a *top secret* meeting⟩ **2** : containing information that is very important to the safety and defense of a nation ⟨*top secret* messages⟩

top·side \'täp-ˌsīd\ *adv* : on or onto the deck of a ship

top·soil \-ˌsȯil\ *n* : surface soil usually including the rich upper layer in which plants have most of their roots and which the farmer turns over in plowing

top·spin \-ˌspin\ *n* : a forward spinning motion of a ball

top·stitch \-ˌstich\ *vb* : to make a line of stitches on the outside of a garment near a seam

top·sy–tur·vy \ˌtäp-sē-'tər-vē\ *adv* : UPSIDE DOWN — **topsy–turvy** *adj*

toque \'tōk\ *n* : a woman's small hat usually without a brim

tor \'tȯ(ə)r\ *n* : a high rocky hill

To·rah \'tōr-ə, 'tȯr-; 'tȯi-rə\ *n* **1** : the wisdom and law contained in Jewish Scripture and other sacred writings and in oral tradition **2** : a scroll containing the first five

toque

books of the Old Testament used in a synagogue for religious services

torch \'tȯ(ə)rch\ *n* **1** : a flaming light made of something that burns brightly and usually is carried in the hand **2** : something that guides or gives light or heat like a torch **3** : any of various portable devices for producing a hot flame — compare BLOWTORCH **4** *chiefly British* : FLASHLIGHT

torch·light \-ˌlīt\ *n* : the light given by torches

tore *past of* [3]TEAR

to·re·ador \'tȯr-ē-ə-ˌdȯ(ə)r, 'tōr-, 'tär-\ *n* : a person who fights bulls : a performer in a bullfight

to·re·ro \tə-'re(ə)r-ō\ *n, pl* **-ros** : TOREADOR

[1]**tor·ment** \'tȯr-ˌment\ *n* **1** : extreme pain or distress of body or mind **2** : a cause of suffering in mind or body

[2]**tor·ment** \tȯr-'ment, 'tȯr-ˌment\ *vb* **1** : to cause severe suffering of body or mind to **2** : to cause worry, distress, or trouble to : HARASS — **tor·men·tor** \tȯr-'ment-ər, 'tȯr-ˌment-\ *n*

torn *past participle of* [3]TEAR

tor·na·do \tȯr-'nād-ō\ *n, pl* **-does** *or* **-dos** : a violent destructive whirling wind accompanied by a funnel-shaped cloud that moves in a narrow path over the land

[1]**tor·pe·do** \tȯr-'pēd-ō\ *n, pl* **-does** **1** : a thin cylindrical self-propelled submarine weapon **2** : a small firework that explodes when thrown against a hard object

Word History The Latin verb *torpēre,* meaning "to be numb," gave rise to the noun *torpedo,* "numbness." This noun was borrowed into English in the 16th century to refer to a long round fish that gave a numbing electric shock to anyone who touched it. This fish was also called an electric ray, a crampfish, or a numbfish. In the early 19th century, the American inventor Robert Fulton developed a floating device that exploded when it touched a ship. He called this device a *torpedo* because it reminded him of the electric ray. Since then the torpedo has been modernized and is fired at its target. Although it still looks somewhat like the fish, its effects can certainly be more than numbing. [from Latin *torpedo,* literally "numbness," from *torpēre* "to be numb" — related to TORPID]

[2]**torpedo** *vb* **-doed; do·ing** \tȯr-'pēd-ə-wiŋ\ : to hit or sink with or as if with a torpedo

torpedo boat *n* : a small very fast boat for firing torpedoes

tor·pid \'tȯr-pəd\ *adj* **1 a** : having lost motion or the power of exertion or feeling **b** : exhibiting or characterized by topor ⟨a bear *torpid* in winter sleep⟩ **2** : having too little energy or strength : APATHETIC [from Latin *torpidus* "having lost motion or power of moving or feeling, numb," from *torpēre* "to be numb" — related to TORPEDO; see *Word History* at TORPEDO]

tor·por \'tȯr-pər\ *n* **1 a** : temporary loss or suspension of motion or feeling **b** : a state of lowered bodily activity (as during hibernation) that is a response to an unfavorable environmental condition (as cold or drought) **2** : APATHY

tor·rent \'tȯr-ənt, 'tär-\ *n* **1** : a rushing stream of a liquid ⟨a *torrent* of rain⟩ **2** : a mountain stream or its channel **3** : a sudden rush like a stream of liquid ⟨a *torrent* of criticism⟩ [from French *torrent* "a violent stream of liquid," from Latin *torrent-, torrens* (same meaning), from *torrens* (adjective) "burning, flowing with great force," derived from *torrēre* "to heat so as to dry up or burn" — related to TORRID; see *Word History* at TORRID]

tor·ren·tial \tȯ-'ren-chəl, tə-\ *adj* : relating to or resembling a torrent ⟨*torrential* rains⟩ — **tor·ren·tial·ly** \-'rench-(ə-)lē\ *adv*

tor·rid \'tȯr-əd, 'tär-\ *adj* : very hot and usually dry — **tor·rid·ly** *adv*

Word History The Latin verb *torrēre,* meaning "to heat so as to dry up or burn," gave rise to two quite different English words. They are *torrid* and *torrent.* The Latin adjective *torridus*, meaning "dried or burnt by heat," was formed from *torrēre*. It became our *torrid*. Another Latin adjective, *torrens*, meaning "scorching, burning," was also formed from *torrēre*. It, however, gained a second sense of "flowing with great force and speed, rushing." This second sense led to the use of *torrens* as a noun for "a rushing or violent stream." This noun was borrowed into English as *torrent*. It came to refer not only to rushing water, but also to any kind of outpouring, such as of words, information, sounds, or feelings. [from Latin *torridus* "dried or burnt by heat, torrid," derived from *torrēre* "to heat so as to dry up or burn" — related to TORRENT]

torrid zone *n* : the area or region between the Tropic of Cancer and the Tropic of Capricorn — compare FRIGID ZONE, TEMPERATE ZONE

tor·sion \'tȯr-shən\ *n* **1** : the act or process of turning or twisting **2** : the state of being twisted

torsion bar *n* : a long metal piece in an automobile suspension that has one end firmly attached to the frame and the other twisted and connected to the axle and that acts as a spring

tor·so \'tȯr-sō\ *n, pl* **torsos** *or* **tor·si** \-ˌsē\ : the human body except for the head, arms, and legs

torte \'tȯrt-ə, 'tȯ(ə)rt\ *n, pl* **tortes** *or* **tor·ten** \'tȯrt-ᵊn\ : a rich cake

tor·tel·li·ni \ˌtȯrt-ə-'lē-nē\ *n, pl* **tortellini** *also* **tortellinis** : pasta in the form of little ring-shaped cases containing a filling (as of meat or cheese)

tor·ti·lla \tȯr-'tē-(y)ə\ *n* : a thin round of unleavened cornmeal or wheat flour bread [American Spanish, literally "little cake," from Spanish *torta* "cake"]

tor·toise \'tȯrt-əs\ *n* : ²TURTLE; *esp* : a land-dwelling turtle

¹tor·toise·shell \'tȯrt-əs-ˌshel, -əsh-ˌshel\ *n* **1** : a spotted hornlike substance that covers the shell of some turtles and is used especially formerly to make ornamental objects **2** : any of several showy butterflies

²tortoiseshell *adj* **1** : made of or resembling tortoiseshell especially in spotted brown and yellow coloring **2** : of, relating to, or being a color pattern of the domestic cat that consists of patches of black, orange, and light yellow

tor·tu·ous \'tȯrch-(ə-)wəs\ *adj* : having many twists and turns — **tor·tu·ous·ly** *adv*

¹tor·ture \'tȯr-chər\ *n* **1** : distress of body or mind **2** : the causing of great pain especially to punish or to obtain a confession [from French *torture* "causing of intense pain or agony," from Latin *tortura* "act of twisting," from earlier *tortus*, past participle of *torquēre* "to twist" — related to DISTORT, EXTORT, RETORT]

²torture *vb* **tor·tured; tor·tur·ing** \'tȯrch-(ə-)riŋ\ **1** : to cause great suffering to **2** : to punish or force someone to do or say something by causing great pain — **tor·tur·er** \'tȯr-chər-ər\ *n*

tor·tur·ous \'tȯrch-(ə-)rəs\ *adj* : causing great pain — **tor·tur·ous·ly** *adv*

To·ry \'tȯr-ē, 'tȯr-\ *n, pl* **Tories 1** : ²CONSERVATIVE **2** : an American on the side of the British during the American Revolution — **Tory** *adj*

> **Word History** In the 17th century, many of the Irish had their property taken from them by the English. Some of them lived by plundering English settlements and robbing English soldiers. Such an outlaw was called a *tóraidhe* in Gaelic, an early language of Ireland. This word literally meant "one who is pursued" and "robber." Later, this term was also applied to an armed Irish supporter of the Roman Catholic faith. In English the word was shortened to *Tory* and was used for a member of the conservative political party in England. Tories strongly supported the authority of the monarch. During the American Revolution, the term *Tory* was used for an American who supported British authority rather than

independence. [from *tóraidhe*, a word in Irish Gaelic, the original language of Ireland, meaning "robber, pursued man"]

toss \'tȯs, 'täs\ *vb* **1** : to throw or swing to and fro or up and down ⟨waves *tossed* the ship about⟩ **2** : to throw with a quick light motion ⟨*toss* a ball into the air⟩ **3** : to lift with a sudden motion ⟨*toss* the head⟩ **4** : to be thrown about rapidly ⟨the river surged and *tossed*⟩ **5** : to move about restlessly ⟨*toss* in one's sleep⟩ **6** : to stir or mix lightly ⟨*toss* a salad⟩ **7** : to drink quickly **synonyms** see THROW — **toss** *n*

toss–up \-ˌəp\ *n* : something that offers no clear choice ⟨it's a *toss-up* who will win⟩

tos·ta·da \tō-'städ-ə\ *n* : a fried tortilla [Mexican Spanish *tostada*, a feminine form of *tostado* "fried," from Spanish *tostado* "toasted"]

tot \'tät\ *n* : a small child

¹to·tal \'tōt-ᵊl\ *adj* **1** : of or relating to the whole of something ⟨a *total* eclipse of the sun⟩ **2** : making up the whole ⟨the *total* amount⟩ **3** : being such to the fullest degree ⟨*total* ruin⟩ **4** : making use of every means to do something ⟨*total* war⟩

²total *n* **1** : a product of addition : SUM **2** : an entire amount

³total *vb* **to·taled** *or* **to·talled; to·tal·ing** *or* **to·tal·ling 1** : ADD **3 2** : to amount to ⟨donations *totaled* $120⟩ **3** : to make a total wreck of ⟨*totaled* the car⟩

to·tal·i·tar·i·an \(ˌ)tō-ˌtal-ə-'ter-ē-ən\ *adj* : of or relating to a political system in which the government has complete control over the people — **to·tal·i·tar·i·an·ism** \-ē-ə-ˌniz-əm\ *n*

to·tal·i·ty \tō-'tal-ət-ē\ *n, pl* **-ties 1** : a combined amount : SUM, WHOLE **2** : the quality or state of being total : ENTIRETY ⟨rejected the scheme in its *totality*⟩

to·tal·ly \'tōt-ᵊl-ē\ *adv* **1** : in a total manner : WHOLLY **2** : as a whole

tote \'tōt\ *vb* **tot·ed; tot·ing** : to carry by hand — **tot·er** *n*

tote bag *n* : a large handbag

tote board *n* : an electrically operated board at a racetrack on which betting odds and race results are posted

to·tem \'tōt-əm\ *n* **1** : an object (as an animal or plant) serving as the emblem of a family or clan **2** : something usually carved or painted to represent a totem — **to·tem·ic** \tō-'tem-ik\ *adj*

totem pole *n* : a pole carved and painted with symbols of totems and set up by Indian tribes of the northwest coast of North America

tot·ter \'tät-ər\ *vb* **1** : to sway or rock as if about to fall **2** : to move unsteadily : STAGGER — **tot·tery** \-ə-rē\ *adj*

tou·can \'tü-ˌkan, tü-'kan\ *n* : any of a family of mostly fruit-eating birds of tropical America with brilliant coloring and a very large but light bill

¹touch \'təch\ *vb* **1** : to feel or handle (as with fingers) especially so as to be aware of by the sense of touch **2 a** : to be or cause to be in contact with something **b** : to be or come next to **3** : to hit lightly **4 a** : to do harm to **b** : to make use of ⟨never *touches* meat⟩ **5** : to refer to in passing : MENTION ⟨the report *touched* upon many important points⟩ **6** : to affect the interest of ⟨a matter that *touches* every parent⟩ **7**

totem pole

: to move emotionally ⟨*touched* by their friend's kindness⟩ — **touch·able** \-ə-bəl\ *adj* — **touch·er** *n*

²**touch** *n* **1** : a light stroke or tap **2** : the act or fact of touching or being touched **3 a** : the special sense by which one is aware of light pressure especially on the skin ⟨soft to the *touch*⟩ **b** : an impression gotten through the sense of touch ⟨the soft *touch* of silk⟩ **4** : a state of contact or communication ⟨keeping in *touch* with friends⟩ **5** : a small amount : TRACE ⟨a *touch* of garlic in the salad⟩

touch and go *adj* : not certain of having a good result ⟨it was *touch and go* there for a while⟩

touch·back \'təch-,bak\ *n* : the act of downing a football behind the goal line after receiving a kick or intercepting a pass

touch·down \'təch-,daun\ *n* **1** : the act of touching a football to the ground behind an opponent's goal **2** : the act of scoring six points in American football by carrying the ball over the opponent's goal line **3** : the act or moment of touching down (as with an airplane or spacecraft)

touch down \(')təch-'daun\ *vb* : to reach the ground : LAND

touch·ing \'təch-iŋ\ *adj* : causing a feeling of tenderness or pity ⟨a *touching* story⟩ — **touch·ing·ly** *adv*

touch·line \'təch-,līn\ *n* : either of the lines that mark the sides of the field of play in rugby and soccer

touch—me—not \'təch-mē-,nät\ *n* : either of two North American impatiens that grow in moist areas

touch off *vb* : to start by or as if by touching with fire ⟨the announcement *touched off* riots⟩

touch pad *n* : a keypad for an electronic device (as a microwave oven) that consists of a flat surface divided into several differently marked areas which are touched to choose options

touch screen *n* : a display screen (as for a computer) on which the user selects options by touching the screen

touch·stone \'təch-,stōn\ *n* **1** : a black stone formerly used to test the purity of gold and silver by the streak left on the stone when rubbed by the metal **2** : a test for judging something

touch—tone \'təch-'tōn, -,tōn\ *adj* : of, relating to, or being a telephone having push buttons that produce tones corresponding to numbers

touch—up \'təch-,əp\ *n* : an act or instance of touching up

touch up \(')təch-'əp\ *vb* : to improve by or as if by small changes : fix the little imperfections of

touchy \'təch-ē\ *adj* **touch·i·er; -est** **1** : easily hurt or insulted **2** : calling for tact or careful handling ⟨a *touchy* subject⟩

¹**tough** \'təf\ *adj* **1 a** : able to take great force : flexible and not brittle ⟨*tough* fibers⟩ **b** : not easily chewed ⟨*tough* meat⟩ **2** : marked by firmness or determination ⟨a *tough* policy⟩ **3** : able to stand hard work and hardship ⟨*tough* soldiers⟩ **4** : hard to influence : STUBBORN ⟨a *tough* bargainer⟩ **5** : very difficult ⟨a *tough* problem⟩ **6** : having much crime or bad behavior ⟨a *tough* neighborhood⟩ **synonyms** see STRONG — **tough·ly** *adv* — **tough·ness** *n*

²**tough** *n* : a tough person : ROWDY

tough·en \'təf-ən\ *vb* **tough·ened; tough·en·ing** \'təf-(ə-)niŋ\ : to make or become tough

tough·ie \'təf-ē\ *n* **1** : ²TOUGH **2** : a hard problem or question

tou·pee \tü-'pā\ *n* : a small wig worn to cover a bald spot

¹**tour** \'tu̇(ə)r, *sense 1 is also* 'tau̇(ə)r\ *n* **1 a** : one's turn in a schedule **b** : a period of time during which one is on duty or in a certain place **2** : a trip usually ending at the point of beginning ⟨a *tour* of the city⟩ **3** : a series of related sports events held regularly at varied locations ⟨the golf *tour*⟩ **synonyms** see JOURNEY

²**tour** *vb* : to make a tour of : travel as a tourist

tour·ism \'tu̇(ə)r-,iz-əm\ *n* : the practice of traveling for

pleasure or the business of encouraging and serving such traveling

tour·ist \'tu̇r-əst\ *n* : a person who travels for pleasure — **tourist** *adj*

tourist class *n* : economy accommodations (as on a ship)

tour·ma·line \'tu̇r-mə-lən, -,lēn\ *n* : a mineral of variable color that makes a striking gem when transparent and cut

tour·na·ment \'tu̇r-nə-mənt *also* 'tər- *or* 'tȯr-\ *n* **1** : a contest of skill and courage between knights wearing armor and fighting with blunted lances or swords **2** : a contest or series of contests played for a championship

tour·ney \'tu̇(ə)r-nē *also* 'tər- *or* 'tȯr-\ *n, pl* **tourneys** : TOURNAMENT

tour·ni·quet \'tu̇r-ni-kət, 'tər-\ *n* : a device (as a band of rubber) used to stop or slow bleeding or blood flow by compressing blood vessels

tou·sle \'tau̇-zəl, -səl\ *vb* **tou·sled; tou·sling** \'tau̇z-(ə-)liŋ, 'tau̇s-\ : to put into disorder by rough handling

tout \'tau̇t, 'tüt\ *vb* : to make much of : PROMOTE

¹**tow** \'tō\ *vb* : to draw or pull along behind [Old English *togian* "to tow"]

²**tow** *n* **1** : a line or rope for towing **2** : an act or instance of towing or the fact or condition of being towed **3** : something (as a barge) that tows or is towed — **in tow** : under guidance or protection ⟨taken *in tow* by a friendly guide⟩

³**tow** *n* **1** : short broken fiber from flax, hemp, or jute used for yarn, twine, or stuffing **2** : yarn or cloth made of tow [Old English *tow-* "spinning"]

to·ward *or* **to·wards** \(')tō(-ə)rd(z), (')tȯ(-ə)rd(z), tə-'wȯrd(z), (')twȯrd(z), (')twōrd(z)\ *prep* **1** : in the direction of ⟨heading *toward* town⟩ **2 a** : along a course leading to ⟨efforts *toward* peace⟩ **b** : in regard to ⟨attitude *toward* life⟩ **3** : so as to face ⟨turn the chair *toward* the window⟩ **4** : not long before : NEAR ⟨*toward* noon⟩ **5** : as part of the payment for ⟨$100 *toward* a new sofa⟩

tow·boat \'tō-,bōt\ *n* **1** : TUGBOAT **2** : a compact shallow-draft boat for pushing barges on inland waterways

¹**tow·el** \'tau̇(-ə)l\ *n* : a cloth or piece of absorbent paper for wiping or drying

²**towel** *vb* **-eled** *or* **-elled; -el·ing** *or* **-el·ling** : to rub or dry with a towel : use a towel to dry off

tow·el·ing *or* **tow·el·ling** \'tau̇-(ə-)liŋ\ *n* : material for towels

¹**tow·er** \'tau̇(-ə)r\ *n* **1** : a tall narrow building or structure that may stand by itself or be attached to a larger structure **2** : CITADEL 1 — **tow·ered** \'tau̇(-ə)rd\ *adj*

²**tower** *vb* : to reach or rise to a great height

tow·er·ing *adj* **1** : rising high : TALL ⟨*towering* mountain peaks⟩ ⟨*towering* skyscrapers⟩ **2** : reaching a high point of strength or force ⟨a *towering* rage⟩ **3** : going beyond proper bounds ⟨*towering* ambitions⟩

tow·head \'tō-,hed\ *n* : a person with very light blond hair

to·whee \'tō-,hē, 'tō-ē, tō-'hē\ *n* : a finch of eastern North America in which the male has a black back, a white belly, and reddish sides; *also* : any of various related birds mostly of the western U.S. and Canada

tow·line \'tō-,līn\ *n* : a line used in towing

town \'tau̇n\ *n* **1 a** : a compactly settled area that is usually larger than a village but smaller than a city **b** : CITY 1 **2** : the people of a town — **town** *adj*

town clerk *n* : an official who keeps the town records

town crier *n* : an official who makes public announcements

town hall *n* : a public building used for offices and meetings of town government

town house *n* : a house connected to the next house by a common sidewall

town·ie \'tau̇-nē\ *n* : a permanent resident of a town

town meeting *n* : a meeting of townspeople to pass laws for the town

towns·folk \\'taùnz-ˌfōk\ *n pl* : TOWNSPEOPLE

town·ship \\'taùn-ˌship\ *n* **1** : a unit of local government in some northeastern and north central states **2** : a division of territory in surveys of U.S. public land containing 36 square miles (about 93 square kilometers)

towns·peo·ple \\'taùnz-ˌpē-pəl\ *n pl* : the people who live in a town or city

tow·path \\'tō-ˌpath, -ˌpȧth\ *n* : a path (as along a canal) traveled especially by animals (as horses or mules) towing boats

tow·rope \-ˌrōp\ *n* : a line used in towing

tow truck *n* : a truck equipped to move or haul wrecked or broken-down vehicles

tox·emia \täk-ˈsē-mē-ə\ *n* : an abnormal condition caused by toxic substances in the blood

tox·ic \\'täk-sik\ *adj* **1** : of, relating to, or caused by a poison or toxin **2** : POISONOUS [from Latin *toxicus* "relating to or caused by a poison," from earlier *toxicum* "poison," from Greek *toxikon* "a poison put on the tips of arrows," from *toxikos* "of a bow and arrows," from *toxon* "bow, arrow" — related to INTOXICATE, TOXIN; see *Word History* at INTOXICATE] — **tox·ic·i·ty** \täk-ˈsis-ət-ē\ *n*

tox·in \\'täk-sən\ *n* : a substance produced by a living organism (as a bacterium) that is very poisonous to other organisms and that usually causes antibody formation — compare ANTITOXIN [derived from Latin *tox-* "poisonous" and English *-in* "chemical compound"; *tox-* from *toxicum* "poison," from Greek *toxikon* "arrow poison," from *toxon* "bow, arrow" — related to INTOXICATE, TOXIC; see *Word History* at INTOXICATE]

tox·oid \\'täk-ˌsòid\ *n* : a toxin of a disease-causing organism treated so as to destroy its poisonous effects while leaving it still capable of causing antibodies to form when it is injected into the body

¹toy \\'tòi\ *n* **1** : something of little or no value or importance **2** : something for a child to play with **3** : something small for its kind; *esp* : an animal of a breed or variety marked by exceptionally small size — **toy** *adj* — **toy·like** \-ˌlīk\ *adj*

²toy *vb* : to amuse oneself as if with a toy

¹trace \\'trās\ *n* **1** : ROAD 2a **2** : a mark left by something that has passed or is past **3** : a very small amount [Middle English *trace* "a course, a mark left by something that passes," from early French *trace* (same meaning), from *tracer* (verb) "to sketch, show by drawn lines," derived from Latin *tractus*, past participle of *trahere* "to pull, drag" — related to ABSTRACT, ATTRACT, ³TRACE, TRAIT]

²trace *vb* **traced; trac·ing 1 a** : ²SKETCH 1 **b** : to form (as letters) carefully **c** : to copy (as a drawing or pattern) by following the lines or letters as seen through a transparent sheet placed over the thing copied **d** : to make a graphic record of by a recording instrument ⟨*trace* the heart action⟩ **2 a** : to follow the footprints, track, or trail of **b** : to study, follow, or show the development and progress of in detail — **trace·able** \\'trā-sə-bəl\ *adj*

³trace *n* : either of two straps, chains, or lines of a harness for attaching a horse to something (as a wagon or plow) to be pulled [Middle English *trais* (plural) "two straps used for connecting a horse to a vehicle to be pulled," from early French *tres*, plural of *trait*, literally "act of pulling," from Latin *tractus*, past participle of *trahere* "to pull, drag" — related to ABSTRACT, ATTRACT, ¹TRACE, TRAIT]

trace element *n* : a chemical element present in tiny amounts; *esp* : one that is used by a living thing and is considered essential to the functions necessary for life

trac·er \\'trā-sər\ *n* **1 a** : a person who traces missing persons or property **b** : an inquiry sent out in tracing a shipment lost in transit **2 a** : ammunition containing a chemical composition to mark the flight of projectiles by a trail of smoke or fire **b** : a substance and especially a labeled element or atom used to trace the course of a chemical or biological process

trac·ery \\'trās-(ə-)rē\ *n, pl* **-er·ies** : ornamental work with many branching lines

tra·chea \\'trā-kē-ə\ *n, pl* **-che·ae** \-kē-ˌē, -kē-ˌī\ *also* **-che·as** *or* **-chea 1** : the main part of the system of tubes by which air passes to and from the lungs in vertebrates — called also *windpipe* **2** : one of the tiny air-carrying tubes that form the respiratory system of most insects and many other land-dwelling arthropods (as spiders) — **tra·che·al** \-kē-əl\ *adj*

tracery

tra·cheid \\'trā-kē-əd, -ˌkēd\ *n* : a long tube-shaped cell that is found in the xylem of plants, is narrower near the ends, has strong thickened walls, and functions in support and in the transport of water and solutions

tra·cho·ma \trə-ˈkō-mə\ *n* : a serious contagious eye disease that is marked by swelling of the conjunctiva, is caused by a bacterium, and often results in blindness if left untreated

trac·ing \\'trā-siŋ\ *n* **1** : the act of one that traces **2** : something that is traced

tracing paper *n* : a thin paper through which something (as a picture) may be traced; *also* : a thin paper for transferring a clothing pattern to cloth

tracing wheel *n* : a small plain or toothed wheel attached to a handle and used on tracing paper to trace a clothing pattern

¹track \\'trak\ *n* **1 a** : a mark left by something that has gone by **b** : PATH 1, TRAIL **c** : a path along which something is recorded (as on magnetic tape) **2 a** : a course laid out for racing **b** : the parallel rails of a railroad **3** : the course along which something moves or progresses **4** : awareness of things or the order in which things happen or ideas come ⟨lose *track* of the time⟩ ⟨keep *track* of expenses⟩ **5** : either of two continuous metal belts on which a vehicle (as a tank or bulldozer) travels **6** : track-and-field sports; *esp* : those performed on a running track — **track·less** \\'trak-ləs\ *adj* — **in one's tracks** : where one is at the moment : on the spot — **on track** : achieving or doing what is necessary or expected

²track *vb* **1 a** : to follow the tracks or traces of : TRAIL ⟨*track* a deer⟩ **b** : to search for until found ⟨*tracking* down the causes of cancer⟩ **2** : to observe the moving path of ⟨*track* a missile with radar⟩ **3** : to make tracks upon or with ⟨*track* up the floor⟩ ⟨*track* mud all over the floor⟩ — **track·er** *n*

track–and–field \ˌtrak-ən-ˈfē(ə)ld\ *adj* : of, relating to, or being sports events (as racing, throwing, and jumping contests) held on a running track and on an enclosed field

track·ball \\'trak-ˌbȯl\ *n* : a ball that is mounted usually in a computer console so as to be only partially exposed and that is rotated to control the movement of a cursor on a display

¹tract \\'trakt\ *n* **1 a** : an indefinite stretch of land ⟨a large *tract* of forest⟩ **b** : a defined area of land ⟨a garden *tract*⟩ **2** : a system of body parts or organs that act together to perform some function ⟨the digestive *tract*⟩

\ə\ abut	\aù\ out	\i\ tip	\ȯ\ saw	\ù\ foot
\ər\ further	\ch\ chin	\ī\ life	\ȯi\ coin	\y\ yet
\a\ mat	\e\ pet	\j\ job	\th\ thin	\yü\ few
\ā\ take	\ē\ easy	\ŋ\ sing	\th\ this	\yù\ cure
\ä\ cot, cart	\g\ go	\ō\ bone	\ü\ food	\zh\ vision

²**tract** *n* : a pamphlet of political or religious ideas and beliefs

trac·ta·ble \'trak-tə-bəl\ *adj* : easily led, taught, or controlled ⟨a *tractable* horse⟩

tract house *n* : a house that is one of a number of very similar houses built on a tract of land

trac·tion \'trak-shən\ *n* **1** : the act of drawing : the state of being drawn **2** : the adhesive friction of a body on a surface on which it moves (as of a wheel on a rail) **3** : a pulling force applied to a skeletal structure (as a broken bone) by using a special device ⟨a *traction* splint⟩; *also* : a state of tension created by such a pulling force ⟨a leg in *traction*⟩

trac·tor \'trak-tər\ *n* **1** : a vehicle that has large rear wheels or moves on tracks and is used especially for pulling farm implements **2** : a short truck with no body used in combination with a trailer for hauling freight

tractor 1

¹**trade** \'trād\ *n* **1** : the business or work in which a person takes part regularly : OCCUPATION **2** : an occupation requiring manual or mechanical skill **3** : the persons working in an occupation, business, or industry **4** : the business of buying and selling items : COMMERCE **5 a** : an act or instance of trading : TRANSACTION **b** : an exchange of property without use of money : SWAP **6** : a firm's customers **7** : TRADE WIND — usually used in plural

²**trade** *vb* **trad·ed; trad·ing 1 a** : to give in exchange for something else **b** : to make an exchange of ⟨*traded* places⟩ **2 a** : to take part in the exchange, purchase, or sale of goods **b** : to deal regularly as a customer

³**trade** *adj* : of, relating to, or used in trade

trade–in \'trād-ˌin\ *n* : something given in trade usually as part payment for a purchase

trade in \(')trād-'in\ *vb* : to turn in as a payment or part payment for a purchase

trade·mark \'trād-ˌmärk\ *n* **1** : a device (as a word) that points clearly to the origin or ownership of merchandise to which it is applied and that is legally reserved for use only by the owner **2** : something that identifies a person or thing — **trademark** *vb*

trade–off \'trād-ˌȯf\ *n* **1** : a balancing of things all of which cannot be had at the same time **2** : a giving up of one thing in return for another

trad·er \'trād-ər\ *n* **1** : a person who trades **2** : a ship engaged in trade

trade route *n* **1** : one of the sea-lanes used by merchant ships **2** : a route followed by traders (as in caravans)

trade school *n* : a secondary school teaching the skilled trades

trades·man \'trādz-mən\ *n* **1** : a worker in a skilled trade : CRAFTSMAN **2** : one who runs a retail store : SHOPKEEPER

trades·peo·ple \-ˌpē-pəl\ *n pl* : people engaged in trade

trade union *n* : LABOR UNION — **trade unionist** *n*

trade wind *n* : a wind blowing almost constantly toward the equator from an easterly direction

trading card *n* : a card that usually has pictures and information about someone or something and is part of a set that is collected by trading with other people

trading post *n* : a station or store of a trader or trading company established in a thinly settled region where local products (as furs) are exchanged for manufactured goods

tra·di·tion \trə-'dish-ən\ *n* **1** : the handing down of information, beliefs, or customs from one generation to another **2** : a belief or custom handed down by tradition [Middle English *tradicioun* "tradition," from early French

tradicion (same meaning) and Latin *tradition-, traditio* "the action of handing over, tradition," — related to TREASON; see *Word History* at TREASON]

tra·di·tion·al \trə-'dish-nəl, -ən-ᵊl\ *adj* **1** : handed down from age to age without writing **2** : based on custom ⟨our *traditional* Thanksgiving dinner⟩ — **tra·di·tion·al·ly** \-ē\ *adv*

tra·duce \trə-'d(y)üs\ *vb* **tra·duced; tra·duc·ing** : ²SLANDER — **tra·duc·er** *n*

¹**traf·fic** \'traf-ik\ *n* **1** : the business of buying and selling : COMMERCE **2** : communication or dealings between persons or groups ⟨had no *traffic* with the enemy⟩ **3 a** : the movement (as of pedestrians or vehicles) through an area or along a route ⟨heavy *traffic* in the kitchen before dinner⟩ ⟨rush-hour *traffic*⟩ **b** : the vehicles, pedestrians, ships, or planes moving along a route **c** : a crowded mass of vehicles ⟨stuck in *traffic*⟩ **4 a** : the passengers or goods carried by train, boat, or airplane **b** : the business of carrying passengers or goods

²**traffic** *vb* **traf·ficked; traf·fick·ing** : to carry on traffic : TRADE, DEAL — **traf·fick·er** *n*

traffic circle *n* : ²ROTARY 2

traffic light *n* : a visual signal (as a system of green, yellow, and red lights) for controlling traffic

traffic signal *n* : a signal (as a traffic light) for controlling traffic

tra·ge·di·an \trə-'jēd-ē-ən\ *n* **1** : a writer of tragedies **2** : an actor of tragic roles

trag·e·dy \'traj-əd-ē\ *n, pl* **-dies 1** : a serious drama with a sorrowful or disastrous conclusion **2** : a disastrous event

Word History Tragedy as a form of drama began in ancient Greece. It developed from the public performances of songs and dances at religious festivals. These festivals were held in honor of Dionysus, the god of wine and fertility. The Greeks called these performances *tragōidia,* which meant literally "goat song." The word came from *tragos,* meaning "goat" and *aeidein,* meaning "to sing." These performances were at first given by a chorus. Later, however, it became popular to have one member of the chorus stand apart from the others and give a spoken introduction to or interpretation of the story. This speaker soon took over a larger and larger role in the performances. In time, this person was joined by more speakers until the dramas came to be like our modern plays with many parts acted out. It is not certain why these performances were named with a word for "goat." One explanation is that a goat was given as a prize to the person presenting the best drama. Another is that the goat was sacred to the god Dionysus and was sacrificed to him at these festivals. The early tragedies were stories of the misfortunes of heroes of legend or history, and that idea of misfortune carries on today in the common meaning of our word *tragedy.* [Middle English *tragedie* "tragedy as a drama," from early French *tragedie* (same meaning), from Latin *tragoedia* (same meaning), from Greek *tragōidia* "a drama about the misfortunes of heroes," literally "goat song," from *tragos* "goat" and *aeidein* "to sing"]

trag·ic \'traj-ik\ *adj* **1** : of, marked by, or expressive of tragedy **2** : dealing with or appearing in tragedy ⟨a *tragic* hero⟩ **3** : very unfortunate : DEPLORABLE ⟨a *tragic* mistake⟩ — **trag·i·cal·ly** \-i-k(ə-)lē\ *adv*

tragic flaw *n* : a defect in the character of a good person (as the hero of a tragedy) that causes his or her destruction

tragi·com·e·dy \ˌtraj-i-'käm-əd-ē\ *n* : a play or situation which blends tragic and comic elements — **tragi·com·ic** \-'käm-ik\ *also* **tragi·com·i·cal** \-i-kəl\ *adj*

¹**trail** \'trā(ə)l\ *vb* **1** : to drag or draw along behind **2** : to lag behind **3 a** : to follow upon the scent or trace of : TRACK ⟨dogs *trailing* a fox⟩ **b** : to follow in the tracks

of : PURSUE ⟨photographers *trailed* the actor⟩ **4** : to hang down or rest on or creep over the ground ⟨*trailing* vines⟩ ⟨a *trailing* skirt⟩ **5** : to form a trail ⟨smoke *trailed* from the chimney⟩ **6** : to become less and less : DWINDLE ⟨the voice *trailed* off⟩ **synonyms** see CHASE

²trail *n* **1** : something that trails or is trailed **2** : a trace or mark left by something that has passed or been drawn along **3 a** : a track made by passage : a beaten path **b** : a path marked to show a route (as through a forest) ⟨hiking *trails*⟩ **c** : an established course or routine ⟨hit the campaign *trail*⟩

trail·blaz·er \'trā(ə)l-ˌblā-zər\ *n* : someone who prepares the way for others who follow: as **a** : PATHFINDER **b** : ¹PIONEER 1

trail·er \'trā-lər\ *n* **1** : one that trails **2 a** : a vehicle designed to be hauled (as by a tractor) **b** : a vehicle designed to serve wherever parked as a dwelling or as a place of business **3** : ²PREVIEW 2

trailing arbutus *n* : a trailing plant of eastern North America that belongs to the heath family and produces fragrant pink or white flowers in early spring — called also *arbutus*

trail mix *n* : a mixture of seeds, nuts, and dried fruit eaten as a snack

¹train \'trān\ *n* **1** : a part of a gown that trails behind the wearer **2** : a number of followers or attendants : RETINUE **3** : a moving file of persons, vehicles, or animals ⟨wagon *train*⟩ **4 a** : an orderly connected series of events, actions, or ideas ⟨*train* of thought⟩ **b** : ²RESULT 1, AFTERMATH **5** : a series of moving machine parts (as gears) for transmitting and modifying motion **6** : a connected line of railroad cars

¹train 1

²train *vb* **1** : to direct the growth of (a plant) usually by bending, pruning, and tying **2 a** : to teach in an art, profession, or trade **b** : to teach (an animal) to obey **3** : to make ready for a test of skill or strength **4** : to aim at an object or target ⟨*trained* their eyes on the horizon⟩ — **train·abil·i·ty** \ˌtrā-nə-ˈbil-ət-ē\ *n* — **train·able** \'trā-nə-bəl\ *adj*

train·ee \trā-'nē\ *n* : a person who is being trained for a job

train·er \'trān-ər\ *n* **1** : one that trains **2** : a person who treats the minor ailments and injuries of the members of an athletic team

train·ing *n* **1** : the course followed by one who trains or is being trained **2** : the knowledge, experience, or condition acquired by one who trains **synonyms** see EDUCATION

training wheels *n pl* : a pair of small wheels connected to the rear axle of a bicycle to help a beginning bicyclist keep balance

traipse \'trāps\ *vb* **traipsed; traips·ing** : to walk or wander about

trait \'trāt\ *n* **1** : a quality that sets one person or thing off from another : PECULIARITY **2** ⟨curiosity is one of her notable *traits*⟩ **2** : an inherited characteristic ⟨dominant and recessive *traits*⟩ [from early French *trait* "the act of pulling," from Latin *tractus*, past participle of *trahere* "to pull, drag" — related to ¹TRACE, ³TRACE]

trai·tor \'trāt-ər\ *n* **1** : one who betrays another's trust or is false to an obligation or duty **2** : one who commits treason [Middle English *traitre* "traitor," from early French *traitre* (same meaning), from Latin *traditor* (same meaning), derived from *tradere* "to hand over, betray" — related to TREASON; see *Word History* at TREASON]

trai·tor·ous \'trāt-ə-rəs, 'trā-trəs\ *adj* **1** : guilty or capable of treason **2** : amounting to treason ⟨*traitorous* acts⟩

tra·jec·to·ry \trə-'jek-t(ə-)rē\ *n, pl* **-ries** : the curve that a body (as a planet in its orbit or a rocket) travels along in space

tram \'tram\ *n* **1** : a cart or wagon running on rails (as in a mine) **2** *chiefly British* : STREETCAR **3** : an overhead cable car

¹tram·mel \'tram-əl\ *n* : something preventing free movement or activity — usually used in plural

²trammel *vb* **-meled** *or* **-melled; -mel·ing** *or* **-mel·ling** \-(ə-)liŋ\ : to prevent or restrict the free movement of

¹tramp \'tramp, *senses 1 & 2 are also* 'trämp, 'trȯmp\ *vb* **1** : to walk heavily **2** : to tread on forcibly and repeatedly **3** : to travel or wander through on foot ⟨*tramp* the streets⟩ — **tramp·er** *n*

²tramp \'tramp, *sense 3 is also* 'trämp, 'trȯmp\ *n* **1** : a homeless wanderer who may beg or steal for a living **2** : a walking trip : HIKE **3** : the sound made by many marching feet **4** : a ship not making regular trips but taking cargo to any port — called also *tramp steamer*

tram·ple \'tram-pəl\ *vb* **tram·pled; tram·pling** \-p(ə-)liŋ\ **1 a** : to tramp or tread heavily so as to bruise, crush, or injure ⟨cattle *trampled* on the young wheat⟩ **b** : to crush, injure, or destroy by or as if by treading ⟨*trampled* the flowers⟩ **2** : to injure or harm by ruthless or heartless treatment ⟨*trampling* on the right of others⟩ — **tram·pler** \-p(ə-)lər\ *n*

tram·po·line \ˌtram-pə-'lēn, 'tram-pə-ˌlēn\ *n* : a canvas sheet supported by springs in a metal frame used for springing and landing in acrobatic tumbling

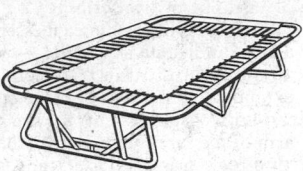

trampoline

trance \'tran(t)s\ *n* **1** : STUPOR 1 **2** : a sleeplike state (as of deep hypnosis) **3** : a state of being so deeply absorbed in something as to be unaware of one's surroundings — **trance·like** \-ˌlīk\ *adj*

tran·quil \'traŋ-kwəl, 'tran-\ *adj* : free from disturbance or turmoil : QUIET **synonyms** see CALM — **tran·quil·ly** \-kwə-lē\ *adv*

tran·quil·ize *also* **tran·quil·lize** \'traŋ-kwə-ˌlīz, 'tran-\ *vb* **-ized** *also* **-lized; -iz·ing** *also* **-liz·ing** : to make or become tranquil or relaxed; *esp* : to ease the nervous tension and anxiety of usually by means of drugs

tran·quil·iz·er *also* **tran·quil·liz·er** \'traŋ-kwə-ˌlī-zər, 'tran-\ *n* : one that tranquilizes; *esp* : a drug used to reduce anxiety and nervous tension

tran·quil·li·ty *or* **tran·quil·i·ty** \tran-'kwil-ət-ē, traŋ-\ *n* : the quality or state of being tranquil

trans- *prefix* **1** : on or to the other side of : across : beyond ⟨*trans*atlantic⟩ **2** : so or such as to change in form or position or transfer ⟨*trans*literate⟩ [derived from Latin *trans*- "across, beyond, so as to change"]

trans·act \tran(t)s-'akt, tranz-\ *vb* **1** : to carry through ⟨*transact* a sale of property⟩ **2** : ²CONDUCT 2, CARRY ON ⟨*transact* business⟩ — **trans·ac·tor** \-'ak-tər\ *n*

trans·ac·tion \tran(t)s-'ak-shən, tranz-\ *n* **1 a** : something transacted; *esp* : a business deal **b** *pl* : the record of the meeting of an organization **2 a** : an act, process, or instance of transacting **b** : an act of communication between two people who influence or change each other

\ə\ **abut**	\au̇\ **out**	\i\ **tip**	\ȯ\ **saw**	\u̇\ **foot**
\ər\ **further**	\ch\ **chin**	\ī\ **life**	\ȯi\ **coin**	\y\ **yet**
\a\ **mat**	\e\ **pet**	\j\ **job**	\th\ **thin**	\yü\ **few**
\ā\ **take**	\ē\ **easy**	\ŋ\ **sing**	\th\ **this**	\yu̇\ **cure**
\ä\ **cot, cart**	\g\ **go**	\ō\ **bone**	\ü\ **food**	\zh\ **vision**

trans·at·lan·tic \ˌtran(t)s-ət-ˈlant-ik, ˌtranz-\ *adj* **1** : crossing or extending across the Atlantic Ocean ⟨a *transatlantic* cable⟩ **2** : located or coming from beyond the Atlantic Ocean ⟨our *transatlantic* friends⟩

trans·bor·der \ˌtran(t)s-ˈbȯrd-ər\ *adj* : crossing or reaching across a border

tran·scend \tran(t)s-ˈend\ *vb* **1** : to rise above or go beyond the limits of : EXCEED **2** : to be greatly superior to : SURPASS

tran·scen·dence \tran(t)s-ˈen-dən(t)s\ *n* : the quality or state of being transcendent

tran·scen·dent \tran(t)s-ˈen-dənt\ *adj* **1** : superior to or going beyond the usual : EXTRAORDINARY **2** : going beyond the limits of ordinary experience

tran·scen·den·tal \ˌtran(t)s-ˌen-ˈdent-ᵊl, -ən-\ *adj* : TRANSCENDENT 2 — **tran·scen·den·tal·ly** \-ᵊl-ē\ *adv*

trans·con·ti·nen·tal \ˌtran(t)s-ˌkänt-ᵊn-ˈent-ᵊl\ *adj* : extending or going across a continent ⟨a *transcontinental* flight⟩

tran·scribe \tran(t)s-ˈkrīb\ *vb* **tran·scribed; tran·scrib·ing** **1 a** : to make a written copy of **b** : to make a copy of (dictated or recorded matter) by hand or on a machine (as a typewriter) **2** : to represent speech sounds with phonetic symbols — **tran·scrib·er** *n*

tran·script \ˈtran(t)s-ˌkript\ *n* **1** : a written, printed, or typed copy **2** : an official copy (as of a student's educational record)

tran·scrip·tion \tran(t)s-ˈkrip-shən\ *n* **1** : an act, process, or instance of transcribing **2** : ¹COPY 1, TRANSCRIPT **3** : the process of forming a messenger RNA molecule using a DNA molecule as a guide — compare TRANSLATION 2

trans·cul·tur·al \tran(t)s-ˈkəlch-(ə-)rəl\ *adj* : involving or extending across two or more cultures

tran·sept \ˈtran(t)s-ˌept\ *n* : the section forming the short arm of a church with a cross-shaped floor plan

¹trans·fer \tran(t)s-ˈfər, ˈtran(t)s-ˌfər\ *vb* **trans·ferred; trans·fer·ring** **1 a** : to pass from one person, place, or situation to another **b** : to cause to pass from one to another **2** : to give over the possession or ownership of **3** : to move to a different place, region, or situation; *esp* : to withdraw from one school to enroll at another **4** : to change from one vehicle or transportation line to another [Middle English *transferren* "to transfer," from Latin *transferre* (same meaning), from *trans-* "across, through" and *ferre* "to bear, carry" — related to ¹DEFER, FERTILE] — **trans·fer·able** \tran(t)s-ˈfər-ə-bəl\ *adj* — **trans·fer·al** \-ˈfər-əl\ *n*

²trans·fer \ˈtran(t)s-ˌfər\ *n* **1** : a giving over of right, title, or interest in property by one person to another **2** : an act, process, or example of transferring **3** : one that transfers or is transferred **4** : a graphic image transferred by contact from one surface to another **5** : a place where a transfer is made (as from trains to ferries) **6** : a ticket permitting a passenger on a bus or train to continue the journey by another route

trans·fer·ence \tran(t)s-ˈfər-ən(t)s\ *n* : an act, process, or example of transferring

transfer RNA \ˈtran(t)s-ˌfər-\ *n* : a relatively small RNA molecule that functions in the transfer of a particular amino acid to a growing protein at the site of protein synthesis during genetic translation — compare MESSENGER RNA

trans·fig·u·ra·tion \ˌ(ˌ)tran(t)s-ˌfig-(y)ə-ˈrā-shən\ *n* **1** : a great change of form or appearance; *esp* : a change that beautifies, glorifies, or makes more spiritual **2** *cap* : a Christian festival celebrating Jesus' transfiguration on the mountain as witnessed by three of his disciples

trans·fig·ure \tran(t)s-ˈfig-yər, *especially British* -ˈfig-ər\ *vb* **-ured; -ur·ing** : to change the form or appearance of and usually make more glorious or ideally beautiful

trans·fix \tran(t)s-ˈfiks\ *vb* **1** : to pierce through with or as if with a pointed weapon **2** : to hold motionless by or as if by piercing ⟨stood *transfixed* by her gaze⟩

trans·form \tran(t)s-ˈfȯ(ə)rm\ *vb* **1 a** : to change completely in composition, structure, or character **b** : to change in outward appearance **2** : to substitute for or change (a mathematical expression) into another using a mathematical rule — **trans·for·ma·tive** \-ˈfȯr-mət-iv\ *adj*

trans·for·ma·tion \ˌtran(t)s-fər-ˈmā-shən, -fȯr-\ *n* : an act, process, or example of transforming or being transformed — **trans·for·ma·tion·al** \-shnəl, -shən-ᵊl\ *adj*

trans·form·er \tran(t)s-ˈfȯr-mər\ *n* : a device for changing an electric current into one of different voltage

trans·fuse \tran(t)s-ˈfyüz\ *vb* **trans·fused; trans·fus·ing** **1 a** : to cause to pass from one to another **b** : to spread through or be filled with ⟨a room *transfused* with light⟩ **2** : to transfer (as blood) into a blood vessel of a person or animal

trans·fu·sion \tran(t)s-ˈfyü-zhən\ *n* **1** : an act, process, or instance of transfusing; *esp* : the process of transfusing a fluid and especially blood into a blood vessel **2** : something transfused

trans·gen·der \tran(t)s-ˈjen-dər\ *adj* : of or relating to people who have a gender identity that is not clearly male or clearly female

trans·gress \tran(t)s-ˈgres, tranz-\ *vb* **1** : to go beyond limits set by : VIOLATE ⟨*transgress* divine law⟩ **2** : to pass beyond or go over a limit or boundary **3** : to violate a command or law [from early French *transgresser* "to transgress," from Latin *transgressus*, past participle of *transgredi* "to step across or beyond," from *trans-* "across, beyond" and *gradi* "to step"] — **trans·gres·sive** \-ˈgres-iv\ *adj* — **trans·gres·sor** \-ˈgres-ər\ *n*

trans·gres·sion \tran(t)s-ˈgresh-ən, tranz-\ *n* : an act, process, or example of transgressing

¹tran·sient \ˈtranch-ənt\ *adj* : not lasting or staying long — **tran·sient·ly** *adv*

synonyms TRANSIENT, TRANSITORY, MOMENTARY, FLEETING mean lasting or staying only a short time. TRANSIENT applies to what is actually short in its duration or stay ⟨a hotel for *transient* guests⟩. TRANSITORY applies to what is by its nature likely to change, pass, or come to an end ⟨fame in the movies is *transitory*⟩. MOMENTARY suggests a quick coming and going as a brief interruption of a more lasting state ⟨my feeling of joy was only *momentary*⟩. FLEETING applies to something that passes very quickly and cannot be brought back ⟨a happy life with only *fleeting* moments of sorrow⟩.

²transient *n* **1** : a temporary guest **2** : a person traveling about usually in search of work

tran·sis·tor \tranz-ˈis-tər, tran(t)s-\ *n* **1** : an electronic device that consists of a small block of a semiconductor (as germanium) with at least three electrodes and is used to control the flow of electricity in electronic equipment (as a radio or computer) **2** : a radio having transistors — called also *transistor radio*

¹tran·sit \ˈtran(t)s-ət, ˈtranz-\ *n* **1** : an act, process, or example of passing through or over : PASSAGE **2** : the transporting of persons or things from one place to another ⟨goods lost in *transit*⟩ **3** : local transportation of people in public vehicles; *also* : the vehicles or system used in such transportation **4** : a surveyor's instrument for measuring angles [from Latin *transitus* "passage, journey," from *transire* "to go across, pass," from *trans-* "across, beyond" and *ire* "to go" — related to ISSUE, ITINERARY]

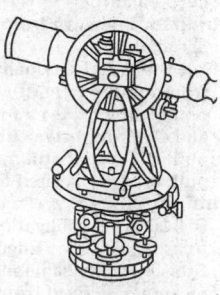
¹transit 4

²transit *vb* : to pass or cause to pass over, through, or across

¹tran·si·tion \tran(t)s-'ish-ən, tranz-\ *n* **1** : a changing from one state, stage, place, or subject to another **2** : a musical passage leading from one section of a piece to another — **tran·si·tion·al** \-'ish-nəl, -'izh-, -ən-°l\ *adj* — **tran·si·tion·al·ly** \-ē\ *adv*

²transition *vb* : to make a transition ⟨*transitioning* to a new school⟩

transition element *n* : any of various metallic elements (as chromium, iron, and nickel) that can form bonds using electrons from two energy levels instead of only one

tran·si·tive \'tran(t)s-ət-iv, 'tranz-; 'tran(t)s-tiv\ *adj* **1** : having or containing a direct object ⟨a *transitive* verb⟩ **2** : of, relating to, or characterized by transition — **tran·si·tive·ly** *adv*

tran·si·to·ry \'tran(t)s-ə-ˌtōr-ē, 'tranz-, -ˌtȯr-\ *adj* : lasting only a short time : SHORT-LIVED, TEMPORARY **synonyms** see TRANSIENT — **tran·si·to·ri·ly** \ˌtran(t)s-ə-'tōr-ə-lē, ˌtranz-, -'tȯr-\ *adv*

trans·late \tran(t)s-'lāt, tranz-\ *vb* **trans·lat·ed; trans·lat·ing** **1** : to change from one place, state, or form to another : TRANSFORM ⟨*translate* ideas into action⟩ **2** : to transport miraculously to heaven without death **3 a** : to change from one language or set of symbols into another ⟨*translate* Japanese into English⟩ **b** : to express in different words : PARAPHRASE **c** : to explain in a clearer way : INTERPRET ⟨needed a lawyer to *translate* the contract⟩ **4** : to be translated **5** : to have as a result — usually used with *into* ⟨believes that more homework will *translate* into better grades⟩ — **trans·lat·able** \-'lāt-ə-bəl\ *adj* — **trans·la·tor** \-'lāt-ər\ *n*

trans·la·tion \tran(t)s-'lā-shən, tranz-\ *n* **1** : an act, process, or product of translating **2** : the process of forming a protein molecule from information contained in a messenger RNA molecule — compare TRANSCRIPTION 3

trans·lit·er·ate \tran(t)s-'lit-ə-ˌrāt, tranz-\ *vb* **-at·ed; -at·ing** : to represent or spell in the characters of another alphabet — **trans·lit·er·a·tion** \(ˌ)tran(t)s-ˌlit-ə-'rā-shən, (ˌ)tranz-\ *n*

trans·lu·cen·cy \tran(t)s-'lü-sən-sē\ *n* : the quality or state of being translucent

trans·lu·cent \tran(t)s-'lüs-°nt; tranz-\ *adj* **1** : clear and pure as if shining from within ⟨a *translucent* lake⟩ **2** : not transparent but clear enough to allow light to pass through ⟨frosted glass is *translucent*⟩

trans·mi·gra·tion \ˌtran(t)s-ˌmī-'grā-shən, ˌtranz-\ *n* : the passing of a soul into another body after death

trans·mis·si·ble \tran(t)s-'mis-ə-bəl, tranz-\ *adj* : capable of being transmitted ⟨*tramsmissible* diseases⟩

trans·mis·sion \tran(t)s-'mish-ən, tranz-\ *n* **1** : an act, process, or example of transmitting **2** : the passage of radio waves in the space between transmitting and receiving stations **3** : the gears by which the power is transmitted from the engine to the axle that gives motion to a motor vehicle **4** : something transmitted

trans·mit \tran(t)s-'mit, tranz-\ *vb* **trans·mit·ted; trans·mit·ting** **1 a** : to transfer from one person or place to another **b** : to pass on by or as if by inheritance **c** : to cause or allow to spread abroad or to another ⟨*transmit* a disease⟩ **2 a** : to pass or cause to pass through space or a material : allow the passage of **b** : to send a signal by radio waves or over a wire [Middle English *transmitten* "to send to another person or place," from Latin *transmittere* (same meaning), from *trans-* "across, to the other side" and *mittere* "to send, throw" — related to EMIT] — **trans·mit·ta·ble** \-'mit-ə-bəl\ *adj* — **trans·mit·tal** \-'mit-°l\ *n*

trans·mit·ter \tran(t)s-'mit-ər, tranz-\ *n* : one that transmits; *esp* : a device that sends out radio or television signals

trans·mu·ta·tion \ˌtran(t)s-myủ-'tā-shən, ˌtranz-\ *n* : an act or example of transmuting or being transmuted; *esp*

: the changing of one element into another (as of base metals into gold or silver)

trans·mute \tran(t)s-'myüt, tranz-\ *vb* **trans·mut·ed; trans·mut·ing** **1** : to change in kind, appearance, or value : CONVERT **2** : to change into another substance or element : to undergo transmutation

trans·oce·an·ic \tran(t)s-ˌō-shē-'an-ik, tranz-\ *adj* **1** : lying or dwelling beyond the ocean ⟨a *transoceanic* land⟩ **2** : crossing or extending across the ocean ⟨a *transoceanic* voyage⟩

tran·som \'tran(t)-səm\ *n* **1** : a horizontal crossbar in a window, over a door, or between a door and a window or fanlight above it **2** : a window above a door or other window built on and commonly hinged to a transom

trans·pa·cif·ic \ˌtran(t)s-pə-'sif-ik\ *adj* **1** : crossing or extending across the Pacific Ocean **2** : located or occurring beyond the Pacific Ocean

trans·par·en·cy \tran(t)s-'par-ən-sē, -'per-\ *n, pl* **-cies** **1** : the quality or state of being transparent **2** : a picture or design on glass, thin cloth, paper, or film viewed by shining light through it or by projection

T transom 1

trans·par·ent \tran(t)s-'par-ənt, -'per-\ *adj* **1 a** : transmitting light so that objects lying beyond are entirely visible **b** : fine or sheer enough to be seen through ⟨*transparent* gauze⟩ **2** : easily detected or understood : OBVIOUS ⟨*transparent* falsehood⟩ — **trans·par·ent·ly** *adv*

tran·spi·ra·tion \ˌtran(t)s-pə-'rā-shən\ *n* : the process by which plants give off water vapor through the stomata in their leaves

tran·spire \tran(t)s-'pī(ə)r\ *vb* **tran·spired; tran·spir·ing** **1** : to pass or give off in the form of water vapor through stomata in leaves **2** : to become known or apparent : become revealed ⟨it *transpired* that we had the wrong address⟩ **3** : to come to pass : HAPPEN ⟨what *transpired* last night⟩

¹trans·plant \tran(t)s-'plant\ *vb* **1** : to dig up and plant in another soil or situation ⟨*transplant* seedlings⟩ **2** : to remove from one place and settle or introduce elsewhere ⟨*transplanted* beavers to other parts of the state⟩ ⟨a New Yorker *transplanted* to the West coast⟩ **3** : to transfer (an organ or tissue) from one part or individual to another — **trans·plan·ta·tion** \ˌtran(t)s-ˌplan-'tā-shən\ *n* — **trans·plant·er** \tran(t)s-'plant-ər\ *n*

²trans·plant \'tran(t)s-ˌplant\ *n* **1** : something or someone transplanted **2** : the act or process of transplanting

¹trans·port \tran(t)s-'pō(ə)rt, -'pȯ(ə)rt\ *vb* **1** : to transfer or convey from one place to another **2** : to fill with delight **3** : to send to a penal colony overseas [Middle English *transporten* "to transport," from early French *transporter* or Latin *transportare* (both, same meaning), from Latin *trans-* "across, through, so as to change" and *portare* "to carry" — related to PORTABLE] — **trans·port·able** \-ə-bəl\ *adj* — **trans·port·er** *n*

²trans·port \'tran(t)s-ˌpō)rt, -ˌpȯ)rt\ *n* **1** : an act or process of transporting : TRANSPORTATION **2** : strong or extremely pleasurable emotion ⟨*transports* of joy⟩ **3 a** : a ship for carrying soldiers or military equipment **b** : a vehicle used to transport persons or goods

\ə\ **abut**	\aủ\ **out**	\i\ **tip**	\ȯ\ **saw**	\ủ\ **foot**
\ər\ **further**	\ch\ **chin**	\ī\ **life**	\ȯi\ **coin**	\y\ **yet**
\a\ **mat**	\e\ **pet**	\j\ **job**	\th\ **thin**	\yü\ **few**
\ā\ **take**	\ē\ **easy**	\ŋ\ **sing**	\th\ **this**	\yủ\ **cure**
\ä\ **cot, cart**	\g\ **go**	\ō\ **bone**	\ü\ **food**	\zh\ **vision**

trans·por·ta·tion \,tran(t)s-pər-'tā-shən\ *n* **1** : an act, process, or instance of transporting or being transported **2** : exile to a penal colony **3 a** : a means or method of transport ⟨was left without *transportation* when the car died⟩ **b** : the public transporting of passengers or goods usually for a price

trans·pose \tran(t)s-'pōz\ *vb* **trans·posed; trans·pos·ing 1** : to change the position, order, or sequence of **2** : to write or perform (a musical composition) in a different key **3** : to bring (a term) from one side of an algebraic equation to the other with change of sign ⟨given the equation *y* = 3 - 2*x*, transpose the 2*x* to get *y* + 2*x* = 3⟩ — **trans·po·si·tion** \,tran(t)s-pə-'zish-ən\ *n*

tran·sub·stan·ti·a·tion \,tran(t)s-əb-,stan-chē-'ā-shən\ *n* : the miraculous change by which according to Roman Catholic and Eastern Orthodox belief the consecrated bread and wine at Mass become the body and blood of Christ while maintaining their appearance

trans·ver·sal \tran(t)s-'vər-səl, tranz-\ *n* : a line that intersects a system of lines

trans·verse \tran(t)s-'vərs, tranz-; 'tran(t)s-,vərs, 'tranz-\ *adj* : lying or being across ⟨*transverse* beams supporting the floor⟩ — **trans·verse·ly** *adv*

transverse wave *n* : a wave in which the vibrating element moves in a direction perpendicular to the direction of advance of the wave

¹trap \'trap\ *n* **1** : a device for catching animals; *esp* : one that catches by springing shut suddenly **2** : something by which one is caught unawares **3 a** : a device for hurling clay pigeons into the air **b** : SAND TRAP **4** : a light usually one-horse carriage with springs **5** : any of various devices for preventing passage of one thing often while allowing something else to proceed; *esp* : a device for drains or sewers consisting of a bend or chamber in which the liquid forms a seal to prevent the passage of sewer gas **6** *pl* : a group of percussion instruments (as in a dance band)

²trap *vb* **trapped; trap·ping 1 a** : to catch in or as if in a trap ⟨*trap* a bird⟩ **b** : to place in a restricted position : CONFINE ⟨was almost *trapped* in the burning building⟩ **2** : to provide or set with a trap **3** : to engage in trapping animals (as for fur) **synonyms** see CATCH — **trap·per** *n*

trap·door \'trap-'dō(ə)r, -'dó(ə)r\ *n* : a lifting or sliding door covering or hiding an opening in a roof, ceiling, or floor

trap–door spider *n* : any of various spiders that build silk-lined underground nests topped with a hinged lid

tra·peze \tra-'pēz\ *n* : a gymnastic or acrobatic device consisting of a short horizontal bar hung from two parallel ropes

trap·e·zoid \'trap-ə-,zȯid\ *n* : a polygon that has four sides and exactly two that are parallel — **trap·e·zoi·dal** \,trap-ə-'zȯid-ᵊl\ *adj*

trap·line \'trap-,līn\ *n* : a line or series of traps especially for fur-bearing animals; *also* : the route along which such traps are set

trapezoid

trap·pings \'trap-iŋz\ *n* **1** : an ornamental covering especially for a horse — usually used in plural **2** *pl* : outward decoration or dress **3** *pl* : outward signs ⟨all the *trappings* of success⟩

trap·shoot·ing \'trap-,shüt-iŋ\ *n* : shooting at clay pigeons sprung into the air from a trap — **trap·shoot·er** \-,shüt-ər\ *n*

tra·pun·to \trə-'pün-tō, -'pün-\ *n, pl* **-tos** : a type of quilting in which a design outlined with a single row of stitches is padded from behind to produce a decorative raised effect

trash \'trash\ *n* **1** : something of little or no value: as **a** : ¹JUNK 2, RUBBISH **b** : silly or worthless talk or works (as

books) **2** : a low or worthless person; *also* : such persons as a group : RABBLE **2** — **trashy** \'trash-ē\ *adj*

trau·ma \'traȯ-mə, 'trȯ-\ *n, pl* **traumas** *also* **trau·ma·ta** \-mə-tə\ **1 a** : a serious bodily injury (as that caused by an accident or violent act) ⟨head *trauma*⟩ **b** : an abnormal psychological or behavioral state resulting from severe mental or emotional stress or injury **2** : a cause of trauma — **trau·mat·ic** \trə-'mat-ik, trȯ-, traȯ-\ *adj*

trau·ma·tize \'traȯ-mə-,tīz, 'trȯ-\ *vb* **-tized; -tiz·ing** : to inflict trauma upon ⟨was *traumatized* by the accident⟩

tra·vail \trə-'vā(ə)l, 'trav-,āl\ *n* **1** : work especially of a painful or difficult nature : TOIL **2** : AGONY 1, TORMENT [Middle English *travail* "hard labor," from early French *travail* (same meaning), from *travailler* (verb) "to torment, labor" — related to TRAVEL; see *Word History* at TRAVEL] — **travail** *vb*

¹trav·el \'trav-əl\ *vb* **-eled** *or* **-elled; -el·ing** *or* **-el·ling** \-(ə-)liŋ\ **1** : to journey from place to place or to a distant place **2** : to move or advance from one place to another ⟨the news *traveled* fast⟩

Word History With our modern cars, ships, and airplanes and our many restaurants and hotels, travel today is not difficult. But in the Middle Ages roads were poor and places to eat and sleep were far apart. Travel was hard, uncomfortable work—even torture. In fact, our word *travel* comes from a Latin word that meant "torture." Many devices were used in the Middle Ages for torture in an effort to force confessions from persons accused of crimes. One of these devices, called in Latin a *tripalium*, gave us our word *travel*. The word *tripalium*, literally "three stakes," was derived from Latin *tri-*, meaning "three" and *palus*, meaning "stake, pale." This word is thought to have been the source of the Latin verb *tripaliare*, meaning "to torture." In early French the word became *travailler*, with both the meaning "to torment" and the meaning "to work hard." This early French word was taken into Middle English as *travailen*, with the meaning "to work hard" and "to travel." In time these two meanings became separated into different words, *travail*, which means "hard work," and *travel*, which means "to go on a trip." [Middle English *travailen* "torment, labor, strive, journey," from early French *travailler* "torment, labor," from an unrecorded Latin verb *tripaliare* "to torture," from Latin *tripalium* "an instrument of torture," literally "three stakes," derived from *tri-* "three" and *palus* "stake, pale" — related to ³PALE, TRAVAIL]

²travel *n* **1 a** : the act or means of traveling ⟨air *travel* is fast⟩ **b** : ¹JOURNEY, TRIP — often used in plural **2** *pl* : an account of one's travels

travel agency *n* : a business that plans and arranges for tours, transportation, and lodgings for travelers — **travel agent** *n*

trav·eled *or* **trav·elled** \'trav-əld\ *adj* **1** : having traveled widely : experienced in travel ⟨a well-*traveled* reporter⟩ **2** : used by travelers ⟨a heavily-*traveled* road⟩

trav·el·er *or* **trav·el·ler** \'trav-(ə-)lər\ *n* : one that travels

traveler's check *n* : a check that is paid for in advance like a money order, that is difficult to forge, and that will be replaced if lost or stolen

trav·el·ing *or* **trav·el·ling** \'trav-(ə-)liŋ\ *adj* **1** : that travels ⟨a troupe of *traveling* actors⟩ **2** : used by or accompanying a traveler ⟨a *traveling* alarm clock⟩ ⟨a *traveling* companion⟩

traveling bag *n* : SUITCASE

traveling salesman *n* : a traveling representative of a business who solicits orders

trav·el·ogue *or* **trav·el·og** \'trav-ə-,lȯg, -,läg\ *n* **1** : an illustrated lecture or film about travel **2** : a piece of writing about travel

tra·vers·al \trə-'vər-səl\ *n* : the act or an instance of traversing

¹**trav·erse** \'tra-vərs\ n **1** : something that crosses or lies across **2** : a curved or zigzag path along the face of a steep slope **3** : the act or an instance of traversing ⟨stopped to rest in their *traverse* of the mountain⟩

²**tra·verse** \trə-'vərs\ vb **tra·versed; tra·vers·ing 1** : to go against : OPPOSE **2 a** : to pass through, across, or over ⟨*traversed* the historic fields⟩ **b** : to lie or extend across ⟨a bridge *traverses* the river⟩ **3** : to make a study of : EXAMINE **4** : to move back and forth or from side to side ⟨pedestrians *traversing* the busy intersection⟩ **5** : to climb or ski at an angle or in a zigzag course

³**trav·erse** \'tra-(,)vərs, trə-'vərs\ adj : lying across : TRANSVERSE

trav·er·tine \'trav-ər-,tēn, -tən\ n : a mineral consisting of a massive usually layered calcium carbonate formed as deposits from spring waters or especially from hot springs

trav·es·ty \'trav-ə-stē\ n, pl **-ties 1** : an imitation that makes crude fun of something **2** : an inferior imitation or likeness ⟨a *travesty* of justice⟩ — **travesty** vb

tra·vois \trə-'vȯi, 'trav-,ȯi\ n, pl **tra·vois** \-'vȯiz, -,ȯiz\ also **tra·voises** \-'vȯiz, -,ȯiz\ : an animal-drawn vehicle made of two crossed trailing poles used by Plains Indians to transport a load

travois

¹**trawl** \'trȯl\ vb : to fish or catch with a trawl

²**trawl** n **1** : a large cone-shaped net dragged along the sea bottom in fishing **2** : SETLINE

trawl·er \'trȯ-lər\ n : a boat used for trawling

tray \'trā\ n : an open container with flat bottom and low rim for holding, carrying, or exhibiting articles — **tray·ful** \-,fúl\ n

treach·er·ous \'trech-(ə-)rəs\ adj **1 a** : guilty of treachery **b** : likely to betray : UNRELIABLE ⟨a *treacherous* memory⟩ **2** : giving a false appearance of safety or solidity ⟨a *treacherous* stretch of bog⟩ — **treach·er·ous·ly** adv

treach·ery \'trech-(ə-)rē\ n, pl **-er·ies 1** : violation of allegiance or of faith and confidence : TREASON **2** : an act of treason

trea·cle \'trē-kəl\ n, chiefly British : MOLASSES

¹**tread** \'tred\ vb **trod** \'träd\; **trod·den** \'träd-ᵊn\ or **trod; tread·ing 1 a** : to step or walk on or over **b** : to walk along : FOLLOW **2** : to beat or press with the feet : TRAMPLE **3 a** : to form by treading : BEAT ⟨*tread* a path⟩ **b** : to perform by stepping or dancing ⟨*tread* a measure⟩ — **tread·er** n — **tread water** : to keep the body nearly upright in the water and the head above water by a treading motion of the feet usually aided by the hands

²**tread** n **1** : a mark made by or as if by treading **2** : the action, manner, or sound of treading or stepping **3 a** : the part of a sole that touches the ground **b** : the part of a wheel or tire that makes contact with a road or rail; esp : the ridges or grooves on the surface of a tire **4** : the horizontal part of a step

¹**trea·dle** \'tred-ᵊl\ n : a lever or other device pressed by the foot to operate a machine

²**treadle** vb **trea·dled; tread·ling** \'tred-liŋ, -ᵊl-iŋ\ : to operate a treadle on a machine

tread·mill \'tred-,mil\ n **1 a** : a device moved by persons treading on steps set around the rim of a wide wheel or by animals walking on an endless belt **b** : a device having an endless belt on which an individual walks or runs in place

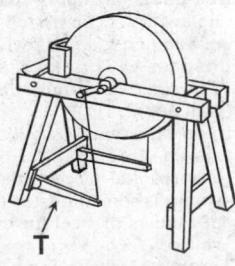

T ¹treadle

for exercise or medical testing **2** : a tiring or monotonous routine

trea·son \'trēz-ᵊn\ n **1** : the betrayal of a trust : TREACHERY **2** : the crime of attempting to overthrow the government of one's country or of attempting to kill or injure the ruler or the ruler's family

Word History The words *treason* and *tradition* both come from the same Latin source. The Latin word *traditio* meant "teaching" or "tradition." These senses developed from its basic meaning, which was "the act of handing something over." Tradition is maintained by passing information from one generation to another. One kind of treason is committed when someone who has been entrusted with secret information passes it on to someone else. The word *tradition* was borrowed directly from the Latin *traditio*. *Treason,* on the other hand, came to us through early French, where *traditio* had changed into the word *traisun*. Middle English *tresoun* "treason," from early French *traisun* (same meaning), from Latin *tradition-, traditio* "the action of handing over, tradition, betrayal," from *tradere* "to hand over, betray," from *tra-, trans-* "across" and *dare* "to give" — related to TRADITION, TRAITOR]

trea·son·able \'trēz-nə-bəl, -ᵊn-ə-bəl\ adj : relating to, consisting of, or involving treason — **trea·son·ably** \-blē\ adv

¹**trea·sure** \'trezh-ər, 'trāzh-\ n **1** : wealth (as money, jewels, or precious metals) stored up or held in reserve **2** : someone or something that is valued highly [Middle English *tresor* "treasure," from early French *tresor* (same meaning), from Latin *thesaurus* "treasure, collection" — related to THESAURUS]

²**treasure** vb **trea·sured; trea·sur·ing** \-(ə-)riŋ\ : to value highly : CHERISH

trea·sur·er \'trezh-rər, 'trezh-ər-ər, 'trāzh-\ n : an officer of a club, business, or government who has charge of money taken in and paid out

treasure trove \-,trōv\ n **1** : treasure of unknown ownership found buried or hidden **2** : a valuable discovery

trea·sury \'trezh-(ə-)rē, 'trāzh-\ n, pl **trea·sur·ies 1 a** : a place in which stores of wealth are kept **b** : the place where collected funds are stored and paid out **2** cap : a government department in charge of finances

¹**treat** \'trēt\ vb **1** : to discuss terms of agreement with : NEGOTIATE ⟨*treat* with the enemy⟩ **2 a** : to have as a subject especially in writing ⟨a book *treating* of crime⟩ **b** : to deal with : HANDLE ⟨roses must be *treated* with care⟩ **3 a** : to pay for another's food or entertainment ⟨I'm *treating* tonight⟩ **b** : to provide with free food, entertainment, or enjoyment ⟨let me *treat* you with lunch⟩ **4** : to handle, use, or act toward in a usually stated way ⟨*treat* a horse cruelly⟩ ⟨*treat* this as top secret⟩ **5** : to give medical or surgical care to ⟨*treat* a patient⟩ ⟨*treat* a cold⟩ **6** : to subject to some action or process to bring about a desired result ⟨*treat* a metal with acid⟩

²**treat** n **1** : an entertainment given without expense to those invited **2** : a usually unexpected or unusual source of pleasure or amusement

trea·tise \'trēt-əs\ n : a book or article examining a subject carefully and completely

treat·ment \'trēt-mənt\ n **1** : the act or manner or an instance of treating someone or something ⟨the antiques require careful *treatment*⟩ **2** : a substance or method used in treating ⟨a beauty *treatment*⟩ ⟨waste *treatment* plant⟩

\ə\ **abut**	\aú\ **out**	\i\ **tip**	\ȯ\ **saw**	\ú\ **foot**
\ər\ **further**	\ch\ **chin**	\ī\ **life**	\ȯi\ **coin**	\y\ **yet**
\a\ **mat**	\e\ **pet**	\j\ **job**	\th\ **thin**	\yü\ **few**
\ā\ **take**	\ē\ **easy**	\ŋ\ **sing**	\th\ **this**	\yú\ **cure**
\ä\ **cot, cart**	\g\ **go**	\ō\ **bone**	\ü\ **food**	\zh\ **vision**

trea·ty \'trēt-ē\ *n, pl* **treaties** : an agreement or arrangement made by negotiation; *esp* : one between two or more states or rulers

¹tre·ble \'treb-əl\ *n* **1 a** : the highest of the four voice parts in vocal music : SOPRANO **b** : a singer or instrument having the highest range **2** : a high-pitched or shrill voice, tone, or sound **3** : the upper half of the musical pitch range — compare ²BASS

²treble *adj* **1 a** : having three parts **b** : triple in number or amount **2 a** : relating to or having the range of a musical treble ⟨*treble* voice⟩ **b** : HIGH-PITCHED, SHRILL — **tre·bly** \'treb-(ə-)lē\ *adv*

³treble *vb* **tre·bled; tre·bling** \'treb-(ə-)liŋ\ : to make or become three times the size, amount, or number

treble clef *n* **1** : a clef that places G above middle C on the second line of the staff **2** : TREBLE STAFF

treble staff *n* : the musical staff carrying the treble clef

¹tree \'trē\ *n* **1 a** : a woody plant that lives for years and has a usually single tall main stem with few or no branches on its lower part **b** : a shrub or herb that has a form like a tree ⟨rose *trees*⟩ ⟨a banana *tree*⟩ **2** : a piece of wood (as a post or pole) put to a particular use of forming part of a structure or device **3** : something shaped like or arranged in a form like a tree; *esp* : a diagram or graph in branching form — compare FACTOR TREE, FAMILY TREE **2** — **tree·less** \-ləs\ *adj* — **tree·like** \-,līk\ *adj*

²tree *vb* **treed; tree·ing** **1** : to drive up or as if up a tree **2** : to furnish or fit with a tree ⟨*tree* an axle⟩

treed \'trēd\ *adj* **1** : driven up a tree ⟨a *treed* animal⟩ **2** : planted or grown with trees : WOODED

tree farm *n* : an area of forest land managed to ensure continuous commercial production — **tree farmer** *n* — **tree farming** *n*

tree fern *n* : a tropical fern with a woody stalk and a top of large often feathery fronds

tree frog *n* : any of numerous often tree-dwelling tailless amphibians (as the spring peeper) that typically have adhesive disks on the toes

tree·hop·per \'trē-,häp-ər\ *n* : any of several small leaping insects that are related to the leafhoppers and feed on sap from branches and twigs

tree house *n* : a structure (as a playhouse) built among the branches of a tree

tree line *n* : TIMBERLINE

tree of heaven : a Chinese tree that is widely planted as a shade and ornamental tree and has leaves divided into many leaflets and ill-smelling male flowers

tree ring *n* : ANNUAL RING

tree toad *n* : TREE FROG

tree·top \'trē-,täp\ *n* **1** : the highest part of a tree **2** *pl* : the height or line marked by the tops of a group of trees

tre·foil \'trē-,foil, 'tref-,oil\ *n* **1** : any of several herbs (as a clover) of the legume family with leaves that have or appear to have three leaflets **2** : an ornament or symbol shaped like a leaf with three parts

trefoil 2

¹trek \'trek\ *vb* **trekked; trek·king** **1** *chiefly South African* : to travel or migrate by ox wagon or in a train of such wagons **2** : to make one's way slowly and painfully [from Afrikaans *trek*, "to travel by ox wagon," from Dutch *trecken* "to haul, pull"] — **trek·ker** *n*

²trek *n* **1** *chiefly South African* : an organized journey or migration of a group of settlers traveling by ox wagon **2** : a slow or difficult journey

trel·lis \'trel-əs\ *n* : a frame of lattice used especially as a screen or a support for climbing plants — **trel·lised** \'trel-əst\ *adj*

trem·a·tode \'trem-ə-,tōd\ *n* : any of a class of parasitic flatworms including the flukes — **trematode** *adj*

¹trem·ble \'trem-bəl\ *vb* **trem·bled; trem·bling** \-b(ə-)liŋ\ **1** : to shake uncontrollably (as with fear or cold) : SHIVER **2** : to move, sound, or happen as if shaken ⟨the building *trembled* from the blast⟩ ⟨my voice *trembled*⟩ **3** : to have strong fear or doubt ⟨I *tremble* to think what might happen⟩ — **trem·bler** \-b(ə-)lər\ *n*

²tremble *n* **1** : a fit or spell of uncontrollable shaking or quivering **2** : a tremor or series of tremors

tre·men·dous \tri-'men-dəs\ *adj* **1** : causing dread, awe, or terror : DREADFUL **2** : astonishing because of great size, excellence, or power ⟨*tremendous* problems⟩ ⟨a writer of *tremendous* talent⟩ **synonyms** see MONSTROUS — **tre·men·dous·ly** *adv*

trem·o·lo \'trem-ə-,lō\ *n, pl* **-los** **1** : the rapid repetition of a musical tone or of alternating tones to produce a rapid wavering sound **2** : a mechanical device in an organ for causing a rapid wavering sound

trem·or \'trem-ər\ *n* **1** : a trembling or shaking usually caused by weakness or disease **2** : a quivering or vibrating motion; *esp* : a small movement of the earth before or after an earthquake

trem·u·lous \'trem-yə-ləs\ *adj* **1** : marked by or affected with trembling or tremors ⟨*tremulous* hands⟩ **2** : FEARFUL **2**, TIMID ⟨a shy *tremulous* person⟩ **3** : caused by or displaying nervousness or shakiness ⟨a *tremulous* smile⟩

trench \'trench\ *n* **1 a** : a long narrow cut in the ground : DITCH **b** : a ditch protected by a bank of earth used to shelter soldiers **2** : a long narrow steep-sided depression in the ocean floor

tren·chant \'tren-chənt\ *adj* **1** : having a sharp edge or point : CUTTING **2** : sharply perceptive : PENETRATING ⟨a *trenchant* view of the situation⟩ **3** : forceful and effective in expressing ideas ⟨a *trechant* analysis⟩ — **tren·chant·ly** *adv*

trench coat *n* : a loose double-breasted raincoat with deep pockets, belt, and straps on the shoulders

tren·cher \'tren-chər\ *n* : a wooden platter for serving food

tren·cher·man \'tren-chər-mən\ *n* : a hearty eater

trench mouth *n* : a destructive infectious inflammation of the mouth caused by bacteria

¹trend \'trend\ *vb* **1** : to extend in a general direction **2** : to show a tendency : INCLINE

²trend *n* **1** : general direction taken ⟨the easterly *trend* of the shoreline⟩ **2 a** : a general tendency or movement ⟨economic *trends*⟩ **b** : a current style or liking ⟨new fashion *trends*⟩

trendy \'tren-dē\ *adj* **trend·i·er; -est** **1** : very fashionable : UP-TO-DATE **2** : marked by passing or shallow appeal or taste

trep·i·da·tion \,trep-ə-'dā-shən\ *n* : a state of alarm or nervousness ⟨approached the abandoned house with *trepidation*⟩

¹tres·pass \'tres-pəs, -,pas\ *n* **1** : ¹SIN, OFFENSE **2** : an unlawful act committed on the person, property, or rights of another; *esp* : unlawful entry on someone else's land

²trespass *vb* **1** : ERR **1**, SIN **2** : to commit a trespass; *esp* : to enter unlawfully upon the land of another — **tres·pass·er** *n*

tress \'tres\ *n* : a long lock of hair

tres·tle \'tres-əl\ *n* **1** : a braced frame consisting usually of a horizontal piece with spreading legs at each end that supports something (as the top of a table) **2** : a structure of timbers or steel for carrying a road or railroad over a valley

T. rex \'tē-'reks\ *n* : TYRANNOSAUR

trey \'trā\ *n, pl* **treys** : a card or dice with three spots

tri- *combining form* **1** : three : having three elements or parts ⟨*tri*angle⟩ **2** : into three ⟨*tri*sect⟩ **3 a** : three times ⟨*tri*weekly⟩ **b** : every third ⟨*tri*monthly⟩ [from Latin *tri-, tres* and Greek *tri-, treis* "three"]

tri·ac·e·tate \(')trī-'as-ə-ˌtāt\ *n* : a textile fiber or fabric made by the chemical addition of acetate groups to cellulose

tri·ad \'trī-ˌad *also* -əd\ *n* **1** : a union or group of three usually closely related persons or things **2** : a chord made up usually of the first, third, and fifth notes of a scale — **tri·ad·ic** \trī-'ad-ik\ *adj*

¹tri·al \'trī-(-ə)l\ *n* **1** : the action or process of testing or trying **2** : the hearing and judgment of a case in court **3** : a test of faith, patience, or strength **4** : an experiment to test quality, value, or usefulness **5** : ²ATTEMPT 1, EFFORT

²trial *adj* **1** : of, relating to, or used in a trial **2** : made or done as a test or experiment ⟨a *trial* run⟩

trial and error *n* : the trying of one thing or another until something succeeds

tri·an·gle \'trī-ˌaŋ-gəl\ *n* **1** : a figure that has three sides and three angles : a polygon that has three sides **2** : a percussion instrument made of a steel rod bent into a triangle open at one corner which is played by striking with a metal rod **3** : a drafting instrument consisting of a thin flat right-angled triangle

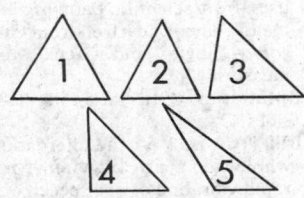

triangle: *1* equilateral, *2* isosceles, *3* scalene, *4* right, *5* obtuse

tri·an·gu·lar \trī-'aŋ-gyə-lər\ *adj* **1** : of, relating to, or having the form of a triangle **2** : having a triangular base or principal surface ⟨a *triangular* pyramid⟩

triangular number *n* : a number (as 3, 6, 10, or 15) that can be represented by that many dots arranged in rows that form a triangle and that for some positive whole number *n* equals the sum of all the whole numbers from 1 to *n* or

$$\frac{n\,(n+1)}{2}$$

tri·an·gu·la·tion \(ˌ)trī-ˌaŋ-gyə-'lā-shən\ *n* : the method in surveying of making measurements and using trigonometry to find where places are located on the earth's surface using points whose exact location is known and especially by constructing a network of triangles

Tri·as·sic \trī-'as-ik\ *adj* : of, relating to, or being the earliest period of the Mesozoic era of geological history marked by the first appearance of dinosaurs; *also* : relating to the corresponding system of rocks — see GEOLOGIC TIME table — **Triassic** *n*

tri·ath·lon \ˌtrī-'ath-ˌlän\ *n* : an athletic contest that is a long-distance race consisting of three phases (as swimming, bicycling, and running)

tri·atom·ic \ˌtrī-ə-'täm-ik\ *adj* : having three atoms in the molecule ⟨ozone is *triatomic* oxygen⟩

trib·al \'trī-bəl\ *adj* : of, relating to, or characteristic of a tribe — **trib·al·ly** \-bə-lē\ *adv*

tribe \'trīb\ *n* **1** : a social group made up of many families, clans, or generations that share the same language, customs, and beliefs **2** : a group of persons with a common character, occupation, or interest **3** : a group of related plants or animals

tribes·man \'trībz-mən\ *n* : a member of a tribe

trib·u·la·tion \ˌtrib-yə-'lā-shən\ *n* **1** : distress or suffering resulting from cruel or unjust treatment or misfortune **2** : a trying experience

tri·bu·nal \trī-'byün-ᵊl, trib-'yün-\ *n* **1** : the seat of a judge **2** : a court of justice **3** : something that decides or determines ⟨the *tribunal* of public opinion⟩

tri·bune \'trib-ˌyün, trib-'yün\ *n* **1** : a Roman official who protected plebeian citizens from unjust action by patrician magistrates **2** : a defender of the people especially against injustice — **tri·bune·ship** \-ˌship\ *n*

¹trib·u·tary \'trib-yə-ˌter-ē\ *adj* **1** : paying tribute to another : SUBJECT **2** : paid or owed as tribute **3** : contributing or adding to something larger or more important; *esp* : flowing into a larger stream or lake

²tributary *n, pl* **-tar·ies** **1** : a ruler or state that pays tribute to a conqueror **2** : a stream flowing into a larger stream or a lake

trib·ute \'trib-ˌyüt, -yət\ *n* **1 a** : a payment made by one ruler or nation to another to show obedience or to obtain peace or protection **b** : a tax to raise money for a tribute **c** : the obligation to pay tribute ⟨nations under *tribute*⟩ **2** : something (as a gift or speech of praise) that is given or performed to show appreciation, respect, or affection ⟨floral *tribute*⟩

trice \'trīs\ *n* : a brief space of time : INSTANT — used chiefly in the phrase *in a trice*

tri·ceps \'trī-ˌseps\ *n, pl* **triceps** : a large muscle along the back of the upper arm that is attached at its upper end by three main parts and that acts to extend the arm at the elbow joint

tri·cer·a·tops \(')trī-'ser-ə-ˌtäps\ *n* : any of a genus of large plant-eating 4-footed Cretaceous dinosaurs with three horns, a bony hood or crest on the neck, and hoofed toes

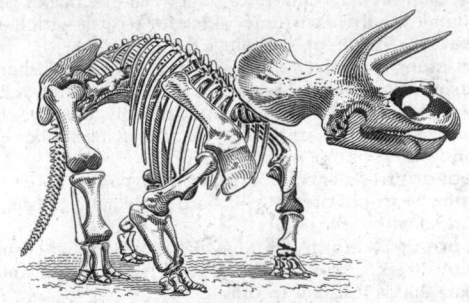

triceratops skeleton

tri·chi·na \trik-'ī-nə\ *n, pl* **tri·chi·nae** \-nē\ *also* **-nas** : a small slender nematode worm which enters the body of flesh-eating mammals (as the hog and human beings) when infected meat is eaten and whose larvae travel to and form cysts in striated muscles causing trichinosis

trich·i·no·sis \ˌtrik-ə-'nō-səs\ *n, pl* **-no·ses** \-'nō-ˌsēz\ : a serious and painful disease caused by trichinae

tricho·mo·ni·a·sis \ˌtrik-ə-mə-'nī-ə-səs\ *n, pl* **-a·ses** \-ˌsēz\ : an infection of the vagina by a protozoan parasite that is marked by itching and a frothy discharge having a bad odor and that also occurs in the male urethra

¹trick \'trik\ *n* **1 a** : an action meant to deceive or cheat **b** : a mischievous act : PRANK **c** : an unwise or childish action **d** : a skillful or clever feat designed to puzzle or amuse ⟨a juggler's *tricks*⟩ **2** : a habitual peculiarity of behavior or manner ⟨a *trick* of speech⟩ **3 a** : a quick or artful way of getting a result : KNACK ⟨the *trick* is to do it quickly⟩ **b** : an instance of getting a desired result ⟨one small adjustment will do the *trick*⟩ **4** : a technical device (as of an art or craft) ⟨*tricks* of the trade⟩ **5** : the cards played in one round of a card game

\ə\ **abut**	\au̇\ **out**	\i\ **tip**	\o̊\ **saw**	\u̇\ **foot**
\ər\ **further**	\ch\ **chin**	\ī\ **life**	\o̊i\ **coin**	\y\ **yet**
\a\ **mat**	\e\ **pet**	\j\ **job**	\th\ **thin**	\yü\ **few**
\ā\ **take**	\ē\ **easy**	\ŋ\ **sing**	\th\ **this**	\yu̇\ **cure**
\ä\ **cot, cart**	\g\ **go**	\ō\ **bone**	\ü\ **food**	\zh\ **vision**

synonyms TRICK, RUSE, WILE, STRATEGEM mean an indirect means to gain an end. TRICK may imply deception, mischief, illusion, and either an evil or harmless end ⟨a *trick* to make you look younger⟩. RUSE stresses an attempt to mislead by a false impression ⟨the *ruses* of smugglers⟩. WILE suggests an attempt to entrap or deceive with false temptations ⟨used all of his *wiles* to gain support⟩. STRATEGEM implies a trick used to entrap, outwit, or surprise an opponent and suggests a more or less carefully laid-out plan ⟨the chess player's *strategems*⟩.

²**trick** *vb* **1** : to deceive with tricks : CHEAT **2** : to dress or decorate especially oddly or ornately ⟨*tricked* out in a gaudy uniform⟩

³**trick** *adj* **1 a** : of or relating to or involving tricks or trickery ⟨*trick* photography⟩ **b** : skilled in or used for tricks ⟨a *trick* horse⟩ **2 a** : somewhat defective and unreliable ⟨a *trick* lock⟩ **b** : inclined to give way unexpectedly ⟨a *trick* knee⟩

trick·ery \'trik-(ə-)rē\ *n, pl* **-er·ies** : the use of tricks to deceive or cheat

trick·le \'trik-əl\ *vb* **trick·led; trick·ling** \-(ə-)liŋ\ **1 a** : to flow or fall in drops ⟨water *trickling* from a leaky faucet⟩ **b** : to flow in a thin slow stream ⟨syrup *trickling* from the bottle⟩ **2 a** : to move or go one by one or little by little ⟨customers *trickled* in⟩ **b** : to slowly grow less ⟨his excitement *trickled* away⟩ — **trickle** *n*

trick or treat *n* : a children's Halloween practice of going around usually in costume asking for treats — **trick–or–treat** *vb* — **trick–or–treat·er** *n*

trick·ster \'trik-stər\ *n* : one who tricks: as **a** : a dishonest person who cheats others by trickery **b** : MAGICIAN 2

tricky \'trik-ē\ *adj* **trick·i·er; -est 1** : likely to use or characterized by tricks or trickery **2** : requiring skill or caution : DIFFICULT ⟨a *tricky* situation⟩

¹**tri·col·or** \'trī-,kəl-ər\ *n* : a flag of three colors

²**tricolor** *or* **tri·col·ored** \'trī-kəl-ərd\ *adj* : having, using, or marked with three colors

tri·corn \'trī-,kȯ(ə)rn\ *adj* : having three horns or corners

tri·cot \'trē-kō, 'trī-kət\ *n* : a knitted fabric (as for underwear) that is resistant to runs

tri·cus·pid valve \(,)trī-'kəs-pəd-\ *n* : a valve on the right side of the heart between the atrium and the ventricle that has three flaps and prevents the backward flow of blood from the ventricle to the atrium

tri·cy·cle \'trī-,sik-əl\ *n* : a three-wheeled vehicle usually moved by pedals

tri·dent \'trīd-ᵊnt\ *n* : a spear with three prongs [from Latin *trident-, tridens* "trident," from *tridens* (adjective) "having three teeth," from *tri-* "three" and *dens* "tooth" — related to DENTAL] — **trident** *adj*

¹**tried** \'trīd\ *past and past participle of* TRY

²**tried** *adj* : found good, faithful, or trustworthy through experience or testing ⟨a *tried* recipe⟩

tried–and–true *adj* : known to be reliable ⟨a *tried-and-true* friend⟩ ⟨a *tried-and-true* remedy⟩

tri·en·ni·al \(')trī-'en-ē-əl\ *adj* **1** : consisting of or lasting for three years **2** : occurring or being done every three years — **triennial** *n* — **tri·en·ni·al·ly** \-ē-ə-lē\ *adv*

¹**tri·fle** \'trī-fəl\ *n* **1** : something of little value or importance **2** : a dessert of sponge cake spread with jam or jelly covered with a custard and whipped cream — **a trifle** : to a small degree : SLIGHTLY ⟨only *a trifle* annoyed⟩

²**trifle** *vb* **tri·fled; tri·fling** \-f(ə-)liŋ\ **1 a** : to talk in a joking manner **b** : to treat someone or something as unimportant **2** : to waste (as time or money) in trifling or on trifles **3** : to handle something idly : TOY — **tri·fler** \-f(ə-)lər\ *n*

tri·fling \'trī-fliŋ\ *adj* **1** : having little meaning or seriousness : FRIVOLOUS ⟨*trifling* talk⟩ **2** : of little value ⟨a *trifling* sum⟩

trig \'trig\ *n* : TRIGONOMETRY

¹**trig·ger** \'trig-ər\ *n* : a movable lever that activates a device when it is squeezed; *esp* : the part of the lock of a firearm that releases the hammer and so fires the gun — **trigger** *adj* — **trig·gered** \-ərd\ *adj*

²**trigger** *vb* **trig·gered; trig·ger·ing** \-(ə-)riŋ\ **1** : to fire by pulling a trigger **2** : to begin, stir up, or set in motion as if by pulling a trigger ⟨the remark that *triggered* the laughter⟩

trig·o·no·met·ric \,trig-ə-nə-'me-trik\ *also* **trig·o·no·met·ri·cal** \-tri-kəl\ *adj* : of, relating to, or involving trigonometry — **trig·o·no·met·ri·cal·ly** \-tri-k(ə-)lē\ *adv*

trigonometric function *n* : any of a group of functions (as the sine, cosine, and tangent) that for an acute angle are most easily expressed as ratios between the sides of a right triangle containing the angle

trig·o·nom·e·try \,trig-ə-'näm-ə-trē\ *n* : a branch of mathematics concerned with the study of the properties of triangles and trigonometric functions and of their practical uses [from scientific Latin *trigonometria*, literally "triangle measurement," derived from Greek *tri-* "three" and Greek *gonia* "angle" and Greek *-metria* "art or science of measuring"]

tri·lat·er·al \(')trī-'lat-ə-rəl, -'la-trəl\ *adj* : having three sides

¹**trill** \'tril\ *n* **1 a** : the alternation of two musical tones a whole step apart **b** : VIBRATO **2** : ¹WARBLE 1 **3 a** : the rapid vibration of one speech organ against another (as of the tip of the tongue against the teeth) **b** : a speech sound produced by a trill

²**trill** *vb* **1** : to utter as or with a trill ⟨*trilled* the letter r⟩ **2** : to play or sing with a trill : QUAVER

tril·lion \'tril-yən\ *n* **1** — see NUMBER table **2** : a very large number ⟨a *trillion* mosquitoes out tonight⟩ — **tril·lion** *adj* — **tril·lionth** \-yən(t)th\ *adj* — **trillionth** *n*

tril·li·um \'tril-ē-əm\ *n* : any of a genus of herbs related to the lilies that have three large leaves arranged around the upright stem at the same level and a single flower with three petals at the end of the stem — called also *wake-robin*

tri·lo·bite \'trī-lə-,bīt\ *n* : any of a group of extinct invertebrate animals that lived in Paleozoic seas, have a body composed of segments and divided lengthwise along the back into three parts, and are classified as arthropods

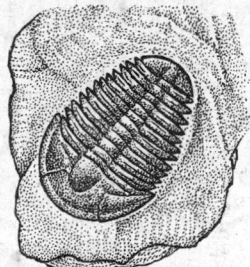

trilobite fossil

tril·o·gy \'tril-ə-jē\ *n, pl* **-gies** : a series of three literary, dramatic, or musical works that are closely related and develop a single theme

¹**trim** \'trim\ *vb* **trimmed; trim·ming 1** : to decorate with ribbons, lace, or ornaments : ADORN ⟨*trim* a Christmas tree⟩ ⟨a jacket *trimmed* with leather⟩ **2** : to defeat in a game or contest **3 a** : to make trim and neat especially by cutting or clipping ⟨*trim* the bushes⟩ ⟨*trimmed* her hair⟩ **b** : to free of excess or unnecessary matter by or as if by cutting ⟨*trim* a steak⟩ ⟨*trim* a budget⟩ **4** : to cause (as a ship) to take the right position in the water by balancing the load carried **5** : to adjust (as an airplane or submarine) for horizontal movement or for motion upward or downward **6** : to adjust (as a sail) to a desired position — **trim·mer** *n*

²**trim** *adj* **trim·mer; trim·mest 1** : ready for service or use **2** : slim and physically fit ⟨keeps *trim* by jogging⟩ **3** : neat, orderly, and compact in line or structure ⟨a *trim* house⟩ **synonyms** see NEAT — **trim·ly** *adv* — **trim·ness** *n*

³**trim** *adv* : in a trim manner : TRIMLY

⁴trim *n* **1** : good or healthy condition : FITNESS **2 a** : material used for ornament or trimming **b** : the woodwork in the finish of a building especially around doors and windows **3 a** : the position of a ship or boat especially with reference to the horizontal **b** : the relation between the plane of a sail and the direction of the ship **c** : the position of an airplane at which it will continue in level flight with no adjustments to the controls **4** : something that is trimmed off or cut out **5** : a haircut that neatens a previous haircut

trim·e·ter \'trim-ət-ər\ *n* : a line of verse consisting of three metrical feet

trim·ming \'trim-iŋ\ *n* **1** : the action of one that trims **2** : a severe defeat or beating **3** : something that trims, ornaments, or completes ⟨*trimmings* for a hat⟩ ⟨turkey with all the *trimmings*⟩

tri·month·ly \(')trī-'mən(t)th-lē\ *adj* : occurring every three months

trin·i·ty \'trin-ət-ē\ *n, pl* **-ties** **1** *cap* : the unity of Father, Son, and Holy Spirit existing as three persons in one Godhead according to some Christian doctrines **2** : TRIAD 1

Trinity Sunday *n* : the eighth Sunday after Easter

trin·ket \'triŋ-kət\ *n* **1** : a small ornament (as a jewel or ring) **2** : a thing of little value

¹tri·no·mi·al \trī-'nō-mē-əl\ *n* : a polynomial that has three terms

²trinomial *adj* : consisting of three mathematical terms

trio \'trē-ō\ *n, pl* **tri·os** **1 a** : a musical composition for three voices or instruments **b** : the performers of a musical trio **2** : a group or set of three

tri·ode \'trī-ōd\ *n* : a vacuum tube with three electrodes

¹trip \'trip\ *n* **1** : an act of causing another to stumble or fall **2 a** : a traveling from one place to another : JOURNEY ⟨a *trip* to Europe⟩ **b** : a brief errand or journey with a purpose that often takes place on a regular basis ⟨a *trip* to the dentist⟩ **3** : ERROR 4, MISSTEP **4 a** : a quick light step **b** : a faltering step : STUMBLE **5 a** : the action of releasing something mechanically **b** : a device (as a catch) for releasing a mechanism **synonyms** see JOURNEY

²trip *vb* **tripped; trip·ping** **1** : to move (as in dancing or walking) with light quick steps **2 a** : to catch one's foot against something so as to stumble ⟨don't *trip* over the rock⟩ **b** : to cause to stumble ⟨someone must have *tripped* him⟩ **3 a** : to make or cause to make a mistake **b** : to catch making a false statement, error, or blunder ⟨questions designed to *trip* her up⟩ **4** : to release or start a device usually by moving a catch ⟨*tripped* the fire alarm⟩

tri·par·tite \(')trī-'pär-ˌtīt\ *adj* **1** : divided into or made of three parts **2** : made between or involving three parties ⟨a *tripartite* treaty⟩

tripe \'trīp\ *n* **1** : stomach tissue of a cud-chewing animal (as a cow) used as food **2** : something poor, worthless, or ridiculous

¹tri·ple \'trip-əl\ *vb* **tri·pled; tri·pling** \'trip-(ə-)liŋ\ **1** : to make or become three times as great or as many : multiply by three ⟨their profits *tripled* last year⟩ **2** : to make a triple in baseball

²triple *n* **1 a** : a triple sum, quantity, or number **b** : a combination, group, or series of three **2** : a hit in baseball that permits a batter to reach third base safely

³triple *adj* **1** : being three times as great or as many **2** : having three units or parts **3 a** : three times repeated **b** : having three full revolutions ⟨a *triple* somersault⟩

triple bond *n* : a chemical bond in which three pairs of electrons are shared by two atoms in a molecule — compare DOUBLE BOND, SINGLE BOND

triple jump *n* : a track-and-field event in which competitors make three jumps in a row after a running start

triple play *n* : a play in baseball by which three base runners are put out

triple point *n* : the condition of temperature and pressure under which the gaseous, liquid, and solid forms of a substance change into each other at equal rates so that the amount of each always remains the same

trip·let \'trip-lət\ *n* **1** : a unit of three lines of verse **2** : a combination, set, or group of three **3** : one of three children or offspring born at one birth **4** : a group of three notes played in the time of two of the same value

¹tri·plex \'trip-ˌleks, 'trī-ˌpleks\ *adj* : ³TRIPLE 2

²triplex *n* : something that has three parts (as an apartment with three floors)

¹trip·li·cate \'trip-li-kət\ *adj* : made in three identical copies

²trip·li·cate \'trip-lə-ˌkāt\ *vb* **-cat·ed; -cat·ing** : to make triple or prepare in triplicate

³trip·li·cate \'trip-li-kət\ *n* : three copies all alike — used with *in* ⟨typed in *triplicate*⟩

tri·ply \'trip-(ə-)lē\ *adv* : in a triple degree, amount, or manner

tri·pod \'trī-ˌpäd\ *n* **1** : something (as a container or stool) resting on three legs **2** : a three-legged stand (as for a camera)

trip·per \'trip-ər\ *n* **1** *chiefly British* : one that takes a trip : TOURIST **2** : a tripping device (as for operating a railroad signal)

trip·ping·ly \'trip-iŋ-lē\ *adv* : in a quick and lively manner

tri·sect \'trī-ˌsekt, trī-'sekt\ *vb* : to divide into three usually equal parts — **tri·sec·tion** \'trī-ˌsek-shən, trī-'sek-\ *n* — **tri·sec·tor** \'trī-ˌsek-tər, trī-'sek-\ *n*

tri·syl·lab·ic \ˌtrī-sə-'lab-ik\ *adj* : having three syllables — **tri·syl·la·ble** \'trī-ˌsil-ə-bəl, (')trī-'sil-\ *n*

trite \'trīt\ *adj* **trit·er; trit·est** : so common that the newness or cleverness has worn off ⟨a *trite* remark⟩ — **trite·ly** *adv* — **trite·ness** *n*

tri·ti·um \'trit-ē-əm, 'trish-ē-\ *n* : a rare radioactive form of hydrogen having atoms with three times the mass of ordinary light hydrogen atoms

tri·ton \'trīt-ᵊn\ *n* : any of various large sea snails with a heavy cone-shaped shell; *also* : the shell of a triton

¹tri·umph \'trī-əm(p)f\ *n, pl* **triumphs** **1** : an ancient Roman ceremony honoring a victorious general **2** : the joy of victory or success **3 a** : a military victory or conquest **b** : any great success ⟨a scientific *triumph*⟩

²triumph *vb* **1** : to celebrate victory or success with much rejoicing **2** : to gain victory : WIN

tri·um·phal \trī-'əm(p)-fəl\ *adj* : of, relating to, or honoring a triumph ⟨a *triumphal* procession⟩

tri·um·phant \trī-'əm(p)-fənt\ *adj* **1** : VICTORIOUS, CONQUERING ⟨*triumphant* armies⟩ **2** : rejoicing for or celebrating victory or success ⟨a *triumphant* shout⟩ — **tri·um·phant·ly** *adv*

tri·um·vir \trī-'əm-vər\ *n* : one of a council or ruling body of three especially in ancient Rome

tri·um·vi·rate \trī-'əm-və-rət\ *n* **1** : government by three persons who share authority and responsibility **2** : the office or term of office of a triumvir **3** : a group of three persons or things having something in common

triv·et \'triv-ət\ *n* **1** : a three-legged stand : TRIPOD **2** : an ornamental metal or ceramic plate used under a hot dish to protect the table

tripod 2

\ə\ **abut**	\au̇\ **out**	\i\ **tip**	\ȯ\ **saw**	\u̇\ **foot**
\ər\ **further**	\ch\ **chin**	\ī\ **life**	\ȯi\ **coin**	\y\ **yet**
\a\ **mat**	\e\ **pet**	\j\ **job**	\th\ **thin**	\yü\ **few**
\ā\ **take**	\ē\ **easy**	\ŋ\ **sing**	\th\ **this**	\yu̇\ **cure**
\ä\ **cot, cart**	\g\ **go**	\ō\ **bone**	\ü\ **food**	\zh\ **vision**

triv·ia \'triv-ē-ə\ *n sing or pl* : unimportant matters or details

triv·i·al \'triv-ē-əl\ *adj* **1** : ²ORDINARY 2, COMMONPLACE **2** : of little worth or importance : INSIGNIFICANT ⟨a *trivial* mistake⟩ — **triv·i·al·ly** \-ē-ə-lē\ *adv*

Word History The words *trivial* and *trivia* can be traced back to the Latin noun *trivium,* meaning "a place where three roads meet." The Latin word was made from *tri-,* meaning "three," and *via* "way, road." The adjective form of *trivium* was *trivialis.* It was used to mean "common, ordinary." This sense probably developed from the notion that road junctions function as meeting places for people to exchange ordinary bits of news. In the 16th century, the adjective *trivial* came to be used in English with the same meaning. In time, this adjective also took on the sense of "of little worth or importance." This is its main meaning today. It wasn't until the 1920s that the word *trivia* began being used for "unimportant matters." This word is the plural form of the Latin word *trivium.* [from Latin *trivialis* "found everywhere, commonplace, trivial," from *trivium* "a place where three roads meet," from *tri-* "three" and *via* "way"]

triv·i·al·i·ty \ˌtriv-ē-'al-ət-ē\ *n, pl* **-ties** **1** : the quality or state of being trivial **2** : something trivial : TRIFLE

¹tri·week·ly \(')trī-'wē-klē\ *adj* **1** : occurring or appearing three times a week **2** : occurring or appearing every three weeks — **triweekly** *adv*

²triweekly *n* : a triweekly publication

tro·chee \'trō-kē\ *n* : a metrical foot consisting of one accented syllable followed by one unaccented syllable (as in *hungry*) — **tro·cha·ic** \trō-'kā-ik\ *adj*

trod *past and past participle of* TREAD

trodden *past participle of* TREAD

Tro·jan \'trō-jən\ *n* : a person born or living in ancient Troy — **Trojan** *adj*

Trojan horse *n* **1** : one intended to undermine or subvert from within **2** : a seemingly useful computer program that contains concealed instructions which when activated perform an illicit or malicious action (as destroying data files) — compare VIRUS 3, WORM 5 [from the large hollow wooden horse filled with Greek soldiers and brought within the walls of Troy as a trick during the Trojan War]

Trojan War *n* : a 10-year war between the ancient Greeks and Trojans

¹troll \'trōl\ *vb* **1 a** : to sing the parts of (as a round) **b** : to sing or recite loudly or merrily **2** : to fish for with a hook and line drawn through the water (as behind a slowly moving boat) [Middle English *trollen* "to cause to move round and round"] — **troll·er** *n*

²troll *n* : a lure or a line with its lure and hook used in trolling

³troll *n* : a dwarf or giant in Scandinavian folklore living in caves or hills [from Norwegian *troll* and Danish *trold,* both meaning "a giant or dwarf of folklore"]

trol·ley *also* **trol·ly** \'träl-ē\ *n, pl* **trolleys** *also* **trollies** **1 a** : a device for carrying current from a wire to an electrically driven vehicle **b** : a streetcar that runs on tracks and gets its electric power through a trolley — called also *trolley car* **2** : a wheeled carriage running on an overhead rail or track

trom·bone \träm-'bōn, (ˌ)trəm-\ *n* : a brass wind instrument with a section that can slide in and out to make different tones [from Italian *trombone,* literally "large trumpet," from *tromba* "trumpet"] — **trom·bon·ist** \-'bō-nəst\ *n*

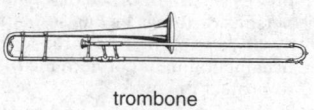

trombone

tromp \'trämp, 'trȯmp\ *vb* : ¹TRAMP 1 ⟨*tromped* from room to room⟩

¹troop \'trüp\ *n* **1 a** : a group of soldiers **b** *pl* : ARMED FORCES, MILITARY **2** : a collection of people or things : COMPANY **3** : a flock of mammals or birds **4** : a unit of Boy Scouts or Girl Scouts under an adult leader

²troop *vb* : to move or gather in crowds

troop·er \'trü-pər\ *n* **1** : a cavalry soldier **2 a** : a police officer who rides a horse **b** : a state police officer

tro·phic \'trō-fik\ *adj* : of or relating to the process of getting and eating food : NUTRITIONAL

tro·phy \'trō-fē\ *n, pl* **trophies** **1** : something taken from the enemy in victory or conquest especially when kept and displayed as proof of one's bravery or victory ⟨took the enemy's flags as *trophies*⟩ **2** : something given in recognition of a victory or as an award for achievement ⟨a golf *trophy*⟩ — **tro·phied** \-fēd\ *adj*

¹trop·ic \'träp-ik\ *n* **1** : either of the two parallels of the earth's latitude that are approximately 23½ degrees north of the equator and approximately 23½ degrees south of the equator **2** *pl, often cap* : the region lying between the two tropics [Middle English *tropik* (noun) "either of the points at which the sun appears furthest from the equator," from Latin *tropicus* (adjective) "of a solstice or equinox," from Greek *tropikos* (same meaning), from *tropē* "turn"; so called because a tropic marks the turning point in the sun's apparent progression up the sky]

²tropic *adj* : TROPICAL

³trop·ic \'trō-pik\ *adj* : of, relating to, or being a tropism ⟨a *tropic* movement of a plant⟩

trop·i·cal \'träp-i-kəl\ *adj* : of, relating to, occurring in, or used in the tropics ⟨a *tropical* island⟩ ⟨*tropical* fruits⟩ — **trop·i·cal·ly** \-k(ə-)lē\ *adv*

tropical aquarium *n* : an aquarium kept at a warm and constant temperature and used especially for tropical fish

tropical fish *n* : any of various small usually brightly colored fishes that occur wild especially in the tropics and are often kept in tropical aquariums

tropical rain forest *n* : RAIN FOREST 1

tropical storm *n* : a cyclone in or originating in the tropics that has very strong winds of less than hurricane strength

Tropic of Cancer : the parallel of latitude that is 23½ degrees north of the equator and is the northernmost latitude reached by the overhead sun

Tropic of Capricorn : the parallel of latitude that is 23½ degrees south of the equator and is the southernmost latitude reached by the overhead sun

tro·pism \'trō-ˌpiz-əm\ *n* : an automatic movement by an organism unable to move about from place to place and especially by a plant that involves a turning or growing toward or away from a stimulus (as light or moisture); *also* : a reflex reaction involving such a movement — compare TAXIS — **tro·pis·tic** \trō-'pis-tik\ *adj*

tro·po·pause \'trōp-ə-ˌpȯz, 'träp-\ *n* : the region at the top of the troposphere

tro·po·sphere \'trōp-ə-ˌsfi(ə)r, 'träp-\ *n* : the portion of the atmosphere which extends from the earth's surface to the bottom of the stratosphere and in which temperature generally decreases rapidly with altitude — **tro·po·spher·ic** \ˌtrōp-ə-'sfi(ə)r-ik, ˌträp-, -'sfer-\ *adj*

¹trot \'trät\ *n* **1** : a moderately fast gait of a four-footed animal (as a horse) in which a front foot and the opposite hind foot move at the same time **2** : a human jogging pace between a walk and a run

²trot *vb* **trot·ted; trot·ting** **1** : to ride, drive, go, or cause to go at a trot **2** : to go along quickly : HURRY

¹troth \'träth, 'trȯth, 'trōth, *or with* th\ *n* **1** : loyal or pledged faithfulness : FIDELITY **2** : one's pledged word; *also* : BETROTHAL

²troth *vb* : BETROTH, PLEDGE

trot·ter \'trät-ər\ *n* : one that trots; *esp* : a standardbred horse trained for harness racing

trou·ba·dour \'trü-bə-ˌdō(ə)r, -ˌdȯ(ə)r, -ˌdú(ə)r\ *n* : a poet=musician of the Middle Ages in France and Italy

¹trou·ble \'trəb-əl\ *vb* **trou·bled; trou·bling** \'trəb-(ə-)liŋ\ **1 a** : to disturb or become disturbed mentally or spiritually : WORRY ⟨her continued absence *troubled* him⟩ **b** : to produce physical disorder in : AFFLICT ⟨*troubled* with weak knees⟩ **c** : to put to exertion or inconvenience ⟨may I *trouble* you for the salt⟩ **2** : to put into confused motion ⟨wind *troubled* the sea⟩ **3** : to make an effort ⟨do not *trouble* to come⟩

²trouble *n* **1 a** : the quality or state of being troubled : MISFORTUNE ⟨help people in *trouble*⟩ **b** : an instance of distress or annoyance ⟨made light of their *troubles*⟩ **2** : disorder or public unrest ⟨labor *trouble*⟩ **3** : a state or condition of distress, annoyance, or difficulty ⟨in big financial *trouble*⟩: as **a** : physical distress or ill health : AILMENT ⟨heart *trouble*⟩ **b** : failure to work properly ⟨engine *trouble*⟩ **c** : a condition of doing something badly or with great difficulty ⟨had *trouble* reading⟩ **4** : an effort made : PAINS ⟨took the *trouble* to write⟩ **5 a** : a cause of distress, annoyance, or inconvenience ⟨don't mean to be any *trouble*⟩ **b** : a negative feature or characteristic ⟨laziness is your biggest *trouble*⟩ **c** : an unpleasant fact ⟨the *trouble* is, I'm broke⟩

trou·ble·mak·er \'trəb-əl-ˌmā-kər\ *n* : a person who causes problems or disagreements

trou·ble·shoot \'trəb-əl-ˌshüt\ *vb* **-shot** \-ˌshät\; **-shoot·ing 1** : to locate trouble and make repairs (as in machinery) **2** : to find a solution to a problem or disagreement

trou·ble·shoot·er \-ˌshüt-ər\ *n* : a person who troubleshoots

trou·ble·some \'trəb-əl-səm\ *adj* **1** : requiring or involving continued or tiring effort, attention, or study : DIFFICULT, BURDENSOME ⟨a *troublesome* task⟩ **2** : giving trouble or anxiety ⟨*troublesome* news⟩ — **trou·ble·some·ly** *adv*

trou·blous \'trəb-(ə-)ləs\ *adj* **1** : full of trouble : STORMY ⟨these *troublous* times⟩ **2** : causing trouble : TROUBLESOME ⟨*troublous* dreams⟩

trough \'trȯf\ *n, pl* **troughs** \'trȯfs, 'trȯvz\ **1** : a long shallow container for the drinking water or feed of domestic animals **2** : a pipe, drain, or channel for water; *esp* : ¹GUTTER 1a **3** : a long and narrow or shallow hollow (as between waves or hills)

trounce \'traun(t)s\ *vb* **trounced; trounc·ing** : to thrash or punish severely; *esp* : to defeat thoroughly

¹troupe \'trüp\ *n* : a company or troop especially of stage performers

²troupe *vb* **trouped; troup·ing 1** : to travel in a troupe **2** : to perform as a member of a theatrical troupe — **troup·er** *n*

trou·ser \'trau-zər\ *adj* : of, relating to, or designed for trousers ⟨*trouser* pockets⟩

trou·sers \'trau-zərz\ *n pl* : PANTS 1

trous·seau \'trü-ˌsō\ *n, pl* **trous·seaux** \-ˌsōz\ *or* **trous·seaus** : the clothes and personal possessions (as household linens) of a bride

trout \'traut\ *n, pl* **trout** *also* **trouts 1** : any of various edible fishes that are mostly smaller than the related salmons, are restricted to cool clear fresh water or spend time at sea before returning to fresh water to breed, and are often speckled with dark colors **2** : any of various fishes that resemble the true trouts

trout 1

¹trow·el \'trau̇(-ə)l\ *n* **1** : a small hand tool consisting of a flat blade with a handle used for spreading and smoothing mortar or plaster **2** : a small hand tool with a curved blade used by gardeners

²trowel *vb* **-eled** *or* **-elled; -el·ing** *or* **-el·ling** : to smooth, mix, or apply with a trowel

troy \'trȯi\ *adj* : expressed in troy weight

troy weight *n* : a series of units of weight based on a pound of 12 ounces and the ounce of 20 pennyweights or 480 grains — see MEASURE table

tru·an·cy \'trü-ən-sē\ *n, pl* **-cies** : an act or an instance of being a truant

tru·ant \'trü-ənt\ *n* **1** : a person who neglects duty **2** : a student who stays out of school without permission — **truant** *adj*

truant officer *n* : a school officer whose duty is to investigate the continued absences of students

truce \'trüs\ *n* **1** : a temporary stopping of fighting (as in a war) **2** : a short rest especially from something unpleasant

¹truck \'trək\ *n* **1** : ²BARTER **2** : goods for barter or for small trade **3** : close association ⟨have no *truck* with such people⟩ **4** : vegetables grown for market **5 a** : small articles of little value **b** : RUBBISH [from earlier *truck* (verb) "to exchange goods, swap," from Middle English *trukken* (same meaning), from early French *troquer* (same meaning)]

²truck *n* : a wheeled vehicle for moving heavy articles [from *truck* "a small wheel," from *truckle* "small wheel, pulley," from Middle English *trokell* "caster, wheel," from Latin *trochlea* "block of pulleys"]

³truck *vb* : to transport on or by truck

truck·er \'trək-ər\ *n* **1** : a person whose business is transporting goods by truck **2** : a truck driver

truck farm *n* : a farm growing vegetables for market — **truck farmer** *n*

truck garden *n* : a garden where vegetables are raised for market

truck·load \'trək-'lōd, -ˌlōd\ *n* : a load or amount that fills or could fill a truck

truc·u·lence \'trək-yə-lən(t)s *also* 'trük-\ *n* : the quality or state of being truculent

truc·u·lent \'trək-yə-lənt *also* 'trük-\ *adj* : ready and willing to fight or quarrel — **tru·cu·lent·ly** *adv*

¹trudge \'trəj\ *vb* **trudged; trudg·ing** : to walk or march steadily and usually with much effort ⟨*trudged* through deep snow⟩ — **trudg·er** *n*

²trudge *n* : a long tiring walk : TRAMP

¹true \'trü\ *adj* **tru·er; tru·est 1** : completely loyal : FAITHFUL **2 a** : agreeing with the facts : ACCURATE ⟨a *true* description⟩ **b** : CONSISTENT **2** ⟨*true* to character⟩ **3** : fully realized or fulfilled ⟨dreams come *true*⟩ **4** : properly so called : GENUINE ⟨lichens have no *true* stems⟩ ⟨*true* love⟩ **5** : placed or formed accurately : EXACT ⟨*true* pitch⟩ **6** : being or holding by right : LEGITIMATE ⟨the *true* owner⟩ **synonyms** see REAL

²true *n* : the quality or state of being accurate (as in adjustment) — used in the phrases *in true* and *out of true*

³true *vb* **trued; true·ing** *also* **tru·ing** : to bring to exactly correct condition as to place, position, or shape ⟨*true* up a board⟩

⁴true *adv* **1** : in agreement with fact : TRUTHFULLY **2** : in an accurate manner : ACCURATELY ⟨the arrow flew straight and *true*⟩ **3** : without variation from type ⟨breed *true*⟩

true–blue \'trü-'blü\ *adj* : very faithful

true bug *n* : ¹BUG 1b

true–false test \'trü-'fôls-\ *n* : a test made up of items that are to be marked as true or false

true seal *n* : HAIR SEAL

truf·fle \'trəf-əl, 'trüf-\ *n* : the dark or light wrinkled fruiting body of a European fungus that grows in the ground; *also* : a fungus that produces truffles

tru·ism \'trü-ˌiz-əm\ *n* : an obvious truth

tru·ly \'trü-lē\ *adv* : in a true manner

¹**trump** \'trəmp\ *n* 1 : a card of a suit any of whose cards will win over a card that is of a different suit; *also* : the suit whose cards are trumps for a particular hand — often used in plural 2 : TRUMP CARD

²**trump** *vb* 1 : to take with a trump ⟨*trump* another player's card⟩ 2 : to play a trump 3 : to get the better of : OUTDO ⟨*trumped* her competitors⟩

trump card *n* 1 : TRUMP 1 2 : something that gives an advantage ⟨the knowledge of her secret was his *trump card*⟩

trumped–up \'trəm(p)-'təp\ *adj* : MADE-UP 1, FALSE ⟨arrested on *trumped-up* charges⟩

trum·pery \'trəm-p(ə-)rē\ *n, pl* **-per·ies** : things of no value — **trumpery** *adj*

¹**trum·pet** \'trəm-pət\ *n*
1 : a wind instrument consisting of a long cylindrical metal tube commonly once or twice curved and ending in a bell 2 : something shaped like a trumpet 3 : a sound like that of a trumpet

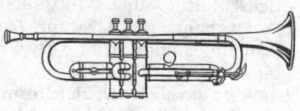

¹trumpet 1

²**trumpet** *vb* 1 : to blow a trumpet 2 : to make a sound like that of a trumpet

trum·pet·er \'trəm-pət-ər\ *n* : a trumpet player

trumpeter swan *n* : a rare large white swan of western North America with a loud low-pitched call

trumpet vine *n* : a North American woody vine with feathery leaves and large usually red trumpet-shaped flowers — called also *trumpet creeper*

¹**trun·cate** \'trəŋ-ˌkāt, 'trən-\ *adj* : having the end square or blunt ⟨a *truncate* leaf⟩

²**truncate** *vb* **trun·cat·ed; trun·cat·ing** : to shorten by or as if by cutting off — **trun·ca·tion** \trəŋ-'kā-shən, trən-\ *n*

trun·cheon \'trən-chən\ *n* : a police officer's club

trun·dle \'trən-dᵊl\ *vb* **trun·dled; trun·dling** \'trən-dliŋ, -dᵊl-iŋ\ 1 : to transport in or as if in a wheeled vehicle : HAUL ⟨*trundled* her off to school⟩ 2 : to move on or as if on wheels ⟨buses *trundling* through the city⟩

trundle bed *n* : a low bed usually on small wheels that can be rolled under a higher bed

trunk \'trəŋk\ *n* 1 a : the main stem of a tree apart from branches or roots b : the body of a person or animal apart from the head, arms, and legs : TORSO c : the main or central part of something ⟨*trunk* of an artery⟩ 2 a : a box or chest for holding

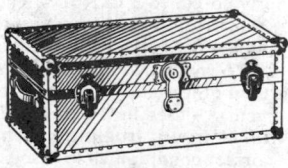

trunk 2a

clothes or other articles especially for traveling b : the enclosed space usually in the rear of an automobile for carrying articles 3 : the long flexible muscular nose of an elephant or a related mammal (as a woolly mammoth) 4 *pl* : men's shorts worn chiefly for sports ⟨swimming *trunks*⟩

¹**truss** \'trəs\ *vb* 1 a : to tie up tightly : BIND b : to tie the wings or legs of for cooking ⟨*truss* a turkey⟩ 2 : to support, strengthen, or stiffen by a truss

²**truss** *n* 1 : a rigid framework of beams, bars, or rods ⟨a *truss* for a roof⟩ 2 : a device worn to hold a hernia in place

¹**trust** \'trəst\ *n* 1 a : firm belief in the character, ability, strength, or truth of someone or something b : a person or thing in which confidence is placed 2 a : confident hope b : financial credit ⟨bought furniture on *trust*⟩ 3 a : property held or managed by one person or organization (as a bank) for the benefit of another b : a combination of firms or corporations formed by a legal agreement; *esp* : one that reduces or threatens to reduce competition 4 a : something (as a public office) held or managed by someone for the benefit of another b : responsibility for safety and well-being

²**trust** *vb* 1 a : to place confidence : DEPEND ⟨*trust* in God⟩ ⟨*trust* to luck⟩ b : to be confident : HOPE 2 : to place in one's care or keeping : ENTRUST ⟨*trusted* him with my car⟩ 3 a : to rely on the truth of : BELIEVE ⟨never *trust* a rumor⟩ b : to place confidence in : rely on ⟨a friend you can *trust*⟩ c : to hope or expect with confidence ⟨*trusts* that a solution will be found soon⟩ 4 : to give financial credit to — **trust·er** *n*

trust company *n* : a corporation (as a bank) organized to act as a trustee

trust·ee \ˌtrəs-'tē\ *n* : a person who has been given responsibility for someone else's property

trust·ee·ship \ˌtrəs-'tē-ˌship\ *n* : the office or job of a trustee

trust·ful \'trəst-fəl\ *adj* : full of trust — **trust·ful·ly** \-fə-lē\ *adv*

trust·ing \'trəs-tiŋ\ *adj* : having trust, faith, or confidence — **trust·ing·ly** *adv*

trust·wor·thy \'trəst-ˌwər-thē\ *adj* : deserving confidence : DEPENDABLE ⟨*trustworthy* information⟩ ⟨a *trustworthy* babysitter⟩ — **trust·wor·thi·ness** \-thē-nəs\ *n*

¹**trusty** \'trəs-tē\ *adj* **trust·i·er; -est** : TRUSTWORTHY, RELIABLE ⟨a Boy Scout's *trusty* pocketknife⟩

²**trusty** \'trəs-tē *also* ˌtrəs-'tē\ *n, pl* **trust·ies** : a convict considered trustworthy and allowed special privileges

truth \'trüth\ *n, pl* **truths** \'trüthz, 'trüths\ 1 : the quality or state of being true 2 : a true or accepted statement 3 : the body of real events or facts 4 : agreement with fact or reality — **in truth** : in fact : ACTUALLY, REALLY

truth·ful \'trüth-fəl\ *adj* : telling or being in the habit of telling the truth — **truth·ful·ly** \-fə-lē\ *adv* — **truth·ful·ness** *n*

truth set *n* : a set in mathematics or logic that contains all the elements which when substituted into a given statement make it true ⟨the equation $x + 7 = 10$ has as its *truth set* the single number 3⟩

¹**try** \'trī\ *vb* **tried; try·ing** 1 : to make an effort to do ⟨I'll *try* to do my best⟩ 2 a : to examine or investigate in a court of law ⟨*try* a case⟩ b : to conduct the trial of 3 a : to put to a test ⟨*try* out something new⟩ ⟨*try* your luck⟩ b : to test to the limit ⟨you're *trying* my patience⟩ 4 : to melt down (as tallow) and obtain in a pure state : RENDER ⟨*try* out whale oil from blubber⟩

²**try** *n, pl* **tries** : an effort to do something : ATTEMPT

try·ing \'trī-iŋ\ *adj* : hard to bear or put up with ⟨these are *trying* times⟩

try on *vb* : to put on (as a garment) in order to test the fit

try·out \'trī-ˌaut\ *n* : a test of the ability (as of an actor or athlete) to fill a part or meet standards

try out \(ˈ)trī-ˈaut\ *vb* : to take part in a tryout especially for a position on an athletic team or a part in a play

try·pano·some \tri-'pan-ə-ˌsōm\ *n* : any of a genus of parasitic protozoans that infect the blood, are usually transmitted by the bite of an insect, and include some that cause serious diseases (as sleeping sickness)

tryp·sin \'trip-sən\ *n* : an enzyme from pancreatic juice that helps to break down proteins

tryp·sin·o·gen \trip-'sin-ə-jən\ *n* : the inactive form of trypsin present in the pancreas

tryp·to·phan \'trip-tə-ˌfan\ *n* : an amino acid that is found in many proteins and is necessary for life but cannot be manufactured by the human body and must be obtained in food

¹tryst \'trist, *especially British* 'trīst\ *n* : a meeting arranged especially by lovers

²tryst *vb* : to make or keep a tryst

try·works \'trī-ˌwərks\ *n* : a brick furnace (as on a whaling ship) for melting down blubber to produce whale oil

tsar *variant of* CZAR

tset·se fly \'(t)set-sē-, 'tet-, '(t)sēt-, 'tēt-\ *n* : any of a genus of two-winged flies found mostly in Africa south of the Sahara Desert and including some forms that pass on disease-causing trypanosomes — called also *tsetse*

T–shirt *also* **tee shirt** \'tē-ˌshərt\ *n* **1** : a cotton undershirt with short sleeves and no collar **2** : a jersey outer shirt designed like a T-shirt

tsk *a t-sound made by suction rather than explosion; often read as* 'tisk\ *interj* — used to express disapproval

tsk–tsk \'tisk-ˌtisk\ *vb* : to express disapproval of someone or something by or as if by uttering tsk

T square *n* : a ruler with a piece fixed at right angles at one end used to draw parallel lines

tsu·na·mi \(t)sù-'näm-ē\ *n* : a great sea wave produced especially by an earthquake or volcanic eruption under the sea : TIDAL WAVE [Japanese, from *tsu* "harbor" + *nami* "wave"]

Tua·reg \'twä-ˌreg\ *n, pl* **Tuareg** *or* **Tuaregs** : a member of a nomadic people of Africa

tu·a·ta·ra \ˌtü-ə-'tär-ə\ *n* : a large spiny reptile of the islands off the coast of New Zealand that looks like a lizard

¹tub \'təb\ *n* **1** : a wide low container **2** : an old or slow boat **3 a** : BATHTUB **b** : BATH 1 **4** : the amount that a tub will hold

²tub *vb* **tubbed; tub·bing** : to wash or bathe in a tub

tu·ba \'t(y)ü-bə\ *n* : a brass musical instrument of lowest pitch with an oval shape and valves for producing different tones

tub·by \'təb-ē\ *adj* **tub·bi·er; -est** : ⁵PLUMP, FLESHY

tube \'t(y)üb\ *n* **1 a** : a slender channel within a plant or animal body : DUCT **b** : a long hollow cylinder; *esp* : one to carry fluids **c** : the part of a wind instrument that connects the mouthpiece with the open end **2** : a soft container shaped something like a tube whose contents (as toothpaste or glue) can be removed by squeezing **3** : INNER TUBE **4** : ELECTRON TUBE **5** : TELEVISION 2 **6** : an article of clothing shaped like a tube ⟨*tube* socks⟩ — **tubed** \'t(y)übd\ *adj* — **tube·like** \'t(y)ü-ˌblīk\ *adj*

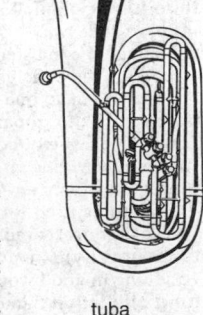

tuba

tube foot *n* : one of the tiny tubes of most echinoderms (as a starfish or sea urchin) that are part of the water-vascular system and are used especially in movement and grasping

tube·less \'t(y)ü-bləs\ *adj* : lacking a tube; *esp* : being a tire that does not depend on an inner tube to keep it airtight

tube nucleus *n* : a nucleus of a pollen grain that is believed to control the growth of the pollen tube

tu·ber \'t(y)ü-bər\ *n* **1** : a short fleshy usually underground stem (as of a potato plant) having tiny scalelike leaves each with a bud at its base that can produce a new plant — compare BULB 1a, CORM **2** : a fleshy root or rhizome that resembles a tuber

tu·ber·cle \'t(y)ü-bər-kəl\ *n* **1** : a small knobby lump or outgrowth especially on a plant or animal **2** : a small diseased growth in an organ or on the skin; *esp* : one caused by tuberculosis

tu·ber·cu·lar \t(y)ù-'bər-kyə-lər\ *adj* : of, relating to, or affected with tuberculosis ⟨a *tubercular* patient⟩

tu·ber·cu·lin \t(y)ù-'bər-kyə-lən\ *n* : a sterile liquid that contains substances taken from the bacterium that causes tuberculosis and is used in the diagnosis of the disease

tuberculin test *n* : a test for sensitivity to tuberculin as a sign of a past or present infection with the bacterium causing tuberculosis

tu·ber·cu·lo·sis \t(y)ù-ˌbər-kyə-'lō-səs\ *n* : a disease of human beings and some other vertebrates caused by a bacterium and usually marked by wasting, fever, and formation of cheesy tubercles that in human beings occur mostly in the lungs — **tu·ber·cu·lous** \t(y)ù-'bər-kyə-ləs\ *adj*

tube·rose \'t(y)ü-ˌbrōz; 't(y)ü-bə-ˌrōz, -bə-ˌrōs\ *n* : an herb related to the agaves and grown for its spike of fragrant white flowers

tu·ber·os·i·ty \ˌt(y)ü-bə-'räs-ət-ē\ *n, pl* **-ties** : a rounded lump; *esp* : one on a bone usually serving for the attachment of muscles or ligaments

tu·ber·ous \'t(y)ü-b(ə-)rəs\ *adj* **1** : consisting of, resembling, or producing a tuber **2** : of, relating to, or being a plant tuber

tube worm *n* : a worm that lives in a tube (as one made of sand grains or calcium carbonate): as **a** : any of various land- or water-dwelling worms that are closely related to the earthworms **b** : any of a group of worms that may grow to be 9 feet (3 meters) long, are related to the earthworms, and live on the ocean floor near openings that give off very hot mineral-rich water

tub·ing \'t(y)ü-bin\ *n* **1** : material in the form of a tube **2** : a series or system of tubes **3** : the sport or activity of riding an inner tube (as down a river or snowy slope)

tu·bu·lar \'t(y)ü-byə-lər\ *adj* **1** : having the form of or consisting of a tube **2** : made or provided with tubes

tu·bule \'t(y)ü-(ˌ)byü(ə)l\ *n* : a small tube; *esp* : a long slender channel in the body of a living thing

¹tuck \'tək\ *vb* **1 a** : to pull up into a fold **b** : to make a tuck in **2** : to put or fit into a snug or safe place ⟨*tucked* their money away in the bank⟩ ⟨our lunch *tucked* in a basket⟩ **3 a** : to push in the loose end of so as to hold tightly ⟨*tuck* in your shirt⟩ **b** : to cover by tucking in bedclothes ⟨a child *tucked* in for the night⟩

²tuck *n* **1** : a fold stitched into cloth (as in a garment) **2** : an act or instance of tucking

tuck·er \'tək-ər\ *vb* **tuck·ered; tuck·er·ing** \'tək-(ə-)rin\ : to cause to tire ⟨*tuckered* out by the hard work⟩

Tues·day \'t(y)üz-dē\ *n* : the third day of the week

Word History The Germanic people who lived in northern Europe in ancient times worshiped many gods. One of the most important of these was a war god whose name in Old English was *Tīw*. The third day of the week was known as *tīwesdæg*, "day of Tiw," in honor of this god. Modern English *Tuesday* comes from Old English *tīwesdæg*. [Old English *tīwesdæg*, literally, "day of Tiw (god of war)"]

tuf·fet \'təf-ət\ *n* : a low seat

¹tuft \'təft\ *n* **1** : a small cluster of long flexible outgrowths (as of hairs, feathers, or blades of grass) that are attached or close together at the base and free at the opposite end **2** : a bunch of soft fluffy threads cut off short and used as ornament — **tuft·ed** \'təf-təd\ *adj*

²tuft *vb* **1** : to provide or decorate with a tuft **2** : to make (as upholstery) firm by stitching through the stuffing here and there

¹tug \'təg\ *vb* **tugged; tug·ging** **1 a** : to pull hard **b** : to move by pulling hard : DRAG **2** : to tow with a tugboat — **tug·ger** *n*

\ə\ **abut**	\aú\ **out**	\i\ **tip**	\ò\ **saw**	\ú\ **foot**
\ər\ **further**	\ch\ **chin**	\ī\ **life**	\òi\ **coin**	\y\ **yet**
\a\ **mat**	\e\ **pet**	\j\ **job**	\th\ **thin**	\yü\ **few**
\ā\ **take**	\ē\ **easy**	\ŋ\ **sing**	\th\ **this**	\yú\ **cure**
\ä\ **cot, cart**	\g\ **go**	\ō\ **bone**	\ü\ **food**	\zh\ **vision**

²tug *n* **1 a** : an act or instance of tugging : PULL **b** : a strong pulling force **2** : a struggle between two people or forces **3** : TUGBOAT

tug-boat \'təg-₁bōt\ *n* : a strongly built powerful boat used for towing and pushing ships

tug-of-war \₁təg-ə(v)-'wȯ(ə)r\ *n, pl* **tugs-of-war 1** : a struggle to win **2** : a contest in which two teams pull against each other at opposite ends of a rope

tu-ition \t(y)ù-'ish-ən\ *n* : money paid for instruction (as at a college)

tu-la-re-mia \₁t(y)ü-lə-'rē-mē-ə\ *n* : a disease especially of rodents, wild rabbits, human beings, and some domestic animals that is caused by a bacterium and passed on by the bites of insects or ticks

tu-lip \'t(y)ü-ləp\ *n* : any of a genus of Eurasian herbs that grow from bulbs, have large lance-shaped leaves, are related to the lilies, and are widely grown for their showy cup-shaped flowers; *also* : the flower or bulb of a tulip

Word History We often think of the tulip as a Dutch flower. The Dutch certainly do grow many tulips, but they first got the plant from Turkey. The Turkish word for the tulip was *tülbent,* meaning literally "turban." Perhaps it was the flower's shape that reminded the Turks of a turban. Or perhaps it was the bright colors and velvety petals. In any case, scientists picking a universal word for the flower chose the scientific Latin *tulipa,* taken from the Turkish word. The word came into English from the scientific Latin and was spelled *tulip.* [from scientific Latin *tulipa* "the tulip," from Turkish *tülbent* "tulip," literally "turban"]

tulip tree *n* : a tall North American timber tree related to the magnolias and having large greenish yellow tulip-shaped flowers and soft white wood used especially for cabinetwork

tulip tree

tulle \'tül\ *n* : a fine netlike fabric used chiefly for veils, evening dresses, or ballet costumes

¹tum-ble \'təm-bəl\ *vb* **tumbled; tum-bling** \-b(ə-)liŋ\ **1 a** : to perform gymnastic feats of rolling and turning **b** : to turn end over end in falling or in flight ⟨the satellite was *tumbling* out of control⟩ **2 a** : to fall suddenly and helplessly **b** : to suffer a sudden downward turn or defeat **3** : to move or go in a hurried or confused way ⟨everyone came *tumbling* out at closing time⟩ **4** : to come to understand ⟨I thought you'd *tumble* to what I meant⟩ **5** : to toss about or together into a confused mass ⟨*tumble* the ingredients lightly⟩

²tumble *n* **1** : a messy state or collection **2** : an act or instance of tumbling

tum-ble-bug \'təm-bəl-₁bəg\ *n* : a large stout-bodied beetle that rolls dung into small balls, buries them in the ground, and lays its eggs in them

tum-ble-down \₁təm-bəl-₁dau̇n\ *adj* : DILAPIDATED ⟨a *tumbledown* shack⟩

tumble dry *vb* **tumble dried; tumble drying** : to dry (as clothes) in a dryer

tum-bler \'təm-blər\ *n* **1** : a person (as an acrobat) who tumbles **2** : a pigeon that often tumbles backward in flight **3** : a drinking glass ⟨a water *tumbler*⟩ **4** : a movable part in a lock that must be adjusted (as by a key) before the lock will open

tum-ble-weed \'təm-bəl-₁wēd\ *n* : a plant that breaks away from its roots in autumn and is blown about by the wind

tu-mid \'t(y)ü-məd\ *adj* : marked by swelling

tum-my \'təm-ē\ *n, pl* **tummies** : ¹STOMACH 1c

tu-mor \'t(y)ü-mər\ *n* : an abnormal mass of tissue that arises from normal tissue cells and serves no useful purpose in the body — **tu-mor-ous** \'t(y)üm-(ə-)rəs\ *adj*

tump-line \'təm-₁plīn\ *n* : a strap placed over the forehead or chest and used to support or help support a pack on the back or to haul a load

tu-mult \'t(y)ü-₁məlt\ *n* **1** : UPROAR ⟨a great *tumult* arose in the stands⟩ **2** : great confusion of mind

tu-mul-tu-ous \t(y)ù-'məlch-(ə-)wəs, -'məl-chəs\ *adj* : being or suggesting a tumult ⟨a *tumultuous* welcome for the astronauts⟩ — **tu-mul-tu-ous-ly** *adv*

tu-mu-lus \'t(y)ü-myə-ləs, 'təm-yə-\ *n, pl* **-li** \-₁lī, -₁lē\ : a mound usually over an ancient grave

tu-na \'t(y)ü-nə\ *n, pl* **tuna** *or* **tunas 1** : any of several mostly large sea fishes (as an albacore or bonito) related to the mackerels and caught for food and sport **2** : the flesh of a tuna especially when canned for use as food — called also *tuna fish*

tuna 1

tun-dra \'tən-drə *also* 'tu̇n-\ *n* : a treeless plain especially of arctic regions having a permanently frozen layer below the surface soil and plant life made up mostly of mosses, lichens, herbs, and very small shrubs

¹tune \'t(y)ün\ *n* **1** : a succession of pleasing musical tones : MELODY **2** : correct musical pitch or consonance ⟨the piano was not in *tune*⟩ **3** : AGREEMENT 1b, HARMONY ⟨in *tune* with the times⟩ **4** : general attitude ⟨changed their *tune* after reading the report⟩

²tune *vb* **tuned; tun-ing 1** : to adjust in musical pitch ⟨*tuned* my guitar⟩ ⟨the orchestra was *tuning* up⟩ **2** : to come or bring into harmony **3** : to adjust a radio or television so that it receives clearly — often used with *in* **4** : to put (as an engine) in good working order — often used with *up*

tune-ful \'t(y)ün-fəl\ *adj* : MELODIOUS, MUSICAL — **tune-ful-ly** \-fə-lē\ *adv*

tune in *vb* **1** : to listen to or view a broadcast ⟨*tune in* next week for the conclusion⟩ **2** : to pay attention to what is happening or to one's surroundings

tune out *vb* : to stop paying attention to what is happening or to one's surroundings ⟨thinking about the work and *tuning* everything else *out*⟩

tun-er \'t(y)ü-nər\ *n* **1** : one that tunes ⟨a piano *tuner*⟩ **2** : something used for tuning; *esp* : the part of a receiving set that converts radio signals into sound or pictures

tune-up \'t(y)ü-₁nəp\ *n* : a general adjustment to get everything in good working order ⟨an engine *tune-up*⟩

tung oil \'təŋ\ *n* : an oil that is obtained from the seeds of any of several trees and especially from an Asian tree widely grown in warm regions and that is used chiefly in quick-drying varnishes and paints and for waterproofing

tung-sten \'təŋ-stən\ *n* : a gray-white heavy hard metallic element that has many characteristics similar to chromium and molybdenum and is used especially for electrical purposes and to harden metal alloys (as steel) — see ELEMENT table [from Swedish *tungsten,* literally "heavy stone," from *tung* "heavy" and *sten* "stone"]

tu-nic \'t(y)ü-nik\ *n* **1** : a usually belted knee-length garment worn by ancient Greeks and Romans **2** : a shirt or jacket reaching to or just below the hips

tu-ni-cate \'t(y)ü-ni-kət, -nə-₁kāt\ *n* : any of a major group of marine chordate animals that are filter feeders having a thick covering layer, a reduced nervous system, and only in the larval stage a notochord

tuning fork *n* : a metal instrument that gives a fixed tone when struck and is useful in tuning musical instruments

¹tun-nel \'tən-ᵊl\ *n* : a passage under the ground — **tun-nel-like** \-ᵊl-₁(l)īk\ *adj*

²**tunnel** *vb* **-neled** *or* **-nelled; -nel·ing** *or* **-nel·ling** \'tən-liŋ, -ᵊl-iŋ\ : to make a tunnel

tunnel vision *n* **1** : narrowing of the field of vision resulting in loss of side vision **2** : a tendency to be extremely focused on something or on a part of something (as a problem or plan) while ignoring other factors

tun·ny \'tən-ē\ *n, pl* **tunnies** *also* **tunny** : TUNA

tuppence *variant of* TWOPENCE

tur·ban \'tər-bən\ *n* **1** : a head covering worn especially by Muslims and made of a long cloth wrapped around the head or around a cap **2** : a woman's small soft hat with no brim — **tur·baned** *or* **tur·banned** \-bənd\ *adj*

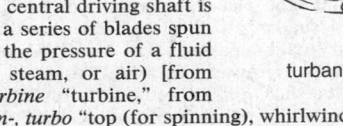

turban 1

tur·bid \'tər-bəd\ *adj* : clouded or discolored by sediment ⟨a *turbid* stream⟩ — **tur·bid·i·ty** \ˌtər-'bid-ət-ē\ *n*

tur·bine \'tər-bən, -ˌbīn\ *n* : an engine whose central driving shaft is fitted with a series of blades spun around by the pressure of a fluid (as water, steam, or air) [from French *turbine* "turbine," from Latin *turbin-, turbo* "top (for spinning), whirlwind"]

tur·bo·jet \'tər-bō-ˌjet\ *n* : an airplane powered by turbojet engines

turbojet engine *n* : a jet engine in which a turbine drives a compressor that supplies air to a burner and hot gases from the burner drive the turbine before being discharged to the rear

tur·bo·prop \'tər-bō-ˌpräp\ *n* : an airplane powered by turboprop engines

turboprop engine *n* : a jet engine that produces power principally through a propeller driven by a turbine but also usually by the rearward discharge of hot exhaust gases

tur·bu·lence \'tər-byə-lən(t)s\ *n* : the quality or state of being turbulent; *esp* : irregular atmospheric motion with up and down currents

tur·bu·lent \'tər-byə-lənt\ *adj* : causing or being in a state of unrest, violence, or disturbance ⟨a *turbulent* relationship⟩ — **tur·bu·lent·ly** *adv*

tu·reen \tə-'rēn, tyù-\ *n* : a deep bowl from which food (as soup) is served

turf \'tərf\ *n* **1 a** : the upper layer of soil bound by grass and plant roots into a thick mat; *also* : a piece of this **b** : an artificial substitute for turf (as on a playing field) **c** : ¹GRASS 3 **2** : the sport or business of horse racing **3** : an area or a place that is or is felt to be under one's control ⟨on my own *turf*⟩

tur·gid \'tər-jəd\ *adj* **1** : being in a swollen state **2** : exhibiting turgor ⟨a *turgid* plant cell⟩

tur·gor \'tər-gər, -ˌgȯ(ə)r\ *n* : the normal state of firmness and tension of living cells

Turk \'tərk\ *n* : a person born or living in Turkey

tur·key \'tər-kē\ *n, pl* **turkeys 1** *pl also* **turkey** : a large North American bird that is related to the domestic chicken and is domesticated in most parts of the world **2** : something that is a failure ⟨the new play was a *turkey*⟩ **3** : a stupid or foolish person

Word History The bird we now call the guinea fowl was once called the *turkey*. *Turkey* was the shortened version of *turkey-cock* and *turkey-hen*. The guinea fowl's

turkey 1

original home was in Africa. However, Europeans discovered that it was good to eat and did well in captivity, so they brought it back to Europe. Some people mistakenly thought that the birds came from Turkey, and the name stuck. Later, when English settlers first arrived in America, they found a large bird living here that was also good to eat. They called this new bird *turkey* because it reminded them of the turkey they were familiar with back in Europe. [from *turkey-cock,* an old word for "guinea fowl," from *Turkey,* a country in Asia Minor; so called because at one time people thought guinea fowl came from Turkey]

tur·key–cock \'tər-kē-ˌkäk\ *n* : a male turkey

turkey vulture *n* : an American vulture with a red head and whitish bill — called also *turkey buzzard*

¹**Turk·ish** \'tər-kish\ *adj* : of or relating to Turkey, the Turks, or Turkish

²**Turkish** *n* : the language of the Turks

Turkish towel *n* : a towel made of cotton terry cloth

tur·mer·ic \'tər-mə-rik *also* 'tü-mə-, 'tyü-\ *n* **1** : an Indian herb related to ginger and having a large yellow underground plant stem **2** : the boiled, dried, and usually ground underground plant stem of turmeric used especially as a flavoring or dye

tur·moil \'tər-ˌmȯil\ *n* : a very confused or disturbed state or condition

¹**turn** \'tərn\ *vb* **1 a** : to move or cause to move around an axis or center : ROTATE, REVOLVE ⟨wheels *turning* slowly⟩ ⟨*turn* a crank⟩ **b** : to bring about a desired end by using a control ⟨*turned* the volume down⟩ **c** : to do by revolving ⟨*turn* handsprings⟩ **d** : to twist out of line or shape : WRENCH ⟨*turn* an ankle⟩ **2 a** : to change in position usually by moving through an arc of a circle ⟨they *turned* and walked away⟩ ⟨*turn* the page⟩ ⟨*turn* a pancake⟩ **b** : to examine as if by turning over : think about ⟨*turned* the problem over in her mind⟩ **3** : to make over (as a garment) by reversing the material and sewing back together ⟨*turn* a collar⟩ **4 a** : to upset the order of ⟨everything was *turned* topsy-turvy⟩ **b** : to set in another and especially opposite direction **5 a** : to change course or direction ⟨the road *turns* to the left⟩ ⟨*turning* to a different subject⟩ **b** : to go around ⟨*turn* a corner⟩ **6** : to direct toward or away from something ⟨we *turned* toward home⟩ **7** : to seek out as a source of something ⟨*turn* to a friend for help⟩ **8 a** : to change or cause to change ⟨water *turned* to ice⟩ ⟨the witch *turned* the prince into a frog⟩ **b** : to cause to spoil : SOUR ⟨the milk had *turned*⟩ **c** : to change in color ⟨leaves *turning* in the fall⟩ **d** : to pass from one state to another : BECOME ⟨hair *turned* gray⟩ ⟨had just *turned* fourteen⟩ **9** : TRANSLATE 3a **10** : to give a rounded form to (as on a lathe) — **turn a hair** : to be or become upset or frightened — **turn heads** : to attract favorable attention — **turn loose** : to set free : let go — **turn one's hand** *or* **turn a hand** : to set to work : apply oneself — **turn one's stomach** : to disgust completely : SICKEN ⟨the foul smell *turned his stomach*⟩ — **turn tail** : to turn away so as to flee — **turn the other cheek** : to respond to injury or unkindness with patience — **turn the tables** : to bring about a switch in the positions or fortunes of two opposing people or sides — **turn the trick** : to bring about the desired result — **turn turtle** : OVERTURN 1

²**turn** *n* **1** : the action or an act of turning about a center **2 a** : a change or changing of direction, course, or position ⟨a left *turn*⟩ ⟨the *turn* of the tide⟩ **b** : a place where something turns ⟨at the *turn* of the road⟩ **c** : a change or

\ə\ **abut**	\au̇\ **out**	\i\ **tip**	\ȯ\ **saw**	\u̇\ **foot**
\ər\ **further**	\ch\ **chin**	\ī\ **life**	\ȯi\ **coin**	\y\ **yet**
\a\ **mat**	\e\ **pet**	\j\ **job**	\th\ **thin**	\yü\ **few**
\ā\ **take**	\ē\ **easy**	\ŋ\ **sing**	\th\ **this**	\yu̇\ **cure**
\ä\ **cot, cart**	\g\ **go**	\ō\ **bone**	\ü\ **food**	\zh\ **vision**

changing of general state or condition ⟨took a *turn* for the better⟩ ⟨a *turn* in the weather⟩ **3** : a short walk or ride ⟨took a *turn* through the park⟩ **4** : an act affecting another ⟨one good *turn* deserves another⟩ **5 a** : a period of action or activity : SPELL ⟨a *turn* as guard⟩ **b** : proper place in a waiting line or time in a schedule ⟨wait your *turn*⟩ **6** : a special purpose ⟨that will serve the *turn*⟩ **7 a** : special quality ⟨a neat *turn* of phrase⟩ **b** : the shape or form in which something is molded : CAST ⟨an odd *turn* of mind⟩ **8** : a single circle or loop (as of rope passed around an object) **9** : natural or special skill ⟨a *turn* for languages⟩ — **at every turn** : on every occasion : all the time : CONSTANTLY — **by turns** : one after another — **in turn** : one after the other in order — **out of turn 1** : not in order ⟨play *out of turn*⟩ **2** : at a wrong time or place ⟨talking *out of turn*⟩ — **to a turn** : precisely right : PERFECTLY

turn·about \\'tər-nə-ˌbau̇t\\ *n* : a change from one direction or one way of thinking or acting to the opposite

turn·around \\'tər-nə-ˌrau̇nd\\ *n* **1** : TURNABOUT **2** : the time needed for one complete cycle or round trip from start to destination and back

turn around *vb* **1** : to act in a sudden, different, or surprising manner ⟨he just *turned around* and left home⟩ **2** : to change for the better ⟨*turned* her life *around*⟩

turn away *vb* : to refuse to let in : send away ⟨all the seats were sold and a large crowd had to be *turned away*⟩

turn back *vb* **1** : to go in the reverse direction : RETURN ⟨*turned back* for home⟩ **2** : to stop the advance of : CHECK ⟨*turned back* the enemy⟩

turn·coat \\'tərn-ˌkōt\\ *n* : a person on one side who goes over to the other

turn down *vb* **1** : to fold back or down **2** : to lower by turning a control ⟨*turn down* the heat⟩ **3** : ¹REJECT 1 ⟨*turned down* the job⟩

turn·er \\'tər-nər\\ *n* : one that turns; *esp* : a kitchen tool for lifting and turning foods

turn in *vb* **1** : to give up or hand back ⟨*turned in* the art supplies when I was finished⟩ **2** : to hand over to authorities ⟨the escaped prisoner *turned* himself *in*⟩ **3** : ¹DO 1a ⟨*turned in* a fine job⟩ **4** : to go to bed

turning point *n* : a point (as in an action or situation) where an important change occurs

tur·nip \\'tər-nəp\\ *n* **1** : either of two herbs related to cabbage with thick edible roots: **a** : one with usually white roundish roots and leaves that are cooked as a vegetable when young and tender **b** : RUTABAGA **2** : the root of a turnip

turn·off \\'tər-ˌnȯf\\ *n* **1** : a place where one turns off (as from a road) **2** : something that causes loss of interest or enjoyment ⟨the music was a *turnoff*⟩

turn off \\ˌtər-'nȯf, 'tər-\\ *vb* **1** : to turn aside ⟨*turned off* onto a side road⟩ **2** : to stop by or as if by turning a control ⟨*turn off* the light⟩ ⟨*turn* the alarm *off*⟩ **3** : to cause dislike or loss of interest ⟨that sort of thing *turns* me *off*⟩

turn on \\(')tər-'nȯn, -'nän\\ *vb* **1** : to cause to work by or as if by turning a control ⟨*turn* the water *on*⟩ ⟨*turn on* the computer⟩ **2** : to cause interest or enjoyment ⟨the kind of music that *turns* me *on*⟩ — **turn–on** *n*

turn·out \\'tər-ˌnau̇t\\ *n* : the number of people who attend or who do something (as vote) ⟨a good *turnout* at the meeting⟩ ⟨expected a light voter *turnout*⟩

turn out \\ˌtər-'nau̇t, 'tər-\\ *vb* **1** : to put or empty out of a container **2** : to make by or as if by machine ⟨the factory *turns out* automobiles⟩ ⟨*turns out* a new story every

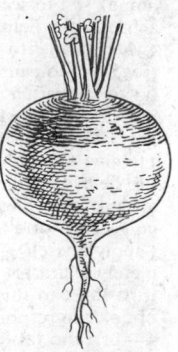

turnip 1

month⟩ **3** : TURN OFF 2 ⟨who *turned out* the light?⟩ **4** : to come or go out from home ⟨thousands *turned out* to see them⟩ **5** : to prove to be ⟨it *turned out* to be only the cat⟩ ⟨of course, I *turned out* to be right⟩

turn·over \\'tər-ˌnō-vər\\ *n* **1** : an act or the action of turning over **2** : a filled pastry with one half of the crust turned over the other **3 a** : movement (as of people) into, through, and out of a place **b** : the purchase, sale, and replacement of a stock of goods (as in a store) **c** : the number of persons hired to replace those leaving

turn over \\ˌtər-'nō-vər, 'tər-\\ *vb* **1** : to shift in position from upright to upside down **2 a** : to give to another to take care of : HAND OVER **b** : to lose possession of ⟨*turned* the ball *over* three times⟩ **3** *of one's stomach* : to feel sick **4** : to begin or cause to begin to run ⟨*turned over* the engine⟩ — **turn over a new leaf** : to make a change for the better

turn·pike \\'tərn-ˌpīk\\ *n* **1** : a road one must pay to use **2** : a main road

Word History In the Middle Ages, a spiked barrier would sometimes be placed on a road or bridge to protect against sudden attack. The barrier would have to be turned to allow passage. The Middle English word for such a barrier was *turnepike*. This word was formed from the verb *turnen*, meaning "to turn," and the noun *pike*, meaning "a sharp-tipped weapon." With a slight change in spelling, *turnpike* later came to be used as the word for a simple gate placed across a road. In order to pass through the turnpike, travelers would have to pay a fee or toll. A road on which these tollgates were found was called a *turnpike road*. Such a road in time became known simply as a *turnpike*. [Middle English *turnepike* "a turning frame bearing spikes that is used as a barrier," from *turnen* "to turn" and *pike* "a pointed weapon"]

turn·stile \\-ˌstīl\\ *n* : a post having arms which turn around that is set in an entrance or exit so that persons can pass through only on foot one by one

turn·ta·ble \\-ˌtā-bəl\\ *n* **1** : a platform that can be turned around **2** : a round flat plate that turns a phonograph record

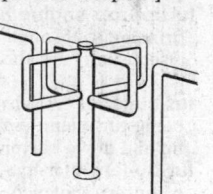

turnstile

turn up *vb* **1** : to be found or happen usually unexpectedly **2** : to raise by or as if by using a control ⟨*turn up* the heat⟩ **3** : ARRIVE 1 ⟨*turned up* late⟩ — **turn up one's nose** : to show scorn

tur·pen·tine \\'tər-pən-ˌtīn\\ *n* **1** : a mixture of oil and resin obtained from pines and some related trees **2** : an oil made from turpentine and used especially as a solvent and paint thinner

tur·quoise \\'tər-ˌk(w)ȯiz\\ *n* **1** : a blue, bluish green, or greenish gray mineral that contains copper and aluminum, takes a high polish, and is used in jewelry **2** : a light greenish blue [Middle English *turkeys* "turquoise," from early French *turkeise* (same meaning), derived from *turkeis*, literally "Turkish (stone)"; so called because it was first brought to Europe from a part of Turkey]

tur·ret \\'tər-ət, 'tə-rət, tu̇r-ət\\ *n* **1** : a little tower often at a corner of a building **2** : a low usually rotating structure (as in a tank, warship, or airplane) in which guns are mounted

¹tur·tle \\'tərt-ᵊl\\ *n, archaic* : TURTLEDOVE [Old English *turtla* "turtledove," from Latin *turtur* (same meaning)]

²turtle *n, pl* **turtles** *also* **turtle** : any of an order of land, freshwater, and marine reptiles with a toothless horny beak and a bony shell which encloses the body and into which the head, legs, and tail usually may be withdrawn [derived from French *tortue* "tortoise, turtle," from Latin *tartaruchus* "of Tartarus (part of Hades reserved for the wicked)," from Greek *tartarouchos* (same meaning)]

tur·tle·dove \'tərt-ᵊl-ˌdəv\ *n* : any of several small wild African and Eurasian pigeons noted for cooing

tur·tle·neck \-ˌnek\ *n* **1** : a high turned-over collar (as of a sweater) **2** : a garment (as a sweater) with a turtleneck

turves *plural of* TURF

¹**tusk** \'təsk\ *n* **1** : a very long large tooth (as of an elephant, walrus, or boar) that sticks out when the mouth is closed and is used especially for digging food or as a weapon **2** : a tooth-shaped part — **tusked** \'təskt\ *adj*

²**tusk** *vb* : to dig up or gash with a tusk

tusk·er \'təs-kər\ *n* : an animal with tusks; *esp* : a male elephant with two normally developed tusks

¹**tus·sle** \'təs-əl\ *vb* **tus·sled; tus·sling** \'təs-(ə-)liŋ\ : SCUFFLE 1

²**tussle** *n* **1** : a physical contest or struggle **2** : a rough argument or a struggle against difficult odds

tus·sock \'təs-ək\ *n* : a compact bunch especially of grass or sedge; *also* : an area of raised solid ground in a marsh or bog that is bound together by plant roots — **tus·socky** \-ə-kē\ *adj*

tussock moth *n* : any of numerous dull-colored moths that usually have wingless females and larvae with long tufts of hair

tu·te·lage \'t(y)üt-ə-lij\ *n* **1** : an act of guarding or protecting : GUARDIANSHIP **2** : INSTRUCTION

¹**tu·tor** \'t(y)üt-ər\ *n* : a person who has the responsibility of instructing and guiding another

²**tutor** *vb* : to teach usually individually

¹**tu·to·ri·al** \t(y)ü-'tōr-ē-əl, -'tor-\ *adj* : of or relating to a tutor or a tutorial

²**tutorial** *n* : a paper, book, film or computer program that gives practical information about a subject

tu·tu \'tü-tü\ *n* : a short skirt that extends out and is worn by a ballerina [French *tutu* "ballerina skirt," from baby talk *tutu* "backside"]

tux \'təks\ *n* : TUXEDO

tux·e·do \ˌtək-'sēd-ō\ *n, pl* **-dos** *or* **-does** : a suit for men to be worn on special occasions

Word History Tuxedo can be traced back to the name of a village in southeastern New York. In the 1880s, an area called Tuxedo Park, near the village of Tuxedo, became a popular vacation community. It was here, around the turn of the century, that young men began wearing a new kind of dress jacket. The new style was soon called *tuxedo*. [named for *Tuxedo* Park, a resort in New York State, where the jacket first became popular]

TV \(ˈ)tē-ˈvē\ *n* : TELEVISION

TV dinner \ˌtē-ˌvē-\ *n* : a quick-frozen packaged dinner that requires only heating before it is served

twad·dle \'twäd-ᵊl\ *n* : silly idle talk

twain \'twān\ *n* **1** : TWO 1 **2** : two persons or things : COUPLE, PAIR

¹**twang** \'twaŋ\ *n* **1** : a harsh quick ringing sound **2** : nasal speech

²**twang** *vb* **twanged; twang·ing** \'twaŋ-iŋ\ **1** : to sound or cause to sound with a twang **2** : to speak with a nasal twang

¹**'twas** \'twoz, 'twäz\ : it was

tweak \'twēk\ *vb* **1** : to pinch and pull with a sudden jerk and twist **2** : to make small adjustments in or to ⟨*tweak* the controls⟩ **3** : to injure slightly — **tweak** *n*

tweed \'twēd\ *n* **1** : a rough woolen cloth **2** *pl* : tweed clothing (as a suit)

tweedy \'twēd-ē\ *adj* : of or resembling tweed

¹**tween** \'twēn\ *prep* : ¹BETWEEN

²**tween** *n* : ¹PRETEEN

¹**tweet** \'twēt\ *n* **1** : a chirping sound **2** : a post made on the Twitter online message service

²**tweet** *vb* **1** : CHIRP **2** : to post a message to the Twitter online message service

tweet·er \'twēt-ər\ *n* : a small loudspeaker that responds only to high sound frequencies and produces sounds of high pitch — compare WOOFER

twee·zers \'twē-zərz\ *n pl* : a small instrument that is used like pincers in grasping or pulling something

twelfth \'twelf(t)th\ *n* — see NUMBER table — **twelfth** *adj or adv*

Twelfth Day *n* : EPIPHANY

Twelfth Night *n* : the evening or sometimes the eve of Epiphany

twelve \'twelv\ *n* **1** — see NUMBER table **2** *cap* : the twelve original disciples of Jesus **3** : the 12th in a set or series — **twelve** *adj or pron*

twelve·month \-ˌmən(t)th\ *n* : YEAR

twen·ti·eth \'twent-ē-əth\ *n* — see NUMBER table — **twentieth** *adj or pron*

twen·ty \'twent-ē\ *n, pl* **twenties** — see NUMBER table — **twenty** *adj or pron*

twen·ty–twen·ty \ˌtwent-ē-'twent-ē\ *adj* : having normal visual sharpness — often written 20/20

twenty–two \ˌtwent-ē-'tü\ *n* **1** : a firearm cartridge of .22 caliber **2** : a firearm of .22 caliber

twerp \'twərp\ *n* : a silly or unimportant person

twice \'twīs\ *adv* : two times ⟨use it *twice*⟩ ⟨*twice* as large⟩

twid·dle \'twid-ᵊl\ *vb* **twid·dled; twid·dling** \'twid-liŋ, -ᵊl-iŋ\ : to rotate lightly or idly ⟨*twiddle* one's thumbs⟩

twig \'twig\ *n* : a small shoot or branch usually without its leaves — **twig·gy** \'twig-ē\ *adj*

twi·light \'twī-ˌlīt\ *n* : the period or the light from the sky between full night and sunrise or between sunset and full night

¹**twill** \'twil\ *n* : a way of weaving cloth that produces a pattern of diagonal lines

²**twill** *vb* : to make (cloth) with a twill weave

¹**twin** \'twin\ *adj* **1** : born with one other or as a pair at one birth ⟨my *twin* brother⟩ ⟨*twin* girls⟩ **2 a** : made up of two similar, related, or connected members or parts **b** : being one of a pair ⟨a *twin* city⟩

²**twin** *vb* **twinned; twin·ning** : to produce or give birth to twins

³**twin** *n* : either of two offspring produced at a birth — compare FRATERNAL TWIN, IDENTICAL TWIN

twin bed *n* **1** : either of a pair of single beds that match **2** : a bed that is big enough for only one person

¹**twine** \'twīn\ *n* : a string made of two or more strands twisted together

²**twine** *vb* **twined; twin·ing** **1 a** : to twist together **b** : INTERLACE **2** : to coil or cause to coil around a support

¹**twinge** \'twinj\ *vb* **twinged; twing·ing** \'twin-jiŋ\ *or* **twinge·ing** : to affect with or feel a sudden sharp pain

²**twinge** *n* **1** : a sudden sharp stab of pain **2** : moral or emotional distress ⟨a *twinge* of regret⟩

¹**twin·kle** \'twiŋ-kəl\ *vb* **twin·kled; twin·kling** \-k(ə-)liŋ\ **1** : to shine or cause to shine with a flickering or sparkling light **2** : to appear bright with amusement ⟨his eyes *twinkled*⟩ **3** : to move or flutter rapidly — **twin·kler** \-k(ə-)lər\ *n*

²**twinkle** *n* **1** : a very short time **2** : ²SPARKLE 1, FLICKER — **twin·kly** \-k(ə-)lē\ *adj*

twin·kling \'twiŋ-kliŋ\ *n* : INSTANT ⟨was back in a *twinkling*⟩

twin–size \'twin-ˌsīz\ *adj* : having a size of 39 inches by 75 inches (about 1.0 by 1.9 meters) ⟨a *twin-size* bed⟩

¹**twirl** \'twər(-ə)l\ *vb* : to turn or cause to turn rapidly ⟨*twirl* a baton⟩ — **twirl·er** *n*

²**twirl** *n* : an act of twirling

¹**twist** \'twist\ *vb* **1** : to unite by winding one thread, strand, or wire around another **2** : ²TWINE 2 **3 a** : to turn so as to sprain or hurt ⟨*twisted* my ankle⟩ **b** : to change the

\ə\ **abut**	\au̇\ **out**	\i\ **tip**	\ȯ\ **saw**	\u̇\ **foot**
\ər\ **further**	\ch\ **chin**	\ī\ **life**	\ȯi\ **coin**	\y\ **yet**
\a\ **mat**	\e\ **pet**	\j\ **job**	\th\ **thin**	\yü\ **few**
\ā\ **take**	\ē\ **easy**	\ŋ\ **sing**	\th\ **this**	\yu̇\ **cure**
\ä\ **cot, cart**	\g\ **go**	\ō\ **bone**	\ü\ **food**	\zh\ **vision**

meaning of ⟨*twisted* the facts⟩ **c** : to pull off, rotate, or break by a turning force ⟨*twisted* a small branch off the tree⟩ **4** : to follow a winding course

²twist *n* **1** : a thread, yarn, or cord made by twisting two or more strands together **2** : an act of twisting : the state of being twisted **3** : a spiral turn or curve **4** : a strong personal tendency : BENT **5** : a changing of meaning **6** : something (as a plan of action) that is both surprising and strange

twist·er \'twis-tər\ *n* **1** : one that twists **2 a** : TORNADO **b** : WATERSPOUT 2

twist tie *n* : a tie used for closing or securing (as a plastic bag) by twisting the ends together

¹twitch \'twich\ *vb* **1** : to move or pull with a sudden motion : JERK **2** : ²QUIVER **3** : to undergo a brief muscular contraction ⟨his hand *twitched*⟩

²twitch *n* **1** : an act of twitching **2 a** : a brief contraction of muscle fibers **b** : a slight jerk of a body part

¹twit·ter \'twit-ər\ *vb* **1** : to make a series of chirping sounds **2** : to talk in a chattering fashion **3** : to make or become very nervous and upset

²twitter *n* **1** : a nervous upset state **2** : the chirping of birds **3** : a light chattering

twixt \'twikst\ *or* ²**twixt** *prep* : ¹BETWEEN [earlier English *twix*, short for *betwix* or *betwixt*]

two \'tü\ *n, pl* **twos** **1** — see NUMBER table **2** : the second in a set or series — **two** *adj or pron*

two–bit \,tü-'bit\ *adj* : not important or valuable

two bits *n sing or pl* : the value of a quarter of a dollar

two–by–four \,tü-bə-'fō(ə)r, -'fȯ(ə)r\ *n* : a piece of lumber sawed to approximately 2 by 4 inches (5 by 10 centimeters)

2–D \'tü-'dē\ *n* : a two-dimensional form ⟨displayed in *2-D*⟩ — **2–D** *adj*

two–dimensional *adj* : of, relating to, or having two dimensions (as length and width)

two–faced \'tü-'fāst\ *adj* : behaving in a false way that hides one's real feelings or plans

two·fold \-,fōld, -'fōld\ *adj* : twice as great or as many — **twofold** *adv*

2, 4–D \,tü-,fȯr-'dē, -,fȯr-\ *n* : a white compound used as a weed killer

two–hand·ed \'tü-'han-dəd\ *adj* **1** : used with both hands ⟨a *two-handed* sword⟩ **2** : requiring two persons ⟨a *two-handed* saw⟩

two·pence *or* **tup·pence** \'təp-ən(t)s, *U.S. also* 'tü-,pen(t)s\ *n* : the sum of two pence

two·some \'tü-səm\ *n* : a group of two persons or things

two–toed sloth \,tü-,tōd-\ *n* : any of a genus of sloths that have two claws on each front foot and three on each back foot — compare THREE-TOED SLOTH

two–way *adj* **1** : moving or acting or allowing movement or action in either direction ⟨*two-way* traffic⟩ ⟨a *two-way* street⟩ **2 a** : involving two persons or groups ⟨communication is a *two-way* process⟩ **b** : made to send and receive messages ⟨a *two-way* radio⟩

two–wheel·er \-'hwē-lər, -'wē-\ *n* : a 2-wheeled vehicle (as a bicycle)

two–winged fly \,tü-,wiŋ(d)-\ *n* : any of a large order of insects (as the housefly, mosquitoes, and gnats) that produce often headless, eyeless, and legless larvae and that usually use the front wings for flying and have the back wings reduced to balancers

ty·coon \tī-'kün\ *n* : a very wealthy and powerful business person [Japanese *taikun* "shogun"]

tyer *variant of* ³TIER

tying *present participle of* TIE

tyke *also* **tike** \'tīk\ *n* : a small child

tympani *variant of* TIMPANI

tym·pan·ic membrane \tim-'pan-ik-\ *n* : EARDRUM

tym·pa·num \'tim-pə-nəm\ *n, pl* **-na** \-nə\ *also* **-nums** **1**

: EARDRUM **2** : a thin membrane of an insect covering an organ of hearing and transmitting vibrations produced by sound waves to it

¹type \'tīp\ *n* **1 a** : a rectangular block usually of metal with a raised letter or number from which an inked print is made **b** : a set of letters or figures that are used for printing or the letters or figures printed by them **2 a** : the special things by which members of a group are set apart from other groups ⟨horses of the draft *type*⟩ **b** : a particular kind, class, or group ⟨a seedless *type* of orange⟩ ⟨I don't like people of that *type*⟩

¹type 1a

²type *vb* **typed; typ·ing 1** : to write with a keyboard (as on a typewriter or computer) **2** : to identify as belonging to a type

type·write \'tī-,prīt\ *vb* **-wrote; -writ·ten; -writ·ing** : ²TYPE 1

type·writ·er \'tī-,prīt-ər\ *n* : a machine that prints letters or figures when a person pushes its keys down

type·writ·ing \'tī-,prīt-iŋ\ *n* **1** : the use of a typewriter **2** : printing done with a typewriter

¹ty·phoid \'tī-,fȯid, (')tī-'fȯid\ *adj* : of, relating to, or being typhoid fever

²typhoid *n* : TYPHOID FEVER

typhoid fever *n* : a disease that is caused by a bacterium, is characterized especially by fever, diarrhea, weakness, headache, and an inflamed intestine, and is passed from one person to another in contaminated food or water

ty·phoon \tī-'fün\ *n* : a hurricane occurring in the region of the Philippines or the China Sea

ty·phus \'tī-fəs\ *n* : any of various diseases caused by bacteria that are rickettsias: as **a** : a severe disease that is marked by high fever, muscle and joint pain, cough, intense headache, and red rash, and that is passed on especially by body lice **b** : a mild disease that is marked by fever, headache, and red rash and is passed on by fleas

typhus fever *n* : TYPHUS

typ·i·cal \'tip-i-kəl\ *adj* : combining or showing the special characteristics of a group or kind ⟨a *typical* school lunch⟩ — **typ·i·cal·ly** \-k(ə-)lē\ *adv*

typ·i·fy \'tip-ə-,fī\ *vb* **-fied; -fy·ing 1** : REPRESENT 2 **2** : to have or include the special or main characteristics of

typ·ist \'tī-pəst\ *n* : a person who types especially as a job

ty·ran·ni·cal \tə-'ran-i-kəl, tī-\ *also* **ty·ran·nic** \-'ran-ik\ *adj* : of, relating to, or characteristic of a tyrant or tyranny ⟨a *tyrannical* ruler⟩ ⟨*tyrannical* rule⟩ — **ty·ran·ni·cal·ly** \-'ran-i-k(ə-)lē\ *adv*

tyr·an·nize \'tir-ə-,nīz\ *vb* **-nized; -niz·ing** : to act like a tyrant — **tyr·an·niz·er** *n*

ty·ran·no·saur \tə-'ran-ə-,sȯ(ə)r, tī-\ *n* : a very large North American flesh-eating dinosaur of the Cretaceous period that had small forelegs and walked on its hind legs

ty·ran·no·sau·rus \tə-,ran-ə-'sȯr-əs, (,)tī-\ *n* : TYRANNOSAUR

tyr·an·nous \'tir-ə-nəs\ *adj* : TYRANNICAL — **tyr·an·nous·ly** *adv*

tyr·an·ny \'tir-ə-nē\ *n, pl* **-nies 1** : a government in which all power is in the hands of a single ruler **2** : harsh, cruel, and severe government or conduct **3** : a tyrannical act

ty·rant \'tī-rənt\ *n* **1** : a ruler who has no legal limits on his or her power by law or constitution **2 a** : a ruler who exercises total power harshly or cruelly **b** : a person who uses authority or power harshly

tyre *chiefly British variant of* TIRE

ty·ro \'tī-rō\ *n, pl* **tyros** : a beginner in learning

tzar *variant of* CZAR

U

u \'yü\ *n, often cap* : the 21st letter of the English alphabet

ubiq·ui·tous \yü-'bik-wət-əs\ *adj* : existing or being everywhere at the same time : constantly encountered : WIDESPREAD ⟨a *ubiquitous* fashion⟩ — **ubiq·ui·tous·ly** *adv* — **ubiq·ui·tous·ness** *n* — **ubiq·ui·ty** \-wət-ē\ *n*

U–boat \'yü-'bōt\ *n* : a German submarine

ud·der \'əd-ər\ *n* 1 : a large bag-shaped organ (as of a cow) consisting of two or more mammary glands enclosed in a common pouch but with each having a separate nipple 2 : a mammary gland

UFO \,yü-(,)ef-'ō\ *n, pl* **UFO's** *or* **UFOs** \-'ōz\ : an unidentified flying object; *esp* : FLYING SAUCER

ugh *often read as* 'əg *or* 'ək *or* 'ə\ *interj* — used for various sounds that express disgust or horror

ug·li·fy \'əg-li-,fī\ *vb* **-fied; -fy·ing** : to make ugly

ug·ly \'əg-lē\ *adj* **ug·li·er; -est** 1 : horrid or unpleasant especially to the sight : UNSIGHTLY, HIDEOUS 2 : [1]OFFENSIVE 3, REPULSIVE ⟨*ugly* habits⟩ 3 a : likely to cause bother or discomfort : TROUBLESOME ⟨an *ugly* situation⟩ b : QUARRELSOME ⟨an *ugly* disposition⟩ — **ug·li·ness** *n*

ugly duckling *n* : a person or thing that seems unpromising but later develops great beauty, talent, or worth

ukase \yü-'kās, -'kāz; 'yü-,kāz, ü-'käz\ *n* : a ruling especially of a Russian emperor or government

uke \'yük\ *n* : UKULELE

Ukrai·ni·an \yü-'krā-nē-ən\ *n* 1 : a person born or living in Ukraine 2 : the language of the Ukrainian people — **Ukrainian** *adj*

uku·le·le \,yü-kə-'lā-lē, ,ü-\ *n* : a usually four-stringed small guitar popularized in Hawaii

ukulele

Word History In the 19th century, a former British army officer named Edward Purvis lived in Hawaii as an official at the royal court. Purvis is said to have been given the Hawaiian nickname of 'ukulele, which means "jumping flea," because he was small and lively. In 1879 Portuguese immigrants arrived in the Hawaiian Islands. They brought several of their native instruments, among them a small four-stringed guitar. Purvis liked this new instrument. He quickly learned to play it. In time the small guitar became a favorite, and it took the nickname of the man who had made it popular. [from Hawaiian 'ukulele "ukulele," literally, "jumping flea," from 'uku "flea" + *lele* "jumping"]

ul·cer \'əl-sər\ *n* : a slow-healing open sore in which tissue breaks down

ul·cer·ate \'əl-sə-,rāt\ *vb* **-at·ed; -at·ing** : to cause or become affected with an ulcer ⟨an *ulcerated* wound⟩

ul·cer·a·tion \,əl-sə-'rā-shən\ *n* 1 : the process of forming or state of having an ulcer 2 : ULCER

ul·na \'əl-nə\ *n, pl* **ul·nae** \-nē\ *or* **ulnas** : the bone on the little-finger side of the human forearm; *also* : a corresponding part of the forelimb of vertebrates — **ul·nar** \-nər\ *adj*

ul·ster \'əl-stər\ *n* : a long loose heavy overcoat

ul·te·ri·or \,əl-'tir-ē-ər\ *adj* : kept hidden in order to achieve a particular result ⟨*ulterior* motives⟩

ul·ti·ma \'əl-tə-mə\ *n* : the last syllable of a word

[1]ul·ti·mate \'əl-tə-mət\ *adj* 1 a : [1]FARTHEST ⟨the *ultimate* reaches of the universe⟩ b : last in a progression : FINAL c : [1]EXTREME 1 ⟨the *ultimate* sacrifice⟩ 2 : arrived at as the last result ⟨the *ultimate* damage of the hurricane⟩ 3 a : [1]BASIC 1 ⟨*ultimate* control⟩ b : incapable of further division or separation : ELEMENTAL ⟨*ultimate* particles⟩ 4 : being the greatest : MAXIMUM ⟨the *ultimate* speed of an airplane⟩ — **ultimate** *n* — **ul·ti·mate·ly** *adv*

[2]ultimate *n* : ULTIMATE FRISBEE

Ultimate Frisbee *n, often not cap* : a game played between two teams in which a plastic disk is advanced by being thrown from player to player — called also *ultimate*

ul·ti·ma·tum \,əl-tə-'māt-əm, -'mät-\ *n, pl* **-tums** *or* **-ta** \-ə\ : a demand that if rejected will bring about an end of peaceful talks and could lead to forceful action

ul·tra \'əl-trə\ *adj* : going beyond others : EXTREME

ultra- *prefix* 1 : beyond : exceeding the range or limits of ⟨*ultra*violet⟩ 2 : more than is usual ⟨*ultra*modern⟩ [derived from Latin *ultra* "beyond"]

ul·tra·high frequency \,əl-trə-'hī-\ *n* : any radio frequency in the range between 300 and 3000 megahertz — abbreviation *UHF*

ul·tra·light \'əl-trə-,līt\ *adj* : very light in mass or weight ⟨an *ultralight* alloy⟩ ⟨an *ultralight* sweater⟩

ul·tra·ma·rine \,əl-trə-mə-'rēn\ *n* : a vivid blue

ul·tra·mod·ern \,əl-trə-'mäd-ərn\ *adj* : very modern in idea, style, or direction — **ul·tra·mod·ern·ist** \-ər-nəst\ *n*

ul·tra·son·ic \,əl-trə-'sän-ik\ *adj* : relating to or being vibrations that are of the same kind as sound waves but have too high a frequency to be heard by the human ear — **ul·tra·son·i·cal·ly** \-'sän-i-k(ə-)lē\ *adv*

ul·tra·sound \'əl-trə-,saùnd\ *n* 1 : ultrasonic vibrations 2 : the use of ultrasound for medical diagnosis or treatment and especially a technique involving the formation of a two-dimensional image used for examining internal body structures and detecting abnormalities in the body

ul·tra·vi·o·let \,əl-trə-'vī-ə-lət\ *adj* 1 : located beyond the visible spectrum at its violet end and having a wavelength shorter than those of visible light but longer than those of X-rays 2 : relating to, producing, or using ultraviolet radiation — **ultraviolet** *n*

ul·va \'əl-və\ *n* : SEA LETTUCE

um *a prolonged* m *sound*, əm\ *interj* — used to express hesitation ⟨well, *um*, I don't know⟩

um·bel \'əm-bəl\ *n* : a flat-topped or ball-shaped flower cluster (as in the carrot) in which the stalks of the individual flowers all grow from about the same point on the main stem like the ribs of an umbrella

um·ber \'əm-bər\ *n* 1 : an artist's pigment that is either greenish brown or reddish brown 2 : a medium to dark brown or yellowish brown — **umber** *adj*

umbel

\ə\ abut	\aù\ out	\i\ tip	\ò\ saw	\ù\ foot
\ər\ further	\ch\ chin	\ī\ life	\òi\ coin	\y\ yet
\a\ mat	\e\ pet	\j\ job	\th\ thin	\yü\ few
\ā\ take	\ē\ easy	\ŋ\ sing	\th\ this	\yù\ cure
\ä\ cot, cart	\g\ go	\ō\ bone	\ü\ food	\zh\ vision

um·bil·i·cal cord \ˌəm-'bil-i-kəl-\ *n* : a cord that contains blood vessels and connects the navel of a fetus with the placenta of the mother

um·bil·i·cus \ˌəm-'bil-i-kəs\ *n, pl* **-bil·i·ci** \-'bil-ə-ˌkī, -ˌkē, -ˌsī\ *or* **-bil·i·cus·es** : NAVEL

um·bra \'əm-brə\ *n, pl* **umbras** *or* **um·brae** \-brē, -ˌbrī\ **1** : a shaded area **2** : the cone-shaped part of the shadow of a celestial body from which the light of the sun is completely blocked

um·brage \'əm-brij\ *n* : RESENTMENT, OFFENSE ⟨take *umbrage* at a remark⟩

um·brel·la \ˌəm-'brel-ə\ *n* **1** : a collapsible covering for protection against weather consisting of fabric stretched over a hinged frame coming out from a center pole; *esp* : a small one for carrying in the hand **2** : something resembling an umbrella in shape or purpose [from Italian *ombrella* "umbrella," from Latin *umbella,* literally, "little shade," from *umbra* "shade, shadow"]

Um·bri·an \'əm-brē-ən\ *n* : a member of a people of ancient Italy occupying Umbria — **Umbrian** *adj*

umi·ak \'ü-mē-ˌak\ *n* : an open Eskimo boat made of an open frame covered with hide

umiak

um·laut \'ùm-ˌlaùt, 'üm-\ *n* **1** : the change of a vowel brought about by a following sound **2** : a diacritical mark ¨ placed especially over a German vowel to indicate umlaut

um·pire \'əm-ˌpī(ə)r\ *n* **1** : one having authority to decide an argument or a question **2** : an official in a sport (as baseball) who rules on plays — **umpire** *vb*

Word History From the Latin word *par,* meaning "equal," came the early French word *per,* which also meant "equal." *Per* was combined with the prefix *non-, nom-,* meaning "not," to form the early French word *nomper,* which meant "without equal." *Nomper* came into Middle English as a noun, *noumpere.* The meaning of *noumpere* was "a person who is not equal, a person who has authority over others." Many people who heard the words *a noumpere* thought they were actually hearing *an oumpere.* Because of that misunderstanding, the letter *n* in time came to be dropped from *noumpere.* Other changes over the course of many years have given us the modern word *umpire.* [Middle English *oumpere,* an altered form of *noumpere* "one having authority to decide an issue or dispute," from early French *nounpier, nompere* (adjective) "single, odd, without equal," from *non-, nom-* "not" and *per* "equal," from Latin *par* "equal" — related to COMPARE, PAIR, PAR, PEER]

ump·teen \'əm(p)-'tēn, ˌəm(p)-\ *adj* : numerous but not fixed in amount ⟨*umpteen* million things to do⟩

¹un- \ˌən, 'ən\ *prefix* **1** : not ⟨*un*skilled⟩ ⟨*un*kindness⟩ **2** : opposite of : contrary to ⟨*un*constitutional⟩ ⟨*un*godly⟩ [Old English *un-* "not"]

²un- *prefix* **1** : do the opposite of : reverse ⟨*un*dress⟩ **2** : remove a specified thing from ⟨*un*burden⟩ [Old English *un-, on-,* an altered form of *and-* "against"]

unabsorbed	unadventurous	unambitious
unabsorbent	unadvertised	unamusing
unacademic	unaesthetic	unanchored
unaccented	unaffectionate	unannounced
unaccepted	unaffiliated	unanswered
unacclimated	unaffordable	unanticipated
unaccredited	unafraid	unapologetic
unachieved	unaggressive	unapparent
unacquainted	unaided	unappeased
unadaptable	unair–conditioned	unappetizing
unadapted	unalike	unappreciated
unadjusted	unaltered	unappreciative
unadmirable	unambiguous	unapproved

unarmored	unconfined	undismayed
unarticulated	unconfirmed	undisputable
unartistic	unconfuse	undisputed
unashamed	uncongenial	undissolved
unaspiring	unconnected	undistinguished
unassailed	unconquered	undisturbed
unassigned	unconsecrated	undivided
unassisted	unconsolidated	undomestic
unassociated	uncontaminated	undomesticated
unathletic	uncontested	undoubtable
unattainable	uncontradicted	undramatic
unattended	uncontrolled	undrinkable
unauthentic	unconverted	undyed
unauthorized	unconvinced	uneager
unavailable	unconvincing	uneaten
unawakened	uncooked	uneconomic
unbaptized	uncooperative	unedifying
unbeloved	uncoordinated	unembarrassed
unbleached	uncorrectable	unemotional
unblemished	uncorrected	unemphatic
unbranded	uncorrupt	unenclosed
unbreakable	uncountable	unendurable
unbridgeable	uncourageous	unenforceable
unbridged	uncreative	unenforced
unbruised	uncredited	unenlarged
unbrushed	uncrippled	unenterprising
unburied	uncritical	unenthusiastic
unburnable	uncritically	unenthusiastically
unburned	uncrowded	unescapable
unburnt	uncultivated	unessential
unbusinesslike	uncultured	unethical
unbusy	uncured	unexamined
unbuttered	uncurious	unexceptional
uncalibrated	uncurtained	unexcited
uncalled	uncustomary	unexciting
uncanceled	undamaged	unexcused
uncapitalized	undamped	unexpended
uncared–for	undated	unexpired
uncaring	undecidable	unexplainable
uncarpeted	undecipherable	unexplained
uncataloged	undeciphered	unexploded
uncatchable	undeclared	unexplored
uncaught	undecorated	unexposed
uncelebrated	undefeated	unexpressed
uncensored	undefended	unexpurgated
uncensured	undefiled	unextraordinary
uncertified	undefinable	unfaltering
unchallenged	undefined	unfashionable
unchallenging	undemanding	unfelt
unchanged	undemocratic	unfeminine
unchaperoned	undenominational	unfenced
unchecked	undependable	unfermented
unchristened	undescribable	unfertile
unclaimed	undeserved	unfertilized
uncleaned	undeserving	unfilled
unclear	undesired	unfiltered
unclouded	undetectable	unflattering
uncluttered	undetected	unfocused
uncoated	undetermined	unforced
uncoiled	undeterred	unforeseeable
uncollected	undeveloped	unforeseen
uncollectible	undigested	unforested
uncolored	undignified	unforgivable
uncombed	undiluted	unforgiving
uncombined	undiminished	unframed
uncomic	undimmed	unfree
uncommercial	undiplomatic	unfrozen
uncompassionate	undisciplined	unfulfilled
uncompensated	undisclosed	unfunny
uncompleted	undiscovered	unfurnished
uncomplicated	undiscriminating	unfussy
unconcealed	undisguised	ungentle

ungentlemanly
unglazed
ungoverned
ungraceful
ungracefully
ungraded
ungrammatical
unguided
unhampered
unharmed
unharvested
unhatched
unhealed
unheated
unheeded
unheeding
unhelpful
unheroic
unhesitating
unhindered
unhomogenized
unhonored
unhopeful
unhoused
unhurt
unidentifiable
unidentified
unidiomatic
unilluminating
unimaginable
unimaginably
unimaginative
unimpaired
unimpeded
unimportant
unimposing
unimpressed
unimpressive
unincorporated
unindexed
unindustrialized
uninfected
uninflected
uninfluenced
uninformative
uninformed
uninhabitable
uninhabited
uninitiated
uninjured
uninoculated
uninspected
uninspired
uninspiring
uninstructed
uninstructive
uninsulated
uninsured
unintegrated
unintelligible
unintelligibly
unintended
unintentional
unintentionally
uninteresting
uninterrupted
uninvited
uninviting
uninvolved
unjoined
unjointed
unjustifiable

unjustified
unkept
unlabeled
unladylike
unlamented
unleavened
unlicensed
unlikable
unlined
unlit
unliterary
unlivable
unlovable
unloved
unloving
unmalicious
unmaliciously
unmanageable
unmapped
unmarked
unmarketable
unmasculine
unmatched
unmeasurable
unmeasured
unmelodious
unmentioned
unmindful
unmixed
unmodified
unmotivated
unmounted
unmovable
unmusical
unnamed
unneeded
unnewsworthy
unnoticeable
unnoticed
unobjectionable
unobservable
unobserved
unobstructed
unobtainable
unofficial
unofficially
unopened
unopposed
unordered
unoriginal
unowned
unpainted
unpalatable
unpardonable
unpasteurized
unpatriotic
unpaved
unpeeled
unperceived
unperceptive
unperformed
unpersuasive
unperturbed
unplanned
unplayable
unpleased
unpleasing
unplowed
unpoetic
unpolarized
unpolished
unpolluted

unposed
unprejudiced
unpremeditated
unprepared
unpreparedness
unprepossessing
unpressed
unprivileged
unprocessed
unproductive
unprogrammed
unprogressive
unprompted
unprovable
unproved
unproven
unprovoked
unpruned
unpunished
unquenchable
unquestioned
unraised
unranked
unrated
unreachable
unready
unrealistic
unrealized
unreasonable
unreasonableness
unrecognizable
unrecognized
unreconcilable
unreconciled
unrecorded
unrecoverable
unrecyclable
unredeemable
unredeemed
unrefined
unreflective
unreformed
unregistered
unregulated
unrehearsed
unrelated
unreliable
unrelieved
unreluctant
unremarkable
unremarkably
unremembered
unremovable
unrepeatable
unrepentant
unrepentantly
unreported
unrepresented
unrequited
unresistant
unresolvable
unresolved
unresponsive
unrestful
unrestricted
unreturnable
unrevealed
unreviewed
unrevised
unrewarded
unrewarding
unrhymed

unrhythmic
unripened
unromantic
unromantically
unruled
unrushed
unsafe
unsaid
unsalable
unsalaried
unsalted
unsanctioned
unsanitary
unsatisfactorily
unsatisfactoriness
unsatisfactory
unsatisfied
unsatisfying
unscarred
unscented
unscreened
unsealed
unseasoned
unseaworthy
unsecured
unseeded
unsegmented
unselected
unsensational
unsent
unsentimental
unseparated
unserved
unsexual
unshaded
unshakable
unshaken
unshapely
unshared
unsharp
unshaven
unshorn
unsigned
unsinkable
unsized
unskillful
unslaked
unsmiling
unsociable
unsoiled
unsold
unsoldierly

unsolicited
unsolicitous
unsolvable
unsolved
unsorted
unsounded
unsown
unspecialized
unspecifiable
unspecific
unspecified
unspectacular
unspent
unspiritual
unsplit
unspoiled
unspoilt
unspoken
unsportsmanlike
unstained
unsterile
unsterilized
unstinted
unstrained
unstratified
unstructured
unstylish
unsubdued
unsubstantiated
unsubtle
unsubtly
unsuitable
unsuited
unsullied
unsupervised
unsupportable
unsupported
unsure
unsurpassable
unsurpassed
unsurprised
unsuspected
unsuspecting
unsuspicious
unsustainable
unsweetened
unsympathetic
unsystematic
untainted
untalented
untamable
untamed

untanned
untarnished
untaxed
unteachable
untended
untested
unthreatening
unthrifty
untilled
untiring
untraceable
untraditional
untrained
untranslated
untraveled
untraversed
untreated
untrimmed
untroubled
untrusting
untrustworthy
untwisted
untypical
unusable
unvaccinated
unvaried
unvarying
unventilated
unverifiable
unvulcanized
unwanted
unwarranted
unwashed
unwatchable
unwavering
unweaned
unwearable
unweathered
unwed
unweighted
unwelcome
unwilled
unwomanly
unwon
unworkable
unworked
unworn
unworried
unwounded
unwoven
unwrinkled

un·abashed \ˌən-ə-'basht\ *adj* : not abashed : not embarrassed or ashamed — **un·abash·ed·ly** \-'bash-əd-lē\ *adv*

un·abat·ed \ˌən-ə-'bāt-əd\ *adj* : not abated : at full strength or force — **un·abat·ed·ly** *adv*

un·able \ˌən-'ā-bəl, 'ən-\ *adj* : not able : INCAPABLE

un·abridged \ˌən-ə-'brijd\ *adj* **1** : not abridged : COMPLETE ⟨an *unabridged* reprint of a novel⟩ **2** : complete of its class : not based on one larger ⟨an *unabridged* dictionary⟩

un·ac·cept·able \ˌən-ik-'sep-tə-bəl, -ak-\ *adj* : not acceptable : not pleasing or welcome — **un·ac·cept·ably** \-blē\ *adv*

un·ac·com·mo·dat·ed \ˌən-ə-'käm-ə-ˌdāt-əd\ *adj* : not accommodated : UNPROVIDED

\ə\ **abut**	\aů\ **out**	\i\ **tip**	\ò\ **saw**	\ů\ **foot**	
\ər\ **further**	\ch\ **chin**	\ī\ **life**	\òi\ **coin**	\y\ **yet**	
\a\ **mat**	\e\ **pet**	\j\ **job**	\th\ **thin**	\yü\ **few**	
\ā\ **take**	\ē\ **easy**	\ŋ\ **sing**	\th\ **this**	\yů\ **cure**	
\ä\ **cot, cart**	\g\ **go**	\ō\ **bone**	\ü\ **food**	\zh\ **vision**	

un·ac·com·pa·nied \ˌən-ə-ˈkəmp-(ə-)nēd\ *adj* : not accompanied; *esp* : being without instrumental accompaniment

un·ac·count·able \ˌən-ə-ˈkaùnt-ə-bəl\ *adj* **1** : INEXPLICABLE, STRANGE **2** : not to be called to account : not responsible — **un·ac·count·ably** \-blē\ *adv*

un·ac·count·ed \ˌən-ə-ˈkaùnt-əd\ *adj* : not accounted : UNEXPLAINED — often used with *for* ⟨their absence was *unaccounted* for⟩

un·ac·cus·tomed \ˌən-ə-ˈkəs-təmd\ *adj* **1** : UNUSUAL, UNFAMILIAR ⟨*unaccustomed* scenes⟩ **2** : not used to something : not accustomed ⟨*unaccustomed* to travel⟩

un·adorned \ˌən-ə-ˈdò(ə)rnd\ *adj* : not adorned : lacking decoration : SIMPLE

un·adul·ter·at·ed \ˌən-ə-ˈdəl-tə-ˌrāt-əd\ *adj* : not adulterated : PURE, UNMIXED ⟨*unadulterated* foods⟩ ⟨*unadulterated* beauty⟩ ⟨*unadulterated* happiness⟩

un·ad·vised \ˌən-əd-ˈvīzd\ *adj* : done without proper consideration

un·af·fect·ed \ˌən-ə-ˈfek-təd\ *adj* **1** : not influenced or changed mentally, physically, or chemically **2** : free from false behavior intended to impress others : GENUINE — **un·af·fect·ed·ly** *adv* — **un·af·fect·ed·ness** *n*

un·alien·able \ˌən-ˈāl-yə-nə-bəl, -ˈā-lē-ə-nə-\ *adj* : INALIENABLE

un·aligned \ˌən-ˌəl-ˈīnd\ *adj* : not associated with other nations

un·al·loyed \ˌən-ˌəl-ˈòid\ *adj* : not alloyed : UNMIXED, PURE ⟨*unalloyed* metals⟩ ⟨*unalloyed* happiness⟩

un·al·ter·able \ˌən-ˈòl-t(ə-)rə-bəl, ˈən-\ *adj* : not capable of being altered or changed ⟨*unalterable* opposition⟩ — **un·al·ter·ably** \-blē\ *adv*

un–Amer·i·can \ˌən-ə-ˈmer-ə-kən\ *adj* : not American

unan·i·mous \yu̇-ˈnan-ə-məs\ *adj* **1** : being of one mind : agreeing completely ⟨the councillors were *unanimous* in their approval of the report⟩ **2** : agreed to by all ⟨a *unanimous* vote⟩ — **una·nim·i·ty** \ˌyü-nə-ˈnim-ət-ē\ *n* — **unan·i·mous·ly** \yu̇-ˈnan-ə-məs-lē\ *adv*

un·an·swer·able \ˌən-ˈan(t)s-(ə-)rə-bəl, ˈən-\ *adj* : not answerable; *esp* : IRREFUTABLE ⟨the arguments were *unanswerable*⟩

un·ap·peal·ing \ˌən-ə-ˈpē-liŋ\ *adj* : not appealing : UNATTRACTIVE

un·ap·peas·able \ˌən-ə-ˈpē-zə-bəl\ *adj* : not to be appeased : IMPLACABLE

un·apt \ˌən-ˈapt, ˈən-\ *adj* **1** : UNSUITABLE, INAPPROPRIATE ⟨an *unapt* quotation⟩ **2** : not accustomed and not likely ⟨*unapt* to run from danger⟩ **3** : not qualified or skilled ⟨*unapt* students⟩ — **un·apt·ly** \-ˈap-(t)lē\ *adv*

un·arm \ˌən-ˈärm, ˈən-\ *vb* : DISARM 1

un·armed \ˌən-ˈärmd, ˈən-\ *adj* : not armed or armored ⟨*unarmed* civilians⟩; *also* : not using or involving a weapon ⟨*unarmed* robbery⟩

un·asked \ˌən-ˈas(k)t, ˈən-\ *adj* **1** : not asked ⟨*unasked* questions⟩ **2** : not asked for ⟨*unasked* advice⟩

un·as·sail·able \ˌən-ə-ˈsā-lə-bəl\ *adj* : not assailable : not open to doubt, attack, or question — **un·as·sail·ably** \-blē\ *adv*

un·as·ser·tive \ˌən-ə-ˈsərt-iv\ *adj* : not assertive : MODEST, SHY

un·as·sum·ing \ˌən-ə-ˈsü-miŋ\ *adj* : not pretentious : MODEST ⟨an *unassuming* manner⟩ ⟨an *unassuming* neighborhood⟩ — **un·as·sum·ing·ly** *adv*

un·at·tached \ˌən-ə-ˈtacht\ *adj* **1** : not attached **2** : not married or engaged

un·at·trac·tive \-ˈtrak-tiv\ *adj* : not attractive : PLAIN — **un·at·trac·tive·ly** *adv* — **un·at·trac·tive·ness** *n*

un·avail·ing \ˌən-ə-ˈvā-liŋ\ *adj* : of no use : not successful : FUTILE — **un·avail·ing·ly** *adv*

un·avoid·able \ˌən-ə-ˈvòid-ə-bəl\ *adj* : not avoidable : INEVITABLE ⟨the accident was *unavoidable*⟩ — **un·avoid·ably** \-blē\ *adv*

¹**un·aware** \ˌən-ə-ˈwa(ə)r, -ˈwe(ə)r\ *adv* : UNAWARES

²**unaware** *adj* : not aware : IGNORANT — **un·aware·ness** *n*

un·awares \ˌən-ə-ˈwa(ə)rz, -ˈwe(ə)rz\ *adv* **1** : without knowing : UNINTENTIONALLY **2** : without warning : by surprise ⟨taken *unawares*⟩

un·backed \ˌən-ˈbakt, ˈən-\ *adj* **1** : not backed **2** : lacking support or aid ⟨a plan *unbacked* by the voters⟩

un·bal·ance \ˌən-ˈbal-ən(t)s\ *vb* : to put out of balance

un·bal·anced \ˌən-ˈbal-ən(t)st\ *adj* **1** : not in a state of balance **2** : not completely sane **3** : not adjusted so as to make credits equal to debits ⟨an *unbalanced* account⟩

un·bar \ˌən-ˈbär, ˈən-\ *vb* **-barred; -bar·ring** : to remove a bar from : UNBOLT

un·bear·able \ˌən-ˈbar-ə-bəl, ˈən-, -ˈber-\ *adj* : greater than can be borne ⟨*unbearable* pain⟩ — **un·bear·ably** \-blē\ *adv*

un·beat·able \ˌən-ˈbēt-ə-bəl\ *adj* : not capable of being defeated

un·beat·en \ˌən-ˈbēt-ᵊn\ *adj* **1** : not pounded, beaten, or whipped **2** : not defeated

un·beau·ti·ful \-ˈbyüt-i-fəl\ *adj* : not beautiful : UNATTRACTIVE — **un·beau·ti·ful·ly** \-f(ə-)lē\ *adv*

un·be·com·ing \ˌən-bi-ˈkəm-iŋ\ *adj* : not becoming ⟨an *unbecoming* dress⟩; *esp* : UNSUITABLE, IMPROPER ⟨*unbecoming* conduct⟩ — **un·be·com·ing·ly** *adv*

un·be·knownst \ˌən-bi-ˈnōn(t)st\ *also* **un·be·known** \-ˈnōn\ *adj* : happening without one's knowledge : UNKNOWN ⟨events *unbeknownst* to me⟩

un·be·lief \ˌən-bə-ˈlēf\ *n* : the withholding or absence of belief : DOUBT

un·be·liev·able \ˌən-bə-ˈlē-və-bəl\ *adj* **1** : too unlikely for belief ⟨an *unbelievable* story⟩ **2** : very significant or impressive ⟨made an *unbelievable* catch in center field⟩ — **un·be·liev·ably** \-blē\ *adv*

un·be·liev·er \ˌən-bə-ˈlē-vər\ *n* **1** : one who does not believe in a particular religious faith : INFIDEL **2** : one who does not believe : DOUBTER — **un·be·liev·ing** \-ˈlē-viŋ\ *adj* — **un·be·liev·ing·ly** *adv*

un·bend \ˌən-ˈbend\ *vb* **-bent** \-ˈbent\; **-bend·ing** **1** : to free from being bent : make or become straight **2** : RELAX **3**

un·bend·ing \ˌən-ˈben-diŋ\ *adj* **1** : INFLEXIBLE 2, RESOLUTE **2** : not relaxed and easy in manner : ALOOF

un·bi·ased \ˌən-ˈbī-əst, ˈən-\ *adj* : free from bias; *esp* : IMPARTIAL, UNPREJUDICED ⟨an *unbiased* opinion⟩

un·bid·den \ˌən-ˈbid-ᵊn\ *also* **un·bid** \-ˈbid\ *adj* : not bidden : UNASKED, UNINVITED ⟨she barged in *unbidden*⟩

un·bind \ˌən-ˈbīnd\ *vb* **-bound** \-ˈbaùnd\; **-bind·ing** **1** : UNFASTEN, UNTIE, LOOSE **2** : to set free : RELEASE

un·blush·ing \ˌən-ˈbləsh-iŋ\ *adj* : not blushing **2** : UNABASHED, SHAMELESS ⟨*unblushing* greed⟩ — **un·blush·ing·ly** *adv*

un·bolt \ˌən-ˈbōlt, ˈən-\ *vb* : to open or unfasten by withdrawing a bolt

un·born \ˌən-ˈbò(ə)rn\ *adj* : not born; *esp* : still to appear : FUTURE ⟨*unborn* generations⟩

un·bos·om \ˌən-ˈbúz-əm\ *vb* **1** : to give expression to : DISCLOSE, REVEAL **2** : to reveal one's thoughts or feelings

un·bound \ˌən-ˈbaùnd\ *adj* **1 a** : not fastened or tied up ⟨*unbound* hair⟩ **b** : not kept within bounds ⟨*unbound* spirit⟩ **2** : not having a binding ⟨an *unbound* book⟩

un·bound·ed \ˌən-ˈbaùn-dəd\ *adj* : having no bounds or limits ⟨*unbounded* space⟩ ⟨*unbounded* enthusiasm⟩

un·bowed \ˌən-ˈbaùd, ˈən-\ *adj* **1** : not bowed down ⟨*unbowed* heads⟩ **2** : not conquered ⟨*unbowed* by failure⟩

un·braid \ˌən-ˈbrād\ *vb* : UNRAVEL 1

un·branched \ˌən-ˈbrancht\ *adj* : free from or not divided into branches ⟨a tree with a straight *unbranched* trunk⟩ ⟨a leaf with *unbranched* veins⟩

un·bri·dled \ˌən-ˈbrīd-ᵊld\ *adj* : UNRESTRAINED, UNGOVERNED ⟨*unbridled* enthusiasm⟩

un·bro·ken \ˌən-ˈbrō-kən\ *adj* **1** : not broken : WHOLE **2** : not tamed; *esp* : not trained for use ⟨*unbroken* colts⟩ **3** : not interrupted : CONTINUOUS ⟨an *unbroken* row of trees⟩ ⟨*unbroken* sleep⟩

un·buck·le \ˌən-ˈbək-əl\ *vb* : to unfasten the buckle of (as a belt)

un·budg·ing \ˌən-ˈbəj-iŋ\ *adj* : not budging : resisting movement or change — **un·budg·ing·ly** *adv*

un·built \ˌən-ˈbilt\ *adj* **1** : not yet built ⟨an *unbuilt* house⟩ **2** : not built on ⟨an *unbuilt* plot⟩

un·bur·den \ˌən-ˈbərd-ᵊn\ *vb* **1** : to free or bring relief from a burden **2** : to free oneself from (as cares)

un·but·ton \ˌən-ˈbət-ᵊn\ *vb* : to unfasten the buttons of (as a garment)

un·but·toned \ˌən-ˈbət-ᵊnd\ *adj* **1 a** : not buttoned **b** : not provided with buttons **2** : free and unrestricted in action or expression ⟨the musician's *unbuttoned* energy⟩

un·cage \ˌən-ˈkāj, ˈən-\ *vb* : to release from or as if from a cage

un·called–for \ˌən-ˈkȯl(d)-ˌfȯ(ə)r\ *adj* **1** : not called for : UNNECESSARY **2 a** : not justified ⟨your jealousy is *uncalled-for*⟩ **b** : IMPOLITE, RUDE ⟨*uncalled-for* comments⟩

un·can·ny \ˌən-ˈkan-ē\ *adj* **1** : MYSTERIOUS **2** : being beyond what is normal ⟨an *uncanny* sense of direction⟩ — **un·can·ni·ly** \-ˈkan-ᵊl-ē\ *adv* — **un·can·ni·ness** \-ˈkan-ē-nəs\ *n*

un·cap \ˌən-ˈkap\ *vb* : to remove a cap or covering from

un·ceas·ing \ˌən-ˈsē-siŋ\ *adj* : never ceasing : CONTINUOUS, INCESSANT — **un·ceas·ing·ly** *adv*

un·cer·e·mo·ni·ous \ˌən-ˌser-ə-ˈmō-nē-əs\ *adj* : acting without or lacking ordinary courtesy : ABRUPT ⟨an *unceremonious* departure⟩ — **un·cer·e·mo·ni·ous·ly** *adv*

un·cer·tain \ˌən-ˈsərt-ᵊn, ˈən-\ *adj* **1** : not definite or fixed ⟨an *uncertain* quantity⟩ **2 a** : not sure ⟨*uncertain* of the truth⟩ **b** : not known for sure ⟨an *uncertain* claim⟩ **3** : likely to change : not dependable ⟨*uncertain* weather⟩ — **un·cer·tain·ly** *adv*

un·cer·tain·ty \ˌən-ˈsərt-ᵊn-tē\ *n* **1** : lack of certainty **2** : something that is uncertain **synonyms** see DOUBT

un·chain \ˌən-ˈchān, ˈən-\ *vb* : to free by or as if by removing a chain : set loose

un·change·able \ˌən-ˈchān-jə-bəl\ *adj* : not changing or to be changed : IMMUTABLE ⟨*unchangeable* facts⟩ — **un·change·able·ness** *n* — **un·change·ably** \-blē\ *adv*

un·chang·ing \ˌən-ˈchān-jiŋ\ *adj* : not changing or capable of change : CONSTANT ⟨*unchanging* beliefs⟩

un·charged \ˌən-ˈchärjd\ *adj* : having no electric charge

un·char·i·ta·ble \ˌən-ˈchar-ət-ə-bəl\ *adj* : not charitable; *esp* : severe in judging others ⟨*uncharitable* comments⟩ — **un·char·i·ta·ble·ness** *n* — **un·char·i·ta·bly** \-blē\ *adv*

un·chart·ed \ˌən-ˈchärt-əd\ *adj* : not recorded or located on a map, chart, or plan : UNKNOWN ⟨vast *uncharted* wilderness⟩

un·chaste \ˌən-ˈchāst\ *adj* : not chaste : lacking in chastity — **un·chas·ti·ty** \-ˈchas-tət-ē\ *n*

un·chris·tian \ˌən-ˈkris-chən\ *adj* **1** : not of the Christian faith **2 a** : not suitable to or like a Christian **b** : UNCIVILIZED, BARBAROUS

un·civ·il \ˌən-ˈsiv-əl\ *adj* **1** : not civilized : BARBAROUS **2** : lacking in courtesy : ILL-MANNERED ⟨*uncivil* remarks⟩

un·civ·i·lized \ˌən-ˈsiv-ə-ˌlīzd\ *adj* **1** : not civilized : lacking culture or refinement **2** : far from civilization : WILD

un·clad \ˌən-ˈklad\ *adj* : not clothed : UNDRESSED, NAKED

un·clasp \ˌən-ˈklasp\ *vb* : to release from a clasp

un·clas·si·fied \ˌən-ˈklas-ə-ˌfīd\ *adj* : not classified; *esp* : not requiring special treatment for purposes of security ⟨*unclassified* documents⟩

un·cle \ˈən-kəl\ *n* **1** : the brother of one's father or mother **2** : the husband of one's aunt

un·clean \ˌən-ˈklēn\ *adj* **1** : not pure and innocent : WICKED **2** : prohibited by religious law for use or contact **3** : ¹DIRTY 1, FILTHY — **un·clean·ness** \-ˈklēn-nəs\ *n*

un·clean·ly \ˌən-ˈklen-lē\ *adj* : UNCLEAN 1, DIRTY — **un·clean·li·ness** *n*

un·clench \ˌən-ˈklench\ *vb* : to open from a clenched position : RELAX ⟨*unclenched* my hands⟩

Un·cle Sam \ˌəŋ-kəl-ˈsam\ *n* **1** : the U.S. government thought of or represented as a person **2** : the American nation or people

Uncle Tom \-ˈtäm\ *n* : a black person eager to win the approval of white people and willing to cooperate with them [from *Uncle Tom,* name of a slave in the novel *Uncle Tom's Cabin* by Harriet Beecher Stowe]

un·clinch \ˌən-ˈklinch\ *vb* : UNCLENCH

un·cloak \ˌən-ˈklōk\ *vb* **1** : to remove a cloak or cover from **2** : REVEAL 1, UNMASK

un·clog \ˌən-ˈkläg, -ˈklȯg\ *vb* : to free from a difficulty or obstruction

un·close \ˌən-ˈklōz\ *vb* : ²OPEN 1a

un·clothe \ˌən-ˈklōth\ *vb* : to strip of clothes or a covering

un·coil \ˌən-ˈkȯi(ə)l, ˈən-\ *vb* : to release or become released from a coiled state : UNWIND

un·com·fort·able \ˌən-ˈkəm(p)(f)-tə(r)-bəl, -ˈkəm(p)-fə(r)t-ə-bəl, ˈən-\ *adj* **1** : causing discomfort ⟨an *uncomfortable* chair⟩ **2** : feeling discomfort : UNEASY — **un·com·fort·ably** \-blē\ *adv*

un·com·mit·ted \ˌən-kə-ˈmit-əd\ *adj* : not committed; *esp* : not pledged to a particular belief, allegiance, or program ⟨*uncommitted* voters⟩

un·com·mon \ˌən-ˈkäm-ən, ˈən-\ *adj* **1** : not ordinarily found or experienced : UNUSUAL ⟨not *uncommon* to catch a cold⟩ **2** : EXTRAORDINARY, REMARKABLE, EXCEPTIONAL ⟨has *uncommon* ability⟩ — **un·com·mon·ly** *adv* — **un·com·mon·ness** \-ən-nəs\ *n*

un·com·mu·ni·ca·tive \ˌən-kə-ˈmyü-nə-ˌkāt-iv, -ni-kət-\ *adj* : not tending to talk or give out information : RESERVED

un·com·pet·i·tive \ˌən-kəm-ˈpet-ət-iv\ *adj* : not competitive : unable to compete — **un·com·pet·i·tive·ness** *n*

un·com·plain·ing \ˌən-kəm-ˈplā-niŋ\ *adj* : not complaining : PATIENT ⟨*uncomplaining* acceptance⟩ — **un·com·plain·ing·ly** *adv*

un·com·pli·men·ta·ry \ˈən-ˌkäm-plə-ˈment-ə-rē, -ˈmen-trē\ *adj* : not complimentary ⟨an *uncomplimentary* remark⟩

un·com·pro·mis·ing \ˌən-ˈkäm-prə-ˌmī-ziŋ\ *adj* : not making or accepting a compromise : UNYIELDING — **un·com·pro·mis·ing·ly** *adv*

un·con·cern \ˌən-kən-ˈsərn\ *n* : lack of care or interest : INDIFFERENCE ⟨*unconcern* for world problems⟩

un·con·cerned \ˌən-kən-ˈsərnd\ *adj* **1** : not involved : not having a part or interest **2** : not anxious or upset : free of worry — **un·con·cern·ed·ly** \-ˈsər-nəd-lē\ *adv*

un·con·di·tion·al \ˌən-kən-ˈdish-nəl, -ˈdish-ən-ᵊl\ *adj* : not limited : ABSOLUTE, UNQUALIFIED ⟨*unconditional* surrender⟩ — **un·con·di·tion·al·ly** \-ē\ *adv*

un·con·quer·able \ˌən-ˈkäŋ-k(ə-)rə-bəl, ˈən-\ *adj* : incapable of being conquered or overcome ⟨*unconquerable* difficulties⟩ — **un·con·quer·ably** \-blē\ *adv*

un·con·scio·na·ble \ˌən-ˈkänch-(ə-)nə-bəl\ *adj* **1** : not guided or controlled by conscience ⟨an *unconscionable* villain⟩ **2** : not being in agreement with what is right or just : UNREASONABLE, EXCESSIVE — **un·con·scio·na·bly** \-blē\ *adv*

¹un·con·scious \ən-'kän-chəs, 'ən-\ *adj* **1** : not aware ⟨*unconscious* of having made a mistake⟩ **2** : having lost consciousness ⟨knocked *unconscious* by a fall⟩ **3** : not realized : not consciously done ⟨an *unconscious* mistake⟩ ⟨*unconscious* humor⟩ — **un·con·scious·ly** *adv* — **un·con·scious·ness** *n*

²unconscious *n* : the part of one's mental life of which one is not aware but which may influence behavior

un·con·sid·ered \ən-kən-'sid-ərd\ *adj* **1** : not considered or worth consideration **2** : not resulting from consideration or study ⟨*unconsidered* opinions⟩

un·con·sti·tu·tion·al \ən-kän(t)-stə-'t(y)üsh-nəl, -ən-ᵊl\ *adj* : not according to or agreeing with the constitution of a state or society — **un·con·sti·tu·tion·al·i·ty** \-ˌt(y)ü-shə-'nal-ət-ē\ *n* — **un·con·sti·tu·tion·al·ly** \-'t(y)üsh-nə-lē, -ən-ᵊl-ē\ *adv*

un·con·trol·la·ble \ən-kən-'trō-lə-bəl\ *adj* : incapable of being controlled : UNGOVERNABLE — **un·con·trol·la·bly** \-blē\ *adv*

un·con·ven·tion·al \ən-kən-'vench-nəl, -ən-ᵊl\ *adj* : not conventional : not bound by or in agreement with convention ⟨*unconventional* behavior⟩ — **un·con·ven·tion·al·i·ty** \-ˌven-chə-'nal-ət-ē\ *n* — **un·con·ven·tion·al·ly** \-'vench-nə-lē, -ən-ᵊl-ē\ *adv*

un·cork \ən-'kȯ(ə)rk, 'ən-\ *vb* **1** : to draw a cork from **2 a** : to release from a sealed or shut up state ⟨*uncork* a surprise⟩ **b** : to let go : RELEASE ⟨*uncork* a wild pitch⟩

un·count·ed \ən-'kaunt-əd\ *adj* **1** : not counted ⟨a stack of *uncounted* bills⟩ **2** : too many to be counted : INNUMERABLE

un·cou·ple \ən-'kəp-əl\ *vb* **-cou·pled; -cou·pling** \-'kəp-(ə-)liŋ\ : DISCONNECT ⟨*uncouple* railroad cars⟩

un·couth \ən-'küth\ *adj* **1** : strange, awkward, and clumsy in shape or appearance **2** : vulgar in conduct or speech : RUDE

un·cov·er \ən-'kəv-ər\ *vb* **1** : to make known : DISCLOSE, REVEAL ⟨*uncover* a plot⟩ **2** : to expose to view by removing some covering ⟨*uncover* the ruins of an ancient city⟩ **3 a** : to take the cover from ⟨*uncover* the box⟩ **b** : to remove the hat from **c** : to take off one's hat as a sign of respect

un·cov·ered \ən-'kəv-ərd\ *adj* : not covered or supplied with a covering

un·cre·at·ed \ən-krē-'āt-əd\ *adj* **1** : not occurring by creation : ETERNAL **2** : not yet created

un·cross \ən-'krȯs\ *vb* : to change from a crossed position ⟨*uncrossed* my legs⟩

un·crown \ən-'kraun\ *vb* : to take the crown from : DEPOSE, DETHRONE

unc·tion \'əŋ(k)-shən\ *n* **1** : the act of anointing as a ceremony of healing **2** : exaggerated earnestness of language or manner

unc·tu·ous \'əŋ(k)-chə-(wə)s, 'əŋ(k)sh-wəs\ *adj* **1** : smooth and greasy like an ointment : OILY **2** : too smooth, polite, and agreeable in speech or manner — **unc·tu·ous·ly** *adv* — **unc·tu·ous·ness** *n*

un·curl \ən-'kər(-ə)l, 'ən-\ *vb* : to make or become straightened out from a curled or coiled position

un·cut \ən-'kət, 'ən-\ *adj* **1** : not cut down or cut into **2** : not shaped by cutting ⟨an *uncut* diamond⟩ **3** : not having the folds of the leaves slit ⟨*uncut* books⟩ **4** : not shortened ⟨an *uncut* text⟩

un·daunt·ed \ən-'dȯnt-əd, -'dänt-\ *adj* : not discouraged or frightened : FEARLESS — **un·daunt·ed·ly** *adv*

un·de·ceive \ən-di-'sēv\ *vb* : to free from deception or error

un·de·cid·ed \ən-di-'sīd-əd\ *adj* **1** : not yet decided : not settled ⟨the question is still *undecided*⟩ **2** : not having decided : uncertain what to do ⟨still *undecided* about it⟩ — **un·de·cid·ed·ly** *adv*

un·de·mon·stra·tive \ən-di-'män(t)-strət-iv\ *adj* : not demonstrative : RESERVED

un·de·ni·able \ən-di-'nī-ə-bəl\ *adj* **1** : plainly true : INCONTESTABLE **2** : positively excellent or genuine — **un·de·ni·ably** \-blē\ *adv*

¹un·der \'ən-dər\ *adv* **1** : in or into a position below or beneath something ⟨the duck surfaced, then went *under* again⟩ **2** : below some quantity, level, or average ⟨ten dollars or *under*⟩ — often used in combination ⟨*under*played the part⟩ **3** : in or into a losing, lower, or unconscious state or condition ⟨kept my disappointment *under*⟩ ⟨put the patient *under* for surgery⟩ **4** : so as to be covered or hidden ⟨turned *under* by the plow⟩

²un·der \ˌən-dər, 'ən-\ *prep* **1** : below or beneath and topped or sheltered by ⟨*under* sunny skies⟩ ⟨*under* a tree⟩ ⟨wearing a sweater *under* my jacket⟩ **2 a** : bound by the authority or guidance of ⟨served *under* the general⟩ **b** : affected or influenced by the action or result of ⟨the disease is *under* treatment⟩ **3** : within the group or division of ⟨*under* this heading⟩ **4 a** : less or lower than (as in size, amount, or rank) ⟨all masses *under* 90 kilograms⟩ ⟨nobody *under* a colonel⟩ **b** : below the required level of ⟨*under* legal age⟩

³un·der \'ən-dər\ *adj* **1 a** : lying or placed below — often used in combination ⟨the sea's *under*currents⟩ ⟨the *under*side of a car⟩ **b** : facing or bulging downward — often used in combination ⟨the *under*surface of a leaf⟩ **2** : lower in position or authority : SUBORDINATE — often used in combination ⟨the *under*secretary of defense⟩ **3** : lower than usual, proper, or desired in amount or quality — often used in combination ⟨*under*nourished children⟩

un·der·achiev·er \ən-də-rə-'chē-vər\ *n* : one (as a student) that fails to do as well as expected

un·der·ac·tive \ən-də-'rak-tiv\ *adj* : having an abnormally low level of activity ⟨an *underactive* gland⟩

un·der·age \ən-də-'rāj\ *adj* : of less than mature or legal age

¹un·der·arm \ən-də-ˌrärm\ *adj* **1** : ²UNDERHAND **2** ⟨an *underarm* toss⟩ **2** : placed under or on the underside of the arm ⟨*underarm* seams⟩

²un·der·arm \ən-də-ˌrärm\ *adv* : with an underarm motion

³un·der·arm \'ən-də-ˌrärm\ *n* **1** : ARMPIT **2** : the part of a garment that covers the underside of the arm

un·der·bel·ly \'ən-dər-ˌbel-ē\ *n* : the underpart of a body or mass ⟨the *underbelly* of a bomber⟩; *also* : an area open to attack or damage ⟨the army's *underbelly*⟩

un·der·bid \ən-dər-'bid\ *vb* **-bid; -bid·ding** **1** : to bid less than a competing bidder **2** : to bid too low (as in cards) — **un·der·bid·der** *n*

un·der·body \'ən-dər-ˌbäd-ē\ *n* : the lower part or underside of something (as an animal or car)

un·der·bred \ən-dər-'bred\ *adj* : marked by lack of good breeding : ILL-BRED

un·der·brush \'ən-dər-ˌbrəsh\ *n* : shrubs and small trees growing among large trees : UNDERGROWTH

un·der·car·riage \'ən-dər-ˌkar-ij\ *n* **1** : a supporting structure or underside (as of an automobile) **2** : the landing gear of an airplane

U undercarriage 2

un·der·charge \ən-dər-'chärj\ *vb* : to charge too little ⟨was *undercharged* by the salesclerk⟩ — **un·der·charge** \'ən-dər-ˌchärj\ *n*

un·der·class·man \ən-dər-'klas-mən\ *n* : a student in the first or second year of a four-year high school or college

un·der·clothes \'ən-dər-ˌklō(th)z\ *n pl* : UNDERWEAR

un·der·cloth·ing \-ˌklō-thiŋ\ *n* : UNDERWEAR

un·der·coat \-ˌkōt\ *n* **1** : a coat or jacket worn under another **2** : a growth of short hair or fur partly concealed by a longer growth of usually coarse hairs ⟨a dog's *under-coat*⟩ **3** : a coat of paint under another — **undercoat** *vb*

un·der·cov·er \-ˌkəv-ər\ *adj* : acting or performed in secret ⟨an *undercover* scheme⟩; *esp* : employed or engaged in spying or secret investigation ⟨an *undercover* agent⟩ — **undercover** *adv*

un·der·cur·rent \-ˌkər-ənt, -ˌkə-rənt\ *n* **1** : a current below the upper currents or surface ⟨*undercurrents* of water⟩ **2** : a hidden current of opinion or feeling often different from the one openly shown

¹**un·der·cut** \ˌən-dər-ˈkət\ *vb* **-cut; -cut·ting** **1** : to cut away the underpart of something or material beneath something **2** : to offer to sell at lower prices than or to work for lower wages than ⟨*undercut* a competitor⟩ **3** : to strike so as to give a backspin or height to the shot ⟨a tennis player *undercutting* the ball⟩

²**un·der·cut** \ˈən-dər-ˌkət\ *n* : the action or result of undercutting

un·der·de·vel·oped \ˌən-dər-di-ˈvel-əpt\ *adj* **1** : not developed normally or enough ⟨*underdeveloped* muscles⟩ **2** : having a low level of industrial production and standard of living ⟨the *underdeveloped* nations⟩

un·der·dog \ˈən-dər-ˌdȯg\ *n* : the loser or predicted loser in a struggle

un·der·done \ˌən-dər-ˈdən\ *adj* : not thoroughly cooked : RARE

un·der·draw·ers \ˈən-dər-ˌdrȯ(-ə)rz\ *n pl* : UNDERPANTS

un·der·dress \ˌən-dər-ˈdres\ *vb* : to dress more simply or informally than is appropriate for an occasion

un·der·es·ti·mate \ˌən-də-ˈres-tə-ˌmāt\ *vb* **1** : to estimate as being less than the actual size, quantity, or number ⟨*underestimate* the cost of a new building⟩ **2** : to place too low a value on : UNDERRATE ⟨*underestimate* an opponent⟩ — **un·der·es·ti·mate** \-mət\ *n* — **un·der·es·ti·ma·tion** \-ˌres-tə-ˈmā-shən\ *n*

un·der·ex·pose \ˌən-də-rik-ˈspōz\ *vb* : to expose for less time than is needed ⟨the film was *underexposed*⟩ — **un·der·ex·po·sure** \-ˈspō-zhər\ *n*

un·der·feed \ˌən-dər-ˈfēd\ *vb* **-fed** \-ˈfed\; **-feed·ing** : to feed with too little food

un·der·foot \-ˈfu̇t\ *adv* **1** : under the feet ⟨flowers trampled *underfoot*⟩ **2** : close about one's feet : in the way ⟨a puppy always *underfoot*⟩

un·der·fur \ˈən-dər-ˌfər\ *n* : the thick soft undercoat of fur lying beneath the longer and coarser hair of a mammal

un·der·gar·ment \ˈən-dər-ˌgär-mənt\ *n* : a garment to be worn under another

un·der·gird \ˌən-dər-ˈgərd\ *vb* : to make secure : brace up : STRENGTHEN ⟨a life *undergirded* by religion⟩

un·der·go \ˌən-dər-ˈgō\ *vb* **-went** \-ˈwent\; **-gone** \-ˈgȯn *also* -ˈgän\; **-go·ing** \-ˈgō-iŋ\ **1** : ENDURE 2 ⟨*undergo* an operation⟩ **2** : to pass through : EXPERIENCE ⟨*undergoing* a change⟩

un·der·grad·u·ate \ˌən-dər-ˈgraj-(ə-)wət, -ə-ˌwāt\ *n* : a student at a college or university who has not yet received a degree

¹**un·der·ground** \ˌən-dər-ˈgrau̇nd\ *adv* **1** : below the surface of the ground ⟨an *underground* passage⟩ **2** : in or into hiding or secret operation ⟨the political party went *underground*⟩

²**un·der·ground** \ˈən-dər-ˌgrau̇nd\ *n* **1** : a space under the surface of the ground; *esp* : SUBWAY 2 **2** : a secret political group; *esp* : an organized body working in secret to overthrow a government or an occupying power

³**un·der·ground** \ˈən-dər-ˌgrau̇nd\ *adj* **1** : being, growing, operating, or located below the surface of the ground ⟨an *underground* stream⟩ **2** : conducted secretly

Underground Railroad *n* : a system of cooperation in the U.S. before 1863 by which slaves were secretly helped to reach the North or Canada

un·der·growth \ˈən-dər-ˌgrōth\ *n* : low growth on the

floor of a forest including seedlings and saplings, shrubs, and herbs

¹**un·der·hand** \ˈən-dər-ˌhand\ *adv* **1** : in an underhand or secret manner **2** : with an underhand motion ⟨throw *underhand*⟩

²**underhand** *adj* **1** : done in secret or so as to deceive : SLY ⟨*underhand* methods⟩ **2** : performed with the hand kept below the level of the shoulder ⟨an *underhand* pitch⟩

un·der·hand·ed \ˌən-dər-ˈhan-dəd\ *adj or adv* : ¹UNDERHAND, ²UNDERHAND 1 — **un·der·hand·ed·ly** *adv* — **un·der·hand·ed·ness** *n*

un·der·lay \ˌən-dər-ˈlā\ *vb* **-laid** \-ˈlād\; **-lay·ing** **1** : to cover, line, or cross the bottom of ⟨shingles *underlaid* with tar paper⟩ **2** : to raise or hold up by something laid under — **un·der·lay** \ˈən-dər-ˌlā\ *n*

un·der·lie \ˌən-dər-ˈlī\ *vb* **-lay** \-ˈlā\; **-lain** \-ˈlān\; **-ly·ing** \-ˈlī-iŋ\ **1** : to lie or be located under **2** : to form the foundation of : SUPPORT ⟨ideas *underlying* the revolution⟩

un·der·line \ˈən-dər-ˌlīn, ˌən-dər-ˈlīn\ *vb* **1** : to draw a line under : UNDERSCORE **2** : EMPHASIZE — **un·der·line** \ˈən-dər-ˌlīn\ *n*

un·der·ling \ˈən-dər-liŋ\ *n* : one who is under the orders of another : SUBORDINATE

un·der·ly·ing \ˌən-dər-ˌlī-iŋ\ *adj* **1** : lying under or below ⟨the *underlying* rock⟩ **2** : ¹FUNDAMENTAL 1

un·der·mine \ˌən-dər-ˈmīn\ *vb* **1** : to dig out or wear away the earth beneath ⟨*undermine* a wall⟩ **2** : to weaken or ruin secretly or gradually ⟨*undermine* a government⟩

un·der·most \ˈən-dər-ˌmōst\ *adj* : lowest in position compared to others — **undermost** *adv*

¹**un·der·neath** \ˌən-dər-ˈnēth\ *prep* **1** : right under ⟨wore their bathing suits *underneath* their clothes⟩ **2** : under the control of

²**underneath** *adv* **1** : under or below an object or an outside part ⟨soaked through the jacket to the shirt *underneath*⟩ **2** : on the lower side ⟨a pot blackened *underneath*⟩

un·der·nour·ished \ˌən-dər-ˈnər-isht, -ˈnə-risht\ *adj* : supplied with too little food for health and growth — **un·der·nour·ish·ment** \-ˈnər-ish-mənt, -ˈnə-rish-\ *n*

un·der·pants \ˈən-dər-ˌpan(t)s\ *n pl* : short or long pants worn under an outer garment

un·der·part \-ˌpärt\ *n* : a part lying on the lower side (as of a bird or mammal)

un·der·pass \-ˌpas\ *n* : a passage underneath something (as for a road passing under another road)

un·der·pay \ˌən-dər-ˈpā\ *vb* **-paid** \-ˈpād\; **-pay·ing** : to pay too little

un·der·pin \-ˈpin\ *vb* **1** : to give support to ⟨*underpin* an argument with evidence⟩ **2** : to form part of, strengthen, or replace the foundation of ⟨*underpin* a structure⟩

underpass

un·der·pin·ning \ˈən-dər-ˌpin-iŋ\ *n* **1** : the foundation used for support of a structure **2** : ¹PROP, SUPPORT **3** : a person's legs — usually used in plural

un·der·play \ˌən-dər-ˈplā\ *vb* : to handle carefully; *esp* : to play a role without much force

un·der·priv·i·leged \-ˈpriv-(ə-)lijd\ *adj* : having fewer privileges than others : POOR

\ə\ **abut**	\au̇\ **out**	\i\ **tip**	\ȯ\ **saw**	\u̇\ **foot**
\ər\ **further**	\ch\ **chin**	\ī\ **life**	\ȯi\ **coin**	\y\ **yet**
\a\ **mat**	\e\ **pet**	\j\ **job**	\th\ **thin**	\yü\ **few**
\ā\ **take**	\ē\ **easy**	\ŋ\ **sing**	\th\ **this**	\yu̇\ **cure**
\ä\ **cot, cart**	\g\ **go**	\ō\ **bone**	\ü\ **food**	\zh\ **vision**

un·der·pro·duc·tion \-prə-'dək-shən\ *n* : the production of less than enough to satisfy the demand or of less than the usual supply

un·der·rate \ˌən-də(r)-'rāt\ *vb* : to rate too low : UNDERVALUE

un·der·score \'ən-dər-ˌskō(ə)r, -ˌskó(ə)r\ *vb* **1** : to draw a line under : UNDERLINE **2** : EMPHASIZE — **underscore** *n*

un·der·sea \'ən-dər-ˌsē\ *adj* **1** : being or carried on under the sea or under the surface of the sea ⟨*undersea* oil deposits⟩ ⟨*undersea* warfare⟩ **2** : designed for use under the surface of the sea ⟨*undersea* fleet⟩

un·der·sec·re·tary \ˌən-dər-'sek-rə-ˌter-ē\ *n* : a secretary right under a principal secretary ⟨*undersecretary* of state⟩

un·der·sell \ˌən-dər-'sel\ *vb* **-sold** \-'sōld\; **-sell·ing** : to sell articles cheaper than ⟨*undersell* a competitor⟩

un·der·shirt \'ən-dər-ˌshərt\ *n* : a collarless undergarment for the upper body

un·der·shorts \-ˌshórts\ *n pl* : underpants for men or boys

un·der·side \'ən-dər-ˌsīd, ˌən-dər-'sīd\ *n* : the side or part lying underneath

un·der·signed \'ən-dər-ˌsīnd\ *n, pl* **undersigned** : one who signs his or her name at the end of a document ⟨the *undersigned* testifies⟩ ⟨the *undersigned* all agree⟩

un·der·sized \ˌən-dər-'sīzd\ *adj* : smaller than is usual or standard ⟨*undersized* fruit⟩

un·der·skirt \'ən-dər-ˌskərt\ *n* : a skirt worn under an outer skirt; *esp* : ¹PETTICOAT

un·der·stand \ˌən-dər-'stand\ *vb* **-stood** \-'stúd\; **-stand·ing** **1 a** : to get the meaning of : COMPREHEND **b** : to have thorough acquaintance with ⟨*understand* the arts⟩ **2** : to have reason to believe : GATHER, INFER ⟨I *understand* that they will arrive today⟩ **3** : to take as meaning something not openly made known : INTERPRET, EXPLAIN ⟨*understand* the letter to be a refusal⟩ **4** : to have a sympathetic attitude ⟨my cousin doesn't *understand* about these things⟩ **5** : to supply in thought as if expressed ⟨"to be married" is commonly *understood* after the word "engaged"⟩ — **un·der·stand·able** \-'stan-də-bəl\ *adj* — **un·der·stand·ably** \-blē\ *adv*

¹**un·der·stand·ing** \ˌən-dər-'stan-diŋ\ *n* **1** : knowledge and ability to judge : INTELLIGENCE ⟨a person of *understanding*⟩ **2 a** : agreement of opinion or feeling **b** : something agreed to by both sides and entered into silently or without ceremony ⟨an *understanding* between two nations over trade⟩ **3** : one's belief about something based upon what is known **4** : SYMPATHY

²**understanding** *adj* : having or showing understanding : TOLERANT, SYMPATHETIC ⟨you seem very *understanding*⟩ — **un·der·stand·ing·ly** \-diŋ-lē\ *adv*

un·der·state \ˌən-dər-'stāt\ *vb* **1** : to represent as less than is the case ⟨*understate* taxable income⟩ **2** : to state mildly especially on purpose — **un·der·state·ment** \-mənt\ *n*

un·der·stat·ed \ˌən-dər-'stāt-əd\ *adj* : expressed or done in a quiet or simple fashion

un·der·stood \ˌən-dər-'stúd\ *adj* **1** : fully known **2** : agreed upon **3** : IMPLICIT 1

un·der·sto·ry \'ən-dər-ˌstōr-ē, -ˌstór-\ *n* : the layer of plants and especially the trees and shrubs between the forest canopy and the ground cover

un·der·study \'ən-dər-ˌstəd-ē, ˌən-dər-'stəd-ē\ *vb* : to study another actor's part in order to be his or her substitute in an emergency — **understudy** *n*

un·der·sur·face \'ən-dər-ˌsər-fəs\ *n* : UNDERSIDE

un·der·take \ˌən-dər-'tāk\ *vb* **-took** \-'túk\; **-tak·en** \-'tā-kən\; **-tak·ing** **1** : to take upon oneself as a task : enter upon ⟨*undertake* a journey⟩ **2** : to take on as a duty : AGREE, CONTRACT ⟨*undertake* to deliver a package⟩

un·der·tak·er \'ən-dər-ˌtā-kər\ *n* : a person whose business is to prepare the dead for burial or cremation and to take charge of funerals

un·der·tak·ing \'ən-dər-ˌtā-kiŋ, ˌən-dər-'tā-kiŋ; *sense 1b is* 'ən-dər-ˌtā-kiŋ *only*\ *n* **1 a** : the act of a person who undertakes something **b** : the business of an undertaker **2** : something undertaken

un·der·throw \-ˌthrō\ *vb* : to throw (a ball or pass) short of the intended receiver in football

un·der·tone \'ən-dər-ˌtōn\ *n* **1** : a low or quiet tone **2** : a faint color as seen through and changing another color

un·der·tow \'ən-dər-ˌtō\ *n* : a current beneath the surface of the water that moves away from or along the shore while the surface water above it moves toward the shore

un·der·val·ue \ˌən-dər-'val-yü\ *vb* **1** : to value below the real worth **2** : to set little value on — **un·der·val·u·a·tion** \-ˌval-yə-'wā-shən\ *n*

un·der·wa·ter \'ən-dər-ˌwót-ər, -ˌwät-\ *adj* : lying, growing, worn, performed, or operating below the surface of the water ⟨*underwater* plants⟩ ⟨an *underwater* cave⟩ — **un·der·wa·ter** \-'wót-, -'wät-\ *adv*

under way *adv* **1** : in or into motion ⟨a ship getting *under way*⟩ **2** : in progress ⟨preparations are *under way*⟩

un·der·wear \'ən-dər-ˌwa(ə)r, -ˌwe(ə)r\ *n* : clothing or an article of clothing worn next to the skin and under other clothing

un·der·weight \ˌən-dər-'wāt\ *adj* : weighing less than what is normal, average, or necessary

underwent *past of* UNDERGO

un·der·wood \'ən-dər-ˌwúd\ *n* : UNDERBRUSH

un·der·world \'ən-dər-ˌwərld\ *n* **1** : the place of the souls of the dead **2** : the side of the earth opposite to one **3** : the world of organized crime

un·der·write \'ən-də(r)-ˌrīt, ˌən-də(r)-'rīt\ *vb* **-wrote** \-ˌrōt, -'rōt\; **-writ·ten** \-ˌrit-ᵊn, -'rit-ᵊn\; **-writ·ing** \-ˌrīt-iŋ, -'rīt-\ **1** : to write under or at the end of something else **2** : to set one's name to (an insurance policy) and thereby agree to insure against specified loss or damage **3** : to agree to **4 a** : to agree to purchase (as security issue) usually on a fixed date at a fixed price with a plan of distribution to the public **b** : to guarantee financial support of ⟨*underwrite* an expedition⟩ — **un·der·writ·er** \'ən-də(r)-ˌrīt-ər\ *n*

un·de·sir·able \ˌən-di-'zī-rə-bəl\ *adj* : not desirable : UNWANTED — **un·de·sir·abil·i·ty** \-ˌzī-rə-ˌbil-ət-ē\ *n* — **undesirable** *n* — **un·de·sir·able·ness** \-'zī-rə-bəl-nəs\ *n* — **un·de·sir·ably** \-blē\ *adv*

un·de·vi·at·ing \ˌən-'dē-vē-ˌāt-iŋ, 'ən-\ *adj* : keeping a true course : UNSWERVING

un·dies \'ən-dēz\ *n pl* : UNDERWEAR; *esp* : women's underwear

un·di·rect·ed \ˌən-də-'rek-təd, -ˌdī-\ *adj* : not directed ⟨*undirected* efforts⟩

un·do \ˌən-'dü, 'ən-\ *vb* **-did** \-'did\; **-done** \-'dən\; **-do·ing** \-'dü-iŋ\ **1** : to make or become unfastened or loosened : OPEN, UNTIE ⟨*undo* a knot⟩ **2** : to destroy the effect of : NULLIFY, REVERSE **3 a** : to cause the ruin of ⟨your stubbornness *undid* you⟩ ⟨*undone* by greed⟩ **b** : to disturb the calmness of : UPSET ⟨she's come *undone*⟩ — **un·do·er** *n*

un·do·ing \ˌən-'dü-iŋ\ *n* **1** : an act or instance of unfastening **2 a** : ¹RUIN 1 ⟨parental neglect helped lead to their *undoing*⟩ **b** : a cause of ruin ⟨my quick temper was my *undoing*⟩ **3** : REVERSAL, ANNULMENT

un·done \ˌən-'dən\ *adj* : not done ⟨an *undone* task⟩

un·doubt·ed \ˌən-'daút-əd\ *adj* : not doubted or open to doubt : CERTAIN ⟨*undoubted* proof of guilt⟩ — **un·doubt·ed·ly** *adv*

un·drape \ˌən-'drāp, 'ən-\ *vb* : to strip of drapery : UNCOVER, UNVEIL

un·dreamed \-'drem(p)t, -'drēmd\ *also* **un·dreamt** \-'drem(p)t\ *adj* : not dreamed : not thought of ⟨advances in science *undreamed* of a few years ago⟩

¹**un·dress** \ˌən-'dres\ *vb* : to remove the clothes or covering of : STRIP, DISROBE

²**undress** *n* **1** : ordinary dress **2** : a state of nudity

un·dressed \,ən-'drest, 'ən-\ *adj* **1** : partially dressed or wearing clothing that is ordinary or unsuitable **2** : not fully processed or finished ⟨*undressed* hides⟩ **3** : not cared for or tended ⟨an *undressed* wound⟩ ⟨*undressed* fields⟩

un·due \,ən-'d(y)ü\ *adj* **1** : not due **2** : EXCESSIVE ⟨*undue* profit⟩

un·du·lant \'ən-jə-lənt, 'ən-d(y)ə-\ *adj* : rising and falling in waves

undulant fever *n* : a human disease that is caused by a bacterium and is marked by weakness, chills, weight loss, and a fever that comes and goes and is passed on by contact with infected domestic animals

un·du·late \'ən-jə-,lāt, 'ən-d(y)ə-\ *vb* **-lat·ed; -lat·ing** **1** : to form or move in waves : FLUCTUATE **2** : to rise and fall in volume, pitch, or rhythm **3** : to present a wavy appearance [from Latin *undula* "small wave," derived from earlier *unda* "wave"]

un·du·la·tion \,ən-jə-'lā-shən, ,ən-d(y)ə-\ *n* **1** : the action of undulating **2** : a wavy appearance or form : WAVINESS

un·du·ly \,ən-'d(y)ü-lē, 'ən-\ *adv* : in an undue manner; *esp* : EXCESSIVELY ⟨*unduly* upset⟩

un·dy·ing \,ən-'dī-iŋ\ *adj* : not dying : IMMORTAL, PERPETUAL ⟨*undying* gratitude⟩

un·earned \,ən-'ərnd, 'ən-\ *adj* : not gained by labor, service, or skill ⟨*unearned* income⟩

un·earth \,ən-'ərth, 'ən-\ *vb* **1** : to drive or draw from the earth : dig up ⟨*unearth* buried treasure⟩ **2** : to bring to light : DISCOVER ⟨*unearth* a secret⟩

un·earth·ly \,ən-'ərth-lē, 'ən-\ *adj* **1** : not of or belonging to the earth ⟨*unearthly* terrain⟩ **2** : SUPERNATURAL 2, WEIRD, TERRIFYING ⟨an *unearthly* scream⟩ — **un·earth·li·ness** *n*

un·easy \,ən-'ē-zē\ *adj* **1** : not easy in manner : AWKWARD ⟨*uneasy* among strangers⟩ **2** : disturbed by pain or worry : RESTLESS ⟨rain made the crew *uneasy*⟩ — **un·eas·i·ly** \-'ēz-ə-lē\ *adv* — **un·eas·i·ness** \-'ē-zē-nəs\ *n*

un·ed·u·cat·ed \,ən-'ej-ə-,kāt-əd\ *adj* : seriously lacking in education and especially in formal schooling **synonyms** see IGNORANT

un·em·ploy·able \,ən-im-'ploi-ə-bəl\ *adj* : not capable of being employed; *esp* : not capable of holding a job — **unemployable** *n*

un·em·ployed \,ən-im-'ploid\ *adj* **1** : not being used ⟨*unemployed* tools⟩ **2** : not employed : having no job ⟨*unemployed* workers⟩ — **unemployed** *n*

un·em·ploy·ment \,ən-im-'ploi-mənt\ *n* : the state of being out of work

un·end·ing \,ən-'en-diŋ, 'ən-\ *adj* : having no ending : ENDLESS — **un·end·ing·ly** *adv*

un·equal \,ən-'ē-kwəl, 'ən-\ *adj* **1 a** : not of the same measurement, quantity, or number as another **b** : not like or not the same as another in value or worth **2** : ¹VARIABLE 3, UNEVEN **3** : badly balanced or matched ⟨an *unequal* fight⟩ **4** : INADEQUATE, INSUFFICIENT ⟨*unequal* to the task⟩ — **un·equal·ly** \-kwə-lē\ *adv*

un·equaled *or* **un·equalled** \,ən-'ē-kwəld, 'ən-\ *adj* : not equaled : UNPARALLELED ⟨an artist of *unequaled* talent⟩

un·equiv·o·cal \,ən-i-'kwiv-ə-kəl\ *adj* : leaving no doubt : CLEAR, UNAMBIGUOUS ⟨an *unequivocal* refusal⟩ — **un·equiv·o·cal·ly** \-k(ə-)lē\ *adv*

un·err·ing \,ən-'e(ə)r-iŋ, -'ər-, 'ən-\ *adj* : making no errors : CERTAIN, UNFAILING — **un·err·ing·ly** *adv*

un·even \,ən-'ē-vən, 'ən-\ *adj* **1** : not even : not level or smooth : RUGGED, RAGGED ⟨large *uneven* teeth⟩ ⟨*uneven* handwriting⟩ **2** : varying from the straight or parallel **3** : not constant : IRREGULAR ⟨*uneven* earnings⟩ **4** : varying in quality ⟨an *uneven* performance⟩ — **un·even·ly** *adv* — **un·even·ness** *n*

un·event·ful \,ən-i-'vent-fəl\ *adj* : not eventful : lacking happenings that are interesting or worth noting ⟨an *uneventful* vacation⟩ — **un·event·ful·ly** \-fə-lē\ *adv*

un·ex·am·pled \,ən-ig-'zam-pəld\ *adj* : having no example or match : UNPRECEDENTED ⟨an *unexampled* record of achievement⟩

un·ex·cep·tion·able \,ən-ik-'sep-sh(ə-)nə-bəl\ *adj* : UNIMPEACHABLE

un·ex·pect·ed \,ən-ik-'spek-təd\ *adj* : not expected : UNFORESEEN ⟨an *unexpected* happening⟩ — **un·ex·pect·ed·ly** *adv* — **un·ex·pect·ed·ness** *n*

un·fad·ing \,ən-'fād-iŋ\ *adj* **1** : not losing color or freshness **2** : not losing value or effectiveness — **un·fad·ing·ly** *adv*

un·fail·ing \,ən-'fā-liŋ, 'ən-\ *adj* **1** : not likely to fail : CONSTANT, UNFLAGGING ⟨*unfailing* support⟩ **2** : not likely to run out or be used up : EVERLASTING, INEXHAUSTIBLE ⟨an *unfailing* supply⟩ **3** : INFALLIBLE 2 ⟨the *unfailing* mark of an amateur⟩ — **un·fail·ing·ly** *adv*

un·fair \,ən-'fa(ə)r, 'ən-, -'fe(ə)r\ *adj* **1** : not fair, honest, or just : UNJUST, DISHONEST ⟨an *unfair* trial⟩ **2** : not fair in doing business ⟨*unfair* to workers⟩ — **un·fair·ly** *adv* — **un·fair·ness** *n*

un·faith·ful \,ən-'fāth-fəl, 'ən-\ *adj* **1** : not observing vows, allegiance, or duty : DISLOYAL ⟨an *unfaithful* friend⟩ **2** : not faithful to marriage vows **3** : INACCURATE ⟨an *unfaithful* translation⟩ — **un·faith·ful·ly** \-fə-lē\ *adv* — **un·faith·ful·ness** *n*

un·fa·mil·iar \,ən-fə-'mil-yər\ *adj* **1** : not well-known : STRANGE ⟨an *unfamiliar* place⟩ **2** : not well acquainted ⟨*unfamiliar* with the subject⟩ — **un·fa·mil·iar·i·ty** \-,mil-'yar-ət-ē, -,mil-ē-'(y)ar-\ *n*

un·fas·ten \,ən-'fas-ᵊn\ *vb* : to make loose: as **a** : UNPIN, UNBUCKLE **b** : UNDO 1 ⟨*unfasten* a button⟩ **c** : DETACH ⟨*unfasten* the boat from its moorings⟩

un·fath·om·able \,ən-'fath-ə-mə-bəl\ *adj* : not capable of being fathomed: **a** : IMMEASURABLE **b** : impossible to understand

un·fa·vor·able \,ən-'fāv-(ə-)rə-bəl\ *adj* **1** : expressing disapproval ⟨*unfavorable* comments⟩ **2** : likely to make difficult or unpleasant ⟨*unfavorable* weather for a camping trip⟩ — **un·fa·vor·ably** \-blē\ *adv*

un·feel·ing \,ən-'fē-liŋ\ *adj* **1** : lacking feeling : INSENSATE **2** : lacking kindness or sympathy : HARDHEARTED, CRUEL — **un·feel·ing·ly** *adv* — **un·feel·ing·ness** *n*

un·feigned \,ən-'fānd\ *adj* : not false or pretended : GENUINE ⟨an *unfeigned* interest in people⟩ — **un·feigned·ly** \-'fā-nəd-lē, -'fān-dlē\ *adv*

un·fet·ter \,ən-'fet-ər\ *vb* : to free from fetters ⟨*unfetter* the prisoner⟩

un·fil·ial \,ən-'fil-ē-əl, 'ən-, -'fil-yəl\ *adj* : not observing the duties of a child to a parent — **un·fil·ial·ly** *adv*

un·fin·ished \,ən-'fin-isht\ *adj* : not finished; *esp* : not brought to the desired state ⟨*unfinished* furniture⟩

¹**un·fit** \,ən-'fit\ *adj* **1** : UNSUITABLE ⟨food that is *unfit* to eat⟩ **2** : not qualified : INCAPABLE, INCOMPETENT ⟨removed *unfit* candidates by testing⟩ **3** : physically or mentally unhealthy ⟨*unfit* for army service⟩

²**unfit** *vb* : to make unfit : DISABLE, DISQUALIFY

un·flag·ging \,ən-'flag-iŋ\ *adj* **1** : not flagging : TIRELESS ⟨*unflagging* enthusiasm⟩ **2** : UNRELENTING 2 — **un·flag·ging·ly** *adv*

un·flap·pa·ble \,ən-'flap-ə-bəl\ *adj* : not easily upset or panicked : unusually calm

un·fledged \,ən-'flejd, 'ən-\ *adj* **1** : not feathered or ready for flight **2** : not fully developed : IMMATURE ⟨an *unfledged* writer⟩

\ə\ **abut**	\au̇\ **out**	\i\ **tip**	\ȯ\ **saw**	\u̇\ **foot**
\ər\ **further**	\ch\ **chin**	\ī\ **life**	\ȯi\ **coin**	\y\ **yet**
\a\ **mat**	\e\ **pet**	\j\ **job**	\th\ **thin**	\yü\ **few**
\ā\ **take**	\ē\ **easy**	\ŋ\ **sing**	\t̲h̲\ **this**	\yu̇\ **cure**
\ä\ **cot, cart**	\g\ **go**	\ō\ **bone**	\ü\ **food**	\zh\ **vision**

un·flinch·ing \ˌən-ˈflin-chiŋ\ adj : not flinching or shrinking : STEADFAST — **un·flinch·ing·ly** adv

un·fold \ˌən-ˈfōld\ vb **1 a** : to spread or cause to spread or straighten out from a folded position or arrangement ⟨unfolded the map⟩ **b** : UNWRAP **2** : ²BLOOM 1 **3** : DEVELOP 1a ⟨as the story unfolds⟩ **4** : to open out or cause to open out gradually to the view or understanding ⟨new technology unfolds before us⟩

un·for·get·ta·ble \ˌən-fər-ˈget-ə-bəl\ adj : not to be forgotten : lasting in memory — **un·for·get·ta·bly** \-blē\ adv

un·formed \ˌən-ˈfȯ(ə)rmd\ adj **1** : not arranged in regular shape, order, or relations; esp : SHAPELESS **2** : IMMATURE, UNDEVELOPED ⟨an unformed thought⟩

¹un·for·tu·nate \ˌən-ˈfȯrch-(ə-)nət\ adj **1 a** : not fortunate : UNLUCKY **b** : showing, accompanied by, or resulting in misfortune ⟨an unfortunate experience⟩ ⟨unfortunate investments⟩ **2 a** : UNSUITABLE, INFELICITOUS ⟨an unfortunate choice of words⟩ **b** : DEPLORABLE 1 ⟨an unfortunate lack of taste⟩ — **un·for·tu·nate·ly** adv

²unfortunate n : an unfortunate person

un·found·ed \ˌən-ˈfaùn-dəd, ˈən-\ adj : lacking a sound base : GROUNDLESS ⟨unfounded suspicions⟩

un·fre·quent·ed \ˌən-frē-ˈkwent-əd, ˌən-ˈfrē-kwənt-, ˈən-\ adj : not often visited or traveled over

un·friend \ˌən-ˈfrend\ vb : to remove (someone) from a list of designated friends on a person's social networking website

un·friend·ly \ˌən-ˈfren-(d)lē\ adj **1** : not friendly or kind : HOSTILE ⟨an unfriendly greeting⟩ **2** : not agreeable ⟨an unfriendly environment⟩ — **un·friend·li·ness** n

un·fruit·ful \ˌən-ˈfrüt-fəl\ adj **1** : not bearing fruit or offspring **2** : not producing a desired result ⟨unfruitful efforts⟩

un·furl \ˌən-ˈfər(-ə)l\ vb : to loose from a furled state : open or spread : UNFOLD ⟨unfurl sails⟩ ⟨unfurl a flag⟩

un·gain·ly \ˌən-ˈgān-lē\ adj : CLUMSY 1a, AWKWARD — **un·gain·li·ness** n

un·glued \ˌən-ˈglüd\ adj **1** : emotionally upset : DISTRAUGHT **2** : in a state of complete failure

un·god·ly \ˌən-ˈgäd-lē also -ˈgȯd-\ adj **1 a** : denying God : IMPIOUS, IRRELIGIOUS **b** : SINFUL, WICKED **2** : OUTRAGEOUS ⟨gets up at an ungodly hour⟩ — **un·god·li·ness** n

un·gov·ern·able \ˌən-ˈgəv-ər-nə-bəl\ adj : not capable of being governed, guided, or controlled ⟨an ungovernable temper⟩ **synonyms** see UNRULY

un·gra·cious \ˌən-ˈgrā-shəs\ adj **1** : not courteous : RUDE ⟨ungracious treatment⟩ **2** : not pleasing : DISAGREEABLE ⟨an ungracious task⟩ — **un·gra·cious·ly** adv — **un·gra·cious·ness** n

un·grate·ful \ˌən-ˈgrāt-fəl, ˈən-\ adj **1** : not thankful for favors ⟨an ungrateful child⟩ **2** : not pleasing : DISAGREEABLE ⟨an ungrateful task⟩ — **un·grate·ful·ly** \-fə-lē\ adv — **un·grate·ful·ness** n

un·ground·ed \ˌən-ˈgraùn-dəd\ adj **1** : UNFOUNDED, BASELESS **2** : not instructed or informed

un·guard·ed \ˌən-ˈgärd-əd\ adj **1** : open to attack : UNPROTECTED **2** : not cautious : UNWARY ⟨unguarded comments⟩ — **un·guard·ed·ly** adv

un·guent \ˈəŋ-gwənt, ˈən-; ˈən-jənt\ n : a soothing or healing salve : OINTMENT

¹un·gu·late \ˈəŋ-gyə-lət, ˈən-, -ˌlāt\ adj **1** : having hooves **2** : of or relating to the ungulates

²ungulate n : any of a group of typically plant-eating 4-footed hoofed mammals (as cows, sheep, pigs, horses, camels, and rhinoceroses)

un·hal·lowed \ˌən-ˈhal-ōd, ˈən-\ adj : UNHOLY, UNCONSECRATED ⟨unhallowed ground⟩

un·hand \ˌən-ˈhand, ˈən-\ vb : to remove the hand from : let go

un·hand·some \ˌən-ˈhan(t)-səm\ adj : not handsome: as **a** : not beautiful : HOMELY **b** : UNBECOMING, UNSEEMLY ⟨an unhandsome habit⟩ **c** : lacking in courtesy or taste

: RUDE ⟨used unhandsome language⟩ — **un·hand·some·ly** adv

un·handy \ˌən-ˈhan-dē\ adj **1** : hard to handle : INCONVENIENT **2** : lacking in skill : AWKWARD

un·hap·py \ˌən-ˈhap-ē\ adj **1** : not fortunate : UNLUCKY ⟨the result of an unhappy mistake⟩ **2** : not cheerful : SAD, MISERABLE **3** : INAPPROPRIATE ⟨an unhappy color combination⟩ — **un·hap·pi·ly** \-ˈhap-ə-lē\ adv — **un·hap·pi·ness** \-ˈhap-i-nəs\ n

un·har·ness \ˌən-ˈhär-nəs\ vb : to remove a harness from ⟨unharness a horse⟩

un·health·ful \ˌən-ˈhelth-fəl\ adj : UNHEALTHY 1

un·healthy \ˌən-ˈhel-thē\ adj **1** : not conducive to good health : not healthful ⟨an unhealthy climate⟩ **2** : not in good health : SICKLY, DISEASED **3 a** : RISKY, UNSOUND **b** : INJURIOUS, BAD — **un·health·i·ly** \-thə-lē\ adv — **un·health·i·ness** \-thē-nəs\ n

un·heard \ˌən-ˈhərd\ adj **1** : not heard by the ear **2** : not given a hearing

un·heard–of \-ˌəv, -ˌäv\ adj : previously unknown : UNPRECEDENTED ⟨moving at unheard-of speeds⟩

un·hinge \ˌən-ˈhinj\ vb **1** : UNSETTLE 2, DISRUPT ⟨a mind unhinged by grief⟩ **2** : to remove (as a door) from the hinges

un·hitch \ˌən-ˈhich\ vb : to free from or as if from being hitched

un·ho·ly \ˌən-ˈhō-lē, ˈən-\ adj : not holy : PROFANE, WICKED — **un·ho·li·ness** n

un·hook \ˌən-ˈhùk\ vb **1** : to remove from a hook **2** : to unfasten the hooks of

un·horse \ˌən-ˈhȯ(ə)rs\ vb : to cause to fall from a horse : OVERTHROW, UNSEAT

un·hur·ried \ˌən-ˈhər-ēd, -ˈhə-rēd\ adj : not hurried : LEISURELY ⟨an unhurried pace⟩ — **un·hur·ried·ly** adv

uni·cam·er·al \ˌyü-ni-ˈkam-(ə-)rəl\ adj : having or consisting of a single legislative body

uni·cel·lu·lar \ˌyü-ni-ˈsel-yə-lər\ adj : having or consisting of a single cell ⟨unicellular microorganisms⟩

uni·corn \ˈyü-nə-ˌkȯ(ə)rn\ n : an imaginary animal generally represented with the body and head of a horse and a single horn in the middle of the forehead [Middle English unicorne "unicorn," from early French unicorne (same meaning), derived from Latin unicornis "having one horn," from uni- "one" and cornu "horn" — related to ³CORN, UNIVERSE]

uni·cy·cle \ˈyü-ni-ˌsī-kəl\ n : a vehicle having a single wheel and usually moved forward by pedals

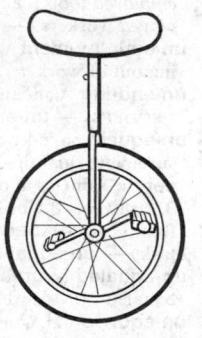

unicycle

¹uni·form \ˈyü-nə-ˌfȯrm\ adj **1** : not varying ⟨uniform temperature⟩ **2** : of the same form with others ⟨uniform procedures in the courts⟩ — **uni·form·ly** adv

²uniform vb : to dress with a uniform

³uniform n : uniform dress worn by members of a particular group (as an army or a police force)

uni·for·mi·tar·i·an·ism \ˌyü-nə-ˌfȯr-mə-ˈter-ē-ə-ˌniz-əm\ n : a principle in geology that states that processes going on in nature at the present time can explain geological changes in the past

uni·for·mi·ty \ˌyü-nə-ˈfȯr-mət-ē\ n, pl **-ties** : the quality or state or an instance of being uniform

uniform resource locator n : URL

uni·fy \ˈyü-nə-ˌfī\ vb **-fied; -fy·ing** : UNITE 1a — **uni·fi·ca·tion** \ˌyü-nə-fə-ˈkā-shən\ n

uni·lat·er·al \ˌyü-ni-ˈlat-ə-rəl, -ˈla-trəl\ adj : done or carried out by only one of two or more parties ⟨unilateral disarmament⟩ — **uni·lat·er·al·ly** \-ē\ adv

un·im·peach·able \ˌən-im-ˈpē-chə-bəl\ *adj* : not impeachable : not to be doubted or questioned : IRREPROACHABLE ⟨an *unimpeachable* reputation⟩ ⟨information from an *unimpeachable* source⟩ — **un·im·peach·ably** \-blē\ *adv*

un·in·hib·it·ed \ˌən-in-ˈhib-ət-əd\ *adj* : not inhibited; *esp* : marked by an open showing of feelings and informal behavior ⟨an *uninhibited* party⟩ — **un·in·hib·it·ed·ly** *adv*

un·in·stall \ˌən-in-ˈstòl\ *vb* : to remove (software) from a computer system especially by using a specially designed program

un·in·tel·li·gent \ˌən-in-ˈtel-ə-jənt\ *adj* : lacking intelligence : UNWISE, STUPID ⟨an *unintelligent* use of your money⟩ — **un·in·tel·li·gent·ly** *adv*

un·in·ter·est·ed \ˌən-ˈint-ə-ˌres-təd, ˈən-; -ˈin-trəs-, -ˌtres-; -ˈint-ərs-, -ˈint-ə-rəs-\ *adj* : not interested : not paying attention

union \ˈyün-yən\ *n* **1 a** : an act or instance of uniting two or more things into one ⟨the *union* of Scotland and England⟩ ⟨*union* of a man and woman in marriage⟩ **b** : COMBINATION 1 ⟨the *union* of science and technology to solve modern problems⟩ **2 a** : something (as a nation) formed by a combining of parts or members **b** : LABOR UNION **c** : the mathematical set that contains all of the elements which are included in at least one of two or more sets ⟨the *union* of the set {1, 2, 3} and the set {3, 4, 5} is the set {1, 2, 3, 4, 5}⟩ **3** : a device for connecting parts (as pipes)

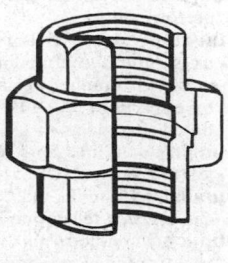

union 3

Union *adj* : of, relating to, or being the side favoring the federal union in the American Civil War ⟨the *Union* army⟩

union·ism \ˈyün-yə-ˌniz-əm\ *n* **1** : the principle or policy of forming or keeping a union **2** *cap* : support of a strong federal union before or during the American Civil War **3** : a theory or policy that supports labor unions — **union·ist** \-yə-nəst\ *n, often cap*

union·ize \ˈyün-yə-ˌnīz\ *vb* **-ized; -iz·ing** : to form into a labor union — **union·i·za·tion** \ˌyün-yə-nə-ˈzā-shən\ *n*

union jack *n* **1** : a flag consisting of the part of a national flag that signifies union; *esp* : a U.S. flag consisting of a blue field with one white star for each state **2** *cap U&J* : the state flag of the United Kingdom

union suit *n* : an undergarment with shirt and pants in one piece

unique \yü-ˈnēk\ *adj* **1 a** : being the only one of its kind **b** : PECULIAR 1 **2** : very unusual : NOTABLE ⟨his talent is *unique*⟩ **3** : being the one and only possible result of one or more mathematical operations ⟨a *unique* solution⟩; *also* : having only one possible result ⟨addition of integers is *unique*⟩ — **unique·ly** *adv* — **unique·ness** *n*

uni·sex \ˈyü-nə-ˌseks\ *adj* : suitable or designed for both males and females ⟨*unisex* clothing⟩

uni·sex·u·al \ˌyü-nə-ˈseksh-(ə-)wəl, -ˈsek-shəl\ *adj* **1** : having only male or only female sex organs **2** : UNISEX

uni·son \ˈyü-nə-sən, -zən\ *n* **1** : sameness of musical pitch **2** : the condition of being tuned or sounded at the same pitch or at an octave ⟨sing in *unison* rather than in harmony⟩ **3** : exact agreement : ACCORD ⟨all are in *unison* on the next move⟩ [from early French *unisson* "having the same musical pitch," from Latin *unisonus* "having the same sound," from *uni-* "one" (from *unus* "one") and *sonus* "a sound" — related to ³SOUND, UNITE]

¹unit \ˈyü-nət\ *n* **1 a** : the first and smallest natural number : ONE **b** : a single quantity regarded as a whole in calcula-

tion **2** : a definite quantity (as of length, time, or value) used as a standard of measurement ⟨the dollar is the *unit* of U.S. money⟩ **3 a** : a single thing or person or group that is a part of a whole **b** : a part or arrangement of parts performing one function ⟨a train drawn by two diesel *units*⟩ **c** : a part of a school course with a central theme

²unit *adj* : being, relating to, or measuring one unit of ⟨*unit* length⟩ ⟨*unit* angle⟩

uni·tard \ˈyü-nə-ˌtärd\ *n* : a close-fitting one-piece garment for the torso and legs and often for the arms and feet [*uni-* "one" + *-tard* (as in *leotard*)]

uni·tar·i·an \ˌyü-nə-ˈter-ē-ən\ *n, often cap* : one who believes that God exists only in one person — **unitarian** *adj, often cap* — **uni·tar·i·an·ism** \-ē-ə-ˌniz-əm\ *n, often cap*

uni·tary \ˈyü-nə-ˌter-ē\ *adj* **1 a** : of or relating to a unit **b** : based on or marked by unity or units **2** : having the character of a unit : WHOLE

unite \yù-ˈnīt\ *vb* **unit·ed; unit·ing** **1 a** : to put or come together to form a single unit **b** : to cause to cling together ⟨*unite* two pieces of wood⟩ **c** : to link by a legal or moral bond **2** : to become one or as if one ⟨two elements *unite* to form a compound⟩ **3** : to join in action : act as if one ⟨*unite* in song⟩ [Middle English *uniten* "to unite," from early French *uniter* (same meaning), from Latin *unitus,* past participle of *unire* "to unite, make into one," from earlier *unus* "one" — related to INCH, OUNCE, UNISON] **synonyms** see JOIN — **unit·er** *n*

unit·ed \yù-ˈnīt-əd\ *adj* **1** : made one : COMBINED **2** : relating to or produced by joint action ⟨a *united* drive against drug abuse⟩ **3** : being in agreement : HARMONIOUS ⟨a *united* family⟩ — **unit·ed·ly** *adv*

unit·ize \ˈyü-nət-ˌīz\ *vb* **-ized; -iz·ing** : to form into a unit

units digit *n* : the numeral (as 6 in 456) occupying the units place

units place *n* : the place immediately to the left of the decimal point in a number expressed in the Arabic system of writing numbers — called also *ones place*

uni·ty \ˈyü-nət-ē\ *n, pl* **-ties** **1** : the quality or state of being one **2** : the state of those that are in full agreement : HARMONY **3 a** : a mathematical quantity or combination of quantities treated as equivalent to one in a calculation ⟨called the distance between earth and the sun *unity* and calculated other distances as multiples⟩ **b** : IDENTITY ELEMENT **4** : the combination or arrangement of parts in a work of art or literature that produces a total effect

¹uni·valve \ˈyü-ni-ˌvalv\ *adj* : having a shell made up of only one piece

²univalve *n* : a univalve mollusk shell or a mollusk having such a shell

uni·ver·sal \ˌyü-nə-ˈvər-səl\ *adj* **1** : including or covering all or a whole without limit or exception ⟨*universal* human characteristics⟩ **2** : present or existing everywhere or under all conditions ⟨the family is a *universal* social unit⟩ **3 a** : including or involving a major part or the greatest portion ⟨*universal* customs⟩ **b** : very broad in range ⟨a *universal* genius⟩ **4** : adapted or adjustable to meet varied requirements (as of use, shape, or size) ⟨a *universal* wrench⟩ — **uni·ver·sal·ly** \-s(ə-)lē\ *adv*

universal donor *n* : a person with blood group O blood which can be donated to any recipient

uni·ver·sal·i·ty \ˌyü-nə-(ˌ)vər-ˈsal-ət-ē\ *n* : the quality or state of being universal (as in range, occurrence, or appeal)

uni·ver·sal·ize \ˌyü-nə-ˈvər-sə-ˌlīz\ *vb* **-ized; -iz·ing** : to

\ə\ abut	\aú\ out	\i\ tip	\ò\ saw	\ú\ foot
\ər\ further	\ch\ chin	\ī\ life	\òi\ coin	\y\ yet
\a\ mat	\e\ pet	\j\ job	\th\ thin	\yü\ few
\ā\ take	\ē\ easy	\ŋ\ sing	\th\ this	\yù\ cure
\ä\ cot, cart	\g\ go	\ō\ bone	\ü\ food	\zh\ vision

make universal : GENERALIZE — **uni·ver·sal·i·za·tion** \-₁vər-sə-lə-'zā-shən\ *n*

universal joint *n* : a shaft coupling capable of transmitting rotation from one shaft to another not in a straight line with it

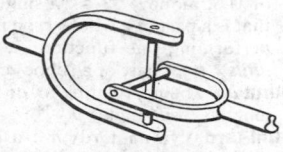

universal joint

Universal Product Code *n* : a bar code that identifies a product's type and price for entry into a computer or cash register (as at a supermarket checkout)

universal recipient *n* : a person with blood group AB blood who can receive blood from any donor

universal resource locator *n* : URL

universal set *n* : a set that contains all elements relating to a particular discussion or problem

uni·verse \'yü-nə-₁vərs\ *n* **1** : the whole body of things observed or assumed : COSMOS **2** : UNIVERSAL SET [from Latin *universum* "whole body of things that exist," from *universus* "whole, entire," literally, "turned into one," from *uni-* "one" and *versus* "turned toward," from *vertere* "to turn" — related to ANNIVERSARY, CONVERSE, UNICORN, VERSATILE]

uni·ver·si·ty \₁yü-nə-'vər-sət-ē, -'vər-stē\ *n, pl* **-ties** : a school that offers courses leading to a degree (as a bachelor's, master's, or doctoral degree) and where research is done

un·just \₁ən-'jəst, 'ən-\ *adj* : not just : UNFAIR ⟨an *unjust* way of picking the winner⟩ — **un·just·ly** *adv* — **un·just·ness** \-'jəs(t)-nəs\ *n*

un·kempt \₁ən-'kem(p)t\ *adj* **1** : not combed **2** : lacking in order or neatness : UNTIDY

un·kind \₁ən-'kīnd\ *adj* : not kind or sympathetic ⟨an *unkind* remark⟩ — **un·kind·ly** *adv* — **un·kind·ness** \-'kīn(d)-nəs\ *n*

un·kind·ly \₁ən-'kīn-(d)lē\ *adj* : UNKIND — **un·kind·li·ness** *n*

un·know·able \₁ən-'nō-ə-bəl, 'ən-\ *adj* : not knowable ⟨some facts in the case may remain *unknowable*⟩

un·know·ing \₁ən-'nō-iŋ\ *adj* : not knowing — **un·know·ing·ly** *adv*

¹un·known \₁ən-'nōn\ *adj* : not known; *also* : having an unknown value ⟨an *unknown* quantity⟩

²unknown *n* **1** : something that is unknown **2** : a symbol (as *x*, *y*, or *z*) representing a quantity whose value is unknown ⟨an equation with two *unknowns*⟩

un·lace \₁ən-'lās, 'ən-\ *vb* : to loose by undoing a lacing

un·lade \₁ən-'lād\ *vb* **-lad·ed; -laded** *or* **-lad·en** \-'lād-ᵊn\; **-lad·ing** **1** : to take the load or cargo from **2** : UNLOAD 1a

un·lash \₁ən-'lash\ *vb* : to untie the lashing of : LOOSE, UNDO

un·latch \₁ən-'lach\ *vb* **1** : to open or loose by lifting the latch **2** : to become loosed or opened

un·law·ful \₁ən-'lò-fəl, 'ən-\ *adj* : not lawful : being against the law : ILLEGAL — **un·law·ful·ly** \-f(ə-)lē\ *adv* — **un·law·ful·ness** \-fəl-nəs\ *n*

un·lead·ed \₁ən-'led-əd\ *adj* : not mixed with lead or lead compounds ⟨*unleaded* gasoline⟩

un·learn \₁ən-'lərn\ *vb* : to put out of one's knowledge or memory

un·learned \₁ən-'lər-nəd *for sense 1*, ₁ən-'lərnd *for senses 2 & 3*\ *adj* **1** : not learned : UNEDUCATED, ILLITERATE ⟨a good but *unlearned* man⟩ **2** : not learned by study : not known ⟨lessons *unlearned* by many⟩ **3** : not learned by previous experience ⟨breathing is *unlearned* behavior⟩

un·leash \₁ən-'lēsh\ *vb* : to free from or as if from a leash ⟨*unleash* a dog⟩ ⟨the storm *unleashed* its fury⟩

un·less \ən-₁les, ₁ən-, *in some contexts* ᵊn-, ᵊm-, *or* ᵊŋ-\ *conj* : except on the condition that : if not ⟨she will fail *unless* she works harder⟩

un·let·tered \₁ən-'let-ərd, 'ən-\ *adj* **1** : not having knowledge especially of the kind gained from books **2** : ILLITERATE 1 *synonyms* see IGNORANT

¹un·like \₁ən-'līk, 'ən-\ *adj* **1** : marked by differences ⟨people are all *unlike*⟩ **2** : UNEQUAL 1a ⟨contributed *unlike* amounts⟩ — **un·like·ness** *n*

²unlike *prep* **1** : different from ⟨feeling completely *unlike* a hero⟩ **2** : not typical of ⟨it was *unlike* her to be late⟩ **3** : in a different manner from ⟨behaving *unlike* all the other children⟩

un·like·li·hood \₁ən-'lī-klē-₁hùd, 'ən-\ *n* : the quality or state of being unlikely

un·like·ly \₁ən-'lī-klē, 'ən-\ *adj* **1** : not likely : IMPROBABLE ⟨an *unlikely* story⟩ **2** : likely to fail : UNPROMISING ⟨an *unlikely* place for fishing⟩ — **un·like·li·ness** *n*

un·lim·ber \₁ən-'lim-bər, 'ən-\ *vb* : to prepare for action or performance

un·lim·it·ed \₁ən-'lim-ət-əd, 'ən-\ *adj* **1** : lacking any controls ⟨*unlimited* freedom⟩ **2** : ¹INFINITE 1 ⟨there is an *unlimited* number of natural numbers⟩ **3** : not bounded by exceptions : UNDEFINED ⟨an *unlimited* and unconditional surrender⟩

un·link \₁ən-'liŋk, 'ən-\ *vb* : to unfasten the links of : SEPARATE, DISCONNECT

un·list·ed \₁ən-'lis-təd, 'ən-\ *adj* : not appearing on a list ⟨an *unlisted* telephone number⟩

un·load \₁ən-'lōd, 'ən-\ *vb* **1 a** : to take away or off : REMOVE ⟨*unload* cargo from a hold⟩ **b** : to take a load from ⟨*unload* a ship⟩; *also* : to rid or set free : UNBURDEN ⟨*unload* your mind of worries⟩ **2** : to get rid of or be freed of a load or burden ⟨the ship is *unloading* now⟩ **3** : to sell in large quantities : DUMP ⟨*unload* surplus goods⟩

un·lock \₁ən-'läk, 'ən-\ *vb* **1** : to open or unfasten through release of a lock ⟨*unlock* the door⟩ ⟨the chest won't *unlock*⟩ **2** : to set free : RELEASE ⟨*unlock* a flood of emotions⟩ **3** : to make known ⟨scientists *unlocking* the secrets of nature⟩

un·looked–for \₁ən-'lùkt-₁fò(ə)r, 'ən-\ *adj* : UNEXPECTED ⟨an *unlooked-for* bonus⟩

un·loose \₁ən-'lüs, 'ən-\ *vb* **1** : to make looser : RELAX ⟨*unloose* a grip⟩ **2** : to set free ⟨the new rules *unloosed* a flood of complaints⟩

un·loos·en \₁ən-'lüs-ᵊn, 'ən-\ *vb* : UNLOOSE

un·love·ly \₁ən-'ləv-lē, 'ən-\ *adj* : having no charm or appeal : DISAGREEABLE ⟨an *unlovely* story about betrayal⟩

un·lucky \₁ən-'lək-ē, 'ən-\ *adj* **1** : marked by bad luck or failure ⟨an *unlucky* day⟩ **2** : likely to bring misfortune ⟨an *unlucky* number⟩ **3** : having or meeting with misfortune ⟨*unlucky* people⟩ **4** : causing distress or regret — **un·luck·i·ly** \-'lək-ə-lē\ *adv* — **un·luck·i·ness** \-'lək-ē-nəs\ *n*

un·make \₁ən-'māk, 'ən-\ *vb* **-made** \-'mād\; **-mak·ing** **1** : to cause to disappear : DESTROY ⟨a reputation can be quickly *unmade*⟩ **2** : to remove from rank or office : DEPOSE

un·man \₁ən-'man, 'ən-\ *vb* : to deprive of vigor or courage

un·man·ly \₁ən-'man-lē, 'ən-\ *adj* : not manly: as **a** : being of weak character : COWARDLY **b** : EFFEMINATE

un·manned \₁ən-'mand, 'ən-\ *adj* : having no crew aboard ⟨an *unmanned* spacecraft⟩

un·man·ner·ly \₁ən-'man-ər-lē, 'ən-\ *adj* : IMPOLITE — **unmannerly** *adv*

un·mar·ried \₁ən-'mar-ēd\ *adj* : not married: **a** : not now or previously married **b** : being divorced or widowed

un·mask \₁ən-'mask, 'ən-\ *vb* : to strip of a mask or a disguise : EXPOSE ⟨*unmask* a traitor⟩

un·men·tion·able \₁ən-'mench-(ə-)nə-bəl, 'ən-\ *adj* : not fit or proper to be talked about

un·mer·ci·ful \₁ən-'mər-si-fəl, 'ən-\ *adj* : not merciful : MERCILESS, CRUEL — **un·mer·ci·ful·ly** \-f(ə-)lē\ *adv*

un·mis·tak·able \ˌən-mə-ˈstā-kə-bəl, ˈən-\ *adj* : not capable of being mistaken or misunderstood : CLEAR, OBVIOUS — **un·mis·tak·ably** \-blē\ *adv*

un·mit·i·gat·ed \ˌən-ˈmit-ə-ˌgāt-əd, ˈən-\ *adj* **1** : not lessened or made less severe ⟨*unmitigated* poverty⟩ **2** : ABSOLUTE, DOWNRIGHT ⟨an *unmitigated* liar⟩

un·mor·al \ˌən-ˈmȯr-əl, -ˈmär-, ˈən-\ *adj* : having no moral quality or relation : being neither moral nor immoral — **un·mor·al·ly** \-ə-lē\ *adv*

un·moved \ˌən-ˈmüvd, ˈən-\ *adj* **1** : not moved : remaining in the same place **2** : holding to the same position ⟨*unmoved* by their arguments⟩ **3** : not disturbed emotionally ⟨*unmoved* by the sad news⟩

un·muf·fle \ˌən-ˈməf-əl, ˈən-\ *vb* : to free from something that muffles

un·muz·zle \ˌən-ˈməz-əl, ˈən-\ *vb* : to remove a muzzle from

un·nat·u·ral \ˌən-ˈnach-(ə-)rəl, ˈən-\ *adj* **1** : not following nature or a normal course of events **2 a** : not being in agreement with normal feelings or behavior **b** : lacking ease and naturalness — **un·nat·u·ral·ly** \-ˈnach-(ə-)rə-lē, -ˈnach-ər-lē\ *adv* — **un·nat·u·ral·ness** \-ˈnach-(ə-)rəl-nəs\ *n*

un·nec·es·sar·i·ly \ˌən-ˌnes-ə-ˈser-ə-lē\ *adv* **1** : not by necessity ⟨spent money *unnecessarily*⟩ **2** : to an unnecessary degree ⟨an *unnecessarily* harsh punishment⟩

un·nec·es·sary \ˌən-ˈnes-ə-ˌser-ē, ˈən-\ *adj* : not necessary

un·nerve \ˌən-ˈnərv, ˈən-\ *vb* **-nerved; -nerv·ing** : to deprive of nerve, courage, or self-control ⟨the accident *unnerved* me⟩

un·num·bered \ˌən-ˈnəm-bərd, ˈən-\ *adj* **1** : COUNTLESS **2** : not having an identifying number ⟨*unnumbered* pages⟩

un·ob·tru·sive \ˌən-əb-ˈtrü-siv, -ziv\ *adj* : not obtrusive or bold : INCONSPICUOUS — **un·ob·tru·sive·ly** *adv*

un·oc·cu·pied \ˌən-ˈäk-yə-ˌpīd, ˈən-\ *adj* **1** : not busy : UNEMPLOYED **2** : not occupied : EMPTY

un·or·ga·nized \ˌən-ˈȯr-gə-ˌnīzd, ˈən-\ *adj* : not organized: as **a** : not formed or brought into an ordered whole **b** : not organized into unions ⟨*unorganized* labor⟩

un·or·tho·dox \ˌən-ˈȯr-thə-ˌdäks, ˈən-\ *adj* : not orthodox : not usual ⟨a tennis player with an *unorthodox* serve⟩

un·pack \ˌən-ˈpak, ˈən-\ *vb* **1** : to separate and remove things packed **2** : to open and remove the contents of ⟨*unpack* a trunk⟩

un·paid \ˌən-ˈpād\ *adj* **1** : not paid ⟨an *unpaid* volunteer⟩ **2** : not paying a salary ⟨an *unpaid* position⟩

un·paired \ˌən-ˈpa(ə)rd, -ˈpe(ə)rd, ˈən-\ *adj* : not paired; *esp* : not matched or mated ⟨an *unpaired* shoe⟩

un·par·al·leled \ˌən-ˈpar-ə-ˌleld, -ləld, ˈən-\ *adj* : having no parallel; *esp* : having no equal or match : UNSURPASSED ⟨a scene of *unparalleled* beauty⟩

un·par·lia·men·ta·ry \ˌən-ˌpär-lə-ˈment-ə-rē, -ˌpärl-yə-, -ˈmen-trē\ *adj* : not being in agreement with parliamentary practice

un·pile \ˌən-ˈpī(ə)l, ˈən-\ *vb* : to take or pull out from a pile

un·pin \ˌən-ˈpin, ˈən-\ *vb* : to remove a pin from : UNFASTEN

un·pleas·ant \ˌən-ˈplez-ᵊnt, ˈən-\ *adj* : not pleasant : not friendly or agreeable : DISPLEASING — **un·pleas·ant·ly** *adv* — **un·pleas·ant·ness** *n*

un·plug \ˌən-ˈpləg, ˈən-\ *vb* **1** : to remove (as an electric plug) from a socket or opening **2** : to disconnect from an electric circuit by removing a plug ⟨*unplug* the television⟩

un·plugged \ˌən-ˈpləgd, ˈən-\ *adj* : ACOUSTIC 2 ⟨an *unplugged* performance⟩

un·plumbed \ˌən-ˈpləmd, ˈən-\ *adj* **1** : not tested or measured with a plumb line **2** : not explored completely ⟨many *unplumbed* areas in science⟩

un·po·lit·i·cal \ˌən-pə-ˈlit-i-kəl\ *adj* : not interested or active in politics

un·pop·u·lar \ˌən-ˈpäp-yə-lər, ˈən-\ *adj* : not popular : disliked by many people — **un·pop·u·lar·i·ty** \ˌən-ˌpäp-yə-ˈlar-ət-ē\ *n*

un·prec·e·dent·ed \ˌən-ˈpres-ə-ˌdent-əd, ˈən-\ *adj* : having no precedent : not done or experienced before ⟨an *unprecedented* achievement⟩

un·pre·dict·able \ˌən-pri-ˈdik-tə-bəl\ *adj* : not predictable — **un·pre·dict·abil·i·ty** \-ˌdik-tə-ˈbil-ət-ē\ *n* — **un·pre·dict·ably** \-ˈdik-tə-blē\ *adv*

un·pre·tend·ing \ˌən-pri-ˈtend-iŋ\ *adj* : UNPRETENTIOUS

un·pre·ten·tious \ˌən-pri-ˈten-chəs\ *adj* : not pretentious : not showy : SIMPLE, MODEST ⟨pleasant but *unpretentious* homes⟩ — **un·pre·ten·tious·ly** *adv*

un·prin·ci·pled \ˌən-ˈprin(t)-s(ə-)pəld, -sə-bəld, ˈən-\ *adj* : lacking moral principles : UNSCRUPULOUS

un·print·able \ˌən-ˈprint-ə-bəl, ˈən-\ *adj* : unfit to be printed

un·pro·fes·sion·al \ˌən-prə-ˈfesh-nəl, -ᵊn-ᵊl\ *adj* : not professional; *esp* : not up to the standards of one's profession — **un·pro·fes·sion·al·ly** \-ē\ *adv*

un·prof·it·able \ˌən-ˈpräf-ət-ə-bəl, -ˈpräf-tə-bəl, ˈən-\ *adj* : not profitable — **un·prof·it·ably** \-blē\ *adv*

un·prom·is·ing \ˌən-ˈpräm-ə-siŋ, ˈən-\ *adj* : appearing unlikely to prove worthwhile or successful — **un·prom·is·ing·ly** *adv*

un·pro·tect·ed \ˌən-prə-ˈtek-təd\ *adj* **1** : lacking protection or defense ⟨*unprotected* troops⟩ ⟨skin *unprotected* from the sun's rays⟩ **2** : performed without the use of birth control to prevent pregnancy; *also* : performed without the use of a condom to prevent the spread of a sexually transmitted disease ⟨*unprotected* sex⟩

un·qual·i·fied \ˌən-ˈkwäl-ə-ˌfīd, ˈən-\ *adj* **1** : not fit : not having required qualifications ⟨*unqualified* for the job⟩ **2** : not having any exceptions : ABSOLUTE ⟨an *unqualified* denial⟩ — **un·qual·i·fied·ly** \-ˌfī(-ə)d-lē\ *adv*

un·ques·tion·able \ˌən-ˈkwes-chə-nə-bəl, -ˈkwesh-, *in rapid speech* -ˈkwesh-nə-; ˈən-\ *adj* : not questionable : INDISPUTABLE ⟨*unquestionable* evidence⟩ — **un·ques·tion·ably** \-blē\ *adv*

un·ques·tion·ing \ˌən-ˈkwes-chə-niŋ, -ˈkwesh-, ˈən-\ *adj* : not questioning : accepting without thinking or doubting ⟨*unquestioning* obedience⟩ — **un·ques·tion·ing·ly** *adv*

un·qui·et \ˌən-ˈkwī-ət, ˈən-\ *adj* **1** : not quiet : AGITATED, TURBULENT **2** : UNEASY 2 — **un·qui·et·ly** *adv* — **un·qui·et·ness** *n*

un·quote \ˈən-ˌkwōt\ *n* — used orally to mark the end of a direct quotation

un·rav·el \ˌən-ˈrav-əl, ˈən-\ *vb* **1** : to separate the threads of : DISENTANGLE ⟨*unravel* a snarl⟩ **2** : SOLVE ⟨*unravel* a mystery⟩ **3** : to become unraveled

un·read \ˌən-ˈred, ˈən-\ *adj* **1** : not read ⟨an *unread* book⟩ **2** : not well informed through reading : UNEDUCATED

un·read·able \ˌən-ˈrēd-ə-bəl, ˈən-\ *adj* **1** : too dull or unattractive to read ⟨a long, *unreadable* essay⟩ **2** : ILLEGIBLE ⟨*unreadable* handwriting⟩

un·re·al \ˌən-ˈrē(-ə)l, -ˈri(-ə)l, ˈən-\ *adj* **1** : not real, actual, or genuine : ILLUSORY **2** : FANTASTIC 2

un·re·al·i·ty \ˌən-rē-ˈal-ət-ē\ *n* **1 a** : the quality or state of being unreal : NONEXISTENCE ⟨an air of *unreality* about the place⟩ **b** : something unreal or imaginary : FIGMENT **2** : inability to deal with reality

un·rea·soned \ˌən-ˈrēz-ᵊnd\ *adj* : not founded on reason or reasoning ⟨*unreasoned* fears⟩ ⟨an *unreasoned* decision⟩

\ə\ **abut**	\aů\ **out**	\i\ **tip**	\ȯ\ **saw**	\ů\ **foot**
\ər\ **further**	\ch\ **chin**	\ī\ **life**	\ȯi\ **coin**	\y\ **yet**
\a\ **mat**	\e\ **pet**	\j\ **job**	\th\ **thin**	\yü\ **few**
\ā\ **take**	\ē\ **easy**	\ŋ\ **sing**	\th\ **this**	\yů\ **cure**
\ä\ **cot, cart**	\g\ **go**	\ō\ **bone**	\ü\ **food**	\zh\ **vision**

un·rea·son·ing \ˌən-'rēz-niŋ, -ᵊn-iŋ, 'ən-\ *adj* : not reasoning; *esp* : not using or showing the use of reason as a guide or control ⟨*unreasoning* fear⟩

un·reel \ˌən-'rē(ə)l, 'ən-\ *vb* : to unwind from or as if from a reel

un·re·gen·er·ate \ˌən-ri-'jen-(ə-)rət\ *adj* : not feeling or showing sorrow or the willingness to reform ⟨an *unregenerate* criminal⟩

un·re·lent·ing \ˌən-ri-'lent-iŋ\ *adj* **1** : not softening or giving in easily : HARD, STERN **2** : not letting up or weakening in energy or pace ⟨our *unrelenting* struggle for freedom⟩ — **un·re·lent·ing·ly** *adv*

un·re·mit·ting \ˌən-ri-'mit-iŋ\ *adj* : not stopping : UNCEASING ⟨*unremitting* pain⟩

un·re·served \ˌən-ri-'zərvd\ *adj* **1** : not held in reserve : not kept back ⟨*unreserved* enthusiasm⟩ **2** : having or showing no reserve in manner or speech — **un·re·serv·ed·ly** \-'zər-vəd-lē\ *adv*

un·rest \ˌən-'rest, 'ən-\ *n* : lack of rest : a disturbed or uneasy state : TURMOIL

un·re·strained \ˌən-ri-'strānd\ *adj* **1** : not restrained : not held back ⟨*unrestrained* praise for the political candidate⟩ **2** : free of outside forces or limits

un·re·straint \ˌən-ri-'strānt\ *n* : lack of restraint

un·righ·teous \ˌən-'rī-chəs, 'ən-\ *adj* **1** : not righteous : SINFUL, WICKED **2** : UNJUST — **un·righ·teous·ly** *adv* — **un·righ·teous·ness** *n*

un·ripe \ˌən-'rīp, 'ən-\ *adj* : not ripe : IMMATURE ⟨*unripe* fruit⟩

un·ri·valed *or* **un·ri·valled** \ˌən-'rī-vəld, 'ən-\ *adj* : having no rival : INCOMPARABLE, UNEQUALED ⟨a palace of *unrivaled* magnificence⟩

un·roll \ˌən-'rōl, 'ən-\ *vb* **1** : to unwind a roll of : open out ⟨*unroll* a carpet⟩ **2** : DISCLOSE ⟨the government *unrolled* a new program⟩ **3** : to become unrolled or spread out : UNFOLD ⟨a view of mountains *unrolled* before them⟩

un·round \ˌən-'raùnd, 'ən-\ *vb* : to pronounce a sound without or with decreased rounding of the lips — **un·round·ed** *adj*

un·ruf·fled \ˌən-'rəf-əld, 'ən-\ *adj* **1** : not upset or disturbed ⟨a speaker *unruffled* by noisy children⟩ **2** : not ruffled : SMOOTH ⟨*unruffled* water⟩

un·ruly \ˌən-'rü-lē, 'ən-\ *adj* **un·rul·i·er; -est** : not yielding easily to rule or restriction : UNCONTROLLABLE ⟨an *unruly* temper⟩ ⟨an *unruly* horse⟩

   synonyms UNRULY, UNGOVERNABLE, WILLFUL, HEAD-STRONG mean not yielding to discipline or control. UN-RULY suggests a lack of self-control or control by others and also often suggests bad behavior ⟨*unruly* children broke the lamp⟩. UNGOVERNABLE suggests either a loss of control or an inability to be controlled by oneself or by others ⟨sometimes an *ungovernable* rage comes over them⟩. WILLFUL suggests a strong determination to have one's own way ⟨a *willful* disregard for the rights of others⟩. HEADSTRONG suggests stubbornness and lack of patience with suggestions, advice, or control by others ⟨a *headstrong* refusal to listen to experienced workers⟩.

un·sad·dle \ˌən-'sad-ᵊl, 'ən-\ *vb* : to remove the saddle from a horse

un·sat·u·rat·ed \ˌən-'sach-ə-ˌrāt-əd, 'ən-\ *adj* : not saturated: as **a** : capable of absorbing or dissolving more of something ⟨an *unsaturated* solution⟩ **b** : able to form products by combining chemically with other substances; *esp* : containing double or triple bonds between carbon atoms ⟨an *unsaturated* fat⟩

un·saved \ˌən-'sāvd, 'ən-\ *adj* : not saved; *esp* : not rescued from eternal punishment

un·sa·vory \ˌən-'sāv-(ə-)rē, 'ən-\ *adj* **1** : having little or no taste **2** : having a bad taste or smell **3** : morally bad

un·say \ˌən-'sā, 'ən-\ *vb* **-said** \-'sed\; **-say·ing** \-'sā-iŋ\ : to take back something said : RETRACT

un·scathed \ˌən-'skāthd, 'ən-\ *adj* : completely unharmed : not injured

un·schooled \ˌən-'sküld, 'ən-\ *adj* : not schooled : UN-TAUGHT, UNTRAINED

un·sci·en·tif·ic \ˌən-ˌsī-ən-'tif-ik\ *adj* : not scientific: as **a** : not being in agreement with the principles and methods of science ⟨an *unscientific* poll⟩ **b** : not showing scientific knowledge or familiarity with scientific methods ⟨an *unscientific* explanation⟩ — **un·sci·en·tif·i·cal·ly** \-'tif-i-k(ə-)lē\ *adv*

un·scram·ble \ˌən-'skram-bəl, 'ən-\ *vb* : to make orderly or clear again ⟨trying to *unscramble* a mix-up with the test scores⟩ ⟨*unscramble* a radio message⟩

un·screw \ˌən-'skrü, 'ən-\ *vb* **1** : to remove the screws from **2** : to loosen or withdraw by turning ⟨*unscrew* a lightbulb⟩

un·scru·pu·lous \ˌən-'skrü-pyə-ləs, 'ən-\ *adj* : not scrupulous : UNPRINCIPLED — **un·scru·pu·lous·ly** *adv* — **un·scru·pu·lous·ness** *n*

un·seal \ˌən-'sē(ə)l, 'ən-\ *vb* : to break or remove the seal of

un·sea·son·able \ˌən-'sēz-nə-bəl, -'sēz-ᵊn-ə-\ *adj* **1** : happening or coming at the wrong time : UNTIMELY ⟨an *unseasonable* visit⟩ **2** : not normal for the season of the year ⟨*unseasonable* weather⟩ — **un·sea·son·ably** \-blē\ *adv*

un·seat \ˌən-'sēt, 'ən-\ *vb* **1** : to throw from one's seat especially on horseback **2** : to remove from a place or position; *esp* : to remove from political office

un·seem·ly \ˌən-'sēm-lē, 'ən-\ *adj* : not seemly : not polite or proper ⟨*unseemly* arguing in public⟩

un·seen \ˌən-'sēn, 'ən-\ *adj* : not seen : INVISIBLE

un·seg·re·gat·ed \ˌən-'seg-ri-ˌgāt-əd, 'ən-\ *adj* : not segregated; *esp* : free from racial segregation

un·self·ish \ˌən-'sel-fish, 'ən-\ *adj* : not selfish : GENEROUS — **un·self·ish·ly** *adv* — **un·self·ish·ness** *n*

un·set·tle \ˌən-'set-ᵊl, 'ən-\ *vb* **1** : to move or loosen from a settled state **2** : to make uneasy ⟨change *unsettles* him⟩

un·set·tled \ˌən-'set-ᵊld, 'ən-\ *adj* **1** : not settled : not fixed (as in position or nature) ⟨*unsettled* weather⟩ **2** : not calm : DISTURBED ⟨*unsettled* waters⟩ **3** : not decided in mind : UNDETERMINED ⟨*unsettled* about what to do⟩ **4** : not paid ⟨an *unsettled* account⟩ **5** : not lived in by settlers ⟨an *unsettled* region⟩

un·shaped \ˌən-'shāpt, 'ən-\ *adj* : not shaped; *esp* : not finished to final form ⟨an *unshaped* timber⟩ ⟨*unshaped* ideas⟩

un·shap·en \ˌən-'shā-pən, 'ən-\ *adj* : UNSHAPED

un·sheathe \ˌən-'shēth, 'ən-\ *vb* : to draw from or as if from a sheath ⟨*unsheathe* a sword⟩

un·ship \ˌən-'ship, 'ən-\ *vb* **1** : to remove from a ship **2** : to remove or become removed from position ⟨*unship* an oar⟩

un·shod \ˌən-'shäd, 'ən-\ *adj* **1** : BAREFOOT **2** : not shod ⟨an *unshod* horse⟩

un·sight·ly \ˌən-'sīt-lē, 'ən-\ *adj* : unpleasant to the sight : UGLY ⟨an *unsightly* scar⟩ — **un·sight·li·ness** *n*

un·skilled \ˌən-'skild, 'ən-\ *adj* **1** : not skilled; *esp* : not skilled in a branch of work : lacking mechanical training ⟨an *unskilled* worker⟩ **2** : not requiring skill ⟨*unskilled* jobs⟩ **3** : marked by lack of skill ⟨an *unskilled* painting⟩

un·sling \ˌən-'sliŋ, 'ən-\ *vb* **-slung** \-'sləŋ\; **-sling·ing** \-'sliŋ-iŋ\ : to remove from being slung

un·snap \ˌən-'snap, 'ən-\ *vb* : to loosen or free by or as if by undoing a snap

un·snarl \ˌən-'snär(-ə)l, 'ən-\ *vb* : to remove a snarl in

un·so·cial \ˌən-'sō-shəl, 'ən-\ *adj* : having or showing a lack of desire for the company of others

un·so·phis·ti·cat·ed \ˌən(t)-sə-'fis-tə-ˌkāt-əd\ *adj* **1** : not sophisticated ⟨was still innocent and *unsophisticated*⟩ **2** : not complex : PLAIN, SIMPLE ⟨*unsophisticated* designs⟩ — **un·so·phis·ti·ca·tion** \-ˌfis-tə-'kā-shən\ *n*

un·sought \ˌən-ˈsȯt, ˈən-\ *adj* : not searched for or asked for ⟨*unsought* advice⟩

un·sound \ˌən-ˈsau̇nd, ˈən-\ *adj* **1** : not healthy or whole ⟨an *unsound* horse⟩ **2** : not mentally normal : not wholly sane ⟨of *unsound* mind⟩ **3** : not firmly made, placed, or fixed ⟨an *unsound* structure⟩ **4** : not based on truth or logic ⟨*unsound* arguments⟩ — **un·sound·ly** \-ˈsau̇n(d)-lē\ *adv* — **un·sound·ness** \-ˈsau̇n(d)-nəs\ *n*

un·spar·ing \ˌən-ˈspa(ə)r-iŋ, -ˈspe(ə)r-, ˈən-\ *adj* **1** : not merciful or forgiving : HARD, RUTHLESS ⟨*unsparing* attacks⟩ **2** : not stingy : LIBERAL ⟨*unsparing* in their gifts to charity⟩ — **un·spar·ing·ly** *adv*

un·speak·able \ˌən-ˈspē-kə-bəl, ˈən-\ *adj* **1** : impossible to express in words ⟨*unspeakable* beauty of the sunset⟩ **2** : extremely bad ⟨*unspeakable* conduct⟩ — **un·speak·ably** \-blē\ *adv*

un·spot·ted \ˌən-ˈspät-əd, ˈən-\ *adj* **1** : not spotted : free from spot or stain **2** : free from moral stain ⟨an *unspotted* record in public office⟩

un·sta·ble \ˌən-ˈstā-bəl, ˈən-\ *adj* **1** : not stable : not firm or fixed : FLUCTUATING ⟨*unstable* prices⟩ ⟨an *unstable* tower⟩ ⟨*unstable* weather⟩ **2** : readily changing in chemical composition or physical state or properties (as by breaking down into parts) ⟨an *unstable* atomic nucleus⟩

un·steady \ˌən-ˈsted-ē, ˈən-\ *adj* : not steady : UNSTABLE — **un·steadi·ly** \-ˈsted-ᵊl-ē\ *adv* — **un·steadi·ness** \-ˈsted-ē-nəs\ *n*

un·stick \ˌən-ˈstik, ˈən-\ *vb* **-stuck** \-ˈstək\; **-stick·ing** : to free from being stuck or bound

un·stint·ing \ˌən-ˈstint-iŋ, ˈən-\ *adj* : giving or being given freely or generously ⟨*unstinting* praise⟩ — **un·stint·ing·ly** *adv*

un·stop \ˌən-ˈstäp, ˈən-\ *vb* **1** : to free from blockage : OPEN ⟨*unstop* a drain⟩ **2** : to remove a stopper from

un·strap \ˌən-ˈstrap, ˈən-\ *vb* : to remove or loosen a strap from

un·stressed \ˌən-ˈstrest, ˈən-\ *adj* **1** : not bearing a stress or accent ⟨*unstressed* syllables⟩ **2** : not stressed

un·string \ˌən-ˈstriŋ, ˈən-\ *vb* **-strung** \-ˈstrəŋ\; **-string·ing** \-ˈstriŋ-iŋ\ **1** : to loosen or remove the strings of **2** : to remove from a string ⟨*unstrung* the beads⟩ **3** : to damage mentally or emotionally ⟨*unstrung* by bad news⟩

un·stud·ied \ˌən-ˈstəd-ēd, ˈən-\ *adj* : not studied or planned with a certain effect in mind : NATURAL, UNFORCED ⟨moved with an *unstudied* grace⟩

un·sub·stan·tial \ˌən(t)-səb-ˈstan-chəl\ *adj* : lacking substance, firmness, or strength

un·suc·cess·ful \ˌən(t)-sək-ˈses-fəl\ *adj* : not successful : not having or producing success — **un·suc·cess·ful·ly** \-fə-lē\ *adv*

un·suit·able \ˌən-ˈsüt-ə-bəl, ˈən-\ *adj* : not suitable or fitting : UNBECOMING, INAPPROPRIATE — **un·suit·ably** \-blē\ *adv*

un·sung \ˌən-ˈsəŋ, ˈən-\ *adj* **1** : not sung **2** : not celebrated or praised (as in song or verse) ⟨*unsung* heroes⟩

un·swerv·ing \ˌən-ˈswər-viŋ, ˈən-\ *adj* **1** : not swerving or turning aside **2** : ¹STEADY 3a ⟨*unswerving* loyalty⟩

un·sym·met·ri·cal \ˌən(t)-sə-ˈme-tri-kəl\ *adj* : not symmetrical : ASYMMETRIC

un·tan·gle \ˌən-ˈtaŋ-gəl, ˈən-\ *vb* **1** : to remove a tangle from : DISENTANGLE ⟨*untangle* a knot⟩ **2** : to straighten out : RESOLVE ⟨*untangle* a mystery⟩

un·tapped \ˌən-ˈtapt\ *adj* **1** : not tapped ⟨an *untapped* keg⟩ **2** : not drawn upon or used ⟨as yet *untapped* markets⟩

un·taught \ˌən-ˈtȯt, ˈən-\ *adj* **1** : not instructed or trained : IGNORANT **1** : ¹NATURAL 1 ⟨*untaught* animal behavior⟩

un·ten·a·ble \ˌən-ˈten-ə-bəl, ˈən-\ *adj* **1** : not able to be defended ⟨an *untenable* position⟩ **2** : not able to be occupied ⟨*untenable* apartments⟩

un·teth·er \ˌən-ˈteth-ər, ˈən-\ *vb* : to free from a tether

un·think·able \ˌən-ˈthiŋ-kə-bəl, ˈən-\ *adj* : not to be thought of or considered as possible ⟨*unthinkable* cruelty⟩

un·think·ing \ˌən-ˈthiŋ-kiŋ, ˈən-\ *adj* **1** : not thinking : INATTENTIVE, THOUGHTLESS ⟨*unthinking* people who litter the streets⟩ **2** : not having the power of thought — **un·think·ing·ly** *adv*

un·thought–of \ˌən-ˈthȯt-ˌəv, -ˌäv, ˈən-\ *adj* : not thought of : not considered : not imagined

un·thread \ˌən-ˈthred, ˈən-\ *vb* **1** : to draw or take out a thread from **2** : to loosen the threads or connections of **3** : to make one's way through ⟨*unthread* a maze⟩

un·throne \ˌən-ˈthrōn, ˈən-\ *vb* **-throned; -thron·ing** : to remove from or as if from a throne

un·ti·dy \ˌən-ˈtīd-ē, ˈən-\ *adj* **1** : not neat : CARELESS **2 a** : not neatly organized or carried out **b** : marked by a lack of neatness — **un·ti·di·ly** \-ˈtīd-ᵊl-ē\ *adv* — **un·ti·di·ness** \-ˈtīd-ē-nəs\ *n*

un·tie \ˌən-ˈtī, ˈən-\ *vb* **-tied; -ty·ing** *or* **-tie·ing** **1** : to free from something that ties or fastens : UNBIND ⟨*untie* a horse⟩ **2 a** : to undo the knotted parts of ⟨*untied* her scarf⟩ **b** : to straighten out : RESOLVE ⟨*untie* a traffic jam⟩ **3** : to become loosened or unbound ⟨the strings *untied* easily⟩

¹un·til \ən-ˌtil, -tᵊl, -ˌtel, ˌən-, *in some contexts* ᵊn-, ᵊm-, *or* ᵊŋ-\ *prep* **1** : up to the time of ⟨stayed *until* morning⟩ **2** : BEFORE **3** ⟨doesn't open *until* ten⟩

²until *conj* : up to the time that ⟨played *until* it got dark⟩ ⟨ran *until* I was breathless⟩

un·time·ly \ˌən-ˈtīm-lē, ˈən-\ *adj* **1** : occurring or done before the expected, natural, or proper time : PREMATURE ⟨*untimely* death⟩ **2** : coming at the wrong time ⟨an *untimely* joke⟩

un·ti·tled \ˌən-ˈtīt-ᵊld, ˈən-\ *adj* : not named ⟨an *untitled* poem⟩

un·to \ˌən-tə, ˈən-tü\ *prep* : ¹TO

un·told \ˌən-ˈtōld, ˈən-\ *adj* **1** : not told : not revealed ⟨*untold* secrets⟩ ⟨a story yet *untold*⟩ **2** : not counted : VAST, NUMBERLESS ⟨*untold* wealth⟩

¹un·touch·able \ˌən-ˈtəch-ə-bəl, ˈən-\ *adj* **1 a** : not to be touched or handled **b** : not to be criticized or controlled **2** : lying beyond the reach

²untouchable *n* : one that is untouchable; *esp* : a member of the lowest social class in India

un·touched \ˌən-ˈtəcht\ *adj* **1** : not touched or handled **2** : not described or dealt with **3 a** : not tasted **b** : being in the first state or condition ⟨an *untouched* wilderness⟩

un·to·ward \ˌən-ˈtō(ə)rd, ˈən-, -ˈtȯ(ə)rd, ˌən-tə-ˈwȯ(ə)rd\ *adj* **1** : hard to manage : STUBBORN, WILLFUL ⟨an *untoward* child⟩ **2** : causing trouble : UNLUCKY ⟨an *untoward* accident⟩

un·tried \ˌən-ˈtrīd, ˈən-\ *adj* **1** : not tested or proved by experience or trial ⟨*untried* soldiers⟩ **2** : not yet tried in court ⟨a long list of *untried* cases⟩

un·trod·den \ˌən-ˈträd-ᵊn\ *also* **un·trod** \-ˈträd\ *adj* : not trod : UNTRAVERSED

un·true \ˌən-ˈtrü, ˈən-\ *adj* **1** : not faithful : DISLOYAL **2** : not meeting a standard of correctness : not level or exact **3** : not agreeing with the facts : FALSE ⟨an *untrue* statement⟩ — **un·tru·ly** \-ˈtrü-lē\ *adv*

un·truth \ˌən-ˈtrüth, ˈən-\ *n* **1** : lack of truthfulness : FALSITY **2** : something that is untrue : FALSEHOOD, LIE

un·truth·ful \ˌən-ˈtrüth-fəl, ˈən-\ *adj* : not containing or telling the truth : FALSE, INACCURATE ⟨*untruthful* reports⟩ — **un·truth·ful·ly** \-fə-lē\ *adv* — **un·truth·ful·ness** *n*

\ə\ **abut**	\au̇\ **out**	\i\ **tip**
\ər\ **further**	\ch\ **chin**	\ī\ **life**
\a\ **mat**	\e\ **pet**	\j\ **job**
\ā\ **take**	\ē\ **easy**	\ŋ\ **sing**
\ä\ **cot, cart**	\g\ **go**	\ō\ **bone**

\ȯ\ **saw**	\u̇\ **foot**
\ȯi\ **coin**	\y\ **yet**
\th\ **thin**	\yü\ **few**
\th\ **this**	\yu̇\ **cure**
\ü\ **food**	\zh\ **vision**

un·tuck \ˌən-ˈtək, ˈən-\ vb : to free from a tuck or from being tucked up

un·tu·tored \ˌən-ˈt(y)üt-ərd, ˈən-\ adj : having no formal learning or training

un·twine \ˌən-ˈtwīn, ˈən-\ vb 1 : to unwind the twisted or tangled parts of : DISENTANGLE 2 : to remove by unwinding 3 : to become untangled or unwound

un·twist \ˌən-ˈtwist, ˈən-\ vb 1 : to separate the twisted parts of : UNTWINE 2 : to become untwined

un·used \ˌən-ˈyüzd, ˈən-, in the phrase "unused to" usually -ˈyüs(t)\ adj 1 : not accustomed ⟨unused to crowds⟩ 2 a : not having been used before ⟨an unused paintbrush⟩ b : not being in use : IDLE c : available for future use ⟨unused vacation time⟩

un·usu·al \ˌən-ˈyüzh-(ə-)wəl, -ˈyü-zhəl\ adj : not usual : UNCOMMON, RARE — **un·usu·al·ly** \-ē\ adv — **un·usu·al·ness** n

un·ut·ter·able \ˌən-ˈət-ə-rə-bəl, ˈən-\ adj 1 : not capable of being pronounced 2 : not capable of being put into words : INEXPRESSIBLE ⟨unutterable sorrow⟩ — **un·ut·ter·ably** \-blē\ adv

un·val·ued \ˌən-ˈval-yüd, -yəd, ˈən-\ adj 1 : not important or prized : DISREGARDED 2 : not having an estimated value ⟨a box of unvalued goods⟩

un·var·nished \ˌən-ˈvär-nisht, ˈən-\ adj 1 : not adorned or exaggerated : PLAIN ⟨the unvarnished truth⟩ 2 : not varnished

un·veil \ˌən-ˈvā(ə)l, ˈən-\ vb 1 a : to remove a veil or covering from ⟨unveil a statue⟩ b : DISCLOSE, REVEAL ⟨unveiled their plans⟩ 2 : to throw off a veil

un·voiced \ˌən-ˈvoist, ˈən-\ adj 1 : not actually said : UNSPOKEN ⟨an unvoiced agreement⟩ 2 : VOICELESS 2

un·war·rant·able \ˌən-ˈwȯr-ənt-ə-bəl, -ˈwär-, ˈən-\ adj : not justifiable : INEXCUSABLE

un·wary \ˌən-ˈwa(ə)r-ē, -ˈwe(ə)r-, ˈən-\ adj : not alert : easily fooled or surprised : HEEDLESS, GULLIBLE ⟨the unwary buyer⟩ — **un·wari·ly** \-ˈwar-ə-lē, -ˈwer-\ adv — **un·wari·ness** \-ˈwar-ē-nəs, -ˈwer-\ n

un·wea·ried \ˌən-ˈwi(ə)r-ēd, ˈən-\ adj : not tired or bored : FRESH

un·well \ˌən-ˈwel, ˈən-\ adj : being in poor health : AILING, SICK

un·whole·some \ˌən-ˈhōl-səm, ˈən-\ adj : bad for the well-being of the body, mind, or soul : UNHEALTHY ⟨unwholesome food⟩

un·wieldy \ˌən-ˈwē-l-dē, ˈən-\ adj : not easily handled or managed because of size or weight : AWKWARD, CUMBERSOME ⟨an unwieldy tool⟩

un·will·ing \ˌən-ˈwil-iŋ, ˈən-\ adj : not willing — **un·will·ing·ly** adv — **un·will·ing·ness** n

un·wind \ˌən-ˈwīnd, ˈən-\ vb **-wound** \-ˈwaůnd\; **-wind·ing** 1 a : to cause to uncoil : wind off b : to become uncoiled or untangled 2 : to make or become free of tension : RELAX ⟨wanted to unwind after a hard day⟩

un·wise \ˌən-ˈwīz, ˈən-\ adj : not wise : FOOLISH — **un·wise·ly** adv

un·wit·ting \ˌən-ˈwit-iŋ, ˈən-\ adj 1 : not intended : INADVERTENT ⟨an unwitting mistake⟩ 2 : not knowing : UNAWARE — **un·wit·ting·ly** adv

un·wont·ed \ˌən-ˈwȯnt-əd, -ˈwōnt-, ˈən-\ adj : being out of the ordinary : RARE, UNUSUAL

un·world·ly \ˌən-ˈwər(-ə)l-dlē, -ˈwərl-lē, ˈən-\ adj 1 : not of this world; esp : SPIRITUAL 1 2 : not wise in the ways of the world : UNSOPHISTICATED — **un·world·li·ness** \-ˈwərl-(d)lē-nəs\ n

un·wor·thy \ˌən-ˈwər-thē, ˈən-\ adj : lacking in excellence or worth : UNDESERVING — **un·wor·thi·ly** \-thə-lē\ adv — **un·wor·thi·ness** \-thē-nəs\ n

un·wrap \ˌən-ˈrap, ˈən-\ vb : to remove the wrapping from

un·writ·ten \ˌən-ˈrit-ᵊn, ˈən-\ adj 1 : not put in writing : ORAL, TRADITIONAL ⟨an unwritten law⟩ 2 : containing no writing : BLANK ⟨unwritten pages⟩

un·yield·ing \ˌən-ˈyē(ə)l-diŋ, ˈən-\ adj 1 : not soft or flexible : HARD 2 : marked by firmness or stubbornness

un·yoke \ˌən-ˈyōk, ˈən-\ vb 1 : to free from a yoke ⟨unyoke oxen⟩ 2 : to take apart : DISCONNECT

un·zip \ˌən-ˈzip, ˈən-\ vb **-zipped; -zip·ping** : to open by means of a zipper

¹up \ˈəp\ adv 1 a : in or to a higher position or level; esp : away from the center of the earth ⟨held up my hand⟩ b : from beneath a surface (as ground or water) ⟨pulling up weeds⟩ c : from below the horizon ⟨watched the moon come up⟩ d : in or into an upright position ⟨stand up⟩ e : out of bed ⟨stayed up late⟩ 2 : with greater force ⟨speak up⟩ 3 a : in or into a better or more advanced state ⟨worked our way up in the world⟩ b : at an end ⟨our time was up⟩ c : in or into a state of greater activity ⟨stir up a fire⟩ d : to or at a greater rate, speed, or amount ⟨prices went up⟩ 4 a : into existence, evidence, or knowledge ⟨the missing ring turned up⟩ b : into consideration ⟨brought the matter up⟩ 5 : into possession or control ⟨gave himself up⟩ 6 : ENTIRELY, COMPLETELY ⟨eat it up⟩ ⟨the house burned up⟩ 7 : in or into storage ⟨lay up supplies⟩ ⟨put our boat up for the winter⟩ 8 : so as to arrive or approach ⟨came up the drive⟩ 9 : in or into parts ⟨tear up paper⟩ 10 : to a stop ⟨pull up⟩ ⟨drew up at the curb⟩ 11 : for each side ⟨score was 15 up⟩

²up adj 1 a : risen above the horizon or ground ⟨the sun was up⟩ b : being out of bed c : higher than usual ⟨the river is up⟩ ⟨prices are up⟩ d : raised so as to be open : LIFTED ⟨windows are up⟩ e : put together : BUILT ⟨the house is up⟩ f : grown above a surface ⟨the corn is up⟩ g : moving or going upward ⟨the up escalator⟩ 2 a : being on one's feet and busy ⟨was eager to be up and doing⟩ b : well prepared ⟨the team was up for the game⟩ c : going on : taking place ⟨find out what is up⟩ 3 : well informed ⟨always up on the news⟩ 4 : being ahead of an opponent ⟨was three games up in the series⟩ 5 a : presented for or under consideration ⟨up for reelection⟩ b : charged before a court ⟨was up for robbery⟩ c : being the one whose turn it is ⟨you're up next⟩ — **up to** 1 : capable of performing or dealing with ⟨feels up to the role⟩ 2 : engaged in ⟨what are they up to⟩ 3 : being the responsibility of ⟨it's up to me⟩

³up \(ˌ)əp, ˈəp\ prep 1 : to, toward, or at a higher point of ⟨up the hill⟩ 2 a : toward the beginning of ⟨going up the river⟩ b : toward the northern or upper end or part of ⟨sailed up the coast⟩ 3 : along the course of ⟨walking up the street⟩

⁴up \ˈəp\ n 1 : an upward course or slope 2 : a period or state of success ⟨had had my ups and downs⟩

⁵up vb **upped** or in sense 1 **up; upped; up·ping; ups** or in sense 1 **up** 1 : to act suddenly or surprisingly ⟨up and left town⟩ 2 : to rise from a lying or sitting position 3 : to move or cause to move upward : ASCEND, RAISE ⟨upped the prices⟩

up–and–down adj 1 : marked by alternate upward and downward movement, action, or surface 2 : ¹PERPENDICULAR 1

¹up·beat \ˈəp-ˌbēt\ n : an unaccented beat in a musical measure; esp : the last beat of the measure

²upbeat adj : OPTIMISTIC, CHEERFUL ⟨a story with an upbeat ending⟩

up·braid \ˌəp-ˈbrād\ vb : to criticize or scold severely

up·bring·ing \ˈəp-ˌbriŋ-iŋ\ n : the process or way of bringing up and training ⟨had a strict upbringing⟩

up·com·ing \ˌəp-ˈkəm-iŋ\ adj : coming soon

¹up–coun·try \ˈəp-ˌkən-trē\ adj : of or relating to the interior of a country or a region — **up–country** \ˈəp-\ n

²up–coun·try \ˈəp-ˈkən-trē\ adv : to or in the interior of a country or a region

¹up·date \ˌəp-ˈdāt\ vb : to bring up to date

²up·date \ˈəp-ˌdāt\ n 1 : an act or instance of updating 2 : an up-to-date version, account, or information

up·draft \'əp-ˌdraft, -ˌdrȧft\ *n* : an upward movement of gas (as air)

up·end \ˌə-'pend\ *vb* : to set, stand, or rise on end

¹up·grade \'əp-ˌgrād\ *n* **1** : an upward grade or slope **2** : ²RISE 4 ⟨crime has been on the *upgrade*⟩

²up·grade \'əp-ˌgrād, ˌəp-'grād\ *vb* **1** : to raise to a higher grade or position **2** : to improve or replace especially software or a device for increased usefulness — **up·grad·abil·i·ty** *or* **up·grade·abil·i·ty** \ˌəp-ˌgrād-ə-'bil-ət-ē\ *n* — **up·grad·able** *or* **up·grade·able** \ˌəp-'grād-ə-bəl\ *adj*

up·heav·al \ˌəp-'hē-vəl, (ˌ)ə-'pē-\ *n* **1** : the action or an instance of heaving or lifting up from beneath especially of part of the earth's crust **2** : an instance of violent disorder or change ⟨emotional *upheaval*⟩

¹up·hill \'əp-'hil\ *adv* **1** : in an upward direction **2** : against difficulties

²up·hill \ˌəp-ˌhil\ *adj* **1** : being on high ground **2** : going up : ASCENDING **3** : DIFFICULT 1 ⟨an *uphill* struggle⟩

up·hold \(ˌ)əp-'hōld\ *vb* **-held** \-'held\; **-hold·ing** **1** : to give support to ⟨promise to *uphold* the law⟩ **2 a** : to keep elevated **b** : to lift up — **up·hold·er** *n*

up·hol·ster \(ˌ)əp-'hōl-stər, (ˌ)ə-'pōl-\ *vb* **-stered; -ster·ing** \-st(ə-)riŋ\ : to provide with or as if with upholstery — **up·hol·ster·er** \-stər-ər\ *n*

up·hol·stery \(ˌ)əp-'hōl-st(ə-)rē, (ˌ)ə-'pōl-\ *n, pl* **-ster·ies** : materials (as fabric, padding, and springs) used to make a soft covering especially for a seat

up·keep \'əp-ˌkēp\ *n* : the act or cost of maintaining in good condition : MAINTENANCE

up·land \'əp-lənd, -ˌland\ *n* : high land especially at some distance from the sea — **upland** *adj*

¹up·lift \(ˌ)əp-'lift\ *vb* **1** : to lift up : ELEVATE **2** : to improve the spiritual, mental, or social condition of

²up·lift \'əp-ˌlift\ *n* **1** : an act, process, or result of uplifting; *esp* : the uplifting of a part of the earth's surface **2** : moral or social improvement or a movement to make such improvement

up·load \ˌəp-'lōd, 'əp-ˌ\ *vb* : to transfer (information) from a computer to a remote computer or other device

up·most \'əp-ˌmōst\ *adj* : being in the highest or most important position

up·on \ə-'pȯn, -'pän, -(ˌ)pən\ *prep* : ¹ON

upped *past and past participle of* UP

¹up·per \'əp-ər\ *adj* **1** : higher in physical position, rank, or order ⟨the *upper* lip⟩ ⟨*upper* management⟩ **2** : being the smaller and more restricted branch of a two-house legislature **3** *cap* : of, relating to, or being a later geologic period or formation ⟨the *Upper* Cretaceous period⟩ **4** : being toward the interior : further inland ⟨the *upper* Amazon⟩ **5** : NORTHERN ⟨*upper* New York state⟩

²upper *n* **1** : the parts of a shoe or boot above the sole **2** : an upper tooth or set of teeth **3** : an upper berth

³upper *n* : a stimulant drug; *esp* : AMPHETAMINE

up·per·case \ˌəp-ər-'kās\ *adj* : ¹CAPITAL 2 — **uppercase** *n*

upper class *n* : the highest class in society — **upper–class** *adj*

up·per·class·man \ˌəp-ər-'klas-mən\ *n* : a student in the third or fourth year of a four-year college or a high school

upper crust *n* : the highest social class or group

up·per·cut \'əp-ər-ˌkət\ *n* : a swinging blow (as in boxing) directed upward with a bent arm — **uppercut** *vb*

upper hand *n* : the position of being ahead or in control

up·per·most \'əp-ər-ˌmōst\ *adv* : in or into the highest or most prominent position — **uppermost** *adj*

upping *present participle of* UP

up·pish \'əp-ish\ *adj* : UPPITY

up·pi·ty \'əp-ət-ē\ *adj* : acting as if better or more important than others : ARROGANT

up·raise \(ˌ)ə-'prāz\ *vb* : to raise or lift up : ELEVATE

¹up·right \'əp-ˌrīt\ *adj* **1 a** : ¹VERTICAL 2 ⟨an *upright* posture⟩ **b** : having the main axis or a main part perpendicu-

lar **2** : living by high moral standards : HONORABLE — **up·right·ness** *n*

synonyms UPRIGHT, HONEST, JUST mean having or showing a great concern for what is right. UPRIGHT suggests having high moral standards in all areas of life ⟨an *upright* person whose life was an example to the whole town⟩. HONEST suggests dealing with others in a fair and truthful way ⟨an *honest* merchant who would not cheat anyone⟩. JUST stresses that one's fairness comes from conscious choice and is practiced steadily ⟨a *just* principal who knows she must treat all students equally⟩.

²upright *n* **1** : an upright or vertical position **2** : something upright

upright piano *n* : a piano whose strings run vertically

up·rise \ˌə-'prīz\ *vb* **up·rose** \-'prōz\; **up·ris·en** \-'priz-ᵊn\; **up·ris·ing** \-'prī-ziŋ\ **1** : to rise to a higher position **2** : to get up (as from sleep or a sitting position)

up·ris·ing \'əp-ˌrī-ziŋ\ *n* : an act or instance of rising up **synonyms** see REBELLION

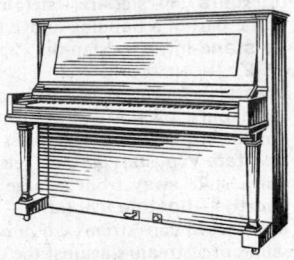
upright piano

up·riv·er \'əp-'riv-ər\ *adv or adj* : toward or at a point nearer the start of a river

up·roar \'əp-ˌrō(ə)r, -ˌrȯ(ə)r\ *n* : a state of commotion, excitement, or violent disturbance

Word History The *-roar* part of the word *uproar* has no connection with the sounds made by some animals and crowds. The first use of *uproar* was as the translation of the Dutch word *oproer,* meaning "uprising, rebellion, revolt." Thus, the first meaning of *uproar* was the same as the Dutch meaning of *oproer.* Nowadays, this sense of *uproar* is no longer used. Because people thought that the *roar* of *uproar* referred to loud cries and sounds, they began to use the word to mean "a noisy disturbance or commotion." This is the sense of *uproar* that has survived. [from Dutch *oproer* "revolt, uprising," from *op* "up" and *roer* "motion"; the English spelling and meaning influenced by the similarity of the English *roar* to Dutch *roer*]

up·roar·i·ous \ˌə-'prōr-ē-əs, -'prȯr-\ *adj* **1** : marked by uproar **2** : extremely funny — **up·roar·i·ous·ly** *adv*

up·root \(ˌ)ə-'prüt, -'pru̇t\ *vb* : to remove by or as if by pulling up by the roots ⟨*uproot* a vine⟩ ⟨families *uprooted* by war⟩

¹up·set \(ˌ)əp-'set\ *vb* **-set; -set·ting** **1** : to force or be forced out of the usual position : OVERTURN **2 a** : to worry, anger, or cause unhappiness to ⟨the news *upset* me⟩ **b** : to make somewhat ill ⟨spicy food *upsets* my stomach⟩ **3 a** : to throw into disorder **b** : to defeat unexpectedly

²up·set \'əp-ˌset\ *n* **1** : an act or result of upsetting : a state of being upset **2 a** : a minor illness ⟨a stomach *upset*⟩ **b** : a period of worry or unhappiness

³up·set \(ˌ)əp-'set\ *adj* : emotionally disturbed or shaken up ⟨was too *upset* to talk⟩

up·shot \'əp-ˌshät\ *n* : final result : OUTCOME

up·side down \ˌəp-ˌsīd-'daun\ *adv* **1** : with the upper part underneath and the lower part on top **2** : in or into great disorder — **upside–down** *adj*

\ə\ **abut**	\au̇\ **out**	\i\ **tip**	\ȯ\ **saw**	\u̇\ **foot**
\ər\ **further**	\ch\ **chin**	\ī\ **life**	\ȯi\ **coin**	\y\ **yet**
\a\ **mat**	\e\ **pet**	\j\ **job**	\th\ **thin**	\yü\ **few**
\ā\ **take**	\ē\ **easy**	\ŋ\ **sing**	\th\ **this**	\yu̇\ **cure**
\ä\ **cot, cart**	\g\ **go**	\ō\ **bone**	\ü\ **food**	\zh\ **vision**

upside–down cake *n* : a cake baked with a layer of fruit (as pineapple) on the bottom and served fruit side up

up·si·lon \'yüp-sə-ˌlän, 'əp-, -lən\ *n* : the 20th letter of the Greek alphabet — Y or υ

¹**up·stage** \'əp-ˌstāj\ *adv or adj* : toward or at the part of the stage or set farthest from the audience or the motion=picture or television camera

²**up·stage** \ˌəp-'stāj\ *vb* : to steal attention away from ⟨children *upstaging* adult performers⟩

¹**up·stairs** \'əp-ˌsta(ə)rz, -'ste(ə)rz\ *adv* **1** : up the stairs : to or on a higher floor **2** : to or at a higher position or level

²**up·stairs** \'əp-ˌsta(ə)rz, -'ste(ə)rz\ *adj* : located on an upper floor ⟨the *upstairs* bedroom⟩

³**up·stairs** \'əp-'sta(ə)rz, -'ste(ə)rz; 'əp-ˌsta(ə)rz, -ˌste(ə)rz\ *n* : the part of a building above the ground floor

up·stand·ing \ˌəp-'stan-diŋ, 'əp-ˌstan-\ *adj* **1** : ¹VERTICAL **2** : ¹HONEST 3

up·start \'əp-ˌstärt\ *n* : a person who has risen suddenly (as from a low position to wealth or power); *esp* : one who makes a great show of success

up·state \'əp-ˌstāt\ *adj* : of, relating to, or typical of a part of a state away from a large city and especially to the north — **upstate** *n or adv*

up·stream \'əp-'strēm\ *adv or adj* : at or toward the beginning of a stream : against the current ⟨salmon swimming *upstream*⟩

up·stroke \'əp-ˌstrōk\ *n* : an upward stroke (as of a pen)

up·surge \'əp-ˌsərj\ *n* : a rapid or sudden rise ⟨an *upsurge* of popularity⟩

up·sweep \'əp-ˌswēp\ *vb* **-swept** \-ˌswept\; **-sweep·ing** : to sweep upward : curve or slope upward — **upsweep** *n*

up·swept \'əp-ˌswept\ *adj* : swept upward ⟨an *upswept* hairdo⟩

up·swing \'əp-ˌswiŋ\ *n* : an upward swing; *esp* : a marked increase or improvement (as in activity) ⟨business is on the *upswing*⟩

up·take \'əp-ˌtāk\ *n* **1** : ¹UNDERSTANDING 1, COMPREHENSION ⟨quick on the *uptake*⟩ **2** : a process especially in a living organism of absorbing and combining with something ⟨oxygen *uptake*⟩

up·tight \'əp-'tīt, (ˌ)əp-'tīt, ˌəp-ˌtīt\ *adj* : being tense, nervous, or uneasy

up·tilt \ˌəp-'tilt\ *vb* : to tilt upward

up to *prep* **1** : as far as a named part or place ⟨sank *up to* my hips⟩ **2** : in accordance with ⟨the game was not *up to* our standards⟩ **3 a** : to the limit of ⟨come in sizes *up to* 10⟩ **b** : as many or as much as ⟨carry *up to* 10 tons⟩ **4** : ¹UNTIL, TILL ⟨from dawn *up to* dusk⟩

up–to–date *adj* **1** : coming up to the present time ⟨*up-to-date* maps⟩ **2** : knowing, being, or making use of what is new or modern ⟨*up-to-date* methods⟩ — **up–to–date·ness** *n*

up·town \'əp-'taùn\ *adv* : toward, to, or in the upper part of a town ⟨took the bus *uptown*⟩ — **uptown** *adj*

up·trend \'əp-ˌtrend\ *n* : a rise especially in business or activity

¹**up·turn** \'əp-ˌtərn, ˌəp-'tərn\ *vb* **1** : to turn up or over ⟨an *upturned* boat⟩ **2** : to turn or direct upward ⟨*upturned* faces⟩

²**up·turn** \'əp-ˌtərn\ *n* : an upward turning (as toward better conditions or higher prices)

¹**up·ward** \'əp-wərd\ *or* **up·wards** \-wərdz\ *adv* **1** : in a direction from lower to higher ⟨the land rises *upward*⟩ **2** : toward a higher or better condition ⟨worked my way *upward* in the business⟩ **3** : toward a greater amount or higher number, degree, or rate ⟨prices shot *upward*⟩

²**upward** *adj* : directed toward or located in a higher place or level : ASCENDING — **up·ward·ly** *adv*

upwards of *also* **upward of** *adv* : more than ⟨*upwards of* half a million people⟩

up·well·ing \ˌəp-'wel-iŋ\ *n* : the process or an example of rising or appearing to rise to the surface and flowing outward; *esp* : the process of movement of deeper cooler layers of ocean water that are often rich in nourishing substances to the surface

up·wind \'əp-'wind\ *adv or adj* : in the direction from which the wind is blowing

ura·cil \'yùr-ə-ˌsil, -səl\ *n* : a pyrimidine base that is one of the four bases coding hereditary information in RNA — compare ADENINE, CYTOSINE, GUANINE, THYMINE

ura·ni·nite \yù-'rā-nə-ˌnīt\ *n* : a mineral that is a black oxide of uranium, contains also various metals (as thorium and lead), and is the chief ore of uranium

ura·ni·um \yò-'rā-nē-əm\ *n* : a silvery heavy radioactive metallic element — see ELEMENT table

Word History The ancient Greek word *ouranos* meant "sky, heaven." It was fitting, then, for the Greeks to name their god of heaven *Ouranos* and their muse of astronomy *Ourania*. In Latin these names became *Uranus* and *Urania*. Uranus was the father of the god Saturn and the grandfather of Jupiter. In 1781 the English astronomer Sir William Herschel discovered by telescope the seventh planet of our solar system. It was the custom to name planets after Roman gods. Following this custom, the German astronomer Johann Bode suggested the name *Uranus* for this planet. It seemed a good idea since the fifth planet was called Jupiter and the sixth was Saturn. Eight years after the discovery of Uranus, the German chemist Martin Klaproth discovered a new element. He called it *uranium* after the new planet Uranus. [scientific Latin; named for the planet Uranus, from Latin *Uranus*, name of the god of heaven]

uranium hexa·flu·o·ride \-ˌhek-sə-'flù(-ə)r-ˌīd\ *n* : a compound of uranium and fluorine that is used in one major process for the separation of uranium 235 from ordinary uranium

uranium 238 *n* : the most stable form of uranium that has an atomic mass number of 238, breaks down in a series of nuclear changes into a form of lead, and can absorb neutrons and then go through a series of nuclear transformations to change into a form of plutonium

uranium 235 *n* : a light form of uranium of mass number 235 that when bombarded with neutrons splits rapidly into smaller atoms with the release of neutrons and atomic energy

Ura·nus \'yùr-ə-nəs, yù-'rā-\ *n* : the planet seventh in order from the sun — see PLANET table

ur·ban \'ər-bən\ *adj* : of, relating to, typical of, or being a city ⟨*urban* life⟩ ⟨an *urban* area⟩

ur·bane \ˌər-'bān\ *adj* : very polite and smooth in manner — **ur·ban·i·ty** \-'ban-ət-ē\ *n*

ur·ban·ite \'ər-bə-ˌnīt\ *n* : one living in a city

ur·ban·ize \'ər-bə-ˌnīz\ *vb* **-ized; -iz·ing** **1** : to cause to have an urban appearance ⟨*urbanized* areas⟩ **2** : to cause to take on an urban way of life ⟨*urbanized* the peasant population⟩ — **ur·ban·i·za·tion** \ˌər-bə-nə-'zā-shən\ *n*

urban renewal *n* : a construction program for replacing or restoring old or run-down buildings in an urban area

urban sprawl *n* : the spreading of urban structures into areas surrounding a city

ur·chin \'ər-chən\ *n* **1** : a mischievous child **2** : SEA URCHIN

-ure *n suffix* **1** : act : process : being ⟨expos*ure*⟩ **2** : office : function; *also* : body performing (such) a function ⟨legislat*ure*⟩ [derived from Latin *-ura* (noun suffix) "-ure"]

urea \yù-'rē-ə\ *n* : a soluble nitrogen-containing compound that is the chief solid substance in the urine of mammals and is an end product of protein breakdown

ure·ter \'yùr-ət-ər\ *n* : a tube that carries urine from a kidney to the bladder or cloaca

ure·thra \yù-'rē-thrə\ *n, pl* **-thras** *or* **ure·thrae** \-thrē\ : a canal that in most mammals carries off urine from the bladder and in the male serves as a passage for the release of semen from the body — **ure·thral** \-thrəl\ *adj*

¹urge \ˈərj\ *vb* **urged; urg·ing** **1** : to ask for or support earnestly ⟨continually *urging* reform⟩ **2** : to try to persuade ⟨*urge* a guest to stay longer⟩ **3** : to force or drive to some course or activity (as greater speed) ⟨riders *urging* their horses on⟩

²urge *n* **1** : the act or process of urging **2** : a strong desire especially to achieve a goal ⟨the *urge* to win⟩

ur·gen·cy \ˈər-jən-sē\ *n* : the quality or state of being urgent

ur·gent \ˈər-jənt\ *adj* **1 a** : calling for immediate attention : PRESSING ⟨an *urgent* need for food⟩ **b** : indicating an urgent desire or need ⟨an *urgent* manner⟩ **2** : urging very earnestly — **ur·gent·ly** *adv*

uric \ˈyu̇(ə)r-ik\ *adj* : of, relating to, or found in urine

uric acid *n* : a white odorless nitrogen-containing acid that is present only in small quantities in the urine of mammals but is the chief form in which nitrogen is eliminated from the body especially of birds, reptiles, and insects

uri·nal \ˈyu̇r-ən-ᵊl\ *n* : a container for receiving urine; *also* : a place for urinating

uri·nal·y·sis \ˌyu̇r-ə-ˈnal-ə-səs\ *n, pl* **-nal·y·ses** \-ə-ˌsēz\ : the analysis of urine

uri·nary \ˈyu̇r-ə-ˌner-ē\ *adj* **1** : relating to, occurring in, affecting, or making up the organs of the urinary tract **2** : of, relating to, or used for urine

urinary tract *n* : the body organs and passages through which urine passes and which consist of the tubes and cavity of the kidney, the ureters, the bladder, and the urethra

uri·nate \ˈyu̇r-ə-ˌnāt\ *vb* **-nat·ed; -nat·ing** : to release or give off urine — **uri·na·tion** \ˌyu̇r-ə-ˈnā-shən\ *n*

urine \ˈyu̇r-ən\ *n* : waste material that is secreted by the kidneys, is rich in the end products of protein breakdown, and is usually a yellowish liquid in mammals but semisolid in birds and reptiles

URL \ˌyu̇-ˌär-ˈel, ˈərl\ *n* : an address (as of a document or website) on the Internet [*uniform resource locator* or *universal resource locator*]

urn \ˈərn\ *n* **1** : a container that has the form of a vase on a base and often is used for keeping the ashes of the dead **2** : a closed vessel usually with a faucet for serving a hot beverage ⟨coffee *urn*⟩

Ur·sa Ma·jor \ˌər-sə-ˈmā-jər\ *n* : the northern group of stars that is the easiest to pick out, is located near the north pole of the heavens, and contains the stars forming the Big Dipper two of which are in a line pointing in the direction of the North Star — called also *Great Bear*

Ursa Mi·nor \-ˈmī-nər\ *n* : the group of stars that includes the north pole of the heavens and the stars which form the Little Dipper with the North Star at the tip of the handle — called also *Little Bear*

urn 2

us \(ˈ)əs\ *pron, objective case of* WE

us·able \ˈyü-zə-bəl\ *adj* : suitable or fit for use ⟨usable waste⟩

us·age \ˈyü-sij, -zij\ *n* **1 a** : usual practice or procedure **b** : the way in which words and phrases are actually used **2 a** : the action of using : USE ⟨increasing *usage* of the nation's highways⟩ **b** : manner of treating ⟨restaurant dishes receive rough *usage*⟩ **synonyms** see HABIT

USB \ˌyü-(ˌ)es-ˈbē\ *n* : a system for connecting a computer to another device (as a printer, keyboard, or mouse) by using a special kind of cord [*Universal Serial Bus*]

¹use \ˈyüs\ *n* **1 a** : the act or practice of using something : APPLICATION ⟨put knowledge to *use*⟩ **b** : the fact or state of being used ⟨a dish in daily *use*⟩ **c** : way of using ⟨the proper *use* of tools⟩ **2 a** : the privilege or benefit of using something ⟨gave me the *use* of their car⟩ **b** : the ability or power to use something (as a limb) ⟨after the operation you'll again have the *use* of your leg⟩ **3 a** : a particular service or end ⟨no *use* in crying all the time⟩ **b** : the quality of being useful ⟨old clothes that are still of some *use*⟩ **c** : a reason or need to use ⟨took only what he had *use* for⟩ **4** : LIKING ⟨had no *use* for modern art⟩

²use \ˈyüz\ *vb* **used** \ˈyüzd, *in the phrase* "used to" *usually* ˈyüst\; **us·ing** \ˈyü-ziŋ\ **1** : to put into action or service : EMPLOY ⟨pronunciations *used* by different people⟩ ⟨*used* care in handling the antiques⟩ **2** : to take into the body regularly ⟨never *uses* tobacco⟩ **3** : to carry out an action by means of : UTILIZE ⟨*use* caution⟩ **4** : to make use of : CONSUME 2 ⟨the car *uses* a lot of gas⟩ **5** : to behave toward : TREAT ⟨*used* the prisoners cruelly⟩ **6** — used in the past tense with *to* to show a former practice, fact, or state ⟨claims winters *used* to be harder⟩ — **us·er** \ˈyü-zər\ *n*

used \ˈyüzd, *in the phrase* "used to" *usually* ˈyüst\ *adj* **1** : employed in accomplishing something ⟨a much *used* excuse⟩ **2** : that has been used; *esp* : SECONDHAND 2a ⟨*used* cars⟩ **3** : having the habit of doing or experiencing ⟨is *used* to flying⟩

use·ful \ˈyüs-fəl\ *adj* **1** : capable of being put to use : USABLE ⟨*useful* scraps of material⟩ **2** : having practical value ⟨a *useful* invention⟩ — **use·ful·ly** \-fə-lē\ *adv* — **use·ful·ness** *n*

use·less \ˈyüs-ləs\ *adj* : having or being of no use — **use·less·ly** *adv* — **use·less·ness** *n*

user name *n* : a sequence of characters that identifies a user when logging onto a computer or website — called also *user ID*

use up *vb* : to make complete use of : EXHAUST ⟨*used up* all the supplies⟩

¹ush·er \ˈəsh-ər\ *n* : a person who leads other persons to seats (as in a theater or at a wedding)

²usher *vb* **ush·ered; ush·er·ing** **1** : to lead to a place **2** : to cause to enter : INTRODUCE ⟨*usher* in a new era⟩

usu·al \ˈyüzh-(ə-)wəl, ˈyüzh-əl\ *adj* : done, found, or used in the ordinary course of events : NORMAL, REGULAR ⟨less than the *usual* fee⟩ ⟨the *usual* route to work⟩ — **usu·al·ly** \ˈyüzh-(ə-)wə-lē, ˈyüzh-(ə-)lē, *in rapid speech* ˈyüz-lē\ *adv*

usu·rer \ˈyü-zhər-ər, ˈyüzh-rər\ *n* : one who lends money especially at a very high rate of interest

usu·ri·ous \yu̇-ˈzhu̇r-ē-əs, -ˈzu̇r-\ *adj* : practicing, involving, or being usury ⟨*usurious* interest⟩

usurp \yu̇-ˈsərp *also* -ˈzərp\ *vb* : to seize and hold by force or without right ⟨*usurp* power from the king⟩

usu·ry \ˈyüzh-(ə-)rē\ *n, pl* **usu·ries** **1** : the lending of money with an interest charge for its use **2** : a rate of interest that is very high or higher than the usual rate

uten·sil \yu̇-ˈten(t)-səl\ *n* **1** : a device or container used in a household and especially a kitchen **2** : an article serving a useful purpose ⟨writing *utensils*⟩ **synonyms** see IMPLEMENT

uter·ine \ˈyüt-ə-ˌrīn, -rən\ *adj* : of, relating to, or affecting the uterus ⟨the *uterine* lining⟩ ⟨*uterine* cancer⟩

uter·us \ˈyüt-ə-rəs\ *n, pl* **uter·us·es** *or* **uteri** \-ˌrī\ : the muscular organ of a female mammal in which the young develop before birth — called also *womb*

\ə\ **abut**	\au̇\ **out**	\i\ **tip**	\ȯ\ **saw**	\u̇\ **foot**
\ər\ **further**	\ch\ **chin**	\ī\ **life**	\ȯi\ **coin**	\y\ **yet**
\a\ **mat**	\e\ **pet**	\j\ **job**	\th\ **thin**	\yü\ **few**
\ā\ **take**	\ē\ **easy**	\ŋ\ **sing**	\th\ **this**	\yu̇\ **cure**
\ä\ **cot, cart**	\g\ **go**	\ō\ **bone**	\ü\ **food**	\zh\ **vision**

util·i·tar·i·an \(ˌ)yü-ˌtil-ə-ˈter-ē-ən\ *adj* **1** : of or relating to utility **2** : aiming at usefulness rather than beauty ⟨*utilitarian* furniture⟩

¹util·i·ty \yü-ˈtil-ət-ē\ *n, pl* **-ties** **1** : the quality or state of being useful : USEFULNESS **2** : something useful or designed for use **3 a** : PUBLIC UTILITY **b** : a public service (as power or water) provided by a public utility **4** : a program designed to perform or aid in especially routine actions (as copying files or editing text) on a computer

²utility *adj* **1** : capable of serving as a substitute in various roles or positions ⟨*utility* infielder⟩ **2** : being of a usable but poor quality ⟨*utility* beef⟩ **3** : serving chiefly for usefulness rather than beauty : UTILITARIAN **4** : designed for general use ⟨*utility* bag⟩

uti·lize \ˈyüt-ᵊl-ˌīz\ *vb* **-lized; -liz·ing** : to make use of especially for a certain job — **uti·li·za·tion** \ˌyüt-ᵊl-ə-ˈzā-shən\ *n*

ut·most \ˈət-ˌmōst, *especially Southern* -məst\ *adj* **1** : located at the farthest or most distant point **2** : of the greatest or highest degree, quantity, number, or amount ⟨a matter of the *utmost* urgency⟩ [Old English *ūtmest* "outermost," from *ūt* "out" and *-mest* (a superlative adjective suffix similar to *-est*)] — **utmost** *n*

uto·pia \yù-ˈtō-pē-ə\ *n* **1** *often cap* : a place of ideal perfection especially in laws, government, and social conditions **2** : an impractical scheme for social improvement — **uto·pi·an** \-pē-ən\ *adj or n*

Word History In 1516 the English statesman Sir Thomas More published a book that compared the condition of his England to that of a perfect and imaginary country, *Utopia*. Everything that was wrong in England was perfect in Utopia. More was trying to show how people could live together in peace and happiness if they only did what he thought was right. But the name he gave his imaginary country showed that he did not really believe perfection could ever be reached. *Utopia* means, literally, "no place," since it was formed from the Greek *ou,* meaning "no, not," and *topos,* "place." Since More's time, *utopia* has come to mean "a place of ideal perfection." Over the years many books similar to *Utopia* have been written, and many plans for perfect societies proposed, most of them impractical. *Utopia* has also come to mean any such scheme or plan. [from *Utopia,* name of an imaginary ideal country in a book *Utopia* written by Sir Thomas More 1478–1535 English statesman and author; from Greek *ou* "not, no" and Greek *topos* "place"]

¹ut·ter \ˈət-ər\ *adj* : complete in extent or degree : TOTAL ⟨an *utter* impossibility⟩ ⟨*utter* strangers⟩ — **ut·ter·ly** *adv*

²utter *vb* **1** : to send forth usually as a sound ⟨*uttered* a laugh⟩ **2** : to express in words ⟨forced to *utter* the truth⟩

ut·ter·ance \ˈət-ə-rən(t)s\ *n* **1** : something uttered; *esp* : an oral or written statement **2** : the action of uttering with the voice : SPEECH **3** : power, style, or manner of speaking

ut·ter·most \ˈət-ər-ˌmōst\ *adj* : UTMOST **2** — **uttermost** *n*

uvu·la \ˈyü-vyə-lə\ *n, pl* **-las** *or* **uvu·lae** \-ˌlē, -ˌlī\ : the small fleshy fingerlike part hanging down from the back part of the roof of the mouth

V

v \ˈvē\ *n, pl* **v's** *or* **vs** *often cap* **1** : the 22nd letter of the English alphabet **2** : five in Roman numerals

va·can·cy \ˈvā-kən-sē\ *n, pl* **-cies** **1** : something (as an office or hotel room) that is vacant **2** : empty space **3** : the state of being vacant

va·cant \ˈvā-kənt\ *adj* **1** : not filled, used, or lived in ⟨a *vacant* house⟩ **2** : free from duties or care ⟨a few *vacant* hours⟩ **3** : showing lack of thought ⟨a *vacant* stare⟩ — **va·cant·ly** *adv*

va·cate \ˈvā-ˌkāt, vā-ˈkāt\ *vb* **va·cat·ed; va·cat·ing** : to leave vacant

¹va·ca·tion \vā-ˈkā-shən, və-\ *n* **1** : a period during which activity (as of a school) is stopped for a time **2** : a period spent away from home or business in travel or amusement

²vacation *vb* **-tioned; -tion·ing** \-sh(ə-)niŋ\ : to take or spend a vacation — **va·ca·tion·er** \-sh(ə-)nər\ *n*

va·ca·tion·ist \vā-ˈkā-sh(ə-)nəst\ *n* : a person taking a vacation

va·ca·tion·land \vā-ˈkā-shən-ˌland\ *n* : a place where many people go on vacation

vac·ci·nate \ˈvak-sə-ˌnāt\ *vb* **-nat·ed; -nat·ing** : to give a vaccine to usually by injection — **vac·ci·na·tor** \-ˌnāt-ər\ *n*

vac·ci·na·tion \ˌvak-sə-ˈnā-shən\ *n* **1** : the act of vaccinating **2** : the scar left by vaccinating

vac·cine \vak-ˈsēn, ˈvak-ˌsēn\ *n* : a preparation of killed, weakened, or fully infectious microbes that is given (as by injection) to produce or increase immunity to a particular disease

Word History Toward the end of the 18th century, Edward Jenner, an English physician, made an important discovery. He observed that dairymaids who had the disease cowpox did not get smallpox, a much more serious disease. Working from this observation, he injected a person with material taken from another person's cowpox sores. He found out that this injection protected that person against the dreaded smallpox. He reported these findings in an article in which he used the Latin translation of *cowpox, variolae vaccinae.* The Latin word *vaccinae* was formed from the adjective *vaccinus* meaning "of or relating to cows." This word, in turn, was based on the noun *vacca,* meaning "cow." The cowpox material used for injections was then called *vaccine.* The injection itself was called *vaccination.* From this noun we created the verb *vaccinate* and the noun *vaccinator.* [from Latin *vaccinus* (adjective) "of or from cows," from *vacca* "cow" — related to BUCKAROO, VAQUERO]

vac·il·late \ˈvas-ə-ˌlāt\ *vb* **-lat·ed; -lat·ing** : to hesitate between courses or opinions : be unable to choose — **vac·il·la·tion** \ˌvas-ə-ˈlā-shən\ *n* — **vac·il·la·tor** \ˈvas-ə-ˌlāt-ər\ *n*

va·cu·ity \va-ˈkyü-ət-ē, və-\ *n, pl* **-ities** **1** : an empty space **2** : the quality or state of being vacuous

vac·u·ole \ˈvak-yə-ˌwōl\ *n* : a cavity in bodily tissues or in the cytoplasm of a cell that is usually filled with fluid — **vac·u·o·lar** \ˌvak-yə-ˈwō-lər, -ˌlär\ *adj*

vac·u·ous \ˈvak-yə-wəs\ *adj* : lacking ideas or intelligence — **vac·u·ous·ly** *adv*

¹vac·u·um \ˈvak-yüm, -yù-əm, -yəm\ *n, pl* **vac·u·ums** *or* **vac·ua** \-yə-wə\ **1 a** : a space completely empty of matter **b** : a space from which most of the air has been removed (as by a pump) **2** : VACUUM CLEANER [from Latin *vacuum* "emptiness," from *vacuus* "empty"]

²vacuum *adj* : of, containing, producing, or using a partial vacuum ⟨the *vacuum* method of making coffee⟩

³vacuum *vb* : to use a vacuum cleaner on

vacuum bottle *n* : THERMOS

vacuum cleaner *n* : an electrical appliance for cleaning (as floors or rugs) by suction

vac·u·um–packed \ˌvak-yüm-ˈpakt, -yu̇-əm-, -yəm-\ *adj* : having much of the air removed before being sealed

vacuum pump *n* : a pump for removing gas from an enclosed space

vacuum tube *n* : an electron tube from which most of the air has been removed

¹**vag·a·bond** \ˈvag-ə-ˌbänd\ *adj* : moving from place to place without a fixed home [Middle English *vagabond* "moving about with no fixed home," from early French *vacabund* (same meaning), from Latin *vagabundus* (same meaning), from *vagari* "to wander about" — related to EXTRAVAGANT]

²**vagabond** *n* : a person who leads a vagabond life

va·ga·ry \ˈvā-gə-rē; və-ˈge(ə)r-ē, -ˈga(ə)r-\ *n, pl* **-ries** : an odd or unpredictable idea or happening

va·gi·na \və-ˈjī-nə\ *n, pl* **-nas** *also* **-nae** \-nē\ : a canal that leads from the uterus to the outside opening of the female sex organs — **vag·i·nal** \ˈvaj-ən-ᵊl\ *adj*

va·gran·cy \ˈvā-grən(t)-sē\ *n, pl* **-cies** : the state or action of being vagrant

¹**va·grant** \ˈvā-grənt\ *n* : a person who has no steady job and wanders from place to place

²**vagrant** *adj* **1** : wandering about from place to place **2** : having no fixed course ⟨*vagrant* breezes⟩

vague \ˈvāg\ *adj* **vagu·er**; **vagu·est** **1** : not clearly expressed ⟨a *vague* answer⟩ **2** : not clearly understood or sensed ⟨only a *vague* idea of where we were⟩ **3** : not clearly outlined : INDISTINCT, SHADOWY ⟨*vague* figures in the mist⟩ — **vague·ly** *adv* — **vague·ness** *n*

vain \ˈvān\ *adj* **1** : having no success : USELESS ⟨a *vain* attempt to escape⟩ **2** : proud of one's looks or abilities — **vain·ly** *adv* — **vain·ness** *n* — **in vain 1** : without success **2** : in an unholy way

vain·glo·ri·ous \(ˈ)vān-ˈglȯr-ē-əs, -ˈglȯr-\ *adj* : being vain and boastful : showing vainglory — **vain·glo·ri·ous·ly** *adv* — **vain·glo·ri·ous·ness** *n*

vain·glo·ry \ˈvān-ˌglȯr-ē, -ˌglȯr-\ *n* : too much pride especially in what one has done

va·lance \ˈval-ən(t)s, ˈvāl-\ *n* : a short drapery or wood or metal frame (as across the top of a window)

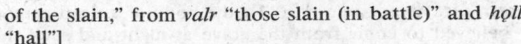

V valance

vale \ˈvā(ə)l\ *n* : VALLEY

vale·dic·to·ri·an \ˌval-ə-ˌdik-ˈtōr-ē-ən, -ˈtȯr-\ *n* : the student usually of the highest rank in a graduating class who gives the farewell speech at graduation ceremonies

vale·dic·to·ry \ˌval-ə-ˈdik-t(ə-)rē\ *adj* : of or relating to a leaving : expressing a farewell

va·lence \ˈvā-lən(t)s\ *n* : the combining power of an atom as shown by the number of electrons in its outermost energy level that are lost, gained, or shared in the formation of chemical bonds

val·en·tine \ˈval-ən-ˌtīn\ *n* **1** : a sweetheart given something as a sign of affection on Valentine's Day **2** : a gift or greeting sent or given on Valentine's Day

Valentine's Day *also* **Valentine Day** *n* : February 14 observed in honor of St. Valentine and as a time for exchanging valentines

va·let \ˈval-ā, va-ˈlā, ˈval-ət\ *n* **1** : a male servant who takes care of a man's clothes and does personal services **2** : a hotel employee who does personal services for guests

Val·hal·la \val-ˈhal-ə\ *n* : the hall of Odin in Norse mythology to which the Valkyries take heroes killed in battle [derived from an early Norse word *Valhǫll*, literally "hall of the slain," from *valr* "those slain (in battle)" and *hǫll* "hall"]

¹**val·iant** \ˈval-yənt\ *adj* **1** : boldly brave **2** : done with courage : HEROIC — **val·iant·ly** *adv*

²**valiant** *n* : a valiant person

val·id \ˈval-əd\ *adj* **1** : legally binding **2** : founded on truth or fact ⟨a *valid* argument⟩ — **val·id·ly** *adv*

val·i·date \ˈval-ə-ˌdāt\ *vb* **-dat·ed; -dat·ing** : to make valid — **val·i·da·tion** \ˌval-ə-ˈdā-shən\ *n*

va·lid·i·ty \və-ˈlid-ət-ē, va-\ *n* : the quality or state of being valid

va·lise \və-ˈlēs\ *n* : SUITCASE

Val·kyr·ie \val-ˈkir-ē\ *n* : any of the maidens in Norse mythology who take slain heroes to Valhalla

val·ley \ˈval-ē\ *n, pl* **valleys** : an area of lowland between ranges of hills or mountains

val·or \ˈval-ər\ *n* : personal bravery in the face of danger **synonyms** see COURAGE

val·or·ous \ˈval-ə-rəs\ *adj* : having or showing valor : BRAVE

¹**val·u·able** \ˈval-yə-(wə-)bəl\ *adj* **1** : worth a large amount of money ⟨a *valuable* necklace⟩ **2** : of great use or service ⟨*valuable* advice⟩ — **val·u·able·ness** *n* — **val·u·ably** \-blē\ *adv*

²**valuable** *n* : a possession (as a jewel) of great value — usually used in plural

val·u·a·tion \ˌval-yə-ˈwā-shən\ *n* : the value placed on something

¹**val·ue** \ˈval-yü\ *n* **1** : a fair return in goods, services, or money for something exchanged **2** : the amount of money something is worth **3** : worth, utility, or importance in comparison with something else **4** : a numerical quantity that is assigned or is found by calculation or measurement ⟨find the *value* of x⟩ **5** : the length of time a musical note is to be held **6** : the lightness or darkness of a color **7** : something (as a belief) that is valuable or desirable — **val·ue·less** \-yü-ləs, -yə-\ *adj*

²**value** *vb* **val·ued; valu·ing** **1** : to estimate the worth of ⟨was *valued* at $200⟩ **2** : to think highly of ⟨*values* your advice⟩ — **valu·er** \-yə-wər\ *n*

value judgment *n* : a judgment assigning a value (as good or bad) to something

valve \ˈvalv\ *n* **1** : a bodily structure (as in a vein or the heart) that closes temporarily to prevent passage of material or that allows movement of a fluid in one direction only **2 a** : a mechanical device by which the flow of liquid, gas, or loose material in bulk may be controlled by a movable part; *also* : the movable part of such a device **b** : a device in a brass musical instrument for quickly changing the tube length in order to make the tone higher or lower **3** : one of the separate pieces that make up the shell of some animals (as clams) and are often hinged **4** : one of the pieces into which a ripe seed capsule or pod separates — **valved** \ˈvalvd\ *adj*

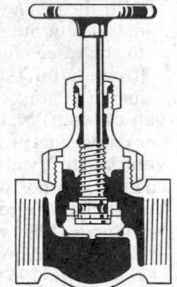

valve 2a

val·vu·lar \ˈval-vyə-lər\ *adj* : of, relating to, or affecting a valve especially of the heart ⟨*valvular* heart disease⟩

\ə\ **abut**	\au̇\ **out**	\i\ **tip**	\ȯ\ **saw**	\u̇\ **foot**
\ər\ **further**	\ch\ **chin**	\ī\ **life**	\ȯi\ **coin**	\y\ **yet**
\a\ **mat**	\e\ **pet**	\j\ **job**	\th\ **thin**	\yü\ **few**
\ā\ **take**	\ē\ **easy**	\ŋ\ **sing**	\th\ **this**	\yu̇\ **cure**
\ä\ **cot, cart**	\g\ **go**	\ō\ **bone**	\ü\ **food**	\zh\ **vision**

vam·pire \'vam-ˌpī(ə)r\ *n* **1** : the body of a dead person believed to come from the grave at night and suck the blood of sleeping persons **2** : VAMPIRE BAT

vampire bat *n* : any of three bats of Mexico and Central and South America that feed on blood especially of domestic animals and sometimes carry and pass on diseases (as rabies); *also* : any of several other bats that do not feed on blood but are sometimes said to do so

¹**van** \'van\ *n* : VANGUARD [a shortened form of *vanguard*]

²**van** *n* **1** : a usually closed wagon or truck for transporting goods or animals **2** : an enclosed motor vehicle shaped like a box that is used for a variety of purposes and has rear or side doors and side panels often with windows [a shortened form of *caravan* "vehicle"]

vampire bat

va·na·di·um \və-'nād-ē-əm\ *n* : a grayish metallic element found combined in minerals and used especially to form alloys (as of steel) — see ELEMENT table

Van Al·len belt \va-ˌnal-ən-, və-\ *n* : a belt of high-energy charged particles that surrounds the earth in the magnetosphere [named for James A. *Van Allen* born 1914 American physicist]

van·dal \'van-dᵊl\ *n* **1** *cap* : a member of a Germanic people overrunning Gaul, Spain, and northern Africa in the fourth and fifth centuries A.D. **2** : a person who destroys or damages property on purpose

Word History The Vandals were a Germanic people who originally lived in northern Europe. In the fourth and fifth centuries, however, other barbarian peoples, especially the Huns, forced the Vandals to migrate westward and southward through what are now the lands of France and Spain. They finally settled in northern Africa. But as they migrated, the Vandals did not just pass through an area. They destroyed many cities and towns. They probably were no worse than other barbarians, but they became widely known for destruction. This probably happened because they invaded and looted the city of Rome in 455. They destroyed or ruined much of what they could not take with them. The Vandals were later defeated by the Roman army but their bad reputation caused their name to be used for "a deliberately destructive person." [from Latin *Vandalii* (plural) "The Vandals"; of Germanic origin]

van·dal·ism \'van-dᵊl-ˌiz-əm\ *n* : intentional destruction or damage to property

van·dal·ize \'van-dᵊl-ˌīz\ *vb* **-ized; -iz·ing** : to destroy or damage property on purpose

Van de Graaff generator \ˌvan-də-ˌgraf-\ *n* : a device for producing high voltages by building up charge in the inside of a hollow sphere [named for Robert J. *Van de Graaff* 1901–1967 American physicist]

Van·dyke \van-'dīk\ *n* : a trim pointed beard

vane \'vān\ *n* **1** : a movable device attached to something high to show which way the wind is blowing **2** : a thin flat or curved object that is rotated about an axis by a flow of fluid (as air or water) or that rotates to cause a fluid to flow or that changes the direction of a flow of fluid ⟨the *vanes* of a windmill⟩ **3** : the web or flat expanded part of a feather — **vaned** \'vānd\ *adj*

van·guard \'van-ˌgärd\ *n* **1** : the troops moving at the head of an army **2** : the forefront of an action or movement [Middle English *vauntgard* "the troops moving at the head of an army," from early French *vantgarde, avantgarde* (same meaning), derived from *avant-* "fore-, in front" and *garde* "guard"]

va·nil·la \və-'nil-ə, -'nel-\ *n* : a flavoring made from the long pods of a tropical American climbing orchid; *also* : this orchid or one of the same genus

vanilla bean *n* : the long pod of a vanilla orchid

van·ish \'van-ish\ *vb* : to pass from sight or existence — **van·ish·er** *n*

vanishing cream *n* : a cosmetic like cold cream but less greasy

vanishing point *n* : a point at which parallel lines seem to meet (as in a drawing)

van·i·ty \'van-ət-ē\ *n, pl* **-ties** **1** : something that is vain **2** : the quality or fact of being vain **3 a** : ³COMPACT 1 **b** : DRESSING TABLE

van·quish \'van-kwish, 'van-\ *vb* : to defeat and gain control of completely **synonyms** see CONQUER — **van·quish·er** *n*

van·tage \'vant-ij\ *n* : a position giving advantage or a wide view

vantage point *n* : POINT OF VIEW

vap·id \'vap-əd\ *adj* : being dull or uninteresting — **vap·id·ly** *adv*

va·por \'vā-pər\ *n* **1** : fine particles of matter (as fog or smoke) floating in the air and clouding it **2** : a substance in the gaseous state

va·por·ize \'vā-pə-ˌrīz\ *vb* **-ized; -iz·ing** : to turn from a liquid or solid into vapor — **va·por·i·za·tion** \ˌvā-pə-rə-'zā-shən\ *n*

va·por·iz·er \'vā-pə-ˌrī-zər\ *n* : a device that vaporizes something (as water or a liquid containing medicine)

va·por·ware \'vā-pər-ˌwa(ə)r, -ˌwe(ə)r\ *n* : a computer-related product that has been widely advertised but has not and may never become available

vapour *chiefly British variant of* VAPOR

va·que·ro \vä-'ke(ə)r-ō\ *n, pl* **-ros** : COWBOY [from Spanish *vaquero* "cowboy," from *vaca* "cow," from Latin *vacca* "cow" — related to BUCKAROO, VACCINE; see *Word History* at VACCINE]

vari·abil·i·ty \ˌver-ē-ə-'bil-ət-ē, ˌvar-\ *n* : the quality or fact of being variable

¹**vari·able** \'ver-ē-ə-bəl, 'var-\ *adj* **1** : able to change : likely to be changed : CHANGEABLE ⟨winds light and *variable*⟩ **2** : having the characteristics of a variable **3** : not true to the usual or normal type : ABERRANT ⟨a *variable* species of wheat⟩ — **vari·able·ness** \'ver-ē-ə-bəl-nəs, 'var-\ *n* — **vari·ably** \-blē\ *adv*

²**variable** *n* **1 a** : a quantity that may take on any one of a set of values **b** : a mathematical symbol representing a variable **2** : something that is variable **3** : a factor in a scientific experiment that may be subject to change ⟨controlled all *variables* except temperature⟩

variable star *n* : a star whose brightness changes usually in more or less regular periods

vari·ance \'ver-ē-ən(t)s, 'var-\ *n* **1** : the quality or state of being variable or variant : DIFFERENCE ⟨yearly *variance* in growth⟩ **2** : the fact or state of being in disagreement : DISPUTE **3** : the square of the standard deviation — **at variance** : not in harmony or agreement

¹**vari·ant** \'ver-ē-ənt, 'var-\ *adj* : differing from others of its kind or class

²**variant** *n* **1** : an individual that shows variation from a type or norm **2** : one of two or more different spellings or pronunciations of the same word

vari·a·tion \ˌver-ē-'ā-shən, ˌvar-\ *n* **1 a** : a change in form, position, or condition **b** : amount of change or difference **2** : the repeating of a musical passage with a change in

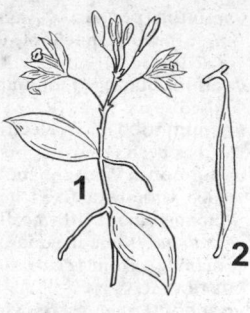
1 vanilla orchid, *2* vanilla bean

rhythm, tune, harmony, or key ⟨*variations* on a theme by Haydn⟩ **3 a** : change in the characteristics that are usual for a species or group **b** : an individual or group showing variation — **vari·a·tion·al** \-shnəl, -shən-ᵊl\ *adj*

vari·col·ored \'ver-i-ˌkəl-ərd, 'var-\ *adj* : having various colors ⟨*varicolored* marble⟩

var·i·cose \'var-ə-ˌkōs\ *adj* : abnormally swollen or made larger or wider ⟨*varicose* veins⟩

var·ied \'ver-ēd, 'var-\ *adj* **1** : having many forms or types : DIVERSE **2** : VARIEGATED 1 — **var·ied·ly** *adv*

var·ie·gat·ed \'ver-ē-ə-ˌgāt-əd, 'ver-i-ˌgāt-, 'var-\ *adj* **1** : having patches, stripes, or marks of different colors ⟨*variegated* flowers⟩ **2** : full of variety ⟨a *variegated* career⟩

va·ri·ety \və-'rī-ət-ē\ *n, pl* **-et·ies 1** : the quality or state of having different forms or types **2** : a number or collection of different things : ASSORTMENT **3 a** : something differing from others of the class to which it belongs **b** : any of various groups of plants or animals within a species that are separated from other groups by characteristics not constant enough or too unimportant to separate species

variety meat *n* : an edible part (as the liver or tongue) of a slaughter animal other than skeletal muscle

variety show *n* : entertainment made up of separate performances (as dances and songs) that follow one another

variety store *n* : a retail store carrying a variety of goods

var·i·ous \'ver-ē-əs, 'var-\ *adj* **1** : of different kinds **2** : different one from another : UNLIKE ⟨animals as *various* as cat and mouse⟩ **3** : having many different characteristics ⟨spring is a *various* season⟩ **4** : made up of an indefinite number greater than one ⟨stopped at *various* places along the way⟩ — **var·i·ous·ly** *adv* — **var·i·ous·ness** *n*

var·let \'vär-lət\ *n* : a dishonest or tricky person

var·mint \'vär-mənt\ *n* **1** : an animal that is considered a pest **2** : an unlikable person : RASCAL

¹var·nish \'vär-nish\ *n* **1 a** : a liquid that when spread and allowed to dry on a surface forms a hard shiny typically transparent coating **b** : the covering or shiny coating given by varnish **2** : false outward appearance

²varnish *vb* : to cover with or as if with varnish

var·si·ty \'vär-sət-ē, -stē\ *n, pl* **-ties** : the main team representing a college, school, or club in contests [an altered form of *versity*, itself an old, shortened form of *university*]

varve \'värv\ *n* : a pair of layers of alternately finer and coarser silt or clay believed to be deposited annually in a body of still water

vary \'ver-ē, 'var-\ *vb* **var·ied; vary·ing 1** : to make a minor or partial change in **2** : to give variety to **3** : to show or undergo change **4 a** : to be different **b** : to change in bodily structure or function away from what is usual for members of a group — **vary·ing·ly** \-iŋ-lē\ *adv*

varying hare *n* : SNOWSHOE HARE

vas·cu·lar \'vas-kyə-lər\ *adj* : of or relating to a tube or channel for carrying a body fluid (as blood of an animal or sap of a plant) or to a system of such channels or tubes; *also* : supplied with or made up of such channels or tubes ⟨a *vascular* system⟩ ⟨*vascular* tissue⟩

vascular bundle *n* : a unit of the vascular system of a higher plant (as a fern or flowering plant) consisting usually of xylem and phloem together with parenchyma cells and fibers

vascular plant *n* : a plant having a specialized system for carrying fluids that includes xylem and phloem

vascular ray *n* : a band of tissue in a root or stem of a vascular plant that looks in cross section like a spoke of a wheel and that carries fluids along a radius away from the center of the root or stem

vas·cu·lum \'vas-kyə-ləm\ *n* : an often cylinder-shaped box usually of metal that is used for the temporary storage of plants collected in the field

vas def·er·ens \'vas-'def-ə-rənz, -ˌrenz\ *n, pl* **va·sa def·er·en·tia** \ˌvā-zə-ˌdef-ə-'ren-ch(ē-)ə\ : a bodily tube especially in a higher vertebrate that serves to carry sperm

vase \'vās, 'vāz\ *n* : an often round container of greater depth than width used chiefly for ornament or for flowers

Vas·e·line \'vas-ə-ˌlēn, ˌvas-ə-'lēn\ *trademark* — used for petroleum jelly

vas·sal \'vas-əl\ *n* : a person in the Middle Ages who received protection and land from a lord in return for loyalty and service

vast \'vast\ *adj* : very great in extent, size, amount, degree, or intensity ⟨a *vast* stretch of desert⟩ ⟨*vast* knowledge⟩ **synonyms** see ENORMOUS — **vast·ly** *adv* — **vast·ness** \'vas(t)-nəs\ *n*

vasty \'vas-tē\ *adj* **vast·i·er; -est** : VAST, IMMENSE

vat \'vat\ *n* : a large container (as a tub) especially for holding liquids in manufacturing processes

vaude·ville \'vȯd(-ə)-vəl, 'väd-, 'vȯd-, -ˌvil\ *n* : theatrical entertainment made up of a variety of songs, dances, and comic acts

Word History In the 15th century, a number of humorous songs became popular in France. The songs were said to have been written by a man who lived in the valley of the River Vire, which is located in northwest France. The songs became known as *chansons de vau de Vire*, meaning "songs of the valley of Vire." Other people were soon writing and performing similar songs. Before long, people no longer connected such songs with the valley of Vire. The name *chansons de vau de Vire* was shortened to one word, *vaudevire*. Further changes in spelling and pronunciation have given us the modern word *vaudeville*, which refers not only to humorous songs, but also to other forms of popular entertainment. [from French *vaudeville* "a humorous song or skit," derived from early French *vaudevire* "a song that makes fun of something," from *chansons de vau de Vire* "songs of the valley of Vire"]

¹vault \'vȯlt\ *n* **1 a** : an arched structure of stone or concrete forming a ceiling or roof **b** : an arch or dome suggesting a vault ⟨the *vault* of the sky⟩ **2** : a room or compartment for storage or safekeeping ⟨a bank *vault*⟩ **3** : a burial chamber

¹vault 1a

²vault *vb* : to leap or leap over with the aid of the hands or a pole — **vault·er** *n*

³vault *n* : an act of vaulting : LEAP

vaunt·ed \'vȯnt-əd, 'vänt-\ *adj* : much praised or boasted about ⟨the team's *vaunted* offense⟩

VCR \ˌvē-(ˌ)sē-'är\ *n* : a device for recording (as television programs) on videocassettes and playing them back [*videocassette recorder*]

've \v, əv\ *vb* : HAVE ⟨we've been there⟩

veal \'vē(ə)l\ *n* : a young calf or its flesh for use as meat

vec·tor \'vek-tər\ *n* **1** : a quantity that has magnitude and direction and that is usually represented by a line segment with the given direction and with a length representing the magnitude **2** : an organism (as an insect) that carries and passes on a disease-causing microbe

\ə\ **abut**	\au̇\ **out**	\i\ **tip**	\ȯ\ **saw**	\u̇\ **foot**
\ər\ **further**	\ch\ **chin**	\ī\ **life**	\ȯi\ **coin**	\y\ **yet**
\a\ **mat**	\e\ **pet**	\j\ **job**	\th\ **thin**	\yü\ **few**
\ā\ **take**	\ē\ **easy**	\ŋ\ **sing**	\th\ **this**	\yu̇\ **cure**
\ä\ **cot, cart**	\g\ **go**	\ō\ **bone**	\ü\ **food**	\zh\ **vision**

vee·jay \\'vē-ˌjā\\ *n* : an announcer of a program (as on television) that features music videos

veer \\'vi(ə)r\\ *vb* : to change direction or course ⟨the highway *veers* inland at this point⟩ — **veer** *n*

veg·an \\'vē-gən\\ *n* : a strict vegetarian who does not use animals or dairy products for food — **vegan** *adj* — **veg·an·ism** \\'vē-gə-ˌniz-əm\\ *n*

¹veg·e·ta·ble \\'vej-tə-bəl, 'vej-ət-ə-bəl\\ *adj* **1** : of, relating to, consisting of, or growing like plants ⟨*vegetable* growth⟩ **2** : made from, obtained from, or containing plants or plant products ⟨*vegetable* soup⟩

²vegetable *n* **1** : ²PLANT 1 **2** : a leafy plant (as the cabbage, bean, or potato) usually without woody tissue grown for an edible part that is usually eaten as part of a meal; *also* : such an edible part

vegetable oil *n* : an oil obtained from plant parts and especially from seeds or fruits

¹veg·e·tar·i·an \\ˌvej-ə-'ter-ē-ən\\ *n* **1** : a person who refrains from eating meat and lives on a diet made up of vegetables, fruits, grains, nuts, and sometimes eggs or dairy products **2** : HERBIVORE

²vegetarian *adj* **1** : of or relating to vegetarians **2** : consisting wholly of vegetables ⟨a *vegetarian* diet⟩

veg·e·tar·i·an·ism \\ˌvej-ə-'ter-ē-ə-ˌniz-əm\\ *n* : the theory and practice of living on a vegetarian diet

veg·e·tate \\'vej-ə-ˌtāt\\ *vb* **-tat·ed; -tat·ing** **1** : to live or grow in the manner of a plant **2** : to lead a lazy life by doing little but eating and growing **3** : to establish plant life in or on ⟨*vegetated* hillsides⟩

veg·e·ta·tion \\ˌvej-ə-'tā-shən\\ *n* **1** : the act or process of vegetating **2** : dull or inactive living ⟨a life of tranquil *vegetation*⟩ **3** : plant life or cover (as of an area)

veg·e·ta·tive \\'vej-ə-ˌtāt-iv\\ *adj* **1** : of, relating to, or functioning in nutrition and growth rather than reproduction **2** : of, relating to, or involving reproduction by other than sexual means — **veg·e·ta·tive·ly** *adv*

veg·gie \\'vej-ē\\ *n* : VEGETABLE

veggie burger *n* : a patty chiefly of vegetable-derived protein used as a meat substitute; *also* : a sandwich containing such a patty

ve·he·mence \\'vē-ə-mən(t)s\\ *n* : the quality or state of being vehement

ve·he·ment \\'vē-ə-mənt\\ *adj* **1** : showing great force or energy ⟨a *vehement* wind⟩ **2** : highly emotional ⟨*vehement* patriotism⟩ **3** : forcibly expressed ⟨*vehement* denials⟩ — **ve·he·ment·ly** *adv*

ve·hi·cle \\'vē-ˌ(h)ik-əl, 'vē-ə-kəl\\ *n* **1** : a means by which something is passed along, expressed, achieved, or shown ⟨movies are *vehicles* of ideas⟩ **2** : something used to transport persons or goods ⟨a space *vehicle*⟩

ve·hic·u·lar \\vē-'hik-yə-lər\\ *adj* : of, relating to, or designed for vehicles

¹veil \\'vā(ə)l\\ *n* **1** : a piece of cloth or net worn usually by women over the head and shoulders and sometimes over the face **2** : something that covers or hides like a veil ⟨lift the *veil* of secrecy⟩

²veil *vb* : to cover with or as if with a veil

vein \\'vān\\ *n* **1** : a long narrow opening in rock filled with mineral matter ⟨a *vein* of gold⟩ **2 a** : one of the blood vessels that carry blood from the capillaries back to the heart **b** : one of the vascular bundles forming the framework of a leaf **c** : one of the thickened ribs that stiffen the wings of an insect **3** : a wavy band or streak (as of a different color or texture) ⟨a marble with greenish *veins*⟩ **4** : a style of expression ⟨stories in a romantic *vein*⟩

veined \\'vānd\\ *adj* : marked with or as if with veins : having venation ⟨a *veined* leaf⟩

vein·ing \\'vā-niŋ\\ *n* : a pattern of veins : VENATION

Vel·cro \\'vel-krō\\ *trademark* — used for a nylon fabric that can be fastened to itself

veld *or* **veldt** \\'felt, 'velt\\ *n* : an area of grassy land with few trees or shrubs especially in southern Africa

vel·lum \\'vel-əm\\ *n* **1** : a fine-grained lambskin, kidskin, or calfskin prepared especially for writing on or for binding books **2** : a strong cream-colored paper resembling vellum — **vellum** *adj*

ve·loc·i·pede \\və-'läs-ə-ˌpēd\\ *n* : a lightweight wheeled vehicle (as a tricycle), propelled by the rider — used especially of early forms

ve·loc·i·ty \\və-'läs-ət-ē, -'läs-tē\\ *n, pl* **-ties** **1** : quickness of motion : SPEED ⟨the *velocity* of sound⟩ **2** : the rate of change of position along a straight line with respect to time **3** : rate of occurrence or action ⟨the *velocity* of political change⟩

ve·lour \\və-'lu(ə)r\\ *n* : a fabric resembling velvet

vel·vet \\'vel-vət\\ *n* **1** : a fabric with short soft raised fibers **2** : the soft skin covering the developing antler of a deer — **velvet** *adj*

vel·ve·teen \\ˌvel-və-'tēn\\ *n* : a fabric resembling velvet

vel·vety \\'vel-vət-ē\\ *adj* : soft, smooth, or thick like velvet ⟨*velvety* leaves⟩

ve·na ca·va \\ˌvē-nə-'kā-və\\ *n, pl* **ve·nae ca·vae** \\ˌvē-ni-'kā-vē\\ : one of the large veins by which the blood is returned to the right atrium of the heart in an air-breathing vertebrate

ve·nal \\'vēn-ᵊl\\ *adj* **1** : willing to take bribes ⟨*venal* officials⟩ **2** : influenced by bribery : CORRUPT ⟨*venal* conduct⟩ — **ve·nal·i·ty** \\vi-'nal-ət-ē\\ *n* — **ve·nal·ly** \\'vēn-ᵊl-ē\\ *adv*

ve·na·tion \\vē-'nā-shən, vē-\\ *n* : an arrangement or system of veins ⟨the *venation* of the hand⟩ ⟨the *venation* of a leaf⟩

venation

vend \\'vend\\ *vb* : to offer for sale (as in a vending machine) : SELL — **vend·er** *n*

ven·det·ta \\ven-'det-ə\\ *n* **1** : a feud between different families **2** : a series of acts marked by bitter hostility and motivated by a desire for revenge ⟨waged a personal *vendetta* against those who opposed his candidacy⟩

vending machine *n* : a machine from which one may get merchandise after putting in coins

ven·dor \\'ven-dər\\ *n* : one that sells : SELLER

¹ve·neer \\və-'ni(ə)r\\ *n* **1** : a thin layer of wood bonded to other wood usually to provide a finer surface or a stronger structure **2** : a protective or ornamental facing (as of brick)

²veneer *vb* : to cover with a veneer

ven·er·a·ble \\'ven-ər(-ə)-bəl, 'ven-rə-bəl\\ *adj* **1** : deserving to be venerated — often used as a religious title **2** : deserving honor or respect ⟨a *venerable* leader⟩ **3** : impressive by reason of age ⟨*venerable* pines⟩

ven·er·ate \\'ven-ə-ˌrāt\\ *vb* **-at·ed; -at·ing** : to show deep respect for ⟨*venerated* their ancestors⟩

ven·er·a·tion \\ˌven-ə-'rā-shən\\ *n* **1** : the act of venerating : the state of being venerated **2** : a feeling of deep respect

ve·ne·re·al \\və-'nir-ē-əl\\ *adj* : resulting from or contracted during sexual intercourse ⟨a *venereal* infection⟩

venereal disease *n* : a contagious disease (as gonorrhea or syphilis) that is usually acquired through sexual intercourse with someone who already has it

ve·ne·tian blind \\və-ˌnē-shən-\\ *n* : a blind having thin horizontal slats that can be adjusted to keep out light or to let light come in between them

ven·geance \\'ven-jən(t)s\\ *n* : punishment given in return for an injury or offense : RETRIBUTION

venge·ful \\'venj-fəl\\ *adj* : wanting revenge — **venge·ful·ly** \\-fə-lē\\ *adv* — **venge·ful·ness** *n*

ve·nial \'vē-nē-əl, -nyəl\ *adj* : not being a serious offense : FORGIVABLE ⟨a *venial* sin⟩

ven·i·son \'ven-ə-sən *also* -ə-zən\ *n* : the flesh of a deer used as food [Middle English *venison* "the flesh of a game animal hunted for food," from early French *veneisun* "flesh of hunted animals, venison," from Latin *venation-, venatio,* "hunting," from *venari* "to hunt"]

Venn diagram \'ven-\ *n* : a diagram that uses overlapping circles to show collections of mathematical elements and what they have in common

ven·om \'ven-əm\ *n* **1** : poison produced by some animals (as a snake, scorpion, or bee) and passed to a victim usually by biting or stinging **2** : ¹SPITE, MALICE

ven·om·ous \'ven-ə-məs\ *adj* : having or producing venom ⟨*venomous* snakes⟩ — **ven·om·ous·ly** *adv*

ve·nous \'vē-nəs\ *adj* **1** : of, relating to, or full of veins ⟨a *venous* rock⟩ **2** : being blood which has passed through the capillaries, given up oxygen to the tissues, and become loaded with carbon dioxide

¹vent \'vent\ *vb* **1 a** : to provide with an outlet **b** : to serve as an outlet for ⟨chimneys *vent* smoke⟩ **2** : to give expression to ⟨*vented* her frustration on her sister⟩

²vent *n* **1** : an opening (as a flue) for the escape of a gas or liquid or for the relief of pressure **2** : an opportunity or means of release : OUTLET ⟨his writing gives *vent* to his pent-up feelings⟩

³vent *n* : an opening in the lower part of a seam (as of a jacket or skirt)

ven·ti·late \'vent-ᵊl-ˌāt\ *vb* **-lat·ed; -lat·ing 1** : to discuss freely and openly ⟨*ventilate* a complaint⟩ **2 a** : to expose to air and especially to a current of fresh air ⟨*ventilate* stored grain⟩ **b** : to provide with ventilation ⟨*ventilate* a room with fans⟩

ven·ti·la·tion \ˌvent-ᵊl-'ā-shən\ *n* **1** : the act or process of ventilating **2** : circulation of air ⟨a room with good *ventilation*⟩ **3** : a system or means of providing fresh air

ven·ti·la·tor \'vent-ᵊl-ˌāt-ər\ *n* **1** : a device for letting in fresh air or driving out bad or stale air **2** : RESPIRATOR 2

ven·tral \'ven-trəl\ *adj* **1** : of or relating to the belly : ABDOMINAL **2** : being or located on or near the surface of the body that in human beings is the front but in most other animals is the lower surface ⟨a fish's *ventral* fins⟩ — **ven·tral·ly** \-trə-lē\ *adv*

ven·tri·cle \'ven-tri-kəl\ *n* **1** : a chamber of the heart which receives blood from an atrium and from which blood is forced into the arteries **2** : one of the cavities in the brain that are continuous with the central canal of the spinal cord

ven·tril·o·quist \ven-'tril-ə-kwəst\ *n* : a person skilled in speaking in such a way that the voice seems to come from a source other than the speaker [from Latin *ventriloquus* "ventriloquist," from *ventr-, venter* "stomach, belly" and *loqui* "to speak"; so called from the early belief that the voice is produced in the ventriloquist's stomach] — **ven·tril·o·quism** \-ˌkwiz-əm\ *n*

¹ven·ture \'ven-chər\ *vb* **ven·tured; ven·tur·ing** \'vench-(ə-)riŋ\ **1** : to expose to risk ⟨*ventured* a dollar on the lottery⟩ **2** : to face the risks and dangers of ⟨*ventured* the stormy sea⟩ **3** : to offer at the risk of being criticized ⟨*venture* an opinion⟩ ⟨*venture* to disagree⟩ **4** : to go ahead in spite of danger ⟨*ventured* down the cliff⟩ — **ven·tur·er** \'vench-(ə-)rər\ *n*

²venture *n* : an undertaking involving chance, risk, or danger; *esp* : a speculative business enterprise

ven·ture·some \'ven-chər-səm\ *adj* **1** : tending to take risks ⟨*venturesome* explorers⟩ **2** : involving risk : RISKY, DANGEROUS ⟨a *venturesome* journey⟩ **synonyms** see ADVENTUROUS — **ven·ture·some·ness** *n*

ven·tur·ous \'vench-(ə-)rəs\ *adj* : VENTURESOME

ven·ue \'ven-ˌyü\ *n* **1** : the place in which a trial is held **2** : LOCALE; *also* : a place where events of a specific type are held ⟨sport *venues*⟩

ve·nule \'ven-yü(ə)l, 'vēn-\ *n* : a small vein; *esp* : one of the minute veins connecting blood capillaries with larger veins

Ve·nus \'vē-nəs\ *n* : the planet second in order from the sun — see PLANET table

Venus flytrap *or* **Venus's–flytrap** *n* : an insect-eating plant that grows along the Carolina coast and has the tip of each leaf formed into an insect trap

Venus's flower–basket *or* **Venus flower basket** *n* : a tube-shaped sponge with a delicate glassy silica-containing skeleton

ve·ra·cious \və-'rā-shəs\ *adj* **1** : telling the truth : TRUTHFUL, HONEST **2** : being truthful or accurate ⟨a *veracious* account of the events⟩ — **ve·ra·cious·ly** *adv*

ve·rac·i·ty \və-'ras-ət-ē\ *n, pl* **-ties 1** : devotion to the truth : TRUTHFULNESS ⟨questioned the *veracity* of the witness⟩ **2** : agreement with truth or fact ⟨described it with *veracity*⟩

ve·ran·da *or* **ve·ran·dah** \və-'ran-də\ *n* : a long open porch usually with a roof

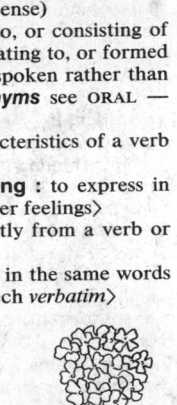

Venus flytrap

verb \'vərb\ *n* : a word that is usually the grammatical center of a predicate and expresses an act, occurrence, or state of being and that in various languages is inflected (as for agreement with the subject or for tense)

¹ver·bal \'vər-bəl\ *adj* **1** : of, relating to, or consisting of words ⟨*verbal* instructions⟩ **2** : of, relating to, or formed from a verb ⟨a *verbal* adjective⟩ **3** : spoken rather than written ⟨a *verbal* agreement⟩ **synonyms** see ORAL — **ver·bal·ly** \-bə-lē\ *adv*

²verbal *n* : a word that combines characteristics of a verb with those of a noun or adjective

ver·bal·ize \'vər-bə-ˌlīz\ *vb* **-ized; -iz·ing** : to express in words ⟨found it difficult to *verbalize* her feelings⟩

verbal noun *n* : a noun derived directly from a verb or verb stem

ver·ba·tim \(ˌ)vər-'bāt-əm\ *adv or adj* : in the same words : word for word ⟨wrote down the speech *verbatim*⟩

ver·be·na \(ˌ)vər-'bē-nə\ *n* : any of a genus of numerous plants including some that are often grown in gardens for their showy spikes of white, pink, red, or blue flowers

ver·bi·age \'vər-bē-ij\ *n* : many words and especially many hard words used to say very little

ver·bose \(ˌ)vər-'bōs\ *adj* : using more words than are needed ⟨a *verbose* reply⟩ — **ver·bose·ly** *adv* — **ver·bose·ness** *n* — **ver·bos·i·ty** \-'bäs-ət-ē\ *n*

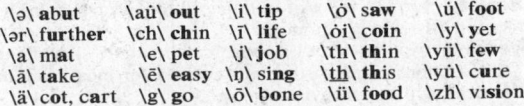

verbena

verb phrase *n* : a verb consisting of a past or present participle preceded by one or more helping verbs

ver·dant \'vərd-ᵊnt\ *adj* : green with growing plants ⟨*verdant* fields⟩ — **ver·dant·ly** *adv*

ver·dict \'vər-(ˌ)dikt\ *n* **1** : the decision reached by a jury **2** : an opinion held or expressed : JUDGMENT [Middle English *verdit, verdict* "a decision by a jury," derived from early French *veir* "true" and *dit* "saying, formal pronouncement"; *veir* from Latin *verus* "true" and *dit* from Latin *dictum* "formal pronouncement," derived from *dicere* "to say" — related to DICTATE, VERIFY, VERY]

ver·dure \'vər-jər\ *n* : green vegetation

¹**verge** \'vərj\ *n* : something that borders, limits, or bounds : EDGE ⟨walking on the grassy *verge* at the side of a country road⟩ **2** : BRINK 2, THRESHOLD ⟨the company was on the *verge* of bankruptcy⟩

²**verge** *vb* **verged; verg·ing** : to come near to being ⟨courage *verging* on recklessness⟩

verg·er \'vər-jər\ *n* : a minor church official

verier *comparative of* VERY

veriest *superlative of* VERY

ver·i·fi·able \'ver-ə-ˌfī-ə-bəl\ *adj* : able to be verified — **ver·i·fi·ably** \-blē\ *adv*

ver·i·fi·ca·tion \ˌver-ə-fə-'kā-shən\ *n* : the act or process of verifying : the state of being verified

ver·i·fy \'ver-ə-ˌfī\ *vb* **-fied; -fy·ing** : to prove or check the truth, accuracy, or reality of ⟨*verify* the claim⟩ [Middle English *verifien* "to establish the truth of," from early French *verifier* (same meaning), from Latin *verificare* (same meaning), from earlier *verus* "true" — related to VERDICT, VERY] — **ver·i·fi·er** \-ˌfī(-ə)r\ *n*

ver·i·ly \'ver-ə-lē\ *adv* : in fact : CERTAINLY

veri·si·mil·i·tude \ˌver-ə-sə-'mil-ə-ˌt(y)üd\ *n* : the appearance of being true or real

ver·i·ta·ble \'ver-ət-ə-bəl\ *adj* : ACTUAL, TRUE — often used to stress the appropriateness of a metaphor ⟨a *veritable* mountain of papers⟩ — **ver·i·ta·bly** \-blē\ *adv*

ver·i·ty \'ver-ət-ē\ *n, pl* **-ties** **1** : the quality or state of being true or real **2** : something (as a statement) that is true : FACT **3** : the quality or state of being truthful or honest : VERACITY

ver·mi·cel·li \ˌvər-mə-'chel-ē, -'sel-\ *n* : a pasta that is thinner than spaghetti [from Italian *vermicelli* "pasta similar to but thinner than spaghetti," literally, "little worms," from *verme* "worm," from Latin *vermis* "worm" — related to VERMIN; see *Word History* at VERMIN]

ver·mic·u·lite \(ˌ)vər-'mik-yə-ˌlīt\ *n* : any of various minerals that result usually from the expansion of small grains of mica at high temperatures to give a lightweight highly water-absorbent material

ver·mi·form appendix \'vər-mə-ˌfȯrm-\ *n* : APPENDIX 2

ver·mil·ion *also* **ver·mil·lion** \vər-'mil-yən\ *n* : a bright reddish orange

ver·min \'vər-mən\ *n, pl* **vermin** : small common harmful or objectionable animals (as fleas or mice) that are difficult to get rid of

Word History The word *vermin* is used for any small harmful or annoying insect or animal that is difficult to get rid of or control. Fleas, lice, mice, rats, and even rabbits when they destroy gardens have been called vermin. However, the word *vermin* comes from a Latin word for a creature that is not usually thought of as troublesome. The word is *vermis*, meaning "worm." The word *vermicelli*, which English borrowed from Italian, can also be traced back to the Latin *vermis*. The Italians used this word for "thin spaghetti" because the strands look like "little worms," which is what *vermicelli* means literally. [Middle English *vermin* "small animal pests," from early French *vermin* (same meaning), derived from Latin *vermis* "worm" — related to VERMICELLI]

ver·mouth \vər-'müth\ *n* : a wine flavored with herbs

¹**ver·nac·u·lar** \və(r)-'nak-yə-lər\ *adj* : of, relating to, or using ordinary especially spoken language

²**vernacular** *n* **1** : ordinary spoken language rather than literary language **2** : a common name of a plant or animal in contrast to its taxonomic name

ver·nal \'vərn-°l\ *adj* : of, relating to, or occurring in the spring ⟨the *vernal* equinox⟩

ver·ni·er \'vər-nē-ər\ *n* : a short scale made to slide along the divisions of an instrument marked for measuring or indicating parts of divisions

vernier caliper *n* : a measuring device that consists of a main scale with a fixed jaw and a sliding jaw with an attached vernier

ver·sa·tile \'vər-sət-°l\ *adj* : able to do many different kinds of things [from French *versatile* or Latin *versatilis*, both meaning "versatile, able to change," derived from Latin *versari* "to turn, change, reside (in a place)," from *vertere* "to turn" — related to CONVERSE, REVERSE, UNIVERSE, VERTICAL, VICE VERSA] — **ver·sa·til·i·ty** \ˌvər-sə-'til-ət-ē\ *n*

verse \'vərs\ *n* **1** : a line of writing in which words are arranged in a rhythmic pattern **2** : writing in which words are arranged in a rhythmic pattern **3** : STANZA **4** : one of the short parts of a chapter of the Bible

versed \'vərst\ *adj* : having knowledge or skill as a result of experience or study ⟨well *versed* in history⟩

ver·si·fi·ca·tion \ˌvər-sə-fə-'kā-shən\ *n* : the making of verses

ver·si·fy \'vər-sə-ˌfī\ *vb* **-fied; -fy·ing** : to write or turn into verse — **ver·si·fi·er** \-ˌfī(-ə)r\ *n*

ver·sion \'vər-zhən\ *n* **1** : a translation especially of the Bible ⟨the Douay *version*⟩ ⟨the King James *version*⟩ **2** : an account or description from one point of view ⟨your *version* of what happened⟩ **3** : a form or variant of a type or original ⟨an experimental *version* of the car⟩

ver·sus \'vər-səs, -səz\ *prep* **1** : AGAINST 1a ⟨the champion *versus* the challenger⟩ **2** : in contrast to or as the alternative of ⟨the tastiness of store-bought *versus* homemade cookies⟩

ver·te·bra \'vərt-ə-brə\ *n, pl* **-brae** \-ˌbrā, -brē, -brə\ *or* **-bras** : one of the sections of bone or cartilage that make up the spinal column

ver·te·bral \(ˌ)vər-'tē-brəl, 'vərt-ə-\ *adj* : of, relating to, or made up of vertebrae : SPINAL

vertebral column *n* : BACKBONE 1

¹**ver·te·brate** \'vərt-ə-brət, -ˌbrāt\ *adj* **1** : having a spinal column **2** : of or relating to the vertebrates

vertebra

²**vertebrate** *n* : any of a large group of chordates comprising animals (as mammals, birds, reptiles, amphibians, and fishes) typically having a bony or cartilaginous backbone which replaces the notochord, a distinct head containing a brain which arises as an enlarged part of the nerve cord, and an internal usually bony skeleton and including some primitive forms (as lampreys) in which the backbone is absent and the notochord persists throughout life

ver·tex \'vər-ˌteks\ *n, pl* **ver·ti·ces** \'vərt-ə-ˌsēz\ *also* **ver·tex·es** **1** : the point of a figure that is opposite to and farthest from its base ⟨the *vertex* of a triangle⟩ **2** : the point where the two sides of an angle meet or where three or more edges of a polyhedron (as a cube) meet

vertex 2

¹**ver·ti·cal** \'vərt-i-kəl\ *adj* **1** : directly overhead **2** : going straight up or down from a level surface **3** : of or relating to persons of higher or lower standing ⟨a *vertical* social order⟩ [from early French *vertical* or Latin *verticalis*, both meaning "relating to a vertex, at the highest point overhead," from earlier Latin *vertic-*, *vertex* "top, highest point, pole (turning point), whirl," from *vertere* "to turn" — related to CONVERSE, REVERSE, UNIVERSE, VERSATILE] — **ver·ti·cal·ly** \-k(ə-)lē\ *adv*

²**vertical** *n* **1** : something (as a line or plane) that is vertical **2** : a vertical direction

vertical angle *n* : either of a pair of angles that have the same vertex and are on opposite sides of two intersecting straight lines

vertical file *n* : a collection especially of pamphlets maintained (as in a library) for reference

ver·ti·go \'vərt-i-ˌgō\ *n, pl* **-goes** *or* **-gos**　**1** : a sensation in which a person or a person's surroundings seem to whirl dizzily　**2** : a confused or bewildered state of mind

verve \'vərv\ *n* : lively enthusiasm

¹very \'ver-ē\ *adj* **ver·i·er; -est**　**1** : being actual or real　**2 a** : ²EXACT 1, PRECISE ⟨the *very* heart of the city⟩　**b** : exactly suitable or necessary ⟨the *very* thing for the purpose⟩　**3** : ²MERE, BARE ⟨the *very* thought terrified them⟩　**4** : exactly the same ⟨the *very* one I saw yesterday⟩ [Middle English *verray, verry* "true, real," from early French *verai* (same meaning), derived from Latin *verus* "true" — related to VERDICT, VERIFY]

²very *adv*　**1** : in actual fact : TRULY ⟨told the *very* same story⟩　**2** : to a great degree : EXTREMELY ⟨a *very* hot day⟩

very high frequency *n* : a radio frequency in the range between 30 and 300 megahertz — abbreviation *VHF*

ves·i·cle \'ves-i-kəl\ *n* : a small cavity, cyst, or blister usually filled with fluid

ves·pers \'ves-pərz\ *n pl, often cap* : a late afternoon or evening church service

ves·sel \'ves-əl\ *n*　**1** : a hollow utensil (as a cup or bowl) for holding something　**2** : a craft bigger than a rowboat for navigation of the water; *esp* : ¹SHIP 1　**3 a** : a tube or canal (as a vein or artery) in which a body fluid is contained and carried or circulated　**b** : a tube in the xylem of a vascular plant through which water passes

¹vest \'vest\ *vb*　**1** : to place or give into the possession or control of some person or authority ⟨powers *vested* in the presidency⟩　**2** : to clothe in vestments [Middle English *vesten* "to give into the possession or control of someone," from early French *vestir* "to dress with clothes, to give power or authority to," from Latin *vestire* "to clothe," from *vestis* "clothing, garment"]

²vest *n*　**1** : a sleeveless garment usually worn under a suit coat　**2** : a protective garment (as a life preserver) that reaches to the waist　**3** : a knitted undershirt for women [from French *veste* "robe, garment," from Italian *veste* (same meaning), from Latin *vestis* "clothing, garment"]

²vest 1

ves·ti·bule \'ves-tə-ˌbyü(ə)l\ *n* : a hall or room between the outer door and the inside part of a building

ves·tige \'ves-tij\ *n*　**1 a** : a trace, mark, or visible sign left by something (as an ancient city or a condition or practice) vanished or lost ⟨*vestiges* of lost civilizations⟩　**b** : the smallest quantity or trace ⟨not a *vestige* of regret⟩　**2** : a small and imperfectly developed bodily part or organ that is the remains of one that was more fully developed in an earlier stage of the individual, in a past generation, or in a closely related form [from French *vestige* "sign of something vanished or lost," from Latin *vestigium* "footprint" — related to INVESTIGATE] — **ves·ti·gial** \ve-'stij-(ē-)əl\ *adj*

vest·ment \'ves(t)-mənt\ *n* : an outer garment especially for wear during ceremonies or by an official

ves·try \'ves-trē\ *n, pl* **vestries** : a room in a church building for sacred furnishings (as vestments)

¹vet \'vet\ *n* : VETERINARIAN, VETERINARY

²vet *n* : VETERAN

vetch \'vech\ *n* : any of a genus of twining herbs of the legume family that include plants used to feed domestic animals and to improve soil

vet·er·an \'vet-ə-rən, 've-trən\ *n*　**1** : a person who has had long experience (as in politics or the arts)　**2** : a former member of the armed forces especially during wartime — **veteran** *adj*

Veterans Day *n* : November 11 observed as a legal holiday in the U.S. in honor of the veterans of U.S. wars

vet·er·i·nar·i·an \ˌvet-ə-rən-'er-ē-ən, ˌve-trən-, ˌvet-ⁿn-\ *n* : a person who is qualified and has been given the authority to treat diseases and injuries of animals

¹vet·er·i·nary \'vet-ə-rən-ˌer-ē, 've-trən-, 'vet-ⁿn-\ *adj* : of, relating to, or being the medical care of animals ⟨*veterinary* medicine⟩

²veterinary *n, pl* **-naries** : VETERINARIAN

¹ve·to \'vēt-ō\ *n, pl* **vetoes**　**1** : a forbidding of something by a person in authority　**2 a** : the power of the head of a government to prevent a bill passed by a legislature from becoming law　**b** : the use of such authority [from Latin *veto* "I forbid," from *vetare* "to forbid"]

²veto *vb* : PROHIBIT 1; *esp* : to use one's power of veto — **ve·to·er** \-ˌō-(ə)r\ *n*

vex \'veks\ *vb* **vexed** *also* **vext; vex·ing**　**1** : to bring trouble, distress, or worry to ⟨*vexed* by thoughts of what could have been⟩　**2** : to annoy continually with little irritations ⟨*vexed* by the children⟩

vex·a·tion \vek-'sā-shən\ *n*　**1** : the quality or state of being vexed : IRRITATION　**2** : the act of vexing : ANNOYANCE　**3** : a cause of trouble or worry

vex·a·tious \vek-'sā-shəs\ *adj* : causing vexation : ANNOYING, DISTRESSING ⟨*vexatious* delays⟩ — **vex·a·tious·ly** *adv* — **vex·a·tious·ness** *n*

vexing *adj* : causing or likely to cause vexation : VEXATIOUS ⟨a *vexing* problem⟩

via \ˌvī-ə, ˌvē-ə\ *prep* : by way of ⟨entered *via* the back door⟩

vi·a·ble \'vī-ə-bəl\ *adj*　**1** : capable of living; *esp* : capable of surviving outside the mother's womb ⟨a *viable* human fetus⟩　**2** : capable of growing or developing ⟨*viable* seeds⟩ ⟨*viable* eggs⟩　**3 a** : capable of being put into practice : WORKABLE ⟨a *viable* solution to the problem⟩　**b** : capable of succeeding ⟨a *viable* candidate⟩ — **vi·a·bil·i·ty** \ˌvī-ə-'bil-ət-ē\ *n*

via·duct \'vī-ə-ˌdəkt\ *n* : a bridge for carrying a road or railroad over something (as a gorge or a highway)

vi·al \'vī-(ə)l\ *n* : a small container (as for medicines) made usually of glass or plastic

vi·and \'vī-ənd\ *n*　**1** : an article of food　**2** *pl* : food supplies

vi·at·i·cum \vī-'at-i-kəm, vē-\ *n, pl* **-cums** *or* **-ca** \-kə\　**1** : the Christian Eucharist given to a person in danger of death　**2** : money or supplies for a journey

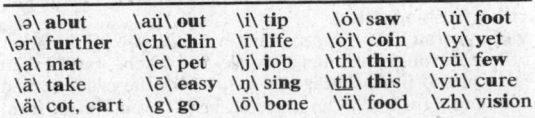

viaduct

vibe \'vīb\ *n* : VIBRATION 3 — usually used in plural ⟨got bad *vibes* from him⟩

vibes \'vībz\ *n pl* : VIBRAPHONE

vi·bran·cy \'vī-brən-sē\ *n* : the quality or state of being vibrant

vi·brant \'vī-brənt\ *adj*　**1 a** : vibrating rapidly　**b** : having or giving a sense of life, vigor, or activity ⟨a *vibrant* personality⟩　**2** : sounding as a result of vibration : RESO-

\ə\ **abut**	\au̇\ **out**	\i\ **tip**	\ȯ\ **saw**	\u̇\ **foot**
\ər\ **further**	\ch\ **chin**	\ī\ **life**	\ȯi\ **coin**	\y\ **yet**
\a\ **mat**	\e\ **pet**	\j\ **job**	\th\ **thin**	\yü\ **few**
\ā\ **take**	\ē\ **easy**	\ŋ\ **sing**	\th\ **this**	\yu̇\ **cure**
\ä\ **cot, cart**	\g\ **go**	\ō\ **bone**	\ü\ **food**	\zh\ **vision**

NANT ⟨a *vibrant* voice⟩ **3** : BRIGHT 2 ⟨a *vibrant* orange⟩ — **vi·brant·ly** *adv*

vi·bra·phone \'vī-brə-ˌfōn\ *n* : a musical instrument resembling the xylophone but having metal bars and devices for increasing the vibrations — **vi·bra·phon·ist** \-ˌfō-nəst\ *n*

vi·brate \'vī-ˌbrāt\ *vb* **vi·brat·ed; vi·brat·ing** : to move or cause to move back and forth or from side to side rapidly so as to produce a quivering effect or sound ⟨guitar strings *vibrate* when plucked⟩

vi·bra·tion \vī-'brā-shən\ *n* **1 a** : a rapid motion of the particles of an elastic body or substance back and forth (as when a stretched cord produces a musical tone or molecules in the air transmit sounds to the ear) **b** : the action of vibrating : the state of being vibrated **2** : a trembling motion ⟨*vibration* of a house caused by a passing truck⟩ **3** : a feeling or impression that someone or something gives off — usually used in plural ⟨good *vibrations*⟩ — **vi·bra·tion·al** \-shnəl, -shən-ᵊl\ *adj*

vibraphone

vi·bra·to \vi-'brät-ō, vī-\ *n, pl* **-tos** : a slightly trembling effect given to vocal or instrumental tone by slight and rapid variations in pitch

vi·bra·tor \'vī-ˌbrāt-ər\ *n* : one that vibrates or causes vibration

vi·bra·to·ry \'vī-brə-ˌtōr-ē, -ˌtȯr-\ *adj* : consisting of, capable of, or causing vibration

vi·bur·num \vī-'bər-nəm\ *n* : any of a genus of widely distributed shrubs or small trees that are related to the honeysuckles and have white or sometimes pink flowers in broad clusters

vic·ar \'vik-ər\ *n* **1** : a minister in charge of a church who serves under the authority of another minister **2** : a church official who takes the place of or represents a higher official

vic·ar·age \'vik-(ə-)rij\ *n* : a vicar's home

vi·car·i·ous \vī-'ker-ē-əs, və-, -'kar-\ *adj* **1** : serving or acting for another **2** : done or suffered for the benefit of someone else ⟨a *vicarious* sacrifice⟩ **3** : sharing in someone else's experience through the use of the imagination or sympathetic feelings ⟨*vicarious* joy⟩ — **vi·car·i·ous·ly** *adv* — **vi·car·i·ous·ness** *n*

vice \'vīs\ *n* **1 a** : evil conduct or habits : WICKEDNESS **b** : a moral fault or weakness ⟨dishonesty was his *vice*⟩ **2** : an unimportant fault ⟨eating too much candy is my *vice*⟩ **3** : behavior that is unwanted in a domestic animal (as pulling out feathers by a bird) **synonyms** see OFFENSE

vice- \(')vīs, ˌvīs\ *prefix* : one that takes the place of [derived from Latin *vice*, a form of *vicis* "a change, another's place or role or job"]

vice admiral *n* : a naval commissioned officer with a rank just below that of admiral

vice presidency *n* : the office of vice president

vice president *n* : an official whose rank is next below that of the president and who takes the place of the president when necessary

vice·re·gal \(')vīs-'rē-gəl\ *adj* : of or relating to a viceroy or viceroyalty — **vice·re·gal·ly** \-gə-lē\ *adv*

vice·roy \'vīs-ˌrȯi\ *n* **1** : the governor of a country or province who represents the sovereign **2** : a black and orange North American butterfly resembling but smaller than the monarch

vi·ce ver·sa \ˌvī-si-'vər-sə, (')vīs-'vər-\ *adv* : with the order turned around ⟨exchange money for tokens, rather than *vice versa*⟩ [from Latin *vice versa* "with the order turned around," from *vice* "in place of, instead" and *versa,* form

of *versus* "turned," from *vertere* "to turn" — related to CONVERSE, REVERSE, VERSATILE]

vi·cin·i·ty \və-'sin-ət-ē\ *n, pl* **-ties** **1** : a surrounding area or district ⟨in the *vicinity* of her home⟩ **2** : an approximate amount, extent, or degree : NEIGHBORHOOD ⟨walks in the *vicinity* of 20 miles a week⟩

vi·cious \'vish-əs\ *adj* **1 a** : likely to do evil : WICKED **b** : of the nature of evil : IMMORAL **2** : very dangerous ⟨a *vicious* dog⟩ **3** : having or showing hateful feelings ⟨*vicious* gossip⟩ — **vi·cious·ly** *adv* — **vi·cious·ness** *n*

vicious circle *n* : a situation or condition that endlessly repeats itself — called also *vicious cycle*

vi·cis·si·tude \və-'sis-ə-ˌt(y)üd, vī-\ *n* : a surprising or irregular change

vic·tim \'vik-təm\ *n* **1** : a living being offered as a sacrifice in a religious rite **2** : an individual injured or killed (as by disease or accident) **3** : a person cheated, fooled, or harmed by another

vic·tim·ize \'vik-tə-ˌmīz\ *vb* **-ized; -iz·ing** : to make a victim of especially by cheating

vic·tor \'vik-tər\ *n* : one that defeats an enemy or opponent : WINNER

vic·to·ria \vik-'tōr-ē-ə, -'tȯr-\ *n* : a low four-wheeled carriage with a folding top and a raised seat in front for the driver [named in honor of *Victoria* 1819–1901 queen of England]

victoria

Vic·to·ri·an \vik-'tōr-ē-ən, -'tȯr-\ *adj* : of, relating to, or typical of the reign of Queen Victoria of England or of the literature, art, and tastes of her time

vic·to·ri·ous \vik-'tōr-ē-əs, -'tȯr-\ *adj* : having won a victory ⟨a *victorious* candidate⟩ — **vic·to·ri·ous·ly** *adv*

vic·to·ry \'vik-t(ə-)rē\ *n, pl* **-ries** **1** : the overcoming of an enemy or opponent **2** : success in a struggle

¹vict·ual \'vit-ᵊl\ *n* **1** : food fit for humans **2** *pl* : supplies of food : PROVISIONS

²victual *vb* **-ualed** *or* **-ualled; -ual·ing** *or* **-ual·ling** **1** : to supply with food **2** : to store provisions

vict·ual·ler *or* **vict·ual·er** \'vit-ᵊl-ər\ *n* : one that supplies provisions (as to an army or a ship)

vi·cu·ña *or* **vi·cu·na** \vi-'kün-yə, vī-; vī-'k(y)ü-nə, və-\ *n* **1** : a wild cud-chewing animal of the Andes that is related to the llama and alpaca **2** : the wool of the vicuña

¹vid·eo \'vid-ē-ˌō\ *n* **1** : TELEVISION **2** : VIDEOTAPE: **a** : a recording of a movie or television program for playing through a television set **b** : a videotaped performance of a song **3** : a recording similar to a videotape but stored in digital form (as on an optical disk or a computer's hard drive)

vicuña 1

²video *adj* **1** : relating to or used in the sending or receiving of television images ⟨a *video* channel⟩ — compare ¹AUDIO 2b **2** : being, relating to, or involving images on a television screen or computer display ⟨a *video* terminal⟩

video camera *n* : a camera that records video and usually audio; *esp* : CAMCORDER

vid·eo·cas·sette \ˌvid-ē-ō-kə-'set\ *n* **1** : a case containing videotape for use with a VCR **2** : a recording (as of a movie) on a videocassette

videocassette recorder *n* : VCR

vid·eo·disc *or* **vid·eo·disk** \\'vid-ē-ō-ˌdisk\\ *n* **1** : a disc similar to a phonograph record on which programs have been recorded for playback on a television set; *also* : OPTICAL DISK **2** : a recording (as of a movie) on a videodisc

video game *n* : a game played with images on a video screen

vid·e·og·ra·phy \\ˌvid-ē-ē-'äg-rə-fē\\ *n* : the practice or art of recording images with a video camera — **vid·e·og·ra·pher** \\-fər\\ *n*

vid·eo·phone \\'vid-ē-ə-ˌfōn\\ *n* : a telephone equipped for transmission of a picture as well as sound so that users can see each other

¹vid·eo·tape \\'vid-ē-ō-ˌtāp\\ *n* : a recording of visual images and sound (as of a television production) made on magnetic tape; *also* : the magnetic tape used for such a recording

²videotape *vb* : to make a videotape of ⟨*videotape* a show⟩

videotape recorder *n* : a device for recording on videotape — called also *video recorder*

vie \\'vī\\ *vb* **vied; vy·ing** \\'vī-iŋ\\ : to strive to win over another : CONTEND ⟨candidates *vying* with each other for the voter's support⟩ — **vi·er** \\'vī-(ə)r\\ *n*

Viet·cong \\vē-'et-'käŋ, -'kȯŋ\\ *n, pl* **Vietcong** : a guerrilla soldier in the Vietnamese Communist movement from the late 1950s to 1975 [from the Vietnamese phrase *Viêt Nam công-san* "Vietnam communist"]

Viet·nam·ese \\vē-ˌet-nə-'mēz, ˌvyet-, vē-ət-, ˌvēt-, -nä-, -nä, -'mēs\\ *n, pl* **Vietnamese** **1** : a person born or living in Vietnam **2** : the official language of Vietnam — **Vietnamese** *adj*

¹view \\'vyü\\ *n* **1 a** : the act of seeing or examining **b** : a brief study or description ⟨a *view* of foreign literature⟩ **2** : OPINION 1 ⟨state your *views*⟩ **3** : all that can be seen from a certain point ⟨a house with a *view* of the lake⟩ **4** : range of vision ⟨out of *view*⟩ **5** : GOAL 2 ⟨with a *view* to winning honors⟩ **6** : the foreseeable future ⟨no hope in *view*⟩ **7** : a picture of a place — **in view of** : in regard to

²view *vb* **1** : ¹SEE 1a ⟨*view* a film⟩ **2** : to look at carefully : STUDY ⟨*view* an exhibit on birds⟩ — **view·able** \\-ə-bəl\\ *adj*

view·er \\'vyü-ər\\ *n* : one that views; *esp* : an optical device used in viewing ⟨a *viewer* for slides⟩

view·find·er \\'vyü-ˌfīn-dər\\ *n* : a device on a camera that shows the view to be included in the picture

view·point \\-ˌpȯint\\ *n* : POINT OF VIEW

vig·il \\'vij-əl\\ *n* **1 a** : the day before a religious feast **b** : prayers or religious services held in the evening or at night — usually used in plural **2** : an act or period of staying awake at times when one normally would be sleeping ⟨an all-night *vigil* spent awaiting her return⟩ **3** : an act or period of attentive watching : WATCH ⟨kept *vigil* at the bedside of his ill son⟩

vig·i·lance \\'vij-ə-lən(t)s\\ *n* : the quality or state of being vigilant

vig·i·lant \\'vij-ə-lənt\\ *adj* : alert to signs of danger — **vig·i·lant·ly** *adv*

vig·i·lan·te \\ˌvij-ə-'lant-ē\\ *n* : a member of a group of volunteers who decide on their own to stop crime and to punish criminals

vi·gnette \\vin-'yet, vēn-\\ *n* : a brief description in words : SKETCH

vig·or \\'vig-ər\\ *n* **1** : active strength or energy of body or mind **2** : active strength or force

vig·or·ous \\'vig-(ə-)rəs\\ *adj* **1** : having vigor : ROBUST ⟨*vigorous* youth⟩ ⟨a *vigorous* plant⟩ **2** : done with force and energy ⟨a *vigorous* protest⟩ — **vig·or·ous·ly** *adv* — **vig·or·ous·ness** *n*

synonyms VIGOROUS, ENERGETIC, STRENUOUS mean having or showing great life and force. VIGOROUS suggests active strength and unfailing freshness and health ⟨people who are still *vigorous* in old age⟩. ENERGETIC suggests an ability to take lots of activity ⟨*energetic* travelers always going places⟩. STRENUOUS suggests the making or meeting of hard and challenging demands ⟨tough athletes doing *strenuous* exercise⟩.

Vi·king \\'vī-kiŋ\\ *n* : one of the Scandinavians who raided or invaded the coasts of Europe in the 8th to 10th centuries

vile \\'vī(ə)l\\ *adj* **vil·er** \\'vī-lər\\; **vil·est** \\-ləst\\ **1 a** : morally bad ⟨*vile* deeds⟩ **b** : physically ugly ⟨*vile* living quarters⟩ **2** : of little worth **3** : very or completely bad ⟨a *vile* temper⟩ ⟨*vile* weather⟩ — **vile·ly** \\'vī(ə)l-lē\\ *adv* — **vile·ness** *n*

vil·i·fy \\'vil-ə-ˌfī\\ *vb* **-fied; -fy·ing** : to speak of as wicked — **vil·i·fi·ca·tion** \\ˌvil-ə-fə-'kā-shən\\ *n* — **vil·i·fi·er** \\'vil-ə-ˌfī(-ə)r\\ *n*

vil·la \\'vil-ə\\ *n* **1** : a country estate **2** : a large expensive house usually located in the country

vil·lage \\'vil-ij\\ *n* **1** : a place somewhat smaller than a town **2** : the people living in a village

vil·lag·er \\'vil-ij-ər\\ *n* : a person living in a village

vil·lain \\'vil-ən\\ *n* **1** : VILLEIN **2** : an evil person : SCOUNDREL **3** : a character in a story or play who opposes the hero

vil·lain·ess \\'vil-ə-nəs\\ *n* : a woman who is a villain

vil·lain·ous \\'vil-ə-nəs\\ *adj* **1** : typical of a villain ⟨*villainous* attacks⟩; *also* : WICKED ⟨a *villainous* enemy⟩ **2** : very objectionable ⟨*villainous* living conditions⟩ — **vil·lain·ous·ly** *adv*

vil·lainy \\'vil-ə-nē\\ *n, pl* **-lain·ies** : conduct or actions of or typical of a villain

vil·lein \\'vil-ən, 'vil-ˌān, vil-'ān\\ *n* **1** : a free peasant **2** : an unfree peasant having the status of a slave to a feudal lord

vil·lus \\'vil-əs\\ *n, pl* **vil·li** \\'vil-ˌī, -ē\\ : one of the tiny finger-shaped processes of the mucous membrane of the small intestine through which digested food is absorbed

vim \\'vim\\ *n* : robust energy and enthusiasm

vin·ai·grette \\ˌvin-i-'gret\\ *n* : a sauce made of oil, vinegar, and seasonings and used especially on salads, cold meats, or fish

vin·ci·ble \\'vin-sə-bəl\\ *adj* : capable of being overcome or subdued ⟨*vincible* obstacles⟩

vin·cu·lum \\'viŋ-kyə-ləm\\ *n, pl* **-lums** *or* **-la** \\-lə\\ : a straight horizontal mark placed over two or more members of a compound mathematical expression and equivalent to parentheses or brackets around them (as in $a–\overline{b–c}=a–[b–c]$)

vin·di·cate \\'vin-də-ˌkāt\\ *vb* **-cat·ed; -cat·ing** **1** : to free from blame or guilt ⟨evidence that will *vindicate* me⟩ **2** : CONFIRM 4 ⟨later discoveries *vindicated* the claim⟩ — **vin·di·ca·tion** \\ˌvin-də-'kā-shən\\ *n* — **vin·di·ca·tor** \\'vin-də-ˌkāt-ər\\ *n*

vin·dic·tive \\vin-'dik-tiv\\ *adj* **1** : likely to seek revenge ⟨a *vindictive* person⟩ **2** : intended to cause pain or anguish : SPITEFUL ⟨*vindictive* remarks⟩ — **vin·dic·tive·ly** *adv* — **vin·dic·tive·ness** *n*

¹vine \\'vīn\\ *n* **1** : GRAPE 2 **2 a** : a plant whose stem requires support and which climbs by tendrils or twining or creeps along the ground; *also* : the stem of a vine **b** : any of various plants (as a tomato) that resemble vines but lack a special means for climbing [Middle English *vine* "grape, a climbing plant," from early French *vigne* (same meaning), from Latin *vinea* "vine, vineyard," derived from *vinum* "wine" — related to VINEGAR, VINTAGE]

²vine *vb* **vined; vin·ing** : to form or grow in the manner of a vine

vin·e·gar \\'vin-i-gər\\ *n* : a sour liquid obtained from cider,

\\ə\\ abut	\\au̇\\ out	\\i\\ tip	\\ȯ\\ saw	\\u̇\\ foot
\\ər\\ further	\\ch\\ chin	\\ī\\ life	\\ȯi\\ coin	\\y\\ yet
\\a\\ mat	\\e\\ pet	\\j\\ job	\\th\\ thin	\\yü\\ few
\\ā\\ take	\\ē\\ easy	\\ŋ\\ sing	\\th\\ this	\\yu̇\\ cure
\\ä\\ cot, cart	\\g\\ go	\\ō\\ bone	\\ü\\ food	\\zh\\ vision

wine, or malt and used to flavor or preserve foods [Middle English *vinegre* "vinegar," from early French *vin egre* (same meaning), literally, "sour wine," from *vin* "wine" and *egre* "sharp, sour, eager"; *vin* from Latin *vinum* "wine" and *egre* from Latin *acer* "sharp, sour, spirited" — related to EAGER, VINE, VINTAGE]

vinegar eel *n* : a tiny nematode worm often found in vinegar that has not been pasteurized or other fermenting vegetable substances

vinegar fly *n* : DROSOPHILA

vin·e·gary \'vin-i-g(ə-)rē\ *adj* : resembling vinegar : SOUR

vine·yard \'vin-yərd\ *n* : a field of grapevines

vin·tage \'vint-ij\ *n* **1 a** : the grapes or wine produced during one season **b** : ¹WINE 1 **2** : a period in which something was made or was begun ⟨a violin of 1820 *vintage*⟩ [Middle English *vintage*, an altered form of *vendage* "the grapes picked during a season," from early French *vendage*, *vendenge* (same meaning), from Latin *vindemia* (same meaning), from *vinum* "wine, grapes" and *demere* "to take off" — related to VINE, VINEGAR] — **vintage** *adj*

vint·ner \'vint-nər\ *n* : a person who makes or sells wine

viny \'vī-nē\ *adj* **vin·i·er; -est** : of, relating to, or resembling vines ⟨*viny* plants⟩

vi·nyl \'vīn-ᵊl\ *n* **1** : a chemical obtained from ethylene by the removal of one hydrogen atom **2** : a polymer of a vinyl compound or a product (as a textile fiber) made from such a polymer

vi·ol \'vī(-ə)l\ *n* : an old stringed instrument like the violin

¹vi·o·la \vī-'ō-lə, vē-\ *n* : VIOLET 1a; *esp* : any of various garden plants that have white, yellow, purple, or variously colored flowers and that resemble but are smaller than the related pansies

²vi·o·la \vē-'ō-lə\ *n* : a stringed musical instrument like a violin but slightly larger and lower in pitch

vi·o·late \'vī-ə-ˌlāt\ *vb* **-lat·ed; -lat·ing** **1** : to fail to keep or observe : BREAK ⟨*violate* the law⟩ **2** : to do harm or damage to **3** : to treat with great disrespect ⟨*violate* a house of worship⟩ **4** : DISTURB 1a ⟨don't *violate* their privacy⟩ — **vi·o·la·tor** \-ˌlāt-ər\ *n*

vi·o·la·tion \ˌvī-ə-'lā-shən\ *n* : an act or an instance of violating : the state of being violated

vi·o·lence \'vī-ə-lən(t)s\ *n* **1** : the use of force in a way that harms a person or property **2** : great force or energy especially of a destructive kind ⟨the *violence* of the storm caused great fear⟩

vi·o·lent \'vī-ə-lənt\ *adj* **1** : marked by great force or sudden activity ⟨a *violent* attack of coughing⟩ ⟨*violent* storms⟩ **2 a** : especially furious or emotional ⟨a *violent* denial of guilt⟩ **b** : INTENSE 1 ⟨*violent* pain⟩ **3** : caused by force ⟨a *violent* death⟩ **4 a** : acting with or characterized by harmful physical force : exercising or marked by violence ⟨a *violent* person⟩ ⟨*violent* actions⟩ **b** : having a tendency to carry out acts of violence ⟨*violent* prison inmates⟩ — **vi·o·lent·ly** *adv*

vi·o·let \'vī-ə-lət\ *n* **1 a** : any of a genus of mostly herbs that often produce showy fragrant flowers in the spring and small closed self-pollinated flowers without petals in the summer **b** : any of several plants of other genera — compare DOGTOOTH VIOLET **2** : a reddish blue

vi·o·lin \ˌvī-ə-'lin\ *n* **1** : a stringed musical instrument with four strings that is usually held against the shoulder under the chin and played with a bow **2** : VIOLINIST

vi·o·lin·ist \ˌvī-ə-'lin-əst\ *n* : a violin player

violet 1a

vi·o·lon·cel·lo \ˌvī-ə-lən-'chel-ō, ˌvē-\ *n* : CELLO

VIP \ˌvē-ˌī-'pē\ *n, pl* **VIPs** \-'pēz\ : a person of great importance or fame [from *v*ery *i*mportant *p*erson]

vi·per \'vī-pər\ *n* **1** : any of a family of poisonous snakes having heavy bodies, broad heads, and hollow tube-shaped fangs and including Old World snakes and the pit vipers **2** : any snake that is poisonous or that is believed to be poisonous

vi·per·ine \'vī-pə-ˌrīn\ *adj* : of, relating to, or resembling a viper

vi·per·ous \'vī-pə-rəs\ *adj* **1** : VIPERINE **2** : having the qualities attributed to a viper : SPITEFUL, MALEVOLENT

vi·ra·go \və-'rāg-ō, -'räg-; 'vir-ə-ˌgō\ *n, pl* **-goes** *or* **-gos** : a scolding quarrelsome woman

vi·ral \'vī-rəl\ *adj* **1** : of, relating to, or caused by a virus ⟨a *viral* infection⟩ **2** : quickly and widely spread or popularized especially by person-to-person electronic communication ⟨a *viral* video⟩

vir·eo \'vir-ē-ˌō\ *n, pl* **-e·os** : any of various small insect-eating American songbirds that are chiefly olive-green or grayish in color

¹vir·gin \'vər-jən\ *n* : a person who has not had sexual intercourse

²virgin *adj* **1** : being a virgin **2** : not soiled ⟨*virgin* snow⟩; *esp* : not altered by human activity ⟨*virgin* soil⟩ **3** : being used or worked for the first time ⟨*virgin* wool⟩

¹vir·gin·al \'vər-jən-ᵊl, 'vərj-nəl\ *adj* : of, relating to, characteristic of, or suitable for a virgin; *esp* : CHASTE 1 — **vir·gin·al·ly** \-ē\ *adv*

²virginal *n* : a musical instrument resembling a small piano with no legs

Vir·gin·ia creeper \vər-ˌjin-yə-, -ˌjin-ē-ə-\ *n* : a common North American climbing vine related to the grape and having leaves with five leaflets and bluish black berries — called also *woodbine*

Virginia reel *n* : an American dance in which two lines of couples face each other and in which all couples in turn do a series of movements

vir·gin·i·ty \(ˌ)vər-'jin-ət-ē\ *n, pl* **-ties** : the quality or state of being virgin

Virgo \'vər-gō, 'vi(ə)r-\ *n* **1** : a group of stars between Leo and Libra usually pictured as a young woman **2 a** : the sixth sign of the zodiac — see ZODIAC table **b** : a person whose sign of the zodiac is Virgo

Virginia creeper

vir·ile \'vir-əl, 'vi(ə)r-ˌīl\ *adj* **1 a** : having the nature, powers, or qualities of an adult male : MASCULINE **b** : having traditionally masculine qualities especially to a noticeable degree **2 a** : VIGOROUS 1, ENERGETIC **b** : MASTERFUL 1, FORCEFUL [from early French *viril* "having the qualities of a man," from Latin *virilis* (same meaning), from *vir* "man, male" — related to VIRTUE]

vi·ril·i·ty \və-'ril-ət-ē\ *n* : the quality or state of being virile

vi·rol·o·gy \vī-'räl-ə-jē\ *n* : a branch of science concerned with viruses and diseases caused by viruses — **vi·rol·o·gist** \vī-'räl-ə-jəst\ *n*

vir·tu·al \'vərch-(ə-)wəl, 'vər-chəl\ *adj* : being in effect but not in fact or name ⟨a *virtual* dictator⟩ — **vir·tu·al·ly** \-ē\ *adv*

virtual reality *n* : an artificial environment which is experienced through sights and sounds provided by a computer and in which one's actions partly decide what happens in the environment

vir·tue \'vər-chü\ *n* **1** : conduct that agrees with what is morally right **2** : a particular moral quality ⟨justice and charity are *virtues*⟩ **3** : a desirable quality : MERIT ⟨the *virtues* of country life⟩ [Middle English *vertu*, *virtu* "behavior that fits with what is right or moral," from early French *virtu* (same meaning), from Latin *virtus* "strength, virtue, manly quality," from *vir* "man, male" — related to VIRILE] — **by virtue of** *or* **in virtue of** : through the force of : by authority of

vir·tu·os·i·ty \ˌvər-chə-ˈwäs-ət-ē\ *n, pl* **-ties** : great performing ability in the fine arts

vir·tu·o·so \ˌvər-chə-ˈwō-sō, -zō\ *n, pl* **-sos** *or* **-si** \-sē, -zē\ : a person who excels in the performance of an art; *esp* : a skilled musician — **virtuoso** *adj*

vir·tu·ous \ˈvərch-(ə-)wəs\ *adj* : having or showing moral virtue — **vir·tu·ous·ly** *adv* — **vir·tu·ous·ness** *n*

vir·u·lence \ˈvir-(y)ə-lən(t)s\ *n* : the quality or state of being virulent

vir·u·lent \ˈvir-(y)ə-lənt\ *adj* **1 a** : marked by a rapid, severe, and often deadly course ⟨a *virulent* infection⟩ **b** : able to overcome or break down the defenses of the body ⟨a *virulent* germ⟩ **2** : extremely poisonous : NOXIOUS **3** : full of hate : SPITEFUL — **vir·u·lent·ly** *adv*

vi·rus \ˈvī-rəs\ *n, pl* **vi·rus·es** **1** : any of a large group of very tiny infectious agents that are too small to be seen with the ordinary light microscope but can often be seen with the electron microscope, that are usually regarded as nonliving complex molecules, that have an outside coat of protein around a core of RNA or DNA, that can grow and multiply only in living cells, and that cause important diseases in plants and animals including human beings — compare FILTERABLE VIRUS **2** : a disease or illness caused by a virus **3** : a computer program that is usually hidden within another seemingly harmless program and that produces copies of itself and inserts them into other programs and usually performs a malicious action (as destroying data) — compare TROJAN HORSE 2, WORM 5 [from Latin *virus* "poison, venom, secretion"]

¹vi·sa \ˈvē-zə *also* -sə\ *n* : a mark on a passport that is a sign of approval and permission for a traveler to go ahead

²visa *vb* **vi·saed** \-zəd, -səd\; **vi·sa·ing** \-zə-iŋ, -sə-\ : to give a visa to

vis·age \ˈviz-ij\ *n* **1** : the face; *also* : an expression of the face **2** : the outward appearance of a person, animal, or thing

viscera *plural of* VISCUS

vis·cer·al \ˈvis-ə-rəl\ *adj* **1** : felt in or as if in the viscera ⟨a *visceral* belief⟩ **2** : of, relating to, or being the viscera ⟨*visceral* organs⟩ — **vis·cer·al·ly** \-rə-lē\ *adv*

vis·cid \ˈvis-əd\ *adj* : VISCOUS

vis·cos·i·ty \vis-ˈkäs-ət-ē\ *n, pl* **-ties** : the quality or state of being viscous; *esp* : the characteristic of a fluid that resists flow ⟨an oil of high *viscosity*⟩

vis·count \ˈvī-ˌkaůnt\ *n* : a British nobleman ranking below an earl and above a baron

vis·count·ess \ˈvī-ˌkaůnt-əs\ *n* **1** : the wife or widow of a viscount **2** : a woman holding the rank of viscount

vis·cous \ˈvis-kəs\ *adj* **1** : having the characteristic of stickiness **2** : having or marked by viscosity

vis·cus \ˈvis-kəs\ *n, pl* **vis·cera** \ˈvis-ə-rə\ : an organ located inside of the body; *esp* : one (as the heart, liver, or intestine) located in the large cavity of the main part of the body

vise \ˈvīs\ *n* : any of various tools with two jaws for holding work that close usually by a screw or lever — **vise·like** *adj*

vise

vis·i·bil·i·ty \ˌviz-ə-ˈbil-ət-ē\ *n* **1** : the quality or state of being visible **2** : the degree of clearness of the atmosphere

vis·i·ble \ˈviz-ə-bəl\ *adj* **1** : capable of being seen ⟨stars *visible* to the naked eye⟩ **2** : eas-

ily seen or understood : OBVIOUS ⟨no *visible* means of support⟩ — **vis·i·bly** \-blē\ *adv*

¹vi·sion \ˈvizh-ən\ *n* **1 a** : something seen in the mind (as during a dream) **b** : a vivid picture created by the imagination **c** : GHOST **2 a** : the act or power of imagination **b** : unusual ability to think or plan ahead ⟨people with *vision* building for the future⟩ **3 a** : the act or power of seeing : SIGHT **b** : the sense by which the qualities of an object (as color, shape, and size) are perceived through a process in which light rays entering the eye are transformed into signals that pass to the brain **4** : something seen; *esp* : a lovely or charming sight [Middle English *vision* "something seen in a dream or trance," from early French *vision* (same meaning), from Latin *vision-, visio* (same meaning), derived from *vidēre* "to see" — related to CLAIRVOYANCE, EVIDENT, PROVIDE, SUPERVISE, VISIT]

²vision *vb* **vi·sioned**; **vi·sion·ing** \ˈvizh-niŋ, -ə-niŋ\ : IMAGINE 1 ⟨couldn't *vision* it happening⟩

¹vi·sion·ary \ˈvizh-ə-ˌner-ē\ *adj* **1** : resembling a vision especially in being impractical ⟨*visionary* plans for underwater cities⟩ **2** : likely to dream or imagine

²visionary *n, pl* **-ar·ies** **1** : a person whose ideas or plans are impractical : DREAMER **2** : a person who sees visions : SEER **3** : one having unusual foresight and imagination ⟨a *visionary* in the field of computer animation⟩

¹vis·it \ˈviz-ət\ *vb* **vis·it·ed** \ˈviz-ət-əd, ˈviz-təd\; **vis·it·ing** \ˈviz-ət-iŋ, ˈviz-tiŋ\ **1** : to go to see in order to comfort or help ⟨*visit* the sick⟩ **2 a** : to pay a call upon as an act of friendship or courtesy **b** : to go or come to see on business **c** : to live with for a time as a guest **3** : to go to for pleasure ⟨*visit* the zoo⟩ **4** : to make a visit or frequent or regular visits **5** : ¹CHAT 1 ⟨enjoys *visiting* with the neighbors⟩ [Middle English *visiten* "to go to a person especially to give comfort," from early French *visiter* (same meaning), derived from Latin *visere* "to go to see," from *vidēre* "to see" — related to VISION]

²visit *n* **1** : a brief stay : CALL ⟨a *visit* with friends⟩ **2** : a stay as a guest ⟨a weekend *visit*⟩ **3** : a journey to and brief stay at a place especially for a particular purpose ⟨a *visit* to the museum⟩ **4** : an official or professional call (as of a doctor to treat a patient)

vis·i·tant \ˈviz-ət-ənt, ˈviz-tənt\ *n* : one that visits; *esp* : a visitor from another world

vis·i·ta·tion \ˌviz-ə-ˈtā-shən\ *n* : an instance of visiting; *esp* : a visit by an important person for a reason (as an inspection)

vis·i·tor \ˈviz-ət-ər, ˈviz-tər\ *n* : one (as a guest or tourist) that visits

vi·sor *also* **vi·zor** \ˈvī-zər\ *n* **1** : a movable front upper piece on a helmet **2** : a projecting part (as on a cap or headband) to protect or shade the eyes — **vi·sored** \-zərd\ *adj*

vis·ta \ˈvis-tə\ *n* **1** : a distant view through an opening or along an avenue : PROSPECT **2** : a mental view over a long period of time

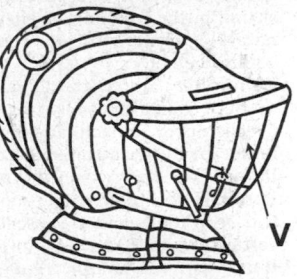

V visor 1

¹vi·su·al \ˈvizh-(ə-)wəl, ˈvizh-əl\ *adj* **1** : of, relating to, or used in vision ⟨*visual* organs⟩ **2** : received by sight ⟨*visual* impressions⟩ **3**

\ə\ **abut**	\aů\ **out**	\i\ **tip**	\ȯ\ **saw**	\ů\ **foot**	
\ər\ **further**	\ch\ **chin**	\ī\ **life**	\ȯi\ **coin**	\y\ **yet**	
\a\ **mat**	\e\ **pet**	\j\ **job**	\th\ **thin**	\yü\ **few**	
\ā\ **take**	\ē\ **easy**	\ŋ\ **sing**	\th\ **this**	\yů\ **cure**	
\ä\ **cot, cart**	\g\ **go**	\ō\ **bone**	\ü\ **food**	\zh\ **vision**	

: VISIBLE 1 ⟨*visual* objects⟩ 4 : of, relating to, or using visual aids ⟨a *visual* presentation⟩ — **vi·su·al·ly** \-ē\ *adv*

²**visual** *n* : something (as a picture, chart, or film) that appeals to the sight and is used to illustrate, demonstrate, or advertise — usually used in plural

visual aid *n* : an instructional device (as a chart, map, or model) that appeals chiefly to vision; *esp* : an educational movie or filmstrip

visual field *n* : the entire space visible at a given instant without moving the eyes — called also *field of vision*

vi·su·al·i·za·tion \ˌvizh-(ə-)wə-lə-ˈzā-shən, ˌvizh-ə-lə-\ *n* 1 : the formation of visual mental images 2 : the act or process of putting into visual form

vi·su·al·ize \ˈvizh-(ə-)wə-ˌlīz, ˈvizh-ə-ˌlīz\ *vb* **-ized; -iz·ing** : to make visible; *esp* : to form a mental image of

visual purple *n* : a red or purple pigment in the retina of various vertebrates including human beings that is sensitive to dim light and functions in night vision

vi·tal \ˈvīt-ᵊl\ *adj* 1 : concerned with or necessary to the continuation of life ⟨the heart and lungs are *vital* organs⟩ 2 : full of vitality : ANIMATED 3 : characteristic of life or of living things ⟨*vital* activities⟩ 4 : destructive of life : FATAL ⟨a *vital* wound⟩ 5 : of first importance ⟨a *vital* clue⟩ [Middle English *vital* "alive, full of life, relating to life," from Latin *vitalis* "of life," from *vita* "life"] — **vi·tal·ly** \-ᵊl-ē\ *adv*

vital capacity *n* : the breathing capacity of the lungs expressed as the number of cubic inches or cubic centimeters of air that can be forcibly exhaled after one full act of breathing in

vi·tal·i·ty \vī-ˈtal-ət-ē\ *n, pl* **-ties** 1 a : the property by which the living can be separated from the nonliving : LIFE b : capacity to live and develop 2 : energy of mind or body 3 a : the ability to last b : lively and animated spirit

vi·tal·ize \ˈvīt-ᵊl-ˌīz\ *vb* **-ized; -iz·ing** : to give vitality to ⟨the good news *vitalized* his supporters⟩

vi·tals \ˈvīt-ᵊlz\ *n pl* 1 : vital organs (as the heart and liver) 2 : essential parts

vital signs *n* : the pulse rate, body temperature, number of breaths taken per minute, and often blood pressure of a person

vital statistics *n pl* : statistics about births, deaths, marriages, health, and disease

vi·ta·min \ˈvīt-ə-mən\ *n* : any of various substances that are necessary in very small amounts to the nutrition of most animals and some plants, that are important to the control of growth and development by activating and assisting in the function of enzymes, and that are present naturally in many foods or in some cases are produced within the body

vitamin A *n* : any of several vitamins or a mixture of them that are found especially in green and orange vegetables (as carrots or spinach) and animal products (as egg yolk, butter, or liver) and are needed especially for good vision

vitamin B *n* 1 : VITAMIN B COMPLEX 2 : THIAMINE

vitamin B complex *n* : a group of vitamins that are found widely in foods and are essential for normal function of certain enzymes and for growth — called also *B complex*

vitamin B₁ \-ˈbē-ˈwən\ *n* : THIAMINE

vitamin B₆ \-ˈbē-ˈsiks\ *n* : PYRIDOXINE; *also* : a closely related compound

vitamin B₁₂ \-ˈbē-ˈtwelv\ *n* : a member of the vitamin B complex that contains cobalt, occurs especially in liver, and is needed for normal blood formation, nerve function, and growth; *also* : any of several other compounds with similar activity

vitamin B₂ \-ˈbē-ˈtü\ *n* : RIBOFLAVIN

vitamin C *n* : a vitamin that is present especially in citrus fruits, tomatoes, and green vegetables and is needed by the body to prevent scurvy — called also *ascorbic acid*

vitamin D *n* : any of several vitamins that are needed for normal bone and tooth structure, and are found especially in fish-liver oils, egg yolk, and milk or are produced in response to ultraviolet light

vitamin E *n* : any of various oily liquid compounds that can be dissolved in fats, are found especially in plants, and are necessary in the body to prevent infertility and the breakdown of muscles

vitamin K *n* : any of several vitamins that are needed in order for blood to clot properly

vi·tel·line membrane \vī-ˈtel-ən-, -ˌēn-, -ˌin-\ *n* : a membrane that encloses an egg and that in mammals is a thick transparent noncellular layer

vi·ti·ate \ˈvish-ē-ˌāt\ *vb* **-at·ed; -at·ing** 1 : to harm the quality of : SPOIL ⟨grammatical errors *vitiated* the impact of her writing⟩ 2 : to destroy the effect or force of ⟨fraud *vitiates* a contract⟩ — **vi·ti·a·tion** \ˌvish-ē-ˈā-shən\ *n*

vit·re·ous humor \ˈvi-trē-əs-\ *n* : the clear colorless transparent jelly that fills the eyeball behind the lens

vit·ri·ol \ˈvi-trē-əl\ *n* : something (as written or spoken words) thought to be as harsh and burning as acid

vit·tles \ˈvit-ᵊlz\ *n pl* : VICTUALS

vi·tu·per·ate \vī-ˈt(y)ü-pə-ˌrāt, və-\ *vb* **-at·ed; -at·ing** : to criticize harshly : SCOLD

vi·tu·per·a·tion \(ˌ)vī-ˌt(y)ü-pə-ˈrā-shən\ *n* : lengthy harsh bitter criticism or abuse

vi·va·ce \vē-ˈväch-ā, -ē\ *adv or adj* : in a brisk spirited manner — used as a direction in music

vi·va·cious \və-ˈvā-shəs *also* vī-\ *adj* : full of life and good spirits *synonyms* see LIVELY — **vi·va·cious·ly** *adv* — **vi·va·cious·ness** *n*

vi·vac·i·ty \və-ˈvas-ət-ē *also* vī-\ *n* : the quality or state of being vivacious

vi·var·i·um \vī-ˈvar-ē-əm, -ˈver-\ *n, pl* **-ia** \-ē-ə\ *or* **-i·ums** : a terrarium used especially for small animals

viv·id \ˈviv-əd\ *adj* 1 : very strong or bright ⟨a *vivid* red⟩ 2 : having the appearance of vigorous life ⟨a *vivid* sketch of the children⟩ 3 : producing a strong or clear impression : SHARP; *esp* : producing distinct mental pictures ⟨a *vivid* description⟩ 4 : acting clearly and powerfully ⟨a *vivid* imagination⟩ *synonyms* see GRAPHIC — **viv·id·ly** *adv* — **viv·id·ness** *n*

viv·i·fy \ˈviv-ə-ˌfī\ *vb* **-fied; -fy·ing** 1 : to put life into : ANIMATE ⟨rains *vivified* the parched land⟩ 2 : to make vivid — **viv·i·fi·ca·tion** \ˌviv-ə-fə-ˈkā-shən\ *n*

vi·vip·a·rous \vī-ˈvip-(ə-)rəs, və-\ *adj* : giving birth to living young from within the body rather than laying eggs ⟨nearly all mammals and some reptiles are *viviparous*⟩

vivi·sec·tion \ˌviv-ə-ˈsek-shən\ *n* : the operating or experimenting on a living animal for scientific or medical study

vix·en \ˈvik-sən\ *n* : a female fox

viz·ard \ˈviz-ərd, -ˌärd\ *n* : a mask for disguise or protection

vi·zier \və-ˈzi(ə)r\ *n* : a high official in a Muslim country

vizor *variant of* VISOR

VJ \ˈvē-ˌjā\ *n* : VEE JAY

vlog \ˈvlȯg, ˈväg\ *n* : a blog that also contains recorded video [from *video* and b*log*]

vo·cab \ˈvō-ˌkab\ *n* : VOCABULARY

vo·cab·u·lary \vō-ˈkab-yə-ˌler-ē\ *n, pl* **-lar·ies** 1 : a list or collection of words defined or explained 2 : a stock of words used in a language, by a group or individual, or in relation to a subject

¹**vo·cal** \ˈvō-kəl\ *adj* 1 : uttered by the voice : ORAL 2 : composed or arranged for or sung by the human voice ⟨*vocal* music⟩ 3 : speaking freely or loudly : OUTSPOKEN ⟨a *vocal* opponent of the new law⟩ 4 : of, relating to, or resembling the voice — **vo·cal·ly** \-kə-lē\ *adv*

²**vocal** *n* 1 : a vocal sound 2 : a piece of vocal music

vocal cords *n pl* : either of two pairs of elastic folds of tissue in the larynx of which the lower pair produce the voice when air exhaled from the lungs causes them to vibrate

vo·cal·ic \vō-ˈkal-ik\ *adj* **1** : marked by or consisting of vowels **2** : of, relating to, or functioning as a vowel

vo·cal·ist \ˈvō-kə-ləst\ *n* : ¹SINGER

vo·cal·i·za·tion \ˌvō-kə-lə-ˈzā-shən\ *n* : an act, process, or instance of vocalizing

vo·cal·ize \ˈvō-kə-ˌlīz\ *vb* **-ized; -iz·ing** : to give voice to; *esp* : ¹SING 1a — **vo·cal·iz·er** \ˈvō-kə-ˌlī-zər\ *n*

vo·ca·tion \vō-ˈkā-shən\ *n* **1** : a strong desire or leaning for a certain career or course of action; *esp* : a divine call to the religious life **2 a** : the work a person regularly does : OCCUPATION **b** : the persons in a particular occupation [Middle English *vocacioun* "a strong inclination to a particular course of action or way of life," from early French *vocaciun* (same meaning), from Latin *vocation-, vocatio* "summons," derived from *vocare* "to call" — related to ADVOCATE, PROVOKE, REVOKE]

vo·ca·tion·al \vō-ˈkā-shnəl, -shən-ᵊl\ *adj* **1** : of, relating to, or concerned with a vocation **2** : of, relating to, or involved in training in a skill or trade to be followed as a career ⟨*vocational* school⟩ — **vo·ca·tion·al·ly** \-ē\ *adv*

vo·cif·er·ate \vō-ˈsif-ə-ˌrāt\ *vb* **-at·ed; -at·ing** : to cry out loudly : SHOUT

vo·cif·er·ous \vō-ˈsif-(ə-)rəs\ *adj* : making a loud outcry : NOISY, CLAMOROUS — **vo·cif·er·ous·ly** *adv*

vod·ka \ˈväd-kə\ *n* : a colorless alcoholic liquor [Russian, literally, "little water," from *voda* "water"]

vogue \ˈvōg\ *n* **1** : the quality or state of being popular **2** : a period in which something is popular or in fashion **3** : something in fashion at a particular time — **vogue** *adj*

¹voice \ˈvȯis\ *n* **1 a** : sound produced by vertebrates in the larynx or syrinx; *esp* : sound so produced by human beings (as in speaking) **b** : the power of speaking ⟨lost my *voice*⟩ **2 a** : musical sound produced by the vocal cords **b** : the ability to sing ⟨a singer with a great *voice*⟩ **c** : ¹SINGER ⟨one of the finest *voices* of our time⟩ **d** : one of the melodic parts in a vocal or instrumental composition **e** : condition of the vocal organs for singing ⟨in good *voice*⟩ **3** : a sound like a vocal sound ⟨the *voice* of the cricket⟩ **4** : a medium of expression ⟨the newspaper was the *voice* of optimism⟩ **5 a** : wish, choice, or opinion openly or formally expressed ⟨the law was passed despite many opposing *voices*⟩ **b** : the right to express a wish, choice, or opinion ⟨students want a *voice* in school affairs⟩ **6** : a grammatical form showing the relation between the subject of a verb and the action which the verb expresses — **with one voice** : in total agreement

²voice *vb* **voiced; voic·ing** **1** : to express in words ⟨*voice* a complaint⟩ **2** : to vibrate the vocal cords in pronouncing ⟨*voice* a consonant⟩

voice box *n* : LARYNX

voiced \ˈvȯist\ *adj* **1** : having a voice especially of a specified kind — often used in combination ⟨soft-*voiced*⟩ **2** : uttered with the vocal cords vibrating ⟨a *voiced* consonant like \v\⟩

voice·less \ˈvȯi-sləs\ *adj* **1** : having no voice **2** : not voiced ⟨a *voiceless* consonant like \f\⟩ — **voice·less·ness** *n*

voice mail *n* : an electronic communication system in which spoken messages are recorded for later playback to the intended recipient; *also* : such a message

voice–over \ˈvȯi-ˌsō-vər\ *n* : the voice in a film or television program of a person who is heard but not seen or not seen actually talking

¹void \ˈvȯid\ *adj* **1** : containing nothing : EMPTY ⟨*void* space⟩ **2** : being without something specified : DEVOID ⟨a person *void* of common sense⟩ **3** : of no legal force or effect ⟨a *void* contract⟩

²void *n* **1** : empty space **2** : a feeling of want or hollowness

³void *vb* : to make void ⟨*void* a contract⟩

voile \ˈvȯi(ə)l\ *n* : a soft sheer fabric used for summer dresses and for curtains

vol·a·tile \ˈväl-ət-ᵊl\ *adj* **1** : easily becoming a vapor at a fairly low temperature ⟨a *volatile* solvent⟩ **2** : likely to change suddenly or quickly ⟨a *volatile* temper⟩ ⟨the stock market is *volatile*⟩ — **vol·a·til·i·ty** \ˌväl-ə-ˈtil-ət-ē\ *n*

vol·ca·nic \väl-ˈkan-ik, vȯl- *also* -ˈkän-\ *adj* **1 a** : of, relating to, or produced by a volcano ⟨a *volcanic* eruption⟩ **b** : made of materials from volcanoes ⟨*volcanic* dust⟩ **2** : explosively violent ⟨a *volcanic* rage⟩

vol·ca·no \väl-ˈkā-nō, vȯl-\ *n, pl* **-noes** *or* **-nos** : a vent in the earth's crust from which melted or hot rock and steam come out; *also* : a hill or mountain composed entirely or in part of the material thrown out

Word History The ancient Greeks and Romans had many gods and goddesses. Each of these deities was in charge of a special kind of work or an aspect of nature. Many of the happenings in nature were explained in myth as the actions of one or more of these gods or goddesses. The Roman god of fire was known as *Vulcanus* in Latin (*Vulcan* in English). He was thought to live inside Mount Etna, a volcano on the island of Sicily. Vulcan was a giant who worked as a blacksmith, forging the thunderbolts for Jupiter, king of the gods. The smoke and occasional fiery rocks and lava that came from Mount Etna were thought to be from Vulcan's forge. That is how his name came to be applied to a mountain that sometimes spews forth fire and smoke. [from Italian or Spanish; Italian *vulcano* "volcano," from Spanish *vulcán*, from Latin *Volcanus, Vulcanus* "Vulcan (Roman god of fire)"]

vole \ˈvōl\ *n* : any of various small rodents that are closely related to the lemmings and muskrats but in general look like fat mice or rats and that are sometimes harmful to crops

vole

vo·li·tion \vō-ˈlish-ən, və-\ *n* : the act or power of making one's choices or decisions : WILL ⟨they do not do this of their own *volition*⟩ — **vo·li·tion·al** \-ˈlish-nəl, -ən-ᵊl\ *adj*

¹vol·ley \ˈväl-ē\ *n, pl* **volleys** **1** : a group of missiles (as arrows or bullets) passing through the air **2** : a firing of a number of weapons (as rifles) at the same time **3** : a bursting forth of many things at once ⟨a *volley* of praise⟩ **4** : the act of volleying

²volley *vb* **vol·leyed; vol·ley·ing** **1** : to shoot in a volley **2** : to hit an object (as a ball) while it is in the air before it touches the ground

vol·ley·ball \ˈväl-ē-ˌbȯl\ *n* : a game played by volleying a large air-filled ball over a net; *also* : the ball used to play this game

volt \ˈvōlt\ *n* : a unit of electrical potential difference and electromotive force equal to the difference in potential between two points in a conducting wire carrying a constant current of one ampere when the power used between these two points is equal to one watt

volt·age \ˈvōl-tij\ *n* : potential difference measured in volts

\ə\ **abut**	\au̇\ **out**	\i\ **tip**	\ȯ\ **saw**	\u̇\ **foot**
\ər\ **further**	\ch\ **chin**	\ī\ **life**	\ȯi\ **coin**	\y\ **yet**
\a\ **mat**	\e\ **pet**	\j\ **job**	\th\ **thin**	\yü\ **few**
\ā\ **take**	\ē\ **easy**	\ŋ\ **sing**	\th\ **this**	\yu̇\ **cure**
\ä\ **cot, cart**	\g\ **go**	\ō\ **bone**	\ü\ **food**	\zh\ **vision**

vol·ta·ic \väl-'tā-ik, vōl-, vȯl-\ *adj* : of, relating to, or producing direct electric current by chemical action (as in a battery) : GALVANIC ⟨*voltaic* cell⟩

volt·me·ter \'vōlt-,mēt-ər\ *n* : an instrument for measuring in volts the difference in potential between different points of an electrical circuit

vol·u·ble \'väl-yə-bəl\ *adj* : having a smooth and fast flow of words in speaking **synonyms** see TALKATIVE — **vol·u·bil·i·ty** \,väl-yə-'bil-ət-ē\ *n* — **vol·u·bly** \'väl-yə-blē\ *adv*

vol·ume \'väl-yəm, -yüm\ *n* **1** : ¹BOOK 2a **2** : one of a series of books forming a complete work or collection ⟨the fifth *volume* of an encyclopedia⟩ **3** : an amount of space as measured in cubic units ⟨the *volume* of a container⟩ **4** : a large amount : MASS ⟨*volumes* of smoke⟩ ⟨a *volume* of criticism poured in⟩ **5** : the degree of loudness of a sound ⟨turn up the *volume*⟩

Word History The earliest books were written on long rolls made from a plant called papyrus. The Roman name for such a roll was *volumen,* a word which came from the verb *volvere,* meaning "to roll." Later, books were made of a material called parchment, which, unlike papyrus, could be folded and bound together. This advance made it unnecessary to use rolls anymore. The French word *volume,* which came from the Latin *volumen,* was originally used to refer to papyrus rolls but later was used for bound books as well. The French word was borrowed into English in the 14th century. By the 16th century, *volume* had also come to mean "the size (of a book)." This meaning led to a more general sense, "the quantity or amount (of anything)." In the 19th century, *volume* acquired still another meaning, "the strength or loudness of a sound." [Middle English *volume* "a book, a scroll of papyrus," from early French (same meaning), from Latin *volumen* "roll, scroll," from *volvere* "to roll" — related to REVOLVE]

vo·lu·mi·nous \və-'lü-mə-nəs\ *adj* **1 a** : having or marked by great volume or bulk : LARGE ⟨a *voluminous* discharge of lava⟩ **b** : FULL 3b ⟨*voluminous* curtains⟩ **2** : filling or capable of filling a large volume or several volumes ⟨*voluminous* research⟩ — **vo·lu·mi·nous·ly** *adv* — **vo·lu·mi·nous·ness** *n*

vol·un·tari·ly \,väl-ən-'ter-ə-lē\ *adv* : of one's own free will ⟨admitted *voluntarily* that he was guilty⟩

¹vol·un·tary \'väl-ən-,ter-ē\ *adj* **1** : done, given, or made with one's own free will ⟨*voluntary* assistance⟩ **2** : not accidental : INTENTIONAL ⟨*voluntary* manslaughter⟩ **3** : of, relating to, or controlled by the will ⟨*voluntary* behavior⟩

synonyms VOLUNTARY, INTENTIONAL, DELIBERATE, WILLING mean done or brought about of one's own will. VOLUNTARY suggests free choice ⟨joining the club is *voluntary*⟩ or control by the will ⟨*voluntary* blinking of the eyes⟩. INTENTIONAL suggests that something is done for a reason and only after some thought ⟨*intentional* misbehavior⟩. DELIBERATE suggests that one is fully aware of what one is doing and of the likely results of the action ⟨a *deliberate* insult⟩. WILLING suggests a readiness and eagerness to go along with the wishes of another ⟨*willing* obedience⟩.

²voluntary *n, pl* **-tar·ies** : a musical piece played usually on the organ at a religious service

voluntary muscle *n* : muscle (as most striated muscle) that is under voluntary control

¹vol·un·teer \,väl-ən-'ti(ə)r\ *n* : a person who volunteers for a service

²volunteer *adj* : being, consisting of, or engaged in by volunteers ⟨a *volunteer* fire department⟩ ⟨*volunteer* activities⟩

³volunteer *vb* **1** : to offer voluntarily ⟨*volunteered* my services⟩ **2** : to offer oneself as a volunteer ⟨*volunteered* to do the job⟩

vo·lup·tuous \və-'ləp-chə(-wə)s\ *adj* : giving pleasure to the senses — **vo·lup·tuous·ly** *adv* — **vo·lup·tuous·ness** *n*

vol·vox \'väl-,väks\ *n* : any of a genus of single-celled green algae with flagella that form ball-shaped colonies

¹vom·it \'väm-ət\ *n* : an act of throwing up the contents of the stomach through the mouth; *also* : the matter thrown up

²vomit *vb* : to throw up the contents of the stomach through the mouth — **vom·it·er** *n*

volvox

voo·doo \'vüd-ü\ *n, pl* **voo·doos** **1** : a religion that is based on African ancestor worship and practiced chiefly in Haiti **2** : a person who deals in spells and magic [from Louisiana French *voudou* "voodoo"; of African origin] — **voodoo** *adj*

voo·doo·ism \'vüd-(,)ü-,iz-əm\ *n* **1** : VOODOO 1 **2** : the practice of witchcraft — **voo·doo·ist** \'vüd-ü-əst\ *n*

vo·ra·cious \vȯ-'rā-shəs, və-\ *adj* **1** : having a huge appetite : RAVENOUS ⟨*voracious* fish⟩ **2** : very eager ⟨a *voracious* reader⟩ — **vo·ra·cious·ly** *adv* — **vo·rac·i·ty** \-'ras-ət-ē\ *n*

vor·tex \'vȯr-,teks\ *n, pl* **vor·ti·ces** \'vȯrt-ə-,sēz\ *also* **vor·tex·es** : a mass of whirling fluid forming a cavity in the center toward which things are drawn : WHIRLPOOL

vor·ti·cel·la \,vȯrt-ə-'sel-ə\ *n, pl* **vor·ti·cel·lae** \-'sel-ē\ *or* **-cellas** : any of a genus of ciliates that look like a bell on the end of a stalk

vo·ta·ry \'vōt-ə-rē\ *n, pl* **-ries** : a devoted follower; *esp* : a devout or eager worshipper

¹vote \'vōt\ *n* **1 a** : a formal expression of opinion or will (as by ballot in an election) **b** : the result reached by voting **c** : ¹BALLOT 1 **2** : the general opinion expressed by voters ⟨the *vote* is to lower taxes⟩ **3** : the right to cast a vote : SUFFRAGE ⟨gave women the *vote*⟩ **4 a** : the act or process of voting ⟨bring the issue to a *vote*⟩ **b** : a method of voting ⟨a voice *vote*⟩ **5 a** : VOTER **b** : a group of voters with a common interest or quality ⟨the farm *vote*⟩ — **vote·less** \-ləs\ *adj*

²vote *vb* **vot·ed; vot·ing** **1** : to express one's wish or choice by a vote : cast a vote **2** : to elect, decide, pass, defeat, grant, or make legal by a vote **3** : to declare by general agreement **4** : to put forth as a suggestion ⟨I *vote* we all go home⟩

vot·er \'vōt-ər\ *n* : one that votes or has the legal right to vote

voting machine *n* : a mechanical device for recording and counting votes cast in an election

vo·tive \'vōt-iv\ *adj* : consisting of or expressing a vow, wish, or desire ⟨a *votive* prayer⟩

votive candle *n* **1** : a candle lit in devotion or gratitude **2** : a small squat candle — called also *votive*

vouch \'vaúch\ *vb* **1** : to give a guarantee ⟨*vouch* for the truth of a story⟩ **2** : to supply supporting evidence or testimony

vouch·er \'vaú-chər\ *n* **1** : one who vouches for another **2** : a paper that records a business dealing (as payment of a bill or credit for a future purchase)

vouch·safe \vaúch-'sāf, 'vaúch-,sāf\ *vb* **vouch·safed; vouch·saf·ing** : to grant as a special favor

¹vow \'vaú\ *n* : a solemn promise or statement

²vow *vb* **1** : to make a vow or as a vow **2** : to bind or make holy by a vow

vow·el \'vaú(-ə)l\ *n* **1** : a speech sound produced without obstruction or audible friction in the mouth **2** : a letter (as *a, e, i, o, u,* and sometimes *y*) representing a vowel

¹voy·age \'vȯi-ij, 'vȯ(-)ij\ *n* : a journey especially by water from one place or country to another

²voyage *vb* **voy·aged; voy·ag·ing** : to take a trip : TRAVEL — **voy·ag·er** *n*

vul·ca·nize \'vəl-kə-ˌnīz\ *vb* **-nized; -niz·ing** : to treat rubber or similar plastic material chemically in order to give it useful properties (as elasticity or strength)

vul·gar \'vəl-gər\ *adj* **1** : generally used, applied, or accepted **2** : of or relating to common speech : ¹VERNACULAR ⟨the *vulgar* name of a plant⟩ **3** : of or relating to the common people ⟨the *vulgar* opinion of the time⟩ **4 a** : lacking in good manners or taste : COARSE ⟨a loud *vulgar* belch⟩ **b** : morally crude **c** : tastelessly showy : PRETENTIOUS **5** : offensive in language : OBSCENE ⟨a *vulgar* joke⟩— **vul·gar·ly** *adv*

vul·gar·ism \'vəl-gə-ˌriz-əm\ *n* : a vulgar expression

vul·gar·i·ty \ˌvəl-'gar-ət-ē\ *n, pl* **-ties** **1** : the quality or state of being vulgar **2** : something vulgar

vul·gar·ize \'vəl-gə-ˌrīz\ *vb* **-ized; -iz·ing** : to make vulgar

Vul·gate \'vəl-ˌgāt\ *n* : a Latin version of the Bible authorized and used by the Roman Catholic Church

vul·ner·a·ble \'vəln-(-ə)rə-bəl, 'vəl-nər-bəl\ *adj* **1** : capable of being physically or emotionally wounded **2** : open to attack or damage ⟨a *vulnerable* position⟩ — **vul·ner·a·bil·i·ty** \ˌvəln-(-ə)rə-'bil-ət-ē\ *n*

vul·ture \'vəl-chər\ *n* **1** : any of various large birds that feed mostly on animals found dead and that are related to the hawks and eagles but have weaker claws and the head usually naked **2** : a greedy or predatory person

vul·va \'vəl-və\ *n, pl* **vul·vae** \-ˌvē, -ˌvī\ : the parts of the female genital organs that are on the outside of the body

vying *present participle of* VIE

W

w \'dəb-əl-(ˌ)yü, -yə, 'dəb-(-ə)-yə\ *n, often cap* : the 23rd letter of the English alphabet

Wac \'wak\ *n* : a member of a U.S. Army unit created for women during World War II and discontinued in the 1970s

wacky \'wak-ē\ *adj* **wacki·er; -est** : ODD 5, CRAZY — **wacki·ly** \'wak-ə-lē\ *adv* — **wacki·ness** \'wak-ē-nəs\ *n*

¹wad \'wäd\ *n* **1** : a small mass, bundle, or tuft ⟨a *wad* of cotton⟩ **2** : a soft pad or plug used to hold a powder charge in a gun or cartridge **3 a** : a roll of paper money **b** : a large amount (as of money) ⟨spent a *wad* on clothes⟩

²wad *vb* **wad·ded; wad·ding** **1** : to form into a wad or wadding ⟨*wad* up a handkerchief⟩ **2** : to stuff or line with soft material

wad·ding \'wäd-iŋ\ *n* **1** : wads or material for making wads **2** : a soft mass or sheet of fibers used for stuffing or padding

¹wad·dle \'wäd-ᵊl\ *vb* **wad·dled; wad·dling** \'wäd-liŋ, -ᵊl-iŋ\ **1** : to walk with short steps swaying from side to side ⟨ducks *waddling* to the water⟩ **2** : to move slowly and awkwardly ⟨the big boat *waddled* upstream⟩ — **wad·dler** \-lər, -ᵊl-ər\ *n*

²waddle *n* : an awkward swaying walk

wade \'wād\ *vb* **wad·ed; wad·ing** **1** : to step in or through a substance (as water, mud, or sand) that is thicker than air **2 a** : to move or proceed slowly or with difficulty ⟨*wade* through a dull book⟩ **b** : to attack or work energetically ⟨*waded* into their chores⟩ **3** : to pass or cross by wading ⟨*wade* a stream⟩

wad·er \'wād-ər\ *n* **1** : one that wades **2** : WADING BIRD **3** *pl* : high waterproof boots or trousers for wading

wa·di \'wäd-ē\ *n* : the bed or valley of a stream in regions of southwestern Asia and northern Africa that is usually dry except during the rainy season

wading bird *n* : any of various long-legged birds (as herons, storks, and ibises) that wade in water in search of food

Waf \'waf\ *n* : a member of the women's branch of the U.S. Air Force formed after World War II and discontinued in the 1970s

wa·fer \'wā-fər\ *n* **1 a** : a thin crisp cake or cracker **b** : a round thin piece of bread used in the sacrament of Communion **2** : something (as a piece of candy or a computer chip) resembling a wafer especially in thin round form

waf·fle \'wäf-əl, 'wȯf-\ *n* : a crisp cake with an indented crust made by cooking batter in a waffle iron

waffle iron *n* : a cooking utensil with two hinged metal parts that shut upon each other to make a grid-shaped pattern on a waffle being cooked

¹waft \'wäft, 'waft\ *vb* : to move or be moved lightly by or as if by the action of wind or waves

²waft *n* : a slight breeze : PUFF

¹wag \'wag\ *vb* **wagged; wagging** : to move or swing to and fro or up and down especially with quick jerky movements ⟨the dog *wagged* its tail⟩ ⟨*wagged* his finger as he scolded⟩ [Middle English *waggen* "to be in motion, move about"] — **wag·ger** *n*

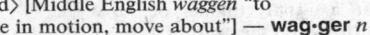

waffle iron

²wag *n* : a wagging movement

³wag *n* : JOKER 1, WIT [probably a shortened form of obsolete *waghalter* "a person who should be hanged"]

¹wage \'wāj\ *vb* **waged; wag·ing** **1** : to engage in or carry on ⟨*wage* war⟩ ⟨*wage* a campaign⟩ **2** : to be in the process of occurring ⟨the battle *waged* for several hours⟩

²wage *n* **1** : a payment for work or services usually calculated on an hourly, daily, or piecework basis — often used in plural **2** *sing or pl* : something given or received because of one's actions : REWARD

¹wa·ger \'wā-jər\ *n* **1** : something (as a sum of money) risked on an uncertain event : BET **2** : something (as the outcome of a game or race) on which a bet is made : GAMBLE

²wager *vb* **wa·gered; wa·ger·ing** \'wāj-(-ə)riŋ\ : to bet on the outcome of a contest or question — **wa·ger·er** \'wā-jər-ər\ *n*

wage scale *n* : a list of wage rates for related tasks; *also* : the general level of wages for an area or region

wag·gery \'wag-ə-rē\ *n, pl* **-ger·ies** **1** : mischievous fun **2** : JEST 1; *esp* : PRACTICAL JOKE

\ə\ **abut**	\au̇\ **out**	\i\ **tip**	\ȯ\ **saw**	\u̇\ **foot**
\ər\ **further**	\ch\ **chin**	\ī\ **life**	\ȯi\ **coin**	\y\ **yet**
\a\ **mat**	\e\ **pet**	\j\ **job**	\th\ **thin**	\yü\ **few**
\ā\ **take**	\ē\ **easy**	\ŋ\ **sing**	\th\ **this**	\yu̇\ **cure**
\ä\ **cot, cart**	\g\ **go**	\ō\ **bone**	\ü\ **food**	\zh\ **vision**

wag·gish \'wag-ish\ *adj* : displaying or done in a spirit of good-humored mischief ⟨*waggish* pranks⟩

wag·gle \'wag-əl\ *vb* **wag·gled; wag·gling** \-(ə-)liŋ\ : ¹WAG — **waggle** *n*

wag·on \'wag-ən\ *n* **1 a** : a usually four-wheeled vehicle for transporting goods or passengers; *esp* : one drawn by animals **b** : PATROL WAGON **2** : a low four-wheeled ve- hicle with an open rect- angular body for the play or use of a child **3** : STATION WAGON — **wag·on·er** \'wag-ə-nər\ *n* — **on the wagon** : choosing not to drink alcoholic beverages

wagon 1a

wa·gon·load \'wag-ən-ˌlōd\ *n* **1** : a load that fills or could fill a wagon ⟨a *wagonload* of apples⟩ **2** : a very large amount ⟨a *wagonload* of choices⟩

waif \'wāf\ *n* : a stray person or animal; *esp* : a homeless child

¹wail \'wā(ə)l\ *vb* **1** : to express sorrow by mournful cries : LAMENT **2** : to make a sound like a mournful cry **3** : to express dissatisfaction : COMPLAIN — **wail·er** \'wā-lər\ *n*

²wail *n* **1** : a long cry or sound of grief or pain **2** : a sound like a wail ⟨the *wail* of a siren⟩

wain \'wān\ *n* : a heavy wagon or two-wheeled cart for farm use

wain·scot \'wān-skət, -ˌskōt, -ˌskät\ *n* **1** : a usually pan- eled wooden lining of the wall of a room **2** : the lower three or four feet (about one meter) of an interior wall when finished differently from the rest

wain·scot·ing *or* **wain·scot·ting** \'wān-ˌskōt-iŋ, -ˌskät-, -skət-\ *n* **1** : WAINSCOT **2** : material used to line a surface with wainscot

waist \'wāst\ *n* **1 a** : the usually nar- rowed part of the body between the chest and hips **b** : the narrow front part of the abdomen of some insects (as a wasp) **2** : the central portion of something that is usually thinner or narrower than the ends ⟨the *waist* of a ship⟩ ⟨the *waist* of a violin⟩ **3** : a gar- ment or the part of a garment that covers the body from the neck to the waist — **waist·ed** \'wā-stəd\ *adj*

waist·band \'wās(t)-ˌband\ *n* : a band (as of trousers or a skirt) fitting around the waist

waist·coat \'wes-kət, 'wās(t)-ˌkōt\ *n, chiefly British* : ²VEST 1

waist·line \'wāst-ˌlīn\ *n* **1 a** : WAIST 1a **b** : body circumference at the waist **2** : the part of a garment surrounding the waist

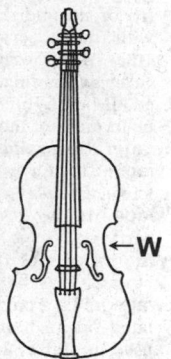

W waist 2

¹wait \'wāt\ *vb* **1 a** : to remain in place in readiness or ex- pectation of something : AWAIT ⟨*wait* your turn⟩ ⟨*wait* for orders⟩ **b** : to pause to let someone catch up ⟨hey, *wait* for me⟩ **2** : POSTPONE, DELAY ⟨*wait* dinner for a guest⟩ **3** : to serve as a waiter or waitress ⟨*wait* tables⟩ ⟨*wait* at a luncheon⟩ — **wait on** *also* **wait upon 1 a** : to work for as a servant **b** : to supply the wants of : SERVE ⟨*wait on* a customer⟩ **2** : to make a formal call on **3** : to wait for — **wait up** : to delay going to bed : stay up ⟨I'll be late; don't *wait up*⟩

²wait *n* **1 a** : a hidden position : AMBUSH — used chiefly in the expression *lie in wait* **b** : a state of watchful expecta- tion **2** : an act or period of waiting ⟨a long *wait* in line⟩

wait·er \'wāt-ər\ *n* : one that waits; *esp* : a person who waits tables (as in a restaurant)

waiting list *n* : a list containing names of people who are waiting (as for admission to an organization or school)

waiting room *n* : a room or area (as in a doctor's office) for the use of persons (as patients) waiting

wait–list \'wāt-ˌlist\ *vb* : to put on a waiting list

wait·per·son \'wāt-ˌpərs-ᵊn\ *n* : a waiter or waitress

wait·ress \'wā-trəs\ *n* : a woman who waits tables (as in a restaurant) — **waitress** *vb*

wait·staff \'wāt-ˌstaf\ *n* : a staff of servers at a restaurant

waive \'wāv\ *vb* **waived; waiv·ing 1** : to give up claim to ⟨*waived* her right to answer⟩ **2** : to let pass ⟨*waive* the fee⟩ **3** : to dismiss with or as if with a wave of the hand ⟨*waived* the problem aside⟩

waiv·er \'wā-vər\ *n* **1** : the act of intentionally giving up a right, claim, or privilege **2** : a document containing a declaration of a waiver

¹wake \'wāk\ *vb* **woke** \'wōk\ *also* **waked** \'wākt\; **wo·ken** \'wō-kən\ *or* **waked** *also* **woke; wak·ing 1** : to be or remain awake **2** : to stand watch over (as a dead body); *esp* : to hold a wake over **3** : to arouse from or as if from sleep : AWAKE — often used with *up* [from Old English *wacan* "to awake" and Old English *wacian* "to be awake"] — **wak·er** *n*

²wake *n* : a time before a dead person is buried when people gather to remember him or her and often to view the body

³wake *n* **1** : a track or path left by a moving body (as a ship) in the water **2** : AFTERMATH 2 [of Germanic origin] — **in the wake of 1** : close behind and following the same course **2** : as a result of

wake·ful \'wāk-fəl\ *adj* : not sleeping or able to sleep — **wake·ful·ly** \-fə-lē\ *adv* — **wake·ful·ness** *n*

wak·en \'wā-kən\ *vb* **wak·ened; wak·en·ing** \'wāk- (ə-)niŋ\ : AROUSE 1

wake–rob·in \'wā-ˌkräb-ən\ *n* : TRILLIUM

wake–up call *n* **1** : something (as a telephone call from a hotel employee to a guest) that serves to wake up a sleep- er **2** : something that serves to alert a person to a prob- lem, danger, or need

Wal·dorf salad \ˌwȯl-ˌdȯrf-\ *n* : a salad usually containing apples, celery, nuts, and mayonnaise [named for the *Wal- dorf*-Astoria Hotel in New York City]

wale \'wā(ə)l\ *n* : a narrow raised surface or ridge; *esp* : one of a series of even ribs on a fabric (as corduroy)

¹walk \'wȯk\ *vb* **1** : to move or cause to move along on foot at a natural slow gait ⟨*walk* to town⟩ ⟨*walk* a horse up a hill⟩ **2** : to pass over, through, or along by walking ⟨*walk* the streets⟩ **3** : to perform or accomplish by walking ⟨*walk* guard⟩ **4** : to take or cause to take first base with a base on balls — **walk off with 1** : ¹STEAL **2** : to win or gain especially without difficulty ⟨*walked off with* the state championship⟩ — **walk over** : to disregard the wishes or feelings of

²walk *n* **1** : a going on foot ⟨go for a *walk*⟩ **2** : a place, path, or course for walking **3** : distance to be walked ⟨it's a long *walk*⟩ **4 a** : manner of living : CONDUCT, BEHAV- IOR **b** : social or economic status ⟨various *walks* of life⟩ **5 a** : manner of walking **b** : a way of moving by a four- footed animal in which there are always at least two feet on the ground; *esp* : a slow way of moving by a horse in which the feet strike the ground in the sequence of left hind foot, left front foot, right hind foot, right front foot **6** : BASE ON BALLS — **walk in the park** : an easy or plea- surable experience : PICNIC

walk·able \'wȯ-kə-bəl\ *adj* : capable of or suitable for be- ing walked ⟨a very *walkable* city⟩ ⟨a *walkable* distance⟩

walk·er \'wȯ-kər\ *n* **1** : one that walks **2** : something used in walking; *esp* : a framework that supports a baby learn- ing to walk or an infirm or disabled person

walk·ie–talk·ie \ˌwȯ-kē-'tȯ-kē\ *n* : a small portable radio set for receiving and sending messages

walk–in \ˌwȯ-kin\ *adj* : large enough to be walked into ⟨a *walk-in* closet⟩

walking stick *n* **1** : a stick used in walking **2** : STICK INSECT

Walk·man \'wòk-mən, -,man\ *trademark* — used for a small portable audio player listened to by means of headphones or earphones

walk·out \'wò-,kaut\ *n* **1** : ²STRIKE 2a **2** : the action of leaving a meeting or organization as an expression of disapproval

walk out \(')wò-'kaut\ *vb* **1** : to go on strike **2** : to leave suddenly often as an expression of disapproval — **walk out on** : ¹ABANDON 3, DESERT

walk–up \'wò-,kəp\ *n* : an apartment or office building without an elevator — **walk–up** *adj*

walk·way \'wò-,kwā\ *n* : a path or passageway for pedestrians ⟨a *walkway* over the busy street⟩

¹**wall** \'wòl\ *n* **1** : a structure (as of brick or stone) meant to enclose or shut off a space; *esp* : a side of a room or building **2** : something resembling a wall; *esp* : something that acts as a barrier or defense ⟨a tariff *wall*⟩ **3** : a layer of material that encloses space ⟨the heart *wall*⟩ ⟨the *walls* of a container⟩ — **walled** \'wòld\ *adj*

²**wall** *vb* **1** : to provide, separate, or surround with or as if with a wall ⟨*wall* in the garden⟩ **2** : to close off an opening with or as if with a wall ⟨*wall* up a door⟩

wal·la·by \'wäl-ə-bē\ *n, pl* **wallabies** *also* **wallaby** : any of various small or medium-sized kangaroos

wallaby

wall·board \'wòl-,bō(ə)rd, -,bó(ə)rd\ *n* : a building material (as of wood pulp, gypsum, or plastic) made in large stiff sheets and used especially for inside walls and ceilings

wal·let \'wäl-ət\ *n* **1** : a bag or sack for carrying things on a journey **2** : a small flat folding pocketbook with compartments (as for coins, paper money, and cards); *also* : BILLFOLD

wall·eye \'wò-,lī\ *n* : a large vigorous North American freshwater food and sport fish with large eyes that is related to the perches but resembles the true pike — called also *walleyed pike*

wall·flow·er \'wòl-,flau(-ə)r\ *n* : a person who from shyness or unpopularity remains alone (as at a dance)

¹**wal·lop** \'wäl-əp\ *n* **1** : a powerful blow or impact **2** : the ability to hit hard

²**wallop** *vb* **1** : to beat thoroughly : TROUNCE **2** : to hit with force : SOCK — **wal·lop·er** *n*

¹**wal·low** \'wäl-ō\ *vb* **1** : to roll about in or as if in deep mud ⟨elephants *wallowing* in the river⟩ **2** : to devote oneself to something pleasurable **3** : to become or remain helpless ⟨allowed them to *wallow* in their ignorance⟩ — **wal·low·er** \'wäl-ə-wər\ *n*

²**wallow** *n* **1** : an act of wallowing **2** : a muddy or dust-filled area where animals wallow

wall·pa·per \'wòl-,pā-pər\ *n* : decorative paper for covering the walls of a room — **wallpaper** *vb*

Wall Street \'wòl-\ *n* : the powerful financial interests that control or influence the U.S. economy [from *Wall Street* in New York City, site of a major stock trading exchange]

wall–to–wall *adj* **1** : covering the entire floor ⟨*wall-to-wall* carpeting⟩ **2** : filling an entire space ⟨a beach that was *wall-to-wall* sunbathers⟩

wal·nut \'wòl-(,)nət\ *n* **1 a** : an edible nut of any of a genus of trees related to the hickories; *esp* : the large nut of a Eurasian tree **b** : a tree that produces walnuts — compare BLACK WALNUT **c** : the usually reddish to dark brown wood of a walnut that is widely used for cabinetwork and veneers **2** : a medium reddish brown

Word History Long before walnut trees were introduced into England, they were cultivated for their tasty nuts in southern Europe. The nut tree native to the more northern areas of Europe was the hazel. In order to tell apart the native hazelnut and the less familiar walnut, Old English called the walnut *wealhhnutu,* which means "foreign nut." This word is a compound of *wealh,* "foreigner" and *hnutu* "nut." The Old English word *wealh* has supplied us with another word as well. While *wealh* meant "foreigner" in a general sense, it was applied specifically by the Anglo-Saxon invaders of Britain to the native people they found living on the island. *Wealh* gave rise to the modern forms *Welsh, Welshman,* and *Welshwoman.* [Old English *wealhhnutu,* literally "foreign nut," from *Wealh* "Welshman, foreigner" + *hnutu* "nut" — related to WELSH]

Wal·pur·gis Night \väl-'pùr-gəs-\ *n* : the evening before May 1 on which witches were believed to gather [named for Saint *Walburga* (German *Walpurgis*) died 779 an English saint whose feast day falls on May Day]

wal·rus \'wòl-rəs, 'wäl-\ *n, pl* **walrus** *or* **wal·rus·es** : a large mammal of cold northern seas that is related to the seals and has long ivory tusks, a tough wrinkled hide with a thick layer of blubber below, stiff whiskers, and flippers used in swimming, diving, and moving about on land

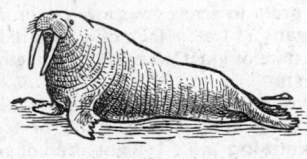
walrus

¹**waltz** \'wòl(t)s\ *n* : a ballroom dance in ³/₄ time with strong accent on the first beat; *also* : music for a waltz

²**waltz** *vb* **1 a** : to dance a waltz **b** : to dance a waltz with **2 a** : to proceed easily and successfully : BREEZE ⟨*waltzed* through the test⟩ **b** : to approach boldly ⟨can't just *waltz* up and introduce ourselves⟩

wam·pum \'wäm-pəm\ *n* **1** : beads of polished shells formerly used by North American Indians as money and ornaments **2** : MONEY 1 [from *wamponpeag,* a word in an American Indian language literally meaning "white strings"]

wan \'wän\ *adj* **wan·ner; wan·nest 1 a** : ¹PALE 1b, SICKLY ⟨a *wan* complexion⟩ **b** : lacking vitality : FEEBLE **2** : ¹DIM 1, FAINT ⟨a *wan* light⟩ **3** : showing little effort : LANGUID ⟨a *wan* smile⟩ — **wan·ly** *adv* — **wan·ness** \'wän-nəs\ *n*

wand \'wänd\ *n* **1** : a slender rod used in performing magic **2** : a light rod or tube

wan·der \'wän-dər\ *vb* **wan·dered; wan·der·ing** \-d(ə-)riŋ\ **1** : to move about without a purpose **2** : to follow a winding course : MEANDER **3 a** : to get off the right course : STRAY ⟨*wandered* away⟩ **b** : to lose one's normal mental concentration ⟨her mind *wandered*⟩ — **wander** *n* — **wan·der·er** \-dər-ər\ *n*

synonyms WANDER, ROAM, RAMBLE, MEANDER mean to move about from place to place without a reason or plan. WANDER suggests that one does not follow a fixed course while moving about ⟨the nomads *wandered* in the desert for hundreds of years⟩. ROAM suggests a carefree wandering over a wide area often for pleasure ⟨I *roamed* over the hills and through the meadows⟩. RAMBLE suggests that one wanders in a careless way and without concern for where one goes ⟨tourists *rambling* through the park⟩. MEANDER suggests following a winding

\ə\ **abut**	\aú\ **out**	\i\ **tip**	\ò\ **saw**	\ú\ **foot**
\ər\ **further**	\ch\ **chin**	\ī\ **life**	\òi\ **coin**	\y\ **yet**
\a\ **mat**	\e\ **pet**	\j\ **job**	\th\ **thin**	\yü\ **few**
\ā\ **take**	\ē\ **easy**	\ŋ\ **sing**	\th\ **this**	\yú\ **cure**
\ä\ **cot, cart**	\g\ **go**	\ō\ **bone**	\ü\ **food**	\zh\ **vision**

course and may also suggest moving lazily ⟨the young-sters *meandered* on the way home⟩.

wandering Jew *n* : any of several creeping or trailing plants often grown for their showy leaves

wan·der·lust \'wän-dər-,ləst\ *n* : strong longing to travel

¹wane \'wān\ *vb* **waned; wan·ing 1** : to grow gradually smaller or less ⟨the moon *wanes*⟩ **2** : to lose power, prosperity, or influence ⟨the nation *waned* as its commerce declined⟩ **3** : to draw toward an end ⟨summer is *waning*⟩

²wane *n* **1** : the act or process of waning **2** : a period or time of waning; *esp* : the period from the full phase of the moon to the new moon

wan·gle \'waŋ-gəl\ *vb* **wan·gled; wan·gling** \-g(ə-)liŋ\ : to achieve or obtain by sly, tricky, or indirect methods ⟨*wangled* a free ticket to the show⟩

¹want \'wȯnt *also* 'wänt, 'wənt\ *vb* **1** : to be without : LACK ⟨this coat is *wanting* a button⟩ **2** : to feel or have the need of : REQUIRE ⟨our house *wants* painting⟩ **3** : to desire, wish, or long for something ⟨*wanted* a chance to play⟩ **4** : OUGHT **2** ⟨you *want* to be very careful⟩ **5** : to seek in order to arrest ⟨was *wanted* for murder⟩

²want *n* **1 a** : a lack of a required or usual amount **b** : a state of great poverty **2** : something wanted : NEED, DE-SIRE

want ad *n* : a newspaper advertisement stating that something (as an employee, job, or item) is wanted

¹want·ing *adj* **1** : not present or noticeable : ABSENT, LACKING **2 a** : falling below standards or expectations **b** : lacking in ability : DEFICIENT

²wanting *prep* **1** : ¹WITHOUT **2a** ⟨a book *wanting* a cover⟩ **2** : ¹MINUS **1** ⟨a month *wanting* two days⟩

wan·ton \'wȯnt-ᵊn, 'wänt-\ *adj* **1** : FRISKY, PLAYFUL ⟨a *wanton* kitten⟩ **2** : INDECENT, LEWD **3 a** : MERCILESS, INHUMANE ⟨*wanton* cruelty⟩ **b** : being without just cause : MALICIOUS ⟨a *wanton* attack⟩ **4** : UNRESTRAINED **1**, EXTRAVAGANT ⟨a life of *wanton* luxury⟩ — **wan·ton·ly** *adv* — **wan·ton·ness** \-ᵊn-nəs\ *n*

wa·pi·ti \'wäp-ət-ē\ *n, pl* **wapiti** *or* **wapitis** : ELK **2**

¹war \'wȯ(ə)r\ *n* **1 a** : a state or period of armed hostile conflict between states, nations, or groups **b** : the science of warfare **2 a** : a state of hostility, antagonism, or conflict **b** : a struggle between opposing forces or for a particular goal ⟨a *war* on disease⟩

²war *vb* **warred; war·ring 1** : to engage in warfare ⟨*war-ring* nations⟩ **2** : to be in conflict

¹war·ble \'wȯr-bəl\ *n* **1** : low pleasing sounds forming a melody **2** : the action of warbling : TRILL

²warble *vb* **war·bled; war·bling** \-b(ə-)liŋ\ **1** : to sing with trills **2** : to express by warbling

war·bler \'wȯr-blər\ *n* **1** : one that warbles **2 a** : any of numerous small Old World songbirds many of which are noted for their melodious song and which are closely related to the thrushes **b** : any of numerous small brightly colored American songbirds with a usually weak and unmusical song

war·bon·net \'wȯr-,bän-ət\ *n* : a long feathered ceremonial American Indian headdress

war cry *n* : a cry or yell used by fighters in battle

¹ward \'wȯ(ə)rd\ *n* **1** : the action or process of guarding or of being under guard; *esp* : CUSTODY **1 2 a** : a division in a hospital; *esp* : a large room in a hospital where a number of patients stay **b** : a division (as a cell or block) of a prison **3** : an electoral or administrative division of a city **4** : a person (as a child) under the protection of a court or guardian

warbonnet

²ward *vb* **1** : to keep watch over : GUARD **2** : to turn aside : DEFLECT — usually used with *off* ⟨*ward* off a cold⟩

¹-ward \wərd\ *also* **-wards** \wərdz\ *adj suffix* **1** : that moves, tends, faces, or is directed toward ⟨wind*ward*⟩ **2** : that occurs or is located in the direction of ⟨rear*ward*⟩ [Old English *-weard* (adjective suffix) "being or moving in the direction of"]

²-ward *or* **-wards** *adv suffix* **1** : in a (specified) direction ⟨rear*wards*⟩ ⟨after*ward*⟩ **2** : toward a (specified) point, position, or area ⟨sky*ward*⟩

war·den \'wȯrd-ᵊn\ *n* **1** : one who has charge or care of something : GUARDIAN, KEEPER **2** : the governor of a town, district, or fortress **3** : an official charged with special duties or with the enforcement of specified laws or regulations ⟨game *warden*⟩ ⟨air-raid *warden*⟩ **4** : an official in charge of a prison **5 a** : a lay officer of an Episcopal parish **b** : any of various British college officials

ward·er \'wȯrd-ər\ *n* : WATCHMAN, WARDEN

ward·robe \'wȯr-,drōb\ *n* **1** : a room, closet, or chest where clothes are kept **2** : a collection of clothes (as of one person or for one activity)

ward·room \'wȯr-,drüm, -,drum\ *n* : the space in a warship assigned to the officers except the captain as living quarters or a dining room

ware \'wa(ə)r, 'we(ə)r\ *n* **1 a** : manufactured articles or products of art or craft : GOODS — often used in combination ⟨tin*ware*⟩ **b** : an article of merchandise ⟨peddlers hawking their *wares*⟩ **2** : items (as dishes) made from fired clay : POTTERY ⟨earthen*ware*⟩

ware·house \'wa(ə)r-,haús, 'we(ə)r-\ *n* : a building for the storage of goods — **ware·house·man** \-,haù-smən\ *n*

war·fare \'wȯr-,fa(ə)r, -,fe(ə)r\ *n* **1 a** : military fighting between enemies : WAR **b** : activity undertaken by one country or group to weaken or destroy another ⟨economic *warfare*⟩ **2** : a struggle between competitors : CONFLICT ⟨industrial *warfare*⟩

war·head \'wȯ(ə)r-,hed\ *n* : the section of a missile containing the charge

war–horse \'wȯ(ə)r-,hȯ(ə)rs\ *n* **1** : a horse used in war : CHARGER **2** : a veteran soldier or politician

warier *comparative of* WARY

wariest *superlative of* WARY

war·like \'wȯ(ə)r-,līk\ *adj* **1** : fond of war ⟨*warlike* people⟩ **2** : of, relating to, or used in war ⟨*warlike* preparations⟩

war·lock \'wȯ(ə)r-,läk\ *n* : a man who practices witchcraft : SORCERER, WIZARD

war·lord \'wȯ(ə)r-,lȯ(ə)rd\ *n* **1** : an important military leader **2** : a military leader who governs an area by force

¹warm \'wȯ(ə)rm\ *adj* **1 a** : having or giving off heat to a moderate or adequate degree ⟨*warm* food⟩ ⟨a *warm* stove⟩ **b** : serving to keep in heat (as of the body) ⟨*warm* clothes⟩ **c** : feeling or causing sensations of heat ⟨*warm* from exertion⟩ ⟨a long *warm* walk⟩ **2 a** : showing or marked by strong feeling : ARDENT ⟨a *warm* hug⟩ **b** : marked by tense excitement or anger ⟨a *warm* political campaign⟩ **3** : marked by or tending toward injury, distress, or pain ⟨gave the enemy a *warm* reception⟩ **4 a** : newly made : FRESH ⟨a *warm* scent⟩ **b** : near to a goal, answer, or object sought ⟨not there yet but getting *warm*⟩ **5** : of a color in the range yellow to orange to red — **warm·ly** *adv* — **warm·ness** *n*

²warm *vb* **1** : to make or become warm ⟨*warm* yourself in front of the fire⟩ **2 a** : to give a feeling of warmth or pleasure to ⟨it *warms* my heart to see you⟩ **b** : to experience feelings of affection or pleasure ⟨*warmed* to her young guests⟩ **3** : to reheat for eating ⟨*warm* over some potatoes⟩ **4 a** : to make or become ready for action or performing by doing special exercises or actions beforehand ⟨swimmers *warm* up before a race⟩ **b** : to become increasingly interested or enthusiastic ⟨a speaker *warm-ing* to his topic⟩

warm–blood·ed \'worm-'bləd-əd\ *adj* **1** : able to keep up a relatively high and constant body temperature that is mostly independent of that of the surrounding environment ⟨birds and mammals are *warm-blooded*⟩ **2** : warm in feeling — **warm–blood·ed·ness** *n*

warm·er \'wor-mər\ *n* : one that warms; *esp* : a device for keeping something warm ⟨a foot *warmer*⟩

warm front *n* : an advancing edge of a warm air mass

warm–heart·ed \'wo(ə)rm-'härt-əd\ *adj* : marked by warmth of feeling — **warm·heart·ed·ness** *n*

warming pan *n* : a long-handled covered pan filled with hot coals and used to warm beds in earlier times

war·mon·ger \'wo(ə)r-,mən-gər, -,mäŋ-\ *n* : one who urges or attempts to stir up war — **war·mon·ger·ing** \-g(ə-)riŋ\ *n*

warmth \'wo(ə)rm(p)th\ *n* **1** : the quality or state of being warm in temperature **2 a** : the quality or state of being warm in feeling ⟨enjoyed the *warmth* of their praise⟩ **b** : a glowing effect produced by the use of warm colors

warm–up \'wor-,məp\ *n* **1** : the act or an instance of warming up **2** : a practice or set of exercises done before a game, contest, or workout

warn \'wo(ə)rn\ *vb* **1 a** : to give notice to beforehand especially of danger or evil **b** : to give advice to : COUNSEL **2** : to order to go or stay away ⟨*warned* us off their land⟩ — **warn·er** *n*

warn·ing \'wor-niŋ\ *n* **1** : the act of warning : the state of being warned ⟨he had *warning* of his illness⟩ **2** : something that warns ⟨storm *warnings*⟩ — **warning** *adj* — **warn·ing·ly** *adv*

warning coloration *n* : bright color patterns on an animal (as an insect) that serve to warn possible predators that the animal is undesirable as prey (as by being poisonous or bad-tasting)

¹warp \'wo(ə)rp\ *n* **1** : a series of yarns going lengthwise in a loom and crossed by the woof **2** : a twist or curve in something once flat or straight ⟨a *warp* in a door⟩

²warp *vb* **1 a** : to turn or twist out of shape **b** : to cause to judge, choose, or act wrongly : PERVERT **2** : to arrange so as to form a warp ⟨*warp* yarns⟩ — **warp·er** *n*

war·path \'wo(ə)r-,path, -,påth\ *n* : the route taken by a group of American Indians on their way to fight the enemy — **on the warpath** : ready to fight or argue

warp knit *n* : a knit fabric produced by a machine in which the knitting is done with the yarns running in a lengthwise direction — compare WEFT KNIT — **warp knitting** *n*

¹war·rant \'wor-ənt, 'wär-\ *n* **1** : evidence or a reason for thinking, deciding, or doing something : JUSTIFICATION **2** : evidence of permission; *esp* : a legal paper giving an officer the power to carry out the law **3** : a certificate of appointment issued to an officer of lower rank than a commissioned officer

²warrant *vb* **1** : to declare or insist with certainty ⟨I'll *warrant* they know the answer⟩ **2** : to guarantee something to be as it appears or is represented to be **3** : to give legal or official approval to : AUTHORIZE **4** : to call for : REQUIRE ⟨this report *warrants* careful study⟩ — **war·rant·able** \-ə-bəl\ *adj* — **war·ran·tor** \,wor-ən-'tò(ə)r, ,wär-, -ənt-ər\ *n*

warrant officer *n* : a military or naval officer with any of the ranks between those of commissioned officers and those of noncommissioned officers; *esp* : a warrant officer of lowest rank

war·ran·ty \'wor-ənt-ē, 'wär-\ *n, pl* **-ties** : a written statement guaranteeing the good condition of a product and stating the maker's responsibility for the repair or replacement of faulty parts

warred *past and past participle of* WAR

war·ren \'wor-ən, 'wär-\ *n* : a place where rabbits breed

warring *present participle of* WAR

war·rior \'wor-yər; 'wor-ē-ər, 'wär-ē-\ *n* : a person who is or has been in warfare

war·ship \'wo(ə)r-,ship\ *n* : a ship armed for combat

wart \'wo(ə)rt\ *n* **1** : a small hard growth on the skin often caused by a virus **2** : something that sticks out (as on a plant) and resembles a wart — **warty** \'wort-ē\ *adj*

wart·hog \'wo(ə)rt-,hog, -,häg\ *n* : a wild African hog with large tusks and in the male two pairs of rough warty growths on the face

warthog

war·time \'wo(ə)r-,tīm\ *n* : a period when a war is going on

wary \'wa(ə)r-ē, 'we(ə)r-\ *adj* **wari·er; -est** : very cautious; *esp* : being on guard against danger or trickery ⟨*wary* of strangers⟩ **synonyms** see CAREFUL — **wari·ly** \'war-ə-lē, 'wer-\ *adv* — **wari·ness** \'war-ē-nəs, 'wer-\ *n*

was *past 1st & 3rd singular of* BE

¹wash \'wȯsh, 'wäsh\ *vb* **1** : to clean with water and usually a cleaning substance (as soap or detergent) ⟨*wash* clothes⟩ ⟨*wash* your hands⟩ **2 a** : to wet thoroughly with liquid **b** : to pass water over or through especially so as to carry off material from the surface or interior **3** : to flow along or splash or overflow against ⟨waves *wash* the shore⟩ **4** : to pour or flow in a stream or current ⟨the river *washes* against its banks⟩ **5** : to move or carry by the action of water ⟨several trees were *washed* away by the flood⟩ **6** : to cover or smear lightly with a liquid (as whitewash or varnish) **7** : to run water over in order to separate out valuable matter ⟨*wash* sand for gold⟩ **8** : to hold up under washing ⟨this dress *washes* well⟩ **9** : to stand a test for truthfulness ⟨that story won't *wash*⟩ **10** : to be worn away by washing ⟨the heavy rain caused the bridge to *wash* out⟩

²wash *n* **1** : the act or process or an instance of washing **2** : articles to be or being washed **3 a** : a piece of ground washed by the sea or river **b** *Western* : the dry bed of a stream **4** : worthless especially liquid waste : REFUSE **5 a** : a thin coat of paint (as watercolor) **b** : a liquid used for coating a surface (as a wall) or for washing **6** : material carried along or deposited by running water **7 a** : BACKWASH **b** : a disturbance in the air produced by the passage of a wing or propeller

³wash *adj* : WASHABLE ⟨*wash* fabric⟩

wash·able \'wȯsh-ə-bəl, 'wäsh-\ *adj* : capable of being washed without damage ⟨a *washable* silk⟩ — **wash·abil·i·ty** \,wȯsh-ə-'bil-ət-ē, ,wäsh-\ *n*

wash–and–wear *adj* : of, relating to, or being a fabric or garment needing little or no ironing after washing

wash·ba·sin \'wȯsh-,bās-ᵊn, 'wäsh-\ *n* : WASHBOWL

wash·board \'wȯsh-,bō(ə)rd, 'wäsh-, -,bȯ(ə)rd\ *n* : a grooved board to scrub clothes on

wash·bowl \-,bōl\ *n* : a large bowl for water that is used to wash one's hands and face

wash·cloth \-,klȯth\ *n* : a cloth for washing one's face and body

washed–out \'wȯsh-'taut, 'wäsh-\ *adj* **1** : faded in color **2** : empty of life or energy : EXHAUSTED

washed–up \'wȯsh-'təp, 'wäsh-\ *adj* : no longer successful, popular, or needed

\ə\ **abut**	\au̇\ **out**	\i\ **tip**	\ȯ\ **saw**	\u̇\ **foot**
\ər\ **further**	\ch\ **chin**	\ī\ **life**	\ȯi\ **coin**	\y\ **yet**
\a\ **mat**	\e\ **pet**	\j\ **job**	\th\ **thin**	\yü\ **few**
\ā\ **take**	\ē\ **easy**	\ŋ\ **sing**	\th\ **this**	\yu̇\ **cure**
\ä\ **cot, cart**	\g\ **go**	\ō\ **bone**	\ü\ **food**	\zh\ **vision**

wash·er \\'wȯsh-ər, 'wäsh-\ *n* **1** : a ring (as of metal) used to make something fit tightly or to prevent rubbing **2** : one that washes; *esp* : WASHING MACHINE

wash·er·wom·an \\'wȯsh-ər-,wu̇m-ən, 'wäsh-\ *n* : a woman who takes in washing

wash·ing \\'wȯsh-iŋ, 'wäsh-\ *n* : articles washed or to be washed

washing machine *n* : a machine used especially for washing clothes and household linen

washing soda *n* : a transparent crystalline sodium carbonate combined chemically with water

Washington's Birthday *n* **1** : February 22 formerly observed as a legal holiday in most states of the U.S. **2** : the third Monday in February observed as a legal holiday in most states of the U.S. — called also *Presidents' Day*

wash·out \\'wȯsh-,au̇t, 'wäsh-\ *n* **1 a** : the washing away of earth (as from a road) **b** : a place where earth is washed away **2** : a complete failure

wash out \(')wȯsh-'au̇t, (')wäsh-\ *vb* **1** : to fade or cause to fade by or as if by laundering **2** : to exhaust the strength or energy **3** : to fail to measure up to a standard **4** : to destroy by the force or action of water

wash·room \\'wȯsh-,rüm, 'wäsh-, -,ru̇m\ *n* : a room with sinks and toilets : LAVATORY

wash·stand \-,(s)tand\ *n* **1** : a stand holding articles for washing one's face and hands **2** : WASHBOWL

wash·tub \-,təb\ *n* : a tub for washing or soaking clothes

wash up *vb* **1** : to wash one's face and hands **2** : to bring to an end the force or value of ⟨a scandal would *wash* you *up* as a sports hero⟩ **3** : to be deposited by or as if by waves ⟨seaweed *washed up* on the shore⟩

wasn't \\'wəz-ᵊnt, 'wäz-\ : was not

wasp \\'wäsp, 'wȯsp\ *n* : any of numerous winged insects related to the bees and ants that have a slender body with the abdomen attached by a narrow stalk and that in females and workers are usually capable of giving a very painful sting

wasp

WASP *or* **Wasp** *n, sometimes disparaging* : an American of northern European and Protestant background

wasp·ish \\'wäs-pish, 'wȯs-\ *adj* **1** : easily annoyed : SNAPPISH **2** : like a wasp in form; *esp* : very thin — **wasp·ish·ly** *adv* — **wasp·ish·ness** *n*

wasp waist *n* : a very slender waist — **wasp–waist·ed** \\'wäsp-'wā-stəd, 'wȯsp-\ *adj*

¹was·sail \\'wäs-əl *also* wä-'sā(ə)l\ *n* **1** : an early English toast to someone's health **2** : wild drinking : REVELRY [Middle English *wæs hæil, washayl,* "a toast to someone's health," from early Norse *ves heill* "be well," from *heill* "healthy" — related to ³HAIL, ¹HALE]

²wassail *vb* **1** : to go on a wild drinking spree : CAROUSE **2** : to drink to the health of

was·sail·er \\'wä-sə-lər *also* wä-'sā-lər\ *n* : one that carouses : REVELER

wast \wəst, (')wäst\ *archaic past 2nd singular of* BE

wast·age \\'wā-stij\ *n* : loss, decrease, or destruction of something (as by use, decay, erosion, or leakage); *esp* : wasteful or avoidable loss of something valuable

¹waste \\'wāst\ *n* **1 a** : a region that has few people or is empty of most signs of life : DESERT **b** : uncultivated land **2 a** : the act or an instance of wasting **b** : the state of being wasted **3 a** : material left over, rejected, or thrown away **b** : an unwanted product obtained in the course of

a manufacturing or chemical process **c** : material (as carbon dioxide in the lungs or urine in the kidneys) produced in and of no further use to the living body

²waste *vb* **wast·ed; wast·ing** **1** : to destroy completely **2** : to wear away or grow smaller gradually **3** : to spend carelessly or uselessly : SQUANDER **4** : to lose or cause to lose weight, strength, or energy ⟨illness caused her to *waste* away⟩

³waste *adj* **1** : being wild and without people or crops : DESOLATE, BARREN **2** : being in a ruined condition **3** : thrown away as worthless after being used **4** : of no further use to a person, animal, or plant ⟨means by which the body gives off *waste* materials⟩

waste·bas·ket \\'wās(t)-,bas-kət\ *n* : an open container for trash and especially wastepaper

waste·ful \\'wāst-fəl\ *adj* : given to or marked by waste : PRODIGAL ⟨a *wasteful* use of our natural resources⟩ — **waste·ful·ly** \-fə-lē\ *adv* — **waste·ful·ness** *n*

waste·land \\'wāst-,land\ *n* **1** : land that is not cultivated or not fit for the cultivation of crops **2** : an ugly often ruined place or area

waste·pa·per \\'wās(t)-'pā-pər\ *n* : paper thrown away as used, not needed, or not fit for use

wast·er \\'wā-stər\ *n* : one that uses or uses up carelessly or needlessly

wast·rel \\'wā-strəl\ *n* : SPENDTHRIFT

¹watch \\'wäch, 'wȯch\ *vb* **1** : to stay awake especially during the night (as at the bedside of a sick person) **2** : to be on the alert or on the lookout **3** : to keep guard ⟨*watch* outside the door⟩ **4** : to keep one's eyes on : keep in view ⟨*watch* a game⟩ **5** : to keep in view so as to prevent harm or warn of danger ⟨*watch* a brush fire carefully⟩ **6** : to keep oneself informed about ⟨*watch* his career⟩ **7** : to be on the alert for the chance to make use of ⟨*watched* her opportunity and took it⟩ — **watch·er** *n*

²watch *n* **1 a** : the act of keeping awake to guard, protect, or attend **b** : a state of alert and continuous attention ⟨a tornado *watch*⟩ **c** : close observation ⟨kept a *watch* over the prisoner⟩ **2 a** : WATCHMAN **b** : a body of watchmen **3 a** : a period during which a part of a ship's company is on duty **b** : the part of a ship's company on duty during a watch **4** : a portable timepiece designed to be worn (as on the wrist) or carried in the pocket

watch·dog \\'wäch-,dȯg, 'wȯch-\ *n* **1** : a dog kept to guard property **2** : one that guards against loss, waste, theft, or dishonesty

watch·ful \\'wäch-fəl, 'wȯch-\ *adj* : continually on the lookout especially for danger — **watch·ful·ly** \-fə-lē\ *adv* — **watch·ful·ness** *n*

watch·mak·er \\'wäch-,mā-kər, 'wȯch-\ *n* : one that makes or repairs watches or clocks — **watch·mak·ing** \-kiŋ\ *n*

watch·man \-mən\ *n* : a person assigned to watch : GUARD

watch out *vb* : to be on the lookout ⟨*watch out* for cars⟩

watch·tow·er \\'wäch-,tau̇(-ə)r, 'wȯch-\ *n* : a tower for a lookout

watch·word \-,wərd\ *n* **1** : a secret word used as a signal or password **2** : a motto used as a slogan or cry for common support

¹wa·ter \\'wȯt-ər, 'wät-\ *n* **1** : the liquid that descends from the clouds as rain, forms streams, lakes, and seas, and is a major part of all living material and that is an odorless and tasteless compound having two atoms of hydrogen and one atom of oxygen per molecule **2** *pl* : an area of seawater bordering on and under the control of a country ⟨sailing Canadian *waters*⟩ **3** : travel or transportation on water ⟨came by *water*⟩ **4** : the level of water at a particular state of the tide : TIDE **5** : a liquid containing or resembling water; *esp* : a watery fluid (as tears, urine, or sap) formed or circulating in a living body — **wa·ter·less** \-ləs\ *adj*

²water *vb* **1** : to wet or supply with water ⟨*water* horses⟩ ⟨*water* the lawn⟩ **2** : to weaken by or as if by the addition of water ⟨someone *watered* down the punch⟩ **3** : to form or give off water or watery matter (as tears or saliva) ⟨smog makes my eyes *water*⟩

water bed *n* : a bed whose mattress is a plastic bag filled with water

water beetle *n* : any of numerous oval flattened beetles (as a whirligig beetle) that are found in water and swim by means of their fringed hind legs which act together as oars

wa·ter·bird \'wȯt-ər-ˌbərd\ *n* : a swimming or wading bird

water blister *n* : a blister containing clear watery fluid

wa·ter·borne \-ˌbōrn, -ˌbȯrn\ *adj* : supported, carried, or passed on by water ⟨*waterborne* diseases⟩

wa·ter·buck \'wȯt-ər-ˌbək, 'wät-\ *n, pl* **waterbuck** *or* **waterbucks** : an African antelope commonly found near streams or wet areas

water beetle

water buffalo *n* : an Asian buffalo that is often domesticated and somewhat resembles a large ox

water bug *n* : any of various insects that live in or near water or in moist places

water chestnut *n* : a whitish crunchy vegetable used especially in Chinese cooking that is the peeled underground stem of an Asian sedge; *also* : the sedge or its underground stem

water clock *n* : a device or machine for measuring time by the fall or flow of water

water closet *n* **1** : a compartment or room with a toilet bowl **2** : a toilet bowl with its fixtures

wa·ter·col·or \'wȯt-ər-ˌkəl-ər, 'wät-\ *n* **1** : a paint whose liquid part is water **2** : a picture painted with watercolor **3** : the art of painting with watercolor — **wa·ter·col·or·ist** \-ˌkəl-ə-rəst\ *n*

wa·ter·course \-ˌkō(ə)rs, -ˌkȯ(ə)rs\ *n* **1** : a channel in which water flows **2** : a stream of water (as a river or brook)

wa·ter·craft \-ˌkraft\ *n* : craft for water transportation

wa·ter·cress \-ˌkres\ *n* : a plant that is related to the mustards and the cabbage, grows especially in clear running water, and has crisp peppery-tasting leaves used especially in salads; *also* : the leaves of a watercress

water cycle *n* : HYDROLOGIC CYCLE

wa·ter·er \'wȯt-ər-ər, 'wät-\ *n* : one that waters ⟨an automatic plant *waterer*⟩

wa·ter·fall \'wȯt-ər-ˌfȯl, 'wät-\ *n* : a fall of water usually from a great height

water flea *n* : any of various small active dark or brightly colored freshwater crustaceans (as a daphnia)

wa·ter·fowl \'wȯt-ər-ˌfau̇l, 'wät-\ *n, pl* **-fowl** *also* **-fowls** : a bird that is found in or near water; *esp* : a swimming bird (as a duck or goose) often hunted as game

wa·ter·front \-ˌfrənt\ *n* : land or a section of a town bordering on a body of water

water gas *n* : a poisonous flammable gaseous mixture that consists chiefly of carbon monoxide and hydrogen, that is usually made by blowing air and then steam over red-hot coke or coal, and that is used as a fuel

water glass *n* : a glass container (as a drinking glass) for holding water

water hole *n* : a natural hole or hollow containing water especially for drinking

water hyacinth *n* : a floating water plant often clogging waterways in the southern U.S.

water ice *n* : a frozen dessert of water, sugar, and flavoring

water jump *n* : an obstacle (as in a steeplechase) consisting of a pool, stream, or ditch of water

water lily *n* : any of a family of water plants with rounded floating leaves and usually showy flowers

wa·ter·line \'wȯt-ər-ˌlīn, 'wät-\ *n* : a line marked on the outside of a ship that matches the surface of the water when the ship floats evenly

wa·ter·logged \'wȯt-ər-ˌlȯgd, 'wät-, -ˌlägd\ *adj* : so filled or soaked with water as to be heavy or hard to manage ⟨a *waterlogged* boat⟩

water lily

¹wa·ter·mark \'wȯt-ər-ˌmärk, 'wät-\ *n* **1** : a mark that shows the height to which water has risen **2** : a mark (as the maker's name or trademark) made in paper during manufacture and visible when the paper is held up to the light

²watermark *vb* : to mark with a watermark

wa·ter·mel·on \'wȯt-ər-ˌmel-ən, 'wät-\ *n* **1** : a large oblong or rounded fruit with a hard outer shell, a sweet red juicy pulp, and usually many seeds **2** : a widely grown African vine of the gourd family that produces watermelons

water moccasin *n* : a poisonous pit viper of the southern U.S. that is closely related to the copperhead — called also *cottonmouth, cottonmouth moccasin*

water ouzel *n* : DIPPER 2

water park *n* : an amusement park with pools and wetted slides for recreation

water moccasin

water pistol *n* : a toy pistol designed to squirt a stream of water

water polo *n* : a game similar to soccer that is played in water by teams of swimmers

wa·ter·pow·er \'wȯt-ər-ˌpau̇(-ə)r, 'wät-\ *n* : the power of moving water used to run machinery (as for generating electricity)

¹wa·ter·proof \-ˌprüf\ *adj* : not letting water through; *esp* : covered or treated with a material to prevent penetration by water

²waterproof *n, chiefly British* : RAINCOAT

³waterproof *vb* : to make waterproof

water rat *n* : a rodent that is found in or near water

wa·ter–re·pel·lent \ˌwȯt-ə(r)-ri-ˈpel-ənt, ˌwät-\ *adj* : treated with a finish that resists but does not completely prevent penetration by water

wa·ter–re·sis·tant \-ri-ˈzis-tənt\ *adj* : WATER-REPELLENT

wa·ter·shed \'wȯt-ər-ˌshed, 'wät-\ *n* **1** : a dividing ridge (as a mountain range) separating one drainage area from others **2** : the area that drains into a river or lake

water–ski \-ˌskē\ *vb* : to ski on water while being towed by a speedboat — **wa·ter–ski·er** *n*

water ski *n* : a ski used in water-skiing

\ə\ **abut**	\au̇\ **out**	\i\ **tip**	\ȯ\ **saw**	\u̇\ **foot**
\ər\ **further**	\ch\ **chin**	\ī\ **life**	\ȯi\ **coin**	\y\ **yet**
\a\ **mat**	\e\ **pet**	\j\ **job**	\th\ **thin**	\yü\ **few**
\ā\ **take**	\ē\ **easy**	\ŋ\ **sing**	\th\ **this**	\yu̇\ **cure**
\ä\ **cot, cart**	\g\ **go**	\ō\ **bone**	\ü\ **food**	\zh\ **vision**

wa·ter·slide \-ˌslīd\ *n* : a continuously wetted chute (as at an amusement park) down which people slide into a pool

water snake *n* : any of various snakes found in or near fresh waters and feeding largely on water-dwelling animals

water spaniel *n* : a rather large spaniel of either of two breeds with heavy curly coats

wa·ter·spout \'wȯt-ər-ˌspaȯt, 'wät-\ *n* 1 : a pipe for carrying off water from a roof 2 : a column of rotating wind extending from a cloud down to a cloud of spray torn up from the surface of a body of water by the winds

water strider *n* : any of various long-legged bugs that move about swiftly on the surface of the water

water table *n* : the upper limit of the portion of the ground completely soaked with water

wa·ter·tight \ˌwȯt-ər-'tīt, ˌwät-\ *adj* 1 : made to keep water out ⟨a *watertight* compartment⟩ 2 : allowing no possibility for doubt or uncertainty ⟨a *watertight* case against the accused⟩

water vapor *n* : water in a gaseous form especially when below boiling temperature and spread through the atmosphere

water–vascular system *n* : a system of vessels in echinoderms containing a circulating watery fluid that is used especially for the movement of tentacles and tube feet

wa·ter·way \'wȯt-ər-ˌwā, 'wät-\ *n* 1 : a channel for water 2 : a body of water through which ships can travel

wa·ter·weed \-ˌwēd\ *n* : any of various water plants (as elodea) usually with small flowers

wa·ter·wheel \-ˌhwēl, -ˌwēl\ *n* : a wheel made to turn by a flow of water against it

water wings *n pl* : an air-filled device to give support to the body of a swimmer

wa·ter·works \'wȯt-ər-ˌwərks, 'wät-\ *n pl* : a system of reservoirs, pumps, and pipes for supplying water (as to a city)

wa·tery \'wȯt-ə-rē, 'wät-\ *adj* 1 **a** : consisting of or filled with water ⟨a *watery* hole⟩ **b** : containing or giving out water or a thin liquid ⟨a *watery* mixture⟩ ⟨*watery* eyes⟩ 2 : being like water especially in thinness, sogginess, paleness, or lack of taste ⟨*watery* lemonade⟩ ⟨*watery* soup⟩

waterwheel

watt \'wät\ *n* : a unit of power equal to the work done at the rate of one joule per second [named for James *Watt* 1736–1819 Scottish engineer]

watt·age \'wät-ij\ *n* : amount of power expressed in watts

¹**wat·tle** \'wät-ᵊl\ *n* : a framework of poles interwoven with slender branches or reeds and used in building; *also* : material for such a framework — **wat·tled** \-ᵊld\ *adj*

²**wattle** *vb* **wat·tled; wat·tling** \'wät-liŋ, -ᵊl-iŋ\ 1 : to form or build of or with wattle 2 **a** : to weave (as branches) together to form wattle **b** : to unite or make solid by weaving together light flexible material

³**wattle** *n* : a fleshy flap of skin hanging usually from the neck (as of a bird)

¹**wave** \'wāv\ *vb* **waved; wav·ing** 1 : to float or shake in an air current : FLUTTER ⟨flags *waving* in the breeze⟩ 2 : to signal or salute with the hand or with something held in it 3 : BRANDISH ⟨*waved* a pistol and made threats⟩ 4 : to move before the wind with a wavelike motion ⟨a field of *waving* grain⟩ 5 : to follow or cause to follow a curving line or take a wavy form ⟨*waved* her hair⟩

²**wave** *n* 1 : a moving ridge on the surface of water 2 : a wavelike formation or shape ⟨a *wave* in the hair⟩ 3 : the action or process of making wavy or curly 4 : a waving motion ⟨a *wave* of the hand⟩ 5 : a steady flowing movement ⟨a *wave* of color swept the speaker's face⟩ 6 : a sudden or rapid increase ⟨a *wave* of buying⟩ 7 : a disturbance similar to a wave in water that transfers energy progressively from point to point ⟨a light *wave*⟩ 8 : a period of hot or cold weather — **wave·like** \-ˌlīk\ *adj*

Wave \'wāv\ *n* : a woman serving in the navy

wave·length \'wāv-ˌleŋ(k)th\ *n* 1 : the distance (as from crest to crest) in the line of advance of a wave from any one point to the next corresponding point 2 : a certain line of thought or behavior that reveals a common understanding ⟨coworkers who are on the same *wavelength*⟩

wave·let \'wāv-lət\ *n* : a little wave : RIPPLE

wave pool *n* : a large swimming pool with a machine that produces waves

wa·ver \'wā-vər\ *vb* **wa·vered; wa·ver·ing** \'wāv-(ə-)riŋ\ 1 : to go back and forth between choices 2 : to weave or sway to and fro 3 : to move unsteadily — **wa·ver·er** \'wā-vər-ər\ *n*

wavy \'wā-vē\ *adj* **wav·i·er; wav·i·est** : having or moving in waves ⟨*wavy* hair⟩ — **wav·i·ness** \-vē-nəs\ *n*

¹**wax** \'waks\ *n* 1 : a yellowish moldable substance produced by bees and used by them for making the honeycomb — called also *beeswax* 2 : any of various substances like the wax of bees [Old English *weax* "wax produced by bees"] — **wax·like** \'wak-ˌslīk\ *adj*

²**wax** *vb* : to treat or rub with wax

³**wax** *vb* 1 : to grow larger, stronger, fuller, or more numerous 2 : BECOME 1 ⟨*waxed* angry as I heard the story⟩ [Old English *weaxan* "to increase"]

wax bean *n* : a kidney bean with pods that are yellow when ripe for use as snap beans

waxed paper *or* **wax paper** *n* : paper treated with wax to make it resistant to water and grease and used especially as a wrapping

wax·en \'wak-sən\ *adj* : of or like wax

wax museum *n* : a place where wax figures (as of famous persons) are exhibited

wax myrtle *n* : any of several trees or shrubs with fragrant leaves; *esp* : an evergreen shrub or small tree of the eastern U.S. that produces small hard berries with a thick coating of white wax used for candles — compare BAYBERRY 1

wax·wing \'wak-ˌswiŋ\ *n* : any of a genus of American and Eurasian birds that are mostly brown or gray with a showy crest, velvety feathers, and sometimes red waxy material on the tip of the lower wing feathers

wax·work \-ˌswərk\ *n* 1 : a figure in wax usually of a person 2 *pl* : WAX MUSEUM

waxy \'wak-sē\ *adj* **wax·i·er; -est** 1 : full of or covered with wax ⟨a *waxy* surface⟩ ⟨*waxy* berries⟩ 2 : resembling wax : WAXEN ⟨a *waxy* complexion⟩ — **wax·i·ness** *n*

waxwing

¹**way** \'wā\ *n* 1 **a** : a track for travel : PATH **b** : an opening for passage (as through a crowd or a gate) ⟨no *way* out⟩ 2 **a** : a course traveled : ROUTE **b** : DIRECTION 3 ⟨come this *way*⟩ ⟨the wrong *way*⟩ 3 **a** : a course of action ⟨chose the easy *way*⟩ **b** : opportunity or power of doing as one pleases ⟨have your own *way*⟩ **c** : POSSIBILITY 1 ⟨there are no two *ways* about it⟩ 4 **a** : the manner in which something is done or happens ⟨this *way* of thinking⟩ ⟨a new *way* of painting⟩ **b** : a noticeable part or detail ⟨a good

worker in many *ways*⟩ **c** : ¹STATE 1a ⟨the *way* things are⟩ **5** : a particular or typical manner of behavior ⟨it's just his *way*⟩ ⟨has a nice *way* with his pets⟩ **6 a** : ¹DISTANCE 1b ⟨a short *way* down the road⟩ **b** : progress along a course ⟨earning her *way* through school⟩ ⟨made her *way* with difficulty⟩ **7** : LOCALITY ⟨visit when you are out our *way*⟩ **8** : CATEGORY 1 ⟨get what you need in the *way* of supplies⟩ — **by the way** : aside or apart from that : INCI-DENTALLY ⟨*by the way*, did you hear what happened to-day?⟩ — **by way of** **1** : for the purpose of ⟨mentioned her *by way of* example⟩ **2** : by the route through : VIA — **in one's way** *also* **in the way** **1** : in or along one's course **2** : in a position to hinder or obstruct — **on the way** *or* **on one's way** : moving along in one's course : in prog-ress ⟨we were *on our way* home⟩ — **out of the way** **1** : IMPROPER ⟨said nothing *out of the way* during dinner⟩ **2** : in or to a place away from public view ⟨found a cottage that was *out of the way*⟩ **3** : brought to an end : done fully ⟨got his homework *out of the way*⟩

²**way** *adv* **1 a** : ¹FAR 1 ⟨is *way* ahead of the class⟩ **b** : ¹FAR 2 ⟨ate *way* too much⟩ **c** : ²VERY 2 ⟨*way* cool⟩ **2** : all the way ⟨pull the switch *way* back⟩

way·far·er \'wā-ˌfar-ər, -ˌfer-\ *n* : a traveler especially on foot — **way·far·ing** \-ˌfar-iŋ, -ˌfer-\ *adj*

way·lay \'wā-ˌlā\ *vb* **-laid** \-ˌlād\; **-lay·ing** : to attack from a hiding place

way–out \'wā-'aut\ *adj* : very unusual or odd ⟨*way-out* ideas⟩

-ways \ˌwāz\ *adv suffix* : in such a way, course, direction, or manner ⟨side*ways*⟩ [derived from Middle English *way* "course, route"]

way·side \'wā-ˌsīd\ *n* : the side or border of a road or path — **wayside** *adj*

way station *n* : a station or stopping place along a line of travel (as a railroad line)

way·ward \'wā-wərd\ *adj* **1** : tending to do as one pleases : DISOBEDIENT ⟨*wayward* children⟩ **2** : not following a rule or regular course of action — **way·ward·ly** *adv* — **way·ward·ness** *n*

we \(ˈ)wē\ *pron* **1** : I and one or more others **2** : I — used by a monarch or an editor or writer

weak \'wēk\ *adj* **1 a** : lacking physical strength **b** : easily upset or nauseated ⟨a *weak* stomach⟩ **2** : not able to stand much weight, pressure, or strain ⟨a *weak* rope⟩ **3 a** : lacking strength of mind or character **b** : resulting from or showing a lack of mental or moral firmness ⟨a *weak* policy⟩ **4** : not rich in some usual or important element ⟨*weak* tea⟩ **5** : not able to stand the test of logic ⟨a *weak* argument⟩ **6** : lacking skill or ability ⟨*weak* in math⟩ **7** : lacking in force of expression ⟨a *weak* writing style⟩ **8** : not having or using authority ⟨*weak* government⟩ **9** : of, relating to, or being a verb or verb conjugation that forms the past tense and past participle by adding the suf-fix *-ed* or *-d* or *-t* **10** : of, relating to, or being the lightest of three levels of stress in pronunciation ⟨a *weak* syllable⟩ **11** : ionizing only slightly in solution ⟨*weak* acids⟩ — **weak·ly** *adv*

　synonyms WEAK, FEEBLE, FRAIL mean not strong enough to stand pressure or hard effort. WEAK can be used of either a temporary or permanent loss of strength or power ⟨felt *weak* after the illness⟩ ⟨I have *weak* lungs⟩. FEEBLE stresses very great and pitiful weakness ⟨an old *feeble* dog⟩. FRAIL can be used of a person who since birth has had a delicate body ⟨a *frail* child always getting sick⟩ or of any kind of fragile construction ⟨a *frail* antique chair⟩.

weak·en \'wē-kən\ *vb* **weak·ened; weak·en·ing** \'wēk-(ə-)niŋ\ : to make or become weak or weaker

weak·fish \'wēk-ˌfish\ *n* : a common fish of the eastern coast of the U.S. that is an important food and sport fish; *also* : any of several related fishes used for food

weak force *n* : a fundamental force experienced by ele-mentary particles that causes some forms of radioactivity and also causes some types of particles to break down into other particles

weak·ling \'wē-kliŋ\ *n* : one that is weak in body, charac-ter, or mind — **weakling** *adj*

weak·ly \'wē-klē\ *adj* **weak·li·er; -est** : not strong or healthy

weak–mind·ed \'wēk-'mīn-dəd\ *adj* **1** : lacking in judg-ment or good sense **2** : FEEBLEMINDED

weak·ness \'wēk-nəs\ *n* **1** : the quality or state of being weak **2** : a weak point : FAULT, DEFECT ⟨a person with few *weaknesses*⟩ **3 a** : a special desire or fondness ⟨has a *weakness* for chocolate⟩ **b** : an object of special desire or fondness ⟨movies are my *weakness*⟩

¹**weal** \'wē(ə)l\ *n* : a sound or prosperous state : WELL=BEING [Old English *wela* "healthy state"]

²**weal** *n* : WELT [an altered form of *wale* "a streak or ridge made on the skin from a blow"]

wealth \'welth\ *n* **1** : a great amount of money or posses-sions : AFFLUENCE **2** : a large amount or number : PRO-FUSION ⟨a *wealth* of detail⟩

wealthy \'wel-thē\ *adj* **wealth·i·er; -est** **1** : having wealth : RICH **2** : marked by plenty : ABUNDANT — **wealth·i·ness** \-thē-nəs\ *n*

wean \'wēn\ *vb* **1** : to get a child or young animal used to food other than its mother's milk **2** : to turn (one) away from something long desired or followed ⟨*wean* a person from a bad habit⟩

weap·on \'wep-ən\ *n* **1** : something (as a gun, knife, or club) used to injure, defeat, or destroy **2** : something with which one fights or struggles against another

weap·on·ry \'wep-ən-rē\ *n* : weapons as a whole

¹**wear** \'wa(ə)r, 'we(ə)r\ *vb* **wore** \'wō(ə)r, 'wȯ(ə)r\; **worn** \'wō(ə)rn, 'wȯ(ə)rn\; **wear·ing** **1 a** : to use as an article of clothing, adornment, or assistance ⟨*wears* blue jeans all the time⟩ ⟨*wears* glasses⟩ **b** : to carry on the person ⟨*wear* a watch⟩ **2** : to have or show an appearance of ⟨*wore* a happy smile⟩ **3 a** : to damage, destroy, or make less by use or by scraping or rubbing ⟨*wore* the shoes to pieces⟩ **b** : to produce gradually by wearing ⟨*wear* a hole in the rug⟩ **c** : to tire or weaken : FATIGUE ⟨soldiers *worn* by the strain of war⟩ **4** : to stand up under use ⟨a silk that *wears* well⟩ **5 a** : to lessen or end with the passage of time ⟨the effect of the medicine *wore* off⟩ ⟨the day *wore* on⟩ **b** : to reach a certain condition gradually ⟨the blade *wore* dull⟩ — **wear·er** *n*

²**wear** *n* **1 a** : the act of wearing : USE **b** : the state of being worn **2** : clothing or an article of clothing usually of a particular kind or for a special occasion or use ⟨chil-dren's *wear*⟩ **3** : wearing quality : durability under use **4** : the result of wearing or use ⟨a carpet showing signs of *wear*⟩

wear·able \'war-ə-bəl, 'wer-\ *adj* : capable of being worn : suitable to be worn — **wear·abil·i·ty** \ˌwar-ə-'bil-ət-ē, ˌwer-\ *n*

wear and tear *n* : the loss or damage that occurs to some-thing in the course of normal use

wea·ri·some \'wir-ē-səm\ *adj* : causing weariness : TIRE-SOME ⟨a *wearisome* lecture⟩ — **wea·ri·some·ly** *adv* — **wea·ri·some·ness** *n*

wear out *vb* **1** : to tire gradually ⟨*worn out* from exercis-ing⟩ **2** : to make or become useless by wear

¹**wea·ry** \'wi(ə)r-ē\ *adj* **wea·ri·er; -est** **1** : worn out in strength, energy, or freshness **2** : showing or marked by

\ə\ **abut**	\aú\ **out**	\i\ **tip**	\ȯ\ **saw**	\ú\ **foot**
\ər\ **further**	\ch\ **chin**	\ī\ **life**	\ȯi\ **coin**	\y\ **yet**
\a\ **mat**	\e\ **pet**	\j\ **job**	\th\ **thin**	\yü\ **few**
\ā\ **take**	\ē\ **easy**	\ŋ\ **sing**	\th\ **this**	\yú\ **cure**
\ä\ **cot, cart**	\g\ **go**	\ō\ **bone**	\ü\ **food**	\zh\ **vision**

weariness **3** : having one's patience, interest, or pleasure exhausted ⟨*weary* of their attacks⟩ **4** : WEARISOME — **wea·ri·ly** \'wir-ə-lē\ *adv* — **wea·ri·ness** \'wir-ē-nəs\ *n*

²**weary** *vb* **wea·ried; wea·ry·ing** : to become or make weary **synonyms** see TIRE

wea·sel \'wē-zəl\ *n, pl* **weasels 1** *or pl* **weasel** : any of various small slender active mammals that are related to the minks, eat small animals (as mice and birds), and in northern regions turn white in winter — compare ERMINE 1 **2** : a sneaky, untrustworthy, or dishonest person

weasel 1

weasel word *n* : a word used in order to mislead a person or to avoid a straight answer

¹**weath·er** \'weth-ər\ *n* **1** : the state of the atmosphere in regard to heat or cold, wetness or dryness, calm or storm, clearness or cloudiness **2** : disagreeable atmospheric conditions ⟨stormy *weather*⟩ — **under the weather** : somewhat ill or drunk

²**weather** *vb* **weath·ered; weath·er·ing** \'weth-(ə-)riŋ\ **1** : to change by exposure to the weather ⟨shingles *weathered* to a silvery gray⟩ **2** : to bear up against and come safely through ⟨*weather* a storm⟩

³**weather** *adj* : ¹WINDWARD

weath·er–beat·en \'weth-ər-,bēt-ᵊn\ *adj* **1** : toughened or colored by the weather ⟨a *weather-beaten* face⟩ **2** : worn or damaged by exposure to the weather ⟨a *weather-beaten* old barn⟩

weath·er·cock \-,käk\ *n* : a weather vane shaped like a rooster

weath·er·ing \'weth-(ə-)riŋ\ *n* : the action of the forces of nature that changes the color, texture, composition, or form of exposed objects; *esp* : the physical and chemical breakdown of earth materials at or near the earth's surface

weath·er·man \'weth-ər-,man\ *n* : a person who reports and forecasts the weather : METEOROLOGIST

weath·er·per·son \-,pərs-ᵊn\ *n* : WEATHERMAN

weath·er·proof \,weth-ər-'prüf\ *adj* : able to stand up under exposure to weather — **weatherproof** *vb*

weather station *n* : a station for taking, recording, and reporting observations of the weather

weather strip *n* : a strip of material used to seal a door or window around the edges — called also *weather stripping* — **weath·er–strip** *vb*

weather vane *n* : VANE 1

¹**weave** \'wēv\ *vb* **wove** \'wōv\ *or* **weaved** \'wēvd\ *or* **wo·ven** \'wō-vən\ *or* **weaved; weav·ing** **1 a** : to form by lacing together strands of material; *esp* : to make on a loom by lacing together threads going lengthwise with threads going crosswise ⟨*weave* cloth⟩ **b** : to form into a fabric ⟨*weave* wool into tweeds⟩ **2** : ¹SPIN 2b ⟨a caterpillar *weaves* a cocoon⟩ **3 a** : to make by or as if by lacing together parts ⟨*wove* an exciting adventure tale⟩ **b** : to insert as a part : work in ⟨*weave* a moral into a tale⟩ **4** : to move back and forth or from side to side ⟨*weaving* his way through a crowd of holiday shoppers⟩

²**weave** *n* : a pattern or method of weaving

weav·er \'wē-vər\ *n* **1** : one that weaves **2** : WEAVER BIRD

weaver bird *n* : any of numerous Old World birds that resemble finches and usually build a complicated nest by weaving together plant materials

¹**web** \'web\ *n* **1** : a fabric on a loom or in the process of being removed from a loom **2 a** : COBWEB 1b, SPIDERWEB **b** : a network of threads spun especially by the larvae of various insects (as tent caterpillars) and usually serving as a nest or shelter **c** : something that catches and holds one ⟨spies caught in a *web* of plots⟩ **3** : a membrane of an animal or plant; *esp* : one uniting toes (as of many waterbirds) **4** : NETWORK 2 **5** *cap* : WORLD WIDE WEB

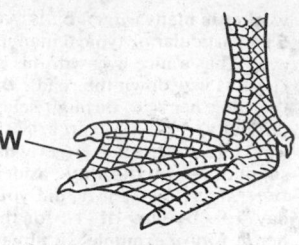

*W*¹web 3

²**web** *vb* **webbed; web·bing** **1** : to make or form a web **2** : to cover or provide with webs or a web

webbed \'webd\ *adj* : having or being toes or fingers joined by webs ⟨the *webbed* feet of ducks⟩

web·bing \'web-iŋ\ *n* : a strong closely woven tape used especially for straps, harness, or upholstery

web·cam \'web-,kam\ *n, often cap* : a camera used in transmitting live images over the World Wide Web

web–foot·ed \'web-'fut-əd\ *adj* : having webbed feet

web·i·sode \'web-ə-,sōd\ *n* : an episode (as of a television series) that is shown over the Internet instead of being broadcast [from World Wide *Web* and ep*isode*]

web·mas·ter \-,mas-tər\ *n* : a person responsible for the creation or maintenance of a website especially for a company or organization

Web page *n* : the information found at a single World Wide Web address

web·site \'web-,sīt\ *n* : a group of World Wide Web pages usually containing links to each other and made available online by an individual, company, or organization

wed \'wed\ *vb* **wed·ded** *also* **wed; wed·ding** **1** : to take, give, or join in marriage : MARRY **2** : to unite firmly as if by marriage

we'd \(,)wēd\ : we had : we should : we would

wed·ding \'wed-iŋ\ *n* : a marriage ceremony usually with accompanying festivities : NUPTIALS

¹**wedge** \'wej\ *n* **1** : a piece of wood or metal with a pointed edge used especially to split wood or rocks and to lift heavy weights **2** : something (as a piece of pie or land) shaped like a triangle **3 a** : something (as a policy or action) that causes a separation or break ⟨the decision drove a *wedge* between them⟩ **b** : something that serves to open the way for an action or development

²**wedge** *vb* **wedged; wedg·ing** **1** : to fasten or tighten by or as if by driving in a wedge **2 a** : to press or force into a narrow space ⟨*wedged* a stick into the crack⟩ **b** : to force (one's way) into or through ⟨*wedged* his way into the crowd⟩ **3** : to separate or force apart with or as if with a wedge

*W*¹wedge 1

wed·lock \'wed-,läk\ *n* : the state of being married

Wednes·day \'wenz-dē\ *n* : the fourth day of the week

Word History Many gods were worshiped by the Germanic people who lived in northern Europe in ancient times. The chief of all the Germanic gods was one who is now usually called *Odin*. His name in Old English was *Woden,* and the fourth day of the week was called *wōdnesdæg,* "day of Woden," or "Woden's day" in his honor. The Old English *wōdnesdæg* eventually became the

Modern English *Wednesday*. [Old English *wōdnesdæg*, literally, "Woden's day"]

wee \'wē\ *adj* **1** : very small : TINY **2** : very early ⟨the *wee* hours of the morning⟩

¹weed \'wēd\ *n* : a plant that tends to grow thickly where it is not wanted and to choke out more desirable plants

²weed *vb* **1** : to remove weeds from ⟨*weed* a garden⟩ **2** : to get rid of (something unwanted) ⟨*weed* out the troublemakers⟩ — **weed·er** *n*

weeds \'wēdz\ *n pl* : mourning clothes

weedy \'wēd-ē\ *adj* **1** : full or consisting of weeds ⟨a *weedy* field⟩ **2** : like a weed especially in having strong rapid growth **3** : very skinny

week \'wēk\ *n* **1 a** : seven days in a row ⟨was sick for a *week*⟩ **b** : a period of seven days beginning with Sunday and ending with Saturday ⟨the last *week* of the month⟩ **2** : the working or school days of the calendar week

week·day \'wēk-ˌdā\ *n* : a day of the week except Sunday or except Saturday and Sunday

¹week·end \'wē-ˌkend\ *n* : the end of the week; *esp* : the period between the close of one working or school week and the beginning of the next

²weekend *vb* : to spend the weekend at a specified place

¹week·ly \'wē-klē\ *adj* **1** : occurring, done, produced, or published every week **2** : figured by the week ⟨a *weekly* wage⟩ — **weekly** *adv*

²weekly *n, pl* **weeklies** : a weekly publication

weep \'wēp\ *vb* **wept** \'wept\; **weep·ing** **1** : to show emotion and especially sorrow by shedding tears : CRY **2** : to give off liquid slowly or in drops : OOZE ⟨a tree *weeping* sap⟩ — **weep·er** *n*

weep·ing \'wē-piŋ\ *adj* **1** : TEARFUL **2** : having slender drooping branches

weeping willow *n* : an Asian willow with slender drooping branches

wee·vil \'wē-vəl\ *n* : any of a family of mostly small beetles that have the head long and usually curved downward to form a snout bearing the jaws at the tip and that include many that feed on and are very harmful to plants or plant products (as nuts, fruit, and grain) especially as larvae — called also *snout beetle*; compare BOLL WEEVIL — **wee·vily** *or* **wee·vil·ly** \'wēv-(ə-)lē\ *adj*

weevil

weft \'weft\ *n* **1 a** : ¹WOOF 1 **b** : yarn used for the woof **2 a** : woven fabric **b** : an article of woven fabric

weft knit *n* : a knit fabric in which the knitting is done with the yarns running in a crosswise or circular direction (as in ordinary hand knitting) — compare WARP KNIT — **weft knitting** *n*

weigh \'wā\ *vb* **1 a** : to find the heaviness of ⟨*weighed* the bag of onions on a scale⟩ **b** : to have weight or a certain weight ⟨he *weighs* 200 pounds⟩ **2 a** : to consider carefully : PONDER ⟨*weigh* your chances of winning⟩ **b** : to be important : COUNT ⟨the evidence will *weigh* heavily against him⟩ **3** : to raise before sailing ⟨*weigh* anchor⟩ **4** : to measure on or as if on a scale ⟨*weigh* out several pounds of rice⟩ **5** : to press down with or as if with a weight ⟨her worries *weigh* heavily on her⟩ — **weigh·er** *n*

¹weight \'wāt\ *n* **1 a** : the amount that something weighs **b** : the standard amount that something should weigh ⟨fined for selling meat under *weight*⟩ **2 a** : a quantity or portion weighing usually a certain amount ⟨equal *weights* of flour and butter⟩ **b** : a heavy object (as a metal ball) used in athletic exercises and contests **3 a** : a unit (as a pound or kilogram) of weight or mass — see MEASURE

table; see METRIC SYSTEM table **b** : an object (as a piece of metal) of known weight for balancing a scale in weighing other objects **4 a** : something heavy : LOAD **b** : a heavy object used to hold, press down, or balance something else ⟨clock *weights*⟩ **5** : a mental or emotional burden ⟨had a *weight* on my conscience⟩ **6** : the force with which a body is attracted toward the earth or a heavenly body by gravitation **7 a** : the importance given to something ⟨opinions that carry *weight*⟩ **b** : the greater or more impressive part ⟨the *weight* of the evidence is for a verdict of guilty⟩

²weight *vb* **1** : to load or make heavy with a weight **2** : to trouble with a burden ⟨*weighted* down with cares⟩

weight·less \'wāt-ləs\ *adj* : having little weight : lacking apparent gravitational pull — **weight·less·ness** *n*

weight lifter *n* : one who lifts barbells in competition or as an exercise — **weight lifting** *n*

weighty \'wāt-ē\ *adj* **weight·i·er**; **-est** **1** : having much weight : HEAVY **2 a** : of much importance : SERIOUS ⟨*weighty* problems⟩ **b** : showing seriousness : SOLEMN ⟨a *weighty* expression on her face⟩ **3** : having the power to influence or persuade ⟨*weighty* arguments⟩ — **weight·i·ly** \'wāt-ᵊl-ē\ *adv* — **weight·i·ness** *n*

wei·ma·ra·ner \ˌvī-mə-'rän-ər, 'wī-mə-ˌrän-ər\ *n* : any of a German breed of large gray short-haired sporting dogs [German, from *Weimar*, a city in Germany]

weir \'wa(ə)r, 'we(ə)r, 'wi(ə)r\ *n* **1** : a fence set in a stream to catch fish **2** : a dam in a stream to raise the water level or change the direction and course of its flow

weird \'wi(ə)rd\ *adj* **1** : of, relating to, or caused by witchcraft or magic **2** : very unusual or strange : FANTASTIC — **weird·ly** *adv* — **weird·ness** *n*

Word History The belief in some form of fate, a force that cannot be explained, predicted, or controlled, has been a part of many cultures. When people understood very little of the laws of nature, such a belief may have helped to make it easier to live with life's misfortunes even if it did not make life any more comfortable. The Old English word for "fate" was *wyrd*. When the English began translating Latin works, they used this word for the Roman Fates, goddesses who were believed to control the events in human lives. When the Fates were described as "weird sisters," the first use of *weird* as an adjective occurred. People practicing witchcraft were thought to be controlling the *wyrd*, and in time the Modern English word *weird* came to refer to things that seemed to happen by magic or that were strange, unusual, or mysterious. [Old English *wyrd* (noun) "fate"]

weirdo \'wi(ə)rd-ō\ *n, pl* **weird·os** : a strange person

¹wel·come \'wel-kəm\ *interj* — used to greet a guest or newcomer upon arrival

²welcome *vb* **wel·comed; wel·com·ing** **1** : to greet in a warm and friendly manner **2** : to receive or accept with pleasure ⟨*welcomes* a challenge⟩ — **wel·com·er** *n*

³welcome *adj* **1** : received gladly ⟨a *welcome* visitor⟩ **2** : giving pleasure : PLEASING ⟨*welcome* news⟩ **3** : willingly permitted to do, have, or enjoy something ⟨anyone is *welcome* to use the pool⟩ **4** — used in the phrase "You're welcome" as a reply to an expression of thanks

⁴welcome *n* : a friendly greeting or reception

¹weld \'weld\ *vb* **1** : to join pieces of metal or plastic by heating and allowing the edges to flow together or by hammering or pressing together **2** : to join as if by welding ⟨*welded* together in friendship⟩ **3** : to become or be capable of being welded ⟨certain metals *weld* easily⟩ — **weld·er** *n*

\ə\ **abut**	\aů\ **out**	\i\ **tip**	\ȯ\ **saw**	\ů\ **foot**
\ər\ **further**	\ch\ **chin**	\ī\ **life**	\ȯi\ **coin**	\y\ **yet**
\a\ **mat**	\e\ **pet**	\j\ **job**	\th\ **thin**	\yü\ **few**
\ā\ **take**	\ē\ **easy**	\ŋ\ **sing**	\t͟h\ **this**	\yů\ **cure**
\ä\ **cot, cart**	\g\ **go**	\ō\ **bone**	\ü\ **food**	\zh\ **vision**

²**weld** *n* **1** : a welded joint **2** : union by welding

wel·fare \'wel-ˌfa(ə)r, -ˌfe(ə)r\ *n* **1** : the state of doing well especially in relation to happiness, well-being, or success ⟨must look out for your own *welfare*⟩ **2 a** : aid in the form of money or necessities for people in need **b** : a program through which such aid is distributed — **welfare** *adj*

welfare state *n* : a social system in which the government takes on much of the responsibility for the individual and group welfare of its people

¹**well** \'wel\ *n* **1** : a source of supply ⟨was a *well* of information⟩ **2** : a hole made in the earth to reach a natural deposit (as of water, oil, or gas) **3** : an open space extending up through floors of a structure (as for a staircase) **4** : something suggesting a well

²**well** *vb* : to rise to the surface and flow out

³**well** *adv* **bet·ter** \'bet-ər\; **best** \'best\ **1** : so as to be right : in a satisfactory way ⟨did *well* on the test⟩ **2** : in a friendly or generous way ⟨they always speak *well* of you⟩ **3** : in a skillful or expert manner ⟨plays the trumpet *well*⟩ **4** : by as much as possible : COMPLETELY ⟨we are *well* aware of the problem⟩ **5** : with reason or courtesy ⟨cannot *well* refuse⟩ **6** : in such a way as to be pleasing : as one would wish ⟨everything has gone *well* this week⟩ **7** : without trouble ⟨we could *well* afford it⟩ **8** : in a thorough manner ⟨shake *well* before using⟩ **9** : in a familiar manner ⟨knew them *well*⟩ **10** : by quite a lot ⟨was *well* ahead⟩ ⟨*well* over a million⟩ — **as well 1** : in addition : ALSO ⟨other features *as well*⟩ **2** : with the same result ⟨might *as well* tell them now⟩

⁴**well** *interj* **1** — used to begin a conversation or continue one that was interrupted **2** — used to express surprise or doubt

⁵**well** *adj* **1** : being in a satisfactory or good state ⟨all is *well*⟩ **2** : free or recovered from ill health : HEALTHY ⟨he's not a *well* man⟩ **3** : FORTUNATE 1 ⟨it was *well* that we left⟩

we'll \(ˌ)wē(ə)l\ : we shall : we will

well–be·ing \'wel-'bē-iŋ\ *n* : the state of being happy, healthy, or prosperous : WELFARE

well·born \-'bȯrn\ *adj* : coming from a good family : of gentle or noble birth

well·bred \-'bred\ *adj* : having or showing good manners : POLITE

well–dis·posed \-dis-'pōzd\ *adj* : having a good disposition

well–done \-'dən\ *adj* **1** : done right **2** : cooked thoroughly ⟨a *well-done* steak⟩

well–fixed \-'fikst\ *adj* : having plenty of money or property ⟨his family was *well-fixed*⟩

well–found·ed \-'faun-dəd\ *adj* : based on good reasons

well·head \'wel-ˌhed\ *n* : the top of or a structure built over a well

well–heeled \'wel-'hē(ə)ld\ *adj* : having plenty of money

well–known \'wel-'nōn\ *adj* : known by many people

well–mean·ing \-'mē-niŋ\ *adj* : having or based on good intentions

well·ness \-nəs\ *n* : the quality or state of being in good health especially as an actively sought goal ⟨lifestyles that promote *wellness*⟩

well–nigh \-'nī\ *adv* : ALMOST, NEARLY

well–off \-'ȯf\ *adj* : being in good condition or in a good situation **2** : WELL-TO-DO

well–read \-'red\ *adj* : well informed by much reading

well–round·ed \-'raun-dəd\ *adj* : including many details or much variety ⟨a *well-rounded* education⟩

well–spo·ken \-'spō-kən\ *adj* **1** : having a good command of language : speaking well and especially courteously **2** : spoken in a fitting and proper manner ⟨*well-spoken* words⟩

well·spring \'wel-ˌspriŋ\ *n* **1** : a source of continual supply **2** : FOUNTAINHEAD 1

well–to–do \ˌwel-tə-'dü\ *adj* : having plenty of money and possessions : PROSPEROUS

well–wish·er \'wel-ˌwish-ər, -'wish-\ *n* : a person who wishes good fortune to another

Welsh \'welsh *also* 'welch\ *n* **1 Welsh** *pl* : people born or living in Wales **2** : the Celtic language of the Welsh people [Old English *Wealh* "Welshman, foreigner"; of Celtic origin — related to WALNUT; see *Word History* at WALNUT] — **Welsh** *adj*

Welsh cor·gi \-'kȯr-gē\ *n* : a Welsh dog that has a foxy head, short legs, and long body and occurs in two breeds: **a** : CARDIGAN WELSH CORGI **b** : PEMBROKE WELSH CORGI

Welsh corgi b

Welsh·man \'welsh-mən\ *n* : a person born or living in Wales

Welsh rabbit *n* : melted cheese served over toast or crackers

Welsh rare·bit \-'ra(ə)r-bət, -'re(ə)r-\ *n* : WELSH RABBIT

Welsh springer spaniel *n* : any of a breed of red and white or orange and white springer spaniels

welt \'welt\ *n* : a ridge or lump raised on the skin (as by a blow)

¹**wel·ter** \'wel-tər\ *vb* **wel·tered; wel·ter·ing** \-t(ə-)riŋ\ **1** : to twist or roll one's body about **2** : to rise and fall or toss about in or with waves **3** : to become deeply sunk or bogged down ⟨*weltered* in misery⟩

²**welter** *n* **1** : a state of wild confusion **2** : a confused jumble ⟨a *welter* of information⟩

wel·ter·weight \'wel-tər-ˌwāt\ *n* : a boxer in a weight division having an upper limit of 147 pounds

wen \'wen\ *n* : a cyst formed by blocking a skin gland and filled with fatty material

wench \'wench\ *n* **1** : a young woman : GIRL **2** : a female servant

wend \'wend\ *vb* : to go one's way : PROCEED ⟨*wending* their way home⟩

went *past of* GO

wept *past and past participle of* WEEP

were *past 2nd sing, past pl, or past subjunctive of* BE

we're \(ˌ)wi(ə)r, (ˌ)wər\ : we are

weren't \(')wərnt, 'wər-ənt\ : were not

were·wolf \'wi(ə)r-ˌwu̇lf, 'we(ə)r-, 'wər-\ *n, pl* **were·wolves** \-ˌwu̇lvz\ : a person changed or able to change into a wolf

Word History Many countries have legends about people who changed into savage wolflike creatures. Often these people were thought to keep their human shape during the day. At night, however, they were transformed into hungry monsters that killed and then ate their human victims. A full moon was sometimes seen as the force that turned people into werewolves. People who changed into these monsters were thought to have inherited the condition or to have been bitten by another werewolf. No one is sure how these stories got started or why so many different groups of people believed in them. We are sure, though, that Modern English *werewolf* comes from Old English *werwulf*, a compound of *wer*, meaning "man," and *wulf*, "wolf." [Old English *werwulf* "werewolf," from *wer* "man" and *wulf* "wolf"]

wert \(')wərt\ *archaic past 2nd singular of* BE

¹**west** \'west\ *adv* : to or toward the west

²**west** *adj* **1** : situated toward or at the west ⟨the *west* entrance⟩ **2** : coming from the west ⟨a *west* wind⟩

³west *n* **1** : the direction of sunset : the compass point opposite to east **2** *cap* : regions or countries west of a point that is mentioned or understood

west·bound \'wes(t)-ˌbau̇nd\ *adj* : going west ⟨a *west-bound* train⟩

west·er \'wes-tər\ *vb* **west·ered; west·er·ing** \-t(ə-)riŋ\ : to turn or move westward

¹west·er·ly \'wes-tər-lē\ *adv or adj* **1** : toward the west ⟨the ship sailed *westerly*⟩ ⟨a *westerly* direction⟩ **2** : from the west ⟨the wind blew *westerly*⟩ ⟨a *westerly* breeze⟩

²westerly *n, pl* **-lies** : a wind blowing from the west

¹west·ern \'wes-tərn\ *adj* **1** *cap* : of, relating to, or resembling that of the West **2** : lying toward or coming from the west ⟨a *western* storm⟩

²western *n* : a story, film, or radio or television show about life in the western U.S. in the last part of the 19th century

West·ern·er \'wes-tə(r)-nər\ *n* : a person born or living in the West (as of the U.S.)

western hemisphere *n, often cap W&H* : the half of the earth including North America, South America, and surrounding waters

western hemlock *n* : a hemlock of commercial importance as a timber tree that ranges from Alaska to California; *also* : its wood

western omelet *n,* : an omelet made with chopped ham, green pepper, and onion

western saddle *n, often cap W* : a large saddle having a deep broad seat and a high front and back

West Highland white terrier *n* : any of a breed of small white long-haired terriers developed in Scotland

¹west·ward \'wes-twərd\ *adv or adj* : toward the west — **west·wards** \-twərdz\ *adv*

²westward *n* : westward direction or part

¹wet \'wet\ *adj* **wet·ter; wet·test** **1** : containing, covered with, or soaked with liquid (as water) **2** : RAINY ⟨*wet* weather⟩ **3** : not yet dry ⟨*wet* paint⟩ — **wet·ly** *adv* — **wet·ness** *n* — **all wet** : completely wrong : MISTAKEN

²wet *n* **1** : ¹WATER 1 **2** : MOISTURE **3** : rainy weather : RAIN

³wet *vb* **wet** *or* **wet·ted; wet·ting** **1** : to make or become wet **2** : to urinate in or on ⟨*wet* his pants⟩

wet blanket *n* : one that discourages or puts an end to enthusiasm or pleasure

wet·land \'wet-ˌland\ *n* : land or areas (as marshes or swamps) having much soil moisture — usually used in plural

wet suit *n* : a rubber suit for swimmers that traps a layer of water against the body to save body heat (as while swimming in cold water)

we've \(ˌ)wēv\ : we have

¹whack \'hwak, 'wak\ *vb* : to hit or cut with a hard noisy blow ⟨*whacked* the ball into left field⟩ — **whack·er** *n*

²whack *n* **1** : a hard noisy blow; *also* : its sound **2** : ²TRY, ATTEMPT ⟨take a *whack* at it⟩ — **out of whack** : not in good working order or shape ⟨the compass was *out of whack*⟩

¹whack·ing \'hwak-iŋ, 'wak-\ *adj* : very big ⟨a *whacking* sum of money⟩

²whacking *adv* : ²VERY 1 ⟨a *whacking* good story⟩ ⟨a *whacking* big diamond⟩

¹whale \'hwā(ə)l, 'wā(ə)l\ *n, pl* **whales** *or* **whale** : a water-dwelling mammal (as a humpback whale or a killer whale) that is a cetacean of usually very large size with a torpedo-shaped body, front limbs modified into flippers but no hind limbs, and a tail flattened and extended to the sides as flukes and that usually breathes through an opening on top of the head — compare BALEEN WHALE, TOOTHED WHALE **2** : something large enough to catch attention ⟨it made a *whale* of a difference⟩ [Old English *hwæl* "whale"]

²whale *vb* **whaled; whal·ing** : to hunt whales

³whale *vb* **whaled; whal·ing** **1** : THRASH 2a **2** : to hit hard ⟨*whaled* the ball⟩ [origin unknown]

whale·boat \'hwā(ə)l-ˌbōt, 'wā(ə)l-\ *n* : a long narrow rowboat formerly used by whalers for hunting whales

whale·bone \-ˌbōn\ *n* : BALEEN

whalebone whale *n* : BALEEN WHALE

whale oil *n* : an oil obtained from the blubber of whales and formerly used especially in lamps

whal·er \'hwā-lər, 'wā-\ *n* : a person or ship that hunts for whales

whale shark *n* : a harmless shark of warm waters that feeds chiefly on plankton, may sometimes grow to a length of up to 60 feet (18.3 meters), and is the largest known fish

whale shark

wharf \'hwȯrf, 'wȯrf\ *n, pl* **wharves** \'hwȯrvz, 'wȯrvz\ *also* **wharfs** : a structure built on the shore at which ships can load and unload

¹what \(')hwät, (')hwət, (')wät, (')wət\ *pron* **1 a :** which thing or things ⟨*what* happened?⟩ **b :** which sort of thing or person ⟨*what* is this?⟩ ⟨*what* are they — doctors?⟩ **2** — used to ask one to repeat something said but not properly heard or understood ⟨you said *what?*⟩ **3** — used to express surprise or excitement ⟨*what*, no breakfast?⟩ **4** — used to direct attention to something that the speaker is about to say ⟨you know *what?*⟩ **5 :** that which ⟨do *what* you're told⟩ · **6 :** ¹WHATEVER 1 ⟨say *what* you will⟩ — **what for :** ¹WHY — **what have you :** ¹WHATNOT — **what if 1 :** what would happen if ⟨*what if* they find out?⟩ **2 :** what does it matter if ⟨so *what if* they do? I don't care⟩

²what *adv* **1 :** in what way : HOW ⟨*what* does it matter?⟩ **2** — used before one or more phrases that tell a cause ⟨*what* with school and sports, she kept busy⟩

³what *adj* **1 a** — used to ask about the identity of a person, object, or matter ⟨*what* books do you read⟩ **b :** how remarkable or surprising ⟨*what* an idea⟩ **2 :** ²WHATEVER 1

¹what·ev·er \hwät-'ev-ər, (ˌ)hwət-, wät-, (ˌ)wət-\ *pron* **1** : anything that ⟨take *whatever* you need⟩ **2** : no matter what ⟨*whatever* you do, don't cheat⟩ **3** : ¹WHAT 1b — used to express surprise or bewilderment ⟨*whatever* made you think that⟩

²whatever *adj* **1** : any and all : any . . . that ⟨take *whatever* action is needed⟩ **2** : of any kind at all ⟨no food *whatever*⟩

¹what·not \'hwät-ˌnät, 'hwət-, 'wät-, 'wət-\ *pron* : any of various other things that might also be mentioned ⟨hummingbirds and hawks and owls and *whatnot*⟩

²whatnot *n* : a light open set of shelves

what·so·ev·er \ˌhwät-sə-'wev-ər, ˌhwət-, ˌwät-, ˌwət-\ *pron or adj* : WHATEVER

wheat \'hwēt, 'wēt\ *n* **1** : a cereal grain that can be made into a fine white flour used mostly in breads, baked goods (as cakes and crackers), and pastas (as macaroni or spaghetti) and that is used in animal feeds **2** : any of a genus of grasses grown in most temperate areas for the wheat they produce; *esp* : a grass with long dense flower spikes and white to dark red grains that is the chief source of wheat and is known only in cultivation

wheat·en \'hwēt-ⁿn, 'wēt-\ *adj* : containing or made from wheat ⟨*wheaten* bread⟩

\ə\ **abut**	\au̇\ **out**	\i\ **tip**	\ȯ\ **saw**	\u̇\ **foot**
\ər\ **further**	\ch\ **chin**	\ī\ **life**	\ȯi\ **coin**	\y\ **yet**
\a\ **mat**	\e\ **pet**	\j\ **job**	\th\ **thin**	\yü\ **few**
\ā\ **take**	\ē\ **easy**	\ŋ\ **sing**	\th\ **this**	\yu̇\ **cure**
\ä\ **cot, cart**	\g\ **go**	\ō\ **bone**	\ü\ **food**	\zh\ **vision**

wheat germ *n* : the embryo of the wheat kernel separated in milling and used especially as a source of vitamins and protein

wheat rust *n* : a harmful disease of wheat caused by rust fungi; *also* : a fungus causing a wheat rust

whee *interj* — used to express delight or high spirits

whee·dle \'hwēd-ºl, 'wēd-\ *vb* **whee·dled; whee·dling** \'hwēd-liŋ, -ºl-iŋ, 'wēd-\ **1** : to get (someone) to think or act a certain way by flattering or coaxing ⟨*wheedled* them into agreeing⟩ **2** : to gain or get by coaxing or flattering ⟨*wheedled* money from his friend⟩

¹wheel \'hwē(ə)l, 'wē(ə)l\ *n* **1** : a disk or circular frame turning on a central point **2** : a device (as a bicycle or potter's wheel) whose main part is a wheel **3** : something resembling a wheel (as in being round) ⟨a *wheel* of cheese⟩ **4** : a curving or circular movement **5** : a moving or essential part of something compared to a machine ⟨the *wheels* of government⟩ **6** : a person of importance ⟨he was a big *wheel* in town⟩ **7** *pl, slang* : AUTOMOBILE ⟨he borrowed my *wheels* for an upcoming date⟩ — **wheeled** \'hwē(ə)ld, 'wē(ə)ld\ *adj*

²wheel *vb* **1** : to turn on or as if on a central point : REVOLVE **2** : to change direction as if turning on a central point ⟨*wheeled* about to face her opponent⟩ **3** : to move in a circle or curve **4** : to carry or move on wheels or in a vehicle ⟨*wheel* a load into the barn⟩ — **wheel and deal** : to make deals or do business especially in a clever or energetic manner

wheel and axle *n* : a simple machine consisting of a grooved wheel turned by a cord or chain with a firmly attached axle (as for winding up a weight) together with supports

wheel·bar·row \'hwē(ə)l-ˌbar-ō, 'wē(ə)l-\ *n* : a small cart that has two handles and usually one wheel, is used for carrying small loads, and is usually pushed

wheel·base \-ˌbās\ *n* : the distance between the front and rear axles of a motor vehicle

wheel·chair \-ˌche(ə)r, -ˌcha(ə)r\ *n* : a chair with wheels used especially by sick, injured, or disabled people to get about

wheel·er \'hwē-lər, 'wē-\ *n* : one of a team of horses that pulls from the position nearest the front wheels of a wagon

wheel·house \-ˌhau̇s\ *n* : PILOTHOUSE

¹wheeze \'hwēz, 'wēz\ *vb* **wheezed; wheez·ing** **1** : to breathe with difficulty especially with a whistling sound **2** : to make a sound like wheezing

²wheeze *n* : a wheezing sound

wheezy \'hwē-zē, 'wē-\ *adj* **wheez·i·er; -est** **1** : tending to wheeze ⟨a *wheezy* infant⟩ **2** : making or having the sound of wheezing ⟨a *wheezy* cough⟩ ⟨*wheezy* old cars⟩

whelk \'hwelk, 'welk, 'wilk\ *n* : any of numerous large marine snails; *esp* : one used for food in Europe

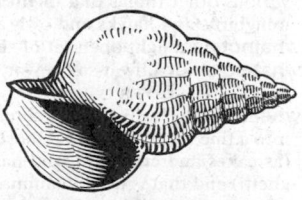

whelk

whelm \'hwelm, 'welm\ *vb* : OVERWHELM 2

¹whelp \'hwelp, 'welp\ *n* **1** : one of the young of a flesh-eating animal and especially a dog **2** : a young person

²whelp *vb* : to give birth to whelps

¹when \(ˈ)hwen, hwən, (ˈ)wen, wən\ *adv* **1** : at what time ⟨*when* will you return⟩ **2** : at or during which time ⟨a time *when* things were upset⟩

²when *conj* **1 a** : at or during the time that : WHILE ⟨went fishing *when* we were on vacation⟩ **b** : just at the moment that ⟨left *when* the bell rang⟩ **c** : every time that ⟨my mouth waters *when* I see food⟩ **2** : in the event that : IF ⟨*when* players cheat, they are disqualified⟩ **3** : in spite of the fact that : ALTHOUGH ⟨went outside *when* she should have done her chores⟩

³when \ˌhwen, ˌwen\ *pron* : what or which time ⟨since *when* have you known that⟩

¹whence \(ˈ)hwen(t)s, (ˈ)wen(t)s\ *adv* : from what place, source, or cause ⟨*whence* come all these doubts⟩

²whence *conj* : from or out of which place, source, or cause ⟨the land *whence* they came⟩

¹when·ev·er \hwe-'nev-ər, hwə-, we-, wə-\ *conj* : at any or every time that ⟨stop *whenever* you wish⟩

²whenever *adv* : at whatever time ⟨come tomorrow or *whenever*⟩

when·so·ev·er \ˌhwen(t)-sə-ˌwev-ər, ˌwen(t)-\ *conj* : WHENEVER

¹where \(ˈ)hwe(ə)r, (ˈ)hwa(ə)r, (ˌ)hwər, (ˈ)we(ə)r, (ˈ)wa(ə)r, (ˌ)wər\ *adv* **1** : at, in, or to what place ⟨*where* are we going⟩ **2** : at, in, or to what situation, position, direction, or circumstances ⟨*where* will this course of action lead⟩

²where *conj* **1 a** : at, in, or to what place ⟨knows *where* the house is⟩ **b** : at, in, or to what situation, position, direction, or circumstances ⟨see *where* that behavior leads⟩ **2** : ²WHEREVER 1 ⟨sit *where* you please⟩ **3** : at, in, or to which place ⟨the town *where* we live⟩ **4 a** : at, in, or to the place at, in, or to which ⟨stay *where* you are⟩ **b** : in a situation or circumstances in which ⟨no good *where* careful work is needed⟩

³where \'hwe(ə)r, 'hwa(ə)r, 'we(ə)r, 'wa(ə)r\ *n* : what place, source, or cause ⟨*where* are you from⟩

¹where·abouts \-ə-ˌbau̇ts\ *also* **where·about** \-ˌbau̇t\ *adv* : about where ⟨*whereabouts* is the house⟩

²whereabouts *n sing or pl* : the place where a person or thing is ⟨do you know their *whereabouts*⟩

where·as \hwer-'az, hwar-, wer-, war-, (ˌ)hwər-, (ˌ)wər-\ *conj* **1** : in view of the fact that : SINCE **2** : while just the opposite ⟨water puts out fire, *whereas* gasoline feeds it⟩

where·at \-'at\ *conj* **1** : at or toward which **2** : as a result of which

where·by \hwe(ə)r-'bī, hwa(ə)r-, we(ə)r-, wa(ə)r-, (ˌ)hwər-, (ˌ)wər-\ *conj* : by, through, or in agreement with which

¹where·fore \'hwe(ə)r-ˌfō(ə)r, 'hwa(ə)r-, 'we(ə)r-, 'wa(ə)r-, -ˌfȯ(ə)r\ *adv* **1** : for what reason or purpose : WHY **2** : THEREFORE

²wherefore *n* : an answer or statement giving an explanation : REASON ⟨the whys and *wherefores*⟩

where·from \-ˌfrəm, -ˌfräm\ *conj* : from which

¹where·in \hwer-'in, hwar-, wer-, war-, (ˌ)hwər-, (ˌ)wər-\ *adv* : in what : in what way ⟨*wherein* was I wrong⟩

²wherein *conj* : in which ⟨the city *wherein* we live⟩

where·of \-'əv, -'äv\ *conj* **1** : of what ⟨knows *whereof* she speaks⟩ **2** : of which or whom ⟨wrote many books *whereof* the best are lost⟩

where·on \-'ȯn, -'än\ *conj* : on which ⟨the base *whereon* the vase rests⟩

where·so·ev·er \'hwer-sə-ˌwev-ər, 'hwar-, 'wer-, 'war-\ *conj* : WHEREVER 1

where·up·on \'hwer-ə-ˌpȯn, 'hwar-, 'wer-, 'war-, -ˌpän\ *conj* **1** : on which **2** : and then : at which time

¹wher·ev·er \hwer-'ev-ər, hwar-, wer-, war-, (ˌ)hwər-, (ˌ)wər-\ *adv* : ¹WHERE 1 — used in questions expressing surprise or bewilderment ⟨*wherever* did you get that hat⟩

²wherever *conj* **1** : at, in, or to whatever place ⟨succeeds *wherever* he goes⟩ **2** : in any situation in which ⟨*wherever* it is possible, I try to help⟩

where·with \'hwe(ə)r-ˌwith, 'hwa(ə)r-, 'we(ə)r-, 'wa(ə)r-, -ˌwith\ *conj* : with or by means of which ⟨we lack tools *wherewith* to repair the damage⟩

where·with·al \'hwe(ə)r-with-ˌȯl, 'hwa(ə)r-, 'we(ə)r-, 'wa(ə)r-, -with-\ *n* : WEALTH 1, RESOURCES; *esp* : MONEY 1b ⟨the *wherewithal* to buy a house⟩

whet \'hwet, 'wet\ *vb* **whet·ted; whet·ting** **1** : to sharpen by rubbing on or with something (as a stone) ⟨*whet* a knife⟩ **2** : to make keen : STIMULATE ⟨*whet* the appetite⟩

wheth·er \'hweth-ər, 'weth-, (ˌ)hweth-ər, (ˌ)weth-\ *conj* **1 a** : if it is or was true that ⟨ask *whether* they are going⟩ **b** : if it is or was better ⟨uncertain *whether* to go or stay⟩ **2** — used to introduce two or more situations of which only one can occur ⟨*whether* we succeed or fail, we must try⟩ ⟨we're going *whether* or not you come⟩

whet·stone \'hwet-ˌstōn, 'wet-\ *n* : a stone for sharpening blades

whew *often read as* 'hwü, 'wü, 'hyü; *the interjection is a whistle ending with a voiceless* ü\ *n* : a sound somewhat like a whistle used chiefly to express amazement, discomfort, or relief

whey \'hwā, 'wā\ *n* : the watery part of milk that separates after the milk has soured and thickened especially in the process of making cheese — compare CURD 1

¹which \(')hwich, (')wich\ *adj* **1** : being what one or ones ⟨*which* tie should I wear⟩ ⟨knew *which* people had paid⟩ **2** : WHICHEVER ⟨it will not fit, turn it *which* way you like⟩

²which *pron* **1** : what one or ones out of a group ⟨*which* of those houses do you live in⟩ ⟨they are swimming or canoeing, I don't know *which*⟩ **2** : WHICHEVER ⟨take *which* you like⟩ **3** — used to introduce a clause referring to something other than human beings ⟨the books *which* we bought⟩

¹which·ev·er \hwich-'ev-ər, wich-\ *pron* : whatever one or ones out of a group ⟨*whichever* you prefer⟩

²whichever *adj* : being whatever one or ones out of a group : no matter which ⟨*whichever* way you go⟩

¹whiff \'hwif, 'wif\ *n* **1** : a quick puff or slight gust ⟨a *whiff* of air⟩ **2** : a small quantity of odor, gas, or smoke that is breathed in

²whiff *vb* **1** : to blow out or away in small amounts **2** : to breathe in an odor

whif·fle·tree \'hwif-əl-(ˌ)trē, 'wif-\ *n* : the swinging bar that connects an animal harness to a vehicle (as a cart) or a plow — called also *whippletree*

Whig \'hwig, 'wig\ *n* **1** : a member or supporter of a British political group of the late 17th through early 19th centuries trying to lessen the power of the monarch and to increase the power of the parliament **2** : an American supporting independence from Great Britain during the American Revolution **3** : a member or supporter of a 19th century American political party formed to oppose the Democrats

¹while \'hwī(ə)l, 'wī(ə)l\ *n* **1** : a period of time ⟨stay here for a *while*⟩ **2** : time and effort used ⟨worth your *while*⟩

²while *conj* **1 a** : during the time that ⟨take a nap *while* I'm out⟩ **b** : as long as ⟨enjoy life *while* we can⟩ **2** : in spite of the fact that : ALTHOUGH ⟨*while* respected, the mayor is not liked⟩

³while *vb* **whiled; whil·ing** : to cause to pass pleasantly or without boredom ⟨*while* away the time⟩

¹whi·lom \'hwī-ləm, 'wī-\ *adv, archaic* : FORMERLY

²whilom *adj* : FORMER ⟨your *whilom* friends⟩

whilst \'hwī(ə)lst, 'wī(ə)lst\ *conj, chiefly British* : ²WHILE

whim \'hwim, 'wim\ *n* : an odd or sudden wish, desire, or change of mind

¹whim·per \'hwim-pər, 'wim-\ *vb* **whim·pered; whim·per·ing** \-p(ə-)riŋ\ : to utter weak interrupted cries ⟨*whimpered* in pain⟩

²whimper *n* : a whimpering cry

whim·si·cal \'hwim-zi-kəl, 'wim-\ *adj* **1** : full of whims : CAPRICIOUS ⟨a *whimsical* person always going off somewhere⟩ **2** : resulting from or marked by whim : ERRATIC ⟨*whimsical* behavior⟩ — **whim·si·cal·i·ty** \ˌhwim-zə-'kal-ət-ē, ˌwim-\ *n* — **whim·si·cal·ly** \'hwim-zi-k(ə-)lē, 'wim-\ *adv*

whim·sy *also* **whim·sey** \'hwim-zē, 'wim-\ *n, pl* **whim·sies** *also* **whimseys 1** : WHIM, CAPRICE **2** : the quality or state of being whimsical or fanciful ⟨the designer's new line of swimwear showed a touch of *whimsy*⟩ **3** : an imaginative or fantastic object or creation especially in a piece of writing or art

¹whine \'hwīn, 'wīn\ *vb* **whined; whin·ing 1** : to make a shrill troubled cry or a similar sound ⟨the electric saw *whined* as it cut the wood⟩ **2** : to complain with or as if with a whine ⟨always *whining* about his chores⟩ — **whin·er** *n* — **whin·ing·ly** \'hwī-niŋ-lē, 'wī-\ *adv*

²whine *n* **1** : a whining cry or sound **2** : a complaint uttered with or as if with a whine — **whiny** \'hwī-nē, 'wī-\ *adj*

¹whin·ny \'hwin-ē, 'win-\ *vb* **whin·nied; whin·ny·ing** : to neigh especially in a low or gentle manner

²whinny *n, pl* **whinnies** : the neigh of a horse especially when low or gentle

¹whip \'hwip, 'wip\ *vb* **whipped; whip·ping 1** : to move, snatch, or jerk quickly and forcefully ⟨*whip* out a camera⟩ **2** : to strike with something long and thin or flexible **3** : to overcome thoroughly : DEFEAT **4** : to stir up : INCITE ⟨*whip* up enthusiasm⟩ **5** : to produce in a hurry ⟨*whipped* up a satisfying meal⟩ **6** : to beat into a thick fluffy mass ⟨*whip* cream⟩ **7** : to flap about in a lively manner ⟨sails *whipped* in the strong wind⟩ — **whip·per** *n*

²whip *n* **1** : a flexible tool for whipping **2 a** : a dessert made by whipping some part of the mixture **b** : a kitchen utensil used in whipping **3** : a whipping motion — **whip·like** \'hwip-ˌlīk, 'wip-\ *adj*

whip·cord \'hwip-ˌkȯ(ə)rd, 'wip-\ *n* **1** : a thin tough braided cord **2** : a strong cloth with fine diagonal ridges

whip·lash \-ˌlash\ *n* **1** : the lash of a whip **2** : injury resulting from a sudden sharp jerking movement of the head and neck (as of a person in a car that is struck from behind by another car)

whip·per·snap·per \'hwip-ər-ˌsnap-ər, 'wip-\ *n* : a small, unimportant, or overly confident person

whip·pet \'hwip-ət, 'wip-\ *n* : any of a breed of small swift slender dogs that are often used for hunting small animals or racing

whip·ping boy *n* : SCAPEGOAT

whip·ple·tree \'hwip-əl-(ˌ)trē, 'wip-\ *n* : WHIFFLETREE

whip–poor–will \'hwip-ər-ˌwil, ˌhwip-ər-'wil, 'wip-, ˌwip-\ *n* : an insect-eating bird of the eastern U.S. and Canada that is active at night and has a loud repeated call which sounds like its name

whip-poor-will

¹whir *also* **whirr** \'hwər, 'wər\ *vb* **whirred; whir·ring** : to fly, turn, or move rapidly with a buzzing sound ⟨ceiling fans *whirred* overhead⟩

²whir *also* **whirr** *n* : a fluttering or vibrating sound made by something in rapid motion ⟨the *whir* of machinery⟩

¹whirl \'hwər(-ə)l, 'wər(-ə)l\ *vb* **1** : to move or drive in a circle or curve especially with force or speed ⟨cars *whirling* around the track⟩ **2 a** : to turn rapidly in circles : SPIN **b** : to turn abruptly : WHEEL ⟨*whirled* around in surprise⟩ **3** : to move or go quickly ⟨*whirled* down the street⟩ **4** : to become dizzy : REEL ⟨my head is *whirling*⟩ — **whirl·er** \'hwər-lər, 'wər-\ *n*

²whirl *n* **1 a** : a rapid whirling movement **b** : something whirling ⟨a *whirl* of dust⟩ **2 a** : a state of busy movement : BUSTLE ⟨a *whirl* of activity⟩ **b** : a confused mental state **3** : an experimental attempt : TRY ⟨gave it a *whirl*⟩

\ə\ **abut**		\au̇\ **out**	\i\ **tip**	\ȯ\ **saw**	\u̇\ **foot**
\ər\ **further**		\ch\ **chin**	\ī\ **life**	\ȯi\ **coin**	\y\ **yet**
\a\ **mat**		\e\ **pet**	\j\ **job**	\th\ **thin**	\yü\ **few**
\ā\ **take**		\ē\ **easy**	\ŋ\ **sing**	\th\ **this**	\yu̇\ **cure**
\ä\ **cot, cart**		\g\ **go**	\ō\ **bone**	\ü\ **food**	\zh\ **vision**

whirl·i·gig \'hwər-li-ˌgig, 'wər-\ *n* **1** : a toy that has a whirling motion **2** : something that continuously whirls or changes

whirligig beetle *n* : any of a family of beetles that live mostly on the surface of water where they swim about in circles

whirl·pool \'hwər-(ə)l-ˌpül, 'wər-(ə)l-\ *n* **1** : water moving rapidly in a circle with a hollow in the center into which floating objects are drawn : EDDY **2** : WHIRLPOOL BATH

whirlpool bath *n* : a bath in which all or part of the body is exposed to forceful whirling currents of hot water

¹**whirl·wind** \-ˌwind\ *n* : a small windstorm of rapidly rotating air

²**whirlwind** *adj* : resembling a whirlwind especially in speed or force ⟨a *whirlwind* campaign⟩ ⟨a *whirlwind* romance⟩

whirly·bird \'hwər-lē-ˌbərd, 'wər-\ *n* : HELICOPTER

whish \'hwish, 'wish\ *vb* : to move with a whizzing or swishing sound — **whish** *n*

¹**whisk** \'hwisk, 'wisk\ *n* **1** : a quick brush or sweep ⟨a *whisk* of the hand⟩ **2** : a small kitchen utensil used for beating food **3** : WHISK BROOM

²**whisk** *vb* **1** : to move easily and quickly ⟨squirrels *whisked* up the trees⟩ **2** : to move or carry briskly ⟨*whisked* the children off to bed⟩ **3** : to mix or fluff up by or as if by beating with a whisk ⟨*whisk* eggs⟩ **4** : to brush or wipe off lightly ⟨*whisk* the lint off your skirt⟩

whisk broom *n* : a small broom with a short handle

whis·ker \'hwis-kər, 'wis-\ *n* **1 a** : a hair of the beard **b** *pl* : the part of the beard growing on the sides of the face or on the chin **2** : one of the long hairs or bristles growing near the mouth of an animal (as a cat or mouse) — **whis·kered** \-kərd\ *adj*

¹whisk 2

whis·key *or* **whis·ky** \'hwis-kē, 'wis-\ *n, pl* **whiskeys** *or* **whiskies** : an alcoholic liquor made from grain (as rye, corn, or barley) [from *uisce beatha,* a phrase in Irish (the ancient language of Ireland) and *isuge beatha,* a phrase in Scottish Gaelic (the ancient language of Scotland), both meaning literally "water of life"]

¹**whis·per** \'hwis-pər, 'wis-\ *vb* **whis·pered; whis·per·ing** \-p(ə-)riŋ\ **1** : to speak very softly or under the breath **2** : to tell or utter by whispering ⟨*whisper* a secret⟩ **3** : to make a series of little noises ⟨*whispering* leaves⟩ — **whis·per·er** \-pər-ər\ *n*

²**whisper** *n* **1** : something said by or as if by whispering; *esp* : ¹RUMOR ⟨*whispers* of scandal⟩ **2** : an act or instance of whispering **3** : a barely noticeable amount : HINT ⟨showed only a *whisper* of concern⟩

whis·pery \'hwis-p(ə-)rē, 'wis-\ *adj* : resembling a whisper ⟨a *whispery* voice⟩

whist \'hwist, 'wist\ *n* : a card game for four players in two partnerships

¹**whis·tle** \'hwis-əl, 'wis-\ *n* **1** : a device making a shrill sound ⟨tin *whistle*⟩ ⟨steam *whistle*⟩ **2 a** : a shrill clear sound made by forcing air through puckered lips **b** : a sound or signal produced by a whistle or as if by whistling

²**whistle** *vb* **whis·tled; whis·tling** \'hwis-(ə-)liŋ, 'wis-\ **1** : to make a whistle through puckered lips **2** : to move, pass, or go with a shrill sound ⟨an arrow *whistled* by me⟩ **3** : to blow or sound a whistle ⟨the teakettle *whistled*⟩ **4** : to utter by whistling ⟨*whistle* a tune⟩ — **whis·tler** \'hwis-(ə-)lər, 'wis-\ *n*

whit \'hwit, 'wit\ *n* : the smallest part or particle : BIT ⟨cared not a *whit* about money⟩

¹**white** \'hwīt, 'wīt\ *adj* **whit·er; whit·est 1 a** : having no color **b** : of the color of new snow or milk **c** : light or pale in color ⟨*white* hair⟩ ⟨lips *white* with fear⟩ **d** : pale gray : SILVERY **2** : of, relating to, or being a member of a group or race having light skin **3** : unmarked by writing or printing : BLANK **4** : not intended to cause harm ⟨a

white lie⟩ ⟨*white* magic⟩ **5** : marked by the presence of snow ⟨a *white* Christmas⟩ — **white·ness** *n*

²**white** *n* **1** : the color of fresh snow **2** : a white or light-colored thing or part (as the material around the yolk of an egg or the white part of the eyeball) **3** : one that is or approaches the color white: as **a** : white clothing ⟨washed a load of *whites*⟩ **b** *pl* : TEETH — used in the phrase *pearly whites* **4** : a person belonging to a light-skinned race

white ant *n* : TERMITE

white blood cell *n* : a colorless blood cell (as a lymphocyte) that lacks hemoglobin and contains a nucleus — called also *leukocyte, white blood corpuscle, white cell, white corpuscle*

white·board \'hwīt-ˌbō(ə)rd, -ˌbȯ(ə)rd, 'wīt-\ *n* : a hard smooth white surface used for writing or drawing on with markers

white·cap \'hwīt-ˌkap, 'wīt-\ *n* : the top of a wave breaking into foam — usually used in plural

white cedar *n* **1** : either of two trees related to the cypresses: **a** : an evergreen swamp tree of the eastern coast of the U.S. **b** : a common arborvitae especially of eastern Canada and the northeastern U.S. **2** : the wood of a white cedar

white chocolate *n* : a sweet food made with cocoa butter, sugar, milk, and flavorings

white clover *n* : a Eurasian clover with heads of white flowers that is widely used in grass-seed mixtures and is an important source of nectar for honey bees

white–collar \'hwīt-ˌkäl-ər, 'wīt-\ *adj* : of, relating to, or being a member of the class of workers (as clerks and salespersons) whose duties do not require the wearing of work clothes

white crappie *n* : an edible silvery North American sunfish that is often stocked in small ponds

white dwarf *n* : a small whitish star of low brightness that has a mass approximately equal to that of the sun but that is many times more dense

white elephant *n* : something requiring much care and expense and giving little profit or enjoyment [so called from the fact that in India and neighboring countries, light-colored elephants are treated as sacred and kept without being put to work]

white·fish \'hwīt-ˌfish, 'wīt-\ *n* : any of various freshwater food fishes related to the salmons and trouts and mostly greenish above and silvery white below

white flag *n* : a flag of plain white used as a flag of truce or as a sign of surrender

white gold *n* : a pale mixture of gold especially with nickel or palladium that resembles platinum in appearance

white goods *n pl* **1** : articles of cloth (as sheets, towels, or curtains) used in the bedroom, bathroom, or kitchen **2** : major household appliances (as stoves and refrigerators) that typically are white-colored

white·head \'hwīt-ˌhed, 'wīt-\ *n* : a small whitish lump in the skin caused by the fluid given off by an oil gland when the canal leading from the gland is blocked

white lead *n* : a heavy white poisonous carbonate of lead used formerly as a coloring matter in exterior paints

white matter *n* : whitish nerve tissue especially of the brain and spinal cord that consists largely of nerve fibers enclosed in a fatty material and that lies under the gray matter

whit·en \'hwīt-ᵊn, 'wīt-\ *vb* **whit·ened; whit·en·ing** \-ᵊn-iŋ, -niŋ\ : to make or become white or whiter — **whit·en·er** \-nər, -ᵊn-ər\ *n*

white noise *n* **1** : an even mixture of sound waves extending over a wide frequency range **2** : a constant background noise; *esp* : one that drowns out other sounds

white oak *n* : any of various oaks with acorns that mature in one year; *also* : the hard, strong wood of a white oak that lasts well and is not easily rotted by water

white pages *n pl* : the section of a telephone directory that lists individuals and businesses alphabetically

white pepper *n* : a seasoning with a sharp flavor that is prepared by grinding the fruit of the Indian pepper after the black outer husk is removed

white pine *n* : a tall-growing pine of eastern North America with long needles in clusters of five; *also* : its wood

white–pine blister rust *n* : a harmful disease of white pine caused by a rust fungus; *also* : this fungus

white potato *n* : POTATO 2b

white rice *n* : rice from which outer covering and seed coat have been removed

white sauce *n* : a sauce made from seasoned milk, cream, or broth and thickened with flour

white shark *n* : GREAT WHITE SHARK

white·tail \'hwīt-ˌtāl, 'wīt-\ *n* : WHITE-TAILED DEER

white–tailed deer \ˌhwīt-ˌtāl-'dī(ə)r, ˌwīt-\ *n* : a North American deer that has a rather long tail which is white on the underside and antlers which arch forward — called also *whitetail deer*

white·throat \'hwīt-ˌthrōt, 'wīt-\ *n* : WHITE-THROATED SPARROW

white–throat·ed spar·row \ˌhwīt-ˌthrōt-əd-, ˌwīt-\ *n* : a common brown sparrow of eastern North America with black and white stripes on the top of its head and with a white patch on its throat

white-tailed deer

¹white·wash \'hwīt-ˌwȯsh, -ˌwäsh, 'wīt-\ *vb* **1** : to whiten with whitewash **2 a** : to explain away or cover up ⟨refused to *whitewash* the scandal⟩ **b** : to clear of a charge of wrongdoing by offering excuses, hiding facts, or conducting a careless investigation ⟨accused the city council of *whitewashing* the mayor⟩ **3** : to prevent an opponent in a game or contest from scoring — **white·wash·er** *n*

²whitewash *n* **1** : a mixture (as of lime and water) for whitening a surface **2** : a clearing or covering up of wrongdoing

white water *n* : rough foamy water (as in rapids or waterfalls)

whith·er \'hwith-ər, 'with-\ *adv* : to what place or situation ⟨*whither* will they go⟩

whit·ish \'hwīt-ish, 'wīt-\ *adj* : somewhat white

whit·low \'hwīt-ˌlō, 'wīt-\ *n* : a deep inflammation of a finger or toe usually with pus and located especially near the end or around the nail

Whit·sun·day \'hwit-ˌsən-dē, -sən-ˌdā, 'wit-\ *n* : PENTECOST 2 [Old English *hwīta sunnandæg*, literally "white Sunday"; probably so called from the fact that at this season there were many people who were newly baptized and who wore white robes]

Whit·sun·tide \'hwit-sən-ˌtīd, 'wit-\ *n* : the week beginning with Whitsunday; *esp* : the first three days of this week

whit·tle \'hwit-ᵊl, 'wit-\ *vb* **whit·tled; whit·tling** \-liŋ, -ᵊl-iŋ\ **1 a** : to shave or cut off chips from the surface of wood with a knife **b** : to shape or form by so shaving or cutting **2** : to reduce gradually : PARE ⟨*whittle* down expenses⟩ — **whit·tler** \-lər, -ᵊl-ər\ *n*

¹whiz *or* **whizz** \'hwiz, 'wiz\ *vb* **whizzed; whiz·zing 1** : to hum, buzz, or hiss like a speeding object (as an arrow or ball) passing through air **2** : to fly, pass, or move swiftly with a buzzing sound ⟨cars *whizzing* by⟩ [probably coined in imitation of the sound of a speeding object going by] — **whiz·zer** *n*

²whiz *or* **whizz** *n, pl* **whiz·zes** : a humming, buzzing, or hissing sound

³whiz *n, pl* **whiz·zes** : WIZARD 2 ⟨a math *whiz*⟩ [probably a shortened and altered form of *wizard*]

whiz–bang \'hwiz-ˌbaŋ, 'wiz-\ *adj* : EXCELLENT, FIRST-CLASS ⟨a *whiz-bang* mechanic⟩

who \(')hü, ü\ *pron* **1** : what or which person or persons ⟨*who* was elected president⟩ ⟨find out *who* did it⟩ **2** : used to introduce a clause that talks about a person or persons ⟨my father, *who* was a lawyer⟩

whoa \'wō, 'hō, 'hwō\ *imperative verb* **1** — used as a command to an animal to stop pulling or moving **2** : step or slow a course of action or a line of thought : pause to consider or reconsider — often used to express a strong reaction (as alarm or astonishment)

who·dun·it \hü-'dən-ət\ *n* : a detective or mystery story presented as a novel, play, or motion picture

who·ev·er \hü-'ev-ər\ *pron* : whatever person ⟨*whoever* wants to come along must be ready⟩

¹whole \'hōl\ *adj* **1** : being in healthy or sound condition : free from sickness or injury : WELL ⟨your care made me *whole* again⟩ **2 a** : having all its proper parts or elements : COMPLETE ⟨*whole* grain⟩ ⟨*whole* milk⟩ **b** : not cut up or in pieces ⟨a *whole* roast chicken⟩ **3** : not divided or scattered ⟨your *whole* attention⟩ **4** : being the total or full amount or extent of something ⟨owns the *whole* island⟩ **5** : each or all of the ⟨the *whole* 10 days⟩ [Old English *hāl* "healthy" — related to ¹HALE]

²whole *n* **1** : a complete amount or sum **2** : something whole or entire ⟨the *whole* of an apple⟩ — **in whole** : to the full or entire extent : WHOLLY — **on the whole 1** : in view of all the facts : all things considered ⟨*on the whole* you did a good job⟩ **2** : in general : in most cases ⟨children *on the whole* have more energy than adults⟩

whole·heart·ed \'hōl-'härt-əd\ *adj* : not lacking in enthusiasm, determination, or devotion : HEARTY ⟨*wholehearted* effort⟩ — **whole·heart·ed·ly** *adv* — **whole·heart·ed·ness** *n*

¹whole hog *n* : the whole way or farthest limit : ALL ⟨go the *whole hog* and invite all your friends⟩

² whole hog *adv* : to the fullest extent : COMPLETELY ⟨accepted *whole hog* their explanation of events⟩

whole language *n* : a method of teaching reading and writing that emphasizes learning whole words and phrases by encountering them in written or printed work rather than by the method of phonics

whole note *n* : a musical note equal to one measure of four beats

whole number *n* : any of the set of nonnegative integers; *also* : INTEGER

whole rest *n* : a musical rest equal in time to a whole note

¹whole·sale \'hōl-ˌsāl\ *n* : the sale of goods in large quantity usually for resale (as by a store owner)

²wholesale *adj* **1** : of, relating to, or engaged in the sale of goods in quantity for resale ⟨a *wholesale* grocer⟩ ⟨*wholesale* prices⟩ **2** : done on a large scale : GENERAL ⟨*wholesale* changes in the team's roster⟩ — **wholesale** *adv*

³wholesale *vb* **whole·saled; whole·sal·ing** : to sell usually in large amounts for resale — **whole·sal·er** *n*

whole·some \'hōl-səm\ *adj* **1** : helping to keep or improve the good condition of the mind, body, or spirit ⟨a *wholesome* environment⟩ **2** : sound in body, mind, or morals : HEALTHY ⟨a *wholesome* family movie⟩ *synonyms* see HEALTHFUL — **whole·some·ly** *adv* — **whole·some·ness** *n*

\ə\ **abut**	\au̇\ **out**	\i\ **tip**	\o̅\ **saw**	\u̇\ **foot**
\ər\ **further**	\ch\ **chin**	\ī\ **life**	\ȯi\ **coin**	\y\ **yet**
\a\ **mat**	\e\ **pet**	\j\ **job**	\th\ **thin**	\yü\ **few**
\ā\ **take**	\ē\ **easy**	\ŋ\ **sing**	\th\ **this**	\yu̇\ **cure**
\ä\ **cot, cart**	\g\ **go**	\ō\ **bone**	\ü\ **food**	\zh\ **vision**

whole step *n* : the basic unit of measurement of the difference in pitch between two tones equal to that between a C and the D just above it

whole wheat *adj* : made from or containing wheat kernels that were ground in their entirety ⟨*whole wheat* bread⟩

whol·ly \'hōl-(l)ē\ *adv* **1** : to the full or entire extent : COMPLETELY ⟨a *wholly* different view⟩ **2** : to the exclusion of other things : SOLELY ⟨a book devoted *wholly* to sports cars⟩

whom \(')hüm, üm\ *pron, objective case of* WHO

whom·ev·er \hü-'mev-ər\ *pron, objective case of* WHOEVER

whom·so·ev·er \,hüm-sə-'wev-ər\ *pron, objective case of* WHOSOEVER

¹whoop \'hüp, 'hùp, *least frequently for sense 2* 'hwùp *or* 'hwûp\ *vb* **1** : to shout or call loudly and energetically especially in enthusiasm or enjoyment ⟨the children *whooped* with joy⟩ **2** : to make the sound that follows an attack of coughing in whooping cough — **whoop it up 1** : to celebrate loudly : CAROUSE **2** : to stir up enthusiasm

²whoop *n* **1** : a whooping sound **2** : a loud booming cry of a bird (as an owl or crane)

whoop·ee \'hwùp-,ē, 'wùp-; 'hwü-,pē, 'hü-, 'wü-\ *interj* — used to express delight or high spirits

whooping cough *n* : a disease especially of children that is caused by a bacterium and is marked by severe attacks of coughing often followed by a high-pitched gasping intake of breath — called also *pertussis*

whooping crane *n* : a large white nearly extinct North American crane that has a loud trumpeting call

whoops *variant of* OOPS

¹whoosh \'hwüsh, 'wüsh, 'hwùsh, 'wùsh\ *n* : a swift or explosive rush; *also* : the sound created by such a rush

whooping crane

²whoosh *vb* : to pass or move along with a whoosh ⟨cars *whooshing* along the highway⟩

whop·per \'hwäp-ər, 'wäp-\ *n* **1** : something unusually large **2** : a monstrous lie

whop·ping \'hwäp-iŋ, 'wäp-\ *adj* : extremely large ⟨got a *whopping* increase in his allowance⟩; *also* : INCREDIBLE ⟨a *whopping* success⟩

whore \'hō(ə)r, 'hù(ə)r\ *n* : ²PROSTITUTE

whorl \'hwȯr(-ə)l, 'wȯr(-ə)l, 'hwər(-ə)l, 'wər(-ə)l\ *n* **1** : a row of similar parts (as leaves or petals) in a circle around a point and especially a stem **2** : something that whirls or winds around a center ⟨a *whorl* of smoke⟩ **3** : one of the turns of a shell (as of a snail) having just one valve **4** : a fingerprint in which the central ridges on the skin turn through at least one complete circle

whorled \'hwȯr(-ə)ld, 'wȯr(-ə)ld, 'hwər(-ə)ld, 'wər(-ə)ld\ *adj* : having or arranged in whorls ⟨*whorled* leaves⟩

¹whose \(')hüz, üz\ *adj* : of or relating to whom or which ⟨*whose* bag is it⟩ ⟨the book *whose* cover is torn⟩

²whose *pron, sing or pl* : whose one : whose ones ⟨*whose* is it⟩ ⟨*whose* were they⟩

who·so \'hü-,sō\ *pron* : WHOEVER

who·so·ev·er \,hü-sə-'wev-ər\ *pron* : WHOEVER

¹why \(')hwī, (')wī\ *adv* : for what cause or reason ⟨*why* did you do it⟩

²why *conj* **1** : the cause or reason for which ⟨know *why* you did it⟩ **2** : for which : on account of which ⟨the reason *why* she did it⟩

³why \'hwī, 'wī\ *n, pl* **whys** : ¹REASON 1a ⟨explained the *whys* and wherefores of the sudden price increase⟩

⁴why \(,)wī, (,)hwī\ *interj* — used to express surprise, indecision, approval, disapproval, or impatience ⟨*why*, I didn't know that⟩

wick \'wik\ *n* : a cord, strip, or ring of loosely woven material through which a liquid (as wax or oil) is drawn to the top in a candle, lamp, or oil stove for burning

wick·ed \'wik-əd\ *adj* **1** : morally bad : EVIL **2** : given to mischief : ROGUISH ⟨a *wicked* glance⟩ **3 a** : very unpleasant ⟨a *wicked* odor⟩ **b** : causing or likely to cause harm or trouble ⟨a *wicked* storm⟩ — **wick·ed·ly** *adv* — **wick·ed·ness** *n*

wick·er \'wik-ər\ *n* **1** : a flexible twig (as of a willow) **2** : WICKERWORK — **wicker** *adj*

wick·er·work \-,wərk\ *n* : something (as a basket or chair) made of interlaced flexible twigs or branches

wick·et \'wik-ət\ *n* **1** : a small gate or door; *esp* : one in or near a larger one **2** : a small window (as at a ticket office) through which one does business **3** : either of the two sets of three rods topped by two crosspieces at which the ball is bowled in cricket **4** : an arch or hoop (as of wire) through which a ball is hit in croquet

wick·i·up \'wik-ē-,əp\ *n* : a cone-shaped hut used by American Indians of the western and southwestern U.S. and consisting of a rough frame covered with reed mats, grass, or branches

wickiup

¹wide \'wīd\ *adj* **wider; wid·est 1 a** : covering a large area ⟨the whole *wide* world⟩ **b** : extending over, reaching, or affecting a vast area : EXTENSIVE ⟨*wide* publicity⟩ **c** : not limited : COMPREHENSIVE ⟨a job calling for *wide* experience⟩ ⟨a *wide* assortment⟩ **2 a** : measured across or at right angles to length ⟨cloth 40 feet *wide*⟩ **b** : having a great measure across : BROAD ⟨a *wide* river⟩ **c** : opened as far as possible **3 a** : extending or fluctuating considerably between limits ⟨a *wide* variation⟩ **b** : far from the thing in question ⟨a charge *wide* of the truth⟩ — **wide·ly** *adv* — **wide·ness** *n*

²wide *adv* **1** : over a great distance or extent : WIDELY ⟨searched far and *wide*⟩ **2 a** : so as to leave much space between ⟨placed *wide* apart⟩ **b** : so as to clear by a wide distance ⟨ran *wide* around the left end⟩ **3** : to the fullest extent : COMPLETELY ⟨opened his eyes *wide*⟩

wide–awake \,wīd-ə-'wāk\ *adj* **1** : fully awake **2** : ¹ALERT 1b

wide–eyed \'wīd-'īd\ *adj* **1** : having the eyes wide open especially with wonder or astonishment **2** : NAIVE 2

wide-mouthed \-'maŭthd, -'maŭtht\ *adj* **1** : having a wide mouth ⟨*widemouthed* jars⟩ **2** : having one's mouth opened wide (as in awe)

wid·en \'wīd-³n\ *vb* **wid·ened; wid·en·ing** \'wīd-niŋ, -³n-iŋ\ : to make or become wide or wider : BROADEN

wide·spread \'wīd-'spred\ *adj* **1** : scattered or found over a wide area ⟨*widespread* interest in the election⟩ **2** : spread out over a wide area ⟨*widespread* wings⟩

¹wid·ow \'wid-ō\ *n* : a woman whose husband has died — **wid·ow·hood** \-,hùd\ *n*

²widow *vb* : to cause to become a widow or widower ⟨*widowed* by war⟩

wid·ow·er \'wid-ə-wər\ *n* : a man whose wife has died

width \'width, 'witth\ *n* **1** : the measurement of the short or shorter side of something : BREADTH **2** : largeness of area or range **3** : a measured piece of material ⟨a *width* of cloth⟩ ⟨a *width* of lumber⟩

wield \'wē(ə)ld\ *vb* **1** : to put (as a tool) to good use ⟨*wield* a broom⟩ **2** : to use one's authority by means of ⟨*wield* influence⟩ **synonyms** see HANDLE — **wield·er** *n*

wie·ner \'wē-nər, 'wē-nē\ *n* : FRANKFURTER [from German *Wienerwurst* "Vienna sausage," from *Vienna*, capital of Austria]

wife \'wīf\ *n, pl* **wives** \'wīvz\ **1** *dialect* : WOMAN 1 **2** : a female partner in a marriage

wife·ly \'wī-flē\ *adj* : of, relating to, or suitable for a wife

Wi-Fi \'wī-'fī\ *certification mark* — used to certify the ability of wireless computer networking devices to communicate with each other

wig \'wig\ *n* : a manufactured covering of natural or artificial hair for the head

wi·geon *or* **wid·geon** \'wij-ən\ *n, pl* **wigeon** *or* **wigeons** *or* **widgeon** *or* **widgeons** : any of several freshwater ducks with a large white patch on each wing

wig·gle \'wig-əl\ *vb* **wig·gled; wig·gling** \-(ə-)liŋ\ **1** : to move to and fro with quick jerky or shaking motions : JIGGLE ⟨*wiggled* my toes⟩ **2** : to move along with twisting and turning movements : WRIGGLE — **wiggle** *n*

wig·gler \'wig-(ə-)lər\ *n* **1** : a larva or pupa of a mosquito — called also *wriggler* **2** : one that wiggles

wig·gly \'wig-(ə-)lē\ *adj* **wig·gli·er; -est** **1** : tending to wiggle ⟨a *wiggly* worm⟩ **2** : WAVY ⟨*wiggly* lines⟩

wight \'wīt\ *n* : a living being : CREATURE; *esp* : HUMAN BEING

¹wig·wag \'wig-,wag\ *vb* **-wagged; -wag·ging** : to signal especially by a flag or light waved according to a code

²wigwag *n* : the art or practice of wigwagging

wig·wam \'wig-,wäm\ *n* : a hut used by the American Indians of the Great Lakes region and eastward usually having an arched frame of poles covered with bark, rush mats, or hides

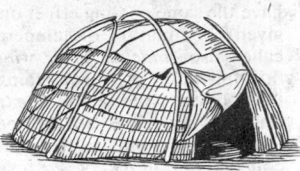

wigwam

¹wild \'wī(ə)ld\ *adj* **1 a** : living in a state of nature and not under human control and care ⟨*wild* animals⟩ **b** : growing or produced without human aid and care ⟨*wild* honey⟩ **c** : of or relating to wild organisms ⟨the *wild* state⟩ **2** : not inhabited or cultivated ⟨*wild* land⟩ **3 a** : not being under control ⟨*wild* rage⟩ ⟨a *wild* young stallion⟩ **b** : marked by disturbance and confusion ⟨a *wild* night⟩ **c** : going beyond what is usual : FANTASTIC ⟨*wild* colors⟩ ⟨*wild* ideas⟩ **4** : not civilized : SAVAGE **5** : being far off the intended course ⟨a *wild* pitch⟩ **6** : having no basis in fact ⟨a *wild* guess⟩ **7** : able to represent any card designated by the holder ⟨poker with deuces *wild*⟩ — **wild·ly** \'wī(ə)l-(d)lē\ *adv* — **wild·ness** \'wī(ə)l(d)-nəs\ *n*

²wild *n* : WILDERNESS

³wild *adv* **1** : in a wild manner : WILDLY **2** : without rules or control ⟨running *wild*⟩

wild boar *n* : an Old World wild hog from which most domestic swine have been developed

wild boar

wild carrot *n* : QUEEN ANNE'S LACE

wild·cat \'wī(ə)l(d)-,kat\ *n, pl* **wildcats** *or* **wildcat** **1** : any of various small or medium-sized cats (as the lynx or ocelot) **2** : a savage quick-tempered person

wil·de·beest \'wil-də-,bēst\ *n, pl* **wildebeest** *also* **wildebeest** : either of two large African antelopes with a head like that of an ox, a short mane, a long tail, and horns that curve downward and outward — called also *gnu*

wil·der·ness \'wil-dər-nəs\ *n* : an area in which few people live that is not used for farming and is more or less in its natural state

wild·fire \'wī(ə)l(d)-,fī(ə)r\ *n* : an uncontrollable fire that destroys a wide area

wild·flower \-,flau̇-(ə)r\ *n* : the flower of a wild plant or the plant bearing it

wild·fowl \-,fau̇l\ *n* : a bird and especially a waterfowl (as a wild duck) hunted as game

wild geranium *n* : a geranium of the eastern U.S. and Canada with rosy purple flowers

wild–goose chase *n* : a complicated or lengthy and usually unsuccessful pursuit or search

wild·life \'wī(ə)l-,(d)līf\ *n* : nonhuman living things and especially wild animals living in their natural environment

wild rice *n* : a tall North American grass that grows in water and produces an edible grain; *also* : the grain

Wild West *n* : the western U.S. in its frontier period characterized by roughness and lawlessness

wild·wood \'wī(ə)l-,(d)wu̇d\ *n* : woodland untouched by human activity

¹wile \'wī(ə)l\ *n* **1** : a trick intended to deceive or trap **2** : skill in tricking : GUILE **synonyms** see TRICK

²wile *vb* **wiled; wil·ing** : to lure by or as if by a magic spell

¹will \wəl, (ə)l, ᵊl, (')wil\ *vb, past* **would** \wəd, (ə)d, (')wu̇d\; *present sing & pl* **will** **1** : ¹WISH 1 ⟨call it what you *will*⟩ **2** — used as a helping verb to express (1) desire, willingness, or in negative sentences refusal ⟨*will* you have another⟩ ⟨no one *would* do it⟩ ⟨they *won't* stop⟩, (2) regular or usual action ⟨*will* get angry over nothing⟩, (3) future action ⟨tomorrow we *will* go shopping⟩, (4) capacity or ability ⟨the back seat *will* hold three people⟩, (5) determination or willfulness ⟨I *will* go despite the weather⟩, (6) inevitability ⟨accidents *will* happen⟩, or (7) a command ⟨you *will* do as I say⟩

²will \'wil\ *n* **1** : firm desire or determination ⟨the *will* to win⟩ **2** : the desire or choice especially of someone in power or authority ⟨the king's *will*⟩ **3** : the process or power of wishing, choosing, desiring, or intending **4** : the power of control over one's own actions or emotions ⟨has an iron *will*⟩ **5** : a legal document that instructs how a person's property is to be divided after death

³will \'wil\ *vb* **1** : to leave by or as if by a will : BEQUEATH ⟨*willed* the house to his daughter⟩ **2** : to bring about by an act of choice ⟨*willed* herself to sleep⟩ **3** : ¹ORDER 2a ⟨it will happen if God *wills* it⟩ **4** : to cause or change by an act of will ⟨*willed* herself to succeed⟩ **5** : to decide on by choice ⟨went wherever they *willed*⟩

willed \'wild\ *adj* : having a will especially of a certain kind ⟨strong-*willed*⟩

will·ful *or* **wil·ful** \'wil-fəl\ *adj* **1** : stubbornly determined to have one's own way ⟨a *willful* child⟩ **2** : done deliberately : INTENTIONAL ⟨*willful* obedience⟩ **synonyms** see UNRULY — **will·ful·ly** \-fə-lē\ *adv* — **will·ful·ness** *n*

wil·lies \'wil-ēz\ *n pl* : a fit of nervousness : JITTERS ⟨gives me the *willies*⟩

will·ing \'wil-iŋ\ *adj* **1** : feeling no objection : READY ⟨*willing* to go⟩ **2** : prompt to act or respond ⟨*willing* workers⟩ **3** : done, made, or given by choice ⟨a *willing* sacrifice⟩ **synonyms** see ¹VOLUNTARY — **will·ing·ly** *adv* — **will·ing·ness** *n*

wil·li·waw \'wil-i-,wȯ\ *n* : a sudden violent gust of cold

\ə\ **abut**	\au̇\ **out**	\i\ **tip**	\ȯ\ **saw**	\u̇\ **foot**
\ər\ **further**	\ch\ **chin**	\ī\ **life**	\ȯi\ **coin**	\y\ **yet**
\a\ **mat**	\e\ **pet**	\j\ **job**	\th\ **thin**	\yu̇\ **few**
\ā\ **take**	\ē\ **easy**	\ŋ\ **sing**	\th\ **this**	\yu̇\ **cure**
\ä\ **cot, cart**	\g\ **go**	\ō\ **bone**	\ü\ **food**	\zh\ **vision**

land air common along mountainous coasts of high latitudes

will–o'–the–wisp \ˌwil-ə-thə-'wisp\ *n* **1** : a light that sometimes appears in the night over marshy ground **2** : a false or unreachable goal

wil·low \'wil-ō\ *n* : any of a genus of trees and shrubs that often have narrow leaves, produce catkins for flowers, and include some used for their wood, for making baskets, or as ornamentals — **wil·low·like** \-ˌlīk\ *adj*

wil·lowy \'wil-ə-wē\ *adj* **1** : having many willows ⟨a *willowy* valley⟩ **2** : resembling a willow; *esp* : gracefully tall and slender ⟨a *willowy* young dancer⟩

will·pow·er \'wil-ˌpau̇(-ə)r\ *n* : strong determination ⟨the temptation tested her *willpower*⟩

wil·ly–nil·ly \ˌwil-ē-'nil-ē\ *adv or adj* **1** : by force : without choice ⟨rushed us along *willy-nilly*⟩ **2** : in an unpredictable manner ⟨children running about *willy–nilly*⟩ [an altered form of the phrase *will I nill I* or *will ye nill ye*; *nill*, an ancient negative form of *will*, from Old English *nyllan*, a combination of *ne* "not" and *wyllan* "to wish, will"]

¹wilt \wəlt, (')wilt\ *archaic present 2nd singular of* WILL

²wilt \'wilt\ *vb* **1** : to lose or cause to lose freshness and become limp : DROOP ⟨*wilting* roses⟩ **2** : to grow weak or faint ⟨was *wilting* after hours of dancing⟩

³wilt \'wilt\ *n* : a plant disease (as one caused by a fungus) marked by wilting of the soft parts of the plant

wily \'wī-lē\ *adj* **wil·i·er; -est** : full of deceit : TRICKY ⟨a *wily* opponent⟩ **synonyms** see CUNNING — **wil·i·ness** *n*

wimp \'wimp\ *n* : a weak and timid person — **wimpy** \'wim-pē\ *adj*

wim·ple \'wim-pəl\ *n* : a cloth covering worn over the head and around the neck and chin by women in earlier times and by some nuns today

¹win \'win\ *vb* **won** \'wən\; **win·ning** **1** : to achieve victory in a contest ⟨I always dream of *winning*⟩ **2** : to get especially by effort or fortune ⟨*won* praise for my hard work⟩ **3 a** : to gain in or as if in battle or contest ⟨*won* the championship⟩ **b** : to be the victor in ⟨*won* the war⟩ **4** : to make friendly or favorable to oneself or one's cause ⟨*won* the voters with her warm sense of humor⟩

²win *n* : VICTORY; *esp* : first place in a horse race

wince \'win(t)s\ *vb* **winced; winc·ing** : to shrink back (as from pain) : FLINCH ⟨the cut on my leg caused me to *wince*⟩ ⟨the crowd *winced* when the skater fell on the ice⟩ — **wince** *n*

winch \'winch\ *n* : a machine that has a roller on which a rope, cable, or chain is wound for pulling or lifting

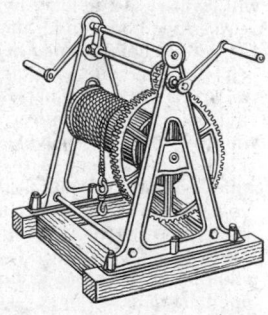

winch

¹wind \'wind\ *n* **1** : a movement of air **2** : something that has force or influence ⟨the changing *winds* of political opinion⟩ **3** : BREATH 2a ⟨the fall knocked the *wind* out of me⟩ **4** : gas produced in the stomach or the intestines **5** : something unimportant; *esp* : idle words **6 a** : air carrying a scent (as of a hunter or game) **b** : slight information especially about something secret ⟨got *wind* of our plans⟩ **7** *pl* : the wind instruments of a band or orchestra **8** : the direction from which the wind is blowing [Old English *wind* "the natural movement of air"] — **in the wind** : about to happen : ASTIR, AFOOT

²wind *vb* **1** : to get a scent of ⟨the dogs *winded* game⟩ **2** : to cause to be out of breath ⟨the long climb *winded* us⟩ **3** : to allow to rest so as to recover breath ⟨*wind* a horse⟩

³wind \'wīnd, 'wind\ *vb* **wind·ed** \'wīn-dəd, 'win-\ *or* **wound** \'wau̇nd\; **wind·ing** : to sound by blowing ⟨*wind* a horn⟩

⁴wind \'wīnd\ *vb* **wound** \'wau̇nd\ *also* **wind·ed; wind·ing** **1** : to move in a series of twists and turns ⟨a river *winding* through the valley⟩ **2** : ENTANGLE 2 **3 a** : to encircle or cover with something flexible **b** : to coil completely or repeatedly about an object : TWINE ⟨*wind* thread on a spool⟩ **4** : to lift, pull, move, or operate by means of a rope, cable, or chain and a winch ⟨*wind* up a pail⟩ **5** : to tighten the spring of ⟨*wind* a clock⟩ ⟨*wind* up a toy train⟩ [Old English *windan* "to twist, move with force"] — **wind·er** *n*

⁵wind \'wīnd\ *n* : something curved or twisted : BEND

⁶wind \'wind\ *adj* : of or relating to wind instruments ⟨the *wind* section of an orchestra⟩

wind·age \'win-dij\ *n* **1** : the influence of the wind in turning the course of a bullet or shell **2** : the amount of turning aside caused by the wind

windbag *n* : a person who talks a lot without saying anything important

wind–blown \'win(d)-ˌblōn\ *adj* : blown or looking as if blown by the wind ⟨*windblown* seeds⟩ ⟨*windblown* streets⟩

wind·break \-ˌbrāk\ *n* : something (as a growth of trees) that serves as a shelter from the wind

Wind·break·er \-ˌbrā-kər\ *trademark* — used for a jacket made of material that can resist the wind

wind·burn \-ˌbərn\ *n* : skin irritation caused by wind — **wind·burned** \-ˌbərnd\ *adj*

wind·chill \-ˌchil\ *n* : a still-air temperature that would have the same cooling effect on exposed human flesh as a given combination of temperature and wind speed — called also *windchill factor, windchill index*

wind·fall \-ˌfȯl\ *n* **1** : something (as a tree or fruit) blown down by the wind **2** : an unexpected gift, gain, or help

wind·flow·er \-ˌflau̇(-ə)r\ *n* : ANEMONE 1

¹wind·ing \'wīn-diŋ\ *n* **1** : material (as wire) wound or coiled about an object **2** : a single turn of wound material

²winding *adj* : marked by winding: as **a** : having a noticeable curved or spiral form ⟨a *winding* staircase⟩ **b** : having a course that winds ⟨a *winding* road⟩

wind·ing–sheet \-ˌshēt\ *n* : a sheet used to wrap a corpse for burial : SHROUD

wind instrument *n* : a musical instrument (as a flute or horn) sounded by the vibration of a stream of air and especially by the player's breath

wind·jam·mer \'win(d)-ˌjam-ər\ *n* : a sailing ship

wind·lass \'win-dləs\ *n* : a winch used especially on ships for pulling and lifting

wind·mill \'win(d)-ˌmil\ *n* : a mill or a machine (as for pumping water) worked by the wind turning sails or vanes at the top of a tower

win·dow \'win-dō\ *n* **1** : an opening in a wall for letting in light or air **2** : WINDOWPANE **3** : an opening in a partition or wall through which business is conducted ⟨a bank teller's *window*⟩ **4** : a period of time during which a certain condition exists ⟨a *window* of opportunity⟩ **5** : any of the areas into which a computer display may be divided and on which distinctly different types of information are displayed — **win·dow·less** *adj*

Word History The English word *window* comes from an early Norse word *vindauga*. *Vindauga* was formed by a combination of *vindr*, meaning "wind," and *auga*, meaning "eye." *Vindauga* could be translated as "wind's eye." A window can be thought of

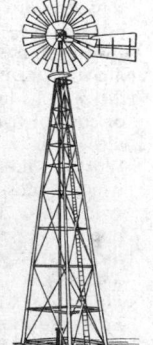

windmill

as an eye, or hole, through which the wind can enter. [from early Norse *vindauga,* literally "wind's eye," from *vindr* "wind" and *auga* "eye"]

window box *n* : a box for growing plants in or by a window

win·dow·pane \'win-dō-ˌpān\ *n* : a pane in a window

window shade *n* : a shade or curtain for a window

win·dow–shop \'win-dō-ˌshäp, -də-\ *vb* : to look at the displays in store windows without going inside to buy — **win·dow–shop·per** *n*

win·dow·sill \-ˌsil\ *n* : the horizontal piece at the bottom of a window

wind·pipe \'win(d)-ˌpīp\ *n* : TRACHEA 1

wind·row \'win-ˌ(d)rō\ *n* **1** : hay raked up into a row to dry **2** : a row of something (as sand or dry leaves) heaped up by or as if by the wind

wind shear *n* : a radical shift in wind speed and direction that occurs over a very short distance

wind·shield \'win(d)-ˌshēld\ *n* : a clear screen (as of glass) in front of the riders of a vehicle

wind·storm \-ˌstȯ(ə)rm\ *n* : a storm with strong wind and little or no rain

wind·swept \-ˌswept\ *adj* : disturbed by or as if by wind ⟨a *windswept* beach⟩

wind tunnel *n* : a passage like a tunnel through which air is blown at a known speed to investigate air flow around an object (as an airplane part or model) placed in the passage

¹wind·up \'wīn-ˌdəp\ *n* **1 a** : the act of bringing to an end **b** : a last act or part : FINISH **2** : a series of motions (as swinging the arms over the head) made by a pitcher prior to releasing a pitch

²windup *adj* : having a spring wound by hand ⟨*windup* toys⟩

wind up \(ˈ)wīn-ˈdəp\ *vb* **1** : to bring or come to a conclusion : END ⟨let's *wind up* the meeting quickly⟩ **2** : to arrive in a place, situation, or state ⟨*wound up* losing the game⟩ ⟨*wound up* as millionaires⟩ **3** : to make a windup in pitching a baseball

¹wind·ward \'win-(d)wərd\ *adj* : moving or placed toward the direction from which the wind is blowing

²windward *n* : the side or direction from which the wind is blowing ⟨sail to *windward*⟩

windy \'win-dē\ *adj* **wind·i·er; -est** **1** : having strong winds ⟨a *windy* prairie⟩ **2** : marked by or given to too much talk ⟨a *windy* speaker⟩ — **wind·i·ness** *n*

¹wine \'wīn\ *n* **1** : an alcoholic beverage made from fermented grape juice **2** : an alcoholic beverage made from the usually fermented juice of fruits (as peaches or berries) other than grapes **3** : a dark red color

²wine *vb* **wined; win·ing** **1** : to drink wine **2** : to provide with wine ⟨*wined* and dined my friends⟩

¹wing \'wiŋ\ *n* **1** : one of the movable feathered or membranous paired appendages by means of which a bird, bat, or insect flies **2** : an extension or part resembling a wing in shape, appearance, or position; *esp* : a flat or broadly expanded plant or animal part ⟨a stem with woody *wings*⟩ **3** : an

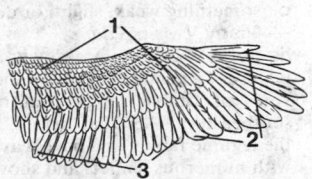

wing 1: 1 covering feathers, 2 primary feathers, 3 secondary feathers

extension from the side of an armchair **4** : a part that extends from the side of an airplane **5** : the act or manner of flying : FLIGHT **6** : a part sticking out from a main part ⟨the rear *wing* of the house⟩ **7** *pl* : the area at the side of the stage out of sight of the audience **8** : one of the positions or players on each side of a center position or line **9**

: a particular group within an organization : FACTION **10** : a unit of a military force and especially an air force — **winged** \'wiŋd, 'wiŋ-əd\ *adj* — **wing·like** \-ˌlīk\ *adj* — **on the wing** : in flight : FLYING — **under one's wing** : under one's protection : in one's care

²wing *vb* **1** : to pass through in flight **2** : to go with or as if with wings : FLY **3** : to wound in the wing ⟨*wing* a duck⟩; *also* : to wound without killing ⟨*wing* a deer⟩ **4** : to do or perform without preparation or guidelines ⟨*wing* it⟩

wing case *n* : ELYTRON

wing chair *n* : an upholstered armchair with a high back and side sections

wing·less \'wiŋ-ləs\ *adj* : having no wings or wings that are not fully developed ⟨*wingless* insects⟩

wing·span \'wiŋ-ˌspan\ *n* : the distance between the tips of a pair of wings (as of a bird or an airplane)

wing·spread \-ˌspred\ *n* : WINGSPAN; *esp* : the distance between the tips of the fully extended wings of a bird, bat, or insect

¹wink \'wiŋk\ *vb* **1** : to close and open one eye quickly as a signal or hint ⟨saw her friend *wink* and knew it was time to go⟩ **2** : to close and open the eyes quickly : BLINK **3** : to avoid seeing or noting something ⟨*wink* at a parking violation⟩ **4** : to gleam or shine on and off : TWINKLE

²wink *n* **1** : a brief period of sleep : NAP ⟨catching a *wink*⟩ **2 a** : a hint or sign given by winking **b** : an act of winking **3** : the time of a wink : INSTANT ⟨quick as a *wink* she did the job⟩

win·ner \'win-ər\ *n* : one that wins

¹win·ning \'win-iŋ\ *n* **1** : the act of one that wins : VICTORY **2** : something won; *esp* : money won in a game or contest — usually used in plural

²winning *adj* **1 a** : of, relating to, or used for or in the act of winning ⟨the *winning* ticket⟩ **b** : successful especially in competition ⟨a *winning* team⟩ **2** : tending to please or delight ⟨a *winning* personality⟩ — **win·ning·ly** *adv*

win·now \'win-ō\ *vb* **1 a** : to remove by a current of air the parts separated from grain in threshing **b** : to expose grain to a current of air to remove waste **2** : to sort or separate as if by winnowing ⟨*winnowed* the group of contestants down to five finalists⟩ — **win·now·er** \'win-ə-wər\ *n*

win·some \'win(t)-səm\ *adj* **1** : having a charming or pleasing quality ⟨a *winsome* smile⟩ **2** : CHEERFUL 1a ⟨a *winsome* mood⟩ — **win·some·ly** *adv* — **win·some·ness** *n*

¹win·ter \'wint-ər\ *n* **1** : the season between autumn and spring usually including in the northern half of the globe the months of December, January, and February **2** : YEAR 2 ⟨happened many *winters* ago⟩ **3** : a time or season of idleness or decay

²winter *vb* **win·tered; win·ter·ing** \'wint-ə-riŋ, 'win-triŋ\ **1** : to pass or live through the winter ⟨the cattle *wintered* on the range⟩ **2** : to keep, feed, or manage during the winter ⟨*winter* livestock⟩

³winter *adj* **1** : of, relating to, or suitable for winter ⟨*winter* clothes⟩ **2** : sown in autumn and harvested in the following spring or summer ⟨*winter* wheat⟩

win·ter·green \'wint-ər-ˌgrēn\ *n* **1 a** : a low evergreen plant of the heath family with white bell-shaped flowers and spicy red berries — called also *checkerberry* **b** : an oil from the wintergreen or its flavor **2** : any of several plants related to the wintergreen

win·ter·ize \'wint-ə-ˌrīz\ *vb* **-ized; -iz·ing** : to make ready for winter ⟨*winterize* the car⟩

\ə\ **abut**	\au̇\ **out**	\i\ **tip**	\ȯ\ **saw**	\u̇\ **foot**
\ər\ **further**	\ch\ **chin**	\ī\ **life**	\ȯi\ **coin**	\y\ **yet**
\a\ **mat**	\e\ **pet**	\j\ **job**	\th\ **thin**	\yü\ **few**
\ā\ **take**	\ē\ **easy**	\ŋ\ **sing**	\t̲h̲\ **this**	\yu̇\ **cure**
\ä\ **cot, cart**	\g\ **go**	\ō\ **bone**	\ü\ **food**	\zh\ **vision**

win·ter–kill \'wint-ər-ˌkil\ *vb* : to cause the death of (as a plant) through the effects of winter and especially cold; *also* : to die as a result of the effects of winter conditions and especially cold

winter melon *n* : any of several muskmelons (as a casaba or honeydew melon) with smooth rind and sweet white or greenish flesh that keeps well

winter squash *n* : any of various hard-shelled squashes (as an acorn squash) that keep well in storage

win·ter·time \'wint-ər-ˌtīm\ *n* : the winter season

win·try \'win-trē\ *adj* **win·tri·er; -est 1** : of, relating to, or typical of winter ⟨*wintry* weather⟩ **2** : not warm and friendly : CHEERLESS ⟨a *wintry* welcome⟩ — **win·tri·ness** *n*

¹**wipe** \'wīp\ *vb* **wiped; wip·ing 1** : to clean or dry by rubbing ⟨*wipe* dishes⟩ **2** : to remove by or as if by rubbing ⟨*wipe* away tears⟩ **3** : to pass or draw over a surface ⟨*wiped* my hand across my forehead⟩ — **wip·er** *n*

²**wipe** *n* **1** : an act or instance of wiping **2** : something used for wiping

wipe·out \'wīp-ˌaùt\ *n* **1** : complete destruction **2** : a fall or crash caused usually by losing control ⟨*wipeouts* on the downhill ski course are common⟩ **3** : total or final defeat ⟨couldn't bear to watch the team's *wipeout*⟩

wipe out *vb* **1** : to destroy completely ⟨crops *wiped out* by flooding⟩ **2** : to fall or crash usually as a result of losing control ⟨the surfer *wiped out*⟩

¹**wire** \'wī(ə)r\ *n* **1 a** : metal in the form of a usually flexible thread or slender rod **b** : a thread or rod of metal **2 a** : a line of wire for conducting electrical current **b** : a telephone or telegraph wire or system **c** : TELEGRAM, CABLEGRAM **3 a** : the finish line of a race **b** : the final moment ⟨the game came down to the *wire*⟩ — **wire·like** \-ˌlīk\ *adj* — **under the wire 1** : at the finish line **2** : at the last moment — **wire to wire** *or* **from wire to wire** : from start to finish

²**wire** *vb* **wired; wir·ing 1** : to provide or equip with wire or electricity ⟨*wire* a house⟩ **2** : to bind, string, or mount with wire **3** : to send or send word to by telegraph ⟨*wire* me some money right away⟩

wired *adj* **1** : reinforced or bound with wire ⟨a *wired* container⟩ **2** : having a netting or fence of wire ⟨a *wired* pen for chickens⟩ **3** : extremely excited ⟨were *wired* after their victory⟩

wire grass *n* : any of various grasses or rushes having wiry stems or leaves

wire·haired \'wī(ə)r-'ha(ə)rd, -'he(ə)rd\ *adj* : having a stiff wiry outer coat of hair ⟨a *wirehaired* dog⟩

¹**wire·less** \'wī(ə)r-ləs\ *adj* **1** : having no wire or wires **2** : of or relating to radio communications ⟨a *wireless* phone⟩

²**wireless** *n* **1** : communication at a distance involving signals transmitted by radio waves rather than over wires **2** *chiefly British* : ¹RADIO

wireless telegraphy *n* : telegraphy carried on by radio waves and without connecting wires — called also *wireless telegraph*

wire service *n* : a news organization that sends out news stories by wire to subscribers (as newspapers)

¹**wire·tap** \'wī(ə)r-ˌtap\ *vb* : to tap a telephone or telegraph wire to get information — **wire·tap·per** *n*

²**wiretap** *n* : the act or an instance of wiretapping

wire·worm \'wī(ə)r-ˌwərm\ *n* : the slender hard-coated larva of various click beetles that is often destructive to plant roots

wiring *n* **1** : the act of providing or using wire **2** : a system of wires; *esp* : an arrangement of wires used for electric distribution

wiry \'wī(ə)r-ē\ *adj* **wir·i·er** \'wī-rē-ər\; **wir·i·est 1** : resembling wire in form and flexibility ⟨*wiry* stems⟩ **2** : being slender yet strong and muscular ⟨a *wiry* physique⟩

wis·dom \'wiz-dəm\ *n* **1 a** : learning acquired over a period of time : KNOWLEDGE **b** : ability to see beneath the surface of things : INSIGHT **c** : good sense : JUDGMENT **2** : a wise attitude, belief, or course of action

Wisdom *n* — see BIBLE table

Wisdom of Sol·o·mon \-'säl-ə-mən\ — see BIBLE table

wisdom tooth *n* : the last tooth of the full set of teeth on each side of the upper and lower jaw in a human being

¹**wise** \'wīz\ *n* : MANNER 2b — used in such phrases as *in any wise, in no wise, in this wise* [Old English *wīse* "way, manner"]

²**wise** *adj* **wis·er; wis·est 1** : having or showing wisdom, good sense, or good judgment : SENSIBLE ⟨a *wise* person⟩ ⟨a *wise* investment⟩ **2** : having special or secret information : INFORMED ⟨I was *wise* to their plans⟩ **3** : boldly rude or disrespectful : IMPUDENT [Old English *wīs* "showing good judgment or intelligence"] — **wise·ly** *adv*

³**wise** *vb* **wised; wis·ing** : to make or become informed or smart — used with *up* ⟨*wise up* if you want to get ahead⟩

-wise \ˌwīz\ *adv combining form* **1 a** : in the manner of **b** : in the position or direction of ⟨slant*wise*⟩ ⟨clock*wise*⟩ **2** : with regard to : in respect of [derived from Old English *wīse* "manner"]

wise·acre \'wī-ˌzā-kər\ *n* : SMART ALECK [a modified form of early Dutch *wijssegger* "one who is thought to be able to foretell events"]

wise·crack \'wīz-ˌkrak\ *n* : a clever, smart, or joking remark — **wisecrack** *vb* — **wise·crack·er** *n*

wise guy \'wīz-ˌgī\ *n* : SMART ALECK

¹**wish** \'wish\ *vb* **1** : to have a desire : long for : WANT ⟨*wish* you were here⟩ ⟨*wish* for a puppy⟩ **2** : to form or express a desire concerning ⟨*wished* them a happy New Year⟩ **3** : to request by expressing a desire ⟨I *wish* you to go now⟩ — **wish·er** *n*

²**wish** *n* **1 a** : an act or instance of wishing or desire ⟨a *wish* to travel⟩ **b** : an object of desire : GOAL ⟨I got my *wish* — a good score on the test⟩ **2** : a wishing of good fortune ⟨sends her best *wishes*⟩

wish·bone \'wish-ˌbōn\ *n* : a bone in front of a bird's breastbone that is shaped like a V and consists chiefly of two fused clavicles

wish·ful \'wish-fəl\ *adj* **1** : having a wish : DESIROUS **2** : based on wishes rather than fact ⟨*wishful* thinking⟩ — **wish·ful·ly** \-fə-lē\ *adv* — **wish·ful·ness** *n*

wish list *n* : a list of desired but often realistically unobtainable items ⟨a *wish list* of equipment for the school's gymnasium⟩

wishy–washy \'wish-ē-ˌwȯsh-ē, -ˌwäsh-\ *adj* : lacking spirit, courage, or determination : WEAK ⟨*wishy-washy* leadership⟩

wisp \'wisp\ *n* **1** : a small bunch of hay or straw **2 a** : a thin piece or strand **b** : a faint streak ⟨a *wisp* of smoke⟩ **c** : something weak, slight, or delicate ⟨a *wisp* of a smile⟩ — **wispy** \'wis-pē\ *adj*

wis·te·ria \wis-'tir-ē-ə\ *also* **wis·tar·ia** \-'tir-ē-ə *also* -'ter-\ *n* : any of a genus of mostly woody vines of China, Japan, and the southeastern U.S. that belong to the legume family and have leaves with numerous leaflets and showy blue, white, purple, or rose flowers in long hanging clusters [named for Caspar *Wistar* 1761–1818 American physician]

wist·ful \'wist-fəl\ *adj* : feeling or showing a timid desire ⟨a *wistful* look on his face⟩ — **wist·ful·ly** \-fə-lē\ *adv* — **wist·ful·ness** *n*

¹**wit** \'wit\ *vb* **wist** \'wist\; **wit·ting;** *present 1st & 3rd sing* **wot** \'wät\ *archaic* : KNOW, LEARN [Old English *witan* "to know"]

wisteria

²wit *n* **1** : ability to think or reason : INTELLIGENCE **2 a** : normal mental state — usually used in plural ⟨scared out of my *wits*⟩ **b** : practical good judgment ⟨had the *wit* to leave quickly⟩ **3 a** : a talent for making clever and usually amusing remarks **b** : cleverly amusing remarks; *also* : one noted for making such remarks [Old English *wit* "mind"] — **at one's wit's end** *or* **at one's wits' end** : at a loss for a means of solving a problem

witch \'wich\ *n* **1** : a person believed to have magic powers **2** : a mean or ugly old woman

witch·craft \-ˌkraft\ *n* : the use of sorcery or magic

witch doctor *n* : a person usually in a primitive society who uses magic to treat sickness and to fight off evil spirits

witch·ery \'wich-(ə-)rē\ *n, pl* **-er·ies 1** : WITCHCRAFT **2** : a power to charm or fascinate

witch ha·zel \'wich-ˌhā-zəl\ *n* **1** : any of a genus of shrubs or small trees that produce usually yellow flowers with very thin petals in late fall or early spring; *esp* : one of eastern North America that blooms in the fall **2** : a soothing alcoholic lotion made from the bark of the witch hazel [from *witch*, an old name for any of several trees with branches that bend easily, from Old English *wice* (same meaning)]

witch–hunt \-ˌhənt\ *n* **1** : a searching out and persecution of persons accused of witchcraft **2** : the searching out and deliberate harassment of those (as political opponents) with unpopular views

witch·ing \'wich-iŋ\ *adj* : of, relating to, or suitable for witchcraft ⟨the *witching* hour⟩

with \(')with, (')with\ *prep* **1 a** : in opposition to : AGAINST ⟨fought *with* his sister⟩ **b** : FROM 2 ⟨parting *with* friends⟩ **2** : in shared relation to ⟨talking *with* a friend⟩ ⟨trade *with* other countries⟩ **3** : in regard to : TOWARD ⟨angry *with* her⟩ ⟨on friendly terms *with* all nations⟩ **4 a** : compared to ⟨on equal terms *with* the others⟩ **b** : on the side of ⟨voted *with* the majority⟩ **c** : as well as ⟨I can debate *with* the best of them⟩ **5 a** : in the judgment or opinion of ⟨it's all right *with* me⟩ **b** : in the experience or practice of ⟨*with* them a promise is a real duty⟩ **6 a** : by means of ⟨write *with* a pen⟩ **b** : because of ⟨danced *with* joy⟩ **7** : having or showing as a manner of action or an accompanying fact ⟨spoke *with* vigor⟩ ⟨stood there *with* my hat on⟩ **8 a** : in possession of : HAVING ⟨animals *with* horns⟩ **b** : marked by ⟨a person *with* a hot temper⟩ **9 a** : in the company of ⟨went to the movies *with* us⟩ **b** : having or including as a part ⟨costs $5 *with* the tax⟩ ⟨tea *with* lemon⟩ **10 a** : at the same time as ⟨rose *with* the sun⟩ **b** : in proportion to ⟨the pressure varies *with* the depth⟩ **11** : in the possession or care of ⟨left the money *with* your mother⟩ **12** : in spite of ⟨*with* all her cleverness, she failed⟩ **13** : in the direction of ⟨cut *with* the grain of the fabric⟩

with·al \with-ˈȯl, with-\ *adv* **1** : together with this : BESIDES **2** : on the other hand : NEVERTHELESS

with·draw \with-ˈdrȯ, with-\ *vb* **-drew** \-ˈdrü\; **-drawn** \-ˈdrȯn\; **-draw·ing** \-ˈdrȯ(-)iŋ\ **1** : to take back or away : draw away : REMOVE ⟨*withdraw* money from the bank⟩ **2 a** : to call back : RECALL ⟨*withdrew* the charge of theft⟩ **b** : to take back (one's words) : RETRACT **3** : to go away : RETREAT ⟨*withdrew* to the country⟩

with·draw·al \with-ˈdrȯ(-ə)l, with-\ *n* **1** : an act or instance of withdrawing; *esp* : a removal of money from a bank account **2 a** : the stopping of the use or giving of a drug and especially a habit-forming drug **b** : the group of often painful physical and emotional symptoms that occur when use of a habit-forming drug is stopped

with·drawn \with-ˈdrȯn, with-\ *adj* **1** : removed from immediate or easy approach : ISOLATED ⟨*withdrawn* mountain communities⟩ **2** : not socially active or interested : INTROVERTED ⟨a shy and *withdrawn* child⟩

withe \'with, 'with, 'wīth\ *n* : a slender flexible branch or twig

with·er \'with-ər\ *vb* **with·ered**; **with·er·ing** \-(ə-)riŋ\ **1** : to shrivel from or as if from loss of bodily moisture and especially sap ⟨the crops *withered* during the drought⟩ **2** : to lose liveliness, force, or freshness ⟨support for the candidate *withered*⟩

with·ers \'with-ərz\ *n pl* : the ridge between the shoulder bones of a horse; *also* : a corresponding part in other four-footed animals (as dogs)

with·hold \with-ˈhōld, with-\ *vb* **-held** \-ˈheld\; **-hold·ing** **1** : to hold back : RESTRAIN ⟨*withhold* an angry response⟩ **2** : to refuse to grant, give, or allow ⟨*withhold* permission⟩ **3** : to deduct (withholding tax) from income — **with·hold·er** *n*

withholding tax *n* : a deduction (as from one's wages) taken at a source of income (as one's employer) as an advance payment of income tax

¹with·in \with-ˈin, with-\ *adv* **1** : in or into the interior : INSIDE **2** : inside oneself : INWARDLY ⟨look *within* for imaginative ideas⟩

²within *prep* **1** : in or into the inner part of ⟨*within* the house⟩ **2** : not beyond the bounds or limits of ⟨*within* sight⟩

³within *n* : an inner place or area

with–it \'with-ət\ *adj* : very aware of what is up-to-date and in fashion

¹with·out \with-ˈau̇t, with-\ *prep* **1 a** : ⁴OUTSIDE 1 ⟨they stood *without* the castle gates⟩ **b** : out of the range or limits of ⟨not *without* our capabilities⟩ **2 a** : not having : in the absence of ⟨*without* food⟩ **b** : not accompanied by or showing ⟨spoke *without* thinking⟩

²without *adv* **1** : on the outside **2** : with something lacking or absent ⟨learn to do *without*⟩

³without *n* : an outer place or area

with·stand \with-ˈstand, with-\ *vb* **-stood** \-ˈstu̇d\; **-standing** : to stand against : RESIST; *esp* : to oppose successfully

wit·less \'wit-ləs\ *adj* : lacking wit : FOOLISH — **wit·lessly** *adv* — **wit·less·ness** *n*

¹wit·ness \'wit-nəs\ *n* **1** : TESTIMONY 1 ⟨bear false *witness*⟩ **2** : one who gives evidence especially before a court of law **3 a** : one present at an action (as a wedding) who can testify to its having taken place **b** : one who has personal knowledge or experience of something **4** : something serving as evidence or proof : SIGN

²witness *vb* **1** : to give testimony to : TESTIFY **2** : to act as legal witness of ⟨*witness* a document⟩ **3** : to be or give proof of ⟨their actions *witness* their guilt⟩ **4** : to have personal knowledge of : see for oneself ⟨had *witnessed* the accident⟩

witness stand *n* : an area from which a witness gives evidence in a court

wit·ted \'wit-əd\ *adj* : having wit or understanding — used in combination ⟨quick-*witted*⟩

wit·ti·cism \'wit-ə-ˌsiz-əm\ *n* : a witty saying

witting *adj* **1** : aware of something : CONSCIOUS ⟨a *witting* participant⟩ **2** : done deliberately : INTENTIONAL ⟨a *witting* mistake⟩

wit·ting·ly \'wit-iŋ-lē\ *adv* : with knowledge or awareness of what one is doing : CONSCIOUSLY ⟨you *wittingly* insulted them⟩

wit·ty \'wit-ē\ *adj* **wit·ti·er**; **-est** : marked by or full of wit : AMUSING ⟨a *witty* writer⟩ ⟨a *witty* remark⟩ — **wit·ti·ly** \'wit-ᵊl-ē\ *adv* — **wit·ti·ness** \'wit-ē-nəs\ *n*

wives *plural of* WIFE

wiz \'wiz\ *n* : WIZARD 2

\ə\ abut	\au̇\ out	\i\ tip	\ȯ\ saw	\u̇\ foot
\ər\ further	\ch\ chin	\ī\ life	\ȯi\ coin	\y\ yet
\a\ mat	\e\ pet	\j\ job	\th\ thin	\yü\ few
\ā\ take	\ē\ easy	\ŋ\ sing	\th\ this	\yu̇\ cure
\ä\ cot, cart	\g\ go	\ō\ bone	\ü\ food	\zh\ vision

wiz·ard \\'wiz-ərd\\ *n* **1** : a person skilled in magic : SORCERER, MAGICIAN **2** : a very clever or skillful person ⟨computer *wizards*⟩ [Middle English *wysard* "wise man, a person skilled in magic," from *wis, wys* "wise," from Old English *wis* "wise"]

wiz·ard·ry \\'wiz-ə(r)-drē\\ *n, pl* **-ries** **1** : the art or practices of a wizard : SORCERY **2 a** : a seemingly magical power or influence ⟨the *wizardry* of modern computers⟩ **b** : extraordinary skill or ability ⟨athletic *wizardry*⟩

wiz·en \\'wiz-ᵊn\\ *vb* **wiz·ened; wiz·en·ing** : to become shrunken or wrinkled often as a result of aging

¹wob·ble \\'wäb-əl\\ *vb* **wob·bled; wob·bling** \\-(ə-)liŋ\\ **1 a** : to move or cause to move with a jerky rocking or side-to-side motion ⟨the baby's head *wobbled* from side to side⟩ **b** : ¹TREMBLE 1 ⟨a voice that *wobbles*⟩ **2** : WAVER 1 ⟨his opinion *wobbled*⟩ — **wob·bler** \\'wäb-(ə-)lər\\ *n* — **wob·bly** \\-(ə-)lē\\ *adj*

²wobble *n* : a wobbling action or movement ⟨the wheel had a bad *wobble*⟩

woe \\'wō\\ *n* **1** : great suffering from loss, misfortune, or trouble **2** : ²TROUBLE 1b ⟨economic *woes*⟩ **synonyms** see SORROW

woe·be·gone \\'wō-bi-ˌgòn *also* -ˌgän\\ *adj* **1** : showing great woe, sorrow, or misery ⟨*woebegone* faces⟩ **2** : being in a sad state ⟨a *woebegone* village⟩

woe·ful \\'wō-fəl\\ *adj* **1** : full of woe ⟨a *woeful* tale⟩ **2** : involving or bringing woe ⟨a *woeful* occurrence⟩ **3** : pitifully bad ⟨*woeful* ignorance⟩ — **woe·ful·ly** \\-f(ə-)lē\\ *adv* — **woe·ful·ness** \\-fəl-nəs\\ *n*

wok \\'wäk\\ *n* : a large bowl-shaped cooking utensil used especially in making Chinese food [Chinese]

woke *past and past participle of* WAKE

woken *past participle of* WAKE

wold \\'wōld\\ *n* : a high plain or hilly area usually without woods

¹wolf \\'wùlf\\ *n, pl* **wolves** \\'wùlvz\\ **1** *pl also* **wolf** : any of several large bushy-tailed mammals with ears standing straight up that resemble the related dogs, that prey on other animals, and that often live and hunt in packs; *esp* : GRAY WOLF — compare COYOTE, JACKAL **2** : a person who resembles a wolf in fierceness — **wolf·ish** \\'wùl-fish\\ *adj* — **wolf·like** \\'wùl-ˌflīk\\ *adj*

¹wolf 1

²wolf *vb* : to eat greedily : DEVOUR ⟨*wolfed* down the sandwiches⟩

wolf dog *n* **1** : any of various large dogs formerly kept for hunting wolves **2** : a hybrid offspring of a wolf and a domestic dog

wolf·hound \\'wùlf-ˌhaùnd\\ *n* : any of several large dogs used especially formerly in hunting large animals (as wolves)

wol·fram \\'wùl-frəm\\ *n* : TUNGSTEN

wol·fram·ite \\'wùl-frə-ˌmīt\\ *n* : a brownish or grayish black mineral that contains tungsten in combination with iron, manganese, and oxygen and that is used as a source of tungsten

wolf spider *n* : any of various active wandering spiders of which most do not build a web but chase and catch their prey

wol·ver·ine \\ˌwùl-və-'rēn\\ *n, pl* **wolverines** *also* **wolverine** : a mostly dark brown mammal with shaggy fur that is related to the weasels, martens, and sables, eats flesh, and is found chiefly in northern forests

wom·an \\'wùm-ən\\ *n, pl* **wom·en** \\'wim-ən\\ **1** : an adult female person **2** : WOMANKIND **3** : a woman who is a servant or attendant [Old English *wīfman* "a female person," from *wīf* "woman, wife" and *man* "person"]

wom·an·hood \\'wùm-ən-ˌhùd\\ *n* **1** : the state of being a woman **2** : qualities associated with women **3** : WOMANKIND

wom·an·ish \\'wùm-ə-nish\\ *adj* **1** : typical of a woman **2** : UNMANLY a

wom·an·kind \\'wùm-ən-ˌkīnd\\ *n* : female human beings : women especially as distinguished from men

wom·an·like \\'wùm-ən-ˌlīk\\ *adj* : resembling or typical of a woman : WOMANLY

wom·an·ly \\'wùm-ən-lē\\ *adj* : marked by qualities typical of a woman

womb \\'wüm\\ *n* **1** : UTERUS **2** : a place where something is begun or developed

wom·bat \\'wüm-ˌbat\\ *n* : any of several stocky burrowing Australian marsupials that resemble small bears

wom·en·folk \\'wim-ən-ˌfòk\\ *also* **wom·en·folks** \\-ˌfōks\\ *n pl* : women especially of one family or group

women's rights *n pl* : legal, political, and social rights for women equal to those of men

¹won *past and past participle of* WIN

²won \\'wòn\\ *n, pl* **won** **1** : the basic unit of money of North Korea and South Korea **2** : a coin or bill representing one won

¹won·der \\'wən-dər\\ *n* **1** : something extraordinary or surprising : MARVEL ⟨the pyramid is a *wonder* of ancient Egypt⟩ **2 a** : a feeling (as awe, astonishment, or uncertainty) caused by something extraordinary, mysterious, or new to one's experience **b** : the quality of exciting wonder ⟨the charm and *wonder* of the scene⟩

²wonder *vb* **won·dered; won·der·ing** \\-d(ə-)riŋ\\ **1** : to feel surprise or amazement **2** : to have curiosity or doubt ⟨I always *wondered* about that⟩ — **won·der·er** \\-dər-ər\\ *n*

wonder drug *n* : a usually newly discovered drug capable of producing a noticeable and favorable change in a patient's condition — called also *miracle drug*

won·der·ful \\'wən-dər-fəl\\ *adj* **1** : exciting wonder : MARVELOUS ⟨a sight *wonderful* to behold⟩ **2** : unusually good : ADMIRABLE ⟨having a *wonderful* time⟩ — **won·der·ful·ly** \\-f(ə-)lē\\ *adv*

won·der·land \\'wən-dər-ˌland, -lənd\\ *n* : a place filled with wonders or surprises ⟨a scenic *wonderland*⟩

won·der·ment \\'wən-dər-mənt\\ *n* **1** : AMAZEMENT **2** : curiosity about something

won·drous \\'wən-drəs\\ *adj* : WONDERFUL ⟨a *wondrous* place⟩ — **wondrous** *adv, archaic* — **won·drous·ly** *adv* — **won·drous·ness** *n*

¹wont \\'wònt, 'wōnt\\ *adj* : being in the habit of doing ⟨got up early as he is *wont* to do⟩

²wont *n* : usual custom

won't \\(')wōnt, 'wənt\\ : will not

wont·ed \\'wònt-əd, 'wōnt-\\ *adj* : CUSTOMARY **2** ⟨acted with their *wonted* politeness⟩

woo \\'wü\\ *vb* **1** : to try to gain the love of : COURT **2** : to seek to gain or bring about ⟨political candidates *wooing* public support⟩

¹wood \\'wùd\\ *n* **1** : a dense growth of trees usually smaller than a forest — often used in plural ⟨a thick *woods* runs along the ridge⟩ **2** : a hard fibrous substance that is basically xylem and makes up the greater part of the stems, branches, and roots of trees or shrubs beneath the bark; *also* : this material prepared for some use (as burning or building) **3** : something made of wood; *esp* : a golf club having a wooden head — **out of the woods** : clear of danger or difficulty

²wood *adj* **1** : WOODEN 1 **2** : suitable for cutting or working wood ⟨*wood* chisels⟩ **3** *or* **woods** \\'wùdz\\ : living, growing, or existing in woods

wood alcohol *n* : METHANOL

wood·bine \\'wùd-ˌbīn\\ *n* **1** : a woody climbing Eurasian honeysuckle **2** : VIRGINIA CREEPER

wood·block \\'wùd-ˌbläk\\ *n* : WOODCUT

wood–carv·er \\-ˌkär-vər\\ *n* : a person who carves objects of wood — **wood carv·ing** \\-viŋ\\ *n*

wood·chop·per \\-ˌchäp-ər\\ *n* : one that chops wood and especially chops down trees

wood·chuck \\-ˌchək\\ *n* : a stocky marmot mostly of Alaska, Canada, and the northeastern U.S. — called also *groundhog*

woodchuck

wood·cock \\-ˌkäk\\ *n, pl* **wood·cocks** *or* **woodcock** : a brownish woodland game bird that has a long bill and is related to the snipes; *also* : a related and similar bird of Eurasia

wood·craft \\-ˌkraft\\ *n* **1** : knowledge about the woods and how to take care of oneself in them **2** : skill in working with or making things of wood

wood·cut \\-ˌkət\\ *n* **1** : a printing surface having a raised design carved from a block of wood **2** : a print from a woodcut

wood·cut·ter \\-ˌkət-ər\\ *n* : one that cuts wood especially as an occupation

wood duck *n* : a showy American duck which nests in the hollowed-out spaces of trees and the male of which has a large crest on the head and feathers colored with green, black, purple, white, and brown

wood·ed \\'wùd-əd\\ *adj* : covered with trees

wood·en \\'wùd-ᵊn\\ *adj* **1** : made of wood ⟨a *wooden* spoon⟩ **2** : lacking in spirit, ease, or charm ⟨written in a *wooden* style⟩ — **wood·en·ly** *adv* — **wood·en·ness** \\-ᵊn-(n)əs\\ *n*

wood engraving *n* **1** : a printing surface consisting of a design cut into a block of wood **2** : a print from a wood engraving

wood frog *n* : a common North American frog that is found mostly in moist woodlands and is dark brown, yellowish brown, or pink with a black stripe on each side of the head

¹wood·land \\'wùd-lənd, -ˌland\\ *n* : land covered with trees and shrubs : FOREST

²woodland *adj* **1** : growing, living, or occurring in woodland ⟨a *woodland* bird⟩ **2** : of, relating to, or made up of woodland ⟨*woodland* areas⟩

wood·lot \\'wùd-ˌlät\\ *n* : an area of trees kept usually to meet fuel and lumber needs

wood louse *n* : a small flat grayish crustacean that is an isopod, lives in damp places (as under stones, fallen leaves, and rotting logs), and is often capable of rolling its body into a ball — called also *pill bug, sow bug*

wood·man \\'wùd-mən\\ *n* : WOODSMAN

wood·peck·er \\-ˌpek-ər\\ *n* : any of numerous brightly marked birds with strong claws and stiff tail feathers used in climbing or resting on tree trunks, a long flexible tongue, and a very hard bill used to drill into trees to get insects for food and to dig out holes for nesting

wood·pile \\-ˌpīl\\ *n* : a pile of wood and especially firewood

wood rat *n* : any of numerous soft-furred rodents of North and Central America that have furry tails, large ears, and a tendency to hoard food and debris — compare PACK RAT

woodpecker

wood·shed \\-ˌshed\\ *n* : a shed for storing wood and especially firewood

woods·man \\'wùdz-mən\\ *n* : a person who visits or works in the woods; *esp* : one skilled in woodcraft

wood sorrel *n* : any of a genus of herbs with acid sap, leaves having leaflets, and flowers with five petals; *esp* : a stemless herb having leaves with three leaflets that is sometimes considered to be the original shamrock

woodsy \\'wùd-zē\\ *adj* **woods·i·er**; **-est** : of, relating to, or suggestive of woods ⟨a *woodsy* smell⟩

wood·wind \\'wùd-ˌwind\\ *n* **1** : one of a group of musical instruments including flutes, clarinets, oboes, bassoons, and sometimes saxophones — compare BRASS INSTRUMENT, PERCUSSION INSTRUMENT, STRINGED INSTRUMENT **2** *pl* : the woodwind instruments of a band or orchestra — **woodwind** *adj*

wood·work \\-ˌwərk\\ *n* : work made of wood; *esp* : interior fittings (as window frames or stairways) of wood

wood·work·ing \\-ˌwər-kiŋ\\ *n* : the act, process, or occupation of working with wood — **wood·work·er** \\-kər\\ *n*

woody \\'wùd-ē\\ *adj* **wood·i·er**; **-est 1** : having or covered with trees ⟨a *woody* piece of land⟩ **2** : of or containing wood or wood fibers ⟨*woody* plant tissue⟩ **3** : characteristic of or similar to wood ⟨a *woody* texture⟩

woo·er \\'wü-ər\\ *n* : one that woos : SUITOR

¹woof \\'wùf, 'wüf\\ *n* **1** : the threads that cross the warp in a woven fabric **2** : a woven fabric or its texture [Middle English *oof* "threads, crossing the warp," from Old English *ōwef* (same meaning), from *ō-* "on" (from *on*) and *-wef* (related to *web* "web" and *wefan* "to weave")]

²woof \\'wùf\\ *vb* : to make the sound of a woof

³woof *n* : a deep harsh sound made by a dog [a word created in imitation of the sound]

woof·er \\'wùf-ər\\ *n* : a loudspeaker larger than a tweeter that responds only to low sound frequencies and produces sounds of low pitch — compare TWEETER

wool \\'wùl\\ *n* **1** : the soft wavy or curly usually thick undercoat of various mammals and especially the sheep **2** : a fabric or garment made of wool **3** : material that resembles a mass of wool — **wooled** \\'wùld\\ *adj*

¹wool·en *or* **wool·len** \\'wùl-ən\\ *adj* **1** : made of wool **2** : of or relating to the manufacture or sale of woolen products

²woolen *or* **woollen** *n* **1** : a fabric made of wool **2** : garments of woolen fabric — usually used in plural

wool·gath·er·ing \\'wùl-ˌgath-(ə-)riŋ\\ *n* : the act of daydreaming

¹wool·ly *also* **wooly** \\'wùl-ē\\ *adj* **wool·li·er**; **-est 1 a** : of, relating to, or bearing wool ⟨*woolly* animals⟩ **b** : resembling wool **2** : marked by mental confusion ⟨*woolly* thinking⟩ **3** : marked by roughness or disorder ⟨the wild and *woolly* West⟩ — **wool·li·ness** *n*

²wool·ly *also* **wooly** *or* **wool·ie** \\'wùl-ē\\ *n, pl* **wool·lies** : a woolen garment; *esp* : underclothing of knitted wool — usually used in plural

woolly bear *n* : any of various rather large very hairy moth caterpillars; *esp* : one that is the larva of a tiger moth

woolly mammoth *n* : an extinct mammal that was a heavy-coated mammoth of cold northern regions and is known from fossils, from the drawings of prehistoric human beings, and from entire dead frozen bodies dug up in Siberia

woo·zy \\'wü-zē\\ *adj* **woo·zi·er**; **-est** : slightly dizzy, nauseous, or weak

Worces·ter·shire sauce \\'wùs-tər-ˌshir-, -shər-\\ *n* : a sauce whose ingredients include soy sauce, vinegar, and

\\ə\\ **abut**	\\aù\\ **out**	\\i\\ **tip**	\\ȯ\\ **saw**	\\ù\\ **foot**
\\ər\\ **further**	\\ch\\ **chin**	\\ī\\ **life**	\\ȯi\\ **coin**	\\y\\ **yet**
\\a\\ **mat**	\\e\\ **pet**	\\j\\ **job**	\\th\\ **thin**	\\yü\\ **few**
\\ā\\ **take**	\\ē\\ **easy**	\\ŋ\\ **sing**	\\th\\ **this**	\\yù\\ **cure**
\\ä\\ **cot, cart**	\\g\\ **go**	\\ō\\ **bone**	\\ü\\ **food**	\\zh\\ **vision**

garlic — called also *Worcestershire* [from *Worcestershire*, England, where it was originally made]

¹word \'wərd\ *n* **1** : a sound or combination of sounds that has meaning and is spoken by a human being **2** : a written or printed letter or letters standing for a spoken word **3** : a brief remark or conversation ⟨could I have a *word* with you⟩ **4** : ¹ORDER 5b ⟨give the *word* to begin⟩ **5** : NEWS 1 ⟨any *word* on how they are⟩ **6** : ¹PROMISE 1 ⟨I give you my *word*⟩ **7** : a remark or conversation uttered in anger — usually used in plural ⟨*words* were exchanged and a fight broke out⟩ — **good word 1** : a favorable statement ⟨put in a *good word* for me⟩ **2** : good news ⟨what's the *good word*⟩ — **in a word** : in short — **in so many words 1** : in exactly those words ⟨implied that such behavior was unacceptable but didn't say so *in so many words*⟩ **2** : in plain straightforward language ⟨told him *in so many words* that he wasn't welcome⟩ — **of few words** : not saying more than is necessary ⟨a man *of few words*⟩ — **of one's word** : that can be relied on to keep a promise ⟨a woman *of her word*⟩

²word *vb* : to express in words : PHRASE ⟨*worded* their request with great care⟩

word·age \'wərd-ij\ *n* : a quantity or number of words

word·book \'wərd-ˌbùk\ *n* : VOCABULARY 1, DICTIONARY

word–for–word *adj* : being in or following the exact words : VERBATIM ⟨a *word-for-word* translation⟩

word for word *adv* : in the exact words : VERBATIM ⟨repeated the message *word for word*⟩

word·ing \'wərd-iŋ\ *n* : the way in which something is put into words

word·less \'wərd-ləs\ *adj* **1** : not expressed in or having words ⟨a *wordless* picture book⟩ **2** : SILENT 1, SPEECHLESS ⟨sat *wordless* throughout the meeting⟩ — **word·less·ly** *adv* — **word·less·ness** *n*

word of mouth : spoken communication

word order *n* : the order or arrangement of words in a phrase, clause, or sentence

word·play \'wərd-ˌplā\ *n* : wit that is based on the clever use of words

word processing *n* : the production of typewritten documents (as business letters) with automated and usually computerized equipment for preparing text

word processor *n* : a keyboard-operated terminal usually with a video display and a magnetic storage device for use in word processing; *also* : software (as for a computer system) to perform word processing

wordy \'wərd-ē\ *adj* **word·i·er; -est** : using or containing too many words — **word·i·ly** \'wərd-ᵊl-ē\ *adv* — **word·i·ness** \'wərd-ē-nəs\ *n*

wore *past of* WEAR

¹work \'wərk\ *n* **1 a** : the use of one's strength or ability to get something done or to achieve a result : LABOR, TOIL **b** : the work done as one's regular job; *also* : the place of one's employment ⟨didn't go to *work* today⟩ **c** : something to be done : TASK ⟨have *work* to do⟩ **2** : the energy used when a force is applied over a given distance **3 a** : something that results from a particular manner or method of working, operating, or devising ⟨careful police *work*⟩ **b** : something that results from the use or shaping of a particular material ⟨porcelain *work*⟩ **4** : a fortified structure (as a fort or trench) **5** *pl* : a place where industrial labor is done : PLANT, FACTORY ⟨cement *works*⟩ **6** *pl* : the working or moving parts of a mechanical device ⟨the *works* of a watch⟩ **7** : something produced by hard work or skill ⟨a writer's first *work*⟩ **8** : manner of working : WORKMANSHIP ⟨careless *work*⟩ **9** *pl* **a** : everything available, possessed, or belonging ⟨a hamburger with the *works*⟩ **b** : the harshest treatment possible ⟨gave him the *works*⟩ [Old English *werc, weorc* "work, activity directed toward accomplishing something"] — **at work 1** : doing work : BUSY; *esp* : taking part in one's regular occupation **2** : having effect : OPERATING ⟨medicine *at work* in the

body⟩ — **in the works** : in process of preparation, development, or completion ⟨a plan for change is now *in the works*⟩ — **out of work** : without a regular job

²work *adj* **1** : used for work ⟨a *work* elephant⟩ **2** : suitable for wear while working ⟨*work* clothes⟩

³work *vb* **worked** \'wərkt\ *or* **wrought** \'rȯt\; **work·ing 1** : to bring about : EFFECT ⟨*work* a cure⟩ **2 a** : to prepare by stirring or shaping ⟨*work* dough⟩ **b** : to bring into a desired form by a manufacturing process ⟨*work* cold steel⟩ **3** : to set or keep in motion or operation ⟨a pump *worked* by hand⟩ **4** : to solve by reasoning or figuring ⟨*work* an arithmetic problem⟩ **5 a** : to cause to labor ⟨*worked* the crew hard⟩ **b** : to make use of : EXPLOIT ⟨*work* a mine⟩ **6** : to pay for with labor ⟨*work* off a debt⟩ **7 a** : to get into or out of a state or position by stages ⟨*worked* the boat loose⟩ **b** : CONTRIVE 3, ARRANGE ⟨*work* it so that you can leave soon⟩ **8** : EXCITE 1, PROVOKE ⟨*worked* myself into a rage⟩ **9 a** : to make an effort especially for a long period **b** : to perform a task requiring extended effort or repeated operations **c** : to perform work regularly for wages ⟨*works* in advertising⟩ **10** : to function or operate properly ⟨hinges *work* better with oil⟩ **11** : to produce a desired effect : SUCCEED ⟨my plan *worked*⟩ **12** : to move gradually into a certain position or state ⟨the knot *worked* loose⟩ [Old English *wyrcan* "to create, cause to happen, shape"] — **work on** : to try to influence or persuade ⟨*working on* them to change their votes⟩

synonyms WORK, LABOR, TOIL mean to exert oneself at a physical or mental task. WORK applies to any effort, pleasant or not, that achieves a goal ⟨*worked* to discover a cure⟩. LABOR applies especially to physical work that is often hard and unpleasant ⟨*labored* for weeks to harvest all the crops⟩. TOIL applies to work that is long, hard, and very tiring ⟨*toiled* all day in the hot sun⟩.

work·able \'wər-kə-bəl\ *adj* **1** : capable of being worked **2** : FEASIBLE ⟨a *workable* solution to the problem⟩

work·a·day \'wər-kə-ˌdā\ *adj* : EVERYDAY ⟨*workaday* clothes⟩ ⟨*workaday* activities⟩

work·bench \'wərk-ˌbench\ *n* : a bench on which work is done

work·book \-ˌbùk\ *n* : a book of problems or practice examples for a student to use as part of a course of study

work·day \-ˌdā\ *n* **1** : a day on which work is performed **2** : the period of time in a day during which work is performed — **workday** *adj*

worked up *adj* : emotionally excited ⟨all *worked up* over the football game⟩

work·er \'wər-kər\ *n* **1 a** : one that works **b** : a member of the working class **2** : one of the members of a colony of social ants, bees, wasps, or termites that are only partially developed sexually and that perform most of the labor and protective duties of the colony

work·force \'wərk-ˌfō(ə)rs, -ˌfȯ(ə)rs\ *n* : the workers of a specific activity or business ⟨the factory's *workforce*⟩

work·horse \'wərk-ˌhó(ə)rs\ *n* **1** : a horse used for hard work (as on a farm) **2 a** : a person who does most of the work of a group task **b** : something that is useful, durable, or dependable

work·house \'wərk-ˌhaùs\ *n* **1** *British* : POORHOUSE **2** : a place where persons who have committed minor wrongdoings are kept

¹work·ing \'wər-kiŋ\ *n* : the manner of functioning or operating : OPERATION — usually used in plural ⟨the inner *workings* of the motion picture industry⟩

²working *adj* **1 a** : doing work especially for a living ⟨*working* people⟩ **b** : being in an operating state ⟨a *working* model⟩ **2** : good enough to allow work to be done ⟨a *working* majority⟩ ⟨a *working* arrangement⟩

working class *n* : the class of people who work for wages usually in manual labor — **working–class** *adj*

work·ing·man \'wər-kiŋ-ˌman\ *n* : one who works for wages usually at manual labor or in industry

work·load \'wərk-ˌlōd\ *n* **1** : the amount of work or of working time expected or assigned ⟨students with a heavy *workload*⟩ **2** : the amount of work performed or capable of being performed usually within a specific period ⟨a machine's *workload*⟩

work·man \'wərk-mən\ *n* **1** : WORKINGMAN **2** : a skilled worker (as an electrician or carpenter)

work·man·like \'wərk-mən-ˌlīk\ *adj* : worthy of a good worker ⟨did a *workmanlike* job on the boat⟩

work·man·ship \'wərk-mən-ˌship\ *n* **1** : the art or skill of a workman : CRAFTSMANSHIP **2** : the quality of a piece of work ⟨the excellent *workmanship* of the desk⟩

work·out \'wər-ˌkaut\ *n* : a practice or exercise to test or improve one's fitness especially in athletics

work out \ˌwər-'kaut\ *vb* **1** : to bring about by effort or by clearing up difficulties **2 a** : SOLVE ⟨*work* out a math problem⟩ **b** : DEVELOP 2 ⟨*work out* a plan⟩ **3** : to be successful ⟨our plans for reorganization *worked out*⟩ **4** : to perform athletic exercises to improve one's fitness ⟨*working out* at the gym⟩

work·room \'wər-ˌkrüm, -ˌkrum\ *n* : a room used especially for manual work

work·shop \'wərk-ˌshäp\ *n* **1** : a shop where manufacturing or the production of handicrafts is carried on **2** : WORKROOM **3** : a usually brief educational program for a small group of people that focuses especially on techniques and skills in a particular field

work up *vb* **1** : to stir up ⟨*worked up* support for the project⟩ **2** : to produce by mental or physical work ⟨*worked up* a sweat at the gym⟩

work·week \'wərk-ˌwēk\ *n* : the hours or days of work in a calendar week ⟨a 40-hour *workweek*⟩ ⟨a 5-day *workweek*⟩

world \'wər(-ə)ld\ *n* **1** : the earth and all the people and things upon it **2** : people in general : HUMANITY **3** : the system of created things : UNIVERSE **4** : the concerns of the earth and human affairs as distinguished from heaven and the life to come **5** : human society ⟨withdraw from the *world*⟩ **6** : a class of persons sharing a common interest or activity ⟨the musical *world*⟩ **7** : a part or section of the earth and the people who live in it **8** : the scene of one's life and action ⟨living in your own little *world*⟩ **9** : a great number or amount ⟨a *world* of troubles⟩ **10** : a heavenly body (as a planet) especially if lived upon — **in the world** : among many possibilities : EVER ⟨what *in the world* is it⟩ — **out of this world** : very good : SUPERB

world beat *n* : WORLD MUSIC — **world–beat** *adj*

world–class *adj* : being of the highest degree of excellence in the world ⟨a *world-class* athlete⟩

world·ling \'wər(-ə)l-dliŋ, 'wərl-liŋ\ *n* : a person busy with the affairs of this world

world·ly \'wər(-ə)l-dlē, 'wərl-lē\ *adj* **1** : of, relating to, or concerned with the affairs of this world rather than with spiritual affairs **2** : WORLDLY-WISE — **world·li·ness** *n*

world·ly–wise \'wərl-dlē-ˌwīz, -lē-\ *adj* : wise as to things and ways of this world

world music *n* : popular music based on non-Western musical traditions and often having a danceable rhythm — **world–music** *adj*

world war *n* : a war involving all or most of the chief nations of the world; *esp, cap both Ws* : either of two such wars of the 20th century

world·wide \'wər(-ə)l-'dwīd\ *adj* : going all over the world — **worldwide** *adv*

World Wide Web *n* : a part of the Internet designed to allow easier navigation of the network through the use of text and graphics that link to other documents

¹worm \'wərm\ *n* **1 a** : EARTHWORM **b** : any of various long creeping or crawling animals (as a grub or tapeworm) that usually have soft bodies **2** : a person who is

hated or pitied : WRETCH **3** *pl* : infection with or disease caused by parasitic worms **4** : something in the form of a coil **5** : a usually small self-contained and self-replicating computer program that invades computers on a network and usually performs a destructive action — compare TROJAN HORSE 2, VIRUS 3 — **worm·like** \-ˌlīk\ *adj*

²worm *vb* **1** : to obtain by cleverness or trickery or by pleading or persuading ⟨*wormed* the truth out of him⟩ **2** : to move, go, or work slowly in the manner of a worm ⟨*wormed* out of the trap⟩ ⟨*wormed* my way into a job⟩ **3** : to rid (as a dog) of parasitic worms

worm·er \'wər-mər\ *n* : a drug used to destroy parasitic worms in an animal

worm gear *n* : a mechanical linkage consisting of a short rotating screw whose threads fit together with the teeth of a gearwheel

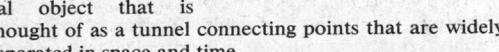

worm gear

worm·hole \'wərm-ˌhōl\ *n* **1** : a hole or passage made by a worm **2** : a hypothetical object that is thought of as a tunnel connecting points that are widely separated in space and time

worm·wood \'wərm-ˌwud\ *n* **1** : a European plant that is related to the daisies and yields a bitter dark green oil **2** : something bitter or painful ⟨it was *wormwood* for him to accept charity⟩

wormy \'wər-mē\ *adj* **worm·i·er; -est** **1** : containing, swarming with, or damaged by worms ⟨*wormy* soil⟩ ⟨*wormy* flour⟩ **2** : resembling or suggestive of a worm ⟨*wormy* creatures⟩

worn *past participle of* WEAR

worn–out \'wō(ə)r-'naut, 'wo(ə)r-\ *adj* **1** : useless from long or hard wear ⟨*worn-out* skates⟩ **2** : very weary ⟨*worn-out* shoppers⟩

wor·ried \'wər-ēd, 'wə-rēd\ *adj* : having worries : marked by or showing worry ⟨very *worried* about the test⟩ ⟨a *worried* look⟩ — **wor·ried·ly** *adv*

wor·ri·some \'wər-ē-səm, 'wə-rē-\ *adj* **1** : causing worry ⟨*worrisome* news⟩ **2** : given to worrying ⟨*worrisome* parents⟩

¹wor·ry \'wər-ē, 'wə-rē\ *vb* **wor·ried; wor·ry·ing** **1** : to shake and tear or mangle with the teeth ⟨a puppy *worrying* an old shoe⟩ **2** : to make anxious or upset ⟨his absence *worried* his friends⟩ **3** : to feel or express great concern : FRET ⟨*worrying* about her health⟩ — **wor·ri·er** *n*

²worry *n, pl* **worries** **1** : ANXIETY 1 **2** : a cause of anxiety : TROUBLE

wor·ry·wart \'wər-ē-ˌwort, 'wə-rē-\ *n* : a person who worries without reasonable cause

¹worse \'wərs\ *adj, comparative of* BAD *or of* ILL **1** : of poorer quality, value, or condition ⟨that car is in *worse* shape than the one you sold⟩ **2 a** : more unfavorable, unpleasant, or painful ⟨a *worse* punishment⟩ **b** : more faulty, unsuitable, or incorrect ⟨can't imagine *worse* ideas⟩ **c** : less skillful or efficient ⟨*worse* than any mechanic I know⟩ **3** : being in poorer health ⟨the child was *worse* the next day⟩ **4** : bad or evil in greater degree ⟨whether stealing is *worse* than cheating⟩

²worse *n* **1** : something worse ⟨threatened detention and

\ə\ **abut**	\au\ **out**	\i\ **tip**	\o\ **saw**	\u\ **foot**
\ər\ **further**	\ch\ **chin**	\ī\ **life**	\oi\ **coin**	\y\ **yet**
\a\ **mat**	\e\ **pet**	\j\ **job**	\th\ **thin**	\yu\ **few**
\ā\ **take**	\ē\ **easy**	\ŋ\ **sing**	\th\ **this**	\yu\ **cure**
\ä\ **cot, cart**	\g\ **go**	\ō\ **bone**	\ü\ **food**	\zh\ **vision**

worse⟩ **2** : a greater degree of ill or badness ⟨a turn for the *worse*⟩

³**worse** *adv, comparative of* BAD *or* BADLY *or of* ILL : in a worse manner : to a worse extent or degree ⟨slept *worse* than ever⟩

wors·en \'wərs-ᵊn\ *vb* **wors·ened; wors·en·ing** \'wərs-niŋ, -ᵊn-iŋ\ : to make or become worse ⟨the weather *worsened*⟩

¹**wor·ship** \'wər-shəp\ *n* **1** *chiefly British* : an important person — used as a title for some officials **2 a** : great respect toward a divine being or supernatural power **b** : the outward showing of such respect **3** : too great admiration or devotion ⟨*worship* of money⟩ [Middle English *worshipe* "worthiness, respect, reverence paid to a divine being," from Old English *weorthscipe* "worthiness, respect," from *weorth* "worth, worthy" and *-scipe* "-ship (quality, condition)"]

²**worship** *vb* **-shipped** *also* **-shiped; -ship·ping** *also* **-ship·ing** **1** : to honor or respect as a divine being or supernatural power **2** : to treat with too great respect, honor, or devotion : IDOLIZE ⟨*worshipped* popular singers⟩ **3** : to perform or take part in worship — **wor·ship·per** *or* **wor·ship·er** *n*

wor·ship·ful \'wər-shəp-fəl\ *adj* : giving worship

¹**worst** \'wərst\ *adj, superlative of* BAD *or of* ILL **1** : most bad, evil, or ill ⟨his *worst* habit⟩ **2 a** : most unfavorable, unpleasant, or painful ⟨the *worst* problem imaginable⟩ **b** : most unsuitable, faulty, unattractive, or ill-conceived ⟨has the *worst* manners⟩ **c** : least skillful or efficient ⟨the *worst* plumber you can hire⟩ **3** : most wanting in quality, value, or condition ⟨farmed the *worst* land⟩ — **the worst way** : very much ⟨wanted a new bicycle in *the worst way*⟩

²**worst** *adv, superlative of* BAD *or* BADLY *or of* ILL **1** : to the greatest degree of badness ⟨sings *worst*⟩ **2** : to the greatest degree ⟨needed help *worst*⟩

³**worst** *n* **1** : one that is worst ⟨always chooses the *worst*⟩ **2** : the greatest degree of ill or badness ⟨if worse comes to *worst*⟩

⁴**worst** *vb* : to get the better of : DEFEAT ⟨*worsted* his opponents⟩

wor·sted \'wus-təd, 'wər-stəd\ *n* **1** : a smooth compact yarn from long wool fibers **2** : a fabric made from worsted yarns [named for *Worsted* (now *Worstead*) a village in England where the fabric was made] — **worsted** *adj*

wort \'wərt, 'wȯ(ə)rt\ *n* : a sweet liquid that is drained from mash made from crushed malt or grain meal and that is fermented to make beer and whiskey

¹**worth** \'wərth\ *prep* **1 a** : equal in value to ⟨the vase is *worth* $200⟩ **b** : having possessions or income equal to ⟨an actress *worth* millions⟩ **2** : deserving of ⟨well *worth* the effort⟩ **3** : capable of ⟨ran for all I was *worth*⟩

²**worth** *n* **1 a** : value in terms of money ⟨furniture of little *worth*⟩ **b** : the equivalent of a certain amount or figure ⟨five dollars *worth* of gas⟩ **2** : the value of something measured by its qualities ⟨an experience of great *worth*⟩ **3** : EXCELLENCE 1

worth·less \'wərth-ləs\ *adj* **1 a** : lacking worth : VALUELESS **b** : USELESS ⟨*worthless* to continue searching⟩ **2** : deserving of hatred or pity ⟨a *worthless* coward⟩ — **worth·less·ly** *adv* — **worth·less·ness** *n*

worth·while \'wərth-'hwī(ə)l, -'wī(ə)l\ *adj* **1** : being worth the time or effort spent ⟨*worthwhile* preparations⟩ **2** : WORTHY 1a

¹**wor·thy** \'wər-thē\ *adj* **wor·thi·er; -est** **1 a** : having worth or value ⟨a *worthy* cause⟩ **b** : HONORABLE 1 ⟨*worthy* candidates⟩ **2** : having enough value or excellence ⟨a student *worthy* of the prize⟩ — **wor·thi·ly** \-thə-lē\ *adv* — **wor·thi·ness** \-thē-nəs\ *n*

²**worthy** *n, pl* **worthies** : a worthy person

wot *present 1st & 3rd singular of* WIT

would \wəd, əd, d, (')wu̇d\ *vb, past of* WILL **1** : strongly desire : WISH ⟨I *would* I were young again⟩ **2** — used as

a helping verb to express (1) preference or willingness ⟨I *would* sooner die than face them⟩, (2) wish or intent ⟨those who *would* forbid free access to books⟩, (3) plan or intention ⟨said they *would* come⟩, (4) custom or usual behavior ⟨we *would* meet often for lunch⟩, (5) consent or choice ⟨*would* put it off if they could⟩, (6) possibility ⟨if they were coming, they *would* be here now⟩, (7) completion of a statement of desire, request, or advice ⟨I wish that you *would* go⟩, or (8) probability or likelihood in past or present time ⟨*would* have won if she had not tripped⟩ **3** : COULD ⟨the pitcher *would* hold two liters⟩ **4** — used as a helping verb to word a polite request or to show doubt or uncertainty ⟨*would* you please help us⟩ ⟨the explanation *would* seem satisfactory⟩ **5** : SHOULD ⟨knew I *would* enjoy the trip⟩ ⟨*would* be glad to know the answer⟩

would–be \'wu̇d-,bē\ *adj* : desiring, intending, or pretending to be ⟨a *would-be* poet⟩

wouldn't \'wu̇d-ᵊnt\ : would not

wouldst \wədst, (')wu̇dst, wətst\ *archaic past 2nd singular of* WILL

¹**wound** \'wünd\ *n* **1** : an injury involving cutting or breaking of bodily tissue (as by violence, accident, or surgery) **2** : an injury to a person's feelings

²**wound** *vb* **1** : to hurt by cutting or breaking bodily tissue ⟨the broken glass *wounded* several people⟩ **2** : to hurt the feelings or pride of ⟨his remark *wounded* her⟩

³**wound** \'wau̇nd\ *past and past participle of* WIND

¹**wound·ed** \'wün-dəd\ *n pl* : persons that have been wounded

²**wounded** *adj* : injured, hurt by, or suffering from a wound ⟨a *wounded* leg⟩ ⟨*wounded* feelings⟩

wove *past of* WEAVE

woven *past participle of* WEAVE

wrack \'rak\ *n* : violent or total destruction : RUIN

wraith \'rāth\ *n* **1** : GHOST **2** : a bodiless appearance : SHADOW

¹**wran·gle** \'raŋ-gəl\ *vb* **wran·gled; wran·gling** \-g(ə-)liŋ\ **1** : to have an angry quarrel **2** : to take part in an argument **3** : to herd and care for livestock and especially horses on the range

²**wrangle** *n* : an angry, noisy, or lengthy dispute or quarrel

wran·gler \'raŋ-g(ə-)lər\ *n* **1** : a person who quarrels **2** : a ranch hand who takes care of the saddle horses

¹**wrap** \'rap\ *vb* **wrapped; wrap·ping** **1 a** : to cover especially by winding or folding ⟨*wrap* a baby in a blanket⟩ **b** : to enclose and prepare (as for transportation or storage) ⟨*wrap* a package⟩ **c** : ¹EMBRACE 1 ⟨*wrapped* her in my arms⟩ **d** : to coil, fold, or draw about something ⟨*wrap* a rubber band around the sticks⟩ **2 a** : to envelop closely or completely : SURROUND ⟨houses *wrapped* in mist⟩ **b** : to involve completely : ENGROSS ⟨they were *wrapped* up in studying for exams⟩ **3** : to finish filming or recording ⟨*wrap* a movie⟩

²**wrap** *n* **1 a** : a covering that encloses something : WRAPPER **b** : material for wrapping ⟨plastic *wrap*⟩ **2** : an article of clothing that may be wrapped around a person; *esp* : a warm loose outer garment (as a coat or shawl) **3** *pl* : SECRECY 2 ⟨a plan kept under *wraps*⟩ **4** : the completion of a schedule or session for filming or recording

wrap·around \'rap-ə-,rau̇nd\ *adj* **1** : made to be wrapped around the body ⟨a *wraparound* skirt⟩ **2** : made to curve from the front around to the side ⟨*wraparound* sunglasses⟩

wrap·per \'rap-ər\ *n* **1** : a covering or enclosure for something **2** : one that wraps **3** : a garment worn wrapped around the body

wrap·ping \'rap-iŋ\ *n* : WRAPPER 1

wrap–up \'rap-,əp\ *n* : a summarizing report

wrap up \(')rap-'əp\ *vb* **1** : SUMMARIZE, SUM UP **2** : to bring to a conclusion ⟨quickly *wrapped* up the meeting⟩

3 : to guarantee the success of : CINCH ⟨*wrapped up* the nomination⟩

wrath \'rath\ *n* **1** : violent anger **2** : punishment for sin or crime — *synonyms* see ANGER

wrath·ful \'rath-fəl\ *adj* **1** : filled with wrath : very angry **2** : showing wrath ⟨a *wrathful* expression⟩ — **wrath·ful·ly** \-fə-lē\ *adv* — **wrath·ful·ness** *n*

wreak \'rēk\ *vb* : to bring down in or as if in punishment ⟨*wreak* revenge on the enemy⟩ ⟨the storm *wreaked* destruction⟩

wreath \'rēth\ *n, pl* **wreaths** \'rēthz, 'rēths\ : something twisted or woven into a circular shape ⟨a *wreath* of flowers⟩

wreathe \'rēth\ *vb* **wreathed; wreath·ing** **1** : to form into a wreath **2** : to crown, decorate, or cover with or as if with a wreath ⟨ivy *wreathed* the pole⟩

¹**wreck** \'rek\ *n* **1** : goods cast upon the land by the sea after a shipwreck **2** : ¹SHIPWRECK 2 **3** : the action of wrecking **4** : a destructive crash ⟨was injured in a car *wreck*⟩ **5** : the broken remains of something wrecked or ruined **6** : something in a state of ruin or decay ⟨the old house was a *wreck*⟩ **7** : a person in poor health or spirits

²**wreck** *vb* **1 a** : to reduce to a state of ruin by or as if by violence ⟨a country *wrecked* by war⟩ ⟨jealousy *wrecked* their friendship⟩ **b** : ²SHIPWRECK 2 **2** : to damage or ruin by a wreck ⟨*wrecked* the car⟩

wreck·age \'rek-ij\ *n* **1 a** : the act of wrecking **b** : the state of being wrecked **2** : the remains of a wreck

wreck·er \'rek-ər\ *n* **1 a** : one that searches for or works on the wrecks of ships **b** : TOW TRUCK **2** : one that wrecks

wren \'ren\ *n* **1** : any of a family of small mostly brown singing birds with short rounded wings and a short tail that points upward **2** : any of various small singing birds resembling the true wrens in size and habits

wren 1

¹**wrench** \'rench\ *vb* **1** : to move with a violent twist **2** : to pull, strain, or tighten with violent twisting or force **3** : to injure by a violent twisting or straining ⟨*wrenched* my knee while playing football⟩ **4** : to snatch forcibly : WREST

²**wrench** *n* **1 a** : a violent twisting or pull **b** : a sharp twist or sudden jerk that strains muscles or ligaments; *also* : the injury caused by this **2** : a tool for holding, twisting, or turning (as nuts and bolts)

wrest \'rest\ *vb* **1** : to pull, force, or move by violent wringing or twisting movements **2** : to gain by or as if by force or violence ⟨*wrest* power from the king⟩

¹**wres·tle** \'res-əl\ *vb* **wres·tled; wres·tling** \-(ə-)liŋ\ **1** : to struggle with and try to throw down an opponent **2** : to compete against in wrestling **3** : to struggle for control (as of something difficult) — **wres·tler** \'res-lər\ *n*

²**wrestle** *n* : the action or an instance of wrestling

wres·tling \'res-liŋ\ *n* : the sport in which two contestants wrestle each other

wretch \'rech\ *n* **1** : a miserable unhappy person **2** : a mean or evil person

wretch·ed \'rech-əd\ *adj* **1** : very miserable or unhappy **2** : causing misery or distress ⟨that *wretched* accident⟩ **3** : deserving of hatred or disgust ⟨a *wretched* trick⟩ **4** : very poor in quality or ability ⟨*wretched* work⟩ — **wretch·ed·ly** *adv* — **wretch·ed·ness** *n*

¹**wrig·gle** \'rig-əl\ *vb* **wrig·gled; wrig·gling** \-(ə-)liŋ\ **1** : to twist or move to and fro like a worm : SQUIRM ⟨*wriggle* in one's chair⟩ ⟨*wriggle* one's toes⟩ **2** : to move along by twisting and turning ⟨the eel *wriggled* its way upstream⟩

²**wriggle** *n* **1** : a short or quick twisting motion **2** : a formation or marking having a winding or twisting course or appearance

wrig·gler \'rig-(ə-)lər\ *n* : one that wriggles; *esp* : WIGGLER 1

wright \'rīt\ *n* : a worker especially in wood — usually used in combination

wring \'riŋ\ *vb* **wrung** \'rəŋ\; **wring·ing** \'riŋ-iŋ\ **1** : to squeeze or twist especially so as to make dry or to rid of moisture or liquid ⟨*wring* wet clothes⟩ **2** : to get by or as if by twisting or pressing ⟨*wring* the truth out of them⟩ **3** : to twist into an unnatural shape or appearance with a forcible or violent motion ⟨*wring* a chicken's neck⟩ **4** : to cause pain to as if by wringing : TORMENT ⟨their troubles *wrung* our hearts⟩

wring·er \'riŋ-ər\ *n* : one that wrings; *esp* : a machine or device for squeezing out liquid or moisture ⟨clothes *wringer*⟩

¹**wrin·kle** \'riŋ-kəl\ *n* **1** : a crease or small fold on a surface (as of the skin or a piece of cloth) **2** : a clever or new method, trick, or idea — **wrin·kly** \-k(ə-)lē\ *adj*

²**wrinkle** *vb* **wrin·kled; wrin·kling** \-k(ə-)liŋ\ : to develop or cause to develop wrinkles

wrist \'rist\ *n* : the joint or the region of the joint between the human hand and the arm; *also* : a corresponding part of a lower animal

wrist·band \'ris(t)-ˌband\ *n* : a band or a part of a sleeve encircling the wrist

wrist·let \'ris(t)-lət\ *n* : WRISTBAND; *esp* : a close-fitting knitted band at the end of a glove or sleeve

wrist·watch \'ris-ˌtwäch\ *n* : a small watch attached to a bracelet or strap to fasten about the wrist

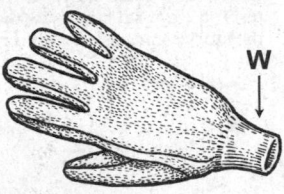

W wristlet

writ \'rit\ *n* **1** : something written : WRITING ⟨Holy *Writ*⟩ **2** : a written legal order signed by a court officer

write \'rīt\ *vb* **wrote** \'rōt\; **writ·ten** \'rit-ᵊn\ *also* **writ** \'rit\; **writ·ing** \'rīt-iŋ\ **1** : to form letters or words on a surface with an instrument (as a pen or pencil) ⟨learn to read and *write*⟩ **2** : to form the letters or the words of (as on paper) ⟨*write* your name⟩ ⟨*write* a check⟩ **3** : to spell in writing ⟨words *written* alike but pronounced differently⟩ **4** : to express in writing ⟨*write* what you felt about the experience⟩ **5 a** : to make up and set down for others to read ⟨*write* a book⟩ **b** : to compose music **6** : to write a letter to ⟨*write* your senator⟩ **7** : to communicate by letter ⟨*writes* that they are coming⟩ **8** : to transfer information in a computer to a storage area or output device

write–in \'rīt-ˌin\ *n* **1** : a vote cast by writing in the name of a candidate **2** : a candidate whose name is written in

write in *vb* : to insert (a name not listed on a ballot or voting machine) in an appropriate space

write off *vb* **1** : to take off the books : enter as a loss or expense ⟨*write off* a bad debt⟩ **2** : to consider to be lost ⟨the candidate has already *written off* the southern states⟩; *also* : DISMISS **3** ⟨*wrote off* my losing as bad luck⟩

\ə\ **abut**		\aů\ **out**	\i\ **tip**	\ò\ **saw**	\ů\ **foot**
\ər\ **further**		\ch\ **chin**	\ī\ **life**	\òi\ **coin**	\y\ **yet**
\a\ **mat**		\e\ **pet**	\j\ **job**	\th\ **thin**	\yü\ **few**
\ā\ **take**		\ē\ **easy**	\ŋ\ **sing**	\th\ **this**	\yů\ **cure**
\ä\ **cot, cart**		\g\ **go**	\ō\ **bone**	\ü\ **food**	\zh\ **vision**

writ·er \'rīt-ər\ *n* : one that writes especially as a business or occupation

writer's block *n* : a usually temporary psychological condition in which a writer is unable to proceed with a piece of writing

writer's cramp *n* : a painful contraction of the muscles of the hand or fingers brought on by too much use in writing

write–up \'rīt-ˌəp\ *n* : a written account (as in a newspaper); *esp* : a flattering article

write up \(')rīt-'əp\ *vb* **1** : to write an account of : DESCRIBE **2** : to report (a person) especially for some violation of law or rules

writhe \'rīth\ *vb* **writhed; writh·ing** : to twist and turn this way and that ⟨*writhe* in pain⟩

writ·ing \'rīt-iŋ\ *n* **1** : the act or process of one that writes: as **a** : the formation of letters to express words and ideas : HANDWRITING 1 **b** : the art or practice of literary or musical composition **2** : something (as a letter or book) that is written or printed **3** : a style or form of composition **4** : the occupation of a writer

writing paper *n* : paper that has a smooth surface so that it can be written on with ink

Writ·ings \'rīt-iŋz\ *n* — see BIBLE table

¹wrong \'ròŋ\ *n* **1** : a harmful, unfair, or unjust act **2** : something that is wrong : wrong principles, practices, or conduct ⟨know right from *wrong*⟩ **3** : the state, position, or fact of being or doing wrong ⟨in the *wrong*⟩

²wrong *adj* **1** : not according to the moral standard : SINFUL, IMMORAL **2** : not agreeing with proper behavior ⟨it was *wrong* not to thank the hostess⟩ **3** : not suitable ⟨wore the *wrong* clothes for a wedding⟩ **4** : not according to truth or facts : INCORRECT ⟨a *wrong* answer on the test⟩ **5** : not satisfactory ⟨there's something *wrong* about the story's ending⟩ **6** : not in agreement with one's needs,

intentions, or expectations ⟨took the *wrong* bus⟩ **7** : made so as to be placed down or under and not to be seen ⟨the *wrong* side of a fabric⟩ — **wrong** *adv* — **wrong·ly** *adv* — **wrong·ness** *n*

³wrong *vb* **wronged; wrong·ing** \'ròŋ-iŋ\ **1** : to do wrong to : INJURE, HARM **2** : to make unjust remarks about

wrong·do·er \'ròŋ-ˌdü-ər\ *n* : a person who does wrong and especially moral wrong — **wrong·do·ing** \-'dü-iŋ\ *n*

wrong·ful \'ròŋ-fəl\ *adj* **1** : ²WRONG 1 ⟨a *wrongful* act⟩ **2** : UNLAWFUL ⟨*wrongful* possession of another's property⟩ — **wrong·ful·ly** \-fə-lē\ *adv* — **wrong·ful·ness** *n*

wrong·head·ed \'ròŋ-'hed-əd\ *adj* : stubborn in clinging to wrong opinion or principles — **wrong·head·ed·ly** *adv* — **wrong·head·ed·ness** *n*

wrote *past of* WRITE

wroth \'ròth *also* 'ròth\ *adj* : filled with wrath : ANGRY

¹wrought \'ròt\ *past and past participle of* WORK

²wrought *adj* **1** : worked into shape by skill or effort ⟨a carefully *wrought* report⟩ **2** : decorated with fancy designs **3** : beaten into shape by tools : HAMMERED ⟨*wrought* metals⟩ **4** : very excited ⟨gets *wrought* up over nothing⟩

wrought iron *n* : a commercial form of iron that is tough but soft and that can be hammered and shaped

wrung *past and past participle of* WRING

wry \'rī\ *adj* **wry·er** \'rī(-ə)r\; **wry·est** \'rī-əst\ **1** : bent, twisted, or turned usually abnormally to one side ⟨a *wry* nose⟩ **2 a** : expressing irony ⟨a *wry* smile⟩ **b** : cleverly humorous ⟨a *wry* remark⟩ — **wry·ly** *adv* — **wry·ness** *n*

wy·an·dotte \'wī-ən-ˌdät\ *n* : any of a U.S. breed of medium-sized domestic chickens raised especially for meat and eggs

WYSIWYG *n* : a computer display generated by word-processing software that shows exactly how a printout of the document will appear

X

¹x \'eks\ *n, often cap* **1** : the 24th letter of the English alphabet **2** : ten in Roman numerals **3** : an unknown quantity

²x *vb* **x–ed** *also* **x'd** *or* **xed** \'ekst\; **x–ing** *or* **x'ing** \'ek-siŋ\ **1** : to mark with an *x* **2** : to cancel with a series of *x*'s

X \'eks\ *adj, of a motion picture* : of such a nature that admission is denied to persons under a certain age (as 17) — used before the adoption of *NC-17*

x–ax·is \'ek-ˌsak-səs\ *n* : the horizontal axis in a plane coordinate system along which or parallel to which abscissas are measured — compare Y-AXIS

X chromosome *n* : a sex chromosome that is associated with femaleness and usually occurs paired in each female cell and single in each male cell in organisms (as human beings) in which the male normally has two unlike sex chromosomes — compare Y CHROMOSOME

x–co·or·di·nate \ˌeks-kō-'òrd-nət, -ᵊn-ət\ *n* : ABSCISSA

xe·bec \'zē-ˌbek, zi-'bek\ *n* : a usually three-masted Mediterranean sailing ship with long overhanging bow and stern

xe·non \'zē-ˌnän, 'zen-ˌän\ *n* : a heavy colorless gaseous element that occurs in air in minute quantities and is used especially in specialized electric lamps — see ELEMENT table

xebec

xe·no·pho·bia \ˌzen-ə-'fō-bē-ə, ˌzēn-\ *n* : fear of foreigners or foreign things [from Greek *xeno-* "strange, foreign" (from *xenos* "foreigner") and English *phobia* "an exaggerated fear"]

xe·ric \'zir-ik, 'zer-\ *adj* : requiring little moisture ⟨*xeric* woodlands⟩ ⟨a *xeric* plant⟩

xe·rog·ra·phy \zə-'räg-rə-fē, zir-'äg-\ *n* : a process for copying printed material by the action of light on an electrically charged surface in which the image is developed with a powder — **xe·ro·graph·ic** \ˌzir-ə-'graf-ik\ *adj*

xe·ro·phyte \'zir-ə-ˌfīt\ *n* : a plant (as an agave, cactus, sagebrush, or yucca) suited for growth in dry or desert conditions — **xe·ro·phyt·ic** \ˌzir-ə-'fit-ik\ *adj*

xe·rox \'zir-ˌäks, 'zē-ˌräks\ *vb* : to copy or make a copy on a xerographic copier

Xe·rox \'zir-ˌäks, 'zē-ˌräks\ *trademark* — used for a xerographic copier

xi \'zī, 'ksī\ *n* : the 14th letter of the Greek alphabet — Ξ or ξ

x–in·ter·cept \'ek-'sint-ər-ˌsept\ *n* : the abscissa of a point where a line or curve intersects the x-axis — compare Y-INTERCEPT

Xmas \'kris-məs *also* 'ek-sməs\ *n* : CHRISTMAS [from *X*, a symbol for Jesus Christ, and *-mas*, from *Christmas*; the *X* is from the Greek letter *X* "chi," the first letter in the Greek word *Christos* "Christ"]

x–ray \'eks-ˌrā\ *vb, often cap X* : to examine, treat, or photograph with X-rays

X–ray \'eks-,rā\ *n* **1** : an electromagnetic radiation of an extremely short wavelength that is able to penetrate various thicknesses of solids and to act on photographic film as light does **2** : a photograph taken by the use of X-rays — **X–ray** *adj*

Word History In 1895, a German scientist, Wilhelm Conrad Röntgen, was experimenting with an electric current passing through a vacuum in a glass tube. He found that a piece of material that glows only when electricity passes through it began to glow even though it was not inside the tube. Röntgen tried to shield the material from the tube. However, he found that the material glowed even when it was shielded by paper or wood. Only a shield of metal stopped the glowing. He guessed that an unknown invisible ray created inside the glass tube was causing this to happen. Since he knew nothing about this mysterious ray, Röntgen called it *X-Strahl* in German, which translates as *X-ray* in English. He was using the letter *x*, which had long been used in mathematics for an unknown value. [from German *X-Strahl* "X-ray," from the use of *x* to represent an unknown value]

xy·lem \'zī-ləm, -,lem\ *n* : a tissue of higher plants that carries water and dissolved materials upward, functions also in support and storage, lies deeper inside the plant than the phloem, and usually makes up the woody parts (as of a plant stem) — compare PHLOEM

xy·lo·phone \'zī-lə-,fōn\ *n* : a musical instrument consisting of a series of wooden bars varying in length and sounded by striking with two wooden hammers [from Greek *xylo-* "wood, of wood" (from *xylon* "wood") and English *-phone* "sound, a sound-producing device"] — **xy·lo·phon·ist** \-,fō-nəst\ *n*

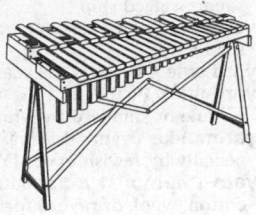
xylophone

Y

y \'wī\ *n*, *pl* **y's** *or* **ys** *often cap* : the 25th letter of the English alphabet

Y \'wī\ *n* **1** : YMCA **2** : YWCA

¹-y *also* **-ey** \ē\ *adj suffix* **-i·er; -i·est 1 a** : marked by : full of ⟨blossom*y*⟩ ⟨dirt*y*⟩ ⟨mudd*y*⟩ ⟨clay*ey*⟩ **b** : composed of ⟨ic*y*⟩ ⟨wax*y*⟩ **c** : like : like that of ⟨hom*ey*⟩ ⟨wintr*y*⟩ ⟨stag*y*⟩ **2 a** : tending to ⟨sleep*y*⟩ ⟨chatt*y*⟩ **b** : causing or performing (a certain) action ⟨tear*y*⟩ [Old English *-ig* (adjective suffix) "having the character of"]

²-y \ē\ *n suffix*, *pl* **-ies 1** : state : condition : quality ⟨jealous*y*⟩ **2** : activity, place of business, or goods dealt with ⟨grocer*y*⟩ ⟨laundr*y*⟩ **3** : whole body or group ⟨soldier*y*⟩ [derived from Greek *-ia* (noun suffix) "state, condition, quality"]

³-y *n suffix*, *pl* **-ies** : instance of a (certain) action ⟨entreat*y*⟩ ⟨inquir*y*⟩ [derived from Latin *-ium* (noun suffix) "an instance of a certain action"]

⁴-y — see -IE

¹yacht \'yät\ *n* : a fairly small ship used for pleasure cruising or racing

Word History In the 16th century, the Dutch were being attacked by pirates and smugglers who managed to escape after their raids because their ships were much faster than the heavy warships used by the Dutch. To solve the problem, the Dutch began building smaller, sleeker, faster craft. This new kind of craft was called a *jaght* (later spelled *jacht*) in Dutch. The word was derived from the Dutch phrase *jachtschip*, literally meaning "hunting ship." In 1660, the Dutch East India Company presented one of these boats to England's King Charles II. He used it for a pleasure boat rather than for chasing pirates. Soon, other wealthy Englishmen wanted boats just like the king's. The style was then copied and improved over the years. The name for this craft also went through a number of changes over the years, from the original *jaght*, taken from the Dutch, to the *yacht* spelling we have today. [from obsolete Dutch *jaght* (now *jacht*), short for *jachtschip*, literally, "hunting ship"]

²yacht *vb* : to race or cruise in a yacht

yacht·ing *n* : the sport of racing or cruising in a yacht

yachts·man \'yät-smən\ *n* : a person who owns or sails a yacht

ya·hoo \yä-'hü\ *interj* : YIPPEE

yak \'yak\ *n*, *pl* **yaks** *also* **yak** : a large long-haired wild or domesticated ox of Tibet and nearby elevated parts of central Asia

yam \'yam\ *n* **1** : an edible starchy root that is an important food in tropical areas; *also* : a plant producing yams **2** : a sweet potato with moist usually orange flesh

yak

yam·mer \'yam-ər\ *vb* **yam·mered; yam·mer·ing** \-(ə-)riŋ\ : to utter repeated cries of sorrow, distress, or complaint

¹yank \'yaŋk\ *n* : a strong sudden pull : JERK

²yank *vb* : to pull suddenly or forcefully

Yank \'yaŋk\ *n* : YANKEE

Yan·kee \'yaŋ-kē\ *n* **1** : a person born or living in New England **2** : a person born or living in the northern U.S. **3** : a person born or living in the U.S.

Ya·no·ma·mi \,yän-ō-'mäm-ē\ *n*, *pl* **Yanomami** : a member of the native people living in the rain forests of southern Venezuela and northern Brazil

¹yap \'yap\ *vb* **yapped; yap·ping 1** : to bark in yaps : YELP **2** : to talk sharply or continuously

²yap *n* : a quick shrill bark : YELP

¹yard \'yärd\ *n* **1 a** : a small often enclosed area open to the sky and next to a building **b** : the grounds of a building (as the grassy area around a house) **2 a** : an enclosure for livestock **b** : an area with its buildings and equipment set aside for a particular activity ⟨a navy *yard*⟩ **c** : a system of railroad tracks for keeping and repairing cars [Old English *geard* "an enclosed space, yard"]

²yard *n* **1** : any of various units of measure; *esp* : a unit of

\ə\ **abut**	\aú\ **out**	\i\ **tip**	\ò\ **saw**	\ú\ **foot**	
\ər\ **further**	\ch\ **chin**	\ī\ **life**	\òi\ **coin**	\y\ **yet**	
\a\ **mat**	\e\ **pet**	\j\ **job**	\th\ **thin**	\yü\ **few**	
\ā\ **take**	\ē\ **easy**	\ŋ\ **sing**	\th\ **this**	\yù\ **cure**	
\ä\ **cot, cart**	\g\ **go**	\ō\ **bone**	\ü\ **food**	\zh\ **vision**	

length equal in the U.S. to 0.9144 meter — see MEASURE table **2** : a long pole tapered toward the ends that supports and spreads the top of a sail [Old English *gierd* "twig, measure"]

yard·age \'yärd-ij\ *n* **1** : a total number of yards **2** : the length or size of something measured in yards

yard·arm \'yärd-,ärm\ *n* : either end of the yard of a square-rigged ship

yard·mas·ter \-,mas-tər\ *n* : the person in charge of a railroad yard

yard sale *n* : GARAGE SALE

yard·stick \-,stik\ *n* **1** : a measuring stick a yard long **2** : a rule or standard by which something is measured

yar·mul·ke \'yäm-ə-kə, 'yär-məl-\ *n* : a skullcap worn especially by Jewish males [Yiddish *yarmlke* "yarmulke"]

¹yarn \'yärn\ *n* **1 a** : a natural or manufactured fiber (as cotton, wool, or rayon) formed as a continuous strand for use in knitting or weaving **b** : a similar strand of another material (as metal, glass, or plastic) **2** : an interesting or exciting story

²yarn *vb* : to tell a yarn

yaw \'yò\ *vb* : to turn suddenly from a straight course : SWERVE, VEER ⟨heavy seas made the ship *yaw*⟩ — **yaw** *n*

yawl \'yòl\ *n* : a sailboat having two masts with the shorter one behind the rudder

¹yawn \'yòn, 'yän\ *vb* **1** : to open wide : GAPE **2** : to open the mouth wide and take a deep breath usually as a reaction to being tired or bored — **yawn·er** *n*

²yawn *n* : an opening of the mouth wide while taking a deep breath often as an involuntary reaction

yawl

¹yawp *or* **yaup** \'yòp\ *vb* : to make a loud harsh noise

²yawp *also* **yaup** *n* : a loud harsh noise

yaws \'yòz\ *n sing or pl* : a tropical contagious skin disease especially of children caused by a bacterium that is a spirochete

y–ax·is \'wī-,ak-səs\ *n* : the vertical axis in a plane coordinate system along which or parallel to which ordinates are measured — compare X-AXIS

Y chromosome *n* : a sex chromosome that is associated with maleness and occurs only in male cells paired with an X chromosome in organisms (as human beings) in which the male normally has two unlike sex chromosomes — compare X CHROMOSOME

yclept \i-'klept\ *or* **ycleped** \-'klēpt, -'klept\ *adj, archaic* : being named : CALLED [Old English *geclipod,* past participle of *clipian* "to cry out, name"]

y–co·or·di·nate \,wī-kō-'òrd-nət, -³n-ət\ *n* : ORDINATE

¹ye \(')yē\ *pron* : YOU 1 [Old English *gē* "you"]

²ye \yē, yə, *or like* THE\ *definite article, archaic* : THE ⟨*Ye* Olde Gifte Shoppe⟩ [an altered form of Old English *þē* "the"; because the handwritten forms of þ and y in old manuscripts looked much alike, early printers used *y* when the obsolete þ was not available]

¹yea \'yā\ *adv* **1** : ¹YES 1 — used in oral voting **2** — used to give special force to a phrase that follows ⟨most people, *yea* everyone, would agree with that⟩

²yea *n* **1** : a vote in favor of something **2** : a person casting a yea vote

yeah \'ye-ə, 'ya-ə\ *adv* : ¹YES

year \'yi(ə)r\ *n* **1** : the period of about 365¼ days required for the earth to make one complete trip around the sun **2** : a period of 365 days or in leap year 366 days beginning

January 1 **3** : a period of time usually shorter than a calendar year ⟨a school *year* of nine months⟩

year·book \-,bůk\ *n* **1** : a book published yearly **2** : a school publication recording the history and activities of a graduating class

year·ling \'yi(ə)r-lin\ *n* **1** : one and especially an animal that is a year old or in the second year after birth **2** : a racehorse between January 1st of the year after the year in which it was born and the next January 1st — **yearling** *adj*

year·ly \'yi(ə)r-lē\ *adj* **1** : occurring, made, done, or produced every year : ANNUAL **2** : calculated in terms of one year — **yearly** *adv*

yearn \'yərn\ *vb* **1** : to desire eagerly **2** : to feel tenderness or sympathy — **yearn·er** *n*

  synonyms YEARN, LONG, PINE mean to desire something very much. YEARN suggests an eager desire along with restless, painful feelings ⟨*yearning* to go home⟩. LONG suggests wanting something with one's whole heart and often striving to get it as well ⟨*longing* to succeed as a writer⟩. PINE suggests that one grows weak while continuing to want something that one will never have ⟨*pining* away for an absent friend⟩.

yearn·ing *n* : a tender or eager longing

year–round \'yi(ə)r-'raůnd, 'yiə-'raůnd\ *adj* : being in operation for the whole year ⟨a *year-round* resort⟩

yeast \'yēst, 'ēst\ *n* **1 a** : a one-celled fungus that produces alcohol during the process of fermentation; *also* : any of various similar fungi **b** : a yellowish foamy material that may occur on the surface of sweet liquids (as fruit juices) undergoing fermentation and that consists chiefly of yeast cells and carbon dioxide **c** : a commercial product containing living yeast cells that is used mostly in the making of alcoholic beverages and as a leaven especially in baking bread **2** : something that causes motion or activity — **yeasty** \'yē-stē, 'ē-stē\ *adj*

¹yell \'yel\ *vb* **1** : to utter a loud cry, scream, or shout **2** : to give a cheer usually as part of a crowd — **yell·er** *n*

²yell *n* **1** : ²SCREAM 1, SHOUT **2** : a cheer used especially in schools or colleges to encourage athletic teams

¹yel·low \'yel-ō\ *adj* **1 a** : of the color yellow **b** : yellowish from age, disease, or discoloring **2** : COWARDLY 1 — **yellow** *vb* — **yel·low·ness** *n*

²yellow *n* **1** : a color like that of ripe lemons **2** : something yellow or yellowish

yellow fever *n* : an infectious disease of warm regions (as sub-Saharan Africa) that is marked by fever, headache, muscle aches, yellowness of the skin, and sometimes death and that is caused by a virus transmitted by a mosquito

yel·low·ham·mer \'yel-ō-,ham-ər, 'yel-ə-\ *n* : YELLOW= SHAFTED FLICKER

yel·low·ish \'yel-ə-wish\ *adj* : somewhat yellow

yellow jack *n* : YELLOW FEVER

yellow jacket *n* : any of various small social wasps with yellow markings that commonly nest in the ground and can sting repeatedly and painfully

yellow pages *n pl, often cap* *Y&P* : the section of a telephone directory that lists businesses and professional firms by category and includes advertising

yellow perch *n* : ³PERCH 1

yel·low–shaft·ed flicker \,yel-ō-,shaf-təd-, ,yel-ə-\ *n* : a flicker of the form found in the more eastern parts of

yellow-shafted flicker

North America that is golden yellow on the underside of the tail and wings, has a red mark on the back of the neck, and in the male has a black streak on each side of the base of the bill — called also *yellowhammer*

¹yelp \'yelp\ *n* : a sharp quick shrill bark or cry ⟨the *yelps* of turkeys⟩ [Middle English *yelpen* "to boast, cry out," from Old English *gielpan* "to boast, exult"]

²yelp *vb* : to utter a yelp or a similar sound ⟨he *yelped* in pain⟩ ⟨heard the dog *yelping* again⟩ — **yelp·er** *n*

¹yen \'yen\ *n, pl* **yen 1** : the basic unit of money of Japan **2** : a coin worth one yen

²yen *n* : an intense desire : LONGING

yeo·man \'yō-mən\ *n* **1 a** : a servant in a royal or noble household **b** : a naval petty officer who works as a clerk **2** : a small landowning farmer

yeo·man·ly \'yō-mən-lē\ *adj* : becoming to a yeoman : STURDY, LOYAL

yeo·man·ry \'yō-mən-rē\ *n* : a body of yeomen

-yer — see ²-ER

yer·ba ma·té \,yer-bə-'mä-,tā, ,yər-\ *n* : MATÉ

¹yes \'yes, 'yeu̇, 'e-(y)ə\ *are three of many variants\ adv* **1** — used to express agreement ⟨are you ready? *Yes*, I am⟩ **2** — used to correct or contradict what another has said ⟨don't say that! *Yes*, I will⟩ **3** — used to introduce a phrase with greater force or clearness ⟨we are glad, *yes*, very glad to see you⟩ **4** — used to show interest or attention ⟨*yes*, what is it you want⟩

²yes \'yes\ *n* : a positive reply

ye·shi·va *also* **ye·shi·vah** \yə-'shē-və\ *n, pl* **yeshivas** *or* **ye·shi·vot** \-,shē-'vōt(h)\ : a Jewish school especially for religious instruction

yes–man \'yes-,man\ *n* : a person who agrees with every opinion or suggestion of a boss

¹yes·ter·day \'yes-tərd-ē\ *adv* **1** : on the day before today **2** : at a time not long past

²yesterday *n* **1** : the day next before the present **2** : recent time : time not long past

yes·ter·year \'yes-tər-,yi(ə)r\ *n* **1** : last year **2** : the recent past

¹yet \(')yet\ *adv* **1 a** : in addition : BESIDES ⟨gives *yet* another reason⟩ **b** : ³EVEN 4 ⟨a *yet* higher speed⟩ **2 a** : up to now : so far ⟨hasn't done much *yet*⟩ **b** : at this time : so soon as now ⟨not time to go *yet*⟩ **c** : ³STILL 2 ⟨is *yet* a new country⟩ **d** : at a later time ⟨may *yet* see the light⟩ **3** : NEVERTHELESS ⟨strong, *yet* not strong enough⟩

²yet *conj* : despite that fact : BUT ⟨bought more milk *yet* it was not enough for everyone⟩

ye·ti \'yet-ē, 'yāt-\ *n* : ABOMINABLE SNOWMAN

yew \'yü\ *n* **1** : any of a genus of evergreen trees and shrubs that are gymnosperms with short stiff flattened needlelike leaves and seeds having a red juicy covering **2** : the wood of a yew; *esp* : the heavy fine-grained wood of an Old World yew that is used especially for bows and small articles

Yid·dish \'yid-ish\ *n* : a language that began among the Jews of eastern Europe and is based on German and written in the Hebrew alphabet [from Yiddish *yidish*, a shortened form of *yidish daytsh*, literally

yew 1

"Jewish German (language)," derived from early German *jüdisch* "Jewish" and *diutsch* "the German language"] — **Yiddish** *adj*

¹yield \'yē(ə)ld\ *vb* **1** : to give up possession of on claim or demand : SURRENDER **2** : to give oneself up to a liking, temptation, or habit **3 a** : to bear as a natural product ⟨trees that *yield* fruit⟩ **b** : to produce as a result of effort

⟨this soil should *yield* good crops⟩ **c** : to return as profit or interest **4** : to bring good results **5** : to give up and stop fighting ⟨will not *yield* to their enemy⟩ **6** : to give way to urging, persuasion, or pleading **7** : to give way under physical force so as to bend, stretch, or break **8** : to admit that someone else is better — **yield·er** \'yēl-dər\ *n*

synonyms YIELD, SUBMIT, SURRENDER mean to give way to someone or something that one can no longer oppose. YIELD applies to any kind of giving way or giving in (as to physical force, argument, or persuasion) ⟨the roof *yielded* to the heavy load of snow⟩ ⟨she refused to *yield* to the pressure to change her vote⟩. SUBMIT stresses giving in to the will of another and going against one's own wishes ⟨*submitted* to the plan but under protest⟩. SURRENDER applies to a total giving in and the placing of oneself at the mercy of another ⟨finally the lord of the castle *surrendered* it to the enemy⟩.

²yield *n* : something yielded : PRODUCT; *esp* : the amount or quantity produced or returned ⟨a high *yield* of wheat per acre⟩

yield·ing \'yēl-diŋ\ *adj* **1** : not rigid or stiff : FLEXIBLE ⟨a *yielding* mass⟩ **2** : tending to give in to the wishes of another ⟨a cheerful *yielding* nature⟩

y–in·ter·cept \'wī-'int-ər-,sept\ *n* : the ordinate of a point where a line or curve intersects the y-axis — compare X-INTERCEPT

yip \'yip\ *vb* **yipped; yip·ping** : to bark sharply, quickly, and often continuously ⟨the poodle ran around *yipping*⟩; *also* : to utter a short sharp cry ⟨*yipped* with joy⟩ — **yip** *n*

yip·pee \'yip-ē\ *interj* — used to express delight or triumph

YMCA \,wī-,em-(,)sē-'ā\ *n* : an international organization that promotes the spiritual, intellectual, social, and physical welfare originally of young Christian men [*Young Men's Christian Association*]

YMHA \,wī-,em-,ā-'chä\ *n* : an international organization that promotes the spiritual, intellectual, social, and physical welfare originally of young Jewish men [*Young Men's Hebrew Association*]

yo·del \'yōd-ᵊl\ *vb* **-deled** *or* **-delled; -del·ing** *or* **-del·ling** \'yōd-liŋ, -ᵊl-iŋ\ : to sing while frequently going back and forth between the range of one's natural voice and a higher range; *also* : to shout or call in this manner — **yodel** *n* — **yo·del·er** \'yōd-lər, -ᵊl-ər\ *n*

yo·ga \'yō-gə\ *n* **1** *cap* : a Hindu philosophy teaching that by holding back the activity of one's body, mind, and will one can know one's true self and be free **2** : a system of exercises for gaining bodily or mental control and well-being

yo·gi \'yō-gē\ *also* **yo·gin** \-gən, -,gin\ *n* **1** : a person who practices yoga **2** *cap* : a follower of Yoga

yo·gurt *also* **yo·ghurt** \'yō-gərt\ *n* : a slightly acidic semisolid food that is often flavored and sweetened and is made of milk that has been soured by the addition of bacteria

¹yoke \'yōk\ *n, pl* **yokes 1 a** : a wooden bar or frame by which two work animals (as oxen) are joined at their heads or necks for pulling a plow or load **b** : a frame fitted to a person's shoulders to carry a load in two equal portions **c** : a clamp or brace that holds or unites two parts **2** *pl usu* **yoke** : two animals yoked together **3 a** : something that brings about a state of hardship, pain, or slavery **b** : SLAVERY 2a **4** : a fitted or shaped piece at the top of a skirt or at the shoulder of a garment

\ə\ **abut**	\au̇\ **out**	\i\ **tip**	\ȯ\ **saw**	\u̇\ **foot**
\ər\ **further**	\ch\ **chin**	\ī\ **life**	\ȯi\ **coin**	\y\ **yet**
\a\ **mat**	\e\ **pet**	\j\ **job**	\th\ **thin**	\yü\ **few**
\ā\ **take**	\ē\ **easy**	\ŋ\ **sing**	\th\ **this**	\yu̇\ **cure**
\ä\ **cot, cart**	\g\ **go**	\ō\ **bone**	\ü\ **food**	\zh\ **vision**

²yoke *vb* **yoked; yok·ing** **1** : to put a yoke on **2** : to attach (a work animal) to something ⟨*yoke* a horse to a cart⟩ **3** : to join as if by a yoke **4** : to put to work

yoke·fel·low \'yōk-ˌfel-ō\ *n* : a close companion

yo·kel \'yō-kəl\ *n* : a country person with little education or experience

yolk \'yōk, 'yelk *also* 'yōlk\ *n* **1** : the yellow inner mass of stored food in the egg of a bird or reptile **2** : the material stored in an animal ovum that supplies food material to the developing embryo

Yom Kip·pur \ˌyōm-ki-'pu̇r, -yōm-, -yäm-, -'kip-ər\ *n* : a Jewish holiday observed in September or October with fasting and prayer as ways of making up for sins

¹yon \'yän\ *adj* : ²YONDER

²yon *adv* **1** : ¹YONDER **2** : ¹THITHER ⟨hither and *yon*⟩

yond \'yänd\ *adv, archaic* : ¹YONDER

¹yon·der \'yän-dər\ *adv* : at or to that place : over there

²yonder *adj* **1** : more distant ⟨the *yonder* side of the river⟩ **2** : being at a distance within view ⟨*yonder* hills⟩

yore \'yō(ə)r, 'yȯ(ə)r\ *n* : time long past — usually used in the phrase *of yore*

York·shire pudding \'yȯ(ə)rk-ˌshi(ə)r-, -shər-\ *n* : batter made from eggs, flour, and milk and baked in meat drippings

Yorkshire terrier *n* : any of a breed of small toy terriers with long straight silky hair that is mostly bluish gray but tan on the head and chest

you \('ˌ)yü, yə, yē\ *pron* **1** : the one or ones spoken to ⟨can I pour *you* a cup of tea⟩ ⟨*you* are my friends⟩ **2** : ³ONE 2 ⟨*you* never know what will happen⟩

you–all \('ˌ)yü-'ȯl, 'yü-ˌȯl, 'yȯl\ *pron, chiefly Southern* : YOU — usually used in addressing two or more persons

you'd \(ˌ)yüd, (ˌ)yu̇d, yəd\ : you had : you would

you'll \(ˌ)yü(ə)l, (ˌ)yu̇l, yəl\ : you shall : you will

¹young \'yəŋ\ *adj* **youn·ger** \'yəŋ-gər\; **youn·gest** \'yəŋ-gəst\ **1 a** : being in the early stage of life, growth, or development **b** : ¹JUNIOR 1a **2** : lacking in experience **3** : recently come into being : NEW ⟨*young* rock strata⟩ **4** : of, relating to, or having the characteristics of youth or a young person ⟨*young* at heart⟩ — **young·ness** \'yəŋ-nəs\ *n*

²young *n pl* **1** : young persons : YOUTH ⟨music that appeals to the *young*⟩ **2** : immature or recently born offspring ⟨a bear and her *young*⟩ — **with young** : PREGNANT 1 — used of animals

youn·gest \'yəŋ-gəst\ *n* : the least old member especially of a family

young·ish \'yəŋ-ish\ *adj* : somewhat young

young·ster \'yəŋ(k)-stər\ *n* **1** : a young person : YOUTH **2** : CHILD 2a

your \yər, ('ˌ)yu̇(ə)r, ('ˌ)yō(ə)r, ('ˌ)yȯ(ə)r\ *adj* **1** : of or relating to you or yourself or yourselves ⟨*your* house⟩ ⟨*your* contributions⟩ ⟨*your* friends⟩ **2** : of or relating to one ⟨when you face the north, east is at *your* right⟩ **3** — used before a title of honor in address ⟨*your* Honor⟩

you're \yər, (ˌ)yu̇(ə)r, (ˌ)yō(ə)r, (ˌ)yȯ(ə)r\ : you are

yours \'yu̇(ə)rz, 'yō(ə)rz, 'yȯ(ə)rz\ *pron* : your one : your ones — often used with an adverb and as part of the closing of a letter ⟨*yours* truly⟩

your·self \yər-'self\ *pron* **1 a** : that one that is you ⟨don't hurt *yourself*⟩ ⟨carry them *yourself*⟩ **b** : your normal or healthy self ⟨you're not *yourself* today⟩ **2** : ONESELF

your·selves \yər-'selvz\ *pron pl* **1** : those identical ones that are you **2** : your normal or healthy selves

youth \'yüth\ *n, pl* **youths** \'yüthz, 'yüths\ **1** : the time of life when one is young; *esp* : the period between childhood and adulthood **2 a** : a young man **b** : young people ⟨the *youth* of today⟩ — usually used with a plural verb **3** : the quality or state of being young

youth·ful \'yüth-fəl\ *adj* **1** : of, relating to, or suitable for youth **2** : being young and not yet mature **3** : having the freshness and energy of youth ⟨*youthful* grandparents⟩ — **youth·ful·ly** \-fə-lē\ *adv* — **youth·ful·ness** *n*

youth hostel *n* : HOSTEL 2

you've \(ˌ)yüv, yəv\ : you have

yowl \'yau̇(ə)l\ *vb* : to utter a loud long often mournful cry or howl ⟨the cats were *yowling* all night⟩ — **yowl** *n*

yo-yo \'yō-ˌyō\ *n, pl* **yo-yos** **1** : a thick divided disk that is made to fall and rise to the hand by unwinding and rewinding on a string **2** : ¹FOOL 1

yt·ter·bi·um \i-'tər-bē-əm\ *n* : a metallic element that occurs in several minerals — see ELEMENT table

yt·tri·um \'i-trē-əm\ *n* : a metallic element that occurs in minerals along with other similar uncommon elements — see ELEMENT table

yu·an \'yü-ən, yu̇-'än\ *n, pl* **yuan** **1** : the basic unit of money in China **2** : a coin or bill worth one yuan

yuc·ca \'yək-ə\ *n* : any of a genus of plants that are related to the agaves, grow in warm dry regions mostly of western North America, have long pointed often stiff leaves, and produce a tall stiff stalk with whitish flowers

yucky \'yək-ē\ *adj* **yuck·i·er; -est** : DISAGREEABLE, DISTASTEFUL

yule \'yü(ə)l\ *n, often cap* : CHRISTMAS

Yule log *n* : a large log formerly put on the hearth on Christmas Eve as the foundation of the fire

yule·tide \'yü(ə)l-ˌtīd\ *n, often cap* : the Christmas season

yum·my \'yəm-ē\ *adj* : very pleasing especially to the taste

yurt \'yu̇(ə)rt\ *n* : a light round tent of skins or felt used by nomads in central Asia [from Russian *yurta* "a domed tent, yurt"; of Turkish origin]

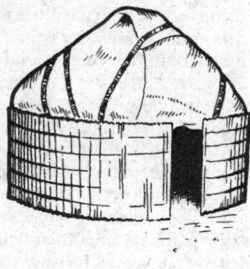

yurt

YWCA \ˌwī-ˌdəb-əl-yü-(ˌ)sē-'ā\ *n* : an international organization that promotes the spiritual, intellectual, social, and physical welfare originally of young Christian women [*Young Women's Christian Association*]

YWHA \ˌwī-ˌdəb-əl-yü-ˌā-'chä\ *n* : an international organization that promotes the spiritual, intellectual, social, and physical welfare originally of young Jewish women [*Young Women's Hebrew Association*]

Z

z \'zē, *British & Canadian* 'zed\ *n, pl* **z's** *or* **zs** *often cap* **1** : the 26th and last letter of the English alphabet **2** : a brief nap ⟨catch some *z's* before dinner⟩

Zach·a·ri·as \ˌzak-ə-'rī-əs\ *n* : ZECHARIAH

¹za·ny \'zā-nē\ *n, pl* **zanies** **1** : ¹CLOWN 2 **2** : a silly or foolish person

²zany *adj* **za·ni·er; -est** **1** : being, typical of, or resembling a zany **2** : fantastically crazy ⟨a *zany* movie⟩ — **za·ni·ly** \'zā-nə-lē, 'zān-ᵊl-ē\ *adv* — **za·ni·ness** \'zā-nē-nəs\ *n*

zap \'zap\ *vb* **zapped; zap·ping** **1** : to destroy or kill by or as if by shooting **2** : to hit suddenly and forcefully

zeal \'zē(ə)l\ *n* : eager desire in going for a goal

zeal·ot \'zel-ət\ *n* : a zealous person; *esp* : an overly zealous supporter

zeal·ous \'zel-əs\ *adj* : filled with or showing zeal : marked by passionate support for a person, cause, or ideal — **zeal·ous·ly** *adv* — **zeal·ous·ness** *n*

ze·bra \'zēb-rə\ *n, pl* **zebras** *also* **zebra** **1** : any of several hoofed plant-eating African mammals that are related to the horse, have a hide striped in black or dark brown and white or buff, and are swift runners **2** : a small Indian fish with blue and silver stripes that is often kept in tropical aquariums

ze·bu \'zē-b(y)ü\ *n* : any of various breeds of domestic oxen developed in India that have a large fleshy hump over the shoulders and loose skin with hanging folds and that are able to withstand the harmful effects of heat and insect attack

Zech·a·ri·ah \ˌzek-ə-'rīə\ *n* — see BIBLE table

zed \'zed\ *n, chiefly British* : the letter z

ze·nith \'zē-nəth\ *n* **1** : the point in the heavens directly overhead **2** : the highest point

zebu

Zeph·a·ni·ah \ˌzef-ə-'nī-ə\ *n* — see BIBLE table

zeph·yr \'zef-ər\ *n* **1** : a breeze from the west **2** : a gentle breeze

zep·pe·lin \'zep-(ə-)lən\ *n* : a long cylindrical passenger balloon that has a metal frame and is driven through the air by engines carried on its underside

¹ze·ro \'zē-rō, 'zi(ə)r-ō\ *n, pl* **zeros** *also* **zeroes** **1** : the numerical symbol 0 meaning the absence of all magnitude or quantity — see NUMBER table **2 a** : a point (as on a scale) from which measurements are made **b** : a value or reading of zero; *esp* : the temperature shown by the zero mark on a thermometer **3** : something or someone of no importance **4** : the lowest point

²zero *adj* **1 a** : of, relating to, or being a zero **b** : having no size or quantity ⟨*zero* growth⟩ **2** : showing no change in the word form ⟨"sheep" is a noun with a *zero* plural⟩

³zero *vb* **1** : to find out or adjust the zero of (as a balance) **2** : to aim or concentrate on a target or goal ⟨*zero* in on my problems with algebra⟩

zero gravity *n* : the state or condition of lacking apparent gravitational pull : WEIGHTLESSNESS

zero hour *n* **1** : the hour at which a military action is scheduled to start **2** : a moment of crisis

zest \'zest\ *n* **1** : a piece of the peel of a citrus fruit (as an orange or lemon) used as a flavoring **2** : a quality that increases enjoyment ⟨added *zest* to the performance⟩ **3** : keen enjoyment : RELISH ⟨has a *zest* for life⟩ — **zest·ful** \-fəl\ *adj* — **zest·ful·ly** \-fə-lē\ *adv* — **zest·ful·ness** *n* — **zesty** \'zes-tē\ *adj*

Word History *Zest* was borrowed into English in the 17th century from the French *zest* (now spelled *zeste*), meaning "an orange or lemon peel." Where the French got the word we do not know. The peels of oranges and lemons are sometimes used to add flavor to food and drinks. The earliest uses of *zest* in English refer to the peel of such fruit used in this way. By the early 18th century, however, *zest* had developed another meaning. It was used to refer to a quality that adds enjoyment to something, in the same way that the *zest* of an orange or lemon adds flavor to food. [from obsolete French *zest* (now *zeste*) "orange or lemon peel used for flavoring"]

ze·ta \'zāt-ə\ *n* : the sixth letter of the Greek alphabet — Z or ζ

¹zig·zag \'zig-ˌzag\ *n* : one of a series of short sharp turns, angles, or changes in a course; *also* : something having the form or appearance of such a series

²zigzag *adv* : in or by a zigzag path or course

³zigzag *adj* : having short sharp turns or angles

⁴zigzag *vb* **zig·zagged; zig·zag·ging** : to form, move along, or consist of a zigzag course

zilch \'zilch\ *n* : ³NOTHING, ZERO

zil·lion \'zil-yən\ *n* : a large number ⟨*zillions* of ants⟩

zinc \'ziŋk\ *n* : a bluish white metallic element that is commonly found in minerals and is used especially in alloys and as a protective coating for iron and steel — see ELEMENT table

zinc oxide *n* : a white substance that is used as a white pigment, is added to rubber, and is used in medical and cosmetic preparations (as ointments and sunblocks)

zinc sulfide *n* : a white to yellowish compound used especially as a white coloring matter

zinc white *n* : a white coloring matter that consists of a compound made up of zinc and oxygen

zing \'ziŋ\ *n* **1** : a shrill humming sound **2** : a lively or energetic quality ⟨a musical show with lots of *zing*⟩

zin·nia \'zin-ē-ə, 'zin-yə, 'zēn-\ *n* : any of a genus of tropical American composite herbs having long-lasting flowers

Zi·on·ism \'zī-ə-ˌniz-əm\ *n* : an international effort working in the beginning for a Jewish homeland and later for the support of Israel — **Zi·on·ist** \-nəst\ *adj or n*

¹zip \'zip\ *vb* **zipped; zip·ping** **1** : to move or act with speed and energy **2** : to travel with a sharp hissing or humming sound **3** : to add energy, interest, or life to — often used with *up* [a word created to imitate the sound of an object speeding past]

²zip *n* **1** : a sudden sharp hissing sound **2** : VIM, ENERGY

³zip *vb* **zipped; zip·ping** : to close or open with a zipper [from *zipper*]

⁴zip *n* : ¹ZERO 1 ⟨won the game 7–*zip*⟩ [origin unknown]

⁵zip *n, often cap Z&I&P* : ZIP CODE

zip code *n* : a number that identifies each postal delivery area in the U.S.

zip gun *n* : a crude homemade pistol

\ə\ **abut**	\au̇\ **out**	\i\ **tip**	\ȯ\ **saw**	\u̇\ **foot**	
\ər\ **further**	\ch\ **chin**	\ī\ **life**	\ȯi\ **coin**	\y\ **yet**	
\a\ **mat**	\e\ **pet**	\j\ **job**	\th\ **thin**	\yü\ **few**	
\ā\ **take**	\ē\ **easy**	\ŋ\ **sing**	\th\ **this**	\yu̇\ **cure**	
\ä\ **cot, cart**	\g\ **go**	\ō\ **bone**	\ü\ **food**	\zh\ **vision**	

zip line *n* : a cable hung above a slope to which a pulley and harness are attached for a rider

zip·per \'zip-ər\ *n* : a fastener consisting of two rows of metal or plastic teeth on strips of tape and a sliding piece that closes an opening by drawing the teeth together [from *Zipper*, a former trademark] — **zip·pered** \-ərd\ *adj*

zip·py \'zip-ē\ *adj* **zip·pi·er; -est** : full of zip : BRISK, SNAPPY

zir·con \'zər-ˌkän, -kən\ *n* : a mineral that consists of a silicate of zirconium and occurs usually as brown or grayish crystals or sometimes as transparent forms which are used as gems

zir·co·ni·um \ˌzər-'kō-nē-əm\ *n* : a steel-gray strong metallic element with a high melting point that is used especially in combination with other metals — see ELEMENT table

zit \'zit\ *n, slang* : PIMPLE [origin unknown]

zith·er \'zith-ər, 'zith-\ *n* : a stringed instrument with thirty to forty tuned strings that are plucked with the fingers or with a pick

zi·ti \'zēt-ē\ *n, pl* **ziti** : medium-sized tube-shaped pasta [Italian, plural of *zito* "a piece of tubular pasta," probably short for *maccheroni di zita*, literally, "bride's macaroni"]

zither

zlo·ty \'zlȯt-ē, zə-'lȯt-ē\ *n, pl* **zlotys** \-ēz\ **1** : the basic unit of money of Poland **2** : a coin worth one zloty

zo·di·ac \'zōd-ē-ˌak\ *n* **1** : an imaginary belt in the heavens that includes the apparent paths of most of the planets and is divided into 12 star groups or signs **2** : a figure showing the signs of the zodiac [Middle English *zodiac* "zodiac," from Latin *zodiacus* (same meaning), derived from Greek *zōidion* "carved or painted figure, sign of the zodiac," from *zōion* "living being, animal, figure"] — **zo·di·a·cal** \zō-'dī-ə-kəl\ *adj*

zom·bie *also* **zom·bi** \'zäm-bē\ *n* : a person who is believed to have died and been brought back to life without speech or free will [Louisiana Creole or Haitian Creole *zonbi*, of Bantu origin]

zon·al \'zōn-ᵊl\ *adj* : of, relating to, or having the form of a zone ⟨a *zonal* boundary⟩

¹zone \'zōn\ *n* **1** : any of five great divisions of the earth's surface with respect to latitude and temperature **2** : a region or area set off from surrounding or neighboring parts **3** : one of the sections of an area or territory created for a particular purpose **4** : an area on a playing field

²zone *vb* **zoned; zon·ing** : to divide into zones; *esp* : to divide (as a city) into sections for different purposes (as manufacturing)

zoo \'zü\ *n, pl* **zoos** : a garden or park where living usually wild animals are kept for showing to the public

zoo·keep·er \-ˌkē-pər\ *n* : a person who keeps or cares for animals in a zoo

zoo·log·i·cal \ˌzō-ə-'läj-i-kəl\ *adj* : of, relating to, or concerned with zoology

zoological garden *n* : ZOO

zoological park *n* : ZOO

zo·ol·o·gist \zō-'äl-ə-jəst, zə-'wäl-\ *n* : a person who specializes in zoology

zo·ol·o·gy \zō-'äl-ə-jē, zə-'wäl-\ *n* : a branch of biology concerned with the animal kingdom and animal life

¹zoom \'züm\ *vb* **1** : to speed along with a loud low hum or buzz ⟨cars *zooming* down the highway⟩ **2** : to gain altitude quickly ⟨the rocket *zoomed* into the sky⟩

²zoom *n* **1** : an act or process of zooming **2** : a zooming sound

zoom lens *n* : a lens on a camera or projector in which the size of the image can be continuously changed while the image remains in focus

zoo·plank·ton \ˌzō-ə-'plaŋ(k)-tən, -ˌtän\ *n* : plankton that is composed of animals

Zo·ro·as·tri·an \ˌzȯr-ə-'was-trē-ən\ *adj* : of or relating to the Persian prophet Zoroaster or the religion founded by him and marked by belief in a great war between good and evil in the universe — **Zoroastrian** *n* — **Zo·ro·as·tri·an·ism** \-trē-ə-ˌniz-əm\ *n*

zounds \'z(w)aún(d)z, 'z(w)ün(d)z\ *interj* — used as a mild oath

zuc·chi·ni \zù-'kē-nē\ *n, pl* **-ni** *or* **-nis** : a smooth cylinder-shaped usually dark green summer squash; *also* : a plant that bears zucchini

Zu·lu \'zü-lü\ *n, pl* **Zulu** *or* **Zulus** : a member of a Bantu-speaking people of South Africa — **Zulu** *adj*

Zu·ni \'zü-nē\ *also* **Zu·ñi** \'zün-yē\ *n, pl* **Zuni** *or* **Zunis** *also* **Zuñi** *or* **Zuñis** : an American Indian people of western New Mexico

zwie·back \'swē-ˌbak, 'swī-, 'zwē-, 'zwī-, -ˌbäk\ *n* : a usually sweet bread made with eggs that is baked and then sliced and toasted until dry and crisp

zy·de·co \'zīd-ə-ˌkō\ *n* : popular music of southern Louisiana that combines tunes of French origin with elements of Caribbean music and blues

zy·gote \'zī-ˌgōt\ *n* : a cell formed by the union of two sex cells; *also* : the developing individual produced from such a cell — **zy·got·ic** \zī-'gät-ik\ *adj*

SIGNS OF THE ZODIAC

NO.	NAME	SYMBOL	SUN ENTERS[1]
1	Aries the Ram	♈	March 21
2	Taurus the Bull	♉	April 20
3	Gemini the Twins	♊	May 21
4	Cancer the Crab	♋	June 22
5	Leo the Lion	♌	July 23
6	Virgo the Virgin	♍	August 23
7	Libra the Balance	♎	September 23
8	Scorpio the Scorpion	♏	October 24
9	Sagittarius the Archer	♐	November 22
10	Capricorn the Goat	♑	December 22
11	Aquarius the Water Bearer	♒	January 20
12	Pisces the Fishes	♓	February 19

[1] Though no longer astronomically accurate, these traditional dates continue to be used in astrology.

Abbreviations
AND SYMBOLS FOR CHEMICAL ELEMENTS

Most of these abbreviations have been entered according to one standard form. There is, however, variation in the use of periods and of capital letters (as *mph, m.p.h., Mph,* and *MPH*). Therefore, stylings other than those given in this dictionary are often acceptable.

a absent, acre, alto, answer, are, area, atto-
A ace, ampere, argon
Å angstrom unit
AA associate in arts
AAA American Automobile Association
A and M agricultural and mechanical
AB able-bodied seaman, Alberta, bachelor of arts [modern Latin *artium baccalaureus*]
abbr abbreviation
ABC American Broadcasting Companies
abl ablative
abp archbishop
abs absolute, abstract
ABS antilock braking system
abstr abstract
ac account, acre
Ac actinium
AC air-conditioning, alternating current, before Christ [Latin *ante Christum*], area code
acad academic, academy
acc, accus accusative
accel accelerando
acct account, accountant
act active, actor, actual
ACT Australian Capital Territory
AD after date, Alzheimer's disease, anno Domini
ADC aide-de-camp, Aid to Dependent Children
addn addition
adj adjective, adjutant
ad loc to or at the place [Latin *ad locum*]
ADM admiral
admin administration, administrative
adv adverb
advt advertisement
aero aerodynamic
AF air force, audio frequency
AFDC Aid to Families with Dependent Children

AFL–CIO American Federation of Labor and Congress of Industrial Organizations
Afr Africa, African
Ag silver [Latin *argentum*]
agcy agency
agr, agric agricultural, agriculture
agt agent
AI artificial intelligence
AK Alaska
aka also known as
Al aluminum
AL Alabama, American League
Ala Alabama
Alas Alaska
Alb Albania, Albanian
alc alcohol
ald alderman
alg algebra
alk alkaline
alt alternate, altitude
Alta Alberta
a.m., A.M. ante meridiem
Am America, American, americium
AM master of arts [modern Latin *artium magister*]
amb ambassador
amdt amendment
Amer America, American
AmerInd American Indian
Amn airman
amt amount
amu atomic mass unit
anat anatomical, anatomy
anc ancient
ann annual
anon anonymous, anonymously
ans answer
ant antonym
Ant Antarctica
anthrop anthropology
AP Associated Press
APB all points bulletin
APO army post office
approx approximate, approximately
appt appointment
Apr April
apt apartment, aptitude

aq aqua, aqueous
ar arrival, arrive
Ar Arabic, argon
AR Arkansas
Arab Arabian, Arabic
arch architect, architectural, architecture
arith arithmetic
Ariz Arizona
Ark Arkansas
arr arranged, arrival, arrive
art article, artificial
ARV American Revised Version
As arsenic
AS American Samoa, Anglo-Saxon
ASAP as soon as possible
ASL American Sign Language
assn association
assoc associate, associated, association
asst assistant
ASV American Standard Version
At astatine
Atl Atlantic
atm atmosphere, atmospheric
at no atomic number
att attached, attention, attorney
attn attention
attrib attributive, attributively
atty attorney
at wt atomic weight
Au gold [Latin *aurum*]
AU astronomical unit
Aug August
Aus Austria, Austrian
Austral Australia
auth author
aux auxiliary verb
av avenue, average, avoirdupois
AV audiovisual, Authorized Version
avdp avoirdupois
ave avenue
avg average
awd all-wheel drive
AZ Arizona

b bachelor, back, bass, bat, billion, bishop, book, born
B Bible, boron
Ba barium
BA bachelor of arts, batting average
bal balance
Bart baronet
BBC British Broadcasting Corporation
bbl barrel, barrels
BBQ barbeque
BBS bulletin board system
BC before Christ, British Columbia
bcc blind carbon copy
BCE before the Christian Era, before the Common Era
bd board, bound
bd ft board foot
bdl, bdle bundle
Be beryllium
Belg Belgian, Belgium
bet between
bf boldface
bg background, bag
Bh bohrium
Bi bismuth
bib Bible, biblical
biog biographer, biographical, biography
biol biologic, biological, biologist, biology
bk bank, book, break
Bk berkelium
bkt basket, bracket
bl bale, barrel, black, blue
bldg building
blk black, block
blvd boulevard
BM basal metabolism, bowel movement
BMI body mass index
BMR basal metabolic rate
BO best offer, body odor, box office
bor borough
bp baptized, birthplace, bishop
BP batting practice, before the present, blood pressure, blueprint, boiling point

bpl birthplace

BPW Board of Public Works

br branch, brown

Br Britain, British, bromine

Braz Brazil, Brazilian

brb be right back

brig brigade, brigadier

Brit Britain, British

BS, BSc bachelor of science

BSA Boy Scouts of America

bskt basket

Bt baronet

BTW by the way

bu bureau, bushel

Bulg Bulgaria, Bulgarian

bull bulletin

bur bureau

bus business

BVM Blessed Virgin Mary

BWI British West Indies

bx box

BX base exchange

c calorie, carat, cent, centi-, centimeter, century, chapter, circa, circumference, contralto, copyright, cubic, cup, curie

C capacitance, carbon, Celsius, centigrade

ca circa

Ca calcium

CA California

CAD computer-aided design

cal small calorie

Cal California, large calorie

Calif California

Can, Canad Canada, Canadian

canc canceled

C & W country and western

cap capital, capitalize, capitalized

caps capitals, capsule

Capt captain

cat catalog

CATV cable television, community antenna television

Cb columbium

CBC Canadian Broadcasting Corporation

CBS Columbia Broadcasting System

cc cubic centimeter

cd candela, candle, cord

Cd cadmium

CD civil defense

CDR commander

CDT central daylight time

Ce cerium

CE Christian Era, Common Era

cent centigrade, central, century

cert certificate, certification, certified, certify

cf compare [Latin *confer*]

Cf californium

CF cystic fibrosis

CFC chlorofluorocarbon

cg centigram

CG coast guard

cgs centimeter-gram-second

ch chapter, church

chap chapter

chem chemical, chemist, chemistry

chg change, charge

Chin Chinese

chm, chmn chairman

CIA Central Intelligence Agency

C in C commander in chief

cir circle, circuit, circular, circumference

CIS Commonwealth of Independent States

civ civil, civilian, civilization

CJ chief justice

ck cask, check

cl centiliter, class, clause

Cl chlorine

clk clerk

cm centimeter

Cm curium

Cmdr commander

Cn copernicium

CNA certified nurse's aid

CNMI Commonwealth of the Northern Mariana Islands

CNN Cable News Network

CNS central nervous system

co company, county

Co cobalt

CO Colorado, commanding officer

c/o care of

COD cash on delivery, collect on delivery

col colonial, colony, color, colored, column, counsel

Col colonel, Colorado

Colo Colorado

com commercial organization

comm commander, commission, committee, commonwealth, community

comp comparative, compensation, compiled, compiler, composition, compound, comprehensive, comptroller

conc concentrated

cond condition, conductivity

conf conference, confidential

Confed Confederate

cong congress, congressional

conj conjunction

Conn Connecticut

cons consonant

const constant, constitution, constitutional, construction

constr construction

cont containing, contents, continent, continental, continued, control

contr contract, contraction, contralto

CORE Congress of Racial Equality

corp corporal, corporation

corr correct, corrected, correction

cos companies, cosine, counties

cp compare

CP candlepower, chemically pure, Communist Party

CPA certified public accountant

cpd compound

Cpl corporal

CPO chief petty officer

CPR cardiopulmonary resuscitation

CPS cycles per second

cr credit, creditor

Cr chromium

cresc crescendo

crit critical, criticism, criticized

CRT cathode ray tube

cryst crystalline, crystallized

Cs cesium

CS civil service

CSA Confederate States of America

csc cosecant

C-Span cable-satellite public affairs network

CST central standard time

ct carat, cent, count, court

CT central time, certified teacher, computed tomography, computerized tomography, Connecticut

ctn carton, cotangent

ctr center, counter

cu cubic

Cu copper [Latin *cuprum*]

cur currency, current

CV cardiovascular

cwt hundredweight

cyl cylinder

CZ Canal Zone

d date, daughter, day, dead, deceased, depart, departure, diameter; pence, penny [Latin *denarius, denarii*]

D Democrat, deuterium, doctor

DA district attorney

dag dekagram

dal, daL dekaliter

dam dekameter

Dan Danish

DAR Daughters of the American Revolution

dB decibel

Db dubnium

dbl, dble double

DC da capo, direct current, District of Columbia

DDS doctor of dental surgery

DE Delaware

dec deceased, decrease

Dec December

def definite, definition

deg degree

del delegate, delegation

Del Delaware

Den Denmark

dent dental, dentist, dentistry

dep deposit

dept department

der, deriv derivation, derivative

dg decigram

dia, diam diameter

diag diagonal, diagram

dial dialect

dict dictionary

dif, diff difference

dil dilute

dir direction, director

disc discount

dist distance, district

div divided, dividend, division, divorced

dl deciliter

DL disabled list

dm decimeter

DMD doctor of dental medicine [Latin *dentariae medicinae doctor*]

DMV Department of Motor Vehicles

dn down

DO doctor of osteopathy

DOA dead on arrival

DOB date of birth

doc document

dom domestic, dominion

DOS disk operating system

doz dozen

DP data processing

dpi dots per inch

dpt department

dr dram, drive, drum

Dr doctor

Ds darmstadtium

DS dal segno

DSL digital subscriber line

DST daylight saving time

DTP diphtheria, tetanus, pertussis

Du Dutch

dup duplex, duplicate

DV Douay Version

DVM doctor of veterinary medicine

DVR digital video recorder

dwt pennyweight

Dy dysprosium

dz dozen

e east, eastern, edge

E energy, English, error, excellent

ea each

EB eastbound

EC European Community

eccl ecclesiastic, ecclesiastical

ecol ecological, ecology

econ economics, economist, economy

Ecua Ecuador

ed edited, edition, editor, education

EDT eastern daylight time

edu educational institution

educ education, educational

EEO equal employment opportunity

e.g. for example [Latin *exempli gratia*]

Eg Egypt, Egyptian

EHF extremely high frequency

el, elev elevation

elec electric, electrical, electricity

elem elementary

ELF extremely low frequency

EM electromagnetic, electron microscope

EMS emergency medical service

enc enclosure

ency, encyc encyclopedia

ENE east-northeast

eng engine, engineer, engineering

Eng England, English

ENS ensign

env envelope

EPA Environmental Protection Agency

EPO erythropoietin

eq equal, equation

Er erbium

ER earned run, emergency room

ERA earned run average, Equal Rights Amendment

Es einsteinium

ESE east-southeast

Esk Eskimo

ESL English as a second language

esp especially

ESPN Entertainment and Sports Programming Network

Esq, Esqr esquire

est established, estimate, estimated

EST eastern standard time

ET eastern time

ETA estimated time of arrival

et al and others [Latin *et alii*]

etc. et cetera

ETD estimated time of departure

Eu europium

EU European Union

Eur Europe, European

eval evaluation

evap evaporate

ex example, executive, extra

exc excellent, except

exp expense, export, express

expt experiment

exptl experimental

ext extension, exterior, extra

f and the following one [*following*], failure, false, female, feminine, focal length, folio, forte, frequency, from

F Fahrenheit, fluorine, French, Friday

Fah, Fahr Fahrenheit

FAQ frequently asked question

fath fathom

FBI Federal Bureau of Investigation

FD fire department

FDA Food and Drug Administration

Fe iron [Latin *ferrum*]

Feb February

fem female, feminine

ff and the following ones [*following*], fortissimo

FICA Federal Insurance Contributions Act

fig figure

fin finish

Finn Finnish

fl fluid

FL, Fla Florida

fl dr fluid dram

Flem Flemish

fl oz fluid ounce

Fm fermium

FOB free on board

for foreign, forestry

4WD four-wheel drive

fp freezing point

fpm feet per minute

FPO fleet post office

fps feet per second, foot-pound-second

fr father, friar, from

Fr France, francium, French, Friday

freq frequency, frequent, frequently

FRG Federal Republic of Germany

Fri Friday

frt freight

frwy freeway

FSH follicle-stimulating hormone

ft feet, foot, fort

ft lb foot-pound

F2F face-to-face

fut future

fwd foreword, forward

FWD front-wheel drive

FYI for your information

g acceleration of gravity, good, gram, gravity

G German, giga-

Ga gallium, Georgia

GA Georgia

gal gallon

gar garage

GB gigabyte, Great Britain

GCD greatest common divisor

GCF greatest common factor

Gd gadolinium

Ge germanium

gen general, genitive

geog geographic, geographical, geography

geol geologic, geological, geology

geom geometric, geometrical, geometry

ger gerund

Ger German, Germany

GHz gigahertz

gi gill

GI gastrointestinal, general issue, government issue

Gib, Gibr Gibraltar

Gk Greek

gm gram

GM general manager, genetically modified

GMT Greenwich mean time

GNP gross national product

GOP Grand Old Party (Republican)

gov government, governmental organization, governor

govt government

gp group

GP general practice, general practitioner

GPA grade point average

GPO general post office

GQ general quarters

gr grade, grain, gram, gravity, gross

Gr Greece, Greek

gro gross

GSA Girl Scouts of America

GSUSA Girl Scouts of the United States of America

gt great

Gt Brit Great Britain

GU Guam

GUI graphical user interface

h hard, hardness, height, hit, hour, husband

H heroin, hydrogen

ha hectare

HAST Hawaii-Aleutian standard time

hd head

HD heavy-duty

HDTV high-definition television

He helium

Heb Hebrew

hf half

Hf hafnium

HF high frequency

hg hectogram

Hg mercury [Latin *hydrargyrum*, literally, water silver]

hgt height

hgwy highway

HI Hawaii

hist historian, historical, history

hl hectoliter

hm hectometer

HM Her Majesty, Her Majesty's, His Majesty, His Majesty's

HMS Her Majesty's ship, His Majesty's ship

Ho holmium

hon honor, honorable, honorary

hor horizontal

hort horticultural, horticulture

hosp hospital

hp horsepower

HP high pressure

HQ headquarters

hr here, hour

HR home run, House of Representatives

HRH Her Royal Highness, His Royal Highness

Hs hassium

HS high school

ht height

HT high-tension

Hung Hungarian, Hungary

HVAC heating, ventilating, and air-conditioning; heating, ventilation, and air-conditioning

hwy highway

Hz hertz

i initial, intransitive, island, isle

I electric current, Indian, interstate, iodine, Israeli

Ia, IA Iowa

ICU intensive care unit

ID Idaho, identification

i.e. that is [Latin *id est*]

IL, Ill Illinois

ill, illus, illust illustrated, illustration

IM instant message

IMHO in my humble opinion

imp imperative, imperfect

in inch

In Indium

IN Indiana

inc incomplete, incorporated, increase

ind independent, index, industrial, industry

Ind Indian, Indiana

indef indefinite

indic indicative

inf infantry, infinitive

INP International News Photo

INRI Jesus of Nazareth, King of the Jews [Latin *Iesus Nazarenus Rex Iudaeorum*]

INS Immigration and Naturalization Service

inst instant, institute, institution, institutional

instr instructor

int interest, intermediate, international, intransitive

interj interjection

interrog interrogative

intrans intransitive

I/O input/output

IOC International Olympic Committee

IP innings pitched, Internet protocol

Ir iridium, Irish

IR infrared

Ire Ireland

irreg irregular

IRS Internal Revenue Service

is island, isle

ISBN International Standard Book Number

ISP Internet service provider

Isr Israel, Israeli

It Italian, Italy

IT information technology

ital italic, italicized

Ital Italian

IU international unit

IV intravenous, intravenously

IWW Industrial Workers of the World

J joule

Jam Jamaica

Jan January

JC junior college

jct junction

JD juvenile delinquent

JP justice of the peace

Jpn Japan, Japanese

Jr junior

jt, jnt joint

jun junior

junc junction

juv juvenile

JV junior varsity

k karat, kindergarten, knit, kosher — often enclosed in a circle

K kelvin, kilometer, potassium [Latin *kalium*]

Kan, Kans Kansas

KB kilobyte

kc kilocycle

KC Kansas City

kcal kilocalorie

kc/s kilocycles per second

kg kilogram

kHz kilohertz

KIA killed in action

kJ kilojoule

KJV King James Version

KKK Ku Klux Klan

kl kiloliter

km kilometer

kPa kilopascal

kph kilometers per hour

Kr krypton

KS Kansas

kt karat, knot

kV kilovolt

kW kilowatt

kWh kilowatt-hour

Ky, KY Kentucky

l large, left, line, liter

L Latin, long, loss, losses

La lanthanum, Louisiana

LA law agent, Los Angeles, Louisiana

Lab Labrador

lang language

lat latitude

Lat Latin

lb pound [Latin *libra*]

lc lowercase

LCD least common denominator, lowest common denominator

LCM least common multiple, lowest common multiple

LD learning disability, learning disabled, lethal dose

leg legal, legato, legislative, legislature

LEM lunar excursion module, lunar module

LF low frequency

lg large, long

LGBT lesbian, gay, bisexual, and transgender

LH left hand, luteinizing hormone

Li lithium

LI Long Island

lib liberal, librarian, library

lieut lieutenant

liq liquid

lit liter, literal, literally

ll lines

LLD doctor of laws [Latin *legum doctor*]

LM lunar module

ln lane

LNG liquefied natural gas

Lond London

long longitude

loq he speaks, she speaks [Latin *loquitur*]

LPG liquefied petroleum gas

Lr lawrencium

LS left side

LSI large-scale integrated circuit, large-scale integration

Lt lieutenant

ltd limited

ltr letter

Lu lutetium

lv leave

m male, married, masculine, mass, meter, mile, milli-, minute, noon [Latin *meridies*], thousand [Latin *mille*]

M medium, mega-, monsieur

ma milliampere

MA Massachusetts, master of arts [Latin *magister artium*]

mach machine, machinery, machinist

mag magazine, magnetism

Maj major

man manual

Man Manitoba

manuf manufacturer

Mar March

masc masculine

Mass Massachusetts

MAT master of arts in teaching

math mathematical, mathematician

mb millibar

Mb megabit

MB megabyte

Mbps megabits per second

mc megacycle

MC member of Congress

Md Maryland, mendelevium

MD doctor of medicine [Latin *medicinae doctor*], Maryland, muscular dystrophy

mdse merchandise

Me Maine

ME Maine

meas measure

mech mechanic, mechanical

med medical, medicine, medieval, medium

mem member, memorial

MeV million electron volts

Mex Mexican, Mexico

mf mezzo forte

MF medium frequency, microfiche

mfd manufactured

mfg manufacturing

mfr manufacturer

mg milligram

Mg magnesium

mgmt, mgt management

mgr manager, monseigneur, monsignor

MHz megahertz

mi mile, miles

MI, Mich Michigan

MIA missing in action

mil military

min minimum, minute, minutes

Minn Minnesota

misc miscellaneous

Miss Mississippi

MKS meter-kilogram-second

ml milliliter

MLB Major League Baseball

Mlle mademoiselle [French]

Mlles mesdemoiselles [French]

MLS Major League Soccer

mm millimeter

MM messieurs [French]

Mme madame [French]

MMes mesdames [French]

Mn manganese

MN magnetic north, Minnesota

mo month

Mo Missouri, molybdenum

MO Missouri

mol molecular, molecule

mol wt molecular weight

Mon Monday

Mont Montana

mos months

MP melting point

mpg miles per gallon

mph miles per hour

MRE meals ready to eat

mRNA messenger RNA

ms millisecond

MS manuscript, master of science, Mississippi, multiple sclerosis

msec millisecond

MSG monosodium glutamate

msgr monsignor

MSS manuscripts

MST mountain standard time

mt mount, mountain

Mt meitnerium

MT metric ton, Montana, mountain time

mus museum, music

MVP most valuable player

mya million years ago

n neuter, neutron, north, northern, note, noun

N newton, nitrogen

Na sodium [Latin *natrium*]

NA North America, not applicable, not available

NAACP National Association for the Advancement of Colored People

NASA National Aeronautics and Space Administration

natl, nat'l national

NATO North Atlantic Treaty Organization

nav naval, navigation

Nb niobium

NB New Brunswick, northbound

NBC National Broadcasting Company

NBS National Bureau of Standards

NC no charge, North Carolina

Nd neodymium

ND, N Dak North Dakota

Ne neon

NE Nebraska, New England, northeast

Neb, Nebr Nebraska

neg negative

Neth Netherlands

neut neuter

Nev Nevada

NF, Nfld Newfoundland

NG national guard, no good

NH New Hampshire

Ni nickel

NIST National Institute of Standards and Technology

NJ New Jersey
NL National League, New-foundland and Labrador
nm nanometer, nautical mile
NM, N Mex New Mexico
NNE north-northeast
NNW north-northwest
no north, northern, number [Latin *numero*]
No nobelium
nom nominative
Nor Norway, Norwegian
Nov November
NOW National Organization for Women
NO$_x$ nitrogen oxide
Np neptunium
NP noun phrase
ns nanosecond
NS Nova Scotia
NT New Testament, Northwest Territories
NTP normal temperature and pressure
num numeral
NV Nevada
NW northwest
NWT Northwest Territories
NY New York
NYC New York City
NZ New Zealand
o ocean, ohm
O Ohio, oxygen
OAS Organization of American States
obj object, objective
obs obsolete
occas occasionally
Oct October
OD officer of the day
OF outfield
off office, officer, official
OH Ohio
OJ orange juice
OK, Okla Oklahoma
ON, Ont Ontario
op operation, operative, operator, opportunity, opus
OPEC Organization of Petroleum Exporting Countries
opp opposite
opt optical, optician, optional
OR operating room, Oregon
ord order
Ore, Oreg Oregon
org organization
orig original, originally
Os osmium
OS operating system
OT Old Testament, overtime
oz ounce, ounces [obsolete Italian *onza* (now *onica*)]
p page, pages, participle, past, pint
P phosphorus, pressure
Pa pascal, Pennsylvania, protactinium

PA Pennsylvania, personal assistant, public address
Pac Pacific
Pan Panama
para paragraph
part participle, particular
pass passenger, passive
pat patent
path, pathol pathological, pathology
payt payment
pb paperback
Pb lead [Latin *plumbum*]
PB personal best
PB&J peanut butter and jelly
PBS Public Broadcasting Service
PC Peace Corps, percent, percentage, political correctness, politically correct, postcard
pct percent, percentage
pd paid
Pd palladium
PD police department
PE physical education
PEI Prince Edward Island
pen peninsula
Penn, Penna Pennsylvania
per period, person
perf perfect
perh perhaps
perp perpendicular
pers person, personal
Pers Persia, Persian
PFC, Pfc private first class
pg page
pharm pharmaceutical, pharmacist, pharmacy
PhD doctor of philosophy [Latin *philosophiae doctor*]
photog photography
phr phrase
phys physical, physics
physiol physiologist, physiology
PI Philippine Islands, private investigator
PIN personal identification number
pizz pizzicato
pk park, peak, peck, pike
pkg package
PKU phenylketonuria
pkwy parkway
pl place, plural
pls please
p.m., P.M. post meridiem
Pm promethium
pmt payment
Po polonium
PO post office
Pol Poland, Polish
pop population
Port Portugal, Portuguese
pos position, positive
poss possessive, possible
pp pages, past participle, pianissimo
ppd postpaid, prepaid

PPS an additional postscript [Latin *post postscriptum*]
PPV pay-per-view
PQ Province of Quebec
pr pair, price, printed
Pr praseodymium
PR Puerto Rico
pred predicate
pref preface, prefix
prep preparatory, preposition
pres present, president
prev previous, previously
prf proof
prim primary, primitive
prin principal, principle
prob probably, problem
prod product, production
prof professional
pron pronoun, pronunciation
prop property, proposition, proprietor
Prot Protestant
prov province
PS postscript [Latin *postscriptum*], public school
pseud pseudonym
PST Pacific standard time
psych psychology
psychol psychological
pt part, pint, point
Pt platinum
PT Pacific time, physical therapy, physical training
PTA Parent-Teacher Association
PTO Parent-Teacher Organization, please turn over
PTV public television
Pu plutonium
pub public
pwt pennyweight
PX post exchange
q quart, queen, question
QED which was to be demonstrated [Latin *quod erat demonstrandum*]
qr quarter
qt quantity, quart
qu, ques question
Que Quebec
quot quotation
r radius, rate, resistance, right
R rabbi, regular, Republican, river
Ra radium
rad radius
R & B rhythm and blues
R & D research and development
Rb rubidium
RBC red blood cell
RC Red Cross, Roman Catholic
rd road, rod
RD rural delivery
RDA recommended daily allowance, recommended dietary allowance

Re rhenium
rec receipt, record, recording, recreation, recreational
rec'd received
ref reference
reg region, regular
rel relative, religion, religious
rep representative, republic
Rep Republican
repl replace, replacement
rept report
req request, require, required
res residence, resident
rev review, revised, revolution
Rev reverend
Rf rutherfordium
RF radio frequency
RFD rural free delivery
RFID radio-frequency identification
Rg roentgenium
Rh rhodium
RH right hand, right-hander
RI Rhode Island
rit ritardando
riv river
rm room
Rn radon
Rom Roman, Romania, Romanian
ROTC Reserve Officers' Training Corps
RP relief pitcher, Republic of the Philippines
rpm revolutions per minute
rps revolutions per second
RR railroad, rural route
RS right side
RSV Revised Standard Version
RSVP please reply [French *répondez s'il vous plaît*]
rt right, route
rte route
Ru ruthenium
Russ Russia, Russian
RV Revised Version
rwy, ry railway
s saint, second, small
S satisfactory, south, southern, sulfur
SA Salvation Army, South Africa, South America
SASE self-addressed stamped envelope
Sask Saskatchewan
sat satellite, saturated
Sat Saturday
sb substantive
Sb antimony [Latin *stibium*]
SB bachelor of science [scientific Latin *scientiae baccalaureus*], southbound
sc science
Sc scandium, Scots, Scottish
SC small capitals, South Carolina

Scand Scandinavia, Scandinavian
sch school
sci science, scientific
Scot Scotland, Scottish
SD, S Dak South Dakota
Se selenium
SE southeast
SEATO Southeast Asia Treaty Organization
sec secant, second, secondary, secretary, section
secy secretary
sel select, selected, selection
sem seminar, seminary
sen senate, senator, senior
Sept, Sep September
ser serial, series, service
sergt sergeant
serv service
sf, sfz sforzando
SF sacrifice fly, science fiction, square feet, square foot
Sg seaborgium
Sgt sergeant
sh share
Si silicon
SI International System of Units [French *Système International d'Unités*]
sin sine
sing singular
sm small
Sm samarium
SM master of science [scientific Latin *scientiae magister*]
Sn tin [Latin *stannum*]
so south, southern
SO strikeout
soc social, society
sociol sociologist, sociology
soph sophomore
sp special, species, specific, spelling
Sp Spain, Spanish
Span Spanish
SPCA Society for the Prevention of Cruelty to Animals
SPCC Society for the Prevention of Cruelty to Children
spec special, specifically
specif specific, specifically
SpEd, SPED special education
sp gr specific gravity
spp species *(pl)*
sq square
Sr senior, senor, sister, strontium
Sra senora
SRO standing room only
Srta senorita

SS saints, Social Security, steamship
SSE south-southeast
ssp subspecies
SSR Soviet Socialist Republic
SSS Selective Service System
SSW south-southwest
st state
St saint, street
ST standard time
sta station
Ste saint (female) [French *sainte*]
STEM science, technology, engineering, and mathematics
stud student
sub subscription, suburb
subj subject, subjunctive
suff sufficient, suffix
Sun Sunday
sup superior
supp supplement
supt superintendent
surg surgeon, surgery, surgical
Sw, Swed Sweden, Swedish
SW southwest, southwestern
Switz Switzerland
sym symmetrical
syn synonym, synonymy
syst system
t metric ton, tablespoon, teaspoon, temperature, tense, ton, transitive, true
T tritium, T-shirt
Ta tantalum
tan tangent
tb tablespoon, tablespoonful
Tb terbium
TBA to be announced
tbs, tbsp tablespoon, tablespoonful
Tc technetium
TD touchdown
TDD telecommunications device for the deaf
Te tellurium
tech technical, technically, technological, technology
TEFL teaching English as a foreign language
tel telephone
temp temporary
Tenn Tennessee
ter terrace
terr territory
Tex Texas
TGIF thank God it's Friday
Th thorium, Thursday
Thurs, Thur, Thu Thursday
Ti titanium
Tl thallium
TLC tender loving care

Tm thulium
TM trademark
tn ton, town
TN Tennessee
tnpk turnpike
tot total
tp township
tpk, tpke turnpike
trans transitive, translated, transmission, transportation
trib tributary
TSH thyroid-stimulating hormone
tsp teaspoon, teaspoonful
TTY teletypewriter
Tues, Tue, Tu Tuesday
Turk Turkey, Turkish
TVA Tennessee Valley Authority
TX Texas
u unit
U university, unsatisfactory, uranium
UHF ultrahigh frequency
UK United Kingdom
ult ultimo
UN United Nations
UNESCO United Nations Educational, Scientific, and Cultural Organization
UNICEF United Nations Children's Fund [*United Nations International Children's Emergency Fund*, its former name]
univ university
UPC Universal Product Code
UPI United Press International
US United States
USA United States Army, United States of America
USAF United States Air Force
USCG United States Coast Guard
USDA United States Department of Agriculture
USMC United States Marine Corps
USN United States Navy
USO United Service Organizations
USPS United States Postal Service
USS United States ship
USSR Union of Soviet Socialist Republics
usu usual, usually
USVI United States Virgin Islands
UT Utah
UV ultraviolet
v velocity, verb, verse, very, victory, voltage, volume
V vanadium, violence, violent, volt

Va Virginia
VA Veterans Administration, Virginia
var variant, various
vb verb, verbal
VD venereal disease
Ven venerable
vert vertical
VFW Veterans of Foreign Wars
VG very good
VHF very high frequency
vi verb intransitive
VI Virgin Islands
vis visual
VISTA Volunteers in Service to America
viz namely [Latin *videlicet*]
vol volume, volunteer
VP verb phrase, vice president
vs versus
vt verb transitive
Vt, VT Vermont
vv verses
w water, week, weight, white, wide, width, wife, with
W tungsten [German *wolfram*], watt, west, western
WA Washington
Wash Washington
WB westbound
WBC white blood cell
WC water closet
We, Wed Wednesday
wh white
WH watt-hour
WHO World Health Organization
WI, Wis, Wisc Wisconsin
wk week, work
WNW west-northwest
w/o without
WPM words per minute
WSW west-southwest
wt weight
WV, W Va West Virginia
WW world war
www World Wide Web
WY, Wyo Wyoming
Xe xenon
XL extra large, extra long
XS extra small
y yard, year
Y yttrium
Yb ytterbium
yd yard
YK Yukon Territory
YOB year of birth
yr year, your
YT Yukon Territory
Yug Yugoslavia
z zero
Zn zinc
zool zoological, zoology
ZPG zero population growth
Zr zirconium

Biographical, Biblical, and Mythological Names

This section is a listing of the names of important figures from recorded history, biblical tradition, classical mythology, popular legend, and current events. Figures from the Bible, myth, or legend are clearly identified as such. In cases where figures have alternate names, they are entered under the name by which they are best known. The part of the name shown in boldface type is either the family name or the common shorter name for that figure. The dates following the name or pronunciation are the birth and death dates. Other dates in the entry refer to the dates of a particular office, honor, or achievement. Italicized names within an entry refer to a person's nickname, original name, title, or other name.

Aar·on \'ar-ən, 'er-\ brother of Moses and high priest of the Hebrews in the Bible

Aaron Hank 1934–   *Henry Louis Aaron* American baseball player

Abel \'ā-bəl\ son of Adam and Eve and brother of Cain in the Bible

Abra·ham \'ā-brə-ˌham\ patriarch and founder of the Hebrew people in the Bible; also revered by Muslims

Achil·les \ə-'kil-ēz\ hero of the Trojan War in Greek mythology

Ad·am \'ad-əm\ the 1st man in biblical tradition

Ad·ams \'ad-əmz\ Abigail 1744–1818 née *Smith* American writer; wife of John Adams

Adams Ansel Easton 1902–1984 American photographer

Adams John 1735–1826 2nd president of the U.S. (1797–1801)

Adams John Quin·cy \'kwin-zē, 'kwin(t)-sē\ 1767–1848 6th president of the U.S. (1825–29); son of John and Abigail Adams

Adams Samuel 1722–1803 patriot in the American Revolution

Ad·dams \'ad-əmz\ Jane 1860–1935 American social worker; Nobel Prize winner (1931)

Ado·nis \ə-'dän-əs, -'dō-nəs\ beautiful youth in Greek mythology who is loved by Aphrodite

Ae·ne·as \i-'nē-əs\ Trojan hero in Greek and Roman mythology

Ae·o·lus \'ē-ə-ləs\ god of the winds in Greek mythology

Aes·chy·lus \'es-kə-ləs, 'ēs-\ 525–456 B.C. Greek dramatist

Aes·cu·la·pi·us \ˌes-kyə-'lā-pē-əs\ god of medicine in Roman mythology — compare ASCLEPIUS

Ae·sop \'ē-ˌsäp, -səp\ legendary Greek writer of fables

Ag·a·mem·non \ˌag-ə-'mem-ˌnän, -nən\ leader of the Greeks during the Trojan War in Greek mythology

Ag·nes \'ag-nəs\ Saint *died* 304 A.D. Christian martyr

Ahab \'ā-ˌhab\ king of Israel in the 9th century B.C. and husband of Jezebel

Ajax \'ā-ˌjaks\ hero in Greek mythology who kills himself because the armor of Achilles is awarded to Odysseus during the Trojan War

Alad·din \ə-'lad-ᵊn\ youth in the *Arabian Nights' Entertainments* who acquires a magic lamp and ring

Al·bright \'ȯl-ˌbrīt\ Madeleine 1937–   née *Korbel* American (Czech-born) diplomat; U.S. secretary of state (1997–2001)

Al·cott \'ȯl-kət, 'al-, -ˌkät\ Louisa May 1832–1888 American author

Al·ex·an·der \ˌal-ig-'zan-dər, ˌel-\ name of eight popes: especially **VI** 1431–1503 (pope 1492–1503)

Alexander the Great 356–323 B.C. *Alexander III* king of Macedonia (336–323)

Al·fred \'al-frəd, -fərd\ 849–899 *Alfred the Great* king of the West Saxons (871–899)

Ali Ba·ba \ˌal-ē-'bäb-ə\ woodcutter in the *Arabian Nights' Entertainments* who enters the cave of the Forty Thieves by using the password *Sesame*

Al·len \'al-ən\ Ethan 1738–1789 American Revolutionary soldier

Amerigo Vespucci — see VESPUCCI

Am·herst \'am-(ˌ)ərst\ Jeffery 1717–1797 Baron *Amherst* British general in America

Amund·sen \'äm-ən-sən\ Roald 1872–1928 Norwegian explorer and discoverer of the South Pole (1911)

An·a·ni·as \ˌan-ə-'nī-əs\ early Christian in the Bible struck dead for lying

An·der·sen \'an-dər-sən\ Hans Christian 1805–1875 Danish writer of fairy tales

An·der·son \'an-dər-sən\ Marian 1897–1993 American contralto

An·ge·lou \'an-jə-ˌlō\ Maya 1928–2014 originally *Marguerite Johnson* American author

Anne \'an\ 1665–1714 queen of Great Britain (1702–14)

An·tho·ny \'an(t)-thə-nē\ Susan Brownell 1820–1906 American suffragist

An·tig·o·ne \an-'tig-ə-nē\ daughter of Oedipus and Jocasta in Greek mythology

An·to·ny \'an-tə-nē\ Mark *about* 82–30 B.C. *Mark Anthony*; *Marcus An·to·ni·us* \an-'tō-nē-əs\ Roman general and triumvir (43–30)

Aph·ro·di·te \ˌaf-rə-'dīt-ē\ goddess of love and beauty in Greek mythology — compare VENUS

Apol·lo \ə-'päl-ō\ god of sunlight, prophecy, music, and poetry in Greek and Roman mythology

Ap·ple·seed \'ap-əl-ˌsēd\ Johnny 1774–1845 originally *John Chap·man* \'chap-mən\ American pioneer

\ə\ **abut**		\aů\ **out**	\i\ **tip**	\ȯ\ **saw**	\ů\ **foot**
\ər\ **further**		\ch\ **chin**	\ī\ **life**	\ȯi\ **coin**	\y\ **yet**
\a\ **mat**		\e\ **pet**	\j\ **job**	\th\ **thin**	\yü\ **few**
\ā\ **take**		\ē\ **easy**	\ŋ\ **sing**	\th\ **this**	\yů\ **cure**
\ä\ **cot, cart**		\g\ **go**	\ō\ **bone**	\ü\ **food**	\zh\ **vision**

Aqui·nas \ə-'kwī-nəs\ Saint Thomas 1224 (or 1225)–1274 Italian theologian

Ar·chi·me·des \ˌär-kə-'mēd-ēz\ *about* 287–212 B.C. Greek mathematician and inventor

Ares \'a(ə)r-ēz, 'e(ə)r-\ god of war in Greek mythology — compare MARS

Ar·is·toph·a·nes \ˌar-ə-'stäf-ə-ˌnēz\ *about* 450–*about* 388 B.C. Greek playwright

Ar·is·tot·le \'ar-ə-ˌstät-ᵊl\ 384–322 B.C. Greek philosopher

Arm·strong \'ärm-ˌstrȯŋ\ Lance 1971– American cyclist

Armstrong Louis 1901–1971 *Satch·mo* \'sach-ˌmō\ American jazz musician

Armstrong Neil Alden 1930–2012 American astronaut and 1st man on the moon (1969)

Ar·nold \'ärn-ᵊld\ Benedict 1741–1801 American Revolutionary general and traitor

Ar·te·mis \'ärt-ə-məs\ goddess of the moon, wild animals, and hunting in Greek mythology — compare DIANA

Ar·thur \'är-thər\ legendary king of the Britons whose story is based on traditions of a 6th century military leader — **Ar·thu·ri·an** \är-'th(y)ùr-ē-ən\ *adj*

Arthur Chester Alan 1829–1886 21st president of the U.S. (1881–85)

As·cle·pi·us \ə-'sklē-pē-əs\ god of medicine in Greek mythology — compare AESCULAPIUS

As·tor \'as-tər\ John Jacob 1763–1848 American (German-born) fur trader and capitalist

Athe·na \ə-'thē-nə\ *or* **Athe·ne** \-nē\ goddess of wisdom in Greek mythology — compare MINERVA

At·las \'at-ləs\ Titan in Greek mythology forced to bear the heavens on his shoulders

At·ti·la \ə-'til-ə, 'at-ᵊl-ə\ 406?–453 A.D. king of the Huns

At·tucks \'at-əks\ Crispus 1723?–1770 American patriot

Au·du·bon \'ȯd-ə-ˌbän, -bən\ John James 1785–1851 American (Haitian-born) artist and naturalist

Au·gus·tine \'ȯ-gə-ˌstēn; ȯ-'gəs-tən, ə-\ Saint 354–430 A.D. church father; bishop of Hippo (396–430)

Au·gus·tus \ȯ-'gəs-təs, ə-\ *or* **Caesar Augustus** *or* **Oc·ta·vi·an** \äk-'tā-vē-ən\ 63 B.C.–14 A.D. first Roman emperor (27 B.C.–14 A.D.)

Au·ro·ra \ə-'rōr-ə, ȯ-'rȯr-, -'rȯr-\ goddess of the dawn in Roman mythology — compare EOS

Aus·ten \'ȯs-tən, 'äs-\ Jane 1775–1817 English author

Bac·chus \'bak-əs\ — see DIONYSUS

Bach \'bäk̲, 'bäk\ Johann Sebastian 1685–1750 German composer and organist

Ba·con \'bā-kən\ Francis 1561–1626 English philosopher and author

Ba·den–Pow·ell \ˌbād-ᵊn-'pō-əl\ Robert Stephenson Smyth 1857–1941 Baron *Baden-Powell* British general and founder of Boy Scout movement

Baf·fin \'baf-ən\ William *about* 1584–1622 English navigator

Bal·boa \bal-'bō-ə\ Vasco Núñez de 1475–1519 Spanish explorer and discoverer of Pacific Ocean (1513)

Baltimore Lord — see George CALVERT

Bal·zac \'bȯl-ˌzak, 'bal-\ Honoré de 1799–1850 French author

Ba·rab·bas \bə-'rab-əs\ prisoner in the Bible released in preference to Jesus at the demand of the multitude

Bar·num \'bär-nəm\ P. T. 1810–1891 *Phineas Taylor Barnum* American showman

Bar·rie \'bar-ē\ Sir James Matthew 1860–1937 Scottish author

Bar·thol·di \bär-'täl-dē, -'tȯl-, -'thäl-, -'thȯl-\ Frédéric-Auguste 1834–1904 French sculptor of the Statue of Liberty

Bar·ton \'bärt-ᵊn\ Clara 1821–1912 founder of American Red Cross Society

Beau·re·gard \'bōr-ə-ˌgärd, 'bȯr-\ Pierre Gustave Toutant 1818–1893 American Confederate general

Beck·et \'bek-ət\ Saint Thomas *about* 1118–1170 *Thomas à Becket* archbishop of Canterbury (1162–70)

Bee·tho·ven \'bā-ˌtō-vən\ Ludwig van 1770–1827 German composer

Bell \'bel\ Alexander Graham 1847–1922 American (Scottish-born) inventor of the telephone

Ben·e·dict \'ben-ə-ˌdikt\ name of 16 popes: especially **XIV** 1675–1758 (pope 1740–58); **XV** 1854–1922 (pope 1914–22); **XVI** 1927– (pope 2005–13)

Be·nét \bə-'nā\ Stephen Vincent 1898–1943 American author

Ben·ja·min \'benj-(ə-)mən\ youngest son of Jacob and ancestor of one of the 12 tribes of Israel in the Bible

Be·o·wulf \'bā-ə-ˌwùlf\ legendary warrior and hero of the Old English poem *Beowulf*

Be·ring \'bi(ə)r-iŋ, 'be(ə)r-\ Vitus 1681–1741 Danish navigator and explorer for Russia

Ber·lin \(ˌ)bər-'lin\ Irving 1888–1989 American (Russian-born) composer

Ber·ners-Lee \'bər-nərz-'lē\ Sir Timothy John 1955– British inventor

Ber·ni·ni \bər-'nē-nē\ Gian Lorenzo 1598–1680 Italian sculptor, architect, and painter

Bes·se·mer \'bes-ə-mər\ Sir Henry 1813–1898 English engineer and inventor

Be·thune \bə-'th(y)ün\ Mary 1875–1955 née *McLeod* American educator

Bi·den \'bī-dᵊn\ Joseph Robinette, Jr. 1942– vice president of the U.S. (2009–17)

Bi·zet \bē-'zā\ Georges 1838–1875 originally *Alexandre-César-Léopold Bizet* French composer

Black Hawk \'blak-ˌhȯk\ 1767–1838 American Indian chief

Black·well \'blak-ˌwel, -wəl\ Elizabeth 1821–1910 American (English-born) physician

Blair \'bla(ə)r, 'ble(ə)r\ Tony 1953– *Anthony Charles Lynton Blair* British prime minister (1997–2007)

Blake \'blāk\ William 1757–1827 English poet and artist

Bloom·er \'blü-mər\ Amelia 1818–1894 née *Jenks* American social reformer

Boc·cac·cio \bō-'käch-(ē-ˌ)ō\ Giovanni 1313–1375 Italian author

Bohr \'bō(ə)r, 'bȯ(ə)r\ Niels 1885–1962 Danish physicist; Nobel Prize winner (1922)

Bo·leyn \bù-'lin, 'bùl-ən\ Anne 1507?–1536 2nd wife of Henry VIII and mother of Elizabeth I of England

Bo·lí·var Si·món \sē-ˌmōn-bə-'lē-ˌvär, ˌsī-mən-'bäl-ə-vər\ 1783–1830 South American liberator

Bon·i·face \'bän-ə-fəs, -ˌfäs\ name of nine popes: especially **VIII** *about* 1235 (or 1240)–1303 (pope 1294–1303)

Boone \'bün\ Daniel 1734–1820 American pioneer

Booth \'büth\ John Wilkes 1838–1865 American actor; assassin of Abraham Lincoln

Bo·re·as \'bōr-ē-əs, 'bȯr-\ god of the north wind in Greek mythology

Bot·ti·cel·li \ˌbät-ə-'chel-ē\ Sandro 1445–1510 Italian painter

Bow·ie \'bü-ē, 'bō-\ Jim 1796–1836 *James Bowie* American popular hero of the Texas revolution

Boyle \'bȯi(ə)l\ Robert 1627–1691 English physicist and chemist

Brad·bury \'brad-ˌber-ē, -b(ə-)rē\ Ray Douglas 1920–2012 American author

Brad·dock \'brad-ək\ Edward 1695–1755 British general

Brad·ford \'brad-fərd\ William 1590–1657 Pilgrim leader

Brad·street \'brad-ˌstrēt\ Anne *about* 1612–1672 American poet

Bra·dy \'brād-ē\ Mathew B. 1823?–1896 American photographer

Brahe \'brä; 'brä-hē, -hə\ Tycho 1546–1601 Danish astronomer

Brah·ma \\'bräm-ə\\ creator god of the Hindu sacred triad — compare SHIVA, VISHNU

Brahms \\'brämz\\ Johannes 1833–1897 German composer

Braille \\'brā(ə)l, 'brī\\ Louis 1809–1852 French blind teacher of the blind

Bran·deis \\'bran-,dīs, -,dīz\\ Louis Dembitz 1856–1941 American jurist

Brant \\'brant\\ Joseph 1742–1807 *Thayendanegea* Mohawk Indian chief

Braun \\'braún\\ Wernher von 1912–1977 American (German-born) engineer

Brezh·nev \\'brezh-,nef\\ Leonid Ilyich 1906–1982 Russian politician; president of the U.S.S.R. (1960–64; 1977–82)

Bron·të \\'bränt-ē, 'brän-,tā\\ family of English writers: Charlotte 1816–1855 and her sisters Emily 1818–1848 and Anne 1820–1849

Brooks \\'brúks\\ Gwendolyn Elizabeth 1917–2000 American poet

Brown \\'braún\\ (James) Gordon 1951–   British prime minister (2007–10)

Brown John 1800–1859 American abolitionist

Brow·ning \\'braú-niŋ\\ Elizabeth Barrett 1806–1861 English poet; wife of Robert Browning

Browning Robert 1812–1889 English poet

Brue·ghel \\'brü-gəl, 'bröi-\\ Pieter *about* 1525–1569 Flemish painter

Bru·tus \\'brüt-əs\\ Marcus Junius 85–42 B.C. Roman politician; one of Julius Caesar's assassins

Bry·an \\'brī-ən\\ William Jennings 1860–1925 American lawyer and politician

Bu·chan·an \\byü-'kan-ən, bə-\\ James 1791–1868 15th president of the U.S. (1857–61)

Buck \\'bək\\ Pearl S. 1892–1973 née *Sydenstricker* American author; Nobel Prize winner (1938)

Bud·dha \\'büd-ə, 'bùd-\\ *about* 563–*about* 483 B.C. originally *Siddhartha Gautama* Indian founder of Buddhism

Buffalo Bill — see William Frederick CODY

Bun·yan \\'bən-yən\\ John 1628–1688 English preacher and author

Bunyan Paul — see PAUL BUNYAN

Bur·bank \\'bər-,baŋk\\ Luther 1849–1926 American horticulturist

Bur·goyne \\(,)bər-'góin, 'bər-,góin\\ John 1722–1792 British general in America

Burns \\'bərnz\\ Robert 1759–1796 Scottish poet

Burn·side \\'bərn-,sīd\\ Ambrose Everett 1824–1881 American general

Burr \\'bər\\ Aaron 1756–1836 vice president of the U.S. (1801–5)

Bush \\'búsh\\ George (Herbert Walker) 1924–   41st president of the U.S. (1989–93)

Bush George W. 1946–   *George Walker Bush* 43rd president of the U.S. (2001–09); son of the preceding

By·ron \\'bī-rən\\ Lord 1788–1824 *George Gordon Byron*, 6th Baron *Byron* English poet

Cab·ot \\'kab-ət\\ John *about* 1450–*about* 1499 originally *Giovanni Ca·bo·to* \\kä-'bōt-ō\\ Italian navigator; explored coast of North America for England

Cabot Sebastian 1476?–1557 English navigator; son of John Cabot

Ca·bri·ni \\kə-'brē-nē\\ Saint Frances Xavier 1850–1917 *Mother Cabrini* 1st American (Italian-born) saint (1946)

Cae·sar \\'sē-zər\\ (Gaius) Julius 100?–44 B.C. Roman general, political leader, and writer

Cain \\'kān\\ son of Adam and Eve and brother of Abel in the Bible

Calamity Jane \\-'jān\\ 1852?–1903 *Martha Jane Burk* \\'bərk\\ née *Can·nary* \\'kan-ə-rē\\ American frontier figure

Cal·houn \\kal-'hün\\ John Caldwell 1782–1850 American politician; vice president of the U.S. (1825–32)

Ca·lig·u·la \\kə-'lig-yə-lə\\ 12–41 A.D. Roman emperor (37–41)

Cal·li·ope \\kə-'lī-ə-,pē\\ muse of heroic poetry in Greek mythology

Cal·vert \\'kal-vərt\\ George 1580?–1632 Baron *Baltimore* English colonist in America

Cal·vin \\'kal-vən\\ John 1509–1564 *Jean Calvin* or *Cau·vin* \\kō-'vaⁿ\\ French theologian and reformer

Ca·nute \\kə-'n(y)üt\\ *died* 1035 *Canute the Great* Danish king of England (1016–35); of Denmark (1018–35); of Norway (1028–35)

Car·ne·gie \\'kär-nə-gē, kär-'neg-ē\\ Andrew 1835–1919 American (Scottish-born) industrialist and philanthropist

Car·roll \\'kar-əl\\ Lewis 1832–1898 pseudonym of *Charles Lutwidge Dodg·son* \\'däd-sən\\ English author and mathematician

Car·son \\'kärs-ᵊn\\ Kit 1809–1868 *Christopher Carson* American frontiersman and guide

Carson Rachel Louise 1907–1964 American scientist and writer

Car·ter \\'kärt-ər\\ Jimmy 1924–   originally *James Earl Carter, Jr.* 39th president of the U.S. (1977–81); Nobel Prize winner (2002)

Car·tier \\kär-'tyā, 'kärt-ē-,ā\\ Jacques 1491–1557 French navigator; explored Saint Lawrence River

Ca·ru·so \\kə-'rü-sō, -zō\\ En·ri·co \\en-'rē-kō\\ 1873–1921 Italian tenor

Car·ver \\'kär-vər\\ George Washington 1861?–1943 American agricultural chemist and agronomist

Ca·sa·no·va \\,kaz-ə-'nō-və, ,kas-\\ Giovanni Giacomo 1725–1798 Italian adventurer

Cas·san·dra \\kə-'san-drə\\ daughter of Priam in Greek mythology who is endowed with the gift of prophecy but fated never to be believed

Cas·satt \\kə-'sat\\ Mary 1845–1926 American painter

Cas·tro \\'kas-trō, 'käs-\\ (Ruz) \\'rüs\\ Fi·del \\fē-'del\\ 1926– Cuban leader (1959–2008)

Castro (Ruz) Raúl Modesto 1931–   Cuban leader (2008–   ); brother of Fidel Castro

Cath·er \\'kath-ər\\ Willa 1873–1947 American author

Cath·er·ine \\'kath-(ə-)rən\\ name of 1st, 5th, and 6th wives of Henry VIII of England: Catherine of Aragon 1485–1536; Catherine Howard 1520?–1542; Catherine Parr 1512–1548

Catherine I 1684–1727 wife of Peter the Great; empress of Russia (1725–27)

Catherine II 1729–1796 *Catherine the Great* empress of Russia (1762–96)

Catherine de Mé·di·cis \\-də-,mā-də-'sēs\\ 1519–1589 Italian *Ca·te·ri·na de' Me·di·ci* \\,kät-ā-'rē-nə-dā-'med-ē-chē\\ queen consort of Henry II of France (1547–59) and regent of France (1560–74)

Cav·en·dish \\'kav-ən-(,)dish\\ Henry 1731–1810 English scientist

Ce·ci·lia \\sə-'sēl-yə, -'sil-\\ Saint *flourished* 3rd century A.D. Christian martyr; patron saint of music

Ce·res \\'si(ə)r-,ēz\\ goddess of agriculture in Roman mythology — compare DEMETER

Cer·van·tes \\sər-'van-,tēz\\ Miguel de 1547–1616 Spanish author

Cé·zanne \\sā-'zan\\ Paul 1839–1906 French painter

Cha·gall \\shə-'gäl, -'gal\\ Marc 1887–1985 Russian painter in France

Cham·plain \\(')sham-'plān\\ Samuel de 1567–1635 French explorer in America; founder of Quebec

Chap·lin \\'chap-lən\\ Charlie 1889–1977 Sir *Charles Spencer Chaplin* British actor and producer

Chapman John — see Johnny APPLESEED

\\ə\\ abut	\\aú\\ out	\\i\\ tip	\\ó\\ saw	\\ú\\ foot
\\ər\\ further	\\ch\\ chin	\\ī\\ life	\\ói\\ coin	\\y\\ yet
\\a\\ mat	\\e\\ pet	\\j\\ job	\\th\\ thin	\\yü\\ few
\\ā\\ take	\\ē\\ easy	\\ŋ\\ sing	\\th\\ this	\\yú\\ cure
\\ä\\ cot, cart	\\g\\ go	\\ō\\ bone	\\ü\\ food	\\zh\\ vision

Char·le·magne \'shär-lə-ˌmän\ 742–814 A.D. *Charles the Great* or *Charles I* Frankish king (768–814); emperor of the West (800–814)

Charles \'chär(-ə)lz\ name of 10 kings of France: especially **II** 823–877 A.D. *Charles the Bald* (reigned 840–77); Holy Roman emperor (875–77); **IV** 1294–1328 *Charles the Fair* (reigned 1322–28); **V** 1337–1380 *Charles the Wise* (reigned 1364–80); **VI** 1368–1422 *Charles the Mad* or *the Beloved* (reigned 1380–1422); **VII** 1403–1461 *Charles the Well-Served* or *the Victorious* (reigned 1422–61); **IX** 1550–1574 (reigned 1560–74); **X** 1757–1836 (reigned 1824–30)

Charles name of two kings of Great Britain: **I** 1600–1649 (reigned 1625–49); **II** 1630–1685 (reigned 1660–85) son of Charles I

Charles V 1500–1558 Holy Roman emperor (1519–56); king of Spain as *Charles I* (1516–56)

Charles Edward Stuart — see Charles Edward STUART

Charles Mar·tel \mär-'tel\ *about* 688–741 A.D. Frankish ruler (719–41); grandfather of Charlemagne

Cha·ryb·dis \kə-'rib-dəs, shə-, chə-\ whirlpool off the coast of Sicily thought of in Greek mythology as a monster

Chau·cer \'chò-sər\ Geoffrey *about* 1342–1400 English poet

Cha·vez \'chä-vəs, -ˌvez\ Cesar Estrada 1927–1993 American labor leader

Che·khov \'chek-ˌòf, -ˌòv\ Anton Pavlovich 1860–1904 Russian author

Che·ney \'chē-nē\ Richard Bruce 1941– vice president of the U.S. (2001–09)

Cheops — see KHUFU

Ches·ter·ton \'ches-tərt-ᵊn\ G. K. 1874–1936 *Gilbert Keith Chesterton* English author

Cho·pin \'shō-ˌpan\ Frédéric François 1810–1849 Polish pianist and composer

Chou En–lai or **Zhou Enlai** \'jō-'en-'lī\ 1898–1976 Chinese Communist politician; premier (1949–76)

Christ Jesus — see JESUS

Chris·tie \'kris-tē\ Dame Agatha 1890–1976 née *Miller* English author

Chur·chill \'chər-ˌchil, 'chərch-ˌhil\ Sir Winston Leonard Spencer 1874–1965 British prime minister (1940–45; 1951–55) Nobel Prize winner (1953)

Clark \'klärk\ George Rogers 1752–1818 American soldier and frontiersman

Clark William 1770–1838 American explorer (with Meriwether Lewis)

Clay \'klā\ Henry 1777–1852 American politician

Clemens Samuel Langhorne — see Mark TWAIN

Cle·o·pa·tra \ˌklē-ə-'pa-trə, -'pā-, -'pä-\ 69–30 B.C. queen of Egypt (51–30)

Cleve·land \'klēv-lənd\ (Stephen) Grover 1837–1908 22nd and 24th president of the U.S. (1885–89; 1893–97)

Clin·ton \'klin-tᵊn\ Hillary Rodham 1947– neé *Rodham* U.S. secretary of state (2009–13); wife of William Clinton

Clinton William Jefferson 1946– *Bill Clinton* 42nd president of the U.S. (1993–2001)

Cly·tem·nes·tra \ˌklīt-əm-'nes-trə\ wife of Agamemnon in Greek mythology

Cobb \'käb\ Ty 1886–1961 *Tyrus Raymond Cobb* American baseball player

Co·chise \kō-'chēs\ 1812?–1874 Apache Indian chief

Co·dy \'kōd-ē\ William Frederick 1846–1917 *Buffalo Bill* American hunter, guide, and showman

Co·han \'kō-ˌhan\ George Michael 1878–1942 American actor and composer

Cole·ridge \'kōl-rij, 'kō-lə-rij\ Samuel Taylor 1772–1834 English poet

Co·lette \kò-'let\ 1873–1954 originally *Sidonie-Gabrielle Colette* French author

Co·lum·bus \kə-'ləm-bəs\ Christopher 1451–1506 Italian navigator and discoverer of America for Spain (1492)

Con·fu·cius \kən-'fyü-shəs\ 551–479 B.C. Chinese philosopher

Con·rad \'kän-ˌrad\ Joseph 1857–1924 British (Ukrainian-born of Polish parents) author

Con·sta·ble \'kən(t)-stə-bəl, 'kän(t)-\ John 1776–1837 English painter

Con·stan·tine I \'kän(t)-stən-ˌtēn, -ˌtīn\ *after* 280–337 A.D. *Constantine the Great* Roman emperor (306–37)

Cook \'kùk\ Captain James 1728–1779 English navigator

Coo·lidge \'kü-lij\ (John) Calvin 1872–1933 30th president of the U.S. (1923–29)

Coo·per \'kü-pər, 'kùp-ər\ James Fen·i·more \'fen-ə-ˌmō(ə)r, -ˌmò(ə)r\ 1789–1851 American author

Co·per·ni·cus \kō-'pər-ni-kəs\ Nicolaus 1473–1543 Polish astronomer

Cop·land \'kō-plənd\ Aaron 1900–1990 American composer

Cop·ley \'käp-lē\ John Sin·gle·ton \'siŋ-gəl-tən\ 1738–1815 American portrait painter

Corn·plan·ter \'kòrn-ˌplan-tər\ *about* 1732–1836 *John O'Bail* Seneca Indian leader of partly European ancestry

Corn·wal·lis \kòrn-'wäl-əs\ Charles 1738–1805 1st Marquess *Cornwallis* British general in America

Co·ro·na·do \ˌkòr-ə-'näd-ō, ˌkär-\ Francisco Vásquez de *about* 1510–1554 Spanish explorer of southwestern U.S.

Cor·tés \kòr-'tez, 'kòr-ˌtez\ Hernán or Hernando 1485–1547 Spanish conqueror of Mexico

Cous·teau \kü-'stō\ Jacques-Yves 1910–1997 French marine explorer

Crane \'krān\ Stephen 1871–1900 American author

Crazy Horse \'krā-zē-ˌhòrs\ 1842?–1877 *Ta-sunko-witko* Sioux Indian chief

Crock·ett \'kräk-ət\ *Davy* 1786–1836 *David Crockett* American frontiersman

Crom·well \'kräm-ˌwel, 'kròm-, -wəl\ Oliver 1599–1658 English general and political leader; lord protector of England (1653–58)

Cro·nus \'krō-nəs, 'krän-əs\ Titan in Greek mythology overthrown by his son Zeus

Cum·mings \'kəm-iŋz\ Edward Estlin 1894–1962 known as *e. e. cummings* American poet

Cu·pid \'kyü-pəd\ god of love in Roman mythology — compare EROS

Cu·rie \kyù-'rē, 'kyù(ə)r-ē\ Marie 1867–1934 née *Sklodow·ska* \sklə-'dòf-skə\ French (Polish-born) chemist; Nobel Prize winner (1903, 1911)

Curie Pierre 1859–1906 French chemist; husband of Marie Curie; Nobel Prize winner (1903)

Cus·ter \'kəs-tər\ George Armstrong 1839–1876 American general

Cy·ra·no de Ber·ge·rac \ˌsir-ə-ˌnō-də-'ber-zhə-ˌrak\ Savinien 1619–1655 French playwright

Cy·rus II \'sī-rəs\ *about* 585–*about* 529 B.C. *Cyrus the Great* king of Persia (*about* 550–529)

Dae·da·lus \'ded-ᵊl-əs, 'dēd-\ builder in Greek mythology of the Cretan labyrinth and inventor of wings by which he and his son Icarus escape imprisonment

Da·lí \'dä-lē, dä-'lē\ Salvador 1904–1989 Spanish painter

Dal·ton \'dòlt-ᵊn\ John 1766–1844 English chemist and physicist

Da·na \'dā-nə\ Richard Henry 1815–1882 American author

Dan·aë \'dan-ə-ˌē\ imprisoned princess in Greek mythology whom Zeus visits as golden rain; mother of Perseus

Dan·iel \'dan-yəl\ prophet in the Bible who is held captive in Babylon and delivered from a den of lions

Dan·te \'dän-tā, 'dan-, -tē\ 1265–1321 *Dante Ali·ghie·ri* \ˌal-ə-'gyer-ē\ Italian poet

Dare \'da(ə)r, 'de(ə)r\ Virginia 1587–? 1st child born in America of English parents

Da·ri·us I \də-'rī-əs\ 550–486 B.C. *Darius the Great* king of Persia (522–486)

Dar·row \'dar-ō\ Clarence Seward 1857–1938 American lawyer

Dar·win \'där-wən\ Charles Robert 1809–1882 English naturalist

Da·vid \'dā-vəd\ a youth in the Bible who slays Goliath and succeeds Saul as king of Israel

Da·vis \'dā-vəs\ Jefferson 1808–1889 president of the Confederate States of America (1861–65)

Davis Miles 1926–1991 American jazz musician

Debs \'debz\ Eugene Victor 1855–1926 American socialist and labor organizer

De·bus·sy \,deb-yü-'sē, ,däb-; də-'byü-sē\ (Achille-) Claude 1862–1918 French composer

De·ca·tur \di-'kāt-ər\ Stephen 1779–1820 American naval officer

De·foe \di-'fō\ Daniel 1660–1731 English author

De·gas \də-'gä\ (Hilaire-Germain-) Edgar 1834–1917 French painter

de Gaulle \di-'gōl, -'gól\ Charles (-André-Marie-Joseph) 1890–1970 French general; president of Fifth Republic (1958–69)

De·li·lah \di-'lī-lə\ mistress and betrayer of Samson in the Bible

De·me·ter \di-'mēt-ər\ goddess of agriculture in Greek mythology — compare CERES

de Mille \də-'mil\ Agnes George 1905–1993 American dancer and choreographer

De·mos·the·nes \di-'mäs-thə-,nēz\ 384–322 B.C. Athenian orator and statesman

Demp·sey \'demp-sē\ Jack 1895–1983 originally *William Harrison Dempsey* American boxer

Des·cartes \dā-'kärt\ René 1596–1650 French mathematician and philosopher

de So·to \di-'sōt-ō\ Hernando *about* 1496–1542 Spanish explorer in America

Dew·ey \'d(y)ü-ē\ George 1837–1917 American admiral

Dewey John 1859–1952 American philosopher and educator

Dewey Melvil 1851–1931 American librarian

Di·ana \dī-'an-ə\ ancient Italian goddess of the forest and of childbirth who was identified with Artemis by the Romans

Dick·ens \'dik-ənz\ Charles (John Huffam) 1812–1870 pseudonym *Boz* \'bäz, 'bōz\ English author

Dick·in·son \'dik-ən-sən\ Emily Elizabeth 1830–1886 American poet

Di·do \'dīd-ō\ legendary queen of Carthage who falls in love with Aeneas and kills herself when he leaves her

Di·Mag·gio \də-'mäzh-ē-ō, -'maj-\ Joe 1914–1999 *Joseph Paul DiMaggio* American baseball player

Di·o·ny·sus \,dī-ə-'nī-səs, -'nē-\ god of wine and ecstasy in classical mythology

Dis·ney \'diz-nē\ Walt 1901–1966 *Walter Elias Disney* American film producer and cartoonist

Dis·rae·li \diz-'rā-lē\ Benjamin 1804–1881 Earl of *Beaconsfield* \'bē-kənz-,fēld\ British politician and author; prime minister (1868; 1874–80)

Dix \'diks\ Dorothea Lynde 1802–1887 American social reformer

Dodgson Charles Lutwidge — see Lewis CARROLL

Donne \'dən\ John 1572–1631 English poet and clergyman

Don Qui·xote \,dän-kē-'(h)ōt-ē, ,dän-; dän-'kwik-sət\ idealistic and impractical hero of Cervantes' *Don Quixote*

Dos·to·yev·sky \,däs-tə-'yef-skē, -'yev-\ Fyodor Mikhaylovich 1821–1881 Russian novelist

Doug·las \'dəg-ləs\ Stephen Arnold 1813–1861 American politician

Doug·lass \'dəg-ləs\ Frederick 1817–1895 American abolitionist

Doyle \'dói(ə)l\ Sir Arthur Co·nan \'kō-nən\ 1859–1930 British physician and author

Drake \'drāk\ Sir Francis 1540 (or 1543)–1596 English navigator, explorer, and admiral

Drei·ser \'drī-sər, -zər\ Theodore 1871–1945 American author

DuBois \d(y)ü-'bóis\ W.E.B. 1868–1963 *William Edward Burghardt* American educator and writer

Du·mas \d(y)ü-'mä, 'd(y)ü-,mä\ Alexandre 1802–1870 *Dumas père* \'pe(ə)r\ French author

Dumas Alexandre 1824–1895 *Dumas fils* \'fēs\ French author

Dun·can \'dəŋ-kən\ Isadora 1877–1927 American dancer

Dü·rer \'d(y)ùr-ər\ Albrecht 1471–1528 German painter and engraver

Dy·lan \'di-lən\ Bob 1941– originally *Robert Allen Zimmerman* American singer and songwriter

Ea·kins \'ā-kənz\ Thomas 1844–1916 American artist

Ear·hart \'e(ə)r-,härt, 'i(ə)r-\ Amelia 1897–1937 American aviator

Earp \'ərp\ Wyatt 1848–1929 American frontiersman and lawman

Ed·dy \'ed-ē\ Mary Baker 1821–1910 American founder of the Christian Science religious faith

Ed·i·son \'ed-ə-sən\ Thomas Alva 1847–1931 American inventor

Ed·ward \'ed-wərd\ name of eight post-Norman kings of England: **I** 1239–1307 *Edward Longshanks* (reigned 1272–1307); **II** 1284–1327 (reigned 1307–27); **III** 1312–1377 (reigned 1327–77); **IV** 1442–1483 (reigned 1461–70; 1471–83); **V** 1470–1483 (reigned 1483); **VI** 1537–1553 (reigned 1547–53) son of Henry VIII and Jane Seymour; **VII** 1841–1910 (reigned 1901–10) son of Queen Victoria; **VIII** 1894–1972 (reigned 1936; abdicated) *Duke of Windsor* son of George V

Ein·stein \'īn-,stīn\ Albert 1879–1955 American (German-born) physicist; Nobel Prize winner (1921)

Ei·sen·how·er \'īz-ᵊn-,haù(-ə)r\ Dwight David 1890–1969 American general; 34th president of the U.S. (1953–61)

Elec·tra \i-'lek-trə\ sister of Orestes in Greek mythology who aids him in avenging their father's murder

Eli·jah \i-'lī-jə\ Hebrew prophet of the 9th century B.C.

El·i·on \'el-ē-ən\ Gertrude Belle 1918–1999 American pharmacologist; Nobel Prize winner (1988)

El·i·ot \'el-ē-ət, 'el-yət\ George 1819–1880 pseudonym of *Mary Ann Evans* English author

Eliot T. S. 1888–1965 *Thomas Stearns Eliot* British (American-born) poet and critic; Nobel Prize winner (1948)

Eliz·a·beth I \i-'liz-ə-bəth\ 1533–1603 queen of England (1558–1603); daughter of Henry VIII and Anne Boleyn

Elizabeth II 1926– queen of the United Kingdom (1952–); daughter of George VI

El·ling·ton \'e-liŋ-tən\ Duke 1899–1974 originally *Edward Kennedy Ellington* American bandleader and composer

Em·er·son \'em-ər-sən\ Ralph Waldo 1803–1882 American essayist and poet

En·dym·i·on \en-'dim-ē-ən\ beautiful youth in Greek mythology loved by the goddess of the moon

Eos \'ē-,äs\ goddess of the dawn in Greek mythology — compare AURORA

Ep·i·cu·rus \,ep-i-'kyùr-əs\ 341–270 B.C. Greek philosopher

Er·ik the Red \'er-ik\ *flourished* 10th century originally *Erik Thorvaldson* Norwegian explorer of Greenland coast (*about* 986); father of Leif Eriksson

Eriksson Leif — see LEIF ERIKSSON

Eros \'e(ə)r-,äs, 'i(ə)r-\ god of love in Greek mythology — compare CUPID

Esau \'ē-(,)só\ son of Isaac and Rebekah and elder twin brother of Jacob in the Bible

\ə\ **abut**	\aù\ **out**	\i\ **tip**	\ó\ **saw**	\ù\ **foot**
\ər\ **further**	\ch\ **chin**	\ī\ **life**	\ói\ **coin**	\y\ **yet**
\a\ **mat**	\e\ **pet**	\j\ **job**	\th\ **thin**	\yü\ **few**
\ā\ **take**	\ē\ **easy**	\ŋ\ **sing**	\th\ **this**	\yù\ **cure**
\ä\ **cot, cart**	\g\ **go**	\ō\ **bone**	\ü\ **food**	\zh\ **vision**

Es·ther \'es-tər\ Hebrew woman in the Bible who as the queen of Persia delivers her people from destruction

Eu·clid \'yü-kləd\ *flourished about* 300 B.C. Greek mathematician

Eu·rip·i·des \yu̇-'rip-ə-ˌdēz\ *about* 484–406 B.C. Greek playwright

Eu·ro·pa \yu̇-'rō-pə\ princess in Greek mythology who was carried off by Zeus disguised as a white bull

Eu·ryd·i·ce \yu̇-'rid-ə-sē\ wife of Orpheus in Greek mythology

Eve \'ēv\ the 1st woman in biblical tradition; wife of Adam

Eze·kiel \i-'zē-kyəl, -kē-əl\ Hebrew prophet of the 6th century B.C.

Fahr·en·heit \'far-ən-ˌhīt, 'fär-\ Daniel Gabriel 1686–1736 German physicist

Far·a·day \'far-ə-ˌdā, -əd-ē\ Michael 1791–1867 English chemist and physicist

Far·ra·gut \'far-ə-gət\ David Glasgow 1801–1870 American admiral

Faulk·ner \'fȯk-nər\ William 1897–1962 American author; Nobel Prize winner (1949)

Faust \'fau̇st\ *or* **Fau·stus** \'fau̇-stəs, 'fȯ-\ magician in German legend who sells his soul to the devil for knowledge and power

Fawkes \'fȯks\ Guy 1570–1606 English conspirator

Fer·di·nand \'fərd-ᵊn-ˌand\ **V** of Castile *or* **II** of Aragon 1452–1516 *Ferdinand the Catholic* king of Castile (1474–1504); of Aragon (1479–1516); of Naples (1504–16); founder of the Spanish monarchy; husband of Isabella I

Fer·mi \'fe(ə)r-mē\ Enrico 1901–1954 American (Italian-born) physicist; Nobel Prize winner (1938)

Fiel·ding \'fē(ə)l-diŋ\ Henry 1707–1754 English author

Fill·more \'fil-ˌmō(ə)r, -ˌmȯ(ə)r\ Millard 1800–1874 13th president of the U.S. (1850–53)

Fitz·ger·ald \fits-'jer-əld\ Ella 1917–1996 American singer

Fitzgerald F. Scott 1896–1940 *Francis Scott Key Fitzgerald* American author

Flem·ing \'flem-iŋ\ Sir Alexander 1881–1955 British bacteriologist; Nobel Prize winner (1945)

Flo·ra \'flōr-ə, 'flȯr-\ goddess of flowers in Roman mythology

Flying Dutchman legendary Dutch mariner condemned to sail the seas until Judgment Day

Ford \'fō(ə)rd, 'fȯ(ə)rd\ Gerald Rudolph 1913–2006 38th president of the U.S. (1974–77)

Ford Henry 1863–1947 American automobile manufacturer

Fos·sey \'fȯs-ē\ Dian 1932–1985 American zoologist

Fos·ter \'fȯs-tər, 'fäs-\ Stephen Collins 1826–1864 American songwriter

Fran·cis \'fran(t)-səs\ 1936– originally *Jorge Mario Bergoglio* pope (2013–)

Francis of As·si·si \-əv-ə-'sis-ē, -'sē-zē, -'sē-sē, -'siz-ē\ Saint 1181 (or 1182)–1226 Italian friar; founder of Franciscan order

Fran·co \'fräŋ-kō, 'fraŋ-\ Francisco 1892–1975 Spanish general, dictator, and head of Spanish state (1936–75)

Frank \'fraŋk, 'fräŋk\ Anne 1929–1945 German-born diarist during the Holocaust

Frank·lin \'fraŋ-klən\ Benjamin 1706–1790 American patriot, author, and inventor

Fred·er·ick I \'fred-(ə-)rik\ *about* 1123–1190 *Frederick Bar·ba·ros·sa* \ˌbär-bə-'räs-ə, -'rȯs-\ Holy Roman emperor (1152–90)

Frederick II 1712–1786 *Frederick the Great* king of Prussia (1740–86)

Fré·mont \'frē-ˌmänt\ John Charles 1813–1890 American general and explorer

French \'french\ Daniel Chester 1850–1931 American sculptor

Freud \'froid\ Sigmund 1856–1939 Austrian neurologist; founder of psychoanalysis

Fried·man \'frēd-mən\ Milton 1912–2006 American economist

Frig·ga \'frig-ə\ *or* **Frigg** wife of Odin and goddess of married love and the hearth in Norse mythology

Frost \'frȯst\ Robert Lee 1874–1963 American poet

Ful·ler \'fu̇l-ər\ (Richard) Buckminster 1895–1983 American engineer and architect

Fuller (Sarah) Margaret 1810–1850 American author and reformer

Ful·ton \'fu̇lt-ᵊn\ Robert 1765–1815 American inventor

Ga·bri·el \'gā-brē-əl\ one of the four archangels named in Hebrew tradition — compare MICHAEL, RAPHAEL, URIEL

Ga·ga·rin \gə-'gär-ən\ Yu·ry \'yü(ə)r-ē\ Alekseyevich 1934–1968 Russian astronaut; 1st man in space (1961)

Gage \'gāj\ Thomas 1721–1787 British general in America

Gal·a·had \'gal-ə-ˌhad\ knight of the Round Table in medieval legend who finds the Holy Grail

Gal·a·tea \ˌgal-ə-'tē-ə\ female figure sculpted by Pygmalion in Greek mythology and given life by Aphrodite in answer to the sculptor's prayer

Ga·len \'gā-lən\ 129–*about* 216 A.D. Greek physician and writer

Ga·li·leo \ˌgal-ə-'lē-ō, -'lā-\ 1564–1642 *Galileo Ga·li·lei* \ˌgal-ə-'lā-ˌē\ Italian astronomer and physicist

Gall \'gȯl\ 1840?–1894 Sioux Indian leader

Ga·ma \'gam-ə, 'gäm-\ Vasco da *about* 1460–1524 Portuguese navigator and explorer

Gan·dhi \'gän-dē, 'gan-\ Indira 1917–1984 Indian prime minister (1966–77; 1980–84); daughter of Jawaharlal Nehru

Gandhi Mohandas Karamchand 1869–1948 *Ma·hat·ma* \mə-'hät-mə, -'hat-\ *Gandhi* Indian leader

Gar·cía Már·quez \gär-'sē-ə-'mär-ˌkäs\ Gabriel 1927–2014 Colombian author

Gar·field \'gär-ˌfēld\ James Abram 1831–1881 20th president of the U.S. (1881)

Gar·i·bal·di \ˌgar-ə-'bȯl-dē\ Giuseppe 1807–1882 Italian patriot

Gar·ri·son \'gar-ə-sən\ William Lloyd 1805–1879 American abolitionist

Gates \'gāts\ Bill 1955– *William Henry Gates III* American computer software manufacturer

Gau·guin \gō-gan\ (Eugène-Henri-) Paul 1848–1903 French painter

Gau·ta·ma Bud·dha — see BUDDHA

Geh·rig \'ger-ig\ Lou 1903–1941 *Henry Louis Gehrig* American baseball player

Gehry \'ger-ē\ Frank Owen 1929– American (Canadian-born) architect

Gei·sel \'gī-zəl\ Theodor Seuss 1904–1991 pseudonym *Dr. Seuss* \'süs\ American author and illustrator

Gen·ghis Khan \ˌjeŋ-gə-'skän, ˌgeŋ-\ *about* 1162–1227 Mongol conqueror

George \'jȯ(ə)rj\ name of six kings of Great Britain: **I** 1660–1727 (reigned 1714–27); **II** 1683–1760 (reigned 1727–60); **III** 1738–1820 (reigned 1760–1820); **IV** 1762–1830 (reigned 1820–30); **V** 1865–1936 (reigned 1910–36); **VI** 1895–1952 (reigned 1936–52) father of Elizabeth II

Ge·ron·i·mo \jə-'rän-ə-ˌmō\ 1829–1909 Apache Indian leader

Gersh·win \'gərsh-wən\ George 1898–1937 American composer

Gid·e·on \'gid-ē-ən\ Hebrew hero in the Bible

Gil·bert \'gil-bərt\ Sir William Schwenck 1836–1911 English librettist and poet; collaborator with Sir Arthur Sullivan

Gins·burg \'ginz-ˌbərg\ Ruth Bader 1933– American jurist

Glad·stone \'glad-ˌstōn, *chiefly British* -stən\ William Ewart 1809–1898 British prime minister (1868–74; 1880–85; 1886; 1892–94)

Glass \'glas\ Philip 1937– American composer

Glenn \\'glen\\ John Herschel 1921–   American astronaut and politician; 1st American to orbit the earth (1962)

Go·di·va \\gə-'dī-və\\ an English gentlewoman who in legend rode naked through Coventry to save its citizens from a tax

Goe·thals \\'gō-thəlz\\ George Washington 1858–1928 American engineer who directed the building of the Panama Canal

Goe·the \\'gə(r)-tə\\ Johann Wolfgang von 1749–1832 German author

Gogh, van \\van-'gō, -'gäk, -'kȯk\\ Vincent Willem 1853–1890 Dutch painter

Gol·ding \\'gōl-diŋ\\ William Gerald 1911–1993 English writer; Nobel Prize winner (1983)

Go·li·ath \\gə-'lī-əth\\ Philistine giant who is killed by David in the Bible

Gom·pers \\'gäm-pərz\\ Samuel 1850–1924 American (British-born) labor leader

Goo·dall \\'gu̇d-ˌȯl\\ Jane 1934–   British zoologist

Good·year \\'gu̇d-ˌyi(ə)r, 'gu̇j-ˌi(ə)r\\ Charles 1800–1860 American inventor

Gore \\'gō(ə)r, 'gȯ(ə)r\\ Albert, Jr. 1948–   vice president of the U.S. (1993–2001); Nobel Prize winner (2007)

Gor·gas \\'gȯr-gəs\\ William Crawford 1854–1920 American army surgeon

Go·ya (y Lu·cien·tes) \\'gȯi-ə-ˌē-lü-sē-'en-ˌtās\\ Francisco José de 1746–1828 Spanish painter

Gra·ham \\'grā-əm, 'gra(-ə)m\\ Martha 1893–1991 American dancer and choreographer

Grant \\'grant\\ Ulysses 1822–1885 originally *Hiram Ulysses Grant* American general; 18th president of the U.S. (1869–77)

Gre·co, El \\el-'grek-ō\\ 1541–1614 *Doménikos Theotokópoulos* Spanish (Cretan-born) painter

Gree·ley \\'grē-lē\\ Horace 1811–1872 American journalist and politician

Greene \\'grēn\\ (Henry) Graham 1904–1991 British author

Greene Nathanael 1742–1786 American Revolutionary general

Greg·o·ry \\'greg-(ə-)rē\\ name of 16 popes: especially **I** Saint *about* 540–604 A.D. *Gregory the Great* (pope 590–604); **VII** Saint *about* 1020–1085 (pope 1073–85); **XIII** 1502–1585 (pope 1572–85)

Grey \\'grā\\ Lady Jane 1537–1554 queen of England for nine days (1553)

Grey Zane 1872–1939 American novelist

Grieg \\'grēg\\ Edward Hagerup 1843–1907 Norwegian composer

Grimm \\'grim\\ Jacob 1785–1863 and his brother Wilhelm 1786–1859 German philologists and folklorists

Gue·va·ra \\ge-'vär-ə, gä-\\ Che 1928–1967 originally *Ernesto Guevara* Cuban (Argentine-born) revolutionary leader

Guin·e·vere \\'gwin-ə-ˌvi(ə)r\\ legendary wife of King Arthur and lover of Lancelot

Gu·ten·berg \\'güt-ᵊn-ˌbərg\\ Johannes *about* 1400–1468 German inventor of printing method from movable type

Ha·des \\'hād-ˌēz\\ — see PLUTO

Ha·dri·an \\'hā-drē-ən\\ 76–138 A.D. Roman emperor (117–138)

Ha·gar \\'hā-ˌgär, -gər\\ mistress of Abraham and mother of Ishmael in the Bible

Hai·le Se·las·sie \\ˌhī-lē-sə-'las-ē, -'läs-\\ 1892–1975 emperor of Ethiopia (1930–36; 1941–74)

Hale \\'hā(ə)l\\ Edward Everett 1822–1909 American author

Hale Nathan 1755–1776 American Revolutionary hero

Hal·ley \\'hal-ē, 'hā-lē\\ Edmond *or* Edmund 1656–1742 English astronomer and mathematician

Hal·sey \\'hȯl-sē, -zē\\ William Frederick 1882–1959 American admiral

Ham·il·ton \\'ham-əl-tən\\ Alexander 1755–1804 American political leader

Ham·mu·ra·bi \\ˌham-ə-'räb-ē\\ *died about* 1750 B.C. king of Babylon (*about* 1792–50)

Han·cock \\'han-ˌkäk\\ John 1737–1793 American Revolutionary patriot

Han·del \\'han-dᵊl\\ George Frideric 1685–1759 British (German-born) composer

Han·dy \\'han-dē\\ W. C. 1873–1958 *William Christopher Handy* American blues musician and composer

Han·ni·bal \\'han-ə-bəl\\ 247–183? B.C. Carthaginian general

Har·ding \\'härd-iŋ\\ Warren Gamaliel 1865–1923 29th president of the U.S. (1921–23)

Har·dy \\'härd-ē\\ Thomas 1840–1928 English author

Har·per \\'här-pər\\ Stephen (Joseph) 1959–   Canadian prime minister (2006–   )

Har·ri·son \\'har-ə-sən\\ Benjamin 1833–1901 23rd president of the U.S. (1889–93); grandson of William Henry Harrison

Harrison William Henry 1773–1841, 9th president of the U.S. (1841)

Harte \\'härt\\ Bret 1836–1902 originally *Francis Brett Harte* American author

Har·vey \\'här-vē\\ William 1578–1657 English physician and anatomist

Haw·king \\'hȯ-kiŋ\\ Stephen William 1942–   British physicist

Haw·thorne \\'hȯ-ˌthȯ(ə)rn\\ Nathaniel 1804–1864 American author

Haydn \\'hīd-ᵊn\\ Franz Joseph 1732–1809 Austrian composer

Hayes \\'hāz\\ Rutherford Birchard 1822–1893 19th president of the U.S. (1877–81)

Hearst \\'hərst\\ William Randolph 1863–1951 American newspaper publisher

Hec·tor \\'hek-tər\\ son of Priam and Hecuba; Trojan hero slain by Achilles in Greek mythology

Hec·u·ba \\'hek-yə-bə\\ wife of Priam in Greek mythology

Hel·en of Troy \\ˌhel-ə-nəv-'trȯi\\ wife of Menelaus whose abduction by Paris in Greek mythology causes the Trojan War

He·li·os \\'hē-lē-əs, -ōs\\ god of the sun in Greek mythology — compare SOL

Hem·ing·way \\'hem-iŋ-ˌwā\\ Ernest Miller 1899–1961 American author; Nobel Prize winner (1954)

Hen·ry \\'hen-rē\\ name of eight kings of England: **I** 1068–1135 (reigned 1100–35); **II** 1133–1189 (reigned 1154–89); **III** 1207–1272 (reigned 1216–72); **IV** 1366–1413 (reigned 1399–1413); **V** 1387–1422 (reigned 1413–22); **VI** 1421–1471 (reigned 1422–61; 1470–71); **VII** 1457–1509 (reigned 1485–1509); **VIII** 1491–1547 (reigned 1509–47)

Henry name of four kings of France: **I** *about* 1008–1060 (reigned 1031–60); **II** 1519–1559 (reigned 1547–59); **III** 1551–1589 (reigned 1574–89); **IV** 1553–1610 *Henry of Navarre* (reigned 1589–1610)

Henry O. 1862–1910 pseudonym of *William Sydney Porter* American author

Henry Patrick 1736–1799 American patriot and orator

Hen·son \\'hən(t)-sən\\ Matthew Alexander 1866–1955 American arctic explorer

He·phaes·tus \\hi-'fes-təs, -'fēs-\\ god of fire and of metalworking in Greek mythology — compare VULCAN

He·ra \\'hir-ə, 'hē-rə\\ sister and wife of Zeus and goddess of women and marriage in Greek mythology — compare JUNO

Her·cu·les \\'hər-kyə-ˌlēz\\ *or* **Her·a·cles** \\'her-ə-ˌklēz\\ hero in Greek mythology noted for his strength and for performing 12 labors imposed on him by Hera

\\ə\\ **abut**	\\au̇\\ **out**	\\i\\ **tip**	\\ȯ\\ **saw**	\\u̇\\ **foot**
\\ər\\ **further**	\\ch\\ **chin**	\\ī\\ **life**	\\ȯi\\ **coin**	\\y\\ **yet**
\\a\\ **mat**	\\e\\ **pet**	\\j\\ **job**	\\th\\ **thin**	\\yü\\ **few**
\\ā\\ **take**	\\ē\\ **easy**	\\ŋ\\ **sing**	\\th\\ **this**	\\yu̇\\ **cure**
\\ä\\ **cot, cart**	\\g\\ **go**	\\ō\\ **bone**	\\ü\\ **food**	\\zh\\ **vision**

Her·maph·ro·di·tus \(ˌ)hər-ˌmaf-rə-'dīt-əs\ son of Hermes and Aphrodite who in Greek mythology is joined with a nymph into one body

Her·mes \'hər-mēz\ god of commerce, eloquence, invention, travel, and theft who serves as herald and messenger of the other gods in Greek mythology — compare MER·CURY

Her·od \'her-əd\ 73–4 B.C. *Herod the Great* Roman king of Judea (37–4)

Herod An·ti·pas \'ant-ə-ˌpas, -pəs\ 21 B.C.–39 A.D. Roman governor of Galilee (4 B.C.–39 A.D.); son of Herod the Great

Her·schel \'hər-shəl\ Sir (Frederick) William 1738–1822 originally *Friedrich Wilhelm Herschel* British (German-born) astronomer

Hey·er·dahl \'hā-ər-ˌdäl, 'hī-\ Thor 1914–2002 Norwegian explorer and author

Hi·a·wa·tha \ˌhī-ə-'wȯ-thə, ˌhē-ə-, -'wäth-ə\ legendary Iroquois Indian chief

Hick·ok \'hik-ˌäk\ Wild Bill 1837–1876 originally *James Butler Hickok* American frontiersman and U.S. marshal

Hi·dal·go (y Cos·ti·lla) \ē-'thäl-gō-ē-kȯ-'stē-yä\ Miguel 1753–1811 Mexican priest and revolutionary leader

Hil·ton \'hilt-ᵊn\ James 1900–1954 English novelist

Hip·poc·ra·tes \hip-'äk-rə-ˌtēz\ *about* 460–*about* 377 B.C. *father of medicine* Greek physician

Hi·ro·hi·to \ˌhir-ō-'hē-tō\ 1901–1989 emperor of Japan (1926–89)

Hitch·cock \'hich-ˌkäk\ Sir Alfred Joseph 1899–1980 British film director

Hit·ler \'hit-lər\ Adolf 1889–1945 German (Austrian-born) chancellor and dictator (1933–45)

Hodg·kin \'häj-kin\ Dorothy Mary 1910–1994 née *Crowfoot* British physicist; Nobel Prize winner (1964)

Holmes \'hōmz, 'hōlmz\ Oliver Wendell 1809–1894 American physician and author

Holmes Oliver Wendell, Jr. 1841–1935 American jurist; son of the preceding

Ho·mer \'hō-mər\ *flourished* 9th *or* 8th century B.C. Greek epic poet — **Ho·mer·ic** \hō-'mer-ik\ *adj*

Homer Winslow 1836–1910 American painter

Hooke \'hu̇k\ Robert 1635–1703 English scientist

Hoo·ver \'hü-vər\ Herbert Clark 1874–1964 31st president of the U.S. (1929–33)

Hoover John Edgar 1895–1972 American criminologist; director of the Federal Bureau of Investigation (1924–72)

Hop·per \'häp-ər\ Edward 1882–1967 American artist

Hopper Grace 1906–1992 née *Murray* American admiral, mathematician, and computer scientist

Hou·di·ni \hü-'dē-nē\ Harry 1874–1926 originally *Erik Weisz* American magician

Hous·ton \'(h)yü-stən\ Sam 1793–1863 *Samuel Houston* American politician; president of the Republic of Texas (1836–38; 1841–44)

Howe \'hau̇\ Elias 1819–1867 American inventor

Howe Julia 1819–1910 née *Ward* American suffragist and reformer

Hud·son \'həd-sən\ Henry *about* 1565–1611 English navigator and explorer

Hughes \'hyüz *also* 'yüz\ (James) Langston 1902–1967 American author

Hus·sein I \hü-'sān\ 1935–1999 king of Jordan (1952–99)

Hussein Saddam 1937–2006 president of Iraq (1979–2003)

Hutch·in·son \'həch-ə(n)-sən\ Anne 1591–1643 née *Marbury* English colonist and religious leader in America

Hutchinson Thomas 1711–1780 American colonial administrator

Hux·ley \'hək-slē\ Aldous Leonard 1894–1963 English author

Hy·men \'hī-mən\ god of marriage in Greek mythology

Ib·sen \'ib-sən, 'ip-\ Henrik 1828–1906 Norwegian playwright and poet

Ic·a·rus \'ik-ə-rəs\ son of Daedalus who in Greek mythology falls into the sea when the wax of his artificial wings melts as he flies too near the sun

Ig·na·tius \ig-'nā-sh(ē-)əs\ Saint 1491–1556 *Ignatius of Loy·o·la* \lȯi-'ō-lə\ Spanish soldier and priest; founded the Society of Jesus (Jesuits)

In·no·cent \'in-ə-sənt\ name of 13 popes: especially **II** *died* 1143 (pope 1130–43); **III** 1160 (or 1161)–1216 (pope 1198–1216); **IV** *died* 1254 (pope 1243–54); **XI** 1611–1689 (pope 1676–89)

Ir·ving \'ər-viŋ\ Washington 1783–1859 American author

Isaac \'ī-zik, -zək\ son of Abraham and father of Jacob in the Bible

Is·a·bel·la I \ˌiz-ə-'bel-ə\ 1451–1504 queen of Castile (1474–1504) and of Aragon (1479–1504); wife of Ferdinand V of Castile

Isa·iah \ī-'zā-ə\ Hebrew prophet of the 8th century B.C.

Ish·ma·el \'ish-(ˌ)mā-əl, -mē-\ outcast son of Abraham and Hagar in the Bible

Ives \'īvz\ Charles Edward 1874–1954 American composer

Jack·son \'jak-sən\ Andrew 1767–1845 American general; 7th president of the U.S. (1829–37)

Jackson Thomas Jonathan 1824–1863 *Stonewall Jackson* American Confederate general

Ja·cob \'jā-kəb\ son of Isaac and Rebekah and younger twin brother of Esau in the Bible

James \'jāmz\ one of the 12 apostles in the Bible

James *the Less* one of the 12 apostles in the Bible

James name of two kings of Great Britain: **I** 1566–1625 (reigned 1603–25); king of Scotland as *James VI* (reigned 1567–1625); **II** 1633–1701 (reigned 1685–88)

James Henry 1843–1916 British (American-born) author

Ja·nus \'jā-nəs\ god of gates and doors and of all beginnings in Roman mythology and that is pictured with two opposite faces

Ja·son \'jās-ᵊn\ hero in Greek mythology noted for his successful quest of the Golden Fleece

Jay \'jā\ John 1745–1829 American jurist and statesman; 1st chief justice of the U.S. Supreme Court (1789–95)

Jef·fer·son \'jef-ər-sən\ Thomas 1743–1826 3rd president of the U.S. (1801–09) — **Jef·fer·so·nian** \ˌjef-ər-'sō-nē-ən, -nyən\ *adj*

Jem·i·son \'jem-ə-sən\ Mae 1956–　　American astronaut

Jer·e·mi·ah \ˌjer-ə-'mī-ə\ Hebrew prophet of the 7th–6th century B.C.

Je·sus \'jē-zəs, -zəz\ *or* **Jesus Christ** \'krīst\ *about* 6 B.C.–*about* 30 A.D. source of the Christian religion and Savior in the Christian faith

Jez·e·bel \'jez-ə-ˌbel\ queen of Israel and wife of Ahab who is noted for her wickedness in the Bible

Joan of Arc \ˌjō-nə-'värk\ Saint *about* 1412–1431 *the Maid of Orléans* French national heroine

Job \'jōb\ man in the Bible who has many sufferings but keeps his faith

Jobs \'jäbz\ Steven Paul 1955–2011 American computer entrepreneur

Jo·cas·ta \jō-'kas-tə\ queen of Thebes in Greek mythology who unknowingly marries her son Oedipus

John \'jän\ one of the 12 apostles believed to be the author of the fourth Gospel, three Epistles, and the Book of Revelation

John name of 21 popes: especially **XXIII** 1881–1963 (pope 1958–63)

John 1167–1216 *John Lack·land* \'lak-ˌland\ king of England (1199–1216)

John Paul name of 2 popes: especially **II** 1920–2005 (pope 1975–2005)

John·son \'jän(t)-sən\ Andrew 1808–1875 17th president of the U.S. (1865–69)

Johnson Lyndon Baines 1908–1973 36th president of the U.S. (1963–69)

Johnson Samuel 1709–1784 *Dr. Johnson* English lexicographer and author

John the Baptist Saint, 1st century A.D. prophet and baptizer of Jesus in the Bible

Jol·liet *or* **Jo·liet** \zhól-ˈyā, ˌjō-lē-ˈet\ Louis 1645–1700 French-Canadian explorer in America

Jo·nah \ˈjō-nə\ Hebrew prophet who in the Bible spends three days in the belly of a great fish

Jones \ˈjōnz\ John Paul 1747–1792 American (Scottish-born) naval officer

Jop·lin \ˈjäp-lən\ Scott 1868–1917 American composer

Jor·dan \ˈjȯrd-ən\ Michael 1963–   American basketball player

Jo·seph \ˈjō-zəf *also* -səf\ son of Jacob in the Bible who rises to high office in Egypt after being sold into slavery by his brothers

Joseph Chief *about* 1840–1904 Nez Percé Indian chief

Joseph Saint, husband of Mary, the mother of Jesus, in the Bible

Josh·ua \ˈjäsh-(ə-)wə\ Hebrew leader in the Bible who succeeds Moses during the settlement of the Israelites in Canaan

Juan Car·los \ˈ(h)wän-ˈkär-ˌlōs\ 1938–   king of Spain (1975–2014)

Juá·rez \ˈhwär-əs, ˈwär-\ Benito Pablo 1806–1872 president of Mexico (1861–65; 1867–72)

Ju·dah \ˈjüd-ə\ son of Jacob and ancestor of one of the 12 tribes of Israel in the Bible

Ju·das \ˈjüd-əs\ *or* **Judas Is·car·i·ot** \-is-ˈkar-ē-ət\ one of the 12 apostles and the betrayer of Jesus in the Bible

Ju·no \ˈjü-nō\ queen of heaven, wife of Jupiter, and goddess of light, women, and marriage in Roman mythology — compare HERA

Ju·pi·ter \ˈjü-pət-ər\ chief god, husband of Juno, and god of light, of the sky and weather, and of the state in Roman mythology — compare ZEUS

Kalb \ˈkälp, ˈkalb\ Johann 1721–1780 Baron *de Kalb* \di-ˈkalb\ German general in American Revolutionary army

Ka·me·ha·me·ha I \kə-ˌmā-ə-ˈmā-hä\ 1758?–1819 *Kamehameha the Great* originally *Pai·ea* \pī-ˈä-ə\ Hawaiian king (1795–1819)

Keats \ˈkēts\ John 1795–1821 English poet

Kel·ler \ˈkel-ər\ Helen Adams 1880–1968 American deaf and blind lecturer and author

Kel·vin \ˈkel-vən\ 1st Baron 1824–1907 *William Thomson* British mathematician and physicist

Ken·ne·dy \ˈken-əd-ē\ John Fitzgerald 1917–1963 35th president of the U.S. (1961–63)

Kennedy Robert Francis 1925–1968 American politician; attorney general of the U.S. (1961–64); brother of John F. Kennedy

Ke·o·kuk \ˈkē-ə-ˌkək\ 1780?–1848 American Indian chief

Key \ˈkē\ Francis Scott 1779–1843 American lawyer; author of "The Star-Spangled Banner"

Keynes \ˈkānz\ John Maynard 1883–1946 1st Baron *Keynes of Tilton* British economist

Khayyám Omar — see OMAR KHAYYÁM

Khru·shchev \krúsh-ˈ(ch)ȯf, -ˈ(ch)ȯv, -ˈ(ch)ef\ Ni·ki·ta \nə-ˈkēt-ə\ Sergeyevich 1894–1971 premier of U.S.S.R. (1958–64)

Khu·fu \ˈkü-fü\ *or Greek* **Che·ops** \ˈkē-ˌäps\ *flourished* 25th century B.C. king of Egypt and pyramid builder

Kidd \ˈkid\ William *about* 1645–1701 *Captain Kidd* Scottish pirate

King \ˈkiŋ\ Billie Jean 1943–   American tennis player

King Martin Luther, Jr. 1929–1968 American minister and civil rights leader; Nobel Prize winner (1964)

Kip·ling \ˈkip-liŋ\ Rud·yard \ˈrəd-yərd, ˈrəj-ərd\ 1865–1936 English author; Nobel Prize winner (1907)

Kis·sin·ger \ˈkis-ᵊn-jər\ Henry Alfred 1923–   American (German-born) government official; U.S. secretary of state (1973–77); Nobel Prize winner (1973)

Knox \ˈnäks\ John *about* 1514–1572 Scottish religious reformer

Koch \ˈkȯk, ˈkȯḵ\ Robert 1843–1910 German bacteriologist; Nobel Prize winner (1905)

Koś·ciusz·ko \ˌkäs-ē-ˈəs-ˌkō, kȯsh-ˈchûsh-kō\ Tadeusz 1746–1817 Polish patriot and general in American Revolutionary army

Krish·na \ˈkrish-nə\ god worshipped in later Hinduism

Ku·blai Khan \ˌkü-blə-ˈkän, -ˌblī-\ 1215–1294 founder of Mongol dynasty in China; grandson of Genghis Khan

La·fa·yette \ˌläf-ē-ˈet, ˌlaf-\ Marquis de 1757–1834 French general in American Revolutionary army

La·ius \ˈlā-(y)əs, ˈlī-əs\ king of Thebes who in Greek mythology is killed by his son Oedipus

Lan·ce·lot \ˈlan(t)s-ə-ˌlät\ legendary knight of the Round Table and lover of Queen Guinevere

Lange \ˈlaŋ\ Dorothea 1895–1965 American photographer

La Salle \lə-ˈsal\ Sieur de 1643–1687 *René-Robert Cavelier* French explorer in America

La·voi·sier \ləv-ˈwäz-ē-ˌā\ Antoine-Laurent 1743–1794 French chemist

Law·rence \ˈlȯr-ən(t)s, ˈlär-\ Thomas Edward 1888–1935 *Lawrence of Arabia* British archaeologist, soldier, and author

Laz·a·rus \ˈlaz-(ə-)rəs\ brother of Mary and Martha who in the Bible is raised by Jesus from the dead

Lazarus beggar in the biblical parable of the rich man and the beggar

Le·da \ˈlēd-ə\ Spartan princess in Greek mythology who is courted by Zeus in the form of a swan

Lee \ˈlē\ Ann 1736–1784 English mystic; founder of Shaker society in the U.S.

Lee Henry 1756–1818 *Light-Horse Harry* American general

Lee Robert Edward 1807–1870 American Confederate general; son of the preceding

Leeu·wen·hoek \ˈlā-vən-ˌhúk\ Antonie van 1632–1723 Dutch naturalist

Leif Er·iks·son \ˌlā-ˈver-ik-sən, ˌlē-ˈfer-\ *or* **Er·ics·son** *flourished* 1000 Norwegian explorer; son of Erik the Red

Le·nin \ˈlen-ən\ 1870–1924 originally *Vladimir Ilyich Ulyanov* \ül-ˈyän-əf, -ˌóf, -ˌóv\ Russian Communist leader

Leo \ˈlē-ō\ name of 13 popes: especially **I** Saint *died* 461 A.D. *Leo the Great* (pope 440–61); **III** Saint *died* 816 (pope 795–816); **XIII** 1810–1903 (pope 1878–1903)

Le·o·nar·do da Vin·ci \ˌlē-ə-ˈnärd-,ōd-ə-ˈvin-chē, ˌlā-, -ˈvēn-\ 1452–1519 Italian painter, sculptor, architect, and engineer

Lew·is \ˈlü-əs\ C. S. 1898–1963 *Clive Staples Lewis* British author

Lewis John Llewellyn 1880–1969 American labor leader

Lewis Meriwether 1774–1809 American explorer (with William Clark)

Lewis (Harry) Sinclair 1885–1951 American author; Nobel Prize winner (1930)

Lin·coln \ˈliŋ-kən\ Abraham 1809–1865 16th president of the U.S. (1861–65)

Lind·bergh \ˈlin(d)-ˌbərg\ Charles Augustus 1902–1974 American aviator

Lin·nae·us \lə-ˈnē-əs, -ˈnā-\ Carolus 1707–1778 *Carl von Linné* \lə-ˈnā\ Swedish botanist

Lis·ter \ˈlis-tər\ Joseph 1827–1912 English surgeon and medical scientist

Liszt \ˈlist\ Franz 1811–1886 Hungarian pianist and composer

Liv·ing·stone \ˈliv-iŋ-stən\ David 1813–1873 Scottish missionary and explorer in Africa

\ə\ **abut**	\aú\ **out**	\i\ **tip**	\ȯ\ **saw**	\ù\ **foot**
\ər\ **further**	\ch\ **chin**	\ī\ **life**	\ȯi\ **coin**	\y\ **yet**
\a\ **mat**	\e\ **pet**	\j\ **job**	\th\ **thin**	\yü\ **few**
\ā\ **take**	\ē\ **easy**	\ŋ\ **sing**	\th̲\ **this**	\yù\ **cure**
\ä\ **cot, cart**	\g\ **go**	\ō\ **bone**	\ü\ **food**	\zh\ **vision**

Lon·don \\'lən-dən\\ Jack 1876–1916 *John Griffith London* American writer

Long·fel·low \\'loŋ-ˌfel-ō\\ Henry Wads·worth \\'wädz-(ˌ)wərth\\ 1807–1882 American poet

Lou·is \\'lü-ē, 'lü-əs\\ name of 18 kings of France: especially **IX** Saint 1214–1270 (reigned 1226–70); **XI** 1423–1483 (reigned 1461–83); **XII** 1462–1515 (reigned 1498–1515); **XIII** 1601–1643 (reigned 1610–43); **XIV** 1638–1715 (reigned 1643–1715); **XV** 1710–1774 (reigned 1715–74); **XVI** 1754–1793 (reigned 1774–92; guillotined); **XVII** 1785–1795 (reigned in name 1793–95); **XVIII** 1755–1824 (reigned 1814–15; 1815–24)

Lou·is \\'lü-əs\\ Joe 1914–1981 originally *Joseph Louis Barrow* American boxer

Low \\'lō\\ Juliette 1860–1927 née *Gordon* American founder of the Girl Scouts

Low·ell \\'lō-əl\\ Amy 1874–1925 American poet

Lowell James Russell 1819–1891 American author

Luke \\'lük\\ physician and companion of the apostle Paul believed to be the author of the third Gospel and the Book of Acts

Lu·ther \\'lü-thər\\ Martin 1483–1546 German Reformation leader

Ly·on \\'lī-ən\\ Mary 1797–1849 American educator

Mac·Ar·thur \\mə-'kär-thər\\ Douglas 1880–1964 American general

Mac·don·ald \\mək-'dän-ᵊld\\ Sir John Alexander 1815–1891 Canadian statesman; 1st prime minister of Dominion of Canada (1867–73; 1878–91)

Ma·chi·a·vel·li \\ˌmak-ē-ə-'vel-ē\\ Niccolò 1469–1527 Italian political philosopher

Ma·cy \\'mā-sē\\ Anne Sullivan 1866–1936 née *Sullivan* American educator; teacher of Helen Keller

Mad·i·son \\'mad-ə-sən\\ James 1751–1836 4th president of the U.S. (1809–17)

Ma·gel·lan \\mə-'jel-ən\\ Ferdinand *about* 1480–1521 Portuguese navigator and explorer

Mah·ler \\'mäl-ər\\ Gustav 1860–1911 Austrian composer

Mal·colm X \\ˌmal-kə-'meks\\ 1925–1965 originally *Malcolm Little* American civil rights leader

Man·dela \\man-'del-ə\\ Nelson Rolihlahla 1918–2013 South African political activist; president of South Africa (1994–99); Nobel Prize winner (1993)

Ma·net \\ma-'nā, mä-\\ Édouard 1832–1883 French painter

Mann \\'man\\ Horace 1796–1859 American educator

Mao Ze·dong *or* **Mao Tse-tung** \\ˌmaü(d)-zə-'dùŋ, ˌmaüt-sə-\\ 1893–1976 Chinese Communist; leader of People's Republic of China (1949–76)

Mar·co·ni \\mär-'kō-nē\\ Guglielmo 1874–1937 Italian physicist and inventor; Nobel Prize winner (1909)

Marco Polo — see POLO

Ma·rie An·toi·nette \\mə-'rē-ˌan-t(w)ə-'net\\ 1755–1793 wife of Louis XVI of France

Mar·i·on \\'mer-ē-ən, 'mar-ē-\\ Francis 1732?–1795 *the Swamp Fox* American commander in Revolution

Mark \\'märk\\ evangelist believed to be the author of the second Gospel

Mark Antony — see ANTONY

Mar·quette \\mär-'ket\\ Jacques 1637–1675 *Père* \\ˌpir, ˌper\\ *Marquette* French-born Jesuit missionary and explorer in America

Mars \\'märz\\ god of war in Roman mythology — compare ARES

Mar·shall \\'mär-shəl\\ George Catlett 1880–1959 American general and diplomat; Nobel Prize winner (1953)

Marshall John 1755–1835 American jurist; chief justice of the U.S. Supreme Court (1801–35)

Marshall Thurgood 1908–1993 American jurist

Mar·tha \\'mär-thə\\ sister of Lazarus and Mary and friend of Jesus in the Bible

Mar·tin \\'märt-ᵊn\\ Saint 316–397 *Martin of Tours* \\-'tù(ə)r\\ patron saint of France

Martin Paul 1938–   prime minister of Canada (2003–06)

Marx \\'märks\\ Karl 1818–1883 German political philosopher and socialist

Mary \\'me(ə)r-ē, 'ma(ə)r-ē, 'mā-rē\\ *Saint Mary*; *Virgin Mary* mother of Jesus ·

Mary sister of Lazarus and Martha in the Bible

Mary I 1516–1558 *Mary Tudor*; *Bloody Mary* queen of England (1553–58)

Mary II 1662–1694 joint British sovereign with William III (1689–94)

Mary Mag·da·lene \\-'mag-də-ˌlən, -ˌlēn\\ woman in the Bible who is healed of evil spirits by Jesus and who later sees the risen Christ

Mary, Queen of Scots 1542–1587 *Mary Stuart* queen of Scotland (1542–67)

Mas·sa·soit \\ˌmas-ə-'sóit\\ *died* 1661 American Indian chief

Math·er \\'ma-thər, 'math-\\ Cotton 1663–1728 American religious leader and author

Mather Increase 1639–1723 American minister and author; father of Cotton Mather

Ma·tisse \\ma-'tēs\\ Henri 1869–1954 French painter

Mat·thew \\'math-yü\\ apostle believed to be the author of the first Gospel

Mau·pas·sant \\ˌmō-pə-'sänt\\ (Henri-René-Albert-) Guy de 1850–1893 French author

Mays \\'māz\\ Willie Howard 1931–   American baseball player

Mc·Au·liffe \\mə-'kól-əf\\ Christa Corrigan 1948–1986 American teacher; 1st private citizen in space (1986)

Mc·Car·thy \\mə-'kär-thē\\ Joseph Raymond 1908–1957 American politician

Mc·Clel·lan \\mə-'klel-ən\\ George Brinton 1826–1885 American general

Mc·Clin·tock \\mə-'klin-tək\\ Barbara 1902–1992 American botanist; Nobel Prize winner (1983)

Mc·Cor·mick \\mə-'kór-mik\\ Cyrus Hall 1809–1884 American inventor

Mc·Kin·ley \\mə-'kin-lē\\ William 1843–1901 25th president of the U.S. (1897–1901)

Mead \\'mēd\\ Margaret 1901–1978 American anthropologist

Meade \\'mēd\\ George Gordon 1815–1872 American Civil War general

Mea·ny \\'mē-nē\\ George 1894–1980 American labor leader

Me·dea \\mə-'dē-ə\\ woman with magic powers in Greek mythology who helps Jason to win the Golden Fleece and who kills her children when he leaves her

Me·di·ci \\'me-də-chē\\ Lorenzo de' 1449–1492 *Lorenzo the Magnificent* Florentine statesman, ruler, and patron of the arts

Médicis Catherine de — see CATHERINE DE MÉDICIS

Me·du·sa \\mi-'dü-sə\\ Gorgon in Greek mythology slain by Perseus

Me·ir \\me-'i(ə)r\\ Golda 1898–1978 prime minister of Israel (1969–74)

Mel·ville \\'mel-ˌvil\\ Herman 1819–1891 American author

Men·del \\'men-dᵊl\\ Gregor Johann 1822–1884 Austrian botanist

Men·dels·sohn (-Bar·thol·dy) \\'men-dᵊl-sən(-bär-'tól-dē)\\ (Jakob Ludwig) Felix 1809–1847 German composer

Men·e·la·us \\ˌmen-ᵊl-'ā-əs\\ king of Sparta, brother of Agamemnon, and husband of Helen of Troy in Greek mythology

Meph·is·toph·e·les \\ˌmef-ə-'stäf-ə-ˌlēz\\ chief devil in the Faust legend

Mer·ca·tor \\(ˌ)mər-'kāt-ər\\ Gerardus 1512–1594 originally *Gerhard Kremer* Flemish cartographer

Mer·cu·ry \\'mər-kyə-rē, -k(ə)rē\\ god of commerce, eloquence, travel, and theft who serves as messenger of the other gods in Roman mythology — compare HERMES

Mer·kel \\'mer-kəl\\ Angela Dorothea 1954–   née *Kasner* chancellor of Germany (2005–   )

Mer·lin \\'mər-lən\\ prophet and magician in the legend of King Arthur

Met·a·com \\'met-ə-ˌkäm\\ *or* **King Philip** *about* 1638–1676 *Met·a·com·et* \\ˌmet-ə-'käm-ət\\ American Indian chief; son of Massasoit

Mi·chael \\'mī-kəl\\ one of the four archangels named in Hebrew tradition — compare GABRIEL, RAPHAEL, URIEL

Mi·chel·an·ge·lo \\ˌmī-kə-'lan-jə-ˌlō, ˌmik-ə-'lan-, ˌmē-kə-'län-\\ 1475–1564 Italian sculptor, painter, architect, and poet

Mi·das \\'mīd-əs\\ legendary king having the power to turn everything he touched into gold

Mil·lay \\mil-'ā\\ Edna St. Vincent 1892–1950 American poet

Mil·ler \\'mil-ər\\ Arthur 1915–2005 American playwright

Milne \\'mil(n)\\ A. A. 1882–1956 *Alan Alexander Milne* English author

Mil·ton \\'milt-ᵊn\\ John 1608–1674 English poet

Mi·ner·va \\mə-'nər-və\\ goddess of wisdom in Roman mythology — compare ATHENA

Mi·no·taur \\'min-ə-ˌto(ə)r, 'mī-nə-\\ monster in Greek mythology shaped half like a man and half like a bull

Min·u·it \\'min-yə-wət\\ Peter *about* 1580–1638 Dutch colonial administrator in America

Mitch·ell \\'mich-əl\\ Maria 1818–1889 American astronomer

Mo·lière \\mōl-'ye(ə)r, 'mōl-ˌye(ə)r\\ 1622–1673 originally *Jean-Baptiste Poquelin* French actor and playwright

Mo·net \\mō-'nā\\ Claude 1840–1926 French painter

Mon·roe \\mən-'rō\\ James 1758–1831 5th president of the U.S. (1817–25)

Mont·calm (de Saint-Vé·ran) \\mänt-'käm(-də-ˌsan-vā-'rän), -'kälm-\\ Marquis de 1712–1759 *Louis-Joseph de Montcalm-Grozon* French field marshal in Canada

Mon·tes·so·ri \\ˌmänt-ə-'sōr-ē, -'sor-\\ Maria 1870–1952 Italian physician and educator

Mon·te·zu·ma II \\ˌmänt-ə-'zü-mə\\ 1466–1520 last Aztec emperor of Mexico (1502–20)

Moore \\'mō(ə)r, 'mo(ə)r, 'mu(ə)r\\ Marianne Craig 1887–1972 American poet

More \\'mō(ə)r, 'mo(ə)r\\ Sir Thomas 1478–1535 *Saint Thomas More* English public official and author

Mor·gan \\'mor-gən\\ J. P. 1837–1913 *John Pierpont Morgan* American financier

Mor·ri·son \\'mor-ə-sən\\ Toni 1931–   originally *Chloe Anthony Wofford* American novelist; Nobel Prize winner (1993)

Morse \\'mo(ə)rs\\ Samuel Finley Breese 1791–1872 American artist and inventor

Mo·ses \\'mō-zəz *also* -zəs\\ Hebrew prophet and lawgiver who in the Bible freed the Israelites from slavery in Egypt

Moses Grandma 1860–1961 *Anna Mary Moses* née *Robertson* American painter

Mott \\'mät\\ Lucretia 1793–1880 American reformer

Mo·zart \\'mōt-ˌsärt\\ Wolfgang Amadeus 1756–1791 Austrian composer

Mu·ham·mad \\mō-'ham-əd, -'häm- *also* mü-\\ *about* 570–632 A.D. Arab prophet and founder of Islam

Mun·ro \\ˌ(ˌ)mən-'rō\\ Alice 1931–   née *Laidlaw* Canadian writer; Nobel Prize winner (2013)

Mus·so·li·ni \\ˌmü-sə-'lē-nē, ˌmus-ə-\\ Be·ni·to \\bə-'nēt-ō\\ 1883–1945 *Il Du·ce* \\ēl-'dü-chā\\ Italian fascist premier (1922–43)

Na·po·leon I \\nə-'pōl-yən, -'pō-lē-ən\\ *or* **Napoleon Bo·na·parte** \\'bō-nə-ˌpärt\\ 1769–1821 French general and emperor of the French (1804–15) — **Na·po·le·on·ic** \\nə-ˌpō-lē-'än-ik\\ *adj*

Nar·cis·sus \\när-'sis-əs\\ beautiful youth in Greek mythology who pines away for love of his own reflection and is then turned into the narcissus flower

Nash \\'nash\\ Ogden 1902–1971 American poet

Na·tion \\'nā-shən\\ Car·ry \\'kar-ē\\ Amelia 1846–1911 née *Moore* American temperance agitator

Nav·ra·ti·lo·va \\ˌnav-rə-tə-'lō-və\\ Martina 1956– American (Czech born) tennis player

Neb·u·cha·drez·zar II \\ˌneb-(y)ə-kə-'drez-ər\\ *or* **Neb·u·chad·nez·zar** \\-kəd-'nez-\\ *about* 630–562 B.C. Chaldean king of Babylon (605–562)

Neh·ru \\'ne(ə)r-ˌü, 'nā-rü\\ Ja·wa·har·lal \\jə-'wä-hər-ˌläl\\ 1889–1964 Indian nationalist; 1st prime minister of the Republic of India (1947–64)

Nel·son \\'nel-sən\\ Horatio 1758–1805 Viscount *Nelson* British admiral

Nem·e·sis \\'nem-ə-səs\\ goddess of reward and punishment in Greek mythology

Nep·tune \\'nep-ˌt(y)ün\\ god of the sea in Roman mythology — compare POSEIDON

Ne·ro \\'nē-ˌrō, 'ni(ə)r-ō\\ 37–68 A.D. Roman emperor (54–68)

Nev·el·son \\'nev-əl-sən\\ Louise 1899–1988 American (Russian-born) sculptor

New·ton \\'n(y)üt-ᵊn\\ Sir Isaac 1642–1727 English mathematician and physicist

Nich·o·las \\'nik-(ə-)ləs\\ Saint *flourished* 4th century A.D. Christian bishop

Nicholas I 1796–1855 czar of Russia (1825–55)

Nicholas II 1868–1918 czar of Russia (1894–1917)

Night·in·gale \\'nīt-ᵊn-ˌgāl, -iŋ-\\ Florence 1820–1910 *Lady of the Lamp* English nurse and philanthropist

Ni·ke \\'nī-kē\\ goddess of victory in Greek mythology

Ni·o·be \\'nī-ə-bē\\ bereaved mother in Greek mythology who while weeping for her slain children is turned into a stone from which her tears continue to flow

Nix·on \\'nik-sən\\ Richard Mil·hous \\'mil-ˌhaus\\ 1913–1994 37th president of the U.S. (1969–74)

No·ah \\'nō-ə\\ biblical builder of the ark in which he, his family, and two animals of every kind survive the Flood

No·bel \\nō-'bel\\ Alfred Bernhard 1833–1896 Swedish manufacturer, inventor, and philanthropist

Nor·man \\'nor-mən\\ Jessye 1945–   American soprano

Oak·ley \\'ōk-lē\\ Annie 1860–1926 originally *Phoebe Anne Oakley Moses* American sharpshooter

Oba·ma \\ō-'bäm-ə\\ Ba·rack \\bə-'räk\\ Hussein, Jr. 1961–44th president of the U.S. (2009–17)

Oce·anus \\ō-'sē-ə-nəs\\ Titan who rules over a great river encircling the earth in Greek mythology

O'·Con·nor \\ō-'kän-ər\\ (Mary) Flannery 1925–1964 American writer

O'Connor Sandra Day 1930–   American jurist

Odin \\'ōd-ᵊn\\ *or* **Wo·den** \\'wōd-ᵊn\\ chief god, god of war, and patron of heroes in Norse mythology

Odys·seus \\ō-'dis-ē-əs, -'dis-yəs, -'dish-əs, -'dish-ˌüs\\ *or* **Ulys·ses** \\yu-'lis-ēz\\ king of Ithaca and hero in Greek mythology who after the Trojan war wanders for 10 years

Oe·di·pus \\'ed-ə-pəs, 'ēd-\\ son of Laius and Jocasta who in Greek mythology kills his father and marries his mother not knowing their identity

Ogle·thorpe \\'ō-gəl-ˌthorp\\ James Edward 1696–1785 English general and founder of Georgia

O'·Keeffe \\ō-'kēf\\ Georgia 1887–1986 American painter

Olaf V \\'ō-ləf, -ˌläf; 'ü-ˌlaf\\ 1903–1991 king of Norway (1957–91)

Omar Khay·yám \\ˌō-ˌmär-ˌkī-'(y)äm, ˌō-mər-, -'(y)am\\ 1048–1131 Persian poet and astronomer

O'·Neill \\ō-'nē(ə)l\\ Eugene Gladstone 1888–1953 American playwright; Nobel Prize winner (1936)

\\ə\\ **a**but	\\au\\ **ou**t	\\i\\ **ti**p	\\o\\ **saw**	\\u\\ **foo**t
\\ər\\ f**ur**ther	\\ch\\ **ch**in	\\ī\\ **li**fe	\\oi\\ **coi**n	\\y\\ **y**et
\\a\\ m**a**t	\\e\\ p**e**t	\\j\\ **j**ob	\\th\\ **th**in	\\yü\\ f**ew**
\\ā\\ t**a**ke	\\ē\\ **ea**sy	\\ŋ\\ si**ng**	\\<u>th</u>\\ **th**is	\\yu\\ **cu**re
\\ä\\ c**o**t, c**a**rt	\\g\\ **g**o	\\ō\\ b**o**ne	\\ü\\ f**oo**d	\\zh\\ vi**si**on

Or·pheus \'ȯr-ˌfyüs, -fē-əs\ poet and musician in Greek mythology who almost rescues his wife Eurydice from Hades by charming Pluto and Persephone with his lyre

Or·well \'ȯr-ˌwel, -wəl\ George 1903–1950 pseudonym of *Eric Arthur Blair* English author — **Or·well·ian** \ȯr-'wel-ē-ən\ *adj*

Osce·o·la \ˌäs-ē-'ō-lə, ˌō-sē-\ *about* 1804–1838 Seminole Indian chief

Otis \'ōt-əs\ James 1725–1783 American Revolutionary patriot

Ov·id \'äv-əd\ 43 B.C.–17 A.D.? Roman poet

Ow·en \'ō-ən\ Robert 1771–1858 Welsh social reformer

Ow·ens \'ō-ənz\ Jesse 1913–1980 originally *James Cleveland Owens* American track-and-field athlete

Paine \'pān\ Thomas 1737–1809 American (English-born) political philosopher and author

Pan \'pan\ god of pastures, flocks, and shepherds in Greek mythology who is usually represented as having the legs, ears, and horns of a goat

Pan·do·ra \pan-'dōr-ə, -'dȯr-\ woman in Greek mythology who out of curiosity opens a box and lets loose all of the evils that trouble humans

Pank·hurst \'paŋk-ˌhərst\ Emmeline 1858–1928 née *Goulden* English suffragist

Par·is \'par-əs\ son of Priam whose abduction of Helen of Troy in Greek mythology leads to the Trojan War

Park·man \'pärk-mən\ Francis 1823–1893 American historian

Parks \'pärks\ Rosa 1913–2005 née *McCauley* American civil rights activist

Pas·cal \pas-'kal\ Blaise 1623–1662 French mathematician and philosopher

Pas·ter·nak \'pas-tər-ˌnak\ Boris Leonidovich 1890–1960 Russian author; Nobel Prize winner (1958)

Pas·teur \pas-'tər\ Louis 1822–1895 French chemist and microbiologist

Pat·rick \'pa-trik\ Saint *flourished* 5th century A.D. apostle and patron saint of Ireland

Pat·ton \'pat-ᵊn\ George Smith 1885–1945 American general

Paul \'pȯl\ Saint *died about* 67 A.D. Christian missionary and author of several New Testament epistles — **Pauline** \'pȯ-ˌlīn\ *adj*

Paul name of six popes: especially **III** 1468–1549 (pope 1534–49); **V** 1552–1621 (pope 1605–21); **VI** 1897–1978 (pope 1963–78)

Paul Bun·yan \'pȯl-'bən-yən\ giant lumberjack in American folklore

Pau·ling \'pȯ-liŋ\ Linus Carl 1901–1994 American chemist; Nobel Prize winner (1954, 1962)

Pav·lov \'päv-ˌlȯf, 'pav-, -ˌlȯv\ Ivan Petrovich 1849–1936 Russian physiologist; Nobel Prize winner (1904)

Pa·vlo·va \'pav-lə-və, pav-'lō-və\ Anna 1881–1931 Russian ballerina

Pea·ry \'pi(ə)r-ē\ Robert Edwin 1856–1920 American arctic explorer

Pe·cos Bill \ˌpā-kəs-'bil\ cowboy in American folklore known for his extraordinary feats

Peg·a·sus \'peg-ə-səs\ winged horse in Greek mythology

Pei \'pā\ Ieoh Ming 1917– American (Chinese-born) architect

Pence \'pens\ Mike 1959– *Michael Richard Pence* vice pres. of the U.S. (2017–)

Penn \'pen\ William 1644–1718 English Quaker leader and founder of Pennsylvania

Per·i·cles \'per-ə-ˌklēz\ *about* 495–429 B.C. Athenian political leader

Per·ry \'per-ē\ Matthew Calbraith 1794–1858 American commodore

Perry Oliver Hazard 1785–1819 American naval officer; brother of the preceding

Per·seph·o·ne \pər-'sef-ə-nē\ daughter of Zeus and Demeter who in Greek mythology is abducted by Pluto to rule with him over the underworld

Per·seus \'pər-ˌsüs, -sē-əs\ son of Zeus and Danaë and slayer of Medusa in Greek mythology

Per·shing \'pər-shiŋ, -zhiŋ\ John Joseph 1860–1948 American general

Pe·ter \'pēt-ər\ Saint *died about* 64 A.D. originally *Si·mon* \'sī-mən-\ one of the 12 apostles in the Bible

Peter I 1672–1725 *Peter the Great* czar of Russia (1682–1725)

Phil·ip \'fil-əp\ Saint, one of the 12 apostles in the Bible

Philip King — see METACOM

Philip name of six kings of France: especially **II** *or* **Philip Augustus** 1165–1223 (reigned 1179–1223); **IV** 1268–1314 *Philip the Fair* (reigned 1285–1314); **VI** 1293–1350 (reigned 1328–50)

Philip name of five kings of Spain: especially **II** 1527–1598 (reigned 1556–98); **V** 1683–1746 (reigned 1700–46)

Philip II 382–336 B.C. king of Macedonia (359–336); father of Alexander the Great

Pi·cas·so \pi-'käs-ō, -'kas-\ Pablo 1881–1973 Spanish painter and sculptor in France

Pic·card \pi-'kär(d)\ Auguste 1884–1962 and his son Jacques 1922–2008 Swiss scientists and developers of the bathyscaphe

Pick·ett \'pik-ət\ George Edward 1825–1875 American Confederate general

Pierce \'pi(ə)rs\ Franklin 1804–1869 14th president of the U.S. (1853–57)

Pi·late \'pī-lət\ Pon·tius \'pän-chəs, 'pən-chəs\ *died after* 36 A.D. Roman governor of Judea (26–36)

Pin·ker·ton \'piŋ-kər-tən\ Allan 1819–1884 American (Scottish-born) detective

Pis·sar·ro \pə-'sär-ō\ Camille 1830–1903 French (West Indian-born) painter

Pitt \'pit\ William 1759–1806 *The Younger Pitt* English prime minister (1783–1801; 1804–06)

Pi·us \'pī-əs\ name of 12 popes: especially **VII** 1742–1823 (pope 1800–23); **IX** 1792–1878 (pope 1846–78); **X** Saint 1835–1914 (pope 1903–14); **XI** 1857–1939 (pope 1922–39); **XII** 1876–1958 (pope 1939–58)

Pi·zar·ro \pə-'zär-ō\ Francisco *about* 1475–1541 Spanish conqueror of Peru

Pla·to \'plāt-ō\ *about* 428–348 (*or* 347) B.C. Greek philosopher

Plu·to \'plüt-ō\ god of the underworld in Greek mythology

Po·ca·hon·tas \ˌpō-kə-'hänt-əs\ *about* 1595–1617 American Indian friend of the colonists at Jamestown; daughter of Powhatan

Poe \'pō\ Edgar Allan 1809–1849 American author

Polk \'pōk\ James Knox 1795–1849 11th president of the U.S. (1845–49)

Po·lo \'pō-lō\ Mar·co \'mär-kō\ *about* 1254–1324 Venetian merchant and traveler

Poly·phe·mus \ˌpäl-ə-'fē-məs\ Cyclops in Greek mythology who is blinded by Odysseus

Ponce de Le·ón \ˌpän(t)-sə-ˌdā-lē-'ōn, ˌpän(t)s-də-'lē-ən\ Juan 1460–1521 Spanish explorer of Florida (1513)

Pon·ti·ac \'pänt-ē-ˌak\ *about* 1720–1769 Ottawa Indian chief

Por·ter \'pōrt-ər, 'pȯrt-\ Cole Albert 1891–1964 American composer and songwriter

Porter Katherine Anne 1890–1980 American author

Porter William Sydney — see O. HENRY

Po·sei·don \pə-'sīd-ᵊn\ god of the sea in Greek mythology — compare NEPTUNE

Pot·ter \'pät-ər\ (Helen) Beatrix 1866–1943 British author and illustrator

Pound·mak·er \'paùnd-ˌmāk-ər\ 1826–1886 Cree Indian chief

Pow·ha·tan \ˌpaů-ə-'tan, paů-'hat-ᵊn\ 1550?–1618 American Indian chief of a confederacy of Algonquian-speaking tribes; father of Pocahontas

Pres·ley \'pres-lē, 'prez-\ Elvis Aaron 1935–1977 American popular singer

Pri·am \'prī-əm, -ˌam\ king of Troy during the Trojan War in Greek mythology

Price \'prīs\ (Mary) Leontyne 1927–   American soprano

Pro·me·theus \prə-'mē-th(y)üs, -thē-əs\ Titan in Greek mythology who is punished by Zeus for stealing fire from heaven and giving it to humans

Pro·teus \'prō-ˌt(y)üs, 'prōt-ē-əs\ sea god in Greek mythology who is capable of assuming different forms

Ptol·e·my \'täl-ə-mē\ name of 15 kings of Egypt 323–30 B.C.

Ptolemy *flourished* 2nd century A.D. Greco-Egyptian astronomer, geographer, and mathematician in Alexandria

Puc·ci·ni \pü-'chē-nē\ Giacomo 1858–1924 Italian composer

Pu·las·ki \pə-'las-kē, pyü-\ Kazimierz 1747–1779 Polish soldier in American Revolutionary army

Pu·lit·zer \'půl-ət-sər, 'pyü-lət-sər\ Joseph 1847–1911 American (Hungarian-born) journalist

Pyg·ma·lion \pig-'māl-yən, -'mā-lē-ən\ sculptor in Greek mythology who creates Galatea

Py·thag·o·ras \pə-'thag-ə-rəs, pī-\ *about* 580–*about* 500 B.C. Greek philosopher and mathematician

Ra \'rä, 'rȯ\ god of the sun and chief deity of ancient Egypt

Ra·leigh *or* **Ra·legh** \'rȯl-ē, 'räl- *also* 'ral-\ Sir Walter 1554?–1618 English navigator and writer

Ram·ses \'ram-ˌsēz\ *or* **Ram·e·ses** \'ram-ə-ˌsēz\ name of 12 kings of Egypt: especially **II** (reigned 1279–1213 B.C.); **III** (reigned 1187–1156 B.C.)

Ran·dolph \'ran-ˌdälf\ Asa Philip 1889–1979 American labor and civil rights leader

Ra·pha·el \'raf-ē-əl, 'rā-fē-\ one of the four archangels named in Hebrew tradition — compare GABRIEL, MICHAEL, URIEL

Ra·pha·el \'raf-ē-əl, 'rā-fē-, 'räf-ē-\ 1483–1520 originally *Raffaello Sanzio* or *Santi* Italian painter

Ras·pu·tin \ra-'sp(y)üt-ᵊn, -'spůt-\ Grigory Yefimovich 1872–1916 Russian mystic

Ra·vel \rə-'vel, ra-\ (Joseph) Maurice 1875–1937 French composer

Rea·gan \'rā-gən *also* 'rē-\ Ronald Wilson 1911–2004 40th president of the U.S. (1981–89)

Re·bek·ah \ri-'bek-ə\ wife of Isaac and mother of Jacob in the Bible

Red Cloud \'red-ˌklaůd\ 1822–1909 Sioux Indian chief

Red Jack·et \'red-ˌjak-ət\ 1758?–1830 *Sa·go·ye·wa·tha* \sä-ˌgoi-(y)ə-'wäth-ə\ Seneca Indian chief

Reed \'rēd\ Walter 1851–1902 American army surgeon

Rem·brandt \'rem-ˌbrant *also* -ˌbränt\ 1606–1669 *Rembrandt (Harmenszoon) van Rijn* Dutch painter

Rem·ing·ton \'rem-iŋ-tən\ Frederic 1861–1909 American painter and sculptor

Re·mus \'rē-məs\ son of Mars who in Roman mythology is killed by his twin brother Romulus

Re·noir \'ren-ˌwär, rən-'wär\ (Pierre-) Auguste 1841–1919 French painter

Re·vere \ri-'vi(ə)r\ Paul 1735–1818 American patriot and silversmith

Rich·ard \'rich-ərd\ name of three kings of England: **I** 1157–1199 *Richard the Lion-Hearted* (reigned 1189–99); **II** 1367–1400 (reigned 1377–99); **III** 1452–1485 (reigned 1483–85)

Ride \'rīd\ Sally Kristen 1951–2012 American astronaut; 1st American woman in space (1983)

Rob·erts \'räb-ərts\ John Glover, Jr. 1955–   American jurist; chief justice U.S. Supreme Court (2005–   )

Rob·in Good·fel·low \ˌräb-ən-'gůd-ˌfel-ō\ mischievous elf in English folklore

Rob·in Hood \'räb-ən-ˌhůd\ legendary English outlaw who gave to the poor what he stole from the rich

Rob·in·son \'räb-ən-sən\ Edwin Arlington 1869–1935 American poet

Robinson Jackie 1919–1972 *Jack Roosevelt Robinson* American baseball player; 1st black player in the major leagues (1947–56)

Rob·in·son Cru·soe \ˌräb-ə(n)-sən-'krü-sō\ shipwrecked sailor in Daniel Defoe's *Robinson Crusoe* who lives for many years on a desert island

Ro·cham·beau \ˌrō-ˌsham-'bō\ Comte de 1725–1807 French general in American Revolution

Rocke·fel·ler \'räk-i-ˌfel-ər, 'räk-ˌfel-\ John Davison 1839–1937 and his son John Davison, Jr. 1874–1960 American oil magnates and philanthropists

Ro·din \'rō-ˌdan\ (François-)Auguste(-René) 1840–1917 French sculptor

Ro·ma·nov \rō-'män-əf, 'rō-mə-ˌnäf\ Michael 1596–1645 1st czar (1613–45) of Russian Romanov dynasty (1613–1917)

Rom·u·lus \'räm-yə-ləs\ son of Mars in Roman mythology who is the twin brother of Remus and the founder of Rome

Rönt·gen *or* **Roent·gen** \'rent-gən, 'rənt-, -jən\ Wilhelm Conrad 1845–1923 German physicist; Nobel Prize winner (1901)

Roo·se·velt \'rō-zə-vəlt (*Roosevelts' usual pronunciation*), -ˌvelt *also* 'rü-\ (Anna) Eleanor 1884–1962 American lecturer and writer; wife of Franklin Delano Roosevelt

Roosevelt Franklin Del·a·no \'del-ə-ˌnō\ 1882–1945 32nd president of the U.S. (1933–45)

Roosevelt Theodore 1858–1919 26th president of the U.S. (1901–09); Nobel Prize winner (1906)

Ross \'rȯs\ Betsy 1752–1836 née *Griscom* reputed maker of 1st American flag

Ros·si·ni \rȯ-'sē-nē, rə-\ Gioacchino Antonio 1792–1868 Italian composer

Row·ling \'rō-liŋ\ J. K. 1965–   *Joanne Kathleen Rowling* British author

Ru·bens \'rü-bənz\ Peter Paul 1577–1640 Flemish painter

Ru·dolph \'rü-ˌdȯlf, -ˌdälf\ Wilma Glodean 1940–1994 American athlete

Rus·sell \'rəs-əl\ Bertrand Arthur William 1872–1970 3rd Earl *Russell* English mathematician and philosopher; Nobel Prize winner (1950)

Ruth \'rüth\ woman in the Bible who was one of the ancestors of King David

Ruth Babe 1895–1948 *George Herman Ruth* American baseball player

Ruth·er·ford \'rəth-ə(r)-fərd, 'rəth-\ Ernest 1871–1937 Baron *Rutherford* British physicist; Nobel Prize winner (1908)

Sa·bin \'sā-bin\ Albert Bruce 1906–1993 American (Polish-born) physician and microbiologist

Sac·a·ga·wea \ˌsak-ə-jə-'wē-ə, -'wä-ə\ 1786?–1812 Shoshone Indian guide to Lewis and Clark

Sa·dat \sə-'dat, -'dät\ Anwar el- 1918–1981 president of Egypt (1970–81); Nobel Prize winner (1978)

Sa·gan \'sā-gən\ Carl Edward 1934–1996 American astronomer and science writer

Saint Nicholas — see NICHOLAS, SANTA CLAUS

Sal·in·ger \'sal-ən-jər\ J. D. 1919–2010 *Jerome David Salinger* American author

\ə\ abut	\aů\ out	\i\ tip	\ȯ\ saw	\ů\ foot
\ər\ further	\ch\ chin	\ī\ life	\ȯi\ coin	\y\ yet
\a\ mat	\e\ pet	\j\ job	\th\ thin	\yü\ few
\ā\ take	\ē\ easy	\ŋ\ sing	\th̲\ this	\yů\ cure
\ä\ cot, cart	\g\ go	\ō\ bone	\ü\ food	\zh\ vision

Salk \\'sók, 'sólk\\ Jonas Edward 1914–1995 American physician and medical researcher

Sa·lo·me \\sə-'lō-mē\\ niece of Herod Antipas who in the Bible is given the head of John the Baptist as a reward for her dancing

Sa·mo·set \\'sam-ə-ˌset, sə-'mäs-ət\\ *died about* 1653 American Indian leader

Sam·son \\'sam(p)-sən\\ powerful Hebrew hero in the Bible who fights against the Philistines but is betrayed by Delilah

Sam·u·el \\'sam-yə(-wə)l\\ Hebrew judge in the Bible who appoints Saul and then David king

Sand·burg \\'san(d)-ˌbərg\\ Carl 1878–1967 American author

Sang·er \\'saŋ-ər\\ Margaret 1883–1966 née *Higgins* American birth-control activist

San·ta Claus \\'sant-ē-ˌklóz, 'sant-ə-\\ plump white-bearded and red-suited old man in modern folklore who delivers presents to good children at Christmastime

Sap·pho \\'saf-ō\\ *flourished about* 610–*about* 580 B.C. Greek poet

Sa·rah \\'ser-ə, 'sar-ə, 'sä-rə\\ wife of Abraham and mother of Isaac in the Bible

Sar·gent \\'sär-jənt\\ John Singer 1856–1925 American painter

Sat·urn \\'sat-ərn\\ god of agriculture in Roman mythology

Saul \\'sól\\ first king of Israel in the Bible

Saul *or* **Saul of Tar·sus** \\-'tär-səs\\ the apostle Paul in the Bible

Sche·her·a·zade \\shə-ˌher-ə-'zäd(-ə), -'zäd(-ē)\\ fictional wife of a sultan and narrator of the tales in the *Arabian Nights' Entertainments*

Schin·dler \\'shind-lər\\ Oskar 1908–1974 German humanitarian during the Holocaust

Schu·bert \\'shü-bərt, -ˌbərt\\ Franz Peter 1797–1828 Austrian composer

Schu·mann \\'shü-ˌmän, -mən\\ Clara 1819–1896 née *Wieck* \\'vēk\\ German pianist and composer; wife of Robert Schumann

Schumann Robert Alexander 1810–1856 German composer

Schweit·zer \\'shwīt-sər, 'swīt-, 'shvīt-\\ Albert 1875–1965 French theologian, philosopher, physician, and music scholar; Nobel Prize winner (1952)

Scott \\'skät\\ Dred \\'dred\\ 1795?–1858 American slave

Scott Robert Falcon 1868–1912 British polar explorer

Scott Sir Walter 1771–1832 Scottish author

Scott Winfield 1786–1866 American general

Scyl·la \\'sil-ə\\ nymph in Greek mythology who is changed into a monster and inhabits a cave opposite the whirlpool Charybdis off the coast of Sicily

Se·at·tle \\sē-'at-ᵊl\\ 1786?–1866 American Indian chief

Se·le·ne \\sə-'lē-nē\\ goddess of the moon in classical mythology

Se·quoy·ah *or* **Se·quoia** \\si-'kwói-ə\\ *about* 1760–1843 *George Guess* Cherokee Indian scholar

Ser·ra \\'ser-ə\\ Junípero 1713–1784 Spanish missionary in Mexico and California

Se·ton \\'sēt-ᵊn\\ Saint Elizabeth Ann 1774–1821 *Mother Seton* née *Bayley* American religious leader

Seu·rat \\sə-'rä\\ Georges 1859–1891 French painter

Sew·ard \\'sü-ərd, 'sü-(-ə)rd\\ William Henry 1801–1872 American politician; U.S. secretary of state (1861–69)

Shack·le·ton \\'shak-əl-tən\\ Sir Ernest Henry 1874–1922 British polar explorer

Shake·speare \\'shāk-ˌspi(ə)r\\ William 1564–1616 English playwright and poet

Shaw \\'shó\\ George Bernard 1856–1950 British playwright; Nobel Prize winner (1925)

Shaw Robert Gould 1837–1863 American soldier

Shel·ley \\'shel-ē\\ Mary Woll·stone·craft \\'wúl-stən-ˌkraft\\ 1797–1851 née *Godwin* English novelist; wife of Percy Bysshe Shelley

Shelley Percy Bysshe \\'bish\\ 1792–1822 English poet

Shep·ard \\'shep-ərd\\ Alan Bartlett, Jr. 1923–1998 American astronaut; 1st American in space (1961)

Sher·i·dan \\'sher-əd-ᵊn\\ Philip Henry 1831–1888 American general

Sher·lock Holmes \\'shər-ˌläk-'hōmz, -'hōlmz\\ detective in stories by Sir Arthur Conan Doyle

Sher·man \\'shər-mən\\ John 1823–1900 American statesman

Sherman William Tecumseh 1820–1891 American general

Shi·va \\'shiv-ə, 'shē-və\\ *or* **Si·va** \\'shiv-ə, 'siv-; 'shē-və, 'sē-\\ god of destruction and regeneration in the Hindu sacred triad — compare BRAHMA, VISHNU

Sieg·fried \\'sig-ˌfrēd, 'sēg-\\ hero in Germanic legend who kills a dragon guarding a gold hoard

Si·mon \\'sī-mən\\ *or* **Simon the Zealot** one of the 12 apostles in the Bible

Sind·bad the Sailor \\'sin-ˌbad-\\ citizen of Baghdad whose adventures are narrated in the *Arabian Nights' Entertainments*

Sis·y·phus \\'sis-ə-fəs\\ king of Corinth who in Greek mythology is condemned to roll a heavy stone up a hill in Hades only to have it roll down again as it nears the top

Sit·ting Bull \\ˌsit-iŋ-'búl\\ *about* 1831–1890 Sioux Indian chief

Siva — see SHIVA

Smith \\'smith\\ Adam 1723–1790 Scottish economist

Smith Bessie 1894?–1937 American blues singer

Smith John *about* 1580–1631 English colonist in America

Smith Joseph 1805–1844 American founder of the Mormon Church

Soc·ra·tes \\'säk-rə-ˌtēz\\ *about* 470–399 B.C. Greek philosopher

Sol \\'säl\\ god of the sun in Roman mythology — see HELIOS

Sol·o·mon \\'säl-ə-mən\\ son of David and 10th-century B.C. king of Israel noted for his wisdom

Soph·o·cles \\'säf-ə-ˌklēz\\ *about* 496–406 B.C. Greek playwright

So·to·may·or \\ˌsō-tō-ˌmī-'ór, -ˌmä-\\ Sonia Maria 1954– American jurist

Sou·sa \\'sü-zə, 'sü-sə\\ John Philip 1854–1932 American bandmaster and composer

Spar·ta·cus \\'spärt-ə-kəs\\ *died* 71 B.C. Roman slave and gladiator; leader of a slave rebellion

Sphinx \\'sfiŋ(k)s\\ monster in Greek mythology having a lion's body, wings, and the head and bust of a woman

Spiel·berg \\'spēl-ˌbərg\\ Steven 1947– American film director, writer, and producer

Squan·to \\'skwän-tō\\ *died* 1622 American Indian friend of the Pilgrims

Sta·lin \\'stäl-ən, 'stal-, -ˌēn\\ Joseph 1879–1953 Soviet Communist party leader (1922–53), premier (1941–53), and dictator

Stan·dish \\'stan-dish\\ Myles *or* Miles 1584?–1656 American colonist

Stan·ley \\'stan-lē\\ Sir Henry Morton 1841–1904 British explorer in Africa

Stan·ton \\'stant-ᵊn\\ Elizabeth Cady 1815–1902 née *Cady* American suffragist

Stein \\'stīn\\ Gertrude 1874–1946 American author

Stein·beck \\'stīn-ˌbek\\ John Ernst 1902–1968 American author; Nobel Prize winner (1962)

Steu·ben \\'st(y)ü-bən, 'shtói-\\ Baron Friedrich Wilhelm von 1730–1794 Prussian-born general in American Revolution

Ste·ven·son \\'stē-vən-sən\\ Adlai Ewing 1900–1965 American politician

Stevenson Robert Louis Balfour 1850–1894 Scottish author

Sto·ker \'stō-kər\ Bram 1847–1912 *Abraham Stoker* Irish author

Stowe \'stō\ Harriet Beecher 1811–1896 American author

Stra·di·va·ri \ˌstrad-ə-'vär-ē, -'var-, -'ver-\ Antonio 1644?–1737 Italian violin maker

Strauss \'straus, 'shtraus\ Johann 1804–1849 and his sons Johann, Jr. 1825–1899 and Josef 1827–1870 Austrian composers

Strauss Richard 1864–1949 German composer

Stra·vin·sky \strə-'vin-skē\ Igor 1882–1971 American (Russian-born) composer

Stu·art \'st(y)ü-ərt, 'st(y)ú(-ə)rt\ Charles Edward 1720–1788 *the Young Pretender; Bonnie Prince Charlie* claimant to the British throne

Stuart Gilbert Charles 1755–1828 American painter

Stuart Jeb 1833–1864 *James Ewell Brown Stuart* American Confederate general

Stuy·ve·sant \'stī-və-sənt\ Peter *about* 1610–1672 Dutch colonial administrator in America

Sul·li·van \'səl-ə-vən\ Sir Arthur Seymour 1842–1900 English composer; collaborator with Sir William Gilbert

Sullivan Louis Henri 1856–1924 American architect

Sum·ner \'səm-nər\ Charles 1811–1874 American politician

Sun Yat–sen \'sún-'yät-'sen\ 1866–1925 Chinese statesman

Sut·ter \'sət-ər, 'sü-tər\ John Augustus 1803–1880 American (German-born) pioneer in California

Swift \'swift\ Jonathan 1667–1745 English (Irish-born) author

Synge \'siŋ\ John Millington 1871–1909 Irish playwright

Taft \'taft\ William Howard 1857–1930 27th president of the U.S. (1909–13); chief justice of the U.S. Supreme Court (1921–30)

Ta·gore \tə-'gór\ Ra·bin·dra·nath \rə-'bin-drə-ˌnät\ 1861–1941 Indian poet; Noble Prize winner (1913)

Tall·chief \'tól-ˌchēf\ Maria 1925–2013 American dancer

Tan \'tan\ Amy 1952–   American novelist

Ta·ney \'tó-nē\ Roger Brooke 1777–1864 American jurist; chief justice of the U.S. Supreme Court (1836–64)

Tan·ta·lus \'tant-ᵊl-əs\ king in Greek mythology who is condemned to stand up to his chin in a pool of water in Hades and beneath fruit-laden boughs only to have the water or fruit go out of reach at each attempt to drink or eat

Tay·lor \'tā-lər\ Zachary 1784–1850 American general; 12th president of the U.S. (1849–50)

Tchai·kov·sky \chī-'kóf-skē, chə-, -'kóv-\ Pyotr Ilich 1840–1893 Russian composer

Te·cum·seh \tə-'kəm(p)-sə, -sē\ 1768–1813 Shawnee Indian chief

Tek·a·kwitha \ˌtek-ə-'kwith-ə\ Ka·teri \'kä-tə-rē\ 1656–1680 *Lily of the Mohawks* beatified Mohawk Indian religious

Ten·ny·son \'ten-ə-sən\ Alfred 1809–1892 Baron *Tennyson* known as *Alfred, Lord Tennyson* English poet

Te·re·sa \tə-'rē-sə, -'rā-\ Mother 1910–1997 beatified Albanian religious in India; Nobel Prize winner (1979)

Teresa of Ávi·la \'äv-i-lə\ Saint 1515–1582 Spanish nun and mystic

Tes·la \'tes-lə\ Nikola 1856–1943 American (Croatian-born) electrical engineer and inventor

Thatch·er \'thach-ər\ Margaret Hilda 1925–2013 Baroness *Thatcher of Kesteven* née *Roberts* British prime minister (1979–90)

The·seus \'thē-ˌsüs, -sē-əs\ hero in Greek mythology who kills the Minotaur and conquers the Amazons

Thom·as \'täm-əs\ apostle in the Bible who demanded proof of Jesus' resurrection

Thomas à Becket — see Saint Thomas BECKET

Thomas Aquinas Saint — see AQUINAS

Thor \'thò(ə)r\ god of thunder, weather, and crops in Norse mythology

Tho·reau \thə-'rō, thò-; 'thór-ō\ Henry David 1817–1862 American author

Thorpe \'thórp\ Jim 1888–1953 *James Francis Thorpe* American athlete

Thur·ber \'thər-bər\ James Grover 1894–1961 American author

Ti·be·ri·us \tī-'bir-ē-əs\ 42 B.C.–37 A.D. Roman emperor (14–37)

Tocque·ville \'tōk-ˌvil, 'tók-, 'täk-, -ˌvēl, -vəl\ Alexis (-Charles-Henri Clérel) de 1805–1859 French politician and author

Tol·kien \'tòl-ˌkēn, 'tól-, 'täl-\ J. R. R. 1892–1973 *John Ronald Reuel Tolkien* British author

Tol·stoy \tól-'stói, tōl-'stói, täl-'stói, 'tól-ˌstói, 'tōl-ˌstói, 'täl-ˌstói\ Leo 1828–1910 Count *Lev Nikolayevich Tolstoy* Russian author

Tou·louse–Lau·trec \tü-ˌlüz-lō-'trek\ Henri de 1864–1901 French painter

Trots·ky \'trät-skē, 'tròt-\ Leon 1879–1940 originally *Lev Davidovich Bronstein* Russian Communist leader

Tru·man \'trü-mən\ Harry S. 1884–1972 33rd president of the U.S. (1945–53)

Trump \'trəmp\ Donald J. 1946–   *Donald John Trump* 45th pres. of the U.S. (2017–   )

Truth \'trüth\ Sojourner 1797?–1883 American abolitionist

Tub·man \'təb-mən\ Harriet *about* 1820–1913 American abolitionist

Tur·ner \'tər-nər\ Joseph Mallord William 1775–1851 English painter

Tut·ankh·a·men \ˌtü-ˌtaŋ-'käm-ən, -ˌtäŋ-\ originally *Tut·ankh·a·ten* \-'kät-ᵊn\ *about* 1370–1352 B.C. king of Egypt (1361–1352)

Twain \'twān\ Mark 1835–1910 pseudonym of *Samuel Langhorne Clem·ens* \'klem-ənz\ American author

Tweed \'twēd\ William Marcy 1823–1878 *Boss Tweed* American politician

Ty·ler \'tī-lər\ John 1790–1862 10th president of the U.S. (1841–45)

Ulysses — see ODYSSEUS

Ura·nus \'yùr-ə-nəs, yù-'rā-\ the sky personified as a god· and father of the Titans in Greek mythology

Ur·ban \'ər-bən\ name of eight popes: especially **II** *about* 1035–1099 (pope 1088–99)

Uri·el \'yùr-ē-əl\ one of the four archangels named in Hebrew tradition — compare GABRIEL, MICHAEL, RAPHAEL

Val·en·tine \'val-ən-ˌtīn\ Saint, 3rd century Christian martyr

Van Bu·ren \van-'byùr-ən, vən-\ Martin 1782–1862 8th president of the U.S. (1837–41)

Van Dyck *or* **Van·dyke** \van-'dīk, vən-\ Sir Anthony 1599–1641 Flemish painter

van Gogh Vincent — see GOGH, VAN

Ve·láz·quez \və-'las-kəs\ Diego Rodríguez de Silva 1599–1660 Spanish painter

Ve·nus \'vē-nəs\ goddess of love and beauty in Roman mythology — compare APHRODITE

Ver·di \'ve(ə)rd-ē\ Giuseppe 1813–1901 Italian composer

Ver·meer \vər-'me(ə)r, -'mi(ə)r\ Jan *or* Johannes 1632–1675 Dutch painter

Verne \'vərn\ Jules 1828–1905 French author

Ves·puc·ci \ve-'spü-chē\ Ame·ri·go \ˌäm-ə-'rē-gō\ 1454–1512 Latin *Amer·i·cus Ves·pu·cius* \ə-'mer-ə-kəs-ˌves-\

\ə\ abut	\aú\ out	\i\ tip	\ó\ saw	\ú\ foot
\ər\ further	\ch\ chin	\ī\ life	\ói\ coin	\y\ yet
\a\ mat	\e\ pet	\j\ job	\th\ thin	\yü\ few
\ā\ take	\ē\ easy	\ŋ\ sing	\th\ this	\yù\ cure
\ä\ cot, cart	\g\ go	\ō\ bone	\ü\ food	\zh\ vision

'pyü-sh(ē-)əs\ Italian navigator for Spain and namesake of America

Vic·to·ria \vik-'tōr-ē-ə, -'tór-\ 1819–1901 *Alexandrina Victoria* queen of the United Kingdom of Great Britain and Ireland (1837–1901)

Vinci, da Leonardo — see LEONARDO DA VINCI

Vir·gil *also* **Ver·gil** \'vər-jəl\ 70–19 B.C. Roman poet

Vish·nu \'vish-nü\ god of preservation in the Hindu sacred triad — compare BRAHMA, SHIVA

Vol·ta \'vōl-tə, 'väl-, 'vól-\ Alessandro 1745–1827 Italian physicist

Vol·taire \vōl-'ta(ə)r, vól-, väl-, -'te(ə)r\ 1694–1778 originally *François-Marie Arouet* French author

Vul·can \'vəl-kən\ god of fire and metalworking in Roman mythology — compare HEPHAESTUS

Wag·ner \'väg-nər\ (Wilhelm) Ri·chard \'rik-ˌärt, 'riḵ-\ 1813–1883 German composer

Walk·er \'wòk-ər\ Alice Malsenior 1944–   American writer

Wal·len·berg \'wäl-ən-ˌbərg\ Raoul 1912–1947? Swedish diplomat and hero of the Holocaust

War·hol \'wòr-ˌhòl, -ˌhōl\ Andy 1928–1987 originally *Andrew Warhola* American artist and filmmaker

War·ren \'wòr-ən, 'wär-\ Earl 1891–1974 American jurist; chief justice of the U.S. Supreme Court (1953–69)

Wash·ing·ton \'wòsh-iŋ-tən, 'wäsh-\ Book·er \'bùk-ər\ Tal·ia·ferro \'täl-ə-vər\ 1856–1915 American educator

Washington George 1732–1799 American general; 1st president of the U.S. (1789–97)

Watt \'wät\ James 1736–1819 Scottish inventor

Wayne \'wān\ Anthony 1745–1796 *Mad Anthony* American general

Web·ster \'web-stər\ Daniel 1782–1852 American politician

Webster Noah 1758–1843 American lexicographer

Wel·ling·ton \'wel-iŋ-tən\ Duke of 1769–1852 *Arthur Wellesley; the Iron Duke* British general and statesman

Wells \'welz\ H. G. 1866–1946 *Herbert George Wells* English author and historian

Wel·ty \'wel-tē\ Eudora 1909–2001 American writer

Wes·ley \'wes-lē, 'wez-\ John 1703–1791 English founder of Methodism

Wes·ting·house \'wes-tiŋ-ˌhaùs\ George 1846–1914 American inventor and industrialist

Whar·ton \'hwòrt-ᵊn, 'wòrt-\ Edith 1862–1937 née *Jones* American author

Whis·tler \'hwis-lər, 'wis-\ James (Abbott) McNeill 1834–1903 American artist

Whit·man \'hwit-mən, 'wit-\ Walt 1819–1892 American poet

Whit·ney \'hwit-nē, 'wit-\ Eli 1765–1825 American inventor

Whit·ti·er \'hwit-ē-ər, 'wit-\ John Greenleaf 1807–1892 American poet

Wie·sel \vē-'zel\ Elie 1928–   American (Romanian-born) writer; Nobel Prize winner (1986)

Wilde \'wī(ə)ld\ Oscar 1854–1900 Irish author

Wil·der \'wīl-dər\ Thornton Niven 1897–1975 American author

Wil·liam \'wil-yəm\ name of four kings of England: **I** *about* 1028–1087 *William the Conqueror* (reigned 1066–87); **II**

about 1056–1100 *William Ru·fus* \'rü-fəs\ (reigned 1087–1100); **III** 1650–1702 (reigned 1689–1702); **IV** 1765–1837 (reigned 1830–37)

Wil·liam Tell \ˌwil-yəm-'tel\ legendary Swiss patriot commanded to shoot an apple off his son's head

Wil·liams \'wil-yəmz\ Roger 1603?–1683 English colonist; founder of Rhode Island

Williams Ted 1918–2002 *Theodore Samuel Williams* American baseball player

Williams Tennessee 1911–1983 originally *Thomas Lanier Williams* American playwright

Williams Venus 1980–   and her sister Serena 1981–American tennis players

Wil·son \'wil-sən\ Edward Osborne 1929–   American biologist

Wilson (Thomas) Wood·row \'wùd-ˌrō\ 1856–1924 28th president of the U.S. (1913–21); Nobel Prize winner (1919)

Win·throp \'win(t)-thrəp\ John 1588–1649 first governor of Massachusetts Bay Colony

Woden — see ODIN

Woll·stone·craft \'wùl-stən-ˌkraft\ Mary 1759–1797 English feminist and writer; mother of Mary Wollstonecraft Shelley

Woods \'wùdz\ Tiger 1975–   *Eldrick Woods* American golfer

Woolf \'wùlf\ Virginia 1882–1941 English author

Words·worth \'wərdz-(ˌ)wərth\ William 1770–1850 English poet

Wo·vo·ka \wō-'vō-kə\ 1858?–1932 *Jack Wilson* Paiute Indian mystic

Wren \'ren\ Sir Christopher 1632–1723 English architect

Wright \'rīt\ Frank Lloyd 1867–1959 American architect

Wright Or·ville \'òr-vəl\ 1871–1948 and his brother Wilbur 1867–1912 American pioneers in aviation

Wright Richard 1908–1960 American author

Wy·eth \'wī-əth\ Andrew Newell 1917–2009 American painter

Xi Jin·ping \'shē-'jin-'piŋ\ 1953–   general secretary of Chinese Communist Party (2012–   ); president of China (2013–   )

Yeats \'yāts\ William Butler 1865–1939 Irish author

Yel·tsin \'yelt-sən\ Boris Nikolayevich 1931–2007 president of Russia (1990–99)

York \'yòrk\ Alvin Cullum 1887–1964 American hero in World War I

Young \'yəŋ\ Brig·ham \'brig-əm\ 1801–1877 American Mormon leader

Za·har·i·as \zə-'har-ē-əs\ Babe Didrikson 1914–1956 *Mildred Ella Zaharias* née *Didrikson* American athlete

Za·pa·ta \sä-'pä-tä\ Emiliano 1879–1919 Mexican revolutionary

Zech·a·ri·ah \ˌzek-ə-'rī-ə\ Hebrew prophet of the 6th century B.C.

Zeng·er \'zeŋ-(g)ər\ John Peter 1697–1746 American (German-born) journalist and printer

Zeph·y·rus \'zef-ə-rəs\ god of the west wind in Greek mythology

Zeus \'züs\ chief god, ruler of the sky and weather, and husband of Hera in Greek mythology — compare JUPITER

Geographical Names

This section contains definitions of names of current, historical, and mythological places likely to be of interest to the student. It adds to the general vocabulary by entering many adjectives and nouns formed from these names, such as **Florentine** at **Florence** and **Libyan** at **Libya**.

In the entries the letters Ⓝ, Ⓔ, Ⓢ, and Ⓦ singly or in combination indicate direction and are not part of the name. They may represent either the direction (as *north*) or the adjective derived from it (as *northern*); thus, west-northwest of Santiago appears as ⓌⓃⓌ of Santiago and southern California appears as Ⓢ California. The only other special abbreviations used in this section are U.S. for United States, and U.S.S.R. for Union of Soviet Socialist Republics.

Ab·er·deen \ˌab-ər-'dēn\ city ⓃⒺ Scotland — **Ab·er·do·ni·an** \-'dō-nē-ən\ *adj or n*

Ab·i·djan \ˌab-i-'jän\ city, seat of government of Cote d'Ivoire

Ab·i·lene \'ab-ə-ˌlēn\ city ⓃⓌ central Texas

Abu Dha·bi \ˌäb-ü-'däb-ē\ city, capital of United Arab Emirates

Abu·ja \ä-'bü-jä\ city, central Nigeria; its capital since 1991

Ab·ys·sin·ia \ˌab-ə-'sin-ē-ə, -'sin-yə\ — see ETHIOPIA — **Ab·ys·sin·i·an** \-ē-ən, -yən\ *adj or n*

Aca·dia \ə-'kād-ē-ə\ *or French* **Aca·die** \ä-kȧ-dē\ NOVA SCOTIA — an early name — **Aca·di·an** \-ē-ən\ *adj or n*

Aca·pul·co \ˌäk-ə-'pül-kō, ˌak-\ city & port Ⓢ Mexico on the Pacific

Ac·cra \ə-'krä\ city & port, capital of Ghana

Acon·ca·gua \ˌak-ən-'käg-wə, ˌäk-, -əŋ-\ mountain 22,834 ft. (6960 m.) Ⓦ Argentina; highest in the Andes & in Western Hemisphere

Ad·dis Aba·ba \ˌad-ə-'sab-ə-bə\ city, capital of Ethiopia

Ad·e·laide \'ad-ᵊl-ˌād\ city, capital of South Australia

Aden \'äd-ᵊn, 'ād-, 'ad-\ city & port Ⓢ Yemen; formerly capital of People's Democratic Republic of Yemen

Aden, Gulf of arm of Indian Ocean between Yemen (Arabia) & Somalia (Africa)

Ad·i·ron·dack \ˌad-ə-'rän-ˌdak\ mountains ⓃⒺ New York; highest Mount Marcy 5344 ft. (1629 m.)

Ad·mi·ral·ty \'ad-mə-rəl-tē, -mrəl-\ **1** island ⓈⒺ Alaska **2** islands Ⓦ Pacific Ⓝ of New Guinea; part of Papua New Guinea

Adri·at·ic Sea \ˌā-drē-'at-ik, ˌad-rē-\ arm of Mediterranean between Italy & Balkan Peninsula

Ae·ge·an Sea \i-'jē-ən\ arm of Mediterranean between Asia Minor & Greece

Af·ghan·i·stan \af-'gan-ə-ˌstan\ country Ⓦ Asia Ⓔ of Iran; capital, Kabul

Af·ri·ca \'af-ri-kə\ continent Ⓢ of the Mediterranean

Agana — see HAGATNA

Agra \'äg-rə, 'ag-\ city Ⓝ India Ⓢ Ⓢ Ⓔ of Delhi

Aguas·ca·lien·tes \ˌäg-wäs-ˌkäl-'yen-ˌtās\ city central Mexico ⓃⒺ of Guadalajara

Agul·has, Cape \ə-'gəl-əs\ cape Republic of South Africa; most southerly point of Africa, at 34° 52′ Ⓢ latitude

Ahag·gar \ə-'häg-ər, ˌä-hə-'gär\ mountains Ⓢ Algeria in Ⓦ central Sahara

Ah·mad·a·bad \'äm-əd-ə-ˌbäd\ city Ⓦ India Ⓝ of Bombay

Ak·ron \'ak-rən\ city ⓃⒺ Ohio

Al·a·bama \ˌal-ə-'bam-ə\ state ⓈⒺ U.S.; capital, Montgomery — **Al·a·bam·i·an** \-'bam-ē-ən\ *or* **Al·a·bam·an** \-'bam-ən\ *adj or n*

Alas·ka \ə-'las-kə\ **1** peninsula Ⓢ Ⓦ Alaska Ⓢ Ⓦ of Cook Inlet **2** state of U.S. in Ⓝ Ⓦ North America; capital, Juneau **3** mountain range Ⓢ Alaska extending from Alaska Peninsula to Yukon boundary — **Alas·kan** \-kən\ *adj or n*

Alaska, Gulf of inlet of Pacific off Ⓢ Alaska between Alaska Peninsula on Ⓦ & Alexander Archipelago on Ⓔ

Al·ba·nia \al-'bā-nē-ə, -nyə\ country Ⓢ Europe in Balkan Peninsula on Adriatic; capital, Tirane

Al·ba·ny \'ȯl-bə-nē\ city, capital of New York

Al·be·marle Sound \'al-bə-ˌmärl\ inlet of the Atlantic in ⓃⒺ North Carolina

Al·bert, Lake \'al-bərt\ lake Ⓔ Africa between Uganda & Democratic Republic of the Congo in course of the Nile

Al·ber·ta \al-'bərt-ə\ province Ⓦ Canada; capital, Edmonton — **Al·ber·tan** \-'bərt-ᵊn\ *adj or n*

Al·bu·quer·que \'al-b(y)ə-ˌkər-kē\ city central New Mexico

Al·ca·traz \'al-kə-ˌtraz\ island California in San Francisco Bay

Al·da·bra \'al-də-brə\ island ⓃⓌ Indian Ocean Ⓝ of Madagascar; belongs to Seychelles

Al·der·ney \'ȯl-dər-nē\ island in English Channel — see CHANNEL 2

Alep·po \ə-'lep-ō\ city Ⓝ Syria

Aleu·tian \ə-'lü-shən\ islands Ⓢ Ⓦ Alaska extending 1700 mi. (2735 km.) Ⓦ from Alaska Peninsula

Al·ex·an·der \ˌal-ig-'zan-dər, ˌel-\ archipelago ⓈⒺ Alaska

Al·ex·an·dria \ˌal-ig-'zan-drē-ə, ˌel-\ **1** city Ⓝ Virginia Ⓢ of District of Columbia **2** city Ⓝ Egypt on the Mediterranean — **Al·ex·an·dri·an** \-drē-ən\ *adj or n*

Al·ge·ria \al-'jir-ē-ə\ country ⓃⓌ Africa on Mediterranean; capital, Algiers — **Al·ge·ri·an** \-ē-ən\ *adj or n*

Al·giers \al-'ji(ə)rz\ city, capital of Algeria — **Al·ge·rine** \ˌal-jə-'rēn\ *adj or n*

Al·lah·a·bad \'al-ə-hə-ˌbad, -ˌbäd\ city Ⓝ India on the Ganges

Al·le·ghe·ny \ˌal-ə-'gā-nē\ **1** river 325 mi. (523 km.) long Ⓦ Pennsylvania & Ⓢ Ⓦ New York **2** mountains of Appalachian system Ⓔ U.S. in Pennsylvania, Maryland, Virginia, & West Virginia

Al·len·town \'al-ən-ˌtaun\ city Ⓔ Pennsylvania

Al·ma·ty \ˌal-'mä-tē\ *or* **Al·ma–Ata** \ˌal-mə-ə-'tä\ city, former capital of Kazakhstan

\ə\ **abut**	\au̇\ **out**	\i\ **tip**	\ȯ\ **saw**	\u̇\ **foot**
\ər\ **further**	\ch\ **chin**	\ī\ **life**	\ȯi\ **coin**	\y\ **yet**
\a\ **mat**	\e\ **pet**	\j\ **job**	\th\ **thin**	\yü\ **few**
\ā\ **take**	\ē\ **easy**	\ŋ\ **sing**	\th\ **this**	\yu̇\ **cure**
\ä\ **cot, cart**	\g\ **go**	\ō\ **bone**	\ü\ **food**	\zh\ **vision**

Alps \\'alps\\ mountain system central Europe — see MONT BLANC

Al·tai or **Al·tay** \\'al-ˌtī\\ mountain system central Asia between Mongolia & W̲ China & between Kazakhstan & Russia

Ama·ga·sa·ki \\ˌam-ə-gə-'säk-ē\\ city Japan in W̲ central Honshu

Am·a·ril·lo \\ˌam-ə-'ril-ō, -ə\\ city N̲W̲ Texas

Am·a·zon \\'am-ə-ˌzän, -zən\\ river 3900 mi. (6275 km.) long N̲ South America flowing from Peruvian Andes into Atlantic in N̲ Brazil

Amer·i·ca \\ə-'mer-ə-kə\\ 1 either continent (**North America** or **South America**) of Western Hemisphere 2 or **the Amer·i·cas** \\-kəz\\ lands of Western Hemisphere including North, Central, & South America & West Indies 3 UNITED STATES OF AMERICA — **American** adj or n

American Falls — see NIAGARA FALLS

American Samoa or **Eastern Samoa** islands S̲W̲ central Pacific; capital, Pago Pago (on Tutuila Island)

Am·man \\a-'män, -'man\\ city, capital of Jordan

Am·ster·dam \\'am(p)-stər-ˌdam\\ city, official capital of the Netherlands

Amur \\ä-'mu̇(ə)r\\ river 1780 mi. (2784 km.) long E̲ Asia flowing into the Pacific & forming part of boundary between China & Russia

An·a·heim \\'an-ə-ˌhīm\\ city S̲W̲ California E̲ of Long Beach

An·a·to·lia \\ˌan-ə-'tō-lē-ə, -'tōl-yə\\ — see ASIA MINOR — **An·a·to·li·an** \\-'tō-lē-ən, -'tōl-yən\\ adj or n

An·chor·age \\'aŋ-k(ə-)rij\\ city S̲ central Alaska

An·da·man \\'an-də-mən, -ˌman\\ 1 islands India in Bay of Bengal S̲ of Myanmar & N̲ of Nicobar Islands 2 sea arm of Bay of Bengal S̲ of Myanmar — **An·da·man·ese** \\ˌan-də-mə-'nēz, -'nēs\\ adj or n

An·des \\'an-dēz\\ mountain system W̲ South America extending from Panama to Tierra del Fuego — see ACONCAGUA — **An·de·an** \\'an-(ˌ)dē-ən, an-'dē-\\ adj — **An·dine** \\'an-ˌdēn, -ˌdīn\\ adj

An·dor·ra \\an-'dȯr-ə, -där-ə\\ country S̲W̲ Europe in E̲ Pyrenees between France & Spain; capital, Andorra la Vella — **An·dor·ran** \\-ən\\ adj or n

An·dros \\'an-drəs\\ island, largest of Bahamas

An·gel Falls \\ˌän-jəl\\ waterfall 3212 ft. (979 m.) S̲E̲ Venezuela; world's highest waterfall

Ang·kor \\'aŋ-ˌkȯ(ə)r\\ ruins of ancient city N̲W̲ Cambodia

An·gle·sey \\'aŋ-gəl-sē\\ island N̲W̲ Wales

An·go·la \\aŋ-'gō-lə, an-\\ country S̲W̲ Africa S̲ of mouth of Congo River; until 1975 a dependency of Portugal; capital, Luanda — **An·go·lan** \\-lən\\ adj or n

An·i·ak·chak Crater \\ˌan-ē-'ak-ˌchak\\ volcanic crater S̲W̲ Alaska on Alaska Peninsula; 6 mi. (10 km.) in diameter

An·ka·ra \\'aŋ-kə-rə, äŋ-\\ city, capital of Turkey in N̲ central Anatolia

An·nap·o·lis \\ə-'nap-(ə-)ləs\\ city, capital of Maryland

Ann Ar·bor \\an-'är-bər\\ city S̲E̲ Michigan

An·shan \\'än-'shän\\ city N̲E̲ China

An·ta·nan·a·ri·vo \\ˌan-tə-ˌnan-ə-'rē-vō\\ city, capital of Madagascar

Ant·arc·ti·ca \\(')ant-'ärk-ti-kə, -'ärt-i-\\ body of land around the South Pole; plateau covered by great ice cap

An·ti·gua \\an-'tē-gə\\ island West Indies in the Leewards; with Barbuda forms independent **Antigua and Barbuda**; capital, Saint John's

An·til·les \\an-'til-ēz\\ the West Indies except for the Bahamas — see GREATER ANTILLES, LESSER ANTILLES — **An·til·le·an** \\-'til-ē-ən\\ adj

An·trim \\'an-trəm\\ 1 district E̲ Northern Ireland 2 town in Antrim district

Ant·werp \\'ant-ˌwərp\\ city N̲ Belgium

Aomen — see MACAO

Aoraki — see COOK (Mount)

Ap·en·nines \\'ap-ə-ˌnīnz\\ mountain chain Italy extending length of the peninsula; highest peak Monte Corno (N̲E̲ of Rome) 9560 ft. (2897 m.) — **Ap·en·nine** \\-ˌnīn\\ adj

Apia \\ə-'pē-ə\\ town, capital of Samoa

Apo, Mount \\'äp-ō\\ volcano Philippines in S̲E̲ Mindanao 9692 ft. (2954 m.); highest peak in the Philippines

Ap·pa·la·chia \\ˌap-ə-'lā-chə, -'lach-ə, -'lā-shə\\ region E̲ U.S. including Appalachian Mountains from S̲ central New York to central Alabama

Ap·pa·la·chian Mountains \\ˌap-ə-'lā-ch(ē-)ən, -'lach-(ē)-ən, -'lā-sh(ē-)ən\\ mountain system E̲ North America extending from S̲ Quebec to central Alabama — see MITCHELL (Mount)

Aqa·ba, Gulf of \\'äk-ə-bə, 'ak-\\ arm of Red Sea E̲ of Sinai Peninsula

Aquid·neck \\ə-'kwid-ˌnek\\ or **Rhode** island S̲E̲ Rhode Island in Narragansett Bay

Ara·bia \\ə-'rā-bē-ə\\ peninsula of S̲W̲ Asia including Saudi Arabia, Yemen, Oman, & Persian Gulf States

Ara·bi·an Sea \\ə-'rā-bē-ən\\ N̲W̲ section of Indian Ocean between Arabia & India

Ar·a·fu·ra \\ˌar-ə-'fu̇r-ə\\ sea between N̲ Australia & W̲ New Guinea

Ar·al Sea \\'ar-əl\\ inland sea W̲ Asia between Kazakhstan & Uzbekistan; now split into sections and only a fraction of its pre-1960 size

Ar·a·rat \\'ar-ə-ˌrat\\ mountain 16,946 ft. (5165 m.) E̲ Turkey near border of Iran

Arc·tic \\'ärk-tik, 'ärt-ik\\ 1 ocean N̲ of Arctic Circle 2 Arctic regions 3 archipelago N̲ Canada in Nunavut & Northwest Territories

Ar·da·bil or **Ar·de·bil** \\ˌär-də-'bēl\\ city N̲W̲ Iran

Ards \\'ärdz\\ district E̲ Northern Ireland

Are·ci·bo \\ˌä-rā-'sē-bō\\ city & port N̲ Puerto Rico

Ar·gen·ti·na \\ˌär-jən-'tē-nə\\ country S̲ South America between the Andes & the Atlantic; capital, Buenos Aires — **Argentine** \\'är-jən-ˌtēn, -ˌtīn\\ adj or n — **Ar·gen·tin·ean** or **Ar·gen·tin·i·an** \\ˌär-jən-'tin-ē-ən\\ adj or n

Ar·gos \\'är-ˌgäs, -gəs\\ ancient Greek city-state S̲ Greece

Ar·i·zo·na \\ˌar-ə-'zō-nə\\ state S̲W̲ U.S.; capital, Phoenix — **Ar·i·zo·nan** \\-nən\\ or **Ar·i·zo·nian** \\-nē-ən, -nyən\\ adj or n

Ar·kan·sas \\'är-kən-ˌsȯ; 1 is also är-'kan-zəs\\ 1 river 1450 mi. (2334 km.) long S̲W̲ central U.S. flowing S̲E̲ into the Mississippi 2 state S̲ central U.S.; capital, Little Rock — **Ar·kan·san** \\är-'kan-zən\\ adj or n

Ar·ling·ton \\'är-liŋ-tən\\ city N̲ Texas

Ar·magh \\är-'mä, 'är-ˌ\\ 1 district S̲ Northern Ireland 2 town central Armagh district

Ar·me·nia \\är-'mē-nē-ə, -nyə\\ 1 region W̲ Asia in mountainous area S̲E̲ of Black Sea & S̲W̲ of Caspian Sea divided between Iran, Turkey, & Armenia (country) 2 country W̲ Asia; capital, Yerevan; a republic of U.S.S.R. 1936–91

Arn·hem Land \\'ärn-ˌhem, 'är-nəm\\ region N̲ Australia on N̲ coast of Northern Territory

Ar·no \\'är-nō\\ river 150 mi. (241 km.) long central Italy flowing through Florence

Aru·ba \\ə-'rü-bə\\ Dutch island in Caribbean Sea off coast of N̲W̲ Venezuela

Ar·va·da \\är-'vad-ə\\ city N̲ central Colorado N̲W̲ of Denver

Ash·ga·bat \\'äsh-gə-ˌbät\\ or **Ashkh·a·bad** \\'ash-kə-ˌbad, -ˌbäd\\ city, capital of Turkmenistan

Asia \\'ā-zhə, -shə\\ continent of Eastern Hemisphere N̲ of the Equator — see EURASIA

Asia Mi·nor \\-'mī-nər\\ or **Anatolia** peninsula in modern Turkey between Black Sea on N̲ & the Mediterranean on S̲

As·ma·ra \\az-'mär-ə, -'mar-ə\\ city, capital of Eritrea

As·syr·ia \\ə-'sir-ē-ə\\ ancient empire W̲ Asia extending along the middle Tigris & over foothills to the E̲ — **As·syr·i·an** \\-ən\\ adj or n

As·ta·na \ä-stä-'nä\ city, capital of Kazakhstan since 1997

Asun·ción \ə-ˌsün(t)-sē-'ōn, (ˌ)ä-\ city, capital of Paraguay on Paraguay River

As·wân \a-'swän, ä-\ city Ⓢ Egypt on the Nile near site of **Aswân High Dam**

Ata·ca·ma \ˌat-ə-'käm-ə\ desert Ⓝ Chile

Atchaf·a·laya \(ə-)ˌchaf-ə-'lī-ə\ river 225 mi. (362 km.) long Ⓢ Louisiana flowing Ⓢ into Gulf of Mexico

Ath·a·bas·ca \ˌath-ə-'bas-kə\ river 765 mi. (1231 km.) long ⓃⒺ Alberta flowing into **Lake Athabasca** on Alberta–Saskatchewan border

Ath·ens \'ath-ənz\ **1** city ⓃⒺ Georgia **2** city, capital of Greece — **Athe·nian** \ə-'thē-nē-ən, -nyən\ adj or n

At·lan·ta \ət-'lant-ə, at-\ city, capital of Georgia

At·lan·tic \ət-'lant-ik, at-\ ocean separating North America & South America from Europe & Africa; often divided into **North Atlantic** and **South Atlantic** — **Atlantic** adj

At·las \'at-ləs\ mountains ⓃⓌ Africa extending from Ⓢ Ⓦ Morocco to Ⓝ Tunisia

At·ti·ca \'at-i-kə\ ancient state Ⓔ Greece; chief city Athens — **At·tic** \'at-ik\ adj

Auck·land \'ò-klənd\ city Ⓝ New Zealand on ⓃⓌ North Island

Au·gus·ta \ò-'gəst-ə, ə-\ **1** city Ⓔ Georgia **2** city, capital of Maine

Au·ro·ra \ə-'rōr-ə, ò-, -'ror-\ **1** city Ⓝ Ⓔ central Colorado **2** city Ⓝ Ⓔ Illinois

Auschwitz — see OSWIECIM

Aus·tin \'òs-tən, 'äs-\ city, capital of Texas

Aus·tral·asia \ˌòs-trə-'lā-zhə, ˌäs-, -'lā-shə\ Australia (including Tasmania), New Zealand, & Melanesia — **Aus·tral·asian** \-zhən, -shən\ adj or n

Aus·tra·lia \ò-'strāl-yə, ä-, ə-\ **1** continent of Eastern Hemisphere Ⓢ Ⓔ of Asia **2** independent country including continent of Australia & island of Tasmania; capital, Canberra — **Aus·tra·lian** \-yən\ adj or n

Australian Alps mountain range Ⓢ Ⓔ Australia in Ⓔ Victoria & Ⓢ Ⓔ New South Wales; part of Great Dividing Range

Australian Capital Territory district Ⓢ Ⓔ Australia including two areas, one containing Canberra (capital of Australia) & the other on Jervis Bay (inlet of the South Pacific); surrounded by New South Wales

Aus·tria \'òs-trē-ə, 'äs-\ country central Europe; capital, Vienna — **Aus·tri·an** \-ən\ adj or n

Aus·tria–Hun·ga·ry \-'həŋ-gə-rē\ country 1867–1918 central Europe including Bohemia, Moravia, Bukovina, Transylvania, Galicia, and what are now Austria, Hungary, Slovenia, Crotia, & part of Ⓝ Ⓔ Italy — **Aus·tro–Hun·gar·i·an** \ˌòs-(ˌ)trō-ˌhəŋ-'gar-ē-ən, ˌäs-, -'ger-\ adj or n

Aus·tro·ne·sia \ˌòs-trə-'nē-zhə, ˌäs-, -'nē-shə\ **1** islands of the South Pacific **2** area extending from Madagascar through Malay Peninsula & Malay Archipelago to Hawaii & Easter Island — **Aus·tro·ne·sian** \-zhən, -shən\ adj or n

Avon \'ā-vən, 'av-ən, in the U.S. also 'ā-ˌvän\ river 96 mi. (154 km.) long central England flowing Ⓦ Ⓢ Ⓦ into the Severn

Ayers Rock — see ULURU

Ayles·bury \'ālz-b(ə-)rē\ town Ⓢ Ⓔ central England

Ayr \'a(ə)r, 'e(ə)r\ or **Ayr·shire** \-ˌshiər, -shər\ former county Ⓢ Ⓦ Scotland

Azer·bai·jan \ˌaz-ər-ˌbī-'jän, ˌäz-\ country Ⓦ Asia & Ⓢ Ⓔ Europe bordering on Caspian Sea; capital, Baku; a republic of U.S.S.R. 1936–91 — **Azer·bai·ja·ni** \-ē\ adj or n

Azores \'ā-ˌzō(ə)rz, -'zō(ə)rz; ə-'zō(ə)rz, -'zò(ə)rz\ islands North Atlantic belonging to Portugal & lying 800 mi. (1287 km.) Ⓦ of Portuguese coast — **Azor·e·an** \ā-'zōr-ē-ən, ə-, -'zòr-\ adj or n

Bab·y·lon \'bab-ə-lən, -ˌlän\ ancient city, capital of Babylonia; site 55 mi. (89 km.) Ⓢ of Baghdad near the Euphrates — **Bab·y·lo·nian** \ˌbab-ə-'lō-nyən, -nē-ən\ adj or n

Bab·y·lo·nia \ˌbab-ə-'lō-nyə, -nē-ə\ ancient country Ⓦ Asia in valley of lower Euphrates and Tigris rivers; capital, Babylon — **Bab·y·lo·nian** \-nyən, -nē-ən\ adj or n

Bac·tria \'bak-trē-ə\ ancient country Ⓦ Asia in present Ⓝ Ⓔ Afghanistan — **Bac·tri·an** \-ən\ adj or n

Badlands barren region Ⓢ Ⓦ South Dakota & ⓃⓌ Nebraska

Baf·fin \'baf-ən\ **1** bay of the Atlantic between Ⓦ Greenland & Ⓔ Baffin Island **2** island Ⓝ Ⓔ Canada in Arctic Archipelago Ⓝ of Hudson Strait

Bagh·dad \'bag-ˌdad\ city, capital of Iraq on the Tigris

Ba·guio \ˌbäg-ē-'ō\ city, former summer capital of the Philippines in ⓃⓌ central Luzon

Ba·ha·mas \bə-'häm-əz, by outsiders also -'hä-məz\ islands in Ⓝ Atlantic Ⓢ Ⓔ of Florida; an independent country; capital, Nassau — **Ba·ha·mi·an** \-'hä-mē-ən, -'häm-ē-ən\ or **Ba·ha·man** \-'hä-mən, -'häm-ən\ adj or n

Bahia — see SALVADOR

Bah·rain \bä-'rän\ islands in Persian Gulf off coast of Arabia; an independent country; capital, Manama — **Bah·raini** \-'rā-nē\ adj or n

Bai·kal, Lake or **Lake Bay·kal** \bī-'käl\ lake Russia, in mountains Ⓝ of Mongolia

Ba·ja California \ˌbä-(ˌ)hä\ peninsula ⓃⓌ Mexico Ⓦ of Gulf of California

Ba·ku \bä-'kü\ city, capital of Azerbaijan on Ⓦ coast of Caspian Sea

Bal·a·ton \'bal-ə-ˌtän, 'bòl-ə-ˌtōn\ lake Ⓦ Hungary

Bal·boa Heights \(ˌ)bal-ˌbō-ə\ town Panama; formerly the center of administration for Canal Zone

Ba·li \'bäl-ē\ island Indonesia off Ⓔ end of Java — **Ba·li·nese** \ˌbäl-i-nēz, ˌbal-, -'nēs\ adj or n

Bal·kans \'bòl-kənz\ **1** or **Balkan Mountains** mountains Ⓝ Bulgaria extending from Serbia border to Black Sea; highest 7793 ft. (2375 m.) **2** or **Balkan Peninsula** peninsula Ⓢ Ⓔ Europe between Adriatic & Ionian seas on the Ⓦ & Aegean & Black seas on the Ⓔ **3** or **Balkan States** countries occupying the Balkan Peninsula: Slovenia, Croatia, Bosnia and Herzegovina, Macedonia, Serbia, Kosovo, Montenegro, Romania, Bulgaria, Albania, Greece, Turkey (in Europe)

Bal·ly·cas·tle \ˌbal-ē-'kas-əl\ town Ⓝ Northern Ireland

Bal·ly·me·na \ˌbal-ē-'mē-nə\ district Ⓝ Ⓔ central Northern Ireland

Bal·ly·mon·ey \ˌbal-ē-'mən-ē\ district Ⓝ central Northern Ireland

Bal·tic Sea \'bòl-tik\ arm of the Atlantic Ⓝ Europe Ⓔ of Scandinavian Peninsula

Bal·ti·more \'bòl-tə-ˌmō(ə)r, -ˌmò(ə)r; 'bòl-(tə-)mər\ city Ⓝ central Maryland

Ba·lu·chi·stan \bə-ˌlü-chə-'stan, -'stän; bə-'lü-chə-\ arid region Ⓢ Asia in Ⓢ Ⓦ Pakistan & Ⓢ Ⓔ Iran

Ba·ma·ko \ˌbäm-ə-'kō\ city, capital of Mali on the Niger

Ban·bridge \ban-'brij\ district Ⓢ Ⓔ central Northern Ireland

Ban·dar Se·ri Be·ga·wan \ˌbən-dər-ˌser-ē-bə-'gä-wən\ town, capital of Brunei

Ban·dung \'bän-ˌdúŋ\ city Indonesia in Ⓦ Java Ⓢ Ⓔ of Jakarta

Ban·ga·lore \'baŋ-gə-ˌlō(ə)r, -ˌlò(ə)r\ or **Ben·ga·lu·ru** \'beŋ-gə-ˌlü-rü\ city Ⓢ India Ⓦ of Madras

Bang·kok \'baŋ-ˌkäk, baŋ-'käk\ city, capital of Thailand

Ban·gla·desh \ˌbäŋ-glə-'desh, ˌbaŋ-, -'däsh\ country Ⓢ Asia Ⓔ of India; formerly part of Pakistan; an independent state since 1971; capital, Dhaka — see EAST PAKISTAN — **Ban·gla·deshi** \-ē\ adj or n

Ban·gor \'baŋ-ˌgòr, 'ban-\ town Ⓔ Northern Ireland

Ban·gui \bäŋ-'gē\ city, capital of Central African Republic

\ə\ **abut**	\aú\ **out**	\i\ **tip**	\ò\ **saw**	\ú\ **foot**
\ər\ **further**	\ch\ **chin**	\ī\ **life**	\òi\ **coin**	\y\ **yet**
\a\ **mat**	\e\ **pet**	\j\ **job**	\th\ **thin**	\yü\ **few**
\ä\ **take**	\ē\ **easy**	\ŋ\ **sing**	\th\ **this**	\yú\ **cure**
\ä\ **cot, cart**	\g\ **go**	\ō\ **bone**	\ü\ **food**	\zh\ **vision**

Ban·jul \\'bän-,jül\\ *or formerly* **Bath·urst** \\'bath-(,)ərst\\ city & port, capital of Gambia

Bao·tou *or* **Pao–t'ou** \\'baú-'tō\\ city N̄ China

Bar·ba·dos \\bär-'bād-əs, -ōz, -äs, -ōs\\ island West Indies in Lesser Antilles Ē of Windward Islands; an independent country since 1966; capital, Bridgetown — **Bar·ba·di·an** \\-'bād-ē-ən\\ *adj or n*

Bar·bu·da \\bär-'büd-ə\\ island West Indies; part of independent Antigua and Barbuda

Bar·ce·lo·na \\,bär-sə-'lō-nə\\ city N̄Ē Spain on the Mediterranean; chief city of Catalonia

Bar·king and Dag·en·ham \\'bär-kiŋ-ənd-'dag-ə-nəm\\ borough of Ē Greater London, England

Bar·na·ul \\,bär-nə-'ül\\ city S̄ Russia

Bar·net \\'bär-nət\\ borough of N̄ Greater London, England

Bar·ran·qui·lla \\,bar-ən-'kē-(y)ə\\ city N̄ Colombia

Barren Grounds treeless plains N̄ Canada W̄ of Hudson Bay

Bar·row, Point \\'bar-ō\\ most northerly point of Alaska & of U.S. at about 71°25′ N̄ latitude

Ba·si·lan \\bä-'sē-,län\\ island S̄ Philippines

Bas·il·don \\'baz-əl-dən\\ town S̄Ē England

Basque Country autonomous region N̄ Spain

Bass \\'bas\\ strait separating Tasmania & continent of Australia

Basse·terre \\bas-'te(ə)r, bäs-\\ seaport Saint Kitts, capital of Saint Kitts and Nevis

Basutoland — see LESOTHO

Batavia — see JAKARTA

Bathurst — see BANJUL

Bat·on Rouge \\,bat-ᵊn-'rüzh\\ city, capital of Louisiana

Ba·var·ia \\bə-'ver-ē-ə, -'var-\\ *or German* **Bay·ern** \\'bī-ᵊrn\\ state S̄Ē Germany bordering on Czech Republic & Austria — **Ba·var·i·an** \\bə-'ver-ē-ən, -'var-\\ *adj or n*

Ba·ya·mon \\,bī-ə-'mōn\\ city N̄Ē central Puerto Rico

Beau·fort \\'bō-fərt\\ sea consisting of part of Arctic Ocean N̄Ē of Alaska & N̄W̄ of Canada

Beau·mont \\'bō-,mänt\\ city S̄Ē Texas

Bech·u·a·na·land \\,bech-(ə-)'wän-ə-,land\\ **1** region S̄ Africa N̄ of Orange River **2** — see BOTSWANA

Bed·ford·shire \\'bed-fərd-,shi(ə)r, -shər\\ *or* **Bedford** county Ē England

Bedloe's — see LIBERTY

Bei·jing \\'bā-'jiŋ\\ *or* **Pe·king** \\'pē-'kiŋ, 'pā-\\ city, capital of China

Bei·rut \\bā-'rüt\\ city, capital of Lebanon

Be·la·rus \\,bē-lə-'rüs, ,byel-ə-\\ country central Europe; capital, Minsk — **Be·la·ru·si·an** \\-'rü-sē-ən, -'rəsh-ən\\ *or* **Be·la·rus·sian** \\'rəsh-ən\\ *adj or n*

Belau — see PALAU

Be·lém \\bə-'lem\\ city N̄ Brazil

Bel·fast \\'bel-,fast, bel-'fast\\ city, capital of Northern Ireland

Belgian Congo — see CONGO 2

Bel·gium \\'bel-jəm\\ *or French* **Bel·gique** \\bel-zhēk\\ *or Flemish* **Bel·gië** \\'bel-gē-ə\\ country W̄ Europe; capital, Brussels — **Bel·gian** \\'bel-jən\\ *adj or n*

Bel·grade \\'bel-,grād, -,gräd, -,grad\\ *or* **Beo·grad** \\'beù-,gräd\\ city, capital of Serbia on the Danube

Be·lize \\bə-'lēz\\ *or formerly* **British Honduras** country Central America on the Caribbean; capital, Belmopan — **Be·liz·ean** \\-'lē-zē-ən\\ *adj or n*

Belize City seaport Ē Belize

Belle·vue \\'bel-,vyü\\ city W̄ Washington Ē of Seattle

Bel·mo·pan \\,bel-mō-'pan\\ city, capital of Belize

Be·lo Ho·ri·zon·te \\'bā-lō-,hòr-ə-'zänt-ē, 'bel-ō-, -,här-\\ city Ē Brazil N̄ of Rio de Janeiro

Be·lo·rus·sia \\,bel-ō-'rəsh-ə, ,byel-\\ *or* **Bye·lo·rus·sia** \\bē-,el-ō-, ,byel-ō-\\ former republic of U.S.S.R.; became independent Belarus in 1991 — **Belorussian** *adj or n*

Ben·gal \\ben-'gòl, beŋ-\\ region S̄ Asia including delta of Ganges & Brahmaputra rivers; divided between Bangladesh & India

Bengal, Bay of arm of Indian Ocean between India & Myanmar

Bengaluru — see BANGALORE

Be·nin \\bə-'nin, -'nēn; 'ben-ən\\ *or formerly* **Da·ho·mey** \\də-'hō-mē\\ country W̄ Africa on Gulf of Guinea; capital, Porto-Novo; seat of government, Cotonou — **Ben·i·nese** \\bə-,nin-'ēz, -,nēn-; ,ben-i-'nēz, -'nēs\\ *adj or n*

Ben Nev·is \\ben-'nev-əs\\ mountain 4406 ft. (1343 m.) W̄ Scotland in the Grampians; highest in Great Britain

Beograd — see BELGRADE

Ber·gen \\'bər-gən, 'be(ə)r-\\ city & port S̄W̄ Norway

Be·ring \\'bi(ə)r-iŋ, 'be(ə)r-\\ **1** sea arm of the North Pacific between Alaska & N̄Ē Siberia **2** strait at narrowest point 53 mi. (85 km.) wide between North America (Alaska) and Asia (Russia)

Berke·ley \\'bər-klē\\ city W̄ California on San Francisco Bay N̄ of Oakland

Berk·shire \\'bərk-,shi(ə)r, -,shər\\ hills W̄ Massachusetts; highest point Mount Greylock 3491 ft. (1064 m.)

Ber·lin \\(,)bər-'lin\\ city, capital of Germany; divided 1945–90 into **East Berlin** (capital of East Germany) & **West Berlin** (city of West Germany lying within East Germany) — **Ber·lin·er** \\-'lin-ər\\ *n*

Ber·mu·da \\(,)bər-'myüd-ə\\ islands W̄ Atlantic Ē̄S̄Ē of Cape Hatteras; a British colony; capital, Hamilton — **Ber·mu·dan** \\-'myüd-ᵊn\\ *or* **Ber·mu·di·an** \\-'myüd-ē-ən\\ *adj or n*

Bern \\'bərn, 'be(ə)rn\\ city, capital of Switzerland — **Ber·nese** \\(,)bər-'nēz, -'nēs\\ *adj or n*

Bes·sa·ra·bia \\,bes-ə-'rā-bē-ə\\ region S̄Ē Europe now chiefly in Moldova — **Bes·sa·ra·bi·an** \\-bē-ən\\ *adj or n*

Beth·le·hem \\'beth-li-,hem, -lē-həm, -lē-əm\\ town of ancient Palestine in Judaea; the present-day town is S̄W̄ of Jerusalem in the West Bank

Bev·er·ly Hills \\,bev-ər-lē-'hilz\\ city S̄W̄ California within city of Los Angeles

Bex·ley \\'bek-slē\\ borough of Ē Greater London, England

Bho·pal \\bō-'päl\\ city N̄ central India

Bhu·tan \\bü-'tan, -'tän\\ country S̄ Asia in the Himalayas on N̄Ē border of India; capital, Thimphu — **Bhu·ta·nese** \\,büt-ᵊn-'ēz, -'ēs\\ *adj or n*

Bi·ki·ni \\bə-'kē-nē\\ atoll W̄ Pacific in Marshall Islands

Bil·lings \\'bil-iŋz\\ city S̄ central Montana; largest in state

Bi·lox·i \\bə-'lək-sē, -'läk-\\ city & port S̄Ē Mississippi on Gulf of Mexico

Bi·o·ko \\bē-'ō-kō\\ *or formerly* **Fer·nan·do Póo** \\fər-,nan-(,)dō-'pō\\ island portion of Equatorial Guinea in Gulf of Guinea

Bir·ken·head \\'bər-kən-,hed, ,bər-kən-'\\ borough N̄W̄ England on the Mersey opposite Liverpool

Bir·ming·ham \\'bər-miŋ-,ham, *British usually* -miŋ-əm\\ **1** city N̄ central Alabama **2** city W̄ central England

Bis·cay, Bay of \\'bis-,kā, -kē\\ inlet of the Atlantic between W̄ coast of France & N̄ coast of Spain

Bish·kek \\bish-'kek\\ *or 1926–91* **Frunze** \\'frün-zə\\ city, capital of Kyrgyzstan

Bis·marck \\'biz-,märk\\ **1** city, capital of North Dakota **2** archipelago W̄ Pacific N̄ of Ē end of New Guinea

Bis·sau \\bis-'aú\\ city, capital of Guinea-Bissau

Bi·thyn·ia \\bə-'thin-ē-ə\\ ancient country N̄W̄ Asia Minor bordering on Sea of Marmara and Black Sea — **Bi·thyn·i·an** \\-ē-ən\\ *adj or n*

Bit·ter·root \\'bit-ər-,rüt, -,rùt\\ range of the Rockies along Idaho–Montana boundary

Black·burn \\'blak-bərn\\ town N̄W̄ England

Black Forest forested mountain region Germany along Ē bank of the upper Rhine

Black Hills mountains W̄ South Dakota & N̄Ē Wyoming

Black·pool \\'blak-,pül\\ town N̄W̄ England on Irish Sea

Black Sea *or ancient* **Pon·tus Eux·i·nus** \\'pänt-əs-,yük-'sī-nəs\\ sea between Europe & Asia connected with Aegean Sea through the Bosporus, Sea of Marmara, & Dardanelles

Blanc, Mont — see MONT BLANC

Blan·tyre \'blan-ˌtīr\ city Ⓢ Malawi

Bloem·fon·tein \'blüm-fən-ˌtān, -ˌfän-\ city Republic of South Africa, judicial capital of the country

Blue Ridge Ⓔ range of the Applachians Ⓔ U.S. extending from Ⓢ Pennsylvania to Ⓝ Georgia

Bodh Ga·ya \'bōd-'gī-ə\ village ⓃⒺ India; one of the holiest sites of Buddhism

Boe·o·tia \bē-'ō-sh(ē-)ə\ ancient state Ⓔ central Greece ⓃⓌ of Attica; chief ancient city, Thebes — **Boe·o·tian** \bē-'ō-shən\ adj or n

Bo·go·tá \ˌbō-gə-'tò, -'tä\ city, capital of Colombia

Bo Hai or **Po Hai** \'bō-'hī\ or **Gulf of Chih·li** \'chē-lē, 'jir-\ arm of Yellow Sea ⓃⒺ China

Bo·he·mia \bō-'hē-mē-ə\ region Ⓦ Czech Republic; once a kingdom; chief city, Prague

Bo·hol \bō-'hòl\ island Ⓢ central Philippines

Boi·se \'bòi-sē, -zē\ city, capital of Idaho

Bo·liv·ia \bə-'liv-ē-ə\ country Ⓦ central South America; administrative capital, La Paz; constitutional capital, Sucre — **Bo·liv·i·an** \-ē-ən\ adj or n

Bo·lo·gna \bə-'lōn-yə\ city Ⓝ Italy

Bol·ton \'bōlt-n\ town ⓃⓌ England

Bom·bay \bäm-'bā\ or **Mum·bai** \'məm-ˌbī\ city & port Ⓦ India

Bonn \'bän, 'bòn\ city Germany on the Rhine ⓈⒺ of Cologne; formerly capital of West Germany

Boo·thia \'bü-thē-ə\ peninsula Ⓝ Canada Ⓦ of Baffin Island; its Ⓝ tip is most northerly point in mainland North America

Bor·neo \'bòr-nē-ˌō\ island Malay Archipelago ⓈⓌ of the Philippines; divided between Brunei, Indonesia, and Malaysia

Bos·nia \'bäz-nē-ə\ region Ⓢ Europe; with Herzegovina forms independent **Bosnia and Herzegovina**; capital, Sarajevo — **Bos·ni·an** \-nē-ən\ adj or n

Bos·po·rus \'bäs-p(ə-)rəs\ or ancient **Bosporus Thra·ci·us** \-'thrā-sh(ē-)əs\ strait 18 mi. (29 km.) long between Turkey in Europe & Turkey in Asia connecting Sea of Marmara & Black Sea

Bos·ton \'bò-stən\ city, capital of Massachusetts — **Bos·to·nian** \bò-'stō-nē-ən, -nyən\ adj or n

Bot·a·ny Bay \'bät-ᵊn-ē, 'bät-nē\ inlet of South Pacific ⓈⒺ Australia in New South Wales Ⓢ of Sydney

Both·nia, Gulf of \'bäth-nē-ə\ arm of Baltic Sea between Sweden & Finland

Bo·tswa·na \bät-'swän-ə\ country Ⓢ Africa; formerly (as Bechuanaland) dependent on Britain; now independent; capital, Gaborone

Boul·der \'bōl-dər\ city Ⓝ central Colorado

Boulder Dam — see HOOVER DAM

Bourne·mouth \'bōrn-məth, 'bòrn-, 'bùrn-\ town Ⓢ England on English Channel

Brad·ford \'brad-fərd\ city Ⓝ England

Brah·ma·pu·tra \ˌbräm-ə-'p(y)ü-trə\ river about 1800 mi. (2900 km.) long Ⓢ Asia flowing from the Himalayas in Tibet to Ganges Delta

Bra·sí·lia \brə-'zil-yə\ city, capital of Brazil

Bra·ti·sla·va \ˌbrat-ə-'släv-ə, ˌbrät-\ city on the Danube; capital of Slovakia

Bra·zil \brə-'zil\ country Ⓔ & central South America; capital, Brasília — **Bra·zil·ian** \brə-'zil-yən\ adj or n

Braz·za·ville \'braz-ə-ˌvil, 'bräz-ə-ˌvēl\ city, capital of Republic of the Congo on Ⓦ bank of lower Congo River

Bre·men \'brem-ən, 'brā-mən\ city & port ⓃⓌ Germany

Bren·ner \'bren-ər\ pass 4495 ft. (1370 m.) high in the Alps between Austria & Italy

Brent \'brent\ borough of Ⓦ Greater London, England

Bret·on, Cape \kāp-'bret-ᵊn, kə-'bret-, -'brit-\ cape Canada; most easterly point of Cape Breton Island & of Nova Scotia

Bridge·port \'brij-ˌpō(ə)rt, -ˌpò(ə)rt\ city ⓈⓌ Connecticut on Long Island Sound

Bridge·town \'brij-ˌtaùn\ city, capital of Barbados

Brigh·ton \'brīt-ᵊn\ town Ⓢ England on English Channel

Bris·bane \'briz-bən, -ˌbän\ city & port Ⓔ Australia; capital of Queensland

Bris·tol \'bris-tᵊl\ **1** city & port ⓈⓌ England **2** channel between Ⓢ Wales & ⓈⓌ England

Brit·ain \'brit-ᵊn\ **1** the island of Great Britain **2** UNITED KINGDOM

British Columbia province Ⓦ Canada on Pacific coast; capital, Victoria

British Commonwealth — see COMMONWEALTH, THE

British Empire former empire consisting of Great Britain & the British dominions & dependencies

British Guiana — see GUYANA

British Honduras — see BELIZE

British Indian Ocean Territory British colony in Indian Ocean consisting of Chagos Archipelago

British Isles island group Ⓦ Europe consisting of Great Britain, Ireland, & nearby islands

British Virgin Islands Ⓔ islands of Virgin Islands; a British possession

British West Indies islands of the West Indies belonging to the Commonwealth & including Jamaica, Trinidad and Tobago, & Bahamas & Cayman Islands, Windward Islands, Leeward Islands, & British Virgin Islands

Brit·ta·ny \'brit-ᵊn-ē\ region ⓃⓌ France ⓈⓌ of Normandy

Brom·ley \'bräm-lē\ borough of ⓈⒺ Greater London, England

Bronx \'brä(ŋ)ks\ or **The Bronx** borough of New York City ⓃⒺ of Manhattan

Brook·lyn \'bruk-lən\ borough of New York City at ⓈⓌ end of Long Island

Brooks Range \'bruks\ mountains Ⓝ Alaska

Browns·ville \'braùnz-ˌvil\ city Ⓢ Texas on the Rio Grande

Bru·nei \bru-'nī, 'brü-ˌnī\ country ⓃⒺ Borneo; formerly under British authority; capital, Bandar Seri Begawan — **Bru·nei·an** \brü-'nī-ən\ adj or n

Brus·sels \'brəs-əlz\ city, capital of Belgium

Bu·cha·rest \'b(y)ü-kə-ˌrest\ city, capital of Romania

Buck·ing·ham·shire \'bək-iŋ-əm-ˌshi(ə)r, -shər, U.S. also -iŋ-ˌham-\ or **Buckingham** county ⓈⒺ central England

Bu·da·pest \'büd-ə-ˌpest also 'byüd-, 'bùd-, -ˌpesht\ city, capital of Hungary

Bue·nos Ai·res \ˌbwā-nə-'sa(ə)r-ēz, ˌbō-nə-, -'se(ə)r-, -'sī(ə)r-\ city, capital of Argentina

Buf·fa·lo \'bəf-ə-ˌlō\ city Ⓦ New York on Lake Erie

Bu·jum·bu·ra \ˌbü-jəm-'bùr-ə\ city, capital of Burundi

Bu·ko·vi·na \ˌbü-kə-'vē-nə\ region Ⓔ central Europe in foothills of Ⓔ Carpathians of ⓃⒺ Romania & Ⓦ Ukraine

Bul·gar·ia \ˌbəl-'gar-ē-ə, bùl-, -'ger-\ country ⓈⒺ Europe on Black Sea; capital, Sofia — **Bulgarian** adj or n

Bull Run \'bùl-'rən\ stream ⓃⒺ Virginia

Bun·ker Hill \ˌbəŋ-kər\ height in Boston, Massachusetts

Bur·bank \'bər-ˌbaŋk\ city ⓈⓌ California

Bur·gun·dy \'bər-gən-dē\ region Ⓔ France — **Bur·gun·di·an** \(ˌ)bər-'gən-dē-ən\ adj or n

Bur·ki·na Fa·so \bùr-ˌkē-nə-'fä-sō\ or formerly **Upper Volta** \'vōl-tə, 'vòl-\ country Ⓦ Africa Ⓝ of Cote d'Ivoire, Ghana, & Togo; capital, Ouagadougou

Bur·ling·ton \'bər-liŋ-tən\ city ⓃⓌ Vermont; largest in state

Bur·ma \'bər-mə\ — see MYANMAR — **Burmese** adj or n

Bu·run·di \bù-'rün-dē\ country Ⓔ central Africa; capital, Bujumbura — see RUANDA-URUNDI — **Bu·run·di·an** \-dē-ən\ adj or n

Busan — see PUSAN

Bute \'byüt\ island [SW] Scotland in Firth of Clyde

Butte \'byüt\ city [SW] Montana

Byelorussia — see BELORUSSIA

By·zan·tine Empire \'biz-ᵊn-ˌtēn, 'bīz-, -ˌtīn; bə-'zan-ˌtēn, -tīn, bī-\ empire of [SE] & [S] Europe and [W] Asia from 4th to 15th century

By·zan·ti·um \bə-'zan-sh(ē-)əm, -'zant-ē-əm\ ancient city on site of modern Istanbul

Cabo Verde — see CAPE VERDE

Caer·nar·von \kär-'när-vən\ town & seaport [NW] Wales

Ca·guas \'käg-ˌwäs\ town [E] central Puerto Rico

Cai·ro \'kī-rō\ city, capital of Egypt — **Cai·rene** \kī-'rēn\ adj or n

Ca·la·bria \kə-'lä-brē-ə, -'läb-rē-\ district of ancient Italy consisting of area forming heel of Italian Peninsula — **Ca·la·bri·an** \kə-'lä-brē-ən, -'läb-rē-\ adj or n

Cal·cut·ta \kal-'kət-ə\ or **Kol·ka·ta** \kōl-'kät-ä\ city [E] India on Hugli River — **Cal·cut·tan** \-'kət-ᵊn\ adj or n

Cal·e·do·nia \ˌkal-ə-'dō-nyə, -nē-ə\ — see SCOTLAND — **Cal·e·do·nian** \-nyən, -nē-ən\ adj or n

Cal·ga·ry \'kal-gə-rē\ city [SW] Alberta, Canada

Ca·li \'käl-ē\ city [W] Colombia

Cal·i·for·nia \ˌkal-ə-'fòr-nyə\ state [SW] U.S.; capital, Sacramento — **Cal·i·for·nian** \-nyən\ adj or n

California, Gulf of arm of the Pacific [NW] Mexico

Cal·va·ry \'kalv-(ə-)rē\ place outside ancient Jerusalem where Jesus was crucified

Cambay, Gulf of — see KHAMBAT (Gulf of)

Cam·bo·dia \kam-'bōd-ē-ə\ or **Kam·pu·chea** \ˌkam-pə-'chē-ə\ or 1970–75 **Khmer Republic** \kə-'me(ə)r-\ country [SE] Asia in [S] Indochina; capital, Phnom Penh — **Cam·bo·di·an** \-ən\ adj or n

Cambria — see WALES

Cam·bridge \'kām-brij\ **1** city [E] Massachusetts [W] of Boston **2** city [E] England

Cam·bridge·shire \'kām-brij-ˌshi(ə)r, -shər\ or **Cambridge** \'kām-brij\ county [E] England

Cam·den \'kam-dən\ borough of [N] Greater London, England

Cam·er·oon or French **Cam·er·oun** \ˌkam-ə-'rün\ country [W] Africa; capital, Yaoundé — **Cam·er·oo·nian** \-'rü-nē-ən, -rü-nyən\ adj or n

Ca·mi·guin \ˌkam-ə-'gēn\ island Philippines, off [N] coast of Mindanao

Ca·naan \'kā-nən\ the part of ancient Palestine between Jordan River & Mediterranean Sea — sometimes *Canaan* refers to all of ancient Palestine — **Ca·naan·ite** \'kā-nə-ˌnīt\ adj or n

Can·a·da \'kan-ə-də\ country [N] North America; capital, Ottawa — **Ca·na·di·an** \kə-'nād-ē-ən\ adj or n

Canadian Falls — see NIAGARA FALLS

Canadian Shield or **Lau·ren·tian Plateau** \lò-'ren-chən\ plateau region [E] Canada & [N] U.S. extending from Mackenzie River basin [E] to Davis Strait & [S] to [S] Quebec, [S] central Ontario, [NE] Minnesota, [N] Wisconsin, [NW] Michigan, and [NE] New York including the Adirondacks

Canal Zone or **Panama Canal Zone** strip of territory Panama leased to U.S. for Panama Canal; ceased to exist as a political entity 1979 but remained under U.S. control through 1999

Ca·nary \kə-'ne(ə)r-ē\ islands in the Atlantic off [NW] coast of Africa belonging to Spain

Ca·nav·er·al, Cape \kə-'nav-(ə-)rəl\ or 1963–73 **Cape Ken·ne·dy** \'ken-ə-dē\ cape [E] Florida in the Atlantic on Canaveral Peninsula [E] of Indian River

Can·ber·ra \'kan-b(ə-)rə, -ˌber-ə\ city, capital of Australia in Australian Capital Territory

Cannes \'kan, 'kän\ port [SE] France; site of an annual international film festival

Can·ter·bury \'kant-ə(r)-ˌber-ē, -b(ə-)rē\ city [SE] England

Canton — see GUANGZHOU

Cape Bret·on Island \ˌkāp-'bret-ᵊn-, kə-'bret-, -'brit-\ island [NE] Nova Scotia

Cape Coral city [SW] Florida

Cape Horn — see HORN (Cape)

Cape of Good Hope — see GOOD HOPE (Cape of)

Cape Province or **Cape of Good Hope** or before 1910 **Cape Colony** former province [S] Republic of South Africa; capital, Cape Town

Cape Town \'kāp-ˌtaùn\ city, legislative capital of Republic of South Africa and formerly capital of Cape Province

Cape Verde \'vərd\ or **Ca·bo Ver·de** \ˌkä-bü-'verd-ə\ islands in the North Atlantic off [W] Africa; an independent country; capital, Praia; until 1975 belonged to Portugal — **Cape Verd·ean** \'vər-dē-ən\ adj or n

Cape York Peninsula \'yò(ə)rk\ peninsula [NE] Australia in [N] Queensland

Ca·pri \ka-'prē, kə-; 'käp-rē, 'kap-\ island Italy [S] of Bay of Naples

Ca·ra·cas \kə-'rak-əs, -'räk-\ city, capital of Venezuela

Car·diff \'kärd-əf\ city, capital of Wales

Ca·rib·be·an Sea \ˌkar-ə-'bē-ən, kə-'rib-ē-\ arm of the Atlantic; on [N] & [E] are the West Indies, on [S] is South America, & on [W] is Central America — **Caribbean** adj

Car·lisle \kär-'līl, 'kär-ˌ\ city [NW] England

Carls·bad Caverns \'kär(-ə)lz-ˌbad\ series of caves [SE] New Mexico

Car·mar·then \kär-'mär-thən, kə(r)-\ port [S] Wales

Car·o·li·na \ˌkar-ə-'lī-nə\ English colony on [E] coast of North America founded 1663 & divided 1729 into North Carolina & South Carolina (the **Carolinas**) — **Car·o·lin·i·an** \-'lin-e-ən\ adj or n

Ca·ro·li·na \kär-ə-'lē-nə\ city [NE] Puerto Rico

Car·o·line \'kar-ə-ˌlīn, -lən\ islands [W] Pacific [E] of [S] Philippines comprising Palau & the Federated States of Micronesia; formerly part of Trust Territory of the Pacific Islands

Car·pa·thi·an \kär-'pā-thē-ən\ mountains [E] central Europe along boundary between Slovakia & Poland & in [N] & central Romania; highest Gerlachovsky 8711 ft. (2655 m.)

Car·pen·tar·ia, Gulf of \ˌkär-pən-'ter-ē-ə, -tar-\ inlet of Arafura Sea [N] of Australia

Car·rick·fer·gus \ˌkar-ik-'fər-gəs\ district [E] Northern Ireland

Car·roll·ton \'kar-əl-tən\ city [N] Texas

Car·son City \'kärs-ᵊn\ city, capital of Nevada

Car·thage \'kär-thij\ ancient city [N] Africa [NE] of modern Tunis; capital of an empire that once included much of [NW] Africa, [E] Spain, & Sicily — **Car·tha·gin·ian** \ˌkär-thə-'jin-yən, -'jin-ē-ən\ adj or n

Ca·sa·blan·ca \ˌkas-ə-'blaŋ-kə, ˌkaz-\ city [W] Morocco on the Atlantic

Cas·cade Range \(')kas-'kād\ mountains [NW] U.S. in Washington, Oregon, & [N] California — see RAINIER (Mount)

Cas·per \'kas-pər\ city central Wyoming

Cas·pi·an Sea \'kas-pē-ən\ salt lake between Europe and Asia about 90 ft. (27 m.) below sea level

Cas·tile \kas-'tē(ə)l\ or Spanish **Cas·ti·lla** \kä-'stē-yä\ region & ancient kingdom central & [N] Spain

Cast·le·reagh \'kas-əl-ˌrā\ district [E] Northern Ireland

Cas·tries \'kas-ˌtrēz, -ˌtrēs\ seaport, capital of Saint Lucia

Cat·a·lo·nia \ˌkat-ᵊl-'ō-nyə, -nē-ə\ region [NE] Spain bordering on France & the Mediterranean; chief city, Barcelona — **Cat·a·lo·nian** \-'ō-nyən, -nē-ən\ adj or n

Ca·thay \kath-'ā\ an old name for China

Cats·kill \'kat-ˌskil\ mountains in Appalachian system [SE] New York [W] of the Hudson

Cau·ca·sus \'kò-kə-səs\ mountain system [SE] Europe between Black & Caspian seas in Russia, Georgia, Azerbaijan, & Armenia

Cay·enne \kī-'en, kā-\ city, capital of French Guiana

Cay·man \(')kā-'man, 'kā-mən\ islands West Indies [NW] of Jamaica; a British colony

Ce·bu \sā-'bü\ island [E] central Philippines

Ce·dar Rapids \'sēd-ər\ city [E] Iowa

Cel·tic Sea \'kel-tik, 'sel-\ inlet of the Atlantic in British Isles [SE] of Ireland, [SW] of Wales, & [W] of [SW] England

Central African Republic country [N] central Africa; capital, Bangui

Central America narrow portion of North America from [S] border of Mexico to South America — **Central American** adj or n

Central Valley valley of Sacramento & San Joaquin rivers in California between Sierra Nevada & Coast Ranges

Cey·lon \si-'län, sā-\ **1** island in Indian Ocean off [S] India **2** — see SRI LANKA — **Cey·lon·ese** \,sā-lə-'nēz, ,sē-lə-, ,sel-ə-, -'nēs\ adj or n

Chad \'chad\ country [N] central Africa; capital, N'Djamena — **Chad·ian** \'chad-ē-ən\ adj or n

Chad, Lake shallow lake [N] central Africa at junction of boundaries of Chad, Niger, & Nigeria

Cha·gos Archipelago \'chä-gəs\ island group central Indian Ocean; forms British Indian Ocean Territory — see DIEGO GARCIA

Chal·dea \kal-'dē-ə\ ancient region [SW] Asia on Euphrates River & Persian Gulf — **Chal·de·an** \-'dē-ən\ adj or n

Cham·pagne \sham-'pān\ region [NE] France

Champlain, Lake \sham-'plān\ lake between New York & Vermont extending [N] into Quebec

Chan·di·garh \'chən-dē-gər\ city [N] India [N] of Delhi

Chan·dler \'chand-lər\ city [SW] central Arizona

Chang \'chäŋ\ or traditionally **Yang·tze** \'yaŋ-'sē, 'yaŋ(k)t-'sē\ river 3965 mi. (6380 km.) long central China flowing into East China Sea

Chang·chun \'chäŋ-'chùn\ city [NE] China

Chang·sha \'chäŋ-'shä\ city [SE] central China

Channel 1 — see SANTA BARBARA 2 **2** islands in English Channel including Jersey, Guernsey, & Alderney & belonging to United Kingdom

Charles \'chär(ə)lz\ river 47 mi. (76 km.) long [E] Massachusetts flowing into Boston harbor

Charles, Cape cape [E] Virginia [N] of entrance to Chesapeake Bay

Charles·ton \'chärl-stən\ **1** seaport [SE] South Carolina **2** city, capital of West Virginia

Char·lotte \'shär-lət\ city [S] North Carolina

Charlotte Ama·lie \ə-'mäl-yə\ city, capital of Virgin Islands of the U.S.; on island of Saint Thomas

Char·lottes·ville \'shär-ləts-,vil, -vəl\ city central Virginia

Char·lotte·town \'shär-lət-,taùn\ city, capital of Prince Edward Island, Canada

Chat·ta·noo·ga \,chat-ə-'nü-gə, ,chat-ᵊn-'ü-\ city [SE] Tennessee

Chech·nya \chech-'nyä\ area of [SE] Russia in Europe; capital, Grozny

Chelms·ford \'chelmz-fərd, 'chemz-\ town [SE] England

Che·lya·binsk \chel-'yä-bən(t)sk\ city [W] Russia

Cheng–chou — see ZHENGZHOU

Cheng·du or **Ch'eng–tu** \'chəŋ-'dü\ city [SW] central China

Chennai — see MADRAS

Cher·no·byl \chər-'nō-bəl\ or **Chor·no·byl** \chôr-\ site [N] Ukraine of town abandoned after 1986 nuclear accident

Ches·a·peake \'ches-(ə-),pēk\ city [SE] Virginia

Chesapeake Bay inlet of the Atlantic in Virginia & Maryland

Chesh·ire \'chesh-ər, -,iər\ or **Ches·ter** \'ches-tər\ county [W] England bordering on Wales

Chester city [NW] England

Chev·i·ot \'chev-ē-ət, 'chē-vē-ət\ hills along English–Scottish border

Chey·enne \shī-'an, -'en\ city, capital of Wyoming

Chi·ba \'chē-bä\ city [E] Japan in Honshu on Tokyo Bay [E] of Tokyo

Chi·ca·go \shə-'käg-ō, -'kòg-\ city & port [NE] Illinois on Lake Michigan — **Chi·ca·go·an** \-'käg-ə-wən, -'kòg-\ n

Chi·chén It·zá \chə-,chen-ət-'sä\ ruined Mayan city [SE] Mexico in Yucatán Peninsula

Chich·es·ter \'chich-əs-tər\ city [S] England

Ch'i–ch'i–ha–erh — see QIQIHAR

Chihli, Gulf of — see BO HAI

Chi·le \'chil-ē\ country [SW] South America; capital, Santiago — **Chil·ean** \'chil-ē-ən, chə-'lā-ən\ adj or n

Chim·bo·ra·zo \,chim-bə-'räz-ō, ,shim-\ mountain 20,561 ft. (6267 m.) [W] central Ecuador

Chi·na \'chī-nə\ **1** country [E] Asia; capital, Beijing — see TAIWAN **2** sea, section of the [W] Pacific; divided at Taiwan strait into East China & South China seas

Chin–chou or **Chinchow** — see JINZHOU

Chi·si·nau \,kē-shē-'naù\ or **Ki·shi·nev** \'kish-i-,nef\ city central Moldova; its capital

Chit·ta·gong \'chit-ə-,gäŋ, -,gòŋ\ city [SE] Bangladesh on Bay of Bengal

Chong·qing or **Ch'ung–ch'ing** \'chùŋ-'chiŋ\ or **Chungking** \'chùŋ-'kiŋ\ city [SW] central China

Christ·church \'krīs(t)-,chərch\ city New Zealand on [E] coast of South Island

Christ·mas \'kris-məs\ island [E] Indian Ocean [SW] of Java; governed by Australia

Chu·la Vis·ta \,chü-lə-'vis-tə\ city [SW] California [S] of San Diego

Chuuk \'chùk\ or **Truk** \'trək, 'trùk\ islands [W] Pacific in the central Carolines; part of the Federated States of Micronesia

Cin·cin·na·ti \,sin(t)-sə-'nat-ē, -'nat-ə\ city [SW] Ohio

Ci·u·dad Jua·rez \,sē-ü-thäd-'hwär-əs, -'wär-\ city Mexico on Texas border

Ciudad Trujillo — see SANTO DOMINGO

Clarks·ville \'klärks-,vil\ city [N] Tennessee [NW] of Nashville

Clear·wa·ter \'klir-,wòt-ər, -,wät-\ city [W] Florida [NW] of Saint Petersburg

Cleve·land \'klēv-lənd\ city & port [NE] Ohio on Lake Erie

Clyde \'klīd\ river 106 mi. (171 km.) long [SW] Scotland flowing into **Firth of Clyde** (estuary)

Coast Mountains mountain range [W] British Columbia, Canada; the [N] continuation of Cascade Range

Coast Ranges chain of mountain ranges [W] North America extending along Pacific coast [W] of Sierra Nevada & Cascade Range & through Vancouver Island into [S] Alaska to Kenai Peninsula & Kodiak Island

Cod, Cape \-'käd\ peninsula [SE] Massachusetts

Coim·ba·tore \,kóim-bə-'tōr, -'tòr\ city [S] India

Cole·raine \kōl-'rān, 'kōl-,\ **1** district [N] Northern Ireland **2** port in Coleraine district

Co·logne \kə-'lōn\ city [W] Germany on the Rhine

Co·lom·bia \kə-'ləm-bē-ə\ country [NW] South America; capital, Bogotá — **Co·lom·bi·an** \-bē-ən\ adj or n

Co·lom·bo \kə-'ləm-bō\ city, capital of Sri Lanka

Col·o·ra·do \,käl-ə-'rad-ō, -'räd-\ **1** river 1450 mi. (2334 km.) long [SW] U.S. & [NW] Mexico flowing from [N] Colorado into Gulf of California **2** desert [SE] California **3** plateau region [SW] U.S. [W] of Rocky Mountains **4** state [W] U.S.; capital, Denver — **Col·o·rad·an** \-'rad-ᵊn, -'räd-\ or **Co·lo·ra·do·an** \-'rad-ə-wən, -'räd-\ adj or n

Colorado Springs city central Colorado [E] of Pikes Peak

Co·lum·bia \kə-'ləm-bē-ə\ **1** river 1214 mi. (1953 km.) long [SW] Canada & [NW] U.S. flowing [S] & [W] from [SE] British Columbia into the Pacific **2** plateau in Columbia River basin in [E] Washington, [E] Oregon, & [SW] Idaho **3** city, capital of South Carolina

\ə\ abut	\aù\ out	\i\ tip	\ò\ saw	\ù\ foot
\ər\ further	\ch\ chin	\ī\ life	\òi\ coin	\y\ yet
\a\ mat	\e\ pet	\j\ job	\th\ thin	\yü\ few
\ā\ take	\ē\ easy	\ŋ\ sing	\th\ this	\yù\ cure
\ä\ cot, cart	\g\ go	\ō\ bone	\ü\ food	\zh\ vision

Co·lum·bus \kə-'ləm-bəs\ **1** city W̲ Georgia **2** city, capital of Ohio

Com·mon·wealth, the \'käm-ən-ˌwel(t)th\ *or* **Commonwealth of Nations** *or formerly* **British Commonwealth** the United Kingdom & most of the countries formerly dependent on it

Commonwealth of Independent States association of the former constituent republics of the U.S.S.R. except for Lithuania, Latvia, & Estonia; Georgia withdrew 2009

Com·o·ros \'käm-ə-ˌrōz\ islands off S̲E̲ Africa N̲W̲ of Madagascar; formerly a French possession; an independent country (except for Mayotte Island remaining French) since 1975; capital, Moroni

Con·a·kry \'kän-ə-krē\ city, capital of Guinea

Con·cord \'käŋ-kərd\ **1** city W̲ California **2** town E̲ Massachusetts N̲W̲ of Boston **3** city, capital of New Hampshire

Confederate States of America *or* **the Confederacy** the 11 Southern states that seceded from the U.S. in 1860 and 1861

Con·go \'käŋ-gō\ **1** *or* **Zaire** \zä-'i(ə)r\ river over 2700 mi. (4344 km.) long W̲ Africa flowing into the Atlantic **2** *or officially* **Democratic Republic of the Congo** *or 1971–97* **Zaire** *or 1908–60* **Belgian Congo** country central Africa consisting of most of Congo River basin E̲ of lower Congo River; capital, Kinshasa **3** *or officially* **Republic of the Congo** country W̲ central Africa W̲ of lower Congo River; capital, Brazzaville — **Con·go·lese** \ˌkäŋ-gə-'lēz, -'lēs\ *adj or n*

Con·nacht \'kän-ˌȯt\ province W̲ Ireland

Con·nect·i·cut \kə-'net-i-kət\ **1** river 407 mi. (655 km.) long N̲E̲ U.S. flowing S̲ from N̲ New Hampshire into Long Island Sound **2** state N̲E̲ U.S.; capital, Hartford

Constantinople — *see* ISTANBUL

Continental Divide line of highest points of land separating the waters flowing W̲ from those flowing N̲ or E̲ and extending S̲S̲E̲ from N̲W̲ Canada across W̲ U.S. through Mexico & Central America to South America where it joins the Andes Mountains

Cook \'kuk\ **1** inlet of the Pacific S̲ Alaska W̲ of Kenai Peninsula **2** islands South Pacific S̲W̲ of Society Islands belonging to New Zealand **3** strait New Zealand between North Island & South Island

Cook, Mount *or Maori* **Ao·ra·ki** \au̇-'rä-kē\ mountain 12,349 ft. (3764 m.) New Zealand in N̲ central South Island in Southern Alps; highest in New Zealand

Cooks·town \'kuks-ˌtau̇n\ district central Northern Ireland

Co·pen·ha·gen \ˌkō-pən-'hā-gən, -'häg-ən\ city, capital of Denmark

Cor·al Sea \'kȯr-əl, 'kär-\ arm of the W̲ Pacific N̲E̲ of Australia

Coral Springs city S̲E̲ Florida

Cór·do·ba \'kȯrd-ə-bə, -ə-və\ city N̲ central Argentina

Cor·inth \'kȯr-ən(t)th, 'kär-\ **1** region of ancient Greece **2** ancient city, its capital; site S̲W̲ of present city of Corinth — **Co·rin·thi·an** \kə-'rin(t)-thē-ən\ *adj or n*

Corinth, Gulf of inlet of Ionian Sea central Greece N̲ of the Peloponnese

Cork \'kȯ(ə)rk\ city S̲ Ireland

Corn·wall \'kȯrn-ˌwȯl, -wəl\ *or since 1974* **Cornwall and Isles of Scil·ly** \'sil-ē\ county S̲W̲ England

Co·ro·na \kə-'rō-nə\ city S̲W̲ California E̲ of Los Angeles

Cor·pus Chris·ti \ˌkȯr-pə-'skris-tē\ city & port S̲ Texas

Cor·reg·i·dor \kə-'reg-ə-ˌdȯ(ə)r\ island Philippines at entrance to Manila Bay

Cor·si·ca \'kȯr-si-kə\ island France in the Mediterranean N̲ of Sardinia — **Cor·si·can** \'kȯr-si-kən\ *adj or n*

Cos·ta Me·sa \ˌkōs-tə-'mā-sə\ city S̲W̲ California

Costa Ri·ca \-'rē-kə\ country Central America between Nicaragua & Panama; capital, San José — **Cos·ta Ri·can** \-'rē-kən\ *adj or n*

Côte d'Ivoire \ˌkōt-dē-'vwär\ *or English* **Ivory Coast** country W̲ Africa on Gulf of Guinea; official capital, Yamoussoukro; seat of government, Abidjan

Co·to·nou \ˌkō-tō-'nü\ city & port S̲ Benin; national seat of government

Cots·wold \'kät-ˌswōld\ hills S̲W̲ central England

Cov·en·try \'kəv-ən-trē, 'kəv-\ city central England

Cow·pens \'kau̇-ˌpenz\ town N̲W̲ South Carolina

Craig·av·on \krā-'gav-ən\ district central Northern Ireland

Cra·ter \'krāt-ər\ lake 1932 ft. (589 m.) deep S̲W̲ Oregon in Cascade Range — *see* MAZAMA (Mount)

Crete \'krēt\ island Greece in E̲ Mediterranean — **Cre·tan** \'krēt-ᵊn\ *adj or n*

Cri·mea \krī-'mē-ə, krə-\ peninsula S̲E̲ Europe extending into Black Sea — **Cri·me·an** \krī-'mē-ən, krə-\ *adj*

Cro·atia \krō-'ā-sh(ē-)ə\ country S̲E̲ Europe; capital, Zagreb; a republic of Yugoslavia 1946–91 — **Croat** *n*

Croy·don \'krȯid-ᵊn\ borough of S̲ Greater London, England

Cu·ba \'kyü-bə\ island in the West Indies; an independent country; capital, Havana — **Cu·ban** \-bən\ *adj or n*

Cum·ber·land \'kəm-bər-lənd\ river 687 mi. (1106 km.) long S̲ Kentucky & N̲ Tennessee

Cumberland Gap pass through Cumberland Plateau N̲E̲ Tennessee

Cumberland Plateau mountain region E̲ U.S.; part of S̲ Appalachian Mountains extending from S̲ West Virginia to N̲E̲ Alabama

Cum·bria \'kəm-brē-ə\ county N̲W̲ England

Cum·bri·an \-ən\ mountains N̲W̲ England chiefly in Cumbria county

Cu·par \'kü-pər\ town E̲ Scotland

Cu·ri·ti·ba \ˌkur-ə-'tē-bə\ city S̲ Brazil S̲W̲ of São Paulo

Cush \'kəsh, 'ku̇sh\ ancient country N̲E̲ Africa in upper Nile valley S̲ of Egypt — **Cush·ite** \-ˌīt\ *n* — **Cush·it·ic** \ˌkəsh-'it-ik, ku̇sh-\ *adj*

Cuz·co \'kü-skō\ city S̲ central Peru

Cymru — *see* WALES

Cy·prus \'sī-prəs\ island E̲ Mediterranean S̲ of Turkey; an independent country, but since 1974 partitioned along Greek and Turkish ethnic lines; capital, Nicosia — **Cyp·ri·ot** \'sip-rē-ət, -rē-ˌät\ *or* **Cyp·ri·ote** \-ˌōt, -ət\ *adj or n*

Cy·re·na·ica \ˌsir-ə-'nā-ə-kə, ˌsī-rə-\ ancient region N̲ Africa on coast W̲ of Egypt; capital, Cyrene — **Cy·re·na·ican** \-kən\ *adj or n*

Czecho·slo·va·kia \ˌchek-ə-slō-'väk-ē-ə, -'vak-\ former country central Europe; capital, Prague; since 1993 divided into the independent states of the Czech Republic & Slovakia — **Czecho·slo·vak** \-'slō-ˌväk, -ˌvak\ *adj or n* — **Czecho·slo·va·ki·an** \-slō-'väk-ē-ən, -'vak-\ *adj or n*

Czech Republic country central Europe; capital, Prague

Daegu — *see* TAEGU

Daejeon — *see* TAEJON

Dahomey — *see* BENIN

Dairen — *see* DALIAN

Da·kar \'dak-ˌär, də-'kär\ city, capital of Senegal

Da·ko·ta \də-'kōt-ə\ **1** *or* **James** \'jāmz\ river 710 mi. (1143 km.) long North Dakota & South Dakota flowing S̲ into the Missouri **2** territory 1861–89 N̲W̲ U.S. divided 1889 into states of North Dakota & South Dakota (the **Da·ko·tas** \də-'kōt-əz\)

Da·lian \'dä-'lyen\ *or* **Ta–lien** \'dä-'lyen\ *or* **Lü·da** *or* **Lü–ta** \'lü-'dä\ *or* **Dai·ren** \'dī-'ren\ city N̲E̲ China

Dal·las \'dal-əs, -is\ city N̲E̲ Texas

Dal·ma·tia \dal-'mā-sh(ē-)ə\ region W̲ Balkan Peninsula on the Adriatic — **Dal·ma·tian** \-shən\ *adj or n*

Da·ly City \'dā-lē\ city W̲ California S̲ of San Francisco

Da·mas·cus \də-'mas-kəs\ city, capital of Syria

Dan·ube \'dan-yüb\ river 1771 mi. (2850 km.) long S̲ Europe flowing from S̲W̲ Germany into Black Sea — **Da·nu·bi·an** \da-'nyü-bē-ən\ *adj*

Dar·da·nelles \ˌdärd-ᵊn-'elz\ *or* **Hel·les·pont** \'hel-ə-ˌspänt\ strait [NW] Turkey connecting Sea of Marmara & the Aegean

Dar es Sa·laam \ˌdär-ˌes-sə-'läm\ city, historic capital of Tanzania

Dar·ling \'där-liŋ\ river about 1700 mi. (2735 km.) long [SE] Australia flowing [SW] into the Murray

Dar·win \'där-wən\ city Australia, capital of Northern Territory

Da·vao \'däv-ˌaù, dä-'vaú\ city [S] Philippines in [E] Mindanao on Davao Gulf

Dav·en·port \'dav-ən-ˌpō(ə)rt, -ˌpȯ(ə)rt\ city [E] Iowa

Da·vis \'dā-vəs\ strait between [SW] Greenland & [E] Baffin Island connecting Baffin Bay & the Atlantic

Day·ton \'dāt-ᵊn\ city [SW] Ohio

Dead Sea \'ded\ salt lake between Israel & Jordan; 1312 ft. (400 m.) below sea level

Death Valley \'deth\ dry valley [E] California & [S] Nevada containing lowest point in U.S. (282 ft. *or* 86 m. below sea level)

Dec·can \'dek-ən, -ˌan\ plateau region [S] India

Del·a·ware \'del-ə-ˌwa(ə)r, -ˌwe(ə)r, -wər\ **1** river 296 mi. (476 km.) long [E] U.S. flowing [S] from [S] New York into Delaware Bay **2** state [E] U.S.; capital, Dover — **Del·a·war·ean** *or* **Del·a·war·ian** \ˌdel-ə-'war-ē-ən, -'wer-\ *adj or n*

Delaware Bay inlet of the Atlantic between [SW] New Jersey & [E] Delaware

Del·hi \'del-ē\ city [N] India — see NEW DELHI

De·los \'dē-ˌläs\ island Greece — **De·lian** \'dē-lē-ən, 'dēl-yən\ *adj or n*

Del·phi \'del-ˌfī\ ancient town central Greece on [S] slope of Mt. Parnassus

Democratic Republic of the Congo — see CONGO 2

De·na·li \də-'näl-ē\ *or* **Mc·Kin·ley, Mount** \mə-'kin-lē\ mountain 20,320 ft. (6194 m.) [S] central Alaska in Alaska Range; highest in U.S. & North America

Den·mark \'den-ˌmärk\ country [E] Europe occupying most of Jutland & neighboring islands; capital, Copenhagen

Den·ver \'den-vər\ city, capital of Colorado

Der·by \'där-bē, *chiefly in the U.S.* 'dər-bē\ city [N] central England

Der·by·shire \'där-bē-ˌshi(ə)r, -shər, *U.S. also* 'dər-\ *or* **Derby** county [N] central England

Der·ry \'der-ē\ *or* **Lon·don·der·ry** \ˌlən-dən-'der-ē; 'lən-dən-ˌder-ē, -d(ə-)rē\ **1** district [NW] Northern Ireland **2** seaport [NW] Northern Ireland

Des Moines \di-'mȯin\ city, capital of Iowa

De·troit \di-'trȯit\ **1** river 31 mi. (50 km.) long between [SE] Michigan & Ontario connecting Lake Saint Clair & Lake Erie **2** city [SE] Michigan

Dev·on \'dev-ən\ *or* **De·von·shire** \-ˌshi(ə)r, -shər\ county [SW] England

Dha·ka \'dak-ə, 'däk-\ city, capital of Bangladesh

Die·go Gar·cia \dē-ˌā-gō-ˌgär-'sē-ə\ island in Indian Ocean; chief island of Chagos Archipelago

Di·li \'dil-ē\ city & port [N] Timor, capital of East Timor

Di·nar·ic Alps \də-ˌnar-ik\ range of the [E] Alps in [W] Slovenia, [W] Croatia, Bosnia and Herzegovina, & Montenegro

District of Co·lum·bia \kə-'ləm-bē-ə\ federal district [E] U.S. coextensive with city of Washington

Djakarta — see JAKARTA

Dji·bou·ti \jə-'büt-ē\ **1** country [E] Africa on Gulf of Aden **2** city, its capital

Dni·pro·pe·trovs'k *or* **Dne·pro·pe·trovsk** \də-ˌnye-prə-pē-'trȯfsk\ city [E] central Ukraine

Dodge City \'däj\ city [S] Kansas on Arkansas River

Do·do·ma \dō-'dō-mä\ city, [NE] central Tanzania, the nation's legislative capital

Do·ha \'dō-hä\ city & port, capital of Qatar on Persian Gulf

Dom·i·ni·ca \ˌdäm-ə-'nē-kə\ island West Indies in the Leeward Islands; an independent country; capital, Roseau

Do·min·i·can Republic \də-ˌmin-i-kən\ country West In-

dies in [E] Hispaniola; capital, Santo Domingo — **Dominican** *adj or n*

Don \'dän\ river 1224 mi. (1969 km.) long [S] Russia in Europe

Do·nets'k \də-'netsk, -'nyetsk\ city [E] Ukraine

Dor·ches·ter \'dȯr-chə-stər, -ˌches-tər\ town [S] England

Dor·set \'dȯr-sət\ *or* **Dor·set·shire** \-ˌshi(ə)r, -shər\ county [S] England on English Channel

Dort·mund \'dȯ(ə)rt-ˌmùnt, -mənd\ city [W] Germany in the Ruhr

Dou·a·la \dü-'ä-lə\ seaport [W] Cameroon

Dou·ro \'dōr-ü, 'dȯr-\ *or Spanish* **Due·ro** \'dwe(ə)r-ō\ *or ancient* **Du·ri·us** \'d(y)ùr-ē-əs\ river 556 mi. (895 km.) long [N] Spain & [N] Portugal flowing into the Atlantic

Do·ver \'dō-vər\ city, capital of Delaware

Dover, Strait of channel between [SE] England & [N] France; the most easterly section of English Channel

Down \'daùn\ district [SE] Northern Ireland

Dow·ney \'daù-nē\ city [SW] California [SE] of Los Angeles

Down·pat·rick \daùn-'pa-trik\ town [E] Northern Ireland

Dra·kens·berg \'dräk-ənz-ˌbərg\ mountain range [E] Republic of South Africa & Lesotho; highest peak Thabana Ntlenyana 11,425 ft. (3482 m.)

Dres·den \'drez-dən\ city [E] Germany

Dub·lin \'dəb-lən\ *or ancient* **Eb·la·na** \'eb-lə-nə\ city, capital of Ireland

Dud·ley \'dəd-lē\ town [W] central England

Duis·burg \'dü-əs-ˌbərg; 'd(y)üz-ˌbərg\ city [W] Germany at junction of Rhine & Ruhr rivers

Du·luth \də-'lüth\ city & port [NE] Minnesota

Dum·fries \ˌdəm-'frēs\ burgh [S] Scotland

Dun·dee \ˌdən-'dē\ city [E] Scotland

Dun·gan·non \dən-'gan-ən\ district [W] Northern Ireland

Dur·ban \'dər-bən\ city and seaport [E] Republic of South Africa

Dur·ham \'dər-əm, 'də-rəm, 'dùr-əm\ **1** city [N] central North Carolina **2** county [N] England on North Sea **3** city in [N] England

Du·shan·be \d(y)ü-'sham-bə, -'shäm-\ city, capital of Tajikistan

Düs·sel·dorf \'d(y)üs-əl-ˌdȯrf\ city [W] Germany on the Rhine

Ea·ling \'ē-liŋ\ borough of [W] Greater London, England

East An·glia \aŋ-glē-ə\ region [E] England

East China Sea — see CHINA

Eas·ter \'ē-stər\ island [SE] Pacific about 2000 mi. (3200 km.) [W] of Chilean coast; belongs to Chile

Eastern Cape province [SE] Republic of South Africa

Eastern Desert desert [E] Egypt between the Nile & Red Sea

Eastern Ghats \'gȯts\ chain of low mountains [SE] India along coast

Eastern Hemisphere the half of the earth [E] of the Atlantic Ocean including Europe, Asia, Australia, & Africa

Eastern Roman Empire the Byzantine Empire from 395 to 474

Eastern Samoa — see AMERICAN SAMOA

East Germany the former German Democratic Republic — see GERMANY

East Indies the Malay Archipelago — **East Indian** *adj or n*

East London city [S] Republic of South Africa

East Pakistan the former [E] division of Pakistan consisting of [E] portion of Bengal; now the independent country of Bangladesh

East River strait [SE] New York connecting upper New York Bay & Long Island Sound and separating Manhattan & Long Island

\ə\ **abut**	\aù\ **out**	\i\ **tip**	\ȯ\ **saw**	\ù\ **foot**
\ər\ **further**	\ch\ **chin**	\ī\ **life**	\ȯi\ **coin**	\y\ **yet**
\a\ **mat**	\e\ **pet**	\j\ **job**	\th\ **thin**	\yü\ **few**
\ā\ **take**	\ē\ **easy**	\ŋ\ **sing**	\th\ **this**	\yù\ **cure**
\ä\ **cot, cart**	\g\ **go**	\ō\ **bone**	\ü\ **food**	\zh\ **vision**

East Sea — see JAPAN (Sea of)

East Sus·sex \'səs-iks, *U.S. also* -ˌeks\ county SE England

East Timor *or* **Ti·mor–Leste** \'tē-ˌmȯr-'lesh-ˌtä, tē-'mȯr-\ country SE Asia on E Timor; capital, Dili

Eblana — see DUBLIN

Ebro \'ā-brō\ river 565 mi. (909 km.) long NE Spain flowing into the Mediterranean

Ec·ua·dor \'ek-wə-ˌdȯ(ə)r\ country W South America; capital, Quito — **Ec·ua·dor·an** \ˌek-wə-'dȯr-ən, -'dōr-\ *or* **Ec·ua·dor·ean** *or* **Ec·ua·dor·ian** \-ē-ən\ *adj or n*

Ed·in·burgh \'ed-ᵊn-ˌbər-ə, -ˌbə-rə, -b(ə)rə\ city, capital of Scotland

Ed·mon·ton \'ed-mən-tən\ city, capital of Alberta, Canada

Edo — see TOKYO

Edom \'ēd-əm\ ancient country SW Asia S of Judaea & Dead Sea — **Edom·ite** \'ēd-ə-ˌmīt\ *n*

Egypt \'ē-jəpt\ country NE Africa & Sinai Peninsula of SW Asia bordering on Mediterranean & Red seas; capital, Cairo

Eire — see IRELAND

Elam \'ē-ləm\ ancient country SW Asia at head of Persian Gulf E of Babylonia — **Elam·ite** \'ē-lə-ˌmīt\ *n*

Elbe \'el-bə, 'elb\ river 720 mi. (1159 km.) long N Czech Republic & NE Germany flowing NW into North Sea

El·bert, Mount \'el-bərt\ mountain 14,433 ft. (4399 m.) W central Colorado; highest in Colorado & the Rocky Mountains

El·brus, Mount \el-'brüz, -'brüs\ mountain 18,510 ft. (5642 m.) Russia; highest in the Caucasus & in Europe

El·burz \el-'bu̇(ə)rz\ mountains N Iran

Eliz·a·beth \i-'liz-ə-bəth\ city NE New Jersey

Elles·mere \'elz-ˌmi(ə)r\ island N Canada in Nunavut

Ellice — see TUVALU

El Mon·te \el-'män-tē\ city SW California E of Los Angeles

El Paso \el-'pas-ō\ city W Texas on Rio Grande

El Sal·va·dor \el-'sal-və-ˌdȯ(ə)r, -ˌsal-və-'dȯ(ə)r\ country Central America bordering on the Pacific; capital, San Salvador

Ely, Isle of \'ē-lē\ area of high ground amid marshes in East Anglia, England

En·field \'en-ˌfēld\ borough of N Greater London, England

En·gland \'iŋ-glənd *also* 'iŋ-lənd\ country S Great Britain; a division of United Kingdom; capital, London

English Channel arm of the Atlantic between S England & N France

En·nis·kil·len \ˌen-ə-'skil-ən\ town SW Northern Ireland in Fermanagh district

Ephra·im \'ē-frē-əm\ **1** hilly region N Jordan E of Jordan River **2** — see ISRAEL — **Ephra·im·ite** \'ē-frē-ə-ˌmīt\ *n*

Equatorial Guinea *or formerly* **Spanish Guinea** country W Africa including Mbini & Bioko; capital, Malabo

Erie \'i(ə)r-ē\ **1** city & port NW Pennsylvania **2** canal New York between Hudson River at Albany & Lake Erie at Buffalo; built 1817–25; now superseded by New York State Barge Canal

Erie, Lake lake E central North America in U.S. & Canada; one of the Great Lakes

Er·in \'er-ən\ poetic name of Ireland

Er·i·trea \ˌer-ə-'trē-ə, -'trā-\ country NE Africa; capital, Asmara — **Er·i·tre·an** \-ən\ *adj or n*

Escaut — see SCHELDE

Es·con·di·do \ˌes-kən-'dēd-ō\ city SW California N of San Diego

Es·fa·han \ˌes-fə-'hän, -'han\ *or* **Is·fa·han** \ˌis-\ *or formerly* **Is·pa·han** \ˌis-pə-\ city W central Iran

Española — see HISPANIOLA

Es·sen \'es-ᵊn\ city W Germany in the Ruhr

Es·sex \'es-iks\ county SE England on North Sea

Es·to·nia \e-'stō-nē-ə, -nyə\ country E Europe on Baltic Sea; capital, Tallinn; a republic of U.S.S.R. 1940–91 — **Es·to·nian** \-nē-ən, -nyən\ *adj or n*

eThe·kwi·ni \'e-te-ˌkwē-nē\ municipality Republic of South Africa including the city of Durban

Ethi·o·pia \ˌē-thē-'ō-pē-ə\ *or historically* **Ab·ys·sin·ia** \ˌab-ə-'sin-yə, -'sin-ē-ə\ country E Africa; capital, Addis Ababa — **Ethi·o·pi·an** \-pē-ən\ *adj or n*

Et·na, Mount \'et-nə\ volcano 10,902 ft. (3323 m.) Italy in NE Sicily

Etru·ria \i-'trur-ē-ə\ ancient country central peninsula of Italy

Eu·gene \yü-'jēn\ city W Oregon

Eu·phra·tes \yu̇-'frāt-ēz\ river 1700 mi. (2736 km.) long SW Asia flowing from E Turkey & uniting with the Tigris to form the Shatt al Arab

Eur·asia \yu̇-'rā-zhə, -shə\ landmass consisting of Europe & Asia — **Eur·asian** \-zhən, -shən\ *adj or n*

Eu·rope \'yu̇r-əp\ continent of the Eastern Hemisphere between Asia & the Atlantic

European Union *or formerly* **European Community** economic, scientific, & political organization consisting of Belgium, France, Italy, Luxembourg, Netherlands, Germany, Denmark, Greece, Ireland, United Kingdom, Spain, Portugal, Austria, Finland, Sweden, Cyprus, Czech Republic, Estonia, Hungary, Latvia, Lithuania, Malta, Poland, Slovakia, Slovenia, Bulgaria, Romania, & Croatia

Ev·ans·ville \'ev-ənz-ˌvil\ city SW Indiana

Ev·er·est, Mount \'ev-(ə-)rəst\ mountain 29,035 ft. (8850 m.) S Asia in the Himalayas on border between Nepal & Tibet; highest in the world

Ev·er·glades \'ev-ər-ˌglādz\ swamp region S Florida now partly drained

Ex·e·ter \'ek-sət-ər\ city SW England

Faer·oe *or* **Far·oe** \'fa(ə)r-ō, 'fe(ə)r-\ islands NE Atlantic NW of the Shetlands belonging to Denmark — **Faero·ese** *or* **Faro·ese** \ˌfar-ō-'wēz, ˌfer-, -'wēs\ *adj or n*

Fair·banks \'fa(ə)r-ˌbaŋks, 'fe(ə)r-\ city E central Alaska

Fai·sa·la·bad \ˌfī-ˌsäl-ə-'bäd, -ˌsal-ə-'bad\ *or formerly* **Ly·all·pur** \lē-ˌäl-'pu̇(ə)r\ city NE Pakistan W of Lahore

Falk·land Islands \'fȯ(l)-klənd\ *or Spanish* **Is·las Mal·vi·nas** \ˌēz-läz-mäl-'vē-näs\ island group S Atlantic E of S end of Argentina; a British colony; capital, Stanley

Far East the countries of E Asia & the Malay Archipelago — usually thought to consist of Asian countries bordering the Pacific but sometimes also India, Sri Lanka, Bangladesh, Tibet, & Myanmar — **Far Eastern** *adj*

Far·go \'fär-gō\ city E North Dakota; largest in state

Faroe — see FAEROE

Fay·ette·ville \'fā-ət-ˌvil, 'fed-vəl\ city SE central North Carolina

Fear, Cape \'fi(ə)r\ cape SE North Carolina at mouth of **Cape Fear River**

Fer·man·agh \fər-'man-ə\ district SW Northern Ireland

Fernando Póo — see BIOKO

Fès \'fes\ *or* **Fez** \'fez\ city N central Morocco

Fi·ji \'fē-jē\ islands SW Pacific; an independent country; capital, Suva — **Fi·ji·an** \-jē-ən\ *adj or n*

Fin·land \'fin-lənd\ country NE Europe; capital, Helsinki — **Fin·land·er** *n*

Flan·ders \'flan-dərz\ **1** region W Belgium & N France on North Sea **2** semiautonomous region W Belgium

Flat·tery, Cape \'flat-ə-rē\ cape NW Washington at entrance to Strait of Juan de Fuca

Flint \'flint\ city SE Michigan

Flor·ence \'flȯr-ən(t)s, 'flär-\ *or Italian* **Fi·ren·ze** \fē-'rent-sä\ *or ancient* **Flo·ren·tia** \flə-'ren-chə, -chē-ə\ city central Italy — **Flor·en·tine** \'flȯr-ən-ˌtēn, 'flär-, -ˌtīn\ *adj or n*

Flor·i·da \'flȯr-əd-ə, 'flär-\ state SE U.S.; capital, Tallahassee — **Flor·id·i·an** \flə-'rid-ē-ən\ *or* **Flor·i·dan** \'flȯr-əd-ᵊn, 'flär-\ *adj or n*

Florida, Straits of channel between Florida Keys on NW & Cuba & Bahamas on S & E connecting Gulf of Mexico & the Atlantic

Florida Keys chain of islands off S tip of Florida

Foochow — see FUZHOU

For·a·ker, Mount \'fòr-i-kər, 'fär-\ mountain 17,400 ft. (5304 m.) S central Alaska in Alaska Range

For·mo·sa \fòr-'mō-sə, fər-, -zə\ — see TAIWAN — **For·mo·san** \-'mōs-ᵊn, -'mōz-\ adj or n

For·ta·le·za \ˌfòrt-ᵊl-'ā-zə\ city & port NE Brazil on the Atlantic

Fort Col·lins \'käl-ənz\ city N Colorado

Fort–de–France \ˌfòrd-ə-'fräns\ city West Indies, capital of Martinique on W coast

Forth \'fō(ə)rth, 'fó(ə)rth\ river 116 mi. (187 km.) long S central Scotland flowing E into North Sea through **Firth of Forth**

Fort Knox \'näks\ military reservation N central Kentucky; location of U.S. Gold Bullion Depository

Fort Lau·der·dale \'lòd-ər-ˌdāl\ city SE Florida

Fort Wayne \'wān\ city NE Indiana

Fort Worth \'wərth\ city NE Texas

Fox \'fäks\ islands SW Alaska in the E Aleutians

Foxe Basin \'fäks\ inlet of the Atlantic N Canada in E Nunavut W of Baffin Island

France \'fran(t)s\ country W Europe between the English Channel & the Mediterranean; capital, Paris

Frank·fort \'fraŋk-fərt\ city, capital of Kentucky

Frank·furt \'fraŋk-fərt, 'frän-ˌfú(ə)rt\ or in full **Frankfurt am Main** \-(ˌ)äm-'mīn\ or **Frankfort on the Main** city W Germany on Main River

Frank·lin \'fraŋ-klən\ former district N Canada in Northwest Territories including Arctic Archipelago & Boothia & Melville peninsulas

Fra·ser \'frā-zər, -zhər\ river 850 mi. (1368 km.) long Canada in S central British Columbia flowing into the Pacific

Fred·er·ic·ton \'fred-(ə-)rik-tən\ city, capital of New Brunswick, Canada

Free State or formerly **Or·ange Free State** \'är-inj, 'òr-, -ənj\ province E central Republic of South Africa

Free·town \'frē-ˌtaùn\ city, capital of Sierra Leone

Fre·mont \'frē-mänt\ city W California

French Guiana country N South America on the Atlantic; an overseas division of France; capital, Cayenne

French Indochina — see INDOCHINA

Fres·no \'frez-nō\ city S central California SE of San Francisco

Fri·sian Islands \'frizh-ən, 'frē-zhən\ island group N Europe in North Sea; divided between Netherlands, Germany, & Denmark

Frunze — see BISHKEK

Fu·ji, Mount \'fü-jē\ or **Fu·ji·ya·ma** \ˌfü-jē-'(y)äm-ə\ mountain 12,388 ft. (3776 m.) Japan in S central Honshu; highest in Japan

Fu·ku·o·ka \ˌfü-kə-'wō-kə\ city Japan in N Kyushu

Ful·ler·ton \'fúl-ərt-ᵊn\ city SW California

Fu·na·fu·ti \ˌfü-nə-'füt-ē\ city, capital of Tuvalu

Fun·dy, Bay of \'fən-dē\ inlet of the Atlantic SE Canada between New Brunswick & Nova Scotia

Fu·shun \'fü-'shùn\ city NE China E of Shenyang

Fu·zhou \'fü-'jō\ or **Foo·chow** \'fü-'jō, -'chaù\ city & port SE China

Ga·bon \ga-'bōn\ country W Africa on the Equator; capital, Libreville — **Gab·o·nese** \ˌgab-ə-'nēz, -'nēs\ adj or n

Ga·bo·rone \ˌgäb-ə-'rōn\ city, capital of Botswana

Gads·den Purchase \'gadz-dən\ area of land S of Gila River in present Arizona & New Mexico purchased 1853 by the U.S. from Mexico

Ga·lá·pa·gos Islands \gə-'läp-ə-gəs, -'lap-\ island group Ecuador in the Pacific 600 mi. (965 km.) W of South America

Ga·la·tia \gə-'lā-sh(ē-)ə\ ancient country central Asia Minor in region around modern Ankara, Turkey — **Ga·la·tian** \-shən\ adj or n

Ga·li·cia \gə-'lish-(ē-)ə\ **1** region E central Europe now divided between Poland & Ukraine **2** region NW Spain on the Atlantic — **Ga·li·cian** \-'lish-ən\ adj or n

Gal·i·lee \'gal-ə-ˌlē\ hilly region N Israel — **Gal·i·le·an** \ˌgal-ə-'lē-ən\ adj or n

Galilee, Sea of or modern **Lake Ti·be·ri·as** \tī-'bir-ē-əs\ or biblical **Lake of Gen·nes·a·ret** \gə-'nes-ə-ˌret, -rət\ lake N Israel on Syrian border; crossed by Jordan River

Gam·bia \'gam-bē-ə\ country W Africa; capital, Banjul — **Gam·bi·an** \-bē-ən\ adj or n

Gan·ges \'gan-jēz\ river 1550 mi. (2494 km.) long N India flowing from Himalayas SE & E to unite with the Brahmaputra and empty into Bay of Bengal through **Ganges Delta** — see HUGLI — **Gan·get·ic** \gan-'jet-ik\ adj

Gao·xiong \'gaù-'shyùŋ\ or **Kao–hsiung** \'kaù-'shyùŋ, 'gaù-\ city & port SW Taiwan

Garden Grove city SW California

Gar·land \'gär-lənd\ city NE Texas NNE of Dallas

Ga·ronne \gə-'rän, -'ròn\ river 355 mi. (571 km.) long SE France flowing NW

Gary \'ga(ə)r-ē, 'ge(ə)r-ē\ city NW Indiana on Lake Michigan

Gas·co·ny \'gas-kə-nē\ region SW France — **Gas·con** \'gas-kən\ adj or n

Gas·pé \gas-'pā, 'gas-ˌpā\ peninsula SE Quebec E of mouth of the Saint Lawrence — **Gas·pe·sian** \ga-'spē-zhən\ adj or n

Gaul \'gòl\ or Latin **Gal·lia** \'gal-ē-ə\ ancient country W Europe chiefly consisting of region occupied by modern France & Belgium but at one time including also Po valley in N Italy

Gau·teng \'gaù-ˌteŋ\ province central NE Republic of South Africa

Ga·za Strip \'gäz-ə\ district NE Sinai Peninsula on the Mediterranean

Gee·long \jə-'lòŋ\ city & port SE Australia in S Victoria

Ge·ne·va \jə-'nē-və\ city SW Switzerland on Lake Geneva — **Ge·ne·van** \-vən\ adj or n — **Gen·e·vese** \ˌjen-ə-'vēz, -'vēs\ adj or n

Geneva, Lake lake on border between SW Switzerland & E France; crossed by the Rhone

Gennesaret, Lake of — see GALILEE (Sea of)

Gen·oa \'jen-ə-wə\ or Italian **Ge·no·va** \'je-nō-vä\ city & port NW Italy — **Gen·o·ese** \ˌjen-ə-'wēz, -'wēs\ or **Gen·o·vese** \-ə-'vēz, -'vēs\ adj or n

George·town \'jó(ə)rj-ˌtaùn\ **1** a W section of Washington, District of Columbia **2** city & port, capital of Guyana

Geor·gia \'jòr-jə\ **1** state SE U.S.; capital, Atlanta **2** or **Republic of Georgia** country SW Asia on Black Sea S of Caucasus Mountains; capital, Tbilisi; a republic of U.S.S.R. 1936–91 — **Geor·gian** \'jòr-jən\ adj or n

Georgia, Strait of channel Canada & U.S. between Vancouver Island & main part of British Columbia NW of Puget Sound

Georgian Bay inlet of Lake Huron in S Ontario

Ger·man·town \'jər-mən-ˌtaùn\ a NW section of Philadelphia, Pennsylvania

Ger·ma·ny \'jərm-(ə-)nē\ country central Europe bordering on North & Baltic seas; capital, Berlin; divided 1946–90 into two independent states: **Federal Republic of Germany** (capital, Bonn) & **German Democratic Republic** (capital, East Berlin)

Get·tys·burg \'get-ēz-ˌbərg\ town S Pennsylvania

Gha·na \'gän-ə, 'gan-ə\ or formerly **Gold Coast** country W Africa on Gulf of Guinea; capital, Accra — **Gha·na·ian** \gä-'nā-ən, ga-, -yən; -'nī-ən\ or **Gha·ni·an** \'gän-ē-ən, 'gän-yən, 'gan-\ adj or n

Ghats \'gòts\ two mountain chains S India — see EASTERN GHATS, WESTERN GHATS

\ə\ abut	\aú\ out	\i\ tip	\ó\ saw	\ú\ foot
\ər\ further	\ch\ chin	\ī\ life	\ói\ coin	\y\ yet
\a\ mat	\e\ pet	\j\ job	\th\ thin	\yü\ few
\ā\ take	\ē\ easy	\ŋ\ sing	\th\ this	\yú\ cure
\ä\ cot, cart	\g\ go	\ō\ bone	\ü\ food	\zh\ vision

Ghent \'gent\ city NW central Belgium

Gi·bral·tar \jə-'brȯl-tər\ British colony on S coast of Spain including Rock of Gibraltar

Gibraltar, Rock of cape on S coast of Spain in Gibraltar at E end of Strait of Gibraltar

Gibraltar, Strait of passage between Spain & Africa connecting the Atlantic & the Mediterranean

Gi·la \'hē-lə\ river 630 mi. (1014 km.) long SW New Mexico and S Arizona flowing W into the Colorado

Gil·bert \'gil-bərt\ town SW central Arizona

Gilbert and El·lice Islands \'el-əs\ island group W Pacific; until 1976 a British colony; now divided into the independent states of Kiribati and Tuvalu

Gil·e·ad \'gil-ē-əd\ mountain region of NE ancient Palestine E of Jordan River; now in NW Jordan — **Gil·e·ad·ite** \-ē-ə-ˌdīt\ n

Gi·za \'gē-zə\ city N Egypt on the Nile SW of Cairo

Gla·cier Bay \ˌglā-shər\ inlet SE Alaska at S end of Saint Elias Range

Glas·gow \'glas-kō, 'glas-gō, 'glaz-gō\ city S central Scotland on the Clyde — **Glas·we·gian** \glas-'wē-jən\ adj or n

Glen·dale \'glen-ˌdāl\ 1 city central Arizona NW of Phoenix 2 city S California NE of Los Angeles

Glouces·ter \'gläs-tər, 'glȯs-\ city SW central England

Glouces·ter·shire \'gläs-tər-ˌshi(ə)r, 'glȯs-, -shər\ or **Gloucester** county SW central England

Goa \'gō-ə\ district W India on Malabar coast belonging to Portugal before 1962

Goat Island island W New York in Niagara River — see NIAGARA FALLS

Go·bi \'gō-bē\ desert E central Asia in Mongolia & N China

Godthab — see NUUK

Godwin Austen — see K2

Go·lan Heights \ˌgō-ˌlän, -lən\ hilly region NE of Sea of Galilee

Gol·con·da \gäl-'kän-də\ ruined city central India W of Hyderabad

Gold Coast 1 — see GHANA 2 coast region W Africa on N shore of Gulf of Guinea E of Cote d'Ivoire

Golden Gate strait W California connecting San Francisco Bay with Pacific Ocean

Good Hope, Cape of \ˌgu̇d-'hōp\ cape S Republic of South Africa on SW coast of Western Cape province

Gorki — see NIZHNIY NOVGOROD

Go·te·borg \ˌyərt-ə-'bȯr-ē\ city & port SW Sweden

Gram·pi·an \'gram-pē-ən\ hills N central Scotland

Grand Banks shallow area in the W North Atlantic SE of Newfoundland

Grand Canyon gorge of Colorado River NW Arizona

Grand Canyon of the Snake — see HELLS CANYON

Grande, Rio — see RIO GRANDE

Grand Prairie city N central Texas W of Dallas

Grand Rapids city SW Michigan

Graz \'gräts\ city S Austria

Great Australian Bight wide bay on S coast of Australia

Great Barrier Reef coral reef Australia off NE coast

Great Basin region W U.S. between Sierra Nevada & Wasatch Range including most of Nevada & parts of California, Idaho, Utah, Wyoming, & Oregon; has no drainage to ocean

Great Bear lake Canada in Northwest Territories draining through Great Bear River into Mackenzie River

Great Brit·ain \'brit-ᵊn\ 1 island W Europe NW of France consisting of England, Scotland, & Wales 2 UNITED KINGDOM

Great Dividing Range mountain system E Australia extending S from Cape York Peninsula into Tasmania — see KOSCIUSKO (Mount)

Greater An·til·les \an-'til-ēz\ group of islands of the West Indies including Cuba, Hispaniola, Jamaica, & Puerto Rico — see LESSER ANTILLES

Greater London metropolitan county SE England consisting of City of London & 32 surrounding boroughs

Greater Manchester metropolitan county NW England including city of Manchester

Greater Sud·bury or **Sudbury** \'səd-ˌber-ē, -b(ə-)rē\ city SE Ontario, Canada

Great Lakes chain of five lakes (Superior, Michigan, Huron, Erie, & Ontario) central North America in U.S. & Canada

Great Plains elevated plains region W central U.S. & W Canada E of the Rockies; extending from W Texas to NE British Columbia & NW Alberta

Great Rift Valley basin SW Asia & E Africa extending with several breaks from valley of the Jordan S to central Mozambique

Great Salt lake N Utah having salty waters & no outlet

Great Slave lake NW Canada in S Northwest Territories drained by Mackenzie River

Great Smoky mountains between W North Carolina & E Tennessee; highest Clingmans Dome 6643 ft. (2025 m.)

Greece \'grēs\ country S Europe at S end of Balkan Peninsula; capital, Athens

Green \'grēn\ 1 mountains E North America in the Appalachians extending from S Quebec S through Vermont into W Massachusetts 2 river 730 mi. (1175 km.) long W U.S. flowing from W Wyoming S into the Colorado in SE Utah

Green Bay 1 inlet of NW Lake Michigan 120 mi. (193 km.) long in NW Michigan & NE Wisconsin 2 city NE Wisconsin on Green Bay

Green·land \'grēn-lənd, -ˌland\ island in the North Atlantic off NE North America belonging to Denmark; capital, Nuuk

Greens·boro \'grēnz-ˌbər-ə, -ˌbə-rə\ city N central North Carolina

Green·wich \'grin-ij, 'gren-, -ich\ borough of SE Greater London, England

Green·wich Village \ˌgren-ich, ˌgrin-, -ij\ section of New York City in Manhattan on lower W side

Gre·na·da \grə-'nād-ə\ island West Indies in S Windward Islands; an independent country; capital, Saint George's

Gren·a·dines, The \ˌgren-ə-'dēnz\ islands West Indies in central Windward Islands; divided between Grenada & Saint Vincent and the Grenadines

Groz·ny \'grȯz-nē, 'gräz-\ city S Russia in Europe; capital of Chechnya

Gua·da·la·ja·ra \ˌgwäd-ə-lə-'här-ə\ city W central Mexico

Gua·dal·ca·nal \ˌgwäd-ᵊl-kə-'nal, ˌgwäd-ə-kə-\ island W Pacific in the SE Solomons

Gua·dal·qui·vir \ˌgwäd-ᵊl-'kwiv-ər, -ki-'vi(ə)r\ river 408 mi. (656 km.) long S Spain flowing into the Atlantic

Gua·de·loupe \'gwäd-ᵊl-ˌüp\ two islands separated by a narrow channel in West Indies in central Leeward Islands; an overseas division of France

Guam \'gwäm\ island W Pacific in S Marianas belonging to U.S.; capital, Hagatna — **Gua·ma·ni·an** \gwä-'mä-nē-ən\ adj or n

Gua·na·ba·ra Bay \ˌgwän-ə-'bar-ə, -'bär-\ inlet of the Atlantic SE Brazil on which city of Rio de Janeiro is located

Guang·zhou \'gwäŋ-'jō\ or **Can·ton** \'kan-ˌtän, kan-'\ city & port SE China

Guan·tá·na·mo Bay \gwän-'tän-ə-ˌmō\ inlet of the Caribbean in SE Cuba; site of U.S. naval station

Gua·te·ma·la \ˌgwät-ə-'mäl-ə\ 1 country Central America 2 or **Guatemala City** city, its capital — **Gua·te·ma·lan** \-'mäl-ən\ adj or n

Gua·ya·quil \ˌgwī-ə-'kē(ə)l, -'kil\ city & port W Ecuador

Guay·na·bo \gwī-'nä-bō\ city NE central Puerto Rico

Guern·sey \'gərn-zē\ island in English Channel — see CHANNEL 2

Gui·a·na \gē-'an-ə, -'än-ə; gī-'an-ə\ region N South America on the Atlantic; includes Guyana, French Guiana, Suriname, & nearby parts of Brazil & Venezuela — **Gui·a·nan** \-ən\ adj or n

Guin·ea \'gin-ē\ **1** region W Africa on the Atlantic extending along coast from Gambia to Angola **2** country W Africa N of Sierra Leone & Liberia; capital, Conakry — **Guin·ean** \'gin-ē-ən\ adj or n

Guinea, Gulf of arm of the Atlantic W central Africa

Guin·ea–Bis·sau \ˌgin-ē-bis-'aù\ country W Africa; an independent state since 1974; capital, Bissau

Gui·yang \'gwē-'yäŋ\ or **Kuei–yang** \'gwä-'yäŋ\ city S China

Gulf States states of U.S. bordering on Gulf of Mexico: Florida, Alabama, Mississippi, Louisiana, and Texas

Gulf Stream warm current of the Atlantic Ocean flowing from Gulf of Mexico NE along coast of U.S. to Nantucket Island and from there eastward

Guy·ana \gī-'an-ə\ or formerly **British Guiana** country N South America on the Atlantic; independent since 1970; capital, Georgetown — **Guy·a·nese** \ˌgī-ə-'nēz, -'nēs\ adj or n

Gwangju — see KWANGJU

Hack·ney \'hak-nē\ borough of Greater London, England

Ha·des \'hād-(ˌ)ēz\ underground abode of the dead in Greek mythology

Ha·gat·na \hə-'gät-nyə\ or formerly **Aga·na** \ä-'gän-yä\ town, capital of Guam

Hague, The \thə-'häg\ city SW Netherlands; national seat of government

Haidarabad — see HYDERABAD

Hai·kou \'hī-'kō\ city & port SE China

Hai·phong \'hī-'fòŋ\ city & port N Vietnam

Hai·ti \'hāt-ē\ **1** — see HISPANIOLA **2** country West Indies in W Hispaniola; capital, Port-au-Prince — **Hai·tian** \'hā-shən\ adj or n

Ha·le·a·ka·la Crater \ˌhäl-ē-ˌäk-ə-'lä\ crater over 2500 ft. (762 m.) deep Hawaii in E Maui

Hal·i·fax \'hal-ə-ˌfaks\ municipality & port, capital of Nova Scotia, Canada

Ham·burg \'ham-ˌbərg, 'häm-ˌbù(ə)rg\ city N Germany on the Elbe — **Ham·burg·er** \-ˌbər-gər, -ˌbùr-\ n

Ham·hung or **Ham·heung** \'häm-ˌhùŋ\ city E central North Korea

Ham·il·ton \'ham-əl-tən, -əlt-ᵊn\ **1** town, capital of Bermuda **2** city & port, S Ontario, Canada on Lake Ontario

Ham·mer·smith and Ful·ham \'ham-ər-ˌsmith-ənd-'fùl-əm\ borough of SW Greater London, England

Hamp·shire \'ham(p)-ˌshi(ə)r, -shər\ county S England on English Channel

Hamp·ton \'ham(p)-tən\ city SE Virginia

Hampton Roads channel SE Virginia through which James River flows into Chesapeake Bay

Hang·zhou \'häŋ-'jō\ or **Hang·chow** \'haŋ-'chaù, 'häŋ-'jō\ or **Hang–chou** \'häŋ-'jō\ city E China

Han·ni·bal \'han-ə-bəl\ city NE Missouri on the Mississippi River

Han·no·ver or **Han·o·ver** \'han-ˌō-vər, 'han-ə-vər; German hä-'nō-vər\ city N central Germany

Ha·noi \ha-'nòi, hə-, hä-\ city, capital of Vietnam

Ha·ra·re \hə-'rä-rä\ or formerly **Salis·bury** \'sòlz-ˌber-ē, -b(ə-)rē\ city, capital of Zimbabwe

Har·bin \'här-bən, här-'bin\ or **Ha–erh–pin** \'hä-'er-'bin\ city NE China

Har·in·gey \'har-iŋ-ˌgā\ borough of N Greater London, England

Har·lem \'här-ləm\ section of New York City in N Manhattan

Har·ris·burg \'har-əs-ˌbərg\ city, capital of Pennsylvania

Har·row \'har-ō\ borough of NW Greater London, England

Hart·ford \'härt-fərd\ city, capital of Connecticut

Hat·ter·as, Cape \'hat-ə-rəs, 'ha-trəs\ cape, North Carolina on **Hatteras Island**

Ha·vana \hə-'van-ə\ city, capital of Cuba

Hav·ant \'hav-ənt\ town S England

Ha·ver·ing \'hāv-(ə-)riŋ\ borough of NE Greater London, England

Ha·waii \hə-'wä-(y)ē, -'wī-, -'wò-\ **1** or **Ha·wai·ian Islands** or formerly **Sand·wich Islands** \ˌsan-(d)wich-\ group of islands central Pacific belonging to U.S. **2** island, largest of the group **3** state of U.S. consisting of Hawaiian Islands except Midway; capital, Honolulu

Hay·ward \'hā-wərd\ city W California SE of Oakland

Heb·ri·des \'heb-rə-ˌdēz\ islands W Scotland in the North Atlantic consisting of **Outer Hebrides** (to W) and **Inner Hebrides** (to E) — **Heb·ri·de·an** \ˌheb-rə-'dē-ən\ adj or n

Hel·e·na \'hel-ə-nə\ city, capital of Montana

Hellespont — see DARDANELLES

Hells Canyon \'helz\ or **Grand Canyon of the Snake** canyon of Snake River on Idaho–Oregon boundary

Hel·sin·ki \'hel-ˌsiŋ-kē, hel-'siŋ-\ city, capital of Finland

Hen·der·son \'hen-dər-sən\ city S Nevada

Henry, Cape \'hen-rē\ cape E Virginia S of entrance to Chesapeake Bay

Hert·ford·shire \'här-fərd-ˌshi(ə)r, -shər, also 'härt-, in the U.S. also 'hərt-\ or **Hertford** county SE England

Her·ze·go·vi·na \ˌhert-sə-gō-'vē-nə, ˌhərt-, -'gō-və-nə\ region S Europe S of Bosnia; now part of Bosnia and Herzegovina

Hi·a·le·ah \ˌhī-ə-'lē-ə\ city SE Florida

Hi·ber·nia \hī-'bər-nē-ə\ — see IRELAND — **Hi·ber·ni·an** \-ən\ adj or n

Hi·ga·shi·ōsa·ka \hē-ˌgä-shē-ō-'säk-ə\ city Japan in S Honshu E of Osaka

High·lands \'hī-lən(d)z\ the mountainous N part of Scotland lying N & W of the Lowlands

High Plains the Great Plains especially from Nebraska southward

Hil·ling·don \'hil-iŋ-dən\ borough of W Greater London, England

Hi·ma·la·yas, the \ˌhim-ə-'lā-əz, hə-'mäl-(ə-)yəz\ or **the Himalaya** mountain system S Asia on border between India & Tibet and in Kashmir, Nepal, & Bhutan — see EVEREST (Mount) — **Hi·ma·la·yan** \ˌhim-ə-'lā-ən, hə-'mäl-(ə-)yən\ adj

Hin·du Kush \ˌhin-(ˌ)dü-'kùsh, -'kəsh\ mountain range central Asia SW of the Pamirs on border of Kashmir and in Afghanistan

Hin·du·stan \ˌhin-(ˌ)dü-'stan, -də-, -'stän\ **1** a name for N India **2** the subcontinent of India **3** the country of India

Hi·ro·shi·ma \ˌhir-ə-'shē-mə, hə-'rō-shə-mə\ city Japan in SW Honshu on Inland Sea

His·pan·io·la \ˌhis-pən-'yō-lə\ or Spanish **Es·pa·ño·la** \ˌes-ˌpän-'yō-lə\ or formerly **Hai·ti** \'hāt-ē\ island West Indies in Greater Antilles divided between Haiti on W & Dominican Republic on E

Ho·bart \'hō-ˌbärt\ city Australia, capital of Tasmania

Ho Chi Minh City \ˌhō-ˌchē-'min, -ˌshē-\ or formerly **Sai·gon** \sī-'gän, 'sī-ˌgän\ city S Vietnam

Hoh·hot \'hō-'hōt\ or **Hu·he·hot** \'hü-ˌhā-'hōt\ city N China, capital of Inner Mongolia

Hok·kai·do \hä-'kīd-ō\ island N Japan N of Honshu

\ə\ **abut**	\aù\ **out**	\i\ **tip**	\ò\ **saw**	\ù\ **foot**
\ər\ **further**	\ch\ **chin**	\ī\ **life**	\òi\ **coin**	\y\ **yet**
\a\ **mat**	\e\ **pet**	\j\ **job**	\th\ **thin**	\yü\ **few**
\ā\ **take**	\ē\ **easy**	\ŋ\ **sing**	\t̲h̲\ **this**	\yù\ **cure**
\ä\ **cot, cart**	\g\ **go**	\ō\ **bone**	\ü\ **food**	\zh\ **vision**

Hol·land \'häl-ənd\ **1** county of Holy Roman Empire bordering on North Sea & consisting of area now forming part of W Netherlands **2** — see NETHERLANDS — **Holland·er** \-ən-dər\ *n*

Hol·ly·wood \'häl-ē-ˌwu̇d\ **1** section of Los Angeles, California, NW of downtown district **2** city SE Florida

Holy Land lands roughly equivalent to ancient Palestine and including holy sites of Jewish, Christian, & Islamic religions

Holy Roman Empire empire consisting mainly of German and Italian territories and existing from 9th or 10th century to 1806

Hon·du·ras \hän-'d(y)u̇r-əs\ country Central America; capital, Tegucigalpa — **Hon·du·ran** \-ən\ *adj or n*

Hong Kong \'häŋ-ˌkäŋ, -'käŋ; 'hȯŋ-ˌkȯŋ, -'kȯŋ\ *or Chinese* **Xiang·gang** \'shyäŋ-ˌgäŋ\ special administrative region China on SE coast including Hong Kong Island & Jiulong Peninsula; formerly a British colony with Victoria as capital

Ho·ni·a·ra \ˌhō-nē-'är-ə\ town, capital of Solomon Islands

Ho·no·lu·lu \ˌhän-ᵊl-'ü-lü, ˌhōn-ᵊl-\ city, capital of Hawaii on Oahu

Hon·shu \'hän-shü\ island Japan; largest of the group

Hood, Mount \'hu̇d\ mountain 11,235 ft. (3424 m.) NW Oregon in Cascade Range

Hoo·ver Dam \ˌhü-vər\ *or* **Boul·der Dam** \ˌbōl-dər\ dam 726 ft. (221 m.) high in Colorado River between Arizona & Nevada — see MEAD (Lake)

Hor·muz, Strait of \'hȯr-ˌməz, hȯr-'müz\ strait connecting Persian Gulf & Gulf of Oman

Horn, Cape \'hȯ(ə)rn\ cape S Chile on an island in Tierra del Fuego; the most southerly point of South America at 56° S latitude

Horseshoe Falls — see NIAGARA FALLS

Houns·low \'hau̇nz-ˌlō\ borough of SW Greater London, England

Hous·ton \'(h)yü-stən\ city SE Texas

How·rah \'hau̇-rə\ city E India on Hugli River opposite Calcutta

Hsi·an — see XI'AN

Huang *or* **Hwang** \'hwäŋ\ *or* **Yellow** river about 3396 mi. (5464 km.) long N China flowing into Bo Hai

Hud·ders·field \'həd-ərz-ˌfēld\ town N England NE of Manchester

Hud·son \'həd-sən\ **1** river 306 mi. (492 km.) long E New York flowing S **2** bay, inlet of the Atlantic in N Canada **3** strait NE Canada connecting Hudson Bay & the Atlantic

Hu·gli *or* **Hoo·ghly** \'hü-glē\ river 120 mi. (193 km.) long E India flowing S into Bay of Bengal; most westerly channel of the Ganges in its delta

Huhehot — see HOHHOT

Hull \'həl\ *or* **Kings·ton upon Hull** \'kiŋ(k)-stən\ city & port N England

Hun·ga·ry \'həŋ-g(ə-)rē\ country central Europe; capital, Budapest

Hunt·ing·ton Beach \'hənt-iŋ-tən\ city SW California

Hunts·ville \'hən(t)s-ˌvil, -vəl\ city N Alabama

Hu·ron, Lake \-'(h)yu̇r-ən, '(h)yu̇(ə)r-ˌän\ lake E central North America in U.S. & Canada; one of the Great Lakes

Hy·der·abad \'hīd-(ə-)rə-ˌbad, -ˌbäd\ **1** *or* **Hai·dar·abad** *same*\ city S central India **2** city SE Pakistan

Iba·dan \i-'bäd-ᵊn, -'bad-\ city SW Nigeria

Ibe·ri·an \ī-'bir-ē-ən\ peninsula SW Europe occupied by Spain & Portugal

Ice·land \'ī-slənd, -ˌsland\ island SE of Greenland between Arctic & Atlantic oceans; an independent country; capital, Reykjavik — **Ice·land·er** \-ˌslan-dər, -slən-dər\ *n*

Ida·ho \'īd-ə-ˌhō\ state NW U.S.; capital, Boise — **Ida·ho·an** \ˌīd-ə-'hō-ən\ *adj or n*

Igua·çú *or* **Igua·zú** \ˌē-gwə-'sü\ river 745 mi. (1199 km.) long S Brazil flowing W

IJs·sel *or* **Ijs·sel** \'ī-səl\ river 70 mi. (113 km.) long E Netherlands flowing out of Rhine N into IJsselmeer

IJs·sel·meer \ˌī-səl-'me(ə)r\ *or* **Lake Ijs·sel** freshwater lake N Netherlands separated from North Sea by a dike; part of former Zuider Zee (inlet of North Sea)

Ilium — see TROY

Il·li·nois \ˌil-ə-'nȯi *also* -'nȯiz\ state N central U.S.; capital, Springfield — **Il·li·nois·an** \-'nȯi-ən, -'nȯiz-ᵊn\ *adj or n*

Il·lyr·ia \il-'lir-ē-ə\ ancient country S Europe and Balkan Peninsula on the Adriatic — **Il·lyr·i·an** \-ē-ən\ *adj or n*

Im·pe·ri·al Valley \im-'pir-ē-əl\ valley SE corner of California & partly in Baja California, Mexico

In·chon *or* **In·cheon** \'in-ˌchän\ city South Korea on Yellow Sea

In·de·pen·dence \ˌin-də-'pen-dən(t)s\ city W Missouri E of Kansas City

In·dia \'in-dē-ə\ **1** subcontinent S Asia S of the Himalayas between Bay of Bengal & Arabian Sea **2** country consisting of major portion of the subcontinent; capital, New Delhi **3** *or* **Indian Empire** before 1947 those parts of the subcontinent of India under British rule or protection

In·di·an \'in-dē-ən\ ocean E of Africa, S of Asia, W of Australia, & N of Antarctica

In·di·ana \ˌin-dē-'an-ə\ state E central U.S.; capital, Indianapolis — **In·di·an·an** \-'an-ən\ *or* **In·di·an·i·an** \-'an-ē-ən\ *adj or n*

In·di·a·nap·o·lis \ˌin-dē-ə-'nap-(ə-)ləs\ city, capital of Indiana

Indian River lagoon 165 mi. (266 km.) long E Florida between main part of the state & coastal islands

Indian Territory former territory S U.S. in present state of Oklahoma

In·dies \'in-dēz\ **1** EAST INDIES **2** WEST INDIES

In·do·chi·na \'in-(ˌ)dō-'chī-nə\ **1** peninsula SE Asia including Myanmar, Malay Peninsula, Thailand, Cambodia, Laos, & Vietnam **2** *or* **French Indochina** former country SE Asia consisting of area now forming Cambodia, Laos, & Vietnam — **In·do–Chi·nese** \-chī-'nēz, -'nēs\ *adj or n*

In·do·ne·sia \ˌin-də-'nē-zhə, -shə\ country SE Asia in Malay Archipelago consisting of Sumatra, Java, S & E Borneo, Sulawesi, W New Guinea, & many smaller islands; capital, Jakarta — see NETHERLANDS EAST INDIES — **In·do·ne·sian** \-zhən, -shən\ *adj or n*

In·dore \in-'dō(ə)r, -'dȯ(ə)r\ city W central India

In·dus \'in-dəs\ river 1800 mi. (2897 km.) long S Asia flowing from Tibet NW & SSW through Pakistan into Arabian Sea

In·gle·wood \'iŋ-gəl-ˌwu̇d\ city SW California

In·land Sea \'in-ˌland, -lənd\ inlet of the Pacific in SW Japan between Honshu on N and Shikoku and Kyushu on S

Inner Hebrides — see HEBRIDES

Inner Mon·go·lia \män-'gōl-yə, mäŋ-, -'gō-lē-ə\ region N China

Inside Passage protected shipping route between Puget Sound, Washington, & Skagway, Alaska

In·ver·ness \ˌin-vər-'nes\ town NW Scotland

Io·ni·an \ī-'ō-nē-ən\ **1** sea, arm of the Mediterranean between SE Italy & W Greece **2** islands W Greece in Ionian Sea

Io·wa \'ī-ə-wə\ state N central U.S.; capital, Des Moines — **Io·wan** \-wən\ *adj or n*

Ips·wich \'ip-(ˌ)swich\ town SE England

Iqa·lu·it \ē-'käl-ü-ət\ town Canada, capital of Nunavut on Baffin Island

Iran \i-'rän, -'ran; ī-'ran\ *or formerly by outsiders* **Per·sia** \'pər-zhə\ country SW Asia; capital, Tehran — **Irani** \i-'rän-ē, -'ran-\ *adj or n* — **Ira·nian** \ir-'ā-nē-ən, -'an-ē-, -'än-ē-\ *adj or n*

Iraq \i-'räk, -'rak\ country SW Asia in Mesopotamia; capital, Baghdad — **Iraqi** \-'räk-ē, -'rak-\ *adj or n*

Ire·land \ˈī(ə)r-lənd\ **1** *or Latin* **Hi·ber·nia** \hī-ˈbər-nē-ə\ island Ⓦ Europe in the North Atlantic; one of the British Isles **2** *or* **Ei·re** \ˈer-ə\ country occupying major portion of Ireland (island); capital, Dublin

Irish Sea \ˈīr-ish\ arm of the North Atlantic between Great Britain & Ireland

Ir·kutsk \i(ə)r-ˈkütsk, ˌər-\ city Ⓢ Russia near Lake Baikal

Ir·ra·wad·dy \ˌir-ə-ˈwäd-ē\ river 1300 mi. (2092 km.) long Myanmar flowing Ⓢ into Bay of Bengal

Ir·tysh \i(ə)r-ˈtish, ˌər-\ river over 2600 mi. (4180 km.) long central Asia flowing ⓃⓌ & Ⓝ from Altai Mountains in China, through Kazakhstan, & into Ⓦ central Russia

Ir·vine \ˈər-ˌvīn\ city ⓈⓌ California

Ir·ving \ˈər-viŋ\ city ⓃⒺ Texas ⓃⓌ of Dallas

Isfahan — see ESFAHAN

Is·lam·a·bad \is-ˈläm-ə-ˌbäd, iz-ˈlam-ə-ˌbad\ city, capital of Pakistan

Islas Malvinas — see FALKLAND ISLANDS

Isle of Man — see MAN (Isle of)

Isle of Wight \-ˈwīt\ island and administrative subdivision of Ⓢ England in English Channel

Isle Roy·ale \(ˈ)ī(ə)l-ˈròi(-ə)l\ island Michigan in Lake Superior

Isles of Scilly 1 — see CORNWALL AND ISLES OF SCILLY **2** — see SCILLY (Isles of)

Is·ling·ton \ˈiz-liŋ-tən\ borough of Ⓝ Greater London, England

Ispahan — see ESFAHAN

Is·ra·el \ˈiz-rē-əl, -rā-əl, -rəl\ **1** kingdom in ancient Palestine consisting of lands occupied by the Hebrew people **2** *or* **Ephra·im** \ˈē-frē-əm\ the Ⓝ part of the Hebrew kingdom after about 933 B.C. **3** country ⓈⓌ Asia; established 1948; capital, Jerusalem — **Is·rae·li** \iz-ˈrā-lē\ *adj or n*

Is·tan·bul \ˌis-tən-ˈbül, -ˌtäm-, -ˌtam-, -ˌtän-\ *or formerly* **Con·stan·ti·no·ple** \ˌkän-ˌstant-ᵊn-ˈō-pəl\ city ⓃⓌ Turkey on the Bosporus & Sea of Marmara; former capital of Turkey

Is·tria \ˈis-trē-ə\ peninsula in Croatia & Slovenia extending into the Ⓝ Adriatic — **Is·tri·an** \-trē-ən\ *adj or n*

It·a·ly \ˈit-ᵊl-ē\ country Ⓢ Europe including a boot-shaped peninsula and the islands of Sicily and Sardinia; capital, Rome

Itas·ca, Lake \ī-ˈtas-kə\ lake ⓃⓌ central Minnesota; source of the Mississippi

Ivory Coast — see COTE D'IVOIRE — **Ivor·i·an** \(ˌ)ī-ˈvòr-ē-ən\ *adj or n* — **Ivory Coast·er** \ˈkōs-tər\ *n*

Iwo Ji·ma \ˌē-(ˌ)wō-ˈjē-mə\ *or* **Io To** \ˌē-(ˌ)ō-ˈtō\ island Japan in Ⓦ Pacific ⓈⓈⒺ of Tokyo

Izhevsk \ˈē-ˌzhefsk\ city Ⓦ Russia

Iz·mir \iz-ˈmi(ə)r\ *or formerly* **Smyr·na** \ˈsmər-nə\ city Ⓦ Turkey

Iz·ta·pa·la·pa \ˌēs-tä-pä-ˈläp-ä\ former municipality Ⓢ central Mexico; now part of Mexico City

Jack·son \ˈjak-sən\ city, capital of Mississippi

Jack·son·ville \ˈjak-sən-ˌvil\ city ⓃⒺ Florida

Jai·pur \ˈjī-ˌpùr\ city ⓃⓌ India

Ja·kar·ta *or* **Dja·kar·ta** \jə-ˈkär-tə\ *or formerly* **Ba·ta·via** \bə-ˈtā-vē-ə\ city, capital of Indonesia in ⓃⓌ Java

Ja·mai·ca \jə-ˈmā-kə\ island West Indies in Greater Antilles; an independent country; capital, Kingston — **Ja·mai·can** \-kən\ *adj or n*

James \ˈjāmz\ **1** — see DAKOTA **2** river 340 mi. (547 km.) long Virginia flowing Ⓔ into Chesapeake Bay

James Bay the Ⓢ extension of Hudson Bay between ⓃⒺ Ontario & Ⓦ Quebec

James·town \ˈjām-ˌstaùn\ ruined village Ⓔ Virginia on James River; first permanent English settlement in America (1607)

Jam·shed·pur \ˈjäm-ˌshed-ˌpù(ə)r\ city Ⓔ India

Ja·pan \jə-ˈpan, ji-, ja-\ country Ⓔ Asia consisting of Honshu, Hokkaido, Kyushu, Shikoku, & other islands in the Ⓦ Pacific; capital, Tokyo

Japan, Sea of *also* **East Sea** arm of the Pacific between Japan & main part of Asia

Ja·va \ˈjäv-ə, ˈjav-ə\ island Indonesia ⓈⓌ of Borneo; chief city, Jakarta — **Ja·van** \-ən\ *adj or n* — **Ja·va·nese** \ˌjav-ə-ˈnēz, jäv-, -ˈnēs\ *n*

Jef·fer·son City \ˈjef-ər-sən\ city, capital of Missouri

Jer·sey \ˈjər-zē\ island in English Channel — see CHANNEL 2 — **Jer·sey·ite** \-zē-ˌīt\ *n*

Jersey City city ⓃⒺ New Jersey on Hudson River

Je·ru·sa·lem \jə-ˈrü-s(ə-)ləm, -ˈrüz-(ə-)ləm\ city ⓃⓌ of Dead Sea divided 1948–67 between Israel & Jordan; capital of Israel since 1950 & formerly of ancient kingdom of Israel

Jid·da *or* **Jid·dah** \ˈjid-ə\ *or* **Jed·da** *or* **Jed·dah** \ˈjed-ə\ city Ⓦ Saudi Arabia on Red Sea

Ji·lin \ˈjē-ˈlin\ *or* **Ki·rin** \ˈkē-ˈrin\ city ⓃⒺ China

Ji·nan *or* **Tsi·nan** \ˈjē-ˈnän\ city Ⓔ China

Jin·zhou *or* **Chin–chou** *or* **Chin·chow** \ˈjin-ˈjō\ city ⓃⒺ China

Jiu·long \ˈjü-ˈlòŋ\ *or* **Kow·loon** \ˈkaù-ˈlün\ **1** peninsula ⓈⒺ China in Hong Kong opposite Hong Kong Island **2** city on Jiulong Peninsula

Jo·han·nes·burg \jō-ˈhan-əs-ˌbərg, -ˈhän-\ city ⓃⒺ Republic of South Africa

Jo·li·et \ˌjō-lē-ˈet\ city ⓃⒺ Illinois

Jor·dan \ˈjòrd-ᵊn\ **1** river 200 mi. (322 km.) long Israel & Jordan flowing Ⓢ from Syria into Dead Sea **2** country ⓈⓌ Asia in ⓃⓌ Arabia; capital, Amman — **Jor·da·ni·an** \jòr-ˈdā-nē-ən\ *adj or n*

Juan de Fu·ca, Strait of \ˌ(h)wän-də-ˈfyü-kə\ strait 100 mi. (161 km.) long between Vancouver Island, British Columbia, & Olympic Peninsula, Washington

Juba \ˈjü-bə, -ˌbä\ town, capital of South Sudan

Ju·daea *or* **Ju·dea** \jü-ˈdē-ə, -ˈdā-\ region of ancient Palestine forming its Ⓢ division under Persian, Greek, & Roman rule — **Ju·de·an** *also* **Ju·dae·an** \-ən\ *adj or n*

Jugoslavia — see YUGOSLAVIA

Ju·neau \ˈjü-nō, jü-ˈnō\ city, capital of Alaska

Ju·ra \ˈjùr-ə\ mountain range extending along boundary between France & Switzerland Ⓝ of Lake Geneva

Jut·land \ˈjət-lənd\ **1** peninsula Ⓝ Europe extending into North Sea and consisting of main part of Denmark & Ⓝ portion of Germany **2** the main part of Denmark

Ka·bul \ˈkäb-əl, kä-ˈbül\ city, capital of Afghanistan

Ka Lae \kä-ˈlä-ä\ *or* **South Cape** *or* **South Point** most southerly point of Hawaii & of U.S.

Kal·a·ha·ri \ˌkal-ə-ˈhär-ē\ desert region Ⓢ Africa Ⓝ of Orange River in Ⓢ Botswana & ⓃⓌ Republic of South Africa

Kalgan — see ZHANGJIAKOU

Ka·li·man·tan \ˌkal-ə-ˈman-ˌtan, ˌkäl-ə-ˈmän-ˌtän\ **1** BORNEO — its Indonesian name **2** the Ⓢ & Ⓔ portion of Borneo belonging to Indonesia; formerly part of Netherlands East Indies

Ka·li·nin·grad \kə-ˈlē-nən-ˌgrad\ *or German* **Kö·nigs·berg** \ˈkā-nigz-ˌbərg, *German* ˈkȫ-niks-ˌberk\ city & port Ⓝ Europe on the Baltic in a part of Russia separated from the rest of the country

Kam·chat·ka \kam-ˈchat-kə\ peninsula 750 mi. (1207 km.) long Ⓔ Russia

Kam·pa·la \käm-ˈpäl-ə\ city, capital of Uganda

Kampuchea — see CAMBODIA

Kan·da·har \ˈkän-də-ˌhär\ city ⓈⒺ Afghanistan

Ka·no \ˈkän-ō\ city Ⓝ central Nigeria

Kan·pur \ˈkän-ˌpù(ə)r\ city Ⓝ India on the Ganges

Kan·sas \ˈkan-zəs\ state Ⓦ central U.S.; capital, Topeka — **Kan·san** \-zən\ *adj or n*

\ə\ abut	\aù\ out	\i\ tip	\ò\ saw	\ù\ foot
\ər\ further	\ch\ chin	\ī\ life	\òi\ coin	\y\ yet
\a\ mat	\e\ pet	\j\ job	\th\ thin	\yü\ few
\ā\ take	\ē\ easy	\ŋ\ sing	\th\ this	\yù\ cure
\ä\ cot, cart	\g\ go	\ō\ bone	\ü\ food	\zh\ vision

Kansas City 1 city \boxed{NE} Kansas bordering on Kansas City, Missouri **2** city \boxed{W} Missouri

Kao·hsiung — see GAOXIONG

Ka·ra·chi \kə-'räch-ē\ city \boxed{S} Pakistan on Arabian Sea

Karaganda — see QARAGHANDY

Kar·a·ko·ram Pass \,kär-ə-'kŏr-əm, -'kȯr-\ mountain pass \boxed{NE} Kashmir in **Karakoram Range** (system connecting the Himalayas with the Pamirs)

Ka·re·lia \kə-'rē-lē-ə, -'rēl-yə\ region \boxed{NE} Europe in Finland & Russia — **Ka·re·lian** \-'rē-lē-ən, -'rēl-yən\ adj or n

Ka·roo or **Kar·roo** \kə-'rü\ plateau region \boxed{W} Republic of South Africa \boxed{W} of Drakensberg Mountains

Kash·mir \'kash-,mi(ə)r, 'kazh-, kash-'mi(ə)r, kazh-'mi(ə)r\ disputed territory \boxed{N} subcontinent of India; claimed by India & Pakistan — **Kash·miri** \kash-'mi(ə)r-ē, kazh-\ adj or n

Ka·thi·a·war \,kät-ē-ə-'wär\ peninsula \boxed{W} India \boxed{N} of Gulf of Khambat

Kath·man·du or **Kat·man·du** \,kat-,man-'dü\ city, capital of Nepal

Kat·mai, Mount \'kat-,mī\ volcano 6715 ft. (2047 m.) \boxed{S} Alaska on Alaska Peninsula

Kat·te·gat \'kat-i-,gat\ arm of North Sea between Sweden & \boxed{E} coast of Jutland Peninsula of Denmark

Kau·ai \kä-'wī\ island Hawaii \boxed{NW} of Oahu

Kau·nas \'kaú-nəs, -,näs\ city central Lithuania

Ka·wa·sa·ki \,kä-wə-'säk-ē\ city Japan in \boxed{E} Honshu \boxed{S} of Tokyo

Ka·zakh·stan also **Ka·zak·stan** \kə-,zak-'stan; kə-,zäk-'stän, ,kä-\ country \boxed{NW} central Asia; capital, Astana; a republic (**Ka·zakh Soviet Socialist Republic** \kə-,zak, -,zäk-\ ) of U.S.S.R. 1936–91 — **Kazakh** also **Ka·zak** n

Ka·zan \kə-'zan, -'zän(-yə)\ city \boxed{W} Russia

Kee·wa·tin \kē-'wät-ᵊn\ former district \boxed{N} Canada in \boxed{E} Northwest Territories \boxed{NW} of Hudson Bay; area now part of Nunavut

Ke·me·ro·vo \'kem-ə-rə-və, -,rō-və, -rə-,vō\ city \boxed{S} central Russia

Ke·nai \'kē-,nī\ peninsula \boxed{S} Alaska \boxed{E} of Cook Inlet

Kennedy, Cape — see CANAVERAL (Cape)

Ken·sing·ton and Chel·sea \'ken-ziŋ-tən-ən-'chel-sē, 'ken(t)-siŋ-\ borough of \boxed{W} Greater London, England

Kent \'kent\ county \boxed{SE} England — **Kent·ish** \'kent-ish\ adj

Ken·tucky \kən-'tək-ē\ state \boxed{E} central U.S.; capital, Frankfort — **Ken·tuck·i·an** \-ē-ən\ adj or n

Ken·ya \'ken-yə, 'kēn-\ **1** mountain 17,058 ft. (5199 m.) central Kenya **2** country \boxed{E} Africa \boxed{S} of Ethiopia; capital, Nairobi — **Ken·yan** \-yən\ adj or n

Key West \'kē-'west\ city \boxed{SW} Florida on Key West (island)

Kha·ba·rovsk \kə-'bär-əfsk\ city \boxed{SE} Russia

Kham·bat, Gulf of \'kəm-bət\ or **Gulf of Cam·bay** \kam-'bā\ inlet of Arabian Sea India \boxed{N} of Bombay

Khar·kiv \'kär-kəf, 'kar-\ or **Khar·kov** \'kär-,kȯf, -,kȯv, -kəf\ city \boxed{NE} Ukraine

Khar·toum \kär-'tüm\ city, capital of Sudan

Khmer Republic — see CAMBODIA

Khy·ber \'kī-bər\ pass 33 mi. (53 km.) long on border between Afghanistan & Pakistan

Ki·bo \'kē-bō\ mountain peak 19,340 ft. (5895 m.) of Kilimanjaro \boxed{NE} Tanzania; highest point in Africa

Kiel — see NORD-OSTSEE

Ki·ev \'kē-,(y)ef, -,(y)ev, -(y)əf\ or Ukrainian **Kyiv** \'kyē-ü\ city, capital of Ukraine

Ki·ga·li \ki-'gäl-ē\ city, capital of Rwanda

Ki·lau·ea \,kē-,laú-'ā-ə\ volcanic crater Hawaii on Hawaii Island on \boxed{E} slope of Mauna Loa

Kil·i·man·ja·ro \,kil-ə-mən-'jär-ō, -'jar-\ mountain \boxed{NE} Tanzania; highest in Africa — see KIBO

Kil·lar·ney, Lakes of \kil-'är-nē\ three lakes \boxed{SW} Ireland

Kings·ton \'kiŋ-stən\ city & port, capital of Jamaica

Kingston upon Hull — see HULL

Kingston upon Thames borough of \boxed{SW} Greater London, England

Kings·town \'kiŋ-,staún\ seaport, capital of Saint Vincent and the Grenadines

Kin·sha·sa \kin-'shäs-ə\ city, capital of Democratic Republic of the Congo

Kirghiz Republic or **Kirgiz Republic** — see KYRGYZSTAN

Ki·ri·bati \'kir-ə-,bas\ island group \boxed{W} Pacific; an independent country; capital, Tarawa

Kirin — see JILIN

Kirk·wall \'kər-,kwȯl\ town and port \boxed{N} Scotland, capital of Orkney Islands

Kishinev — see CHISINAU

Ki·ta·kyu·shu \kē-'tä-kē-'ü-shü\ city Japan in \boxed{N} Kyushu

Kitch·e·ner \'kich-(ə-)nər\ city \boxed{SE} Ontario, Canada

Kit·ty Hawk \'kit-ē-,hȯk\ town \boxed{E} North Carolina

Klon·dike \'klän-,dīk\ region \boxed{NW} Canada in central Yukon in valley of Klondike River

Knox·ville \'näks-,vil, -vəl\ city \boxed{E} Tennessee

Ko·be \'kō-bē, -,bā\ city Japan in \boxed{S} Honshu

Ko·di·ak \'kōd-ē-,ak\ island \boxed{S} Alaska \boxed{E} of Alaska Peninsula

Ko·la \'kō-lə\ peninsula \boxed{NW} Russia

Königsberg — see KALININGRAD

Ko·rea \kə-'rē-ə, especially South kō-\ country \boxed{E} Asia between Yellow Sea & East Sea (Sea of Japan); capital, Seoul; divided after World War II at 38th parallel of latitude into independent countries of **North Korea** (capital, Pyongyang) & **South Korea** (capital, Seoul) — **Korean** adj or n

Ko·ror \'kȯr-,ȯr\ town, former capital of Palau

Kos·ci·us·ko, Mount \,käz-ē-'əs-kō\ mountain 7310 ft. (2228 m.) \boxed{SE} Australia in \boxed{SE} New South Wales; highest in Great Dividing Range & in Australia

Ko·so·vo \'kȯ-sō-,vō, 'käs-ō-\ country \boxed{S} Europe in Balkan Peninsula; capital, Pristina; an autonomous province of Serbia 1946–2008

Kowloon — see JIULONG

Krak·a·tau \,krak-ə-'taú\ or **Krak·a·toa** \-'tō-ə\ island & volcano Indonesia between Sumatra & Java

Kra·kow \'kräk-,aú, 'krak-, 'kräk-, -ō, Polish 'kräk-,üf\ city \boxed{S} Poland

Kras·no·dar \'kras-nə-,där\ city \boxed{SW} Russia

Kras·no·yarsk \,kras-nə-'yärsk\ city \boxed{S} central Russia

Kry·vyy Rih \kri-'vē-'rik\ or **Kri·voy Rog** \,kriv-,ȯi-'rȯg, -'rȯk\ city \boxed{SE} central Ukraine

K2 \'kā-'tü\ or **God·win Aus·ten** \,gäd-wə-'nȯs-tən, -'näs-tən\ mountain 28,250 ft. (8611 m.) \boxed{N} Kashmir in Karakoram Range; second highest in the world

Kua·la Lum·pur \,kwäl-ə-'lúm-,pù(ə)r, -'ləm-\ city, capital of Malaysia

Kuei·yang — see GUIYANG

Kun·lun \'kün-lün\ mountain system \boxed{W} China extending \boxed{E} from the Pamirs; highest peak Muztag 25,340 ft. (7724 m.)

Kun·ming \'kún-'miŋ\ city \boxed{S} China

Kur·di·stan \,kúr-də-'stan, ,kər-, -'stän; 'kər-də-,\ region \boxed{SW} Asia chiefly in \boxed{E} Turkey, \boxed{NW} Iran, & \boxed{N} Iraq — **Kurd** \'kú(ə)rd, 'kərd\ n — **Kurd·ish** \-ish\ adj

Ku·ril or **Ku·rile** \'kyúr-,ēl, 'kúr-; kyú-'rē(ə)l, kù-\ islands Russia in \boxed{W} Pacific between Kamchatka Peninsula & Hokkaido Island

Ku·wait \kə-'wāt\ **1** country \boxed{SW} Asia in Arabia at head of Persian Gulf **2** city, its capital — **Ku·waiti** \-'wāt-ē\ adj or n

Kuybyshev — see SAMARA

Kuz·netsk Basin \kúz-'netsk\ or **Kuz·bas** or **Kuz·bass** \'kúz-,bas\ basin \boxed{S} central Russia

Kwa·ja·lein \'kwäj-ə-lən, -,lān\ island \boxed{W} Pacific in Marshall Islands

Kwang·ju or **Gwang·ju** \'gwän-jü\ city \boxed{SW} South Korea

Kwa·Zu·lu–Na·tal \kwä-'zü-lü-nä-'täl\ province E Republic of South Africa

Kyiv — see KIEV

Kyo·to \kē-'ōt-ō\ city Japan in W central Honshu; formerly capital of Japan

Kyr·gyz·stan \ˌkir-gi-'stan, -'stän; 'kir-gi-ˌ\ country W central Asia; capital, Bishkek; a republic (**Kir·giz Republic** or **Kir·ghiz Republic** \(ˌ)kir-'gēz\) of U.S.S.R. 1936–91

Kyu·shu \kē-'ü-shü\ island Japan S of W end of Honshu

Lab·ra·dor \'lab-rə-ˌdȯ(ə)r\ **1** peninsula E Canada between Hudson Bay & the Atlantic divided between the provinces of Quebec & Newfoundland and Labrador **2** the part of the peninsula belonging to the province of Newfoundland and Labrador — **Lab·ra·dor·ean** or **Lab·ra·dor·ian** \ˌlab-rə-'dȯr-ē-ən, -'dōr-\ adj or n

Lac·ca·dive \'lak-ə-ˌdēv, -ˌdīv\ islands India in Arabian Sea N of Maldive Islands

Lacedaemon — see SPARTA

La·co·nia \lə-'kō-nē-ə, -nyə\ ancient country S Greece in SE Peloponnese; capital, Sparta — **La·co·nian** \-nē-ən, -nyən\ adj or n

La·fay·ette \ˌlaf-ē-'et, ˌläf-\ city S Louisiana

La·gos \'lä-ˌgäs\ city, former capital of Nigeria

La·hore \lə-'hō(ə)r, -'hȯ(ə)r\ city E Pakistan

Lake District region NW England containing many lakes & mountains

Lake·wood \'lā-ˌkwu̇d\ city central Colorado

Lam·beth \'lam-bəth, -ˌbeth\ borough of S Greater London, England

La·nai \lə-'nī\ island Hawaii W of Maui

Lan·ca·shire \'laŋ-kə-ˌshi(ə)r, -shər\ or **Lan·cas·ter** \'laŋ-kə-stər\ county NW England — **Lan·cas·tri·an** \laŋ-'kas-trē-ən, lan-\ adj or n

Lan·cas·ter \'laŋ-kə-stər; 'lan-ˌkas-tər, 'laŋ-\ **1** city SW California NE of Los Angeles **2** city NW England

Land's End \'lan(d)-'zend\ cape SW England; most westerly point of England, at 5° 41′ W longitude

Lan·sing \'lan(t)-siŋ\ city, capital of Michigan

Lan·zhou or **Lan–chou** \'län-'jō\ city W China

Laos \'laus, 'lā-ˌäs, 'lä-ōs\ country SE Asia in Indochina NE of Thailand; capital, Vientiane — **Laotian** adj or n

La Paz \lə-'paz, -'päz, -'päs\ city, administrative capital of Bolivia

Lap·land \'lap-ˌland, -lənd\ region N Europe above the Arctic Circle in N Norway, N Sweden, N Finland, & Kola Peninsula of Russia — **Lap·land·er** \-ˌlan-dər, -lən-\ n

La·re·do \lə-'rā-(ˌ)dō\ city S Texas on the Rio Grande

Larne \'lärn\ district NE Northern Ireland

Las·sen Peak \'las-ᵊn\ volcano 10,457 ft. (3187 m.) N California at S end of Cascade Range

Las Ve·gas \läs-'vā-gəs\ city SE Nevada

Latin America 1 Spanish America and Brazil **2** all of the Americas S of the U.S. — **Latin–American** adj — **Latin American** n

Latin Quarter section of Paris, France S of the Seine

Lat·via \'lat-vē-ə\ country E Europe on Baltic Sea; capital, Riga; a republic of U.S.S.R. 1940–91

Lau·ren·tian Mountains \lȯ-'ren-chən\ hills E Canada in S Quebec N of the Saint Lawrence on S edge of Canadian Shield

Laurentian Plateau — see CANADIAN SHIELD

La·val \lə-'val\ city S Quebec NW of Montreal

Law·rence \'lȯr-ən(t)s, 'lär-\ city NE corner of Massachusetts

League of Nations political organization established at the end of World War I; replaced by United Nations 1946

Leb·a·non \'leb-ə-nən, -ˌnän\ **1** mountains Lebanon (country) running parallel to coast **2** country SW Asia on the Mediterranean; capital, Beirut — **Leb·a·nese** \ˌleb-ə-'nēz, -'nēs\ adj or n

Leeds \'lēdz\ city N England

Lee·ward Islands \'lē-wərd\ **1** islands Hawaii extending WNW from main islands of the group **2** islands South Pacific in W Society Islands **3** islands West Indies in N Lesser Antilles extending from Virgin Islands (on N) to Dominica (on S)

Le Ha·vre \lə-'hävrᵉ\ city N France on English Channel

Leh·man Caves \'lē-mən\ limestone caverns E Nevada

Leices·ter \'les-tər\ city central England ENE of Birmingham

Leices·ter·shire \'les-tər-ˌshi(ə)r, -shər\ or **Leicester** county central England

Lein·ster \'len(t)-stər\ province E Ireland

Leip·zig \'līp-sig, -sik\ city E Germany

Le·na \'lē-nə, 'lā-\ river about 2700 mi. (4345 km.) long E Russia, flowing NE & N from mountains W of Lake Baikal into Arctic Ocean

Leningrad — see SAINT PETERSBURG 2

Le·ón \lā-'ōn\ city central Mexico

Ler·wick \'lər-(ˌ)wik, 'le(ə)r-\ town and port N Scotland in the Shetlands

Le·so·tho \lə-'sō-tō, -'sü-(ˌ)tü\ country S Africa surrounded by Republic of South Africa; formerly British territory of **Ba·su·to·land** \bə-'süt-ə-ˌland\, now an independent country; capital, Maseru

Lesser Antilles islands in the West Indies including Virgin Islands, Leeward Islands, & Windward Islands, Barbados, Trinidad, Tobago, & islands in the S Caribbean N of Venezuela — see GREATER ANTILLES

Le·vant \lə-'vant\ the countries bordering on the E Mediterranean — **Lev·an·tine** \'lev-ən-ˌtīn, -ˌtēn, lə-'van-\ adj or n

Lew·es \'lü-əs\ town S England

Lew·i·sham \'lü-ə-shəm\ borough of SE Greater London, England

Lewis with Har·ris \ˌlü-ə-swəth-'har-əs, -swəth-\ island NW Scotland in Outer Hebrides

Lex·ing·ton \'lek-siŋ-tən\ **1** city NE central Kentucky **2** town NE Massachusetts

Ley·te \'lāt-ē\ island Philippines S of Samar

Lha·sa \'läs-ə, 'las-\ city SW China, capital of Tibet

Li·be·ria \lī-'bir-ē-ə\ country W Africa on the North Atlantic; capital, Monrovia — **Li·be·ri·an** \-ē-ən\ adj or n

Lib·er·ty \'lib-ərt-ē\ or formerly **Bed·loe's** \'bed-ˌlōz\ island SE New York; site of the Statue of Liberty

Li·bre·ville \'lē-brə-ˌvil, -ˌvē(ə)l\ city, capital of Gabon

Lib·ya \'lib-ē-ə\ **1** the part of Africa N of the Sahara & just W of Egypt — an ancient name **2** N Africa W of Egypt — an ancient name **3** country N Africa on the Mediterranean W of Egypt; capital, Tripoli — **Lib·y·an** \'lib-ē-ən\ adj or n

Libyan desert N Africa W of the Nile in Libya, Egypt, & Sudan

Liech·ten·stein \'lik-tən-ˌstīn, -ˌshtīn\ country W Europe between Austria & Switzerland; capital, Vaduz — **Liech·ten·stein·er** \-ˌstī-nər, -ˌshtī-\ n

Lif·fey \'lif-ē\ river 50 mi. (80 km.) long E Ireland

Li·gu·ria \lə-'gyu̇r-ē-ə\ region NW Italy on Ligurian Sea; capital, Genoa — **Li·gu·ri·an** \-ē-ən\ adj or n

Ligurian Sea arm of the Mediterranean N of Corsica

Li·lon·gwe \li-'lȯŋ-wā\ city, capital of Malawi

Li·ma \'lē-mə\ city, capital of Peru

Lim·a·vady \ˌlim-ə-'vad-ē\ district NW Northern Ireland

Lim·po·po \lim-'pō-pō\ **1** river 1000 mi. (1609 km.) long Africa flowing from Republic of South Africa into Indian Ocean in Mozambique **2** or formerly **Northern** province NE Republic of South Africa

\ə\ **abut**	\au̇\ **out**	\i\ **tip**	\ȯ\ **saw**	\u̇\ **foot**	
\ər\ **further**	\ch\ **chin**	\ī\ **life**	\ȯi\ **coin**	\y\ **yet**	
\a\ **mat**	\e\ **pet**	\j\ **job**	\th\ **thin**	\yü\ **few**	
\ā\ **take**	\ē\ **easy**	\ŋ\ **sing**	\th\ **this**	\yu̇\ **cure**	
\ä\ **cot, cart**	\g\ **go**	\ō\ **bone**	\ü\ **food**	\zh\ **vision**	

Lin·coln \'liŋ-kən\ **1** city, capital of Nebraska **2** city E England

Lin·coln·shire \'liŋ-kən-ˌshi(ə)r, -shər\ *or* **Lincoln** county E England

Line \'līn\ islands Kiribati S of Hawaii; formerly divided between U.S. & United Kingdom

Lis·bon \'liz-bən\ *or Portuguese* **Lis·boa** \lēzh-'vō-ə\ city, capital of Portugal

Lis·burn \'liz-(ˌ)bərn\ district E Northern Ireland

Lith·u·a·nia \ˌlith-(y)ə-'wā-nē-ə, -nyə\ country E Europe; capital, Vilnius; a republic of U.S.S.R. 1940–91

Lit·tle Rock \'lit-ᵊl-ˌräk\ city, capital of Arkansas

Liv·er·pool \'liv-ər-ˌpül\ city NW England

Li·vo·nia \lə-'vō-nē-ə, -nyə\ city SE Michigan

Lju·blja·na \lē-ˌü-blē-'än-ə\ city, capital of Slovenia

Llan·drin·dod Wells \hlan-'drin-ˌdód-, lan-\ town E Wales

Lla·no Es·ta·ca·do \'lan-(ˌ)ō-ˌes-ta-'käd-ō, 'län-\ *or* **Staked Plain** \'stāk(t)-\ plateau region SE New Mexico & NW Texas

Lo·bam·ba \lō-'bäm-bə\ town, legislative capital of Swaziland

Lodz \'lüj, 'lädz\ city central Poland WSW of Warsaw

Lo·fo·ten \'lō-ˌfōt-ᵊn\ islands NW Norway

Lo·gan, Mount \'lō-gən\ mountain 19,551 ft. (5959 m.) NW Canada in Saint Elias Range; highest in Canada & second highest in North America

Loire \lə-'wär\ river 634 mi. (1020 km.) long central France flowing NW & W into Bay of Biscay

Lo·mé \lō-'mā\ city, capital of Togo

Lo·mond, Loch \-'lō-mənd\ lake S central Scotland

Lon·don \'lən-dən\ **1** city SE Ontario, Canada **2** city, capital of England & of United Kingdom on the Thames; consists of **City of London** & Greater London metropolitan county — **Lon·don·er** \-də-nər\ *n*

Londonderry — see DERRY

Long Beach city SW California S of Los Angeles

Long Island island 118 mi. (190 km.) long SE New York S of Connecticut

Long Island Sound inlet of the Atlantic between Connecticut & Long Island, New York

Lon·gueuil \lòŋ-'gā(ə)l\ city Canada in S Quebec E of Montreal

Lor·raine \lə-'rān, lò-\ region NE France

Los An·ge·les \lò-'san-jə-ləs *also* -'saŋ-g(ə-)ləs\ city SW California

Lou·ise, Lake \lü-'ēz\ lake SW Alberta, Canada

Lou·i·si·ana \lù-ˌē-zē-'an-ə, ˌlü-ə-zē-, ˌlü-zē-\ state S U.S.; capital, Baton Rouge — **Lou·i·si·an·ian** \-'an-ē-ən, -'an-yən\ *or* **Lou·i·si·an·an** \-'an-ən\ *adj or n*

Louisiana Purchase area W central U.S. between Rocky Mountains & the Mississippi purchased 1803 from France

Lou·is·ville \'lü-i-ˌvil, -vəl\ city N Kentucky on the Ohio River

Low Countries region W Europe consisting of modern Belgium, Luxembourg, & the Netherlands

Low·ell \'lō-əl\ city NE Massachusetts NW of Boston

Lower 48 the continental states of the U.S. excluding Alaska

Low·lands \'lō-lən(d)z, -ˌlan(d)z\ the central & E part of Scotland

Lu·an·da \lü-'an-də\ city, capital of Angola

Lub·bock \'ləb-ək\ city NW Texas

Lu·bum·ba·shi \ˌlü-büm-'bäsh-ē\ city SE Democratic Republic of the Congo

Luck·now \'lək-ˌnaù\ city N India ESE of Delhi

Lüda *or* **Lü–ta** — see DALIAN

Lu·ray Caverns \'lü-ˌrā, lü-'rā\ series of caves N Virginia

Lu·sa·ka \lü-'säk-ə\ city, capital of Zambia

Lü·shun \'lü-'shún\ *or* **Port Ar·thur** \'är-thər\ seaport NE China; part of greater Dalian

Lu·ton \'lüt-ᵊn\ town SE central England

Lux·em·bourg *or German* **Lux·em·burg** \'lək-səm-ˌbərg, 'lúk-səm-ˌbú(ə)rg\ **1** country W Europe bordered by Belgium, France, & Germany **2** city, its capital — **Lux·em·bourg·er** \-ˌbər-gər, -ˌbúr-\ *n* — **Lux·em·bourg·ian** \ˌlək-səm-'bər-gē-ən, ˌlúk-səm-'búr-\ *adj*

Lu·zon \lü-'zän\ island N Philippines

L'viv \lə-'vē-ü, -'vēf\ *or* **L'vov** \lə-'vóf, -'vòv\ *or Polish* **Lwów** \lə-'vúf, -'vüv\ city W Ukraine

Lyallpur — see FAISALABAD

Lyd·ia \'lid-ē-ə\ ancient country W Asia Minor on the Aegean — **Lyd·i·an** \-ē-ən\ *adj or n*

Lynn \'lin\ city NE corner of Massachusetts

Lyon \'lyòⁿ\ *or* **Ly·ons** \lē-'ōⁿ, 'lī-ənz\ city SE central France

Ma·cao *or Portuguese* **Ma·cau** \mə-'kaù\ *or Chinese* **Ao·men** \'aù-'mən\ **1** special administrative region on coast of SE China W of Hong Kong **2** city, its capital — **Mac·a·nese** \ˌmak-ə-'nēz, -'nēs\ *n*

Mac·e·do·nia \ˌmas-ə-'dō-nyə, -nē-ə\ **1** region S Europe in Balkan Peninsula in NE Greece, the former Yugoslav section & now independent country of Macedonia, & SW Bulgaria including territory of ancient kingdom of Macedonia (**Mac·e·don** \'mas-əd-ən, -ə-ˌdän\ ) **2** independent country S central Balkan Peninsula; capital, Skopje; a former republic of Yugoslavia — **Mac·e·do·nian** \ˌmas-ə-'dō-nyən, -nē-ən\ *adj or n*

Mac·gil·li·cud·dy's Reeks \mə-ˌgil-ə-ˌkəd-ēz-'rēks\ mountains SW Ireland; highest Carrantuohill 3414 ft. (1041 m.)

Ma·chu Pic·chu \ˌmäch-ü-'pēk-chü\ site SE Peru of ancient Inca city

Mac·ken·zie \mə-'ken-zē\ **1** river 1120 mi. (1802 km.) long NW Canada flowing from Great Slave Lake NW into Beaufort Sea **2** former district NW Canada in Northwest Territories in basin of Mackenzie River; area now split between Northwest Territories & Nunavut

Mack·i·nac, Straits of \'mak-ə-ˌnak, -ˌnó\ channel N Michigan connecting Lake Huron & Lake Michigan

Ma·con \'mā-kən\ city central Georgia

Mad·a·gas·car \ˌmad-ə-'gas-kər\ *or formerly* **Mal·a·gasy Re·public** \ˌmal-ə-ˌgas-ē\ island country W Indian Ocean off SE Africa; capital, Antananarivo — **Mad·a·gas·can** \ˌmad-ə-'gas-kən\ *adj or n*

Ma·dei·ra \mə-'dir-ə, -'der-\ **1** river 2013 mi. (3239 km.) long W Brazil flowing NE into the Amazon **2** islands in the North Atlantic N of the Canary Islands belonging to Portugal **3** island; chief of the Madeira group — **Ma·dei·ran** \-ən\ *adj or n*

Ma·di·nat ash Sha'b \mə-'dē-ˌnət-ash-'shab\ city S Yemen

Mad·i·son \'mad-ə-sən\ city, capital of Wisconsin

Ma·dras \mə-'dras, -'dräs\ *or* **Chen·nai** \'chen-ˌī\ city SE India

Ma·drid \mə-'drid\ city, capital of Spain

Ma·du·rai \ˌmäd-ə-'rī\ city S India

Ma·gel·lan, Strait of \mə-'jel-ən\ strait at S end of South America between mainland & Tierra del Fuego

Magh·er·a·felt \'mär-ə-ˌfelt, 'mak-ə-rə-ˌfelt\ district central Northern Ireland

Maid·stone \'mād-stən, -ˌstōn\ town SE England

Main \'mīn, 'mān\ river 325 mi. (523 km.) long S central Germany flowing W into the Rhine

Maine \'mān\ state NE U.S.; capital, Augusta — **Main·er** \'mā-nər\ *n*

Ma·jor·ca \mə-'jòr-kə, -'yòr-\ *or Spanish* **Ma·llor·ca** \mə-'yòr-kə\ island Spain in W Mediterranean — **Ma·jor·can** \-'jòr-kən, -'yòr-\ *adj or n*

Ma·ju·ro \mə-'jür-ō\ atoll W Pacific; contains capital of Marshall Islands

Mal·a·bar Coast \'mal-ə-ˌbär\ region SW India on Arabian Sea

Ma·la·bo \mä-'lä-bō\ city, capital of Equatorial Guinea

Ma·lac·ca, Strait of \mə-'lak-ə, -'läk-\ channel between Ⓢ Malay Peninsula & island of Sumatra

Ma·la·wi \mə-'lä-wē, -'laú-ē\ *or formerly* **Ny·asa·land** \nī-'as-ə-,land, nē-\ country Ⓢ Ⓔ Africa on Lake Malawi; an independent state since 1964; capital, Lilongwe — **Ma·la·wi·an** \-ən\ *adj or n*

Malawi, Lake *or* **Lake Ny·asa** \nī-'as-ə, nē-\ lake Ⓢ Ⓔ Africa in Malawi, Mozambique, & Tanzania

Ma·lay \mə-'lā, 'mā-lā\ **1** archipelago Ⓢ Ⓔ Asia including Sumatra, Java, Borneo, Sulawesi, Moluccas, & Timor; usually thought to include the Philippines & sometimes New Guinea **2** peninsula Ⓢ Ⓔ Asia divided between Thailand & Malaysia (country)

Ma·laya \mə-'lā-ə, mä-\ **1** the Malay Peninsula **2** former country Ⓢ Ⓔ Asia on Malay Peninsula; since 1963 part of Malaysia

Ma·lay·sia \mə-'lā-zh(ē-)ə, -sh(ē-)ə\ **1** the Malay Archipelago **2** the Malay Peninsula & Malay Archipelago **3** country Ⓢ Ⓔ Asia, a union of Malaya, Sabah, Sarawak, & (until 1965) Singapore; capital, Kuala Lumpur — **Ma·lay·sian** \mə-'lā-zhən, -shən\ *adj or n*

Mal·dives \'mȯl-,dēvz, -,dīvz\ islands in Indian Ocean Ⓢ of the Laccadives; formerly under British protection; since 1965 an independent country; capital on **Ma·le Atoll** \'mäl-ē\ — **Mal·div·i·an** \mȯl-'div-ē-ən\ *adj or n*

Ma·li \'mäl-ē, 'mal-ē\ country Ⓦ Africa; capital, Bamako — **Ma·li·an** \-ē-ən\ *adj or n*

Mal·ta \'mȯl-tə\ islands in the Mediterranean Ⓢ of Sicily; a former British colony; an independent country since 1964; capital, Valletta — **Maltese** *adj or n*

Malvinas, Islas — see FALKLAND ISLANDS

Mam·moth Cave \,mam-əth\ limestone caverns Ⓢ Ⓦ central Kentucky

Man, Isle of \'man\ island British Isles in Irish Sea; has own legislature & laws

Ma·na·gua \mə-'näg-wə\ city, capital of Nicaragua

Ma·na·ma \mə-'nam-ə\ city, capital of Bahrain

Man·ches·ter \'man-,ches-tər, -chə-stər\ **1** city Ⓢ central New Hampshire; largest in state **2** city Ⓝ Ⓦ England in Greater Manchester

Man·chu·ria \man-'chùr-ē-ə\ region Ⓝ Ⓔ China Ⓢ of the Amur — **Man·chu·ri·an** \man-'chùr-ē-ən\ *adj or n*

Man·hat·tan \man-'hat-ᵊn, mən-\ **1** island Ⓢ Ⓔ New York in New York City **2** borough of New York City consisting chiefly of Manhattan Island

Ma·nila \mə-'nil-ə\ city, capital of Philippines in Ⓦ Luzon

Man·i·to·ba \,man-ə-'tō-bə\ province central Canada; capital, Winnipeg — **Man·i·to·ban** \-'tō-bən\ *adj or n*

Man·i·tou·lin \,man-ə-'tü-lən\ island 80 mi. (129 km.) long Ⓢ Ontario in Lake Huron

Ma·pu·to \mä-'pü-tō\ city, capital of Mozambique

Mar·a·cai·bo \,mar-ə-'kī-bō\ city Ⓝ Ⓦ Venezuela

Maracaibo, Lake extension of a gulf of the Caribbean Ⓝ Ⓦ Venezuela

Mar·a·thon \'mar-ə-,thän, -thən\ plain Ⓔ Greece Ⓝ Ⓔ of Athens

Mar·i·ana \,mar-ē-'an-ə, ,mer-\ islands Ⓦ Pacific Ⓝ of Caroline Islands; comprise Commonwealth of Northern Mariana Islands & Guam

Mariana Trench ocean trench Ⓦ Pacific extending from Ⓢ Ⓔ of Guam to Ⓝ Ⓦ of Mariana Islands; deepest in world

Ma·rin·du·que \,mar-ən-'dü-kā, ,mär-\ island central Philippines

Maritime Provinces the Canadian provinces of New Brunswick, Nova Scotia, & Prince Edward Island & sometimes thought to include Newfoundland and Labrador

Ma·ri·u·pol' \,mar-ē-'ü-,pȯl\ *or 1949–89* **Zhda·nov** \zhə-'dän-əf\ city Ⓔ Ukraine

Mar·ma·ra, Sea of \'mär-mə-rə\ sea Ⓝ Ⓦ Turkey connected with Black Sea by the Bosporus & with Aegean Sea by the Dardanelles

Marne \'märn\ river 325 mi. (523 km.) long Ⓝ Ⓔ France flowing Ⓦ into the Seine

Mar·que·sas \mär-'kā-zəz, -zəs, -səz, -səs\ islands South Pacific belonging to France — **Mar·que·san** \-zən, -sən\ *adj or n*

Mar·ra·kech \mə-'räk-ish, ,mar-ə-'kesh\ city central Morocco

Mar·seille \mär-'sā\ *or* **Mar·seilles** \mär-'sā, -'sā(ə)lz\ *or ancient* **Mas·sil·ia** \mə-'sil-ē-ə\ city Ⓢ Ⓔ France

Mar·shall Islands \'mär-shəl\ islands Ⓦ Pacific Ⓔ of the Carolines; formerly part of Trust Territory of the Pacific Islands; an independent republic in association with U.S.; capital, Majuro — **Mar·shall·ese** \,mär-shə-'lēz, -'lēs\ *adj or n*

Mar·tha's Vineyard \,mär-thəz\ island Ⓢ Ⓔ Massachusetts off Ⓢ Ⓦ coast of Cape Cod Ⓦ Ⓝ Ⓦ of Nantucket

Mar·ti·nique \,märt-ᵊn-'ēk\ island West Indies in the Windward Islands; an overseas division of France; capital, Fort-de-France

Mary·land \'mer-ə-lənd\ state Ⓔ U.S.; capital, Annapolis — **Mary·land·er** \-lən-dər, -,lan-\ *n*

Mas·ba·te \,mäz-'bät-ē\ island central Philippines

Mas·e·ru \'maz-ə-,rü\ city, capital of Lesotho

Mash·had \mə-'shad\ city Ⓝ Ⓔ Iran

Ma·son–Dix·on Line \,mās-ᵊn-'dik-sən\ boundary between Maryland & Pennsylvania; was in part boundary between free & slave states

Masqat — see MUSCAT

Mas·sa·chu·setts \,mas(-ə)-'chü-səts, -zəts\ state Ⓝ Ⓔ U.S.; capital, Boston

Mat·a·be·le·land \,mat-ə-'bē-lē-,land\ region Ⓢ Ⓦ Zimbabwe

Mat·lock \'mat-,läk\ town Ⓝ England

Mat·ter·horn \'mat-ər-,hȯ(ə)rn, 'mät-\ mountain 14,691 ft. (4478 m.) on border between Switzerland & Italy

Maui \'maú-ē\ island Hawaii Ⓝ Ⓦ of Hawaii Island

Mau·na Kea \,maú-nə-'kā-ə\ extinct volcano 13,796 ft. (4205 m.) Hawaii in Ⓝ central Hawaii Island

Mau·na Loa \,maú-nə-'lō-ə\ volcano 13,680 ft. (4170 m.) Hawaii in Ⓢ central Hawaii Island

Mau·re·ta·nia *or* **Mau·ri·ta·nia** \,mȯr-ə-'tā-nē-ə, ,mär-, -nyə\ ancient country Ⓝ Ⓦ Africa in modern Morocco & Ⓦ Algeria — **Mau·re·ta·ni·an** \-nē-ən, -nyən\ *adj or n*

Mauritania country Ⓝ Ⓦ Africa on the Atlantic Ⓝ of Senegal River; capital, Nouakchott — **Mauritanian** *adj or n*

Mau·ri·tius \mȯ-'rish-(ē-)əs\ island in Indian Ocean Ⓔ of Madagascar; an independent country; capital, Port Louis — **Mau·ri·tian** \-'rish-ən\ *adj or n*

May, Cape \'mā\ cape Ⓢ New Jersey at entrance to Delaware Bay

Ma·yon, Mount \mä-'yōn\ volcano 8077 ft. (2462 m.) Philippines in Ⓢ Ⓔ Luzon

Ma·yotte \mä-'yät\ island Comoros; a French dependency

Ma·za·ma, Mount \mə-'zäm-ə\ prehistoric mountain Ⓢ Ⓦ Oregon the collapse of whose top formed Crater Lake

Mba·bane \,em-bə-'bän-ā\ town, capital of Swaziland

Mbi·ni \em-'bē-nē\ *or formerly* **Río Mu·ni** \,rē-ō-'mü-nē\ mainland portion of Equatorial Guinea

Mc·Al·len \mə-'kal-ən\ city Ⓢ Texas

McKinley, Mount — see DENALI

Mead, Lake \'mēd\ reservoir Ⓝ Ⓦ Arizona & Ⓢ Ⓔ Nevada formed by Hoover Dam in Colorado River

Mec·ca \'mek-ə\ city Ⓦ Saudi Arabia containing the Great Mosque of Islam

\ə\ abut	\aú\ out	\i\ tip	\ȯ\ saw	\ù\ foot
\ər\ further	\ch\ chin	\ī\ life	\ȯi\ coin	\y\ yet
\a\ mat	\e\ pet	\j\ job	\th\ thin	\yü\ few
\ā\ take	\ē\ easy	\ŋ\ sing	\th\ this	\yù\ cure
\ä\ cot, cart	\g\ go	\ō\ bone	\ü\ food	\zh\ vision

Me·dan \mā-'dän\ city Indonesia in [N] Sumatra

Me·de·llín \med-ᵊl-'ēn, ˌmā-thə-'yēn\ city [NW] Colombia

Me·di·na \mə-'dē-nə\ city [W] Saudi Arabia

Med·i·ter·ra·nean \ˌmed-ə-tə-'rā-nē-ən, -nyən\ sea 2300 mi. (3700 km.) long between Europe & Africa connecting with the Atlantic through Strait of Gibraltar

Me·kong \'mā-'kòŋ, -'käŋ\ river 2600 mi. (4184 km.) long [SE] Asia flowing from [E] Tibet [S] & [SE] into South China Sea in [S] Vietnam

Mel·a·ne·sia \ˌmel-ə-'nē-zhə, -shə\ islands of the Pacific [NE] of Australia & [S] of Micronesia including Bismarck, the Solomons, Vanuatu, New Caledonia, & the Fijis

Mel·bourne \'mel-bərn\ city [SE] Australia, capital of Victoria

Mel·e·ke·ok \'mel-ə-ˌkā-ˌók\ town, capital of Palau

Me·los or **Mi·los** \'mē-ˌläs\ island Greece

Mel·ville \'mel-ˌvil\ 1 island [N] Canada, split between Northwest Territories & Nunavut 2 peninsula Canada in Nunavut

Mem·phis \'mem(p)-fəs\ 1 city [SW] Tennessee 2 ancient city [N] Egypt [S] of modern Cairo

Mem·phre·ma·gog, Lake \ˌmem-fri-'mā-ˌgäg\ lake on border between Canada (Quebec) & U.S. (Vermont)

Men·do·ci·no, Cape \ˌmen-də-'sē-nō\ cape [NW] California

Mer·cia \'mər-sh(ē-)ə\ ancient Anglo-Saxon kingdom central England — **Mer·cian** \'mər-shən\ adj or n

Mer·sey \'mər-zē\ river 70 mi. (113 km.) long [NW] England flowing [NW] & [W] into Irish Sea

Mer·sey·side \'mər-zē-ˌsīd\ metropolitan county [NW] England; includes Liverpool

Mer·ton \'mərt-ᵊn\ borough of [SW] Greater London, England

Me·sa \'mā-sə\ city [S] central Arizona

Me·sa·bi Range \mə-'säb-ē\ region [NE] Minnesota that contains iron ore

Mes·o·po·ta·mia \ˌmes-(ə-)pə-'tā-mē-ə, -myə\ 1 region [SW] Asia between Euphrates & Tigris rivers 2 the entire Tigris-Euphrates valley — **Mes·o·po·ta·mian** \-mē-ən, -myən\ adj or n

Mes·quite \mə-'skēt\ city [NE] Texas [E] of Dallas

Meuse \'myüz, 'mə(r)z\ river 580 mi. (933 km.) long [W] Europe flowing from [NE] France into North Sea in the Netherlands

Mex·i·co \'mek-si-ˌkō\ 1 country [S] North America 2 or **Mexico City** city, its capital — **Mexican** adj or n

Mexico, Gulf of inlet of the Atlantic [SE] North America

Mi·ami \mī-'am-ē, -'am-ə\ city & port [SE] Florida

Miami Beach city [SE] Florida

Mich·i·gan \'mish-i-gən\ state [N] central U.S.; capital, Lansing — **Mich·i·gan·der** \ˌmish-i-'gan-dər\ n — **Mich·i·ga·ni·an** \-ə-'gā-nē-ən, -'gan-ē-\ n — **Mich·i·gan·ite** \'mish-i-gə-ˌnīt\ n

Michigan, Lake lake [N] central U.S.; one of the Great Lakes

Mi·cro·ne·sia \ˌmī-krə-'nē-zhə, -shə\ islands of the [W] Pacific [E] of the Philippines & [N] of Melanesia including Caroline, Kiribati, Mariana, & Marshall groups — **Mi·cro·ne·sian** \-zhən, -shən\ adj or n

Micronesia, Federated States of islands [W] Pacific in the Carolines; part of former Trust Territory of the Pacific Islands; a republic in association with U.S.; capital, Palikir

Middle East the countries of [SW] Asia & [N] Africa — usually thought to include the countries extending from Libya on the [W] to Afghanistan on the [E] — **Middle Eastern** adj

Mid·dles·brough \'mid-ᵊlz-brə\ town [N] England

Middle West — see MIDWEST

Mid·i·an \'mid-ē-ən\ ancient region [NW] Arabia [E] of Gulf of Aqaba — **Mid·i·an·ite** \-ē-ə-ˌnīt\ n

Mid·lands \'mid-lən(d)z\ the central counties of England

Mid·way \'mid-ˌwā\ islands central Pacific in Hawaiian group 1300 mi. (2092 km.) [WNW] of Honolulu belonging to U.S.; not included in state of Hawaii

Mid·west \ˌmid-'west\ or **Middle West** region [N] central U.S. including area around Great Lakes & in upper Mississippi valley from Ohio on the [E] to North Dakota, South Dakota, Nebraska, & Kansas on the [W] — **Mid·wes·tern** \ˌmid-'wes-tərn\ or **Middle Western** — **Mid·wes·tern·er** \ˌmid-'wes-tə(r)-nər\ or **Middle Westerner** n

Mi·lan \mə-'lan, -'län\ or Italian **Mi·la·no** \mi-'län-ō\ city [NW] Italy — **Mil·a·nese** \ˌmil-ə-'nēz, -'nēs\ adj or n

Mil·wau·kee \mil-'wò-kē\ city [SE] Wisconsin on Lake Michigan

Mi·nas Basin \ˌmī-nəs\ bay central Nova Scotia; [NE] extension of Bay of Fundy

Min·da·nao \ˌmin-də-'nä-ō, -'naú\ island [S] Philippines

Min·do·ro \min-'dòr-ō, -'dòr-\ island central Philippines

Min·ne·ap·o·lis \ˌmin-ē-'ap-(ə-)ləs\ city [SE] Minnesota

Min·ne·so·ta \ˌmin-ə-'sōt-ə\ state [N] central U.S.; capital, Saint Paul — **Min·ne·so·tan** \-'sōt-ᵊn\ adj or n

Mi·nor·ca \mə-'nòr-kə\ island Spain in [W] Mediterranean — **Mi·nor·can** \mə-'nòr-kən\ adj or n

Minsk \'min(t)sk\ city, capital of Belarus

Mis·sis·sau·ga \ˌmīs-ə-'sòg-ə\ city Canada in [S] Ontario

Mis·sis·sip·pi \ˌmis-(ə-)'sip-ē\ 1 river 2340 mi. (3765 km.) long central U.S. flowing into Gulf of Mexico — see ITASCA (Lake) 2 state [S] U.S.; capital, Jackson

Mis·sou·ri \mə-'zùr-ē, -'zùr-ə\ 1 river 2466 mi. (3968 km.) long [W] U.S. flowing from [SW] Montana to the Mississippi in [E] Missouri (state) 2 state central U.S.; capital, Jefferson City — **Mis·sou·ri·an** \-'zùr-ē-ən\ adj or n

Mitch·ell, Mount \'mich-əl\ mountain 6684 ft. (2037 m.) [W] North Carolina in the Appalachians; highest in U.S. [E] of the Mississippi

Mo·bile \mō-'bē(ə)l, 'mō-ˌbēl\ city [SW] Alabama on **Mobile Bay** (inlet of Gulf of Mexico)

Mo·des·to \mə-'dəs-tō\ city central California

Mog·a·di·shu \ˌmäg-ə-'dish-ü, -'dēsh-\ or **Mog·a·di·scio** \-ō\ city, capital of Somalia

Mo·hawk \'mō-ˌhòk\ river [E] central New York flowing into the Hudson

Mo·hen·jo Da·ro \mō-ˌhen-jō-'där-ō\ prehistoric city in valley of the Indus [NE] of modern Karachi, Pakistan

Mo·ja·ve or **Mo·ha·ve** \mə-'häv-ē\ desert [S] California [SE] of [S] end of Sierra Nevada

Mold \'mōld\ town [NE] Wales

Mol·da·via \mäl-'dā-vē-ə, -vyə\ 1 region [E] Europe in [NE] Romania & Moldova 2 former republic of U.S.S.R. bordered by Ukraine, Black Sea, & Romania; became independent (as Moldova) 1991 — **Mol·da·vian** \-vē-ən, -vyən\ adj or n

Mol·do·va \mäl-'dō-və, mól-\ country [E] Europe in [E] Moldavia region; capital, Chisinau — **Mol·do·van** \-vən\ adj or n

Mol·o·kai \ˌmäl-ə-'kī, ˌmō-lə-\ island Hawaii [ESE] of Oahu

Mo·luc·cas \mə-'lək-əz\ islands Indonesia [E] of Sulawesi — **Mo·luc·ca** \mə-'lək-ə\ adj — **Mo·luc·can** \-ən\ adj or n

Mom·ba·sa \mäm-'bäs-ə\ city & port [S] Kenya

Mo·na·co \'män-ə-ˌkō also mə-'näk-ō\ country [W] Europe on Mediterranean coast of France; capital, Monaco — **Mo·na·can** \'män-ə-kən, mə-'näk-ən\ adj or n — **Mon·e·gasque** \ˌmän-i-'gask\ n

Mon·go·lia \män-'gōl-yə, mäŋ-, -'gō-lē-ə\ 1 region [E] Asia [E] of Altai Mountains; includes Gobi Desert 2 country [E] Asia consisting of major portion of Mongolia region; capital, Ulaanbaatar

Mo·non·ga·he·la \mə-ˌnän-gə-'hē-lə, -ˌnäŋ-gə-, -'hā-lə\ river [N] West Virginia & [SW] Pennsylvania

Mon·ro·via \mən-'rō-vē-ə\ city, capital of Liberia

Mon·tana \män-'tan-ə\ state [NW] U.S.; capital, Helena — **Mon·tan·an** \-ən\ adj or n

Mont Blanc \'mōⁿ-'bläⁿ(k)\ mountain 15,771 ft. (4807 m.) [SE] France on Italian border; highest in the Alps

Mon·te·ne·gro \ˌmän-tə-ˈnē-(ˌ)grō, -ˈnā-\ country Ⓢ Europe on the Adriatic Sea; capital, Podgorica; a republic of Yugoslavia 1946–92

Mon·ter·rey \ˌmänt-ə-ˈrā\ city ⓃⒺ Mexico

Mon·te·vi·deo \ˌmänt-ə-və-ˈdā-ō, -ˈvid-ē-ˌō\ city, capital of Uruguay

Mont·gom·ery \(ˌ)mən(t)-ˈgəm-(ə-)rē, män(t)-, -ˈgäm-\ city, capital of Alabama

Mont·pe·lier \mänt-ˈpēl-yər, -ˈpil-\ city, capital of Vermont

Mon·tre·al \ˌmän-trē-ˈol, ˌmən-\ city Ⓢ Quebec, Canada on **Montreal Island** in the Saint Lawrence

Mont·ser·rat \ˌmän(t)-sə-ˈrat\ island British West Indies in the Leeward Islands

Mo·ra·via \mə-ˈrā-vē-ə\ region Ⓔ Czech Republic — **Mo·ra·vi·an** \mə-ˈrā-vē-ən\ *adj or n*

Mo·re·no Valley \mə-ˈrē-nō\ city Ⓢ California

Mo·roc·co \mə-ˈräk-ō\ country ⓃⓌ Africa; a kingdom; capital, Rabat — **Mo·roc·can** \-ˈräk-ən\ *adj or n*

Mo·ro·ni \mó-ˈrō-nē\ city, capital of Comoros

Mos·cow \ˈmäs-ˌkaú, -kō\ *or Russian* **Mos·kva** \mäsk-ˈvä\ city, capital of Russia & formerly of U.S.S.R.

Mo·selle \mō-ˈzel\ river about 340 mi. (545 km.) long Ⓔ France & Ⓦ Germany

Moyle \ˈmói(ə)l\ district Ⓝ Northern Ireland

Mo·zam·bique \ˌmō-zəm-ˈbēk\ **1** channel ⓈⒺ Africa between Mozambique (country) & Madagascar **2** country ⓈⒺ Africa; capital, Maputo — **Mo·zam·bi·can** \-ˈbē-kən\ *adj or n*

Mpu·ma·lan·ga \əm-ˌpü-mä-ˈläŋ-gə\ province ⓃⒺ Republic of South Africa

Mukden — see SHENYANG

Mul·tan \múl-ˈtän\ city ⓃⒺ Pakistan ⓈⓌ of Lahore

Mumbai — see BOMBAY

Mu·nich \ˈmyü-nik\ *or German* **Mün·chen** \ˈm(y)ün-kən\ city Ⓢ Germany in Bavaria

Mun·ster \ˈmən(t)-stər\ province Ⓢ Ireland

Mur·cia \ˈmər-sh(ē-)ə\ region & ancient kingdom ⓈⒺ Spain — **Mur·cian** \-shən\ *adj or n*

Mur·ray \ˈmər-ē, ˈmə-rē\ river 1609 mi. (2589 km.) long ⓈⒺ Australia flowing Ⓦ from Ⓔ Victoria into Indian Ocean in South Australia — see DARLING

Mur·rum·bidg·ee \ˌmər-əm-ˈbij-ē, ˌmə-rəm-\ river almost 1000 mi. (1609 km.) long ⓈⒺ Australia in New South Wales flowing Ⓦ into the Murray

Mus·cat \ˈməs-ˌkät, -ˌkat, -kət\ *or* **Mas·qat** \ˈmäs-ˌkät\ city Ⓔ Arabia, capital of Oman

Myan·mar \ˈmyän-ˌmär\ *or* **Bur·ma** \ˈbər-mə\ country ⓈⒺ Asia; capital, Nay Pyi Taw; historic capital, Yangon (Rangoon)

My·ce·nae \mī-ˈsē-nē\ ancient city Ⓢ Greece in ⓃⒺ Peloponnese

My·sore \mī-ˈsō(ə)r, -ˈsó(ə)r\ city Ⓢ India

Nab·a·taea *or* **Nab·a·tea** \ˌnab-ə-ˈtē-ə\ ancient Arab kingdom ⓈⒺ of Palestine — **Nab·a·tae·an** *or* **Nab·a·te·an** \-ˈtē-ən\ *adj or n*

Na·goya \nə-ˈgói-ə, ˈnäg-ə-ˌyä\ city Japan in Ⓢ central Honshu

Nag·pur \ˈnäg-ˌpú(ə)r\ city Ⓔ central India

Nai·ro·bi \nī-ˈrō-bē\ city, capital of Kenya

Na·mib·ia \nə-ˈmib-ē-ə\ *or formerly* **South–West Africa** country ⓈⓌ Africa on the Atlantic; capital, Windhoek — **Na·mib·ian** \-ən\ *adj or n*

Nan·chang \ˈnän-ˈjäŋ\ city ⓈⒺ China

Nan·jing \ˈnän-ˈjiŋ\ *or* **Nan·king** \ˈnan-ˈkiŋ, ˈnän-\ city Ⓔ China

Nan·tuck·et \nan-ˈtək-ət\ island ⓈⒺ Massachusetts Ⓢ of Cape Cod

Na·per·ville \ˈnā-pər-ˌvil\ city ⓃⒺ Illinois Ⓦ of Chicago

Na·ples \ˈnā-pəlz\ *or Italian* **Na·po·li** \ˈnäp-ə-lē\ *or ancient* **Ne·ap·o·lis** \nē-ˈap-ə-ləs\ city Ⓢ Italy on Bay of Naples — **Ne·a·pol·i·tan** \ˌnē-ə-ˈpäl-ət-ᵊn\ *adj or n*

Nar·ra·gan·sett Bay \ˌnar-ə-ˈgan(t)-sət\ inlet of the Atlantic ⓈⒺ Rhode Island

Nash·ville \ˈnash-ˌvil, -vəl\ city, capital of Tennessee

Nas·sau \ˈnas-ˌó\ city, capital of Bahamas

Na·tal \nə-ˈtal, -ˈtäl\ former province Ⓔ Republic of South Africa

Na·u·ru \nä-ˈü-rü\ island Ⓦ Pacific Ⓢ of the Equator; formerly a shared British, New Zealand, & Australian trust territory; an independent country since 1968 — **Na·u·ru·an** \-ˈü-rə-wən\ *adj or n*

Nay Pyi Taw *or* **Nay·pyi·daw** \ˈnep-yē-ˌdó\ city, capital of Myanmar

Naz·a·reth \ˈnaz-(ə-)rəth\ town of ancient Palestine in central Galilee; now a city of Ⓝ Israel

N'Dja·me·na \en-ˈjäm-ə-nə\ city, capital of Chad

Neagh, Lough \läk-ˈnä\ lake Northern Ireland

Near East the countries of ⓃⒺ Africa & ⓈⓌ Asia — **Near Eastern** *adj*

Ne·bras·ka \nə-ˈbras-kə\ state central U.S.; capital, Lincoln — **Ne·bras·kan** \-kən\ *adj or n*

Neg·ev \ˈneg-ˌev\ desert region Ⓢ Israel

Ne·gro \ˈnā-grō, ˈne-\ river 1400 mi. (2253 km.) long Ⓔ Colombia & Ⓝ Brazil flowing into the Amazon

Ne·gros \ˈnā-(ˌ)grōs\ island central Philippines

Ne·pal \nə-ˈpol, -ˈpäl, -ˈpal\ country Asia on ⓃⒺ border of India in the Himalayas; capital, Kathmandu — **Nep·a·lese** \ˌnep-ə-ˈlēz, -ˈlēs\ *adj or n* — **Ne·pali** \nə-ˈpól-ē, -ˈpäl-, -ˈpal-\ *adj or n*

Ness, Loch \ˈnes\ lake ⓃⓌ Scotland

Neth·er·lands \ˈneth-ər-lən(d)z\ **1** *or the Netherlands or Dutch* **Ne·der·land** \ˈnäd-ər-ˌlänt\ *also* **Holland** country ⓃⓌ Europe on North Sea; a kingdom; capital, Amsterdam; seat of government, The Hague **2** LOW COUNTRIES — a historical usage — **Neth·er·land** \ˈneth-ər-lənd\ *adj* — **Neth·er·land·er** \-ˌlan-dər, -lən-\ *n* — **Neth·er·land·ish** \-dish\ *adj*

Netherlands Antilles islands of the West Indies, formerly an overseas territory of the Netherlands; capital, Willemstad

Netherlands Indies former Dutch possessions in the East Indies including Indonesia

Ne·va \ˈnē-və, ˈnā-\ river 40 mi. (64 km.) long Ⓦ Russia; flows through Saint Petersburg

Ne·vada \nə-ˈvad-ə, -ˈväd-ə\ state Ⓦ U.S.; capital, Carson City — **Ne·vad·an** \-ˈvad-ᵊn, -ˈväd-ᵊn\ *adj or n*

Ne·vis \ˈnē-vəs\ island West Indies in the Leeward Islands — see SAINT KITTS

New Amsterdam town founded 1625 on island of Manhattan by the Dutch; renamed New York 1664 by the British

New·ark \ˈn(y)ü-ərk, ˈn(y)ú(-ə)rk\ city ⓃⒺ New Jersey Ⓦ of New York City

New Britain island Ⓦ Pacific in Bismarck group

New Bruns·wick \-ˈbrənz-(ˌ)wik\ province ⓈⒺ Canada; capital, Fredericton

New Cal·e·do·nia \-ˌkal-ə-ˈdō-nyə, -nē-ə\ island ⓈⓌ Pacific ⓈⓌ of Vanuatu; an overseas department of France; capital, Nouméa

New·cas·tle \ˈn(y)ü-ˌkas-əl\ city ⓈⒺ Australia in Ⓔ New South Wales

Newcastle *or* **New·cas·tle up·on Tyne** \n(y)ü-ˈkas-əl-ə-ˌpón-ˈtīn\ city Ⓝ England

New Del·hi \-ˈdel-ē\ city, capital of India Ⓢ of Delhi

New England section of ⓃⒺ U.S. consisting of states of Maine, New Hampshire, Vermont, Massachusetts, Rhode

\ə\ abut	\aú\ out	\i\ tip	\ó\ saw	\ú\ foot
\ər\ further	\ch\ chin	\ī\ life	\ói\ coin	\y\ yet
\a\ mat	\e\ pet	\j\ job	\th\ thin	\yü\ few
\ā\ take	\ē\ easy	\ŋ\ sing	\th\ this	\yú\ cure
\ä\ cot, cart	\g\ go	\ō\ bone	\ü\ food	\zh\ vision

Island, & Connecticut — **New En·gland·er** \\'iŋ-glən-dər *also* 'iŋ-lən-\ *n*

New·found·land \\'n(y)ü-fən-(d)lənd, -,(d)land; ,n(y)ü-fən-'(d)land\ island Canada in the Atlantic — **New·found·land·er** \-(d)lən-dər, -'(d)lan-dər\ *n*

Newfoundland and Labrador province Ⓔ Canada consisting of Newfoundland Island and Labrador; capital, Saint John's

New France the possessions of France in North America before 1763

New Guin·ea \\'gin-ē\ **1** island Ⓦ Pacific Ⓝ of Ⓔ Australia divided between Indonesia & independent Papua New Guinea **2** the Ⓝ Ⓔ portion of the island of New Guinea together with some nearby islands; now part of Papua New Guinea — **New Guin·e·an** \-'gin-ē-ən\ *adj or n*

New·ham \\'n(y)ü-əm\ borough of Ⓔ Greater London, England

New Hamp·shire \\'ham(p)-shər, -,shi(ə)r\ state Ⓝ Ⓔ U.S.; capital, Concord — **New Hamp·shire·man** \-mən\ *n* — **New Hamp·shir·ite** \-,īt\ *n*

New Ha·ven \-'hā-vən\ city Ⓢ Connecticut

New Hebrides — see VANUATU

New Jer·sey \\'jər-zē\ state Ⓔ U.S.; capital, Trenton — **New Jer·sey·an** \-ən\ *n* — **New Jer·sey·ite** \-,īt\ *n*

New Mex·i·co \\'mek-si-,kō\ state Ⓢ Ⓦ U.S.; capital, Santa Fe — **New Mex·i·can** \-si-kən\ *adj or n*

New Neth·er·land \-'neth-ər-lənd\ former Dutch colony (1613–64) North America along Hudson & lower Delaware rivers; capital, New Amsterdam

New Or·leans \-'or-lē-ənz, -'orl-(y)ənz, -,(,)or-'lēnz\ city Ⓢ Ⓔ Louisiana

New·port \\'n(y)ü-,pō(ə)rt, -,po(ə)rt\ **1** town Ⓢ England in Isle of Wight **2** city Ⓢ Ⓔ Wales

Newport News \,n(y)ü-,pōrt-'n(y)üz, -,port-, -pərt-\ city Ⓢ Ⓔ Virginia

New Prov·i·dence \-'präv-əd-ən(t)s, -ə-,den(t)s\ island Ⓝ Ⓦ central Bahamas; chief town, Nassau

New·ry and Mourne \\'n(y)ü(ə)r-ē-ənd-'morn\ district Ⓢ Northern Ireland

New South Wales state Ⓢ Ⓔ Australia; capital, Sydney

New Spain former Spanish possessions in North America, Central America, West Indies, & the Philippines; capital, Mexico City

New Sweden former Swedish colony (1638–55) North America on Ⓦ bank of Delaware River

New·town·ab·bey \,n(y)üt-ᵊn-'ab-ē\ district Ⓔ Northern Ireland

New·town·ards \,n(y)üt-ᵊn-'ärdz\ town Ⓔ Northern Ireland

Newtown Saint Bos·wells \sənt-'bäz-wəlz, -sänt-\ village Ⓢ Scotland

New World the Western Hemisphere including North America and South America

New York \\'yo(ə)rk\ **1** state Ⓝ Ⓔ U.S.; capital, Albany **2** *or* **New York City** city Ⓢ Ⓔ New York (state) — **New York·er** \\'yor-kər\ *n*

New York State Barge Canal — see ERIE

New Zea·land \\'zē-lənd\ country Ⓢ Ⓦ Pacific Ⓔ Ⓢ Ⓔ of Australia; capital, Wellington — **New Zea·land·er** \-lən-dər\ *n*

Ni·ag·a·ra Falls \(,)nī-'ag-(ə-)rə\ falls New York & Ontario in **Niagara River** (flowing Ⓝ from Lake Erie into Lake Ontario); divided by Goat Island into Horseshoe, or Canadian, Falls (158 ft. or 48 m. high) & American Falls (167 ft. or 51 m. high)

Nia·mey \nē-'äm-ā, nyä-'mā\ city, capital of Niger

Ni·caea \nī-'sē-ə\ *or* **Nice** \\'nīs\ ancient city Ⓦ Bithynia; site at modern village in Ⓝ Ⓦ Turkey — **Ni·cae·an** \nī-'sē-ən\ *adj or n* — **Ni·cene** \\'nī-,sēn, nī-'sēn\ *adj*

Ni·ca·ra·gua \,nik-ə-'räg-wə\ **1** lake about 100 mi. (160 km.) long Ⓢ Nicaragua **2** country Central America; capital, Managua — **Ni·ca·ra·guan** \-wən\ *adj or n*

Nice \\'nēs\ city & port Ⓢ Ⓔ France on the Mediterranean

Nic·o·bar \\'nik-ə-,bär\ islands India in Bay of Bengal Ⓢ of the Andamans

Nic·o·sia \,nik-ə-'sē-ə\ city, capital of Cyprus

Ni·ger \\'nī-jər, nē-'zher\ **1** river 2600 mi. (4184 km.) long Ⓦ Africa flowing into Gulf of Guinea **2** country Ⓦ Africa Ⓝ of Nigeria; capital, Niamey — **Ni·ger·ien** \,nī-jir-ē-'en, nē-'zher-ē-ən\ *adj or n* — **Ni·ger·ois** \,nē-zhər-'wä, -zher-\

Ni·ge·ria \nī-'jir-ē-ə\ country Ⓦ Africa on Gulf of Guinea; capital, Abuja — **Ni·ge·ri·an** \-ē-ən\ *adj or n*

Nii·hau \\'nē-,haú\ island Hawaii Ⓦ Ⓢ Ⓦ of Kauai

Nile \\'nī(ə)l\ river 4160 mi. (6693 km.) long Ⓔ Africa flowing from Lake Victoria in Uganda Ⓝ into the Mediterranean in Egypt

Nil·gi·ri \\'nil-gə-rē\ hills Ⓢ India

Nin·e·veh \\'nin-ə-və\ ancient city, capital of Assyria; ruins in Iraq on the Tigris

Nip·i·gon, Lake \\'nip-ə-,gän\ lake Canada in Ⓦ Ontario Ⓝ of Lake Superior

Nizh·niy Nov·go·rod \,nizh-nē-'näv-gə-,räd, -'nov-gə-rət\ *or 1932–89* **Gor·ki** \\'gor-kē\ city Ⓦ Russia

Nord–Ost·see \\'nort-'ost-,zä\ *or* **Kiel** \\'kēl\ canal 61 mi. (98 km.) long Ⓝ Germany across base of Jutland Peninsula connecting Baltic Sea & North Sea

Nor·folk \\'nor-fək, *in the U.S. also* -,fok\ **1** city & port Ⓢ Ⓔ Virginia **2** county Ⓔ England on North Sea

Nor·man·dy \\'nor-mən-dē\ region Ⓝ Ⓦ France Ⓝ Ⓔ of Brittany

North 1 river, estuary of the Hudson between Ⓝ Ⓔ New Jersey & Ⓢ Ⓔ New York **2** sea, arm of the Atlantic Ⓔ of Great Britain **3** island Ⓝ New Zealand

North·al·ler·ton \nor-'thal-ərt-ᵊn\ town Ⓝ England

North America continent of Western Hemisphere Ⓝ Ⓦ of South America & Ⓝ of the Equator — **North American** *adj or n*

North·amp·ton \north-'(h)am(p)-tən\ city central England

North·amp·ton·shire \north-'(h)am(p)-tən-,shi(ə)r, -shər\ *or* **Northampton** county central England

North Cape cape New Zealand at Ⓝ end of North Island

North Car·o·li·na \,kar-ə-'lī-nə\ state Ⓔ U.S.; capital, Raleigh — **North Car·o·lin·ian** \-'lin-ē-ən, -'lin-yən\ *adj or n*

North Da·ko·ta \də-'kōt-ə\ state Ⓝ U.S.; capital, Bismarck — **North Da·ko·tan** \-'kōt-ᵊn\ *adj or n*

North Down district Ⓔ Northern Ireland

Northern — see LIMPOPO 2

Northern Cape province Ⓦ Republic of South Africa

Northern Cook \\'kúk\ islands Ⓢ central Pacific Ⓝ of Cook Islands

Northern Hemisphere the half of the earth that lies Ⓝ of the Equator

Northern Ireland region Ⓝ Ireland comprising 26 districts of Ulster; a division of United Kingdom; capital, Belfast

Northern Mar·i·ana Islands \,mar-ē-'an-ə-, ,mer-\ islands Ⓦ Pacific; commonwealth in association with U.S.; capital, Saipan

Northern Rhodesia — see ZAMBIA

Northern Territory territory Ⓝ & central Australia; capital, Darwin

North Korea — see KOREA

North Las Vegas city Ⓢ Ⓔ Nevada

North Slope region Ⓝ Alaska between Brooks Range & Arctic Ocean

North·um·ber·land \nor-'thəm-bər-lənd\ county Ⓝ England — **North·um·bri·an** \-'thəm-brē-ən\ *adj or n*

North·um·bria \nor-'thəm-brē-ə\ ancient country Great Britain in what is now Ⓝ England and Ⓢ Scotland — **North·um·bri·an** \-brē-ən\ *adj or n*

North Vietnam — see VIETNAM

North West province Ⓝ Republic of South Africa

Northwest Passage sea passage between North Atlantic & North Pacific along Ⓝ coast of North America

Northwest Territories territory NW Canada consisting of the area of the mainland north of 60° between Yukon & Nunavut; capital, Yellowknife

North York former city Canada in SE Ontario; now part of Toronto

North Yorkshire county N England

Nor·walk \'nôr-ˌwòk\ city SW California SE of Los Angeles

Nor·way \'nó(ə)r-ˌwä\ country N Europe in Scandinavia; a kingdom; capital, Oslo

Nor·wich \'nó(ə)r-(ˌ)wich; 'nòr-ich, 'när-\ city E England

Not·ting·ham \'nät-iŋ-əm, in the U.S. also -ˌham\ city N central England

Not·ting·ham·shire \'nät-iŋ-əm-shi(ə)r, -shər, in the U.S. also -ˌham-\ or **Nottingham** county N central England

Nouak·chott \nů-'äk-ˌshät\ city, capital of Mauritania

Nou·méa \nü-'mā-ə\ city, capital of New Caledonia

No·va Sco·tia \ˌnō-və-'skō-shə\ province SE Canada; capital, Halifax — **No·va Sco·tian** \-'skō-shən\ adj or n

No·vo·kuz·netsk \ˌnō-(ˌ)vō-kùz-'netsk\ city S Russia in Asia

No·vo·si·birsk \ˌnō-(ˌ)vō-sə-'bi(ə)rsk\ city S Russia in Asia

Nu·bia \'n(y)ü-bē-ə\ region NE Africa in Nile valley in S Egypt & N Sudan — **Nu·bian** \-bē-ən\ adj or n

Nu·ku·a·lo·fa \ˌnü-kə-wə-'lò-fə\ seaport, capital of Tonga

Nu·mid·ia \n(y)ü-'mid-ē-ə\ ancient country N Africa E of Mauretania in modern Algeria — **Nu·mid·i·an** \-ē-ən\ adj or n

Nu·na·vut \'nü-nə-ˌvüt\ semiautonomous territory NE Canada; capital, Iqaluit

Nu·rem·berg \'nùr-əm-ˌbərg, 'nyùr-\ or German **Nürn·berg** \'nuern-ˌberk\ city S Germany

Nuuk \'nük\ or Danish **Godt·hab** \'gòt-ˌhòp\ town, capital of Greenland on SW coast

Nyasa, Lake — see MALAWI (Lake)

Nyasaland — see MALAWI

Oa·hu \ə-'wä-hü\ island Hawaii; site of Honolulu

Oak·land \'ō-klənd\ city W California on San Francisco Bay E of San Francisco

Ob' \'äb, 'òb\ river over 2250 mi. (3620 km.) long W Russia in Asia flowing NW & N into Arctic Ocean

Oce·a·nia \ˌō-shē-'an-ē-ə, -'ā-nē-ə\ lands of the central & S Pacific: Micronesia, Melanesia, Polynesia including New Zealand, & sometimes Australia & Malay Archipelago — **Oce·a·ni·an** \-'an-ē-ən, -'ā-nē-\ adj or n

Ocean·side \'ō-shən-ˌsīd\ city SW California NNW of San Diego

Oder \'ōd-ər\ or **Odra** \'ò-drä\ river about 565 mi. (909 km.) long central Europe flowing from Silesia NW into Baltic Sea; forms part of boundary between Poland & Germany

Odes·sa \ō-'des-ə\ city & port S Ukraine on Black Sea

Ohio \ō-'hī-ō\ **1** river about 981 mi. (1578 km.) long E U.S. flowing from W Pennsylvania into the Mississippi **2** state E central U.S.; capital, Columbus — **Ohio·an** \ō-'hī-ə-wən\ adj or n

Oka·ya·ma \ˌō-kə-'yäm-ə\ city Japan in W Honshu on Inland Sea

Okee·cho·bee, Lake \ˌō-kə-'chō-bē\ lake S central Florida

Oke·fe·no·kee \ˌō-kə-fə-'nō-kē\ swamp SE Georgia & NE Florida

Okhotsk, Sea of \ō-'kätsk\ inlet of the North Pacific E Russia in Asia

Oki·na·wa \ˌō-kə-'nä-wə, -'naù-ə\ **1** islands Japan in central Ryukyus **2** island, chief of group — **Oki·na·wan** \-'nä-wən, -'naù-ən\ adj or n

Okla·ho·ma \ˌō-klə-'hō-mə\ state S central U.S.; capital, Oklahoma City — **Okla·ho·man** \-mən\ adj or n

Oklahoma City city, capital of Oklahoma

Old·ham \'ōl-dəm\ city NW England

Old Point Comfort cape SE Virginia N of entrance to Hampton Roads

Ol·du·vai Gorge \'ōl-də-ˌvī\ canyon N Tanzania SE of Serengeti Plain; site of fossil beds

Old World the half of the earth to the E of the Atlantic Ocean including Europe, Asia, and Africa & especially the continent of Europe

Olym·pia \ə-'lim-pē-ə, ō-\ **1** city, capital of Washington **2** plain S Greece in NW Peloponnese

Olym·pic \ə-'lim-pik, ō-\ mountains NW Washington on Olympic Peninsula; highest Mt. Olympus 7965 ft. (2428 m.)

Olym·pus \ə-'lim-pəs, ō-\ mountains NE Greece

Omagh \'ō-mə\ **1** district W Northern Ireland **2** town in Omagh district

Oma·ha \'ō-mə-ˌhò, -ˌhä\ **1** city E Nebraska on Missouri River **2** beach NW France in Normandy

Oman \ō-'män, -'man\ country SW Asia in SE Arabia; a sultanate; capital, Muscat — **Omani** \ō-'män-ē, -'man-\ adj or n

Oman, Gulf of arm of Arabian Sea between Oman & SE Iran

Omsk \'òm(p)sk, 'äm(p)sk\ city SW Russia in Asia

On·tar·io \än-'ter-ē-ō, -'tar-\ **1** city SW California **2** province E Canada; capital, Toronto — **On·tar·i·an** \-ē-ən\ adj or n

Ontario, Lake lake E central North America in U.S. & Canada; one of the Great Lakes

Oporto — see PORTO

Oran \ò-'rän\ city & port NW Algeria

Or·ange \'òr-inj, 'är-, -ənj\ **1** city SW California **2** river 1300 mi. (2092 km.) long S Africa flowing W from Drakensberg Mountains into the Atlantic

Orange Free State — see FREE STATE

Or·e·gon \'òr-i-gən, 'är-, -ˌgän\ state NW U.S.; capital, Salem — **Or·e·go·nian** \ˌòr-i-'gō-nē-ən, är-, -nyən\ adj or n

Oregon Trail pioneer route to the NW U.S. about 2000 mi. (3225 km.) long from Missouri to Washington

Ori·no·co \ˌòr-ə-'nō-kō, ˌòr-\ river 1336 mi. (2150 km.) long Venezuela flowing into the Atlantic

Ork·ney \'òrk-nē\ islands N Scotland

Or·lan·do \òr-'lan-dō\ city central Florida

Osa·ka \ō-'säk-ə\ city Japan in S Honshu

Osh·a·wa \'äsh-ə-ˌwä\ city SE Ontario, Canada on Lake Ontario ENE of Toronto

Os·lo \'äz-lō, 'äs-\ city, capital of Norway

Os·wie·cim \ˌòsh-'fyen-chēm\ or German **Ausch·witz** \'aùsh-ˌvits\ town S Poland W of Krakow

Ot·ta·wa \'ät-ə-ˌwä, -wə, -ˌwò\ **1** river 696 mi. (1120 km.) E Canada in SE Ontario & S Quebec flowing E into the Saint Lawrence **2** city, capital of Canada in SE Ontario on Ottawa River

Ottoman Empire \'ät-ə-mən\ former Turkish sultanate in SE Europe, W Asia, & N Africa

Oua·ga·dou·gou \ˌwäg-ə-'dü-ˌgü\ city, capital of Burkina Faso

Outer Hebrides — see HEBRIDES

Over·land Park \'ō-vər-lənd\ city NE Kansas S of Kansas City

Ox·ford \'äks-fərd\ city central England

Ox·ford·shire \'äks-fərd-ˌshi(ə)r, -shər\ or **Oxford** county central England

Ox·nard \'äk-ˌsnärd\ city SW California

Ozark Plateau \'ō-ˌzärk\ or **Ozark Mountains** eroded plateau N Arkansas, S Missouri, & NE Oklahoma with E extension into S Illinois

\ə\ abut	\aù\ out	\i\ tip	\ò\ saw	\ù\ foot
\ər\ further	\ch\ chin	\ī\ life	\òi\ coin	\y\ yet
\a\ mat	\e\ pet	\j\ job	\th\ thin	\yü\ few
\ā\ take	\ē\ easy	\ŋ\ sing	\th\ this	\yù\ cure
\ä\ cot, cart	\g\ go	\ō\ bone	\ü\ food	\zh\ vision

Pa·cif·ic \pə-'sif-ik\ ocean extending from Arctic Circle to the Equator (**North Pacific**) and from the Equator to the Antarctic regions (**South Pacific**) & from Ⓦ North America & Ⓦ South America to Ⓔ Asia & Australia — **Pacific** adj

Pacific Islands, Trust Territory of the grouping of islands in Ⓦ Pacific formerly under U.S. administration: the Carolines & the Marshalls

Pacific Rim the countries bordering on or located in the Pacific Ocean — used especially of Asian countries on the Pacific

Pa·dang \'pä-,däŋ\ city Indonesia in Ⓦ Sumatra

Pa·dre \'päd-rē, 'pad-\ island 113 mi. (182 km.) long Ⓢ Texas in Gulf of Mexico

Pa·go Pa·go \,päŋ-(g)ō-'päŋ-(g)ō, ,päg-ō-'päg-ō\ town, capital of American Samoa on Tutuila Island

Painted Desert region Ⓝ central Arizona

Pak·i·stan \'pak-i-,stan, ,päk-i-'stän\ country Ⓢ Asia Ⓝ Ⓦ of India; until 1971 included also an Ⓔ division Ⓔ of India; capital, Islamabad — see EAST PAKISTAN — **Pak·i·stani** \-'stan-ē, -'stän-ē\ adj or n

Pa·lau \pə-'laú\ or **Be·lau** \bə-\ island group Ⓦ Pacific in the Ⓦ Carolines; an independent country since 1994; capital, Melekeok — **Pa·lau·an** \pə-'laú-ən\ n

Pa·la·wan \pə-'lä-wən, -,wän\ island Ⓦ Philippines between South China & Sulu seas

Pa·lem·bang \,päl-əm-'bäŋ\ city Indonesia in Ⓢ Ⓔ Sumatra

Pa·ler·mo \pə-'ler-mō, -'le(ə)r-\ city Italy, capital of Sicily

Pal·es·tine \'pal-ə-,stīn, -,stēn\ region Ⓢ Ⓦ Asia dating back to ancient times with unofficial, disputed, & fluctuating boundaries, but extending from Ⓔ coast of the Mediterranean up to or beyond the Jordan River — **Pal·es·tin·ian** \,pal-ə-'stin-ē-ən, -'stin-yən\ adj or n

Pa·li·kir \,päl-ē-'kir\ town, capital of Federated States of Micronesia on Pohnpei Island

Pal·i·sades \,pal-ə-'sādz\ line of high cliffs 15 mi. (24 km.) long on Ⓦ bank of the Hudson in Ⓢ Ⓔ New York & Ⓝ Ⓔ New Jersey

Palm·dale \'päm-,dāl, 'pälm-\ city Ⓢ Ⓦ California Ⓝ Ⓔ of Los Angeles

Pa·mirs \pə-'mi(ə)rz\ elevated mountainous region central Asia in Ⓔ Tajikistan & on borders of China, India, Pakistan, & Afghanistan; many peaks over 20,000 ft. (6096 m.)

Pam·li·co Sound \'pam-li-,kō\ inlet of the North Atlantic Ⓔ North Carolina between main part of the state & offshore islands

Pan·a·ma \'pan-ə-,mä, -,mȯ, ,pan-ə-'mä, -'mȯ\ **1** country Ⓢ Central America **2** or **Panama City** city, its capital on the Pacific **3** canal 40 mi. (64 km.) long Panama connecting Atlantic & Pacific oceans — **Pan·a·ma·ni·an** \,pan-ə-'mä-nē-ən\ adj or n

Panama, Isthmus of or formerly **Isthmus of Dar·i·en** \,dar-ē-'en\ strip of land central Panama connecting North America & South America

Panama Canal Zone — see CANAL ZONE

Pa·nay \pə-'nī\ island central Philippines

Pan·gaea \pan-'jē-ə\ ancient supercontinent that included almost all of Earth's land area

Pan·mun·jom or **Pan·mun·jeom** \,pän-,mún-'jəm\ village on North Korea–South Korea border

Pao·t'ou — see BAOTOU

Pap·ua, Territory of \'pap-yə-wə, 'päp-ə-wə\ former British territory consisting of Ⓢ Ⓔ New Guinea & offshore islands; now part of Papua New Guinea

Papua New Guinea country Ⓢ Ⓦ Pacific combining former territories of Papua & New Guinea; formerly a United Nations trust territory governed by Australia; independent since 1975; capital, Port Moresby

Par·a·guay \'par-ə-,gwī, -,gwä\ **1** river 1584 mi. (2549 km.) long central South America flowing from Brazil Ⓢ into the Paraná in Paraguay **2** country central South America; capital, Asunción — **Par·a·guay·an** \,par-ə-'gwī-ən, -'gwä-\ adj or n

Par·a·mar·i·bo \,par-ə-'mar-ə-,bō\ city, capital of Suriname

Pa·ra·ná \,par-ə-'nä\ river about 2500 mi. (4022 km.) long central South America flowing Ⓢ from Brazil into Argentina

Pa·ri·cu·tin \pə-'rē-kə-,tēn\ **1** former village Mexico **2** volcano on site of former village of Paricutin

Par·is \'par-əs\ city, capital of France — **Pa·ri·sian** \pə-'rizh-ən, -'rēzh-\ adj or n

Par·nas·sus \pär-'nas-əs\ mountain central Greece

Par·os \'par-,äs, 'per-\ island Greece — **Par·i·an** \'par-ē-ən, 'per-\ adj

Par·ra·mat·ta \,par-ə-'mat-ə\ city Ⓢ Ⓔ Australia in New South Wales Ⓝ Ⓦ of Sydney

Par·thia \'pär-thē-ə\ ancient country Ⓢ Ⓦ Asia in Ⓝ Ⓔ modern Iran — **Par·thi·an** \-thē-ən\ adj or n

Pas·a·de·na \,pas-ə-'dē-nə\ **1** city Ⓢ Ⓦ California Ⓔ of Glendale **2** city Ⓢ Ⓔ Texas

Pat·a·go·nia \,pat-ə-'gō-nyə, -nē-ə\ region South America Ⓢ of about 40° Ⓢ latitude in Ⓢ Argentina & Ⓢ tip of Chile; sometimes thought to include Tierra del Fuego — **Pat·a·go·nian** \-nyən, -nē-ən\ adj or n

Pat·er·son \'pat-ər-sən\ city Ⓝ Ⓔ New Jersey

Pat·mos \'pat-məs\ island Greece Ⓢ Ⓢ Ⓦ of Samos

Pat·na \'pət-nə\ city Ⓝ Ⓔ India on the Ganges

Pearl Harbor inlet Hawaii on Ⓢ coast of Oahu Ⓦ of Honolulu

Peking — see BEIJING

Pe·li·on \'pē-lē-ən\ mountain 5089 ft. (1551 m.) Ⓝ Ⓔ Greece

Pel·o·pon·nese \'pel-ə-pə-,nēz, -,nēs\ or **Pel·o·pon·ni·sos** \,pel-ə-pə-'nē-səs\ peninsula forming Ⓢ part of mainland of Greece

Pem·broke Pines \'pem-,brōk\ city Ⓢ Ⓔ Florida

Pen·nine Chain \'pen-,īn\ mountains Ⓝ England; highest Cross Fell 2930 ft. (893 m.)

Penn·syl·va·nia \,pen(t)-səl-'vā-nyə, -nē-ə\ state Ⓔ U.S.; capital, Harrisburg

People's Democratic Republic of Yemen — see YEMEN

Pe·o·ria \pē-'ȯr-ē-ə, -'ōr-\ **1** town Ⓢ Ⓦ central Arizona **2** city Ⓝ central Illinois

Per·ga·mum \'pər-gə-məm\ or **Per·ga·mus** \-məs\ ancient Greek kingdom including most of Asia Minor; at its height 263–133 B.C.; capital, Pergamum (in what is now Ⓦ Turkey)

Perm \'pərm, 'pe(ə)rm\ city Ⓔ Russia in Europe

Pernambuco — see RECIFE

Persia — see IRAN

Per·sian Gulf \'pər-zhən\ arm of Arabian Sea between Iran & Arabia

Perth \'pərth\ city, capital of Western Australia

Pe·ru \pə-'rü\ country Ⓦ South America; capital, Lima — **Pe·ru·vi·an** \pə-'rü-vē-ən\ adj or n

Pe·ter·bor·ough \'pēt-ər-,bər-ə, -,bə-rə, -b(ə-)rə\ city central England

Pe·tra \'pē-trə, 'pe-trə\ ancient city Ⓝ Ⓦ Arabia; site in Ⓢ Ⓦ Jordan

Petrograd — see SAINT PETERSBURG 2

Phil·a·del·phia \,fil-ə-'del-fyə, -fē-ə\ city Ⓢ Ⓔ Pennsylvania — **Phil·a·del·phian** \-fyən, -fē-ən\ adj or n

Phil·ip·pines \,fil-ə-'pēnz, 'fil-ə-,pēnz\ island group approximately 500 mi. (805 km.) off Ⓢ Ⓔ coast of Asia; an independent country; capital, Manila — **Phil·ip·pine** \-'pēn, -,pēn\ adj

Phnom Penh \(pə-)'nȯm-'pen, (pə-)'näm-\ city, capital of Cambodia

Phoe·ni·cia \fi-'nish-(ē-)ə, -'nēsh-\ ancient country Ⓢ Ⓦ Asia on the Mediterranean in modern Syria & Lebanon

Phoe·nix \'fē-niks\ city, capital of Arizona

Phry·gia \'frij-(ē-)ə\ ancient country Ⓦ central Asia Minor

Pied·mont \'pēd-ˌmänt\ plateau region Ⓔ U.S. Ⓔ of the Appalachians between ⓈⒺ New York & ⓃⒺ Alabama — **Pied·mon·tese** \ˌpēd-mən-'tēz, -(ˌ)män-, -'tēs\ *adj or n*

Pierre \'pi(ə)r\ city, capital of South Dakota

Pie·ter·mar·itz·burg \ˌpēt-ər-'mar-əts-ˌbərg\ city Ⓔ Republic of South Africa

Pikes Peak \'pīks\ mountain 14,110 ft. (4301 m.) Ⓔ central Colorado in a range of the Rockies

Pin·dus \'pin-dəs\ mountains Ⓦ Greece; highest point 8136 ft. (2480 m.)

Pi·sa \'pē-zə\ city Ⓦ central Italy Ⓦ of Florence

Pit·cairn \'pit-ˌka(ə)rn, -ˌke(ə)rn\ island South Pacific; a British colony

Pitts·burgh \'pits-ˌbərg\ city ⓈⓌ Pennsylvania

Plac·id, Lake \'plas-əd\ lake ⓃⒺ New York

Pla·no \'plā-nō\ city ⓃⒺ Texas Ⓝ of Dallas

Plov·div \'plov-ˌdif, -ˌdiv\ city Ⓢ Bulgaria

Plym·outh \'plim-əth\ **1** town ⓈⒺ Massachusetts **2** city & port ⓈⓌ England

Po \'pō\ river 405 mi. (652 km.) Ⓝ Italy flowing into the Adriatic

Pod·go·ri·ca \'pod-ˌgor-ēt-sä\ city, capital of Montenegro

Po Hai — see BO HAI

Pohn·pei \'pōn-ˌpā\ island Ⓦ Pacific in the Ⓔ Carolines; part of Federated States of Micronesia

Po·land \'pō-lənd\ country central Europe on Baltic Sea; capital, Warsaw — **Pole** *n*

Pol·y·ne·sia \ˌpäl-ə-'nē-zhə, -shə\ islands of the central & Ⓢ Pacific including Hawaii, the Line, Tonga, Cook, & Samoa islands, & often New Zealand among others

Pom·er·a·nia \ˌpäm-ə-'rā-nē-ə, -nyə\ region Ⓝ Europe on Baltic Sea; formerly in Germany, now mostly in Poland

Po·mo·na \pə-'mō-nə\ city ⓈⓌ California Ⓔ of Los Angeles

Pom·peii \päm-'pā, -'pā-ē\ ancient city Ⓘ Italy ⓈⒺ of Naples destroyed 79 A.D. by eruption of Vesuvius — **Pom·pe·ian** \-'pā-ən\ *adj or n*

Pon·ce \'pon(t)-sä\ city Ⓢ Puerto Rico

Pon·ta Del·ga·da \ˌpän-tə-del-'gäd-ə, -'gad-\ city & port Portugal, largest in the Azores

Pont·char·train, Lake \'pän-chər-ˌtrān, ˌpän-chər-'trān\ lake ⓈⒺ Louisiana Ⓝ of New Orleans

Pon·tus \'pänt-əs\ **1** ancient country ⓃⒺ Asia Minor **2** *or* **Pontus Euxinus** — see BLACK SEA — **Pon·tic** \'pänt-ik\ *adj or n*

Poole \'pül\ town Ⓢ England on English Channel

Po·po·ca·te·petl \ˌpō-pə-ˌkat-ə-'pet-ᵊl\ volcano 17,887 ft. (5452 m.) ⓈⒺ central Mexico

Port Arthur — see LÜSHUN

Port–au–Prince \ˌpōrt-ō-'prin(t)s, ˌport-\ city, capital of Haiti

Port Jack·son \'jak-sən\ inlet of South Pacific ⓈⒺ Australia in New South Wales; harbor of Sydney

Port·land \'pōrt-lənd, 'port-\ **1** city ⓈⓌ Maine; largest in state **2** city ⓃⓌ Oregon

Port Lou·is \'lü-əs, 'lü-ē, lú-'ē\ city, capital of Mauritius

Port Mores·by \'mō(ə)rz-bē, 'mó(ə)rz-\ city, capital of Papua New Guinea

Por·to \'pór-tü\ *or* **Opor·to** \ō-'pórt-ō\ city & port ⓃⓌ Portugal

Por·to Ale·gre \ˌpōrt-ō-ə-'leg-rə, ˌpórt-\ city & port Ⓢ Brazil

Port of Spain city ⓃⓌ Trinidad, capital of Trinidad and Tobago

Por·to–No·vo \ˌpōrt-ə-'nō-vō, ˌpórt-\ city, capital of Benin

Port Phil·lip Bay \'fil-əp\ inlet of South Pacific ⓈⒺ Australia in Victoria; harbor of Melbourne

Port Said \sä-'ēd, 'sīd\ city & port ⓃⒺ Egypt on the Mediterranean at Ⓝ end of the Suez Canal

Ports·mouth \'pōrt-sməth, 'pórt-\ **1** city ⓈⒺ Virginia **2** city Ⓢ England

Por·tu·gal \'pōr-chi-gəl, 'pór-\ country ⓈⓌ Europe; capital, Lisbon

Portuguese India former Portuguese possession on Ⓦ coast of India; became part of India 1962

Port–Vi·la \ˌpór-'vē-lä, -vē-'lä\ *or* **Vi·la** \'vē-lä, vē-'lä\ city, capital of Vanuatu

Po·to·mac \pə-'tō-mək, -mik\ river 287 mi. (462 km.) long flowing from West Virginia into Chesapeake Bay and forming boundary between Maryland & Virginia

Pough·keep·sie \pə-'kip-sē, pō-\ city & river port ⓈⒺ New York on the Hudson

Po·wys \'pō-əs\ administrative subdivision Ⓔ central Wales

Prague \'präg\ *or Czech* **Pra·ha** \'prä-hä\ city, capital of Czech Republic & formerly of Czechoslovakia

Praia \'prī-ə\ town, capital of Cape Verde

Prairie Provinces the Canadian provinces of Alberta, Manitoba, & Saskatchewan

Pres·ton \'pres-tən\ town ⓃⓌ England

Pre·to·ria \pri-'tōr-ē-ə, -'tor-\ city Republic of South Africa, administrative capital of the country in municipality of Tshwane

Prib·i·lof \'prib-ə-ˌlof\ islands Alaska in Bering Sea

Prince Ed·ward Island \ˌed-wərd\ island ⓈⒺ Canada in Gulf of Saint Lawrence; a province; capital, Charlottetown

Prince Ru·pert's Land \'rü-pərts\ historical region Ⓝ & Ⓦ Canada consisting of drainage basin of Hudson Bay granted 1670 by King Charles II to Hudson's Bay Company

Prince·ton \'prin(t)-stən\ town Ⓦ central New Jersey

Prín·ci·pe \'prin(t)-sə-pə\ island Ⓦ Africa in Gulf of Guinea — see SÃO TOMÉ AND PRÍNCIPE

Pris·ti·na \'prēsh-tē-ˌnä\ town, capital of Kosovo

Pro·vence \prə-'vän(t)s\ region ⓈⒺ France on the Mediterranean

Prov·i·dence \'präv-əd-ən(t)s, -ə-ˌden(t)s\ city, capital of Rhode Island

Pro·vo \'prō-vō\ city Ⓝ central Utah

Prud·hoe Bay \'prü-dō\ inlet of Beaufort Sea Ⓝ Alaska

Prus·sia \'prəsh-ə\ former kingdom &, later, state Germany; capital, Berlin — **Prus·sian** \-ən\ *adj or n*

Pueb·lo \pü-'eb-lō, 'pweb-, pyü-'eb-\ city ⓈⒺ central Colorado ⓈⓈⒺ of Colorado Springs

Puer·to Ri·co \ˌpōrt-ə-'rē-kō, ˌport-, ˌpwert-\ island West Indies Ⓔ of Hispaniola; a self-governing commonwealth associated with U.S.; capital, San Juan — **Puer·to Ri·can** \-'rē-kən\ *adj or n*

Pu·get Sound \ˌpyü-jət\ arm of the North Pacific Ⓦ Washington

Pu·ne \'pü-nə\ city Ⓦ India, ⒺⓈⒺ of Bombay

Pun·jab \ˌpən-'jäb, -'jab, 'pen-ˌjäb, -ˌjab\ region in Pakistan & ⓃⓌ India in valley of the Indus

Pu·san \'pü-ˌsän\ *or* **Bu·san** \'bü-\ city ⓈⒺ South Korea

Pyong·yang *or* **Pyeong·yang** \'pyóŋ-ˌyaŋ, 'pyəŋ-, -ˌyäŋ\ city, capital of North Korea

Pyr·e·nees \'pir-ə-ˌnēz\ mountains on French–Spanish border extending from Bay of Biscay to the Mediterranean; highest Pico de Aneto 11,168 ft. (3404 m.)

Qa·ra·ghan·dy \ˌkär-ə-'gän-dē\ *or* **Ka·ra·gan·da** \-də\ city central Kazakhstan

Qa·tar \'kät-ər, 'gät-, 'gət-\ independent country Ⓔ Arabia on peninsula extending into Persian Gulf; capital, Doha — **Qa·tari** \kə-'tär-ē, gə-\ *adj or n*

Qing·dao \'chiŋ-'daú\ *or* **Tsing·tao** \'chiŋ-'daú, '(t)siŋ-\ city & port Ⓔ China

Qi·qi·har \'chē-'chē-'här\ *or* **Ch'i–ch'i–ha–erh** \'chē-'chē-'hä-'ər\ city ⓃⒺ China

Que·bec \kwi-'bek, ki-\ *or French* **Qué·bec** \kā-'bek\ **1** province E Canada **2** city, its capital, on the Saint Lawrence — **Que·bec·er** *or* **Que·beck·er** \kwi-'bek-ər, ki-\ *n*

Queens \'kwēnz\ borough of New York City on Long Island E of Brooklyn

Queens·land \'kwēnz-ˌland, -lənd\ state NE Australia; capital, Brisbane — **Queens·land·er** \-ər\ *n*

Que·zon City \'kā-ˌsȯn\ city Philippines in Luzon; formerly capital of the country

Qui·to \'kē-tō\ city, capital of Ecuador

Ra·bat \rə-'bät\ city, capital of Morocco

Rai·nier, Mount \rə-'ni(ə)r, rā-\ mountain 14,410 ft. (4392 m.) W central Washington; highest in Cascade Range

Raj·pu·ta·na \ˌräj-pə-'tän-ə\ *or* **Ra·ja·sthan** \'räj-ə-ˌstän\ region NW India S of Punjab

Ra·leigh \'rȯ-lē, 'räl-ē\ city, capital of North Carolina

Ran·cho Cu·ca·mon·ga \'ran-chō-ˌkü-kə-'məŋ-gə\ city SW California

Rand — *see* WITWATERSRAND

Range·ley Lakes \'rānj-lē\ chain of lakes W Maine & N New Hampshire

Rangoon — *see* YANGON

Ra·wal·pin·di \ˌrä-wəl-'pin-dē, raȯl-'pin-, rȯl-'pin-\ city NE Pakistan NNW of Lahore

Read·ing \'red-iŋ\ town S England

Re·ci·fe \rə-'sē-fə\ *or formerly* **Per·nam·bu·co** \ˌpər-nəm-'b(y)ü-kō, ˌper-nəm-'bü-\ city NE Brazil

Red \'red\ **1** river 1018 mi. (1638 km.) long flowing E on Oklahoma–Texas boundary and into the Atchafalaya & the Mississippi in Louisiana **2** sea between Arabia & NE Africa

Red·bridge \'red-(ˌ)brij\ borough of NE Greater London, England

Re·gi·na \ri-'jī-nə\ city, capital of Saskatchewan, Canada

Re·no \'rē-nō\ city NW Nevada

Republic of the Congo — *see* CONGO 3

Ré·union \rē-'yün-yən\ island W Indian Ocean; an overseas division of France; capital, Saint-Denis

Reyk·ja·vik \'rāk-(y)ə-ˌvik, -ˌvēk\ city, capital of Iceland

Rhine \'rīn\ river 820 mi. (1320 km.) long W Europe flowing from SE Switzerland to North Sea in the Netherlands — **Rhen·ish** \'ren-ish, 'rē-nish\ *adj*

Rhine·land \'rīn-ˌland, -lənd\ *or German* **Rhein·land** \'rīn-ˌlänt\ the part of Germany W of the Rhine — **Rhine·land·er** \'rīn-ˌlan-dər, -lən-\ *n*

Rhode Is·land \rō-'dī-lənd\ **1** *or officially* **Rhode Island and Providence Plantations** state NE U.S.; capital, Providence **2** — *see* AQUIDNECK ISLAND — **Rhode Island·er** \-lən-dər\ *n*

Rhodes \'rōdz\ island Greece in the SE Aegean

Rhodesia — *see* ZIMBABWE

Rhone \'rōn\ river 505 mi. (813 km.) long Switzerland & SE France

Rich·mond \'rich-mənd\ **1** — *see* STATEN ISLAND 2 **2** city, capital of Virginia

Richmond upon Thames borough of SW Greater London, England

Ri·ga \'rē-gə\ city, capital of Latvia

Rio RIO DE JANEIRO

Rio de Ja·nei·ro \'rē-ō-ˌdā-zhə-'ne(ə)r-ō, -ˌdē-, -də-, -jə-'ne(ə)r-ō\ city SE Brazil on Guanabara Bay

Rio Grande \ˌrē-(ˌ)ō-'grand(-ē)\ *or Mexican* **Rio Bra·vo** \-'bräv-ō\ river 1885 mi. (3034 km.) long SW U.S., forming part of U.S.–Mexico boundary, and flowing into Gulf of Mexico

Río Muni — *see* MBINI

Riv·er·side \'riv-ər-ˌsīd\ city S California

Riv·i·era \ˌriv-ē-'er-ə\ coast region SE France & NW Italy

Ri·yadh \rē-'(y)äd\ city, capital of Saudi Arabia

Ro·a·noke \'rō-(ə-)ˌnōk\ city W Virginia

Roanoke Island island North Carolina S of entrance to Albemarle Sound

Rob·son, Mount \'räb-sən\ mountain 12,972 ft. (3954 m.) W Canada in E British Columbia; highest in the Canadian Rockies

Roch·es·ter \'räch-ə-stər, 'räch-ˌes-tər\ city W New York

Rock·ford \'räk-fərd\ city N Illinois

Rocky Mountains \'räk-ē\ *or* **the Rock·ies** \'räk-ēz\ mountains W North America extending SE from N Alaska to central New Mexico — *see* ELBERT (Mount), ROBSON (Mount)

Roman Empire the empire of ancient Rome

Ro·ma·nia \rō-'mā-nē-ə, -nyə\ *or* **Ru·ma·nia** \rü-\ country SE Europe on Black Sea; capital, Bucharest

Rom·blon \räm-'blōn\ island group central Philippines

Rome \'rōm\ **1** *or Italian* **Ro·ma** \'rō-mä\ city, capital of Italy **2** the Roman Empire

Ro·sa·rio \rō-'zär-ē-ˌō, -'sär-\ city E central Argentina on the Paraná

Ro·seau \rō-'zō\ seaport, capital of Dominica

Ros·tov-on-Don \rē-'stȯf-ˌän-'dän, -'stȯv-, -ˌȯn-\ city S Russia in Europe

Ros·well \'räz-ˌwel, -wəl\ city SE New Mexico

Ro·ta \'rōt-ə\ island W Pacific in the Marianas

Rot·ter·dam \'rät-ər-ˌdam\ city & port SW Netherlands

Ru·an·da–Urun·di \rü-ˌän-də-ü-'rün-dē\ former trust territory E central Africa bordering on Lake Tanganyika and administered by Belgium; divided into Burundi & Rwanda 1962

Rudolf, Lake — *see* TURKANA (Lake)

Ruhr \'rü(ə)r\ **1** river 146 mi. (235 km.) long W Germany flowing NW & N to the Rhine **2** industrial district W Germany E of the Rhine in valley of Ruhr River

Rumania — *see* ROMANIA

Rupert's Land PRINCE RUPERT'S LAND

Rush·more, Mount \'rəsh-ˌmō(ə)r, -ˌmȯ(ə)r\ mountain 5600 ft. (1707 m.) W South Dakota in Black Hills

Rus·sia \'rəsh-ə\ **1** former empire largely having the same boundaries as U.S.S.R.; capital, Petrograd (Saint Petersburg) **2** UNION OF SOVIET SOCIALIST REPUBLICS **3** country E Europe & N Asia; capital, Moscow; a republic **(Russian Soviet Federated Socialist Republic)** of U.S.S.R. 1922–91

Ru·the·nia \rü-'thē-nyə, -nē-ə\ region W Ukraine W of the N Carpathians — **Ru·the·nian** \rü-'thē-nyən, -nē-ən\ *adj or n*

Ru·wen·zo·ri \ˌrü-(w)ən-'zōr-ē, -'zȯr-\ mountain group E central Africa between Uganda & Democratic Republic of the Congo; highest Mount Margherita 16,763 ft. (5109 m.)

Rwan·da *or formerly* **Ru·an·da** \rü-'än-də\ country E central Africa, until 1962 part of Ruanda–Urundi trust territory; capital, Kigali — **Rwan·dan** \-dən\ *adj or n*

Ryu·kyu \rē-'(y)ü-k(y)ü\ islands Japan extending in an arc from Kyushu, Japan, to Taiwan, China — **Ryu·kyu·an** \-ˌ(y)ü-'k(y)ü-ən\ *adj or n*

Saar \'sär, 'zär\ **1** river about 150 mi. (241 km.) long Europe flowing from E France to W Germany **2** *or* **Saarland** \'sär-ˌland, 'zär-\ region W Europe in valley of Saar River between France & Germany

Sa·bah \'säb-ə\ part of Malaysia in NE Borneo

Sac·ra·men·to \ˌsak-rə-'ment-ō\ **1** river 382 mi. (615 km.) long N California flowing S into Suisun Bay **2** city, capital of California

Sag·ue·nay \'sag-ə-ˌnā, ˌsag-ə-'nā\ river 105 mi. (169 km.) long Canada in S Quebec flowing E into the Saint Lawrence

Sa·ha·ra \sə-'har-ə, -'her-, -'här-\ desert region N Africa extending from Atlantic coast to Red Sea — **Sa·ha·ran** \-ən\ *adj*

Sa·hel \'sa-hil, sə-'hil\ the S fringe of the Sahara

Saigon — *see* HO CHI MINH CITY

Saint Al·bans \'ȯl-bənz\ city SE England

Saint Cath·a·rines \'kath-(ə-)rənz\ city Canada in SE Ontario

Saint Christopher — see SAINT KITTS

Saint Clair, Lake \'kla(ə)r, 'kle(ə)r\ lake SE Michigan & SE Ontario connected by **Saint Clair River** (40 mi. or 64 km. long) with Lake Huron & draining by Detroit River into Lake Erie

Saint Croix \sänt-'krȯi, sənt-\ **1** river 129 mi. (208 km.) long Canada & U.S. on border between New Brunswick & Maine **2** island West Indies; largest of Virgin Islands of the U.S.

Saint Eli·as, Mount \ˌsänt-ᵊl-'ī-əs\ mountain 18,008 ft. (5489 m.) on Alaska–Yukon boundary in **Saint Elias Range**

Saint George's \'jȯr-jəz\ town, capital of Grenada

Saint George's Channel channel British Isles between SW Wales & Ireland

Saint Gott·hard \sänt-'gät-ərd, -'gäth-, sənt-\ **1** pass S central Switzerland in Saint Gotthard Range of the Alps **2** road tunnel 10 mi. (16 km.) long near Saint Gotthard Pass

Saint He·le·na \ˌsänt-ᵊl-'ē-nə, ˌsänt-hə-'lē-\ island South Atlantic; a British colony

Saint Hel·ens \sänt-'hel-ənz, sənt-\ town NW England ENE of Liverpool

Saint Helens, Mount volcano S Washington

Saint John \sänt-'jän, sənt-\ city & port Canada in New Brunswick

Saint John's \sänt-'jänz, sənt-\ **1** city, capital of Antigua and Barbuda **2** city, capital of Newfoundland and Labrador, Canada

Saint Kitts \sänt-'kits\ or **Saint Chris·to·pher** \-'kris-tə-fər\ island West Indies in the Leeward Islands; with Nevis forms independent **Saint Kitts and Nevis**; capital, Basseterre (on Saint Kitts)

Saint Law·rence \sänt-'lȯr-ən(t)s, sənt-, -'lär-\ **1** river 760 mi. (1223 km.) long E Canada in Ontario & Quebec bordering on U.S. in New York and flowing from Lake Ontario NE into the **Gulf of Saint Lawrence** (inlet of the Atlantic) **2** seaway Canada & U.S. in and along the Saint Lawrence between Lake Ontario & Montreal

Saint Lou·is \sänt-'lü-əs, sənt-\ city E Missouri on the Mississippi

Saint Lu·cia \sänt-'lü-shə, sənt-\ island West Indies in the Windwards S of Martinique; an independent country; capital, Castries

Saint Paul \'pȯl\ city, capital of Minnesota

Saint Pe·ters·burg \'pēt-ərz-ˌbərg\ **1** city W Florida **2** or 1914–24 **Pet·ro·grad** \'pe-trə-ˌgrad, -ˌgräd\ or 1924–91 **Le·nin·grad** \'len-ən-ˌgrad, -ˌgräd\ city W Russia in Europe

Saint Thom·as \'täm-əs\ island West Indies, one of Virgin Islands of the U.S.; chief town, Charlotte Amalie

Saint Vin·cent \sänt-'vin(t)-sənt, sənt-\ island West Indies in the central Windward Islands; with N Grenadines forms independent **Saint Vincent and the Grenadines**; capital, Kingstown (on Saint Vincent)

Sai·pan \sī-'pan, -'pän; 'sī-ˌpan, -ˌpän\ island W Pacific in S central Marianas; contains capital of Northern Mariana Islands

Sa·kai \(')sä-'kī\ city Japan in S Honshu

Sa·kha·lin \'sak-ə-ˌlēn, -lən; ˌsak-ə-'lēn\ island SE Russia in W Pacific N of Hokkaido, Japan; until 1945 divided between Japan & U.S.S.R.

Sal·a·mis \'sal-ə-məs\ **1** ancient city Cyprus on E coast **2** island Greece off Attica

Sa·lem \'sā-ləm\ city, capital of Oregon

Sal·ford \'sȯl-fərd\ urban area NW England

Sa·li·nas \sə-'lē-nəs\ city W California

Salisbury — see HARARE

Salop — see SHROPSHIRE

Salt Lake City city, capital of Utah

Sal·va·dor \'sal-və-ˌdȯ(ə)r, ˌsal-və-'dȯ(ə)r\ or **Ba·hia** \bä-'ē-ə\ city NE Brazil on the Atlantic — **Sal·va·dor·an** \ˌsal-və-'dȯr-ən, -'dōr-\ or **Sal·va·dor·ean** or **Sal·va·dor·ian** \-ē-ən\ adj or n

Sal·ween \'sal-ˌwēn\ river about 1500 mi. (2415 km.) long SE Asia flowing from Tibet S into Bay of Bengal in Myanmar

Sa·mar \'säm-ˌär\ island central Philippines

Sa·ma·ra \sə-'mär-ə\ or 1935–91 **Kuy·by·shev** \'kwē-bə-ˌshef, -ˌshev\ city W Russia, on the Volga

Sam·ar·qand or **Sam·ar·kand** \'sam-ər-ˌkand\ city E Uzbekistan

Sam·ni·um \'sam-nē-əm\ ancient country S central Italy — **Sam·nite** \'sam-ˌnīt\ adj or n

Sa·moa \sə-'mō-ə\ **1** islands SW central Pacific N of Tonga; divided at longitude 171° W into American Samoa (or Eastern Samoa) & independent Samoa **2** or formerly **Western Samoa** islands Samoa W of 171° W; an independent country since 1962; capital, Apia — **Sa·mo·an** \-ən\ adj or n

Sa·mos \'sā-ˌmäs\ island Greece in the Aegean off coast of Turkey — **Sa·mi·an** \-mē-ən\ adj or n

San·aa or **Sana** \'san-ˌä, san-'ä\ city SW Arabia, capital of Yemen & formerly of Yemen Arab Republic

San An·dre·as Fault \ˌsan-an-'drā-əs\ zone of faults in California extending from N coast SE toward head of Gulf of California

San An·to·nio \ˌsan-ən-'tō-nē-ˌō\ city S Texas

San Ber·nar·di·no \ˌsan-ˌbər-nə(r)-'dē-nō\ city S California

San Buenaventura — see VENTURA

San Di·ego \ˌsan-dē-'ā-gō\ coastal city SW California

Sand·wich \'san-(ˌ)(d)wich\ town SE England

Sandwich Islands — see HAWAII

San Fran·cis·co \ˌsan-frən-'sis-kō\ city W California on San Francisco Bay & Pacific Ocean

San Joa·quin \ˌsan-wä-'kēn, -wȯ-\ river 350 mi. (563 km.) long central California flowing NW into the Sacramento

San Jo·se \ˌsan-ə-'zā\ city W California SE of San Francisco

San Jo·sé \ˌsan-ə-'zā, -ō-'zā, -hō-'zā\ city, capital of Costa Rica

San Juan \san-'hwän, -'wän\ city, capital of Puerto Rico

San Ma·ri·no \ˌsan-mə-'rē-nō\ **1** small country S Europe surrounded by Italy ENE of Florence near Adriatic Sea **2** town, its capital — **Sam·mar·i·nese** \ˌsam-ˌmar-ə-'nēz, -'nēs\ n — **San Mar·i·nese** \ˌsan-\ adj or n

San Pe·dro Su·la \san-ˌpā-ˌdrō-'sü-lə\ city NW Honduras

San Sal·va·dor \san-'sal-və-ˌdȯ(ə)r\ **1** island central Bahamas **2** city, capital of El Salvador

San·ta Ana \ˌsant-ə-'an-ə\ city SW California ESE of Long Beach

San·ta Bar·ba·ra \-'bär-b(ə-)rə\ **1** city S California **2** or **Channel** islands California off SW coast

San·ta Clara \-'klar-ə, -'kler-ə\ city W California NW of San Jose

San·ta Cla·ri·ta \-klə-'rēt-ə\ city S California N of Los Angeles

San·ta Fe \ˌsant-ə-'fā\ city, capital of New Mexico

Santa Fe Trail pioneer route to the SW U.S. about 1200 mi. (1930 km.) long used especially 1821–80 from vicinity of Kansas City, Missouri, to Santa Fe, New Mexico

San·ta Ro·sa \ˌsan-tə-'rō-zə\ city W California N of San Francisco

San·ti·a·go \ˌsant-ē-'äg-ō, ˌsänt-\ city, capital of Chile

\ə\ abut	\au̇\ out	\i\ tip	\ȯ\ saw	\u̇\ foot
\ər\ further	\ch\ chin	\ī\ life	\ȯi\ coin	\y\ yet
\a\ mat	\e\ pet	\j\ job	\th\ thin	\yü\ few
\ā\ take	\ē\ easy	\ŋ\ sing	\th\ this	\yu̇\ cure
\ä\ cot, cart	\g\ go	\ō\ bone	\ü\ food	\zh\ vision

San·to Do·min·go \ˌsant-əd-ə-'miŋ-gō\ *or formerly* **Ci·u·dad Tru·ji·llo** \sē-ù-ˌthä-trü-'hē-(y)ō, ˌsē-ù-ˌdad-\ city, capital of Dominican Republic

São Pau·lo \ˌsä-ō-'pau̇-lō\ city SE Brazil

São To·mé \ˌsä-ō-tō-'mä\ town, capital of São Tomé and Príncipe

São Tomé and Príncipe country W Africa; formerly a Portuguese colony; became independent 1975; capital, São Tomé

Sap·po·ro \'säp-ə-ˌrō; sə-'pōr-ō, -'pór-\ city Japan on W Hokkaido

Sa·ra·je·vo \'sär-ə-yə-ˌvō\ city SE central Bosnia and Herzegovina, its capital

Sa·ra·tov \sə-'rät-əf\ city W Russia, on the Volga

Sa·ra·wak \sə-'rä-(ˌ)wä(k), -ˌwak\ part of Malaysia in N Borneo

Sar·din·ia \sär-'din-ē-ə, -'din-yə\ island Italy in the Mediterranean S of Corsica — **Sar·din·ian** \-'din-ē-ən, -'din-yən\ *adj or n*

Sar·gas·so Sea \sär-ˌgas-ō\ area of nearly still water in the North Atlantic lying chiefly between 20° & 35° latitude & 30° & 70° W longitude

Sas·katch·e·wan \sə-'skach-ə-wən, sa-, -ˌwän\ province W Canada; capital, Regina

Sas·ka·toon \ˌsas-kə-'tün\ city central Saskatchewan, Canada

Sau·di Ara·bia \ˌsauḋ-ē-ə-'rä-bē-ə, ˌsȯd-ē-, sä-ˌüd-ē-\ country SW Asia occupying largest part of Arabian Peninsula; a kingdom; capital, Riyadh — **Saudi** *adj or n* — **Saudi Arabian** *adj or n*

Sault Sainte Ma·rie Canals \ˌsü-(ˌ)sänt-mə-'rē\ *or* **Soo Canals** \ˌsü\ three ship canals, two in U.S. (Michigan) & one in Canada (Ontario), at rapids in river connecting Lake Superior & Lake Huron

Sa·vaii \sə-'vī-ˌē\ island, largest in independent Samoa

Sa·van·nah \sə-'van-ə\ city & port E Georgia

Sa·voy \sə-'vȯi\ *or French* **Sa·voie** \sȧ-vwȧ\ region SE France SW of Switzerland bordering on Italy — **Sa·voy·ard** \sə-'vȯi-ˌärd, sav-ˌȯi-'ärd; ˌsav-wä-'yär(d)\ *adj or n*

Sca·fell Pike \ˌskȯ-'fel\ mountain 3210 ft. (978 m.) NW England; highest in Cumbrian Mountains & in England

Scan·di·na·via \ˌskan-də-'nä-vē-ə, -vyə\ 1 peninsula N Europe occupied by Norway & Sweden 2 Denmark, Norway, Sweden, & sometimes also Iceland & Finland — **Scan·di·na·vian** \-vē-ən, -vyən\ *adj or n*

Scar·bor·ough \'skär-ˌbər-ə, -b(ə-)rə\ former city Canada in SE Ontario; now part of Toronto

Schel·de \'skel-də\ *or* **Scheldt** \'skelt\ *or* **Es·caut** \e-'skō\ river 270 mi. (434 km.) long W Europe flowing from N France through Belgium into North Sea in Netherlands

Schuyl·kill \'skü-kᵊl, 'skül-ˌkil\ river 131 mi. (211 km.) long SE Pennsylvania flowing SE into the Delaware River at Philadelphia

Scil·ly, Isles of \'sil-ē\ island group SW England off Land's End

Sco·tia \'skō-shə\ SCOTLAND — the Medieval Latin name

Scot·land \'skät-lənd\ *or Latin* **Cal·e·do·nia** \ˌkal-ə-'dō-nyə, -nē-ə\ country N Great Britain; a division of United Kingdom; capital, Edinburgh

Scotts·dale \'skäts-ˌdäl\ city SW central Arizona E of Phoenix

Scyth·ia \'sith-ē-ə, 'sith-\ ancient area of Europe & Asia N & NE of Black Sea & E of Aral Sea — **Scyth·i·an** \-ē-ən\ *adj or n*

Se·at·tle \sē-'at-ᵊl\ city & port W Washington

Seine \'sān, 'sen\ river 480 mi. (772 km.) long N France flowing NW into English Channel

Sel·kirk \'sel-ˌkərk\ range of the Rocky Mountains SE British Columbia, Canada; highest peak, 11,555 ft. (3522 m.)

Se·ma·rang \sə-'mär-ˌäŋ\ city Indonesia in central Java

Sen·dai \(ˌ)sen-'dī\ city Japan in NE Honshu

Sen·e·ca Falls \'sen-i-kə\ village W central New York

Sen·e·gal \ˌsen-i-'gȯl\ 1 river 1015 mi. (1633 km.) long W Africa flowing W into the North Atlantic 2 country W Africa; capital, Dakar — **Sen·e·ga·lese** \ˌsen-i-gə-'lēz, -'lēs\ *adj or n*

Seoul \'sōl\ city, capital of South Korea

Ser·bia \'sər-bē-ə\ country S Europe in the Balkans; capital, Belgrade

Serbia and Montenegro *or 1992–2003* **Yugoslavia** former country S Europe; capital, Belgrade

Ser·en·ge·ti Plain \ˌser-ən-'get-ē\ area N Tanzania

Seven Hills the seven hills upon and about which was built the city of Rome, Italy

Sev·ern \'sev-ərn\ river 210 mi. (338 km.) long Wales & England flowing from E central Wales into Bristol Channel

Se·ville \sə-'vil\ *or Spanish* **Se·vi·lla** \sā-'vē-(y)ä\ city SW Spain

Sey·chelles \sā-'shel(z)\ islands W Indian Ocean NE of Madagascar; formerly a British colony; became independent 1976; capital, Victoria — **Sey·chel·lois** \ˌsā-shəl-'wä\ *n*

Shang·hai \shaŋ-'hī\ municipality & port E China

Shan·non \'shan-ən\ river 230 mi. (370 km.) long W Ireland flowing S & W into the North Atlantic

Shar·on, Plain of \'sher-ən\ region Israel on the coast

Shas·ta, Mount \'shas-tə\ mountain 14,162 ft. (4316 m.) N California in Cascade Range

Shatt al Ar·ab \ˌshat-ˌal-'ar-əb\ river 120 mi. (193 km.) long SE Iraq formed by flowing together of Euphrates & Tigris rivers and flowing SE into Persian Gulf

Shef·field \'shef-ˌēld\ city N England

Shen·an·do·ah \ˌshen-ən-'dō-ə, ˌshan-ə-'dō-ə\ valley Virginia between the Allegheney & Blue Ridge mountains

Shen·yang \'shən-'yäŋ\ *or traditionally* **Muk·den** \'mu̇k-dən, 'mək-; mu̇k-'den\ city NE China; chief city of Manchuria

Sher·brooke \'shər-ˌbru̇k\ city Quebec, Canada E of Montreal

Sher·wood Forest \ˌshər-ˌwu̇d\ ancient royal forest central England

Shet·land \'shet-lənd\ islands N Scotland NE of the Orkneys

Shi·jia·zhuang *or* **Shih–chia–chuang** \ˌshi(ə)r-jē-'äj-ˌwäŋ, ˌshē-jē-\ city NE China

Shi·ko·ku \shi-'kō-kü\ island S Japan E of Kyushu

Shi·raz \shi-'räz\ city SW central Iran

Shreve·port \'shrēv-ˌpō(ə)rt, -ˌpȯ(ə)rt\ city NW Louisiana on Red River

Shrews·bury \'sh(r)üz-ˌber-ē, 'shrōz-\ town W England

Shrop·shire \'shräp-shər, -ˌshir\ *or 1974–80* **Sal·op** \'sal-əp\ county W England bordering on Wales

Shu·ma·gin \'shü-mə-gən\ islands SW Alaska S of Alaska Peninsula

Siam — see THAILAND

Siam, Gulf of — see THAILAND (Gulf of)

Si·be·ria \sī-'bir-ē-ə\ region N Asia in Russia between the Urals & the North Pacific — **Si·be·ri·an** \-ē-ən\ *adj or n*

Sic·i·ly \'sis-(ə-)lē\ *or Italian* **Si·ci·lia** \sē-'chēl-yä\ island S Italy SW of toe of peninsula of Italy; capital, Palermo — **Si·cil·ian** \sə-'sil-yən\ *adj or n*

Si·er·ra Le·one \sē-ˌer-ə-lē-'ōn, ˌsir-ə-\ country W Africa on the North Atlantic; capital, Freetown — **Si·er·ra Le·on·ean** \-'ō-nē-ən\ *adj or n*

Si·er·ra Ma·dre \sē-ˌer-ə-'mäd-rē\ mountain system Mexico including **Sierra Madre Oc·ci·den·tal** \-ˌäk-sə-ˌden-'täl\ range W of the central plateau, **Sierra Madre Ori·en·tal** \-ˌōr-ē-ˌen-'täl, -ˌȯr-\ range E of the plateau, & **Sierra Madre del Sur** \-ˌdel-'sü(ə)r\ range to the S

Si·er·ra Ne·va·da \-nə-'vad-ə, -'väd-\ 1 mountain range E California & W Nevada — see WHITNEY (Mount) 2 mountain range S Spain; highest peak Mulhacén 11,410 ft. (3478 m.), highest in Spain

Sik·kim \'sik-əm, -,im\ former country SE Asia on S slope of the Himalayas between Nepal & Bhutan; part of India (country) since 1975; capital, Gangtok

Si·le·sia \sī-'lē-zh(ē-)ə, -sh(ē-)ə, sə-\ region E central Europe in valley of the upper Oder; formerly chiefly in Germany now chiefly in E Czech Republic & SW Poland — **Si·le·sian** \-zh(ē-)ən, -sh(ē-)ən\ adj or n

Silk Road or **Silk Route** ancient trade route that extended from China to the Mediterranean

Sim·coe, Lake \'sim-kō\ lake Canada in SE Ontario

Si·mi Valley \sē-'mē\ city SW California W of Los Angeles

Si·nai \'sī-,nī\ **1** mountain on Sinai Peninsula where, according to the Bible, the Law was given to Moses **2** peninsula, extension of continent of Asia NE Egypt between Red Sea & the Mediterranean

Sin·ga·pore \'siŋ-(g)ə-,pō(ə)r, -,pó(ə)r\ **1** island off S end of Malay Peninsula; an independent country **2** city, its capital — **Sin·ga·por·ean** \,siŋ-(g)ə-'pōr-ē-ən, -'pór-\ adj or n

Sinkiang Uighur — see XINJIANG UYGUR

Sioux Falls \'sü\ city SE South Dakota; largest in state

Skag·ge·rak \'skag-ə-,rak\ arm of North Sea between S Norway & N Denmark

Skag·way \'skag-wā\ city SE Alaska N of Juneau

Skop·je \'skóp-,yā\ city, capital of independent Macedonia

Sla·vo·nia \slə-'vō-nē-ə, -nyə\ region E Croatia — **Sla·vo·ni·an** \-nē-ən, -nyən\ adj or n

Slo·va·kia \slō-'väk-ē-ə, -'vak-\ country central Europe; capital, Bratislava; formerly part of Czechoslovakia

Slo·ve·nia \slō-'vē-nē-ə, -nyə\ country S Europe; capital, Ljubljana; a republic of Yugoslavia 1946–91

Smyrna — see IZMIR

Snake \'snāk\ river NW U.S. flowing from NW Wyoming into the Columbia in SE Washington

Snow·don \'snód-ᵊn\ massif 3560 ft. (1085 m.) in **Snow·do·nia** \snō-'dō-nē-ə, -nyə\ (mountainous district) NW Wales; highest point in Wales

So·ci·e·ty \sə-'sī-ət-ē\ islands South Pacific belonging to France; chief island, Tahiti

So·fia \'sō-fē-ə, 'só-, sō-'fē-\ city, capital of Bulgaria

So·ho \'sō-,hō\ district of central London, England

So·li·hull \,sō-li-'həl\ town central England

Sol·o·mon \'säl-ə-mən\ **1** islands W Pacific E of New Guinea divided between Papua New Guinea & independent **Solomon Islands** (capital, Honiara) **2** sea, arm of Coral Sea W of the Solomons

So·ma·lia \sō-'mäl-ē-ə, sə-, -'mäl-yə\ country E Africa on Gulf of Aden & Indian Ocean; capital, Mogadishu — **So·ma·li·an** \-'mäl-ē-ən, -'mäl-yən\ adj or n

So·ma·li·land \sō-'mäl-ē-,land, sə-\ region E Africa consisting of Somalia, Djibouti, & part of E Ethiopia — **So·ma·li** \sō-'mäl-ē\ n

Som·er·set \'səm-ər-,set, -sət\ or **Som·er·set·shire** \-,shi(ə)r, -shər\ county SW England

So·nor·an \sə-'nór-ən, -'nór-\ or **Sonora** desert SW U.S. & NW Mexico

Soo Canals — see SAULT SAINTE MARIE CANALS

South island S New Zealand

South Africa, Republic of country S Africa; formerly (as **Union of South Africa**) a British dominion; became independent 1961; administrative capital, Pretoria; legislative capital, Cape Town; judicial capital, Bloemfontein — **South African** adj or n

South America continent of Western Hemisphere SE of North America and chiefly S of the Equator — **South American** adj or n

South·amp·ton \saùth-'(h)am(p)-tən\ city S England

South Australia state S Australia; capital, Adelaide — **South Australian** adj or n

South Bend \'bend\ city N Indiana

South Cape or **South Point** — see KA LAE

South Car·o·li·na \,kar-ə-'lī-nə\ state SE U.S.; capital, Columbia — **South Car·o·lin·i·an** \-'lin-ē-ən, -'lin-yən\ adj or n

South China Sea — see CHINA

South Da·ko·ta \də-'kōt-ə\ state NW central U.S.; capital, Pierre — **South Da·ko·tan** \-'kōt-ᵊn\ adj or n

South·end–on–Sea \,saù-,thend-,än-'sē, -,ón-\ seaside resort SE England E of London

Southern Alps mountain range New Zealand in W South Island extending almost the length of the island

Southern Hemisphere the half of the earth that lies S of the Equator

Southern Rhodesia — see ZIMBABWE

South Korea — see KOREA

South Seas the areas of the Atlantic, Indian, & Pacific oceans in the Southern Hemisphere

South Shields \'shē(ə)l(d)z\ seaport N England

South Sudan country E Africa formed from the S part of Sudan 2011; capital, Juba

South Vietnam — see VIETNAM

South·wark \'səth-ərk, 'saùth-wərk\ borough of S Greater London, England

South–West Africa territory Africa; under administration of Union (later Republic) of South Africa 1919–90 — see NAMIBIA

South Yorkshire metropolitan county N England

Soviet Central Asia portion of central & SW Asia formerly belonging to U.S.S.R. and including Kirghiz, Tadzhik, Turkmen, & Uzbek soviet socialist republics & sometimes thought to also include Kazakh Soviet Socialist Republic

Soviet Russia — see UNION OF SOVIET SOCIALIST REPUBLICS

Soviet Union — see UNION OF SOVIET SOCIALIST REPUBLICS

So·we·to \sō-'wät-ō, -'wet-\ residential area NE Republic of South Africa adjoining SW Johannesburg

Spain \'spān\ country SW Europe on Iberian Peninsula; a kingdom; capital, Madrid

Spanish America **1** the Spanish-speaking countries of America **2** the parts of America settled and formerly governed by the Spanish

Spanish Guinea — see EQUATORIAL GUINEA

Spanish Sahara — see WESTERN SAHARA

Spar·ta \'spärt-ə\ or **Lac·e·dae·mon** \,las-ə-'dē-mən\ ancient city S Greece in Peloponnese; capital of Laconia

Spo·kane \spō-'kan\ city E Washington

Spring·field \'spriŋ-,fēld\ **1** city, capital of Illinois **2** city SW Massachusetts **3** city SW Missouri

Sri Lan·ka \(')srē-'läŋ-kə, (')shrē-\ or formerly **Cey·lon** \si-'län, sā-\ country having the same boundaries as island of Ceylon; capital, Colombo — **Sri Lan·kan** \-kən\ adj or n

Sri·na·gar \sri-'nəg-ər\ city N India

Staf·ford \'staf-ərd\ town W central England

Staf·ford·shire \'staf-ərd-,shi(ə)r, -shər\ or **Stafford** county W central England

Staked Plain — see LLANO ESTACADO

Stam·ford \'stam(p)-fərd\ city SW Connecticut

Stan·ley \'stan-lē\ town, capital of Falkland Islands

Stat·en Island \'stat-ᵊn\ **1** island SE New York SW of mouth of the Hudson **2** or formerly **Rich·mond** \'rich-mənd\ borough of New York City including Staten Island

Sterling Heights city SE Michigan

Stir·ling \'stər-liŋ\ town central Scotland

Stock·holm \'stäk-,hō(l)m\ city, capital of Sweden

Stock·port \'stäk-,pō(ə)rt, -,pó(ə)rt\ town NW England

\ə\ abut	\aù\ out	\i\ tip	\ò\ saw	\ú\ foot
\ər\ further	\ch\ chin	\ī\ life	\ói\ coin	\y\ yet
\a\ mat	\e\ pet	\j\ job	\th\ thin	\yü\ few
\ā\ take	\ē\ easy	\ŋ\ sing	\th\ this	\yú\ cure
\ä\ cot, cart	\g\ go	\ō\ bone	\ü\ food	\zh\ vision

Stock·ton \'stäk-tən\ city central California

Stoke–on–Trent \ˌstō-ˌkòn-'trent, -ˌkän-\ city central England

Stone Mountain mountain 1686 ft. (514 m.) NW Georgia E of Atlanta

Stor·no·way \'stòr-nə-ˌwā\ seaport NW Scotland; chief town of Lewis with Harris Island

Stra·bane \strə-'ban\ district W Northern Ireland

Strom·bo·li \'sträm-bə-lē\ volcano 2500 ft. (758 m.) Italy on **Stromboli Island** in Tyrrhenian Sea

Stutt·gart \'shtút-ˌgärt, 'stút-, 'stət-\ city SW Germany

Styx \'stiks\ chief river of Hades in Greek mythology

Süchow — see XUZHOU

Su·cre \'sü-krā\ city, constitutional capital of Bolivia

Su·dan \sü-'dan, -'dän\ 1 region N Africa S of the Sahara between the Atlantic & the upper Nile 2 country NE Africa S of Egypt; capital, Khartoum — **Su·da·nese** \ˌsüd-ᵊn-'ēz, -'ēs\ adj or n

Sudbury — see GREATER SUDBURY

Suez, Gulf of arm of Red Sea

Suez, Isthmus of isthmus NE Egypt between Mediterranean & Red seas connecting Africa & Asia

Suez Canal canal 100 mi. (161 km.) long NE Egypt across the Isthmus of Suez

Suf·folk \'səf-ək\ county E England on North Sea

Sui·sun Bay \sə-'sün\ inlet of San Francisco Bay, W central California

Su·la·we·si \ˌsü-lə-'wä-sē\ island Indonesia E of Borneo

Su·lu \'sü-lü\ 1 archipelago SW Philippines SW of Mindanao 2 sea W Philippines

Su·ma·tra \sü-'mä-trə\ island W Indonesia S of Malay Peninsula — **Su·ma·tran** \-trən\ adj or n

Su·mer \'sü-mər\ the S division of ancient Babylonia — **Su·me·ri·an** \sü-'mer-ē-ən, -'mir-\ adj or n

Sun·belt \'sən-ˌbelt\ region S & SW U.S.

Sun·da \'sün-də\ strait between Java & Sumatra

Sun·der·land \'sən-dər-lənd\ seaport N England

Sun·ny·vale \'sən-ē-ˌvāl\ city W California

Sun Valley resort center central Idaho

Su·pe·ri·or, Lake \sü-'pir-ē-ər\ lake E central North America in U.S. & Canada; largest of the Great Lakes

Su·ra·ba·ya \ˌsùr-ə-'bī-ə\ city Indonesia in NE Java

Su·ri·na·me \ˌsùr-ə-'näm-ə\ country S South America between Guyana & French Guiana; formerly a territory of the Netherlands; became independent 1975; capital, Paramaribo — **Su·ri·nam·er** \'sùr-ə-ˌnäm-ər, ˌsùr-ə-'näm-\ n — **Su·ri·nam·ese** \ˌsùr-ə-nə-'mēz, -'mēs\ adj or n

Sur·rey \'sər-ē, 'sə-rē\ city Canada in SW British Columbia

Sut·ton \'sət-ᵊn\ borough of S Greater London, England

Su·va \'sü-və\ seaport, capital of Fiji on Viti Levu Island

Sverdlovsk — see YEKATERINBURG

Swan·sea \'swän-zē\ city & port SE Wales

Swa·zi·land \'swäz-ē-ˌland\ country SE Africa between Republic of South Africa & Mozambique; an independent kingdom; capital, Mbabane — **Swa·zi** \'swäz-ē\ adj or n

Swe·den \'swēd-ᵊn\ country N Europe in Scandinavia bordering on Baltic Sea; a kingdom; capital, Stockholm

Swit·zer·land \'swit-sər-lənd\ country W Europe in the Alps; capital, Bern

Syd·ney \'sid-nē\ city SE Australia, capital of New South Wales

Syr·a·cuse \'sir-ə-ˌkyüs, -ˌkyüz\ city central New York

Syr·ia \'sir-ē-ə\ 1 ancient region SW Asia bordering on the Mediterranean 2 former French mandate (1920–44) including present Syria & Lebanon 3 country S of Turkey; capital, Damascus — **Syr·i·an** \'sir-ē-ən\ adj or n

Syrian Desert desert region between Mediterranean coast & the Euphrates in N Saudi Arabia, SE Syria, W Iraq, & NE Jordan

Ta·ble Bay harbor of Cape Town, Republic of South Africa

Ta·briz \tə-'brēz\ city NW Iran

Ta·co·ma \tə-'kō-mə\ city & port W Washington S of Seattle

Tae·gu \'tā-gü\ or **Dae·gu** \'dā-\ city SE South Korea

Tae·jon \'tā-ˌjən\ or **Dae·jeon** \'dā-\ city central South Korea NW of Taegu

Ta·gus \'tā-gəs\ or Spanish **Ta·jo** \'tä-hō\ or Portuguese **Te·jo** \'tä-zhü\ river 626 mi. (1007 km.) long Spain & Portugal flowing W into the North Atlantic

Ta·hi·ti \tə-'hēt-ē\ island South Pacific in Society Islands

Tai·bei \'tī-'bā\ or **Tai·pei** \-'pā, -'bā\ city, capital of (Nationalist) China in N Taiwan

Taichung — see TAIZHONG

T'ai·nan \'tī-'nän\ city SW Taiwan

Tai·wan \'tī-'wän\ or formerly **For·mo·sa** \fòr-'mō-sə, fər-, -zə\ 1 island off SE coast of Asia; since 1949 seat of government of (Nationalist) Republic of China; capital, Taibei 2 strait between Taiwan & mainland of China connecting East China & South China seas — **Tai·wan·ese** \ˌtī-wə-'nēz, -'nēs\ adj or n

Tai·yuan \'tī-yü-'än\ city N China

Tai·zhong \'tī-'jùn\ or **Tai·chung** \'tī-'chùn\ city W Taiwan

Ta·jik·i·stan \tä-ˌjik-i-'stan, -'stän, -ˌjik-ə-ˌ, -'jēk-\ country W central Asia bordering on China & Afghanistan; capital, Dushanbe; a republic (**Ta·dzhik Soviet Socialist Republic** \tä-'jik-, -'jēk-\ or **Ta·dzhik·i·stan** \same as TAJIKISTAN\ ) of U.S.S.R. 1929–91

Ta·kli·ma·kan or **Ta·kla Ma·kan** \ˌtäk-lə-mə-'kän\ desert W China

Ta–lien — see DALIAN

Tal·la·has·see \ˌtal-ə-'has-ē\ city, capital of Florida

Tal·linn \'tal-ən, 'täl-\ city, capital of Estonia

Tam·pa \'tam-pə\ city W Florida on **Tampa Bay** (inlet of Gulf of Mexico)

Tan·gan·yi·ka \ˌtan-gən-'yē-kə, ˌtaŋ-gən-, -gə-'nē-\ former country E Africa; since 1964 part of Tanzania

Tanganyika, Lake lake E Africa between Tanzania & Democratic Republic of the Congo

Tang·shan \'däŋ-'shän, 'täŋ-\ city NE China

Tan·za·nia \ˌtan-zə-'nē-ə, ˌtän-\ country E Africa on Indian Ocean; formed 1964 by union of Tanganyika & Zanzibar; legislative capital, Dodoma; historic capital, Dar es Salaam — **Tan·za·ni·an** \-'nē-ən\ adj or n

Ta·ra·wa \tə-'rä-wə, 'tar-ə-ˌwä\ island central Pacific, contains capital of Kiribati

Tar·ry·town \'tar-ē-ˌtaùn\ village SE New York

Tar·sus \'tär-səs\ ancient city of S Asia Minor; now a city in S Turkey

Tash·kent \tash-'kent\ city, capital of Uzbekistan

Tas·man Sea \'taz-mən\ the part of the South Pacific between SE Australia & New Zealand

Tas·ma·nia \taz-'mā-nē-ə, -nyə\ or earlier **Van Die·men's Land** \van-'dē-mənz\ island SE Australia S of Victoria; a state; capital, Hobart — **Tas·ma·nian** \-nē-ən, -nyən\ adj or n

Ta·try \'tä-trē\ or **Ta·tra** \'tä-trə\ mountains N Slovakia & S Poland in central Carpathian Mountains

Taun·ton \'tònt-ᵊn, 'tänt-, 'tant-\ town SW England

Tbi·li·si \tə-'bil-ə-sē\ or **Tif·lis** \'tif-ləs, tə-'flēs\ city, capital of Republic of Georgia

Te·gu·ci·gal·pa \tə-ˌgü-sə-'gal-pə\ city, capital of Honduras

Teh·ran \ˌtā-'ran, -'rän\ city, capital of Iran; at foot of S slope of Elburz Mountains

Tel Aviv \ˌtel-ə-'vēv\ or officially **Tel Aviv–Ya·fo** \-'yä-fō\ city W Israel on the Mediterranean

Tem·pe \'tem-ᵊpē\ city S central Arizona

Ten·nes·see \ˌten-ə-'sē\ 1 river 652 mi. (1049 km.) long in Tennessee, N Alabama, & W Kentucky 2 state E central U.S.; capital, Nashville — **Ten·nes·se·an** or **Ten·nes·see·an** \-ən\ adj or n

Te·noch·ti·tlan \tā-ˌnóch-tē-ˈtlän\ ancient name of Mexico City

Tex·as \ˈtek-səs, -siz\ state ⑤ U.S.; capital, Austin — **Tex·an** \-sən\ adj or n

Texas Panhandle the ◻NW projection of land in Texas

Thai·land \ˈtī-ˌland, -lənd\ or formerly **Si·am** \sī-ˈam\ country ◻SE Asia on Gulf of Thailand; capital, Bangkok — **Thai·land·er** \ˈtī-ˌlan-dər, -lən-dər\ n

Thailand, Gulf of or formerly **Gulf of Siam** arm of South China Sea between Indochina & Malay Peninsula

Thames \ˈtemz\ river over 200 mi. (322 km.) long ⑤ England flowing ◻E from the Cotswolds into the North Sea

Thar \ˈtär\ desert ◻E Pakistan & ◻NW India (country) ◻E of Indus River

Thebes \ˈthēbz\ **1** or **The·bae** \ˈthē-bē\ ancient city ⑤ Egypt on the Nile **2** ancient city ◻E Greece ◻NNW of Athens — **The·ban** \ˈthē-bən\ adj or n

Thes·sa·lo·ní·ki \ˌthes-ə-lō-ˈnē-kē\ city ◻N Greece

Thim·phu \thim-ˈpü\ city, capital of Bhutan

Thousand Islands island group Canada & U.S. in the Saint Lawrence River in Ontario & New York

Thousand Oaks city ◻SW California ◻W of Los Angeles

Thrace \ˈthrās\ or ancient **Thra·cia** \ˈthrā-sh(ē-)ə\ region ◻SE Europe in Balkan Peninsula ◻N of the Aegean now divided between Greece & Turkey; in ancient times extended ◻N to the Danube — **Thra·cian** \ˈthrā-shən\ adj or n

Thunder Bay city & port ◻SW Ontario, Canada on Lake Superior

Thur·rock \ˈthər-ək, ˈthə-rək\ former urban district ◻SE England

Tian·jin \tē-ˈän-ˈjin\ or **Tien·tsin** \tē-ˈen(t)-ˈsin\ city ◻NE China ◻SE of Beijing

Tian Shan or **Tien Shan** \tē-ˈen-ˈshän, tē-ˈän-\ mountain system central Asia extending ◻NE from Pamirs

Ti·ber \ˈtī-bər\ or Italian **Te·ve·re** \ˈtā-vā-rā\ or ancient **Ti·ber·is** \ˈtī-bə-rəs\ river 252 mi. (405 km.) long central Italy flowing through Rome into Tyrrhenian Sea

Tiberias, Lake — see GALILEE (Sea of)

Ti·bes·ti \tə-ˈbes-tē\ mountains ◻N central Africa in central Sahara in ◻NW Chad; highest 11,204 ft. (3415 m.)

Ti·bet \tə-ˈbet\ or **Xi·zang** \ˈshē-ˈzäŋ\ region ◻SW China on high plateau (average altitude 16,000 ft. or 4877 m.) ◻N of the Himalayas; capital, Lhasa

Tier·ra del Fue·go \tē-ˈer-ə-ˌdel-f(y)ù-ˈā-gō\ **1** island group off ⑤ South America **2** chief island of the group; divided between Argentina & Chile

Tiflis — see TBILISI

Ti·gris \ˈtī-grəs\ river 1180 mi. (1899 km.) long Turkey & Iraq flowing ◻SSE and uniting with the Euphrates to form the Shatt al Arab

Ti·jua·na \tē-ə-ˈwän-ə, tē-ˈwän-\ city ◻NW Mexico on the U.S. border

Tim·buk·tu \ˌtim-ˌbək-ˈtü\ or **Tom·bouc·tou** \ˌtōn-bük-ˈtü\ town Mali near Niger River

Ti·mor \ˈtē-ˌmó(ə)r, tē-ˈmó(ə)r\ island Indonesia ◻SE of Sulawesi; ◻W half formerly belonged to Netherlands and is now part of Indonesia; ◻E half belonged to Portugal until 1975, was annexed by Indonesia 1976, and gained independence 2002 as East Timor

Timor–Leste — see EAST TIMOR

Ti·ra·ne or **Ti·ra·na** \ti-ˈrän-ə\ city, capital of Albania

Ti·rol or **Ty·rol** \tə-ˈrōl; ˈtī-ˌrōl, tī-ˈrōl; ˈtir-əl\ or Italian **Ti·ro·lo** \tē-ˈró-lō\ region in ◻E Alps in ◻W Austria & ◻NE Italy — **Ti·ro·le·an** or **Ty·ro·le·an** \tə-ˈrō-lē-ən, tī-; ˌtir-ə-ˈlē-, ˌtī-rə-ˈlē-\ or **Ti·ro·lese** or **Ty·ro·lese** \ˌtir-ə-ˈlēz, ˌtī-rə-, -ˈlēs\ adj or n

Ti·ti·ca·ca, Lake \ˌtit-i-ˈkäk-ə\ lake on Bolivia–Peru boundary at altitude of 12,500 ft. (3810 m.)

To·ba·go \tə-ˈbā-gō\ island West Indies ◻NE of Trinidad; part of independent Trinidad and Tobago — **To·ba·go·ni·an** \ˌtō-bə-ˈgō-nē-ən, -nyən\ n

To·go \ˈtō-gō\ country ◻W Africa on Gulf of Guinea; capital, Lomé — **To·go·lese** \ˌtō-gə-ˈlēz, -ˈlēs\ adj or n

To·kyo \ˈtō-kē-ˌō\ or formerly **Edo** \ˈē-ˌdō\ city, capital of Japan in ◻SE Honshu on Tokyo Bay — **To·kyo·ite** \ˈtō-kē-(ˌ)ō-ˌīt\ n

To·le·do \tə-ˈlēd-ō, -ˈlēd-ə\ city ◻NW Ohio

Tol'·yat·ti \tól-ˈyät-ē\ city ◻W Russia; ◻NW of Samara

Ton·ga \ˈtäŋ-(g)ə\ islands ◻SW Pacific ◻E of Fiji Islands; a kingdom; capital, Nukualofa — **Ton·gan** \-(g)ən\ adj or n

Ton·kin, Gulf of \ˈtäŋ-kən, ˈtän-ˈkin\ arm of South China Sea ◻E of ◻N Vietnam

To·pe·ka \tə-ˈpē-kə\ city, capital of Kansas

Tor·bay \(ˈ)tór-ˈbā\ urban area ◻SW England

To·ron·to \tə-ˈränt-ō, -ˈränt-ə\ city, capital of Ontario, Canada

Tor·rance \ˈtór-ən(t)s, ˈtär-\ city ◻SW California

Tor·res \ˈtór-əs\ strait between New Guinea & Cape York Peninsula, Australia

Tou·louse \tù-ˈlüz\ city ◻SW France

Tower Hamlets borough of ◻E Greater London, England

To·yo·na·ka \ˌtói-ə-ˈnäk-ə\ city Japan on Honshu; a suburb of Osaka

Trans·vaal \tran(t)s-ˈväl, tranz-\ former province ◻NE Republic of South Africa

Tran·syl·va·nia \ˌtran(t)s-əl-ˈvā-nyə, -nē-ə\ region ◻W Romania — **Tran·syl·va·nian** \-nyən, -nē-ən\ adj or n

Transylvanian Alps a ⑤ extension of Carpathian Mountains in central Romania

Tren·ton \ˈtrent-ᵊn\ city, capital of New Jersey

Trin·i·dad \ˈtrin-ə-ˌdad\ island West Indies off ◻NE coast of Venezuela; with Tobago forms (since 1962) the independent country of **Trinidad and Tobago**; capital, Port of Spain — **Trin·i·da·di·an** \ˌtrin-ə-ˈdād-ē-ən, -ˈdad-\ adj or n

Trip·o·li \ˈtrip-ə-lē\ **1** city & port ◻NW Lebanon **2** city & port, capital of Libya

Tris·tan da Cu·nha \ˌtris-tən-də-ˈkü-nə, -nyə\ island South Atlantic, chief of the Tristan da Cunha Islands (part of British colony of Saint Helena)

Tri·van·drum \triv-ˈan-drəm\ city ⑤ India

Tro·bri·and \ˈtrō-brē-ˌänd\ islands ◻SW Pacific in Solomon Sea belonging to Papua New Guinea

Trois–Ri·vieres \ˌtrwä-ri-ˈvyer\ city ⑤ Quebec, Canada

Trond·heim \ˈträn-ˌhäm\ city & port central Norway

Troy \ˈtrói\ or **Il·i·um** \ˈil-ē-əm\ or **Tro·ja** \ˈtrō-jə, -yə\ ancient city ◻NW Asia Minor ◻SW of the Dardanelles

Truk — see CHUUK

Tru·ro \ˈtrù(ə)r-ō\ city ◻SW England

Trust Territory of the Pacific Islands — see PACIFIC ISLANDS (Trust Territory of the)

Tshwa·ne \ˈchwä-nä\ municipality Republic of South Africa including the city of Pretoria

Tsinan — see JINAN

Tsingtao — see QINGDAO

Tuc·son \tü-ˈsän, ˈtü-ˌsän\ city ◻SE Arizona

Tu·la \ˈtü-lə\ city ◻W Russia ⑤ of Moscow

Tul·sa \ˈtəl-sə\ city ◻NE Oklahoma

Tu·nis \ˈt(y)ü-nəs\ city, capital of Tunisia

Tu·ni·sia \t(y)ü-ˈnē-zh(ē-)ə, -ˈnizh-(ē-)ə\ country ◻N Africa on the Mediterranean ◻E of Algeria; capital, Tunis — **Tu·ni·sian** \-ˈnē-zh(ē-)ən, -ˈnizh-(ē-)ən\ adj or n

Tu·rin \ˈt(y)ùr-ən, t(y)ù-ˈrin\ city ◻NW Italy on the Po

Tur·kana, Lake \tər-ˈkan-ə\ or **Lake Ru·dolf** \ˈrü-ˌdólf, -ˌdälf\ lake ◻N Kenya in Great Rift Valley

\ə\ abut	\aù\ out	\i\ tip	\ó\ saw	\ù\ foot
\ər\ further	\ch\ chin	\ī\ life	\ói\ coin	\y\ yet
\a\ mat	\e\ pet	\j\ job	\th\ thin	\yü\ few
\ā\ take	\ē\ easy	\ŋ\ sing	\th\ this	\yù\ cure
\ä\ cot, cart	\g\ go	\ō\ bone	\ü\ food	\zh\ vision

Tur·key \'tər-kē\ country W Asia & SE Europe between Mediterranean & Black seas; capital, Ankara — **Turk** n

Turk·men·i·stan \(ˌ)tərk-ˌmen-ə-'stan, -'stän; -'men-ə-ˌ\ country central Asia; capital, Ashkhabad; a republic (**Turk·men Soviet Socialist Republic** \'tərk-mən\) of U.S.S.R. 1925–91 — **Turk·me·ni·an** \ˌtərk-'mē-nē-ən\ adj

Turks and Cai·cos \ˌtərk-sən-'kā-kəs\ two groups of islands West Indies at SE end of Bahamas; a British colony

Tu·tu·ila \ˌtüt-ə-'wē-lə\ island South Pacific, chief of American Samoa group

Tu·va·lu \tü-'väl-ü, -'vär-\ or formerly **El·lice** \'el-əs\ islands W Pacific N of Fiji; an independent country; capital, Funafuti — see GILBERT AND ELLICE ISLANDS

Tyne and Wear \'tī-nən-'(d)wi(ə)r\ metropolitan county N England

Tyre \'tī(ə)r\ ancient city, capital of Phoenicia; now a town of S Lebanon — **Tyr·i·an** \'tir-ē-ən\ adj or n

Tyrol — see TIROL

Tyr·rhe·ni·an Sea \tə-'rē-nē-ən\ the part of the Mediterranean SW of Italy, N of Sicily, & E of Sardinia & Corsica

Ufa \ü-'fä\ city W Russia NE of Samara

Ugan·da \yü-'gan-də, -'gän-, -'gän-\ country E Africa N of Lake Victoria; capital, Kampala — **Ugan·dan** \-dən\ adj or n

Ukraine \yü-'krān, 'yü-ˌkrān\ country E Europe on N coast of Black Sea; capital, Kiev; a republic of U.S.S.R. 1923–91 — **Ukrai·ni·an** \yü-'krā-nē-ən\ adj or n

Ulaan·baa·tar or **Ulan Ba·tor** \ˌü-ˌlän-'bä-ˌtȯ(ə)r\ city, capital of Mongolia

Ul·san \'ül-sän\ city SE South Korea

Ul·ster \'əl-stər\ 1 region N Ireland (island) consisting of Northern Ireland & N Ireland (country) 2 province N Ireland (country) 3 NORTHERN IRELAND

Ulu·ru \ü-'lü-rü\ or **Ayers Rock** \'erz\ outcrop central Australia in SW Northern Territory

Um·bria \'əm-brē-ə\ region central Italy in the Apennines

Un·ga·va \ˌən-'gav-ə\ 1 bay, inlet of Hudson Strait NE Canada 2 peninsula region NE Canada in N Quebec

Union of South Africa — see SOUTH AFRICA (Republic of)

Union of Soviet Socialist Republics or **Soviet Union** or **Soviet Russia** country 1922–91 E Europe & N Asia; a union of 15 now independent republics; capital, Moscow

United Arab Emirates country E Arabia on Persian Gulf; composed of seven emirates; capital, Abu Dhabi

United Kingdom or in full **United Kingdom of Great Britain and Northern Ireland** country W Europe in British Isles consisting of England, Scotland, Wales, Northern Ireland, Channel Islands, & Isle of Man; capital, London

United Nations political organization established in 1945 with headquarters in New York City

United States of America or **United States** country North America bordering on Atlantic, Pacific, & Arctic oceans & including Hawaii; capital, Washington

Upper Volta — see BURKINA FASO

Ural \'yùr-əl\ 1 mountains Russia & Kazakhstan extending about 1640 mi. (2640 km.); usually thought of as dividing line between Europe & Asia; highest about 6214 ft. (1894 m.) 2 river over 1500 mi. (2414 km.) long Russia & Kazakhstan flowing from S end of Ural Mountains into Caspian Sea

Uru·guay \'(y)ùr-ə-ˌgwī, 'yùr-ə-ˌgwä\ 1 river about 1000 mi. (1609 km.) long SE South America 2 country SE South America; capital, Montevideo — **Uru·guay·an** \ˌ(y)ùr-ə-'gwī-ən, ˌyùr-ə-'gwä-\ adj or n

Ürüm·qi \'ūē-'rüm-'chē\ or **Urum·chi** \ù-'rùm-chē, ˌùr-əm-'chē\ city NW China

Us·pa·lla·ta \ˌü-spə-'yät-ə, -'zhät-\ mountain pass S South America in the Andes between Argentina & Chile

Utah \'yü-ˌtȯ, -ˌtä\ state W U.S.; capital, Salt Lake City — **Utah·an** \-ˌtȯ(-ə)n, -ˌtä(-ə)n\ adj or n — **Utahn** \-ˌtȯ(-ə)n, -ˌtä(-ə)n\ n

Uz·bek·i·stan \(ˌ)ùz-ˌbek-i-'stan, -'stän; -'bek-i-ˌ\ country W central Asia between Aral Sea & Afghanistan; capital, Tashkent; a republic (**Uz·bek Soviet Socialist Republic** \'ùz-ˌbek, 'əz-; üz-'\) of U.S.S.R. 1924–91

Va·duz \vä-'düts\ town, capital of Liechtenstein

Val·dez \val-'dēz\ city & port S Alaska

Va·len·cia \və-'len-ch(ē-)ə, -'len(t)-sē-ə\ 1 region & ancient kingdom E Spain 2 city, its capital, on the Mediterranean

Val·le·jo \və-'lā-ō\ city W California

Valley Forge locality SE Pennsylvania

Val·let·ta \və-'let-ə\ city, capital of Malta

Van·cou·ver \van-'kü-vər\ 1 city SW Washington on Columbia River opposite Portland, Oregon 2 island W Canada in SW British Columbia 3 city & port SW British Columbia, Canada

Van Diemen's Land — see TASMANIA

Van·u·atu \ˌvan-ˌwä-'tü, ˌvän-, -'wä-ˌtü\ or formerly **New Heb·ri·des** \-'heb-rə-ˌdēz\ islands SW Pacific W of Fiji; formerly under shared British and French administration; became independent 1980; capital, Port-Vila

Va·ra·na·si \və-'rä-nə-sē\ city N India

Vat·i·can City \ˌvat-i-kən\ independent state within Rome, Italy; created 1929 as headquarters for the Pope

Ven·e·zu·e·la \ˌven-əz(-ə)-'wā-lə, -'wē-\ country N South America; capital, Caracas — **Ven·e·zu·e·lan** \-lən\ adj or n

Ven·ice \'ven-əs\ or Italian **Ve·ne·zia** \və-'net-sē-ə\ city N Italy on islands in Lagoon of Venice — **Ve·ne·tian** \və-'nē-shən\ adj

Ven·tu·ra \ven-'tùr-ə, -'tyùr-\ or officially **San Buen·a·ven·tu·ra** \ˌsan-ˌbwen-ə-ˌven-\ city & port SW California

Ve·ra·cruz \ˌver-ə-'krüz, -'krüs\ city E Mexico

Ver·mont \vər-'mänt\ state NE U.S.; capital, Montpelier — **Ver·mont·er** \-ər\ n

Ve·ro·na \və-'rō-nə\ city N Italy W of Venice

Ve·su·vi·us \və-'sü-vē-əs\ volcano about 4190 ft. (1277 m.) S Italy near Bay of Naples

Vicks·burg \'viks-ˌbərg\ city W Mississippi

Vic·to·ria \vik-'tȯr-ē-ə, -'tȯr-\ 1 city, capital of British Columbia, Canada on Vancouver Island 2 island N Canada in Arctic Archipelago 3 state SE Australia; capital, Melbourne 4 city & port, Hong Kong; served as capital of Hong Kong colony 5 seaport, capital of Seychelles — **Vic·to·ri·an** \-ē-ən\ adj or n

Victoria, Lake lake E Africa in Tanzania, Kenya, & Uganda

Vi·en·na \vē-'en-ə\ or German **Wien** \'vēn\ city, capital of Austria on the Danube — **Vi·en·nese** \ˌvē-ə-'nēz, -'nēs\ adj or n

Vien·tiane \(')vyen-'tyän\ city, capital of Laos

Vie·ques \vē-'ā-kās\ island Puerto Rico off E end of main island

Viet·nam \vē-'et-'näm, vyet-, ˌvē-ət-, -'nam\ country SE Asia in Indochina; capital, Hanoi; established 1945–46 & divided 1954–75 at 17th parallel into the independent states of **North Vietnam** (capital, Hanoi) & **South Vietnam** (capital, Saigon) — **Viet·nam·ese** \vē-ˌet-nə-'mēz, ˌvyet-, ˌvē-ət-, ˌvēt-, -na-, -nä-, -'mēs\ adj or n

Vila — see PORT-VILA

Vi·la No·va de Ga·ia \'vē-lə-ˌnȯ-və-dē-'gī-ə\ city NW Portugal

Vil·ni·us \'vil-nē-əs\ city, capital of Lithuania

Vin·land \'vin-lənd\ a portion of the coast of North America visited & so-called by Norse voyagers about 1000 A.D.; thought to be located along the North Atlantic in what is now E or NE Canada

Vir·gin·ia \vər-'jin-yə, -'jin-ē-ə\ state E U.S.; capital, Richmond — **Vir·gin·ian** \-yən, -ē-ən\ adj or n

Virginia Beach city SE Virginia

Virginia City locality W Nevada

Vir·gin Islands \ˌvər-jən\ island group West Indies E of Puerto Rico — see BRITISH VIRGIN ISLANDS; VIRGIN ISLANDS OF THE UNITED STATES

Virgin Islands of the United States the W islands of the Virgin Islands; capital, Charlotte Amalie (on Saint Thomas)

Vi·sa·yan \və-ˈsī-ən\ islands central Philippines

Vish·a·kha·pat·nam \vi-ˌshäk-ə-ˈpət-nəm\ *or* **Vis·a·kha·pat·nam** \-ˌsäk-\ city E India

Vis·tu·la \ˈvis(h)-chə-lə, ˈvis-tə-lə\ river over 660 mi. (1062 km.) long Poland flowing N from the Carpathians

Vi·ti Le·vu \ˌvēt-ē-ˈlev-ü\ island SW Pacific; largest of the Fiji group

Vlad·i·vos·tok \ˌvlad-ə-və-ˈstäk, -ˈväs-ˌtäk\ city & port SE Russia on an inlet of Sea of Japan

Voj·vo·di·na \ˈvoi-vȯ-ˌdē-nä\ autonomous province N Serbia

Vol·ga \ˈväl-gə, ˈvȯl-, ˈvōl-\ river about 2300 mi. (3700 km.) long W Russia; longest river in Europe

Vol·go·grad \ˈväl-gə-ˌgrad, ˈvȯl-, ˈvōl-\ city S Russia in Europe, on the Volga

Vol·ta \ˈväl-tə, ˈvȯl-\ river about 300 mi. (485 km.) long Ghana flowing from **Lake Volta** (reservoir) into Gulf of Guinea

Vo·ro·nezh \və-ˈrȯ-nish\ city S central Russia in Europe

Vosges \ˈvōzh\ mountains NE France on W side of Rhine valley; highest 4672 ft. (1424 m.)

Wa·co \ˈwā-kō\ city central Texas

Wad·den·zee \ˌväd-ᵊn-ˈzā\ inlet of the North Sea N Netherlands

Wake \ˈwāk\ island North Pacific; U.S. territory

Wake·field \ˈwāk-ˌfēld\ city N England

Wa·la·chia *or* **Wal·la·chia** \wä-ˈlā-kē-ə\ region S Romania between Transylvanian Alps & the Danube

Wales \ˈwā(ə)lz\ *or Welsh* **Cym·ru** \ˈkəm-ˌrē\ *or Latin* **Cam·bria** \ˈkam-brē-ə\ principality SW Great Britain; a division of United Kingdom; capital, Cardiff

Wal·lo·nia \wä-ˈlō-nē-ə\ semiautonomous region S Belgium

Wal·sall \ˈwȯl-ˌsȯl, -səl\ town W central England

Wal·tham Forest \ˌwȯl-thəm\ borough of NE Greater London, England

Wands·worth \ˈwän(d)z-(ˌ)wərth\ borough of SW Greater London, England

War·ley \ˈwȯr-lē\ town W central England

War·ren \ˈwȯr-ən, ˈwär-\ city SE Michigan

War·saw \ˈwȯr-ˌsȯ\ *or Polish* **War·sza·wa** \vär-ˈshäv-ə\ city, capital of Poland

War·wick \ˈwär-ik\ town central England

War·wick·shire \ˈwär-ik-ˌshi(ə)r, -shər\ *or* **Warwick** county central England

Wa·satch \ˈwȯ-ˌsach\ range of the Rockies SE Idaho & N central Utah; highest Mount Timpanogos 12,008 ft. (3660 m.), in Utah

Wash·ing·ton \ˈwȯsh-iŋ-tən, ˈwäsh-\ **1** state NW U.S.; capital, Olympia **2** city, capital of U.S.; having the same boundaries as District of Columbia and often referred to as **Washington, D.C.** — **Wash·ing·to·nian** \ˌwȯsh-iŋ-ˈtō-nē-ən, ˌwäsh-, -nyən\ *adj or n*

Washington, Mount mountain 6288 ft. (1916 m.) N New Hampshire; highest in White Mountains

Wa·ter·bury \ˈwȯt-ə(r)-ˌber-ē, ˈwät-\ city W central Connecticut

Wed·dell \wə-ˈdel, ˈwed-ᵊl\ sea consisting of part of the South Atlantic

Wei·mar Republic \ˈvī-ˌmär\ the German republic 1919–33

Wel·land \ˈwel-ənd\ canal 27 mi. (44 km.) long SE Ontario connecting Lake Erie & Lake Ontario

Wel·ling·ton \ˈwel-iŋ-tən\ city, capital of New Zealand

Wes·sex \ˈwes-iks\ ancient kingdom S England; capital, Winchester

West Bank area Middle East W of Jordan River; occupied by Israel since 1967 with parts having been transferred to Palestinian administration since 1993

West Brom·wich \-ˈbrəm-ij, -ˈbräm-, -ich\ town W central England

West Co·vi·na \kō-ˈvē-nə\ city SW California

Western Australia state W Australia; capital, Perth — **Western Australian** *adj or n*

Western Cape province SW Republic of South Africa

Western Ghats chain of low mountains SW India

Western Hemisphere the half of the earth lying W of the Atlantic Ocean comprising North America, South America, & surrounding waters

Western Isles area of W Scotland consisting of the Outer Hebrides — see HEBRIDES

Western Sahara *or formerly* **Spanish Sahara** territory NW Africa; occupied by Morocco

Western Samoa — see SAMOA

West Germany the former Federal Republic of Germany — see GERMANY

West Indies islands lying between SE North America & N South America & consisting of the Greater Antilles, Lesser Antilles, & Bahamas — **West Indian** *adj or n*

West Midlands metropolitan county W central England; includes Birmingham

West·min·ster \ˈwes(t)-ˌmin(t)-stər\ **1** city N central Colorado NW of Denver **2** *or* **City of Westminster** borough of W central Greater London, England

West Pakistan the former W division of Pakistan having the same boundaries as present-day Pakistan

West·pha·lia \wes(t)-ˈfāl-yə, -ˈfā-lē-ə\ region W Germany E of the Rhine — **West·pha·lian** \-ˈfāl-yən, -ˈfā-lē-ən\ *adj or n*

West Point U.S. military post SE New York on Hudson River N of New York City

West Quod·dy Head \ˌkwäd-ē\ cape; most easterly point of Maine & of the Lower 48

West Sus·sex \ˈsəs-iks\ county SE England

West Valley City city N Utah S of Salt Lake City

West Virginia state E U.S.; capital, Charleston — **West Virginian** *adj or n*

West York·shire \ˈyȯrk-ˌshi(ə)r, -shər\ metropolitan county NW England including city of Wakefield

White sea NW Russia in Europe

White·horse \ˈhwīt-ˌhȯrs, ˈwīt-\ city, capital of Yukon, Canada

White Mountains mountains N New Hampshire in the Appalachians — see WASHINGTON (Mount)

Whit·ney, Mount \ˈhwit-nē, ˈwit-\ mountain 14,495 ft. (4418 m.) SE central California in Sierra Nevada; highest in U.S. outside of Alaska

Wich·i·ta \ˈwich-ə-ˌtȯ\ city S Kansas

Wichita Falls city N Texas

Wien — see VIENNA

Wight, Isle of — see ISLE OF WIGHT

Wil·lem·stad \ˈvil-əm-ˌstät\ city, formerly capital of Netherlands Antilles

Wil·liams·burg \ˈwil-yəmz-ˌbərg\ city SE Virginia

Wil·ming·ton \ˈwil-miŋ-tən\ city N Delaware; largest in state

Wilt·shire \ˈwilt-ˌshi(ə)r, ˈwil-chər, ˈwilt-shər\ county S England

Win·ches·ter \ˈwin-ˌches-tər, -chə-stər\ city S England

Win·der·mere \ˈwin-də(r)-ˌmi(ə)r\ lake NW England in Lake District

Wind·hoek \ˈvint-ˌhu̇k\ city, capital of Namibia

\ə\ abut	\au̇\ out	\i\ tip	\ȯ\ saw	\u̇\ foot
\ər\ further	\ch\ chin	\ī\ life	\ȯi\ coin	\y\ yet
\a\ mat	\e\ pet	\j\ job	\th\ thin	\yü\ few
\ā\ take	\ē\ easy	\ŋ\ sing	\th\ this	\yu̇\ cure
\ä\ cot, cart	\g\ go	\ō\ bone	\ü\ food	\zh\ vision

Wind·sor \'win-zər\ city S Ontario, Canada

Wind·ward Islands \'win-dwərd\ islands West Indies in the S Lesser Antilles extending S from Martinique but not including Barbados, Tobago, or Trinidad

Win·ni·peg \'win-ə-ˌpeg\ city, capital of Manitoba, Canada

Winnipeg, Lake lake S central Manitoba, Canada

Win·ni·pe·sau·kee, Lake \ˌwin-ə-pə-'sȯ-kē\ lake central New Hampshire

Win·ston–Sa·lem \ˌwin(t)-stən-'sā-ləm\ city N central North Carolina

Wis·con·sin \wis-'kän(t)-sən\ state N central U.S.; capital, Madison — **Wis·con·sin·ite** \-sə-ˌnīt\ n

Wit·wa·ters·rand \'wit-ˌwȯt-ərz-ˌrand, -ˌwät-, -ˌränd, -ˌränt\ or **Rand** \'rand, 'ränd, 'ränt\ ridge of gold-bearing rock NE Republic of South Africa

Wol·lon·gong \'wu̇l-ən-ˌgäŋ, -ˌgȯŋ\ city SE Australia in E New South Wales S of Sydney

Wol·ver·hamp·ton \'wu̇l-vər-ˌham(p)-tən\ town W central England NW of Birmingham

Worces·ter \'wu̇s-tər\ **1** city E central Massachusetts **2** city W central England

Wran·gell, Mount \'raŋ-gəl\ volcano 14,163 ft. (4317 m.) S Alaska in **Wrangell Mountains**

Wro·claw \'vrȯt-ˌsläf, -ˌsläv\ city SW Poland in Silesia

Wu·han \'wü-'hän\ city E central China

Wu·xi or **Wu–hsi** \'wü-'shē\ city E China

Wy·o·ming \wī-'ō-miŋ\ state NW U.S.; capital, Cheyenne — **Wy·o·ming·ite** \-miŋ-ˌīt\ n

Xi'·an or **Hsi–an** \'shē-'än, -'an\ city E central China

Xianggang — see HONG KONG

Xin·jiang Uy·gur or **Sin–kiang Ui·ghur** \'shin-jē-'äŋ-'wē-gər\ region W China between the Kunlun & Altai mountains

Xizang — see TIBET

Xu·zhou \'shü-'jō\ or **Sü·chow** \'shü-'jō, 'sü-; 'sü-'chau̇\ city E China

Yak·i·ma \'yak-ə-ˌmȯ\ city S central Washington

Ya·lu \'yäl-ü\ river 500 mi. (804 km.) long China (SE Manchuria region) & North Korea

Ya·mous·sou·kro \ˌyä-mü-'sü-krō\ town, official capital of Cote d'Ivoire

Yan·gon \ˌyän-'gōn\ or formerly **Ran·goon** \ran-'gün, raŋ-\ city, historic capital of Myanmar

Yangtze — see CHANG

Yaoun·dé \yau̇n-'dā\ city, capital of Cameroon

Yap \'yap, 'yäp\ island W Pacific in the W Carolines

Ya·ren \'yä-ren\ district of Nauru where government offices are located

Ya·ro·slavl \ˌyär-ə-'släv-əl\ city central Russia in Europe, NE of Moscow

Yaz·oo \ya-'zü, 'yaz-ü\ river W central Mississippi

Ye·ka·te·rin·burg \yi-ˌkat-ə-rən-ˌbȯrg, -'kät-, -ˌbȯrk\ or **1924–91 Sverd·lovsk** \sverd-'lȯfsk\ city W Russia, in central Ural Mountains

Yellow 1 — see HUANG **2** sea, section of East China Sea between N China, North Korea, & South Korea

Yel·low·knife \'yel-ō-ˌnīf\ town, capital of Northwest Territories, Canada

Ye·men \'yem-ən\ country S Arabia bordering on Red Sea & Gulf of Aden; capital, Sanaa; before 1990 divided into the independent states of **Yemen Arab Republic** (capital, Sanaa) & **People's Democratic Republic of Yemen** (capital, Aden) — **Ye·me·ni** \'yem-ə-nē\ adj or n — **Ye·men·ite** \-ə-ˌnīt\ adj or n

Ye·ni·sey or **Ye·ni·sei** \ˌyi-ni-'sā\ river over 2500 mi. (4022 km.) long central Russia, flowing N into Arctic Ocean

Ye·re·van \ˌyer-ə-'vän\ city, capital of Armenia

Yo·ko·ha·ma \ˌyō-kə-'häm-ə\ city Japan in SE Honshu on Tokyo Bay S of Tokyo

Yon·kers \'yäŋ-kərz\ city SE New York N of New York City

York \'yȯ(ə)rk\ city N England

York, Cape cape NE Australia in Queensland at N tip of Cape York Peninsula

Yo·sem·i·te Falls \yō-ˌsem-ət-ē\ waterfall E California; includes two falls, the upper 1430 ft. (436 m.) & the lower 320 ft. (98 m.)

Youngs·town \'yəŋ-ˌstau̇n\ city NE Ohio

Yu·ca·tán \ˌyü-kə-'tan, -'tän\ peninsula SE Mexico & N Central America including Belize & N Guatemala

Yu·go·sla·via or earlier **Ju·go·sla·via** \ˌyü-gō-'släv-ē-ə\ **1** former country S Europe including Serbia, Montenegro, Slovenia, Croatia, Bosnia and Herzegovina, & Macedonia; capital, Belgrade **2** — see SERBIA AND MONTENEGRO — **Yu·go·slav** \ˌyü-gō-'släv, -'slav\ or **Yu·go·sla·vi·an** \-'släv-ē-ən\ adj or n

Yu·kon \'yü-ˌkän\ **1** river 1979 mi. (3185 km.) long NW Canada & Alaska flowing into Bering Sea **2** territory NW Canada; capital, Whitehorse

Yu·ma \'yü-mə\ city SW corner of Arizona on the Colorado

Za·greb \'zäg-ˌreb\ city, capital of Croatia

Zaire \zä-'i(ə)r also 'zī(ə)r\ **1** river in Africa — see CONGO 1 **2** country in Africa — see CONGO 2 — **Zair·ean** or **Zair·ian** \zä-'ir-ē-ən\ adj or n

Zam·be·zi or **Zam·be·si** \zam-'bē-zē\ river about 1700 mi. (2735 km.) long SE Africa flowing from NW Zambia into Mozambique Channel

Zam·bia \'zam-bē-ə\ country S Africa N of the Zambezi; formerly (as **Northern Rhodesia**) dependent on Britain; became independent 1964; capital, Lusaka — **Zam·bi·an** \-ən\ adj or n

Zan·zi·bar \'zan-zə-ˌbär\ island Tanzania off NE Tanganyika coast; formerly a sultanate; became independent 1963; united 1964 with Tanganyika forming Tanzania

Za·po·rizh·zhya \ˌzäp-ə-'rēzh-zhyə\ or **Za·po·ro·zh'ye** \ˌzäp-ə-'rȯ-zhə\ city SE Ukraine

Zetland — see SHETLAND

Zhang·jia·kou \'jäŋ-jē-'ä-'kō\ or **Kal·gan** \'kal-'gan\ city NE China NW of Beijing

Zhdanov — see MARIUPOL'

Zheng·zhou or **Cheng–chou** \'jəŋ-'jō\ city NE central China

Zim·ba·bwe \zim-'bäb-wē, -wä\ or formerly **Rho·de·sia** \rō-'dē-zhə, -zhē-ə\ country S Africa S of Zambezi River; capital, Harare — **Zim·ba·bwean** \-ən\ adj or n

Zui·der Zee \ˌzīd-ər-'zā, -'zē\ — see IJSSELMEER

Zu·lu·land \'zü-(ˌ)lü-ˌland\ territory E Republic of South Africa on Indian Ocean

Zu·rich \'zu̇(ə)r-ik\ city N Switzerland

Signs and Symbols

Astronomy

☉	the sun; Sunday	♃	Jupiter; Thursday
○ or ☽	the moon; Monday	♄ or ♄	Saturn; Saturday
●	new moon	♅, ⛢, or ♅	Uranus
☽, ☾, or)	first quarter	♆, ♆, or ♆	Neptune
○	full moon	♇	Pluto
☾, ☾, or (	last quarter	☄	comet
☿	Mercury; Wednesday	✳ or ✶	fixed star
♀	Venus; Friday		(for astrological symbols see ZODIAC table)
⊕ or ♁	Earth		
♂	Mars; Tuesday		

Biology

○	a female individual—used chiefly in inheritance charts	P_1	parental generation usually consisting of two or more different pure strains
□	a male individual—used chiefly in inheritance charts	F_1	first filial generation, offspring of a mating between different P_1 strains
♀	female	F_2	second filial generation, offspring of an $F_1 \times F_1$ mating
♂ or ♂	male		
×	crossed with; hybrid		

Business and Finance

@	at; each ⟨4 apples @ 5¢ = 20¢⟩	℔	pound; pounds
P	principal	%	percent
i, r	rate of interest	‰	per thousand
n	number of periods (as of interest) and especially years	©	copyrighted
		®	registered trademark
/ or ℔	per	$	dollars
c/o	care of	¢	cents
#	number if it precedes a numeral ⟨track #3⟩; pounds if it follows ⟨a 5 # sack of sugar⟩	£	pounds

Chemistry

+	signifies "plus," "and," "together with"—used between the symbols of substances brought together for, or produced by, a reaction; placed to the right of a symbol above the line, it signifies a charge of positive electricity: Ca^{++} or Ca^{2+} denotes the ion of calcium, which carries two positive charges	≡	signifies a triple bond or a triple negative charge
−	signifies a charge of negative electricity when placed to the right of a symbol above the line: Cl^- denotes a chlorine ion carrying a negative charge	:	—used to indicate an unshared pair of electrons (as :NH_3); also sometimes used to indicate a double bond (as in CH_2:CH_2)
−	signifies a single bond—used between the symbols of elements or groups which unite to form a compound: (as H–O–H for H_2O)	( )	marks groups within a compound [as in $C_6H_4(CH_3)_2$, which contains two methyl groups (CH_3)]
·	—used to separate parts of a compound regarded as loosely joined (as $CuSO_4 \cdot 5H_2O$); the centered dot is also used to denote the presence of a single unpaired electron (as H·)	=	gives or forms
		→	gives, leads to, or is converted to
		⇆	forms and is formed from
		↓	indicates precipitation of the substance
		↑	indicates that the substance is released as a gas
=	indicates a double bond; placed to the right of a symbol above the line, it signifies two charges of negative electricity (as $SO_4^=$, the negative ion of sulfuric acid, carrying two negative charges)	Δ	indicates that heat is required or produced
		1, 2, etc.	—used to indicate various quantities (as mass number ⟨^{12}C⟩, atomic number ⟨$_6C$⟩, number of atoms or groups ⟨(C_6H_5)$_2$⟩, or quantity of electric charge ⟨Ca^{2+}⟩)
		I, II, III, etc.	—used to indicate oxidation state ⟨Fe^{III}⟩
		Z	atomic number
			(for element symbols see ELEMENT table)

Computers

?	symbol used especially to represent any single character in a keyword search (as in a search for "f?n" to find *fan, fin,* and *fun*)
*	symbol used especially to represent zero or more characters in a keyword search (as in a search for "key*" to find *key, keys, keyed, keying,* etc.)
@	at sign—used to introduce the domain name in an e-mail address
:-) *and* :-(etc.	emoticons (e.g., smile, frown, etc.)
/ *or* \	—used to introduce or separate parts of a computer address
.	dot—used to separate parts of a computer address or file name
⟨ ⟩	—used to enclose tags in a markup language (as ⟨title⟩Dictionary⟨/title⟩)

Mathematics

+	plus; positive ⟨$a + b = c$⟩—also used to indicate omitted figures or an approximation
−	minus; negative
±	plus or minus; positive or negative ⟨the square root of $4a^2$ is $\pm 2a$⟩ ⟨an age of 120,000 years ±12,000⟩
×	multiplied by; times ⟨$6 \times 4 = 24$⟩—also indicated by placing a dot between the factors ⟨$6 \cdot 4 = 24$⟩ or by writing the factors one after the other, often enclosed in parentheses ⟨(4)(5)(3) = 60⟩ ⟨$-4abc$⟩
÷ *or* :	divided by ⟨$24 \div 6 = 4$⟩—also indicated by writing the divisor under the dividend with a line between ⟨$\frac{24}{6} = 4$⟩ or by writing the divisor after the dividend with a slash between ⟨3/8⟩
E	times 10 raised to an indicated exponent ⟨$4.52E5 = 4.52 \times 10^5$⟩—used especially in electronic displays
=	equals ⟨$6 + 2 = 8$⟩
≠ *or* ╪	is not equal to
>	is greater than ⟨6 > 5⟩
<	is less than ⟨3 < 4⟩
≧ *or* ≥	is greater than or equal to
≦ *or* ≤	is less than or equal to
≯	is not greater than
≮	is not less than
≈	is approximately equal to
≡	is identical to
~	is similar to; the negation of; the negative of
≅	is congruent to
∝	varies directly as; is proportional to
:	is to; the ratio of
∴	therefore
∞	infinity
∠	angle; the angle ⟨∠ ABC⟩
∟	right angle ⟨∟ *ABC*⟩
⊥	the perpendicular; is perpendicular to ⟨AB ⊥ CD⟩
∥	parallel; is parallel to ⟨AB ∥ CD⟩
⊙ *or* ○	circle
⌒	arc of a circle
△	triangle
□	square
▭	rectangle
√ *or* √	root—used without an index to indicate a square root (as in $\sqrt{4} = 2$) or with an index above the sign to indicate a higher degree (as in $\sqrt[3]{3}$, $\sqrt[3]{7}$); also denoted by a fractional index at the right of a number whose denominator expresses the degree of the root ⟨$3^{1/3} = \sqrt[3]{3}$⟩
( )	parentheses
[ ]	brackets
{ }	braces
	—used to indicate associated quantities and the order of operations
―	(when placed above quantities) vinculum
s	standard deviation of a sample taken from a population
σ	standard deviation of a population
s^2	variance of a sample from a population
σ^2	variance
Σ	sum; summation ⟨$\sum_{i=1}^{n} x_i = x_1 + x_2 + \ldots + x_n$⟩
$\bar{x}$	arithmetic mean of a sample of a variable x
μ	(1) micrometer (2) arithmetic mean of a population
P	probability
π	pi; the number 3.14159265+; the ratio of the circumference of a circle to its diameter
Π	product ⟨$\prod_{i=1}^{n} x_i = (x_1)(x_2) \ldots (x_n)$⟩
!	factorial ⟨$n! = n(n-1)(n-2) \ldots 1$⟩
e *or* ϵ	(1) the number 2.7182818+; the base of the natural system of logarithms (2) the eccentricity of a conic section
i	the positive square root of minus one $\sqrt{-1}$
n	an unspecified number (as an exponent) especially when integral
°	degree ⟨60°⟩
′	minute; foot ⟨30′⟩—also used to distinguish between different values of the same variable or between different variables (as a', a'', a''')
″	second; inch ⟨30″⟩
0, 1, 2, 3, etc.	—used as exponents placed above and at the right of an expression to indicate that it is raised to a power whose degree is indicated by the figure ⟨a^0 equals 1⟩ ⟨a^1 equals a⟩ ⟨a^2 is the square of a⟩
−1, −2, −3, etc.	—used as exponents placed above and at the right of an expression to indicate that the reciprocal of the expression is raised to the power whose degree is indicated by the figure ⟨a^{-1} equals $1/a$⟩ ⟨a^{-2} equals $1/a^2$⟩
θ	angle or measure of an angle
f	function
f^{-1}	the inverse of the function f
$|z|$	the absolute value of z
$[x]$	the greatest integer not greater than x
∍ *or* :	such that ⟨choose a and $b \ni a + b = 6$⟩
∃	there exists ⟨$\exists\, a \ni a + 2 = 4$⟩
∀	for every, for all ⟨$\forall\, a \ni a$ is a real number, $a^2 \geq 0$⟩

∪	union of two sets	∈ *or* ε	is an element of
∩	intersection of two sets	∉	is not an element of
⊂	is included in, is a subset of	Λ *or* 0 *or* ∅ *or*	
⊃	contains as a subset	{ }	empty set, null set

Miscellaneous

&	and	☩ *or* +	—used in some service books to indicate
&c	et cetera, and so forth		where the sign of the cross is to be made;
" *or* "	ditto marks		also used by certain Roman Catholic and
/	slash (*or* diagonal)—used to mean "or" (as		Anglican prelates as a sign of the cross pre-
	in *and/or*), "and/or" (as in *dead/wounded*),		ceding their signatures
	"per" (as in *feet/second*); used to indicate end	℞	take—used on prescriptions; prescription;
	of a line of verse; used to separate the figures		treatment
	of a date (4/4/73)	☠	poison
☞	index *or* fist	☢ *or* ☢	radiation, radioactive materials
†	died—used especially in genealogies	☢	fallout shelter
☧	monogram from Greek XP signifying Christ	⊕	peace
Ⓤ *or* Ⓚ	kosher certification	x *or* ×	by ⟨3 × 5 cards⟩
✡	Magen David	♺	recycle, recyclable
℟	response		
✽	—used in Roman Catholic and Anglican ser-		
	vice books to divide each verse of a psalm,		
	indicating where the response begins		

Physics

α	alpha particle	q	charge; quark
β	beta particle, beta ray	X	power of magnification
γ	gamma ray, photon		
λ	wavelength		
μ	micro-; micron; permeability		**CIRCUIT ELEMENTS**
ν	frequency; neutrino		
σ	conductivity; cross section; surface tension	⊣⊢ *or* ⊣⊪	DC power, battery
Ω	ohm	⊖	AC power, generator
Å	angstrom	⊣⊢	capacitor
c	speed of light	⌁	resistor
e	electron; electronic charge	⌁	inductor
n	neutron	⌁	switch
p	proton	⩎ *or* ⊥	grounded connection

Reference Marks

*	asterisk *or* star	‖	parallels
†	dagger	¶ *or* ⁋	paragraph
§	section *or* numbered clause		

Weather

◎	calm	∞	haze
○	clear	≡	fog
◑	cloudy (partly)	◗	hurricane
●	cloudy (completely overcast)	⊖	tropical storm
┽	drifting or blowing snow	●	rain
'	drizzle	⑊	sandstorm or dust storm
▲▲▲	front, cold	∇	shower(s)
⌢⌢⌢	warm	∀̇	shower of rain
▲⌢▲⌢	occluded	⁂	snow
⌄⌄	stationary	℞	thunderstorm

A Handbook of Style

Punctuation

Punctuation marks give readers important clues about how combinations of words should be read and understood. Some uses of punctuation marks in American English are discussed and illustrated in the following pages.

Apostrophe   '

1. The apostrophe is used to indicate the possessive of nouns and indefinite pronouns (*anyone, someone,* etc.). The possessive of singular nouns and plural nouns that do not end in an *s* or *z* sound is usually formed by adding *-'s.*

the boy's mother	the child's skates
women's voices	people's ideas

The possessive of plural nouns ending in an *s* or *z* sound is usually formed by adding only an apostrophe.

dogs' leashes	birds' migrations

2. The apostrophe is used to mark a spot where a letter or digit has been left out of a contracted word or numeral.

didn't	they're
she'd	class of '03
in the '90s	

Colon   :

1. The colon introduces a part of the sentence that identifies something that comes before it.

That year Dad's old obsession was replaced with a new one: jazz.

The problem is this: We don't have enough chairs.

2. The colon introduces a list or series.

Three countries were represented: Britain, France, and Belgium.

3. The colon introduces a part of the sentence that explains, illustrates, clarifies, or restates what has gone before.

Dawn was breaking: the distant peaks were already glowing with the sun's first rays.

4. The colon introduces a long quotation that is not enclosed in quotation marks but is indented to set it off from the rest of the text.

The *Rumpole* series has been well described as follows:

Horace Rumpole often wins cases despite the disdain of his more aristocratic colleagues. Fond of

cheap wine ("Château Thames Embankment") and . . . .

A colon may also be used before a quotation that is enclosed by quotation marks and is not indented.

The inscription reads: "To our favorite teacher, Mr. Richards."

5. The colon follows the salutation in formal letters.

Dear Judge Wright:

Ladies and Gentlemen:

Comma   ,

1. The comma separates independent clauses (parts of a sentence that could stand as sentences on their own) that are joined by a coordinating conjunction (such as *and, but, or, nor, so*).

She left a message, and he called her back that afternoon.

The trial lasted for nine months, but the jury took only four hours to reach its verdict.

Occasionally, the comma is also used to separate very short clauses that are not joined by conjunctions.

She came, she saw, she conquered.

2. The comma sometimes sets off adverbial clauses and phrases that begin or interrupt a sentence.

When we heard the news, we whooped with joy.

The teacher, having taken attendance, told us to take out our homework.

If the sentence can be easily read without a comma, the comma may be left out.

In January the roof fell in.

As cars age they become less valuable.

3. The comma sets off words and phrases that suggest a transition or introduce examples, such as *indeed, however, furthermore, namely,* and *for example*.

Indeed, no one seemed to have heard of him.

The mystery, however, remains unsolved.

She plans to visit two countries, namely, Mexico and Belize.

4. The comma sets off contrasting expressions within a sentence.

> This project will take six months, not six weeks.

5. The comma separates items in a series. Many writers leave out the comma before the last item in a series whenever this would not result in confusion.

> Men, women, and children crowded aboard the train.
>
> *or*
>
> Men, women and children crowded aboard the train.
>
> Her job required her to pack quickly, to travel often, and to have no personal life.
>
> *or*
>
> Her job required her to pack quickly, to travel often and to have no personal life.

6. The comma separates two or more adjectives that modify a noun.

> in a calm, reflective manner
>
> the harsh, damp, piercing wind

The comma is not used between two adjectives when the first adjective modifies the combination of the second adjective plus the noun it modifies.

> the lone bald eagle
>
> a good used car

7. The comma is used to set off material that is not an essential part of the sentence but provides additional information.

> We visited Gettysburg, site of the famous battle.
>
> A cherished landmark, the Hotel Sandburg was spared.
>
> Its author, Maria Olevsky, was an expert diver.

8. The comma separates a direct quotation from a phrase identifying its speaker or source.

> She answered, "I'm leaving."
>
> "I suspect," Bob observed, "we'll be hearing more."

The comma is left out when the quotation ends with a question mark or exclamation point.

> "How about another game?" Elaine piped up.

It is usually left out when the quoted phrase itself is the subject or object of the larger sentence.

> "Absolutely not" was the reply she received.

9. The comma sets off mild interjections and words used to address someone directly.

> Ah, that's my idea of an excellent dinner.
>
> Well, what have we here?
>
> The facts, my friend, are very different.
>
> You may go if you wish, Sam.

10. The comma comes before a question that has been added to a statement or command.

> That's obvious, isn't it?

11. The comma is used to avoid confusion that might arise from words placed side by side.

> Under Mr. James, Madison High School flourished.
>
> To Mary, Jane was someone special.

12. The comma is used to group numerals into units of three to separate thousands, millions, and so on.

> 2,000 case histories
>
> a fee of $12,500
>
> numbering 3,450,000

It is not, however, used in street addresses, page numbers, and four-digit years.

> 12537 Wilshire Blvd.
>
> page 1415
>
> in 3000 B.C.

13. The comma separates a name from a title or degree.

> Sandra H. Cobb, Vice President
>
> Lee Herman Melville, M.D.

It is also often used to separate a name from the abbreviations *Jr.* and *Sr.*

> Douglas Fairbanks, Jr.   *or*   Douglas Fairbanks Jr.

14. A comma sets off elements of a place name or address (except for zip codes).

> On the way to Austin, Texas, our car broke down.
>
> Write to Bureau of the Census, Washington, DC 20233.

15. A comma separates the day from the year in dates.

> The Continental Congress approved the Declaration of Independence on July 4, 1776.

When only the month and year are given, the comma is usually left out.

> The Wright brothers finally succeeded in keeping an airplane aloft for a few seconds in December 1903.

16. A comma follows the salutation in informal correspondence.

> Dear Aunt Sarah,

It also follows the word or words that conventionally come before the signature of a letter.

> Sincerely yours,

— Dash

1. The dash marks an abrupt change or break in a sentence.

> The students seemed happy enough with the new plan, but the parents—there was the problem.

2. The dash is often used in place of commas or parentheses to set off material that is not essential but provides additional information.

The new law will prevent corporations—large and small—from buying influence with campaign contributions.

3. The dash introduces a list.

He speaks three languages—English, French, and Spanish.

4. The dash introduces a part of the sentence that defines something that comes before it.

The motion was tabled—that is, removed indefinitely from consideration.

5. The dash often precedes the information identifying the source of a quotation, either immediately after the quotation or on the next line.

No one can make you feel inferior without your consent.—Eleanor Roosevelt

or

No one can make you feel inferior without your consent.

—Eleanor Roosevelt

Ellipsis . . .

1. The ellipsis is used when one or more words have been left out of a quotation.

We the People of the United States . . . do ordain and establish this Constitution for the United States of America.

2. The ellipsis indicates faltering speech or an unfinished sentence.

"I mean . . . " he stammered, "like . . . How?"

Exclamation Point   !

The exclamation point ends an emphatic phrase, sentence, or interjection.

Without a trace!

There is no alternative!

Encore!

Hyphen   -

1. The hyphen is often used to link elements in compound words.

secretary-treasurer	take-up
fleet-footed	light-year
middle-of-the-road	quick-freeze

2. The hyphen is used in writing out compound numbers between 21 and 99.

forty-one years old

one hundred forty-one

his forty-first birthday

3. The hyphen is used between numbers and dates with the meaning "(up) to and including."

pages 128-34

the years 1995-99

4. The hyphen is often used with the meaning *to, and, or versus.*

the New York-Paris flight

the Lincoln-Douglas debates

a final score of 7-2

5. The hyphen marks a division of a word at the end of a line.

In 1979 smallpox, formerly a great scourge, was declared eradicated by the World Health Organization.

Parentheses   ( )

1. Parentheses can be used to enclose a sentence or a part of a sentence that provides additional information or helps make something clearer.

The discussion was held in private. (The results are still confidential.)

Although we like the restaurant (their pizza is the best), we haven't been there in several months.

Nominations for club officers (president, vice president, treasurer, and secretary) were approved.

Four computers (all outdated models) were replaced.

I'll get back to you tomorrow (Friday).

The diagram (Fig. 3) illustrates the parts of the body.

2. Parentheses enclose numbers or letters indicating individual items in a series.

The clouds in the illustration are (1) cirrus, (2) cumulus, and (3) stratus.

3. Parentheses enclose abbreviations that follow their spelled-out forms, or spelled-out forms that follow their abbreviations.

the Food and Drug Administration (FDA)

the FDA (Food and Drug Administration)

4. Parentheses indicate alternative terms.

Please sign and return the enclosed form(s).

Period   .

1. The period ends a sentence or a sentence fragment that is neither a question nor an exclamation.

The bus left five minutes ago.

She asked if we liked to dance.

He said, "I haven't read that book yet."

Don't forget your homework.

Unlikely. In fact, inconceivable.

2. The period follows most abbreviations and some contractions.

Calif.	e.g.	Dr.
Sept.	p.m.	Jr.
etc.	dept.	Assn.

3. The period is used with a person's initials.

F. Scott Fitzgerald   Robert E. Lee

4. The period follows numerals and letters when used without parentheses in outlines and lists.

I. Pollution
   A. Principal sources
      1. Industrial
      2. Residential
   B. Proposed solutions

?   Question Mark

1. The question mark ends a direct question.

What went wrong?

Was anyone seen in the area after 10 p.m.?

"When do they arrive?" she asked.

The question mark does not follow an indirect question.

He asked when the store normally closed.

2. The question mark indicates uncertainty about a fact.

Homer, the Greek epic poet (9th-8th? cent. B.C.)

" "   Quotation Marks, Double

1. Quotation marks enclose direct quotations.

"I'm leaving," she whispered. "This could last forever."

He asked, "What went wrong?"

"Mom, we tried that already!" they said in unison.

Quotation marks do not enclose indirect quotations or paraphrases.

She whispered that she was leaving.

2. Quotation marks enclose words or phrases that have been borrowed from others and words or phrases that are very informal or in some way unusual.

They were afraid the patient had "stroked out"—or had had a stroke.

They required a "biodata summary"—that is, a résumé.

He called himself "emperor," but he was really just a dictator.

3. Quotation marks enclose titles of songs, poems, short stories, essays, chapters of books, episodes of radio and television programs, and articles in newspapers and magazines.

the article "In Search of Sleep" in *Newsweek*

"The Death of the Hired Man" by Robert Frost

Poe's "The Murders in the Rue Morgue"

Thoreau's famous essay "Civil Disobedience"

The Jungle Book's ninth chapter, "Rikki-tikki-tavi"

M*A*S*H's finale, "Goodbye, Farewell and Amen"

4. Quotation marks are used with other punctuation marks as follows: A period or comma is placed inside the quotation marks. A colon or semicolon is placed outside them. A dash, question mark, or exclamation point is placed inside the quotation marks when it punctuates the quoted matter only, but outside when it punctuates the whole sentence.

He smiled and said, "I'm happy for you."

"Too easy," she shot back.

There was only one real "issue": noise.

She spoke of her "little cottage in the country"; she might better have called it a mansion.

"I can't see how—" he started to say.

Saturdays there were dances—"sock hops"—in the gym.

He asked, "When did she leave?"

Did you say "Australia"?

She leaped into the air with a joyful "Hooray!"

Save us from his "mercy"!

' '   Quotation Marks, Single

Single quotation marks enclose quotations within quotations.

The witness said, "I distinctly heard him say, 'Don't be late,' and then I heard the door close."

;   Semicolon

1. The semicolon links independent clauses (parts of a sentence that could stand as sentences on their own) when they are joined without a coordinating conjunction.

Cream the butter and sugar; add the eggs and beat well.

The river overflowed its banks; roads vanished; freshly plowed fields turned into lakes.

2. The semicolon joins two clauses when the second includes a word or phase like *however, indeed, thus, in that case, as a result,* or *on the other hand.*

It won't be easy to sort out the facts; a decision must be made, however.

The show started an hour late; as a result, many people requested refunds.

3. The semicolon is often used before introductory expressions such as *for example, that is,* and *namely*.

We were fairly successful; that is, we raised more than a thousand dollars.

4. The semicolon separates phrases or items in a series when they contain commas.

The assets include $22 million in land, buildings, and equipment; $34 million in cash and investments; and $8 million in inventory.

The exhibition will travel to Washington, D.C.; Concord, N.H.; Portland, Ore.; and Oakland, Cal.

The votes against were: Megan's group, 8; Brandon's group, 2; Jake's group, 6.

5. The semicolon is placed outside quotation marks and parentheses.

They again demanded "complete freedom"; the demand was again rejected.

She likes rock and roll (the louder the better); he prefers classical.

Slash   /

1. The slash sometimes stands for *or* or *and/or*.

his/her

2. The slash sometimes stands for *to* or *and*.

1998/99   *or*   1998-99

the May/June issue   *or*   the May-June issue

3. The slash sometimes stands for *per* or *to*.

400,000 tons/year

price/earnings ratio

29 mi/gal

4. The slash separates parts of a date or fraction.

on 9/21/01

a 7/8-mile course

5. The slash is used as a part of some abbreviations.

w/o [*for* without]

c/o [*for* care of]

6. The slash is used in Internet addresses.

http://www.Merriam-Webster.com/

Plurals

1. The plurals of most English words are formed by adding *-s* or *-es* to the singular; *-es* is added when the noun ends in *-s, -x, -z, -ch,* or *-sh.*

dog	→ dogs	tax	→ taxes
race	→ races	blitz	→ blitzes
voter	→ voters	branch	→ branches
book	→ books	dish	→ dishes
grass	→ grasses		

2. The plurals of words that follow other patterns are given at the appropriate entries in the main section of this dictionary.

army	→ armies	passerby	→ passersby
woman	→ women	alumnus	→ alumni
ox	→ oxen	elf	→ elves
foot	→ feet	sheep	→ sheep
phenomenon	→ phenomena		

Capitals and Italics

Words and phrases are capitalized or italicized to indicate that they have special significance in particular situations. The following rules and examples describe some of the most common uses of capitals and italics.

Beginnings

1. The first word of a sentence or sentence fragment is capitalized.

The play lasted nearly three hours.

How are you feeling?

So many people, so many opinions.

Bravo!

2. The first word of a direct quotation is capitalized. However, if the quotation is interrupted in mid-sentence, the second part does not begin with a capital.

Hart repeated, "We can only stay a few minutes."

"We can only stay a few minutes," repeated Hart, "but we'll come back tomorrow."

3. The first word of a line of poetry is traditionally capitalized. However, in modern poetry the line beginnings are often lowercased. The poem's original capitalization should always be kept.

Heart, do not bruise the breast
That sheltered you so long;
Beat quietly, strange guest.
　　　　　　　—Edna St. Vincent Millay

A free bird leaps
on the back of the wind

and floats downstream
till the current ends
and dips his wings
in the orange sun rays
and dares to claim the sky
                    —Maya Angelou

4. In a letter, the first word of the salutation and the first of the words that conventionally come before the signature are capitalized.

Dear Catherine:

To whom it may concern:

Sincerely yours,

Proper Nouns and Adjectives

1. Names of persons and places, organizations and their members, conferences and councils, and historical periods and events are capitalized. If you are not sure if something should be capitalized or not, look it up in a dictionary or encyclopedia.

Noah Webster	Yalta Conference
Christa McAuliffe	Council of Trent
New York City	Bronze Age
the Rotary Club	World War II
all Rotarians	Boston Tea Party

2. Words formed from proper nouns are often capitalized. Look up the word in the dictionary when you are not sure.

Bunsen burner

Gregorian calendar

People

3. Words designating languages, nationalities, peoples, races, religious groups, and tribes are capitalized. Designations based on skin color are usually lowercased.

Spanish	Iroquois
Spaniards	Asians
Muslims	blacks and Hispanics

4. Titles that come before the name of a person and epithets or nicknames used instead of a name are capitalized.

President Lincoln

Honest Abe

King Henry VIII

Titles following a name or used alone are usually lowercased.

Henry VIII, king of England

Marcia Ramirez, president of Logex Corp.

Logex Corp.'s president

5. Words of family relationship that come before a person's name or are used in place of it are capitalized; otherwise they are lowercased.

Uncle Fred	Mother's birthday
Cousin Julia	my mother's birthday

Religious Terms

6. Words designating the Supreme Being are capitalized.

Allah

the Almighty

Brahma

in the eyes of God

Jehovah

Plural references to deities are lowercased, however.

the angry gods

7. Personal pronouns referring to the Supreme Being are often capitalized in religious writing.

God gave His Son

Scientific Terms

8. Names of planets and their satellites, stars, constellations, and other specific celestial objects are capitalized. However, the words *sun, earth,* and *moon* are usually lowercased unless they occur with other astronomical names.

Jupiter	Mars, Venus, and Earth
the North Star	life on earth
Ursa Major	voyage to the moon

9. Names of geological time divisions are capitalized. The generic terms that follow them are lowercased.

Mesozoic era

Paleocene epoch

Quaternary period

the Upper Cretaceous

Time Periods

10. Names of days of the week, months, and holidays and holy days are capitalized.

Tuesday

January

Veterans Day

Yom Kippur

Easter

Names of the seasons are lowercased.

winter

Titles of Works

11. The first word in the title of a book, magazine, newspaper, play, movie, work of art, or long poem or musical composition is capitalized. The other words in the title are also capitalized, except for articles (*a, an, the*), coordinating conjunctions (*and, or, but,* etc.), short prepositions (*by, of, on, to,* etc.) and the *to* of infinitives. Prepositions of four or more letters are often capitalized. The entire title is italicized. (Some other kinds of titles are enclosed in quotation marks rather than italicized; see "Quotation Marks, Double" on p. 1005.)

Of Mice and Men

Sports Illustrated

USA Today

Miller's *The Crucible*

Lawrence of Arabia

Monet's *Water-Lily Pool*

Eliot's *The Waste Land*

Trademarks

12. Registered trademarks, service marks, and brand names are capitalized.

Coke	Kleenex	Frisbee
Walkman	Band-Aid	Levi's

Transportation

13. Names of ships, airplanes, and space vehicles are capitalized and italicized.

Titanic	*Challenger*
Spirit of St. Louis	*Apollo 13*

14. Names of train lines, types of aircraft, and space programs are capitalized but not italicized.

Metroliner	Concorde
Boeing 727	Pathfinder Program

Other Styling Conventions

1. Italics are often used for letters referred to as letters, words referred to as words, and numerals referred to as numerals.

The *g* in *align* is silent.

The word *slogan* evolved from Scottish Gaelic, the ancient language of Scotland.

The first *2* and the last *0* are barely legible.

2. Foreign words and phrases are italicized.

"The cooking here is *wunderbar!*"